The Consumer Credit and Sales
Legal Practice Series

UNFAIR AND DECEPTIVE ACTS AND PRACTICES

Sixth Edition

Jonathan Sheldon
Carolyn L. Carter

Contributing Authors: Stephen Gardner, Elizabeth De Armond,
Anthony Rodriguez

National Consumer Law Center
77 Summer Street, 10th Floor   Boston, MA 02110   www.consumerlaw.org

About NCLC

The National Consumer Law Center, a nonprofit corporation founded in 1969, assists consumers, advocates, and public policy makers nationwide who use the powerful and complex tools of consumer law to ensure justice and fair treatment for all, particularly those whose poverty renders them powerless to demand accountability from the economic marketplace. For more information, go to www.consumerlaw.org.

Ordering NCLC Publications

Order securely online at www.consumerlaw.org, or contact Publications Department, National Consumer Law Center, 77 Summer Street, Boston, MA 02110, (617) 542-9595, FAX: (617) 542-8028, e-mail: publications@nclc.org.

Training and Conferences

NCLC participates in numerous national, regional, and local consumer law trainings. Its annual fall conference is a forum for consumer rights attorneys from legal services programs, private practice, government, and nonprofit organizations to share insights into common problems and explore novel and tested approaches that promote consumer justice in the marketplace. Contact NCLC for more information or see our web site.

Case Consulting

Case analysis, consulting and co-counseling for lawyers representing vulnerable consumers are among NCLC's important activities. Administration on Aging funds allow us to provide free consulting to legal services advocates representing elderly consumers on many types of cases. Massachusetts Legal Assistance Corporation funds permit case assistance to advocates representing low-income Massachusetts consumers. Other funding may allow NCLC to provide very brief consultations to other advocates without charge. More comprehensive case analysis and research is available for a reasonable fee. See our web site for more information at www.consumerlaw.org.

Charitable Donations and Cy Pres *Awards*

NCLC's work depends in part on the support of private donors. Tax-deductible donations should be made payable to National Consumer Law Center, Inc. For more information, contact Suzanne Cutler of NCLC's Development Office at (617) 542-8010 or scutler@nclc.org. NCLC has also received generous court-approved *cy pres* awards arising from consumer class actions to advance the interests of class members. For more information, contact Robert Hobbs (rhobbs@nclc.org) or Rich Dubois (rdubois@nclc.org) at (617) 542-8010.

Comments and Corrections

Write to the above address to the attention of the Editorial Department or e-mail consumerlaw@nclc.org.

About This Volume

This is the Sixth Edition of *Unfair and Deceptive Acts and Practices* with a 2004 companion CD-Rom. The Sixth Edition and 2004 CD-Rom supersede all prior editions, supplements, and CDs, which should all be discarded. Continuing developments can be found in periodic updates to this volume and in NCLC REPORTS, *Deceptive Practices & Warranties Edition*.

Cite This Volume As

National Consumer Law Center, Unfair and Deceptive Acts and Practices (6th ed. 2004).

Attention

This publication is designed to provide authoritative information concerning the subject matter covered. Always use the most current edition and supplement, and use other sources for more recent developments or for special rules for individual jurisdictions. This publication cannot substitute for the independent judgment and skills of an attorney or other professional. Non-attorneys are cautioned against using these materials to conduct a lawsuit without advice from an attorney and are cautioned against engaging in the unauthorized practice of law.

Copyright

ISBN 1-931697-63-9 (this volume)
ISBN 0-943116-10-4 (Series)

Library of Congress Control Number 2004114741

About the Authors

Jonathan Sheldon has been an NCLC staff attorney writing on deceptive practices law, automobile fraud, leasing, and other consumer law topics since 1976. Previously he was a staff attorney with the Federal Trade Commission. His publications include *Unfair and Deceptive Acts and Practices* (1982, 1988, 1991, 1997, 2001), *Consumer Warranty Law* (1997, 2001), *Automobile Fraud* (1998, 2003), *Consumer Class Actions* (5th ed. 1999), *Consumer Arbitration Agreements* (2001, 2002, 2003, 2004), *Repossessions and Foreclosures* (1982, 1988, 1995, 1999), *Credit Discrimination* (1st ed. 1993), and *Fair Credit Reporting* (2d ed. 1988).

Carolyn L. Carter is of counsel with NCLC, and was formerly co-director of Legal Services, Inc., in Gettysburg, Pennsylvania, and formerly was director of the Law Reform Office of Cleveland Legal Aid Society. She is the editor of *Pennsylvania Consumer Law*, editor of the First Edition of *Ohio Consumer Law*, co-author of *Unfair and Deceptive Acts and Practices* (1997, 2001), *Consumer Warranty Law* (1997, 2001), *Repossessions and Foreclosures* (5th ed. 2002), *Automobile Fraud* (2d ed. 2003), contributing author to *Fair Debt Collection* (5th ed. 2004), *Truth in Lending* (5th ed. 2003) and *The Cost of Credit* (2d ed. 2000), and the 1992 recipient of the Vern Countryman Consumer Law Award.

Stephen Gardner is Director of Litigation for the Center for Science in the Public Interest and of counsel to NCLC. Previously, he was assistant dean of clinical education at Southern Methodist University School of Law, assistant attorney general in both Texas and New York, students' attorney at the University of Texas, and a legal aid attorney at what is now Texas Rio Grande Legal Services.

Elizabeth De Armond is on the faculty of Chicago-Kent College of Law, where her research focuses on consumer law and privacy issues. She has contributed frequently to NCLC publications and is a co-author of the 2004 supplement to *Fair Credit Reporting* as well as a contributing author to *Automobile Fraud* (2d ed. 2003), *Consumer Warranty Law* (2d ed. 2000), and *Fair Credit Reporting* (5th ed. 2002). Previously, she was in private practice in Texas and a clerk for Judge Cornelia Kennedy of the United States Court of Appeals for the Sixth Circuit.

Anthony Rodriguez is an NCLC staff attorney, and previously served as the Director of the Massachusetts Attorney General's Disability Rights Project and as an Assistant Attorney General in the Consumer Protection and Civil Rights Divisions, where he litigated UDAP, telemarketing, credit repair, housing discrimination and public accommodations cases. He is co-author of *Fair Credit Reporting* (5th ed. 2002) and contributing author to *Credit Discrimination* (3d ed. 2002).

Acknowledgments: We are particularly grateful to Denise Lisio for editorial supervision, Nathan Day for editorial assistance, Shannon Halbrook for production assistance, Shirlron Williams for assistance with cite and fact checking, Mary McLean for indexing, Xylutions for typesetting services, and Neil Fogarty of Law Disks for developing the CD-Rom.

A large number of people also assisted with this edition, including Olivia Wein on utility issues, Thomas Grande for the *qui tam* section, Deanne Loonin on student loans and other topics, Eric Carlson on long term care, Cathy Lesser Mansfield on holder in due course issues, Mark Budnitz on banking issues, and also to Dmitry Feofanov, Michael Donovan, and Robert Eppes for a number of substantive contributions. Thanks also to Elizabeth Ryan, Allen Agnitti, Kurt Terwilliger, Steve Boyajian, and Mary Kingsley for legal research and writing.

This Sixth Edition builds on the prior five editions and eighteen annual supplements. As such, this edition is indebted to the efforts of over 100 individuals who contributed to this project starting over two decades ago. There are now too many people to list here, but a collective thanks to everyone. We also want to express our appreciation to the many state attorneys general and private attorneys for, over the years, sending in cases, regulations, and interpretations on their states' UDAP statutes. We also want to thank Morton Needelman for starting us on this path over thirty years ago.

What Your Library Should Contain

The Consumer Credit and Sales Legal Practice Series contains 16 titles, updated annually, arranged into four libraries, and designed to be an attorney's primary practice guide and legal resource in all 50 states. Each manual includes a CD-Rom allowing pinpoint searches and the pasting of text into a word processor.

Debtor Rights Library

2004 Seventh Edition with CD-Rom, Including Law Disks' Bankruptcy Forms

Consumer Bankruptcy Law and Practice: the definitive personal bankruptcy manual, with step-by-step instructions from initial interview to final discharge, and including consumers' rights as creditors when a merchant or landlord files for bankruptcy. Appendices and CD-Rom contain over 130 annotated pleadings, bankruptcy statutes, rules and fee schedules, an interview questionnaire, a client handout, and software to complete the latest versions of petitions and schedules.

2004 Fifth Edition with CD-Rom

Fair Debt Collection: the basic reference in the field, covering the Fair Debt Collection Practices Act and common law, state statutory and other federal debt collection protections. Appendices and companion CD-Rom contain sample pleadings and discovery, the FTC's Official Staff Commentary, *all* FTC staff opinion letters, and summaries of reported and unreported cases.

2002 Fifth Edition, 2004 Supplement, and 2004 CD-Rom

Repossessions and Foreclosures: unique guide to VA, FHA and other types of home foreclosures, servicer obligations, motor vehicle and mobile home repossessions, threatened seizures of household goods, tax and other statutory liens, and automobile lease and rent-to-own default remedies. The CD-Rom reprints relevant UCC provisions and numerous key federal statutes, regulations, and agency letters, summarizes hundreds of state laws, and includes over 150 pleadings covering a wide variety of cases.

2002 Second Edition, 2004 Supplement, and 2004 CD-Rom

Student Loan Law: student loan debt collection and collection fees; discharges based on closed school, false certification, failure to refund, disability, and bankruptcy; tax intercepts, wage garnishment, and offset of social security benefits; repayment plans, consolidation loans, deferments, and non-payment of loan based on school fraud. CD-Rom and appendices contain numerous forms, pleadings, interpretation letters and regulations.

2004 Third Edition with CD-Rom

Access to Utility Service: the only examination of consumer rights when dealing with regulated, de-regulated, and unregulated utilities, including telecommunications, terminations, billing errors, low-income payment plans, utility allowances in subsidized housing, LIHEAP, and weatherization. Includes summaries of state utility regulations.

Credit and Banking Library

2003 Fifth Edition, 2004 Supplement, and 2004 CD-Rom

Truth in Lending: detailed analysis of *all* aspects of TILA, the Consumer Leasing Act, and the Home Ownership and Equity Protection Act (HOEPA). Appendices and the CD-Rom contain the Acts, Reg. Z, Reg. M, and their Official Staff Commentaries, numerous sample pleadings, rescission notices, and two programs to compute APRs.

2002 Fifth Edition, 2004 Supplement, and 2004 CD-Rom

Fair Credit Reporting: the key resource for handling any type of credit reporting issue, from cleaning up blemished credit records to suing reporting agencies and creditors for inaccurate reports. Covers credit scoring, privacy issues, identity theft, the FCRA, the new FACT Act, the Credit Repair Organizations Act, state credit reporting and repair statutes, and common law claims.

2002 Second Edition, 2004 Supplement, and 2004 CD-Rom

Consumer Banking and Payments Law: unique analysis of consumer law (and NACHA rules) as to checks, money orders, credit, debit, and stored value cards, and banker's right of setoff. Also extensive treatment of electronic records and signatures, electronic transfer of food stamps, and direct deposits of federal payments. The CD-Rom and appendices reprint relevant agency interpretations and pleadings.

2000 Second Edition, 2004 Supplement, and 2004 CD-Rom

The Cost of Credit: Regulation and Legal Challenges: a one-of-a-kind resource detailing state and federal regulation of consumer credit in all fifty states, federal usury preemption, explaining credit math, and how to challenge excessive credit charges and credit insurance. The CD-Rom includes a credit math program and hard-to-find agency interpretations.

2002 Third Edition, 2004 Supplement, and 2004 CD-Rom

Credit Discrimination: analysis of the Equal Credit Opportunity Act, Fair Housing Act, Civil Rights Acts, and state credit discrimination statutes, including reprints of all relevant federal interpretations, government enforcement actions, and numerous sample pleadings.

Consumer Litigation Library

2004 Fourth Edition with CD-Rom

Consumer Arbitration Agreements: numerous successful approaches to challenge the enforceability of a binding arbitration agreement, the interrelation of the Federal Arbitration Act and state law, class actions in arbitration, collections via arbitration, the right to discovery, and other topics. Appendices and CD-Rom include sample discovery, numerous briefs, arbitration service provider rules and affidavits as to arbitrator costs.

2002 Fifth Edition, 2004 Supplement, and 2004 CD-Rom

Consumer Class Actions: A Practical Litigation Guide: makes class action litigation manageable even for small offices, including numerous sample pleadings, class certification memoranda, discovery, class notices, settlement materials, and much more. Includes contributions from seven of the most experienced consumer class action litigators around the country.

2004 CD-Rom with Index Guide: ALL pleadings from ALL NCLC Manuals, including Consumer Law Pleadings Numbers One through Ten

Consumer Law Pleadings on CD-Rom: Over 1000 notable recent pleadings from all types of consumer cases, including predatory lending, foreclosures, automobile fraud, lemon laws, debt collection, fair credit reporting, home improvement fraud, rent to own, student loans, and lender liability. Finding aids pinpoint the desired pleading in seconds, ready to paste into a word processing program.

Deception and Warranties Library

2004 Sixth Edition with CD-Rom

Unfair and Deceptive Acts and Practices: the only practice manual covering all aspects of a deceptive practices case in every state. Special sections on automobile sales, the federal racketeering (RICO) statute, unfair insurance practices, and the FTC Holder Rule.

2003 Second Edition, 2004 Supplement, and 2004 CD-Rom

Automobile Fraud: examination of title law, odometer tampering, lemon laundering, sale of salvage and wrecked cars, undisclosed prior use, prior damage to new cars, numerous sample pleadings, and title search techniques.

2001 Second Edition, 2004 Supplement, and 2004 CD-Rom

Consumer Warranty Law: comprehensive treatment of new and used car lemon laws, the Magnuson-Moss Warranty Act, UCC Articles 2 and 2A, mobile home, new home, and assistive device warranty laws, FTC Used Car Rule, tort theories, car repair and home improvement statutes, service contract and lease laws, with numerous sample pleadings.

NCLC's CD-Roms

Every NCLC manual comes with a companion CD-Rom featuring pop-up menus, PDF format, Internet-style navigation of appendices, indices, and bonus pleadings, hard-to-find agency interpretations and other practice aids. Documents can be copied into a word processing program. Of special note is *Consumer Law in a Box*:

December 2004 CD-Rom

Consumer Law in a Box: a CD-Rom combining *all* documents and software from 16 other NCLC CD-Roms. Quickly pinpoint a document from thousands found on the CD through keyword searches and Internet-style navigation, links, bookmarks, and other finding aids.

Other NCLC Publications for Lawyers

issued 24 times a year

NCLC REPORTS covers the latest developments and ideas in the practice of consumer law.

2003 First Edition with CD-Rom

The Practice of Consumer Law: Seeking Economic Justice: contains an essential overview to consumer law and explains how to get started in a private or legal services consumer practice. Packed with invaluable sample pleadings and practice pointers for even experienced consumer attorneys.

2002 First Edition with CD-Rom

STOP Predatory Lending: A Guide for Legal Advocates: provides a roadmap and practical legal strategy for litigating predatory lending abuses, from small loans to mortgage loans. The CD-Rom contains a credit math program, pleadings, legislative and administrative materials, and underwriting guidelines.

National Consumer Law Center Guide Series

are books designed for consumers, counselors, and attorneys new to consumer law:

2002 Edition

NCLC Guide to Surviving Debt: a great overview of consumer law. Everything a paralegal, new attorney, or client needs to know about debt collectors, managing credit card debt, whether to refinance, credit card problems, home foreclosures, evictions, repossessions, credit reporting, utility terminations, student loans, budgeting, and bankruptcy.

2002 Edition

NCLC Guide to Mobile Homes: what consumers and their advocates need to know about mobile home dealer sales practices and an in-depth look at mobile home quality and defects, with 35 photographs and construction details.

2002 Edition

NCLC Guide to Consumer Rights for Immigrants: an introduction to many of the most critical consumer issues faced by immigrants, including international wires, check cashing and banking, *notario* and immigration consultant fraud, affidavits of support, telephones, utilities, credit history discrimination, high-cost credit, used car fraud, student loans and more.

2000 Edition

Return to Sender: Getting a Refund or Replacement for Your Lemon Car: Find how lemon laws work, what consumers and their lawyers should know to evaluate each other, investigative techniques and discovery tips, how to handle both informal dispute resolution and trials, and more.

Visit **www.consumerlaw.org** to order securely online or for more information on all NCLC manuals and CD-Roms, including the full tables of contents, indices, listings of CD-Rom contents, and **web-based searches of the manuals' full text.**

National Consumer Law Center ▪ 77 Summer Street ▪ 10th Floor ▪ Boston MA ▪ 02110
(617) 542-9595 ▪ FAX (617) 542-8028 ▪ publications@nclc.org
Order securely online at www.consumerlaw.org

Finding Aids and Search Tips

The Consumer Credit and Sales Legal Practice Series presently contains sixteen volumes, ten supplements, and sixteen companion CD-Roms—all constantly being updated. The Series includes over 10,000 pages, 100 chapters, 100 appendices, and over 1000 pleadings, as well as hundreds of documents found on the CD-Roms, but not found in the books. Here are a number of ways to pinpoint in seconds what you need from this array of materials.

Internet-Based Searches

www.consumerlaw.org

Electronically search every chapter and appendix of all sixteen manuals and their supplements: go to www.consumerlaw.org/keyword and enter a case name, regulation cite, or other search term. You are instantly given the book names and page numbers of any of the NCLC manuals containing that term.

www.consumerlaw.org

Current indexes, tables of contents, and CD-Rom contents for all sixteen volumes are found at www.consumerlaw.org. Just click on *The Consumer Credit and Sales Legal Practice Series* and scroll down to the book you want. Then click on that volume's index, contents, or CD-Rom contents.

Finding Material on NCLC's CD-Roms

Consumer Law in a Box CD-Rom

Electronically search all sixteen NCLC CD-Roms, including thousands of agency interpretations, all NCLC appendices and almost 1000 pleadings: use Acrobat's search button* in NCLC's *Consumer Law in a Box CD-Rom* (this CD-Rom is free to set subscribers) to find every instance that a keyword appears on any of our sixteen CD-Roms. Then, with one click, go to that location to see the full text of the document.

CD-Rom accompanying this volume

Electronically search the CD-Rom accompanying this volume, including pleadings, agency interpretations, and regulations. Use Acrobat's search button* to find every instance that a keyword appears on the CD-Rom, and then, with one click, go to that location on the CD-Rom. Or just click on subject buttons until you navigate to the document you need.

Finding Pleadings

Consumer Law Pleadings on CD-Rom and Index Guide

Search five different ways for the right pleading from over 1000 choices: use the *Index Guide* accompanying *Consumer Law Pleadings on CD-Rom* to search for pleadings by type, subject, publication title, name of contributor, or contributor's jurisdiction. The guide also provides a summary of the pleading once the right pleading is located. *Consumer Law Pleadings on CD-Rom* and the *Consumer Law in a Box CD-Rom* also let you search for all pleadings electronically by subject, type of pleading, and by publication title, giving you instant access to the full pleading in Word and/or PDF format once you find the pleading you need.

Using This Volume to Find Material in All Sixteen Volumes

This volume

The Quick Reference at the back of this volume lets you pinpoint manual sections or appendices where over 1000 different subject areas are covered.

* Users of NCLC CD-Roms should become familiar with "search," a powerful Acrobat tool, distinguished from "find," another Acrobat feature that is far slower and less powerful than "search." The Acrobat 5 "search" icon is a pair of binoculars with paper in the background, while the "find" icon is a pair of binoculars without the paper. Acrobat 6 uses one icon, a pair of binoculars, that brings you to a menu with several search options.

Summary Contents

Contents

Chapter 3 Demonstrating That a Practice Is a UDAP Violation

Chapter 4 General Principles as to UDAP Violations

Chapter 6 Liability of Various Parties

Chapter 7 Litigating UDAP Cases

Chapter 8 Private UDAP Remedies

Chapter 9 Other Private Remedies

CD-Rom Contents

UDAP Pleadings by Type

Unfair and Deceptive Acts and Practices

- Credit Insurance Claims
- Credit Report, Unauthorized Access
- *Debt Collection*
  - Harassment, Collector's Use of Attorney's Name
  - Harassment, Collection Agency Litigation Abuses
  - Harassment of Debtor's Relative
  - Debt Collectors Seeking Attorney Fees, Unauthorized Practice of Law
- Distant Forum Abuse
- *Forced Placed Automobile Insurance*
  - Vendor's Single Interest Insurance (IL) (*Consumer Class Actions*, Appendix D.7)
  - Forced Placed Automobile Insurance (CA)
  - Forced Placed Automobile Insurance, Class Action (N.M.)
- Foreclosure, False Threat of
- *FTC Holder Rule*
  - FTC Holder Rule as Basis for Bank's Liability for Used Car Fraud
  - FTC Holder Rule, Lender's Failure to Include Satellite Dish (*Consumer Class Actions*, Appendix D.6)
  - FTC Holder Rule, Lender's Failure to Include Used Car Financing, Motion for Leave
  - FTC Holder Rule, Lender's Failure to Include Used Car Financing
- Furniture Sales, Failure to Deliver
- *Home Improvement*
  - Home Improvement Fraud, Class Action (*Consumer Class Actions*, Appendix D.2)
  - Home Improvement Fraud (VA)
  - Home Improvement Finance Scheme, Class Action
  - Home Improvement Scheme with Bank's Involvement
  - Scheme to Defraud Elderly Homeowner
- Home Solicitation Sale Cancellation
- Infertility Clinic Practices
- Labeling of Diet Supplement
- Land Installment Sales
- *Landlord-Tenant*
  - Defenses and Counterclaims Challenging Lease
  - Eviction via Utility Shutoff
  - Challenge of Eviction Process, Class Action
- Lender's Improvident Extension of Credit
- Loan Flipping
- *Mandatory Arbitration*
  - Included in Credit Card "Stuffer"
  - Included in Long-Distance Carrier Correspondence
- *Mobile Homes*
  - Mobile Home Parks, Uninhabitable Conditions
  - Mobile Home Sales, Eviction via Conversion of Mobile Home Park
  - Mobile Home Sales, Damages and Cancellation
  - Mobile Home Sales and Defects, Suit Against Dealer & Financer
  - Mobile Home Sales and Defects, Suit Against Dealer & Manufacturer
- *Mortgages*
  - Misrepresentation of Savings from Refinancing
  - Mortgage Loans and Foreclosure Defense, Loan Scheme Involving Multiple Parties
  - Mortgage Loans and Foreclosure Defense, Challenging Mortgage in Chapter 13
  - Mortgage Servicer Abuses, Class Complaint

Unfair and Deceptive Acts and Practices

Used Car Fraud

Jury Instructions

Labeling of Diet Supplements

Odometer Fraud and Threat of Violent Repossession

Used Car Fraud

Predatory Mortgage Lending

Request for Findings and Rulings, JNOV

Auto Pawn

Labeling of Diet Supplements, JNOV

Mandatory Arbitration Included in Long Distance Carrier Correspondence

Mortgage Loans and Foreclosure Defense

Payday Loans

Scheme to Defraud Elderly Homeowner

Requests for Attorney Fees

Debt Collection Case, Seeking Fees Exceeding Damages

Mortgage Loans and Foreclosure Defense, Motion for Allowance of Fees in Bankruptcy Court

Support for Catalyst Award in UDAP Case Despite *Buckhannon*

Time Share Litigation, Support for Fees and Discovery of Defendants' Fees

Appellate Briefs

Bank's Wrongful Setoff of Exempt Funds

Distant Forum Abuse

Lemon New Car

FTC Holder Rule Preserving Consumer Claims That Are Less Than Rescission

Certiorari *and Petitions for Review*

Distant Forum Abuse, Answer to Petition for Review

Distant Forum Abuse, Opposition to Petition for Writ of *Certiorari*

Cy Pres *Remedy*

Cy Pres Remedy, Credit Card Deception, Class Action

Telephones, Telemarketing

Federal Telemarketing and Consumer Fraud and Abuse Prevention Act (Appendix D.1.1)

Federal Telephone Disclosure and Dispute Resolution Act (Appendix D.1.2)

Federal Restrictions on Use of Telephone Equipment (Appendix D.1.3)

Federal Regulation of Carrier Offering of Pay-Per-Call Services (Appendix D.1.4)

FTC Telemarketing Sales Rule

Telemarketing Sales Rule, *amended by* 68 Fed. Reg. 4580 (Jan. 29, 2003) (Appendix D.2.1)

Telemarketing Sales Rule, Statement of Basis and Purpose, 68 Fed. Reg. 4580 (Jan. 29, 2003)

Proposed Changes to FTC Telemarketing Sales Rule (Jan. 30, 2002)

Old Telemarketing Sales Rule

Old Telemarketing Sales Rule, Statement of Basis and Purpose (60 Fed. Reg. 43841, Aug. 23, 1995)

Telephone Disclosure and Dispute Resolution Rule (Appendix D.2.2)

Restrictions on Telephone Solicitation (Appendix D.2.3)

Summaries of State Telemarketing and State "900 Number" Statutes (Appendix E)

Massachusetts Rulings Regarding Telephone Disconnect for Non-Payment of Long Distance

RICO: Federal, State

Federal RICO Statute (Appendix C.1.1)

Useful Addresses, Web Links

Unfair and Deceptive Acts and Practices Appendices on CD-Rom

Word Files on CD-Rom

Search This Manual

Search This Manual's Appendices, Plus All Other Documents on This CD-Rom
Limit Search Only to the Current File You Are Using on the CD-Rom
Search Chapters and Appendices of This Manual
Summary Contents of This Manual
Table of Contents of This Manual
Index of This Manual
CD-Rom Contents for This Manual
Contents of Other NCLC Manuals

Search All Manuals

Contents of NCLC Publications

Internet-Based Keyword Search of All NCLC Manuals
Detailed and Summary Tables of Contents for Each Manual
Short Description of Each Manual's Features with Link to Manual's Detailed Index
Short Index to Major Topics Covered in the 16-Volume Series
Descriptions of Other NCLC Books for Lawyers and Consumers
Features of *Consumer Law in a Box* (16 CD-Roms Combined into One Master CD-Rom)
Printer-Friendly 3-Page Description of All NCLC Publications, Latest Supplements
Printer-Friendly 25-Page Brochure Describing All NCLC Publications
Printer-Friendly Order Form for All NCLC Publications
Order Securely On-line

Consumer Education Brochures, Books

Legal and General Audience Books Available to Order from NCLC
- *The Practice of Consumer Law*
- *STOP Predatory Lending: A Guide for Legal Advocates, with CD-Rom*
- *Return to Sender: Getting a Refund or Replacement for Your Lemon Car*
- *The NCLC Guide to Surviving Debt*, 2002 Edition
- *The NCLC Guide to Consumer Rights for Immigrants*
- *The NCLC Guide to Mobile Homes*
- Printer-Friendly Order Form
- Order Securely On-line

Brochures for Consumers on This CD-Rom
- General Consumer Education Brochures
- *Consumer Concerns for Older Americans*
- *Immigrant Justice in the Consumer Marketplace*

Order NCLC Publications, CD-Roms

NCLC Manuals and CD-Roms
Order Publications On-line
Printer-Friendly Order Form
Consumer Law in a Box CD-Rom
Credit Math, Bankruptcy Forms Software
Printer-Friendly Publications Brochure
NCLC Newsletters
Case Assistance
Conferences, Training
Books for Lawyers, Consumers
Consumer Education Pamphlets
Consumer Web Links

About NCLC, About This CD-Rom

Adobe Acrobat Reader 5 & 6.0.1

Chapter 1 First Considerations

1.1 What Is "UDAP"

All fifty states, the District of Columbia, Puerto Rico, Guam, and the Virgin Islands have enacted at least one statute with broad applicability to most consumer transactions, aimed at preventing consumer deception and abuse in the marketplace.[1] Many of these statutes are patterned after the language found in Section 5(a)(1) of the Federal Trade Commission (FTC) Act[2] which prohibits "unfair or deceptive acts or practices." The term "UDAP" is an acronym for this prohibition.

"UDAP" will be used in this manual somewhat imprecisely to refer to all state consumer statutes of general applicability, as listed in Appendix A, *infra*, whether the legislation proscribes unfair, unconscionable, deceptive, misleading, or even simply fraudulent practices. This terminological convenience is necessitated by the lack of any other common name for such statutes. These statutes are referred to in different states as consumer protection acts, consumer sales acts, unfair trade practices acts, deceptive and unfair trade practices acts, deceptive consumer sales acts, deceptive trade practices acts, and consumer fraud acts. In addition, commentators often call these statutes "Little FTC Acts," although this name is only precise for those statutes that parallel the FTC Act and prohibit "unfair methods of competition and unfair or deceptive acts or practices."

Most UDAP statutes were enacted in the ten-year span of the mid-1960s to the mid-1970s, but significant amendments and even some new statutes have been enacted since that period, and there continues to be legislative activity in this area. UDAP statutes apply to most consumer transactions and provide a flexible and practical consumer remedy for many abuses. These statutes are particularly important because, while the Federal Trade Commission Act is often viewed as sharply limiting the doctrine of *caveat emptor*,[3] the Act provides only FTC enforcement and not state or private enforcement. State UDAP statutes, by incorporating the FTC Act concepts of deception and unfairness and by providing significant state and private remedies, allow for widespread redress of marketplace misconduct and abuse of consumers.

A UDAP action is a statutory cause of action rather than a tort or contract action, although it has characteristics of both. It may be necessary for some purposes, such as determining what statute of limitations applies, however, to classify a UDAP claim as either tort or contract.[4]

Legislatures and courts have been careful to guarantee that UDAP statutes are broad and flexible, so that they can apply to creative, new forms of abusive business schemes in almost all types of consumer transactions.[5] Even when UDAP statutes enumerate specifically prohibited practices, most statutes also prohibit other unfair, unconscionable, and/or deceptive practices in more general terms. UDAP statutes typically do not require proof of the seller's fraudulent intent or knowledge. In some cases, consumer reliance, damage, or even actual deception is not a prerequisite to a UDAP action. Thus a UDAP claim is a far easier cause of action to prove than common law fraud.

In addition, almost all UDAP statutes authorize private damage actions. In order to encourage private litigation and deter merchant misconduct, many provide such special private remedies as attorney fees for prevailing consumers and punitive, treble, or minimum damage awards. The advisability of a UDAP action requires a close analysis of the

1 *See* Appx. A, *infra*.

2 15 U.S.C. § 45(a)(1).

3 Legal historians point out that *caveat emptor*, or let the buyer beware, is not an ancient doctrine. Medieval economic concepts included a "just price" and "a sound price warranting a sound commodity." The prices of many goods and services were fixed, allowing courts to examine contracts for their fairness independently of the terms agreed upon. However, emerging 19th-century commercial notions of markets, speculation, and business bargains gradually ended notions of contractual fairness apart from the original intent of the bargaining parties. Notions of the sanctity of contracts and *caveat emptor* thus only reached full development in the 19th century. At about the same time, the common law action of Trespass on the Case in the Nature of Deceit that applied even to negligent misrepresentations was replaced by common law actions for deceit or fraud that required defendant's knowledge of the falsity and intent to deceive. *See, e.g.*, Horwitz, *The Historical Foundation of Modern Contract Law*, 87 Harv. L. Rev. 917 (1974).

4 *See, e.g.*, Baldassari v. Public Fin. Trust, 369 Mass. 33, 337, N.E.2d 701 (1975); Standard Register Co. v. Bolton-Emerson, Inc., 38 Mass. App. Ct. 545, 649 N.E.2d 791 (1995).

5 *See, e.g.*, Luskin's, Inc. v. Consumer Protection Div., 353 Md. 335, 726 A.2d 702 (1999); Fletcher v. Don Foss of Cleveland, Inc., 90 Ohio App. 3d 82, 628 N.E.2d 60 (1993); Miller v. Keyser, 90 S.W.3d 712 (Tex. 2002). *See generally* § 2.1.3, *infra*.

facts and possible recoveries compared with the costs of litigation. UDAP statutes often provide a practical remedial approach for consumer complaints, as well as counterclaims and defenses to collection actions.

The breadth of UDAP statutes and lack of precise definition as to which practices are prohibited by them may discourage private litigation. However, this manual will describe a large body of Federal Trade Commission rules, guides and cases, state regulations and cases, statutory provisions, and other materials that can provide clear guidance in initiating most UDAP claims. Moreover, it is when a specific abusive practice has not been previously prohibited by statute or common law that a UDAP statute should be most relied upon. The broad, expansive, developing nature of UDAP statutes is their unique strength. Where a practice does not fall precisely under a debt collection act, state or federal credit legislation, warranty law, or other statutes, UDAP statutes can provide an all-purpose remedy. Almost any abusive business practice aimed at consumers is at least arguably a UDAP violation, unless the trade practice falls clearly outside the scope of the statute.

1.2 About This Manual

This manual encourages attorneys facing a collection action or dealing with a consumer's complaint to evaluate the applicability and practicality of a UDAP claim. Chapter 2 analyzes the scope of UDAP statutes and whether they are displaced by other state or federal laws. Chapters 3 through 5 are a guide to determining whether specific practices involve UDAP violations. Chapter 3 describes approaches to researching UDAP precedent, and Chapter 4 summarizes UDAP precedent of more general applicability.

Chapter 5 sets out UDAP precedent dealing with specific types of sellers or types of practices: extenders of credit, debt collectors, insurers, car dealers and repair shops, real estate sales, home improvement contracts, landlord-tenant practices, mobile home sale and parks, utilities and communications, home solicitation sales, telemarketing, health spas, buyers clubs, membership campgrounds, health care providers, funerals, *notarios* and other non-attorney providers of legal services, business opportunities, work at home schemes, pyramid schemes, and many others. The chapter discusses not only UDAP approaches in these areas, but also analyzes relevant FTC rules and other state laws such as Unfair Insurance Practices statutes, home solicitation sales statutes, and telemarketing statutes. It includes extensive investigation and discovery tips for automobile sales and future service contract transactions. Fraud by vocational schools, while discussed in Chapter 5, is treated in more detail in NCLC's *Student Loan Law* (2d ed. 2002 and Supp.).

Chapter 6 discusses the parties that may be liable for a UDAP claim and strategies for reaching a deep pocket. Chapter 7 covers UDAP litigation issues—is there a private right of action, statutes of limitation, retroactive application of statutory amendments, requirements as to damage, public interest, and notice, jurisdictional and constitutional questions, pleading and framing UDAP claims, discovery and factual investigation, trials, and settlement. It also addresses constitutional challenges to UDAP statutes that defendants may raise in litigation.

Chapter 8 discusses private UDAP remedies, including actual damages, statutory damages, multiple damages, injunctive and other equitable relief, attorney fees, and the effect of arbitration agreement on these remedies. Arbitration agreements are such an important issue, cutting across all areas of consumer law, that a separate NCLC manual, *Consumer Arbitration Agreements* (4th ed. 2004), is devoted to this topic. In Chapter 9 the manual addresses other private remedies for consumer abuses, such as the federal RICO statute, state RICO statutes, and cancellation and rescission under tort and contract law theories. Chapter 10 analyzes state UDAP enforcement remedies.

Appendix A is a statute-by-statute analysis of all state UDAP statutes and regulations. Appendix B reprints key Federal Trade Commission Rules. Appendix C reprints the federal RICO statute and summarizes state RICO legislation; Appendix D reprints several federal statutes and regulations dealing with telemarketing; and Appendix E analyzes state telemarketing statutes. Appendix F reprints portions of UCC Articles 3 and 9 that are relevant to the analysis of a creditor's holder-in-due-course status. Appendix G lists the many sample pleadings found on the companion CD-Rom, and Appendix H lists useful websites.

A unique feature of this manual is its companion CD-Rom, which contains the index, all the appendices, a quick reference to the complete NCLC series of legal practice manuals, the full text of or weblinks to most states' UDAP regulations, FTC interpretive letters and selected items from the regulatory history of key FTC rules, and over a hundred sample UDAP pleadings.

Another unique feature of this manual is web-based text searching. The search engine is located at www.consumerlaw.org. Clicking on "Keyword Search" brings up a screen that allows the user to search for any term or phrase in NCLC's manuals. The search can be confined to a single manual, or can extend to all NCLC's manuals. The search engine will indicate the pages in the manual where the term or phrase appears.

This function is not only the best way to locate the discussion of a particular topic, but is also an excellent way to find out where a particular case, statute, or regulation is discussed in NCLC's manuals. The search instructions explain how to use wildcards and how to search for phrases, for one term that is near another term, for either of two terms, and for one term that is not on the same page as another term.

This manual should be used in conjunction with its most current cumulative supplement; NCLC typically releases annual cumulative supplements. NCLC REPORTS, *Deceptive Practices & Warranties Edition* provides even more current UDAP developments.

Unreported cases with Clearinghouse numbers cited in NCLC manuals are available through the Sargent Shriver National Center on Poverty Law, 50 E. Washington St., Suite 500, Chicago, IL 60602, telephone 1-800-621-3256 or (312) 263-3830, fax (312) 263-3846, e-mail admin@povertylaw.org. Many documents are available on their website, www.povertylaw.org. There is a $60.00 annual access charge plus $10.00 per copy plus shipping for hard copies. Non-subscribers can order individual documents for $10.00 plus shipping.

1.3 General Preparation for UDAP Clients

There are a number of steps attorneys can take, *before* the client appears, to prepare themselves to press UDAP claims successfully. To stay abreast of the law, in addition to referring to this manual,[6] the attorney should keep a file of the most current version of the state's UDAP statute(s)[7] and all previous versions, indicating when they were superseded. California, Delaware, Georgia, Hawaii, Illinois, Maine, Minnesota, Nebraska, Ohio, Oklahoma, and Utah have two UDAP statutes, so both should be consulted. The attorney should collect relevant legislative history[8] and keep current on legislative developments.

Many state attorney general offices compile and publish case summaries, attorney general opinions, regulations, and enforcement proceedings. It is helpful to keep a file of these materials and new reported and unreported UDAP decisions.[9] Remember that UDAP decisions may appear in West's Bankruptcy Reporter and other federal reporters, as well as a state's own reporter system.

As with other forms of legal research, the Internet is an increasingly important resource for UDAP precedent. For example, the FTC has its own website at www.ftc.gov. An extraordinary site is found at www.consumerworld.org. Another useful site is www.advertisinglaw.com. NCLC's own site is found at www.consumerlaw.org. These are only a sampling of the many relevant sites that are continually being developed relating to UDAP and other consumer law.[10]

Manuals or texts on a particular state's consumer protection laws have also been published in several states. These include Stern, *Business and Professional Code Section 17200 Practice* (TRG Press 2003) (available from TRG press, One Embarcadero Center, Suite 2600, San Francisco, CA 94111, telephone (415) 398-3344, fax (415) 956-0439); Langer, Morgan & Belt, *The Connecticut Unfair Trade Practices Act* (1994) (available from Connecticut Law Tribune, 201 Ann St., Hartford, CT 06103, telephone 860-527-7900) (currently out of print); Greaney, *Chapter 93A Rights and Remedies* (1989 with 1999 Supp.) (available from Massachusetts Continuing Legal Education, Inc., 10 Winter Pl., Boston, MA 02108-4751, telephone (617) 482-2205, fax (617) 482-9498); Newman & Imholz, *Caveat Venditor* (2d ed. 1994) (available from Julius Blumberg, Inc., 62 White St., New York, NY 10013, telephone (212) 431-5000) (New York law); Williams, *Ohio Consumer Law* (West 2004 ed.) (available from West, 610 Opperman Dr., Eagan, MN 55123, telephone 1-800-344-5009); Carter, *Pennsylvania Consumer Law* (2d ed. 2003 and Supp.) (available from George T. Bisel Co., 710 S. Washington Square, Philadelphia, PA 19106, telephone 1-800-247-3526); Alderman, *The Lawyer's Guide to the Texas Deceptive Trade Practices Act* (2d ed., with annual supplement) (available from Lexis Law Publishing, 1275 Broadway, Albany, NY 12204, telephone 1-800-223-1940); Moll and Alderman, *Alderman's Texas Commercial and Consumer Laws Annotated* (2004 ed., with new edition published every year) (available from Imprimatur Press, 2351 West Northwest Highway, Suite 3297, Dallas, TX 75220, telephone 1-800-811-6725); Bragg and Curry, *DTPA Forms and Practice Guide* (James Publ'g Co. 1999) (Texas law) (available from James Publishing, 3505 Cadillac Ave., Suite H, Costa Mesa, CA 92626, telephone (800) 440-4780 or (714) 755-5450); Texas Practice Guide Series, Vol. 28A, *Texas Consumer Law Handbook* (West Publ'g Co. 1999) (available from Houston Bar Association, 1001 Fanin, Suite 1300, Houston, TX 77002, telephone (713) 759-1133, fax (713) 759-1710). Several state attorney general offices or consumer protection departments have also prepared handbooks that may be available to practitioners, or may post helpful materials on a website.

6 This manual has been cited in over 80 law review and journal articles, and in a number of reported decisions, including: Guillermerty v. Secretary of Educ., 241 F. Supp. 2d 727 (E.D. Mich. 2002); Bird v. John Chezik Homerun, Inc., 2000 WL 49333 (W.D. Mo. Jan. 18, 2000); Crews v. Altavista Motors, Inc., 65 F. Supp. 2d 388 (W.D. Va. 1999); Fisher v. Bristol-Meyers Squibb Co., 181 F.R.D. 365 (N.D. Ill. 1998); Washington Mutual Bank v. Superior Court, 82 Cal. Rptr. 2d 564 (Cal. App. 1999); Walter v. Hall, 940 P.2d 991 (Colo. App. 1996); Luskins, Inc. v. Consumer Protection Division, 726 A.2d 702 (Md. 1999); Doody v. Worthington, 1991 WL 757571 (Ohio Mun. Apr. 10, 1991); Patterson v. Beall, 19 P.3d 839 (Okla. 2000); Walls v. American Tobacco Co., 11 P.3d 626 (Okla. 2000); Singleton v. Stokes Motors, Inc., 595 S.E.2d 461 (S.C. 2004); Gansevoort v. Russell, 949 S.W.2d 293 (Tenn. 1997); Alduridi v. Community Trust Bank, N.A., 1999 WL 969644 (Tenn. App. Oct. 26, 1999); State v. International Collection Service, Inc., 594 A.2d 426 (Vt. 1991).

7 *See* Appx. A, *infra*.

8 *See* § 3.4.2, *infra*.

9 *See* § 3.4.3.1, *infra*.

10 *See* Appendix H, *infra* for a list of useful websites.

Research materials that are helpful for keeping track of FTC developments include Title 16 of the *Code of Federal Regulations* (CFR) for existing FTC rules and guides;[11] the *Federal Register* for new rules, guides, enforcement statements, consent orders, and other actions;[12] NCLC REPORTS, *Deceptive Practices and Warranty Edition* for recent developments; and *CCH Trade Regulation Reporter* for both recent developments and older precedent. Copies of the FTC rules most frequently applicable to UDAP cases are found in Appendices B and D, *infra*, and on the companion CD-Rom to this volume. The CD-Rom also includes selected administrative history documents and FTC interpretative letters for these rules.

NCLC offers several other manuals that focus in more detail on specific unfair or deceptive practices or on litigation issues common to many types of consumer cases:

- National Consumer Law Center, *Automobile Fraud* (2d ed. 2003 and Supp.), which analyzes federal and state laws regulating odometers, lemon laundering, title branding, and disclosure of damage, as well as warranty, fraud, and UDAP approaches to the sale of vehicles with rollbacks, concealed wreck or flood damage, undisclosed prior use, grey market origin, or other negative history.
- National Consumer Law Center, *Student Loan Law* (2d ed. 2002 and Supp.), a unique resource on trade school fraud and student loan debt.
- National Consumer Law Center, *Consumer Arbitration Agreements* (4th ed. 2004), a detailed exploration of challenges to arbitration agreements, including sample briefs and discovery both in hard copy and on the companion CD-Rom.
- National Consumer Law Center, *Consumer Class Actions* (5th ed. 2002 and Supp.), a practical guide to class actions, including dozens of sample complaints, discovery, motions, briefs, class notices, and settlement papers, both in hard copy and on the companion CD-Rom.

Legal Services programs often offer consumer law training sessions on a state, regional or national basis that include presentations on UDAP issues. State bar associations or the state attorney general's office may offer similar programs. Experienced attorneys should develop in-house training programs for new attorneys and acquaint them with the uses of the UDAP statute and the availability of this manual.

Another way to expand the knowledge and use of UDAP statutes is to participate in educational programs to inform the bar and judges as to the expansive use and legislative intent behind the state's UDAP statute. Attorneys should also consider joining the consumer section of the state bar association and participating in any newsletter or other publications of that section. Another idea is to write or encourage others to write law review articles or a consumer law manual that interprets the state UDAP statute and that can be cited in later cases. It is helpful to develop a working relationship with the state attorney general's consumer protection division, the local or state consumer protection agency, and the regional office of the Federal Trade Commission, thus keeping abreast of recent case decisions and consumer problems.

Expert witnesses are often critical to a UDAP case, but they may be difficult to find. It is helpful to locate expert witnesses in areas of common consumer abuse, such as automobile condition and home improvements, in advance of actual cases. The attorney can also gather other helpful factual material, such as standards for various consumer goods and services promulgated by governmental bodies and trade organizations.

1.4 Determining Whether There Is a UDAP Approach to the Client's Problem

1.4.1 Transactions Amenable to a UDAP Approach

In all situations where the client comes to the attorney with a consumer problem, the attorney should consider whether there is a UDAP "angle"—there usually is. The attorney should look for UDAP approaches to "non-consumer" cases as well, such as landlord-tenant cases,[13] migrant farm worker cases,[14] nursing home, HMO, or assisted living facility cases,[15] mobile home park cases,[16] and the provision of unregulated fuels[17] or utility service.[18]

Automobile and mobile home repair, warranty, sale, and lease practices are typically covered by UDAP statutes.[19] So are home improvement scams,[20] door-to-door sales,[21] mail order problems,[22] telemarketing,[23] unsolicited goods,[24] insurance sales, and refusals to pay insurance benefits.[25] Real

11 These materials can also generally be found on the FTC's website, www.ftc.gov.

12 The Federal Register is available on-line at www.access.gpo.gov/nara/.

13 *See* §§ 2.2.6, 5.5.2, *infra.*

14 *See* §§ 2.2.7, 5.5.4, *infra.*

15 *See* §§ 5.11.3, 5.11.4, 5.11.5, *infra.*

16 *See* §§ 2.2.6, 5.5.1, *infra.*

17 *See* § 5.6.8, *infra.*

18 *See* § 5.6.8, *infra.*

19 *See* § 5.4, *infra.*

20 *See* § 5.6.1, *infra.*

21 *See* § 5.8.2, *infra.*

22 *See* § 5.8.1, *infra.*

23 *See* § 5.9, *infra.*

24 *See* § 5.8.4, *infra.*

25 *See* §§ 2.3.1, 5.3, *infra.*

estate sales, campground resorts, shell homes, timeshares, and other realty related practices are usually also covered.[26]

UDAP statutes usually apply to a host of abuses at the default or collection stages of a credit transaction:

- Collection practices by a collection agency or creditor;[27]
- Collection suits in inconvenient venues;[28]
- Sewer service or other abuse of process;[29]
- Repossession;[30] and
- Foreclosure.[31]

UDAP statutes also usually apply to innumerable abusive credit practices:

- Credit terms;
- Finance company or bank practices;
- Credit finders and credit repair companies;
- Loan brokers;
- Consumer reporting agencies;
- Pawnbrokers;
- Credit card practices;
- Loan flipping;
- Refinancings;
- Debt consolidations, fraudulent credit counseling or debt adjusting, mortgage loans, and mortgage assistance scams.[32]

UDAP statutes may apply to contracts written in an overly complex manner or in a language not spoken in the sales transaction, warranty and contract misrepresentations, and even breaches of contract or warranties.[33] Attorneys should pay special attention to harsh terms found in standard form contracts. The FTC and the courts are developing an unfairness theory that prohibits many overreaching terms in consumer contracts.[34] Thus forfeiture of deposits or harsh cancellation penalties may be unfair.[35]

UDAP counterclaims are often a consumer's best defense to a creditor's collection action on a health spa, membership campground, buying club, or other future-service related contract[36] as well as loans and credit sales. Usually employment agency scams, phony employment opportunity offers, or over-inflated business opportunity, franchise, or investment schemes can be remedied by a UDAP claim.[37]

26 *See* §§ 2.2.5, 2.2.6, 2.2.8, 5.5, *infra*.
27 *See* §§ 2.2.2, 5.1.1, 5.1.1.5, *infra*.
28 *See* § 5.1.1.4, *infra*.
29 *See* § 5.1.1.4, *infra*.
30 *See* §§ 2.2.2, 5.1.1.5, *infra*.
31 *Id.*
32 *See* §§ 2.2.1, 5.1, *infra*.
33 *See* § 5.2, *infra*.
34 *See* § 5.2.3, *infra*.
35 *See* §§ 5.1.1.2, 5.1.1.3, 5.2.3, *infra*.
36 *See* § 5.10, *infra*.
37 *See* § 5.13, *infra*.

1.4.2 Look at All Aspects of a Transaction

Whatever type of problem the consumer client first discusses, the attorney should explore potential UDAP violations in all aspects of the transaction—advertising, sales presentations, the consummation of the sale, the credit terms, the seller's performance, and subsequent debt collection practices. For example, if a client complains of debt collection harassment, examine not only the collection practices, but also the underlying sales transaction and the credit terms. If the client's concern involves sales misrepresentations, also investigate the credit terms and collection tactics. If a client is being sued for a deficiency after a car repossession, UDAP counterclaims may involve the original car sale, subsequent warranty performance on the car, the credit terms, debt collection practices, and repossession techniques.

As a result, in every case, whether the client is being sued or wishes to sue a seller, the attorney should determine whether there are abusive debt collection practices, simulation of legal process, deceptive collection letters or notices, other collection misrepresentations, or abuse of legal process. Review the credit documents in search of unfair or oppressive credit terms or creditor remedies.

Also consider the underlying sales transaction from which the consumer debt arose. Was there deception in advertising or sales representations, was what was promised never delivered, was the price unconscionable, was the contract unfair on its face, or did the seller do anything else unfair or deceptive? Also do not forget to consider the seller's media advertising and sales brochures, even if a case primarily involves oral misrepresentations made by the seller to the client. If the sale conforms to the sales documents, the advocate should explore for deceptive oral claims. Remember that ambiguous statements, half-truths, and literally true statements can deceive.[38] Claims inconsistent with written sales documents may not be actionable under a contract theory, but are under a UDAP theory.[39] Make sure to review the relevant sections of Chapter 5, *infra*, that detail common deceptive practices found in particular types of transactions.

Even where the consumer is not being sued by the original seller, but only by an assignee or a creditor to whom the seller referred the consumer, the consumer can raise all defenses and UDAP counterclaims that the consumer could have raised against the seller.[40] The consumer should also consider bringing the seller in as a third party defendant.

1.4.3 Apply UDAP Standards Expansively

UDAP liability may exist if the consumer was in any way misled in the sales transaction, taking into account the

38 *See* § 4.2.13, *infra*.
39 *See* § 4.2.15, *infra*.
40 *See* § 6.6, *infra*.

consumer's level of sophistication.[41] Intent, scienter, bad faith, even actual reliance often need not be shown.[42] Even if nothing stated was deceptive, the seller may be liable if something important was not stated, that is, if there was a material nondisclosure.[43] This is just as deceptive as a misrepresentation. Silence can be deceptive.

Look to see if a UDAP statute specifically prohibits a practice. Also consider if the practice violates a state's UDAP regulations or other state or federal law,[44] or is just plain deceptive.

If the practice is not specifically prohibited by a statute or regulation and the practice is not deceptive, many state UDAP statutes also proscribe unfair or unconscionable conduct. Oppressive sales techniques, unfair adhesion contract provisions, overreaching creditor remedies, and similarly one-sided or abusive practices can then be challenged as unfair or unconscionable practices.[45]

This manual, particularly in Chapters 4 and 5, *infra*, details numerous UDAP cases finding specific practices unfair or deceptive. But remember that UDAP statutes should be liberally and expansively applied to new forms of merchant misconduct.[46] UDAP statutes are meant to remedy marketplace imbalances, and serious consumer abuses of almost any form are arguably UDAP violations.[47] That a particular practice has never been prohibited should not deter an attorney from pursuing a UDAP case.

1.5 Alternatives to a UDAP Action

While a practitioner's first instinct should always be to look for a UDAP approach to a case, the attorney should not neglect alternative claims. Such claims may provide superior remedies or federal court jurisdiction. In other cases, where a UDAP statute's scope, statute of limitations, or other limitation may prevent a UDAP claim, alternative claims are a necessity.

One of the most important alternative claims for general patterns of fraud or collection of an unlawful debt is the federal RICO statute. A federal RICO claim will allow federal court jurisdiction and provide treble damages and attorney fees. A state RICO claim may provide similar remedies or even punitive damages. But a RICO case is complex and should be undertaken only after careful consideration. The application of federal and state RICO statutes to consumer fraud is analyzed in Chapter 9 of this manual.[48]

41 *See* § 4.2.11, *infra.*
42 *See* §§ 4.2.4, 4.2.5, 4.2.6, 4.2.12, *infra.*
43 *See* § 4.2.14, *infra.*
44 *See* § 3.2, *infra.*
45 *See* §§ 4.3, 4.4, *infra.*
46 *See* §§ 2.1.3, 3.1.2, *infra.*
47 *See* § 3.3.4, *infra.*
48 *See* §§ 9.2, 9.3, *infra.*

Other alternatives (or additional counts) to a UDAP case are claims of common law fraud, breach of contract, breach of warranty, rescission, restitution, revocation of acceptance, cancellation, violation of a credit repair statute, or unjust enrichment.[49] Common law fraud and other tort remedies are important because they allow a punitive damages claim. Misrepresentation as a contract *defense* is often overlooked, but this defense may not require a showing of intent or knowledge, as would an affirmative claim of fraud.

At the time of the interview, the attorney should obtain permission from the client to report the deceptive practices to a government agency. If litigation is not feasible, the attorney can explore this other avenue.[50]

1.6 Determining Whether a UDAP Claim Should Be Pursued

In a case of first impression, how compelling the facts are may have an important impact on the development of UDAP law in the state. Similarly, the opposing attorney, the defendant, and the court deciding the case may all have an important impact on the case's outcome and thus the creation of UDAP precedent.

In collection cases, if a UDAP count is not brought as a counterclaim, state compulsory counterclaim rules may foreclose the consumer's subsequent assertion of the claim. UDAP counterclaims to collection actions often require only a minimum of effort before trial and can create favorable settlements where the counterclaim is well founded and alleges a clear violation of the statute. Of course, if a case goes to trial, extensive and early preparation is critical.

Attorneys should consider whether the statute provides for attorney fees and multiple, minimum, or punitive damages.[51] If the UDAP statute does not authorize punitive damages, adding a common law deceit count will usually make punitive damages available. The size of the seller's potential exposure will affect the defendant's willingness to settle. Of course, the certainty that the seller's practice is indeed a UDAP violation is also important. The nature of the opposing counsel and the defendant will also determine the course of settlement negotiations.

Where a consumer complaint involves a small amount of damage, the deception is not widespread or egregious, and the issues are essentially factual, not legal, the consumer may decide to go to small claims court on his or her own. An attorney can assist the client in drafting a complaint and other documents necessary for the small claims court action. Another option is referring the client to a consumer action group or similar self-help consumer organization.

49 *See* §§ 9.5, 9.6, *infra.*
50 The addresses of various governmental agencies can be found on the companion CD-Rom to this volume.
51 *See* §§ 8.4.1, 8.4.2, 8.4.3, 8.8, *infra.*

Sending a forceful demand letter to the seller before drafting a complaint may result in a favorable settlement offer, eliminating the need to determine whether to pursue a case to litigation. However, some advocates believe that demand letters tip a litigant's hand too early. Some states require a demand letter before a UDAP claim can be filed.

If the debt is roughly equal to the possible UDAP recovery, and the client has stopped paying the debt, one course of action is to await a collection action, bringing UDAP counterclaims at that time. If the UDAP statute of limitations is an issue, the consumer attorney must be clear about state courts' treatment of recoupment claims before advising this approach.[52] In addition, a recoupment claim can not exceed the amount being sought on the debt, which may diminish the consumer's potential recovery where treble or punitive damages are available. Bringing an affirmative suit may also be a stronger posture for a litigant in front of the court.

The attorney should determine if a class action is a practical way to pursue a case even if an individual case is not feasible. Statutory damages or multiple damages for each class member and attorney fees make a class action attractive, particularly since it is often easier to show a common UDAP fact pattern than a common pattern in a common law fraud case. Standard form contracts, media advertising, print claims, widespread nondisclosure, or standardized sales pitches may make a UDAP class action appropriate.[53]

52 *See* § 7.3.4, *infra*.

53 *See* § 8.5, *infra*.

Chapter 2 UDAP Scope

2.1 General Principles

2.1.1 Determining a UDAP Statute's Scope

A preliminary issue that must be considered in each UDAP case is whether the challenged practice is within the statute's scope. While a UDAP statute's greatest utility is its general applicability, in a surprising number of cases the statute may not apply. UDAP scope varies from state to state, but in some states the UDAP statute will not apply to credit, debt-collection, landlord-tenant, realty, securities or business opportunity practices. Some statutes also exempt from coverage insurance companies, utilities, banks, or other regulated industries.

It is critical to examine closely all provisions in the state UDAP statute to determine its scope. Even though the statute may broadly prohibit all deceptive practices "in trade or commerce" in one section, the statute, in important operative sections, may further limit the scope of private actions or certain private remedies by the use of such terms as "consumer," "supplier," "consumer transaction," "sale," or "goods or services."

The scope of these terms, including "trade or commerce," may be further narrowed by the statute's definition of that term. Consequently, a UDAP statute's definitional section, usually at the beginning or end of the statute, is often critical in analyzing scope issues. Other statutes may also contain a broader definition of a term used in the UDAP statutes and courts may adopt that definition.[1]

UDAP statutes typically also include a section exempting certain practices, such as those permitted by law, or exempting certain merchants, such as insurance companies, banks, or printers and publishers who disseminate advertisements without knowledge of the deception. Statutes may exempt companies regulated by state agencies or regulated by a specific section of the state's code, requiring reference to this other code section.

The first step then is to read the statute itself carefully. The current versions of all state UDAP statutes are summarized at Appendix A, *infra*, along with links to websites that have the full text of the statutes. Since the most common aspect of a UDAP statute to be amended is its scope, a careful analysis requires use of both the most up-to-date version of the statute, and the version of the statute in force at the time of the challenged practice. Since courts will generally not retroactively apply amendments affecting a UDAP statute's scope, UDAP coverage issues are determined by the version of the statute in effect at the time of the challenged practice.[2]

In using out-of-state case law to interpret the scope of one's own UDAP statute, remember that courts in these cases are interpreting different scope provisions. Make sure to compare the correct version of the other state's statute. An out-of-state case may be interpreting a version of its state UDAP statute no longer in effect, since controversial court decisions often trigger remedial amendments to UDAP statutes' scope provisions.

This chapter analyzes scope issues in five categories. Section 2.1 sets forth general principles for analyzing the scope of UDAP statutes and examines judicial interpretations of common statutory terms, such as "trade or commerce," "goods," "merchandise," "services," and "personal, family, or household use." Section 2.2 addresses whether certain generic types of transactions are outside the scope of some UDAP statutes, including transactions involving:

- Credit;[3]
- Debt collection;[4]
- No actual sale[5] or post-sale practices;[6]
- Real property, mobile homes, and landlord-tenant relations;[7]
- Migrant farmworker camps,[8] and campground and other club memberships;[9]
- Pyramid sales, franchises, investments and securities, work-at-home schemes, and business opportunities;[10]

1 Watkins v. Alvey, 549 N.E.2d 74 (Ind. Ct. App. 1990) (using pyramid sales statute's broader definition of "supplier" in UDAP suit against pyramid promoter).

2 *See* § 7.4, *infra.*

3 *See* § 2.2.1, *infra.*

4 *See* § 2.2.2, *infra.*

5 *See* § 2.2.3, *infra.*

6 *See* § 2.2.4, *infra.*

7 *See* §§ 2.2.5, 2.2.6, *infra.*

8 *See* § 2.2.7, *infra.*

9 *See* § 2.2.8, *infra.*

10 *See* § 2.2.9, *infra.*

- Employer/employee relations and internal business disputes;[11] and
- Personal injury suits.[12]

Section 2.3 examines whether certain types of sellers fall outside certain UDAP statutes' coverage:

- Insurance companies;[13]
- Utilities;[14]
- Those regulated by other statutes and regulations;[15]
- Nonmerchants,[16] nonprofit organizations,[17] government and quasi-government agencies;[18]
- Printers and the media;[19]
- Wholesalers and other indirect parties;[20]
- Lawyers,[21] medical professionals,[22] and other professionals;[23] and
- Out-of-state transactions.[24]

Section 2.4 considers whether unusual types of consumers are covered by UDAP statutes, including:

- Recipients of insurance payments, third-party beneficiaries, donees, assignees, and other third parties;[25]
- Deceased consumers;[26]
- Loan guarantors;[27]
- Out-of-state residents;[28]
- Merchants, corporations, and government entities;[29] and
- Investigators.[30]

Section 2.5 analyzes whether certain federal laws or actions preempt state UDAP claims.

2.1.2 Burden of Proof

UDAP complaints should allege that the consumer transaction is covered by the UDAP statute. The consumer will have the burden of proving that the UDAP statute applies.[31] For example, where a statute applies only to "consumers," the plaintiff must allege facts which show the plaintiff to be a person within the statutory definition of "consumer."[32] Unless there is a factual dispute, the question of "consumer" status is a question of law.[33] Nevertheless, a court may infer that the plaintiff is a "consumer" from the totality of the pleadings,[34] or find that facts prove the plaintiff to be a consumer even though it was never pleaded.[35] On the other hand, the burden of claiming a specific exemption from the UDAP statute will be on the party claiming that exemption.[36]

2.1.3 Liberal Construction of UDAP Scope Sections

The rule that UDAP statutes are remedial and must be liberally construed applies to the scope sections of the statute just as much as to its substantive provisions.[37] Defi-

11 *See* § 2.2.10, *infra.*
12 *See* § 2.2.11, *infra.*
13 *See* § 2.3.1, *infra.*
14 *See* § 2.3.2, *infra.*
15 *See* § 2.3.3, *infra.*
16 *See* § 2.3.4, *infra.*
17 *See* § 2.3.5, *infra.*
18 *See* § 2.3.6, *infra.*
19 *See* § 2.3.7, *infra.*
20 *See* § 2.3.8, *infra.*
21 *See* § 2.3.9, *infra.*
22 *See* § 2.3.10, *infra.*
23 *See* § 2.3.11, *infra.*
24 *See* § 2.3.12, *infra.*
25 *See* § 2.4.1, *infra.*
26 *See* § 2.4.2, *infra.*
27 *See* § 2.4.3, *infra.*
28 *See* § 2.4.4, *infra.*
29 *See* § 2.4.5, *infra.*
30 *See* § 2.4.6, *infra.*

31 Gapas v. Hambleton, 1980 Ohio App. LEXIS 11295 (Nov. 20, 1980); Farmers & Merchants State Bank v. Ferguson, 617 S.W.2d 918 (Tex. 1981); St. John v. Barker, 638 S.W.2d 239 (Tex. App. 1982).

32 Fireman's Fund Ins. Co. v. Murchison, 937 F.2d 204 (5th Cir. 1991) (Texas law); Winkler v. Interim Servs., Inc., 36 F. Supp. 2d 1026 (M.D. Tenn. 1999); Cameron v. Terrell & Garrett, Inc., 618 S.W.2d 535 (Tex. 1981); GTE Mobilnet of South Texas Ltd. P'ship v. Telecell Cellular, Inc., 955 S.W.2d 286 (Tex. App. 1997); Clary Corp. v. Smith, 949 S.W.2d 452 (Tex. App. 1997); Apple Imports, Inc. v. Koole, 945 S.W.2d 895 (Tex. App. 1997); Taylor v. GWR Operating Co., 820 S.W.2d 908 (Tex. App. 1991); River Oaks Townhomes Owners' Ass'n v. Bunt, 712 S.W.2d 529 (Tex. App. 1986); Reed v. Israel National Oil Co., 681 S.W.2d 228 (Tex. App. 1984). *Cf.* Mendoza v. American National Ins. Co., 932 S.W.2d 605 (Tex. App. 1996) (although consumer status is necessary under Texas UDAP, plaintiff need not prove consumer status to sue under Texas UNIP).

33 Great Plains Trust Co. v. Morgan Stanley Dean Witter & Co., 313 F.3d 305 (5th Cir. 2002); Apple Imports, Inc. v. Koole, 945 S.W.2d 895 (Tex. App. 1997); Clary Corp. v. Smith, 949 S.W.2d 452 (Tex. App. 1997); GTE Mobilnet of South Texas Ltd. P'ship v. Telecell Cellular, Inc., 955 S.W.2d 286 (Tex. App. 1997); Garner v. Corpus Christi National Bank, 944 S.W.2d 469 (Tex. App. 1997).

34 Reed v. Israel National Oil Co., 681 S.W.2d 228 (Tex. App. 1984); Ridco v. Sexton, 623 S.W.2d 792 (Tex. Civ. App. 1981).

35 Reed v. Israel National Oil Co., 681 S.W.2d 228 (Tex. App. 1984); Lubbock Mortgage & Inv. Co. v. Thomas, 626 S.W.2d 611 (Tex. Civ. App. 1981).

36 Turner v. Johnson & Johnson, 549 F. Supp. 807 (D. Mass. 1982); Eckman v. Centennial Sav. Bank, 784 S.W.2d 672 (Tex. 1990); Challenge Transportation Inc. v. J-Gem Transportation Inc., 717 S.W.2d 115 (Tex. App. 1986).

37 *See, e.g.*, Smith v. Commercial Banking Corp., 866 F.2d 576 (3d Cir. 1989) (Pa. law); Daly v. Harris, 215 F. Supp. 2d 1098 (D. Haw. 2002); Rachoza v. Gallas & Schultz, 1998 U.S. Dist. LEXIS 5018 (D. Kan. Mar. 23, 1998); Nichols Motorcycle Supply Inc. v. Dunlop Tire Corp., 913 F. Supp. 1088 (N.D. Ill. 1995); Iadanza v. Mather, 820 F. Supp. 1371 (D. Utah 1993); Chalfin v. Beverly Enterprises, Inc., 741 F. Supp. 1162 (E.D. Pa.

nitions in the UDAP statute are to be construed in light of the statute's remedial purpose to protect the public.[38] This argument has particular strength in those states where the legislative history shows that the UDAP statute was intended to be among the strongest consumer protection laws in the nation.[39] UDAP statutes that are broadly written apply to "virtually all economic activity."[40] Exceptions to UDAP statutes must be narrowly construed.[41] Thus, even though the consumer has the burden of proving that the UDAP statute applies, the court should adopt a liberal interpretation of the statute's scope and should resolve any doubts in favor of coverage.

Where a UDAP statute's scope section uses the term "includes," other items are includable, though not specifically enumerated.[42] Unless there is a clear legislative intent to exempt a transaction, the practice is subject to the UDAP statute.[43] Texas courts, for example, have repeatedly stressed that it is the relationship of the consumer to the transaction, and not the relationship of the consumer to the defendant, that determines whether the Texas UDAP statute applies.[44]

2.1.4 Interpretations of "Trade or Commerce"

A number of UDAP statutes patterned after the FTC Act cover any practice in "trade or commerce." As a general rule, "trade or commerce" is a broad term applying to

1989); State v. O'Neill Investigations, Inc., 609 P.2d 520 (Alaska 1980); Schnall v. Hertz Corp., 78 Cal. App. 4th 1144, 93 Cal. Rptr. 2d 439 (2000); Showpiece Homes Corp. v. Assurance Co. of Am., 38 P.3d 47 (Colo. 2001); Hall v. Walter, 969 P.2d 224 (Colo. 1998); Norman Gershman's Things to Wear, Inc. v. Mercedez-Benz of N. Am., 558 A.2d 1066 (Del. Super. Ct. 1989); Schauer v. Gen. Motors Acceptance Corp., 819 So. 2d 809 (Fla. App. 2002); People *ex rel.* Daley v. Datacom Sys. Corp., 146 Ill. 2d 1, 585 N.E.2d 51 (1991); Scott v. Association for Childbirth at Home International, 88 Ill. 2d 279, 430 N.E.2d 1012 (1982); Bank One Milwaukee v. Sanchez, 336 Ill. App. 3d 319, 783 N.E.2d 217 (2003); Carter v. Mueller, 120 Ill. App. 3d 314, 457 N.E.2d 1335 (1983); State v. Brotherhood Bank & Trust Co., 649 P.2d 419 (Kan. Ct. App. 1982); Slaney v. Westwood Auto, Inc., 366 Mass. 688, 322 N.E.2d 768 (1975); Forton v. Laszar, 239 Mich. App. 711, 609 N.W.2d 850 (2000); Price v. Long Realty, Inc., 199 Mich. App. 461, 502 N.W.2d 337 (1993); Boubelik v. Liberty State Bank, 553 N.W.2d 393 (Minn. 1996) (UDAP statute must be construed liberally, but loans not covered; the next year, the legislature amended the statute to include loans); Kavky v. Herbalife Int'l, 359 N.J. Super. 497, 820 A.2d 677 (App. Div. 2003); Blatterfein v. Larken Assocs., 323 N.J. Super. 167, 732 A.2d 555 (App. Div. 1999); New Mea Constr. Corp. v. Harper, 203 N.J. Super. 486, 497 A.2d 534 (App. Div. 1985); Polonetsky v. Better Homes Depot, Inc., 185 Misc. 2d 282, 712 N.Y.S.2d 801 (Sup. Ct. 2000), *rev'd*, 279 A.D.2d 418, 720 N.Y.S.2d 59 (2001) (holding that city UDAP ordinance did not cover real estate sales), *rev'd, complaint reinstated*, 97 N.Y.2d 46, 760 N.E.2d 1274 (2001) (real estate sale that was bound up with services was covered by city UDAP ordinance); Connolly v. Wecare Distributors, Inc., 143 Misc. 2d 637, 541 N.Y.S.2d 163 (Sup. Ct. 1989), *aff'd mem.*, 152 A.D.2d 965, 544 N.Y.S.2d 758 (4th Dept. 1989); State *ex rel.* Montgomery v. Purchase Plus Buyer's Group, Inc., 2002 Ohio App. LEXIS 1966 (Apr. 25, 2002); Elder v. Fischer, 717 N.E.2d 730 (Ohio App. 1998); Broadnax v. Greene Credit Serv., 118 Ohio App. 3d 881, 694 N.E.2d 167 (1997); Chiropractic Clinic of Solon v. Kutsko, 92 Ohio App. 3d 608, 636 N.E.2d 422 (1994); Celebrezze v. Howard, 77 Ohio App. 3d 387, 602 N.E.2d 665 (1991); Commonwealth v. Monumental Properties, Inc., 459 Pa. 450, 329 A.2d 812 (1974); Myint v. Allstate Ins. Co., 970 S.W.2d 920 (Tenn. 1998); Skinner v. Steele, 730 S.W.2d 335 (Tenn. Ct. App. 1987); Miller v. Keyser, 90 S.W.3d 712 (Tex. 2002); E.F. Hutton & Co. v. Youngblood, 708 S.W.2d 865 (Tex. App. 1986); Kieft v. Becker, 58 Va. Cir. 171 (2002); Elkins v. Microsoft Corp., 817 A.2d 9 (Vt. 2002) (UDAP statute intended to have "as broad a reach as possible"); State v. Custom Pools, 556 A.2d 72 (Vt. 1988). *But see* Levine v. First Nat'l Bank of Commerce, 845 So. 2d 1189 (La. App. 2003) (applying "reasonably strict" construction to UDAP statute's scope provision).

38 Scott v. Association for Childbirth at Home International, 88 Ill. 2d 279, 430 N.E.2d 1012 (1982); Lemelledo v. Beneficial Management Corp., 150 N.J. 255, 696 A.2d 546 (1997); New Mea Constr. Corp. v. Harper, 203 N.J. Super. 486, 497 A.2d 534 (App. Div. 1985); Saenz Motors v. Big H. Auto Auction, Inc., 665 S.W.2d 756 (Tex. 1984).

39 Boyes v. Greenwich Boat Works, Inc., 27 F. Supp. 2d 543 (D.N.J. 1998); Moran, Shuster, Carignan & Knierim v. August, 43 Conn. Supp. 431, 657 A.2d 736 (1994), *aff'd on other grounds*, 232 Conn. 756, 657 A.2d 229 (1995); Zorba Contractors, Inc. v. Housing Authority of City of Newark, 282 N.J. Super. 430, 660 A.2d 550 (1995).

40 Karlin v. IVF Am., Inc., 93 N.Y.2d 282, 712 N.E.2d 662 (1999).

41 Edmonds v. John L. Scott Real Estate, Inc., 942 P.2d 1072 (Wash. Ct. App. 1997).

42 State *ex rel.* Nixon v. Estes, 108 S.W.3d 795 (Mo. App. 2003) (definition that trade or commerce "includes" certain activities is term of enlargement rather than limitation); Zorba Contractors, Inc. v. Housing Authority of City of Newark, 282 N.J. Super. 430, 660 A.2d 550 (1995).

43 Normand Josef Enterprises v. Connecticut Bank, 230 Conn. 486, 646 A.2d 1289 (1994); Barry v. N.J. State Highway Authority, 245 N.J. Super. 302, 585 A.2d 420 (1990); Elder v. Fischer, 717 N.E.2d 730 (Ohio App. 1998); Culbreth v. Lawrence J. Miller, Inc., 328 Pa. Super. 374, 477 A.2d 491 (1984); Fancher v. Benson, 580 A.2d 51 (Vt. 1990).

44 Chamrad v. Volvo Cars of N. Am., 145 F.3d 671 (5th Cir. 1998) (Texas law); Park v. Nova Container Freight Station, 1998 U.S. Dist. LEXIS 15551 (N.D. Tex. Sept. 23, 1998); United States v. Sullivan, 1998 WL 223709 (N.D. Tex. 1998); Insurance Co. of N. Am. v. Morris, 981 S.W.2d 667 (Tex. 1998); Moritz v. Bueche, 980 S.W.2d 849 (Tex. App. 1998); Hendricks v. Grant Thornton International, 973 S.W.2d 348 (Tex. App. 1998); Segura v. Abbott Laboratories, Inc., 873 S.W.2d 399 (Tex. App. 1994), *rev'd on other grounds*, 907 S.W.2d 503 (Tex. 1995); Parkway Co. v. Woodruff, 857 S.W.2d 903 (Tex. App. 1993); Hedley Feedlot, Inc. v. Weatherly Trust, 855 S.W.2d 826 (Tex. App. 1993); D/FW Commercial Roofing Co. v. Mehra, 854 S.W.2d 182 (Tex. App. 1993); 3Z Corp. v. Stewart Title Guar. Co., 851 S.W.2d 933 (Tex. App. 1993); First State Bank v. Keilman, 851 S.W.2d 914 (Tex. App. 1993).

almost any profit-oriented transaction.[45] A definition that trade or commerce "includes" certain activities is a term of enlargement rather than limitation.[46]

Banking and other credit activities are in "trade or commerce,"[47] as are debt collection efforts.[48] There is not even a requirement that there be a purchase.[49] Companies that offer to buy individuals' structured settlements for cash are engaged in trade or commerce.[50] "Trade or commerce" also applies to post-sale activities, and not just practices to induce a sale.[51] Refusing to pay insurance claims is in "trade or commerce."[52] Lawyers, doctors and other professionals are also in trade or commerce, at least as to the entrepreneurial aspects of the professions.[53] A UDAP statute applies to people who "find" missing heirs for a fee.[54]

"Trade or commerce" is not limited to transactions in personalty, but also includes real estate transactions,[55] mobile home space rentals, and residential lease practices.[56] A company's initial start-up steps after its incorporation are in trade or commerce.[57] A company is in trade or commerce when it acquires a beach club and attempts to terminate consumers' memberships in the club.[58]

On the other hand, some courts find the isolated sale of real estate[59] or other property[60] by a nonmerchant—for example, a family's sale of its own home—or lease practices involving an owner-occupied two-family home[61] as not being in "trade or commerce." A federal court in Connecticut has gone one step farther and found a corporation's sale of real estate not to be in trade or commerce where the corporation was not in the business of selling real estate.[62] A disappointed seller can not sue a consumer for changing his mind about whether to buy, because the consumer is not engaged in trade or commerce.[63] Nor does how a company maintains its own private land involve trade or commerce.[64] A consensual romantic relationship between two adults is not in trade or commerce even though the parties may have met in the course of a business transaction.[65]

There are also questions whether charitable organizations, other nonprofits, governmental entities, or quasi-governmental entities are in "trade or commerce."[66] In determining whether a transaction occurs in enough of a business context to be in "trade or commerce," Massachusetts courts consider the nature of the transaction, the character of the parties and their activities, and whether the transaction was motivated by personal or business reasons.[67] The relationship between condominium unit owners and the condominium's volunteer governing board is a private one that is not in trade or commerce.[68] The Hawaii Supreme Court has cited the Massachusetts criteria with approval.[69] The following practices have been held not within the scope of a UDAP statute: political campaign practices;[70] the activities of citizens and a neighborhood in opposing a developer's plan to build a shopping center;[71] the submission of a bid to a county for the right to provide ambulance service and charge user fees to local residents who made 911 emergency calls;[72] a city's contracting to have a fire truck repaired;[73]

45 *See* Food Lion, Inc. v. Capital Cities/ABC, Inc., 951 F. Supp. 1233 (M.D.N.C. 1996); Phillips v. A Triangle Women's Health Clinic, Inc., 573 S.E.2d 600 (N.C. App. 2002) (" 'commerce' comprehends intercourse for the purpose of trade in any form").

46 State *ex rel.* Nixon v. Estes, 108 S.W.3d 795 (Mo. App. 2003) (term includes in-state defendant's transactions with out-of-state consumers even though definition only mentions acts directly or indirectly affecting Missourians).

47 *See* § 2.2.1.4, *infra.*

48 *See* § 2.2.2, *infra.*

49 *See* § 2.2.3.1, *infra.*

50 *In re* Wiggins, 273 B.R. 839, 856 (Bankr. D. Idaho 2001).

51 *See* § 2.2.4, *infra.*

52 *See* § 2.3.1, *infra.*

53 *See* §§ 2.3.9–2.3.11, *infra.*

54 Guess v. Brophy, 164 Ill. App. 3d 75, 517 N.E.2d 693 (1987).

55 *See* § 2.2.5.1, *infra.*

56 *See* § 2.2.6.1, *infra.*

57 Hanover Ins. Co. v. Sutton, 46 Mass. App. Ct. 153, 705 N.E.2d 279 (1999).

58 Baker v. Chavis, 410 S.E.2d 600 (S.C. Ct. App. 1991).

59 *See* § 2.2.5.1.3, *infra.*

60 *See* § 2.3.4, *infra.*

61 *See* § 2.2.6.3, *infra.*

62 Cornerstone Realty, Inc. v. Dresser Rand Co., 993 F. Supp. 107 (D. Conn. 1998). *Accord* Brandewiede v. Emery Worldwide, 890 F. Supp. 79 (D. Conn. 1994) (claim regarding overnight delivery service's lease of aircraft dismissed), *aff'd without op.*, 66 F.3d 308 (2d Cir. 1995); Arawana Mills Co. v. United Technologies Corp., 795 F. Supp. 1238 (D. Conn. 1992) (no UDAP claim for lessee's conduct as a lessee where it was not in business of being a lessee).

63 Gulf S. Bus. Sys. & Consultants, Inc. v. State, 625 So. 2d 697 (La. Ct. App. 1993).

64 Foggie v. CSX Transportation, Inc., 431 S.E.2d 587 (S.C. 1993).

65 Korper v. Weinstein, 783 N.E.2d 877 (Mass. App. 2003).

66 *See* §§ 2.3.5, 2.3.6, *infra. See also* Malone v. Topsail Area Jaycees, Inc., 439 S.E.2d 192 (N.C. Ct. App. 1994).

67 Poznik v. Massachusetts Medical Professional Ins. Ass'n, 417 Mass. 48, 628 N.E.2d 1 (1994); Comets Community Youth Center v. Town of Natick, 778 N.E.2d 1038 (Mass. App. 2002) (town's lease of skating rink for local youth not covered); Miller v. Risk Management Foundation, 36 Mass. App. Ct. 411, 632 N.E.2d 841 (1994).

68 Office One, Inc. v. Lopez, 437 Mass. 113, 769 N.E.2d 749 (2002). *See also* Rafalowski v. Old County Rd., 245 Conn. 504, 714 A.2d 675 (1998) (management of condominium association is not trade or commerce); Berish v. Bornstein, 437 Mass. 252, 770 N.E.2d 961 (2002) (UDAP statute does not apply to suit by condo owners' association against developer); Eisenberg v. Phoenix Ass'n Management, Inc., 777 N.E.2d 1265 (Mass. App. 2002) (condominium management company's preparation of form for buyer's bank not in any trade or business).

69 Cieri v. Leticia Query Realty, Inc., 905 P.2d 29 (Haw. 1995).

70 O'Conner v. Superior Court (Wyman), 177 Cal. App. 3d 1013, 223 Cal. Rptr. 357 (1986); Del Tufo v. National Republican Senatorial Committee, 248 N.J. Super. 684, 591 A.2d 1040 (1991).

71 Saylor v. Valles, 63 P.3d 1152 (N.M. App. 2002).

72 Northwest Strategies v. Buck Medical Servs., 927 F. Supp. 1343 (W.D. Wash. 1996).

73 Middleboro Fire Apparatus, Inc. v. City of Haverhill, 60 Mass. App. Ct. 1127, 806 N.E.2d 472 (Mass. App. Ct. 2004).

and the operations of a court, which provides services to the public, but does not sell its services.[74]

One case, open to some criticism, has held that once a lawsuit has been filed against a seller, the matter is subject to the control of the courts, and no longer in "trade or commerce."[75] But a later decision from the same court cuts back significantly on this decision, holding that a collection agency's violations of the Collection Agency Act after filing suit are actionable under the UDAP statute.[76]

Similarly, courts have found the administration of an estate to be a private affair so that it does not involve trade or commerce.[77] But a scheme to defraud workers' compensation insurers is in trade or commerce even though the malefactors use adversarial workers' compensation litigation to accomplish their ends.[78] Massachusetts' UDAP statute does not allow one entity to sue a neighboring landowner when there is no transactional business relationship between them.[79] A seller of land is not a "consumer" under Tennessee's UDAP statute and can not bring a UDAP claim against neighboring landowners for placing signs that allegedly interfered with the sale. The placement of such signs does not fall within the definition of trade or commerce.[80] A bank can not be sued when its only involvement with the plaintiff was as holder of funds belonging to a third party that the plaintiff sued.[81] A trademark licensor who did not advertise, sell, rent, lease, distribute, or manufacture the product was likewise not in trade or commerce as defined by Connecticut's UDAP statute.[82] Nor are academic research and publication in trade or commerce, because they are not entrepreneurial.[83] A manufacturer's handling of hazardous waste has also been held not within trade or commerce, particularly where the company was not in the hazardous waste business.[84]

74 Keenan v. Allan, 889 F. Supp. 1320 (E.D. Wash. 1995), *aff'd*, 91 F.3d 1275 (9th Cir. 1996).

75 Blake v. Federal Way Cycle Center, 40 Wash. App. 302, 698 P.2d 578 (1985).

76 Evergreen Collectors v. Holt, 60 Wash. App. 151, 803 P.2d 10 (1991) (litigation practices of collection agencies could be in trade or commerce).

77 Edinburg v. Cavers, 22 Mass. App. Ct. 212, 492 N.E.2d 1171 (1986); Garrett v. Lovel, 16 Mass. App. Ct. 325, 450 N.E.2d 1121 (1983).

78 St. Paul Fire & Marine Ins. Co. v. Ellis & Ellis, 262 F.3d 53 (1st Cir. 2001) (Mass. law). *See also* Tsagaroulis v. Federal Home Loan Mortg. Corp., 2001 U.S. Dist. LEXIS 18235 (D. Mass. Oct. 23, 2001) (where baseless litigation arises out of a preexisting business relationship, it is in trade or commerce).

79 John Boyd Co. v. Boston Gas Co., 775 F. Supp. 435 (D. Mass. 1991); Cash Energy, Inc. v. Weiner, 768 F. Supp. 892 (D. Mass. 1991).

80 Wagner v. Fleming, 2004 WL 32379 (Tenn. Ct. App. Jan. 6, 2004) (unpublished, citation limited).

81 Arthur D. Little, Inc. v. East Cambridge Savings Bank, 35 Mass. App. Ct. 734, 625 N.E.2d 1383 (1994).

82 Burkert v. Petrol Plus of Naugatuck, Inc., 579 A.2d 26 (Conn. 1990).

83 Johnson v. Schmitz, 119 F. Supp. 2d 90 (D. Conn. 2000).

84 Sealy Connecticut, Inc. v. Litton Indus., Inc., 989 F. Supp. 120 (D. Conn. 1997); Bernbach v. Timex Corp., 989 F. Supp. 403 (D. Conn. 1996).

2.1.5 Interpretations of "Goods"

Many UDAP statutes apply to the sale of "goods," and a key question will be whether a particular transaction involves "goods." Where the UDAP statute itself does not contain a definition of "goods," some UDAP cases refer to the definitions in the Uniform Commercial Code, sections 2-105 and 9-102(a)(44) (formerly 9-105).[85]

Most cases find that money is not considered a "good."[86] Similarly, an intangible property right has been found to be neither a "good" nor a "service."[87] However, receipt of services collateral to an intangible will bring the transaction within a UDAP statute's scope if the collateral services are an important object of the transaction, and not merely incidental to it.[88]

85 Allgrant v. Evergreen Valley Nurseries Ltd. P'ship, 126 F.3d 178 (3d Cir. 1997) (holding that securities are not goods); Riverside National Bank v. Lewis, 603 S.W.2d 169 (Tex. 1980).

86 Grass v. Credito Mexicano, S.A., 797 F.2d 220 (5th Cir. 1986) (Texas law) (certificate of deposit is not goods); Idaho First National Bank v. Wells, 100 Idaho 256, 596 P.2d 429 (1979); Haeger v. Johnson, 25 Or. App. 131, 548 P.2d 532 (1976) (a loan is not the sale of goods or services); English v. Fischer, 660 S.W.2d 521 (Tex. 1983) (proceeds of insurance policy are not goods); Riverside National Bank v. Lewis, 603 S.W.2d 169 (Tex. 1980) (goods does not include money); Henry v. Cullum Cos., 891 S.W.2d 789 (Tex. App. 1995) (grocery store slip and fall case could not be brought under Texas UDAP because goods sought did not form the basis of the complaint and because the use of store floors was not a "service" within the meaning of Texas UDAP statute); Hand v. Dean Witter Reynolds, Inc., 889 S.W.2d 483 (Tex. App. 1994) (commodity option contract neither good nor service). *But see* Dominguez v. Brackey Enterprises, Inc., 756 S.W.2d 788 (Tex. App. 1988) (goods include money); *cf.* Villegas v. Transamerica Fin. Servs., 147 Ariz. 100, 708 P.2d 781 (Ct. App. 1985) ("merchandise" includes money).

87 Ashlar Fin. Servs. Corp. v. Sterling Fin. Co. 2002 WL 206439 (N.D. Tex. Feb. 8, 2002) (contract for future sales commissions is neither a "good" or a "service"); Stroud v. Meister, 2001 U.S. Dist. LEXIS 13282 (N.D. Tex. Aug. 22, 2001) (joint venture agreement); Barnes v. Omnitrition Intern., Inc., 2001 WL 194757 (N.D. Tex. Feb. 22, 2001) (distributorship agreement); Hendricks v. Thornton, 973 S.W.2d 348 (Tex. App. 1998) (securities); Kinnard v. Circle K Stores Inc., 966 S.W.2d 613 (Tex. App. 1998) (lottery ticket); Fisher Controls International, Inc. v. Gibbons, 911 S.W.2d 135 (Tex. App. 1995). *But see In re* Wiggins, 273 B.R. 839 (Bankr. D. Idaho 2001) (Idaho statute includes intangibles as goods).

88 Canfield v. Bank One, Texas, N.A., 51 S.W.3d 828, 45 U.C.C. Rep. Serv. 2d 571 (Tex. App. 2001) (financial counseling collateral to checking account is within UDAP statute); Insurance Co. of N. Am. v. Morris, 928 S.W.2d 133 (Tex. App. 1996).

Living property, such as a horse, is a "good."[89] Whether real estate is a good is discussed in § 2.2.5.1.2, *infra,* but the construction of a structure on land is a sale of goods even though the structure will ultimately become part of the real estate.[90]

2.1.6 Interpretations of "Merchandise"

Several states, including Delaware, Missouri, New Jersey, and North Dakota, use the term "merchandise" in the scope sections of their UDAP statutes. Minnesota also uses the term in one of its UDAP statutes.[91] Each of these statutes defines "merchandise" as including various types of property such as goods, services, realty, commodities, and intangibles.[92] "Merchandise" is thus a broader term than "goods." For example, while money may not be a "good,"[93] Arizona finds money to be merchandise under a statutory definition that includes both tangible property and intangibles.[94] An offer of consumer credit is "merchandise" under New Jersey's definition, as is the sale of insurance.[95] The sale of information about low-cost credit cards also involves merchandise.[96] Similarly, while courts are split as to whether a real estate sale involves "goods," it almost invariably is found to include "merchandise."[97] The sale of an existing business entity is not, however, the sale of "merchandise."[98]

Merchandise, defined in the New Jersey UDAP statute as a service "offered to the public," does not encompass pet burials where a veterinarian did not offer to perform this service and only performed this function when requested by pet owners.[99] New Jersey courts also have held that turnpike tokens sold by the Highway Authority are not merchandise because there is only a single seller, they are not sold for profit, and they represent prepayment for the right to enjoy a government service.[100] Showing a reluctance to apply New Jersey's UDAP statute in a purely business context, a court has also held that transit car design services provided by one large corporation to another were not "merchandise."[101] Nonetheless, New Jersey's definition requires the merchandise to be offered to the public for sale, but does not require it to be for personal, family, or household purposes. Accordingly, the sale of a franchise that is too small to be covered by the state Franchise Practices Act is "merchandise" as long as it is offered to the general public.[102]

2.1.7 Interpretations of "Services"

The definition of the term "service" is very important in determining the scope of UDAP statutes. Many transactions can be brought within a UDAP statute's scope if "services" is defined broadly.

Texas courts define services as "action or use that furthers some end or purpose: conduct or performance that assists or benefits someone or something; deeds useful or instrumental toward some object."[103] To meet this definition, the party allegedly performing services must engage in some activity on behalf of another.[104] A UDAP plaintiff need only seek or

See also White v. Mellon Mortg. Co., 995 S.W.2d 795 (Tex. App. 1999) (activity related to a loan is UDAP "services" only if the activity is an objective of the transaction).

89 Scholtz v. Sigel, 601 S.W.2d 516 (Tex. Civ. App. 1980); Fancher v. Benson, 580 A.2d 51 (Vt. 1990). *But see* Cohen v. North Ridge Farms, Inc., 712 F. Supp. 1265 (E.D. Ky. 1989) (purchase of thoroughbred horse is not purchase of consumer goods).

90 Parr v. Tagco Indus., 620 S.W.2d 200 (Tex. Civ. App. 1981); § 2.2.5.2, *infra. See also* Crystal v. West & Callahan, 328 Md. 318, 614 A.2d 560 (1992) (home improvement contract involves both goods and services).

91 Minn. Stat. §§ 325F.69, 325F.68. *See* Twardy v. L.B. Sales, Inc., 2000 Minn. App. LEXIS 636 (June 27, 2000) (unpublished, limited precedent) (characterizing definition as "broad"; used cars are clearly covered).

92 Freeman Health Sys. v. Wass, 124 S.W.3d 504 (Mo. App. 2004) ("merchandise" includes medical services).

93 *See* § 2.1.5, *supra.*

94 Villegas v. Transamerica Fin. Servs., 147 Ariz. 100, 708 P.2d 781 (Ct. App. 1985); Clingerman v. Ford Motor Credit Co., Clearinghouse No. 50,427 (Ariz. Super. Ct. Nov. 1, 1994) (ruling on motion to dismiss). *But see* Boubelik v. Liberty State Bank, 553 N.W.2d 393 (Minn. 1996) (a loan is not "merchandise" so not covered by Minnesota's UDAP statute; statute has since been amended to include loans).

95 Lemelledo v. Beneficial Management Corp., 150 N.J. 255, 696 A.2d 546 (1997).

96 State v. Sgillo, 176 Ariz. 148, 859 P.2d 771 (Ct. App. 1993).

97 *See* § 2.2.5.1, *infra.*

98 Waste Mfg. & Leasing Corp. v. Hambicki, 900 P.2d 1220 (Ariz. Ct. App. 1995).

99 Annunziata v. Miller, 241 N.J. Super. 275, 574 A.2d 1021 (Ch. Div. 1990).

100 Barry v. N.J. State Highway Authority, 245 N.J. Super. 302, 585 A.2d 420 (1990); Schlichtman v. N.J. Highway Authority, 243 N.J. Super. 464, 579 A.2d 1275 (Law Div. 1990).

101 R.J. Longo Constr. v. Transit Am., 921 F. Supp. 1295 (D.N.J. 1996); *see also* Bracco Diagnostics Inc. v. Bergen Brunswig Drug Co., 226 F. Supp. 2d 557 (D.N.J. 2002) (services provided by wholesaler to manufacturer not "merchandise").

102 Kavky v. Herbalife Int'l, 359 N.J. Super. 497, 820 A.2d 677 (App. Div. 2003); Morgan v. Air Brook Limousine, 211 N.J. Super. 84, 510 A.2d 1197 (Law Div. 1986). *But see* J & R Ice Cream Corp. v. California Smoothie Licensing Corp., 31 F.3d 1259 (3d Cir. 1994). *See generally* § 2.2.9.2, *infra.*

103 Riverside National Bank v. Lewis, 603 S.W.2d 169 (Tex. 1980); Van Zandt v. Forth Worth Press, 359 S.W.2d 893, 895 (Tex. 1962); Fortner v. Fannin Bank in Windom, 634 S.W.2d 74 (Tex. App. 1982).

104 Ashlar Fin. Servs. Corp. v. Sterling Fin. Co. 2002 WL 206439 (N.D. Tex. Feb. 8, 2002) (contract for future sales commissions is neither a "good" or a "service"); La Sara Grain Co. v. First National Bank, 673 S.W.2d 558 (Tex. 1984); Riverside National Bank v. Lewis, 603 S.W.2d 169 (Tex. 1980); Henry v. Cullum Cos., 891 S.W.2d 789 (Tex. App. 1995) (grocery store slip and fall case could not be brought under Texas UDAP because goods sought did not form the basis of the complaint and because the use of store floors was not a "service" within the meaning of Texas UDAP statute); Hand v. Dean Witter Reynolds, Inc., 889 S.W.2d 483 (Tex. App. 1994) (commodity option contract neither good nor service).

acquire services; a third party can pay for them.[105] A UDAP plaintiff does not, in fact, have to acquire services—it is enough merely to seek them.[106] The owner of a towed vehicle is a "consumer" as to the towing company, even though the towing services were involuntarily obtained.[107] A Vermont court has defined service as "to furnish and supply something needed or desired."[108]

One court has drawn an overly-fine distinction between "services" that are covered and those that are not, holding that a plaintiff who contracted for services can not sue for wrongful suspension of the services, but only for problems with the services themselves.[109] Because this decision would eliminate a UDAP claim for the deceptive failure to provide a service, it appears to be in error. However, the distinction the court drew could be explained by the "mere breach of contract" theory.[110]

Courts have found the following "services" subject to UDAP statutes: the construction of a home;[111] home improvements;[112] heating, ventilation, maintenance, and water supply provided in connection with the lease of an apartment;[113] renting out mobile home lots, maintaining utilities and roads within the park, and removing snow and garbage;[114] a contract giving the consumer the option to buy football season tickets;[115] an heir-finding service;[116] the provision of credit insurance in connection with a loan;[117] other forms of insurance;[118] insurance adjusting;[119] suretyship;[120] repair and maintenance services on a leased car;[121] campground memberships;[122] management services provided by a general partner to people who purchase limited partnerships in a business venture;[123] tax and investment advice and brokerage service;[124] accounting services;[125] legal services;[126] checking account services and other bank services;[127] mortgage brokering;[128] termite inspection and prevention;[129] educational services at a paralegal school;[130] and collection services performed by a collection agency to collect unpaid parking tickets.[131] Solicitation for and provision of antiabortion counseling services are covered by a UDAP statute because the organization advertised, distributed pamphlets, and provided various services, even though no money was paid, and even though the group tried to liken itself to a nonprofit entity expressing political views.[132] Whether a loan is a service as defined by UDAP statutes is discussed in §§ 2.2.1.2 and 2.2.1.3, *infra*.

2.1.8 Interpretations of "Personal, Family, or Household Use"

2.1.8.1 General

Many UDAP statutes cover only consumer transactions or actions by consumers, and define consumer as a person using a good or service for "personal, family, or household use." Interpretations of other consumer protection statutes that use the terms "personal, family, or household use,"

105 Arthur Andersen & Co. v. Perry Equip. Corp., 945 S.W.2d 812 (Tex. 1997).

106 Nast v. State Farm Fire and Cas. Co., 82 S.W.3d 114 (Tex. App. 2002).

107 Lonergan v. A.J.'s Wrecker Serv. of Dallas, Inc., 1999 U.S. Dist. LEXIS 10494 (N.D. Tex. July 6, 1999).

108 Lavinia v. Howard Bank, Clearinghouse No. 26,015 (Vt. Super. Ct. 1976).

109 Brittan Communications Intern. Corp. v. Southwestern Bell Tel. Co., 313 F.3d 899 (5th Cir. 2002) (Texas law).

110 *See* 5.2.5, *infra*.

111 New Mea Constr. Corp. v. Harper, 203 N.J. Super. 486, 497 A.2d 534 (App. Div. 1985); Precision Homes, Inc. v. Cooper, 671 S.W.2d 924 (Tex. App. 1984).

112 Crystal v. West & Callahan, 328 Md. 318, 614 A.2d 560 (1992) (home improvement contract involves both goods and services).

113 Carter v. Mueller, 120 Ill. App. 3d 314, 457 N.E.2d 1335 (1983).

114 People *ex rel.* Fahner v. Hedrich, 108 Ill. App. 3d 83, 438 N.E.2d 924 (1982).

115 Yocca v. Pittsburgh Steelers Sports, Inc., 806 A.2d 936 (Pa. Commw. Ct. 2002), *rev'd on other grounds,* 2004 WL 1618851 (Pa. July 20, 2004).

116 Guess v. Brophy, 164 Ill. App. 3d 75, 517 N.E.2d 693 (1987).

117 Juarez v. Bank of Austin, 659 S.W.2d 139 (Tex. App. 1983).

118 *See* § 2.3.1, *infra*. Showpiece Homes Corp. v. Assurance Co. of Am., 38 P.3d 47 (Colo. 2001); Lang v. Consumers Ins. Serv., Inc., 583 N.E.2d 1147 (Ill. App. Ct. 1991).

119 Culbreth v. Lawrence J. Miller, Inc., 328 Pa. Super. 374, 477 A.2d 491 (1984).

120 Associated Indem. Corp. v. CAT Contracting, Inc., 918 S.W.2d 580 (Tex. App. 1996).

121 Edwards v. William H. Porter, Inc., 1991 Del. Super. LEXIS 315 (July 26, 1991), *aff'd on other grounds*, 616 A.2d 838 (Del. 1992).

122 *See* § 2.2.8, *infra*.

123 Marshall v. Quinn-L Equities, Inc., 704 F. Supp. 1384 (N.D. Tex. 1988).

124 Dominguez v. Brackey Enterprises, Inc., 756 S.W.2d 788 (Tex. App. 1988); E.F. Hutton & Co. v. Youngblood, 708 S.W.2d 865 (Tex. App. 1986).

125 Lyne v. Arthur Andersen & Co., 772 F. Supp. 1064 (N.D. Ill. 1991).

126 Nottingham v. General Am. Communications, Corp., 811 F.2d 873 (5th Cir. 1987) (Texas law); Cuyler v. Minns, 60 S.W.3d 209 (Tex. App. 2001) (client could sue even though attorneys decided not to bill her for their service). *Accord* Banks v. Department of Consumer & Regulatory Affairs, 634 A.2d 433 (D.C. 1993) ("legal services" performed by a non-lawyer are covered by UDAP statute).

127 First Federal Savings & Loan Ass'n v. Ritenour, 704 S.W.2d 895 (Tex. App. 1986); Farmers & Merchants State Bank v. Ferguson, 605 S.W.2d 320 (Tex. Civ. App. 1980), *modified on other grounds*, 617 S.W.2d 918 (Tex. 1981).

128 Allan v. M&S Mortgage Co., 359 N.W.2d 238 (Mich. Ct. App. 1984).

129 Warren v. LeMay, 142 Ill. App. 3d 550, 491 N.E.2d 464 (1986).

130 Malone v. Academy of Court Reporting, 64 Ohio App. 3d 588, 582 N.E.2d 54 (1990).

131 People *ex rel.* Daley v. Datacom Sys. Corp., 146 Ill. 2d 1, 585 N.E.2d 51 (1991).

132 Mother & Unborn Baby Care, Inc. v. State, 749 S.W.2d 533 (Tex. App. 1988), *cert. denied*, 490 U.S. 1090 (1989).

such as the Truth in Lending Act,[133] the Fair Debt Collection Practices Act,[134] the Magnuson-Moss Warranty Act,[135] and the Uniform Commercial Code,[136] are useful precedent for interpretation of the same language in UDAP statutes. Moreover, extensive state UDAP case law now interprets these terms. Unfortunately, there is little uniformity from state to state. Perhaps this is because the terms are not used in the Federal Trade Commission Act and the FTC has not interpreted their meaning for purposes of the FTC Act.

Where a use is part consumer and part commercial, courts find the transaction to be a consumer one.[137] As long as a UDAP statute does not limit its scope to individuals, that a commercial entity is purchasing property for consumer purposes does not detract from the fact that it is for consumer purposes.[138]

2.1.8.2 Is the Test Objective or Subjective?

In determining whether a transaction is for "personal, family or household purposes," a key question is whether the court will use the consumer's subjective individual intent in purchasing goods, or a more objective standard, such as whether most purchases of that item are for personal, family, or household uses. Oregon courts determine whether an item is for personal, family, or household use by asking not what the individual subjective motivation is, but whether the product is customarily bought by a substantial number of consumers for such use.[139] Thus, even though a used car may in fact be purchased to start a delivery business, if most used car purchases are for personal purposes, the car sale would be covered. Similarly, since advice concerning the investment of money customarily is for a commercial use, even a small, individual investor is not a "consumer."[140]

Other courts hold the opposite, determining that the actual purpose of the purchase, not the type of goods purchased, is controlling.[141] A Florida court has ruled that where a person is in the business of reselling used cars, the person could not bring an action for the repair of a car meant for resale.[142] (In 1993, Florida repealed the requirement that the transaction be for personal, family, or household use.) A Pennsylvania court found that a condominium association's purchase of a replacement roof involved a purchase for personal, family, or household purposes.[143] The purpose of the purchase, not the type of goods purchased, is determinative. The condominium association is also not a business purchaser, but acts in a representative capacity for individual consumers.[144] The Eleventh Circuit, interpreting Alabama law, has ruled that where a consumer purchases a car with the intent of eventually reselling it, but also with the intent to use it personally until that time, it is a factual question as to which is the buyer's primary purpose.[145] Where a purchase has both a business purpose and a personal, family, or household purpose, it is a factual question which purpose is primary.[146]

For purposes of the subjective test, whether a transaction is for personal, family, or household use is generally decided based upon the parties' intentions at the time they enter into the transaction, regardless of any later change in the use of the item.[147] The parties' objective manifestations of their intent at the time of the transaction will control over their actual subjective intent.[148]

An Ohio court looked at the relative skill and sophistication of the parties in determining that an "investor" in a pyramid scheme entered it for personal, family, or house-

133 15 U.S.C. § 1602(h). *See* National Consumer Law Center, Truth in Lending § 2.2.3 (4th ed. 1999 and Supp.).

134 15 U.S.C. § 1692a(5). *See* National Consumer Law Center, Fair Debt Collection § 4.4.2 (5th ed. 2003 and Supp.).

135 15 U.S.C. § 2301. *See* National Consumer Law Center, Consumer Warranty Law Ch. 2 (5th ed. 2004).

136 U.C.C. § 9-102(a)(23) (former 9-109(A)).

137 Marascio v. Campanella, 298 N.J. Super. 491, 689 A.2d 852 (App. Div. 1997) (commercially owned, unoccupied property that is part residential and part commercial still covered by UDAP statute).

138 Id. See generally § 2.4.5.2, infra.

139 Searle v. Exley Express, Inc., 278 Or. 535, 564 P.2d 1054 (1977); Miller v. Hubbard-Wray, 53 Or. App. 531, 633 P.2d 1 (1981); *see also* F.D.S. Marine, L.L.C. v. Shaver Transp. Co., 2001 U.S. Dist. LEXIS 7800 (D. Or. Mar. 29, 2001), *adopted by* 2001 U.S. Dist. LEXIS 7787 (D. Or. May 25, 2001).

140 Roach v. Mead, 301 Or. 383, 722 P.2d 1229 (1986).

141 *See, e.g.*, Valley Forge Towers S. Condominium v. Ron-Ike Foam Insulators, Inc., 574 A.2d 641 (Pa. Super. Ct. 1990), *aff'd without op.*, 605 A.2d 798 (Pa. 1992).

142 Heindel v. Southside Chrysler-Plymouth, Inc., 476 So. 2d 266 (Fla. Dist. Ct. App. 1985); *see also In re* Sterling Foster & Co., Securities Litigation, 222 F. Supp. 2d 216, 286, 287 (E.D.N.Y. 2002) (purchases for purposes of resale are excluded); U.S. Fin. Group v. Horizon Management, 476 So. 2d 771 (Fla. Dist. Ct. App. 1985). *But see* Lou Bachrodt Chevrolet, Inc. v. Savage, 570 So. 2d 306 (Fla. Dist. Ct. App. 1990) (purchase of car for commercial use is still a "consumer transaction").

143 Valley Forge Towers S. Condominium v. Ron-Ike Foam Insulators, Inc., 574 A.2d 641 (Pa. Super. Ct. 1990), *aff'd without opinion,* 605 A.2d 798 (Pa. 1992).

144 *Id.*

145 Harrison v. Jones, 880 F.2d 1279 (11th Cir. 1989) (Alabama law).

146 Harrison v. Jones, 880 F.2d 1279 (11th Cir. 1989) (Alabama law); Robertson v. State Farm Fire & Casualty Co., 890 F. Supp. 671 (E.D. Mich. 1995) (where plaintiff's primary focus was commercial aspects of purchase, it was not a consumer transaction).

147 *In re* Pettit, 18 B.R. 8 (Bankr. E.D. Ark. 1981); Morris v. Osmose Wood Preserving, 340 Md. 519, 667 A.2d 624 (1995) (plywood purchased by commercial builder was not a consumer good at time of sale); Linthicum v. Archambault, 379 Mass. 381, 398 N.E.2d 482 (1979) (use of house as rental property not covered, even though owner later lived in the house also); Tomes v. George P. Ballas Leasing, Inc., 1986 Ohio App. LEXIS 8463 (Sept. 30, 1986) (lease of van for business use not covered by UDAP statute even though it was actually used primarily for personal use); Commercial Credit Equipment Corp. v. Carter, 516 P.2d 767 (Wash. 1973).

148 Tomes v. George P. Ballas Leasing, Inc., 1986 Ohio App. LEXIS 8463 (Sept. 30, 1986).

hold purposes rather than business purposes.[149] The court was also swayed by the fact that the consumer was not in the pyramid scheme business, and had entered into only one such transaction.

The Minnesota UDAP statute is not restricted to consumer transactions, although the intent of the legislature was to protect consumers.[150] Thus, the sale of a restaurant business should be viewed as a consumer transaction covered by the statute where the buyer intended to operate the business rather than resell it.[151] The court, however, also decided to allow private UDAP actions only if they benefited the public, so deception that did not affect others in a one-time sale of a business was not actionable.

2.1.8.3 Interpretations Unique to Particular States

In 1990, a Michigan appellate court defined "personal" as relating to a person, and then looked to the UDAP statute's definition of a person. Thus, it found a law firm to be a "person," and furnishings for a law firm were, therefore, primarily for "personal" use.[152] A later decision by the same court rejects this interpretation, holding that business purchases are not for "personal" purposes.[153]

Where a UDAP statute's scope is defined as "trade or commerce involving the sale of goods primarily for consumer purposes," this phrase refers to the goods being primarily for consumer purposes and not the "trade or commerce" being primarily for consumer purposes.[154] The consumer must use the particular goods primarily for consumer purposes; it is not necessary that the seller's overall business deals primarily with consumers.[155]

If a statute defines "personal, family, and household use," that definition will be determinative. The Kansas statute defines a "consumer" to include someone who purchases goods for agricultural purposes, and thus applies to a farmer purchasing livestock from another farmer.[156] But a purchase for purposes of resale is not a consumer transaction.[157]

In Vermont a consumer is "one who does not purchase for resale in the ordinary course of business," so a person purchasing only one car for investment is a "consumer."[158] A farmer who purchases items for agricultural use is also a consumer under Vermont's law, whether or not the farm is conducted as a trade or business.[159] But a federal court has interpreted Maryland's statute as not applying to a commercial farming corporation, even though its definition of "consumer" goods includes those used for agricultural purposes.[160] A Louisiana court finds that purchase of a heavy-duty, special order truck for commercial use falls within the scope of a UDAP statute that applies to transactions in the "consumer interest," defined as affecting the economic welfare of a consumer.[161]

In Georgia, covered transactions must occur within the context of the consumer marketplace.[162] In determining whether a transaction meets this test, the courts consider the medium through which the act or practice is introduced into the stream of commerce and the market on which the act or practice is reasonably intended to impact. An auto dealer's discounting of a credit contract to a financing company was held not to be a consumer transaction, where the price to the consumer was not raised and the consumer was not affected by the discount.[163]

2.1.8.4 Listing of Consumer Transactions

Courts usually are liberal in finding that a transaction is for personal, family, or household purposes. A home sale is for consumer purposes where the house had been purchased for the owner's son and his wife to live in.[164] A consumer contracted for a real estate agent's services for "personal, family or household purposes" when the consumer sold property even though the consumer was not residing in the property at the time.[165] A real estate broker's or salesperson's sale of a residence is a consumer transaction.[166]

A condominium association's purchase of a replacement roof[167] and an absentee landlord's purchase of propane for

149 Celebrezze v. Howard, 77 Ohio App. 3d 387, 602 N.E.2d 665 (1991).

150 Ly v. Nystrom, 615 N.W.2d 302 (Minn. 2000).

151 *Id.*

152 Catallo Assocs., Inc. v. MacDonald & Goren, P.C., 465 N.W.2d 29 (Mich. Ct. App. 1990).

153 Jackson County Hog Producers v. Consumers Power Co., 592 N.W.2d 112 (Mich. App. 1999). *Accord* Robertson v. State Farm Fire & Casualty Co., 890 F. Supp. 671 (E.D. Mich. 1995); Passalacqua Corp. v. AIG Claim Servs., Inc., 2002 Mich. App. LEXIS 90 (Jan. 29, 2002).

154 Noggles v. Battle Creek Wrecking, Inc., 153 Mich. App. 363, 395 N.W.2d 322 (1986). *Accord* Robertson v. State Farm Fire & Casualty Co., 890 F. Supp. 671 (E.D. Mich. 1995).

155 Noggles v. Battle Creek Wrecking, Inc., 153 Mich. App. 363, 395 N.W.2d 322 (1986). *See also* Rodriguez v. Berrybrook Farms, Inc., 672 F. Supp. 1009 (W.D. Mich. 1987).

156 Musil v. Hendrich, 6 Kan. App. 2d 196, 627 P.2d 367 (1981).

157 Roberts v. Shawnee Mission Ford, 2003 WL 22143727 (D. Kan. Aug. 20, 2003).

158 Poulin v. Ford Motor Co., 513 A.2d 1168 (Vt. 1986).

159 Mainline Tractor & Equipment Co. v. Nutrite Co., 937 F. Supp. 1095 (D. Vt. 1996).

160 Pig Improvement Co. v. Middle States Holding Co., 943 F. Supp. 392 (D. Del. 1996).

161 Barrios v. Associates Commercial Corp., 481 So. 2d 702 (La. Ct. App. 1985).

162 Chancellor v. Gateway Lincoln-Mercury, 502 S.E.2d 799 (Ga. App. Ct. 1998). *See* § 7.5.3.6, *infra*.

163 Chancellor v. Gateway Lincoln-Mercury, 502 S.E.2d 799 (Ga. App. Ct. 1998).

164 Pointer v. Edward L. Kuhs, Co., 678 S.W.2d 836 (Mo. Ct. App. 1984).

165 *Id.*

166 Cieri v. Leticia Query Realty, Inc., 905 P.2d 29 (Haw. 1995).

167 Valley Forge Towers S. Condominium v. Ron-Ike Foam Insulators, Inc., 574 A.2d 641 (Pa. Super. Ct. 1990).

tenants' "use or benefit"[168] are consumer transactions. The purchase of a valuable antique for display in one's home or office is a transaction for personal, family, or household use, unless the consumer regularly buys such items for resale.[169]

The purchase by a professional driver of a part for his truck has been found to be for a consumer purpose,[170] as has the purchase of a used car by a self-employed craftsman from a dealer.[171] Driving a car to and from work is for "personal" reasons.[172] The parents of a 4H student are "consumers" with respect to services offered by a livestock show.[173]

The sale of insurance and various services to assist a person in setting up a home-based business was a consumer transaction where the program was marketed as a way to reduce the buyer's personal income tax liability.[174] A pyramid scheme is a consumer transaction.[175] The purchase of brokerage services for one's personal portfolio is also a consumer transaction.[176] Similarly, investment advice is covered by the Texas UDAP statute.[177]

An interesting Ohio decision deals with a two-part transaction, in which a property manager gave a repair worker a check (a business transaction), but then stopped payment on it. In the meantime, however, the repair worker negotiated the check at a grocery store to satisfy a consumer debt. A collection agency then tried to collect the amount of the check from the property manager. Since the collection agency was trying to collect the consumer debt—the worker's debt to the grocery store—its activities were covered by the state UDAP statute.[178] Another two-part transaction, in which a contractor agreed to do home improvement work in exchange for being allowed to dump excavated dirt from a commercial road construction project on the consumer's land, also met the Ohio standard for a consumer transaction.[179]

168 Barrett v. Adirondack Bottled Gas Corp., 487 A.2d 1074 (Vt. 1984).

169 Adam A. Wechsler & Son, Inc. v. Klank, 561 A.2d 1003 (D.C. 1989).

170 Meyer v. Diesel Equip. Co., 1 Kan. App. 2d 574, 570 P.2d 1374 (1977).

171 Lou Bachrodt Chevrolet, Inc. v. Savage, 570 So. 2d 306 (Fla. Dist. Ct. App. 1990).

172 Couto v. Gibson, Inc., 1992 Ohio App. LEXIS 756 (Feb. 26, 1992).

173 Houston Livestock Show and Rodeo, Inc. v. Hamrick, 125 S.W.3d 555 (Tex. App. 2003).

174 Hofstetter v. Fletcher, 905 F.2d 897 (6th Cir. 1988) (Ohio law).

175 Celebrezze v. Howard, 77 Ohio App. 3d 387, 602 N.E.2d 665 (1991).

176 Denison v. Kelly, 759 F. Supp. 199 (M.D. Pa. 1991).

177 Wingate v. Acree, 2003 WL 1922569 (Tex. App. Apr. 24, 2003).

178 Broadnax v. Greene Credit Serv., 118 Ohio App. 3d 881, 694 N.E.2d 167 (1997).

179 Williams v. Edwards, 129 Ohio App. 3d 116, 717 N.E.2d 368 (1998).

2.1.8.5 Transactions Not Found to Be for Consumer Purposes

Courts have found the following transactions not to be for personal, family, or household use:

- The purchase of a hay baler for use on a family farm;[180]
- Insurance for a dairy farm, even though it also covered the family's residence and personal property;[181]
- The purchase of a truck as an investment and for the buyer's son to use in his employment as a freight hauler;[182]
- Ownership of a house for use as a rental property;[183]
- Roofing material purchased by a builder, even though it was later used on consumers' roofs;[184]
- The making of business loans;[185]
- The purchase of computer software that is suitable only for business applications;[186]
- A doctor's purchase of pedicle screws to insert in patients during surgery[187] and a patient's purchase of a medical device for a doctor to use during surgery;[188]
- Services to repair an oil well that supplied the consumer's individual home fuel needs but also produced oil that the consumer sold;[189]
- Requesting medical records for use in litigation;[190]

180 Miller v. Hubbard-Wray, 53 Or. App. 531, 633 P.2d 1 (1981).

181 Robertson v. State Farm Fire & Casualty Co., 890 F. Supp. 671 (E.D. Mich. 1995).

182 Searle v. Exley Express, Inc., 278 Or. 535, 564 P.2d 1054 (1977). *Accord In re* Jenkins, 249 B.R. 532 (Bankr. W.D. Mo. 2000) (trucker's purchase of Kenworth truck for his occupation).

183 Linthicum v. Archambault, 379 Mass. 381, 398 N.E.2d 482 (1979). *See also* DiLucido v. Terminix International, Inc., 676 A.2d 1237 (Pa. Super. 1996) (purchase of extermination services for rental property is not consumer transaction). *But see* Barrett v. Adirondack Bottled Gas Corp., 487 A.2d 1074 (Vt. 1984) (landlord's purchase of propane for tenants' use is consumer transaction).

184 Morris v. Osmose Wood Preserving, 340 Md. 519, 667 A.2d 624 (1995); *accord* Bindra v. Michael Bowman & Assocs., Inc., 58 Va. Cir. 47, 2001 WL 1829999 (2001) (stucco).

185 Dinjian v. Dinjian, 22 Mass. App. Ct. 589, 495 N.E.2d 882 (1986) (Massachusetts statute later amended to cover such transactions).

186 Barazatto v. Intelligent Sys., Inc., 40 Ohio App. 3d 117, 532 N.E.2d 148 (1987).

187 Balderston v. Medtronic Sofamor Danek, Inc., 285 F.3d 238 (3d Cir. 2002).

188 Herzog v. Arthrocare Corp., 2003 WL 1785795, at *10 (D. Me. Mar. 21, 2003) (reasoning that the consumer did not himself use or possess the device).

189 Temple Oil & Gas Co. v. Henning, 2002 WL 31689331 (Ohio App. Nov. 22, 2002).

190 Slobin v. Henry Ford Health Care, 666 N.W.2d 632 (Mich. 2003); McShane v. Recordex Acquisition Corp., 2003 WL 22805233 (Pa. Com. Pleas Nov. 14, 2003). *But see* Mermer v. Medical Correspondence Servs., 115 Ohio App. 3d 717, 686 N.E.2d 296 (1996).

- Investment advice;[191]
- The purchase of securities;[192]
- Former franchisees who complained only about intangible property rights, not about any specific goods or services;[193]
- Brokerage services for formation of an international joint venture;[194]
- Investment in a franchise by a company owned by the plaintiffs;[195]
- Political solicitations;[196]
- A debt for taxes;[197]
- An auto dealer's purchase of an individual's trade-in vehicle for purposes of resale;[198]
- An auto dealer's discounting of a credit contract to a financing company, where the price was not raised and the consumer was not affected by the discount;[199]
- Residual beneficiaries under a will who could not show any producing cause of damages;[200] and
- A person who sought a $1 million line of credit but who did not prove that he actually sought or acquired the goods (here, cattle) allegedly desired.[201]

2.1.8.6 Texas Case Law Defining "Consumer Transaction": "Consumer" Not Limited to "Personal, Family or Household Purposes"

Texas courts have found that a wide variety of persons are consumers with respect to the Texas UDAP statute, which does not contain a "personal, family, or household use" limitation. Texas UDAP claims were permitted as to:

- Makers of a note who had asked the defendant bank to investigate the creditworthiness of the co-makers;[202]
- Purchasers for resale;[203]
- Purchasers of a home;[204]
- Legatees, as to the guardian and the temporary administrator;[205]
- Purchasers of a burial plot for others (who were moved after interment);[206]
- Indigents who obtained emergency medical services without consideration;[207]
- Persons seeking financing to buy a car;[208]
- A trust that brought an action against a feedlot for losses sustained in a cattle feeding venture;[209]
- A person whose vehicle was stolen while it was in the shop for repairs;[210]
- A corporation that sought and acquired accounting services that were paid for by someone else;[211]
- A contestant at a county fair steer show;[212]
- An oil rig worker who was injured on the rig;[213]
- A partner, with respect to misrepresentations made and actions taken prior to formation of the partnership;[214]
- A car buyer, with respect to a trade-in, as well as the car purchased;[215]
- A person injured on a ride at an amusement park;[216]
- A car lessee, with respect to repairs to the car;[217]
- A person who purchased a distributorship;[218]
- A corporation that purchased a radio station;[219]
- The corporate executor of estate;[220]
- Students of a defunct law school, as against the father of the law school manager;[221]
- The purchaser of services from a third party, as to

---

191 Roach v. Mead, 301 Or. 383, 722 P.2d 1229 (1986).

192 *In re* Sterling Foster & Co., Securities Litigation, 222 F. Supp. 2d 216, 286, 287 (E.D.N.Y. 2002).

193 Meineke Discount Muffler v. Jaynes, 999 F.2d 120 (5th Cir. 1993) (Texas law).

194 Shaw Indus., Inc. v. Brett, 884 F. Supp. 1054 (M.D. La. 1994).

195 Lui Ciro, Inc. v. Ciro, Inc., 895 F. Supp. 1365 (D. Haw. 1995); *see also* Wheeling, Inc. v. Stelle, 2000 U.S. Dist. LEXIS 8628 (E.D. Mich. May 30, 2000) (investment in business).

196 Del Tufo v. National Republican Senatorial Committee, 248 N.J. Super. 684, 591 A.2d 1040 (1991).

197 Teel v. Panarella, 16 Pa. D. & C.4th 271 (1993).

198 Roberts v. Shawnee Mission Ford, 2003 WL 22143727 (D. Kan. Aug. 20, 2003).

199 Chancellor v. Gateway Lincoln-Mercury, 502 S.E.2d 799 (Ga. App. Ct. 1998).

200 Thompson v. Vinson & Elkins, 859 S.W.2d 617 (Tex. App. 1993).

201 First State Bank of Canadian, Texas v. McMordie, 861 S.W.2d 284 (Tex. App. 1993).

202 F.D.I.C. v. F&A Equipment Leasing, 854 S.W.2d 681 (Tex. App. 1993).

203 Hedley Feedlot, Inc. v. Weatherly Trust, 855 S.W.2d 826 (Tex. App. 1993).

204 Parkway Co. v. Woodruff, 857 S.W.2d 903 (Tex. App. 1993).

205 Coble Wall Trust Co. v. Palmer, 859 S.W.2d 475 (Tex. App. 1993).

206 Hines v. Evergreen Cemetery Ass'n, 865 S.W.2d 266 (Tex. App. 1993).

207 Wheeler v. Yettie Kersting Memorial Hosp., 866 S.W.2d 32 (Tex. App. 1993).

208 Megason v. Red River Employees Federal Credit Union, 868 S.W.2d 871 (Tex. App. 1993).

209 Hedley Feedlot, Inc. v. Weatherly Trust, 855 S.W.2d 826 (Tex. App. 1993).

210 Sears, Roebuck & Co. v. Wilson, 963 S.W.2d 166 (Tex. App. 1998) (vehicle was stolen before repairs were started); Bown v. Longo, 909 S.W.2d 618 (Tex. App. 1995).

211 Arthur Andersen & Co. v. Perry Equipment Corp., 945 S.W.2d 812 (Tex. 1997).

212 Galveston County Fair & Rodeo, Inc. v. Kauffman, 910 S.W.2d 129 (Tex. App. 1995).

213 Mote v. Oryx Energy Co., 910 F. Supp. 291 (E.D. Tex. 1995).

214 Clary Corp. v. Smith, 949 S.W.2d 452 (Tex. App. 1997).

215 Apple Imports, Inc. v. Koole, 945 S.W.2d 895 (Tex. App. 1997).

216 Sells v. Six Flags Over Texas, Inc., 1997 U.S. Dist. LEXIS 23747 (N.D. Tex. Aug. 14, 1997).

217 LaBella v. Charlie Thomas, Inc., 942 S.W.2d 127 (Tex. App. 1997).

218 Clary Corp. v. Smith, 949 S.W.2d 452 (Tex. App. 1997).

219 Mason v. F.D.I.C., 888 F. Supp. 799 (S.D. Tex. 1995).

220 NationsBank of Texas v. Akin, Gump, Hauer & Feld, L.L.P., 979 S.W.2d 385 (Tex. App. 1998).

221 Moritz v. Bueche, 980 S.W.2d 849 (Tex. App. 1998).

misrepresentations made by the third party's insurer;[222]

- Purchasers of a home, with respect to the private mortgage insurance they acquired in connection with the purchase;[223]
- Wrongful actions that occurred after the transaction was completed;[224]
- A landlord, as to a utility company that supplied electricity to tenants;[225]
- Electric utility customers, who paid bills directly to the utility company;[226] and
- A physician seeking professional liability insurance.[227]

On the other hand, an employee of a subcontractor that was providing services to the defendant can not bring a Texas UDAP claim arising out of an on-the-job injury.[228] A shopper injured in a slip-and-fall at a Wal-Mart does not have a UDAP claim based on the use of the floors in the store.[229] A terminated employee can not bring a UDAP action against the employer.[230] An employee can not bring an action based on a purchase by the employer unless the employer's primary purpose was to benefit the employee, and not the employer's business.[231] Not surprisingly, the seller in a transaction is not a "consumer" with respect to its buyer.[232]

The widow of a man murdered at a motel that promoted its safety, and even used a "dummy" video monitor camera, can not bring a UDAP action, in the absence of evidence that the dead man was aware of the deceptive safety claims.[233] The shareholder of a company can not bring his own UDAP action, simply because the company itself could.[234] An insurance company can not sue as a "consumer" in the place of its subrogee insured, even if it sues in the name of the insured.[235] A person can not sue his ex-spouse's lawyer under the UDAP statute for the work that lawyer performed for his ex-spouse.[236] A shopper wrongfully accused of shoplifting the item he had just purchased is not a "consumer," because the anti-theft device was not part of the goods or services he bought.[237]

An independent insurance agent is not a "consumer" with respect to the insurer.[238] However, an agent can sue for UNIP violations, and bootstrap UDAP claims under the UNIP violation.[239] Lottery players are not "consumers."[240] Investors are not "consumers" of the services of a security dealer's accounting firm.[241] Nor are they "consumers" with respect to a surety's prescreening and investment counseling, but they are "consumers" with respect to that surety's credit enhancement services.[242] A vehicle purchaser's fiancẽ, who did not participate in the purchase of the vehicle, was not a "consumer," because the vehicle was not purchased for his use nor was there evidence of any intent to benefit the fiancẽ.[243] For a beneficiary of a transaction to have "consumer" status, the transaction must have been specifically required by, or intended to benefit, that beneficiary.[244] A beneficiary of an estate is not a "consumer," with respect to the lawyer for the executor.[245] An insurer that was, at least, an incidental beneficiary of a transaction is not a "consumer."[246]

In an inexplicable decision, one Texas intermediate court held that a homeowner is not a "consumer" with respect to a pool safety alarm because her intended purchase was the installation of the pool (including a safety alarm) rather than just the alarm itself.[247] Not to be outdone, another Texas

222 Park v. Nova Container Freight Station, 1998 U.S. Dist. LEXIS 15551 (N.D. Tex. Sept. 23, 1998).

223 Bennett v. Bank United, 114 S.W.3d 75 (Tex. App. July 11, 2003).

224 Houston Livestock Show and Rodeo, Inc. v. Hamrick, 125 S.W.3d 555 (Tex. App. 2003).

225 Henderson v. Central Power & Light Co., 977 S.W.2d 439 (Tex. App. 1998).

226 Bailey v. Gulf States Utilities Co., 27 S.W.3d 713 (Tex. App. 2000).

227 Herrin v. Medical Protective Co., 89 S.W.3d 301 (Tex. App. 2002).

228 Nabors Loffland Drilling Co. v. Martinez, 894 S.W.2d 70 (Tex. App. 1995).

229 Rojas v. Wal-Mart Stores, 857 F. Supp. 533 (N.D. Tex. 1994). *See also* Ramirez v. H.E. Butt Grocery Co., 909 S.W.2d 62 (Tex. App. 1995).

230 Figueroa v. West, 902 S.W.2d 701 (Tex. App. 1995).

231 Banzhaf v. ADT Sec. Sys. Southwest, Inc., 28 S.W.3d 180 (Tex. App. 2000) (employee does not have standing to sue burglar alarm company hired by employer, when employer's purpose was to protect its property and not its employees); Clark Equipment Co. v. Pitner, 923 S.W.2d 117 (Tex. App. 1996).

232 Flameout Design & Fabrication, Inc. v. Pennzoil Caspian Corp., 994 S.W.2d 830 (Tex. App. 1999).

233 Cianfichi v. White House Motor Hotel, 921 S.W.2d 440 (Tex. App. 1996).

234 Mason v. F.D.I.C., 888 F. Supp. 799 (S.D. Tex. 1995); Kenneth H. Hughes Interests, Inc. v. Westrup, 879 S.W.2d 229 (Tex. App. 1994).

235 Trimble v. Itz, 1995 Tex. App. LEXIS 1056 (1995).

236 McDuffie v. Blassingame, 883 S.W.2d 329 (Tex. App. 1994).

237 McClung v. Wal-Mart, 866 F. Supp. 306 (N.D. Tex. 1994).

238 Metropolitan Life Ins. Co. v. Haney, 987 S.W.2d 236 (Tex. App. 1999) (agent who used software sold by insurer to another agent is not a "consumer" of the software because the insurer's goal was to increase sales, not benefit its agents); Tweedell v. Hochheim Prairie Farm Mut. Ins. Ass'n, 1 S.W.3d 304 (Tex. App. 1999) (although agent is not a UDAP "consumer," the agent has standing to sue the insurer for UNIP violations).

239 Crown Life Ins. Co. v. Casteel, 22 S.W.3d 378 (Tex. 2000); Tweedell v. Hochheim Prairie Farm Mut. Ins. Ass'n, 1 S.W.3d 304 (Tex. App. 1999).

240 Kinnard v. Circle K Stores Inc., 966 S.W.2d 613 (Tex. App. 1998).

241 Hendricks v. Thornton, 973 S.W.2d 348 (Tex. App. 1998).

242 Insurance Co. of N. Am. v. Morris, 981 S.W.2d 667 (Tex. 1998).

243 Chamrad v. Volvo Cars of N. Am., 145 F.3d 671 (5th Cir. 1998).

244 Cook-Pizzi v. Van Waters & Rogers, Inc., 94 S.W.3d 636 (Tex. App. 2002).

245 Frost National Bank v. Heafner, 12 S.W.3d 104 (Tex. App. 1999); Querner v. Rindfuss, 966 S.W.2d 661 (Tex. App. 1998).

246 Burroughs v. APS Int'l, Ltd., 93 S.W.3d 155 (Tex. App. May 30, 2002).

247 Lukasik v. San Antonio Blue Haven Pools, Inc., 21 S.W.3d 394 (Tex. App. 2000).

court of appeals held that a tenant has no UDAP claim for the wrongful exercise of a landlord's lien because the lien was not based on the lease of the property,[248] and that a claim for the refusal to issue a warranty on an installed roof does not arise out of the purchase of the roof and installation services.[249] These three cases involve an almost-willful ignorance of consumer transactions, and should not be extended beyond their facts, or even to other Texas courts of appeal.

2.1.9 No Requirement for Media Advertisement

Courts reject the argument occasionally made by sellers that UDAP statutes apply only to media advertising, and that oral misrepresentations alone are not actionable.[250]

2.1.10 UDAP Liability Where Party Outside UDAP Statute's Scope

A party can still be liable under a state UDAP statute in some situations even where that party falls outside the statute's scope. For example, even if certain entities do not fall within a UDAP statute's scope, they may be liable for UDAP violations they committed as part of a conspiracy with covered entities.[251]

Similarly, a party may be derivatively liable for the UDAP violation of another party. For example, a holder of a promissory note containing the FTC Holder Notice[252] is subject to all UDAP claims that the consumer can raise against the seller, even if the holder is not covered by the UDAP statute. The very promissory note states that the holder is subject to all claims the consumer can raise against the seller.[253]

248 Koch v. Griffith-Stroud Constr. & Leasing Co., 2004 WL 555617 (Tex. App. Mar. 23, 2004).

249 Roof Sys., Inc. v. Johns Manville Corp., 130 S.W.3d 430 (Tex. App. 2004).

250 *See* Bonn v. Haubrich, 123 Wis. App. 168, 366 N.W.2d 503 (1985); *see also* State v. Automatic Merchandisers, 64 Wis. 2d 659, 221 N.W.2d 683 (1974).

251 Camp, Dresser & McKee, Inc. v. Steimle & Assocs., Inc., 652 So. 2d 44 (La. Ct. App. 1995); Strahan v. Louisiana Dep't of Agriculture & Forestry, 645 So. 2d 1162 (La. Ct. App. 1994); Anton v. Merrill Lynch, 36 S.W.3d 251 (Tex. App. 2001).

252 *See* § 6.6, *infra.*

253 Nations Credit v. Pheanis, 102 Ohio App. 3d 71, 656 N.E.2d 998 (1995) (mobile home financer held liable under FTC rule for UDAP violations of mobile home dealer). *See also* § 2.2.1.5, *infra.*

2.2 Exempted Transactions

2.2.1 Credit

2.2.1.1 General

Although it would appear strange for UDAP statutes to apply to the sale of goods and services, but not to the credit practices used to finance those goods or services, in a number of jurisdictions this issue will be raised. Thus, UDAP practitioners must pay special attention where a challenged practice involves banking, credit terms, loan practices, or other financing activities. The issue's resolution often is determined by the exact language of the state's statute. Keep in mind what one federal court has indicated is the underlying policy consideration: "only an artificially restrictive construction would hold that the statute applies broadly to practices utilized to effect a sale, but can not reach the practices utilized in its financing."[254]

2.2.1.2 Does a Credit Transaction Involve "Goods or Services"?

Where a UDAP statute limits coverage to transactions involving "goods or services," most courts hold that this language encompasses credit transactions.[255] For example, a

254 Garland v. Mobil Oil Corp., 340 F. Supp. 1095 (N.D. Ill. 1972).

255 Smith v. Commercial Banking Corp., 866 F.2d 576 (3d Cir. 1989) (Penn. law); Stafford v. Cross Country Bank, 262 F. Supp. 2d 776 (W.D. Ky. 2003) (credit is a service); Apgar v. Homeside Lending, Inc. (*In re* Apgar), 291 B.R. 665, 684 (E.D. Pa. 2003) (mortgage loan is service); Flores v. Shapiro & Kreisman, 246 F. Supp. 2d 427 (E.D. Pa. 2002) (covers loans that finance goods or services for personal use); Hogan v. Valley National Fin. Servs. Co., Clearinghouse No. 40,428 (D. Colo. Feb. 1, 1995) (denying motion to dismiss and holding that a loan is a "service" covered by Colorado's UDAP law); Jackson v. Culinary School of Washington, 788 F. Supp. 1233 (D.D.C. 1992) (denying motion to dismiss), *dismissed on summary judgment on other grounds*, 811 F. Supp. 714 (D.D.C. 1993), *aff'd in part, rev'd and remanded in part on other grounds*, 27 F.3d 573 (1994) (reversing, on *de novo* review, district court's decision to issue declaratory judgment on state law issues), *vacated*, 515 U.S. 1139 (1995) (appeals court should have used abuse of discretion standard to review district court's decision to issue declaratory judgment on state law issues), *on remand*, 59 F.3d 254 (D.C. Cir. 1995) (remanding for district court to exercise its discretion about whether to issue declaratory judgment on state law issues); McTeer v. Provident Life & Acc. Ins., 712 F. Supp. 512 (D.S.C. 1989); *In re* Wiggins, 273 B.R. 839 (Bankr. D. Idaho 2001) (purchase of structured settlement annuity for cash is covered); Andrews v. Fleet Real Estate Funding Corp. (*In re* Andrews), 78 B.R. 78 (Bankr. E.D. Pa. 1987); Russell v. Fidelity Consumer Discount Co. (*In re* Russell), 72 B.R. 855 (Bankr. E.D. Pa. 1987); Villegas v. Transamerica Fin. Servs., 147 Ariz. 100, 708 P.2d 781 (Ct. App. 1985); Poquonnock Avenue Assocs. v. Society For Savings, Clearinghouse No. 31,045 (Conn.

Vermont court has ruled that a bank loan is a service since "service means to furnish and supply something needed or desired. . . . Thus anyone supplying money, a need, would be one who serves."[256] Similarly, a Connecticut court has ruled that giving and collecting loans is a "distribution of services or property."[257]

An Arizona appellate court has held that the UDAP statute applies to a loan refinancing, since money is an "object," "goods," or "commodity" and the right to repayment is an "intangible."[258] In addition, the Arizona court found that a loan is a "sale."[259] Tennessee's UDAP statute, which covers advertising or distribution of any service or other thing of value, covers loans of money.[260] Similarly, a federal court has interpreted South Carolina's statute as covering a mortgage loan since there is a sale of the present use of money for a promise to repay in the future.[261]

Texas courts have developed some fine distinctions about whether credit and banking activities are the purchase of a "good" or "service." A straight loan is not the purchase of a "good," since the term is defined as a "tangible chattel bought for use."[262] Seeking a loan is not "acquiring services," defined as "work or labor."[263] These rulings that a straight loan is not covered by the Texas UDAP statute are significantly narrowed by holdings that loans whose proceeds are used to purchase something are covered by the UDAP statute.

The Texas Supreme Court has ruled that a credit extension in conjunction with a retail sale is covered because the transaction involves the purchase of goods, even though the purchaser does not buy the goods from the creditor.[264] The same is true for the financing of a home sale.[265] Thus where

Super. Ct. 1980); State v. Brotherhood Bank & Trust, 649 P.2d 419 (Kan. Ct. App. 1982) (home mortgages and other forms of credit); Pennsylvania Bankers Ass'n v. Commonwealth, 58 Pa. Commw. 170, 427 A.2d 730 (1981); Lavinia v. Howard Bank, Clearinghouse No. 26,015 (Vt. Super. Ct. 1976); *see also* Williams v. First Government Mortgage & Investors Corp., 176 F.3d 497 (D.C. Cir. 1999) (same); Fielder v. Credit Acceptance Corp., 19 F. Supp. 2d 966 (W.D. Mo. 1998), *vacated and remanded, in part, on other grounds*, 188 F.3d 1031 (8th Cir. 1999), *later opinion*, 98 F. Supp. 2d 1104 (W.D. Mo. 2000) (summary judgment for lender on TILA claim; state claims remanded to state court); Saler v. Hurvitz (*In re* Saler), 84 B.R. 45 (Bankr. E.D. Pa. 1988); Jungkurth v. Eastern Fin. Servs., Inc. (*In re* Jungkurth), 74 B.R. 323 (Bankr. E.D. Pa. 1987); DeBerry v. First Gov't Mortg. & Investors Corp., 743 A.2d 699 (D.C. 1999) (prohibition of unconscionable terms in sales or leases applies to mortgage loan); Entriken v. Motor Coach Federal Credit Union, 845 P.2d 93 (Mont. 1992); Baird v. Norwest Bank, 843 P.2d 327 (Mont. 1992); Lemelledo v. Beneficial Management Corp., 150 N.J. 255, 696 A.2d 546 (1997) (offer of consumer credit is "merchandise"). *Cf.* Nienke v. Norman Gray, Ltd., 857 P.2d 446 (Colo. Ct. App. 1993) (appellate court found UDAP challenge to loan not frivolous, since issue of whether loan covered by "goods or services" not established in Colorado). *But see* Barber v. National Bank of Alaska, 815 P.2d 857 (Alaska 1991); York v. InTrust Bank, 265 Kan. 271, 962 P.2d 405 (1998) (implying that banking may not be covered in general, but finding coverage where bank subdivided and developed real property); Boubelik v. Liberty State Bank, 553 N.W.2d 393 (Minn. 1996) (bank loans are not "merchandise" so are not covered by UDAP statute; statute has since been amended to include loans) (after this decision, the Minnesota legislature amended the UDAP statute to explicitly include loans within its scope); Epstein v. Goldome FSB, 49 Pa. D. & C.3d 551 (C.P. Delaware Cty. 1987).

256 Lavinia v. Howard Bank, Clearinghouse No. 26,015 (Vt. Super. Ct. 1976).

257 Poquonnock Avenue Assocs. v. Society For Savings, Clearinghouse No. 31,045 (Conn. Super. Ct. 1980).

258 Villegas v. Transamerica Fin. Servs., 147 Ariz. 100, 708 P.2d 781 (Ct. App. 1985). *Accord In re* Wiggins, 273 B.R. 839 (Bankr. D. Idaho 2001) (exchange of structured settlement annuity for cash is covered; "goods" includes intangibles); Clingerman v. Ford Motor Credit Co., Clearinghouse No. 50,427 (Ariz. Super. Ct. Nov. 1, 1994) (ruling on motion to dismiss).

259 Villegas v. Transamerica Fin. Servs., 147 Ariz. 100, 708 P.2d 781 (Ct. App. 1985).

260 Turner v. E-Z Check Cashing, 35 F. Supp. 2d 1042, 1051 (M.D. Tenn. 1999).

261 McTeer v. Provident Life & Acc. Ins., 712 F. Supp. 512 (D.S.C. 1989).

262 Riverside National Bank v. Lewis, 603 S.W.2d 169 (Tex. 1980); Brown v. Bank of Galveston, National Ass'n, 930 S.W.2d 140 (Tex. App. 1996), *aff'd on other grounds*, 963 S.W.2d 511 (Tex. 1998); Bank of El Paso v. T.O. Stanley Boot Co., 809 S.W.2d 279 (Tex. App. 1991); Smith v. United States National Bank, 767 S.W.2d 820 (Tex. App. 1989); *see also* Federal Sav. & Loan Ins. v. Kralj, 968 F.2d 500 (5th Cir. 1992) (Texas law); La Sara Grain Co. v. First National Bank, 673 S.W.2d 558 (Tex. 1984); Baskin v. Mortgage & Trust, Inc., 837 S.W.2d 743 (Tex. App. 1992); Henderson v. Texas Commerce Bank-Midland, 837 S.W.2d 778 (Tex. App. 1992); White Budd Van Ness P'ship v. Major-Gladys Drive Joint Venture, 798 S.W.2d 805 (Tex. App. 1990); Fuller v. Preston State Bank, 667 S.W.2d 214 (Tex. App. 1984).

263 Clardy Mfg. Co. v. Marine Midland Bus. Loans, Inc., 88 F.3d 347 (5th Cir. 1996); Bank of El Paso v. T.O. Stanley Boot Co., 809 S.W.2d 279 (Tex. App. 1991); Riverside National Bank v. Lewis, 603 S.W.2d 169 (Tex. 1980); *see also* White Budd Van Ness P'ship v. Major-Gladys Drive Joint Venture, 798 S.W.2d 805 (Tex. App. 1990); Fortner v. Fannin Bank in Windom, 634 S.W.2d 74 (Tex. App. 1982).

264 Knight v. International Harvester Credit Corp., 627 S.W.2d 382 (Tex. 1982); *see also* MBank Fort Worth, N.A. v. Trans Meridian, Inc., 820 F.2d 716 (5th Cir. 1987) (Texas law); Security Bank v. Dalton, 803 S.W.2d 443 (Tex. App. 1991); Irizarry v. Amarillo Pantex Federal Credit Union, 695 S.W.2d 91 (Tex. App. 1985); First Texas Savings Ass'n v. Stiff Properties, 685 S.W.2d 703 (Tex. App. 1984).

265 First Texas Savings Ass'n v. Stiff Properties, 685 S.W.2d 703 (Tex. App. 1984); Dickinson State Bank v. Ogden, 624 S.W.2d 214 (Tex. Civ. App. 1981); *see also* Holland Mortg. & Invest. Corp. v. Bone, 751 S.W.2d 515 (Tex. App. 1987) (at least where seller and bank have some form of "tie-in," loan to pay for home construction is covered). *But cf.* Maginn v. Norwest Mortg., Inc., 919 S.W.2d 164 (Tex. App. 1996) (ignoring the fact that the transaction at issue was a mortgage loan, the court reviewed the services rendered in connection with the mortgage

the financing of a sale is really the same transaction as the sale itself, unfair provisions in the credit agreement fall within the UDAP statute's scope.[266] Similarly, a credit union's loan practices are actionable where the loan proceeds go to purchase an automobile.[267] A dispute over seller's points in the purchase price of a home also involves the purchase of goods or services.[268]

The Texas Supreme Court has also ruled that the UDAP statute applies to a foreclosure performed by the assignee of the credit-seller.[269] The statutory language "consumers of goods or services" applies to all persons who try to enjoy the benefits of a sales transaction, even if the deceptive practice happens well after the acquisition of services, and even if the individual engaging in the deceptive practices was not the original credit-seller.[270]

In fact, there is a question in Texas whether any type of loan is now excluded because a careful consumer attorney can describe virtually any loan as one where proceeds are used to purchase something. Most lenders will certainly know the purposes to which the loan proceeds will be put. Nevertheless, the distinction between a straight loan and a credit sale may still have some vitality because some Texas courts are requiring a tie-in between the seller of the goods or services and the lender, such as the seller referring the consumer to the lender.[271] The lender may be so inextricably intertwined in a transaction as to bring the lender as well as the seller, under the UDAP statute.[272] Other courts also require the UDAP claim to relate to the goods or services being purchased.[273] For example, misrepresentations related to collecting a student loan do not form the basis for a UDAP claim because the UDAP-related transaction was the initial loan for education.[274]

A few courts do find that credit transactions are outside the scope of "goods and services." An Oregon court has ruled that the extension of consumer credit by a small loan company is not a sale of goods or services.[275] According to the same court, a loan broker's deception regarding its services is actionable under the UDAP statute, but its representations about the attributes of the loan itself are not.[276] Massachusetts' highest court has interpreted that state's UDAP statute, since amended in the pertinent sections, to exclude mortgagors as not being purchasers of the use of the money.[277] The Alaska Supreme Court held a mortgage loan not to be either a "good" or a "service."[278] The Idaho Supreme Court finds signing a personal guarantee for a loan to a corporation not a "purchase of goods" and thus not covered.[279] A court interpreting the Alabama statute finds a mortgage loan not to involve goods or services because the Alabama UDAP statute exempts banks, and the court viewed this exemption as an indication of legislative intent that the statute does not apply to loans generally.[280] Even if

---

loan and concluded that all services were incidental to, and not an objective of, the transaction, so borrowers did not have standing to bring a UDAP claim).

266 Knight v. International Harvester Credit Corp., 627 S.W.2d 382 (Tex. 1982); Griffith v. Porter, 817 S.W.2d 131 (Tex. App. 1991).

267 Irizarry v. Amarillo Pantex Federal Credit Union, 695 S.W.2d 91 (Tex. App. 1985).

268 William P. Terrell, Inc. v. Miller, 697 S.W.2d 454 (Tex. App. 1985).

269 Flenniken v. Longview Bank & Trust Co., 661 S.W.2d 705 (Tex. 1984). *But see* English v. Fischer, 649 S.W.2d 83 (Tex. App. 1982), *rev'd on other grounds*, 660 S.W.2d 521 (Tex. 1983) (Texas act does not apply to acceleration of mortgage note).

270 Flenniken v. Longview Bank & Trust Co., 661 S.W.2d 705 (Tex. 1984). After *Flennikin*, Texas UDAP claims were permitted as to makers of a note who had asked the defendant bank to investigate the creditworthiness of the co-makers, F.D.I.C. v. F&A Equipment Leasing, 854 S.W.2d 681 (Tex. App. 1993); purchasers of a home, Parkway Co. v. Woodruff, 857 S.W.2d 903 (Tex. App. 1993); and persons seeking financing to buy a car, Megason v. Red River Employees Federal Credit Union, 868 S.W.2d 871 (Tex. App. 1993). However, a person who sought a $1 million line of credit, but who did not prove that he actually sought or acquired the goods (here, cattle) allegedly desired was denied UDAP remedies. First State Bank of Canadian, Texas v. McMordie, 861 S.W.2d 284 (Tex. App. 1993).

271 Holland Mortg. & Invest. Corp. v. Bone, 751 S.W.2d 515 (Tex. App. 1987); Wynn v. Kensington Mortg. & Fin. Corp., 697 S.W.2d 47 (Tex. App. 1985).

272 Ford v. City State Bank of Palacios, 44 S.W.3d 121 (Tex. App. 2001); Norwest Mortgage, Inc. v. Salinas, 999 S.W.2d 846 (Tex. App. 1999).

273 *See* Wellborn v. Sears, Roebuck & Co., 970 F.2d 1420 (5th Cir. 1992) (Texas law).

274 Holeman v. Landmark Chevrolet Corp., 989 S.W.2d 395 (Tex. App. 1999).

275 Haeger v. Johnson, 25 Or. App. 131, 548 P.2d 532 (1976). A subsequent amendment to expand the term "sale" in the Oregon UDAP statute to include "rental or otherwise" was found not to be intended to overrule Haeger v. Johnson, and consumer credit remains outside the scope of the Oregon statute. Lamm v. Amfac Mortgage Corp., 44 Or. App. 203, 605 P.2d 730 (1980). *Accord* Carey v. Lincoln Loan Co., 165 Or. App. 657, 998 P.2d 724 (2000). *See also* Roach v. Mead, 301 Or. 383, 722 P.2d 1229 (1986), in which the Oregon Supreme Court ruled that the UDAP statute did not cover an attorney who gave advice about business lending. The intermediate appellate court had ruled that ruled that credit was not covered, 139 Or. App. 119, 911 P.2d 936 (1996). By contrast, the supreme court based its ruling on the fact that the transaction was a business rather than a consumer transaction, suggesting some doubt about the intermediate appellate court's rationale.

276 Cullen v. Investment Strategies, Inc., 139 Or. App. 119, 911 P.2d 936 (1996).

277 Murphy v. Charlestown Savings Bank, 380 Mass. 738, 405 N.E.2d 954 (1980). The court apparently did not consider whether the mortgagor had purchased a service, but found the loan to be only a product, the use of the money. *See also* Dance v. Taunton Sav. Bank, 385 Mass. 1, 429 N.E.2d 1129 (1982). *Accord* Shawmut Community Bank v. Zagami, 411 Mass. 807, 586 N.E.2d 962 (1992) (interpreting pre-amendment statute).

278 Barber v. National Bank of Alaska, 815 P.2d 857 (Alaska 1991).

279 Idaho First National Bank v. Wells, 100 Idaho 256, 596 P.2d 429 (1979).

280 Deerman v. Federal Home Loan Mortgage Corp., 955 F. Supp. 1393 (N.D. Ala. 1997), *aff'd without op.*, 140 F.3d 1043 (11th Cir. 1998).

a state exempts lending in general, a bank is covered by the UDAP statute when it subdivides and sells lots in a real estate development.[281]

2.2.1.3 Services in Connection with a Loan or Banking Are "Goods or Services"

No matter which way a court rules on whether a credit extension is a "service," there should be little doubt that services in connection with the loan are covered.[282] Thus a mortgage broker sells the service of procuring loans,[283] and credit counseling and debt pooling services are in trade or commerce.[284] The sale of advice on low-cost credit cards involves the sale of merchandise, defined to include services.[285] A company that purchases individuals' structured settlements in exchange for cash, and that promises financial planning and other services, is engaged in the sale of services.[286]

A bank's sale of credit insurance in conjunction with a loan is a service.[287] A bank's provision of check cashing activities for a fee is also a service, allowing a consumer to challenge the bank's improper dishonoring of a check.[288] Even if a loan is not covered by a state's statute, the bank's collateral activity of agreeing to process the title papers is a service since the activity is of benefit to both parties, and the service is purchased with part of the loan payment.[289]

A Texas court has ruled that it is a factual issue whether a passbook savings account involves a service, the court noting that the bank assesses a "service charge."[290] Similarly, where purchase of a certificate of deposit entitles the consumer to free financial counseling services from the bank, a service is involved.[291] Opening an IRA account involves purchase of a service from an IRA trustee.[292] Purchasing a traveler's check involves purchase of services, including free replacement of lost checks.[293] A factual question exists on whether a "service" has been purchased where the consumer alleges that, by obtaining a bank loan, he also purchased financial advice on where and when to obtain financing and how to structure the loan.[294] However, a Texas court has held that services related to a loan are subject to the UDAP statute only if those services were one of the actual objectives of the transaction, and not merely incidental to the loan.[295]

An Oregon appellate decision makes unusually fine distinctions regarding UDAP coverage of mortgage brokers. According to that court, mortgage brokers are covered by the state UDAP statute. Nondisclosure or misrepresentation by the broker is not actionable under UDAP, however, if it relates solely to the loan's attributes, since Oregon's UDAP statute would exempt the creditor itself from liability for such acts. If the nondisclosure or misrepresentation relates to the broker's services or the cost of those services, it is actionable under the UDAP statute.[296]

2.2.1.4 Credit Is in "Trade or Commerce"

Courts have little problem finding that credit practices are included in the term "trade or commerce." Consequently,

281 York v. InTrust Bank, 265 Kan. 271, 962 P.2d 405 (1998).

282 Phillips v. Dukes (Matter of Dukes), 24 B.R. 404 (Bankr. E.D. Mich. 1982); Allan v. M&S Mortgage Co., 359 N.W.2d 238 (Mich. Ct. App. 1984); Riverside National Bank v. Lewis, 603 S.W.2d 169 (Tex. 1980); *see also* Stogsdill v. Cragin Federal Bank, 645 N.E.2d 564 (Ill. App. Ct. 1995) (banking services, including cashing of checks, are covered by UDAP statute); Fortner v. Fannin Bank in Windom, 634 S.W.2d 74 (Tex. App. 1982); Lubbock Mortgage & Inv. Co. v. Thomas, 626 S.W.2d 611 (Tex. Civ. App. 1981). The issue applies to real estate and securities transactions and those cases are also supportive of the inclusion of credit services; *see* §§ 2.2.5.2, 2.2.9.3, *infra*.

283 Phillips v. Dukes (Matter of Dukes), 24 B.R. 404 (Bankr. E.D. Mich. 1982); Allan v. M&S Mortgage Co., 359 N.W.2d 238 (Mich. Ct. App. 1984); Cullen v. Investment Strategies, Inc., 139 Or. App. 119, 911 P.2d 936 (1996); Lubbock Mortgage & Inv. Co. v. Thomas, 626 S.W.2d 611 (Tex. Civ. App. 1981).

284 Commonwealth v. Legal Credit Counselors, Inc., Clearinghouse No. 41,271 (Mass. Super. Ct. 1983).

285 State v. Sgillo, 176 Ariz. 148, 859 P.2d 771 (Ct. App. 1993).

286 *In re* Wiggins, 273 B.R. 839 (Bankr. D. Idaho 2001).

287 Bennett v. Bank United, 114 S.W.3d 75 (Tex. App. July 11, 2003); Juarez v. Bank of Austin, 659 S.W.2d 139 (Tex. App. 1983). *But see* English v. Fischer, 660 S.W.2d 521 (Tex. 1983) (UDAP statute does not apply to creditor's failure to turn over insurance proceeds to the debtor).

288 La Sara Grain Co. v. First National Bank, 673 S.W.2d 558 (Tex. 1984); Farmers & Merchants State Bank v. Ferguson, 605 S.W.2d 320 (Tex. Civ. App. 1980), *modified on other grounds*, 617 S.W.2d 918 (Tex. 1981); *see also* Bank One, Texas, N.A. v. Taylor, 970 F.2d 16 (5th Cir. 1992) (Texas law); *In re* Wernly, 91 B.R. 702 (Bankr. E.D. Pa. 1988); Security Bank v. Dalton, 803 S.W.2d 443 (Tex. App. 1991); Plaza National Bank v. Walker, 767 S.W.2d 276 (Tex. App. 1989) (a consumer's savings account with bank involves a purchase of "services").

289 Fortner v. Fannin Bank in Windom, 634 S.W.2d 74 (Tex. App. 1982).

290 Netterville v. Interfirst Bank, 718 S.W.2d 921 (Tex. App. 1986). *But see* Genico Distrib. Inc. v. First National Bank, 616 S.W.2d 418 (Tex. Civ. App. 1981) (making a deposit does not involve a service).

291 First Federal Savings & Loan Ass'n v. Ritenour, 704 S.W.2d 895 (Tex. App. 1986). *But see* Grass v. Credito Mexicano, S.A., 797 F.2d 220 (5th Cir. 1986) (Texas law) (purchasing a certificate of deposit does not involve service; no discussion of counseling services as part of transaction); First State Bank v. Chesshir, 613 S.W.2d 61 (Tex. Civ. App. 1981), *aff'd as reformed*, 634 S.W.2d 742 (Tex. App. 1982) (same).

292 McDade v. Texas Commerce Bank, 822 S.W.2d 713 (Tex. App. 1991).

293 Thomas C. Cook, Inc. v. Rowhanion, 774 S.W.2d 679 (Tex. App. 1989).

294 Herndon v. First National Bank of Tulia, 802 S.W.2d 396 (Tex. App. 1991).

295 White v. Mellon Mortg. Co., 995 S.W.2d 795 (Tex. App. 1999).

296 Cullen v. Investment Strategies, Inc., 139 Or. App. 119, 911 P.2d 936 (1996).

banking and credit activities are covered by UDAP statutes that apply broadly to "trade or commerce."[297]

2.2.1.5 Specific Statutory Exemptions

In some states, other statutory language is determinative of the UDAP statute's applicability to credit-related activities. In some states, courts hold that credit falls within an exemption for transactions regulated by an agency, but most states reject this interpretation.[298] Louisiana has a blanket exemption for chartered banks.[299] Maine's banking laws exempt banks and credit unions from its UDAP statute.[300] Ohio's UDAP statute explicitly exempts "financial institutions" and "dealers in intangibles."[301] An Ohio court has ruled that a finance company or bank providing standard forms and discounting promissory notes for the seller was not a supplier "engaged in the business of affecting or soliciting consumer transactions," but was a dealer in "intangibles," and thus specifically exempted from the Ohio UDAP statute.[302] A payday lender was also held to be a dealer in intangibles.[303] Similarly, an Ohio bank that financed a car sale was exempt as a "financial institution" from Ohio's UDAP statute.[304] But another lender did not meet the criteria for the statutory exemption because it did not maintain an office in Ohio.[305] Further, this exemption does not protect a financial institution or dealer in intangibles from derivative liability, under the FTC's rule on Preservation of Consumers' Claims and Defenses, for UDAP violations committed by the merchant that dealt with the consumer.[306] Mortgage loans in Ohio may also be exempt as real estate transactions unless the transaction also involves goods or services.[307]

A 2002 amendment to New Hampshire's UDAP statute exempts trade or commerce that is subject to the jurisdiction of the state banking commissioner, the financial institutions regulators of other states, or federal banking regulators who have authority to regulate unfair or deceptive practices.[308]

2.2.1.6 Does Other Legislation Occupy the Field of Credit Regulation?

2.2.1.6.1 FTC Act

A final problem with UDAP coverage of credit practices is possible preemption by other credit statutes or regulatory schemes.[309] The Federal Trade Commission regulates some of the credit market but does not regulate unfair banking practices, which is reserved for the federal regulatory agencies, such as the Federal Reserve Board and the Comptroller of the Currency, that regulate these financial institutions. But even though the FTC Act does not apply to banks, and even though state courts are guided by the FTC Act in interpreting state UDAP statutes, the FTC's scope does not prevent UDAP statutes from applying to banks.[310] Indeed, while banks are not directly subject to the FTC Act, the FTC still

297 Morse v. Mutual Fed. Sav. & Loan Ass'n, 536 F. Supp. 1271 (D. Mass. 1982); *In re* Rodriguez, 218 B.R. 764 (Bankr. E.D. Pa. 1998); Petersen v. State Employees Credit Union (*In re* Kittrell), 115 B.R. 873 (Bankr. M.D.N.C. 1990); Hawaii Community Fed. Credit Union v. Keka, 94 Haw. 213, 11 P.3d 1 (2000); Perez v. Citicorp Mortgage, Inc., 703 N.E.2d 518 (Ill. App. Ct. 1998) (mortgage lenders are covered); Stogsdill v. Cragin Federal Bank, 645 N.E.2d 564 (Ill. App. Ct. 1995) (UDAP statute covers banking practices; declining to follow Estate of Szorek, 194 Ill. App. 3d 750, 551 N.E.2d 697 (1990)); Bankier v. First Federal Savings & Loan Ass'n, 588 N.E.2d 391 (Ill. App. Ct. 1992); Mid-American National Bank v. First Savings & Loan Ass'n, 161 Ill. App. 531, 515 N.E.2d 176 (1987); Exchange National Bank v. Farm Bureau Life Ins. Co., 108 Ill. App. 3d 212, 438 N.E.2d 1247 (1982); Raymer v. Bay State National Bank, 384 Mass. 310, 424 N.E.2d 515 (1981); Pennsylvania Bankers Ass'n v. Commonwealth, 58 Pa. Commw. 170, 427 A.2d 730 (1981); *see also* Johnson v. Phoenix Mut. Life Ins. Co., 300 N.C. 247, 266 S.E.2d 610 (1980) (loan finder is in "trade or commerce," but debt collection practices are not); Brooks v. Creech, 2003 WL 174805 (Tenn. App. Jan. 28, 2003) (Tenn. UDAP statute covers loans; court does not specify rationale).

298 *See* §§ 2.2.1.6, 2.3.3, *infra.*

299 Bank One v. Colley, 294 F. Supp. 2d 864 (M.D. La. 2003); Blanchard & Co. v. Barrick Gold Corp., 2003 WL 22071173 (E.D. La. Sept. 3, 2003); Traina v. NationsBank, 2001 U.S. Dist. LEXIS 14612 (E.D. La. Sept. 7, 2001). *See also* § 2.2.1.6.2, *infra.*

300 Me. Rev. Stat. Ann. tit. 9-B, § 244. *See* Shapiro v. Haenn, 190 F. Supp. 2d 64 (D. Me. 2002).

301 Ohio Rev. Code § 1345.01(A) (referring to § 5725.01).

302 Brown v. Willard, 5 Ohio Op. 3d 195 (Ct. App. 1977). *See* Ohio Consumer Law § 2.8 (2002 ed.) for further discussion of coverage of creditors under Ohio's UDAP statute.

303 King v. Cashland, Inc., 2001 Ohio App. LEXIS 3943 (Sept. 1, 2000).

304 Vannoy v. Capital Lincoln-Mercury Sales, Inc., 88 Ohio App. 3d 138, 623 N.E.2d 177 (1993).

305 Hanlin v. Ohio Builders & Remodelers, 212 F. Supp. 2d 752 (S.D. Ohio 2002).

306 Hanlin v. Ohio Builders & Remodelers, 2001 WL 1678864 (S.D. Ohio Dec. 26, 2001) (if contract contains Holder Notice then lender has derivative liability for contractor's UDAP violations; lender may be liable if home improvement contract was submitted to it even though not assigned to it), *later op. at* 212 F. Supp. 2d 752 (S.D. Ohio 2002) (lender not derivatively liable for contractor's UDAP violations where Holder Notice not in loan contract and lender was unaware it was in original home improvement contract); Milchen v. Bob Morris Pontiac-GMC Truck, 113 Ohio App. 3d 190, 680 N.E.2d 698 (1996); Nations Credit v. Pheanis, 102 Ohio App. 3d 71, 656 N.E.2d 998 (1995).

307 Hanlin v. Ohio Builders & Remodelers, 212 F. Supp. 2d 752 (S.D. Ohio 2002) (closing services not enough). *See* § 2.2.5, *infra.*

308 N.H. Rev. Stat. Ann. § 358-A:3, *as amended, effective* July 17, 2002.

309 *See generally* §§ 2.3.3, *supra*, 2.5.2, *infra.*

310 Normand Josef Enterprises v. Connecticut Bank, 230 Conn. 486, 646 A.2d 1289 (1994); Raymer v. Bay State National Bank, 384 Mass. 310, 424 N.E.2d 515 (1981); Farmers & Merchant State Bank v. Ferguson, 605 S.W.2d 320 (Tex. Civ. App. 1980), *modified on other grounds*, 617 S.W.2d 918 (Tex. 1981). *But see* Idaho First National Bank v. Wells, 100 Idaho 256, 596 P.2d 429 (1979).

plays a leadership role in defining what conduct by banks is unfair and deceptive. Whenever the FTC promulgates a rule the federal banking agencies must adopt a substantially similar regulations within sixty days unless they make certain specified findings.[311]

2.2.1.6.2 Federal and state banking laws

Whether federal banking laws preempt state UDAP statutes as a matter of federal law is analyzed in § 2.5.3, *infra*. As a matter of state law, the UDAP statutes of Arizona,[312] Arkansas,[313] Connecticut,[314] and Pennsylvania[315] courts interpret their UDAP statutes not to be displaced by state and federal credit regulation. The New Jersey Supreme Court has held that the extension of credit by a finance company is subject to the UDAP statute despite substantial regulation by the state department of banking.[316] The court held that the UDAP statute's recognition of cumulative remedies and its empowerment of citizens as private attorneys general showed the legislative intent "to enlarge fraud-fighting authority." The court noted:

> That legislative intent is readily inferable from the ongoing need for consumer protection and the salutary benefits to be achieved by expanding enforcement authority and enhancing remedial redress. When remedial power is concentrated in one agency, underenforcement may result because of lack of resources, concentration on other agency responsibilities, lack of expertise, agency capture by regulated parties, or a particular ideological bent by agency decisionmakers. . . . Underenforcement by an administrative agency may be even more likely where, as in this case, the regulated party is a relatively powerful business entity while the class protected by the regulation tends to consist of low-income persons with scant resources, lack of knowledge about their rights, inexperience in the regulated area, and insufficient understanding of the prohibited practice.[317]

The majority view is that language exempting "authorized practices" does not exempt practices not authorized under the state credit statute.[318] It protects the regulated entity only from liability for specifically authorized activities, rather than giving it a blanket exemption from the UDAP statute.[319] But the Nebraska Supreme Court has interpreted the statutory exemption for actions regulated by state agencies to exclude finance company practices regulated by the installment sales act[320] and by the banking and finance agency.[321] The Rhode Island Supreme Court has interpreted its UDAP statute's exclusion of "actions or transactions permitted under laws administered by" a state or federal regulatory body to exclude a national bank's deceptive credit card solicitations because of the authority of the Office of the Comptroller of the Currency to enforce Truth in Lending standards and the FTC Act's prohibition against unfair and deceptive acts.[322] Michigan's UDAP statute exempts transactions or conduct specifically authorized under laws administered by a regulatory board.[323] And in Tennessee the remedies allowed by state usury statutes displace any UDAP remedies for credit overcharges by industrial loan and thrift companies, although they still face potential UDAP liability for acts other than overcharges.[324]

Of course, where a UDAP statute exempts practices regulated by the banking commissioner, and the bank commissioner regulates bank loan collection activity, a bank's

---

311 15 U.S.C. § 57(a)(f). *See* Normand Josef Enterprises v. Connecticut Bank, 230 Conn. 486, 646 A.2d 1289 (1994).

312 Madsen v. Western Am. Mortg. Co., 694 P.2d 1228 (Ariz. Ct. App. 1985) (state mortgage brokers act does not displace UDAP statute); Villegas v. Transamerica Fin. Servs., 147 Ariz. 100, 708 P.2d 781 (Ct. App. 1985) (same).

313 State *ex rel.* Bryant v. R&A Investment, 985 S.W.2d 299 (Ark. 1999) (state constitution's regulation of usury does not prevent UDAP claim against usurious credit scheme).

314 Normand Josef Enterprises v. Connecticut Bank, 230 Conn. 486, 646 A.2d 1289 (1994) (federal and state regulation of banking industry does not give it blanket exemption from UDAP statute).

315 Safeguard Inv. Corp. v. Colville, 44 Pa. Commw. 417, 404 A.2d 720 (1979) (UDAP statute not displaced by state usury regulation); Commonwealth *ex rel.* Zimmerman v. Nickel, 26 Pa. D. & C.3d 115 (C.P. Mercer Cty. 1983) (Truth in Lending Act does not prevent application of UDAP statute to creditor).

316 Lemelledo v. Beneficial Management Corp., 150 N.J. 255, 696 A.2d 546 (1997). *Cf.* Westervelt v. Gateway Fin. Serv., 190 N.J. Super. 615, 464 A.2d 1203 (Super. Ct. Ch. Div. 1983) (holding state second mortgage law to preempt UDAP statute).

317 Lemelledo v. Beneficial Management Corp., 150 N.J. 255, 696 A.2d 546, 553 (1997).

318 State v. Brotherhood Bank & Trust, 649 P.2d 419 (Kan. Ct. App. 1982); Ashlock v. Sunwest Bank, 107 N.M. 100, 753 P.2d 346 (1988) (permitted practices exemption does not create blanket exemption for banks, nor does federal law preempt application of UDAP statute); Commonwealth *ex rel.* Zimmerman v. Nickel, 26 Pa. D. & C.3d 115 (C.P. Mercer Cty. 1983); Vogt v. Seattle-First National Bank, 117 Wash. 2d 541, 817 P.2d 1364 (1991) (permitted practices exemption does not make UDAP statute inapplicable to banks).

319 Aurora Firefighter's Credit Union v. Harvey, 163 Ill. App. 3d 915, 516 N.E.2d 1028 (1987).

320 Kuntzelman v. Avco Fin. Servs., 206 Neb. 130, 291 N.W.2d 705 (1980).

321 McCaul v. American Sav. Co., 213 Neb. 841, 331 N.W.2d 795 (1983); *see also* Hydroflo Corp. v. First National Bank, 349 N.W.2d 615 (Neb. 1984); Little v. Gillette, 218 Neb. 271, 354 N.E.2d 147 (1984).

322 Chavers v. Fleet Bank, 2004 WL 249605 (R.I. Feb. 11, 2004). *See* § 2.3.3.2, *infra*.

323 Mich. Comp. Laws § 445.904(1)(a). *See* Dressel v. Ameribank, 247 Mich. App. 133, 635 N.W.2d 328 (2000) (defendant bank's acts violated Savings Bank Act, so fell within an exception to UDAP statute's exclusion of banks), *rev'd on other grounds*, 664 N.W.2d 151 (Mich. 2003) (finding no violation of Savings Bank Act).

324 Hathaway v. First Family Fin. Servs., 1 S.W.3d 634 (Tenn. 1999).

practices collecting a loan are exempt.[325] However, even where most banking activities are thus exempted, a bank's credit card activities are not exempt where the credit card activities are not in the banking commissioner's jurisdiction.[326] Further precedent concerning preemption by regulatory action is detailed in later sections.[327]

2.2.1.6.3 *Effect of Truth in Lending Act*

A few UDAP statutes exempt "those aspects of a consumer transaction which are regulated by the Federal Consumer Credit Protection Act, 15 U.S.C. § 1601."[328] This language prevents use of the UDAP statute to bring an action alleging Truth in Lending, Fair Credit Billing, Consumer Leasing, federal wage garnishment, or Equal Credit Opportunity Act violations. UDAP actions in these states can still challenge other aspects of the credit transaction not specifically covered by the federal legislation.[329]

As a general rule, the Truth in Lending Act does not preempt a UDAP action.[330] But some courts, mostly in Illinois, find that, where the Truth in Lending Act requires certain disclosures, the UDAP statute can not require additional disclosure.[331] These courts generally reason that the more limited disclosure has been "authorized" by an agency and the UDAP statute exempts practices authorized by an agency. The Seventh Circuit has reconciled these cases by concluding that the Illinois UDAP statute will not impose higher disclosure requirements than those that are sufficient to satisfy federal regulations, but that this exemption will not protect statements that are in technical compliance with federal regulations but are still so misleading or deceptive that federal law itself might not regard them as adequate.[332] Accordingly, where the credit terms in a transaction are correctly disclosed for purposes of Truth in Lending, hiding the true cost of the credit in other ways or deceiving the consumers in ways outside the loan documents is not "authorized" by the Truth in Lending Act.[333] If the practice which is the subject of the UDAP claim is not the actual Truth in Lending disclosure, the practice is not "permitted" by Truth in Lending.[334] Merely because a party does not violate federal law does not immunize it from UDAP liability.[335]

---

325 Scott v. Bank of Coushatta, 512 So. 2d 356 (La. 1987); Preferred Inv. Corp. v. Neucere, 592 So. 2d 889 (La. Ct. App. 1991); Fidelity Bank & Trust Co. v. Hammons, 540 So. 2d 461 (La. Ct. App. 1989).

326 Bank of New Orleans & Trust Co. v. Phillips, 415 So. 2d 973 (La. Ct. App. 1982).

327 *See* §§ 2.3.3, 2.5, *infra.*

328 *See, e.g.,* Ala. Code § 8-19-7(4); Va. Code Ann. § 59.1-199.

329 *See* § 2.3.3.2, *infra.*

330 *See* § 2.5.3.8, *infra.*

331 Najieb v. William Chrysler-Plymouth, 2002 WL 31906466 (N.D. Ill. Dec. 31, 2002) (failure to disclose that yo-yo sale was conditional is not UDAP violation because TILA does not require this disclosure); Jenkins v. Mercantile Mortgage Co., 231 F. Supp. 2d 737 (N.D. Ill. 2002); Fillinger v. Willowbrook Ford, Inc., 1999 U.S. Dist. LEXIS 3629 (N.D. Ill. Mar. 22, 1999) (assignee's protection from TILA liability for false disclosure of upcharge does not necessarily insulate it from UDAP liability if it actively participated in the fraud); Franks v. Rockenbach Chevrolet Sales, Inc., 1999 U.S. Dist. LEXIS 3367 (N.D. Ill. Mar. 15, 1999); Wiskup v. Liberty Buick Co., 953 F. Supp. 958 (N.D. Ill. 1997); Allen v. Aronson Furniture Co., 971 F. Supp. 1259 (N.D. Ill. 1997); Walker v. Wallace Auto Sales, Inc., 1997 U.S. Dist. LEXIS 14508 (N.D. Ill. Sept. 12, 1997), *rev'd on other grounds,* 155 F.3d 927 (7th Cir. 1998); Taylor v. Quality Hyundai, Inc., 932 F. Supp. 218 (N.D. Ill. 1996), *aff'd in part and rev'd in part on other grounds,* 150 F.3d 689 (7th Cir. 1998); Hernandez v. Buick Co., 910 F. Supp. 422 (N.D. Ill. 1996), *rev'd on other grounds sub nom.* Gibson v. Bob Watson Chevrolet-Geo, Inc., 112 F.3d 283 (7th Cir. 1997); April v. Union Mortgage Co., 709 F. Supp. 809 (N.D. Ill. 1989); Chancellor v. Gateway Lincoln-Mercury, 502 S.E.2d 799 (Ga. App. Ct. 1998) (no UDAP claim for nondisclosure of auto dealer's discounting of credit contract to financing company, where TILA does not require disclosure); Robinson v. Toyota Motor Credit Corp., 201 Ill. 2d 403, 778 N.E.2d 951, 266 Ill. Dec. 879 (2002) (recognizing that UDAP statute may require disclosures beyond TILA, but not shown here); Jarvis v. South Oak Dodge, Inc., 201 Ill. 2d 81, 773 N.E.2d 641, 265 Ill. Dec. 877 (2002) (TIL assignee liability limitations shield assignee from liability for salesman's misrepresentations regarding matters on which TILA requires disclosures); Jackson v. S. Holland Dodge, Inc., 197 Ill. 2d 39, 258 Ill. Dec. 79, 755 N.E.2d 462 (2001) (assignee not liable for TIL violation that is not apparent on face of disclosure statement, unless it actively participated in the fraud); Lanier v. Associates Fin., Inc., 114 Ill. 2d 1, 499 N.E.2d 440 (1986); Hill v. St. Paul Fed. Bank, 329 Ill. App. 3d 705, 768 N.E.2d 322 (2002); Beckett v. H&R Block, Inc., 714 N.E.2d 1033 (Ill. App. Ct. 1999) (if disclosures are sufficient under TILA, they are sufficient under UDAP); Aurora Firefighter's Credit Union v. Harvey, 163 Ill. App. 3d 915, 516 N.E.2d 1028 (1987). *See also* Cunningham v. Equicredit Corp., 256 F. Supp. 2d 785 (N.D. Ill. 2003) (where TIL disclosure is inaccurate, consumer can base UDAP claim on it); Weatherman v. Gary-Wheaton Bank, 186 Ill. 2d 472, 713 N.E.2d 543 (1999) (where RESPA permitted aggregate disclosure and lender did not mischaracterize charge, failure to disclose charge separately was not UDAP violation).

332 Bober v. Glaxo Wellcome P.L.C., 246 F.3d 934 (7th Cir. 2001).

333 Therrien v. Resource Fin. Group, Inc., 704 F. Supp. 322 (D.N.H. 1989); Chandler v. Am. Gen. Fin., Inc., 329 Ill. App. 3d 729, 768 N.E.2d 60 (2002); Harvey v. Ford Motor Credit Co., 8 S.W.3d 273 (Tenn. App. 1999) (compliance with TIL disclosure rules does not defeat UDAP claim that dealer concealed financing kickback). *See also* Knapp v. Americredit Fin. Servs., Inc., 245 F. Supp. 2d 841 (S.D. W. Va. 2003) (finance company's involvement in scheme to add hidden finance charges, involving false pay stubs, false down payments, and an acquisition fee, not preempted by TILA).

334 Heastie v. Community Bank, 690 F. Supp. 716 (N.D. Ill. 1988); Chandler v. Am. Gen. Fin., Inc., 329 Ill. App. 3d 729, 768 N.E.2d 60 (2002). *See also* Fidelity Fin. Servs. v. Hicks, 214 Ill. App. 3d 398, 574 N.E.2d 15 (1991) (even if interest rate had been authorized by state law, consumer would still have UDAP claim for deception). *But see* Najieb v. William Chrysler-Plymouth, 2002 WL 31906466 (N.D. Ill. Dec. 31, 2002) (failure to disclose that yo-yo sale was conditional is not UDAP violation because TILA does not require this disclosure).

335 Jenkins v. Mercantile Mortgage Co., 231 F. Supp. 2d 737 (N.D. Ill. Sept. 27, 2002).

2.2.1.7 Derivative Liability Under Holder Rule Regardless of UDAP Statute's Coverage

Even if a UDAP statute exempts creditors, this should only insulate creditors from UDAP liability for their own misconduct. The FTC's Holder Rule subjects assignees and related creditors to claims and defenses including UDAP claims arising from the *seller's* misconduct.[336] The seller's misconduct typically is covered by the UDAP statute, and then the creditor is derivatively liable for those damages. The fact that the creditor is exempt from the UDAP statute has no bearing on its derivative liability for UDAP claims against the seller.[337]

2.2.2 Debt Collection

A UDAP statute that applies to conduct "in trade or commerce" can be used to challenge debt collection activities.[338] At one point, the North Carolina Supreme Court ruled that the term "in the conduct of any trade or commerce" did not include debt collection, but instead only applied to activities surrounding the formation of the sales contract.[339] The North Carolina legislature promptly amended the statute to expressly cover debt collection activities.[340] An unpublished federal court decision[341] holds that debt collection abuses are too attenuated from the actual sale for the Minnesota UDAP statute to apply, but it has not been followed or even cited by any court.

Pennsylvania courts find that debt collection activities are "in trade or commerce" even where this term is defined as the sale of services or property.[342] A federal court has reached the same result in a repossession case interpreting similar language in the South Carolina UDAP statute.[343] But a Florida court and the Tennessee Supreme Court have decided that post-sale repossession practices do not relate to the original sale and are thus not covered.[344]

The Montana Supreme Court finds that collecting on a bank loan comes within the UDAP statute's coverage of sales of services.[345] A federal court, interpreting Illinois law, reaches the same conclusion.[346] The Idaho Supreme Court finds that debt collection practices, even by an assignee of the original credit-seller, involve the "sale of goods and services."[347] It is the connection with the original sale that makes the subsequent collection covered by the UDAP statute; if the debt was not based on the sale of goods or services, the subsequent debt collection practices would not be covered.[348] A federal court in Arizona takes a more narrow view of that state's statute, however, holding that it did not cover false allegations made in a repossession complaint against a person who was not the original buyer.[349] A Minnesota court exempted loan servicers because a former version of the state UDAP statute did not cover loans, but the statute has now been amended to list loans explicitly.[350]

336 *See* § 6.6, *infra*. *See also* Williams v. ITT Fin. Servs., 1997 Ohio App. LEXIS 2721 (June 25, 1997), *aff'd on other grounds*, 83 Ohio St. 3d 464, 700 N.E.2d 859 (1998), *cert. denied*, 526 U.S. 1051 (1999); Nations Credit v. Pheanis, 102 Ohio App. 3d 71, 656 N.E.2d 998 (1995) (mobile home financer held liable under FTC rule for UDAP violations of mobile home dealer). *But see* Vannoy v. Capital Lincoln-Mercury Sales, Inc., 88 Ohio App. 3d 138, 623 N.E.2d 177 (1993) (bank not liable for seller's post-sale UDAP violations; no discussion of FTC rule).

337 *See* Williams v. ITT Fin. Servs., 1997 Ohio App. LEXIS 2721, *aff'd*, 700 N.E.2d 859 (Ohio 1998) (June 25, 1997), *aff'd on other grounds*, 83 Ohio St. 3d 464, 700 N.E.2d 859 (1998), *cert. denied*, 526 U.S. 1051 (1999).

338 Asch v. Teller, Levit & Silvertrust, P.C., 2003 WL 22232801 (N.D. Ill. Sept. 26, 2003) (ICFA); Flamm v. Sarner & Assocs., 2002 WL 31618443 (E.D. Pa. Nov. 6, 2002); Brown v. C.I.L., Inc., 1996 U.S. Dist. LEXIS 4053, Clearinghouse No. 51,255 (N.D. Ill. 1996) (Illinois UDAP statute applies to misrepresentations in collection of a debt even though they do not affect the consumer's decision to enter into the loan); Zanni v. Lippold, Clearinghouse No. 39,435D (C.D. Ill. 1986); Wagner v. American National Educ. Corp., 1983 U.S. Dist. LEXIS 10287 (D. Conn. Dec. 30, 1983); *In re* Scrimpsher, 17 B.R. 999 (Bankr. N.D.N.Y. 1982); State v. O'Neill Investigations, Inc., 609 P.2d 520 (Alaska 1980); Poquonnock Avenue Assocs. v. Society For Savings, Clearinghouse No. 31,045 (Conn. Super. Ct. 1980); Schauer v. Gen. Motors Acceptance Corp., 819 So. 2d 809 (Fla. App. 2002); People *ex rel.* Daley v. Datacom Sys., Inc., 146 Ill. 2d 1, 585 N.E.2d 51 (1991); Davis Lake Community Ass'n v. Feldmann, 530 S.E.2d 865 (N.C. App. 2000) (debt collection is in trade or commerce). *See also* Holley v. Gurnee Volkswagen & Oldsmobile, Inc., 2001 U.S. Dist. LEXIS 7274 (N.D. Ill. Jan. 4, 2001) (repossession is in trade or commerce).

339 State *ex rel.* Edminsten v. J.C. Penney Co., 292 N.C. 311, 233 S.E.2d 895 (1977).

340 1977 N.C. Sess. Laws 747 §§ 1, 2. *See also* Davis Lake Community Ass'n v. Feldmann, 530 S.E.2d 865 (N.C. App. 2000) (debt collection is in trade or commerce under current version of statute). *Cf.* Friday v. United Dominion Realty Trust, Inc., 575 S.E.2d 532 (N.C. App. 2003) (where landlord met definition of debt collector, remedy limitation in debt collection section of UDAP statute applied).

341 Baribeau v. Orthopedic Surgeons, Ltd., 1997 U.S. Dist. LEXIS 23426 (D. Minn. Feb. 18, 1997).

342 Daniels v. Baritz, 2003 WL 21027238 (E.D. Pa. Apr. 30, 2003); Flores v. Shapiro & Kreisman, 246 F. Supp. 2d 427 (E.D. Pa. 2002); Pennsylvania Bankers Ass'n v. Commonwealth, 58 Pa. Commw. 170, 427 A.2d 730 (1981); Pennsylvania Retailers Ass'n v. Lazin, 57 Pa. Commw. 232, 426 A.2d 712 (1981).

343 *In re* Daniel, 137 B.R. 884 (D.S.C. 1992).

344 City of Cars, Inc. v. Simms, 526 So. 2d 119 (Fla. Dist. Ct. App. 1988); Pursell v. First Am. National Bank, 937 S.W.2d 838 (Tenn. 1996).

345 Baird v. Norwest Bank, 843 P.2d 327 (Mont. 1992); *see also* Entriken v. Motor Coach Federal Credit Union, 845 P.2d 93 (Mont. 1992).

346 Asch v. Teller, Levit & Silvertrust, P.C., 2003 WL 22232801 (N.D. Ill. Sept. 26, 2003) (Ill. DTPA).

347 *In re* Western Acceptance Corp., 788 P.2d 214 (Idaho 1990).

348 *Id.*

349 Walker v. Gallegos, 167 F. Supp. 2d 1105 (D. Ariz. 2001).

350 Rossbach v. FBS Mortg. Corp., 1998 WL 156303 (Minn. App. Apr. 7, 1998) (unpublished, citation limited) (interpreting former version of Minn. Stat. § 325F.68).

Ohio considers debt collection a covered practice, finding collectors to be "suppliers" engaged in the business of affecting consumer transactions.[351] Ohio's statute specifically applies to practices occurring "before, during, or after the transaction."[352] The statute is intended to apply to consumer contracts until they are terminated or until the debt is fully paid, and that the purpose of the act would be defeated if a seller could escape the act's proscriptions by transferring the debt to an agent.[353] The Kansas Supreme Court similarly finds, despite an arguably conflicting legislative history, that even an independent debt collection agency is a "supplier," where "supplier" is defined to include those who "enforce consumer transactions."[354] But two unpublished Oklahoma decisions, interpreting language similar to Ohio's, find that debt collection is not covered.[355] These decisions, by relying primarily on the fact that the statute does not specifically mention debt collection, fail to accord proper weight to the explicit coverage of acts occurring after the transaction is entered into. Another decision finds debt collectors exempt on the ground that they are not involved in consumer transactions or consumer-related activities with the debtors.[356] The decision wrongly reads a limitation into the statute, which does not require the consumer to have a contractual relationship with the defendant.

A separate issue is whether other regulation of collectors preempts UDAP coverage of collection practices. State and federal banking laws did not preempt Pennsylvania's former debt collection regulation (now replaced by a statute).[357] But issues arise as to whether the state attorney general and consumers can enforce the regulations against banks where the state banking department is vested with exclusive enforcement authority regarding state chartered banks and the Comptroller of the Currency has exclusive authority regarding nationally chartered banks.[358] A further discussion of whether other state regulation displaces UDAP coverage can be found in § 2.3.3, *infra*.

Another issue is whether the UDAP statute applies to a collector hired by a municipality, state, or other government agency. Another section discusses whether government agencies themselves are liable under the UDAP statute for their own acts,[359] but a private collection agency collecting for a government entity should be subject to a UDAP claim,[360] as long as the debt itself arises from a covered transaction.[361]

2.2.3 Where There Is No "Purchase"

2.2.3.1 Where Transaction Involves No "Purchase"

A sale need not be completed for liability to attach under a UDAP statute, particularly where statutory language specifically defines a covered consumer transaction to include "solicitations to supply products"[362] or applies the statute to someone who "seeks" to purchase goods.[363] In addition, a purchase is not necessary where a statute applies broadly to any practice in "trade or commerce."[364] The activity is still

351 Celebrezze v. United Research, Inc., 19 Ohio App. 49, 482 N.E.2d 1260 (1984); Bennett v. Tri-State Collection Serv., Clearinghouse No. 27,062 (C.P. Cuyahoga Cty., Ohio 1976). *Cf.* Schroyer v. Frankel, 197 F.3d 1170 (6th Cir. 1999) (attorney debt collector would be subject to Ohio UDAP statute except that he was not regularly engaged in the business of collecting consumer debts, as debt collection was only a minor part of his law practice). *But see* Oak Hill Inv. Co. v. Jablonski, 78 Ohio App. 3d 643, 605 N.E.2d 998 (1992) (landlord's report of a debt to a credit bureau is not a consumer transaction; note that, as discussed in § 2.2.6.1, *infra*, landlords themselves are not covered by Ohio's UDAP statute).

352 Ohio Rev. Code § 1345.02(A); *see* Celebrezze v. United Research, Inc., 19 Ohio App. 49, 482 N.E.2d 1260 (1984); Santiago v. S.S. Kresge Co., 2 Ohio Op. 3d 54 (C.P. Cuyahoga Cty. 1976).

353 Celebrezze v. United Research, Inc., 19 Ohio App. 49, 482 N.E.2d 1260 (1984); Liggins v. May Co., 44 Ohio Misc. 81, 337 N.E.2d 816 (C.P. Cuyahoga Cty. 1975).

354 State *ex rel.* Miller v. Midwest Serv. Bureau, Inc., 229 Kan. 322, 623 P.2d 1343 (1981). *Accord* Rachoza v. Gallas & Schultz, 1998 U.S. Dist. LEXIS 5018 (D. Kan. Mar. 23, 1998).

355 Melvin v. Credit Collections, Inc., 2001 WL 34047943 (W.D. Okla. Apr. 5, 2001); Melvin v. Nationwide Debt Recovery, 2000 WL 33950122 (W.D. Okla. Aug. 24, 2000).

356 Okla. *ex rel.* Board of Regents v. Greer, 205 F. Supp. 2d 1273 (W.D. Okla. 2001).

357 Pennsylvania Bankers Ass'n v. Commonwealth, 58 Pa. Commw. 170, 427 A.2d 730 (1981).

358 *Id.*

359 *See* § 2.3.6, *infra*.

360 People *ex rel.* Daley v. Datacom Sys., Inc., 146 Ill. 2d 1, 585 N.E.2d 51 (1991).

361 Teel v. Panarella, 16 Pa. D. & C.4th 271 (1993) (debt for taxes not covered by Pennsylvania's former UDAP regulation, so collection activities not covered; the regulation has now been replaced by a statute, 73 Pa. Stat. § 2270.3, that explicitly covers collection of certain local tax debts)).

362 State v. Classic Pool & Patio, 777 N.E.2d 1162 (Ind. App. 2002); Swarthout v. Mut. Serv. Life Ins. Co., 632 N.W.2d 741 (Minn. App. 2001) (attempt to make sale covered); McDonald v. Bedford Datsun, 59 Ohio App. 3d 38, 570 N.E.2d 299 (1989); Weaver v. J.C. Penney, Inc., 53 Ohio App. 2d 165, 372 N.E.2d 633, 6 Ohio Op. 3d 270 (1977); Brashears v. Sight 'N Sound Appliance Centers, Inc., 981 P.2d 1270 (Okla. App. 1999) (UDAP statute covers offering for sale, so allows suit for bait and switch tactics even for consumers who ultimately purchased elsewhere).

363 Zanakis-Pico v. Cutter Dodge, Inc., 47 P.3d 1222 (Haw. 2002); Sherman Simon Enterprises, Inc. v. Lorac Serv. Corp., 724 S.W.2d 13 (Tex. 1987); Bohls v. Oakes, 75 S.W.3d 473 (Tex. App. 2002); Houston v. Mike Black Auto Sales, Inc., 788 S.W.2d 696 (Tex. App. 1990); Lawson v. Commercial Credit Bus. Loans, 690 S.W.2d 679 (Tex. App. 1985); Martin v. Lou Poliquin Enterprises, Inc., 696 S.W.2d 180 (Tex. App. 1985). *But see In re* Grant, 182 B.R. 709 (E.D. Pa. 1995) (Pennsylvania's UDAP statute gives private cause of action only to those who enter into a purchase or lease).

364 Miller v. Risk Management Foundation, 36 Mass. App. Ct. 411, 632 N.E.2d 841 (1994). *But see* Kramer v. Pollock-Krasner

in trade or commerce. Colorado's highest court interprets "consumer" in its UDAP statute to include not only a person who has purchased merchandise but also someone who has been exposed to the defendant's violations and has undertaken other activities in reliance upon them.[365] A North Carolina court interpreted its UDAP statute to apply to a law firm's claim that a political candidate's campaign ads defamed it.[366] Where a UDAP statute extends a private cause of action not just to consumers but to anyone aggrieved by an unfair or deceptive practice, a person who bought nothing from the defendant but whose photograph was misappropriated by the defendant has standing to sue.[367] Even where a literal reading of the UDAP statute would exclude non-sale transactions, the act, interpreted as a whole, has been extended to cover them.[368] The fact that a contract is void due to other state law violations does not make the UDAP statute inapplicable to the transaction.[369] A "purchase of goods or services" does not require a completed purchase, but does require more than just a contemplated transaction or some preliminary negotiations.[370]

A charitable solicitation is covered by a UDAP statute that applies to "the distribution of anything of value," at least where a sweepstakes or a gift to the donor is involved.[371] Similarly, the sale of advertising space and promotional items by a charitable organization brings it within the UDAP statute.[372] A deceptive sweepstakes offer is made "in connection with the sale of merchandise" and relates to the "character or quality" of goods within the meaning of Minnesota's Consumer Fraud Act and false advertising statute where the sweepstakes practices are directly connected to the sale of merchandise.[373] But a political advertisement seeking donations was not covered by New York's UDAP statute.[374]

If there is no purchase and no solicitation to purchase, certain UDAP statutes have been found not to apply, such as when an anti-abortion group that advertised itself as an abortion clinic accepted no payment upon counseling a telephone caller,[375] or when a contest involved no purchase.[376] A Pennsylvania court found a credit union's provision of credit life insurance to a borrower not to be covered by the UDAP statute because there was no separate charge for the insurance.[377] The court should have looked at the transaction as a whole, and found UDAP coverage because there was a charge for the loan itself.

Courts have found that a UDAP statute did not apply because there was no "purchase" where a dealer loaned a car to the consumer free of charge,[378] where a seller agreed to reserve a car for a consumer without deposit, but later sold that car to someone else,[379] and where a home buyer sought a creditor's permission to assume the seller's mortgage, but did not make any payments to the creditor.[380] A therapy patient who received free services, and in fact was paid an honorarium, in return for agreeing to be videotaped, could not press a UDAP claim.[381] Nor could a budding author whose manuscript and scientific funding proposals

Foundation, 890 F. Supp. 250 (S.D.N.Y. 1995) (auction house's refusal to accept a painting for auction not covered by New York's UDAP statute); Cash Energy, Inc. v. Weiner, 768 F. Supp. 892 (D. Mass. 1991) (no trade or commerce where two landowners have not entered into any transactions with each other).

365 Hall v. Walter, 969 P.2d 224 (Colo. 1998). *But cf.* Rhino Linings USA, Inc. v. Rocky Mountain Rhino Lining, Inc., 62 P.3d 142 (Colo. 2003) (plaintiff can not base UDAP claim on representation made to third party that did not induce that party to act).

366 Boyce & Isley v. Cooper, 568 S.E.2d 893 (N.C. App. 2002). *But see* Lawrence v. Trans Union L.L.C., 296 F. Supp. 2d 582 (E.D. Pa. 2003) (consumer could not assert UDAP claim against credit reporting agency with which she had entered into no sale or lease transaction).

367 Gritzke v. M.R.A. Holding, L.L.C., 2002 WL 32107540 (N.D. Fla. Mar. 15, 2002).

368 Brashears v. Sight N Sound Appliance Centers, Inc., 981 P.2d 1270 (Okla. App. 1999) (allowing bait and switch claim even for consumers who ultimately purchased elsewhere); Anderson v. Havins, 595 S.W.2d 147 (Tex. Civ. App. 1980). *But see* Lauria v. Wright, 805 S.W.2d 344 (Mo. Ct. App. 1991).

369 Griffin v. Security Pacific Automotive Fin. Servs. Corp., 33 F. Supp. 2d 926 (D. Kan. 1998); Antle v. Reynolds, 15 S.W.3d 762 (Mo. App. 2000).

370 Haskin v. Glass, 102 Idaho 785, 640 P.2d 1186 (1982); *see also* Braucher v. Mariemont Auto, 2002 WL 1393570 (Ohio App. June 28, 2002) (unpublished, citation limited) (statute that covers "transfers" of goods covers yo-yo sale in which buyer took delivery but seller did not transfer title).

371 State *ex rel.* Preate v. Watson & Hughey Co., 563 A.2d 1276 (Pa. Commw. Ct. 1989). *But see* Brzica v. Trustees of Dartmouth College, 791 A.2d 990 (N.H. 2002).

372 State *ex rel.* Preate v. Pennsylvania Chiefs of Police, 572 A.2d 256 (Pa. Commw. Ct. 1990). *But see* Del Tufo v. National Republican Senatorial Committee, 248 N.J. Super. 684, 591 A.2d 1040 (1991) (solicitation for political contribution not covered even though solicitor promises to list donor's name in a publication).

373 State *ex rel.* Hatch v. Publishers Clearing House, Clearinghouse No. 53,567 (D. Minn. June 12, 2000).

374 Mastercard Int'l Inc. v. Nader 2000 Primary Committee, Inc., 2004 WL 434404 (S.D.N.Y. Mar. 8, 2004).

375 Bonacci v. SOUL, 11 Pa. D. & C.3d 259 (C.P. Phila. Cty. 1979). *Accord In re* Grant, 182 B.R. 709 (E.D. Pa. 1995) (no private cause of action where plaintiff was only prospective purchaser of storage space). *But see* Mother & Unborn Baby Care, Inc. v. State, 749 S.W.2d 533 (Tex. App. 1988), *cert. denied*, 490 U.S. 1090 (1989) (antiabortion counseling service covered where it advertises and provides pamphlets and various services, even though no money is received in exchange).

376 Gottlieb v. Tropicana Hotel and Casino, 109 F. Supp. 2d 324 (E.D. Pa. 2000); Rutherford v. Whataburger, 601 S.W.2d 441 (Tex. Civ. App. 1980); Hall v. Bean, 582 S.W.2d 263 (Tex. Civ. App. 1979).

377 Carlotti v. Employees of General Electric Federal Credit Union, 717 A.2d 564 (Pa. Super. 1998).

378 Mongeau v. Borlen, 11 Mass. App. Ct. 1031, 419 N.E.2d 1386 (1981).

379 Jackson v. Charlie's Chevrolet, 664 S.W.2d 675 (Mo. Ct. App. 1984).

380 Longview Savings & Loan Ass'n v. Nabours, 673 S.W.2d 357 (Tex. App. 1984).

381 Bass v. Hendrix, 931 F. Supp. 523 (S.D. Tex. 1996).

were rejected.[382] A federal court has held that Minnesota's UDAP statute did not apply to a company's negotiation of an agreement that prevented an individual from exercising stock options for a period of time after an initial public offering, because of an insufficient nexus to any sale.[383] The Texas statute includes both purchasers and those who seek to acquire goods or services by purchase or lease, but one court has held that this only includes individuals who have a good faith intention and the capacity to purchase.[384]

A court has held a dealership's replacement of the consumer's license plate frames with frames advertising its name when it performed recall work on her vehicle to be separate from and only incidental to the consumer transaction, i.e., the warranty repair work, and therefore exempt from UDAP coverage.[385] Payment of a parking ticket does not involve a purchase so the payor is not a consumer under the Illinois UDAP statute.[386] Registering a horse with a nonprofit association that maintains records of the bloodlines of purebred horses is not a transaction in trade or commerce.[387] A speeding truck is not engaged in trade or commerce with an accident victim.[388] Likewise, an employee injured by a defective vehicle owned by an employer is not one who seeks to acquire goods or services and is thus not a covered consumer under the UDAP statute.[389] A shoplifter, whether inadvertent or intentional, is not a consumer within the meaning of a state UDAP statute.[390] Likewise, courts have held that, while a cable TV company acts in trade or commerce when it sells goods or services to consumers, its assertion of claims against people who allegedly pirated satellite TV signals was not in trade or commerce, and the alleged piraters did not have standing to bring UDAP claims against the company.[391] But a creditor who took negative action against an identity theft victim was covered by the UDAP statute even though only the imposter had actually entered into the transaction, since the creditor treated the victim as the purchaser.[392] But another court held that an individual could not bring a UDAP claim against a company that had wrongfully sued her on a contract she did not sign, as she had not engaged in any transaction with the company.[393] A sheriff who mistakenly seized the plaintiffs' property when executing upon another person's debt was not acting in trade or commerce, as he had no commercial relationship with the plaintiffs.[394]

A barter transaction, in which something of value other than money is exchanged, should fall within the UDAP definition of "sale" unless the statute specifies that a sale must involve the payment of money. The only court known to consider this question, however, decided it under statutory language that covered not just sales and leases but also other "transfers."[395] A Delaware court has reached the dubious conclusion that a car lease may not be covered under a statute applying to the "sale" of goods or services.[396] Only the provision of services accompanying the lease made the transaction covered.[397]

One lower court has given an inappropriately narrow reading to a UDAP remedy by holding that a consumer could not sue a merchant who had falsely advertised a price savings, because the consumer did not enter into a transaction with that merchant, but ultimately bought the item elsewhere.[398] This decision went beyond the statutory requirement that there be a purchase and improperly added a requirement that the purchase be from the UDAP defendant. A New Jersey court has ruled that a person may be able to bring a UDAP suit for false advertising even though he did not enter into a transaction with the defendant, as long as he was a bona fide consumer who responded to the advertisement with an intent to buy the item.[399]

---

382 Slaby v. Fairbridge, 3 F. Supp. 2d 22 (D.D.C. 1998).

383 Flora v. Firepond, Inc., 260 F. Supp. 2d 780 (D. Minn. 2003).

384 *See* Jones v. Star Houston, Inc., 45 S.W.3d 350 (Tex. App. 2001); Holeman v. Landmark Chevrolet Corp., 989 S.W.2d 395 (Tex. App. 1999).

385 Richards v. Beechmont Volvo, 127 Ohio App. 3d 188, 711 N.E.2d 1088 (1998).

386 Norton v. City of Chicago, 267 Ill. App. 3d 507, 642 N.E.2d 839 (1994) (case notes that state's attorney may have broader standing). *Cf.* People *ex rel.* Daley v. Datacom, 146 Ill. 2d 1, 585 N.E.2d 51, 165 Ill. Dec. 655 (1991) (company that collected past-due parking tickets for a city was engaged in trade or commerce and could be sued by AG).

387 Snow v. American Morgan Horse Ass'n, Inc., 686 A.2d 1168 (N.H. 1996).

388 Swenson v. Yellow Transportation, Inc., 2004 WL 1068880 (D. Mass. Apr. 12, 2004).

389 Clark Equipment Co. v. Pitner, 923 S.W.2d 117 (Tex. App. 1996); Hernandez v. Kasco Ventures, Inc., 832 S.W.2d 629 (Tex. App. 1992).

390 Serpico v. Menard, 927 F. Supp. 276 (N.D. Ill. 1996).

391 DirecTV, Inc. v. Karpinsky, 269 F. Supp. 2d 918 (E.D. Mich. 2003), *vacated in part on other grounds*, 274 F. Supp. 2d 918 (E.D. Mich. 2003); DirecTV, Inc. v. Shea, 2003 WL 23200250 (W.D. Mich. Oct. 20, 2003) (one of a series of seven related cases).

392 Stafford v. Cross Country Bank, 262 F. Supp. 2d 776 (W.D. Ky. 2003).

393 SWA, Inc. v. Straka, 2003 WL 21434637 (Ohio App. June 19, 2003) (unpublished, citation limited).

394 Cady v. Marcella, 49 Mass. App. Ct. 334, 729 N.E.2d 1125 (2000).

395 Williams v. Edwards, 129 Ohio App. 3d 116, 717 N.E.2d 368 (1998); *see also* Geinko v. KPMG L.L.P., 2002 WL 31867708 (N.D. Ill. Dec. 20, 2002) (sale of business in exchange for stock is a purchase of stock).

396 Edwards v. William H. Porter, Inc., 1991 Del. Super. LEXIS 315 (Feb. 14, 26, 1991), *aff'd on other grounds*, 616 A.2d 838 (Del. 1992). *Contra* Demitropoulos v. Bank One Milwaukee, N.A., 915 F. Supp. 1399 (N.D. Ill. 1996) (applying the explicit coverage of leases in Wisconsin's UDAP statute).

397 Edwards v. William H. Porter, Inc., 1991 Del. Super. LEXIS 315 (Feb. 14, 1991), *aff'd on other grounds*, 616 A.2d 838 (Del. 1992).

398 Lauer v. McKean Corp., 2 Pa. D. & C.4th 394 (Pa. C.P. 1989).

399 Grauer v. Norman Chevrolet Geo, 321 N.J. Super. 547, 729 A.2d 522 (Law Div. 1998) (denying motion for summary judgment). *But see* Arsenault v. PNC Mortg. Corp., 2002 U.S. App. LEXIS 6248 (6th Cir. Apr. 1, 2002) (unpublished, citation

There is no "practice related to a purchase" where the seller of one item told the buyer at a later date that the buyer did not need a second item.[400] However, where a consumer purchased and took delivery of a new vehicle in reliance upon his insurance agent's incorrect statement that the new vehicle would be covered by the consumer's existing insurance, the consumer had a UDAP claim against the agent even though no sale of insurance occurred.[401] The misrepresentations occurred in relation to a sale—the sale of the vehicle.

A ward is not one who "acquires goods or services" and thus can not bring a UDAP action against a guardian who converts the ward's property.[402] Other relationships not covered by UDAP because the plaintiff did not seek or acquire goods or services from the defendant are: (1) the guarantor of a child's loan;[403] (2) a landowner, with respect to a natural gas company's easement;[404] (3) an estate beneficiary;[405] (4) an employee, with respect to retirement benefits;[406] (5) a subcontractor, with respect to a surety;[407] (6) an insured, with respect to a reinsurer[408] or an adjuster;[409] (7) a casino patron whose attempt to place a bet was refused;[410] (8) a consumer, with respect to a credit reporting agency that was reporting erroneous information about her;[411] (9) a prison inmate who sued the Department of Corrections because it had given an exclusive contract to a certain company to provide telecommunications services to inmates;[412] and (10) a prison inmate, whose claim is against a state-provided counsel who provided free legal advice.[413]

Less clear is the situation where a seller, who would ordinarily charge, does not charge for its services. A court found no UDAP coverage when a repair shop failed to fix a car but did not charge for the work.[414] Other courts, however, find the UDAP statute applies where the consumer purchased services, and the seller decided not to charge for those services after it discovered its own UDAP violation,[415] or where a seller negligently failed to either provide or charge for requested services.[416] Otherwise, a seller could avoid UDAP damages which exceed the purchase price by refunding the purchase price. A consumer is also covered by the UDAP statute where the consumer has paid for services, even though the seller never receives payment because a middleman has absconded with the money[417] or the consumer stops payment on a check or money order.

A transaction may be covered, even though the consumer never requested the offered service, where one was performed and charged for. Thus "purchase of goods and services" may include unrequested towing services.[418] Likewise, a tenant "acquires goods or services" from a moving and storage company where a sheriff hires the company to move out an evicted tenant's possessions from an apartment.[419]

A Washington Supreme Court decision allows a physician to bring a UDAP action against a drug manufacturer even though it was the physician's patient who purchased the drug. The physician's reputation was damaged where the manufacturer did not fully disclose all relevant facts about the drug to the physician.[420]

2.2.3.2 Where Purchase Is Not from UDAP Defendant

Where there is a sale, there is no requirement that the consumer purchase the good or service from the defen-

limited) (Ky. law) (consumer had no claim against bank that refused to make loan on the terms it advertised, where UDAP statute requires a purchase or lease).

400 Zeller v. Northorp King Co., 125 Wis. 2d 31, 370 N.W.2d 809 (Ct. App. 1985).

401 Lang v. Consumers Ins. Serv., Inc., 583 N.E.2d 1147 (Ill. App. Ct. 1991).

402 Kilgore Fed. Sav. & Loan v. Donnelly, 624 S.W.2d 933 (Tex. Civ. App. 1981).

403 Plumley v. Landmark Chevrolet, Inc., 122 F.3d 308 (5th Cir. 1997).

404 Hall v. Lone Star Gas Co., 954 S.W.2d 174 (Tex. App. 1997).

405 Vinson & Elkins v. Moran, 946 S.W.2d 381 (Tex. App. 1997).

406 Garner v. Corpus Christi National Bank, 944 S.W.2d 469 (Tex. App. 1997), *cert. denied*, 525 U.S. 965 (1998).

407 Universal Sur. of Am. v. Central Elec. Enterprises & Co., 956 S.W.2d 627 (Tex. App. 1997).

408 Keightley v. Republic Ins. Co., 946 S.W.2d 124 (Tex. App. 1997), *rev'd and remanded by stipulation due to settlement*, 1997 Tex. App. LEXIS 3950 (Tex. July 24, 1997).

409 Janik v. City of Dallas, 1997 WL 538758 (N.D. Tex. 1997). *See also* Thomas v. Harford Mut. Ins. Co., 2003 WL 21742143 (Del. Super. July 25, 2003) (unpublished, citation limited) (insured could not assert UDAP claim against case manager hired by insurer, because relationship too attenuated), *vacated in part on other grounds*, 2003 WL 21742143 (Del. Super. July 25, 2003).

410 Ziglin v. Players MH, L.P., 36 S.W.3d 786 (Mo. App. 2001).

411 Lawrence v. Trans Union L.L.C., 296 F. Supp. 2d 582 (E.D. Pa. 2003).

412 Bowers v. T-Netix, 837 A.2d 608 (Pa. Commw. Ct. 2003).

413 Rayford v. Maselli, 73 S.W.3d 410 (Tex. App. 2002).

414 Exxon Corp. v. Dunn, 581 S.W.2d 500 (Tex. Civ. App. 1980).

415 E.F. Hutton & Co. v. Youngblood, 708 S.W.2d 865 (Tex. App. 1986); *see also* Sherman Simon Enterprises, Inc. v. Lorac Serv. Corp., 724 S.W.2d 13 (Tex. 1987); Cuyler v. Minns, 60 S.W.3d 209 (Tex. App. 2001) (client may sue attorneys even though they decided not to bill her).

416 Martin v. Lou Poliquin Enterprises, Inc., 696 S.W.2d 180 (Tex. App. 1985); McCrann v. Klaneckey, 667 S.W.2d 924 (Tex. App. 1984).

417 Joseph v. PPG Indus., Inc., 674 S.W.2d 862 (Tex. App. 1984).

418 Estep v. Johnson, 123 Ohio App. 3d 307, 704 N.E.2d 58 (1998); Coker v. Burghardt, 833 S.W.2d 306 (Tex. App. 1992); Allied Towing Serv. v. Mitchell, 833 S.W.2d 577 (Tex. App. 1992); Nelson v. Schanzer, 788 S.W.2d 81 (Tex. App. 1990); Waters v. Hollie, 642 S.W.2d 90 (Tex. App. 1982). *But see* River Oaks Townhomes Owners' Ass'n v. Bunt, 712 S.W.2d 529 (Tex. App. 1986); Northside Auto Storage v. Allstate Ins. Co., 684 S.W.2d 185 (Tex. App. 1984).

419 Nelson v. Schanzer, 788 S.W.2d 81 (Tex. App. 1990).

420 Washington State Physicians Ins. Exchange & Ass'n v. Fisons Corp., 122 Wash. 2d 299, 858 P.2d 1054 (1993).

dant.[421] A mortgagor is a consumer of "goods or services" and can bring an action against a mortgagee's assignee even for actions engaged in by the assignee many years after the original mortgage transaction.[422] One is a consumer not by one's relation to the defendants, but by the terms of the original transaction. A consumer is a person who enjoys the benefits of a transaction, even if there was no initial contractual relationship between the consumer and defendant.[423] An appraiser who conspired with a seller to issue inflated appraisals for properties was subject to the Maryland UDAP statute even though he provided no goods or services directly to the consumer, because his deception so infected the transaction that it was deemed to be committed as part of the sale.[424]

The Idaho Supreme Court holds that debt collection practices, even by an assignee of the original credit-seller, involve the "sale of goods and services."[425] It is the connection with the original sale that makes the subsequent collection covered by the UDAP statute; if the debt was not based on the sale of goods or services, the subsequent collection practices would not be covered.[426] But a body shop is not responsible for warranty problems between the consumer and the car's manufacturer or seller, even where the shop transmits communications between them.[427]

Many UDAP statutes give a private cause of action to any person who suffers damage due to a UDAP violation.[428] This language allows a UDAP suit even by a person who never dealt with the defendant, but who was harmed by the defendant's unfair or deceptive acts toward others. For example, a landowner could bring a UDAP suit against a developer who falsely represented to buyers that they had the right to go across the landowner's property to reach their lots.[429] The increased unauthorized traffic across the land caused damage to the landowner. Likewise, a Washington court permitted an insurer to bring a UDAP suit against a chiropractor who submitted false bills and reports to support an insured party's fabricated accident claim, as it was injured by the defendant's UDAP violations.[430] A Virginia court allowed a consumer to sue a licensed contractor that allowed its name to be used on a building permit for the consumer's home, even though the contractor never had any contact with the consumer and did not work on the home.[431] But a Massachusetts appellate court has held that investors had no commercial relationship with, and therefore no UDAP claim against, an accountant who issued a favorable report on a company in which they invested.[432] The court suggested that the result might be different if the accountant had volunteered assurances to the investors, or had known that this specific group of people would rely on the report. Similarly, a federal court has held that Minnesota's UDAP statute did not cover shareholders who sold their shares to the defendant, because they were sellers rather than purchasers.[433]

2.2.3.3 Where Someone Other Than Consumer Pays

One can be a consumer of services even if one does not pay for them.[434] A consumer purchasing a house can sue a realtor, even though the buyer does not pay the realtor's commission.[435] A consumer can sue a pest inspector for misrepresenting that a home was free of insect infestation even though the inspector reported only to the seller and broker.[436]

421 *See* §§ 2.3.8, 4.2.15.3, *infra*.

422 Flenniken v. Longview Bank & Trust Co., 661 S.W.2d 705 (Tex. 1984); *see also* Kennedy v. Sale, 689 S.W.2d 890 (Tex. 1985). *But cf.* Connolly v. People's Life Ins. Co., 294 S.C. 355, 364 S.E.2d 475 (Ct. App. 1988) (assignee's wrongful refusal to discharge mortgage is not sale of goods or services and thus not covered), *rev'd*, 299 S.C. 348, 384 S.E.2d 738 (1989) (appellate court should not have addressed issue not presented to it and state supreme court refuses to consider issue).

423 Birchfield v. Texarkana Memorial Hosp., 747 S.W.2d 361 (Tex. 1987); Flenniken v. Longview Bank & Trust Co., 661 S.W.2d 705 (Tex. 1984); Parker v. Carnahan, 772 S.W.2d 151 (Tex. App. 1989). *But see* Moody Nat. Bank v. Texas City Development Ltd., Co., 46 S.W.3d 373, 44 U.C.C. Rep. Serv. 2d 261 (Tex. App. 2001).

424 Hoffman v. Stamper, 843 A.2d 153 (Md. Spec. App. 2004).

425 *In re* Western Acceptance Corp., 788 P.2d 214 (Idaho 1990).

426 *Id.*

427 Farrell v. General Motors Corp., 249 Kan. 231, 845 P.2d 538 (1991).

428 *See* § 7.5.2.1, *infra*.

429 Rhino Linings USA, Inc. v. Rocky Mountain Rhino Lining, Inc., 62 P.3d 142 (Colo. 2003) (plaintiff can not base UDAP claim on representation made to third party that did not induce that party to act); Hall v. Walter, 969 P.2d 224 (Colo. 1998).

430 State Farm Fire & Cas. Co. v. Huynh, 92 Wash. App. 454, 962 P.2d 854 (1998).

431 Kieft v. Becker, 58 Va. Cir. 171 (2002). *See also* Shannon v. Boise Cascade Corp., 208 Ill. 2d 517, 805 N.E.2d 213 (Ill. 2004) (UDAP claim possible if manufacturer's deception causes builder to install defective product in consumer's home, even if no misrepresentations made directly to consumer).

432 Spencer v. Doyle, 50 Mass. App. Ct. 6, 733 N.E.2d 1082 (2000). *See also* Thomas v. Harford Mut. Ins. Co., 2003 WL 21742143 (Del. Super. July 25, 2003) (unpublished, citation limited) (insured could not assert UDAP claim against case manager hired by insurer, because relationship too attenuated), *vacated in part on other grounds*, 2003 WL 21742143 (Del. Super. July 25).

433 Popp Telcom, Inc. v. American Sharecom, Inc., 2003 WL 1610789 (D. Minn. Mar. 20, 2003).

434 Arthur Andersen & Co. v. Perry Equipment Corp., 945 S.W.2d 812 (Tex. 1997); Birchfield v. Texarkana Memorial Hosp., 747 S.W.2d 361 (Tex. 1987); Kennedy v. Sale, 689 S.W.2d 890 (Tex. 1985); Perez v. Kirk & Carrigan, 822 S.W.2d 261 (Tex. App. 1992); Dickson Distribution Co. v. LeJune, 662 S.W.2d 693 (Tex. App. 1983).

435 Cameron v. Terrell & Garrett, Inc., 618 S.W.2d 535 (Tex. 1981); Manchac v. Pace, 608 S.W.2d 314 (Tex. Civ. App. 1980). *See also* § 4.2.15.3, *infra* (privity issues).

436 Raudebaugh v. Action Pest Control, Inc., 59 Or. App. 166, 650 P.2d 1006 (1982). *But see* Nei v. Boston Survey Consultants,

An insured can sue an insurance agent even though the insurance was purchased directly from an insurance company.[437] The insured can also sue an insurance agent for incorrectly advising that further insurance was not needed, when that misrepresentation was made in connection with the purchase of a vehicle from an automobile dealer.[438]

A builder has been found liable for representations made to the first owner of a house where an action is brought by a subsequent owner based on those representations.[439] A prior dealer in the chain of title of a vehicle with concealed wreck damage also meets Virginia's definition of a supplier, which includes sellers, lessors, manufacturers, and distributors.[440] A home purchaser is a consumer of a company's service of administering a homeowner's warranty program even though the warranty administrator contracted only with the home builder and not the consumer.[441] Moreover, a child is a consumer where she acquired services, and the seller sold the services, even if someone else paid for the services.[442] A client was allowed to sue her attorneys even though the attorneys decided not to bill for service.[443]

But there are limits. Texas courts have refused to treat a passenger in a car as a consumer regarding the purchase of the car[444] or someone who borrows a product as a consumer who "acquires" that product.[445] A relative who used a car without the owners' consent could not assert a claim against their insurance company under the District of Columbia UDAP law.[446] A physician who purchased pedicle screws to insert in patients did not buy them for his own personal, family, or household use, and could not assert UDAP claims as the purchasing agent for the ultimate consumers.[447] A person who wants to assume a mortgage at no cost is not one who seeks goods or services, so can not challenge the terms of the original mortgage that limit such assumptions.[448] One court held that an inmate who received free legal advice from an inmate's counsel office could not bring a UDAP claim because he did not prove that he sought or acquired services.[449] So this decision is in conflict with most opinions.[450] A Colorado court has held that an insured does not have standing to assert a UDAP claim against a physician who was retained by an insurance company to examine her.[451]

2.2.4 Post-Sale Activities

The term "trade or commerce" includes post-sale activities, and not just practices designed to induce a sale.[452] Failure to pay out on an insurance claim is thus within "trade or commerce"—if a legislature wished to limit the statute's scope to just sales activity, it would have done so specifically.[453]

388 Mass. 320, 446 N.E.2d 681 (1983) (while no requirement that parties have privity of contract, surveyor did not have to disclose significance of true report to consumer where surveyor had no business relation with consumer); Spencer v. Doyle, 50 Mass. App. Ct. 6, 733 N.E.2d 1082 (2000) (investors had no commercial relationship with accountant who issued favorable report on company, so could not assert UDAP claim); Elia v. Erie Ins. Exchange, 398 Pa. Super. 433, 581 A.2d 209 (1990) (insured did not purchase goods or services from doctor who examined him for insurance company, so had no claim under Pennsylvania's UDAP statute).

437 Kennedy v. Sale, 689 S.W.2d 890 (Tex. 1985).

438 Lang v. Consumers Ins. Serv., Inc., 583 N.E.2d 1147 (Ill. App. Ct. 1991).

439 Galbraith v. McLaughlin, 44 Pa. D. & C.3d 70 (C.P. Erie Cty. 1986). *But see* Chattin v. Cape May Greene, Inc., 216 N.J. Super. 618, 524 A.2d 841 (App. Div. 1987), *aff'd*, 591 A.2d 943 (N.J. 1991); Taylor v. Burk, 722 S.W.2d 226 (Tex. App. 1986).

440 Merriman v. Auto Excellence, Inc., 55 Va. Cir. 330 (2001).

441 HOW Ins. v. Patriot Fin. Servs., 786 S.W.2d 533 (Tex. App. 1990).

442 Birchfield v. Texarkana Memorial Hosp., 747 S.W.2d 361 (Tex. 1987).

443 Cuyler v. Minns, 60 S.W.3d 209 (Tex. App. 2001).

444 Rodriguez v. Ed Hicks Imports, 767 S.W.2d 187 (Tex. App. 1989).

445 Kitchener v. T.C. Trailers, Inc., 715 F. Supp. 798 (S.D. Tex. 1988).

446 Athridge v. Aetna Cas. & Sur. Co., 163 F. Supp. 2d 38, 56 (D.D.C. 2001).

447 Balderston v. Medtronic Sofamor Danek, Inc., 285 F.3d 238 (3d Cir. 2002).

448 Longview Savings & Loan Ass'n v. Nabours, 673 S.W 2d 357 (Tex. App. 1984).

449 Rayford v. Maselli, 73 S.W.3d 410 (Tex. App. 2002).

450 *See* § 2.2.3.1, *infra*.

451 Martinez v. Lewis, 942 P.2d 1219 (Colo. Ct. App. 1996), *aff'd on other grounds*, 969 P.2d 213 (Colo. 1998).

452 Holley v. Gurnee Volkswagen & Oldsmobile, Inc., 2001 U.S. Dist. LEXIS 7274 (N.D. Ill. Jan. 4, 2001) (covers repossession); Zanni v. Lippold, Clearinghouse No. 39,435D (C.D. Ill. 1986); Wagner v. American National Educ. Corp., 1983 U.S. Dist. LEXIS 10287 (D. Conn. Dec. 30, 1983); *In re* Scrimpsher, 17 B.R. 999 (Bankr. N.D.N.Y. 1982); State v. O'Neill Investigations, Inc., 609 P.2d 520 (Alaska 1980); Poquonnock Avenue Assocs. v. Society For Savings, Clearinghouse No. 31,045 (Conn. Super. Ct. 1980); People *ex rel.* Daley v. Datacom Sys., Corp., 176 Ill. App. 3d 697, 531 N.E.2d 839 (1988), *aff'd*, 146 Ill. 2d 1, 585 N.E.2d 51 (1991); Mosley & Mosley Builders, Inc. v. Landin Ltd., 389 S.E.2d 576 (N.C. Ct. App. 1990); 3Z Corp. v. Stewart Title Guar. Co., 851 S.W.2d 933 (Tex. App. 1993); Salois v. Mutual of Omaha Ins. Co., 90 Wash. 2d 355, 581 P.2d 1349 (1978); *see also* Ranger County Mut. Ins. Co. v. Guinn, 608 S.W.2d 730 (Tex. Civ. App. 1980). *But see* Coffey v. Fort Wayne Pools, Inc., 24 F. Supp. 2d 671 (N.D. Tex. 1998); Lexington Ins. Co. v. Bennett Evans Grain Co., 642 F. Supp. 78 (S.D. Tex. 1986); Norman Gershman's Things to Wear, Inc. v. Mercedez-Benz of N. Am., 558 A.2d 1066 (Del. Super. Ct. 1989) (post-sale misrepresentations dealing with car repair not covered); State *ex rel.* Edminsten v. J.C. Penney Co., 292 N.C. 311, 233 S.E.2d 895 (1977) (note that legislature expanded UDAP coverage after this decision); Key Co. v. Fameco Distributors, Inc., 292 S.C. 524, 357 S.E.2d 476 (Ct. App. 1987); American Ins. Co. v. Reed, 626 S.W.2d 898 (Tex. App. 1982).

453 Salois v. Mutual of Omaha Ins. Co., 90 Wash. 2d 355, 581 P.2d 1349 (1978); *see also* Showpiece Homes Corp. v. Assurance Co. of Am., 38 P.3d 47 (Colo. 2001) (UDAP statute covers post-sale activities, including insurance claims settlement practices, ex-

Even when a UDAP statute applies more narrowly to the sale of goods and services, this should include the post-sale behavior of continuing to promise delivery where the merchant knows that delivery can not be made,[454] and the seller's post-sale warranty compliance practices.[455] The seller's subsequent repair attempts are covered even though there is no charge for the repair attempts. The consumer could have brought an action immediately and should not be penalized for letting the seller attempt to make repairs.[456] Misrepresentations that prevent a consumer from exercising a cancellation right are also just as actionable as misrepresentations that induce the consumer to sign the contract.[457] However, one court has held that pre-approval of surgery by an insurer, followed by refusal to pay, does not give rise to a UDAP claim, in the absence of proof that the consumer would not have had the surgery without the pre-approval.[458]

The Third Circuit has found that the "sale of goods and services" applies not just to practices to induce a purchase, but to post-consummation dealings between the mortgagee and the consumer.[459] Debt collection practices are also found to involve the sale of goods and services.[460] Insurance adjusting practices after the initial sale of insurance are also covered.[461]

There is little question that post-sale behavior is covered in Ohio because the statute applies to practices occurring "before, during, or after the transaction."[462] Idaho's statute is identical.[463] In New Jersey, post-sale behavior is covered because the statute applies to "the subsequent performance of such person."[464] The UDAP statute should also apply to those who take assignments of credit agreements.[465] Where a UDAP statute applies to practices "in connection with" a sale, the statute applies to post-sale activity.[466] The Tennessee Supreme Court has, however, held that a bank's sale of a repossessed vehicle was not covered by the state UDAP statute because it did not affect "advertising, offering for sale, lease or rental, or distribution" of goods, services, or other property.[467] And a federal court in Rhode Island held that a reseller's misdeeds while trying to negotiate a release of claims with a buyer, occurring long after the transaction had been completed, was not in trade or commerce.[468]

2.2.5 *Real Property and Mobile Homes*

2.2.5.1 Are Real Estate Sales Covered?

2.2.5.1.1 Real estate sales involve "trade or commerce," "property," and "merchandise"

States divide on whether real estate is covered by their UDAP statutes. The actual wording of the statute may be determinative.

---

cept for substantive prohibitions that have an explicit temporal limitation).

454 Wilman v. Ewen, 230 Kan. 262, 634 P.2d 1061 (1981).

455 Melody Home Mfg. Co. v. Barnes, 741 S.W.2d 349 (Tex. 1987); North Star Dodge Sales, Inc. v. Luna, 653 S.W.2d 892 (Tex. App. 1983), *aff'd in part, rev'd in part on other grounds*, 667 S.W.2d 115 (Tex. 1984); *see also* Jeep Eagle Sales Corp. v. Mack Massey Motors, Inc., 814 S.W.2d 167 (Tex. App. 1991). *But see* Sather v. State Farm Fire & Cas. Ins. Co., 2002 Minn. App. LEXIS 277 (Mar. 12, 2002) (unpublished, citation limited) (insurance claim denial not covered by portion of UDAP statute that relates to practices in connection with sale).

456 Melody Home Mfg. Co. v. Barnes, 741 S.W.2d 349 (Tex. 1987).

457 American Commercial Colleges, Inc. v. Davis, 821 S.W.2d 450 (Tex. App. 1991).

458 Provident Am. Ins. Co. v. Castaneda, 988 S.W.2d 189 (Tex. 1999).

459 Smith v. Commercial Banking Corp., 866 F.2d 576 (3d Cir. 1989) (Pennsylvania law). *See also* Griffith v. Porter, 817 S.W.2d 131 (Tex. App. 1991).

460 *See* § 2.2.2, *supra*.

461 P.I.A. Michigan City v. National Porges Radiator, 789 F. Supp. 1421 (N.D. Ill. 1992); Culbreth v. Lawrence J. Miller, Inc., 328 Pa. Super. 374, 477 A.2d 491 (1984).

462 Ohio Rev. Code § 1345.02(A). *See* Celebrezze v. United Research, Inc., 19 Ohio App. 49, 482 N.E.2d 1260 (1984); Santiago v. S.S. Kresge Co., 2 Ohio Op. 3d 54 (C.P. Cuyahoga Cty. 1976); Liggins v. May Co., 44 Ohio Misc. 81, 337 N.E.2d 816 (C.P. Cuyahoga Cty. 1975); Couto v. Gibson, Inc., 1992 Ohio App. LEXIS 756 (Feb. 26, 1992) (post-sale settlement practices).

463 Idaho Code § 48-603C(1). *See In re* Wiggins, 273 B.R. 839 (Bankr. D. Idaho 2001).

464 N.J. Stat. Ann. § 56:802. *See* 49 Prospect St. Tenants Ass'n v. Sheva Gardens, 227 N.J. Super. 449, 547 A.2d 1134 (App. Div. 1988); New Mea Constr. Corp. v. Harper, 203 N.J. Super. 486, 497 A.2d 534 (App. Div. 1985). *Cf.* Annunziata v. Miller, 241 N.J. Super. 275, 574 A.2d 1021 (Ch. Div. 1990) ("subsequent performance" applies to the seller's affirmative representation of a future act it will perform, and not to "friendly assurances" by a veterinarian that pets would be securely buried on his property).

465 Jackson v. Culinary School of Washington, 788 F. Supp. 1233 (D.D.C. 1992) (denying motion to dismiss), *dismissed on summary judgment on other grounds*, 811 F. Supp. 714 (D.D.C. 1993), *aff'd in party, rev'd and remanded in part on other grounds*, 27 F.3d 573 (1994) (reversing, on *de novo* review, district court's decision to issue declaratory judgment on state law issues), *vacated on other grounds*, 515 U.S. 1139 (1995) (appeals court should have used abuse of discretion standard to review district court's decision to issue declaratory judgment on state law issues), *on remand*, 59 F.3d 254 (D.C. Cir. 1995) (remanding for district court to exercise its discretion about whether to issue declaratory judgment on state law issues).

466 Lony v. E.I. duPont de Nemours & Co., 821 F. Supp. 956 (D. Del. 1993). *But see* Walker v. Gallegos, 167 F. Supp. 2d 1105 (D. Ariz. 2001) (false allegations that creditor made in repossession complaint against person who was not original buyer are too attenuated from sale or advertisement of merchandise to be covered).

467 Pursell v. First Am. National Bank, 937 S.W.2d 838 (Tenn. 1996).

468 McElheny v. Trans Nat'l Travel, Inc., 165 F. Supp. 2d 190 (D.R.I. 2001).

Courts consistently hold that the sale of real estate is in "trade or commerce."[469] Similarly, UDAP statutes that cover the sale of "merchandise" cover the sale of real estate.[470] Real estate sales are also covered by a UDAP statute that applies to "property."[471] Obviously, if a statute explicitly applies to real estate transactions, the statute can be used to challenge such transactions.[472]

2.2.5.1.2 Does real estate sale involve "goods or services"?

Courts are split as to whether real estate is within the scope of UDAP statutes that require that a transaction involve "consumer goods or services." Florida courts, while finding that the state statute generally applies to real estate, have found that real estate was outside the scope of a former provision applying only to "goods, consumer services and intangibles."[473] Texas courts, while finding that the sale of real property is "trade or commerce" within the statute's scope, hold that a real estate purchaser is not a "consumer," depriving the purchaser of certain remedies.[474] However, a subsequent amendment to the Texas statute has

469 Cieri v. Leticia Query Realty, Inc., 905 P.2d 29 (Haw. 1995) (a broker or salesperson's sale of real estate involves trade or commerce); City of Aurora v. Green, 126 Ill. App. 3d 684, 467 N.E.2d 610 (1984); Beard v. Gress, 90 Ill. App. 3d 622, 413 N.E.2d 448 (1980); Muss v. Driskell, Clearinghouse No. 47,931 (Ky. Ct. App. Sept. 20, 1991); Forton v. Laszar, 239 Mich. App. 711, 609 N.W.2d 850 (2000) (builder who constructed and sold home is in trade or commerce); Price v. Long Realty, Inc., 199 Mich. App. 461, 502 N.W.2d 337 (1993); Gilmore v. Bradgate Assocs., Inc., 604 A.2d 555 (N.H. 1992) (condominium sellers and developers not excluded by New Hampshire statute's exemption for acts otherwise permitted under laws administered by a regulatory agency; note, however, that the court adopted a broader interpretation of the statutory exemption language in Averill v. Cox, 761 A.2d 1083 (N.H. 2000), a case involving a UDAP claim against an attorney; *see* discussion in § 2.3.3.3.2, *infra*); Gennari v. Weichert Co. Realtors, 288 N.J. Super. 504, 672 A.2d 1190 (App. 1996); Hofstad v. Fairfield Communities, Inc., 595 S.E.2d 813 (N.C. Ct. App. 2004); Adams v. Moore, 385 S.E.2d 799 (N.C. Ct. App. 1989); Douglas v. Doub, 383 S.E.2d 423 (N.C. Ct. App. 1989); Opsahl v. Pinehurst, Inc., 344 S.E.2d 68 (N.C. Ct. App. 1986); Kim v. Professional Bus. Brokers, Ltd., 328 S.E.2d 296 (N.C. Ct. App. 1985) (sale of motel); Rosenthal v. Perkins, 42 N.C. App. 449, 257 S.E.2d 63 (1979); Best v. Hammill Quinlan Realty Co., 18 Pa. D. & C.3d 31 (C.P. Washington Cty. 1980); Edmondson v. Coates, 1992 Tenn. App. LEXIS 466, Clearinghouse No. 51,276 (Tenn. App. 1992); Stagner v. Friendswood Dev. Co., 620 S.W.2d 103 (Tex. 1981) (real property is in trade or commerce, but a purchaser is not a consumer); Cape Conroe Ltd. v. Specht, 525 S.W.2d 215 (Tex. Civ. App. 1975); McRae v. Bolstad, 676 P.2d 496 (Wash. 1984). *Cf.* Munn v. Thornton, 956 P.2d 1213 (Alaska 1998) (declining to address lower court's ruling that UDAP statute did not apply to real property transactions). *See also* Davis Lake Community Ass'n v. Feldmann, 530 S.E.2d 865 (N.C. App. 2000) (collection of homeowners association dues and assessments is in trade or commerce). *But see* Webb v. Theriot, 704 So. 2d 1211 (La. App. 1997) (lease and sublease of hunting property not within trade or commerce; court does not state rationale).

470 Menuskin v. Williams, 940 F. Supp. 1199 (E.D. Tenn. 1996), *aff'd on this ground*, 145 F.3d 755 (6th Cir. 1998); Stephenson v. Capano Dev. Inc., 462 A.2d 1069 (Del. 1983); Fulkerson v. MHC Operating Ltd., 2002 WL 32067510 (Del. Super. Sept. 24, 2002) (unpublished, citation limited) (Del. Consumer Fraud Act covers lease of mobile home park lots); Nash v. Hoopes, 332 A.2d 411 (Del. Super. Ct. 1975); Schimmer v. H.W. Freeman Constr. Co., 607 S.W.2d 767 (Mo. Ct. App. 1980) (real property is merchandise, but private action requires sale of "goods and services" that does not include real property); New Mea Constr. Corp. v. Harper, 203 N.J. Super. 486, 497 A.2d 534 (App. Div. 1985) (home builder's practice of using substandard material involves "merchandise" and is thus covered). *But cf.* Katz v. Schachter, 251 N.J. Super. 467, 598 A.2d 923 (1991) (court states that New Jersey's UDAP statute did not cover real estate prior to its 1976 amendment).

Note that the above cited Delaware cases interpret the Delaware Consumer Fraud Act, Del. Code Ann. tit. 6, § 2511, *not* the Delaware version of the Uniform Deceptive Trade Practices Act (UDTPA), Del. Code Ann. tit. 6, § 2531. The UDTPA does not apply to the sale of real estate. *See* Stephenson v. Capano Dev. Inc., 462 A.2d 1069 (Del. 1983); State *ex rel.* Brady v. Wellington Homes, Inc., 2003 WL 22048231 (Del. Super. Aug. 20, 2003) (unpublished, citation limited) ("merchandise" in Deceptive Trade Practices Act does not include real estate even though it is defined to include real estate in Delaware's other UDAP statute).

471 Cornerstone Realty, Inc. v. Dresser Rand Co., 993 F. Supp. 107 (D. Conn. 1998); Iadanza v. Mather, 820 F. Supp. 1371 (D. Utah 1993).

472 Birnberg v. Milk Street Residential Assocs. Ltd. P'ship, 2003 WL 151929 (N.D. Ill. Jan. 21, 2003) (where statute covers sales of real estate, it covers sale of interest in limited partnership whose only asset was real estate); Menuskin v. Williams, 940 F. Supp. 1199 (E.D. Tenn. 1996); Klotz v. Underwood, 563 F. Supp. 335 (E.D. Tenn. 1982), *aff'd*, 709 F.2d 1504 (6th Cir. 1983); Hall v. Walter, 969 P.2d 224 (Colo. 1998) (statute covers real property transactions); Murphy v. Berlin Constr. Co., 1999 Del. Super. LEXIS 5 (Jan. 12, 1999) (Delaware defines "merchandise" to include real estate); Benik v. Hatcher, 358 Md. 507, 750 A.2d 10 (2000) (noting 1976 amendment that brought certain real property transactions, including residential leases, under UDAP statute); Strawn v. Canuso, 140 N.J. 43, 657 A.2d 420 (1995), *aff'g* 271 N.J. Super. 88, 638 A.2d 141 (1994); Byrne v. Weichert Realtors, 290 N.J. Super. 126, 675 A.2d 235 (1996) (New Jersey UDAP statute applies to real estate professionals who represent non-professional sellers); Brooks v. Creech, 2003 WL 174805 (Tenn. App. Jan. 28, 2003); Carter v. Gugliuzzi, 716 A.2d 17 (Vt. 1998); Grube v. Daun, 173 Wis. 2d 30, 496 N.W.2d 106 (Ct. App. 1992).

473 Kingswharf Ltd. v. Kranz, 545 So. 2d 276 (Fla. Dist. Ct. App. 1989); State *ex rel.* Herring v. Murdock, 345 So. 2d 759 (Fla. Dist. Ct. App. 1977). *See also* Fendrich v. RBF, L.L.C., 842 So. 2d 1076 (Fla. Dist. Ct. App. 2003) (applying UDAP statute to real estate purchase transaction); Larry Kent Homes, Inc. v. Empire of Am. FSA, 474 So. 2d 868 (Fla. Dist. Ct. App. 1985); Brown v. Gardens By The Sea Condominium Ass'ns, 424 So. 2d 181 (Fla. Dist. Ct. App. 1983); State v. DeAnza Corp., 416 So. 2d 1173 (Fla. Dist. Ct. App. 1982).

474 Stagner v. Friendswood Dev. Co., 620 S.W.2d 103 (Tex. 1981); Gage v. Langford, 615 S.W.2d 934 (Tex. Civ. App. 1981); Ferguson v. Beal, 588 S.W.2d 651 (Tex. Civ. App. 1979); Cape Conroe Ltd. v. Specht, 525 S.W.2d 215 (Tex. Civ. App. 1975).

been interpreted as making real estate purchasers "consumers."[475] And a more recent law, the Residential Construction Liability Act, by its terms applies instead of the UDAP statute to the extent of a conflict between the requirements of the two acts.[476]

The Kentucky UDAP statute covers "any property," specifically including real property, but a consumer has a private cause of action only in cases of a purchase or lease of goods or services.[477] A federal court has held that the sale of a piece of land formerly used for railroad purposes was not covered.[478] A state appellate decision, without citing any statutory language, holds that a single sale of a home by a builder was not covered.[479] This second decision is particularly questionable since the builder clearly provided services as well as real estate.

While the Missouri UDAP statute applies to "merchandise," defined to include real property, a private action can only be brought by purchasers of "goods or services," which has been found not to include real estate.[480] Alaska,[481] the District of Columbia,[482] and a New Mexico appellate court[483] have also concluded that real estate is not "consumer goods or services." However, the District of Columbia Code was subsequently amended to list real estate transactions as an example of a good or service, thereby legislatively overruling the negative decision.[484] In Hawaii, a real estate sale is not considered a sale of goods or services, but it is considered a "personal investment," which can be the subject of a UDAP suit under the Hawaii statute.[485]

Pennsylvania courts hold that real estate sales involve the sale of consumer goods or services.[486] Illinois courts have found a legislative intent to include real estate within the UDAP statute's scope even though a literal reading of the definition of "consumer"—one who purchases goods, services or real estate situated outside the state[487]—would exclude sale of real estate within the state.[488] A Colorado court examined the UDAP statute as a whole and considered its broad purpose, and concluded that, even though "goods or services" is not explicitly defined to include realty, real property should fall within this definition.[489] New York's highest court has held that, even though it might not apply to a simple sale of a house, a New York City UDAP-type ordinance applied to a seller of homes who promoted the sale of overpriced homes, promised repairs, claimed FHA involvement, steered buyers to affiliated banks and lawyers who would not alert them to the problems in the transaction, and threatened to withhold down payments.[490]

Other courts have found that the legislative intent was not to include real estate. This result has been reached where the statute specifically includes only real estate situated out of state[491] or where the legislature first defeated an amendment that would have expanded the statute to specifically cover real estate and then adopted the amendment, but only after the challenged conduct had occurred.[492] Indiana's UDAP statute covers real estate transactions, but only the attorney

475 *See* Chastain v. Koance, 700 S.W.2d 579 (Tex. 1985); Thedford v. Missouri Pacific R. Co., 929 S.W.2d 39 (Tex. App. 1996); *see also* Norwood Builders Inc. v. Toler, 609 S.W.2d 861 (Tex. Civ. App. 1981); Anderson v. Havins, 595 S.W.2d 147 (Tex. Civ. App. 1980).

476 F & S Constr., Inc. v. Saidi, 2003 WL 23005013 (Tex. App. Dec. 24, 2003).

477 Ky. Rev. Stat. §§ 367.110, 367.220.

478 Aud v. Illinois Central R. Co., 955 F. Supp. 757 (W.D. Ky. 1997) (land does not constitute "goods" as it is not moveable; plaintiffs also failed to show that sale was for personal, family, or household use).

479 Craig v. Keene, 32 S.W.3d 90 (Ky. App. 2000).

480 Lauria v. Wright, 805 S.W.2d 344 (Mo. Ct. App. 1991); Callicoat v. Acuff Homes, Inc., 723 S.W.2d 565 (Mo. Ct. App. 1987) (construction and sale of residence not covered); Hutchings v. Valhalla Cemetery, 622 S.W.2d 296 (Mo. Ct. App. 1981) (sale of burial space does not involve goods or services); Schimmer v. H.W. Freeman Constr. Co., 607 S.W.2d 767 (Mo. Ct. App. 1980). *But see* Pointer v. Edward L. Kuhs, Co., 678 S.W.2d 836 (Mo. Ct. App. 1984) (real estate agent services involve "services" covered by statute).

481 State v. First National Bank of Anchorage, 660 P.2d 406 (Alaska 1982).

482 Owens v. Curtis, 432 A.2d 737 (D.C. 1981). *But see* Lawson v. Nationwide Mortgage Corp., 628 F. Supp. 804 (D.D.C. 1986) (suggesting *Owens* be limited to real estate sales from one consumer to another); Kinner, Drymalski, and Barry, *Application of the District of Columbia Consumer Protection Procedures Act of 1976 to Residential Real Estate Transactions; A Critical Look at Owens v. Curtis*, 32 Cath. U.L. Rev. 851 (1983) (criticizing *Owens* and suggesting it be limited to real estate sales from one consumer to another).

483 McElhannon v. Ford, 73 P.3d 827 (N.M. App. 2003) (sale of completed home).

484 *See* DeBerry v. First Gov't Mortgage & Investors Corp., 170 F.3d 1105 (D.C. Cir. 1999) (discussing legislative history and finding real estate transactions covered), *certified question answered affirmatively*, 743 A.2d 699 (D.C. 1999) (unconscionability provision applies to real estate transactions).

485 Cieri v. Leticia Query Realty, Inc., 905 P.2d 29 (Haw. 1995).

486 *In re* Bryant, 111 B.R. 474 (E.D. Pa. 1990); Gabriel v. O'Hara, 534 A.2d 488 (Pa. Super. Ct. 1987); Commonwealth v. Percudani, 844 A.2d 35 (Pa. Commw. Ct. 2004); Anderson v. Kessler, 32 Pa. D. & C.3d 623 (C.P. Allegheny Cty. 1984).

487 815 Ill. Comp. Stat. Ann. § 505/1(b), (c).

488 Warren v. LeMay, 142 Ill. App. 3d 550, 491 N.E.2d 464 (1986); Beard v. Gress, 90 Ill. App. 3d 622, 413 N.E.2d 448 (1980); *see also* Riley v. Fair & Co. Realtors, 150 Ill. App. 3d 597, 502 N.E.2d 45 (1986) (UDAP applies to realtors); People *ex rel.* Fahner v. Hedrich, 108 Ill. App. 3d 83, 438 N.E.2d 924 (1982).

489 People *ex rel.* MacFarlane v. Alpert Corp., 660 P.2d 1295 (Colo. Ct. App. 1982).

490 Polonetsky v. Better Homes Depot, 97 N.Y.2d 46, 760 N.E.2d 1274 (2001).

491 Hunter v. Haun, 210 Kan. 11, 449 P.2d 1087 (1972) (the Kansas statute now covers real estate sales. *See* Heller v. Martin, 782 P.2d 1241 (Kan. Ct. App. 1989)).

492 Neveroski v. Blair, 141 N.J. Super. 365, 358 A.2d 473 (App. Div. 1976). *But cf.* Blatterfein v. Larkin Assocs., 323 N.J. Super. 167, 732 A.2d 555 (App. Div. 1999) (New Jersey UDAP now applies to real estate); Arroyo v. Arnold-Baker & Assoc., 206 N.J. Super. 294, 502 A.2d 106 (1985) (same).

general may bring an action, and then only if the defendant acted with intent to defraud or mislead.[493] Ohio's statute, which does not cover real estate transactions,[494] nonetheless covers the personal property or services portion of a mixed transaction involving both the transfer of personal property or services and the transfer of real property.[495] One court has, however, held that the settlement services provided by a real estate lender did not make the transaction a mixed transaction.[496]

2.2.5.1.3 The isolated sale of real estate by owner

A number of state courts have ruled that, even where real estate sales are generally covered, the isolated sale of real estate by a nonmerchant is not covered.[497] This should be viewed as an attempt to keep consumer-to-consumer sales transactions outside the UDAP statute's scope, and not an attempt to exclude all real estate practices from the state's coverage.[498] Even though a court may dismiss the homeowner as a UDAP defendant, the case against the homeowner's realtor and termite inspector should go forward.[499] North Carolina courts have found the UDAP statute to cover home sales by a licensed home contractor[500] or a home-

493 McKinney v. State, 693 N.E.2d 65 (Ind. 1998).

494 Heritage Hills, Inc. v. Deacon, 49 Ohio St. 3d 80, 551 N.E.2d 125 (1990) (interpreting "an item of goods, an intangible, or a service" not to include real estate).

495 Brown v. Liberty Clubs, Inc., 45 Ohio St. 3d 191, 543 N.E.2d 783 (1989) (membership campground sale). *But see* Colburn v. Baier Realty & Auctioneers, Inc., 2003 WL 22931379 (Ohio App. Dec. 12, 2003) (unpublished, citation limited) (agreement with auctioneer to sell real property not covered).

496 Hanlin v. Ohio Builders & Remodelers, 212 F. Supp. 2d 752 (S.D. Ohio 2002).

497 Baghdady v. Baghdady, 2003 WL 202436 (2d Cir. Jan. 29, 2003) (unpublished, citation limited); Cinalli v. Kane, 191 F. Supp. 2d 601 (E.D. Pa. 2002) (N.J. law); Young v. Joyce, 351 A.2d 857 (Del. 1975); Waller v. Scheer, 175 Ga. App. 1, 332 S.E.2d 293 (1985); Zeeman v. Black, 156 Ga. App. 82, 273 S.E.2d 910 (1980); Kleczek v. Jorgensen, 328 Ill. App. 3d 1012, 767 N.E.2d 913, 263 Ill. Dec. 187 (2002) (home sold by builder was not an isolated sale even though he claimed it was his residence); Provenzale v. Forister, 318 Ill. App. 3d 869, 743 N.E.2d 676, 252 Ill. Dec. 808 (2001); Carrera v. Smith, 713 N.E.2d 1282 (Ill. App. Ct. 1999); Eickmeyer v. Blietz Organization, Inc., 671 N.E.2d 795 (Ill. App. Ct. 1996); Strauss v. Cruz, 631 N.E.2d 468 (Ill. App. Ct. 1994) (1990 amendment to Illinois UDAP statute, providing that proof of public injury, pattern, or effect on consumers is not required, has no effect on exclusion of individuals selling their own homes); Zimmerman v. Northfield Real Estate, Inc., 156 Ill. App. 3d 154, 510 N.E.2d 409 (1987); A.J.'s Automotive Sales, Inc. v. Freet, 725 N.E.2d 955 (Ind. App. 2000) (definition of "supplier" required that seller regularly engage in or solicit consumer transactions); Haas v. Deal, 2002 WL 31376445 (Mich. App. Oct. 22, 2002); Snierson v. Scruton, 145 N.H. 73, 761 A.2d 1046 (2000) (isolated sale of real estate is not in trade or commerce); Hughes v. DiSalvo, 729 A.2d 422 (N.H. 1999) (isolated sale of former residence by owner not covered, nor is lease of former residence while attempting to sell it); Chase v. Dorais, 448 A.2d 390 (N.H. 1982); Strawn v. Canuso, 140 N.J. 43, 657 A.2d 420 (1995); Stephenson v. Warren, 136 N.C. App. 768, 525 S.E.2d 809 (2000); Dairs v. Sellers, 443 S.E.2d 879 (N.C. Ct. App. 1994); Johnson v. Beverly-Hanks & Assoc., 388 S.E.2d 584 (N.C. Ct. App. 1990); Blackwell v. Dorosko, 377 S.E.2d 814 (N.C. Ct. App. 1989); Robertson v. Boyd, 88 N.C. App. 437, 363 S.E.2d 672 (1988); Rosenthal v. Perkins, 42 N.C. App. 449, 257 S.E.2d 63 (1979); Ganzevoort v. Russell, 949 S.W.2d 293 (Tenn. 1997); Gage v. Seaman, 1999 Tenn. App. LEXIS 114 (Feb. 23, 1999); Murvin v. Cofer, 968 S.W.2d 304 (Tenn. App. 1997); Allen v. Anderson, 16 Wash. App. 446, 557 P.2d 24 (1976); *see also* Cornerstone Realty, Inc. v. Dresser Rand Co., 993 F. Supp. 107 (D. Conn. 1998) (Connecticut UDAP statute does not apply to business' sale of real estate where the business is not generally in the business of selling property); Iadanza v. Mather, 820 F. Supp. 1371 (D. Utah 1993); Lawson v. Nationwide Mortgage Corp., 628 F. Supp. 804 (D.D.C. 1986); Neihaus v. Maxwell, 766 N.E.2d 556 (Mass. App. 2002) (one-time rental of single-family home by owner while temporarily living overseas not in trade or commerce); Byrne v. Weichert Realtors, 286 N.J. Super. 523, 675 A.2d 235 (1996) (New Jersey UDAP statute does not cover non-professional sellers of real estate, but does cover real estate professionals who sell homes for one-time sellers); DiBernardo v. Mosley, 206 N.J. Super. 371, 502 A.2d 1166 (App. Div. 1986); *cf.* Heller v. Martin, 782 P.2d 1241 (Kan. Ct. App. 1989) (real estate agency employee's sale of own home covered where seller regularly sells real estate); Adams v. Moore, 385 S.E.2d 799 (N.C. Ct. App. 1989) (consumer must be allowed to show that defendant buys and sells homes as a business). *Cf.* Jackson v. Manasquan Savings Bank, 638 A.2d 165 (N.J. Super. 1993) (sale of home by a commercial entity—a bank—is covered by UDAP statute). *But see* Beshada v. Millard Realty, 2004 WL 60321 (Mich. App. Jan. 13, 2004) (unpublished, citation limited) (purchaser of single older home to rehabilitate and resell for profit is in trade or commerce); Bhatti v. Buddand, 400 S.E.2d 440 (N.C. 1991) (North Carolina's Supreme Court takes no position on middle-level court of appeals-created "homeowner's exception"; state supreme court rules, in any event, that "homeowner's exception" does not apply where no evidence that property being sold is the seller's residence); Gabriel v. O'Hara, 534 A.2d 488 (Pa. Super. Ct. 1987) (house sale by one consumer to another is covered); Edwards v. Bruce, 1996 Tenn. App. LEXIS 403 (Tenn. App. 1996) (sale of real estate by owner covered by UDAP statute).

498 *See* Lawson v. Nationwide Mortgage Corp., 628 F. Supp. 804 (D.D.C. 1986) (suggesting Owens v. Curtis, 432 A.2d 737 (D.C. 1981)), be limited to real estate sales from one consumer to another); Snierson v. Scruton, 145 N.H. 73, 761 A.2d 1046 (2000) (isolated sale of real estate by owner is exempt, but realtor who engages in deception or misleading acts while conducting its business is covered); Bhatti v. Buddand, 400 S.E.2d 440 (N.C. 1991); Adams v. Moore, 385 S.E.2d 799 (N.C. Ct. App. 1989); Kinner, Drymalski, and Barry, *Application of the District of Columbia Consumer Protection Procedures Act of 1976 to Residential Real Estate Transactions; A Critical Look at Owens v. Curtis*, 32 Cath. U.L. Rev. 851 (1983) (criticizing Owens, *supra*, and suggesting it be limited to real estate sales from one consumer to another).

499 Robertson v. Boyd, 88 N.C. App. 437, 363 S.E.2d 672 (1988). *But see* Canario v. Gunn, 751 N.Y.S.2d 310 (App. Div. Dec. 9, 2002) (misrepresentation by real estate agent in connection with single sale of unique real estate does not meet New York's consumer orientation test).

500 Rucker v. Huffman, 99 N.C. App. 137, 392 S.E.2d 419 (1990),

owner who has a real estate license and receives a referral fee in connection with the sale,[501] even though sales between private parties are not covered. Similarly, the Vermont Supreme Court holds that a real estate broker is a seller engaged in trade or commerce, and is covered by the UDAP statute, regardless of whether the sale is between private parties.[502] The fact that the broker never holds title to the property does not mean that the broker is not a seller.[503]

2.2.5.1.4 *Special consideration for mobile home sales*

UDAP coverage of mobile home sales will likely depend not only on the wording of the UDAP statute, but also on the nature of the mobile home sale and other state law. Even where a UDAP statute only applies to the sale of "consumer goods," there should be little question that a mobile home purchased from a dealer on the dealer's lot is covered, since a mobile home is clearly a movable consumer good.[504]

Almost as clear is the treatment of the sale of a home that is sited in a mobile home park or that must be moved to another location. Even if the statute does not apply to real estate sales, since the consumer is purchasing a movable "good" without land, the UDAP statute should apply. Uniform Commercial Code § 2-105(1) indicates that "goods" include "identified things attached to realty as described in the section on goods to be severed from realty (section 2-107)." State law treating this transaction, for other purposes, as involving personalty should also be helpful in showing the UDAP statute applies.

Where the mobile home is semi-permanently affixed to and sold with the land, however, courts may treat it the same as a real estate sale. That is, the court will apply the UDAP statute to the mobile home sale only if the court would apply the statute to a real estate sale. On the other hand, since the home is movable, the consumer can argue that the transaction should be bifurcated into a land sale and the sale of personalty. Especially if state law treats a mobile home as personalty for purposes of taxes or foreclosures, the court should be willing to bifurcate the transaction and apply the UDAP statute to the mobile home sale even where it would not to a real estate sale.

2.2.5.2 Services, Personalty Related to Real Estate Are Covered

Even if a UDAP statute does not apply to the sale of real estate, UDAP remedies may still apply to services related to real estate sales, such as false promises that the seller will make repairs on a purchased home if problems arise,[505] or a seller's failure to remedy defects in a home.[506] Likewise, contracting for the construction of a home or an improvement to existing property is not a real estate purchase, but rather purchase of a service or a chattel, even if the construction work is affixed to the real estate.[507] The Texas Residential Construction Liability Act did not prevent a UDAP claim where there was no conflict between the two laws.[508]

The UDAP statute also applies to the sale of carpeting and other accessories sold with the land,[509] and to misrepresentations by a realtor (who offers a service), even though the consumer does not pay the realtor.[510] A real estate appraiser

---

distinguishing Robertson v. Boyd, 88 N.C. App. 437, 363 S.E.2d 672 (1988).

501 Dairs v. Sellers, 443 S.E.2d 879 (N.C. Ct. App. 1994).

502 Carter v. Gugliuzzi, 716 A.2d 17 (Vt. 1998).

503 *Id.*

504 *See* U.C.C. § 2-105(1); *see also* cases cited at National Consumer Law Center, Consumer Warranty Law § 15.2.1 (2d ed. 2001 and Supp.).

505 Woods v. Littleton, 554 S.W.2d 662 (Tex. 1977); Jim Walter Homes Inc. v. Mora, 622 S.W.2d 878 (Tex. Civ. App. 1981); Jim Walter Homes Inc. v. White, 617 S.W.2d 767 (Tex. Civ. App. 1981); Holifield v. Coronado Building, Inc., 594 S.W.2d 214 (Tex. Civ. App. 1980).

506 MacDonald v. Mobley, 555 S.W.2d 916 (Tex. Civ. App. 1977).

507 State *ex rel.* Brady v. Wellington Homes, Inc., 2003 WL 22048231 (Del. Super. Aug. 20, 2003) (unpublished, citation limited) (DTPA interpretation); Grove v. Huffman, 634 N.E.2d 1184 (Ill. App. Ct. 1994) (builder is not exempted from UDAP statute by exception for realtors); Pierce v. Drees, 607 N.E.2d 726 (Ind. Ct. App. 1993); Forton v. Laszar, 239 Mich. App. 711, 609 N.W.2d 850 (2000) (UDAP statute does not exclude real property); Suttle v. DeCesare, 2003 WL 21291053 (Ohio App. June 5, 2003) (unpublished, citation limited); Lump v. Best Door & Window, Inc., 2002 Ohio App. LEXIS 1381 (Mar. 27, 2002); Worshil v. Smythe Cramer Co., 2001 Ohio App. LEXIS 4172 (Sept. 10, 2001) (services portion of real estate transaction covered, but promotion and marketing services provided to builder rather than buyer are not); Byers v. Coppel, 2001 Ohio App. LEXIS 3846 (Aug. 24, 2001); Inserra v. J.E.M. Building Corp., 2000 Ohio App. LEXIS 5447 (Nov. 22, 2000); Williams v. Edwards, 129 Ohio App. 3d 116, 717 N.E.2d 368 (1998) (contract for improvements to real property is a sale or transfer of services for personal use, so is covered by Ohio's UDAP statute); Rose v. Zaring Homes, Inc., 122 Ohio App. 3d 739, 702 N.E.2d 952 (1997) (Ohio's UDAP statute covers construction of home even though sale of land is exempt); Precision Homes, Inc. v. Cooper, 671 S.W.2d 924 (Tex. App. 1984) (construction of a home); Parr v. Tagco Indus., 620 S.W.2d 200 (Tex. Civ. App. 1981) (construction of a grain facility). *See also* McKinney v. State, 693 N.E.2d 65 (Ind. 1998) (construction contracts are not subject to Indiana UDAP statute's restrictions on actions arising from real estate transactions, even though consumer also buys the building lot); Leduc v. Rotar, 2004 WL 298979 (Mich. App. Feb. 17, 2004) (unpublished, citation limited) (defendant's sideline home improvement business could be in trade or commerce). *But see* Callicoat v. Acuff Homes, Inc., 723 S.W.2d 565 (Mo. Ct. App. 1987) (construction and sale of residence was not a service, but was a sale of realty, excluded from UDAP coverage); Kanu v. George Development, Inc., 2002 WL 31630745 (Ohio App. Nov. 22, 2002) (unpublished, citation limited) (construction of home not covered).

508 Sanders v. Construction Equity, Inc., 42 S.W.3d 364 (Tex. App. 2001).

509 Deltona Corp. v. Jannetti, 392 So. 2d 976 (Fla. Dist. Ct. App. 1981).

510 Cameron v. Terrell & Garrett, Inc., 618 S.W.2d 535 (Tex. 1981);

is also subject to UDAP coverage.[511] A UDAP statute applies to a debt consolidation loan taking real estate as collateral.[512]

Where a transaction is covered by the UDAP statute, even if real estate in general is not, damages can be recovered not only for inadequacies in the goods or services added to the property, but also for the decreased value of the land. UDAP scope provisions apply to what type of action may be brought, not to the scope of damages.[513] But the consumer will have to show that the UDAP violation involved the services, and not just the sale of real estate.[514]

2.2.6 Residential Leases; Mobile Home Parks

2.2.6.1 Coverage

UDAP statutes whose scope is limited only by the "trade or commerce" standard may be used to challenge mobile home space rentals[515] and residential lease practices.[516] Moreover, "sale or distribution of . . . any property" includes the lease of an apartment. This interpretation is based on the economic reality that renting a house is a consumer transaction, that a lease is nearly identical to a sale, and that rental housing is in need of regulation.[517] Illinois courts similarly find landlord-tenant practices to involve both the distribution of "services" and of "any property . . . real, personal or mixed," and that a tenant is a "consumer" within the meaning of the act.[518] Where "merchandise" is defined to include real estate, it includes the lease of mobile home park lots.[519] Similarly mobile home tenants are "consumers" covered by a UDAP statute.[520] A Minnesota appellate court has found a UDAP statute applying to sale of services or real estate to apply to landlord actions in renting residential property.[521] A Texas court has reached a similar holding.[522] A statute applying to unfair practices "in business" applies to large-scale landlords' rental practices.[523]

The Utah UDAP statute, which covers "sale [or] lease . . . of goods, services, or other property, both tangible and intangible," covers landlord-tenant transactions,[524] unless the particular aspect of the statute is covered by a more

Manchac v. Pace, 608 S.W.2d 314 (Tex. Civ. App. 1980); *see also* Pointer v. Edward L. Kuhs, Co., 678 S.W.2d 836 (Mo. Ct. App. 1984) (real estate agent services involve "services" covered by statute).

511 Sampen v. Dabrowski, 584 N.E.2d 493 (Ill. App. Ct. 1991).

512 Lawson v. Nationwide Mortgage Corp., 628 F. Supp. 804 (D.D.C. 1986).

513 Precision Homes, Inc. v. Cooper, 671 S.W 2d 924 (Tex. App. 1984).

514 Rose v. Zaring Homes, Inc., 122 Ohio App. 3d 739, 702 N.E.2d 952 (1997) (consumer could bring UDAP claim only if complaints related to developer's construction of home rather than to sale of lot); Baskin v. Mortgage & Trust, Inc., 837 S.W.2d 743 (Tex. App. 1992).

515 People *ex rel.* Fahner v. Testa, 112 Ill. App. 3d 834, 445 N.E.2d 1249 (1983); People *ex rel.* Fahner v. Hedrich, 108 Ill. App. 3d 83, 438 N.E.2d 924 (1982); Commonwealth v. DeCotis, 366 Mass. 234, 316 N.E.2d 748 (1974); Stanley v. Moore, 439 S.E.2d 250 (N.C. Ct. App. 1994), *denial of treble damages rev'd*, 454 S.E.2d 225 (N.C. 1995); Marshall v. Miller, 47 N.C. App. 530, 268 S.E.2d 97 (1980); Laxson v. Lenger, 6 Pa. D. & C.4th 175 (C.P. 1990); Ethridge v. Hwang, 105 Wash. App. 447, 20 P.3d 958 (2001) (coverage under "trade or business" standard).

516 Travieso v. Gutman, Mintz, Baker & Sonnenfeldt, P.C., 1995 U.S. Dist. LEXIS 17804 (E.D.N.Y. Nov. 16, 1995); Connelly v. New Haven Hous. Auth., 8 Conn. L. Trib. No. 31 (Super. Ct. 1982); Conaway v. Prestia, CVN-803-76 (Conn. Super. Ct. 1981), *aff'd*, 191 Conn. 484, 464 A.2d 847 (1983); McGrath v. Mishara, 386 Mass. 74, 434 N.E.2d 1215 (1982); Frazier v. Priest, 141 Misc. 2d 775, 534 N.Y.S.2d 846 (N.Y.C. Ct. 1988); Pierce v. Reichard, 593 S. E. 2d 787 (N.C. Ct App. 2004); Friday v. United Dominion Realty Trust, Inc., 575 S.E.2d 532 (N.C. App. 2003); Creekside Apartments v. Poteat, 446 S.E.2d 826 (N.C. App. 1994); Stanley v. Moore, 439 S.E.2d 250 (N.C. App. 1994), *denial of treble damages rev'd*, 454 S.E.2d 225 (N.C. 1995); Allen v. Simmons, 99 N.C. App. 636, 394 S.E.2d 478 (1990); Mosley & Mosley Builders, Inc. v. Landin Ltd., 389 S.E.2d 576 (N.C. App. 1990); Love v. Pressley, 34 N.C. App. 503, 239 S.E.2d 574 (1977), *appeal dismissed*, 294 N.C. 441, 241 S.E.2d 843 (1978); *see also* Electronic World, Inc. v. Barefoot, 570 S.E.2d 225 (N.C. App. 2002) (lease of commercial property is covered); Kent v. Humphries, 50 N.C. App. 580, 275 S.E.2d 176 (1981); Brief of the Federal Trade Comm'n as Amicus Curiae, Commonwealth v. Monumental Properties, Inc., Clearinghouse No. 45,904 (Pa. submitted 1974) (FTC Act applies to leases of realty and personalty); Burbach v. Investors Management Corp., 484 S.E.2d 119 (S.C. App. 1997); *cf.* Cotton v. Stanley, 86 N.C. App. 534, 358 S.E.2d 692 (1987). *But see* Jackson & Assocs., Ltd. v. Christi, 1991 Tenn. App. LEXIS 638, Clearinghouse No. 51,283 (Tenn. App. 1991) (letter terminating residential lease was not a consumer transaction); State v. Schwab, 693 P.2d 108 (Wash. 1985).

517 Commonwealth v. Monumental Properties, Inc., 459 Pa. 450, 329 A.2d 812 (1974); *see also In re* Clark, 96 B.R. 569 (Bankr. E.D. Pa. 1989); *In re* Clarkson, 105 B.R. 266 (Bankr. E.D. Pa. 1989); Aponte v. Aungst (*In re* Aponte), 82 B.R. 738 (Bankr. E.D. Pa. 1988).

518 Anast v. Commonwealth Apartments, 956 F. Supp. 792 (N.D. Ill. 1997); Petrauskas v. Wexenthaller Realty Mgmt., Inc., 186 Ill. App. 3d 820, 542 N.E.2d 902 (1989); Carter v. Mueller, 120 Ill. App. 3d 314, 457 N.E.2d 1335 (1983).

519 Fulkerson v. MHC Operating Ltd., 2002 WL 32067510 (Del. Super. Sept. 24, 2002) (unpublished, citation limited).

520 People *ex rel.* Fahner v. Testa, 112 Ill. App. 3d 834, 445 N.E.2d 1249 (1983); People *ex rel.* Fahner v. Hedrich, 108 Ill. App. 3d 83, 438 N.E.2d 924 (1982). *Accord* Brown v. Veile, 198 Ill. App. 3d 513, 555 N.E.2d 1227 (1990).

521 Love v. Amsler, 441 N.W.2d 555 (Minn. Ct. App. 1989).

522 Myers v. Ginsburg, 735 S.W.2d 600 (Tex. App. 1987). *See also* 49 Prospect St. Tenants Ass'n v. Sheva Gardens, 227 N.J. Super. 449, 547 A.2d 1134 (App. Div. 1988).

523 Weller v. Department of Agriculture, Trade & Consumer Protection, No. 78-813 (Wis. Ct. App. 1980), *aff'd*, 109 Wis. 2d 665, 327 N.W.2d 172 (1982).

524 Woodhaven Apartments v. Washington, 942 P.2d 918 (Utah 1997). *See also* Wade v. Jobe, 818 P.2d 1006 (Utah 1991) (stating in dictum that UDAP statute covers landlord-tenant transactions).

specific state statute such as the Utah Fit Premises Act.[525] Ohio's highest court has, however, found an apartment rental not to be the provision of a "service," and thus not covered by the UDAP statute.[526]

Of course, the exact statutory language may be determinative. Rental of real property is explicitly included in the Maryland,[527] Michigan,[528] and New Jersey[529] UDAP statutes. Maryland's highest court has, however, limited the applicability of its UDAP statute to the formation of the landlord-tenant relationship, so it does not apply to acts or omissions during the term of the lease.[530]

The Missouri Supreme Court has ruled that residential tenants can not use the UDAP statute where the statute explicitly excludes private actions dealing with real estate.[531] Virginia amended its UDAP statute in 1994 to exclude aspects of consumer transactions that are covered by its Landlord and Tenant Act, unless the landlord's act is fraudulent or a misrepresentation.[532]

A court held that, since a former version of the Florida UDAP statute did not apply to real estate, it did not apply to mobile home lot leases either.[533] The language on which that court relied has since been deleted from the statute,[534] so it should now be clear that it covers lot leases as well as other real estate transactions. Even before the amendment of the statute, another court held that it applied to landlord-tenant transactions because the state attorney general had enacted UDAP regulations (now repealed) covering those transactions.[535]

525 Carlie v. Morgan, 922 P.2d 1 (Utah 1996).

526 Heritage Hills, Ltd. v. Deacon, 49 Ohio St. 3d 80, 551 N.E.2d 125 (1990). *But cf.* Brown v. Liberty Clubs, Inc., 45 Ohio St. 3d 191, 543 N.E.2d 783 (1989) (membership campground sale was mixed transaction involving both the transfer of personal property or services and the transfer of real estate, so was covered).

527 Md. Comm. L. Code §§ 13-301, 13-303; Richwind v. Brunson, 335 Md. 661, 645 A.2d 1147 (1994).

528 Smolen v. Dahlman Apartments, Ltd., 338 N.W.2d 892 (Mich. Ct. App. 1983); *see also* Rodriguez v. Berrybrook Farms, Inc., 672 F. Supp. 1009 (W.D. Mich. 1987).

529 *In re* Cohen, 191 B.R. 599 (D.N.J. 1996), *aff'd on other grounds*, 106 F.3d 52 (3d Cir. 1997), *aff'd*, 523 U.S. 213 (1998); 316 49 St. Assocs. Ltd. v. Galvez, 269 N.J. Super. 481, 635 A.2d 1013 (1994).

530 Richwind v. Brunson, 335 Md. 661, 645 A.2d 1147 (1994) (case involves non-disclosure of dangerous housing conditions; one of court's rationales is that the landlord should not be responsible for nondisclosure of conditions that arise during the lease term, since landlord may be ignorant of them); Scroggins v. Dahne, 335 Md. 688, 645 A.2d 1160 (1994). *See also* Benik v. Hatcher, 750 A.2d 10, 21–22 (Md. 2000) (explaining *Richwind*).

531 Detling v. Edelbrock, 671 S.W.2d 265 (Mo. 1984).

532 Va. Code § 59.1-199.

533 State v. De Anza Corp., 416 So. 2d 1173 (Fla. Dist. Ct. App. 1982).

534 Fla. Stat. § 501.203, *as amended by* Laws 1993, c. 93-38, § 2, eff. June 30, 1993.

535 Kingston Square Tenants v. Tuskegee Gardens, 792 F. Supp. 1566 (S.D. Fla. 1992).

2.2.6.2 Does Other State Regulation of Landlord-Tenant Relations Displace UDAP Coverage?

Three courts have ruled that a state's comprehensive landlord-tenant legislation displaces the UDAP statute's applicability to landlord-tenant issues.[536] On the other hand, courts have found UDAP actions not displaced by New Jersey's,[537] New York's,[538] or Wisconsin's[539] landlord-tenant legislation; Massachusetts' landlord-tenant statute even though that statute specifically regulates the challenged practice;[540] various Maryland landlord-tenant laws;[541] or Vermont's Residential Rental Agreements Act.[542] On the other hand, the Connecticut Supreme Court held that HUD regulation of low-income housing displaced the UDAP statute, so tenants could not assert habitability claims under the UDAP statute against a municipal housing authority.[543] An employee's occupancy of an apartment as part of the employment relationship was also not subject to the Connecticut UDAP statute.[544]

In Connecticut, a mobile home statute not only does not displace, but is enforceable through, the state's UDAP statute.[545] In Washington State, mobile home park tenants can bring suit under the UDAP statute even though parks are extensively regulated by a separate law.[546] In North Carolina, tenants can recover UDAP treble damages for wrongful eviction even though the state's Ejectment of Residential

536 Chelsea Plaza Homes, Inc. v. Moore, 226 Kan. 430, 601 P.2d 1100 (1979); Heritage Hills, Ltd. v. Deacon, 49 Ohio St. 3d 80, 551 N.E.2d 125 (1990); Carlie v. Morgan, 922 P.2d 1 (Utah 1996) (new statute providing specific remedies for uninhabitable premises displaced any UDAP coverage as to the same practices); State v. Schwab, 693 P.2d 108 (Wash. 1985) (landlord-tenant act recently enacted provides adequate private remedies including attorney fees; court also seems to hold that there never was a legislative intent that the UDAP statute apply to landlord-tenant cases, ignoring the fact that the UDAP statute applies to all practices in trade or commerce). *See also* Property Exchange & Sales, Inc. v. King, 863 S.W.2d 12 (Mo. Ct. App. 1993) (state law dealing with security deposits displaces UDAP applicability to security deposits related claim).

537 49 Prospect St. Tenants Ass'n v. Sheva Gardens, 227 N.J. Super. 449, 547 A.2d 1134 (App. Div. 1988).

538 Weiner v. People *ex rel.* Abrams, 119 Misc. 2d 970, 464 N.Y.S.2d 919 (Sup. Ct. 1983) (New York City Rent Stabilization law does not displace UDAP).

539 Weller v. Department of Agriculture, Trade & Consumer Protection, No. 78-813 (Wis. Ct. App. 1980), *aff'd*, 109 Wis. 2d 665, 327 N.W.2d 178 (1982).

540 McGrath v. Mishara, 386 Mass. 74, 434 N.E.2d 1215 (1982).

541 State v. Connelly, Clearinghouse No. 40,634 (Md. Cir. Ct. Baltimore Cty. 1985).

542 Bisson v. Ward, 628 A.2d 1256 (Vt. 1993).

543 Connelly v. New Haven Hous. Auth., 213 Conn. 354, 567 A.2d 1212 (1990).

544 Muniz v. Kravis, 59 Conn. App. 704, 757 A.2d 1207 (2000).

545 Gibbs v. Southeastern Inv. Corp., 705 F. Supp. 738 (D. Conn. 1989).

546 Ethridge v. Hwang, 105 Wash. App. 447, 20 P.3d 958 (2001).

Tenants Act[547] explicitly excludes treble damages.[548] Issues of statutory conflict and whether practices regulated by other statutes are excluded from UDAP coverage are discussed in more detail in § 2.3.3, *infra*.

2.2.6.3 UDAP Coverage Where Building Is Owner Occupied

One other area where courts may find landlord practices not covered by a UDAP statute is where the landlord is an owner-occupant, and thus not in "business." Massachusetts courts find a landlord occupying a two- or three-family house to have a primarily personal objective, and consequently the landlord's practices are not in trade or commerce.[549]

2.2.7 Migrant Farmworker Camps

In a unique case with far-reaching implications, a federal court has ruled that migrant farmworkers are tenants and can bring a UDAP action concerning migrant camp conditions since rental housing is covered by the state UDAP statute.[550] Even if the housing is theoretically "free," the UDAP statute still applies.[551]

2.2.8 Campground and Other Membership Clubs

In a typical campground membership contract, the consumer purchases a lifetime undivided right to use certain campground facilities.[552] Campground memberships have been held to be a "service"[553] and "merchandise,"[554] and thus covered by UDAP statutes. The Ohio Supreme Court has ruled that, while Ohio's UDAP statute does not apply to "pure" real estate transactions, the awarding of a "gift" of steak knives to prospective customers of a membership campground made the transaction "mixed," so the entire transaction was covered.[555] A company is in "trade or commerce" where it acquires a beach club and attempts to terminate consumers' memberships in the club.[556]

2.2.9 Pyramid Sales, Franchises, Securities, Business Opportunities

2.2.9.1 Pyramid Sales

An Indiana appellate court has found a pyramid sale scheme to be covered where the Indiana UDAP statute applied to "suppliers," defined to include a person who solicits consumer transactions.[557] The Indiana UDAP statute has since been amended to apply explicitly to pyramid sales.[558] An Ohio court finds a pyramid scheme to involve a consumer transaction, not a business investment, and so is covered by the Ohio UDAP statute.[559] Alabama also finds a pyramid sales scheme to involve the sale of goods, and is thus covered under its UDAP statute.[560]

2.2.9.2 Franchises and Other Investments

Courts usually find that the sale of a franchise to a franchisee is covered by the UDAP statute. Federal courts have interpreted the Connecticut statute as applying to franchise sales because the franchise is a "commodity or thing of value," and thus within the statute's "trade or commerce" definition.[561] A North Carolina court has reached a similar conclusion.[562] Colorado's statute, which defines "property" to include intangible property, applies to the sale of franchises, and franchisees are "consumers" because they are purchasers of the franchise.[563] Oregon's UDAP statute was amended to include franchises and dis-

547 N.C. Gen. Stat. § 42-25.9(a).

548 Stanley v. Moore, 454 S.E.2d 225 (N.C. 1995).

549 Billings v. Wilson, 397 Mass. 614, 493 N.E.2d 187 (1986); Sayah v. Hatzipetro, 397 Mass. 1004, 492 N.E.2d 1131 (1986); Neihaus v. Maxwell, 766 N.E.2d 556 (Mass. App. 2002) (one-time rental of single-family home by owner while temporarily living overseas not in trade or commerce); Young v. Patukonis, 24 Mass. App. Ct. 907, 506 N.E.2d 1164 (1987). *See also* 49 Prospect St. Tenants Ass'n v. Sheva Gardens, 227 N.J. Super. 449, 547 A.2d 1134 (App. Div. 1988) (issue not relevant where 55-unit building is involved).

550 Rodriguez v. Berrybrook Farms, Inc., 672 F. Supp. 1009 (W.D. Mich. 1987).

551 *Id. Contra* DeBruyn Produce Co. v. Romero, 202 Mich. App. 92, 508 N.W.2d 150 (1993).

552 *See* § 5.10.5, *infra*.

553 Commonwealth *ex rel.* Zimmerman v. Nickel, 26 Pa. D. & C.3d 115 (C.P. Mercer Cty. 1983).

554 State *ex rel.* Webster v. Missouri Trails Resort Corp., 627 F. Supp. 86 (E.D. Mo. 1985).

555 Brown v. Liberty Clubs, Inc., 45 Ohio St. 3d 191, 543 A.2d 783 (1989).

556 Baker v. Chavis, 410 S.E.2d 600 (S.C. Ct. App. 1991).

557 Watkins v. Alvey, 549 N.E.2d 74 (Ind. Ct. App. 1990).

558 Ind. Code § 24-5-0.5-2(3)(B).

559 Celebrezze v. Howard, 77 Ohio App. 3d 387, 602 N.E.2d 665 (1991).

560 Sheehan v. Bowden, 572 So. 2d 1211 (Ala. 1990).

561 Aurigemma v. Arco Petroleum Products Co., 734 F. Supp. 1025 (D. Conn. 1990); Bailey Employment Sys., Inc. v. Hahn, 545 F. Supp. 62 (D. Conn. 1982), *aff'd without op.*, 723 F.2d 895 (2d Cir. 1983).

562 Olivetti Corp. v. Ames Bus. Sys., Inc., 344 S.E.2d 82 (N.C. Ct. App. 1986).

563 Rocky Mt. Rhino Lining, Inc. v. Rhino Linings USA, Inc., 37 P.3d 458 (Colo. App. 2001), *cert. granted*, 2002 Colo. LEXIS 56 (Jan. 14, 2002), *vacated on other grounds*, 62 P.3d 142 (Colo. 2003).

tributorships specifically,[564] but a court has interpreted the statute not to apply to a company's termination of a distributorship.[565]

Both Arizona[566] and New Jersey[567] courts hold that their statutes apply to franchise sales because the sales involve "merchandise." On the other hand, a Minnesota case finds that deception regarding the terms of a distributorship is not covered by the UDAP statute, because there is no nexus between the alleged fraud and the sale of merchandise.[568] Pennsylvania[569] and Texas[570] courts hold that the offer of a franchise constitutes offering of "goods or services" covered by the statute. A distributorship also involves the purchase of goods and services and is covered by the Texas UDAP statute.[571] However, the Texas statute excludes the purchase of a wholly-intangible property right, so one court concluded that the right to act as a sales representative was not covered.[572] Courts interpreting the Louisiana UDAP statute disagree on the question.[573]

An Illinois court found that while franchisees are not "consumers" (the statute was subsequently amended to make them consumers[574]), a franchise is an "intangible," and the statute would thus apply to the sale of such an intangible if the purchaser is a "consumer."[575] However, even where a statute covers franchise sales and business opportunities, the UDAP legislation may not apply to purely commercial activities such as the sale of a machine to a grocery store.[576]

A Kentucky court has distinguished between private actions and those initiated by the state. The Kentucky UDAP statute specifies that private actions must involve purchases for family, personal or household purposes.[577] Since the attorney general's use of the UDAP statute is not so restricted, the state can bring an action to protect such nonconsumers as purchasers of business opportunities or participants in an employment offer.[578] An Ohio court concluded that, while franchises are listed in its UDAP statute, individuals who bought a franchise could not bring a UDAP suit because the purchase was not for personal, family, or household use.[579] An argument against this interpretation is that it appears to render the statute's reference to franchises meaningless.

Where a UDAP statute applies to consumers who purchase goods or services for personal, family, or household purposes, a private person who lends money to commercial developers is not a consumer.[580] Moreover, an investor may be found not to be a consumer.[581]

2.2.9.3 Securities Transactions

While one Texas court has ruled that the Texas statute that applies to "goods" and "tangible chattels" does not apply

564 Or. Rev. Stat. § 646.605(6).

565 Lund v. Arbonne International, Inc., 132 Or. App. 87, 887 P.2d 817 (1994).

566 Flower World of Am., Inc. v. Wenzel, 122 Ariz. 319, 594 P.2d 1015 (Ct. App. 1978).

567 Kavky v. Herbalife Int'l, 359 N.J. Super. 497, 820 A.2d 677 (App. Div. 2003) (sale of franchise that it is offered to the general public is covered by UDAP statute if it is too small to be covered by state Franchise Practices Act); Morgan v. Air Brook Limousine, 211 N.J. Super. 84, 510 A.2d 1197 (Law Div. 1986). *But see* J&R Ice Cream Corp. v. California Smoothie Licensing Corp., 31 F.3d 1259 (3d Cir. 1994) (declining to follow *Morgan*; holding franchises not covered by New Jersey UDAP statute); Christy v. We the People Forms & Serv. Centers USA, Inc., 213 F.R.D. 235 (D.N.J. 2003) (following *J&R Ice Cream*); Waterloo v. Gutter Protection Sys. Co. v. Absolute Gutter Protection, 64 F. Supp. 2d 398 (D.N.J. 1999) (following *J&R Ice Cream*). *But cf.* A.H. Meyers & Co. v. CNA Ins. Co., 2004 WL 180417 (3d Cir. Jan. 29, 2004) (unpublished, citation limited) (insurance agency agreement is not merchandise).

568 Banbury v. Omnitrition International, Inc., 533 N.W.2d 876 (Minn. App. 1995); *see also* Tisdell v. ValAdCo, 2002 WL 31368336 (Minn. App. Oct. 16, 2002) (unpublished, citation limited) (commercial farmer's investment in agricultural cooperative not covered).

569 Commonwealth v. Mirror World, Inc., Clearinghouse No. 26,022 (C.P. Phila. Cty., Pa. 1973).

570 Nelson v. Data Terminal Sys., Inc., 762 S.W.2d 744 (Tex. App. 1988); Texas Cookie Co. v. Hendricks & Peralta, Inc., 747 S.W.2d 873 (Tex. App. 1988); Wheeler v. Box, 671 S.W.2d 75 (Tex. App. 1984).

571 Clary Corp. v. Smith, 949 S.W.2d 452 (Tex. App. 1997).

572 Fisher Controls International, Inc. v. Gibbons, 911 S.W.2d 135 (Tex. App. 1995).

573 *Compare* Jarrell v. Carter, 577 So. 2d 120 (La. App. 1991) (allowing suit by person who wanted to buy distributorship from defendants) *with* Watercraft Management v. Mercury Marine, 191 F. Supp. 2d 709 (M.D. La. 2001) (distributor can not bring suit against parent company); Hamilton v. Business Partners, Inc., 938 F. Supp. 370 (E.D. La. 1996) (distributor can not bring suit against parent company); National Gypsum Co. v. Ace Wholesale, Inc., 738 So. 2d 128 (La. App. 1999) (same).

574 *See* Bixby's Food Sys., Inc. v. McKay, 985 F. Supp. 802 (N.D. Ill. 1997); Onesti v. Thomas McKinnon Securities, Inc., 619 F. Supp. 1262 (N.D. Ill. 1985) (securities are "merchandise"); Heinhold Commodities Inc. v. McCarty, 513 F. Supp. 311 (N.D. Ill. 1979) (purchasers of investment services and commodities futures are consumers under amended Illinois UDAP statute).

575 People *ex rel.* Scott v. Cardet International, Inc., 24 Ill. App. 3d 740, 321 N.E.2d 386 (1974). A court interpreting the new Illinois Act has ruled that the Act applies even to a chain letter scheme. *See* People *ex rel.* Fahner v. Walsh, 122 Ill. App. 3d 481, 461 N.E.2d 78 (1984).

576 Graham v. Kold Kist Beverage, Inc., 43 Or. App. 1037, 607 P.2d 759 (1979).

577 Ky. Rev. Stat. § 367.220.

578 Commonwealth *ex rel.* Stephens v. North Am. Van Lines, 600 S.W.2d 459 (Ky. Ct. App. 1979).

579 Yo-Can, Inc. v. Yogurt Exchange, Inc., 778 N.E.2d 80 (Ohio App. 2002).

580 Dinjian v. Dinjian, 22 Mass. App. Ct. 589, 495 N.E.2d 882 (1986) (UDAP statute has since been amended to cover such transactions).

581 National Union Fire Ins. Co. v. Arioli, 941 F. Supp. 646 (E.D. Mich. 1996) (Michigan law); Roach v. Mead, 301 Or. 383, 722 P.2d 1229 (1986).

to stock certificates,[582] the Fifth Circuit finds the sale of a fractional interest in oil and gas leases is a sale of a "good."[583] A Minnesota court holds that investment contracts are covered because they are "commodities" and "intangibles."[584] In Illinois[585] and Tennessee,[586] securities transactions are covered for the same reasons. New York appellate courts have agreed that that state's UDAP statute covers securities transactions.[587] A Washington appellate court, while not directly addressing coverage questions, has reversed the dismissal of investors' UDAP claims against underwriters whose misrepresentations allegedly inflated the price of a company's stock.[588] A California appellate court holds that the state Unfair Competition Law applies to securities transactions and is not preempted by federal law.[589] Two Arkansas cases on the question reach opposite conclusions.[590]

The Third Circuit, predicting how Pennsylvania courts will rule, holds that securities transactions are not covered by the Pennsylvania UDAP statute, at least where the transaction involves a company's valuation of its own securities and not a broker's sale of securities.[591] Earlier district court decisions finding the statute to apply to securities brokers should still be good law.[592] The Third Circuit has also affirmed a district court decision that the New Jersey UDAP statute does not apply to securities.[593] An unreported Minnesota decision reaches the same conclusion about its statute.[594]

If a court finds that the sale of securities is not covered by the UDAP statute, the consumer can still use the UDAP statute to challenge services related to the sale of the securities. Investment counseling leading later to the purchase of stock on a commission basis[595] and other services in connection with the sale of securities[596] involve the sale of a "service" and thus fall within a UDAP statute's scope. Financial advice offered in an investment opportunity is a "service" even if the consumer pays someone else; in addition, the broker offers "services" in putting an investment deal together.[597] A court may be particularly swayed by a brokerage's advertising itself as a "full service" broker.[598] Similarly, even if a UDAP statute can not be applied to a securities transaction, it should apply where a broker absconds with the investor's money before investing it in securities.[599]

---

582 Swenson v. Engelstad, 626 F.2d 421 (5th Cir. 1980) (Texas law); Portland Savings & Loan Ass'n v. Bevill, Bresler & Shulman Government Securities, Inc., 619 S.W.2d 241 (Tex. Civ. App. 1981); *see also* Marshall v. Quinn-L Equities, Inc., 704 F. Supp. 1384 (N.D. Tex. 1988).

583 MBank Fort Worth, N.A. v. Trans Meridian, Inc., 820 F.2d 716 (5th Cir. 1987) (Texas law); *see also In re* Gas Reclamation, Inc. Securities Litigation, 659 F. Supp. 493 (S.D.N.Y. 1987) (Texas law) (gas reclamation units are tangible chattels constituting both goods as well as securities under applicable laws); Frizzell v. Cook, 790 S.W.2d 41 (Tex. App. 1990); Vick v. George, 671 S.W.2d 541 (Tex. App. 1983), *rev'd on other grounds*, 686 S.W.2d 99 (Tex. 1984). *But see* Swenson v. Engelstad, 626 F.2d 421 (5th Cir. 1980) (Texas law).

584 LeSage v. Norwest Bank Calhoun-Isles, 409 N.W.2d 536 (Minn. Ct. App. 1987); *see also* Meyer v. Dygert, 156 F. Supp. 2d 1081 (D. Minn. 2001) (UDAP statute covers junior mortgage notes that state commerce commissioner characterized as securities); *In re* Professional Fin. Management, Ltd., 703 F. Supp. 1388 (D. Minn. 1989); Jenson v. Touche Ross & Co., 335 N.W.2d 720 (Minn. 1983).

585 Lyne v. Arthur Anderson & Co., 772 F. Supp. 1064 (N.D. Ill. 1991). *See also* Endo v. Albertine, 812 F. Supp. 1479 (N.D. Ill. 1993); Preston v. Kruezer, 641 F. Supp. 1163 (N.D. Ill. 1986); Evanston Bank v. Conticommodity Servs., Inc., 623 F. Supp. 1014 (N.D. Ill. 1985).

586 Stevenson v. J.C. Bradford & Co. (*In re* Cannon), 230 B.R. 546 (Bankr. W.D. Tenn. 1999) (purchase and sale of commodities futures contracts are covered), *rev'd on other grounds*, 277 F.3d 838 (6th Cir. 2002).

587 Scalp & Blade, Inc. v. Advest, Inc., 722 N.Y.S.2d 639 (App. Div. 2001); B.S.L. One Owners' Corp. v. Key International Mfg., Inc., 640 N.Y.S.2d 135 (App. Div. 1996); Breakwaters Townhomes v. Breakwaters of Buffalo, 207 A.D.2d 963, 616 N.Y.S.2d 829 (App. Div. 1994). *But see* Morris v. Gilbert, 649 F. Supp. 1491 (E.D.N.Y. 1986); *In re* Dean Witter Managed Futures Ltd. P'ship Litig., 282 A.D.2d 271, 724 N.Y.S.2d 149 (2001).

588 Reale v. Ernst & Young, L.L.P., 101 Wash. App. 1037 (2000).

589 Roskind v. Morgan Stanley Dean Witter & Co., 80 Cal. App. 4th 345, 95 Cal. Rptr. 2d 258 (2000).

590 *Compare* New Equity Sec. Holders Committee for Golden Gulf, Ltd. v. Phillips, 97 B.R. 492 (E.D. Ark. 1989) (applying UDAP statute to securities fraud) *with* Robertson v. White, 633 F. Supp. 954 (W.D. Ark. 1986) (also points out that Arkansas UDAP statute explicitly excludes practices regulated by state securities commission), *aff'd on other grounds*, 856 F.2d 52 (8th Cir. 1988).

591 Algrant v. Evergreen Valley Nurseries Ltd. Partners, 126 F.3d 178 (3d Cir. 1997) (Pa. law). *See also* Perry v. Markman Capital Management, Inc., 2002 WL 31248038 (E.D. Pa. Oct. 4, 2002); Baker v. Summit Bank, 64 F. Supp. 2d 466 (E.D. Pa. 1999) (following *Algrant*; UDAP statute covers case if fraud relates to the transaction rather than the specific security).

592 Merrill Lynch, Pierce, Fenner & Smith v. Masland, 878 F. Supp. 710 (M.D. Pa. 1995); Denison v. Kelly, 759 F. Supp. 199 (M.D. Pa. 1991).

593 Nicholas v. Saul Stone & Co., 224 F.3d 179, 190 (3d Cir. 2000), *aff'g* 1998 U.S. Dist. LEXIS 22977 (D.N.J. June 30, 1998).

594 Tisdell v. ValAdCo, 2002 WL 31368336 (Minn. App. Oct. 16, 2002) (unpublished, citation limited).

595 E.F. Hutton & Co. v. Youngblood, 708 S.W.2d 865 (Tex. App. 1986).

596 Nottingham v. General Am. Communications, Corp., 811 F.2d 873 (5th Cir. 1987) (Texas law); Lyne v. Arthur Anderson & Co., 772 F. Supp. 1064 (N.D. Ill. 1991) (accounting services offered in connection with sale of securities are "merchandise" under Illinois UDAP statute); Marshall v. Quinn-L Equities, Inc., 704 F. Supp. 1384 (N.D. Tex. 1988). *But see* Denison v. Kelly, 759 F. Supp. 199 (M.D. Pa. 1991).

597 Dominguez v. Brackey Enterprises, Inc., 756 S.W.2d 788 (Tex. App. 1988).

598 E.F. Hutton & Co. v. Youngblood, 708 S.W.2d 865 (Tex. App. 1986).

599 French by Pickard v. Wilgus, 742 F. Supp. 434 (M.D. Tenn. 1990). *But see* Miller v. Fahnestock & Co., 2000 WL 34001922 (Kan. Dist. Ct. Aug. 3, 2000) (where UDAP statute excludes

However, some courts completely reject the application of UDAP statutes to securities cases. Massachusetts' highest court has resolved a conflict among federal courts interpreting the Massachusetts statute[600] by finding two grounds for rejecting UDAP application to securities cases.[601] First, the court found that the FTC does not regulate securities fraud and prior Massachusetts cases finding UDAP coverage in areas not regulated by the FTC pertained only to areas of special state control such as insurance and banking. Second, shortly after enacting the relevant UDAP provision, the Massachusetts legislature also enacted a comprehensive state securities fraud regulatory scheme including a private remedy for damages and attorney fees.[602] The Massachusetts legislature did not approve of these interpretations and amended the UDAP statute to explicitly cover securities and commodities cases.[603]

While the Massachusetts Supreme Judicial Court's view has been legislatively overturned, courts in a number of other states have adopted the position taken by Massachusetts courts that securities fraud is not covered. This includes courts interpreting the Connecticut,[604] Florida,[605] Georgia,[606] Hawaii,[607] Louisiana,[608] Maine,[609] Michigan,[610] New Jersey,[611] New York,[612] North Carolina,[613] Ohio,[614] Oklahoma,[615] and Tennessee[616] UDAP statutes. The New Hampshire legislature amended the state UDAP statute in 2002 to exclude trade or commerce that is subject to the jurisdiction of the state director of securities or federal securities regulators who have authority to regulate unfair or deceptive practices.[617] A Kansas court, relying on its UDAP statute's explicit exclusion of sales of securities,

---

sales of securities, it does not cover stockbroker's theft of consumer's investment).

600 *Compare* Conkling v. Moseley, Hallgarten, Estabrook & Weeden, 575 F. Supp. 760 (D. Mass. 1983); Sweeney v. Keystone Provident Life Ins. Co., 578 F. Supp. 31 (D. Mass. 1983) (no UDAP action) *with* Hickey v. Howard, 598 F. Supp. 1105 (D. Mass. 1984); Pettigrew v. Oppenheimer & Co., 582 F. Supp. 98 (D. Mass. 1984); Redstone v. Goldman Sachs & Co., 583 F. Supp. 74 (D. Mass. 1984); Mitchelson v. Aviation Simulation Technology, 582 F. Supp. 1 (D. Mass. 1983) (UDAP action allowed).

601 Cabot Corp. v. Baddour, 394 Mass. 720, 477 N.E.2d 399 (1985); *see also* Levine v. Tucker, Anthony & R.L. Day, Inc., 395 Mass. 1004, 479 N.E.2d 694 (1985).

602 Mass. Gen. Laws Ann. ch. 110A.

603 1987 Mass Acts 664, amending Mass. Gen. Laws ch. 93A, §§ 1, 4, 9.

604 United Components, Inc. v. Wdowiak, 239 Conn. 259, 684 A.2d 693 (1996); Russell v. Dean Witter Reynolds, Inc., 200 Conn. 172, 510 A.2d 972 (1986). *Accord* Seeman v. Arthur Andersen & Co., 896 F. Supp. 250 (D. Conn. 1995). *See also* Caraluzzi v. Prudential Securities, Inc., 824 F. Supp. 1206 (N.D. Ill. 1993) (Conn. law); Andreo v. Friedlander, Gaines, Cohen, 660 F. Supp. 1362 (D. Conn. 1987).

605 Rogers v. Cisco Sys., Inc., 268 F. Supp. 2d 1305 (N.D. Fla. 2003) (construing Fla. statute to be consistent with FTC Act); Crowell v. Morgan Stanley Dean Witter Servs. Co., 87 F. Supp. 2d 1287 (S.D. Fla. 2000).

606 Taylor v. Bear Stearns & Co., 572 F. Supp. 667 (N.D. Ga. 1983);

607 Bulgo v. Munoz, 853 F.2d 710 (9th Cir. 1988) (Haw. law); Spinner Corp. v. Princeville Dev. Corp., 849 F.2d 388 (9th Cir. 1988) (Hawaii law); Nakamoto v. Hartley, 758 F. Supp. 1357 (D. Haw. 1991).

608 Smith v. Cooper/T. Smith Corp., 846 F.2d 325 (5th Cir. 1988) (Louisiana law); Stephenson v. Paine Webber Jackson & Curtis, Inc., 839 F.2d 1095 (5th Cir.) (Louisiana law), *reh'g denied*, 849 F.2d 901 (5th Cir. 1988), *cert. denied*, 488 U.S. 926 (1988); Moore v. A.G. Edwards & Sons, Inc., 631 F. Supp. 138 (E.D. La. 1986); Feiber v. Cassidy, 723 So. 2d 1101 (La. App. 1998); Taylor v. First Jersey Securities, Inc., 533 So. 2d 1383 (La. Ct. App. 1988), *cert. denied*, 538 So. 2d 593 (La. 1989).

609 Wyman v. Prime Discount Securities, 819 F. Supp. 79 (D. Me. 1993).

610 Wheeling, Inc. v. Stelle, 2000 U.S. Dist. LEXIS 8628 (E.D. Mich. May 30, 2000); Vennittilli v. Primerica, Inc., 943 F. Supp. 793 (E.D. Mich. 1996) (Michigan law); Silverman v. Niswonger, 761 F. Supp. 464 (E.D. Mich. 1991); Mercer v. Jaffe, Snider, Reiff & Heuer, P.C., 730 F. Supp. 74 (W.D. Mich. 1990); Mercer v. Jaffe, Snider, Reiff & Heuer, P.C., 713 F. Supp. 1019 (W.D. Mich. 1989); *see also* Caproni v. Prudential Securities, Inc., 15 F.3d 614 (6th Cir. 1994) (Michigan law).

611 Waterloo v. Gutter Protection Sys. Co. v. Absolute Gutter Protection, 64 F. Supp. 2d 398 (D.N.J. 1999); Nicholas v. Saul Stone & Co., 1998 WL 34111036 (D.N.J. June 30, 1998), *aff'd*, 224 F.3d 179, 190 (3d Cir. 1999); Bramblewood Investors, Inc. v. C&G Assocs., 262 N.J. Super. 96, 619 A.2d 1332 (1992).

612 *In re* Sterling Foster & Co., Securities Litigation, 222 F. Supp. 2d 216, 286, 287 (E.D.N.Y. 2002); Spirit Partners v. Audiohighway.com, 2000 U.S. Dist. LEXIS 7236 (S.D.N.Y. May 25, 2000); Fesseha v. TD Waterhouse Investor Servs., 305 A.D.2d 268, 761 N.Y.S.2d 22 (2003); Smith v. Triad Mfg. Group, Inc., 255 A.D.2d 962, 681 N.Y.S.2d 710 (1998).

613 McPhail v. Wilson, 733 F. Supp. 1011 (W.D.N.C. 1990); Hajmm Co. v. House of Raeford Farms, Inc., 328 N.C. 578, 403 S.E.2d 483 (1991); Skinner v. E.F. Hutton & Co., 314 N.C. 267, 333 S.E.2d 236 (1985); Sterner v. Penn, 159 N.C. App. 626, 583 S.E.2d 670 (N.C. Ct. App. 2003); Allen v. Ferrera, 540 S.E.2d 761 (N.C. App. 2000); Ward v. Zabady, 354 S.E.2d 369 (N.C. Ct. App. 1987); *see also* City National Bank v. American Com. Fin. Corp., 801 F.2d 714 (4th Cir. 1986) (North Carolina law); Linder v. Durham Hosiery Mills, Inc., 761 F.2d 162 (4th Cir. 1985) (North Carolina law); Weft, Inc. v. G.L. Inv. Assoc., 630 F. Supp. 1138 (E.D.N.C. 1986); *aff'd without op.*, 822 F.2d 56 (4th Cir. 1987); Oberlin Capital v. Slavin, 554 S.E.2d 840 (N.C. App. 2001) (commercial loan agreement, which granted lender the right to purchase stock in the borrower and which was intended to supply short-term capital, is not in trade or commerce); Bache Halsey Stuart, Inc. v. Hunsucker, 38 N.C. App. 414, 248 S.E.2d 567 (1978).

614 Huang v. E*Trade Group, Inc., 151 Ohio App. 3d 363, 784 N.E.2d 151 (2003).

615 Robertson v. White, 633 F. Supp. 954 (W.D. Ark. 1986) (Oklahoma law) (also points out that Arkansas UDAP statute explicitly excludes practices regulated by state securities commission).

616 Joyner v. Triple Check Fin. Serv., 782 F. Supp. 364 (W.D. Tenn. 1991); Hardy v. First Am. Bank, N.A., 774 F. Supp. 1078 (M.D. Tenn. 1991); French by Pickard v. Wilgus, 742 F. Supp. 434 (M.D. Tenn. 1990); Nichols v. Merrill, Lynch, Pierce, Fenner & Smith, 706 F. Supp. 1309 (M.D. Tenn. 1989); DePriest v. 1717-19 West End Assocs., 951 S.W.2d 769 (Tenn. App. 1997).

617 N.H. Rev. Stat. Ann. § 358-A:3, *as amended, effective* July 17, 2002.

holds that the statute does not cover a stockbroker's theft of a consumer's investment.[618]

In considering a UDAP claim on behalf of investors, care must be taken to distinguish between rights of the corporation which an individual investor can enforce only through a derivative suit, and violations of duties owed directly to the shareholder, which can be redressed by an individual suit.[619]

2.2.9.4 Work at Home Schemes and Other Personal Business Opportunities

Work-at-home schemes and other deceptive business opportunities are promoted on a vast scale.[620] Some sellers advertise these schemes in the employment want ads as if they were job opportunities. Their targets are unemployed and underemployed individuals who want to better their lives.

Many UDAP statutes explicitly include the sale of franchises or business opportunities in their definition of covered transactions.[621] In other states, the question will be whether the scheme falls within the general coverage language of the UDAP statute. There should be no question of coverage in the states where business transactions are generally covered.[622] Work-at-home and business opportunity schemes also clearly fall within the definition of "trade or commerce."[623]

Some UDAP statutes restrict their coverage to "goods and services" or "merchandise." If these definitions include intangibles, sale of a business opportunity is covered.[624] Even if they do not, the seller promises at least some services in almost all business opportunities. Many involve goods as well, such as equipment to use in the business, samples, or products to sell. As a result, sales of business opportunities may be covered even in states that do not cover intangibles.[625] A business opportunity that involves commissions for recruiting new members may be covered as an "award by chance" under Ohio's UDAP statute, as money paid into the scheme does not generate a return by its use in some productive capacity, but depends only on the solicitation of new members.[626]

A business opportunity falls within the broad New Jersey[627] and Arizona[628] definitions of "merchandise." It also meets the Connecticut definition of goods, which includes any "commodity or thing of value."[629]

A common pattern is for the UDAP statute to apply only to consumer transactions, or to restrict its private cause of action to "consumers." Some courts have defined "consumer" to require that the purchase not be for resale. Using such a definition, a New York court held that unsophisticated individuals who had been recruited as independent cosmetic distributors were consumers.[630] Even though they were not the end-users of the products they bought for resale, they were the end-users of the distributorships. In addition, many plaintiffs bought cosmetics that they were never able to sell, so they became the *de facto* end-users.[631] Likewise, the Minnesota Supreme Court has concluded that the sale of a restaurant business should be viewed as a consumer transaction covered by the statute where the buyer intended to operate the business rather than resell it.[632]

---

618 Miller v. Fahnestock & Co., 2000 WL 34001922 (Kan. Dist. Ct. Aug. 3, 2000).

619 Mann v. Kemper Fin. Cos., 618 N.E.2d 317 (Ill. App. Ct. 1992).

620 *See* § 5.13.1, *infra.*

621 *See, e.g.*, Barman v. Union Oil Co., 2000 U.S. Dist. LEXIS 14157 (D. Or. Sept. 8, 2000), *aff'd in part, rev'd in part, remanded, on other grounds*, 2002 U.S. App. LEXIS 20764 (9th Cir. Sept. 26, 2002); Akers v. Bonifasi, 629 F. Supp. 1212 (M.D. Tenn. 1985); *see also* Black v. Dept. of Legal Affairs, 353 So. 2d 655 (Fla. App. 1977) (under former Florida definition of "consumer transaction," must show that buyer had not engaged in the business in the past); Lund v. Arbonne International, Inc., 887 P.2d 817 (Or. App. 1994) (declining to decide whether sale of business opportunity must be for personal, family, or household use to be covered by UDAP statute). *But see* Yo-Can, Inc. v. Yogurt Exchange, Inc., 778 N.E.2d 80 (Ohio App. 2002) (even though statute states that it covers sale of franchises, court finds no coverage because sale was not for personal, family, or household use).

622 *See* § 2.4.5.2, *supra.*

623 Aurigemma v. Arco Petroleum Prods. Co., 734 F. Supp. 1025 (D. Conn. 1990); Sheehan v. Bowden, 572 So. 2d 1211 (Ala. 1990) (promotion of pyramid scheme falls within "trade or commerce"); Connolly v. Wecare Distribs., Inc., 143 Misc. 2d 637, 541 N.Y.S.2d 163 (Sup. Ct. 1989) (sale of cosmetic distributorship to unsophisticated buyer after public recruitment campaign is "business, trade, or commerce"), *aff'd without op.*, 544 N.Y.S.2d 758 (4th Dept. 1989).

624 People *ex rel.* Scott v. Cardet International, 24 Ill. App. 3d 740, 321 N.E.2d 386 (1974) (distributorship is an intangible).

625 Clary Corp. v. Smith, 949 S.W.2d 452 (Tex. App. 1997); Nelson v. Data Terminal Sys., Inc., 762 S.W.2d 744 (Tex. App. 1988); Texas Cookie Co. v. Hendricks & Peralta, Inc., 747 S.W.2d 873 (Tex. App. 1988). *See* § 2.2.9.2, *supra.*

626 State *ex rel.* Montgomery v. Purchase Plus Buyer's Group, Inc., 2002 WL 723707 (Ohio App. Apr. 25, 2002) (unpublished, citation limited).

627 Morgan v. Air Brook Limousine, Inc., 211 N.J. Super. 84, 510 A.2d 1197 (Law. Div. 1986).

628 Flower World of Am., Inc. v. Wenzel, 122 Ariz. 319, 594 P.2d 1015 (Ct. App. 1978).

629 Bailey Employment Sys., Inc. v. Hahn, 545 F. Supp. 62 (D. Conn. 1982).

630 Connolly v. Wecare Distribs., Inc., 143 Misc. 2d 637, 541 N.Y.S.2d 163 (Sup. Ct. 1989), *aff'd without op.*, 544 N.Y.S.2d 758 (4th Dept. 1989); *see also* Akgul v. Prime Time Transportation, Inc., 293 A.D.2d 631, 741 N.Y.S.2d 553 (2002) (franchise marketing scheme meets New York's consumer impact requirement).

631 *See also* State *ex rel.* Montgomery v. Purchase Plus Buyer's Group, Inc., 2002 Ohio App. LEXIS 1966 (Apr. 25, 2002) (UDAP statute applied where distributors were encouraged to use the product).

632 Ly v. Nystrom, 615 N.W.2d 302 (Minn. 2000) (the court concluded that the UDAP statute did not cover the transaction,

Other UDAP statutes define a "consumer transaction" as one for "personal, family, or household use." Since fraudulent work-at-home and business opportunity schemes are usually promoted as a means of personal growth and enhancement of income through personal effort, they should be considered to be for personal use.[633] The Sixth Circuit dealt with a scheme that was promoted as a way to reduce personal income tax liability by setting up a home-based business, but was really a cover for selling life insurance. Since the focus of the sales pitch was on reducing the individual's personal income taxes, the transaction was for personal rather than business use.[634]

In arguing that a business opportunity scheme is covered by a UDAP statute, it is important to stress the liberal construction required of the statute[635] and the seller's practice of targeting unsophisticated individuals.[636] It may also be helpful to focus not just on the business opportunity itself, but on any incidental goods or services.

Whether or not the UDAP statute covers the transaction, the practitioner should investigate whether the buyer's or seller's state has a specific law regulating the sale of business opportunities.[637] The state's pyramid sales law should also be checked carefully to see whether it might cover the transaction.[638] RICO and fraud claims are also possibilities.[639]

2.2.10 *Employer-Employee and Internal Business Disputes*

Employees and business partners are generally unsuccessful in their efforts to bring UDAP actions against their employers or partners. Courts are antagonistic to these types of UDAP actions, holding that UDAP statutes do not apply to employer-employee relations,[640] to practices between a

---

however, because it was a one-shot sale that did not affect the public). *See also* Rocky Mt. Rhino Lining, Inc. v. Rhino Linings USA, Inc., 37 P.3d 458 (Colo. App. 2001) (sale of franchise is "property" covered by UDAP statute), *rev'd on other grounds*, 62 P.3d 142 (Colo. 2003) (transaction did not meet public impact test and is not deceptive; finding it unnecessary to address coverage issue).

633 *See* State *ex rel.* Celebrezze v. Howard, 602 N.E.2d 665 (Ohio App. 1991) (pyramid scheme covered by UDAP statute where victim's purpose was to acquire greater personal wealth, not to begin a new business venture). *See also* Sheehan v. Bowden, 572 So. 2d 1211 (Ala. 1990) (recruitment to enter pyramid scheme is consumer transaction; statute requires personal, family, or household use but court does not discuss this requirement); Meyer v. Diesel Equipment Co., 570 P.2d 1374 (Kan. App. 1977) (repair of truck that consumer drove for a living is a consumer transaction). *Cf.* People *ex rel.* Scott v. Cardet International, 24 Ill. App. 3d 740, 321 N.E.2d 386 (1974) (court states that it would probably find that purchase of a franchise for purposes other than resale is a consumer transaction, except for subsequent legislative amendment which court construes as indication that previous version of statute did not cover such sales); Yo-Can, Inc. v. Yogurt Exchange, Inc., 778 N.E.2d 80 (Ohio App. 2002) (sale of franchise not covered because not for personal, family, or household use); State *ex rel.* Montgomery v. Purchase Plus Buyer's Group, Inc., 2002 Ohio App. LEXIS 1966 (Apr. 25, 2002) (unpublished, citation limited) (business opportunity that involves ordering goods and then reselling them may not be covered, but if compensation depends on recruiting new members it is covered). *But cf.* State *ex rel.* Montgomery v. Purchase Plus Buyer's Group, Inc., 2002 WL 723707 (Ohio App. Apr. 25, 2002) (unpublished, citation limited) (business opportunity covered by UDAP statute only to extent it involved members' purchase of goods for their own use or recruitment of new members, not resale of goods); Searle v. Exley Express, 564 P.2d 1054 (Or. 1977) (purchase of commercial truck as family investment and to provide employment for buyer's son might be for personal, family, or household use if subjective test used, but court applies objective test).

634 Hofstetter v. Fletcher, 905 F.2d 897 (6th Cir. 1988).

635 *See* § 2.1.3, *supra*; *see also* State *ex rel.* Montgomery v. Purchase Plus Buyer's Group, Inc., 2002 Ohio App. LEXIS 1966 (Apr. 25, 2002) (unpublished, citation limited).

636 *See* Connolly v. Wecare Distribs., Inc., 143 Misc. 2d 637, 541 N.Y.S.2d 163 (Sup. Ct. 1989) (stressing defendant's targeting of unsophisticated individuals), *aff'd without op.*, 544 N.Y.S.2d 758 (4th Dept. 1989); State *ex rel.* Celebrezze v. Howard, 602 N.E.2d 665 (Ohio App. 1991).

637 *See e.g.*, Conn. Gen. Stats. § 36b-60 *et seq.*; Fla. Stat. Ann. § 559.80 *et seq.*; Ga. Code Ann. § 10-1-410 *et seq.*; 815 Ill. Comp. Stat. Ann. § 602/5-1; Ind. Code Ann. § 24-5-8-1 *et seq.*; Iowa Code ch. 523B; Ky. Rev. Stat. § 367.801 *et seq.*; La. Rev. Stat. § 51:1821 *et seq.*; Me. Rev. Stat. Ann. tit. 32, ch. 69-B; Md. Bus. Reg. Code Ann. § 14-101 *et seq.*; N.C. Gen. Stat. § 66-94; Ohio Rev. Code ch. 1334; 71 Okla. Stat. § 801; S.C. Code Ann. § 39-57-10 *et seq.*; S.D. Codified Laws § 37-25A-1 *et seq.*; Tex. Bus. & Com. Code § 41.001 *et seq.*; Utah Code Ann. § 13-15-1 *et seq.*; Wash. Rev. Code § 19.110.010.

638 *See* § 5.13.3, *infra*.

639 *See* Ch. 9, *infra*.

640 Foraste v. Brown University, 248 F. Supp. 2d 71 (D.R.I. 2003) (dispute regarding ownership of copyright to work produced while an employee); Jon-Don Prods., Inc. v. Malone, 2003 WL 1856420 (D.N.H. Apr. 10, 2003); Bollinger v. Tanner Cos., 2003 WL 1824836 (E.D. La. Apr. 7, 2003) (former employee can not sue because she is neither consumer nor business competitor); Keckhafer v. Prudential Ins. Co., 2002 WL 31185866 (D. Minn. Oct. 1, 2002); Hart v. Verizon Communications, Inc., 2002 WL 31027429 (D. Mass. Sept. 11, 2002); Grasso v. Forrest Edward Employment Servs., 2002 U.S. Dist. LEXIS 8598 (S.D.N.Y. May 15, 2002); Drybrough v. Acxiom Corp., 172 F. Supp. 2d 366 (D. Conn. 2001) (reneging on promises that induced employee to give up valuable accounts as part of a job promotion); Dotson v. Sears, Roebuck & Co., 2001 U.S. Dist. LEXIS 13171 (W.D.N.C. Feb. 23, 2001) (termination of employee not covered); Carrabus v. Schneider, 119 F. Supp. 2d 221 (E.D.N.Y. 2000) (hiring practices not covered), *aff'd*, 2001 U.S. App. LEXIS 14197 (2d Cir. June 20, 2001); McMahon v. Digital Equip. Corp., 944 F. Supp. 70 (D. Mass. 1996) (even where employer acts as self-insurer and employee's claim deals with insurance claim against employer), *rev'd on other grounds*, 162 F.3d 28 (1st Cir. 1998); Whelan v. Intergraph Corp., 889 F. Supp. 15 (D. Mass. 1995) (UDAP statute does not cover claims arising from recruitment or employment of worker); Donovan v. Digital Equip. Corp., 883 F. Supp. 775 (D.N.H. 1994); Powderly v. Metrabyte Corp., 866 F. Supp. 39 (D. Mass. 1994) (Mass. law) (no coverage even if employment ended before act occurred); Evan v. Certified Engineering &

seller and its representatives,[641] to employer-independent contractor relations,[642] to practices between a company and one of its executives,[643] to internal partnership matters,[644] to disputes between shareholders and joint venturers about the control of a business,[645] to disputes between the beneficiary of a trust and the trustee,[646] or to grievances by a stockholder against a corporation as to the internal governance of the corporation.[647] A Connecticut appellate court held that an employee's occupancy of an employer-supplied apartment as part of the job was outside the scope of the UDAP statute even though landlord-tenant matters were covered.[648]

On the other hand, the North Carolina Supreme Court found that an employer can use the UDAP statute to challenge a former employee's violation of a covenant not to

---

Testing Co., 834 F. Supp. 488 (D. Mass. 1993); Fickes v. Sun Expert, Inc., 762 F. Supp. 998 (D. Mass. 1991); Bolen v. Paragon Plastics, Inc., 754 F. Supp. 221 (D. Mass. 1990) (but an independent contractor may be covered); Wilson v. Wilson-Cook Medical, Inc., 720 F. Supp. 533 (M.D.N.C. 1989); Hoffman v. Optima Sys., Inc., 683 F. Supp. 865 (D. Mass. 1988); Kintner v. Nidec-Torin Corp., 662 F. Supp. 112 (D. Conn. 1987); Banerjee v. Roberts, 641 F. Supp. 1093 (D. Conn. 1986); Mitchelson v. Aviation Simulation Technology, 582 F. Supp. 1 (D. Mass. 1983); United Components, Inc. v. Wdowiak, 239 Conn. 259, 684 A.2d 693 (1996); Quimby v. Kimberly-Clark Corp., 28 Conn. App. 660, 613 A.2d 838 (1992); Smith v. 2001 South Dixie Highway, Inc., 2004 WL 1057794 (Fla. Dist. Ct. App. May. 12, 2004) (employee can not bring UDAP claim against employer who terminated her, contrary to statute, for buying a vehicle from a competing dealership, since goal of suit is job reinstatement); Larson v. Tandy Corp., 187 Ga. App. 893, 371 S.E.2d 663 (1988); Feldstein v. Guinan, 148 Ill. App. 3d 610, 499 N.E.2d 535 (1986) (physician's relationship to employer involves practice of medicine not trade or commerce): Thibaut v. Thibaut, 607 So. 2d 587 (La. Ct. App. 1992); Falmouth Ob-Gyn Assocs., Inc. v. Abisla, 417 Mass. 176, 629 N.E.2d 291 (1994); Anzalone v. Massachusetts Bay Transportation Authority, 403 Mass. 119, 526 N.E.2d 246 (1988); Manning v. Zuckerman, 388 Mass. 8, 444 N.E.2d 1262 (1983); Weeks v. Harbor National Bank, 388 Mass. 141, 445 N.E.2d 605 (1983); O'Connell v. Bank of Boston, 37 Mass. App. Ct. 416, 640 N.E.2d 513 (1994) (employer's initiation of theft investigation and criminal charges against employees not covered); Dorfman v. TDA Indus., Inc., 16 Mass. App. Ct. 714, 455 N.E.2d 457 (1983); Winslow v. Corporate Express, Inc., 364 N.J. Super. 128, 834 A.2d 1037 (App. Div. 2003) (merchandise salesman's claims against employer not covered); American Marble Corp. v. Crawford, 84 N.C. App. 86, 351 S.E.2d 848 (1987); Buie v. Daniel International Corp., 56 N.C. App. 445, 289 S.E.2d 118 (1982); Davenport v. Island Ford, Lincoln, Mercury, Inc., 465 S.E.2d 737 (S.C. App. 1995); Figueroa v. West, 902 S.W.2d 701 (Tex. App. 1995); Bundy v. University of Wisconsin, 220 Wis. 2d 357, 582 N.W.2d 504 (App. 1998) (unpublished limited precedent opinion, text available on LEXIS at 1998 Wisc. App. LEXIS 600) (UDAP statute does not cover fraudulent representations that induced plaintiff to enter into employment contract). *See also* Bass v. Hendrix, 931 F. Supp. 523 (S.D. Tex. 1996) (patient's agreement that her therapy sessions could be filmed, for which she was paid an honorarium, was not a consumer transaction); Barlow v. McLeod, 666 F. Supp. 222 (D.D.C. 1986), *aff'd without op.*, 861 F.2d 303 (D.C. Cir. 1988) (loan by prospective employee to employer not covered); Lucey v. Southeast Texas Emergency Physicians Assoc., 802 S.W.2d 300 (Tex. App. 1990). *Cf.* Larsen Chelsey Realty Co. v. Larsen, 232 Conn. 480, 656 A.2d 1009 (1995) (declining to reach issue of whether UDAP statute covers employer-employee matters); Schinkel v. Maxi-Holding, Inc., 30 Mass. App. Ct. 41, 565 N.E.2d 1219 (1991) (court defers question whether a consultant's claim falls into the exemption for employer-employee transactions); Quality Auto Parts v. Bluff City Buick, 876 S.W.2d 818 (Tenn. App. 1994) (declining to rule on coverage question). *But see* Brassford v. CNA, Inc., Clearinghouse No. 40,632 (D. Conn. 1982); Wilkenson v. Times Mirror Corp., 264 Cal. Rptr. 194 (Ct. App. 1989).

641 Cooperman v. R.G. Barry Corp., 775 F. Supp. 1211 (D. Minn. 1991); W.A. Offshore Equip. Co. v. Parmatic Filter Corp., 767 F. Supp. 125 (E.D. La. 1991); Barille v. Sears Roebuck & Co., 682 N.E.2d 118 (Ill. App. Ct. 1997) (claims by former insurance agent against insurance company not covered); Durling v. King, 554 S.E.2d 1 (N.C. App. 2001) (suit for commissions).

642 Benoit v. Landry, Lyons & Whyte Co., 31 Mass. App. Ct. 948, 580 N.E.2d 1053 (1991). *But see* Bolen v. Paragon Plastics, Inc., 754 F. Supp. 221 (D. Mass. 1990) (independent contractor may be covered); Linkage Corp. v. Trustees of Boston University, 425 Mass. 1, 679 N.E.2d 191 (1997) (independent contractor covered).

643 Gil v. Metal Serv. Corp., 412 So. 2d 706 (La. Ct. App. 1982); Edinburg v. Cavers, 22 Mass. App. Ct. 212, 492 N.E.2d 1171 (1986).

644 Bank v. Leroux (*In re* Curran), 157 B.R. 500 (Bankr. D. Mass. 1993); Moran, Shuster, Carignan & Knierim v. August, 43 Conn. Supp. 431, 657 A.2d 736 (1994), *aff'd on other grounds*, 232 Conn. 756, 657 A.2d 229 (1995) (dispute between law firm and its former partner not covered by UDAP statute); Zimmerman v. Bogoff, 402 Mass. 650, 524 N.E.2d 849 (1988); Newton v. Moffie, 13 Mass. App. Ct. 462, 434 N.E.2d 656 (1982); Miami Subs Corp. v. Murray Family Trust, 703 A.2d 1366 (N.H. 1997) (UDAP statute does not apply to partnership disputes).

645 Fickes v. Sun Expert, Inc., 762 F. Supp. 998 (D. Mass. 1991); First Enterprises, Ltd. v. Cooper, 425 Mass. 344, 680 N.E.2d 1163 (1997) (dispute between parties to the same venture not covered); Szalla v. Locke, 421 Mass. 448, 657 N.E.2d 1267 (1995) (UDAP statute does not apply to dispute between the two parties to a joint venture); Miami Subs Corp. v. Murray Family Trust, 703 A.2d 1366 (N.H. 1997) (UDAP statute does not apply to joint venture disputes). *See also* Ansin v. River Oaks Furniture, Inc., 105 F.3d 745 (1st Cir. 1997), *cert. denied*, 522 U.S. 818 (1997) (Massachusetts law). *But see* Fink v. Golenbock, 238 Conn. 183, 680 A.2d 1243 (1996) (upholding UDAP claim by half-owner of corporation that other owner set up another corporation to usurp its business).

646 Steele v. Kelley, 46 Mass. App. Ct. 712, 710 N.E.2d 973 (1999).

647 Dash v. Wayne, 700 F. Supp. 1056 (D. Haw. 1988); Riseman v. Orion Research, Inc., 475 N.E.2d 398 (Mass. 1985); Kurker v. Hill, 44 Mass. App. Ct. 184, 689 N.E.2d 833 (1998). *See also* White Cliffs Community Ass'n v. Ranieri, 1999 Mass. Super. LEXIS 285 (Aug. 4, 1999) (applying rule against UDAP coverage of intra-business disputes to dispute between condominium governing body and unit owners); Eisenberg v. Phoenix Ass'n Management, Inc., 1999 Mass. Super. LEXIS 310 (July 23, 1999) (applying rule against UDAP coverage of intra-business disputes to dispute between community association and its members). *But see* Wilson v. Wilson-Cook Medical, Inc., 720 F. Supp. 533 (M.D.N.C. 1989).

648 Muniz v. Kravis, 59 Conn. App. 704, 757 A.2d 1207 (2000).

compete.[649] It has also allowed a UDAP suit against an employee who fraudulently sold his employer products from companies he owned, without disclosing his ownership interest, holding that his status as an employee did not protect him from UDAP liability.[650] The Connecticut Supreme Court found its state UDAP statute to apply to the tortious conduct of an employee who acts outside the scope of his employment relationship to aid a competitor.[651] The same court has also found that acts occurring after the end of an employment relationship can be trade or commerce for UDAP purposes.[652] Massachusetts' highest court concluded that an employee can make a UDAP claim for injuries he sustained due to the malfunctioning of a machine his employer purchased from another company.[653] A federal court applying Minnesota law has held that a former employee can seek injunctive relief under one of the state's UDAP statutes against her former employer's unauthorized use of her name.[654] The California Supreme Court has allowed employees to sue their employer for unpaid overtime wages under that state's broad unfair competition law.[655]

The South Dakota Supreme Court adopted an interesting approach in a 1996 case involving an employer who was defrauding consumers by mislabeling products. The court held that a salesperson had standing to sue the employer for the damages to his income and business reputation that he suffered because of his employer's fraud.[656]

In addition, the line of cases that finds employer-employee and similar practices outside the scope of a state UDAP statute should be clearly distinguished from cases dealing with franchises or with business or employment opportunity schemes. The employer-employee cases do not affect consumers, the public, or competitors. But clearly bogus business or employment opportunity schemes targeted at the general public are a different matter altogether.[657]

2.2.11 Personal Injury Suits

In few states, the UDAP statute specifically exempts personal or bodily injury suits from its scope.[658] Where such actions are not explicitly exempted, courts are split about whether the UDAP statute can be used to recover such injury.

An Oregon court dismissed a suit against an auto dealer where the consumer sought relief for personal injuries resulting from a car accident. The court ruled that other legal remedies were adequate.[659] A Hawaii court took the similar position that the UDAP statute could not be utilized in a products liability case,[660] and a Tennessee court refused to apply a UDAP statute to a wrongful death case.[661]

The Connecticut Supreme Court interprets the exclusivity provision of its Product Liability Act to bar claims for

649 United Laboratories, Inc. v. Kuykendall, 322 N.C. 643, 370 S.E.2d 375 (1988). *See also* Eli Research, Inc. v. United Communications Group, L.L.C., 312 F. Supp. 2d 748 (M.D.N.C. 2004) (denying motion to dismiss UDAP claim where former employer alleged that former employees stole trade secrets); Nursing Enterprises v. Marr, 719 So. 2d 524 (La. App. 1998) (without deciding, court assumes that UDAP statute applies to case holding that former employer did not have UDAP claim for former employee's creation of competing business); Wyatt v. PO2, Inc., 651 So. 2d 359 (La. Ct. App. 1995) (court considers UDAP claim against former employee for competing, but rules against plaintiff on merits); Informix, Inc. v. Rennell, 41 Mass. App. Ct. 161, 668 N.E.2d 1351 (1996); Ausley v. Bishop, 133 N.C. App. 210, 515 S.E.2d 72 (1999) (allowing UDAP claim for acts after employment relationship terminated). *But see* Falmouth Ob-Gyn Assocs., Inc. v. Abisla, 417 Mass. 176, 629 N.E.2d 291 (1994) (former employer can not bring UDAP claim against former employee for violating covenant not to compete); *cf.* Dalton v. Camp, 353 N.C. 647, 548 S.E.2d 704 (2001) (no UDAP claim where employee did not have fiduciary duty, did not buy or sell for employer, and no aggravating circumstances).

650 Sara Lee Corp. v. Carter, 351 N.C. 27, 519 S.E.2d 308 (1999).

651 Larsen Chelsey Realty Co. v. Larsen, 232 Conn. 480, 656 A.2d 1009 (1995). *Accord* Ostrowski v. Avery, 243 Conn. 355, 703 A.2d 117 (1997) (UDAP statute applies to employees who usurped corporate opportunity); Hanover Ins. Co. v. Sutton, 46 Mass. App. Ct. 153, 705 N.E.2d 279 (1999) (UDAP claim allowed against former employee who usurped company's business opportunity). *But see* United Components, Inc. v. Wdowiak, 239 Conn. 259, 684 A.2d 693 (1996) (UDAP statute does not cover claim that corporate officer diverted accounts to a competitor).

652 Larsen Chelsey Realty Co. v. Larsen, 232 Conn. 480, 656 A.2d 1009 (1995); *see also* Jewell v. Medical Protective Co., 2003 WL 226823332 (D. Conn. Oct. 30, 2003).

653 Maillet v. ATF-Davidson Co., 552 N.E.2d 95 (Mass. 1990).

654 Kovatovich v. K-Mart Corp., 88 F. Supp. 2d 975 (D. Minn. 1999).

655 Cortez v. Purolator Air Filtration Prods. Co., 23 Cal. 4th 163, 999 P.2d 706 (2000). *See also* Bureerong v. Uvawas, 922 F. Supp. 1450 (C.D. Cal. 1996) (violations of federal and state labor laws are California UDAP violations); Hudgins v. Neiman Marcus Group, Inc., 34 Cal. App. 4th 1109, 41 Cal. Rptr. 2d 46 (1995) (employer's violation of wage payment law is a UDAP violation; no discussion of coverage issues).

656 Moss v. Guttormson, 1996 S.D. 76, 551 N.W.2d 14 (1996).

657 *See* Multi Technology v. Mitchell Management Sys., Inc., 25 Mass. App. Ct. 333, 518 N.E.2d 854 (1988) (relationship of business and employment agency is not employer-employee relationship, and thus is not exempt from UDAP statute); § 2.2.9.4, *supra*; *see also* Akgul v. Prime Time Transportation, Inc., 293 A.D.2d 631, 741 N.Y.S.2d 553 (2002) (franchise marketing scheme meets New York's consumer impact requirement); § 2.2.9, *supra*. *But cf.* Moore v. Eggers Consulting Co., 562 N.W.2d 534 (Neb. 1997) (where Nebraska UDAP statute excludes sale of labor, an employment recruiter was held not covered by the UDAP statute).

658 *See* Appx. A, *infra*.

659 Gross-Haentjens v. Leckenby, 38 Or. App. 313, 589 P.2d 1209 (1979). *See also* Allen v. G.D. Searle & Co., 708 F. Supp. 1142 (D. Or. 1989) (following *Gross-Haentjens* in finding no UDAP claim for personal injuries).

660 Beerman v. Toro Mfg. Corp., 1 Haw. App. 111, 615 P.2d 749 (1980). *See also* Blowers v. Eli Lilly and Co., 100 F. Supp. 2d 1265 (D. Haw. 2000).

661 Kirksey v. Overton Pub. Inc., 804 S.W.2d 68 (Tenn. Ct. App. 1990).

personal injury, death, or property damage that are caused by the defective product, but a claim for financial injury—the higher price the plaintiff paid because of the defendant's deception—is not barred.[662] In cases outside the product liability field, Connecticut courts allow UDAP suits for personal injury if the acts complained of have an entrepreneurial or business aspect.[663] The Washington Supreme Court finds that, since the statute requires injury to business or property, UDAP claims can not remedy personal injuries.[664]

On the other hand, many courts find a UDAP statute applicable to personal injury claims, including courts interpreting the California,[665] Colorado,[666] Illinois,[667] Massachusetts,[668] and Minnesota[669] UDAP statutes. In addition, a series of Texas cases holds that UDAP remedies are available for any personal injury where that damage would be recoverable at common law and where the damage was caused by a UDAP violation.[670] But there must be proof of a UDAP violation, and not just enough to prove a personal injury claim.[671]

Where a consumer can not seek UDAP remedies in a product liability action, the consumer can still obtain UDAP remedies for other related unfair or deceptive conduct arising in the same transaction.[672] However, the Texas Products Liability Act can bar a UDAP claim arising out of the same claims as a products liability claim (here, smoking and nicotine addiction).[673]

2.2.12 The Texas Exemption for Large Transactions

Most UDAP statutes cover transactions regardless of their size. The Texas UDAP statute was, however, amended in 1995 to exempt transactions and projects that involve total consideration by the consumer of more than $500,000.[674] The large transaction cap only applies to consideration—an award of damages can far exceed that amount without any effect.[675] Transactions and projects arising out of a written contract and involving more than $100,000 in total consideration by the consumer are also exempt if the consumer is represented by independent legal counsel.[676] Neither exception applies if the transaction involves the consumer's home.

2.3 Exempted Sellers

2.3.1 Insurance Companies

2.3.1.1 Does the UDAP Statute Apply to Insurance Practices?

In general, UDAP statutory coverage extends to the sale of insurance by brokers, agents, and insurance companies. Insurance sales are certainly within trade or commerce,[677] as

662 Gerrity v. R.J. Reynolds Tobacco Co., 263 Conn. 120, 818 A.2d 769 (2003). *But cf.* Mountain West Helicopter v. Kaman Aerospace Corp., 2004 WL 574720 (D. Conn. Mar. 9, 2004) (product liability statute governs UDAP claim for damage to property caused by defective product).

663 Simms v. Candela, 45 Conn. Supp. 267, 711 A.2d 778 (Super. Ct. 1998) (UDAP claim allowed for personal injury to tenant caused by housing conditions).

664 Washington State Physicians Ins. Exchange & Ass'n v. Fisons Corp., 122 Wash. 2d 299, 858 P.2d 1054 (1993). *See also* Ass'n of Wash. Pub. Hosp. Dists. v. Philip Morris, Inc., 241 F.3d 696 (9th Cir. 2001) (Wash. law) (hospitals can not sue tobacco companies for expenses caused by personal injuries of patients they deceived); Stevens v. Hyde Athletic Indus., Inc., 54 Wash. App. 366, 773 P.2d 871 (1989) (same).

665 Maurer v. Cerkvenik-Anderson Travel, Inc., 181 Ariz. 294, 890 P.2d 69 (App. 1994) (California UDAP statute allows recovery for death of tourist caused by travel agency's failure to disclose risks of trip).

666 *In re* Air Crash Disaster at Stapleton International, 720 F. Supp. 1505 (D. Colo. 1989).

667 Duncavage v. Allen, 147 Ill. App. 3d 88, 497 N.E.2d 433 (1986) (death claim allowed to proceed).

668 Maillet v. AFT-Davidson Co., 552 N.E.2d 95 (Mass. 1990) (product liability UDAP suit). *But cf.* Swenson v. Yellow Transportation, Inc., 2004 WL 1068880 (D. Mass. Apr. 12, 2004) (lack of relationship between truck driver and accident victim precludes UDAP claim because the wrongful conduct did not arise in business context).

669 Kociemba v. G.D. Searle & Co., 680 F. Supp. 1293 (D. Minn. 1988).

670 Pope v. Rollins Protective Serv. Co., 703 F.2d 197 (5th Cir. 1983); Keller Indus., Inc. v. Reeves, 656 S.W.2d 221 (Tex. App. 1983); Mahan Volkswagen Inc. v. Hall, 648 S.W.2d 324 (Tex. App. 1982); *see also* Birchfield v. Texarkana Memorial Hosps., 747 S.W.2d 361 (Tex. 1987); International Armament Corp. v. King, 674 S.W.2d 413 (Tex. App. 1984), *aff'd*, 686 S.W.2d 595 (Tex. 1985); *cf.* Ahn v. Texaco, Inc., 756 S.W.2d 63 (Tex. App. 1988) (advertising not related to injury). *But cf.* Tex. Civ. Prac. & Rem. Code § 74.004 (formerly Tex. Rev. Civ. Stat. Ann. art. 4590i, § 12.01(a) (Vernon)) (no UDAP action allowed against health care providers for personal injury claims based on negligence); Quinn v. Memorial Medical Center, 764 S.W.2d 915 (Tex. App. 1989) (interpreting Tex. Rev. Civ. Stat. Ann. art. 4590i, § 12.01(a) (Vernon)). But note that the remedies provisions of the Texas UDAP statute have been amended since these decisions to limit personal injury claims in certain situations.

671 Litton Indus. Prod. v. Gammage, 668 S.W.2d 319 (Tex. 1984); Cianfichi v. White House Motor Hotel, 921 S.W.2d 441 (Tex. App. 1996); *see also* Pizzaloto v. Hoover Co., 486 So. 2d 124 (La. Ct. App. 1986).

672 Pomianawski v. Merle Norman Cosmetics Inc., 507 F. Supp. 435 (S.D. Ohio 1980) (Ohio law).

673 Davis *ex rel.* Davis v. R.J. Reynolds Tobacco, Inc., 231 F.3d 928 (5th Cir. 2000).

674 Tex. Bus. & Com. Code Ann. § 17.49(g). *See* Space Maker Designs, Inc. v. Weldon F. Stump and Co., 2003 WL 21251743 (N.D. Tex. Mar. 28, 2003).

675 Hannover Life Reassurance Co. of America v. Baker, Lowe, Fox Ins. Marketing, Inc., 2001 U.S. Dist. LEXIS 20468 (N.D. Tex. Dec. 10, 2001).

676 Tex. Bus. & Com. Code Ann. § 17.49(f).

677 Sparks v. Allstate Ins. Co., 98 F. Supp. 2d 933 (W.D. Tenn.

are insurance broker practices.[678] The sale of insurance constitutes the "sale of property and services"[679] or "merchandise"[680] under state UDAP statutes.

2000) (Tennessee definitions of "trade," "commerce," and "consumer transaction" encompass post-sale insurance claim settlement practices).

678 MacGillvory v. W. Dana Bartlett Ins. Agency, 14 Mass. App. Ct. 52, 436 N.E.2d 964 (1982).

679 Hofstetter v. Fletcher, 905 F.2d 897 (6th Cir. 1988) (exclusion of insurance sales by Ohio's home solicitation sales statute did not affect UDAP statute's coverage; UDAP coverage also found since insurance sale was only part of a total package of goods and services); Force v. ITT Hartford Life & Annuity Ins. Co., 4 F. Supp. 2d 843 (D. Minn. 1998); Yourman v. People's Security Life Ins. Co., 992 F. Supp. 696 (D.N.J. 1998); P.I.A. Michigan City v. National Porges Radiator, 789 F. Supp. 1421 (N.D. Ill. 1992); Maduff v. Life Ins. Co. of Virginia, 657 F. Supp. 437 (N.D. Ill. 1987); Aabye v. Security-Connecticut Life Ins. Co., 586 F. Supp. 5 (N.D. Ill. 1984); Doyle v. St. Paul Fire & Marine Ins. Co., 583 F. Supp. 554 (D. Conn. 1984); Philadelphia Mfgs. Mut. Ins. Co. v. Gulf Forge Co., 555 F. Supp. 519 (S.D. Tex. 1982); Showpiece Homes Corp. v. Assurance Co. of Am., 38 P.3d 47 (Colo. 2001) (insurance qualifies as both "services" and "property"); Griswold v. Union Labor Life Ins. Co., 186 Conn. 507, 442 A.2d 920 (1982); Lang v. Consumers Ins. Serv., Inc., 583 N.E.2d 1147 (Ill. App. Ct. 1991); Petersen v. Allstate Ins. Co., 171 Ill. App. 3d 909, 525 N.E.2d 1094 (1988); McCarter v. State Farm Mut. Auto Ins. Co., 473 N.E.2d 1015 (Ill. App. Ct. 1985); Fox v. Industrial Casualty Ins. Co., 98 Ill. App. 3d 543, 424 N.E.2d 839 (1981); Stevens v. Motorists Mut. Ins. Co., 759 S.W.2d 819 (Ky. 1988); Morton v. Bank of the Bluegrass, 18 S.W.3d 353 (Ky. App. 1999); Dodd v. Commercial Union Ins. Co., 373 Mass. 72, 365 N.E.2d 802 (1977); Pearce v. American Defender Life Ins. Co., 343 S.E.2d 174 (N.C. 1986); Phillips v. Integon, 319 S.E 2d 673 (N.C. Ct. App. 1984) (insurance is a good, defined as a thing of value); Pekular v. Eich, 513 A.2d 427 (Pa. Super. Ct. 1986); Commonwealth v. Allstate Ins. Co., 729 A.2d 135 (Pa. Commw. 1999) (insurance companies are covered); Deetz v. Nationwide Mut. Ins. Co., 20 Pa. D. & C.3d 499 (C.P. Dauphin Cty. 1981) (insurance is product or service); Skinner v. Steele, 730 S.W.2d 335 (Tenn. Ct. App. 1987) (sale of annuity is a purchase of "intangible property or anything of value" and thus is covered by certain prohibitions in Tennessee UDAP statute); *In re* Stifel, Nicholaus & Co., Clearinghouse No. 38,906 (Tenn. Ch. Ct. 1984) (same); Allstate Ins. Co. v. Kelly, 680 S.W.2d 595 (Tex. App. 1984); McCrann v. Klaneckey, 667 S.W.2d 924 (Tex. App. 1984); Ranger County Mut. Ins. Co. v. Guinn, 608 S.W.2d 730 (Tex. Civ. App. 1980) (insurance is a service); Dairyland County Mut. Ins. Co. v. Harrison, 578 S.W.2d 186 (Tex. Civ. App. 1979). *But see* Van Holt v. Liberty Mut. Fire Ins. Co., 163 F.3d 161 (3d Cir. 1998) (holding, as alternate ground for denial of UDAP claim, that New Jersey UDAP statute does not cover payment of insurance benefits); Burley v. Homeowners Warranty Corp., 773 F. Supp. 844 (S.D. Miss. 1990); Wilder v. Aetna Life & Casualty Ins. Co., 140 Vt. 16, 433 A.2d 309 (1981) (insurance is in "trade or commerce," but, particularly where consumer is accident victim and not purchaser of the policy, no "purchase of goods or services").

680 Parkhill v. Minnesota Mut. Life Ins. Co., 995 F. Supp. 983 (D. Minn. 1998) (insurance is "merchandise" where merchandise includes intangibles); Lemelledo v. Beneficial Management Corp., 150 N.J. 255, 696 A.2d 546 (1997).

One court, however, has held that a state-created assigned claims plan that does not have a seller/consumer relationship with the insured does not involve the sale of property or services.[681] Massachusetts' highest court finds that statutorily mandated nonprofit organizations that fund claims against insolvent insurance companies[682] or that assure the availability of malpractice insurance[683] are not covered by the state's UDAP statute.

Most UDAP insurance cases do not relate to the sale of insurance, but to an insurer's refusal to pay a claim. Refusing to pay insurance claims is a practice in "trade or commerce,"[684] as are practices by insurance adjusters.[685] Similarly, insurance claims practices[686] and those of insurance adjusters[687] are "in connection with the purchase of goods or services." Whether a claimant who did not purchase the insurance (such as an accident victim) can bring a UDAP action against the insurer is discussed in § 2.4.1, *infra*.

2.3.1.2 Statutory Exemptions for Insurance Companies

Even if a state UDAP statute would seem to apply to insurance sales or claims practices, some state UDAP statutes explicitly exempt insurance or insurance companies. For example, the Illinois UDAP statute exempts deceptive

681 Edkin v. Travellers Companies, 3 Pa. D. & C.4th 557 (C.P. 1988).

682 Barrett v. Massachusetts Insurers Insolvency Fund, 412 Mass. 774, 592 N.E.2d 1317 (1992).

683 Poznik v. Massachusetts Medical Professional Ins. Ass'n, 417 Mass. 48, 628 N.E.2d 1 (1994).

684 Layton v. Liberty Mut. Fire Ins. Co., 530 F. Supp. 285 (E.D. Pa. 1981), *UDAP claim dismissed on other grounds*, 577 F. Supp. 1 (E.D. Pa. 1983); Dimarzo v. American Mut. Ins. Co., 389 Mass. 85, 449 N.E.2d 1189 (1983); Pearce v. American Defender Life Ins. Co., 343 S.E.2d 174 (N.C. 1986); *see also* Deetz v. Nationwide Mut. Ins. Co., 20 Pa. D. & C.3d 499 (C.P. Dauphin Cty. 1981). *But cf.* Morrison v. Toys R Us, Inc., 441 Mass. 451, 806 N.E.2d 388 (Mass. 2004) (retailer that self-insures is not engaged in trade or commerce as to claims brought by customers for personal injuries so is not subject to UDAP liability for its claims settlement practices).

685 Miller v. Risk Management Foundation, 36 Mass. App. Ct. 411, 632 N.E.2d 841 (1994).

686 P.I.A. Michigan City v. National Porges Radiator, 789 F. Supp. 1421 (N.D. Ill. 1992); Allstate Ins. Co. v. Kelly, 680 S.W.2d 595 (Tex. App. 1984). *But see* Rosell v. Farmers Texas County Mut. Ins. Co., 642 S.W.2d 278 (Tex. App. 1982); American Ins. Co. v. Reed, 626 S.W.2d 898 (Tex. Civ. App. 1981). *Rosell* and *Reed*, *supra*, were probably overturned by Flenniken v. Longview Bank & Trust Co., 661 S.W.2d 705 (Tex. 1983).

687 Elder v. Coronet Ins. Co., 201 Ill. App. 3d 733, 558 N.E.2d 1312 (1990); Culbreth v. Lawrence J. Miller, Inc., 328 Pa. Super. 374, 477 A.2d 491 (1984). *But see* Elia v. Erie Ins. Exchange, 398 Pa. Super. 433, 581 A.2d 209 (1990) (where a UDAP statute's coverage is limited to purchases of goods or services, an insured does not have a UDAP claim against a doctor who examined him for an insurance company).

information by an insurance producer or company concerning the sale, placement, renewal, cancellation, or terms of insurance unless the insurance producer has actual knowledge of the deception.[688] This exemption was enacted, however, as part of a tort reform act that the state supreme court declared unconstitutional in its entirety.[689]

An initial question in any case where a statutory exemption for insurance transactions is raised is whether the product that has been marketed as insurance actually is insurance. The elements normally present in an insurance contract are an insurable interest, a risk of loss, an assumption of the risk by the insurer, a general scheme to distribute the loss among the larger group of persons bearing similar risks, and the payment of a premium for the assumption of risk.[690] For example, a Florida decision holds that the sale of non-filing insurance by a creditor did not fall under the statutory exemption for insurance transactions because the creditor did not have an insurable interest, the insurance company assumed no risk of loss, and the "insurance" did not result in distribution of risk over a larger group.[691]

New Hampshire has interpreted its exemption for "trade or commerce otherwise permitted under laws as administered by any regulatory board" to exempt insurance companies.[692] In 2002, the legislature amended the statute to codify this conclusion.[693] In Michigan, the supreme court interpreted an exemption for "a transaction or conduct specifically authorized under laws administered by a regulatory board or officer" to preclude a fraudulent practices claim against an insurance company, because its forms were filed with and approved by the state Insurance Department.[694] However, the court interpreted another section of the statute to allow a private party to file a UDAP action for a violation of the state's Unfair Insurance Practices statute. The result was that private parties could bring UDAP claims against insurance companies that violated the UNIP statute, but the attorney general could not bring UDAP claims against insurance companies. Soon afterward, the legislature overruled the decision by amending the statute to provide that it does not apply to or create a cause of action for a UNIP violation.[695] Two Delaware lower court opinions interpret the state Consumer Fraud Act to preclude the state, but not consumers, from suing insurers.[696] An unpublished Minnesota appellate decision finds a nonprofit health service corporation (Blue Cross) not to be subject to the UDAP statute, where the legislature explicitly provided that some similar organizations were covered but was silent as to Blue Cross.[697]

Louisiana courts hold certain insurance practices exempt if the UDAP statute excludes actions "regulated under laws administered by the insurance commissioner," or similar language.[698] The South Carolina UDAP statute provides that it does not apply to practices covered by the state's unfair and deceptive insurance practices statute, but may apply to improper claims practices.[699] In addition, some state insurance statutes specifically indicate that, for certain lines of insurance or certain types of insurers, the insurance code offers an exclusive remedy, preempting the state UDAP statute.[700]

688 815 Ill. Comp. Stat. 505/10b(6).

689 Best v. Taylor Machine Works, 689 N.E.2d 1057 (Ill. 1997).

690 Guaranteed Warranty Corp. v. State *ex rel.* Humphrey, 23 Ariz. App. 327, 533 P.2d 87 (1975); W.S. Badcock Corp. v. Myers, 696 So. 2d 776 (Fla. Dist. Ct. App. 1997); Professional Lens Plan, Inc. v. Department of Ins., 387 So. 2d 548 (Fla. App. Ct. 1980). *See also* Russ, Couch on Insurance 3d § 1.6 (West 1997).

691 W.S. Badcock Corp. v. Myers, 696 So. 2d 776 (Fla. Dist. Ct. App. 1997).

692 Bell v. Liberty Mut. Ins. Co., 146 N.H. 190, 776 A.2d 1260 (2001). *See also* Surge Resources, Inc. v. Barrow Group, 2003 WL 1193012 (D.N.H. Mar. 12, 2003) (finding insurer exempt even if it is unlicensed).

693 N.H. Rev. Stat. Ann. § 358-A:3, *as amended, effective* July 17, 2002.

694 McClain v. Coverdell & Co., 272 F. Supp. 2d 631 (E.D. Mich. 2003) (applying pre-amendment version of statute to find insurer covered); Smith v. Globe Life Ins., 597 N.W.2d 28 (Mich. 1999) (overruling Kekel v. Allstate Ins. Co., 144 Mich. App. 379, 375 N.W.2d 455 (1985) and Bell v. League Life Ins. Co., 149 Mich. App. 481, 387 N.W.2d 154 (1986)).

695 Mich. Comp. Laws § 445.904, effective Mar. 1, 2001.

696 Crowhorn v. Nationwide Mut. Ins. Co., 2001 Del. Super. LEXIS 358 (Apr. 26, 2001); Mentis v. Delaware Am. Life Ins. Co., 1999 Del. Super. LEXIS 419 (July 28, 1999).

697 Rothenberg v. Milne, 2000 Minn. App. LEXIS 1207 (Dec. 5, 2000) (unpublished, citation limited).

698 LeMarie v. Lone Star Life Ins. Co., 2000 U.S. Dist. LEXIS 8285 (E.D. La. June 7, 2000), *aff'd without op.*, 265 F.3d 1059 (5th Cir. 2001); West v. Fireman's Fund Ins. Co., 683 F. Supp. 156 (E.D. La. 1988); O.K. Lumber Co. v. Providence Washington Ins. Co., 759 P.2d 523 (Alaska 1988); Ferguson v. United Ins. Co. of Am., 163 Ga. App. 282, 293 S.E.2d 736 (1982); Irwin Rogers Ins. Agency, Inc. v. Murphy, 122 Idaho 270, 833 P.2d 128 (Ct. App. 1992); Phillips v. Patterson Ins. Co., 813 So. 2d 1191 (La. App. 2002); Southern General Agency, Inc. v. Safeway Ins. Co., 769 So. 2d 606 (La. App. 2000); A-I Nursery v. United Teacher Assocs., 682 So. 2d 929 (La. App. 1996) (no UDAP cause of action for submission of false insurance claim); Alarcon v. Aetna-Cas. & Surety Co., 538 So. 2d 696 (La. Ct. App. 1989); Comeaux v. Pennsylvania General Ins. Co., 490 So. 2d 1191 (La. Ct. App. 1986). *But see* Lamarque v. Mass. Indemnity & Life Ins. Co., 794 F.2d 197 (5th Cir. 1986) (Louisiana law) (it would be circular to say insurance commissioner preempts UDAP coverage because commissioner only gets power from UDAP statute).

699 *See* Trustees of Grace Episcopal Church v. Charleston Ins. Co., 868 F. Supp. 128 (D.S.C. 1994). *Cf.* Colonial Life & Accident Ins. Co. v. American Family Life Assurance Co., 846 F. Supp. 454 (D.S.C. 1994).

700 Arnold v. National County Mut. Fire Ins. Co., 725 S.W.2d 165 (Tex. 1987) (county mutual insurance companies); McNeil v. McDavid Ins. Agency, 594 S.W.2d 198 (Tex. Civ. App. 1980) (same); Mobile County Mut. Ins. Co. v. Jewell, 555 S.W.2d 903 (Tex. Civ. App. 1977) (same); Deeter v. Safeway Stores, Inc., 50 Wash. App. 67, 747 P.2d 1103 (1987) (workers' compensation legislation says it is exclusive remedy; consequently, UDAP is preempted). *But see* Vacanti v. State Compensation Ins. Fund, 24 Cal. 4th 800, 14 P.3d 234 (2001) (exclusive remedy provi-

Even where a UDAP statute states that "nothing required or permitted to be done pursuant to the insurance code is a violation" of the UDAP statute, unfair cancellation procedures,[701] illegal rebates to creditors,[702] and other unfair or deceptive practices are actionable under the UDAP statute because the insurance code certainly does not require or permit such practices. In fact, while the Washington UDAP statute exempts acts permitted by the insurance department, Washington courts find a violation of the state's insurance law to be a *per se* UDAP violation.[703]

2.3.1.3 State Insurance Code Displacement of UDAP Applicability

A frequently litigated issue is whether a state UDAP statute applies to insurance practices where those practices are already regulated by the state insurance code, but where the UDAP statute does not explicitly exempt insurance companies. Insurers often argue that the state insurance statute prohibiting unfair and deceptive insurance practices (the UNIP statute),[704] displaces UDAP coverage.

The federal McCarran-Ferguson Act prohibits federal regulation of insurance practices to the extent that states regulate the practices.[705] UNIP statutes were enacted to oust FTC and other federal jurisdiction over unfair and deceptive insurance practices; they were not enacted as a replacement for state UDAP statutes, which did not even exist at the time. The fact that state UNIP statutes preempt action by the FTC does not mean that the scope of state UDAP statutes should be similarly limited, even though FTC standards are guides for interpreting state UDAP statutes.[706]

Further, UNIP statutes do not provide consumers with much relief from unfair and deceptive insurance practices. They do not offer an explicit private remedy, usually do not even authorize the insurance commissioner to order restitution, and in fact may only authorize administrative actions if those actions are in the public interest. Such a scheme does not offer an adequate remedy to individual injured insureds and should not preempt their right to seek such a remedy through a UDAP action.

Consequently, the majority of cases find that the state UNIP statute or other insurance regulation does *not* displace applicability of the state UDAP statute.[707] A minority of

sion does not bar UDAP suit against workers' compensation carriers for conspiracy to mishandle claims, although claims regarding mere mishandling of claims are barred); ABC Truck Rental & Leasing Co. v. Southern County Mut. Ins. Co., 662 S.W.2d 132 (Tex. App. 1983) (county mutual insurance companies not excluded except as specified in insurance code).

701 Rounds v. Union Bankers, 22 Wash. App. 613, 590 P.2d 1286 (1979). *See also* Dimarzo v. American Mut. Ins. Co., 389 Mass. 85, 449 N.E.2d 1189 (1983) (unfair settlement offer not exempt by "transactions permitted by agency" language). *But see* State v. Piedmont Funding Corp., 382 A.2d 819 (R.I. 1978).

702 State *ex rel.* Stratton v. Gurley Motor Co., 105 N.M. 803, 737 P.2d 1180 (Ct. App. 1987).

703 Salois v. Mutual of Omaha Ins. Co., 90 Wash. 2d 355, 581 P.2d 1349 (1978). The legislature has now codified this holding. *See* Escalante v. Sentry Ins., 49 Wash. App. 375, 743 P.2d 832 (1987).

704 "UNIP" statutes are described in more detail at § 5.3.2, *infra.*

705 15 U.S.C. § 1012(b).

706 Dodd v. Commercial Union Ins. Co., 373 Mass. 72, 365 N.E.2d 802 (1977).

707 Loe v. State Farm Ins. Cos., 1998 U.S. App. LEXIS 24457 (9th Cir. Sept. 25, 1998) (UDAP claim under Cal. Bus. & Prof. Code § 17200 can be based on acts that would violate UNIP statute, even though there is no cause of action for UNIP violations); Jenkins v. Commonwealth Land Title Ins. Co., 95 F.3d 791 (9th Cir. 1996) (Haw. law) (overruling Genovia v. Jackson National Life Ins. Co., 795 F. Supp. 1036 (D. Haw. 1992)); Riordan v. Nationwide Mut. Fire Ins. Co., 977 F.2d 47 (2d Cir. 1992) (New York law); Hangarter v. Paul Revere Life Ins. Co., 236 F. Supp. 2d 1069 (N.D. Cal. 2002); Force v. ITT Hartford Life & Annuity Ins. Co., 4 F. Supp. 2d 843 (D. Minn. 1998); Parkhill v. Minnesota Mut. Life Ins. Co., 995 F. Supp. 983 (D. Minn. 1998); Yourman v. People's Security Life Ins. Co., 992 F. Supp. 696 (D.N.J. 1998); Greenspan v. Allstate Ins. Co., 937 F. Supp. 288 (S.D.N.Y. 1996); Donaldson v. Liberty Mut. Ins. Co., 947 F. Supp. 429 (D. Haw. 1996); WVG v. Pacific Ins. Co., 707 F. Supp. 70 (D.N.H. 1986); Barr Co. v. Safeco Ins. Co. of Am., 583 F. Supp. 248 (N.D. Ill. 1984); Ray v. United Family Life Ins. Co., 430 F. Supp. 1353 (W.D.N.C. 1977); Quelimane Co. v. Stewart Title Guaranty Co., 77 Cal. Rptr. 2d 709, 960 P.2d 513 (1998) (insurance code does not displace coverage of title insurance companies under Cal. Bus. & Prof. Code § 17200 except for matters relating to rate setting); State Farm Fire & Cas. Co. v. Superior Court, 45 Cal. App. 4th 1093, 53 Cal. Rptr. 2d 229 (1996) (UDAP claim under Cal. Bus. & Prof. Code § 17200 can be based on acts that would violate UNIP statute, even though there is no cause of action for UNIP violations); Mead v. Burns, 199 Conn. 651, 509 A.2d 11 (1986); Griswold v. Union Labor Life Ins. Co., 186 Conn. 507, 442 A.2d 920 (1982) (state insurance act does not provide private right of action, so no adequate administrative remedy); Grand Ventures, Inc. v. Whaley, 622 A.2d 655 (Del. Super. Ct. 1993), *aff'd on other grounds*, 632 A.2d 63 (Del. 1993); Marshall v. W&L Enterprises Corp., 360 So. 2d 1147 (Fla. Dist. Ct. App. 1978); Fox v. Industrial Casualty Ins. Co., 98 Ill. App. 3d 543, 424 N.E.2d 839 (1981) (but UDAP claim may be unavailable for insurer's mere failure to pay a claim with no accompanying misrepresentations); Stevens v. Motorists Mut. Ins. Co., 759 S.W.2d 819 (Ky. 1988); Dodd v. Commercial Union Ins. Co., 373 Mass. 72, 365 N.E.2d 802 (1977); New Mexico Life Ins. Guaranty Ass'n v. Quinn & Co., 111 N.M. 750, 809 P.2d 1278 (1991); State *ex rel.* Stratton v. Gurley Motor Co., 105 N.M. 803, 737 P.2d 1180 (Ct. App. 1987); Paterson v. Globe Am. Casualty Co., 101 N.M. 541, 685 P.2d 396 (Ct. App. 1984); Hart v. Moore, 587 N.Y.S.2d 477 (Sup. Ct. 1992); Pearce v. American Defender Life Ins. Co., 343 S.E.2d 174 (N.C. 1986); Golden Rule Ins. Co. v. Long, 113 N.C. App. 187, 439 S.E.2d 599 (1993); Phillips v. Integon Corp., 319 S.E.2d 673 (N.C. Ct. App. 1984); Ellis v. Smith-Broadhurst Inc., 48 N.C. App. 180, 268 S.E.2d 271 (1980); Commonwealth v. Allstate Ins. Co., 729 A.2d 135 (Pa. Commw. 1999); Myint v. Allstate Ins. Co., 970 S.W.2d 920 (Tenn. 1998); Strainer v. Steele, 730 S.W.2d 335 (Tenn. Ct. App. 1987); Vail v. Texas Farm Bureau Mut. Ins. Co., 754 S.W.2d 129 (Tex. 1988). *See also* Kentucky Central Life Ins. Co. v. LeDuc, 814 F. Supp. 832 (N.D. Cal. 1992); Farmers Ins. Exchange v. Superior Court (The People), 6 Cal. Rptr. 2d 487, 826 P.2d 730 (1992) (UDAP claim not preempted, but

states hold otherwise.[708]

Pennsylvania case law in this area is particularly copious and complex. The Pennsylvania UNIP statute contains no provision either stating or implying that it represents the exclusive means by which an insurer's unfair or deceptive acts are to be penalized, and thus courts recognize that the Pennsylvania UNIP statute is not in conflict with the Pennsylvania UDAP statute.[709] An insured may maintain a private cause of action under the Pennsylvania UDAP statute even though the allegations in the complaint fall within the purview of acts and practices prohibited by the UNIP statute.[710] The UNIP statute also does not preclude an insured from pursuing a cause of action against an insurer for common law fraud and deceit.[711]

Although the Pennsylvania UNIP statute does not preempt an insured from bringing a UDAP action, several cases hold that an insured's UDAP claim can not be based merely on an insurer's violations of the UNIP statute.[712] These cases hold that the plaintiff's UDAP claim must be based on something other than the fact that the UNIP statute has been violated. The UNIP statute can be enforced only by the State Insurance Commissioner and not by way of private action. Thus, where the determination of an insured's UDAP claim necessarily requires an inquiry into whether the insurer has committed a UNIP violation, the UDAP claim falls outside of the court's jurisdiction.

The consumer must show instead why the alleged practice specifically violates the state UDAP statute, not the state UNIP statute.[713] Not every practice violating the UNIP

court may determine, as matter of primary jurisdiction, that it will defer to insurance department resolution of an issue). A court finding that there is no private cause of action that can be implied into the UNIP statute does not prevent UDAP application to the insurance practice. Kiewit Constr. Co. v. Westchester Fire Ins. Co., 878 F. Supp. 298 (D. Mass. 1995); Leo v. State Farm Mut. Auto Ins. Co., 908 F. Supp. 254 (E.D. Pa. 1995) (court may take UNIP statute into account in interpreting UDAP prohibitions); Manufacturers Life Ins. Co. v. Superior Court, 10 Cal. 4th 257, 895 P.2d 56 (1995); Dierkes v. Blue Cross & Blue Shield, 991 S.W.2d 662 (Mo. 1999) (insurance code did not displace common law claims against insurer that imposed rate increases that had not been approved by insurance department); Thomas v. Northwestern National Ins. Co., 973 P.2d 804 (Mont. 1998) (construing UNIP statute not to preclude assertion of claims for negligence, bad faith, and breach of fiduciary duty).

708 *In re* Prudential Ins. Co. of Am. Sales Practices Litigation, 975 F. Supp. 584 (D.N.J. 1996); Showpiece Homes Corp. v. Assurance Co. of Am., 38 P.3d 47 (Colo. 2001); Morris v. American Family Mut. Ins. Co., 386 N.W.2d 233 (Minn. 1986); Britton v. Farmers Ins. Group, 721 P.2d 303 (Mont. 1986); Pierzga v. Ohio Casualty Group of Ins. Co., 208 N.J. Super. 40, 504 A.2d 1200 (1986); Johnson v. Lincoln National Life Ins. Co., 69 Ohio App. 3d 249, 590 N.E.2d 761 (1990); State *ex rel.* Blue Cross & Blue Shield Mut. v. Carroll, 21 Ohio App. 3d 263, 487 N.E.2d 576 (1985) (insurance department has primary and initial regulatory jurisdiction over deceptive advertising); Chandler v. Prudential Ins. Co., 715 S.W.2d 615 (Tenn. Ct. App. 1986) (bad faith penalty statute exclusive remedy for practices regulated by it); *see also* Persian Galleries, Inc. v. Transcontinental Ins. Co., 38 F.3d 253 (6th Cir. 1994) (Tennessee bad faith penalty statute displaces UDAP remedy for bad faith refusal to pay claim, but not for other acts such as deceptive sale of annuity); Textron Fin. Corp. v. Nat'l Union Fire Ins. Co., 2002 Cal. App. Unpub. LEXIS 6131 (June 28, 2002) (unpublished, citation limited) (plaintiff can not avoid lack of private UNIP cause of action by recasting claim as UDAP violation); General Accident Ins. Co. v. Blank, 873 S.W.2d 580 (Ky. Ct. App. 1993) (no UDAP applicability to dispute covered by a state's detailed administrative mechanism to resolve workers' compensation claims).

709 Great W. Life Assurance Co. v. Levithan, 834 F. Supp. 858 (E.D. Pa. 1993); Margolies v. State Farm Fire and Cas. Co., 810 F. Supp. 637 (E.D. Pa. 1992); Hardy v. Pennock Ins. Agency, Inc., 365 Pa. Super. 206, 529 A.2d 471 (Pa. Super. Ct. 1987); Pekular v. Eich, 355 Pa. Super. 276, 513 A.2d 427 (Pa. Super. Ct. 1986); Dezaiffe v. State Farm Fire & Casualty Co., 42 Pa. D. & C.3d 133 (C.P. Clearfield Cty. 1985); Culbreth v. Lawrence J. Miller, Inc., 328 Pa. Super. 374, 477 A.2d 491 (Pa. Super. Ct. 1984). *See generally* Carter, Pennsylvania Consumer Law § 2.5.6.2 (Geo. T. Bisel Co. 2d ed. 2003 and Supp.).

710 Smith v. Nationwide Mut. Ins. Co., 935 F. Supp. 616 (W.D. Pa. 1996); Great W. Life Assurance Co. v. Levithan, 834 F. Supp. 858 (E.D. Pa. 1993); MacFarland v. U.S. Fidelity & Guar. Co., 818 F. Supp. 108 (E.D. Pa. 1993); Margolies v. State Farm Fire and Cas. Co., 810 F. Supp. 637 (E.D. Pa. 1992); Lombardo v. State Farm Mut. Auto. Ins. Co., 800 F. Supp. 208 (E.D. Pa. 1992); Henry v. State Farm Ins. Co., 788 F. Supp. 241 (E.D. Pa. 1992); Brownell v. State Farm Mut. Ins. Co., 757 F. Supp. 526 (E.D. Pa. 1991); Fay v. Erie Ins. Group, 723 A.2d 712 (Pa. Super. 1999); Hardy v. Pennock Ins. Agency, Inc., 365 Pa. Super. 206, 529 A.2d 471 (1987); Wright v. North Am. Life Assurance Co., 372 Pa. Super. 272, 539 A.2d 434 (1988); Pekular v. Eich, 355 Pa. Super. 276, 513 A.2d 427 (Pa. Super. Ct. 1986); Culbreth v. Lawrence J. Miller, Inc., 328 Pa. Super. 374, 477 A.2d 491 (Pa. Super. Ct. 1984) (UDAP action against insurance adjusters representing insured not preempted by state unfair practices act or by state statute regulating such insurance adjusters); Dezaiffe v. State Farm Fire & Casualty Co., 42 Pa. D. & C.3d 133 (C.P. Clearfield Cty. 1985). *But see* Williams v. State Farm Mut. Auto Ins. Co., 763 F. Supp. 121 (E.D. Pa. 1991) (refusing to follow Hardy and Pekular; no UDAP cause of action for unfair claim settlement practices); Layton v. Liberty Mut. Fire Ins. Co., 577 F. Supp. 1 (E.D. Pa.), *aff'd without op.*, 725 F.2d 668 (3d Cir. 1983).

711 Lombardo v. State Farm Mut. Auto. Ins. Co., 800 F. Supp. 208 (E.D. Pa. 1992); Henry v. State Farm Ins. Co., 788 F. Supp. 241 (E.D. Pa. 1992); Gordon v. Pennsylvania Blue Shield, 378 Pa. Super. 256, 548 A.2d 600 (1988); Wright v. North Am. Life Assurance Co., 372 Pa. Super. 272, 539 A.2d 434 (1988); Hardy v. Pennock Ins. Agency, Inc., 365 Pa. Super. 206, 529 A.2d 471 (1987); Pekular v. Eich, 355 Pa. Super. 276, 513 A.2d 427 (1986).

712 Smith v. Nationwide Mut. Ins. Co., 935 F. Supp. 616 (W.D. Pa. 1996); Parasco v. Pacific Indem. Co., 870 F. Supp. 644 (E.D. Pa. 1994); Lombardo v. State Farm Mut. Auto. Ins. Co., 800 F. Supp. 208 (E.D. Pa. 1992); Fay v. Erie Ins. Group, 723 A.2d 712 (Pa. Super. 1999); Gordon v. Pennsylvania Blue Shield, 378 Pa. Super. 256, 548 A.2d 600 (1988); Fair v. State Farm Mut. Ins., 18 Pa. D. & C.4th 78 (C. P. Lancaster 1992).

713 Horowitz v. Federal Kemper Life Assur. Co., 57 F.3d 300 (3d Cir. 1995); Smith v. Nationwide Mut. Ins. Co., 935 F. Supp. 616 (W.D. Pa. 1996); Aetna Cas. & Sur. Co. v. Ericksen, 903 F. Supp. 836 (M.D. Pa. 1995); Parasco v. Pacific Indem. Co., 870

statute is unfair or deceptive, so a mere refusal to pay an insurance claim, for example, may not necessarily be unfair and deceptive.[714] To avoid a successful motion to dismiss, the consumer's complaint must specifically describe some misfeasance that violates the UDAP statute.[715] Nevertheless, the consumer may be able to use the UNIP statute to help interpret what practices are unfair or deceptive under the UDAP statute.[716]

2.3.1.4 The Filed Rate Doctrine and Primary Jurisdiction

The filed rate doctrine,[717] which precludes challenges to rates that have been approved by a regulatory body, poses related issues. A federal court applied this doctrine to preclude a challenge to a hurricane deductible for homeowners insurance because it had been filed with the insurance commissioner.[718] A Kentucky case applied the doctrine to bar the attorney general's claim for damages caused by an insurer's inflated health insurance rates, which had been filed with and approved by the Department of Insurance.[719] But the doctrine should be limited to ratemaking, and should not protect insurers from claims regarding other practices such as deceptive marketing or claims adjustment.[720] Where a case involves issues within the special competence of the insurance department, the court may also apply the doctrine of primary jurisdiction and dismiss or suspend the case to enable the department to consider the issues.[721]

2.3.2 Utilities

UDAP actions against utilities have been dismissed when the UDAP statute specifically exempts utilities,[722] when an adequate administrative remedy is available before the Public Utilities Commission (PUC),[723] and when the defendant municipal utility is a nonprofit corporation.[724] An exemption for actions "permitted by law" does not operate as a general

---

F. Supp. 644 (E.D. Pa. 1994); MacFarland v. U.S. Fidelity & Guar. Co., 818 F. Supp. 108 (E.D. Pa. 1993); Lombardo v. State Farm Mut. Auto. Ins. Co., 800 F. Supp. 208 (E.D. Pa. 1992); Brownell v. State Farm Mut. Ins. Co., 757 F. Supp. 526 (E.D. Pa. 1991); Gordon v. Pennsylvania Blue Shield, 378 Pa. Super. 256, 548 A.2d 600 (1988).

714 Horowitz v. Federal Kemper Life Assur. Co., 57 F.3d 300 (3d Cir. 1995); MacFarland v. U.S. Fidelity & Guar. Co., 818 F. Supp. 108 (E.D. Pa. 1993); Lombardo v. State Farm Mut. Auto. Ins. Co., 800 F. Supp. 208 (E.D. Pa. 1992); Gordon v. Pennsylvania Blue Shield, 378 Pa. Super. 256, 548 A.2d 600 (1988). *See also* Aetna Cas. & Sur. Co. v. Ericksen, 903 F. Supp. 836 (M.D. Pa. 1995) (insurer's refusal to defend and indemnify plaintiff in state court action).

715 *See, e.g.*, Smith v. Nationwide Mut. Ins. Co., 935 F. Supp. 616 (W.D. Pa. 1996) (court did not dismiss plaintiff's UDAP claim because complaint could be construed as alleging that an improper post-loss investigation was performed); Parasco v. Pacific Indem. Co., 870 F. Supp. 644 (E.D. Pa. 1994) (plaintiff's UDAP claim not dismissed where complaint contained allegations that insurer conducted its post-loss investigation in an unfair and unobjective manner and misrepresented the nature of its contractual obligations); Brownell v. State Farm Mut. Ins. Co., 757 F. Supp. 526 (E.D. Pa. 1991) (plaintiff alleged misfeasance where complaint contained allegations that insurer had undertaken an affirmative course of action to defraud her of benefits and misrepresented to her that medical care available for her injuries).

716 Leo v. State Farm Mut. Auto Ins. Co., 908 F. Supp. 254 (E.D. Pa. 1995). *See also* Romano v. Nationwide Mut. Fire Ins. Co., 435 Pa. Super. 545, 646 A.2d 1228 (1994) (approving use of UNIP statute as an aid in interpreting an ambiguity in Pennsylvania's bad faith statute, 42 Pa. Cons. Stat. Ann. § 8371). *Cf.* Smith v. Nationwide Mut. Ins. Co., 935 F. Supp. 616 (W.D. Pa. 1996) (*Romano* and *Leo* inapplicable because plaintiffs here made no assertion that reference to the UNIP statute was necessary to resolve an ambiguity in the UDAP statute); Parasco v. Pacific Indem. Co., 870 F. Supp. 644 (E.D. Pa. 1994) (*Romano* inapplicable because plaintiffs here did not argue that resort to the UNIP statute was warranted due to an ambiguity in the UDAP statute).

717 *See* § 5.6.10.1.1, *infra*, for a discussion of the filed rate doctrine in the context of telecommunication services.

718 Allen v. State Farm Fire & Cas. Co., 59 F. Supp. 2d 1217 (S.D. Ala. 1999); Richardson v. Standard Guar. Ins., 2002 WL 972181 (N.J. Super. Law Div. May 13, 2002) (unpublished, citation limited).

719 Commonwealth *ex rel.* Chandler v. Anthem Ins. Cos., 8 S.W.3d 48 (Ky. App. 1999).

720 Loe v. State Farm Ins. Cos., 1998 U.S. App. LEXIS 24457 (9th Cir. Sept. 25, 1998) (applying California law). *See also* American Bankers Ins. Co. v. Alexander, 818 So. 2d 1073 (Miss. 2001) (claim regarding scheme to defraud customers by obtaining force-placed insurance at high rates not barred).

721 Irvin v. Liberty Life Ins. Co., 2001 U.S. Dist. LEXIS 2935 (E.D. La. Mar. 12, 2001); Richardson v. Standard Guar. Ins., 2002 WL 972181 (N.J. Super., Law Div., May 13, 2002) (unpublished, citation limited). *See* § 2.3.3.6.2, *infra*.

722 Canterbury v. Columbia Gas, 2001 WL 1681132 (S.D. Ohio Sept. 25, 2001) (supplier of natural gas exempt); State *ex rel.* Guste v. Council of New Orleans, 309 So. 2d 290 (La. 1975); Brice v. AT&T Communications, Inc., 32 P.3d 885 (Okla. App. 2001) (UDAP statute could not be applied to telephone company billing dispute because of exemption for acts or transactions regulated by state corporations commission); Haning v. Rutland Furniture, Inc., 115 Ohio App. 3d 61, 684 N.E.2d 713 (1996) (Ohio's exemption for gas companies applies to propane dealers); Tanner Electric Coop. v. Puget Sound Power & Light Co., 911 P.2d 1301 (Wash. 1996). *See also* N.H. Rev. Stat. Ann. § 358-A:3 (exempting trade or commerce that is subject to jurisdiction of state public utilities commission).

723 Daaleman v. Elizabethtown Gas Co., 142 N.J. Super. 531, 362 A.2d 70 (Law Div. 1976).

724 Haberman v. Washington Public Power Supply Sys., 109 Wash. 2d 107, 744 P.2d 1032 (1987); Washington Natural Gas Co. v. Public Utility District No. 1, 77 Wash. 2d 94, 459 P.2d 633 (1969). *But see* Keene Inc. v. Boston Water & Sewer Comm'n, Civ. Action No. 50133 (Mass. Super. Ct. Suffolk Cty. 1981). The UDAP coverage of municipal corporations is discussed in more detail in § 2.3.6, *infra*.

exemption for regulated utility companies, however, but only for those actions that the regulatory body has specifically authorized.[725]

State law may give the PUC exclusive jurisdiction over some types of disputes against utility companies.[726] But activities beyond the purview of the PUC have been found covered by the UDAP statute.[727] Further, utilities such as electric cooperatives that are not regulated by the PUC will generally be covered by the UDAP statute.[728] As states deregulate utility services, more utilities may find themselves subject to the UDAP statute.[729] Moreover, even where the PUC has primary jurisdiction, a UDAP action may be maintained if the PUC is powerless to grant the relief sought[730] or has not exercised its jurisdiction.[731]

Even though a company's rates are regulated by the PUC, misrepresentations concerning those rates may be challenged under the UDAP statute.[732] Consumers may also be able to challenge a utility's failure to provide services for which it charged, if those charges were built into rates approved by the PUC.[733] However, the "filed tariff" doctrine may prevent assertion of claims that are contrary to the utility's filed tariff.[734] Courts may also defer to the PUC for an initial adjudication of the issues under the doctrine of primary jurisdiction.[735]

2.3.3 *Regulated Industries*

2.3.3.1 Determining Whether Other State Regulation Bars a UDAP Action

One of the most complex and important issues involving UDAP statute coverage is the relation of UDAP statutes to practices regulated or permitted by other laws. Although the issue becomes acute when challenging insurance, utility, or credit practices, it is also relevant to UDAP claims against car dealers, repair services, vocational schools, landlords, and any other seller regulated by other state or federal law.

The fact that a business entity has a license from some governmental agency does not, of course, establish that it has acted without deception or unfairness.[736] The question is whether the state UDAP statute applies to this type of transaction or this type of dealer, or whether other regulation displaces the UDAP statute's applicability.

The initial step in determining a UDAP statute's applicability to otherwise regulated practices is a careful analysis of the version of the state's UDAP statute in effect at the time of the challenged practice. This will determine if the statute explicitly excludes practices permitted by law, regulated by other law, or regulated by a government agency, or contains similar language. As will be described below, the exact language of such provisions is important. The absence of any such provision simplifies, but does not eliminate, the issue.

The second step, whether such a statutory provision is found or not, is to determine if the seller is specifically regulated by other law. If so, carefully analyze how extensively that statute regulates the seller's practices in general, and the challenged practices in particular, and what kinds of remedies the statute affords to the state and private litigants as to the wrong being challenged in the UDAP action.

725 Andrade v. Johnson, 345 S.C. 216, 546 S.E.2d 665 (S.C. App. 2001), *rev'd on other grounds*, 588 S.E.2d 588 (S.C. 2003). *See* § 2.3.3, *infra*.

726 Higgins v. Columbia Gas, 736 N.E.2d 92 (Ohio App. 2000) (PUC has exclusive jurisdiction over claim that utility company wrongfully terminated service at landlord's request). *But see* Wernikoff v. RCN Telecom Servs., 341 Ill. App. 3d 89, 791 N.E.2d 1195, 274 Ill. Dec. 784 (2003) (after rate deregulation, Ill. Commerce Comm'n does not have jurisdiction over claim that telecommunications provider overcharged).

727 Penny v. Southwestern Bell Tel. Co., 906 F.2d 183 (5th Cir. 1990) (Texas law); Qwest Corp. v. Kelly, 59 P.3d 789 (Ariz. App. 2002) (court has jurisdiction to hear claim for damages and injunctive relief against utility that deceptively sold inside wire maintenance plans that consumers did not need); Wernikoff v. RCN Telecom Servs., 341 Ill. App. 3d 89, 791 N.E.2d 1195, 274 Ill. Dec. 784 (2003); Perron v. Treasurer of the City of Woonsocket, 403 A.2d 252 (R.I. 1979).

728 Granbois v. Big Horn County Elec. Coop., Inc., 986 P.2d 1097 (Mont. 1999) (consumer protection portion of UDAP statute covers electric cooperatives, although they are exempt from the anti-competitive portions).

729 *See, e.g.*, D.J. Hopkins, Inc. v. G.T.E. Northwest, Inc., 947 P.2d 1220 (Wash. App. 1997) (local telephone company's deceptive billing practices were exempt from post-amendment UDAP statute; although the company was partially deregulated, billing practices remained regulated). *See also* § 5.6.10.1.2, *infra*.

730 Penny v. Southwestern Bell Tel. Co., 906 F.2d 183 (5th Cir. 1990) (Texas law); Southwestern Bell Tel. Co. v. Nash, 586 S.W.2d 647 (Tex. Civ. App. 1979).

731 People *ex rel.* Orloff v. Pacific Bell, 31 Cal. 4th 1132, 7 Cal. Rptr. 3d 315, 80 P.3d 201 (2003) (interpreting Cal. statutes to allow district attorneys to sue public utilities for deceptive practices unless suit would interfere with a PUC enforcement proceeding).

732 Penny v. Southwestern Bell Tel. Co., 906 F.2d 183 (5th Cir. 1990) (Texas law); Lowell Gas Co. v. Attorney General, 377 Mass. 37, 385 N.E.2d 240 (1979).

733 Wise v. Pacific Gas & Elec. Co., 77 Cal. App. 4th 287, 91 Cal. Rptr. 2d 479 (1999).

734 Henderson v. Central Power & Light Co., 977 S.W.2d 439 (Tex. App. 1998); Kanuco Technology Corp. v. Worldcom Network Servs., Inc., 979 S.W.2d 368 (Tex. App. 1998). *But cf.* State *ex rel.* Hatch v. Worldcom, Inc., 125 F. Supp. 2d 365 (D. Minn. 2000) (filed rate doctrine does not preempt AG suit to enforce UDAP prohibition against false advertising); Qwest Corp. v. Kelly, 59 P.3d 789 (Ariz. App. 2002) (filed rate doctrine, even if recognized in Arizona, not applicable to claim involving deceptive sale of inside wire maintenance plan); Wise v. Pacific Gas & Elec. Co., 77 Cal. App. 4th 287, 91 Cal. Rptr. 2d 479 (1999) (plaintiffs could assert UDAP claim where challenge was not to the rates themselves, but to utility company's failure to deliver services for which it charged). *See* § 5.6.10.1, *infra*.

735 Wise v. Pacific Gas & Elec. Co., 77 Cal. App. 4th 287, 91 Cal. Rptr. 2d 479 (1999). *See generally* § 2.3.3.6.2, *infra*.

736 Hartigan v. Northern Illinois Mortgage Co., 201 Ill. App. 3d 356, 559 N.E.2d 14 (1990).

The final step is to determine whether the existing state regulation of the challenged practice is sufficient to exempt the practice from a UDAP statute's coverage. In making the determination, a factor to keep in mind is the specific nature of the UDAP statute's exemption of regulated practices.

Even where an administrative agency regulates an industry, the question of whether the industry is exempt from UDAP coverage is a matter for the courts, not the agency, to decide.[737]

2.3.3.2 UDAP Statutes Exempting Specific Regulated Entities or All "Regulated Practices"

The most restrictive UDAP language excludes specific types of merchants, such as banks, insurance companies, or lawyers. Such language will, of course, be given effect.[738] Where "banks" are excluded, this has been held to apply to savings and loans.[739] Where financial institutions are excluded, this has been found not only to exempt a financial institution's loan practices, but also its practices related to a lease.[740]

The next most restrictive language excludes practices regulated by other law. Three of the states that use this language have narrowed the exemption significantly in recent years. Washington, which formerly exempted regulated activities in general, still exempts regulated utilities and insurance but otherwise only exempts activities specifically permitted by regulatory bodies.[741] Nebraska exempts regulated activities and transactions, but has eliminated the exception for loan brokers and funeral directors and narrowed it as to insurance.[742] Alaska amended its statute in 1993 to deny the exemption to a wide range of banking transactions.[743] Pre-amendment cases from these states may have some bearing on interpretation of similar language in other states' statutes, but are questionable precedent within the state.

Language excluding regulated practices has been found sufficient to exempt the following types of activities: installment lending by licensed finance companies;[744] the issuance of a certificate of deposit by a state bank;[745] licensed real estate agents allegedly involved in land fraud schemes that violated regulations of a real estate board;[746] insurance practices regulated by the insurance commission;[747] the activities of a regulated utility, even if they violate state utility commission regulations;[748] security dealers regulated by an extensive security act that provided a private right of action;[749] shippers regulated by the Carmack amendment;[750] regulated prepaid health services organizations;[751] a county hospital;[752] and regulated law book publishers.[753]

At least some of these holdings excluding UDAP coverage may be explained by the fact that the very practice challenged under the UDAP statute was specifically regu-

737 Booth v. Consumers Power Co., 573 N.W.2d 333 (Mich. App. 1997) (public utility commission has statutory authority to issue declaratory rulings regarding applicability of the statutes it administers, not UDAP statute).

738 *See* Autin v. Martin, 576 So. 2d 72 (La. Ct. App. 1991); § 2.2.1.5, *supra*.

739 First Fin. Bank FSB v. Butler, 492 So. 2d 503 (La. Ct. App. 1986).

740 Bard v. Society Nat'l Bank, 1998 Ohio App. LEXIS 4187 (Ohio Ct. App. Sept. 10, 1998).

741 Wash. Rev. Code § 19.86.170. *See* Robinson v. Avis Rent A Car Sys., 106 Wash. App. 104, 22 P.3d 818 (2001) (except for transactions regulated by federal power commissioner or state commissioner of insurance, utilities, or transportation, acts are exempt only if agency specifically permitted the act and had statutory authority to do so). *But see* Interstate Production Credit Ass'n v. MacHugh, 61 Wash. App. 403, 810 P.2d 535 (1991) (creditor extending farm credit exempt because closely regulated).

742 Neb. Code § 59-1617.

743 Alaska Stat. § 45.50.481.

744 Kuntzelman v. Avco Fin. Servs., 206 Neb. 130, 291 N.W.2d 705 (1980). *See also* Hydroflo Corp. v. First Nat'l Bank, 349 N.W.2d 615 (Neb. 1984); Little v. Gillette, 218 Neb. 271, 354 N.E.2d 147 (1984); McCaul v. American Sav. Co., 213 Neb. 841, 331 N.W.2d 795 (1983).

745 Wrede v. Exchange Bank of Gibbon, 247 Neb. 907, 531 N.W.2d 523 (1995).

746 Little v. Gillette, 218 Neb. 271, 354 N.E.2d 147 (1984).

747 West v. Fireman's Fund Ins. Co., 683 F. Supp. 156 (E.D. La. 1987); O.K. Lumber Co. v. Providence Washington Ins. Co., 759 P.2d 523 (Alaska 1988); Ferguson v. United Ins. Co. of Am., 163 Ga. App. 282, 293 S.E.2d 736 (1982); Comeaux v. Pennsylvania General Ins. Co., 490 So. 2d 1191 (La. Ct. App. 1986). *But see* Lamarque v. Massachusetts Indemnity & Life Ins. Co., 794 F.2d 197 (5th Cir. 1986) (Louisiana law).

748 Tanner Electric Coop. v. Puget Sound Power & Light Co., 911 P.2d 1301 (Wash. 1996) (construing post-amendment statute); D.J. Hopkins, Inc. v. G.T.E. Northwest, Inc., 947 P.2d 1220 (Wash. App. 1997) (local telephone company's deceptive billing practices were exempt from post-amendment UDAP statute; although the company was partially deregulated, billing practices remained regulated).

749 Kittilson v. Ford, 23 Wash. App. 402, 595 P.2d 944 (1979) (interpreting pre-amendment version), *aff'd*, 608 P.2d 264 (Wash. 1980); *see also* § 2.2.9.3, *supra*.

750 Suarez v. United Van Lines, Inc., 791 F. Supp. 815 (D. Colo. 1992).

751 Washington Osteopathic Medical Ass'n v. King County Medical Serv. Corp., 78 Wash. 2d 577, 478 P.2d 228 (1970). The Washington UDAP statute has been amended to exclude only permitted, not regulated practices, and so this case is not controlling in Washington for actions engaged in after the date of the amendment. *See* Allen v. American Land Research, 25 Wash. App. 914, 611 P.2d 420 (1980), *rev'd on other grounds*, 95 Wash. 2d 841, 631 P.2d 930 (1981).

752 Williamson v. Grant County Public Hosps. District No. 1, 65 Wash. 2d 245, 396 P.2d 879 (1964) (interpreting pre-amendment version of statute).

753 Threthewey v. Bancroft-Whitney Co., 13 Wash. App. 353, 534 P.2d 1382 (1975) (interpreting pre-amendment version of statute).

lated by a government agency.[754] Thus where a UDAP statute specifically exempts regulated practices, the UDAP statute can not be used to challenge a mobile home construction practice that is specifically prohibited by a state agency regulation.[755]

However, challenged practices are not "regulated by other law" where the only law regulating debt collectors does not specifically prohibit the challenged debt collection practices,[756] where the specific challenged practice is not covered by a general regulatory structure,[757] where the Department of Motor Vehicles' discretionary power to refuse to renew a dealer's license is not considered regulation of auto dealership practices,[758] or where the regulatory agency would only derive its authority to regulate a practice from the UDAP statute itself.[759]

Although licensed brokers are regulated, unlicensed practices are not sufficiently regulated to come under the exclusion, even though the eventual sale is regulated.[760] While normal banking operations are regulated by the state banking commission, and thus fall within a UDAP exemption for regulated practices,[761] where a bank's credit card operations are not so regulated, they are subject to a UDAP challenge.[762]

Often UDAP statutes that exempt regulated practices limit the exclusion to practices regulated by *regulatory bodies*. The Federal Trade Commission[763] and the Department of Justice[764] are not regulatory bodies but are enforcement agencies, so that practices coming within the purview of laws enforced by these agencies are not exempt. But one state court (interpreting a somewhat different exemption) found the state's attorney professional conduct committee to be a regulatory board.[765]

A few UDAP statutes exempt "those aspects of a consumer transaction which are regulated by the Federal Consumer Credit Protection Act, 15 U.S.C. § 1601."[766] This prevents use of the UDAP statute to bring an action alleging Truth in Lending, Fair Credit Billing, Consumer Leasing, or Equal Credit Opportunity Act violations. This language does not preempt a UDAP challenge to other aspects of a credit transaction.[767]

2.3.3.3 UDAP Statutes Exempting "Practices Permitted by Law"

2.3.3.3.1 Mainstream precedent

Certain UDAP statutes exclude from UDAP coverage only practices "permitted" by law[768] or "authorized" by a regulatory agency. This language exempts far fewer practices than statutes using the term "regulated," since a practice may be remedied by the UDAP statute where there is an insufficient showing that the particular challenged activity is specifically permitted or authorized by law.[769] An

754 Wrede v. Exchange Bank of Gibbon, 247 Neb. 907, 531 N.W.2d 523 (1995) (Nebraska's exemption only applies if the conduct itself, not just the actor, is regulated); Lidstrand v. Silvercrest Indus., 28 Wash. App. 359, 623 P.2d 710 (1981) (interpreting pre-amendment version of statute).

755 Lidstrand v. Silvercrest Indus., 28 Wash. App. 359, 623 P.2d 710 (1981) (interpreting pre-amendment version of statute).

756 State v. O'Neill Investigations, Inc., 609 P.2d 520 (Alaska 1980).

757 Dick v. Attorney General, 83 Wash. 2d 684, 521 P.2d 702 (1974) (interpreting pre-amendment version of statute).

758 State v. Ralph Williams' N.W. Chrysler Plymouth, Inc., 87 Wash. 2d 298, 553 P.2d 423 (1976) (question was whether plaintiff had adequate remedy at law).

759 Lamarque v. Massachusetts Indemnity & Life Ins. Co., 794 F.2d 197 (5th Cir. 1986) (Louisiana law).

760 Allen v. American Land Research, 95 Wash. 2d 841, 631 P.2d 930 (1981) (interpreting pre-amendment version of statute).

761 *See* Scott v. Bank of Coushatta, 512 So. 2d 356 (La. 1987); Preferred Inv. Corp. v. Neucere, 592 So. 2d 889 (La. Ct. App. 1991); State Bank of Commerce v. Deanco, Inc., 483 So. 2d 1119 (La. Ct. App. 1986).

762 Bank of New Orleans & Trust Co. v. Phillips, 415 So. 2d 973 (La. Ct. App. 1982).

763 State v. Reader's Digest Ass'n, Inc., 81 Wash. 2d 259, 501 P.2d 290 (1972) (interpreting pre-amendment version of statute, but construing language that also appears in amended version).

764 State v. Sterling Theaters Co., 64 Wash. 2d 761, 394 P.2d 226 (1964) (interpreting pre-amendment version of statute, but construing language that also appears in amended version).

765 Rousseau v. Eshleman, 519 A.2d 243 (N.H. 1986) (case interprets former version of statute, which exempted "permitted" practices, not regulated industries; statute has since been amended to exempt only trade or commerce that is subject to the jurisdiction of certain specified agencies, not including attorney professional conduct committee). *Accord* Averill v. Cox, 761 A.2d 1083 (N.H. 2000) (interpreting former version of statute). *See* § 2.3.3.3, *infra*.

766 *See, e.g.*, Ala. Code § 8-19-7(4); Va. Code Ann. § 59.1-199.

767 Graham v. RRR, L.L.C., 202 F. Supp. 2d 483 (E.D. Va. 2002) (Virginia exemption for aspects of transaction that are regulated by Consumer Credit Protection Act precludes claim based on false representation that creditor had agreed to interest rate shown on a contract), *aff'd*, 2003 WL 139432 (4th Cir. Jan. 21, 2003) (unpublished, citation limited); Valley Acceptance Corp. v. Glasby, 337 S.E.2d 291 (Va. 1985).

768 The Washington UDAP statute has been amended to exclude only permitted, not regulated practices, and Washington cases cited in § 2.3.3.2, *supra*, are not determinative for actions engaged in after the date of the amendment. The Washington UDAP statute still exempts practices regulated by the public utility commission and state power commission. *See* D.J. Hopkins, Inc. v. G.T.E. Northwest, Inc., 947 P.2d 1220 (Wash. App. 1997); Allen v. American Land Research, 25 Wash. App. 914, 611 P.2d 420 (1980), *rev'd on other grounds*, 95 Wash. 2d 841, 631 P.2d 930 (1981).

769 Zapka v. Coca-Cola Co., 2001 U.S. Dist. LEXIS 20155 (N.D. Ill. Dec. 3, 2001) (compliance with FDA labeling requirements has no effect on UDAP action alleging deceptive marketing); Blue Cross and Blue Shield v. Philip Morris, Inc., 178 F. Supp. 2d 198 (E.D.N.Y. 2001) (unrelated regulatory supervision does not bar UDAP deception claim), *rev'd in part on other grounds, questions certified by* Blue Cross and Blue Shield v. Philip Morris, Inc., 344 F.3d 211 (2d Cir. 2003); Am. Indian and Alaska Native Cultural and Arts Dev. Inst. v. Daymon &

exemption for actions authorized by other laws does not preclude UDAP application to conduct regulated by these other laws, but only allows the defendant to assert compliance with other laws as a defense.[770] The seller has the burden of showing a practice is permitted.[771]

A regulatory agency's acquiescence to a practice over a period of years does not make the practice "specifically permitted within the statutory authority," and thus the practice can be challenged by the UDAP statute.[772] Not taking action against a company is not the same thing as permitting the company's conduct.[773] The fact that the Federal Trade Commission considered and rejected a trade regulation rule prohibiting certain conduct does not mean such conduct is permitted.[774]

A state insurance law that permits the sale of a certain annuity does not permit deceptive sales of such annuities, so a deceptive sale is not exempt.[775] The existence of a federal regulation controlling permissible fees is not enough if the particular facts of a case mean that regulation does not set fees in that case.[776] The fact that a similar case is pending before a state or federal regulatory agency does not mean

---

Assocs., 1999 U.S. Dist. LEXIS 22380 (D.N.M. June 23, 1999) (exception for "expressly permitted" actions or transactions does not exclude acts by member of regulated profession unless specifically authorized; court notes 1999 amendment that makes this interpretation explicit); Winkler v. Interim Servs., Inc., 36 F. Supp. 2d 1026 (M.D. Tenn. 1999); Robertson v. State Farm Fire & Casualty Co., 890 F. Supp. 671 (E.D. Mich. 1995) (licensure does not authorize deceptive conduct); Nault's Automobile Sales, Inc. v. American Honda Motor Co., 148 F.R.D. 25 (D.N.H. 1993); Wislow v. Wong, 713 F. Supp. 1103 (N.D. Ill. 1989) (UDAP statute applies to securities transactions even though regulated by federal and state agencies); Therrien v. Resource Fin. Group, Inc., 704 F. Supp. 322 (D.N.H. 1989) (bank regulation); WVG v. Pacific Ins. Co., 707 F. Supp. 70 (D.N.H. 1986) (insurance regulation); Globe v. Adolph Coors Co. (*In re* Globe Distributors, Inc.), 111 B.R. 377 (Bankr. D.N.H. 1990) (state's regulation of distributorship termination does not prevent UDAP suit by terminated distributor); Schnall v. Hertz Corp., 78 Cal. App. 4th 1144, 93 Cal. Rptr. 2d 439 (2000) (state statute that explicitly authorized fuel service charges for rental cars and did not specify a ceiling precluded challenge to their unconscionability but not to deceptive manner in which consumers were induced to incur them); Showpiece Homes Corp. v. Assurance Co. of Am., 38 P.3d 47 (Colo. 2001); Aurora Firefighter's Credit Union v. Harvey, 163 Ill. App. 3d 915, 516 N.E.2d 1028 (1987) (state credit union legislation does not authorize challenged practice, so practice is not exempt; only exclude practice from UDAP if conduct is specifically authorized by state law or in compliance with state law); Dimarzo v. American Mut. Ins. Co., 389 Mass. 85, 449 N.E.2d 1189 (1983); York v. Sullivan, 369 Mass. 157, 338 N.E.2d 341 (1975); Commonwealth v. DeCotis, 366 Mass. 234, 316 N.E.2d 748 (1974); DePasquale v. Odgen Suffolk Downs, Inc., 29 Mass. App. Ct. 658, 564 N.E.2d 584 (1990) (racetrack practices that were not specifically regulated by State Racing Commission regulations are subject to UDAP claims); Attorney General v. Diamond Mortgage Co., 414 Mich. 603, 327 N.W.2d 805 (1982) (even though company licensed, no agency authorization to engage in deceptive activity); Price v. Long Realty, Inc., 199 Mich. App. 461, 502 N.W.2d 337 (1993); Ashlock v. Sunwest Bank, N.A., 107 N.M. 100, 753 P.2d 346 (1988); Azar v. Prudential Ins. Co., 68 P.3d 909 (N.M. App. 2003) (exception must be construed narrowly; Insurance Dept.'s approval of policies insufficient); State *ex rel.* Stratton v. Gurley Motor Co., 105 N.M. 803, 737 P.2d 1180 (Ct. App. 1987); People *ex rel.* Spitzer v. Gen. Electric Co., 302 A.D.2d 314, 756 N.Y.S.2d 520 (2003) (affirming finding that product recall letters were deceptive where Consumer Product Safety Comm'n had not approved them); Rathgeber v. James Hemenway, Inc., 69 P.3d 710 (Or. 2003) (providing disclosure form required by statute did not insulate real estate agent from UDAP liability for failure to perform duties promised on the form); Hinds v. Paul's Auto Werkstatt, Inc., 107 Or. App. 63, 810 P.2d 874 (1991); Taylor v. Medenica, 479 S.E.2d 35 (S.C. 1996) (federal and state regulation of medical laboratory does not give it blanket UDAP exemption); Skinner v. Steele, 730 S.W.2d 335 (Tenn. Ct. App. 1987); Driver v. J.C. Bradford & Co., Clearinghouse No. 38,904 (Tenn. Ch. Ct. 1984); Vogt v. Seattle-First Nat'l Bank, 117 Wash. 2d 541, 817 P.2d 1364 (1991); Edmonds v. John L. Scott Real Estate, Inc., 942 P.2d 1072 (Wash. App. 1997) (exception applies only if agency has taken "overt affirmative actions specifically to permit the actions or transactions engaged in"); Sing v. John L. Scott, Inc., 920 P.2d 589 (Wash. App. 1996), *rev'd on other grounds*, 948 P.2d 816 (Wash. 1997). *See also* Vennittilli v. Primerica, Inc., 943 F. Supp. 793 (E.D. Mich. 1996) (holding securities transactions exempt from Michigan UDAP statute; equating "authorized" with "regulated"); Ott v. Baker, 53 Va. Cir. 113, 2000 Va. Cir. LEXIS 424 (May 25, 2000) (excluding medical care on ground that it was authorized by statute); .

770 Shields v. Lefta, Inc., 888 F. Supp. 894 (N.D. Ill. 1995) (compliance with TIL disclosure requirements may be a defense to UDAP liability for nondisclosure or misleading disclosure); Wislow v. Wong, 713 F. Supp. 1103 (N.D. Ill. 1989); Weatherman v. Gary-Wheaton Bank, 186 Ill. 2d 472, 713 N.E.2d 543, 239 Ill. Dec. 12 (1999) (compliance with RESPA disclosure requirements is a defense); Martin v. Heinold Commodities, Inc., 163 Ill. 2d 33, 643 N.E.2d 734 (1994); Investigators, Inc. v. Harvey, 53 Or. App. 586, 633 P.2d 6 (1981).

771 Connelly v. Housing Authority, 213 Conn. 354, 567 A.2d 1212 (1990) (statute placed burden on person claiming exemption); Bierig v. Everett Square Plaza Assocs., 34 Mass. App. Ct. 354, 611 N.E.2d 720 (1993).

772 *In re* Real Estate Litigation, 95 Wash. 2d 297, 622 P.2d 1185 (1980); *see also* State v. Multiple Listing Serv., 95 Wash. 2d 280, 622 P.2d 1190 (1980).

773 Parkhill v. Minnesota Mut. Life Ins. Co., 995 F. Supp. 983 (D. Minn. 1998).

774 Hinds v. Paul's Auto Werkstatt, Inc., 107 Or. App. 63, 810 P.2d 874 (1991). *See also* DeMarco v. Bay Ridge Car World, 169 A.D.2d 808, 565 N.Y.S.2d 176 (1991) (compliance with federal automobile recall notice regulations does not insulate dealer from UDAP suit for failing to disclose that vehicle was subject to recall).

775 Showpiece Homes Corp. v. Assurance Co. of Am., 38 P.3d 47 (Colo. 2001); Skinner v. Steele, 730 S.W.2d 335 (Tenn. Ct. App. 1987); Driver v. J.C. Bradford & Co., Clearinghouse No. 38,904 (Tenn. Ch. Ct. 1984); *In re* Stifel, Nicholaus & Co., Clearinghouse No. 38,906 (Tenn. Ch. Ct. 1984). *See also* Fidelity Fin. Servs. v. Hicks, 214 Ill. App. 3d 398, 574 N.E.2d 15 (1991) (even if transaction permitted under state loan statute, consumer's allegations of deception would properly invoke UDAP coverage).

776 Vogt v. Seattle-First Nat'l Bank, 117 Wash. 2d 541, 817 P.2d 1364 (1991).

that the UDAP action must be stayed pending the outcome of that regulatory determination.[777] A transaction is certainly not permitted by another state law when the transaction violates that law.[778]

The exclusion is further limited by some UDAP statutes that exclude practices only if permitted by a regulatory body or official, not by state law.[779] In that case, there must be an agency that administers a statute to preempt UDAP coverage, not just a statute that regulates an industry.

Of course, if the state or federal agency has specifically approved a practice, the "permitted practices" exception does apply.[780] Similarly, the state agency itself can not be sued under a UDAP statute exempting permitted practices, since the state agency by definition has permitted the practices it has engaged in itself.[781] Where a state statute makes an agreement to pay unenforceable, the Connecticut Supreme Court rejected a UDAP claim against a party that refused to pay on that agreement. The court held that UDAP liability would allow the plaintiff to make an "end run" around the statute that specified the agreement was unenforceable.[782]

Where the Truth in Lending Act requires disclosure, the UDAP statute can not require additional disclosure, because the more limited disclosure is "authorized" by an agency.[783] But even where the credit terms in a transaction are correctly disclosed for purposes of Truth in Lending, a related deceptive practice of hiding the true cost of the credit is not "authorized" by the Truth in Lending Act.[784] If the practice which is the subject of the UDAP claim is not the actual Truth in Lending disclosure, the practice is not "permitted" by Truth in Lending.[785] Merely because a party does not violate federal law does not make it immune from UDAP liability.[786]

2.3.3.3.2 Minority of courts confuse regulated with permitted

An all too common mistake courts have made is to interpret UDAP language exempting "permitted" or "authorized" practices as if the statute exempted "any regulated practice." Usually the problem is that the court for *ad hoc* reasons does not want to apply the UDAP statute to an area that is already extensively regulated. But, instead of just stating that this special form of regulation displaces the UDAP statute,[787] the court latches onto language in the UDAP statute that exempts "permitted" practices, and

777 People *ex rel.* Abrams v. American Direct Indus., Inc., Clearinghouse No. 43,083 (N.Y. Sup. Ct. 1988).

778 Fidelity Fin. Servs. v. Hicks, 214 Ill. App. 3d 398, 574 N.E.2d 15 (1991).

779 *See, e.g.*, Mass. Gen. Laws Ann. ch. 93A, § 3.

780 Bober v. Glaxo Wellcome P.L.C., 246 F.3d 934 (7th Cir. 2001); Cahnmann v. Sprint Corp., 961 F. Supp. 1229 (N.D. Ill. 1997) (charging rates in accord with filed tariff is "specifically authorized"), *aff'd on other grounds*, 133 F.3d 484 (7th Cir. 1998) (affirmance holds that plaintiffs' claim was really a challenge to a telephone tariff, which had to be presented first to the FCC under the primary jurisdiction doctrine); American Home Products Corp. v. Johnson & Johnson, 672 F. Supp. 135 (S.D.N.Y. 1987) (aspirin labels comply with FDA requirements); Trident Nevro Imaging Laboratory v. Blue Cross, 568 F. Supp. 1474 (D.S.C. 1982); Cel-Tech Communications, Inc. v. Los Angeles Cellular Tel. Co., 20 Cal. 4th 163, 973 P.2d 527 (1999); Olszewski v. Scripps Health, 135 Cal. Rptr. 2d 1, 69 P.3d 927 (2003) (no UDAP damages liability for taking action specifically permitted by state statute, even though court holds statute preempted by federal law); First Midwest Bank v. Sparks, 682 N.E.2d 373 (Ill. App. Ct. 1997) (no UDAP liability where state banking law prohibited disclosure); Laing v. Clair Car Connection, 2003 WL 1669624 (Me. Super. Jan. 29, 2003) (granting summary judgment to dealer on UDAP claim where car dealer complied with state law inspection and disclosure requirements); Bierig v. Everett Square Plaza Assocs., 34 Mass. App. Ct. 354, 611 N.E.2d 720 (1993) (statutory scheme expressly permitted, and implicitly required, the acts to which plaintiffs objected); DePasquale v. Odgen Suffolk Downs, Inc., 29 Mass. App. Ct. 658, 564 N.E.2d 584 (1990) (State Racing Commission regulations specifically governing payment of bets to ticket holders preclude UDAP liability for those acts); Valdez v. State, 54 P.3d 71 (N.M. 2002) (UDAP statute does not apply to telephone rates that are within the primary jurisdiction of the state public utility commission); Oregon *ex rel.* Frohnmayer v. Freeman, 131 Or. App. 336, 884 P.2d 878 (1994); Smith v. First Union Nat'l Bank of Tennessee, 958 S.W.2d 113 (Tenn. Ct. App. 1997). *See also* Lanier v. Associates Fin., Inc., 114 Ill. 2d 1, 499 N.E.2d 440 (1986) (use of Rule of 78's, as permitted by state and federal law, can not be challenged by UDAP statute that excludes actions "authorized" by law); State v. Piedmont Funding Corp., 382 A.2d 819 (R.I. 1978) (seller of leverage funding program regulated by both state insurance department and SEC). *Cf.* Rathgeber v. Hemenway, Inc., 69 P.3d 710, 715 (Or. 2003) (no UDAP liability for providing disclosure form required by statute, but seller can be liable for failing to conform to duties disclosed on that form).

781 Rozel Corp. v. Dept. of Public Serv. Regulation, 735 P.2d 282 (Mont. 1987).

782 McCutcheon & Burr, Inc. v. Bernan, 218 Conn. 512, 590 A.2d 438 (1991).

783 *See* § 2.2.1.6.3, *supra*..

784 Therrien v. Resource Fin. Group, Inc., 704 F. Supp. 322 (D.N.H. 1989); Chandler v. Am. Gen. Fin., Inc., 329 Ill. App. 3d 729, 768 N.E.2d 60 (2002). *See also* Knapp v. Americredit Fin. Servs., Inc., 245 F. Supp. 2d 841 (S.D. W. Va. 2003) (finance company's involvement in scheme to add hidden finance charges, involving false pay stubs, false down payments, and an acquisition fee, not preempted by TILA).

785 Heastie v. Community Bank, 690 F. Supp. 716 (N.D. Ill. 1988); Chandler v. Am. Gen. Fin., Inc., 329 Ill. App. 3d 729, 768 N.E.2d 60 (2002). *See also* Fidelity Fin. Servs. v. Hicks, 214 Ill. App. 3d 398, 574 N.E.2d 15 (1991) (even if interest rate had been authorized by state law, consumer would still have UDAP claim for deception). *But see* Najieb v. William Chrysler-Plymouth, 2002 WL 31906466 (N.D. Ill. Dec. 31, 2002) (failure to disclose that yo-yo sale was conditional is not UDAP violation because TILA does not require this disclosure).

786 Jenkins v. Mercantile Mortgage Co., 231 F. Supp. 2d 737 (N.D. Ill. Sept. 27, 2002).

787 See § 2.3.3.5, *infra* for a discussion as to when courts do and do not find UDAP statutes displaced by an extensive regulation of a practice.

holds that this provision exempts all "regulated" practices. This has disastrous effects because the decision is now precedent that all sorts of regulated professions—from automobile dealers to plumbers—are exempted from the UDAP statute.

For example, South Carolina, in its eagerness to exclude securities transactions from UDAP coverage, ruled that the exclusion for "permitted" practices exempted any transaction if the general activity was regulated, unless the opposing party showed that the specific acts were not covered by the exemption.[788] The result was a decade of litigation with inconsistent results.[789]

The South Carolina Supreme Court, finally faced with the realization that exempting regulated activities would exclude *all* automobile sales from the scope of the UDAP statute, and that its reading of "permitted" as "regulated" was causing more confusion than clarity, recanted its position. The court instead ruled that only specifically "permitted" practices are exempt, and the statute otherwise applies to "regulated" activities.[790] As to UDAP coverage of securities transactions (the origin of the whole problem), the South Carolina Supreme Court instead created an *ad hoc* exclusion only for that type of transaction,[791] the same *ad hoc* exclusion that other courts have made when dealing with UDAP coverage of securities transactions.[792]

Despite the South Carolina experience, other courts occasionally still fall into the same trap. The New Hampshire Supreme Court ran into the same problem when it excluded all attorneys from UDAP coverage because they are "regulated," even though the UDAP statute only excludes "trade or commerce otherwise permitted under laws as administered by any regulatory board or officer" acting under state or federal statutory authority.[793] As in South Carolina, this caused great confusion as trial courts resisted such a broad exemption.[794] In 1992, the New Hampshire Supreme Court decided to limit the exclusion for permitted practices only to situations where existing law specifically permits the challenged conduct.[795] While overturning the general rule, the court indicated that attorney practices were probably still exempt.[796]

Eight years later, in another case involving an attorney, the New Hampshire Supreme Court returned to its original interpretation that trade or commerce is exempt if it is subject to comprehensive regulation by an administrative agency, even if the particular transaction or practice is not specifically authorized.[797] The court limited this exemption by stressing that regulation must be comprehensive and must protect consumers from the same deception, fraud, and unfair practices as the UDAP statute; mere licensing requirements, approval of plans or declarations, limited trade provisions, and consumer protection provisions would be insufficient to exempt an area of trade or commerce.[798]

---

788 State *ex rel.* McLeod v. Rhoades, 275 S.C. 104, 267 S.E.2d 539 (1980). *See also* Smith v. Globe Life Ins., 597 N.W.2d 28 (Mich. 1999) (statutory exemption for "transaction or conduct specifically authorized under laws administered by a regulatory board or officer" would preclude fraudulent practices claim against insurance company whose forms are filed with and approved by Insurance Department, but court finds that another section of UDAP statute authorizes private suit for any UNIP violation; note that a later amendment to the statute has eliminated UDAP causes of attention for UNIP violations).

789 *Compare* NCNB Nat'l Bank v. Tiller, 814 F.2d 931 (4th Cir. 1987) (South Carolina law) (exempting all practices regulated by the Comptroller of the Currency); Anderson v. Citizens Bank, 294 S.C. 387, 365 S.E.2d 26 (Ct. App. 1987) (state regulation of banks exempts banking practices from UDAP coverage); Scott v. Mid Carolina Homes, Inc., 293 S.C. 191, 359 S.E.2d 291 (Ct. App. 1987) (while criticizing *Rhoades*, court feels bound by it to find state regulation of mobile homes excludes UDAP coverage of mobile home transactions) *with* McTeer v. Provident Life & Acc. Ins., 712 F. Supp. 512 (D.S.C. 1989) (narrowly interpreting *Rhoades* so as not to apply to area where state generally regulates but does not regulate the specific practice being complained of); Bocook Outdoor Media, Inc. v. Summey Outdoor Advertising, Inc., 294 S.C. 169, 363 S.E.2d 390 (Ct. App. 1987) (while state regulates billboard advertising, it does not regulate aspect of advertising challenged in this action).

790 Ward v. Dick Dyer & Assocs., Inc., 403 S.E.2d 310 (S.C. 1991). *Accord* Andrade v. Johnson, 345 S.C. 216, 546 S.E.2d 665 (App. 2001) (utility company not exempt unless action is specifically authorized), *rev'd on other grounds*, 588 S.E.2d 588 (S.C. 2003). *See also* Camp v. Springs Mortgage Corp., 414 S.E.2d 784 (S.C. Ct. App. 1991).

791 Ward v. Dick Dyer & Assocs., Inc., 403 S.E.2d 310 (S.C. 1991).

792 *See* § 2.2.9.3, *supra*; *see also* Unisys Corp. v. So. Car. Budget and Control Board, 346 S.C. 158, 551 S.E.2d 263 (2001) (creating special exception for transactions under the state's government procurement code, which has exclusive remedy provision).

793 Rousseau v. Eshleman, 519 A.2d 243 (N.H. 1986).

794 *See* Therrien v. Resource Fin. Group, Inc., 704 F. Supp. 322 (D.N.H. 1989) (regulated banking practices covered by UDAP); WVG v. Pacific Ins. Co., 707 F. Supp. 70 (D.N.H. 1986) (regulated insurance practices covered by UDAP); Globe v. Adolph Coors Co. (*In re* Globe Distributors, Inc.), 111 B.R. 377 (Bankr. D.N.H. 1990) (court distinguishes Rousseau v. Eshleman because regulation of attorneys in that case was more extensive than regulation of franchisor-franchisee relationship); Gelinas v. Metropolitan Property & Liability Ins. Co., 131 N.H. 154, 551 A.2d 962 (1988) (court chooses not to decide whether or not to follow Rousseau v. Eshleman for regulated insurance practices).

795 Gilmore v. Bradgate Assocs., Inc., 604 A.2d 555 (N.H. 1992). *See also* Ford Motor Co. v. Meredith Motor Co., 2000 U.S. Dist. LEXIS 13098 (D.N.H. 2000) (following *Gilmore*), *vacated and remanded on other grounds*, 257 F.3d 67 (1st Cir. 2000); Nault's Automobile Sales, Inc. v. American Honda Motor Co., 148 F.R.D. 25 (D.N.H. 1993) (following *Gilmore*).

796 Gilmore v. Bradgate Assocs., Inc., 604 A.2d 555 (N.H. 1992).

797 Averill v. Cox, 761 A.2d 1083 (N.H. 2000). *Accord* Bell v. Liberty Mut. Ins. Co., 146 N.H. 190, 776 A.2d 1260 (2001) (regulation of insurance is comprehensive and protects consumers from same fraud and unfair practices as UDAP statute, so is exempt).

798 *But see* Couture v. G.W.M., Inc., 2002 WL 31962752 (N.H. Super. Dec. 3, 2002) (deceptive yo-yo sales tactics exempt from

In 2002 the state legislature resolved the issue by replacing the exclusion of trade or commerce "otherwise permitted under laws administered by any regulatory board or officer" with an exclusion that specifies that trade or commerce is exempt if it is subject to the jurisdiction of the bank commissioner, the director of securities regulation, the insurance commissioner, the public utilities commission, the director of securities regulation, the financial institutions and insurance regulators of other states, or federal banking or securities regulators who have authority to regulate unfair or deceptive practices.[799] This language draws a brighter line and it is clear that it does not exempt attorneys, car dealers, contractors, or other industries whose regulators are not specifically listed.

A federal court interpreting the Maine UDAP statute has held that conduct regulated by securities laws is "permitted," leaving the potential for much confusion in Maine over the reach of the term "permitted."[800] This case instead should be seen as joining the significant number of courts that have refused to apply the UDAP statute to securities transactions because of the extensive federal and state law already in the area.[801]

A federal court interpreting Georgia law also equated "specifically authorized" with "highly regulated" in searching for a way to avoid applying the state UDAP statute to the quality of care provided by a nursing home.[802] A bankruptcy court has applied this decision to exempt mortgage brokers as a highly-regulated industry because of the federal laws that apply to credit.[803]

The Michigan Supreme Court has held that its statute's exception for transactions or conduct specifically authorized under laws administered by a regulatory body excludes all acts, even deceptive acts, in regulated transactions.[804] Thus, as long as the defendant acts within the scope of its license, it is exempt.[805] A court applying this decision held the UDAP statute inapplicable to the acts of a licensed mortgage lender since it was specifically authorized under Michigan law to make loans.[806] The existence of a statute regulating transfers of title does not, however, mean that transferring title in a way to conceal a car's salvage status is authorized by statute.[807] And a federal court interpreting the Michigan Supreme Court ruling has confined the exclusion to areas of "heavy regulation," so a suit involving breach of a vehicle warranty is not excluded.[808]

In 2004, over a persuasive dissent, the Rhode Island Supreme Court held that its exemption for "actions or transactions permitted under laws administered by" a state or federal regulatory body meant that the state UDAP statute did not apply to a national bank's deceptive credit card solicitations.[809] The authority of the Office of the Comptroller of the Currency to enforce Truth in Lending standards and the FTC Act's prohibition against unfair and deceptive acts were sufficient to give the bank this exemption. The court reaffirmed a two-step analysis that it had announced in earlier cases. First the party claiming an exemption must show that the general activity in question is regulated by a regulatory body or officer. Then the consumer has the burden of showing that the specific acts at issue are not covered by the exemption.[810] The court has also held a construction company exempt because of its regulation by a state board[811] and a seller of a leveraged funding program exempt because of its regulation by the state insurance department and the Securities and Exchange Commission.[812]

Similarly, the Connecticut Supreme Court has refused to apply the UDAP statute to the leasing of subsidized apartments by a municipal housing authority.[813] So far, the only other entity that the court has found exempt is another governmental body, a municipality, in its performance of a highly-regulated governmental function (tax lien foreclosure).[814] The court has ruled that banks do not fall within

---

the UDAP statute because a cause of action exists under the state motor vehicle laws).

799 N.H. Rev. Stat. Ann. § 358-A:3, *as amended, effective* July 17, 2002.

800 Wyman v. Prime Discount Securities, 819 F. Supp. 79 (D. Me. 1993).

801 *See* § 2.2.9.3, *supra*.

802 Brogdon v. National Healthcare Corp., 103 F. Supp. 2d 1322 (N.D. Ga. 2000). *See also See also* Taylor v. Bear Stearns & Co., 572 F. Supp. 667 (N.D. Ga. 1983) (conduct regulated by administrative agency is exempt; securities transactions not covered); Chancellor v. Gateway Lincoln-Mercury, Inc., 233 Ga. App. 38, 502 S.E.2d 799 (1998) (nondisclosure of discount not UDAP violation because Truth in Lending Act does not require its disclosure); Ferguson v. United Ins. Co., 293 S.E.2d 736 (Ga. App. 1982) (insurance transactions exempt because specifically authorized). *See* § 2.3.3.1, *supra*.

803 *In re* Taylor, 292 B.R. 434 (Bankr. N.D. Ga. 2002).

804 Smith v. Globe Life Ins. Co., 460 Mich. 446, 597 N.W.2d 28 (1999). *See also* Timmons v. DeVoll, 2004 WL 345495 (Mich. App. Feb. 24, 2004) (unpublished, citation limited) (licensed realtor is exempt); Beshada v. Millard Realty, 2004 WL 60321 (Mich. App. Jan. 13, 2004) (UDAP statute does not cover FHA appraisal or realtor's conveyance of appraisal to buyers).

805 Winans v. Paul and Marlene, inc., 2003 WL 21540437 (Mich. App. July 8, 2003) (unpublished, citation limited) (licensed builder's construction of residence exempt; strong dissent).

806 Mills v. Equicredit Corp., 294 F. Supp. 2d 903 (E.D. Mich. 2003).

807 Ross v. Bob Saks Toyota, Inc., Clearinghouse No. 53,543 (Mich. Cir. Ct. July 11, 2001).

808 Watson v. Damon Corp., 2002 WL 32059736 (W.D. Mich. Dec. 17, 2002).

809 Chavers v. Fleet Bank, 844 A.2d 666 (R.I. 2004).

810 *Id.* at *3.

811 Kondracky v. Crystal Restoration, Inc., 791 A.2d 482 (R.I. 2002).

812 State v. Piedmont Funding Corp., 382 A.2d 819 (R.I. 1978).

813 Connelly v. Housing Authority, 213 Conn. 354, 567 A.2d 1212 (1990).

814 City of Danbury v. Dana Investment Corp., 249 Conn. 1, 730 A.2d 1128 (1998).

this exemption.[815] That decision stresses that the bank's practices had not been expressly authorized by any regulation, suggesting that in future cases the court will find the mere existence of regulations insufficient to trigger the exemption.

2.3.3.4 Are Permitted Practices Exempt Even Without an Explicit Statutory Exclusion?

Even if a UDAP statute does not specifically exclude acts permitted under law, there is still an argument that practices permitted by law should not be found unfair or deceptive.[816] It would seem unreasonable to penalize a merchant for complying with the law.

Nevertheless, UDAP statutes are not penal, but only remedial. Consumers should be returned to the status quo and merchants should not be able to take unfair advantage of a practice, even if generally allowed by law. Bringing a collection action in an inconvenient venue is a good example of a practice permitted by state law (the state venue statute) that has still been found to violate a state UDAP statute.[817] An insurance company's practice of denying claims based solely on the results of a polygraph examination of the insured has been held to be a UDAP violation, even though the state insurance regulation on the subject did not prohibit the practice.[818]

2.3.3.5 State Law Displacement of UDAP Coverage

2.3.3.5.1 Introduction

If a UDAP statute does not specifically exclude practices regulated by other statutes, a UDAP defendant may still argue that other state or federal laws displace a UDAP statute's coverage. The mere existence of overlap between the UDAP statute and some other state or federal regulatory scheme is not enough to justify displacement.[819] As one court has pointed out, "occupations with high potential for consumer fraud are commonly licensed."[820]

There are actually two separate issues here. The first issue is whether the state legislature intended other state regulation to exclude UDAP application in certain areas. This issue is discussed in this section. The second issue—whether the federal Supremacy Clause requires that certain federal regulation preempt state regulation in that area—is discussed in § 2.5, *infra*.

The New Jersey Supreme Court has enunciated a cogent framework for analyzing whether another state statute displaces UDAP coverage. Given the strong and sweeping remedial purpose of the typical UDAP statute, it should ordinarily be presumed that the UDAP statute applies to a practice.[821] This is particularly true since the rights, remedies, and prohibitions created by UDAP statutes are intended to be cumulative to those created by other sources of law. By authorizing citizens to act as "private attorneys general," the UDAP statute accomplishes the salutary purpose of expanding fraud-fighting authority and avoiding underregulation by overburdened regulatory agencies that may be captured by the powerful economic players they purport to regulate. If there is a conflict between the UDAP statute and another state regulatory scheme, it must be direct, unavoidable, patent, and sharp before the court will conclude that the UDAP statute is displaced. If at all possible, statutes should be construed to be consistent with each other, and one should be held to preempt the other only if there is a manifest inconsistency between them.[822]

2.3.3.5.2 Impact of explicit statutory language on statute's cumulative or exclusive effect

In determining if a state statute displaces that state's UDAP statute, a good starting place is to examine the language of the two statutes at issue. Does the UDAP statute specifically indicate whether its remedies are cumulative with other state statutes? Some UDAP statutes, for example, state "the provisions of this article are in addition to all other

815 Normand Josef Enterprises v. Conn. Nat'l Bank, 230 Conn. 486, 646 A.2d 1289 (1994).

816 *See, e.g.*, Cel-Tech Communications, Inc. v. Los Angeles Cellular Tel. Co., 83 Cal. Rptr. 2d 548, 973 P.2d 527 (1999); Smith v. State Farm Mut. Auto. Ins. Co., 113 Cal. Rptr. 2d 399 (App. 2001) (practices that are mandated by insurance code can not be UDAP violations); Treski v. Kemper Nat'l Ins. Companies, 674 A.2d 1106 (Pa. Super. 1996) (insurer's use of verbatim disclosure required by insurance law did not violate UDAP statute).

817 Spiegel v. FTC, 540 F.2d 287 (7th Cir. 1976), *aff'g* 86 F.T.C. 425 (1975), *modified*, 89 F.T.C. 1974 (1977); J.C. Penney Co., 109 F.T.C. 54 (1987) (consent order); Benny v. Aldens, Inc., Clearinghouse No. 37,522B (Ill. Cir. Ct. 1984); Shubach v. Household Fin. Corp., 375 Mass. 133, 376 N.E.2d 140 (1978); Celebrezze v. United Research, Inc., 19 Ohio App. 3d 49, 482 N.E.2d 1260 (1984); Santiago v. S.S. Kresge Co., 2 Ohio Op. 3d 54 (C.P. Cuyahoga Cty. 1976).

818 Elder v. Coronet Ins. Co., 201 Ill. App. 3d 733, 558 N.E.2d 1312 (1990). *But see* Association of Personnel Consultants v. Green, 580 N.Y.S.2d 635 (Sup. Ct. 1992) (New York statute exempting certain employment agencies from its prohibition preempted city law).

819 Stop Youth Addiction, Inc. v. Lucky Stores, Inc., 17 Cal. 4th 553, 71 Cal. Rptr. 2d 731 (1998); Normand Josef Enterprises v. Connecticut Bank, 230 Conn. 486, 646 A.2d 1289 (1994).

820 Elder v. Fischer, 717 N.E.2d 730 (Ohio App. 1998), quoting Roberts & Martz, Consumerism Comes of Age: Treble Damages and Attorney Fees in Consumer Transactions—The Ohio Consumer Sales Practices Act, 42 Ohio St. L. J. 927, 959 (1981).

821 Lemelledo v. Beneficial Management Corp., 150 N.J. 255, 696 A.2d 546 (1997).

822 Showpiece Homes Corp. v. Assurance Co. of Am., 38 P.3d 47 (Colo. 2001). *See also* Ciardi v. F. Hoffmann-La Roche, Ltd., 436 Mass. 53, 762 N.E.2d 303 (2002).

causes of action, remedies, and penalties," and it has been held that this language prevents displacement.[823] Similarly, if the alternative regulatory scheme specifically states that its remedies are cumulative and not exclusive, the UDAP statute should also apply.[824] If another statute states that it overrides the UDAP statute to the extent of any conflict, it does not prevent a UDAP claim when there is no conflict between the two laws.[825] Conversely, if another, more specific statute explicitly states it is the exclusive remedy, that statute is likely to displace the UDAP statute.[826] Language in the UDAP statute that specifically exempts particular entities is also a strong indication that other entities are not exempt.[827]

UDAP statutes often state that violations of certain enumerated statutes are *per se* UDAP violations. The fact that a specific statutory violation is not among those listed does not show legislative intent to displace UDAP coverage in those areas.[828] UDAP statutes are to be liberally construed,[829] and the legislature can not be expected to catalog every statute that does not override the UDAP statute.

2.3.3.5.3 Jurisdictions that reject displacement

Some jurisdictions generally reject the view that other regulation displaces a UDAP statute's applicability, no matter the extensiveness of the alternative regulatory scheme.[830] For example, Pennsylvania courts hold that a statute that regulates a particular transaction will be held to override the state's UDAP law only if the statute explicitly states that it supplies the exclusive remedy or if the two statutes are in

---

823 State *ex rel.* Corbin v. Pickrell, 136 Ariz. 589, 667 P.2d 1304 (1983); Stop Youth Addiction, Inc. v. Lucky Stores, Inc., 17 Cal. 4th 553, 71 Cal. Rptr. 2d 731 (1998); Cybal v. Atrium Palace Syndicate, 272 N.J. Super. 330, 639 A.2d 1146 (1994); Skinner v. Steele, 730 S.W.2d 335 (Tenn. Ct. App. 1987); Frizzell v. Cook, 790 S.W.2d 41 (Tex. App. 1990). *See also* Elder v. Fischer, 717 N.E.2d 730 (Ohio App. 1998) (UDAP statute's statement that its remedies are cumulative is a factor favoring non-displacement).

824 People *ex rel.* Orloff v. Pacific Bell, 31 Cal. 4th 1132, 7 Cal. Rptr. 3d 315, 80 P.3d 201 (2003) (interpreting Cal. statutes to allow district attorneys to sue public utilities for deceptive practices unless suit would interfere with a PUC enforcement proceeding); Rothschild v. Tyco Int'l (US), Inc., 83 Cal. App. 4th 488, 99 Cal. Rptr. 2d 721 (2000) (state *qui tam* statute which states that its remedies are in addition to those under other laws does not displace UDAP statute); Showpiece Homes Corp. v. Assurance Co. of Am., 38 P.3d 47 (Colo. 2001) (language in insurance code indicated that other remedies were preserved); State *ex rel.* Webster v. Myers, 779 S.W.2d 286 (Mo. Ct. App. 1989); Myint v. Allstate Ins. Co., 970 S.W.2d 920 (Tenn. 1998). *But see* Nobrega v. Edison Glen Assocs., 167 N.J. 520, 772 A.2d 368 (2001) (interpreting ambiguous statutory language in real estate sales statute to displace UDAP statute).

825 Sanders v. Construction Equity, Inc., 42 S.W.3d 364 (Tex. App. 2001).

826 Winterberg v. CNA Ins. Co., 868 F. Supp. 713 (E.D. Pa. 1994) (workers' compensation law provides exclusive remedy and bars UDAP claim); Hughes v. Argonaut Ins. Co., 88 Cal. App. 4th 517, 105 Cal. Rptr. 2d 877 (2001) (workers' compensation system provides exclusive remedy for dispute between worker and workers' compensation insurance provider over how much of tort settlement it can take); Unisys Corp. v. So. Car. Budget and Control Board, 346 S.C. 158, 551 S.E.2d 263 (2001) (exclusive remedy provision of government procurement code bars UDAP claim); Deeter v. Safeway Stores, Inc., 50 Wash. App. 67, 747 P.2d 1103 (1987) (state workers' compensation act explicitly states it is exclusive remedy, and thus preempts UDAP); *see also* Denison v. Kelly, 759 F. Supp. 199 (M.D. Pa. 1991) (securities law does not state that it provides exclusive remedy, so UDAP statute also applies; optional treble damages under UDAP do not conflict with legislative goals in securities law cases). *But see* St. Paul Fire & Marine Ins. Co. v. Ellis & Ellis, 262 F.3d 53 (1st Cir. 2001) (Mass. law) (attorney's scheme to defraud workers' compensation insurers is covered by UDAP statute even though he used adversarial workers' compensation litigation as part of scheme); Penny v. Southwestern Bell Tel. Co., 906 F.2d 183 (5th Cir. 1990) (Texas law) (although public utility commission has exclusive jurisdiction to regulate rates, it does not have exclusive jurisdiction over misrepresentations and deceptive conduct); Vacanti v. State Compensation Ins. Fund, 24 Cal. 4th 800, 14 P.3d 234 (2001) (exclusive remedy provision does not bar UDAP suit against workers' compensation carriers for conspiracy to mishandle claims, although claims regarding mere mishandling of claims are barred).

827 Showpiece Homes Corp. v. Assurance Co. of Am., 38 P.3d 47 (Colo. 2001); Myint v. Allstate Ins. Co., 970 S.W.2d 920 (Tenn. 1998).

828 Showpiece Homes Corp. v. Assurance Co. of Am., 38 P.3d 47 (Colo. 2001); Drouillard v. Keister Williams Newspaper Servs., Inc., 108 N.C. App. 169, 423 S.E.2d 324 (1992); Pruit v. Orr, 991 S.W.2d 312 (Tex. App. 1999) (Smoke Detector Act precludes UDAP-based habitability claim). *See also* United Virginia Bank v. Air-Lift Assocs., 79 N.C. App. 315, 339 S.E.2d 90 (1986); Ellis v. Smith-Broadhurst, Inc., 48 N.C. App. 180, 268 S.E.2d 271 (1980); Edminsten v. Chemical Co., 45 N.C. App. 604, 263 S.E.2d 849 (1980). *But see* Kuhnel v. CNA Ins. Cos., 322 N.J. Super. 568, 731 A.2d 564 (App. Div. 1999) (UDAP statute does not cover claims involving payment of workers' compensation benefits); Daubner v. Firemans' Fund Ins. Co., 31 Pa. D. & C.4th 449 (C.P. Butler 1996) (Workers' Compensation Act is exclusive remedy).

829 *See* § 3.1.2, *infra*.

830 Nault's Automobile Sales, Inc. v. American Honda Motor Co., 148 F.R.D. 25 (D.N.H. 1993); Morse v. Mutual Fed. Sav. & Loan Ass'n of Whitman, 536 F. Supp. 1271 (D. Mass. 1982); Stop Youth Addiction, Inc. v. Lucky Stores, Inc., 17 Cal. 4th 553, 71 Cal. Rptr. 2d 731 (1998); Hewlett v. Squaw Valley Ski Corp., 63 Cal. Rptr. 2d 118 (Ct. App. 1997); McGrath v. Mishara, 386 Mass. 74, 434 N.E.2d 1215 (1982); Lowell Gas Co. v. Attorney General, 377 Mass. 37, 385 N.E.2d 240 (1979); Dodd v. Commercial Union Ins. Co., 373 Mass. 72, 365 N.E.2d 802 (1977); SDK Medical Computer Serv. Corp. v. Professional Operating Management Group, Inc., 371 Mass. 117, 354 N.E.2d 852 (1976); DePasquale v. Odgen Suffolk Downs, Inc., 29 Mass. App. Ct. 658, 564 N.E.2d 584 (1990) (mere regulation of horse racing does not preclude UDAP coverage); Gabriel v. O'Hara, 368 Pa. Super. 383, 534 A.2d 488 (1987); Frizzell v. Cook, 790 S.W.2d 41 (Tex. App. 1990). *See also* Setliff Bros. Serv. v. Bureau of Automotive Repair, 62 Cal. Rptr. 2d 25 (Cal. App. 1997); Midpeninsula Citizens for Fair Hous. v. Westwood Investors, 221 Cal. App. 3d 1377, 271 Cal. Rptr. 99 (1990).

irreconcilable conflict.[831] But while federal and state banking legislation does not preempt a state attorney general from issuing debt collection regulations under the UDAP statute, the state banking department has exclusive authority to enforce those regulations against banks.[832]

The California Supreme Court similarly states that the UDAP statute is only displaced if a later statute is in irreconcilable conflict with the UDAP statute.[833] Even with a specific statutory enforcement scheme for another statute, a parallel UDAP action is still permitted.[834] If the legislature has legitimized specific behavior, that behavior can not be the basis of a claim under California's unfair competition statute.[835] But the legislature's mere failure to prohibit an activity does not provide a safe harbor from suit.[836] California allows UDAP suits to proceed against utility companies unless an award of damages would directly contravene a specific order or decision of the PUC or would undermine a general supervisory or regulatory policy of the PUC.[837]

In New Jersey, the UDAP statute applies unless there is a "direct and unavoidable" and "nearly irreconcilable" conflict with another statute. The conflict must be "patent and sharp, and must not simply constitute a mere possibility of incompatibility."[838] The fact that an industry is highly regulated is irrelevant to coverage under New York's statute.[839]

831 Denison v. Kelly, 759 F. Supp. 199 (M.D. Pa. 1991) (securities transactions are not exempt from UDAP coverage); Gabriel v. O'Hara, 368 Pa. Super. 383, 534 A.2d 488 (1987).

832 Pennsylvania Bankers Ass'n v. Commonwealth, 58 Pa. Commw. 170, 427 A.2d 730 (1981). *See also* Hartigan v. Northern Illinois Mortgage Co., 201 Ill. App. 3d 356, 559 N.E.2d 14 (1990) (remanding case to determine scope of attorney general's enforcement authority over entity licensed by banking commissioner).

833 Stop Youth Addiction, Inc. v. Lucky Stores, Inc., 17 Cal. 4th 553, 71 Cal. Rptr. 2d 731 (1998).

834 *Id.*

835 Cel-Tech Communications, Inc. v. Los Angeles Cellular Tel. Co., 83 Cal. Rptr. 2d 548, 973 P.2d 527 (1999). *See also* Aiello v. First Alliance Mortg. Co. (*In re* First Alliance Mortg. Co.), 280 B.R. 246 (C.D. Cal. 2002); Olszewski v. Scripps Health, 135 Cal. Rptr. 2d 1, 69 P.3d 927 (2003) (no UDAP damages liability for taking action specifically permitted by state statute, even though court holds statute preempted by federal law); Schnall v. Hertz Corp., 78 Cal. App. 4th 1144, 93 Cal. Rptr. 2d 439 (2000).

836 Cel-Tech Communications, Inc. v. Los Angeles Cellular Tel. Co., 83 Cal. Rptr. 2d 548, 973 P.2d 527 (1999).

837 Cundiff v. Bell Atlantic Corp., 101 Cal. App. 4th 1395, 125 Cal. Rptr. 2d 445 (2002) (suit alleging deceptive billing may proceed in court); Wise v. Pacific Gas & Elec. Co., 77 Cal. App. 4th 287, 91 Cal. Rptr. 2d 479 (1999).

838 Lemelledo v. Beneficial Management Corp., 150 N.J. 255, 696 A.2d 546 (1997). *But cf.* Doug Grant, Inc. v. Greate Bay Casino Corp, 232 F.3d 173 (3d Cir. 2000) (pervasive state regulation of casino gambling creates possibility of conflict and UDAP statute is displaced by the state's Casino Control Act).

839 Greenspan v. Allstate Ins. Co., 937 F. Supp. 288 (S.D.N.Y. 1996).

2.3.3.5.4 Other jurisdictions adopt a balancing approach

While certain courts almost never find the UDAP statute displaced by more specific state regulation, other courts adopt a balancing approach. They look to see the legislative intent behind the other state law, how extensive is the regulation,[840] what kind of private remedies are offered by that other state law, and what the other state law says about the specific challenged practice. For this group of courts, a key issue will be whether the state regulation provides adequate relief to an injured consumer, or whether displacement of a UDAP statute would prevent the consumer from being compensated for his or her damages.[841]

Where another state statute establishes detailed rules about the contractual relationship between two parties, courts may be wary of allowing a UDAP claim to alter that relationship.[842] Another factor considered by Connecticut courts is the extent of activity by the FTC and the state consumer protection commissioner in the area.[843]

Thus, adopting this overall balancing approach, a few states hold that a state's UDAP statute is preempted in the landlord-tenant area by the extensive regulation of that state's landlord-tenant act.[844] In California, the state slack-

840 Association of Personnel Consultants v. Green, 580 N.Y.S.2d 635 (Sup. Ct. 1992) (comprehensiveness and detail of state law are factors favoring preemption).

841 Penny v. Southwestern Bell Tel. Co., 906 F.2d 183 (5th Cir. 1990) (Texas law); Skeet v. Sears, Roebuck & Co., 760 F. Supp. 872 (D. Kan. 1991); Quincy Cablesystems, Inc. v. Sully's Bar, Inc., 684 F. Supp. 1138 (D. Mass. 1988); Griswold v. Union Labor Life Ins. Co., 186 Conn. 507, 442 A.2d 920 (1982); Cabot Corp. v. Baddour, 394 Mass. 720, 477 N.E.2d 399 (1985); Attorney General v. Diamond Mortgage Co., 414 Mich. 603, 327 N.W.2d 805 (1982); Westervelt v. Gateway Fin. Serv., 190 N.J. Super. 615, 464 A.2d 1203 (Super. Ct. Ch. Div. 1983); Culbreth v. Lawrence J. Miller, Inc., 328 Pa. Super. 374, 477 A.2d 491 (1984); State v. Schwab, 693 P.2d 108 (Wash. 1985). The line of cases holding that state and federal securities laws preempt a UDAP action in that area can probably be explained by the fact that federal and state securities legislation offer consumers adequate remedies. *See* § 2.2.9.3, *supra*. *See also* Elder v. Fischer, 717 N.E.2d 730 (Ohio App. 1998) (less complete remedies under other statute would be a factor favoring non-displacement).

842 Schnall v. Hertz Corp., 78 Cal. App. 4th 1144, 93 Cal. Rptr. 2d 439 (2000) (state statute that explicitly authorized fuel service charges for rental cars and did not specify a ceiling precluded challenge to their unconscionability but not to deceptive manner in which consumers were induced to incur them); New England Inv. Properties, Inc. v. Spice Realty & Dev. Corp., 31 Conn. App. 682, 626 A.2d 1316 (1993) (state law regulates real estate broker commissions).

843 Normand Josef Enterprises v. Connecticut Bank, 230 Conn. 486, 646 A.2d 1289 (1994).

844 Connelly v. New Haven Hous. Auth., 213 Conn. 354, 567 A.2d 1212 (1990) (HUD regulation preempts public housing tenants' UDAP claims as to habitability); Chelsea Plaza Homes, Inc. v. Moore, 226 Kan. 430, 601 P.2d 1100 (1979); Heritage Hills, Ltd. v. Deacon, 49 Ohio St. 3d 80, 551 N.E.2d 125 (1990); State v. Schwab, 693 P.2d 108 (Wash. 1985); Carlie v. Morgan, 922

fill law which holds only manufacturers, not retailers, liable for slack-fill practices, preempts use of a UDAP statute to attack a retailer's slack-fill practices.[845] A New Jersey appellate decision exempts hospitals providing medical services, citing policy reasons and the state's regulation of hospitals.[846] A special state medical malpractice law setting up a pre-litigation screening panel preempts a UDAP claim based on medical malpractice.[847] A state's odometer law passed subsequent to the Missouri UDAP statute and which provided adequate private remedies was found to preempt UDAP regulation of the specific practices prohibited by the odometer statute.[848] The next year, however, the state legislature overruled this decision by clarifying that the odometer law's remedies were cumulative and in addition to any other remedies.[849] A franchise practices statute enacted after the UDAP statute with slightly different private remedies has been found to preempt the UDAP statute.[850]

Arizona courts at one time followed this approach and found the UDAP statute preempted by a securities regulation act that was comprehensive and detailed, providing a complete administrative enforcement scheme that specifically attacked fraud.[851] The holding in this case no longer applies because the statute[852] was amended in 1981 so that "the provisions of this article are in addition to all other causes of action, remedies, and penalties available to this state."[853] Even before the amendment, the state's regulation of funeral directors did not preempt a UDAP challenge to funeral practices, since the regulation of funeral directors was not directed to fraud or to effective investigation and enforcement of the practices before the court.[854] Similarly, Kansas' landlord-tenant law is a comprehensive statute with adequate private remedies and thus preempts the UDAP statute,[855] but the state regulation of optometrists provides no special private remedies and thus does not preempt a claim against an optometrist.[856]

2.3.3.5.5 *Whichever approach adopted, most UDAP claims are not displaced by other state regulation*

Whether a court rejects displacement of UDAP statutes outright or adopts a balancing approach, most case law finds that the UDAP statute is not displaced by other state regulation. UDAP statutes have been found *not* displaced by the following:

- State insurance codes;[857]
- State regulation of insurance adjusters;[858]
- Federal and state credit statutes;[859]
- Utility regulation;[860]
- Regulation of household movers, freight shippers, and airlines;[861]
- The Uniform Commercial Code;[862]

P.2d 1 (Utah 1996) (holding that Utah's Fit Premises Act displaces UDAP statute for tenant uninhabitability claims). *See also* Property Exchange & Sales, Inc. v. King, 863 S.W.2d 12 (Mo. Ct. App. 1993) (state law relating to lease security deposits, which provides multiple damages, displaces UDAP claim). *But see* Conaway v. Prestia, CVN-803-76 (Conn. Super. Ct. 1981), *aff'd*, 191 Conn. 484, 464 A.2d 847 (1983); State v. Connelly, Clearinghouse No. 40,634 (Md. Cir. Ct. Baltimore Cty. 1985); McGrath v. Mishara, 386 Mass. 74, 434 N.E.2d 1215 (1982); Wiener v. People by Abrams, 119 Misc. 2d 970, 464 N.Y.S.2d 919 (Sup. Ct. 1983); Weller v. Department of Agriculture, Trade & Consumer Protection, No. 78-813 (Wis. Ct. App. 1980), *aff'd*, 109 Wis. 2d 665, 327 N.W.2d 178 (1982). *See generally* § 2.2.6.2, *supra*.

845 Hobby Indus. Ass'n v. Younger, 101 Cal. App. 3d 358, 161 Cal. Rptr. 601 (1980).

846 Hampton Hosps. v. Bresan, 288 N.J. Super. 372, 672 A.2d 725 (App. 1996).

847 Keyser v. St. Mary's Hosps., Inc., 662 F. Supp. 191 (D. Idaho 1987); Bremer v. Community Hosps., 583 N.E.2d 780 (Ind. Ct. App. 1991).

848 Dover v. Stanley, 652 S.W.2d 258 (Mo. Ct. App. 1983).

849 State *ex rel.* Webster v. Myers, 779 S.W.2d 286 (Mo. App. 1989).

850 New Hampshire Auto Dealers v. General Motors Corp., 620 F. Supp. 1150 (D.N.H. 1985); Reiter Oldsmobile, Inc. v. General Motors Corp., 378 Mass. 707, 393 N.E.2d 376 (1979).

851 People *ex rel.* Babbitt v. Green Acres Trust, 127 Ariz. 160, 618 P.2d 1086 (Ct. App. 1980).

852 Ariz. Rev. Stat. Ann. § 44-1533(A).

853 *See* State *ex rel.* Corbin v. Pickrell, 136 Ariz. 589, 667 P.2d 1304 (1983). *See also* Madsen v. Western Am. Mortg. Co., 694 P.2d 1228 (Ariz. Ct. App. 1985); Villegas v. Transamerica Fin. Servs., 147 Ariz. 100, 708 P.2d 781 (Ct. App. 1985).

854 People *ex rel.* Babbitt v. Green Acres Trust, 127 Ariz. 160, 618 P.2d 1086 (Ct. App. 1980).

855 Chelsea Plaza Homes, Inc. v. Moore, 226 Kan. 430, 601 P.2d 1100 (1979).

856 Skeet v. Sears, Roebuck & Co., 760 F. Supp. 872 (D. Kan. 1991).

857 *See* § 2.3.1.3, *supra*.

858 Culbreth v. Lawrence J. Miller, Inc., 328 Pa. Super. 374, 477 A.2d 491 (1984).

859 *See* § 2.2.1.6, *supra*.

860 *See* § 2.3.2, *supra*.

861 Tousley v. North Am. Van Lines, Inc., 752 F.2d 96 (4th Cir. 1985) (South Carolina UDAP statute's exemption for actions permitted under other laws did not preempt UDAP claim for inducing trucker to become owner-operator); American Transfer & Storage Co. v. Brown, 584 S.W.2d 284 (Tex. Civ. App. 1979), *aff'd*, 601 S.W.2d 931 (Tex. 1980); National Van Lines v. Lifshen, 584 S.W.2d 298 (Tex. Civ. App. 1979).*But see* Mendelson v. Trans World Airlines, 466 N.Y.S.2d 168 (Sup. Ct. 1983) (no UDAP violation where carrier complies with CAB required disclosures concerning overbooking). *See also* § 2.5.5, *infra* (discussion of federal preemption).

862 Williams-Garrett v. Murphy, 106 F. Supp. 2d 834 (D.S.C. 2000) (compliance with U.C.C. not a UDAP defense); International Minerals & Mining Co. v. Citicorp N. Am., Inc., 736 F. Supp. 587 (D.N.J. 1990) (UDAP claims in lender liability case not preempted by U.C.C.); D'Angelo v. Miller Yacht Sales, 261 N.J. Super. 683, 619 A.2d 689 (1992); Dreier Co. v. Unitronix Corp., 218 N.J. Super. 260, 527 A.2d 875 (App. Div. 1986); United Virginia Bank v. Air-Lift Assocs., Inc., 339 S.E.2d 90 (N.C. Ct. App. 1986).

- State lemon laws;[863]
- State used car warranty laws;[864]
- Employment agency regulation;[865]
- State regulation of dentists;[866]
- Regulation of nursing homes by the state health department;[867]
- State licensing and regulation of accountants;[868]
- Mobile home park laws;[869]
- Landlord-tenant regulation;[870]
- State real estate board regulation,[871] including a specific statute regulating real estate fraud;[872]
- State securities laws;[873]
- A state statute regulating condominium sales;[874]
- State regulation of community antenna television and cable systems;[875] and
- State antitrust regulation.[876]

2.3.3.6 Exhaustion of Administrative Remedies

2.3.3.6.1 Must consumer exhaust administrative remedies?

Even if a regulatory scheme does not preempt the UDAP statute, some courts may require litigants to exhaust administrative remedies. In some states this issue may be resolved by explicit statutory language. Several UDAP statutes specifically indicate that exhaustion of administrative remedies is not required.[877]

On the other hand, a few UDAP statutes specifically require that complaints first be referred to applicable state regulatory agencies. A Georgia court, however, found this requirement did not apply where the state agency had never prohibited the alleged practice (in this case odometer rollbacks).[878]

Normally, though, there will be no legislative language indicating whether administrative remedies must be exhausted. In that case, courts usually find that exhaustion is not required. The Michigan Supreme Court overturned an appellate decision requiring that a complaint against a real estate broker first be brought before the agency licensing such brokers.[879] The court ruled that where the regulatory body could not provide the requested relief, there was no requirement of exhaustion of administrative remedies. There was no pervasive regulatory scheme which might be thrown out of balance by court review of the facts.[880] A Colorado court held that nursing home residents need not present their complaints about the quality of care to the federal and state agencies administering the Medicare and Medicaid programs, as those agencies did not have the authority to grant the remedy the residents sought.[881]

The Washington Supreme Court agrees that exhaustion of administrative remedies is not required where the agency has neither technical expertise nor authority to grant the requested relief.[882] The West Virginia Supreme Court has

863 Tennessee Attorney General Opinion Letter to Honorable Pam Gaia, Tennessee House of Representatives, Clearinghouse No. 38,905B (Sept. 21, 1984) (although the lemon law requires the consumer to choose which statute to use).

864 Twardy v. L.B. Sales, Inc., 2000 Minn. App. LEXIS 636 (June 27, 2000) (unpublished, limited precedent).

865 Steele v. State *ex rel.* Gorton, 85 Wash. 2d 585, 537 P.2d 782 (1975). *But see* Association of Personnel Consultants v. Green, 580 N.Y.S.2d 635 (Sup. Ct. 1992) (New York City law regulating certain employment agencies preempted by state statute exempting them).

866 Investigators Inc. v. Harvey, 53 Or. App. 586, 633 P.2d 6 (1981).

867 Elder v. Fischer, 717 N.E.2d 730 (Ohio App. 1998). *But see* Brogdon v. National Healthcare Corp., 103 F. Supp. 2d 1322 (N.D. Ga. 2000).

868 Am. Indian and Alaska Native Cultural and Arts Dev. Inst. v. Daymon & Assocs., 1999 U.S. Dist. LEXIS 22380 (D.N.M. June 23, 1999).

869 Ethridge v. Hwang, 105 Wash. App. 447, 20 P.3d 958 (2001).

870 *See* § 2.2.6.2, *supra.*

871 *In re* Real Estate Litigation, 95 Wash. 2d 297, 622 P.2d 1185 (1980); *see also* Attorney General v. Diamond Mortgage Co., 414 Mich. 603, 327 N.W.2d 805 (1982).

872 Manchac v. Pace, 608 S.W.2d 314 (Tex. Civ. App. 1980). *Cf.* Bruce v. Jim Walters Homes, Inc., 943 S.W.2d 121 (Tex. App. 1997) (Texas Residential Construction Liability Act not preemptive of common law fraud).

873 *See* § 2.2.9.3, *supra* (case law in this area is split between displacement and no displacement).

874 Cybul v. Atrium Palace Syndicate, 272 N.J. Super. 330, 639 A.2d 1146 (1994).

875 Quincy Cablesystems, Inc. v. Sully's Bar, Inc., 684 F. Supp. 1138 (D. Mass. 1988).

876 Mack v. Bristol-Myers Squibb Co., 673 So. 2d 100 (Fla. Dist. Ct. App. 1996); Blake v. Abbott Laboratories, Inc., 1996 Tenn. App. LEXIS 184 (Apr. 24, 1996) (state UDAP statute applicable in addition to state antitrust statute to anti-competitive conduct where UDAP statute prohibits "unfair" practices). *Contra* Gaebler v. New Mexico Potash Corp., 676 N.E.2d 228 (Ill. App. Ct. 1996) (price fixing claim had to be brought under state antitrust act, not UDAP statute); Abbott Laboratories, Inc. v. Segura, 907 S.W.2d 503 (Tex. 1995) (consumers could not use Texas UDAP statute to avoid *Illinois Brick*'s application to Texas anti-trust statute). *See generally* § 4.10, *infra.*

877 *See, e.g.,* Mass. Gen. Laws ch. 93A, § 9(6). This statute, as amended, overturns the findings in Nelson v. Blue Shield of Massachusetts, 377 Mass. 746, 387 N.E.2d 589 (1979); Little v. Rosenthal, 382 N.E.2d 1037 (Mass. 1978); Gordon v. Hardware Mut. Casualty Co., 361 Mass. 582, 281 N.E.2d 573 (1972).

878 State v. Meredith Chevrolet, Inc., 145 Ga. App. 8, 244 S.E.2d 15 (1978), *aff'd*, 242 Ga. 294, 249 S.E.2d 87 (1978).

879 Attorney General v. Diamond Mortgage Corp., 414 Mich. 603, 327 N.W.2d 805 (1982), *rev'g* 102 Mich. App. 322, 301 N.W.2d 523 (1981).

880 Attorney General v. Diamond Mortgage Co., 414 Mich. 603, 327 N.W.2d 805 (1982). *See also* Penny v. Southwestern Bell Tel. Co., 906 F.2d 183 (5th Cir. 1990) (Texas law).

881 Salas v. Grancare, Inc., 22 P.3d 568 (Colo. App. 2001).

882 Vogt v. Seattle-First Nat'l Bank, 117 Wash. 2d 541, 817 P.2d 1364 (1991); *In re* Real Estate Litigation, 95 Wash. 2d 297, 622 P.2d 1185 (1980); State v. Multiple Listing Serv., 95 Wash. 2d 280, 622 P.2d 1190 (1980). *But see* Miller v. U.S. Bank of Washington, N.A., 72 Wash. App. 416, 865 P.2d 536 (1994) (Comptroller of Currency has primary jurisdiction of aspects of

ruled that the state public utility commission does not have exclusive jurisdiction over matters concerning maintenance of telephone wires within consumers' homes, so plaintiffs need not exhaust administrative remedies before bringing suit in state court on UDAP and other statutory and common law claims.[883]

A Pennsylvania intermediate appellate court required UDAP plaintiffs to make an administrative complaint to the state Insurance Department before filing a UDAP suit that was based on violations of state insurance laws.[884] A North Carolina court required exhaustion of administrative remedies only in an unusual case where a specialized state board was uniquely equipped to determine whether a workers' compensation insurer's action was correct.[885] Even in the workers' compensation context, though, exhaustion may not be required if the UDAP claims are outside the board's authority.[886] A Georgia appellate court ruled that a plaintiff who alleges insurance code violations in a RICO suit does not necessarily have to exhaust administrative remedies with the state insurance commissioner.[887] But the Texas Supreme Court held that a car dealer had to exhaust administrative remedies where a state statute gave the Motor Vehicle Board exclusive jurisdiction to resolve claims between dealers and manufacturers.[888]

Where a court finds that administrative remedies must first be exhausted, one option is to suspend the lawsuit instead of dismissing it.[889] This option may be particularly appropriate where only the UDAP action (not the administrative proceeding) can award damages, or where dismissal may bar a damage action because the statute of limitations will run.[890]

national banking that it regulates).

883 State *ex rel.* Bell Atlantic v. Ranson, 497 S.E.2d 755 (W. Va. 1997).

884 Moy v. Schreiber Deed Security Co., 572 A.2d 758 (Pa. Super. Ct. 1990). *See also* § 5.3.2.2.3, *infra.*

885 North Carolina Chiropractic Ass'n, Inc. v. Aetna Casualty & Surety Co., 89 N.C. App. 1, 365 S.E.2d 312 (1988). *See also* Johnson v. First Union Corp., 131 N.C. App. 142, 504 S.E.2d 808 (1998) (comprehensive regulatory scheme precludes claims except through workers' compensation system).

886 Golden v. Employers Ins. of Wausau, 981 F. Supp. 467 (S.D. Tex. 1997).

887 Provident Indemnity Life Ins. Co. v. James, 506 S.E.2d 892 (Ga. App. 1998).

888 Subaru of America, Inc. v. David McDavid Nissan, Inc., 84 S.W.3d 212 (Tex. 2002).

889 Subaru of America, Inc. v. David McDavid Nissan, Inc., 84 S.W.3d 212 (Tex. 2002) (auto dealer must exhaust administrative remedies before suing manufacturer); Oh v. AT&T Corp., 76 F. Supp. 2d 551 (D.N.J. 1999).

890 Lowell Gas Co. v. Attorney General, 377 Mass. 37, 385 N.E.2d 240 (1979); J&J Enterprises, Inc. v. Martignetti, 369 Mass. 535, 341 N.E.2d 645 (1976); Frank J. Linhares Co. v. Reliance Ins., 4 Mass. App. Ct. 617, 357 N.E.2d 313 (1976); North Carolina Chiropractic Ass'n, Inc. v. Aetna Casualty & Surety Co., 89 N.C. App. 1, 365 S.E.2d 312 (1988).

2.3.3.6.2 The doctrine of primary jurisdiction

Where an agency has special competence to decide an issue, the doctrine of primary jurisdiction gives the court discretion to delay exercising its jurisdiction until after the administrative agency has determined some aspect of the issues before the court. This is not a requirement that the consumer exhaust the administrative process and there is no requirement that the agency determine the issue in question. The case can always be returned to the court for trial.

For example, the Fifth Circuit found jurisdiction to consider a UDAP claim that a telephone company had engaged in misrepresentations, retaliation, and the use of discriminatory rates even though the state public utility commission had exclusive jurisdiction over rate setting issues.[891] The misrepresentation and retaliation claims were not "rate setting" and the public utility commission had no authority to award damages for past discriminatory rates.[892]

But, while the UDAP claim could proceed, the court was impressed that the public utility commission had special competence to determine whether the rates were discriminatory. The court thus chose to refer that particular issue to the commission to see if the commission would choose to determine the issue. The case would then be returned to the court for a ruling concerning what actions to take if the rates were found discriminatory and to determine the misrepresentation and retaliation claims.[893]

Texas courts apply the doctrine of primary jurisdiction in situations where the court and the administrative agency have concurrent jurisdiction over a UDAP claim.[894] The California Supreme Court has also applied the doctrine of primary jurisdiction to a UDAP action. Even where the basis for a UDAP claim is a violation of the state insurance code, there is no requirement of exhaustion of administrative remedies.[895] But a court in its judgment may determine that a particular issue is best first addressed by the insurance department, and not the courts, particularly where the insurance department is better equipped to resolve the issue than the courts.[896]

891 Penny v. Southwestern Bell Tel. Co., 906 F.2d 183 (5th Cir. 1990) (Texas law); *see also* Oh v. AT&T Corp., 76 F. Supp. 2d 551 (D.N.J. 1999). *See* § 5.6.10, *infra.*

892 Penny v. Southwestern Bell Tel. Co., 906 F.2d 183 (5th Cir. 1990) (Texas law); *see also In re* Methyl Tertiary Butyl Ether Prods. Liab. Litigation, 175 F. Supp. 2d 593 (S.D.N.Y. 2001) (declining to refer UDAP claim involving pollution of wells to primary jurisdiction of environmental protection agencies).

893 Penny v. Southwestern Bell Tel. Co., 906 F.2d 183 (5th Cir. 1990) (Texas law). *Accord* Allen v. State Farm Fire & Cas. Co., 59 F. Supp. 2d 1217 (S.D. Ala. 1999) (dismissing UDAP suit because insurance commissioner had primary jurisdiction).

894 *See, e.g.*, Bur-Cold Express, Inc. v. Parker Hannifin Corp., 808 F. Supp. 553 (S.D. Tex. 1992).

895 Farmers Ins. Exchange v. Superior Court (The People), 6 Cal. Rptr. 2d 487, 826 P.2d 730 (1992).

896 *Id. See also* State Farm Fire & Cas. Co. v. Superior Court, 53 Cal. Rptr. 2d 229 (Ct. App. 1996) (primary jurisdiction does not

In another case arising out of California, the Ninth Circuit noted that the relevant factors are whether application of the policy will (1) enhance court decision-making and efficiency by allowing the court to take advantage of administrative expertise; and (2) help assure uniform application of regulatory laws. The court declined to refer a dispute about life insurance rates for a person with a rare ailment to the insurance commissioner, because the ailment was so rare that uniformity would not be affected.[897]

The West Virginia Supreme Court has used a similar analysis in upholding a trial court's decision to exercise jurisdiction over a UDAP claim involving a telephone company's deceptive tactics in the sale of inside wire maintenance contracts.[898] The decision holds that the relevant factors are whether the question is within the conventional experience of judges; whether the question lies peculiarly within the agency's discretion or requires the exercise of agency expertise; whether there is a danger of inconsistent rulings; and whether a prior application to the agency has been made.[899]

The Washington Supreme Court, listing similar but not identical factors, has ruled that the doctrine does not bar a court from hearing a challenge to deceptive advertising of cellular telephone service rates.[900] Likewise, the Massachusetts Supreme Judicial Court rejected an argument that the state chiropractor registration board had primary jurisdiction over a UDAP claim that a chiropractic group had submitted unreasonable and unnecessary bills to an insurance company.[901] The court noted that questions of deceptive billing do not require agency expertise, and the board could not award the damages relief that the insurance company sought. But a Pennsylvania court has upheld the trial court's decision that the insurance department had primary jurisdiction over a UDAP challenge that affected rates.

The New Mexico Supreme Court affirmed a decision that the state public utility commission had primary jurisdiction over a suit seeking injunctive relief that would have affected telephone rates.[902] A California court has held that a UDAP claim against a utility company falls within the primary jurisdiction of the Public Utility Commission.[903] But another California court declined to defer to the PUC because it did not have jurisdiction to consider UDAP claims.[904] A challenge to deceptive billing practices that enabled telephone companies to collect rental fees for telephones over a 15-year period likewise could proceed in court, as it did not involve rates or matters on which the PUC would have special expertise.[905]

In general, deference to an administrative agency is inappropriate[906] when the issues are outside the agency's special expertise.[907] Deference to an agency's primary jurisdiction is also inappropriate when the agency has already completed all proceedings that relate to the issue before the court.[908]

2.3.4 Nonmerchant Sellers and Isolated Occurrences

Another important scope issue is whether consumers can bring UDAP claims against other consumers, or just against merchants. Most statutes are silent on the issue. Statutes patterned after the Uniform Deceptive Trade Practices Act limit their scope to practices occurring in the course of the seller's "business, vocation or occupation." The Oregon Supreme Court interprets this to apply to practices "which arise out of transactions which are at least indirectly connected with the ordinary and usual course of defendant's business, vocation or occupation."[909] Thus a service station's sale of a used automobile engine is covered by the act.[910] The New Mexico statute requires that a deceptive practice be in the "regular course" of a person's trade or commerce. The statute does not apply to a single, isolated occurrence.[911]

The Nebraska Supreme Court has interpreted its statute, which defines "trade or commerce" as a "sale of assets or services and any commerce directly or indirectly affecting the people of the State of Nebraska," to exclude transactions

require review first by state insurance department of consumer's claim of bad faith in processing a claim). *Accord* Irvin v. Liberty Life Ins. Co., 2001 U.S. Dist. LEXIS 2935 (E.D. La. Mar. 12, 2001).

897 Chabner v. United of Omaha Life Ins. Co., 225 F.3d 1042 (9th Cir. 2000).

898 State *ex rel.* Bell Atlantic v. Ranson, 497 S.E.2d 755 (W. Va. 1997).

899 *Accord* Oh v. AT&T Corp., 76 F. Supp. 2d 551 (D.N.J. 1999); Boldt v. Correspondence Management, Inc., 320 N.J. Super. 74, 726 A.2d 975 (App. Div. 1999).

900 Tenore v. AT&T Wireless Servs., 136 Wash. 2d 322, 962 P.2d 104 (1998), *cert. denied*, 525 U.S. 1171 (1999).

901 Columbia Chiropractic Group, Inc. v. Trust Ins. Co., 430 Mass. 60, 712 N.E.2d 93 (1999).

902 Valdez v. State, 54 P.3d 71 (N.M. 2002).

903 Wise v. Pacific Gas & Elec. Co., 77 Cal. App. 4th 287, 91 Cal. Rptr. 2d 479 (1999).

904 Greenlining Institute v. Pub. Utilities Comm'n, 103 Cal. App. 4th 1324, 127 Cal. Rptr. 2d 736 (2002).

905 Cundiff v. Bell Atlantic Corp., 101 Cal. App. 4th 1395, 125 Cal. Rptr. 2d 445 (2002).

906 Zapka v. Coca-Cola Co., 2001 U.S. Dist. LEXIS 20155 (N.D. Ill. Dec. 3, 2001) (FDA does not have special expertise in marketing of products, so court declines to refer case to it).

907 *Id.*

908 AICCO Inc. v. Ins. Co. of N. Am., 90 Cal. App. 4th 579, 109 Cal. Rptr. 2d 359 (2001).

909 Wolverton v. Stanwood, 278 Or. 341, 563 P.2d 1203 (1977). *See also* Bentley v. Slavik, 663 F. Supp. 736 (S.D. Ill. 1987) (does not apply to sale by nonmerchant).

910 Wolverton v. Stanwood, 278 Or. 341, 563 P.2d 1203 (1977).

911 Klein v. Bronstein (*In re* Klein), 39 B.R. 20 (Bankr. D.N.M. 1984).

with non-merchants.[912] The Minnesota Supreme Court has reached a similar result by reading a public benefit requirement into its statute that creates a private cause of action for consumer protection violations.[913] As a result, there is no private UDAP cause of action for deception in an isolated one-on-one transaction. A few courts find an isolated sale of real estate by its owner not to be "trade or commerce." These decisions generally rely on the legislative intent that the statute redress the imbalance between merchants and consumers, rather than settling private disputes among consumers.[914]

Many courts must interpret the phrase "trade or commerce" to determine whether the UDAP statute covers cases of consumers suing consumers. The Texas Supreme Court holds that "trade or commerce" includes all types of sellers, including a person who has never sold a boat before and who is not in the business of selling.[915] Similarly the Illinois UDAP statute applies even if the defendant is not a merchant.[916] A Michigan case held that a defendant could be in trade or commerce based on a sideline home improvement business.[917]

The most detailed analysis of when a nonmerchant seller is in trade or commerce is provided by Massachusetts case law. Massachusetts limits "trade or commerce" to acts "in a business context," but practices can be in a business context even though not engaged in during the ordinary course of the seller's business.[918] Whether a nonmerchant's participation in an isolated transaction takes place "in a business context" is determined by the nature of the transaction, the character of the parties, the activities engaged in, whether a similar transaction has been undertaken in the past, whether the practice was motivated by personal or by business considerations, and whether the participant played an active part in the scheme.[919] Maine adopts the same rule.[920]

A nonmerchant was found not covered by the Massachusetts UDAP statute where the individual minimally participated in a real estate deal. He was not involved in the negotiation or directly in the receipt of payments, but was brought in as a passive partner by other investors.[921] Similarly, where private sellers, not in the real estate business, did not actively participate in the sale, there was no "business" context.[922]

Where a landlord owns no property other than an owner-occupied multi-family house, the Massachusetts Supreme Judicial Court has ruled that a landlord-tenant dispute is private in nature and does not involve trade or commerce.[923] A series of transactions that were essentially private dealings between brothers, strongly influenced by familial impulses and without effect on the public interest, was not covered by the UDAP statute.[924] But where a non-business person owns several pieces of property, and is involved in a sale which is part of a larger real estate venture, that person is liable under the statute.[925]

Georgia courts seem to be developing a rule that the seller must engage in a volitional act to enter the channels of trade or commerce.[926] A New Jersey court has ruled that the UDAP statute can not be used by a seller to sue a consumer.[927] A Tennessee court, relying on the general purposes of the UDAP statute rather than its broad coverage definitions, has concluded that the statute does not cover the sale of a vehicle by a nonmerchant.[928] Several Illinois courts have expressed the view that if the plaintiff is a consumer of the defendant's goods or services, an isolated transaction is covered, but a plaintiff who is not a consumer must show that the transaction implicates consumer protection concerns.[929]

Ohio's UDAP statute applies only to "suppliers." A supplier must be "engaged in the business of" effecting or soliciting consumer transactions.[930] This phrase connotes continuous or regular activity, rather than a singular or isolated sale.[931] Sale of less than three cars a year does not meet this standard.[932] Nor does a single instance of debt collection.[933] A party is not a supplier where it provides the prize at a raffle but it otherwise does not sell such merchan-

912 Nelson v. Lusterstone Surfacing Co., 258 Neb. 678, 605 N.W.2d 136 (2000).

913 Ly v. Nystrom, 615 N.W.2d 302 (Minn. 2000). *See* § 7.5.3, *infra*.

914 *See* § 2.2.5.1.3, *supra*.

915 Singleton v. Pennington, 606 S.W.2d 682 (Tex. 1980).

916 People *ex rel.* Scott v. Larance, 105 Ill. App. 3d 171, 434 N.E.2d 5 (1982) (odometer tampering case). *See also* Black v. Iovino, 580 N.E.2d 139 (Ill. App. Ct. 1991) (sale of four cars in 15 months brings seller within UDAP statute).

917 Leduc v. Rotar, 2004 WL 298979 (Mich. App. Feb. 17, 2004) (unpublished, citation limited).

918 Lynn v. Nashawaty, 12 Mass. App. Ct. 310, 423 N.E.2d 1052 (1981).

919 Begelfer v. Najarian, 381 Mass. 177, 409 N.E.2d 167 (1980).

920 Binette v. Dyer Library Assoc., 688 A.2d 898 (Me. 1996) (isolated sale in a business context is covered, but nonprofit library association's sale of land was not in a business context).

921 Begelfer v. Najarian, 381 Mass. 177, 409 N.E.2d 167 (1980).

922 Nei v. Burley, 388 Mass. 307, 446 N.E.2d 674 (1983).

923 Billings v. Wilson, 397 Mass. 614, 493 N.E.2d 187 (1986); Sayah v. Hatzipetro, 397 Mass. 1004, 492 N.E.2d 1131 (1986); Young v. Patukonis, 24 Mass. App. Ct. 907, 506 N.E.2d 1164 (1987).

924 Simon v. Simon, 35 Mass. App. Ct. 705, 625 N.E.2d 564 (1994).

925 Rousseau v. Gelinas, 24 Mass. App. Ct. 154, 507 N.E.2d 265 (1987).

926 *See, e.g.*, Regency Nissan, Inc. v. Taylor, 194 Ga. App. 645, 391 S.E.2d 467 (1990).

927 Channel Companies, Inc. v. Britton, 167 N.J. Super. 417, 400 A.2d 1221 (App. Div. 1979).

928 White v. Eastland, 1991 Tenn. App. LEXIS 624, Clearinghouse No. 51,286 (Tenn. App. Aug. 9, 1991).

929 *See* § 2.4.5.2, *infra*.

930 Ohio Rev. Code Ann. § 1345.01(C).

931 LaVeck v. Al's Mustang Stable, 73 Ohio App. 3d 700, 598 N.E.2d 154 (1991).

932 *Id.*

933 Renner v. Derin Acquisition Corp., 111 Ohio App. 3d 326, 676 N.E.2d 151 (1996).

dise.[934] Utah's statute applies only to suppliers who "regularly" engage in consumer transactions, and this has been held to exclude those involved in the isolated sale of real estate.[935]

Hawaii's UDAP statute allows actions to be brought against nonmerchants only if the action is in the public interest. But a *per se* violation of the UDAP statute conclusively shows that the action is in the public interest.[936] Individuals are merchants if they hold themselves out as having special knowledge about the product or service.[937] But a seller of a hotel is not a merchant because it is not a dealer of goods or services, and there is no public interest in the purely private transaction.[938]

The Florida Supreme Court has held that its UDAP statute can be applied to unfair or deceptive acts committed by a single party in a single transaction directed toward a single contract.[939] The court rejected the defendant's argument that the statute's reference to unfair or deceptive "practices" implied that there had to be more of a pattern of misconduct. The statute also referred to unfair or deceptive "acts," and the remedy sections of the statute afforded relief to anyone injured by "a violation" of the statute.

A California court, while not required by the facts in the case before it, added an unusual coverage requirement to one of California's two UDAP statutes.[940] The challenged practice must directly relate to a "primary" part of the seller's business.[941] The California Supreme Court ordered the decision depublished, however, so it has no precedential value.[942]

2.3.5 Nonprofit Organizations and Schools

The FTC Act applies only to a company or other entity organized to carry on business for its own profit or that of its members. This limitation does not flow from the definition of "trade or commerce," but occurs because the FTC Act only applies to acts by a "corporation." The term "corporation" is defined in the FTC Act to include only companies organized to carry on business for profit or for the profit of their members.[943] The FTC does, however, have jurisdiction over for-profit companies that solicit donations to charities.[944]

Consequently, a state UDAP statute not limited to acts by "corporations" should have a broader scope than the FTC Act.[945] This should be the case even if the UDAP statute specifies that courts are to be guided by FTC decisions.[946]

Even the relatively narrow scope of the FTC Act has been found to apply to nonprofit trade associations and even to charitable organizations, such as the American Medical Association, to the extent that they engage in business activities.[947] If a nonprofit organization is really engaged in a profit-making enterprise, it is still covered by the FTC Act; if in form and in fact an enterprise is purely charitable, the enterprise does not fall within the FTC's definition of corporation.[948]

State UDAP statutes do not have the term "corporation" as a key definition, and the issue is rather whether the challenged practice falls within the statute's specific scope. For many states, this will mean whether a transaction is in "trade or commerce" or whether goods or services are sold. Therefore, even a charitable entity engaging in commerce or selling goods or services should be covered.[949] On the other hand, purely charitable enterprises may be found not to involve trade or commerce[950] or the sale of goods or ser-

934 Moore v. Florida Bank of Commerce, 654 F. Supp. 38 (S.D. Ohio 1086), *aff'd without op.*, 833 F.2d 1013 (6th Cir. 1987).

935 Iadanza v. Mather, 820 F. Supp. 1371 (D. Utah 1993).

936 Ai v. Frank Huff Agency Ltd., 61 Haw. 607, 607 P.2d 1304 (1980).

937 Eastern Star, Inc. v. Union Building Materials, 712 P.2d 1148 (Haw. Ct. App. 1985).

938 Kona Hawaiian Assocs. v. Pacific Group, 680 F. Supp. 1438 (D. Haw. 1988).

939 PNR, Inc. v. Beacon Property Management, Inc., 2003 WL 10885751 (Fla. Mar. 13, 2003).

940 Cal. Bus. & Prof. Code § 17200.

941 Starbuck v. Kaiser Found. Health Plan, 275 Cal. Rptr. 444 (Ct. App. 1990).

942 1991 Cal. LEXIS 607, 91 Cal. Daily Op. Serv. 1530, 91 Daily Journal D.A.R. 1993 (Feb. 14, 1991).

943 15 U.S.C. § 44.

944 FTC v. Mitchell Gold, 5 Trade Reg. Rep. (CCH) ¶ 15378 (C.D. Cal. Mar. 6, 2003) (proposed consent decree against for-profit charitable fundraiser who misrepresented amount that went to charities). *See* § 5.9.4.2, *infra*.

945 Mother & Unborn Baby Care, Inc. v. State, 749 S.W.2d 533 (Tex. App. 1988), *cert. denied*, 490 U.S. 1090 (1989).

946 *Id.*

947 *See* American Medical Ass'n v. FTC, 638 F.2d 443 (2d Cir. 1980), *aff'd per curiam* 455 U.S. 676 (1982), *rehearing denied*, 456 U.S. 966 (1982); FTC v. National Comm'n on Egg Nutrition, 517 F.2d 485 (7th Cir. 1975), *cert. denied*, 426 U.S. 919 (1976). *See also* Community Blood Bank, Inc. v. FTC, 405 F.2d 1011 (8th Cir. 1969); Miller v. Risk Management Foundation, 36 Mass. App. Ct. 411, 632 N.E.2d 841 (1994).

948 Community Blood Bank, Inc. v. FTC, 405 F.2d 1011 (8th Cir. 1969).

949 Trustees of Boston University v. ASM Communications, Inc., 33 F. Supp. 2d 66 (D. Mass. 1998) (university was not engaging in trade or commerce when it undertook activities in furtherance of its core mission); Dushkin v. Desai, 18 F. Supp. 2d 117 (D. Mass. 1998) (defendant was engaged in trade or commerce even though he purported to operate a spiritual community, when real purpose was alleged to be financial gain); Linkage Corp. v. Trustees of Boston University, 425 Mass. 1, 679 N.E.2d 191 (1997), *cert. denied*, 522 U.S. 1015 (1997); State *ex rel.* Fisher v. Warren Star Theater, 84 Ohio App. 3d 435, 616 N.E.2d 1192 (1992) (UDAP statute applied without discussion to non-profit corporation and its principal); Mother & Unborn Baby Care, Inc. v. State, 749 S.W.2d 533 (Tex. App. 1988), *cert. denied*, 490 U.S. 1090 (1989).

950 Schiff v. American Ass'n of Retired Persons, 697 A.2d 1193 (D.C. Ct. App. 1997); Poznik v. Massachusetts Medical Professional Ins. Ass'n, 417 Mass. 48, 628 N.E.2d 1 (1994) (nonprofit, statutorily-mandated joint underwriting association is not en-

vices.[951] In Massachusetts, for example, courts will first ask whether the interaction is commercial in nature; an arm's length transaction between two corporations for services in exchange for payment signifies a commercial transaction.[952] Next the court will examine whether the parties were engaged in "trade or commerce," that is, whether they are acting in a "business context."[953] That a party is a nonprofit organization does not conclude the question. If the organization took on the activity in question with a business motivation, "insert[ing] itself into the marketplace," it may well be found to be within the reach of the statute.[954] In contrast, activities considered central to the nonprofit organization's "core" mission will be considered to be outside "trade or commerce," and accordingly outside the scope of the UDAP statute.[955] Courts will also take into account whether the organization undertook the activity pursuant to a "legislative mandate,"[956] as opposed to a voluntary participation in the market.

In other states, the analysis will involve other coverage terms. For example, the Iowa Attorney General has indicated that it believes the Iowa UDAP statute applies to a political action committee (PAC) soliciting campaign contributions.[957] A PAC is a person and the statute explicitly applies to acts by a person in the "solicitation of contributions for charitable purposes."[958] The New Hampshire Supreme Court has held that a college's solicitation of funds is strictly private in nature and is not in trade or commerce.[959]

A UDAP statute should apply to educational institutions. There should be little doubt that a student is a consumer, and students can thus sue as consumers.[960] A childbirth class is "in trade or commerce" and covered by a UDAP statute.[961]

The more difficult question will be whether a school's nonprofit status excludes the school from UDAP coverage. Proprietary, for-profit schools are clearly covered.[962] (A good source of precedent that vocational and other schools that are not strictly charitable institutions are covered by a UDAP statute is the numerous FTC actions against proprietary vocational schools.[963]) A nonprofit religious school, however, has been found exempt because it is not a merchant.[964] A Connecticut trial court has drawn a distinction between the entrepreneurial aspects of a university's activi-

---

gaged in "trade or commerce"); All Seasons Servs. v. Commissioner of Health, 416 Mass. 269, 620 N.E.2d 778 (1993) (publicly operated charitable hospital was not a person engaging in trade or commerce when it contracted for food services); Barrett v. Massachusetts Insurers Insolvency Fund, 412 Mass. 774, 592 N.E.2d 1317 (1992) (statutorily-mandated nonprofit fund that covers claims by insolvent insurers is not engaged in "trade or commerce."); Planned Parenthood Fed'n of Am., Inc. v. Problem Pregnancy, Inc., 398 Mass. 480, 498 N.E.2d 1044 (1986); Hubert v. Melrose-Wakefield Hosps. Assn., 40 Mass. App. Ct. 172, 661 N.E.2d 1347 (1996) (land transaction between individual and nonprofit hospital not covered); Malone v. Topsail Area Jaycees, Inc., 439 S.E.2d 192 (N.C. Ct. App. 1994) (fundraiser for Jaycees not in "trade or commerce").

951 Kozup v. Georgetown University, 663 F. Supp. 1048 (D.D.C. 1987) (American Red Cross blood bank activities do not involve a merchant selling consumer goods).

952 Linkage Corp. v. Trustees of Boston Univ., 425 Mass. 1, 679 N.E.2d 191, 206 (1997) (finding that agreement between satellite unit of university and corporate training business was "commercial" in nature), *cert. denied*, 522 U.S. 1015 (1997).

953 Id.

954 *Id.*, 679 N.E.2d at 208–09 (finding university was "motivated by a strong desire to benefit as much as possible" from the arrangement underlying the suit). *Accord* Trustees of Boston University v. ASM Communications, Inc., 33 F. Supp. 2d 66 (D. Mass. 1998) ("Only if the nonprofit 'goes beyond its ordinary business' and aims instead to generate a profit does it fall within" the UDAP statute). *See also* Dushkin v. Desai, 18 F. Supp. 2d 117 (D. Mass. 1998) (defendant was engaged in trade or commerce even though he purported to operate a spiritual community, when real purpose was alleged to be financial gain; court noted that the defendant's, not the plaintiff's, business motivation governs).

955 Linkage Corp. v. Trustees of Boston Univ., 425 Mass. 1, 679 N.E.2d 191 at 208 (1997). *See also* Trustees of Boston University v. ASM Communications, Inc., 33 F. Supp. 2d 66 (D. Mass. 1998) (holding that university's purchase of term papers from commercial entity, made in the course of investigating academic fraud, was not "trade or commerce": "Nothing could be more central to a university's educational mission than an investigation into student cheating"); Thornton v. Harvard Univ., 2 F. Supp. 2d 89 (D. Mass. 1998) (university's administration of student financial aid program not "trade or commerce"); *cf.* Peabody NE, Inc. v. Town of Marshfield, 426 Mass. 436, 689 N.E.2d 774 (1998) (town did not engage in "trade or commerce" by contracting for the construction of a waste treatment plant).

956 Linkage Corp. v. Trustees of Boston Univ., 425 Mass. 1, 679 N.E.2d 191, 208 (1997) (noting that university was not operating under any "legislative constraints"); Peabody NE, Inc. v. Town of Marshfield, 426 Mass. 436, 689 N.E.2d 774 (1998) (where town had contracted for the construction of a waste treatment plant pursuant to an administrative order issued by a state agency, no "trade or commerce").

957 Letter from Peter Kochenburger, Assistant Attorney General, to the Honorable Roy Taylor, Clearinghouse No. 47,937 (Feb. 13, 1992).

958 Iowa Code § 714.16.

959 Brzica v. Trustees of Dartmouth College, 791 A.2d 990 (N.H. 2002).

960 Scott v. Association for Childbirth at Home Int'l, 88 Ill. 2d 279, 430 N.E.2d 1012 (1981); Brody v. Finch University of Health Sciences, 698 N.E.2d 257 (Ill. App. Ct. 1998).

961 Scott v. Association for Childbirth at Home Int'l, 88 Ill. 2d 279, 430 N.E.2d 1012 (1981). *See also* Linkage Corp. v. Trustees of Boston University, 425 Mass. 1, 679 N.E.2d 191 (1997), *cert. denied*, 522 U.S. 1015 (1997).

962 Alsides v. Brown Institute, 592 N.W.2d 468 (Minn. App. Ct. 1999) (both Minnesota UDAP and UDTPA statutes cover private, proprietary, for-profit schools); Malone v. Academy of Court Reporting, 64 Ohio App. 3d 588, 582 N.E.2d 54 (1990).

963 *See* § 5.10.7, *infra*; National Consumer Law Center, Student Loan Law § 9.3.2 (2d ed. 2002 and Supp.).

964 Save Immaculata v. Immaculata Preparatory School, 514 A.2d 1152 (D.C. App. 1986). *But see* Linkage Corp. v. Trustees of Boston University, 425 Mass. 1, 679 N.E.2d 191 (1997), *cert. denied*, 522 U.S. 1015 (1997).

ties and its professional competence.[965] The UDAP statute covers claims involving entrepreneurial aspects, such as accepting a student's tuition money without telling him he was on the brink of dismissal, but not claims analogous to educational malpractice. Whether public institutions can be sued under a UDAP statute is discussed in § 2.3.6, *infra*.

Another issue is whether any statutory cap on the liability of a nonprofit applies to a UDAP claim. Massachusetts' $20,000 limitation on charitable institutions' tort liability[966] does not apply to such an institution's UDAP liability.[967]

2.3.6 Government and Quasi-Government Agencies as Sellers

UDAP statutes normally define the entities that can be sued under the statute; therefore, the first question is whether a UDAP statute explicitly excludes or includes government agencies as UDAP defendants.[968] Usually, courts will have to interpret ambiguous language. Thus the U.S. Department of Housing and Urban Development acting as a landlord has been found to be a "person" and therefore subject to a UDAP statute.[969]

A Texas court has ruled that the Texas UDAP statute can not be used to sue a municipality.[970] The statute explicitly applies to a municipality bringing an action as a consumer, but is silent as to whether a municipality is a "person" that can be sued under the statute. The court found that this silence indicated that the municipality was exempt because the legislature knew how to explicitly include municipalities within the scope of the statute.[971] An Illinois court has similarly ruled that a municipal corporation is not a "person" subject to its UDAP statute, where the statute explicitly covers domestic and foreign corporations, but is silent as to municipal corporations.[972] On the other hand, a federal court finds Hawaii's UDAP statute, which exempts certain organizations but is silent as to municipalities, broad enough to cover municipalities.[973]

The Montana Supreme court has held that a government entity such as a school district is not a "person" and is not engaging in "business," at least as those terms are used in the antitrust provisions of its Unfair Trade Practices Act.[974] Two California decisions hold that a government entity such as the state lottery commission is not a "person" subject to UDAP suit,[975] but a third decision, relying in part on specific language in the statute authorizing the fund, reaches the opposite conclusion with respect to the state workers' compensation fund.[976] Cities, like states, may not be sued under North Carolina's UDAP statute.[977]

If the state itself does not qualify as a "person" under the statute, its officers are similarly exempt when they are acting in their official capacities.[978] However, a court reporter is subject to a UDAP claim and is not covered by derived judicial immunity.[979]

Where a statute applies to actions in "trade or commerce," courts may consider acts of a governmental agency acting in a governmental capacity not to be in "trade or commerce" and thus exempt.[980] Courts have found munici-

965 Day v. Yale University School of Drama, 2000 Conn. Super. LEXIS 658 (Mar. 7, 2000); *see also* Johnson v. Schmitz, 119 F. Supp. 2d 90 (D. Conn. 2000) (academic research and publication are not in trade or commerce because not entrepreneurial).

966 Mass. Gen. Laws ch. 231, § 85K.

967 Linkage Corp. v. Trustees of Boston University, 425 Mass. 1, 679 N.E.2d 191 (1997), *cert. denied*, 522 U.S. 1015 (1997).

968 *See* City of Danbury v. Dana Investment Corp., 249 Conn. 1, 730 A.2d 1128 (1999) (construing Connecticut UDAP statute's exemption for "actions permitted under law as administered by any regulatory board or officer acting under statutory authority of the state" to exempt a municipality when it foreclosed on tax liens).

969 Pierce v. Dew, 626 F. Supp. 386 (D. Mass. 1986).

970 Kerrville HRH v. City of Kerrville, 803 S.W.2d 377 (Tex. App. 1991). *See also* Gormley v. Port of Port Angeles, 2003 WL 22137351 (Wash. App. Sept. 16, 2003) (unpublished, citation limited) (municipal corporation not subject to Washington UDAP statute).

971 *Id.*

972 DuPage Aviation v. DuPage Airport Authority, 594 N.E.2d 1334 (Ill. App. Ct. 1992).

973 Daly v. Harris, 215 F. Supp. 2d 1098 (D. Haw. 2002).

974 Montana Vending, Inc. v. Coca-Cola Bottling Co., 318 Mont. 1, 78 P.3d 499 (2003).

975 Trinkle v. California State Lottery, 71 Cal. App. 4th 1198, 84 Cal. Rptr. 2d 496 (1999) (Cal. Bus. & Prof. Code § 17200); Janis v. California State Lottery Comm'n, 68 Cal. App. 4th 824, 80 Cal. Rptr. 2d 549 (1998) (Cal. Bus. & Prof. Code § 17200).

976 Notrica v. State Compensation Ins. Fund, 70 Cal. 4th 911, 83 Cal. Rptr. 2d 89 (1999).

977 Rea Constr. Co. v. City of Charlotte, 465 S.E.2d 342 (N.C. App. 1996).

978 Sperry Corp. v. Patterson, 73 N.C. App. 123, 325 S.E.2d 642 (1985).

979 Dallas County v. Halsesy, 87 S.W.3d 552 (Tex. 2002).

980 Daly v. Harris, 215 F. Supp. 2d 1098 (D. Haw. 2002) (municipality not exempt, but charging beach access fee to non-residents may not be in trade or commerce); Boston Housing Authority v. Howard, 427 Mass. 537, 695 N.E.2d 192 (1998) (housing authority is not subject to UDAP statute when it rents out apartments because it is not acting in a business context); Lafayette Place Assocs. v. Boston Redevelopment Authority, 427 Mass. 509, 694 N.E.2d 820 (1998), *cert. denied*, 525 U.S. 1177 (1999) (redevelopment authority not covered because it was motivated by legislative mandate, not business or personal reasons); All Seasons Servs. v. Commissioner of Health, 416 Mass. 269, 620 N.E.2d 778 (1993) (publicly operated charitable hospital was not a person engaging in trade or commerce when it contracted for food services); United States Leasing Corp. v. City of Chicopee, 402 Mass. 228, 521 N.E.2d 741 (1988); Middleboro Fire Apparatus, Inc. v. City of Haverhill, 60 Mass. App. Ct. 1127, 806 N.E.2d 472 (Mass. App. Ct. 2004) (city not engaged in trade or commerce when it contracts for repair of a fire truck); Morton v. Town of Hanover, 43 Mass. App. Ct. 197, 682 N.E.2d 889 (1997) (municipality's operation of water system is not covered by UDAP statute); T. Bedrosian v. Costanza, 1999 Mass. Super. LEXIS 349 (Aug. 19, 1999) (denial of motion to dismiss) (municipality may be subject to UDAP

pal corporations, such as water commissions, irrigation districts, rural electrical cooperatives, public hospitals, and other government-run entities exempt on this ground.[981] A California court found that a county hospital, acting within the county's sovereign powers, was exempt on the theory that express statutory language was necessary to bring a state or its subdivision within the scope of a general statute.[982]

Even if a government agency falls within a UDAP statute's definitions, it may be protected by the state's tort claims act or other sovereign immunity doctrine.[983] But public officials who act beyond the scope of their authority may not be protected. A public official is not immune where the alleged unfair practice is the misuse of public authority to effect a private transaction.[984]

Private entities employed by the government may be subject to UDAP suit even if the government is not. A private collection agency collecting for a government agency should be covered by the UDAP statute,[985] assuming that collection activities are generally within a UDAP statute's scope.[986] However, a private company performing discretionary governmental duties (here, removing dead bodies from a crash scene) under contract may assert official immunity as a defense.[987]

Even if a governmental entity is outside the scope of the UDAP statute, it may still be liable for UDAP violations it committed as part of a conspiracy with other defendants who are within the statute's scope.[988] A government entity holding a loan containing the FTC Holder Notice should generally be subject to all UDAP claims the consumer could bring against the seller.[989]

2.3.7 *Printers and the Media*

The exemption section of most UDAP statutes specifically excludes printers, publishers, and others who disseminate advertisements in good faith.[990] The Pennsylvania Supreme Court has ruled that this exemption applies to printers of lease forms and those who distribute lease forms.[991] If a publisher disseminates an advertisement with knowledge that it is deceptive, the good faith exclusion does not apply, and a UDAP action can be brought against it.[992] This exemption also does not apply to publishers advertising their own product.[993] To underscore this, many state UDAP statutes explicitly exempt only media statements where the media has no direct financial interest in the advertised product.[994]

---

liability when it enters market and engages in trade or commerce); Golden Rule Ins. Co. v. Long, 113 N.C. App. 187, 439 S.E.2d 599 (1993); Sperry Corp. v. Patterson, 73 N.C. App. 123, 325 S.E.2d 642 (1985). *See also* Alger v. Ganick, O'Brien & Sarin, 35 F. Supp. 2d 148 (D. Mass. 1999) (declining to rule on "difficult issue of first impression" whether higher education assistance agency can be a UDAP defendant where it acts pursuant to legislative mandate but has corporate powers and is collecting a debt).

981 Keenan v. Allan, 889 F. Supp. 1320 (E.D. Wash. 1995), *aff'd on other grounds*, 91 F.3d 1275 (9th Cir. 1996) (actions of county, its commissioners, and a court not covered); Connelly v. Housing Authority, 213 Conn. 354, 567 A.2d 1212 (1990) (municipal housing authority not covered); Lazaros v. City of W. Haven, 45 Conn. Super. 11, 697 A.2d 724 (1994) (municipalities are exempt), *aff'd*, 45 Conn. App. 571, 696 A.2d 1304 (1997); Bretton v. State Lottery Comm'n, 41 Mass. App. Ct. 736, 673 N.E.2d 76 (1996) (state lottery commission); Quincy Corp. v. Massachusetts Bay Transportation Authority, Civ. Action No. 39881 (Mass. Super. Ct. Suffolk Cty 1984) (public transportation authority not covered); Camerson v. New Hanover Memorial Hosps., Inc., 293 S.E.2d 901 (N.C. Ct. App. 1982) (municipal hospital not covered); Haberman v. Washington Public Power Supply Sys., 109 Wash. 2d 107, 744 P.2d 1032 (1987) (rural electrical cooperatives are exempt); Washington Natural Gas Co. v. PUD 1, 77 Wash. 2d 94, 459 P.2d 633 (1969) (municipal irrigation district is exempt); Ottgen v. Clover Park Technical College, 928 P.2d 1119 (Wash. App. 1996) (public community college exempt). *See also* Barry v. N.J. State Highway Authority, 245 N.J. Super. 302, 585 A.2d 420 (1990) (highway authority probably not covered). *But see* Keene Inc. v. Boston Water & Sewer Comm'n, Civ. Action No. 50133 (Mass. Super. Ct. Suffolk Cty 1981) (public water commission covered); Kinkopf v. Triborough Bridge & Tunnel Authority, 764 N.Y.S.2d 549 (Civ. Ct. 2003) (E-Z Pass program covered).

982 Community Memorial v. County of Ventura, 50 Cal. App. 4th 199, 56 Cal. Rptr. 2d 732 (1996).

983 Ramapo Brae Condominium Assoc., Inc. v. Bergen County Housing Auth., 328 N.J. Super. 561, 746 A.2d 519 (2000) (housing authority protected by tort claims act), *aff'd per curiam*, 770 A.2d 253 (N.J. 2001); Walker v. Jefferson County, 2003 WL 21505472, at *8 (Ohio App. June 25, 2003) (unpublished, citation limited).

984 Piccuirro v. Gaitenby, 20 Mass. App. Ct. 286, 480 N.E.2d 30 (1985); Leftwich v. Gaines, 521 S.E.2d 717 (N.C. App. 1999) (government official who acts corruptly to profit from information obtained in official capacity is not protected by governmental immunity).

985 People *ex rel.* Daley v. Datacom Sys. Corp., 146 Ill. 2d 1, 585 N.E.2d 51 (1991).

986 *See* § 2.2.2, *supra.*

987 Guerrero v. Tarrant County Mortician Servs. Co., 977 S.W.2d 829 (Tex. App. 1998).

988 Strahan v. Louisiana Dep't of Agriculture & Forestry, 645 So. 2d 1162 (La. Ct. App. 1994).

989 *See* § 6.6, *infra.*

990 *See* Repucci v. Lake Champagne Campground, Inc., 251 F. Supp. 2d 1235 (D. Vt. 2002); Aequitron Medical, Inc. v. CBS, Inc., 964 F. Supp. 704 (S.D.N.Y. 1996); Miller v. Keyser, 90 S.W.3d 712, (Tex. 2002).

991 Commonwealth v. Monumental Properties, Inc., 459 Pa. 450, 329 A.2d 812 (1974).

992 Mother & Unborn Baby Care, Inc. v. State, 749 S.W.2d 533 (Tex. App. 1988), *cert. denied*, 490 U.S. 1090 (1989). *See also* Thomas v. Times Mirror Magazine, Inc., 98 Cal. App. 3d 913, 159 Cal. Rptr. 711 (1979) (not citable; ordered depublished).

993 People *ex rel.* Hartigan v. Maclean Hunter Publishing Corp., 119 Ill. App. 3d 1049, 457 N.E.2d 480 (1983); Mother & Unborn Baby Care, Inc. v. State, 749 S.W.2d 533 (Tex. App. 1988), *cert. denied*, 490 U.S. 1090 (1989).

994 *See, e.g.*, People *ex rel.* Hartigan v. Maclean Hunter Publishing Corp., 119 Ill. App. 3d 1049, 457 N.E.2d 480 (1983).

Where a publisher is covered by a UDAP statute, the publisher is sure to raise the First Amendment, particularly if an injunction is sought. While non-commercial speech has certain protections, advertising, even advertising attempting to sell printed material, will have less protection and deceptive advertising no protection.[995]

2.3.8 *Wholesalers and Other Indirect Parties*

Questions also arise as to whether a UDAP statute can reach practices by wholesalers or manufacturers who do not sell directly to consumers. This may be a critical issue where the retailer dealing directly with the consumer is judgment-proof or is not entirely responsible for the unfair or deceptive practice.

For example, often a car purchaser will not deal with a manufacturer directly. The car will be purchased from a dealer, and the warranty work will be performed by the dealer as the manufacturer's agent under the manufacturer's warranty. Nevertheless, there should be little question that a UDAP action can be brought against both the dealer and the manufacturer where a car is defective.[996]

Privity is a contract or warranty concept and is not required in UDAP actions, so the consumer and the wholesaler or other third party need have no direct contractual relationship.[997] While there is no privity requirement, a transaction must be within the scope of the UDAP statute.

For example, some UDAP statutes can only be used to sue "suppliers." An Ohio court has held that a wholesaler who rolled back odometers is a "supplier" participating in "consumer transactions," since the statute covers practices "in connection with a consumer transaction."[998] A manufacturer is also a "supplier" under the Ohio statute.[999] Similarly, a federal court interpreting the Utah statute found a wholesaler who tampered with odometers to be a "supplier" who engages in consumer transactions, even though the wholesaler never dealt directly with consumers.[1000] An insurance company that acquired title to a wrecked car and then resold it to a dealer without obtaining a salvage title as required by law is subject to suit under Michigan's UDAP statute even though it never made misrepresentations directly to the consumer.[1001] Virginia's definition of supplier covered a secured creditor who auctioned a repossessed car to a dealer without disclosing frame damage, since it was reasonably foreseeable that the car would be sold to a consumer.[1002] An organization that certified "master builders" was a supplier under the Kansas UDAP statute where one of its goals was promotion of the home building industry, and it supplied promotional materials to members and distributed brochures to the general public.[1003]

The Maryland UDAP statute applies to merchants who directly or indirectly sell or offer to sell consumer goods or services. Where a franchisor is actively engaged in assisting franchisees to sell services to consumers, and participates in the deceptive practices, the franchisor is liable under the UDAP statute for the deception involved in the franchisees' sales to consumers.[1004] On the other hand, Maryland's highest court held that homeowners could not bring a UDAP suit against a manufacturer that made and sold building products only to builders, and directed its alleged deceptive practices only to those builders, even though the homeowners were indirectly affected by the manufacturer's deception of the builders.[1005] In a similar vein, a New Jersey court held that its UDAP statute, and in particular a set of regulations

---

995 See § 7.10.2, *infra* for a discussion of UDAP First Amendment issues.

996 *See* DaimlerChrysler Corp. v. Inman, 121 S.W.3d 862 (Tex. App. Nov. 20, 2003); Milt Ferguson Motor Co. v. Zeretzke, 827 S.W.2d 349 (Tex. App. 1991).

997 *See* § 4.2.15.3, *infra*. *See also* U.S. Tire-Tech, Inc. v. Boeran, B.V., 110 S.W.3d 194 (Tex. App. 2003) (privity not required even when UDAP claim based on breach of an express warranty).

998 Brown v. Lancaster Chrysler-Plymouth, Inc., No. 76CV-05-2077, Clearinghouse No. 27,061 (C.P. Franklin Cty., Ohio Oct. 20, 1976). *See also* Garner v. Borcherding Buick, Inc., 84 Ohio App. 3d 61, 616 N.E.2d 283 (1992) (wholesalers who sold galvanized vehicle were "suppliers").

999 Miner v. Jayco, 1999 Ohio App. LEXIS 3944 (Aug. 27, 1999); *see also* Lump v. Best Door & Window, Inc., 2002 Ohio App. LEXIS 1381 (Mar. 27, 2002) (manufacturer who had some direct dealings with the consumer is covered).

1000 State *ex rel.* Wilkinson v. B&H Auto, 701 F. Supp. 201 (D. Utah 1988); *see also* Tandy v. Marti, 213 F. Supp. 2d 935, 938 n.1 (S.D. Ill. 2002) (ultimate consumer buyer can sue wholesaler who sold vehicle to retailer without disclosing damage). *But see* United Pacific Ins. Co. v. Berryhill, 620 So. 2d 1077 (Fla. Dist. Ct. App. 1993) (one dealer selling tampered odometer to another dealer is not a consumer transaction).

1001 Ross v. Bob Saks Toyota, Inc., Clearinghouse No. 53543A (Mich. Cir. Ct. Aug. 1, 2001) (no direct relationship necessary except for substantive prohibitions that require direct oral representations).

1002 Harris v. Universal Ford, Inc., 2001 U.S. Dist. LEXIS 8913 (E.D. Va. Feb. 5, 2001) (magistrate's opinion; case was settled before further rulings were issued). *See also* Merriman v. Auto Excellence, Inc., 55 Va. Cir. 330, 2001 Va. Cir. LEXIS 292 (June 18, 2001) (dealer who sold car to wholesaler, who sold it to another dealer, who sold it to consumer, was "supplier"). *But see* Eubank v. Ford Motor Credit Co., 54 Va. Cir. 170 (2000) (ultimate buyer had no claim against prior lessor who auctioned car to dealer, since sale to dealer was not a consumer transaction); MacConkey v. F.J. Matter Design, Inc., 54 Va. Cir. 1 (2000) (manufacturer that sold siding to subcontractor, who installed it on consumer's home, is outside UDAP statute).

1003 Alexander v. Certified Master Builders Corp., 1 P.3d 899 (Kan. 2000).

1004 State v. Cottman Transmissions Sys., Inc., 86 Md. App. 714, 587 A.2d 1190 (1991). *Accord* Williams v. Purdue Phama Co., 297 F. Supp. 2d 171 (D.D.C. 2003) (similar interpretation of District of Columbia UDAP law).

1005 Morris v. Osmose Wood Preserving, 340 Md. 519, 667 A.2d 624 (1995); *see also* Sergent v. Early Street Properties, 56 Va. 168

governing the format of home improvement contracts, did not apply to a subcontractor who dealt only with the general contractor, not the homeowners.[1006]

Texas courts have said that it is the consumer's relationship to the transaction, not to the defendant, that determines whether a defendant is subject to a UDAP claim.[1007] All those who seek to enjoy the benefits of the transaction are subject to UDAP liability.[1008] A consumer may bring a UDAP claim if he or she is the beneficiary of the good or service, regardless of who pays for it.[1009] However, one Texas intermediate court has required that the consumer be a beneficiary at the time of purchase, and not afterward.[1010] UDAP liability does not attach to a party based on being "inextricably intertwined" with the wrongdoer in the transaction.[1011] The prospective defendant must be tied in some way to the transaction or to the misrepresentation.[1012]

Where a UDAP statute applies to direct or indirect advertising, a consumer may sue a drug company even though the drug company only advertised to doctors.[1013] A manufacturer has also been held liable without such statutory language since the economic benefit accrues to the manufacturer and is ultimately paid for by the consumer.[1014] Similarly a UDAP statute applies to the acts of remote suppliers, including suppliers of component parts, whose products are passed on to a buyer and whose representations are made to or intended to be conveyed to the buyer.[1015] An oil company is responsible for its tire advertising, even if tires are sold through independent retailers.[1016] Where a wholesaler markets useless anti-freeze, an action can be brought on behalf of retail customers against the wholesaler, instead of against the retailers.[1017] A number of courts also hold that consumers can assert price-fixing claims against manufacturers under the state UDAP statute, even though, as indirect parties, they could not assert these claims under state or federal antitrust law.[1018]

Courts have ruled that a consumer who buys a home from another consumer has a UDAP action against the original builder.[1019] An aberrant South Carolina Supreme Court decision, however, holds that people who buy a home from the first owner can not assert UDAP claims against the builder/vendor.[1020] The majority conceded that nothing in the UDAP statute supported this interpretation. A builder is also liable to a building's first consumer purchaser even where there is no direct contract between builder and consumer.[1021] A Delaware court has held that a manufacturer is liable for representations made to a consumer where the action is brought by a subsequent buyer from that consumer.[1022] But a Georgia court came to the opposite conclusion, where the wholesaler had not taken "some volitional act to avail himself of the channels of consumer commerce."[1023]

The Texas UDAP statute was not intended to reach upstream manufacturers and suppliers whose misrepresentations were not communicated to the ultimate consumer. Therefore, homeowners who bought homes with defective polybutylene plumbing could not bring a UDAP claim against the polybutylene pipe manufacturer.[1024] But a manufacturer is still liable for its own misrepresentation about its

---

(2001) (component part used in construction of home not part of a consumer transaction).

1006 Messeka Sheet Metal Co. v. Hodder, 368 N.J. Super. 116, 845 A.2d 646 (App. Div. 2004).

1007 Brown v. Bank of Galveston, Nat'l Ass'n, 930 S.W.2d 140 (Tex. App. 1996); Wheaton Van Lines, Inc. v. Mason, 925 S.W.2d 722 (Tex. App. 1996).

1008 Wheaton Van Lines, Inc. v. Mason, 925 S.W.2d 722 (Tex. App. 1996).

1009 Burnap v. Linnartz, 38 S.W.3d 612 (Tex. App. 2000).

1010 Lukasik v. San Antonio Blue Haven Pools, Inc., 21 S.W.3d 394 (Tex. App. 2000).

1011 Qantel Bus. Sys., Inc. v. Custom Controls Co., 761 S.W.2d 302 (Tex. 1988). *See also* Cogan v. Triad Am. Energy, 944 F. Supp. 1325 (S.D. Tex. 1996).

1012 Brown v. Bank of Galveston, Nat'l Ass'n, 930 S.W.2d 140 (Tex. App. 1996).

1013 Kociemba v. G.D. Searle & Co., 680 F. Supp. 1293 (D. Minn. 1988).

1014 Jones v. Sportelli, 166 N.J. Super. 383, 399 A.2d 1047 (Law Div. 1979); *see also* Haner v. Quincy Farm Chemicals Inc., 29 Wash. App. 93, 627 P.2d 571 (1981), *rev'd on other grounds*, 97 Wash. 2d 753, 649 P.2d 828 (1982).

1015 Perth Amboy Iron Works, Inc. v. American Home Assurance Co., 226 N.J. Super. 200, 543 A.2d 1020 (1988). *See also* Ford Motor Co. Ignition Switch Prods. Liability Litig., 1999 WL 33495352 (D.N.J. July 27, 1999), *as modified on reconsideration*, (July 27, 1999) (upstream component parts supplier is in trade or commerce under Nebraska UDAP statute and is involved in consumer transaction under Oklahoma UDAP statute). *But see* Sergent v. Early Street Properties, 56 Va. Cir. 168 (2001) (component part used in construction of home not part of a consumer transaction); MacConkey v. F.J. Matter Design, Inc., 54 Va. Cir. 1 (2000).

1016 State v. Amoco Oil Co., 97 Wis. 2d 226, 293 N.W.2d 487 (1980).

1017 Edminston v. Chemical Co., 45 N.C. App. 604, 263 S.E.2d 849 (1980).

1018 *See* § 4.10, *infra*.

1019 Galbraith v. McLaughlin, 44 Pa. D. & C.3d 70 (C.P. Erie Cty. 1986). *See also* Tackling v. Shinerman, 42 Conn. Supp. 517, 630 A.2d 1381 (1993) (home buyers may have UDAP claim against appraiser hired by bank); Katz v. Schachter, 251 N.J. Super. 467, 598 A.2d 923 (1991) (purchaser of home may have UDAP claim against persons who dealt with previous owners). *But see* Chattin v. Cape May Greene, Inc., 216 N.J. Super. 618, 524 A.2d 841 (App. Div. 1987); Taylor v. Burk, 722 S.W.2d 226 (Tex. App. 1986).

1020 Reynolds v. Ryland Group, Inc., 340 S.C. 331, 531 S.E.2d 917 (S.C. 2000).

1021 Gennari v. Weichert Co. Realtors, 148 N.J. 582, 691 A.2d 350 (1997). *But see* Reynolds v. Ryland Group, Inc., 340 S.C. 331, 531 S.E.2d 917 (2000) (people who bought home from first owner can not bring UDAP claim against builder/vendor).

1022 Pack & Process, Inc. v. Celotex Corp., 503 A.2d 646 (Del. Super. Ct. 1985).

1023 State v. Meredith Chevrolet, Inc., 145 Ga. App. 8, 244 S.E.2d 15 (1978), *aff'd*, 242 Ga. 294, 249 S.E.2d 87 (1978).

1024 Amstadt v. U.S. Brass Corp., 919 S.W.2d 644 (Tex. 1996); State Indus., Inc. v. Corbitt, 925 S.W.2d 304 (Tex. App. 1996).

products, even if the direct seller made no independent misrepresentations and is not liable.[1025] However, misrepresentation by the manufacturer must be communicated to the consumer.[1026] One Texas intermediate court has held that a third-party's misrepresentations must be communicated directly to the consumer and not merely made to an intermediary.[1027]

The District of Columbia's highest court has ruled that although a merchant does not have to be the actual seller of goods or services, the merchant must be connected with the "supply" side of a consumer transaction. Thus, where a disinterested third party recommends a seller, the UDAP statute does not apply to that third party.[1028] On the other hand, while transactions along the distribution chain that do not involve the ultimate retail consumer may not be consumer transactions, any entity involved in the retail transaction between the final distribution and the ultimate consumer is covered.[1029] Auctioneers are thus covered when they sell to the ultimate consumer, even if they sell the goods for a fee rather than taking title to the goods and reselling them.[1030] A federal district court interpreting the District of Columbia UDAP law holds that it applies to a manufacturer that actively promotes its product to consumers, even though sales occur through retailers.[1031]

Some courts refuse to apply the UDAP statute to a party who has only a remote or tangential connection to the transaction. The Connecticut Supreme Court has held that a municipality had no standing to assert UDAP claims against handgun manufacturers.[1032] The injuries the municipality asserted were too remote from the defendants' misconduct and too derivative of injuries of others. But a federal court in New York allowed homeowners whose wells were polluted by a contaminant in gasoline to bring a UDAP claim against the petroleum companies who had deceptively marketed it to the public even though there was no commercial transaction between the plaintiffs themselves and the companies.[1033]

The issue has arisen particularly often in suits against tobacco companies. A federal court interpreting Connecticut's UDAP statute held that, while privity is not necessary, there must be some connection or nexus—business, consumer, commercial, competitor, or other—between the parties.[1034] It held that a union trust fund did not have such a connection to tobacco companies whose products had caused health problems for the fund's beneficiaries. But a federal court in New York reached the opposite conclusion in upholding a $17,000,000 verdict in an insurer's suit against tobacco companies.[1035] Allowing recovery by victims who had suffered indirect injuries recognized the fact that injuries in the consumer marketplace are diffuse and attenuated. The court noted that private enforcement is not effective when remedies are limited to directly injured consumers, who lack resources to prosecute small claims, or to direct competitors, who in oligopolistic markets shy away from exposing the disadvantages of rival products.[1036] The Second Circuit has now affirmed the district court's conclusion that privity is not required in UDAP actions, but it has certified to the New York Court of Appeals the question whether such claims are too remote to permit recovery under the UDAP statute.[1037]

Applying a rationale similar to the federal district court in New York, a New Jersey appellate court held that a bank was not liable for condominium owners' claims involving other parties' unfair and deceptive practices in connection with the sale of the units.[1038] The bank had acquired the condominium development by foreclosure after the plaintiffs had bought their units, and never made any representations to the plaintiffs that were related to the sale. The court held that the UDAP statute covers remote suppliers, such as suppliers of component parts, but the party must have done something in connection with the sale. Similarly, a court held that a consumer could not assert a UDAP claim against a credit reporting agency that was misreporting information about her, because she had not entered into a sale or lease transaction with it.[1039]

2.3.9 Lawyers

In general, lawyers' activities in providing legal services can be within the scope of a UDAP statute that applies to practices "in trade or commerce."[1040] Many courts also find

1025 Church & Dwight Co. v. Huey, 961 S.W.2d 560 (Tex. App. 1997).

1026 Hou-Tex, Inc. v. Landmark Graphics, 26 S.W.3d 103 (Tex. App. 2000).

1027 Dagley v. Haag Engineering Co., 18 S.W.3d 787 (Tex. App. 2000).

1028 Howard v. Riggs Nat'l Bank, 432 A.2d 701 (D.C. 1981).

1029 Adam A. Wechsler & Son, Inc. v. Klank, 561 A.2d 1003 (D.C. 1989).

1030 *Id.*

1031 Williams v. Purdue Phama Co., 297 F. Supp. 2d 171 (D.D.C. 2003).

1032 Ganim v. Smith & Wesson Corp., 258 Conn. 313, 780 A.2d 98 (2001).

1033 *In re* Methyl Tertiary Butyl Ether Prods. Liab. Litigation, 175 F. Supp. 2d 593 (S.D.N.Y. 2001).

1034 Conn. Pipe Trades Health Fund v. Philip Morris, Inc., 153 F. Supp. 2d 101 (D. Conn. 2001). *See also* § 4.2.15.3, *infra* (discussion of privity of contract and remoteness issue).

1035 Blue Cross and Blue Shield v. Philip Morris, Inc., 2001 U.S. Dist. LEXIS 17354 (E.D.N.Y. Oct. 19, 2001).

1036 *Id.*

1037 Blue Cross and Blue Shield v. Philip Morris, Inc., 344 F.3d 211 (2d Cir. 2003).

1038 O'Loughlin v. Nat'l Community Bank, 338 N.J. Super. 592, 770 A.2d 1185 (2001).

1039 Lawrence v. Trans Union L.L.C., 296 F. Supp. 2d 582 (E.D. Pa. 2003).

1040 St. Paul Fire & Marine Ins. Co. v. Ellis & Ellis, 262 F.3d 53 (1st Cir. 2001) (Mass. law) (attorney's scheme to submit false workers' compensation claims to insurers affects trade or commerce and is covered by UDAP statute); Sears, Roebuck & Co.

that these activities involve a consumer's purchase of "goods or services."[1041]

A number of courts are uncomfortable allowing UDAP claims against attorneys solely for legal malpractice. Consequently, the Supreme Courts of Washington[1042] and Connecticut[1043] and a federal court in Vermont[1044] draw the following distinction. The entrepreneurial aspects of legal practice, such as billing, collecting, and attracting clients are covered. But issues concerning legal competence or legal strategies, such as attorney negligence, are exempt.[1045] A number of other courts hold that an attorney's alleged malpractice is not covered by the UDAP statute.[1046] Illinois, however, rejects the distinction, holding that the state UDAP statute applies neither to the billing practices of a lawyer nor to matters more closely involved with the attorney-client relationship.[1047] Likewise, even without an explicit statutory exemption, the New Jersey Supreme Court has exempted learned professions from its UDAP statute, as long as they are operating in their professional capacities.[1048]

Of course, UDAP applicability to lawyers can be limited by an explicit statutory exemption. Ohio's UDAP statute

---

v. Goldstone & Sudalter, 128 F.3d 10 (1st Cir. 1997) (Mass. law); Bro-Vita, Ltd. v. Rausch, 759 F. Supp. 33 (D. Mass. 1991); Heslin v. Connecticut Law Clinic of Trantolo & Trantolo, 190 Conn. 510, 461 A.2d 938 (1983) (misleading advertising, misrepresentation regarding fees); IBrown v. Gerstein, 460 N.E.2d 1043 (Mass. App. Ct. 1984); Doucette v. Kwiat, 392 Mass. 915, 467 N.E.2d 1374 (1984) (applying without comment UDAP statute to attorneys); *see also* Goldfarb v. Virginia State Bar, 421 U.S. 773 (1975) (attorneys are within trade or commerce for purposes of the Sherman Antitrust Act); Wilson Chemical Co. 64 F.T.C. 168 (1964) (attorney liable under the FTC Act); *Hearings on S. 1984 Before the Senate Comm. on Commerce, Science and Transportation*, 97th Cong., 2d Sess., 32–36 (1982) (FTC letter arguing that professionals must be covered by the FTC Act). *Cf.* Ivey, Barnum & O'Mara v. Indian Harbor Properties, Inc., 190 Conn. 528, 461 A.2d 1369 (1983) (UDAP statute may apply to attorneys, but not here because dispute did not meet former public interest test); Note, *Tolling the Death Knell on the "Learned Profession" Immunity Under the Consumer Protection Act: Short v. Demopolis*, 21 Willimette L.J. 899 (1985).

1041 Kelly v. Nelson, Mullins, Riley & Scarborough, 2002 U.S. Dist. LEXIS 6430 (M.D. Fla. Mar. 20, 2002); Banks v. Department of Consumer & Regulatory Affairs, 634 A.2d 433 (D.C. 1993) (legal services are covered by UDAP statute; case involved a non-lawyer performing services); Reed v. Allison & Perrone, 376 So. 2d 1067 (La. Ct. App. 1979); Camp v. Springs Mortgage Corp., 414 S.E.2d 784 (S.C. Ct. App. 1991); Sample v. Freeman, 873 S.W.2d 470 (Tex. 1994); Haynes & Boone v. Bowser Bouldin, Ltd., 864 S.W.2d 662 (Tex. App. 1993); Johnson v. DeLay, 809 S.W.2d 552 (Tex. App. 1991); Parker v. Carnahan, 772 S.W.2d 151 (Tex. App. 1989); Barnard v. Mecom, 650 S.W.2d 123 (Tex. App. 1983); Lucas v. Nesbitt, 653 S.W.2d 883 (Tex. App. 1983); DeBakey v. Staggs, 605 S.W.2d 631 (Tex. Civ. App. 1980), *aff'd*, 612 S.W.2d 924 (Tex. 1981); *see also* Heath v. Herron, 732 S.W.2d 748 (Tex. App. 1987). *But see* Pucci v. Smith, 711 F. Supp. 916 (N.D. Ill. 1989); Robertson v. White, 633 F. Supp. 954 (W.D. Ark. 1986) (Oklahoma law); Lurz v. Panek, 172 Ill. App. 3d 915, 527 N.E.2d 663 (1988); Guess v. Brophy, 164 Ill. App. 3d 75, 517 N.E.2d 693 (1987) (UDAP does not apply to furnishing of legal services to client); Frahm v. Urkovich, 113 Ill. App. 3d 580, 447 N.E.2d 1007 (1983); Thibaut, Thibaut, Garrett & Bacot v. Smith & Loveless, Inc., 576 So. 2d 532 (La. Ct. App. 1990); Vort v. Hollander, 257 N.J. Super. 56, 607 A.2d 1339 (1992) (attorneys' services are not ordinary commercial sales of goods and services, so are not covered), *questioned by* Waterloov Gutter Protection Sys. Co. v. Absolute Gutter Protection, 64 F. Supp. 2d 398 (D.N.J. 1999) (noting erosion of exemption of professionals); Newton v. Cox, 1992 Tenn. App. LEXIS 758, Clearinghouse No. 51,277 (Tenn. App. 1992) (alternate holding), *rev'd on other grounds*, 878 S.W.2d 105 (Tenn. 1994).

1042 Eriks v. Denver, 824 P.2d 1207 (Wash. 1992); Short v. Demopolis, 691 P.2d 163 (Wash. 1984); Manteufel v. Safeco Ins. Co., 68 P.3d 1093 (Wash. App. 2003) (insured has no UDAP claim against insurer's attorney for claim denial); Whitcombe v. Barr, 2000 Wash. App. LEXIS 1720 (Sept. 5, 2000) (unpublished, citation limited) (collection of fees and withdrawal from case due to nonpayment did not involve entrepreneurial aspect); Meryhew v. Gillingham, 893 P.2d 692 (Wash. Ct. App. 1995) (billing and collecting fees covered, but claims regarding fees collected from a probate estate are barred unless brought before estate is closed). *See also* Quinn v. Connelly, 63 Wash. App. 733, 821 P.2d 1256 (1992) (billing practice covered, but no violation found); Styrk v. Cornerstone Investments, Inc., 61 Wash. App. 463, 810 P.2d 1366 (1991) (closing real estate transactions and acting as escrow agent were commercial activities).

1043 Suffield Dev. Assocs. v. Nat'l Loan Investors, 260 Conn. 766, 802 A.2d 44 (Conn. 2002) (law firm's execution on behalf of its client on judgment owed by plaintiff not entrepreneurial); Beverly Hills Concepts v. Schatz & Schatz, Ribicoff & Kotkin, 247 Conn. 48, 717 A.2d 724 (1998).

1044 Kessler v. Loftus, 994 F. Supp. 240 (D. Vt. 1997).

1045 Zimmerman v. Cohen, 2004 WL 877853 (D. Conn. Apr. 23, 2004); Evanauskas v. Strumpf, 2001 U.S. Dist. LEXIS 14326 (D. Conn. June 27, 2001) (collection activities for client do not involve entrepreneurial aspects, so debtor can not sue creditor's attorney); Campion v. Credit Bureau Servs., Inc., 2000 U.S. Dist. LEXIS 20233 (E.D. Wash. Sept. 19, 2000) (attorney's collection activities are professional rather than entrepreneurial so are exempt); Beverly Hills Concepts v. Schatz & Schatz, Ribicoff & Kotkin, 247 Conn. 48, 717 A.2d 724 (1998) (professional negligence not covered); Eriks v. Denver, 824 P.2d 1207 (Wash. 1992); Haberman v. Washington Public Power Supply Sys., 109 Wash. 2d 107, 744 P.2d 1032 (1987); Quinn v. Connelly, 63 Wash. App. 733, 821 P.2d 1256 (1992). *See also* Ikuno v. Yip, 912 F.2d 306 (9th Cir. 1990) (Washington law) (negligence in instructing client how to act lawfully not covered by UDAP); Demopolis v. People's Nat'l Bank of Washington, 59 Wash. App. 105, 796 P.2d 426 (1990) (lawyer's alleged defamatory allegation against opposing party not covered by UDAP statute).

1046 Schimenti v. Whitman & Ransom, 208 A.D.2d 470, 617 N.Y.S.2d 742 (App. 1994). *See also* Jackson v. Ferrera, 2002 WL 32348328 (E.D. Pa. Apr. 16, 2002) (Pa. UDAP statute does not cover legal malpractice claims); Meyer v. Wagner, 429 Mass. 410, 709 N.E.2d 784 (1999) (garden-variety malpractice was not a UDAP violation); Chipman v. Shocket, 60 Mass. App. Ct. 1109, 800 N.E.2d 726 (Mass. App. Ct. 2003) (unpublished, text available at 2003 WL 22992124).

1047 Cripe v. Leiter, 184 Ill. 2d 185, 703 N.E.2d 100 (1998). *Accord* Wafra Leasing Corp. v. Prime Capital Corp., 204 F. Supp. 2d 1120 (N.D. Ill. 2002).

1048 Macedo v. Dello Russo, 178 N.J. 340, 840 A.2d 238 (2004).

includes an explicit exception for transactions between attorneys and their clients.[1049] An attorney's acts toward third parties on behalf of a client—for example in the debt collection context—should not fall within this exception, however. The Texas UDAP statute was amended in 1995 to include a limited exemption for professionals who provide advice, judgment, an opinion, or a similar professional skill.[1050] Such professionals remain liable for express misrepresentations of material facts and some nondisclosures, unconscionable acts, and breaches of warranty.[1051] Even without an actual attorney-client relationship, the plaintiff may have UDAP "consumer" status.[1052] Texas consumers formerly could raise malpractice-based UDAP claims,[1053] but now can only raise claims that lie outside negligence/malpractice, such as affirmative misrepresentations,[1054] or unconscionable conduct.[1055] One court held that an attorney's affair with his client's wife was not actionable under the UDAP statute, because it was malpractice rather than deceptive or unconscionable.[1056] The Texas Supreme Court has said that general representations of opinion, in particular, are too vague to support UDAP liability.[1057] However, misrepresentations of the law, when stated in detail, may rise above the exclusion of general representations of opinion.[1058]

A North Carolina court has held that an attorney performing professional services falls into the state's exception for members of a learned profession.[1059] As a result, attorney collectors are exempt from UDAP liability for debt collection abuses, but entrepreneurial aspects of the attorney's practice, i.e., acts geared toward the firm's interests rather than its clients', would be covered. The exemption for attorneys does not prevent an attorney from pursuing a UDAP claim, however.[1060]

Even if an attorney's conduct in providing legal services is not covered by a UDAP statute, other attorney conduct can be covered.[1061] It is the lawyer-client relationship that is outside the statute's scope; there is no blanket immunity from deceptive conduct for those graduating from law school.[1062] For example, coverage is more likely if the attorney is fulfilling more than one role, e.g., is acting not just as a lawyer but also as an investor.[1063] If the UDAP statute covers debt collection, an attorney collecting a debt may be covered even if the relationship with his or her own client is exempt.[1064] Moreover, non-lawyers who hold themselves out as providing legal services are covered by UDAP statutes.[1065]

The Massachusetts Supreme Court holds that only the client, or someone acting on a client's behalf, can assert a UDAP claim against an attorney.[1066] Thus, an attorney who prepared a will can not be subjected to a UDAP claim by relatives that the client excluded from inheritance.[1067] On the other hand, the attorney for the administrator of an estate may owe a duty to the heirs akin to that in an attorney-client relationship, and thus be subject to the heirs' UDAP suit.[1068]

Connecticut also holds that a consumer can not maintain a UDAP action against an attorney who represented an opposing party rather than the consumer.[1069] Allowing such UDAP suits would interfere with "the attorney's primary duty of robust representation of the interests of his or her client." A Washington appellate opinion agrees with this analysis.[1070] A court interpreting the District of Columbia UDAP law has held that statements made by a party's attorney in litigation can not be the basis of a UDAP deception claim.[1071]

Another special concern about attorney UDAP coverage is whether the regulation of attorneys by courts or bar associations displaces the applicability of the UDAP statute.

1049 Burke v. Gammarino, 108 Ohio App. 3d 138, 670 N.E.2d 295 (1995).

1050 Tex. Bus. & Com. Code Ann. § 17.49(c).

1051 Nast v. State Farm Fire and Cas. Co., 82 S.W.3d 114 (Tex. App. 2002); James V. Mazuca and Assocs. v. Schumann, 82 S.W.3d 90 (Tex. App. 2002); *cf.* Latham v. Castillo, 972 S.W.2d 66 (Tex. 1998) (interpreting Texas UDAP statute prior to amendment as applying to attorney's unconscionable conduct of misrepresenting that suit would be filed; court distinguishes between legal malpractice of not filing suit within statute of limitations and UDAP claim based on misrepresentation to client that suit had been filed).

1052 Roberts v. Healey, 991 S.W.2d 873 (Tex. App. 1999).

1053 Rodriguez v. Klein, 960 S.W.2d 179 (Tex. App. 1997).

1054 Cadle Co. v. Sweet & Brousseau, P.C., 1998 U.S. Dist. LEXIS 2632 (N.D. Tex. Mar. 3, 1998).

1055 Latham v. Castillo, 972 S.W.2d 66 (Tex. 1998); Ballesteros v. Jones, 985 S.W.2d 485 (Tex. App. 1998). *But see* Goffney v. Rabson, 56 S.W.3d 186 (Tex. App. 2001).

1056 Kahlig v. Boyd, 980 S.W.2d 685 (Tex. App. 1998).

1057 Douglas v. Delp, 987 S.W.2d 879 (Tex. 1999).

1058 Streber v. Hunter, 221 F.3d 701 (5th Cir. 2000).

1059 Reid v. Ayers, 138 N.C. App. 261, 531 S.E.2d 231 (2000).

1060 Boyce & Isley v. Cooper, 568 S.E.2d 893 (N.C. App. 2002).

1061 Pucci v. Litwin, 828 F. Supp. 1285 (N.D. Ill. 1993).

1062 *Id.*

1063 Waterloov Gutter Protection Sys. Co. v. Absolute Gutter Protection, 64 F. Supp. 2d 398 (D.N.J. 1999) (discussing attorney coverage issues but finding it unnecessary to decide them). *See also* Macedo v. Dello Russo, 178 N.J. 340, 840 A.2d 238 (2004) (learned professionals are exempt but not when acting outside professional capacity).

1064 Daniels v. Baritz, 2003 WL 21027238, at *5 (E.D. Pa. Apr. 30, 2003); Rachoza v. Gallas & Schultz, 1998 U.S. Dist. LEXIS 5018 (D. Kan. Mar. 23, 1998).

1065 Banks v. Department of Consumer & Regulatory Affairs, 634 A.2d 433 (D.C. 1993). *See* § 5.12.2, *infra.*

1066 Tetrault v. Mahoney, Hawkes & Goldings, 425 Mass. 456, 681 N.E.2d 1189 (1997).

1067 Miller v. Mooney, 431 Mass. 57, 725 N.E.2d 545 (2000).

1068 McCarthy v. Landry, 42 Mass. App. Ct. 488, 678 N.E.2d 172 (1997).

1069 Jackson v. R.G. Whipple, Inc., 225 Conn. 705, 627 A.2d 374 (1993); Field v. Kearns, 43 Conn. App. 265, 682 A.2d 148 (1996).

1070 Jeckle v. Crotty, 85 P.3d 931 (Wash. App. 2004).

1071 Athridge v. Aetna Cas. & Surety Co., 351 F.3d 1166 (D.C. Cir. 2003).

For example, after finding attorneys to be in trade or commerce, the Connecticut Supreme Court still had to determine whether the state judiciary's pervasive supervision of attorneys prevents application of the UDAP statute to the profession. The court ruled that simultaneous regulation of attorneys by the judiciary and the UDAP statute did not violate the constitutional doctrine of separation of powers, and that the overlap in regulation was reasonable.[1072] The court noted that judicial supervision of the bar does not include a damage remedy for injured clients.

On the other hand, the New Hampshire Supreme Court, in a divided opinion, has exempted lawyers because of specific language in its UDAP statute that the court interpreted as exempting practices regulated by the bar association.[1073] This language has now been replaced with an exemption for trade or commerce that is subject to the jurisdiction of certain specified regulatory agencies, and the bar association is not listed.[1074] The Illinois Supreme Court has also held attorneys exempt.[1075] Federal courts ruling on UDAP issues in Pennsylvania have noted that coverage of attorneys may be inconsistent with the state supreme court's exclusive constitutional authority to regulate the conduct of attorneys, but no court has yet decided the question.[1076] In light of the state supreme court's authority to regulate attorneys, a Delaware court has declined to find attorneys covered by the state UDAP statute without explicit statutory language.[1077]

1072 Heslin v. Connecticut Law Clinic of Trantolo & Trantolo, 190 Conn. 510, 461 A.2d 938 (1983); *see also* Waterloo v. Gutter Protection Sys. Co. v. Absolute Gutter Protection, 64 F. Supp. 2d 398 (D.N.J. 1999) (suggesting that similar question may be an issue in New Jersey); Field v. Kearns, 682 A.2d 148 (Conn. App. 1996); Noble v. Marshall, 23 Conn. App. 227, 579 A.2d 594 (1990); Short v. Demopolis, 691 P.2d 163 (Wash. 1984).

1073 Rousseau v. Eshleman, 519 A.2d 243 (N.H. 1986) (attorneys are regulated by professional conduct committee and thus excluded by statute exempting practices otherwise permitted by regulatory agency; vigorous and detailed dissent that supervision of attorneys by professional conduct committee is not adequate state regulation), *motion for reconsideration denied*, 529 A.2d 862 (N.H. 1987) (concurring opinion distinguishes entrepreneurial aspects of legal profession, that are covered, from malpractice issues cases that are not within UDAP scope). The New Hampshire Supreme Court reaffirmed the holding of this case in Averill v. Cox, 761 A.2d 1083 (N.H. 2000).

1074 N.H. Rev. Stat. Ann. § 358-A:3, *as amended, effective* July 17, 2002.

1075 Cripe v. Leiter, 184 Ill. 2d 185, 703 N.E.2d 100 (1998).

1076 Crossley v. Lieberman, 90 B.R. 682, 695 (E.D. Pa. 1988), *aff'd on other grounds*, 868 F.2d 566 (3d Cir. 1989); Littles v. Lieberman, 90 B.R. 700 (E.D. Pa. 1988). *See* Carter, Pennsylvania Consumer Law § 2.4.3.5 (George T. Bisel Co., Philadelphia 2d ed. 2003 and Supp.) for further discussion of Pennsylvania coverage of attorneys.

1077 Jamgochian v. Prousalis, 2000 Del. Super. LEXIS 373 (Aug. 31, 2000).

2.3.10 Medical Professionals

The FTC considers doctors and other medical professionals to be covered by the FTC Act language of "trade or commerce."[1078] Courts in Connecticut,[1079] the District of Columbia,[1080] Kentucky,[1081] Michigan,[1082] and Washington[1083] hold that the entrepreneurial aspects of medicine are covered by the UDAP statute's "trade or commerce" scope, but actions for negligence or malpractice are not covered because these claims go to competence.[1084] Thus performing a procedure without the patient's informed consent is covered,[1085] but mere professional malpractice or negligence is not.[1086] These courts have noted that "it would be a dangerous form of elitism, indeed, to dole out exemptions to our consumer protection laws merely on the basis of the edu-

1078 See Hearings on S. 1984 Before the Senate Comm. on Commerce, Science and Transportation, 97th Cong., 2d Sess. 32–36 (1982).

1079 Janusaukas v. Fichman, 264 Conn. 796, 826 A.2d 1066 (2003) (doctor's statements regarding level of care not covered; advertisements that are independent of treatment may be entrepreneurial, but these ads were not deceptive); Sherwood v. Danbury Hosp., 252 Conn. 193, 746 A.2d 730 (2000); Haynes v. Yale-New Haven Hosps., 243 Conn. 17, 699 A.2d 964 (1997); Rumbin v. Baez, 52 Conn. App. 487, 727 A.2d 744 (1999) (applying same rule to licensed psychologist and holding that UDAP statute does not apply to claim that services did not meet professional standards).

1080 Dorn v. McTigue, 121 F. Supp. 2d 17 (D.D.C. 2000) (conduct within entrepreneurial, commercial, or business aspect of a physician's practice is covered), *partial summary judgment granted by* 157 F. Supp. 2d 37 (D.D.C. 2001) (doctor's statements about surgery did not have entrepreneurial motivation).

1081 Simmons v. Stephenson, 84 S.W.3d 926 (Ky. App. 2002).

1082 Nelson v. Ho, 564 N.W.2d 482 (Mich. App. 1997).

1083 O'Malley v. Group Health Coop., 2001 Wash. App. LEXIS 2609 (Nov. 26, 2001) (HMO is subject to UDAP suit only if its physicians' omissions were motivated by business concerns rather than negligence); State Farm Fire & Cas. Co. v. Huynh, 92 Wash. App. 454, 962 P.2d 854 (1998); Benoy v. Simons, 66 Wash. App. 56, 831 P.2d 167 (1992); Burnet v. Spokane Ambulance, 54 Wash. App. 162, 772 P.2d 1027 (1989) (extending entrepreneurial vs. malpractice distinction not only to doctors, but also to hospitals); Jaramillo v. Morris, 50 Wash. App. 822, 750 P.2d 1301 (1988); Quimby v. Fine, 45 Wash. App. 175, 724 P.2d 403 (1986).

1084 *See also* Elder v. Fischer, 717 N.E.2d 730 (Ohio App. 1998) (noting distinction between UDAP claims regarding commercial aspects of nursing home care and malpractice-type claims).

1085 Quimby v. Fine, 45 Wash. App. 175, 724 P.2d 403 (1986). *But cf.* Darviris v. Petros, 59 Mass. App. Ct. 323, 795 N.E.2d 1196 (Mass. App. Ct. 2003) (negligent failure to obtain patient's informed consent for a particular surgical procedure was not unfair or deceptive).

1086 Haynes v. Yale-New Haven Hosps., 243 Conn. 17, 699 A.2d 964 (1997); Nelson v. Ho, 564 N.W.2d 482 (Mich. App. 1997); Jaramillo v. Morris, 50 Wash. App. 822, 750 P.2d 1301 (1988). *See also* Physical Therapy & Sports Fitness Assocs. v. Curran, Clearinghouse No. 47,928 (Md. Cir. Ct. Feb. 26, 1992) (note that in 2003 Maryland adopted an explicit exemption for health care providers).

cational level needed to practice a given profession, or for that matter, the impact which the profession has on society's health and welfare."[1087]

New York's highest court holds that there is no blanket UDAP exemption for medical providers.[1088] Accordingly, a UDAP claim could proceed against an *in vitro* fertilization clinic that lured patients by advertising exaggerated success rates. The fact that a plaintiff might have both a UDAP false advertising claim and a claim under New York's informed consent law did not concern the court. While New York does not follow the entrepreneurial/malpractice distinction, the court expects that individual disputes about the quality of care will be weeded out by its rule that UDAP plaintiffs must show an impact on consumers at large. The South Carolina Supreme Court, while not specifically addressing whether physicians are exempt, has held that its UDAP statute does not exclude professionals, and that medical laboratory services are covered.[1089] A federal court has applied the Vermont UDAP statute to a medical laboratory that allegedly misrepresented that it had analyzed a medical sample, finding no exemption for professional services.[1090]

In many states, the language of a particular state UDAP statute is critical because some statutes exempt "learned professions"[1091] or even doctors and dentists explicitly. Ohio's statutory exclusion of physician-patient transactions has been construed to exempt licensed chiropractors as well as medical doctors.[1092] A 2003 amendment to Maryland's UDAP statute prohibits a private cause of action for injuries sustained as a result of professional services provided by a health care provider.[1093] A Texas statute explicitly prohibits UDAP personal injury or death claims against physicians or health care providers where the claim is based on negligence.[1094] But this statute does not exclude UDAP coverage for intentional misrepresentation,[1095] or even for breach of implied warranty, but only for negligence claims.[1096] Where the UDAP claim is truly a separate claim, and not merely a recasting of a negligence claim, the UDAP claim will stand.[1097] But a cause of action in Texas based on failing to inform a patient of the risks of surgery is a negligence claim, and a UDAP action is precluded.[1098] Another court curiously held that a medical provider could be sued under the UDAP statute for breach of warranty or misrepresentations, but only if they were in writing.[1099] The Texas Veterinary Licensing Act provides a similar exemption from the Texas UDAP statute for veterinary negligence.[1100]

Even if a UDAP statute does not specifically exempt medical practitioners, they may fall within a general exemption for regulated industries or practices permitted by other laws. This type of exemption is discussed in § 2.3.3, *supra*. Two courts have found that a state's special medical malpractice statute creating a pre-litigation screening panel preempts UDAP medical malpractice actions.[1101] There is

1087 Haynes v. Yale-New Haven Hosps., 243 Conn. 17, 699 A.2d 964 (1997); Nelson v. Ho, 564 N.W.2d 482 (Mich. App. 1997).

1088 Karlin v. IVF Am., Inc., 93 N.Y.2d 282, 712 N.E.2d 662 (1999).

1089 Taylor v. Medenica, 479 S.E.2d 35 (S.C. 1996).

1090 Bridge v. Corning Life Sciences, Inc., 997 F. Supp. 551 (D. Vt. 1998).

1091 *See* Cohn v. Wilkes General Hosps., 767 F. Supp. 111 (W.D.N.C. 1991), *aff'd on other grounds*, Cohn v. Bond, 953 F.2d 154 (4th Cir. 1991); Phillips v. A Triangle Women's Health Clinic, Inc., 573 S.E.2d 600 (N.C. App. 2002) (North Carolina exemption for learned professions precludes UDAP suit against physician; dissent argues that conduct in question was not a rendering of professional services so should not be exempt); Gaunt v. Pittaway, 139 N.C. App. 778, 534 S.E.2d 660 (2000) (physicians exempt even when making disparaging remarks about other physicians); Abram v. Charter Medical Corp. of Raleigh, Inc., 100 N.C. App. 718, 398 S.E.2d 331 (1990); Wisenbarger v. Gonzales Warm Springs Rehabilitation Hosp., 789 S.W.2d 688 (Tex. App. 1990) (provider of services to cure chemical dependency was involved in exempt "learned profession").

1092 Chiropractic Clinic of Solon v. Kutsko, 92 Ohio App. 3d 608, 636 N.E.2d 422 (1994).

1093 Md. Code Comm. Law § 13-408.

1094 Tex. Civ. Prac. & Rem. Code § 74.004 (formerly Tex. Rev. Civ. Stat. Ann. Art. 4590i, § 12.01(a). *See also* Tex. Bus. & Comm. Code § 17.49(c) (limiting UDAP claims against professionals), (e) (limiting bodily injury claims). *See* Earle v. Ratliff, 998 S.W.2d 882 (Tex. 1999); MacGregor Medical Ass'n v. Campbell, 985 S.W.2d 38 (Tex. 1998); Mulligan v. Beverly-Enterprises Texas Inc., 954 S.W.2d 881 (Tex. App. 1997) (nursing home); *see also* Sorokolit v. Rhodes, 889 S.W.2d 239 (Tex. 1994); Drury v. Baptist Memorial Hosp. Sys., 933 S.W.2d 668 (Tex. App. 1996); Allen v. Tolon, 918 S.W.2d 605 (Tex. App. 1996); Chapman v. Paul R. Wilson, Jr., D.D.S., Inc., 826 S.W.2d 214 (Tex. App. 1992); Wisenbarger v. Gonzales Warm Springs Rehabilitation Hosp., 789 S.W.2d 688 (Tex. App. 1990); Quinn v. Memorial Medical Center, 764 S.W.2d 915 (Tex. App. 1989).

1095 Campbell v. MacGregor Medical Ass'n, 966 S.W.2d 538 (Tex. App. 1997), *rev'd*, 985 S.W.2d 38 (Tex. 1998) (characterizing plaintiff's claim as involving failure to meet standard of care rather than knowing misrepresentation); Rhodes v. Sorokolit, 846 S.W.2d 618 (Tex. App. 1993); Chapman v. Paul R. Wilson, Jr., D.D.S., Inc., 826 S.W.2d 214 (Tex. App. 1992). *But see* Gomez v. Diaz, 57 S.W.3d 573 (Tex. App. 2001); Waters *ex rel.* Walton v. Del-Ky, Inc., 844 S.W.2d 250 (Tex. App. 1992).

1096 Eoff v. Hal & Charlie Peterson Found., 811 S.W.2d 187 (Tex. App. 1991).

1097 Sorokolit v. Rhodes, 889 S.W.2d 239 (Tex. 1994) (UDAP claim allowable if truly separate, not merely recasting of negligence claim); Cobb v. Dallas Fort Worth Medical Center-Grand Prairie, 48 S.W.3d 820 (Tex. App. 2001) (UDAP claims would be allowed for misrepresentations regarding FDA approval of medical device); Wright v. Fowler, 991 S.W.2d 343 (Tex. App. 1999); Nguyen v. Kim, 3 S.W.3d 146 (Tex. App. 1999); *see also* Gormley v. Stover, 907 S.W.2d 448 (Tex. 1995); Walden v. Jeffery, 907 S.W.2d 446 (Tex. 1995); Drennan v. Community Health Inv. Corp., 905 S.W.2d 811 (Tex. App. 1995).

1098 Drennan v. Community Health Inv. Corp., 905 S.W.2d 811 (Tex. App. 1995).

1099 Smith v. Elliott, 68 S.W.3d 844 (Tex. App. 2002).

1100 Williams v. Neutercorp, 1995 Tex. App. LEXIS 833 (1995).

1101 Keyser v. St. Mary's Hosps., Inc., 662 F. Supp. 191 (D. Idaho 1987); Bremer v. Community Hosps., 583 N.E.2d 780 (Ind. Ct. App. 1991).

also a possibility of preemption of some claims by federal statutes that regulate medical devices.[1102]

Some courts tend to resist any UDAP challenge against a physician. Illinois,[1103] New Jersey,[1104] and Pennsylvania[1105] courts have ruled that the state legislature did not intend its UDAP statute to cover physicians even though there is no explicit statutory exclusion. The Pennsylvania court reasoned that inclusion of physicians would imprudently expand their liability for statements about the probable result of treatment that did not succeed. The New Jersey decision relies on policy grounds and the regulation of hospitals by a state agency.

Dentists offer "goods or services" and are also engaged in a "business, vocation, or occupation," so they are covered by the Oregon UDAP statute.[1106] But an Illinois court has extended the judicially-created exemption for physicians to dental care providers, at least those who serve patients at a university dental school clinic.[1107]

Prescription drugs are "merchandise" and their sale is within a UDAP statute's scope.[1108] Medical laboratory services fall within the definition of "trade or commerce."[1109] A federal court has ruled that health care provided by a nursing home is a service primarily for personal, family, or household use and falls within the Pennsylvania UDAP statute's definition of "trade or commerce."[1110] Similarly, an Ohio appellate court has concluded that Ohio's UDAP statute applies to a nursing home's billing practices.[1111] An ambulance service that had generally represented to the public that it had qualified emergency medical personnel who could render aid in emergency conditions can be held liable under a UDAP statute for the death of someone it undertakes to transport to a hospital in response to an emergency call.[1112]

The blood bank activities of the American Red Cross have been held not to involve a sale of consumer goods by a merchant.[1113] Issues as to whether nonprofit institutions (such as hospitals) or municipal corporations (such as municipal hospitals) are covered by a UDAP statute are discussed in other sections.[1114]

2.3.11 Other Professionals

Where a state UDAP statute is found to apply to lawyers or doctors, it should also apply to other professionals. Thus a Texas court has found architects and architectural malpractice to be covered by the UDAP statute.[1115] (However, a statutory amendment five years later exempted those providing professional services from many types of UDAP actions.) The converse, of course, may not be true because of the special treatment courts may give to bar regulation of attorneys or to regulation of the medical profession. Further, the state supreme court does not have exclusive authority over other professions as it does over attorneys under many state constitutions.[1116] For example, accountants and architects[1117] are not exempt from UDAP coverage in Illinois even though the practice of medicine and law may be, because the accounting and architecture professions are not subject to similar policing and regulation.[1118] Nor are accountants exempt in Oregon.[1119] Professional engineers are covered by the Kansas statute.[1120]

The New Jersey Supreme Court excludes learned professionals from its UDAP statute, as long as they are operating in their professional capacities.[1121] If the professional is operating in a different capacity, however, such as an architect who participates in the deceptive marketing of homes, then the UDAP statute applies.[1122]

Some courts draw a distinction between entrepreneurial and professional aspects of a practice. A federal court in Connecticut has held that academic research and publication are not in trade or commerce because they are not entrepreneurial.[1123] A Washington appellate court has held that only

1102 *See* § 2.5.8, *infra.*

1103 Gadson v. Newman, 807 F. Supp. 1412 (C.D. Ill. 1992); Evanston Hosps. v. Crane, 627 N.E.2d 29 (Ill. App. Ct. 1993) (health care aspects as opposed to business aspects of practice of medicine are not covered by UDAP statute).

1104 Hampton Hosps. v. Bresan, 288 N.J. Super. 372, 672 A.2d 725 (App. 1996). *See also* Macedo v. Dello Russo, 178 N.J. 340, 840 A.2d 238 (2004) (creating general exemption for learned professionals).

1105 Foflygen v. R. Zemel, M.D. (P.C.), 615 A.2d 1345 (Pa. Super. Ct. 1992); Gatten v. Merzi, 397 Pa. Super. 148, 579 A.2d 974 (1990).

1106 Investigators Inc. v. Harvey, 53 Or. App. 586, 633 P.2d 6 (1981).

1107 Doe v. Northwestern University, 682 N.E.2d 145 (Ill. App. Ct. 1997), *aff'd on other grounds sub nom.* Majca v. Beekil, 701 N.E.2d 1084, 183 Ill. 2d 407 (1998).

1108 Kociemba v. G.D. Searle & Co., 680 F. Supp. 1293 (D. Minn. 1988).

1109 Taylor v. Medenica, 479 S.E.2d 35 (S.C. 1996).

1110 Chalfin v. Beverly Enterprises, Inc., 741 F. Supp. 1162 (E.D. Pa. 1989); *see also* Lebish v. Whitehall Manor Inc., 57 Pa. D. & C.4th 247 (C.P. 2002) (declining to dismiss UDAP claim against nursing home).

1111 Elder v. Fischer, 717 N.E.2d 730 (Ohio App. 1998).

1112 Townsend v. Catalina Ambulance Co., 857 S.W.2d 791 (Tex. App. 1993).

1113 Kozup v. Georgetown University, 663 F. Supp. 1048 (D.D.C. 1987).

1114 §§ 2.3.5, 2.3.6, *supra.*

1115 White Budd Van Ness P'ship v. Major-Gladys Drive Joint Venture, 798 S.W.2d 805 (Tex. App. 1990).

1116 *See* Moore v. Bird Engineering Co., 41 P.3d 755 (Kan. 2002).

1117 Parkman & Weston Assocs., Ltd. v. Ebenezer A.M.E. Church, 2003 WL 22287358 (N.D. Ill. Sept. 30, 2003).

1118 Wafra Leasing Corp. v. Prime Capital Corp., 204 F. Supp. 1120 (N.D. Ill. 2002); Lyne v. Arthur Anderson & Co., 772 F. Supp. 1064 (N.D. Ill. 1991).

1119 State *ex rel.* Kulongoski v. Cunning, 139 Or. App. 515, 912 P.2d 958 (1996).

1120 Moore v. Bird Engineering Co., 41 P.3d 755 (Kan. 2002).

1121 Macedo v. Dello Russo, 178 N.J. 340, 840 A.2d 238 (2004).

1122 Blatterfein v. Larken, 323 N.J. Super. 167, 732 A.2d 555 (App. Div. 1999).

1123 Johnson v. Schmitz, 119 F. Supp. 2d 90 (D. Conn. 2000).

the entrepreneurial aspects of an auditor's practice are subject to the UDAP statute.[1124] As a result, disappointed investors could not assert a UDAP claim against the accounting firm that had audited the company in which they invested.[1125] A federal court finds that the New Mexico UDAP statute applies at least to the entrepreneurial aspects of the activities of licensed professionals such as accountants.[1126] The Texas UDAP statute provides a limited exemption for professionals who provide advice, judgment, an opinion, or a similar professional skill.[1127] This exemption applies to accountants.[1128] However, investment advice appears to be covered by the UDAP statute, although the defendant did not raise the professional exemption.[1129] North Carolina's exemption for "learned professions" covers architects.[1130]

2.3.12 *Out-of-State Transactions*

A state UDAP statute may specify to which out-of-state transactions it applies. Even if it does not, a court may have to determine whether to apply the statute to transactions that occur primarily out of state.

The Maine UDAP statute formerly exempted sellers where twenty percent of their gross revenue was derived from interstate commerce, except where the transaction occurred primarily within the state. Maine's highest court, applying this exemption for interstate sellers, ruled that Ford Motor Company's car sales practices occur primarily outside of Maine.[1131] Maine's statute now applies to "any trade or commerce directly or indirectly affecting the people of this State," without any exception for sellers involved in interstate commerce.[1132] One court has held that the statute is still inapplicable to acts occurring out of state, but this decision did not take into account the language "directly or indirectly affecting the people of this State."[1133]

The Massachusetts UDAP statute formerly contained a similar exemption, but the exemption now applies only where one business sues another, not where a consumer sues a business.[1134] Thus, while there is extensive precedent in Massachusetts as to when a transaction occurs primarily in that state, the cases are almost all business suing business cases.[1135] Courts applying the Massachusetts test apply a

1124 Reale v. Ernst & Young, L.L.P., 2000 Wash. App. LEXIS 1239 (July 10, 2000).

1125 *See also* Spencer v. Doyle, 50 Mass. App. Ct. 6, 733 N.E.2d 1082 (2000) (accountant who issued favorable report on company not liable to investors, where accountant did not have actual knowledge of a limited group that would rely on the audit).

1126 Am. Indian and Alaska Native Cultural and Arts Dev. Inst. v. Daymon & Assocs., 1999 U.S. Dist. LEXIS 22380 (D.N.M. June 23, 1999).

1127 Tex. Bus. & Com. Code Ann. § 17.49(c). *But see* Cole v. Central Valley Chemicals, Inc., 9 S.W.3d 207 (Tex. App. 1999) (pesticide salesman's representations about product performance were not rendering of a professional service).

1128 *In re* R&C Petroleum, Inc., 236 B.R. 355 (Bankr. E.D. Tex. 1999).

1129 Wingate v. Acree, 2003 WL 1922569 (Tex. App. Apr. 24, 2003).

1130 RCDI Constr. v. Space/Architecture Planning, 2002 U.S. App. LEXIS 640 (4th Cir. Jan. 15, 2002) (unpublished, citation limited).

1131 State *ex rel.* Tierney v. Ford Motor Co., 436 A.2d 866 (Me. 1981).

1132 Me. Rev. Stat. Ann. tit. 5, § 206.

1133 Marshall v. Scotia Prince Cruises Ltd., 2003 WL 22709076 (D. Me. Nov. 17, 2003).

1134 *See* Mass. Gen. Laws ch. 93A, §§ 9, 11. *See also* Back Bay Farm, L.L.C. v. Collucio, 230 F. Supp. 2d 136 (D. Mass. 2002); Amtrol, Inc. v. Tudor Ins. Co., 2002 WL 31194863 (D. Mass. Sept. 10, 2002); Boos v. Abbott Laboratories, 925 F. Supp. 49 (D. Mass. 1996) (Massachusetts locus required only for actions brought under § 11, not § 9).

1135 *See, e.g.*, Zyla v. Wadsworth, Div. of Thomson Corp., 360 F.3d 243 (1st Cir. 2004); M&I Heat Transfer Products, Ltd. v. Gorchev, 141 F.3d 21 (1st Cir. 1998) (transaction did not occur primarily within the state); Camp Creek Hospitality Inns v. Sheraton Franchise, 139 F.3d 1396 (11th Cir. 1997) (Mass. law) (fact that defendant is a Massachusetts corporation is not in itself enough to make transaction occur within Massachusetts); Play Time v. LDDS Metromedia Communications, Inc., 123 F.3d 23 (1st Cir. 1997) (Mass. law) (transaction occurred sufficiently within Massachusetts); Roche v. Royal Bank of Canada, 109 F.3d 820 (1st Cir. 1997); Compagnie de Reassurance v. New England Reinsurance, 57 F.3d 56 (1st Cir. 1995); Clinton Hosps. Ass'n v. Carson Group, Inc., 907 F.2d 1260 (1st Cir. 1990) (Massachusetts law) (corporation's activities held to be primarily and substantially in Massachusetts); Amtrol, Inc. v. Tudor Ins. Co., 2002 WL 31194863 (D. Mass. Sept. 10, 2002) (section 11 suit barred because of insufficient acts in Mass., but business can also bring unfair insurance practices claim under section 9); Henry v. Nat'l Geographic Soc., 147 F. Supp. 2d 16 (D. Mass. 2001) (Mass. UDAP statute did not apply where conduct occurred primarily in D.C.); Citicorp N. Am. v. Ogden Martin Sys., 8 F. Supp. 2d 72 (D. Mass. 1998), *aff'd*, 202 F.3d 454 (1st Cir. 2000); Maltz v. Union Carbide Chemicals & Plastics Co., 992 F. Supp. 286 (S.D.N.Y. 1998) (defendant did not meet burden to show transaction did not occur primarily within the state); Bradley v. Dean Witter Realty Inc., 967 F. Supp. 19 (D. Mass. 1997) (transaction occurred sufficiently within Massachusetts); Arthur D. Little Int'l, Inc. v. Dooyang Corp., 928 F. Supp. 1189 (D. Mass. 1996) (transaction not substantially within Massachusetts); Central Mass. Television Inc. v. Amplicon, Inc., 930 F. Supp. 16 (D. Mass. 1996) (same); American Management Servs., Inc. v. George S. May Int'l Co., 933 F. Supp. 64 (D. Mass. 1996) (same); Wilson Group, Inc. v. Quorum Health Resources, Inc., 880 F. Supp. 416 (D.S.C. 1995) (Massachusetts UDAP claim fails because of dearth of improper conduct alleged there); Lone Star Indus., Inc. v. Lafarge Corp., 882 F. Supp. 482 (D. Md. 1995) (sufficient acts occurred in Massachusetts); Sterling Suffolk Racecourse Ltd. v. Burrillville Racing Ass'n, 802 F. Supp. 662 (D.R.I. 1992) (interpreting Mass. UDAP statute), *aff'd on other grounds*, 989 F.2d 1266 (1st Cir. 1993); Charles River Data Sys. v. Oracle Complex Sys., 788 F. Supp. 54 (D. Mass. 1991); Eastland Bank v. MassBank for Savings, 767 F. Supp. 29 (D.R.I. 1991), *aff'd without op.*, 953 F.2d 633 (1st Cir. 1991); Fink v. DeClassis, 745 F. Supp. 509 (N.D. Ill. 1990) (Massachusetts UDAP statute does not apply where negotiations and alleged misrepresentations occurred in

functional analysis that considers where the defendant committed the alleged unfair or deceptive practices, where the plaintiff received and acted upon the unfair or deceptive statements, and the *situs* of the plaintiff's losses.[1136] The burden is on the defendant to contest application of the Massachusetts UDAP statute.[1137]

Ohio's UDAP statute covers only acts or practices "in this state," thus excluding a mobile home transaction where the manufacture, negotiation and sale all took place in another state.[1138] The Kansas[1139] and New York[1140] statutes and one of Delaware's UDAP statutes[1141] have similar limitations. The New Hampshire UDAP statute likewise applies only to trade or commerce within the state, and one court has held that causing injury in the state by out-of-state conduct is insufficient.[1142]

New York's highest court interprets its UDAP statute to apply where the deceptive act takes place in the state, regardless of the residence of the consumer.[1143] Hatching a deceptive scheme in New York is not enough, though, where the consumers are solicited and make the purchase out of state.[1144] An earlier lower court decision, allowing the state attorney general to seek restitution on behalf of in-state and out-of-state victims of a deceptive scheme marketed from New York, is likely still valid because the actual deceptive conduct, not just the formulation of the scheme, occurred in the state in that case.[1145]

Where a UDAP statute applies only to sales within the state, it is enough if the solicitation was within the state, even though the sale was out of state.[1146] Similarly, where the Maryland UDAP statute does not specify its applicability to out-of-state transactions, a court found coverage where the seller communicated with consumers or potential consumers within the state.[1147] The District of Columbia UDAP statute has been applied to out-of-state mortgage

---

another state); Logan Equip. Corp. v. Simon Aerials, Inc., 736 F. Supp. 1188 (D. Mass. 1990) (court questions whether acts occurred primarily and substantially in Massachusetts); Shawmut Worcester County Bank v. First Am. Bank & Trust, 731 F. Supp. 57 (D. Mass. 1990) (banking activity occurred out-of-state); Evans v. Yegen Assocs., 556 F. Supp. 1219 (D. Mass. 1989); Robyn Lee Yacht Charters, Inc. v. General Motors Corp., 584 F. Supp. 8 (D. Mass. 1984); Turner v. Johnson & Johnson, 549 F. Supp. 807 (D. Mass. 1982); Service Publication, Inc. v. Governman, 396 Mass. 567, 487 N.E.2d 520 (1986); Bushkin Assoc., Inc. v. Raytheon Co., 473 N.E.2d 662 (Mass. 1985); Burnham v. Mark IV Homes, Inc., 387 Mass. 575, 441 N.E.2d 1027 (1982) (transaction primarily within state where modular home manufactured out-of-state, but delivered to buyer in-state); Makino U.S.A., Inc. v. Metlife Capital Credit Corp., 25 Mass. App. Ct. 302, 518 N.E.2d 519 (1988) (primarily within state even though injury may have been suffered out of state); Goldstein Oil Co. v. C.K. Smith Co., 20 Mass. App. Ct. 243, 479 N.E.2d 728 (1985) (seller's nondelivery of product occurs primarily out-of-state where product was to be delivered out-of-state).

1136 Garshman Co. v. General Electric Co., 176 F.3d 1 (1st Cir. 1999); Clinton Hosps. Ass'n v. Corson Group, Inc., 907 F.2d 1260 (1st Cir. 1990); Boston Hides & Furs v. Sumitomo Bank, 870 F. Supp. 1153 (D. Mass. 1994).

1137 Amcel Corp. v. International Executive Sales, Inc., 170 F.3d 32 (1st Cir. 1999); Kansallis Fin. Ltd. v. Fern, 40 F.3d 476 (1st Cir. 1994); Omni-Wave Electronics Corp. v. Marshall Indus., 127 F.R.D. 644 (D. Mass. 1989); Computer Sys. Engineering, Inc. v. Qantel Corp., 571 F. Supp. 1365 (D. Mass. 1983), *aff'd*, 740 F.2d 59 (1st Cir. 1984) (seller did not meet burden of showing the transaction did not occur primarily in Massachusetts where transaction occurred roughly evenly between two states).

1138 Shorter v. Champion Home Bldrs., 776 F. Supp. 333 (N.D. Ohio 1991); *see also* Delahunt v. Cytodyne Technologies, 241 F. Supp. 2d 827 (S.D. Ohio 2003) (UDAP statute does not cover medication sales made outside Ohio).

1139 Sithon Maritime Co. v. Holiday Mansion, 1999 U.S. Dist. LEXIS 3174 (D. Kan. Feb. 16, 1999) (services performed outside state not covered); Kluin v. Am. Suzuki Motor Corp., 56 P.3d 829 (Kan. 2002) (national advertising and communications in response to buyer's calls insufficient where sale took place out of state). *But cf.* Watkins v. Roach Cadillac, Inc., 7 Kan. App. 2d 8, 637 P.3d 458 (1981) (Kansas UDAP statute covers lease to Kansas resident of vehicle registered in Kansas by dealership located partly in Kansas and partly in Missouri, even though contract signed in Missouri).

1140 Goshen v. Mutual Life Ins. Co., 98 N.Y.2d 314, 774 N.E.2d 1190 (2002) (deceptive act, not merely formulation of deceptive scheme, must occur in state, but statute applies to out-of-state residents who make in-state purchases); Wiener v. Unumprovident Corp., 202 F. Supp. 2d 116 (S.D.N.Y. 2002); Padilla v. Payco Gen. Am. Credits, Inc., 161 F. Supp. 2d 264 (S.D.N.Y. 2001) (dismissing claim for debt collection actions taken before debtor moved to New York); Murrin v. Ford Motor Co., 303 A.D.2d 475, 756 N.Y.S.2d 596 (2003) (affirming dismissal of complaint that did not allege that deceptive acts took place in state).

1141 Goodrich v. E.F. Hutton Group, Inc., 542 A.2d 1200 (Del. Ch. Ct. 1988) (statute does not apply where there was no transaction in state and consumers were not in state).

1142 Mueller Co. v. U.S. Pipe & Foundry Co., 2003 WL 22272135 (D.N.H. Oct. 2, 2003).

1143 Goshen v. Mutual Life Ins. Co., 98 N.Y.2d 314, 774 N.E.2d 1190, 1197 (2002). *See also In re* Rey-Willis v. Citibank, N.A., 2004 WL 315267 (S.D.N.Y. Feb. 18, 2004) (New York UDAP statute does not apply to representations made in Florida to Argentine resident by Florida employees of New York bank); Universal Serv. Fund Tel. Billing Practices Litig., 300 F. Supp. 2d 1107, 1151 (D. Kan. 2003) (deception must occur in New York for claim under New York UDAP statute); Padilla v. Payco Gen. Am. Credits, Inc., 161 F. Supp. 2d 264 (S.D.N.Y. 2001) (dismissing claim for debt collection actions taken before debtor moved to New York); Murrin v. Ford Motor Co., 303 A.D.2d 475, 756 N.Y.S.2d 596 (2003) (affirming dismissal of complaint that did not allege that deceptive acts took place in state).

1144 Goshen v. Mutual Life Ins. Co., 98 N.Y.2d 314, 774 N.E.2d 1190, 1197 (2002).

1145 People by Vacco v. Lipsitz, 174 Misc. 2d 571, 663 N.Y.S.2d 468 (Sup. Ct. 1997). *See also* People by Spitzer v. Telehublink, 756 N.Y.S.2d 285 (N.Y. App. Div. 2003) (AG can seek relief for out-of-state residents where part of deceptive scheme occurred in New York).

1146 Watkins v. Roach Cadillac, Inc., 7 Kan. App. 2d 8, 637 P.2d 458 (1981). *But see* Nelson v. Nationwide Mortgage Corp., 659 F. Supp. 611 (D.D.C. 1987) (D.C. UDAP statute does not apply where defendant and transaction occurred out-of-state, even though consumer resided in the District).

1147 Attorney General v. Dickson, 717 F. Supp. 1090 (D. Md. 1989).

companies that loaned money to District of Columbia residents and took a mortgage on District of Columbia property.[1148] Merely engaging in a deceptive practice in the state, however, may not be enough if only out-of-state consumers were solicited.[1149] Where a statute only applies to conduct occurring in that state, the UDAP statute does not apply to out-of-state representations, even if those representations were made by a company headquartered in the same state as the UDAP statute.[1150]

Connecticut's UDAP statute applies to practices in trade or commerce, defined by the statute as sales "in this state," and courts have interpreted this as applying to violations that do not occur within the state but are tied to a form of trade or commerce intimately associated with the state.[1151] Connecticut law may also apply where the UDAP claim is tort-like and the injury was sustained in Connecticut.[1152] But it does not apply to the sale of foreign real estate.[1153]

Where a UDAP statute applies to the conduct of any trade or commerce in part or wholly within the state, it applies to the sale of out-of-state property where the seller advertised in the state, conducted real estate closings in the state and had an office in the state.[1154] The Texas UDAP statute covers any trade or commerce that directly or indirectly affects the people of Texas.[1155] But this language was not broad enough to cover a transaction that was solicited and performed out of state, before the consumer moved to Texas.[1156] The Illinois UDAP statute covers out-of-state acts that affect an Illinois corporation.[1157] But neither it[1158] nor a California UDAP statute[1159] applies to an in-state company's out-of-state practices against out-of-state consumers.

1148 Williams v. Central Money Co., 974 F. Supp. 22 (D.D.C. 1997).

1149 Attorney General v. Dickson, 717 F. Supp. 1090 (D. Md. 1989).

1150 Parkhill v. Minnesota Mut. Life Ins. Co., 995 F. Supp. 983 (D. Minn. 1998).

1151 Uniroyal Chemical Co. v. Drexel Chemical Co., 931 F. Supp. 132 (D. Conn. 1996).

1152 *Id. But see* Mueller Co. v. U.S. Pipe & Foundry Co., 2003 WL 22272135 (D.N.H. Oct. 2, 2003) (causing in-state injury by out-of-state acts insufficient under New Hampshire UDAP statute).

1153 Baghdady v. Baghdady, 2003 WL 202436 (2d Cir. Jan. 29, 2003) (unpublished, citation limited).

1154 Steed Realty v. Oveisi, 823 S.W.2d 195 (Tenn. Ct. App. 1991).

1155 Busse v. Pacific Cattle Feeding Fund #1, LTD., 896 S.W.2d 807 (Tex. App. 1995).

1156 Bass v. Hendrix, 931 F. Supp. 523 (S.D. Tex. 1996).

1157 Nichols Motorcycle Supply Inc. v. Dunlop Tire Corp., 913 F. Supp. 1088 (N.D. Ill. 1995).

1158 Hastings v. Fidelity Mortgage Decisions, Corp., 984 F. Supp. 600 (N.D. Ill. 1997); Oliveira v. Amoco Oil Co., 311 Ill. App. 3d 886, 726 N.E.2d 51, 244 Ill. Dec. 455 (2000), *rev'd in part, vacated in part on other grounds*, 201 Ill. 2d 134, 776 N.E.2d 151, 267 Ill. Dec. 14 (2002).

1159 Norwest Mortgage, Inc. v. Superior Court, 72 Cal. App. 4th 214, 85 Cal. Rptr. 2d 18 (1999).

2.4 Persons Excluded from UDAP Protections

2.4.1 Recipients of Insurance Payments; Third-Party Beneficiaries; Donees; Assignees

2.4.1.1 Introduction

In some cases, the injured "consumer" is not the person who contracted with the seller. Thus issues arise as to whether recipients of gifts, beneficiaries of insurance policies, and others may bring UDAP actions in their own right, as opposed to through the original consumer.

2.4.1.2 Recipients of Insurance Payments

There is a split among courts (often within the same jurisdiction) concerning whether automobile accident victims and others claiming under someone else's insurance policy are consumers who can bring a UDAP action against the insurer. A number of cases hold they can not,[1160] but an

1160 Katz v. Aetna Cas. & Sur. Co., 972 F.2d 53 (3d Cir. 1992) (Penn. law); Hipsky v. Allstate Ins. Co., 304 F. Supp. 2d 284 (D. Conn. 2004); Metropolitan Life Ins. Co. v. Barretto, 178 F. Supp. 2d 745 (S.D. Tex. 2001) (a beneficiary lacks standing to sue under UNIP and is not a "consumer" under UDAP); Lopes v. State Farm Mut. Auto. Ins. Co., 2001 U.S. Dist. LEXIS 2396 (N.D. Tex. Mar. 6, 2001) (although a beneficiary may have UNIP standing, she is not a UDAP "consumer"); Winburn v. Liberty Mut. Ins. Co., 933 F. Supp. 664 (E.D. Ky. 1996); National Union Fire Ins. Co. v. Continental Illinois Corp., 652 F. Supp. 858 (N.D. Ill. 1986); Hunt v. First Ins. Co., 922 P.2d 976 (Haw. Ct. App. 1996); McCarter v. State Farm Mut. Auto Ins. Co., 473 N.E.2d 1015 (Ill. App. Ct. 1985); Anderson v. National Security Fire & Casualty Co., 870 S.W.2d 432 (Ky. Ct. App. 1993); Dodd v. Commercial Union Ins. Co., 373 Mass. 72, 365 N.E.2d 802 (1977); Blackwell v. Citizens Ins. Co., 457 Mich. 662, 579 N.W.2d 889 (1998); Allstate Ins. Co. v. Watson, 876 S.W.2d 145 (Tex. 1994) (reaching this conclusion despite the fact that the law grants a cause of action to "any person" who has sustained actual damages as the result of such an unfair claim settlement practice, and not solely to "an insured"); Rumley v. Allstate Indem. Co., 924 S.W.2d 448 (Tex. App. 1996) (spouse making claim against insurer for injuries arising out of automobile accident caused by negligence of other spouse is a third-party claimant and can not pursue UNIP claim, even though injured spouse is also an insured on the same policy); Watson v. Allstate Ins. Co., 828 S.W.2d 423 (Tex. App. 1991); Russell v. Farmers Texas County Mut. Ins. Co., 642 S.W.2d 278 (Tex. App. 1982); Hi-Line Electric Co. v. Travelers Ins. Co., 587 S.W.2d 488 (Tex. Civ. App. 1979); Russell v. Hartford Casualty Ins. Co., 548 S.W.2d 737 (Tex. Civ. App. 1977); Wilder v. Aetna Life & Casualty Ins. Co., 140 Vt. 16, 433 A.2d 309 (1981); Neigel v. Harrell, 919 P.2d 630 (Wash. App. 1996) (automobile accident victim can not make UDAP claim against insured's insurer); Tank v. State Farm Fire & Casualty Co., 38 Wash. App. 438, 686

almost equal number of cases say they can.[1161]

Statutory language may be critical in the court's resolution of this issue. Beneficiaries of a group health policy purchased by the employer have a UDAP remedy because the beneficiary has "acquired goods or services" as required by the UDAP statute.[1162] Where a UDAP statute applies to "any person," the statute applies to a patient suing a doctor's insurance company.[1163]

An assignee of the insured should be able to bring an action.[1164] Thus where the injured party can not bring a direct UDAP claim against the other party's insurer, consider obtaining an assignment from the insured of that party's UDAP claims against the insurance company.

Similarly a consumer's insurer has been held not the "person injured," and thus unable to bring a UDAP claim in its own right.[1165] The insurer, however, can usually bring an action as the consumer's subrogee after paying the consumer's claim.[1166]

2.4.1.3 Donees

A Florida court has found that an intended beneficiary of a gift is a "consumer;" nothing in the statutory definition of "consumer" limits the term to an immediate purchaser.[1167] But a Texas court found that inheritors of a house could not bring a UDAP action in their own name against the house's original seller.[1168]

2.4.1.4 Third-Party Beneficiaries

A third-party beneficiary of a contract was found entitled to bring a UDAP action where a home purchaser relied on a contract and representations made by a termite exterminator while dealing with the previous owners and the real estate agent.[1169] A tenant could not, however, assert a UDAP claim for a faulty inspection performed by her landlord's insurance company, where the landlord's purpose was to prevent property damage, not to benefit the tenant.[1170] A mortgagor is a third-party beneficiary with standing to sue an insurer that issued a mortgage insurance policy.[1171] A child was a consumer of a garage door opener purchased by his parents for the benefit of the whole family.[1172] But a husband could not bring a UDAP action in his own name as one who "purchases goods or services" against an attorney for deceptive practices relating to the handling of his wife's

---

P.2d 1127 (1984); Green v. Holm, 28 Wash. App. 135, 622 P.2d 869 (1981); Rice v. Life Ins. Co., 25 Wash. App. 479, 609 P.2d 1387 (1980); Bowe v. Eaton, 17 Wash. App. 840, 565 P.2d 826 (1977); Herrig v. Herrig, 844 P.2d 487 (Wyo. 1992). *See also* Celestine v. State Farm Mut. Automobile Ins. Co., 735 So. 2d 1 (La. App. 1998) (UNIP statute's requirement of prompt payment only gives private cause of action to insured, not to third party claimant).

1161 Athridge v. Aetna Cas. & Surety Co., 351 F.3d 1166 (D.C. Cir. 2003); Lopes v. State Farm Mut. Auto. Ins. Co., 2001 U.S. Dist. LEXIS 2396 (N.D. Tex. Mar. 6, 2001) (the intended third-party beneficiary of an insurance contract has standing); Adams v. Rubin, 964 F. Supp. 507 (D. Me. 1997) (Mass. law); Donaldson v. Liberty Mut. Ins. Co., 947 F. Supp. 429 (D. Haw. 1996) (third party beneficiary can bring UDAP suit as long as contracting party is a consumer); Bates v. Jackson Nat'l Life Ins. Co., 927 F. Supp. 1015 (S.D. Tex. 1996) (holding that beneficiaries of life insurance policy have standing to assert violations of Texas Insurance Code); P.I.A. Michigan City v. National Porges Radiator, 789 F. Supp. 1421 (N.D. Ill. 1992); Impex Shrimp & Fish Co. v. Aetna Cas. & Sur. Co., 686 F. Supp. 183 (N.D. Ill. 1985); Hopkins v. Liberty Mut. Ins. Co., 434 Mass. 556, 750 N.E.2d 943 (2001) (by virtue of a legislative amendment, injured parties who are not insureds can make UDAP claims based on UNIP violations); Clegg v. Butler, 424 Mass. 413, 676 N.E.2d 1134 (1997); Hart v. Moore, 587 N.Y.S.2d 477 (Sup. Ct. 1992); Murray v. Nationwide Mut. Ins. Co., 472 S.E.2d 358 (N.C. App. 1996) (distinguishing Wilson v. Wilson and Nationwide Mut. Fire Ins. Co., 121 N.C. App. 662, 468 S.E.2d 495 (1996), and holding that injured party has UDAP claim against tortfeasor's insurance company, at least after liability has been judicially determined); Webb v. International Trucking Co., 909 S.W.2d 220 (Tex. App. 1995) (third-party claimant, who did not meet the "consumer" standing requirement of the Texas UDAP, could nonetheless sue the insurance company for making a misrepresentation covered by the Texas UDAP); Aetna Casualty & Surety Co. v. Martin Surgical Supply Co., 689 S.W.2d 263 (Tex. App. 1985) (third-party beneficiary of insurance contract can sue insurer as long as plaintiff also purchased goods or services forming the basis of the complaint, thus making the plaintiff a consumer under the Texas UDAP statute); Escalante v. Sentry Ins., 49 Wash. App. 375, 743 P.2d 832 (1987) (passenger in automobile accident can bring UDAP action even though he is not the insured); Gould v. Mutual Life Ins. Co., 37 Wash. App. 756, 683 P.2d 207 (1984). *See also* Motorists Mut. Ins. Co. v. Glass, 996 S.W.2d 437 (Ky. 1997) (third party claimants can pursue UNIP claims for failure to make prompt payment of claims).

1162 Kennedy v. Sale, 689 S.W.2d 890 (Tex. 1985); Estate of Small v. Southland Life Ins. Co., 797 S.W.2d 74 (Tex. App. 1990), *rev'd on other grounds*, 806 S.W.2d 800 (Tex. 1991).

1163 Van Dyke v. St. Paul Fire & Marine Ins. Co., 388 Mass. 671, 448 N.E.2d 357 (1983); *see also* Gould v. Mutual Life Ins. Co., 37 Wash. App. 756, 683 P.2d 207 (1984) (beneficiary of policy can bring UDAP action).

1164 Aabye v. Security-Connecticut Life Ins. Co., 586 F. Supp. 5 (N.D. Ill. 1984). *See* § 2.4.1.5, *infra*. *But see* Gringeri v. Maryland Cas. Co., 1998 U.S. Dist. LEXIS 5931 (E.D. Pa. Apr. 28, 1998) (doctor to whom insured assigned right to receive insurance payment can not bring UDAP suit); State Farm Fire & Cas. Co. v. Gandy, 925 S.W.2d 696 (Tex. 1996). *See* § 2.4.1.5, *infra*.

1165 Illinois Farmers Ins. Co. v. Brekke Fireplace, 495 N.W.2d 216 (Minn. Ct. App. 1993).

1166 *Id.*

1167 Warren v. Monahan Beaches Jewelry Center, Inc., 548 So. 2d 870 (Fla. Dist. Ct. App. 1989).

1168 March v. Thiery, 729 S.W.2d 889 (Tex. App. 1987).

1169 Neveroski v. Blair, 141 N.J. Super. 365, 358 A.2d 473 (App. Div. 1976). *Accord* Plumley v. Landmark Chevrolet, Inc., 122 F.3d 308 (5th Cir. 1997) (Texas law).

1170 Prince v. Wright, 541 S.E.2d 191 (N.C. 2000).

1171 Palma v. Verex Assur., Inc., 79 F.3d 1453 (5th Cir. 1996).

1172 Wellborn v. Sears, Roebuck & Co., 970 F.2d 1420 (5th Cir. 1992) (Texas law).

estate. An action, nevertheless, could be brought on behalf of the wife's estate.[1173] A former beneficiary of an IRA can not make a UDAP claim against an investment firm for failure to advise that she had been removed as a beneficiary.

2.4.1.5 Assignees of Consumers' Claims

The North Carolina Supreme Court has ruled that UDAP claims are not assignable.[1174] North Carolina law does not allow the assignment of personal torts, and a UDAP claim is akin to a personal tort.[1175] The court was also strongly influenced by a desire to limit mandatory treble damage recoveries to consumers with limited resources and not to make them available to insurance companies and similarly well-financed parties.[1176]

Reaching the same result by a different path, New Jersey holds that assignees lack standing to bring UDAP suits because they have not suffered a loss themselves.[1177] Two federal courts have similarly ruled that a health care provider could not bring a Pennsylvania UDAP claim against its consumers' insurance company even though it was the assignee of the consumers' rights under their insurance contracts.[1178] The court held that the UDAP statute protected only the purchasers of the goods or services.

The Texas Supreme Court, citing policy reasons, has held that UDAP claims are not assignable.[1179] An earlier federal decision held that an insurance company that was subrogated to its insured's claim could not assume its insured's "consumer" status in order to sue under the UDAP statute.[1180]

On the other hand, the Minnesota Supreme Court has ruled that a health insurer has standing to sue tobacco companies for the increased cost of health care caused by smoking-related illnesses.[1181] The court rejected the companies' claim that the insurer could not sue for costs that were "passed through" to other entities, i.e., the employer subscribers to the health insurance plan. A Washington appellate decision allows an assignee of an insured's UDAP and bad faith claim to sue the insurer.[1182]

2.4.1.6 Other Third Parties

There are other situations in which a third party may attempt to assert the rights of consumers. In one case, a condominium association purchased a roof on behalf of the individual unit owners. The court held that, since the association was acting in a representative capacity, the purchase would be considered to be for "personal, family, or household purposes."[1183] But a federal court refused to extend this holding to allow physicians to bring a UDAP claim against an HMO for acts it took that impeded patient-subscribers' access to health care.[1184] An HMO could sue tobacco companies for losses it suffered due to buyers' health care needs, where the statute allowed suit by any person injured by a UDAP violation.[1185] A labor union was permitted to assert UDAP claims against a health insurer on behalf of its members, even though the statute provided for suit by an injured person "in his own name."[1186] The court construed the language as merely intended to distinguish between consumer suits and those by the attorney general. On the other hand, Rhode Island's statute only allows suit by a person who has purchased or leased goods or services for personal, family, or household use, so a union health and welfare fund could not sue tobacco companies for the health care expenses it incurred due to its members' purchase of tobacco.[1187] A professional photographer could not maintain

---

1173 Levin v. Berley, 728 F.2d 551 (1st Cir. 1984). *See also* Glasgow v. Eagle Pacific Ins. Co., 45 F.3d 1401 (10th Cir. 1995) (wife could not bring action against husband's insurer); Jackson v. R.G. Whipple, Inc., 225 Conn. 705, 627 A.2d 374 (1993) (can not maintain UDAP suit against attorney who represented opposing party); Field v. Kearns, 682 A.2d 148 (Conn. App. 1996) (same).

1174 Investors Title Ins. Co. v. Herzig, 413 S.E.2d 268 (N.C. 1992). *Accord* Horton v. New South Ins. Co., 468 S.E.2d 856 (N.C. Ct. App. 1996).

1175 Investors Title Ins. Co. v. Herzig, 413 S.E.2d 268 (N.C. 1992).

1176 *Id.*

1177 Levy v. Edmund Buick-Pontiac Ltd., 270 N.J. Super. 563, 637 A.2d 600 (1993).

1178 Gemini Physical Therapy & Rehabilitation, Inc. v. State Farm Mut. Automobile Ins. Co., 40 F.3d 63 (3d Cir. 1994); Jack A. Danton, D.O. v. State Farm Mut. Auto Ins. Co., 769 F. Supp. 174 (E.D. Pa. 1991). *Accord* Gringeri v. Maryland Cas. Co., 1998 U.S. Dist. LEXIS 5931 (E.D. Pa. Apr. 28, 1998) (doctor to whom insured assigned right to receive insurance payment can not bring UDAP suit).

1179 PPG Indus., Inc. v. JMB/Houston Centers Partners Ltd. P'ship, 2004 WL 1533274 (Tex. July 9, 2004).

1180 Essex Ins. Co. v. Blount, Inc., 72 F. Supp. 2d 722 (E.D. Tex. 1999); *see also* Reagan Nat'l Advertising v. Lakeway 620 Partners, 2001 Tex. App. LEXIS 4375 (June 29, 2001) (unpublished, citation limited) (same conclusion under Home Solicitation Act).

1181 State *ex rel.* Humphrey v. Philip Morris Inc., 551 N.W.2d 490 (Minn. 1996).

1182 Besel v. Viking Ins. Co., 105 Wash. App. 463, 21 P.3d 293 (2001), *rev'd in part on other issues*, 49 P.3d 887 (Wash. 2002) (reversing disposition of separate bad faith claim; ordering trial court to enter judgment on UDAP claim).

1183 Valley Forge Towers South Condominium v. Ron-Ike Foam Insulators, Inc., 393 Pa. Super. 339, 574 A.2d 641 (1990), *aff'd without op.*, 605 A.2d 798 (Pa. 1992).

1184 Pennsylvania Psychiatric Soc. v. Green Spring Health Servs., Inc., 2000 U.S. Dist. LEXIS 8017 (W.D. Pa. Feb. 15, 2000), *adopted by* 2000 U.S. Dist. LEXIS 7953 (W.D. Pa. Mar. 24, 2000), *rev'd on other grounds*, 280 F.3d 278 (3d Cir. 2002).

1185 Group Health Plan, Inc. v. Philip Morris, Inc., 621 N.W.2d 2 (Minn. 2001).

1186 Am. Medical Ass'n v. United Healthcare Corp., 2003 WL 22004877 (S.D.N.Y. Aug. 22, 2003).

1187 R.I. Laborers' Health & Welfare Fund v. Philip Morris, 99 F. Supp. 2d 174 (D.R.I. 2000). *See also* Blue Cross & Blue Shield v. Philip Morris USA Inc., 344 F.3d 211 (2d Cir. 2003) (certifying question whether remoteness bars UDAP suit to N.Y.

a deception claim against an advertiser who pirated a photograph, because no damage to him was caused by the deception of consumers about whether reproduction of the photograph was authorized.[1188]

A person whose name was forged by a dealership on a consumer contract has standing to bring a claim under the Illinois UDAP statute.[1189] Even though she did not actually contract with the dealership, the dealership's conduct implicated consumer protection concerns, and the UDAP statute affords a private cause of action to "any person" who suffers actual damage due to a violation.

2.4.2 Where Consumer Is Now Deceased

A Texas appellate court has ruled that a UDAP treble damages action survives the consumer's death, even though in Texas punitive damages claims are considered personal and do not survive the plaintiff. The UDAP statute was enacted to expand on the consumer's rights under contract and tort theories. It would be contrary to the legislative intent to make a UDAP claim more difficult to bring than contract or tort claims, both of which survive the consumer's death.[1190] Attorney fees and treble damages are not just punitive, but serve other social goods, and even they should be recoverable by the consumer's estate.[1191] Typically, it is the executor, not the beneficiary, who would have standing to bring a UDAP claim on behalf of the estate, although the beneficiary may be allowed to sue if the executor was involved in the deception.[1192]

Ohio appellate courts have found that rescission[1193] and damages[1194] claims under that state's UDAP statute survive the consumer's death, although a claim for restitution may not survive.[1195] A court has interpreted the South Carolina UDAP statute's provision that a person can bring an action "but not in a representative capacity" to mean that an action by a representative of an estate can not be brought under the statute.[1196]

2.4.3 Loan Guarantors

The Idaho Supreme Court has ruled that a signer of a personal guarantee for a car loan is not a "purchaser of goods" and thus not covered by the Idaho UDAP statute.[1197] A Kansas appellate court finds that an individual who guaranteed a corporation's business loan does not meet the UDAP statute's definition of "consumer."[1198] Of course, statutes that only limit their scope to transactions in "trade or commerce" may not preclude cosigners and other loan guarantors from bringing actions.[1199]

2.4.4 Out-of-State Residents

Unless the statute explicitly provides otherwise,[1200] UDAP statutes apply to practices by in-state sellers affecting out-of-state consumers, since the state has an interest in deceptive acts within its own borders, even if the activities do not affect its citizens.[1201] This confronts a consumer

---

Court of Appeals); A.O. Fox Mem. Hosp. v. Am. Tobacco Co., 302 A.D.2d 413, 754 N.Y.S.2d 368 (2003) (hospital's claim against tobacco companies for unreimbursed costs of health care for smokers entirely derivative and too remote); § 4.2.15.3, *infra*.

1188 Pritikin v. Liberation Publications, Inc., 83 F. Supp. 2d 920 (N.D. Ill. 1999).

1189 Bank One Milwaukee v. Sanchez, 783 N.E.2d 217 (Ill. App. 2003).

1190 Thomes v. Porter, 761 S.W.2d 592 (Tex. App. 1988). *See also* Mahan Volkswagen, Inc. v. Hall, 648 S.W.2d 324 (Tex. App. 1982). *Cf.* Wellborn v. Sears, Roebuck & Co., 970 F.2d 1420 (5th Cir. 1992) (Texas law) (certifying question to Texas Supreme Court because of lack of controlling case law). *But see* Lukasik v. San Antonio Blue Haven Pools, Inc., 21 S.W.3d 394 (Tex. App. 2000); First Nat'l Bank v. Hackworth, 673 S.W.2d 218 (Tex. App. 1984).

1191 Thomes v. Porter, 761 S.W.2d 592 (Tex. App. 1988).

1192 Lefkowitz v. Bank of New York, 2003 WL 22480049 (S.D.N.Y. Oct. 31, 2003).

1193 Nations Credit v. Pheanis, 102 Ohio App. 3d 71, 656 N.E.2d 998 (1995).

1194 Estate of Cattano v. High Touch Homes, Inc., 2002 WL 1290411 (Ohio App. May 24, 2002) (unpublished, citation limited).

1195 Motzer Dodge Jeep Eagle, Inc. v. Ohio Attorney General, 95 Ohio App. 3d 183, 642 N.E.2d 20 (1994).

1196 Faircloth v. Jackie Fine Arts, Inc., 682 F. Supp. 837 (D.S.C. 1988).

1197 Idaho First Nat'l Bank v. Wells, 100 Idaho 256, 596 P.2d 429 (1979). *Accord* First Nat'l Bank of Anthony v. Dunning, 18 Kan. App. 2d 518, 855 P.2d 493 (1993).

1198 CIT Group/Sales Fin., Inc. v. E-Z Pay Used Cars, Inc., 32 P.3d 1197 (Kan. App. 2001).

1199 Anderson v. Rizza Chevrolet, Inc., 9 F. Supp. 2d 908 (N.D. Ill. 1998); Bank One Milwaukee v. Sanchez, 336 Ill. App. 3d 319, 783 N.E.2d 217 (2003) (person whose signature was forged as co-signer has standing); Northwestern Bank v. Roseman, 344 S.E.2d 120 (N.C. Ct. App. 1986), *aff'd without op.*, 354 S.E.2d 238 (1987).

1200 *See, e.g.*, Mich. Comp. Laws Ann. § 445.911. *See also* Highsmith v. Chrysler Credit Corp., 150 B.R. 997 (N.D. Ill. 1993), *aff'd in part and rev'd in part on other grounds*, 18 F.3d 434 (7th Cir. 1994) (disallowing class action by out-of-state residents whose only contact with state whose UDAP statute plaintiffs sought to apply was that payments under allegedly deceptive lease were sent to corporate headquarters there).

1201 *In re* St. Jude Medical, Inc., Silzone Heart Valves Prods. Liability Litig., 2003 WL 1589527 (D. Minn. Mar. 27, 2003) (relying on language that "any person" may sue); Wafra Leasing Corp. v. Prime Capital Corp., 204 F. Supp. 2d 1120 (N.D. Ill. 2002) (consumer of Illinois products and services can bring Illinois UDAP suit); Mlynek v. Household Fin. Co., 2000 U.S. Dist. LEXIS 13783 (N.D. Ill. Sept. 11, 2000) (Florida debt collection statute, like UDAP statute, is not limited to state residents); Boyes v. Greenwich Boat Works, Inc., 27 F. Supp. 2d 543 (D.N.J. 1998) (discussing choice of law principles); Perry v. Household Retail Servs., Inc., 953 F. Supp. 1370 (M.D. Ala.

litigant with two choices of law and two choices of forums. Consumers can bring an action in their own or the seller's state, and can argue that either the consumer's or the seller's UDAP statute applies. Bringing an action in the seller's state may be impractical, but could offer the consumer better UDAP coverage or remedies if the seller's state's UDAP statute applies.[1202]

2.4.5 Merchants; Corporations; Government Entities

2.4.5.1 Seller's Attempt to Treat Consumer as a Commercial Entity

There should be little doubt that a consumer is covered by a UDAP statute, even if the seller attempts to restructure the transaction as a purely commercial one. Where a debtor is forced to incorporate before engaging in a transaction or required to state falsely that the transaction is for business purposes, the individual consumer may still bring a UDAP action, even if a corporation could not otherwise bring an action or the consumer's business purpose would otherwise exempt the transaction. In fact, the very act of forcing the consumer to incorporate or falsely state a business purpose may be a UDAP violation.[1203]

2.4.5.2 Can Businesses Bring UDAP Actions?

UDAP claims by businesses are becoming more common, and can add significantly to the impact of a business suit.[1204] Whether a business can bring a UDAP action will depend on several issues. First, is the UDAP statute limited to sales for "personal, family, or household use"? While the meaning of this phrase is subject to various interpretations,[1205] most business purchases will be excluded if the statute is so limited. Thus this should exclude actions by creditors,[1206] businesses,[1207] and

1996); Demitropoulos v. Bank One Milwaukee, N.A., 915 F. Supp. 1399 (N.D. Ill. 1996) (interpreting Wisconsin UDAP statute); Long v. E.I. duPont de Nemours & Co., 821 F. Supp. 956 (D. Del. 1993); Walmsley v. Mercury Fin. Co., Clearinghouse No. 49,973 (S.D. Fla. Sept. 10, 1993); Fry v. UAL Corp., 136 F.R.D. 626 (N.D. Ill. 1991); Norwest Mortgage, Inc. v. Superior Court, 72 Cal. App. 4th 214, 85 Cal. Rptr. 2d 18 (1999); Millennium Communications & Fulfillment, Inc. v. Attorney General, 761 So. 2d 1256 (Fla. App. 2000) (Florida UDAP statute applies to deceptive acts committing in the state against residents of other states); Iowa *ex rel.* Campbell v. Runza, Clearinghouse No. 50,443 (Iowa Dist. Ct. Jan. 12, 1994); Nesbitt v. American Community Mut. Ins. Co., 236 Mich. App. 215, 600 N.W.2d 427 (1999) (Michigan UDAP statute covers Michigan company's in-state actions toward Ohio residents); State *ex rel.* Nixon v. Estes, 108 S.W.3d 795 (Mo. App. 2003); People by Spitzer v. Telehublink, 756 N.Y.S.2d 285 (App. Div. 2003) (AG can seek relief for out-of-state residents where part of deceptive scheme occurred in New York); Goshen v. Mutual Life Ins. Co., 98 N.Y.2d 314, 774 N.E.2d 1190, 1197 (2002) (deceptive act, not merely formulation of deceptive scheme, must occur in state, but statute applies to out-of-state residents who make in-state purchases); Brown v. Market Dev., Inc., 41 Ohio Misc. 57, 322 N.E.2d 367 (C.P. Hamilton Cty. 1974); Steed Realty v. Oveisi, 823 S.W.2d 195 (Tenn. Ct. App. 1991) (UDAP statute applies to out-of-state sale to out-of-state residents); State v. Premium Underwriters, Clearinghouse No. 49,153 (Tenn. Ch. Ct., Hamilton Cty. Apr. 13, 1993). *See also* Peters v. Northern Trust Co., 1999 U.S. Dist. LEXIS 11179 (N.D. Ill. July 12, 1999) (discussing two lines of cases in Illinois, one holding that non-residents can not sue and the other that non-residents can sue if injured by activity in Illinois); Nichols Motorcycle Supply Inc. v. Dunlop Tire Corp., 913 F. Supp. 1088 (N.D. Ill. 1995) (misrepresentations that affect an Illinois corporation are subject to Illinois UDAP statute even if no effect on Illinois consumers is shown). *But see* Swartz v. Schaub, 818 F. Supp. 1214 (N.D. Ill. 1993) (court takes position that practice of Illinois entity in defending out-of-state resident does not even indirectly affect people of Illinois); Coastal Physician Servs. v. Ortiz, 764 So. 2d 7 (Fla. App. 1999) (disallowing discovery regarding actions against non-residents on theory that Florida UDAP statute does not protect them).

1202 See § 7.6, *infra* for a discussion of choice of laws and choice of forum issues.

1203 McLaughlin Ford, Inc. v. Ford Motor Co., 192 Conn. 558, 473 A.2d 1185 (1984); Allan v. M&S Mortgage Co., 359 N.W.2d 238 (Mich. Ct. App. 1984); Dreier Co. v. Unitronix Corp., 218 N.J. Super. 260, 527 A.2d 875 (App. Div. 1986); *see also* Rutter v. Troy Mortgage Servicing Co., 145 Mich. App. 116, 377 N.W.2d 846 (1985).

1204 Veranda Beach Club v. Western Surety Co., 936 F.2d 1364 (1st Cir. 1991) (double damages of $4 million awarded on UDAP claim in business suit).

1205 *See* § 2.1.8, *supra.*

1206 Independent Communication Network, Inc. v. MCI Telecommunications Corp., 657 F. Supp. 785 (D.D.C. 1987); Toledo Metro Federal Credit Union v. Ted Papenhagan Oldsmobile, 56 Ohio App. 2d 218, 381 N.E.2d 1337 (1978). *See also* Schmueser v. Burkburnett Bank, 937 F.2d 1025 (5th Cir. 1991) (Texas law).

1207 Rhode Island Depositors Economic Protection Corp. v. Hayes, 64 F.3d 22 (1st Cir. 1995) (Rhode Island law); George v. United Kentucky Bank, Inc., 753 F.2d 50 (6th Cir. 1985) (Kentucky law); Babbit Electronics, Inc. v. Dynascan Corp., 38 F.3d 1161 (11th Cir. 1994); World Wrestling Federation Entertainment, Inc. v. Big Dog Holdings, Inc., 280 F. Supp. 2d 413 (W.D. Pa. 2003) (business competitor has no UDAP private cause of action); Magnum Defense, Inc. v. Harbour Group Ltd., 248 F. Supp. 2d 64, 71 (D.R.I. 2003); Roberts v. Shawnee Mission Ford, 2003 WL 22143727 (D. Kan. Aug. 20, 2003) (dealer could not state UDAP claim against person from whom it purchased vehicle); Fare Deals, Ltd. v. World Choice Travel.com, Inc., 180 F. Supp. 2d 678 (D. Md. 2001) (business competitors excluded); Pig Improvement Co. v. Middle States Holding Co., 943 F. Supp. 392 (D. Del. 1996); Scully Signal Co. v. Joyal, 881 F. Supp. 727 (D.R.I. 1995) (Rhode Island UDAP statute); Jack A. Danton, D.O. v. State Farm Mut. Auto Ins. Co., 769 F. Supp. 174 (E.D. Pa. 1991) (medical providers are not "consumers" entitled to bring UDAP suit even though they are assignees of consumer's right to insurance payment); Cohen v. North Ridge Farms, Inc., 712 F. Supp. 1265 (E.D. Ky. 1989) (purchase of thoroughbred horse is not purchase of consumer goods); Layton v. AAMCO Transmissions, Inc., 717 F. Supp. 368 (D. Md. 1989) (suit by franchise buyers); Marra v. Burgdorf Realtors, Inc., 726 F. Supp. 1000 (E.D. Pa. 1989); C-B Ken-

landlords.[1208] On the other hand, statutes that are only limited to practices in "trade or commerce" will allow claims by merchants and others not engaged in transactions for personal or household purposes.[1209]

The other key question is how the UDAP statute defines the entities that can bring an action. If private UDAP actions are limited to "consumers" or "individuals," most business entities will be excluded.[1210] Corpora-

worth, Inc. v. General Motors Corp., 706 F. Supp. 952 (D. Me. 1988); Mazanderm v. Independent Taxi Owners' Ass'n, Inc., 700 F. Supp. 588 (D.D.C. 1988); Waldo v. North Am. Van Lines, Inc., 669 F. Supp. 722 (W.D. Pa. 1987); Bryant Heating & Air Conditioning Corp. v. Carrier Corp., 597 F. Supp. 1045 (S.D. Fla. 1984); Hydro Air of Connecticut, Inc. v. Versa Technologies, Inc., 599 F. Supp. 1119 (D. Conn. 1984); Merv Swing Agency, Inc. v. Graham Co., 579 F. Supp. 429 (E.D. Pa. 1983); Packaging Corp. Int'l v. Travenol Laboratories, Inc., 566 F. Supp. 1480 (S.D. Fla. 1983) (manufacturer/seller of products to merchants not involved in consumer transactions); Morris v. Osmose Wood Preserving, 340 Md. 519, 667 A.2d 624 (1995); Boatel Indus., Inc. v. Hester, 77 Md. App. 284, 550 A.2d 389 (1988); Slobin v. Henry Ford Health Care, 666 N.W.2d 632 (Mich. 2003) (UDAP statute applies only to purchases by consumer; does not apply to acquisition of medical records for use in litigation); Passalacqua Corp. v. AIG Claim Servs., Inc., 2002 Mich. App. LEXIS 90 (Jan. 29, 2002) (does not cover transaction between businesses); Jackson County Hog Producers v. Consumers Power Co., 592 N.W.2d 112 (Mich. App. 1999) (business use is not a "personal" use); Doll v. Major Muffler Center's, Inc., 687 P.2d 48 (Mont. 1984); Ostrander v. Andrew, 2000 Ohio App. LEXIS 2290 (May 31, 2000) (no UDAP coverage where check and receipt were in name of plaintiff's company, and plaintiff did not establish that transaction was actually for her personal use); Barazatto v. Intelligent Sys., Inc., 40 Ohio App. 3d 117, 532 N.E.2d 148 (1987); Kremen v. Ohio Expositions Comm'n, 81 Ohio Misc. 2d 29, 673 N.E.2d 1028 (Ct. of Claims 1996); Bash v. Bell Tel. Co., 601 A.2d 825 (Pa. Super. Ct. 1992); Trackers Raceway, Inc. v. Comstock Agency, Inc., 583 A.2d 119 (Pa. Super. Ct. 1990) (purchase of insurance for commercial purpose is not covered); Girton Mfg. Co. v. Pennsylvania Manufacturers' Ass'n Ins. Co., 11 Pa. D. & C. 4th 13 (C.P. Columbia Cty. 1989); ERI Max Entertainment, Inc. v. Streisand, 690 A.2d 1351 (R.I. 1997); MacConkey v. F.J. Matter Design, Inc., 54 Va. Cir. 1, 2000 Va. Cir. LEXIS 390 (Feb. 8, 2000) (subcontractor's purchase of product from manufacturer to use in construction of home). *Cf.* Jungkurth v. Eastern Fin. Servs., Inc. (*In re* Jungkurth), 74 B.R. 323 (Bankr. E.D. Pa. 1987) (private UDAP remedy available only for consumer transactions, but UDAP statute itself is not so limited). *But see* Florists' Transworld Delivery, Inc. v. Fleurop-Interflora, 261 F. Supp. 2d 837 (E.D. Mich. 2003) (pre-*Slobin* case allowing business vs. business suit because both were engaged in selling consumer goods); John Labatt Ltd. v. Molson Breweries, 853 F. Supp. 965 (E.D. Mich. 1994) (Michigan UDAP statute's "personal, family, or household use" language allows suit by business competitor where dispute involves labeling of consumer product; pre-*Slobin* case); Va. Beach Rehab Specialists, Inc. v. Augustine Medical, Inc., 58 Va. Cir. 379 (2002) (if medical practice purchased product for personal use of its patients, UDAP statute might apply, but not here where the misrepresentations related to Medicare coverage for the product, not to the product itself).

1208 Linthicum v. Archambault, 379 Mass. 381, 398 N.E.2d 482 (1979). *But see* Barrett v. Adirondack Bottled Gas Corp., 487 A.2d 1074 (Vt. 1984) (landlord purchasing item for tenants' use is purchasing consumer goods).

1209 Eastern Mountain Platform Tennis, Inc. v. Sherwin-Williams Co., 40 F.3d 492 (1st Cir. 1994); United Roasters Inc. v. Colgate-Palmolive Co., 649 F.2d 985 (4th Cir. 1981) (North Carolina law); Florists' Transworld Delivery, Inc. v. Fleurop-Interflora, 261 F. Supp. 2d 837 (E.D. Mich. 2003) (two companies that sell consumer goods are engaged in "trade or commerce," so they may bring UDAP claims against each other); Liberty Mut. Ins. Co. v. Employee Resource Management, Inc., 176 F. Supp. 2d 510 (D.S.C. 2001); Action Auto Glass v. Auto Glass Specialists, 2001 U.S. Dist. LEXIS 22127 (W.D. Mich. Aug. 21, 2001); Olin Corp. v. Lambda Electronics, Inc., 39 F. Supp. 2d 912 (E.D. Tenn. 1998); Food Lion, Inc. v. Capital Cities/ABC, Inc., 951 F. Supp. 1233 (M.D.N.C. 1996); John Labatt Ltd. v. Molson Breweries, 853 F. Supp. 965 (E.D. Mich. 1994) (Michigan UDAP statute allows suit by business competitor where dispute involves a consumer product); Sullivan's Wholesale Drug v. Faryl's Pharmacy, 214 Ill. App. 3d 1073, 573 N.E.2d 1370 (1991); A&W Sheet Metal, Inc. v. Berg Mechanical, Inc., 653 So. 2d 158 (La. Ct. App. 1995) (unsuccessful bidder for a construction contract has UDAP claim under statute covering "trade or commerce"); New Orleans Riverwalk Assocs. v. Robert P. Guastella Equities, Inc., 664 So. 2d 151 (La. Ct. App. 1995) (consumers and business competitors may sue under Louisiana's UDAP statute); Jarrell v. Carter, 577 So. 2d 120 (La. Ct. App. 1991); Monroe Medical Clinic v. Hospital Corp. of Am., 522 So. 2d 1362 (La. Ct. App. 1988) (same); Morris v. Rental Tools, Inc., 435 So. 2d 528 (La. Ct. App. 1983) (same); Linthicum v. Archambault, 379 Mass. 381, 398 N.E.2d 482 (1979); Barrows v. Boles, 687 A.2d 979 (N.H. 1996) (implicitly concluding that businesses are covered, but applying higher substantive standard); Jones v. General Motors Corp., 953 P.2d 1104 (N.M. App. 1998); Dalton v. Camp, 353 N.C. 647, 548 S.E.2d 704 (2001); Sara Lee Corp. v. Carter, 351 N.C. 27, 519 S.E.2d 308 (1999) (business is covered by UDAP statute when it purchases goods); United Laboratories, Inc. v. Kuykendall, 322 N.C. 643, 370 S.E.2d 375 (1988); Jennings Glass Co. v. Brummer, 88 N.C. App. 44, 362 S.E.2d 578 (1987); Winston Realty Co. v. G.H.G., Inc., 320 S.E.2d 286 (N.C. Ct. App. 1984) (employer may sue personnel agency); *see also* Gardes Directional Drilling v. U.S. Turnkey Exploration, 98 F.3d 860 (5th Cir. 1996) (businesses may not sue each other under Louisiana UDAP statute unless they are competitors); Church of the Nativity of Our Lord v. WatPro, Inc., 474 N.W.2d 605 (Minn. Ct. App. 1991) (consumer need not be unsophisticated to bring UDAP action), *aff'd on other grounds*, 491 N.W.2d 1 (Minn. 1992).

1210 F.D.S. Marine, L.L.C. v. Shaver Transp. Co., 2001 U.S. Dist. LEXIS 7800 (D. Or. Mar. 29, 2001) (corporation is a "person" that can sue, but here it had no claim because it alleged a substantive violation that required purchase for personal, family, or household use), *adopted by* 230 F. Supp. 2d 1167 (D. Or. 2001); Ulico Cas. Co. v. Professional Indem. Agency, 1999 U.S. Dist. LEXIS 8591 (D.D.C. May 5, 1999) (only consumers can sue under D.C. UDAP code); Classic Car Centre v. Haire Machine Corp., 580 N.E.2d 722 (Ind. Ct. App. 1991) (corporation can not bring UDAP suit in Indiana because private cause of action is limited to individuals); Limestone Farms, Inc. v. Deere & Co., 29 P.3d 457 (Kan. App. 2001) (family farm corporation not covered by UDAP statute, which covers agricultural and consumer transactions by individuals, sole proprietors and, as of 2001, family partnerships). *Cf.* Collegenet, Inc. v. Embark.com, Inc., 2000 U.S. Dist. LEXIS 20752 (D. Or. Dec.

tions[1211] and credit unions[1212] are not defined as consumers or individuals and thus are excluded from bringing UDAP actions in a number of states. The Kansas UDAP statute allows individuals, sole proprietors, and family partnerships, but not corporations, to sue.[1213] Other language in that statute, however, restricts such suits to disputes involving products that the business uses and consumes itself, not goods purchased for resale.[1214] An intermediate appellate court has also held that the statute does not cover an individual's guarantee of a corporate debt.[1215] Other courts will consider a corporation a consumer as long as it is purchasing products or services for its own use. If the product is purchased for resale, then the corporation is not a consumer.[1216] The Tennessee UDAP statute was particularly ambiguous as to whether a corporation can be a "person," but the statute has now been clarified that corporations can be persons and can sue for treble damages.[1217]

Some statutes explicitly include corporations within a statute's scope. For example, the Florida (as of 2001),[1218] Illinois,[1219] Louisiana,[1220] and Oregon[1221] UDAP statutes

15, 2000) (corporation can bring suit, but only if it is consumer of defendant's goods or services), *adopted by* 2001 U.S. Dist. LEXIS 7873 (D. Or. Apr. 4, 2001).

1211 Grantham & Mann v. American Safety Products, 831 F.2d 596 (6th Cir. 1987) (Tennessee law) (corporation is not a natural person; statute has been amended); Delhomme Indus. Inc. v. Houston Beechcraft, 669 F.2d 1049 (5th Cir. 1982) (Kansas law); Paulson, Inc. v. Bromer, Inc., 775 F. Supp. 1329 (D. Haw. 1991); Wynn Oil Co. v. American Way Serv. Corp., 736 F. Supp. 746 (E.D. Mich. 1990); Independent Communications Network, Inc. v. MCI Telecommunications, Corp., 657 F. Supp. 785 (D.D.C. 1987); United States Welding, Inc. v. Burroughs Corp., 615 F. Supp. 554 (D. Colo. 1985); Zerpol Corp. v. DMP Corp., 561 F. Supp. 404 (E.D. Pa. 1983); L.J.S. Co. v. Marks, 480 F. Supp. 241 (S.D. Fla. 1979); American Building Co. v. White, 640 S.W.2d 569 (Tenn. Ct. App. 1982); Manufactured Housing Management v. Tubb, 643 S.W.2d 483 (Tex. Civ. App. 1982). *See also* Clifton Terrace Assoc., Ltd. v. United Technologies, 728 F. Supp. 24 (D.D.C. 1990) (limited partnership worth over $5 million is not consumer). *But see* Dreier Co. v. Unitronix Corp., 218 N.J. Super. 260, 527 A.2d 875 (App. Div. 1986) (consumer is "any person" and a corporation is a person); *cf.* Chilton Air Cooled Engines, Inc. v. Omark Indus., Inc., 721 F. Supp. 151 (M.D. Tenn. 1988), *following* Colyer v. Trew, 1982 Tenn. App. LEXIS 459 (Feb. 12, 1982) (unreported) (corporations can bring injunctive actions under UDAP statute, but not damage actions).

1212 Toledo Metro Federal Credit Union v. Ted Papenhagan Oldsmobile, 56 Ohio App. 2d 218, 381 N.E.2d 1337 (1978).

1213 Sithon Maritime Co. v. Holiday Mansion, 1999 U.S. Dist. LEXIS 3174 (D. Kan. Feb. 16, 1999) (only consumers and sole proprietors can bring UDAP suit). Family partnerships were added to the definition of "consumer" in Kan. Stat. Ann. § 50-624 in 2001.

1214 Wayman v. Amoco Oil, 923 F. Supp. 1322 (D. Kan. 1996), *aff'd without op.*, 145 F.3d 1347 (10th Cir. 1998).

1215 CIT Group/Sales Fin., Inc. v. E-Z Pay Used Cars, Inc., 32 P.3d 1197 (Kan. App. 2001).

1216 *See* Windsor Card Shops, Inc. v. Hallmark Cards, Inc., 957 F. Supp. 562 (D.N.J. 1997); Warren Technology, Inc. v. Hines Interests Ltd. P'ship, 733 So. 2d 1146 (Fla. Dist. Ct. App. 1999) (corporation can be consumer if it is acting in that capacity, but not if it is acting in manufacturing capacity).

1217 ATS Southeast, Inc. v. Carrier Corp., 18 S.W.3d 626 (Tenn. 2000). *See also* Operations Management Int'l, Inc. v. Tengasco, Inc., 35 F. Supp. 2d 1052 (E.D. Tenn. 1999) (Tennessee courts would probably rule that a corporation has standing to sue, but case must involve advertising, offering for sale, or distribution of goods or services); Olin Corp. v. Lambda Electronics, Inc., 39 F. Supp. 2d 912 (E.D. Tenn. 1998); Smith Corona Corp. v. Pelikan, Inc., 784 F. Supp. 452 (M.D. Tenn. 1992) (Tennessee UDAP statute was amended in 1989, and now corporations can be consumers), *aff'd without op.*, 1 F.3d 1252 (Fed. Cir. 1993). *But cf.* New Life Corp. v. Thomas Nelson, Inc., 932 S.W.2d 921 (Tenn. App. 1996) (rejecting business' UDAP suit on other grounds).

1218 Fla. Stat. Ann. § 501.203(7), *as amended by* 2001 Fla. Sess. Law Serv. Ch. 2001-39. *See* Niles Audio Corp. v. OEM Sys. Co., 174 F. Supp. 2d 1315 (S.D. Fla. 2001). The 2001 amendment overruled cases that require a business to have a consumer relationship with the defendant in order to bring a UDAP action, such as Portionpac Chem. Corp. v. Sanitech Sys., Inc., 217 F. Supp. 2d 1238 (M.D. Fla. 2002) (business competitor can not sue); Burger King Corp. v. Ashland Equities, Inc., 161 F. Supp. 2d 1331 (S.D. Fla. 2001) (seller is not a consumer); N.G.L. Travel Assocs. v. Celebrity Cruises, Inc., 764 So. 2d 672 (Fla. App. 2000); Warren Technology, Inc. v. Hines Interests Ltd. P'ship, 733 So. 2d 1146 (Fla. Dist. Ct. App. 1999).

1219 *See* Champion Parts, Inc. v. Oppenheimer Co., 878 F.2d 1003 (7th Cir. 1989) (Illinois law); Hartmarx Corp. v. JBA Int'l, Inc., 2002 U.S. Dist. LEXIS 4294 (N.D. Ill. Mar. 14, 2002) (use of pronoun "he" does not show intent to exclude corporations); Bell Enterprises Venture v. Santanna Natural Gas Corp., 2001 U.S. Dist. LEXIS 23684 (N.D. Ill. Dec. 7, 2001) (business plaintiff that purchased services for consumption rather than resale can bring UDAP suit); Uniroyal Tire Co. v. Mut. Trading Corp., 749 F. Supp. 869 (N.D. Ill. 1990); W.E. O'Neil Constr. Co. v. National Union Fire Ins. Co., 721 F. Supp. 984 (N.D. Ill. 1989); Heritage Ins. Co. v. First Nat'l Bank, 629 F. Supp. 1412 (W.D. Ill. 1986); Evanston Bank v. Conticommodity Servs., Inc., 623 F. Supp. 1014 (N.D. Ill. 1985); Zinser v. Rose, 614 N.E.2d 1259 (Ill. App. Ct. 1993) (business plaintiffs have standing to sue where they suffered injury to reputation); *see also* Tan v. Boyke, 508 N.E.2d 390 (Ill. App. Ct. 1987) (plaintiff need not be a consumer where claim involves realty). *But see* Huss v. Goldman, Sachs & Co., 635 F. Supp. 1227 (N.D. Ill. 1986); National Union Fire Ins. Co. v. Continental Illinois Corp., 652 F. Supp. 858 (N.D. Ill. 1986).

1220 A&W Sheet Metal, Inc. v. Berg Mechanical, Inc., 653 So. 2d 158 (La. Ct. App. 1995); Morris v. Rental Tools, Inc., 435 So. 2d 528 (La. Ct. App. 1983).

1221 Barman v. Union Oil Co., 2000 U.S. Dist. LEXIS 14157 (D. Or. Sept. 8, 2000), *aff'd in part, rev'd in part, remanded, on other grounds*, 2002 U.S. App. LEXIS 20764 (9th Cir. Sept. 26, 2002); Goodyear Tire & Rubber v. Tualatan Tire, 129 Or. App. 206, 879 P.2d 193 (1994), *aff'd in part and rev'd in part on other grounds*, 932 P.2d 1141 (Or. 1997); *see also* F.D.S. Marine, L.L.C. v. Shaver Transp. Co., 2001 U.S. Dist. LEXIS 7800 (D. Or. Mar. 29, 2001) ("person" includes corporation, but substantive violation alleged here requires purchase for personal, family, or household use), *adopted by* 230 F. Supp. 2d 1167 (D. Or. 2001); *cf.* Collegenet, Inc. v. Embark.com, Inc., 2000 U.S. Dist. LEXIS 20752 (D. Or. Dec. 15, 2000) (this corporation can not bring UDAP suit because not a purchaser of competitor's goods or services, but court seems to accept view that corpo-

allow "persons," defined to include corporations, to sue.[1222] But even this may not be enough to counter judicial aversion to UDAP actions brought by businesses. Some Illinois courts hold that the UDAP statute does not apply to a dispute among businesses who are not consumers of each other's services.[1223] Other courts have required businesses suing under the Illinois UDAP statute to show that the defendant's practices are of a type that affects consumers generally,[1224] that the acts have caused public or consumer injury,[1225] or that the plaintiff and the defendant are competitors in the market affected by the defendant's deceptive practices.[1226] 1990 amendments to the Illinois UDAP statute made it clear that proof of a public injury, a pattern, or an effect on consumers generally is not required,[1227] but some Illinois courts still require that, in contract disputes between businesses, UDAP plaintiffs must show that consumer protection concerns are implicated.[1228]

Georgia's UDAP statute was originally interpreted to allow a business to sue if it sustained damage as a con-

rations may be "persons"), *adopted by* 2001 U.S. Dist. LEXIS 7873 (D. Or. Apr. 4, 2001). *But see* Volm v. Legacy Health Sys., Inc., 237 F. Supp. 2d 1166 (D. Or. 2002) (business competitor can not bring UDAP suit).

1222 *See also* Brookings Mun. Utilities, Inc. v. Amoco Chem. Co., 103 F. Supp. 2d 1169 (D.S.D. 2000) (applying UDAP statute to business case without discussion; statute allows "any person who claims to have been adversely affected" to sue).

1223 DeJohn v. The .TV Corp. Int'l, 245 F. Supp. 2d 913 (C.D. Ill. 2003) (purchase for resale not covered); Prime Leasing, Inc. v. Kendig, 332 Ill. App. 3d 300, 773 N.E.2d 84, 265 Ill. Dec. 722 (2002) (relying on definition of "consumer" even though statute affords private cause of action to "any person"); Brown v. Veile, 198 Ill. App. 3d 513, 555 N.E.2d 1227 (1990); Century Universal Enterprises v. Triana Development Corp., 158 Ill. App. 3d 182, 510 N.E.2d 1260 (1987). *See also* Jacobs v. Central Transport, Inc., 891 F. Supp. 1088 (E.D.N.C. 1995) (UDAP claims arising from drivers' lease of vehicles from trucking company not preempted by Interstate Commerce Act and regulations); Continental Assurance Co. v. Commonwealth Edison Co., 551 N.E.2d 1054 (Ill. App. Ct. 1990) (redemption of shares of stock is not a sale or distribution of property, an advertisement, or an offer, and is therefore not covered by Illinois UDAP statute). *Cf.* Stogsdill v. Cragin Federal Bank, 645 N.E.2d 564 (Ill. App. Ct. 1995) (law firm was consumer of bank's checking account services). *But see* Hartmarx Corp. v. JBA Int'l, Inc., 2002 U.S. Dist. LEXIS 4294 (N.D. Ill. Mar. 14, 2002) (showing of consumer nexus is necessary only when business is not a consumer of the other's product).

1224 Champion Parts, Inc. v. Oppenheimer Co., 878 F.2d 1003 (7th Cir. 1989) (Illinois law); Pressalite Corp. v. Matsushita Elec. Corp., 2003 WL 1811530 (N.D. Ill. Apr. 4, 2003) (fact that product is ultimately sold to consumers does not make UDAP statute applicable to manufacturer's purchase of components); Prevue Pet Prods. v. Targeted Media for Medicine, Inc., 2003 WL 22247182 (N.D. Ill. Sept. 29, 2003) (UDAP statute applies where distributor's breach of contract undermined product sold to public); Birnberg v. Milk Street Residential Assocs. Ltd. P'ship, 2003 WL 151929 (N.D. Ill. Jan. 21, 2003); Menasha Corp. v. News America Marketing In-Store, Inc., 238 F. Supp. 1024 (N.D. Ill. 2003); Geinko v. KPMG L.L.P., 2002 WL 31867708 (N.D. Ill. Dec. 20, 2002); Gelco Corp. v. Major Chevrolet, Inc., 2002 WL 31427027 (N.D. Ill. Oct. 30, 2002) (complaint alleging car dealer's fraud on company that financed leases for consumers did not sufficiently allege consumer nexus); Underwriters Laboratories Inc. v. Solarcom L.L.C., 2002 WL 31103476 (N.D. Ill. Sept. 18, 2002) (must implicate consumer protection concerns or involve something more than breach of a business customer's contract); DRL Enterprises, Inc. v. ePartners, Inc., 173 F. Supp. 2d 818 (N.D. Ill. 2001); Web Communications Group, Inc. v. Gateway 2000, Inc., 889 F. Supp. 316 (N.D. Ill. 1995); Bank One Milwaukee v. Sanchez, 783 N.E.2d 217 (Ill. App. 2003); Peter J. Hartman Co. v. Capital Bank & Trust Co., 694 N.E.2d 1108 (Ill. App. Ct. 1998) (must implicate consumer protection concerns); Brody v. Finch University of Health Sciences, 698 N.E.2d 257 (Ill. App. Ct. 1998) (must implicate consumer protection concerns); Doherty v. Kahn, 682 N.E.2d 163 (Ill. App. Ct. 1997); *In re* Estate of Albergo, 656 N.E.2d 97 (Ill. App. Ct. 1995) (must be directed to market generally or otherwise implicate consumer protection concerns); Empire Home Servs., Inc. v. Carpet Am., 653 N.E.2d 852 (Ill. App. Ct. 1995); Bankier v. First Federal Savings & Loan Ass'n, 588 N.E.2d 391 (Ill. App. Ct. 1992); Downers Grove Volkswagen v. Wigglesworth, 190 Ill. App. 3d 524, 546 N.E.2d 33 (1989). *But see* We Deliver America v. General Growth Properties, Inc., 2003 WL 22836449 (N.D. Ill. Nov. 21, 2003) (where business is consumer of defendant's product it need not meet consumer nexus test).

1225 First Comics, Inc. v. World Color Press, Inc., 884 F.2d 1033 (7th Cir. 1989) (Illinois law); Hill v. Names & Addresses, Inc., 212 Ill. App. 3d 1065, 571 N.E.2d 1085 (1991) (business must show consumer injury). *Contra* Typographics Plus, Inc. v. I.M. Estrada & Co., 2000 U.S. Dist. LEXIS 10351 (N.D. Ill. July 14, 2000) (business need not show public injury if it is consumer of defendant's business product); W.E. O'Neil Constr. Co. v. National Union Fire Ins. Co., 721 F. Supp. 984 (N.D. Ill. 1989).

1226 Champion Parts, Inc. v. Oppenheimer Co., 878 F.2d 1003 (7th Cir. 1989) (Illinois law); B. Sanfield, Inc. v. Finlay Fine Jewelry Corp., 857 F. Supp. 1241 (N.D. Ill. 1994), *vacated on other grounds*, 168 F.3d 967 (7th Cir. 1999) (holding that business competitor has standing to bring Illinois UDAP claim).

1227 *See* Zinser v. Rose, 614 N.E.2d 1259 (Ill. App. Ct. 1993) (legislature's elimination of public injury requirement applies retroactively).

1228 Birnberg v. Milk Street Residential Assocs. Ltd. P'ship, 2003 WL 151929 (N.D. Ill. Jan. 21, 2003); Nakajima All Co. v. SL Ventures Corp., 2001 U.S. Dist. LEXIS 7535 (N.D. Ill. May 31, 2001) (if plaintiff is not consumer, must show nexus to consumer protection); Williams Elec. Games, Inc. v. Barry, 2001 U.S. Dist. LEXIS 16412 (N.D. Ill. Sept. 17, 2001); Stepan Co. v. Winter Panel Corp., 948 F. Supp. 802 (N.D. Ill. 1996); Brody v. Finch University of Health Sciences, 698 N.E.2d 257 (Ill. App. Ct. 1998) (applying principle to consumer contract between school and its students); Barille v. Sears Roebuck & Co., 682 N.E.2d 118 (Ill. App. Ct. 1997); Lake County Grading Co. v. Advance Mechanical Contractors, 654 N.E.2d 1109 (Ill. App. Ct. 1995). *Cf.* Skyline Int'l Development v. Citibank, 706 N.E.2d 942 (Ill. App. Ct. 1998) (business that is a consumer of other's business product or service need not show public injury). *But see* J.C. Whitney & Co. v. Renaissance Software Corp., 2000 U.S. Dist. LEXIS 6180 (N.D. Ill. Apr. 19, 2000) (consumer nexus need not be shown), *adopted in part, rejected in part, on other grounds*, 98 F. Supp. 2d 981 (N.D. Ill. 2000); Lefebvre Intergraphics, Inc. v. Sanden Machine, Ltd., 946 F. Supp. 1358 (N.D. Ill. 1996) (no such requirement where business is a consumer of other business' goods or services).

sumer.[1229] But it has been amended to limit the definition of "consumer" to natural persons, so companies can not sue at all.[1230] Businesses can sue, however, under Georgia's second UDAP statute, modeled after the Uniform Deceptive Trade Practices Act.[1231] A federal court has interpreted the Virginia UDAP statute as not allowing actions by one competitor against another.[1232]

Courts in other states find a corporation to be a person qualified to bring a UDAP action.[1233] An Idaho court has found nothing in its UDAP statute to exclude actions by businesses; the act thus applies to commercial transactions.[1234] Courts interpreting the Wisconsin UDAP statute reach the same result.[1235] South Carolina's Supreme Court finds a corporation to be a "person" as defined in the state UDAP statute.[1236] A condominium association can bring an action under Pennsylvania's UDAP statute because it falls within the definition of "person," but it can only assert the consumer claims of its members.[1237]

In New York, a party who claims the benefit of the UDAP statute must, at the threshold, charge conduct that is consumer oriented.[1238] New York's highest court has allowed a UDAP suit by a labor union pension fund against a bank where the parties occupied disparate bargaining positions and the bank had provided the standard forms and advice that it supplied to the consuming public at large.[1239] The court refused to apply the UDAP statute, however, to a major university's suit against an insurance company where each side was knowledgeable and received expert advice, and the policy was tailored to meet the university's requirements.[1240] The court held the dispute to be essentially private, arising out of a claim unique to the parties rather than conduct that affects the consuming public at large. Another question is whether a business that has suffered losses because of another company's consumer-oriented conduct—for example, a health insurer that has suffered losses due to treating people who were deceptively induced to smoke—can assert a UDAP claim. It is clear that the insurer's injury results from consumer-oriented acts, but it is not clear whether New York courts will find the claim too remote.[1241]

The Texas UDAP statute is particularly convoluted as to who may bring an action, as several poorly drafted amendments and constant change in the law have resulted in rulings such as one that businesses can sue for deceptive practices involving goods, but not involving services.[1242]

1229 Friedlander v. PDK Labs, Inc., 266 Ga. 180, 465 S.E.2d 670 (1996); Eason Publications, Inc. v. Nationsbank, 458 S.E.2d 899 (Ga. Ct. App. 1995) (UDAP statute does not cover bank's practices concerning commercial checking accounts that are not offered to consumers).

1230 *See* Blue Cross & Blue Shield of Georgia v. Kell, 488 S.E.2d 735 (Ga. App. Ct. 1997).

1231 *In re* Johnston Indus., Inc., 300 B.R. 821 (Bankr. M.D. Ga. 2003).

1232 H.D. Oliver Funeral Apartments, Inc. v. Dignity Funeral Servs., Inc., 964 F. Supp. 1033 (E.D. Va. 1997).

1233 Nault's Automobile Sales, Inc. v. American Honda Motor Co., 148 F.R.D. 25 (D.N.H. 1993); McLaughlin Ford, Inc. v. Ford Motor Co., 192 Conn. 558, 473 A.2d 1185 (1984); Sidney Binder, Inc. v. Jewelers Mut. Ins. Co., 552 N.E.2d 568 (Mass. App. Ct. 1990) (insurance company can bring UDAP suit against insured); Allan v. M&S Mortgage Co., 359 N.W.2d 238 (Mich. Ct. App. 1984); Dreier Co. v. Unitronix Corp., 218 N.J. Super. 260, 527 A.2d 875 (App. Div. 1986). *See also* Chaucer v. Chapman, 1995 Tenn. App. LEXIS 150, Clearinghouse No. 51,285 (Tenn. App. 1995) (assuming without deciding that business can sue, but holding that a establishing a competing business is not a UDAP violation unless activities deceive customers).

1234 Myers v. A.O. Smith Harvestore Products, Inc., 114 Idaho 432, 757 P.2d 695 (Ct. App. 1988).

1235 Stoughton Trailers, Inc. v. Henkel Corp., 965 F. Supp. 1227 (W.D. Wis. 1997); *see also* Gorton v. American Cyanamid Co., 533 N.W.2d 746 (Wis. 1995), *cert. denied*, 516 U.S. 1067 (1996).

1236 Daisy Outdoor Advertising Co. v. Abbott, 473 S.E.2d 47 (S.C. 1996).

1237 Valley Forge Towers South Condominium v. Ron-Ike Foam Insulators, Inc., 574 A.2d 641 (Pa. Super. Ct. 1990), *aff'd without opinion*, 605 A.2d 798 (Pa. 1992).

1238 New York University v. Continental Ins. Co., 87 N.Y.2d 308, 662 N.E.2d 763 (1995); Oswego Laborers' Local 214 Pension Fund v. Marine Midland Bank, 85 N.Y.2d 20, 647 N.E.2d 741 (1995). *See generally* § 7.5.3.8, *infra*.

1239 Oswego Laborers' Local 214 Pension Fund v. Marine Midland Bank, 85 N.Y.2d 20, 647 N.E.2d 741 (1995). *See also* Boule v. Hutton, 328 F.3d 84, 94 (2d Cir. 2003) (business competitors may sue, but only if there is some harm to the public at large); Excellus Health Plan, Inc. v. Tran, 287 F. Supp. 2d 167 (W.D.N.Y. 2003) (allegation that HMO attempted to run competitors out of business, thereby limiting consumers' health care choices, sufficient to withstand motion to dismiss); Capitol Records, Inc. v. Wings Digital Corp., 218 F. Supp. 2d 280 (E.D.N.Y. 2002) (competitors' copyright suit affects consumers because public might believe that infringing copies were authentic).

1240 New York University v. Continental Ins. Co., 87 N.Y.2d 308, 662 N.E.2d 763 (1995). *See also* Perkins School for the Blind v. Maxi-Aids, Inc., 274 F. Supp. 2d 319 (E.D.N.Y. 2003) (trademark infringement claim); Gucci America, Inc. v. Duty Free Apparel, Ltd., 277 F. Supp. 2d 269 (S.D.N.Y. 2003) (not met here); Wells Fargo Bank v. TACA Int'l Airlines, 247 F. Supp. 2d 352 (S.D.N.Y. 2002) (not met here); EUA Cogenex Corp. v. North Rockland Central School Dist., 124 F. Supp. 2d 861 (S.D.N.Y. 2000) (not met here).

1241 Blue Cross & Blue Shield v. Philip Morris USA Inc., 344 F.3d 211 (2d Cir. 2003) (certifying question to N.Y. Court of Appeals).

1242 *See* Big H. Auto Auction, Inc. v. Saenz Motors, 665 S.W.2d 756 (Tex. 1984) (purchase of goods for resale is purchase "for use" and thus covered by statute); Aetna Casualty & Surety Co. v. Martin Surgical Supply Co., 689 S.W.2d 263 (Tex. App. 1985) (plaintiff was purchaser of "goods" even though later sued insurance company for failure to supply "services" in regard to original goods purchase); Gibbs v. Main Bank of Houston, 666 S.W.2d 554 (Tex. App. 1984) (purchase of service in connection with purchase of goods involves goods, and is thus covered); Harwath v. Colwell, 648 S.W.2d 709 (Tex. App. 1982); Dowling v. NADW Marketing Inc., 625 S.W.2d 392 (Tex. Civ. App. 1981); Rotello v. Ring Around Products Inc., 614 S.W.2d 455

More particularly, the Texas statute at one time allowed merchants to bring UDAP claims where goods are purchased "for use," thus covering the purchase of seeds for agricultural use,[1243] cattle for commercial cattle-raising,[1244] pipe for oil drilling,[1245] and the purchase of goods for resale.[1246]

The statute now applies to a corporation that seeks or acquires by purchase or lease goods or services; consequently the statute applies to corporations that are purchasers.[1247] A person who *provides* services is not one who "seeks or acquires services."[1248] An entity seeking a loan for business purposes is also not covered.[1249]

In addition, the Texas statute, as amended, presently requires a business consumer to have under $25 million in assets to qualify under the Texas statute as a business consumer.[1250] But the burden of raising and proving this exemption is on the seller.[1251] The $25 million amount is based on gross assets.[1252] An entity with less than $25 million in assets, but which is controlled by an entity over that limit, is not a "consumer."[1253] An oil rig employee, who was severely injured on the rig, can sue the company that provided safety technicians to the oil rig operator, even though the oil rig operator was itself a corporation with over $25 million in assets and therefore did not itself have standing to sue under the Texas UDAP statute.[1254] A 1995 amendment to the Texas statute also exempts certain large transactions: those that involve total consideration by the consumer of more than $500,000, and those that involve total consideration by the consumer of more than $100,000 if the consumer is represented by independent legal counsel.[1255]

In Hawaii, only consumers, the attorney general, or the director of the office of consumer protection can bring suit for deceptive practices that violate the UDAP statute.[1256] Earlier decisions held that businesses could sue for violation of the statute's unfair competition prohibition,[1257] but a 1999 Hawaii Supreme Court decision held that they could not.[1258] A 2002 legislative amendment appears to have overruled this decision.[1259]

The Massachusetts UDAP statute is bifurcated.[1260] Businesses and individuals who engage in the conduct of any trade or commerce can bring suit under section 11, while consumers can bring suit under section 9.[1261] Section 11 offers somewhat reduced rights and remedies, for example by not affording a UDAP remedy for a violation of the state's unfair insurance practices law.[1262] There are also procedural differences between the two remedies.

Louisiana's UDAP statute covers both consumers and business competitors.[1263] Most decisions interpret it not to

(Tex. Civ. App. 1981) (merchant can recover for defective goods); Bennett v. Imperial Ins. Co., 606 S.W.2d 7 (Tex. Civ. App. 1980) (commercial sale of insurance is sale of service, not goods, and thus not within statute's coverage); Greene v. Bearden Enterprises Inc., 598 S.W.2d 649 (Tex. Civ. App. 1980) (merchant can recover for damage relating to sale of goods, but not relating to provision of services, even though part of same transaction); Ratcliff v. Tronholm, 596 S.W.2d 645 (Tex. Civ. App. 1980); Baldwin v. Calcasieu Lumber Co., 588 S.W.2d 659 (Tex. Civ. App. 1979); Trial v. McCoy, 581 S.W.2d 792 (Tex. Civ. App. 1979); United Postage Corp. v. Kammeyer, 581 S.W.2d 716 (Tex. Civ. App. 1979); Trial v. McCoy, 553 S.W.2d 199 (Tex. Civ. App. 1977); *see also* Crossland v. Canteen Corp., 711 F.2d 714 (5th Cir. 1983) (Texas law) (1973 version of statute excludes any action by corporation).

1243 Rotello v. Ring Around Products Inc., 614 S.W.2d 455 (Tex. Civ. App. 1981).

1244 Hennessey v. Skinner, 698 S.W.2d 382 (Tex. App. 1985).

1245 Reed v. Israel Nat'l Oil Co., 681 S.W.2d 228 (Tex. App. 1984).

1246 Big H. Auto Auction, Inc. v. Saenz Motors, 665 S.W.2d 756 (Tex. 1984); Aetna Casualty & Surety Co. v. Martin Surgical Supply Co., 689 S.W.2d 263 (Tex. App. 1985); Otto Inc. v. Cotton Salvage & Sales Inc., 609 S.W.2d 590 (Tex. Civ. App. 1980). *Contra* South Texas Irrigation Sys. Inc. v. Lockwood Corp., 489 F. Supp. 256 (W.D. Texas 1980).

1247 *See* Mason v. F.D.I.C., 888 F. Supp. 799 (S.D. Tex. 1995); Rentclubs, Inc. v. Transamerican Rental Fin. Corp., 775 F. Supp. 1460 (M.D. Fla. 1991) (Texas law); Sherman Simon Enter. v. Lorac Serv. Corp., 724 S.W.2d 13 (Tex. 1987).

1248 Baker v. Missouri Pacific Truck Lines, Inc., 616 S.W.2d 389 (Tex. Civ. App. 1981).

1249 First Interstate Bank of Bedford v. Bland, 810 S.W.2d 277 (Tex. App. 1991).

1250 Tex. Bus. & Com. Code § 17.45(4). *See* Alcan Aluminum Corp. v. BASF Corp., 2001 U.S. Dist. LEXIS 16807 (N.D. Tex. Oct. 17, 2001), *aff'd without op.*, 2002 U.S. App. LEXIS 16807 (5th Cir. Sept. 30, 2002); Eckman v. Centennial Sav. Bank, 784 S.W.2d 672 (Tex. 1990).

1251 Eckman v. Centennial Sav. Bank, 784 S.W.2d 672 (Tex. 1990). *See also* Compusolve, Inc. v. Urban Engineering Inc., 799 S.W.2d 374 (Tex. App. 1990).

1252 Hugh Symons Group, P.L.C. v. Motorola, Inc., 292 F.3d 466 (5th Cir. 2002).

1253 *Id.*

1254 Mote v. Oryx Energy Co., 910 F. Supp. 291 (E.D. Tex. 1995).

1255 Tex. Bus. & Com. Code Ann. § 17.49(f), (g); Landscape Design and Const., Inc. v. Transport Leasing/Contract, 2002 WL 257573 (N.D. Tex. Feb. 19, 2002). Neither exception applies if the transaction involves the consumer's home, however. *See generally* § 2.2.12, *supra*.

1256 Lui Ciro, Inc. v. Ciro, Inc., 895 F. Supp. 1365 (D. Haw. 1995); Aquarian Fdn. v. Ass'n of Apt. Owners, 44 P.3d 285 (Haw. 2001); Hough v. Pacific Ins. Co., 927 P.2d 858 (Haw. 1996); Molokai Advertiser-News v. Anderson, 2000 Haw. App. LEXIS 208 (Nov. 29, 2000).

1257 Star Markets, Ltd. v. Texaco, Inc., 945 F. Supp. 1344 (D. Haw. 1996); Lui Ciro, Inc. v. Ciro, Inc., 895 F. Supp. 1365 (D. Haw. 1995).

1258 Robert's Haw. School Bus, Inc. v. Laupahoehoe Transp. Co., 91 Haw. 224, 982 P.2d 853 (1999). *Accord* Molokai Advertiser-News v. Anderson, 2000 Haw. App. LEXIS 208 (Nov. 29, 2000).

1259 2002 Haw. Laws Act 229, *adding* Haw. Rev. Stat. § 480-2(e).

1260 *See* Mass. Gen. Laws Ann. ch. 93A, §§ 9, 11.

1261 Continental Ins. Co. v. Bahnan, 216 F.3d 150 (1st Cir. 2000); John Beaudette, Inc. v. Sentry Ins., 94 F. Supp. 2d 77 (D. Mass. 1999).

1262 John Beaudette, Inc. v. Sentry Ins., 94 F. Supp. 2d 77 (D. Mass. 1999).

1263 Blanchard & Co. v. Barrick Gold Corp., 2003 WL 22071173

cover business parties that are not competitors.[1264]

In Connecticut, the UDAP statute covers transactions between one business and another, and corporations can bring UDAP suits.[1265] Minnesota's "Consumer Protection; Products and Sales" statute[1266] protects not just consumers, but also non-consumers.[1267] Even Minnesota's Consumer Fraud Act protects not only individual consumers, but also businesses, religious institutions and other groups.[1268] However, to support a private cause of action the plaintiff must show that the cause of action benefits the public, i.e., that misrepresentations were made to others.[1269] A commercial farmer's investment in an agricultural cooperative is not covered.[1270]

In New Jersey, the UDAP statute applies to merchandise sales to businesses.[1271] Several courts have, however, limited UDAP coverage to businesses that "use economic goods, thereby diminishing or destroying their utilities."[1272] Where a dealer buys a product at wholesale and sells it at retail, it is not a consumer because it does not diminish or destroy the utility of the product.[1273] Another New Jersey

---

(E.D. La. Sept. 3, 2003) (finding plaintiff to be a business competitor of defendants); Sears, Roebuck & Co. v. Danny Williams Plumbing, Inc., 1999 U.S. Dist. LEXIS 6965 (E.D. La. May 3, 1999); Camp, Dresser & McKee, Inc. v. Steimle & Assocs., Inc., 652 So. 2d 44 (La. Ct. App. 1995).

1264 Tubos de Acero v. Am. Int'l Investment Corp., 292 F.3d 471 (5th Cir. 2002); Gardes Directional Drilling v. U.S. Turnkey Exploration Co., 98 F.3d 860 (5th Cir. 1996) (predicting that Louisiana Supreme Court will rule that right to bring UDAP suit extends only to consumers and business competitors); Specialty Diving v. Master Builders, Inc., 2003 WL 22416381 (E.D. La. Oct. 22, 2003); Becnel v. Whirley Indus., Inc., 2003 WL 22852215 (E.D. La. Nov. 26, 2003); Cashman Equipment Corp. v. Acadian Shipyard, Inc., 2002 WL 1433876 (E.D. La. June 28, 2002); Watercraft Management v. Mercury Marine, 191 F. Supp. 2d 709 (M.D. La. 2001) (holder of distributorship can not sue parent company); Traina v. NationsBank, 2001 U.S. Dist. LEXIS 14612 (E.D. La. Sept. 7, 2001) (business can only sue competitor, not seller); 5-Star Premium Fin., Inc. v. Wood, 2000 U.S. Dist. LEXIS 15582 (E.D. La. Oct. 16, 2000) (business consumer can not bring UDAP claim); Hamilton v. Business Partners, Inc., 938 F. Supp. 370 (E.D. La. 1996) (distributor is neither a competitor of its parent company nor a consumer of the products it distributes, so can not bring UDAP suit); Sportsman's Cove, Inc. v. Brunswick Corp., 845 So. 2d 1231 (La. Ct. App. 2003) (distributor can not bring UDAP claim against manufacturer); National Gypsum Co. v. Ace Wholesale, Inc., 738 So. 2d 128 (La. Ct. App. 1999) (distributor can not bring UDAP claim against supplier). *See also* Levine v. First Nat'l Bank of Commerce, 845 So. 2d 1189 (La. Ct. App. 2003) (UDAP statute is limited to business competitors and direct consumers, so buyers of home can not bring UDAP claim against seller's mortgage company, with whom buyers had no legal relationship); Monroe Medical Clinic v. Hospital Corp. of Am., 622 So. 2d 760 (La. Ct. App. 1993) (holding that UDAP plaintiff must be a consumer or business competitor, but interpreting competitor broadly to include potential competitors). *But see* Jesco Constr. Corp. v. NationsBank Corp., 107 F. Supp. 2d 715 (E.D. La. 2000) (company can bring UDAP claim against bank for failing to lend it money); Plaquemine Marine, Inc. v. Mercury Marine, 859 So. 2d 110 (La. Ct. App. 2003) (need not be consumer or business competitor); Wood v. Collins, 725 So. 2d 531 (La. Ct. App. 1998) (unsuccessful bidder can bring UDAP suit against successful bidder; court states broadly that right to sue is not limited to consumers and competitors); A&W Sheet Metal, Inc. v. Berg Mechanical, Inc., 653 So. 2d 158 (La. Ct. App. 1995) (unsuccessful bidder can not bring suit against company that solicited bids); Jarrell v. Carter, 577 So. 2d 120 (La. Ct. App. 1991) (allowing suit by person who wanted to buy distributorship from defendants; court states that right to bring UDAP suit is not limited to business consumers and competitors).

1265 Macomber v. Travelers Prop. & Cas. Corp., 261 Conn. 620, 804 A.2d 180, 195 (2002); Service Road Corp. v. Quinn, 241 Conn. 630, 698 A.2d 258 (1997); Larsen Chelsey Realty Co. v. Larsen, 232 Conn. 480, 656 A.2d 1009 (1995); Roncari Dev. v. GMG Enterprises, 45 Conn. Super. 408, 718 A.2d 1025 (1997) (competitor or other business person may bring UDAP suit).

1266 Minn. Stat. § 325F.67.

1267 Kronebusch v. MVBA Harvestore Sys., 488 N.W.2d 490 (Minn. Ct. App. 1992).

1268 Ly v. Nystrom, 615 N.W.2d 302 (Minn. 2000); Church of the Nativity of Our Lord v. Watpro, 491 N.W.2d 1 (Minn. 1992). *See also* Hutchinson Utilities Comm'n v. Curtiss-Wright Corp., 775 F.2d 231 (8th Cir. 1985) (municipal utility); Carlock v. Pillsbury Co., 719 F. Supp. 791 (D. Minn. 1989) (group of franchisees); Eager v. Siwek Lumber & Millwork, Inc., 392 N.W.2d 691 (Minn. Ct. App. 1986) (construction contractor). *But see* Gas Aggregation Servs., Inc. v. Howard Avista Energy, L.L.C., 319 F.3d 1060 (8th Cir. 2003) (Act does not apply to sophisticated traders in wholesale, commercial gas market); Stephenson v. Deutsche Bank, 2003 WL 22136062 (D. Minn. Sept. 8, 2003) (Act's substantive provisions do not apply to transactions between sophisticated traders). *But cf.* Popp Telecom, Inc. v. Am. Sharecom, Inc., 2004 WL 360388 (8th Cir. Feb. 17, 2004) (Minn. Prevention of Consumer Fraud Act does not allow seller to sue consumer); Solvay Pharmaceuticals, Inc. v. Global Pharmaceuticals, 298 F. Supp. 2d 880 (D. Minn. 2004) (Consumer Fraud Act does not protect merchants); Martin Lumber & Cedar Co. v. PPG Indus., 223 F.3d 873 (8th Cir. 2000) (holding that Consumer Fraud Act does not cover businesses; decision ignores *Ly*, decided 19 days earlier; also holds that Minn. UTPA does not apply to non-consumers); Antioch Co. v. Scrapbook Borders, Inc., 291 F. Supp. 2d 980 (D. Minn. 2003) (Consumer Fraud Act does not protect sellers).

1269 Ly v. Nystrom, 615 N.W.2d 302 (Minn. 2000). *See* § 7.5.3.4, *infra*. *See also* Gas Aggregation Servs., Inc. v. Howard Avista Energy, L.L.C., 319 F.3d 1060 (8th Cir. 2003) (Act does not apply to sophisticated traders in wholesale, commercial gas market); Stephenson v. Deutsche Bank, 282 F. Supp. 2d 1032 (D. Minn. 2003) (does not apply to transactions between sophisticated traders).

1270 Tisdell v. ValAdCo, 2002 WL 31368336 (Minn. App. Oct. 16, 2002) (unpublished, citation limited).

1271 International Minerals & Mining Co. v. Citicorp N. Am., Inc., 736 F. Supp. 587 (D.N.J. 1990); Coastal Group, Inc. v. Dryvit Sys., Inc., 274 N.J. Super. 171, 643 A.2d 649 (1994); Hundred E. Credit Corp. v. Eric Schuster Corp., 212 N.J. Super. 350, 515 A.2d 246 (App. Div. 1986). *But see* Werner & Pfleiderer Corp. v. Gary Chemical Corp., 697 F. Supp. 808 (D.N.J. 1988).

1272 City Check Cashing, Inc. v. National State Bank, 244 N.J. Super. 304, 582 A.2d 809 (App. Div. 1990).

1273 Lithuanian Commerce Corp. v. Sara Lee Hosiery, 179 F.R.D. 450 (D.N.J. 1998); Arc Networks, Inc. v. Gold Phone Card Co., 333 N.J. Super. 587, 756 A.2d 636 (Law. Div. 2000); City Check Cashing, Inc. v. National State Bank, 244 N.J. Super. 304, 582 A.2d 809 (App. Div. 1990).

court has held that its UDAP statute applies only to merchandise of a type that is sold to the public, and does not apply to a multi-million dollar negotiation for design of an industrial plant.[1274] The services that a wholesaler provides to a manufacturer, such as inventory tracking, are not "merchandise" because they are not of a type offered to the general public.[1275] But large, sophisticated businesses can be considered consumers, and a purchase of an industrial crane can be covered by the UDAP statute if the crane is publicly offered for sale to at least a limited market.[1276] Kansas makes a similar distinction, excluding a business's purchases of goods for resale.[1277]

A federal court interpreting the Colorado UDAP statute has decided that a corporation's claim dealing with a purely commercial matter with no benefit to consumers should not be within the scope of the state UDAP statute.[1278]

In a 1994 case, the New Hampshire Supreme Court refused to apply its UDAP statute to a business transaction because it was dissimilar to the types of transactions covered by the statute's list of prohibited acts and practices.[1279] Seven years later, however, it held that the statute covered business-to-business transactions.[1280] The court held that the statute's list of prohibited acts, all of which related to consumer transactions, was a non-exhaustive list, so did not limit the statute's scope.

Where the UDAP statute allows businesses to sue, they may have to show a greater level of deception or unfairness than is necessary in consumer suits.[1281] For example, many courts have held that Massachusetts businesses bringing UDAP suits must show that the defendant's conduct attained "a level of rascality" that would raise the eyebrow of someone inured to the rough and tumble of the world of commerce.[1282] New Hampshire's Supreme Court has adopted the same standard.[1283] Also, some substantive regulations or parts of the statute may apply only to consumer transactions.[1284] Where a state's UDAP prohibitions cover business transactions, but the UDAP statute grants a private cause of action only to consumers, businesses may still have implied remedies, such as recoupment,[1285] injunction, or reformation or cancellation of contract.

2.4.5.3 Can Government Entities Bring UDAP Claims?

In every state, the attorney general or other agencies can bring state enforcement actions on behalf of the state's citizens, as specified by the UDAP statute. State enforcement is detailed in Chapter 10, *infra*.

A separate issue arises as to whether a government entity can bring a private UDAP action under the private remedy provisions of the statute to remedy injury done directly to

1274 Boc Group v. Lummus Crest, 251 N.J. Super. 271, 597 A.2d 1109 (1990). *Accord* R.J. Longo Constr. v. Transit Am., 921 F. Supp. 1295 (D.N.J. 1996) (New Jersey UDAP statute does not apply to transit car design services provided by one large corporation to another).

1275 Bracco Diagnostics Inc. v. Bergen Brunswig Drug Co., 226 F. Supp. 2d 557 (D.N.J. 2002).

1276 Naporano Iron & Metal Co. v. American Crane Corp., 79 F. Supp. 2d 494 (D.N.J. 1999).

1277 Roberts v. Shawnee Mission Ford, 2003 WL 22143727 (D. Kan. Aug. 20, 2003).

1278 United States Welding, Inc. v. Burroughs Corp., 615 F. Supp. 554 (D. Colo. 1985) (Colorado law). *Contra* Heller v. Lexton-Ancira Real Estate Fund, Ltd., 809 P.2d 1016 (Colo. Ct. App. 1990), *rev'd on other grounds*, 826 P.2d 819 (Colo. 1992).

1279 Roberts v. General Motors Corp., 138 N.H. 532, 643 A.2d 956 (1994).

1280 Milford Lumber Co. v. RCB Realty, 780 A.2d 1259 (N.H. 2001).

1281 Brennan v. Carvel Corp., 929 F.2d 801 (1st Cir. 1991) (Massachusetts law); Madan v. Royal Indemnity Co., 26 Mass. App. Ct. 756, 532 N.E.2d 1214 (1989).

1282 Tagliente v. Himmer, 949 F.2d 1 (1st Cir. 1991) (Massachusetts law); Quaker State Oil Refining v. Garrity Oil Co., 884 F.2d 1510 (1st Cir. 1989) (Massachusetts law); Skinder-Strauss v. Massachusetts Continuing Legal Ed., 914 F. Supp. 665 (D. Mass. 1995); Bio-Vita, Ltd. v. Rausch, 759 F. Supp. 33 (D. Mass. 1991) (common law deceit rose to "level of rascality" required for UDAP liability); Logan Equip. Corp. v. Simon Aerials, Inc., 736 F. Supp. 1188 (D. Mass. 1990) (delays, back-pedaling, and less than total candor did not rise to "level of rascality" necessary to prove UDAP violation in business case); Greenery Rehabilitation Group, Inc. v. Antaramian, 36 Mass. App. Ct. 73, 628 N.E.2d 1291 (1994) (non-disclosure in business transaction did not violate UDAP statute where seller's knowledge unproven). *Cf.* Picciuto v. Dwyer, 32 Mass. App. Ct. 137, 586 N.E.2d 38 (1992) (UDAP statute has established "for businesses as well as for consumers, a path of conduct higher than that trod by the crowd in the past"). The Massachusetts Supreme Judicial Court has termed these formulations "uninstructive," Massachusetts Employers Ins. Exchange v. Propac-Mass, Inc., 420 Mass. 39, 648 N.E.2d 435 (1995), *cert. denied*, 516 U.S. 988 (1995), but courts have continued to use this standard. *See, e.g.*, Suzuki of W. Mass., Inc. v. Outdoor Sports Expo, Inc., 126 F. Supp. 2d 40 (D. Mass. 2001).

1283 Milford Lumber Co. v. RCB Realty, 780 A.2d 1259 (N.H. 2001); Barrows v. Boles, 687 A.2d 979 (N.H. 1996). *Accord* Anheuser-Busch, Inc. v. Caught-on-Bleu, Inc., 2003 WL 21715330, at *6 (D.N.H. July 22, 2003).

1284 F.D.S. Marine, L.L.C. v. Shaver Transp. Co., 2001 U.S. Dist. LEXIS 7800 (D. Or. Mar. 29, 2001) (corporation was a "person" that could sue, but the substantive violation it alleged required purchase for personal, family, or household use), *adopted by* 230 F. Supp. 2d 1167 (D. Or. 2001); Knapp Shoes, Inc. v. Sylvania Shoe Mfg. Corp., 418 Mass. 737, 640 N.E.2d 1101 (1994); Mayville Die & Tool, Inc. v. Weller Mach. Co., 2001 Wisc. App. LEXIS 1224 (Nov. 29, 2001) (unpublished, citation limited) (UDAP statute that prohibits false advertising to the public does not apply to parties that have an ongoing business relationship, i.e., a representation made by a distributor to its supplier).

1285 *In re* Fricker, 115 B.R. 809 (Bankr. E.D. Pa. 1990); Saler v. Hurvitz, 84 B.R. 45 (Bankr. E.D. Pa. 1988); Jungkurth v. Eastern Fin. Serv., 74 B.R. 323 (Bankr. E.D. Pa. 1987). *See generally* the discussion of remedies in business cases at Carter, Pennsylvania Consumer Law § 2.7.4 (George T. Bisel Co. 2d ed. 2003 and Supp.).

that government entity. Where a UDAP statute allows "any person" to bring an action, Massachusetts' highest court has allowed the Boston Housing Authority to bring a UDAP action.[1286] Similarly, the City of Boston is a "person who engages in the conduct of any trade or commerce," and thus can bring a UDAP action under the section pertaining to businesses suing businesses.[1287] A Massachusetts federal court has come to the same conclusion for the United States suing based on injury to itself.[1288] But a local Massachusetts board of health can not bring a UDAP claim under a section of the statute that requires *plaintiffs* to be engaged in trade or commerce.[1289]

The State of North Carolina can sue under that state's UDAP statute.[1290] Likewise, applying the rule of liberal construction, a New Jersey court interpreted its UDAP statute to allow a housing authority to sue, even though the statutory definition of "person" included corporations, business entities, and associations, but not public authorities.[1291] On the other hand, school districts and other "bodies politic" have been held not to be "persons" and therefore not entitled to sue under the Illinois UDAP statute.[1292] While Washington's UDAP statute allows counties, municipalities, and political subdivisions to sue, one unreported decision interprets it not to allow state agencies to sue.[1293]

2.4.6 Investigators

It may be advisable to investigate allegedly fraudulent sellers by making test purchases or sending pre-examined goods to be repaired. Normally those actions would serve as evidence that another purchase involved deception. However, a consumer may wish to bring an action based solely on such test purchases. The issue then arises whether a sale has taken place to trigger use of the UDAP statute. In two cases considering the issue, courts have held that investigators who make test purchases or have test goods repaired are considered consumers so that the attorney general may base a UDAP action on their experience.[1294] In one case, however, while not reaching the question whether investigators could be considered consumers, the Kansas Supreme Court relied heavily on the fact that they were not harmed as support for its conclusion that the sale was not unconscionable as prohibited by the UDAP statute.[1295]

2.5 Conflict with the FTC Act and Other Federal Law

2.5.1 General Principles of Federal Preemption

Sometimes a defendant will argue that a UDAP claim, or a claim under another consumer protection statute or the common law, is preempted by federal law. Preemption is a radical intrusion on state power. In areas that the states have traditionally occupied, their historic police powers are not to be superseded by a federal act unless that is the clear and manifest purpose of Congress, so preemption provisions must be read narrowly.[1296] A federal law that imposes standards on an industry does not implicitly preempt state laws that create remedies by which victims can be compensated.[1297]

Preemption is a question of congressional intent.[1298] There are three types of preemption. First, Congress can express an intent to preempt state law explicitly in the federal statute. This is express preemption. The other two types, conflict and field preemption, are implicit in the

1286 Spence v. Boston Edison Co., 390 Mass. 604, 459 N.E.2d 80 (1983).

1287 City of Boston v. Aetna Life Ins. Co., 399 Mass. 569, 506 N.E.2d 106 (1987).

1288 United States v. United States Trust Co., 660 F. Supp. 1085 (D. Mass. 1986). *See also* Republic of Turkey v. OKS Partners, 797 F. Supp. 64 (D. Mass. 1992). *But cf.* United States v. Roche, 425 F. Supp. 743 (D. Mass. 1977) (United States can not sue in *parens patriae*).

1289 Clean Harbors v. Board of Health, 409 Mass. 834, 570 N.E.2d 987 (1991).

1290 F. Ray Moore Oil Co. v. State, 341 S.E.2d 371 (N.C. Ct. App. 1986).

1291 Zorba Contractors, Inc. v. Housing Authority of City of Newark, 282 N.J. Super. 430, 660 A.2d 550 (1995).

1292 Chicago Board of Ed. v. AC&S, Inc., 131 Ill. 2d 428, 546 N.E.2d 580 (1989).

1293 Rufer v. Abbott Laboratories, 2003 WL 22430193 (Wash. App. Oct. 27, 2003) (unpublished, citation limited).

1294 Brown v. Spitzer Ford, Inc., 11 Ohio Op. 3d 84 (Ct. App. 1978); Brown v. Howe Motor Co., Clearinghouse No. 26,575 (C.P. Butler Cty., Ohio 1977). *Cf.* Stanley v. Wal Mart Stores, Inc., 839 F. Supp. 430 (N.D. Tex. 1993).

1295 State *ex rel.* Stovall v. Confirmed.com, 38 P.3d 707 (Kan. 2002).

1296 Rush Prudential HMO, Inc. v. Moran, 536 U.S. 355, 122 S. Ct. 2151, 153 L. Ed. 2d 375 (2002); Medtronic, Inc. v. Lohr, 518 U.S. 470, 485, 116 S. Ct. 2240, 135 L. Ed. 2d 700 (1996); Cipollone v. Liggett Group, 505 U.S. 504, 112 S. Ct. 2608, 2617, 120 L. Ed. 2d 407 (1992); Mangini v. R.J. Reynolds Tobacco Co., 7 Cal. 4th 1057 (1994); Washington Mut. Bank v. Superior Court, 115 Cal. Rptr. 2d 765 (App. 2002) (consumer protection laws are within the states' traditional police powers so enjoy a heightened presumption against preemption). *But cf.* Buckman Co. v. Plaintiff's Legal Committee, 531 U.S. 341, 121 S. Ct. 1012, 148 L. Ed. 2d 854 (2001) (presumption against preemption is only appropriate in fields that states have traditionally occupied); U.S. v. Locke, 529 U.S. 89, 120 S. Ct. 1135, 146 L. Ed. 2d 69 (2000) (no presumption against preemption in field such as maritime commerce, which the federal government has historically regulated heavily).

1297 Sprietsma v. Mercury Marine, 123 S. Ct. 518, 154 L. Ed. 2d 466 (2002).

1298 Lorillard Tobacco Co. v. Reilly, 533 U.S. 525, 121 S. Ct. 2404, 150 L. Ed. 2d 532 (2001); Medtronic, Inc. v. Lohr, 518 U.S. 470, 485, 116 S. Ct. 2240, 135 L. Ed. 2d 700 (1996); Cipollone v. Liggett Group, 505 U.S. 504, 112 S. Ct. 2608, 2617, 120 L. Ed. 2d 407 (1992).

statute's structure or purpose. Conflict preemption will be found where the state law actually conflicts with the federal law. For example, compliance with both sate and federal law may be a physical impossibility, or the state law may stand as an obstacle to the accomplishment and execution of the full purposes of Congress.[1299] Field preemption exists where the federal law so thoroughly occupies a legislative field as to make reasonable the inference that Congress left no room for states to legislate.[1300]

State law may be preempted not just by a federal statute but also by federal regulations where a federal agency, acting within the scope of its congressionally delegated authority, acts to preempt state law.[1301] The same federal statute may expressly preempt some aspects of state law, and impliedly preempt others.[1302] Where a statute expressly preempts some areas of state law, however, it is a reasonable inference that Congress did not intend to preempt other matters by implication.[1303]

Preemption problems should be identified and addressed before a UDAP case is filed. Careful pleading can reduce preemption problems. If the UDAP claim focuses on aspects or stages of the transaction other than those regulated by the federal law, it may escape preemption. For example, a claim against a van line may avoid Carmack amendment preemption where it focuses on the shipper's misdeeds before the contract was signed.[1304] It is also wise to select UDAP claims that do not conflict with federal standards, and to make the precise substantive claims clear in the pleadings so that the court can see that there is no substantive conflict with federal law.[1305] Preemption may also be avoided if the court finds that the UDAP claim is merely a procedural vehicle for enforcing standards that are consistent with federal law.[1306] Even if a UDAP claim is preempted, alternate claims based on contract or tort may not be.[1307] Preemption is an affirmative defense that is waived if it is not pleaded.[1308]

In a few rare cases, federal law so completely displaces state law that any claim that could have been pleaded as a federal claim is removable to federal court, even if the claim is framed solely as a state law claim. This "complete preemption" doctrine is discussed in § 7.6.5, *infra.*

This section deals with whether, because of the Supremacy Clause, federal law preempts state UDAP statutes in certain areas. Section 2.3.3.5, *supra*, discusses whether, as a matter of *state* law, a state legislature intended UDAP remedies to apply in areas regulated by other federal or state laws. Preemption of state UDAP statutes by the Bankruptcy Code[1309] and the federal Arbitration Act[1310] is discussed in other sections of this manual.

2.5.2 The FTC Act

As a general rule, FTC decisions do not preempt state cases, but serve as guidelines.[1311] Even FTC guides covering a challenged subject area do not preempt state UDAP regulations that conflict with the FTC guides,[1312] or prevent states from finding UDAP violations in practices not prohibited by those guides.[1313] The authority given to the FTC

1299 Barnett Bank of Marion County v. Nelson, 517 U.S. 25, 31, 116 S. Ct. 1103, 134 L. Ed. 2d 237 (1996).

1300 Cipollone v. Liggett Group, 505 U.S. 504, 112 S. Ct. 2608, 2617, 120 L. Ed. 2d 407 (1992).

1301 New York v. Fed. Energy Regulatory Com'n, 535 U.S. 1, 122 S. Ct. 1012, 152 L. Ed. 2d 47 (2002); Lynnbrook Farms v. Smithkline Beecham Corp., 79 F.3d 620 (7th Cir. 1996) (UDAP claims preempted by regulations under the federal Virus-Serums-Toxins Act); Time Warner Cable v. Doyle, 66 F.3d 867 (7th Cir. 1995).

1302 Lorillard Tobacco Co. v. Reilly, 533 U.S. 525, 121 S. Ct. 2404, 150 L. Ed. 2d 532 (2001); Geier v. Am. Honda Motor Co., 529 U.S. 861, 120 S. Ct. 1913, 146 L. Ed. 2d 914 (2000); Dahl v. Charles Schwab & Co., 545 N.W.2d 918 (Minn. 1996), *citing* Freightliner Corp. v. Myrick, 514 U.S. 280, 115 S. Ct. 1483, 1488, 131 L. Ed. 2d 385 (1995).

1303 Lorillard Tobacco Co. v. Reilly, 533 U.S. 525, 121 S. Ct. 2404, 150 L. Ed. 2d 532 (2001); Geier v. Am. Honda Motor Co., 529 U.S. 861, 120 S. Ct. 1913, 146 L. Ed. 2d 914 (2000).

1304 Mesta v. Allied Van Lines Int'l Inc., 695 F. Supp. 63 (D. Mass. 1988). *See generally* § 2.5.5, *infra* (discussion of Carmack amendment preemption). *See also* DeMarco v. Bay Ridge Car World, 169 A.D.2d 808, 565 N.Y.S.2d 176 (1991) (compliance with federal automobile recall notice requirements does not preclude a UDAP suit where the complaint focuses on the dealer's failure to make disclosures at the time of sale).

1305 Mario's Butcher Shop & Food Center, Inc. v. Armour & Co., 574 F. Supp. 653 (N.D. Ill. 1983); Solorzano v. Superior Court, 13 Cal. Rptr. 2d 161 (Ct. App. 1992); *see also* Buckman Co. v. Plaintiff's Legal Committee, 531 U.S. 341, 348, 121 S. Ct. 1012, 1020, 148 L. Ed. 2d 854, 861 (2001) (noting that state law causes of action that parallel federal safety requirements for medical devices may not be preempted).

1306 Woolridge v. Redman Homes, Inc., 792 F. Supp. 1469 (N.D. Tex. 1991); McCarthy v. Paine Webber, Inc., 618 F. Supp. 933 (N.D. Ill. 1985); Mario's Butcher Shop & Food Center, Inc. v. Armour & Co., 574 F. Supp. 653 (N.D. Ill. 1983).

1307 American Airlines, Inc. v. Wolens, 513 U.S. 219, 115 S. Ct. 817, 130 L. Ed. 2d 715 (1995) (Airline Deregulation Act does not preempt state contract claims); Shupe v. American Airlines, Inc., 893 S.W.2d 305 (Tex. App. 1995) (Airline Deregulation Act does not preempt state law negligence claims).

1308 Brannan v. United Student Aid Funds, 94 F.3d 1260, 1266 (9th Cir. 1996); Sweeney v. Westvaco, 926 F.2d 29, 38–41 (1st Cir. 1991); Dueringer v. Gen. Am. Life Ins. Co., 842 F.2d 127 (5th Cir. 1988).

1309 *See* § 7.6.6, *infra.*

1310 *See* § 7.6.7, *infra.* A detailed discussion of preemption by the Federal Arbitration Act may be found in National Consumer Law Center, Consumer Arbitration Agreements (4th ed. 2004).

1311 *See* § 3.4.5.1 *infra.*

1312 Hinds v. Paul's Auto Werkstatt, Inc., 107 Or. App. 63, 810 P.2d 874 (1991); State v. Amoco Oil Co., 97 Wis. 2d 226, 293 N.W.2d 487 (1980).

1313 Caldor, Inc. v. Heslin, 215 Conn. 590, 577 A.2d 1009 (1990) (state UDAP regulations can go beyond FTC rules and guides); Purity Supreme, Inc. v. Attorney General, 380 Mass. 762, 407 N.E.2d 297 (1980); Hinds v. Paul's Auto Werkstatt, Inc., 107 Or. App. 63, 810 P.2d 874 (1991); State v. American TV & Appli-

to obtain injunctive relief against deceptive practices does not preempt UDAP claims.[1314]

For example, a car dealer's nondisclosure of known defects in an automobile can be a UDAP violation even though the FTC considered and refrained from enacting a version of the FTC Used Car Rule that would have required disclosure of known defects.[1315] Alleged compliance with FTC guides can not be raised as a UDAP defense where a vocational school consulted an FTC attorney with no authority to approve the school's advertising.[1316] The Vermont UDAP statute's requirement that its regulations be consistent with federal law is met even if they provide more protection than FTC rules, as long as they do not stand as an obstacle to the accomplishment of the federal objectives.[1317] The FTC's franchise rule, which requires disclosures when franchises are sold, does not preempt state franchise laws that regulate the relationship between the parties.[1318]

The fact that a similar matter is pending before the FTC is no reason to stay the state UDAP action to await the FTC's decision, even if the UDAP statute requires the state court to defer to the FTC's interpretation of whether a practice is permitted.[1319] In addition, state UDAP case law can prohibit practices not reached by the FTC Act.[1320]

2.5.3 Federal Banking and Credit Disclosure Laws

2.5.3.1 Federal Banking Laws Vary in the Scope of Preemption

When analyzing a defendant's claim that federal banking laws preempt a state UDAP claim, it is important to determine exactly what federal statutes apply to the particular defendant. The scope of preemption varies significantly among the federal banking laws. In some cases the federal banking law only preempts state laws regarding the institution's rates or charges. Preemption then often turns on whether the defendant succeeds in characterizing the consumer's claim as a challenge to rates and charges.

2.5.3.2 National Bank Act

The National Bank Act expressly preempts state limits on interest rates as applied to national banks.[1321] It provides the exclusive cause of action for usury claims against national banks, so any claim regarding excess interest, even if framed solely as a state law violation, necessarily arises under federal law so is removable to federal court under the complete preemption doctrine.[1322]

The National Bank Act also preempts non-usury state laws if they prevent or significantly interfere with the exercise of the bank's federally-granted powers.[1323] In regulations adopted in 2004, however, the Office of the Comptroller of the Currency (OCC) defined a broader scope of preemption, seemingly asserting that state laws are preempted unless their effect on the exercise of national banks' powers is "only incidental."[1324] These regulations govern deposit-taking and mortgage and non-mortgage lending by national banks.

The regulations list state laws regarding contracts, torts, criminal law, the right to collect debts, acquisition and

---

ance, 140 Wis. 2d 353, 410 N.W.2d 596 (Ct. App. 1987), *rev'd on other grounds*, 146 Wis. 2d 292, 430 N.W.2d 709 (1988), *motion to vacate denied*, 151 Wis. 2d 175, 443 N.W.2d 175, 443 N.W.2d 662 (1989); *see also* § 3.4.5.1, *supra*.

1314 Consumer Justice Center v. Olympian Labs, Inc., 99 Cal. App. 4th 1056, 121 Cal. Rptr. 2d 749 (2002).

1315 Hinds v. Paul's Auto Werkstatt, Inc., 107 Or. App. 63, 810 P.2d 874 (1991).

1316 State *ex rel.* Lefkowitz v. Interstate Tractor Trailer Training, Inc., 66 Misc. 2d 678, 321 N.Y.S.2d 147 (Sup. Ct. 1971).

1317 North Am. Enterprises, Inc. v. State of Vermont, Clearinghouse No. 50,442 (Vt. Super. Ct. Oct. 11, 1994). *Accord* Commonwealth v. Amcan Enterprises, 47 Mass. App. Ct. 330, 712 N.E.2d 1205, 1209 n.9 (1999).

1318 H.R.R. Zimmerman Co. v. Tecumseh Prods. Co., 2001 U.S. Dist. LEXIS 1920 (N.D. Ill. Feb. 15, 2001).

1319 Bailey Employment Sys., Inc. v. Hahn, 545 F. Supp. 62 (D. Conn. 1982), *aff'd without op.*, 723 F.2d 895 (2d Cir. 1983); People *ex rel.* Abrams v. American Direct Indus., Inc., Clearinghouse No. 43,083 (N.Y. Sup. Ct. 1988).

1320 *See* § 3.4.5.1, *infra*. *See also* Commonwealth v. Amcan Enterprises, 47 Mass. App. Ct. 330, 712 N.E.2d 1205, 1209 n.9 (1999).

1321 U.S.C. § 85 (allowing national banks, when originating credit, to charge either highest rate allowed by state law or an alternative federal rate). *See* National Consumer Law Center, The Cost of Credit: Regulation and Legal Challenges § 3.4 (2d ed. 2000 and Supp.) (detailed discussion of preemption under § 85).

1322 Beneficial Nat'l Bank v. Anderson, 539 U.S. 1, 123 S. Ct. 2058, 2062, 156 L. Ed. 2d 1 (2003). *But cf.* Jacobs v. ABN AMRO Bank, 2004 WL 869557 (E.D.N.Y. Apr. 21, 2004) (UDAP and other state law claims concerning fax fees are not usury claims so not completely preempted); Freunscht v. Banknorth, 2004 WL 540693 (D.N.H. Mar. 17, 2004) (Nat'l Bank Act does not completely preempt claim that bank violated state retail installment sales act by failing to arrange for refund of credit insurance premium upon borrower's repayment of loan); Delaney v. Bank of Am., 2004 WL 1553518 (N.D. Miss. June 16, 2004) (National Bank Act does not completely preempt fraud claims); Cortazar v. Wells Fargo & Co., 2004 WL 1774219 (N.D. Cal. Aug. 9, 2004) (claim that bank baited consumers with low cost loan and then switched them to high cost loan is not a challenge to legality of rates so complete preemption doctrine does not apply); Wilson v. Bank of Am., 2004 WL 443881 (S.D. Miss. Feb. 20, 2004) (claim that consumers were fraudulently induced to accept high priced loans is not a usury claim so not completely preempted). *See generally* National Consumer Law Center, The Cost of Credit: Regulation and Legal Challenges § 3.4 (2d ed. 2000 and Supp.) (discussion of effect of National Bank Act on state usury law).

1323 Barnett Bank of Marion County v. Nelson, 517 U.S. 25, 31, 116 S. Ct. 1103, 134 L. Ed. 2d 237 (1996) (National Bank Act granting banks the power to sell insurance preempts state law to the contrary).

1324 12 C.F.R. §§ 7.4007(c), 7.4008(e), 7.4009(c)(2), 34.4.

transfer of property, taxation, and zoning as ones that are not preempted as long as they only incidentally affect the exercise of national banks' powers.[1325] In addition, other state laws are not preempted if the OCC determines that their effect is incidental to the bank's exercise of its powers or otherwise consistent with the bank's powers.[1326] The OCC's intent in adopting the regulations was to leave unpreempted state laws that are part of the legal infrastructure that makes it practicable for national banks to conduct their authorized activities and that do not regulate the manner or content of the business of banking.[1327] A court applying the identical standard under a different federal banking law held that the duty to refrain from misrepresentation that a UDAP statute imposed was part of the legal infrastructure that undergirds all contractual and commercial transactions, so was not preempted.[1328]

The OCC regulation does not list state UDAP laws, either among the state laws that are preempted or among those that are generally not preempted. Since UDAP statutes are not directed at the manner or content of banks' lending activities, but apply generally-applicable standards of unfairness and deception to banks and other industries, this formulation of the standard suggests that they should not be preempted. Also, UDAP statutes represent a liberalization of common law fraud; accordingly, since tort law is not preempted UDAP statutes should also not be preempted. As part of these new regulations, however, the OCC also adopted anti-predatory lending standards and incorporated the FTC Act's prohibition of unfair or deceptive acts or practices.[1329] The OCC stated that this action ensured that national banks "are subject to consistent and uniform Federal standards,"[1330] which suggests an intent to displace state UDAP statutes. Nonetheless, in testimony before a House Subcommittee, the OCC's Chief Counsel testified, in response to a question from a subcommittee member, that state UDAP statutes are *not* preempted.[1331] This view is consistent with an OCC advisory letter issued in 2002.[1332] Many pre-2004 cases have held that the federal scheme for regulating national banks is not so extensive as to preempt state law challenges to unfair or deceptive practices by national banks.[1333]

By federal statute, the host state's consumer protection laws apply to a branch of an out-of-state national bank to the same extent as they would apply to a branch of a bank chartered by the host state, unless the Comptroller of the Currency rules otherwise or federal law preempts the appli-

1325 12 C.F.R. §§ 7.4007(c), 7.4008(e), 7.4009(c)(2), 34.4.

1326 *Id.*

1327 69 Fed. Reg. 1904, 1912, 1913 (Jan. 13, 2004). *But see* Abel v. Keybank USA, 313 F. Supp. 2d 720 (N.D. Ohio 2004) (interpreting OCC regulation to preempt state law that subjects lender to claims and defenses that consumer could assert against seller; court fails to consider that this regulation mirrors federal law, i.e., the FTC Holder Rule).

1328 Gibson v. World Sav. & Loan Ass'n, 103 Cal. App. 4th 1291, 128 Cal. Rptr. 2d 19 (2002).

1329 12 C.F.R. §§ 7.4007(b), (c), 34.3(b), (c).

1330 69 Fed. Reg. 1912 (Jan. 13, 2004).

1331 A record of the oral testimony from this hearing is available at http://financialservices.house.gov/hearings.asp?formmode=detail&hearing=273&comm=4. Note that the chief counsel's written testimony does not address the issue: Hearing Before the Subcomm. on Oversight and Investigations, House Comm. on Fin. Servs., 108th Cong. (Jan. 28, 2004) (testimony of Julie Williams, First Senior Deputy Comptroller & Chief Counsel, Office of the Comptroller of the Currency), *available at* http://financialservices.house.gov/media/pdf/012804jw.pdf.

1332 OCC Advisory Letter AL 2002-3 (Mar. 22, 2002) at 3 n.2 ("A number of state laws prohibit unfair or deceptive acts or practices, and such laws may be applicable to insured depository institutions. *See, e.g.*, Cal. Bus. Prof. Code §§ 17200 *et seq.* and 17500 *et seq.*"). This letter is reproduced on the companion CD-Rom to National Consumer Law Center, The Cost of Credit: Regulation and Legal Challenges (2d ed. 2000 and Supp.).

1333 Minn. *ex rel.* Hatch v. Fleet Mortg. Corp., 158 F. Supp. 2d 962 (D. Minn. 2001) (authority of Comptroller of the Currency to regulate national banks does not oust AG of authority to enforce non-banking state laws against a national bank; allowing UDAP claim against bank for sharing customer information with telemarketers to go forward); Perdue v. Crocker Nat'l Bank, 38 Cal. 3d 913, 702 P.2d 503, 216 Cal. Rptr. 345 (1985) (National Bank Act does not preempt UDAP claim that charges imposed on deposit accounts are excessive), *appeal dismissed*, 475 U.S. 1001 (1986); Normand Josef Enters., Inc. v. Conn. Nat'l Bank, 646 A.2d 1289, 1304–05 (Conn. 1994) (application of UDAP statute to national bank not preempted); Ashlock v. Sunwest Bank, 107 N.M. 100, 753 P.2d 346 (1988); Basile v. H & R Block, Inc., 729 A.2d 574, 584 (Pa. Super. 1999) (fact that plaintiffs' excess interest rate claims were preempted did not bar them from recovering excess interest as damages on UDAP claim), *vac'd, remanded on other grounds*, 563 Pa. 359, 761 A.2d 1115 (2000); Household Retail Servs. v. State, 2001 Tex. App. LEXIS 5893 (Aug. 29, 2001) (OCC's exclusive jurisdiction to enforce banking statutes against federally chartered banks does not oust state of authority to enforce its laws regarding non-banking matters, e.g., bank's communications with debtors regarding warranties and cancellation of purchases paid for by bank's credit card); Detonics ".45" Assocs. v. Bank of California, 97 Wash. 2d 351, 644 P.2d 1170 (1982) (National Bank Act does not preempt state statute allowing attorney fees to borrower who won usury case). *See also* James Mitchell & Co. v. Florida Dept. of Ins., 679 So. 2d 334 (Fla. Dist. Ct. App. 1996) (National Bank Act does not preempt state's regulation of insurance agents who sell annuities through banks); Pennsylvania Bankers Ass'n v. Commonwealth, 58 Pa. Commw. 170, 427 A.2d 730 (1981) (while federal banking legislation does not preempt former state UDAP regulation on debt collection, enforcement of that regulation against national banks may be restricted to the Comptroller of the Currency because of federal grant to Comptroller of Currency of regulatory authority over national banks); Vogt v. Seattle-First Nat'l Bank, 117 Wash. 2d 541, 817 P.2d 1364 (1991) (allowing UDAP claim to proceed against national bank for charging excessive fees and breaching fiduciary duty in administering trust; court's analysis is primarily whether state law exempts the bank, but draws on federal preemption analysis). *But see* Miller v. U.S. Bank, N.A., 72 Wash. App. 416, 865 P.2d 536 (1994).

cation of the consumer protection law to a national bank.[1334] In addition, an OCC regulation provides that state laws apply to national bank operating subsidiaries to the same extent that they apply to the parent national bank.[1335]

2.5.3.3 OTS Regulation of Savings and Loan Associations

The federal Home Owners Loan Act (HOLA)[1336] gives the Office of Thrift Supervision (formerly the Federal Home Loan Bank Board) broad authority over federal savings and loan associations. Pursuant to this statute, the Office of Thrift Supervision has adopted regulations asserting its intention to occupy the entire field of lending and deposit regulation for federal savings and loan associations.[1337] The regulation lists a number of specific types of state lending laws that are preempted, but does not include UDAP statutes in the list.[1338] The regulation explicitly preserves state laws of certain types, including contract, commercial, real property, and tort law, to the extent that they only incidentally affect the lending operations of savings and loan associations or are otherwise consistent with OTS's purposes.[1339] Presumably it is consistent with OTS's purposes that savings and loan associations avoid the unfair and deceptive acts and practices that UDAP statutes prohibit.

An OTS opinion letter holds that state UDAP statutes are generally not preempted.[1340] According to OTS's analysis, a UDAP statute may affect lending relationships, but the impact on lending is only incidental to the primary purpose of the statute—the regulation of the ethical practices of all businesses in the state. Since federal savings and loan associations are presumed to interact with their borrowers in a truthful manner, a UDAP statute's prohibition of deception should have no measurable impact on their lending practices.[1341] However, a later OTS opinion letter states that one of the two California UDAP statutes is preempted to the extent that its broad and flexible language is used to set standards for payoff statement fees, specific disclosures, or force-placed insurance.[1342] The letter focuses on the unusually broad and flexible language of the California statute, which OTS felt could create the risk of conflicting rulings by different judges. The letter stresses that it is limited to the effect of the UDAP statute on the three specific issues it discusses, and that the general application of the state UDAP statute to savings and loan associations is not preempted.

Applying these standards, courts have held that the OTS regulation does not preempt:

- State UDAP, contract, and other claims based on the lender's payment of a yield spread premium without disclosing material facts, and its imposition of an inflated tax service fee.[1343] The court noted that the consumers were not claiming that the actual fees charged were unlawful, but were challenging the methods through which the lender imposed them.
- A UDAP claim that a lender had exceeded its contractual authority to force-place insurance, by charging the consumer for insurance and services covering not only the consumer's home but other properties.[1344] The court held that the lender's duties to comply with its contract and to refrain from misrepresentation were principles of general application, part of the legal infrastructure that undergirds all contractual and commercial transactions, so these claims were not preempted.
- A state law requiring a mortgagee to record the satisfaction of a mortgage within ninety days after payoff.[1345] The court held that such a law is a real estate law

1334 12 U.S.C. § 36(f).

1335 12 C.F.R. § 7.4006. *See* Wachovia Bank v. Burke, 319 F. Supp. 2d 275 (D. Conn. 2004) (regulation is reasonable interpretation of National Bank Act and preempts state regulator from requiring operating subsidiary to have state license); Wachovia Bank v. Watters, 2004 WL 1948644 (W.D. Mich. Aug. 30, 2004) (upholding OCC's ouster of state regulators' visitorial powers over state-chartered operating subsidiaries of national banks). OCC's narrative accompanying the regulations describes operating subsidiaries as separately incorporated entities that national banks use to engage in activities that the bank itself is authorized to conduct. 69 Fed. Reg. 1900 (Jan. 13, 2004). *See generally* National Consumer Law Center, The Cost of Credit: Regulation and Legal Challenges § 3.4.6.4 (2004 Supp.).

1336 12 U.S.C. § 1463(a). *See also* National Consumer Law Center, The Cost of Credit: Regulation and Legal Challenges § 3.5 (2004 Supp.).

1337 12 C.F.R. § 560.2(a) (lending regulation); 12 C.F.R. § 557.11 (deposit regulation). *See also* Ansley v. Ameriquest Mortg. Co., 340 F.3d 858 (9th Cir. 2003) (AMTPA does not completely preempt challenge under state credit law and UDAP statute to prepayment penalty).

1338 12 C.F.R. § 560.2(b) (list of state lending laws that are preempted includes those that impose requirements regarding the ability of a creditor to obtain private mortgage insurance, insurance for other collateral, or other credit enhancements; loan-to-value ratios; the terms of credit; loan-related fees; escrow, impound, and similar accounts; access to and use of credit reports; disclosure and advertising laws, specifically including laws requiring specific statements or disclosures in loan documents; processing, origination, servicing, sale, or purchase of, or investment or participation in mortgages).

1339 12 C.F.R. § 560.2(c).

1340 OTS Chief Counsel Letter (Dec. 24, 1996), *reproduced on* companion CD-Rom to National Consumer Law Center, The Cost of Credit: Regulation and Legal Challenges (2d ed. 2000 and Supp.).

1341 *Id.*

1342 OTS Chief Counsel Letter P-99-3 (Mar. 10, 1999), *reproduced on* companion CD-Rom to National Consumer Law Center, The Cost of Credit: Regulation and Legal Challenges (2d ed. 2000 and Supp.).

1343 Michalowski v. Flagstar Bank, 2002 WL 113905 (N.D. Ill. Jan. 25, 2002).

1344 Gibson v. World Sav. & Loan Ass'n, 103 Cal. App. 4th 1291, 128 Cal. Rptr. 2d 19 (2002).

1345 Pinchot v. Charter One Bank, 792 N.E.2d 1105 (Ohio 2003).

and that it only incidentally relates to savings and loan associations' lending operation or practices and is consistent with the goals stated in OTS's regulation. Presumably a UDAP claim based on a statute of this sort would also avoid preemption.

A number of other cases are consistent with these decisions.[1346]

On the other hand, a court held that OTS's regulation preempted a claim that a savings and loan's billing statement was deceptive.[1347] The court held that this claim fell within OTS's explicit preemption of state "disclosure and advertising laws," since the plaintiffs were claiming that the billing statements failed to convey certain information about the amount due. Another court held that the regulation preempted UDAP claims regarding fax fees and a creditor's brief retention of excessive funds when the consumer paid off the loan.[1348] The court held that these claims involved the terms of credit, loan related fees, disclosure and advertising, and disbursements and repayments, which the OTS regulation lists as preempted.

Several courts have also held that a UDAP claim is preempted if it is based on a state banking statute that is itself preempted.[1349] In other words, a UDAP claim can not be used as a vehicle to create liability under a state statute that is preempted by HOLA. But a UDAP claim that is based on the bank's violation of its agreement with the consumer should not be preempted, even if it involves one of the subjects that the OTS regulation lists. Such a claim does not seek to impose requirements regarding a banking function, but only seeks to impose a duty to abide by a contractual obligation.[1350] UDAP claims involving deceptive marketing are also likely to avoid preemption, especially if there are affirmative misrepresentations.

2.5.3.4 Alternative Mortgage Transactions Parity Act

A different federal statute, the Alternative Mortgage Transactions Parity Act (AMTPA),[1351] applies to state housing creditors, defined to include certain depository institutions and other mortgage lenders.[1352] It preempts state laws that restrict non-traditional mortgage terms such as variable interest rates, balloon payments, and negative amortization. The OTS regulations under this statute do not even purport to preempt the field and cover only a few mortgage terms.[1353] A California appellate court has accordingly concluded that a UDAP challenge to deceptive advertisements and misleading transactional documents in a reverse mortgage transaction was not preempted by AMTPA.[1354]

2.5.3.5 Federal Regulation of State-Chartered FDIC-Insured Banks

The Depository Institutions Deregulation and Monetary Control Act of 1980 (DIDA),[1355] establishes the maximum interest rate for loans made by state-chartered, FDIC-insured banks, and expressly preempts conflicting state laws.[1356] Where consumers did not challenge the *rate* of interest, but claimed that a bank misrepresented the nature

---

1346 *See also* Tuxedo Beach Club Corp. v. City Federal Sav. Bank, 749 F. Supp. 635 (D.N.J. 1990) (neither Fin. Institutions Reform, Recovery, and Enforcement Act nor federal regulation of savings and loan associations preempts UDAP claim against bank that is in receivership); Morses v. Mut. Fed. S. & L. Ass'n, 536 F. Supp. 1271 (D. Mass. 1982) (UDAP statute is peripheral to and not in conflict with HOLA; claim regarding wrongful freeze of bank account, wrongful attempted foreclosures, and interference with refinancing not preempted). *Cf.* McKenzie v. Ocwen Fed. Bank, 306 F. Supp. 2d 543 (D. Md. 2004) (HOLA does not completely preempt state law claims because it does not provide an exclusive federal cause of action).

1347 Rosenberg v. Washington Mut. Bank, 369 N.J. Super. 456, 849 A.2d 566 (App. Div. 2004).

1348 Boursiquot v. Citibank F.S.B., 323 F. Supp. 2d 350 (D. Conn. 2004).

1349 Flagg v. Yonkers S. & L. Ass'n, 307 F. Supp. 2d 565 (S.D.N.Y. 2004); Washington Mut. Bank v. Superior Court, 115 Cal. Rptr. 2d 765 (App. 2002) (OTS regulation preempts use of UDAP statute to enforce state statute that restricted pre-closing interest); Laskey v. Downey Sav. & Loan Ass'n, 2002 WL 31721686 (Cal. App. Dec. 5, 2002) (unpublished, citation limited) (affirming dismissal of UDAP claim that was based on a preempted state statute that limited pre-closing interest); Bright v. Washington Mut. Bank, 2002 Cal. App. Unpub. LEXIS 2718 (Cal. App. Mar. 25, 2002) (unpublished, citation limited) (use of UDAP statute to enforce state law restricting amount of hazard insurance is preempted by OTS regulation); Stoneking v. Bank of America, 43 P.3d 1089 (N.M. App. 2002) (OTS regulation preempts state limit on prepayment penalty; court affirms dismissal of UDAP claim based on this state law). *See also* Lopez v. Washington Mut. Bank, 302 F.3d 900 (9th Cir. 2002) (declining to reach question whether UDAP claims preempted, because state banking statute on which UDAP claims were based was preempted), *as amended on denial of rehearing by* 311 F.3d 928 (9th Cir. 2002).

1350 Gibson v. World Sav. & Loan Ass'n, 103 Cal. App. 4th 1291, 128 Cal. Rptr. 2d 19 (2002). *Cf.* Lopez v. World Savings & Loan Ass'n, 130 Cal. Rptr. 2d 42 (App. 2003) (state law that directly restricts payoff statement fees is preempted, but court agrees with *Gibson* that contract-based claims would not be preempted). *But see* Moskowitz v. Washington Mut. Bank, 329 Ill. App. 3d 144, 768 N.E.2d 262, 263 Ill. Dec. 502 (2002) (OTS regulations preempt contract law and UDAP challenge to imposition of fax fees in violation of parties' contract, because payoff statements are integral part of lending process).

1351 U.S.C. §§ 3801–3805.

1352 12 U.S.C. § 3802.

1353 C.F.R. §§ 560.210, 560.220. OTS significantly narrowed the scope of preemption for state housing creditors that are not commercial banks, credit unions, or federal savings associations in 2003 by amending § 560.220.

1354 Black v. Fin. Freedom Senior Funding Corp., 112 Cal. Rptr. 2d 445 (App. 2002).

1355 12 U.S.C. § 1831d.

1356 *See* Cross-County Bank v. Klussman, 2004 WL 966289 (N.D. Cal. Apr. 30, 2004); Bankwest, Inc. v. Baker, 324 F. Supp. 2d

and benefits of its services, placed unauthorized and undisclosed charges on consumers' accounts, breached their agreements with consumers, and wrongfully closed consumers' accounts, DIDA did not preempt the claim.[1357]

In analyzing the scope of preemption for state-chartered financial institutions, the effect of state parity laws must also be considered. Almost all states have parity laws that permit state banks to extend credit under the same rate ceiling or under the same terms and conditions as another type of creditor, such as a federal savings and loan association or national bank.[1358] Where federal law allows a federally-regulated creditor to engage in a specific practice, a state parity law might conceivably be interpreted to allow a state-chartered institution to do so also.

2.5.3.6 Federal Credit Unions

Pursuant to its statutory authority to regulate the rates, terms of repayment, and other conditions of credit extended by federal credit unions, the National Credit Union Administration (NCUA) has adopted a regulation regarding preemption of state law.[1359] According to the regulation, state laws are preempted if they restrict interest rates, late charges, closing costs, other fees, terms of repayment, the amount and purpose of loans, the security for loans, the eligibility of borrowers, or liens on share accounts. The regulation makes it clear that it does not preempt state laws that do not affect these matters.[1360] Further, for matters that are regulated by other federal laws such as the Truth in Lending Act or the Fair Debt Collection Practices Act, NCUA adopts the preemption standards expressed in those laws.[1361] Thus, for example, since the Fair Debt Collection Practices Act expressly preserves state laws that provide greater consumer protections,[1362] state debt collection laws are not preempted by federal credit union law.[1363] Given this relatively narrow scope of preemption, UDAP statutes are unlikely to be preempted except when they are used as a means of enforcing a preempted state law such as one purporting to set a ceiling on federal credit union interest rates.

1333 (N.D. Ga. 2004) (detailed discussion of scope of DIDA preemption).

1357 Cross-County Bank v. Klussman, 2004 WL 966289 (N.D. Cal. Apr. 30, 2004).

1358 *See* National Consumer Law Center, The Cost of Credit: Regulation and Legal Challenges § 3.13 (2004 Supp.).

1359 12 C.F.R. § 701.21, *promulgated pursuant to* 12 U.S.C. § 1757(5).

1360 12 C.F.R. § 701.21(b)(2).

1361 12 C.F.R. § 701.21(b)(3).

1362 15 U.S.C. § 1692n.

1363 *See* NCUA Interpretive Letter 03-0905 (Texas Debt Collection Law), *reproduced on* companion CD-Rom to National Consumer Law Center, The Cost of Credit: Regulation and Legal Challenges (2d ed. 2000 and Supp.).

2.5.3.7 Real Estate Settlement Procedures Act

The Real Estate Settlement Procedures Act (RESPA)[1364] requires disclosures and substantive protections relating to settlement services, escrows, and servicing of mortgage loans. RESPA expressly preempts state laws only to the extent they are inconsistent with it.[1365] State laws that provide greater protection to consumers are not preempted.[1366] However, a RESPA regulation broadly preempts state laws that require certain notices to the borrower.[1367]

Many courts have held that RESPA does not preempt state law claims except where it explicitly so states.[1368] The use of a state UDAP statute as a vehicle for enforcing RESPA's disclosure requirements is not preempted.[1369] Where a contractual provision for calculating the amount a mortgagor places in escrow conflicts with calculations authorized by RESPA, the federal law does not preempt a UDAP action.[1370] The calculations authorized by RESPA merely set outer limits on the amount of money a mortgagor may be required to pay.[1371] Courts interpreting UDAP statutes that exempt practices authorized by other law may find compliance with RESPA's disclosure requirements sufficient to defeat a UDAP claim involving disclosure, however.[1372]

2.5.3.8 Truth in Lending Act

The Truth-in-Lending Act does not preempt UDAP claims.[1373] However, as a matter of *state* law, some courts,

1364 12 U.S.C. § 2601 *et seq. See* National Consumer Law Center, The Cost of Credit: Regulation and Legal Challenges § 11.3 (2d ed. 2000 and Supp.) and National Consumer Law Center, Repossessions and Foreclosures Ch. 19 (5th ed. 2002 and Supp.) for detailed discussions of RESPA.

1365 12 U.S.C. § 2616; 24 C.F.R. § 3500.13(a).

1366 24 C.F.R. § 3500.13(b)(2).

1367 24 C.F.R. § 3500.21(h).

1368 Blair v. Source One Mortgage Servs. Corp., 925 F. Supp. 617 (D. Minn. 1996). *See also* Fardella v. Downey Sav. & Loan Ass'n, 2001 U.S. Dist. LEXIS 6037 (N.D. Cal. May 8, 2001).

1369 Washington Mut. Bank v. Superior Court, 75 Cal. App. 4th 773, 89 Cal. Rptr. 2d 560 (1999). *See* § 5.1.5.2, *infra.*

1370 Attorney General v. Michigan Nat'l Bank, 110 Mich. App. 106, 312 N.W.2d 405 (1981).

1371 *Id.*

1372 Weatherman v. Gary-Wheaton Bank, 186 Ill. 2d 472, 713 N.E.2d 543, 239 Ill. Dec. 12 (1999). *See* § 2.2.1.6, *supra.*

1373 Williams v. First Government Mortgage & Investors Corp., 176 F.3d 497 (D.C. Cir. 1999); Knapp v. Americredit Fin. Servs., Inc., 245 F. Supp. 2d 841 (S.D. W. Va. 2003) (finance company's involvement in scheme to add hidden finance charges, involving false pay stubs, false down payments, and an acquisition fee, not preempted by TILA); Aiello v. First Alliance Mortg. Co. (*In re* First Alliance Mortg. Co.), 280 B.R. 246 (C.D. Cal. 2002) (fact that a defendant is not liable under TILA does not mean that there is no UDAP liability, and TILA does not preempt state UDAP claim); Heastie v. Community Bank, 690 F. Supp. 716 (N.D. Ill. 1988) (no preemption even where TILA regulates credit transaction secured by mortgages on principal dwellings);

primarily in Illinois, have held that a consumer can not base a UDAP claim on a disclosure that complies with TILA.[1374]

2.5.4 Federal Vehicle, Boat, and Mobile Home Standards

The National Traffic and Motor Vehicle Safety Act has an express preemption provision that prohibits states from adopting standards for aspects of motor vehicle performance that are governed by federal standards, unless the state standard is identical to the federal standard.[1375] The state expressly preserves state common law claims.[1376] The statute also implicitly preempts common law tort claims that stand as an obstacle to the accomplishment of the federal objectives.[1377] For example, where the federal objective was to encourage a mix of different types of passive restraint devices, the Act preempted a claim that a manufacturer's design of a vehicle was negligent because it failed to include a particular type of passive restraint system.[1378] Claims involving affirmative misrepresentations and breaches of express warranties are not preempted.[1379] Design defect claims may not be preempted if the allegedly defective design was not specifically allowed under the Act.[1380]

An automobile dealer's compliance with federal automobile recall notice requirements does not insulate it from liability for failure to disclose at the time of sale that the vehicle was subject to recall.[1381] The federal odometer fraud statute does not preempt UDAP claims regarding odometer tampering.[1382]

The Supreme Court has held that the Federal Boat Safety Act, which includes both a preemption provision[1383] and a savings clause for liability at common law or under state law,[1384] does not implicitly preempt state common law claims.[1385] The Court held that the standard-setting role of the federal law was entirely consistent with the preservation of victims' ability to seek compensation for injuries under state law. While the decision only dealt with common law claims, the savings clause applies equally to state statutes, so UDAP claims should be preserved as well.

The National Manufactured Housing Construction and Safety Standards Act preempts state law standards for mobile homes,[1386] but does not preempt most state law claims.[1387]

2.5.5 Federal Transportation and Shipping Laws

The federal Carmack amendment,[1388] which limits liability of carriers of interstate freight shipments, applies to contractual liability, preempts UDAP claims against shippers for loss or damage to goods.[1389] Although case law is

---

Schwartz v. Visa Int'l Corp., 2003 WL 1870370, at *64–65 (Cal. Super. Apr. 7, 2003) (no preemption where TILA is silent); Black v. Fin. Freedom Senior Funding Corp., 112 Cal. Rptr. 2d 445 (App. 2002); State v. Brotherhood Bank & Trust, 649 P.2d 419 (Kan. Ct. App. 1982); Commonwealth *ex rel.* Zimmerman v. Nickel, 26 Pa. D. & C.3d 115 (C.P. Mercer Cty. 1983). *But see* Najieb v. William Chrysler-Plymouth, 2002 WL 31906466 (N.D. Ill. Dec. 31, 2002) (failure to disclose that yo-yo sale was conditional is not UDAP violation because TILA does not require this disclosure). Note that several UDAP statute exemption sections specifically refer to the federal Truth In Lending Act. The meaning of that language is discussed in § 2.3.3.2, *supra*. *See also* §§ 2.2.1.6, 2.3.3.3.1, *supra*.

1374 *See* § 2.2.1.6.3, *supra*.

1375 49 U.S.C. § 30103.

1376 49 U.S.C. § 30103(e).

1377 Geier v. Am. Honda Motor Co., 529 U.S. 861, 120 S. Ct. 1913, 146 L. Ed. 2d 914 (2000).

1378 *Id.*

1379 Chamberlan v. Ford Motor Co., 2004 WL 615090 (N.D. Cal. Mar. 24, 2004); Martin v. Ford Motor Co., 914 F. Supp. 1449 (S.D. Tex. 1996). *See also* Farkas v. Bridgestone/Firestone, Inc., 113 F. Supp. 2d 1107 (W.D. Ky. 2000) (federal recall statute does not completely preempt state claims); Talalai v. Cooper Tire & Rubber Co., 360 N.J. Super. 547, 823 A.2d 888 (Law Div. 2001) (claim for damages due to unreasonably dangerous manufacturing of tires not preempted). *See generally* National Consumer Law Center, Consumer Warranty Law § 1.4.9.4 (2d ed. 2001 and Supp.).

1380 Brewer v. General Motors Corp., 926 S.W.2d 774 (Tex. App. 1996).

1381 DeMarco v. Bay Ridge Car World, 169 A.D.2d 808, 565 N.Y.S.2d 176 (1991). *See also* Farkas v. Bridgestone/Firestone, Inc., 113 F. Supp. 2d 1107 (W.D. Ky. 2000) (federal recall statute does not completely preempt state claims).

1382 49 U.S.C. § 32711 (state statute preempted only if it requires actions inconsistent with federal Odometer Act); *see* State v. Fritz Waidner Sports Cars, 274 S.C. 332, 263 S.E.2d 384 (1980). *See generally* National Consumer Law Center, Automobile Fraud § 4.1.5 (2d ed. 2003 and Supp.).

1383 46 U.S.C. § 4306.

1384 46 U.S.C. § 4311(b).

1385 Sprietsma v. Mercury Marine, 123 S. Ct. 518, 154 L. Ed. 2d 466 (2002).

1386 42 U.S.C. § 5403(d). *See also* 42 U.S.C. § 5409(c) (preserving common law liability).

1387 Richard v. Fleetwood Enterprises, Inc., 4 F. Supp. 2d 650 (E.D. Tex. 1998); Shorter v. Champion Home Bldrs., 776 F. Supp. 333 (N.D. Ohio 1991); Woolridge v. Redman Homes, Inc., 792 F. Supp. 1469 (N.D. Tex. 1991); Redman Homes, Inc. v. Ivy, 920 S.W.2d 664 (Tex. 1996). *See* National Consumer Law Center, Consumer Warranty Law § 15.3.5 (2d ed. 2001 and Supp.).

1388 49 U.S.C. § 14706 (formerly 49 U.S.C. § 20).

1389 Hoskins v. Bekins Van Lines, 343 F.3d 769 (5th Cir. 2003) (Carmack preempts claims for damage by moving company); Great Northern Ins. Co. v. McCollister's Moving & Storage, Inc., 190 F. Supp. 2d 91 (D. Mass. 2001) (Carmack amendment preempts claims against carrier that scrapped computer equipment instead of storing it); Werner v. Lawrence Transportation Sys., Inc., 52 F. Supp. 2d 567 (E.D.N.C. 1998) (Carmack amendment preempts all state claims, including UDAP claim, arising from damage to goods during transit and storage); Schultz v. Auld, 848 F. Supp. 1497 (D. Idaho 1993); Malone v. Mayflower Transit, Inc., 819 F. Supp. 724 (E.D. Tenn. 1993). *Cf.* Kimmel v. Bekins Moving & Storage Co., 210 F. Supp. 2d 850

split, several courts have held that it does not preempt a UDAP action based on misrepresentations before the contract was signed[1390] or even some practices after the contract is signed that cause harm to the person shipping the goods rather than to the goods themselves.[1391] If UDAP claims are preempted, consumers can still assert claims under the Carmack amendment itself.[1392] Also, if the carrier's bill of lading does not comply with its tariff and federal regulations, the Carmack amendment does not limit its liability.[1393] Similarly, misrepresentations about a package's delivery are actionable despite the Warsaw Convention's limitations on contractual liability.[1394]

The Interstate Commerce Act and regulations did not preempt a UDAP action against deceptive recruitment of owner-operators of tractor trailers.[1395] Nor did the Interstate Commerce Act preempt a suit against a common carrier's insurance company by a driver injured in a collision with the common carrier's truck.[1396] However, an express preemption provision of the Interstate Commerce Act[1397] did preempt city regulation of tow truck operators and a consumer's claim based on those regulations.[1398] A Louisiana court has held that a price-fixing claim against trucking companies is preempted by federal law.[1399]

An express preemption provision of the Airline Deregulation Act[1400] preempts state UDAP litigation regarding airline services and fare advertising,[1401] although it does not preempt state contract law[1402] or

(S.D. Tex. 2002) (Carmack amendment completely preempts state law claims against common carrier); Duerrmeyer v. Alamo Moving & Storage One, Corp., 49 F. Supp. 2d 934 (W.D. Tex. 1999) (all state law claims against moving company preempted); Broughton v. Global Van Lines, Inc., 1998 U.S. Dist. LEXIS 10750 (N.D. Tex. July 10, 1998); Simmons v. United Parcel Serv., 924 F. Supp. 65 (W.D. Tex. 1996) (Carmack amendment preempts all state law claims against a common carrier); Suarez v. United Van Lines, Inc., 791 F. Supp. 815 (D. Colo. 1992); Shull v. United Parcel Serv., 4 S.W.3d 46 (Tex. App. 1999) (UDAP claims against delivery service preempted). *See also* Stephenson v. Wheaton Van Lines, Inc., 240 F. Supp. 2d 1161 (D. Kan. 2002) (Carmack amendment completely preempts contract and negligence claims).

1390 Brown v. American Transfer & Storage Co., 601 S.W.2d 931 (Tex. 1980); D.M. Diamond Corp. v. Dunbar Armored, Inc., 124 S.W.3d 655 (Tex. App. Sept. 23, 2003). *But see* Ferrostaal, Inc. v. Seale, 170 F. Supp. 2d 705 (E.D. Tex. 2001), *aff'd without op.*, 273 F.3d 1095 (5th Cir. 2001); Richter v. North Am. Van Lines, Inc., 110 F. Supp. 2d 406 (D. Md. 2000) (UDAP, fraud, and contract claims based on mover's representations regarding how goods would be packed, when they would arrive, etc., are preempted); Schultz v. Auld, 848 F. Supp. 1497 (D. Idaho 1993); Margetson v. United Van Lines, Inc., 785 F. Supp. 917 (D.N.M. 1991); North Am. Van Lines v. Bauerle, 678 S.W.2d 229 (Tex. App. 1984).

1391 Rini v. United Van Lines, Inc., 104 F.3d 502 (1st Cir. 1997) (claims for damage or loss of goods and liability stemming from claims process or claims payment are preempted, but emotional distress or other injury to person shipping the goods would not be preempted)..

1392 *See* 49 U.S.C. §§ 14704, 14706(d), 14708 (attorney fees). *See also* Hoover v. Allied Van Lines, 205 F. Supp. 2d 1232 (D. Kan. 2002); Great Northern Ins. Co. v. McCollister's Moving & Storage, Inc., 190 F. Supp. 2d 91 (D. Mass. 2001) (plaintiff may maintain action under Carmack amendment, but here it is dismissed as untimely); Richter v. North Am. Van Lines, Inc., 110 F. Supp. 2d 406 (D. Md. 2000).

1393 Rohner Gehrig Co. v. Tri-State Motor Transit, 950 F.2d 1079 (5th Cir. 1992).

1394 Imtiaz v. Emery Air Freight, Inc., 728 S.W.2d 897 (Tex. App. 1987).

1395 Tousley v. North Am. Van Lines, Inc., 752 F.2d 96 (4th Cir. 1985) (interpreting former 49 U.S.C. § 11107, now 49 U.S.C. § 14102); Jacobs v. Central Transport, Inc., 891 F. Supp. 1088 (E.D. N.C. 1995). *But cf.* Bur-Cold Express, Inc. v. Parker Hannifin Corp., 808 F. Supp. 553 (S.D. Tex. 1992) (issue as to proper rate submitted under primary jurisdiction doctrine to ICC for initial determination).

1396 Carway v. Progressive County Mut. Ins. Co., 183 B.R. 769 (N.D. Tex. 1995).

1397 49 U.S.C. § 14501.

1398 Whitten v. Vehicle Removal Corp., 56 S.W.3d 293 (Tex. App. 2001) (case discusses contrary decisions).

1399 Beyer v. Acme Truck Line, Inc., 802 So. 2d 798 (La. App. 2001).

1400 49 U.S.C. § 41713 (formerly 49 U.S.C. App. § 1305).

1401 American Airlines, Inc. v. Wolens, 513 U.S. 219, 115 S. Ct. 817, 130 L. Ed. 2d 715 (1995) (interpreting predecessor preemption provision); Morales v. Trans World Airlines, Inc., 504 U.S. 374, 112 S. Ct. 2031, 119 L. Ed 2d 157 (1992) (same); Sam L. Majors Jewelers v. ABX, Inc., 117 F.3d 922 (5th Cir. 1997) (air carrier lost packages of jewelry being shipped); Stone v. Frontier Airlines, Inc., 256 F. Supp. 2d 28 (D. Mass. 2002) (preempts claims based on airlines failure to have defibrillators on board); Federal Express Corp. v. U.S. Postal Serv., 55 F. Supp. 2d 813 (W.D. Tenn. 1999) (claims regarding advertising of air express package services are preempted); Nali v. Northwest Airlines, Inc., 2003 WL 22162315 (Mich. App. Sept. 18, 2003) (unpublished, citation limited) (UDAP claims arising from cancellation of flight); Delta Air Lines, Inc. v. Black, 116 S.W.3d 745 (Tex. 2003); D.M. Diamond Corp. v. Dunbar Armored, Inc., 124 S.W.3d 655 (Tex. App. Sept. 23, 2003); Howell v. Alaska Airlines, Inc., 99 Wash. App. 646, 994 P.2d 901 (2000) (laws relating to price, route, or service are preempted). *See also* Casas v. American Airlines, Inc., 304 F.3d 517 (5th Cir. 2002) (UDAP claim for loss of baggage preempted); Lyn-Lea Travel Corp. v. American Airlines, Inc., 283 F.3d 282 (5th Cir. 2002) (travel agency's UDAP claim against airline for changing commission schedule is preempted); Harpalani v. Air India, Inc., 622 F. Supp. 69 (N.D. Ill. 1985) (Warsaw Convention, not UDAP statute, exclusive remedy for "bumping" of passenger on international flight); Continental Airlines, Inc. v. Kiefer, 920 S.W.2d 274 (Tex. 1996). *Cf.* Wayne v. DHL Worldwide Express, 294 F.3d 1179 (9th Cir. 2002) (Airline Deregulation Act does not completely preempt state claims, but preemption may be defense to state claims). *But see* Brunwasser v. Trans World Airlines, Inc., 541 F. Supp. 1338 (W.D. Pa. 1982) (false advertising claim not preempted by predecessor preemption provision); People v. Western Airlines, Inc., 155 Cal. App. 3d 597, 202 Cal. Rptr. 237 (1984) (CAB does not preempt state challenge to misleading airline fare advertisements); Kings Choice Neckwear, Inc. v. DHL Airways, Inc., 2003 WL 22283814 (S.D.N.Y. Oct. 2, 2003) (Act does not completely preempt UDAP claim regarding air courier fees).

1402 American Airlines, Inc. v. Wolens, 513 U.S. 219, 115 S. Ct. 817, 130 L. Ed. 2d 715 (1995) (interpreting predecessor preemption provision); Delta Air Lines, Inc. v. Black, 116 S.W.3d 745 (Tex.

negligence[1403] claims.

Federal admiralty law principles, although not codified, generally take precedence over conflicting provisions of state UDAP statutes.[1404] Where the dispute is not normally a subject of maritime law, however, the UDAP provision will not be preempted.[1405] The Shippers Act (Federal Maritime Commission) tariff-filing requirements do not preempt a UDAP action based on tariff misrepresentations.[1406]

2.5.6 Federal Communications Laws

Courts have found that UDAP actions are generally not preempted by the Federal Communications Act.[1407] Nonetheless, under the "filed tariff" doctrine, utility tariffs filed

2003); D.M. Diamond Corp. v. Dunbar Armored, Inc., 124 S.W.3d 655 (Tex. App. Sept. 23, 2003); Howell v. Alaska Airlines, Inc., 99 Wash. App. 646, 994 P.2d 901 (2000). *See also* Kingsley v. Lania, 221 F. Supp. 2d 93 (D. Mass. 2002) (contract and UDAP claims not completely preempted).

1403 Stone v. Frontier Airlines, Inc., 256 F. Supp. 2d 28 (D. Mass. 2002) (no preemption of tort claims); Continental Airlines, Inc. v. Kiefer, 920 S.W.2d 274 (Tex. 1996).

1404 Delta Marine, Inc. v. Whaley, 813 F. Supp. 414 (E.D.N.C. 1993) (mandatory UDAP treble damages conflicts with admiralty law principles). *But see* Latman v. Costa Cruise Lines, 758 So. 2d 699 (Fla. App. 2000) (deceptive practices in sale of cruise tickets not preempted).

1405 Southworth Machinery Co. v. F/V Corey Pride, 994 F.2d 37 (1st Cir. 1993) (Mass. law). *Accord* Hull & Co. v. Chandler, 889 S.W.2d 513 (Tex. App. 1994) (Texas UDAP and UDIP).

1406 Zachry-Dillingham v. American President Lines, Ltd., 739 S.W.2d 420 (Tex. App. 1987).

1407 Ting v. AT&T, 319 F.3d 1126 (9th Cir. 2003) (Federal Communications Act does not preempt UDAP challenge to telecommunication contract terms after detariffing); Total TV v. Palmer Communications, Inc., 69 F.3d 298 (9th Cir. 1995) (federal cable TV laws do not preempt California's unfair competition law); Shaw v. AT&T Wireless Servs., Inc., 2001 U.S. Dist. LEXIS 6589 (N.D. Tex. May 18, 2001); Valdes v. Qwest Communications Int'l, 147 F. Supp. 2d 116 (D. Conn. 2001) (UDAP, fraud, and negligence claims regarding "slamming" not preempted by Federal Telecommunications Act); Iowa v. U.S. Cellular Corp., 2000 WL 33915909 (S.D. Iowa Aug. 7, 2000); A.S.I. Worldwide Communications Corp. v. Worldwide Communications Corp., 115 F. Supp. 2d 201 (D.N.H. 2000) (UDAP and other state claims not preempted, but many are barred by filed rate doctrine); State *ex rel.* Stovall v. Home Cable Inc., 35 F. Supp. 2d 783 (D. Kan. 1998) (FCC regulation about installation of antennas does not preempt UDAP claims that satellite system seller misrepresented quality, features, and costs); Texas v. Synchronal Corp., 800 F. Supp. 1456 (W.D. Tex. 1992); Quincy Cablesystems, Inc. v. Sully's Bar, Inc., 684 F. Supp. 1138 (D. Mass. 1988) (federal regulation of cable systems does not preempt UDAP coverage); Bruss Co. v. Allnet Communication Servs., Inc., 606 F. Supp. 401 (N.D. Ill. 1985); Union Ink Co. v. AT&T Corp., 352 N.J. Super. 617, 801 A.2d 361 (App. Div. 2002) (claims regarding misrepresentation of cellular service provider's facilities not preempted); Oncor Communications v. State of New York, 165 Misc. 2d 262, 626 N.Y.S.2d 369 (Sup. 1995), *aff'd*, 218 A.D.2d 60, 636 N.Y.S.2d 176 (1996) (common law claims concerning pre-subscription practices of interexchange carriers not preempted); Bryceland v. AT&T Corp. 2002 WL 31688961 (Tex. App. Dec. 3, 2002) (no preemption of UDAP claims against wireless providers for failure to provide service as promised); Tenore v. AT&T Wireless Servs., 136 Wash. 2d 322, 962 P.2d 104 (1998), *cert. denied*, 525 U.S. 1171 (1999) (claims regarding advertising of cellular phone service not preempted). *See also* Gattegno v. Sprint Corp., 297 F. Supp. 2d 372 (D. Mass. 2003) (no complete preemption of state UDAP claims arising from wireless carrier's deceptive billing); State *ex rel.* Nixon v. Nextel West Corp., 248 F. Supp. 2d 885 (E.D. Mo. 2003) (Federal Communications Act does not completely preempt claim that cell phone company deceptively characterized charges on bills); Moriconi v. AT&T Wireless PCS, 280 F. Supp. 2d 867 (E.D. Ark. 2003) (Federal Communications Act does not completely preempt UDAP claim against wireless telecommunications provider); Cedar Rapids Cellular Tel. v. Miller, 2000 WL 34030836 (N.D. Iowa Sept. 15, 2000) (Federal Communications Act does not completely preempt claims under state credit laws against wireless provider); Time Warner Entertainment Co. v. Federal Communications Comm'n, 56 F.3d 151 (D.C. Cir. 1995) (federal cable TV laws do not preempt all state negative option billing prohibitions); Gilmore v. Southwestern Bell Mobile Sys., Inc., 156 F. Supp. 2d 916 (N.D. Ill. 2001) (challenge to mobile phone rates is completely preempted but nondisclosure and deceit claims are not preempted); Crump v. Worldcom, Inc., 128 F. Supp. 2d 549 (W.D. Tenn. 2001) (no complete preemption of claims regarding misleading telephone ads); Iowa v. U.S. Cellular Corp., 2000 U.S. Dist. LEXIS 21656 (S.D. Iowa Aug. 7, 2000) (Federal Communications Act does not so completely preempt state claims as to allow removal to federal court); Weinberg v. Sprint Corp., 165 F.R.D. 431 (D.N.J. 1996) (UDAP claim regarding advertisements' failure to disclose billing practices not completely preempted), *op. after remand to state court*, 801 A.2d 281 (N.J. 2002) (filed rate doctrine prevents plaintiff from establishing ascertainable loss, so no UDAP claim). *But see* Cahnmann v. Sprint Corp., 133 F.3d 484 (7th Cir. 1998), *cert. denied*, 524 U.S. 952 (1998) (consumer's contract, fraud, and UDAP claims barred by Communications Act); Time Warner Cable v. Doyle, 66 F.3d 867 (7th Cir. 1995) (federal cable regulation preempts Wisconsin UDAP statute); Alport v. Sprint Corp., 2003 WL 22872134 (N.D. Ill. Dec. 4, 2003) (challenge to rates is completely preempted); Gilmore v. Southwestern Bell Mobile Sys., 2001 U.S. Dist. LEXIS 19850 (N.D. Ill. Nov. 29, 2001) (fraud-type claim that cellular telephone service provider charged fee without performing service is preempted); Vermont v. Oncor Communications, 166 F.R.D. 313 (D. Vt. 1996) (FCA completely preempts UDAP claim regarding "slamming"); Gelb v. AT&T, 813 F. Supp. 1022 (S.D.N.Y. 1993) (federal common law fraud claims preempt UDAP claim); Ball v. GTE Mobilnet, 81 Cal. App. 4th 529, 96 Cal. Rptr. 2d 801 (2000) (provision effective Aug. 7, 1995 that preempts state rate and entry regulation of wireless phone service prevents claims attacking rates after that date, but not non-disclosure claims); Naevus Int'l, Inc. v. AT&T Corp., 283 A.D.2d 171, 724 N.Y.S.2d 721 (2001) (complaint that wireless service quality is poor is an attack on rates so is preempted, but UDAP and fraud claims relating to unlawful acts and false advertising are not). *But cf.* TPS Utilicom Servs., Inc. v. AT&T Corp., 223 F. Supp. 2d 1089 (C.D. Cal. 2002) (FCA preempts competitor's UDAP claim regarding access to wireless licenses); Hardy v. Clairdom Communications Group, Inc., 937 P.2d 1128 (Wash. Ct. App. 1997) (Federal Communications Act preempts all state claims except those that address obligations different from those created under the Act).

with the state[1408] or federal government[1409] may prevent a consumer from enforcing rights that conflict with the filed tariffs.[1410] As telecommunication companies are deregulated, this defense will be less available.[1411] The Cable Television Consumer Protection Act expressly preempts inconsistent state laws,[1412] but it generally does not preempt UDAP claims.[1413]

2.5.7 Federal Securities and Commerce Laws

In enacting federal securities law, Congress intended to subject the securities industry to state regulation that is not inconsistent with the federal law. State laws are expressly preempted, however, if they conflict with federal securities laws or regulations, and impliedly preempted if compliance with both state and federal law would be impossible, or if the state law presents an obstacle to the accomplishment of the purpose of the federal law.[1414] The Securities Litigation Uniform Standards Act[1415] prohibits class actions asserting state law claims regarding certain types of securities fraud.[1416]

Courts have held that the Federal Copyright Act and patent laws do not preempt UDAP statutes when they are used to prevent deception of the public,[1417] but do preempt UDAP in suits between businesses regarding copying of products.[1418] The same rule applies in cases involving trademarks.[1419] As long as a UDAP claim does not specifically

1408 Kanuco Technology Corp. v. Worldcom Network Servs., Inc., 979 S.W.2d 368 (Tex. App. 1998).

1409 Henderson v. Central Power & Light Co., 977 S.W.2d 439 (Tex. App. 1998); *see also* Bastien v. AT&T Wireless Servs., 205 F.3d 983 (7th Cir. 2000) (challenge to rates is completely preempted); Gilmore v. Southwestern Bell Mobile Sys., Inc., 156 F. Supp. 2d 916 (N.D. Ill. 2001) (same).

1410 *See also* § 5.6.10.1, *infra.*

1411 *See* Ting v. AT&T, 319 F.3d 1126 (9th Cir. 2003) (because of detariffing, state law controls contract formation with telecommunications company). *See also* § 5.6.10, *infra*; National Consumer Law Center, Access to Utility Service § 2.8.2 (2d ed. 2001 and Supp.).

1412 47 U.S.C. § 556.

1413 47 U.S.C. § 521 *et seq.* Parker v. Time Warner Entertainment Co., 1999 U.S. Dist. LEXIS 18883 (E.D.N.Y. Nov. 8, 1999); Kentucky v. Comcast Cable, 881 F. Supp. 285 (W.D. Ky. 1995). *But see* Bass v. Prime Cable of Chicago, Inc., 284 Ill. App. 3d 116, 674 N.E.2d 43 (1996) (claims relating to rates are preempted).

1414 Dahl v. Charles Schwab & Co., 545 N.W.2d 918 (Minn. 1996) (federal law preempts UDAP claims regarding "order flow payments"); *see also* State v. Justin, 2003 WL 23269283 (N.Y. Sup. Ct. Nov. 29, 2003) (federal law does not preempt claim regarding broker-dealer's supervision of salespeople). *Cf.* State v. Justin, 237 F. Supp. 2d 368 (W.D.N.Y. 2002) (federal law does not completely preempt UDAP and other state claims based on fraudulent sale of investment opportunity). *But cf.* Roskind v. Morgan Stanley Dean Witter & Co., 80 Cal. App. 4th 345, 95 Cal. Rptr. 2d 258 (2000) (federal securities law does not preempt UDAP claims).

1415 15 U.S.C. §§ 77p(b), 78bb(f).

1416 Patenaude v. Equitable Life Assurance Soc., 290 F.3d 1020 (9th Cir. 2002) (UDAP claim alleging misrepresentation in sale of variable annuity is preempted); Rowinski v. Salomon Smith Barney, Inc., 2003 WL 22740976 (M.D. Pa. Nov. 20, 2003) (UDAP claim regarding investment analysis services is preempted); Winne v. Equitable Life Assurance Soc., 2003 WL 22434215 (S.D.N.Y. Oct. 27, 2003) (UDAP claim alleging deception regarding variable annuity's penalty withdrawal fee preempted by SLUSA even though scienter not an element of UDAP claim and annuity purchased before SLUSA's enactment); Kenneth Rothschild Trust v. Morgan Stanley Dean Witter, 199 F. Supp. 2d 993 (C.D. Cal. 2002); Feitelberg v. Merrill Lynch & Co., 234 F. Supp. 2d 1043 (N.D. Cal. 2002); Riley v. Merrill Lynch, Pierce, Fenner & Smith, Inc., 168 F. Supp. 2d 1352 (M.D. Fla. 2001) (federal statute precludes class UDAP claims regarding securities fraud), *aff'd*, 292 F.3d 1334 (11th Cir. 2002). *Cf.* Spielman v. Merrill Lynch, Pierce, Fenner & Smith, Inc., 332 F.3d 116, 123 (2d Cir. 2003) (discussing SLUSA but finding order remanding case to state court not reviewable on appeal); Green v. Ameritrade, 279 F.3d 590 (8th Cir. 2002) (claim against provider of on-line stock price information not preempted because acts were not in connection with sale or purchase of covered security). *But cf.* Gray v. Seaboard Securities, Inc., 241 F. Supp. 2d 213 (N.D.N.Y. 2003) (claim that brokerage firms used misrepresentation to obtain plaintiff's business not preempted, but claim of misrepresentation of value of securities is).

1417 Pritikin v. Liberation Publications, Inc., 83 F. Supp. 2d 920 (N.D. Ill. 1999); Nash v. CBS, 704 F. Supp. 823 (N.D. Ill. 1989), *aff'd on other grounds*, 899 F.2d 1537 (7th Cir. 1990); Bicentennial Comm'n v. Olde Bradford Co., 26 Pa. Commw. 636, 365 A.2d 172 (1976).

1418 Nintendo of Am., Inc. v. Aeropower Co., Ltd., 34 F.3d 246 (4th Cir. 1994); Inconbazzar, L.L.C. v. America Online, Inc., 308 F. Supp. 2d 630 (M.D.N.C. 2004); Vesture Corp. v. Thermal Solutions, Inc., 284 F. Supp. 2d 290 (M.D.N.C. 2003) (state UDAP claim preempted by federal patent law); Collezione Europa U.S.A. v. Hillsdale House, Ltd., 243 F. Supp. 3d 444 (M.D.N.C. 2003) (the nature of the UDAP action must be qualitatively different from a copyright infringement claim); John G. Danielson, Inc. v. Winchester-Conant Props., Inc., 186 F. Supp. 2d 1 (D. Mass. 2002) (UDAP claims that are equivalent to copyright claims are preempted), *aff'd on other grounds*, 322 F.3d 26 (1st Cir. 2003); Henry v. Nat'l Geographic Soc., 147 F. Supp. 2d 16 (D. Mass. 2001); Qualey v. Caring Center of Slidell, 942 F. Supp. 1074 (E.D. La. 1996); Skinder-Strauss v. Massachusetts Continuing Legal Ed., 914 F. Supp. 665 (D. Mass. 1995); Nash v. CBS, 704 F. Supp. 823 (N.D. Ill. 1989), *aff'd on other grounds*, 899 F.2d 1537 (7th Cir. 1990); Klitzner Indus., Inc. v. H.K. James & Co., 535 F. Supp. 1249 (E.D. Pa. 1982); Chicago Style Productions v. Chicago Sun Times, 313 Ill. App. 3d 45, 728 N.E.2d 1204, 245 Ill. Dec. 847 (2000); Bicentennial Comm'n v. Olde Bradford Co., 26 Pa. Commw. 636, 365 A.2d 172 (1976). *But see* Broadway Theatre Corp. v. Buena Vista Pictures Distribution, 2002 WL 32502100 (D. Conn. Sept. 19, 2002) (Copyright Act does not prohibit regulation of unfair competition, even if the competition touches upon copyrighted material).

1419 State v. Directory Publishing Servs., Inc., 1996 Minn. App. LEXIS 62 (Jan. 9, 1996) (unpublished and non-precedential under Minnesota rules).

conflict with the Commodity Exchange Act[1420] or the Federal Petroleum Marketing and Practices Act,[1421] the UDAP claim is not preempted.

A finding that a UDAP statute applies to in-state sellers dealing with out-of-state consumers does not create a conflict with the federal mail fraud statutes or other federal laws, nor does it create an undue burden on interstate commerce.[1422] In one area, insurance, due to the McCarran-Ferguson Act,[1423] state law overrides conflicting federal law unless the federal law specifically relates to the business of insurance.[1424]

2.5.8 Federal Health Care Laws

One court has held that the federal Hill-Burton Act's requirement that hospitals provide some free health care does not preempt a UDAP claim that a hospital deceptively concealed its Hill-Burton obligation and billed patients for care that should have been free.[1425] A Connecticut court agreed, holding that allowing a state action for conduct which also violates the Hill-Burton Act would not interfere with or undermine federal objectives.[1426] But another court ruled that the Act preempts a similar UDAP claim against a hospital, where the plaintiff was seeking an order preventing the hospital from charging her for particular medical care.[1427]

The federal law[1428] regulating the enrollment practices that HMOs use in recruiting Medicare patients does not preempt a UDAP challenge to deceptive enrollment practices by a particular HMO.[1429] Nor was a UDAP challenge to a health plan's marketing materials preempted by the Medicare statute.[1430] The administrative review scheme for denial of Medicare benefits does not displace traditional tort remedies—such as complaints about the quality of care, marketing problems, and forced disenrollment—that do not seek payment of a claim.[1431] But another court has held UDAP claims against an HMO preempted by the Federal Employees Health Benefits Act.[1432] The COBRA provisions of the Public Health Service Act, which require group health care plans to offer continuation coverage, do not preempt state law claims.[1433]

A California court holds that Medicare provider cost reporting and reimbursement is so completely regulated by federal law that it ousts UDAP claims.[1434] As a result, a union could not bring a UDAP suit to challenge a hospital's inclusion of anti-union expenses in its reimbursement submissions to the Medicare program. But a claim that nursing homes had failed to pay wage increases that the state funded on a pass-through basis was not preempted by the Medicare laws as it did not deal with Medicare cost reimbursement.[1435]

The medical device amendments to the Food and Drug Act explicitly preempt state law "requirements" with respect to devices intended for human use that are different from or in addition to federal requirements.[1436] State law requirements are only preempted, however, if they relate to the safety or effectiveness of the device or to any other matter included in a requirement applicable to the device

1420 McCarthy v. Paine Webber, Inc., 618 F. Supp. 933 (N.D. Ill. 1985); Taylor v. Bear Stearns Co., 572 F. Supp. 667 (N.D. Ga. 1983); *see also* Nattrass v. Rosenthal & Co., 641 S.W.2d 675 (Tex. App. 1982). *But see* Saul Stone & Co. v. Browning, 615 F. Supp. 20 (N.D. Ill. 1985).

1421 Shell Oil Co. v. Wentworth, 822 F. Supp. 878 (D. Conn. 1993); Carson v. Texaco, 621 F. Supp. 1518 (M.D. La. 1985). *But see* Mehdi-Kashi v. Exxon Mobil Corp., 2002 WL 32052603 (S.D. Tex. Jan. 7, 2002) (preemption if conduct complies with PMPA).

1422 New York v. Feldman, 210 F. Supp. 2d 294 (S.D.N.Y. 2002) (federal antitrust laws do no preempt application of UDAP statute to in-state price-fixing activity that affects out-of-state customers); Conte & Co. v. Stephan, 713 F. Supp. 1382 (D. Kan. 1989) (federal regulation of mails does not preempt UDAP statute); Bazarian v. Harris, No. 1:88-CV-232 MHS (N.D. Ga. Feb. 22, 1989) (unpublished); Commonwealth *ex rel.* Cowan v. Telcom Directories, Inc., 806 S.W.2d 638 (Ky. 1991) (mail fraud laws do not preempt state UDAP claims); State *ex rel.* Nixon v. Telco Directory Publishing, 863 S.W.2d 596 (Mo. 1993); Brown v. Market Dev., Inc., 41 Ohio Misc. 57, 322 N.E.2d 367, 68 Ohio Op. 2d 276 (C.P. Hamilton Cty. 1974). *See also* Jacobs v. Central Transport, Inc., 891 F. Supp. 1088 (E.D.N.C. 1995) (UDAP claims arising from drivers' lease of vehicles from trucking company not preempted by Interstate Commerce Act and regulations).

1423 15 U.S.C. § 1012(b).

1424 Barnett Bank of Marion Cty. v. Nelson, 517 U.S. 25, 116 S. Ct. 1103, 134 L. Ed. 2d 237 (1996); Mitchell v. Florida Dept. of Ins., 679 So. 2d 334 (Fla. Dist. Ct. App. 1996) (applying McCarran-Ferguson "reverse preemption" rule to uphold state's regulation of insurance agents).

1425 Flagstaff Medical Center, Inc. v. Sullivan, 773 F. Supp. 1325 (D. Ariz. 1991), *rev'd on other grounds*, 962 F.2d 879 (9th Cir. 1992) (court agrees that claims not preempted).

1426 Yale New Haven Hosps. v. Mitchell, 683 A.2d 1362 (Conn. Super. Ct. 1995).

1427 White v. Moses Taylor Hosp., 763 F. Supp. 776 (M.D. Pa. 1991).

1428 42 U.S.C. § 1395mm.

1429 Solorzano v. Superior Court, 13 Cal. Rptr. 2d 161 (Ct. App. 1992).

1430 Palmer v. St. Joseph Healthcare P.S.O., Inc., 77 P.3d 560 (N.M. App. 2003) (construing express preemption provision), *review granted*, 77 P.3d 278 (N.M. 2003).

1431 McCall v. Pacificare of Cal., Inc., 25 Cal. 4th 412, 21 P.3d 1189 (2001).

1432 Fink v. Delaware Valley HMO, 612 A.2d 485 (Pa. Super. Ct. 1992) (federal worker's UDAP and other state tort claims against HMO are preempted by 5 U.S.C. §§ 8901 *et seq.* as inconsistent with HMO contract).

1433 Radici v. Associated Ins. Cos., 217 F.3d 737 (9th Cir. 2000).

1434 Congress of Cal. Seniors v. Catholic Healthcare West, 87 Cal. App. 4th 491, 104 Cal. Rptr. 2d 655 (2001).

1435 Macque-Garcia v. Dominican Santa Cruz Hosp., 2001 U.S. Dist. LEXIS 4866 (N.D. Cal. Apr. 16, 2001).

1436 21 U.S.C. § 360k(a). *See generally* National Consumer Law Center, Consumer Warranty Law § 1.4.9 (2d ed. 2001 and Supp.).

under federal law.[1437] The United States Supreme Court has interpreted this language not to preempt state law claims of negligent design, manufacturing, labeling, and failure to warn, at least in the case of a device that was grandfathered in rather than subjected to the FDA's full pre-market review procedure.[1438] Courts have found broader preemption for devices that have undergone the FDA's full review.[1439] The federal law does not, however, preempt the use of state common law claims as a vehicle for enforcing the federal standards.[1440] In addition to express preemption, the medical device amendments impliedly preempt "fraud on the FDA" claims.[1441] A preemption provision similar to that in the medical device amendments applies to claims regarding medications approved by the Food and Drug Administration.[1442] But federal laws regarding nutritional supplements do not preempt state deceptive advertising claims.[1443]

2.5.9 ERISA

The Employee Retirement Income Security Act of 1974 (ERISA) has a broad preemption provision[1444] that has been held to preclude many UDAP and similar claims that relate to employee benefit plans.[1445] In addition, ERISA provides

1437 *Id.*

1438 Medtronic, Inc. v. Lohr, 518 U.S. 470, 116 S. Ct. 2240, 135 L. Ed. 2d 700 (1996). *Cf.* Buckman Co. v. Plaintiffs' Legal Committee, 531 U.S. 341, 121 S. Ct. 1012, 148 L. Ed. 2d 854 (2001) (state law claims of fraud on FDA in processing of obtaining approval to market grandfathered device are preempted).

1439 *See* Worthy v. Collagen Corp., 967 S.W.2d 360 (Tex. 1998) (UDAP and other state claims regarding design, manufacture, and labeling of device that went through full premarket review are preempted), *cert. denied*, 524 U.S. 954 (1998). *But see* Haidak v. Collagen Corp., 67 F. Supp. 2d 21 (D. Mass. 1999) (full premarket review did not result in specific enough requirements to preempt state negligence, warranty, and UDAP claims).

1440 Medtronic, Inc. v. Lohr, 518 U.S. 470, 116 S. Ct. 2240, 135 L. Ed. 2d 700 (1996); Worthy v. Collagen Corp., 967 S.W.2d 360 (Tex. 1998) (UDAP and other state claims regarding design, manufacture, and labeling of device that went through full premarket review are preempted, but claims that parallel the federal process are not), *cert. denied*, 524 U.S. 954 (1998); *see also* Buckman Co. v. Plaintiff's Legal Committee, 531 U.S. 341, 348, 121 S. Ct. 1012, 1020, 148 L. Ed. 2d 854, 861 (2001) (noting that state law causes of action that parallel federal safety requirements for medical devices may not be preempted).

1441 Buckman Co. v. Plaintiff's Legal Committee, 531 U.S. 341, 348, 121 S. Ct. 1012, 1020, 148 L. Ed. 2d 854, 861 (2001).

1442 Solvay Pharmaceuticals, Inc. v. Global Pharmaceuticals, 298 F. Supp. 2d 880 (D. Minn. 2004) (claim that manufacturer misrepresented its drug as generic equivalent of competitor's is not preempted); Kanter v. Warner-Lambert Co., 99 Cal. App. 4th 780, 122 Cal. Rptr. 2d 72 (2002). *See also* N.J. Citizen Action v. Schering-Plough Corp., 367 N.J. Super. 8, 842 A.2d 174 (App. Div. 2003) (no UDAP claim to the extent drug ads are subject to FDA oversight).

1443 Consumer Justice Center v. Olympian Labs, Inc., 99 Cal. App. 4th 1056, 121 Cal. Rptr. 2d 749 (2002).

1444 29 U.S.C. § 1144. *See* Pilot Life Ins. Co. v. Dedeaux, 481 U.S. 41, 46, 107 S. Ct. 1549, 95 L. Ed. 2d 39 (1987) (describing ERISA preemption provisions as "deliberately expansive").

1445 Mayeaux v. La. Health Serv. & Indem. Co., 376 F.3d 420 (5th Cir. 2004) (state law tort claims preempted); Dudley Supermarket, Inc. v. Transamerica Life Ins. & Annuity Co., 302 F.3d 1 (1st Cir. 2002) (malpractice claim against fiduciary who provided advice to ERISA plan administrator is preempted); Darcangelo v. Verizon Communications, Inc., 292 F.3d 181 (4th Cir. 2002) (ERISA preempts breach of contract claims but not claims based on plan administrator's actions that are unrelated to plan administration); Gilbert v. Alta Health & Life Ins. Co., 276 F.3d 1292 (11th Cir. 2001) (ERISA preemption applies to sole shareholder and bars statutory bad faith claim); Harris v. Harvard Pilgrim Health Care, Inc., 208 F.3d 274 (1st Cir. 2000) (claim that health plan's lien recovery policies and procedures violated UDAP statute is preempted); Bast v. Prudential Ins. Co., 150 F.3d 1003 (9th Cir. 1998) (UDAP and state insurance code claims against insurance coverage for delay in approving coverage under ERISA plan are preempted), *cert. denied*, 528 U.S. 870, 120 S. Ct. 170, 145 L. Ed. 2d 144 (1999); Hubbard v. Blue Cross & Blue Shield Ass'n, 42 F.3d 942 (5th Cir. 1995) (preemption of claim that insurance company used "secret guidelines" on coverage, but no preemption of UDAP false advertising claims); Hogan v. Kraft Foods, 969 F.2d 142 (5th Cir. 1992) (Texas law); Dwyer v. UNUM Life Ins. Co., 2003 WL 22844234 (N.D. Ill. Dec. 1, 2003) (ERISA preempts UDAP and other claims even though plan participant was independent contractor rather than employee); Baylor University Medical Center v. Western Growers Assurance Trust, 2003 WL 21528676 (N.D. Tex. July 3, 2003) (UDAP claim completely preempted, but misrepresentation claim is not); Blum v. Spectrum Restaurant Group, Inc., 2003 WL 1889036 (E.D. Tex. Apr. 14, 2003); Burgos v. Group & Pension Administrators, Inc., 286 F. Supp. 2d 812 (S.D. Tex. 2003); Jones v. Texas Health Choice, L.C., 2003 WL 302217 (E.D. Tex. Feb. 7, 2003); Caraveo v. Nielsen Media Research, Inc., 2003 WL 169767 (S.D.N.Y. Jan. 22, 2003); Dobner v. Health Care Serv. Corp., 2002 WL 1348910 (N.D. Ill. June 19, 2002) (UDAP claim that insurer misrepresented benefits is preempted); Erwin v. Texas Health Choice, L.C., 187 F. Supp. 2d 661 (N.D. Tex. 2002) (ERISA preempts common law bad faith claims); Pachuta v. Unumprovident Corp., 242 F. Supp. 2d 752 (D. Haw. 2002); Miller v. Aetna Healthcare, 2001 U.S. Dist. LEXIS 20801 (E.D. Pa. Dec. 12, 2001) (claim for benefits due under plan); St. Luke's Episcopal Hosp. Corp. v. Stevens Transport Inc., 172 F. Supp. 2d 837 (S.D. Tex. 2001); Andrews-Clarke v. Lucent Technologies, Inc., 157 F. Supp. 2d 93 (D. Mass. 2001) (claim that decedent did not receive the medical treatment to which he was entitled under the plan is preempted); Brandner v. UNUM Life Ins. Co., 152 F. Supp. 2d 1219 (D. Nev. 2001) (claim for benefits relates to ERISA plan, so is preempted); Murphy v. Metropolitan Life Ins. Co., 152 F. Supp. 2d 755 (E.D. Pa. 2001) (ERISA preempts UDAP and bad faith insurance claims); Tuohig v. Principal Ins. Group, 134 F. Supp. 2d 148 (D. Mass. 2001) (ERISA preempts UDAP claim for damages caused to employee's spouse by denial of employee's claim); Richardson v. Aetna Life Ins. Co., 2001 U.S. Dist LEXIS 21483 (N.D. Tex. Dec. 26, 2001); Magallon-Laffey v. Sun Life Assur. Co. of Canada, 2001 U.S. Dist. LEXIS 13252 (N.D. Tex. Aug. 28, 2001); Page v. Unum Life Ins. Co. of America, 2001 WL 294252 (N.D. Tex. Mar. 23, 2001); Alfaro v. Leather Center, Inc., 2001 U.S. Dist. LEXIS 2082 (N.D. Tex. Feb. 20, 2001); Aguirre v. Badgett, 2001 WL 694489 (W.D. Tex. Feb. 7, 2001); Norman v. Paul Revere Life Ins. Co., 2000 U.S. Dist. LEXIS 21478 (W.D.

its own enforcement mechanism.[1446] The Supreme Court has held that this ERISA enforcement remedy, even though it has a number of significant limitations,[1447] wholly displaces state law causes of action.[1448] As a result, ERISA is one of the few federal statutes to which the doctrine of complete preemption applies. A complaint that pleads state claims that could have been pleaded as ERISA claims is removable to federal court.[1449]

While ERISA's preemptive scope is broad, fraudulent inducement-type claims[1450] and other claims that are only

Wash. May 12, 2000) (UDAP, contract, fiduciary duty, negligence, and fraud claims are preempted but claims under bad faith insurance statute are not); Shackelford v. Continental Cas. Co., 96 F. Supp. 2d 738 (W.D. Tenn. 2000) (UNIP and UDAP claims based on employer's deceptive statement that employee would receive disability benefits is essentially a claim for benefits and is preempted, but claim based on employer's contemporaneous promise of a consulting job is not); Biondo v. Life Ins. Co. of N. Am., 116 F. Supp. 2d 872 (E.D. Mich. 2000) (ERISA preempts contract, UDAP, and UNIP claims; UNIP assessment of interest on late payment of claim does not fall within savings clause for laws regulating insurance); Norris v. Continental Cas. Co., 2000 U.S. Dist. LEXIS 9163 (E.D. Pa. June 29, 2000) (ERISA preempts UDAP and UNIP claims); Lewis v. Aetna U.S. Healthcare, Inc., 78 F. Supp. 2d 1202 (N.D. Okla. 1999) (ERISA preempts claim for breach of contract based on employee benefit plan, but bad faith claim falls within savings clause so is not preempted); Belanger v. Healthsource of Maine, 66 F. Supp. 2d 70 (D. Me. 1999) (state law claims that amount to alternative mechanisms to enforce rights under ERISA plan are preempted); Salameh v. Provident Life & Acc. Ins. Co., 23 F. Supp. 2d 704 (S.D. Tex. 1998) (claims for denial of benefits preempted); Witten v. Pacificare of Texas, Inc., 1998 U.S. Dist. LEXIS 1889 (N.D. Tex. Feb. 11, 1998) (claims for misrepresentation of policy and denial of benefits preempted); Hollander v. Paul Revere Life Ins. Co., 1998 U.S. Dist. LEXIS 22732 (S.D.N.Y. Apr. 17, 1998) (UDAP and UNIP claims regarding insurer's refusal to pay claim under employer-provided disability insurance are preempted); Spillers v. Webb, 979 F. Supp. 494 (S.D. Tex. 1997); Timmons v. Special Ins. Servs., 984 F. Supp. 997 (E.D. Tex. 1997), *aff'd without op.*, 167 F.3d 537 (5th Cir. 1998); Hartford Life & Acc. Ins. Co. v. Eterna Benefits L.L.C., 1997 U.S. Dist. LEXIS 18670 (N.D. Tex. Nov. 17, 1997); Hermann Hosp. v. Pan Am. Life Ins. Co., 932 F. Supp. 899 (S.D. Tex. 1996) (preemption of hospital's claim against ERISA plan administrator for misrepresenting pay benefits); Gabner v. Metropolitan Life Ins. Co., 938 F. Supp. 1295 (E.D. Tex. 1996) (preemption of plan participant's claim for misrepresenting cost of conversion insurance policy); Ryan v. Fallon Community Health Plan, 921 F. Supp. 34 (D. Mass. 1996); Bailey-Gates v. Aetna Life Ins. Co., 890 F. Supp. 73 (D. Conn. 1994) (ERISA preempts UDAP claim against employee's health insurance provider for damages resulting from managed care system's denial of benefits); Cox v. Blue Cross & Blue Shield of Michigan, 869 F. Supp. 501 (E.D. Mich. 1994); National Alcoholism Programs v. Palm Springs Hosps. Employee Benefit Plan, 825 F. Supp. 299 (S.D. Fla. 1993); Dipietro-Kay v. Interactive Benefits Corp., 825 F. Supp. 459 (D. Conn. 1993); DeGrooth v. General Dynamics Corp., 837 F. Supp. 485 (D. Conn. 1993); Anderson v. Humana, Inc., 820 F. Supp. 368 (N.D. Ill. 1993), *aff'd*, 24 F.3d 889 (7th Cir. 1994); Charlton Memorial Hosp. v. Foxboro Co., 818 F. Supp. 456 (D. Mass. 1993); Pariseau v. Albany Int'l Corp., 822 F. Supp. 843 (D. Mass. 1993); Camire v. Aetna Life Ins. Co., 822 F. Supp. 846 (D.N.H. 1993); Oaks Psychiatric Hosp. v. American Heritage Life Ins. Co., 814 F. Supp. 553 (W.D. Tex. 1993); State Street Bank & Trust Co. v. Mutual Life Ins. Co. of New York, 811 F. Supp. 915 (S.D.N.Y. 1993); Optimal Health Care Servs., Inc. v. Travelers Ins. Co., 791 F. Supp. 163 (E.D. Tex. 1992); Nechero v. Provident Life & Acc. Ins. Co., 795 F. Supp. 374 (D.N.M. 1992); Cote v. Durham Life Ins. Co., 754 F. Supp. 18 (D. Conn. 1991); Altieri v. Cigna Dental Health, Inc., 753 F. Supp. 61 (D. Conn. 1990) (ERISA preempts suit against health plan but not suit against health provider); Fischman v. Blue Cross & Blue Shield of Conn., 755 F. Supp. 528 (D. Conn. 1990) (ERISA preempts claims for negligence, bad faith, infliction of emotional distress, and violation of Unfair Insurance Practices Act); McManus v. Travelers Health Network of Texas, 742 F. Supp. 377 (W.D. Tex. 1990); Worthington v. Metropolitan Life Ins. Co., 688 F. Supp. 298 (S.D. Tex. 1987); Provience v. Valley Clerks Trust Fund, 509 F. Supp. 388 (E.D. Cal. 1981); Yardley v. U. S. Healthcare, Inc., 698 A.2d 979 (Del. Super. Ct. 1996) (ERISA bars claim under UNIP statute), *aff'd without op.*, 693 A.2d 1083 (Del. 1997); Curry v. Cincinnati Equitable Ins. Co., 834 S.W.2d 701 (Ky. Ct. App. 1992); Cathey v. Metropolitan Life Ins. Co., 805 S.W.2d 387 (Tex. 1991); Manahan v. Meyer, 862 S.W.2d 130 (Tex. App. 1993); Hepler v. CBS, Inc., 696 P.2d 596 (Wash. Ct. App. 1985). *See also* Christenson v. Mutual Life Ins. Co., 950 F. Supp. 179 (N.D. Tex. 1996) (although state UNIP statute does not regulate the business of insurance and is therefore preempted, state law prohibiting discrimination in providing insurance is not preempted). *But see* Hobbs v. Blue Cross & Blue Shield of Alabama, 276 F.3d 1236 (11th Cir. 2001) (claim by providers that they were wrongly excluded from ERISA plan is not preempted because providers have no standing to bring ERISA suit); Memorial Hosp. Sys. v. Northbrook Life Ins. Co., 904 F.2d 236 (5th Cir. 1990) (Texas law) (no preemption for hospital's UDAP claim that employer and insurer misrepresented employee's insurance coverage); Glynn v. Bankers Life and Casualty Co., 297 F. Supp. 2d 424 (D. Conn. 2003); Taylor v. Carter, 948 F. Supp. 1290 (W.D. Tex. 1996) (no preemption if plaintiff has no standing to sue under ERISA for state-law-based claims); Forest Springs Hosp. v. Illinois New Car & Truck Dealers Ass'n Employees Ins. Trust, 812 F. Supp. 729 (S.D. Tex. 1993) (ERISA does not preempt common-law misrepresentation claim by hospital against ERISA plan administrators, but ERISA does preempt hospital's equitable estoppel claim against administrators because such a claim is tantamount to a claim for benefits).

1446 29 U.S.C. § 1132(a). *See* Sundown Ranch, Inc. v. General American Life Ins. Co., 2001 U.S. Dist. LEXIS 10083 (N.D. Tex. July 17, 2001).

1447 Aetna Health Inc. v. Davila, 124 S. Ct. 2488, 2503 (2004) (Ginsburg, J., concurring); Andrews-Clarke v. Lucent Technologies, Inc., 157 F. Supp. 2d 93 (D. Mass. 2001) (ERISA creates cause of action to recover benefits due or to clarify or enforce rights under the plan, but not for damages).

1448 Aetna Health Inc. v. Davila, 124 S. Ct. 2488, 2494–96 (2004); Pilot Life Ins. Co. v. Dedeaux, 481 U.S. 41, 46, 107 S. Ct. 1549, 1555, 95 L. Ed. 2d 39 (1987).

1449 Aetna Health Inc. v. Davila, 124 S. Ct. 2488, 2494–96 (2004). *See* § 7.6.5, *infra*.

1450 Woodworker's Supply, Inc. v. Principal Mut. Life Ins. Co., 170 F.3d 985 (10th Cir. 1999) (employer's claim that insurance company fraudulently induced contract not preempted; decision identifies four categories of claims that are preempted); Hubbard v. Blue Cross & Blue Shield Ass'n, 42 F.3d 942 (5th Cir. 1995) (preemption of claim that insurance company used "se-

peripherally related to ERISA[1451] may escape preemption. In addition, some employees are not covered by ERISA even though they have benefit plans, and their UDAP claims are unaffected by ERISA.[1452]

In addition, ERISA has a savings clause, which provides that "nothing in this title shall be construed to exempt or relieve any person from any law of any state which regulates insurance."[1453] According to revised criteria announced by the Supreme Court in 2003, a law "regulates insurance" for purposes of ERISA if it (1) is specifically directed toward entities engaged in insurance, and (2) substantially affects the risk pooling arrangement between the insurer and the insured.[1454] The Supreme Court has broadly defined this latter criterion: as long as the law alters the scope of permissible bargains between the insurer and the insured, it affects the risk pooling arrangements.[1455] For example, a law that required HMOs to abide by an independent medical review when deciding whether to approve a claim fell within the savings clause.[1456]

State Unfair Insurance Practices (UNIP) laws[1457] and other restrictions on insurers may fall within the savings clause and avoid preemption.[1458] However, in 2004 the

---

cret guidelines" on coverage, but no preemption of UDAP false advertising claims); Daniels v. Bursey, 2003 WL 22053580 (N.D. Ill. Sept. 3, 2003); Almond v. Berretta, 2002 WL 1784645 (W.D. Tenn. June 26, 2002) (claim against agent who procured ERISA plan for company not preempted); Giannetti v. Mahoney, 218 F. Supp. 2d 8 (D. Mass. 2002); Aetna U.S. Healthcare Inc. v. Maltz, 1999 U.S. Dist. LEXIS 6708 (S.D.N.Y. May 4, 1999) (UDAP claims regarding quality of care and misrepresentation in plan's promotional and advertising announcements not preempted); Stetson v. PFL Ins. Co., 16 F. Supp. 2d 28 (D. Me. 1998) (ERISA does not preempt claim that insurance agent and insurer misrepresented plan's coverage when marketing plan, before plaintiff's employer adopted it, where plaintiff sought compensatory and punitive damages rather than plan benefits); Hardy v. Fisher, 901 F. Supp. 228 (E.D. Tex. 1995) (claims for misrepresentations of group insurance policy are not sufficiently "related to" ERISA for preemption); Adorno v. Nitzkin, 828 F. Supp. 42 (N.D. Ill. 1993) (no preemption by ERISA for claims based on agent's actions in inducing consumer to surrender existing insurance policy to join ERISA plan); Napoletano v. Cigna Healthcare of Conn., 238 Conn. 216, 680 A.2d 127 (1996) (patients' claim that health care network misrepresented features of the plan are not preempted); Finderne Management Co. v. Barrett, 355 N.J. Super. 170, 809 A.2d 842 (App. Div. 2002) (employers' claim that insurers, insurance agent, tax advisor, and plan administrator misrepresented tax consequences of plan not preempted); McDonald v. Houston Brokerage, Inc., 928 S.W.2d 633 (Tex. App. 1996) (no preemption of claim by employer and beneficiaries for misrepresentation of cost of replacement policy used to fund the plan).

1451 Roark v. Humana, Inc., 307 F.3d 298 (5th Cir. 2002) (state law claim against HMO for medical necessity decision); Darcangelo v. Verizon Communications, Inc., 292 F.3d 181 (4th Cir. 2002) (ERISA does not preempt UDAP and other claims based on plan administrator's actions—collection and dissemination of confidential medical information—that were unrelated to plan administration, but does preempt breach of contract claim); Lazorko v. Pennsylvania Hosps., 237 F.3d 242 (3d Cir. 2000) (ERISA preempts UDAP claims that focus on company's administration of employee benefits plan but claim that HMO is vicariously liable for negligence of plan physicians is not preempted); Memorial Hosp. Sys. v. Northbrook Life Ins. Co., 904 F.2d 236 (5th Cir. 1990) (Texas law) (no preemption for hospital's UDAP claim that employer and insurer misrepresented employee's insurance coverage); Southwest Bank v. Management Counsel for Employee Benefits, Inc., 2003 WL 298976 (N.D. Tex. Feb. 10, 2003); Wiener v. Unumprovident Corp., 202 F. Supp. 2d 116 (S.D.N.Y. 2002) (denying motion to dismiss claims regarding employee's individual disability policy in absence of evidence that it was related to her employer-provided group policy); Shackelford v. Continental Cas. Co., 96 F. Supp. 2d 738 (W.D. Tenn. 2000) (UNIP and UDAP claims based on employer's deceptive statement that employee would receive disability benefits is essentially a claim for benefits and is preempted, but claim based on employer's contemporaneous promise of a consulting job is not); Inverness Corp. v. McCullough, 1999 U.S. Dist. LEXIS 19557 (D. Mass. Feb. 24, 1999) (ERISA claim not preempted where plaintiffs are not plan participants, beneficiaries, or fiduciaries, and do not seek plan benefits; dispute arose out of investments made by trustee on behalf of plan); Altieri v. Cigna Dental Health, Inc., 753 F. Supp. 61 (D. Conn. 1990) (ERISA preempts suit against health plan but not suit against health provider); Napoletano v. Cigna Healthcare of Conn., 238 Conn. 216, 680 A.2d 127 (1996) (doctors' claims regarding improper termination from network are not preempted); Gulf Coast Alloy Welding, Inc. v. Legal Sec. Life Ins. Co., 981 S.W.2d 239 (Tex. App. 1998) (misrepresentation of policy and denial of benefits are peripheral to ERISA and thus not preempted). *See also* Lazorko v. Pennsylvania Hosps., 237 F.3d 242 (3d Cir. 2000) (claims challenging soundness of medical decision by health care provider rather than administration of plan are not completely preempted).

1452 *See, e.g.*, 29 U.S.C. § 1003(b)(1), (2) (exempting government and public agency employees and church employees). *See* White v. Provident American Ins. Co., 2002 WL 1432575 (N.D. Tex. June 28, 2002) (ERISA does not completely preempt state law claim unless plaintiff has standing to sue as participant on beneficiary of ERISA plan); Macro v. Independent Health Ass'n, 180 F. Supp. 2d 427 (W.D.N.Y. 2001) (school district plan is governmental plan). *See generally* Michael J. Bidard and Ricardo Echeverria, The Erosion of ERISA Preemption of Bad Faith Liability Actions, *The Consumer Advocate* vol. 6, issue 2 at 29 (National Ass'n of Consumer Advocates Mar./Apr. 2000). *But see* Gilbert v. Alta Health & Life Ins. Co., 276 F.3d 1292 (11th Cir. 2001) (ERISA preemption applies to sole shareholder of company).

1453 29 U.S.C. § 1144(b)(20)(A).

1454 Kentucky Ass'n. of Health Plans, Inc. v. Miller, 538 U.S. 329, 123 S. Ct. 1471, 1479, 155 L. Ed. 2d 468 (2003) (repudiating prior decisions' adoption of factors used under McCarran-Ferguson Act). *See also* Elliot v. Fortis Benefits Ins. Co., 337 F.3d 1138 (9th Cir. 2003) (analyzing changes in Supreme Court's analysis of ERISA savings clause).

1455 Ky. Ass'n of Health Plans, Inc. v. Miller, 538 U.S. 329, 123 S. Ct. 1471, 1477–78, 155 L. Ed. 2d 468 (2003).

1456 Rush Prudential HMO, Inc. v. Moran, 536 U.S. 355, 122 S. Ct. 2151, 153 L. Ed. 2d 375 (2002). *See also* UNUM Life Ins. Co. v. Ward, 526 U.S. 358, 119 S. Ct. 1380, 143 L. Ed. 2d 462 (1999) (state law governing whether insurer must cover claims submitted late is not preempted).

1457 *See* § 5.3.2, *infra*.

1458 *Not Preempted*: Baylor University Medical Center v. Western

Supreme Court stated that "any state-law cause of action that duplicates, supplements, or supplants the ERISA civil enforcement remedy conflicts with the clear congressional intent to make the ERISA remedy exclusive and is therefore preempted."[1459] The court specifically applied this rule to laws regulating insurance: "[E]ven a state law that can arguably be characterized as 'regulating insurance' will be pre-empted if it provides a separate vehicle to assert a claim for benefits outside of, or in addition to, ERISA's remedial scheme."[1460] Thus, it appears that while UNIP and other insurance laws may impose duties on ERISA plan providers, those duties would only be enforceable through an action under ERISA. The Supreme Court's decisions appear to foreclose consumers from asserting claims directly under UNIP or other insurance laws if those laws would give them broader remedies than ERISA.[1461]

Growers Assurance Trust, 2003 WL 21528676 (N.D. Tex. July 3, 2003); Macro v. Independent Health Assn., 180 F. Supp. 2d 427 (W.D.N.Y. 2001) (claim based on insurance law that required coverage of certain conditions is not preempted; issue is complete preemption); Norman v. Paul Revere Life Ins. Co., 2000 U.S. Dist. LEXIS 21478 (W.D. Wash. May 12, 2000) (bad faith insurance statute regulates insurance even though it does not spread risk, so ERISA does not preempt claim under that statute, but UDAP, contract, breach of fiduciary duty, negligence, and fraud claims are preempted); Lewis v. Aetna U.S. Healthcare, Inc., 78 F. Supp. 2d 1202 (N.D. Okla. 1999) (ERISA preempts claim for breach of contract based on employee benefit plan, but common law bad faith claim falls within savings clause so is not preempted; issue is complete preemption); Graves v. Blue Cross, 688 F. Supp. 1405 (N.D. Cal. 1988) (ERISA does not preempt UNIP action even when it offers remedies beyond ERISA's; issue is complete preemption); Mayfield v. Hartford Life Ins. Co., 699 F. Supp. 605 (W.D. Tex. 1988) (same); Denette v. Life of Indiana Ins. Co., 693 F. Supp. 959 (D. Colo. 1988) (ERISA preempts some but not all UNIP claims); Clothesrigger, Inc. v. GTE Corp., 191 Cal. App. 3d 605, 236 Cal. Rptr. 605 (1987).

Preempted: Barber v. UNUM Life Ins. Co., 2004 WL 1964500 (3d Cir. Sept. 7, 2004) (bad faith insurance statute is not a law regulating insurance so does not fall within savings clause); Walker v. Southern Co. Servs., Inc., 279 F.3d 1289 (11th Cir. 2002) (ERISA preempts statutory bad faith claim); Hotz v. Blue Cross & Blue Shield, 292 F.3d 57 (1st Cir. 2002) (Mass. unfair insurance practices statute, enforceable through UDAP statute, imposes standards that are generally applicable to other industries so does not fall within Savings Clause); Gilbert v. Alta Health & Life Ins. Co., 276 F.3d 1292 (11th Cir. 2001) (ERISA preempts statutory bad faith claim); Tri-State Machine, Inc. v. Nationwide Life Ins. Co., 33 F.3d 309 (4th Cir. 1994) (UNIP claim does not avoid preemption by falling within ERISA's savings clause for state statutes regulating the business of insurance); Dwyer v. UNUM Life Ins. Co., 2003 WL 22844234 (N.D. Ill. Dec. 1, 2003) (Illinois vexatious refusal statute does not regulate insurance so is preempted); Pachuta v. Unumprovident Corp., 242 F. Supp. 2d 752 (D. Haw. 2002) (UDAP, contract, and bad faith tort claims preempted); Chamblin v. Reliance Standard Life Ins. Co., 168 F. Supp. 2d 1168 (N.D. Cal. 2001) (magistrate's decision) (concluding that it is bound by 9th Cir. precedent despite intervening Supreme Court decision); Coffman v. Metropolitan Life Ins. Co., 138 F. Supp. 2d 764 (S.D. W. Va. 2001) (following 4th Cir. case and finding UNIP claim preempted despite intervening Supreme Court decisions); Brandner v. UNUM Life Ins. Co., 152 F. Supp. 2d 1219 (D. Nev. 2001) (UNIP statute does not fall within Savings Clause, partly because it imposes same duties on insurers as common law imposes on all contracts and because existence of any other remedies is inconsistent with ERISA); Murphy v. Metropolitan Life Ins. Co., 152 F. Supp. 2d 755 (E.D. Pa. 2001) (ERISA preempts UDAP and bad faith insurance claims); Shackelford v. Continental Cas. Co., 96 F. Supp. 2d 738 (W.D. Tenn. 2000) (UNIP and UDAP claims based on employer's deceptive statement that employee would receive disability benefits is essentially a claim for benefits and is preempted, but claim based on employer's contemporaneous promise of a consulting job is not); Chiroff v. Life Ins. Co., 142 F. Supp. 2d 1360 (S.D. Fla. 2000) (statutory bad faith claim preempted because does not relate to business of insurance and providing alternate remedy conflicts with ERISA); Chilton v. Prudential Ins. Co., 124 F. Supp. 2d 673 (M.D. Fla. 2000) (claim that employer provided disability insurance policy with terms that differed from representations does not fall within savings clause), *aff'd without op.*, 2001 WL 1711209 (11th Cir. Dec. 17, 2001); Norris v. Continental Cas. Co., 2000 U.S. Dist. LEXIS 9163 (E.D. Pa. June 29, 2000) (ERISA preempts UDAP and UNIP claims); Biondo v. Life Ins. Co. of N. Am., 116 F. Supp. 2d 872 (E.D. Mich. 2000) (ERISA preempts contract, UDAP, and UNIP claims; UNIP assessment of interest on late payment of claim does not fall within savings clause for laws regulating insurance); Hollander v. Paul Revere Life Ins. Co., 1998 U.S. Dist. LEXIS 22732 (S.D.N.Y. Apr. 17, 1998) (UDAP and UNIP claims regarding insurer's refusal to pay claim under employer-provided disability insurance are preempted); Fischman v. Blue Cross & Blue Shield of Conn., 755 F. Supp. 528 (D. Conn. 1990) (ERISA preempts claims for negligence, bad faith, infliction of emotional distress, and violation of Unfair Insurance Practices Act); Yardley v. U.S. Healthcare, Inc., 698 A.2d 979 (Del. Super. Ct. 1996) (ERISA bars claim under UNIP statute), *aff'd without op.*, 693 A.2d 1083 (Del. 1997); *see also* Glynn v. Bankers Life and Casualty Co., 297 F. Supp. 2d 424 (D. Conn. 2003) (UDAP cause of action conflicts directly with civil enforcement provisions of ERISA and therefore is preempted notwithstanding savings clause); Christenson v. Mutual Life Ins. Co., 950 F. Supp. 179 (N.D. Tex. 1996) (although state UNIP statute does not regulate the business of insurance and is therefore preempted, state law prohibiting discrimination in providing insurance is not preempted). *Cf.* Dobner v. Health Care Serv. Corp., 2002 WL 1348910 (N.D. Ill. June 19, 2002) (UDAP statute is not specifically directed toward insurance so does not escape preemption).

1459 Aetna Health Inc. v. Davila, 124 S. Ct. 2488, 2495 (2004).

1460 *Id.* at 2500. *See also* Rush Prudential HMO, Inc. v., Moran, 536 U.S. 355, 122 S. Ct. 2151, 153 L. Ed. 2d 375 (2002) (holding state insurance law not preempted; stressing that it did not create new cause of action or new form of relief, but just provided procedures for determining the ERISA benefits to which HMO member was entitled); Pilot Life Ins. Co. v. Dedeaux, 481 U.S. 41, 46, 107 S. Ct. 1549, 1555, 95 L. Ed. 2d 39 (1987) (cause of action provided by ERISA is exclusive remedy when beneficiary asserts improper processing of claim for benefits).

1461 Barber v. UNUM Life Ins. Co., 2004 WL 1964500 (3d Cir. Sept. 7, 2004) (ERISA preempts claim under bad faith insurance statute because it provides additional remedies); Elliot v. Fortis Benefits Ins. Co., 337 F.3d 1138 (9th Cir. 2003) (UNIP claim probably meets *Ky. Ass'n* requirement of affecting risk allocation, but it is still preempted because it allows remedies beyond ERISA's); Kidneigh v. UNUM Life Ins. Co., 345 F.3d 1182

2.5.10 Federal Tobacco Regulation

Courts have differed about whether the Federal Cigarette Labeling and Advertising Act[1462] preempts UDAP damages claims based on manufacturers' unfair and deceptive methods of promoting and selling cigarettes.[1463] But it does preempt UDAP regulations that restrict cigarette advertising near schools.[1464]

2.5.11 Other Federal Statutes

Courts have found that UDAP actions are generally *not* preempted by:

- Federal regulation of lotteries by mail;[1465]
- The Wool Products Labeling Act (15 U.S.C. § 68);[1466]
- The Federal Hazardous Substances Act;[1467]
- The Higher Education Act;[1468]
- FDA requirements regarding labeling of foods;[1469]
- The Miller Act, which governs the payment rights of persons who supply labor and materials for federal construction projects;[1470]
- The Federal Emergency Management Agency's National Flood Insurance Program.[1471]
- The Ship Mortgage Act;[1472] and
- The Federal Crop Insurance Act.[1473]

On the other hand, the following federal statutes contain explicit preemption provisions that courts usually find bar at least some UDAP claims:

- The Federal Insecticide, Fungicide, and Rodenticide Act, 17 U.S.C. §§ 136–136y;[1474]

(10th Cir. 2003) (bad faith insurance claim does not fall within Savings Clause; also preempted because it affords additional remedy); Bonnell v. Bank of America, 284 F. Supp. 2d 1284 (D. Kan. 2003) (UNIP claim preempted because it allows remedies beyond ERISA's).

1462 15 U.S.C. §§ 1331, 1334 (prohibiting states from imposing any requirement or prohibition with respect to advertising or promotion of cigarettes that are labeled as required by federal law).

1463 Blue Cross & Blue Shield v. Philip Morris USA Inc., 344 F.3d 211 (2d Cir. 2003) (no preemption where claim is based on affirmative misrepresentation rather than non-disclosure); Castano v. American Tobacco Co., 870 F. Supp. 1425 (E.D. La. 1994). *But see* Sanchez v. Liggett & Myers, Inc., 187 F.3d 486 (5th Cir. 1999) (smoker's UDAP claim against cigarette manufacturer preempted); American Tobacco Co. v. Grinnell, 951 S.W.2d 420 (Tex. 1997) (claims for UDAP damages for failure to disclose risks and for deceptive advertising are preempted).

1464 Lorillard Tobacco Co. v. Reilly, 533 U.S. 525, 121 S. Ct. 2404, 150 L. Ed. 2d 532 (2001). *But cf.* Mangini v. R.J. Reynolds Tobacco Co., 7 Cal. 4th 1057, 31 Cal. Rptr. 2d 358, 875 P.2d 73 (1994) (pre-*Lorillard* case holding that UDAP suit seeking injunction against advertisements targeting minors was not preempted).

1465 State v. Reader's Digest Ass'n, Inc., 81 Wash. 2d 259, 501 P.2d 290 (1972). *See also* State v. Sterling Theaters Co., 64 Wash. 2d 761, 394 P.2d 226 (1964); Ritholz v. Ammon, 240 Wis. 578, 4 N.W.2d 173 (1942).

1466 State *ex rel.* Redden v. Discount Fabrics, 289 Or. 375, 615 P.2d 1034 (1980).

1467 Cole v. Sunnyside Corp., 610 N.W.2d 511 (Wis. App. 2000) (preemption inappropriate when there is a question whether label complied with federal statute).

1468 Morgan v. Markerdowne Corp., 976 F. Supp. 301 (D.N.J. 1997); Williams v. National School of Health Technology, Inc., 836 F. Supp. 273 (E.D. Pa. 1993), *aff'd without op.*, 37 F.3d 1491 (3d Cir. 1994); Jackson v. Culinary School of Washington, 788 F. Supp. 1233 (D.D.C. 1992) (denying motion to dismiss), *dismissed on summary judgment on other grounds*, 811 F. Supp. 714 (D.D.C. 1993), *aff'd in party, rev'd and remanded in part on other grounds*, 27 F.3d 573 (1994) (reversing, on *de novo* review, district court's decision to issue declaratory judgment on state law issues), *vacated*, 515 U.S. 1139 (1995) (appeals court should have used abuse of discretion standard to review district court's decision to issue declaratory judgment on state law issues), *on remand*, 59 F.3d 254 (D.C. Cir. 1995) (remanding for district court to exercise its discretion about whether to issue declaratory judgment on state law issues). *But see* Wilson v. Chism, 665 N.E.2d 446 (Ill. App. Ct. 1996) (claim that school violated UDAP statute by falsely certifying that students met HEA's ability-to-benefit standard is preempted). *Cf.* Cliff v. Payco General American Credits, Inc., 363 F.3d 1113 (11th Cir. 2004) (state debt collection act not preempted by HEA; declines to follow *Brannan*). *But cf.* Brannan v. United Student Aid Funds, 94 F.3d 1260 (9th Cir. 1996) (state debt collection statute (not UDAP statute) preempted by student loan collection regulations adopted under HEA); Washkoviak v. Student Loan Marketing Ass'n, 849 A.2d 37 (D.C. 2004) (UDAP claim regarding nondisclosure of late charges is preempted by HEA's specific exemption of student loans from state law disclosure requirements, but claim regarding affirmative misrepresentation may survive).

1469 Morelli v. Weider Nutrition Group, 275 A.D.2d 607, 712 N.Y.S.2d 551 (2000) (interpreting express preemption provision of 21 U.S.C. § 343-1 not to preempt claims regarding misrepresentation of nutritional content of product where plaintiffs claim defendants violated the federal statute). *Cf.* Nagel v. Twin Laboratories, Inc., 109 Cal. App. 4th 39, 134 Cal. Rptr. 2d 420 (2003) (affirming dismissal of defendant's challenge under anti-SLAPP suit law to; label can be deceptive even if it complies with FDA requirements). *But see* Cohen v. McDonald's Corp., 808 N.E.2d 1 (Ill. App. 2004) (UDAP claim preempted by 21 U.S.C. § 343-1 where it would have required court to create nutritional labeling requirements beyond FDA's). *But cf.* Anthony v. Country Life Mfg., 2002 WL 31269621 (N.D. Ill. Oct. 9, 2002), *aff'd*, 2003 WL 21540975 (7th Cir. July 2, 2003) (unpublished, citation limited) (FDA nutritional supplement rules preempt claim that it was UDAP violation to market product containing ingredients not approved by FDA).

1470 U.S. on behalf of Polied Environmental Servs., Inc. v. Incor Group, Inc., 238 F. Supp. 2d 456 (D. Conn. 2002) (Miller Act does not provide exclusive remedy, so does not preclude UDAP claim).

1471 Richmond Printing L.L.C. v. Director Fed. Emergency Mgmt. Agency, 2003 WL 21697457 (5th Cir. July 21, 2003).

1472 Duzich v. Marine Office of Am. Corp., 980 S.W.2d 857 (Tex. App. 1998).

1473 Halfmann v. USAG Ins. Servs., Inc., 118 F. Supp. 2d 714 (N.D. Tex. 2000).

1474 Dow Agrosciences L.L.C. v. Bates, 332 F.3d 323 (5th Cir. 2003) (FIFRA preempts UDAP-based breach of warranty claims

- The Railway Labor Act;[1475]
- The Longshore and Harbor Workers' Compensation Act;[1476] and
- The National Flood Insurance Program.[1477]

While the Clean Air Act has a preemption provision for motor vehicle emission control,[1478] it does not preempt a claim that a gasoline additive leaked into the ground from gas station storage tanks and other sources and polluted homeowners' well water.[1479] The federal laws regulating animal vaccines[1480] preempt claims based on packaging and labeling that seek to enforce standards different from or in addition to the federal standards, but not claims based on violation of the federal standards or on the manufacturer's voluntary promotional representations about the product's effectiveness.[1481] The federal laws governing the U.S. Postal Service preempt a manufacturer's UDAP challenge to the Postal Service's procurement decisions.[1482]

---

based on advertising and marketing, if those claims merely repeat FIFRA-protected label claims); Dahlman Farms, Inc. v. FMC Corp., 240 F. Supp. 2d 1012 (D. Minn. 2002) (FIFRA preempts claims based both on false statements on label and advertisements that repeated those statements). *But see* Kuiper v. American Cyanamid Co., 913 F. Supp. 1236 (E.D. Wis. 1996); Uniroyal Chemical Co. v. Drexel Chemical Co., 931 F. Supp. 132 (D. Conn. 1996) (Connecticut UDAP claim regarding pesticide registration in the U.K. not preempted); American Cyanamid Co. v. Geye, 79 S.W.3d 21 (Tex. 2002) (FIFRA does not preempt UDAP claims based on a label representation EPA has chosen not to review); Cole v. Central Valley Chemicals, Inc., 9 S.W.3d 207 (Tex. App. 1999) (no preemption of UDAP claims by farmer against herbicide seller based on seller's misrepresentations of performance, not product labeling). *But cf.* Peterson v. BASF Corp., 675 N.W.2d 57 (Minn. 2004) (claim that manufacturer's statements, not part of label, misrepresented uses that EPA had approved is not preempted). *See generally* National Consumer Law Center, Consumer Warranty Law § 1.4.9 (2d ed. 2001 and Supp.).

1475 Edelman v. Western Airlines, Inc., 892 F.2d 839 (9th Cir. 1989) (UDAP claim for wrongful discharge preempted).

1476 Hetzel v. Bethlehem Steel Corp., 50 F.3d 360 (5th Cir. 1995) (UDAP claim by worker who applied for and received compensation benefits under the Act is preempted; to permit UDAP-based relief along with benefits under the Act would conflict with federal policies).

1477 Jamal v. Travelers Lloyds of Texas Ins. Co., 129 F. Supp. 2d 1024 (S.D. Tex. 2001); Stapleton v. State Farm Fire & Cas. Co., 11 F. Supp. 2d 1344 (M.D. Fla. 1998); *see also* Messa v. Omaha Prop. & Cas. Ins. Co., 122 F. Supp. 2d 513 (D.N.J. 2000) (federal flood insurance law preempts state bad faith claims regarding settlement practices but not claims regarding fraud in sale of policies).

1478 42 U.S.C. § 7545(c)(4)(A).

1479 *In re* Methyl Tertiary Butyl Ether Prods. Liab. Litigation, 175 F. Supp. 2d 593 (S.D.N.Y. 2001).

1480 Viruses, Serums, Toxin, and Analogous Products Act, 21 U.S.C. §§ 151–159. *See* 57 Fed. Reg. 38758 (Aug. 27, 1992) (preemption statement of Animal and Plant Health Inspection Service).

1481 Symens v. Smithkline Beecham Corp., 152 F.3d 1050 (8th Cir. 1998); Lynbrook Farms v. Smithkline Beecham Corp., 79 F.3d 620 (7th Cir. 1996); Behrens v. United Vaccines, Inc., 189 F. Supp. 2d 945 (D. Minn. 2002).

1482 Flamingo Indus. (USA) Ltd. v. U.S. Postal Serv., 302 F.3d 985 (9th Cir. 2002).

Chapter 3 Demonstrating That a Practice Is a UDAP Violation

3.1 Getting Started

3.1.1 *How to Use This Manual to Prove a Violation*

Deception, unfairness, and unconscionability are broad and evolving standards that arguably apply to almost every consumer abuse. Consequently, consumer attorneys should always consider the applicability of a UDAP claim when a consumer complains of merchant, creditor, landlord, or other marketplace misconduct. In addition, a UDAP counterclaim may be appropriate in defending a collection action if an investigation uncovers abuse in the underlying sales transaction, the credit terms, or collection practices.

This chapter presents a methodology for demonstrating to a court that a practice is a UDAP violation. This chapter also evaluates the sources of precedent available for any UDAP case. Consumer attorneys should be familiar with this chapter as a conceptual framework no matter what type of UDAP action they bring.

The next two chapters will detail the specific holdings of existing UDAP precedent. Chapter 4 explains UDAP precedent of general applicability to most consumer transactions—when is a practice unfair, deceptive, or unconscionable, and types of deceptive misrepresentations and practices that are common to many types of cases. Chapter 5 provides a detailed analysis of existing UDAP precedent for specific types of transactions, from automobile sales to health spas, from debt collection procedures to landlord-tenant problems, from adhesion contracts to insurance.

In other words, Chapter 3 provides a conceptual framework and practical tips for researching UDAP precedent and for using this precedent in demonstrating a UDAP violation. Chapters 4 and 5 offer a research shortcut, by summarizing UDAP case law, guides, rules, and related materials. But attention to Chapters 4 and 5 by themselves can not substitute for a careful reading of Chapter 3.

3.1.2 *Expansive, Liberal Application of UDAP Statutes*

Because of the ever-changing characteristics of the marketplace and consumer abuse, consumer litigants may challenge practices that have not previously been definitively ruled deceptive. In these contexts, UDAP statutes should be applied expansively and liberally to protect consumers and reach innovative forms of marketplace misconduct.

There is ample precedent for so treating UDAP statutes. State UDAP statutes are broadly written with few limitations on covered practices, in order to be used to the utmost degree to eradicate all forms of unfair and deceptive practices.[1] UDAP statutes should be interpreted liberally to effect their object, to eradicate deception, to protect consumers, and to correct marketplace imbalances.[2] The law is remedial legislation and should be construed liberally.[3] Even

---

1 Hinchliffe v. American Motors Corp., 440 A.2d 810 (Conn. 1981); *aff'd per curiam*, 470 A.2d 1216 (1984); Falcon Associates, Inc. v. Cox, 699 N.E.2d 203 (Ill. App. Ct. 1998); American Buyers Club v. Hayes, 46 Ill. App. 3d 270, 361 N.E.2d 1383 (1977); Strahan v. Louisiana Dep't of Agriculture & Forestry, 645 So. 2d 1162 (La. Ct. App. 1994).

2 Sellinger v. Freeway Motor Home Sales, Inc., 110 Ariz. 573, 521 P.2d 1119 (1974); Young v. Joyce, 351 A.2d 857 (Del. 1975); Connick v. Suzuki Motor Co., 174 Ill. 2d 482, 675 N.E.2d 584 (1996); Perlman v. Time, Inc., 64 Ill. App. 3d 190, 380 N.E.2d 1040 (1978); American Buyers Club v. Hayes, 46 Ill. App. 3d 270, 361 N.E.2d 1383 (1977); State *ex rel.* Guste v. Crossroads Gallery, Inc., 357 So. 2d 1381 (La. Ct. App. 1978); State v. Hudson Furniture Co., 165 N.J. Super. 518, 398 A.2d 900 (App. Div. 1979); Kugler v. Banner Pontiac-Buick, Opel, Inc., 120 N.J. Super. 572, 295 A.2d 385 (Ch. Div. 1972); Fletcher v. Don Foss of Cleveland, Inc., 90 Ohio App. 3d 82, 628 N.E.2d 60 (1993); Commonwealth v. Monumental Properties, Inc., 459 Pa. 450, 329 A.2d 812 (1974); Commonwealth v. Handicapped Industries, Inc., No. 74-1131-09-5, Clearinghouse No. 26,027 (C.P. Bucks Cty., Pa. 1977); Elkins v. Microsoft Corp., 817 A.2d 9 (Vt. 2002) (UDAP statute intended to have "as broad a reach as possible"); Dick v. Attorney General, 83 Wash. 2d 684, 521 P.2d 702 (1974); Hockley v. Hargitt, 82 Wash. 2d 337, 510 P.2d 1123 (1973); State v. Ralph Williams' North West Chrysler Plymouth, Inc., 82 Wash. 2d 265, 510 P.2d 233 (1973); Testo v. Russ Dunmire Oldsmobile, Inc., 16 Wash. App. 39, 554 P.2d 349 (1976).

3 Hanson Hams, Inc. v. HBH Franchise Co., 2003 WL 22768687 (S.D. Fla. Nov. 7, 2003); Salmeron v. Highlands Ford Sales,

though civil penalties or multiple damages are authorized, the legislation is still remedial, not penal, and should be liberally construed.[4] By using a general prohibition and not attempting to define deception, the legislature attempts to give the statutory protection broad scope and prevent evasion of its provisions.[5] As with fraud, deception "is infinite in variety. The fertility of man's invention in devising new schemes of fraud is so great, that the courts have always

Inc., 271 F. Supp. 2d 1314 (D.N.M. 2003); Lozada v. Dale Baker Oldsmobile, Inc., 136 F. Supp. 2d 719 (W.D. Mich. 2001); Lorenzetti v. Jolles, 120 F. Supp. 2d 181 (D. Conn. 2000); *In re* Bryant, 111 B.R. 474 (E.D. Pa. 1990); Heastie v. Community Bank, 727 F. Supp. 1133 (N.D. Ill. 1989); *In re* Wiggins, 273 B.R. 839 (Bankr. D. Idaho 2001); *In re* Derienzo, 254 B.R. 334 (Bankr. M.D. Pa. 2000); *In re* Milbourne, 108 B.R. 522 (Bankr. E.D. Pa. 1989); State v. O'Neill Investigations, Inc., 609 P.2d 520 (Alaska 1980); Dunlap v. Jimmy GMC Tucson Inc., 136 Ariz. 338, 666 P.2d 83 (App. Ct. 1983); State *ex rel.* Bryant v. R & A Investment, 985 S.W.2d 299 (Ark. 1999); Wang v. Massey Chevrolet, 97 Cal. App. 4th 856, 118 Cal. Rptr. 2d 770 (2002); Schnall v. Hertz Corp., 93 Cal. Rptr. 2d 439 (Cal. App. 2000); Showpiece Homes Corp. v. Assurance Co. of Am., 38 P.3d 47 (Colo. 2001); Ganim v. Smith and Wesson Corp., 258 Conn. 313, 780 A.2d 98 (2001); Willow Springs Condominium Ass'n v. Seventh BRT Development Corp., 245 Conn. 1, 717 A.2d 77 (1998); Service Road Corp. v. Quinn, 241 Conn. 630, 698 A.2d 258 (1997); Hinchliffe v. American Motors Corp., 440 A.2d 810 (Conn. 1981), *aff'd per curiam*, 470 A.2d 1216 (1984); Lester v. Resort Camplands Int'l, Inc., 27 Conn. App. 59, 605 A.2d 550 (1992); Yale New Haven Hospital, Inc. v. Mitchell, 662 A.2d 178 (Conn. Super. Ct. 1995); State *ex rel.* Brady v. Publishers Clearing House, 787 A.2d 111 (Del. Ch. 2001); State *ex rel.* Brady v. Gardiner, 2000 Del. Super. LEXIS 208 (June 5, 2000); Norman Gershman's Things to Wear, Inc. v. Mercedes-Benz of North America, 558 A.2d 1066 (Del. Super. Ct. 1989), *aff'd on other grounds*, 596 A.2d 1358 (Del. 1991); W.S. Badcock Corp. v. Myers, 696 So. 2d 776 (Fla. Dist. Ct. App. 1996); Cummings v. Warren Henry Motors, Inc., 648 So. 2d 1230 (Fla. Dist. Ct. App. 1995); Catrett v. Landmark Dodge, Inc., 253 Ga. App. 639, 560 S.E.2d 101 (2002); Hawaii Community Fed. Credit Union v. Keka, 94 Haw. 213, 11 P.3d 1 (2000); *In re* Western Acceptance Corp., 788 P.2d 214 (Idaho 1990); Bank One Milwaukee v. Sanchez, 783 N.E.2d 217 (Ill. App. Ct. 2003) ("there is a clear mandate from the Illinois legislature that the courts of this State utilize the Act to the utmost degree in eradicating all forms of deceptive and unfair business practices and grant appropriate remedies to injured persons"); Falcon Associates, Inc. v. Cox, 699 N.E.2d 203 (Ill. App. Ct. 1998); Carl Sandburg Village v. First Condominium Dev. Co., 197 Ill. App. 3d 948, 557 N.E.2d 246 (1990); Johnston v. Anchor Organization, 621 N.E.2d 137 (Ill. App. Ct. 1993); Breckenridge v. Cambridge Homes, Inc., 616 N.E.2d 615 (Ill. App. Ct. 1993); People *ex rel.* Hartigan v. Lann, 587 N.E.2d 521 (Ill. App. Ct. 1992); Kennedy v. First Nat'l Bank, 551 N.E.2d 1002 (Ill. App. Ct. 1990); Ray v. Ponca/Universal Holdings, Inc., 913 P.2d 209 (Kan. App. 1995); Porras v. Bell, 18 Kan. App. 2d 569, 857 P.2d 676 (1993); Lowell Gas Co. v. Attorney General, 377 Mass. 37, 385 N.E.2d 240 (1979); Forton v. Laszar, 2000 Mich. App. LEXIS 38 (Feb. 22, 2000); Boubelik v. Liberty State Bank, 553 N.W.2d 393, 402 (Minn. 1996) (note that holding regarding coverage of banks has been superseded by statute); State *ex rel.* Ashcroft v. Marketing Unlimited, 613 S.W.2d 440 (Mo. Ct. App. 1981); Cox v. Sears, Roebuck & Co., 138 N.J. 2, 647 A.2d 454 (1994); Leon v. Rite Aid Corp., 340 N.J. Super. 462, 774 A.2d 764 (App. Div. 2001); Division of Consumer Affairs v. General Electric Co., 244 N.J. Super. 349, 582 A.2d 831 (App. Div. 1990); Levin v. Lewis, 179 N.J. Super. 193, 431 A.2d 157 (App. Div. 1981); Sulner v. General Accident Fire & Life Assurance Corp., 471 N.Y.S.2d 794 (Sup. Ct. 1984); Holley v. Coggin Pontiac, 43 N.C. App. 229, 259 S.E.2d 1 (1979); Einhorn v. Ford Motor Co., 48 Ohio St. 3d 27, 29, 548 N.E.2d 933 (1990); Credit Acceptance Corp. v. Banks, 1999 Ohio App. LEXIS 6058 (Dec. 16, 1999); Renner v. Derin Acquisition Corp., 111 Ohio App. 3d 326, 676 N.E.2d 151 (1996); Motzer Jeep Eagle, Inc. v. Ohio Attorney General, 95 Ohio App. 3d 183, 642 N.E.2d 20 (1994); State *ex rel.* Fisher v. Rose Chevrolet, 82 Ohio App. 3d 520, 612 N.E.2d 782 (1992); Charlie's Dodge, Inc. v. Celebrezze, 72 Ohio App. 3d 744, 596 N.E.2d 486 (1991); Renner v. Proctor & Gamble Co., 54 Ohio App. 3d 79, 561 N.E.2d 959 (1988); Liggins v. May Co., 53 Ohio Misc. 21, 373 N.E.2d 404 (C.P. Cuyahoga Cty. 1977), *related decision*, 44 Ohio Misc. 81, 337 N.E.2d 816 (C.P. Cuyahoga Cty. 1975); Brown v. Market Development, Inc., 41 Ohio Misc. 57, 322 N.E.2d 367 (C.P. Hamilton Cty. 1974); Commonwealth v. Monumental Properties, Inc., 459 Pa. 450, 329 A.2d 812 (1974); Commonwealth v. Percudani, 844 A.2d 35 (Pa. Commw. Ct. 2004); Commonwealth *ex rel.* Fisher v. Percudani, 825 A.2d 743 (Pa. Commw. Ct. 2003); Dibble v. Penn State Geisinger Clinic Inc., 42 Pa. D. & C.4th 225, 1999 Pa. D. & C. LEXIS 7 (C.P. 1999); State *ex rel.* McLeod v. Brown, 294 S.E.2d 781 (S.C. 1982); Young v. Century Lincoln-Mercury, Inc., 396 S.E.2d 105 (S.C. Ct. App. 1989); Haverlah v. Memphis Aviation, Inc., 674 S.W.2d 297 (Tenn. Ct. App. 1984); Miller v. Keyser, 90 S.W.3d 712 (Tex. 2002). *See also* §§ 2.1.3, *supra* (liberal construction of scope sections), 8.1, *infra* (liberal construction of remedies). *But see* Levine v. First Nat'l Bank of Commerce, 845 So. 2d 1189 (La. App. 2003) (applying "reasonably strict" construction to UDAP statute's scope provision); National Gypsum Co. v. Ace Wholesale, Inc., 738 So. 2d 128 (La. App. 1999) (strictly construing UDAP private cause of action provision). *But cf.* Gath v. M/A-Com, Inc., 802 N.E.2d 521 (Mass. 2003) (declining on policy grounds to recognize UDAP claim for spoliation of evidence).

4 State v. O'Neill Investigations, Inc., 609 P.2d 520 (Alaska 1980); Lingar v. Live-In Companions, Inc., 300 N.J. Super. 22, 692 A.2d 61 (App. Div. 1997).

5 Hanson Hams, Inc. v. HBH Franchise Co., 2003 WL 22768687 (S.D. Fla. Nov. 7, 2003) (concept of unfairness and deception is "extremely broad"); State *ex rel.* Bryant v. R & A Investment, 985 S.W.2d 299 (Ark. 1999) (catchall prohibition is not too vague for enforcement; statute must be broad to respond to fraud); Sportsmen's Boating Corp. v. Hensley, 192 Conn. 747, 474 A.2d 780 (1984); Simms v. Candela, 45 Conn. Super. 267, 711 A.2d 778 (1998) ("unfair trade practice statutes are to be interpreted dynamically rather than statically."); Clement v. St. Charles Nissan, Inc., 103 S.W.3d 898 (Mo. App. 2003); State *ex rel.* Webster v. Eisenbeis, 775 S.W.2d 276 (Mo. Ct. App. 1989); State *ex rel.* Danforth Independence Dodge, Inc., 494 S.W.2d 362 (Mo. Ct. App. 1973); Truex v. Ocean Dodge, Inc., 219 N.J. Super. 44, 529 A.2d 1017 (App. Div. 1987); Skeer v. EMK Motors, Inc., 187 N.J. Super. 465, 455 A.2d 508 (App. Div. 1982); New York Public Interest Research Group v. Insurance Information Institute, 140 Misc. 2d 920, 531 N.Y.S.2d 1002 (Sup. Ct. 1988), *aff'd*, 554 N.Y.S.2d 590 (1st Dept. 1990); Johnson v. Phoenix Mut. Life Ins. Co., 300 N.C. 247, 266 S.E.2d 610 (1980); Pennington v. Singleton, 606 S.W.2d 682 (Tex. 1980).

declined to define it . . . reserving to themselves the liberty to deal with it under whatever form it may present itself."[6]

UDAP statutes are designed to permit courts to proscribe new forms of deception,[7] encompassing wrongful business conduct in whatever context such activity might occur.[8] The law should be found broadly applicable to consumer transactions and should be construed in a manner consistent with economic reality.[9] A UDAP statute "is a statute of broad impact whose basic policy is to ensure an equitable relationship between consumers and persons engaged in business."[10] Thus, in enacting UDAP statutes, legislatures are raising the standards which the public has the right to expect from all business enterprises.[11] Judge Learned Hand, in describing the FTC's mission, was also explaining the purpose of state UDAP statutes when he said the role of the FTC is "to discover and make explicit those unexpressed standards of fair dealing which the conscience of the community may progressively develop."[12]

In some states, legislative history shows that the UDAP statute was intended to be among the strongest consumer protection laws in the nation.[13] It should be particularly easy in these states to argue that all doubts should be resolved in favor of the broadest interpretation of the statute.

6 Kerr, Fraud & Mistake 1 (7th ed. 1952) quoted approvingly in Kugler v. Koscot Interplanetary, Inc., 120 N.J. Super. 216, 293 A.2d 682 (Ch. Div. 1972); Cavette v. Mastercard International, Inc., 282 F. Supp. 2d 813 (W.D. Tenn. 2003). *See also* Cel-Tech Communications, Inc. v. Los Angeles Cellular Tel. Co., 83 Cal. Rptr. 2d 548, 973 P.2d 527 (1999); Barquis v. Merchants Collection Ass'n, 7 Cal. 3d 94, 496 P.2d 817, 101 Cal. Rptr. 745 (1972); Showpiece Homes Corp. v. Assurance Co. of Am., 38 P.3d 47 (Colo. 2001); Carl Sandburg Village v. First Condominium Dev. Co., 197 Ill. App. 3d 948, 557 N.E.2d 246 (1990); Commonwealth v. Monumental Properties, Inc., 459 Pa. 450, 329 A.2d 812 (1974).

7 Garland v. Mobil Oil Corp., 340 F. Supp. 1095 (N.D. Ill. 1972).

8 Barquis v. Merchants Collection Ass'n, 7 Cal. 3d 94, 496 P.2d 817, 101 Cal. Rptr. 745 (1972); State *ex rel.* Nixon v. Estes, 108 S.W.3d 795 (Mo. App. 2003).

9 Commonwealth v. Monumental Properties, Inc., 459 Pa. 450, 329 A.2d 812 (1974).

10 Veranda Beach Club v. Western Surety Co., 936 F.2d 1364 (1st Cir. 1991), *quoting* Heller v. Silverbranch Constr. Corp., 376 Mass. 621, 382 N.E.2d 1065, 1069 (1978). *Accord* State *ex rel.* Easley v. Rich Food Servs., Inc., 535 S.E.2d 84 (N.C. App. 2000).

11 *In re* Brandywine Volkswagen, Ltd., 312 A.2d 632 (Del. 1973); *see also* Lorenzetti v. Jolles, 120 F. Supp. 2d 181 (D. Conn. 2000) (UDAP statute makes practices actionable even if they are not in violation of any common law duty).

12 FTC v. Standard Education Society, 86 F.2d 692 (2d Cir. 1936), *rev'd in part*, 382 U.S. 112 (1937).

13 Moran, Shuster, Carignan & Knierim v. August, 43 Conn. Supp. 431, 657 A.2d 736 (1994), *aff'd on other grounds*, 232 Conn. 756, 657 A.2d 229 (1995); Zorba Contractors, Inc. v. Housing Authority of City of Newark, 282 N.J. Super. 430, 660 A.2d 550 (1995); Scott v. Mayflower Home Improvement Corp., 363 N.J. Super. 145, 831 A.2d 564 (Law Div. 2001).

3.2 *Per Se* Violations

3.2.1 Pleading Per Se *Violations*

The first step in showing that a practice is a UDAP violation is to determine if it is an automatic or "*per se*" UDAP violation. A *per se* or automatic UDAP violation occurs when a practice violates a specific UDAP guideline, and violation of that guideline automatically is a UDAP violation. Always try to prove that a practice is a *per se* violation, because the court will not have to determine whether a practice falls within a broad but not precisely defined notion of deception or unfairness. All the court will have to do is determine if the practice occurred is that described in the specific guideline. Courts have less discretion interpreting statutes with specific requirements than with expansive and dynamic terms such as deception and unfairness. In addition, sellers, creditors and other potential defendants usually settle quickly on terms favorable to the consumer if they are caught violating a clear-cut standard.

While automatic, *per se* violations should always be alleged where applicable, it is imperative to also *plead independently that the practice is generally unfair and/or deceptive*. Courts may find that a practice, no matter how unfair or deceptive, does not fit precisely into a specific *per se* prohibition. Without an independent claim of general deception or unfairness, the case will be lost. If both the *per se* violation and a general claim of deception or unfairness are pleaded, the consumer's attorney minimizes the chances of the case being dismissed before trial. Even if a *per se* claim is dismissed, the case is more likely to go to trial on the factual issue of whether the seller or creditor's practices fall within the broad prohibition of unfairness or deception.

For example, if a consumer challenges practices relating to the lease of an apartment, the consumer might allege a violation of a specific prohibition in the UDAP statute against "sellers" engaging in deceptive pricing, or the consumer might allege that the state's landlord-tenant legislation has been violated and that violation of this other statute is a *per se* UDAP violation. The court might find that while the UDAP statute applies generally to residential leases, the specific statutory prohibition against deceptive pricing relied upon in the complaint applies only to "sellers" narrowly, and not to landlords. The court might also find for technical reasons that the state landlord-tenant legislation has not been violated. Neither of these holdings should prevent the court from finding that, nevertheless, this practice violates the UDAP statute's general prohibition of deceptive practices. In this case, if the consumer had alleged only a *per se* violation, without alleging the practice was also independently deceptive, the entire case would have been dismissed.

3.2.2 Per Se *Violations Enumerated in the UDAP Statute*

3.2.2.1 Most UDAP Statutes Prohibit Specific Enumerated Practices

The first place to look for *per se* violations is in the list of enumerated prohibitions found in the UDAP statute itself. Most state UDAP statutes[14] prohibit itemized practices in what is sometimes called the statute's "laundry list" of enumerated deceptive practices. There is no substitute for simply reading the statute to see which prohibitions are enumerated. Because of the enormous variation from state to state, this manual will not analyze individual state UDAP laundry lists. This should not be a cue to ignore these prohibitions, but instead is an indication of how important it is for attorneys to examine their own UDAP statutes directly.

A consumer complainant is always on firmer footing if a challenged practice can be shaped to fall within one of the UDAP statute's enumerated prohibitions. If the court finds that the challenged practice falls within the itemized prohibition, then the practice *per se* violates the statute.[15] Since most state UDAP statutes are based on one of several model acts,[16] many states include similar items in these lists of specific prohibitions, so decisions from other states may help in interpreting the statutory language.

The simplicity of alleging a laundry list violation should not lull the practitioner into a false sense of security.[17] Always add an additional allegation that the practice is generally unfair or deceptive, in case the court finds for a technical reason that the practice does not fall within the enumerated prohibition specified in the statute's laundry list.

3.2.2.2 Practices Outside Specific UDAP Prohibitions Are Still UDAP Violations

The existence of a statutory laundry list does not foreclose challenges to practices not included in this list, nor does it prevent challenges to practices that fall just outside the definition of a specific statutory prohibition. Courts consistently hold that a statute's itemized prohibitions do not exhaust or limit the practices that violate a UDAP statute, and that other acts can also be unfair or deceptive.[18] UDAP statutes are not limited to specific enumerated practices since they are designed to permit the courts to prohibit new kinds of deception as novel practices arise.[19] Since "fraud is infinite," restricting the act's prohibitions to specifically enumerated practices would allow the statute to be "eluded by new schemes which the fertility of man's invention would contrive."[20]

3.2.3 Per Se *Violations of State UDAP Regulations*

Practices violating a state's UDAP regulations are another form of *per se* UDAP violation. Any violation of a UDAP regulation is a *per se* violation of the statute.[21] There is no

14 *See* Appx. A, *infra*.

15 *See* Rotello v. Ring Around Products Inc., 614 S.W.2d 455 (Tex. Civ. App. 1981).

16 *See* § 3.4.2, *infra* (discussion of legislative history of UDAP statutes).

17 *See* § 3.2.1, *supra*.

18 Minnesota *ex rel.* Hatch v. Fleet Mortg. Corp., 158 F. Supp. 2d 962 (D. Minn. 2001) (catchall prohibition is not limited to practices similar to enumerated practices); Garland v. Mobil Oil Corp., 340 F. Supp. 1095 (N.D. Ill. 1972); State v. O'Neill Investigation, Inc., 609 P.2d 520 (Alaska 1980); Showpiece Homes Corp. v. Assurance Co., 38 P.3d 47, 54 (Colo. 2001); District Cablevision Ltd. P'ship v. Bassin, 828 A.2d 714, 723 (D.C. 2003); Milford Lumber Co. v. RCB Realty, 780 A.2d 1259 (N.H. 2001); Lump v. Best Door & Window, Inc., 2002 Ohio App. LEXIS 1381 (Mar. 27, 2002); Commonwealth v. Monumental Properties, Inc., 459 Pa. 450, 329 A.2d 812 (1974); Myint v. Allstate Ins. Co., 970 S.W.2d 920 (Tenn. 1998); Ancira GMC Trucks and Motor Homes, Inc. v. Motor Vehicle Bd., 1999 Tex. App. LEXIS 6908 (Sept. 10, 1999). *See also* Showpiece Homes Corp. v. Assurance Co. of Am., 38 P.3d 47 (Colo. 2001). *Cf.* Jon-Don Prods., Inc. v. Malone, 2003 WL 1856420 (D.N.H. Apr. 10, 2003) (statutory list is non-exclusive, but other acts must be of same type). *But see* Coors v. Security Life of Denver Ins. Co., 2003 WL 22019815 (Colo. App. Aug. 28, 2003) (treating *Showpiece Homes* as *dictum* and declining to follow it; list of deceptive trade practices at Colo. Rev. Stat. § 6-1-105 is exclusive).

However, the Texas UDAP laundry list is exclusive. A private plaintiff can not sue under the broad prohibition of false, misleading, and deceptive acts and practices. Griffith v. Levi Strauss & Co., 85 F.3d 185 (5th Cir. 1996). The broad prohibition language is enforceable only by the attorney general. Tex. Bus. & Com. Code §§ 17.46(a), 17.47.

19 Garland v. Mobil Oil Corp., 340 F. Supp. 1095 (N.D. Ill. 1972). *See* § 3.1.2, *supra*.

20 State *ex rel.* Bryant v. R & A Investment, 985 S.W.2d 299 (Ark. 1999) (catchall was added because legislature could not be expected to envision every conceivable violation); Elder v. Coronet Ins. Co., 201 Ill. App. 3d 733, 558 N.E.2d 1312 (1990) (insurance company's practice violates UDAP statute even though insurance regulation on the subject did not prohibit the practice); Wood v. Collins, 725 So. 2d 531 (La. App. 1998) (rejecting argument that a violation of another statute is a UDAP violation only when the other statute so states); State *ex rel.* Webster v. Eisenbeis, 775 S.W.2d 276 (Mo. Ct. App. 1989) (purpose of general language is to "prevent easy evasions"); Commonwealth v. Monumental Properties, Inc., 459 Pa. 450, 329 A.2d 812, 826 n.4 (1974).

21 *In re* Belile, 209 B.R. 658 (Bankr. E.D. Pa. 1997); Jungkurth v. Eastern Fin. Servs., Inc., 74 B.R. 323 (Bankr. E.D. Pa. 1987); A. Secondino & Son, Inc. v. LoRicco, 215 Conn. 336, 576 A.2d 464 (1990); United Consumers Club, Inc. v. Attorney General, 119 Ill. App. 3d 701, 456 N.E.2d 856 (1983); Purity Supreme, Inc. v. Attorney General, 380 Mass. 762, 407 N.E.2d 297 (1980); Slaney v. Westwood Auto, Inc., 366 Mass. 688, 322 N.E.2d 768 (1975); Fenwick v. Kay Am. Jeep, Inc., 371 A.2d 13

defense that regulations have been substantially complied with or that complete compliance is impossible. Exceptions for substantial compliance or determinations that compliance is impossible are for the rulemaking authority to make, not the court.[22] A merchant's good faith does not excuse technical noncompliance.[23] A seller's lack of awareness of a UDAP regulation is no defense.[24] UDAP regulations are to be liberally construed.[25]

More than half the states authorize a state agency to promulgate UDAP regulations.[26] Most of these states have adopted regulations, some more extensively than others, that define with more specificity than the statute itself what particular actions violate the UDAP statute.[27] UDAP regulations are discussed in more detail in § 3.4.4, *infra*.

3.2.4 Finding of Common Law Fraud Necessitates Finding a UDAP Violation

The elements of common law fraud are more stringent than deception. If a court or jury finds for the consumer on a common law fraud count, and if the challenged practice is within the scope of a UDAP statute, the court must, as a matter of law, find a UDAP violation.[28]

3.2.5 UDTPA Violations as Per Se *UDAP Violations*

In Delaware, Georgia, Hawaii, Illinois, Maine, Nebraska, Ohio and Oklahoma, consumer attorneys should argue that a violation of the state's UDAP statute modeled after the Uniform Deceptive Trade Practices Act (UDTPA)[29] is a *per se* violation of the state's other UDAP statute. (Because UDTPA-type statutes do not have private damage remedies,[30] it is usually preferable to bring the action under other state UDAP statutes.) Thus a practice prohibited by the laundry list found in the UDTPA-type statute can be remedied by the state's other UDAP statute. Illinois' other UDAP statute, in fact, explicitly states that a violation of any of the enumerated deceptive practices in the Illinois UDTPA[31] is a *per se* violation of Illinois' other UDAP statute.[32] In the other states listed with both a UDTPA and another UDAP statute, courts should come to the same conclusion, since the UDTPA's laundry list is a legislative

---

(N.J. 1977); Leon v. Rite Aid Corp., 340 N.J. Super. 462, 774 A.2d 764 (App. Div. 2001); Huffmaster v. Robinson, 221 N.J. Super. 315, 534 A.2d 435 (Law Div. 1986); State v. Hudson Furniture Co., 165 N.J. Super. 516, 398 A.2d 900 (App. Div. 1979); Pet Dealers Ass'n v. Division of Consumer Affairs, 149 N.J. Super. 235, 373 A.2d 688 (App. Div. 1977); Martin v. Bullinger, 43 Ohio App. 3d 136, 539 N.E.2d 681 (1988); Peasley v. Clark, 1980 Ohio App. LEXIS 9809 (May 30, 1980) (failure to follow regulation regarding repairs entitled consumer to statutory damages even though regulation was new and shop spent much time on the repairs); Brown v. Deacon's Chrysler Plymouth, Inc., 14 Ohio Op. 3d 436 (Ct. App. 1979); Brown v. Spitzer Ford, Inc., 11 Ohio Op. 3d 84 (Ct. App. 1978); Weaver v. J.C. Penney Co., 53 Ohio App. 2d 165, 372 N.E.2d 633 (1977); Huff & Morse, Inc. v. Riordon, 118 Wis. 2d 1, 345 N.W.2d 504 (Ct. App. 1984); High Tech Heating & Air Conditioning, Inc. v. O'Connell, 206 Wis. 2d 677, 588 N.W.2d 706 (App. 1996) (unpublished and non-precedential, text available on LEXIS at 1996 Wisc. App. LEXIS 1417); State v. Menard, 121 Wis. 2d 199, 358 N.W.2d 813 (Ct. App. 1984); *see also* State v. Fonk's Mobile Home Park & Sales, 343 N.W.2d 820 (Wis. Ct. App. 1983) ("rule" and "order" are synonymous, and violation can be enjoined). *But see* State v. Dakotas Retail Hardware Ass'n, 279 N.W.2d 360 (Minn. 1979) (Minnesota UDAP statute specifies that UDAP rules provide only guidance to the courts).

22 Brown v. Deacon's Chrysler Plymouth, Inc., 14 Ohio Op. 3d 436 (Ct. App. 1979).

23 Huffmaster v. Robinson, 221 N.J. Super. 315, 534 A.2d 435 (Law Div. 1986); State v. Hudson Furniture Co., 165 N.J. Super. 516, 398 A.2d 900 (App. Div. 1979).

24 Fate v. Dick Callendar Buick, 1986 Ohio App. LEXIS 6878 (May 23, 1986).

25 Ganson v. Vaughn, 135 Ohio App. 3d 689, 735 N.E.2d 483 (1999).

26 *See* Appx. A, "State Remedies," *infra*.

27 *See* Appx. A, "State UDAP Regulations," *infra*.

28 Bond Leather Co. v. Q.T. Shoe Mfg. Co., 764 F.2d 928 (1st Cir. 1985) (Massachusetts law); Atlantic Purchasers, Inc. v. Aircraft Sales, Inc., 705 F.2d 712 (4th Cir. 1983) (North Carolina law); Volumetrics Medical Imaging, Inc. v. ATL Ultrasound, Inc., 2003 WL 21650004 (M.D.N.C. July 10, 2003); Computer Sys. Engineering, Inc. v. Quantel Corp., 571 F. Supp. 1365 (D. Mass. 1983), *aff'd*, 740 F.2d 59 (1st Cir. 1984); Pack & Process, Inc. v. Celotex Corp., 503 A.2d 646 (Del. Super. Ct. 1985); Zimmerman v. Northfield Real Estate, 156 Ill. App. 3d 154, 510 N.E.2d 409 (1986); Carter v. Mueller, 120 Ill. App. 3d 314, 457 N.E.2d 1335 (1983); Yost v. Millhouse, 373 N.W.2d 826 (Minn. Ct. App. 1985); Winston Realty Co. v. G.H.G. Inc., 331 S.E.2d 677 (N.C. 1985); Hardy v. Toler, 288 N.C. 303, 218 S.E.2d 342 (1975); State Properties, L.L.C. v. Ray, 574 S.E.2d 180 (N.C. Ct. App. 2002); Douglas v. Doub, 383 S.E.2d 423 (N.C. Ct. App. 1989); Jennings Glass Co. v. Brummer, 88 N.C. App. 44, 362 S.E.2d 578 (1987); Webb v. Triad Appraisal & Adjustment & Servs., Inc., 352 S.E.2d 859 (N.C. Ct. App. 1987).

29 *See* § 3.4.2.4, *infra*. Minnesota also has a UDTPA and a UDAP statute, but the consumer's private cause of action is created by a separate statute that applies equally to both, so there is no need to incorporate one into the other.

30 *See* Appx. A, *infra*. *See also* § 7.2.3, *infra*.

31 815 Ill. Comp. Stat. Ann. § 510/1 *et. seq.*

32 815 Ill. Comp. Stat. Ann. § 505/2. *See also* Pain Prevention Lab v. Electronic Waveform Labs, 657 F. Supp. 1486 (N.D. Ill. 1987); Wheeler v. Sunbelt Tool Co., 181 Ill. App. 3d 1088, 537 N.E.2d 1332 (1989); Duncavage v. Allen, 147 Ill. App. 3d 88, 497 N.E.2d 433 (1986); Crinkley v. Dow Jones & Co., 67 Ill. App. 3d 869, 385 N.E.2d 714 (1978). These cases find that a violation of Ill. Rev. Stat. ch. 121 1/2 § 311 (the codification of the Illinois UDTPA statute at the time) is a *per se* violation of Ill. Rev. Stat. ch. 121 1/2 § 262 (the codification at the time of Illinois' other UDAP statute). These two statutes have since been recodified at 815 Ill. Comp. Stat. Ann. §§ 510 and 505, respectively.

enumeration of deceptive practices, and since the other state UDAP statute prohibits deception.[33]

3.2.6 *Violation of the FTC Act, Other Laws Where the Statute Itself States a Violation Is Unfair or Deceptive*

A number of federal and state laws specifically indicate in the statute itself that a violation of the statute is an unfair or deceptive practice.[34] This should be a clear signal to a court that a violation of such a statute is a *per se* state UDAP violation. Thus a violation of the federal Fair Debt Collection Practices Act has been found to be a *per se* UDAP violation.[35]

Similarly, a violation of an FTC rule should be a *per se* state UDAP violation. An FTC rule defines with specificity unfair and deceptive practices and practices that are required to prevent such unfair and deceptive practices.[36] The rule itself will say that it is unfair or deceptive to engage in enumerated practices. While there is no private right of action under the FTC Act for violation of an FTC rule,[37] there should be a private right of action under the state UDAP statute because violation of an FTC rule is a *per se* violation of the state UDAP statute.[38]

Many state statutes do not merely state that a violation is an unfair or deceptive practice, but state that a violation constitutes a violation of the state UDAP statute. Such language leaves no room for doubt about the availability of a UDAP cause of action. The fact that a consumer protection statute may not itself provide for a private cause of action is irrelevant if it states that a violation constitutes a violation of the state UDAP statute; then the consumer has a private cause of action under the UDAP statute to redress the violation.[39] The Illinois UDAP statute provides that a violation of the state's Retail Installment Sales Act is a UDAP violation, but only if the violation is willful and material or the seller has committed three or more Retail Installment Sales Act violations in a year.[40]

3.2.7 *Violations of Other State, Federal Laws as* Per Se *UDAP Violations*

3.2.7.1 Importance of Finding Violations of Other Laws *Per Se* UDAP Violations

A critical issue is whether a violation of another statute, particularly one meant to protect the public, is a *per se* UDAP violation. Other consumer protection laws, especially when agency regulations and local ordinances are included, often have very specific requirements and prohibitions that can add concreteness to a UDAP claim.[41] A finding that a violation of federal or state law is a *per se* UDAP violation can open up one of the most effective uses of a UDAP statute.

Such a finding means that all state and federal laws intended to protect the public will incorporate UDAP remedies—often including attorney fees, treble damages or statutory damages. Indeed, a violation of a statute that does not create a private cause of action at all can be the basis of a UDAP claim.[42] These extra remedies are particularly

33 Witt v. Aetna United States Healthcare, Inc., 2000 U.S. Dist. LEXIS 13264 (D. Me. Sept. 14, 2000); Norman Gershman's Things to Wear, Inc. v. Mercedez-Benz of North America, 558 A.2d 1066 (Del. Super. Ct. 1989); *aff'd on other grounds*, 596 A.2d 1358 (Del. 1991); Kukui Nuts of Hawaii, Inc. v. R. Baird & Co., 789 P.2d 501 (Haw. Ct. App. 1990). *But see* Grand Ventures, Inc. v. Whaley, 632 A.2d 63 (Del. 1993) (discussing the distinctions between the injuries which Delaware's two statutes are designed to redress).

34 For example, Washington State has enacted at least 65 statutes that explicitly state that a violation is a UDAP violation. *See* Washington, Public Interest and Unfair or Deceptive Trade Practice, *Per se* violations of Ch. 19.86 RCW—Consumer Protection Act, Clearinghouse No. 51,965 (17 pp.) (Rev. Feb. 1995).

35 *See* § 3.2.7.3.6, *infra.*

36 15 U.S.C. § 57a(a)(1).

37 *See* § 9.1, *infra.*

38 Idaho Consumer Protection Regulations, Idaho Admin. Code § 04.02.01.033 (FTC rule violation is *per se* UDAP violation); Nieman v. DryClean U.S.A. Franchise Co., 178 F.3d 1126 (11th Cir. 1999) (Florida UDAP statute defines violation of FTC rules, including Franchise Rule, as violation), *cert. denied*, 528 U.S. 1118 (2000); Aurigemma v. Arco Petroleum Products Co., 734 F. Supp. 1025 (D. Conn. 1990) (violation of FTC Franchise rule is *per se* violation of Connecticut's UDAP statute); Morgan v. Air Brook Limousine, Inc., 211 N.J. Super. 84, 510 A.2d 1197 (Law Div. 1986) (violation of the FTC Franchise Rule is a *per se* deceptive and unconscionable practice); *see also* Texas Cookie Co. v. Hendricks & Peralta, Inc., 747 S.W.2d 873 (Tex. App. 1988) (deceptive to fail to disclose information required by FTC Franchise Rule). *But see* Zhang v. Southeastern Fin. Group, Inc., 980 F. Supp. 787 (E.D. Pa. 1997) (violation of FTC Credit Practices Rule did not amount to a violation of Pennsylvania's UDAP statute where Pennsylvania courts have consistently upheld confessions of judgment in consumer credit transactions); Leblanc v. Belt Center, Inc., 509 So. 2d 134 (La. Ct. App. 1987) (violation of FTC Franchise Rule not *per se* UDAP violation); *In re* Rice Lake Auto, Inc., 1989 Minn. App. LEXIS 178 (Feb. 21, 1989) (unpublished opinion) (failure to post Buyers Guide on used cars in violation of FTC rule not a state UDAP violation where state enacted similar law at later date).

39 McCoy v. MTI Vacations, Inc., 650 N.E.2d 605 (Ill. App. Ct. 1995); State v. Thompson, 2003 WL 1442417 (Tenn. Ct. App. Mar. 20, 2003) (unpublished, citation limited) (violation of the state's Health Club Act is *per se* violation of Consumer Protection Act).

40 Weather-Seal-Nu-Sash v. Marx, 596 N.E.2d 780 (Ill. App. Ct. 1992).

41 *See, e.g.*, Hammer v. Nikol, 659 A.2d 617 (Pa. Commw. 1995) (towing company's demand for fees in violation of city ordinance one factor in finding UDAP violation).

42 Hangarter v. Paul Revere Life Ins. Co., 2001 U.S. Dist. LEXIS 17975 (N.D. Cal. Sept. 21, 2001); Kasky v. Nike, Inc., 27 Cal. 4th 939, 45 P.3d 243, 119 Cal. Rptr. 2d 296, 303 (2002); Schnall

helpful in challenging violations of state landlord-tenant legislation, insurance laws, credit and collection legislation, and warranty laws, where private remedies are often limited or do not include attorney fees.

It is also always prudent to argue that the conduct causing the statutory violation is itself unfair or deceptive. The court may reject the *per se* approach or find no statutory violation, but still find that the conduct is unfair or deceptive.

The fact that some state statutes explicitly state that a violation constitutes a UDAP violation does not mean that violations of other statutes can not also be found to be UDAP violations.[43] The specific language that a violation constitutes a UDAP violation merely removes the court's discretion to decide whether a violation is a UDAP violation.[44]

3.2.7.2 UDAP Scope Issues May Limit Applicability of *Per Se* Approach

The enormous utility of a *per se* approach to violation of other state laws has one significant limitation. The challenged practice must be within the scope of the UDAP statute. There can be no *per se* UDAP violation for a violation of the landlord-tenant code if landlord practices are outside the scope of a particular UDAP statute. Similarly, if a state's courts find that the legislature intended for the state's insurance legislation to displace a UDAP statute's applicability to insurance practices, a violation of the insurance legislation is not a UDAP violation.

As a general rule, consumer transactions are within a UDAP statute's scope, and courts will not find that other state law displaces the UDAP statute's applicability. Nevertheless this issue should be examined whenever a litigant considers challenging a violation of another state law as a UDAP violation. Scope issues are treated in Chapter 2, *supra*. In particular, issues about whether certain other state regulations *preclude* a UDAP action are detailed in § 2.3.3, *supra*.

v. Hertz Corp., 93 Cal. Rptr. 2d 439 (Cal. App. 2000); Stevens v. Superior Court, 75 Cal. App. 4th 594, 89 Cal. Rptr. 2d 370 (1999); Yale New Haven Hospital, Inc. v. Mitchell, 662 A.2d 178 (Conn. Super. Ct. 1995). *But see* § 3.2.7.3.6, *infra*.

43 State *ex rel.* Stovall v. Confirmed.com, 38 P.3d 707 (Kan. 2002); Wood v. Collins, 725 So. 2d 531 (La. App. 1998). *But see* Darviris v. Petros, 59 Mass. App. Ct. 323, 795 N.E.2d 1196 (Mass. App. Ct. 2003) (violation of informed consent law is not a *per se* UDAP violation where other sections of same law are explicitly declared to be UDAP violations).

44 *Id.*

3.2.7.3 Precedent Finding Violations of Other Laws to Be *Per Se* UDAP Violations

3.2.7.3.1 *California, the District of Columbia, and Nevada UDAP statutes explicitly adopt and Texas UDAP statute explicitly rejects* per se *approach*

One of California's two UDAP statutes prohibits not only unfair or deceptive conduct, but also unlawful business conduct.[45] Thus the statute itself specifies that a violation of another statute is a *per se* UDAP violation. The state's courts find that such unlawful business activity includes anything that can properly be called a business practice and that at the same time is forbidden by law.[46] Even though the violation is an isolated act, it is still a *per se* UDAP violation.[47] At one time the California statute applied to a business practice, but now it applies to an act or practice. A violation of a federal statute[48] or another state's law[49] can be enough to trigger a violation of this California UDAP statute. Even though another statute provides its own enforcement mechanism, a violation of that statute is still a *per se* UDAP violation.[50]

45 Cal. Bus. & Prof. Code § 17,200 (West).

46 Summit Tech. v. High-Line Medical Instruments Co., 933 F. Supp. 918 (C.D. Cal. 1996); Microsoft Corp. v. A-Tech Corp., 855 F. Supp. 308 (C.D. Cal. 1994) (Cal. law); Cel-Tech Communications, Inc. v. Los Angeles Cellular Tel. Co., 83 Cal. Rptr. 2d 548, 973 P.2d 527 (1999); Stevens v. Superior Court, 75 Cal. App. 4th 594, 89 Cal. Rptr. 2d 370 (1999) (violation of insurance licensing statute); Farmers Ins. Exchange v. Superior Court, 2 Cal. 4th 377, 826 P.2d 730 (1992); Perdue v. Crocker Nat'l Bank, 38 Cal. 3d 913, 702 P.2d 503, 216 Cal. Rptr. 345 (1985); Committee on Children's Television, Inc. v. General Foods Corp., 35 Cal. 3d 197, 673 P.2d 660, 197 Cal. Rptr. 783, (1983); People v. McKale, 25 Cal. 3d 626, 602 P.2d 731, 159 Cal. Rptr. 811 (1979); Barquis v. Merchants Collection Ass'n, 7 Cal. 3d 94, 496 P.2d 817, 101 Cal. Rptr. 745 (1972); Hodgins v. Neiman Marcus Group, Inc., 34 Cal. App. 4th 1109, 41 Cal. Rptr. 2d 46 (1995); Cisneros v. U.D. Registry, 39 Cal. App. 4th 548, 46 Cal. Rptr. 2d 233 (1995); Hernandez v. Stabach, 145 Cal. App. 3d 309, 193 Cal. Rptr. 350 (1983); Hobby Industry Ass'n v. Younger, 101 Cal. App. 3d 358, 161 Cal. Rptr. 601 (1980). *But cf.* Bank of America v. Lallana, 64 Cal. Rptr. 2d 168 (Ct. App. 1997) (mere defective repossession notice is not a UDAP violation, but seeking a deficiency where the notice is defective is a UDAP violation), *superseded by, aff'd on other issues*, 19 Cal. 4th 203, 77 Cal. Rptr. 2d 910, 960 P.2d 1133 (1999).

47 Hangarter v. Paul Revere Life Ins. Co., 236 F. Supp. 2d 1069 (N.D. Cal. 2002).

48 Citizens for a Better Environment v. Union Oil of California, 996 F. Supp. 934 (N.D. Cal. 1997).

49 Schwartz v. Upper Deck Co., 967 F. Supp. 405 (S.D. Cal. 1997), *vacated on other grounds*, 104 F. Supp. 2d 1228 (S.D. Cal. 2000), *aff'd sub nom. Chaset v. Fleet/Skybox Int'l*, 300 F.3d 1083 (9th Cir. 2002).

50 Committee on Children's Television, Inc. v. General Foods Corp., 35 Cal. 3d 197, 673 P.2d 660, 197 Cal. Rptr. 783 (1983); People v. McKale, 25 Cal. 3d 626, 602 P.2d 731, 159 Cal. Rptr. 811 (1980); Barquis v. Merchants Collection Ass'n, 7 Cal. 3d

Conversely, the UDAP statute provides a remedy even if the other statute does not, as long as the other statute does not expressly bar enforcement via the UDAP statute.[51] But the reference to acts made illegal by other statutes is not a limitation on the UDAP statute's scope. Practices that are not made unlawful by another statute are still UDAP violations if they are unfair or fraudulent.[52]

The District of Columbia's UDAP statute provides a cause of action to any person seeking relief from "a trade practice in violation of a law of the District of Columbia."[53] The District's highest court has held that this language means that trade practices that violate other laws, including the common law, fall within the purview of the UDAP statute.[54]

Nevada's UDAP statute provides that a person engages in a deceptive trade practice by knowingly violating a state or federal statute or regulation relating to the sale or lease of goods or services.[55] On the other hand, the Texas legislature has specifically rejected finding a violation of another law as a *per se* UDAP violation unless the other law so declares.[56] Violations of FTC rules may nonetheless serve to establish violations of the Texas UDAP statute.[57]

3.2.7.3.2 Illinois UDAP statute has unique treatment for violation of credit statutes

The Illinois UDAP statute provides that any person who in one year commits three or more violations of certain specified credit statutes, including the Consumer Finance Act, the Consumer Installment Loan Act, the Motor Vehicle Retail Installment Sales Act, the Interest Act, or the wage garnishment and assignment laws, as determined in a civil or criminal proceeding, has engaged in a *per se* UDAP violation.[58] In addition, any person who in a judicial proceeding is found to have willfully and materially violated a state credit statute has committed a *per se* UDAP violation.[59]

3.2.7.3.3 State UDAP regulations finding statutory violations to be per se *UDAP violations*

Massachusetts and Missouri UDAP regulations specify that a violation of any federal or state statute intended to protect the public is a *per se* UDAP violation. For example, the Massachusetts regulation rules that it is *per se* unfair or deceptive to fail to comply with existing statutes, rules, or regulations meant for the protection of the public's health, safety, or welfare.[60] The regulation has survived a challenge based upon constitutional and statutory arguments.[61] Consequently, Massachusetts courts have little trouble finding a violation of other law a *per se* UDAP violation, simply pointing to the attorney general's regulation.[62] The attorney

---

94, 496 P.2d 817, 101 Cal. Rptr. 745 (1972); People *ex rel.* Lockyer v. Fremont Life Ins. Co., 104 Cal. App. 4th 508, 128 Cal. Rptr. 2d 463, 469 (2002) (UDAP remedies are cumulative to those imposed under other law); People v. Hill, 66 Cal. App. 3d 320, 136 Cal. Rptr. 30 (1977); People v. K. Sakai Co., 56 Cal. App. 3d 531, 128 Cal. Rptr. 563 (1976).

51 Hangarter v. Paul Revere Life Ins. Co., 2001 U.S. Dist. LEXIS 17975 (N.D. Cal. Sept. 21, 2001); Kasky v. Nike, Inc., 27 Cal. 4th 939, 45 P.3d 243, 119 Cal. Rptr. 2d 296, 303 (2002); Schnall v. Hertz Corp., 93 Cal. Rptr. 2d 439 (Cal. App. 2000); Stevens v. Superior Court, 75 Cal. App. 4th 594, 89 Cal. Rptr. 2d 370 (1999).

52 Cel-Tech Communications, Inc. v. Los Angeles Cellular Tel. Co., 83 Cal. Rptr. 2d 548, 973 P.2d 527 (1999). *See also* Klussman v. Cross-Country Bank, 2002 U.S. Dist. LEXIS 9387 (N.D. Cal. May 10, 2002), *vacated, remanded on other grounds*, 2003 WL 22088801 (9th Cir. Sept. 8, 2003).

53 D.C. Code § 28-3905(k)(1).

54 District Cablevision Ltd. P'ship v. Bassin, 828 A.2d 714 (D.C. 2003).

55 Nev. Rev. Stat. § 598.0923.

56 Tex. Bus. & Comm. Code § 17.43 (Vernon).

57 Howery v. Allstate Ins. Co., 243 F.3d 912 (5th Cir. 2001) (Texas law).

58 815 Ill. Comp. Stat. § 505/2E. *See* Weather-Seal-Nu-Sash v. Marx, 231 Ill. App. 3d 871, 596 N.E.2d 780, 173 Ill. Dec. 156 (1992).

59 815 Ill. Comp. Stat. § 505/2F.

60 Massachusetts Consumer Protection Regulations, 940 Mass. Reg. § 3.16. *Cf.* Sweeney v. Resolution Trust Corp., 16 F.3d 1 (1st Cir. 1994) (Massachusetts law) (banking regulation not meant to protect consumers, so violation of regulation not *per se* UDAP violation).

61 Commonwealth v. Mass. CRINC, Clearinghouse No. 40,637 (Mass. Super. Ct. 1984).

62 Dolan v. Schreiber & Assocs., 2002 U.S. Dist. LEXIS 6005 (D. Mass. Mar. 19, 2002) (FDCPA); Martin v. Sands, 62 F. Supp. 2d 196 (D. Mass. 1999) (regulations have the force of substantive law and make an FDCPA violation a UDAP violation); Wood v. General Motors Corp., 673 F. Supp. 1108 (D. Mass. 1987) (breach of implied warranty is *per se* UDAP violation); Tavares v. Sprunk (*In re* Tavares), 298 B.R. 195 (Bankr. D. Mass. 2003) (criminal usury statute); American Shooting Sports Council v. Attorney General, 429 Mass. 871, 711 N.E.2d 899 (1999) (recognizing attorney general's authority to promulgate regulations implementing other statutes); Calimlim v. Foreign Car Center, Inc., 392 Mass. 228, 467 N.E.2d 443 (1984) (violation of UCC warranty provisions is *per se* UDAP violation); Poncz v. Loftin, 607 N.E.2d 765 (Mass. App. Ct. 1993) (UDAP violation where landlord violates state Sanitary Code requirement that agreement for tenant to pay for heat and hot water be in writing); Montanez v. Bagg, 24 Mass. App. 954, 510 N.E.2d 298 (1987) (landlord-tenant law violation *per se* UDAP); Piccuirro v. Gaitenby, 20 Mass. App. 286, 480 N.E.2d 30 (1985) (violation of environmental code regulation *per se* UDAP violation); Goldstein Oil Co. v. C.K. Smith Co., 20 Mass. App. 243, 479 N.E.2d 728 (1985); MacGillvory v. W. Dana Bartlett, Ins. Agency, 14 Mass. App. 52, 436 N.E.2d 964 (1982); McGonagle v. Home Depot USA, Inc. 2002 WL 31956999 (Mass. Super. Nov. 26, 2002) (UDAP violation when store violates department of revenue regulation that prohibits taxes on amount of discount that is deducted from price of goods when consumer uses a coupon); Dannenmaier v. Brown, Clearinghouse No. 35,755 (Mass. Boston Housing Ct. 1983). *But see* Swenson v. Yellow Transportation, Inc., 2004 WL 1068880 (D. Mass. Apr. 12, 2004) (violation of the Federal Motor Carrier Safety Act regulation is not *per se* UDAP violation because the regulation

general, by promulgating a brief regulation, has effectively incorporated state UDAP remedies into virtually all Massachusetts and federal statutes. The UDAP regulation only applies to consumer transactions, not business-to-business transactions.[63]

Missouri has adopted a similar regulation.[64] It is unfair for any person to violate state or federal law intended to protect the public and where the violation presents a risk of or causes substantial injury to consumers.[65]

Mississippi now has a regulation that finds it a UDAP violation to violate any federal or state law, any FTC consent decree where the seller is a party to the decree, or any judicial order where the seller is a party or otherwise subject to the decree.[66] An Idaho regulation makes it a *per se* UDAP violation to violate any FTC rule or order, the Truth in Lending Act, or any state law that identifies conduct in trade or commerce as unfair or deceptive.[67]

3.2.7.3.4 Courts may determine that statutory violations are per se *UDAP violations*

Courts in Delaware,[68] New York,[69] North Carolina,[70] and Pennsylvania[71] also accept this *per se* approach, without the benefit of an attorney general regulation. The First Circuit also appears to adopt this approach for the New Hampshire UDAP statute.[72] A federal court interpreting the Hawaii UDAP statute also finds a Truth in Lending violation to be a *per se* UDAP violation.[73] Some Connecticut cases find violations of other statutes to be *per se* UDAP violations,[74] while other Connecticut cases hold that the circumstances surrounding the violation must be individually analyzed.[75]

Washington was the first state to hold squarely that a violation of another state statute is a *per se* UDAP viola-

---

is not directed to protection of consumers); Tavares v. Sprunk, 298 B.R. 195 (Bankr. D. Mass. 2003); Darviris v. Petros, 59 Mass. App. Ct. 323, 795 N.E.2d 1196 (Mass. App. Ct. 2003) (violation of informed consent law is not a *per se* UDAP violation where other sections of same law are explicitly declared to be UDAP violations); Lewis v. Walcott, 47 Mass. App. Ct. 394, 713 N.E.2d 394 (1999) (violation of rent control ordinance, without more, is not UDAP violation).

63 Knapp Shoes, Inc. v. Sylvania Shoe Mfg. Corp., 418 Mass. 737, 640 N.E.2d 1101 (1994); *In re* First New England Dental Centers, Inc., 291 B.R. 229 (Bankr. D. Mass. 2003).

64 15 Mo. Code Regs. § 60-8.090.

65 *But cf.* Ports Petroleum Co. v. Nixon, 37 S.W.3d 237 (Mo. 2001) (UDAP statute's remedies could not be applied to a statute that prohibited anti-competitive price-cutting).

66 Miss. Reg. 24-000-002 R12.

67 Idaho Consumer Protection Regulations, Idaho Admin. Code § 04.02.01.033.

68 Diamond Rental Center v. Rogers, Clearinghouse No. 43,670 (Del. J.P. Ct. Kent Cty. 1988).

69 *In re* Scrimpsher, 17 B.R. 999 (Bankr. N.D.N.Y. 1982).

70 Winston Realty Co. v. G.H.G. Inc., 331 S.E.2d 677 (N.C. 1985); State *ex rel.* Edminsten v. Zim Chemical Co., 45 N.C. App. 604, 263 S.E.2d 849 (1980). *See also* Stanley v. Moore, 454 S.E.2d 225 (N.C. 1995) (violation of Ejectment of Residential Tenants Act may be a UDAP violation).

71 *In re* Fricker, 115 B.R. 809 (Bankr. E.D. Pa. 1990); *In re* Stewart, 93 B.R. 878 (Bankr. E.D. Pa. 1988); *In re* Koresko, 91 B.R. 689 (Bankr. E.D. Pa. 1988); Russell v. Fidelity Consumer Discount Co., 72 B.R. 855 (Bankr. E.D. Pa. 1987); Moy v. Schreiber Deed Security Co., 572 A.2d 758 (Pa. Super. Ct. 1990) (violation of insurance laws may constitute UDAP violation, but consumer must first utilize Insurance Department complaint procedures); Gabriel v. O'Hara, 368 Pa. Super. 383, 534 A.2d 488, 494 n.20 (1988); Commonwealth v. Tolleson (I), 14 Pa. Commw. 72, 321 A.2d 664 (1971); Commonwealth *ex rel.* Zimmerman v. Nickel, 26 Pa. D. & C.3d 115 (C.P. Mercer Cty 1983); Iron & Glass Bank v. Franz, 9 Pa. D. & C.3d 419 (C.P. 1978); Commonwealth v. Armstrong, 74 Pa. D. & C.2d 579 (C.P. Phila. Cty. 1974). *But see* Griffin v. Allstate Ins. Co., 44 Pa. D. & C.4th 261, 1999 Phila. Cty. Rptr. LEXIS 22 (C.P. 1999) (no UDAP claim for violation of motor vehicle insurance statute that does not provide a remedy; allowing a UDAP remedy would permit insureds to opt for greater coverage after an accident, and interfere with statutory goal of cost containment).

72 Chronaik v. Golden Inv. Corp., 983 F.2d 1140 (1st Cir. 1993) (N.H. law).

73 Burnett v. Ala Moana Pawn Shop, Clearinghouse No. 46,771 (D. Haw. 1991), *aff'd*, 3 F.3d 1261 (9th Cir. 1993). *But see* Riopta v. Amresco Residential Mortgage Corp., 101 F. Supp. 2d 1326 (D. Haw. 1999).

74 U.S. on behalf of Polied Environmental Servs., Inc. v. Incor Group, Inc., 238 F. Supp. 2d 456 (D. Conn. 2002) (violation of state Miller Act); Hildabrand v. Difeo Partnership, Inc., 89 F. Supp. 2d 202 (D. Conn. 2000) (violation of Consumer Leasing Act would be a UDAP violation, but not shown here); Gibbs v. Southeastern Invest. Corp., 705 F. Supp. 738 (D. Conn. 1989) (violation of Mobile Home Act treated as UDAP violation); Tillquist v. Ford Motor Credit Co., 714 F. Supp. 607 (D. Conn. 1989) (violation of state banking regulations on collection practices is a UDAP violation); Dial Corp. v. Manghnani Inv. Corp., 659 F. Supp. 1230 (D. Conn. 1987); Wagner v. American Nat'l Educ. Corp., 1983 U.S. Dist. LEXIS 10287 (D. Conn. Dec. 30, 1983); Woronecki v. Trappe, 228 Conn. 574, 637 A.2d 783 (1994) (statute stated that a violation was unfair or deceptive practice); Graham v. Connecticut Nat'l Bank, Clearinghouse No. 36,598 (Conn. Super. Ct. 1983). *See also* Yale New Haven Hospital, Inc. v. Mitchell, 662 A.2d 178 (Conn. Super. Ct. 1995) (acts that violate the Federal Hill-Burton Act may create UDAP cause of action even if there is no private cause of action under the federal law; court's language suggests that some further analysis is required to determine if the federal law violation rises to the level of a UDAP violation).

75 Locascio v. Imports Unlimited, Inc., 309 F. Supp. 2d 267 (D. Conn. 2004) (finding violation of state title law to be UDAP violation after three-prong unfairness analysis); Jacobs v. Healey Ford-Subaru, Inc., 231 Conn. 707, 652 A.2d 496 (1995) (violation of retail installment sales act is not a *per se* UDAP violation); Gaynor v. Union Trust Co., 216 Conn. 458, 582 A.2d 190 (1990) (inadvertent failure to provide fully accurate redemption notice not a UDAP violation); Noble v. Marshall, 23 Conn. App. 227, 579 A.2d 594 (1990) (attorney's violation of Rules of Professional Responsibility does not give rise to a UDAP violation); Gibbs v. Mase, 11 Conn. App. 289, 526 A.2d 7 (1987) (breach of warranty not *per se* UDAP violation); Hunter v. Am. Honda Fin. Corp., 2000 Conn. Super. LEXIS 885 (Apr. 3, 2000) (isolated, inadvertent provision of 9-days rather than 10-days notice in violation of repossession statute not unfair).

tion.[76] The Washington Supreme Court applied a two-fold test to determine if violation of another statute is a *per se* UDAP violation: whether the practice is illegal or unlawful and whether it is against public policies as declared by the legislature or judiciary.[77]

Washington case law as to *per se* UDAP violations is now confusing, and is generally only of reference to Washington practitioners. It is clear that it is a *per se* violation in Washington to violate a statute whose violation the legislature has declared to constitute an unfair or deceptive act.[78] This is even the case where that other statute was enacted before the UDAP statute, such as the state's insurance legislation.[79] Less clear is the impact of a statutory violation where the legislation has not declared a violation of that statute to be unfair or deceptive. (Whether a statutory violation is a *per se* UDAP violation should not be confused with the separate question whether an action asserting that violation is in the public interest. Washington courts are in a small minority requiring that UDAP actions be in the public interest. A practice is *per se* in the *public interest* only if a statute is violated where that statute has a specific legislative declaration that the statute has a public interest impact.[80])

3.2.7.3.5 Courts that reject the per se *approach*

A few courts in other states have rejected the *per se* approach, finding no UDAP violation where there is only a technical disclosure violation of another law;[81] where the other law provides no private remedy;[82] or for warranty law violations which would effectively supplant UCC Article 2 with state UDAP law.[83] Iowa and Tennessee courts have

76 State v. Reader's Digest Ass'n, Inc., 81 Wash. 2d 259, 501 P.2d 290 (1972); *see also* Federated Am. Ins. Co. v. Strong, 102 Wash. 2d 665, 687 P.2d 68 (1984); Levy v. North American Co. for Life Ins., 90 Wash. 2d 846, 586 P.2d 845 (1978); Salois v. Mutual of Omaha Ins. Co., 90 Wash. 2d 355, 581 P.2d 1349 (1978); Sherwood v. Bellevue Dodge, Inc., 35 Wash. App. 741, 669 P.2d 1258 (1983); Rounds v. Union Bankers Ins. Co., 22 Wash. App. 613, 590 P.2d 1286 (1979).

77 Salois v. Mutual of Omaha Ins. Co., 90 Wash. 2d 355, 581 P.2d 1349 (1978); State v. Reader's Digest Ass'n, Inc., 81 Wash. 2d 259, 501 P.2d 290 (1972).

78 Industrial Indemnity Co. v. Kallevig, 114 Wash. 2d 907, 792 P.2d 520 (1990); Hangman Ridge Training Stables, Inc. v. Safeco Title Ins. Co., 105 Wash. 2d 778, 719 P.2d 531 (1986); Urban v. Mid-Century Ins., 905 P.2d 404 (Wash. App. 1995) (violation of unfair insurance practices statute or regulation is a *per se* UDAP violation).

79 Industrial Indemnity Co. v. Kallevig, 114 Wash. 2d 907, 792 P.2d 520 (1990).

80 Hangman Ridge Training Stables, Inc. v. Safeco Title Ins. Co., 105 Wash. 2d 778, 719 P.2d 531 (1986). *See* § 7.5.3.2, *infra*.

81 Anthony v. Country Life Mfg., L.L.C., 2003 WL 21540975 (7th Cir. July 2, 2003) (unpublished, citation limited) (nutrition bar manufacturer's inclusion of ingredient not approved by FDA as food additive not unfair practice where FDA had approved it as nutritional supplement, it was not dangerous, and it was clearly disclosed on label); Morales v. Walker Motors Sales, Inc., 162 F. Supp. 2d 786 (S.D. Ohio 2000) (failure to use type size specified by Holder Rule not material, so not a UDAP violation); Riopta v. Amresco Residential Mortgage Corp., 101 F. Supp. 2d 1326 (D. Haw. 1999) (failure to provide properly dated TIL rescission notice not a UDAP violation, as it was technical violation and did not create likelihood of confusion since deadline for rescission was stated elsewhere in the notice); Lamb v. M&M Assocs., 1998 U.S. Dist. LEXIS 13773 (S.D. Ohio Sept. 1, 1998) (failure to include validation notice required by FDCPA is not UDAP violation); Hawaii Community Fed. Credit Union v. Keka, 94 Haw. 213, 11 P.3d 1 (2000) (TIL violation is not automatically a UDAP violation; court must examine each case); Mid-America Nat'l Bank v. First Sav. & Loan Ass'n, 161 Ill. App. 3d 531, 515 N.E.2d 176 (1987) (disclosure violation of National Flood Act not *per se* UDAP violation); Holmes v. No. 2 Galesburg Crown Fin. Corp., 77 Ill. App. 3d 785, 396 N.E.2d 583, 33 Ill. Dec. 194 (1979); Celebrezze v. Fred Godard Ford, 27 Ohio App. 3d 301, 500 N.E.2d 881 (1985) (Consumer Leasing Act violation not *per se* UDAP violation); Griffin v. Allstate Ins. Co., 44 Pa. D. & C.4th 261, 1999 Phila. Cty. Rptr. LEXIS 22 (C.P. 1999) (no UDAP claim for violation of motor vehicle insurance statute that does not provide a remedy; allowing a UDAP remedy would permit insureds to opt for greater coverage after an accident, and interfere with statutory goal of cost containment).

82 Conboy v. AT&T Corp., 241 F.3d 242 (2d Cir. 2001) (no UDAP remedy for violation of state debt collection law, which state's highest court has construed not to provide a private cause of action); Hodges v. Koons Buick Pontiac GMC, Inc., 180 F. Supp. 2d 786 (E.D. Va. 2001) (failure to display buyer's order required by state law not UDAP violation); Nigh v. Koons Buick Pontiac GMC, Inc., 143 F. Supp. 2d 535 (E.D. Va. 2001) (no UDAP remedy for violation of statute that created its own comprehensive scheme of administrative remedies and did not afford a private cause of action), *aff'd on other grounds*, 319 F.3d 119 (4th Cir. 2003), *cert. granted on other issues*, 124 S. Ct. 1144 (2004); Tirado v. "Z" Frank, Inc., 522 F. Supp. 405 (N.D. Ill. 1981) (since only the state can bring motor vehicle installment sales act claims, no finding whether motor vehicle act has been violated, so no UDAP violation); Arca v. Colonial Bank & Trust Co., 637 N.E.2d 687 (Ill. App. Ct. 1994) (Consumer Fraud Act does not create private cause of action for violation of Motor Vehicle Retail Installment Sales Act where it is only enforceable by AG and state's attorney; violations can constitute common law fraud); Miles v. Shauntee, 664 S.W.2d 512 (Ky. 1984) (where there is no private action for housing code violations, such violations can not be *per se* UDAP violations); Griffin v. Allstate Ins. Co., 44 Pa. D. & C.4th 261, 1999 Phila. Cty. Rptr. LEXIS 22 (C.P. 1999) (no UDAP claim for violation of motor vehicle insurance statute that does not provide a remedy; allowing a UDAP remedy would permit insureds to opt for greater coverage after an accident, and interfere with statutory goal of cost containment).

83 Gibbs v. Mase, 11 Conn. App. 289, 526 A.2d 7 (1987) (breach of warranty not *per se* UDAP violation); Hershenson v. Lake Champlain Motors, Inc., 139 Vt. 219, 424 A.2d 1075 (1981) (warranty violation is not *per se* UDAP violation). *See also* Coffey v. Peoples Mortgage & Loan, 408 So. 2d 1153 (La. Ct. App. 1981) (violation of technical usury requirement is not *per se* violation); Holmes v. American States Ins. Co., 1 P.3d 552 (Utah 2000) (violation of motor vehicle statute would not be enough to establish UDAP violation, which must be proven on its own merits).

refused to allow plaintiffs to bring a UDAP challenge to a violation of the state cooling-off statute where that statute has its own enforcement scheme.[84] The Kansas Supreme Court has held that the illegal sale of medications over the Internet without a physical examination is not unconscionable without evidence of deception or unequal bargaining power.[85] A New Jersey court rejected the creative argument that acts inconsistent with a consumer leasing statute enacted after the transaction in question should be a *per se* UDAP violation because it demonstrated the legislature's view of what acts were unconscionable.[86]

A court has found that a statutory violation was not a *per se* UDAP violation where the seller had a meritorious but eventually unsuccessful argument that the statute was unconstitutional.[87] Similarly, a violation caused by a party's misinterpretation of a statute that had not yet been construed by the courts may not be a UDAP violation.[88] Consequently, consumer litigants bringing a case of first impression in a jurisdiction are advised to limit claims of *per se* UDAP violations to cases based on statutory violations that also involve serious consumer abuses, rather than purely technical violations of other statutes.[89]

84 State *ex rel.* Miller v. Santa Rosa Sales, 475 N.W.2d 210 (Iowa 1991); Laymance v. Vaughn, 857 S.W.2d 36 (Tenn. Ct. App. 1993).

85 State *ex rel.* Stovall v. DVM Enters., Inc., 62 P.3d 653 (Kan. 2003); State *ex rel.* Stovall v. ConfiMed.com, 272 Kan. 1313, 38 P.3d 707 (2002).

86 Biederman v. Mitsubishi Motors Credit of Am., Inc., 332 N.J. Super. 583, 753 A.2d 1251 (Law. Div. 2000).

87 Eamiello v. Liberty Mobile Home Sales, Inc., 208 Conn. 620, 546 A.2d 805 (1988).

88 Mangone v. U-Haul Int'l, 7 P.3d 189 (Colo. App. 1999) (rental vehicle company's sale of insurance without license could not be UDAP violation where legislature had not clearly specified that license was required); Stern v. Norwest Mortg., 179 Ill. 2d 160, 688 N.E.2d 99, 227 Ill. Dec. 762 (1997); Exeter v. GEICO Gen. Ins. Co., 2001 Wash. App. LEXIS 2630 (Dec. 3, 2001) (use of non-original equipment manufacturer [non-OEM] parts for repair estimates under auto insurance policy not a UDAP violation where it was an arguable interpretation of existing insurance law).

89 In Lookbill v. Mom's Mobile Homes, Inc., 16 Wash. App. 817, 559 P.2d 600 (1977), the court held that the failure to comply with the Retail Installment Act's disclosure requirements was not a *per se* UDAP violation where the evidence was insufficient to establish that the practice was injurious to the public. While this holding may be overturned by Salois v. Mutual of Omaha Ins. Co., 90 Wash. 2d 355, 581 P.2d 1349 (1978), it is indicative of courts' reluctance to award UDAP remedies for purely technical violations of other statutes. *See also* Pagani v. BT II, Ltd. Partnership, 24 Conn. App. 739, 592 A.2d 397 (1991) (a single proven instance of violation of state health regulations did not make a restaurant liable under UDAP for serving tainted food to an individual).

3.2.7.3.6 Examples of statutory violations found to be per se *UDAP violations*

Examples of statutes and regulations whose violation has been found to be a *per se* UDAP violation include:

- The state debt collection act or the federal Fair Debt Collection Practices Act;[90]
- The state insurance law[91] or state insurance licensing

90 Becker v. Montgomery, Lunch, 2003 WL 23335929 (N.D. Ohio Feb. 26, 2003) (FDCPA violations are UDAP violations); Irwin v. Mascott, 112 F. Supp. 2d 937 (N.D. Cal. 2000); Pabon v. Recko, 122 F. Supp. 2d 311 (D. Conn. 2000) (a violation of the state's Creditor's Collection Practices Act could constitute a violation of public policy and thereby form the basis for a UDAP claim); Watkins v. Peterson Enterprises, Inc., 57 F. Supp. 2d 1102 (E.D. Wash. 1999); Wagner v. American Nat'l Educ. Corp., 1983 U.S. Dist. LEXIS 10287 (D. Conn. Dec. 30, 1983); *In re* Scrimpsher, 17 B.R. 999 (Bankr. N.D.N.Y. 1982) (violation of Federal Fair Debt Collection Practices Act is automatic UDAP violation); GreenPoint Credit Corp. v. Perez, 75 S.W.3d 40 (Tex. App. 2002) (Texas Debt Collection Act expressly provides that a violation of that Act, in addition to allowing that Act's remedies, is a violation of the Texas UDAP statute), *vacated without op. pursuant to settlement*, 2003 Tex. LEXIS 50 (Tex. Apr. 24, 2003); Evergreen Collectors v. Holt, 60 Wash. App. 151, 803 P.2d 10 (1991); Connelly v. Puget Sound Collections, Inc., 16 Wash. App. 62, 553 P.2d 1354 (1976). *But see* Conboy v. AT&T Corp., 241 F.3d 242 (2d Cir. 2001) (violation of N.Y. debt collection statute is not N.Y. UDAP violation); King v. Int'l Data Servs., 2002 WL 32345923 (D. Haw. Aug. 5, 2002) (questioning whether FDCPA violation is necessarily a UDAP violation where state has adopted a separate debt collection law); Lamb v. M&M Assocs., 98 U.S. Dist. LEXIS 13773 (S.D. Ohio Sept. 1, 1998) (failure to include validation notice required by FDCPA is not UDAP violation).

91 Continental Ins. Co. v. Bahnan, 216 F.3d 150 (1st Cir. 2000) (consumers, but not business plaintiffs, can claim UNIP violation as Massachusetts UDAP violation); Peckham v. Continental Cas. Ins. Co., 895 F.2d 830 (1st Cir. 1990) (Mass. law); Hangarter v. Paul Revere Life Ins. Co., 2001 U.S. Dist. LEXIS 17975 (N.D. Cal. Sept. 21, 2001); Walts v. First Union Mortgage Corp., 686 N.Y.S.2d 428 (App. Div. 1999) (state mortgage insurance law); McKinnon v. International Fidelity Ins. Co., 704 N.Y.S.2d 774, 182 Misc. 2d 517 (N.Y. Sup. Ct. 1999) (state bail bond statute); Gabriel v. O'Hara, 368 Pa. Super. 383, 534 A.2d 488, 494 n.20 (1988); Hayden v. Mutual of Enumclaw Ins. Co., 141 Wash. 2d 55, 1 P.3d 1167 (2000) (insurance regulation); Industrial Indemnity Co. v. Kallevig, 114 Wash. 2d 907, 792 P.2d 520 (1990); Federated Am. Ins. Co. v. Strong, 102 Wash. 2d 665, 687 P.2d 68 (1984); Levy v. North American Co. for Life Ins., 90 Wash. 2d 846, 586 P.2d 845 (1978); Salois v. Mutual of Omaha Ins. Co., 90 Wash. 2d 355, 581 P.2d 1349 (1978); Anderson v. State Farm Mut. Ins. Co., 2 P.3d 1029 (Wash. App. 2000); Foltz v. Crum and Forster Personal Ins., 2000 Wash. App. LEXIS 677 (Apr. 24, 2000) (unreported, citation limited, full text available at 2000 Wash. App. LEXIS 1109); Evergreen Int'l, Inc. v. American Cas. Co., 52 Wash. App. 548, 761 P.2d 964 (1988); Rounds v. Union Bankers Ins. Co., 22 Wash. App. 613, 590 P.2d 1286 (1979). *See also* § 5.3.2.2.1, *infra* (violations of state unfair insurance practices laws as UDAP violations). *But see* Mackinac v. Arcadia Nat'l Life Ins. Co., 648 N.E.2d 237 (Ill. App. Ct. 1995) (failure to

laws; [92]
- State registration laws;[93]
- A state statute requiring a three-day cooling-off period for door-to-door sales;[94]
- The Telephone Consumer Protection Act's prohibition against junk faxes;[95]
- The federal Nutritional Labeling and Education Act;[96]
- The California Labor Code;[97]
- State and federal credit reporting laws;[98]
- Laws dealing with health and safety of tenants;[99]
- The Truth in Lending Act;[100]
- The Real Estate Settlement Procedures Act;[101]
- UCC repossession requirements,[102] or UCC warranty requirements;[103]
- The federal Lanham Act (trademark infringement);[104]
- Federal securities laws;[105]
- The state's proscription of lotteries by constitution and criminal statute;[106]
- The state's real estate broker's law;[107]
- State credit and usury laws;[108]

---

send credit insurance policy or certificate to consumer, contrary to state law, not a UDAP violation where defendants did not intend to induce plaintiff's reliance); Griffin v. Allstate Ins. Co., 44 Pa. D. & C.4th 261, 1999 Phila. Cty. Rptr. LEXIS 22 (C.P. 1999) (no UDAP claim for violation of motor vehicle insurance statute that does not provide a remedy; allowing a UDAP remedy would permit insureds to opt for greater coverage after an accident, and interfere with statutory goal of cost containment).

92 MacGillvary v. W. Dana Bartlett Ins. Agency, 14 Mass. App. 52, 436 N.E.2d 964 (1982).

93 Commonwealth v. Tolleson (I), 14 Pa. Commw. 72, 321 A.2d 664 (1971); Commonwealth v. Armstrong, 74 Pa. D. & C.2d 579 (C.P. Phila. Cty. 1974). *See also* § 4.7.8, *infra*.

94 Brown v. Banks, No. 944618, Clearinghouse No. 27,065 (Ohio C.P. Cuyahoga Cty. 1976). *But see* Laymance v. Vaughn, 857 S.W.2d 36 (Tenn. Ct. App. 1993).

95 Grady v. St. Cloud Mortg. Co., 2003 WL 21190993 (Ohio C.P. Mar. 7, 2003) (unpublished, citation limited).

96 Morelli v. Weider Nutrition Group, Inc., 712 N.Y.S.2d 551 (App. Div. 2000).

97 Hodgins v. Neiman Marcus Group, Inc., 34 Cal. App. 4th 1109, 41 Cal. Rptr. 2d 46 (1995).

98 Mendoza v. Experian Information Solutions, Inc., 2003 WL 2005832 (S.D. Tex. Mar. 25, 2003); Crane v. Trans Union, L.L.C., 282 F. Supp. 2d 311 (E.D. Pa. 2003); Cisneros v. U.D. Registry, 39 Cal. App. 4th 548, 46 Cal. Rptr. 2d 233 (1995); Commonwealth v. Source One Assocs., 436 Mass. 118, 763 N.E.2d 42 (2002).

99 Connelly v. New Haven Housing Authority, 8 Conn. L. Trib. No. 31 (Conn. Super. Ct. 1982), *rev'd on other grounds*, 213 Conn. 354, 567 A.2d 1212 (1990); Hardy v. Griffin, 41 Conn. Supp. 283, 569 A.2d 49 (Super. Ct. 1989) (lead paint restrictions); Miles v. Shauntee, 664 S.W.2d 512 (Ky. 1984) (where there is no private action for housing code violations, such violations can not be *per se* UDAP violations); Montanez v. Bagg, 24 Mass. App. 954, 510 N.E.2d 298 (1987); L'Esperance v. Benware, 830 A.2d 675 (Vt. 2003) (renting out house that did not comply with health and safety codes was UDAP violation). *But cf.* State v. Schwab, 693 P.2d 108 (Wash. 1985) (state landlord-tenant law with adequate private remedies preempts UDAP statute).

100 Herrara v. North & Kimball Group, Inc., 2002 U.S. Dist. LEXIS 2640 (N.D. Ill. Feb. 15, 2002) (TIL violation for which defendant would have TIL liability is also a UDAP violation); Burnett v. Ala Moana Pawn Shop, Clearinghouse No. 46,771 (D. Haw. 1991), *aff'd*, 3 F.3d 1261 (9th Cir. 1993); Cheshire Mortgage Servs., Inc. v. Montes, 223 Conn. 80, 612 A.2d 1130 (1992); W. S. Badcock Corp. v. Myers, 696 So. 2d 776 (Fla. Dist. Ct. App. 1997); Sims v. First Consumers Nat'l Bank, 303 A.D.2d 288, 758 N.Y.S.2d 284 (2003); Commonwealth *ex rel.* Zimmerman v. Nickel, 26 Pa. D. & C.3d 115 (C.P. Mercer Cty. 1983). *See also* Chow v. Aegis Mortg. Corp., 286 F. Supp. 2d 956 (N.D. Ill. Oct. 7, 2003) (inconsistent and potentially misleading TIL and RESPA disclosures may be UDAP violation); Hildabrand v. Difeo Partnership, Inc., 89 F. Supp. 2d 202 (D. Conn. 2000) (violation of Consumer Leasing Act would be a UDAP violation, but not shown here); Sims v. First Consumers Nat'l Bank, 303 A.D.2d 288, 758 N.Y.S.2d 284 (2003) (disclosure that is not clear and conspicuous as required by TILA may also be deceptive under state UDAP statute). *But see* Riopta v. Amresco Residential Mortgage Corp., 101 F. Supp. 2d 1326 (D. Haw. 1999) (TIL violation is not *per se* UDAP violation); Williams v. Gelt Fin. Corp., 232 B.R. 629, 642 (Bankr. E.D. Pa. 1999) (TIL violation not a *per se* UDAP violation without evidence of pervasive illegal conduct), *aff'd on other grounds*, 237 B.R. 590 (E.D. Pa. 1999); Pittman v. Allright Mortg. Co., 165 B.R. 586, 589 (Bankr. D. Md. 1994) (declining to hold that a technical violation of TILA was a *per se* violation); Hawaii Community Fed. Credit Union v. Keka, 94 Haw. 213, 11 P.3d 1, 17 n.15 (2000) (TIL violation is not automatically a UDAP violation; court must examine each case); Celebrezze v. Fred Godard Ford, Inc., 27 Ohio App. 3d 301, 303-04, 500 N.E.2d 881 (1985) (TIL violation is not always a UDAP violation).

101 *See* § 5.1.5.2, *infra*.

102 Graham v. Connecticut Nat'l Bank, Clearinghouse No. 36,598 (Conn. Super. Ct. 1983); Sherwood v. Bellevue Dodge, Inc., 35 Wash. App. 741, 669 P.2d 1258 (1983).

103 Wood v. General Motors Corp., 673 F. Supp. 1108 (D. Mass. 1987) (breach of implied warranty is *per se* UDAP); Calimlim v. Foreign Car Center, Inc., 392 Mass. 228, 467 N.E.2d 443 (1984); Goldstein Oil Co. v. C.K. Smith Co., 20 Mass. App. 243, 479 N.E.2d 728 (1985); *see also* Mikos v. Chrysler Corp., 158 Mich. App. 781, 404 N.W.2d 783 (1987). *But see* Gibbs v. Mase, 11 Conn. App. 289, 526 A.2d 7 (1987); Hershenson v. Lake Champlain Motors, Inc., 139 Vt. 219, 424 A.2d 1075 (1981).

104 Dial Corp. v. Manghnani Inv. Corp., 659 F. Supp. 1230 (D. Conn. 1987) (violation of 15 U.S.C. § 1114(1) *per se* UDAP violation).

105 Roskind v. Morgan Stanley Dean Witter & Co., 80 Cal. App. 4th 345, 95 Cal. Rptr. 2d 258 (2000).

106 State v. Reader's Digest Ass'n, Inc., 81 Wash. 2d 259, 501 P.2d 290 (1972).

107 Seligman v. First Nat'l Invest., Inc., 184 Ill. App. 3d 1053, 540 N.E.2d 1057 (1989). *But see* People *ex rel.* Daley v. Grady, 192 Ill. App. 3d 330, 548 N.E.2d 764 (1989).

108 Tavares v. Sprunk, 298 B.R. 195 (Bankr. D. Mass. 2003) (violation of state usury law is UDAP violation under Mass. UDAP regulation); *In re* Arsenault, 184 B.R. 864 (Bankr. D.N.H. 1995); *In re* Koresko, 91 B.R. 689 (Bankr. E.D. Pa. 1988); *In re* Stewart, 93 B.R. 878 (Bankr. E.D. Pa. 1988); Russell v. Fidelity Consumer Discount Co., 72 B.R. 855 (Bankr. E.D. Pa. 1987); Cheshire Mortgage Servs., Inc. v. Montes, 223 Conn. 80, 612 A.2d 1130 (1992); Diamond Rental Center v.

- State pawnshop laws;[109]
- A state's home improvement contractor law;[110]
- State motor vehicle title laws;[111]
- State lemon laundering laws;[112]
- A state civil commitment statute;[113]
- A state criminal law prohibiting debt pooling;[114]
- The FTC's Holder Rule;[115]
- The FTC's Cooling Off Period for Door-to-Door Sales Rule;[116]
- The FTC's Franchising Rule;[117]
- The FTC's Credit Practices Rule;[118]

Rogers, Clearinghouse No. 43,670 (Del. J.P. Ct. Kent Cty. 1988); Arca v. Colonial Bank & Trust Co., 637 N.E.2d 687 (Ill. App. Ct. 1994) (Consumer Fraud Act does not create private cause of action for violation of Motor Vehicle Retail Installment Sales Act where it is only enforceable by AG and state's attorney; violations can constitute common law fraud); Coffey v. Peoples Mortgage & Loan, 408 So. 2d 1153 (La. Ct. App. 1981) (violation of technical usury requirement is not *per se* violation); Nelson v. Associates Fin. Servs. Co., 659 N.W.2d 635 (Mich. App. 2003); Lemelledo v. Beneficial Management Corp., 289 N.J. Super. 489, 674 A.2d 582 (App. Div. 1996), *aff'd*, 150 N.J. 255, 696 A.2d 546 (1997) (violation of Consumer Loan Act protection against insurance packing is evidence of UDAP violation); Kidd v. Delta Funding Corp., 2000 N.Y. Misc. LEXIS 29 (Sup. Ct. Feb. 22, 2000) (creditor's imposition of illegal fees, and implicit representation that it was entitled to them, is deceptive), *denial of lender's motion for summary judgment aff'd*, 299 A.D.2d 457, 751 N.Y.S.2d 267 (2002); Safeguard Invest. Corp. v. Commonwealth by Colville, 44 Pa. Commw. 417, 404 A.2d 720 (1979); Commonwealth *ex rel.* Zimmerman v. Nickel, 26 Pa. D. & C.3d 115 (C.P. Mercer Cty. 1983). *See also* Chroniak v. Golden Inv. Corp., 983 F.2d 1140 (1st Cir. 1993) (N.H. law). *But see* Homziak v. Gen. Elec. Capital Warranty Corp., Clearinghouse No. 54,551 (Pa. C.P. Ct. May 21, 2001) (Motor Vehicle Sales Finance Act violation is not necessarily a UDAP violation); Bowman Plumbing, Heating & Elec., Inc. v. Logan, 59 Va. Cir. 446 (2002).

109 Keith v. Howerton, 2001 Tenn. App. LEXIS 646 (Aug. 28, 2001).

110 *In re* Armstrong, 288 B.R. 404 (E.D. Pa. 2003); Woronecki v. Trappe, 228 Conn. 574, 637 A.2d 783 (1994).

111 Locascio v. Imports Unlimited, Inc., 309 F. Supp. 2d 267 (D. Conn. 2004) (withholding title certificate, which would have revealed that car was rebuilt); Ramirez v. C.L.A.S., Inc., 2000 Mass. App. Div. LEXIS 6 (Jan. 13, 2002) (prohibition of sale of vehicle without a visible VIN); Nelson v. Assocs. Fin. Servs. Co., 659 N.W.2d 635 (Mich. App. 2002) (limits on prepayment penalties); Holiday Recreational Industries, Inc. v. Manheim Servs. Corp., 599 N.W.2d 179 (Minn. App. 1999) (affirming award of UDAP treble damages for violation of salvage title requirements; title branding requirements are contained in the state UDAP statute); Viene v. Concours Auto Sales, Inc., 787 S.W.2d 814 (Mo. App. 1990) (seller committed UDAP violation by failing to obtain inspection certificate required by salvage vehicle statute and misrepresenting that it had the certificate and that vehicle had passed inspection). *But see* Holmes v. American States Ins. Co, 2000 UT App. 85, 1 P.3d 552 (2000) (even if seller had violated title branding statute, court indicates it would not hold that alone to be a UDAP violation; court also finds buyer, a business purchaser, not covered by UDAP statute). *See generally* National Consumer Law Center, Automobile Fraud Ch. 6 (2d ed. 2003 and Supp.).

112 Alexander v. DaimlerChrysler Corp., 2004 WL 179369 (N.C. Super. Jan. 30, 2004). *See* National Consumer Law Center, Automobile Fraud Ch. 6 (2d ed. 2003 and Supp.).

113 Wingate v. Ridgeview Institute, Inc., 504 S.E.2d 714 (Ga. App. 1998) (false imprisonment of patient in alcohol rehabilitation facility, in violation of state commitment law and facility's internal discharge procedures, may be UDAP violation), *rev'd in part on other grounds*, 271 Ga. 512, 520 S.E.2d 445 (1999) (finding no violation of civil commitment laws).

114 *In re* Fricker, 115 B.R. 809 (Bankr. E.D. Pa. 1990).

115 *See* Iron & Glass Bank v. Franz, 9 Pa. D. & C.3d 419 (C.P. Allegheny Cty. 1978). *See* § 6.6.4.4.2, *infra.*

116 16 C.F.R. Part 429. *See* Swiss v. Williams, 445 A.2d 486, 184 N.J. Super. 243 (1982) (conclusion that plaintiff violated the New Jersey UDAP statute was buttressed by reference to federal legislation and FTC Cooling Off Period Rule regulating the same subject matter, which designates conduct engaged in by plaintiff, as an "unfair and deceptive act or practice"); Eastern Roofing and Aluminum Co. v. Brock, 320 S.E.2d 22, 70 N.C. App. 431 (1984) (failure to comply with rule constituted an unfair and deceptive act in violation of state UDAP statute). *See also* Collins v. Kingsmen Enterprises, Inc., 1995 WL 23345 (Ohio App. Jan. 19, 1995) (noting that Ohio provision is modeled after FTC rule and should be interpreted consistently).

117 16 C.F.R. Part 436. *See* Nieman v. Dryclean U.S.A. Franchise Co., Inc., 178 F.3d 1126 (11th Cir. 1999) (holding that violation of FTC Franchising Rule would be violation of Florida UDAP statute, but finding no cause of action because transaction occurred outside of U.S.); Aurigemma v. Arco Petroleum Products Co., 734 F. Supp. 1025 (D. Conn. 1990) (violation of FTC Franchise Rule is *per se* violation of Connecticut's UDAP statute); Morgan v. Airbrook Limousine, 510 A.2d 1197, 211 N.J. Super. 84 (1986) (failure of franchisor to provide franchisee with a rule disclosure statement was a *per se* unconscionable commercial practice in violation of state UDAP statute); Texas Cookie Co. v. Hendricks & Peralta, 747 S.W.2d 873 (Tex. App. 1988) (deceptive to fail to disclose information required by FTC Franchise Rule). *See also* Dollar Sys., Inc. v. Avcar Leasing Sys., Inc. 673 F. Supp. 1493 (C.D. Cal. 1987) (not finding *per se* violation but noting similarities between state requirements and FTC rule); Mark Fistos, *Per Se Violations of the Florida Deceptive And Unfair Trade Practices Act*, 76-May Fla. B.J. 62 (May 2002). *But see* Leblanc v. Belt Center, Inc., 509 So. 2d 134 (La. Ct. App. 1987) (violation of FTC Franchise Rule not *per se* UDAP violation).

118 16 C.F.R. Part 444. *Cf.* Provident Fin. Co. of North Carolina, Inc. v. Rowe, 399 S.E.2d 368, 101 N.C. App. 367 (1991) (in reversing dismissal of UDAP counterclaims, court did not reach the issue of whether violation of FTC rule is *per se* violation of UDAP statute, but noted that FTC rule declares certain practices to be unfair and deceptive, and UDAP statute and Consumer Finance Act generally prohibit unfair and deceptive trade practices; court remanded for determination of whether violation of FTC Credit Practices Rule is a violation of UDAP statute). *But see* Zhang v. Southeastern Fin. Group, Inc., 980 F. Supp. 787 (E.D. 1997) (violation of FTC rule prohibiting confession of judgment provisions did not violate Pennsylvania UDAP statute; Pennsylvania courts "routinely" uphold and enforce confessed judgments in connection with consumer transactions). *But cf.* Ken-Mar Fin. v. Harvey, 368 S.E.2d 646, 90 N.C. App. 362 (1988) (violation of FTC Credit Practices Rule not a UDAP violation because rule not in effect at time contract was entered into).

- The FTC's Used Car Rule;[119] and
- The FTC's Funeral Practices Rule.[120]

3.2.7.4 Arguing That a Statutory Violation Is a *Per Se* UDAP Violation

3.2.7.4.1 Violation of another statute as an unfair practice

In addition to the weight of case law precedent, there are many other reasons why courts should adopt the position that a violation of other state law is a *per se* UDAP violation. Where a state UDAP statute prohibits "unfair" practices, and not just "deceptive" practices, FTC and federal court authority indicates that a state court should find most state statutory violations to be *per se* "unfair." If conduct that is not proscribed by any statute may be found unfair under a UDAP statute, conduct squarely within the prohibitions of a consumer protection statute surely meets the unfairness standard.[121]

The current FTC definition of unfairness is that a practice is unfair if it:

- Causes substantial consumer injury;
- Not outweighed by countervailing benefits to consumers or competition;
- That could not be reasonably avoided by consumers.[122]

Under this definition, a violation of a state or federal statute should be unfair, particularly where the statutory violation causes consumer injury. (That is, there may be an argument that a mere technical violation with no resulting injury is not unfair.) There is no countervailing benefit to consumers or to competition to have companies violate state or federal law. Consumers are not reasonably expected to avoid law violations. State and federal law violations should thus almost always be unfair practices.

Many courts interpreting unfairness under state UDAP statutes do not use the current FTC unfairness definition, but use the old FTC "*S&H*" standard for determining when a practice is unfair.[123] Under this standard the following criteria are used to determine if a practice is unfair:

- Whether the practice offends public policy. Is it within at least the penumbra of some common law, statutory, or other established concept of unfairness?
- Whether the practice is immoral, unethical, oppressive, or unscrupulous.
- Whether the practice causes substantial injury to the consumer.

Under those criteria, statutory violations are also unfair, as they are certainly within the penumbra of a statutory concept of unfairness and offending the public policy embodied in the law violated. The Connecticut Supreme Court has followed this analysis in concluding that Truth in Lending and usury violations constitute UDAP violations, relying heavily on the legislative history of those statutes.[124]

The fact that a statutory violation is unfair under both the FTC's current unfairness approach and the "*S&H*" criteria is useful for consumer litigants in two ways. First, it gives solid support to the argument that a violation of state law meant to protect the public is a *per se* UDAP violation. But even if a court does not want to adopt a *per se* approach, the FTC unfairness analysis strongly supports a finding that a statutory law violation in the facts of a particular case is an unfair trade practice.

To be safe, consumer litigants should plead not only that the statutory violation is a *per se* UDAP violation, but that it is also an unfair practice. The consumer can then explain how the specific injury caused by the specific law violation fits within either the "*S&H*" unfairness standard or the FTC's current unfairness interpretation. In addition, the consumer should argue that the conduct that caused the

---

119 16 C.F.R. Part 455. *See* Barnes v. Holliday, 1990 WL 269884 (Conn. Super. June 6, 1990) (failure to comply with FTC Used Car Rule was a violation of Connecticut UDAP statute); Buskirk v. Harrell, 2000 WL 943782, *5 (Ohio App. June 28, 2000) (failure to post Buyers Guide in violation of Used Car Rule is violation of Ohio UDAP statute, which requires the court to give weight to FTC orders and rules); Cummins v. Dave Fillmore Car Co., 1987 WL 19186 (Ohio App. Oct. 27, 1987); Rubin v. Gallery Auto Sales, 1997 WL 1068459, *5 (Ohio Com. Pl. June 9, 1997) (failure to complete and display Buyer's Guide as required by FTC Used Car Rule is a violation of Ohio UDAP statute); Milton v. Riverside Auto Exchange, Clearinghouse No. 55453 (Montgomery County Court, Ohio, Aug. 27, 1991) (UDAP statute allows rescission of used car sale where seller did not post Buyer's Guide). *See also* § 3.4.5.1, *infra* (general discussion of precedential value of FTC interpretations). *But see* *In re* Rice Lake Auto, Inc., 1989 Minn. App. LEXIS 178 (Feb. 21, 1989) (unpublished opinion) (failure to post Buyers Guide on used cars in violation of FTC rule not a state UDAP violation where state enacted similar law at later date).

120 16 C.F.R. Part 453. *See* North Haven Funeral Home, Inc. v. Sortito, 1995 WL 630996 (Conn. Super. Oct. 19, 1995) (furnishing funeral goods and services without accurate written information as to the cost for each specific item before such goods are purchased or services rendered is an unfair or deceptive act or practice under FTC rule and is violation of Connecticut UDAP statute).

121 Keith v. Howerton, 2001 Tenn. App. LEXIS 646 (Aug. 28, 2001); *In re* Arsenault, 184 B.R. 864 (Bankr. D.N.H. 1995); Yale New Haven Hospital, Inc. v. Mitchell, 683 A.2d 1362 (Conn. Super. Ct. 1995) (Hill-Burton Act).

122 *See* § 4.3.2, *infra.*

123 *See* § 4.3.3.5, *infra.*

124 Cheshire Mortgage Servs., Inc. v. Montes, 223 Conn. 80, 612 A.2d 1130 (1992). *But see* Carroll v. Butterfield Health Care, Inc., 2003 WL 22462604 (N.D. Ill. Oct. 29, 2003) (weighing factors but finding violation of Medicaid Act not UDAP violation).

statutory violation is unfair and deceptive in its own right. This alleviates any danger that the court may find that the conduct does not violate the statute or that a statutory violation is not unfair.

A good example of this is a state UDAP action against a pawn shop charging a 240% interest rate and not clearly disclosing this.[125] The court found the pawnshop's Truth in Lending violation to be a *per se* UDAP violation. As alternative grounds, the court found that charging 240% interest was excessive and thus unfair, whether or not TIL or state usury laws were violated. The court also found that the failure to disclose the 240% interest rate would confuse a consumer as to the true nature of the transaction and was thus deceptive.[126]

Another helpful argument can sometimes be based on the purpose section of a statute. Many laws include a preliminary provision that recites the purposes of the law or legislative findings about the conditions that create a need for the law. If a statute says that it was enacted to prevent unfair or deceptive acts, then surely a violation is a UDAP violation.

A court may hesitate to hold that a seller is subject to UDAP remedies for violating a statute that does not itself provide any private remedies.[127] It is important to go beyond the mere fact that the statute does not provide its own remedy, and ask whether a UDAP remedy would be inconsistent with the goals of the statute. Only in rare instances will allowing the consumer a UDAP remedy be inconsistent with the other statute.[128]

3.2.7.4.2 Violation of another statute as deceptive practice

In states whose UDAP statute only prohibits deceptive practices, consumers are in a different position in arguing for a *per se* standard. It is deceptive for a seller to fail to disclose that its conduct violates state or federal law.[129] In addition, it can be argued that a seller who violates federal or state law has confused the consumer as to his or her legal rights,[130] or has misrepresented the seller's legal rights.[131] Further, by entering into a transaction, the seller makes an implicit or explicit representation that its conduct is legal, which is deceptive if in fact it is violating the law.[132]

Again, the consumer litigant should argue both that the statutory violation is *per se* deceptive, and, even if it is not, that the conduct causing the statutory violation is deceptive in its own right. It may also be possible to uncover deceptive tactics that the seller used to induce the consumer to enter into such a disadvantageous transaction.[133]

3.3 Proving UDAP Claims Without *Per Se* Violations

3.3.1 Introduction

In many situations, an unscrupulous practice does not specifically violate an enumerated prohibition in the UDAP statute, a UDAP regulation, or some other statute. The practice may still be a UDAP violation, but the consumer litigant must take extra steps to demonstrate liability to the court. When a practice must be proved deceptive or unfair without the aid of a *per se* theory, the consumer litigant should adopt a three-step approach.

---

125 Burnett v. Ala Moana Pawn Shop, Clearinghouse No. 46,771 (D. Haw. 1991), *aff'd*, 3 F.3d 1261 (9th Cir. 1993). *But see* Riopta v. Amresco Residential Mortgage Corp., 101 F. Supp. 2d 1326 (D. Haw. 1999) (TIL violation not *per se* UDAP violation, given technical nature of violation and fact that TILA, unlike UDAP statute, is a strict liability statute).

126 Burnett v. Ala Moana Pawn Shop, Clearinghouse No. 46,771 (D. Haw. 1991), *aff'd*, 3 F.3d 1261 (9th Cir. 1993).

127 *See* § 3.2.7.3.4, *supra*.

128 *See, e.g.*, Griffin v. Allstate Ins. Co., 44 Pa. D. & C.4th 261, 1999 Phila. Cty. Rptr. LEXIS 22 (C.P. 1999) (detailed analysis of how providing UDAP remedy for violation of motor vehicle insurance statute that does not provide a remedy would permit insureds to opt for greater coverage after an accident, and interfere with statutory goal of cost containment).

129 FTC v. Canada Prepaid Legal Servs., Inc., 5 Trade Reg. Rep. (CCH) ¶ 24,839 (D. Wash. Dec. 11, 2000) (TRO against company that failed to disclose illegality of its sale of bonds); Karst v. Goldberg, 623 N.E.2d 1348 (Ohio App. 1993) (deceptive not to disclose that satellite dish's unscrambling device violated federal law). *But cf.* Hauschildt v. Beneficial Wisconsin, Inc., 2003 WL 23289788 (W.D. Wis. Dec. 17, 2003) (charging for credit life insurance in excess of statutory cap not deceptive; no indication that plaintiff argued that silence was misleading).

130 Demitropoulos v. Bank One, 924 F. Supp. 894 (N.D. Ill. 1996); State *ex rel.* Miller v. Pace, 677 N.W.2d 761 (Iowa 2004) (failure to disclose that securities and seller are unregistered is deceptive); State *ex rel.* Nixon v. Beer Nuts, 29 S.W.3d 828 (Mo. App. 2000) (failure to disclose illegality of sale of alcohol); Iron & Glass Bank v. Franz, 9 Pa. D. & C.3d 419, Clearinghouse No. 31,037 (C.P. Allegheny Cty. 1978). *See also* Nelson v. Associates Fin. Servs. Co., 659 N.W.2d 635 (Mich. App. 2003). *But see* Conboy v. AT&T Corp., 241 F.3d 242 (2d Cir. 2001) (abusive collection calls not a violation of UDAP statute's prohibition of deception).

131 Keith v. Howerton, 2001 Tenn. App. LEXIS 646 (Aug. 28, 2001).

132 Demitropoulos v. Bank One, 924 F. Supp. 894 (N.D. Ill. 1996); Benik v. Hatcher, 358 Md. 507, 750 A.2d 10 (2000); Golt v. Phillips, 308 Md. 1, 517 A.2d 328 (1986); Bisson v. Ward, 628 A.2d 1256 (Vt. 1993) (by renting out apartment, landlord impliedly represented to tenant that it was in compliance with law). *But see* Miller v. Pacific Shore Funding, 224 F. Supp. 2d 977 (D. Md. 2002) (settlement statement was not implicit representation that listed fees were legal); *cf.* Delaware Solid Waste Authority v. Eastern Shore Environmental, Inc., 2002 Del. Ch. LEXIS 34 (Mar. 28, 2002) (no violation where company was in fact operating lawfully).

133 *See* § 5.1.6.3, *infra*.

3.3.2 Develop the Facts

The most critical aspect of any UDAP case is to develop the facts. Unfairness is a question of fact for the jury or, in a non-jury case, the judge to decide.[134] Too often consumer attorneys rely on one specific representation or practice to build a case. A careful investigation of advertising, written promotional materials, oral claims, key facts not disclosed, sales techniques, training provided to seller employees, contract terms, credit terms, and collection practices often demonstrates a whole range of systematic, widespread, unscrupulous practices.

Relying on just one part of the scheme as the basis of a UDAP action harms a consumer's case in two regards. By putting all the consumer's eggs in one basket, the chances of the action being dismissed at the summary judgment stage or lost because of credibility or evidentiary issues at trial are greatly increased. Conversely, allegations of numerous oral misrepresentations, deceptions in written materials, and unfair contract terms and sales techniques will almost certainly survive a summary judgment challenge.

Second, painting a broader and more detailed picture will influence the judge and jury to the consumer's benefit. Intent, scienter, bad faith, or a widespread pattern are not necessary elements to a UDAP case, but they are helpful in convincing a court or jury to award an adequate remedy. Strong evidence concerning one deceptive practice may increase the credibility of the consumer's evidence as to other practices and undermine the defense, particularly where the defense involves a denial of the occurrence of any deceptive practices. Putting on a broader case may also make it easier to locate additional victims as corroborating witnesses.[135]

3.3.3 Practice-Specific Precedent

The second step, after fully developing the facts, is to produce for the court specific precedent that holds the exact practice or some similar practice to be a UDAP violation. Courts may feel uneasy dealing with broad statutes generally prohibiting deception or unfairness, or even the UDAP standards developed by the FTC, federal and state courts. To the extent that cases factually on point exist, it is always helpful to provide the court with this precedent.

Possible sources of this precedent are a state's UDAP regulations and case law, FTC rules, guides, and cases, and case law and regulations from other states; these sources of precedent are evaluated in § 3.4, *infra*. Chapter 5 analyzes in detail all of this precedent as it applies to specific transactions and practices—from automobile repair to health spas, from mobile home parks to debt collection, from adhesion contracts to insurance problems. Chapter 4 analyzes precedent prohibiting certain deceptive practices that are found in a number of different types of transactions—such as deceptive pricing, quality misrepresentations, high pressure sales, and failure to deliver.

3.3.4 Point Out General UDAP Standards

3.3.4.1 Introduction

The third step in showing a UDAP violation is to explain to the court how the practice violates the UDAP statute's general standards of deception or unfairness. By impressing the court with the broad, flexible standards of unfairness and deception,[136] the consumer's specific precedent will be that much more compelling, and the consumer can still show that a challenged practice is a UDAP violation even where the practice has never been challenged before or where there is not specific precedent.[137] The existence of a listing of itemized prohibitions in a UDAP statute does not foreclose challenges to practices that are not included or that fall just outside the definition of a specific statutory prohibition.[138]

FTC and state guides and rules will also define with specificity certain unfair or deceptive practices. Even if a practice is closely related to the subject matter of a rule or guide, but not specifically prohibited by the rule, the court can still find the practice falls within the general standards of unfairness and deception.[139] An FTC announcement that particular conduct is clearly violative of the FTC Act does not mean that all other conduct is permitted. State courts will even go beyond what the FTC was willing to do, ruling a practice deceptive where the FTC specifically decided a practice was not necessarily unfair or deceptive.[140]

---

134 DeMotses v. Leonard Schwartz Nissan, 22 Conn. App. 464, 578 A.2d 144 (1990); Edart Truck Rental v. B. Swirsky & Co., 23 Conn. App. 137, 579 A.2d 133 (1990); Wood v. Collins, 725 So. 2d 531 (La. App. 1998) (court has broad discretion to determine unfairness). *See* § 7.9.2.3, *infra.*

135 See §§ 7.7–7.9, *infra*, for additional tips for pleading and presenting UDAP cases.

136 *See* § 3.1.2, *supra.*

137 Allied Grape Growers v. Bronco Wine Co., 203 Cal. App. 3d 432, 249 Cal. Rptr. 872 (1988) (seller can be liable for UDAP violation even if no precedent exists).

138 *See* § 3.2.2.2, *supra.*

139 Brown v. LaSalle Northwest Nat'l Bank, 820 F. Supp. 1078 (N.D. Ill. 1993).

140 Ramson v. Layne, 668 F. Supp. 1162 (N.D. Ill. 1987) (state UDAP law goes beyond FTC consent order); Bailey Employment Sys. Inc. v. Hahn, 545 F. Supp. 62 (D. Conn. 1982); People *ex rel.* Hartigan v. Unimax, Inc., 168 Ill. App. 3d 718, 523 N.E.2d 26, *appeal denied*, 122 Ill. 2d 593, 530 N.E.2d 263 (1988); Perlman v. Time, Inc., 64 Ill. App. 3d 190, 380 N.E.2d 1040 (1978); Purity Supreme, Inc. v. Attorney General, 380 Mass. 762, 407 N.E.2d 297 (1980). *See also* Brown v. LaSalle Northwest Nat'l Bank, 820 F. Supp. 1078 (N.D. Ill. 1993).

3.3.4.2 Deception as a Broad Standard

The general principle that UDAP statutes should be expansively and liberally applied indicates that deception is a broad standard.[141] The most important factor in determining whether a practice is deceptive is not whether precedent has found the same practice to be deceptive, but whether the sales activity or representations have the tendency to mislead unsophisticated consumers. Courts should examine the totality of the sales transaction, including the manner and context in which representations are made. They should consider the vulnerability of the consumer and they should determine whether the practice has the capacity to deceive the actual consumer, not whether the practice would mislead a particularly sophisticated buyer. The broad language of a UDAP statute indicates that the legislation is not limited to precise acts which can be readily catalogued.[142]

The UDAP standard of deception in most states does not require actual deception, only that a practice has a capacity or is likely to deceive.[143] Ambiguous, partially true, even literally true statements can be deceptive.[144] Subsequent clarification does not prevent deception.[145] The parol evidence rule, disclaimers, and other contract or even tort defenses do not apply to a deception claim.[146] The UDAP statute's deception standard is violated even if the deceptive claim is subsequently clarified or contradicted by other statements or documents. A practice can be common throughout an industry and still be deceptive.[147] The failure to disclose a material fact is deceptive.[148] Thus silence is deceptive. Vulnerable consumers are specially considered in determining whether a practice misleads.[149]

The UDAP deception standard is broad enough to cover acts that are unintentional,[150] done in good faith,[151] or stopped once the seller discovers them to be deceptive.[152] The seller's state of mind is not the real issue, nor is whether a statement is literally true or false determinative.[153]

Consequently, consumer attorneys should actively investigate all claims and representations made to the consumer, and determine what material facts were not disclosed. Deception standards are examined in more detail at Chapter 4, *infra*.

3.3.4.3 Unfairness and Unconscionability as Evolving, Expansive Concepts

Over thirty UDAP statutes prohibit unfair practices and about ten UDAP statutes proscribe unconscionable acts.[154] Neither of these standards is precisely defined. Instead they are expansive, evolving concepts that can be used to challenge novel forms of consumer abuse. The lack of precedent should not discourage consumers from aggressively utilizing these concepts.[155]

The United States Supreme Court has found unfairness to be a broader standard than deception and has noted with approval the following criteria for determining whether a practice is unfair:

- Whether the practice offends public policy: whether it is within at least the penumbra of some common law, statutory, or other established concept of unfairness.
- Whether the practice is immoral, unethical, oppressive, or unscrupulous.
- Whether the practice causes substantial injury to consumers.[156]

The FTC unfairness standard in recent years has become even more flexible. A practice is unfair if it causes substantial consumer injury that the consumer could not reasonably have avoided and the injury is not outweighed by countervailing benefits to competition.[157]

Consumer litigants can thus apply the unfairness standard to practices that violate public policy, situations where a seller or creditor has disproportionate market power compared to the consumer, contexts where there are imbalances in knowledge between the seller and buyer, one-sided provisions in adhesion contracts, and cases of high-pressure or oppressive sales tactics.[158] Unfairness is a developing concept and should be treated as such by consumer litigants.

Unconscionability is a standard similar to unfairness, and it is just as open-ended. A practice may be unconscionable if unfair advantage is taken of a consumer's experience or

---

141 Thacker v. Menard, Inc., 105 F.3d 382 (7th Cir. 1997) (Illinois law) ("broad protective philosophy"); Gennari v. Weichert Co. Realtors, 148 N.J. 582, 691 A.2d 350 (1997); People of State of New York v. Apple Health & Sports Clubs, Ltd., Inc., 206 A.D.2d 266, 613 N.Y.S.2d 868 (1994).

142 *See* § 3.1.2, *supra*.

143 Skinder-Strauss v. Massachusetts Continuing Legal Education, 914 F. Supp. 665 (D. Mass. 1995). *See also* Cobb v. Monarch Fin. Co., 913 F. Supp. 1164 (N.D. Ill. 1995) (to be deceptive under Illinois UDAP statute, a practice need only be misleading, but it is necessary to show both deception and unfairness); § 4.2.9, *infra*.

144 *See* § 4.2.13, *infra*.

145 *See* § 4.2.17, *infra*.

146 *See* §§ 4.2.15, 4.2.16, *infra*.

147 *See* § 4.2.8, *infra*.

148 *See* § 4.2.14, *infra*.

149 *See* § 4.2.11, *infra*.

150 *See* §§ 4.2.4, 4.2.5, *infra*.

151 *See* § 4.2.6, *infra*.

152 *See* § 4.2.7, *infra*.

153 *See* § 4.2.13, *infra*.

154 *Id.*

155 *See, e.g.*, People v. James, 122 Cal. App. 3d 25, 177 Cal. Rptr. 110 (1981).

156 FTC v. Sperry & Hutchinson Co., 405 U.S. 233 (1972).

157 See § 4.3, *infra* for a more detailed discussion of these forms of unfairness.

158 *Id.*

capacity, if the merchant knows of the consumer's inexperience or inability to receive anticipated benefits, if goods are grossly overpriced or agreements substantially one-sided, if consumers are required to waive legal rights, or if agreements contain terms prohibited by law.[159] Courts and legislatures have been careful not to limit the concept of unconscionability in order to allow it to be applied to novel forms of consumer oppression. Unfairness and unconscionability are examined in more detail at Chapter 4, *infra*.

3.4 Sources of UDAP Precedent and Guidelines

3.4.1 The Statute

Helpful in establishing a practice as a UDAP violation are state and FTC case law, guides, rules, and related materials finding the same or similar practices to be deceptive, unfair, or unconscionable. This section will describe and evaluate these sources of UDAP rulings and offer various research suggestions.

The first source of guidance in a UDAP case must be the statute itself. All state UDAP statutes are summarized in Appendix A, *infra*. Of course, practitioners must not merely rely on the summary of their own statute, but must have a copy of the most recent version of the statute and analyze it. They also must have the version of the statute that was in effect at the time of the challenged practice. Subsequent amendments typically are not retroactively applied.[160] Links to the current versions of state UDAP statutes are included in Appendix A, *infra*, and on the companion CD-Rom to this volume.

It is important to scrutinize the statute for several reasons. Available remedies must be determined to make sure the UDAP count is worth pursuing. The statute's scope must always be checked to see if it applies to the challenged practice, particularly where the practice involves credit, real estate or rentals, professionals, insurance, business opportunities, or regulated industries.[161] Procedural preconditions, such as notice letters, must be examined.

Most especially, what the statute prohibits must be examined. Does the statute also prohibit unfair practices, or just deceptive practices? Is there a laundry list of enumerated prohibitions and is there also a catch-all phrase at the end of the itemized prohibition? What does the catch-all phrase prohibit? Is there an intent or knowledge requirement for any of the enumerated prohibitions?

159 See § 4.4, *infra* for a more detailed discussion of unconscionability.

160 *See* § 7.4, *infra*.

161 *See* Ch. 2, *supra*.

3.4.2 Legislative History; Model Statutes

3.4.2.1 General

State legislative history for a UDAP statute is often sparse. This can be expanded to some extent by the legislative history of the model legislation upon which a UDAP statute is based. Local law reviews written at the time of enactment are often helpful to courts in determining the legislature's objectives.

3.4.2.2 Unfair Trade Practices and Consumer Protection Law

Many state UDAP statutes are patterned after the Unfair Trade Practices and Consumer Protection Law, developed by the Federal Trade Commission in conjunction with the Committee on Suggested State Legislation of the Council of State Governments. The Unfair Trade Practices and Consumer Protection Law offers three alternative versions, giving states an option concerning which trade practices are prohibited. The central prohibition of unfair and deceptive acts and practices in Alternative #1 is patterned exactly after section 45 of the Federal Trade Commission Act and prohibits unfair methods of competition and unfair or deceptive acts and practices. Fourteen states have enacted this version.[162]

Alternative #2, prohibiting false, misleading or deceptive practices, is not presently adopted in its exact form by any state, but a few UDAP statutes bear some resemblance to it.[163] Alternative #3 enumerates thirteen specific prohibited practices, including "any other practice that is unfair or deceptive."[164] Nine states have enacted statutes similar to

162 Conn. Gen. Stat. § 42-110b; Fla. Stat. Ann. § 501.204 (West) (also includes unconscionability); Haw. Rev. Stat. § 480-2; 815 Ill. Comp. Stat. 505/2 (includes additional language); La. Rev. Stat. Ann. § 51:1405 (West); Me. Rev. Stat. Ann., tit. 5, § 207 (West); Mass. Gen. Laws Ann. ch. 93A, § 2; Mont. Code Ann. § 30-14-103; Neb. Rev. Stat. § 59-1602; N.C. Gen. Stat. § 75-1.1; S.C. Code Ann. § 39-5-20 (Law. Co-op.); Vt. Stat. Ann. tit. 9, § 2453; Wash. Rev. Code § 19.86.020; W. Va. Code § 46A-6-104.

163 For example, Ky. Rev. Stat. § 367.170 and Tex. Bus. & Com. Code Ann. tit. 2, § 17.46 (Vernon) were originally patterned after this alternative but have since been amended in important respects.

164 The first 12 enumerated practices deal with: passing off; approval; affiliation; geographic origin; characteristics, uses, benefits or quantities; altered or used goods; standard, quality or grade; disparagement; bait and switch; unavailability of advertised goods; deceptive pricing; and other conduct leading to confusion or misunderstanding. These itemized practices are largely derived from an earlier model law, the Uniform Deceptive Trade Practices Act, adopted in 1964 by the National Conference on Uniform Laws. *See* § 3.4.2.4, *infra*. The addition of the thirteenth item, "any other unfair or deceptive practice," makes this alternative similar to the first alternative of the Unfair

the third alternative but itemize additional or different prohibited practices and use varying language concerning the statute's applicability to other unfair or deceptive practices.[165]

A number of other state UDAP statutes are patterned directly after the Federal Trade Commission Act itself, and not the model Unfair Trade Practices and Consumer Protection Law.[166] Utah has a statute prohibiting "unfair methods of competition" dating from 1937, thus antedating even the 1938 Wheeler Lea amendments to the FTC Act that added the prohibition against unfair or deceptive practices.[167]

Consequently, drafting comments and other legislative history of the Unfair Trade Practices and Consumer Protection Law may prove relevant to interpreting many state UDAP statutes. There are two major sources of these drafting comments: Federal Trade Commission explanations of the proposed legislation as forwarded to the Council of State Governments[168] and publications by the Council of State Governments that largely adopted the FTC proposal.[169]

3.4.2.3 Uniform Consumer Sales Practices Act

The National Conference of Commissioners on Uniform State Laws and the American Bar Association have adopted the Uniform Consumer Sales Practices Act.[170] This uniform act, which differs from all three versions of the Unfair Trade Practices and Consumer Protection Law, has been adopted in three states.[171] The drafting comments for this model act may also prove helpful.[172]

3.4.2.4 Uniform Deceptive Trade Practices Act

A third model act, the Uniform Deceptive Trade Practices Act, was adopted in 1964 and revised in 1966 by the National Conference on Uniform Laws.[173] One or the other version is presently law in seven states[174] and forms the basis for UDAP statutes in six other states.[175] Both versions of the model law have accompanying drafting comments.[176]

3.4.2.5 Consumer Fraud Acts and Other Models

Seven states have enacted a different form of legislation, called Consumer Fraud Acts. While some of these statutes have since been amended to prohibit unfair or unconscionable acts, as originally drafted they prohibit "deception, fraud, false pretense, false promise, misrepresentation or knowing concealment, suppression or omission of any material fact with intent that others rely."[177]

The remaining state UDAP statutes borrow from various models and include their own special features.[178] Even statutes listed here as following uniform or model acts usually depart in important respects from the model.

Trade Practices and Consumer Protection Law, although arguably somewhat more restrictive.

165 Alaska Stat. § 45.50.471; Ga. Code Ann. § 10-1-393; Idaho Code § 48-603; Md. Com. Law Code Ann. §§ 13-101, 13-301; Miss. Code Ann. 75-24-5; N.H. Rev. Stat. Ann. § 358A:2; Pa. Stat. Ann. tit. 73, §§ 201-2(4), 201-3; R.I. Gen. Laws §§ 6-13.1-1, 6-13.1-2; Tenn. Code Ann. § 47-18-104.

166 Cal. Civ. Code § 1750 and Cal. Bus. & Prof. Code § 17200; Wis. Stat. § 100.20.

167 Utah Code Ann. § 13-5-2.5.

168 Letter from FTC Chairman Dixon to Phillip Hughes, Deputy Director, Bureau of the Budget, Clearinghouse No. 31,035A (Apr. 23, 1969). *See also* FTC News Release, *FTC Proposes That States Enact Laws* (July 7, 1966), reproduced on the companion CD-Rom to this volume.

169 Council of State Governments, 1970 Suggested State Legislation, Unfair Trade Practices and Consumer Protection Cases—Revision (Vol. XXIX), Clearinghouse No. 31,035B, reproduced on the companion CD-Rom to this volume.

170 The model act and drafting comments are reprinted in 7A Uniform Laws Annotated Pt. 1 71 (2002) and also Council of State Governments, 1973 Suggested State Legislation (Vol. XXXII), Clearinghouse No. 31,036.

171 Ohio Rev. Code Ann. § 1345.01 (since amended to prohibit unfair practices also); Utah Code Ann. § 13-11-1. In addition, Kan. Stat. Ann. § 50-624 follows the model act in most respects.

172 *See* National Conference of Commissioners on Unfair State Laws, Uniform Consumer Sales Practices Act with prefatory Note and Comments, Clearinghouse No. 43,087 (1972), reproduced on the companion CD-Rom to this volume. The drafting comments are also printed in 7A Uniform Laws Annotated Pt. 1 71 (2002).

173 *See* 7A Uniform Laws Annotated Part 1 (1999) for the text, case law, and comments concerning the model act.

174 Del. Code Ann. tit. 6, § 2531; Ga. Code Ann. § 10-1-370; Haw. Rev. Stat. ch. 481A; 815 Ill. Comp. Stat. § 510/1; Me. Rev. Stat. Ann. tit. 10, § 1211; Ohio Rev. Code Ann. § 4165.01; Okla. Stat. Ann. tit. 78, § 51.

175 Colo. Rev. Stat. § 6-1-101; Minn. Stat. Ann. § 325D.43 (one of several UDAP-type statutes); Neb. Rev. Stat. § 87-301 (one of two UDAP statutes); Nev. Rev. Stat. § 598.0903; N.M. Stat. Ann. § 57-12-1; Or. Rev. Stat. § 646.605.

176 *See* 7A Uniform Laws Annotated Part 1 281, 322 (1999 and Supp.) (the UDTPA has been withdrawn from recommendation as of 2000 because it is "obsolete").

177 Ariz. Rev. Stat. Ann. § 44-1522; Ark. Stat. Ann. § 4-88-108; Del. Code. Ann. tit. 6, § 2513; Iowa Code § 714.16; Mo. Rev. Stat. § 407.020; N.J. Stat. Ann. § 56:8-2; N.D. Cent. Code § 51-15-02. *See also* the Illinois Consumer Fraud Act, 815 Ill. Comp. Stat. § 505/2. The Iowa Consumer Fraud Act was in part patterned after the Illinois Consumer Fraud Act. *See* State *ex rel.* Miller v. Hydro Mag Ltd., 436 N.W.2d 617 (Iowa 1989).

178 UDAP statutes not previously cited in this section and falling into this category are: D.C. Code § 28-3901; Ind. Code Ann. § 24-5-0.5-1; Mich. Comp. Laws § 445.901; N.Y. Gen. Bus. Law § 349; S.D. Comp. Laws Ann. § 37-24-1; Va. Code § 59.1-196; Wyo. Stat. § 40-12-101.

3.4.3 State UDAP Case Law

3.4.3.1 Keeping Up with In-State UDAP Cases

Attorneys with consumer caseloads should consider keeping an up-to-date digest of their state's own UDAP case law. For some states, such as Massachusetts, California, Connecticut, Illinois, New York, Pennsylvania, Texas, Ohio, and Washington, such a digest will be quite an undertaking due to the large number of cases. But in these states, the attorney general's consumer protection division or a private publisher often has already prepared such a digest.[179] State annotated statutes and practice digests are other good research shortcuts. A Commerce Clearing House (CCH) publication also gives the full text and a brief summary of each state's law.[180] This manual also summarizes all states' UDAP case law as it relates to particular topics.

Often the most useful state precedent will be unreported lower court cases, where the trial court rules on whether a particular practice is deceptive, unlike appellate court decisions which may be limited to procedural questions. Moreover, in some states there are large numbers of favorable trial court decisions based on attorney general actions. Since an injunction against the challenged practice is the only remedy sought, defendants usually do not appeal the judgment, and it may not even be reported.

Even more common are UDAP cases initiated by the attorney general that are settled by a court-approved agreement. It is certainly useful to argue that a practice is a UDAP violation when the same or nearby court has already approved an agreement by which another seller has agreed to stop a practice that the attorney general considers deceptive. The consumer protection division of the attorney general's office may collect these consent agreements and unreported UDAP decisions.

In addition, consumer litigants, in appropriate cases, should encourage courts to write and report decisions. If a decision can not be officially reported, it can still be submitted to computerized databases such as Lexis or Westlaw. Offices should retain a central file of a state's reported and unreported UDAP decisions and settlements. Important decisions should be sent to the Sargent Shriver National Center on Poverty Law for inclusion in their case bank,[181] and to the National Consumer Law Center, to the attention of "UDAP Manual."

179 See § 1.3, *supra* for a listing of these resources.

180 State Unfair Trade Practices Law (CCH).

181 50 E. Washington St., Suite 500, Chicago IL 60602, 1-800-621-3256, FAX (312) 263-3846, e-mail admin@povertylaw.org, website www.povertylaw.org.

3.4.3.2 Other States' UDAP Case Law

For many UDAP issues, a jurisdiction will have no case law on point, particularly since there is an almost infinite number of potentially deceptive practices. Moreover, typical appellate court reported decisions concern questions of procedure or remedy and may not make an explicit holding as to whether the challenged practice itself is deceptive.

An alternative source of precedent is case law interpreting other states' UDAP statutes.[182] Some care must be taken because statutes vary from state to state, but most state statutes are patterned after one of only a few model statutes, and virtually every UDAP statute prohibits deceptive practices.[183] Only a few statutes proscribe "fraud," and fraud in this context has been interpreted as virtually synonymous with "deception."[184] Statutes that also proscribe "unconscionable" or "unfair" practices are broader in scope than those limited to deceptive practices. Even in these states, most challenged practices are found to violate the deception standard, with the courts rarely relying on unfairness or unconscionability.

While out-of-state case law is useful in determining if a practice violates a UDAP statute, greater care must be utilized in using out-of-state case law as precedent for issues involving statutory scope because these statutory provisions vary significantly from state to state. The relevance of other states' cases dealing with scope issues must be determined by a careful analysis of the case, the statutory language it is interpreting, and the parallel language in one's own state statute.

The best source for other states' UDAP case law is this manual, with its periodic updates. Readers are encouraged to submit reported and unreported cases to the Center, to the attention of "UDAP Manual."

Unreported cases and certain other documents are cited in this manual by a "Clearinghouse" number. The National Center on Poverty Law (formerly the National Clearinghouse for Legal Services) retains copies of these documents, organized by Clearinghouse number. Clearinghouse cases may be ordered from this organization for $10 per copy plus actual delivery costs.[185]

Particularly if an unreported case is very recent, determine whether the case has now been reported. If the case is still unreported, attorneys will have to follow their own court rules on citing unpublished cases.

182 *See, e.g.*, Showpiece Homes Corp. v. Assurance Co. of Am., 38 P.3d 47 (Colo. 2001) (finding other states' UDAP decisions persuasive).

183 *See* § 3.4.2, *supra*.

184 *See* § 4.2.3, *infra*.

185 National Center on Poverty Law, 50 E. Washington St., Suite 500, Chicago IL 60602, 1-800-621-3256, FAX (312) 263-3846, e-mail admin@povertylaw.org. The organization also offers annual subscriptions to its website, www.povertylaw.org. Subscribers can download documents directly from the website.

3.4.4 State UDAP Regulations

3.4.4.1 Authority and Procedure to Enact Regulations

For certain states, the first source of UDAP precedent to be consulted is the state UDAP regulations promulgated by the attorney general's office or other state agency. Better than half the states authorize a state agency to promulgate UDAP regulations.[186] A statute that authorizes enactment of regulations "necessary for the enforcement and administration" of the UDAP statute permits the state to promulgate substantive regulations that define with specificity what practices are unfair or deceptive.[187] The Massachusetts Supreme Judicial Court has interpreted the state attorney general's rulemaking authority to include restrictions on the sale of dangerous and defective products, and has upheld most of the provisions of a handgun regulation.[188] In most states where UDAP rulemaking authority is granted, the state has enacted such regulations, some more extensively than others.[189] Certain local agencies, such as the New York City Department of Consumer Affairs, have also enacted UDAP regulations. Links to state UDAP regulations, where available, are found in Appendix A, *infra*, and on the companion CD-Rom to this volume.

UDAP regulations define specific prohibited practices, thereby providing notice of actions violating the act. The effect is to mitigate possible vagueness in a statute whose prohibition of unfair or deceptive practices is left open-ended to encompass new practices.[190] UDAP defendants are still liable for deceptive acts that are not specified in the regulations.[191] Regulations may also require merchants to take certain actions, where the failure to so act is ruled deceptive.

UDAP regulations have consistently been upheld as valid delegation of legislative authority, as not unconstitutionally vague, and as not violative of equal protection guarantees.[192] There is no separation of powers problem when an executive agency exercises rulemaking powers.[193] UDAP rules are entitled to a presumption of validity.[194] Where the UDAP statute allows the state to adopt future FTC rules, but does not mandate that it do so, this is not an unconstitutional delegation of powers to the FTC.[195]

Rulemaking procedures are usually specified by the state administrative procedures act or by another state statute. Federal Trade Commission procedures, such as statements of facts supporting the decision, need not be followed.[196] And while state procedural requirements must be complied with, courts will not place unreasonable demands on the rulemaking authority that would place form over substance.[197]

Courts will not interfere with the expert judgment of the state attorney general or other state agency except where the remedy selected has no reasonable relation to the unlawful practices found to exist.[198] At least one court has found the judicial standard in reviewing a regulation is whether it bears a reasonable relation to the goal of consumer protection.[199]

3.4.4.2 Precedential Effect of UDAP Regulations

A violation of a UDAP regulation is normally a *per se* UDAP violation.[200] There is no defense that regulations

186 *See* Appx. A, "State Remedies," *infra*. *But see* Kauer v. Amemiya, 56 Haw. 182, 532 P.2d 664 (1975); Minnesota-Dakotas Retail Hardware Ass'n v. State, 279 N.W.2d 360 (Minn. 1979).

187 Pennsylvania Retailers Ass'n v. Lazin, 57 Pa. Commw. 232, 426 A.2d 712 (1981).

188 American Shooting Sports Council v. Attorney General, 429 Mass. 871, 711 N.E.2d 899 (1999).

189 *See* Appx. A, "State UDAP Regulations," *infra*.

190 Purity Supreme, Inc. v. Attorney General, 380 Mass. 762, 407 N.E.2d 297 (1980).

191 Dep't of Legal Affairs v. Father & Son Moving & Storage, 643 So. 2d 22 (Fla. Dist. Ct. App. 1994).

192 United Companies Lending Corp. v. Sargeant, 20 F. Supp. 2d 192 (D. Mass. 1998); Pennsylvania Mortgage Bankers Ass'n v. Zimmerman, 664 F. Supp. 186 (M.D. Pa. 1987); Caldor, Inc. v. Heslin, 215 Conn. 590, 577 A.2d 1009 (1990); Department of Legal Affairs v. Rogers, 329 So. 2d 257 (Fla. 1976); United Consumers Club, Inc. v. Attorney General, 119 Ill. App. 3d 701, 456 N.E.2d 856 (1983); Purity Supreme, Inc. v. Attorney General, 380 Mass. 762, 407 N.E.2d 297 (1980); Commonwealth v. Mass. CRINC, Clearinghouse No. 40,637 (Mass. Super. Ct. July 24, 1984); T & W Chevrolet v. Darvial, 641 P.2d 1368 (Mont. 1982); Barry v. Arrow Pontiac, Inc., 100 N.J. 57, 494 A.2d 804 (1985); Fenwick v. Kay Am. Jeep, Inc., 72 N.J. 372, 371 A.2d 13 (1977); Pet Dealers Ass'n v. Division of Consumer Affairs, 149 N.J. Super. 235, 373 A.2d 688 (App. Div. 1977); Brown v. Barnum & Crow, Inc., 22 Ohio Op. 3d 24 (Lucas Cty. C.P. 1980); Brown v. United Laboratories of America, Inc., Clearinghouse No. 27,056 (Ohio C.P. Portage Cty. 1975); Thorn Americas, Inc. v. Vermont Attorney General, Clearinghouse No. 51,957 (Vt. Super. Ct. Mar. 7, 1997); HM Distributors of Milwaukee, Inc. v. Department of Agriculture, 55 Wis. 2d 261, 198 N.W.2d 598 (1972); State v. Fonk's Mobile Home Park & Sales, 343 N.W.2d 820 (Wis. Ct. App. 1983); Cacchione v. State, Clearinghouse No. 36,594 (Wis. Cir. Ct. Dane Cty. Jan. 1984). *But see* Christie v. Dalwig Inc., 136 Vt. 597, 396 A.2d 1385 (1979) (regulation defining as a UDAP violation any failure to honor a warranty is too broad a regulation).

193 Pennsylvania Retailers Ass'n v. Lazin, 57 Pa. Commw. 232, 426 A.2d 712 (1981).

194 Vermont v. Gene Rosenberg, Clearinghouse No. 50,445 (Vt. Super. Ct. Apr. 26, 1995).

195 T & W Chevrolet v. Darvial, 641 P.2d 1368 (Mont. 1982).

196 Purity Supreme, Inc. v. Attorney General, 380 Mass. 762, 407 N.E.2d 297 (1980).

197 Celebrezze v. Fred Godard Ford, Inc., 27 Ohio App. 3d 301, 500 N.E.2d 881 (1985).

198 Caldor, Inc. v. Heslin, 215 Conn. 590, 577 A.2d 1009 (1990).

199 Purity Supreme, Inc. v. Attorney General, 380 Mass. 762, 407 N.E.2d 297 (1980).

200 Jungkurth v. Eastern Fin. Servs., Inc., 74 B.R. 323 (Bankr. E.D.

have been substantially complied with or that complete compliance is impossible. Exceptions for substantial compliance or determinations that compliance is impossible are for the rulemaking authority to make, not the court.[201] A merchant's good faith does not excuse technical noncompliance.[202]

But Minnesota gives its UDAP rules more limited weight, finding them not "legislative," but "administrative." Its rules are interpretive rules that specify the acts that the agency considers to violate the statute, but they do not have the force or effect of law.[203] Minnesota is atypical in that the rulemaking authority is not found in the UDAP statute, but in legislation giving supplemental powers to the state consumer protection board. The rules are treated as statements of agency policy, whose weight is determined by the court on a case-by-case basis.

Contrast the Minnesota case with Illinois' UDAP statute that gives the attorney general power to "promulgate such rules and regulations as may be necessary, which rules and regulations shall have the force of laws."[204] An Illinois appellate court has held that such rules are not interpretive so as only to guide a court, but are legislative in that they have the force of law.[205] Moreover, even though the Illinois rulemaking authority is enunciated in the UDAP provision dealing with the attorney general's investigatory powers, such rulemaking authority goes to substantive and not just procedural issues.[206] In reaching this result, the court relied in part on a similar New Jersey case,[207] a federal circuit court decision giving the FTC rulemaking authority,[208] and the remedial nature of the state UDAP statute.

UDAP regulations can be more useful as precedent than case law because regulations precisely define specific prohibited practices in common areas of consumer abuse. By contrast, judicial decisions reflect the courts' reluctance to rule on issues that need not be determined to resolve the case before them. UDAP regulations are to be liberally construed.[209]

The authority of one state's UDAP regulations as precedent in another state is unclear. Since regulations are definitive interpretations of one state's UDAP statute, out-of-state regulations are arguably as compelling a precedent as out-of-state case law. Since many states have no regulations, and only a relatively few have extensive ones, the greatest use of UDAP regulations may be as precedent in other states. Taking the UDAP regulations of all the states as one body of law produces an impressive delineation of specific deceptive practices.[210] States which have enacted UDAP regulations include Alaska, Connecticut, Florida, Georgia, Hawaii, Idaho, Illinois, Iowa, Kentucky, Louisiana, Maine, Maryland, Massachusetts, Michigan, Mississippi, Missouri, Montana, Nevada, New Jersey, New Mexico, North Dakota, Ohio, Oregon, Pennsylvania, Rhode Island, Utah, Vermont, West Virginia, and Wisconsin. States with particularly extensive regulations include Connecticut, Idaho, Massachusetts, New Jersey, Ohio, and Wisconsin.

UDAP regulations are most easily obtained from the state's administrative code. If not available there, other sources include the state's secretary of state, attorney general office's consumer protection division, state consumer protection agency, or from a comparable state agency. Many states have posted their regulations on a website, and links to those websites are included in Appendix A, *infra*, and on the companion CD-Rom to this volume. The CD-Rom also includes copies of a limited number of states' regulations, and Appendix A, *infra*, lists the topics that each state's regulations address. The National Consumer Law Center also attempts to keep a current collection and readers are encouraged to forward new regulations to the Center, to the attention of "UDAP Manual." This manual, at Chapters 4 and 5 refers to applicable state regulations in its discussion of UDAP precedent by subject area.

Some state attorneys general issue statements of enforcement policy, advisory letters, or guidelines pursuant to a

---

Pa. 1987); A. Secondino & Son, Inc. v. LoRicco, 215 Conn. 336, 576 A.2d 464 (1990); United Consumers Club, Inc. v. Attorney General, 119 Ill. App. 3d 701, 456 N.E.2d 856 (1983); Purity Supreme, Inc. v. Attorney General, 380 Mass. 762, 407 N.E.2d 297 (1980); Slaney v. Westwood Auto, Inc., 366 Mass. 688, 322 N.E.2d 768 (1975); Fenwick v. Kay Am. Jeep, Inc., 371 A.2d 13 (N.J. 1977); Huffmaster v. Robinson, 221 N.J. Super. 315, 534 A.2d 435 (Law Div. 1986); State v. Hudson Furniture Co., 165 N.J. Super. 516, 398 A.2d 900 (App. Div. 1979); Pet Dealers Ass'n v. Division of Consumer Affairs, 149 N.J. Super. 235, 373 A.2d 688 (App. Div. 1977); Martin v. Bullinger, 43 Ohio App. 3d 136, 539 N.E.2d 681 (1988); Brown v. Deacon's Chrysler Plymouth, Inc., 14 Ohio Op. 3d 436 (Ct. App. 1979); Brown v. Spitzer Ford, Inc., 11 Ohio Op. 3d 84 (Ct. App. 1978); Weaver v. J.C. Penney Co., 53 Ohio App. 2d 165, 372 N.E.2d 633 (1977); State v. Menard, 121 Wis. 2d 199, 358 N.W.2d 813 (1984); Huff & Morse, Inc. v. Riordon, 345 N.W.2d 504 (Wis. Ct. App. 1984); *see also* State v. Fonk's Mobile Home Park & Sales, 343 N.W.2d 820 (Wis. Ct. App. 1983) ("rule" and "order" are synonymous, and violation can be enjoined). *But see* Minnesota-Dakotas Retail Hardware Ass'n v. State, 279 N.W.2d 360 (Minn. 1979) (Minnesota UDAP statute specifies that UDAP rules provide only guidance to the courts).

201 Brown v. Deacon's Chrysler Plymouth, Inc., 14 Ohio Op. 3d 436 (Ct. App. 1979).

202 Huffmaster v. Robinson, 221 N.J. Super. 315, 534 A.2d 435 (Law Div. 1986); State v. Hudson Furniture Co., 165 N.J. Super. 516, 398 A.2d 900 (App. Div. 1979).

203 Minnesota-Dakotas Retail Hardware Ass'n v. State, 279 N.W.2d 360 (Minn. 1979).

204 815 Ill. Comp. Stat. § 505/4.

205 United Consumers Club v. Attorney General, 119 Ill. App. 3d 701, 456 N.E.2d 856 (1983).

206 *Id.*

207 Fenwick v. Kay Am. Jeep, Inc. 72 N.J. 372, 371 A.2d 13 (1977).

208 National Petroleum Refiners Ass'n v. FTC, 482 F.2d 672 (D.C. Cir. 1973).

209 Ganson v. Vaughn, 135 Ohio App. 3d 689, 735 N.E.2d 483 (1999).

210 *See* Appx. A, "State UDAP Regulations," *infra*, and citations to UDAP regulations in Chapters 4, 5 *infra*.

UDAP statute. Practitioners should contact their state attorney general's office and obtain a complete set of such less formal guides. Again, to the extent NCLC has received these enforcement statements, they have been included in Chapters 4 and 5, *infra*, in the appropriate subject area.

3.4.5 FTC Cases, Other Guidelines

3.4.5.1 FTC Cases, Other Guidelines Are Important Sources of UDAP Precedent

FTC case law is another important source of UDAP interpretations, particularly since there are many federal circuit court decisions interpreting the FTC Act. Congress established the Federal Trade Commission in 1914 to prevent "unfair methods of competition," and expanded this mission in 1938 by amending section 5(a)(1) of the FTC Act to prohibit "unfair or deceptive acts or practices."

Most state UDAP statutes are modeled after the FTC Act, as amended,[211] and, because of this "parentage," most state UDAP statutes declare that "it is the intent of the legislature that in construing . . . this Act the courts will be guided by the interpretations given by the Federal Trade Commission and the federal courts to Section 5(a)(1) of the Federal Trade Commission Act (15 U.S.C. 45(a)(1))."[212] In states with this statutory provision, courts show great deference to FTC decisions and other FTC guidelines when interpreting the state UDAP statute.[213] This deference applies to the determination of what conduct is prohibited by a state UDAP statute, not to questions such as who may sue or what remedies are available, as the FTC Act does not afford a private cause of action, and so provides nothing on which interpretation of these questions can be based.[214] Practices outside the scope of the FTC Act, such as deceptive insurance practices, are not necessarily outside the scope of the state UDAP statute.[215]

Courts also show great deference to FTC actions in interpreting UDAP statutes where the statute does not expressly refer to the precedential value of FTC decisions.[216] Courts find a legislative intent that FTC decisions be used to

211 *See* § 3.4.2.2, *supra*.

212 *See* Appx. A, "Precedential Value of FTC Interpretations," *infra*.

213 McKeown Distributors, Inc. v. Gyp-Crete Corp., 618 F. Supp. 632 (D. Conn. 1985); *In re* Diamond Mortgage Corp. (Aramowicz v. Bridges), 118 B.R. 575 (Bankr. N.D. Ill. 1989); State v. O'Neill Investigations, Inc., 609 P.2d 520 (Alaska 1980); State v. Marsden, Clearinghouse No. 27,048 (Alaska Super. Ct. 1977); Madsen v. Western Am. Mortgage Co., 694 P.2d 1228 (Ariz. Ct. App. 1985); People *ex rel.* Nelson v. Superior Court (Kempton), 20 Ariz. App. 591, 514 P.2d 1042 (1973); McLaughlin Ford, Inc. v. Ford Motor Co., 192 Conn. 558, 473 A.2d 1185 (1984); Davis v. Powertel, Inc., 776 So. 2d 971 (Fla. App. 2000); Dep't of Legal Affairs v. Father & Son Moving & Storage, 643 So. 2d 22 (Fla. Dist. Ct. App. 1994); Urling v. Helms Exterminators, Inc., 468 So. 2d 451 (Fla. Dist. Ct. App. 1985); Rollins, Inc. v. Heller, 454 So. 2d 580 (Fla. Dist. Ct. App. 1984); Kukui Nuts of Hawaii, Inc. v. R. Baird & Co., 789 P.2d 501 (Haw. Ct. App. 1990); Rosa v. Johnson, 651 P.2d 1228 (Haw. Ct. App. 1982); *In re* Western Acceptance Corp., 788 P.2d 214 (Idaho 1990); Fitzgerald v. Chicago Title & Trust Co., 380 N.E.2d 790 (Ill. 1978); People *ex rel.* Fahner v. Walsh, 122 Ill. App. 3d 481, 461 N.E.2d 78 (1984); Gour v. Daray Motors, 373 So. 2d 571 (La. Ct. App. 1979); Ciardi v. F. Hoffmann-La Roche, Ltd., 436 Mass. 53, 762 N.E.2d 303 (2002); Leardi v. Brown, 394 Mass. 151, 474 N.E.2d 1094 (1985); Schubach v. Household Fin. Corp., 375 Mass. 133, 376 N.E.2d 140 (1978); Nader v. Citron, 372 Mass. 96, 360 N.E.2d 870 (1977); PMP Associates, Inc. v. Globe Newspaper Co., 366 Mass. 593, 321 N.E.2d 915 (1975); Slaney v. Westwood Auto, Inc., 366 Mass. 688, 322 N.E.2d 768 (1975); Commonwealth v. Decotis, 366 Mass. 234, 316 N.E.2d 748 (1974); Thomas v. Sun Furniture & Appliance Co., 61 Ohio App. 2d 78, 399 N.E.2d 567, 11 Ohio Op. 3d 26 (1978); Santiago v. S.S. Kresge Co., 2 Ohio Op. 3d 54 (C.P. Cuyahoga Cty. 1976); State *ex rel.* McLeod v. C&L Corp., 313 S.E.2d 334 (S.C. Ct. App. 1984); Spradling v. Williams, 566 S.W.2d 561 (Tex. 1978); State v. Credit Bureau of Laredo, 530 S.W.2d 288 (Tex. 1975); Wesware, Inc. v. State, 488 S.W.2d 844 (Tex. Civ. App. 1972); Elkins v. Microsoft Corp., 817 A.2d 9 (Vt. 2002) (statute requires deference to interpretations of FTC Act, not federal antitrust laws); State v. Packard, Clearinghouse No. 27,066 (Vt. Super. Ct. 1977); Lightfoot v. MacDonald, 86 Wash. 2d 331, 544 P.2d 88 (1976); Testo v. Russ Dunmire Oldsmobile, Inc., 16 Wash. App. 39, 554 P.2d 349 (1976). *See also* Plath v. Schonrock, 64 P.3d 984 (Mont. 2003) (citing rule that FTC interpretations should be given weight). *But see* Vargas v. Allied Fin. Co., 545 S.W.2d 231 (Tex. App. 1976).

214 Elkins v. Microsoft Corp., 817 A.2d 9 (Vt. 2002).

215 Raymer v. Bay State Nat'l, 384 Mass. 310, 424 N.E.2d 515 (1981); Dodd v. Commercial Union Ins. Co., 373 Mass. 72, 365 N.E.2d 802 (1977); Farmers & Merchants State Bank of Krum v. Ferguson, 605 S.W.2d 320 (Tex. Civ. App. 1980), *modified on other grounds*, 617 S.W.2d 918 (Tex. 1981).

216 *In re* Scrimpsher, 17 B.R. 999 (Bankr. N.D.N.Y. 1982); People *ex rel.* Mosk v. National Research, 201 Cal. App. 2d 765, 20 Cal. Rptr. 516 (1962); People *ex rel.* Dunbar v. Gym of America, Inc., 177 Colo. 97, 493 P.2d 660 (1972); People *ex rel.* Lefkowitz v. Colorado State Christian College, 76 Misc. 2d 50, 346 N.Y.S.2d 482 (Sup. Ct. 1973); Marshall v. Miller, 302 N.C. 539, 276 S.E.2d 397 (1981); Johnson v. Phoenix Mut. Life Ins. Co., 300 N.C. 247, 266 S.E.2d 610 (1980); Hardy v. Toler, 288 N.C. 303, 218 S.E.2d 342 (1975); Commonwealth *ex rel.* Zimmerman v. Nickel, 26 Pa. D. & C.3d 115 (C.P. Mercer Cty. 1983); Commonwealth v. Flick, Clearinghouse No. 26,032 (Pa. Commw. Ct. 1978); Americans Be Independent v. Commonwealth, 14 Pa. Commw. Ct. 179, 321 A.2d 721 (1974); Commonwealth v. Hush-Tone Industries, Inc., 4 Pa. Commw. 1, Clearinghouse No. 26,025 (1971); Commonwealth v. Handicapped Industries, Inc., Clearinghouse No. 26,027 (Pa. C.P. Bucks Cty., 1977); Commonwealth v. Programmed Learning Sys., Inc., Clearinghouse No. 26,019 (Pa. C.P. Allegheny Cty. 1975); Commonwealth v. Empire Express, Inc., 28 Erie County L.J. 27, Clearinghouse No. 11,129 (Pa. C.P. Erie Cty., 1972); Commonwealth v. Gold Bond Industries, Inc., Clearinghouse No. 26,208 (Pa. C.P. Allegheny Ct. 1972). *But see* State *ex rel.* Edminsten v. J.C. Penney Co., 292 N.C. 311, 233 S.E.2d 895 (N.C. 1977) (declining to follow interpretations that FTC Act covered debt collection; legislature amended statute promptly afterwards to make coverage clear).

interpret state UDAP acts based upon the similarity of the federal and state statutes and the fact that UDAP statutes are patterned after the FTC Act.[217] Further, courts refuse to distinguish a state UDAP statute from the FTC Act, rejecting the argument that the FTC Act is enforced at the administrative level, while a UDAP statute is directly enforced in the courts.[218] In interpreting their own state statutes, state courts should also give weight to rulings other than adjudicated decisions interpreting the FTC Act, such as FTC advisory opinions.[219]

FTC decisions are particularly helpful in showing:

- How a practice works;
- How the practice is deceptive or unfair;
- How consumers are misled or harmed; and
- How even truthful statements can be misleading.

Nevertheless, FTC decisions are guiding, not binding. Courts often make this distinction to avoid finding that the UDAP statute requires unswerving adherence to as yet to be decided FTC cases and thus involving an improper delegation of legislative authority.[220]

In the event that the FTC finds a practice not to violate the FTC Act, the state court can still independently evaluate whether the practice violates the state UDAP standard.[221] Even if an FTC rule is pending, a state UDAP statute can still be used to prohibit the same practice.[222] States are not forbidden from adopting rules more restrictive than those of the FTC.[223] Certainly, consulting an FTC staff attorney with no authority to approve a company's representations is no defense to a state UDAP action.[224]

The extent to which state courts as a practical matter will be guided by FTC interpretations will depend on the status of the FTC ruling. Certainly, federal appellate court decisions will be accorded great weight. In addition, courts interpreting state UDAP statutes should closely follow FTC federal court enforcement actions, administrative decisions, administrative law judges' decisions, and rules and guides.[225] An Idaho UDAP regulation indicates that a seller's violation of an FTC consent order or any other judgment or order involving the FTC is a *per se* UDAP violation.[226]

3.4.5.2 Types of FTC Cases

It is important to understand the different forms of FTC precedent. The FTC often will issue an administrative complaint against an individual company. If a settlement is not reached, the Commission can pursue its complaint before an FTC administrative law judge who makes findings of fact and law, and orders such relief as is appropriate and authorized. Either the Commission staff or the respondent can appeal the administrative law judge's "initial decision" to the Commission. If neither party appeals, the Commission adopts the administrative law judge's order as final, unless the Commission places the matter on its own docket, *sua sponte*. Respondents, but not the FTC staff, can appeal Commission decisions to a United States circuit court of appeals. Either the respondent or the FTC can then seek *certiorari* from the United States Supreme Court. Orders do not become final until all appeals are exhausted.

Although the numbers have diminished in recent years, the FTC has issued a large number of administrative decisions since 1938 interpreting what practices are unfair or deceptive. Even excluding the many antitrust cases the Commission initiates, the number of consent agreements is in the thousands, and the number of Commission decisions in the hundreds, with a large number of federal appellate court decisions and a handful of Supreme Court rulings. This makes FTC case law a significant source of interpretations of deception and unfairness.

In 1975, the FTC's enforcement authority was enlarged to allow it to bypass the administrative route and to go immediately into federal court in certain situations to seek preliminary injunctions, restitution, and civil penalties.[227]

217 Guste v. Demars, 330 So. 2d 123 (La. Ct. App. 1976); People *ex rel.* Lefkowitz v. Colorado State Christian College, 76 Misc. 2d 50, 346 N.Y.S.2d 482 (Sup. Ct. 1973); Johnson v. Phoenix Mut. Life Ins. Co., 300 N.C. 247, 266 S.E.2d 610 (1980); Hardy v. Toler, 288 N.C. 303, 218 S.E.2d 342 (1975); Commonwealth v. Hush-Tone Industries, Inc., 4 Pa. Commw. 1, Clearinghouse No. 26,025 (Pa. Commw. Ct. 1971); Commonwealth *ex rel.* Zimmerman v. Nickel, 26 Pa. D. & C.3d 115 (C.P. Mercer Cty. 1983); Wesware, Inc. v. State, 488 S.W.2d 844 (Tex. Civ. App. 1972); State v. Packard, Clearinghouse No. 27,066 (Vt. Super. Ct. 1977).

218 People *ex rel.* Dunbar v. Gym of America, Inc., 177 Colo. 97, 493 P.2d 660 (1972).

219 PMP Assocs., Inc. v. Globe Newspaper Co., 366 Mass. 593, 321 N.E.2d 748 (1975).

220 Department of Legal Affairs v. Rogers, 329 So. 2d 257 (Fla. 1976); State v. Reader's Digest Ass'n, Inc., 81 Wash. 2d 259, 501 P.2d 290 (1972); *see also* State v. Goodyear Tire & Rubber Co., 128 Ariz. 483, 626 P.2d 1115 (App. Ct. 1981); T & W Chevrolet v. Darvial, 641 P.2d 1368 (Mont. 1982).

221 Ramson v. Layne, 668 F. Supp. 1162 (N.D. Ill. 1987); Bailey Employment Sys. Inc. v. Hahn, 545 F. Supp. 62 (D. Conn. 1982), *aff'd without op.*, 723 F.2d 895 (2d Cir. 1983); People *ex rel.* Hartigan v. Unimax, Inc., 168 Ill. App. 3d 718, 523 N.E.2d 26 (1988); Perlman v. Time, Inc., 64 Ill. App. 3d 190, 380 N.E.2d 1040 (1978).

222 Bailey Employment Sys. Inc. v. Hahn, 545 F. Supp. 62 (D. Conn. 1982); People *ex rel.* Abrams v. American Direct Industries, Inc., Clearinghouse No. 43,083 (N.Y. Sup. Ct. 1988).

223 Caldor, Inc. v. Heslin, 215 Conn. 590, 577 A.2d 1009 (1990); Purity Supreme, Inc. v. Attorney General, 380 Mass. 762, 407 N.E.2d 297 (1980); Hinds v. Paul's Auto Werkstatt, Inc., 107 Or. App. 63, 810 P.2d 874 (1991).

224 State *ex rel.* Lefkowitz v. Interstate Tractor Trailor Training, Inc., 66 Misc. 2d 678, 321 N.Y.S.2d 147 (Sup. Ct. 1971).

225 *See* notes 213 and 216, *supra*.

226 Idaho Consumer Protection Regulations, Idaho Admin. Code § 04.02.01.033.

227 15 U.S.C. §§ 53, 57b. *See* FTC v. Gem Merchandising Corp., 87 F.3d 466 (11th Cir. 1996) (holding that FTC Act allows court to

While the FTC now frequently uses this authority to go directly into federal courts, these actions usually result in restraining orders, injunctions, or settlements, with few federal court decisions interpreting what practices are in fact unfair or deceptive.

3.4.5.3 Precedential Value of FTC Consent Agreements

The precedential value of the thousands of FTC consent agreements and court settlements requires some explanation. Strictly speaking, an FTC consent order or settlement does not adjudicate disputed issues of fact and does not decide a disputed issue of law. The respondent does not admit any wrongdoing but, for settlement purposes only, agrees not to perform certain acts or agrees to meet certain requirements in the future.

Nevertheless, courts use FTC consent agreements as guidance in interpreting state UDAP statutes. Relatively few FTC cases are actually adjudicated, and ignoring consent agreements forecloses the use of the bulk of FTC activity in preventing unfair or deceptive acts. Often the Commission challenges an existing industry-wide practice as unfair or deceptive by suing the major industry members. These companies usually sign consent agreements or settlements and other companies informally cease the practice. In reality, the Commission has determined that a practice violates the FTC Act, has obtained consent orders from a number of companies, and informal agreement from the industry that the practice is unfair or deceptive, and has succeeded in limiting the practice. While there is no adjudicated order, for all practical purposes, the Commission and industry consider the practice unfair or deceptive.

Thus the United States Supreme Court has held that an FTC construction "is entitled to great weight . . . even though it was applied in cases settled by consent rather than in litigation."[228] The Alaska Supreme Court has similarly held that "adjudications which are resolved by consent decree constitute an administrative interpretation of the FTC Act which have clear precedential value."[229] The Idaho UDAP regulations indicate that a seller's violation of an FTC consent order is a *per se* state UDAP violation.[230]

There are good reasons for these rulings. In many important areas of consumer abuse, the only guidance from the Commission will be consent agreements. While a consent agreement is not an adjudicated decision, it still shows that the FTC has made a policy decision in the area. A consent agreement includes an FTC complaint that alleges that certain acts have taken place and that these acts are unfair or deceptive. The respondent, while not admitting or denying that these acts have taken place, consents to an order prohibiting the respondent from engaging in the challenged acts in the future.

There are two further arguments that courts should seek guidance from FTC consent agreements to interpret state UDAP statutes. The FTC complaint, while stating that it has reason to believe that certain practices have taken place, unconditionally states that certain practices are unfair or deceptive if they did take place. Thus the complaint provides an unambiguous FTC interpretation of what practices the Commission believes to be unfair or deceptive. Second, consent agreements indicate practices the Commission would prohibit if the matter went to adjudication. The Commission complaint and proposed order are negotiated during the settlement process, so the consent agreement provides a less sweeping statement of unfair or deceptive practices than a final adjudicated order might.

3.4.5.4 Comparing the FTC Act and the State UDAP Statutes

One problem in using FTC case law is that the decisions do not directly interpret state UDAP statutes, but instead interpret the FTC Act prohibition of "unfair or deceptive acts or practices." Some state UDAP statutes are identically worded, but others do not even proscribe unfair practices. Thus FTC cases finding a practice illegal may not be useful in some states if the FTC decision is based on an unfairness theory.[231] In practice, this is not an important problem because few FTC cases rely on the unfairness standard alone but also prohibit the challenged activity as deceptive. Even when a decision uses the term "unfair or deceptive," a careful reading of the case usually indicates that the Commission has based its ruling on a finding of deception.

Occasionally a state UDAP statute will have a more limited standard of deception than the FTC's.[232] However, this more restrictive state deception standard normally relates to additional elements of proof, such as intent, actual deception, damage, or reliance. The state deception standard is usually not further limited if these elements are met, so the types of practices prohibited should be the same at the state and FTC levels. While an attorney should always be aware of peculiarities of a state's UDAP statute, FTC case law is almost always applicable as guidance to courts interpreting the state statute.

order restitution and disgorgement, and payment of unclaimed consumer redress funds into U.S. Treasury).

228 FTC v. Mandel Bros., 359 U.S. 385 (1959) (citations omitted).

229 State v. O'Neill Investigations, Inc., 609 P.2d 520 (Alaska 1980).

230 Idaho Consumer Protection Regulations, Idaho Admin. Code § 04.02.01.033.

231 *See* Richardson Ford Sales, Inc. v. Johnson, 676 P.2d 1344 (N.M. Ct. App. 1984).

232 *See* § 4.2, *infra*.

3.4.5.5 Researching FTC Case Law

FTC case law is not easy to research by subject matter. For most purposes, the best approach to FTC case law is to use Chapters 4 and 5 of this manual to find citations to FTC cases within each topic area.

The Commission compiles all its decisions and orders in *FTC Decisions*. This reporting service includes consent orders, initial administrative law judge decisions, and Commission decisions adopting or modifying the initial decisions. FTC actions decided by courts are not compiled in this reporter. Initial decisions are reported only after the Commission adopts or modifies them, and in the volume covering the date of the full commission action, not the date of the administrative law judge decision. There is often a considerable lag time between Commission decisions and release of the bound reports. The Commission decisions are not updated with a loose-leaf supplement, but individual copies of specified, recent FTC issuances can be obtained from: Public Reference Branch, Federal Trade Commission, 600 Pennsylvania Ave., N.W., Room 130, Washington, D.C. 20580, 202-326-2222.

Complaints, consent agreements, initial decisions, Commission decisions, proposed rules, staff reports, and other public documents are available. Those requesting information will be charged for the direct costs to search for and duplicate documents; however, the first 100 pages of duplication and the first two hours of search time are furnished without charge.[233] Thereafter, reproduction costs are 14 cents per page, and fees for search and review are assessed on a quarter-hourly basis. The exact fees charged by the agency are calculated periodically and are available from the Public Reference Branch, Federal Trade Commission, 600 Pennsylvania Avenue, N.W., Room 130, Washington, DC 20580.[234] Legal services attorneys and others can write to the Deputy Executive Director for Planning and Information, Federal Trade Commission, Washington, DC 20580, to request waiver of the copying costs because such charges are not in the public interest.[235] Recent Commission decisions are available to all requesters without charge while supplies last.[236]

Many recent documents are available on the FTC website, www.ftc.gov, including the text of rules and guides, complaints, decisions, and orders from 1996 on, advisory opinions on the pay-per-call and franchise rule, news releases from 1995 on, and information about various FTC initiatives. The *Code of Federal Regulations* and the text of the *Federal Register* from 1994 on are available on-line at www.gpoaccess.gov.

Citations to *FTC Decisions* are by volume and page (*e.g.*, 80 F.T.C. 210), but complaints and orders obtained from the Commission are numbered by a different system. Preliminary investigations have seven-digit numbers, whose first two digits indicate the year they are initiated (*e.g.*, 792 4351 was initiated in 1979). Matters in adjudication are given four-digit docket numbers, in chronological order of initiation of the adjudication (*e.g.*, Docket No. 8039). Consent orders are given four-digit numbers in order of their issuance preceded by the letter "C" (*e.g.*, C-2041).

The Commerce Clearing House (CCH) *Trade Regulation Reporter* provides tables that allow conversion of docket numbers to *FTC Decisions* citations and conversion of both these numbering schemes to the CCH *Trade Regulation Reporter's* own system that indexes and digests FTC administrative actions by subject. The *Trade Regulation Reporter* provides a loose-leaf service of excerpts and summaries of FTC decisions and orders and has also developed a topical index. This reporter is also the best source for summaries of FTC actions in federal courts.

Lexis and Westlaw are other methods of researching FTC administrative case law. Each offers several databases with FTC materials, such as Commission decisions, consent orders, FTC press releases, and FTC news. Since these databases contain all recent FTC materials, including antitrust cases and purely procedural orders, search requests must be carefully drafted to produce manageable search results.

Lexis and Westlaw also contain the complete text of nearly all federal court cases, and search requests can easily be developed to seek FTC cases dealing with unfair and deceptive practices. *United States Code Annotated*, at 15 U.S.C.A. § 45, summarizes federal court cases interpreting that section of the FTC Act. Another method of researching federal interpretations of the FTC Act is to shepardize its statutory citation.

To be practical, research efforts dealing with FTC case law, whether they involve administrative or federal court decisions, must be sharply limited to cases interpreting the "unfair or deceptive practices" standard found in section 5 of the FTC Act.[237] Approximately half of FTC decisions dealing with section 5 are antitrust cases brought under the section's prohibition of unfair methods of competition. Other FTC cases do not deal with section 5 at all, but are brought pursuant to such specialized statutes as those dealing with credit, warranties, debt collection, hobby protection, textile and fur labeling, and food and drug advertising. FTC cases interpreting these statutes will not be precise precedent for UDAP statutes.

233 16 C.F.R. § 4.8(b)(3).

234 16 C.F.R. § 4.8(b)(6).

235 16 C.F.R. § 4.8(e)(1)–(2) (procedure for requesting fee waiver).

236 16 C.F.R. § 4.8(b)(5).

237 *Id.*

3.4.5.6 FTC Trade Regulation Rules, Guides, and Other Statements

FTC rules, guides, and other materials are another important source of guidance in interpreting state UDAP statutes. The Commission has issued a number of Trade Regulation Rules (TRRs) defining unfair or deceptive practices. Of particular importance are TRRs concerning Credit Practices,[238] Used Cars,[239] Funerals,[240] Cooling-Off Periods for Door-to-Door Sales,[241] Preservation of Consumers' Claims and Defenses,[242] Mail Order Merchandise,[243] the Use of Negative-Option Plans,[244] Franchising and Business Opportunity Ventures,[245] and Home Insulation.[246]

Proposed TRRs are accompanied by extensive staff reports, and a hearing officer may also have issued a report. These documents analyze consumer abuses in an industry and may explain why such practices are unfair or deceptive, detailing legal arguments and citing case law. Final TRRs are accompanied by useful statements of basis and purpose in the *Federal Register*. The FTC staff also issues enforcement guidelines and staff interpretation letters concerning TRRs.

TRRs in some respects are the most useful source of FTC guidelines. They define with specificity unfair or deceptive practices and generally concern important areas of consumer abuse. The Federal Trade Commission Act imposes special remedies for TRR violations, allowing the FTC to seek civil penalties and restitution immediately in federal district court. The only issue in such a proceeding is whether the rule has been violated, not the appropriateness of the TRR. Trade Regulation Rules are also enacted after lengthy proceedings allowing all parties extensive opportunity to present their views. Thus, TRRs are definitive statements of practices that are unfair or deceptive and that the federal government will take strong measures to combat. State courts should show great deference to FTC TRRs.[247]

TRRs do more than just define unfair or deceptive acts. They often detail affirmative requirements merchants must follow to prevent unfair or deceptive practices. Until a state court is comfortable using FTC TRRs as precedent, consumer attorneys may be well advised to challenge not only technical violations of TRRs' affirmative requirements, but rather, to use the TRRs as precedent for challenges to abusive sales practices which are in themselves unfair or deceptive.

The FTC has also issued a number of guides that state the Commission's interpretation of what types of practices are unfair or deceptive. These guides are not as specific as TRRs, the proceedings to enact them are not so extensive, and no special remedies result from violations of a guide. Guides are essentially comprehensive advisory opinions warning sellers that the Commission deems certain practices unfair or deceptive. Sellers engaging in such practices may find themselves the subject of an FTC complaint. As FTC guidelines for what practices are unfair or deceptive, they are also helpful guidelines for state court proceedings. Guides have been enacted in various important areas,[248] such as deceptive pricing,[249] bait advertising,[250] guarantees,[251] private vocational and home study schools,[252] and fuel economy advertising for new automobiles.[253] A number of older "Trade Practice Rules," not to be confused with "Trade Regulation Rules," have also been enacted, but are largely rescinded.

Finally, the Commission and its staff issue advisory opinions, enforcement statements, and informal staff opinions. FTC advisory opinions are normally given in response to a merchant's request for an opinion as to whether a certain action the merchant is contemplating pursuing violates the FTC Act. Consumers can also seek an advisory opinion. The FTC Rules of Procedure indicate that any person may request advice "with respect to a course of action which the requesting party proposes to pursue."[254] In this case, the consumer would be pursuing the course of action of bringing a state UDAP action, and would be seeking advice to determine whether the challenged practice violates the FTC Act.

The Commission rules call for a response from either the Commission or the staff where the matter involves a substantial or novel question or the matter is of significant public interest.[255] Consumers seeking such opinions should carefully follow FTC procedures[256] and be prepared to pursue aggressively their right to seek such advice.

In addition to more formal advisory opinions, the FTC issues numerous informal staff opinion letters, usually relating to the interpretation of its trade regulation rules. Again, these letters almost exclusively respond to inquiries from industry representatives, but consumer representatives have the same right. Often the best place to start is to

238 16 C.F.R. § 444, *reprinted in* Appx. B.1, *infra*.
239 16 C.F.R. § 455, *reprinted in* Appx. B.6, *infra*.
240 16 C.F.R. § 453, *reprinted in* Appx. B.5, *infra*.
241 16 C.F.R. § 429, *reprinted in* Appx. B.3, *infra*.
242 16 C.F.R. § 433, *reprinted in* Appx. B.2, *infra*.
243 16 C.F.R. § 435, *reprinted in* Appx. B.4, *infra*.
244 16 C.F.R. § 425.
245 16 C.F.R. § 436.
246 16 C.F.R. § 460.
247 *See* §§ 3.2.6, 3.2.7.3.6, *supra*.

248 In 1995 the FTC rescinded its guides for the mail order insurance industry, 16 C.F.R. § 234, and against debt collection deception, 16 C.F.R. § 237, because it concluded that they were no longer useful in light of the passage of other consumer protection laws. 60 Fed. Reg. 40262, 40263 (Aug. 8, 1995).
249 16 C.F.R. § 233.
250 16 C.F.R. § 238.
251 16 C.F.R. § 239.
252 16 C.F.R. § 254.
253 16 C.F.R. § 259.
254 16 C.F.R. § 1.1(a).
255 *Id.*
256 16 C.F.R. § 1.2.

informally telephone an FTC staff attorney specializing in the subject area at issue. If the telephone conversation is supportive, a written response should be requested and used in court.

Six TRRs are reprinted in Appendix B, *infra* and are included on the companion CD-Rom to this volume. All FTC TRRs, guides, and advisory opinions are compiled in Volume 16 of the *Code of Federal Regulations*.[257] The *Code of Federal Regulations* is revised annually, and kept current by the *Federal Register*. To determine whether a Code volume has been amended since its revision date, consult the List of CFR Sections Affected (monthly pamphlet) and the Cumulative List of Parts Affected which appears in the Reader Aids section of the daily *Federal Register*. These two lists will identify the *Federal Register* page number of the latest amendment of any given rule. Recent updates are also reported in CCH *Trade Regulation Reporter*, and can be found both in Westlaw and Lexis.

Chapters 4 and 5 of this manual also include FTC guides and TRRs in their synopses of selected subject areas. Accompanying FTC TRRs are very helpful statements of basis and purpose, and also staff reports, staff enforcement guidelines, and informal opinion letters. These are not found in the *Code of Federal Regulations* and should be obtained from the Public Reference Branch at the FTC. Statements of basis and purpose and enforcement guidelines are also published in the *Federal Register*. Recent FTC statements can also be found on its website, www.ftc.gov, and recent issues of the *Federal Register* are available on-line at www.gpoaccess.gov and through Lexis and Westlaw, and many libraries have older issues on microfilm.

257 For administrative interpretations, general policy statements and enforcement policy statements, and administrative opinions and rulings, see 16 C.F.R. Part 14. For guides and trade practice rules, see 16 C.F.R. Parts 17–24, 228-260. For trade regulation rules, see 16 C.F.R. Parts 400–460.

Chapter 4 General Principles as to UDAP Violations

4.1 Introduction

This chapter provides a synopsis of precedent interpreting the terms "unfair," "deceptive," "fraudulent," and "unconscionable" as delineated in the FTC Act and state UDAP statutes. The chapter also analyzes other general precedent that is applicable to many different types of unlawful practices, such as precedent dealing with deceptive pricing, misrepresentations about the product's quality or the seller's identity, high pressure sales, and slow delivery.

Chapter 5 enumerates UDAP violations organized by specific type of transaction, such as automobile repair, debt collection, landlord tenant, and credit repair. Chapter 3 provides a conceptual framework and methodology as to how to demonstrate a UDAP violation, and evaluates the sources of UDAP precedent. Consequently, readers should use both this chapter and the next to determine UDAP precedent relating to their case, and also be familiar with the concepts spelled out in Chapter 3, *supra*.

4.2 Deception, Statutory Fraud

4.2.1 Per Se *Deception*

Most of this section will analyze how practices fall within the broad, expansive definition of "deception." However, certain specific practices are *per se* deceptive. That is, if the practice is within certain guidelines, it is automatically deceptive, and the court need not determine whether the practice falls within the general parameters of "deception." The most important example of a *per se* deceptive practice is a practice specifically prohibited by the UDAP statute itself. Some, but not all, UDAP statutes have a "laundry list" of prohibited practices plus a catch-all phrase prohibiting other deceptive practices. While most UDAP cases will turn on the definition of the catch-all phrase, some cases can be won simply by showing that the practice violates one of the enumerated specific prohibitions. Violations of UDAP statutes' laundry lists are discussed in another section.[1]

A second source of enumerated prohibitions in about half the states is state UDAP regulations. A violation of these regulations will be a *per se* UDAP violation.[2] A third source for some states is the laundry list found in the state's version of the Uniform Deceptive Trade Practices Act (UDTPA). Some states have enacted two UDAP statutes, one patterned after the UDTPA, containing a laundry list of deceptive practices, but providing only an injunctive, not a damage remedy for their violation. Consider using the UDTPA laundry list as a source of *per se* violations of the *other* state UDAP statute. The UDTPA-type statute's laundry list is a legislative itemization of deceptive practices, and consumers should be able to argue that a violation of that laundry list is *per se* deceptive under the state's other UDAP statute.[3] It is also recognized in many states that a violation of an FTC rule or a state or federal statute meant to protect the public is a *per se* UDAP violation.[4]

Finally, courts will hold, as long as a practice is within a UDAP statute's scope, that if the practice violates common law fraud standards it is *per se* deceptive.[5] Deception is a more inclusive standard than common law fraud, so if a practice is fraudulent, it is automatically deceptive.

One caution about claiming that a practice is *per se* deceptive. Always add an additional count claiming that the practice also falls within the more general definition of deception. If for some technical reason the court throws out the *per se* claim at the summary judgment stage, the general claim of deception should still go to trial as long as sufficient facts are alleged to raise the issue of whether the practice falls within the general definition of deception. The rest of this section analyzes that general definition of deception.

4.2.2 Relationship of Deception to Unfairness, Unconscionability

Many state UDAP statutes prohibit both deceptive and unfair practices or both deceptive and unconscionable practices. The consumer need not show that a practice is both unfair or unconscionable and also deceptive. The practice need be only one *or* the other.

1 *See* § 3.2.2, *supra*.

2 *See* § 3.2.3, *supra*, for a more detailed discussion of *per se* violations of UDAP regulations. *See* Appx. A, *infra*, for a listing of state UDAP regulations.

3 *See* § 3.2.5, *supra*.

4 *See* § 3.2.7, *supra*.

5 *See* § 3.2.4, *supra*.

As will be described in §§ 4.3 and 4.4, unfairness and unconscionability are different concepts than deception. A practice can be unfair even if it is not deceptive—a merchant with overbearing market power may be very explicit about how it will take unfair advantage of a consumer. Similarly, even if a court finds a practice not to be unfair, the court can still find the practice to be deceptive.[6] Some courts have held that there is an implicit representation in every transaction that the transaction is legal.[7] Then, if the transaction in fact violates another law, it is not only unfair but also deceptive. This argument is helpful in states that prohibit only deceptive, but not unfair acts.

4.2.3 Comparison of Deception with Fraud, Misleading Practices

4.2.3.1 Comparison with Common Law Fraud

Virtually all state UDAP statutes prohibit deceptive practices. "Deception" is a broader, more flexible standard of actionable merchant misconduct than the traditional remedy of common law fraud. In its most restrictive interpretation,[8] common law fraud requires proof of five elements:

- A false representation, usually of fact;
- Reliance on the representation by plaintiff;
- Damage as a result of the reliance;
- "Scienter," that is, the defendant's knowledge of the falsity; and
- Defendant's intentional misrepresentation seeking reliance.

The modern concept of deception, as shaped by federal court interpretations of the Federal Trade Commission Act,[9] substantially eliminates these proof requirements. To show deception under the FTC Act, intent, scienter, actual reliance or damage, and even actual deception are unnecessary. All that is required is proof that a practice has a tendency or capacity to deceive even a significant minority of consumers.[10] In addition, while common law fraud often must be proven with clear, convincing evidence, the UDAP standard is likely to be just a preponderance of the evidence.[11] Since the UDAP standard is less stringent than fraud, proof of common law fraud constitutes proof of a UDAP violation as long as the UDAP coverage requirements are met.[12]

The definition of deception for purposes of the FTC Act does not always apply in all respects to private actions alleging deception under state UDAP statutes. It is, however, a good indication of the flexibility of the deception concept. UDAP statutes clearly provide more flexible remedies for consumer abuse than was previously available under common law,[13] since deception liberalizes the traditional elements for the torts of fraud or deceit.[14] The essence

6 Bristol Technology, Inc. v. Microsoft Corp., 114 F. Supp. 2d 59 (D. Conn. 2000), *as modified by* 127 F. Supp. 2d 61 (D. Conn. 2000), *vacated pursuant to settlement by* 250 F.3d 152 (2d Cir. 2001); Cobb v. Monarch Fin. Co., 913 F. Supp. 1164 (N.D. Ill. 1995); State v. United States Steel Corp., 919 P.2d 294 (Haw. 1996).

7 *See* § 3.2.7.4, *supra.*

8 There are significant state variations concerning the necessary elements for common law fraud, deceit, or negligent misrepresentation. *See* § 9.6.3, *infra* for a more detailed discussion of common law fraud and other tort actions.

9 15 U.S.C. § 45.

10 The FTC's policy statement setting forth its current standard is included as an appendix to its decision in *In re* Cliffdale Assocs., Inc., 103 F.T.C. 110 (1984). The Comptroller of the Currency, which enforces the FTC Act against national banks, has adopted the FTC's standard. *See* OCC Advisory Letter 2002-3, *Guidance on Unfair or Deceptive Acts or Practices* (Mar. 22, 2002). *See also* OCC Advisory Letter 2003-2, *Guidelines for National Banks to Guard Against Predatory and Abusive Lending Practices* (Feb. 21, 2003) (applying analysis to predatory lending practices).

11 *See* § 7.9.1.1, *infra.*

12 Siegel v. Levy Organization Dev. Co., 153 Ill. 2d 534, 607 N.E.2d 194 (1992); Miller v. William Chevrolet/Geo, Inc., 326 Ill. App. 3d 642, 762 N.E.2d 1 (2001); Washington Courte Condominium Ass'n v. Washington-Golf Corp., 267 Ill. App. 3d 790, 643 N.E.2d 199 (1994).

13 Associated Investment Co. v. Williams Assocs., 230 Conn. 148, 645 A.2d 505 (1994); Harkala v. Wildwood Realty, Inc., 200 Ill. App. 3d 447, 558 N.E.2d 195 (1990); Carl Sandburg Village v. First Condominium Dev. Co., 197 Ill. App. 3d 948, 557 N.E.2d 246 (1990); Heller v. Silverbranch Constr. Corp., 376 Mass. 621, 382 N.E.2d 1065 (1978); Group Health Plan v. Philip Morris, Inc., 621 N.W.2d 2 (Minn. 2001) (legislative intent was to make it easier to sue for consumer fraud, so reliance not required); Fletcher v. Don Foss of Cleveland, Inc., 90 Ohio App. 3d 82, 628 N.E.2d 60 (1993).

14 Bandura v. Orkin Exterminating Co., 865 F.2d 816 (7th Cir. 1988) (Illinois law); Fisher v. Quality Hyundai, Inc., 2002 U.S. Dist. LEXIS 407 (N.D. Ill. Jan. 8, 2002) (UDAP statute provides broader protections than common law); Meyer v. Dygert, 156 F. Supp. 2d 1081 (D. Minn. 2001); Celex Group, Inc. v. Executive Gallery, Inc., 877 F. Supp. 1114 (N.D. Ill. 1995) (UDAP statute provides "far broader protection"); Riordan v. Nationwide Mut. Fire Ins. Co., 756 F. Supp. 732 (S.D.N.Y. 1990); April v. Union Mortgage Co., 709 F. Supp. 809 (N.D. Ill. 1989); *In re* Tapper, 123 B.R. 594 (Bankr. N.D. Ill. 1991); Peery v. Hansen, 120 Ariz. 266, 585 P.2d 574 (1978); State v. McLeod, Clearinghouse No. 50,412 (Ark. Ch. Ct., Pulaski Cty. Nov. 23, 1993); Mass. Mut. Life Ins. Co. v. Superior Court, 97 Cal. App. 4th 1282, 119 Cal. Rptr. 2d 190, 195 (2002); Webster v. Board of Dental Examiners, 17 Cal. 2d 534, 110 P.2d 992 (1941); Saunders v. Superior Court, 27 Cal. App. 4th 832, 33 Cal. Rptr. 2d 438 (1994); Hinchliffe v. American Motors Corp., 440 A.2d 810 (Conn. 1981); State *ex rel.* Brady v. Publishers Clearing House, 787 A.2d 111 (Del. Ch. 2001); State *ex rel.* Brady v. Gardiner, 2000 Del. Super. LEXIS 208 (June 5, 2000); Wirt v. Matthews, 2002 WL 31999339 (Del. Com. Pleas Apr. 9, 2002), *disposing of motion for reargument of* 2002 WL 31999360 (Del. Com. Pleas Feb. 7, 2002) (unpublished, citation limited); W.S. Badcock Corp. v. Myers, 696 So. 2d 776 (Fla. Dist. Ct. App. 1997), *review denied*, 698 So. 2d 840 (Fla. 1997); Urling v. Helms Exterminators, Inc., 468 So. 2d 451 (Fla. Dist. Ct. App.

of deception is not evil intent,[15] negligent merchant behavior,[16] or even breach of an agreement,[17] but misleading of consumers by a merchant's statements, silence, or actions.

4.2.3.2 Statutory Fraud; Misleading Practices

A few state UDAP statutes do not prohibit "deceptive" acts, but proscribe "misleading" or "fraudulent" practices.[18] Nevertheless, the standards developed for "deception" also apply to these related concepts. "Misleading" and "deceptive" are identical in meaning. While common law fraud and deception are very different, statutory fraud, *i.e.*, fraud as prohibited by a state UDAP statute, is interpreted as being akin to deception.[19] Consumers invoking UDAP statutes that prohibit fraud, but not deception, should, with some caution, use the principles developed in this section to interpret statutory fraud as well.

Until 1997, the catchall provision of the Pennsylvania UDAP statute prohibited "other fraudulent conduct." In interpreting that prohibition a Pennsylvania court recognized the distinction between common law fraud and statutory fraud, and adopted "any kind of artifice employed by one person to deceive another" as a definition of statutory fraud.[20] The Third Circuit, applying this same section of the Pennsylvania UDAP law, stated that the defendant's conduct was to be measured against the elements of common law fraud, but interpreted that term broadly to require "fair and aboveboard treatment" and to prohibit taking "undue advantage" of the consumer.[21] A number of Pennsylvania cases similarly interpreted this statutory fraud provision broadly,[22] although there was also a substantial opposing

---

1985); Rollins, Inc. v. Heller, 454 So. 2d 580 (Fla. Dist. Ct. App. 1984); Campbell v. Beak, 568 S.E.2d 801 (Ga. App. 2002) (scienter and intent unnecessary); Chandler v. Am. Gen. Fin., Inc., 329 Ill. App. 3d 729, 768 N.E.2d 60 (2002) (one goal of UDAP statute was to give protection broader than that afforded by common law fraud); Ciampi v. Ogden Chrysler Plymouth, Inc., 634 N.E.2d 448 (Ill. App. Ct. 1994); Breckenridge v. Cambridge Homes, Inc., 616 N.E.2d 615 (Ill. App. Ct. 1993); Zinser v. Rose, 614 N.E.2d 1259 (Ill. App. Ct. 1993); Totz v. Continental DuPage Acura, 602 N.E.2d 1374 (Ill. App. Ct. 1992); Bankier v. First Federal Savings & Loan Ass'n, 588 N.E.2d 391 (Ill. App. Ct. 1992); Duran v. Leslie Oldsmobile, 594 N.E.2d 1355 (Ill. App. Ct. 1992); Rubin v. Marshall Field & Co., 597 N.E.2d 688 (Ill. App. Ct. 1992) (judgment for consumers on UDAP claim is not inconsistent with judgment against them on common law fraud claim); State *ex rel.* Miller v. Pace, 677 N.W.2d 761 (Iowa 2004); Kattar v. Demoulas, 433 Mass. 1, 739 N.E.2d 246 (2000); Mass. Farm Bureau Federation v. Blue Cross, 403 Mass. 722, 532 N.E.2d 660 (1989); Heller v. Silverbranch Constr. Corp., 376 Mass. 621, 382 N.E.2d 1065 (1978); Slaney v. Westwood Auto, Inc., 366 Mass. 688, 322 N.E.2d 768 (1975); Billingham v. Dornemann, 771 N.E.2d 166 (Mass. App. 2002) (application of common law fraud restrictions to UDAP claim was error); State *ex rel.* Webster v. Milbourn, 759 S.W.2d 862 (Mo. Ct. App. 1988); State *ex rel.* Ashcroft v. Marketing Unlimited, 613 S.W.2d 440 (Mo. Ct. App. 1981); Gaidon v. Guardian Life Ins. Co., 704 N.Y.S.2d 177, 725 N.E.2d 598 (N.Y. 1999) (UDAP statute "contemplates conduct that does not necessarily rise to the level of fraud"), *later op. at* 96 N.Y.2d 201, 750 N.E.2d 1078 (2001) (UDAP statute "encompasses a far greater range of claims" than common law fraud); Broder v. MBNA Corp., 281 A.D.2d 369, 722 N.Y.S.2d 524 (2001) (dismissal of fraud claim does not require dismissal of UDAP claim); Hardy v. Toler, 288 N.C. 303, 218 S.E.2d 342 (1975); Rosenthal v. Perkins, 42 N.C. App. 449, 257 S.E.2d 63 (1979); Funk v. Montgomery AMC/Jeep/Renault, 66 Ohio App. 3d 815, 586 N.E.2d 1113 (1990); Inman v. Ken Hyatt Chrysler Plymouth, Inc., 294 S.C. 240, 363 S.E.2d 691 (1988); State *ex rel.* McLeod v. Brown, 294 S.E.2d 781 (S.C. 1982); Dowd v. Imperial Chrysler-Plymouth, Inc., 381 S.E.2d 212 (S.C. Ct. App. 1989); Lien v. Couch, 993 S.W.2d 53 (Tenn. App. 1998) (UDAP statute is broader than common law fraud); Miller v. Keyser, 90 S.W.3d 712 (Tex. 2002); Smith v. Baldwin, 611 S.W.2d 611 (Tex. 1980); Winey v. William E. Dailey, Inc., 636 A.2d 744 (Vt. 1993) (UDAP statute provides a much broader right than common law fraud); Parker-Smith v. Sto Corp., 262 Va. 432, 551 S.E.2d 615 (2001) (construing false advertising statute); 15 Mo. Code State Regs. §§ 60-9.020, 60-9.040 (definition of deception states that common law fraud elements are not required).

15 *See* § 4.2.4, *infra*.

16 *See* § 4.2.16, *infra*.

17 *See* § 4.2.15, *infra*.

18 *See* Appx. A, *infra*.

19 State *ex rel.* Lefkowitz v. Interstate Tractor Trailer Training, Inc., 66 Misc. 2d 678, 321 N.Y.S.2d 147 (Sup. Ct. 1971); State *ex rel.* Lefkowitz v. Bevis Indus., Inc., 63 Misc. 2d 1088, 314 N.Y.S.2d 60 (Sup. Ct. 1970); Celestino v. Mid-American Indem. Ins. Co., 883 S.W.2d 310 (Tex. App. 1994); State v. Packard, Clearinghouse No. 27,066 (Vt. Super. Ct. 1977); *see also* People *ex rel.* Fahner v. American Buyer's Club, 115 Ill. App. 3d 759, 450 N.E.2d 904 (1983).

20 Chatham Racquet Club v. Commonwealth, 561 A.2d 354 (Pa. Commw. Ct. 1989); Commonwealth *ex rel.* Zimmerman v. NALCO, 108 Pa. Commw. 300, 529 A.2d 1157 (1987).

21 Smith v. Commercial Banking Corp., 866 F.2d 576 (3d Cir. 1989) (Pennsylvania law). *See also In re* Fricker, 115 B.R. 809 (Bankr. E.D. Pa. 1990) (unconscionable, opportunistic loan practices amount to fraudulent conduct).

22 *In re* Bryant, 111 B.R. 474 (E.D. Pa. 1990); *In re* Milbourne, 108 B.R. 522 (Bankr. E.D. Pa. 1989); Commonwealth v. Monumental Properties, Inc., 459 Pa. 450, 329 A.2d 812 (1974); Pirozzi v. Penske-Olds-Cadillac-GMS, 605 A.2d 373 (Pa. Super. Ct. 1992) (applying "other fraudulent conduct" prohibition to nondisclosure of damage to a vehicle); Culbreth v. Lawrence J. Miller, Inc. 328 Pa. Super. 374, 477 A.2d 491 (1984); Kromm v. P&W Excavating Co., 11 Franklin 99 (Pa. C.P. 1992); Commonwealth *ex rel.* Zimmerman v. Nickel, 26 D. & C.3d 115 (Pa. C.P. Mercer Cty 1983). *Cf.* Pennsylvania v. Burns, 663 A.2d 308 (Pa. Commw. 1995) (declining to address issue of whether common law fraud is required, because contractor's actions amounted to fraud); Commonwealth of Pennsylvania v. Diversified Chemicals, Inc., Clearinghouse No. 50,440 (Pa. C.P. Oct. 6, 1994); Nelson v. Stine, Davis & Peck Ins., 7 Pa. D. & C.4th 415 (C.P. 1990) (complaint must allege intentional misconduct; fraud requires some intentional and deceitful practice, or at least some implication of intentional misrepresentation). *See generally* the discussion of Pennsylvania cases at Carter, Pennsylvania Consumer Law § 2.5.4.2.1 (George T. Bisel Co., Philadelphia 1997 and Supp.).

view.[23] The issue became moot in 1997, when the legislature revised the catchall to prohibit "other fraudulent or deceptive conduct."[24]

4.2.4 Intent Unnecessary

4.2.4.1 Intent Generally Not Required

The FTC definition of deception does not require intent; a practice is deceptive even if there is no intent to deceive.[25] Unless a state UDAP statute specifically provides otherwise, intent is not necessary under state UDAP statutes either.[26]

23 Booze v. Allstate Ins. Co., 750 A.2d 877 (Pa. Super. Ct. 2000) (interpreting pre-amendment language); Sewak v. Lockhart, 699 A.2d 755 (Pa. Super. Ct. 1997) (stating that proof of fraud is required under former version of statute); DiLucido v. Terminix Int'l, Inc., 676 A.2d 1237 (Pa. Super. Ct. 1996); Prime Meats, Inc. v. Yochim, 619 A.2d 769 (Pa. Super. Ct. 1993); Burkholder v. Cherry, 607 A.2d 745 (Pa. Super. Ct. 1992) (UDAP claim rejected because "fraud" not shown; no definition of fraud); Rizzo v. Michener, 584 A.2d 973 (Pa. Super. Ct. 1990) (equating statutory fraud with common law fraud); Hammer v. Nikol, 659 A.2d 617 (Pa. Commw. Ct. 1995); Laxson v. Lenger, 6 Pa. D. & C.4th 175 (C.P. 1990) (equating statutory fraud with common law fraud). *See also* Com. *ex rel.* Fisher v. Percudani, 825 A.2d 743 (Pa. Commw. Ct. 2003).

24 Flores v. Shapiro & Kreisman, 246 F. Supp. 2d 427 (E.D. Pa. 2002); Patterson v. Chrysler Fin. Co. (*In re* Patterson), 263 B.R. 82 (Bankr. E.D. Pa. 2001) (legislature's addition of word "deceptive" means that catchall prohibition now includes conduct other than fraud); 73 Pa. Stat. § 201-2(4)(xxi); Com. *ex rel.* Fisher v. Percudani, 825 A.2d 743 (Pa. Commw. Ct. 2003); Commonwealth *ex rel.* Fisher v. Allstate Ins. Co., Clearinghouse No. 53,561 (Pa. Commw. Ct. Jan. 18, 2001) (catchall no longer requires fraud but only a material representation that is likely to mislead consumers acting reasonably under the circumstances); Weiler v. SmithKline Beecham Corp., 53 Pa. D. & C.4th 449, 2001 Pa. D. & C. LEXIS 154 (C.P. Oct. 8, 2001). *See also* Santana Prods., Inc. v. Bobrick Washroom Equipment, Inc., 249 F. Supp. 2d 463 (M.D. Pa. 2003) (unlike fraud, UDAP claim does not require intent or actual reliance); Sheppard v. GMAC Mortg. Corp., 299 B.R. 753 (Bankr. E.D. Pa. 2003) (proof of causation still required after amendments); Seth William Goren, *A Pothole on the Road to Recovery: Reliance and Private Class Actions Under Pennsylvania's Unfair Trade Practices and Consumer Protection Law*, 107 Dickinson Law Rev. 1 (Summer 2002) (discussing history of Pa. catchall provision). *But cf.* Johnson v. Robinson (*In re* Johnson), 292 B.R. 821, 825 (Bankr. E.D. Pa. 2003) (citing pre-amendment decisions for proposition that common law fraud is required). *But see* Cheatle v. Katz, 2003 WL 21250583 (E.D. Pa. Apr. 1, 2003) (stating without analysis that fraud is still required; since plaintiffs sufficiently alleged fraud the issue was moot).

25 FTC v. Algoma Lumber Co., 291 U.S. 67 (1934); FTC v. Amy Travel Service, Inc., 875 F.2d 564 (7th Cir. 1989) (intent unnecessary even for action for monetary redress); Orkin Exterminating Co. v. FTC, 849 F.2d 1354 (11th Cir. 1988), *cert. denied*, 488 U.S. 1041 (1989); Chrysler Corp. v. FTC, 561 F.2d 357 (D.C. Cir. 1977); Beneficial Corp. v. FTC, 542 F.2d 611 (3d Cir. 1976); Doherty, Clifford, Steers & Shenfield, Inc. v. FTC, 392 F.2d 921 (6th Cir. 1968); Montgomery Ward & Co. v. FTC, 379 F.2d 666 (7th Cir. 1967); Regina Corp. v. FTC, 322 F.2d 765 (3d Cir. 1963); Feil v. FTC, 285 F.2d 879 (9th Cir. 1960); Gimbel Bros., Inc. v. FTC, 116 F.2d 578 (2d Cir. 1941).

26 *Alaska*: State v. O'Neill Investigations, Inc., 609 P.2d 520 (Alaska 1980).
Arkansas: State v. McLeod, Clearinghouse No. 50,412 (Ark. Ch. Ct., Pulaski Cty. Nov. 23, 1993).
California: Chern v. Bank of America, 15 Cal. 3d 866, 544 P.2d 1310, 127 Cal. Rptr. 110 (1976); Hewlett v. Squaw Valley Ski Corp., 63 Cal. Rptr. 2d 118 (Ct. App. 1997); State Farm Fire & Cas. Co. v. Superior Court, 53 Cal. Rptr. 2d 229 (Ct. App. 1996).
Connecticut: Associated Investment Co. v. Williams Assocs., 230 Conn. 148, 645 A.2d 505 (1994); Cheshire Mortgage Servs., Inc. v. Montes, 223 Conn. 80, 612 A.2d 1130 (1992).
Delaware: Stephenson v. Capano, Dev. Inc., 462 A.2d 1069 (Del. 1983).
District of Columbia: Smith v. Brown & Williamson Tobacco Corp., 108 F. Supp. 2d 12 (D.D.C. 2000).
Georgia: Campbell v. Beak, 568 S.E.2d 801 (Ga. App. Ct. 2002); Crown Ford, Inc. v. Crawford, 473 S.E.2d 554 (Ga. App. Ct. 1996); Regency Nissan, Inc. v. Taylor, 194 Ga. App. 645, 391 S.E.2d 467 (1990).
Idaho: State *ex rel.* Kidwell v. Master Distributors, Inc., 101 Idaho 447, 615 P.2d 116 (1980).
Illinois: Chow v. Aegis Mortg. Corp., 286 F. Supp. 2d 956 (N.D. Ill. Oct. 7, 2003) (innocent misrepresentation is violation); Cripe v. Leiter, 184 Ill. 2d 185, 703 N.E.2d 100 (1998) (intent to deceive unnecessary; innocent misrepresentations can be UDAP violations); Falcon Assocs., Inc. v. Cox, 699 N.E.2d 203 (Ill. App. Ct. 1998); Roche v. Fireside Chrysler-Plymouth, 600 N.E.2d 1218 (Ill. App. Ct. 1992); Rubin v. Marshall Field & Co., 597 N.E.2d 688 (Ill. App. Ct. 1992) (innocent or negligent misrepresentations are UDAP violations); Hoke v. Beck, 587 N.E.2d 4 (Ill. App. Ct. 1992) (intent that consumer rely on information must be shown, but not intent to deceive); People *ex rel.* Hartigan v. Knecht Servs., 216 Ill. App. 3d 843, 575 N.E.2d 1378 (1991); Doll v. Bernard, 578 N.E.2d 1053 (Ill. App. Ct. 1991) (innocent misrepresentation violates UDAP if it is material); Harkala v. Wildwood Realty, Inc., 200 Ill. App. 3d 447, 558 N.E.2d 195 (1990); Carl Sandburg Village v. First Condominium Dev. Co., 197 Ill. App. 3d 948, 557 N.E.2d 246 (1990) (negligent innocent misrepresentations are actionable under UDAP); Warren v. LeMay, 142 Ill. App. 3d 550, 491 N.E.2d 464 (1986).
Indiana: McKinney v. State, 693 N.E.2d 65 (Ind. 1998) (intent need not be shown except when seeking to meet statute's definition of "incurable" deceptive act).
Iowa: State *ex rel.* Miller v. Pace, 677 N.W.2d 761 (Iowa 2004) (intent to deceive need not be shown, just intent that others rely).
Kansas: Moore v. Bird Engineering Co., 41 P.3d 755 (Kan. 2002) (intent not required except for substantive prohibitions that specifically make it an element); Swanston v. McConnell Air Force Base Federal Credit Union, 8 Kan. App. 2d 538, 661 P.2d 826 (1983); Bell v. Kent-Brown Chevrolet Co., 1 Kan. App. 2d 131, 561 P.2d 907 (1977) (refusing to read an intent requirement into UDAP statute; the legislature later added an intent requirement to some substantive prohibitions). *But cf.* Griffin v. Security Pacific Automotive Fin. Servs., 33 F. Supp. 2d 926 (D. Kan. 1998) (statutory language requires willfulness for misrepresentations or omissions); Gonzales v. Associates Fin. Service Co., 967 P.2d 312 (Kan. 1998) (willfulness required).
Louisiana: Industrias Magromer Cueros y Pieles v. Louisiana Bayou Furs Inc., 293 F.3d 912 (5th Cir. 2002) (statute does not require intent to obtain an advantage or cause a loss); Thomas

Thus, a state court has concluded that to require proof of intent "would effectively emasculate the act and contradict its fundamental purpose," which is to avoid common law fraud proof requirements.[27] Innocent misrepresentations are actionable under UDAP statutes.[28] Even where a UDAP statute prohibits fraudulent, but not deceptive, practices,

J. Sibley v. National Union Fire Ins., 921 F. Supp. 1526 (E.D. Tex. 1996) (intent probably not required under Louisiana UDAP statute).

Maine: State v. Bob Chambers Ford, Inc., 522 A.2d 362 (Me. 1987) (state action); Bartner v. Carter, 405 A.2d 194 (Me. 1979).

Massachusetts: Bond Leather Co. v. Q.T. Shoe Mfg. Co., 764 F.2d 928 (1st Cir. 1985) (Massachusetts law); Giannasca v. Everett Aluminum Inc., 13 Mass. App. Ct. 208, 431 N.E.2d 596 (1982); Jeffco Fibres Inc. v. Dario Diesel Service, Inc., 13 Mass. App. Ct. 1029, 433 N.E.2d 918 (1982); MacGillivary v. W. Dana Bartlett Ins. Agency, 14 Mass. App. Ct. 52, 436 N.E.2d 964 (1982).

Minnesota: Freeman v. A & J Auto MN, Inc., 2003 WL 22136807 (Minn. App. Sept. 16, 2003) (unpublished, citation limited); Church of the Nativity of Our Lord v. WatPro, Inc., 474 N.W.2d 605 (Minn. Ct. App. 1991).

New Hampshire: Kowalski v. Cedars of Portsmouth Condominium Ass'n, 769 A.2d 344 (N.H. 2001) (deception is actionable whether or not it is deliberate).

New Jersey: Gennari v. Weichert Co. Realtors, 148 N.J. 582, 691 A.2d 350 (1997); Fenwick v. Kay Am. Jeep, Inc., 72 N.J. 372, 371 A.2d 13 (1977); Leon v. Rite Aid Corp., 340 N.J. Super. 462, 774 A.2d 674 (App. Div. 2001) (intent and knowledge unnecessary except for omissions); Jiries v. BP Oil, 294 N.J. Super. 225, 682 A.2d 1241 (Law Div. 1996); Chattin v. Cape May Greene, Inc., 243 N.J. Super. 590, 581 A.2d 91 (App. Div. 1990) (acts of omission must, however, be "knowing" under New Jersey's UDAP statute), *aff'd*, 124 N.J. 520, 591 A.2d 943 (1991); D'Ercole Sales, Inc. v. Fruehauf Corp., 206 N.J. Super. 11, 501 A.2d 990 (App. Div. 1985); Miller v. American Family Publishers, 284 N.J. Super. 67, 663 A.2d 643 (Chancery Div. 1995) (intent not an element for affirmative UDAP violations, although omissions must be knowing).

New Mexico: Page & Wirtz Constr. Co. v. Solomon, 110 N.M. 206, 794 P.2d 349 (1990); Richardson Ford Sales, Inc. v. Johnson, 676 P.2d 1344 (N.M. Ct. App. 1984).

New York: Riordan v. Nationwide Mut. Fire Ins. Co., 756 F. Supp. 732 (S.D.N.Y. 1990) (showing of intent or recklessness unnecessary, but may be considered for treble damages or attorney fees); Small v. Lorillard Tobacco Co., 94 N.Y.2d 43, 720 N.E.2d 892 (1999); Oswego Laborers' Local 214 Pension Fund v. Marine Midland Bank, 85 N.Y.2d 20, 647 N.E.2d 741 (1995); People v. Wilco Energy Corp., 284 A.D.2d 469, 728 N.Y.S.2d 471 (2001); People of State of New York v. Apple Health & Sports Clubs, Ltd., Inc., 206 A.D.2d 266, 613 N.Y.S.2d 868 (1994); State *ex rel.* Abrams v. Abandoned Funds Information Center, Inc., 129 Misc. 2d 614, 493 N.Y.S.2d 907 (Sup. Ct. 1985).

North Carolina: United Roasters Inc. v. Colgate-Palmolive Co., 649 F.2d 985 (4th Cir. 1981) (North Carolina law); Marshall v. Miller, 302 N.C. 539, 276 S.E.2d 397 (1981); Torrance v. AS&L Motors, 459 S.E.2d 67 (N.C. Ct. App. 1995); Forbes v. Par Ten Group, Inc., 99 N.C. App. 587, 394 S.E.2d 643 (1990). *But cf.* Erler v. Aon Risks Servs., Inc. 540 S.E.2d 65 (N.C. App. 2000) (applying general standards of unfairness to find that this particular unintentional misrepresentation was not a UDAP violation).

Ohio: Rose v. Zaring Homes, Inc., 122 Ohio App. 3d 739, 702 N.E.2d 952 (1997); Renner v. Derin Acquisition Corp., 111 Ohio App. 3d 326, 676 N.E.2d 151 (1996), *review denied*, 77 Ohio St. 3d 1480, 673 N.E.2d 142 (1996); Janos v. Murduck, 109 Ohio App. 3d 583, 672 N.E.2d 1021 (1996); Hubbard v. Bob McDorman Chevrolet, 104 Ohio App. 3d 621, 662 N.E.2d 1102 (1995); Karst v. Goldberg, 623 N.E.2d 1348 (Ohio App. 1993) (intent unnecessary for deception claims, but scienter must be shown to establish unconscionable act); Fletcher v. Don Foss of Cleveland, Inc., 90 Ohio App. 3d 82, 628 N.E.2d 60 (1993); Frey v. Vin Devers, Inc., 80 Ohio App. 3d 1, 608 N.E.2d 796 (1992); D&K Roofing, Inc. v. Pleso, 77 Ohio App. 3d 181, 601 N.E.2d 561 (1991); Funk v. Montgomery AMC/Jeep/Renault, 66 Ohio App. 3d 815, 586 N.E.2d 1113 (1990); Robinson v. McDougal, 62 Ohio App. 3d 253, 575 N.E.2d 469 (1988); Thomas v. Sun Furniture & Appliance Co., 61 Ohio App. 2d 78, 399 N.E.2d 567, 11 Ohio Op. 3d 26 (1978).

Pennsylvania: Santana Prods., Inc. v. Bobrick Washroom Equipment, Inc., 249 F. Supp. 2d 463, 499 (M.D. Pa. 2003); Andrews v. Fleet Real Estate Funding Corp., 78 B.R. 78 (Bankr. E.D. Pa. 1987); Commonwealth *ex rel.* Zimmerman v. Nickel, 26 Pa. D. & C.3d 115 (C.P. Mercer Cty. 1983).

South Carolina: Young v. Century Lincoln-Mercury, Inc., 396 S.E.2d 105 (S.C. Ct. App. 1990); State *ex rel.* McLeod v. C&L Corp., 313 S.E.2d 334 (S.C. Ct. App. 1984).

Tennessee: Shah v. Racetrac Petroleum Co., 338 F.3d 557 (6th Cir. 2003) (Tenn. law); Menuskin v. Williams, 145 F.3d 755 (6th Cir. 1998) (Tennessee law); Smith v. Scott Lewis Chevrolet, Inc., 843 S.W.2d 9 (Tenn. Ct. App. 1992).

Texas: Miller v. Keyser, 90 S.W.3d 712 (Tex. 2002); Smith v. Baldwin, 611 S.W.2d 611 (Tex. 1980); Pennington v. Singleton, 606 S.W.2d 682 (Tex. 1980); Barnett v. Coppell North Texas Court, Ltd., 123 S.W.3d 804 (Tex. App. 2003); Herrin v. Medical Protective Co., 89 S.W.3d 301 (Tex. App. 2002); Williams v. Trail Dust Steak House, Inc., 727 S.W.2d 812 (Tex. App. 1987).

Vermont: Jordan v. Nissan North America, Inc., 2004 WL 595413 (Vt. Mar. 26, 2004); Carter v. Gugliuzzi, 716 A.2d 17 (Vt. 1998) (only intent to publish the statement, not intent to deceive, is necessary); Poulin v. Ford Motor Co., 513 A.2d 1168 (Vt. 1986); Winton v. Johnson & Dix Fuel Corp., 515 A.2d 371 (Vt. 1986).

Washington: Hangman Ridge Training Stables, Inc. v. Safeco Title Ins. Co., 105 Wash. 2d 778, 719 P.2d 531 (1986); Bowers v. Transamerican Title Ins. Co., 675 P.2d 193 (Wash. 1983); Haner v. Quincy Farm Chemical Inc., 97 Wash. 2d 753, 649 P.2d 828 (1982); Hertzog v. WebTV Networks, 2002 WL 1609032 (Wash. App. July 22, 2002) (unpublished, citation limited).

Wisconsin: State v. Clausen, 105 Wis. 2d 231, 313 N.W.2d 819 (1982); State v. Stepniewski, 105 Wis. 2d 261, 314 N.W.2d 98 (1982).

27 Thomas v. Sun Furniture & Appliance Co., 61 Ohio App. 2d 78, 399 N.E.2d 567 (1978).

28 Chow v. Aegis Mortg. Corp., 286 F. Supp. 2d 956 (N.D. Ill. 2003); Limberopoulos v. First Midwest Bank, 2002 WL 1163733 (N.D. Ill. May 31, 2002); Arenson v. Whitehall Convalescent & Nursing Home, 880 F. Supp. 1202 (N.D. Ill. 1995); Griffin v. Universal Cas. Co., 654 N.E.2d 694 (Ill. App. Ct. 1995); Mackinac v. Arcadia Nat'l Life Ins. Co., 648 N.E.2d 237 (Ill. App. Ct. 1995); Washington Courte Condominium Ass'n v. Washington-Golf Corp., 267 Ill. App. 3d 790, 643 N.E.2d 199 (1994); Ciampi v. Ogden Chrysler Plymouth, Inc., 634 N.E.2d 448 (Ill. App. Ct. 1994). *But see* Elson v. State Farm Fire & Cas. Co., 691 N.E.2d 807 (Ill. App. Ct. 1998) (innocent misrepresentations not actionable).

intent has been found to be unnecessary.[29] Negligence that is or results in an unfair or deceptive practice creates UDAP liability.[30]

The strongest indication of courts' willingness to find deception without intent is their awarding mandatory treble damages for unintentional violations. Thus the Texas Supreme Court has overruled an appellate court that would have implied an intent requirement where the court was mandated to award treble damages for any UDAP violation.[31] The North Carolina Supreme Court has similarly overturned an appellate court, and ruled that intent need not be shown, even when damages are automatically trebled.[32] A California court has found that civil penalties awarded for negligent misrepresentation are not unconstitutional.[33] A UDAP criminal prosecution may not even need to prove the seller's intent.[34] The New Jersey Supreme Court has divided UDAP violations into three categories: omissions, affirmative acts, and violations of UDAP regulations. Proof of knowledge and intent is necessary only where the violation consists of an omission.[35]

29 State *ex rel.* Lefkowitz v. Interstate Tractor Trailer Training, Inc., 66 Misc. 2d 678, 321 N.Y.S.2d 147 (Sup. Ct. 1971); State *ex rel.* Lefkowitz v. Bevis Indus., Inc., 63 Misc. 2d 1088, 314 N.Y.S. 2d 60 (Sup. Ct. 1970). *But see* Chatham Racquet Club v. Commonwealth, 541 A.2d 51 (Pa. Commw. Ct. 1988) (must show something more than unintentional misunderstanding of seller's contractual rights).

30 South Atlantic Ltd. P'ship v. Riese, 284 F.3d 518 (4th Cir. 2002) (N.C. law); Grove v. Huffman, 634 N.E.2d 1184 (Ill. App. Ct. 1994); Squeri v. McCarrick, 32 Mass. App. Ct. 203, 588 N.E.2d 22 (1991); Reed v. Wally Conard Constr., Inc., 1999 Tenn. App. LEXIS 681 (Oct. 13, 1999) (builder's negligent misrepresentation about placement of house on lot is UDAP violation); Brandon v. Winnett, 1995 Tenn. App. LEXIS 508, Clearinghouse No. 51,279 (Tenn. App. 1995) (negligent misrepresentation is a UDAP violation. *See also* Bonaccoloto v. Coca-Cola Enters., 1999 U.S. Dist. LEXIS 22732 (D. Mass. Feb. 11, 1999) (negligence can be basis for UDAP liability if it is or results in unfair or deceptive acts or practice, but not shown here). *But see* Aiken v. Hancock, 115 S.W.3d 26 (Tex. App. 2003) (negligent statements are not a UDAP violation). *But cf.* Skyline Int'l Development v. Citibank, 706 N.E.2d 942 (Ill. App. Ct. 1998) (inadvertent isolated misstatement between businesses not a UDAP violation).

31 Pennington v. Singleton, 606 S.W.2d 682 (Tex. 1980), *rev'g* 568 S.W.2d 367 (Tex. Civ. App. 1977).

32 Marshall v. Miller, 302 N.C. 539, 276 S.E.2d 397 (1981), *rev'g* 47 N.C. App. 530, 268 S.E.2d 97 (1980).

33 People v. Superior Court (Olson), 96 Cal. App. 3d 181, 157 Cal. Rptr. 628 (1979).

34 State v. Clausen, 105 Wis. 2d 231, 313 N.W.2d 819 (1982); State v. Stepniewski, 105 Wis. 2d 261, 314 N.W.2d 98 (1982). *But cf.* People v. Watts, 181 Ill. 2d 133, 692 N.E.2d 315 (1998) (presumption of intent makes criminal home repair fraud statute unconstitutional).

35 Cox v. Sears, Roebuck & Co., 138 N.J. 2, 647 A.2d 454 (1994). *See also* Ramanadham v. N.J. Mfg. Ins. Co., 188 N.J. Super. 30, 455 A.2d 1134 (App. Div. 1982).

4.2.4.2 Where Statute Explicitly Requires Proof of Intent

Some state UDAP statutes specifically require that there be an intent that the prohibited act be relied upon by others.[36] Courts interpret this requirement narrowly and do not require that an intent to deceive or make untrue statements be shown, only an intent that the act be relied upon by others.[37] Thus, even innocent misrepresentations may be actionable if the party intends the consumer to rely on them.[38] A party is presumed to intend the necessary consequences of his or her own actions or omissions.[39] A dealer's

36 *See* Northwestern Public Service v. Union Carbide, 236 F. Supp. 2d 966 (D.S.D. 2002); Wafra Leasing Corp. v. Prime Capital Corp., 204 F. Supp. 2d 1120 (N.D. Ill. 2002) (dismissing UDAP claim because accountants did not intend third parties to rely on their report); Fisher v. Quality Hyundai, Inc., 2002 U.S. Dist. LEXIS 407 (N.D. Ill. Jan. 8, 2002) (requirement satisfied by dealer's intent that finance company rely on its misrepresentations, which harmed the consumer); State *ex rel.* Brady v. 3-D Auto World, Inc., 2000 Del. Super. LEXIS 17 (Jan. 19, 2000) (plaintiff must show that defendant intended that others rely on omission); Tudor v. Jewel Food Stores, Inc., 681 N.E.2d 6 (Ill. App. Ct. 1997); Totz v. Continental DuPage Acura, 602 N.E.2d 1374 (Ill. App. Ct. 1992) (intent that consumer rely on nondisclosure must be shown under Illinois UDAP statute; circumstantial evidence is satisfactory); State *ex rel.* Miller v. Pace, 677 N.W.2d 761 (Iowa 2004); Porras v. Bell, 18 Kan. App. 2d 569, 857 P.2d 676 (1993) (certain provisions in statute require intent); Slowinski v. Valley Nat'l Bank, 264 N.J. Super. 172, 624 A.2d 85 (1993); Ji v. Palmer, 333 N.J. Super. 451, 755 A.2d 1221 (App. Div. 2000) (only knowing omissions are UDAP violations); Rathgeber v. Hemenway, Inc., 69 P.3d 710 (Or. 2003) (for private cause of action, Oregon requires showing of willfulness, *i.e.*, that defendant knew or should have known, at time of representations, that they would not be carried out); Scott v. Western Int'l, Surplus Sales, Inc., 267 Or. 512, 517 P.2d 661 (1973); Sanders v. Francis, 277 Or. 593, 561 P.2d 1003 (1971); Luedeman v. Tri-West Constr. Co., 39 Or. App. 401, 592 P.2d 281 (1979); State v. GAF Corp., 760 P.2d 310 (Utah 1988) (noting legislature's addition of intent requirement in 1985). *See also* Forrest v. P&L Real Estate Investment Co., 134 Md. App. 371, 759 A.2d 1187 (2000) (parts of Maryland UDAP statute require scienter but others do not); Clark v. Ourisman Fairfax, Inc., 2002 WL 1941132 (Va. Cir. Ct. May 29, 2002) (interpreting bona fide error defense of Va. UDAP statute).

37 Chow v. Aegis Mortg. Corp., 286 F. Supp. 2d 956 (N.D. Ill. 2003); Roberts v. Rohrman, 909 F. Supp. 545 (N.D. Ill. 1995); *In re* Brandywine Volkswagen, Ltd., 312 A.2d 632 (Del. 1973); Nash v. Hoopes, 332 A.2d 411 (Del. Super. Ct. 1975); Siegel v. Levy Organization Dev. Co., 153 Ill. 2d 534, 607 N.E.2d 194 (1992); Falcon Assocs., Inc. v. Cox, 699 N.E.2d 203 (Ill. App. Ct. 1998); Griffin v. Universal Cas. Co., 654 N.E.2d 694 (Ill. App. Ct. 1995); Breckenridge v. Cambridge Homes, Inc., 616 N.E.2d 615 (Ill. App. Ct. 1993); Carl Sandburg Village v. First Condominium Dev. Co., 197 Ill. App. 3d 948, 557 N.E.2d 246 (1990); State *ex rel.* Miller v. Pace, 677 N.W.2d 761 (Iowa 2004).

38 Falcon Assocs., Inc. v. Cox, 699 N.E.2d 203 (Ill. App. Ct. 1998).

39 Carl Sandburg Village v. First Condominium Dev. Co., 197 Ill. App. 3d 948, 557 N.E.2d 246 (1990).

misrepresentation to a finance company that it had authority to enter into a financing contract on behalf of the consumer, and its false statements to a credit reporting agency, satisfied this criterion even though the representations were not made to the consumer.[40]

Other courts similarly interpret a UDAP statute's intent standard as a requirement that the seller intends to do the act, not that the seller intends to deceive.[41] Even where a court finds that the consumer must show the seller's intent to deceive, this has been given a liberal interpretation so that the failure to sell goods as advertised has been found to create a rebuttable presumption of an intent to violate the law.[42] A pattern of misrepresentations also shows an intent to deceive.[43] Finally, note that, even where a UDAP statute requires that intent be shown to prove a violation of certain provisions (such as a "laundry list" of prohibited deceptive practices), other provisions may not require proof of intent (*e.g.*, unconscionability).[44]

4.2.5 Knowledge Unnecessary

4.2.5.1 Knowledge Generally Not Required

As a corollary to the FTC finding that an evil motive or intent to deceive is unnecessary,[45] it follows that knowledge of a statement's falsity, "scienter," is not a necessary element for an FTC finding of deception. State courts similarly interpret their state UDAP statutes,[46] even when a statute prohibits fraudulent, but not deceptive, practices.[47]

---

40 Fisher v. Quality Hyundai, Inc., 2002 U.S. Dist. LEXIS 407 (N.D. Ill. Jan. 8, 2002).

41 State *ex rel.* Corbin v. Tolleson, 160 Ariz. 385, 773 P.2d 490 (Ct. App. 1989); State v. Goodyear Tire & Rubber Co., 128 Ariz. 483, 626 P.2d 1115 (Ct. App. 1981); York v. InTrust Bank, 265 Kan. 271, 962 P.2d 405 (1998) (statute's requirement that defendant's use of deceptive tactic be willful does not require showing that defendant intended to violate the statute); Ashlock v. Sunwest Bank, N.A., 107 N.M. 100, 753 P.2d 346 (1988). *But cf.* Griffin v. Security Pacific Automotive Fin. Servs. Corp., 33 F. Supp. 2d 926 (D. Kan. 1998) (interpreting Kansas willfulness requirement to require a designed purpose or intent to do wrong or cause injury).

42 State v. Packard, Clearinghouse No. 27,066 (Vt. Super. Ct. 1977). *But see* Bidwell v. German Motors, 41 Colo. App. 284, 586 P.2d 1003 (1978).

43 Dix v. American Bankers Life Assurance Co., 429 Mich. 410, 415 N.W.2d 206 (1987).

44 *See* Wade v. Jobe, 818 P.2d 1006 (Utah 1991).

45 *See* § 4.2.4.1, *supra*.

46 *Alabama*: *In re* Russell, 181 B.R. 616 (M.D. Ala. 1995) (liability shown where dealer should have been aware of damage to vehicle). *But see* Strickland v. Kafko Mfg., Inc., 512 So. 2d 714 (Ala. 1987).
Arizona: Cearley v. Wieser, 151 Ariz. 293, 727 P.2d 346 (Ct. App. 1986).
Arkansas: State v. McLeod, Clearinghouse No. 50,412 (Ark. Ch. Ct., Pulaski Cty. Nov. 23, 1993).
Connecticut: Webb Press Servs. v. New London Motors, 203 Conn. 342, 525 A.2d 57 (1987); Prishwalko v. Bob Thomas Ford, Inc., 33 Conn. App. 575, 636 A.2d 1383 (1994) (innocent misrepresentation of odometer reading is a UDAP violation).
Georgia: Campbell v. Beak, 568 S.E.2d 801 (Ga. App. Ct. 2002); Crown Ford, Inc. v. Crawford, 473 S.E.2d 554 (Ga. App. Ct. 1996).
Illinois: Thacker v. Menard, Inc., 105 F.3d 382 (7th Cir. 1997) (Illinois law); Roberts v. Rohrman, 909 F. Supp. 545 (N.D. Ill. 1995) (dealer may be liable for unknowingly making incorrect odometer disclosure); Martin v. Heinold Commodities, Inc., 163 Ill. 2d 33, 643 N.E.2d 734 (1994); Duran v. Leslie Oldsmobile, 594 N.E.2d 1355 (Ill. App. Ct. 1992); Totz v. Continental DuPage Acura, 602 N.E.2d 1374 (Ill. App. Ct. 1992) (innocent misrepresentation of material fact is a UDAP violation); Sohaey v. Van Cura, 607 N.E.2d 253 (Ill. App. Ct. 1992) (innocent misrepresentations violate UDAP statute); Hoke v. Beck, 587 N.E.2d 4 (Ill. App. Ct. 1992) (representation made in complete ignorance of its truth or falsity violates UDAP). *But see* Weis v. State Farm Mut. Auto. Ins. Co., 333 Ill. App. 3d 402, 776 N.E.2d 309, 267 Ill. Dec. 172 (2002) (no UDAP violation where insurer unknowingly passed along another entity's deceptive statement).
Indiana: *But see* McKinney v. State, 693 N.E.2d 65 (Ind. 1998) (noting that ten of Indiana's definitions of deceptive acts require showing that defendant knew or should have known).
Iowa: State *ex rel.* Miller v. Pace, 677 N.W.2d 761 (Iowa 2004).
Kansas: Bell v. Kent-Brown Chevrolet Co., 1 Kan. App. 2d 131, 561 P.2d 907 (1977) (refusing to read a knowledge requirement into UDAP statute; the legislature later added a knowledge requirement to most substantive prohibitions). *But see* Morton Buildings, Inc. v. Cronister, 2000 WL 34001923 (Kan. Dist. Ct. Aug. 3, 2000) (knowledge necessary where this requirement was incorporated into substantive prohibition).
Maryland: Golt v. Phillips, 308 Md. 1, 517 A.2d 328 (1986). *See also* Benik v. Hatcher, 358 Md. 507, 750 A.2d 10 (2000) (knowledge is required for certain non-disclosure violations, but knowledge can be imputed by duties under housing code; case can also be framed as violation of other subsections that do not require knowledge); Forrest v. P&L Real Estate Investment Co., 134 Md. App. 371, 759 A.2d 1187 (2000) (parts of Maryland UDAP statute require scienter but others do not). *But see* Luskin's, Inc. v. Consumer Protection Div., 353 Md. 335, 726 A.2d 702 (1999) (scienter is required for certain violations).
Massachusetts: Equitable Life Assurance Soc. v. Porter-Englehart, 867 F.2d 79 (1st Cir. 1989) (Massachusetts law); Barden v. HarperCollins Publishers, Inc., 863 F. Supp. 41 (D. Mass. 1994) (publisher not liable under Massachusetts UDAP statute for unknowing inclusion of incorrect information in book); Slaney v. Westwood Auto, Inc., 366 Mass. 688, 322 N.E.2d 768 (1975); Graves v. R.M. Packer Co., 45 Mass. App. Ct. 760, 702 N.E.2d 21 (1998); Acushnet Federal Credit Union v. Roderick, 26 Mass. App. Ct. 604, 530 N.E.2d 1243 (1988); Glickman v. Brown, 21 Mass. App. Ct. 229, 486 N.E.2d 737 (1985) (UDAP violation for negligent misrepresentation of fact the truth of which reasonably can be ascertained).
Minnesota: *See also In re* Professional Fin. Mgmt., Ltd., 703 F. Supp. 1388 (D. Minn. 1989) (no scienter necessary, just some culpability, such as negligence).
New Jersey: Gennari v. Weichert Co. Realtors, 148 N.J. 582, 691 A.2d 350 (1997) (unknowing misrepresentation of fact creates UDAP liability if it is mutual and made to induce purchase); Leon v. Rite Aid Corp., 340 N.J. Super. 462, 774 A.2d 674 (App. Div. 2001) (intent and knowledge unnecessary except for omissions). *But cf.* Ji v. Palmer, 333 N.J. Super. 451, 755 A.2d 1221 (App. Div. 2000) (only knowing omissions are UDAP violations).

An agent is liable for its misrepresentations, even where only the principal, and not the agent, had any knowledge of the truth or falsity of the representations.[48] Courts, however, may take a different approach where the agent or seller is merely accused of failing to disclose material facts. Some courts find agents or sellers are not liable for failing to disclose facts they do not know.[49] A dealer's lack of awareness of a UDAP regulation is not a defense.[50] If a seller elects to make an affirmative representation, it will be liable for a UDAP violation if that representation turns out to be untrue or deceptive, even in a situation where affirmative disclosure is not required and even if the seller had no actual knowledge of the falsity.[51]

4.2.5.2 Where Proof of Seller's Knowledge Is Required

Some UDAP statutes explicitly require knowledge, either generally or for some substantive prohibitions,[52] or for enhanced damages.[53] If a scienter requirement is found, it is construed liberally. Thus, a court has ruled that statements made in an absolute and unqualified manner without any knowledge are the same as knowingly made false statements.[54] Knowledge may be shown by the seller's failure to test a modification to a product's design or by a failure to disclose design flaws.[55] Knowledge may also be established by circumstantial evidence.[56] Similarly, where a seller is reckless as to the truth or falsity of a representation, this is sufficient willfulness.[57] Several courts find a violation if the seller knew or should have known of the statement's falsity.[58] A knowledge requirement was met where a company official did not know of an error in advertising, but would have discovered it if he had examined company records more carefully. The official was found to have a duty to investigate.[59] A promise to perform under a contract in the future is a UDAP violation, if it is made without intention of performance.[60]

The Oregon UDAP statute requires private litigants to show that the violation was willful, *i.e.*, the person committing the violation knew or should have known that the conduct was a violation.[61] The Oregon Supreme Court

---

New Mexico: *But see* Stevenson v. Louis Dreyfus Corp., 112 N.M. 97, 811 P.2d 1308 (1991).

North Carolina: *See also* Forbes v. Par Ten Group, Inc., 99 N.C. App. 587, 394 S.E.2d 643 (1990); Bernard v. Central Carolina Truck Sales, Inc., 314 S.E.2d 582 (N.C. Ct. App. 1984).

Ohio: Erie Shore Builders v. Leimbach, 2001 Ohio App. LEXIS 3158 (July 13, 2001); Karst v. Goldberg, 623 N.E.2d 1348 (Ohio App. 1993) (intent unnecessary for deception claims, but scienter must be shown to establish unconscionable act); *see also* Karst v. Goldberg, 88 Ohio App. 3d 413, 623 N.E.2d 1348 (1993); D&K Roofing, Inc. v. Pleso, 77 Ohio App. 3d 181, 601 N.E.2d 561 (1991); Funk v. Montgomery AMC/Jeep/Renault, 66 Ohio App. 3d 815, 586 N.E.2d 1113 (1990).

Pennsylvania: Andrews v. Fleet Real Estate Funding Corp., 78 B.R. 78 (Bankr. E.D. Pa. 1987).

South Carolina: *In re* Daniel, 137 B.R. 884 (D.S.C. 1992). *See also* Clarkson v. Orkin Exterminating Co., 761 F.2d 189 (4th Cir. 1985) (South Carolina law).

Tennessee: *See also* Smith v. Scott Lewis Chevrolet, Inc., 843 S.W.2d 9 (Tenn. Ct. App. 1992). *But cf.* Shepherd v. Weather Shield Mfg., Inc., 2000 Tenn. App. LEXIS 559 (July 31, 2000) (not UDAP violation to sell defective windows where seller was unaware of defect).

Texas: Miller v. Keyser, 90 S.W.3d 712 (Tex. 2002). *See also* Sergeant Oil & Gas Co. v. National Maintenance & Repair, 861 F. Supp. 1351 (S.D. Tex. 1994); Robinson v. Preston Chrysler-Plymouth, Inc., 633 S.W.2d 500 (Tex. 1982) (deceptive to make affirmative misstatements without knowledge of falsity, but not deceptive for sellers to fail to disclose facts of which seller is not aware); State v. Credit Bureau of Laredo, 530 S.W.2d 288 (Tex. 1975); Henry S. Miller Co. v. Bynum, 797 S.W.2d 51 (Tex. App. 1990).

Utah: *But see* Rawson v. Conover, 20 P.3d 876 (Utah 2001) (knowing or intentional deception is required because of 1985 amendment to statute); State v. GAF Corp., 760 P.2d 310 (Utah 1988) (interpreting pre-1985 version of statute, which has since been amended to require intent to deceive).

47 State *ex rel.* Lefkowitz v. Interstate Tractor Trailer Training, Inc., 66 Misc. 2d 678, 321 N.Y.S.2d 147 (Sup. Ct. 1971).

48 *See* Cameron v. Terrell & Garrett, Inc., 618 S.W.2d 535 (Tex. 1981); Henry S. Miller Co. v. Bynum, 797 S.W.2d 51 (Tex. App. 1990). *See* § 4.2.5.2, *infra*.

49 Robinson v. Preston Chrysler-Plymouth, Inc., 633 S.W.2d 500 (Tex. 1982). *But see* Golt v. Phillips, 308 Md. 1, 517 A.2d 328 (1986). *See generally* § 4.2.14.3.4, *infra*.

50 Fate v. Dick Callendar Buick, 1986 Ohio App. LEXIS 6878 (May 23, 1986).

51 First Title Co. of Waco v. Garrett, 860 S.W.2d 74 (Tex. 1993); Camden Mach. & Tool, Inc. v. Cascade Co., 870 S.W.2d 304 (Tex. App. 1993); 3Z Corp. v. Stewart Title Guar. Co., 851 S.W.2d 933 (Tex. App. 1993).

52 Northwestern Public Service v. Union Carbide, 236 F. Supp. 2d 966 (D.S.D. 2002).

53 *See* § 8.4.2.3.1, *infra*.

54 People v. Lynam, 253 Cal. App. 2d 959, 61 Cal. Rptr. 800 (1967).

55 Bayliner Marine Corp. v. Elder, 994 S.W.2d 439 (Tex. App. 1999) (defective boat).

56 Etheridge v. Oak Creek Mobile Homes, Inc., 989 S.W.2d 412 (Tex. App. 1999) (defective mobile home).

57 Montanez v. Bagg, 24 Mass. App. Ct. 954, 510 N.E.2d 298 (1987) (sufficient willfulness to award treble damages).

58 People v. Lynam, 253 Cal. App. 2d 959, 61 Cal. Rptr. 800 (1967); Rhino Linings USA, Inc. v. Rocky Mountain Rhino Lining, Inc., 62 P.3d 142 (Colo. 2003) (knowledge requirement can be satisfied by recklessness); Nash v. Hoopes, 332 A.2d 411 (Del. Super. Ct. 1975); McKinney v. State, 693 N.E.2d 65 (Ind. 1998) (statutory definition adopts "knew or should have known" standard); Scott v. Western Int'l Surplus Sales, Inc., 267 Or. 512, 517 P.2d 661 (1973). *See also* Stevenson v. Louis Dreyfus Corp., 112 N.M. 97, 811 P.2d 1308 (1991). *Contra* Parkway Co. v. Woodruff, 901 S.W.2d 434 (Tex. 1995). *But cf.* Woodlands Land Development Co., L.P. v. Jenkins, 48 S.W.3d 415 (Tex. App. 2001) (actual awareness in state real estate fraud statute means that a defendant knows an act is deceptive but acts nonetheless).

59 People v. Forest E. Olson, Inc., 137 Cal. App. 3d 137, 186 Cal. Rptr. 804 (1982). *See also In re* Wiggins, 273 B.R. 839 (Bankr. D. Idaho 2001).

60 Kuehnhoefer v. Welch, 893 S.W.2d 689 (Tex. App. 1995).

61 Rathgeber v. Hemenway, Inc., 69 P.3d 710, 715 (Or. 2003)

interpreted this as requiring a showing that a real estate agent knew, at the time of making a representation about his services, that he would not perform as promised.[62] A single act of misconduct can support a finding that the actor did not intend to act in accord with the promise.[63]

Knowledge may be inferred from the circumstances.[64] Moreover, the knowledge of officials will be imputed to the corporation.[65] Similarly, an automobile dealer's knowledge was imputed to his salesman since the dealer had the duty to see that his salesman had whatever knowledge was chargeable to the dealer.[66] Where a seller promises to build a home in a certain fashion, a knowledge requirement is met where the seller knowingly builds the home differently, even if the seller did not know its original promise was false at the time it made the promise.[67] Where a UDAP statute allows civil penalties when the seller "knew or should have known that the conduct was a violation," no more is required than proof of ordinary negligence as shown by the preponderance of the evidence, and the common law fraud standard of clear and convincing evidence does not apply.[68]

4.2.6 Despite Good Faith Efforts

A seller's good faith efforts do not prevent a practice from being deceptive under the FTC Act.[69] For example, it is not a defense that the seller acted in good faith upon the advice of counsel.[70] State courts also agree that good faith is not controlling.[71] Moreover, the consumer need not show that the seller acted in bad faith to establish a UDAP violation.[72]

A Texas court has upheld the constitutionality of a former provision of its UDAP statute that permitted a bona fide error defense only in class actions.[73] Where there is a statutory defense for "bona fide error," this defense applies only to clerical errors, such as typographical errors or mistakes in computing numbers, not to a seller's other unintentional misrepresentations.[74] Ohio's bona fide error

(quoting Or. Rev. Stat. § 646.605(10)).

62 *Id.*

63 *Id.*

64 K.C. Roofing Co. v. Abundis, 940 S.W.2d 375 (Tex. App. 1997).

65 *In re* Wiggins, 273 B.R. 839 (Bankr. D. Idaho 2001); People v. Forest E. Olson, Inc., 137 Cal. App. 3d 137, 186 Cal. Rptr. 804 (1982); Green Tree Acceptance, Inc. v. Holmes, 803 S.W.2d 458 (Tex. App. 1991).

66 *In re* Brandywine Volkswagen, Ltd., 312 A.2d 632 (Del. 1973). *See also* Green Tree Acceptance, Inc. v. Holmes, 803 S.W.2d 458 (Tex. App. 1991).

67 Jim Walter Homes, Inc. v. Valencia, 690 S.W.2d 239 (Tex. 1985); *accord* Am. Indian and Alaska Native Cultural and Arts Development Inst. v. Daymon & Assocs., 1999 U.S. Dist. LEXIS 22380 (D.N.M. June 23, 1999) (misrepresentation can become false due to later events). *But see* Swarthout v. Mut. Serv. Life Ins. Co., 632 N.W.2d 741 (Minn. App. 2001) (no UDAP claim where insurance agent's statements about which doctors he would contact were rendered false only after he made them, when other employees altered plaintiff's release).

68 State *ex rel.* Redden Discount Fabrics, 289 Or. 375, 615 P.2d 1034 (1980).

69 Orkin Exterminating Co. v. FTC, 849 F.2d 1354 (11th Cir. 1988), *cert. denied*, 488 U.S. 1041 (1989); Chrysler Corp. v. FTC, 561 F.2d 357 (D.C. Cir. 1977); Doherty, Clifford, Steers & Shenfield, Inc. v. FTC, 392 F.2d 921 (6th Cir. 1968); Montgomery Ward & Co. v. FTC, 379 F.2d 666 (7th Cir. 1967); Koch v. FTC, 206 F.2d 311 (6th Cir. 1953); FTC v. U.S. Sales Corp., 785 F. Supp. 737 (N.D. Ill. 1992); FTC v. Pharmtech Research, Inc., 576 F. Supp. 294 (D.D.C. 1983).

70 FTC v. Amy Travel Service, Inc., 875 F.2d 564 (7th Cir. 1989); Orkin Exterminating Co. v. FTC, 849 F.2d 1354 (11th Cir. 1988), *cert. denied*, 488 U.S. 1041 (1989).

71 *In re* Cohen, 191 B.R. 599 (D.N.J. 1996), *aff'd on other grounds*, 106 F.3d 52 (3d Cir. 1997), *aff'd*, 523 U.S. 213 (1998); Francoline v. Klatt, 26 Conn. App. 203, 600 A.2d 8 (1991); People *ex rel.* Hartigan v. Maclean Hunter Publishing Corp., 119 Ill. App. 3d 1049, 457 N.E.2d 480 (1983); Courtney v. Bassano, 1999 ME 101, 733 A.2d 973 (Me. 1999); Bartner v. Carter, 405 A.2d 194 (Me. 1979); Gennari v. Weichert Co. Realtors, 148 N.J. 582, 691 A.2d 350 (1997); Cox v. Sears, Roebuck & Co., 138 N.J. 2, 647 A.2d 454 (1994); Huffmaster v. Robinson, 221 N.J. Super. 315, 534 A.2d 435 (Law. Div. 1986); Gray v. North Carolina Ins. Underwriting Assn., 352 N.C. 61, 529 S.E.2d 676 (2000); Pearce v. American Defender Life Ins. Co., 343 S.E.2d 174 (N.C. 1986); Marshall v. Miller, 302 N.C. 539, 276 S.E.2d 397 (1981); Forbes v. Par Ten Group, Inc., 99 N.C. App. 587, 394 S.E.2d 643 (1990); Myers v. Liberty Lincoln-Mercury, Inc., 89 N.C. App. 335, 365 S.E.2d 663 (1988); Boyle v. Daimler Chrysler Corp., 2002 WL 1881157 (Ohio App. Aug. 16, 2002) (unpublished, citation limited) (bona fide error not a defense to liability; only precludes attorney fees and damages in excess of actual damages); Andrews v. Scott Pontiac Cadillac GMC, Inc., 71 Ohio App. 3d 613, 594 N.E.2d 1127 (1991); Peasley v. Clark, Clearinghouse No. 46,643 (Ohio Ct. App. 1980); Commonwealth v. Hush-Tone Indus., Inc., 4 Pa. Commw. 1 (1971); Commonwealth v. Programmed Learning Sys., Inc., Clearinghouse No. 26,019 (Pa. C.P. Allegheny Cty. 1975); Commonwealth v. Gold Bond Indus., Inc., Clearinghouse No. 26,028 (Pa. C.P. Allegheny Cty. 1973); Miller v. Soliz, 648 S.W.2d 734 (Tex. App. 1983) (practice can be unconscionable even despite seller's good faith); United Postage Corp. v. Kammeyer, 581 S.W.2d 716 (Tex. Civ. App. 1979); Crawford Chevrolet, Inc. v. McLerty, 519 S.W.2d 656 (Tex. Civ. App. 1975); Winton v. Johnson & Dix Fuel Corp., 515 A.2d 371 (Vt. 1986); Testo v. Russ Dunmire Oldsmobile, Inc., 16 Wash. App. 39, 554 P.2d 349, (1976); *see also* Hurst v. Sears, Roebuck & Co., 647 S.W.2d 249 (Tex. 1983) (misrepresentation unconscionable even though impossible for seller to comply with representation). *Cf.* Watkins v. Peterson Enterprises, Inc., 57 F. Supp. 2d 1102 (E.D. Wash. 1999) (good faith not a defense to deception but is a defense to unfairness).

72 Equitable Life Assurance Society v. Porter-Englehart, 867 F.2d 79 (1st Cir. 1989) (Mass. law); April v. Union Mortgage Co., 709 F. Supp. 809 (N.D. Ill. 1989); State v. United States Steel Corp., 919 P.2d 294 (Haw. 1996) (plaintiff claiming deception need not show that defendant's act was immoral, unethical, oppressive, or unscrupulous); Torrance v. AS&L Motors, 459 S.E.2d 67 (N.C. Ct. App. 1995).

73 Crawford Chevrolet, Inc. v. McLerty, 519 S.W.2d 656 (Tex. Civ. App. 1975).

74 Fleck v. Custom Sound Co., 1981 Ohio App. LEXIS 14162 (Dec. 31, 1981); Katz v. G.C. Murphy Co., 1979 Ohio App. LEXIS 8976 (Jan. 31, 1979); Stendebach v. Campbell, 665 S.W.2d 557 (Tex. App. 1984); *see also* Andrews v. Scott Pontiac Cadillac GMC, Inc., 71 Ohio App. 3d 613, 594 N.E.2d 1127

defense relieves the supplier of liability only for attorney fees, multiple damages and statutory damages, not actual damages.[75]

4.2.7 Despite Cessation of Practice

The cessation by the seller of the deceptive practice at the time of the suit is no defense under the FTC Act.[76] While this defense is irrelevant to a private damage action,[77] it may have to be considered in a private action seeking an injunction only.[78] Nonetheless, state courts agree that cessation of the practice does not moot an injunctive action.[79] Injunctions are issued to prohibit practices like those already committed. If an injunctive suit were dismissed because of the defendant's cessation of the practice, the seller would be free to revert to its identical deceptive practice or a related one at no additional risk. Nor does a defendant's offer to refund the consumer's money after suit has been filed, without offering to pay attorney fees recoverable under the UDAP statute, moot a case.[80]

4.2.8 Despite Industrywide Practice

It is no defense to a deception claim under the FTC Act that the challenged practice is engaged in throughout an industry or is "customary" business conduct.[81] State UDAP case law also follows this approach.[82] For example, the practice of quoting, as a "per annum" rate, interest computed on the basis of a 360-day year violates California's UDAP statute even though it is a "customary" business practice within the banking community.[83] Improperly calculating late charges is a UDAP violation even though the

---

(1991) (where UDAP violation occurred as a result of a company policy, existence of the policy did not establish bona fide error defense); Green v. USA Energy Consultants, 1986 Ohio App. LEXIS 8309 (Sept. 18, 1986) (defendant could not establish the bona fide error defense simply by blaming another corporation); Allstate Ins. Co. v. Kelly, 680 S.W.2d 595 (Tex. App. 1984). *But cf.* Clark v. Ourisman Fairfax, Inc., 2002 WL 1941132 (Va. Cir. Ct. May 29, 2002) (interpreting bona fide error defense in dictum to excuse unintentional misrepresentations). *See also* the cases discussing the bona fide error defense in the Truth in Lending Act and the Fair Debt Collection Practice Act, at National Consumer Law Center, Truth in Lending § 7.4.3 (5th ed. 2003 and Supp.) and National Consumer Law Center, Fair Debt Collection § 7.5 (5th ed. 2004).

75 Boyle v. Daimler Chrysler Corp., 2002 WL 1881157 (Ohio App. Aug. 16, 2002) (unpublished, citation limited).

76 Beneficial Corp. v. FTC, 542 F.2d 611 (3d Cir. 1976); Fedders Corp. v. FTC, 529 F.2d 1398 (2d Cir. 1976), *cert. denied*, 429 U.S. 818 (1976); Diener's, Inc. v. FTC, 494 F.2d 1132 (D.C. Cir. 1974); P.F. Collier & Son Corp. v. FTC, 427 F.2d 261 (6th Cir.), *cert. denied*, 400 U.S. 926 (1970); Cotherman v. FTC, 417 F.2d 587 (5th Cir. 1969); Libby Owens Ford Glass Co. v. FTC, 352 F.2d 415 (6th Cir. 1965); Carter Products, Inc. v. FTC, 323 F.2d 523 (5th Cir. 1963); International Harvester Co., 104 F.T.C. 949 (1984). Of course, if there is no likelihood of resumption of the challenged practice, the FTC may find there is no public interest in the proceeding with an action solely seeking to enjoin future practices.

77 Cybal v. Atrium Palace Syndicate, 272 N.J. Super. 330, 639 A.2d 1146 (App. Div. 1994) (return of consumer's deposit shortly before arbitration did not moot UDAP claim for attorney fees); State v. A.N.W. Seed Corp., 116 Wash. 2d 39, 802 P.2d 1353 (1991). *See also* Hart v. Moore, 587 N.Y.S.2d 477 (Sup. Ct. 1992).

78 Wiginton v. Pacific Credit Corp., 2 Haw. App. 435, 634 P.2d 111 (1981); MET-Rx USA, Inc. v. Shipman, 62 S.W.3d 807 (Tex. App. 2001) (consumer can not seek only prospective declaratory or injunctive relief when he does not plan to purchase goods from the defendant again).

79 State v. Goodyear Tire & Rubber Co., 128 Ariz. 483, 626 P.2d 1115 (Ct. App. 1981); People *ex rel.* Babbitt v. Green Acres Trust, 127 Ariz. 160, 618 P.2d 1086 (Ct. App. 1980); Wiginton v. Pacific Credit Corp., 2 Haw. App. 435, 634 P.2d 111 (1981) (private action); Commonwealth *ex rel.* Stephens v. Isaacs, 577 S.W.2d 617 (Ky. App. 1979); Consumer Protection Div. v. Consumer Publishing Co., 304 Md. 731, 501 A.2d 48 (1986); Lowell Gas Co. v. Attorney General, 377 Mass. 37, 385 N.E.2d 240 (1979); People *ex rel.* Spitzer v. Network Assocs., Inc., 195 Misc. 2d 384, 758 N.Y.S.2d 466, 469 (2003) (suit by AG); People *ex rel.* Abrams v. Robbins, Clearinghouse No. 50,409 (N.Y. Sup. Ct. Mar. 14, 1994); State v. Midland Equities of New York, Inc., 117 Misc. 2d 203, 458 N.Y.S.2d 126 (Sup. Ct. 1982); People *ex rel.* Lefkowitz v. Therapeutic Hypnosis, Inc., 83 Misc. 2d 1068, 374 N.Y.S.2d 576 (Sup. Ct. 1975); State *ex rel.* McLeod v. Brown, 294 S.E.2d 781 (S.C. 1982); State v. Ralph Williams' N.W. Chrysler Plymouth, Inc., 87 Wash. 2d 298, 553 P.2d 423 (1976); State v. Ralph Williams' N.W. Chrysler Plymouth, Inc., 82 Wash. 2d 265, 510 P.2d 233 (1973); Weller v. Department of Agriculture, Trade & Consumer Protection, No. 78-813 (Wis. Ct. App. 1980), *aff'd*, 109 Wis. 2d 665, 327 N.W.2d 178 (1982); *see also* People v. Wilco Energy Corp., 284 A.D.2d 469, 728 N.Y.S.2d 471 (2001) (cessation does not moot suit by AG).

80 Larobina v. Home Depot, USA, Inc., 821 A.2d 283 (Conn. App. 2003) (noting that encouraging consumers to walk away from deceptive practices would impair statute's goal of deterrence); Bates v. William Chevrolet/Geo, Inc., 785 N.E.2d 53 (Ill. App. 2003). *See also* Kiley v. Petsmart, 80 P.3d 1179 (Kan. App. 2003) (allowing UDAP claim to proceed even though seller offered to replace mismarked used goods with new). *But cf.* Huss v. Sessler Ford, Inc., 343 Ill. App. 3d 835, 799 N.E.2d 444 (Ill. App. 2003) (pre-suit offer of refund moots case).

81 Moog Indus., Inc. v. FTC, 355 U.S. 411 (1958); United Biscuit Co. v. FTC, 350 F.2d 615 (7th Cir. 1965), *cert. denied*, 383 U.S. 926 (1966); Sterling Drug, Inc., 102 F.T.C. 395 (1983); Peacock Buick, Inc., 86 F.T.C. 1532 (1976). *See also* Encyclopedia Britannica v. FTC, 605 F.2d 964 (7th Cir. 1979).

82 Andrews v. Fleet Real Estate Funding Corp., 78 B.R. 78 (Bankr. E.D. Pa. 1987); Chern v. Bank of Am., 15 Cal. 3d 866, 544 P.2d 1310, 127 Cal. Rptr. 110 (1976); People v. Cappuccio, Inc., 204 Cal. App. 3d 750, 251 Cal. Rptr. 657 (1988); People v. Casa Blanca Convalescent Homes, 206 Cal. Rptr. 164 (Ct. App. 1984); Halloran's v. Spillane's Servicecenter, Inc., 41 Conn. Supp. 484, 587 A.2d 176 (1990); Commonwealth v. DeCotis, 366 Mass. 234, 316 N.E.2d 748 (1974); Commonwealth v. Gold Bond Indus., Inc., Clearinghouse No. 26,028 (Pa. C.P. Allegheny Cty. 1973); Huff & Morse, Inc. v. Riordan, 345 N.W.2d 504 (Wis. Ct. App. 1984).

83 Chern v. Bank of Am., 15 Cal. 3d 866, 544 P.2d 1310, 127 Cal. Rptr. 110 (1976).

practice is traditional in the industry.[84] It is no defense that none of a state's auto repair shops comply with a written authorization regulation.[85] Commercial impracticability is not a defense.[86]

4.2.9 Actual Deception Unnecessary; Likelihood or Capacity for Deception Sufficient

The Federal Trade Commission can order a company to cease and desist a practice without finding that consumers were actually deceived. Actual deception is unnecessary, and all that need be shown is that the practice has the "capacity" or "tendency" to deceive.[87] Consumer testimony is not essential; only the challenged practice must be described.[88]

Since the 1980s, the FTC has abandoned its capacity to deceive standard in favor of a "likely" to deceive standard.[89] It appears that this standard is intended to be somewhat, but not much more restrictive than the capacity to deceive standard.[90] It is hard to imagine a private UDAP claim turning on whether the claim has a "tendency or capacity" or is just "likely" to deceive consumers. For example, several decisions have stated that a practice was deceptive under either the tendency or capacity to mislead standard or the likely to mislead standard.[91] Some decisions find no real difference between the two standards.[92]

The Ninth Circuit has held that the new standard places a greater burden of proof on the FTC, and that any violation of the new standard necessarily violates the old one.[93] Consequently, the seller is not prejudiced if a court uses the new and not the old standard.

It is unclear whether the FTC's current standard has any precedential effect for state UDAP cases since existing United States Supreme Court and United States circuit court precedent is still restricted to the capacity to deceive standard.[94] To date, most courts interpreting state UDAP statutes

84 Andrews v. Fleet Real Estate Funding Corp., 78 B.R. 78 (Bankr. E.D. Pa. 1987).

85 Huff & Morse, Inc. v. Riordan, 345 N.W.2d 504 (Wis. Ct. App. 1984).

86 People v. Wilco Energy Corp., 284 A.D.2d 469, 728 N.Y.S.2d 471 (2001).

87 FTC v. Colgate-Palmolive Co., 380 U.S. 374 (1965); FTC v. Raladam Co., 316 U.S. 149 (1942); FTC v. Algoma Lumber Co., 291 U.S. 67 (1934); FTC v. Royal Milling Co., 288 U.S. 212 (1933); American Home Products Corp. v. FTC, 695 F.2d 681 (3d Cir. 1982); Trans World Accounts, Inc. v. FTC, 594 F.2d 212 (9th Cir. 1979); Beneficial Corp. v. FTC, 542 F.2d 611 (3d Cir. 1976); Resort Car Rental Sys., Inc. v. FTC, 518 F.2d 962 (9th Cir.), *cert. denied sub nom.* Mackenzie v. United States 423 U.S. 827 (1975); Montgomery Ward & Co. v. FTC, 379 F.2d 666 (7th Cir. 1967); Benrus Watch Co. v. FTC, 352 F.2d 313 (8th Cir. 1965); FTC v. Sterling Drug, 317 F.2d 669 (2d Cir. 1963); U.S. Retail Credit Ass'n, Inc. v. FTC, 300 F.2d 212 (4th Cir. 1962); FTC v. Think Achievement Corp., 144 F. Supp. 2d 993 (N.D. Ind. 2000), *aff'd in part, rev'd in part on other grounds*, 312 F.3d 259 (7th Cir. 2002). *See* Commonwealth *ex rel.* Fisher v. Allstate Ins. Co., Clearinghouse No. 53,561 (Pa. Commw. Ct. Jan. 18, 2001).

88 FTC v. Colgate-Palmolive Co., 380 U.S. 374 (1965); Simeon Mgmt. Corp. v. FTC, 579 F.2d 1137 (9th Cir. 1978); Resort Car Rental Sys., Inc. v. FTC, 518 F.2d 962 (9th Cir. 1975), *cert. denied sub nom.* Mackenzie v. United States, 423 U.S. 827 (1975); Floersheim v. FTC, 411 F.2d 874 (9th Cir. 1969), *cert. denied*, 396 U.S. 1002 (1970); Montgomery Ward & Co. v. FTC, 379 F.2d 666 (7th Cir. 1967); Carter Products, Inc. v. FTC, 323 F.2d 523 (5th Cir. 1963); Murray Space Shoe Corp. v. FTC, 304 F.2d 270 (2d Cir. 1962); Feil v. FTC, 285 F.2d 879 (9th Cir. 1960); Kraft, Inc., 5 Trade Reg. Rep. (CCH) ¶ 22937 (F.T.C. Dkt. 9208 1991); MacMillan Inc., 96 F.T.C. 208 (1980); *see also* Consumer Protection Div. v. Consumer Publishing Co., 304 Md. 731, 501 A.2d 48 (1986).

89 FTC v. Consumer Alliance, Inc., 2003 WL 22287364, at *4 (N.D. Ill. Sept. 30, 2003); FTC v. Gill, 71 F. Supp. 2d 1030 (C.D. Cal. 1999), *aff'd*, 265 F.3d 944 (9th Cir. 2001); Cliffdale Assocs., 103 F.T.C. 110 (1984); International Harvester Co., 104 F.T.C. 949 (1984); Thompson Medical Co., 104 F.T.C. 648 (1984), *aff'd*, 791 F.2d 189 (D.C. Cir. 1986), *cert. denied*, 479 U.S. 1086 (1987); *see also* FTC v. Wilcox, 926 F. Supp. 1091 (S.D. Fla. 1995); Letters by Chairman Miller to Honorable Bob Packwood, Chairman, Committee on Commerce, Science and Transportation, U.S. Senate (Oct. 14, 1983), and to Honorable John Dingell, Chairman, Committee on Energy and Commerce, U.S. House (Oct. 14, 1983).

90 *See* Southwest Sunsites, Inc. v. FTC, 785 F.2d 1431 (9th Cir. 1986). *Cf.* Kraft, Inc., 5 Trade Reg. Rep. (CCH) ¶ 22937 (F.T.C. Dkt. 9208 1991) (no proof of actual deception needed); Commonwealth v. Amcan Enterprises, 47 Mass. App. Ct. 330, 712 N.E.2d 1205 (1999) (new standard is rooted in established precedent and is not a radical change in policy).

91 Massachusetts v. Amcan Enterprises, Inc., 1996 Mass. Super. LEXIS 609 (Mar. 20, 1996), *aff'd as modified*, Commonwealth v. Amcan Enterprises, 47 Mass. App. Ct. 330, 712 N.E.2d 1205 (1999); Pekular v. Eich, 513 A.2d 427 (Pa. Super. Ct. 1986) (result the same whether court uses "tendency or capacity" standard or "likely to deceive" standard); Poulin v. Ford Motor Co., 513 A.2d 1168 (Vt. 1986).

92 Gray v. North Carolina Ins. Underwriting Assn., 352 N.C. 61, 529 S.E.2d 676 (2000); DeBondt v. Carlton Motorcars, Inc., 342 S.C. 254, 536 S.E.2d 399 (2000); *see also* Kasky v. Nike, Inc., 27 Cal. 4th 939, 45 P.3d 243, 119 Cal. Rptr. 2d 296, 304 (2002) ("capacity, likelihood, or tendency to deceive" sufficient).

93 Southwest Sunsites, Inc. v. FTC, 785 F.2d 1431 (9th Cir. 1986).

94 *See* note 87, *supra*. In addition, the use of these new standards in FTC decisions has been somewhat forced, since the standards seem to have no impact on the cases' holdings, and discussions of the new standards arguably are just dicta. *See* Cliffdale Assocs., 103 F.T.C. 110 (1984); International Harvester Co., 104 F.T.C. 949 (1984); Thompson Medical Co., 104 F.T.C. 648 (1984), *aff'd*, 791 F.2d 189 (D.C. Cir. 1986), *cert. denied*, 479 U.S. 1086 (1987).

Even if the FTC statements in these cases are treated as more than just dicta, it is doubtful if this has an impact on state UDAP cases. The numerous U.S. circuit courts of appeal decisions and several U.S. Supreme Court decisions contradicting the FTC standard should control the legal standard, since FTC decisions are subject to review by these appellate courts. According to the U.S. Supreme Court, "in the last analysis the words 'deceptive practices' set forth a legal standard and they must get their final meaning from judicial construction." FTC v. Colgate-Palmolive

continue to use the capacity to deceive and not the likely to deceive standard, both for actions brought by the state[95] and for private actions.[96] This standard is valid and does not conflict with federal law.[97]

Co., 380 U.S. 374, 385 (1965). To the extent the FTC standards are less encompassing than that adopted by the circuit courts, courts interpreting state UDAP statutes are likely to view the FTC as not exercising its full statutory authority.

95 State v. O'Neill Investigations, Inc., 609 P.2d 520 (Alaska 1980); State v. McLeod, Clearinghouse No. 50,412 (Ark. Ch. Ct., Pulaski Cty. Nov. 23, 1993); People v. Dollar Rent-a-Car Sys., Inc., 211 Cal. App. 3d 119, 259 Cal. Rptr. 191 (1989); People v. Toomey, 157 Cal. App. 3d 1, 203 Cal. Rptr. 642 (1984); State *ex rel.* Kidwell v. Master Distributors, Inc., 101 Idaho 447, 615 P.2d 116 (1980); People *ex rel.* Fahner v. Walsh, 122 Ill. App. 3d 481, 461 N.E.2d 78 (1984); State *ex rel.* Miller v. Hydro Mag, Ltd., 436 N.W.2d 617 (Iowa 1989); State v. Koscot Interplanetary, Inc., 212 Kan. 668, 512 P.2d 416 (1973); Telcom Directories, Inc. v. Commonwealth *ex rel.* Cowan, 833 S.W.2d 848 (Ky. Ct. App. 1991); Consumer Protection Div. v. Consumer Publishing Co., 304 Md. 731, 501 A.2d 48 (1986); State v. Directory Publishing Servs., Inc., 1996 Minn. App. LEXIS 62 (Jan. 9, 1996) (unpublished, non-precedential); State *ex rel.* Humphrey v. Dynasty Sys. Corp., Clearinghouse No. 36,591 (Minn. Dist. Ct. 1983); Cox v. Sears, Roebuck & Co., 138 N.J. 2, 647 A.2d 454 (1994); Kugler v. Romain, 58 N.J. 522, 279 A.2d 640 (1971); Kugler v. Koscot Interplanetary, Inc., 120 N.J. Super. 216, 293 A.2d 682 (Ch. Div. 1972); People *ex rel.* Spitzer v. Gen. Electric Co., 302 A.D.2d 314, 756 N.Y.S.2d 520 (2003) (Exec. Law. § 63(12)); People by Spitzer v. Network Assocs., Inc., 195 Misc. 2d 384, 758 N.Y.S.2d 466 (2003) (referring to certain terms of software licensing agreement as "rules and regulations" is deceptive because it implies that they are imposed by some external authority); People *ex rel.* Lefkowitz v. Volkswagen of Am., Inc., 47 A.D.2d 868, 366 N.Y.S.2d 157 (1975); State *ex rel.* Abrams v. Abandoned Funds Information Center, Inc., 129 Misc. 2d 614, 493 N.Y.S.2d 907 (Sup. Ct. 1985); State v. Management Transition Resources, Inc., 454 N.Y.S.2d 513 (Sup. Ct. 1982); Wachovia Bank & Trust v. Carrington Dev. Assocs., 459 S.E.2d 17 (N.C. Ct. App. 1995); Creekside Apartments v. Poteat, 446 S.E.2d 826 (N.C. Ct. App. 1994) (capacity to deceive average consumer); Commonwealth v. Hush-Tone Indus., Inc., 4 Pa. Commw. 1 (1971); Commonwealth *ex rel.* Zimmerman v. Nickel, 26 Pa. D. & C.3d 115 (C.P. Mercer Cty. 1983); Commonwealth v. Programmed Learning Sys., Inc., Clearinghouse No. 26,019 (Pa. C.P. Allegheny Cty. 1975); Commonwealth v. Armstrong, 74 Pa. D. & C.2d 579 (C.P. Phila. Cty. 1974); State *ex rel.* McLeod v. Brown, 294 S.E.2d 781 (S.C. 1984); State v. Packard, Clearinghouse No. 27,066 (Vt. Super. Ct. 1977); State v. Ralph Williams' N.W. Chrysler Plymouth, Inc., 87 Wash. 2d 298, 553 P.2d 423 (1976); State v. American TV & Appliance, 140 Wis. 2d 353, 410 N.W.2d 596 (Ct. App. 1987), *rev'd on other grounds*, 430 N.W.2d 709 (Wis. 1988). *But cf.* State *ex rel.* Nixon v. Telco Directory Publishing, 863 S.W.2d 596 (Mo. 1993) (holding that Missouri UDAP statute addresses only actual deception, not capacity to deceive; subsequent to this holding the Missouri attorney general adopted regulations incorporating the capacity to deceive standard, Mo. Code State Regs. tit. 15, §§ 60-7.020, 60-9.020, 9.030). *But see* Millennium Communications & Fulfillment, Inc. v. Attorney General, 761 So. 2d 1256 (Fla. App. 2000) (adopting "likely to deceive" standard).

96 Clarkson v. Orkin Exterminating Co., 761 F.2d 189 (4th Cir. 1985) (South Carolina law); Daenzer v. Wayland Ford, Inc., 2002 WL 1050209, 2002 U.S. Dist. LEXIS 8409 (E.D. Mich. May 7, 2002) (probability of confusion or misunderstanding sufficient); Top Rank, Inc. v. Gutierrez, 236 F. Supp. 2d 637 (W.D. Tex. 2001); Basnight v. Diamond Developers, Inc., 146 F. Supp. 2d 754 (M.D.N.C. 2001); Aurigemma v. Arco Petroleum Products Co., 734 F. Supp. 1025 (D. Conn. 1990); *In re* Daniel, 137 B.R. 884 (D.S.C. 1992); Committee on Children's Television, Inc. v. General Foods Corp., 35 Cal. 3d 197, 197 Cal. Rptr. 783, 673 P.2d 660 (1983) (actual deception unnecessary under Cal. Bus. & Prof. Code § 17,200 to obtain private injunction or where restitution necessary to prevent unfair practice); Fletcher v. Security Pacific Nat'l Bank, 23 Cal. 3d 442, 591 P.2d 51, 153 Cal. Rptr. 28 (1979); Chern v. Bank of Am., 15 Cal. 3d 866, 544 P.2d 1310, 127 Cal. Rptr. 110 (1976); Rhino Linings USA, Inc. v. Rocky Mountain Rhino Lining, Inc., 62 P.3d 142 (Colo. 2003); Hawaii Community Fed. Credit Union v. Keka, 94 Haw. 213, 11 P.3d 1 (2000); Eastern Star, Inc. v. Union Building Materials, 712 P.2d 1148 (Haw. Ct. App. 1985); Claybourne v. Imsland, 414 N.W.2d 449 (Minn. Ct. App. 1987) (Uniform Deceptive Trade Practices Act-type statute does not require actual deception); Gennari v. Weichert Co. Realtors, 148 N.J. 582, 691 A.2d 350 (1997) (whether consumer plaintiffs were in fact misled is irrelevant); Miller v. American Family Publishers, 284 N.J. Super. 67, 663 A.2d 643 (Chancery Div. 1995); Hyland v. Zuback, 146 N.J. Super. 407, 370 A.2d 20 (App. Div. 1976); Pearce v. American Defender Life Ins. Co., 343 S.E.2d 174 (N.C. 1986); Torrance v. AS&L Motors, 459 S.E.2d 67 (N.C. Ct. App. 1995); Blackwell v. Dorosko, 383 S.E.2d 670 (N.C. Ct. App. 1989); Pekular v. Eich, 513 A.2d 427 (Pa. Super. Ct. 1986) (result the same whether "tendency or capacity" standard or FTC's new "likely to deceive" standard used); Inman v. Ken Hyatt Chrysler Plymouth, Inc., 294 S.C. 240, 363 S.E.2d 691 (1988); Young v. Century Lincoln-Mercury, Inc., 396 S.E.2d 105 (S.C. Ct. App. 1990); Bekins Moving & Storage Co. v. Williams, 947 S.W.2d 568 (Tex. App. 1997); Travis v. Washington Horse Breeders Ass'n, 111 Wash. 2d 396, 759 P.2d 418 (1988); Hangman Ridge Training Stables, Inc. v. Safeco Title Ins. Co., 105 Wash. 2d 778, 719 P.2d 531 (1986); Haner v. Quincy Farm Chemicals, Inc., 97 Wash. 2d 753, 649 P.2d 828 (1982); Hertzog v. WebTV Networks, 2002 WL 1609032 (Wash. App. July 22, 2002) (unpublished, citation limited); Robinson v. Avis Rent A Car Sys., Inc., 106 Wash. App. 104, 22 P.3d 818 (2001); Gruetzke v. Rodgers, 2001 Wash. App. LEXIS 1879 (Aug. 10, 2001) (unpublished, citation limited) (capacity to deceive sufficient, but not shown here); Dwyer v. J.I. Kislak Mortgage Corp., 103 Wash. App. 542, 13 P.3d 240 (2000); *see also* Chandler v. Am. Gen. Fin., 329 Ill. App. 3d 729, 768 N.E.2d 60 (2002) (ad is deceptive if it is likely or has capacity to deceive); Glazewski v. Allstate Ins. Co., 126 Ill. App. 3d 401, 466 N.E.2d 1151 (1984), *rev'd on other grounds*, 483 N.E.2d 1263 (Ill. 1985). *But see* Lavie v. Procter & Gamble Co., 105 Cal. App. 4th 496, 129 Cal. Rptr. 2d 486 (2003); Mass. Mut. Life Ins. Co. v. Superior Court, 97 Cal. App. 4th 1282, 119 Cal. Rptr. 2d 190, 195 (2002) (reciting "likely to deceive" standard); Bartner v. Carter, 405 A.2d 194 (Me. 1979); Knapp v. Potamkin Motors Corp., 253 N.J. Super. 502, 602 A.2d 302 (1991) (individual consumer must show actual deception and resulting damage to meet New Jersey's "ascertainable loss" requirement, although suits by attorney general are not so limited); Kraus v. Visa Int'l Serv. Ass'n, 304 A.D.2d 408, 756 N.Y.S.2d 853 (2003) (requiring showing that conduct is likely to mislead a reasonable consumer acting reasonably under the circumstances); Motzer Jeep Eagle, Inc. v. Ohio Attorney General, 95 Ohio App. 3d 183, 642 N.E.2d 20 (1994) (act is deceptive if it

Thus, while lack of actual damage may be an independent bar to private relief,[98] and while most cases will want to show actual damage, state UDAP statutes have been interpreted so that an individual plaintiff need not show he or she was actually deceived, but only that the practice has a tendency to deceive.[99] Nevertheless, since it should not be difficult, it would seem wise also to plead and make some showing of actual deception in a private damage action.

In a class action, however, actual deception may be difficult to prove, and the capacity-to-deceive standard will prove particularly useful. The California Supreme Court, to deter future UDAP violations and to foreclose retention of ill-gotten gains, allows restitution for each class member even though there is no evidence that each class member is deceived. The remedy is based on the policy that "protection of unwary consumers from being duped by unscrupulous sellers is an exigency of the utmost priority in contemporary society."[100]

Often the advertisement or statement itself is sufficient proof of its deceptive nature.[101] Evidence from a number of consumers who have been deceived is also helpful.[102] Survey evidence should ordinarily be unnecessary.[103]

has the likelihood of inducing a state of mind in the consumer that is not in accord with the facts); Shaver v. Standard Oil Co., 89 Ohio App. 3d 52, 623 N.E.2d 602 (1993) (same); Frey v. Vin Devers, Inc., 80 Ohio App. 3d 1, 608 N.E.2d 796 (1992) (same); Funk v. Montgomery AMC/Jeep/Renault, 66 Ohio App. 3d 815, 586 N.E.2d 1113 (1990) (same); State *ex rel.* Celebrezze v. Ferraro, 63 Ohio App. 3d 168, 578 N.E.2d 492 (1989) (same).

97 State v. Directory Publishing Servs., Inc., 1996 Minn. App. LEXIS 62 (Jan. 9, 1996) (unpublished, non-precedential).

98 *See* Shannon v. Boise Cascade Corp., 208 Ill. 2d 517, 805 N.E.2d 213 (Ill. 2004) (no proximate causation unless plaintiff was actually deceived); Knapp v. Potamkin Motors Corp., 253 N.J. Super. 502, 602 A.2d 302 (1991); § 7.5.2, *infra*.

99 Prata v. Superior Court, 91 Cal. App. 4th 1128, 111 Cal. Rptr. 2d 296 (2001); Schnall v. Hertz Corp., 78 Cal. App. 4th 1144, 93 Cal. Rptr. 2d 439 (2000); Rhino Linings USA, Inc. v. Rocky Mountain Rhino Lining, Inc., 62 P.3d 142 (Colo. 2003); Hawaii Community Fed. Credit Union v. Keka, 94 Haw. 213, 11 P.3d 1 (2000); Eshaghi v. Hanley Dawson Cadillac Co., 214 Ill. App. 3d 995, 574 N.E.2d 760 (1991); Sutton v. Viking Oldsmobile Nissan, Inc., 611 N.W.2d 60 (Minn. App. 2000), *appeal after remand* 2001 WL 856250 (Minn. App. July 31, 2001) (consumer alleged "legal nexus" between misconduct and injury, sufficient to support private action, with allegations that he would have bargained or refused the deal had he known that dealer kept significant portion of sum allegedly paid to another for service plan).

100 Fletcher v. Security Pacific Nat'l Bank, 23 Cal. 3d 442, 591 P.2d 51, 153 Cal. Rptr. 28 (1979); *accord* Mass. Mut. Life Ins. Co. v. Superior Court, 97 Cal. App. 4th 1282, 119 Cal. Rptr. 2d 190 (2002) (following *Fletcher*); *see also* Vasquez v. Superior Court, 4 Cal. 3d 800, 484 P.2d 964, 94 Cal. Rptr. 796 (1971).

101 Brockey v. Moore, 107 Cal. App. 4th 86, 131 Cal. Rptr. 2d 746 (2003).

102 *Id.*

103 *Id*; Consumer Advocates v. Echostar Satellite Corp., 113 Cal. App. 4th 1351, 8 Cal. Rptr. 3d 22 (2003).

4.2.10 Puffing as a Defense

"Puffing" is an exaggeration that is incredible and not taken seriously by the listener or reader. Puffing is a common defense to FTC actions, although usually not a successful one.[104] To prove that a claim is mere puffing, the seller will have to show that the exaggerated claim is harmless, purely fanciful, or a spoof, calculated to amuse and with *no* capacity to deceive.[105] Thus a practice was found to be only puffing since it was not likely to "dupe even the most gullible consumer."[106] An imprecise or vague representation is mere opinion and not actionable.[107]

104 FTC v. Colgate-Palmolive Co., 380 U.S. 374 (1965); J.B. Williams Co. v. FTC, 381 F.2d 884 (6th Cir. 1967); Double Eagle Lubricants, Inc. v. FTC, 360 F.2d 268 (10th Cir. 1965); Mohr v. FTC, 272 F.2d 401 (9th Cir. 1959), *cert. denied*, 362 U.S. 920 (1960); Niresk Indus., Inc. v. FTC, 278 F.2d 337 (7th Cir.), *cert. denied*, 364 U.S. 883 (1960); E.F. Drew & Co. v. FTC, 235 F.2d 735 (2d Cir. 1956), *cert. denied*, 352 U.S. 969 (1957); Charles of the Ritz Distributors Corp. v. FTC, 143 F.2d 676 (2d Cir. 1944); FTC v. U.S. Sales Corp., 785 F. Supp. 737 (N.D. Ill. 1992).

105 FTC v. Colgate-Palmolive Co., 380 U.S. 374 (1965); Goodman v. FTC, 244 F.2d 584 (9th Cir. 1957); People *ex rel.* Hartigan v. Maclean Hunter Publishing Corp., 119 Ill. App. 3d 1049, 457 N.E.2d 1023 (1983). *See also* Haskell v. Time, Inc., 857 F. Supp. 1392 (E.D. Cal. 1994) (vague, subjective claims that would deceive no reasonable consumer do not violate California's Unfair Business Practices Act).

106 State v. Marsden, Clearinghouse No. 27,048 (Alaska Super. Ct. 1977); *see also* Webb Press Servs. v. New London Motors, Inc., 205 Conn. 479, 533 A.2d 1211 (1987); Autohaus, Inc. v. Aguilar, 794 S.W.2d 459 (Tex. App. 1990) (over a dissent, a claim that a Mercedes-Benz is the best-engineered car in the world and probably would not have mechanical difficulties found to be mere puffing).

107 Bologna v. Allstate Ins. Co., 138 F. Supp. 2d 310 (E.D.N.Y. 2001) ("you're in good hands with Allstate" is puffing); Nigh v. Koons Buick Pontiac GMC, Inc., 143 F. Supp. 2d 535 (E.D. Va. 2001) (statement that car did not look like it had been in any accidents was not actionable under UDAP statute because not unambiguous), *aff'd on other grounds*, 319 F.3d 119 (4th Cir. 2003), *cert. granted on other issues*, 124 S. Ct. 1144 (2004); Viches v. MLT, Inc., 124 F. Supp. 2d 1092 (E.D. Mich. 2000) (representation that vacation would be "worry-free"); Consumer Advocates v. Echostar Satellite Corp., 113 Cal. App. 4th 1351, 8 Cal. Rptr. 3d 22 (2003) (claim that system provided "crystal clear" video and "CD quality audio" not actionable); Rodio v. Smith, 123 N.J. 345, 587 A.2d 621 (1991) ("you're in good hands with Allstate" is puffing); Williams v. Heuser Chiropractic, 2004 WL 100462 (Tex. App. Jan. 21, 2004) (correctly stating the test for puffery but incorrectly applying the test to precise representations); Munters Corp. v. Swissco Young Indus., Inc., 100 S.W.2d 292 (Tex. App. 2002) (good statement of test for puffery); Bank One, Texas, N.A. v. Little, 978 S.W.2d 272 (Tex. App 1998); Lambert v. Downtown Garage, Inc., 553 S.E.2d 714 (Va. 2001) (statements that car was in "excellent condition" and that damage to it was not serious were puffing and not UDAP violations, at least where the parties dealt on equal terms and buyer was unusually knowledgeable about car's actual condition); State v. American TV & Appliance, 146 Wis. 2d 292, 430 N.W.2d 709 (1988) (statements that products are

A more conservative approach examined (1) the specificity of the misrepresentation, (2) the comparative knowledge of the buyer and seller, and (3) whether the representation pertained to a past, current, or future event or condition. The court concluded that a bank's promotion of its "tradition of excellence" and of its policy that it "knows its customer" was not specific enough to constitute a representation or warranty.[108]

A claim is not puffing where the claim promises a specific act, or where the claim's truth or falsity can be determined.[109] A statement is puffing only when it is an expression of opinion, not a representation of a fact.[110] A false statement regarding a future event can be a UDAP violation.[111] A seller is not permitted to ascribe virtues to a product that it does not possess.[112] It is not an adequate defense that "puffing" is widespread in an industry.[113]

4.2.11 Vulnerable Consumers Specially Considered

4.2.11.1 The FTC Standard

In determining under the FTC Act whether a practice has a capacity or tendency to deceive,[114] federal courts and the FTC historically have considered whether the ignorant, the unthinking, the credulous, and the least sophisticated consumer would be deceived.[115] The FTC Act does not make an

"best" and "finest" not UDAP violations).

108 Humble Nat'l Bank v. DCV, Inc., 933 S.W.2d 224 (Tex. App. 1996).

109 Consumer Advocates v. Echostar Satellite Corp., 113 Cal. App. 4th 1351, 8 Cal. Rptr. 3d 22 (2003) (promise of 50 channels and 7-day schedule); Miller v. William Chevrolet/Geo, Inc., 326 Ill. App. 3d 642, 762 N.E.2d 1 (2001) (statement that car was "executive driven" is factual, not puffing); Novartis Corp., 5 Trade Reg. Rep. (CCH) ¶ 24,614, F.T.C. Dkt. 9279 (May 27, 1999), *aff'd*, 223 F.3d 783 (D.C. Cir. 2000).

110 Thacker v. Menard, Inc., 105 F.3d 382 (7th Cir. 1997) (Illinois law); Graham v. RRR, L.L.C., 202 F. Supp. 2d 483 (E.D. Va. 2002) (salesman's statement that he would see what he could do about getting lower rate was not a representation of fact), *aff'd*, 2003 WL 139432 (4th Cir. Jan. 21, 2003) (unpublished, citation limited); Repucci v. Lake Champagne Campground, Inc., 251 F. Supp. 2d 1235 (D. Vt. 2002) (statements that campground was well-maintained and premier were opinions and could not be basis of UDAP claim); Transclean Corp. v. Bridgewood Servs., Inc., 77 F. Supp. 2d 1045 (D. Minn. 1999) (ad is not puffing if it describes specific or absolute characteristics or specific, measurable claims of product superiority based on product testing); Abele v. Bayliner Marine Corp., 11 F. Supp. 2d 955 (N.D. Ohio 1997) (finding some representations to be puffing, but not others); Petri v. Gatlin, 997 F. Supp. 956 (N.D. Ill. 1997); Better Living, Inc., 54 F.T.C. 648 (1959); Lynas v. Williams, 454 S.E.2d 570 (Ga. Ct. App. 1995) (subjective, non-specific statements that consumer would be extremely pleased and stunned with the work were puffing); Connick v. Suzuki Motor Co., Ltd., 275 Ill. App. 3d 705, 656 N.E.2d 170 (1995) (advertisements that car "never lets you down," "is a funmobile," "handles differently" than ordinary car, and has a "nifty, go-getter engine" are mere puffery), *aff'd in relevant part*, 675 N.E.2d 584 (Ill. 1996); *In re* Estate of Albergo, 656 N.E.2d 97 (Ill. App. Ct. 1995); Evanston Hosp. v. Crane, 627 N.E.2d 29 (Ill. App. Ct. 1993) (hospital's description of its high quality care was puffing); Breckenridge v. Cambridge Homes, Inc., 616 N.E.2d 615 (Ill. App. Ct. 1993) (statements that home would be "perfect" and built with "expert workmanship" and "custom quality" were puffery); Sohaey v. Van Cura, 607 N.E.2d 253 (Ill. App. Ct. 1992) (statements of opinion or statements regarding future or contingent events, expectations, or probabilities are not UDAP violations); Totz v. Continental DuPage Acura, 602 N.E.2d 1374 (Ill. App. Ct. 1992) (statement that car was in perfect condition and that the only defect was an inoperable radio was a statement of fact, not puffery); McGraw v. Loyola Ford, Inc., 124 Md. App. 560, 723 A.2d 502 (1999) (assertion that vehicle was most outstanding value on lot was puffing); Gennari v. Weichert Co. Realtors, 148 N.J. 582, 691 A.2d 350 (1997); Rodio v. Smith, 123 N.J. 345, 587 A.2d 621 (1991) (statement that consumer is "in good hands" with insurer is puffery); N.J. Citizen Action v. Schering-Plough Corp., 367 N.J. Super. 8, 842 A.2d 174 (App. Div. 2003) (drug manufacturer's statement that "you . . . can lead a normal nearly symptom free life again" is puffery and not a UDAP violation); Lingar v. Live-In Companions, Inc., 300 N.J. Super. 22, 692 A.2d 61 (App. Div. 1997); Koagel v. Ryan Homes, Inc., 167 A.D. 2d 822, 562 N.Y.S.2d 312 (1990) (real estate agent's inaccurate projection of future real estate taxes not actionable under UDAP statute); Vallery v. Bermuda Star Line, Inc., 141 Misc. 2d 395, 532 N.Y.S.2d 965 (N.Y. City Civ. Ct. 1988); Dowling v. NADW Marketing, Inc., 631 S.W.2d 726 (Tex. 1982); Milt Ferguson Motor Co. v. Zeretzke, 827 S.W.2d 349 (Tex. App. 1991); Key v. Lewis Aquatech Pool Supply, Inc., 58 Va. Cir. 344, 2002 WL 920936 (2002) (statement that company was premier pool builder in area); State v. American TV & Appliance, 146 Wis. 2d 292, 430 N.W.2d 709 (1988) (general statement that product is the best is mere puffery); *see also* Wheeler v. Box, 671 S.W.2d 75 (Tex. App. 1984). *Cf.* Randazzo v. Harris Bank Palatine, 262 F.3d 663 (7th Cir. 2001) (interpreting Illinois UDAP statute, in case involving large commercial loan and unusual facts, to prohibit misrepresentation of facts but not erroneous representations regarding interpretation of legal documents); Hill v. Jay Pontiac, Inc., 191 Ga. App. 258, 381 S.E.2d 417 (1989) (court seems to confuse common law fraud and UDAP standards as to puffing); Chandler v. Gene Messer Ford, Inc., 81 S.W.3d 493 (Tex. App. 2002) (car salesman's claims that car model was safer than other models is "puffing").

111 Parker-Smith v. Sto Corp., 262 Va. 432, 551 S.E.2d 615 (2001) (construing false advertising statute).

112 Totz v. Continental DuPage Acura, 602 N.E.2d 1374 (Ill. App. Ct. 1992).

113 Commonwealth v. Gold Bond Indus., Inc., Clearinghouse No. 26,028 (Pa. C.P. Allegheny Cty. 1973). *But see* Tagliente v. Himmer, 949 F.2d 1 (1st Cir. 1991) (exaggeration excused in business case as widespread in industry).

114 *See* § 4.2.9, *supra*.

115 FTC v. Standard Education Society, 302 U.S. 112 (1937); Standard Oil Co. of California v. FTC, 577 F.2d 653 (9th Cir. 1978); Stauffer Laboratories, Inc. v. FTC, 343 F.2d 75 (9th Cir. 1965); FTC v. Sterling Drug, Inc., 317 F.2d 669 (2d Cir. 1963); Exposition Press, Inc. v. FTC, 295 F.2d 869 (2d Cir. 1961), *cert. denied*, 370 U.S. 917 (1962); Royal Oil Co. v. FTC, 262 F.2d 741 (4th Cir. 1959); Charles of the Ritz Distributors Corp. v. FTC, 143 F.2d 676 (2d Cir. 1944); Aronberg v. FTC, 132 F.2d

exception for extravagant claims.[116] While it may not be enough if only an insignificant and unrepresentative segment of the public is misled, a practice can be deceptive even if most consumers are not misled and only especially vulnerable consumers are deceived.

The FTC in the 1980s modified its credulous and unsophisticated consumer standard. The FTC now looks to see whether the intended audience is deceived when it is behaving reasonably for that audience in the circumstances. If a practice affects or is directed primarily to a particular group, the FTC examines reasonableness from the perspective of that group.[117] A claim is not deceptive if it is unreasonably misunderstood by a very small and unrepresentative segment of the audience to whom the claim was directed.[118] The current FTC standard—particularly for national advertising—would seem to depart from the FTC's credulous and vulnerable standard. Even for national advertising, however, it is enough if an advertisement misleads a significant minority of reasonable consumers.[119]

Moreover, under the current FTC approach, if a practice affects or is directed primarily at a vulnerable group or individual, reasonableness should be evaluated from the perspective of that group or individual. Thus this standard will have minimal impact on a private action based on oral representations. Finally, the FTC still looks at the overall, net impression of a representation to see how it should reasonably be interpreted, including determining if there are implied claims and determining from extrinsic evidence how consumers in fact perceive a representation.[120]

165 (7th Cir. 1942); General Motors Corp. v. FTC, 114 F.2d 33 (2d Cir. 1940).

116 FTC v. Tashman, 318 F.3d 1273 (11th Cir. 2003).

117 Kraft, Inc., 5 Trade Reg. Rep. (CCH) ¶ 22937 (F.T.C. Dkt. 9208 1991); Cliffdale Assocs., 103 F.T.C. 110 (1984); International Harvester Co., 104 F.T.C. 949 (1984); Thompson Medical Co., 104 F.T.C. 648 (1984), *aff'd*, 791 F.2d 189 (D.C. Cir. 1986), *cert. denied*, 479 U.S. 1086 (1987). *See also* Letters by Chairman Miller to Honorable Bob Packwood, Chairman, Committee on Commerce, Science and Transportation, U.S. Senate (Oct. 14, 1983); and to Honorable John Dingell, Chairman, Committee on Energy and Commerce, U.S. House (Oct. 14, 1983); Brockey v. Moore, 107 Cal. App. 4th 86, 131 Cal. Rptr. 2d 746 (2003) (applying same standard under state UDAP statute).

118 Removatron Int'l Corp., 111 F.T.C. 206 (1988), *aff'd on other grounds*, 884 F.2d 1489 (11th Cir. 1989).

119 Novartis Corp., 5 Trade Reg. Rep. (CCH) ¶ 24,614, F.T.C. Dkt. 9279 (May 27, 1999), *aff'd*, 223 F.3d 783 (D.C. Cir. 2000); Kraft, Inc., 5 Trade Reg. Rep. (CCH) ¶ 22937 (F.T.C. Dkt. 9208 1991).

120 Novartis Corp., 5 Trade Reg. Rep. (CCH) ¶ 24,614, F.T.C. Dkt. 9279 (May 27, 1999), *aff'd*, 223 F.3d 783 (D.C. Cir. 2000); FTC v. Think Achievement Corp., 144 F. Supp. 2d 993 (N.D. Ind. 2000), *aff'd in relevant part, rev'd in part on other grounds*, 312 F.3d 259 (7th Cir. 2002); Removatron Int'l Corp., 111 F.T.C. 206 (1988), *aff'd on other grounds*, 884 F.2d 1489 (11th Cir. 1989); *see also* Thompson Medical Co., 104 F.T.C. 648 at 788 (1984), *aff'd*, 791 F.2d 189 (D.C. Cir. 1986), *cert. denied*, 479 U.S. 1086 (1987); Cliffdale Assocs., Inc., 103 F.T.C. 110, 164–166 (1988); Bristol-Meyers Co., 102 F.T.C. 21, 319 (1983), *aff'd*, 738 F.2d 554 (2d Cir. 1984), *cert. denied*, 469 U.S. 1189 (1985).

4.2.11.2 State UDAP Case Law

Cases under many state UDAP statutes still follow the federal court decisions and the old FTC standard in finding that the test is whether a practice has a tendency to mislead even a minority of consumers, not whether the average person would be deceived; UDAP statutes safeguard the vast multitude which includes the ignorant, the unthinking and the credulous.[121] "If unfair trade practitioners could

121 Top Rank, Inc. v. Gutierrez, 236 F. Supp. 2d 637 (W.D. Tex. 2001); Aurigemma v. Arco Petroleum Products Co., 734 F. Supp. 1025 (D. Conn. 1990) (capacity to deceive is measured by effect on least sophisticated); Madsen v. Western Am. Mortg. Co., 694 P.2d 1228 (Ariz. Ct. App. 1985); McGraw v. Loyola Ford, Inc., 124 Md. App. 560, 723 A.2d 502 (1999) (capacity to deceive ordinary consumer, not reasonable consumer, is the test); DeSantis v. Sears, Roebuck & Co., 543 N.Y.S.2d 228 (App. Div. 1989) (deception is measured by its effect on the unthinking and credulous); People *ex rel.* Lefkowitz v. Volkswagen of Am., Inc., 47 A.D. 2d 868, 366 N.Y.S.2d 157 (1975); Vallery v. Bermuda Star Line, Inc., 141 Misc. 2d 395, 532 N.Y.S.2d 965 (N.Y. City Civ. Ct. 1988); Quinn v. Aetna Life & Cas. Co., 96 Misc. 2d 545, 409 N.Y.S.2d 473 (Sup. Ct. 1978); Geismar v. Abraham & Strauss, 109 Misc. 2d 495, 439 N.Y.S.2d 1005 (Dist. Ct. 1981); Commonwealth v. Hush-Tone Indus., Inc., 4 Pa. Commw. 1 (1971); RRTM Restaurant Corp. v. Keeping, 766 S.W.2d 804 (Tex. App. 1988); Chrysler-Plymouth City Inc. v. Guerrero, 620 S.W.2d 700 (Tex. Civ. App. 1981); Barnhouse Motors Inc. v. Godfrey, 577 S.W.2d 378 (Tex. Civ. App. 1979); Spradling v. Williams, 553 S.W.2d 143 (Tex. Civ. App. 1977), *aff'd*, 566 S.W.2d 561 (Tex. 1978); *cf.* Paces Ferry Dodge, Inc. v. Thomas, 174 Ga. App. 642, 331 S.E.2d 4 (1985) (consumer's failure to test drive new car no defense to UDAP action); Dwyer v. J.I. Kislak Mortgage Corp., 103 Wash. App. 542, 13 P.3d 240 (2000) (practice is deceptive if it has capacity to deceive a substantial number of consumers). *But cf.* Workmon v. Publishers Clearing House, 118 F.3d 457 (6th Cir. 1997) (Michigan law) (consumer who misread contest advertising as stating that he had in fact won ten million dollars was not acting reasonably; court in effort to dismiss suit for $10 million failed to consider whether the advertisement was a deceptive scheme to sell magazines preying on the unsophisticated). *But see* Freeman v. Time, Inc., 68 F.3d 285 (9th Cir. 1995) (adopting reasonable consumer standard under California's Unfair Business Practices Act, unless advertising campaign targets vulnerable consumers); Arizona Cartridge Remanufacturers Ass'n v. Lexmark Int'l, Inc., 290 F. Supp. 2d 1034, 1041 (N.D. Cal. 2003) (under reasonable consumer standard, if representation is targeted to sophisticated group it will be evaluated from their vantage point); Berrios v. Sprint Corp., 1998 U.S. Dist. LEXIS 6579 (E.D.N.Y. Mar. 16, 1998) (holding that statement must be objectively deceptive, not just deceptive to the least sophisticated consumer); Haskell v. Time, Inc., 857 F. Supp. 1392 (E.D. Cal. 1994) (adopting "reasonable consumer" standard for evaluating deceptive advertising under California Unfair Business Practices Act); Lavie v. Procter & Gamble Co., 105 Cal. App. 4th 496, 129 Cal. Rptr. 2d 486 (2003) (reasonable consumer standard applies unless seller targets vulnerable consumers); Caldor, Inc. v. Heslin, 215 Conn. 590, 577 A.2d 1009 (1990) (court recites new FTC standard in decision upholding state UDAP regulation on deceptive rebate advertising); Zee-

escape liability upon showing that their victims were careless, gullible, or otherwise inattentive to their own interests, the Act would soon be a dead letter."[122] This focus is particularly appropriate when the seller has targeted unsophisticated members of the public.[123]

More specifically, the sufferers of diseases have been found to be especially credulous, and advertisements directed to them are subject to close scrutiny.[124] Courts also buttress findings of deception referring to the consumers' inability to speak English,[125] lack of education,[126] bad credit,[127] low income,[128] naiveté,[129] fright or confusion,[130] and minority group status.[131] Another court found that subtle psychological techniques, such as "sympathy presentations" that goods were made by handicapped labor, would have the capacity to deceive.[132]

man v. Black, 156 Ga. App. 82, 273 S.E.2d 910 (1980) (consumer must use due diligence to ascertain if representations false) (the authors believe this case misconstrues the legislative intent in enacting the UDAP statute); Luskin's, Inc. v. Consumer Protection Div., 353 Md. 335, 726 A.2d 702 (1999) (following new FTC standard and adopting reasonable unsophisticated consumer standard); Leon v. Rite Aid Corp., 340 N.J. Super. 462, 774 A.2d 674 (App. Div. 2001) (if ad does not violate specific UDAP regulation, test is whether it is misleading to average consumer); Miller v. American Family Publishers, 284 N.J. Super. 67, 663 A.2d 643 (Chancery Div. 1995) (practice is deceptive if it is misleading to the average consumer); Andre Strishak & Assocs. v. Hewlett Packard Co., 752 N.Y.S.2d 400 (App. Div. 2002) (practice is deceptive if it is likely to mislead reasonable consumer acting reasonably under the circumstances); Gaidon v. Guardian Life Ins. Co., 704 N.Y.S.2d 177, 725 N.E.2d 598 (N.Y. 1999) (adopting reasonable consumer standard), *aff'd on other grounds*, 96 N.Y.2d 201, 750 N.E.2d 1078 (2001); Commonwealth *ex rel.* Fisher v. Allstate Ins. Co., Clearinghouse No. 53,561 (Pa. Commw. Ct. Jan. 18, 2001) (adopting FTC's current view).

122 Winston Realty Co. v. GHG, Inc., 320 S.E.2d 286 (N.C. Ct. App. 1984), *aff'd*, 331 S.E.2d 677 (N.C. 1985); *see also* Lavie v. Procter & Gamble Co., 105 Cal. App. 4th 496, 129 Cal. Rptr. 2d 486 (2003) (adopting reasonable consumer standard, but reasonable consumer need not be wary or suspicious of advertising claims).

123 Brockey v. Moore, 107 Cal. App. 4th 86, 131 Cal. Rptr. 2d 746 (2003).

124 Belmont Laboratories v. FTC, 103 F.2d 538 (3d Cir. 1939); Commonwealth v. Hush-Tone Indus. Inc., 4 Pa. Commw. 1 (1971).

125 People v. Conway, 42 Cal. App. 3d 875, 117 Cal. Rptr. 251 (1974).

126 People v. Conway, 42 Cal. App. 3d 875, 117 Cal. Rptr. 251 (1974); Kugler v. Romain, 58 N.J. 522, 279 A.2d 640 (1971).

127 Sims v. First Consumers Nat'l Bank, 303 A.D.2d 288, 758 N.Y.S.2d 284 (2003).

128 Kugler v. Romain, 58 N.J. 522, 279 A.2d 640 (1971).

129 *Id.*

130 Brown v. Banks, Clearinghouse No. 27,065 (Ohio C.P. Cuyahoga Cty. 1976) (soliciting repair contracts for fire-damaged residences while fire was in progress and consumers were confused or frightened).

131 *Id.*

132 Commonwealth v. Handicapped Indus., Inc., Clearinghouse No. 26,027 (Pa. C.P. Bucks Cty. 1977).

Contributory negligence is not a defense to a UDAP action.[133] That is, the burden is not on the consumer to ferret out deception or remedy the situation where the seller has engaged in deception.[134] The merchant has a responsibility not to deceive even the credulous or unsophisticated.

Consequently, in presenting a UDAP case, one should concentrate not only on the deceptive nature of the practice, but also on the vulnerability of the consumer. A practice not deceptive to the average consumer in the normal context can still be found deceptive to certain consumers or in certain sales contexts. It may be particularly important to emphasize this in a case tried before a judge, because a judge, used to careful analysis, might not be personally deceived by a claim. It must be explained to the judge that less sophisticated consumers may not examine the fine point, may not question ambiguous language, and may be more impressed by the overall message than by the literal meaning of a claim.

4.2.12 *Materiality May Be Presumed and Reliance Is Unnecessary*

4.2.12.1 Introduction

At common law, to establish a fraud claim the consumer must prove that the misrepresentation was material and that he or she justifiably relied upon it. These requirements are significant impediments to fraud claims, particularly in class actions. Reliance, especially justifiable reliance, can be difficult to prove, and a requirement of showing reliance would complicate a private UDAP action.

Fortunately, the FTC and many courts in FTC Act and UDAP cases have held that reliance need not be shown, or may be presumed. Materiality likewise may be presumed.

4.2.12.2 The FTC Standard

The FTC standard is that while materiality is important, the Commission can infer materiality and does not need independent evidence in most situations.[135] Under the current standard, materiality can be presumed whenever:

133 *See* § 4.2.16, *infra*.

134 Sullivan's Wholesale Drug v. Faryl's Pharmacy, Inc., 214 Ill. App. 3d 1073, 573 N.E.2d 1370 (1991) (consumers can not be expected to check supplier's records to learn truth regarding price of goods sold); Rose v. Zaring Homes, Inc., 122 Ohio App. 3d 739, 702 N.E.2d 952 (1997) (consumer's failure to inspect does not defeat UDAP claim).

135 Thompson Medical Co., 104 F.T.C. 648 (1984), *aff'd*, 791 F.2d 189 (D.C. Cir. 1986), *cert. denied*, 479 U.S. 1086 (1987). *See also* Novartis Corp., 5 Trade Reg. Rep. (CCH) ¶ 24,614, F.T.C. Dkt. 9279 (May 27, 1999), *aff'd*, 223 F.3d 783 (D.C. Cir. 2000); FTC v. Wilcox, 926 F. Supp. 1091 (S.D. Fla. 1995). Cases under an earlier version of the FTC's standard include FTC v. Colgate-Palmolive Co., 380 U.S. 374 (1965); FTC v. Raladam Co., 316 U.S. 149 (1942); Simeon Mgmt. Corp. v. FTC, 579 F.2d 1137

- Sellers make express claims;
- Sellers should have known that the consumer would need information not disclosed;
- Sellers intended to make implied claims; or
- Sellers make any claims involving health, safety, purpose, efficacy, cost, durability, performance, warranties, quality, or other areas with which the reasonable consumer would be concerned.[136]

Consequently, the FTC will require a showing of materiality only where sellers should not have known that they were failing to disclose important information or where sellers make *implied* claims concerning issues of little general concern to consumers. Since these categories of deception are rarely presented, a showing of materiality will almost never be required.

For example, the FTC has said that a claim that a product is "new" implies efficacy, and materiality can thus be presumed.[137] A claim that a pain remedy is superior to other products is a material claim.[138]

Once materiality is shown, the FTC also presumes reliance as long as it is shown that the defendant's material misrepresentations were widely disseminated and that consumers purchased the defendant's product.[139] The FTC is not required to present proof of subjective reliance of each individual consumer, as such a requirement would thwart effective prosecution of large consumer redress actions and frustrate the goals of the FTC Act.[140]

4.2.12.3 State UDAP Case Law

4.2.12.3.1 Proof of reliance generally not required

Many courts follow the FTC's lead and hold that proof of actual reliance is not required under state UDAP statutes.[141] For example, UDAP liability may be imposed where a

(9th Cir. 1978); Equifax Inc., 96 F.T.C. 844 (1980), *rev'd in part on other grounds*, 678 F.2d 1047 (11th Cir. 1982).

136 Thompson Medical Co., 104 F.T.C. 648 (1984), *aff'd*, 791 F.2d 189 (D.C. Cir. 1986), *cert. denied*, 479 U.S. 1086 (1987). *See also* Novartis Corp., 5 Trade Reg. Rep. (CCH) ¶ 24,614, F.T.C. Dkt. 9279 (May 27, 1999), *aff'd*, 223 F.3d 783 (D.C. Cir. 2000); FTC v. Wilcox, 926 F. Supp. 1091 (S.D. Fla. 1995).

137 Thompson Medical Co., 104 F.T.C. 648 at 788 (1984), *aff'd*, 791 F.2d 189 (D.C. Cir. 1986), *cert. denied*, 479 U.S. 1086 (1987).

138 Novartis Corp. v. FTC, 223 F.3d 783 (D.C. Cir. 2000).

139 McGregor v. Chierico, 206 F.3d 1378 (11th Cir. 2000); FTC v. Figgie Int'l, Inc., 994 F.2d 595 (9th Cir. 1993); FTC v. Security Rare Coin & Bullion Corp., 931 F.2d 1312 (8th Cir. 1991); FTC v. 1263523 Ontario, Inc., 205 F. Supp. 2d 205 (S.D.N.Y. 2002); FTC v. Windward Marketing, Ltd., 1997 U.S. Dist. LEXIS 17114 (N.D. Ga. Sept. 30, 1997).

140 McGregor v. Chierico, 206 F.3d 1378 (11th Cir. 2000); FTC v. Figgie Int'l, Inc., 994 F.2d 595, 605 (9th Cir. 1993); FTC v. U.S. Oil & Gas Corp., 1987 U.S. Dist. LEXIS 16137 (S.D. Fla. 1987).

141 *Arizona*: Siemer v. Associates First Capital Corp., 2001 U.S. Dist. LEXIS 12810 (D. Ariz. Mar. 29, 2001) (reliance necessary in private UDAP actions but may be established simply by the fact that an individual purchased the product after the misrepresentations were made); State *ex rel.* Corbin v. Tolleson, 160 Ariz. 385, 773 P.2d 490 (Ct. App. 1989); People *ex rel.* Babbitt v. Green Acres Trust, 127 Ariz. 160, 618 P.2d 1086 (Ct. App. 1980).
Arkansas: State v. McLeod, Clearinghouse No. 50,412 (Ark. Ch. Ct., Pulaski Cty. Nov. 23, 1993).
California: Committee on Children's Television, Inc. v. General Foods Corp., 35 Cal. 3d 197, 673 P.2d 660, 197 Cal. Rptr. 783 (1983) (reliance unnecessary under Cal. Bus. & Prof. Code § 17,200 for injunctive action or where restitution necessary to prevent unfair practices); Mass. Mut. Life Ins. Co. v. Superior Court, 97 Cal. App. 4th 1282, 119 Cal. Rptr. 2d 190 (2002) (reliance unnecessary under § 17200; proof of materiality suffices as proof of causation under CLRA); Prata v. Superior Court, 91 Cal. App. 4th 1128, 111 Cal. Rptr. 2d 296 (2001).
Connecticut: Aurigemma v. Arco Petroleum Products Co., 734 F. Supp. 1025 (D. Conn. 1990) (consumer need not prove reliance or that representation was part of basis of bargain); Webb Press Servs. v. New London Motors, Inc., 205 Conn. 479, 533 A.2d 1211 (1987); Hinchliffe v. American Motors Corp., 440 A.2d 810 (Conn. 1981); Meyers v. Cornwell Quality Tools, Inc., 41 Conn. App. 19, 674 A.2d 444 (1996).
Delaware: Stephenson v. Capano Development, Inc., 462 A.2d 1069 (Del. 1983); State *ex rel.* Brady v. 3-D Auto World, Inc., 2000 Del. Super. LEXIS 17 (Jan. 19, 2000) (actual reliance unnecessary, but defendant must have intended that others rely on omission or concealment of material fact); State *ex rel.* Brady v. Gardiner, 2000 Del. Super. LEXIS 208 (June 5, 2000); S&R Assocs. v. Shell Oil Co., 725 A.2d 431 (Del. Super. 1998).
District of Columbia: Wells v. Allstate Ins. Co., 210 F.R.D. 1 (D.D.C. 2002) (2000 amendments eliminated requirement of injury in fact and causation; even before amendments, reliance unnecessary for non-disclosure claim); *cf.* Smith v. Brown & Williamson Tobacco Corp., 108 F. Supp. 2d 12 (D.D.C. 2000) (court does not decide whether reliance is necessary; UDAP claims dismissed because plaintiff showed no causal connection between defendants' nondisclosure of tobacco's dangers and her decision to start and continue smoking).
Florida: Davis v. Powertel, Inc., 776 So. 2d 971 (Fla. App. 2000) (actual reliance unnecessary, both in individual and class actions; plaintiff must show that practice is likely to deceive reasonable consumer). *But see* Rosa v. Amoco Oil Co., 262 F. Supp. 2d 1364 (S.D. Fla. 2003) (business case).
Idaho: State *ex rel.* Kidwell v. Master Distributors, Inc., 101 Idaho 447, 615 P.2d 116 (1980).
Illinois: The Illinois Supreme Court has held that proximate cause, but not reliance, must be shown: Connick v. Suzuki Motor Co., Ltd., 675 N.E.2d 584 (Ill. 1996). Decisions from intermediate appellate courts preceding *Connick* need to be read with *Connick* in mind. *See also* Thacker v. Menard, Inc., 105 F.3d 382 (7th Cir. 1997) (Illinois law); Smith v. Am. Gen. Life & Accident Ins. Co., 2002 U.S. Dist. LEXIS 2154 (N.D. Ill. Feb. 8, 2002), *vacated, remanded on other grounds*, 337 F.3d 888 (7th Cir. 2003); Bixby's Food Sys., Inc. v. McKay, 193 F. Supp. 2d 1053 (N.D. Ill. 2002) (no need to show actual or reasonable reliance); Anderson v. Rizza Chevrolet, Inc., 9 F. Supp. 2d 908 (N.D. Ill. 1998); Arenson v. Whitehall Convalescent & Nursing Home, 164 F.R.D. 659 (N.D. Ill. 1996) (Illinois UDAP statute); Celex Group, Inc. v. Executive Gallery, Inc., 877 F. Supp. 1114 (N.D. Ill. 1995) (reasonable reliance need not be shown); April v. Union Mortgage Co., 709 F. Supp. 809 (N.D. Ill. 1989) (plaintiffs need not show reliance or due

realtor misrepresented the extent of termite damage, even though the buyers conducted an independent inspection by

diligence in ascertaining accuracy of the misstatements); Martin v. Heinold Commodities, Inc., 163 Ill. 2d 33, 643 N.E.2d 734 (1994); Siegel v. Levy Organization Dev. Co., 153 Ill. 2d 534, 607 N.E.2d 194 (1992) (materiality and intent to induce reliance must be shown, but not actual reliance); Chandler v. Am. Gen. Fin., Inc., 329 Ill. App. 3d 729, 768 N.E.2d 60 (2002); Perona v. Volkswagen of Am., Inc., 684 N.E.2d 859 (Ill. App. Ct. 1997) (intent by seller, rather than individual reliance by buyer, is dispositive); Adler v. Wm. Blair & Co., 171 Ill. App. 3d 117, 648 N.E.2d 226, 207 Ill. Dec. 770 (1995); Empire Home Servs., Inc. v. Carpet Am., 653 N.E.2d 852 (Ill. App. Ct. 1995); Adler v. William Blair & Co., 648 N.E.2d 226 (Ill. App. Ct. 1995) (reliance not necessary, but consumer must show that damages were proximately caused by defendant's acts); Zinser v. Rose, 614 N.E.2d 1259 (Ill. App. Ct. 1993) (rejecting contrary holding of Elipas Enterprises v. Silverstein, 243 Ill. App. 3d 230, 612 N.E.2d 9 (1993) that consumer plaintiff must show reliance, even if state need not); Randels v. Best Real Estate, Inc., 612 N.E.2d 984 (Ill. App. Ct. 1993) (reliance need not be shown under Illinois Consumer Fraud Act, but deception must relate to a material fact); Sohaey v. Van Cura, 607 N.E.2d 253 (Ill. App. Ct. 1992); Harkala v. Wildwood Realty, Inc., 200 Ill. App. 3d 447, 558 N.E.2d 195 (1990); Salkeld v. V.R. Bus. Brokers, 192 Ill. App. 3d 663, 548 N.E.2d 1151 (1989). *But see* Elipas Enterprises, Inc. v. Silverstein, 612 N.E.2d 9 (Ill. App. Ct. 1993) (attorney general need not show reasonable reliance under Illinois Consumer Fraud Act, but consumers must).

Iowa: State *ex rel.* Miller v. Hydro Mag, Ltd., 436 N.W.2d 617 (Iowa 1989).

Kansas: Cole v. Hewlett Packard Co., 2004 WL 376471 (Kan. App. Feb. 27, 2004) (unpublished, citation limited) (citing specific statutory language).

Maine: Tungate v. MacLean-Stevens Studios, 714 A.2d 792 (Me. 1998) (plaintiffs must show that practice could reasonably be found to have caused a person to act differently; no UDAP violation where seller's practice did not induce consumers to act to their detriment).

Maryland: State v. Andrews, 73 Md. App. 80, 533 A.2d 282 (1987).

Massachusetts: Heller Fin. v. INA, 410 Mass. 400, 573 N.E.2d 8 (1991) (reliance not necessary, but plaintiff must show causal connection between misrepresentation and injury); International Fidelity Ins. Co. v. Wilson, 387 Mass. 841, 443 N.E.2d 1308 (1983); Slaney v. Westwood Auto, Inc., 366 Mass. 688, 322 N.E.2d 768 (1975); Fraser Engineering Co. v. Desmond, 26 Mass. App. Ct. 99, 524 N.E.2d 110 (1988) (no reliance necessary as long as there is a causal relationship); Zayre Corp. v. Computer Sys. of Am., Inc., 24 Mass. App. Ct. 559, 511 N.E.2d 23 (1987); Glickman v. Brown, 21 Mass. App. Ct. 229, 486 N.E.2d 737 (1985).

Michigan: Dix v. American Bankers Life Assurance Co., 429 Mich. 410, 415 N.W.2d 206 (1987) (individual proof of reliance unnecessary; in class action plaintiffs need only show that a reasonable person would have relied); *accord* Gilkey v. Central Clearing Co., 202 F.R.D. 515 (E.D. Mich. 2001); Gasperoni v. Metabolife, 2000 U.S. Dist. LEXIS 20879 (E.D. Mich. Sept. 27, 2000).

Minnesota: Mulcahy v. Cheetah Learning L.L.C., 2003 WL 21909570 (D. Minn. July 28, 2003) (circumstantial evidence of reliance sufficient, but not shown here); *In re* Lutheran Brotherhood Variable Ins. Prods. Co. Sales Practices Litig., 2003 WL 21737528 (D. Minn. July 22, 2003) (causal nexus not reliance is necessary); *In re* St. Jude Medical, Inc., Calzone Heart Valves Prods. Liability Litig., 2003 WL 1589527 (D. Minn. Mar. 27, 2003) (causal nexus, not reliance, is necessary); Group Health Plan v. Philip Morris, Inc., 621 N.W.2d 2 (Minn. 2001) (private plaintiffs in damages suit need not plead or prove reliance but must prove causation, which may require direct or circumstantial evidence of reliance), *later opinion in related case at* 188 F. Supp. 2d 1122 (D. Minn. 2002) (declining to presume causation and finding plaintiffs' survey evidence insufficiently tied to the plaintiff population and defendants' false advertising to withstand summary judgment), *aff'd in relevant part, remanded in part on other grounds*, 344 F.3d 753 (8th Cir. 2003); State *ex rel.* Humphrey v. Alpine Air Products, Inc., 500 N.W.2d 788 (Minn. 1993) (dicta); Freeman v. A & J Auto MN, Inc., 2003 WL 22136807 (Minn. App. Sept. 16, 2003) (unpublished, citation limited) (not necessary to plead reliance, but necessary to prove reliance in the form of some legal nexus between the injury and the wrongful conduct); Flynn v. Am. Home Prods. Corp., 627 N.W.2d 342 (Minn. App. 2001) (causation has a reliance component, but it can be proven by direct or circumstantial evidence; not shown here). *But see* Parkhill v. Minnesota Mut. Life Ins. Co., 188 F.R.D. 332 (D. Minn. 1999) (concluding that reliance is required for damages claims but not for injunctive relief and restitution), *overruled by* Group Health Plan v. Philip Morris, Inc., 621 N.W.2d 2 (Minn. 2001); Wiegand v. Walker Automotive Groups, Inc., 670 N.W.2d 449 (Minn. App. 2003) (interpreting *Group Health* to require proof of reliance as part of causation), *review granted*, 2004 Minn. LEXIS 10 (Jan. 20, 2004).

Missouri: State *ex rel.* Webster v. Areaco Inv. Co., 756 S.W.2d 633 (Mo. Ct. App. 1988).

New Jersey: Gennari v. Weichert Co. Realtors, 148 N.J. 582, 691 A.2d 350 (1997); Leon v. Rite Aid Corp., 340 N.J. Super. 462, 774 A.2d 674 (App. Div. 2001); Varacallo v. Massachusetts Mut. Life Ins. Co., 332 N.J. Super. 31, 752 A.2d 807 (App. Div. 2000) (causal nexus must be shown, but not reliance); Carroll v. Cellco P'ship, 313 N.J. Super. 488, 713 A.2d 509 (App. Div. 1998) (reliance unnecessary, but must show materiality, an ascertainable loss, and causation); Byrne v. Weichert Realtors, 290 N.J. Super. 126, 675 A.2d 235 (1996). *But see* International Minerals & Mining Co. v. Citicorp N. Am., Inc., 736 F. Supp. 587 (D.N.J. 1990) (commercial borrower has no UDAP claim for its unreasonable reliance on statements predicting loan approval).

New Mexico: Smoot v. Physicians Life Ins. Co., 87 P.3d 545 (N.M. App. 2003) (proof of causation, but not necessarily reliance, is required).

New York: *In re* Methyl Tertiary Butyl Ether Prods. Liab. Litigation, 175 F. Supp. 2d 593 (S.D.N.Y. 2001) (no need to show reliance; sufficient to allege that defendants' misrepresentations about safety of gasoline additives misled the public and that as result of public use of product, plaintiffs' water supply was contaminated); State Street Bank & Trust Co. v. Mut. Life Ins. Co. of New York, 811 F. Supp. 915 (S.D.N.Y. 1993); Stutman v. Chemical Bank, 95 N.Y.2d 24, 731 N.E.2d 608 (2000); Oswego Laborers' Local 214 Pension Fund v. Marine Midland Bank, 85 N.Y.2d 20, 647 N.E.2d 741 (1995) (reliance unnecessary but plaintiffs must show that defendant engaged in a material deceptive act that caused actual harm); Hazelhurst v. Brita Prods. Co., 295 A.D.2d 240, 744 N.Y.S.2d 31 (2002) (reliance not required, but need to show injury prevents class certification here); Kidd v. Delta Funding Corp., 2000 N.Y. Misc. LEXIS 378 (Sup. Ct. Sept. 18, 2000); Bartolomeo v. Runco, 162 Misc. 2d 485, 616 N.Y.S.2d 695 (City Ct. 1994); Giarratano v. Midas Muffler, 630 N.Y.S.2d 656, 27 U.C.C. Rep. 2d 87 (N.Y. City Ct. 1995); Geismar v. Abraham & Strauss, 109

engaging their own inspector.[142] Many of these courts point out that proof of causation is always necessary, but that reliance is not always an essential part of that proof.[143]

In a few states, the UDAP statute requires a showing that the seller intended that the consumer rely on the misrepresentation.[144] This is different from proof that the consumer actually relied on the misrepresentation, however.[145] The difference is particularly significant in class actions, where the seller's intent can be established on a classwide basis, but proof of individual reliance by each class member would be burdensome.

4.2.12.3.2 Small minority require reliance

Proof of reliance is required in a small minority of jurisdictions. Georgia courts, in a strained interpretation, have read reliance into their statute's requirement of causation.[146] A Wisconsin appellate decision assumes that reliance is necessary.[147] In Pennsylvania, an intermediate appellate court had held that reliance is only required for those UDAP claims that it characterized as fraud-based.[148] The state supreme court reversed, holding that the legislature had not intended to dispense with proof of the traditional common law elements of reliance and causation.[149] The statute has been amended

---

Misc. 2d 495, 439 N.Y.S.2d 1005 (Dist. Ct. 1981) (no need for reliance, just that consumer misled in a material way). *See also* Boule v. Hutton, 328 F.3d 84, 94 (2d Cir. 2003). *Cf.* Pelman v. McDonald's Corp., 2003 WL 22052778 (S.D.N.Y. Sept. 3, 2003) (reliance unnecessary for Gen. Bus. Law § 349 claim, but necessary under § 350). *But see* Berrios v. Sprint Corp., 1998 U.S. Dist. LEXIS 6579 (E.D.N.Y. Mar. 16, 1998) (stating that New York requires damage, which carries with it a reliance requirement; this decision should be considered overruled by *Stutman*); Andre Strishak & Assocs. v. Hewlett Packard Co., 752 N.Y.S.2d 400 (App. Div. 2002) (reliance necessary for false advertising claim); Sabater v. Lead Indus. Ass'n, Inc., 183 Misc. 2d 759, 704 N.Y.S.2d 800 (2000) (reliance on misrepresentation is essential for false advertising UDAP claim); Small v. Lorillard Tobacco Co., 94 N.Y.2d 43, 720 N.E.2d 892 (1999) (reliance unnecessary, but plaintiff must show materiality and actual harm).

North Carolina: Cullen v. Valley Forge Life Ins. Co., 589 S.E.2d 423 (N.C. Ct. App. 2003). *But see* Fozard v. Publishers Clearing House, Inc., 1999 U.S. Dist. LEXIS 22994 (M.D.N.C. Apr. 29, 1999) (equating reliance with causation without analysis), *aff'd without op.*, 205 F.3d 1333 (4th Cir. 2000).

Oregon: Sanders v. Francis, 277 Or. 593, 561 P.2d 1003 (1971); *cf.* Feitler v. Animation Collection, Inc., 170 Or. App. 702, 13 P.3d 1044 (2000) (reliance is required as element of causation when plaintiff claims to have relied on seller's express representations).

Tennessee: Harvey v. Ford Motor Credit Co., 1999 Tenn. App. LEXIS 448 (1999) (Tennessee UDAP statute does not require reliance, but proximate causation must be shown).

Texas: The Texas UDAP statute was amended in 1995 to require reliance for deception claims (but not for other UDAP claims): Tex. Bus. & Comm. Code § 17.50(b)(1). *See* McCaskey v. Continental Airlines, Inc., 159 F. Supp. 2d 562 (S.D. Tex. 2001) (reliance required; not shown where airline presented a release but consumer rejected it). Earlier decisions, including Celtic Life Ins. Co. v. Coats, 885 S.W.2d 96 (Tex. 1994) and Weitzel v. Barnes, 691 S.W.2d 598 (Tex. 1985), had refused to read a reliance requirement into the statute.

Vermont: *Cf.* Lalande Air & Water Corp. v. Pratt, 795 A.2d 1233 (Vt. 2002) (declining to reach question whether reliance is necessary for unfairness claim).

West Virginia: State v. Imperial Marketing, 472 S.E.2d 792 (W. Va. 1996) (under W.Va. Prizes and Gifts Act, need only show that deceptive practices are used to affect consumer's decision to purchase).

142 Byrne v. Weichert Realtors, 290 N.J. Super. 126, 675 A.2d 235 (1996).

143 *See, e.g.*, Group Health Plan v. Philip Morris, Inc., 621 N.W.2d 2 (Minn. 2001).

144 Cripe v. Leiter, 184 Ill. 2d 185, 703 N.E.2d 100 (1998); Connick v. Suzuki Motor Co., 174 Ill. 2d 482, 675 N.E.2d 584 (1996) (reliance unnecessary, just that the deception proximately caused the injury and the defendant intended the consumer to rely); People *ex rel.* Hartigan v. E&E Hauling, Inc., 153 Ill. 2d 473, 607 N.E.2d 165 (1992); Tudor v. Jewel Food Stores, Inc., 681 N.E.2d 6 (Ill. App. Ct. 1997); Byrne v. Weichert Realtors, 290 N.J. Super. 126, 675 A.2d 235 (1996) (necessary where deceptive act is nondisclosure).

145 Cozzi Iron & Metal, Inc. v. U.S. Office Equipment, Inc., 250 F.3d 570 (7th Cir. 2001) (Ill. law); Group Health Plan, Inc. v. Philip Morris, Inc., 621 N.W.2d 2 (Minn. 2000); Byrne v. Weichert Realtors, 290 N.J. Super. 126, 675 A.2d 235 (1996) (once plaintiff shows that seller intended that other rely, actual reliance is unnecessary). *But cf.* Oliveira v. Amoco Oil Co., 201 Ill. 2d 134, 776 N.E.2d 151, 267 Ill. Dec. 14 (2002) (no UDAP claim where consumers did not sufficiently allege that they were deceived; causation must be shown).

146 Ford v. Saint Francis Hosp., 490 S.E.2d 415 (Ga. App. Ct. 1997) (no UDAP liability where patient relied on surgeon to select hospital and did not rely on hospital's assurances about its level of care); Crown Ford, Inc. v. Crawford, 473 S.E.2d 554 (Ga. App. Ct. 1996) (justifiable reliance must be shown); Baranco, Inc. v. Bradshaw, 456 S.E.2d 592 (Ga. App. Ct. 1995) (justifiable reliance necessary); Allen v. Remax N. Atlanta, Inc., 213 Ga. App. 644, 445 S.E.2d 774 (1994) (justifiable reliance necessary); Zeeman v. Black, 156 Ga. App. 82, 273 S.E.2d 910 (1980) (strained interpretation of statute finds reasonable reliance necessary).

147 Ricco v. Riva, 669 N.W.2d 193 (Wis. App. 2003).

148 Weinberg v. Sun Co., 740 A.2d 1152 (Pa. Super. 1999) (reliance necessary for fraud-based UDAP claims but not for other claims such as advertising violations); DiLucido v. Terminix Int'l, Inc., 676 A.2d 1237 (Pa. Super. 1996). *See also* Fay v. Erie Ins. Group, 723 A.2d 712 (Pa. Super. 1999) (UDAP claim dismissed for failure to allege reliance on misrepresentations); Basile v. H&R Block, Inc., 729 A.2d 574 (Pa. Super. 1999), (showing of reliance required for UDAP claim against bank, but defendant tax preparer is a fiduciary so reliance is presumed), *vacated, remanded on other grounds*, 563 Pa. 359, 761 A.2d 1115 (Pa. 2000), *appeal after remand*, 777 A.2d 95 (Pa. Super. 2001) (reverses grant of summary judgment to tax preparer; consumers made prima facie showing of confidential relationship).

149 Weinberg v. Sun Co., 565 Pa. 612, 777 A.2d 442 (2001); *see also* Debbs v. Chrysler Corp., 810 A.2d 137 (Pa. Super. 2002) (stating that reliance is required for all Pa. UDAP violations); Aronson v. GreenMountain.com, 809 A.2d 399 (Pa. Super. 2002) (declining to recognize presumption of reliance where plaintiffs did not allege that all class members saw the deceptive ads); Sexton v. PNC Bank, 792 A.2d 602 (Pa. Super. 2002) (dismissal of claim

since the case arose and now makes it clear that not only fraudulent but also deceptive practices are actionable, so perhaps in future cases the court will give less weight to common law fraud requirements.[150] Also, some of the acts listed in the statute's "laundry list," such as performing substandard repairs, failing to comply with a warranty, or including a confession of judgment clause in a contract,[151] are so different from common law fraud that courts are unlikely to find that reliance is a necessary element.[152]

The Washington Supreme Court formerly interpreted its UDAP statute to include a requirement that the defendant's acts induced the plaintiff to act or refrain from acting, causing damage.[153] It construed this requirement liberally, finding inducement even where the deception is only apparent later when the seller does not perform as promised.[154] In 1986, the court reformulated its list of elements for UDAP claims, eliminating mention of inducement.[155] The court has termed it "debatable" whether reliance is still required.[156] A causal link must be shown between the unfair or deceptive act and the plaintiff's damage, however.[157]

4.2.12.3.3 No reliance required in non-disclosure or mis-disclosure cases

There is a particularly strong argument that reliance need not be proven where the seller misstates a disclosure it is legally required to make.[158] It is also especially clear that, where the seller's deceptive act involves failure to disclose rather than an affirmative misrepresentation, the consumer need not show reliance.[159] For example, in one case an insurer sold life insurance to consumers without disclosing that illustrated dividends not only "may" but "probably will" decrease. The court assumed that few consumers would have bought the policy had this material fact been disclosed. It held that the purchase of a policy by a person who was shown the literature would be sufficient to establish *prima facie* proof of causation.[160] Even for common law fraud claims, many courts have held that reliance need not be proven if the fraud involves nondisclosure.[161] The United States Supreme Court has adopted this position in the context of securities fraud, holding that, where the fraud involves a failure to disclose, the plaintiff need only show that the facts withheld were material in the sense that a reasonable investor might have considered them important.[162]

4.2.12.3.4 No reliance required in cases seeking injunctive relief

Almost all courts also agree that a showing of reliance is unnecessary when the plaintiff is seeking injunctive relief. Injunctive relief is designed to prevent future harm or bring ongoing harm to a halt, rather than compensate for past harm.[163] Indeed, some UDAP statutes specify that an injunction can be granted if consumers are likely to be harmed.[164] Even restitution can be ordered in an injunctive action without a showing of reliance.[165]

---

that bank charged illegal fee upheld because plaintiff failed to allege reliance on a representation or conduct).

150 *See* Sheppard v. GMAC Mortg. Corp., 299 B.R. 753 (Bankr. E.D. Pa. 2003) (finding it unnecessary to decide whether reliance is necessary under post-amendment version of statute).

151 73 Pa. Stat. § 201-2(4).

152 *See* Seth William Goren, A Pothole on the Road to Recovery: Reliance and Private Class Actions Under Pennsylvania's Unfair Trade Practices and Consumer Protection Law, 107 Dickinson Law Rev. 1 (Summer 2002). *But see* Amendolia v. Rothman, 2003 WL 23162389 (E.D. Pa. Dec. 8, 2003) (stating without elaboration that reliance is necessary for Pa. UDAP claims); Debbs v. Chrysler Corp., 810 A.2d 137 (Pa. Super. 2002) (stating that reliance is required for all Pa. UDAP violations).

153 Anhold v. Daniels, 94 Wash. 2d 40, 614 P.2d 184 (1980).

154 Eastlake Constr. Co. v. Hess, 686 P.2d 465 (Wash. 1984).

155 Hangman Ridge Training Stables, Inc. v. Safeco Title Ins. Co., 105 Wash. 2d 778, 719 P.2d 531 (1986).

156 Pickett v. Holland Am. Line-Westours, Inc., 35 P.3d 351 (Wash. 2001).

157 Hangman Ridge Training Stables, Inc. v. Safeco Title Ins. Co., 105 Wash. 2d 778, 719 P.2d 531 (1986). *See also* Pickett v. Holland Am. Line-Westours, Inc., 35 P.3d 351 (Wash. 2001) (causal link must be shown; whether reliance is necessary is "debatable"); McLaughlin v. Watercraft Int'l, 1997 Wash. App. LEXIS 1476 (Sept. 2, 1997) (equating causal link with reliance).

158 Tri-West Constr. v. Hernandez, 43 Or. App. 961, 607 P.2d 1375 (1979).

159 Wells v. Allstate Ins. Co., 210 F.R.D. 1 (D.D.C. 2002); Lipinski v. Martin J. Kelly Oldsmobile, Inc., 325 Ill. App. 3d 1139, 759 N.E.2d 66 (2001); Varacallo v. Massachusetts Mut. Life Ins. Co., 332 N.J. Super. 31, 752 A.2d 807 (App. Div. 2000); Cope v. Metro Life Ins. Co., 82 Ohio St. 3d 426, 696 N.E.2d 1001 (1998) (claims under Del. UDAP statute and common law claims); Sanders v. Francis, 277 Or. 593, 561 P.2d 1003 (1977); Tri-West Constr. v. Hernandez, 43 Or. App. 961, 607 P.2d 1375 (1979); *see also* Cannon v. Cherry Hill Toyota, Inc., 161 F. Supp. 2d 362 (D.N.J. 2001) (unnecessary to show reliance where omission is knowing); Gasperoni v. Metabolife Int'l Inc., 2000 U.S. Dist. LEXIS 20879 (E.D. Mich. Sept. 27, 2000) (for fraudulent omission claim, plaintiff must only show defendant's intent to induce reliance, not actual reliance). *But see* Fink v. Ricoh Corp., 365 N.J. Super. 520, 839 A.2d 942 (Law. Div. 2003) (distinguishing *Vacarello*); Debbs v. Chrysler Corp., 810 A.2d 137 (Pa. Super. 2002).

160 Varacallo v. Massachusetts Mut. Life Ins. Co., 332 N.J. Super. 31, 752 A.2d 807 (App. Div. 2000).

161 Murray v. Sevier, 156 F.R.D. 235, 248–9 n.11 (D. Kan. 1994); Varacallo v. Massachusetts Mut. Life Ins. Co., 332 N.J. Super. 31, 752 A.2d 807 (App. Div. 2000); Adams v. Little Missouri Minerals Ass'n, 143 N.W.2d 659, 684–5 (N.D. 1966); Cope v. Metro Life Ins. Co., 82 Ohio St. 3d 426, 696 N.E.2d 1001 (1998) (claims under Del. UDAP statute and common law claims).

162 Affiliated Ute Citizens v. U.S., 406 U.S. 128 (1972).

163 Committee on Children's Television, Inc. v. General Foods Corp., 35 Cal. 3d 197, 673 P.2d 660, 197 Cal. Rptr. 783 (1983).

164 *See* §§ 8.6.3.1, 8.6.3.2, *infra*.

165 Committee on Children's Television, Inc. v. General Foods Corp., 35 Cal. 3d 197, 673 P.2d 660, 197 Cal. Rptr. 783 (1983).

4.2.12.3.5 Where reliance required, it need not be reasonable reliance

Even the minority of courts that require reliance generally do not require a showing that the consumer's reliance was reasonable or justiciable. Consumers still may have an action if they relied on the representations when they should not have, that is, when they should have known the statements were false.[166] The reliance element may be satisfied even where the consumers have been given corrected information before contractual performance is consummated, if the original false information was an inducement to enter into the contract.[167]

4.2.12.3.6 Presumption of reliance where misrepresentations are material

In place of a requirement of reliance, many courts adopt a presumption of reliance if the misrepresentations were material.[168] Since many decisions approve this approach under the FTC Act,[169] it is equally appropriate for actions under state UDAP statutes, which were modeled on the FTC Act. Circumstantial evidence is sufficient to give rise to an inference or presumption of reliance.[170] Reliance may be established simply by the fact that an individual purchased the product after the misrepresentations were made.[171]

4.2.12.4 Requirement That Representation Be Material

Even though proof of reliance is not required, courts may require a showing that a misrepresentation or omission is material.[172] Illinois cases define a fact as material when the

166 Parks v. Macro Dynamics, Inc., 121 Ariz. 517, 591 P.2d 1005 (App. Ct. 1979); Peery v. Hansen, 120 Ariz. App. 266, 585 P.2d 574 (App. Ct. 1978); Duran v. Leslie Oldsmobile, 594 N.E.2d 1355 (Ill. App. Ct. 1992) (diligence in ascertaining truth of seller's statements not required; note that a later decision, Connick v. Suzuki Motor Co., Ltd., 675 N.E.2d 584 (Ill. 1996) holds that reliance is not even an element); Sutton v. Viking Oldsmobile Nissan, Inc., 611 N.W.2d 60 (Minn. App. June 2, 2000) (misrepresentation is a UDAP violation even if consumer knows the truth), *vacated, remanded*, 623 N.W.2d 247 (Minn. 2001) (remanding for reconsideration in light of Group Health Plan v. Philip Morris, Inc., 621 N.W.2d 2 (2001), which holds that private plaintiffs in damage suit need not prove reliance but must prove causation), *appeal after remand,* 2001 WL 856250 (Minn. App. July 31, 2001) (consumer alleged "legal nexus" between misconduct and injury, sufficient to support private action, with allegations that he would have bargained or refused the deal had he known that dealer kept significant portion of sum allegedly paid to another for service plan). *But see* Rosa v. Amoco Oil Co., 262 F. Supp. 2d 1364 (S.D. Fla. 2003) (business case); Massachusetts Laborers' Health & Welfare Fund v. Philip Morris, Inc., 62 F. Supp. 2d 236 (D. Mass. 1999) (cigarette smokers' UDAP claims barred because they could not show reasonable reliance on tobacco companies' false safety claims that were communicated through same mass media that carried countervailing information from other sources); Hoffman v. Stamper, 843 A.2d 153 (Md. Spec. App. 2004) (reliance necessary for recovery; shown here); Asbury v. Lagonia-Sherman, L.L.C., 2002 WL 31306691 (Tenn. App. Oct. 15, 2002) (unpublished, citation limited); Lunde v. Chase, 224 Wis. 2d 642, 590 N.W.2d 282 (Wis. App. 1999) (unpublished limited precedent opinion, text available on LEXIS at 1999 Wisc. App. LEXIS 1) (no liability where buyer learned true facts before entering into contract); Georgia cases cited in § 4.2.12.3.2, *supra*. *But cf.* Gruetzke v. Rodgers, 2001 Wash. App. LEXIS 1879 (Aug. 10, 2001) (unpublished, citation limited) (document that would not have deceived reasonable consumer did not meet "capacity to deceive" standard). *See* § 4.6.1, *infra*.

167 Sonnenberg v. Security Mgmt., 325 Md. 117, 599 A.2d 820 (1992).

168 Vasquez v. Superior Court, 4 Cal. 3d 800, 814, 484 P.2d 964 (1971); Mass. Mut. Life Ins. Co. v. Superior Court, 97 Cal. App. 4th 1282, 119 Cal. Rptr. 2d 190 (2002) (evidence of materiality is sufficient proof that misrepresentations were the cause of the harm suffered by buyers); Amato v. General Motors Corp., 11 Ohio App. 3d 124, 463 N.E.2d 625 (1982). *See also* Sykes v. AT&T Co., 179 F.R.D. 342 (S.D. Ga. 1998) (RICO suit); *In re* American Continental/Lincoln S&L Securities Litigation, 140 F.R.D. 425 (D. Ariz. 1992) (securities fraud suit); Smith v. MCI Telecommunications Corp., 124 F.R.D. 665, 679 (D. Kan. 1989) (employees' reliance on documents that spelled out their commission structure can be presumed). *See generally* National Consumer Law Center, Consumer Class Actions: A Practical Litigation Guide § 9.3.4.2 (5th ed. 2002 and Supp.). *But see* Group Health Plan v. Philip Morris, Inc., 188 F. Supp. 2d 1122 (D. Minn. 2002) (rejecting argument that there should be a presumption of causation), *aff'd in relevant part, remanded in part on other grounds*, 344 F.3d 753 (8th Cir. 2003); Aronson v. GreenMountain.com, 809 A.2d 399 (Pa. Super. 2002) (no presumption without allegation that class members actually saw the ads).

169 *See* § 4.2.12.2, *supra.*

170 *In re* Lutheran Brotherhood Variable Ins. Prods. Co. Sales Practices Litig., 2003 WL 21737528 (D. Minn. July 22, 2003) (evidence that defendant intended customers to rely and observed that they were relying is sufficient to withstand summary judgment); Dix v. American Bankers Life Assurance Co., 429 Mich. 410, 415 N.W.2d 206 (1987); Sutton v. Viking Oldsmobile Nissan, Inc., 2001 Minn. App. LEXIS 866 (July 31, 2001) (unpublished, limited precedent); Pyles v. Johnson, 143 Ohio App. 3d 720, 758 N.E.2d 1182 (2001); Amato v. General Motors Corp., 11 Ohio App. 3d 124, 463 N.E.2d 625 (1982).

171 Siemer v. Associates First Capital Corp., 2001 U.S. Dist. LEXIS 12810 (D. Ariz. Mar. 29, 2001).

172 Wells v. Allstate Ins. Co., 210 F.R.D. 1 (D.D.C. 2002) (reliance unnecessary but materiality required for non-disclosure claim); Markarian v. Conn. Mut. Life Ins. Co., 202 F.R.D. 60 (D. Mass. 2001) (vanishing premium case; materiality can not be presumed); HVAW Ltd. P'ship v. American Motorists Ins. Co., 968 F. Supp. 1178 (N.D. Tex. 1997) (misrepresentation must be "material"); Doll v. Bernard, 578 N.E.2d 1053 (Ill. App. Ct. 1991) (materiality must be shown, at least where misrepresentation is innocent). *But see* Sutton v. Viking Oldsmobile Nissan, Inc., 611 N.W.2d 60 (Minn. App. June 2, 2000) (misrepresentation is a violation even if it is not material, as long as seller intended others to rely on it), *vacated, remanded*, 623 N.W.2d 247 (Minn. 2001) (remanding for reconsideration in light of

plaintiff would have acted differently had he or she been aware of the information, or it concerned the type of information upon which he or she would be expected to rely in making a decision to act.[173]

4.2.12.5 Relationship of Reliance to Causation

Of course, whether or not a showing of reliance is required, plaintiffs seeking damages must prove causation, or as many courts term it, a causal connection to the UDAP violation.[174] Reliance and causation are twin concepts, often intertwined, but not identical,[175] and in some circumstances reliance can be an element of causation.[176] Nonetheless, a causal connection can be established in many circumstances without proof of reliance.

An example of a case finding a causal connection without reliance is *Stutman v. Chemical Bank*,[177] in which a bank had promised no prepayment charge, but then assessed a charge when the consumers sought to prepay the note. The bank argued that the consumers should have to show that they entered into the loan in reliance on the promise that there would be no prepayment charge. The New York Court of Appeals disagreed, holding that causation was shown by the fact that, because of the bank's deception, they were forced to pay a charge that they had been led to believe was not required. Likewise, a North Carolina court held that an insurance company's repudiation of its insurance contract and its representation that no insurance coverage had ever existed was a UDAP violation regardless of whether the plaintiff relied on the misrepresentation.[178]

In another case,[179] a contractor had given the consumers incorrect information about their right to rescind. The consumers did not have to prove that they relied on that information, but only that they lost money because they had not been able to prevent the contractor from starting work.

In another case, where a cruise company billed for "port charges" as if they were a pass-through of government taxes and fees, a Florida appellate court held that reliance and damages were sufficiently shown by the fact that consumers parted with their money after receiving the bill.[180] The fact that the consumer paid no attention to that term of the bill, and paid the bill willingly, was irrelevant.[181]

Where reliance is a necessary element of causation, it may be established by circumstantial evidence that shows a relationship between the deception and the claimed dam-

---

Group Health Plan v. Philip Morris, Inc., 621 N.W.2d 2 (Minn. 2001), which holds that private plaintiffs in damage suit need not prove reliance but must prove causation), *appeal after remand* 2001 WL 856250 (Minn. App. July 31, 2001) (consumer alleged "legal nexus" between misconduct and injury, sufficient to support private action, with allegations that he would have bargained or refused the deal had he known that dealer kept significant portion of sum allegedly paid to another for service plan). *But cf.* Arizona Cartridge Remanufacturers Ass'n v. Lexmark Int'l, Inc., 290 F. Supp. 2d 1034 (N.D. Cal. 2003) (not clear that showing of materiality is required under § 17200).

173 *In re* Limberopoulos, 2004 WL 528005 (N.D. Ill. Mar. 16, 2004) (finding bank's omission not to be material); Lipinski v. Martin J. Kelly Oldsmobile, Inc., 325 Ill. App. 3d 1139, 759 N.E.2d 66 (2001); *see also* Hartmarx Corp. v. JBA Int'l, Inc., 2002 U.S. Dist. LEXIS 4294 (N.D. Ill. Mar. 14, 2002) (finding alleged representations material); Connick v. Suzuki Motor Co., Ltd., 675 N.E.2d 584 (Ill. 1996) (interpreting statutory language making it a UDAP violation to fail to disclose a material fact); Wood v. Detroit Memorial Park Ass'n, 2001 WL 1654940 (Mich. App. Dec. 21, 2001) (defining "material" as "so substantial and important as to influence the party to whom it is made"); Azar v. Prudential Ins. Co., 68 P.3d 909 (N.M. App. 2003) (similar definition).

174 Perry v. American Tobacco Co., Inc., 324 F.3d 845 (6th Cir. 2003) (increase in health insurance premiums due to smokers in pool of insureds not recoverable from tobacco companies because causation too remote); Cozzi Iron & Metal, Inc. v. U.S. Office Equipment, Inc., 250 F.3d 570 (7th Cir. 2001) (Ill. law); Markarian v. Conn. Mut. Life Ins. Co., 202 F.R.D. 60 (D. Mass. 2001) (vanishing premium case; must prove "but for" causation); Connick v. Suzuki Motor Co., Ltd., 675 N.E.2d 584 (Ill. 1996) (need not prove reliance, but must show proximate cause; not shown as to post-sale statements since they could not have caused plaintiff's damage); Oliveira v. Amoco Oil Co., 201 Ill. 2d 134, 776 N.E.2d 151, 267 Ill. Dec. 14 (2002); Heller Fin. v. INA, 410 Mass. 400, 573 N.E.2d 8 (1991); Group Health Plan v. Philip Morris, Inc., 621 N.W.2d 2 (Minn. 2001); Varacallo v. Mass. Mut. Life Ins. Co., 332 N.J. Super. 31, 752 A.2d 807 (App. Div. 2000); Sanders v. Francis, 277 Or. 593, 561 P.2d 1003 (1977). *See also* Wiginton v. Pacific Credit Corp., 2 Haw. App. 435, 634 P.2d 111 (1981) (plaintiff must show that the violation induced the injury).

175 Stutman v. Chemical Bank, 95 N.Y.2d 24, 731 N.E.2d 608 (2000). *Accord* Smoot v. Physicians Life Ins. Co., 87 P.3d 545 (N.M. App. 2003); Sanders v. Francis, 277 Or. 593, 561 P.2d 1003 (1977).

176 Flock v. Scripto-Tokai Corp., 319 F.3d 231 (5th Cir. 2003); Miller v. William Chevrolet/Geo, Inc., 326 Ill. App. 3d 642, 762 N.E.2d 1 (2001) (plaintiffs need not show reliance but must show proximate cause, which requires proof that the misrepresentation occurred before plaintiff acted and that no intervening cause broke the chain); Sutton v. Viking Oldsmobile Nissan, Inc., 2001 Minn. App. LEXIS 866 (July 31, 2001) (unpublished, limited precedent); Tucker v. Boulevard at Piper Glen, 150 N.C. App. 150, 564 S.E.2d 248 (2002); Feitler v. Animation Collection, Inc., 170 Or. App. 702, 13 P.3d 1044 (2000) (reliance is required as element of causation when plaintiff claims to have relied on seller's express representations); TKO, Ltd. v. Wayne Manternach & Grayfield Dev., 222 Wis. 2d 623, 587 N.W.2d 456 (Wis. App. 1998) (unpublished limited precedent opinion, text available on LEXIS at 1998 Wisc. App. LEXIS 1227 (proof of reliance may be necessary to show causal connection).

177 95 N.Y.2d 24, 731 N.E.2d 608 (2000).

178 Cullen v. Valley Forge Life Ins. Co., 589 S.E.2d 423 (N.C. Ct. App. 2003).

179 Tri-West Constr. Co. v. Hernandez, 43 Or. App. 961, 607 P.2d 1375 (1979).

180 Latman v. Costa Cruise Lines, 758 So. 2d 699 (Fla. App. 2000). *See also* Pickett v. Holland Am. Line-Westours, Inc., 6 P.3d 63 (Wash. App. 2000), *rev'd on other grounds*, 35 P.3d 351 (Wash. 2001).

181 Latman v. Costa Cruise Lines, 758 So. 2d 699 (Fla. App. 2000).

ages.[182] Causation may also be proven by expert testimony. The Minnesota Supreme Court has used Lanham Act cases as an analogy, citing cases that allow proof of consumer confusion through circumstantial evidence such as surveys or consumer reaction tests.[183]

Several courts take the view that the plaintiff must show that the false representation is likely to make a difference in the purchasing decision.[184] If a consumer has actual knowledge of facts that a seller failed to disclose, the failure can not be a producing cause of damages under the Texas UDAP statute.[185] Where it is difficult to show actual reliance, a court has dispensed with proof of individual reliance as long as a reasonable person would have relied upon the representation.[186] Casting a gimlet eye on UDAP claims by criminals, Texas courts hold that a criminal's conduct is the sole cause of his punishment, so that no malpractice or UDAP claims may be brought.[187]

182 Group Health Plan v. Philip Morris, Inc., 621 N.W.2d 2 (Minn. 2001).

183 *See* Group Health Plan, Inc. v. Phillip Morris USA, Inc., 344 F.3d 753 (8th Cir. 2003) (using Lanham Act cases as analogy, but finding evidence of causation insufficient).

184 Anderson v. Rizza Chevrolet, Inc., 9 F. Supp. 2d 908 (N.D. Ill. 1998) (must show deception proximate cause of injury); Bercoon, Weiner, Glide & Brooke v. Manufacturer's Hanover Trust Co., 818 F. Supp. 1152 (N.D. Ill. 1993); Parks v. Macro Dynamics, Inc., 121 Ariz. 517, 591 P.2d 1005 (App. Ct. 1979); Peery v. Hansen, 120 Ariz. 266, 585 P.2d 574 (App. Ct. 1978); Massey v. Thomaston Ford Mercury, 196 Ga. App. 278, 395 S.E.2d 663 (1990); People *ex rel.* Hartigan v. E&E Hauling, Inc., 153 Ill. 2d 473, 607 N.E.2d 165 (1992) (must show a connection between the deceptive act and the injury); Affrunti v. Village Ford Sales, Inc., 597 N.E.2d 1242 (Ill. App. Ct. 1992); Totz v. Continental DuPage Acura, 602 N.E.2d 1374 (Ill. App. Ct. 1992); Lehrman v. South Chicago Cable, Inc., 210 Ill. App. 3d 346, 569 N.E.2d 99 (1991); Butitta v. First Mortgage Corp., 578 N.E.2d 116 (Ill. App. Ct. 1991); Mack v. Plaza DeWitt Ltd. P'ship, 137 Ill. App. 3d 343, 484 N.E.2d 900 (1985); City of Aurora v. Green, 126 Ill. App. 3d 684, 467 N.E.2d 610 (1984); Maloney v. Sargisson, 18 Mass. App. Ct. 341, 465 N.E.2d 296 (1984); Butler v. Caldwell & Cook, Inc., 122 A.D.2d 559, 505 N.Y.S.2d 288 (1986); Bello v. Cablevision Sys. Corp., 587 N.Y.S.2d 1 (App. Div. 1992); Caldwell v. Pop's Home Inc., 54 Or. App. 104, 634 P.2d 471 (1981); Terry v. Hoden-Dhein Enterprises Ltd., 48 Or. App. 763, 618 P.2d 7 (1980); Commonwealth v. Hush-Tone Indus., Inc., 4 Pa. Commw. 1 (1971); McCrea v. Cubilla Condominium Corp., 685 S.W.2d 755 (Tex. App. 1985). *But see* Weinberg v. Sun Oil Co., 565 Pa. 612, 777 A.2d 442 (2001) (distinguishing between attorney general suits and private suits, which require reliance as element of causation).

185 Gill v. Boyd Distribution Center, 64 S.W.3d 601 (Tex. App. 2001).

186 Latman v. Costa Cruise Lines, 758 So. 2d 699 (Fla. App. 2000) (class action); Dix v. American Bankers Life Assurance Co., 429 Mich. 410, 415 N.W.2d 206 (1987). *See also* FTC v. Windward Marketing, Ltd., 1997 U.S. Dist. LEXIS 17114 (N.D. Ga. Sept. 30, 1997) (reliance presumed once FTC shows that defendant made materials misrepresentations that were widely disseminated and that consumers purchased the product).

187 Golden v. McNeal, 78 S.W.3d 488 (Tex. App. 2002).

4.2.13 Ambiguous but Literally True Statements, Partial Truths, and Pictures Can Be Deceptive

Literally true statements can be deceptive.[188] A literally true statement may have implications that are deceptive. Literal truthfulness is only the beginning of deception analysis which then proceeds to analyze the implication of the statement.

Deception can be accomplished through innuendo and not just outright false statements.[189] Advertisements or other representations can contain implied claims, and if these implied claims are false, the advertisement is deceptive even

188 Ambrose v. New England Ass'n of Schools and Colleges, 252 F.3d 488 (1st Cir. 2001); American Home Products Corp. v. FTC, 695 F.2d 681 (3d Cir. 1982); L.G. Balfour Co. v. FTC, 442 F.2d 1 (7th Cir. 1971); FTC v. Sterling Drug, Inc., 317 F.2d 669 (2d Cir. 1963); Exposition Press, Inc. v. FTC, 295 F.2d 869 (2d Cir. 1961); Royal Oil Co. v. FTC, 262 F.2d 741 (4th Cir. 1959); Kalwajtys v. FTC, 237 F.2d 654 (7th Cir. 1956), *cert. denied*, 352 U.S. 1025 (1957); Aronberg v. FTC, 132 F.2d 165 (7th Cir. 1942); Ford Motor Co. v. FTC, 120 F.2d 175 (6th Cir. 1941); Kleczek v. Jorgensen, 328 Ill. App. 3d 1012, 767 N.E.2d 913, 263 Ill. Dec. 187 (2002) (statement that builder had received no notice of plumbing violations deceptive where inspector had orally informed him of violations); M&W Gear Co. v. A.W. Dynamometer Inc., 97 Ill. App. 3d 904, 424 N.E.2d 356 (1981); Commonwealth v. Fall River Motor Sales, Inc., 409 Mass. 302, 565 N.E.2d 1205 (1991); Leardi v. Brown, 394 Mass. 151, 474 N.E.2d 1094 (1985); Miller v. American Family Publishers, 284 N.J. Super. 67, 663 A.2d 643 (Chancery Div. 1995) (deceptive implications in solicitations for publisher's sweepstakes); Johnson v. Phoenix Mut. Life Ins. Co., 300 N.C. 247, 266 S.E.2d 610 (1980); State *ex rel.* Fisher v. Rose Chevrolet, 82 Ohio App. 3d 520, 612 N.E.2d 782 (1992) (non-direct answer to consumer's question about car's prior use was deceptive where it concealed prior use as rental car); DeBondt v. Carlton Motorcars, Inc., 342 S.C. 254, 536 S.E.2d 399 (App. 2000); Young v. Century Lincoln-Mercury, Inc., 396 S.E.2d 105 (S.C. Ct. App. 1990); Parker-Smith v. Sto Corp., 262 Va. 432, 551 S.E.2d 615 (2001) (construing false advertising statute).

189 Regina Corp. v. FTC, 322 F.2d 765 (3d Cir. 1963); Bakers Franchise Corp. v. FTC, 302 F.2d 258 (3d Cir. 1962); Bockenstette v. FTC, 134 F.2d 369 (10th Cir. 1943); Minnesota *ex rel.* Hatch v. Fleet Mortg. Corp., 158 F. Supp. 2d 962 (D. Minn. 2001) (promoting "free trial period" while obscuring fact that monthly charges will be assessed unless consumer cancels is deceptive); FTC v. Think Achievement Corp., 144 F. Supp. 2d 993 (N.D. Ind. 2000), *aff'd in relevant part, rev'd in part on other grounds*, 312 F.3d 259 (7th Cir. 2002); Thompson Medical Co., 104 F.T.C. 648 (1984), *aff'd*, 791 F.2d 189 (D.C. Cir. 1986), *cert. denied*, 479 U.S. 1086 (1987); MacMillan, Inc., 96 F.T.C. 208 (1980); Brockey v. Moore, 107 Cal. App. 4th 86, 131 Cal. Rptr. 2d 746 (2003); Chandler v. Am. Gen. Fin., Inc., 329 Ill. App. 3d 729, 768 N.E.2d 60 (2002) (ads that created impression that new loan was offered, when lender actually intended only to offer refinancing, could be deceptive); Cole v. Sunnyside Corp., 234 Wis. 2d 149, 610 N.W.2d 511 (App. 2000) (advertising a product to homeowners carries implicit representation that it is safe for household use). *See also* Feil v. FTC, 285 F.2d 879 (9th Cir. 1960); Aronberg v. FTC, 132 F.2d 165 (7th Cir. 1942); FTC v. Wilcox, 926 F. Supp. 1091 (S.D. Fla. 1995).

if the explicit claims are true.[190] Implied claims are present if consumers acting reasonably in the circumstances interpret the advertisement as containing that message.[191]

To determine the meaning of implied claims, the FTC looks at the content of the whole representation, the juxtaposition of various phrases therein, the nature of the claim, and the surrounding circumstances. Extrinsic evidence will be considered where the implied meaning can not be determined from a facial examination of the claim.[192]

The Seventh Circuit in the *Kraft* case reaffirmed this principle, that even literally true statements can be deceptive.[193] In *Kraft*, the company's advertisements claimed that cheese slices had five ounces of milk and that the cheese slices were thus concentrated with calcium. The ad had a subscript indicating that a cheese slice has 70% of the calcium of five ounces of milk. The ad was thus literally true. Nevertheless, the Seventh Circuit upheld the FTC's conclusion that consumers would likely assume, after reviewing the advertisement, that a Kraft cheese slice had five ounces of milk worth of calcium, when in fact 30% of the calcium was lost in processing.

The *Kraft* analysis has obvious implications for other consumer transactions. For example, consider a car dealer who claims that the previous owner took excellent care of the car and, in small print in the sales contract, states that the vehicle contains replacement parts. The dealer's statements might be literally true, even if the replacement parts were necessary because the car had been totaled, if the accident was not the fault of the prior owner. Nevertheless, the fact that the car is mostly replacement parts is contrary to the dealer's implied message. Following *Kraft*, the consumer should have a UDAP claim.

A practice is deceptive if a consideration of the entire representation, and not just the specific explicit claim, finds the statement deceptive.[194] Such an interpretation may be found even if the literal meaning is not deceptive.[195] Of

190 Novartis Corp., 5 Trade Reg. Rep. (CCH) ¶ 24,614, F.T.C. Dkt. 9279 (May 27, 1999), *aff'd*, 223 F.3d 783 (D.C. Cir. 2000); Kraft, Inc., 5 Trade Reg. Rep. (CCH) ¶ 22937 (F.T.C. Dkt. 9208 1991); Removatron Int'l Corp., 111 F.T.C. 206 (1988), *aff'd on other grounds*, 884 F.2d 1489 (11th Cir. 1989); Latman v. Costa Cruise Lines, 758 So. 2d 699 (Fla. App. 2000) (cruise line's use of term "port charges" implicitly represents that the charge is a pass-through); Beltz v. Dings, 27 Kan. App. 2d 507, 6 P.3d 424 (2000); *see also* Thompson Medical Co., 104 F.T.C. 648 at 788 (1984), *aff'd*, 791 F.2d 189 (D.C. Cir. 1986), *cert. denied*, 479 U.S. 1086 (1987); Cliffdale Assocs., Inc., 103 F.T.C. 110, 164–166 (1988); Bristol-Meyers Co., 102 F.T.C. 21, 31 (1983), *aff'd*, 738 F.2d 554 (2d Cir. 1984), *cert. denied*, 469 U.S. 1189 (1985); Miller v. American Family Publishers, 284 N.J. Super. 67, 663 A.2d 643 (Chancery Div. 1995) (deceptive implications in solicitations for publisher's sweepstakes). *But see* Nigh v. Koons Buick Pontiac GMC, Inc., 143 F. Supp. 2d 535 (E.D. Va. 2001) (statement that car did not look like it had been in any accidents not a representation because not unambiguous), *aff'd on other grounds*, 319 F.3d 119 (4th Cir. 2003), *cert. granted on other issues*, 124 S. Ct. 1144 (2004); Kaplan v. Cablevision, Inc., 671 A.2d 716 (Pa. Super. 1996) (refusing to find that provision of uninterrupted service is an implied term of cable TV service contract).

191 Kraft, Inc., 5 Trade Reg. Rep. (CCH) ¶ 22937 (F.T.C. Dkt. 9208 1991); Removatron Int'l Corp., 111 F.T.C. 206 (1988), *aff'd on other grounds*, 884 F.2d 1489 (11th Cir. 1989); Prata v. Superior Court, 91 Cal. App. 4th 1128, 111 Cal. Rptr. 2d 296 (2001); *see also* Thompson Medical Co., 104 F.T.C. 648 at 788 (1984), *aff'd*, 791 F.2d 189 (D.C. Cir. 1986), *cert. denied*, 479 U.S. 1086 (1987); Cliffdale Assocs., Inc., 103 F.T.C. 110, 164–166 (1988); Bristol-Meyers Co., 102 F.T.C. 21, 31 (1983), *aff'd*, 738 F.2d 554 (2d Cir. 1984), *cert. denied*, 469 U.S. 1189 (1985).

192 Thompson Medical Co., 104 F.T.C. 648 at 788 (1984), *aff'd*, 791 F.2d 189 (D.C. Cir. 1986), *cert. denied*, 479 U.S. 1086 (1987).

193 *See* Kraft, Inc. v. FTC, 970 F.2d 311 (7th Cir. 1992).

194 American Home Products Corp. v. FTC, 695 F.2d 681 (3d Cir. 1982); National Bakers Servs., Inc. v. FTC, 329 F.2d 365 (7th Cir. 1964); FTC v. Sterling Drug, Inc., 317 F.2d 669 (2d Cir. 1963); Murray Space Shoe Corp. v. FTC, 304 F.2d 270 (2d Cir. 1962); Elliot Knitwear v. FTC, 266 F.2d 787 (2d Cir. 1959); Koch v. FTC, 206 F.2d 311 (6th Cir. 1953); Aronberg v. FTC, 132 F.2d 165 (7th Cir. 1942); Ford Motor Co. v. FTC, 120 F.2d 175 (6th Cir. 1941); FTC v. Cyberspace.com, L.L.C., 2002 WL 32060289 (W.D. Wash. July 10, 2002) (fine print on back of check stating that cashing it created a contract for Internet services); FTC v. Medicor, 217 F. Supp. 2d 1048 (C.D. Cal. 2002) (statement that "results may vary" did not save ad since consumers could still reasonably believe that illustrated results were typical); FTC v. Think Achievement Corp., 144 F. Supp. 2d 993 (N.D. Ind. 2000), *aff'd in relevant part, rev'd in part on other grounds*, 312 F.3d 259 (7th Cir. 2002); FTC v. Gill, 71 F. Supp. 2d 1030 (C.D. Cal. 1999), *aff'd on other grounds*, 265 F.3d 944 (9th Cir. 2001); FTC v. U.S. Sales Corp., 785 F. Supp. 737 (N.D. Ill. 1992); FTC v. Alantex Assocs., 1987-2 Trade Cases ¶ 67,788 (S.D. Fla. 1987); FTC v. Pharmtech Research, Inc., 576 F. Supp. 294 (D.D.C. 1983); Kraft, Inc., 5 Trade Reg. Rep. (CCH) ¶ 22937 (F.T.C. Dkt. 9208 1991); Removatron Int'l Corp., 111 F.T.C. 206 (1988), *aff'd on other grounds*, 884 F.2d 1489 (11th Cir. 1989); Thompson Medical Co., 104 F.T.C. 648 (1984), *aff'd*, 791 F.2d 189 (D.C. Cir. 1986), *cert. denied*, 479 U.S. 1086 (1987); Bristol-Myers Co., 102 F.T.C. 21 (1983), *aff'd*, 738 F.2d 554 (2d Cir. 1984), *cert. denied*, 469 U.S. 1189 (1985); Great Atlantic & Pacific Tea Co., 85 F.T.C. 601 (1975); Madsen v. Western Am. Mortg. Co., 694 P.2d 1228 (Ariz. Ct. App. 1985); Garcia v. Overland Bond & Investment Co., 282 Ill. App. 3d 486, 668 N.E.2d 199 (1996); Leardi v. Brown, 394 Mass. 151, 474 N.E.2d 1094 (1985); Commonwealth v. Amcan Enterprises, 47 Mass. App. Ct. 330, 712 N.E.2d 1205 (1999); Johnson v. Hewlett Packard Co., 2002 WL 1050426 (Minn. App. May 22, 2002) (unpublished, citation limited) (it is a factual question whether it was deceptive not to disclose that ink cartridge had less ink than standard cartridge); Gaidon v. Guardian Life Ins. Co., 96 N.Y.2d 201, 750 N.E.2d 1078 (2001) (disclaimers insufficient to dispel deception created by misleading illustrations); Commonwealth *ex rel.* Zimmerman v. Nickel, 26 Pa. D. & C.3d 115 (C.P. Mercer Cty. 1983); Jordan v. Nissan North America, Inc., 2004 WL 595413 (Vt. Mar. 26, 2004); State v. Burlison, 38 Wash. App. 487, 685 P.2d 1115 (1984).

195 American Home Products Corp. v. FTC, 695 F.2d 681 (3d Cir. 1983); Bristol-Myers Co., 102 F.T.C. 21 (1983), *aff'd*, 738 F.2d 554 (2d Cir. 1984), *cert. denied*, 469 U.S. 1189 (1985); J.B. Williams Co. v. FTC, 381 F.2d 884 (6th Cir. 1967); Madsen v. Western Am. Mortg. Co., 694 P.2d 1228 (Ariz. Ct. App. 1985); Leardi v. Brown, 394 Mass. 151, 474 N.E.2d 1094 (1985); State v. Burlison, 38 Wash. App. 487, 685 P.2d 1115 (1984).

course, courts should not freely speculate that the public will place a patently absurd interpretation on an advertisement.[196] However, representations capable of being interpreted in a misleading way should be construed against the advertiser.[197] A statement or omission may convey more than one reasonable meaning, and if one of those meanings is deceptive, it violates the UDAP statute.[198] A seller commits a deceptive act by giving the consumer a contract that promises performance in one clause, but then renders that promise meaningless by another clause.[199]

Conduct can be deceptive,[200] as can pictures.[201] A website can be considered an advertisement for purposes of a UDAP statute.[202] Thus for television advertising, the court should look at the implied meaning of visual and audio imagery, and not just at the words of an advertisement.[203] It is also deceptive to package and name a product in a way that resembles a different product.[204]

4.2.14 Failure to Disclose

4.2.14.1 Overview

One of the most important uses of a UDAP statute is to attack the failure to disclose material facts. Where sellers do not make affirmative misrepresentations or it is difficult to prove oral misrepresentations, the key to a UDAP case often is the claim that the seller did not disclose important information.

It is usually easier to prove that something was not said than prove what was actually said. Where a class action is involved, it is certainly easier to prove the seller never told anyone an important fact than it is to prove what was said to each class member.[205] It will be hard for a court to say as a matter of law that a fact is not material and need not be disclosed; consequently, a consumer's claim of deception based upon the failure to disclose should be allowed to go to trial.[206]

In a surprising number of situations where the consumer is having difficulty explaining what was deceptive about the seller's conduct, the solution is found in detailing what was *not* said, what important information was not disclosed to the consumer. For example, a finance company offers to refinance a loan at far worse terms than are available elsewhere, but the complexity of the transaction is such that the consumer does not understand this. The best approach may be to claim it is deceptive for the creditor to fail to

196 Standard Oil Co. of California v. FTC, 577 F.2d 653 (9th Cir. 1978); Bellinger v. Hewlett-Packard Co., 2002 Ohio App. LEXIS 1573 (Apr. 10, 2002) (representation that printer included ink cartridge is not implicit representation about size of cartridge). *See also* Cole v. Hewlett Packard Co., 2004 WL 376471 (Kan. App. Feb. 27, 2004) (unpublished, citation limited) (consumer failed to show that fact that ink cartridge was half-full was material); Andre Strishak & Assocs. v. Hewlett-Packard Co., 2001 N.Y. Misc. LEXIS 350 (Sup. Ct. July 13, 2001) (advertising that printer includes an ink cartridge does not implicitly represent that it is the larger of two sizes).

197 Simeon Mgmt. Corp. v. FTC, 579 F.2d 1137 (9th Cir. 1978); Resort Car Rental Sys., Inc. v. FTC, 518 F.2d 962 (9th Cir.), *cert. denied sub nom.* Mackenzie v. United States, 423 U.S. 827 (1975); Continental Wax Corp. v. FTC, 330 F.2d 475 (2d Cir. 1964); Country Tweeds, Inc. v. FTC, 326 F.2d 144 (2d Cir. 1964); Ward Laboratories, Inc. v. FTC, 276 F.2d 952 (2d Cir.), *cert. denied*, 364 U.S. 827 (1960); Gelb v. FTC, 144 F.2d 580 (2d Cir. 1944); Removatron Int'l Corp., 111 F.T.C. 206 (1988), *aff'd on other grounds*, 884 F.2d 1489 (11th Cir. 1989); MacMillan Inc., 96 F.T.C. 208 (1980).

198 Porter & Dietsch Inc. v. FTC, 605 F.2d 294 (7th Cir. 1979); Chrysler Corp. v. FTC, 561 F.2d 357 (D.C. Cir. 1977); Magnaflo Co. v. FTC, 343 F.2d 318 (D.C. Cir. 1965); Giant Food, Inc. v. FTC, 322 F.2d 977 (D.C. Cir. 1963), *cert. denied*, 376 U.S. 967 (1964); Murray Space Shoe Corp. v. FTC, 304 F.2d 270 (2d Cir. 1962); Rhodes Pharmacal Co. v. FTC, 208 F.2d 382 (7th Cir. 1953), *modified by reinstating Commission's order*, 348 U.S. 940 (1953); Carter Products, Inc. v. FTC, 186 F.2d 821 (7th Cir. 1951); Jordan v. Nissan North America, Inc., 2004 WL 595413 (Vt. Mar. 26, 2004); FTC v. Pharmtech Research, Inc., 576 F. Supp. 294 (D.D.C. 1983); Bristol-Myers Co., 102 F.T.C. 21 (1983), *aff'd*, 738 F.2d 554 (2d Cir. 1984), *cert. denied*, 469 U.S. 1189 (1985); National Comm'n on Egg Nutrition, 88 F.T.C. 89 (1976), *aff'd*, 570 F.2d 157 (7th Cir. 1977), *cert. denied*, 439 U.S. 821 (1978); Merck & Co., 69 F.T.C. 525, *aff'd sub nom.* Doherty, Clifford, Steers & Shenfield, Inc. v. FTC, 392 F.2d 921 (6th Cir. 1968); Madsen v. Western Am. Mortg. Co., 694 P.2d 1228 (Ariz. Ct. App. 1985); Williams v. Bruno Appliance & Furniture Mart, 62 Ill. App. 3d 219, 379 N.E.2d 52 (1978); Broder v. MBNA Corp., 281 A.D.2d 369, 722 N.Y.S.2d 524 (2001); Broder v. MBNA Corp., 722 N.Y.S.2d 524 (App. Div. 2001) (fine-print statement that creditor "may" use unfavorable method of allocating payments is ambiguous and may be UDAP violation); Carter v. Gugliuzzi, 716 A.2d 17 (Vt. 1998).

199 Fendrich v. RBF, L.L.C., 842 So. 2d 1076 (Fla. Dist. Ct. App. 2003).

200 Cambridge Plating Co. v. NAPCO, Inc., 876 F. Supp. 326 (D. Mass. 1995), *aff'd in part, vacated in part on other grounds*, 85 F.3d 752 (1st Cir. 1996). *But cf.* Jones v. Davenport, 2001 Ohio App. LEXIS 226 (Jan. 26, 2001) (middleman's use of manufacturer's sample to help buyer select desired color of brick was not a representation that brick would match that color).

201 FTC v. Colgate-Palmolive Co., 380 U.S. 374 (1965); Sterling Drug Inc. v. FTC, 741 F.2d 1146 (9th Cir. 1984); United States Ass'n of Credit Bureaus, Inc. v. FTC, 299 F.2d 220 (7th Cir. 1962); Keele Hair & Scalp Specialists, Inc. v. FTC, 275 F.2d 18 (5th Cir. 1960); Erickson v. FTC, 272 F.2d 318 (7th Cir. 1959); Cambridge Plating Co. v. NAPCO, Inc., 876 F. Supp. 326 (D. Mass. 1995) (submission of inaccurate drawings of wastewater treatment system was deceptive), *aff'd in part, vacated in part on other grounds*, 85 F.3d 752 (1st Cir. 1996).

202 Minnesota *ex rel.* Hatch v. Fleet Mortg. Corp., 158 F. Supp. 2d 962 (D. Minn. 2001). *See also* § 4.2.14.3.9, *infra*.

203 American Home Products Corp. v. FTC, 695 F.2d 681 (3d Cir. 1983).

204 Canandaigua Wine Co., 114 F.T.C. 348 (1991) (consent order) (bottle shape and color, and names of flavors, resembled wine cooler drinks).

205 *See, e.g.*, Mass. Mut. Life Ins. Co. v. Superior Court, 97 Cal. App. 4th 1282, 119 Cal. Rptr. 2d 190 (2002).

206 *See* Packard v. KC One, Inc., 727 S.W.2d 435 (Mo. Ct. App. 1987).

disclose that preferable terms are available elsewhere.[207] Also consider a case where a dealer sells a car "as is," keeps to itself known defects, but makes no explicit claims as to quality. A useful UDAP claim is that the dealer must disclose known defects.

There are three ways of showing that the failure to disclose is deceptive. Some UDAP statutes or regulations specifically prohibit the nondisclosure of material facts.[208] Examine the statutory or regulatory language closely to see if the nondisclosure must be intentional.[209] Second, failing an explicit statutory or regulatory prohibition, courts consistently hold that nondisclosure can be deceptive. Finally, in states where the UDAP statute also prohibits unfair practices, it is prudent to add that the nondisclosure is "unfair," and not just deceptive.

4.2.14.2 The FTC Standard

According to federal courts interpreting the FTC Act, representations are deceptive if necessary qualifications are not made, if material facts are not disclosed, or if these disclosures or qualifications are too inconspicuous.[210] "To tell less than the whole truth is a well known method of deception."[211] Even if proper disclosures are made in writing, if a sales presentation effectively obscures the meaning of those disclosures, the total representation is deceptive.[212] The public is not under any duty to make a reasonable inquiry into undisclosed aspects of an advertisement.[213] When a seller makes absolute claims, the seller must disclose if the claims are open to question, particularly where verification rests with the seller, and consumers would otherwise assume the claim is unqualified.[214]

The FTC has also proffered a complex analysis, not adopted by any federal court interpreting the FTC Act or any court interpreting a state UDAP statute, of when a failure to disclose is unfair and when it is deceptive.[215] It is deceptive to say half the truth and omit the rest, to omit qualifying information necessary to prevent the statement from creating a misleading impression, or to remain silent if this, under the circumstances, constitutes a false implied representation.[216] Such an implied representation can be created from a product's physical appearance, the circumstances of the transaction, and consumer expectations as to the minimum standards of a good. For example, failure to disclose that a product is not reasonably fit for its intended use and is not free of gross safety hazards is deceptive.[217]

On the other hand, a "pure omission"—the seller's silence with no explicit or implied meaning to that silence—is not "deceptive," but it may be "unfair." To determine whether a "pure omission" is unfair, the FTC applies its standard unfairness criteria: whether there is substantial consumer injury that is not outweighed by the benefits to

207 *See In re* Milbourne, 108 B.R. 522 (Bankr. E.D. Pa. 1989).

208 Statutes prohibiting nondisclosure are listed at Appx. A, *infra*. UDAP regulations prohibiting nondisclosure are detailed § 4.2.14.3.2, *infra*.

209 Even though the Texas UDAP statute now specifically prohibits the failure to disclose material facts, such a prohibition is also implicit within the statute's general prohibition of deception. Thus the failure to disclose is deceptive even in transactions antedating the amendment creating the specific itemized prohibition. Robinson v. Preston Chrysler-Plymouth, Inc., 633 S.W.2d 500, 502 n.1 (Tex. 1982); Pairett v. Gutierrez, 969 S.W.2d 512 (Tex. App. 1998); Kahlig v. Boyd, 980 S.W.2d 685 (Tex. App. 1998); Aetna Cas. & Surety Co. v. Martin Surgical Supply Co., 689 S.W.2d 263 (Tex. App. 1985); Gibbs v. Main Bank of Houston, 666 S.W.2d 554 (Tex. App. 1984); Cobb v. Dunlap 656 S.W.2d 550 (Tex. App. 1983). But the information must be withheld in order to induce the consumer to enter into that transaction. Bradford v. Vento, 48 S.W.3d 749 (Tex. 2001).

210 FTC v. Brown & Williamson Tobacco Corp., 778 F.2d 35 (D.C. Cir. 1985) (small print disclosure can not save deceptive general claim); Sterling Drug, Inc. v. FTC, 741 F.2d 1146 (9th Cir. 1984); American Home Products Corp. v. FTC, 695 F.2d 681 (3d Cir. 1982); Simeon Mgmt. Corp. v. FTC, 579 F.2d 1137 (9th Cir. 1978) (weight loss clinic's ads deceptive although they contained no false facts but did not disclose that the injection of a drug found not safe and effective for obesity was part of clinic's program); J.B. Williams Co. v. FTC, 381 F.2d 884 (6th Cir. 1967) (Geritol ads must disclose that iron deficiency anemia is not the cause of most tiredness); Benrus Watch Co. v. FTC, 352 F.2d 313 (8th Cir. 1965), *cert. denied*, 384 U.S. 939 (1966) (failing to disclose $1.00 service charge to repair "guaranteed" watch); Brite Mfg. Co. v. FTC, 347 F.2d 477 (D.C. Cir. 1965); Waltham Watch Co. v. FTC, 318 F.2d 28 (7th Cir. 1963), *cert. denied*, 375 U.S. 944 (1964) (fail to disclose Waltham clocks no longer manufactured by Waltham Watch Co. and fail to disclose the county of origin); *In re* Sydney Floersheim, 316 F.2d 423 (9th Cir. 1963); Spencer Gifts, Inc. v. FTC, 302 F.2d 267 (3d Cir. 1962); Theodore Kagen Corp. v. FTC, 283 F.2d 371 (D.C. Cir. 1960), *cert. denied*, 365 U.S. 843 (1961); Feil v. FTC, 285 F.2d 879 (9th Cir. 1960); Ward Laboratories, Inc. v. FTC, 276 F.2d 952 (2d Cir.), *cert. denied*, 364 U.S. 827 (1960); Keele Hair & Scalp Specialists, Inc. v. FTC, 275 F.2d 18 (5th Cir. 1960); Kerran v. FTC, 265 F.2d 246 (10th Cir. 1959), *cert. denied*, 361 U.S. 818 (1961); Royal Oil Co. v. FTC, 262 F.2d 741 (4th Cir. 1959); American Life & Accident Ins. Co. v. FTC, 225 F.2d 289 (2d Cir. 1955); Mary Muffet Inc. v. FTC, 194 F.2d 504 (2d Cir. 1952); Haskelite v. FTC, 127 F.2d 765 (7th Cir. 1942); MacMillan Inc., 96 F.T.C. 208 (1980); FTC v. P.M.C.S., Inc., 21 F. Supp. 2d 187 (E.D.N.Y. 1998) (omission of material information from advertisement, even if advertisement does not contain falsehoods, may be an unfair or deceptive act).

211 P. Lorillard Co. v. FTC, 186 F.2d 52 at 58 (4th Cir. 1950). *See also* Benrus Watch Co. v. FTC, 352 F.2d 313 (8th Cir. 1965), *cert. denied*, 384 U.S. 939 (1966); Bennett v. FTC, 200 F.2d 362 (D.C. Cir. 1952); Bockenstette v. FTC, 134 F.2d 369 (10th Cir. 1943).

212 Horizon Corp., 97 F.T.C. 464 (1981).

213 Resort Car Rental Sys., Inc. v. FTC, 518 F.2d 962 (9th Cir.), *cert. denied sub nom.* Mackenzie v. United States, 423 U.S. 827 (1975).

214 American Home Products Corp., 98 F.T.C. 136 (1981), *aff'd*, 695 F.2d 681 (3d Cir. 1983); *see also* National Comm'n on Egg Nutrition, 88 F.T.C. 89 (1976), *aff'd*, 570 F.2d 157 (7th Cir. 1977), *cert. denied*, 439 U.S. 821 (1978).

215 International Harvester Co., 104 F.T.C. 949 (1984).

216 *Id.*

217 *Id.*

competition and that the consumer could not reasonably have avoided the practice.[218] In a nondisclosure case, consumers can not be expected to avoid something where they have not been told the information needed to act reasonably.[219] Consequently, a pure omission is unfair if the consumer benefit from the disclosure of information outweighs the disclosure costs.

Examples the FTC provides as to "unfair" nondisclosure include the failure to disclose hidden safety hazards and information on the product's fitness for its intended use.[220] The FTC states that unfairness can be found even where the injury is limited to a small number of people, particularly since the costs of disclosure are usually minimal.[221]

4.2.14.3 State UDAP Precedent

4.2.14.3.1 General standards

Cases under state UDAP statutes do not utilize such a complex analysis, but have little difficulty finding the failure to disclose to be deceptive. In scrutinizing a seller's practices, courts demand the "most literal truthfulness" and both actual words and their net impression must be considered.[222] A seller's knowledge may be proven by circumstantial evidence.[223] Literal truths and half-truths that avoid material facts are deceptive.[224] For example, a credit card statement disclosure that past-due accounts would incur a service charge, when no such charge was being imposed for past-due balances of less than $25, violates the Illinois UDAP Act.[225] Likewise, a non-direct answer to a consumer's question about a vehicle's prior use was deceptive where it concealed that the vehicle had been previously owned by a rental car company.[226]

An omission is considered material if a significant number of unsophisticated consumers of the goods or services would attach importance to the information in deciding on a course of action.[227] The standard for materiality may also include a subjective test, where the seller knows that the consumer, because of some peculiarity, is particularly susceptible to an omission or misrepresentation.[228] Whether an omission is material is a question of fact.[229]

Under a state UDAP statute it can be deceptive to disclose facts too late, such as just as the consumer is signing the agreement.[230] A party entering into a contract with a consumer makes an implicit representation that it will follow all laws that are in effect at the time of the agreement. Its failure to disclose its noncompliance with law is deceptive.[231]

There are limits on the duty to disclose. A number of states make nondisclosure a UDAP violation only if the defendant intended that others rely on the omission.[232] Illinois courts hold that, where federal law governs disclosures, the UDAP statute will not be construed to require additional or different disclosures.[233] The Wisconsin Supreme Court has held that non-disclosure is not a violation of a prohibition in one of its two UDAP statutes that only forbids false "assertion[s], representations[s], or statement[s] of fact."[234] In cases involving nondisclosure it is wiser to rely on more general prohibitions of unfair and deceptive practices, if possible.

---

218 *See* § 4.3.2, *supra*.

219 For examples, consumers can not reasonably avoid a safety hazard even though that safety hazard would occur only when consumers used a product in violation of its safety instructions. Consumers could not reasonably avoid the safety hazard where the manufacturer failed to disclose *why* the violation of safety instructions was dangerous. International Harvester Co., 104 F.T.C. 949 (1984).

220 International Harvester Co., 104 F.T.C. 949 (1984) (see text accompanying n.49, explaining somewhat greater scope of unfairness prohibition).

221 *Id.*

222 State *ex rel.* Guste v. Alaska Overseas, Inc., No. 8718, Clearinghouse No. 26,208 (La. Ct. App. 1977).

223 Fernandez v. Schultz, 15 S.W.3d 648 (Tex. App. 2000). *See also* Etheridge v. Oak Creek Mobile Homes, Inc., 989 S.W.2d 412 (Tex. App. 1999).

224 V.S.H. Realty, Inc. v. Texaco, Inc., 757 F.2d 411 (1st Cir. 1985) (Massachusetts law); Commonwealth v. Handicapped Indus., Inc., Clearinghouse No. 26,027 (Pa. C.P. Bucks Cty. 1977); Commonwealth v. Foster, Clearinghouse No. 26,031 (Pa. C.P. Allegheny Cty. 1974); 15 Mo. Code State Regs. §§ 60-9.090, 60-9.110. *But see* Hubbard v. Bob McDorman Chevrolet, 104 Ohio App. 3d 621, 662 N.E.2d 1102 (1995) (mere evasiveness is not the same as a misrepresentation).

225 Garland v. Mobil Oil Corp., 340 F. Supp. 1095 (N.D. Ill. 1972).

226 State *ex rel.* Fisher v. Rose Chevrolet, 82 Ohio App. 3d 520, 612 N.E.2d 782 (1992).

227 Cole v. Hewlett Packard Co., 2004 WL 376471 (Kan. App. Feb. 27, 2004) (unpublished, citation limited) (fact is material if reasonable person would attach importance to it in determining course of action); Green v. H&R Block, Inc., 355 Md. 488, 735 A.2d 1039 (1999); State v. Cottman Transmissions Sys., Inc., 86 Md. App. 714, 587 A.2d 1190 (1991). *See also* Carter v. Gugliuzzi, 716 A.2d 17 (Vt. 1998) (objective standard for materiality is what a reasonable person would regard as important in making a decision).

228 Carter v. Gugliuzzi, 716 A.2d 17 (Vt. 1998).

229 Green v. H&R Block, Inc., 355 Md. 488, 735 A.2d 1039 (1999) (jury question).

230 Phillips v. Dukes (Matter of Dukes), 24 B.R. 404 (Bankr. E.D. Mich. 1982); Robinson v. Avis Rent A Car Sys., Inc., 106 Wash. App. 104, 22 P.3d 818 (2001).

231 Demitropoulos v. Bank One, Milwaukee, N.A., 924 F. Supp. 894 (N.D. Ill. 1996).

232 *See* § 4.2.14.3.5, Appx. A, *infra*.

233 *See, e.g.*, Hill v. St. Paul Fed. Bank, 329 Ill. App. 3d 705, 768 N.E.2d 322 (2002). *But cf.* Robinson v. Toyota Motor Credit Corp., 201 Ill. 2d 403, 775 N.E.2d 951, 266 Ill. Dec. 879 (2002) (recognizing that UDAP statute may require disclosures beyond TILA, but not shown here). *See generally* § 2.3.3.3.2, *supra*.

234 Tietsworth v. Harley-Davidson, Inc., 677 N.W.2d 233 (Wis. 2004) (construing Wis. Stat. § 100.18(1)).

4.2.14.3.2 State regulations

Massachusetts' UDAP regulations declare as deceptive the failure to disclose any fact which, if disclosed, might have influenced the buyer not to enter into the transaction.[235] It is also deceptive to fail to disclose additional relevant information if the failure has the capacity, tendency, or effect of deceiving buyers in any material respect.[236] Similarly, Idaho's UDAP regulations prohibit omitting a material or relevant fact which directly or by implication has the capacity and tendency or effect of deceiving buyers or prospective buyers.[237] Mississippi's regulation prohibits the omission of a material or relevant fact where this has the tendency to mislead a consumer acting reasonably under the circumstances.[238] Missouri's UDAP regulations prohibit omission of material facts in broad terms.[239]

A number of other state UDAP regulations prohibit the failure to conspicuously disclose limitations or conditions to offers.[240] Ohio regulations require limitations to offers to be easily legible and in close proximity to the claim being limited and to precede immediately or follow oral claims; the regulations enumerate nine examples.[241] The Oregon Attorney General has issued a rule specifying when disclosures are clear and conspicuous.[242]

Massachusetts UDAP regulations also have detailed standards as to when disclosures are clear and conspicuous, including type-size requirements and special requirements for audio, video, and catalog disclosures.[243] Georgia and Illinois UDAP statutes require specific disclosures when advertising in the yellow pages is sold.[244] Many other state UDAP regulations also require specific disclosures for certain types of transactions.

4.2.14.3.3 Special duty to disclose for fiduciaries

At common law, a party with a fiduciary relationship to an individual has a duty to disclose information to the individual. For example, trustees, attorneys, income agents, and financial advisors have a special duty of disclosure apart from any UDAP requirement. Whether parties such as loan brokers and creditors are considered fiduciaries is discussed in another manual.[245]

As a result, UDAP nondisclosure standards should be particularly strict for fiduciaries.[246] For example, where there is a fiduciary relationship between an insurance agent and the insured, and the agent knows or should know that the insured has a misunderstanding about the terms of the policy, the agent has a duty to speak to correct the misunderstanding.[247]

Similarly, brokers must disclose if they have a financial interest in a sale,[248] and "investment counselors" must

---

235 Ramirez v. C.L.A.S., Inc., 2000 Mass. App. Div. LEXIS 6 (Jan. 13, 2002) (failure to disclose that vehicle lacked visible VIN and could not be legally driven until state provided replacement VIN); Massachusetts Consumer Protection Regulations, Mass. Regs. Code tit. 940, § 3.16.

236 Massachusetts Consumer Protection Regulations, Mass. Regs. Code tit. 940, § 3.05, General Misrepresentations, and § 3.16, General. *See also* Homsi v. C.H. Babb Co., 10 Mass. 474, 409 N.E.2d 219 (1980); Mongeau v. Boutelle, 10 Mass. App. Ct. 246, 407 N.E.2d 352 (1980); Mass. Regs. Code tit. 940, § 6.04(2) (disclosure of material representation in retail advertising).

237 Idaho Consumer Protection Regulations, Idaho Admin. Code 04.02.01.030, False, Misleading or Deceptive Conduct in General.

238 Code Miss. Rules 24 000 002 Rule 9.

239 15 Mo. Code State Regs. §§ 60-7.030, 60-9.110, 60-9.090.

240 Connecticut Regulations for the Department of Consumer Protection, Conn. Agencies Regs. § 42-110b-22, Offer Conditions; Haw. Admin. Code § 16-303-5(c); Idaho Consumer Protection Regulations, Idaho Admin. Code § 04.02.01.040, Disclosure of Conditions in Offer; Code Miss. Rules 24-000-002 Rule 16; N.J. Admin. Code § 13:45A-26A.7(a)(4) (motor vehicle sales); Ohio Attorney General Consumer Protection Rules, Ohio Admin. Code § 109:4-3-02, Exclusions and Limitations in Advertisements; Utah Admin. Rules 152-11-2, Exclusions and Limitations in Advertisement; Code Vt. Rules 06 031 001 Rule 103.03. *See* Feinberg v. Red Bank Volvo, 331 N.J. Super. 506, 752 A.2d 720 (App. Div. 2000) (advertising special financing terms without stating that they were available only if buyer passed credit check violated regulation).

241 Ohio Attorney General Consumer Protection Rules, Ohio Admin. Code 109:4-3-02, Exclusions and Limitations in Advertisements.

242 Or. Admin. Rule 137-020-0020 (definition of clear and conspicuous), 137-020-0015 (incorporating definition).

243 Mass. Regs. Code tit. 940, § 6.01. *See also* Commonwealth v. Boston Scandals, Inc., Clearinghouse No. 49,155 (Mass. Super. Ct. 1991) (preliminary injunction) (disclosure relating to savings claim on video shall appear in video part of advertisement in type no less than 14 scan lines in height and so that contrasts with background, shall not be a footnote or asterisk and shall remain on screen full length of the savings claim; audio savings claims will be accompanied by audio disclaimer as integral part of the claim each time claim is made with same prominence, clarity, decibel level, and pacing as the savings claims).

244 Ga. Code Ann. § 10-1-393.1(10); Disc Jockey Referral Network, Ltd. v. Ameritech Publishing of Illinois, 596 N.E.2d 4 (Ill. App. Ct. 1992). *See also* Commonwealth v. Amcan Enterprises, 47 Mass. App. Ct. 330, 712 N.E.2d 1205 (1999) (solicitations for ads in limited-circulation yellow pages were deceptive); State v. Directory Publishing Servs., Inc., 1996 Minn. App. LEXIS 62 (Jan. 9, 1996) (unpublished and non-precedential under Minnesota rules) (sale of "yellow pages" ads without disclosure that telephone directory has limited distribution was deceptive).

245 National Consumer Law Center, The Cost of Credit: Regulation and Legal Challenges § 11.9 (2d ed. 2000 and Supp.).

246 Industrial General Corp. v. Sequoia Pacific Sys., 44 F.3d 40 (1st Cir. 1995) (UDAP duty to disclose would have existed if defendant had been fiduciary).

247 Kron Medical Corp. v. Collier Cob & Assoc., 107 N.C. App. 331, 420 S.E.2d 192 (1992).

248 Kirkruff v. Wisegarver, 697 N.E.2d 406 (Ill. App. Ct. 1998); Seligman v. First Nat'l Invest., Inc., 184 Ill. App. 3d 1053, 540 N.E.2d 1057 (1989); Wilkinson v. Smith, 31 Wash. App. 1, 639 P.2d 768 (1982). *But see* Abernathy v. Squires Realty Co., 55 N.C. App. 354, 285 S.E.2d 325 (1982) (broker does not have to disclose that he is working on normal commission).

disclose material facts about real estate they recommend buying.[249] It is also deceptive to fail to disclose that credit insurance prices are inflated, where there is a fiduciary relationship between the credit insurance seller and consumer.[250]

Maryland's highest court has held that a tax return preparer may have a principal-agent relationship with customers that requires it to disclose kickbacks it receives when it processes refund anticipation loans.[251] Even without a fiduciary duty, disclosure would be required under the UDAP statute if the information is material.[252]

4.2.14.3.4 Must the non-disclosure be knowing?

There are limits as to when the failure to disclose is a UDAP violation. Several UDAP statutes explicitly require that non-disclosure be knowing or intentional.[253] Some other courts imply the same requirements into the statute; sellers need not disclose information they do not know and should not have known.[254] This view has a certain amount of appeal, until one considers that there is no intent or knowledge requirement for affirmative misrepresentations. The same should be true where the deception arises not through the seller's explicit claims, but by the deceptive implication of the seller's silence. That the seller did not know the information to be disclosed should be no defense,

249 Allen v. American Land Research, 95 Wash. 2d 841, 631 P.2d 930 (1981).

250 *In re* Dickson, 432 F. Supp. 752 (W.D.N.C. 1977). *But cf.* Green v. Paradise Pontiac, 19 Ohio App. 3d 219, 483 N.E.2d 1213 (1984) (no duty to disclose where no fiduciary relationship).

251 Green v. H&R Block, Inc., 355 Md. 488, 735 A.2d 1039 (1999). *But see* Carnegie v. H&R Block, Inc., 703 N.Y.S.2d 27 (App. Div. 2000) (tax return preparer that handles refund anticipation loan does not have fiduciary duty to customer).

252 Green v. H&R Block, Inc., 355 Md. 488, 735 A.2d 1039 (1999).

253 *See In re* Cohen, 191 B.R. 599 (D.N.J. 1996) (New Jersey UDAP statute requires that omissions be knowing, with intent that others rely on them, resulting in ascertainable damages, but knowledge and intent are not required in the case of affirmative acts), *aff'd on other grounds*, 106 F.3d 52 (3d Cir. 1997), *aff'd*, 523 U.S. 213 (1988); Sergeant Oil & Gas Co. v. National Maintenance & Repair, 861 F. Supp. 1351 (S.D. Tex. 1994) (relying on Texas UDAP statute that specifically imposes knowledge requirement for failure to disclose violations); Harkala v. Wildwood Realty, Inc., 200 Ill. App. 3d 447, 558 N.E.2d 195 (1990) (Illinois UDAP statute amended to exculpate real estate broker for unknowing failure to disclose hidden defects); Strawn v. Canuso, 140 N.J. 43, 657 A.2d 420 (1995); Varacallo v. Massachusetts Mut. Life Ins. Co., 332 N.J. Super. 31, 752 A.2d 807 (App. Div. 2000); Ji v. Palmer, 333 N.J. Super. 451, 755 A.2d 1221 (App. Div. 2000) (only knowing omissions are UDAP violations); Miller v. American Family Publishers, 284 N.J. Super. 67, 663 A.2d 643 (Chancery Div. 1995); Chattin v. Cape May Greene, Inc., 243 N.J. Super. 590, 581 A.2d 91 (1990), *aff'd*, 124 N.J. 520, 591 A.2d 943 (1991) (New Jersey UDAP statute imposed liability only where failure to disclose is knowing); Richardson Ford Sales, Inc. v. Johnson, 676 P.2d 1344 (N.M. Ct. App. 1984) (seller must be aware of nondisclosure where UDAP statute explicitly applies only to claims "knowingly made"); Robinson v. Preston Chrysler-Plymouth Inc., 633 S.W.2d 500 (Tex. 1982) (dealer did not know new car had been in accident); Colonial County Mut. Ins. Co. v. Valdez, 30 S.W.3d 514 (Tex. App. 2000); Nwaigwe v. Prudential Property & Cas. Ins. Co., 27 S.W.3d 558 (Tex. App. 2000); Celestino v. Mid-American Indem. Ins. Co., 883 S.W.2d 310 (Tex. App. 1994) (absent fraud, no affirmative duty to disclose terms of plainly-worded contract); Wright v. Lewis, 777 S.W.2d 520 (Tex. App. 1989); Pfeiffer v. Ebby Halliday Real Estate, Inc., 747 S.W.2d 887 (Tex. App. 1988) (relying on Texas UDAP statute that specifically imposes knowledge requirement for failure to disclose violation); Stewart Title Guaranty Co. v. Cheatham, 764 S.W.2d 315 (Tex. App. 1988) (same); Wyatt v. Petrila, 752 S.W.2d 683 (Tex. App. 1988) (same); Lambert v. Downtown Garage, Inc., 553 S.E.2d 714 (Va. 2001) (note that case involved unusually knowledgeable buyer). *See also* Sidco Products Marketing, Inc. v. Gulf Oil Corp., 858 F.2d 1095 (5th Cir. 1988) (Texas law); Hubbard v. Bob McDorman Chevrolet, 104 Ohio App. 3d 621, 662 N.E.2d 1102 (1995) (Ohio UDAP rule imposes no duty to disclose motor vehicle defects unless seller knows of them). *Cf.* Benik v. Hatcher, 358 Md. 507, 750 A.2d 10 (2000) (discussing when knowledge not required).

254 Szczubelek v. Cendant Mortg. Corp., 215 F.R.D. 107 (D.N.J. 2003); Griffin v. Security Pacific Automotive Fin. Servs., 33 F. Supp. 2d 926 (D. Kan. 1998) (omission must be willful); Hayes v. Hambruch, 841 F. Supp. 706 (D. Md. 1994), *aff'd*, 1995 U.S. App. LEXIS 22272 (4th Cir. 1995); Siudyla v. Chemexec Relocation Sys., Inc., 23 Conn. App. 180, 579 A.2d 578 (1990) (no UDAP violation where real estate seller was not in position to make representations about the property and so advised buyer); Greenberg v. United Airlines, 206 Ill. App. 3d 40, 563 N.E.2d 1031 (1990) (no UDAP violation for airline to fail in 1981 to disclose unforeseen changes in frequent flyer program that it instituted in 1988); Munjal v. Baird & Warner, 138 Ill. App. 3d 172, 485 N.E.2d 855 (1985); Inniss v. Methot Buick-Opel, Inc., 506 A.2d 212 (Me. 1986); Sternberger v. Kettler Bros., 123 Md. App. 303, 718 A.2d 619 (1998); Underwood v. Risman, 414 Mass. 96, 605 N.E.2d 832 (1993) (mere reason to suspect lead paint hazard did not create duty to disclose); Nei v. Burley, 388 Mass. 307, 446 N.E.2d 674 (1983) (broker did not disclose facts about property broker did not know); Fernandes v. Rodrigue, 38 Mass. App. Ct. 926, 646 N.E.2d 414 (1995); Greenery Rehabilitation Group, Inc. v. Antaramian, 36 Mass. App. Ct. 73, 628 N.E.2d 1291 (1994) (business transaction); Massachusetts v. Elan Medical Laboratories, Inc., 33 Mass. App. Ct. 71, 596 N.E.2d 376 (1992); Sargent v. Koulisas, 29 Mass. App. Ct. 956, 560 N.E.2d 569 (1990); Judge v. Blackfin Yacht Corp., 357 N.J. Super. 418, 815 A.2d 537, 541 (App. Div. 2003); Ramsey v. Keever's Used Cars, 92 N.C. App. 187, 374 S.E.2d 135 (1988); Schneider v. Miller, 73 Ohio App. 3d 335, 597 N.E.2d 175 (1991); Ganzevoort v. Russell, 949 S.W.2d 293 (Tenn. 1997); Trinity Universal Ins. Co. v. Bleeker, 966 S.W.2d 489 (Tex. 1998); Steptoe v. True, 38 S.W.3d 213 (Tex. App. 2001); McFarland v. Associated Brokers, 977 S.W.2d 427 (Tex. App. 1998); Erwin v. Smiley, 975 S.W.2d 335 (Tex. App. 1998); Wilson v. John Daugherty Realtors, Inc., 981 S.W.2d 723 (Tex. App. 1998); Key v. Lewis Aquatech Pool Supply, Inc., 58 Va. Cir. 344, 2002 WL 920936 (2002) (nondisclosure not a UDAP violation where it was not deliberately deceptive); Hertzog v. WebTV Networks, 2002 WL 1609032 (Wash. App. July 22, 2002) (unpublished, citation limited) (seller has duty to disclose material facts which are known to the seller but not easily discoverable by the buyer; no duty to disclose unverified and possibly inaccurate information).

just as it is no defense that the seller did not know a claim is deceptive.[255] One of the underlying justifications for a UDAP statute is that the seller is in a better position to bear the loss of a deceptive sales transaction and is in a better position to prevent or correct the deception. This purpose should remain the same, even if the nondisclosure was unintentional and unknowing.

Even if a court adopts a requirement that for a nondisclosure to be actionable it must be a knowing nondisclosure, it should clearly be deceptive for a seller's agent to fail to disclose material facts in a situation where the agent was unaware, but the seller was aware, of those facts.[256] A company is chargeable with the composite knowledge of all its officers and employees acting within the scope of their duties, and it does not matter that any particular agent does not know the representation is false.[257] Further, when there is a statutory or regulatory duty to disclose certain information, failure to disclose it is evidence of a UDAP violation even if the defendant is unaware of the information that is required to be disclosed.[258] The seller may also have a duty under a law or regulation to investigate and discover certain facts, in which case knowledge will be imputed.[259]

255 State *ex rel.* Miller v. Pace, 677 N.W.2d 761 (Iowa 2004); Golt v. Phillips, 308 Md. 1, 517 A.2d 328 (1986).

256 *See* Brandt v. Olympia Constr., Inc., 16 Mass. App. Ct. 913, 449 N.E.2d 1231 (1983); Chandler v. Gene Messer Ford, Inc., 81 S.W.3d 493 (Tex. App. 2002). *See also* Oswego Laborers' Local 214 Pension Fund v. Marine Midland Bank, 85 N.Y.2d 20, 623 N.Y.S.2d 529, 647 N.E.2d 741 (1995) (disclosure probably required where business alone has material information that is relevant to the consumer).

257 Gem City Motors, Inc. v. Minton, 109 Ga. App. 842, 137 S.E.2d 522 (1964) (affirming judgment for plaintiff in action where salesman told plaintiff car had been used as a demonstrator, but in fact it had been sold to a prior customer who had traded it back in); Brown v. New Plaza Pontiac Co., 719 S.W.2d 468 (Mo. App. 1986) (knowledge held by personnel in used car and service departments imputed to dealership); Gray v. Green Lincoln Mercury Mazda, Inc., 16 Phila. 411, 1987 Phila. Cty. Rptr. LEXIS 43 (Pa. C.P. Oct. 13, 1987) (prior owner's report of accident to dealer's agents when trading car in attributed to dealer); Barton v. Superior Motors, Inc., 309 S.C. 491, 424 S.E.2d 524 (App. 1992) (finding that dealer had duty of disclosure where its body shop had repaired car, but no UDAP liability because buyer failed to prove diminution in value). *See also* Harris v. M&S Toyota, Inc., 575 So. 2d 74 (Ala. 1991) (if some of the defendant's employees were aware of concealing paint work done to car, did not matter that a specific salesperson was unaware). *But see* Wilson v. Huntsville Chrysler, Plymouth, Dodge, Inc., 1999 Tex. App. LEXIS 3834 (Aug. 29, 1996) (upholding jury verdict finding no liability even for non-disclosure even though dealership knew of flood damage; basis for jury's conclusion not entirely clear). *See generally* National Consumer Law Center, Automobile Fraud § 7.4.2 (2d ed. 2003 and Supp.).

258 Binette v. Dyer Library Assoc., 688 A.2d 898 (Me. 1996).

259 Benik v. Hatcher, 358 Md. 507, 750 A.2d 10 (2000).

4.2.14.3.5 Must the seller intend that others rely on the omission?

Some UDAP statutes specify that a failure to disclose is deceptive if there is an intent that others rely upon the omission.[260] For example, New Jersey makes an omission a violation of its UDAP statute if a fact is material and the defendant acted knowingly and with the intent that others rely on the omission.[261] This intent relates to the seller intending that consumers *rely* on the omission, not that the seller intends to deceive the consumer. Where a termite inspector's report contains material omissions, the mere submission of the report demonstrates the requisite intent since the very purpose of the report is for consumers to rely upon it.[262]

Intent should be presumed when the information was (1) material, (2) known to the defendant, and (3) not disclosed by the defendant.[263] On the other hand, if the failure to disclose has no identified impact on the consumer, a court is less likely to find a UDAP violation.[264]

4.2.14.3.6 Must the seller have an independent duty of disclosure?

A few courts have held that a failure to disclose is a UDAP violation only if the defendant had a duty to disclose the information.[265] A duty to disclose may arise from a

260 *See, e.g.*, State *ex rel.* Brady v. 3-D Auto World, Inc., 2000 Del. Super. LEXIS 17 (Jan. 19, 2000); Chandler v. Gene Messer Ford, Inc., 81 S.W.3d 493 (Tex. App. 2002).

261 N.J. Stat. Ann. § 56:8-2 (West). *See* Fenwick v. Kay Am. Jeep, Inc., 72 N.J. 372, 37 A.2d 13 (1977); Varacallo v. Massachusetts Mut. Life Ins. Co., 332 N.J. Super. 31, 752 A.2d 807 (App. Div. 2000) (causal nexus must be shown, but not reliance).

262 Warren v. LeMay, 142 Ill. App. 3d 550, 491 N.E.2d 464 (1986). *But see* Heller v. Martin, 782 P.2d 1241 (Kan. Ct. App. 1989) (no showing of intent, as required by statute).

263 Jones v. Ray Ins. Agency, 59 S.W.3d 739 (Tex. App. 2001).

264 *See* Mackinac v. Arcadia Nat'l Life Ins. Co., 648 N.E.2d 237 (Ill. App. Ct. 1995); Kellerman v. Mar-Rue Realty & Builders, Inc., 132 Ill. App. 3d 300, 476 N.E.2d 1259 (1985); Nwaigwe v. Prudential Property & Cas. Ins. Co., 27 S.W.3d 558 (Tex. App. 2000).

265 Industrial General Corp. v. Sequoia Pacific Sys., 44 F.3d 40 (1st Cir. 1995) ("duty to disclose should be limited to situations which even at common law sometimes required disclosure"); Vigilante v. Phoenix Mut. Life Ins. Co., 755 F. Supp. 25 (D. Mass. 1991) (insurance company did not have duty to disclose agent's criminal past to insurance commissioner or policy holders); Miller v. Guimares, 78 Conn. App. 760, 829 A.2d 422 (Conn. App. Ct. 2003); Murphy v. Berlin Constr. Co., 1999 Del. Super. LEXIS 5 (Jan. 12, 1999) (no duty to disclose without pre-existing relationship or partial disclosure); Mackinac v. Arcadia Nat'l Life Ins. Co., 648 N.E.2d 237 (Ill. App. Ct. 1995) (automobile dealer had no duty to disclose restrictions on credit disability insurance policy). *See also* Normand Josef Enterprises v. Connecticut Bank, 230 Conn. 486, 646 A.2d 1289 (1994); First Midwest Bank v. Sparks, 682 N.E.2d 373 (Ill. App. Ct. 1997) (no UDAP liability where state banking law prohibited

fiduciary relationship, from partial disclosure, or from superior knowledge.[266] Better-reasoned decisions do not require any independent duty of disclosure, but hold it a UDAP violation for a seller to fail to disclose material facts that it knows but that are not reasonably discoverable by the buyer.[267]

4.2.14.3.7 Must the consumer investigate?

A substantial body of decisions holds that a UDAP claim is not affected by the consumer's negligence or lack of due care.[268] Any other holding would be inconsistent with the purpose of UDAP statutes to protect vulnerable, unsophisticated consumers.[269] Nevertheless, a Georgia court has taken the remarkable position that where information is concealed, making the scope of insurance coverage ambiguous, it is the *consumer's* responsibility to inquire as to what coverage is being offered and to thus resolve the ambiguity.[270] The Georgia court describes the sale of credit insurance in a consumer car sale as an "arm's length business transaction," and consequently views the consumer as being fully responsible to ferret out any misrepresentation or ambiguity in the transaction. This anomalous result can be chiefly attributed to the overly restrictive view Georgia courts take toward the state UDAP statute,[271] and also to some extent to the court's failure to appreciate the actual manner in which credit insurance is sold in the marketplace.

disclosure). *Cf.* Barstad v. Stewart Title Guar. Co., 145 Wash. 2d 528, 39 P.3d 984 (2002). *But see* cases cited in § 4.2.14.3.3, *supra*; *cf.* Forrest v. P&L Real Estate Investment Co., 134 Md. App. 371, 759 A.2d 1187 (2000) (superior knowledge creates duty to disclose).

266 Smith v. General Motors Corp., 979 S.W.2d 127 (Ky. App. Ct. 1998) (discussion in context of fraud analysis). *See* §§ 4.2.14.3.3, *supra* (fiduciaries' disclosure duties), 9.5.9.1, *infra* (fraudulent concealment).

267 South Atlantic Ltd. P'ship v. Riese, 284 F.3d 518, 537, 538 (4th Cir. 2002) (N.C. law); Minnesota *ex rel.* Hatch v. Fleet Mortg. Corp., 158 F. Supp. 2d 962 (D. Minn. 2001); Cambridge Plating Co. v. NAPCO, Inc., 876 F. Supp. 326 (D. Mass. 1995), *aff'd in part, vacated in part on other grounds*, 85 F.3d 752 (1st Cir. 1996); Celex Group, Inc. v. Executive Gallery, Inc., 877 F. Supp. 1114 (N.D. Ill. 1995); Lipinski v. Martin J. Kelly Oldsmobile, Inc., 325 Ill. App. 3d 1139, 759 N.E.2d 66 (2001); Connick v. Suzuki Motor Co., 174 Ill. 2d 482, 675 N.E.2d 584 (1996) (UDAP claim need not be based on common law duty to disclose); Totz v. Continental DuPage Acura, 602 N.E.2d 1374 (Ill. App. Ct. 1992); Green v. H&R Block, Inc., 355 Md. 488, 735 A.2d 1039 (1999) (tax return preparer must disclose material information if it would be important to a significant number of unsophisticated consumers, regardless of whether it has a fiduciary duty); Griffith v. Centex Real Estate FCorp., 93 Wash. App. 202, 969 P.2d 486 (1998).

268 *See* §§ 4.2.15.6, 4.2.16.1, *infra.*

269 *See* § 4.2.11, *supra.*

270 Credithrift of Am., Inc. v. Whitley, 190 Ga. App. 833, 380 S.E.2d 489 (1989).

271 *See* § 4.2.17.3, *infra.*

A later decision, while citing these earlier cases, is more generous in finding exceptions to which particular transactions can fit.[272]

An Illinois court has held that it is not a UDAP violation to fail to disclose that a village ordinance would require the buyers of a home to hook up the home's sewer system to the village's sewer system.[273] The court reasoned that the existence of the ordinance was a law that was a matter of public knowledge. The Texas Supreme Court has found that a seller need not disclose its policy of enforcing rights that its contract clearly provides.[274]

4.2.14.3.8 Specific nondisclosure holdings

UDAP judicial decisions and regulations have held that nondisclosure of the following matters violates the UDAP statute:

Defects and dangerous conditions:

- Dangerous conditions in vehicles and real estate;[275]

272 Heard v. Sexton, 243 Ga. App. 462, 532 S.E.2d 156 (2000). *But see* Fregeau v. Hall, 196 Ga. App. 493, 396 S.E.2d 241 (1990) (in absence of fiduciary relationship or other special circumstances, no UDAP liability where plaintiff failed to examine insurance application and verify that he had received the coverage sought).

273 Randels v. Best Real Estate, Inc., 612 N.E.2d 984 (Ill. App. Ct. 1993); *see also* Eff v. Slusher, 2000 Mich. App. LEXIS 2151 (May 19, 2000) (unpublished, limited precedent) (not a UDAP violation to fail to disclose easement that was recorded in registry of deeds). *But see* § 4.2.15.6, *infra.*

274 DeWitt County Electric Coop., Inc. v. Parks, 1 S.W.3d 96 (Tex. 1999).

275 Outboard Marine Corp. v. Superior Court (Howarth), 52 Cal. App. 3d 30, 124 Cal. Rptr. 852 (1975); Connick v. Suzuki Motor Co., 174 Ill. 2d 482, 675 N.E.2d 584 (1996) (danger of jeep tipping over); Perona v. Volkswagen of Am., Inc., 684 N.E.2d 859 (Ill. App. Ct. 1997) (failure to disclose that vehicle was susceptible to unintended acceleration); Benik v. Hatcher, 358 Md. 507, 750 A.2d 10 (2000) (failure to disclose lead paint, contrary to housing ordinance, is UDAP violation even if landlord is unaware of condition); Mackesy v. Fotopoulos, 2002 WL 971812 (Mass. App. May 7, 2002); Strawn v. Canuso, 140 N.J. 43, 657 A.2d 420 (1995) (failure to disclose existence of closed toxic landfill near home); Nobrega v. Edison Glen Assocs., 327 N.J. Super. 414, 743 A.2d 864 (App. Div. 2000) (failure to disclose existence of toxic waste site near home is still UDAP violation despite statutory amendments), *modified on other grounds*, 772 A.2d 368 (N.J. 2001); DeMarco v. Bay Ridge Car World, 169 A.D.2d 808, 565 N.Y.S.2d 176 (1991) (failure to disclose that vehicle was vulnerable to engine compartment fires); *see also* International Harvester Co., 104 F.T.C. 949 (1984) (failure to disclose hidden safety hazard in placing fuel tanks in front of operator). *But cf.* Romeo v. Pittsburgh Assocs., 787 A.2d 1027 (Pa. Super. 2001) (UDAP statute does not require baseball stadium to warn patrons of danger of being hit by foul ball; warning on back of ticket would be sufficient in any event).

- Safety risks on tours marketed by a travel agency;[276]
- Any defect in a car that would make a difference to the consumer,[277] even if the car is sold "as is";[278]
- Damage that a new car had suffered in transit and which had been repaired;[279]
- Known material defects in the sale of land,[280] the fact that the property was subject to foreclosure,[281] that a lot was not suitable for sewage disposal,[282] that inspectors had orally informed the seller of violations,[283] or that there were drainage problems;[284] and
- Defects in equipment being sold or installed.[285]

The relevant history or origin of goods:
- A vehicle's collision or lemon history;[286]
- A vehicle's past use as a racing car[287] or rental car;[288]
- A vehicle's odometer reading;[289] and
- A product's "gray market" origin, *i.e.*, its manufacture in a foreign country for sale and use outside the United States.[290]

Title problems:
- Liens on a piece of property to be purchased;[291]
- A contractor's lack of an ownership interest in vacant land to be developed and the fact that the consumers would have to pay additional money for it;[292] and
- A cloud on a boat's title (even though the seller believed the lien to be invalid and unenforceable).[293]

Potential future price increases:
- A landlord's application to HUD for rent increases that would affect prospective tenants of subsidized housing;[294]
- An insurance company's method for determining whether a surcharge would be necessary on an underfunded insurance plan;[295]
- A life insurance company's knowledge that the market was unlikely to support the dividends it projected;[296] and
- A bank's right to reinstate a fee at any time for a checking account that it had represented as free.[297]

Information about the background of the company or its staff:
- The lack of expertise of an investment opportunity company's sales staff;[298]
- The attrition rates of franchisees and the involvement of the franchisor in several lawsuits for fraud;[299]
- A long-distance telephone service provider's identity and its use of "knock off" numbers similar to competitors' numbers;[300]

---

276 Maurer v. Cerkvenik-Anderson Travel, Inc., 181 Ariz. 294, 890 P.2d 69 (App. 1994).

277 Perona v. Volkswagen of Am., Inc., 684 N.E.2d 859 (Ill. App. Ct. 1997) (failure to disclose susceptibility to unintended acceleration); Totz v. Continental DuPage Acura, 602 N.E.2d 1374 (Ill. App. Ct. 1992) (failure to disclose that car had suffered extensive damage in an accident); Vercher v. Ford Motor Co., 527 So. 2d 995 (La. Ct. App. 1988); Slaney v. Westwood Auto, Inc., 366 Mass. 688, 322 N.E.2d 768 (1975) (or engine); Mahan Volkswagen, Inc. v. Hall, 648 S.W.2d 324 (Tex. App. 1982) (treble personal injuries awarded for failure to disclose defective brakes).

278 V.S.H. Realty, Inc. v. Texaco, Inc., 757 F.2d 411 (1st Cir. 1985) (Massachusetts law); Automobile Trader v. Simmons, 22 Ohio Op. 3d 149 (Ct. App. 1981); Hatfield v. D.D. Sullivan Inc., No. 111813 (Or. Civ. Ct. Marion Cty. 1980); Metro Ford Truck Sales, Inc. v. Davis, 709 S.W.2d 785 (Tex. App. 1986). *See also* §§ 5.4.6.8.1 (nondisclosure of defects), 5.4.6.6.3 (nondisclosure of vehicle's collision history), *infra*.

279 Pirozzi v. Penske-Olds-Cadillac-GMS, 605 A.2d 373 (Pa. Super. Ct. 1992).

280 Robinson v. McReynolds, 52 Wash. App. 635, 762 P.2d 1166 (1988). *But cf.* Levine v. Kramer Group, 354 N.J. Super. 397, 807 A.2d 264 (App. Div. 2002) (UDAP statute does not require disclosure of transient social conditions, here an unbalanced neighbor, that might affect value of property).

281 Nash v. Hoopes, 332 A.2d 411 (Del. Super. Ct. 1975).

282 Catucci v. Ouellette, 25 Conn. App. 56, 592 A.2d 962 (1991).

283 Kleczek v. Jorgensen, 328 Ill. App. 3d 1012, 767 N.E.2d 913, 263 Ill. Dec. 187 (2002) (seller stated he had received no written notices).

284 Heller v. Silverbranch Constr. Corp., 376 Mass. 621, 382 N.E.2d 1065 (1978); *see also* McRae v. Bolstad, 101 Wash. 2d 161, 676 P.2d 496 (1984).

285 Cambridge Plating Co. v. NAPCO, Inc., 876 F. Supp. 326 (D. Mass. 1995), *aff'd in part, vacated in part on other grounds*, 85 F.3d 752 (1st Cir. 1996); Sargent v. Koulisas, 29 Mass. App. Ct. 956, 560 N.E.2d 569 (1990) (poor condition of equipment and inadequate electric service).

286 *See* §§ 5.4.6.6.3, 5.4.6.7, *infra*.

287 Testo v. Russ Dunmire Oldsmobile, Inc., 16 Wash. App. 39, 554 P.2d 349 (1976). *See also* § 5.4.6.4, *infra*.

288 Salmeron v. Highlands Ford Sales, Inc., 271 F. Supp. 2d 1314 (D.N.M. 2003).

289 Gordon v. Stickney, 2000 Del. Super. LEXIS 209 (May 11, 2000).

290 State v. Edwards (*In re* Edwards), 233 B.R. 461 (Bankr. D. Idaho 1999) (tractor).

291 Gibbs v. Main Bank of Houston, 666 S.W.2d 554 (Tex. App. 1984) (claim against title insurance company).

292 Miller v. Guimaraes, 78 Conn. App. 760, 829 A.2d 422 (Conn. Ct. App. 2004).

293 Standing v. Midgett, 850 F. Supp. 396 (E.D.N.C. 1993).

294 York v. Sullivan, 369 Mass. 157, 338 N.E.2d 341 (1975).

295 Woodworker's Supply, Inc. v. Principal Mut. Life Ins. Co., 170 F.3d 985 (10th Cir. 1999).

296 Varacallo v. Massachusetts Mut. Life Ins. Co., 332 N.J. Super. 31, 752 A.2d 807 (2000) (vanishing premium case); *see also* Mass. Mut. Life Ins. Co. v. Superior Court, 97 Cal. App. 4th 1282, 119 Cal. Rptr. 2d 190 (2002) (certifying class action).

297 Giummo v. Citibank, N.A., 107 Misc. 2d 895, 436 N.Y.S.2d 172 (Civ. Ct., N.Y. City Ct. 1981).

298 State *ex rel.* Corbin v. Goodrich, 151 Ariz. 118, 726 P.2d 215 (Ct. App. 1986).

299 Aurigemma v. Arco Petroleum Products Co., 734 F. Supp. 1025 (D. Conn. 1990) (failure to disclose potential loss of franchise due to lease termination violates FTC Franchise Rule and Connecticut UDAP statute); Bailey Employment Sys., Inc. v. Hahn, 545 F. Supp. 62 (D. Conn. 1982), *aff'd without op.*, 723 F.2d 895 (2d Cir. 1983).

300 Drizin v. Spring Corp., 3 A.D.3d 388, 771 N.Y.S.2d 82 (2004) (company failed to disclose its identity to consumers who

- A supplier's financial difficulties that were likely to interfere with performance of the contract;[301] and
- Various law violations by a company's corporate officers.[302]

Illegality of the transaction:
- The lack of a required license or registration;[303] and
- The illegality of a securities transaction.[304]

Kickbacks or secret relationships with other parties:
- The fact that a dealer would receive a commission on a credit insurance sale;[305]
- A kickback that a tax return preparer would receive from the lender if the customer took out a refund anticipation loan;[306]
- An upcharge on an extended warranty[307] or a yield spread premium;[308]
- The relationship between realtors and title insurance companies that paid kickbacks through sham intermediary companies;[309]
- A home inspection company's business philosophy of soft-pedaling defects it found, in order to avoid killing home sales and antagonizing the realtors from whom it got referrals;[310] and
- A company's affiliation with another company that had previously worked on a home.[311]

Availability of lower price or less expensive alternatives:
- The availability of cheaper credit insurance than that offered by the dealer and the fact that excessive premiums were charged;[312]
- That a new loan would be much less expensive than refinancing an old loan;[313]
- That a car had been advertised at a lower price,[314] or that unjustifiably large dealer preparation costs were being charged;[315] and
- The manufacturer's suggested list price for a car.[316]

Material information about financing or payment terms:
- The interest rate or other credit terms;[317]

mistakenly dialed knock-off number).

301 Van Vels v. Premier Athletic Center, 1998 U.S. Dist. LEXIS 10993 (W.D. Mich. 1998) (deceptive to sell three-year health spa contracts without informing consumers of company's financial problems that will likely prevent delivery of services); Commonwealth v. Windsor of Dracut, Inc., Clearinghouse No. 52,034 (Mass. Super. Ct. Aug. 20, 1997) (failure to disclose to people making deposits with a function hall that premises were about to be foreclosed upon); Temborius v. Slatkin, 157 Mich. App. 587, 403 N.W.2d 821 (1986) (failure to disclose that dealer is in financial difficulty and that consumer's payment might not be forwarded to the distributor). *But cf.* Judge v. Blackfin Yacht Corp., 357 N.J. Super. 418, 815 A.2d 537 (App. Div. 2003) (no duty to disclose manufacturer's bankruptcy where no evidence that it would interfere with performance of obligations).

302 State *ex rel.* Corbin v. Goodrich, 151 Ariz. 118, 726 P.2d 215 (Ct. App. 1986). *But see* Vigilante v. Phoenix Mut. Life Ins. Co., 755 F. Supp. 25 (D. Mass. 1991) (insurance company did not have duty to disclose agent's criminal past to insurance commissioner or policy holders).

303 State *ex rel.* Miller v. Pace, 677 N.W.2d 761 (Iowa 2004) (unregistered securities sold by unregistered seller); Golt v. Phillips, 308 Md. 1, 517 A.2d 328 (1986) (unlicensed rental premises).

304 FTC v. Canada Prepaid Legal Servs., Inc., 5 Trade Reg. Rep. ¶ 24,839 (D. Wash. Dec. 11, 2000) (TRO against telemarketing company that failed to disclose that its sale of bonds was illegal); State *ex rel.* Miller v. Pace, 677 N.W.2d 761 (Iowa 2004).

305 Browder v. Hanley Dawson Cadillac Co., 62 Ill. App. 3d 623, 379 N.E.2d 1206 (1978). *But see* Chabraja v. Avis Rent-A-Car Sys., Inc., 549 N.E.2d 872 (Ill. App. Ct. 1989) (car rental company is not required to tell consumers that "collision damage waiver" may duplicate their existing insurance coverage); Green v. Paradise Pontiac, 19 Ohio App. 3d 219, 483 N.E.2d 1213 (1984) (no duty to disclose).

306 Green v. H&R Block, Inc., 355 Md. 488, 735 A.2d 1039 (1999). *But see* Murphy v. Berlin Constr. Co., 1999 Del. Super. LEXIS 5 (Jan. 12, 1999) (builder did not violate UDAP statute by failing to disclose that he paid a commission to realtor who referred customer); Tungate v. MacLean-Stevens Studios, 714 A.2d 792 (Me. 1998) (no UDAP claim for school photo company's failure to disclose commission paid to school, where amount was insubstantial and total price was accurately disclosed).

307 Cannon v. Cherry Hill Toyota, Inc., 161 F. Supp. 2d 362 (D.N.J. 2001) (violates New Jersey UDAP requirement of disclosure of terms of any warranty or service contract offered by dealer).

308 Smith v. Precision Chevrolet, Clearinghouse No. 52,495 (N.J. Super. Aug. 19, 1999) (misstatement of amounts paid to others for credit insurance and extended warranty).

309 Gardner v. First Am. Title Ins. Co., 2001 U.S. Dist. LEXIS 21839 (D. Minn. Dec. 10, 2001) (denial of motion to dismiss).

310 Herner v. HouseMaster of Am., Inc., 349 N.J. Super. 89, 793 A.2d 55 (App. Div. 2002) (unconscionability finding).

311 Swiger v. Terminix Int'l Co., 1995 Ohio App. LEXIS 2826 (June 28, 1995).

312 Browder v. Hanley Dawson Cadillac Co., 62 Ill. App. 3d 623, 379 N.E.2d 1206 (1978). *But see* Chabraja v. Avis Rent-A-Car Sys., Inc., 549 N.E.2d 872 (Ill. App. Ct. 1989) (car rental company is not required to tell consumers that "collision damage waiver" may duplicate their existing insurance coverage); Green v. Paradise Pontiac, 19 Ohio App. 3d 219, 483 N.E.2d 1213 (1984) (no duty to disclose).

313 *In re* Milbourne, 108 B.R. 522 (Bankr. E.D. Pa. 1989); Chandler v. Am. Gen. Fin., Inc., 329 Ill. App. 3d 729, 768 N.E.2d 60 (2002).

314 Affrunti v. Village Ford Sales, Inc., 597 N.E.2d 1242 (Ill. App. Ct. 1992); Sanders v. Francis, 277 Or. 593, 561 P.2d 1003 (1977).

315 State v. Ralph Williams' N.W. Chrysler Plymouth, Inc., 87 Wash. 2d 298, 553 P.2d 423 (1976).

316 Ciampi v. Ogden Chrysler Plymouth, Inc., 634 N.E.2d 448 (Ill. App. Ct. 1994).

317 Burnett v. Ala Moana Pawn Shop, Clearinghouse No. 46,771 (D. Haw. 1991), *aff'd*, 3 F.3d 1261 (9th Cir. 1993). *See also* All-State Indus. of North Carolina v. FTC, 423 F.2d 423 (4th Cir. 1970), *cert. denied*, 400 U.S. 828 (1970) (failure to disclose

- The charge for early withdrawal of funds from an annuity policy;[318]
- A bank's intention, contrary to the UCC, not to pay interest on the consumer's security deposit for an automobile lease;[319] and
- A merchant's policy of not refunding deposits.[320]

Consumers' rights:

- Rescission rights;[321] and
- Statutory tenant remedies.[322]

Repair and warranty problems:

- The unavailability of service for a product;[323]
- The lack of a warranty on a product;[324]
- That significant costs for parts would be charged for repairs under a warranty;[325]
- That the job a repairman had started had already taken substantially longer than estimated;[326] and
- The diagnostic information and price estimates learned from an external inspection of a vehicle (where nondisclosure induced the consumer to agree to a more expensive internal inspection.[327]

Material limits on products or services:

- The limited coverage offered by an insurance policy;[328]
- The harsh and unfair claims settlement practices of an insurance company that was selling a policy;[329]
- The fact that registration of an Internet domain name would not give the owner exclusive use and control of the name;[330]
- The limited, business-to-business distribution of a telephone directory in which "yellow pages" advertising was sold;[331] and
- The inapplicability of promised energy tax credits to nonresidents.[332]

Other information:

- That a consumer was entitled to coverage under an insurance policy;[333]
- The fact that an inside wiring maintenance contract is not regulated by the utility commission, that the customer can hire another company to repair inside wires, that the customer may not be responsible for those repairs, and that they may only have to be repaired every fourteen years;[334] and
- Deficiencies in a medical laboratory that resulted in inaccurate reading of Pap tests.[335]

4.2.14.3.9 Disclosures in on-line transactions

Many FTC rules and guides, as well as many state UDAP statutes and regulations, require specific disclosures in advertisements and other sales materials, or prohibit certain claims unless specific disclosures are made. The FTC takes the position that its rules and guides apply to on-line sales materials just as they apply to traditional advertisements.[336] The FTC considers on-line sales materials to be encompassed in the terms "written," "writing," "printed," and

---

that note or contract could be sold); Tashof v. FTC, 437 F.2d 707 (D.C. Cir. 1970) (failure to disclose credit terms and charges); Garland v. Mobil Oil Corp., 340 F. Supp. 1095 (N.D. Ill. 1972) (disclosing that past due accounts would incur service charge, when no such charge was imposed for balances under $25); Prata v. Superior Court, 91 Cal. App. 4th 1128, 111 Cal. Rptr. 2d 296 (2001) (advertising "90 days same as cash" but requiring monthly payments in order to avoid finance charges).

318 People *ex rel.* Lockyer v. Fremont Life Ins. Co., 104 Cal. App. 4th 508, 128 Cal. Rptr. 2d 463 (2002).

319 Demitropoulos v. Bank One, Milwaukee, N.A., 924 F. Supp. 894 (N.D. Ill. 1996).

320 Riley v. Enterprise Furniture Co., 54 Ohio Misc. 1, 375 N.E.2d 821, 7 Ohio Op. 3d 271 (Mun. Ct. Sylvania 1977).

321 Swiss v. Williams, 184 N.J. Super. 243, 445 A.2d 486 (Dist. Ct. Mercer County 1982).

322 Commonwealth v. Monumental Properties, Inc., 459 Pa. 450, 329 A.2d 812 (1974) (landlord's use of form lease).

323 Connecticut Regulations for the Department of Consumer Protection, Conn. Agencies Regs. § 42-110b-22, Offer Conditions.

324 Aubrey's R.V. Center, Inc. v. Tandy Corp., 46 Wash. App. 595, 731 P.2d 1124 (1987).

325 Brooks v. Midas-International Corp., 47 Ill. App. 3d 266, 361 N.E.2d 815 (1977).

326 Hyland v. Zuback, 146 N.J. Super. 407, 370 A.2d 20 (App. Div. 1976).

327 State v. Cottman Transmissions Sys., Inc., 86 Md. App. 714, 587 A.2d 1190 (1991).

328 Glazewski v. Allstate Ins. Co., 126 Ill. App. 3d 401, 466 N.E.2d 1151 (1984), *rev'd in relevant part on other grounds*, 483 N.E.2d 1263 (Ill. 1985).

329 Elder v. Coronet Ins. Co., 201 Ill. App. 3d 733, 558 N.E.2d 1312 (1990). *See also* Kron Medical Corp. v. Collier Cob & Assoc., 107 N.C. App. 331, 420 S.E.2d 192 (1992).

330 Zurakov v. Register.com, Inc., 304 A.D.2d 176, 760 N.Y.S.2d 13 (2003).

331 State v. Smith, Clearinghouse No. 51,273 (Minn. App. 1996) (unpublished and non-precedential under Minnesota rules); State v. Directory Publishing Servs., Inc., 1996 Minn. App. LEXIS 62 (Jan. 9, 1996) (unpublished and non-precedential under Minnesota rules). *See also* Commonwealth v. Amcan Enterprises, 47 Mass. App. Ct. 330, 712 N.E.2d 1205 (1999) (solicitations for ads in limited-circulation yellow pages were deceptive).

332 Winton v. Johnson & Dix Fuel Corp., 515 A.2d 371 (Vt. 1986).

333 Aetna Cas. & Surety Co. v. Martin Surgical Supply Co., 689 S.W.2d 263 (Tex. App. 1985).

334 Commonwealth *ex rel.* Zimmerman v. Bell Tel. Co., 121 Pa. Commw. 642, 551 A.2d 602 (1988).

335 Massachusetts v. Elm Medical Laboratories, Inc., 33 Mass. App. Ct. 71, 596 N.E.2d 376 (1992).

336 FTC, Dot Com Disclosures (2000), *available at* www.ftc.gov. *See* FTC v. Direct Marketing Concepts, Inc., 2004 WL 1399185, at *7 (D. Mass. June 23, 2004); FTC v. Crescent Publ'g Group, Inc., 2001 WL 128444, at *2–*3 (S.D.N.Y. Feb. 16, 2001); FTC v. Five Star Auto Club, Inc., 2000 WL 1609798 (S.D.N.Y. June 12, 2000). *See also* Leslie Anne Fair, *Advertising Enforcement in the New Media Age*, 1207 Practicing Law Inst. 267, 301 (Oct. 2000) (compiling enforcement actions by the FTC against on-line advertisers).

"direct mail," as used in its rules.[337] In evaluating whether an on-line disclosure is clear and conspicuous, the FTC will consider:

- The placement of the disclosure in the advertisement;
- The proximity of the disclosure to the relevant claim;
- The prominence of the disclosure;
- Whether items in other parts of the advertisement distract attention from the disclosure;
- Whether the advertisement is so lengthy that the disclosure needs to be repeated;
- Whether disclosures in audio messages are presented in an adequate volume and cadence and whether visual disclosures appear for a sufficient duration; and
- Whether the language of the disclosure is understandable to the intended audience.[338]

When issuing a preliminary injunction restraining a pornographic website operator from deceiving visitors, one court elaborated on the FTC's definition of clear and conspicuous. In order to be considered clear and conspicuous, on-line disclosures must meet the following requirements:

- The disclosure must provide material information about the proposed transaction such that a reasonable consumer "would perceive and understand the disclosure in the context of the entire advertisement."
- "The disclosure must assume that consumers do not read an entire website, just as they do not read every word on a printed page."
- "[T]he disclosure shall be unavoidable and shall be presented prior to the consumer incurring any financial obligation."
- Nothing in the advertisement can conflict with the disclosure or interfere with the consumer's understanding of it.[339]

4.2.14.3.10 Electronic disclosures

Many state and federal laws require certain documents, such as a Truth in Lending disclosure statement or change of terms notice or a notice of the right to cancel a door-to-door sale, to be given to consumers in writing. The federal Electronic Signatures in Global and National Commerce Act (E-Sign)[340] allows most documents to be provided electronically rather than in writing, as long as both parties consent. The federal law allows electronic provision of such documents even when the transaction is otherwise conducted face-to-face. This creates the opportunity for sellers and creditors to obscure required information by providing it electronically.

E-Sign's primary safeguard is a very specific consent procedure that the seller or lender must follow when asking a consumer to agree to receive a document electronically that the law would otherwise require to be delivered in writing. Prior to consenting, the consumer must be given a clear and conspicuous statement of:

- Any right or option to get the copy of the contract in non-electronic form;
- The right to withdraw consent and the procedures for and consequences of doing so;
- What transactions the consumer's consent applies to;
- The procedures for updating the information needed to contact the consumer electronically; and
- How, after consenting to electronic provision of the information, the consumer may get a paper copy, and whether any fee will be imposed.[341]

The consumer must also be given a statement of the hardware and software requirements for access to and retention of electronic records.[342]

Most importantly, the consumer must also either give consent electronically to receive the document electronically, or must confirm consent electronically.[343] In either case, the consent or confirmation of consent must be done "in a manner that reasonably demonstrates that the consumer can access information in the electronic form that will be used to provide the information that is the subject of the consent."[344] This means that the consumer must demonstrate, not just affirm, that he or she has access to the equipment and programs necessary to receive, open, and read electronic documents from the creditor.[345] The creditor

337 FTC, Dot Com Disclosures (2000), *available at* www.ftc.gov. *See* FTC v. Direct Marketing Concepts, Inc., 2004 WL 1399185, at *7 (D. Mass. June 23, 2004); FTC v. Crescent Publ'g Group, Inc., 2001 WL 128444, at *2–*3 (S.D.N.Y. Feb. 16, 2001); FTC v. Five Star Auto Club, Inc., 2000 WL 1609798, at *2 (S.D.N.Y. June 12, 2000).

338 FTC, Dot Com Disclosures (2000), *available at* www.ftc.gov.

339 FTC v. Crescent Publ'g Group, Inc., 2001 WL 128444, at *2–*3 (S.D.N.Y. Feb. 16, 2001). *See also* Zurakov v. Register.com, Inc., 304 A.D.2d 176, 760 N.Y.S.2d 13, 16–17 (2003) (reversing dismissal of UDAP complaint alleging that defendant concealed important contractual terms among hundreds of pages of disclosures on website).

340 15 U.S.C. § 7001 *et seq.* This statute is discussed in more detail in National Consumer Law Center, The Cost of Credit: Regulation and Legal Challenges § 9.2.10 (2d ed. 2000 and Supp.) and Consumer Banking and Payments Law Ch. 9 (2d ed. 2002 and Supp.).

341 15 U.S.C. § 7001(c)(1)(B).

342 15 U.S.C. § 7001(c)(1)(C)(i).

343 15 U.S.C. § 7001(c)(1)(C)(ii).

344 *Id. See* Statement of Sens. Hollings, Wyden and Sarbanes, 106th Cong., 2d Session, 146 Cong. Rec. S. 5224 (June 15, 2000) ("The Act requires that consumers consent electronically—or confirm their consent electronically—in either case, in a manner that allows the consumer to test his capacity to access and retain the electronic records that will be provided to him").

345 *See* Comments of Sen. Wyden, 106th Cong., 2d Session, 146 Cong. Rec. S. 5216 (June 15, 2000) ("Reasonably demonstrates means just that. It means the consumer can prove his or her

has to inform the consumer and go through the consent procedures again if it changes its hardware or software requirements for accessing or retaining its electronic records.[346]

Unscrupulous dealers are likely to try to evade these requirements through use of dealer-owned Palm Pilots or in-house terminals. This would hardly meet the requirement of "reasonably demonstrat[ing] that the consumer can access information in electronic form." Merely consenting on the dealer's computer should not be sufficient since the consumer can not independently access the disclosure.

There is one significant proviso to these federal requirements: states can opt out of them by enacting a uniform version of the Uniform Electronic Transactions Act (UETA) or another state law that is consistent with E-Sign and does not favor any particular electronic technology.[347] Assuming that a state has not opted out of E-Sign, if a seller provides a document electronically without going through these requirements, and other law requires the document to be provided in writing, then the seller is subject to whatever penalties that other law provides. In addition, there is substantial authority that violation of another statute is a UDAP violation,[348] so violation of E-Sign's consumer consent requirements should be a UDAP violation as well.

Even if a court declines to hold that any violation of another statute is a *per se* UDAP violation, it is likely to find deceptive a seller's attempt to obscure important disclosures by providing them electronically to a person who could not retrieve them. The Department of Commerce has issued a report to Congress that details the deficiencies of electronic communications as compared to delivery of paper documents by postal mail.[349] While electronic communication has advantages in some situations, there are significant concerns about universal access, reliability, retention, and portability of records, authentication and integrity of documents, privacy, and security. For example, throughout its history, the postal service has had a mandate for universal delivery to every household. By contrast, electronic mail delivery is offered primarily through private organizations, requires specialized telecommunications equipment, and is not universally mandated. Many households in the United States have no access to the Internet in their homes or elsewhere. Even if a household has Internet access, electronic messages are easily lost, misdirected, corrupted, intercepted, mistakenly deleted as spam, or bounced back due to a malfunctioning firewall.

UDAP principles developed in other situations apply to sellers and creditors who obscure disclosures by providing them electronically. Many cases hold that contract terms that are hidden in incomprehensible fine print are unconscionable and unenforceable.[350] The analysis of unfairness that the FTC spelled out in adopting the Credit Practices Rule also applies well to this situation: obscuring important information by providing it electronically to consumers who can not receive electronic documents causes substantial injury that consumers can not reasonably avoid and is not outweighed by countervailing benefits to consumers or to competition.[351]

4.2.15 Contract Defenses Do Not Apply to UDAP Cases

4.2.15.1 Deception Is Not Based on Breach of Contract

UDAP statutes are broader than contract or tort law and dispense with many of the elements of those claims.[352] A UDAP claim is not based on the contract, but on oral and other misrepresentations.[353] Consequently, deception can be found where there is no breach of contract or warranty.[354] For the same reason, as detailed in the following sections, contract and common law defenses generally do *not* apply to UDAP claims.

---

ability to access the electronic information that will be provided. It means the consumer, in response to an electronic vendor enquiry, actually opens an attached document sent electronically by the vendor and confirms that ability in an e-mail response. . . . It is not sufficient for the consumer merely to tell the vendor in an e-mail that he or she can access the information in the specified formats.") *See* National Consumer Law Center, Consumer Banking and Payments Law § 9.4.6.2 (2004 Supp.).

346 15 U.S.C. § 7001(c)(1)(D).

347 15 U.S.C. § 1002(a). *See* National Consumer Law Center, Consumer Banking and Payments Law § 9.5.5 (2004 Supp.) for a detailed discussion and a state-by-state analysis of this opt-out provision.

348 *See* § 3.2.7, *supra*.

349 Department of Congress, National Telecommunications and Information Administration, Report to Congress on Electronic Signatures in Global and National Commerce Act, Section 105(a) (June 2000).

350 *See* § 4.4.9.1, *infra*.

351 *See* § 5.2.3, *infra*.

352 Kattar v. Demoulas, 433 Mass. 1, 739 N.E.2d 246 (2000).

353 Sergeant Oil & Gas Co. v. National Maintenance & Repair, 861 F. Supp. 1351 (S.D. Tex. 1994); Rhino Linings USA, Inc. v. Rocky Mountain Rhino Lining, Inc., 62 P.3d 142 (Colo. 2003); Dixon v. Bryan, 1998 Tenn. App. LEXIS 847 (Dec. 15, 1998) (signing contract that listed someone else as seller does not bar buyer's UDAP claim that defendant misrepresented himself as owner); Hedley Feedlot, Inc. v. Weatherly Trust, 855 S.W.2d 826 (Tex. App. 1993); Shenandoah Assoc. v. J&K Properties, 741 S.W.2d 470 (Tex. App. 1987). *See also* Chrysler Corp. v. Schiffer, 736 So. 2d 538 (Ala. 1999) (waiver saying that purchaser accepts car even if it has minor damage that has been repaired is ineffective where damage was not minor); Morris v. Mack's Used Cars, 824 S.W.2d 538 (Tenn. 1992). *But see* Vera v. North Star Dodge Sales, Inc., 989 S.W.2d 13 (Tex. App. 1998) (waiver of claims in post-transaction settlement is permitted).

354 Heller v. Silverbranch Constr. Corp., 376 Mass. 621, 382 N.E.2d 1065 (1978); Prestwick Golf Club, Inc. v. Prestwick Ltd. P'ship, 503 S.E.2d 184 (S.C. Ct. App. 1998).

4.2.15.2 Parol Evidence Rule

The parol evidence rule, which generally prohibits the introduction of oral or written representations extrinsic to a contract to vary, add to, or contradict the terms of the contract, does not apply to UDAP claims.[355] Any other interpretation would be, in effect, a ruling that the written contract operated as a waiver of the protections of the UDAP statute, which would be contrary to public policy.[356] In a UDAP case, the representations are not introduced to vary or contradict the terms of the contract, but rather to establish a misrepresentation or deception.[357]

Oral representations, made before or after a contract is entered into, can be admitted to prove an unfair or deceptive practice, even if the contract contains a merger clause or expressly disclaims any oral representations,[358] or where goods are sold "as is."[359] Thus, for example, where a salesman misrepresented a used car's mileage, the misrepresentation was admissible to prove a UDAP violation, even though the sales contract expressly stated that the actual mileage was unknown and that the odometer reading was not a factor in the purchase of the car.[360] Such representations are not only admissible but may form the basis for a UDAP claim.[361]

4.2.15.3 Privity of Contract

The concept of privity of contract is irrelevant to UDAP claims, since they are not based on contract. Instead, whether a consumer can sue a particular defendant is a question of interpretation of terms in the UDAP statute.

For example, many states allow any person who is injured by a UDAP violation to sue. Courts interpret these statutes not to require the plaintiff and defendant to be in privity as long as the defendant's UDAP violation caused the plaintiff's injury.[362] The fact that a wholesaler's sale to a retailer

355 Casas v. American Airlines, Inc., 304 F.3d 517 (5th Cir. 2002); Wang v. Massey Chevrolet, 97 Cal. App. 4th 856, 118 Cal. Rptr. 2d 770 (2002); Lester v. Resort Camplands Int'l, Inc., 27 Conn. App. 59, 605 A.2d 550 (1992) (application of parol evidence rule to UDAP case rejected on other grounds); Torrance v. AS&L Motors, 459 S.E.2d 67 (N.C. Ct. App. 1995); Love v. Keith, 383 S.E.2d 674 (N.C. Ct. App. 1989); Burton v. Elsea, Inc., 1999 Ohio App. LEXIS 6401 (Dec. 27, 1999); Peterman v. Waite, 1980 Ohio App. LEXIS 13565 (June 25, 1980) (seller's misrepresentation that vehicle was in excellent condition was required to be included in the contract under Ohio UDAP rule); Mike Castrucci Ford Sales, Inc. v. Krull, Clearinghouse No. 53,534 (C.P. Clermont County, Ohio 2001); Prestwick Golf Club, Inc. v. Prestwick Ltd. P'ship, 503 S.E.2d 184 (S.C. Ct. App. 1998) (deceptive inducement can be basis of UDAP liability even if inducement does not become part of contract); Weitzel v. Barnes, 691 S.W.2d 598 (Tex. 1985); Downs v. Seaton, 864 S.W.2d 553 (Tex. App. 1993); Brown Foundation Repair & Consulting, Inc. v. McGuire, 711 S.W.2d 349 (Tex. App. 1986). *See also* Bates v. William Chevrolet/Geo, Inc., 785 N.E.2d 53 (Ill. App. 2003) (affirming fraud judgment where car salesman represented that consumer's signature on contract was mere formality and not binding); Crawford v. Bill Swad Chevrolet, Inc., 2000 Ohio App. LEXIS 4221 (Sept. 19, 2000) (parol evidence admissible when fraud is alleged; case also involved UDAP violations); Dixon v. Bryan, 1998 Tenn. App. LEXIS 847 (Dec. 15, 1998) (signing contract that listed someone else as seller does not bar buyer's UDAP claim that defendant misrepresented himself as owner). *But see* Vezina v. Nautilus Pools, Inc., 27 Conn. App. 810, 610 A.2d 1312 (1992) (parol evidence rule applied to at least some claims in a UDAP case). *But cf.* Davis v. G N Mortg. Corp., 244 F. Supp. 2d 950 (N.D. Ill. 2003) (UDAP claim fails because of lack of proof; court also generally stresses reasons it favors parol evidence rule).

356 Wang v. Massey Chevrolet, 97 Cal. App. 4th 856, 118 Cal. Rptr. 2d 770 (2002).

357 Couto v. Gibson, Inc., 1992 Ohio App. LEXIS 756 (Feb. 26, 1992)Villarreal v. Elizondo, 831 S.W.2d 474 (Tex. App. 1992); Honeywell v. Imperial Condominium Ass'n, 716 S.W.2d 75 (Tex. App. 1986).

358 Hofstad v. Fairfield Communities, Inc., 595 S.E.2d 813 (N.C. Ct. App. 2004) (rule that all prior negotiations and representations are merged into the writing does not apply to UDAP claim); Teague Motor Co. v. Rowton, 84 Or. App. 72, 733 P.2d 93 (1987); DeWitt County Electric Coop., Inc. v. Parks, 1 S.W.3d 96 (Tex. 1999); Watkins v. Hammerman & Gainer, 814 S.W.2d 867 (Tex. App. 1991). *See also* Shah v. Racetrac Petroleum Co., 338 F.3d 557 (6th Cir. 2003) (Tenn. law); § 4.2.15.4, *infra*.

359 Torrance v. AS&L Motors, 459 S.E.2d 67 (N.C. App. 1995). *See also* § 4.2.15.4, *infra*.

360 Twardy v. L.B. Sales, Inc., 2000 Minn. App. LEXIS 636 (June 27, 2000) (unpublished, citation limited).

361 Weitzel v. Barnes, 691 S.W.2d 598 (Tex. 1985); Downs v. Seaton, 864 S.W.2d 553 (Tex. App. 1993).

362 Tandy v. Marti, 213 F. Supp. 2d 935 (N.D. Ill. 2002); *In re* Methyl Tertiary Butyl Ether Prods. Liab. Litigation, 175 F. Supp. 2d 593 (S.D.N.Y. 2001) (plaintiffs could assert UDAP claim against gasoline manufacturers who sold gasoline to the public with additives that leaked into plaintiffs' water supply); Reisman v. KPMG Peat Marwick L.L.P., 965 F. Supp. 165 (D. Mass. 1997); Boos v. Abbott Laboratories, 925 F. Supp. 49 (D. Mass. 1996); Hall v. Walter, 969 P.2d 224 (Colo. 1998); Shannon v. Boise Cascade Corp., 208 Ill. 2d 517, 805 N.E.2d 213 (Ill. 2004) (UDAP claim possible if manufacturer's deception causes builder to install defective product in consumer's home, even if no misrepresentations made directly to consumer); Elder v. Coronet Ins. Co., 201 Ill. App. 3d 733, 558 N.E.2d 1312 (1990) (statute allows suit against "any person," so suit could be brought against insurance claim service company); Ciardi v. F. Hoffmann-La Roche, Ltd., 436 Mass. 53, 762 N.E.2d 303 (2002); Kattar v. Demoulas, 739 N.E.2d 246 (Mass. 2000) (participant at meetings between parties may be liable for his business associates' UDAP violations); Maillet v. ATF-Davidson Co., 552 N.E.2d 95 (Mass. 1990) (injured employee of purchaser may sue); Standard Register Co. v. Bolton-Emerson, Inc., 38 Mass. App. Ct. 545, 649 N.E.2d 791 (1995); Remsburg v. Docusearch, Inc., 816 A.2d 1001 (N.H. 2003); Katz v. Schachter, 251 N.J. Super. 467, 598 A.2d 923 (1991); Vitolo v. Dow Corning Corp., 166 Misc. 2d 717, 634 N.Y.S.2d 362 (1995), *aff'd on other issues*, 651 N.Y.S.2d 104 (1996); U.S. Tire-Tech, Inc. v. Boeran, B.V., 110 S.W.3d 194 (Tex. App. 2003) (privity not required even when UDAP claim based on breach of an express warranty); Bohls v. Oakes, 75 S.W.3d 473 (Tex. App. 2002); Oakwood Mobile Homes, Inc. v. Cabler, 73

is not itself a sale to a consumer is irrelevant.[363] In Ohio[364] and Florida,[365] the question is not whether there is privity of contract, but whether the defendant meets the broad statutory definition of "supplier." Virginia's UDAP statute can be analyzed similarly.[366] Texas requires that the plaintiff be a consumer, meaning that the plaintiff must seek or acquire goods or services by purchase or lease, and these must be the basis of the claim.[367] Privity is unnecessary, as standing is established by the consumer's relationship to the transaction, not by a contractual relationship with the defendant.[368] Although the Kentucky Supreme Court has not yet spoken, some lower courts in Kentucky have held that privity is necessary for a UDAP claim.[369] Nonetheless, despite the lack of privity, a victim of identity theft was allowed to assert a claim under the Kentucky UDAP statute against a bank that was dunning him for a debt incurred by an imposter.[370]

Where a UDAP statute is silent on the question, courts should not read a privity requirement into it.[371] This is especially true since UDAP statutes were intended to broaden the remedies that pre-existing tort and contract law

S.W.3d 363 (Tex. App. 2002); Long Distance Intern., Inc. v. Telefonos De Mexico, S.A., 2002 Tex. App. LEXIS 1839 (Tex. App. Mar. 13, 2002), *op. withdrawn and appeal dismissed at request of parties due to settlement*, 2002 Tex. App. LEXIS 6330 (Aug. 30, 2002). *See also* Knapp v. Americredit Fin. Servs., Inc., 245 F. Supp. 2d 841 (S.D. W. Va. 2003) (defendant is subject to UDAP statute even though it did not deal directly with consumers); Richie v. Bank of Am. Auto Fin. Corp., 2002 Cal. App. Unpub. LEXIS 6077 (June 28, 2002) (unpublished, citation limited) (allowing car buyer to assert UDAP claim against prior owner who auctioned car to dealer who sold it to buyer); Elkins v. Microsoft Corp., 817 A.2d 9 (Vt. 2002). *But see* Reynolds v. Ryland Group, Inc., 340 S.C. 331, 531 S.E.2d 917 (2000) (concluding, without any specific statutory authority, that subsequent purchaser of home can not bring UDAP suit against builder-vendor). *But cf.* Schwartz v. Visa Int'l Corp., 2003 WL 1870370 (Cal. Super. Apr. 7, 2003) (privity is required for unconscionability claims that are based on contract).

363 Tandy v. Marti, 213 F. Supp. 2d 935, 938 n.1 (N.D. Ill. 2002). *But see* Murray v. Dryvit Sys., Inc., 2002 WL 32072493 (Va. Cir. July 15, 2002) (manufacturer's sale of stucco to contractor not a consumer transaction so not covered by UDAP statute even though it was installed in consumer's home).

364 Patterson v. Central Mills, Inc., 112 F. Supp. 2d 681 (N.D. Ohio 2000) (manufacturer can be held liable as supplier despite lack of privity); Miner v. Jayco, 1999 Ohio App. LEXIS 3944 (Aug. 27, 1999) (manufacturer is supplier); Garner v. Borcherding Buick, Inc., 84 Ohio App. 3d 61, 616 N.E.2d 283 (1992).

365 Warren v. Monahan Beaches Jewelry Ctr., Inc., 548 So. 2d 870 (Fla. Dist. Ct. App. 1989).

366 Harris v. Universal Ford, Inc., 2001 U.S. Dist. LEXIS 8913 (E.D. Va. Feb. 5, 2001) (magistrate's opinion; case was settled before further rulings were issued) (secured creditor that auctioned a repossessed vehicle to dealer without disclosing frame damage was a supplier because it could reasonably foresee that car would be resold to a consumer); Kieft v. Becker, 2002 Va. Cir. LEXIS 33 (Jan. 31, 2002) (licensed contractor that allowed its name to be used on building permit but never dealt with consumer is subject to UDAP statute). *But see* Murray v. Dryvit Sys., Inc., 2002 WL 32072493 (Va. Cir. July 15, 2002) (manufacturer's sale of stucco to contractor not a consumer transaction so not covered by UDAP statute even though it was installed in consumer's home); Eubank v. Ford Motor Credit Co., 54 Va. Cir. 172 (2000) (ultimate buyer had no claim against prior lessor who auctioned car to dealer, since sale to dealer was not a consumer transaction).

367 Flenniken v. Longview Bank & Trust Co., 661 S.W.2d 701 (Tex. 1983).

368 *Id. See also* Wellborn v. Sears, Roebuck & Co., 970 F.2d 1420 (5th Cir. 1992) (Texas law); Bass v. Hendrix, 931 F. Supp. 523 (S.D. Tex. 1996); Mote v. Oryx Energy Co., 910 F. Supp. 291 (E.D. Tex. 1995); Kennedy v. Sale, 689 S.W.2d 890 (Tex. 1985) (claim against insurance agent); Stagner v. Friendswood Dev. Co., 620 S.W.2d 103 (Tex. 1981); Elite Towing v. Hernandez, 2001 Tex. App. LEXIS 1971 (Mar. 28, 2001); Clary Corp. v. Smith, 949 S.W.2d 452 (Tex. App. 1997); Howell Crude Oil Co. v. Donna Refinery Partners, Ltd., 928 S.W.2d 100 (Tex. App. 1996); Mendoza v. American Nat'l Ins. Co., 932 S.W.2d 605 (Tex. App. 1996); Inglish v. Union State Bank, 911 S.W.2d 829 (Tex. App. 1995); Gilbreath v. White, 903 S.W.2d 851 (Tex. App. 1995); Thompson v. Vinson & Elkins, 859 S.W.2d 617 (Tex. App. 1993); D/FW Commercial Roofing Co. v. Mehra, 854 S.W.2d 182 (Tex. App. 1993). *But cf.* Amstadt v. U.S. Brass Corp., 919 S.W.2d 644 (Tex. 1996) (upstream manufacturer whose misrepresentations were not communicated to the ultimate purchaser not subject to UDAP statute because did not have sufficient connection to the sale); State Farm Fire & Cas. Co. v. Gandy, 925 S.W.2d 696 (Tex. 1996) (alleged tortfeasor's attempt to assign his DTPA claim against his insurance company to victim is ineffective); Parkway Co. v. Woodruff, 901 S.W.2d 434 (Tex. 1995) (DTPA prohibits breach of warranty, but does not create warranties; no warranty arose because parties never contracted with each other).

369 Kentucky Laborers District Council Health & Welfare Trust Fund v. Hill & Knowlton, Inc., 24 F. Supp. 2d 755 (W.D. Ky. 1998) (using absence of privity as basis for denying union fund's claim against tobacco companies for expenses caused due to members' illnesses; court notes that consumers may have remedy under a separate statute, Ky. Rev. Stat. Ann. § 446.070, even if privity is lacking); Anderson v. Nat'l Sec. Fire & Cas. Co., 870 S.W.3d 432 (Ky. App. 2000) (third party claimant can not assert UDAP claim against consumer's insurance company because of lack of privity); Sparks v. Re/Max Allstar Realty, Inc., 37 S.W.3d 343 (Ky. App. 2000) (buyer had no UDAP claim against prior owner of car whose husband falsely told buyer it had never been wrecked); Skilcraft Sheetmetal, Inc. v. Kentucky Machinery, Inc., 836 S.W.2d 907 (Ky. App. 1992) (buyer of wheel loader can not bring UDAP suit against person who repaired it for previous owner).

370 Stafford v. Cross Country Bank, 262 F. Supp. 2d 776 (W.D. Ky. 2003) (distinguishing its own prior decision because here bank claimed consumer was in privity and this consumer fell within class protected by UDAP statute).

371 Lyne v. Arthur Anderson & Co., 772 F. Supp. 1064 (N.D. Ill. 1991); Warren v. Monahan Beaches Jewelry Ctr., Inc., 548 So. 2d 870 (Fla. Dist. Ct. App. 1989); Ross v. Bob Saks Toyota, Inc., Clearinghouse No. 53,543A (Mich. Cir. Ct. July 11, 2001) (some of the substantive prohibitions of Michigan UDAP statute may have an implicit privity requirement, but others do not); Prince v. Wright, 141 N.C. App. 262, 541 S.E.2d 191 (2000); Valley Forge Towers S. Condominium v. Ron-Ike Foam Insulators, Inc., 574 A.2d 641 (Pa. Super. Ct. 1990), *aff'd without op.*, 605 A.2d 798 (Pa. 1992); Elkins v. Microsoft Corp., 817 A.2d 9 (Vt. 2002).

provided for consumers.[372] Thus, under the North Carolina UDAP standard, the question is not whether the parties were in privity but whether the defendant's acts affected commerce, a criterion expressly required by the statute.[373] Many other courts have employed similar reasoning to conclude that privity is unnecessary.[374]

Even though privity is not required, many courts do require that the defendant have some relationship or contact with the consumer, and some deny a UDAP cause of action if the relationship is too remote.[375] In analyzing remoteness, the Connecticut Supreme Court identifies the factors as: the difficulty of determining the amount of the plaintiff's damages attributable to the wrongdoing as opposed to other independent causes; the complexity of apportioning damages among plaintiffs at different levels of remoteness, in order to avoid a double recovery; and whether there are other more directly injured parties who can remedy the harm without these complications.[376]

4.2.15.4 Disclaimers, Merger Clauses, Limitations on Liability or Remedies, and Other Contract Clauses

Allowing creditors to escape UDAP liability by placing restrictive terms in written contracts would facilitate fraud and make UDAP laws a dead letter. It would also fly in the face of research showing that few American adults can understand and use typical contract terms and disclosures.[377]

A contract provision that "no agreement between salesman and customer [is] binding on the company" or otherwise disclaiming oral representations does not defeat a UDAP action against a salesman's misrepresentations.[378]

---

372 *See, e.g.*, Raudebaugh v. Action Pest Control, Inc., 59 Or. App. 166, 650 P.2d 1006 (1982) (inspector who provided false inspection report to owner for submission to public agency is liable to individual who relies on report in buying house; tort concepts should not be grafted onto UDAP statute); Elkins v. Microsoft Corp., 817 A.2d 9 (Vt. 2002); Merriman v. Auto Excellence, Inc., 55 Va. Cir. 330, 2001 Va. Cir. LEXIS 292 (June 18, 2001). *See generally* § 4.2.3.1, *supra*.

373 Prince v. Wright, 141 N.C. App. 262, 541 S.E.2d 191 (2000); J.M. Westall & Co. v. Windswept View, 97 N.C. App. 71, 387 S.E.2d 67 (1990) (UDAP violations tend to involve buyer/seller relationships but can include other types of commercial relationships, including those outside of contract).

374 Ford Motor Co. Ignition Switch Prods. Liability Litig., 1999 WL 33495352 (D.N.J. July 27, 1999), *as modified on reconsideration*, (July 27, 1999) (upstream component parts supplier is in trade or commerce under Nebraska UDAP statute and is involved in consumer transaction under Oklahoma UDAP statute); Tackling v. Shinerman, 42 Conn. Supp. 517, 630 A.2d 1381 (1993) (UDAP suit may be maintained against appraiser with whom consumer had no contract, if reliance and harm were reasonably foreseeable); Heatherly v. Merrimack Mut. Fire Ins. Co., 43 S.W.3d 911 (Tenn. App. 2000) (privity requirement is inapplicable to UDAP suit); Elkins v. Microsoft Corp., 817 A.2d 9 (Vt. 2002); Merriman v. Auto Excellence, Inc., 55 Va. Cir. 330, 2001 Va. Cir. LEXIS 292 (June 18, 2001) (privity unnecessary as long as defendant meets definition of supplier; prior dealer in chain of title of vehicle with concealed wreck damage can be liable to ultimate consumer notwithstanding lack of privity). *See also* Waterbury Petroleum Products, Inc. v. Canaan Oil & Fuel Co., 193 Conn. 208, 477 A.2d 988 (1984) (privity was required until 1979 amendments eliminated it).

375 *See, e.g.*, Conn. Pipe Trades Health Fund v. Philip Morris, Inc., 153 F. Supp. 2d 101 (D. Conn. 2001) (must be some connection or nexus—business, consumer, commercial, competitor, or other—between the parties; union trust fund could not assert UDAP claim against tobacco companies whose products caused health problems for fund's beneficiaries); Vacco v. Microsoft Corp., 260 Conn. 59, 793 A.2d 1048 (2002) (indirect purchasers too remote to bring UDAP claim based on manufacturer's monopolization); Jackson v. R.G. Whipple, Inc., 627 A.2d 374 (Conn. 1993) (although privity is not required, CUTPA is not formless, and plaintiff must have some type of consumer relationship with the person who caused harm); Peleschak v. Verex Assurance, Inc., 651 N.E.2d 562 (Ill. App. Ct. 1995) (no UDAP liability where mortgage insurance company made no representations to plaintiff and had no contact with her); Nei v. Boston Survey Consultants, 388 Mass. 320, 446 N.E.2d 681 (1983) (while privity not necessary, appraiser who was hired to report to property owner does not have UDAP liability to buyer for failing to include explanation of findings); A.O. Fox Mem. Hosp. v. Am. Tobacco Co., 302 A.D.2d 413, 754 N.Y.S.2d 368 (2003) (hospital's claim against tobacco companies for unreimbursed costs of health care for smokers entirely derivative and too remote); Prince v. Wright, 141 N.C. App. 262, 541 S.E.2d 191 (2000) (plaintiff could not sue insurance company that inspected property for her landlord because inspection did not affect commerce); Nava v. Central Power and Light, 2000 Tex. App. LEXIS 5972 (Aug. 31, 2000) (unpublished, citation limited) (privity not required, but tenant's relationship to landlord's utility company too remote). *See also* Messeka Sheet Metal Co. v. Hodder, 368 N.J. Super. 116, 845 A.2d 646 (App. Div. 2004) (UDAP statute and regulations governing format of home improvement contracts did not apply to subcontractor who dealt only with general contractor). *Cf.* Blue Cross & Blue Shield v. Philip Morris USA Inc., 344 F.3d 211 (2d Cir. 2003) (certifying question whether remoteness bars UDAP suit to N.Y. Court of Appeals). *But cf.* Allstate Ins. Co. v. Siegel, 312 F. Supp. 2d 260 (D. Conn. 2004) (connection or nexus sufficient between insurer and physician who submitted fraudulent invoices for evaluation and treatment of insureds); Ciardi v. F. Hoffmann-La Roche, Ltd., 436 Mass. 53, 762 N.E.2d 303 (2002) (rejecting argument that indirect purchaser was too remote).

376 Vacco v. Microsoft Corp., 260 Conn. 59, 793 A.2d 1048 (2002).

377 Alan M. White and Cathy Lesser Mansfield, Literacy and Contract, 13 *Stanford Law and Policy Review* 233 (2003).

378 Thacker v. Menard, Inc., 105 F.3d 382 (7th Cir. 1997) (Illinois law); Attaway v. Tom's Auto Sales, Inc., 144 Ga. App. 813, 242 S.E.2d 740 (1978); Billingham v. Dornemann, 771 N.E.2d 166 (Mass. App. 2002); State *ex rel.* Webster v. Areaco Inv. Co., 756 S.W.2d 633 (Mo. Ct. App. 1988); Gaidon v. Guardian Life Ins. Co., 704 N.Y.S.2d 177, 725 N.E.2d 598 (N.Y. 1999) (merger clauses and contractual disclaimers do not defeat UDAP claim), *aff'd on other grounds*, 96 N.Y.2d 201, 750 N.E.2d 1078 (2001) (statute of limitations); Oakwood Mobile Homes, Inc. v. Cabler, 73 S.W.3d 363 (Tex. App. 2002). *But see* Sparks v. RE/Max Allstar Realty, Inc., 55 S.W.3d 343 (Ky. App. 2000) (consumer had no UDAP claim against appraiser where clause stated that appraisal was solely for benefit of mortgage company and that consumer should not rely on it); Wiegand v. Walker Automotive Groups, Inc., 670 N.W.2d 449 (Minn. App. 2003), *review*

This position is especially strong if the consumer has signed an order form or other binding document in reliance on the oral statements, and is only later presented with additional documents that disclose the true facts.[379] In addition, a merger clause that the contract is the complete agreement has no effect on a UDAP claim.[380] Courts reach these same conclusions even when dealing with common law fraud rather than UDAP claims.[381] Ohio courts hold that it is a UDAP violation to fail to include oral representations in the written contract.[382]

Disclaimers and disclosures in advertisements do not defeat a deception claim when they are phrased and presented in a way that does not draw the reader's attention away from the deceptive statements.[383] Nor does a waiver of all warranties defeat a consumer's misrepresentation claim.[384] Oral deception[385] and price unconscionability[386] are not cured by an "as is" disclaimer. It is deceptive to fail to disclose material facts even where a product is sold "as is."[387]

Of course, if a UDAP claim is merely based on a warranty breach and not on the seller's deception, a valid warranty disclaimer defeating the breach of warranty claim will also defeat the UDAP claim.[388] But even in a warranty-based claim, the "as is" clause will not preclude a UDAP claim unless, construed in light of the nature of the transaction and the totality of circumstances, it clearly and unambiguously demonstrates the buyer's agreement to rely solely on his or her own inspection.[389] A court-created implied warranty of

granted, 2004 Minn. LEXIS 10 (Jan. 20, 2004); Nagle v. No. Central Life Ins. Co., 2002 Minn. App. LEXIS 31 (Jan. 8, 2002) (unpublished, citation limited); Tucker v. Boulevard at Piper Glen, 150 N.C. App. 150, 564 S.E.2d 248 (2002) (clause that buyer is not relying on any oral representations negated reliance and defeats UDAP claim).

379 Duran v. Leslie Oldsmobile, 594 N.E.2d 1355 (Ill. App. Ct. 1992).

380 McEvoy Travel Bureau, Inc. v. Norton Co., 408 Mass. 704, 563 N.E.2d 188 (1990) (contract found not to represent parties' complete understanding); Teague Motor Co. v. Rowten, 84 Or. App. 72, 733 P.2d 93 (1987); DeWitt County Electric Coop., Inc. v. Parks, 1 S.W.3d 96 (Tex. 1999). *See also* J.C. Whitney & Co. v. Renaissance Software Corp., 2000 U.S. Dist. LEXIS 6180 (N.D. Ill. Apr. 19, 2000) (fraud claim not necessarily barred by integration clause), *adopted in part, dismissed without prejudice on other grounds*, 98 F. Supp. 2d 981 (N.D. Ill. 2000); Mike Castrucci Ford Sales, Inc. v. Krull, Clearinghouse No. 53,534 (C.P. Clermont County, Ohio 2001). *But see* McCartin v. Westlake, 36 Mass. App. Ct. 221, 630 N.E.2d 283 (1994) (buyers in business transaction could not base UDAP claim on statements made during negotiations but not incorporated into written contract).

381 *See* National Consumer Law Center, Consumer Warranty Law § 5.15.1 (2d ed. 2001 and Supp.); National Consumer Law Center, Automobile Fraud § 7.8.2 (2d ed. 2003 and Supp.).

382 Lump v. Best Door & Window, Inc., 2002 Ohio App. LEXIS 1381 (Mar. 27, 2002).

383 FTC v. Medicor, 217 F. Supp. 2d 1048 (C.D. Cal. 2002) (statement that "results may vary" did not save ad since consumers could still reasonably believe that illustrated results were typical); Garcia v. Overland Bond & Investment Co., 282 Ill. App. 3d 486, 668 N.E.2d 199 (1996); Miller v. American Family Publishers, 284 N.J. Super. 67, 663 A.2d 643 (Chancery Div. 1995). *See also* Thacker v. Menard, Inc., 105 F.3d 382 (7th Cir. 1997) (Illinois law); FTC v. Cyberspace.com, L.L.C., 2002 WL 32060289 (W.D. Wash. July 10, 2002) (fine print on back of check stating that cashing it created a contract for Internet services).

384 Campbell v. Beak, 568 S.E.2d 801 (Ga. App. 2002); Goshen v. Mut. Life Ins. Co., 98 N.Y.2d 314, 774 N.E.2d 1190, 1197 (2002); Murray v. D&J Motor Co., 958 P.2d 823 (Okla. App. 1998); Morris v. Mack's Used Cars, 824 S.W.2d 538 (Tenn. 1992); Smith v. Levine, 911 S.W.2d 427 (Tex. App. 1995); Mercedes-Benz of N. Am. v. Dickenson, 720 S.W.2d 844 (Tex. App. 1986).

385 Lou Bachrodt Chevrolet, Inc. v. Savage, 570 So. 2d 306 (Fla. Dist. Ct. App. 1990); Automobile Trader v. Simmons, 22 Ohio Op. 3d 149 (Ct. App. 1981) (oral deception not excluded by "as is" disclaimer); Morris v. Mack's Used Cars, 824 S.W.2d 538 (Tenn. 1992); Weitzel v. Barnes, 691 S.W.2d 598 (Tex. 1985).

386 Wyatt v. Petrila, 752 S.W.2d 683 (Tex. App. 1988).

387 V.S.H. Realty, Inc. v. Texaco, Inc., 757 F.2d 411 (1st Cir. 1985) (Massachusetts law); Automobile Trader v. Simmons, 22 Ohio Op. 3d 149 (Ct. App. 1981); Hatfield v. D.D. Sullivan, Inc., No. 1813 (Or. Cir. Ct. Marion Cty. 1980); Smith v. Scott Lewis Chevrolet, Inc., 843 S.W.2d 9 (Tenn. Ct. App. 1992); Smith v. Levine, 911 S.W.2d 427 (Tex. App. 1995); Metro Ford Truck Sales, Inc. v. Davis, 709 S.W.2d 785 (Tex. App. 1986). *See also* Streeks, Inc. v. Diamond Hill Farms, Inc., 258 Neb. 581 (2000), 605 N.W.2d 110 (affirming fraudulent concealment verdict despite disclaimer where seller failed to disclose information about basic defect). *But see* American Eagle Ins. Co. v. United Techs. Corp., 51 F.3d 468 (5th Cir. 1995) (a U.C.C. disclaimer of implied warranties also disclaims any Texas UDAP implied warranties); Prudential Ins. Co. of Am. v. Jefferson Assocs., 896 S.W.2d 156 (Tex. 1995) (as-is clause does not operate as a waiver, but does constitute the consumer's confirmation that no warranty exists, thus negating causation where the UDAP claim is based on breach of warranty); Bynum v. Prudential Residential Servs., Ltd. P'ship, 2003 WL 22456111 (Tex. App. Oct. 30, 2003).

388 American Eagle Ins. Co. v. United Technologies Corp., 51 F.3d 468 (5th Cir. 1995); Canal Electric Co. v. Westinghouse Electric Co., 406 Mass. 369, 548 N.E.2d 182 (1990); Helena Chemical Co. v. Wilkins, 47 S.W.3d 486 (Tex. 2001); Schlumberger Technology Corp. v. Swanson, 959 S.W.2d 171 (Tex. 1997); Prudential Ins. Co. of Am. v. Jefferson Assocs., 896 S.W.2d 156 (Tex. 1995); Smith v. Radam, Inc., 51 S.W.3d 413, 45 U.C.C. Rep. Serv. 2d 796 (Tex. App. 2001); Materials Marketing Corp. v. Spencer, 40 S.W.3d 172, 43 U.C.C. Rep. Serv. 2d 1131 (Tex. App. 2001) (since implied warranty was not created by UDAP, it could be disclaimed); Arthur's Garage, Inc. v. Racal-Chubb Sec. Sys., Inc., 997 S.W.2d 803 (Tex. App. 1999); Singleton v. LaCoure, 712 S.W.2d 757 (Tex. App. 1986). *See* Centex Homes v. Buecher, 95 S.W.3d 266 (Tex. 2002) (implied warranty of good workmanship for new home may be waived if agreement details manner and quality of work desired). *See also* § 4.9.3, *infra*, and National Consumer Law Center, Consumer Warranty Law (2d ed. 2001 and Supp.) for a detailed analysis of warranty law.

389 Woodlands Land Dev. Co. v. Jenkins, 48 S.W.3d 415 (Tex. App. 2001) ("as is" clause in boilerplate provisions that were not negotiated does not preclude reliance on misrepresentations); Fletcher v. Edwards, 26 S.W.3d 66 (Tex. App. 2000) (agreement does not preclude recovery if consumer was fraudulently in-

habitability in the sale of a new house can only be waived in unique circumstances, if buyer buys a "problem" house with express and full knowledge of the defects.[390]

Courts generally hold that contractual limitations on liability[391] and remedies[392] are unenforceable as to UDAP claims. The rule may be different for commercial parties, however.[393] Including a clause that makes a contract's promises illusory may itself be deceptive.[394]

The Texas UDAP statute includes broad statutory restrictions on waivers of rights under the statute, which apply to limitations on liability and remedies.[395] The Kansas UDAP statute specifically prohibits clauses that limit remedies provided by law for breach of implied warranties of fitness and merchantability,[396] but it only applies to goods, not services.[397]

A contract clause may also make the seller's contract ambiguous, which many decisions hold is deceptive.[398] UDAP principles may also require prominent disclosure of a burdensome contract clause.[399]

4.2.15.5 Voluntary Payment Doctrine

Under the common law doctrine of voluntary payment, money paid with full knowledge of the facts generally can

duced to enter into it); Pairett v. Gutierrez, 969 S.W.2d 512 (Tex. App. 1998); Smith v. Levine, 911 S.W.2d 427 (Tex. App. 1995) (causation not negated where buyers testified they relied on seller's representations regarding condition of house and believed "as is" clause referred only to possible future problems). *Cf.* Larsen v. Carlene Langford & Assocs., Inc., 41 S.W.3d 245 (Tex. App. 2001) ("as-is" clause negated essential reliance element of UDAP claim).

390 Centex Homes v. Buecher, 95 S.W.3d 266 (Tex. 2002).

391 Cummings v. HPG Int'l, Inc., 244 F.3d 16 (1st Cir. 2001) (Mass. law) (party can not induce a contract by fraudulent representation and then use contractual devices to escape liability); Cambridge Plating Co. v. NAPCO, Inc., 876 F. Supp. 326 (D. Mass. 1995) (contractual bar to consequential damages is inapplicable to UDAP claim), *aff'd in part, vacated on other grounds*, 85 F.3d 752 (1st Cir. 1996); Rollins, Inc. v. Heller, 454 So. 2d 580 (Fla. Dist. Ct. App. 1984); Smith v. Scott Lewis Chevrolet, Inc., 843 S.W.2d 9 (Tenn. Ct. App. 1992); Keyes v. Bollinger, 31 Wash. App. 286, 640 P.2d 1077 (1982); McCullough v. Lewensohn, 221 Wis. 2d 595, 586 N.W.2d 698 (Wis. App. 1998) (unpublished limited precedent opinion, text available on LEXIS at 1998 Wisc. App. LEXIS 980) (contractual disclaimer does not affect liability for misrepresentation; commercial case). *See also* Tex. Bus. & Com. Code Ann. § 17.42 (waiver permitted in restricted circumstances). *But see* Vickes v. MLT, Inc., 124 F. Supp. 2d 1092 (E.D. Mich. 2000) (because of exculpatory clause in contract, seller's general assurances did not override general rule that tour operator is not vicariously liable for hotel's negligence); Lee v. C.D.E. Home Inspection Co., 2002 WL 1938248 (Ohio App. Aug. 22, 2002) (buyers bound by disclaimer regarding scope of home inspection where they accepted report and used it in negotiations). The Federal Arbitration Act may preempt the application of a UDAP nonwaiver provision that would otherwise invalidate a waiver of the right to a judicial determination. This issue is discussed in detail in National Consumer Law Center, Consumer Arbitration Agreements § 2.2.1 (4th ed. 2004).

392 Capitol Cadillac Olds, Inc. v. Roberts, 813 S.W.2d 287 (Ky. 1991); Ford Motor Co. v. Mayes, 575 S.W.2d 480 (Ky. Ct. App. 1978); O'Briant v. Rollins, Inc., 2001 Mich. App. LEXIS 1451 (June 15, 2001) (unpublished, limited precedent) (dictum); Roelle v. Orkin Exterminating Co., 2000 Ohio App. LEXIS 5141 (Nov. 7, 2000); Fletcher v. Don Foss of Cleveland, 628 N.E.2d 60 (Ohio App. 1993); Couto v. Gibson, Inc., 1992 Ohio App. LEXIS 756 (Feb. 26, 1992) (requirement that seller be notified of problems within 20 days). *See also* Bolton-Emerson, Inc., 38 Mass. App. Ct. 545, 649 N.E.2d 791 (1995) (remedy limitation inapplicable to tort-like UDAP claim even between commercial parties). *But see* Kruger v. Subaru of Am., Inc., 996 F. Supp. 451 (E.D. Pa. 1998) (where UDAP claim based solely on breach of warranty, limitation on remedy clause found valid for purposes of warranty claim); Lefebvre Intergraphics, Inc. v. Sanden Machine, Ltd., 946 F. Supp. 1358 (N.D. Ill. 1996) (enforcing waiver of consequential damages in commercial party's UDAP claim).

393 Canal Electric Co. v. Westinghouse Electric Co., 406 Mass. 369, 548 N.E.2d 182 (1990) (limitation of liability valid where it allocated risks between two commercially sophisticated parties and the UDAP claim merely duplicated a breach of warranty claim). *See also* Winter Panel Corp. v. Reichhold Chemicals, Inc., 823 F. Supp. 963 (D. Mass. 1993) (UDAP claim was based on misrepresentation, not duplication of breach of warranty claim, so limitation of liability clause was unenforceable); Boston Helicopter Charter, Inc. v. Agusta Aviation Corp., 767 F. Supp. 363, 377 (D. Mass. 1991) (contractual bar on consequential damages can bar UDAP claim that duplicates warranty claim); Chestnut Hill Dev. Corp. v. Otis Elevator Co., 653 F. Supp. 927 (D. Mass. 1987) (enforcing remedy limitation in commercial UDAP claim based on breach of warranty); Beacon Hill Civic Ass'n v. Ristorante Toscano, 662 N.E.2d 1015 (Mass. 1996) ("we ordinarily would not effectuate a consumer's waiver of rights" under UDAP statute).

394 Fendrich v. RBF, L.L.C., 842 So. 2d 1076 (Fla. Dist. Ct. App. 2003). *See* § 5.2.7.3.1, *infra* (illusory warranties).

395 High Plains Natural Gas Co. v. Warren Petroleum Co., 875 F.2d 284 (10th Cir. 1989) (Texas law); Bakhico Co. v. Shasta Beverages, Inc., 1998 U.S. Dist. LEXIS 14266 (N.D. Tex. Sept. 3, 1998) (waiver of right to seek indemnity from third party unenforceable); First Title Co. of Waco v. Garrett, 860 S.W.2d 74 (Tex. 1993); Southwestern Bell Tel. Co. v. FDP Corp., 811 S.W.2d 572 (Tex. 1991); Arthur's Garage, Inc. v. Racal-Chubb Sec. Sys., 997 S.W.2d 803 (Tex. App. 1999); Ciba-Geigy Corp. v. Stephens, 871 S.W.2d 317 (Tex. App. 1994); Rickey v. Houston Health Club, Inc., 863 S.W.2d 148 (Tex. App. 1993); Reliance Universal, Inc. v. Sparks Industrial, 688 S.W.2d 890 (Tex. App. 1985); Martin v. Lou Poliquin Enterprises, Inc., 696 S.W.2d 180 (Tex. App. 1985).

396 Kan. Stat. Ann. § 50-639. *See* Corral v. Rolling Protective Servs. Co., 240 Kan. 678, 732 P.2d 1260 (1987); *cf.* State *ex rel.* Stovall v. DVM Enters., Inc., 62 P.3d 653 (Kan. 2003) (release of liability was not a warranty disclaimer so was not prohibited; seeking a warranty disclaimer would not be *per se* unconscionable but just a factor).

397 Moler v. Melzer, 942 P.2d 643 (Kan. App. 1997).

398 *See* § 4.2.13, *supra.*

399 *See* § 4.2.14.1, *supra.*

not be recovered, even if the demand is unlawful.[400] In theory, the rule ensures that a party with a legal claim asserts it at the first opportunity, before making payment, thereby allowing other parties to respond or adjust their positions accordingly.[401] The doctrine developed in tandem with the view that the courts would not grant relief for a mistake of law.[402] Historically, the doctrine has been applied where the parties involved were more or less on equal terms.[403] Many, but not all, jurisdictions have adopted the doctrine as a general rule of law for contract and tort claims.[404]

There is a strong argument that the voluntary payment doctrine is entirely inapplicable to UDAP claims. UDAP statutes were intended to expand and liberalize common law rules, which often left consumers without a remedy.[405] UDAP statutes generally are written to cover all deception, including not just misrepresentation of fact but also misrepresentation of law. To deny consumers a UDAP remedy because they paid a bill after learning of the deception would ignore the disparity in bargaining power that UDAP statutes were intended to address, since consumers are often rightly fearful of the consequences of unilateral nonpayment. In many states, the UDAP statute or a state debt collection law specifically prohibits billing for amounts not actually owed, clearly demonstrating a legislative intent that consumers have remedies for these practices.[406]

Even if the voluntary payment doctrine applies to UDAP claims, it is subject to a number of limitations that should make it inapplicable in most cases. First, a payment can not be voluntary if it is induced by fraud, extortion or other wrongful conduct.[407] These factors will almost always be present in UDAP cases.

Second, the doctrine only bars recovery of payments made under a mistake of law. Payments made under a mistake of fact are usually recoverable.[408] Thus, where a consumer pays for a service or product based on a misrepresentation by the seller, there can be no voluntary payment defense. The payment is based on a mistake of fact. For example, in a Michigan case brought by customers of a lawn care service challenging overcharges and surcharges contained in their bills, the court held that the customers' UDAP claims were not barred by the voluntary payment doctrine, because their payments, made in response to overbilling, were based on a mistake of fact.[409] Even a mistake of fact that is due to the consumer's failure to investigate defeats the voluntary payment doctrine.[410] The party raising voluntary payment as a defense has the burden of proving that the opposing party had knowledge of all material facts.[411] Even if the payment was made under a mistake of law, courts may make an exception where the application of the bar would lead to an inequitable result and a party would be unjustly enriched.[412] The Indiana Supreme Court holds that the

---

400 Jenkins v. Concorde Acceptance Corp., 802 N.E.2d 1270 (Ill. App. 2003), *app. granted*, 2004 Ill. LEXIS 583 (Mar. 24, 2004). *See* Randazzo v. Harris Bank Palatine, 262 F.3d 663 (7th Cir. 2001); Progressive Mich. Ins. Co. v. United Wis. Life Ins. Co., 84 F. Supp. 2d 848, 854 (E.D. Mich. 2000); Cotton v. Med-Cor Health Information Solutions, Inc., 472 S.E.2d 92, 221 Ga. App. 609 (1996); Durant v. Servicemaster, 159 F. Supp. 2d 977, 981 (Mich. 2001); Criterion Ins. Co. v. Fulgham, 247 S.E.2d 404, 406, 407 (Va. 1978); Putnam v. Time Warner Cable, 255 Wis. 2d 447, 649 N.W.2d 626 (2001).

401 Randazzo v. Harris Bank Palatine, 262 F.3d 663, 668 (7th Cir. 2001) (discussing history and development of the doctrine). *See also* Illinois Glass Co. v. Chicago Tel. Co., 234 Ill. 535, 539, 85 N.E. 100 (1908) (company that acquiesced in rate increase, knowing that it was in excess of that allowed by law, and made payments for years, could not later sue to recover payments).

402 *See* Putnam v. Time Warner Cable, 255 Wis. 2d 447, 649 N.W.2d 626 (2001); Stephen L. Camp, *The Voluntary Payment Doctrine in Georgia*, 16 Ga. L. Rev. 893 (Summer 1982).

403 *See* Putnam v. Time Warner Cable, 255 Wis. 2d 447, 649 N.W.2d 626 (2001); Stephen L. Camp, *The Voluntary Payment Doctrine in Georgia*, 16 Ga. L. Rev. 893 (Summer 1982). *See also* Illinois Glass Co. v. Chicago Tel. Co., 234 Ill. 535, 539, 85 N.E. 100 (1908).

404 *See* § 9.7.5.4, *infra*.

405 *See* § 4.2.3.1, *supra*.

406 *Cf.* Scott v. Fairbanks Capital Corp., 284 F. Supp. 2d 880 (S.D. Ohio 2003) (recognizing that voluntary payment doctrine would be inconsistent with Fair Debt Collection Practices Act). *But see* Westfall v. Chase Lincoln First Bank, 258 A.D.2d 299, 685 N.Y.S.2d 181 (1999) (applying voluntary payment doctrine to UDAP claim for mortgage overcharges).

407 Buechin v. Ogden Chrysler-Plymouth, Inc., 159 Ill. App. 3d 237, 250, 251, 511 N.E.2d 1330 (Ill. 1987) (where seller committed fraud in misrepresenting used car as "new," buyer did not waive claims by paying for car after learning of fraud); Williams v. Consolvo, 237 Va. 608, 615, 379 S.E.2d 333 (1989). *Cf.* Jenkins v. Concorde Acceptance Corp., 802 N.E.2d 1270 (Ill. App. 2003) (voluntary payment doctrine applies even though plaintiffs alleged UDAP violations, since UDAP statute eliminates many fraud elements), *app. granted*, 2004 Ill. LEXIS 583 (Mar. 24, 2004).

408 Durant v. Servicemaster, 159 F. Supp. 2d 977, 981 (Mich. 2001); Williams v. Consolvo, 237 Va. 608, 615, 379 S.E.2d 333 (1989) (party who paid noteholder on advice of counsel when not obliged to do so, had knowledge of facts and was therefore a volunteer). *See* Applied Solutions, Inc. v. Plews/Edelmann, 2003 WL 21800410 (N.D. Ill. July 31, 2003) (business purchaser of services is covered).

409 Durant v. Servicemaster, 159 F. Supp. 2d 977, 981 (Mich. 2001) (citing Wilson v. Newman, 463 Mich. 435, 617 N.W.2d 318, 320, 321 (2000)); Shield Benefit Administrators Inc. v. University of Mich. Bd. of Regents, 225 Mich. App. 467, 571 N.W.2d 556 (1997). *But see* Dillon v. U-A Columbia Cablevision of Westchester, Inc., 100 N.Y.2d 525, 760 N.Y.S.2d 726, 790 N.E.2d 1155 (2003) (voluntary payment defense bars challenge to cable TV late fees even though bills mischaracterized them as "administrative fees").

410 *Id.*; Montgomery Ward Co. v. Williams, 330 Mich. 275, 47 N.W.2d 607, 611, 612 (1951) (insurance company made voluntary payment under policy). *But cf.* Randazzo v. Harris Bank Palatine, 262 F.3d 663, 670 (7th Cir. 2001) (finding a payment to be voluntary where paying party made mistake as to his legal rights under the contract because he had not read the contract).

411 Slobin v. Henry Ford Healthcare, 2002 WL 1482690, at *5 (Mich. App. July 9, 2002) (unpublished, citation limited), *rev'd on other grounds*, 666 N.W.2d 632 (Mich. 2003).

412 Criterion, Ins. Co. v. Fulgham, 247 S.E.2d 404, 406, 407 (Va.

voluntary payment doctrine applies only when the consumer pays in the face of a recognized uncertainty as to the existence or extent of the obligation, so the doctrine does not apply if the consumer was unaware of the illegality of the charge.[413]

Third, payments made under duress or compulsion are not subject to the voluntary payment defense.[414] The rationale underlying this exception is that a party under duress or threat of loss can not be expected to resort to litigation to assert a claim prior to payment.[415] Duress can be physical duress, where a person makes a payment to prevent personal injury or property damage.[416] Duress can also be economic duress, where a payment is made to prevent injury to a business or significant financial loss.[417] For example, in a class action challenging a telephone company's method of calculating a city tax charged to business customers in their monthly bills, the court rejected the phone company's argument that the claims were barred by the voluntary tax payment doctrine.[418] The implicit and real threat that telephone service would be disconnected if bills were not paid amounted to compulsion because of the potentially "disastrous effects to business" that would be caused by a loss of telephone service.[419] Likewise, in a case against a car dealer for failure to disclose that a car sold as new had in fact been previously owned by another, the court held that the purchaser did not waive her UDAP claims by continuing to pay for the car after learning of the fraud.[420] The buyer was not aware of the fraud at the time the contract was signed, and discontinuing payments she was obligated to make under the contract would have been prejudicial.[421] Compulsion or duress has also been established where the product or service paid for is a necessity, and is not reasonably available from other sources.[422] Some courts bar the doctrine if nonpayment will result in the loss of any goods or services.[423]

Consumers seeking to establish duress as an exception to the voluntary payment doctrine should focus not only on the threat of loss of the item or service for which payment was demanded, but also on other potential consequences of non-payment. For example, withholding payment is likely to result in an adverse entry on a consumer's credit report, which can impair the consumer's ability to get credit or cost the consumer thousands of dollars in higher interest payments. Also, withholding payment may make it impossible

1978) (allowing insurance company that paid claim for amounts not covered by policy because of a mistake of law to recover payment; otherwise insured would be unjustly enriched).

413 Time Warner Entertainment Co. v. Whiteman, 802 N.E.2d 886 (Ind. 2004).

414 *See* Randazzo v. Harris Bank Palatine, 262 F.3d 663, 668 n.1 (7th Cir. 2001) (lengthy discussion of circumstances that may constitute duress).

415 *See* Williams v. Consolvo, 237 Va. 608, 615, 379 S.E.2d 333 (1989) (no threat of loss, so party should have raised claims before payment); Vick v. Siegel, 191 Va. 731, 62 S.E.2d 899 (1951) (trustee demanded unlawful fee for releasing deed of trust, landowner paid fee to avoid losing buyer, court held that payment not voluntary because landowner did not have time and opportunity to challenge the fee by litigation; if he had done so he might have lost the sale).

416 *See* Randazzo v. Harris Bank Palatine, 262 F.3d 663, 668 n.1 (7th Cir. 2001).

417 *See* Getto v. City of Chicago, 86 Ill. 2d 39, 55 Ill. Dec. 519, 426 N.E.3d 844 (1981); Illinois Glass Co. v. Chicago Tel. Co., 234 Ill. 535, 539, 85 N.E. 100 (1908) (not finding duress but discussing rules); *see also* Randazzo v. Harris Bank Palatine, 262 F.3d 663, n.1 (7th Cir. 2001) (discussing cases where potential injury to business or financial interests constituted duress).

418 Getto v. City of Chicago, 86 Ill. 2d 39, 55 Ill. Dec. 519, 426 N.E.3d 844 (1981). The voluntary tax payment doctrine holds that taxes voluntarily paid can not be recovered even if the tax is illegal, absent a statute authorizing recovery.

419 *Id.* at 51 (even though telephone company had not actually threatened termination, customers' belief that service would be terminated was enough). *See also* Ross v. City of Geneva, 71 Ill. 2d 27, 15 Ill. Dec. 658, 373 N.E.2d 1342 (1978) (noting that termination of electric service would be disastrous for a business, court ruled, "[c]onfronted with the choice of payment of the surcharge or termination of [electrical] service, plaintiff, in making the payment, acted with prudence and is not barred (by the voluntary-payment doctrine) from recovery of the sums paid."). *But see* Dreyfus v. Ameritech Mobile Communications, Inc., 700 N.E.2d 162 (Ill. 1998) (cellular telephone services are not a necessity and service was available from other sources, so payment of bill containing challenged charge was not made under duress, and voluntary payment doctrine barred recovery).

420 Buechin v. Ogden Chrysler-Plymouth, Inc., 159 Ill. App. 3d 237, 250, 251, 511 N.E.2d 1330 (Ill. 1987).

421 *Id.* at 251.

422 *See* Geary v. Dominick's Finer Foods, Inc., 129 Ill. 2d 389, 135 Ill. Dec. 848, 544 N.E.2d 344 (1989) (payment of tax on sanitary napkins not voluntary because these products are necessities which could not be purchased without paying the tax); Getto v. City of Chicago, 86 Ill. 2d 39, 52, 55 Ill. Dec. 519, 426 N.E.3d 844 (1981) (telephone as a necessity); Ross v. City of Geneva, 71 Ill. 2d 27, 15 Ill. Dec. 658, 373 N.E.2d 1342 (1978) (electric service as necessity). *See also* Johnson v. City of Brockton, 391 N.E.2d 940, 942, 8 Mass. App. Ct. 80 (1979) (driver's education classes so important for teenagers that payment is considered to be involuntary). *But cf.* Corbett v. Devon Bank, 12 Ill. App. 3d 559, 299 N.E.2d 521 (Ill. 1973) (no compulsion where plaintiffs could have obtained motor vehicle license directly from the state without the objectionable charge). *But see* Hassen v. Mediaone of Greater Fla., Inc., 751 So. 2d 1289, 1290 (Fla. Dist. Ct. App. 2000) (payment deemed voluntary unless circumstances present compulsion of such a degree as to "impose a necessity of payment sufficient to overcome the mind and will of a person of ordinary firmness"); Dreyfus v. Ameritech Mobile Communications, Inc., 700 N.E.2d 162, 167 (Ill. 1998) ("the existence of a reasonable alternative source precludes any arguments about whether a particular product or service constitutes a necessity"); Smith v. Prime Cable of Chicago, 276 Ill. App. 3d 843, 213 Ill. Dec. 304, 658 N.E.2d 1325, 1332, 1333 (1995) (cable television not a necessity).

423 Time Warner Entertainment Co. v. Whiteman, 802 N.E.2d 886 (Ind. 2004).

for the consumer to go through with another transaction, such as the sale or purchase of a home.[424]

In some jurisdictions, paying under protest is evidence that the payment was not voluntary,[425] although the court may hold that it is not conclusive evidence.[426] Initiating a lawsuit to stop a party from imposing an illegal fee may constitute sufficient protest to establish that the fee was not paid voluntarily.[427]

4.2.15.6 Unclean Hands or Lack of Care by the Consumer

The consumer's failure to test drive a new car is no defense to a UDAP action.[428] Nor is the consumer's failure to inspect for termite damage a defense to an action for misrepresentation concerning a report that a home is termite free.[429] A consumer has no duty to investigate the accuracy of advertisements.[430] Fraudulently inducing a consumer to sign a contract is a UDAP violation even if reading the contract would have revealed the terms to the consumer.[431] The fact that the consumer could have found correct information in public records is not a defense.[432] A consumer's payment for a product, after the seller's demand, does not waive the consumer's right to subsequently bring a UDAP action.[433]

That the consumer has unclean hands is not a defense to a UDAP action.[434] A policyholder's false answers in an insurance application do not create a defense to a UDAP claim based on the agent's own misrepresentations, even if they would create a defense to a contract claim.[435]

4.2.15.7 Post-Transaction Waivers

Signing another document after the deception is apparent does not waive the consumer's right to sue for a UDAP violation.[436] Nevertheless, accord and satisfaction may be a valid defense to a UDAP claim.[437]

4.2.15.8 Other Contract Defenses

UDAP claims are also not barred by:

- Estoppel;[438]
- The statute of frauds;[439] and

---

424 *See* Negrin v. Norwest Mortg., 263 A.D.2d 39, 700 N.Y.S.2d 184, 193 (1999) (homeowner's voluntary payment of junk fees for mortgage payoff statement is not a defense; "[a]ny reasonable person would conclude, as the plaintiff did, that the only sane thing to do was to pay the charges rather than jeopardize the closing and the sale of her condominium"). *Accord* Dougherty v. North Fork Bank, 753 N.Y.S.2d 130 (App. Div. 2003).

425 Putnam v. Time Warner Cable, 255 Wis. 2d 447, 649 N.W.2d 626 (2001). *See also* Boykin v. Smart Corp., 669 So. 2d 939 (Ala. Ct. App. 1995) (patients' payments for photocopies of medical records without protest were voluntary and not recoverable). *But see* Cotton v. Med-Cor Health Information Solutions, Inc., 221 Ga. App. 609, 472 S.E.2d 92 (1996) (payment under protest does not preserve claim under Georgia's codification of voluntary payment doctrine); Williams v. Consolvo, 237 Va. 608, 615, 379 S.E.2d 333 (1989) (payment under protest does not save claim).

426 Dreyfus v. Ameritech Mobile Communications, Inc., 700 N.E.2d 162, 166 (Ill. 1998). *Cf.* Randazzo v. Harris Bank Palatine, 262 F.3d 663, 670 (7th Cir. 2001) (protest is particularly strong evidence of duress, but plaintiff's "protest" was not the assertion of a legal right but simply an appeal to defendant's business judgment).

427 Johnson v. City of Brockton, 391 N.E.2d 940, 942, 8 Mass. App. Ct. 80 (1979) ("[a]t no time did the plaintiffs abandon their position or acquiesce in the city's demand for payment").

428 Paces Ferry Dodge, Inc. v. Thomas, 174 Ga. App. 642, 331 S.E.2d 4 (1985).

429 Robertson v. Boyd, 88 N.C. App. 437, 363 S.E.2d 672 (1988). *See also* Little v. Stogner, 592 S.E.2d 5 (N.C. App. 2004) (jury may find consumer's reliance reasonable for purposes of fraud claim even though the truth was available in public records); Smith v. Levine, 911 S.W.2d 427 (Tex. App. 1995).

430 Sauvey v. Ford, 2003 WL 21386282 (Ohio App. June 13, 2003) (unpublished, citation limited). *See also* § 4.2.16.1, *infra.*

431 Schauer v. Gen. Motors Acceptance Corp., 819 So. 2d 809 (Fla. App. 2002).

432 Ojeda de Toca v. Wise, 748 S.W.2d 449 (Tex. 1988); ECC Parkway Joint Venture v. Baldwin, 765 S.W.2d 504 (Tex. App. 1989). *Cf.* Capiccioni v. Brennan Naperville, Inc., 339 Ill. App. 3d 927, 791 N.E.2d 553 (2003) (reversing dismissal of case where consumers alleged they contacted local official to verify seller's representation about school district boundaries); Gilmore v. Kowalkiewicz, 234 Ill. App. 3d 522, 600 N.E.2d 492 (1992) (buyer entitled to rely on seller's representation that home could be used for dental office, where ordinance was so unclear that buyer would not have learned the truth by reviewing it). *But cf.* Rendels v. Best Real Estate, Inc., 243 Ill. App. 3d 801, 612 N.E.2d 984 (1993) (failure to disclose existence of ordinance requiring hookup to sewer system not a UDAP violation where seller disclosed that city sewers were available and an assessment was possible and buyer did not inquire further); Eff v. Slusher, 2000 Mich. App. LEXIS 2151 (May 19, 2000) (unpublished, limited precedent) (not a UDAP violation to fail to disclose easement that was recorded in registry of deeds).

433 Negrin v. Norwest Mortgage, Inc., 700 N.Y.S.2d 184 (App. Div. 1999) (plaintiff did not waive UDAP claim by paying disputed fees, which was her only choice if she wanted to sell condo); Kennemore v. Bennett, 755 S.W.2d 89 (Tex. 1988). *See* § 4.2.15.5, *supra.*

434 Chow v. Aegis Mortg. Corp., 286 F. Supp. 2d 956 (N.D. Ill. 2003) (unclean hands is an equitable defense that is inapplicable to actions at law for money damages); Davis v. Wholesale Motors, Inc., 949 P.2d 1026 (Haw. App. 1997).

435 Tidelands Life Ins. Co. v. Franco, 711 S.W.2d 728 (Tex. App. 1986).

436 Teague Motor Co. v. Rowton, 84 Or. App. 72, 733 P.2d 93 (1987).

437 Jenkins v. Steakley Bros. Chevrolet Co., 712 S.W.2d 587 (Tex. App. 1986).

438 ARA Automotive Group v. Central Garage, Inc., 124 F.3d 720 (5th Cir. 1997); Kuehnhoefer v. Welch, 893 S.W.2d 689 (Tex. App. 1995) (estoppel is not a defense to a UDAP claim).

439 McClure v. Duggan, 674 F. Supp. 211 (N.D. Tex. 1987); Gaidon

- The doctrine that a contract is merged in the deed.[440]

The fact that a contract is void due to other state law violations does not make the UDAP statute inapplicable to the transaction.[441]

4.2.16 Tort Defenses Do Not Apply to Deception Claim

4.2.16.1 Contributory Negligence and Other Tort Doctrines

A UDAP claim is a statutory action, not a tort.[442] Consequently, tort defenses are inapplicable.

Deception can be found where there is no negligence.[443] A consumer's contributory negligence is not a defense to a UDAP claim.[444] For example, the consumer's failure to inspect for termite damage is not a defense to a consumer's claim concerning misrepresentations regarding a home's termite damage.[445] A UDAP claim can not be defeated because the consumer failed to use diligence in ascertaining the accuracy of the defendant's misstatements.[446] Nor is it relevant to a UDAP claim that a party to an at-will contract does not incur tort liability by terminating the contract.[447] The "learned intermediary" doctrine may limit a drug manufacturer's UDAP liability to a consumer for the effects of a drug prescribed by a physician, however.[448]

4.2.16.2 Economic Loss Rule Generally Does Not Apply to UDAP Claims

The economic loss rule, followed in most jurisdictions, restricts claims for economic damages in tort to situations in which a plaintiff has suffered either personal injury or damage to property other than damage to the defective goods themselves.[449] Under the rule, a plaintiff who can claim only economic damages without being able to show any personal or property injury will not be allowed to bring a tort action for the loss, and must look to contract, warranty, and statutory actions instead. Courts use the rule to separate contract law, "which is designed to enforce the expectancy interests of the parties," from tort law, "which imposes a duty of reasonable care and thereby encourages citizens to avoid causing physical harm to others."[450] Supporters also reason that parties to a contract have the opportunity to allocate their risks in their agreement and therefore do not need tort law to give them additional protection and compensation for a breach of contract.[451] Yet another argument

v. Guardian Life Ins. Co., 272 A.D. 2d 60, 707 N.Y.S.2d 166 (2000), *aff'd on other issues*, 96 N.Y.2d 201 (2001). *See also* Fraser Engineering Co. v. Desmond, 26 Mass. App. Ct. 99, 524 N.E.2d 110 (1988). *But cf.* Big Red, L.L.C. v. Davines S.P.A., 2002 U.S. App. LEXIS 4582 (4th Cir. Mar. 21, 2002) (unpublished, citation limited) (N.C. law) (enforceable agreement not a prerequisite to a UDAP claim, but fact that commercial entities terminated their negotiations without entering into a contract complying with statute of frauds is a factor in finding no UDAP violation); Madan v. Royal Indemnity Co., 26 Mass. App. Ct. 756, 532 N.E.2d 1214 (1989) (to allow UDAP suit for breach of an oral contract to lease real estate, without unfairness or deception, would undermine the statute of frauds).

440 Alvarado v. Bolton, 749 S.W.2d 47 (Tex. 1988); ECC Parkway Joint Venture v. Baldwin, 765 S.W.2d 504 (Tex. App. 1989).

441 Griffin v. Security Pacific Automotive Fin. Servs. Corp., 33 F. Supp. 2d 926 (D. Kan. 1998).

442 Kailin v. Armstrong, 643 N.W.2d 132 (Wis. App. 2002).

443 Heller v. Silverbranch Constr. Corp., 376 Mass. 621, 382 N.E.2d 1065 (1978); Gennari v. Weichert Co. Realtors, 148 N.J. 582, 691 A.2d 350 (1997).

444 Miller v. William Chevrolet/Geo, Inc., 326 Ill. App. 3d 642, 762 N.E.2d 1 (2001); Winston Realty Co. v. G.H.G., Inc., 314 N.C. 90, 331 S.E.2d 677 (1985); Forbes v. Par Ten Group, Inc., 99 N.C. App. 587, 394 S.E.2d 643 (1990); Robertson v. Boyd, 88 N.C. App. 437, 363 S.E.2d 672 (1988); *see also* Paces Ferry Dodge, Inc. v. Thomas, 174 Ga. App. 642, 331 S.E.2d 4 (1985); Schenck v. Ebby Halliday Real Estate, 803 S.W.2d 361 (Tex. App. 1990) (contributory negligence available only to extent explicitly allowed by statute). *But see* Delta Chevrolet, Inc. v. Wells, 187 Ga. App. 694, 371 S.E.2d 250 (1988); Gennari v. Weichert Co. Realtors, 148 N.J. 582, 691 A.2d 350 (1997) (applying state contributory negligence statute to UDAP claim). *But cf.* Campbell v. Beak, 568 S.E.2d 801 (Ga. App. 2002) (buyer's failure to exercise the diligence warranted by the circumstances may be defense, but is jury question); Hayes v. Osterman Jewelers, Inc., 2002 Ohio App. LEXIS 1868 (Apr. 19, 2002) (no UDAP violation in construing ambiguous statement as request for credit insurance where charges were clearly disclosed on consumer's monthly bill).

445 Robertson v. Boyd, 88 N.C. App. 437, 363 S.E.2d 672 (1988).

446 Miller v. William Chevrolet/Geo, Inc., 326 Ill. App. 3d 642, 762 N.E.2d 1 (2001); Duran v. Leslie Oldsmobile, 594 N.E.2d 1355 (Ill. App. Ct. 1992); Sohaey v. Van Cura, 607 N.E.2d 253 (Ill. App. Ct. 1992). *See also* § 4.2.15.6, *supra.*

447 Sullivan's Wholesale Drug v. Faryl's Pharmacy, Inc., 214 Ill. App. 3d 1073, 573 N.E.2d 1370 (1991).

448 *In re* Norplant Contraceptive Products Litigation, 165 F.3d 374 (5th Cir. 1999); Wyeth-Ayerst Laboratories Co. v. Medrano, 28 S.W.3d 87 (Tex. App. 2000). *See also* N.J. Citizen Action v. Schering-Plough Corp., 367 N.J. Super. 8, 842 A.2d 174 (App. Div. 2003) (declining to impose learned intermediary doctrine, but finding no UDAP violation where ultimate consumer is not free to act on manufacturer's advertising claims, but may only obtain prescription drug from physician). *Cf.* Perez v. Wyeth Laboratories, Inc., 161 N.J. 1, 734 A.2d 1245 (1999) (abandoning learned intermediary defense to tort claims where drug manufacturer advertises directly to consumers, but compliance with FDA labeling requirements creates rebuttable presumption that manufacturer has fulfilled duty to warn).

449 *See* National Consumer Law Center, Consumer Warranty Law § 12.2 (2d ed. 2001 and Supp.).

450 Casa Clara Condo. Ass'n v. Charley Toppino & Sons, Inc., 620 So. 2d 1244, 1246 (Fla. 1993).

451 East River S.S. Corp. v. Transamerica Delaval, Inc., 476 U.S. 858, 872, 873 (1986) ("[c]ontract law, and the law of warranty in particular, is well suited to commercial controversies of the sort involved in this case because the parties may set the terms of their own agreements"); Werwinski v. Ford Motor Co. 286

cited in favor of the economic loss rule is that it encourages the purchaser to assume or to insure against the risk of economic loss.[452]

Exceptions to the general rule exist. Most courts will not apply the economic loss rule to bar claims that the defendant fraudulently induced the transaction.[453] These courts reason that the purpose of the rule, to limit parties to contract remedies, is not promoted when fraud has undermined the consumer's ability to freely negotiate the terms and remedies of the contract.[454] Nonetheless, a significant number of cases have held that the economic loss rule will bar even those tort claims based on a contract induced by fraud, especially where the contract itself refers to the subject matter of the fraudulent representations.[455]

The rule has generally been used to bar only tort claims; most courts have held that the economic loss rule does not apply to UDAP claims.[456] UDAP claims are exempt from the economic loss rule because the rule is judicial, not legislative, and must give way to a specific legislative policy pronouncement allowing damages for economic loss.[457] In other words, by enacting a remedy for economic losses suffered by reason of an act deemed wrongful by the statute, the legislature has effectively preempted the economic loss rule for those cases covered by the act. To apply the economic loss rule to UDAP claims would effectively eviscerate the statute. The legislature could hardly have intended that the rule would bar the very claims the UDAP statute created.[458]

F.3d 661, 680 (3d Cir. 2002) (arguing that plaintiffs do not need additional tort remedies if they can be made whole under contract law); *In re* StarLink Corn Prods. Liab. Litig., 212 F. Supp. 2d 828, 839 (N.D. Ill. 2002); Prent Corp. v. Martek Holdings, Inc., 618 N.W.2d 201, 207, 46 U.C.C. Rep. 2d 68 (Wis. Ct. App. 2000) (buyers of software could have bargained for recovery of consequential damages).

452 *See, e.g.*, *In re* StarLink Corn Products Liab. Litig., 212 F. Supp. 2d 828, 839 (N.D. Ill. 2002); Budgetel Inns, Inc. v. Micros Sys., Inc., 8 F. Supp. 2d 1137, 1149 (E.D. Wis. 1998); Kailin v. Armstrong, 643 N.W.2d 132, 144 (Wis. Ct. App. 2002).

453 *See, e.g.*, Medline Indus. Inc. v. Maersk Med. Ltd., 230 F. Supp. 2d 857, 876–68 (N.D. Ill. 2002) (economic loss doctrine did not bar claim based on fraudulent inducement, notwithstanding that allegedly false statement was also in the contract); Geneva Pharm. Tech. Corp. v. Barr Labs., Inc., 201 F. Supp. 2d 236, 287, 288 (S.D.N.Y. 2002); HTP, Ltd v. Lineas Aereas Costarricenses, S.A., 685 So. 2d 1239, 1239, 1240 (Fla. 1996); Hinton v. Brooks, 820 So. 2d 325, 328 (Fla. Ct. App. 2001) (allowing home buyers' fraud counterclaim in foreclosure action); *In re* Chicago Flood Litig., 680 N.E.2d 265, 275 (Ill. 1997) (listing exceptions to economic loss rule); Minn. Stat. § 604.10(e) (economic loss rule does not bar tort actions based on fraud or intentional misrepresentation); Phoenix Controls, Inc. v. Eisenmann Corp., 644 N.W.2d 293 (table), 2002 WL 436367, at *4 (Wis. Ct. App. 2002); Kailin v. Armstrong, 643 N.W.2d 132, 145 (Wis. Ct. App. 2002); Douglas-Hanson Co. v. BF Goodrich Co., 598 N.W.2d 262, 268 (Wis. Ct. App. 1999), *aff'd*, 233 Wis. 2d 276, 607 N.W.2d 621 (2000). *See also* Duncan v. Kasim, Inc., 810 So. 2d 968, 970 (Fla. Ct. App. 2002) (conversion and civil theft claims arose outside the terms of the contract and therefore were not barred by the rule); Digicorp, Inc. v. Ameritech Corp., 662 N.W.2d 652 (Wis. 2003) (recognizing fraud in inducement as exception to economic loss doctrine, limited to misrepresentations occurring before contract formation that are not interwoven into the contract).

454 *See, e.g.*, Budgetel Inns, Inc. v. Micros Sys., Inc., 8 F. Supp. 2d 1137, 1138 (E.D. Wis. 1998) ("[d]ue diligence can not ensure against intentional dishonesty"); HTP, Ltd v. Lineas Aereas Costarricenses, S.A., 685 So. 2d 1239, 1239, 1240 (Fla. 1996) (arguing that "the interest protected by fraud is society's need for true factual statements in important human relationships, primarily commercial or business relationships"); Kailin v. Armstrong, 643 N.W.2d 132, 145 (Wis. Ct. App. 2002); Douglas-Hanson Co. v. BF Goodrich Co. 598 N.W.2d 262, 268 (Wis. Ct. App. 1999), *aff'd*, 233 Wis. 2d 276, 607 N.W.2d 621 (2000).

455 *See, e.g.*, Werwinski v. Ford Motor Co., 286 F.3d 661, 680 (3d Cir. 2002) (economic loss doctrine applies to fraudulent concealment claims); Hoseline, Inc. v. U.S.A. Diversified Prods., Inc., 40 F.3d 1198, 1200 (11th Cir. 1994) (rule barred buyer's civil theft and fraud claims alleging that seller had misrepresented the amount of product); Excess Risk Underwriters, Inc. v. Lafayette Life Ins. Co., 208 F. Supp. 2d 1310, 1318, 1319 (S.D. Fla. 2002) (ruling that defendant's fraudulent inducement claim was not separate and distinct from the terms of the contract itself); Nelson Distrib., Inc. v. Stewart Warner Indus. Balancers, 808 F. Supp. 684, 688 (D. Minn. 1992) (rule barred buyer's fraudulent inducement claim); Robinson Helicopter Co. v. Dana Corp., 2003 WL 164734, at *12–*14 (Cal. Ct. App. Jan. 24, 2003) (fraud allegations were so intertwined with contract performance that plaintiff could not allege separate damages, therefore economic loss ruled applied to intentional fraud claim), *review granted, opinion superseded*, 68 P.3d 344 (Cal. 2003); Tietsworth v. Harley-Davidson, Inc., 677 N.W.2d 233 (Wis. 2004).

456 Samuels v. King Motor Co. of Ft. Lauderdale, 782 So. 2d 489 (Fla. App. 2001); Invo Florida, Inc. v. Somerset Venturer, Inc., 751 So. 2d 1263, 1267 (Fla. Ct. App. 2000); Comptech Int'l v. Milam Commerce Park Ltd., 753 So. 2d 1219 (Fla. App. 1999); Delgado v. J.W. Courtesy Pontiac GMC-Truck, 693 So. 2d 602 (Fla. App. 1997); Sarkis v. Pafford Oil Co., 697 So. 2d 524, 528 (Fla. Ct. App. 1997); Oppenheimer v. York Int'l, 2002 WL 31409949 (Pa. Ct. Com. Pl. Oct. 25, 2002) (economic loss rule does not apply to intentional torts or to UDAP claims based on an alleged intentional misrepresentation); Zwieran v. General Motors Corp., 58 Pa. D. & C.4th 251, 2002 WL 31053835 (Pa. Ct. Com. Pl. Sept. 11, 2002) (economic loss rule did not apply to UDAP claim); Kailin v. Armstrong, 643 N.W.2d 132 (Wis. App. 2002). *See* National Consumer Law Center, Consumer Warranty Law Ch. 12 (2d ed. 2001 and Supp.) (discussion of economic loss rule). *See also* Sebago, Inc. v. Beazer East, Inc., 18 F. Supp. 2d 70 (D. Mass. 1998) (striking plaintiff's negligence and strict liability claims on economic loss rule grounds, but allowing claim under Massachusetts consumer protection statute); Tietsworth v. Harley-Davidson, Inc., 661 N.W.2d 450 (Wis. Ct. App. 2003) (UDAP statute may be used to redress a purely economic loss), *rev'd on other grounds*, 677 N.W.2d 233 (Wis. 2004).

457 Delgado v. J.W. Courtesy Pontiac GMC-Truck, 693 So. 2d 602, 611 (Fla. Ct. App. 1997).

458 *See* Oppenheimer v. York Int'l, 2002 WL 31409949, at *6 (Oct. 25, 2002) (economic loss rule does not apply to intentional torts or to UDAP claims based on an alleged intentional misrepresentation); Zwieran v. General Motors Corp., 58 Pa. D. & C.4th 251, 2002 WL 31053835, at *7 (Pa. Ct. Com. Pl. Sept. 11, 2002)

Nonetheless, in *Werwinski v. Ford Motor Co.*,[459] the Third Circuit held that the rule barred claims for economic loss for breach of warranty that were asserted under Pennsylvania's UDAP statute.[460] According to the court, Pennsylvania is in the minority that applies the economic loss doctrine to fraud claims,[461] statutory fraud is sufficiently similar to common law fraud that it should be bound by the same common law rules. Trial courts,[462] even including a district court in the Third Circuit,[463] have refused to apply the decision to UDAP claims, and in a later decision, the Third Circuit itself has retreated from its ruling.[464] In addition to the Third Circuit, courts in Connecticut[465] and Wisconsin[466] have used the economic loss rule to bar warranty-type claims asserted under UDAP statutes in commercial cases. The rule and its exceptions are discussed in detail in National Consumer Law Center, *Consumer Warranty Law* §§ 12.2.2–12.2.6 (2d ed. 2001 and Supp.).

(economic loss rule did not apply to UDAP claim). *See also* FTC v. Pantron I Corp., 33 F.3d 1088 (9th Cir. 1994) (economic loss rule would defeat purpose of FTC Act).

459 286 F.3d 661, 674 (3d Cir. 2002) (Pennsylvania law).

460 Cases from Pennsylvania state courts allowing economic loss damages for UDAP violations include: McCauslin v. Reliance Furniture Co., 751 A.2d 683 (Pa. Super. 2000); Sewart v. Lockhart, 699 A.2d 755 (Pa. Super. 2000); Johnson v. Hyundai Motor Am., 698 A.2d 631 (Pa. Super. 1997); Oppenheimer v. York Int'l, 2002 WL 31409949 (Pa. Com. Pl. Oct. 25, 2002) (explicitly rejecting *Werwinski*).

461 *But see* Aikens v. Balt. & Ohio R. Co., 501 A.2d 277 (Pa. Super. 1985) (in adopting economic loss doctrine for negligence, court states that it does not apply to intentional torts); Teledyne Tech. Inc. v. Freedom Forge Corp., 2002 WL 748898, at *19 (Pa. Ct. Com. Pl. Apr. 19, 2002) (economic loss doctrine does not apply to intentional misrepresentation); Paola Amico v. Radius Communications, 2001 WL 1807924 (Pa. Ct. Com. Pl. Jan. 9, 2001) (economic loss doctrine does not apply to fraud).

462 Oppenheimer v. York Int'l, 2002 WL 31409949 (Pa. Ct. Com. Pl. Oct. 25, 2002) (economic loss rule does not apply to intentional torts or to UDAP claims based on an alleged intentional misrepresentation); Zwieran v. General Motors Corp., 58 Pa. D. & C.4th 251, 2002 WL 31053835 (Pa. Ct. Com. Pl. Sept. 11, 2002) (economic loss rule did not apply to UDAP claim based on allegedly defective front car seats). *See also* Becker v. Chicago Title Ins. Co., 2004 WL 228672, at *13 (E.D. Pa. Feb. 4, 2004) (declining to apply economic loss doctrine to UDAP claim at motion to dismiss stage).

463 O'Keefe v. Mercedes-Benz USA, 214 F.R.D. 266 (E.D. Pa. 2003).

464 Samuel-Bassett v. Kia Motors America, Inc., 357 F.3d 392, 400, 401 n.5 (3d Cir. 2004) (noting that briefing in *Werwinski* had been inadequate and suggesting that district court reexamine question on remand).

465 Flagg Energy Dev. Corp. v. General Motors Corp., 709 A.2d 1075, 1088 (Conn. 1998) (economic loss rule barred plaintiff's claims under Connecticut unfair trade practices act, where claims depended on same facts as contract claims).

466 Weather Shield Mfg., Inc. v. PPF Indus., Inc., 1998 WL 469913, at *4 (W.D. Wis. June 11, 1998) (treating statutory fraud claim as barred by economic loss rule).

4.2.17 Subsequent Clarification Does Not Prevent Deception

4.2.17.1 Subsequent Disclosures Can Not Correct Earlier Deceptive Claims

A practice is deceptive even if subsequently clarified.[467] Point of sale disclosure is not sufficient to clarify deceptive media advertising.[468] It is deceptive to place statements in a product's instruction manual at variance with advertising claims.[469] Even small print accompanying and clarifying a claim can not save a misleading representation.[470] Interest rate disclosures of a "per annum" rate based on a 360-day year is deceptive even though the higher, 365-day APR is subsequently disclosed.[471]

Subsequent disclosure on a label can not correct failure to disclose the same information in advertising.[472] If advertising is at variance with the nature of an airline flight, the advertising is deceptive even if the flight meets all federal regulations.[473] Even where the certificate of title and other written documents reveal the proper age of a vehicle, con-

467 Idaho Admin. Code § 04.02.01.041; Code Miss. Rules of 24 000 002 Rule 17; Resort Car Rental Sys., Inc. v. FTC, 518 F.2d 962 (9th Cir.), *cert. denied sub nom.* Mackenzie v. United States, 423 U.S. 827 (1975); Exposition Press, Inc. v. FTC, 295 F.2d 869 (2d Cir. 1961), *cert. denied*, 370 U.S. 917 (1962); Carter Products, Inc. v. FTC, 186 F.2d 821 (7th Cir. 1951); FTC v. Gill, 71 F. Supp. 2d 1030 (C.D. Cal. 1999), *aff'd on other grounds*, 265 F.3d 944 (9th Cir. 2001); MacMillan Inc., 96 F.T.C. 208 (1980); Madsen v. Western Am. Mortg. Co., 694 P.2d 1228 (Ariz. Ct. App. 1984); DeWitt County Electric Coop., Inc. v. Parks, 1 S.W.3d 96 (Tex. 1999).

468 Prata v. Superior Court, 91 Cal. App. 4th 1128, 111 Cal. Rptr. 2d 296 (2001); State v. Amoco Oil Co., 97 Wis. 2d 226, 293 N.W.2d 487 (1980); Robinson v. Avis Rent A Car Sys., Inc., 106 Wash. App. 104, 22 P.3d 818 (2001); Office of the Attorney General of the State of Tennessee, Opinion No. 98-026, 1998 Tenn. AG LEXIS 26 (Jan. 26, 1998) (later proper disclosure can not cure inaccurate odometer disclosure). *See also* Code Miss. Rules 24 000 002 Rule 11 (statements contradicting a contract or other written statement are deceptive).

469 Sears Roebuck & Co., 95 F.T.C. 406 (1980); *see* Gasperoni v. Metabolife, 2000 U.S. Dist. LEXIS 20879 (E.D. Mich. Sept. 27, 2000) (providing accurate supplemental information elsewhere does not cure inaccurate label); *also* Montgomery Ward Co., 70 F.T.C. 52 (1966), *aff'd*, 379 F.2d 666 (7th Cir. 1967).

470 FTC v. Brown & Williamson Tobacco Corp., 778 F.2d 35 (D.C. Cir. 1985).

471 Chern v. Bank of Am., 15 Cal. 3d 866, 544 P.2d 1310, 127 Cal. Rptr. 110 (1976). *But see* Heidt v. Potamkin Chrysler Plymouth Inc., 181 Ga. App. 903, 354 S.E.2d 440 (1987) (consumer should have read contract which contradicted oral claims).

472 Thompson Medical Co., 104 F.T.C. 648 (1984), *aff'd*, 791 F.2d 189 (D.C. Cir. 1986), *cert. denied*, 479 U.S. 1086 (1987); American Home Products Corp., 98 F.T.C. 136 (1981), *aff'd*, 695 F.2d 681 (3d Cir. 1983); *see also* Carter Products Inc. v. FTC, 186 F.2d 821 (7th Cir. 1951).

473 Brunwasser v. Trans World Airlines, Inc., 541 F. Supp. 1338 (W.D. Pa. 1982). *See* § 2.5.5, *supra* (federal preemption issues).

flicting prior oral claims are deceptive.[474] Oral misrepresentations concerning insurance policy coverage are not cured by proper disclosure in the insurance policy.[475] Lulling the victim into a false sense of security through oral misrepresentations is deceptive even if the written contract has truthful disclosures.[476]

The failure to disclose information can not be cured by proper disclosure where that disclosure is not timely. Disclosure of important missing information just as the contract is being signed does not prevent the previous failure to disclose from being deceptive.[477] Recording of material information at the registry of deeds does not cure failure to point out that information to the consumer, even where the consumer is expected to perform a title search before purchasing the home.[478] Even where misrepresentations in a real estate sale were corrected prior to closing, the buyer may still bring a UDAP action for damages.[479] That an offer is correctly represented in certain written material does not prevent a UDAP challenge to misrepresentations and omissions concerning that offer occurring elsewhere in the transaction.[480]

4.2.17.2 Subsequent Consumer Conduct or Other Occurrence Can Not Cure Deception

Signing another document after the deception is apparent does not waive the consumer's right to sue for a UDAP violation.[481] When a consumer leased a used car represented as new, discovered that the car was used, but still purchased it at the end of the lease term, the consumer did not waive his right to bring a UDAP action for the original deception.[482] Similarly, when a car proved not to be as represented, and the consumer first revoked acceptance, but then reaccepted the car and continued to use it, the consumer still had a UDAP claim, even if he lost rights under the Uniform Commercial Code.[483]

A tenant's ability to view an apartment does not cure a landlord's failure to disclose that the apartment is unlicensed.[484] An incorrect statement regarding the law is not cured by a subsequent law change that brings the statement into conformity with the new law.[485] Postponement of a foreclosure sale does not sufficiently cure the lack of notice of that sale, where that lack of notice was found to be a UDAP violation.[486]

Knowing about defects, yet going ahead with a home closing, did not foreclose subsequent UDAP claims in one case. The extent of the problems were not known at the closing, other problems were not apparent, and the homeowner was told that certain defects would be repaired.[487] Likewise, the buyers' independent investigation of a builder did not relieve their real estate broker of liability for misrepresentations about the home.[488] Their investigation did not give them reason to think they should not rely on the broker's statements, and proof of actual deception is unnecessary in any event.

4.2.17.3 The Georgia Exception

Georgia middle-level appellate courts adopt a position at variance with other jurisdictions and at variance with established FTC precedent.[489] They find that contract terms that clearly state certain aspects of a transaction cure prior oral misrepresentations about those aspects of the transaction. The consumer has the responsibility to read the contract and

474 Gonzalez v. Global Truck & Equip. Inc., 625 S.W.2d 348 (Tex. Civ. App. 1981).

475 Glazewski v. Allstate Ins. Co., 126 Ill. App. 3d 401, 466 N.E.2d 1151 (1984). *See also* Marshall v. Citicorp Mortgage Inc., 601 So. 2d 669 (La. Ct. App. 1992).

476 Miller v. William Chevrolet/Geo, Inc., 326 Ill. App. 3d 642, 762 N.E.2d 1 (2001).

477 Heastie v. Community Bank, 690 F. Supp. 716 (N.D. Ill. 1988); Phillips v. Dukes (Matter of Dukes), 24 B.R. 404 (Bankr. E.D. Mich. 1982); *see also* Miller v. William Chevrolet/Geo, Inc., 326 Ill. App. 3d 642, 762 N.E.2d 1 (2001) (disclosures after contract signed have no effect). *But see* Sheppard v. GMAC Mortg. Corp., 299 B.R. 753 (Bankr. E.D. Pa. 2003) (no UDAP violation where consumers were aware that final terms were different from those originally described).

478 Ojeda de Toca v. Wise, 748 S.W.2d 449 (Tex. 1988).

479 Sonnenberg v. Security Mgmt., 325 Md. 117, 599 A.2d 820 (1992). *But see* McGraw v. Loyola Ford, Inc., 124 Md. App. 560, 723 A.2d 502 (1999) (no violation where dealer made correct oral disclosure and also corrected erroneous written disclosure); Lunde v. Chase, 224 Wis. 2d 642, 590 N.W.2d 282 (Wis. App. 1999) (unpublished limited precedent opinion, text available on LEXIS at 1999 Wisc. App. LEXIS 1) (no UDAP liability where buyer learned true facts before entering into contract).

480 Staub v. Outdoor World Corp., Clearinghouse No. 45,940 (Pa. C.P. Lancaster Cty. 1987).

481 Teague Motor Co. v. Rowton, 84 Or. App. 72, 733 P.2d 93 (1987). *See also* Myers v. Liberty Lincoln-Mercury, Inc., 89 N.C. App. 335, 365 S.E.2d 663 (1988) (consumer signing sham document whose very nature was misrepresented to consumer does not cure misrepresentation in first contract signed by consumer).

482 Wilkins v. Roach Cadillac, Inc., 7 Kan. App. 2d 8, 637 P.2d 458 (1981).

483 Greene v. Waddell, 657 S.W.2d 589 (Ky. Ct. App. 1983).

484 Golt v. Phillips, 308 Md. 1, 517 A.2d 328 (1986).

485 Winton v. Johnson & Dix Fuel Corp., 515 A.2d 371 (Vt. 1986).

486 Smith v. Commercial Banking Corp., 866 F.2d 576 (3d Cir. 1989) (Pennsylvania law).

487 Masure v. Donnelly, 962 F.2d 128 (1st Cir. 1992) (Maine law).

488 Gennari v. Weichert Co. Realtors, 148 N.J. 582, 691 A.2d 350 (1997).

489 Boynton v. State Farm Mut. Automobile Ins. Co., 207 Ga. App. 756, 429 S.E.2d 304 (1993); Rivergate Corp. v. McIntosh, 421 S.E.2d 737 (Ga. App. 1992) (failure to read auto lease agreement bars claim that dealer misrepresented terms); Castellana v. Conyers Toyota, Inc., 200 Ga. App. 161, 407 S.E.2d 64 (1991); Creditthrift of Am., Inc. v. Whitley, 190 Ga. App. 833, 380 S.E.2d 489 (1989); Delta Chevrolet, Inc. v. Wells, 187 Ga. App. 694, 371 S.E.2d 250 (1988).

ferret out inconsistencies in the seller's oral statements. If the consumer is not sophisticated and aggressive enough in protecting himself or herself from fraud, the seller is absolved from its misrepresentations. In effect, sellers have *carte blanche* to lie to consumers as long as information is eventually provided whereby a diligent consumer could discover the truth. Even these Georgia courts, however, recognize this approach does not apply if the seller engaged in practices to prevent the consumer from reading the contract prior to signing.[490]

4.2.18 Immediate Customer's Deception Unnecessary

A practice can be deceptive even if the immediate customer is not deceived.[491] A dealer's misrepresentation to a finance company that it had authority to enter into a financing contract on behalf of the consumer, and its false statements to a credit reporting agency, would be a UDAP violation even though the representations were not made to the consumer.[492] A wholesaler's labeling or advertising is actionable even though the wholesaler's customers (retailers) are not deceived, but only consumers are. Privity of contract is not required to bring a UDAP action.[493] Thus, where a developer misrepresented to buyers that they would have access across a landowner's property, resulting in damage to the landowner due to unauthorized entry, the landowner could assert a UDAP claim against the developer even though there was no claim that any of the misrepresentations had been directed to the landowner.[494] Likewise, homeowners whose well water was polluted by additives in gasoline could sue the manufacturer even though the pollution was caused primarily by other consumers' purchase of the gasoline in reliance on the manufacturer's advertisements.[495] And a consumer may have a UDAP claim against a manufacturer whose deception causes a builder to install a defective product on the consumer's home, even if the deceptive statements are communicated only to the builder.[496] But a federal court interpreting the Kansas UDAP statute held that a bank's misrepresentation to a debt collector that the consumer owed a debt was not a violation because it was made in connection with the commercial transaction between the bank and the collector, not in connection with a consumer transaction.[497]

An area of growing importance is the issue of whether home inspectors, land surveyors, termite inspectors or other experts hired to report to the seller or broker can be liable to a purchaser if the report contains misrepresentations or fails to disclose important information. In one case a court found a pest inspector liable to a consumer for misrepresentations that a home was free of insect infestation even though the inspector reported only to the seller and broker.[498] But another case, while recognizing that there was no requirement that parties in a UDAP action have privity of contract, held that a surveyor did not have to disclose the significance of a true report to the consumer where the land survey company was not working for the consumer and had no business relationship with the consumer.[499] Civil conspiracy claims should be considered as a way of bringing in parties who enable fraudulent transactions to proceed but do not themselves deal directly with the consumer.[500]

In a highly interesting case, a distributor was found to have a duty to warn consumers that the retailer the consumers were doing business with was having financial difficulties. The distributor should have warned consumers that the retailer might not forward their payment to the distributor, leaving them holding the bag.[501] Query whether aluminum siding manufacturers or distributors have the same responsibility to warn consumers about fly-by-night aluminum siding installers.

4.2.19 Oral Deceptions and Not Just Advertised Deceptions Are Actionable

There is no merit to the argument occasionally made by sellers that UDAP statutes apply only to media advertising, and that oral representations not preceded by media adver-

490 Rivergate Corp. v. McIntosh, 205 Ga. App. 189, 421 S.E.2d 737 (1992); Creditthrift of Am., Inc. v. Whitley, 190 Ga. App. 833, 380 S.E.2d 489 (1989); Delta Chevrolet, Inc. v. Wells, 187 Ga. App. 694, 371 S.E.2d 250 (1988).

491 FTC v. Winsted Hosiery Co., 258 U.S. 483 (1922); Marietta Mfg. Co. v. FTC, 50 F.2d 641 (7th Cir. 1931); Prata v. Superior Court, 91 Cal. App. 4th 1128, 111 Cal. Rptr. 2d 296 (2001); Seligman v. First Nat'l Inv., Inc., 184 Ill. App. 3d 1053, 540 N.E.2d 1057 (1989) (deception does not require someone to be actually deceived, under explicit provisions of Illinois law).

492 Fisher v. Quality Hyundai, Inc., 2002 U.S. Dist. LEXIS 407 (N.D. Ill. Jan. 8, 2002).

493 *See* § 4.2.15.3, *supra*.

494 Hall v. Walter, 969 P.2d 224 (Colo. 1998).

495 *In re* Methyl Tertiary Butyl Ether, 175 F. Supp. 2d 593 (S.D.N.Y. 2001).

496 Shannon v. Boise Cascade Corp., 208 Ill. 2d 517, 805 N.E.2d 213 (Ill. 2004).

497 Lowe v. Surpas Resource Corp., 253 F. Supp. 2d 1209 (D. Kan. 2003).

498 Raudebaugh v. Action Pest Control, Inc., 59 Or. App. 166, 650 P.2d 1006 (1982).

499 Nei v. Boston Survey Consultants, 388 Mass. 320, 446 N.E.2d 681 (1983). *See also* Estep v. Johnson, 123 Ohio App. 3d 307, 704 N.E.2d 58 (1998) (towing company's misrepresentation to state motor vehicle department, which enabled it to sell consumer's car, was not a UDAP violation because it did not deceive the consumer).

500 *See* §§ 5.5.5.5, 5.5.5.6, 6.5.2.3, *infra*.

501 Temborius v. Slatkin, 157 Mich. App. 587, 403 N.W.2d 821 (1986).

tising are not actionable.[502] However, one court has held that the statements must be made in a sales promotion context, so testimony before Congress can not be the basis of a UDAP claim.[503] And one of Wisconsin's UDAP statutes, its false advertising statute, applies only to statements made to the public, so does not cover private communications made to a party with whom the seller has already contracted.[504]

4.2.20 Money-Back Guarantee Does Not Sanitize Fraud

Sometimes a defendant argues that because it offered a money-back guarantee its misrepresentations are not actionable. A number of courts have rejected this theory.[505] Fraud artists know that many consumers will not seek a refund even when the product turns out to be worthless: they will have lost the receipt or the seller's address, will be unsure of their right to a refund, or will be too busy or embarrassed. Few consumers would buy a product knowing it was worthless and that therefore they would have to get a refund of the purchase price.

502 Barnett v. Coppell North Texas Court, Ltd., 123 S.W.3d 804 (Tex. App. 2003); Grube v. Daun, 173 Wis. 2d 30, 496 N.W.2d 106 (Ct. App. 1992); Bonn v. Haubrich, 123 Wis. App. 168, 366 N.W.2d 503 (1985). *See also* State v. Automatic Merchandisers, 64 Wis. 2d 659, 221 N.W.2d 683 (1974). *But see* Commonwealth v. Percudani, 844 A.2d 35 (Pa. Commw. Ct. 2004) (mistakenly interpreting one subsection of UDAP statute's list of prohibited practices to apply only to advertisements). *But cf.* Mayville Die & Tool, Inc. v. Weller Mach. Co., 2001 Wisc. App. LEXIS 1224 (Nov. 29, 2001) (unpublished, citation limited) (UDAP statute that prohibits false advertising to the public can apply to representations made to an individual but not to parties that have an ongoing business relationship, *i.e.*, a representation made by a distributor to its supplier).

503 Group Health Plan, Inc. v. Philip Morris Inc., 68 F. Supp. 2d 1064 (D. Minn. 1999) (tobacco executives' statements to Congress, even if deceptive, could not be basis of UDAP claim).

504 Kailin v. Armstrong, 643 N.W.2d 132 (Wis. App. 2002).

505 FTC v. Think Achievement Corp., 312 F.3d 259 (7th Cir. 2002); FTC v. Pantron I Corp., 33 F.3d 1088, 1103 (9th Cir. 1994) ("Because even many unsatisfied customers will not take advantage of a money-back guarantee, a company which has engaged in consumer fraud would be able to retain a significant portion of the proceeds simply by making a largely illusory money-back offer."); FTC v. SlimAmerica, Inc., 77 F. Supp. 2d 1263, 1273 (S.D. Fla. 1999); Mountz v. Global Vision Prods., Inc., 770 N.Y.S.2d 603 (Sup. Ct. 2003). *See also* Montgomery Ward & Co. v. FTC, 379 F.2d 666, 671 (7th Cir. 1967) (a general company policy of a money-back guarantee can not excuse false advertising, as "[a]nything might then be advertised as long as unsatisfied customers were returned their money"). *See also* Kiley v. Petsmart, 80 P.3d 1179 (Kan. App. 2003) (allowing UDAP claim to proceed even though seller offered to replace mismarked used goods with new); Goshen v. Mut. Life Ins., 98 N.Y.2d 314, 774 N.E.2d 1190, 1197, 746 N.Y.S.2d 858 (2002) (consumers stated UDAP claim even though seller offered 30-day trial period), *rev'g in relevant part* Scott v. Bell Atlantic Corp., 282 A.D.2d 180, 726 N.Y.S.2d 60 (2001) (finding no UDAP violation in light of free trial period for services and right to cancel without obligation).

4.3 Unfairness

4.3.1 General

Many state UDAP statutes, patterning themselves after the FTC Act, prohibit not only deceptive but also "unfair" acts or practices. This unfairness standard reaches various abusive business practices that are not deceptive. While deception is a broad standard, particularly when the failure to disclose is aggressively challenged as a deceptive practice, certain practices do not mislead, but only take advantage of consumers. In states providing a private right of action for unfair practices, consumers are given a highly flexible remedy that can be used innovatively.[506]

When courts formulate general standards as to what practices are unfair, there is a surprising amount of variation. The FTC uses an unfairness standard it adopted in 1980 and that Congress codified in 1994. A few courts utilize this standard as well. Most state courts use what is known as the "*S&H*" standard of unfairness developed by the FTC in the 1960s and 1970s. Moreover, individual states sometimes develop their own unique definitions of unfairness. These varying general standards are set out at § 4.3.2, *infra* (the current FTC standard), and at §§ 4.3.3, 4.3.5–4.3.7, *infra* (various standards under state UDAP statutes).

The rest of this section is devoted to specific types of practices that are found to be unfair:

- Unfair provisions in adhesion contracts;[507]
- Systematic breaches of contracts;[508]
- Coercive high-pressure sales and collection tactics;[509]
- Taking advantage of disparate knowledge;[510]
- Taking advantage of a vulnerable group;[511]
- Illegal conduct;[512]
- Misuse of a special status;[513]
- Taking advantage of an emergency situation;[514] and
- Unconscionable conduct.[515]

506 *See* Curtis Mfg. Co. v. Plastic-Clip Corp., 888 F. Supp. 1212 (D.N.H. 1994) (New Hampshire UDAP statute's list of unfair and deceptive acts is non-exhaustive, and the facts can establish that other conduct is unfair).

507 *See* § 4.3.4, *infra.*

508 *See* § 4.3.5, *infra.*

509 *See* § 4.3.6, *infra.*

510 *See* § 4.3.7, *infra.*

511 *See* § 4.3.8, *infra.*

512 *See* § 4.3.9, *infra.*

513 *See* § 4.3.10, *infra.*

514 *See* § 4.3.11, *infra.*

515 *See* §§ 4.3.12, 4.4, *infra.*

4.3.2 The Current FTC Unfairness Standard

4.3.2.1 Standard Enacted by Congress in 1994

The FTC's 1994 Reauthorization Act defines those unfair practices that the FTC can declare unlawful:

> The Commission shall have no authority [through FTC adjudications or rulemaking] to declare unlawful an act or practice on the grounds that such act or practice is unfair unless the act or practice causes or is likely to cause substantial injury to consumers which is not reasonably avoidable by consumers themselves and not outweighed by countervailing benefits to consumers or to competition. In determining whether an act or practice is unfair, the Commission may consider established public policies as evidence to be considered with all other evidence. Such public policy considerations may not serve as a primary basis for such determination.[516]

The Senate Report provides the most extensive legislative history of this provision:

> This section is intended to codify, as a statutory limitation on unfair acts or practices, the principles of the FTC's December 17, 1980, policy statement on unfairness, reaffirmed by a letter from the FTC dated March 5, 1982. Since the FTC's policy statement itself is based on the FTC's decided cases and rules, this section codifies existing law.
>
> * * *
>
> Consumer injury may be "substantial" under this section if a relatively small harm is inflicted on a large number of consumers or if a greater harm is inflicted on a relatively small number of consumers. In accordance with the FTC's December 17, 1980, letter, substantial injury is not intended to encompass merely trivial or speculative harm. In most cases, substantial injury would involve monetary or economic harm or unwarranted health and safety risks. Emotional impact and more subjective types of harm alone are not intended to make an injury unfair.
>
> In determining whether a substantial consumer injury is outweighed by the countervailing benefits of a practice, the Committee does not intend that the FTC quantify the detrimental and beneficial effects of the practice in every case. In many instances, such a numerical benefit-cost analysis would be unnecessary; in other cases, it may be impossible. This section would require, however, that the FTC carefully evaluate the benefits and costs of each exercise of its unfairness authority, gathering and considering reasonably available evidence.[517]

As stated in the above-quoted Senate Report, the congressionally-mandated unfairness standard is a codification of the unfairness standard the Commission itself adopted in a December 17, 1980 letter from the five commissioners to the Consumer Subcommittee of the Senate Committee on Commerce, Science and Transportation,[518] and in a "Companion Statement on the Commission's Consumer Unfairness Jurisdiction" dated March 5, 1982.[519] That standard has also been utilized in a number of FTC cases and rules,[520] and has been approved by the D.C. Circuit and the Eleventh Circuit.[521] The Comptroller of the Currency, which enforces the FTC Act against national banks, has adopted the FTC's standard.[522]

4.3.2.2 Substantial Consumer Injury

To be unfair under the FTC Act, an act or practice must cause or be "likely to cause" substantial injury to consumers.[523] Substantial injury must not be trivial or merely speculative harm, but will usually involve monetary harm or unwarranted health and safety risks.[524] Emotional or other

516 The Federal Trade Commission Act Amendments of 1994, Pub. L. No. 103-312 § 9, *adding a new* 15 U.S.C. § 45(n) (Aug. 26, 1994).

517 Sen. Rep. No. 130, 103d Cong., 2d Sess. 12 (1994), *reprinted in* 1994 U.S.C.C.A.N. 1787–88; *see also* H. Conf. Rep. No. 617, 103d Cong., 2d Sess. 11 (1994), *reprinted in* 1994 U.S.C.C.A.N. 1797.

518 Reauthorization of the Federal Trade Commission Before the Senate Comm. on Commerce, Science and Transportation, 97th Cong., 2d Sess. 23 (1982).

519 *Id.* at 28; *see also* Michael M. Greenfield, *Unfairness Under Section 5 of the FTC Act and Its Impact on State Law*, 46 Wayne L. Rev. 1869 (Winter 2000) (history of FTC's policy statement).

520 *See* §§ 4.3.4–4.3.10, *infra.*

521 Orkin Exterminating Co. v. FTC, 849 F.2d 1354 (11th Cir. 1988), *cert. denied*, 488 U.S. 1041 (1989); American Fin. Servs. Ass'n v. FTC, 767 F.2d 957 (D.C. Cir. 1985), *cert. denied*, 475 U.S. 1011 (1986); *see also* FTC v. Atlantex Assocs., 1987-2 Trade Cases ¶ 67,788 (S.D. Fla. 1987).

522 OCC Advisory Letter 2002-3, Guidance on Unfair or Deceptive Acts or Practices (Mar. 22, 2002). *See also* OCC Advisory Letter 2003-2, Guidelines for National Banks to Guard Against Predatory and Abusive Lending Practices (Feb. 21, 2003) (applying unfairness analysis to predatory lending practices).

523 15 U.S.C. § 45(n).

524 Sen. Rep. No. 130, 103d Cong., 2d Sess. 12 (1994), *reprinted in* 1994 U.S.C.C.A.N. 1787–88; *see also* H. Conf. Rep. No. 617, 103d Cong., 2d Sess. 11 (1994), *reprinted in* 1994 U.S.C.C.A.N. 1797; Reauthorization of the Federal Trade Commission Before the Senate Comm. on Commerce, Science and Transportation, 97th Cong., 2d Sess. 23, 25, 29 (1982), *citing to* Philip Morris Inc., 82 F.T.C. 16 (1973); Tungate v. MacLean-Stevens Studios, 1998 ME 162, 714 A.2d 792 (Me. 1998) (price differential as small as $1.25 caused by undisclosed commission is not a substantial injury under UDAP statute).

subjective harm alone will not ordinarily make a practice unfair,[525] although invasion of privacy may be a substantial injury.[526] Consumer injury may be "substantial" if a relatively small harm is inflicted on a large number of consumers or if a greater harm is inflicted on a relatively small number of consumers.[527]

It is significant that this definition refers to a practice that causes "or is *likely* to cause" injury. Risk of harm is thus sufficient; there need not be actual proof of injury, and the injury need not yet have occurred.[528]

The nature of the seller's actions or culpability is not the issue, but rather it is the extent of the injury to consumers. For example, the D.C. Circuit rejected creditor arguments that "unfairness" is limited to situations of seller misconduct or overreaching, such as practices involving seller deception, coercion, or withholding of material information.[529] The court pointed to the FTC's Holder Rule[530] as precedent for the FTC's authority to find unfair an allocation of post-purchase remedies.

Even when the seller does nothing wrong, a practice can be unfair "where the seller takes advantage of an existing obstacle which prevents free consumer choice from effectuating a self-correcting market."[531] The D.C. Circuit found such an imperfect market in the extension of consumer credit because consumers can not bargain over the contract's creditor remedies and because creditors have no incentive to compete on the basis of the creditor remedies offered. A creditor remedy can thus be unfair even if it does not result from the creditor's deception, coercion, or nondisclosure, as long as the remedy causes substantial consumer injury.

525 Sen. Rep. No. 130, 103d Cong., 2d Sess. 12 (1994), *reprinted in* 1994 U.S.C.C.A.N. 1787–88; *see also* H. Conf. Rep. No. 617, 103d Cong., 2d Sess. 11 (1994), *reprinted in* 1994 U.S.C.C.A.N. 1797.

526 FTC v. ReverseAuction.com, Inc., 5 Trade Reg. Rep. (CCH) ¶ 24,688 (D.D.C. Jan. 6, 2000) (company caused substantial injury by harvesting consumers' personal information from a competitor's website and then sending them deceptive unsolicited e-mail solicitations; two Commissioners dissent on ground that invasion of privacy via unsolicited e-mail messages is insufficient to constitute substantial injury).

527 *Id. Accord* Orkin Exterminating Co. v. FTC, 849 F.2d 1354, 1365 (11th Cir. 1988); FTC v. J.K. Publications, Inc., 99 F. Supp. 2d 1176 (C.D. Cal. 2000); FTC v. Windward Marketing, Ltd., 1997 U.S. Dist. LEXIS 17114 (N.D. Ga. Sept. 30, 1997).

528 *See also* Reauthorization of the Federal Trade Commission Before the Senate Comm. on Commerce, Science and Transportation, 97th Cong., 2d Sess. 23, 25, n.12 (1982).

529 American Fin. Servs. Ass'n v. FTC, 767 F.2d 957 (D.C. Cir. 1985), *cert. denied*, 475 U.S. 1011 (1986).

530 16 C.F.R. § 433.

531 American Fin. Servs. Ass'n v. FTC, 767 F.2d 957 (D.C. Cir. 1985), *cert. denied*. 475 U.S. 1011 (1986).

4.3.2.3 Injury that Consumer Can Not Avoid

To be unfair under the FTC Act, the practice must not only cause substantial consumer injury, but also the injury must not be "reasonably avoidable by consumers themselves."[532] The Commission has explained that consumers can not reasonably avoid injury when the merchant's sales practices unreasonably create or take advantage of an obstacle to the free exercise of consumer decision-making.

Such unfair practices may include withholding important information from consumers, overt coercion, or exercising undue influence over highly susceptible classes of purchasers.[533] Another example of injury that can not be avoided is a provision in a standard form contract that is common to the whole industry and which can not be negotiated.[534] Consumers can not avoid an injury if the seller does not afford them a free and informed choice that enables them to avoid the unfair practices.[535] A consumer accommodation program that provides relief from an unauthorized price increase only to customers who complain does not provide a reasonable opportunity for consumers to avoid injury.[536]

By contrast, a state court applying a similar principle has held that overcharges resulting from errors by an electronic scanner are not unfair practices, where the store issues a receipt that enables the consumer to check the scanner's accuracy, and offers a money-back guarantee if the scanned price differs from the shelf price.[537] Because of these safeguards, consumers have alternatives other than paying the incorrectly scanned prices. Likewise, failure to explain a small-print contract provision may not be unfair where the clause is located directly above the signature line and the consumer has a copy of the contract a week before signing it.[538]

4.3.2.4 Injury Not Outweighed by the Benefits to Consumers or Competition

An unfair practice under the FTC Act is one that is "not outweighed by countervailing benefits to consumers or to

532 15 U.S.C. § 45(n).

533 Reauthorization of the Federal Trade Commission Before the Senate Comm. on Commerce, Science and Transportation, 97th Cong., 2d Sess. 23, 26, 28, 29 (1982). *See* FTC v. Crescent Publishing Group, Inc., 129 F. Supp. 2d 311 (S.D.N.Y. 2001) (inconspicuousness of disclosure of end of free portion of services made charges not reasonably avoidable).

534 American Fin. Servs. Ass'n v. FTC, 767 F.2d 957 (D.C. Cir. 1985), *cert. denied*, 475 U.S. 1011 (1986).

535 FTC v. J.K. Publications, Inc., 99 F. Supp. 2d 1176 (C.D. Cal. 2000).

536 Orkin Exterminating Co. v. FTC, 849 F.2d 1354, 1365 (11th Cir. 1988).

537 Tudor v. Jewel Food Stores, Inc., 681 N.E.2d 6 (Ill. App. Ct. 1997).

538 Bangor Publishing Co. v. Union Street Market, 706 A.2d 595 (Me. 1998).

competition."[539] Congress did not intend that the FTC "quantify the detrimental and beneficial effects of the practice in every case."[540] Instead, Congress expects the Commission to "carefully evaluate the benefits and costs . . . gathering and considering reasonably available evidence."[541] The fact that some customers are satisfied with a defendant's services is not a benefit that outweighs the harm caused by deceptive enrollment and billing practices.[542] A state court applying this standard, however, held that an insurer could not assert an unfair practices claim against an insurance adjuster because there is a countervailing benefit in preserving the adjuster's primary duty to the insured.[543]

4.3.2.5 Relation to Public Policy

The FTC Act specifies that, in determining if a practice is unfair, "the Commission may consider established public policies as evidence to be considered with all other evidence. Such public policy considerations may not serve as a primary basis for such determination."[544] In other words, Congress did not want the FTC to outlaw various practices simply as a matter of public policy—the practice must cause substantial harm that can not be avoided. But public policy can be a factor in measuring the amount of injury and weighing that injury against the countervailing benefits to consumers and competition.

While proof of consumer injury alone is sufficient to show a practice is unfair, that the practice violates public policy helps to prove the consumer injury. The violation of public policy by a practice indicates the magnitude of the consumer injury, or can even be a dispositive legislative or judicial determination that a practice causes substantial consumer injury.[545] For example, the FTC did not assess the factual evidence of consumer injury in holding that a creditor's suing consumers in an inconvenient venue was unfair because the Commission utilized a due process analogy to find the practice violated public policy. Similarly, a creditor's failure to turn over repossession surpluses violates the UCC, and is thus unfair.[546]

539 15 U.S.C. § 45(n). *See* Orkin Exterminating Co. v. FTC, 849 F.2d 1354 (11th Cir. 1988) (unauthorized fee increase without increase in level or quality of service meets standard).

540 Sen. Rep. No. 130, 103d Cong., 2d Sess. 12 (1994), *reprinted in* 1994 U.S.C.C.A.N. 1787–88; *see also* H. Conf. Rep. No. 617, 103d Cong., 2d Sess. 11 (1994), *reprinted in* 1994 U.S.C.C.A.N. 1797.

541 Sen. Rep. No. 130, 103d Cong., 2d Sess. 12 (1994), *reprinted in* 1994 U.S.C.C.A.N. 1787–88; *see also* H. Conf. Rep. No. 617, 103d Cong., 2d Sess. 11 (1994), *reprinted in* 1994 U.S.C.C.A.N. 1797.

542 FTC v. Crescent Publishing Group, Inc., 129 F. Supp. 2d 311 (S.D.N.Y. 2001).

543 Calandro v. Allstate Ins. Co., 63 Conn. App. 602, 778 A.2d 212 (2001).

544 Pub. L. No. 103-312 § 9, *adding a new* 15 U.S.C. § 45(n).

545 Reauthorization of the Federal Trade Commission Before the Senate Comm. on Commerce, Science and Transportation, 97th Cong., 2d Sess. 23, 26 (1982).

4.3.3 Unfairness Standards under State UDAP Statutes

4.3.3.1 Unfairness Broader than Deception

Unfairness, for purposes of state UDAP statutes (as it is for purposes of the FTC Act[547]) is not limited to traditional notions of deception or fraud, but encompasses other types of wrongful business conduct.[548] A defendant may violate a UDAP prohibition of unfair practices without making any misrepresentations.[549] It is not necessary to show intent to deceive.[550] Unfairness is not limited to "unfair methods of competition," that is, anti-competitive conduct.[551] Conduct can be unfair even though it is permitted by statute or common law principles.[552]

A small aberrant line of cases has developed in one jurisdiction. The Illinois Supreme Court ruled in *Laughlin v. Evanston Hospital*[553] that the UDAP prohibition of unfair acts and practices can not be used as a means of enforcing federal antitrust legislation. The court stated that the reach of the UDAP statute was intended to be limited to "conduct that defrauds or deceives consumers or others."[554] Two

546 *Id.* at 27.

547 FTC v. Sperry & Hutchinson Co., 405 U.S. 233, 244–45 (1972) (unfairness is broader than deception).

548 State v. O'Neill Investigations, Inc., 609 P.2d 520 (Alaska 1980); Barquis v. Merchants Collection Ass'n, 7 Cal. 3d 94, 496 P.2d 817, 101 Cal. Rptr. 745 (1972); Cherick Distributors, Inc. v. Polar Corp., 41 Mass. App. Ct. 125, 669 N.E.2d 218 (1996); Farm Bureau Fed'n v. Blue Cross, 403 Mass. 722, 532 N.E.2d 660 (1989); Service Publications, Inc. v. Goverman, 396 Mass. 567, 487 N.E.2d 520 (1986); Slaney v. Westwood Auto, Inc., 366 Mass. 688, 322 N.E.2d 768 (1975); Patterson v. Beall, 19 P.3d 839 (Okla. 2000) (unfair act was a UDAP violation even though not deceptive).

549 State *ex rel.* Hartigan v. Commonwealth Mortgage Corp., 732 F. Supp. 885 (N.D. Ill. 1990); People *ex rel.* Hartigan v. Knecht Servs., 216 Ill. App. 3d 843, 575 N.E.2d 1378 (1991).

550 Jacobs v. Healey Ford-Subaru, Inc., 231 Conn. 707, 652 A.2d 496 (1995) (but court finds no UDAP violation in light of unique circumstances of particular case, including defendant's lack of bad faith or willfulness).

551 Barquis v. Merchants Collection Ass'n, 7 Cal. 3d 94, 496 P.2d 817, 101 Cal. Rptr. 745 (1972); HM Distributors of Milwaukee, Inc. v. Department of Agriculture, 55 Wis. 2d 261, 198 N.W.2d 598 (1972).

552 Broadway Theatre Corp. v. Buena Vista Pictures Distribution, 2002 WL 32502100 (D. Conn. Sept. 19, 2002) (a practice that is not outlawed by antitrust laws does not necessarily preclude that practice from UDAP statute's reach as "unfair"); Schubach v. Household Fin. Corp., 375 Mass. 133, 376 N.E.2d 140 (1978).

553 133 Ill. 2d 374, 550 N.E.2d 986 (1990).

554 *Id.* at 550 N.E.2d 993. This holding that UDAP antitrust actions

federal district courts have taken this language out of context and ruled that unfair acts are no longer actionable under the Illinois UDAP statute unless deception is shown also.[555]

This conclusion ignores other language in *Laughlin* that the Illinois UDAP statute prohibits overreaching as well as fraudulent conduct. Most Illinois appellate courts have continued to apply the "*S&H*" unfairness definition in UDAP cases,[556] and have confined *Laughlin* to antitrust cases.[557]

4.3.3.2 Primacy of State Statutory Language and Intent and State Regulations

The definition of unfairness under a state UDAP statute is primarily guided by that statute's own definition (if any), by the state's legislative intent in enacting the UDAP statute, and by state regulations promulgated under the UDAP statute. Only secondarily does the FTC's definition of unfairness have precedential value in interpreting a state UDAP statute.

For example, Oklahoma has enacted a statutory definition of unfairness.[558] Missouri's UDAP regulations adopt a definition of unfairness that requires both substantial injury and acts that are unethical, unscrupulous, oppressive, or offensive to public policy.[559] In Hawaii, the legislative committee recommending enactment of an unfairness standard[560] quoted from the legislative history of the FTC standard for unfair methods of competition:

> It is impossible to frame definitions which embrace all unfair practices. There is no limit to human inventiveness in this field. Even if all known practices were specifically defined and prohibited, it would be at once necessary to begin over again. If Congress were to adopt the method of definition, it would undertake an endless task.[561]

4.3.3.3 Precedential Effect of Congress' 1994 Definition of Unfairness in Interpreting State UDAP Statutes

The FTC's 1994 Reauthorization Act defines those unfair practices that the FTC can declare unlawful.[562] The implication of this amendment for court interpretations of the unfairness standard under *state* UDAP statutes is far from clear, since the 1994 amendment limits the FTC's authority to challenge certain practices, but does not define the term "unfairness" generally.

Moreover, the legislative history takes pains to indicate that the amendment to the FTC Act should have no effect on the development of the unfairness concept under state statutes:

> The Committee is aware that State attorneys general have expressed a concern that the limitation on unfairness in this section may be construed to affect provisions in State statutes or State case law.
>
> Since the mid-1960s, virtually every State has enacted statutes prohibiting deceptive practices, while many States also prohibit unfair practices. These State consumer protection acts are enforced almost exclusively through recourse to State courts. Many of the statutes direct courts to be guided by interpretations of the FTC Act. In other States, the courts have interpreted these laws consistently with developments under Federal law. State courts have applied the unfairness standard in a variety of contexts, including unconscionable pricing practices, high pressure sales tactics, uninhabitable living conditions in leased premises, and abusive debt collection practices.
>
> The Committee intends no effect on those or other developments under State law. This section represents a consensus view of an appropriate codification of Federal standards, undertaken after careful assessment of the FTC's past activities. The Committee's action should not be understood as suggesting that the criteria in this section are necessarily suitable in the further development of State unfairness law or that the FTC's future construction of these criteria delimits in any way the range of State decisionmaking. Sound principles of federalism limit the impact of this section to the FTC only.[563]

---

must involve deception is clearly in the minority. *See, e.g.*, Mack v. Bristol-Myers Squibb Co., 673 So. 2d 100 (Fla. Dist. Ct. App. 1996).

555 Cobb v. Monarch Fin. Co., 913 F. Supp. 1164 (N.D. Ill. 1995); Kedziora v. Citicorp Nat'l Servs., Inc., 780 F. Supp. 516 (N.D. Ill. 1991).

556 Perez v. Citicorp Mortgage, Inc., 301 Ill. App. 3d 413, 703 N.E.2d 518 (1998); Saunders v. Michigan Ave. Nat'l Bank, 278 Ill. App. 3d 307, 662 N.E.2d 602 (1996); Griffin v. Universal Cas. Co., 274 Ill. App. 3d 1056, 654 N.E.2d 694, 211 Ill. Dec. 232 (1995); People *ex rel.* Hartigan v. Knecht Servs., 216 Ill. App. 3d 843, 575 N.E.2d 1378 (1991); Ekl v. Knecht, 585 N.E.2d 156 (Ill. App. Ct. 1991); Elder v. Coronet Ins. Co., 201 Ill. App. 3d 733, 558 N.E.2d 1312 (1990).

557 Sullivan's Wholesale Drug v. Faryl's Pharmacy Inc., 214 Ill. App. 3d 1073, 573 N.E.2d 1370 (1991).

558 Okla. Stat. Ann. tit. 15, § 752(14). *See* Patterson v. Beall, 19 P.3d 839 (Okla. 2000).

559 15 Mo. Code State Regs. § 60-8.020. *See* Ports Petroleum Co. v. Nixon, 37 S.W.3d 237 (Mo. 2001) (violation of statute prohibiting price-cutting not a UDAP violation despite regulation because it protects competition, not consumers).

560 Conf. Rep. No. 267, 3d Leg., Reg. Sess., House Journal at 600 (1965), *cited* in Robert's Waikiki U-Drive v. Budget Rent-A-Car, 491 F. Supp. 1199 (D. Haw. 1980).

561 H.R. Conf. Rep. No. 1142, 63 Cong., 2d Sess. at 19 (1914).

562 *See* § 4.3.2, *supra*.

563 Sen. Rep. No. 130, 103d Cong., 2d Sess. 13 (1994), *reprinted in* 1994 U.S.C.C.A.N. 1788.

Moreover, as described in § 4.3.3.4, *infra*, most courts have seemed uninterested in adopting the FTC's unfairness definition announced by the FTC in 1980, and which Congress in 1994 codified into federal law. Instead, courts interpreting state UDAP statutes mostly rely on the FTC's old "*S&H*" standard[564] or on their own jurisprudence.

4.3.3.4 State UDAP Use of "*S&H*" Unfairness Definition in Lieu of the Current FTC Definition

At the time of the early development of state UDAP case law in the 1960s and 1970s, the FTC utilized the "*S&H*" definition of unfairness: whether the practice is within the penumbra of common law, statutory, or other established concepts of fairness; whether it is immoral, unethical, oppressive, or unscrupulous; and whether it causes substantial injury.[565] In 1980, the FTC amended this definition to adopt the standard that is essentially codified now in the FTC Act.[566]

Nevertheless, most courts in interpreting state UDAP statutes do not apply this current FTC unfairness definition. Instead, they continue to use the "*S&H*" standard.[567] Connecticut courts are a limited exception to this rule. A number of Connecticut UDAP cases either utilize the current FTC unfairness definition or use that definition as a refinement of the term "substantial injury" under the "*S&H*" definition.[568] But even Connecticut courts more often (and more

564 This standard is described in § 4.3.3.5, *infra*.

565 *See* § 4.3.3.5, *infra*.

566 *See* § 4.3.2, *supra*.

567 *Alaska*: State v. Grogan, 628 P.2d 570 (Alaska 1981).
California: Informix Software, Inc. v. Oracle Corp., 927 F. Supp. 1283 (N.D. Cal. 1996). *But cf.* Cel-Tech Communications, Inc. v. Los Angeles Cellular Tel. Co., 20 Cal. 4th 163, 973 P.2d 527 (1999) (disapproving "*S&H*" unfairness definition in UDAP cases involving antitrust violations); People *ex rel.* Lockyer v. Fremont Life Ins. Co., 104 Cal. App. 4th 508, 128 Cal. Rptr. 2d 463, 470 n.4 (2002) (analyzing California Supreme Court unfairness definition). *See also* § 4.3.3.7, *infra*.
Florida: Hanson Hams, Inc. v. HBH Franchise Co., 2003 WL 22768687 (S.D. Fla. Nov. 7, 2003); Kelly v. Nelson, Mullins, Riley & Scarborough, 2002 U.S. Dist. LEXIS 6430 (M.D. Fla. Mar. 20, 2002); PNR, Inc. v. Beacon Property Mgmt., Inc., 842 So. 2d 773 (Fla. 2003); McClendon v. Metropolitan Mortgage Co., Clearinghouse No. 43,703G (Fla. Cir. Ct. Dade Cty. May 20, 1988).
Hawaii: Roberts' Waikiki U-Drive v. Budget Rent-A-Car, 491 F. Supp. 1199 (D. Haw. 1980) (interpreting Hawaii law); Hawaii Community Fed. Credit Union v. Keka, 94 Haw. 213, 11 P.3d 1 (2000); Ai v. Frank Huff Agency Ltd., 61 Haw. 607, 607 P.2d 1304 (1980); Rosa v. Johnson, 651 P.2d 1228 (Haw. Ct. App. 1982); Eastern Star, Inc. v. Union Building Materials, 712 P.2d 1148 (Haw. Ct. App. 1985).
Illinois: Robinson v. Toyota Motor Credit Corp., 201 Ill. 2d 403, 775 N.E.2d 951, 266 Ill. Dec. 879 (2002); Ekl v. Knecht, 585 N.E.2d 156 (Ill. App. Ct. 1991); People *ex rel.* Hartigan v. Knecht Servs., 216 Ill. App. 3d 843, 575 N.E.2d 1378 (1991); Elder v. Coronet Ins. Co., 201 Ill. App. 3d 733, 558 N.E.2d 1312 (1990); People *ex rel.* Fahner v. Walsh, 122 Ill. App. 3d 481, 461 N.E.2d 78 (1984). *See also* Tudor v. Jewel Food Stores, Inc., 681 N.E.2d 6 (Ill. App. Ct. 1997) (to be unfair, defendant's conduct must violate public policy, be so oppressive that consumer has little alternative but to submit, and substantially injure the consumer); Michael M. Greenfield, *Unfairness Under Section 5 of the FTC Act and Its Impact on State Law*, 46 Wayne L. Rev. 1869, 1909–16 (Winter 2000).
Louisiana: Surgical Care Center v. Hospital Serv. Dist., 309 F.3d 836 (5th Cir. 2002); Specialty Diving v. Master Builders, Inc., 2003 WL 22416381 (E. D. La. Oct. 22, 2003); Wood v. Collins, 725 So. 2d 531 (La. Ct. App. 1998); Thomas v. Busby, 670 So. 2d 603 (La. Ct. App. 1996); Camp, Dresser & McKee, Inc. v. Steimle & Assocs., Inc., 652 So. 2d 44 (La. Ct. App. 1995); Vercher v. Ford Motor Co., 527 So. 2d 995 (La. Ct. App. 1988); Gautreau v. Southern Milk Sales, Inc., 509 So. 2d 495 (La. Ct. App. 1987); Moore v. Goodyear Tire & Rubber Co., 364 So. 2d 630 (La. Ct. App. 1978).
Massachusetts: Pepsi-Cola Metropolitan Bottling Co. v. Checkers, Inc., 754 F.2d 10 (1st Cir. 1985) (Massachusetts law); Farm Bureau Federation v. Blue Cross, 403 Mass. 722, 532 N.E.2d 660 (1989); Purity Supreme, Inc. v. Attorney General, 380 Mass. 762, 407 N.E.2d 297 (1980); PMP Assocs., Inc. v. Globe Newspaper Co., 366 Mass. 593, 321 N.E.2d 915 (1975); Ellis v. Safety Ins. Co., 41 Mass. App. Ct. 630, 672 N.E.2d 979 (1996); Wasserman v. Agnastopoulos, 22 Mass. App. Ct. 672, 497 N.E.2d 19 (1986); Piccuirro v. Gaitenby, 20 Mass. App. Ct. 286, 480 N.E.2d 30 (1985); *see also* Michael M. Greenfield, *Unfairness Under Section 5 of the FTC Act and Its Impact on State Law*, 46 Wayne L. Rev. 1869, 1924–30 (Winter 2000).
Minnesota: State *ex rel.* Humphrey v. Directory Publishing Servs., Inc., 1996 Minn. App. LEXIS 62 (Jan. 9, 1996).
New Hampshire: Curtis Mfg. Co. v. Plastic-Clip Corp., 888 F. Supp. 1212 (D.N.H. 1994); Milford Lumber Co. v. RCB Realty, 780 A.2d 1259 (N.H. 2001).
North Carolina: South Atlantic Ltd. P'ship v. Riese, 284 F.3d 518 (4th Cir. 2002) (N.C. law); Basnight v. Diamond Developers, Inc., 146 F. Supp. 2d 754 (M.D.N.C. 2001); *In re* Bozzano, 183 B.R. 735 (Bankr. M.D.N.C. 1995); Gray v. North Carolina Ins. Underwriting Assn., 352 N.C. 61, 529 S.E.2d 676 (2000); Marshall v. Miller, 302 N.C. 539, 276 S.E.2d 397 (1981); Johnson v. Phoenix Mut. Life Ins. Co., 300 N.C. 247, 266 S.E.2d 610 (1980); Lake Mary Ltd. P'ship v. Johnston, 551 S.E.2d 546 (N.C. Ct. App. 2001); Murray v. Nationwide Mut. Ins. Co., 472 S.E.2d 358 (N.C. Ct. App. 1996); Wachovia Bank & Trust v. Carrington Dev. Assocs., 459 S.E.2d 17 (N.C. Ct. App. 1995); Torrance v. AS&L Motors, 459 S.E.2d 67 (N.C. Ct. App. 1995); Creekside Apartments v. Poteat, 446 S.E.2d 826 (N.C. Ct. App. 1994); Barbee v. Atlantic Marine Sales & Service, Inc., 115 N.C. App. 641, 446 S.E.2d 117 (1993); Process Components, Inc. v. Baltimore Aircoil Co., 89 N.C. App. 649, 366 S.E.2d 907, *aff'd*, 323 N.C. 620, 374 S.E.2d 116 (1988); Morris v. Bailey, 358 S.E.2d 120 (N.C. Ct. App. 1987); Lee v. Payton, 313 S.E.2d 247 (N.C. Ct. App. 1984); *see also* Dalton v. Camp, 353 N.C. 647, 548 S.E.2d 704 (2001) (defining unfair as "unethical or unscrupulous").
Rhode Island: Ames v. Oceanside Welding & Towing Co., 767 A.2d 677 (R.I. 2001).
South Carolina: DeBondt v. Carlton Motorcars, Inc., 342 S.C. 254, 536 S.E.2d 399 (App. 2000).

568 Dow & Condon, Inc. v. Anderson, 203 Conn. 475, 525 A.2d 935 (1987); Webb Press Servs. v. New London Motors, Inc., 205 Conn. 479, 533 A.2d 1211 (1987); McLaughlin Ford, Inc. v. Ford Motor Co., 192 Conn. 558, 473 A.2d 1185 (1984); Hudson

recently) apply the "*S&H*" definition with no mention of the current FTC definition.[569] Outside of Connecticut, only a few courts apply the current FTC unfairness definition to state UDAP statutes.[570]

4.3.3.5 The "*S&H*" Standard Described

The "*S&H*" standard, which is chiefly utilized in interpreting unfairness pursuant to state UDAP statutes, is described in the landmark 1972 United States Supreme Court case, *FTC v. Sperry and Hutchinson Company* (*S&H*). There, the court found unfairness to be a broader standard than deception.[571] The court noted with approval the FTC's use[572] of the following criteria for determining whether a practice is unfair:

- Whether the practice offends public policy. Is it within at least the penumbra of some common law, statutory, or other established concept of unfairness?
- Whether the practice is immoral, unethical, oppressive, or unscrupulous.
- Whether the practice causes substantial injury to consumers.

The consumer need not establish all three prongs of the standard.[573] Instead, while the court may consider all three prongs, evidence concerning just one prong may be sufficient to show a practice is unfair.[574] A practice may thus be

---

United Bank v. Cinnamon Ridge Corp., 81 Conn. App. 557, 845 A.2d 417 (Conn. App. Ct. 2004); Calandro v. Allstate Ins. Co., 63 Conn. App. 602, 778 A.2d 212 (2001); Vezina v. Nautilus Pools, Inc., 27 Conn. App. 810, 610 A.2d 1312 (1992); *see also* United States *ex rel.* Balf v. Casle Corp., 895 F. Supp. 420 (D. Conn. 1995); Chem-Tek, Inc. v. General Motors Corp., 816 F. Supp. 123 (D. Conn. 1993); Carpentino v. Transport Ins. Co., 609 F. Supp. 556 (D. Conn. 1985); *In re* Kellogg, 166 B.R. 504 (Bankr. D. Conn. 1994); Williams Ford v. Hartford Courant Co., 232 Conn. 559, 657 A.2d 212 (1995) (contributory negligence bars UDAP unfairness claim in business case).

569 Locascio v. Imports Unlimited, Inc., 309 F. Supp. 2 267 (D. Conn. 2004); Journal Publishing Co. v. Hartford Courant Co., 261 Conn. 673, 804 A.2d 823 (2002); Macomber v. Travelers Prop. & Cas. Corp., 261 Conn. 620, 804 A.2d 180 (2002); Willow Springs Condominium Ass'n v. Seventh BRT Development Corp., 245 Conn. 1, 717 A.2d 77 (1998); Larsen Chelsey Realty Co. v. Larsen, 232 Conn. 480, 656 A.2d 1009 (1995); Jacobs v. Healey Ford-Subaru, Inc., 231 Conn. 707, 652 A.2d 496 (1995); Moran, Shuster, Carignan & Knierim v. August, 43 Conn. Supp. 431, 657 A.2d 736 (1994), *aff'd on other grounds*, 232 Conn. 756, 657 A.2d 229 (1995) (former law partner's denial that he owed a debt was not an unfair practice); Normand Josef Enterprises v. Connecticut Bank, 230 Conn. 486, 646 A.2d 1289 (1994); Associated Investment Co. v. Williams Assocs., 230 Conn. 148, 645 A.2d 505 (1994); Cheshire Mortgage Servs., Inc. v. Montes, 223 Conn. 80, 612 A.2d 1130 (1992); A-G Foods, Inc. v. Pepperidge Farm, Inc., 216 Conn. 200, 579 A.2d 69 (1990); Sanghavi v. Paul Revere Life Ins. Co., 214 Conn. 303, 572 A.2d 307 (1990); Daddonna v. Liberty Mobile Home Sales, Inc., 209 Conn. 243, 550 A.2d 1061 (1988); Norwich Sav. Soc. v. Caldrello, 38 Conn. App. 859, 663 A.2d 415 (1995); Prishwalko v. Bob Thomas Ford, Inc., 33 Conn. App. 575, 636 A.2d 1383 (1994) (Connecticut follows "*S&H*" standard, but any ascertainable loss satisfies injury requirement); Lester v. Resort Camplands Int'l, Inc., 27 Conn. App. 59, 605 A.2d 550 (1992); Krawiec v. Blake Manor Dev. Co., 26 Conn. App. 601, 602 A.2d 1062 (1992); Francoline v. Klatt, 26 Conn. App. 203, 600 A.2d 8 (1991); Edart Truck Rental v. B. Swirsky & Co., 23 Conn. App. 137, 579 A.2d 133 (1990); Noble v. Marshall, 23 Conn. App. 227, 579 A.2d 594 (1990); Siudyla v. Chemexec Relocation Sys., Inc., 23 Conn. App. 180, 579 A.2d 578 (1990); DeMotses v. Leonard Schwartz Nissan, 22 Conn. App. 464, 578 A.2d 144 (1990); Yale New Haven Hosp., Inc. v. Mitchell, 662 A.2d 178 (Conn. Super. Ct. 1995); *see also* Omega Engineering, Inc. v. Eastman Kodak Co., 908 F. Supp. 1084 (D. Conn. 1995); Brandewiede v. Emery Worldwide, 890 F. Supp. 79 (D. Conn. 1994), *aff'd without op.*, 66 F.3d 308 (2d Cir. 1995); Retail Service Assocs. v. Conagra Pet Products Co., 759 F. Supp. 976 (D. Conn. 1991); Aurigemma v. Arco Petroleum Products Co., 734 F. Supp. 1025 (D. Conn. 1990); Gibbs v. Southeastern Invest. Corp., 705 F. Supp. 738 (D. Conn. 1989); McKeown Distributors, Inc. v. Gyp-Crete Corp., 618 F. Supp. 632 (D. Conn. 1985); Michael M. Greenfield, *Unfairness Under Section 5 of the FTC Act and Its Impact on State Law*, 46 Wayne L. Rev. 1869, 1915–23 (Winter 2000).

570 Tungate v. MacLean-Stevens Studios, 1998 ME 162, 714 A.2d 792 (Me. 1998) (relying on FTC's new standard to bar UDAP claim where amount of damage was small); Bangor Publishing Co. v. Union Street Market, 706 A.2d 595 (Me. 1998) (Maine standard for unfairness requires that injury not be reasonably avoidable by consumers or outweighed by countervailing benefits to consumers or competition); Legg v. Castruccio, 100 Md. App. 748, 642 A.2d 906 (1994) (relying on the FTC's current unfairness standards to bar private causes of action for injuries that were insubstantial, reasonably avoidable, or outweighed by countervailing benefits to consumers, but recognizing that a private cause of action would exist for violation of a clear public policy, even if consumer injury were unclear); Swiger v. Terminix Int'l Co., 1995 Ohio App. LEXIS 2826 (June 28, 1995) (reciting current FTC unfairness definition as part of analysis of nondisclosure); Blake v. Federal Way Cycle Center, 40 Wash. App. 302, 698 P.2d 578 (1985).

571 405 U.S. 233, 244–45 (1972).

572 *See* Statement of Basis and Purpose of the FTC Trade Regulation Rule, Unfair or Deceptive Advertising and Labeling of Cigarettes in Relation to the Health Hazards of Smoking, 16 C.F.R. Part 408, 29 Fed. Reg. 8355 (1964), since rescinded.

573 Journal Publishing Co. v. Hartford Courant Co., 261 Conn. 673, 804 A.2d 823 (2002); Macomber v. Travelers Prop. & Cas. Corp., 261 Conn. 620, 804 A.2d 180 (2002); Cheshire Mortgage Servs., Inc. v. Montes, 223 Conn. 80, 612 A.2d 1130 (1992); Robinson v. Toyota Motor Credit Corp., 201 Ill. 2d 403, 775 N.E.2d 951, 266 Ill. Dec. 879 (2002).

574 *See* Aurigemma v. Arco Petroleum Products Co., 734 F. Supp. 1025 (D. Conn. 1990); Sorisio v. Lenox, Inc., 701 F. Supp. 950 (D. Conn.), *aff'd*, 863 F.2d 195 (2d Cir. 1988); Carpentino v. Transport Ins. Co., 609 F. Supp. 556 (D. Conn. 1985); Jacobs v. Healey Ford-Subaru, Inc., 231 Conn. 707, 652 A.2d 496 (1995); Normand Josef Enterprises v. Connecticut Bank, 230 Conn. 486, 646 A.2d 1289 (1994); Daddonna v. Liberty Mobile Home Sales, Inc., 209 Conn. 243, 550 A.2d 1061 (1988); McLaughlin Ford, Inc. v. Ford Motor Co., 192 Conn. 558, 473 A.2d 1185 (1984); Meyers v. Cornwell Quality Tools, Inc., 41 Conn. App. 19, 674 A.2d 444 (1996); Prishwalko v. Bob Thomas Ford, Inc., 33 Conn. App. 575, 636 A.2d 1383 (1994); Krawiec v. Blake Manor Dev. Co., 26 Conn. App. 601, 602 A.2d 1062 (1992);

a UDAP violation if it violates public policy.[575] A practice need not be prohibited by other law to be unfair.[576]

4.3.3.6 Differences Between the "*S&H*" and the Current FTC Standard

To some extent, distinctions between the "*S&H*" standard and the current FTC definition of unfairness may have little practical effect. Unfairness is a question of fact for the jury or, in a non-jury case, the judge.[577] The facts of a case will be more dispositive than the standard utilized.

In addition, the three prongs of the "*S&H*" definition are not that much different from the current FTC definition. The "*S&H*" definition looks at three factors: whether the practice is within the penumbra of common law, statutory, or other established concepts of fairness; whether it is immoral, unethical, oppressive, or unscrupulous; and whether it causes substantial injury. The first factor is somewhat akin to the current FTC definition's acknowledgment of public policy concerns.[578]

The second factor, whether conduct is immoral, unethical, oppressive, or unscrupulous, has proven to be largely duplicative of the other two unfairness criteria. Unethical or oppressive conduct almost always injures consumers or violates public policy.[579] The third factor in the "*S&H*" definition (substantial injury) is identical to the current FTC definition.

The FTC definition explicitly considers whether consumers can avoid the injury and whether there are countervailing benefits to competition, while these factors are not explicitly included in the "*S&H*" definition. Nevertheless, courts are unlikely to ignore these factors even under the "*S&H*" definition.[580]

4.3.3.7 Alternative State Definitions

As described in § 4.3.3.2, *supra*, a few state UDAP statutes or regulations explicitly define unfairness. In addition, courts in a few states have developed their own law as to unfairness. The California courts utilize their own standard, a standard that is similar, but somewhat different, than the new FTC standard. Unfairness is determined by weighing the practice's impact on the victim compared with its business justification.[581]

Massachusetts adopts the "*S&H*" standard when a consumer sues a business, but some courts utilize a more restrictive standard where one business sues another business. These courts require a showing that the objectionable conduct attained "a level of rascality that would raise an eyebrow of someone inured to the rough and tumble of the world of commerce."[582] North Carolina recognizes the FTC

Gibbs v. Mase, 11 Conn. App. 289, 526 A.2d 7 (1987); McClendon v. Metropolitan Mortgage Co., Clearinghouse No. 43,703G (Fla. Cir. Ct. Dade Cty. May 20, 1988). *But see* Golembiewski v. Hallberg Ins. Agency, Inc., 635 N.E.2d 452 (Ill. App. Ct. 1994) (must meet standards of all three prongs); Jones v. Universal Cas. Co., 630 N.E.2d 94 (Ill. App. Ct. 1994) (all three prongs must be proven).

575 Vezina v. Nautilus Pools, Inc., 27 Conn. App. 810, 610 A.2d 1312 (1992).

576 Smith v. State Farm Mut. Auto. Ins. Co., 113 Cal. Rptr. 2d 399 (App. 2001).

577 Krawiec v. Blake Manor Dev. Co., 26 Conn. App. 601, 602 A.2d 1062 (1992); DeMotses v. Leonard Schwartz Nissan, 22 Conn. App. 464, 578 A.2d 144 (1990); Edart Truck Rental v. B. Swirsky & Co., 23 Conn. App. 137, 579 A.2d 133 (1990). *See also* Patterson v. Beall, 19 P.3d 839 (Okla. 2000) (whether specific conduct meets broad statutory definition of unfairness is a fact question to be decided by courts on case-by-case basis). *But see* Francoline v. Klatt, 26 Conn. App. 203, 600 A.2d 8 (1991) (in some cases, facts found may be so egregious as to require a conclusion that as a matter of law, they violate public policy).

578 *See* § 4.3.2.5, *supra.*

579 Reauthorization of the Federal Trade Commission Before the Senate Comm. on Commerce, Science and Transportation, 97th Cong., 2d Sess. 23, 28 (1982).

580 *See* Tudor v. Jewel Food Stores, Inc., 681 N.E.2d 6 (Ill. App. Ct. 1997) (in determining unfairness, court considers whether consumer lacked meaningful choice).

581 Testan v. Carlsen Motor Cars, Inc., 2002 Cal. App. LEXIS 1837 (Feb. 19, 2002) (unpublished, citation limited) (applying *Cel-Tech* standard to consumer claim; concept of unfairness must be tethered to some legislatively declared policy); Smith v. State Farm Mut. Auto. Ins. Co., 113 Cal. Rptr. 2d 399 (App. 2001); Olsen v. Breeze, Inc., 48 Cal. App. 4th 608, 55 Cal. Rptr. 2d 818 (1996); State Farm Fire & Cas. Co. v. Superior Court, 45 Cal. App. 4th 1093, 53 Cal. Rptr. 2d 229 (1996) (court must weigh the utility of the defendant's conduct against the gravity of the harm to the alleged victim); Saunders v. Superior Court, 27 Cal. App. 4th 832, 33 Cal. Rptr. 2d 438 (1994) ("unfair" means any practice whose harm to the victim outweighs its benefits). *See also* People *ex rel.* Lockyer v. Fremont Life Ins. Co., 104 Cal. App. 4th 508, 128 Cal. Rptr. 2d 463 (2002) (discussing *Cel-Tech* standard; a deceptive or sharp practice is unfair); Searle v. Wyndham Int'l, Inc., 102 Cal. App. 4th 1327, 126 Cal. Rptr. 2d 231 (2002) (hotel's failure to disclose to guests that 17% room service charge was paid to the server is not unfair); Walker v. Countrywide Home Loans, Inc., 98 Cal. App. 4th 1158, 121 Cal. Rptr. 2d 79 (2002) (imposing fees on homeowners for drive-by inspections of home after mortgage default not unfair in light of usefulness of inspections); Cel-Tech Communications, Inc. v. Los Angeles Cellular Tel. Co., 83 Cal. Rptr. 2d 548, 973 P.2d 527 (1999) (adopting definition of unfairness under § 17200 for antitrust purposes). *But see* People v. Casa Blanca Convalescent Homes, 206 Cal. Rptr. 164 (Ct. App. 1984) (applying the "*S&H*" standard).

582 *See, e.g.,* Suzuki of W. Mass., Inc. v. Outdoor Sports Expo, Inc., 126 F. Supp. 2d 40 (D. Mass. 2001); General Electric v. Lyon, 894 F. Supp. 544 (D. Mass. 1995); Mass Cash Register, Inc. v. Comtrex Sys. Corp., 901 F. Supp. 404 (D. Mass. 1995); Credit Data of Cent. Massachusetts, Inc. v. TRW, Inc., 37 Mass. App. Ct. 442, 640 N.E.2d 499 (1994); Doliner v. Brown, 21 Mass. App. Ct. 692, 489 N.E.2d 1036 (1986); Levings v. Forbes & Wallace, Inc., 8 Mass. App. Ct. 498, 396 N.E.2d 149 (1979). *But see* Mass. Employees Ins. Exchange v. Propac-Mass., Inc., 420

standard, but also holds that a party is guilty of an unfair act or practice when it engages in conduct which amounts to an inequitable assertion of its power or position.[583]

4.3.4 Application of Unfairness to Adhesion Contracts

4.3.4.1 FTC Credit Practices Rule

The most important application of the FTC's current unfairness analysis to adhesion contracts is found in the Statement of Basis and Purpose of the FTC's Credit Practices Rule.[584] The FTC begins with its three-step analysis: an unfair practice is one that (1) causes substantial injury; (2) is not outweighed by any countervailing benefits to consumers or competition; and (3) consumers themselves could not reasonably have avoided the resulting injury. The Statement of Basis and Purpose then details how this three-part test applies to certain provisions commonly found in consumer credit contracts.

Taking the third element first, the FTC concludes that consumers can not reasonably avoid creditor remedies found in standard form credit agreements:

> The economic exigencies of extending credit to large numbers of consumers each day make standardization a necessity. . . .
>
> Consumers have limited incentives to search out better remedial provisions in credit contracts. The substantive similarities of contracts from different creditors mean that search is less likely to reveal a different alternative. Because remedies are relevant only in the event of default, and default is relatively infrequent, consumers reasonably concentrate their search on such factors as interest rates and payment terms. Searching for credit contracts is also difficult, because contracts are written in obscure technical language, do not use standardized terminology, and may not be provided before the transaction is consummated. Individual creditors have little incentive to provide better terms and explain their benefits to consumers, because a costly education effort would be required with all creditors sharing the benefits. Moreover, such a campaign might differentially attract relatively high risk borrowers. [Footnote omitted]
>
> For these reasons, the Commission concludes that consumers can not reasonably avoid the remedial provisions themselves. Nor can consumers, having signed a contract, avoid the harsh consequences of remedies by avoiding default. When default occurs, it is most often a response to events such as unemployment or illness that are not within the borrower's control. Thus consumers can not reasonably avoid the substantial injury these creditor remedies may inflict.[585]

Consequently, an adhesive creditor remedy is unfair if it causes substantial injury not outweighed by countervailing benefits.

The Statement of Basis and Purpose gives useful examples of how certain prohibited creditor remedies cause substantial injury, both economic and emotional. The Statement also notes that all debtors, and not just defaulting consumers, suffer harm from harsh creditor remedies because even non-defaulting debtors live under the threat of the severe remedies. The ban on a creditor remedy protects these consumers in the same way as an insurance policy.

In considering the countervailing benefits of creditor remedies, the Statement points out that one must consider the marginal benefit of a particular creditor remedy, and not the benefit of creditor remedies in general. That is, what is the extra benefit to competition of a particular remedy assuming the creditor still has a varied arsenal of other remedies to choose from, such as repossession, suit, garnishment, acceleration, and direct collection contacts? Based on this analysis, the FTC found the mere inclusion in standard form credit contracts of six different provisions to be an unfair trade practice.[586] The D.C. Circuit has upheld the FTC's unfairness analysis as it applies to creditor remedies and the Credit Practices Rule.[587] The D.C. Circuit found that the free market does not operate properly in the drafting of standard form credit agreements, so that credit provisions that cause substantial consumer injury not outweighed by contributing benefits to competition can be ruled unfair.[588]

4.3.4.2 Other Precedent

In *AMREP Corp.*[589] and *Horizon Corp.*[590] the Commission also reiterated the three-fold test for determining if there is substantial consumer injury (substantial injury, not outweighed by countervailing benefits, that consumers could not reasonably avoid). The Commission found a forfeiture clause in an adhesion contract which caused

Mass. 39, 648 N.E.2d 435 (1995) (terming the rascality formulation "uninstructive"). *See* § 2.4.5.2, *supra*.

583 South Atlantic Ltd. P'ship v. Riese, 284 F.3d 518 (4th Cir. 2002) (N.C. law); Walker v. Sloan, 137 N.C. App. 387, 529 S.E.2d 236 (2000).

584 49 Fed. Reg. 7744 (Mar. 1, 1984). The Credit Practices Rule is codified at 16 C.F.R. § 444, *reprinted at* Appx. B.1, *infra*, and analyzed at § 5.1.1.2, *infra*.

585 *Id.*

586 *Id.*

587 American Fin. Servs. Ass'n v. FTC, 767 F.2d 957 (D.C. Cir. 1985), *cert. denied*, 475 U.S. 1011 (1986).

588 *Id.*

589 102 F.T.C. 1362 (1983), *aff'd*, 768 F.2d 1171 (10th Cir. 1985).

590 97 F.T.C. 464 (1981).

cancellation resulting in the consumers losing all amounts paid to be unfair.[591] On the other hand, the Commission also found that, where there was no evidence that consumers were chilled from asserting their rights, an integration clause (excluding oral representations from being considered as part of the contract) was not unfair because it did not foreclose consumers' legal remedies.

The FTC has found other creditor practices unfair under its earlier "*S&H*" standard, since the seller or creditor has disproportionate market power compared to the consumer. "Where one party to a transaction enjoys a substantial advantage with respect to the consumers with whom he deals, it is appropriate for the Commission to determine whether the dominant party is using an overabundance of market power or commercial advantage in an inequitable manner."[592] Thus, the holder-in-due course status in consumer transactions is unfair.[593] A state court has also found a hospital's standard form contract to be unfair where the contract requires patients to pay collection costs, particularly where there is no relationship between the charge and the actual collection claim.[594]

4.3.5 Systematic Breach of Contract as Unfair

The FTC has also utilized its current unfairness standard in challenging a company's systematic breach of its consumer contracts. In *Orkin Exterminating Co.*,[595] the FTC found it unfair for a seller to systematically breach its standard form contracts. Orkin's contracts specified annual reinspections at a fixed price, but, due to rising costs, Orkin raised its reinspection fees.

Applying the FTC's three-part unfairness standard, the Commission had little difficulty finding Orkin's breach of contract to cause substantial harm, with no countervailing benefits to consumers or competition, and that consumers could not reasonably avoid or mitigate the breach. Alternative suppliers of reinspections would be more costly than Orkin's originally promised price. Consequently, the FTC ruled that, as a matter of law, this breach was an unfair trade practice, even though no deception or bad faith was involved. No evidence of materiality was needed; any breach of a provision in a standard form contract is a material unfair practice. The Eleventh Circuit affirmed the opinion, upholding the three-part unfairness standard and its application to the facts in *Orkin*.[596] A Louisiana court found the same practice to be unfair.[597]

FTC Chairman Oliver—considered by many to have the most restrictive view of the FTC Act—was troubled by the Commission's opinion because he correctly saw that it would encourage consumer attorneys to bring UDAP actions for attorney fees and treble damages for sellers' mere breach of contract. In a separate opinion (not joined by any other Commissioner), Chairman Oliver attempted to distinguish two types of breach of contract cases.

In one type of case, the injured party can adequately protect itself by bringing a breach of contract lawsuit, such as where the injury is large and the injured party is a business. In that context a mere breach without more would not be unfair. Where a consumer's damages are too small to make viable a breach of contract action, then the seller's breach of contract would be unfair under the FTC Act. In *Orkin* each consumer was damaged about $40, and Oliver found the breach to be unfair because many injured consumers could not otherwise protect themselves.

Oliver's view, although not FTC law, may be reflective of some judges' resentment against awarding treble damages when one business sues another business for a mere breach of contract. Oliver's opinion also reinforces the *Orkin* holding that a seller's systematic breach of a standard form contract provision is unfair even if no deception or bad faith is involved, where each individual consumer's loss is so small or knowledge so incomplete that it is unlikely most consumers would bring a breach of contract action.

A Missouri UDAP regulation adopts the *Orkin* standard and makes it an unfair practice to unilaterally breach unambiguous provisions of consumer contracts.[598] It has also been found to be unfair for a campground to unilaterally change the terms of the membership agreements to consumers' disadvantage where the major justification was to increase campground profits.[599] It is a UDAP violation to disregard known contractual obligations in order to destroy the rights of the other party or secure benefits for the breaching party.[600]

591 *But cf.* Boyd v. Berrier, 2001 Tenn. App. LEXIS 538 (July 26, 2001) (forfeiture clause in contract for sale of mobile home lots to buyer who rented them out to others was not unfair).

592 Statement of Basis and Purpose of the FTC Trade Regulation Rule Concerning Preservation of Consumers' Claims and Defenses, 16 C.F.R. Part 433, 40 Fed. Reg. 524, 533 (1975).

593 FTC Trade Regulation Rule Concerning Preservation of Consumers' Claims and Defenses, 16 C.F.R. Part 433, *reprinted at* Appx. B.2, *infra*.

594 Bondanza v. Peninsula Hosp. & Medical Center, 23 Cal. 3d 260, 590 P.2d 22, 152 Cal. Rptr. 446 (1979). *But cf.* Robinson v. Toyota Motor Credit Corp., 201 Ill. 2d 403, 775 N.E.2d 951, 266 Ill. Dec. 879 (2002) (lease terms not unfair where no evidence of oppressiveness or lack of meaningful choice).

595 108 F.T.C. 263 (1986), *aff'd*, 849 F.2d 1354 (11th Cir. 1988).

596 Orkin Exterminating Co. v. FTC, 849 F.2d 1354 (11th Cir. 1988), *cert. denied*, 488 U.S. 1041 (1989).

597 State *ex rel.* Guste v. Orkin Exterminating Co., 528 So. 2d 198 (La. Ct. App. 1988).

598 15 Mo. Code State Regs. § 60-8.070.

599 Lester v. Resort Camplands Int'l Inc., 27 Conn. App. 59, 605 A.2d 550 (1992). *See also* § 5.2.5, *infra*.

600 Nasco, Inc. v. Public Storage, Inc., 29 F.3d 28 (1st Cir. 1994); Massachusetts Employers Ins. Exchange v. PropacMass, 420 Mass. 39, 648 N.E.2d 435 (1995); Anthony's Pier Four v. HBC Assocs., 411 Mass. 451, 583 N.E.2d 806 (1991). *But cf.* Adams v. G.J. Creel & Sons, Inc., 465 S.E.2d 84 (S.C. 1995) (no UDAP

State cases have also found related practices unfair. It is unfair to negotiate an arrangement, knowing that the debtor will take actions in reliance on the negotiated agreement, and then back out of the deal before it is put in writing, claiming the agent did not have authority to speak for the principal.[601] A defendant's refusal to carry through on an assurance that the plaintiff would be paid from insurance proceeds is also unfair.[602]

4.3.6 Coercive High-Pressure Sales and Collection Tactics

High-pressure sales tactics are unfair trade practices. Examples include intimidation, coercion, personal disparagement, emphasizing social difficulties, refusing to let customers leave until they sign contracts, using relays of salesmen until the consumer succumbs, preventing consumers from taking the time to consider a decision and its consequences, and dismantling equipment and refusing to reassemble it unless the consumer purchases the service.[603] Coercive conduct in itself can be an adequate basis for finding a practice unfair,[604] such as refusing to return a down payment unless the consumer agrees to forfeit part of it.[605] Unfairness can be found where one party refuses to pay monies lawfully owed to intentionally exert undue pressure on another.[606]

The practice of bringing consumer collection actions in inconvenient or distant forums is "patently offensive to clearly articulated public policy, intended to guarantee all citizens a meaningful opportunity to defend themselves in court," even when the creditor operates within the state's venue laws.[607] Also unfair is a creditor's unlawful repossession of the debtor's property,[608] or a repair shop's vandalization of the consumer's property when the consumer complained and refused to pay a repair bill.[609] A repairman who threatens to turn off a consumer's water and undo repair work unless the consumer pays a bill immediately commits an unfair practice.[610]

4.3.7 Taking Advantage of Disparate Knowledge

Unfairness can be based not only on disproportionate bargaining power, but also on imbalances of knowledge. It is unfair for a seller to make claims without adequate substantiation for those claims.

> With the development and proliferation of highly complex and technical products, there is often no practical way for consumers to ascertain the truthfulness of affirmative product claims prior to buying and using the product. . . . Given the imbalance of knowledge and resources between a business enterprise and each of its customers, economically it is more rational and imposes far less cost on society to require a manufacturer to confirm his affirmative product claims rather than impose a burden upon each individual consumer to test, investigate, or experiment for himself.[611]

The FTC has also found unfair certain non-deceptive "pure omissions." That is, even where a seller's nondisclosure is not deceptive, it can still be unfair where the threefold unfairness test is met.[612] It is particularly easy to satisfy this unfairness test in the case of nondisclosures because the cost to businesses of disclosure is so slight, and because it is difficult for consumers to reasonably avoid the unfairness where the essence of their complaint is that they have not been informed of the problem.

---

violation to charge different prices to different customers, where contract did not forbid this).

601 Wasserman v. Agnastopoulos, 22 Mass. App. Ct. 672, 497 N.E.2d 19 (1986).

602 Fraser Engineering Co. v. Desmond, 26 Mass. App. Ct. 99, 524 N.E.2d 110 (1988).

603 Carpets "R" Us, Inc., 87 F.T.C. 303 (1976); Wilbanks Carpet Specialists, Inc., 84 F.T.C. 510 (1974); Tri-State Carpets, Inc., 84 F.T.C. 1078 (1974); Arthur Murray Studio, 78 F.T.C. 401 (1971), *aff'd*, 458 F.2d 622 (5th Cir. 1972); Household Sewing Machine Co., 76 F.T.C. 207 (1969); Holland Furnace Co. v. FTC, 55 F.T.C. 55 (1958), *aff'd*, 295 F.2d 302 (7th Cir. 1961).

604 Monroe Medical Clinic, Inc. v. Hospital Corp. of Am., 522 So. 2d 1362 (La. Ct. App. 1988); Love v. Keith, 383 S.E.2d 674 (N.C. Ct. App. 1989); Wilder v. Squires, 315 S.E.2d 63 (N.C. Ct. App. 1984); 15 Mo. Code State Regs. § 60-8.050 (use of duress or undue influence is unfair). *But cf.* Robinson v. Toyota Motor Credit Corp., 201 Ill. 2d 403, 775 N.E.2d 951, 266 Ill. Dec. 879 (2002) (lack of coercion is one factor in finding terms not unfair); Hoke v. Young, 89 N.C. App. 569, 366 S.E.2d 548 (1988) (facts do not establish coercion).

605 Wilder v. Squires, 315 S.E.2d 63 (N.C. Ct. App. 1984). *See also* Bertassi v. Allstate Ins. Co., 402 Mass. 366, 522 N.E.2d 949 (1988) (unfair to coerce consumer to sign waiver by refusing to pay rightfully owed insurance settlement); Love v. Keith, 383 S.E.2d 674 (N.C. Ct. App. 1989) (unfair to try to coerce release of escrow funds by wrongfully refusing to enroll home in warranty program). *But cf.* Farrell v. General Motors Corp., 249 Kan. 231, 845 P.2d 538 (1991) (not unconscionable to ask for release as part of generous settlement offer).

606 Pepsi-Cola Metro. Bottling Co. v. Checkers, Inc., 754 F.2d 10 (1st Cir. 1985) (Massachusetts law); Wilder v. Squires, 315 S.E.2d 63 (N.C. Ct. App. 1984).

607 Spiegel v. FTC, 540 F.2d 287 (7th Cir. 1976). *Accord* Barquis v. Merchants Collection Ass'n, 7 Cal. 3d 94, 496 P.2d 817, 101 Cal. Rptr. 745 (1972); Schubach v. Household Fin. Corp., 375 Mass. 133, 376 N.E.2d 140 (1978). *See also* § 5.1.1.4, *infra*; National Consumer Law Center, Fair Debt Collection § 11.3.4 (5th ed. 2004).

608 Moore v. Goodyear Tire & Rubber Co., 364 So. 2d 630 (La. Ct. App. 1978).

609 State v. Grogan, 628 P.2d 570 (Alaska 1981).

610 Ekl v. Knecht, 585 N.E.2d 156 (Ill. App. Ct. 1991).

611 Pfizer Inc., 81 F.T.C. 23 (1972) (dismissing complaint).

612 International Harvester Co., 104 F.T.C. 949 (1984). *See* § 4.2.14.2, *supra*.

In one case, the FTC found it unfair for a manufacturer to warn against use of a product in a certain fashion, but fail to explain why the violation of the manufacturer's safety instructions could be dangerous (*i.e.*, cause a gas tank explosion).[613] In other words, the FTC said that consumers could not reasonably avoid the safety hazard, even though the manufacturer's safety instructions warned against such behavior, unless consumers were informed of the risk of explosion. Similarly, where a pawn shop structured a loan so that the interest rate was 240% per year without clearly disclosing this, a federal court found this to be unfair.[614]

4.3.8 *Taking Advantage of a Vulnerable Group*

A 1933 United States Supreme Court case, interpreting "unfair methods of competition,"[615] has found unfair the sale of candy involving games of chance because the practice exploits a category of consumers—children—who are unable to protect themselves and because the amount of candy received for the purchase price depends on chance or a lottery, long deemed contrary to public policy.[616] Thus, in determining unfairness, one should consider not only public policy, but the vulnerability of the consumers involved. Under a Missouri UDAP regulation it is unfair to charge an inflated price for merchandise by taking advantage of a person's physical or mental impairment or hardship caused by extreme temporary conditions.[617]

Another vulnerable group is homeowners with marginal credit histories whom many lenders avoid, leaving a vacuum where predatory lending can develop. Responding to these concerns, a Massachusetts UDAP regulation prohibits as unfair any closed-end, non-purchase money mortgage loan rates or terms which significantly deviate from industry-wide standards or which are otherwise unconscionable.[618] A federal court decision has upheld this regulation in a case where the mortgage lender was charging ten points.[619] Even though Massachusetts law explicitly allows lenders to charge any number of points they choose, as long as that number is disclosed,[620] a UDAP regulation can still limit those points as unfair and deceptive.

The court measured the Massachusetts regulation and the lender's charging of ten points against the FTC's unfairness definition: substantial injury, not outweighed by the benefits to competition, and that could not be reasonably avoided by the consumer. The court found that all three aspects of this definition were met. The consumer injury was substantial—the points being charged. The court also found no adequate business justification for the practice, even though the lender argued that the alternative to charging high points was either to raise the mortgage rate or abandon the subprime market. The court disagreed, pointing out that other lenders servicing the same market charged five points or less, and that adding points to a loan increased the loan's APR, instead of reducing it.

The court also rejected the argument that market forces would take care of any problem, and the court thus found that consumers could not reasonably avoid the abuses. The court examined in some detail how market forces had failed to handle the subprime mortgage needs in certain geographic areas and for particular types of consumers. The court found that mortgage redlining and reverse redlining had led to both a vacuum of legitimate credit and an onslaught of predatory lenders.

4.3.9 *Illegal Conduct*

It is not hard to see how illegal conduct could easily fit under either the "*S&H*" or the FTC's current unfairness standards. The FTC has found unfair the practice of retaining surpluses from the sale of repossessed automobiles.[621] The practice is contrary to public policy as enunciated by the Uniform Commercial Code, oppressing victimized consumers and causing substantial injury measured by the money withheld. It is similarly unfair to retain credit balances owed to consumer debtors.[622]

It is unfair to keep the benefits of unlawful acts.[623] A landlord commits a UDAP violation by renting residential premises in which there is lead paint that exceeds statutory limits, because such an act is contrary to the public policy embodied in those statutes.[624] The unauthorized use of cable

613 *Id.*

614 Burnett v. Ala Moana Pawn Shop, Clearinghouse No. 46,771 (D. Haw. 1991), *aff'd*, 3 F.3d 1261 (9th Cir. 1993).

615 The FTC Act was subsequently amended to prohibit "unfair practices."

616 FTC v. Keppel & Bros., 291 U.S. 304 (1933).

617 15 Mo. Code State Regs. § 60-8.030.

618 Mass. Reg. Code tit. 940, § 8.06(6).

619 United Companies Lending Corp. v. Sargeant, 20 F. Supp. 2d 192 (D. Mass. 1998).

620 Mass. Gen. Laws ch. 183, § 63.

621 Ford Motor Co. (Francis Ford), 94 F.T.C. 564 (1979), *rev'd on other grounds*, 673 F.2d 1008 (9th Cir. 1981), *cert. denied*, 459 U.S. 999 (1982).

622 *Genesco*, 89 F.T.C. 451 (1977).

623 Jay Norris Inc., 91 F.T.C. 751 (1978), *aff'd*, 598 F.2d 1244 (2d Cir. 1979), *cert. denied*, 444 U.S. 980 (1980); Koscot Interplanetary, Inc., 86 F.T.C. 1106 (1975); Universal Credit Acceptance Corp., 82 F.T.C. 570 (1973), *rev'd in part sub nom.* Heater v. FTC, 503 F.2d 321 (9th Cir. 1974); Heastie v. Community Bank, 690 F. Supp. 716 (N.D. Ill. 1988) (knowingly accepting benefits of fraudulent conduct is unfair); Conaway v. Prestia, 191 Conn. 484, 464 A.2d 847 (1983) (unfair to receive rent from unlicensed rental); Golt v. Phillips, 308 Md. 1, 517 A.2d 328 (1986).

624 Hardy v. Griffin, 41 Conn. Supp. 283, 569 A.2d 49 (1989). *Accord* Creekside Apartments v. Poteat, 446 S.E.2d 826 (N.C. Ct. App. 1994) (landlord's maintenance of apartment in violation of housing codes was an unfair practice).

TV transmissions is unfair.[625] Kickbacks paid by real estate title insurers to mortgagee creditors are also actionable as unfair trade practices.[626]

Systematically overcharging a customer for two years is unfair.[627] A creditor who threatens criminal acts to collect a debt commits an unfair practice.[628] Demanding payment for a service never performed is an unfair practice.[629] A company commits an unfair act by going through a competitor's dumpster and publicizing information it uncovers, contrary to state laws against trespass and scavenging.[630] Racial harassment is an unfair business practice.[631] While simple rude or boorish behavior on the part of merchants is not a UDAP violation, if the conduct of a merchant repeatedly frightens, terrorizes, or physically endangers the public it is an unfair practice.[632] A state UDAP regulation finds unfair any violation of the duty of good faith.[633]

Attempts to circumvent legal requirements can also be unfair. The FTC has found unfairness under the "*S&H*" standard where drug advertising circumvents a Food and Drug Administration prohibition, thus offending public policy.[634] It is unfair for a creditor to scheme to avoid state exemption laws protecting retirement accounts by giving the impression those accounts are not exempt, obtaining a debtor's signature authorizing any payments out of the retirement account to go directly to the creditor, and then convincing the debtor to take money out of the retirement account.[635]

One of the most important applications of the FTC unfairness approach will be to find violations of federal or state law meant to protect the public and other forms of illegal conduct to be unfair. In effect, UDAP remedies will be incorporated into these other laws because a violation of these laws will also violate a UDAP statute's "unfairness" prohibition. To the extent a violation of one of these other laws causes substantial consumer injury, the three-part test should be met. There is no benefit to consumers or competitors in a company's violation of state or federal laws, and consumers can not be expected to avoid a company's law violations. Furthermore, the very fact that the state has prohibited a practice is a legislative determination that the practice causes substantial consumer injury. Violations of other state laws as UDAP violations are more thoroughly discussed in an earlier section.[636]

4.3.10 Misuse of Special Status

It is unfair for a person to use an official position to obtain favorable government action to the detriment of the consumer where the official has a financial interest in the matter.[637] It is unfair for a creditor to conspire with a home seller to avoid the seller's obligations under a purchase and sale agreement by denying the buyer's mortgage application too late for the buyer to find alternative financing.[638] It is unfair to take a loan application, mortgage and note, record the mortgage, and then disapprove the loan, but nonetheless refuse to satisfy the mortgage unless the consumer pays a broker fee and other charges.[639]

A bank, while acting as an escrow agent, acts unfairly by failing to answer letters, failing to pay interest as required, failing to account for the money, and intentionally disregarding its fiduciary duty.[640] It is also unfair for a broker to arrange, solely for the broker's own personal gain, to sell a business at a lower price than available from other potential buyers.[641] An insurance company commits an unfair trade practice by engaging in conduct that manifests an inequitable assertion of power or position.[642] A nursing home may commit a UDAP violation by billing patients the full price for drugs, while accepting a 15% kickback from the drug supplier.[643]

The FTC has also ruled as unfair the obtaining of tax preparation data and the use of it to solicit loans. While this practice does not run afoul of any statute, the inherent

625 Quincy Cablesystems, Inc. v. Sully's Bar, Inc., 684 F. Supp. 1138 (D. Mass. 1988).

626 Fitzgerald v. Chicago Title & Trust Co., 72 Ill. 2d 179, 380 N.E.2d 790, 20 Ill. Dec. 581 (1978).

627 Sampson-Bladen Oil Co. v. Walters, 356 S.E.2d 805 (N.C. Ct. App. 1987). *Cf.* Tudor v. Jewel Food Stores, Inc., 681 N.E.2d 6 (Ill. App. Ct. 1997) (overcharges resulting from errors by electronic scanner not unfair practice where store issued receipt allowing consumer to check prices and offered money-back guarantee in case of error).

628 Ekl v. Knecht, 585 N.E.2d 156 (Ill. App. Ct. 1991).

629 Patterson v. Beall, 19 P.3d 839 (Okla. 2000).

630 Camp, Dresser & McKee, Inc. v. Steimle & Assocs., Inc., 652 So. 2d 44 (La. Ct. App. 1995).

631 Ellis v. Safety Ins. Co., 41 Mass. App. Ct. 630, 672 N.E.2d 979 (1996). *See also* King v. First, 46 Mass. App. Ct. 372, 705 N.E.2d 1172 (1999) (plaintiff must pursue state administrative remedies before bringing UDAP claim of racial discrimination in housing).

632 State v. Shattuck, 747 A.2d 174 (Me. 2000).

633 15 Mo. Code State Regs. § 60-8.040.

634 Simeon Mgmt. Corp., 87 F.T.C. 1184 (1976), *aff'd*, 579 F.2d 1137 (9th Cir. 1978).

635 Petersen v. State Employees Credit Union (*In re* Kittrell), 115 B.R. 873 (Bankr. M.D.N.C. 1990). *See also* 316 49 St. Assocs. Ltd. v. Galvez, 269 N.J. Super. 481, 635 A.2d 1013 (1994) (use of phony lease-purchase option to evade rent control ordinance may be unconscionable).

636 *See* §§ 3.2.6, 3.2.7, *supra*.

637 Piccuirro v. Gaitenby, 20 Mass. App. Ct. 286, 480 N.E.2d 30 (1985).

638 Pedwell v. First Union Nat'l Bank, 51 N.C. App. 237, 275 S.E.2d 565 (1981).

639 McClendon v. Metropolitan Co., Clearinghouse No. 43,703G (Fla. Cir. Ct. Dade Cty. May 20, 1988).

640 United States v. U.S. Trust Co., 660 F. Supp. 1085 (D. Mass. 1986).

641 Dow & Condon, Inc. v. Anderson, 203 Conn. 475, 525 A.2d 935 (1987).

642 Murray v. Nationwide Mut. Ins. Co., 472 S.E.2d 358 (N.C. App. 1996).

643 Sullivan's Wholesale Drug v. Faryl's Pharmacy, Inc., 214 Ill. App. 3d 1073, 573 N.E.2d 1370 (1991).

confidentiality of tax data makes the practice violative of public policy. "Those who engage in commercial conduct which is contrary to a generally recognized public value are violating the FTC Act, notwithstanding that no other specific statutory strictures apply."[644] An insurance company's exclusive reliance upon the results of a polygraph test to deny the insured's claim, otherwise proper on its face, is unfair.[645]

4.3.11 Taking Advantage of an Emergency Situation

There is a growing body of law concerning merchants' price gouging in emergency situations. A number of states have statutes or regulations prohibiting price gouging for at least certain necessities during emergencies.[646] The New York statute prohibiting unconscionably excessive prices during market disruptions has survived constitutional challenge[647] and has been successfully applied to the sale of electric generators following a hurricane, where the generators were priced generally 5% to 30% above retail, with a few sales 60% above retail.[648]

Even where a state statute or regulation does not specifically prohibit price gouging during emergencies, a strong argument can be made that the practice is a UDAP violation. It should be a UDAP violation for a seller to take unfair advantage of an emergency to significantly increase prices where the seller's costs have not similarly increased.

Most state UDAP statutes prohibit "unfair practices." Federal courts and the Federal Trade Commission define "unfair" as causing substantial consumer injury not outweighed by countervailing benefits to competition and which the consumer could not reasonably avoid.[649] Price gouging in an emergency situation certainly meets these criteria. There is no benefit to competition for a seller to use the consumer's lack of choice to exert unfair advantage in an emergency situation. Charging exorbitant prices in an emergency may also violate a UDAP prohibition against unconscionable practices.[650]

4.3.12 Unconscionable Practices as Unfair Practices

Unconscionable practices are also unfair. Since case law dealing with unconscionability[651] is almost as extensive as that dealing with unfairness, unconscionability standards are useful in interpreting unfairness. UDAP cases have found it unfair to charge unconscionably high prices.[652] The inclusion of unconscionable terms in standardized agreements is an unfair practice.[653] A Connecticut appellate court, finding that a loan transaction was procedurally and substantively unconscionable, concluded that these facts established that the lender also violated the state UDAP statute.[654]

Massachusetts and Missouri regulations state that unconscionable acts are unfair or deceptive.[655] A New Jersey court has gone one step further and found that deception and fraud, as used in a UDAP statute, are interchangeable with

644 Beneficial Corp., 86 F.T.C. 119 (1975), *aff'd*, 542 F.2d 611 (3d Cir. 1976).

645 Elder v. Coronet Ins. Co., 201 Ill. App. 3d 733, 558 N.E.2d 1312 (1990).

646 Ala. Code § 8-31-3 (violation is UDAP violation); Ark. Code Ann. §§ 4-88-301–4-88-305 (part of UDAP statute); Fla. Stat. Ann. § 501.160, *et seq.* (violation is UDAP violation but statute explicitly denies private cause of action); Ga. Code Ann. §§ 10-1-393.4(a) (part of UDAP statute), 38-3-3 (defining emergency); Idaho Code § 48-603(19) (part of UDAP statute but no private cause of action is available for violations of this prohibition); Miss. Code Ann. § 75-24-25 (any unjustified price increase for any product is a violation during a state of emergency); N.Y. Gen. Bus. Law § 396-r; Tex. Bus. & Com. Code Ann. § 17.46(b)(27) (part of UDAP statute); Va. Code §§ 59.1-526–59.1-529 (violation is UDAP violation but Va. Code § 59.1-529 vests enforcement exclusively in public authorities); Conn. Agencies Regs. § 42-110b-29; Iowa Admin Code ch. 30, § 61-31.1(714), Excessive Prices; Mass. Regs. Code tit. 940, § 3.18; 15 Mo. Code State Regs. §§ 60-8.010, 60-8.030.

647 People v. Two Wheel Corp., 128 A.D.2d 507, 512 N.Y.S.2d 439 (1987) (statute not overly vague), *aff'd on other grounds*, 71 N.Y.2d 693, 530 N.Y.S.2d 46, 525 N.E.2d 692 (1988).

648 People v. Two Wheel Corp., 71 N.Y.2d 693, 530 N.Y.S.2d 46, 525 N.E.2d 692 (1988).

649 *See* § 4.3.2, *supra*.

650 *See* § 4.4, *infra*.

651 *See* § 4.4, *infra*.

652 *In re* Wernly, 91 B.R. 702 (Bankr. E.D. Pa. 1988) ($1156 fee to cash $11,171 Social Security check); Murphy v. McNamara, 36 Conn. Supp. 183, 416 A.2d 170 (Super. Ct. 1979) (lease of a RV set with option to buy at more than double retail value); People *ex rel.* Hartigan v. Knecht Servs., 216 Ill. App. 3d 843, 575 N.E.2d 1378 (1991) (charging unconscionably high prices for little or no services where consumer has no real alternatives, and after advertising "minimum charge"); Lane v. Fabert, 178 Ill. App. 3d 698, 533 N.E.2d 546 (1989); Korn v. Avis Rent-A-Car, 8 Pa. D. & C.3d 640 (C.P. Phila. Cty. 1977) (charging unconscionably high price for collision damage waiver may be unfair practice that violates state UDAP statute); State v. Ralph Williams' N.W. Chrysler Plymouth, Inc., 87 Wash. 2d 298, 553 P.2d 423 (1976). *But see* Saunders v. Michigan Avenue Nat'l Bank, 662 N.E.2d 602 (Ill. App. Ct. 1996) (charging unconscionably high price, without showing of other unfair tactics, is generally insufficient to establish UDAP unfairness claim).

653 People v. McKale, 25 Cal. 3d 626, 634–37, 159 Cal. Rptr. 811, 602 P.2d 731 (1979) (inclusion of illegal terms in mobile home park agreement was unfair even if park had not enforced them); People *ex rel.* Lockyer v. Fremont Life Ins. Co., 104 Cal. App. 4th 508, 128 Cal. Rptr. 2d 463, 470 (2002).

654 Family Fin. Servs., Inc. v. Spencer, 41 Conn. App. 754, 677 A.2d 479 (1996).

655 Mass. Consumer Protection Regulations, Mass. Regs. Code tit. 940, § 3.16, General (acts that are oppressive or unconscionable in any respect); 15 Mo. Code State Regs. § 60-8.080 (unconscionable acts, practices, or contract terms are unfair practices).

unconscionability, even though the statute does not mention unconscionability or unfairness.[656]

4.4 Unconscionability

4.4.1 Importance of Unconscionability Standard

Seventeen state UDAP statutes prohibit unconscionable practices.[657] The FTC Act does not use the word "unconscionable." Unconscionability as a UDAP concept appears to be an alternative to unfairness, since only a few UDAP statutes[658] proscribe both unconscionable and unfair practices. A prohibition of unconscionability may also be found in a state predatory lending statute.

The unconscionability concept is important even in states that do not explicitly proscribe unconscionable practices, since unconscionability has been held to violate UDAP statutes that specifically prohibit only unfair or even only deceptive practices.[659] Thus unconscionability standards have relevance to the seventeen UDAP statutes prohibiting unconscionable practices, and to the large number of other UDAP statutes that proscribe unfair acts, and perhaps even to those few statutes that only prohibit deceptive practices.

The term "unconscionability" should be interpreted liberally to effectuate the public purpose of UDAP statutes.[660] The Kansas Supreme Court holds that whether an action is unconscionable is a question of law for the court, but since it is highly dependent on the facts, a reviewing court will afford considerable deference to the sound discretion of the trial court.[661]

4.4.2 Definitions of Unconscionability in UDAP Statutes and Regulations

Many UDAP statutes and regulations themselves provide one source of unconscionability standards. For example, the Kansas, Ohio, and Utah UDAP statutes are based on the Uniform Consumer Sales Practices Act, adopted by the National Conference of Commissioners on Uniform State Laws and the American Bar Association. That uniform act states that in determining whether a practice is unconscionable, the court should consider circumstances which the supplier had reason to know, such as:

- That the supplier took advantage of the inability of the consumer to protect his or her interests reasonably because of physical infirmity, ignorance,[662] illiteracy,[663] inability to understand the language of an agreement, or similar factors;
- That when the consumer transaction was entered into, the price grossly exceeded the price at which similar property or services were readily obtainable in similar transaction by like consumers;
- That when the consumer transaction was entered into, the consumer was unable to receive a substantial benefit from the subject of the transaction;
- That when the consumer transaction was entered into, there was no reasonable probability of payment of the obligation in full by the consumer;[664]
- That the transaction the supplier induced the consumer to enter into was excessively one-sided in favor of the supplier; or
- That the supplier made a misleading statement of opinion on which the consumer was likely to rely to his or her detriment.[665]

This is a non-exhaustive list of factors and does not prevent the court from finding other conduct unconscionable.[666] Whether a UDAP statute is based on this uniform law or not, these standards and the drafting comments interpreting them should guide courts in determining whether a practice is unconscionable and thus whether it is also unfair.

Statutory definitions of unconscionability are also found in other state UDAP statutes and regulations. For example, Idaho's UDAP statute prohibits unconscionable practices and specifies four factors to consider in determining unconscionability: the first, second, and fifth factors found in the Uniform Consumer Sales Practices Act, and whether the conduct "would outrage or offend the public con-

656 Kugler v. Romain, 58 N.J. 522, 279 A.2d 640 (1971).

657 Ala. Code § 8-19-5(27); Ark. Code. Ann. § 4-88-107; D.C. Code Ann. § 28-3904(r); Fla. Stat. Ann. § 501.204; Idaho Code Ann. § 48-603C; Ind. Code. Ann. § 24-5-0.5-1; Kan. Stat. Ann. § 50-627; Ky. Rev. Stat. § 367.170; Mich. Comp. Laws § 445.903; Neb. Rev. Stat. § 87-303.01; N.J. Stat. Ann. § 56:8-2; N.M. Stat. Ann. § 57-12-3; N.Y. Exec. Law § 63(12); Ohio Rev. Code Ann. § 1345.03; Or. Rev. Stat. § 646.607; Tex. Bus. & Com. Code Ann. tit. 2, § 17.50; Utah Code Ann. § 13-11-5.

658 Fla. Stat. Ann. § 501.204; Mich. Comp. Laws § 445.903; N.M. Stat. Ann. § 57-12-3; Ohio Rev. Code Ann. §§ 1345.02, 1345.03; Or. Rev. Stat. §§ 646.607, 646.608(1)(u).

659 *See* § 4.3.12, *supra*.

660 Associates Home Equity Servs., Inc. v. Troup, 343 N.J. Super. 254, 778 A.2d 529 (App. Div. 2001).

661 State *ex rel.* Stovall v. DVM Enters., Inc., 62 P.3d 653 (Kan. 2003).

662 *See* Ford v. Brewer, 1986 Ohio App. LEXIS 9790 (Dec. 9, 1986) (definition of unconscionability refers to ignorance in general, not ignorance of a given, limited subject matter).

663 *See* Williams v. First Gov't Mortgage & Investors Corp., 225 F.3d 738 (D.C. Cir. 2000) (plaintiff had sixth grade education and was only semi-literate).

664 *Id.*

665 The model act and drafting comments are reprinted in 7A Uniform Laws Annotated and also Council of State Governments, 1973 Suggested State Legislation (Vol. XXXII), Clearinghouse No. 31,036, and are also reproduced on the companion CD-Rom to this volume.

666 State *ex rel.* Stovall v. Confirmed.com, 38 P.3d 707 (Kan. 2002).

science."[667] A Mississippi UDAP regulation instructs courts to consider the first, second, fourth, and sixth of these factors, plus "whether the supplier has refused, without justification, to make a cash refund unless another return policy is posted."[668] The Texas UDAP statute defines unconscionability as taking advantage of an individual's lack of knowledge, ability, experience, or capacity to a grossly unfair degree.[669] A former version of the statute also made gross disparity between price and value unconscionable. Under that version, gross disparity could be shown by economic loss alone, and there was no need to show intent or a specific misrepresentation.[670]

In making a finding of unconscionability, the court considers the entire transaction and not just its inception.[671] Unconscionability is determined under an objective standard, and the defendant's intent is irrelevant.[672] The reference to the seller's knowledge in some state UDAP definitions of unconscionability may imply a *scienter* requirement, however.[673] In these states, actual knowledge may be inferred where objective manifestations indicate that the seller acted with knowledge.[674] A seller is indisputably aware of the terms of its own form contract.[675]

4.4.3 UDAP Case Law Defining Unconscionability

There is also UDAP case law interpreting the concept of unconscionability. New Jersey courts define unconscionability as the absence of good faith, honesty in fact, and observance of fair dealing.[676] A practice can be unconscionable even though it is not listed in the statute.[677]

A seller's good faith or bona fide error does not necessarily defeat an unconscionability claim.[678] Similarly, there is no intent requirement for an unconscionability claim.[679] The Texas Supreme Court has discussed unconscionability as defined by the Texas UDAP statute—taking advantage of an individual's knowledge to a grossly unfair degree or, under a now-repealed provision, creating a gross disparity between the value received and the consideration paid. While finding no intent requirement, the court did emphasize that "gross" implied not just a slight but a significant unfairness or disparity.[680] A later case defines "gross" as "glaringly noticeable, flagrant, complete, and unmitigated."[681]

Unconscionability can be demonstrated without the showing of even one specific misrepresentation.[682] This can avoid or preclude squabbling about whether a particular statement was or was not made. As defined by the Kansas Supreme Court, however, a finding of unconscionable contract terms requires some element of deceptive bargaining conduct as well as unequal bargaining power.[683]

4.4.4 Taking Advantage of Vulnerable Consumers

The unconscionability standard should be applied with particular force when a professional seller is seeking the

667 Idaho Code Ann. § 48-603C. *See also* Or. Rev. Stat. § 646.605 (listing first, third, and fourth factors in definition of "unconscionable tactics"); S.C. Code § 37-5-108 (listing first, second, and third UCSPA factors, plus two others).

668 Code Miss. Rules 24 000 002 Rule 69.

669 Tex. Bus. & Com. Code Ann. § 17.45; Allison v. Fire Ins. Exchange, 98 S.W.3d 227 (Tex. App. 2002) (unconscionability does not equate with misrepresentation).

670 Johnston v. McKinney Am., Inc., 9 S.W.3d 271 (Tex. App. 1999).

671 Jones v. Ray Ins. Agency, 59 S.W.3d 739 (Tex. App. 2001).

672 Top Rank, Inc. v. Gutierrez, 236 F. Supp. 2d 637 (W.D. Tex. 2001).

673 Karst v. Goldberg, 88 Ohio App. 3d 413, 623 N.E.2d 1348 (1993) (proof of scienter is necessary to show unconscionability under Ohio's UDAP statute); State *ex rel.* Celebrezze v. Ferraro, 63 Ohio App. 3d 168, 578 N.E.2d 492 (1989). *But see* Insurance Co. of N. Am. v. Morris, 981 S.W.2d 667 (Tex. 1998).

674 *In re* Wiggins, 273 B.R. 839 (Bankr. D. Idaho 2001) (citing defendant's lack of due diligence in pursuing information); Karst v. Goldberg, 88 Ohio App. 3d 413, 623 N.E.2d 1348 (1993); Celebrezze v. Ferraro, 63 Ohio App. 3d 168, 578 N.E.2d 492 (1989).

675 Celebrezze v. Ferraro, 63 Ohio App. 3d 168, 578 N.E.2d 492 (1989).

676 Cox v. Sears, Roebuck & Co., 138 N.J. 2, 647 A.2d 454 (1994); Meshinsky v. Nichols Yacht Sales, Inc., 110 N.J. 464, 541 A.2d 1063 (1988); Associates Home Equity Servs., Inc. v. Troup, 343 N.J. Super. 254, 778 A.2d 529 (App. Div. 2001); *see also In re* Fleet, 95 B.R. 319 (E.D. Pa. 1989) (New Jersey law); Herner v. HouseMaster of Am., Inc., 349 N.J. Super. 89, 793 A.2d 55 (App. Div. 2002) (home inspection service soft-pedaled defects in order to avoid killing sales and antagonizing realtors from whom it got its referrals).

677 State *ex rel.* Stovall v. Confirmed.com, 38 P.3d 707 (Kan. 2002).

678 Miller v. Soliz, 648 S.W.2d 734 (Tex. App. 1983) (failure to credit down payment is unconscionable even though done in good faith or as bona fide error); *see also* Franks v. Associated Air Center, Inc., 663 F.2d 583 (5th Cir. 1981) (interpreting Texas law) (no need to show bad intent); Chastain v. Koonce, 700 S.W.2d 579 (Tex. 1985) (no need to show intent); Hurst v. Sears Roebuck & Co., 647 S.W.2d 249 (Tex. 1983) (failure to get building permit and home repairs inspected by city unconscionable even though this was impossible to do).

679 Williams v. Trail Dust Steak House, Inc., 727 S.W.2d 812 (Tex. App. 1987).

680 Chastain v. Koonce, 700 S.W.2d 579 (Tex. 1985). *See also* Dwight's Discount Vacuum Cleaner City, Inc. v. Scott Fetzer Co., 860 F.2d 646 (5th Cir. 1988) (Texas law), *cert. denied*, 490 U.S. 1108 (1989); Brown v. Galleria Area Ford, Inc., 752 S.W.2d 114 (Tex. 1988); Pfeiffer v. Ebby Halliday Real Estate, Inc., 747 S.W.2d 887 (Tex. App. 1988); Wyatt v. Petrila, 752 S.W.2d 683 (Tex. App. 1988).

681 State Farm Lloyds v. Nicolau, 951 S.W.2d 444 (Tex. 1997).

682 Wheeler v. Yettie Kersting Memorial Hosp., 866 S.W.2d 32 (Tex. App. 1993).

683 State *ex rel.* Stovall v. DVM Enters., Inc., 62 P.3d 653 (Kan. 2003); State *ex rel.* Stovall v. Confirmed.com, 38 P.3d 707 (Kan. 2002).

trade of those most subject to exploitation—the uneducated, the inexperienced, and people of low incomes.[684] Knowingly taking advantage of the consumer's confusion or frightened state of mind is unconscionable.[685] It is likewise unconscionable to take advantage of the inability of consumers to protect their interests because of an impairment,[686] the number and complexity of the documents,[687] or the inability to understand the language of the agreement[688] or technical terms.[689] Targeting a sales approach at minority groups and consumers of limited educational and economic means (such as those with incomes less than a certain amount a year)[690] or the use of duress to force a consumer to agree to a transaction[691] contribute to the unconscionability of a practice. A home improvement contractor's unworkmanlike performance can be unconscionable where the contractor takes advantage of the consumer's ignorance concerning the service allegedly offered.[692] An attorney's failure to take even the simplest steps toward performing the service paid for by his client is unconscionable because the attorney takes advantage of the consumer's lack of knowledge, ability, experience and capacity to a grossly unfair degree.[693]

UDAP decisions also hold unconscionable:

- Failing to determine whether a consumer possessed the aptitude and abilities necessary to successfully benefit from a business opportunity;[694]
- Inducing a brain-damaged 20-year-old to sell his structured settlement for a steeply discounted cash payment, while failing to follow up on information that would have disclosed his impairment;[695]
- Filing a groundless suit in a distant forum against a mentally impaired individual as a means of intimidation;[696]
- Inducing a disabled, aging, semi-literate man to place a mortgage on his home for a loan he had no reasonable probability of repaying;[697] and
- Taking advantage of an annuity recipient's diminished mental capacity and inability to understand the language and complexities of an assignment agreement, and dealing with the recipient's brother-in-law while knowing that he was not the appropriate legal representative.[698]

On the other hand, a court has found a sale conscionable, even if the dealer dealt with an "ignorant" buyer, if the buyer was protected by an accompanying friend who participated in the sale.[699]

4.4.5 Price Unconscionability

A substantial body of case law holds that a seller commits a UDAP violation by charging unconscionably high prices.[700] Selling a car for a higher-than-advertised price to

684 Associates Home Equity Servs., Inc. v. Troup, 343 N.J. Super. 254, 778 A.2d 529 (App. Div. 2001) (quoting from Kugler v. Romain, 58 N.J. 522, 543, 279 A.2d 640 (1971)).

685 Brown v. Banks, Clearinghouse No. 27,065 (Ohio C.P. Cuyahoga Cty. 1976) (seller solicited home repair job while house was still burning).

686 *In re* Wiggins, 273 B.R. 839 (Bankr. D. Idaho 2001).

687 *Id.* (complex 78-page document, in small type, requiring 30 signatures, with many substantive waivers, was excessively one-sided and unconscionable); Associates Home Equity Servs., Inc. v. Troup, 343 N.J. Super. 254, 778 A.2d 529 (App. Div. 2001).

688 316 49 St. Assocs. Ltd. v. Galvez, 269 N.J. Super. 481, 635 A.2d 1013 (1994).

689 Williams v. First Gov't Mortgage & Investors Corp., 225 F.3d 738 (D.C. Cir. 2000) (failure to explain mortgage terms to semi-literate man); Preston v. Kelsey, 1986 Ohio App. LEXIS 6703 (May 9, 1986) (seller acted unconscionably and violated UDAP statute by orally misrepresenting consumer's contract rights and taking advantage of his lack of business acumen); Brown v. Lyons, 43 Ohio Misc. 14, 332 N.E.2d 380, 72 Ohio Op. 2d 216 (C.P. Hamilton Cty. 1974).

690 Kugler v. Romain, 58 N.J. 522, 279 A.2d 640 (1971); Associates Home Equity Servs., Inc. v. Troup, 343 N.J. Super. 254, 778 A.2d 529 (App. Div. 2001).

691 Charping v. Light, 578 S.W.2d 462 (Tex. Civ. App. 1979).

692 Thrall v. Renno, 695 S.W.2d 84 (Tex. App. 1985). *But cf.* Roelle v. Orkin Exterminating Co., 2000 Ohio App. LEXIS 5141 (Nov. 7, 2000) (mere incompetence is not unconscionable).

693 DeBakey v. Staggs, 605 S.W.2d 631 (Tex. Civ. App. 1980).

694 Woo v. Great Southwestern Acceptance Corp., 565 S.W.2d 290 (Tex. Civ. App. 1978).

695 *In re* Wiggins, 273 B.R. 839 (Bankr. D. Idaho 2001).

696 *Id.*

697 Williams v. First Gov't Mortgage & Investors Corp., 225 F.3d 738 (D.C. Cir. 2000); Stone Street Servs., Inc. v. Daniels, 2000 WL 1909373 (E.D. Pa. Dec. 29, 2000) (unconscionable to take advantage of person's diminished capacity and inability to understand agreement); *see also* Associates Home Equity Servs., Inc. v. Troup, 343 N.J. Super. 254, 778 A.2d 529 (App. Div. 2001) (reversing summary judgment for lender).

698 Stone Street Servs., Inc. v. Daniels, 2000 WL 1909373 (E.D. Pa. Dec. 29, 2000).

699 Clayton v. McCary, 426 F. Supp. 248 (N.D. Ohio 1976).

700 Franks v. Associated Air Center, Inc., 663 F.2d 583 (5th Cir. 1982) (interpreting Texas law) (basing repair bill on many hours of work when repair should have taken just a few hours and price was grossly disproportionate); *In re* National Credit Mgmt. Group, 21 F. Supp. 2d 424 (D.N.J. 1998) (selling services for exorbitant price violates UDAP unconscionability standard where seller's advertisements were misleading as to nature and value of services); *In re* Fleet, 95 B.R. 319 (E.D. Pa. 1989) (New Jersey law) ($195 to $260 simply to refer debtors in financial distress to attorney where bar association referral service would do so for free); Phillips v. Dukes (Matter of Dukes), 24 B.R. 404 (Bankr. E.D. Mich. 1982) (loan broker charged price grossly in excess of price charged by others); Murphy v. McNamara, 36 Conn. Supp. 183, 416 A.2d 170 (Super. Ct. 1979); Nelson v. Associates Fin. Servs. Co., 659 N.W.2d 635 (Mich. App. 2003) (charging prepayment penalty in violation of Michigan usury law may violate UDAP prohibition against charging grossly excessive price); Slobin v. Henry Ford Health Care, 2002 WL 1482690 (Mich. App. July 9, 2002) (unpublished, citation limited) (price that is double what other

a buyer who had not seen the advertisement is unconscionable.[701] Using a phony lease-purchase option as a means of evading a rent control ordinance[702] or otherwise charging rent in excess of the ordinance is likewise a violation.[703]

A former provision of the Texas UDAP statute provided that a practice was unconscionable if it resulted in a gross disparity between the value received and the consideration paid.[704] Even though this provision has been repealed, decisions interpreting it[705] may be relevant in other states.

providers charge may violate Michigan's specific prohibition against grossly excessive prices), *rev'd on other grounds*, 666 N.W.2d 632 (Mich. 2003); McRaild v. Shepard Lincoln Mercury, 141 Mich. App. 406, 367 N.W.2d 404 (1985) (allowing consumer to trade $43,000 house for $27,000 car is unconscionable); Delaney v. Garden State Auto Park, 318 N.J. Super. 15, 722 A.2d 967 (App. Div. 1999) (charging $2200 for pre-delivery services that cost dealer $85, after consumer had rejected extended warranty that included those same services); Brown v. Silzar, 1981 Ohio App. LEXIS 13616 (Jan. 28, 1981) (excessive price of dance lessons a factor in unconscionability determination); Bruner v. Credit Motors, Inc., Clearinghouse No. 55602 (Toledo Mun. Ct., Lucas County, Ohio, Mar. 22, 1991); Bruner v. Credit Motors, Inc., Clearinghouse No. 53,568 (Ohio Mun. Ct. Aug. 14, 1989); Brown v. Lawyers Tax Service, Inc., Clearinghouse No. 26,059 (Ohio C.P. Hamilton Cty. 1976). *But see In re* Wiggins, 273 B.R. 839 (Bankr. D. Idaho 2001) (buying a structured settlement for a steeply-discounted cash price not unconscionable in and of itself, but court finds unconscionability in light of other factors); Sands v. Ticketmaster-New York, Inc., 207 A.D.2d 687, 616 N.Y.S.2d 362 (App. Div. 1994) (charging high fees not deceptive where fees are fully disclosed). *But cf.* Hatke v. Heartland Homecare Servs., Inc., 2003 WL 22283161 (Kan. App. Oct. 3, 2003) (unpublished) (charging high prices not unconscionable without deceptive bargaining conduct or unequal bargaining power).

701 Hamilton v. Davis Buick Co., Clearinghouse No. 53,569 (Ohio C.P. Ct. June 24, 1980).

702 316 49 St. Assocs. Ltd. v. Galvez, 269 N.J. Super. 481, 635 A.2d 1013 (1994).

703 *In re* Cohen, 191 B.R. 599 (D.N.J. 1996), *aff'd on other grounds*, 106 F.3d 52 (3d Cir. 1997), *aff'd*, 523 U.S. 213 (1998).

704 Tex. Bus. & Comm. Code § 17.45(5), prior to its amendment by Acts 1995, 74th Leg., ch. 414, § 2, eff. Sept. 1, 1995.

705 Brown v. Galleria Area Ford, Inc., 752 S.W.2d 114 (Tex. 1988); Segura v. Abbott Laboratories, Inc., 873 S.W.2d 399 (Tex. App. 1994) (restraining competition in infant formula market and overcharging retail customers), *rev'd on other grounds*, 907 S.W.2d 503 (Tex. 1995); Town East Ford Sales, Inc. v. Gray, 730 S.W.2d 796 (Tex. App. 1987); Miller v. Soliz, 648 S.W.2d 734 (Tex. App. 1983); Vick v. George, 671 S.W.2d 541 (Tex. App. 1983), *aff'd in part, rev'd in part on other grounds*, 686 S.W.2d 99 (Tex. 1984); Butler v. Joseph's Wine Shop, Inc., 633 S.W.2d 926 (Tex. App. 1982); Jim Walter Homes, Inc. v. White, 617 S.W.2d 767 (Tex. Civ. App. 1981); Sam Kane Beef Processors, Inc. v. Manning, 601 S.W.2d 93 (Tex. Civ. App. 1980); State v. Ralph Williams' N.W. Chrysler Plymouth, Inc., 87 Wash. 2d 298, 553 P.2d 423 (1976). *See also* La Chalet Int'l, Inc. v. Nowik, 787 S.W.2d 101 (Tex. App. 1990); Mytel Int'l, Inc. v. Turbo Refrigerating Co., 689 S.W.2d 315 (Tex. App. 1985). *Cf.* Castelli v. Lien, 910 S.W.2d 420 (Tenn. App. 1995).

4.4.6 Unconscionable Performance Practices

Consistently maintaining a pattern of inefficiency and incompetency and continually stalling and evading legal obligations to consumers is unconscionable.[706] Failing to do repair work, while claiming it was done, is unconscionable.[707] Other unconscionable performance practices are:

- Misleading a consumer through continuous stalling over a period of three months into believing that a car would be delivered when the seller had no assurance it would be;[708]
- Delaying for almost a year the installation of windows;[709]
- Delivery by a manufacturer of improper replacement parts;[710]
- Unreasonably refusing to allow a car purchaser to revoke acceptance of a defective car;[711] and
- Recommending a particular car model as suitable for pulling a trailer, and then failing to remedy the situation where the model was not suitable for that purpose.[712]

A Utah Supreme Court involving a landlord's failure to repair an apartment demonstrates why unconscionability after the contract has been negotiated may be easier to establish.[713] At the time the consumer rented an apartment, there was no unconscionable practice in renting a substandard unit because at that time the bargaining power of the landlord and tenants were roughly equal, and the landlord did not know about the unit's problems. But, after the tenants moved in, the relative positions of the two parties changed drastically. The tenants had only a choice between abandoning their home or living in substandard conditions. When the housing violations became evident, it was thus unconscionable for the landlord to fail to correct them. Also

706 Brown v. Lyons, 43 Ohio Misc. 14, 332 N.E.2d 380, 72 Ohio Op. 2d 216 (C.P. Hamilton Cty. 1974).

707 Town East Ford Sales, Inc. v. Gray, 730 S.W.2d 796 (Tex. App. 1987).

708 Wilman v. Ewen, 230 Kan. 262, 634 P.2d 1061 (1981).

709 Sinkfield v. Strong, 34 Ohio Misc. 2d 19, 517 N.E.2d 1051 (Mun. Ct. 1987).

710 Mercedes-Benz of N. Am. v. Dickenson, 720 S.W.2d 844 (Tex. App. 1986).

711 Ford Motor Co. v. Mayes, 575 S.W.2d 480 (Ky. Ct. App. 1978); Town East Ford Sales, Inc. v. Gray, 730 S.W.2d 796 (Tex. App. 1987).

712 Jeep Eagle Sales Corp. v. Mack Massey Motors, Inc., 814 S.W.2d 167 (Tex. App. 1991).

713 Wade v. Jobe, 818 P.2d 1006 (Utah 1991). *Cf.* Woodhaven Apartments v. Washington, 942 P.2d 918 (Utah 1997) (holding that UDAP statute applies to landlord-tenant issues other than habitability, and discussing definition of unconscionability). *But see* Carlie v. Morgan, 922 P.2d 1 (Utah 1996) (characterizing *Jobe* as dictum and holding that UDAP statute does not apply to uninhabitability claims).

unconscionable was the landlord condemning a house as a technique to evict the tenants.[714]

On the other hand, a repairman's failure to perform requested work was not unconscionable where the repairman considered the work unnecessary.[715] Nor was it unconscionable for a repairman to leave a car unattended, unlocked and with the keys in the ignition when delivering the car to another repair shop, even though this resulted in theft of the car.[716]

4.4.7 Unconscionable Collection and Enforcement Practices

It is unconscionable and a UDAP violation to threaten, before judgment, to inform a debtor's employer that the creditor intends to garnish the consumer's wages[717] and to exaggerate the remedies or power of the creditor or collector over the consumer.[718] Filing debt collection suits in distant forums is unconscionable.[719] But retaining a truck after installation of a new part until an earlier disputed bill was paid was not so outrageous and shocking to the conscience to dictate a finding of unconscionability as a matter of law.[720]

4.4.8 Other UDAP Unconscionability Decisions

UDAP case law also defines as unconscionable:

- Accepting money knowing that consumers would receive no substantial benefit;[721]
- Soft-pedaling defects found upon a home inspection in order to avoid killing sales and antagonizing the realtors from whom the inspection company got its referrals;[722]
- Signing a widow up for an $18,000 dance studio contract by using flattery and high pressure sales, then trying to switch her to a $49,000 contract, and upon failing, discouraging her from using the balance of her lessons;[723]
- Miscalculating the pay-off figure on a loan, and then refusing to return the overpayment to the consumer;[724]
- Offering only a credit and not a full refund when the seller's service turned out to be bogus;[725]
- Failing to credit a down payment to a sales contract;[726]
- Knowingly making false statements regarding the financing terms of a transaction;[727]
- Foreclosing on a home where the bank had loaned money to a contractor who absconded with the money, and where the homeowner had never approved the loan;[728]
- Demanding money that was not due, and evicting the consumer for failing to pay it;[729]
- Intentionally resetting a car's odometer;[730] and
- Giving the consumer one-sided contract terms in the form of a warranty that is so riddled with limitations as to be illusory.[731]

On the other hand, courts have rejected unconscionability claims in a number of cases. A sale of Viagra over the Internet without a physical exam, contrary to state law, was not unconscionable where the only purchasers before the court were investigators who had not been deceived or harmed.[732] The Kansas Supreme Court has held that even the on-line sale of a controlled substance—a weight-loss medication—was not unconscionable.[733] The same decision held that an on-line seller of medications did not act unconscionably by requiring buyers to sign a release of liability.[734]

Selling a gift card that could be used like a gift certificate, but charging a $1 monthly fee against it if it was not used after two years, was not unconscionable where the charge

714 Wade v. Jobe, 818 P.2d 1006 (Utah 1991).

715 Hyland v. Zuback, 146 N.J. Super. 407, 370 A.2d 20 (App. Div. 1976).

716 Chandler v. Housholder, 722 S.W.2d 217 (Tex. App. 1986).

717 Bennett v. Tri-State Collection Service, Clearinghouse No. 27,062 (Ohio C.P. Cuyahoga Cty. 1976).

718 *Id.*

719 *In re* Wiggins, 273 B.R. 839 (Bankr. D. Idaho 2001) (filing groundless suit in distant forum against mentally impaired individual as means of intimidation); Santiago v. S.S. Kresge Co., 2 Ohio Op. 3d 54 (C.P. Cuyahoga Cty. 1976).

720 Meyer v. Diesel Equip. Co., 1 Kan. App. 2d 574, 570 P.2d 1374 (1977).

721 Brown v. Silzar, 1981 Ohio App. LEXIS 13616 (Jan. 28, 1981) (inability of consumers to benefit from dance lessons a factor in unconscionability decision); Brown v. Wonderful World Publishing Co., Clearinghouse No. 27,055 (Ohio C.P. Franklin Cty. 1976); Brown v. Lyons, 43 Ohio Misc. 14, 332 N.E.2d 380, 72 Ohio Op. 2d 216 (C.P. Hamilton Cty. 1974).

722 Herner v. HouseMaster of Am., Inc., 349 N.J. Super. 89, 793 A.2d 55 (App. Div. 2002).

723 Bennet v. Bailey, 597 S.W.2d 532 (Tex. Civ. App. 1980). *Accord* Brown v. Silzar, 1981 Ohio App. LEXIS 13616 (Jan. 28, 1981) (unremitting sales pressure to sign up for dance lessons a factor in unconscionability determination).

724 Griffith v. Porter, 817 S.W.2d 131 (Tex. App. 1991).

725 Diversified Human Resources Group v. PB-KBB, 671 S.W.2d 634 (Tex. App. 1984).

726 Miller v. Soliz, 648 S.W.2d 734 (Tex. App. 1983).

727 Smith v. Precision Chevrolet, Clearinghouse No. 52,495 (N.J. Super. Aug. 19, 1999) (misstatement of amounts paid to others for credit insurance and extended warranty).

728 Longview Bank & Trust Co. v. Flenniken, 642 S.W.2d 568 (Tex. App. 1982).

729 Stringer v. Perales, 2003 WL 1848594 (Tex. App. Apr. 10, 2003) (unpublished, citation limited).

730 Wildstein v. Tru Motors, Inc., 227 N.J. Super. 331, 547 A.2d 340 (Law Div. 1988).

731 State *ex rel.* Celebrezze v. Ferraro, 63 Ohio App. 3d 168, 578 N.E.2d 492 (1989).

732 State *ex rel.* Stovall v. Confirmed.com, 38 P.3d 707 (Kan. 2002).

733 State *ex rel.* Stovall v. DVM Enters., Inc., 62 P.3d 653 (Kan. 2003).

734 *Id.*

was disclosed.[735] An insurer's failure to inform its insured of a settlement offer by a third party was not unconscionable, in the absence of evidence that the insured would have accepted the offer.[736] Nor is a mere breach of contract between two parties of equal bargaining power unconscionable.[737] Disparity of bargaining power is not enough to show unconscionability. There must be an attempt to exploit the weaker party.[738]

4.4.9 *Other Sources of Unconscionability Precedent*

4.4.9.1 General

Other sources of precedent for defining unconscionability are cases interpreting the term in the context of the common law,[739] sections 2-302[740] and 2A-108 of the Uniform Commercial Code, and the Uniform Consumer Credit Code (UCCC). UCC and UCCC case law in this area are analyzed in other National Consumer Law Center volumes in this series,[741] but in brief, section 2-302 deals with the lack of meaningful choices and unreasonable terms. While the Code does not define unconscionability, the Official Comment to Section 2-302 enunciates the following test:

> The basic test is whether, in light of the general commercial background and the commercial needs of the particular trade or case, the clauses involved are so one-sided as to be unconscionable . . . at the time of the making of the contract. . . . The principle is one of the prevention of oppression and unfair surprise [citation omitted] and not of disturbance of allocation of risks because of superior bargaining power.

Commentators delineate two forms of UCC unconscionability: procedural and substantive.[742] Procedural unconscionability involves oppression or unfair surprise resulting from consumer ignorance and seller guile, such as the consumer's lack of education and the seller's use of virtually incomprehensible fine-print standard-form contract provisions,[743] or the seller's use of English-language contracts where the seller knows the buyer can not speak English or can not read it.[744] Also unconscionable are binding the buyer to additional written terms after the contract is signed,[745] switching contract documents at the last moment to include non-negotiated, one-sided terms,[746] using one-sided contract terms that are standardized throughout the industry giving the consumer no opportunity to negotiate,[747] rushing the signing at a time when the consumer is vulnerable,[748] and purposefully selecting impoverished consumers to target for sales pitches.[749] It is unconscionable for a creditor to take a

735 Freeman v. Wal-Mart Stores, Inc., 111 Cal. App. 4th 660, 3 Cal. Rptr. 3d 860 (2003).

736 Trinity Universal Ins. Co. v. Bleeker, 966 S.W.2d 489 (Tex. 1998).

737 Group Hosp. Servs., Inc. v. One & Two Brookview Center, 704 S.W.2d 886 (Tex. App. 1986).

738 Wight v. Agristor Leasing, 652 F. Supp. 1000 (D. Kan. 1987).

739 *See, e.g.*, Matthews v. New Century Mortg. Corp., 185 F. Supp. 2d 874 (S.D. Ohio 2002) (denying motion to dismiss); Marin Storage & Trucking, Inc. v. Benco Contracting & Engineering, Inc., 89 Cal. App. 4th 1042, 107 Cal. Rptr. 2d 645 (2001) (setting forth unconscionability principles but finding indemnity clause in commercial contract not to be unconscionable).

740 *In re* Russell, 181 B.R. 616 (M.D. Ala. 1995); Fuentes v. Woodhouse Ford, Inc., 2004 WL 1243589 (Neb. App. June 8, 2004) (unpublished, citation limited) (drawing on non-UDAP unconscionability law to interpret UDAP statute); Wade v. Jobe, 818 P.2d 1006 (Utah 1991) (UCC unconscionability principles applicable to UDAP unconscionability standard).

741 National Consumer Law Center, Consumer Warranty Law § 11.2 (2d ed. 2001 and Supp.) (UCC case law); National Consumer Law Center, The Cost of Credit: Regulation and Legal Challenges § 11.6 (2d ed. 2000 and Supp.).

742 Ting v. AT&T, 319 F.3d 1126 (9th Cir. 2003); Phoenix Leasing Inc. v. Sure Broadcasting, 843 F. Supp. 1379 (D. Nev. 1994), *aff'd mem.*, 89 F.3d 846 (9th Cir. 1996); Maxwell v. Fidelity Fin. Servs., Inc., 184 Ariz. 82, 907 P.2d 51 (1995); Ilkhchooyi v. Best, 37 Cal. App. 4th 395, 45 Cal. Rptr. 2d 766 (1995); Construction Assocs., Inc. v. Fargo Water Equip. Co., 446 N.W.2d 237 (N.D. 1989) (commercial case); Woodhaven Apartments v. Washington, 942 P.2d 918 (Utah 1997) (applying U.C.C. precedent to UDAP analysis); Sosa v. Paulos, 924 P.2d 357 (Utah 1996). *See* Leff, *Unconscionability and the Code—The Emperor's New Clause*, 115 U. Pa. L. Rev. 485 (1967); National Consumer Law Center, Consumer Arbitration Agreements Ch. 4 (3d ed. 2003); White & Summers, 1 Uniform Commercial Code 4.3 (4th ed. 1995).

743 Ting v. AT&T, 319 F.3d 1126 (9th Cir. 2003) (use of bill stuffer that company knew few consumers would notice was procedurally unconscionable); Williams v. Walker-Thomas Furniture Co., 350 F.2d 445 (D.C. Cir. 1965). *See also* Tinsman v. Moline Beneficial Fin. Co., 531 F.2d 815 (7th Cir. 1970); John Deere Leasing Co. v. Blubaugh, 636 F. Supp. 1569 (D. Kan. 1986); Johnson v. Mobil Oil Corp., 415 F. Supp. 264 (E.D. Mich. 1976); Unico v. Owen, 50 N.J. 101, 232 A.2d 405 (1967).

744 Family Fin. Servs. v. Spencer, 677 A.2d 479 (Conn. App. 1996); Brooklyn Union Gas Co. v. Jimenez, 82 Misc. 2d 948, 371 N.Y.S.2d 289 (Civ. Ct. 1975); Kabro Constr. Corp. v. Carire, Pov. L. Rep. (CCH) ¶ 10,808 (Civ. Ct. N.Y. 1970); Jefferson Credit Corp. v. Marcano, 60 Misc. 2d 138, 302 N.Y.S.2d 390 (Civ. Ct. 1969); Central Budget Corp. v. Sanchez, 53 Misc. 2d 620, 279 N.Y.S.2d 391 (Civ. Ct. 1967); Frostifresh Corp. v. Reynoso, 52 Misc. 2d 26, 274 N.Y.S.2d 757 (Dist. Ct. 1966), *rev'd on issue of relief*, 54 Misc. 2d 119, 281 N.Y.S.2d 964 (App. Term 1967).

745 Chrysler Corp. v. Wilson Plumbing Co., 132 Ga. App. 435, 208 S.E.2d 321 (1974).

746 Industralease Automated & Scientific Equip. Corp. v. R.M.E. Enterprises, Inc., 58 A.D.2d 482, 396 N.Y.S.2d 427 (1977).

747 Henningsen v. Bloomfield Motors, Inc., 32 N.J. 358, 161 A.2d 69 (1960); Construction Assocs., Inc. v. Fargo Water Equip. Co., 446 N.W.2d 237 (N.D. 1989) (commercial case).

748 Sosa v. Paulos, 924 P.2d 357 (Utah 1996) (plaintiff was presented with agreement minutes before going into surgery).

749 Williams v. Walker-Thomas Furniture Co., 350 F.2d 445 (D.C. Cir. 1965); Jones v. Star Credit Corp., 59 Misc. 2d 189, 298 N.Y.S.2d 264 (Sup. Ct. 1969).

loan application, mortgage and note, record the mortgage, and then disapprove the loan, but nonetheless refuse to satisfy the mortgage unless the consumer pays a broker fee and other charges.[750]

Substantive unconscionability under the Uniform Commercial Code involves contract terms that are unreasonably, unacceptably, or unfairly harsh. Creditor remedies found unconscionable include cross-collateral[751] or waiver of defense[752] clauses, consent to breach of the peace in self-help repossession,[753] waiver of interest in repossessed personal property unless the creditor is notified,[754] and authorizing venue or jurisdiction in distant forums.[755] Also unconscionable are penalty clauses and excessive liquidated damage clauses.[756] Section 2A-108 of the UCC specifically lists unconscionable conduct in the collection of a claim arising from a lease contract as a basis for relief. Gross disparity between price and value is another form of substantive unconscionability.[757] Alabama courts have identified the following factors in assessing unconscionability: the party's lack of sophistication and/or education; the absence of meaningful choice; contract terms that unreasonably favor one party; unequal bargaining power; and oppressive, one-sided, or patently unfair contract terms.[758]

Courts take differing views about the necessity of proving both procedural and substantive unconscionability. Some courts will require a showing that both types of unconscionability are present.[759] But a weak showing of procedural unconscionability can be compensated for by a strong showing of substantive unconscionability, and vice versa.[760] Other courts will examine the extent of both procedural and substantive unconscionability, but are willing to find a practice unconscionable based exclusively on just procedural, or more commonly, substantive unconscionability.[761]

4.4.9.2 Specific UCC, UCCC, and Common Law Unconscionability Findings

An unconscionability case of special note to consumer debtors is *Besta v. Beneficial Loan Company*.[762] The Eighth Circuit overruled a district court opinion, and instead ruled that the facts required a finding of unconscionability under the Iowa Consumer Credit Code. The core unconscionabil-

750 McClendon v. Metropolitan Mortgage Co., Clearinghouse No. 43,703G (Fla. Cir. Ct. Dade Cty. May 20, 1988).

751 Williams v. Walker-Thomas Furniture Co., 350 F.2d 445 (D.C. Cir. 1965); *In re* Jackson, 9 U.C.C. Rep. 1152 (W.D. Mo. 1971). *But see* Bastaich v. Kenworth Northwest, Inc., 1997 Wash. App. LEXIS 635 (Apr. 28, 1997).

752 Quality Fin. Co. v. Hurley, 337 Mass. 150, 148 N.E.2d 385 (1958); Unico v. Owen, 50 N.J. 101, 232 A.2d 405 (1967).

753 Kosches v. Nichols, 68 Misc. 2d 795, 327 N.Y.S.2d 968 (Civ. Ct. N.Y. 1971).

754 Dean v. Universal CIT Credit Corp., 114 N.J. Super. 132, 275 A.2d 154 (App. Div. 1971).

755 Paragon Homes, Inc. v. Carter, 56 Misc. 2d 463, 288 N.Y.S.2d 817 (Sup. Ct.), *aff'd per curiam*, 30 A.D.2d 1052, 295 N.Y.S.2d 606 (1968).

756 Honey Dew Assocs. v. Bowen Inv., Inc., 81 F. Supp. 2d 352 (D.R.I. 2000), *vacated on other grounds*, 241 F.3d 23 (1st Cir. 2001) (remanding because trail court should have allocated burden of proof to party challenging the clause); John Deere Leasing Co. v. Blubaugh, 636 F. Supp. 1569 (D. Kan. 1986); Glacier Lincoln-Mercury, Inc. v. Freeman, 2 Pov. L. Rep. (CCH) ¶ 12,663 (Alaska Dist. Ct. 1970); Block v. Ford Motor Credit Co., 286 A.2d 228 (D.C. 1972); Magic Valley Truck Brokers, Inc. v. Meyer, 982 P.2d 945 (Idaho App. 1999); Collar City P'ship v. Redemption Church of Christ, 235 A.D.2d 665, 651 N.Y.S.2d 729 (1997); Bogatz v. Case Catering Corp., 86 Misc. 2d 1052, 383 N.Y.S.2d 535 (Civ. Ct. N.Y. 1976); Educational Beneficial, Inc. v. Reynolds, 67 Misc. 2d 739, 324 N.Y.S.2d 813 (Civ. Ct. N.Y. 1971); Kabro Constr. Corp. v. Carire, Pov. L. Rep. (CCH) ¶ 10,808 (Civ. Ct. N.Y. 1970); Holt Chevrolet, Inc. v. Meier, Pov. L. Rep. (CCH) ¶ 10,283 (Wis. Cir. Ct. Dane Cty. 1969). *But see* Woodhaven Apartments v. Washington, 942 P.2d 918 (Utah 1997) (liquidated damages clause in lease was unenforceable as a penalty, but was not shown to be unconscionable).

757 Maxwell v. Fidelity Fin. Servs., 907 P.2d 51 (Ariz. 1995); Murphy v. McNamara, 36 Conn. Supp. 183, 416 A.2d 170 (Super. Ct. 1979); Ahern v. Knecht, 202 Ill. App. 3d 709, 563 N.E.2d 787 (1990) (repair of air conditioner for $762 unconscionable); Sho-Po of Indiana, Inc. v. Brown, 585 N.E.2d 1357 (Ind. App. 1992); American Home Improvement, Inc. v. MacIver, 105 N.H. 435, 201 A.2d 886 (1964); Kugler v. Romain, 279 A.2d 640 (N.J. 1971); Toker v. Perl, 103 N.J. Super. 500, 247 A.2d 701 (Law. Div. 1968), *aff'd on other grounds*, 108 N.J. Super. 129, 260 A.2d 244 (App. Div. 1970); Toker v. Westerman, 113 N.J. Super. 452, 274 A.2d 78 (Dist. Ct. 1970); Rossi v. 21st Century Concepts, Inc., 162 Misc. 2d 932, 618 N.Y.S.2d 182 (Yonkers City Ct. 1994) (sale of overpriced cookware); Frostifresh Corp. v. Reynoso, 52 Misc. 2d 26, 274 N.Y.S.2d 757 (Dist. Ct. 1966), *rev'd on issue of relief*, 54 Misc. 2d 119, 281 N.Y.S.2d 964 (App. Term 1967); Jones v. Star Credit Corp., 59 Misc. 2d 189, 298 N.Y.S.2d 264 (Sup. Ct. 1969); State *ex rel.* Lefkowitz v. ITM, Inc., 52 Misc. 2d 39, 275 N.Y.S.2d 303 (Sup. Ct. 1966). *See also* Perdue v. Crocker Nat'l Bank, 38 Cal. 3d 913, 702 P.2d 503, 216 Cal. Rptr. 345 (1985), *appeal dismissed*, 475 U.S. 1001 (1986). *But see In re* Colin, 136 B.R. 856 (Bankr. D. Or. 1991) (price alone in RTO contract not enough to render leases unconscionable without overreaching).

758 Layne v. Garner, 612 So. 2d 404 (Ala. 1992). A bankruptcy court adopted this standard as the test for UDAP unconscionability in *In re* Russell, 181 B.R. 616 (M.D. Ala. 1995).

759 *See* Roberson v. Money Tree, 954 F. Supp. 1519 (M.D. Ala. 1997) (while loan agreements may amount to adhesion contracts, arbitration clause is not unconscionable because it is not substantively unfair to the consumer); Goodwin v. Ford Motor Credit Co., 970 F. Supp. 1007 (M.D. Ala. 1997) (same with regard to arbitration clause in installment sales contract). *See generally* National Consumer Law Center, Consumer Warranty Law § 11.2.4.5 (2d ed. 2001 and Supp.).

760 *See, e.g.*, Ting v. AT&T, 319 F.3d 1126 (9th Cir. 2003); Myrtle Beach Pipeline Corp. v. Emerson Elec. Co., 843 F. Supp. 1027 (D.S.C. 1993); Rite Color Chemical Co. v. Velvet Textile Co., 411 S.E.2d 645 (N.C. App. 1992). *See also* Hawkland, Uniform Commercial Code Series § 2-302.05 (1984, 1996 Supp.).

761 *See, e.g.*, Maxwell v. Fidelity Fin. Servs., Inc., 907 P.2d 51 (Ariz. 1995); Gillman v. Chase Manhattan Bank, 534 N.E.2d 824 (N.Y. 1988); Sosa v. Paulos, 924 P.2d 357 (Utah 1996).

762 855 F.2d 532 (8th Cir. 1988).

ity was that the lender did not disclose to the consumer that the consumer could have received the same loan proceeds with a three-year loan at a *lower monthly payment* and half the total of payments instead of the six-year loan the lender provided.[763] Since no reasonable person would have chosen the six-year loan with higher monthly payments, the lender should have at least disclosed to the consumer the choice that was available. Other cases have agreed that an extortionate interest rate can make a loan unconscionable.[764]

In another landmark case, the California Supreme Court, in *Perdue v. Crocker National Bank*,[765] decided that allegations that bank charges were more than six times actual costs and thus were unconscionable should survive a motion to dismiss. The court reached this conclusion after a lengthy discussion of situations where price unconscionability may be found. In this case the court was swayed by the fact that the charges resulted from a one-sided transaction where there were not the checks and balances which would inhibit the charging of unconscionable fees. In particular, there was an absence of equal bargaining power, open negotiation, full disclosure, and a contract which fairly sets out the rights and duties of each party.

Another interesting unconscionability case is *John Deere Leasing Co. v. Blubaugh*,[766] where the court refused to enforce unconscionable lease default terms. While UCC Article 2 may not apply to leases, the court applied the UCC unconscionability concept by analogy. The district court judge found the lease default terms unconscionable on both substantive and procedural grounds. The default provisions were found on the back of the contract, in such fine, light print as to be nearly illegible. The legalistic language was difficult to understand, and the definition of "termination value"—key to the default formula—was hidden elsewhere in the contract among a mass of additional terms. The lease itself was a pre-printed adhesion contract presented on a take-it-or-leave-it basis. Finally, there was significant disparity in sophistication and bargaining power between John Deere Leasing and the defendant farmer.

The court also found the default formula substantively unconscionable because it was a penalty clause and not liquidated damages. In particular, the court was offended that the default formula in effect forced the farmer to pay all remaining lease payments, exercise an otherwise voluntary purchase option, and then obtain credit for the sale price the lessor eventually obtains in re-selling the equipment.

A Ninth Circuit decision concluded that contract terms contained in an insert mailed with consumers' telephone bills was procedurally and substantively unconscionable.[767] The telephone company had conducted a study of whether consumers would notice and read the bill stuffer, and proceeded with it even though (or perhaps because) it found that consumers were unlikely to read it. The contract terms were offered on a take-it-or-leave-it basis, and the company told consumers that all other major carriers required the same terms. The terms imposed were also substantively unconscionable, including a prohibition of class actions, a requirement that consumers bear half the fees of arbitration, and a secrecy clause.

A final case, *Hager v. American General Finance*,[768] illustrates the use of a non-UCC unconscionability prohibition. The plaintiffs were unsophisticated and uneducated, and one of them was illiterate. Their income was low, and they were in desperate economic straits due to loss of their possessions in a house fire, so they had grossly inadequate bargaining power and few or no meaningful alternatives. A finance company initially lent them $2500, but refinanced repeatedly, starting just ten days after the original loan. The plaintiffs ended up with a substantial mortgage debt. A federal court denied summary judgment to the lender, holding that there were triable issues of fact as to whether the loan was unconscionable under the West Virginia UCCC.

In cases that do not involve the sale of goods, and so are not covered by the Uniform Commercial Code, judge-made unconscionability doctrines may provide similar protections. Thus, for example, in a Connecticut case a court, drawing on UCC precedent, found a mortgage loan procedurally unconscionable where the borrower had a limited knowledge of English, was uneducated, did not read very well, was unrepresented and rushed at closing, was not informed of important aspects of the transaction until the last minute, and did not have enough income to have a reasonable prospect of paying the debt.[769] The court also found the loan substantively unconscionable because it required a large balloon payment.

763 The longer term loan allowed the creditor to charge higher insurance premiums and take a real estate mortgage which resulted in various additional closing costs.

764 Carboni v. Arrospide, 2 Cal. Rptr. 2d 845 (Ct. App. 1991) (loan held unconscionable where 200% interest rate was charged on $99,000 secured loan); Brown v. C.I.L., Inc., 1996 U.S. Dist. LEXIS 4053 (N.D. Ill. Mar. 29, 1996) (denying motion to dismiss claim that loans with interest rates between 179% and 557% are unconscionable); Cobb v. Monarch Fin. Co., 913 F. Supp. 1164 (N.D. Ill. 1995) (denying motion to dismiss claim that loans with interest rates between 57% and 101% were unconscionable); Johnson v. Cash Store, 116 Wash. App. 833, 68 P.3d 1099 (2003) (upholding default judgment against payday lender).

765 38 Cal. 3d 913, 702 P.2d 503, 216 Cal. Rptr. 345 (1985), *appeal dismissed*, 475 U.S. 1001 (1986). *But cf.* Shadoan v. World Sav. & Loan Ass'n, 268 Cal. Rptr. 207 (Ct. App. 1990) (distinguishing *Perdue* because no allegation of lack of consumer choice and because challenged practice of prepayment penalties authorized by statute).

766 636 F. Supp. 1569 (D. Kan. 1986).

767 Ting v. AT&T, 319 F.3d 1126 (9th Cir. 2003).

768 37 F. Supp. 2d 778 (S.D. W. Va. 1999).

769 Family Fin. Servs., Inc. v. Spencer, 41 Conn. App. 754, 677 A.2d 479 (1996).

4.5 Unsubstantiated Claims

4.5.1 General

It is unfair and deceptive to make unsubstantiated claims, even if the claims later turn out to be true.[770] This is an important principle since it is often difficult to prove a claim to be false, but it may be easier to show that the seller did not have an adequate basis for making a claim at the time it was made.

Unsubstantiated claims violate UDAP statutes on two alternative theories. The deception theory holds that it is deceptive to fail to disclose that a claim is unsubstantiated because every product claim carries with it the representation that "the party making it possesses a reasonable basis for so doing, and that the assertion does not constitute mere surmise or wishful thinking on the advertiser's part."[771]

770 FTC v. Tashman, 318 F.3d 1273 (11th Cir. 2003) (franchisor's sales projections, backed up by nothing, were deceptive); FTC v. Pantron I Corp., 33 F.3d 1088 (9th Cir. 1994); Removatron Int'l Corp. v. FTC, 884 F.2d 1489 (1st Cir. 1989); Jay Norris, Inc. v. FTC, 598 F.2d 1244 (2d Cir. 1979), *cert. denied*, 444 U.S. 980 (1980); Fedders Corp. v. FTC, 529 F.2d 1398 (2d Cir.), *cert. denied*, 429 U.S. 818 (1976); National Dynamics Corp. v. FTC, 492 F.2d 1333 (2d Cir.), *cert. denied*, 419 U.S. 993 (1974); Firestone Tire & Rubber Co. v. FTC, 481 F.2d 246 (6th Cir.), *cert. denied*, 414 U.S. 1112 (1973); FTC v. Vital Living Prods., Inc., 5 Trade Reg. Rep. (CCH) ¶ 15223 (W.D.N.C. Feb. 22, 2002) (proposed consent order; kit purportedly detected anthrax spores); FTC Policy Statement Regarding Advertising Substantiation, 48 Fed. Reg. 30999 (Aug. 2, 1984); Esrim Ve Sheva Holding Corp., Dkt. C-4030, www.ftc.gov/opa/2001/12/fyi0164.htm (Dec. 21, 2001) (consent order); Sears Roebuck Co., 95 F.T.C. 406 (1980); Jay Norris, Inc., 91 F.T.C. 751 (1978), *aff'd*, 598 F.2d 1244 (2d Cir. 1979), *cert. denied*, 444 U.S. 980 (1980); Block Drug Co., 90 F.T.C. 893 (1977); Porter & Dietsch, 90 F.T.C. 770 (1977); Chrysler Corp., 87 F.T.C. 719 (1976); National Comm'n on Egg Nutrition, 88 F.T.C. 89 (1976), *modified*, 570 F.2d 157 (7th Cir. 1977), *cert. denied*, 439 U.S. 821 (1978); National Dynamics Corp., 82 F.T.C. 488 (1973), *aff'd*, 429 F.2d 1333 (2d Cir.), *cert. denied*, 419 U.S. 993 (1974); Firestone Tire & Rubber Co., 81 F.T.C. 398 (1972), *aff'd*, 481 F.2d 246 (6th Cir.), *cert. denied*, 414 U.S. 1112 (1973); Pfizer Corp., 81 F.T.C. 23 (1972) (complaint dismissed); Solar Age Indus., Inc., 109 F.T.C. 23 (1987) (consent order); Walgreen Co., 109 F.T.C. 156 (1987) (consent order); Dancer-Fitzgerald-Sample Inc., 96 F.T.C. 1 (1980) (consent order); Clorox Co., 94 F.T.C. 1 (1979) (consent order); Ford Motor Co., 93 F.T.C. 873 (1979) (consent order); J. Walter Thompson Co., 94 F.T.C. 331 (1979) (consent order); *see also* Novartis Consumer Health, Inc. v. Johnson & Johnson-Merck Consumer Pharmaceuticals Co., 290 F.3d 578 (3d Cir. 2002) (Lanham Act).

771 American Home Products, Corp. v. FTC, 695 F.2d 681 (3d Cir. 1982); National Comm'n on Egg Nutrition, 88 F.T.C. 89, 191 (1976), *modified*, 570 F.2d 157 (7th Cir. 1977), *cert. denied*, 439 U.S. 821 (1978). *See also* National Dynamics Corp., 82 F.T.C. 488 (1973), *aff'd*, 492 F.2d 1333 (2d Cir. 1974), *cert. denied*, 419 U.S. 993 (1974).

The unfairness theory is more direct: it is unfair to make an unsubstantiated claim to a consumer, particularly given the imbalance in knowledge and resources between a business enterprise and consumers. Economically, it is far more reasonable for the manufacturer to substantiate the claim than for each consumer to investigate.[772]

4.5.2 FTC Standards

The FTC has delineated criteria for determining whether an advertiser has a reasonable basis for a claim. Adequate substantiation depends on a case-by-case analysis, but consideration should be given to the following factors:

- The specificity of the claims;
- The nature of the product offered;
- The consequences if the claim is false;
- Consumer reliance on the claim; and
- The accessibility of substantiation data.[773]

The FTC has added two other factors that determine how much substantiation is required to demonstrate a claim's reasonable basis: the benefits of a truthful claim and the amount of substantiation experts think reasonable.[774] The FTC also now requires two well-controlled scientific studies as substantiation where the product involves health and safety and where the claim is of a scientific nature and is difficult for consumers to judge.[775]

The substantiation requirement does not just pertain to claims involving health, safety, or technical issues, but also applies, for example, to claims regarding comparative grocery prices,[776] the merit of educational programs,[777] and products to help disabled people communicate.[778] Claims based on tests are deceptive where they do not reflect the inadequacy of those tests to prove the claim.[779] Even im-

772 Pfizer, Inc., 81 F.T.C. 23 (1972) (complaint dismissed).

773 FTC Policy Statement Regarding Advertising Substantiation, 104 F.T.C. 648, 49 Fed. Reg. 30999 (Aug. 2, 1984); Pfizer, Inc., 81 F.T.C. 23 (1972) (complaint dismissed). *See also* 5 Trade Reg. Rep. (CCH) ¶ 24,832 (Nov. 30, 2000) (denial of petition for rulemaking; FTC reiterates its continued adherence to its substantiation policy).

774 FTC Policy Statement Regarding Advertising Substantiation, 49 Fed. Reg. 30999 (Aug. 2, 1984); Thompson Medical Co., 104 F.T.C. 648 (1984), *aff'd*, 791 F.2d 189 (D.C. Cir. 1986).

775 Thompson Medical Co., 104 F.T.C. 648 (1984), *aff'd*, 791 F.2d 189 (D.C. Cir. 1986). *See also* T-UP, Inc. v. Consumer Protection Div., 801 A.2d 173 (Md. App. 2002); Removatron Int'l Corp., 111 F.T.C. 206 (1988), *aff'd*, 884 F.2d 1489 (11th Cir. 1989).

776 The Kroger Co., 98 F.T.C. 639 (1981).

777 Gateway Educational Products, Inc., 5 Trade Reg. Rep. (CCH) ¶ 23,728 (F.T.C. Dkt. C-3581 1995) (consent order).

778 Louis Bass, Inc., 5 Trade Reg. Rep. (CCH) ¶ 23,729 (F.T.C. Dkt. C-3562, 3563 1995).

779 Unither Phama, Inc., File No. 022-3-36, www.ftc.gov/opa/2003/07/fyi0347.htm (July 29, 2003) (consent order) (substantiation

plied claims about a product must be substantiated.[780] The nature of the claim will affect the type of substantiation required.

Advertisers that make claims based on allegedly scientific surveys can run afoul of a UDAP statute. Where claims are specific, and appear to be based on an adequate survey, the practice is deceptive if the surveys do not meet scientific standards or the results are not accurately and fairly reported.[781] This is so even if the advertiser did not claim to conduct a survey, but where the net impression is one of medical or scientific proof.[782] Even if a test is adequate at the time it was made, intervening events may make it no longer accurate by the time the seller makes advertising claims.[783] But where an advertiser does not imply a scientific basis for the claim, the advertiser need only have a reasonable basis for the claim, even if the scientific community is split as to the validity of the claim.[784]

inadequate because studies did not account for placebo effect and sample size was too small); Med Gen, Inc., Dkt. C-4061, www.ftc.gov/opa/2002/07/fyi0240.htm (July 19, 2002) (consent order) (stiffening substantiation requirement after FTC discovered that company had composed the questions and compiled the results of study); Sears Roebuck Co., 95 F.T.C. 406 (1980); *see also* Standard Oil Co. of California, 84 F.T.C. 1401 (1974), *modified on other grounds*, 577 F.2d 653 (9th Cir. 1978).

780 Novartis Corp., 5 Trade Reg. Rep. ¶ 24,614, F.T.C. Dkt. 9279 (May 27, 1999), *aff'd*, 223 F.3d 783 (D.C. Cir. 2000).

781 Removatron Int'l Corp. v. FTC, 884 F.2d 1489 (1st Cir. 1989); FTC v. Pharmtech Research, Inc., 576 F. Supp. 294 (D.D.C. 1983); J. Walter Thompson USA, Inc., 5 Trade Reg. Rep. (CCH) ¶ 23,861 (F.T.C. C-3622 1995) (consent order) (misrepresentation of survey results); Thompson Medical Co., 104 F.T.C. 648 (1984), *aff'd*, 791 F.2d 189 (D.C. Cir. 1986), *cert. denied*, 479 U.S. 1086 (1987); Cliffdale Assocs., 103 F.T.C. 110 (1984); Bristol-Myers Co., 102 F.T.C. 21 (1983), *aff'd*, 738 F.2d 554 (2d Cir. 1984), *cert. denied*, 469 U.S. 1189 (1985); Sterling Drug, Inc., 102 F.T.C. 395 (1983), *aff'd*, 741 F.2d 1146 (11th Cir. 1984); The Kroger Co., 98 F.T.C. 639 (1981); Litton Indus. Inc., 97 F.T.C. 1 (1981); Amana Refrigerator, Inc., 102 F.T.C. 1262 (1983) (consent order); Ogilvy v. Mather Int'l Inc., 101 F.T.C. 1 (1983) (consent order); J. Walter Thompson Co., 97 F.T.C. 333 (1981) (consent order); Standard Brands Inc., 97 F.T.C. 233 (1981) (consent order); Ted Bates & Co., 97 F.T.C. 220 (1981) (consent order); Teledyne Inc., 97 F.T.C. 320 (1981) (consent order); *see also* T-UP, Inc. v. Consumer Protection Div., 801 A.2d 173 (Md. App. 2002) (rejecting various proffers of substantiation as lacking scientific validity).

782 American Home Products Corp., 98 F.T.C. 136 (1981), *aff'd*, 695 F.2d 681 (3d Cir. 1983); *see also* Bristol-Myers Co., 102 F.T.C. 21 (1983), *aff'd*, 738 F.2d 554 (2d Cir. 1984), *cert. denied*, 469 U.S. 1189 (1985); Sterling Drug, Inc., 102 F.T.C. 395 (1983), *aff'd*, 741 F.2d 1146 (9th Cir. 1984); Porter & Dietsch, 90 F.T.C. 770 (1977).

783 Stihl, Inc., 101 F.T.C. 840 (1983) (consent order) (3-year-old comparison test no longer valid).

784 Bristol-Myers Co., 102 F.T.C. 21 (1983), *aff'd*, 738 F.2d 554 (2d Cir. 1984), *cert. denied*, 469 U.S. 1189 (1985); Sterling Drug, Inc., 102 F.T.C. 395 (1983), *aff'd*, 741 F.2d 1146 (9th Cir. 1984).

4.5.3 State UDAP Precedent

Connecticut was the first state to explicitly include a substantiation requirement in its UDAP regulations—in this case requiring car dealers to have sufficient information upon which a reasonable belief in the truth of their claims can be based.[785] Idaho, Massachusetts, Mississippi, Missouri and Ohio have also enacted UDAP regulations requiring sellers to have substantiation for their claims.[786] Pennsylvania regulations prohibit unsubstantiated automobile advertising.[787] New Mexico and Wisconsin UDAP regulations require sellers to have substantiation of claims that products are recycled, recyclable, or degradable.[788] One of California's UDAP statutes establishes an administrative procedure by which the attorney general and other public authorities can require an advertiser to produce substantiation of its claims.[789] Private plaintiffs can also bring UDAP claims, but they bear both the burden of production and the burden of proof.[790]

The Iowa Supreme Court found unsubstantiated claims about a water conditioner to be actionable under the state's UDAP statute.[791] The Iowa UDAP statute now defines as deceptive advertising the making of an advertised claim where there is no reasonable basis to make that claim.[792] A Maryland case approves the state consumer protection agency's application of the standard to a seller of alternative medical treatments.[793] A South Carolina case has found energy saving claims deceptive using a lack of substantiation theory,[794] and a California court has enjoined unsubstantiated price comparisons.[795]

785 Standards for Advertising and Selling Motor Vehicles, Conn. Agencies Regs. § 42-110b-28.

786 Idaho Consumer Protection Regulations, Idaho Admin. Code 04.02.01.031; 940 Mass. Regs. Code tit. 940, § 6.03(1); Code Miss. Rules 24 000 002 Rule 10; 15 Mo. Code State Regs. § 60-7.040; Ohio Admin. Rule 109:4-3-10.

787 37 Pa. Code § 301.2(6).

788 N.M. Admin. Code tit. 1, §§ 12.2.5.9, .10, .16, .18; Wis. Dep't of Agriculture, Trade & Consumer Protection Rules, Wis. Admin. Code ch. ATCP 137.08, Environmental Labeling of Products.

789 Nat'l Council Against Health Fraud, Inc. v. King Bio Pharmaceuticals, Inc., 107 Cal. App. 4th 1336, 133 Cal. Rptr. 2d 207 (2003) (interpreting Cal. Bus. & Prof. Code § 17508).

790 *Id.*

791 State *ex rel.* Miller v. Hydro Mag, Ltd., 436 N.W.2d 617 (Iowa 1989).

792 Iowa Code § 714.16(2)(a); *see also* State *ex rel.* Miller v. National Dietary Research, Inc., 454 N.W.2d 820 (Iowa 1990).

793 T-UP, Inc. v. Consumer Protection Div., 801 A.2d 173 (Md. App. 2002).

794 State *ex rel.* McLeod v. Whiteside, Clearinghouse No. 38,907 (S.C. C.P. July 17, 1981).

795 People v. Custom Craft Carpets, Inc., 206 Cal. Rptr. 12 (Ct. App. 1984).

4.6 Deceptive Pricing Inducements

4.6.1 Bait and Switch

"Bait and switch" is the advertising of a product without the bona fide intention to sell it ("bait"), for the purpose of establishing contact with a prospective customer in order to "switch" the customer to the purchase of another, usually higher priced product. This is achieved through a variety of practices designed to discourage the sale of the advertised product at the advertised price.[796] Bait-and-switch tactics are most likely to occur with high-ticket items such as cars, appliances, and loans, but can be used for any product. Some switches are so skillfully performed that the consumer quickly forgets the advertised bait.

The FTC has prohibited various forms of this practice in numerous individual cases[797] and through an official FTC Guide.[798] Forms of bait advertising the FTC has prohibited include disparaging an advertised product for the purpose of switching the customer to another product,[799] advertising a product whose actual appearance or performance discourages its purchase by being below the quality implied or represented in the advertising,[800] and refusing to show or sell the advertised product.[801] Other proscribed types of bait advertising include claiming the advertised product is unavailable or failing to have the advertised product available in reasonable quantity[802] and refusing to take orders for delivery within a reasonable time.[803]

Evidence indicating an illegal bait-and-switch scheme includes a relatively low number of sales of the advertised product at the advertised price,[804] the commission structure for the sale of the advertised product compared with other products,[805] and a comparison of the amount of advertising expenditures to the sale of the advertised product.[806]

State regulations are another important source interpreting when bait advertising violates state UDAP acts. A typical regulation rules unfair or deceptive such non-bona fide offers to sell as: refusing to show or sell the product as advertised; disparaging the product or its guarantee, credit

796 Official FTC Synopsis of FTC Decisions Concerning "Bait and Switch" Sales Practices (approved by the Commission Sept. 23, 1975). *See also* Freight Liquidators, 85 F.T.C. 274 (1975); Tashof, 74 F.T.C. 1361 (1968), *aff'd*, 437 F.2d 707 (D.C. Cir. 1970); McGough v. Oakwood Mobile Homes, Inc., 779 So. 2d 793 (La. App. 2000) (non-UDAP case reciting salesman's testimony about use of bait and switch tactics); FTC Guides Against Bait Advertising, 16 C.F.R. Part 238.

797 Tashof v. FTC, 437 F.2d 707 (D.C. Cir. 1970); All-State Indus. of North Carolina v. FTC, 423 F.2d 423 (4th Cir. 1970), *cert. denied*, 400 U.S. 828 (1970); Consumer Products of Am., Inc. v. FTC, 400 F.2d 930 (3d Cir. 1968), *cert. denied*, 393 U.S. 1088 (1969); Better Living, Inc. v. FTC, 259 F.2d 271 (3d Cir. 1958); New Rapids Carpet Center, Inc., 90 F.T.C. 64 (1977); Carpets "R" Us, Inc., 87 F.T.C. 303 (1976); Mut. Constr. Co., 87 F.T.C. 621 (1976); Maryland Carpet Outlet, Inc., 85 F.T.C. 754 (1975); Sir Carpet, Inc., 85 F.T.C. 190 (1975); American Aluminum Corp., 84 F.T.C. 48 (1974), *aff'd per curiam*, 522 F.2d 1278 (5th Cir. 1975), *cert. denied*, 426 U.S. 906 (1976); Wilbanks Carpet Specialists, Inc., 84 F.T.C. 510 (1974); All-State Indus. of North Carolina, Inc., 75 F.T.C. 465 (1969), *aff'd*, 423 F.2d 423 (4th Cir.), *cert. denied*, 400 U.S. 828 (1970); Pati-Port, Inc., 60 F.T.C. 35 (1962), *aff'd*, 313 F.2d 103 (4th Cir. 1963); Sears Roebuck & Co., 89 F.T.C. 229 (1977) (consent order).

798 Guides Against Bait Advertising, 16 C.F.R. Part 238. The FTC has published guidelines for applying the requirements of this and other rules to on-line sales. FTC, Dot Com Disclosures (2000), available on the FTC's website, www.ftc.gov.

799 New Rapids Carpet Center, Inc., 90 F.T.C. 64 (1977); Carpets "R" Us, Inc., 87 F.T.C. 303 (1976); Maryland Carpet Outlet, Inc., 85 F.T.C. 754 (1975); Sir Carpet, Inc., 85 F.T.C. 190 (1975); Wilbanks Carpet Specialists, Inc., 84 F.T.C. 510 (1974); Southern States Distributing Co., 83 F.T.C. 1126 (1973); Seekonk Freezer Meats, Inc., 82 F.T.C. 1025 (1973); Aluminum Indus., Inc., 67 F.T.C. 1 (1965); State v. Quality Meats of Concord, Inc., Clearinghouse No. 44,812 (Alaska Super. Ct. Dec. 28, 1988) (preliminary injunction).

800 Tri-State Carpets, Inc., Docket No. 8945 (1974); Wilbanks Carpet Specialists, Inc., 84 F.T.C. 510 (1974); Seekonk Freezer Meats, Inc., 82 F.T.C. 1025 (1973); Supreme Freezer Meats, Inc., 73 F.T.C. 990 (1968); Consumer Products of Am., Inc., 72 F.T.C. 533 (1967); Consolidated Sewing Machine Corp., 71 F.T.C. 356 (1967); R&B Sewing Machine & Vacuum Cleaner Co., 70 F.T.C. 1463 (1966). *But cf.* State v. American TV & Appliance, Inc., 146 Wis. 2d 292, 430 N.W.2d 709 (1988) (placing an adequate model next to a better model is not bait and switch).

801 Atlantic Constr. & Supply Co., 83 F.T.C. 1449 (1974) (consent order); Turkey Mountain Estates, Inc., 84 F.T.C. 698 (1974) (consent order); Lifetime, Inc., 59 F.T.C. 1231 (1961); Household Sewing Machine Co., 52 F.T.C. 250 (1955). *But see* Ford Motor Credit Co. v. Russell, 519 N.W.2d 460 (Minn. App. 1994) (no bait-and-switch violation where dealer made advertised financing rate available to other customers who had better credit histories).

802 Surdyk's Liquor, Inc. v. MGM Liquor Stores, 83 F. Supp. 2d 1016 (D. Minn. 2000) (applying FTC guide as standard in Lanham Act claim); Holiday Carpets, Inc., 76 F.T.C. 673 (1969); Better Living, Inc., 54 F.T.C. 648 (3d Cir. 1957), *aff'd*, 259 F.2d 271 (3d Cir. 1958); Brown v. Silzar, 1981 Ohio App. LEXIS 13616 (Jan. 28, 1981) (luring customers with advertisement for social club and then selling dance lessons violates bait and switch rule).

803 Southern States Distributing Co., 83 F.T.C. 1126 (1973); Royal Constr. Co., 71 F.T.C. 762 (1967).

804 Wilbanks Carpet Specialists, Inc., 84 F.T.C. 510 (1974); Southern States Distributing Co., 83 F.T.C. 1126 (1973); Tashof, 74 F.T.C. 1361 (1968), *aff'd*, 437 F.2d 707 (D.C. Cir. 1970). *Cf.* State v. American TV & Appliance, 146 Wis. 2d 292, 430 N.W.2d 709 (1988) (relatively low number of sales of advertised product not sufficient by itself to show bait and switch).

805 Wilbanks Carpet Specialists, Inc., 84 F.T.C. 510 (1974); Consumer Products of Am., 72 F.T.C. 533 (1969). *Cf.* State v. American TV & Appliance, 146 Wis. 2d 292, 430 N.W.2d 709 (1988) (commission structure by itself insufficient to show bait and switch).

806 Tashof v. FTC, 437 F.2d 707 (D.C. Cir. 1970); Giant Food Inc. v. FTC, 322 F.2d 977 (D.C. Cir. 1963), *cert. denied*, 376 U.S. 967 (1964); Carpets "R" Us, Inc., 87 F.T.C. 303 (1976); Maryland Carpet Outlet, Inc., 85 F.T.C. 754 (1975); Southern States Distributing Co., 83 F.T.C. 1126 (1973).

terms, availability of service or otherwise; failing to have available at all outlets listed in the advertising a sufficient quantity to meet anticipated demand unless otherwise disclosed; refusing to take orders for delivery within a reasonable period of time; showing or delivering defective or otherwise unusable products for the purpose advertised; and using a sales plan or method of compensation discouraging the sale of the advertised product.[807]

Similarly, several regulations specifically proscribe an attempt to "unsell" the consumer after a completed sale, with the purpose of switching the consumer to other goods.[808] In addition, a number of state UDAP statutes specifically prohibit bait and switch.[809]

Colorado's highest court has found a statutory prohibition of bait advertising not to be unconstitutionally vague.[810] The court found such terms as "disparagement of own services," "tie-in sales," and "advertisement" adequately specific, based on common sense, long-time business and legal usage, and statutory intent. An Illinois court has found a violation of the UDAP statute's prohibition against advertising goods or services with the intent not to sell them as advertised, where a car dealer failed to reveal the advertised price of a car to a walk-in customer.[811] Even without a specific statutory prohibition, bait and switch tactics meet the general UDAP definition of deception.[812]

The Hawaii Supreme Court has ruled that bait and switch tactics are unfair practices as defined by its UDAP statute whether or not the "bait" is communicated through public advertising.[813] Thus, a loan officer's statement early in the process of loan negotiation that a low rate was available could be the basis of a bait and switch claim. Sending solicitations to the consumer that state or imply that a new loan is offered, but then switching the consumer to a much more expensive refinancing of an existing loan, is deceptive.[814]

Damages and causation issues sometimes arise in private suits challenging bait and switch tactics. This issue is discussed in §§ 7.5.2.5.5 and 8.3.5.2, *infra*.

4.6.2 Unavailability of Advertised Items

A practice related to bait and switch is advertising goods of which the seller does not have sufficient quantity to meet anticipated demand. The intent is to lure the buyer to the seller's establishment with bargain advertising for a product that will be out of stock before many customers arrive. These customers will purchase substitute or other goods given the inconvenience of shopping elsewhere once they are at the seller's premises.

The FTC's Retail Food Store Advertising and Marketing Practices Rule[815] prohibits advertised offers of retail food when the store does not have the product readily available or has not ordered enough items in adequate time to meet reasonably anticipated demands.[816] Advertisements must conspicuously disclose all limitations as to the product's availability, *e.g.*, when sold in only certain stores or for a certain period of time. A store can comply by clearly and adequately disclosing in its advertisements that there are limitations on availability, or by offering rain checks or substitute items if supplies run out. The Commission also indicated in its preamble to the Retail Food Store Rule that this principle is applicable in general to the advertising of other commodities.[817]

807 *See, e.g.*, Connecticut Regulations for the Dep't of Consumer Protection, Conn. Agencies Regs. § 42-110b-18, Misleading Advertising, and § 42-110b-20, Bait and Switch; Idaho Consumer Protection Regulations, Idaho Admin. Code 04.02.01.050–.055, Bait and Switch Sales; Louisiana Consumer Protection Division Rules and Regulations, La. Admin. Code tit. 16, pt. III § 507, Bait Advertising; Massachusetts Consumer Protection Regulations, Mass. Regs. Code tit. 940, §§ 3.02, False Advertising, and 6.06, Retail Advertising, Availability of Advertised Products; Code Miss. Rules 024 000 002 Rules 18–22; 15 Mo. Code State Regs. § 60-7.080 and .090; Mont. Admin. Rules ch. 2.61.101(h), (i), (m); Ohio Admin. Code § 109:4-3-03, Bait Advertising; Rules for the Utah Consumer Sales Practices Act, Utah Admin. Rule 152-11-3, Bait Advertising; Code Vt. Rules 06 031 001 Rule 103, Bait Advertising; *see also* Greenbrier Dodge v. May, 155 Ga. App. 892, 273 S.E.2d 186 (1980); *cf.* State v. American TV & Appliance, Inc., 146 Wis. 2d 292, 430 N.W.2d 709 (1988).

808 Idaho Consumer Protection Regulations, Idaho Admin. Code 04.02.01.053, Bait and Switch Sales; Massachusetts Consumer Protection Regulations, 940 Mass. Regs. Code § 3.02, False Advertising; Ohio Admin. Code § 109:4-3-03, Bait Advertising; Code Vt. Rules 06 031 001 Rule 103.02.

809 *See* Garcia v. Overland Bond & Investment Co., 282 Ill. App. 3d 486, 668 N.E.2d 199 (1996) (applying Illinois statutory prohibition); Williams v. Bruno Appliance & Furniture Mart, 62 Ill. App. 3d 219, 379 N.E.2d 52 (1978) (same).

810 People *ex rel.* Dunbar v. Gym of Am., Inc., 177 Colo. 97, 493 P.2d 660 (1972).

811 Affrunti v. Village Ford Sales, Inc., 597 N.E.2d 1242 (Ill. App. Ct. 1992). *See also* Garcia v. Overland Bond & Investment Co., 282 Ill. App. 3d 486, 668 N.E.2d 199 (1996); Motzer Jeep Eagle, Inc. v. Ohio Attorney General, 95 Ohio App. 3d 183, 642 N.E.2d 20 (1994); Collins v. Fred Haas Toyota, 21 S.W.3d 606 (Tex. App. 2000). *See generally* § 5.4.7.2, *infra*.

812 Fendrich v. RBF, L.L.C., 842 So. 2d 1076 (Fla. Dist. Ct. App. 2003).

813 Hawaii Community Fed. Credit Union v. Keka, 94 Haw. 213, 11 P.3d 1 (2000).

814 Chandler v. Am. Gen. Fin., Inc., 329 Ill. App. 3d 729, 768 N.E.2d 60 (2002).

815 16 C.F.R. Part 424.

816 *See also* Kroger Co., 90 F.T.C. 459 (1977) (consent order); Fisher Food, Inc., 90 F.T.C. 473 (1977) (consent order); Food Fair Stores, Inc., 90 F.T.C. 491 (1977) (consent order); Shop-Rite Foods, Inc., 90 F.T.C. 500 (1977) (consent order); Great Atlantic & Pacific Tea Co., 85 F.T.C. 601 (1975); Pay'n Pak Stores, Inc., 87 F.T.C. 99 (1976) (consent order).

817 *See also* General Motors Corp., 93 F.T.C. 860 (1979) (consent order); Zayre Corp., 90 F.T.C. 328 (1977) (consent order); Fred Meyer, Inc., 87 F.T.C. 112 (1976) (consent order).

A number of state UDAP regulations also proscribe advertising unavailable items.[818] Unless otherwise disclosed, all the advertiser's stores within the advertising area must have the product in stock during the period of the advertisement. General disclaimers are not sufficient, but a disclosure of the specific stores carrying the item and the number of items available is adequate.[819] In Ohio, with some exceptions, a seller must offer a rain check when the goods offered on "sale" are sold out.[820] In some states, the offer of "rain checks" or comparable goods will be a mitigating circumstance, but not a complete defense.[821] The FTC requires sellers to disclose in advertising if they offer rain checks.[822]

In addition, a number of state UDAP statutes specifically prohibit advertising unavailable goods. But one court has limited a prohibition against "advertising goods or services with intent not to sell them as advertised" to general advertising claims, not one-on-one representations.[823]

In a long opinion, a Maine trial court closely examined various Sears Roebuck and Co. policies, and found no evidence of deceptive advertisement of unavailable goods.[824] The opinion is very helpful in understanding how large retailers deal with the unavailability issue.

A New York appellate court has held that it was deceptive to advertise that a product was on sale for a certain period, when the seller's entire supply had been depleted before the sale began.[825] The court rejected the seller's argument that it should be excused because it had been allocated an adequate supply that had been depleted by unusually high demand before the sale. The seller must have a reasonable supply at the commencement of the sale.[826]

4.6.3 Deceptive Pricing and Bargain Sales

4.6.3.1 Deceptive Pricing in Comparison to a Reference Price

Deceptive pricing and illegal bargain sales involve a variety of pricing gimmicks that lure consumers into retail premises believing they are getting a bargain when they are not. The basic concept is that it is deceptive for advertisers to compare their own "sale" prices with some other reference prices unless the article on sale and the nature of the reference prices are explicitly identified and the seller can substantiate the reference price.

Such phony sales violate general prohibitions of deceptive conduct in the FTC Act[827] and state UDAP statutes.[828] The FTC has also adopted guidelines on the use of reference prices, which not only spell out specific deceptive practices but also explain why these practices are deceptive.[829] A number of states have similar UDAP regulations.[830] The

818 Alaska Admin. Code tit. 9, § 05.040; Connecticut Regulations for the Dep't of Consumer Protection, Conn. Agencies Regs. § 42-110b-18, Misleading Advertising; Hawaii Rules Relating to Unfair or Deceptive Practices in Advertising, 16 Haw. Admin. Code § 303-7; Idaho Consumer Protection Regulations, Idaho Admin. Code 04.02.01.100–.106, Insufficient Supply/Limitation on Quantity; Ill. Admin. Code tit. 14, 470.310; Louisiana Consumer Protection Division Rules and Regulations, La. Admin. Code tit. 16, pt. III § 507, Bait Advertising, and tit. 46, pt. V. § 701, Bait Advertisement-Motor Vehicles; Massachusetts Consumer Protection Regulations, Mass. Regs. Code tit. 940, § 6.06, Retail Advertising, Availability of Advertised Products; 15 Mo. Code of State Regs. 60-7.080; Mont. Admin. Rules 2.61.101(1)(i); New Jersey Administrative Rules of the Division of Consumer Affairs, N.J. Admin. Code ch. 13:45A-9.2, Advertising and Marketing Practices (1976); Ohio Admin. Code § 109:4-3-03, Bait Advertising; Rules of the Utah Consumer Sales Practices Act, Utah Admin. Rules 152-11-3, Exclusions and Limitations in Advertisement; Code Vt. Rules 06 031 001 Rule 103.

819 Connecticut Regulations for the Dep't of Consumer Protection, Conn. Agencies Regs. § 42-110b-18, Misleading Advertising; Hawaii Rules Relating to Unfair or Deceptive Practices in Advertising, 16 Haw. Admin. Code § 303-7, Unfair or Deceptive Practices in Advertising.

820 Ohio Admin. Code § 109:4-3-03; *see also* Fleck v. Custom Sound Co., 1981 Ohio App. LEXIS 14162 (Dec. 31, 1981); Katz v. G.C. Murphy Co., 1979 Ohio App. LEXIS 8976 (Jan. 31, 1979).

821 Idaho Consumer Protection Regulations, Idaho Admin. Code 04.02.01.100, Insufficient Supply/Limitation on Quantity; Massachusetts Consumer Protection Regulations, Mass. Regs. Code tit. 940, § 6.06, Retail Advertising, Availability of Advertised Products.

822 *See* Kroger Co. 90 F.T.C. 459 (1977) (consent order); Fisher Food, Inc., 90 F.T.C. 473 (1977) (consent order); Food Fair Stores, Inc., 90 F.T.C. 491 (1977) (consent order); Shop-Rite Foods, Inc., 90 F.T.C. 500 (1977) (consent order); Pay'n Pak Stores, Inc., 87 F.T.C. 99 (1976) (consent order).

823 Deer Creek Constr. Co. v. Peterson, 412 So. 2d 1169 (Miss. 1982).

824 Maine v. Sears, Roebuck & Co., Clearinghouse No. 40,629 (Me. Super. Ct. 1985).

825 DeSantis v. Sears, Roebuck & Co., 543 N.Y.S.2d 228 (App. Div. 1989).

826 *Id.*

827 Giant Foods, Inc. v. FTC, 322 F.2d 977 (D.C. Cir. 1963), *cert. denied*, 376 U.S. 967 (1964); Baltimore Luggage Co. v. FTC, 296 F.2d 608 (4th Cir. 1961), *cert. denied*, 369 U.S. 860 (1962); Niresk Indus. v. FTC, 278 F.2d 337 (7th Cir.), *cert. denied*, 364 U.S. 883 (1960); Progress Tailoring Co. v. FTC, 153 F.2d 103 (7th Cir. 1946); Macher v. FTC, 126 F.2d 420 (2d Cir. 1942); Thomas v. FTC, 116 F.2d 347 (10th Cir. 1940); George's Radio & Television Co., 60 F.T.C. 179 (1962); State *ex rel.* Lefkowitz v. Bevis Indus., Inc., 63 Misc. 2d 1088, 314 N.Y.S.2d 60 (Sup. Ct. 1970).

828 State *ex rel.* Kidwell v. Master Distributors, 101 Idaho 447, 615 P.2d 116 (1980); Tennessee Attorney General Opinion Letter to Commissioner of Tennessee Dep't of Commerce and Ins., Clearinghouse No. 38,905 (Jan. 17, 1985).

829 FTC Guides Against Deceptive Pricing, 16 C.F.R. Part 233. *See also* B. Sanfield, Inc. v. Finlay Fine Jewelry Corp., 168 F.3d 967 (7th Cir. 1999) (remanding company's claim with instructions that District Court consider whether competitor violated Illinois and FTC reference price regulations).

830 Code Miss. Rules 24 000 002 Rules 24–30; Nev. Admin. Code ch. 598.200–.290, Regulations of the Department of Commerce,

seller can not seek to mislead the buyer that the he or she is saving the difference between the price fictitiously offered as a comparison and the seller's allegedly lower asking price.[831]

Thus, comparisons with a seller's own former prices must be based on actual bona fide former prices.[832] Nevertheless, it is not always easy to determine when a former price is bona fide. For example, in the jewelry industry it is common to mark prices up as much as five times cost, and at a later date to discount those regular prices. A North Carolina court, after a lengthy trial, held that a former price was bona fide if the retailer offered the merchandise 50% of the time at the higher prices and 25% of total sales must be at such higher prices.[833]

A large retailer with a number of stores can get into trouble by advertising sale prices compared to the retailer's own "regular prices." Where that retailer's individual stores are authorized to offer lower "competitive" prices than the company's "regular" prices, the result is nationally advertised price reductions which are less than advertised for certain individual stores or may be no reduction at all from an individual store's "competitive price."[834] Similarly, a suggested retail price advertised by a manufacturer may be significantly higher than the actual, average, negotiated price. Or a national car manufacturer may offer a sale price which is not actually available in all parts of the country because regional distributors increase the price by adding their own accessories to the advertised models.

Discounted introductory offers or other references to higher future prices must actually be followed by higher prices.[835] Comparisons with competitors' prices must refer

---

Consumer Affairs Division, Comparative Price Advertising; N.D. Admin. Code ch. 10-15-01.

831 FTC Guides Against Deceptive Pricing, 16 C.F.R. Part 233. *See also* B. Sanfield, Inc. v. Finlay Fine Jewelry Corp., 168 F.3d 967 (7th Cir. 1999) (remanding company's claim with instructions that District Court consider whether competitor violated Illinois and FTC reference price regulations).

832 *FTC decisions and guides*: FTC v. Standard Education Society, 302 U.S. 112 (1937); Spiegel Inc. v. FTC, 411 F.2d 481 (7th Cir. 1969); Regina Corp. v. FTC, 322 F.2d 765 (3d Cir. 1963); Niresk Indus., Inc. v. FTC, 278 F.2d 337 (7th Cir.), *cert. denied*, 364 U.S. 883 (1960); Kalwajtys v. FTC, 237 F.2d 654 (7th Cir. 1956), *cert. denied*, 352 U.S. 1025 (1957); Grolier Inc., 91 F.T.C. 315 (1978), *vacated, remanded on other grounds*, 615 F.2d 1215 (9th Cir. 1980), *on remand, reinstated as modified*, 98 F.T.C. 882 (1981); Carpets "R" Us, Inc., 87 F.T.C. 303 (1976); Encyclopedia Britannica, Inc., 87 F.T.C. 421 (1976), *aff'd*, 605 F.2d 964 (1979); Hollywood Carpets Inc., 86 F.T.C. 784 (1975); Certified Building Products Inc., 83 F.T.C. 1004 (1973), *aff'd sub nom.* Thiret v. FTC, 512 F.2d 176 (1975); Arthur Murray Studio, 78 F.T.C. 401 (1971), *aff'd*, 458 F.2d 622 (5th Cir. 1972); Home Centers Inc., 94 F.T.C. 1362 (1979) (consent order).

Interpretation of general UDAP prohibitions: State *ex rel.* Lefkowitz v. Bevis Indus., Inc., 63 Misc. 2d 1088, 314 N.Y.S.2d 60 (Sup. Ct. 1970) (advertising merchandise as "on sale" or "reduced" violates general prohibition of deception if the goods have not been sold recently at the alleged original price).

State regulations:

Alaska: Alaska Admin. Code tit. 9, § 05.020.

Connecticut: Connecticut Regulations for the Dep't of Consumer Protection, Conn. Agencies Regs. §§ 42-110b-10(2), Deceptive Pricing.

Hawaii: Hawaii Rules Relating to Unfair or Deceptive Practices in Advertising, 16 Haw. Admin. Code § 303-4, Unfair or Deceptive Practices in Advertising.

Idaho: Idaho Consumer Protection Regulations, Idaho Admin. Code 04.02.01.060–.062, Deceptive and Comparative Pricing; *see also* State *ex rel.* Kidwell v. Master Distributors, 101 Idaho 447, 615 P.2d 116 (1980) (reversing denial of restitution order where telemarketer misrepresented price as special discount price).

Illinois: Ill. Admin. Code tit. 14, §§ 470.210–.250.

Louisiana: La. Admin. Code tit. 16, pt. III §§ 301–323, Deceptive Pricing; *see also* State *ex rel.* Guste v. Crossroads Gallery, Inc., 357 So. 2d 1381 (La. Ct. App. 1978) (use of higher reference price violates regulation where merchandise was offered at lower price 90% of time).

Massachusetts: Massachusetts Consumer Protection Regulations, Mass. Regs. Code tit. 940, § 6.05, Retail Advertising.

Mississippi: Code Miss. Rules 24 000 002 Rule 25.

Missouri: 15 Mo. Code State Regs. § 60-7.060.

Montana: Mont. Admin. Rules 2.61.101(1)(p).

Nevada: Nev. Admin. Code § 598.200–.290.

New Jersey: New Jersey Administrative Rules of the Division of Consumer Affairs, N.J. Admin. Code ch. 13:45A-9, Advertising and Marketing Practices; *see also* Division of Consumer Affairs v. General Electric Co., 244 N.J. Super. 349, 582 A.2d 831 (App. Div. 1990) (New Jersey rule applies only to retailers, not to manufacturers).

New York: Guggenheimer v. Ginzburg, 43 N.Y.2d 268, 372 N.E.2d 17, 401 N.Y.S.2d 182 (1977) (reversing dismissal of complaint alleging violation of New York City price comparison regulation).

Oregon: Oregon Rules Related to Unlawful Trade Practices, Or. Admin. Rule 137-20-0010, Misleading Price Representations.

Pennsylvania: Pennsylvania Attorney General Guidelines for Use of Reference Prices in Price Reduction Advertisements; Commonwealth v. Mirror World Inc., Clearinghouse No. 26,022 (Pa. C.P. Phila. Cty. 1978); Commonwealth v. Programmed Learning Sys., Inc., Clearinghouse No. 26,019 (Pa. C.P. Cty. Allegheny Cty. 1975).

Vermont: Vermont Consumer Fraud Rules, Code Vt. Rules 06 031 005 Rule 110, Deceptive Pricing; *see also* Vermont v. Gene Rosenberg, Clearinghouse No. 50,445 (Vt. Super. Ct. Apr. 26, 1995) (enforcing Vermont's price comparison rule).

Wisconsin: Wis. Dep't of Agriculture, Trade & Consumer Protection Rules, Wis. Admin. Code. ch. ATCP 124, Price Comparison Advertising.

833 State *ex rel.* Thornburg v. J.C. Penney Co., Clearinghouse No. 49,157 (N.C. Super. Ct. 1992).

834 State v. F.W. Woolworth Co., Clearinghouse No. 36,566 (Md. Cir. Ct. Prince George's Cty. 1983). *See also* State v. F.W. Woolworth Co., Clearinghouse No. 45,901 (Md. Cir. Ct. Prince George's Cty. May 31, 1990) ($100,000 civil penalty).

835 FTC Guides Against Deceptive Pricing, 16 C.F.R. § 233.5; *see also* State *ex rel.* Corbin v. Tucson Public Auction, 147 Ariz. 213, 709 P.2d 570 (Ct. App. 1985) (deceptive to offer rebate if buyer made purchase immediately, where stated price was fictitious); Ill. Admin. Code tit. 14, 470.230; 15 Mo. Code State Regs. § 60-7.060; Oregon Rules Related to Unlawful Trade Practices, Rule 137-20-010, Misleading Price Representations;

to prices at which a substantial number of sales have been made in the same trade area.[836] Specific savings claims substantiated by surveys of competitors' prices may not be adequate where there are scientific flaws in the surveys.[837]

An offer of a price reduction of an unspecified size must be significant, normally at least five or ten percent.[838] Nor can general offers of price reductions apply only to a few items in a store.[839] Thus where advertising refers to discounts on certain products, those discounts must apply to all models of that product unless clearly disclosed otherwise.[840]

"List," "suggested retail," and related price representations must refer to prices at which a substantial number of goods have been sold in the trade area.[841] Manufacturers and wholesalers may not preticket, advertise, or provide the means by which the retailer engages in such deceptive pricing.[842]

4.6.3.2 Other Deceptive Pricing Techniques

Various misrepresentations that goods are "wholesale," "factory-priced," "seconds" or "imperfect," and related deceptive claims have been prohibited.[843] "Below cost" prices must be below the seller's cost to purchase and prepare the item.[844] Giving a buyer $2000 for a trade-in

Wis. Dep't of Agriculture, Trade & Consumer Protection Rules, Wis. Admin. Code ch. ATCP 124, Price Comparison Advertising.

836 Tashof v. FTC, 437 F.2d 707; Hollywood Carpets, Inc., 86 F.T.C. 784 (1975); Home Centers Inc., 94 F.T.C. 1362 (1979) (consent order); People v. Columbia Research Corp., 71 Cal. App. 3d 607, 139 Cal. Rptr. 517 (1977) (interpreting UDAP statute that defined prevailing market price for use in ads); Guggenheimer v. Ginzburg, 43 N.Y.2d 268, 372 N.E.2d 17, 401 N.Y.S.2d 182 (1977) (reversing dismissal of complaint concerning ad for "bargain" price that was higher than competitor's, in violation of New York City UDAP ordinance); FTC Guides Against Deceptive Pricing, 16 C.F.R. § 233.2 (1967); Alaska Admin. Code tit. 9, § 05.030; Connecticut Regulations for the Dep't of Consumer Protection, Conn. Agencies Regs. §§ 42-110b-92–42-110b-142, Deceptive Pricing; Hawaii Rules Relating to Unfair or Deceptive Practices in Advertising, 16 Haw. Admin. Code § 303-6, Unfair or Deceptive Practices in Advertising; Ill. Admin. Code tit. 14, § 470.260; Massachusetts Consumer Protection Regulations, Mass. Regs. Code tit. 940, § 6.05, Retail Advertising; Code Miss. Rules 24 000 02 Rule 26; 15 Mo. Code State Regs. § 60-7.060; Mont. Admin. Rules 8.78.101(1)(p); Nev. Admin. Code § 598.200; Code Vt. Rules 06 031 005 Rule 110, Deceptive Pricing; *see also* Concorde Limousines, Inc. v. Moloney Coachbuilders, Inc., 835 F.2d 541 (5th Cir. 1987) (Texas law); State v. Ralph Williams' N.W. Chrysler Plymouth, Inc., 87 Wash. 2d 298, 553 P.2d 423 (1976) (affirming injunction, civil penalties and other relief against dealer who misrepresented prices as lower than competitors'); Wis. Dep't of Agriculture, Trade & Consumer Protection Rules, Wis. Admin. Code ch. ATCP 124, Price Comparison Advertising.

837 Kroger Co., 98 F.T.C. 639 (1981).

838 Connecticut Regulations for the Dep't of Consumer Protection, Conn. Agencies Regs. § 42-110b-92(d), Deceptive Pricing; Massachusetts Consumer Protection Regulations, Mass. Regs. Code tit. 940, § 6.05, Retail Advertising; Pennsylvania Attorney General Guidelines for Use of Reference Prices in Price Reduction Advertisements; Vermont Consumer Fraud Rules, Code Vt. Rules 06 031 005 Rule 110, Deceptive Pricing.

839 Alaska Admin. Code tit. 9, § 05.050; Hawaii Rules Relating to Unfair or Deceptive Practices in Advertising, 16 Haw. Admin. Code § 303-4, Unfair or Deceptive Practices in Advertising; Idaho Consumer Protection Regulations, Idaho Admin. Code 04.02.01.061, .063, Deceptive and Comparative Pricing; Ill. Admin. Code tit. 14, § 470.240; Massachusetts Consumer Protection Regulations, Mass. Regs. Code tit. 940, § 6.05, Retail Advertising; Code Miss. Rules 24 000 002 Rule 23.

840 Beslity v. Manhattan Honda, 467 N.Y.S.2d 471 (App. Term Ct. 1983).

841 Haleakala Motors Ltd., 88 F.T.C. 753 (1976) (consent order); John Surrey Ltd., 67 F.T.C. 299 (1965); Leonard Margolis, 64 F.T.C. 409 (1964); Spradling v. Williams, 553 S.W.2d 143 (Tex. Civ. App. 1977); FTC Guides Against Deceptive Pricing, 16 C.F.R. § 233.3 (1967); Enforcement Guidelines in letter by Colorado Assistant Attorney General Garth Lucero concerning comparative pricing advertisements, Alpha No. LW CP ZDVYZ, File No. CEN8400366/23 (Feb. 6, 1984); Connecticut Regulations for the Dep't of Consumer Protection, Conn. Agencies Regs. §§ 42-110b-9a to 42-110b-15, Deceptive Pricing; Hawaii Rules Relating to Unfair or Deceptive Practices in Advertising, 16 Haw. Admin. Code § 303-6, Unfair or Deceptive Practices in Advertising; Ill. Admin. Code tit. 14, 470.250; La. Admin. Code tit. 16, pt. III §§ 303, 311, 313, Deceptive Pricing; Massachusetts Consumer Protection Regulations, Mass. Regs. Code tit. 940, § 6.05(6), Retail Advertising; Code Miss. Rules 024 000 002 Rule 27; Code Vt. Rules 06 031 005 Rule 110.03; Tennessee Attorney General opinion letter to Commissioner of Tennessee Dep't of Commerce and Ins., Clearinghouse No. 38,905A (Jan. 17, 1985).

842 Benrus Watch Co. v. FTC, 352 F.2d 313 (8th Cir. 1965), *cert. denied*, 384 U.S. 939 (1966); Rayex Corp. v. FTC, 317 F.2d 290 (2d Cir. 1963); Helbros Watch Co. v. FTC, 310 F.2d 868 (D.C. Cir. 1962); Baltimore Luggage Co. v. FTC, 296 F.2d 608 (4th Cir. 1961); Clinton Watch Co. v. FTC, 291 F.2d 838 (7th Cir. 1961); Raylew Enterprises Inc., 74 F.T.C. 1093 (1968); Crown Publishing, Inc., 66 F.T.C. 1488 (1964); FTC Guides Against Deceptive Pricing, 16 C.F.R. § 233.3 (1967); Massachusetts Consumer Protection Regulations, Mass. Regs. Code tit. 940, § 6.05(6)(b), (9), Retail Advertising. *But see* Division of Consumer Affairs v. General Electric Co., 244 N.J. Super. 349, 582 A.2d 831 (App. Div. 1990) (regulation regarding price reduction advertisements held not to apply to manufacturer).

843 Taylor Mobile Home, Inc., 82 F.T.C. 1145 (1973) (consent order); Commonwealth v. R&W Indus., Inc., Clearinghouse No. 26,021 (Pa. Commw. Ct. 1976); FTC Guides Against Deceptive Pricing, 16 C.F.R. § 233.5 (1967); Alaska Admin. Code tit. 9, 05.030; Connecticut Regulation for the Dep't of Consumer Protection, Conn. Agencies Regs. §§ 42-110b-9a–42-110b-15, Deceptive Pricing; Idaho Consumer Protection Regulations, Idaho Admin. Code 04.02.04.066, Deceptive and Comparative Pricing; La. Admin. Code tit. 16, pt. III § 319, Deceptive Pricing; Massachusetts Consumer Protection Regulations, Mass. Regs. Code tit. 940, § 6.05(12), Retail Advertising; Code Miss. Rules 024 000 002 Rule 28; Code Vt. Rules 06 031 005 Rule 110, Deceptive Pricing. *See also* State *ex rel.* Thornburg v. Wal-Mart Stores, Inc., Clearinghouse No. 45,902 (N.C. Super. Ct. July 18, 1990) (deceptive to name company "Sam's Wholesale Club" where most sales are at retail).

844 Feitler v. Animation Collection, Inc., 170 Or. App. 702, 13 P.3d

vehicle while simultaneously increasing the price of the new vehicle by $2000 is a deceptive representation that a price advantage exists.[845] It is deceptive to "pad" a repair estimate by exaggerating the amount of work that is necessary.[846] Pricing misrepresentations in new car sales are discussed in detail a separate section.[847]

A number of restrictions are placed on going-out-of-business, fire, flood, bankruptcy, and similar types of sales. The special circumstances must be true, prices must be lower than regular, and the seller can not order additional goods for the sale.[848] It may also be deceptive to put goods on "sale" too often; for example, one UDAP regulation prohibits an item being on sale more than four months a year.[849] A "complete liquidation sale" at "bankrupt prices" is deceptive since the general public would mistakenly believe a court-supervised bankruptcy sale was occurring.[850] Sellers must also sell their products at advertised sale prices, even where the price listed was a typographical error.[851] A court has ruled that it is not, however, a UDAP violation to charge a higher price to some buyers to account for commissions, as long as the total price is accurately disclosed.[852]

1044 (2000); Connecticut Regulations for the Dep't of Consumer Protection, Conn. Agencies Regs. §§ 42-110b-9a–42-110b-15, Deceptive Pricing; Massachusetts Consumer Protection Regulations, Mass. Regs. Code tit. 940, § 6.05(12), Retail Advertising.

845 White v. Kent, 47 Ohio App. 3d 105, 547 N.E.2d 386 (1988).

846 Jefferies v. Phillips, 451 S.E.2d 21 (S.C. Ct. App. 1994).

847 *See* § 5.4.7.2, *infra*.

848 Commonwealth v. Mirror World, Inc., Clearinghouse No. 26,022 (Pa. C.P. Phila. Cty. 1978); Hawaii Rules Relating to Unfair or Deceptive Practices in Advertising, 16 Haw. Admin. Code § 303-4, Unfair or Deceptive Practices in Advertising; Idaho Consumer Protection Regulations, Idaho Admin. Code 04.02.01.090–.091; La. Admin. Code tit. 16, pt. III § 513(c), Deceptive Pricing; Massachusetts Consumer Protection Regulations, Mass. Regs. Code tit. 940, § 6.05(5)(c), Retail Advertising; Code Miss. Rules 024 000 002 Rules 40, 41; Ohio Admin. Code § 109:4-3-17, Distress Sales. *But see* State *ex rel.* Spaeth v. Eddy Furniture Co., 386 N.W.2d 901 (N.D. 1986) (not deceptive to add new merchandise when actually going out of business and when newer merchandise on sale at deep discounts); State v. American TV & Appliance, 146 Wis. 2d 292, 430 N.W.2d 709 (1988) (not deceptive to bring additional merchandise into store for close-out sale).

849 Enforcement Guidelines in letter by Colorado Assistant Attorney General Garth Lucero concerning comparative pricing advertisements, Alpha No. LW CP ZDVYZ, File No. CEN8400366/23 (Feb. 6, 1984) (no sales for more than 60 consecutive days; no sales for more than 182 days a year); Massachusetts Consumer Protection Regulations, Mass. Regs. Code tit. 940, §§ 6.04, 6.05, Retail Advertising; Ohio Admin. Code § 109:4-3-17 Distress Sales.

850 State v. Marsden, Clearinghouse No. 27,048 (Alaska Super. Ct. 1977).

851 Geismar v. Abraham & Strauss, 109 Misc. 2d 495, 439 N.Y.S.2d 1005 (Dist. Ct. 1981). *See also* Beslity v. Manhattan Honda, 467 N.Y.S.2d 471 (App. Term 1983); § 4.6.5, *infra*.

852 Tungate v. MacLean-Stevens Studios, 714 A.2d 792 (Me. 1998).

A Connecticut regulation requires sellers who advertise net prices that already reflect a reduction for a manufacturer's rebate to pay consumers the amount of such rebate at the time of purchase.[853] The Connecticut Supreme Court has upheld the Connecticut regulation, finding the advertising of net prices (*i.e.*, after the manufacturer rebate) to be deceptive because the consumer must expend money to obtain the rebate.[854] UDAP issues may also arise where companies advertise rebates but then delay or evade paying them. Fulfillment houses that process rebates may even be paid a percentage of the "slippage," *i.e.*, the rebate checks that are never cashed, so they have an incentive to impede payment of rebates. The Connecticut Supreme Court has also held that it is deceptive for an insurance company to represent that it is purchasing an annuity of a certain value and cost for a tort victim, when actually its cost is less because it receives a secret rebate from the annuity company.[855] Advertising rebates but then delaying them or rejecting them on spurious grounds is deceptive.[856]

Another deceptive pricing technique is to induce a consumer to incur a charge by disclosing it only in incomprehensible language in the agreement. For example, a California court examined a rental car agreement that disclosed refueling charges in such an obscure manner that consumers would be unlikely to act to avoid the charges.[857] The court reversed dismissal of a UDAP complaint that alleged that the manner of disclosing this charge was a UDAP violation. Similar theories may be useful against other businesses, such as credit card issuers, that foster late payment charges by adopting byzantine, obscure payment deadline rules.

4.6.4 Use of the Word "Free"

A special type of deceptive pricing involves the use of the word "free," two-for-one bargains, and similar offers implying that the consumer will get something for nothing. Typically, the "free" offer requires the purchase of another item, or that the consumer sit through a sales presentation or comply with some other condition.

The FTC has adopted a guide stating that when a product or service is offered free with the purchase of another product, the merchant can not recover part of the cost of the free merchandise by marking up the price of the article to be

853 Conn. Agencies Reg. § 42-110b-19.

854 Caldor, Inc. v. Heslin, 215 Conn. 590, 577 A.2d 1009 (1990).

855 Macomber v. Travelers Prop. & Cas. Corp., 261 Conn. 620, 804 A.2d 180 (2002).

856 FTC v. UrbanZ, 5 Trade Reg. Rep. (CCH) ¶ 15428 (E.D.N.Y. June 26, 2003) (proposed consent order); Phillips Electronics N. Am., Dkt. C-4002, www.ftc.gov/opa/2002/10/fyi0254.htm (Oct. 11, 2002) (consent order); Tim R. Wofford (individually and as officer of Okie Corp.), Dkt. C-4061, www.ftc.gov/opa/2002/10/fyi0254.htm (Oct. 11, 2002) (consent order).

857 Schnall v. Hertz Corp., 78 Cal. App. 4th 1144, 93 Cal. Rptr. 2d 439 (2000).

purchased.[858] The guide also requires disclosure of any terms and conditions of free offers.[859] Sellers can not make free offers more than six months a year.[860] State UDAP regulations[861] and cases[862] proscribe similar practices. The FTC has proceeded against a laser surgery clinic that advertised free consultations, but required a $300 non-refundable deposit before advising the consumer about the risks and limitations of the procedure.[863]

Where a UDAP statute requires disclosure in advertising of the total sale price whenever a free item is conditioned on the purchase of another item, the total sale price must be disclosed in all advertisements, not just at the point of sale, no matter how impractical this may be.[864] While Ohio's regulation regarding the use of the word "free" is ambiguous, it has been construed to apply only to "combination" sales—that is, those where the consumer must purchase another item in order to obtain the "free" item.[865] A health spa that advertised two memberships for the price of one violated Ohio's regulation by not conspicuously disclosing the terms and conditions of the offer.[866]

4.6.5 Low Balling; Charging Higher Prices Than Agreed Upon

Another deceptive pricing inducement is sometimes referred to as "low balling." The seller advertises low prices but eventually sells the item for a higher price. Low balling may be used to frustrate a consumer's comparison shopping efforts, particularly where there is no standard price for a standard product, such as car repairs, moving household contents, and home improvements. Low balling is deceptive under both the FTC Act and state UDAP statutes.[867]

It is deceptive to sell goods above their advertised prices.[868] This is the case even if the price listed contains a

---

858 FTC Guide Concerning Use of the Word "Free" and Similar Representations, 16 C.F.R. Part 251 (1971). *See also* FTC v. Mary Carter Paint Co., 382 U.S. 46 (1965); FTC v. Standard Education Society, 302 U.S. 112 (1937); Spiegel Inc. v. FTC, 494 F.2d 59 (7th Cir. 1974); Sunshine Art Studios, Inc. v. FTC, 481 F.2d 1171 (1st Cir. 1973); Kalwajtys v. FTC, 237 F.2d 654 (7th Cir. 1956), *cert. denied*, 352 U.S. 1025 (1957); Encyclopedia Britannica, Inc., 87 F.T.C. 421 (1976), *aff'd*, 605 F.2d 964 (1979).

859 *See also* FTC v. C&L Indus., Inc., 5 Trade Reg. Rep. (CCH) ¶ 23,198 (N.D. Tex. 1992) (consent judgment); FTC v. Precision Mailers, Inc., 5 Trade Reg. Rep. (CCH) ¶ 23,321 (D. Minn. 1993) (consent decree); FTC v. Pioneer Enterprises, Inc., 5 Trade Reg. Rep. (CCH) ¶ 23,292 (D. Nev. 1992) (consent judgment). *See also* Luskin's, Inc. v. Consumer Protection Div., 353 Md. 335, 726 A.2d 702 (1999) (omission of conditions on "free" airfare was deceptive under state UDAP statute's general prohibitions); State *ex rel.* Abrams v. Stevens, 130 Misc. 2d 790, 497 N.Y.S.2d 812 (Sup. Ct. 1985) (nondisclosure of limitations violates general language of New York UDAP statute and FTC guide). The FTC has published guidelines on how on-line sellers should make these disclosures. FTC, Dot Com Disclosures (2000), available on the FTC's website, www.ftc.gov.

860 16 C.F.R. § 251.1(h).

861 Connecticut Regulations for the Dep't of Consumer Protection, Conn. Agencies Regs. § 42-110b-19, Advertising "Free," "Reduced," "Discount," or "Below Cost;" Hawaii Rules Relating to Unfair or Deceptive Practices in Advertising, 16 Haw. Admin. Code § 303-5, Unfair or Deceptive Practices in Advertising; Idaho Consumer Protection Regulations, Idaho Admin. Code 04.02.01.070–.075, Use of Word "Free" and Similar Representations; Ill. Admin. Code tit. 14, 470.280; Massachusetts Consumer Protection Regulation, Mass. Regs. Code tit. 940, § 6.05, Retail Advertising; Code Miss. Rules 24 000 002 Rules 31–36; 15 Mo. Code State Regs. § 60-7.060(7); Mont. Admin. Rules Ch. 2.61.101(1)(o); Ohio Admin. Code § 109:4-3-04, Use of Word "Free," etc; Oregon Administrative Rule 137-020-0015, Misleading Use of "Free" Offers; Oregon Attorney General's Trade Practice Guideline 87-7, "Free" Offers; Rules for the Utah Consumer Sales Practices Act, Utah Admin. Rules 152-11-4, Use of the Word "Free," Etc.

862 *In re* Fravel, 143 B.R. 1001 (Bankr. E.D. Va. 1992) (use of flyer promising free item to entice buyers violated UDAP statute's general prohibitions), *aff'd*, Clearinghouse No. 49,161 (E.D. Va. Jan. 8, 1993); Luskin's, Inc. v. Consumer Protection Div., 353 Md. 335, 726 A.2d 702 (1999) (adopting FTC guide as standard for determining whether advertisements are deceptive under Maryland UDAP statute); People v. Record Clubs of Am., 51 A.D.2d 709, 380 N.Y.S.2d 26 (1976) (misrepresentation of goods as free is violation of general UDAP prohibitions). *But cf.* Fineman v. Citicorp USA, Inc., 137 Ill. App. 3d 1035, 485 N.E.2d 591 (1985) (use of word "free" in credit card travel insurance offer was not deceptive where it was clearly tied to payment of higher membership fee).

863 Laser Vision Institute, L.L.C., File No. 022-3053, and LCA-Vision, Inc., File No. 022-3098, www.ftc.gov/opa/2003/07/fyi0343.htm (July 11, 2003) (consent orders).

864 State v. Amoco Oil Co., 97 Wis. 2d 226, 293 N.W.2d 487 (1980).

865 Renner v. Proctor & Gamble Co., 54 Ohio App. 3d 79, 561 N.E.2d 959 (1988).

866 Mid Am. Acceptance Co. v. Lightle, 63 Ohio App. 3d 590, 579 N.E.2d 721 (1989).

867 FTC v. S.J.A. Society, Inc., 5 Trade Reg. Rep. (CCH) ¶ 24,321 (E.D. Va. 1997) (proposed consent decree). *See* Florida Dep't of Consumer Affairs v. Father & Son Moving & Storage, 643 So. 2d 22 (Fla. Dist. Ct. App. 1994).

868 FTC Rule Concerning Retail Food Store Advertising and Marketing Practices, 16 C.F.R. Part 424 (1971); Commercial Lighting Products, Inc., 95 F.T.C. 750 (1973) (consent order); Market Development, 95 F.T.C. 100 (1980) (representing price as including delivery, but then adding delivery charge); Hiken Furniture Co., 91 F.T.C. 1115 (1978) (consent order); Safeway Stores, 91 F.T.C. 975 (1978) (consent order); Fisher Food, Inc., 90 F.T.C. 473 (1977) (consent order); Food Fair Stores, Inc., 90 F.T.C. 491 (1977) (consent order); Kroger Co., 90 F.T.C. 459 (1977) (consent order); Shop-Rite Foods, Inc., 90 F.T.C. 500 (1977) (consent order); Zayre Corp., 90 F.T.C. 328 (1977) (consent order); Levitz Furniture Corp., 88 F.T.C. 263 (1976) (consent order); Fred Meyer, Inc., 87 F.T.C. 112 (1976) (consent order); Pay'n Pak Stores, Inc., 87 F.T.C. 99 (1976) (consent order); Great Atlantic & Pacific Tea Co., 85 F.T.C. 601 (1975); Main Street Furniture, Inc., 86 F.T.C. 1588 (1975) (consent order); Devine Seafood, Inc. v. Attorney General, 37 Md. App. 439, 377 A.2d 1194 (Ct. Spec. App. 1977); Gaylan v. Dave Towell Cadillac, 15 Ohio Misc. 2d 1, 473 N.E.2d 64 (Mun. Ct. 1984); Sanders v. Francis, 277 Or. 593, 561 P.2d 1003 (1971).

typographical error.[869] Sellers may not coerce customers to pay higher prices than agreed upon.[870] Nor may a merchant deliver without authorization a more expensive product than ordered and demand greater payment.[871] Merchants also can not charge for fictitious government fees that are never turned over to a third party,[872] or charge a sales tax exceeding that required by law.[873]

Another type of prohibited low-balling practice is for a dealer to decrease the agreed upon trade-in value for the consumer's car while also refusing to return the consumer's deposit for the new car. Even if the sales contract specifically allows the dealer to do this, the practice is contrary to oral representations and thus deceptive.[874] Similarly, it is deceptive for an insurer, without authority from the insured, to increase the policy premium.[875]

It is deceptive for a service company to promise annual inspections at a fixed price, and then several years later to increase the price of those inspections.[876] Low-balling can also occur during the provision of repairs or other services where charges are higher than estimated or authorized. Precedent prohibiting these practices is analyzed in other sections.[877]

One common form of low-balling is for a builder to give an unrealistically low estimate for a construction job and then induce the consumer to pay for cost overruns. For example, one appellate court has found a UDAP violation where a home builder made a practice of quoting unrealistically low prices for the cost of erecting homes to entice business, and then involved consumers "in a painful morass of cost overruns and unexpectedly high cash outlays."[878] Household movers must unload interstate shipments upon the consumer's payment of the estimated price plus no more than ten percent in the event of an underestimation.[879]

4.6.6 Consumer Specially Selected or Contest Winner

Another deceptive inducement is to claim to a consumer that he or she is specially selected, is a member of a "test family," or has won a contest and thus will receive a special offer. This is both a method of attracting the consumer's attention—for example, allowing a door-to-door seller to get inside the buyer's home—and a means of misrepresenting that an offer is an exceptionally good one. The FTC holds it deceptive to operate a contest or otherwise specially select consumers when the scheme is really designed to make contact with prospective buyers and special prices are not being offered.[880] These practices also violate state UDAP statutes,[881] and a number of states have UDAP regulations or specific statutes prohibiting these practices.[882] Deceptive contests are described at § 5.13.4, *infra*.

869 Geismar v. Abraham & Strauss, 109 Misc. 2d 495, 439 N.Y.S.2d 1005 (Dist. Ct. 1981); *see also* Beslity v. Manhattan Honda, 467 N.Y.S.2d 471 (App. Term 1983).

870 Truex v. Ocean Dodge, Inc., 219 N.J. Super. 44, 529 A.2d 1017 (App. Div. 1987); Crawford Chevrolet, Inc. v. McLarty, 519 S.W.2d 656 (Tex. Civ. App. 1975). *See also* Taylor Mobile Homes, Inc., 82 F.T.C. 1145 (1973) (consent order) (taking deposit, delaying delivery, then claiming prices have risen and demanding higher price or deposit will be forfeited).

871 State v. Packard, Clearinghouse No. 27,066 (Vt. Super. Ct. 1977).

872 Jim Walter Homes Inc. v. White, 617 S.W.2d 767 (Tex. Civ. App. 1981).

873 People *ex rel.* Hartigan v. Stianos, 475 N.E.2d 1024 (Ill. App. Ct. 1985).

874 State *ex rel.* Redden v. Willamette Recreation Inc., 54 Or. App. 156, 634 P.2d 286 (1981); *see also* Freitag v. Bill Swad Datsun, 3 Ohio App. 3d 83, 443 N.E.2d 988 (1981).

875 St. Paul Fire & Marine Ins. Co. v. Updegrave, 656 P.2d 1130 (Wash. Ct. App. 1983).

876 Orkin Exterminating Co., 108 F.T.C. 263 (1980), *aff'd*, 849 F.2d 1354 (11th Cir. 1988), *cert. denied*, 488 U.S. 1041 (1989); *see also* People v. Wilco Energy Corp., 284 A.D.2d 469, 728 N.Y.S.2d 471 (2001) (deceptive to promise long-term fixed price but then raise prices).

877 *See* §§ 4.9.7, 5.4.1.2, *infra*.

878 Quate v. Caudle, 381 S.E.2d 842 (N.C. Ct. App. 1989).

879 *See* 49 C.F.R. § 375.407.

880 FTC v. Nishika, Ltd., 5 Trade Reg. Rep. (CCH) ¶ 24,001 (D. Nev. 1996) (proposed consent decree); FTC v. Frank LoPinto, 5 Trade Reg. Rep. (CCH) ¶ 23,832 (D. Nev. 1995) (proposed consent decree); FTC v. Hensley Group, 5 Trade Reg. Rep. (CCH) ¶ 22,716 (E.D. Va. Aug. 7, 1989) (preliminary injunction); Hensley Group, F.T.C. Dkt. No. 9230, 5 Trade Reg. Rep. (CCH) ¶ 22,745 (F.T.C. 1990) (consent order); Outdoor World Corp., F.T.C. Dkt. No. 9229, 5 Trade Reg. Rep. (CCH) ¶ 22,780 (F.T.C. 1990) (consent order); Market Dev. Corp. 95 F.T.C. 100 (1980); Richard A. Romain, 77 F.T.C. 837 (1978) (consent order); Household Sewing Machine Co., 76 F.T.C. 207 (1969); Raylew Enterprises, Inc., 74 F.T.C. 1093 (1968); National Housewares, Inc., 73 F.T.C. 287 (1968) (consent order); King Distributing Co., 71 F.T.C. 1300 (1967) (consent order); E.W. Sederstrom, 66 F.T.C. 973 (1964); Herbert Howell, 62 F.T.C. 1240 (1963); Van-R, Inc., 62 F.T.C. 1215 (1963).

881 People v. Columbia Research Corp., 71 Cal. App. 3d 607, 139 Cal. Rptr. 517 (1977); Commonwealth v. General Ionics, Inc., Clearinghouse No. 26,030 (Pa. C.P., Allegheny Cty. 1975), *aff'd without op.*, 365 A.2d 187 (Pa. Commw. Ct. 1976); Commonwealth v. Programmed Learning Sys., Inc., Clearinghouse No. 26,019 (Pa. C.P. Allegheny Cty. 1975).

882 Idaho Admin. Code 04.02.01.080–.082 and 02.04.01.162; Md. Com. Law Code Ann. § 13-305 (forbids prizes contingent upon purchase, with exception for small prizes); Massachusetts Consumer Protection Regulations, Mass. Regs. Code tit. 940, § 3.09, Door-to-Door Sales and Home Improvement Transactions; N.M. Admin. Code § 12.2.2.12; Ohio Admin. Code § 109:4-3-11, Direct Solicitations; Ohio Admin. Code § 109:4-3-06, Prizes; Wis. Dep't of Agriculture, Trade & Consumer Protection Rules, Wis. Admin. Code ch. ATCP 127.14, 127.44, 127.72, Direct Marketing. *See also* Luskin's, Inc. v. Consumer Protection Div., 353 Md. 335, 726 A.2d 702 (1999) (Maryland's statutory restrictions on prize promotions apply only where promoter claims consumer is specially selected, not to promotions disseminated to the public generally through advertisements).

4.6.7 *Conditions or Limitations on Offers*

Offering goods or services to a consumer without disclosing all conditions and limitations on the offer is deceptive.[883] A number of states have UDAP regulations that specifically prohibit this practice.[884] Ohio regulations require limitations on offers to be easily legible and in close proximity to the claim being limited and to precede immediately or follow oral claims.[885] The FTC's telemarketing sales rule requires disclosure, before the consumer pays, of material restrictions, limitations, or conditions to purchase, receive, or use goods,[886] and state telemarketing laws may have similar requirements.[887] An FTC guide also prohibits "free" offers without disclosing all terms, conditions, and obligations upon which receipt of the item is contingent.[888]

883 *See* Value Am., Inc., 5 Trade Reg. Rep. (CCH) ¶ 24,766, F.T.C. Dkt. C-3976 (Sept. 5, 2000) (consent order concerning ads for low-price computers that did not adequately disclose that a three-year Internet service contract was required); Buy.Com, Inc., 5 Trade Reg. Rep. (CCH) ¶ 24,765, F.T.C. Dkt. C-3978 (Sept. 5, 2000) (same); Office Depot, Inc., 5 Trade Reg. Rep. (CCH) ¶ 24,767, F.T.C. Dkt. C-3977 (Sept. 5, 2000) (same); Stephenson v. Capano Development, Inc., 462 A.2d 1069 (Del. 1983); Luskin's, Inc. v. Consumer Protection Div., 353 Md. 335, 726 A.2d 702 (1999).

884 Connecticut Regulations for the Department of Consumer Protection, Conn. Agencies Regs. § 42-110b-22, Offer Conditions; Hawaii Admin. Code § 16-305-5 (terms, conditions, and limitations on "free" offers); Idaho Consumer Protection Regulations, Idaho Admin. Code 04.02.01.040, Disclosure of Conditions in Offer (note that Idaho Admin. Code 04.02.01.041 provides that subsequent disclosure is not a defense); Code Miss. Rules 24-000-002 Rule 16 (note that Code Miss. Rules 24-000-002 Rule 17 provides that subsequent disclosure is not a defense); N.J. Admin. Code § 13:45A-26A.7(a)(4) (motor vehicle sales); Ohio Attorney General Consumer Protection Rules, Ohio Admin. Code 109:4-3-02, Exclusions and Limitations in Advertisements; Utah Admin. Rules 152-11-2, Exclusions and Limitations in Advertisement; Code Vt. Rules 06 031 001 Rule 103.03. *See* Feinberg v. Red Bank Volvo, 331 N.J. Super. 506, 752 A.2d 720 (App. Div. 2000) (advertising special financing terms without stating that they were available only if buyer passed credit check violated regulation).

885 Ohio Attorney General Consumer Protection Rules, Ohio Admin. Code 109:4-3-02, Exclusions and Limitations in Advertisements. *See* Crow v. Fred Martin Motor Co., 2003 WL 1240119 (Ohio App. Mar. 19, 2003) (unpublished, citation limited) (disclosing limitations on 2.9% financing only in small font footnote, and failing to disclose that offer was subject to approved credit, is violation).

886 16 C.F.R. § 310.3(a)(1)(ii).

887 *See* Appx. E, *infra*.

888 16 C.F.R. § 251.1(c). *See* § 4.6.4, *supra*.

4.7 General Misrepresentations Regarding Product and Seller

4.7.1 *Product Characteristics, Uses and Benefits*

It is deceptive to misrepresent a product's nature, characteristics,[889] uses, or benefits,[890] such as a product's durability,[891] maintenance,[892] conformity to specifications,[893] or performance qualities,[894] or to misrepresent test results as to

889 Tufts v. Newmar Corp., 53 F. Supp. 2d 1171 (D. Kan. 1999) (false statement regarding weight of recreational vehicle); Ahlborn v. Daley, 2001 Wash. App. LEXIS 2567 (Nov. 20, 2001) (unpublished, citation limited) (advertising door locks on self-service storage facility and then failing to inform renter that they were not working could be UDAP violation where renter relied on representation, even though renter had signed contract saying that facility was not responsible for loss or damage). *See also* Commonwealth v. Percudani, 844 A.2d 35 (Pa. Commw. Ct. 2004) (false appraisal, made as part of scheme to sell rehabilitated properties at inflated prices, may violate UDAP statute's prohibition of false certification, but prohibition against misrepresentation of sponsorship, uses, benefits, etc., applies only to advertisements).

890 Standard Oil Co. of Cal. v. FTC, 577 F.2d 653 (9th Cir. 1978); Warner Lambert Co. v. FTC, 562 F.2d 749 (D.C. Cir. 1977), *cert. denied*, 435 U.S. 950 (1978); Continental Wax Corp. v. FTC, 330 F.2d 475 (2d Cir. 1964); Charles of the Ritz Distributors Corp. v. FTC, 143 F.2d 676 (2d Cir. 1944); DeBondt v. Carlton Motorcars, Inc., 342 S.C. 254, 536 S.E.2d 399 (App. 2000) (dealer failed to fulfill promise made as part of special promotion to induce sale); Scott v. Noland Co., 1995 Tenn. App. LEXIS 505, Clearinghouse No. 51,282 (Tenn. App. 1995); Parr v. Tagco Indus., 620 S.W.2d 200 (Tex. Civ. App. 1981); FTC Trade Regulation Rule Concerning Household Sewing Machines, 16 C.F.R. Part 401; FTC Guides for Watch Industry, 16 C.F.R. Part 245; Connecticut Regulation for the Dep't of Consumer Protection, Conn. Agencies Regs. § 42-110b-18, Misleading Advertising.

891 Mutual Constr. Co., 87 F.T.C. 621 (1976); American Aluminum Corp., 84 F.T.C. 21 (1974), *aff'd*, 522 F.2d 1278 (5th Cir. 1975), *cert. denied*, 426 U.S. 906 (1976); Certified Building Products, Inc., 83 F.T.C. 1004 (1973), *aff'd sub nom.* Thiret v. FTC, 512 F.2d 176 (10th Cir. 1975); Southern States Distributing Co., 83 F.T.C. 1126 (1973); Better Living, Inc., 54 F.T.C. 648 (1957), *aff'd*, 259 F.2d 271 (1958); Wis. Dep't of Agriculture, Trade & Consumer Protection Rules, Wis. Admin. Code ch. ATCP 110, Home Improvement Trade Practices, Rule 110.02(2).

892 Mutual Constr. Co., 87 F.T.C. 621 (1976).

893 Hartford Accident & Indemnity Co. v. Scarlett Harbor Assocs., 109 Md. App. 217, 674 A.2d 106 (1996); Wiseman v. Kirkman, 2002 WL 31243522 (Ohio App. Oct. 4, 2002) (unpublished, citation limited); Estate of Cattano v. High Touch Homes, Inc., 2002 WL 1290411 (Ohio App. May 24, 2002) (unpublished, citation limited) (modular home did not conform to model consumer was shown).

894 Abele v. Bayliner Marine Corp., 11 F. Supp. 2d 955 (N.D. Ohio 1997) (statements that boat would go more than 40 m.p.h. and that it was unsurpassed for trouble-free operation went beyond puffing and could be UDAP violations); Princeton Graphics Operating v. NEC Home Electronics, 732 F. Supp. 1258

a product's performance.[895] This general principle has wide applicability. Thus, state cases have found UDAP violations when a broker falsely stated a home did not have a leakage problem,[896] or where a car dealer misrepresented a car's condition, mileage, and warranty[897] or that it was identical to an earlier model,[898] Other actionable misrepresentations include a vocational school's inflated job and earnings claims,[899] false representations as to used appliances' performance characteristics,[900] claims that hearing aids are beneficial for those with certain irreversible hearing dysfunctions,[901] promises that a basement could be effectively waterproofed,[902] false claims that a sewer system was in good working order,[903] false representations regarding the layout of a condominium terrace,[904] and misrepresentations concerning a franchise's earning potential.[905] A seller is responsible for verifying the accuracy of the information in the advertisement it places.[906]

State courts have also found deceptive the following representations regarding characteristics, uses and benefits: a misrepresentation that a boat was in good condition[907] or was completely built;[908] that a car engine had eight cylinders;[909] that household goods would be moved according to a particular method that was safe;[910] that certain cookware would promote health;[911] that a condominium would be built according to descriptions in plans;[912] and that refrigerators would work as specified.[913] Other misrepresentations concerning characteristics and benefits include that a property management service would properly inspect and protect managed property,[914] that a set of books was the complete collection of a rare book fancier,[915] that an art collection included all of the originals that were known to exist,[916] and that a record company would offer particular services to an aspiring singer.[917]

A seller misrepresented a mobile home's characteristics in representing it as defect free,[918] as did a seller who failed to disclose that a mobile home could not be kept in the park in which it was situated.[919] So did a pest inspector who claimed a home was free of insect infestation.[920] A burglar alarm installer misrepresented the system's characteristics by claiming that cutting the wires would not disarm the system.[921] Deceptively advertising that a drug has stronger ingredients than aspirin is a misrepresentation of its characteristics.[922] As a general rule, it is a UDAP violation to misrepresent future conditions or the future performance of goods or services.[923] A representation that an insurance policy would last as long as the plaintiff lived was a UDAP violation because it misrepresented the characteristics of the

(S.D.N.Y. 1990) (claim that computer monitor was "compatible" with another company's computer did not meet trade usage of that term and was deceptive); Certified Building Products, Inc., 83 F.T.C. 1004 (1973), *aff'd sub nom.* Thiret v. FTC, 512 F.2d 176 (10th Cir. 1975); Scholtz v. Sigel, 601 S.W.2d 516 (Tex. Civ. App. 1980); Haner v. Quincy Farm Chemicals Inc., 29 Wash. App. 93, 627 P.2d 571 (1981) (false statement that seed had 85% germination rate). *But see* Smaldino v. Larsick, 90 Ohio App. 3d 691, 630 N.E.2d 408 (1993) (no UDAP violation where expert testified that furnace had the performance characteristics the seller claimed); Kaplan v. Cablevision, Inc., 671 A.2d 716 (Pa. Super. 1996) (cable TV company's service interruptions did not violate UDAP statute where its contract did not oblige it to provide uninterrupted service).

895 Mitsushito Electric Corp. of Am., 89 F.T.C. 157 (1977) (consent order); National Dynamics Corp., 82 F.T.C. 488 (1973), *aff'd*, 492 F.2d 1333 (2d Cir.), *cert. denied*, 419 U.S. 993 (1974).

896 Young v. Joyce, 351 A.2d 857 (Del. 1975).

897 Attaway v. Tom's Auto Sales, Inc., 144 Ga. App. 813, 242 S.E.2d 740 (1978); Briggs v. Carol Cars, Inc., 407 Mass. 391, 553 N.E.2d 930 (1990) (UDAP violation to misrepresent car as low-mileage, one-owner, and in good condition and having had certain repairs); Hardy v. Toler, 288 N.C. 303, 218 S.E.2d 342 (1975).

898 Mercedes-Benz of N. Am., Inc. v. Garten, 94 Md. App. 547, 618 A.2d 233 (1993).

899 State *ex rel.* Lefkowitz v. Interstate Tractor Trailer Training, Inc., 66 Misc. 2d 678, 321 N.Y.S.2d 147 (Sup. Ct. 1971).

900 Brown v. Lyons, 43 Ohio Misc. 14, 332 N.E.2d 380, 72 Ohio Op. 2d 216 (C.P. Hamilton Cty. 1974).

901 Commonwealth v. Hush-Tone Indus., Inc., 4 Pa. Commw. 1 (1971).

902 Commonwealth v. Premier Basement Waterproofing Co., Clearinghouse No. 26,020 (Pa. C.P. Erie Cty. 1973).

903 Woods v. Littleton, 554 S.W.2d 662 (Tex. 1977).

904 Siegel v. Levy Organization Dev. Co., 153 Ill. 2d 534, 607 N.E.2d 194 (1992).

905 Woo v. Great Southwestern Acceptance Corp., 565 S.W.2d 290 (Tex. Civ. App. 1978).

906 Sauvey v. Ford, 2003 WL 21386282 (Ohio App. June 13, 2003) (unpublished, citation limited).

907 Pennington v. Singleton, 606 S.W.2d 682 (Tex. 1980).

908 Evans v. Yegen Assocs., 556 F. Supp. 1219 (D. Mass. 1982).

909 Duncan v. Luke Johnson Ford Inc., 603 S.W.2d 777 (Tex. 1980).

910 Brown v. American Transfer & Storage Co., 601 S.W.2d 931 (Tex. 1980).

911 Rossi v. 21st Century Concepts, Inc., 162 Misc. 2d 932, 618 N.Y.S.2d 182 (Yonkers City Ct. 1994).

912 Hartford Accident & Indemnity Co. v. Scarlett Harbor Assocs., 109 Md. App. 217, 674 A.2d 106 (1996).

913 Whirlpool v. Texical, Inc., 649 S.W.2d 55 (Tex. App. 1982).

914 Lerma v. Brecheisen, 602 S.W.2d 318 (Tex. Civ. App. 1980).

915 Mimaco L.L.C. v. Maison Faurie Antiquities, 2000 U.S. App. LEXIS 18335 (10th Cir. July 31, 2000) (unpublished, citation limited).

916 Feitler v. Animation Collection, Inc., 170 Or. App. 702, 13 P.3d 1044 (2000).

917 Brungard v. Caprice Records Inc., 608 S.W.2d 585 (Tenn. Ct. App. 1980).

918 Manufactured Housing Mgmt. v. Tubb, 643 S.W.2d 483 (Tex. App. 1982).

919 Caldwell v. Pop's Homes Inc., 54 Or. App. 104, 634 P.2d 471 (1981).

920 Raudebaugh v. Action Pest Control, Inc., 59 Or. App. 166, 650 P.2d 1006 (1982).

921 Pope v. Rollins Protective Servs. Co., 703 F.2d 197 (5th Cir. 1983).

922 American Home Products Corp., 98 F.T.C. 136 (1981), *aff'd*, 695 F.2d 681 (3d Cir. 1983).

923 Hedley Feedlot, Inc. v. Weatherly Trust, 855 S.W.2d 826 (Tex. App. 1993). *See also* Townsend v. Catalina Ambulance Co., 857 S.W.2d 791 (Tex. App. 1993).

policy.[924] Selling used products as new is described in § 4.9.4, *infra.*

4.7.2 Product Uniqueness

It is deceptive to make false claims as to a product's uniqueness, exclusiveness, or originality, such as that a product is the "only genuine" one, is "unique" or "exclusive," or that the seller possesses exclusive legal rights to, is the sole distributor of, or is the originator of a product.[925]

4.7.3 Product Quality, Composition, Model and Identity

Misrepresentation of a product's model, grade, quality, style, nature, composition, identity, or ingredients is deceptive under FTC decisions,[926] interpretations of state UDAP statutes,[927] and state UDAP regulations.[928] Where goods are not of the quality promised, the consumer need not prove that the seller's nonperformance was intentional, since the doctrine of substantial performance applies to contract, not UDAP, actions.[929] One of the most obvious applications of this principle is that deceptive quality claims as to used cars are UDAP violations.[930] State courts have found quality misrepresentations where a home[931] or mobile home[932] is constructed defectively or a seller does not disclose that a mobile home can not remain in the park in which it is situated.[933] It is also deceptive to mislabel a product,[934] and a trade name itself may be deceptive if it implies ingredients not contained in the product.[935]

4.7.4 Product Safety

It is a UDAP violation to fail to disclose a safety risk in the use of a product which is not apparent to a casual user.[936]

924 Jones v. Ray Ins. Agency, 59 S.W.3d 739 (Tex. App. 2001).

925 Thompson Medical Co., 104 F.T.C. 648 (1984) *aff'd*, 791 F.2d 189 (D.C. Cir. 1986), *cert. denied*, 479 U.S. 1086 (1987); Fedders Corp., 85 F.T.C. 38 (1975), *aff'd*, 529 F.2d 1398 (2d Cir.), *cert. denied*, 429 U.S. 818 (1976); Revere Chemical Corp., 80 F.T.C. 85 (1972).

926 FTC v. Algoma Lumber Co., 291 U.S. 67 (1934); FTC v. Winsted Hosiery Co., 258 U.S. 483 (1922); State v. Edwards (*In re* Edwards), 233 B.R. 461 (Bankr. D. Idaho 1999) (misrepresentation of brand, year, and availability of parts, and failure to disclose that tractor was a "gray market" product); Sovereign Chemical & Petroleum Products, Inc., 104 F.T.C. 478 (1984) (consent order) (misrepresentation of oil viscosity and quality ratings); Frankart Distributors, Inc., 90 F.T.C. 277 (1977) (consent order); Levitz Furniture Corp., 88 F.T.C. 263 (1976) (consent order); J. Kurtz & Sons, Inc., 87 F.T.C. 1300 (1976) (consent order); Carpets "R" Us, Inc., 87 F.T.C. 303 (1976); Southern States Distributing Co., 83 F.T.C. 1126 (1973); Johns-Manville Corp., 31 F.T.C. 262 (1940).

927 Borcherding v. Anderson Remodeling Co., 624 N.E.2d 887 (Ill. App. Ct. 1993) (misrepresentation that remodeling services would be suitable); Edminsten v. Zim Chemical Co., 45 N.C. App. 604, 263 S.E.2d 849 (1980); Wiseman v. Kirkman, 2002 WL 31243522 (Ohio App. Oct. 4, 2002) (unpublished, citation limited) (contracting to install one brand of appliance but installing another and keeping the savings is a UDAP violation); Rotello v. Ring Around Products Inc., 614 S.W.2d 455 (Tex. Civ. App. 1981) (misleading labeling of products).

928 Connecticut Regulations for the Dep't of Consumer Protection, Conn. Agencies Regs. § 42-110b-18, Misleading Advertising (1977); N.M. Admin. Code § 12.5.5 (environmental marketing claims); Wis. Dep't of Agriculture, Trade & Consumer Protection Rules, Wis. Admin. Code ch. ATCP 137 (environmental labeling of products).

929 Smith v. Baldwin, 611 S.W.2d 611 (Tex. 1980).

930 *See* §§ 5.4.6.3–5.4.6.11, *infra*. *See also* Pennington v. Singleton, 606 S.W.2d 682 (Tex. 1980) (false claim that boat is in excellent condition).

931 Jim Walter Homes Inc. v. Chapa, 614 S.W.2d 838 (Tex. Civ. App. 1981).

932 Manufactured Housing Mgmt. v. Tubb, 643 S.W.2d 483 (Tex. App. 1982).

933 Caldwell v. Pop's Homes Inc., 54 Or. App. 104, 634 P.2d 471 (1981).

934 Singh v. Queens Ledger Newspaper Group, 2 A.D.3d 703, 770 N.Y.S.2d 99 (2003) (mislabeling of fiber content of fabric); Galaxy Export Inc. v. Bedford Textile Products Inc., 84 A.D.2d 572, 443 N.Y.S.2d 439 (1981); Haner v. Quincy Farm Chemicals, Inc., 97 Wash. 2d 753, 649 P.2d 828 (1982) (misrepresentation of germination rate of seeds).

935 Ogilvy & Mather Int'l, Inc., 101 F.T.C. 1 (1983) (consent order) (trade name Aspercreme deceptive where does not contain aspirin).

936 McCoy Indus., Inc., 109 F.T.C. 101 (1987) (consent order); Reliance Wood Preserving Inc., 109 F.T.C. 85 (1987) (consent order); Descent Control, Inc., 105 F.T.C. 280 (1985) (consent order); International Harvester Co., 104 F.T.C. 949 (1984); Bayleysuit, Inc., 102 F.T.C. 1285 (1983) (consent order) (survival suits that did not inflate); American Motors Corp., 100 F.T.C. 229 (1982) (consent order) (sharp turns could cause vehicle driver to lose control); Hair Extension of Beverly Hills, Inc., 95 F.T.C. 361 (1980) (consent order); Terrance D. Leska, M.D., 96 F.T.C. 73 (1980) (consent order); Revlon Inc., 89 F.T.C. 1 (1977) (consent order); Miriam Maschek Inc., 85 F.T.C. 536 (1975) (consent order); The New You Inc., 85 F.T.C. 931 (1975) (consent order); FMC Corp., 86 F.T.C. 897 (1975) (consent order); Hercules Inc., 84 F.T.C. 605 (1974) (consent order); Union Carbide Corp., 84 F.T.C. 591 (1974) (consent order); Stupell Originals, Inc., 67 F.T.C. 173 (1965); Fisher & Deritis, 49 F.T.C. 77 (1952); Nuclear Products Co., 49 F.T.C. 229 (1952); Earl Aronberg, 33 F.T.C. 1327 (1941), *aff'd*, 132 F.2d 165 (7th Cir. 1942); American Medicinal Products Inc., 32 F.T.C. 1376 (1941), *aff'd*, 136 F.2d 426 (9th Cir. 1943); Cole v. Sunnyside Corp., 610 N.W.2d 511 (Wis. App. 2000) (store's advertising of product could be found to imply falsely that it was suitable for home use, creating UDAP violation). *See also* Me. Admin. Code § 26-239-102, Dep't of Att'y Gen., Trade Practices and the Sale of Urea Formaldehyde Foam Insulation (requiring health and safety warning; rule will sunset if Consumer Product Safety Commission issues final ruling). *Cf.* Hiner v. Bridgestone/Firestone, Inc., 959 P.2d 1158 (Wash. App. 1998) (failure to warn of product's inherent dangers may be UDAP violation if seller knows of dangers and by failing to reveal them misrepresents product's safety), *aff'd on other grounds*, 138 Wash. 2d 248, 978 P.2d 505 (1999).

Disclosure is required even where the safety hazard only occurs when the consumer does not follow safety instructions.[937] In particular, latent safety hazards relating to flammability must be disclosed.[938] This disclosure must be conspicuous and clear to arrest the eye or attract the attention of an average purchaser or user of the product,[939] and the disclosure must be on packaging and labeling and at the point of sale.[940] Advertising a product to homeowners carries an implicit representation that it is safe for household use.[941]

Automobile safety advertising can not use dummy props to make a car look safe.[942] A New Jersey regulation declares it a UDAP violation to manufacture, distribute, sell, or offer to sell any product contrary to an order of the Consumer Product Safety Commission.[943]

Massachusetts has enacted a UDAP regulation dealing with handgun safety. It prohibits sale of handguns that violate state gun control laws or that are made from inferior materials, and requires childproofing or safety devices and safety warnings.[944] The Massachusetts Supreme Judicial Court has upheld most of this regulation, specifically holding that the attorney general has the authority to restrict the sale of dangerous and defective products.[945]

Representations can not be inconsistent with warnings on labels.[946] Advertising claims involving safety, where the buyer must rely on the manufacturer's technical knowledge, must be supported by scientific tests,[947] and sellers can not claim products are safe to use when the product presents a risk of harm.[948] FTC consent agreements prohibit misrepresentations as to the effectiveness of survival suits,[949] anti-smoke masks,[950] cigarettes,[951] and sun-tanning devices.[952]

Advertising aimed at children is unfair if it shows toys being operated in an unsafe manner.[953] Advertisements depicting unsafe actions, such as a young child driving a tricycle down a traffic thoroughfare, have the capacity to induce behavior involving an unreasonable risk of harm, and are unfair.[954] Even adult products may not contain directions that allow an unsafe use of the product.[955] A court has ordered complete restitution for all purchases of an air purifier that could emit unsafe levels of ozone into the atmosphere with consumers having no way of knowing the level of ozone being produced.[956]

4.7.5 Product Quantity and Size

It is deceptive to misrepresent—through advertising, labels, other claims, use of oversized containers, slack fill, or use of substandard containers—a product's volume, weight, size, or the number of units sold.[957] Most states also have a

937 International Harvester Co., 104 F.T.C. 949 (1984).

938 The Society of the Plastics Industry Inc., 84 F.T.C. 1253 (1974) (consent order); Isidore Sandberg, 49 F.T.C. 1278 (1953); Fisher & Deritis, 49 F.T.C. 77 (1952); Academy Knitted Fabrics Corp., 49 F.T.C. 697 (1952).

939 Cannon Mills, Inc., 55 F.T.C. 1448 (1959); Salyer Refining Co., 54 F.T.C. 1026 (1958); Standard Sewing Equip. Corp., 51 F.T.C. 1012 (1955); Hillman Periodicals Inc., 51 F.T.C. 36 (1954); Nuclear Products, 49 F.T.C. 229 (1952).

940 CEB Products, 85 F.T.C. 565 (1975) (consent order); A. Elcott & Co., 85 F.T.C. 582 (1975) (consent order); Stupell Originals, Inc., 67 F.T.C. 173 (1965); Rudolph Siebort, 49 F.T.C. 1418 (1953); Albert E. Fisher, 49 F.T.C. 77 (1952); Nuclear Products Co., 49 F.T.C. 229 (1952); Clairol Inc. v. Cosmetics Plus, 130 N.J. Super. 81, 325 A.2d 505 (Ch. Div. 1974).

941 Cole v. Sunnyside Corp., 234 Wis. 2d 149, 610 N.W.2d 511 (App. 2000).

942 Volvo N. Am. Corp., 5 Trade Reg. Rep. (CCH) ¶ 23,041 (F.T.C. C-3367 1992) (consent order).

943 N.J. Admin. Code §§ 13:45A-4.1–13:45A-4.3.

944 Massachusetts Consumer Protection Regulations, Mass. Reg. Code tit. 940, § 16, Handgun Sales.

945 American Shooting Sports Council v. Attorney General, 429 Mass. 871, 711 N.E.2d 899 (1999).

946 Farnam Cos. Inc., 96 F.T.C. 862 (1980) (consent order); W.M. Barrad Co., 85 F.T.C. 213 (1975) (consent order).

947 Silver Group, 110 F.T.C. 380 (1988) (consent order); Sun Indus., Inc., 110 F.T.C. 511 (1988) (consent order); Lustrasilk Corp. of Am., 87 F.T.C. 145 (1976) (consent order); Soft Sheen Co., 87 F.T.C. 164 (1976) (consent order); Bridgestone Tire Corp. of Am., 86 F.T.C. 825 (1976) (consent order); Crown Rental Petroleum Corp., 84 F.T.C. 1493 (1974); Lear Siegler, 83 F.T.C. 503 (1973) (consent order); Royal Indus. Inc., 83 F.T.C. 507 (1973) (consent order); Firestone Tire & Rubber Co., 81 F.T.C. 398 (1972), *aff'd*, 481 F.2d 246 (6th Cir.), *cert. denied*, 414 U.S. 1112 (1973); Heinz Kirchner, 63 F.T.C. 1282 (1963); James Tompkins, 63 F.T.C. 1644 (1963).

948 Porter & Dietsch Inc. v. FTC, 605 F.2d 294 (7th Cir. 1979); Silver Group, 110 F.T.C. 380 (1988) (consent order); Sun Indus., Inc., 110 F.T.C. 511 (1988) (consent order); McCoy Indus., Inc., 109 F.T.C. 101 (1987) (consent order); Reliance Wood Preserving, Inc., 109 F.T.C. 85 (1987) (consent order); Farnam Companies Inc., 96 F.T.C. 826 (1980) (consent order); Kettle Moraine Electric Inc., 95 F.T.C. 398 (1980) (consent order); Stupell Originals, Inc., 67 F.T.C. 173 (1965); Nuclear Products Co., 49 F.T.C. 229 (1952); Carter Products Inc., 46 F.T.C. 64 (1949), *aff'd*, 186 F.2d 821 (7th Cir. 1951); Earl Aronberg, 33 F.T.C. 1327 (1941), *aff'd*, 132 F.2d 165; Clairol, Inc., 33 F.T.C. 1450 (1941), *aff'd sub nom.* Gelb v. FTC, 144 F.2d 580 (2d Cir. 1944).

949 Aquanautics Corp., 109 F.T.C. 34 (1987) (consent order); Bayleysuit Inc., 102 F.T.C. 1285 (1983) (consent order).

950 Puritan-Benett Aero Sys. Co., 110 F.T.C. 86 (1987) (consent order); Emergency Devices, Inc., 102 F.T.C. 1713 (1983) (consent order).

951 R.J. Reynolds Tobacco Co., F.T.C. Dkt. No. 9206, 5 Trade Reg. Rep. (CCH) ¶ 22,736 (F.T.C. 1989) (consent order).

952 An-Mar Int'l, Ltd., 112 F.T.C. 72 (1989) (consent order).

953 AMF Inc., 95 F.T.C. 310 (1980) (consent order); Benton & Bowles Inc., 96 F.T.C. 619 (1980) (consent order).

954 Benton & Bowles Inc., 96 F.T.C. 619 (1980) (consent order).

955 Montgomery Ward & Co., 95 F.T.C. 265 (1980).

956 State v. Alpine Air Products, Inc., 500 N.W.2d 788 (Minn. 1993).

957 Corning Glass Works, 92 F.T.C. 861 (1978) (consent order); Owens Illinois Inc., 92 F.T.C. 866 (1978); Hasbro Indus., 86 F.T.C. 1009 (1975) (consent order); Walco Toy Co., 83 F.T.C. 1783 (1974); Avalon Indus., 83 F.T.C. 1728 (1974); Seekonk Freezer Meats, Inc., 82 F.T.C. 1025 (1973); Cattlemen's Freezer

separate statute, regulation, and agency regulating weights and measures.

4.7.6 Product's Method of Manufacture

It is deceptive to misrepresent the method or process by which a product is produced, including false claims that a product is "custom-made," "tailor-made," "hand-made" or "union-made,"[958] or that it was made by handicapped persons.[959] "Indian-made" must be hand-made by Indians who reside within the United States.[960] It is deceptive to falsely represent that food is unprocessed or unfiltered.[961] Vermont has enacted UDAP regulations that define such terms as "local," "locally grown," "native," "farm fresh," and "our own."[962]

The FTC has promulgated a guide for the use of environmental marketing claims.[963] New Mexico and Wisconsin also have UDAP regulations that set standards for representations that a product is made from recycled materials, and require sellers to be able to substantiate such claims.[964]

4.7.7 Seller's and Product's Approval, Affiliation and Endorsement

4.7.7.1 Approval or Affiliation

It is deceptive to misrepresent a product's or seller's approval, affiliation, endorsement, or sponsorship by an individual, company, government agency, or other organization.[965] For example, it is a UDAP violation to misrepresent one's affiliation with the federal government[966] or one's endorsement by the United States[967] or a foreign government.[968] A Mississippi UDAP regulation finds it deceptive for a seller to use any graphics or printing that would lead one incorrectly to believe that the correspondence is from a government agency, public utility, insurance company, reporting agency, collection agency, or law firm.[969] It is deceptive to use a governmental sounding company name, such as United States Consumer Council, along with emblems, seals or other representations of government connection, such as an American eagle emblem.[970] Describing a directory of attorneys as the "official" listing is deceptive when it is actually published by a private entity.[971] A falsely

Meats, Inc., 80 F.T.C. 738 (1972) (consent order); Wolverton v. Stanwood, 278 Or. 341, 563 P.2d 1203 (1977); Cameron v. Terrell & Garrett Inc., 618 S.W.2d 535 (Tex. 1981) (square footage of house); Connecticut Regulations for the Dep't of Consumer Protection, Conn. Agencies Regs. § 42-110b-18, Misleading Advertising (1977).

958 Korber Hats Inc. v. FTC, 311 F.2d 358 (1st Cir. 1962); Progress Tailoring Co. v. FTC, 153 F.2d 103 (7th Cir. 1946); E.B. Muller & Co. v. FTC, 142 F.2d 511 (6th Cir. 1944); Dorfman v. FTC, 144 F.2d 737 (8th Cir. 1944); FTC v. Artloom Corp., 69 F.2d 36 (3d Cir. 1934); Light House Rug Co. v. FTC, 35 F.2d 163 (7th Cir. 1929); United States v. Hindman, 179 F. Supp. 926 (D.N.J. 1960). *See also* Trade Reg. Rep. (CCH) ¶ 7725.

959 Missouri *ex rel.* Nixon v. Audley (*In re* Audley), 268 B.R. 279 (Bankr. D. Kan. 2001) (finding restitution order and penalties nondischargeable).

960 FTC v. Maisel Trading Post Inc., 79 F.2d 127 (10th Cir. 1935); FTC Statement of Enforcement Policies (Apr. 18, 1968).

961 The Perrier Group of Am., Inc., 114 F.T.C. 514 (1991) (consent order).

962 Code Vt. Rules 06 031 016 Rule CF 117, Statements of Origin.

963 16 C.F.R. Part 260.

964 N.M. Admin. Code § 12.5.5; Wis. Dep't of Agriculture, Trade & Consumer Protection Rules, Wis. Admin. Code ch. ATCP 137.

965 Niresk Indus., Inc. v. FTC, 278 F.2d 337 (7th Cir.) *cert. denied*, 364 U.S. 883 (1960); Goodman v. FTC, 244 F.2d 584 (9th Cir. 1957); Buchwalter v. FTC, 235 F.2d 344 (2d Cir. 1956); Steelco Stainless Steel Inc. v. FTC, 187 F.2d 693 (7th Cir. 1951); Full Draw Productions v. Easton Sports, Inc., 85 F. Supp. 2d 1001 (D. Colo. 2000) (false statement about sponsorship by an organization); FTC v. Screen Test USA, 5 Trade Reg. Rep. (CCH) ¶ 24,699 (D.N.J. Jan. 21, 2000) (consent order against company that urged potential customers to check with supposedly independent monitoring organization that was actually a sham related corporation); The Right Start, 5 Trade Reg. Rep. (CCH) ¶ 23,365 (F.T.C. Dkt. C-3444 1993) (consent order); Market Dev. Corp., 95 F.T.C. 100 (1980); Post Institute Sales Corp. v. FTC, 34 F.T.C. 394 (1941); Estee Corp., 102 F.T.C. 1804 (1983) (consent order); People *ex rel.* Hartigan v. Maclean Hunter Publishing Corp., 119 Ill. App. 3d 1049, 457 N.E.2d 480 (1983); State *ex rel.* Stovall v. Cooper, 2001 WL 34117813 (Kan. Dist. Ct. May 15, 2001); Hennessey v. Vanguard Ins. Co., 895 S.W.2d 794 (Tex. App. 1995); Connecticut Regulations for the Dep't of Consumer Protection, Conn. Agencies Regs. § 42-110b-18, Misleading Advertising.

966 Floersheim v. FTC, 411 F.2d 874 (9th Cir. 1969), *cert. denied*, 396 U.S. 1002 (1970); FTC v. Army & Navy Trading Co., 88 F.2d 776 (D.C. Cir. 1937); FTC v. Vocational Guides, Inc., 5 Trade Reg. Rep. (CCH) ¶ 15138 (M.D. Tenn. July 27, 2001) (U.S. Postal Service); FTC v. Robert M. Oliver, 5 Trade Reg. Rep. (CCH) ¶ 24,533 (N.D. Fla. 1998) (consent decree); Hallcraft Jewelers, Inc., 89 F.T.C. 415 (1977) (consent order); Wisen's Inc., 84 F.T.C. 209 (1974) (consent order); Rushing, 59 F.T.C. 1182 (1961), *aff'd*, 320 F.2d 280 (5th Cir. 1963), *cert. denied*, 375 U.S. 986 (1964); James McCorrey, 53 F.T.C. 1 (1956); Capital Service, Inc., 51 F.T.C. 198 (1954); Central Training Institute, Inc., 51 F.T.C. 178 (1954); Don Carnerie, 47 F.T.C. 868 (1951).

967 Removatron Int'l Corp., 111 F.T.C. 206 (1988), *aff'd on other grounds*, 884 F.2d 1489 (11th Cir. 1989); Horizon Corp., 97 F.T.C. 464 (1981); GAC Corp., 84 F.T.C. 163 (1974) (consent order); United Nat'l Life Ins. Co., 75 F.T.C. 200 (1969) (consent order); National Advertising Agency Inc., 74 F.T.C. 616 (1968) (consent order).

968 Ex-Cello Corp., 82 F.T.C. 36 (1975) (consent order).

969 Code Miss. Rules 24 000 002 Rule 13.

970 *In re* Fleet, 95 B.R. 319 (E.D. Pa. 1989) (New Jersey law); *see also* Bennett v. FTC, 200 F.2d 362 (D.C. Cir. 1952); United States Ass'n of Credit Bureaus, Inc., 58 F.T.C. 1044 (1960), *modified*, 299 F.2d 220 (7th Cir. 1962); Capital Service, Inc., 51 F.T.C. 198 (1954); American Extension School, 50 F.T.C. 102 (1953); National Consumer Law Center, Fair Debt Collection §§ 5.5.2, 8.3.10 (5th ed. 2004).

971 Skinder-Strauss v. Massachusetts Continuing Legal Education, 914 F. Supp. 665 (D. Mass. 1995). *See also* FTC v. A. Glann

inflated appraisal may violate this prohibition in that it is a certification that the property is actually worth the selling price.[972]

Other actionable misrepresentations[973] include falsely stating that a corporation is qualified to do business in a state and that the state has approved the company's contracts,[974] that a product was sold under federal grant,[975] or that a company's service was approved by a national accrediting association when that accrediting association was created by the company.[976] It is deceptive to misrepresent compliance with minority business enterprise programs in order to secure a contract.[977] Misrepresenting that employees are disabled[978] or that purchases benefit disabled individuals or a charity[979] is deceptive.

It is deceptive for a home improvement contractor to represent that it would obtain a building permit and get the repairs inspected where it was impossible for the contractor to do so.[980] Also deceptive are collection letters designed to appear to be issued by public officials,[981] claims that a seller of certified copies of deeds is associated with the purchaser's lawyer or recorder of deeds,[982] and use of a name nearly identical to that of a well-known company.[983] It is deceptive to solicit businesses to buy yellow pages listings without disclosing that the seller does not publish the local telephone directory, but only a small business-to-business directory that is not distributed to all telephone subscribers in the area.[984] The seller's use of the words "yellow pages" and the "walking fingers" logo, combined with a local return address, the promise of a "free white page listing," and the reference to an account number gave the strong impression that the solicitation was from the publisher of the local telephone directory.

There is a growing use of infomercials—advertisers purchasing lengthy television spots, and using these spots to sell goods or services in what appears to be news programming. The FTC has accepted consent agreements limiting this practice after the FTC had alleged that it was deceptive to represent that a paid advertisement is an independent consumer or news program.[985]

4.7.7.2 Unlicensed or Unregistered Sellers

Falsely holding oneself out as having a license is a UDAP violation.[986] It is deceptive to advertise oneself as an accountant if not certified,[987] to misrepresent one's approval by the medical profession,[988] to hold oneself out as able to provide legal services if not licensed as an attorney,[989] or to misrepresent that medical approval is unnecessary.[990] Simply doing business while unlicensed or unregistered, without

Braswell, 5 Trade Reg. Rep. (CCH) ¶ 15412 (C.D. Cal. May 27, 2003) (complaint charging that seller deceptively portrayed its magazine as an independent health magazine when it was actually advertising written by seller).

972 Commonwealth v. Percudani, 844 A.2d 35 (Pa. Commw. Ct. 2004).

973 *See also* Commonwealth v. Armstrong, 74 Pa. D. & C.2d 579 (C.P. Phila. Cty. 1974); Commonwealth v. Hawkins, Clearinghouse No. 26,026 (Pa. C.P. Phila. Cty. 1973); Mallery v. Custer, 537 S.W.2d 141 (Tex. Civ. App. 1976).

974 People v. Witzerman, 29 Cal. App. 3d 169, 105 Cal. Rptr. 284 (1972).

975 Kugler v. Romain, 58 N.J. 522, 279 A.2d 640 (1971).

976 FTC v. Affiliated Vendors Ass'n, Inc., 5 Trade Reg. Rep. (CCH) ¶ 15282 (N.D. Tex. July 25, 2002) (proposed consent decree against sham BBB-type organization that was paid by seller); People *ex rel.* Lefkowitz v. Therapeutic Hypnosis, Inc., 83 Misc. 2d 1068, 374 N.Y.S.2d 576 (Sup. Ct. 1975); *see also* Alexander v. Certified Master Builders Corp., 268 Kan. 812, 1 P.2d 899 (2000) (accrediting organization can be liable under UDAP statute for misrepresentations it makes about its members' qualifications). *But cf.* Ambrose v. New England Ass'n of Schools and Colleges, Inc., 252 F.3d 488 (1st Cir. 2001) (claim as to falsity of general statements about accreditation was really a claim for negligent accreditation and could not be maintained).

977 People *ex rel.* Hartigan v. E&E Hauling, Inc., 607 N.E.2d 165 (Ill. 1992).

978 FTC v. Handicapped Indus. Midwest, Inc., 5 Trade Reg. Rep. (CCH) ¶ 24,786 (D. Ariz. Aug. 4, 2000) (stipulated final order).

979 *Id.*; Benckiser Consumer Products, 5 Trade Reg. Rep. (CCH) ¶ 23,992 (F.T.C. C-3659 1996) (consent order).

980 Hurst v. Sears, Roebuck & Co., 647 S.W.2d 249 (Tex. 1983).

981 Liggins v. May Co., 53 Ohio Misc. 21, 373 N.E.2d 404 (C.P. Cuyahoga Cty. 1977). *See also* National Consumer Law Center, Fair Debt Collection §§ 5.5.2, 5.5.12, 8.3.11 (5th ed. 2004).

982 Commonwealth v. Foster, Clearinghouse No. 26,031 (Pa. C.P. Allegheny Cty. 1974).

983 Commonwealth v. Mirror World, Inc., Clearinghouse No. 26,022 (Pa. C.P. Phila. Cty. 1978).

984 Commonwealth v. Amcan Enterprises, 47 Mass. App. Ct. 330, 712 N.E.2d 1205 (1999); State v. Smith, 1996 Minn. App. LEXIS 370, Clearinghouse No. 51,273 (Minn. App. Apr. 2, 1996) (unpublished, non-precedential); State v. Directory Publishing Servs., Inc., 1996 Minn. App. LEXIS 62 (Jan. 9, 1996) (unpublished, non-precedential).

985 Robert Francis, 5 Trade Reg. Rep. (CCH) ¶ 22,920 (F.T.C. Dkt. C-3326 1991) (consent order); Money Money Money, Inc., 5 Trade Reg. Rep. (CCH) ¶ 22,847 (F.T.C. Dkt. C-3308 1990) (consent order); TV Inc., 5 Trade Reg. Rep. (CCH) ¶ 22,827 (F.T.C. Dkt. C-3296 1990) (consent order); Twin Star Production, Inc., 5 Trade Reg. Rep. (CCH) ¶ 22,821 (F.T.C. Dkt. C-3307 1990) (consent order); JS&A Group, Inc., 111 F.T.C. 522 (1989) (consent order).

986 People v. First Fed. Credit Corp., 104 Cal. App. 4th 721, 128 Cal. Rptr. 2d 542 (2002) (real estate license); Tri-West Constr. v. Hernandez, 43 Or. App. 961, 607 P.2d 1375 (1979).

987 People v. Hill, 66 Cal. App. 3d 320, 136 Cal. Rptr. 30 (1977).

988 Richard Foods Corp., 88 F.T.C. 11 (1976) (consent order); Guild Indus. Corp., 86 F.T.C. 693 (1975) (consent order); Eclipse Sleep Products Inc., 81 F.T.C. 125 (1972) (consent order); Forrest A. Jones, 52 F.T.C. 1192 (1956) (consent order); Dahlberg Co., 50 F.T.C. 938 (1954) (consent order); Terry v. Hoden-Dhein Enterprises, Ltd., 48 Or. App. 763, 618 P.2d 7 (1980) (advertisement by denturist, one who works on dentures, failed to disclose that seller was not a dentist or associated with dentist).

989 Banks v. Department of Consumer & Regulatory Affairs, 634 A.2d 433 (D.C. 1993).

990 Nagle, Spillman & Bergman, Inc., 88 F.T.C. 244 (1976) (consent order).

disclosing the illegality, is a UDAP violation, even without any affirmative misrepresentations.[991] Implicit in any advertisement is a representation that the transaction is lawful,[992] which is a misrepresentation if the seller is actually unlicensed or acting in violation of other regulations. In some states out-of-state companies and companies with fictitious names must be registered. It is a UDAP violation to fail to do so and still solicit consumers.[993]

Many courts rule that unlicensed sellers can not collect amounts due, even under a theory of *quantum meruit*.[994] Collecting amounts due without such a right may in itself be an unfair practice.[995] It is deceptive to misrepresent that a seller is bonded.[996] A contract with a party who lacks a required license may also be unenforceable under general contract law principles.[997]

4.7.7.3 Endorsements

A common type of advertising misrepresentation involves personal endorsements. It is deceptive to imply falsely that a third party has endorsed a product or its performance,[998] to alter or selectively quote from an endorsement so that it does not reflect the substance of the endorsement,[999] to represent an endorser as a user of a product when such endorser does not use the product,[1000] or to continue to advertise an endorsement where the endorser no longer endorses the product.[1001] Endorsements must be motivated by a product's performance, not solely by any remuneration to the endorser.[1002]

---

991 Zee-Bar Inc.-N.H. v. Kaplan, 792 F. Supp. 895 (D.N.H. 1992); Circulation Builders, Inc., 87 F.T.C. 81 (1976) (consent order); Stevens v. Superior Court, 75 Cal. App. 4th 594, 89 Cal. Rptr. 2d 370 (1999) (violation of § 17200); Walter v. Hall, 940 P.2d 991 (Colo. Ct. App. 1996) (failure to register as subdivision developer violates UDAP statute's prohibition against sales without obtaining required license or permit), *aff'd on other grounds*, 969 P.2d 224 (Colo. 1998); Barnes v. Holliday, 1990 Conn. Super. LEXIS 392 (June 5, 1990); Boyce v. Hebert, Clearinghouse No. 41,255 (Conn. Super. Ct. Sept. 19, 1985); Banks v. Department of Consumer & Regulatory Affairs, 634 A.2d 433 (D.C. 1993) (non-attorney performing legal services); Anden v. Litinsky, 472 So. 2d 825 (Fla. Dist. Ct. App. 1985); State *ex rel.* Reno v. Barquet, 358 So. 2d 230 (Fla. Dist. Ct. App. 1978); State *ex rel.* Miller v. Pace, 677 N.W.2d 761 (Iowa 2004) (deceptive not to disclose that securities and seller were not registered); Golt v. Phillips, 308 Md. 1, 517 A.2d 328 (1986); Danusis v. Longo, 48 Mass. App. Ct. 254, 720 N.E.2d 470 (1999) (operating mobile home park without license is actionable under UDAP statute) (ruling on motion to amend complaint); State *ex rel.* Nixon v. Beer Nuts, Ltd., 29 S.W.3d 828 (Mo. App. 2000); Sussman v. Grado, 192 Misc. 2d 628, 746 N.Y.S.2d 548 (Dist. Ct. 2002) (acceptance of legal work by unlicensed, independent paralegal was UDAP violation); Brown v. Martz, Case No. CV 81-11-1152 (Ohio C.P. Sutter Cty. May 25, 1982); Commonwealth v. Tolleson (I), 14 Pa. Commw. Ct. 72, 321 A.2d 664 (1974). *See also* Nev. Rev. Stat. § 598.0923(1) (defining unlicensed business activity as deceptive); People by Abrams v. American Motor Club, Inc., 179 A.D.2d 277, 582 N.Y.S.2d 688 (1992); Reusch v. Roob, 234 Wis. 2d 270, 610 N.W.2d 168 (App. 2000) (violation of statute requiring business permit to be posted was UDAP violation, but not actionable because did not cause damage). *But see* Abele v. Bayliner Marine Corp., 11 F. Supp. 2d 955 (N.D. Ohio 1997); *cf.* Mangone v. U-Haul Int'l, Inc., 7 P.3d 189 (Colo. App. 1999) (court will not impose UDAP liability for operating without a license when courts had not made prior ruling that license was required); Mitchell v. Linville, 557 S.E.2d 620 (N.C. App. 2001) (unlicensed construction work may be a UDAP violation, but no recovery where plaintiffs did not show a causal connection to their damages). *See also* § 4.7.8, *infra*.

992 Benik v. Hatcher, 358 Md. 507, 750 A.2d 10 (2000).

993 Stevens v. Superior Court, 75 Cal. App. 4th 594, 89 Cal. Rptr. 2d 370 (1999) (violation of § 17200); Robles v. 4 Brothers Homes, 2003 WL 23312872 (N.Y. City Civ. Ct. Dec. 3, 2003); Burton v. Elsea, Inc., 1999 Ohio App. LEXIS 6401 (Dec. 27, 1999); Daniels v. True, 47 Ohio Misc. 2d 8, 547 N.E.2d 425 (Mun. Ct. 1988) (deceptive to use unregistered name and business address); Bron v. GEM Collections Int'l, Ltd., Case No. 81CV-09-4788 (Ohio C.P. Franklin Cty. June 9, 1983); Celebrezze v. Lloyd, Case No. 82CV-063184 (Ohio C.P. Franklin Cty. May 25, 1983); Brown v. Fetcher Used Cars, Case No. A 82017981 (Ohio C.P. Hamilton Cty. Apr. 27, 1982); Brown v. Martz, Case No. CV 81-11-1152 (Ohio C.P. Sutter Cty. May 25, 1982); Commonwealth v. Flick, 382 A.2d 762 (Pa. Commw. Ct. 1978); Commonwealth v. Armstrong, 74 Pa. D. & C.2d 579 (C.P. Phila. Cty. 1974); Commonwealth v. Empire Express Inc., 28 Erie County L.J. 27, Clearinghouse No. 11,129 (Pa. C.P. Erie Cty. 1972). *But see* Abele v. Bayliner Marine Corp., 11 F. Supp. 2d 955 (N.D. Ohio 1997) (failure to register trade name is not *per se* UDAP violation). *See also* § 4.7.8, *infra*.

994 *See* DeReggi Constr. Co. v. Mate, 130 Md. App. 648, 747 A.2d 743 (2000) (contract of seller who knowingly ignored licensing requirements is unenforceable if law is intended to protect public rather than raise revenue).

995 Golt v. Phillips, 308 Md. 1, 517 A.2d 328 (1986).

996 J.M. Westall & Co. v. Windswept View, 97 N.C. App. 71, 387 S.E.2d 67 (1990).

997 *See* § 9.5.8, *infra*.

998 Niresk Indus., Inc. v. FTC, 278 F.2d 337 (7th Cir.), *cert. denied*, 364 U.S. 883 (1960); Howe v. FTC, 148 F.2d 561 (9th Cir.), *cert. denied*, 326 U.S. 741 (1945); J. Walter Thompson Co., 97 F.T.C. 333 (1981) (consent order); Teledyne Inc., 97 F.T.C. 320 (1981) (consent order); L'Argene Products Co., 73 F.T.C. 16 (1968); Mytinger & Casselbergy Inc., 57 F.T.C. 717 (1960); Neuville Inc., 53 F.T.C. 436 (1956); Ar-Ex Cosmetics, 48 F.T.C. 800 (1952); United States Navy Weekly, Inc., 48 F.T.C. 1347 (1952).

999 Country Tweeds, Inc., 61 F.T.C. 1250 (1962).

1000 Esrim Ve Sheva Holding Corp., 5 Trade Reg. Rep. (CCH) ¶ 15177 (Dec. 17, 2001) (proposed consent order) (company used testimonials where speaker had no experience with the product); R.J. Reynolds Tobacco Co., 46 F.T.C. 706 (1950).

1001 National Dynamics Corp., 82 F.T.C. 488 (1973), *aff'd*, 492 F.2d 1333 (2d Cir.), *cert. denied*, 419 U.S. 993 (1974).

1002 FTC v. Accent Marketing, Inc., 2002 WL 31257708 (S.D. Ala. July 1, 2002) (failure of person listed as reference to disclose his substantial remuneration from company was deceptive); Buckingham Productions, Inc., 3 Trade Reg. Rep. (CCH) ¶ 22,387 (F.T.C. Dkt 9194 1987) (consent order); Cliffdale Assocs., 103 F.T.C. 110 (1984) (must disclose endorser's bias, as where endorser has business relationship with company and is not an independent consumer); American Consumer Inc., 94 F.T.C. 648 (1979) (consent order); C.I. Energy Dev. Inc., 94 F.T.C.

Endorsements by experts must be by experts with adequate qualifications, who are able to support the endorsement by the exercise of their expertise based on an extensive evaluation.[1003] Advertisers can not misrepresent that a product is endorsed by an independent research organization.[1004] Organizational endorsements must be reached by a process sufficient to ensure that the endorsement reflects the organization's collective judgment.[1005]

Advertisers must have a statistical basis for claiming endorsement by a class of individuals.[1006] This statistical basis must comply with scientific survey standards.[1007] Consumer testimonials that do not indicate typical results must disclose that the represented success is rare or unusual.[1008]

Consumer endorsements that state deceptive facts are deceptive even if the testimonials are true.[1009] It is deceptive to say consumer testimonials are typical when they are not, or to say testimonials are current when they are five years old.[1010]

Not just the company but also the endorser may be liable for a deceptive endorsement.[1011] The FTC rules it is deceptive for an endorser to make claims which the endorser should know to be false.[1012] Endorsers have a duty to substantiate the truthfulness of their endorsement and obtain independent and reliable information regarding the financial stability of the company whose product they endorse.[1013] A federal court interpreting a state UDAP statute goes one step further and finds a UDAP violation by an endorser even where the endorser did not know the claims were false.[1014]

One case explores whether someone who appears in advertising is in fact an endorser, and thus subject to the FTC Guide and other precedents dealing with endorsers. The court found a celebrity spokesperson to be an endorser where a consumer reasonably would view the spokesperson as an endorser, even where he never said he was endorsing the product.[1015] The endorser need not be an expert or receive financial benefit from the endorsement.[1016]

4.7.8 Manufacturer's and Seller's Status; Fictitious Names

Misrepresentations as to the nature of the seller or manufacturer are actionable under UDAP statutes.[1017] Illegal

---

1337 (1979) (consent order); Leroy Gordon Cooper, Jr., 94 F.T.C. 674 (1979) (consent order); R.R. Int'l Inc., 94 F.T.C. 1312 (1979) (consent order); Amstar Corp., 83 F.T.C. 659 (1973) (consent order); Beatrice Foods Co., 81 F.T.C. 830 (1972) (consent order).

1003 FTC Guides Concerning Use of Endorsements and Testimonials In Advertising, 16 C.F.R. Part 255; Robert M. Currier, Dkt. C-4067, www.ftc.gov/opa/2002/12/fyi0267.htm (Dec. 20, 2002) (consent order against physician who made infomercials for anti-snoring aid without reasonable basis and without disclosing product's limitations or his relationship with seller); Patricia Wexler, M.D., 115 F.T.C. 849 (1992) (consent order) (order against expert who endorsed hair loss treatment). *See also* SmartScience Laboratories, Inc., 5 Trade Reg. Rep. (CCH) ¶ 24,788, F.T.C. Dkt. C-3980 (Nov. 20, 2000) (consent order); Black & Decker, Inc., F.T.C. No. C-3289, 5 Trade Reg. Rep. (CCH) ¶ 22,758 (F.T.C. 1990) (consent order); National Ass'n of Scuba Diving Schools, Inc., 100 F.T.C. 439 (1982) (consent order); American Consumer Inc., 94 F.T.C. 648 (1979) (consent order); C.I. Energy Dev. Inc., 94 F.T.C. 1337 (1979) (consent order); R.R. Int'l Inc., 94 F.T.C. 1312 (1979) (consent order).

1004 Revco D.S. Inc., 67 F.T.C. 1158 (1965).

1005 FTC Guides Concerning Use of Endorsements and Testimonials In Advertising, 16 C.F.R. § 255.4.

1006 J. Walter Thompson USA, Inc., 5 Trade Reg. Rep. (CCH) ¶ 23,861 (F.T.C. C-3622 1995) (consent order); Lustrasilk Corp. of Am., 87 F.T.C. 145 (1976) (consent order); Perma Strate Co., 87 F.T.C. 155 (1976) (consent order); Softsheen Co., 87 F.T.C. 164 (1976) (consent order).

1007 J. Walter Thompson Co., 97 F.T.C. 333 (1981) (consent order); Litton Indus., Inc., 97 F.T.C. 1 (1981); Teledyne Inc., 97 F.T.C. 320 (1981) (consent order).

1008 Porter & Dietsch Inc. v. FTC, 605 F.2d 294 (7th Cir. 1979).

1009 Cliffdale Assocs., 103 F.T.C. 110 (1984).

1010 *Id.*

1011 FTC v. J. Michael Ernest, 5 Trade Reg. Rep. (CCH) ¶ 15353 (C.D. Cal. Jan. 17, 2003) (consent decree); Ramson v. Layne, 668 F. Supp. 1162 (N.D. Ill. 1987); Aramowicz v. Bridges (*In re* Diamond Mortgage Corp.), 118 B.R. 575 (Bankr. N.D. Ill. 1989); Glass, 95 F.T.C. 246 (1980) (consent order); Leroy Gordon Cooper Jr., 94 F.T.C. 674 (1979) (consent order); Cooga Mooga, Inc., 92 F.T.C. 310 (1978) (consent order); *see also* Alexander v. Certified Master Builders Corp., 268 Kan. 812, 1 P.2d 899 (2000) (accrediting organization can be liable under UDAP statute for misrepresentations it makes about its members' qualifications); § 6.5.1, *infra*. *But see* FTC v. Garvey, 2002 WL 31961462 (C.D. Cal. Oct. 31, 2002) (notice of intended ruling), 2002 WL 31744639 (C.D. Cal. Nov. 25, 2002) (findings of fact and conclusions of law) (pitchman's statements were not endorsements as defined by FTC guide, and no evidence that statements were untrue).

1012 Buckingham Productions, Inc., 106 F.T.C. 115 (1985) (consent order). *But cf.* FTC v. Garvey, 2002 WL 31961462 (C.D. Cal. Oct. 31, 2002) (notice of intended ruling), 2002 WL 31744639 (C.D. Cal. Nov. 25, 2002) (findings of fact and conclusions of law) (endorser not liable where he had used the product and there was no evidence that his statements about his personal experience were false).

1013 FTC v. J. Michael Ernest, 5 Trade Reg. Rep. (CCH) ¶ 15353 (C.D. Cal. Jan. 17, 2003) (consent decree); Aramowicz v. Bridges (*In re* Diamond Mortgage Corp.), 118 B.R. 575 (Bankr. N.D. Ill. 1989) (endorser for investment scheme).

1014 Ramson v. Layne, 668 F. Supp. 1162 (N.D. Ill. 1987).

1015 Aramowicz v. Bridges (*In re* Diamond Mortgage Corp.), 118 B.R. 575 (Bankr. N.D. Ill. 1989).

1016 *Id.*

1017 FTC v. Royal Milling Co., 288 U.S. 212 (1933); Niresk Indus. Inc. v. FTC, 278 F.2d 337 (7th Cir.), *cert. denied*, 364 U.S. 883 (1960); Market Dev. Corp., 95 F.T.C. 100 (1980); Product Testing Co., 64 F.T.C. 857, *aff'd*, 337 F.2d 603 (3d Cir. 1964); Borcherding v. Anderson Remodeling Co., 624 N.E.2d 887 (Ill. App. Ct. 1993) (misrepresentation about company's relationship with another company); Brungard v. Caprice Records Inc., 608 S.W.2d 585 (Tenn. Ct. App. 1980) (misrepresentations concerning the stature of a recording company). *See also* Kinkopf v. Triborough Bridge & Tunnel Authority, 764 N.Y.S.2d 549 (Civ. Ct. 2003) (deceptive not to disclose identity of entity with which consumer was contracting).

practices involve companies misrepresenting themselves as charities,[1018] misrepresenting their geographical location,[1019] and exaggerating their age[1020] or size.[1021] It may be a UDAP violation to set up sham intermediary companies and receive kickbacks from them without disclosing the relationship to consumers.[1022] It is deceptive to misrepresent that the seller is an exclusive distributor, has nationwide distributorships, or has exclusive processes.[1023] State courts have found UDAP violations where a seller falsely described itself as a society of poets while soliciting poems and selling poetry books, or as a society of starving local artists,[1024] or where individuals misrepresented themselves as doctors or qualified hypnotists.[1025] It is deceptive for sales agents to represent that they are estate planning advisors and that their sponsoring organization functions on behalf of senior citizens when in actuality it is a sales organization.[1026]

A common deceptive technique is for door-to-door sellers to claim falsely that they are conducting a survey.[1027] This practice is so prevalent that one state's UDAP regulations requires door-to-door sellers, before saying anything else on entering the consumer's residence, to state that they are selling products and describe the products they are selling.[1028] Vocational or correspondence schools can not represent themselves as employers[1029] or accept "union dues" which are really down payments on tuition.[1030]

It is deceptive to use a fictitious[1031] or unregistered[1032] name (as when a state's Fictitious Names Act requires sellers to register). A trade name can be prohibited as not truly descriptive of the company, where no qualifying statements will wholly eliminate the deception.[1033]

The Illinois Attorney General in an opinion letter has stated that corporations may not incorporate under names which are deceptively similar to existing corporations and that corporations may not assume or advertise using names other than those under which they are incorporated. In particular, a vocational school can not use the name of a store where the only connection is an agreement that school customers can use their store credit cards. Such a practice can be a state UDAP violation.[1034]

Companies have been required to disclose in advertising all names under which they do business,[1035] and sellers can not misrepresent that they are licensed.[1036] It is deceptive for a seller to misrepresent the nature of its supplier,[1037] or that it is bonded.[1038]

It is also deceptive to fail to disclose a product's foreign manufacture, or to make the disclosure inconspicuously.[1039] The FTC has issued a detailed description of its enforcement policy for judging the accuracy of "Made in USA" labels.[1040] It requires that all or virtually all of the product be made in the United States.

4.7.9 Passing Off; Trademarks

It is deceptive to try to pass off one's product as that of another company, or oneself as being another company.[1041]

1018 State *ex rel.* Aschcroft v. Marketing Unlimited, 613 S.W.2d 440 (Mo. Ct. App. 1981); Commonwealth v. Handicapped Indus., Inc., Clearinghouse No. 26,027 (Pa. C.P. Bucks Cty. 1977).

1019 State *ex rel.* Brady v. Preferred Florist Network, Inc., 791 A.2d 8 (Del. Ch. 2001) (use of yellow pages ads that make it appear that company is local may be deceptive under general UDAP prohibitions; part of a specific statutory prohibition struck down as violative of Commerce Clause).

1020 Waltham Watch Co. v. FTC, 318 F.2d 28 (7th Cir. 1963), *cert. denied*, 375 U.S. 944 (1964).

1021 Parliament T.V. Tube Sales, Inc., 59 F.T.C. 127 (1961).

1022 Gardner v. First Am. Title Ins. Co., 2001 U.S. Dist. LEXIS 21839 (D. Minn. Dec. 10, 2001) (denial of motion to dismiss).

1023 Commonwealth v. Mirror World, Inc., Clearinghouse No. 26,022 (Pa. C.P. Phila. Cty. 1978).

1024 Shevin v. Thuotte, 339 So. 2d 253 (Fla. Dist. Ct. App. 1976); Southwest Starving Artists Group, Inc. v. State, 364 So. 2d 1128 (Miss. 1978).

1025 People *ex rel.* Lefkowitz v. Therapeutic Hypnosis Inc., 83 Misc. 2d 1068, 374 N.Y.S.2d 576 (Sup. Ct. 1975).

1026 People *ex rel.* Lockyer v. Fremont Life Ins. Co., 104 Cal. App. 4th 508, 128 Cal. Rptr. 2d 463 (2002).

1027 Commonwealth v. Programmed Learning Sys., Inc., Clearinghouse No. 26,019 (Pa. C.P. Allegheny Cty. 1975). *See also* § 4.8.1, *infra.*

1028 Ohio Admin. Code § 109:4-3-11, Direct Solicitations.

1029 Commonwealth v. Tolleson (I), 14 Pa. Commw. Ct. 72, 321 A.2d 664 (1974).

1030 Commonwealth v. Empire Express, Inc., 28 Erie County L.J. 27, Clearinghouse No. 11,129 (Pa. C.P. Erie Cty. 1972).

1031 State v. Kay, 115 N.H. 696, 350 A.2d 336 (1975); Commonwealth v. Tolleson (I), 14 Pa. Commw. Ct. 72, 321 A.2d 664 (1974); Collegiate Recovery & Credit Assistance Programs, Inc. v. State, 525 S.W.2d 900 (Tex. Civ. App. 1975). *But see* Ganson v. Vaughn, 735 N.E.2d 483 (Ohio App. 1999) (use of unregistered fictitious name is not UDAP violation unless it is a means of subterfuge). *See also* § 4.7.7.2, *supra.*

1032 *See* § 4.7.7.2, *supra.*

1033 Commonwealth v. Handicapped Indus., Inc., Clearinghouse No. 26,027 (Pa. C.P. Bucks Cty. 1977).

1034 Office of the Attorney General of Illinois, 1979 Ill. AG LEXIS 30, 1979 Op. Att'y Gen. Ill. 85 (June 29, 1979).

1035 Commonwealth v. Chanderamani, Clearinghouse No. 26,035 (Pa. C.P. Phila. Cty. 1973).

1036 *See* § 4.7.7.2, *supra.*

1037 F. Ray Moore Oil Co. v. State, 341 S.E.2d 371 (N.C. Ct. App. 1986).

1038 J.M. Westall & Co. v. Windswept View, 97 N.C. App. 71, 387 S.E.2d 67 (1990).

1039 Oxwell Tool Co., 59 F.T.C. 1408 (1961); Kukui Nuts of Haw., Inc. v. R. Baird & Co., 789 P.2d 501 (Haw. Ct. App. 1990).

1040 62 Fed. Reg. 63756 (Dec. 2, 1997); Perrigo Co., Dkt. C-4039, www.ftc.gov/opa/2001/02/fyi0212.htm (Feb. 22, 2002) (consent order against misrepresentation that products were made in USA). *See also* FTC, Complying with the Made in the USA Standard (Dec. 1998), *available at* www.ftc.gov/os/statutes/usajump.htm.

1041 United HealthCare Ins. Co. v. AdvancePCS, 316 F.3d 737 (8th Cir. 2002) (affirming preliminary injunction against competing provider); Brunswick Corp. v. Spinit Reel Co., 832 F.2d 513 (10th Cir. 1987) (Tennessee law); American Airlines, Inc. v. A 1-800-A-M-E-R-I-C-A-N Corp., 622 F. Supp. 673 (N.D. Ill.

Also a UDAP violation is the unauthorized advertising or display of merchandise bearing another company's private label, trade name, or trademark,[1042] or an organization's official seal.[1043] It has been held that a Federal Lanhan Act trademark violation is a *per se* UDAP violation.[1044] Sellers who misrepresent their ownership of the product also violate the "passing off" prohibition.[1045]

4.7.10 Disparaging Competitors

It is unfair and deceptive to disparage the merchandise, services, or business of another by false or misleading representations.[1046] This can entail false statements about a competitor's selling prices, business methods, credit terms, policies, or services,[1047] or the competitor's overall product performance,[1048] use of misleading pictures, demonstrations, or comparisons,[1049] false laboratory claims,[1050] imputing dishonorable conduct to a competitor,[1051] or not selling to customers buying from a competitor.[1052] The North Carolina Supreme Court has found that one business libeling another is a UDAP violation.[1053]

4.8 High-Pressure and Coercive Sales Techniques

4.8.1 UDAP Precedent

UDAP precedent specifies types of high-pressure sales techniques that are unfair or deceptive. Most of the cases deal with door-to-door and resort sales. It is a UDAP violation to begin a sale with a deceptive "door opener." Door openers disguise the main purpose of the visit by such ploys as offering prizes or free booklets,[1054] claims that the seller is conducting a survey,[1055] misrepresentations as to the

---

1985); Lloyd's Furs, Inc., 102 F.T.C. 1828 (1983) (consent order); Perfumeric Lido Inc., 69 F.T.C. 187 (1966); State *ex rel.* Brady v. Preferred Florist Network, Inc., 791 A.2d 8 (Del. Ch. 2001); Unichem Corp. v. Gurtler, 148 Ill. App. 3d 284, 498 N.E.2d 724 (1986); Harrington Mfg. Co. v. Powell Mfg. Co., 38 N.C. App. 393, 248 S.E.2d 739 (1978); Wiseman v. Kirkman, 2002 WL 31243522 (Ohio App. Oct. 4, 2002) (unpublished, citation limited) (contracting to install one brand of appliance but installing another and keeping the savings is a UDAP violation); Commonwealth v. Mirror World, Inc., Clearinghouse No. 26,022 (Pa. C.P. Phila. Cty. 1978). *See also* Heller v. Lexton-Ancira Real Estate Fund, Ltd., 809 P.2d 1016 (Colo. Ct. App. 1990).

1042 Niresk Indus. Inc. v. FTC, 278 F.2d 337 (7th Cir.), *cert. denied*, 364 U.S. 883 (1960); R.J. Toomey Co. v. Toomey, 683 F. Supp. 873 (D. Mass. 1988); J.C. Penney Co. v. Parrish Co., 339 F. Supp. 726 (D. Idaho 1972); Midway Mfg. Co. v. Dirkschneider, 571 F. Supp. 282 (D. Neb. 1983) (Nebraska law); George Luxner, 46 F.T.C. 553 (1950). *See also* State *ex rel.* Anderson v. Reward Corp., 482 N.W.2d 815 (Minn. Ct. App. 1992); Seattle Endeavors, Inc. v. Mastro, 67 Wash. App. 866, 841 P.2d 73 (1992).

1043 Bicentennial Comm'n v. Olde Bradford Co., 26 Pa. Commw. Ct. 636, 365 A.2d 172 (1976).

1044 Dial Corp. v. Manghnani Inv. Corp., 659 F. Supp. 1230 (D. Conn. 1987) (violation of 15 U.S.C. § 1114(1) *per se* UDAP violation).

1045 Walter v. Hall, 940 P.2d 991 (Colo. Ct. App. 1996), *aff'd*, 969 P.2d 224 (Colo. 1998) (falsely representing that buyers would have access to their properties across plaintiff's land).

1046 Action Auto Glass v. Auto Glass Specialists, 2001 U.S. Dist. LEXIS 22127 (W.D. Mich. Aug. 21, 2001); LG Balfour Co., 79 F.T.C. 486 (1971), *aff'd*, 442 F.2d 1 (7th Cir. 1971); LG Balfour Co. 74 F.T.C. 345 (1968); M&W Gear Co. v. A.W. Dynamometer Inc., 97 Ill. App. 3d 904, 424 N.E.2d 356 (1981); Crinkley v. Dow Jones, 67 Ill. App. 3d 869, 385 N.E.2d 714 (1979); Connecticut Regulations for the Dep't of Consumer Protection, Conn. Agencies Regs. § 42-110b-18, Misleading Advertising (1977). *See also* Robb Container Corp. v. Sho-me Co., 566 F. Supp. 1143 (N.D. Ill. 1983); Kirsch Fabric Corp. v. Brookstein Enterprises, 209 Neb. 666, 309 N.W.2d 328 (1981).

1047 LG Balfour Co., 79 F.T.C. 486 (1971), *aff'd*, 442 F.2d 1 (7th Cir. 1971); LG Balfour Co., 74 F.T.C. 345 (1968).

1048 Block Drug Co., 92 F.T.C. 852 (1978) (consent order); Eversharp Inc., 77 F.T.C. 686 (1970) (consent order); Washington Gas & Electric Appliance Co., 75 F.T.C. 540 (1969) (consent order); General Motors Corp., 66 F.T.C. 267 (1964) (consent order).

1049 American Home Products Corp., 81 F.T.C. 579 (1972); Libby Owens Ford Glass Co., 69 F.T.C. 523 (1966).

1050 Sunmaster Electric Products, Inc., 67 F.T.C. 735 (1968).

1051 LG Balfour Co., 74 F.T.C. 345 (1968); Guild Indus. Corp., 86 F.T.C. 693 (1975) (consent order).

1052 Fairchild Camera & Inv. Corp., 68 F.T.C. 846 (1965) (consent order).

1053 Ellis v. Northern Star Co., 388 S.E.2d 127 (N.C. 1990). *Accord* Martin v. Samulis, 24 Conn. App. 85, 585 A.2d 1255 (1991) (false accusations that a business was having financial difficulty violated UDAP).

1054 FTC v. Standard Education Society, 302 U.S. 112 (1937); Grolier, Inc., 91 F.T.C. 315 (1978); Encyclopedia Britannica, Inc., 87 F.T.C. 421 (1976), *vacated, remanded on other grounds*, 615 F.2d 1215 (9th Cir. 1980), *on remand, reinstated as modified*, 98 F.T.C. 882 (1981); Arthur Murray Studio, 78 F.T.C. 401 (1971), *aff'd*, 458 F.2d 622 (5th Cir. 1972); Raylew Enterprises, Inc., 74 F.T.C. 1093 (1968); Fred Astaire Dance Studio, Inc., 64 F.T.C. 1295 (1964).

1055 National Trade Publications Servs., Inc. v. FTC, 300 F.2d 790 (8th Cir. 1962); Goodman v. FTC, 244 F.2d 584 (9th Cir. 1957); Standard Distributors Inc. v. FTC, 211 F.2d 7 (2d Cir. 1954); Grolier Inc., 91 F.T.C. 315 (1978); National Housewares, Inc., 90 F.T.C. 512 (1977), *vacated, remanded on other grounds*, 615 F.2d 1215 (9th Cir. 1980), *on remand, reinstated as modified*, 98 F.T.C. 882 (1981); Encyclopedia Britannica, Inc., 87 F.T.C. 421 (1976), *aff'd*, 605 F.2d 964 (7th Cir. 1979); Raylew Enterprises, Inc., 74 F.T.C. 1093 (1968); Commonwealth v. General Ionics, Inc., Clearinghouse No. 26,030 (C.P. Allegheny Cty., Pa. 1975), *aff'd without op.*, 365 A.2d 187 (Pa. Commw. Ct. 1976); Idaho Admin Code 04.02.01.160–.162; Massachusetts Consumer Protection Regulations, Mass. Regs. Code tit. 940, § 3.09, Door-to-Door Sales & Home Improvement Transactions; Wis. Dep't of Agriculture, Trade & Consumer Protection Rules, Wis. Admin. Code ch. ATCP 127.72, Direct Marketing. *See also* Statement of Basis and Purpose of the FTC's Rule Concerning a Cooling-Off Period for Door-to-Door Sales, 37 Fed. Reg. 22945 (Oct. 26, 1972).

organization the salesperson works for,[1056] claims that the consumer is a contest winner or specially selected for a low price[1057] or is being invited to join a preferred group of buyers,[1058] and representations that the consumer's home will be used as a model.[1059] Several state UDAP regulations require that door-to-door or telephone sales begin by stating the seller's identity, the kind of goods or services being offered, and that door-to-door sellers offer written "identification."[1060]

Misrepresentations that goods can only be purchased door-to-door[1061] or that offers are for a limited time only (for example, you must sign today)[1062] are also deceptive. Sellers must leave the consumer's home promptly when requested to do so.[1063] Salespersons can not misrepresent the length of the sale presentation (for example, requesting five minutes of time, and taking substantially longer),[1064] the salesperson's authority to negotiate a final transaction,[1065] or the buyer's right to cancel.[1066]

The FTC has ruled unfair or deceptive high-pressure sales tactics where consumers are not given adequate time to consider their decision and its consequences.[1067] A classic example of such high-pressure sales involved a dance studio using relays of salesmen and sales pitches, refusing to let consumers out of the studio, and emphasizing the usually elderly consumers' marital or social difficulties.[1068] Other forms of coercion or intimidation are actionable as well, such as dismantling a furnace and refusing to reassemble it without a repair contract.[1069] A scare tactic to sell termite protection is a UDAP violation.[1070] Refusing to pay money lawfully owed in order to exert undue pressure on another[1071] or refusing to return a down payment unless the consumer agrees to forfeit part of it are unfair practices.[1072] Illegal high-pressure sales tactics are not limited to those based on persistence and argumentativeness, but may include subtle psychological techniques such as deceptive "sympathy" presentations concerning handicapped labor.[1073] Playing husband and wife off against each other and telling them that they can not leave until a purchase order is

1056 Publications Servs., Inc. v. FTC, 300 F.2d 790 (8th Cir. 1962); Goodman v. FTC, 244 F.2d 584 (9th Cir. 1957); Equifax, Inc., 96 F.T.C. 844 (1980), *rev'd in part on other grounds*, 678 F.2d 1047 (11th Cir. 1982).

1057 National Housewares, Inc., 90 F.T.C. 512 (1977); Van-R Inc., 62 F.T.C. 1215 (1963); Herbert Howell, 62 F.T.C. 1240 (1963); Idaho Admin. Code 04.02.01.162; Massachusetts Consumer Protection Regulations, Mass. Regs. Code tit. 940, § 3.09, Door-to-Door Sales and Home Improvement Transactions; Ohio Admin. Code § 109:4-3-11, Direct Solicitations; Rules of the Utah Consumer Sales Practices Act, Utah Admin. Rules 152-11-9, Direct Solicitations; Wis. Dep't of Agriculture, Trade & Consumer Protection Rules, Wis. Ad. Code ch. ATCP 127.72, Home Solicitation Selling.

1058 Raylew Enterprises, Inc., 74 F.T.C. 1093 (1968); E.W. Sederstrom, 66 F.T.C. 973 (1964); Budget Fin. Plan v. Superior Court (McDowell), 34 Cal. App. 3d 794, 110 Cal. Rptr. 302 (1973).

1059 Mutual Constr. Co., 87 F.T.C. 621 (1976); American Aluminum Corp., 84 F.T.C. 48 (1974), *aff'd*, 522 F.2d 1278 (5th Cir. 1975) *cert. denied*, 426 U.S. 906 (1976); All-State Indus. of North Carolina Inc., 75 F.T.C. 465 (1969), *aff'd*, 423 F.2d 423 (4th Cir.), *cert. denied*, 400 U.S. 828 (1976); Royal Constr. Co., 71 F.T.C. 762 (1967); Idaho Consumer Protection Regulations, Idaho Admin. Code 04.02.01.130, Repairs and Improvements; Massachusetts Consumer Protection Regulations, Mass. Regs. Code tit. 940, § 3.09, Door-to-Door Sales and Home Improvement Transactions; Ohio Admin. Code § 109:4-3-11, Direct Solicitations; Rules of the Utah Consumer Sales Practices Act, Utah Admin. Rules 152-11-9, Direct Solicitations; Wis. Dep't of Agriculture, Trade & Consumer Protection Rules, Wis. Admin. Code ch. ATCP 110.02, Home Improvement Trade Practices.

1060 Idaho Consumer Protection Regulations, Idaho Admin. Code 04.02.01.160, Unfair Solicitation Practices Other Than Trade Premises; Ohio Admin. Code § 109:4-3-11, Direct Solicitations; Rules of the Utah Consumer Sales Practices Act, Utah Admin. Rules 152-11-9, Direct Solicitations; Wis. Dep't of Agriculture, Trade & Consumer Protection Rules, Wis. Admin. Code ch. ATCP 127.62, Home Solicitation Selling. *See also* P.F. Collier & Son Corp. v. FTC, 427 F.2d 261 (6th Cir.) *cert. denied*, 400 U.S. 926 (1970).

1061 Ohio Admin. Code § 109:4-3-11, Direct Solicitations; Rules of the Utah Consumer Sales Practices Act, Utah Admin. Rules 152-11-9, Direct Solicitations.

1062 Certified Building Products, Inc., 83 F.T.C. 1004 (1973), *aff'd sub nom.* Thiret v. FTC, 512 F.2d 176 (10th Cir. 1975); Southern States Distributing Co., 83 F.T.C. 1126 (1973); Royal Constr. Co., 71 F.T.C. 762 (1967).

1063 Idaho Consumer Protection Regulations, Idaho Admin. Code 04.02.01.161, Unfair Solicitation Practices Other Than Trade Premises; Wis. Dep't of Agriculture, Trade & Consumer Protection Rules, Wis. Admin. Code, ch. ATCP 127.74, Home Solicitation Selling.

1064 Wis. Dep't of Agriculture, Trade & Consumer Protection Rules, Wis. Admin. Code ch. ATCP 127.72, Home Solicitation Selling.

1065 Ohio Admin. Code § 109:4-3-11, Direct Solicitations; Rules of the Utah Consumer Sales Practices Act, Utah Admin. Rules 152-11-9, Direct Solicitations.

1066 Commonwealth v. R&W Indus., Inc., Clearinghouse No. 26,021 (Pa. Commw. Ct. 1976); Ohio Admin. Code § 109:4-3-11, Direct Solicitations.

1067 National Housewares, Inc., 90 F.T.C. 512 (1977); Carpets "R" Us, Inc., 87 F.T.C. 303 (1976); Wilbanks Carpet Specialists, Inc., 84 F.T.C. 510 (1974); Tri-State Carpet Inc., 84 F.T.C. 1078 (1974); Arthur Murray Studio, 78 F.T.C. 401 (1971), *aff'd*, 458 F.2d 622 (5th Cir. 1972); Household Sewing Machine Co., 76 F.T.C. 207 (1969); Holland Furnace Co. v. FTC, 55 F.T.C. 55 (1958), *aff'd*, 295 F.2d 302 (7th Cir. 1961). *See also* Horizon Corp., 97 F.T.C. 464 (1981).

1068 Arthur Murray Studio, 78 F.T.C. 401 (1971), *aff'd*, 458 F.2d 622 (5th Cir. 1972); Brown v. Silzar, 1981 Ohio App. LEXIS 13616 (Jan. 28, 1981).

1069 Holland Furnace Co. v. FTC, 55 F.T.C. 55 (1958), *aff'd*, 295 F.2d 302 (7th Cir. 1961).

1070 Bandura v. Orkin Exterminating Co., 865 F.2d 816 (7th Cir. 1988).

1071 Pepsi-Cola Metro Bottling Co. v. Checkers, Inc., 754 F.2d 10 (11th Cir. 1985) (Massachusetts law); Wilder v. Squires, 315 S.E.2d 63 (N.C. Ct. App. 1984). *See also* Reusch v. Roob, 234 Wis. 2d 270, 610 N.W.2d 168 (App. 2000) (threatening to withhold items already paid for).

1072 Wilder v. Squires, 315 S.E.2d 63 (N.C. Ct. App. 1984).

1073 Commonwealth v. Handicapped Indus., Inc., Clearinghouse No. 26,027 (Pa. C.P. Bucks Cty. 1977).

signed may push sales tactics over the line.[1074] A Michigan court has held that it is not coercive, however, to present a contract for signature only after a home inspection has already been performed and the consumer has spent several hours accompanying the inspector.[1075]

4.8.2 High-Pressure Sales as Unfair Practices

Even where there is no UDAP precedent, high-pressure sales should be attacked as unfair trade practices. Depending on the facts of a case, the high-pressure sale may fit very neatly into the FTC's three-part unfairness definition: a practice causes substantial consumer injury, not authorized by countervailing benefits, that could not be reasonably avoided.[1076] Being sold a good or service that the consumer upon reflection would realize he or she neither wants nor can afford certainly involves substantial consumer injury. It is hard to see the benefit to consumers or competition for one company to sell products not on the basis of price, quality, or service, but on the sophistication and oppressiveness of its commissioned sales staff. High-pressure sales are also designed so that consumers can not reasonably avoid them.[1077] Thus courts find the use of coercion to be unfair. This precedent is detailed at § 4.3.6, *supra*.

4.9 Deceptive Performance Practices

4.9.1 Layaway Plans; Other Deposits

Under a layaway plan, consumers make payments toward the total price of goods in advance, receiving the goods only when the total price is paid. A layaway plan is thus closely related to a deposit to hold merchandise. In either situation, abuses can arise when the consumer stops making payments and wishes a refund, or when the consumer pays in full but does not receive the goods selected, or is required to pay a higher price.

State UDAP regulations and cases prohibit misrepresentations concerning the seller's layaway plan policy and require disclosure in the layaway agreement of the goods to be purchased, the cash price and down payment, and the period during which the offer will be held open for the buyer.[1078] The seller must hold for the buyer the specific goods chosen or an exact duplicate; when payment is made, goods identical to those set aside must be delivered, at the price originally agreed upon.[1079] The buyer has a right to receipts and an itemized statement of the amount paid or owing.[1080]

The seller's policy as to refunds must be conspicuously disclosed,[1081] and, if the consumer ceases making payments, the seller must disclose to the consumer if he or she is entitled to a refund.[1082] The FTC has indicated in a complaint (resulting in a consent agreement) that layaway contract provisions that allow the seller to keep all deposits are adhesive and unfair.[1083]

Not just for layaway plans but for any form of consumer deposit, it is deceptive to misrepresent buyers' cancellation rights or rights to a return of a deposit, or to refuse to return to consumers deposits to which they are entitled.[1084] Ohio's

---

1074 Reusch v. Roob, 234 Wis. 2d 270, 610 N.W.2d 168 (App. 2000).

1075 Starks v. Solomon, 2001 Mich. App. LEXIS 1000 (Mar. 30, 2001) (unpublished, citation limited).

1076 *See* § 4.3.2, *supra*.

1077 See § 4.3.2, *supra* for further discussion of the FTC unfairness definition.

1078 Idaho Consumer Protection Regulations, Idaho Admin. Code 04.02.01.150, Lay-Away Plans; Massachusetts Consumer Protection Regulations, Mass. Regs. Code tit. 940, § 3.12, Lay-Away Plans; Ohio Admin. Code § 109:4-3-07, Deposits; State *ex rel.* Turner v. Limbrecht, 246 N.W.2d 330 (Iowa 1976). *See also* Daniels v. True, 47 Ohio Misc. 2d 8, 547 N.E.2d 425 (Mun. Ct. 1988) (contractor violated UDAP regulation by accepting down payment and then failing to complete the work or make a full refund).

1079 Idaho Consumer Protection Regulations, Idaho Admin. Code 04.02.01.150, Lay-Away Plans; Massachusetts Consumer Protection Regulations, Mass. Regs. Code tit. 940, § 3.12, Lay-Away Plans; Ohio Admin. Code § 109:4-3-07, Deposits; Rules of the Utah Consumer Sales Practices Act, Utah Admin. Rules 152-11-10, Deposits and Refunds.

1080 Idaho Consumer Protection Regulations, Idaho Admin. Code 04.02.01.150, Lay-Away Plans; Massachusetts Consumer Protection Regulations, Mass. Regs. Code tit. 940, § 3.12, Lay-Away Plans.

1081 Heirloom Collection, Inc., 90 F.T.C. 152 (1977) (consent order); Riley v. Enterprise Furniture Co., 54 Ohio Misc. 1, 375 N.E.2d 821, 7 Ohio Op. 3d 271 (Mun. Ct. Sylvania 1977); Bierlein v. Alex's Continental Inn, Inc., 16 Ohio App. 3d 294, 475 N.E.2d 1273 (1984); Idaho Consumer Protection Regulations, Idaho Admin. Code 04.02.01.151, Lay-Away Plans; Massachusetts Consumer Protection Regulations, Mass. Regs. Code tit. 940, § 3.12, Lay-Away Plans; Ohio Admin. Code § 109:4-3-07, Deposits; Rules of the Utah Consumer Sales Practices Act, Utah Admin. Rules 152-11-10, Deposits and Refunds.

1082 Fred Meyer, Inc., 96 F.T.C. 60 (1980) (consent order).

1083 S. Klein Inc., 95 F.T.C. 387 (1980) (consent order).

1084 *In re* Edwards, 233 B.R. 461 (Bankr. D. Idaho 1999) (deceptive to disclose that deposit is nonrefundable only after accepting it); Patry v. Liberty Mobilhome Sales, Inc., 15 Mass. App. Ct. 701, 448 N.E.2d 405 (1983), *aff'd*, 475 N.E.2d 392 (Mass. 1985); Cybul v. Atrium Palace Syndicate, 272 N.J. Super. 330, 639 A.2d 1146 (App. Div. 1994) (condominium seller violated UDAP by insisting that buyers either close title without the required certificate of occupancy or forfeit their deposits); Wilder v. Squires, 315 S.E.2d 63 (N.C. Ct. App. 1984); Commonwealth v. National Apartment Leasing Co., 529 A.2d 1157 (Pa. Commw. Ct. 1987); Commonwealth v. Flick, 382 A.2d 762 (Pa. Commw. Ct. 1978); Leal v. Furniture Barn Inc., 571 S.W.2d 864 (Tex. 1978); State v. Ralph Williams' N.W. Chrysler Plymouth Inc., 82 Wash. 2d 265, 510 P.2d 233 (1973); *see also* Jones v. Wide World of Cars, Inc., 820 F. Supp. 132 (S.D.N.Y. 1993); Paulik v. Coombs, 120 Wis. 2d 431, 355 N.W.2d 357 (Ct. App. 1984). *But see* Banks v. Department of Consumer &

regulation requires that the receipt state the seller's refund policy.[1085] It is also deceptive to attempt to negotiate a deposit check when the seller had promised not to do so, or to sell the consumer's trade-in car immediately to take away the consumer's opportunity to cancel.[1086] It is unconscionable to fail to credit a down payment to a sales contract,[1087] to deny receiving a check and then refuse to return it,[1088] or for an attorney to refuse to turn over money the attorney was holding for the client.[1089]

While UDAP statutes provide a useful remedy in dealing with layaway plan abuses, traditional contract remedies should not be neglected. The layaway plan can be treated as an option contract for a specified period of time, supported by consideration. Seller's damages if a buyer does not exercise the option are equal to the cost to the merchant of not being able to offer the merchandise to another buyer. If the seller does not retain the requested goods for the specified period, the buyer also has a breach of contract action. Under contract law principles, deposits may not always be retained even if the contract provides for such forfeiture. If the deposit exceeds the seller's reasonably foreseeable damages from the buyer's cancellation, then forfeiture of the deposit would be an unenforceable penalty. Some states also have special statutes regulating layaway plans.[1090]

Another possible remedy for layaway plan problems is the Truth in Lending Act. Although the Truth in Lending Act does not generally apply to layaway plans, if the consumer is contractually obligated under state law to continue making payments, then the seller must comply with the Truth in Lending Act.[1091]

A seller can not take a deposit and intermingle it with the seller's other funds, without disclosing to the consumer that the seller is on the verge of closure, if that is the case.[1092]

Regulatory Affairs, 634 A.2d 433 (D.C. 1993) (refusal to return partial payment did not violate UDAP statute, where consumer repudiated the contract soon after paying and defendant never represented that he had performed the services).

1085 Ganson v. Vaughn, 735 N.E.2d 483 (Ohio App. 1999) (seller violated deposit regulation by failing to include refund policy on receipt, even though sign was posted in store and policy was stated in agreement signed at later date).

1086 Mapp v. Toyota World, Inc., 344 S.E.2d 297 (N.C. Ct. App. 1986).

1087 Miller v. Soliz, 648 S.W.2d 734 (Tex. App. 1983).

1088 Butler v. Joseph's Wine Shop, Inc., 633 S.W.2d 926 (Tex. App. 1982).

1089 Barnard v. Mecom, 650 S.W.2d 123 (Tex. App. 1983).

1090 *See, e.g.*, Liverpool v. Baltimore Diamond Exchange, Inc., 799 A.2d 1264 (Md. 2002).

1091 *See* Federal Reserve Board Official Staff Commentary § 226.2(a)(14)-1; *see also* National Consumer Law Center, Truth in Lending § 2.4.9.2 (5th ed. 2003 and Supp.).

1092 Commonwealth v. Windsor of Dracut, Inc., Clearinghouse No. 52,034 (Mass. Super. Ct. Aug. 20, 1997).

4.9.2 Delay and Nondelivery

Delay and nondelivery of mail order sales is discussed in another section.[1093] But deceptive delay and nondelivery are not restricted to mail order sales. Furniture, carpet, and other products purchased in stores or via the Internet are also associated with this problem. Just as with mail order sales, it is a UDAP violation if sellers, when offering prompt delivery, fail to take reasonable action to insure such delivery.[1094]

If delivery can not be made within a reasonable time following the promised date, due to unforeseen circumstances, the FTC requires the seller to give timely notice of the delay, allowing the consumers the option to cancel and receive a full and prompt refund.[1095] Delay and nondelivery are UDAP violations as well,[1096] and many states have UDAP regulations that set specific rules about delivery dates.[1097] New York's Merchandise Delivery Act requires

1093 *See* § 5.8.1, *supra*.

1094 FTC v. Craig Lee Hare, 5 Trade Reg. Rep. (CCH) ¶ 24,497 (S.D. Fla. 1998) (proposed consent decree) (non-delivery of computer ordered via Internet); FTC v. Worldwide Wallcoverings & Blinds, Inc., 5 Trade Reg. Rep. (CCH) ¶ 24,262 (N.D. Ill. 1997) (consent decree); Commonwealth of Pennsylvania v. Diversified Chemicals, Inc., Clearinghouse No. 50,440 (Pa. C.P. Oct. 6, 1994). *See* National Consumer Law Center, Consumer Law Pleadings No. 2, § 7.1 (CD-Rom and Index Guide) for a sample complaint involving non-delivery of furniture, also found on the CD-Rom accompanying this volume.

1095 Jay Norris Inc., 91 F.T.C. 751 (1978), *aff'd*, 598 F.2d 1244 (2d Cir. 1979), *cert. denied*, 444 U.S. 980 (1980); United States v. Star Crest Products of California, Inc., Trade Reg. Rep. (CCH) ¶ 21,923 (C.D. Cal. 1982) (consent order); Joseph Winkler & Co., 46 F.T.C. 107 (1949); Kustom Enterprises, 85 F.T.C. 840 (1975) (consent order); Auslander Decorator Furniture, Inc., 83 F.T.C. 1542 (1973).

1096 Willman v. Ewen, 230 Kan. 262, 634 P.2d 1061 (1981) (seller stalled over three months and misled consumer that could deliver car); Cybul v. Atrium Palace Syndicate, 272 N.J. Super. 330, 639 A.2d 1146 (1994) (condominium seller violated condo sales law, and therefore UDAP statute, by refusing to return buyers' deposits when it could not produce certificates of occupancy by the closing date); State *ex rel.* Lefkowitz v. Bevis Indus., Inc., 63 Misc. 2d 1088, 314 N.Y.S.2d 60 (N.Y. Sup. Ct. 1970) (excessive delay in making refunds when merchandise is unavailable violates general UDAP prohibition against deception); Walker v. Winks Furniture, 640 N.Y.S.2d 428 (Yonkers City Ct. 1996) (false promise of delivery within one week was UDAP violation and violation of state Merchandise Delivery Act); Lump v. Best Door & Window, Inc., 2002 Ohio App. LEXIS 1381 (Mar. 27, 2002); Commonwealth v. Chanderamani, Clearinghouse No. 26,035 (Pa. C.P. Phila. Cty. 1973); Commonwealth v. Hawkins, Clearinghouse No. 26,026 (Pa. C.P. Phila. Cty. 1973); Bob Robertson, Inc. v. Webster, 679 S.W.2d 683 (Tex. App. 1984). *But see* Opsahl v. Pinehurst, Inc., 344 S.E.2d 68 (N.C. Ct. App. 1986).

1097 Idaho Consumer Protection Regulations, Idaho Admin. Code 04.02.01.140, Time of Delivery or Performance, General Rule; Massachusetts Consumer Protection Regulations, Mass. Regs. Code tit. 940, § 3.15(3), Failure to Deliver; New Jersey Administrative Rules of the Division of Consumer Affairs, N.J. Admin. Code ch. 13:45A-5, Household Furniture and Furnishings; Ohio

sellers to disclose an estimated delivery date in writing on the contract.[1098]

It is a UDAP violation to fail to disclose to consumers the option of a full refund where delivery is delayed even if the seller obtains the buyer's permission to deliver late; the buyer should at least know of his or her right to obtain a refund.[1099] Nondelivery is not excused by unavailability unless the quantity in stock was sufficient to meet reasonably anticipated demand.[1100]

Almost a year's delay in installing windows is a UDAP violation.[1101] Even where there are circumstances justifying a delay, a home improvement contractor's completion date is meant to be not just helpful, but reliable. Contractors, based on their experience, should be able to foresee and take account of such delays in establishing a delivery date.[1102] Intent not to deliver when promised is a deceptive practice.[1103] A New Jersey court has ruled, however, that its UDAP regulation covering failure to deliver ordered merchandise was not violated when a merchant made a timely delivery, but the merchandise was defective.[1104]

Admin. Code § 109:4-3-09, Failure to Deliver/Substitution of Goods or Services; Rules for the Utah Consumer Sales Practices Act, Utah Admin. Rules 152-11-8, Substitution of Consumer Commodities; Vermont Consumer Fraud Rules, Code Vt. Rules 06 031 010 Rule 105, Substitution of Products/Failure to Deliver. *See also* State v. Hudson Furniture Co., 165 N.J. Super. 516, 398 A.2d 900 (App. Div. 1979) (applying New Jersey regulation); Brown v. Cole, Clearinghouse No. 27,057 (Ohio C.P. Richland Cty. 1976); Brown v. Wonderful World Publishing Co., Clearinghouse No. 27,055 (Ohio C.P. Franklin Cty. 1976); Brown v. Bredenbeck, 2 Ohio Op. 3d 286 (C.P. Franklin Cty. 1975); Brown v. Lyons, 43 Ohio Misc. 14, 332 N.E.2d 380, 72 Ohio Op. 2d 216 (C.P. Hamilton Cty. 1974); State v. Clausen, 105 Wis. 2d 231, 313 N.W.2d 819 (1982) (UDAP regulation requires home improvement contractor to give notice of delay even if delay excusable).

1098 N.Y. Gen. Bus. Law § 396-u; Walker v. Winks Furniture, 640 N.Y.S.2d 428 (Yonkers City Ct. 1996).

1099 Brooks v. Hurst Buick-Pontiac-Olds-GMC, Inc., 23 Ohio App. 3d 85, 491 N.E.2d 345 (1985) (interpreting UDAP regulation).

1100 Bede Aircraft, Inc., 92 F.T.C. 449 (1978) (consent order).

1101 Daniels v. True, 47 Ohio Misc. 2d 8, 547 N.E.2d 425 (Mun. Ct. 1988) (contractor's delay in starting work and failure to complete work violates UDAP regulation); Sinkfield v. Strong, 34 Ohio Misc. 2d 19, 517 N.E.2d 1051 (Mun. Ct. 1987). *See also* Lump v. Best Door & Window, Inc., 2002 Ohio App. LEXIS 1381 (Mar. 27, 2002) (delay of nearly two months past promised delivery date may be UDAP violation); Janos v. Murduck, 109 Ohio App. 3d 583, 672 N.E.2d 1021 (1996) (error to grant summary judgment to dealer who failed to deliver windows).

1102 Keyes v. Bollinger, 31 Wash. App. 286, 640 P.2d 1077 (1982); *see also* Ybarra v. Saldona, 624 S.W.2d 948 (Tex. Civ. App. 1981).

1103 KuyKendal v. C.O.M.H. Woodburn, Inc., 77 Or. App. 350, 713 P.2d 620 (1986). *See also* Foley v. L&L Int'l, Inc., 88 N.C. App. 710, 364 S.E.2d 733 (1988) (promise to deliver when had never even ordered car).

1104 DiNicola v. Watchung Furniture Country Manor, 232 N.J. Super. 69, 556 A.2d 367 (1989).

4.9.3 Damaged and Defective Goods

It is deceptive not to disclose that goods are damaged or defective.[1105] It is deceptive for a seller to fail to disclose known defects even if a good is sold "as is."[1106] Most of the UDAP case law dealing with sale of defective goods deals with automobiles. These cases are analyzed in a later section,[1107] and should be referred to when analyzing any type of defective product case. Suppliers may be liable, however, if other items they provide, even including household water service, are defective.[1108] Defective goods must be repaired or replaced.[1109] Of course, warranty law provides an additional remedy for defective goods,[1110] and the breach of warranty itself may also be actionable as a UDAP violation.[1111] Concealment of known defects may also constitute fraud.[1112]

4.9.4 Used as New; Prior Use

It is deceptive to fail to disclose that a product is used, reconditioned, rebuilt, or repossessed,[1113] to misrepresent its

1105 La. Admin. Code tit. 16, pt. III § 513, Imperfections, Rejects, and Distressed Goods (1977); W. Va. Code St. R. § 142-6-3; Royal Furniture, 93 F.T.C. 422 (1979) (consent order); Auslander Decorator Furniture, 83 F.T.C. 1542 (1973); Consumers Home Equip. Co., 42 F.T.C. 296 (1947); Vercher v. Ford Motor Co., 527 So. 2d 995 (La. Ct. App. 1988); Calimlim v. Foreign Car Center, Inc., 392 Mass. 228, 467 N.E.2d 443 (1984); Commonwealth v. Commercial Enterprises, Inc., Clearinghouse No. 26,036 (C.P. Erie Cty., Pa. 1972); Manufactured Housing Mgmt. v. Tubb, 643 S.W.2d 483 (Tex. App. 1982); State v. Ralph Williams' N.W. Chrysler Plymouth Inc., 87 Wash. 2d 298, 553 P.2d 423 (1976); State v. Keehn, 74 Wis. 2d 218, 246 N.W.2d 547 (1976). *See also* § 4.2.14, *supra* (general nondisclosure rules).

1106 V.S.H. Realty, Inc. v. Texaco, Inc., 757 F.2d 411 (1st Cir. 1985) (Massachusetts law); Automobile Trader v. Simmons, 22 Ohio Op. 3d 149 (Ct. App. 1981); Hatfield v. D.D. Sullivan Inc., No. 111813 (Or. Civ. Ct. Marion Cty. 1980); Metro Ford Truck Sales, Inc. v. Davis, 709 S.W.2d 785 (Tex. App. 1986). *But see* Erwin v. Smiley, 975 S.W.2d 335 (Tex. App. 1998).

1107 *See* §§ 5.4.6.6, 5.4.6.7, *infra.*

1108 Sternberg v. N.Y. Water Service Corp., 548 N.Y.S.2d 247 (App. Div. 1989).

1109 Royal Furniture, 93 F.T.C. 422 (1979) (consent order); Auslander Decorator Furniture, 83 F.T.C. 1542 (1973); Consumers Home Equip. Co., 42 F.T.C. 296 (1947).

1110 *See* National Consumer Law Center, Consumer Warranty Law (2d ed. 2001 and Supp.).

1111 *See* § 5.2.7.1, *infra.*

1112 *See* §§ 9.5.9, 9.6.3, *infra*, and National Consumer Law Center, Automobile Fraud Ch. 7 (2d ed. 2003 and Supp.).

1113 Kerran v. FTC, 265 F.2d 246 (10th Cir. 1959), *cert. denied sub nom.* Double Eagle Refining Co. v. FTC, 361 U.S. 818 (1966); Mohawk Refining Corp. v. FTC, 263 F.2d 818 (3d Cir. 1959), *cert. denied*, 361 U.S. 814 (1960); Nelson Brothers Furniture Co., 92 F.T.C. 954 (1978) (consent order); Peacock Buick, Inc., 86 F.T.C. 1532 (1975); Sidney Lenet, 50 F.T.C. 207 (1973); Metropolitan Golf Ball Inc., 66 F.T.C. 378 (1964); Slayer

prior use,[1114] or to substitute used or reconditioned merchandise for merchandise represented as new.[1115] A number of states have UDAP regulations that spell out these prohibitions more specifically.[1116] Intent or seller's prior knowledge is irrelevant.[1117] Where a certificate of title and other documents reveal a vehicle's prior use, conflicting oral misrepresentations that the vehicle is new are actionable.[1118] In addition to being a UDAP violation, the sale of used goods as new may also be a breach of warranty.[1119]

A common issue in used as new cases is whether or not the prior use is significant enough to call the goods used.[1120] Even a product damaged in transit from manufacturer to dealer may be considered used.[1121] Certain returned merchandise without defects, however, can be considered unused.[1122] Purchasing a car at the end of lease term, after discovering the car's undisclosed prior use, does not waive the consumer's right to bring a UDAP action.[1123] Misrepresentation of a vehicle's history is discussed in detail in NCLC's *Automobile Fraud* (2d ed. 2003 and Supp.).

4.9.5 Substitution of Displayed Products

It is deceptive to deliver merchandise not identical to floor models or other samples displayed at the time of purchase or to substitute a different product from the one purchased.[1124]

Refining Co., 54 F.T.C. 1026 (1958); Leaco Spring Co., 49 F.T.C. 419 (1953), *aff'd*, No. 11789 (D.C. Cir. June 2, 1953); Bond Trading Co., 46 F.T.C. 626 (1950); Joseph Winkler & Co., 46 F.T.C. 107 (1949); Jacob Swimmer, 35 F.T.C. 178 (1942); Penn-Lub Oil Products Co., 34 F.T.C. 1049 (1942); People v. Conway, 42 Cal. App. 3d 875, 117 Cal. Rptr. 251 (1974); Kiley v. Petsmart, 80 P.3d 1179 (Kan. App. 2003) (allowing UDAP claim to proceed even though seller offered to replace mismarked used goods with new); Bell v. Kent-Brown Chevrolet Co., 1 Kan. App. 2d 131, 561 P.2d 907 (1977); Oster v. Swad Chevrolet, 1982 Ohio App. LEXIS 15049 (June 17, 1982) (dealer violated "used for new" rule by failing to inform buyer that demonstrator vehicle had been used by another dealer); Brown v. Spitzer Ford Inc., 11 Ohio Op. 3d 84 (Ct. App. 1978); Weigel v. Ron Tonkin Chevrolet Co., 298 Or. 127, 690 P.2d 488 (1984); Bodin v. B&L Furniture Co., 42 Or. App. 731, 601 P. 2d 848 (1979); Commonwealth *ex rel.* Biester v. Luther Ford Sales Inc., 60 Pa. Commw. 123, 430 A.2d 1053 (1981); Haverlah v. Memphis Aviation, Inc., 674 S.W.2d 297 (Tenn. Ct. App. 1984); Spradling v. Williams, 566 S.W.2d 561 (Tex. 1978); State v. Packard, Clearinghouse No. 27,066 (Vt. Super. Ct. 1977); *see also* § 5.4.6.3, *infra*. *But cf.* Hodges v. Koons Buick Pontiac GMC, Inc., 180 F. Supp. 2d 786 (E.D. Va. 2001) (describing demonstrator car as new was not UDAP violation when seller told buyer it was a demo, buyer signed odometer statement showing mileage, and buyer knew it was a demo).

1114 Hertz Corp., 88 F.T.C. 238 (1976) (consent order); Sunset Pools v. Schaefer, 869 S.W.2d 883 (Mo. Ct. App. 1994) (failed to disclose product used as a store model); State *ex rel.* Danforth v. Independence Dodge, Inc., 494 S.W.2d 362 (Mo. Ct. App. 1973); Hardy v. Toler, 288 N.C. 303, 218 S.E.2d 342 (1975); Arales v. Furs by Weiss, Inc., 2003 WL 21469131 (Ohio App. June 26, 2003) (unpublished, citation limited) (unfair and deceptive to alter a coat to conceal prior buyer's monogram without telling new buyer); Wolverton v. Stanwood, 278 Or. 341, 563 P.2d 1203 (1977).

1115 Valley Steel Products Co., 47 F.T.C. 230 (1950); Plaza Pontiac v. Shaw, 158 Ga. App. 799, 282 S.E.2d 383 (1981); Arales v. Furs by Weiss, Inc., 1999 Ohio App. LEXIS 125 (Jan. 21, 1999) (plaintiff stated claim where seller sold coat as new when it had been previously bought and returned; it is for jury to make judgment whether coat should be considered used); Abrams v. Mike Salta Pontiac Inc., 51 Or. App. 495, 625 P.2d 1383 (1981); Jack Roach Ford v. De Urdanavia, 659 S.W.2d 725 (Tex. App. 1983) (sale of deteriorated new car).

1116 Connecticut Regulations for the Dep't of Consumer Protection, Conn. Agencies Regs. § 42-110b-18(x), Misleading Advertising (1977); Idaho Consumer Protection Regulations, Idaho Admin. Code 04.02.01.110–.113, Disclosure of Prior Use; Louisiana Consumer Protection Division Rules and Regulations, La. Admin. Code tit. 16, pt. III § 511, Misrepresentation of Old, Used or Secondhand Goods; Massachusetts Consumer Protection Regulations, Mass. Regs. Code tit. 940, § 3.15(1), New For Used; Code Miss. Rules 24 000 002 Rules 48–51; Mont. Admin. Rules 2.61.101(1)(f); Ohio Admin. Code § 109:4-3-08, New for Used; Rules for the Utah Consumer Sales Practices Act, Utah Admin. Rules 152-11-7, New for Used.

1117 Bell v. Kent-Brown Chevrolet Co., 1 Kan. App. 2d 131, 561 P.2d 907 (1977). *See generally* §§ 4.2.4, 4.2.5, *supra*.

1118 Gonzalez v. Global Truck & Equip. Inc., 625 S.W.2d 348 (Tex. Civ. App. 1981).

1119 *See* National Consumer Law Center, Consumer Warranty Law (2d ed. 2001 and Supp.).

1120 See Annotation, What Goods or Property Are "Used," Secondhand or the Like, for Purposes of State Consumer Laws Prohibiting Claims That Such Items Are New, 59 A.L.R.4th 1192 (1988 and Supp.).

1121 Nemore, Nemore & Silverman v. W.A. Austin Chevrolet, D.N.CV. 81 0054979S (Conn. Super. Ct. 1982); Brooks v. Hurst Buick-Pontiac-Olds-GMC, 23 Ohio App. 3d 85, 491 N.E.2d 345 (1985); Pirozzi v. Penske-Olds-Cadillac-GMS, 605 A.2d 373 (Pa. Super. Ct. 1992). *See* § 5.4.7.4, *infra*.

1122 Idaho Consumer Protection Regulations, Idaho Admin. Code 04.02.01.113, Disclosure of Prior Use; Ohio Admin. Code § 109:4-3-08, New For Used.

1123 Wadkins v. Roach Cadillac Inc., 7 Kan. App. 2d 8, 637 P.2d 458 (1981).

1124 National Trade Publications Servs., Inc. v. FTC, 300 F.2d 790 (8th Cir. 1962); Consumers Home Equip. v. FTC, 164 F.2d 972 (6th Cir.), *cert. denied*, 331 U.S. 860 (1947); Royal Furniture, 93 F.T.C. 422 (1979) (consent order); New Process Co., 87 F.T.C. 1359 (1976) (consent order); Tomorrow's Heritage, Inc., 84 F.T.C. 1676 (1974) (consent order); Auslander Decorator Furniture, 83 F.T.C. 1542 (1973); Sunshine Art Studios, Inc., 81 F.T.C. 836 (1972); Star Office Supply Co., 77 F.T.C. 383 (1970); Kiddieland Studio, 44 F.T.C. 49 (1947); Consumer Home Equip. Co., 42 F.T.C. 296 (1946); People v. Conway, 42 Cal. App. 3d 875, 117 Cal. Rptr. 251 (1974); Deltona Corp. v. Janotti, 392 So. 2d 976 (Fla. Dist. Ct. App. 1981); State *ex rel.* Guste v. General Motors Corp., Clearinghouse No. 26,209 (La. Ct. App. Jan. 17, 1978); Kohl v. Silver Lake Motors, Inc., 369 Mass. 795, 343 N.E.2d 375 (1976); Chambless v. Barry Robinson Farm Supply, 667 S.W.2d 598 (Tex. App. 1984); State v. Packard, Clearinghouse No. 27,066 (Vt. Super. Ct. May 3, 1977); Tallmadge v. Aurora Chrysler Plymouth, 25 Wash. App. 90, 605 P.2d 1275 (1979); Massachusetts Consumer Protection Regulations, Mass. Regs. Code tit. 940, § 3.15, Substitution of Products; Ohio Admin. Code § 109:4-3-09, Failure to Deliver/Substitution of Goods; Failure to Deliver/Substitution of Goods.

The availability of this UDAP remedy should not lead consumer litigants to ignore warranty remedies as well.[1125]

4.9.6 Packaging

Oversized boxes or containers can misrepresent the size, dimensions, amount, or quantity of the product contained inside.[1126] Packaged products are deceptive if the product does not reasonably correspond in size with the container or package dimensions, based upon a visual inspection by the trier of fact.[1127] This prohibited practice is sometimes called "slack filling." Similarly deceptive is placing fewer items in a package than appear on the label.[1128] Packaging can also be deceptive if it resembles the packaging for another type of product.[1129]

4.9.7 Repair Practices

A wide range of practices associated with repairs or other services has been found unfair or deceptive. Specific findings concerning auto repair[1130] and home improvement[1131] practices appear elsewhere in this manual. More generally, deceptive repair practices include falsely representing that repairs are needed or misrepresenting that consumer goods are in unsafe or substandard condition, refusing to reassemble goods after dismantling them during a free or low-priced inspection, or making low-price estimates and then proceeding with higher cost repairs without the consumer's permission.[1132] UDAP regulations prohibit merchants from misrepresenting that repairs have been performed,[1133] and such actions would also be a violation of a general prohibition against deceptive conduct.[1134] UDAP regulations prohibit retention of the property repaired after payment is made,[1135] failure to provide an itemized bill indicating parts and labor,[1136] and failure to allow consumers to keep or

1125 *See* National Consumer Law Center, Consumer Warranty Law (2d ed. 2001 and Supp.).

1126 Hasbro Indus., 86 F.T.C. 1009 (1975) (consent order); Milton Bradley Co., 85 F.T.C. 953 (1975) (consent order); Pastime Indus., Inc., 84 F.T.C. 238 (1974) (consent order); EduCards Corp., 83 F.T.C. 1583 (1974) (consent order); Avalon Indus., 83 F.T.C. 1728 (1974); Walco Toy Co., 83 F.T.C. 1783 (1974); Papercraft Corp., 63 F.T.C. 1965 (1963); Pioneer Specialty Co., 39 F.T.C. 188 (1944); United Drug Co., 35 F.T.C. 643 (1942); Burry Biscuit Corp., 33 F.T.C. 89 (1941); Baltimore Paint & Color Works, 9 F.T.C. 242 (1925).

1127 Avalon Indus., 83 F.T.C. 1728 (1974); Papercraft Corp., 63 F.T.C. 1965 (1963).

1128 Corning Glass Works, 92 F.T.C. 861 (1978) (consent order); Owens Illinois, Inc., 92 F.T.C. 866 (1978) (consent order).

1129 Canandaigua Wine Co., 114 F.T.C. 348 (1991) (consent order) (bottle shape and color resembled wine cooler).

1130 *See* § 5.4.1, *infra*.

1131 *See* § 5.6.1, *infra*.

1132 Holland Furnace Co. v. FTC, 295 F.2d 302 (7th Cir. 1961); Aamco Transmission Co., 77 F.T.C. 1559 (1970) (consent order); People *ex rel.* Moore v. Burgess T.V. Service, 36 Colo. App. 19, 534 P.2d 361 (1975) (repairing TV without authorization and refusing to release it without payment is violation of general prohibition against deception); Crown Buick, Inc. v. Bercier, 483 So. 2d 1310 (La. Ct. App. 1986) (performing unnecessary repair work violates general prohibition against deception and unfair practices); Hyland v. Zuback, 146 N.J. Super. 407, 370 A.2d 20 (App. Div. 1976) (exceeding estimate without notifying consumer is violation of general UDAP prohibitions); Wiseman v. Kirkman, 2002 WL 31243522 (Ohio App. Oct. 4, 2002) (unpublished, citation limited) (rerouting plumbing in mistaken belief that it violated state law was UDAP violation). *Cf.* Lehman v. Shroyer, 721 N.E.2d 365 (Ind. App. 1999) (specific provisions of Indiana's UDAP statute requiring bill to conform to estimate did not apply to "ballpark" figure given in a casual setting by contractor).

These practices are also prohibited by statute or regulation in many states: Idaho Consumer Protection Regulations, Idaho Admin. Code 04.02.01.120–.122, 04.02.01.130, Estimates and Repairs and Improvements; Ind. Code Ann. § 24-5-0.5-3(a); Massachusetts Consumer Protection Regulations, Mass. Regs. Code tit. 940, § 3.08(1), Repairs and Services; Code Miss. Rules 024 000 002 Rules 42–45; New Jersey Administrative Rules of the Division of Consumer Affairs, N.J. Admin. Code ch. 13:45A-10, Servicing and Repairing of Home Appliances (1976); Ohio Admin. Code § 109:4-3-05, Repairs and Services; Rules for the Utah Consumer Sales Practices Act, Utah Admin. Rules 152-11-5, Repairs and Services. Cases interpreting these regulations include Martin v. Bullinger, 43 Ohio App. 3d 136, 539 N.E.2d 681 (1988) (must disclose right to estimate before beginning work, even though difficult to do in the circumstances); Brown v. Spitzer Ford, Inc., 11 Ohio Op. 3d 84, 1978 Ohio App. LEXIS 8238 (Ct. App. 1978); Brown v. Barnum & Crow Inc., 22 Ohio Op. 3d 24 (Lucas Cty C.P. 1980); Brown v. Joe Schott Chevrolet, Inc., Clearinghouse No. 27,051 (Ohio C.P. Hamilton Cty. 1976); Brown v. Lyons, 43 Ohio Misc. 14, 332 N.E.2d 380, 72 Ohio Op. 2d 216 (C.P. Hamilton Cty. 1974).

1133 Idaho Consumer Protection Regulations, Idaho Admin. Code 04.02.01.130, Repairs and Improvements; Massachusetts Consumer Protection Regulations, Mass. Regs. Code tit. 940, § 3.08(1)(e), Repairs and Services; Code Miss. Rules 024 000 002 Rule 45; Ohio Admin. Code § 109:4-3-05, Repairs and Services; Rules of the Utah Consumer Sales Practices Act, Utah Admin. Rules 152-11-5, Repairs and Services. *See also* Estate of Cattano v. High Touch Homes, Inc., 2002 WL 1290411 (Ohio App. May 24, 2002) (unpublished, citation limited) (misrepresenting that modular home had been repaired); Perkins v. Stapleton Buick-GMC Truck, Inc., 2001 Ohio App. LEXIS 2651 (June 15, 2001) (repeatedly representing that repairs had been made when they had not been successful would be UDAP violation); Brown v. Joe Schott Chevrolet, Clearinghouse No. 27,051 (Ohio C.P. Hamilton Cty. 1976).

1134 Miner v. Jayco, 1999 Ohio App. LEXIS 3944 (Aug. 27, 1999).

1135 Idaho Consumer Protection Regulations, Idaho Admin. Code 04.02.01.130, Repairs and Improvements.

1136 Idaho Consumer Protection Regulations, Idaho Admin. Code 04.02.01.131, Repairs and Improvements; Massachusetts Consumer Protection Regulations, Mass. Regs. Code tit. 940, § 3.08(1)(h), Repairs and Services; Code Miss. Rules 024 000 002 Rule 46; Ohio Admin. Code § 109:4-3-05, Repairs and Services; Rules of the Utah Consumer Sales Practices Act, Utah Admin. Rules 152-11-5, Repairs and Services. *See also* Brown v. Joe Schott Chevrolet, Clearinghouse No. 27,051 (Ohio C.P. Hamilton Cty. 1976).

inspect replaced parts.[1137] It is an unfair and deceptive practice to employ repair workers guilty of shoddy workmanship and persons with inadequate training and supervision to perform the repair work.[1138] Persistent failure to fix a product despite promises and a warranty is a UDAP violation.[1139]

Regulations in several states require minimum service charges to be disclosed before the repairman visits the consumer's home.[1140] Repairmen can not unnecessarily remove products to the shop for repairs.[1141] A number of states have UDAP regulations that require written estimates upon request before repairs are begun.[1142] Ohio UDAP regulations require the consumer to be given a check-box form on which to indicate whether a written estimate is requested.[1143] It is unfair for a repair shop to vandalize the consumer's property after the consumer complains and refuses to pay the bill.[1144] It was a UDAP violation for a jeweler to sell jewelry without the owner's permission when the owner merely left it to be appraised.[1145]

It is a UDAP violation for a repair shop to pad its bills by charging for labor not performed and parts not used.[1146] Submitting a large repair bill based on many hours of labor where the work should only have taken a few hours may be unconscionable.[1147] Nor can repairmen charge for fictitious government fees that are not turned over to third parties.[1148]

It is deceptive for a contractor to misrepresent its own experience and that it would perform the work itself, when other subcontractors would do the work.[1149] It is similarly deceptive to contract to do repair work where that work can not be done.[1150] But courts have found mere negligent repair work not to be a UDAP violation.[1151] A company that installed a product but did not provide a maintenance or service contract does not violate the UDAP statute by failing to respond to requests for repairs.[1152]

4.9.8 Deceptive Billing Practices

Unscrupulous businesses can increase their income by concealing unauthorized charges amid legitimate charges in their bills. Many consumers will trust the company to bill properly, and pay without questioning the amount of the bill. Billing charges to a credit card without the consumer's consent is unfair and deceptive.[1153] Billing for charges is an

1137 Idaho Consumer Protection Regulations, Idaho Admin. Code 04.02.01.132, Repairs and Improvements; Code Miss. Rules Rule 47; New Jersey Administrative Rules of the Division of Consumer Affairs, N.J. Admin. Code ch. 13:45A-10.3(a)(5), Servicing and Repairing of Home Appliances; Ohio Admin. Code § 109:4-3-05, Repairs and Services; Rules of the Utah Consumer Sales Practices Act, Utah Admin. Rules 152-11-5, Repairs and Services. *See also* Brown v. Bob Kay, 14 Ohio Op. 3d 329 (Ct. App. 1979); Brown v. Deacon's Chrysler Plymouth, Inc., 14 Ohio Op. 3d 436 (Ct. App. 1979); Brown v. Spitzer Ford, Inc., 11 Ohio Op. 3d 84 (Ct. App. 1978).

1138 People *ex rel.* Hartigan v. Knecht Servs., 216 Ill. App. 3d 843, 575 N.E.2d 1378 (1991).

1139 Miner v. Jayco, 1999 Ohio App. LEXIS 3944 (Aug. 27, 1999) (manufacturer may have violated UDAP statute by failing to complete repairs).

1140 Massachusetts Consumer Protection Regulations, Mass. Regs. Code tit. 940, § 3.08(1)(c), Repairs and Services; New Jersey Administrative Rules of the Division of Consumer Affairs, N.J. Admin. Code ch. 13:45A-10.2, Servicing and Repairing of Home Appliances (1976); Ohio Admin. Code 109:4-3-05, Repairs and Services; Rules of the Utah Consumer Sales Practices Act, Utah Admin. Rules 152-11-5, Repairs and Services.

1141 Appliance Product Service, 72 F.T.C. 844 (1967) (consent order). *See also* Rules of the Utah Consumer Sales Practices Act, Utah Admin. Rules 152-11-5, Repairs and Services.

1142 Massachusetts Consumer Protection Regulations, Mass. Regs. Code tit. 940, § 3.08(1)(a), Repairs and Services; New Jersey Administrative Rules of the Division of Consumer Affairs, N.J. Admin. Code ch. 13:45A-10.3(a)(1), Servicing and Repairing of Home Appliances; Ohio Admin. Code § 109:4-3-05, Repairs and Services; Rules for the Utah Consumer Sales Practices Act, Utah Admin. Rules 152-11-5, Repairs and Services. *See also* Burton v. Elsea, Inc., 1999 Ohio App. LEXIS 6401 (Dec. 27, 1999); Albert v. Boatsmith Marine Service & Storage, Inc., 65 Ohio App. 3d 38, 582 N.E.2d 1023 (1989); Martin v. Bullinger, 43 Ohio App. 3d 136, 539 N.E.2d 681 (1988) (violation of Ohio regulation on estimates is a *per se* UDAP violation); Brown v. Spitzer Ford, Inc., 11 Ohio Op. 3d 84 (Ct. App. 1978); Brown v. Barnum & Crow Inc., 22 Ohio Op. 3d 24 (Lucas Cty. C.P. 1980); Brown v. Lyons, 43 Ohio Misc. 14, 332 N.E.2d 380, 72 Ohio Op. 2d 216 (C.P. Hamilton Cty. 1974).

1143 Ohio Admin. Code § 109:4-3-05.

1144 State v. Grogan, 628 P.2d 570 (Alaska 1981).

1145 Williams v. Dodson, 976 S.W.2d 861 (Tex. App. 1998).

1146 Barnes v. Jones Chevrolet Co., 358 S.E.2d 156 (S.C. Ct. App. 1987).

1147 Franks v. Associated Air Center Inc., 663 F.2d 583 (5th Cir. 1981) (interpreting former provision of Texas statute that defined unconscionable to include gross overcharges). *See generally* § 4.4.5, *supra* (price unconscionability).

1148 Jim Walter Homes Inc. v. White, 617 S.W.2d 767 (Tex. Civ. App. 1981).

1149 International Fidelity Ins. Co. v. Wilson, 387 Mass. 841, 443 N.E.2d 1308 (1983).

1150 Watson v. Bettinger, 658 S.W.2d 756 (Tex. App. 1983).

1151 Burdakin v. Hub Motor Co., 183 Ga. App. 90, 357 S.E.2d 839 (1987); Hubbard v. Albuquerque Truck Center, 125 N.M. 153, 958 P.2d 111 (1998) (unsuccessful repair attempts are not UDAP violations unless there is deception); Gatrell v. Kilgore, 1999 Ohio App. LEXIS 6170 (Dec. 22, 1999) (inadequate installation of septic system was not a UDAP violation); Sampson v. Winnie, 2001 Tenn. App. LEXIS 894 (Dec. 11, 2001).

1152 Spiroles v. Simpson Fence Co., 99 Ohio App. 3d 72, 649 N.E.2d 1297 (1994).

1153 FTC v. Consumer Alliance, Inc., 2003 WL 22287364 (N.D. Ill. Sept. 30, 2003); FTC v. Automated Transaction Corp., 5 Trade Reg. Rep. (CCH) ¶ 15206 (S.D. Fla. Jan. 24, 2002) (proposed consent decree); U.S. v. Netpliance, Inc., 5 Trade Reg. Rep. (CCH) ¶ 15125 (W.D. Tex. July 2, 2001) (proposed consent decree); FTC v. Nationwide Information Serv., 5 Trade Reg. Rep. (CCH) ¶ 15158 (W.D. Cal. Oct. 3, 2001) (proposed consent decree); FTC v. Ira Smolev, 5 Trade Reg. Rep. (CCH) ¶ 15167 (S.D. Fla. Oct. 23, 2001); FTC v. Fin. Servs., 5 Trade Reg. Rep. (CCH) ¶ 15173 (Oct. 31, 2001) (proposed consent decree against debiting consumer bank accounts without authorization); FTC v. 9094-5486 Quebec, Inc., 5 Trade Reg. Rep.

implicit representation that the creditor is lawfully entitled to the charges.[1154] The consumer's payment of the charge is sufficient proof of causation.[1155] An appellate court in Washington held that a mortgage lender violated the UDAP statute by including a $50 fee identified as "miscellaneous service charges" in its payoff statement, when under the terms of the loan such a fee could not be required as a condition of release of the mortgage.[1156] Demanding payment for a phony service is an unfair act and a UDAP violation.[1157] Minnesota's UDAP statute explicitly forbids deceptive billing.[1158] Federal postal laws prohibit mailing of simulated bills that are in fact solicitations to purchase[1159] and billing for unordered merchandise.[1160] The FTC's Telemarketing Sales Rule prohibits the submission of billing information for payment without the express informed consent of the consumer.[1161] It has special restrictions for negative option plans[1162] and sales in which a "free trial" is converted into a payment obligation if the consumer does not cancel within the free trial period.[1163] A restitution claim may provide an alternative to a UDAP claim as a means of recovering amounts paid in response to deceptive bills.[1164]

Some fraudulent companies have devised ways of submitting charges to consumers' credit cards, bank accounts, or telephone bills without authorization.[1165] The FTC requires telemarketers to have a customer's express verifiable authorization before submitting billing information for payment.[1166] This requirement applies to all payment methods other than credit cards and debit cards that are subject to federal protections against liability. Even without a specific prohibition, charging a consumer's credit card or other payment mechanism without authorization is unfair and deceptive.[1167] Mischaracterizing a charge or designing bills to conceal its nature is a UDAP violation.[1168] Promoting a "free trial period" while obscuring the fact that monthly charges will be assessed unless the consumer cancels is deceptive.[1169] Often an intermediary who processes fraudulent charges for the seller will be equally liable for consumers' losses.[1170]

(CCH) ¶ 15190 (N.D.N.Y. Dec. 18, 2001) (TRO).

1154 Kidd v. Delta Funding Corp., 2000 N.Y. Misc. LEXIS 29 (Sup. Ct. Feb. 22, 2000) (imposing and collecting fees prohibited by state law is a UDAP violation), *denial of summary judgment aff'd*, 751 N.Y.S.2d 267 (App. Div. 2002) (affirming denial of lender's motion for summary judgment on claim that charging illegal fees and failing to notify consumers of existence and terms of settlement agreement was deceptive). *See also* FTC v. Verity Int'l, Ltd., 194 F. Supp. 2d 270 (S.D.N.Y. 2002) (granting preliminary injunction against Internet billing service that billed telephone line subscribers for rerouted calls as if they were liable for them); Dawson v. Dovenmuehle, 2002 U.S. Dist. LEXIS 5688 (E.D. Pa. Apr. 3, 2002) (denying motion to dismiss); Chisolm v. Transouth Fin. Corp., 194 F.R.D. 538, 561 (E.D. Va. 2000); § 8.5.4.2.7, *infra* (class certification of deceptive billing claims).

1155 Chisolm v. Transouth Fin. Corp., 194 F.R.D. 538, 561 (E.D. Va. 2000) (reliance presumed when consumers made payments after receiving bills); Pickett v. Holland Am. Line-Westours, Inc., 101 Wash. App. 901, 6 P.3d 63 (2000), *rev'd on other grounds*, 35 P.3d 351 (Wash. 2001); *see also* Latman v. Costa Cruise Lines, 758 So. 2d 699 (Fla. App. 2000) (assessment of port charges was deceptive practice when cruise line passed through to the port only a portion of the sum, retaining the rest for itself).

1156 Dwyer v. J.I. Kislak Mortgage Corp., 103 Wash. App. 542, 13 P.3d 240 (2000) (reversing dismissal of class action). *But see* Miller v. Pacific Shore Funding, 224 F. Supp. 2d 977 (D. Md. 2002) (settlement statement was not implicit representation that listed fees were legal).

1157 Chatman v. Fairbanks Capital Corp., 2002 WL 1338492 (N.D. Ill. June 18, 2002) (denying motion to dismiss claim that billing for fictitious property preservation fees was a UDAP violation); Commonwealth v. DeCotis, 316 N.E.2d 748, 754 (Mass. 1974); Patterson v. Beall, 19 P.3d 839 (Okla. 2000).

1158 Minn. Stat. Ann. § 325F.69(4).

1159 39 U.S.C. § 3001(d).

1160 39 U.S.C. § 3009(c). *See* § 5.8.4, *infra*.

1161 16 C.F.R. § 310.4(a)(6), *as amended by* 68 Fed. Reg. 2580 (Jan. 29, 2003). *See* § 5.9.3.8.1, *infra*.

1162 *See* § 5.9.4.7.3, *infra*.

1163 *See* § 5.9.4.7.5, *infra*. *See also* FTC v. Preferred Alliance, Inc., 5 Trade Reg. Rep. (CCH) ¶ 15365 (N.D. Ga. Feb. 12, 2003) (complaint against telemarketers who sold free trial offers that were actually negative option plans that would result in charges if consumer did not cancel); FTC v. Ira Smolev, 5 Trade Reg. Rep. (CCH) ¶ 15167 (S.D. Fla. Oct. 23, 2001) (proposed consent decree ordering $8.3 million in restitution against buyers club that misled consumers into accepting "free" trial memberships, then billed them unless they cancelled).

1164 *See* §§ 8.3.2.4.1, 9.7, *infra*.

1165 *See* FTC v. Verity Int'l, Ltd., 194 F. Supp. 2d 270 (S.D.N.Y. 2002); FTC v. Int'l Telemedia Assocs., Inc., 5 Trade Reg. Rep. (CCH) ¶ 15170 (N.D. Ga. Oct. 31, 2001) (proposed consent decree against defendants who advertised free dating service but then worked with billing aggregator to cram unauthorized per-minute charges onto consumers' phone bills); FTC v. Hold Billing Servs., 5 Trade Reg. Rep. ¶ 24,659 (W.D. Tex. Oct. 6, 1999) (consent decree against company that crammed charges onto consumers' telephone bills for unordered services). *See* § 5.9.2.3.7, *infra*.

1166 16 C.F.R. § 310.3(a)(3), *as amended by* 68 Fed. Reg. 4580 (Jan. 29, 2003). *See* § 5.9.3.8.2, *infra*.

1167 *See* FTC v. Crescent Publ. Group, Inc., 129 F. Supp. 2d 311 (S.D.N.Y. 2001) (unauthorized billing to credit card is violation of FTC Act); FTC v. Hold Billing Servs., 5 Trade Reg. Rep. ¶ 24,659 (W.D. Tex. Oct. 6, 1999) (consent decree against company that crammed charges onto consumers' telephone bills for unordered services).

1168 Schwartz v. Visa Int'l Corp., 2003 WL 1870370 (Cal. Super. Apr. 7, 2003); Pickett v. Holland Am. Line-Westours, Inc., 101 Wash. App. 901, 6 P.3d 63 (2000), *rev'd on other grounds*, 35 P.3d 351 (Wash. 2001).

1169 Minnesota *ex rel.* Hatch v. Fleet Mortg. Corp., 158 F. Supp. 2d 962 (D. Minn. 2001). *See also* Alaska Stat. § 45.45.920 (requiring disclosure of all restrictions on free trial periods and mandating right to cancel without obligation during such periods).

1170 FTC v. Verity Int'l, Ltd., 194 F. Supp. 2d 270 (S.D.N.Y. 2002) (issuing injunction against Internet billing service that treated Internet access calls as international calls and crammed them onto subscriber's phone bill); FTC v. Hold Billing Servs., 5 Trade Reg. Rep. ¶ 24,659 (W.D. Tex. Oct. 6, 1999). *See* §§ 5.9.2.3.7, 5.9.2.7, *infra*.

Nondisclosure of an automatic renewal policy is a UDAP violation.[1171] For transactions conducted by telephone, the FTC's Telemarketing Sales Rule has special disclosure requirements that should be consulted.[1172]

4.10 Anti-Competitive Conduct

4.10.1 Application of UDAP Statutes to Antitrust Cases

This manual focuses on UDAP and other remedies for consumer abuses. It does not deal with antitrust law. Nevertheless, practitioners should note that UDAP statutes may have applicability to price-fixing and other antitrust cases as alternatives or supplements to federal and state antitrust statutes.

UDAP statutes are particularly important since they may provide relief where federal and state antitrust statutes do not. In a Florida case,[1173] a class of consumers who purchased infant formula brought a price-fixing action against the manufacturers. Claims based on the state antitrust statute were dismissed based on the Supreme Court's decision in *Illinois Brick Company v. Illinois*.[1174] That ruling holds that indirect purchasers of a product (such as consumers buying from retailers) can not use the federal antitrust statutes to sue indirect sellers (such as the manufacturers who sold to the retailers) for anti-competitive conduct. Only the retailers have standing to sue the manufacturers.

While *Illinois Brick* dealt with the federal antitrust statutes, Florida courts extend the ruling to the Florida antitrust statute as well. Nevertheless, the appellate court held that *Illinois Brick* does not apply to the Florida UDAP statute—indirect purchasers can sue manufacturers for price-fixing under the state UDAP statute. The scope of the Florida UDAP statute was found to apply explicitly to indirect purchasers, and the rationale behind *Illinois Brick* thus did not control.

Similarly, the Massachusetts Supreme court has concluded that indirect purchasers can assert price-fixing claims against manufacturers and distributors even though *Illinois Brick* would bar the same claims under the federal and state antitrust laws.[1175] The decision stresses the broad language of the UDAP statute, which extends the right to sue to any person who has been injured by unfair or deceptive practices and which does not impose any requirement of privity of contract. The Vermont Supreme Court has reached the same conclusion, rejecting the defendant's argument that the mandate to interpret its UDAP statute in a way consistent with federal decisions under the FTC Act compels a contrary result.[1176]

A federal court has held that the Attorneys General of Alaska, Arkansas, Connecticut, Florida, Idaho, Kentucky, Louisiana, Maine, North Carolina, Oklahoma, South Carolina, Vermont, and West Virginia can assert UDAP restitution claims for indirect purchasers for antitrust violations.[1177] Another court has declined to dismiss claims brought under state UDAP statutes and other non-antitrust statutes by plaintiffs in Arizona, Connecticut, Kentucky, Louisiana, Massachusetts, Ohio, South Carolina, and Vermont.[1178] But the Connecticut[1179] and Texas[1180] supreme courts and lower courts in Nebraska,[1181] New York,[1182] Oklahoma[1183] and Washington[1184] have reached the opposite conclusion, finding indirect purchasers too remote.

Private litigants often have three types of potential claims for antitrust violations: federal laws such as the Sherman and Clayton Acts,[1185] state statutes patterned after these federal laws, and state UDAP statutes. While *Illinois Brick* prevents indirect purchasers from bringing actions under the federal statutes, the *Illinois Brick* decision does not determine whether indirect purchasers can bring actions under state law.[1186]

For state antitrust statutes, it will be up to the nature of that statute and the state legislative intent whether *Illinois Brick* applies.[1187] For states not enacting a separate state

1171 College Resource Mgmt., Inc., 5 Trade Reg. Rep. (CCH) ¶ 15101 (N.D. Tex. May 2, 2001) (proposed consent decree).

1172 *See* § 5.9.4.7.3, *infra*.

1173 *See* Mack v. Bristol-Myers Squibb Co., 673 So. 2d 100 (Fla. Dist. Ct. App. 1996). *Accord In re* Vitamins Antitrust Litigation, 2000 U.S. Dist. LEXIS 7397 (May 9, 2000); *In re* Fla. Microsoft Antitrust Litigation, 2002 WL 31423620 (Fla. Cir. Ct. Aug. 26, 2002).

1174 431 U.S. 720, 97 S. Ct. 2061, 52 L. Ed. 2d 707 (1977).

1175 Ciardi v. F. Hoffmann-La Roche, Ltd., 436 Mass. 53, 762 N.E.2d 303 (2002).

1176 Elkins v. Microsoft Corp., 817 A.2d 9 (Vt. 2002).

1177 Federal Trade Comm'n v. Mylan Laboratories, Inc., 99 F. Supp. 2d 1 (D.D.C. 1999).

1178 *In re* Microsoft Corp. Antitrust Litigation, 127 F. Supp. 2d 702 (D. Md. 2001).

1179 Vacco v. Microsoft Corp., 260 Conn. 59, 793 A.2d 1048 (2002).

1180 Abbott Laboratories, Inc. v. Segura, 907 S.W.2d 503 (Tex. 1995).

1181 Arthur v. Microsoft Corp., 676 N.W.2d 29 (Neb. 2004) (applying *Illinois Brick* to antitrust provisions of state UDAP statute).

1182 Levine v. Abbott Laboratories, Clearinghouse No. 52,047 (N.Y. Sup. Ct. 1996).

1183 Major v. Microsoft Corp., 2002 WL 1585649 (Okla. Dist. Ct. May 24, 2002) (UDAP claim can not avoid *Illinois Brick*), *aff'd*, 60 P.3d 511 (Okla. Civ. App. 2002).

1184 Blewett v. Abbott Laboratories, 86 Wash. App. 782, 938 P.2d 842 (1997).

1185 There is no private right of action under the Federal Trade Commission Act, 15 U.S.C. § 45(a)(1), one of the federal antitrust statutes, which prohibits unfair methods of competition. *See* § 9.1, *infra*.

1186 *See* California v. ARC Am. Corp., 490 U.S. 93, 109 S. Ct. 1661, 104 L. Ed. 2d 86 (1989).

1187 *See* Emergency One, Inc. v. Waterous Co., 23 F. Supp. 2d 959 (E.D. Wis. 1998) (*Illiniois Brick* does not apply to Wisconsin antitrust statute) (*dicta*); McLaughlin v. Abbott Laboratories, Clearinghouse No. 52,048 (Ariz. Super. Ct. 1996) (*Illinois Brick*

antitrust law or where a state's courts find that *Illinois Brick* applies to that statute, then a state UDAP claim provides another potential source of relief for indirect purchasers.

A number of state UDAP statutes explicitly prohibit "unfair methods of competition"[1188] and these statutes are certainly applicable to anti-competitive practices.[1189] However, the term "unfair methods of competition" may not be given the same interpretation in the context of a state UDAP statute as it has been given in the context of the FTC Act. The Illinois Supreme Court has ruled that the Illinois UDAP statute's prohibition of unfair methods of competition does not extend to price discrimination, despite the fact that the same terminology within the FTC Act has been held to reach price discrimination.[1190] Whether a statute allows claims by indirect buyers will turn on its exact language, but in many cases, as in the Florida decision, the UDAP statute will provide a viable claim.[1191]

Other state UDAP statutes do not prohibit unfair methods of competition, but do prohibit unfair practices. In general, any unfair method of competition should be found to be an unfair trade practice.[1192] Defendants may argue that the failure of the UDAP statute to prohibit "unfair methods of competition" evidences a legislative intent to exempt antitrust violations from the state UDAP statute. But a UDAP statute should apply to any unfair practice within the scope of that statute.[1193] However, some courts have declined to apply their UDAP statutes to monopolistic conduct since a separate statutory scheme addresses that area and antitrust violations may not fit within the UDAP statute's framework.[1194]

Other state UDAP statutes only prohibit deceptive practices, but even these statutes may be applicable to certain antitrust violations. Price-fixing, for example, may be not only unfair, but also deceptive.[1195] The failure to disclose important information is deceptive,[1196] and price fixers may also make affirmative claims that are deceptive because of their price fixing—*e.g.*, "we offer the lowest prices" or "we are a name you can trust."

Even where *Illinois Brick* does not limit federal or state antitrust claims, a state UDAP claim may still be preferred as an alternative claim where the plaintiff wants to stay in state court. Federal antitrust claims may be removed to federal court and litigious defendants may even try to remove to federal court a claim based on a state antitrust statute, arguing that the claim is really under federal law or closely related to the federal law. Removal will be harder if the state claim is based on the state UDAP statute instead, since this will not parallel any federal claim allowing a private right of action.[1197]

In addition, a state UDAP statute may reach anti-competitive conduct not prohibited by the federal or state antitrust statutes. "Unfair methods of competition" and "unfair

---

does not apply to Arizona antitrust statute); Blake v. Abbott Laboratories, Inc., 1996 Tenn. App. LEXIS 184 (Apr. 24, 1996) (*Illinois Brick* does not apply to Tennessee antitrust statute). *But see* Levine v. Abbott Laboratories, Clearinghouse No. 52,047 (N.Y. Sup. Ct. 1996) (*Illinois Brick* applies to New York antitrust statute).

1188 *See* Appx. A, *infra*.

1189 Quelimane Co. v. Stewart Title Guaranty Co., 77 Cal. Rptr. 2d 709, 960 P.2d 513 (1998) (UDAP statute prohibiting unlawful, unfair or fraudulent business act or practice can be used to challenge conspiracy in restraint of trade in violation of state antitrust statute); Roncari Dev. v. GMG Enterprises, 45 Conn. Super. 408, 718 A.2d 1025 (1997) (antitrust violations are unfair methods of competition that violate UDAP statute).

1190 Laughlin v. Evanston Hosp., 550 N.E.2d 986 (Ill. 1990) (ruling that extension of UDAP statute to prohibit price discrimination would defeat purposes behind state antitrust statute's deliberate exclusion of price discrimination from its scope). *But see* Jefferson v. Chevron U.S.A., 713 So. 2d 785 (La. App. 1998) (applying UDAP statute to price discrimination claim), *review denied*, 727 So. 2d 441 (La. 1998).

1191 *But see* Gaebler v. New Mexico Potash Corp., 676 N.E.2d 228 (Ill. App. Ct. 1997) (state UDAP statute prohibits unfair methods of competition but court finds that state antitrust law preempts the field).

1192 *See* Execu-Tech Bus. Sys., Inc. v. New Oji Paper Co., 752 So. 2d 582 (Fla. 2000) ("unfair or deceptive acts or practices in the conduct of any trade or commerce" covers price-fixing), *cert. denied*, 121 S. Ct. 58, 148 L. Ed. 2d 25 (2000); Jefferson v. Chevron U.S.A., 713 So. 2d 785 (La. App. 1998) (court interprets the unfair trade practices prohibition of Louisiana UDAP statute to apply to price discrimination; note that statute also prohibits unfair methods of competition). *But cf.* Abbott Laboratories, Inc. v. Segura, 907 S.W.2d 503 (Tex. 1995) (not reaching issue whether price fixing could be unconscionable under Texas UDAP statute; one concurring opinion found conduct not to be unconscionable as that term is defined in Texas UDAP statute). *But see* Berghausen v. Microsoft Corp., 765 N.E.2d 592 (Ind. App. 2002) (affirming dismissal of consumer's UDAP unconscionability claim against indirect seller because it only applies if seller solicits buyer); Johnson v. Microsoft Corp., 155 Ohio App. 3d 626, 802 N.E.2d 712 (2003).

1193 *See* Blake v. Abbott Laboratories, Inc., 1996 Tenn. App. LEXIS 184 (Apr. 24, 1996) (state UDAP statute applicable in addition to state antitrust statute to anti-competitive conduct where UDAP statute prohibits "unfair" practices). *But see* Johnson v. Microsoft Corp., 155 Ohio App. 3d 626, 802 N.E.2d 712 (2003). *But cf.* Journal Publishing Co. v. Hartford Courant Co., 261 Conn. 673, 804 A.2d 823 (2002) (exclusivity provision of contracts between newspapers and comic strip syndicators was not unfair practice).

1194 Davidson v. Microsoft Corp., 143 Md. App. 43, 792 A.2d 336 (2002); Johnson v. Microsoft Corp., 155 Ohio App. 3d 626, 802 N.E.2d 712 (2003); Sherwood v. Microsoft Corp., 2003 WL 21780975 (Tenn. Ct. App. July 31, 2003) (unpublished, citation limited) (precluding indirect purchasers from pursing anticompetitive conduct claims under state UDAP Act).

1195 New York v. Feldman, 210 F. Supp. 2d 294 (S.D.N.Y. 2002) (scheme to rig bids at public auction).

1196 *See* § 4.2.14, *supra*. *But see* Berghausen v. Microsoft Corp., 765 N.E.2d 592 (Ind. App. 2002) (indirect seller's implicit representation of price advantage not a UDAP violation since statute requires representation to be oral or written); Levine v. Abbott Laboratories, Clearinghouse No. 52,047 (N.Y. Sup. Ct. 1996) (price fixing is not a deceptive practice).

1197 *See* Kruse v. DuPont Merck Pharmaceutical Co., 985 F. Supp. 846 (N.D. Ill. 1998).

practices" may be broader and more flexible standards than those found in other antitrust statutes.[1198]

4.10.2 Challenging Consumer Abuses as Anti-Competitive

UDAP statutes' applicability to antitrust matters, on occasion, can be utilized to challenge practices traditionally viewed as "consumer" and not as "antitrust." Tie-ins are perhaps the best example, such as mobile home park operators requiring new tenants to purchase their homes from a particular dealer or to purchase other services from a particular seller.[1199] Another example of a tie-in is the sale of credit property or other insurance tied to the offer of credit.[1200]

Another possible use of antitrust statutes in the consumer context is where industry members agree to institute a deceptive or unfair charge. For example, in Louisiana a class action has successfully alleged that the Louisiana automobile dealership association colluded with the state's automobile dealers, in violation of the federal Clayton Act, to create a separate charge to reimburse dealers for the inventory tax dealers must pay the state. The allegation was not that the dealers had fixed prices, but that they had engaged in concerted action that had an impact on prices. The federal court certified a plaintiff class of all Louisiana car purchasers over a ten-year period and a defendant class of all Louisiana car dealers, and rejected the defendants' summary judgment motions. A settlement was reached valued at several hundred million dollars.[1201]

4.11 Invasion of Privacy

With the growth of the Internet and direct marketing, there is a growing utilization of UDAP law to challenge companies' use of personal information on their customers without disclosing that use to the customers. For example, the FTC has obtained a consent decree from a company that misrepresented the purpose for which it collected personal identifying information from its Internet users, and falsely told consumers that this information would not be released to anyone, but sold the information to marketers.[1202] Another case involved a seller that harvested consumers' personal information from a competitor's website and then sent deceptive unsolicited e-mail messages to those consumers, soliciting their business.[1203] Disclosure of personal information, even if legitimately collected and even if the disclosure is inadvertent, is an unfair practice.[1204] Nebraska's UDAP statute prohibits false or misleading statements in privacy policies that are published on the Internet or otherwise, that relate to the use of personal information submitted by members of the public.[1205] Allegations that a pharmacy that was going out of business sold confidential patient prescription information to another pharmacy, without first notifying the patients and giving them a chance to object, states a UDAP claim.[1206] But a doctor did not commit a UDAP violation by disclosing a patient's medical condition on orders of a federal judge.[1207]

1198 Broadway Theatre Corp. v. Buena Vista Pictures Distribution, 2002 WL 32502100 (D. Conn. Sept. 19, 2002).

1199 *See* § 5.5.1, *infra.*

1200 *See* National Consumer Law Center, The Cost of Credit: Regulation and Legal Challenges § 8.5.2.5.3 (2d ed. 2000 and Supp.). *See also* § 5.3.10, *supra.*

1201 Cook v. Powell Buick, Inc., Clearinghouse No. 52,030 (W.D. La. complaint filed 1994). Documents available through the Clearinghouse number include the First Amended Complaint, Findings and Recommendation (concerning class certification and defendants' motion for partial summary judgment), Proposed Settlement Agreement, and Notice of Settlement.

1202 GeoCities, 5 Trade Reg. Rep. (CCH) ¶ 24,485 (F.T.C. Dkt. No. C-3850 1999) (consent decree). *See also* FTC v. 30 Minute Mortg., Inc., 5 Trade Reg. Rep. (CCH) ¶ 15379 (S.D. Fla. Mar. 14, 2003) (complaint against company that took on-line mortgage application, then sold the information; also misrepresented that site was secure); FTC v. Information Search, Inc., 5 Trade Reg. Rep. (CCH) ¶ 15229 (D. Md. Mar. 8, 2002) (settlement barring pretextual information acquisition and violation of Gramm-Leach-Bliley Act); FTC v. New Millennium Concepts, Inc., 5 Trade Reg. Rep. (CCH) ¶ 15180 (N.D. Ill. Nov. 20, 2001) (company induced consumers to pay fee and give personal information in return for free monthly Internet service; proposed consent decree requires information to be destroyed and $481,172.05 judgment against principal); FTC v. Robert Stout, 5 Trade Reg. Rep. (CCH) ¶ 15144 (D.N.J. Aug. 24, 2001) (proposed consent decree against spammers who collected personal and credit card information by sending e-mail messages to consumers saying they had to register to maintain Internet access); FTC v. ReverseAuction.com, Inc., 5 Trade Reg. Rep. (CCH) ¶ 24,688 (D.D.C. Jan. 6, 2000); Guess?, Inc., File No. 022-3260, www.ftc.gov/opa/2003/08/fyi0348.htm (Aug. 5, 2003) (consent order) (false representation about security of site); Nat'l Research Center for College and University Admissions, Dkt. C-4071, www.ftc.gov/opa/2003/01/fyi0308.htm (Jan. 29, 2003) (consent order) (company collected personal information from high school students, then sold it to commercial marketers); Educational Research Center of Am., Inc., Dkt. C-4079, www.ftc.gov/opa/2003/05/fyi0335.htm (May 9, 2003) (consent order against company that told schools that survey information would be given to colleges but actually sold it primarily to commercial entities); Microsoft Corp., Dkt. C-4069, www.ftc.gov/os/2002/12/miscrsoftdecision.pdf (Dec. 20, 2002) (proposed consent decree) (company misrepresented security of site and its information collection policy). *But see* Smith v. Chase Manhattan Bank, 293 A.D.2d 598, 741 N.Y.S.2d 100 (2002) (sale of plaintiff's personal information to telemarketers and direct mail solicitors, who then offered goods and services, does not constitute actual injury, so no UDAP claim).

1203 FTC v. ReverseAuction.com, Inc., 5 Trade Reg. Rep. (CCH) ¶ 24,688 (D.D.C. Jan. 6, 2000) (consent decree).

1204 Eli Lilly & Co., Dkt. C-4047, www.ftc.gov/opa/2002/05/fyi0235.htm (May 10, 2002) (consent order against company that inadvertently disclosed Prozac users' e-mail addresses).

1205 Neb. Rev. Stat. § 87-302(a)(14).

1206 Anonymous v. CVS Corp., 188 Misc. 2d 616, 728 N.Y.S.2d 333 (Sup. Ct. 2001).

1207 Dubin v. Wakuzawa, 89 Haw. 188, 970 P.2d 496 (1998).

Using deceptive means to obtain private information about consumers' bank accounts for resale is a UDAP violation.[1208] When a company uses a pretext to obtain private information about an individual, usually the caller uses an implicit or explicit misrepresentation about the caller's identity or affiliation. Many state UDAP statutes explicitly prohibit misrepresentation of one's affiliation.[1209] Even in states without this explicit prohibition, pretext calling almost certainly falls within the general definition of deception. Since UDAP statutes generally do not require privity of contract,[1210] a person damaged by a pretext caller's acquisition of personal information can sue even though the caller's contract is with another person.[1211]

The Gramm-Leach-Bliley Act,[1212] which is discussed more fully in a different volume,[1213] requires financial institutions to notify their consumers and customers of their policies regarding disclosure of "nonpublic personal information." The Act also prohibits, with many exceptions, the disclosure of this information to a nonaffiliated third party unless the institution has given the consumer an opportunity to opt out of the disclosure. The Act does not include a private cause of action for consumers, but a violation may be actionable as a UDAP violation.[1214] The FTC has also proceeded against companies that collected information from children in violation of the Children's On-line Privacy Protection Act.[1215]

1208 FTC v. Information Search, Inc., 5 Trade Reg. Rep. (CCH) ¶ 24,906 (D. Md. 2001); FTC v. Guzzetta, 5 Trade Reg. Rep. (CCH) ¶ 24,906 (E.D.N.Y. 2001); FTC v. Paula Garrett, 5 Trade Reg. Rep. (CCH) ¶ 24,906 (S.D. Tex. 2001); Commonwealth v. Source One Assocs., 436 Mass. 118, 763 N.E.2d 42 (2002) (injunction and $500,000 in civil penalties).

1209 Remsburg v. Docusearch, Inc., 816 A.2d 1001 (N.H. 2003).

1210 *See* § 4.2.15.3, *supra*.

1211 Remsburg v. Docusearch, Inc., 816 A.2d 1001 (N.H. 2003).

1212 Pub. L. No. 106-102, 113 Stat. 1338 (Nov. 12, 1999), *codified at* 15 U.S.C. § 6801 *et seq.*

1213 National Consumer Law Center, Fair Credit Reporting § 16.4.1 (5th ed. 2002).

1214 *See* § 3.2.7, *supra*.

1215 15 U.S.C. §§ 6501–6505. *See* U.S. v. Hershey Foods Corp., 5 Trade Reg. Rep. (CCH) ¶ 15370 (M.D. Pa. Feb. 26, 2003) (company collected information through website aimed at children without complying with Act); U.S. v. Ohio Art Co., 5 Trade Reg. Rep. (CCH) ¶ 15245 (N.D. Ohio Apr. 22, 2002) (proposed consent order); FTC v. Am. Pop Corn Co., 5 Trade Reg. Rep. (CCH) ¶ 15215 (N.D. Iowa Feb. 13, 2002); U.S. v. Lisa Frank, Inc., 5 Trade Reg. Rep. (CCH) ¶ 15157 (E.D. Va. Oct. 2, 2001).

Chapter 5 Specific Unfair or Deceptive Practices

5.1 Credit and Collections

5.1.1 Debt Collection, Other Creditor Remedies

5.1.1.1 Debt Collection

5.1.1.1.1 Introduction and important sources of UDAP precedent

The federal Fair Debt Collection Practices Act (FDCPA),[1] state debt collection acts, and common law tort theories provide a number of remedies for debt collection abuses. Another National Consumer Law Center manual[2] analyzes these remedies in detail. A private UDAP action provides yet another approach in those states where debt collection practices are within the UDAP statute's scope.[3]

UDAP claims offer certain advantages over claims under the FDCPA. A UDAP claim can be litigated in state court if the consumer prefers that forum. The UDAP remedy may also provide better relief, such as attorney fees and minimum or multiple damages, than is available under state debt collection practices statutes or common law theories.

An especially significant advantage is that UDAP actions can reach practices outside the scope of the FDCPA. In particular, a UDAP claim can challenge creditors' collection practices, and not just collection agency practices. A UDAP statute may also cover collection of types of debts that are excluded from FDCPA coverage.[4] A creditor may be subject to UDAP liability not only for its own collection practices, but also for failing to oversee the practices of independent collection agencies it hires.[5] The UDAP remedy may also provide better relief, such as attorney fees and minimum or multiple damages, than is available under state debt collection practices statutes or common law theories.

In addition, UDAP debt collection principles can apply to many different forms of collection, such as foreclosures, repossessions, evictions, landlord lockouts, utility company or landlord-induced utility shutoffs.[6] When a practice is unfair or deceptive if engaged in by a debt collector, an analogous practice by a landlord, mobile home park, mortgage holder, utility company, secured party, or other party should equally be unfair or deceptive.

However, in a few states collection practices may be outside the UDAP statute's scope. This coverage issue is examined in another section.[7] There also may be coverage questions if the debt collector is an attorney.[8] In the case of particularly abusive debt collection practices, a tort theory may be the primary approach because of the availability of punitive damages and a jury trial right.

If debt collection practices are within the scope of a state's UDAP statute, there are several important sources of precedent as to whether a particular practice is unfair or deceptive. A few states have UDAP regulations that define certain practices as unfair or deceptive. Activities prohibited by a state's own debt collection practices statute have been found to be *per se* UDAP violations.[9] Courts may also recognize collection agency violations of the FDCPA as *per*

---

1 15 U.S.C. § 1692.

2 National Consumer Law Center, Fair Debt Collection (5th ed. 2004).

3 Yet another option is an action under the federal or state RICO statute for collection of an unlawful debt. *See* § 9.2.3.7, *infra*. *See also* Brown v. C.I.L., Inc., 1996 U.S. Dist. LEXIS 4053 (N.D. Ill. Mar. 29, 1996) (denying defendant's motion to dismiss).

4 People *ex rel.* Daley v. Datacom Sys. Corp., 146 Ill. 2d 1, 585 N.E.2d 51 (1991) (collection of parking ticket debts covered by UDAP statute).

5 *See* American Family Publishers, 58 Fed. Reg. 8762, Clearinghouse No. 47,965 (F.T.C. Dkt. 9240, Feb. 17, 1993) (consent order). *See also* § 6.3.2, *infra*, for further discussion of this case.

6 *See, e.g.*, Clarkson v. DeCaceres, 105 B.R. 266 (Bankr. E.D. Pa. 1989) (deceptive for landlord to sell tenant's property without legal right); *In re* Aponte, 82 B.R. 738 (Bankr. E.D. Pa. 1988) (landlord's termination of heat and hot water).

7 *See* § 2.2.2, *supra*.

8 *See* § 2.3.9, *supra*.

9 Bergs v. Hoover, Bax & Slovacek, L.L.P., 2003 WL 22255679 (N.D. Tex. Sept. 24, 2003); Campion v. Credit Bureau Servs., Inc., 2000 U.S. Dist. LEXIS 20233 (E.D. Wash. Sept. 19, 2000); Wagner v. American Nat'l Educ. Corp., Clearinghouse No. 36,132 (D. Conn. 1984); *In re* Scrimpsher, 17 B.R. 999 (Bankr. N.D.N.Y. 1982); Connelly v. Puget Sound Collections, Inc., 16 Wash. App. 62, 553 P.2d 1354 (1976). Violation of other statutes as *per se* UDAP violations is discussed in more detail at § 3.2.7, *supra*. *But cf.* Conboy v. AT&T Corp., 241 F.3d 242 (2d Cir. 2001) (New York's UDAP statute may incorporate state debt collection statute's prohibitions of deceptive conduct, but does not incorporate prohibitions of abusive conduct).

se deceptive under state UDAP statutes.[10]

Even creditors, whose collection activities are not covered by the FDCPA, may violate the state UDAP statute if they commit acts that would be FDCPA violations if committed by a collection agency. The FTC uses the FDCPA as its standard for determining whether a creditor has violated the FTC Act's general prohibition of unfair and deceptive practices.[11] The FTC has also won a number of consent orders and litigated decisions that further define the standards for deception and unfairness in debt collection. In interpreting their UDAP statutes, many states give great weight to FTC interpretations.[12]

This section will list the various debt collection abuses prohibited by FTC precedent, state UDAP decisions, and state UDAP regulations. The companion CD-Rom to this volume has two sample debt collection complaints that include UDAP counts.[13] The case materials also include discovery requests, a motion to compel discovery, a summary judgment motion, and an appellate brief. In addition, NCLC's *Fair Debt Collection* (5th ed. 2004) contains, in hard copy and on a companion CD-Rom, two additional sample FDCPA complaints, interrogatories, requests for documents, requests for admissions, sample summary judgment brief, sample jury *voir dire* questions, instructions and proposed verdict sheet, and sample documents for award of attorney fees.

5.1.1.1.2 Skip-Tracing

One common debt collection function is to track down debtors who have moved. This practice is pejoratively called skip-tracing. FTC case law and state case law and regulations all prohibit creditors and collection agencies from disguising the purpose for which information is sought while attempting to locate the address of the debtor.[14] Thus collectors can not claim, directly or implicitly, to be from a government agency seeking data for government purposes.[15] Nor can the skip-tracer hold out an inducement to furnish information not in the debtor's interest and which the debtor would otherwise not supply. For example, a collector can not pretend to be seeking information for a survey or for a motion picture part, pretend to have a prepaid package for the debtor, or claim that money will be paid for information.[16] The debt collector must disclose that forms, letters, questionnaires, and similar documents are for purposes of collecting a debt. Obtaining confidential information from banks and credit reporting agencies by impersonating the debtor or bank officers or through other pretexts is a UDAP violation.[17]

A sample complaint raising UDAP and FDCPA claims against a collection attorney who allegedly sought collection information in the guise of taking a survey is included on the companion CD-Rom to this volume.[18]

5.1.1.1.3 Misrepresentations concerning identity and nature of collector

Debt collectors commit UDAP violations if they misrepresent their affiliation or connection with a court or other government agency. It is deceptive for collectors to represent that they are marshals, sheriffs, or other officials, that correspondence comes directly from a government agency, or that a court or other government agency officially sanctions the collection efforts.[19] Nor can debt collection docu-

10 Joseph v. J.J. MacIntyre Cos., 238 F. Supp. 2d 1158 (N.D. Cal. 2002); Irwin v. Mascott, 112 F. Supp. 2d 937 (N.D. Cal. 2000); *In re* Scrimpsher, 17 B.R. 999 (Bankr. N.D.N.Y. 1982) (New York law). *See* § 3.2.7.3.5, *supra*. *But see* Lamb v. M&M Assocs., Inc., 1998 U.S. Dist. LEXIS 13773 (S.D. Ohio Sept. 1, 1998) (failure to include validation notice was not UDAP violation; some but not all FDCPA violations are UDAP violations). *See generally* § 3.2.7.3.5, *supra*.

11 *See* 60 Fed. Reg. 40263 (Aug. 8, 1995). *Cf. In re* Scrimpsher, 17 B.R. 999 (Bankr. N.D.N.Y. 1982) (declining to find creditor's violation of FDCPA to be *per se* violation of New York UDAP statute, but finding acts deceptive on their own; case was decided before FTC's announcement of its use of FDCPA standards for creditors).

12 *See* § 3.4.5, *supra*.

13 These documents are also found on Consumer Law Pleadings No. 2, §§ 11.1, 11.2 (CD-Rom and Index Guide).

14 Mohr v. FTC, 272 F.2d 401 (9th Cir. 1959), *cert. denied*, 362 U.S. 920 (1960); Operation Skip-Locate, Inc., 78 F.T.C. 963 (1971) (consent order); Wm. H. Wise Co., 52 F.T.C. 150 (1956); International Research, 38 F.T.C. 374 (1942); Massachusetts Consumer Protection Regulations, Mass. Regs. Code tit. 940, §§ 7.04, 7.07, Debt Collection; Code Vt. Rules 06 031 004, Rule CF 104.04, Debt Collection.

15 Floersheim v. FTC, 411 F.2d 874 (9th Cir. 1969), *cert. denied*, 396 U.S. 1018 (1970); S. Dean Slough, 70 F.T.C. 1318 (1966), *aff'd*, 396 F.2d 870 (5th Cir. 1968), *cert. denied*, 393 U.S. 1980 (1969). *See also* National Consumer Law Center, Fair Debt Collection § 8.3.11 (5th ed. 2004).

16 Rothschild v. FTC, 200 F.2d 39 (7th Cir. 1952); Dejay Stores Inc. v. FTC, (2d Cir. 1952); Silverman v. FTC, 145 F.2d 751 (9th Cir. 1944).

17 Commonwealth v. Source One Assocs., 436 Mass. 118, 763 N.E.2d 42 (2002).

18 It is also found on Consumer Law Pleadings, No. 2, § 12.1 (CD-Rom and Index Guide).

19 Floersheim v. FTC, 411 F.2d 874 (9th Cir. 1969), *cert. denied*, 396 U.S. 1018 (1970); United States Ass'n of Credit Bureaus v. FTC, 299 F.2d 220 (7th Cir. 1962); Avco Financial Services, 104 F.T.C. 485 (1984) (consent order); Royal Furniture, 93 F.T.C. 422 (1979) (consent order); Pubco Corp., 87 F.T.C. 348 (1976) (consent order); Atlantic Indus., 85 F.T.C. 903 (1975) (consent order); Associated Claims Inc., 80 F.T.C. 74 (1972) (consent order); Operation Skip-Locate Inc., 78 F.T.C. 963 (1971) (consent order); Pilgrim Financial Service, 77 F.T.C. 1138 (1970) (consent order); State Credit Control Board, 70 F.T.C. 1318 (1966); Tuseck Enterprises, Inc., 58 F.T.C. 665 (1961); Allied Information Service, 56 F.T.C. 1615 (1959); Massachusetts Consumer Protection Regulations, Mass. Regs. Code tit. 940, § 7.07, Debt Collection; Code Miss. Rules 24 000 002; Code Vt. Rules 06 031 004, Rule CF 104.04, Debt

ments simulate legal process or other government documents.[20]

It is deceptive for creditors to misrepresent their internal organization, such as by use of fictitious job titles or department designations, that imply that a company has a full-time collection department.[21] Nor can a creditor misrepresent the nature of a collection agency as separate from the seller, such as by using a separate letterhead for its collections, even if the collection agency is incorporated as a distinct business entity, as long as it is controlled by the creditor.[22] It is deceptive for collection agencies or creditors to misrepresent their size or geographical scope,[23] to falsely claim that they have a legal division or in-house attorney,[24] or to use an attorney's letterhead to send out collection letters.[25]

5.1.1.1.4 *Misrepresentations concerning imminency of threatened actions, damage to consumer's credit rating*

Debt collectors may not use simulated telegrams to misrepresent the urgency and importance of collection correspondence.[26] Creditors may not misrepresent that a matter has been or will be referred to a collection agency.[27]

Nor can collectors misrepresent the imminency or probability of legal action. Debt collectors may not threaten that nonpayment "will" result in legal action unless suit is filed in all cases, can not threaten that nonpayment "may" result in litigation unless suit is the ordinary response to nonpayment, and can not threaten that if payment is not made immediately or in a specified number of days, specified action will be initiated, if the determination to take that action at that time has not been made.[28] It is deceptive to

---

Collection; Liggins v. May Co., 53 Ohio Misc. 21, 373 N.E.2d 404 (C.P. Cuyahoga Cty. 1977); State v. Credit Bureau, 530 S.W.2d 288 (Tex. 1975).

20 Floersheim v. FTC, 411 F.2d 874 (9th Cir. 1969), *cert. denied*, 396 U.S. 1018 (1970); Slough v. FTC, 396 F.2d 870 (5th Cir. 1968), *cert. denied*, 393 U.S. 980 (1969); Russey v. Rankin, 911 F. Supp. 1449 (D.N.M. 1995); CTC Collections Inc., 86 F.T.C. 109 (1975) (consent order); Intercontinental Services Corp., 86 F.T.C. 1098 (1975) (consent order); Trans-American Collection, Inc., 83 F.T.C. 525 (1973) (consent order); Neighborhood Periodical Club, 81 F.T.C. 93 (1972) (consent order); State v. O'Neill Investigations, Inc., 609 P.2d 520 (Alaska 1980); Thomas v. Sun Furniture & Appliance Co., 399 N.E.2d 567 (Ohio Ct. App. 1978) (misleading use of post-judgment collection notice); State v. Credit Bureau, 530 S.W.2d 288 (Tex. 1975); Massachusetts Consumer Protection Regulations, Mass. Regs. Code tit. 940, § 7.07, Debt Collection; Code Vt. Rules 06 031 004, Rule CF 104.04, Debt Collection.

21 Slough v. FTC, 396 F.2d 870 (5th Cir. 1968), *cert. denied*, 393 U.S. 980 (1969); Grolier Inc., 91 F.T.C. 315 (1978), *vacated and remanded on other grounds*, 615 F.2d 1215 (9th Cir. 1980); Capax Inc., 91 F.T.C. 1048 (1978); Intercontinental Services Corp., 86 F.T.C. 1098 (1975) (consent order); Helix Marketing Corp., 83 F.T.C. 514 (1973); Code Vt. Rules 06 031 004, Rule CF 104.04, Debt Collection.

22 Wm. H. Wise Co. v. FTC, 246 F.2d 702 (D.C. Cir. 1957), *cert. denied*, 355 U.S. 856 (1957); Providence Washington Ins. Co., 89 F.T.C. 345 (1977); North Am. Collections, Inc., 87 F.T.C. 566 (1976) (consent order); Pubco Corp., 87 F.T.C. 348 (1976) (consent order); Atlantic Indus., 85 F.T.C. 903 (1975) (consent order); Sunshine Art Studios, 81 F.T.C. 836 (1972), *aff'd*, 481 F.2d 1171 (1st Cir. 1973); Pilgrim Financial Services, 77 F.T.C. 1138 (1970) (consent order). To do so also brings a *creditor* (not just collectors) within the coverage of and violates the Fair Debt Collection Practices Act. *See* National Consumer Law Center, Fair Debt Collection § 4.2.4 (5th ed. 2004).

23 Operation Skip-Locate Inc., 78 F.T.C. 963 (1971) (consent order); Mutual Credit Bureau, Inc., 76 F.T.C. 448 (1969) (consent order); Liquidation Corp. of Am., 69 F.T.C. 628 (1966) (consent order); American Retail Board of Trade, 67 F.T.C. 856 (1965) (consent order).

24 Grolier Inc., 91 F.T.C. 315 (1978), *vacated and remanded on other grounds*, 615 F.2d 1215 (9th Cir. 1980); Providence Washington Ins. Co., 89 F.T.C. 345 (1977); Pubco Corp., 87 F.T.C. 348 (1976) (consent order); Trans-American Collections Inc., 83 F.T.C. 525 (1973) (consent order); Associated Claims Inc., 80 F.T.C. 794 (1972) (consent order); Empire Accounts Service Inc., 80 F.T.C. 258 (1972) (consent order); Credit & Investigation Bureau of Maryland, 67 F.T.C. 277 (1965); Wilson Chemical Co., 64 F.T.C. 168 (1964); Code Vt. Rules 06 031 004, Rule CF 104.06, Debt Collection.

25 Grolier Inc., 91 F.T.C. 315 (1978); Intercontinental Services Corp., 86 F.T.C. 1098 (1975) (consent order); Federated Bureau of Installment Credit, 72 F.T.C. 5641 (1966) (consent order); Wilson Chemical Co., 64 F.T.C. 168 (1964); Vermont Consumer Fraud Rules, Rule CF 104, Debt Collection.

26 Trans World Accounts, Inc. v. FTC, 594 F.2d 212 (9th Cir. 1979); *In re* Scrimpsher, 17 B.R. 999 (Bankr. N.D.N.Y. 1982) (New York law); Capax Inc., 91 F.T.C. 1048 (1978); Continental Collections Bureau of Am., 87 F.T.C. 557 (1976) (consent order); North Am. Collections, Inc., 87 F.T.C. 566 (1976) (consent order); Powers Service Inc., 87 F.T.C. 574 (1976) (consent order); Trans Nat'l Credit Corp., 87 F.T.C. 549 (1976) (consent order); United Compucreed Collections Inc., 87 F.T.C. 547 (1976) (consent order).

27 Sunshine Art Studios, 81 F.T.C. 836 (1972), *aff'd*, 481 F.2d 1171 (1st Cir. 1973); Consumer Products of Am., 75 F.T.C. 445 (1968); Consumer Products of Am., 72 F.T.C. 533 (1967); Consolidated Sewing Machine Co., 71 F.T.C. 356 (1966); Parents Magazine Enterprises, Inc., 68 F.T.C. 980 (1965); Wm. H. Wise Co., 53 F.T.C. 408 (1956), *aff'd*, 246 F.2d 702 (D.C. Cir. 1957); Federal Coaching Institute, 49 F.T.C. 1138 (1953).

28 Caputo v. Professional Recovery Servs., Inc., 261 F. Supp. 2d 1249, 1261–62 (D. Kan. 2003); Trans World Accounts, Inc. v. FTC, 594 F.2d 212 (9th Cir. 1979); Avco Financial Services, 104 F.T.C. 485 (1984) (consent order); Hiken Furniture Co., 91 F.T.C. 1115 (1978) (consent order); Capax Inc., 91 F.T.C. 1048 (1978); Providence Washington Ins. Co., 89 F.T.C. 345 (1977); Trans Nat'l Credit Corp., 87 F.T.C. 549 (1976) (consent order); United Compucreed Collections Inc., 87 F.T.C. 547 (1976) (consent order); North Am. Collections, Inc., 87 F.T.C. 566 (1976) (consent order); Continental Collection Bureau of Am., 87 F.T.C. 557 (1976) (consent order); Pubco Corp., 87 F.T.C. 348 (1976) (consent order); Intercontinental Services Corp., 86 F.T.C. 1098 (1975) (consent order); Atlantic Indus. Inc., 85 F.T.C. 903 (1975) (consent order); GC Services Corp., 83 F.T.C. 1521 (1974) (consent order); Trans-American Collections, Inc., 83 F.T.C. 525 (1973) (consent order); Associated Claims Inc., 80 F.T.C. 794 (1972) (consent order); Helix Marketing Corp., 83

threaten a monthly service charge when such a charge is not assessed for delinquent payments.[29]

A creditor or collection agency can not represent falsely that nonpayment will adversely affect a debtor's credit record with a consumer reporting agency or other third parties or misrepresent the effect of nonpayment on the debtor's credit rating.[30] A collection agency engages in a deceptive practice when it misrepresents itself as a credit rating organization, thus falsely linking payment of the debt with the debtor's credit rating.[31] Falsely reporting to a credit reporting agency that a consumer owes a debt is a UDAP violation.[32]

5.1.1.1.5 Misrepresentations as to legal consequences of debt nonpayment

Collectors may not misrepresent the rights, duties, or obligations of any person arising from any federal, state, or local statute or regulation, such as that a debtor is subject to prosecution under the federal mail fraud statutes.[33] Collection letters may not be designed to create fear and take advantage of the consumer's ignorance of legal procedures.[34] Thus, it is deceptive to threaten that nonpayment will lead to garnishment of the debtor's wages, without disclosing that garnishment requires a judicial order,[35] or to threaten falsely that goods can be repossessed,[36] that a lien will be placed on everything the debtor owns,[37] that the consumer can be arrested,[38] or that added attorney, investigatory, or other fees will be assessed.[39] It is deceptive to imply, by the use of the word "judgment," that certain costs have been added to a debt.[40] Conversely, it is deceptive to promise that payment of a certain size will wipe out the debt when this is not the case.[41] It is unfair and deceptive for an assignee to refuse to acknowledge that the FTC Holder Rule makes it liable for claims and defenses that the consumer could assert against the original seller.[42]

It is unfair for a credit union to evade a state law that protects retirement accounts from seizure or use as security.[43] The credit union falsely implied that it had a security

F.T.C. 514 (1973); Wilson Chemical Co., 64 F.T.C. 168 (1964); Massachusetts Consumer Protection Regulations, Mass. Regs. Code tit. 940, § 7.04, Debt Collection; Code Vt. Rules 06 031 004, Rule CF 104.01, Debt Collection; State v. O'Neill Investigations, Inc., 609 P.2d 520 (Alaska 1980); Liggins v. May Co., 53 Ohio Misc. 21, 375 N.E.2d 404 (C.P. Cuyahoga Cty. 1977); Bennett v. Tri-State Collection Service, Clearinghouse No. 27,062 (Ohio C.P. Cuyahoga Cty. 1976).

29 Garland v. Mobil Oil Corp., 340 F. Supp. 1095 (N.D. Ill. 1972).

30 International Masters Publishers, Inc., 109 F.T.C. 9 (1987) (consent order); Capax, Inc., 91 F.T.C. 1048 (1978); Grolier Inc., 91 F.T.C. 315 (1978), *vacated and remanded on other grounds*, 615 F.2d 1215 (9th Cir. 1980); CBS Inc., 90 F.T.C. 9 (1977) (consent order); Pubco Corp., 87 F.T.C. 348 (1976) (consent order); United Compucreed Collections Inc., 87 F.T.C. 547 (1976) (consent order); Continental Collections Bureau of Am., 87 F.T.C. 557 (1976) (consent order); Trans Nat'l Credit Corp., 87 F.T.C. 549 (1976) (consent order); Trans Am. Collections, Inc., 83 F.T.C. 525 (1973) (consent order); State v. O'Neill Investigations, Inc., 609 P.2d 520 (Alaska 1980).

31 United States Credit Rating Bureau Inc., 60 F.T.C. 250 (1962) (consent order).

32 Fisher v. Quality Hyundai, Inc., 2002 U.S. Dist. LEXIS 407 (N.D. Ill. Jan. 8, 2002).

33 Caputo v. Professional Recovery Servs., Inc., 261 F. Supp. 2d 1249, 1261–62 (D. Kan. 2003); Grolier Inc., 91 F.T.C. 315 (1978), *vacated and remanded on other grounds*, 615 F.2d 1215 (9th Cir. 1980); Liggins v. May Co., 53 Ohio Misc. 21, 373 N.E.2d 404 (C.P. Cuyahoga Cty. 1977); Bennett v. Tri-State Collection Service, Clearinghouse No. 27,062 (Ohio C.P. Cuyahoga Cty. 1976); Connelly v. Puget Sound Collections, Inc., 16 Wash. App. 62, 553 P.2d 1354 (1976).

34 Slough v. FTC, 396 F.2d 870 (5th Cir. 1968), *cert. denied*, 393 U.S. 980 (1969); Liggins v. May Co., 53 Ohio Misc. 21, 373 N.E.2d 404, 7 Ohio Op. 3d 164 (C.P. Cuyahoga Cty. 1977).

35 Royal Furniture, 93 F.T.C. 422 (1979) (consent order); Associated Claims Inc., 80 F.T.C. 794 (1972) (consent order); Massachusetts Consumer Protection Regulations, Mass. Regs. Code tit. 940, § 7.04, Debt Collection; Code Vt. Fraud Rules 06 031 004, Rule CF 104.01, Debt Collection.

36 Clarkson v. DeCaceres, 105 B.R. 266 (Bankr. E.D. Pa. 1989) (deceptive for landlord to sell tenant's property without any legal right to do so); Royal Furniture, 93 F.T.C. 422 (1979) (consent order).

37 Caputo v. Professional Recovery Servs., Inc., 261 F. Supp. 2d 1249 (D. Kan. 2003).

38 Calabrese v. CSC Holdings, Inc., 283 F. Supp. 2d 797, 815 (E.D.N.Y. 2003) (denial of motion to dismiss) (deceptive to accuse consumer of stealing cable programming without any definitive proof and state that ordering or possessing a decoder can be basis for civil claim); Turner v. E-Z Check Cashing, 35 F. Supp. 2d 1042 (M.D. Tenn. 1999) (deceptive to represent that nonpayment of payday loan will result in bad check prosecution); Massachusetts Consumer Protection Regulations, Mass. Regs. Code tit. 940, § 7.04, Debt Collection; Code Vt. Rules 06 031 004, Rule CF 104.01, Debt Collection; State v. O'Neill Investigations, Inc., 609 P.2d 520 (Alaska 1980); *see also* Irwin v. Mascott, 112 F. Supp. 2d 937 (N.D. Cal. 2000) (threat to sue writers of NSF checks under statute which imposed civil liability on shoplifters violated UDAP statute); Delaney v. Budget Rent-a-Car, Clearinghouse No. 36,595 (Conn. Super. Ct. 1983) (threats that debtor could lose his driver's license and car registration could be UDAP violation).

39 Hartke v. Illinois Payday Loans, Inc., 1999 U.S. Dist. LEXIS 14937 (C.D. Ill. Sept. 13, 1999) (deceptive to refer to statutory penalties, attorney fees, and costs where bad check statute which authorized them was inapplicable); Massachusetts Consumer Protection Regulations, Mass. Regs. Code tit. 940, § 7.07, Debt Collection; Code Vt. Rules 06 031 004, Rule CF 104.04, Debt Collection; Wiginton v. Pacific Credit Corp., 2 Haw. App. 435, 634 P.2d 111 (1981) (collector notified debtor of attorney fees it would have to pay where such fees were prohibited by state law); Bennett v. Tri-State Collection Service, Clearinghouse No. 27,062 (Ohio C.P. Cuyahoga Cty., 1976).

40 Campion v. Credit Bureau Servs., Inc., 2000 U.S. Dist. LEXIS 20233 (E.D. Wash. Sept. 19, 2000).

41 Jungkurth v. Eastern Financial Services, Inc., 74 B.R. 323 (Bankr. E.D. Pa. 1987).

42 Jaramillo v. Gonzales, 50 P.3d 554 (N.M. 2002). *See also* § 6.6, *infra* (discussion of FTC Holder Rule).

43 Petersen v. State Employees Credit Union (*In re* Kittrell), 115 B.R. 873 (Bankr. M.D.N.C. 1990).

interest in the consumer's retirement account. When the consumer lost his job, the credit union convinced him to transfer money out of his otherwise protected retirement account into his credit union account, where the credit union could seize it.[44]

5.1.1.1.6 Harassment

Also unfair or deceptive are threats of violence, threats to assign the debtor's obligation so that he or she loses claims or defenses or becomes subject to harsh collection efforts, threats to hold the debtor up to ridicule or contempt, use of obscene language, telephone calls that do not disclose the creditor's and telephone caller's identity, and silences that cause the debtor to pay for long-distance telephone calls or other charges.[45] Some state UDAP regulations limit creditors' telephone calls and visits to normal working hours and limit their number at the debtor's residence and at other places.[46] Creditors must obey debtors' requests not to call them at their place of employment and normally may not visit them there.[47] Creditors may not contact the debtor at all if so requested by the debtor's attorney.[48] Threats to make embarrassing contacts with employers, the debtor's family, and others, such as contacting an employer prior to obtaining judgment and informing it that the consumer's wages will be garnished, violate UDAP standards.[49] A Massachusetts UDAP regulation prohibits creditors from seeking post-dated checks or negotiating such instruments before the due date.[50] The federal Fair Debt Collection Practices Act also sets out standards about permissible telephone calls and third-party contacts by collection agencies; these standards should be referred to in bringing a UDAP debt collection challenge.[51]

5.1.1.1.7 Collecting debts or amounts that are not owed

Creditors may not collect interest or expenses beyond those authorized by the credit agreement or law.[52] It is deceptive for collectors to make demand for such nonexistent payment rights as "bad check service charges" where there is no legal obligation for the debtor to pay these charges.[53] Where a consumer agreed to pay "reasonable

44 *Id.*

45 Avco Financial Services, 104 F.T.C. 485 (1984) (consent order); Hearst Corp., 82 F.T.C. 1792 (1973) (consent order); Neighborhood Periodical Club Inc., 81 F.T.C. 93 (1972) (consent order); Massachusetts Consumer Protection Regulations, Mass. Regs. Code tit. 940, §§ 7.04. 7.07, Debt Collection; Code Vt. Rules 06 031 004, Rule CF 104.01, 104.04, Debt Collection; Ekl v. Knecht, 585 N.E.2d 156 (Ill. App. Ct. 1991) (threats to disconnect consumer's water and undo repairs).

46 Massachusetts Consumer Protection Regulations, Mass. Regs. Code tit. 940, § 7.04, Debt Collection; Code Vt. Rules 06 031 004, Rule CF 104.02, Debt Collection. *See also* Clarkson v. DeCaceres, 105 B.R. 266 (Bankr. E.D. Pa. 1989); Aldens Inc., 98 F.T.C. 790 (1981) (consent order).

47 Avco Financial Services, 104 F.T.C. 485 (1984) (consent order); Nosoma Sys. Inc., 88 F.T.C. 458 (1976) (consent order); Intercontinental Services Corp., 86 F.T.C. 1098 (1975) (consent order); Family Publication Service, Inc., 63 F.T.C. 971 (1963) (consent order); Massachusetts Consumer Protection Regulations, Mass. Regs. Code tit. 940, §§ 7.01, 7.04 Debt Collection; Code Vt. Rules 06 031 004, Rule CF 104.02, Debt Collection; Bennett v. Tri-State Collection Service, Clearinghouse No. 27,062 (Ohio C.P. Cuyahoga Cty. 1976).

48 Tillquist v. Ford Motor Credit Co., 714 F. Supp. 607 (D. Conn. 1989); Massachusetts Consumer Protection Regulations, Mass. Regs. Code tit. 940, § 7.04, Debt Collection; Brow v. Stanton, 12 Mass. App. Ct. 992, 429 N.E.2d 60 (1981) (no exceptions to the UDAP regulation that requires collectors, upon the debtor's request, not to contact the debtor, but only the debtor's attorney).

49 G.C. Services Corp., 83 F.T.C. 1521 (1974) (consent order); Illinois Collection Service, 77 F.T.C. 1338 (1970) (consent order); Family Publications Service, Inc., 63 F.T.C. 971 (1963) (consent order); Massachusetts Consumer Protection Regulations, Mass. Regs. Code tit. 940, §§ 7.04, 7.07, Debt Collection; Code Vt. Rules 06 031 004, Rule CF 104.03, Debt Collection; Bennett v. Tri-State Collection Service, Clearinghouse No. 27,062 (Ohio C.P. Cuyahoga Cty. 1976).

50 Massachusetts Consumer Protection Regulations, Mass. Regs. Code tit. 940, §§ 7.08, 7.09, Debt Collection. *See also* G.C. Services, 83 F.T.C. 1521 (1974) (consent order).

51 *See* National Consumer Law Center, Fair Debt Collection Ch. 5 (5th ed. 2004).

52 Campion v. Credit Bureau Servs., Inc., 2000 U.S. Dist. LEXIS 20233 (E.D. Wash. Sept. 19, 2000) (retention of garnished wages without a judicial order, and inclusion of unauthorized costs in affidavit for writ of garnishment, violated state debt collection law and UDAP statute); Ballard v. Equifax Check Servs., Inc., 27 F. Supp. 2d 1201 (E.D. Cal. 1998) (UDAP violation to attempt to collect $20 bad check fee that was not authorized by contract or law); Midwest Studios Inc., 28 F.T.C. 1583 (1939); Code Vt. Rules 06 031 004, Rule CF 104.05, Debt Collection; Fuller v. Pacific Medical Collections, Inc., 891 P.2d 300 (Haw. Ct. App. 1995) (collection of unauthorized interest and attorney fees that are not paid over to the collection attorney violates state debt collection law and UDAP statute); People *ex rel.* Daley v. Datacom Sys. Corp., 176 Ill. App. 3d 697, 531 N.E.2d 839 (1988) (increased amount of parking ticket fine and added costs although fines not officially due); Friday v. United Dominion Realty Trust, Inc., 575 S.E.2d 532 (N.C. App. 2003) (fee not allowed by state landlord-tenant law); Strenge v. Clarke, 89 Wash. 2d 23, 569 P.2d 60 (1977); *see also* Smith v. Keycorp Mortgage Inc., 151 B.R. 870 (N.D. Ill. 1993) (attempt to collect late charges not allowed because of debtor's bankruptcy reorganization); Ai v. Frank Huff Agency Ltd., 61 Haw. 607, 607 P.2d 1304 (1980).

53 Calabrese v. CSC Holdings, Inc., 283 F. Supp. 2d 797 (E.D.N.Y. 2003) (denying motion to dismiss claim that it was deceptive to accuse plaintiffs of theft without definitive proof and state that ordering or possessing cable signal decoder can be basis for civil claim against them, forcing plaintiffs either to pay money or face litigation); *In re* Scrimpsher, 17 B.R. 999 (Bankr. N.D.N.Y. 1982); Davis Lake Community Ass'n, Inc. v. Feldmann, 138 N.C. App. 292, 530 S.E.2d 865 (2000) (demanding attorney fees beyond amount allowed by statute is deceptive). *But see* Varela v. Investors Ins. Holding Corp., 81 N.Y.2d 958, 615 N.E.2d 218 (1993) (no deception in law firm's insistence that opposing parties pay court fee required to satisfy erroneous judgment against them). *Cf.* Lalande Air & Water Corp. v. Pratt,

collection expenses," it is unfair to seek an additional one-third of the debt for such expenses, even if the collection agency charges the creditor that amount, as there is no relationship between that amount and the actual expense of collection.[54] Where state law prohibits creditors from seeking attorney fees, it is a UDAP violation to seek those fees.[55] It is a UDAP violation to fail to credit debtors' payments promptly, while charging them interest on the unpaid balance.[56] A Massachusetts UDAP regulation requires creditors to allow debtors or their attorneys to inspect all relevant documents.[57]

It is deceptive to knowingly sue for more than the amount due.[58] Misrepresenting the amount of a debt is a UDAP violation.[59] It is a UDAP violation for a collector to settle an action, and then, instead of dismissing the case, continue to pursue the matter to collect fees and other costs.[60] It has been found unfair for a merchant to press thousands of claims where the merchant never checked the claims' validity before pursuing them.[61] Seeking to collect debts that are barred by the statute of limitations is a UDAP violation.[62] A Vermont regulation requires creditors to disclose if a debt is barred by the statute of limitations.[63]

Persisting in collection attempts against a person the collector knows does not owe the debt is deceptive.[64] Some companies send goods they know were goods not requested and then aggressively pursue collection efforts. The FTC has negotiated consent orders with a number of such companies, most of which targeted institutions rather than individual consumers for this scam.[65]

Where a collector seeks but does not collect an illegal amount, consumer litigants must give some thought to their actual damages. In some cases, where nothing is paid to the creditor, the consumer may be limited to minimum statutory damages, where available.[66]

A sample UDAP complaint and discovery request involving a creditor's attempts to collect for a credit card debt not owed is included on the companion CD-Rom to this volume.[67]

5.1.1.1.8 Taking illegal actions against the consumer or the consumer's property

It is unfair and deceptive to seize a car unlawfully and tow it away in order to collect an overdue repair bill.[68] A landlord creditor who sold a tenant's property without a valid lien violated Pennsylvania's former UDAP debt collection regulation (now replaced by a statute) by using illegal action to harm another's property.[69] Also unfair and deceptive is a bank's unlawful set-off against a consumer's deposit for a debt owed.[70]

It is unfair to bring a criminal action against a debtor for bounced checks without probable cause to believe that such a crime was committed.[71] It is a UDAP violation to procure a warrant for the consumer's arrest, where the consumer's nonpayment was justified.[72] Illegal repossession and fore-

---

795 A.2d 1233 (Vt. 2002) (mobile home park's demand for rental amount disapproved by rent control commission not unfair where appeal of disapproval was pending and no evidence of retaliation, oppression, etc.).

54 Bondanza v. Peninsula Hosp. & Medical Center, 23 Cal. 3d 260, 590 P.2d. 22, 152 Cal. Rptr. 446 (1979). *See* National Consumer Law Center, Fair Debt Collection § 15.2 (5th ed. 2004).

55 Davis Lake Community Ass'n, Inc. v. Feldmann, 138 N.C. App. 292, 530 S.E.2d 865 (2000); Elsea, Inc. v. Stapleton, 1998 Ohio App. LEXIS 3165 (Ohio Ct. App. July 2, 1998).

56 Asch v. Teller, Levit & Silvertrust, P.C., 2003 WL 22232801 (N.D. Ill. Sept. 26, 2003).

57 Massachusetts Consumer Protection Regulations, Mass. Regs. Code tit. 940, § 7.08, Debt Collection.

58 Chrysler Credit Corp. v. Walker, 488 So. 2d 209 (La. Ct. App. 1986); Davis Lake Community Ass'n, Inc. v. Feldmann, 138 N.C. App. 292, 530 S.E.2d 865 (2000) (demanding attorney fees beyond amount allowed by statute is deceptive); Vaughan v. Kalyvas, 342 S.E.2d 617 (S.C. Ct. App. 1986).

59 Asch v. Teller, Levit & Silvertrust, P.C., 2003 WL 22232801 (N.D. Ill. Sept. 26, 2003).

60 Evergreen Collectors v. Holt, 60 Wash. App. 151, 803 P.2d 10 (1991).

61 Blanchette v. Cataldo, 734 F.2d 869 (1st Cir. 1984) (Massachusetts law) (freight claims agent brought thousands of unvalidated claims concerning slow vegetable shipments against a railroad).

62 Taylor v. Unifund, 1999 U.S. Dist. LEXIS 13651 (N.D. Ill. May 3, 1999); Commonwealth v. Cole, 709 A.2d 994 (Pa. Commw. Ct. 1998) (*citing* Kimber v. Federal Financial Corp., 668 F. Supp. 1480 (M.D. Ala. 1987)).

63 Code Vt. Rules 06 031 004, Rule CF 104.05, Debt Collection.

64 Heard v. Bonneville Billing & Collections, Inc., 2000 U.S. App. LEXIS 14625 (10th Cir. 2000) (unpublished, citation limited); Fisher v. Quality Hyundai, Inc., 2002 U.S. Dist. LEXIS 407 (N.D. Ill. Jan. 8, 2002). *But cf.* Havens-Tobias v. Eagle, 2003 WL 1601461 (Ohio App. Mar. 28, 2003) (unpublished, citation limited) (not deceptive or unfair to sue on bad check, given the facts known to the attorney).

65 FTC v. AKOA, Inc., 5 Trade Reg. Rep. (CCH) ¶ 24,408 (C.D. Cal. 1998) (consent decree); Image Sales & Consultants, Inc., 5 Trade Reg. Rep. (CCH) ¶ 24,442 (N.D. Ill. 1998) (consent decree); The Century Group, 5 Trade Reg. Rep. (CCH) ¶ 24,442 (N.D. Ill. 1998) (consent decree); FTC v. Dean Thomas Corp., 5 Trade Reg. Rep. (CCH) ¶ 24,327 (N.D. Ind. 1997) (stipulated final judgment); FTC v. McGowan, 5 Trade Reg. Rep. (CCH) ¶ 24,248 (D. N.J. 1997) (proposed consent decree).

66 Page & Wirtz Constr. Co. v. Solomon, 110 N.M. 206, 794 P.2d 349 (1990). *See* §§ 7.5.2 (UDAP damage requirements), 8.4.1 (statutory damages), *infra*.

67 It can also be found on the comprehensive, cumulative CD-Rom, National Consumer Law Center, Consumer Law Pleadings, No. 2, § 9.1 (CD-Rom and Index Guide).

68 Hanner v. Classic Auto Body, Inc., 10 Mass. App. Ct. 121, 406 N.E.2d 686 (1980). *See also* § 5.1.1.5.3, *infra*.

69 Clarkson v. DeCaceres, 105 B.R. 266 (Bankr. E.D. Pa. 1989). The regulation has been replaced by 73 Pa. Stat. § 2270.1 *et seq.*

70 Raymer v. Bay State Nat'l Bank, 384 Mass. 310, 424 N.E.2d 515 (1981).

71 Oblon v. G. Fox & Co., Clearinghouse No. 40,643 (Conn. Super. Ct. 1984).

72 Mapp v. Toyota World, Inc., 344 S.E.2d 297 (N.C. Ct. App. 1986).

closure practices as UDAP violations are discussed in §§ 5.1.1.5, 5.1.1.6, *infra*.

5.1.1.2 FTC Credit Practices Rule

5.1.1.2.1 General overview

The most important precedent dealing with unfair remedies used by creditors in enforcing consumer credit contracts is the FTC's Trade Regulation Rule Concerning Credit Practices.[73] The District of Columbia Circuit dismissed a challenge to the rule initiated by a national trade association of finance companies and by several state creditor regulators, and the Supreme Court denied *certiorari*.[74]

Transactions covered by the rule include lease-purchase contracts where the consumer is obligated to pay a specified amount and is permitted to become the owner of the property for little or no additional consideration.[75] The rule also covers creditors such as physicians and contractors who use deferred payment plans.[76] The rule does not, however, cover nonprofit organizations[77] or a city that administers a housing rehabilitation grant program.[78] The rule overrides inconsistent provisions of state law.[79]

The FTC rule prohibits the following six practices:

- Confessions of judgment, *cognovits*, and other waivers of the right to notice and opportunity to be heard in the event of suit (this provision does not apply to executory process in Louisiana);
- The debtor's waiver of protections concerning personal or real property exempt from attachment or execution, such as waiver of a homestead exemption, unless the waiver applies only to property that is the subject of a security interest granted in that credit transaction;[80]
- Assignment of wages or other earnings before judgment;
- Non-purchase money security interests in certain household goods, but creditors can still take security interests in works of art, items acquired as antiques, jewelry (except wedding rings), and electronic entertainment equipment (except one television and one radio);[81]
- Pyramiding late charges by assessing more than one delinquency charge for one late payment (pyramiding late charges for a *missed* payment is not prohibited); and
- Failure to provide cosigners with a specified warning indicating the potential obligations of a cosigner.[82]

The best sources for understanding the FTC's Credit Practices Rule are the FTC's Statement of Basis and Purpose for the rule[83] and, to a lesser extent, the informal FTC staff opinion letters on the rule. All of these documents are reproduced on the companion CD-Rom to this volume.

5.1.1.2.2 Similar FRB, OTS, and NCUA rules for banks

The FTC rule applies to finance companies, retailers, and other creditors within the FTC's jurisdiction. The FTC rule does not apply to most banks. Nevertheless, the Office of Thrift Supervision (OTS) and the Federal Reserve Board (FRB) have enacted analogous rules for savings and loan institutions[84] and for all other banks,[85] respectively. Credit unions are covered by a comparable rule enacted by the National Credit Union Administration (NCUA).[86]

While the rules enacted by these other agencies closely track the FTC rule, there are a number of differences.[87] The

73 16 C.F.R. § 444 (effective Mar. 1, 1985) [*reprinted at* Appx. B.1, *infra*]. *See also* the accompanying Statement of Basis and Purpose, at 49 Fed. Reg. 7740 (Mar. 1, 1984), *reproduced on* the companion CD-Rom to this volume. After reviewing the regulation as required by the Regulatory Flexibility Act the FTC concluded in 1995 that revisions to the rule were not warranted. 60 Fed. Reg. 24805 (May 10, 1995).

74 American Financial Services Ass'n v. FTC, 767 F.2d 957 (D.C. Cir. 1985), *cert. denied*, 475 U.S. 1011 (1986).

75 Green, FTC Informal Staff Opinion Letter (Mar. 16, 1985).

76 Martin, FTC Informal Staff Opinion Letter (July 16, 1987); Shevin, FTC Informal Staff Opinion Letter (Apr. 30, 1986).

77 Marwil, FTC Informal Staff Opinion Letter (May 17, 1985); Lush, FTC Informal Staff Opinion Letter (Mar. 8, 1985).

78 Balaban, FTC Informal Staff Opinion Letter (Nov. 26 1985).

79 Free Bridge Auto Sales v. Fitzgerald, 48 Va. Cir. 1, 1999 Va. Cir. LEXIS 13 (Circ. Ct. 1999).

80 *See* Kaswell, FTC Informal Staff Opinion Letter (Mar. 20, 1985). *See also* U.S. v. Action Loan Co., 5 Trade Reg. Rep. (CCH) ¶ 24,793 (W.D. Ky. Aug. 24, 2000) (proposed consent decree against company that used waiver of exemption clause).

81 *See* United States v. West Capital Financial Services Corp., F.T.C. File No. 922 3306 (S.D. Cal. June 15, 1994) (consent decree) (allegedly took nonpurchase money security interest in household goods; relief includes restitution of all filing fees and related finance charges concerning household goods collateral).

82 The FTC has exempted New York contracts from the co-signer disclosure because state law offers similar or greater protections; *see* 51 Fed. Reg. 28328 (Aug. 7, 1986). *See also* Royal Furniture Co., 93 F.T.C. 422 (1979) (consent order) (failure to disclose rights and obligations to cosigners).

83 49 Fed. Reg. 7740 (Mar. 1, 1984).

84 12 C.F.R. § 535.

85 12 C.F.R. § 227.11–.16.

86 *See* 12 C.F.R. § 706.

87 While the FTC Rule is silent on its applicability to real estate loans, the FRB and OTS Rules do not apply to credit extended for the purchase of real property. The FRB and OTS Rules, however, do apply to credit extended to improve a home or to purchase a mobile home deemed to be personalty under state law. The NCUA, OTS and FRB Rules also give the creditor the added option of including the cosigner notice in the contract and not just in a separate document, and of modifying the notice in some respects. In addition, the definition of "cosigner" and "household goods" have been clarified and limited. The FRB and OTS Rules do not prohibit certain types of *cognovits*, and the FRB Rule allows refinancing of purchase money loans without losing their purchase money characterization.

most important difference is that the FRB, OTS and NCUA rules only prohibit banks and credit unions from entering into credit agreements containing or enforcing the prohibited creditor remedies. The FRB, OTS and NCUA rules do not prohibit a bank or credit union from purchasing consumer credit agreements containing the prohibited terms as long as the financial entity does not enforce the prohibited creditor remedy.

Important materials for interpreting the FRB rule are FRB staff guidelines.[88] These guidelines only apply to bank compliance with the FRB rule, and not to finance companies', retailers', and others' compliance with the similar FTC rule.

5.1.1.2.3 FTC staff letters as precedent

FTC staff letters interpret the Credit Practices Rule very narrowly. For example, while the FTC rule restricts security interests in "household goods," the FTC staff has tried to limit the number of items treated as "household goods." This seems at variance with the intent of the FTC's Statement of Basis and Purpose for the rule, which states that security interests in household goods are unfair because "[d]ebtors lose property which is of great value to them and little value to the creditor . . . Although creditors are entitled to payment, such security interests offer little economic return to creditors at great cost to the debtor."[89] Nonetheless, the FTC staff advises that the term "household goods" does not include many common household items that easily meet the Statement of Basis and Purpose test, such as typewriters, bicycles, sporting goods, books and encyclopedias, gardening equipment, luggage, rugs, and children's car seats.

While the FTC informal staff opinion letters often seem overly restrictive, and are not binding on courts or the FTC itself, it is important for practitioners to be familiar with them. While a party can argue that the letter is wrong, if necessary, courts are likely to give the letter an initial presumption of validity. The following six subsections summarize these FTC letters as they apply to the rule's specific provisions. The letters are reproduced on the companion CD-Rom to this volume.

5.1.1.2.4 Confession of judgment provision

The confession of judgment prohibition applies to instruments executed after a consumer defaults as well as to notes and contracts signed at the time of the transaction.[90] Informal FTC staff opinion letters do distinguish though between judicial proceedings and self-help creditor remedies in applying the ban on confession of judgment clauses. The rule bars the use of a clause waiving the right to a hearing before the creditor gets a repossession order from a magistrate.[91] On the other hand, it does not prohibit a "power of sale" clause that allows a creditor, upon default, to exercise a self-help right to take possession of property and sell it,[92] nor does it prohibit waiver of notice of default.[93] A court has ruled that a confession of judgment provision did not violate the Pennsylvania UDAP statute, even if it would violate the FTC rule,[94] but the Pennsylvania UDAP statute has since been amended to make it clear that confession of judgment clauses are violations.[95] The protections of the confessed judgment prohibition can not be waived by the consumer.[96]

5.1.1.2.5 Waiver of exemption clauses

The rule prohibits contract clauses that waive or limit exemptions for attachment, execution, or other process on the debtor's real or personal property.[97] The prohibition applies not only to property owned by the consumer, but also to property held by or "due" to the consumer, thus covering wages or other debts owed to the consumer.[98] There is an exception for property subject to a security interest executed in connection with the transaction.[99]

5.1.1.2.6 Wage assignments

The rule's prohibition of wage assignments contains an exception for wage assignments that are revocable at the will of the debtor.[100] According to informal FTC staff opinion letters, a creditor may require that revocation of a wage assignment be in writing,[101] but not that it be done a specified number of days before it is given effect.[102] Mandatory irrevocable wage assignments are allowed in the context of payroll deduction plans of the sort used in credit

---

88 50 Fed. Reg. 47036 (Nov. 14, 1985), as updated at 51 Fed. Reg. 39646 (Oct. 30, 1986) and at 53 Fed. Reg. 29225 (Aug. 1988).

89 49 Fed. Reg. 7763 (Mar. 1, 1984).

90 Raver, FTC Informal Staff Opinion Letter (Jan. 22, 1986).

91 Torkildson, FTC Informal Staff Opinion Letter (Apr. 17, 1985); Curlee, FTC Informal Staff Opinion Letter (May 9, 1985).

92 Witzel, FTC Informal Staff Opinion Letter (Mar. 22, 1985); Leverick, FTC Informal Staff Opinion Letter (Mar. 29, 1985) (Arizona "deed of trust" procedure).

93 Clancy, FTC Informal Staff Opinion Letter (Dec. 14, 1988).

94 Zhang v. Southeastern Financial Group, Inc., 980 F. Supp. 787 (E.D. Pa. 1997).

95 73 Pa. Stat. § 201-2(4)(xviii). *See* Commonwealth *ex rel.* Fisher v. Percudani, 825 A.2d 743 (Pa. Commw. Ct. 2003) (refusing to dismiss claim that contractual liquidated damages clause was prohibited confession of judgment clause).

96 Kienzl, FTC Informal Staff Opinion Letter (Sept. 26, 1985).

97 16 C.F.R. § 444.2(a)(2).

98 Free Bridge Auto Sales v. Fitzgerald, 48 Va. Cir. 1, 1999 Va. Cir. LEXIS 13 (Circ. Ct. 1999).

99 16 C.F.R. § 444.2(a)(4).

100 16 C.F.R. § 444.2(a)(3)(i).

101 Torkildson, FTC Informal Staff Opinion Letter (Apr. 17, 1985); Miller, FTC Informal Staff Opinion Letter (Apr. 17, 1985).

102 Wilson, FTC Informal Staff Opinion Letter (July 29, 1986); Torkildson, FTC Informal Staff Opinion Letter (Apr. 17, 1985).

union loans,[103] as long as only part of the debtor's paycheck is taken.[104] Another exception allows assignment of wages that the consumer has already earned;[105] the FTC staff has construed this exception to allow assignment of the portion of his or her monthly salary that the consumer has earned at the time credit is extended.[106]

Wage assignments that predated the rule were not invalidated by it.[107] An employer does not violate the rule by complying with a wage assignment, regardless of its legality under the rule.[108]

5.1.1.2.7 Household goods security interests

Construing the prohibition against non-purchase money, non-possessory security interests in household goods, the FTC staff has indicated that the following items fall within the rule's definition of "household goods":

- Sewing machines;[109]
- Vacuum cleaners;[110]
- Telephones and answering machines;[111]
- Air conditioners;[112]
- Household pets;[113]
- Freezers;[114]
- Floor polishers;[115]
- Patio furniture;[116]
- Ovens, including microwave ovens;[117]
- Dishwashers;[118] and
- Fans, clocks, lamps, toasters and electric can openers.[119]

Duplicate items are protected by the rule, except that only one television and one radio is protected.[120]

The FTC staff has indicated that the following items would not fall within the definition of "household goods":

- Bicycles;[121]
- Typewriters;[122]
- Power tools;[123]
- A butane tank;[124]
- Livestock;[125]
- Barbecue grills;[126]
- Luggage;[127]
- Carpets and rugs;[128]
- A hot tub;[129]
- Fireplace equipment;[130]
- A child's car seat;[131]
- Firearms;[132]
- Camping and sports equipment;[133]
- Hunting and fishing equipment;[134]
- Cameras;[135]

---

103 16 C.F.R. § 444.2(a)(3)(ii); Klewin, FTC Informal Staff Opinion Letter (June 26, 1986); Wilson, FTC Informal Staff Opinion Letter (July 29, 1986); Parker, FTC Informal Staff Opinion Letter (Mar. 29, 1985).

104 Kelley, FTC Informal Staff Opinion Letter (June 17, 1987). *But see* Parker, FTC Informal Staff Opinion Letter (Mar. 29, 1985); Kaswell, FTC Informal Staff Opinion Letter (Mar. 20, 1985) (assignment of entire final paycheck to credit union does not violate Rule).

105 16 C.F.R. § 444.2(a)(3)(iii).

106 Scott, FTC Informal Staff Opinion Letter (Mar. 1, 1985).

107 Treaster, FTC Informal Staff Opinion Letter (Apr. 15 1985).

108 McCarthy, FTC Informal Staff Opinion Letter (Jan. 27, 1986); Patterson, FTC Informal Staff Opinion Letter (June 20, 1985).

109 Scott, FTC Informal Staff Opinion Letter (Aug. 8, 1985).

110 Letter from the Secretary of the Federal Trade Commission to the Honorable Wendell Ford (Mar. 8, 1994), Clearinghouse No. 49,972; Scott, FTC Informal Staff Opinion Letter (Aug. 8, 1985).

111 *But see* Mewhinney, FTC Informal Staff Opinion Letter (Feb. 16, 1989) (Letter 2).

112 Scott, FTC Informal Staff Opinion Letter (Aug. 8, 1985).

113 Scott, FTC Informal Staff Opinion Letter (Mar. 1, 1985).

114 Scott, FTC Informal Staff Opinion Letter (Aug. 8, 1985).

115 *Id.*

116 *Id.*

117 Letter from the Secretary of the Federal Trade Commission to the Honorable Wendell Ford (Mar. 8, 1994), Clearinghouse No. 49,972; Mewhinney, FTC Informal Staff Opinion Letter (Feb. 16, 1989) (Letter 2); Chamness, FTC Informal Staff Opinion Letter (Feb. 11, 1985).

118 Chamness, FTC Informal Staff Opinion Letter (Feb. 11, 1985).

119 Letter from the Secretary of the Federal Trade Commission to the Honorable Wendell Ford (Mar. 8, 1994), Clearinghouse No. 49,972.

120 16 C.F.R. § 444.1(i); Chamness, FTC Informal Staff Opinion Letter (Feb. 11, 1985).

121 Mewhinney, FTC Informal Staff Opinion Letter (Feb. 16, 1989) (Letter 2); Chamness, FTC Informal Staff Opinion Letter (Feb. 11, 1985); Scott, FTC Informal Staff Opinion Letter (Mar. 1, 1985).

122 Chamness, FTC Informal Staff Opinion Letter (Feb. 11, 1985); Geary, FTC Informal Staff Opinion Letter (Mar. 22, 1985); Scott, FTC Informal Staff Opinion Letter (Mar. 1, 1985).

123 Mewhinney, FTC Informal Staff Opinion Letter (Feb. 16, 1989) (Letter 2); Chamness, FTC Informal Staff Opinion Letter (Feb. 11, 1985); Scott, FTC Informal Staff Opinion Letter (Mar. 1, 1985).

124 Scott, FTC Informal Staff Opinion Letter (Aug. 8, 1985).

125 *Id.*

126 *Id.*

127 *Id.*

128 Scott, FTC Informal Staff Opinion Letter (Aug. 8, 1985); Scott, FTC Informal Staff Opinion Letter (Mar. 1, 1985).

129 Scott, FTC Informal Staff Opinion Letter (Aug. 8, 1985).

130 *Id.*

131 *Id.*

132 Mewhinney, FTC Informal Staff Opinion Letter (Feb. 16, 1989) (Letter 2); Geary, FTC Informal Staff Opinion Letter (Mar. 22, 1985); Scott, FTC Informal Staff Opinion Letter (Mar. 1, 1985).

133 Mewhinney, FTC Informal Staff Opinion Letter (Feb. 16, 1989) (Letter 2); Scott, FTC Informal Staff Opinion Letter (Aug. 8, 1985); Scott, FTC Informal Staff Opinion Letter (Mar. 1, 1985).

134 Geary, FTC Informal Staff Opinion Letter (Mar. 22, 1985); Chamness, FTC Informal Staff Opinion Letter (Feb. 11, 1985); Scott, FTC Informal Staff Opinion Letter (Mar. 1, 1985).

135 Mewhinney, FTC Informal Staff Opinion Letter (Feb. 16, 1989) (Letter 2); Geary, FTC Informal Staff Opinion Letter (Mar. 22,

- Musical instruments;[136]
- Home computers and computer equipment;[137]
- Lawn equipment;[138]
- Mechanic and carpenter tools;[139]
- Boats;[140]
- Snowmobiles;[141]
- Stamp and coin collections;[142]
- Stereo equipment;[143]
- Bank deposits;[144]
- Credit insurance proceeds;[145]
- Tape players;[146] and
- VCRs.[147]

The FTC staff considers "personal effects" to be limited to items that an individual would ordinarily carry about on his or her person and possessions of a uniquely personal nature, such as family photographs, personal papers, or a Bible.[148] Where the FTC rule is unclear, state law will determine whether an item is considered furniture or an appliance.[149] A security interest in "fixtures" is permissible even if it includes items that might be considered household goods if they were not attached to the real property.[150]

As mentioned earlier, many of these staff exclusions from the definition of household goods seem at variance with the full Commission's opinion in its Statement of Basis and Purpose for the rule.[151] Consumer attorneys should not view these staff opinions as binding on the courts, but must be aware that creditors may use these letters as justification for their practices.

A creditor who lists a security interest in household goods violates the rule even if a clause in the contract says that the security interest does not apply to non-purchase money consumer loans.[152] The clause might not be clear to all consumers, thus leading them to believe that the creditor had the power to repossess their household goods.

A purchase-money security interest in household goods may be retained when the credit transaction is consolidated or refinanced, even by a new creditor,[153] as long as the new creditor makes a reasonably prudent business judgment that the original transaction complied with the rule.[154] This is true regardless of the number of times the transaction is consolidated or refinanced.[155] A blanket security interest in household goods that was taken before the rule's effective date may not, however, be retained if the transaction is refinanced or renewed after the effective date.[156] A cross-collateralization clause that applies a purchase money security interest in household goods to other extensions of credit does not violate the rule if it is limited to refinancings or consolidations of the original purchase money transaction.[157] But presumably the converse is also true: a cross-collateralization clause that is not limited to refinancings or consolidations does violate the rule.

5.1.1.2.8 *Pyramiding late charges*

The prohibition against pyramiding late charges does not, according to the FTC staff, affect a creditor's choice of accounting methods, as long as the method chosen does not result in the assessment of late charges where the only delinquency is attributable to late charges assessed on earlier installments.[158] The rule does not prevent a creditor from assessing a late charge for each month that an installment remains unpaid.[159] Nor does it dictate which month a late payment is applied to—the month when it was due or the month in which it was actually paid.[160]

1985); Scott, FTC Informal Staff Opinion Letter (Mar. 1, 1985).

136 Mewhinney, FTC Informal Staff Opinion Letter (Feb. 16, 1989) (Letter 2); Geary, FTC Informal Staff Opinion Letter (Mar. 22, 1985); Chamness, FTC Informal Staff Opinion Letter (Feb. 11, 1985); Scott, FTC Informal Staff Opinion Letter (Mar. 1, 1985).

137 Geary, FTC Informal Staff Opinion Letter (Mar. 22, 1985); Scott, FTC Informal Staff Opinion Letter (Mar. 1, 1985).

138 Mewhinney, FTC Informal Staff Opinion Letter (Feb. 16, 1989) (Letter 1); Mewhinney, FTC Informal Staff Opinion Letter (Feb. 16, 1989) (Letter 2); Scott, FTC Informal Staff Opinion Letter (Mar. 1, 1985).

139 Scott, FTC Informal Staff Opinion Letter (Mar. 1, 1985).

140 Scott, FTC Informal Staff Opinion Letter (Mar. 1, 1985).

141 *Id.*

142 Scott, FTC Informal Staff Opinion Letter (Mar. 1, 1985); Geary, FTC Informal Staff Opinion Letter (Mar. 22, 1985).

143 Scott, FTC Informal Staff Opinion Letter (Mar. 1, 1985).

144 Bucchi, FTC Informal Staff Opinion Letter (June 21, 1985).

145 *Id.*

146 Mewhinney, FTC Informal Staff Opinion Letter (Feb. 16, 1989) (Letter 2).

147 *Id.*

148 Scott, FTC Informal Staff Opinion Letter (Aug. 8, 1985); Chamness, FTC Informal Staff Opinion Letter (Feb. 11, 1985); Scott, FTC Informal Staff Opinion Letter (Mar. 1, 1985); Dyer, FTC Informal Staff Opinion Letter (May 1, 1984).

149 Dyer, FTC Informal Staff Opinion Letter (May 1, 1984).

150 Hazlett, FTC Informal Staff Opinion Letter (Apr. 16, 1985).

151 *See* 49 Fed. Reg. 7763 (Mar. 1, 1984).

152 Henry, FTC Informal Staff Opinion Letter (Sept. 27, 1988).

153 Lax, FTC Informal Staff Opinion Letter (Mar. 6, 1987); Feldman, FTC Informal Staff Opinion Letter (Feb. 20, 1985); Wilkinson, FTC Informal Staff Opinion Letter (June 28, 1985); Chamness, FTC Informal Staff Opinion Letter (June 28, 1985).

154 Chamness, FTC Informal Staff Opinion Letter (June 28, 1985).

155 *Id.*

156 Wilkinson, FTC Informal Staff Opinion Letter (June 28, 1985); Chamness, FTC Informal Staff Opinion Letter (June 28, 1985) (security interest may be retained in post-rule refinancing only if original transaction was a purchase money extension of credit).

157 Lax, FTC Informal Staff Opinion Letter (Mar. 6, 1987); Torkildson, FTC Informal Staff Opinion Letter (July 1, 1985); Torkildson, FTC Informal Staff Opinion Letter (Apr. 17, 1985).

158 O'Connell, FTC Informal Staff Opinion Letter (May 31, 1985); Caspo, FTC Informal Staff Opinion Letter (Dec. 21, 1984).

159 Bucchi, FTC Informal Staff Opinion Letter (June 21, 1985); Caspo, FTC Informal Staff Opinion Letter (Dec. 21, 1984).

160 Caspo, FTC Informal Staff Opinion Letter (Dec. 21, 1984).

5.1.1.2.9 Cosigner warning notice

The notice to cosigners required by the rule, warning them of their potential obligations, must be in the form prescribed by the FTC.[161] References to creditor remedies that are not allowed under a particular state's laws may be deleted, however, in order to make the notice accurate.[162] The creditor may add summary identifying information such as the date, account number, name, address, and loan amount,[163] and a signature line,[164] and can print the notice on its letterhead,[165] but should not include any other statements[166] or information about such matters as the creditor's insurance or its national affiliations.[167]

The rule is not violated by including Spanish and English versions[168] or a state law version and the FTC version of the notice[169] on the same sheet. Creditors may also modify the notice by substituting a word such as "buyer" for "borrower" if necessary to make the notice an accurate reflection of the underlying transaction.[170] The type size and style of the notice should be clear and conspicuous.[171]

A person who signs to be liable on someone else's consumer credit contract but does not receive compensation is a cosigner under the rule even if he or she is described as a "buyer" in the contract documents.[172] A person who is to be the co-owner of the property purchased or is to share in its use, however, is not a cosigner.[173] Nonetheless, if a person's signature is obtained after the initial applicant is told that the signature of another person is necessary, that person is a co-signer even if his or her name is also placed on the title documents.[174] In seeking to establish that a person shown as a co-buyer or sole buyer is actually a co-signer, it is helpful to subpoena the dealer's file at the earliest possible moment. Usually it will have a credit application signed by the real principal buyer. Both persons' credit reports should also be obtained, to see if and when the dealer checked their credit records.

A person who merely provides collateral for an extension of credit without becoming obligated on the underlying debt is not considered a cosigner.[175] The same is true where two people apply for a loan together and are both entitled to receive the proceeds.[176] A creditor does not violate the rule by providing the notice to persons involved in the transaction who may not technically be "cosigners," as long as there is no deception.[177]

5.1.1.2.10 Private UDAP actions utilizing the FTC rule

There is generally no private right of action under the FTC Act for a violation of an FTC rule.[178] It seems clear, however, that a consumer can challenge an FTC Credit Practices Rule violation under the almost forty state UDAP statutes that prohibit "unfair" and/or "unconscionable" practices.[179] The rule is an official FTC ruling that use of

161 Moore, FTC Informal Staff Opinion Letter (Mar. 1, 1985).

162 Lozoff, FTC Informal Staff Opinion Letter (May 22, 1986); LaBarfera, FTC Informal Staff Opinion Letter (Nov. 19, 1985); Gwynne, FTC Informal Staff Opinion Letter (Sept. 17, 1985); Gwynne, FTC Informal Staff Opinion Letter (July 12, 1985); Lozoff, FTC Informal Staff Opinion Letter (Mar. 6, 1985); Kinsler, FTC Informal Staff Opinion Letter (Mar. 1, 1985); Kaswell, FTC Informal Staff Opinion Letter (Mar. 20, 1985); Scott, FTC Informal Staff Opinion Letter (Mar. 1, 1985).

163 Topoluk, FTC Informal Staff Opinion Letter (Mar. 10, 1986); Kaswell, FTC Informal Staff Opinion Letter (Mar. 20, 1985); Miller, FTC Informal Staff Opinion Letter (Feb. 25, 1985); Colello, FTC Informal Staff Opinion Letter (July 1, 1985); Gwynne, FTC Informal Staff Opinion Letter (July 12, 1985); Dayton, FTC Informal Staff Opinion Letter (Nov. 18, 1985); Dyer, FTC Informal Staff Opinion Letter (May 1, 1984).

164 Meegan, FTC Informal Staff Opinion Letter (Feb. 19, 1985); Miller, FTC Informal Staff Opinion Letter (Feb. 25, 1985); Colello, FTC Informal Staff Opinion Letter (July 1, 1985); Gwynne, FTC Informal Staff Opinion Letter (July 12, 1985); Dyer, FTC Informal Staff Opinion Letter (May 1, 1984); Feldman, FTC Informal Staff Opinion Letter (July 24, 1984); Caspo, FTC Informal Staff Opinion Letter (Dec. 21, 1984).

165 Meegan, FTC Informal Staff Opinion Letter (Feb. 19, 1985); Miller, FTC Informal Staff Opinion Letter (Feb. 25, 1985); Colello, FTC Informal Staff Opinion Letter (July 1, 1985); Feldman, FTC Informal Staff Opinion Letter (July 24, 1984); Caspo, FTC Informal Staff Opinion Letter (Dec. 21, 1984).

166 Weise, FTC Informal Staff Opinion Letter (Apr. 26, 1985). *But see* Harter, FTC Informal Staff Opinion Letter (June 12, 1987) (statement that creditor is required to give the notice in certain circumstances is allowed).

167 Meegan, FTC Informal Staff Opinion Letter (Feb. 19, 1985).

168 Waterman, FTC Informal Staff Opinion Letter (Apr. 18, 1985).

169 Harter, FTC Informal Staff Opinion Letter (June 12, 1987); Topoluk, FTC Informal Staff Opinion Letter (Mar. 10, 1986); Caspo, FTC Informal Staff Opinion Letter (Dec. 21, 1984).

170 Feldman, FTC Informal Staff Opinion Letter (July 24, 1984).

171 Caspo, FTC Informal Staff Opinion Letter (Dec. 21, 1984).

172 Mintz, FTC Informal Staff Opinion Letter (Dec. 9, 1986); *see* Qualkenbush v. Harris Trust & Sav. Bank, 219 F. Supp. 2d 935 (N.D. Ill. 2002); *see also* definition of "cosigner" at 16 C.F.R. § 444.1(k); Lee v. Nationwide Cassel, L.P., 660 N.E.2d 94 (Ill. App. Ct. 1995) (seller may violate UDAP statute by listing cosigner as co-buyer, contrary to state law), *rev'd in part on other grounds*, 174 Ill. 2d 540, 675 N.E.2d 599 (1996).

173 Riley, FTC Informal Staff Opinion Letter (July 10, 1985); Norskog, FTC Informal Staff Opinion Letter (June 11, 1985); Stodard, FTC Informal Staff Opinion Letter (July 10, 1985); Caspo, FTC Informal Staff Opinion Letter (Dec. 21, 1984) (co-owner of real estate that is to be improved through the credit transaction is a buyer, not a cosigner, even if he or she does not reside there). *See also* Rudolph, FTC Informal Staff Opinion Letter (May 19, 1985) (person who is already obligated on a debt, and then finds another person to buy the property and sign the note, is not a cosigner).

174 FTC, Regulatory Flexibility Act Review of Trade Regulation Rule Concerning Credit Practices, 60 Fed. Reg. 24805, 24806 (May 10, 1995).

175 Lynott, FTC Informal Staff Opinion Letter (Feb. 22, 1985); Witzel, FTC Informal Staff Opinion Letter (Mar. 22, 1985).

176 Witzel, FTC Informal Staff Opinion Letter (Mar. 22, 1985).

177 Miller, FTC Informal Staff Opinion Letter (Feb. 25, 1985).

178 *See* § 9.1, *infra*.

179 *Cf.* Provident Fin. Co. v. Rowe, 101 N.C. App. 367, 399 S.E.2d

certain creditor remedies is an "unfair" trade practice. This FTC ruling guides courts in interpreting what is unfair under a state UDAP statute. Moreover, it may be a *per se* state UDAP violation to violate an FTC rule.[180]

Even in states where the UDAP statute prohibits only "deceptive" practices, it is deceptive for a creditor to violate the rule because including illegal provisions in a credit agreement misrepresents the consumer's legal rights.[181] It is certainly deceptive for a creditor to make false threats that it will utilize remedies that are now outlawed.

Since a contract term prohibited by the FTC rule is unlawful, creditors have no right to enforce that term.[182] A consumer can therefore base a defense on a violation of the Credit Practices Rule, or can bring an affirmative suit to declare a contract provision unenforceable.

The federal Truth in Lending Act (TILA) may provide another remedy where a creditor takes a security interest in violation of the FTC rule. TILA requires disclosure of the security interest, and disclosure of an invalid and unenforceable security interest may be a disclosure violation leading to a significant award of statutory damages and attorney fees.[183]

5.1.1.2.11 Attempts to circumvent FTC Credit Practices Rule

Some creditors seek to circumvent the FTC Credit Practices Rule. In particular, many finance companies have not given up their exorbitant profits from the sale of credit property insurance on household goods collateral. Instead, these companies closely analyze FTC staff opinion letters to determine what types of collateral are not prohibited by the rule's ban on "household goods" collateral. These creditors take non-purchase money security interests in second televisions and radios, and in such items as lawn equipment, tools, stereos, VCR's, jewelry (other than wedding rings), cameras, typewriters, firearms, bicycles, and musical instruments. The creditor then sells credit property insurance on these items.

The values of these items are often exaggerated in the collateral inventory, thus increasing premium costs. In some states, such an exaggerated evaluation may also be used to avoid state legislation prohibiting security interests in items under a specified value. Also closely examine whether the creditor is selling duplicate coverage for items already covered by the debtor's own household insurance policy.

Finance companies wishing to take consumer goods as collateral can no longer identify the property as "all household goods," but must identify each specific item. Many creditors use a preprinted form listing the types of collateral falling outside the FTC rule's definition of "household goods," and then just check appropriate items. For example, a creditor might check "jewelry," "stereo," and "tools." But a valid security agreement must identify collateral with particularity so a sheriff or other party knows precisely what property to seize.[184] It is unlikely that checking boxes on a preprinted form will suffice. Consequently, the security interest would be invalid, attempts or threats to enforce the interest would be actionable, and disclosure of the interest may be deceptive or violate Truth in Lending disclosure requirements.

The FTC staff has also stated that it is unfair and deceptive to try to evade the rule by taking a prohibited security interest in household goods and then later disclaiming that interest in the contract. The creditor listed as security various non-purchase money interests in household goods. Elsewhere, the contract stated that the contract did not take any non-purchase money security interests in household goods if the loan was for personal, family or household purposes. The FTC staff said this should be regarded as an attempt to evade the rule and, as such, is unfair and deceptive.[185]

---

368 (1991) (appellate court returns issue to trial court after UDAP claim was dismissed). *But see* Zhang v. Southeastern Financial Group, Inc., 980 F. Supp. 787 (E.D. Pa. 1997) (violation of FTC rule prohibiting confession of judgment provisions did not violate Pennsylvania UDAP statute; Pennsylvania courts "routinely" uphold and enforce confessed judgments in connection with consumer transactions).

180 *See* § 3.2.7, *supra*.

181 *See* Iron & Glass Bank v. Franz, 9 Pa. D. & C.3d 419 (C.P. Allegheny Cty. 1978); *see also* People v. McKale, 25 Cal. 3d 626, 602 P.2d 731, 159 Cal. Rptr. 811 (1980); Orlando v. Finance One, 369 S.E.2d 882 (W. Va. 1988). *See generally* §§ 3.2.7.4.2, *supra*, § 5.2.8, *infra*.

182 *In re* Raymond, 103 B.R. 846 (Bankr. W.D. Ky. 1989) (security interest unenforceable); Boyer v. ITT Financial Services (*In re* Boyer), 63 B.R. 153 (Bankr. E.D. Mo. 1986) (security interest unenforceable); Free Bridge Auto Sales v. Fitzgerald, 48 Va. Cir. 1, 1999 Va. Cir. LEXIS 13 (Circ. Ct. 1999) (waiver of exemptions unenforceable). *See also* U.S. v. Action Loan Co., Civil No. 3:00CV-511-H (W.D. Ky. Aug. 24, 2000) (consent decree nullifying waivers of exemptions and extinguishing security interests in household goods that violated Credit Practices Rule), *available at* www.ftc.gov/os/2000/08/actionloancon.htm; W. Va. Code § 46A-2-104(a) (providing that no person shall be held liable as cosigner or charged with personal liability for payment in consumer credit sale, lease, or loan, unless creditor gave notice of potential liability).

183 National Consumer Law Center, Truth in Lending § 4.6.7.4 (5th ed. 2003 and Supp.). *But see* Szumny v. Am. Gen. Fin., 246 F.3d 1065 (7th Cir. 2001) (bona fide attempt to describe a security interest in household goods is not TIL violation even if security interest might be invalid under Credit Practices Rule).

184 National Consumer Law Center, Repossessions and Foreclosures § 3.2.7 (5th ed. 2002 and Supp.).

185 FTC Informal Staff Letter of Sandra Wilmore to the Legal Aid Society of Northwest North Carolina (Sept. 27, 1988). *See also* Orlando v. Finance One, 369 S.E.2d 882 (W. Va. 1988) (waiver of exemption rights contrary to state law is deceptive even though contract clause made it inapplicable to these transactions).

5.1.1.3 Challenging Other Creditor Remedies

5.1.1.3.1 Using the FTC unfairness theory, as applied in the Credit Practices Rule

The FTC Credit Practices Rule Statement of Basis and Purpose[186] is significant because it provides an "unfairness" approach which can apply to many kinds of adhesive consumer credit provisions, and not just the six creditor remedies prohibited by the rule. The FTC defines an unfair practice as one that (1) causes substantial injury (including emotional distress); (2) is not outweighed by any countervailing benefits to consumers or competition; and (3) consumers themselves could not reasonably have avoided.[187]

This analysis is further bolstered by the District of Columbia Circuit (D.C. Circuit) opinion upholding the Credit Practices Rule.[188] The D.C. Circuit specifically approved of the FTC's three-part unfairness test, describing this standard as "the most precise definition of unfairness articulated by either the Commission or Congress," and finding that the FTC had properly applied this standard in its Credit Practices Rule.

The D.C. Circuit rejected creditor arguments that "unfairness" is limited to situations of seller misconduct or overreaching, such as practices involving seller deception, coercion, or withholding of material information. The court pointed to the FTC's Holder Rule[189] as precedent for the FTC's authority to correct allocations of post-purchase remedies. Even where the seller does nothing wrong, a practice can be unfair "where the seller takes advantage of an existing obstacle which prevents free consumer choice from effectuating a self-correcting market."

The D.C. Circuit found such an imperfect market in the extension of consumer credit because consumers can not bargain over the contractors' creditor remedies and because creditors have no incentive to compete on the basis of the creditor remedies offered. A creditor remedy can thus be unfair even if it does not result from the creditor's deception, coercion, or non-disclosure, as long as it causes substantial consumer injury, not outweighed by countervailing benefits to competition.

The FTC Statement of Basis and Purpose details how this three part unfairness test applies to consumer credit contracts. Taking the third element first, the FTC concludes that consumers can not reasonably avoid creditor remedies found in standard form credit agreements:

> The economic exigencies of extending credit to large numbers of consumers each day make standardization a necessity. . . .
>
> Consumers have limited incentives to search out better remedial provisions in credit contracts. The substantive similarities of contracts from different creditors mean that a search is less likely to reveal a different alternative. Because remedies are relevant only in the event of default, and default is relatively infrequent, consumers reasonably concentrate their search on such factors as interest rates and payment terms. Searching for credit contracts is also difficult, because contracts are written in obscure technical language, do not use standardized terminology, and may not be provided before the transaction is consummated. Individual creditors have little incentive to provide better terms and explain their benefits to consumers, because a costly education effort would be required with all creditors sharing the benefits. Moreover, such a campaign might differentially attract relatively high risk borrowers.
>
> For these reasons, the Commission concludes that consumers can not reasonably avoid the remedial provisions themselves. Nor can consumers, having signed a contract, avoid the harsh consequences of remedies by avoiding default. When default occurs, it is most often a response to events such as unemployment or illness that are not within the borrower's control. Thus consumers can not reasonably avoid the substantial injury these creditor remedies may inflict.[190]

Consequently, an adhesive creditor remedy is unfair if it causes substantial injury not outweighed by countervailing benefits.

The Statement of Basis and Purpose gives useful examples of how the six prohibited creditor remedies cause substantial injury, both economic and emotional. The Statement also notes that all debtors, and not just defaulting consumers, suffer harm from harsh creditor remedies because even non-defaulting debtors live under the threat of the severe remedies. The ban on a creditor remedy protects these consumers in the same way as an insurance policy.[191]

In considering the countervailing benefits of creditor remedies, the Statement points out that one must consider the marginal benefit of a particular creditor remedy, and not the benefit of creditor remedies in general. That is, what is the extra benefit to competition of a particular remedy assuming the creditor still has a varied arsenal of other remedies to choose from, such as repossession, suit, garnishment, acceleration, and direct collection contacts.[192]

Consider a specific example of how powerful this FTC analysis can be in challenging creditor remedies. Credit contracts typically waive the debtor's right to notice that the note has been accelerated. The FTC has ruled that debtors

186 49 Fed. Reg. 7763 (Mar. 1, 1984).

187 *See* § 4.3.2, *supra*.

188 American Financial Services Ass'n v. FTC, 767 F.2d 957 (D.C. Cir. 1985), *cert. denied*, 475 U.S. 1011 (1986).

189 16 C.F.R. § 433 [*reprinted at* Appx. B.2.1, *infra*].

190 Statement of Basis and Purpose, 49 Fed. Reg. 7744 (Mar. 1, 1984) (footnotes omitted).

191 *Id.*

192 *Id.*

can not avoid this or other creditor remedies. Consequently, the sole issue before a court in determining this practice's unfairness under a state UDAP statute is whether the resulting economic and emotional consequences of unexpected (and sometimes mistaken) acceleration and repossession are outweighed by the benefits of not having to notify the debtor of the acceleration.

That practices relating to these creditor remedies have not yet been found unfair by a final FTC trade regulation rule does not mean that they can not be successfully challenged in a state UDAP case. The FTC Staff Report will be useful in such a challenge, providing legal arguments why these practices are unfair.

The fact that a creditor does not, or claims not to, enforce a particular clause does not mean that its inclusion in the contract is not unfair or deceptive. Such a position would mean that creditors could reap the benefits of the clause's *in terroram* effect on consumers without any consequences.[193]

Of course, one must also determine whether challenges to creditor remedies are within the scope of a UDAP statute. A few UDAP statutes have been interpreted to apply only to sales practices and not to related credit transactions.[194] If credit practices are covered by a UDAP statute, challenges need not be limited to unfair adhesion provisions, but can involve misrepresentations inconsistent with credit agreement provisions, the failure to disclose the complete nature of creditor remedies, or other practices that fall within traditional UDAP notions of deception.

5.1.1.3.2 Case law finding creditor remedies unfair or deceptive

Other sections discuss when debt collection, repossessions, and foreclosures are unfair or deceptive. *See* §§ 5.1.1.1, *supra*, 5.1.1.5, 5.1.1.6, *infra*. This subsection examines when other creditor remedies are unfair or deceptive, including collection fees, waivers of exemption rights, and default penalties.

Creditors sometimes seek to assess debtors an extra charge for the cost of turning an account over to a collection agency. The FTC has sued a creditor for imposing a 20% collection fee on accounts referred to a collection agency, finding that the fee was not authorized by a contractual attorney-fee provision.[195] California's Supreme Court has held that where a credit agreement authorizes collection of additional expenses, it is unfair to seek an additional one-third of the debt for such expenses, even when a collection agency charges the creditor one-third of the debt to collect the debt.[196] It is a UDAP violation to charge a disproportionate late fee that is void as a penalty under common law.[197]

The West Virginia Supreme Court has found deceptive a contractual provision waiving the consumer's rights to exempt certain property from seizure. The waiver was only "to the extent permitted by law," and West Virginia prohibits such a waiver. The creditor argued that the contractual provision was not deceptive because the provision had no effect as it was not "permitted by law." But the court found the provision misleading and likely to cause confusion or misunderstanding.[198]

The FTC has ruled it unfair for creditors to use contract terms that result in an overly harsh penalty (the consumer's loss of the property purchased and default of all previous payments) in the event of default.[199] It is deceptive to calculate late charges in the traditional manner accepted by the industry, if this approach is at variance with the language of the credit agreement. This is the case even if the creditor did not draft the original loan document.[200] Charging excessive late payment penalties has been found to be a UDAP violation.[201] It can also be a UDAP violation to attempt to collect late charges to which a creditor is not entitled because of the debtor's bankruptcy reorganization.[202]

One court has held that it was not a UDAP violation to fail to disclose to debtors the implications of a credit agreement's use of the Rule of 78s to rebate unearned interest where state and federal law explicitly authorized this method.[203] The holding was further supported by an explicit exclusion in the UDAP statute for practices "authorized" by state or federal law.[204]

It is deceptive to advertise "easy credit" and then use harsh credit remedies.[205] A creditor violates a UDAP statute by knowingly conspiring to collect a judgment it knows is unenforceable.[206]

Finally, a number of creditor remedies have been found unconscionable under the Uniform Commercial Code section 2-302. These unconscionable creditor remedies include

193 *See* Baierl v. McTaggart, 245 Wis. 2d 632, 629 N.W.2d 277 (2001) (refusing to allow illegal clause to be severed so that remainder of lease could be enforced). *See generally* § 5.2.3.3, *infra*.

194 *See* § 2.2.1, *supra*.

195 City Stores Co., 90 F.T.C. 415 (1977) (consent order).

196 Bondanza v. Peninsula Hosp. & Medical Center, 23 Cal. 3d 260, 590 P.2d 22, 152 Cal. Rptr. 446 (1979).

197 District Cablevision Ltd. P'ship v. Bassin, 828 A.2d 714 (D.C. 2003).

198 Orlando v. Finance One, 369 S.E.2d 882 (W. Va. 1988).

199 AMREP Corp., 102 F.T.C. 1362 (1983), *aff'd*, 768 F.2d 1171 (10th Cir. 1985); Horizon Corp., 97 F.T.C. 464 (1981); Mutual Home Equip. Co., 87 F.T.C. 606 (1976).

200 Andrews v. Fleet Real Estate Funding Corp., 78 B.R. 78 (Bankr. E.D. Pa. 1987).

201 Cotton v. Stanley, 86 N.C. App. 534, 358 S.E.2d 692 (1987).

202 Smith v. Keycorp Mortgage Inc., 151 B.R. 870 (N.D. Ill. 1993).

203 Lanier v. Associates Fin., Inc., 134 Ill. App. 3d 183, 479 N.E.2d 1227 (1985).

204 815 Ill. Comp. Stat. Ann. § 505/10b(1).

205 Tashof v. FTC, 437 F.2d 707 (D.C. Cir. 1970).

206 Kennedy v. First Nat'l Bank, 551 N.E.2d 1002 (Ill. App. Ct. 1990).

cross-collateral[207] or waiver-of-defense[208] clauses, consent to breach of the peace on self-help repossession,[209] and waiver of the consumer's interest in personal property seized with the collateral unless the creditor is notified.[210] Practices found unconscionable under the UCC can be argued to be unfair or unconscionable pursuant to a UDAP statute.[211]

On the other hand, courts have upheld several established creditor remedies. Massachusetts' highest court refused to find (in a non-consumer case) that self-help repossession was *per se* unfair.[212] A Washington court refused to strike down a due-on-sale clause where there was no showing of oppression or substantial injury.[213] Nor does a bank have a duty to inform depositors that a hold has been placed on their account because of their default on a loan.[214] It is not a UDAP violation for a bank to extend the due date of a loan, even if the extension is concealed from a co-obligor.[215]

5.1.1.4 Abuse of Process, Inconvenient Venue

It is unfair to sue a consumer in an inconvenient venue. A creditor who filed collection suits in Virginia against California debtors committed UDAP violations.[216] Despite a state long-arm statute permitting a mail order firm to sue debtors where the mail order house is located, the Seventh Circuit has upheld an FTC decision stating that the suit must be brought where the debtor lives or signed the contract.[217] Likewise, it is a UDAP violation to file collection suits in improper counties,[218] or in districts other than where the consumer resides or signed the contract, even where the state venue statute authorizes the choice of district.[219] Creditors can not seek to have consumers waive this right to a convenient venue.[220] Attorneys and debt collectors who file collection suits in inconvenient forums also risk liability under the venue abuse provisions of the Fair Debt Collection Practices Act.[221]

Some merchants utilize contracts where small "mom and pop" businesses or consumers purchasing business opportunities consent to being sued in an inconvenient venue. These merchants claim that the FTC, UDAP, and Fair Debt Collection Practices Act precedent does not apply to such "commercial" transactions, only to consumer transaction. Nevertheless, the FTC and seven attorneys general offices have sued Leasecomm Corporation alleging that it is an unfair practice in connection with the financing of a business opportunity to use a venue waiver provision or file a lawsuit in a place other than a small business' residence or where the contract was executed.[222] In a consent agreement, Leasecomm agreed to discontinue the practice.[223]

A creditor who follows a practice of filing collection suits after the statute of limitations has run violates a UDAP

207 Williams v. Walker-Thomas Furniture Co., 350 F.2d 445 (D.C. Cir. 1965); *In re* Jackson, 9 U.C.C. Rep. 1152 (Bankr. W.D. Mo. 1971).

208 Quality Fin. Co. v. Hurley, 337 Mass. 150, 148 N.E.2d 385 (1958); Unico v. Owen, 50 N.J. 101, 232 A.2d 405 (1967).

209 Kosches v. Nichols, 68 Misc. 2d 795, 327 N.Y.S.2d 968 (Civ. Ct. 1971).

210 Dean v. Universal CIT Credit Corp., 114 N.J. Super. 132, 275 A.2d 154 (1971).

211 *See* §§ 4.3.12, 4.4, *supra*.

212 Penney v. First Nat'l Bank of Boston, 385 Mass. 715, 433 N.E.2d 901 (1982).

213 Magney v. Lincoln Mut. Savings Bank, 34 Wash. App. 45, 659 P.2d 537 (1983).

214 Southington Savings Bank v. Rodgers, 40 Conn. App. 23, 668 A.2d 733 (1995).

215 Norwich Savings Society v. Caldrello, 38 Conn. App. 859, 663 A.2d 415 (1995).

216 Yu v. Signet Bank/Virginia, 69 Cal. App. 4th 1377, 82 Cal. Rptr. 3d 304 (1999) (reversing grant of summary judgment to defendant), *decision on later appeal*, 103 Cal. App. 4th 298, 126 Cal. Rptr. 2d 516 (2002) (reaffirming original holding).

217 Spiegel v. FTC, 540 F.2d 287 (7th Cir. 1976), *aff'g* 86 F.T.C. 425 (1975), *request for modification denied*, 89 F.T.C. 174 (1977).

218 Barquis v. Merchants Collection Ass'n, 7 Cal. 3d 94, 496 P.2d 817, 101 Cal. Rptr. 745 (1972); Connecticut Student Loan Found. v. Newtown, Clearinghouse No. 36,596 (Conn. Super. Ct. 1982) (even unintentional filing in wrong venue is UDAP violation); Bank of New Orleans & Trust Co. v. Phillips, 415 So. 2d 973 (La. Ct. App. 1982). *See also* Zanni v. Lippold, Clearinghouse No. 39,435 (C.D. Ill. 1986) (denial of motion to dismiss UDAP action alleging use of improper venue); Community Credit Plan, Inc. v. Johnson, 228 Wis. 2d 30, 596 N.W.2d 799 (1999) (filing replevin suits in inconvenient county, contrary to state venue rules, violated state debt collection statute). *But cf.* Rusk Indus. v. Alexander, 2002 Ohio App. LEXIS 2137 (May 3, 2002) (single instance of venue abuse not a violation; must be a practice).

219 J.C. Penney Co., 109 F.T.C. 54 (1987) (consent order); Marathon Oil Co., 92 F.T.C. 422 (1978) (consent order); S.S. Kresge Co., 90 F.T.C. 222 (1977) (consent order); New Rapids Carpet Center, Inc., 90 F.T.C. 64 (1977); Commercial Service Co., 86 F.T.C. 467 (1975) (consent order); Benny v. Aldens, Inc., Clearinghouse No. 37,522B (Ill. Cir. Ct. 1984); Schubach v. Household Fin. Corp., 375 Mass. 133, 376 N.E.2d 140 (1978); Celebrezze v. United Research, Inc., 19 Ohio App. 3d 49, 482 N.E.2d 1260 (1984); Santiago v. S.S. Kresge Co., 2 Ohio Op. 3d 54 (C.P. Cuyahoga Cty. 1976). *See also* Zanni v. Lippold, 119 F.R.D. 32 (C.D. Ill. 1988) (certifying class action); Sellers v. United Home Food Distributors, Inc., Clearinghouse No. 44,043E (Bankr. W.D. Okla. 1990). *But see* First Nat'l Bank of Commerce v. Brown, 525 So. 2d 672 (La. Ct. App. 1988); Vargas v. Allied Fin. Co., 545 S.W.2d 231 (Tex. App. 1977) (Texas UDAP statute subsequently amended to prohibit venue abuse Vargas allows).

220 West Coast Credit Corp., 84 F.T.C. 1328 (1974) (consent order); *see also* Paragon Homes, Inc. v. Carter, 56 Misc. 2d 463, 288 N.Y.S.2d 817 (Sup. Ct.), *aff'd*, 30 App. Div. 2d 1052, 295 N.Y.S.2d 606 (1968) (Uniform Commercial Code unconscionability). *But see* Carnival Cruise Lines, Inc. v. Shute, 499 U.S. 585, 111 S. Ct. 1522, 113 L. Ed. 2d 622 (1991) (in a non-UDAP case, Court upholds validity, under circumstances of that case, of clause forcing individual to sue corporation in distant forum).

221 15 U.S.C. § 1692i. *See* National Consumer Law Center, Fair Debt Collection § 5.9 (5th ed. 2004.).

222 FTC v. Leasecomm (D. Mass. May 22, 2003) (complaint for injunctive and other equitable relief), available at www.ftc.gov.

223 FTC v. Leasecomm (D. Mass. May 26, 2003) (stipulated final judgment and order), available at www.ftc.gov.

regulation modeled on the federal Fair Debt Collection Practices Act.[224]

Using a confusingly worded summons that gives the defendant inadequate or misleading directions as to proper procedures for responding to a complaint is unfair or deceptive.[225] Another unfair practice is "sewer service," obtaining default judgments because defendants do not actually receive the summonses in a timely fashion.[226]

When a debtor contacts a creditor after receiving a summons and agrees to make payment, and the creditor tells the debtor to ignore the summons, it is unfair for the creditor not to file a notice of discontinuance but instead to obtain a default judgment.[227] A court has also allowed a UDAP action to proceed challenging default judgments obtained through affidavits that failed to disclose that the underlying products were not delivered.[228] It is unfair and deceptive to file legal actions against tenants claiming damages to property and cleaning costs before the tenant has vacated or to falsely allege in suits that attorney fees are due and owing.[229] It is also a UDAP violation to file a false affidavit seeking post-default interest at a rate higher than allowed by the credit agreement.[230] In Connecticut, the filing of a single lawsuit may be a UDAP violation if it is objectively meritless or a "sham."[231]

224 Commonwealth v. Cole, 709 A.2d 994 (Pa. Commw. Ct. 1998) (*citing* Kimber v. Federal Financial Corp., 668 F. Supp. 1480 (M.D. Ala. 1987); regulation has now been replaced by a statute).

225 Commercial Service Co., 86 F.T.C. 467 (1975) (consent order). *See also* Agucha K. v. Montgomery Ward Co., 520 P.2d 1352 (Alaska 1974) (summons failed to inform consumer that written appearance could be filed in distant forum violating due process requirements).

226 New Rapids Carpet Center, Inc., 90 F.T.C. 64 (1977); *In re* Smith, 866 F.2d 576, 59 B.R. 298 (Bankr. E.D. Pa. 1986) (failure to comply with notice provision not UDAP violation in circumstances where no harm to debtor).

227 Royal Furniture Co., 93 F.T.C. 422 (1979) (consent order); Pay'N Save Corp., 86 F.T.C. 688 (1975) (consent order).

228 Olive v. Graceland Sales Corp., 61 N.J. 182, 293 A.2d 658 (1972).

229 Love v. Amsler, Clearinghouse No. 44,805 (Minn. Dist. Ct. Hennepin Cty. July 15, 1988), *aff'd*, 441 N.W.2d 555 (Minn. Ct. App. 1989).

230 Fielder v. Credit Acceptance Corp., 19 F. Supp. 2d 966 (W.D. Mo. 1998), *vacated on other grounds*, 188 F.3d 1031 (8th Cir. 1999) (district court did not have authority to issue injunction requiring creditor to move to have state court judgments amended to delete interest overcharges; remands that portion of case to state court).

231 Nationwide Mut. Ins. Co. v. Bland, 2003 WL 23354137 (D. Conn. Mar. 30, 2003); *see also* Zeller v. Consolini, 59 Conn. App. 545, 563 n.7, 758 A.2d 376 (2000) (no UDAP violation if suit not objectively meritless).

5.1.1.5 Unfair and Deceptive Repossession and Pawnshop Practices

5.1.1.5.1 Unfair contract provisions

Often a seemingly abusive repossession or foreclosure practice is authorized in a consumer credit contract signed by the debtor. A growing body of law finds these contract provisions unfair. The FTC Credit Practices Rule is the most important example, prohibiting non-purchase money security interests in household goods.[232]

The FTC applied its unfairness definition[233] to standard form credit contracts that gave creditors blanket security interests in all the consumer's household goods, allowing creditors to threaten defaulting debtors with repossession of all their personal effects, even if the creditor had no intention of repossessing this property. The FTC found that consumers could not reasonably avoid repossession terms in standard form contracts, so the sole issue was whether the repossession provision caused substantial consumer injury not outweighed by countervailing benefits to consumers or competition.[234] The FTC went on to analyze the consumer injury that this provision creates. The injury was not outweighed by countervailing benefits to competition, particularly since creditors have other remedies available beside repossession to protect their rights (e.g., debt collection activities, court judgments, garnishment). The FTC thus concluded that it is unfair merely to include in a credit contract a security interest in household goods.[235]

The D.C. Circuit specifically upheld this unfairness finding and the United States Supreme Court denied *certiorari*.[236] Consequently, this FTC holding is a definitive statement that this form of repossession practice is unfair. The exact type of household goods whose repossession is prohibited and other more detailed aspects of the FTC rule are discussed at § 5.1.1.2.7, *supra,* and in National Consumer Law Center, *Repossessions and Foreclosures*.[237]

The important points are that security interests in most household goods are unfair, that repossession of such house-

232 16 C.F.R. § 444 (effective Mar. 1, 1985). *See also* 49 Fed. Reg. 7740 (Mar. 1, 1984) for the text of the Statement of Basis and Purpose. The rule was upheld in American Fin. Services Ass'n v. FTC, 767 F.2d 957 (D.C. Cir. 1985), *cert. denied* 475 U.S. 1011 (1986). An analogous rule has been adopted by the Federal Home Loan Bank Board applicable to Savings and Loans. *See* 12 C.F.R. Part 535 (effective Jan. 1, 1986). The Federal Reserve Board has also adopted a similar rule applicable to banks it regulates. *See* 12 C.F.R. § 227.11 to 227.16 (effective Jan. 1, 1986).

233 *See* § 4.3.2, *supra.*

234 *See* Statement of Basis and Purpose, 49 Fed. Reg. 7740 (Mar. 1, 1984).

235 *Id.*

236 American Fin. Services Ass'n v. FTC, 767 F.2d 957 (D.C. Cir. 1985), *cert. denied*, 475 U.S. 1011 (1986).

237 § 3.4.2 (5th ed. 2002 and Supp.).

hold goods is also a UDAP violation, and that the FTC has provided powerful precedent for finding other contract provisions dealing with repossessions to be unfair. For example, there should be little question that a standard form consumer credit contract provision is unfair if it authorizes the creditor to enter the buyer's home and retake property without the debtor's permission or legal process,[238] or if it authorizes the creditor to breach the peace in repossessing property.[239] Consumers should also be able to bring an unfairness challenge to standard form provisions that unreasonably limit a debtor's rights when a creditor mistakenly seizes the debtor's personal property along with repossessed collateral (e.g., tools or fishing rods left in the trunk of a repossessed car).[240]

The FTC analysis can provide a basis for challenging other creditor remedies that are commonplace in today's credit agreements. The standard form contract provision waiving the consumer's right to notice of acceleration and repossession, for example, may be unfair. The sole question is whether the consumer injury from lack of notice outweighs the benefits to creditors of avoiding such notice.

There are limits, of course, as to what type of repossession provisions a court will throw out. For example, a non-consumer debtor failed in an attempt to argue that *any* self-help repossession is *per se* unfair.[241]

5.1.1.5.2 Deceptive contract provisions

Another approach is to challenge contract provisions as deceptive if they violate state law. For example, a contract clause giving the creditor the right to accelerate a note upon default is deceptive where state law limits the creditor's right of acceleration.[242] Where a federal or state law gives the consumer the right to cure a default,[243] the contract is deceptive if it implies the creditor can accelerate and repossess immediately without affording the consumer the opportunity to cure.[244]

A credit union engages in a deceptive practice where the loan documents indicate that a retirement account has been taken as collateral on a loan where state law prohibits such property from being security.[245] This is the case even though other loan documents disclaim any intent by the creditor to take the property as security.[246] This misrepresentation was found to be part of an unfair scheme to encourage debtors to transfer money out of their protected retirement account to the consumer's credit union account where the credit union could legally set-off that money against obligations the consumer owed to the credit union.

5.1.1.5.3 Unfair and deceptive repossession conduct

Certain repossession conduct is clearly unfair and deceptive. It is a UDAP violation to repossess property where the creditor has no right to do so,[247] or for a repair shop to seize a car unlawfully and tow it away from the owner's property where a repair bill is overdue.[248] Moving and storage companies that aid in the eviction of a tenant from an apartment may engage in UDAP violations where they sell the warehoused items before the time specified in the notice to the tenant or fail to act carefully as a bailee, resulting in damage

238 *See also* Mutual Home Equip. Co., 87 F.T.C. 606 (1976) (consent order).

239 *See also* Kosches v. Nichols, 68 Misc. 2d 795, 327 N.Y.S.2d 968 (Civ. Ct. 1971) (unconscionability theory).

240 Dean v. Universal CIT Credit Corp., 114 N.J. Super. 132, 275 A.2d 154 (1971) (unconscionability theory); National Consumer Law Center, Repossessions and Foreclosures § 7.4 (5th ed. 2002 and Supp.).

241 Penney v. First Nat'l Bank, 385 Mass. 715, 433 N.E.2d 901 (1982).

242 Levine v. Baldwin, 23 Ohio Op. 3d 436 (Hamilton Cty. 1981); *see also* § 5.2.8, *infra*.

243 National Consumer Law Center, Repossessions and Foreclosures § 4.8.2 (5th ed. 2002 and Supp.).

244 *Cf.* Quiller v. Barclays Am./Credit, Inc., 727 F.2d 1067, *aff'd on rehearing en banc*, 764 F.2d 1400 (11th Cir. 1985), *cert. denied*, 476 U.S. 1124 (1986) (ability to accelerate "subject to any notice of right to cure" too vague to be understood by debtors). *But cf.* Grant v. General Electric Credit Corp., 764 F.2d 1404 (11th Cir. 1985), *cert. denied*, 476 U.S. 1124 (1986) ("provided that Buyer shall be given notice of right to cure default before seller is permitted to exercise that right" is sufficiently clear).

245 Petersen v. State Employees Credit Union (*In re* Kittrell), 115 B.R. 873 (Bankr. M.D.N.C. 1990).

246 *Id.*

247 Holley v. Gurnee Volkswagen & Oldsmobile, Inc., 2001 U.S. Dist. LEXIS 7274 (N.D. Ill. Jan. 4, 2001) (wrongful repossession involves implicit false representation of right to possession); Graham v. Conn. Nat'l Bank, Clearinghouse No. 36,598 (Conn. Super. Ct. 1983) (violation of RISA and U.C.C. repossession standards is automatic UDAP violation); Bryant v. Sears Consumer Financial Corp., 617 So. 2d 1191 (La. Ct. App. 1993); Jones v. Petty, 577 So. 2d 821 (La. Ct. App. 1991); Cook v. Spillers, 574 So. 2d 464 (La. Ct. App. 1991); Chrysler Credit Corp. v. Walker, 488 So. 2d 209 (La. Ct. App. 1986); Moore v. Goodyear Tire & Rubber Co., 364 So. 2d 630 (La. Ct. App. 1978); Atlas Amalgamated, Inc. v. Castillo, 601 S.W.2d 728 (Tex. Civ. App. 1980); Sherwood v. Bellevue Dodge, Inc., 35 Wash. App. 741, 669 P.2d 1258 (1983); *see also* General Inv. Inc. v. Thomas, 400 So. 2d 1081 (La. Ct. App. 1981); Fair Deal Auto Sales v. Brantley, 24 S.W.3d 543 (Tex. App. 2000); § 5.1.1.6, *infra* (similar cases dealing with unlawful home foreclosures); National Consumer Law Center, Consumer Law Pleadings, No. 2, § 12.2 (CD-Rom and Index Guide) for a complaint and TRO motion in a suit seeking damages, replevin, and an injunction against sale of a wrongfully repossessed boat, also found on the CD-Rom accompanying this volume. *Cf.* Barrios v. Associates Commercial Corp., 481 So. 2d 702 (La. Ct. App. 1985) (seizure not unfair where not wrongful, but pursuant to court order). *But see* Purkett v. Key Bank USA, 2001 U.S. Dist. LEXIS 6126 (N.D. Ill. May 9, 2001) (wrongful repossession not deceptive); Ford Motor Credit Co. v. Corbello, 482 So. 2d 203 (La. Ct. App. 1986).

248 Hanner v. Classic Auto Body, Inc., 10 Mass. App. Ct. 121, 406 N.E.2d 686 (1980).

and theft of the tenant's property.[249]

It is deceptive for a creditor to agree to allow car payments to be made after their due date and then repossess the car before the agreed upon payment date.[250] This is the case despite the fact that the written credit agreement was not amended in writing.[251]

It should also be a UDAP violation for a creditor to agree to delay acceleration until a certain date, and then accelerate the note or repossess the collateral before that date.[252] Similarly, it should be a UDAP violation for a creditor to repossess a vehicle after assuring the consumer that the creditor would soon start receiving payments under the debtor's disability insurance policy, and there was nothing to worry about.[253]

Creditors may not represent or imply that they have a lien when they do not[254] and creditors may not permit a lien to be filed or perfected when the consumer has adhered to his or her contractual obligations.[255] Creditors may not represent that they have a right to a deficiency judgment where state law prohibits deficiencies.[256] Using a debt collection analogy, creditors may not threaten to repossess collateral with no intent to actually repossess that collateral.[257] Breach of the peace during repossession may be a UDAP violation as well as a violation of the Uniform Commercial Code.[258]

Repossessors often use trickery to obtain possession of property (for example, asking the consumer to bring a car in for repairs) or misrepresent that they will not seize property. These actions may violate UDAP statutes. For example, it can be a UDAP violation for a creditor to falsely promise a consumer that it would not repossess property while the consumer went to telephone his attorney.[259]

5.1.1.5.4 Unfair or deceptive practices relating to redemption, collateral sales, deficiencies, and surpluses

The FTC has required creditors to disclose material facts to the debtor concerning the right under state law to redeem repossessed collateral.[260] It is a UDAP violation to promise to return a car and reinstate the contract if the debtor pays the arrears, and then renege.[261] It is a UDAP violation to base a deficiency on a post-default interest rate that exceeds the amount allowed in the contract.[262]

A revolving repossession or "churning" scheme is a classic example of an unfair and deceptive practice.[263] A federal court has certified a class action on RICO, fraud, UCC, UDAP, and other claims against a finance company that allegedly participated in such a scheme.[264] The FTC has also ordered a creditor to cease sham sales to itself to eliminate surpluses owed to the debtor.[265]

There is also a good argument that a violation of the Uniform Commercial Code or other state repossession requirements is a *per se* UDAP violation.[266] Since state

249 Nelson v. Schanzer, 788 S.W.2d 81 (Tex. App. 1990).

250 Villarreal v. Elizondo, 831 S.W.2d 474 (Tex. App. 1992).

251 *Id.*

252 *See* Baird v. Norwest Bank, 843 P.2d 327 (Mont. 1992).

253 *See* Entriken v. Motor Coach Federal Credit Union, 845 P.2d 93 (Mont. 1992).

254 Petersen v. State Employees Credit Union (*In re* Kittrell), 115 B.R. 873 (Bankr. M.D.N.C. 1990) (deceptive for creditor to imply that retirement account was collateral when state law prohibited it); Atlas Amalgamated Inc. v. Castillo, 601 S.W.2d 728 (Tex. Civ. App. 1980). *Cf.* Clarkson v. DeCaceres, 105 B.R. 266 (Bankr. E.D. Pa. 1989) (landlord's sale of tenant's property without a lien was conversion and a UDAP violation). *But see* Gaynor v. Union Trust Co., 216 Conn. 458, 582 A.2d 190 (1990) (inadvertent failure to provide fully accurate redemption notice not a UDAP violation); Zinser v. Uptown Fed. Sav. & Loan, 185 Ill. App. 3d 979, 542 N.E.2d 87 (1989) (not a UDAP violation to repossess without notice of intent to enforce contract strictly, where state cases do not require such notice in all circumstances).

255 Code Miss. Rules 24 000 002, Office of the Attorney General Rule 45(4).

256 Chrysler Corp. (Aurora Chrysler-Plymouth), 97 F.T.C. 107 (1981) (consent order).

257 *See* § 5.1.1.1.4, *supra*; *see also* the discussion of household good security interests in § 5.1.1.2.7, *supra*.

258 *See* Clark v. Auto Recovery Bureau, 889 F. Supp. 543 (D. Conn. 1994) (no breach of peace found, so no UDAP violation); *see also* Smith v. A.B. Bonded Locksmith, Inc., 143 Ohio App. 3d 321, 757 N.E.2d 1242 (2001) (no UDAP claim for entry into home since defendants acted pursuant to valid court order).

259 *In re* Daniel, 137 B.R. 884 (D.S.C. 1992).

260 Chrysler Corp. (Aurora Chrysler-Plymouth), 97 F.T.C. 107 (1981) (consent order); Ford Motor Co., 93 F.T.C. 402 (1979) (consent order), *modified on other grounds*, 109 F.T.C. 116 (1987).

261 Patterson v. Chrysler Fin. Co. (*In re* Patterson) 263 B.R. 82 (Bankr. E.D. Pa. 2001).

262 Fielder v. Credit Acceptance Corp., 19 F. Supp. 2d 966 (W.D. Mo. 1998), *vacated on other grounds*, 188 F.3d 1031 (8th Cir. 1999) (appellate decision holds that district court did not have authority to issue injunction requiring creditor to move to have state court judgments amended to delete interest overcharges; remands that portion of case to state court).

263 *See* National Consumer Law Center, Repossessions and Foreclosures § 10.9.4 (5th ed. 2002 and Supp.).

264 Chisolm v. TranSouth Fin. Corp., 184 F.R.D. 556 (E.D. Va. 1999) (certifying class), *later op. at* 194 F.R.D. 538 (E.D. Va. 2000) (refusing to decertify class and ruling on plaintiffs' trial plans).

265 General Motors Corp., 95 F.T.C. 825 (1980) (consent order), *modified on other grounds*, 110 F.T.C. 165 (1988).

266 *See* Graham v. Conn. Nat'l Bank, Clearinghouse No. 36,598 (Conn. Super. Ct. 1983); § 3.2.7, *supra.*; *cf.* Bank of Am. v. Lallana, 64 Cal. Rptr. 2d 168 (Ct. App. 1997) (mere defective repossession notice is not a UDAP violation, but seeking a deficiency where the notice is defective is a UDAP violation), *aff'd on other issues*, 19 Cal. 4th 203, 77 Cal. Rptr. 2d 910, 960 P.2d 1133 (1999) (affirming holding that notice was deficient). *But see* Williams v. Regency Fin. Corp., 309 F.3d 1045 (8th Cir. 2002) (court wrongly characterizes repossession sale as a transaction that does not affect the consumer, despite fact that it disposes of consumer's property and establishes amount of deficiency); Gaynor v. Union Trust Co., 216 Conn. 458, 582 A.2d 190 (1990) (inadvertent failure to provide fully accurate redemption notice not a UDAP violation).

repossession requirements are very detailed, with numerous notice requirements, this is a ripe source of UDAP violations.[267] For example, the failure to send a statute-mandated notice should not only be a *per se* UDAP violation, but also a deceptive nondisclosure of a material fact.

The FTC has ruled that it is unfair to fail to account for a refund to consumers owed surpluses from the sale of repossessed goods, as required by state law.[268] The FTC has also held that in the sale of repossessed automobiles, the creditor can only retain that portion of the proceeds that will pay off the debt and cover the creditor's out-of-pocket expenses (but not overhead) of a commercially reasonable sale.[269] But the Ninth Circuit has reversed that portion of the decision that specified that the dealer's expenses must be calculated with no provision for overhead or profit. The Ninth Circuit found this to be a departure from existing law and practice, and introduced the unique rationale that the FTC should not make such a change through an individual adjudication, but through rulemaking.[270]

5.1.1.5.5 Pawnbrokers' sale of pawned goods

The FTC has accepted a number of consent agreements dealing with practices of trading posts serving Native Americans. These cases also have applicability to other pawnbroker situations. It is deceptive to fail to give consumers pawn receipts with the correct redemption date and the value of the pawned item. Pawnbrokers can not sell the item before the redemption period and must make restitution for value when the broker is unable to present the pledged item when the consumer effects redemption.[271] Pawnbrokers often fail to provide written notice of the sale of pawned goods, entitling the consumer to statutory damages under UCC § 9-625 (formerly § 9-507).[272] A pawnbroker who accepted monthly payments from the owner after having sold the pledged item committed a UDAP violation even though the owner unwittingly signed a sales contract instead of a pledge agreement.[273]

5.1.1.6 Unfair and Deceptive Foreclosure Practices

Uniform Commercial Code Article 9, state retail installment sales acts, and related state credit legislation regulate seizure of personal property. Special state foreclosure laws regulate seizure of real property. Nevertheless, the UDAP principles for repossessions and foreclosures are the same. Consequently, the discussion in § 5.1.1.5, *supra* should also apply to real estate foreclosures.

In addition, a number of UDAP cases deal specifically with real property foreclosures. It is a UDAP violation for a creditor to attempt to collect on the full note and foreclose on a home when it has no right to do so.[274] A creditor may not improperly add a bad check obligation to a mortgage, freeze a checking account without notice, or unlawfully attempt to foreclose on the home.[275] Falsely claiming that a buyer under a land contract is in default and is subject to eviction is a UDAP violation.[276] A California court, however, held that a lender did not commit a UDAP violation by charging homeowners a fee every month for a drive-by inspection of the property, where state law did not prohibit such fees.[277] Even if a creditor has the legal right to foreclose, it is a UDAP violation to do so for an improper reason, e.g., as retaliation for a refusal to give favorable testimony in another case.[278]

267 *But cf.* Kirby v. Horne Motor Co., 366 S.E.2d 259 (S.C. Ct. App. 1988) (no violation of Article 9 or state law to allow prospective buyer to test drive repossessed car before expiration of prior owner's statutory right to redeem, so no UDAP violation).

268 Chrysler Corp. (Aurora Chrysler-Plymouth), 97 F.T.C. 107 (1981) (consent order); Chrysler Corp., 97 F.T.C. 139 (1981) (consent order); General Motors Corp., 95 F.T.C. 899 (1980) (consent order) *modified on other grounds*, 110 F.T.C. 165 (1988); Ford Motor Co., 93 F.T.C. 402 (1979) (consent order), *modified on other grounds*, 109 F.T.C. 116 (1987); Ford Motor Co. (Francis Ford), 94 F.T.C. 564 (1979), *rev'd on other grounds*, 673 F.2d 1008 (9th Cir. 1982), *cert. denied sub nom.* FTC v. Francis Ford, Inc., 459 U.S. 999 (1982). *See also* State v. Ralph Williams' N.W. Chrysler Plymouth, Inc., 87 Wash. 2d 298, 553 P.2d 423 (1976).

269 Ford Motor Co. (Francis Ford), 94 F.T.C. 564 (1979), *rev'd*, 673 F.2d 1008 (9th Cir. 1982).

270 Ford Motor Co. v. FTC, 673 F.2d 1008 (9th Cir. 1982), *cert. denied sub nom.* FTC v. Francis Ford, Inc., 459 U.S. 999 (1982).

271 Babbitt Brothers Trading Co., 84 F.T.C. 623 (1974) (consent order); Bruce Barnard Co. of Shiprock, Inc., 84 F.T.C. 680 (1974) (consent order); Lower Sunrise Trading Post, 84 F.T.C. 661 (1974) (consent order); McGee Traders, Inc., 84 F.T.C. 689 (1974) (consent order); Keith v. Howerton, 2001 Tenn. App. LEXIS 646 (Aug. 28, 2001) (unreported, citation limited).

272 *See* National Consumer Law Center, Repossessions and Foreclosures § 13.2 (5th ed. 2002 and Supp.).

273 Lane v. Fabert, 178 Ill. App. 3d 698, 533 N.E.2d 546 (1989).

274 Morse v. Mutual Federal Savings & Loan Ass'n of Whitman, 536 F. Supp. 1271 (D. Mass. 1982); Hart v. GMAC Mortgage Corp., 246 B.R. 709 (Bankr. D. Mass. 2000) (UDAP violation for lender to proceed to foreclosure after becoming aware that debtor had complied with payment obligations under forbearance agreement, and to fail to straighten out its accounting of debtor's payments); Longview Bank & Trust Co. v. Flenniken, 661 S.W.2d 705 (Tex. 1984). *Cf.* Ogden v. Dickinson State Bank, 662 S.W.2d 330 (Tex. 1984) (where creditor has legal right to foreclose, no UDAP violation). *But see* Williams v. Resolution GGF OY, 417 Mass. 377, 630 N.E.2d 581 (1994) (bank's misstatement of amount due not a UDAP violation where reliance not alleged).

275 Morse v. Mutual Federal Savings & Loan Ass'n of Whitman, 536 F. Supp. 1271 (D. Mass. 1982).

276 Stringer v. Perales, 2003 WL 1848594 (Tex. App. Apr. 10, 2003) (unpublished, citation limited).

277 Walker v. Countrywide Home Loans, Inc., 98 Cal. App. 4th 1158, 121 Cal. Rptr. 2d 79 (2002).

278 Kattar v. Demoulas, 433 Mass. 1, 739 N.E.2d 246 (2000). *But cf.* Buster v. Moore, 438 Mass. 635, 783 N.E.2d 399 (2003) (no UDAP violation where there was no contract to forbear foreclosure or a bad faith breach of forbearance contract).

Improper service of the foreclosure complaint and the failure to give notice of the intent to foreclose, as required by law, is a UDAP violation.[279] A Georgia homeowner was held to have a state RICO claim against lenders who used a power of sale to sell the home.[280] The predicate acts for the RICO claim were the lenders' conversion of personal property in the home and their alleged interference with the owner's attempts to save the home by paying the balance due.

A court has found a UDAP violation where a home mortgage company locked the debtor out of the home and assumed control of the home without the debtor's permission and without legal process.[281] The mortgage company also violated the UDAP statute by failing to send the required notices of the right to cure and the right to seek emergency mortgage assistance from a state agency.[282]

It is not, however, a UDAP violation for a town to value property at the fair market value for purposes of a tax foreclosure sale, even though it computed the tax based on the higher assessed value, where state law made it clear that interim reassessments were not required.[283] Nor did a bank commit a UDAP violation when it improperly calculated the mortgagors' escrow obligations, misapplied payments to earlier shortfalls, and gave the mortgagors confusing and changing information about the monthly payment amount, even though these errors ultimately led to foreclosure.[284] A bank's failure to follow up on a neighbor's offer to purchase a property was also held not to be a UDAP violation, where the bank learned of the neighbor's interest only a few days before the foreclosure sale.[285] A Georgia court has also held that a home buyer does not have a UDAP claim against a bank that foreclosed without following applicable HUD regulations.[286]

Investigating the transaction that led to the foreclosure often reveals other UDAP claims.[287] Two sample complaints and other pleadings in cases challenging predatory mortgage lending may be found on the companion CD-Rom to this volume.[288]

279 Smith v. Commercial Banking Corp., 866 F.2d 576 (3d Cir. 1989) (Pennsylvania law). *But see* Hull v. Attleboro Savings Bank, 33 Mass. App. Ct. 18, 596 N.E.2d 358 (1992) (no UDAP violation where homeowner received notice).

280 Brown v. Freedman, 474 S.E.2d 73 (Ga. App. 1996).

281 *In re* Rodriguez, 218 B.R. 764 (Bankr. E.D. Pa. 1998).

282 *Id.*

283 Town of Voluntown v. Rytman, 21 Conn. App. 275, 573 A.2d 336 (1990).

284 Ferris v. Federal Home Loan Mortgage Corp., 905 F. Supp. 23 (D. Mass. 1995).

285 Williams v. Resolution GGF OY, 417 Mass. 377, 630 N.E.2d 581 (1994).

286 Krell v. National Mortgage Corp., 214 Ga. App. 503, 448 S.E.2d 248 (1994).

287 *See* §§ 5.1.7. 5.1.8, *infra.*

288 These pleadings are also collected on Consumer Law Pleadings, No. 1, Ch. 7, and No. 2, § 3.3.1 (CD-Rom and Index Guide).

5.1.2 Foreclosure Assistance, Credit Repair, and Credit Counseling

5.1.2.1 Foreclosure Assistance Scams

5.1.2.1.1 Advice, referral, and bankruptcy scams

Some companies use public records to identify those whose homes are being foreclosed, and offer, for a fee, to help save the home. The company may imply it will offer re-financing or other effective techniques to stave off foreclosure. Instead, the company just files a bankruptcy petition for the homeowner or refers the consumer to a bankruptcy attorney. A poorly filed bankruptcy that is dismissed will make matters worse because it will be more difficult for the homeowner to file a bankruptcy properly later. The New York Attorney General has successfully enjoined and obtained a restitution order for all fees received by such a "mortgage consulting firm."[289]

The failure to clearly disclose the nature of the offered service is a UDAP violation.[290] Courts have also found the fees charged to be unconscionable since the same services typically are offered free by a bar association lawyer referral service.[291] The company may also be engaging in the unauthorized practice of law or the improper solicitation of business for an attorney.

To the extent that a company helps the consumer file a bankruptcy, the Bankruptcy Code provides special remedies for a defrauded consumer. Whenever a preparer engages in any unfair, deceptive, or fraudulent act or violates the Bankruptcy Code's provision dealing with bankruptcy petition preparers, the consumer has an action for actual damages plus the greater of $2000 or twice the amount paid the petition preparer, injunctive relief, attorney fees, and costs.[292]

5.1.2.1.2 UDAP claims in sale-leaseback and similar scams

An even more insidious form of "home saver" represents that it can save the home from foreclosure, asking the consumer to sign a pile of papers whose import the consumer typically does not understand. Buried in the paperwork are contracts whereby the consumer sells the home to the home saver, who then leases it back to the consumer.

289 State v. Midland Equities, 117 Misc. 2d 203, 458 N.Y.S.2d 126 (Sup. Ct. 1982). *See also See also* Fleet v. United States Consumer Council, Inc., 53 B.R. 833 (Bankr. E.D. Pa. 1985).

290 *In re* Fleet, 95 B.R. 319 (E.D. Pa. 1989) (New Jersey law); State v. Midland Equities, 117 Misc. 2d 203, 458 N.Y.S.2d 126 (Sup. Ct. 1982).

291 *In re* Fleet, 95 B.R. 319 (E.D. Pa. 1989) (New Jersey law).

292 11 U.S.C. § 110. *See also* NCLC's Consumer Bankruptcy Law and Practice § 15.6 (6th ed. and Supp.).

Sometimes the sale and leaseback is disclosed to the consumer, but with the vague and generally false promise that the consumer can repurchase the home at a future date.

The home saver is subject to an action for fraud, and the whole transaction is certainly a UDAP violation.[293] The description of the homesaver's services is deceptive,[294] and the terms of the sale-leaseback are so extremely one-sided as to be unfair or unconscionable.[295]

In a private UDAP suit involving a sale-leaseback scheme, a debtor who lost her home to a homesaver won as damages the amount of equity in the home, which the court then trebled.[296] Another court awarded $50,000 punitive damages in a similar sale and lease-back situation based on fraud, breach of fiduciary duty, and UDAP violations.[297] The FTC obtained a preliminary injunction against a similar scam.[298] In another case, a court found a UDAP violation where a consumer, with no one to counsel her, whose sole source of income was Aid to Families with Dependent Children, was pressured into a financing scheme that she did not understand and that was disadvantageous.[299] A District of Columbia trial court found that a homesaver committed numerous deceptive and unconscionable acts. These included failure to disclose the appraised value of the home and that he was the other contracting party and would profit personally from the transaction; presenting himself as helping the homeowner save her home, when his real intention was to acquire the home for a pittance; and acquiring the home at a grossly disproportionate price from an aged and infirm homeowner.[300]

In another variant of this scheme, entrepreneurs buy delinquent debts before foreclosure begins. Then they contact the homeowner, threaten foreclosure, and by one means or another, acquire control of the property. Firms even offer seminars on these tactics.[301] A Massachusetts court held that a home-saver who followed this pattern may have committed UDAP violations by representing to the homeowner that signing the agreements was a mere formality after the homeowner made it clear that he could not afford the payments.[302]

5.1.2.1.3 Other claims against homesavers

A homesaver transaction, even if disguised as a sale and leaseback, may be subject to Truth in Lending rescission rights.[303] Many of these operators fail to give any TIL disclosures at all.[304]

A few states have statutes specifically directed at homesavers.[305] The state home solicitation sales law, a state or federal telemarketing statute, or a state or federal credit repair organization statute may also apply, depending on how the transaction was solicited and consummated.[306] Another possible cause of action is to seek specific performance of the contract to sell the home back to the homeowner.

Another angle to investigate is whether state real estate or mortgage broker laws require the homesaver to be licensed. Lack of a license may be a UDAP violation, and may make the transaction unenforceable.[307]

5.1.2.1.4 Claims against other parties and against the house

People who perpetrate homesaver frauds often resell the home or cash out its equity promptly after acquiring it. If the homesaver is uncollectible, the homeowner's focus in litigation may need to be on getting title back. Regardless of whether the suit is styled a quiet title action, all parties with potential interests in the property, and their agents, should be joined, including trustees, mortgagees, assignees, settlement agents, and brokers. It may be appropriate to record the homeowner's claim through a *lis pendens* or similar procedure, so that the property can not be transferred again without notice of the claim. The equitable mortgage doctrine may provide additional claims.[308] The attorney for the homeowner should also check the details of the state's formal requirements for deeds, since homesavers often cut corners. The deed may be invalid if it is challenged on formal grounds, but there may be a very short deadline for this type of challenge.

---

293 *See In re* Bryant, 111 B.R. 474 (E.D. Pa. 1990) (consumer recovered treble the equity in the home under a UDAP claim); Jeffries v. The Lewis Group, Clearinghouse No. 47,473F (Ill. Cir. Ct. Cook Cty. Oct. 9, 1991) ($50,000 punitive damages based on fraud, breach of fiduciary duty, and UDAP violations).

294 Bryant v. Woodland (*In re* Bryant), 111 B.R. 474 (Bankr. E.D. Pa. 1990).

295 *See* § 4.4, *supra.*

296 *In re* Bryant, 111 B.R. 474 (E.D. Pa. 1990).

297 Jeffries v. The Lewis Group, Clearinghouse No. 47,473F (Ill. Cir. Ct. Cook Cty. Oct. 9, 1991).

298 R.A. Walker & Associates, Inc., 3 Trade Reg. Rep. (CCH) ¶ 22,080, F.T.C. File No. 832 3227 (D.D.C. 1983) (preliminary injunction).

299 U.S. Home & Realty Corp v. Lehnartz, Clearinghouse No. 43,259 (Mich. Dist. Ct. 1987).

300 Jackson v. Byrd, Clearinghouse No. 55605 (D.C. Super. Apr. 16, 2004).

301 *See* Billingham v. Dornemann, 771 N.E.2d 166 (Mass. App. 2002).

302 *Id.*

303 James v. Ragin, 432 F. Supp. 887 (W.D.N.C. 1977); Long v. Storms, 50 Or. App. 39, 622 P.2d 731 (1981). *See generally* National Consumer Law Center, Truth in Lending § 2.5.3, Ch. 6 (5th ed. 2003 and Supp.) *See also* 55 Am. Jur. 2d Mortgage §§ 73–82 (1971).

304 *See* National Consumer Law Center, Truth in Lending § 2.5.3 (5th ed. 2003 and Supp.) (coverage of sale-leasebacks).

305 *See* Cal. Civ. Code §§ 1695.1 to 1695.17 (home equity purchasers), 2945.1 to 1945.11 (foreclosure consultants).

306 *See* §§ 5.1.2.2, 5.8, 5.9, *infra.*

307 *See* §§ 4.7.7.2, 4.7.8, *supra*, 9.5.8, *infra.*

308 *See* National Consumer Law Center, The Cost of Credit: Regulation and Legal Challenges § 7.5.2.1 (2d ed. 2000 and Supp.).

If the homesaver cashed out the equity in the home through a bank loan, the homeowner's attorney should obtain the loan documents for this and any other loans the homesaver got, the homesaver's credit history, any judgment reports, the title search, and any other information the bank had when it made the loan. These documents may show that the bank was on notice of the fraud. In addition, if the homeowner did not even know that the document being signed was a deed, as is often the case with homesaver frauds, the deed may be void rather than voidable.

It is important to investigate how many other homes the homesaver has acquired in the same manner. This evidence is critical for fraud and punitive damages claims, and will also help show the court that the case is not an ordinary real estate transfer that should be governed by ordinary real estate law.

5.1.2.2 Credit Repair Organizations

5.1.2.2.1 Introduction

Credit repair clinics promise to improve a consumer's credit rating or credit records. These organizations commonly call themselves "credit repair" or "credit service" agencies, "credit clinics," or use similar titles. According to the FTC,[309] these entities tell consumers that for a fee (usually a substantial one, not even counting the 900-number charges sometimes assessed to contact the credit repair agency[310]), they can remove negative items from a credit history. Sometimes, they encourage consumers to establish a new credit identity by using an Employer Identification Number instead of their Social Security number, a seemingly fraudulent and possibly criminal solution to a bad situation. A 2004 FTC Study estimated that, over a one-year period, almost 2.5 million people in the United States fell victim to credit repair scams.[311]

Generally, these agencies do nothing consumers can not do for themselves free of charge.[312] Indeed, consumers may be better positioned to deal with their credit histories by themselves, as many credit bureaus refuse to deal with credit repair agencies. Typically, the "service" provided consists solely of advising consumers to barrage credit reporting agencies with form letters disputing most or all items in their files—letters that the reporting agencies generally ignore as frivolous. Thus, a consumer will have far greater success by drafting individualized letters, which are not as likely to be considered frivolous as a repair agency form, and save paying the repair organization fee.

Credit repair agency abuses are subject to a UDAP approach. The federal Credit Repair Organizations Act and similar state laws offer additional remedies. Federal and state RICO claims are also possible.[313] In addition, the FTC Telemarketing Rule prohibits many specific practices when credit repair services are sold through telephone calls.[314] This section will consider these claims.

5.1.2.2.2 Federal Credit Repair Organizations Act

In many situations, the federal Credit Repair Organizations Act[315] (CROA) provides superior remedies and stronger restrictions than are available under a UDAP statute. This subsection briefly summarizes this Act, which is analyzed more thoroughly in NCLC's *Fair Credit Reporting* Ch. 15 (5th ed. 2002 and Supp.).

The CROA applies to credit repair organizations, defined as any person who performs or offers to perform any service, for a fee or other valuable consideration, for the purpose of improving a consumer's credit record, credit history, or credit rating, or advising or assisting a consumer in such efforts.[316] There are exclusions for certain charitable organizations,[317] creditors restructuring a consumer's debt, and depository institutions.[318]

Credit repair organizations are prohibited under the Act from charging or receiving payment for their services until the service is fully performed.[319] In addition, the CROA provides a three-day right to cancel.[320] No services can be provided until three days after the consumer signs a contract. The contract must include the total of all payments due, a full and detailed description of all services and all guarantees of performance, and other specified information.[321] The CROA also requires separate disclosure of consumer rights

309 FTC v. Giving You Credit, Inc., 5 Trade Reg. Rep. (CCH) ¶ 24,013 (N.D. Ill. 1996) (consent decree).

310 *See* FTC v. Interactive Marketing Concepts, Inc., 5 Trade Reg. Rep. (CCH) ¶ 23,872 (D.N.J. 1995) (proposed consent decree); FTC v. M.D.M. Interests, Inc., 5 Trade Reg. Rep. (CCH) ¶ 23,262 (S.D. Tex. 1992) (consent order); FTC v. Interactive Communications Technology, Inc., 5 Trade Reg. Rep. (CCH) ¶ 23,212 (F.T.C. Dkt. C-3400 1992) (consent order); FTC v. Timmerman, 5 Trade Reg. Rep. (CCH) ¶ 23,046 (D. Md. 1991) (consent order).

311 FTC, Consumer Fraud in the United States: An FTC Survey (2004) at 32.

312 *See* National Consumer Law Center, Fair Credit Reporting Ch. 13 (5th ed. 2002 and Supp.).

313 *See* §§ 9.2, 9.3, *infra*.

314 *See* § 5.9.4.7.4, *infra*.

315 15 U.S.C. §§ 1679–1679j, Pub. L. No. 104-208 § 110 Stat. 3009 (Sept. 30, 1996).

316 15 U.S.C. § 1679a(3)(a). *See* Iosello v. Lexington Law Firm, 2003 WL 21920237 (N.D. Ill. Aug. 7, 2003) (Act covers attorneys who act in the manner of a credit repair organization).

317 Zimmerman v. Cambridge Credit Counseling Corp., 323 F. Supp. 2d 95 (D. Mass. 2004) (IRS classification of defendant as § 501(c)(3) organization is conclusive).

318 15 U.S.C. § 1679a(3).

319 15 U.S.C. § 1679b(b). *See* FTC v. Gill, 265 F.3d 944 (9th Cir. 2001) (law office violated CROA by accepting payment before completing credit repair services).

320 15 U.S.C. § 1679e(a).

321 15 U.S.C. § 1679d.

under the FCRA and CROA.[322] Noncomplying contracts are treated as void and may not be enforced by any court or person.[323] Accordingly, any arbitration clause included in such a contract should have no effect.

The CROA prohibits any person from making false or misleading statements to credit reporting agencies or actual or potential creditors with respect to the consumer's creditworthiness, or advise the consumer to do so.[324] The Act also forbids altering or concealing a consumer's identity or advising a consumer to do so, for the purpose of concealing accurate non-obsolete information from a credit reporting agency or an actual or potential creditor.[325] Untrue or misleading representations of the services of the credit repair organization are also prohibited,[326] as are any acts that constitute or result in a fraud or deception on any person in connection with the offer or sale of a credit repair organization's services.[327] These prohibitions all apply to "any person," so a defendant can be liable even if it does not meet the definition of a credit repair organization.[328] Any waiver of any consumer protection under the Act is void and unenforceable, and the attempt to obtain the waiver is a violation of the Act.[329]

For any violation of the Act, individual consumers or a class of consumers can recover the sum of:

- Actual damages or the amount paid to the organization, whichever is greater;
- Such additional punitive damages as the court may allow; and
- Costs and reasonable attorney fees.[330]

Unlike the other titles of the Consumer Credit Protection Act, the CROA does not contain a specific grant of jurisdiction in the federal district courts. Federal jurisdiction is probably available under the general federal question statute.[331] CROA's statute of limitations is five years from the occurrence of the violation or, where the violation relates to the organization's material and willful failure to disclose, five years from the date the consumer discovers the misrepresentation.[332]

5.1.2.2.3 State credit repair laws

State credit repair statutes provide another important remedy for credit repair abuses.[333] The Credit Repair Organizations Act does not preempt state credit repair statutes, except to the extent the two are inconsistent, and then only to the extent of such inconsistency.[334] Depending on the circumstances and the statute, possible advantages of claims under state credit repair laws are broader coverage than the CROA, different remedies, state instead of federal court jurisdiction, and a bond from which judgments can be collected.

Many state credit repair statutes are significantly broader than the federal statute and cover not only organizations that promise to improve the consumer's credit rating but also those that assist, or offer to assist, in obtaining credit for the consumer. These statutes potentially cover:

- Credit card "finders" that claim to be able to procure credit cards for consumers.[335]
- Loan brokers and mortgage brokers.[336] Most state credit repair statutes exclude licensed real estate brokers and securities brokers, but few exclude loan brokers. The West Virginia Supreme Court, interpreting language that is found in many other states' statutes, has held that a loan broker meets the definition of "credit services organization."[337]
- Tax preparers who offer, for a fee, to arrange refund anticipation loans for their clients. While tax preparers may not disclose any special fee for arranging a refund anticipation loan, most receive a substantial fee in the form of a kickback of part of the borrower's payment to the lender.
- Scholarship location services.[338]

322 15 U.S.C. § 1679c).

323 15 U.S.C. § 1679f(c).

324 15 U.S.C. § 1679b(a)(i).

325 15 U.S.C. § 1679b(a)(2).

326 15 U.S.C. § 1679b(a)(3).

327 15 U.S.C. § 1679b(a)(4).

328 Lacey v. William Chrysler Plymouth Inc., 2004 U.S. Dist. LEXIS 2479 (N. D. Ill. Feb. 20, 2004); Parker v. 1-800 Bar None, 2002 WL 215530 (N.D. Ill. Feb. 12, 2002); Bigalke v. Creditrust Corp., 162 F. Supp. 2d 996, 999 (N.D. Ill. 2001); Vance v. Nat'l Benefit Ass'n, 1999 WL 731763, at *4 (N.D. Ill. Aug. 30, 1999).

329 15 U.S.C. § 1679f.

330 15 U.S.C. § 1679g(a). *See also* FTC v. Gill, 265 F.3d 944 (9th Cir. 2001) (ordering restitution of all amounts paid by consumers, under general authority of FTC Act).

331 28 U.S.C. § 1331.

332 15 U.S.C. § 1679i.

333 *See* National Consumer Law Center, Fair Credit Reporting Appx. B (5th ed. 2002 and Supp.) (state-by-state summaries of state credit repair statutes).

334 15 U.S.C. § 1679j.

335 *See* State v. Schlosser, 79 Ohio St. 3d 329, 681 N.E.2d 911 (1997) (affirming conviction of credit card finder under state RICO statute based on predicate offense of operating unlicensed credit services organization).

336 Lewis v. Delta Funding Corp. (*In re* Lewis), 290 B.R. 541, 555–56 (Bankr. E.D. Pa. 2003) (finding both loan broker and the bank that prepared the non-complying broker contract liable for violation of state credit repair law).

337 Arnold v. United Companies Lending Corp., 511 S.E.2d 854 (W. Va. 1998). *See also* Barker v. Altegra Corp. (*In re* Barker), 251 B.R. 250 (Bankr. E.D. Pa. 2000) (finding that loan broker was covered under Pa. credit repair statute, but basing decision on language that does not appear in most states' statutes).

338 *See* Hatch v. College Resource Mgmt., Clearinghouse No. 53,563 (Minn. Dist. Ct. Oct. 24, 2001) (denying scholarship

- "Home finders" that promise to help people buy homes. These operations often appear in cities and are usually fraudulent.
- "Home savers" that approach homeowners who are in foreclosure and offer to secure financing to enable them to save their homes.

Most of these statutes exempt non-profit organizations; licensed real estate brokers and attorneys when acting within the scope of their licenses; broker-dealers registered with the SEC or CFTC; consumer reporting agencies; credit unions; banks eligible for FDIC or FSLIC insurance; banks and other lenders authorized under federal or state law; and lenders approved by HUD for participation in federal mortgage insurance.[339] A smaller number exempt debt collectors, debt adjusters, mortgage brokers, accountants, holders of other licenses, or other entities.

Typical provisions of these state statutes include:

- A requirement of a written contract that includes a description of the specific services to be provided;[340]
- A right to rescind the contract;
- Bonding and registration requirements;
- Mandatory disclosure of rights under the FCRA;
- Remedies under the state UDAP statute for violations; and
- In many states, a special private cause of action as well, often including punitive damages, statutory damages, or attorney fees.[341]

Creditors and others that are closely involved with the credit services organization—for example, by preparing and securing the consumer's signature on the organization's fee agreement—can be liable along with the organization for violation of the state credit repair law.[342]

5.1.2.2.4 FTC Telemarketing Rule

The FTC Telemarketing Rule applies to credit repair services that are marketed through at least one interstate telephone call without a face-to-face meeting.[343] Since its coverage and exemptions are different from state and federal credit repair laws,[344] it may apply to organizations that are exempt from those laws. It specifically covers cases where the consumer makes the first call to the credit repair clinic in response to an advertisement or a direct mail solicitation.[345] It does not, however, cover 900-number calls to credit repair clinics, because these are regulated by different statutes and rules.[346]

The Telemarketing Rule provides greater consumer protection than the Credit Repair Organizations Act regarding payment for services. The CROA prohibits credit repair organizations from charging or receiving payment for their services until the service is fully performed.[347] The FTC's Telemarketing Rule, on the other hand, prohibits a credit repair clinic from requesting or receiving any payment for its services until it has provided the consumer a credit report, issued at least six months after the credit repair services were provided, that demonstrates that the promised results have been achieved.[348] The Telemarketing Rule also goes beyond the CROA in restricting the use of payment methods such as "telechecks" by which the consumer's bank account is debited through telephone authorization.[349]

The Act under which the rule was promulgated creates a private cause of action for violations of the telemarketing rule, but only where each plaintiff's damages exceed $50,000.[350] In many states a rule violation is a *per se* UDAP violation.[351]

The FTC and state attorneys general have sued many fraudulent credit repair clinics to enforce the prohibition against advance payment.[352] The FTC has also proceeded against companies that deceptively represent they can delete accurate information from a consumer's credit record.[353]

location service's motion for summary judgment and concluding that state credit repair law applies to it).

339 *See* Brown v. Mortgagestar, Inc., 194 F. Supp. 2d 473 (S.D. W. Va. 2002) (HUD-approved lender exempt even though it was acting as broker rather than lender in transaction with plaintiff).

340 *See* Mitchell v. Am. Fair Credit Ass'n, Inc., 99 Cal. App. 4th 1345, 122 Cal. Rptr. 2d 193 (2002) (modification of credit repair contract ineffective where not signed by consumer as required by state credit repair law).

341 *See* National Consumer Law Center, Fair Credit Reporting Appx. B (5th ed. 2002 and Supp.) for an analysis of individual state statutes on credit repair.

342 Lewis v. Delta Funding Corp. (*In re* Lewis), 290 B.R. 541, 555–56 (Bankr. E.D. Pa. 2003). *But see* Allen v. Advanta Fin. Corp., 2002 U.S. Dist. LEXIS 11650 (E.D. Pa. Jan. 3, 2002) (participating in scheme with credit services organization insufficient to create liability).

343 16 C.F.R. §§ 310.2(cc), 310.6(b)(3).

344 *See* § 5.9.4.2, *infra.*

345 16 C.F.R. § 310.6(b)(5), (6). *See* § 5.9.4.2, *infra.*

346 16 C.F.R. § 310.6(b)(1); *see* § 5.9.3, *infra.*

347 15 U.S.C. § 1679b(b).

348 16 C.F.R. § 310.4(a)(2). *See* § 5.9.4.7.4, *infra.*

349 16 C.F.R. § 310.3(a)(3). *See In re* National Credit Mgmt. Group, 21 F. Supp. 2d 424 (D.N.J. 1998) (enjoining credit repair organization's violation of rule; court also finds defendant's failure to disclose all costs violates rule). *See generally* §§ 5.1.10.3, 5.9.4.8.2, *infra.*

350 Telemarketing and Consumer Fraud and Abuse Protection Act, 15 U.S.C. § 6104(a).

351 *See* §§ 3.2.6, 3.2.7, *supra.*

352 *See* § 5.9.4.7.4, *infra.*

353 A few of the FTC's many suits are: FTC v. Gill, 265 F.3d 944 (9th Cir. 2001); FTC v. Donald Quaite, 5 Trade Reg. Rep. (CCH) ¶ 24,495 (N.D. Tex. 1998) (consent decree); FTC v. John Mancini, 5 Trade Reg. Rep. (CCH) ¶ 24,495 (N.D. Tex. 1998); FTC v. Second Federal Credit Inc., 5 Trade Reg. Rep. (CCH) ¶ 24,472 (D. Mass. 1998) (consent decree); FTC v. Frattaroli 5 Trade Reg. Rep. (CCH) ¶ 24,472 (D. Mass. 1998) (consent decree); FTC v. Caluori, 5 Trade Reg. Rep. (CCH) ¶ 24,472 (D. Mass. 1998) (consent decree); Phillips Hall, Inc., 5 Trade Reg. Rep. (CCH) ¶ 24,472 (D. Mass. 1998) (consent decree); FTC v.

5.1.2.2.5 UDAP approaches

Most credit repair abuses should also be state UDAP violations, and the federal Credit Repair Organizations Act explicitly states that state laws are not preempted.[354] Thus a series of FTC and state UDAP cases have held that credit repair clinics may not misrepresent their ability to clean up a person's credit record,[355] the nature of the services they offer,[356] or the legality of the steps they undertake.[357]

5.1.2.2.6 Car dealers and other sellers as regulated by state credit repair laws

A highly significant question is whether car dealerships and other sellers who arrange credit for their customers are covered by the state credit repair law. Since state credit repair laws typically apply not only to organizations that offer to repair a consumer's credit, but also to those that offer to arrange an extension of credit for the consumer, they are broad enough to cover these sellers. If the law applies to these sellers, in most states consumers will have a right to cancel the contract and will be entitled to various disclosures and other protections that sellers usually ignore.

In two states, Illinois and Ohio, the issue of coverage of sellers was litigated successfully in the lower courts but with less success on appeal. The Illinois Supreme Court[358] reversed a lower court's ruling that a contractor was covered by the state credit repair statute when it arranged financing for home improvements. Under the state law, a "credit services organization" was one that provided its services "in return for the payment of money or other valuable consideration." The supreme court held that the contractor did not meet this definition because the consumer had not made a specially earmarked payment, separate from the payment for the home improvements, for the service of arranging credit. In many consumer transactions, however, the seller charges a document preparation fee, receives a kickback from the creditor in the form of a yield spread premium, or pays a bonus from the proceeds of the sale to the employee who arranged the financing. These types of payments may be sufficient to bring a transaction within the scope of a state credit repair statute, at least in other states.[359]

In Ohio, the credit repair statute originally did not specifically exempt car dealers. Also, unlike most state credit repair statutes, it required that the consumer pay money but did not specifically say that the money had to be *for* the credit services. A number of Ohio cases held that dealers who offered to help consumers in arranging for car loans fell within both the explicit language and the intent of the Ohio statute.[360] The first appellate decision on the question, how-

---

CRA Champion Credit Inc., 5 Trade Reg. Rep. (CCH) ¶ 24,425 (W.D. Wash. 1998) (proposed consent decree); FTC v. Maynard, 5 Trade Reg. Rep. (CCH) ¶ 24,213 (D. Ariz. 1997) (proposed consent decree); FTC v. USA Credit Services Inc., 5 Trade Reg. Rep. (CCH) ¶ 24,214 (S.D. Cal. 1997) (proposed consent decree); FTC v. Giving You Credit, Inc., 5 Trade Reg. Rep. (CCH) ¶ 24,244 (N.D. Ill. 1997) (court order); FTC v. Channels, 5 Trade Reg. Rep. (CCH) ¶ 24,175 (C.D. Cal. 1996) (proposed consent decree); FTC v. Ellis, 5 Trade Reg. Rep. (CCH) ¶ 24,179 (C.D. Cal. 1996) (proposed consent decree).

354 15 U.S.C. § 1679j.

355 FTC v. Hartbrodt, 5 Trade Reg. Rep. (CCH) ¶ 23,878 (C.D. Cal. 1995) (consent order); FTC v. Timmerman, 5 Trade Reg. Rep. (CCH) ¶ 23,046 (D. Md. 1991) (consent order); FTC v. S&L Professional Credit Clinic, Inc., 5 Trade Reg. Rep. (CCH) ¶ 22,886 (N.D. Tex. 1990) (permanent injunction); FTC v. Credit Repair, Inc., 5 Trade Reg. Rep. (CCH) ¶ 22,807 (N.D. Ill. 1990) (consent decree); Universal Credit Network, 5 Trade Reg. Rep. (CCH) ¶ 22,812 (F.T.C. File No. 882 3085 1990) (consent order); FTC v. Action Credit Sys., Inc., 3 Trade Reg. Rep. (CCH) ¶ 22,534 (N.D. Cal. 1988) (consent order); FTC v. Roberts, 3 Trade Reg. Rep. (CCH) ¶ 22,535 (D.N.J. 1988) (consent order); Steven Leff, F.T.C. File No. 8823083, 5 Trade Reg. Rep. (CCH) ¶ 22,727 (F.T.C. Sept. 1, 1989) (consent order); State *ex rel.* Thornburg v. International Bus. Services, Clearinghouse No. 44,814 (N.C. Super. Ct. Dec. 9, 1988) (temporary restraining order); FTC v. Consumer Credit Advocates, P.C., 5 Trade Reg. Rep. (CCH) ¶ 24,003 (S.D.N.Y. 1996) (proposed consent decree) (charges against law firms); State *ex rel.* Thornburg v. Ollison, Clearinghouse No. 44,813 (N.C. Super. Ct. Dec. 9, 1988) (temporary restraining order); State v. New Beginning Credit Ass'n Inc., Clearinghouse No. 52,031 (Tenn. Ch. Ct. Jan. 8, 1998). *See also* State v. Second Chance Financial, Clearinghouse No. 50,410 (Tenn. Ch. Ct. Knox Cty. Mar. 31, 1994).

356 *In re* National Credit Mgmt. Group, 21 F. Supp. 2d 424 (D.N.J. 1998).

357 *See* FTC v. Gill, 265 F.3d 944 (9th Cir. 2001) (lawyers' misrepresentation of ability to remove negative information permanently and legally violates FTC Act); FTC v. Clifton W. Cross, 5 Trade Reg. Rep. (CCH) ¶ 15124 (W.D. Tex. June 21, 2001) (proposed consent decree against credit repair website operator who sold instructions for building new credit profile with fake SSN); FTC v. Corzine, 5 Trade Reg. Rep. (CCH) ¶ 23,670 (E.D. Cal. Sept. 12, 1994) (TRO), ¶ 23,715 (proposed consent decree).

358 Midstate Siding & Window Co. v. Rogers, 204 Ill. 2d 314, 789 N.E.2d 1248, 273 Ill. Dec. 816 (2003).

359 *But see* Cannon v. William Chevrolet/Geo, Inc., 341 Ill. App. 3d 674, 794 N.E.2d 843 (2003) (legislature did not intend credit services law to apply to sellers, so car dealer is not covered even though it required consumer to pay 4.5% higher interest rate than bank required and charged documentary fee of $46.88).

360 Hester v. Alan Besco Cars-Trucks, Inc., 1999 Ohio Misc. LEXIS 62 (C.P. Aug. 9, 1999) (summary judgment that Ohio Credit Services Organization Act applied and that dealer had violated the Act); Bailey v. Ford Motor Co., 1999 Ohio Misc. LEXIS 61 (C.P. Aug. 10, 1999) (summary judgment that Ohio Credit Services Organization Act applied to dealer who had arranged a lease, that dealer had violated the Act, and that violation was *per se* UDAP violation); Sannes v. Jeff Wyler Chevrolet, Inc., 107 Ohio Misc. 2d 6, 736 N.E.2d 112 (C.P.), *upheld on reconsideration*, 107 Ohio Misc. 2d 11, 736 N.E.2d 116 (C.P. 1999) (the state's auto dealer association and retail merchant association filed amicus briefs in opposition to the initial decision); Hall v. Jack Walker Pontiac, Toyota, Inc., 1999 Ohio Misc. LEXIS 65 (C.P. Mar. 1, 1999) (magistrate's decision), *adopted by* 1999 Ohio Misc. LEXIS 64 (C.P. Sept. 24, 1999). *But see* Snook v. Ford Motor Co., 755 N.E.2d 380 (Ohio

ever, read into the definition of "buyer" a requirement that the consumer show either payment of a fee specifically for the service of arranging credit or that the cost of this service was included in the price of the vehicle.[361] In the meantime, the Ohio legislature amended the Credit Services Organization Act, effective September 29, 1999, to explicitly exclude car dealers and to specify that an organization was covered only if it accepted a fee specifically for obtaining credit.[362] There is some doubt that the legislation comports with the Ohio Constitution, because it was attached to an unrelated bill.

In some states the question may arise whether dealers and other sellers fall within an exemption for entities that are authorized to extend credit under state or federal laws. Some dealers may hold a license under the state Retail Installment Sales Act or Motor Vehicle Installment Sales Act that allows the dealer to enter into retail installment contracts. Most sellers then assign such contracts to a financing entity.

Such an exemption will not help a seller, such as a home improvement contractor, who merely arranges a direct loan between the consumer and a third-party lender. (The distinction in the documents is that an installment credit contract that is assigned to a creditor will be originally payable to the seller, while in the case of a loan the debt is owed to the lender from the outset.) With a direct loan, the seller itself is not extending credit but merely arranging for a loan from a third party, so will not be covered by its retail installment sales license. The fact that it acts as the lender's agent for the purposes of obtaining the consumer's signature on the loan papers does not mean that it shares in the lender's exemption.[363] Any other conclusion would nullify the application of state credit repair statutes to entities that obtain or offer to obtain extensions of credit for the consumer.

5.1.2.2.7 *Applicability of federal credit repair statute to sellers*

Perhaps even more significant than the potential use of *state* credit repair statutes to cancel car sales and home improvement transactions is the possible applicability of the *federal* Credit Repair Organizations Act.[364] While the federal statute's remedies and requirements are very similar to state credit repair statutes, the existence of the federal statute means that more transactions will be covered by one statute or the other. This is because not every state has enacted a state credit repair statute, and because the federal statute has a different scope than state repair statutes. The federal statute will apply to transactions exempt from a state statute and vice versa.

The federal statute applies (with certain enumerated exceptions not applicable to car dealers or home improvement contractors) to persons who perform or offer to perform a service, for a fee or other valuable consideration, that involves improving or giving advice about how to improve a consumer's credit rating.[365] As such, it does not apply, as many state statutes do, to sellers who merely arrange financing, but applies only to those who promise to improve a consumer's credit rating.

On the other hand, the federal Act exempts depository institutions (e.g., banks), but does not exempt other creditors unless they are assisting the consumer to restructure a debt owed to that creditor.[366] Consequently, even if a state credit repair statute does not apply to car dealers or others that originate and then assign consumer credit contracts, the federal Act will apply to these dealers as long as the dealer held itself out as being able to fix or upgrade the consumer's credit history. Many sellers marketing themselves to lower-income households, such as subprime automobile and home-equity lenders, adopt this very sales technique. Some even advertise in the yellow pages under credit repair.

One case attempting to use the federal statute in this way was not successful where insufficient evidence was found that the dealer had offered to improve the consumer's credit rating.[367] The consumers alleged that the dealer had advertised in the automobile classified section that it would help re-establish consumers' credit, and that the dealer was thus assisting consumers in improving their credit. The federal court, while noting precedent to the contrary, found that the dealer was offering this service ancillary to its primary business of selling vehicles, and that Congress did not intend to include such ancillary financing service in the category of a credit repair organization.[368] Nevertheless, even this court might have ruled otherwise if the advertising was in a credit repair section of a newspaper or yellow pages, instead of in the automotive section.

Another decision holds that, while a car dealership could fit into the definition of a credit repair organization, buyers had no CROA claim where they had not been concerned with their credit and had never seen or heard any ads touting the dealer's credit repair services, even though the dealer had a sign on its premises about helping first-time buyers

App. 2001); Blinkoff v. Ricart Ford, Inc., 2000 Ohio Misc. LEXIS 8 (C.P. Jan. 18, 2000) (consumer's payment of money must be for the credit services, not merely to lease the vehicle). *But cf.* Clark v. D.O.W. Fin. Co., 2000 Del. Super. LEXIS 238 (May 26, 2000) (automotive finance company itself is not a credit services organization as it does not obtain extensions of credit by others for consideration).

361 Snook v. Ford Motor Co., 755 N.E.2d 380 (Ohio App. 2001).

362 Amended Substitute House Bill 283, *adding* Ohio Rev. Code § 4712.01(C)(2)(k) (June 30, 1999, eff. Sept. 29, 1999).

363 Hester v. Alan Besco Cars-Trucks, Inc., 1999 Ohio Misc. LEXIS 62 (C.P. Aug. 9, 1999).

364 15 U.S.C. § 1679.

365 15 U.S.C. § 1679a(3)(A). *See* § 5.1.2.2.2, *supra*.

366 15 U.S.C. § 1679a(3).

367 *Citing* Lovely v. Peffley Ford Inc., No. C-3-97-435 (S.D. Ohio Aug. 25, 1998) (magistrate report and recommendation).

368 Sannes v. Jeff Wyler Chevrolet, Inc., 1999 U.S. Dist. LEXIS 21748 (S.D. Ohio Mar. 31, 1999).

build credit.[369] The court also held that the CROA would apply only if the dealer charged the consumer an additional amount for the credit repair services.[370]

5.1.2.3 Credit Counselors, Debt Settlement, and Debt Elimination

5.1.2.3.1 The credit counseling industry

The credit counseling industry experienced tremendous growth during the 1990s. There were about two hundred agencies nationally in the early 1990s and more than 1000 by 2002.[371] About nine million consumers in financial trouble have some contact with a credit counseling agency each year.[372] Based on the growing number of complaints about these agencies, many consumers will not necessarily find desperately needed assistance, but may instead find themselves even deeper in debt or stuck with a secured consolidation loan.[373]

Initially, most credit counseling agencies were affiliated with the National Foundation for Credit Counseling (NFCC).[374] These agencies generally offered a variety of services. Their feature service, however, was debt management plans (DMPs). Through a DMP, a consumer sends the credit counseling agency a lump sum, which the agency then distributes to the consumer's creditors.

There have been reports of problems with the NFCC agencies over the years. In particular, the agencies were accused of deceptive practices based on their failure to disclose that the vast majority of their funding came from creditors. Through this credit-based funding system, known as "Fair Share," creditors return to the agencies a certain percentage of the funds disbursed to them.[375] In addition, there have been reports over the years that NFCC affiliates and other agencies have been reluctant to inform consumers of bankruptcy rights. Even prior to the huge growth in the industry, credit counseling agencies, both NFCC affiliates and others, have also been accused, among other problems, of failing to timely remit consumer payments to creditors and falling to disclose fees.[376]

These problems have increased in recent years, largely due to changes in the way the industry operates.[377] Newcomers to the industry, including both agencies that are literally new to the field and older agencies that have begun to adopt the business strategies of the newer players, are more likely to offer services mainly by phone or Internet, to steer the vast majority of consumers into DMPs, to sell their services aggressively, and to charge high fees for service. Almost all of these organizations have been granted tax-exempt status by the IRS, but many operate more like "for-profit businesses."[378] Many are involved in a related industry, debt negotiation, which has also been the source of consumer complaints.[379] Some newcomers have engaged in aggressive telemarketing that the FTC has alleged was in violation of the nationwide do-not-call list rule.[380]

5.1.2.3.2 Legal claims

There are a number of possible remedies available to challenge problems with credit counseling. The closest statutory scheme at the federal level is the Credit Repair

369 Wojcik v. Courtesy Auto Sales, Inc., 2002 WL 31663298 (D. Neb. Nov. 25, 2002).

370 *Accord* Oslan v. Collection Bur., 206 F.R.D. 109 (E.D. Pa. 2001).

371 *See* Jennifer Barrett, *Debt Consolidation: Beware Big Fees and Big Promises*, Newsweek On-line, Jan. 3, 2002; National Foundation for Credit Counseling, *Fact Sheet and Industry Background* (June 2003), *available on-line at* www.nfcc.org.

372 Christopher H. Schmitt with Heather Timmons and John Cady, *A Debt Trap for the Unwary*, Business Week, Oct. 29, 2001. In a 2003 Fact Sheet, the National Foundation for Credit Counseling stated that more than one million households contacted NFCC and were given budget counseling.

373 *See generally* National Consumer Law Center and Consumer Federation of America, *Credit Counseling in Crisis*, April 2003. Available on-line at www.nclc.org/initiatives/credit_counseling/content/creditcounselingreport.pdf.

374 The Foundation (NFCC) was formerly known as the National Foundation for Consumer Credit.

375 As a result of a settlement with the FTC in 1999, NFCC now includes in its best practices standards that member agencies must disclose this possible conflict. *See* Stephen Gardner, *Consumer Credit Counseling Services: The Need for Reform and Some Proposals for Change*, Advancing the Consumer Interest vol. 13 Fall 2001/Winter 2002. Fair Share issues are discussed in detail in National Consumer Law Center and Consumer Federation of America, *Credit Counseling in Crisis*, Apr. 2003. Available on-line at www.nclc.org/initiatives/credit_counseling/content/creditcounselingreport.pdf.

376 *See, e.g.*, FTC v. Credit-Care, Inc., 5 Trade Reg. Rep. (CCH). 23,296 (N.D. Ill. 1992) (consent decree) (alleging that Credi-Care kept a significant portion of consumer payments, assessed unfair fees, processed payments so slowly that most accounts became delinquent, and stopped payments on drafts sent to creditors when consumers tried to cancel the agreement); Commonwealth v. Legal Credit Counselors, Inc., Clearinghouse No. 41, 271 (Mass Super. Ct. 1983) (alleging that the agency took unfair advantage of persons in debt, enticing them into believing that creditors would agree to debt pooling arrangements, when many creditors would never agree, and then collecting large up-front fees as well as fees if the debtors was terminated from the services).

377 *See generally* National Consumer Law Center and Consumer Federation of America, *Credit Counseling in Crisis*, Apr. 2003. Available on-line at www.nclc.org/initiatives/credit_counseling/content/creditcounselingreport.pdf; Senate Permanent Subcommittee on Investigations, Committee on Governmental Affairs, *Profiteering in a Non-Profit Industry: Abusive Practices in Credit Counseling* (Mar. 24, 2004), *available at* http://govtaff.senate.gov/_files/032404psistaffreport_creditcounsel.pdf (last visited in Aug. 2004).

378 *See* § 5.1.2.3.3, *infra*.

379 *See* § 5.1.2.3.4, *infra*.

380 *See* www.ftc.gov/opa/2004/07/dmfs.htm (F.T.C. complaints). *See generally* § 5.9.4.6.3, *infra* (discussion of do-not-call rule).

Organizations Act (CROA).[381] The CROA applies only to agencies that offer credit repair services. The definition is broad, encompassing any person who performs or offers to perform any service, for a fee or other valuable consideration, for the express or implied purpose of (i) improving any consumer's credit record, credit history, or credit rating or (ii) providing advice and assistance to any consumer with regard to any activity or service described above.[382] Many credit counseling agencies should fit this definition.

A critical problem with the CROA and its state analogs[383] is that it does not apply to non-profit organizations.[384] Although the vast majority of agencies now charge at least some fees for service, nearly every organization in the industry operates as a non-profit. It may be possible to overcome this hurdle by arguing that a non-profit is a for-profit business in disguise either because it focuses entirely on selling DMPs or because of close connections to for-profit affiliates.[385]

Another possible claim is violation of a state debt pooling law. Many state laws specifically prohibit the business of debt pooling (also known as debt management plans, debt consolidation, budget planning, or debt prorating). With notable exceptions, these state laws are generally ineffective and/or under-enforced. The majority do not specifically provide for private enforcement.[386] Some are contained in the state criminal codes. Where no specific private remedy is provided, violations should be UDAP violations.[387]

State debt pooling laws vary in scope. About half of the states require some type of licensing for agencies providing debt management services.[388] But nearly half of these states

381 15 U.S.C. §§ 1679–1679j. *See* § 5.1.2.2.2, *supra*; National Consumer Law Center, Fair Credit Reporting Ch. 15 (5th ed. 2002 and Supp.).

382 15 U.S.C. § 1679a(3)(A).

383 *See* § 5.1.2.2.2, *supra*; National Consumer Law Center, Fair Credit Reporting Ch. 15 (5th ed. 2002 and Supp.) (discussion of state credit repair organization laws).

384 15 U.S.C. § 1679a(3)(B)(i).

385 For example, a class action lawsuit against Cambridge Credit Counseling is based primarily on alleged violations of the federal CROA. *See* Zimmerman v. Cambridge Credit Counseling Corp. *et al*, Civ. Action 3:03-cv-30261-MAP, Clearinghouse # 55455 (D. Mass. filed Nov. 4, 2003). However, in 2004, the Massachusetts district court rejected Plaintiffs' arguments that the court should examine whether an agency is truly "non-profit" even if it has been granted that status by the IRS. *See* Zimmerman v. Cambridge Credit Counseling Corp., 322 F. Supp. 2d 95 (D. Mass. 2004) (IRS determination of tax-exempt status was dispositive on the issue of whether providers were exempt from the CROA). *See also* Limpert v. Cambridge Credit Counseling, 328 F. Supp. 2d 360 (E.D.N.Y. 2004) (CROA may apply to credit counseling agencies that make representations regarding credit reports, but claims against 501(c)(3) agencies dismissed due to non-profit exemption).

386 In an encouraging sign for consumers, a number of states that have recently passed legislation in this area have included an explicit private right of enforcement for consumers. *See, e.g.*, Kan. S.B. 509, *amending* Kan. Stat. Ann. § 21-4401; Va. Code Ann. § 6.1-363.22. *See also* Me. Rev. Stat. Ann. tit. 32, § 6181. Some states explicitly provide that a violation of the debt management law is a violation of the state UDAP law. Although these provisions are helpful to consumers, violations of these laws should be UDAP violations regardless of whether this explicit language is included.

387 *In re* Fricker, 115 B.R. 809 (Bankr. E.D. Pa. 1990). As with the CROA and state credit repair laws, there may be issues in some states regarding whether the UDAP law applies to non-profit organizations. *See* § 2.3.5, *supra*.

388 Some of the states listed below explicitly exempt non-profits from licensing or registration requirements. Others implicitly exempt at least some non-profit organizations by defining the practice or debt management to include only those organizations that charge fees or receive consideration for services. Thus, the minority of credit counseling agencies that do not charge fees for service are arguably not required to obtain licenses in these states.

Arizona: Ariz. Rev. Stat. § 6-702-716 (exemption from licensing applies to non-profit agencies that do not collect any compensation directly or indirectly. Also requires bonding).

California: Cal. Fin. Code § 12100 *et seq.* (non-profit agencies exempted from licensing, but only if they abide by fee limits and other substantive provisions).

Connecticut: Conn. Gen. Stat. § 36a-655-665 (only non-profits can engage in debt adjusting and must be licensed).

Idaho: Idaho Code § 26-2223 (no exemptions for non-profits).

Illinois: 205 Ill. Comp. Stat. Ann. § 665/2 *et seq.* (non-profits that do not charge implicitly exempted from licensing).

Indiana: Ind. Code § 28-1-29-12 (non-profits explicitly exempted from licensing if they do not charge fees).

Iowa: Iowa Code § 533A.1 *et seq.* (certain non-profits offering free debt management services exempt from licensing, also implicitly exempted if they do not charge).

Kansas: Kan. Stat. Ann. § 21-4402 (non-profits are not exempted from registration requirement). In 2004, Kansas amended its existing debt management law and added a registration requirement, among other substantive provisions.

Louisiana: Louisiana has two laws governing debt adjusting that contradict each other. One law generally prohibits for-profit debt adjusting, but exempts non-profit organizations. La. Rev. Stat. Ann. § 14:331. A second law allows financial planning and management services, but requires the agencies to be licensed. Non-profits engaging in debt management services are exempted from the licensing requirement. La. Rev. Stat. Ann. § 37:2581.

Maine: Me. Rev. Stat. Ann. tit. 17, § 701; Me. Rev. Stat. Ann. tit. 32, § 6172 *et seq.* (only non-profit agencies can operate in the state and must register with state, non-profits that do not charge implicitly exempted).

Maryland: Md. Fin. Inst. § 12-901-12-931 (debt management service providers must be non-profit and must register with the state).

Michigan: Mich. Comp. Laws Ann. § 451.411 *et seq.* (certain non-profits may be exempt from licensing).

Minnesota: Minn. Stat. § 332.13 *et seq.* (non-profits that do not charge fees are explicitly exempt).

Mississippi: Miss. Code Ann. § 81-22-1-81-22-29 (all debt management services providers must be licensed and only non-profits may apply for and receive licenses).

Nebraska: Neb. Rev. Stat. § 69-1201 *et seq.* (non-profits implicitly exempt).

Nevada: Nev. Rev. Stat. § 676.010 *et seq.* (exempts non-profits).

New Hampshire: N.H. Rev. Stat. Ann. § 399-D:1 through D: 27. In 2004, the New Hampshire legislature amended the debt management law. Among other changes, the new law no longer explicitly exempt most non-profits from the licensing requirements. A few states restrict debt management business in the state to non-profits and require these non-profits to be licensed.[389]

The stronger state laws provide regulation beyond licensing and/or regulation. The most common substantive regulations include fee limits and requirements that consumers be given written contracts and that agencies maintain consumer payments in separate trust accounts. In addition, most of the states that require licenses also require agencies to post bonds.

With only a few exceptions, most of the states that have licensing requirements also limit the fees that licensed agencies are allowed to charge. Fee limits vary from state to state. Some states set very specific amounts for start-up and monthly fees. Arizona, for example, sets a ceiling of $39 for retainers and a monthly limit of three-quarters of 1 percent of the consumer's total indebtedness or $50, whichever is less.[390] Certain out-of-pocket expenses may also be charged with debtor approval.[391] California caps fees for enrollment (a one-time fee) at no more than $50 for education and counseling combined in connection with debt management or debt settlement services and a monthly sum not to exceed 6.5 percent of the money disbursed each month, or $20, whichever is less.[392] Other states use percentage limits for monthly fees, based on the level of the consumer's indebtedness (compared to income) or of the total amount of the monthly DMP payment. The percentages allowed are as high as 12 percent or 15 percent in some states. In other states, a maximum dollar cap is used.[393] At least a few states simply limit fees to bona fide and reasonable costs.[394] However, it is more common for states to use the more general standard when regulating fees for counseling and education and to set specific limits when regulating fees for debt management plans.

About twenty states take a different, generally less restrictive, approach. Most of these states generally prohibit debt adjusting, but allow a long list of exceptions. Most important, nearly all of these states exempt non-profit organizations from the general prohibition. Other states do not require licensing, but still limit fees agencies can charge and/or other practices.[395]

In addition to these specific debt management laws, advocates should also consider state credit repair laws and UDAP laws as discussed above. A Massachusetts court found that a debt consolidation service violated the state UDAP statute by promising to stop all bill collectors' calls, when actually some creditors would not agree to the plan but would continue to look to the debtor for money. Furthermore, the debt consolidation service promised to stop interest from accruing but the service charged such large fees that the debtor's payments were often increased. By leading the consumers to believe that creditors would agree to the plan, the debt consolidation service took unfair advantage of consumers and charged large up-front fees.[396] The court also held that it was a UDAP violation not to disclose an initial sixty-day delay in forwarding payments to creditors; the fact that certain creditors would not agree to debt pooling arrangements; the penalties for missed payments and termination; the total number of payments; and the total of fees. Unauthorized practice of law statutes and regulations[397] and

---

exempts non-profits from the licensing requirements. *See* S.B. 498.

New Jersey: N.J. Stat. Ann. §§ 2C:21-19, 17:16G-1 (only non-profits can operate in the state and must be licensed).

New York: N.Y. Gen. Business Law. § 455-457 (general prohibition of budget planning, but licensed non-profits and others including attorneys are exempted); N.Y. Banking Law § 579-587 (budget planner licensing law).

Ohio: Ohio Rev. Code Ann. § 4710.01 *et seq.* In 2004, the Ohio legislature passed significant amendments to the state's debt adjusting law. The changes are effective November 5, 2004.

Oregon: Or. Rev. Stat. § 697.602 *et seq.* (non-profits not exempted from registration).

Rhode Island: R.I. Gen. Law § 5-66-1 (only non-profits may operate in the state and must be licensed). The Rhode Island legislature passed significant amendments to this law in 2004.

South Carolina: S.C. Code Ann. § 40-5-370 (only licensed attorneys may perform debt adjusting).

Vermont: Vt. Stat. Ann. tit. 8, § 4861 (certain non-profits exempted).

Virginia: Va. Code Ann. § 6.1-363.2 through 363.26 (only non-profits allowed and must have license).

Wisconsin: Wis. Stat. § 218.02 (implicit exemption only).

389 *See, e.g.*, Conn. Gen. Stat. § 36-656; Me. Rev. Stat. Ann. tit. 32, § 6172; Md. Fin. Inst. § 12-901 through 12-931; N.J. Stat. Ann. §§ 2C:21-19, 17:16G-2; R.I. Gen. Law § 5-66-1; Va. Code Ann. § 6.1-363.2 through 363.26.

390 Ariz. Rev. Stat. § 6-709.

391 *Id.*

392 Cal. Fin. Code § 12104. The fee limits are higher for debt settlement organizations. The California legislature has been considering amendments that would increase these fee limits.

393 For example, New Jersey sets a fee limit of no more than 1 percent of a consumer's monthly gross income but, in any case, no more than $15. Tennessee's limit is $20. N.J. Stat. Ann. § 17:16G-6; Tenn. Code Ann. § 39-14-142.

394 *See, e.g.*, Guam St. tit. 14, § 7109; R.I. Gen. Laws § 5-66.1-3 (limited to non-profits and costs must not exceed amounts required to defray bona fide expenses).

395 Ark. Code Ann. § 5-63-302; Colo. Rev. Stat. Ann. § 12-14-103 (debt collector law explicitly exempts non-profit credit counselors); Del. Code Ann. tit. 11, § 910; D.C. Code Ann. § 22-1201; Fla. Stat. Ann. § 817.801 through 817.806 (credit counseling), Fla. Stat. Ann. § 559.10 (budget planners); Ga. Code Ann. § 18-5-1; Guam St. tit. 14, § 7101-7106; Haw. Rev. Stat. § 446-3; Ky. Rev. Stat. § 380.010; Mass. Gen. Laws ch. 180, § 4A; Mo. Rev. Stat. § 425.010; Mont. Code Ann. § 31-3-201; N.M. Stat. Ann. § 56-2-1; N.C. Gen. Stat. § 14-423; N.D. Cent. Code §§ 13-06-01 (definitions); 13-07-01-13-07-07; Okla. Stat. tit. 24, § 15; 18 Pa. Cons. Stat. § 7312; S.D. Codified Laws § 22-47-2; Tenn. Code Ann. § 39-14-142; Tex. Fin. Ann. Code § 394.101; Wash. Re. Code § 18.28.010-18.28.9; W. Va. Code § 61-10-23; Wyo. Stat. Ann. § 33-14-101.

396 Commonwealth v. Legal Credit Counselors, Inc., Clearinghouse No. 41, 271 (Mass Super. Ct. 1983).

397 *See* § 5.12.2.4, *infra*.

state loan broker laws[398] may also apply.

Some agencies have argued that they are subject to regulation only in the state in which they are incorporated. For example, in response to a request from a Kansas district attorney that it cease services in the state of Kansas, Cambridge Credit Counseling Corporation claimed that it is only subject to the laws in Massachusetts, its state of incorporation.[399] Although the agency had customers throughout the country, including Kansas, it argued that prosecution under state laws deprived it of its rights under the Commerce Clause. It also argued that the Kansas debt management law is invalid because of the burden imposed on interstate business. A federal district court rejected these arguments, allowing the district attorney to proceed with her request that Cambridge cease doing business in the state.[400]

States have stepped up enforcement throughout 2003 and 2004. The state actions generally raise UDAP claims and in some cases claims based on violations of federal and state telemarketing laws or state debt management laws.[401]

5.1.2.3.3 Abuse of non-profit status

The deference given to organizations with tax-exempt status is especially problematic because the Internal Revenue Service (IRS) has granted this status to many "for-profits in disguise."[402] The vast majority of credit counseling agencies are non-profit organizations. From 1994 through early 2004, 1215 credit counseling agencies applied to the IRS for section 501(c)(3) tax-exempt status.[403] Over 800 of these agencies applied between 2000 and 2003.[404]

A key to improving regulation in this industry is for the IRS and state regulators to aggressively enforce the standards for non-profit eligibility. There are promising signs that the IRS is heading in this direction. First, in January 2003, the IRS released a report signaling the agency's increased awareness of problems with credit counseling agencies.[405] Facing pressure throughout 2003, the IRS, along with the FTC and state regulators, issued a rare joint announcement in October 2003 advising consumers to beware of problems with certain credit counseling organizations.[406] Testifying in Congress in March 2004, IRS Commissioner Mark Everson stated that his agency is examining the tax-exempt status of more than fifty credit counseling organizations.[407]

In the October advisory and subsequent statements, the IRS discusses the standards it uses, or will use, to determine tax-exempt status for credit counseling agencies. Specifically, the agency stated that organizations that only offer debt management plans without significant education and counseling should not qualify for tax-exempt status.[408]

The IRS provided additional guidance on these standards in a 2004 memo.[409] According to the IRS Chief Counsel, it can and should be argued that the new generation of credit counseling organizations does not meet the criteria for exemption set forth in previous revenue rulings and case law because ". . . they are not providing any meaningful education or relief of the poor."[410] The counsel states further that in some cases there may be a basis for arguing for

398 *See* § 5.1.3, *infra.*

399 Cambridge Credit Counseling Corp. v. Foulston, 2003 WL 23279978 (D. Kan. Sept. 25, 2003).

400 *Id.* Cambridge Credit Counseling Corporation is appealing the district court decision. In addition, in 2004, Kansas passed a comprehensive new law regulating debt management agencies. *See* S.B. #509, *amending* Kan. Stat. Ann. § 21-4402.

401 A number of state attorney general offices preceded the FTC in filing suit against AmeriDebt. The Illinois Attorney General's office was the first to sue AmeriDebt, in February 2003, followed by Missouri, Minnesota, and Texas. For a press release describing the Illinois suit filed on February 5, 2003, see www.ag.state.il.us/pressrelease/020503_b.htm; Mo. v. AmeriDebt Inc., Debticated Inc., *available at* http://ago.missouri.gov/lawsuits/2003/091103ameridebt.pdf (filed Sept. 11, 2003). The Minnesota and Texas cases were filed on November 19, 2003. *See also* Commonwealth of Mass. v. Integrated Credit Solutions, Inc. and Flagship Capital Services Corp., Case No.: 1:02-cv-12431-JLT, Clearinghouse No. 55549 (D. Mass. filed Dec. 29, 2002); Cambridge Credit Counseling Corp. v. Foulston, 2003 WL 23279978 (D. Kan. Sept. 25, 2003).

402 Non-profit status is technically a state law concept, making an organization eligible for certain benefits, such as state sales, property, and income tax exemptions. Although most federal tax-exempt organizations are non-profit, organizing as a non-profit at the state level does not automatically grant the organization exemption from federal income tax. The terms "tax-exempt" and "non-profit" organizations or corporations are used interchangeably in this section even though there are some differences between them. For more information, see Internal Revenue Service, "Charities and Non-Profits," and Internal Revenue Service Publication 557, *Tax-Exempt Status for Your Organization*, available at www.irs.gov. Re: tax-exempt vs. non-profit

403 U.S. Senate Permanent Subcommittee on Investigations, Committee on Governmental Affairs, *Profiteering in a Non-Profit Industry: Abusive Practices in Credit Counseling* (Mar. 24, 2004), *available at* http://govt-aff.senate.gov/_files/032404psistaffreport_creditcounsel.pdf (last visited in Aug. 2004).

404 *Id.*

405 Debra Cowen and Debra Kawecki, *Credit Counseling Organizations*, CPE 2004-1 (Jan. 9, 2003), *available at* www.irs.gov/pub/irs-tege/eotopica04.pdf (last visited in Aug. 2004).

406 FTC, IRS and State Regulators Urge Care When Seeking Help from Credit Counseling Organizations (Oct. 13, 2003), *available at* www.irs.gov/newsroom/article/0,,id=114574,00.html (last visited in Aug. 2004).

407 Senate Committee on Governmental Affairs, Profiteering in a Non-Profit Industry: Abusive Practices in Credit Counseling (Mar. 24, 2004) (statement of the Honorable Mark W. Everson), *available at* http://govt-aff.senate.gov/index.cfm?Fuseaction=Hearings.Testimony&HearingID=158&WitnessID=492.

408 *Id.* See also IRS Takes Steps to Ensure Credit Counseling Organizations Comply with Requirements for Tax-Exempt Status FS-2003-17 (Oct. 2003), available at www.irs.gov/newsroom/article/0,,id=114575,00.html (last visited in Mar. 2004).

409 Internal Revenue Service, Chief Counsel Advice Memorandums, CCA 200431023, "IRC Section 501-Exemptoin from Tax on Corporations, Certain Trusts, etc.," July 13, 2004.

410 *Id.*

revocation based on inurement.[411]

In addition, the Federal Trade Commission and a number of state attorney general offices have begun pursuing credit counseling agencies more aggressively, often raising claims related to abuses of non-profit status.[412]

5.1.2.3.4 Debt settlement or negotiation agencies

In contrast to credit counseling agencies that provide debt management services, most debt settlement and debt negotiation agencies are for-profit entities.[413] Negotiation and settlement services differ from debt management services mainly because the debt settlement agencies do not send regular monthly payments to creditors. In fact, they encourage consumers to pay fees to the agency and not pay their creditors. These agencies generally maintain debtor funds in separate accounts, holding the consumer's funds until the agency believes it can settle the entire debt.

There are important distinctions with respect to available legal remedies against debt settlement companies as opposed to credit counselors (or debt management companies). The first key difference is that debt settlement companies are generally for-profit. Thus, there should be no question that the CROA and state analogs apply as long as the threshold definitional requirements are met.[414]

The majority of state debt management laws do not extend to debt settlement companies. However, state UDAP laws should clearly apply. There is also a growing trend, particularly in states that are enacting new legislation in this area, to cover debt settlement agencies in their debt management laws.[415] If the definitions in the state debt management law are sufficiently broad to cover debt settlement, the typical for-profit debt settlement agency will most likely be violating the law in numerous ways. Most clearly, the average debt settlement agency charges fees substantially higher than the fee limits in many state debt management laws.

Federal Trade Commission actions in 2004 highlight many of the problems with debt settlement companies. In one case, the FTC alleged that debt settlement agency Briggs and Baker promised to negotiate reductions in unsecured debt by as much as 75 percent.[416] Consumers who signed up were told to stop making payments to unsecured creditors because creditors would be more likely to settle if the consumer's account was sufficiently delinquent. The FTC raised violations of the federal FTC Act based on alleged misrepresentations and deceptive actions.[417]

The FTC also sued National Consumer Council and related organizations in 2004, claiming violations of the Federal Trade Commission Act, the Telemarketing and Consumer Fraud and Abuse Prevention Act and the Gramm-Leach-Bliley Act.[418] The complaint describes an elaborate scheme fronted by a non-profit agency, National Consumer Council, which allegedly left voice message advertisements on consumers' home answering machines with the goal of generating clients for the its affiliated debt negotiation programs.[419]

5.1.2.3.5 Debt elimination

Some companies promise not just credit counseling, debt payment plans, or debt negotiation, but elimination of debt. Some offer various instruments, such as a "bond for discharge of debt" or "redemption certificate," that the debtor is to present to the creditor and that supposedly force the creditor to relinquish the debt. The Office of the Comptroller of the Currency (OCC), which regulates national banks, has warned banks against these schemes and asserted that creating or presenting such instruments may be a federal crime.[420]

---

411 *Id.*

412 *See* Fed. Trade Comm'n v. AmeriDebt Inc., DebtWorks, Inc., Andris Pukke and Pamela Pukke (D. Md. filed Nov. 19, 2003), *complaint available at* www.ftc.gov/os/caselist/0223171/031119compameridebt.pdf; Fed. Trade Comm'n v. Ballenger Group, L.L.C., and Ballenger Holdings, L.L.C. (D. Md. Filed Nov. 19, 2003), *complaint available at* www.ftc.gov/os/caselist/0223171/031119compballenger.pdf, *stipulated final judgment available at* www.ftc.gov/os/caselist/0223171/031119stipballengerimage.pdf. *See also* www.ag.state.il.us/pressrelease/020503_b.htm (press release describing Illinois AG suit against AmeriDebt); Mo. v. AmeriDebt Inc., Debticated Inc., *available at* http://ago.missouri.gov/lawsuits/2003/091103ameridebt.pdf (filed Sept. 11, 2003); Commonwealth of Mass. v. Integrated Credit Solutions, Inc. and Flagship Capital Servs. Corp., Case No.: 1:02-cv-12431-JLT, Clearinghouse No. 55549 (D. Mass. filed Dec. 29, 2002).

413 There are at least some non-profit agencies that will negotiate settlements for consumers, but these agencies generally do not hold or escrow consumers' monthly payments. Instead, these agencies attempt to negotiate lump-sum pay-offs of a consumer's debts based on funds the consumer already has or can easily obtain.

414 *See* § 5.1.2.2, *supra*.

415 *See, e.g.*, Kan. S.B. 509, *amending* Kan. Stat. Ann. § 21-4402. The California statute exempts non-profit debt settlement agencies from the licensing requirements as long as the agencies charge fees below the required fee limits. Cal. Fin. Code § 12104. However, the majority of debt settlement agencies are for-profit and should not be exempted from licensing even if they did charge fees under the limits.

416 FTC v. Innovative Sys. Tech., Inc., CVO 4-0728 (C.D. Cal. complaint filed Feb. 4, 2004). On the same day the complaint was filed, a stipulated final judgment and order for permanent injunction was filed against defendant Jack Briggs. Both documents are available on the FTC website, www.ftc.gov.

417 Id.

418 FTC v. National Consumer Council, et seq., Case No. SACV-04-0474 CJC On-line: www.ftc.gov/os/2004/05/040423ncccomplaint.pdf. C.D. Ca., complaint filed Apr. 23, 2004.

419 *Id. See also* § 5.9.4.6, *infra* (telemarketing and "Do Not Call" laws).

420 *See* OCC Alert 2003-12 (Oct. 1, 2003), *available at* www.occ.treas.gove/ftp/alert/2003-12.doc.

Another scheme sets up an arbitration that is programmed to produce a ruling that the debt is invalid. This scheme is interesting to consumer advocates because it validates their assertion that if one side—typically the creditor or seller—controls the choice of the arbitrator, the arbitration system can not be relied upon to produce just results. From the point of view of the consumer who has paid for one of these debt elimination techniques, if the technique is unsuccessful the consumer certainly has a UDAP claim for misrepresenting its features, legality, and likelihood of success of the technique.

The federal Credit Repair Organizations Act[421] or a state analog may give the consumer additional claims, as these schemes are often marketed as methods for consumers to improve their credit records.

5.1.3 Loan Brokers

5.1.3.1 General

Misdeeds by loan brokers are often at the bottom of unfair or deceptive lending. Loan brokers' compensation is usually based on the volume, size, or terms of the loans they generate, and they bear little or none of the risk of nonpayment of the loan. As a result, knowing that they will not bear the consequences if the consumer is unable or refuses to pay, unscrupulous brokers use deceptive and unfair tactics to bind consumers to loans. This section deals with deception by loan brokers about their fees and services, special restrictions on advance fees, and challenges to yield spread premiums. Other sections discuss falsified appraisals and credit applications.[422]

It is deceptive for a loan broker, loan finder or credit consultant to misrepresent the likelihood of securing a loan, the terms of the credit, the availability of long-term loans, or the speed with which a loan can be made, or to fail to disclose extra charges for obtaining a loan.[423] It is also deceptive for a loan broker to misrepresent itself as a lender.[424]

Conversely, it is deceptive for an individual to misrepresent himself as a loan broker when in fact he was just an agent of one creditor and the "broker" only contacted that one creditor on behalf of the debtor.[425] In effect, this may be an attempt by the creditor to hide part of the finance charge as a loan broker fee. In a similar case, Virginia's highest court found it deceptive for a lender to charge a broker fee when the consumer applied for a loan from the lender, but the lender placed the loan with the lender's president.[426]

It is deceptive for a loan broker to fail to reveal his charge until minutes before the credit agreement is to be signed (even though the credit agreement has a three-day cooling-off period).[427] It is also deceptive to hide a broker's commission in the loan documents, so that the consumer has to make an extra payment at the closing.[428] Charging a fee of $1130 on a $3500 loan was grossly excessive and unconscionable.[429] It is unfair and deceptive for a creditor to take a loan application, mortgage and note from the applicant, record the mortgage, then disapprove the loan, but refuse to satisfy the mortgage without payment of a broker fee and other charges.[430]

The Pennsylvania Attorney General has issued UDAP regulations that prohibit loan brokers from, among other things, accepting or refinancing a fee where a loan is not procured within the time and at the rate, term, and overall cost as promised.[431] Massachusetts' mortgage-broker and

421 *See* § 5.1.2.2, *supra*.

422 *See* §§ 5.1.4.5, 5.5.5.6, *infra*.

423 State v. Western Capital Corp., 290 N.W.2d 467 (S.D. 1980); FTC v. Puma Indus., Inc., 5 Trade Reg. Rep. (CCH) ¶ 23,654 (E.D. Cal. Aug. 23, 1994) (TRO) ¶ 23,741 (proposed final order) (failure to provide promised loan or refund); Massachusetts Regulations Concerning Mortgage Brokers and Mortgage Lenders, Mass. Regs. Code tit. 940, §§ 8.04 to 8.06. *See also* FTC v. Schwab, 3 Trade Reg. Rep. (CCH) ¶ 22,396 (S.D. Ohio 1986) (consent order); State v. Gartenberg, 488 N.W.2d 496 (Minn. Ct. App. 1992); State *ex rel.* Abrams v. East Coast Auto Consultants Corp., 472 N.Y.S.2d 1010 (Sup. Ct. 1984). *Cf.* Lewis v. Delta Funding Corp. (*In re* Lewis), 290 B.R. 541 (Bankr. E.D. Pa. 2003) (issues of material fact prevent summary judgment on claim that broker and lender violated UDAP statute by failing to advise homeowner of disadvantages of refinancing).

424 Rutter v. Troy Mortgage Servicing Co., 145 Mich. App. 116, 377 N.W.2d 846 (1985); Lubbock Mortgage & Inv. Co. v. Thomas, 626 S.W.2d 611 (Tex. Civ. App. 1981); Massachusetts Regulations Concerning Mortgage Brokers and Mortgage Lenders, Mass. Regs. Code tit. 940, §§ 8.04 to 8.06; *see also* State v. Gartenberg, 488 N.W.2d 496 (Minn. Ct. App. 1992); Valley Acceptance Corp. v. Glasby, 337 S.E.2d 291 (Va. 1985) (deceptive for creditor to take broker fee for placing loan with creditor's president).

425 Phillips v. Dukes (*In re* Dukes), 24 B.R. 404 (Bankr. E.D. Mich. 1982); Massachusetts Regulations Concerning Mortgage Brokers and Mortgage Lenders, Mass. Regs. Code tit. 940, §§ 8.04 to 8.06 (effective Aug. 1, 1992).

426 Valley Acceptance Corp. v. Glasby, 337 S.E.2d 291 (Va. 1985).

427 Phillips v. Dukes (*In re* Dukes), 24 B.R. 404 (Bankr. E.D. Mich. 1982). *See also* Massachusetts Regulations Concerning Mortgage Brokers and Mortgage Lenders, Mass. Regs. Code tit. 940, §§ 8.05, 8.06.

428 Russell v. Fidelity Consumer Discount Co., 72 B.R. 855 (Bankr. E.D. Pa. 1987). *But see* Butitta v. First Mortgage Corp., 578 N.E.2d 116 (Ill. App. Ct. 1991) (no UDAP violation where there was no misrepresentation and debtors did not allege that knowledge of the disputed charges would have made a difference).

429 Russell v. Fidelity Consumer Discount Co., 72 B.R. 855 (Bankr. E.D. Pa. 1987). *See also* Massachusetts Regulations Concerning Mortgage Brokers and Mortgage Lenders, Mass. Regs. Code tit. 940, § 8.06(2), (6).

430 McClendon v. Metropolitan Mortgage Co., Clearinghouse No. 43,703G (Fla. Cir. Ct. Dade Cty. May 20, 1988).

431 Pennsylvania Attorney General Regulations, 37 Pa. Code ch. 305, Loan Broker Trade Practices. Note that Pennsylvania also has a separate mortgage broker law, 63 Pa. Stat. § 456.301 *et seq.*, and that its credit services organization statute, 73 Pa. Stat. § 2181 *et seq.* also applies to certain loan brokers. *See also* State *ex rel.* Hartigan v. Commonwealth Mortgage Corp., 732 F.

mortgage-lender regulations cover various broker misrepresentations and require a set disclosure from all covered brokers.[432] Brokers also can not do business with unlicensed lenders or include undisclosed fees.[433]

The Comptroller of the Currency has issued an advisory letter to the national banks it regulates, cautioning them of the heightened risk that loans originated by brokers and other intermediaries will be abusive.[434] The letter points out that, since these intermediaries do not take on the ultimate credit risk of the loan and are less intensely supervised than banks, they are more likely to be tempted to originate loans that the borrower does not have a reasonable prospect of repaying. The letter advises national banks to establish specific policies and procedures to avoid these loans. In litigating against a bank that acquired an abusive loan through a broker, it may be useful to inquire through discovery whether the bank had such policies and procedures in place.

Loan broker abuses are becoming so widespread that states are beginning to enact special statutes covering such abuses.[435] State credit repair organization statutes may also be worded broadly enough to apply to loan brokers.[436] These statutes may provide their own remedial scheme or violations may be treated as state UDAP violations.[437] In addition, many states require that loan brokers be licensed. Failure of a broker to obtain a proper license may be a state UDAP violation.[438] If the contract with the broker is solicited or signed in the consumer's home, the state home solicitation sales law may provide a right to cancel.[439] In some states loan brokers owe a fiduciary or quasi-fiduciary duty to their borrowers.[440]

Supp. 885 (N.D. Ill. 1990) (UDAP violation for mortgage company to represent falsely that they could close loans within a certain time period); Massachusetts Regulations Concerning Mortgage Brokers and Mortgage Lenders, Mass. Regs. Code tit. 940, §§ 8.04, 8.06.

432 Massachusetts Regulations Concerning Mortgage Brokers and Mortgage Lenders, Mass. Regs. Code tit. 940, §§ 8.04, to 8.06.

433 *Id.*

434 OCC Advisory Letter 2003-3, Avoiding Predatory and Abusive Lending Practices in Brokered and Purchased Loans (Feb. 21, 2003).

435 *See, e.g.*, Ark. Code Ann. § 23-39-401 *et seq.*; Ky. Rev. Stat. §§ 367.380 to .389.

436 *See* § 5.1.2.2.2, *supra*. *See, e.g.*, Lewis v. Delta Funding Corp. (*In re* Lewis), 290 B.R. 541 (Bankr. E.D. Pa. 2003).

437 *Id*; State v. WWJ Corp., 980 P.2d 1257 (Wash. 1999) (assessing $500,000 in UDAP civil penalties for violation of state mortgage broker statute); Opportunity Mgmt. Co. v. Frost, 1999 Wash. App. LEXIS 336 (Feb. 16, 1999) (violation of mortgage broker statute is UDAP violation).

438 *See* § 4.7.7.2, *supra*.

439 Bank of New York v. Kaiser, 2003 WL 23335972 (Ohio Com. Pleas Aug. 16, 2003). *See generally* § 5.8.2, *infra*.

440 *See* National Consumer Law Center, The Cost of Credit: Regulation and Legal Challenges § 11.9.1 (2d ed. 2000 and Supp.).

5.1.3.2 Advance-Fee Brokers

A widespread form of loan broker abuse involves advance fees. The broker takes cash up front from the consumer, promising to find the consumer a loan, but never follows through and never refunds the consumer the fee.

The FTC's Telemarketing Rule prohibits brokers who meet the definition of telemarketer from requesting or receiving payment of any fee in advance of obtaining a loan when the broker has guaranteed or represented a high likelihood of success in obtaining the loan.[441] Some state telemarketing laws have similar prohibitions.[442]

An Oregon UDAP regulation prohibits loan brokers from accepting advance fees unless they first provide the consumer with a written contract with numerous disclosures concerning the broker and the broker's success rate in placing loans. They must also have a written contract from a qualified lender agreeing to make loans if that broker's clients meet specified criteria. Oregon advance-fee brokers must also notify the consumer within fourteen days whether a loan has been accepted or rejected, provide the loan within seven days of acceptance, place all advance fees into an escrow account, and promptly refund such fees if a loan is denied. The regulation also prohibits advertising that claims that most borrowers will qualify for a loan and requires various disclosures in advertising.[443]

Even without more specific prohibitions, a loan broker can not take an advance fee to obtain a loan, and then fail to refund that fee as promised when the broker does not obtain a loan.[444] It is also deceptive to misrepresent that advance payments will be applied to the consumer's loan repayments and to fail to disclose to consumers various non-refundable charges imposed by the loan broker.[445]

Brokers also violate a UDAP statute by promising to put advance fees in an escrow account, only to be drawn down as earned, when in fact the funds remain in the control of the loan broker.[446] The FTC has stopped a loan broker's practice of inviting consumers to call an 800 number that refers them to a 900 number to submit a loan application, where most applicants did not obtain loans but the 900-number charges provided significant income to the broker.[447]

441 16 C.F.R. § 310.4(a)(4). *See also* FTC v. Ideal Credit Referral Services, Ltd., 5 Trade Reg. Rep. (CCH) ¶ 24,253 (W.D. Wash. 1997) (proposed consent decree); FTC v. Amstar Fin. Corp., Inc., 5 Trade Reg. Rep. (CCH) ¶ 24,221 (C.D. Cal. 1997) (proposed consent decree). *See* § 5.9, *supra*.

442 *See* Appx. E, *infra*.

443 Or. Admin. Rules 137-20-0250.

444 *See* State *ex rel.* Montgomery v. Global Financial Assistance, Clearinghouse No. 52,021 (Ohio C.P. Franklin Cty. Sept. 3, 1996).

445 *See* State v. Gartenberg, 488 N.W.2d 496 (Minn. Ct. App. 1992). *See also* Worldwide Credit, Inc., 5 Trade Reg. Rep. (CCH) ¶ 23,628 (F.T.C. File No. 922 3108 1994) (consent order).

446 *See* State *ex rel.* Stenberg v. American Midlands, Inc., 244 Neb. 887, 509 N.W.2d 633 (1994).

447 Delta Financial Services, Inc., 5 Trade Reg. Rep. (CCH) ¶ 23,685

5.1.3.3 Yield Spread Premiums

A widespread practice in both the home mortgage and auto finance industries is charging interest rates that include "yield spread premiums." Lenders provide brokers, car dealers, or other arrangers of credit a range of acceptable interest rates. If the broker arranges the loan at a rate higher than the minimum of that range, then the broker gets to keep all or some of the amount that exceeds the minimum rate. The consumer may have some sense that the loan broker will be paid by the lender, but have no idea that the amount of the loan broker's compensation depends on getting the least favorable terms for the consumer.

Yield spreads in automotive financing are analyzed at 5.4.3.4, *infra*. Most litigation regarding yield spread premiums in home mortgage loans is based on claims under the federal Real Estate Settlement Procedures Act (RESPA).[448] State mortgage broker or loan broker laws may also require disclosure of such fees.[449] It can also be a UDAP violation to fail to disclose to the consumer that the lender is willing to write the loan at a lower interest rate, and that all or some of the amount exceeding that lower rate is being paid to the loan arranger.[450] Paying a yield spread premium to a mortgage broker solely for arranging a higher interest rate on a consumer's loan may be a UDAP violation in and of itself.[451] The consumer's attorney should also look carefully for any express or implied claims that the broker would get the best rate possible for the consumer or would act in the consumer's interest. Such deceptive claims should be UDAP violations.[452]

The creditor often has a high degree of discretion about the size of the yield spread premium and may follow a pattern of charging higher amounts to minority consumers.[453] Such a practice is not only a possible UDAP violation[454] but also violates federal and state discrimination laws.[455]

5.1.4 Improvident Extension of Credit

5.1.4.1 General

A recent case, *City Financial Services v. Smith*,[456] is a small step toward the growth of an important concept, that the improvident extension of credit is an unfair, deceptive or unconscionable practice. Lenders should not make loans when they know that borrowers will not be able to repay them.

Why would a lender do this? Some creditors want to foreclose on the debtor's home or other security. Or a lender may set up a commission structure that encourages its agents to make loans even when they know the money can not be repaid.[457]

City Financial Services made a $3000 loan to Ms. Smith at 22% interest plus $618 in insurance and other charges. Ms. Smith had $574 a month in disability income, was already in default with one loan with City Financial Services, and had over $6700 in other credit card debt. She also had equity in her home, which gave City Financial Services an incentive to make the loan, despite her inability to repay it.

(F.T.C. File No. X-92 0049 1994) (proposed consent order).

448 *See* National Consumer Law Center, The Cost of Credit: Regulation and Legal Challenges § 11.3.1.5 (2d ed. 2000 and Supp.).

449 *See* Opportunity Mgmt. Co. v. Frost, 1999 Wash. App. LEXIS 336 (Feb. 16, 1999) (nondisclosure of lender's kickback of part of origination fee to broker violated state mortgage broker law, which was *per se* UDAP violation).

450 Watson v. CBSK Fin. Group, Inc., 2002 U.S. Dist. LEXIS 6872 (N.D. Ill. Apr. 17, 2002) (denying motion to dismiss UDAP claim that lender failed to disclose impact of yield spread premium on interest rate and overall cost of loan); Michalowski v. Flagstar Bank, 2002 U.S. Dist. LEXIS 1245 (N.D. Ill. Jan. 24, 2002) (paying yield spread premium to mortgage broker solely for arranging higher interest rate may be UDAP violation); Moses v. Citicorp Mortgage, Inc., 982 F. Supp. 897 (E.D.N.Y. 1997) (denying defendant's motion to dismiss claim in home mortgage case). *See also* Besta v. Beneficial Loan Co., 855 F.2d 532 (8th Cir. 1988); Andrews v. Temple Inland Mortg. Corp., 2001 U.S. Dist. LEXIS 23613 (D. Minn. Sept. 24, 2001) (denying motion to dismiss claim that imposition of hidden yield spread premium was UDAP violation); *In re* Milbourne, 108 B.R. 522 (Bankr. E.D. Pa. 1989); Green v. H&R Block, Inc., 355 Md. 488, 735 A.2d 1039 (1999) (failure to disclose that tax return preparer received hidden fees from bank for refund anticipation loans it referred states UDAP claim); National Consumer Law Center, The Cost of Credit: Regulation and Legal Challenges § 11.2.2.6 (2d ed. 2000 and Supp.). *Cf.* Basile v. H&R Block, Inc., 563 Pa. 359, 761 A.2d 1115 (2000) (no agency relationship between tax preparation service and taxpayer/borrower required disclosure of hidden fees, but case remanded to determine if fiduciary relationship existed), *appeal after remand*, 777 A.2d 95 (Pa. Super. 2001) (reversing summary judgment for tax preparer; genuine issue of fact whether relationship was confidential). *But cf.* Melton v. Family First Mortg. Corp., 576 S.E.2d 365 (N.C. App. 2003) (no UDAP violation where no agreement between broker and lender to conceal fact that loan was approved at lower rate than consumer was charged).

451 Michalowski v. Flagstar Bank, 2002 U.S. Dist. LEXIS 1245 (N.D. Ill. Jan. 24, 2002).

452 Fairman v. Schaumburg Toyota, Inc., 1996 U.S. Dist. LEXIS 9669 (N.D. Ill. July 9, 1996).

453 *See* Coleman v. General Motors Acceptance Corp., 196 F.R.D. 315 (M.D. Tenn. 2000), *vacated on other grounds*, 296 F.3d 443 (6th Cir. 2002).

454 *See* §§ 4.3.9, *supra*, 5.1.5.3, *infra*.

455 *See* § 5.4.5.3, *infra*; National Consumer Law Center, Credit Discrimination (3d ed. 2002 and Supp.).

456 Clearinghouse No. 52,489 (Ohio Mun. Ct. Jan. 4, 2000).

457 To increase commissions and retain their arrangements with brokers and sellers who generate business for them, loan approval employees may also agree to accept shaky loans as long as each one is paired with a more solid loan. *See also* Matthews v. New Century Mortg. Corp., 185 F. Supp. 2d 874 (S.D. Ohio 2002) (loan company employees had close personal ties to mortgage brokers whose loan applications they approved).

The court found the loan unconscionable and unenforceable, despite the fact that the lender followed its own underwriting guidelines. The court criticized the guidelines for inflating Ms. Smith's $574 a month disability income to $718 based on the fact that her disability income was tax-free. The court also found the guidelines to produce unreasonable results.

Another recent case, *Opportunity Management Co. v. Frost*,[458] analyzes improvident extension of credit in some detail. There, a Washington intermediate appellate court upheld a jury's verdict that a lender committed a UDAP violation by lending money to a woman it knew did not have the income to repay. Instead, the lender relied on the loan-to-value ratio, i.e., the fact that the value of the property securing the loan was sufficient to repay it.

The court applied the FTC definition of unfairness: whether the practice offends public policy; whether it is immoral, unethical, oppressive, or unscrupulous; and whether it causes substantial injury to consumers.[459] The court held that the jury could reasonably conclude that making the loan based on the value of the collateral was unethical or unscrupulous and caused substantial consumer injury.

The District of Columbia UDAP statute specifies that it is a violation for a lender to make a loan when it knows there is no reasonable probability of repayment in full.[460] The District of Columbia Circuit has upheld a trebled jury verdict where the jury found a mortgage lender had violated that provision.[461] In another case, a federal court held that consumers stated a claim by alleging that the defendants induced them to enter into a home mortgage by submitting an inflated appraisal and misrepresenting that the payments would be affordable.[462]

Another debtor was awarded approximately $3 million in UDAP multiple damages and $100,000 in attorney fees for a lender's misconduct in luring the debtor into a loan the debtor could not afford.[463] By implication and oral statements, the lender gave the debtor the clear impression that future financing would be available. The lender knew the debtor had neither the income nor the assets to repay its initial loan to the debtor, and the lender knew the failure to offer future financing (in this case to allow the debtor to develop the property and so hopefully satisfy the various loan obligations) would spell certain foreclosure.

The court found this scheme—essentially to lure a debtor into a secured loan he could not afford on the implied promise of future financing and then to pull the rug out after the debtor had become obligated—to be unfair and deceptive. The lack of written documents promising such future financing was irrelevant when the lender's conduct and oral statements led the debtor to believe such financing would be forthcoming.

5.1.4.2 UDAP and Other Laws Prohibiting Credit That Consumer Can Not Repay

Other states have statutes that are easily applicable to these practices. The Uniform Consumer Credit Code (1974), adopted in Idaho, Iowa, Kansas, and Maine, and the Uniform Consumer Sales Practices Act, adopted in Ohio, Kansas, and Utah, specify that, in determining whether a practice is unconscionable, the court should consider whether the creditor had reason to know, when the consumer entered into the transaction, that there was no reasonable probability of payment of the obligation in full by the consumer.[464] Mississippi UDAP regulations have a similar definition.[465]

Wisconsin defines unconscionable credit transactions to include ones that require consumers "to unreasonably jeopardize money or property beyond the money or property immediately at issue in the transaction."[466] In other words, it may be unconscionable if a loan unreasonably jeopardizes the consumer's non-purchase money collateral.

Montana has passed a statute that provides a mathematical formula for determining whether a payday loan is unconscionably improvident. A payday loan may be unconscionable if the loan amount exceeds 25% of the consumer's monthly net income. For example, if a consumer's monthly net income is $1500, a payday loan amount can not exceed $375.[467]

5.1.4.3 Applying General UDAP Prohibitions to Improvident Extension of Credit

Even without a specific statutory prohibition, improvident extension of credit violates general UDAP principles of unfairness and deception. A lender that intentionally makes a loan for the reason of seizing the consumer's collateral

458 1999 Wash. App. LEXIS 336 (Feb. 16, 1999).

459 *See* § 4.3, *supra*.

460 D.C. Code § 28-3904(r)(1).

461 Williams v. First Government Mortgage & Investors Corp., 225 F.3d 738 (D.C. Cir. 2000).

462 Vaughn v. Consumer Home Mortg., Inc., 2003 WL 21241669 (E.D.N.Y. Mar. 23, 2003).

463 Sweeney v. Comfed Savings Bank, Clearinghouse No. 45,751 (Mass. Super. Ct. 1991). *But cf.* Wachovia Bank & Trust v. Carrington Dev. Assocs., 459 S.E.2d 17 (N.C. Ct. App. 1995) (no UDAP violation for refusal to disburse additional funds on a construction loan because the borrower has defaulted in paying subcontractors).

464 *See* U.C.C.C. § 5.108(4)(a) (1974); UCSPA § 4(c)(4). Note, however, that Ohio and Utah exclude at least some lenders from coverage. *See* Appx. A, *infra*. *See, e.g.*, Jones v. Novastar Mortg., Inc., 298 B.R. 451 (Bankr. D. Kan. 2003) (issue of fact whether lender extended credit based solely on value of collateral, knowing that borrower could not repay, where borrower claimed to have given accurate income information to broker).

465 Mississippi Rules of Consumer Protection, Office of the Attorney General Rule 69.

466 Wis. Code Ann. § 425.107(3)(f).

467 Mont. Code Ann. § 31-1-723(8).

engages in a UDAP violation. It is certainly deceptive for the lender to fail to disclose to the consumer that it is not making the loan because it believes the consumer will repay the loan, but because it hopes it can take possession of the consumer's home or other property. The practice is also unfair and unconscionable—stealing someone's home does not have a legitimate business justification outweighing the consumer injury.[468]

Similarly, it is deceptive for a lender to represent that a consumer meets the lender's underwriting guidelines for a particular loan where that is not the case or where those guidelines are not real guidelines at all. It is also unfair for a broker or agent of the creditor to falsify, or encourage the consumer to falsify the consumer's credit application, resulting in the extension of an unaffordable loan to the consumer and the potential loss of the home or other collateral.[469]

The consumer may also be able to show that there was deception or fraud as to the loan terms. A creditor who merely takes advantage of the consumer's misunderstanding of how high the payments are or the nature of a balloon payment may commit a UDAP violation.[470]

Even if the lender makes no explicit or implied representations as to a consumer's ability to repay a loan, offering a loan that is obviously beyond the borrower's ability to repay is an unfair practice. The lender is taking advantage of its superior knowledge and expertise[471] and there is no legitimate business justification for such a loan.[472] The unfairness is accentuated where the consumer is especially vulnerable[473] or is facing an emergency need for the loan.[474]

5.1.4.4 Other Claims

An unconscionability claim may be helpful in improvident lending cases.[475] The terms of the loan are substantively unconscionable, when with the borrower is saddled with an unreasonable risk of loss of the collateral while the lender has little or no risk of loss. Probably procedural unconscionability, i.e., oppression or unfair surprise in the manner in which the transaction was consummated, can also be shown. If the transaction is unconscionable, the court may be willing to reform it, for example by reducing the interest or principal so that the payments are affordable.

Congress in 1994 attacked improvident lending with the Home Ownership and Equity Protection Act (HOEPA) that prohibits "a pattern or practice of extending credit to consumers [in covered loans] based on the consumers' collateral without regard to the consumers' repayment ability."[476] This statute applies to certain high-rate, home-secured loans, and requires there to be a pattern or practice of improvident extension of credit. For more details and a sample complaint, see NCLC's *Truth in Lending* Ch. 9 (5th ed. 2003 and Supp.). A sample complaint is also included on the companion CD-Rom to this volume.[477]

For a creditor to purchase or refinance the consumer's principal residence that will be secured by a mortgage on the home, Regulation B under the Equal Credit Opportunity Act requires the creditor to take a written credit application.[478] If the creditor did not take a written application, the borrower has an ECOA claim against the creditor, making actual and punitive damages, declaratory and injunctive relief, and attorney fees available.[479] The absence of a written application is also powerful evidence that the lender made the loan without regard to the consumer's repayment ability. If there is a written application, the borrower's attorney should obtain it through discovery, along with the underwriting worksheets and other documents that the lender used in approving the loan. These may show that the lender had clear warning signs that the consumer could not afford the loan, or that the broker falsified the borrower's credit information.[480]

5.1.4.5 Falsification of Credit Application by Seller or Broker

5.1.4.5.1 Nature of the problem

All too often, a seller or broker falsifies the information on the consumer's credit application as a means of securing an improvident extension of credit from a creditor.[481] This may take the form of manufacturing phony income, recording a fictitious down payment, or representing that a down payment came from the consumer's own funds when actu-

468 *See* §§ 4.3, 4.4, *supra.*

469 *See* § 5.1.4.5, *infra.*

470 *See In re* Barker, 251 B.R. 250 (Bankr. E.D. Pa. 2000) (UDAP violation to sign naive debtor to balloon note without explaining it).

471 *See* § 4.3.7, *supra.*

472 *See* § 4.3.2.4, *supra.*

473 *See* § 4.3.8, *supra.*

474 *See* Hager v. Am. Gen. Fin., Inc., 37 F. Supp. 2d 778 (S.D. W. Va. 1999) (denying lender's motion for summary judgment). *See generally* § 4.3.11, *supra.*

475 *See* § 4.4.9, *supra.*

476 15 U.S.C. § 1639(h); Reg. Z § 226.32(e)(1).

477 The complaint is also included on National Consumer Law Center, Consumer Law Pleadings No. 4, Ch. 2 (CD-Rom and Index Guide).

478 12 C.F.R. §§ 202.5(e), 202.13(a). *See* National Consumer Law Center, Credit Discrimination § 5.4 (3d ed. 2002 and Supp.).

479 15 U.S.C. §§ 1691e, 1692a(g). *See* National Consume Law Center, Credit Discrimination Ch. 11 (3d ed. 2002 and Supp.).

480 *See* § 5.1.4.5, *infra.*

481 *See* Gelco Corp. v. Major Chevrolet, Inc., 2002 WL 31427027 (N.D. Ill. Oct. 30, 2002) (describing "massive pattern of fraud" by car dealer in falsifying consumers' credit information in order to induce assignee to accept contracts); Union Mortg. Co. v. Barlow, 595 So. 2d 1335 (Ala. 1992) (upholding fraud and conspiracy verdicts for consumer; home improvement contractor instructed her and other consumers to misrepresent purpose and use of loan proceeds).

ally it was provided by the seller, inflating the value of a trade-in, or misrepresenting the nature or value of the collateral.[482] Sometimes a seller even falsifies the identity of the consumer by substituting a "straw buyer."

A seller who creates a fictitious down payment typically offsets it by increasing the cash price. A $8000 loan looks less risky to a lender if it is based on a $10,000 cash price with a $2000 down payment than a $8000 cash price with no down payment. This in turn may require the seller to misrepresent to the lender the value of the collateral to support the higher cash price. For example, the dealer may inflate the features found on a car being purchased.

Sellers and brokers often are paid up front once a credit transaction is consummated, usually with no recourse back to them if the consumer defaults. They thus have the incentive to get the deal financed, and are unconcerned about whether the consumer will be able to pay the lender or assignee. Even employees of the assignee or lender may participate in this fraud, since their compensation often depends on the number of transactions they generate.[483] Or the lender may be counting on passing the loan onto the secondary market or recovering from mortgage insurance.

5.1.4.5.2 The consumer's legal claims

Seller or broker practices misrepresenting the credit application are clearly wrongful, and may even violate federal criminal law. Anyone knowingly making a false statement or overvaluing security for the purpose of influencing an action of a federally-insured financial institution is subject to a fine of not more than $1 million or imprisonment of not more than thirty years, or both.[484]

In addition, a broker's or seller's manufacture of fictitious income or down payment information is a UDAP violation.[485] Even though the falsified credit information is typically communicated not to the consumer, but to the creditor, this should not undercut the UDAP claim. Most state UDAP statutes reach practices by parties who do not communicate directly with the consumer.[486]

Credit application misrepresentations may also violate the federal Credit Repair Organizations Act, which prohibits making, or advising a consumer to make, false statements to an actual or potential creditor concerning the consumer's creditworthiness, credit standing, or credit capacity.[487] This prohibition applies to any entity, even those that do not meet the statute's definition of "credit repair organization."[488] The Act has advantages over some UDAP statutes in that it offers a private cause of action for actual damages, punitive damages, and attorney fees, has a five year statute of limitations, explicitly authorizes class actions,[489] and provides federal court jurisdiction. State credit repair laws often have similar prohibitions and similar remedies, if a litigant prefers to stay in state court.[490] In addition, the falsification may be bank fraud, which is a predicate offense under the federal RICO statute.[491]

5.1.4.5.3 Computing the consumer's damages

The court may initially be inclined to view the creditor rather than the consumer as the victim, with the consumer suffering no damage. However, the consumer should be able to establish damage if the income falsification caused the consumer to be locked into an unaffordable transaction.[492] The main consumer injury is that the consumer has obtained a loan where there is a higher probability than normal that the consumer will default. In effect, the dealer has engaged in an improvident extension of credit,[493] and the dealer should be liable for any injury the consumer suffers because of the default. For example, the amount of a deficiency claim against the consumer might be considered actual damages.

Where the dealer increases the vehicle's purchase price to offset a fictitious down payment, the consumer also may become obligated to pay a higher sales tax, or GAP, force-placed, or other insurance premiums may be higher to the extent they are based on the vehicle's higher cash price.

482 Honorable v. Easy Life Real Estate Sys., Inc., 182 F.R.D. 553 (N.D. Ill. 1998); Hoffman v. Stamper, 843 A.2d 153 (Md. Ct. Spec. App. 2004), *review granted*, 851 A.2d 593 (Md. 2004). For more on falsified appraisals, see § 5.5.5.6, *infra*.

483 *See, e.g.*, Knapp v. Americredit Fin. Serv., Inc., 245 F. Supp. 2d 841 (S.D. W. Va. 2003) (testimony supported consumer's allegations that lender trained car dealer to create false paystubs and false down payments).

484 18 U.S.C. § 1014.

485 Haser v. Wright, 2002 WL 31379971 (Mass. Super. Sept. 4, 2002). *See also* Hoffman v. Stamper, 843 A.2d 153 (Md. Ct. Spec. App. 2004) (defendants' involvement in manufacture of documentation about source of down payment funds is UDAP violation), *review granted*, 851 A.2d 593 (Md. 2004).

486 *See* §§ 2.3.8, 4.2.15.3, *supra*.

487 15 U.S.C. § 1679b(a)(1).

488 *Id. See* Lacey v. William Chrysler Plymouth Inc., 2004 U.S. Dist. LEXIS 2479 (N.D. Ill. Feb. 20, 2004). *See also* § 5.1.2.2.2, *supra*; National Consumer Law Center, Fair Credit Reporting Ch. 15 (5th ed. 2002 and Supp.).

489 15 U.S.C. § 1679g.

490 *See* § 5.1.2.2.3, *supra*; National Consumer Law Center, Fair Credit Reporting § 15.3 (5th ed. 2002 and Supp.).

491 18 U.S.C. §§ 1344. *But cf.* Honorable v. Easy Life Real Estate Sys., Inc., 182 F.R.D. 553 (N.D. Ill. 1998) (property flippers' false representation to banks that they had not provided down payments to buyers was bank fraud, but only banks were victims so buyers could not assert RICO claim). *See* § 9.2, *infra* (discussion of federal RICO).

492 *See* § 5.5.5.6, *infra* (discussion of reliance issue in context of falsified appraisals). *See also* Haser v. Wright, 2002 WL 31379971 (Mass. Super. Sept. 4, 2002) (consumers' damage was the deposit they lost when they backed out of transaction after discovering falsification).

493 *See* § 5.1.4, *supra*.

Such injuries are sufficient to allow a UDAP claim to go forward.[494]

Sellers who manipulate the price or terms of a transaction may also run afoul of the Truth in Lending Act, since the increase in price to obtain credit may be viewed as a finance charge. If the TIL violation is one that leads to statutory damages, this can provide a viable consumer remedy, including attorney fees, even where there are not provable actual damages.

A final consumer remedy may be rescission of the whole deal. The agreement to finance and proceed with the sale is based on a misrepresentation, and as such should be rescinded

5.1.4.5.4 Consumer's clean hands

The seller or broker has a lot to lose if its conduct is made public. Often, a lender with an established relationship with a seller or broker will not be happy to learn of such behavior. Nor will state licensing agencies or other regulators. Nevertheless, where the seller or broker is willing to litigate a case and risk disclosure of its practices, the consumer's attorney must act carefully before bringing a claim involving falsification of information provided to a creditor. The consumer's attorney must thoroughly explore whether the consumer was complicit in the falsification. Such acts can amount to bank fraud, a serious criminal offense.[495]

Often, though, the credit application alteration occurs after the consumer signs the document, or the dealer even forges the consumer's signature, so the consumer can not be held responsible for what the dealer does.[496] It is excellent practice, though, when a consumer discovers that a credit application has been altered, to report that alteration immediately to the financer and to government officials, such as the police or the dealer licensing board. In addition, frame the complaint in terms of the misrepresentation directed to the consumer, not to the financer. For example, a seller may claim that the consumer has been approved for financing, without disclosing that this was because the seller had misrepresented the consumer's creditworthiness. Focus on the fact that the seller hid the credit misrepresentations from the consumer as much as from the financer.

494 Knapp v. Americredit Fin. Serv., Inc., 245 F. Supp. 2d 841 (S.D. W. Va. 2003).

495 18 U.S.C. § 1344.

496 *See* Knapp v. Americredit Financial Services, Inc., 245 F. Supp. 2d 841 (S.D. W. Va. 2003); Gelco Corp. v. Major Chevrolet, Inc., 2002 WL 31427027 (N.D. Ill. Oct. 30, 2002).

5.1.5 Violations of Federal and State Credit Laws as UDAP Violations

5.1.5.1 Truth in Lending Violations

The federal Truth in Lending Act and the Consumer Leasing Act require specific disclosures in consumer credit transactions. These laws afford a private cause of action for actual damages and attorney fees. Nonetheless, a UDAP statute's double or treble damages provision may be a better remedy than TILA offers. Further, claims under these federal statutes are subject to a one-year statute of limitations, while most UDAP statutes have longer limitation periods. Some federal courts have also imposed strict requirements for proof of actual damages under TILA, going well beyond the rules usually adopted by courts for consumer protection statutes. For all of these reasons, the consumer may want to assert a creditor's TIL violation as a UDAP violation.

The FTC has specifically held that violations of Federal Reserve Board Regulation Z[497] and the Truth in Lending Act[498] are unfair and deceptive practices under the FTC Act.[499] Oregon and Massachusetts UDAP regulations also specify that a violation of the federal Truth in Lending or Consumer Leasing Acts are *per se* UDAP violations.[500] Courts in many other states have held that a creditor who violates TILA also violates the state UDAP statute.[501] A

497 12 C.F.R. § 226.

498 15 U.S.C. § 1601 *et seq.*

499 Jerry's Ford Sales Inc., 5 Trade Reg. Rep. (CCH) ¶ 23,830 (F.T.C. File No. 932 3240 1995) (proposed consent order) (car dealer failed to disclose balloon payments and other credit terms); Beauty Style Modernizers, Inc., 83 F.T.C. 1761 (1974); Seekonk Freezer Meats, Inc., 82 F.T.C. 1025 (1973); Southern States Distributing Co., 83 F.T.C. 1126 (1973); Charnita, Inc., 80 F.T.C. 892 (1972).

500 Mass. Regs. Code tit. 940, §§ 6.10, 6.11; Oregon Admin. Rules 137-20-0040, Adoption of Federal Credit and Leasing Law.

501 Lozada v. Dale Baker Oldsmobile, 197 F.R.D. 321 (W.D. Mich. 2000) (failure to provide disclosures prior to or at time of signing, contrary to TILA, is UDAP violation); Taylor v. Bob O'Connor Ford, Inc., 1998 U.S. Dist. LEXIS 5095 (N.D. Ill. Apr. 10, 1998); Burnett v. Ala Moana Pawn Shop, Clearinghouse No. 46,771 (D. Haw. 1991), *aff'd*, 3 F.3d 1261 (9th Cir. 1993); Hill v. Allright Mortgage Co., 213 B.R. 934 (Bankr. D. Md. 1996), *aff'd*, 1997 U.S. Dist. LEXIS 21406 (D. Md. July 10, 1997); Cheshire Mortgage v. Montes, 612 A.2d 1130 (Conn. 1992); W.S. Badcock Corp. v. Myers, 696 So. 2d 776 (Fla. Dist. Ct. App. 1997) (misrepresenting non-filing fee as a charge for insurance violated Truth in Lending Act and state UDAP statute); Commonwealth *ex rel.* Zimmerman v. Nickel, 26 Pa. D. & C.3d 115 (C.P. Mercer Cty. 1983) (failure to provide Truth in Lending rescission notice is violation of state UDAP statute); *see also* Barco Auto Leasing Corp. v. House, Clearinghouse No. 40,641 (Conn. Super. Ct. 1983), *aff'd in part, rev'd in part on other grounds*, 202 Conn. 106, 520 A.2d 162 (1987). *But see* Riopta v. Amresco Residential Mortgage Corp., 101 F. Supp. 2d 1326 (D. Haw. 1999) (TIL violation is not *per se* UDAP violation); Williams v. Gelt Fin. Corp., 232 B.R. 629, 642

federal court has allowed a consumer to recover Truth in Lending statutory damages (up to $1000) *plus* UDAP treble damages, calculated as treble the finance charge.[502] If the court views the TIL violation as merely technical, however, it may decline to find that it is a UDAP violation.[503] For this reason, it is best not to rely simply on the fact of the TIL violation, but also to show how that violation contributed to the deception or unfair treatment of the consumer.

5.1.5.2 RESPA Violations

The federal Real Estate Settlement Procedures Act (RESPA) includes important protections for people entering into real estate transactions. However, the statute creates an explicit federal cause of action only for violation of certain of its provisions.[504]

One of RESPA's key requirements is that closing costs and other charges be accurately disclosed in a standard format on a settlement statement. Mortgage lenders often conceal overcharges by mislabeling them on the settlement statement. While RESPA does not provide a private cause of action for this violation, one court has allowed a UDAP claim based on this violation to go forward, holding that such a claim is not preempted by RESPA.[505] Even where RESPA does provide its own remedy, UDAP statutes can provide a parallel cause of action.[506]

5.1.5.3 Discriminatory Extension of Credit

It is a violation of federal and state law to discriminate on a prohibited basis in the granting of credit.[507] For example, it is clearly illegal to charge higher interest rates to African-Americans or Latino-Americans than other consumers.[508] It may also be illegal discrimination to target protected groups for unfair or deceptive credit practices.[509] That is, it may be illegal for a creditor to target minorities as the prime victims of its abusive practices. Discrimination on the basis of race has been documented where companies that extend credit have discretion about the rates to be charged.[510]

A UDAP claim may be an alternative or additional claim to these anti-discrimination statutes, particularly where the claim is that a particular group is being targeted for abusive treatment. For example, in one recent case, a federal court refused to dismiss a consumer's UDAP claim that a credit-seller targeted African-Americans and Latino-Americans for oppressive credit practices.[511] UDAP claims are particularly well-suited to such a situation because the notion is well-established that unsophisticated or vulnerable consumers need special UDAP protection.[512] Targeting a particular group for unfair practices should clearly be unfair.

UDAP claims may also be attractive alternatives to federal anti-discrimination statutes where the consumer wishes to stay in state court, where treble or minimum statutory damages are available, where the group being discriminated against is not one of those protected by the federal statutes, or where the UDAP statute of limitations is more generous to the consumer. UDAP statutes may also be more flexible in that the notion of "unfairness" may be broader than discrimination set out in the federal anti-discrimination statutes. An interesting Washington state case holds that it is a violation of the state anti-discrimination statute, and there-

---

(Bankr. E.D. Pa. 1999) (TILA violation not a *per se* UDAP violation without evidence of pervasive illegal conduct), *aff'd as modified on other grounds*, 237 B.R. 590 (E.D. Pa. 1999); Pittman v. Allright Mortg. Co., 165 B.R. 586, 589 (Bankr. D. Md. 1994) (declining to hold that a technical violation of TILA was a *per se* violation); Hawaii Community Fed. Credit Union v. Keka, 94 Haw. 213, 11 P.3d 1, 17 n.15 (2000) (TIL violation is not automatically a UDAP violation; court must examine each case); Celebrezze v. Fred Godard Ford, Inc., 27 Ohio App. 3d 301, 500 N.E.2d 881 (1985) (violation of FTC rules may be *per se* UDAP violation, but court declines to find that violation of TIL rules is).

502 Burnett v. Ala Moana Pawn Shop, Clearinghouse No. 46,771 (D. Haw. 1991), *aff'd*, 3 F.3d 1261 (9th Cir. 1993).

503 *See* Riopta v. Amresco Residential Mortgage Corp., 101 F. Supp. 2d 1326 (D. Haw. 1999); Pittman v. Allright Mortg. Co., 165 B.R. 586, 589 (Bankr. D. Md. 1994) (declining to hold that a technical violation of TILA was a *per se* violation).

504 The statute affords a private cause of action for violation of the servicer obligations (12 U.S.C. § 2605), the anti-kickback provisions (12 U.S.C. § 2607), the title insurance company steering rules (12 U.S.C. § 2608), the escrow payment rules (§ 2605(g)), and the duty to respond to a qualified written request (§ 2605(e)). *See* National Consumer Law Center, The Cost of Credit: Regulation and Legal Challenges § 11.3 (2d ed. 2000 and Supp.).

505 Washington Mut. Bank v. Superior Court, 75 Cal. App. 4th 773, 89 Cal. Rptr. 2d 560 (1999). *See also* Brazier v. Security Pacific Mortg. Inc., 245 F. Supp. 2d 1136 (W.D. Wash. 2003) (RESPA requirements are incorporated into state UDAP statute).

506 Chow v. Aegis Mortg. Corp., 286 F. Supp. 2d 956 (N.D. Ill. 2003); Jenkins v. Mercantile Mortgage Co., 231 F. Supp. 2d 737 (N.D. Ill. Sept. 27, 2002); Fardella v. Downey Sav. & Loan Ass'n, 2001 WL 492442 (N.D. Cal. May 9, 2001); Gardner v. First Am. Title Ins. Co., 2001 U.S. Dist. LEXIS 21839 (D. Minn. Dec. 10, 2001) (plaintiff's allegations that defendants created sham intermediary companies which paid kickbacks stated both RESPA and UDAP claims); Christakos v. Intercounty Title Co., 196 F.R.D. 496 (N.D. Ill. 2000). *But cf.* Shafer v. GSF Mortg. Corp., 2003 WL 21005793 (Minn. App. May 6, 2003) (unpublished, citation limited) (RESPA violations not admissible as evidence of consumer fraud).

507 *See, e.g.*, 15 U.S.C. § 1691 (Equal Credit Opportunity Act); 42 U.S.C. § 3601 (Fair Housing Act); 42 U.S.C. §§ 1981, 1982, 1988 (Civil Rights Acts). *See generally* National Consumer Law Center, Credit Discrimination (3d ed. 2002 and Supp.).

508 National Consumer Law Center, Credit Discrimination § 8.4 (3d ed. 2002 and Supp.).

509 *See id.* § 4.2.10. *See also* Fairman v. Schaumburg Toyota, Inc., 1996 U.S. Dist. LEXIS 9669 (N.D. Ill. July 9, 1996).

510 Coleman v. General Motors Acceptance Corp., 196 F.R.D. 315 (M.D. Tenn. 2000) (certifying class and denying creditor's motion for summary judgment), *vacated on other grounds*, 296 F.3d 443 (6th Cir. 2002).

511 Fairman v. Schaumburg Toyota, Inc., 1996 U.S. Dist. LEXIS 9669 (N.D. Ill. July 9, 1996).

512 *See* § 4.2.11, *supra*.

fore a *per se* UDAP violation, for a credit union to expel a member because he submitted an affidavit supporting credit union employees in an employment discrimination suit.[513]

5.1.5.4 Violations of State Credit Laws

Most states have laws such as retail installment sales acts, consumer leasing acts and banking laws that regulate credit transactions. These laws often require disclosures, prohibit certain terms and practices, and place substantive limits on terms such as interest rates and late charges.

To the extent that these statutes offer effective consumer remedies, they can stand on their own. But many were enacted decades ago and have been amended only piecemeal since then, without adding effective remedies. In these cases, consumers may be able to enforce the credit law through the state UDAP statute.[514]

Many courts have held that a violation of a state statute meant to protect the public is a *per se* UDAP violation.[515] In addition, some states' UDAP statutes or regulations explicitly state that a violation of any other consumer protection law is a UDAP violation.[516] Some courts do not apply a *per se* rule that violation of a state credit statute is automatically a UDAP violation, but use a balancing analysis based on the FTC definition of unfairness. For these courts, the purposes behind the state credit law and the extent of the harm caused by the violation will be critical.[517]

Violation of a state credit statute's disclosure requirements is a UDAP violation,[518] as is imposition of charges that state law prohibits.[519] For example, violation of a state law prohibiting advance collection of interest is a UDAP violation.[520] Imposition of illegal mortgage processing fees, in violation of New York statutes, which induced consumers to believe they were required to pay them, is deceptive.[521] The Arkansas Supreme Court has found an auto title pawn scheme in violation of the Arkansas Constitution to be an unconscionable practice in violation of the UDAP statute.[522]

Before basing a UDAP claim on a state credit law, the consumer's attorney should make sure that the law has not been preempted by federal law. Federal preemption of state credit laws is discussed in detail in another NCLC manual.[523]

5.1.5.5 Attempts to Evade Credit Legislation

It is deceptive to have a consumer form a corporation to avoid state usury limits on consumer loans.[524] Other schemes to avoid state usury laws may also be actionable.[525] A creditor engages in unfair or deceptive conduct by enter-

513 Galbraith v. TAPCO Credit Union, 946 P.2d 1242 (Wash. App. 1997).

514 *See* Terry v. Community Bank, 255 F. Supp. 2d 817, 823 (W.D. Tenn. 2003) (denial of motion to dismiss) (violation of state usury statute is UDAP violation); *In re* Koresko, 91 B.R. 689 (Bankr. E.D. Pa. 1988); Russell v. Fidelity Consumer Discount Co. (*In re* Russell), 72 B.R. 855 (Bankr. E.D. Pa. 1987) (legislature's enactment of UDAP statute shows intent to provide remedy for violation of state credit laws, so that aggrieved consumers would no longer be left without a remedy).

515 Keith v. Howerton, 2001 Tenn. App. LEXIS 646 (Aug. 28, 2001) (unreported, citation limited) (pawnbroker law); *see also* Kidd v. Delta Funding Corp., 751 N.Y.S.2d 267 (App. Div. 2002) (summary judgment properly denied to lender who charged illegal loan fees and failed to notify consumers of right to refund negotiated as part of settlement with state). *See generally* § 3.2.7, *supra*.

516 *See* §§ 3.2.7.1–3.2.7.3, *supra*.

517 *Compare* Cheshire Mortg. Servs., Inc. v. Montes, 223 Conn. 80, 612 A.2d 1130 (1992) (charging prepaid finance charge exceeding that allowed by state second mortgage law is UDAP violation because of important public policies behind the law and the significant damage to consumer) *with* Jacobs v. Healey Ford-Subaru, Inc., 231 Conn. 707, 652 A.2d 496 (1995) (isolated instance of misinterpretation of repossession provisions of retail installment sales act is not a *per se* UDAP violation); Gaynor v. Union Trust Co., 216 Conn. 458, 582 A.2d 190 (1990) (inadvertent failure to provide fully accurate redemption notice after repossession is not UDAP violation).

518 Chroniak v. Golden Inv. Corp., 983 F.2d 1140 (1st Cir. 1993) (N.H. law); Lozada v. Dale Baker Oldsmobile, 197 F.R.D. 321 (W.D. Mich. 2000); *In re* Stewart, 93 B.R. 878 (Bankr. E.D. Pa. 1988). *But see* Holmes v. No. 2 Galesburg Crown Fin. Corp., 77 Ill. App. 3d 785, 396 N.E.2d 583 (1979) (improper disclosure of security interest violating Ill. Large Loan Act is not a *per se* UDAP violation).

519 Jungkurth v. Eastern Fin. Servs., Inc., 74 B.R. 323 (Bankr. E.D. Pa. 1987) (citing lender's attempt to collect illegal prepayment penalty as one element of UDAP violation); Nelson v. Associates Fin. Servs. Co., 659 N.W.2d 635 (Mich. App. 2003) (prepayment penalty).

520 *In re* Arsenault, 184 B.R. 864 (Bankr. D.N.H. 1995). *See* § 5.1.8.1.1, *infra*. *See also* National Consumer Law Center, Consumer Law Pleadings, No. 2, § 3.3 (CD-Rom and Index Guide) (sample complaint, discovery requests, summary judgment motion, list of evidence, request for findings, briefs on liability and damages, and attorney fee petition, all filed in bankruptcy court in a case raising UDAP and other claims concerning a lender's assessment of illegal charges; these pleadings are also found on the CD-Rom accompanying this volume). *But cf.* Weatherman v. Gary-Wheaton Bank, 186 Ill. 2d 472, 713 N.E.2d 543 (1999) (escrow suspension fee was allowed by state law so was not UDAP violation).

521 Kidd v. Delta Funding Corp., 2000 N.Y. Misc. LEXIS 29 (Sup. Ct. Feb. 22, 2000), *denial of summary judgment aff'd*, 751 N.Y.S.2d 267 (App. Div. 2002).

522 State *ex rel.* Bryant v. R&A Investment Co., 985 S.W.2d 299 (Ark. 1999).

523 National Consumer Law Center, The Cost of Credit: Regulation and Legal Challenges Ch. 3 (2d ed. 2000 and Supp.).

524 Rutter v. Troy Mortgage Servicing Co., 145 Mich. App. 116, 377 N.W.2d 846 (1985); *see also* FTC v. Nationwide Mortgage Co., 5 Trade Reg. Rep. (CCH) ¶ 22,540 (D.D.C. 1988) (consent order); State *ex rel.* Bryant v. R&A Investment Co., 985 S.W.2d 299 (Ark. 1999).

525 State *ex rel.* Bryant v. R&A Investment, 985 S.W.2d 299 (Ark. 1999) (usury in violation of state law is unconscionable); Vaughan v. Kalyvas, 342 S.E.2d 617 (S.C. Ct. App. 1986).

ing into a car "lease" that is really a contract for sale, violating state and federal disclosure laws, disguising the finance charge, creating a large balloon payment at the end, and having a total of payments far exceeding the purchase price of the vehicle.[526] A car pawn scheme has been held to violate a UDAP statute where the pawn was really a loan scheme.[527] A creditor may commit a UDAP violation by listing a cosigner as a co-buyer, contrary to a state law designed to ensure that those who do not actually receive the property are treated only as guarantors.[528]

5.1.6 Exorbitant Credit Charges

5.1.6.1 Credit Costs That Are Grossly in Excess of Those Usually Charged in Market

UDAP statutes that prohibit unfair or unconscionable practices have been successfully applied where the interest or other credit costs are excessive in comparison to those generally available. This approach can reach exorbitant credit charges even when they are legal under state or federal credit statutes

Massachusetts UDAP regulations prohibit, as unfair or deceptive, any closed-end, non-purchase money mortgage loan rates or terms which significantly deviate from industry-wide standards or which are otherwise unconscionable.[529] A detailed federal court decision upholds this regulation in a case where the mortgage lender was charging ten points.[530] Even though Massachusetts law explicitly allows lenders to charge any number of points they choose, as long as that number is disclosed,[531] a UDAP regulation can still limit those points as unfair and deceptive.

Even in states that have no specific prohibition like that in Massachusetts, the court's discussion of the general concept of unfairness should be applicable. The court measured the Massachusetts regulation and the lender's charging of ten points against the FTC's unfairness definition—substantial injury, not outweighed by the benefits to competition, and that could not be reasonably avoided by the consumer.[532] The court found that all three aspects of this definition were met.

The consumer injury was substantial: the points being charged. The court also found no adequate business justification for the practice, even though the lender argued that the alternative to charging high points was either to raise the mortgage rate or abandon the subprime market, where these borrowers are in need of credit to get back on their feet. The court disagreed, pointing out that other lenders serving the same market charged five points or less, and that adding points to a loan increased the loan's APR, instead of reducing it.

The court also upheld, against a constitutional vagueness challenge, the regulation's standard that terms not "significantly deviate" from those of other lenders. Finally, the court ruled that the regulation was not arbitrary or capricious, even if it allowed a challenge to the number of points charged, and even if the lender could circumvent this challenge by charging a higher interest rate instead of the higher number of points.

The court also rejected the argument that market forces would take care of any problem, and the court thus found that consumers could not reasonably avoid the abuses. The court examined in some detail how market forces had failed to handle the subprime mortgage needs in certain geographic areas and for particular types of consumers. The court found that mortgage redlining and reverse redlining had led to both a vacuum of legitimate credit and an onslaught of predatory lenders.[533]

A number of other state UDAP statutes include a general prohibition against charging a price that is grossly in excess of the price at which similar services are sold.[534] These statutes lend themselves well to the Massachusetts analysis. It may also be possible to reach the same result through a non-disclosure argument. A number of courts have found UDAP violations where the creditor steers the consumer to a higher-cost product without disclosing that it also has a lower-cost product available.[535] Like the approaches discussed above, this non-disclosure argument compares what the consumer got to what is readily available in the marketplace, although it focuses on what the creditor itself made available.

5.1.6.2 Other Unfairness or Unconscionability in Credit Charges

The typical state UDAP statute prohibits unfairness as well as deception. Many of these states follow an FTC definition of unfairness that involves, among other things, evaluating whether the practice causes substantial consumer

526 Barco Auto Leasing Corp. v. House, Clearinghouse No. 40,641 (Conn. Super. Ct. Oct. 26, 1983), *aff'd in part, rev'd in part on other grounds*, 202 Conn. 106, 520 A.2d 162 (1987).

527 Commonwealth v. Car Pawn of Virginia, 37 Va. Cir. 412 (1995).

528 Lee v. Nationwide Cassel, L.P., 660 N.E.2d 94 (Ill. App. Ct. 1995), *rev'd in part on other grounds*, 174 Ill. 2d 540, 675 N.E.2d 599 (1996).

529 Mass. Regs. Code tit. 940, § 8.06.

530 United Companies Lending Corp. v. Sargeant, 20 F. Supp. 2d 192 (D. Mass. 1998).

531 Mass. Gen. Laws ch. 183, § 63.

532 *See* § 4.3.2, *supra*.

533 *See also* Honorable v. Easy Life Real Estate Sys., 100 F. Supp. 2d 885 (N.D. Ill. 2000) (detailed analysis of how defendants exploited minority homebuyers by carving out noncompetitive enclave in the market); Associates Home Equity Servs. v. Troup, 343 N.J. Super. 254, 778 A.2d 529 (App. Div. 2001) (describing expert analysis of dual housing market).

534 *See* §§ 4.3.12, 4.4.2 to 4.4.5, *supra*.

535 *See* § 5.1.6.3, *infra*.

injury.[536] In addition, about a third of the states' UDAP statutes prohibit unconscionable practices. Some define certain circumstances that the court should consider in determining whether a transaction is unconscionable. In other states, courts may look to the concept of unconscionability under the Uniform Commercial Code, and evaluate whether the contract terms are unreasonably one-sided and harsh and whether the formation of the contract involved oppression or unfair surprise.[537]

A number of courts have applied these concepts to credit charges. Charging interest of 57% to 101% may be unconscionable, if other facts are consistent with an absence of meaningful choice.[538] In another case, a federal court held that interest rates ranging from 179% to 557% could be found unconscionable, particularly where the plaintiffs are characterized as poor and unsophisticated, with no easy access to credit.[539] A Michigan appellate court held a car dealer to have violated the state UDAP statute by exchanging a $17,000 car and $10,000 in cash for a home worth $43,000.[540] The consumer remained obligated on the home mortgage, and the seller was entitled to repossess the car if the consumer defaulted on the mortgage payments. The court based its ruling on the facts that the seller confused the plaintiff, the consideration the consumer exchanged for the car was grossly excessive, and the seller took advantage of the consumer. A bankruptcy court ruled it deceptive for a creditor to overreach in a loan transaction by charging high fees, unconscionably high interest rates, and illegal prepayment penalties, taking an unconscionable amount of security, and failing to disclose these facts to the unsophisticated borrowers.[541] The court characterized the lender's conduct as gross fraudulent conduct that was intended to and did in fact create confusion and misunderstanding.

A federal court has found a 240% APR implicit in a pawn transaction to be oppressive and thus unfair.[542] The Eighth Circuit, overruling a district court opinion, has found it unconscionable for a finance company to offer a six-year loan to a consumer, where a three-year loan would have had lower monthly payments and a far lower total of payments, and to fail to disclose this fact to the consumer.[543] Failing to disclose to the consumer that a new loan would be less expensive than refinancing an old loan is a UDAP violation.[544]

In a case decided under RICO, but which would be convincing precedent for a UDAP claim, the Seventh Circuit has held that a complaint against a finance company properly alleged mail fraud.[545] The company solicited a debtor to borrow an additional $200, falsely claiming that she was specially selected because she was a good customer. By refinancing the existing loan rather than giving her a new loan, the finance company increased her repayment obligation by $1200 over three years. A debtor may also state a valid UDAP claim by alleging that a creditor has refinanced a loan at significantly higher rates without making this fact clear to the debtor,[546] or by continually refinancing loans in a short time period, with each refinancing putting the consumer in a worse position.[547]

Charging 200% interest on a $99,000 secured loan has been found unconscionable.[548] Also found to be a UDAP violation and breach of a fiduciary duty was a grossly inequitable sale and lease-back scheme that allegedly was designed to help a homeowner pay his mortgage and stave off foreclosure.[549] A court found a UDAP violation where a consumer, with no one to counsel her, and whose sole source of income was Aid to Families with Dependent Children, was pressured into a financing scheme that she did not understand and that was disadvantageous.[550] Obtaining the consumer's signature without giving the consumer an opportunity to read the contract may violate a UDAP prohibition of unfairness or unconscionability.[551]

---

536 *See* § 4.3, *supra*.

537 *See* § 4.4, *supra*.

538 Cobb v. Monarch Fin. Corp., 913 F. Supp. 1164 (N.D. Ill. 1995) (ruling on motion to dismiss).

539 Brown v. C.I.L., Inc., 1996 U.S. Dist. LEXIS 4053 (N.D. Ill. Mar. 29, 1996) (denying defendant's motion to dismiss). *Accord* Hartke v. Illinois Payday Loans, Inc., 1999 U.S. Dist. LEXIS 14937 (C.D. Ill. Sept. 13, 1999) (denying payday lender's motion for summary judgment on claim that unconscionably high interest rates and terms were UDAP violations).

540 McRaild v. Shepard Lincoln-Mercury, 141 Mich. App. 406, 367 N.W.2d 404 (1985).

541 Jungkurth v. Eastern Financial Services, Inc., 74 B.R. 323 (Bankr. E.D. Pa. 1987). *See also* Family Financial Services, Inc. v. Spencer, 41 Conn. App. 754, 677 A.2d 479 (1996).

542 Burnett v. Ala Moana Pawn Shop, Clearinghouse No. 46,771 (D. Haw. 1991), *aff'd*, 3 F.3d 1261 (9th Cir. 1993).

543 Besta v. Beneficial Loan Co., 855 F.2d 532 (8th Cir. 1988) (unconscionability finding under Iowa Consumer Credit Code; higher monthly payment for six-year loan caused by higher credit insurance and closing costs). *See also* Hager v. Am. Gen. Fin., Inc., 37 F. Supp. 2d 778 (S.D. W. Va. 1999) (denying lender's motion for summary judgment under Consumer Credit Act's unconscionability provision where it induced unsophisticated, financially strapped consumers to take out and refinance mortgage loans on disadvantageous terms).

544 *In re* Milbourne, 108 B.R. 522 (Bankr. E.D. Pa. 1989). *See also In re* Barker, 251 B.R. 250 (Bankr. E.D. Pa. 2000) (failure to disclose detrimental effect of refinancing existing mortgage with high-rate loan was UDAP violation).

545 Emery v. American General Fin., Inc., 71 F.3d 1343 (6th Cir. 1995).

546 Villegas v. TransAmerica Financial Services, Inc., 147 Ariz. 100, 708 P.2d 781 (Ct. App. 1985).

547 *See In re* Tucker, 74 B.R. 923 (Bankr. E.D. Pa. 1987).

548 Carboni v. Arrospide, 2 Cal. Rptr. 2d 845 (Ct. App. 1991).

549 Jeffries v. The Lewis Group, Clearinghouse No. 47,473F (Ill. Cir. Ct. Cook Cty. Oct. 9, 1991).

550 U.S. Home & Realty Corp v. Lehnartz, Clearinghouse No. 43,259 (Mich. Dist. Ct. 1987).

551 *Cf.* Matthews v. New Century Mortg. Corp., 185 F. Supp. 2d 874 (S.D. Ohio 2002) (upholding common law unconscionability claim against motion to dismiss).

Courts that have found credit terms unfair or unconscionable often cite not only the terms themselves, but also the consumer's particular vulnerability due to age, inexperience, lack of education, or desperate financial circumstances.[552] These factors are also relevant in applying the Uniform Commercial Code's unconscionability provision.[553] The consumer's attorney should investigate these facts thoroughly, along with any other tactics by which the creditor avoided or delayed meaningful disclosure of the terms of the loan. Even if the legal claim is based solely on the unconscionability of the terms themselves, evidence along these lines will help the trier of fact understand how the consumer was induced to enter into the transaction, and may resolve questions of causation and damages. Expert testimony about how creditors induce consumers to agree to disadvantageous credit terms may be helpful. The consumer may also wish to explore the possibility of testimony from an economist about defects or segmentation that prevent the market from self-correcting.[554]

Another court has ruled that a "debt pooler" violates the state UDAP statute by charging an extremely high interest rate, adding substantial loan broker charges, placement fees, acceptance fees, and attorney fees, and falsely disclosing or failing to disclose important loan terms.[555] A tax preparer's practice of purchasing customers' tax refunds for one-half of the estimated refund has been found a UDAP violation,[556] as has a "borrower program" where the debtor pays one half the debt to the loan program and still remains the primary obligor under the debt, contrary to the program's representations.[557]

Selling credit insurance at inflated premiums, receiving a 25% commission, and failing to disclose these facts is a UDAP violation, where the finance company is in a fiduciary relationship.[558] In this case, the fiduciary relationship was based on a Federal Reserve Board regulation (since repealed)[559] that subsidiaries of bank holding companies have such a relationship when extending credit insurance. Double-charging for costs or fees can be deceptive.[560] The Arkansas Supreme Court has found that an auto title pawn scheme that effectively charged 304% interest was unconscionable and a UDAP violation.[561]

5.1.6.3 Uncovering Deception in Excessive Charge Cases

Cases that involve excessive charges rather than deception are more difficult to attack in jurisdictions where the state UDAP statute only prohibits deception, not unfairness or unconscionability. Even where the statute prohibits unfairness, a court may be reluctant to substitute its judgment for the agreement it perceives the parties as having negotiated. For these reasons, it is helpful if there is evidence of deception as well as unfairness.

The advocate should look at the advertising, the sales pitch, and any promotional material. Are the terms they describe different from the terms that were actually offered? Both explicit and implicit representations are actionable. Baiting the consumer with favorable rates and then switching to higher rates is a UDAP violation.[562] Even if the creditor ultimately made accurate disclosures, there is UDAP precedent that subsequent disclosure does not cure the violation.[563] The consumer may also be able to show that the correct disclosures came at a point when it was too late to shop around for other alternatives, that they came only after non-refundable fees had been paid,[564] or that the creditor deceptively downplayed the final, accurate disclosures.[565]

552 *See, e.g.*, Williams v. First Government Mortgage & Investors Corp., 225 F.3d 738 (D.C. Cir. 2000) (consumer had sixth grade education and was marginally literate); Hager v. Am. Gen. Fin., Inc., 37 F. Supp. 2d 778 (S.D. W. Va. 1999) (denying lender's motion for summary judgment on unconscionability count; consumers were marginally literate, unsophisticated, and financially strapped); *In re* Jungkurth, 74 B.R. 323 (Bankr. E.D. Pa. 1987) (citing borrowers' lack of sophistication).

553 *See* § 4.4.9, *supra*.

554 *See, e.g.*, Honorable v. Easy Life Real Estate Sys., 100 F. Supp. 2d 885 (N.D. Ill. 2000) (fair housing case); United Companies Lending Corp. v. Sargeant, 20 F. Supp. 2d 192 (D. Mass. 1998) (citing AG report and other sources in upholding Massachusetts regulation); Associates Home Equity Servs. v. Troup, 343 N.J. Super. 254, 778 A.2d 529 (App. Div. 2001) (describing expert analysis of dual housing market).

555 *In re* Fricker, 115 B.R. 809 (Bankr. E.D. Pa. 1990). *See also* Williams v. Resolution GGF OY, 417 Mass. 377, 630 N.E.2d 581, 586 (1994) (concurring opinion; dictum).

556 Brown v. Lawyers Tax Service, Inc., Clearinghouse No. 26,059 (Ohio C.P. Hamilton Cty. 1976).

557 Commonwealth v. Armstrong, 74 Pa. D. & C.2d 579 (C.P. Phila. Cty. 1974).

558 *In re* Dickson, 432 F. Supp. 752 (W.D.N.C. 1977).

559 Regulation Y, 12 C.F.R. Part 225 (now repealed).

560 Therrien v. Resource Financial Group, 704 F. Supp. 322 (D.N.H. 1989).

561 State *ex rel.* Bryant v. R&A Investment Co., 985 S.W.2d 299 (Ark. 1999).

562 Hawaii Community Fed. Credit Union v. Keka, 11 P.3d 1 (Haw. 2000) (reversing summary judgment for lender); Chandler v. Am. Gen. Fin., Inc., 329 Ill. App. 3d 729, 768 N.E.2d 60 (2002) (sending solicitations to the consumer that state or imply that a new loan is offered, but then switching the consumer to a much more expensive refinancing of an existing loan, is deceptive).

563 *See* § 4.2.17, *supra*.

564 *See, e.g.*, Opportunity Mgmt. Co. v. Frost, 1999 Wash. App. LEXIS 336 (Feb. 16, 1999) (consumer paid nonrefundable deposit on mobile home after loan broker provided assurance that loan had been approved but before disclosure of specific terms). *See also* Pedwell v. First Union Nat'l Bank, 51 N.C. App. 236, 275 S.E.2d 565 (1981) (deliberate sabotage of sale by denying loan at point that was too late to arrange alternate financing would be UDAP violation).

565 *See, e.g.*, Hawaii Community Fed. Credit Union v. Keka, 11 P.3d 1 (Haw. 2000) (consumer was informed of higher rate at closing, but lender represented that it would be no problem to lower the rate in the future).

Even if everything the creditor said was accurate, did the creditor fail to disclose material facts?[566] In many oppressive credit transactions, the creditor or a broker is secretly profiting from what appear to be pass-through charges. This fact should be considered a material fact that must be disclosed, since it would alert the consumer to the disadvantageous nature of the transaction.[567] Often a broker or seller receives greater compensation if the consumer accepts worse credit terms. Since this gives the broker or seller an interest adverse to the consumer, it is a highly material fact.[568] The court is especially likely to find the failure to disclose this arrangement deceptive if the broker or seller has promised, expressly or implicitly, to find the best rate possible for the consumer.[569] A New York decision upholds the denial of summary judgment on a deception claim to a lender who charged illegal loan fees and then failed to inform consumers of a settlement with the state that entitled them to refunds.[570]

Comparing the terms the consumer was offered with other, less expensive ways of setting up the transaction can be especially fruitful. The broker may have had the option of placing the loan with a less expensive lender, or the lender itself may have had alternate, less expensive loan products available. For example, in *Besta v. Beneficial Loan Co.*,[571] the consumer refinanced a 36-month $1000 loan in order to borrow $500 more. For the refinanced loan, the lender extended the term to 72 months, which enabled it to add larger credit and property insurance premiums and to charge fees for recording security interests. Taking into account the larger premiums, the extra years of interest on the principal, and the fees, the cost of the 72-month loan to the consumer was over twice the cost of the 36-month loan for the same amount and at the same interest rate, and the monthly payment was $5.00 *higher*. The court held that it was unconscionable under the Iowa Consumer Credit Code for the lender to make the 72-month loan without disclosing the 36-month option. Significantly, it reached this conclusion even though the terms of the 72-month loan were perfectly legal in and of themselves. A number of cases have adopted this approach.[572]

Meticulous expert analysis of the terms of the transaction and the undisclosed alternatives is essential for this approach. Documents available through discovery, such as the rate sheets the broker or lender used, and the worksheet showing how the consumer's rates and fees were determined, often reveal that there were alternative loans that were not disclosed to the consumer.

5.1.7 *Deception, Coercion, and Violation of Credit Contract*

5.1.7.1 Misrepresentation of Credit Terms

Misrepresentation that a creditor offers easy credit terms is deceptive, particularly where the seller does not extend credit to persons below prevailing standards of creditworthiness, the down payment or repayment periods are less favorable than ordinary, the credit cost is higher than average, the seller's mark-up on the underlying goods is higher than usual, or the seller has a more vigorous debt collection policy than usual.[573] Promising a "good loan" at 9 1/2% but

566 *See* Weil v. Long Island Savings Bank, 77 F. Supp. 2d 313 (E.D.N.Y. 1999) (concealing true nature of fees would be UDAP violation).

567 *See* Latman v. Costa Cruise Lines, 758 So. 2d 699 (Fla. App. 2000) (port charges imposed by cruise line); Pickett v. Holland Am. Line-Westours, Inc., 101 Wash. App. 901, 6 P.3d 63 (2000) (port charges imposed by cruise line), *rev'd on other grounds*, 35 P.3d 351 (Wash. 2001); *See also* Negrin v. Norwest Mortgage, Inc., 700 N.Y.S.2d 184 (App. Div. 1999) (reversing grant of motion to dismiss on claim that billing for illegal fees violates New York UDAP statute's prohibition against deception). *But see* Green v. Paradise Pontiac, 19 Ohio App. 3d 219, 483 N.E.2d 1213 (1984) (where no fiduciary duty between parties, and no deception, where credit insurance is not required, and where consumer could purchase insurance on his own, no requirement that creditor disclose 32.5% commission).

568 *See* Moses v. Citicorp Mortgage, Inc., 982 F. Supp. 897 (E.D.N.Y. 1997) (allegation that lenders had agreement with brokers not to advise consumer that loan had been approved at lower rates states UDAP claim). *See also* § 5.1.3.3, *supra*.

569 Fairman v. Schaumburg Toyota, Inc., 1996 U.S. Dist. LEXIS 9669 (N.D. Ill. July 10, 1996).

570 Kidd v. Delta Funding Corp., 751 N.Y.S.2d 267 (App. Div. 2002).

571 855 F.2d 532 (8th Cir. 1988).

572 Chandler v. Am. Gen. Fin., Inc., 329 Ill. App. 3d 729, 768 N.E.2d 60 (2002) (sending solicitations to the consumer that state or imply that a new loan is offered, but then switching the consumer to a much more expensive refinancing of an existing loan, is deceptive). *See also In re* Barker, 251 B.R. 250 (Bankr. E.D. Pa. 2000) (failure to disclose detrimental effect of refinancing existing mortgage with high-rate loan was UDAP violation); *In re* Milbourne, 108 B.R. 522 (Bankr. E.D. Pa. 1989) (failure to disclose that a supplemental loan would be less expensive than refinancing was UDAP violation); Browder v. Hanley Dawson Cadillac Co., 62 Ill. App. 3d 623, 379 N.E.2d 1206 (1978) (reversing trial court's dismissal of claim; failure to disclose availability of cheaper credit insurance would be UDAP violation). *But see* Melton v. Family First Mortg. Corp., 576 S.E.2d 365 (N.C. App. 2003) (lender had no duty to recommend that borrower investigate reverse mortgage as alternative to loan, so no UDAP violation).

573 Tashof v. FTC, 437 F.2d 707 (D.C. Cir. 1970); Royal Furniture, 93 F.T.C. 422 (1979) (consent order); Massachusetts Consumer Protection Regulations, Mass. Regs. Code tit. 940, § 3.07, Advertising or Offering to Sell on an "Easy Credit" Basis; State v. Ralph Williams' N.W. Chrysler Plymouth, Inc., 87 Wash. 2d 298, 553 P.2d 423 (1976). *Cf.* Arsenault v. PNC Mortg. Corp., 2000 U.S. Dist. LEXIS 21667 (W.D. Ky. Nov. 3, 2000) (refinancing offer was not deceptive even though rate quoted as available "today" was not available when consumer called a few days later), *aff'd*, 2002 U.S. App. LEXIS 6248 (6th Cir. Apr. 1, 2002) (unpublished, citation limited); Consumer Action v. Wells Fargo Bank, 2002 Cal. App. Unpub. LEXIS 588 (Cal. App. Apr. 30, 2002) (notice of overdraft charge was not deceptive, but employees' scripted misleading statements to custom-

including a variable rate and demand clause has been held *per se* fraudulent.[574] Oral misrepresentations about the terms of a contract are UDAP violations, and the parol evidence rule is inapplicable to such a claim.[575]

Offering low-cost financing when the seller knows that there are conditions and restrictions on its availability is deceptive.[576] A seller may engage in a deceptive practice where it promises to find the consumer the best available financing, but instead looks for financing that will provide it the largest kickback.[577] Sending solicitations to the consumer that state or imply that a new loan is offered, but then switching the consumer to a much more expensive refinancing of an existing loan, is deceptive.[578]

Misrepresenting the interest rate[579] or charging interest rates higher than disclosed is also a UDAP violation.[580] Submitting an inflated appraisal and misrepresenting to consumers that the payments on a loan will be set at an amount they can afford is deceptive.[581] Characterizing a fee as a "loan discount fee" when the fee does not actually reduce the interest rate may be deceptive.[582] It is deceptive to state a finance charge as a certain amount, while hiding some of the finance charge in the cash price—that is, the cash price in the financing document was higher than the cash price found in the original sales agreement.[583] It is deceptive to represent that loan documents are for a 30-year fixed rate loan when actually they are for a 15-year balloon loan.[584] Disclosing the amount of legal fees for a home mortgage transaction, while concealing the fact that the law firm paid kickbacks back to the bank, may be a UDAP violation.[585] Inducing consumers to pay charges by mislabeling them or by billing for them as if they were owed is deceptive.[586]

It is a UDAP violation to misrepresent that a mortgage is not required as a condition of a loan,[587] or that credit insurance is mandatory.[588] Disclosing a security interest greater than that allowed by state law is deceptive.[589] An advertisement offering $99 a month, no money down is deceptive where the creditor offers only one or the other term, but not both.[590] Inducing the consumer to sign a contract by understating the amount of the monthly payment is a UDAP violation.[591] It is also deceptive to misrepresent

ers might be). *But see* Hogan v. Riemer, 35 Mass. App. Ct. 360, 619 N.E.2d 984 (1993) (lender's initial misstatements about payment terms of loan not a UDAP violation where borrower learned the true terms at closing, but did not protest or rescind).

574 Peoples Trust & Savings Bank v. Humphrey, 451 N.E.2d 1104 (Ind. Ct. App. 1983) (foreclosure dismissed, contract reformed, $1000 actual and $40,000 punitive damages awarded). *See also* Hawaii Community Fed. Credit Union v. Keka, 94 Haw. 213, 11 P.3d 1 (2000) (bait-and-switch tactics in loan negotiation violate UDAP statute). *But cf.* Duren v. First Gov't Mortg. & Investors Corp., 2000 U.S. App. LEXIS 15469 (D.C. Cir. June 7, 2000) (unpublished, citation limited) (evidence that borrower was led to believe loan terms were favorable to her is insufficient to show deception).

575 Wang v. Massey Chevrolet, 97 Cal. App. 4th 856, 118 Cal. Rptr. 2d 770 (2002). *See* § 4.2.15.2, *supra*.

576 Illinois Attorney General Consumer Protection Rules, 14 Ill. Admin. Code. §§ 475.620, 475.630; Stephenson v. Capano Dev., Inc., 462 A.2d 1069 (Del. 1983). *But cf.* International Minerals & Mining Corp. v. Citicorp N. Am., Inc., 736 F. Supp. 587 (D.N.J. 1990) (commercial borrower has no UDAP claim for its unreasonable reliance on a lender's statements predicting that a loan would be approved).

577 Fairman v. Schaumburg Toyota, Inc., 1996 U.S. Dist. LEXIS 9669 (N.D. Ill. July 10, 1996). *But see* Beckett v. H&R Block, Inc., 714 N.E.2d 1033 (Ill. App. Ct. 1999) (taking highly literalistic view and finding that disclosure of an amount paid to the bank was correct even though bank kicked back a portion); Shafer v. GSF Mortg. Corp., 2003 WL 21005793 (Minn. App. May 6, 2003) (unpublished, citation limited) (no UDAP violation for broker to place loan with subprime lender to which it was related by common control even though borrower had exemplary credit).

578 Chandler v. Am. Gen. Fin., Inc., 329 Ill. App. 3d 729, 768 N.E.2d 60 (2002).

579 Hauschildt v. Beneficial Wisconsin, Inc., 2003 WL 23289788 (W.D. Wis. Dec. 17, 2003) (misrepresenting amount of loan discount fee); Capitol Builders, Inc., 92 F.T.C. 274 (1978) (consent order); United Builders, Inc., 92 F.T.C. 291 (1978) (consent order); Kleidon v. Rizza Chevrolet, Inc., 173 Ill. App. 3d 116, 527 N.E.2d 374 (1988); Beard v. Gress, 90 Ill. App. 3d 622, 413 N.E.2d 448 (1980).

580 Taylor v. Bob O'Connor Ford, Inc., 1998 U.S. Dist. LEXIS 5095 (N.D. Ill. Apr. 10, 1998). *See also* DBC Financial, 5 Trade Reg. Rep. (CCH) ¶ 24,700 (F.T.C. Dkt. No. C-3931 2000) (consent order against company that falsely advertised ATM card as having free overdraft protection and no fees).

581 Vaughn v. Consumer Home Mortg., Inc., 2003 WL 21241669 (E.D.N.Y. Mar. 23, 2003).

582 Hauschildt v. Beneficial Wisconsin, Inc., 2003 WL 23289788 (W.D. Wis. Dec. 17, 2003) (denial of motion to dismiss). *See* § 5.5.5.6, *infra* (appraisal fraud).

583 Fielder v. Credit Acceptance Corp., 19 F. Supp. 2d 966 (W.D. Mo. 1998), *vacated on other grounds*, 188 F.3d 1031 (8th Cir. 1999) (appellate decision holds that district court did not have authority to issue injunction requiring creditor to move to have state court judgments amended to delete interest overcharges; remands that portion of case to state court).

584 FTC v. OSI Fin. Servs., Inc., 2003 WL 1904013 (N.D. Ill. Apr. 17, 2003) (denying motion to dismiss).

585 Weil v. Long Island Sav. Bank, 77 F. Supp. 2d 313 (E.D.N.Y. 1999) (ruling on motion to dismiss).

586 Latman v. Costa Cruise Lines, 758 So. 2d 699 (Fla. App. 2000); Pickett v. Holland Am. Line-Westours, Inc., 101 Wash. App. 901, 6 P.3d 63 (2000), *rev'd on other grounds*, 35 P.3d 351 (Wash. 2001); Dwyer v. J.I. Kislak Mortgage Corp., 103 Wash. App. 542, 13 P.3d 240 (2000) (reversing summary judgment for lender).

587 Capitol Builders, Inc., 92 F.T.C. 274 (1978) (consent order); United Builders, Inc., 92 F.T.C. 291 (1978) (consent order); Burns v. Walters, Clearinghouse No. 47,843 (Ohio Ct. App. 1984).

588 Hager v. Am. Gen. Fin., Inc., 37 F. Supp. 2d 778 (S.D. W. Va. 1999) (denying lender's motion for summary judgment on fraud claim).

589 Ellis v. Hensley, Clearinghouse No. 27,967, 1979 Ohio App. LEXIS 12025 (Ohio Ct. App. 1979).

590 State v. Terry Buick, Inc., 520 N.Y.S.2d 497 (Sup. Ct. 1987).

591 Conseco Fin. Serv. Corp. v. Hill, 556 S.E.2d 468 (Ga. App. 2001).

the legality of the transaction.[592] It is a UDAP violation to ask the debtor's spouse to sign a new credit agreement because of an error in the first agreement, saying it was a mere formality, when in fact the new agreement increased the finance charge and deleted the credit insurance.[593]

A credit card statement's disclosure of a late charge was deceptive where it was not being charged on balances less than $25.[594] As a result, consumers were induced to pay small balances more promptly than they otherwise would. It is a factual issue whether it was deceptive for a creditor to advertise free credit life insurance where there was a minimum physical condition requirement to be eligible.[595] Disclosing that the creditor "may" use a disadvantageous payment allocation method, when in fact it *will* use that method, may be deceptive.[596] Misrepresenting that the lender imposes no charges for prepayment may be UDAP violation.[597] A UDAP claim also exists for misrepresenting the identity of the lender, manufacturing deceptive closing charges, and misrepresenting the actual recipient of origination fees.[598] It is deceptive to sell a computer software program that falsely shows that it is better to buy a car on credit, and put the cash price of the car in a savings account, than to pay cash for the car.[599]

A lender commits a UDAP violation by representing that it can close on a loan within a certain period when it is extremely unlikely or impossible for it to do so.[600] A members loan association has been restrained from misrepresenting that members are guaranteed to receive large loans right away and that all payments go to a nonprofit fund, and from failing to disclose that membership fees are nonrefundable even if the promised loan is not forthcoming.[601]

It is also deceptive to misrepresent that long-term payment plans are available,[602] and that open-end credit is being offered when only coupon books are available.[603] Creditors can not misrepresent that a consumer loan is a cash advance on a refund of federal income taxes, and that as such it is superior to a normal consumer loan.[604] Also deceptive is to misrepresent a sale and lease-back scheme as a refinancing.[605]

Mortgage lenders often conceal overcharges by mislabeling them on the settlement statement, in violation of the federal Real Estate Settlement Procedures Act (RESPA). While RESPA does not provide a private cause of action for this violation, it is a deceptive act that may be actionable under the state UDAP statute.[606]

5.1.7.2 Nondisclosure of True Credit Terms

5.1.7.2.1 General

It is a UDAP violation to fail to disclose adequately all credit charges, such as not disclosing the annual percentage rate, the dollar credit charge, and the cash price.[607] It is a UDAP violation for the seller to create a hidden finance charge by boosting the price of the product to offset low financing charges.[608] Concealing finance charges in a purportedly zero-interest loan is deceptive.[609] Hiding the true cost of a loan is unfair and deceptive.[610]

---

592 *Id.* (misrepresentation of legality of "straw man" or "buy for" arrangement).

593 Baggett v. Crown Automotive Group, Inc., 1992 WL 108710 (Tenn. Ct. App. May 22, 1992).

594 Garland v. Mobil Oil Corp., 340 F. Supp. 1095 (N.D. Ill. 1972).

595 Swanston v. McConnell Air Force Base Federal Credit Union, 8 Kan. App. 2d 538, 661 P.2d 826 (1983).

596 Broder v. MBNA Corp., 281 A.D.2d 369, 722 N.Y.S.2d 524 (2001).

597 Rumford v. Countrywide Funding Corp., 678 N.E.2d 369 (Ill. App. Ct. 1997); *cf.* Stutman v. Chemical Bank, 95 N.Y.2d 24, 731 N.E.2d 608 (2000) (reliance not required to establish that imposition of prepayment fee contrary to contract is UDAP violation).

598 Terry v. Community Bank, 255 F. Supp. 2d 817 (W.D. Tenn. 2003) (denial of motion to dismiss).

599 Automatic Data Processing, 5 Trade Reg. Rep. (CCH) ¶ 23,049 (F.T.C. 892 3107 1992) (consent order).

600 State *ex rel.* Hartigan v. Commonwealth Mortgage Corp., 732 F. Supp. 885 (N.D. Ill. 1990).

601 Commonwealth *ex rel.* Terry v. United Members Loan Ass'n, Clearinghouse No. 45,936 (Va. Cir. Ct. Nov. 9, 1990).

602 Grolier, 91 F.T.C. 315 (1978), *vacated and remanded on other grounds*, 615 F.2d 1215 (9th Cir. 1980).

603 W.T. Grant Co., 83 F.T.C. 1328 (1974) (consent order).

604 Beneficial Corp. v. FTC, 542 F.2d 611 (3d Cir. 1976).

605 Jeffries v. The Lewis Group, Clearinghouse No. 47,473F (Ill. Cir. Ct. Cook Cty. Oct. 9, 1991); *see also* Brooks v. Creech, 2003 WL 174805 (Tenn. App. Jan. 28, 2003) (deceptive to misrepresent that quitclaim deed was deed of trust).

606 *See* § 5.1.5.2, *supra*.

607 Chroniak v. Golden Inv. Corp., 983 F.2d 1140 (1st Cir. 1993) (N.H. law); Tashof v. FTC, 437 F.2d 707 (D.C. Cir. 1970); Foster v. New Dimensions Funding, Clearinghouse No. 47,070 (D.N.H. Nov. 24, 1992); FTC v. OSI Fin. Servs., Inc., 2003 WL 1904013 (N.D. Ill. Apr. 17, 2003) (denying motion to dismiss claim that lender misrepresented loans as 30-year fixed rate when actually they were 15-year balloon loans); U.S. v. Mercantile Mortg. Co., 5 Trade Reg. Rep. (CCH) ¶ 15275 (N.D. Ill. July 18, 2002) (proposed consent decree against subprime lender who misrepresented or concealed balloon payments); Lester Cotheman, 72 F.T.C. 376 (1968), *aff'd*, 417 F.2d 587 (5th Cir. 1969); Audio Graphic Potomac Corp., 59 F.T.C. 1201 (1961). *See also* Woodworker's Supply, Inc. v. Principal Mut. Life Ins. Co., 170 F.3d 985 (10th Cir. 1999) (UDAP violation for insurer to fail to disclose method for deciding whether surcharge would be necessary, and to sell plan knowing rates were inadequate so surcharge was likely).

608 April v. Union Mortgage Co., 709 F. Supp. 809 (N.D. Ill. 1989) (may violate UDAP statute to inflate cost of services so creditor could retain part of proceeds); *In re* Stewart, 93 B.R. 878 (Bankr. E.D. Pa. 1988).

609 State *ex rel.* Brady v. 3-D Auto World, Inc., 2000 Del. Super. LEXIS 17 (Jan. 19, 2000) (would be deceptive, but seller here may have disclosed the finance charges).

610 Conseco Fin. Serv. Corp. v. Hill, 556 S.E.2d 468 (Ga. App. 2001) (failing to inform buyers of "step interest rate" and removing that page from their copy of contract).

Thus a court found there could be a UDAP violation where a loan represented as having a 21.7% interest rate was actually much more costly. This happened because $11,846 of the loan proceeds was kept by the lender in a "payment escrow account," earning only 5% interest for the consumer, while the consumer was paying 21.7% for the use of that money.[611] It is a UDAP violation for a creditor to base a loan's payments and interest rate on the assumption the creditor will forward the full loan amount immediately to a third party, when in fact the creditor and third party have created an arrangement where the loan amount will go to the third party in two installments.[612] A federal court has also held that the failure to clearly disclose a 240% APR would confuse a consumer as to the true nature of the transaction and was thus deceptive.[613] Charging an above-market price for an appraisal by concealing the lender's share of the fee may be a UDAP violation.[614]

Failing to disclose to the consumer that a new loan would be less expensive than refinancing an old loan is a UDAP violation.[615] Quoting a "*per annum*" rate based on a 360-day year is deceptive even though it is customary practice and even though the actual annual percentage rate (APR) is subsequently disclosed.[616]

A dealer engaged in a deceptive practice by representing the cost of Ford Motor Credit Company (FMCC) financing as 16.5% when FMCC was only charging 14% and the remaining 2.5% would be kept by the dealer if the consumer made all payments owed.[617] Similarly, a credit-seller may engage in a deceptive practice where it promises to find the consumer the best available financing, but fails to disclose that the 24% interest rate is inflated because the credit-seller will keep 5% when it assigns the note to a lender.[618] It is not a UDAP violation for a bank to fail to tell a cosigner about the principal's shaky financial condition, however, where a state banking law prohibits such disclosure.[619]

611 Therrien v. Resource Financial Group, 704 F. Supp. 322 (D.N.H. 1989).

612 Leibert v. Finance Factors Ltd., 788 P.2d 833 (Haw. 1990).

613 Burnett v. Ala Moana Pawn Shop, Clearinghouse No. 46,771 (D. Haw. 1991), *aff'd*, 3 F.3d 1261 (9th Cir. 1993).

614 Szczubelek v. Cendant Mortg. Corp., 215 F.R.D. 107 (D.N.J. 2003).

615 *In re* Milbourne, 108 B.R. 522 (Bankr. E.D. Pa. 1989). *See generally* §§ 5.1.6.2, 5.1.6.3, *supra*.

616 Chern v. Bank of Am., 15 Cal. 3d 866, 544 P.2d 1310, 127 Cal. Rptr. 110 (1976). *But see* Gonzales v. Associates Financial Service Co., 967 P.2d 312 (Kan. 1998) (failing to make clear identification of origination fees for refinancing was not UDAP violation).

617 Adkinson v. Harpeth Ford-Mercury, Inc., 1991 WL 17177, Clearinghouse No. 47,926 (Tenn. Ct. App. Feb. 15, 1991). *See* § 5.1.3.3, *supra*.

618 Fairman v. Schaumburg Toyota, Inc., 1996 U.S. Dist. LEXIS 9669 (N.D. Ill. July 10, 1996).

619 First Midwest Bank v. Sparks, 682 N.E.2d 373 (Ill. App. Ct. 1997).

5.1.7.2.2 Rules requiring disclosure of all material restrictions

The FTC Telemarketing Rule requires disclosure of all material restrictions, limitations or conditions to purchase, receive or use goods or services that are the subject of a sales offer that is covered by the rule.[620] This rule applies to telemarketers who promise to obtain credit cards or arrange other credit for consumers. Failure to disclose material limitations on the use of the offered credit card is a violation of the rule.[621] A number of states have similar requirements in their telemarketing statutes. Even outside the telemarketing context, a UDAP regulation or decision may require the promoter to disclose material limitations on an offer of credit before the consumer pays anything.[622] Concealing restrictions applicable to a credit offer, and then switching the consumer to less attractive terms, may violate a prohibition of bait-and-switch tactics.[623]

5.1.7.3 Coercive Tactics

It is unfair and deceptive for a creditor to take a loan application, mortgage and note from the applicant, record the mortgage, then disapprove the loan, but refuse to satisfy the mortgage unless the consumer pays a broker fee and other charges.[624] Coercing the consumer's payment of spurious charges in order to get a payoff statement so a home can be sold is a UDAP violation.[625] A creditor violates a UDAP statute by rushing the consummation on a credit purchase even though the creditor knew the product was not yet finished and the buyer did not wish to accept the sale on those conditions.[626]

620 16 C.F.R. § 310.3(a)(1)(ii).

621 New York v. Fin. Servs., 930 F. Supp. 865 (W.D.N.Y. 1996) (issuing preliminary injunction).

622 *See* § 4.6.7, *supra*. *But see* Millenium Communications & Fulfillment, Inc. v. Attorney General, 761 So. 2d 1256 (Fla. App. 2000) (finding that postcard soliciting consumers to call for credit card deal was not deceptive even though it omitted material information; consumers were given at least some of the information before paying anything), *later op. at* 800 So. 2d 255 (Fla. App. 2001) (ordering discovery and stating that holding in first decision was merely in context of preliminary injunction and was not a determination on the merits).

623 *See* Hawaii Community Fed. Credit Union v. Keka, 94 Haw. 213, 11 P.3d 1 (2000) (bait-and-switch tactics in loan negotiation violate UDAP statute); *cf.* Rossman v. Fleet Bank, 2000 U.S. Dist. LEXIS 19120 (E.D. Pa. Dec. 29, 2000) (bait-and-switch tactics would not violation TILA if credit card disclosures were accurate at time they were made; court expresses no view on plaintiffs' UDAP claims), *rev'd on other grounds, remanded*, 280 F.3d 384 (3d Cir. 2002).

624 McClendon v. Metropolitan Mortgage Co., Clearinghouse No. 43,703G (Fla. Cir. Ct. Dade Cty. May 20, 1988).

625 Negrin v. Norwest Mortgage, Inc., 700 N.Y.S.2d 184 (App. Div. 1999) (reversing grant of motion to dismiss).

626 Evans v. Yegen Associates, 556 F. Supp. 1219 (D. Mass. 1983).

Coercing a debtor to sign a refinancing agreement may be a UDAP violation.[627] Telling a consumer that her deceased mother would not rest in peace unless the consumer signed a promissory note to repay her mother's debt is unfair and deceptive.[628]

An increasingly frequent tactic is for a car dealer to promise low-cost financing, take the consumer's car in trade, and hand over the new car to the consumer. Then the dealer calls the consumer in and requires a higher interest rate because the first loan was not "approved," threatening to repossess the car if the consumer does not agree. The unfair and deceptive nature of these "yo-yo" sales is discussed in detail in § 5.4.5, *infra*.

Other oppressive creditor practices involve the sale of credit insurance and the "packing" of other forms of insurance with a loan transaction. These issues are discussed in § 5.3.12, *infra*. The companion CD-Rom to this volume includes a number of pleadings, briefs, motions, and discovery requests in cases involving creditor overreaching.[629]

5.1.7.4 Post-Consummation Violation of Credit Terms

Systematic breach of contract is an unfair practice.[630] This principle can be applied to credit transactions. It is a UDAP violation to charge a higher post-default interest rate than that allowed by the credit agreement.[631] It is deceptive to impose and bill for services to preserve the mortgaged property that the lender does not actually perform.[632] Imposing a prepayment charge contrary to the contract is also a UDAP violation where it reveals a pattern of misrepresentation that no fee would be charged.[633] The imposition of fabricated and unlawful fees as a condition of sending a payoff statement is a UDAP violation.[634] Misrepresenting that a lump sum payment will satisfy the balance due is a UDAP violation.[635] It is unconscionable for a creditor to miscalculate the pay-off figure on a loan and then refuse to return the overpayment.[636]

5.1.8 Special Issues in Home Mortgage Loans

5.1.8.1 Negotiation, Closing, and Loan Terms

The Comptroller of the Currency has issued a detailed analysis of why certain mortgage lending practices are predatory and abusive.[637] The OCC states that a fundamental characteristic of predatory lending is the aggressive marketing of credit to prospective borrowers who can not afford to repay it. Typically, such credit is underwritten predominantly on the basis of the foreclosure value of the home. The OCC identifies a variety of other practices that accompany the marketing of abusive loans:

- Loan flipping, i.e., frequent refinancings that result in little or no economic benefit to the borrower and are undertaken with the primary objective of generating fees or prepayment penalties;[638]
- Refinancings of special subsidized mortgages issued by government or non-profit agencies;
- Packing of excessive and hidden fees into the amount financed;
- Using loan terms such as negative amortization to make it harder for borrowers to repay the debt;
- Using balloon payments to conceal the true burden of the refinancing and to force borrowers into costly refinancing transactions or foreclosures;
- Targeting older, financially unsophisticated, or otherwise vulnerable borrowers for inappropriate or excessively expensive credit products;
- Targeting borrowers who could qualify for mainstream credit products and terms;
- Inadequately disclosing the true costs and risks of a loan, and its appropriateness or inappropriateness for the particular borrower;
- Offering single premium credit life insurance; and
- Using mandatory arbitration clauses.

Since the OCC letter states that these practices may be unfair or deceptive under the FTC Act, it is persuasive precedent

627 Vaughan v. Kalyvas, 342 S.E.2d 617 (S.C. Ct. App. 1986).

628 Isla Fin. Servs. v. Sablan, 2001 N. Mar. I. LEXIS 24 (N. Mariana Is. Dec. 14, 2001).

629 These are also found on National Consumer Law Center, Consumer Law Pleadings, No. 1, Chs. 2, 3, 4, 5, 6, 7 (CD-Rom and Index Guide). Additional pleadings may be found in National Consumer Law Center, Consumer Class Actions: A Practical Litigation Guide Appx. D.6 (5th ed. 2002 and Supp.).

630 *See* § 4.3.5, *supra*.

631 Fielder v. Credit Acceptance Corp., 19 F. Supp. 2d 966 (W.D. Mo. 1998), *vacated on other grounds*, 188 F.3d 1031 (8th Cir. 1999) (appellate decision holds that district court did not have authority to issue injunction requiring creditor to move to have state court judgments amended to delete interest overcharges; remands that portion of case to state court).

632 Chatman v. Fairbanks Capital Corp., 2002 WL 1338492 (N.D. Ill. June 18, 2002) (ruling on motion to dismiss).

633 Stutman v. Chemical Bank, 95 N.Y.2d 24, 731 N.E.2d 608 (2000).

634 Negrin v. Norwest Mortgage, Inc., 700 N.Y.S.2d 184 (App. Div. 1999) (reversal of grant of motion to dismiss); *see also* Dawson v. Dovenmuehle, 2002 U.S. Dist. LEXIS 5688 (E.D. Pa. Apr. 3, 2002) (denying motion to dismiss claim that lender intentionally mischaracterized fees on bills).

635 *In re* Jungkurth, 74 B.R. 323 (Bankr. E.D. Pa. 1987).

636 Griffith v. Porter, 817 S.W.2d 131 (Tex. App. 1991).

637 OCC Advisory Letter 2003-2, Guidelines for National Banks to Guard Against Predatory and Abusive Lending Practices (Feb. 21, 2003), available at www.occ.treas.gov/Advlst03.htm.

638 *See* National Consumer Law Center, The Cost of Credit: Regulation and Legal Challenges § 6.1 (2d ed. 2000 and Supp.) (discussion of loan flipping).

that they are UDAP violations as well. A second Comptroller Advisory Letter advises national banks to set clear standards to avoid acquiring predatory loans originated by brokers.[639]

Another source of minimum standards for real estate secured loans is a settlement that a coalition of attorneys general reached with Household Finance Corp. and its related corporation Beneficial Finance. The attorneys general alleged that these companies committed UDAP violations by: (1) splitting a single loan into two transactions, and misrepresenting the benefits of refinancing with split loans, as a means to make high loan-to-value mortgage loans; (2) failing to provide timely and adequate information about the amount and purpose of putative "discount" or "buy-down" points and fees; (3) misrepresenting interest rates by telling borrowers they would achieve a low "effective" interest rate by making biweekly payments; (4) failing to inform borrowers that higher payments, rather than lower rates, were the feature of the biweekly payment plan; (5) insurance packing; (6) misleading consumers about the presence of prepayment penalties; (7) using live checks as bait to solicit high-cost mortgage loans; (8) disguising closed-end credit as open-end credit in order to evade disclosure requirements; (9) accounting practices that treated consumers' loan payments as insufficient, resulting in extra finance charge costs; (10) failing to disclose balloon payments; (11) failing to provide timely payoff information; (12) failing to provide meaningful descriptions of loan terms to non-English speaking borrowers; and (13) refinancing its own or other loans, thereby imposing additional fees and costs, where the new loan provided no net tangible benefit to the consumer. These allegations may be useful in other cases because they represent an interpretation of the state UDAP statute by the state's highest enforcement officer.[640]

To resolve these complaints, Household/Beneficial entered into a universal settlement that created a $484 million consumer redress fund and restricted certain specific practices. This settlement was filed as a consent order in each state.[641] Highlights of the settlement are that it limited loan fees and points to 5% of principal for three years; required that all real estate secured loans provide a net tangible benefit to the borrower; required these lenders to give each borrower the lowest rate available for their loan products, assuming that the borrower's credit qualifies; prohibited prepayment penalties after the first 24 months of the loan; required these lenders to use loan closers who do not report to sales management and whose compensation is not based on the terms of the loan (if the closer is an employee of these lenders, compensation must not be based on the volume of loan closings); banned single premium credit insurance (in which the entire premium is paid at the outset of the loan) on real estate secured loans; limited split loans; limited points and fees when a loan is refinanced within 12 months of the original loan; and required better disclosures.

A creditor committed an unfair practice by conspiring with a home seller to avoid a purchase and sale agreement by stalling, and then refusing to offer the home buyer a mortgage when it was too late for the buyer to find alternative financing.[642] It is unfair and deceptive for a creditor to take a loan application, mortgage, and note from the applicant, record the mortgage, then disapprove the loan, but refuse to satisfy the mortgage without payment of a broker fee and other charges.[643] By contrast, lenders did not commit a UDAP violation by charging "escrow waiver fees" in the good faith, although erroneous, belief that state law allowed it.[644] It can be unconscionable for a creditor not to be ready to close when promised, resulting in the debtor forfeiting the right to purchase a home.[645] Charging an above-market price for an appraisal by concealing the lender's share of the fee may be a UDAP violation.[646]

The Minnesota, Missouri and Texas Attorneys General have issued guidelines for mortgage banking lenders concerning lock-in periods and other mortgage practices.[647] The FTC has accepted a consent agreement from a major mortgage company concerning misrepresentations whether an interest rate was "locked in."[648] Massachusetts has UDAP regulations requiring extensive disclosures by mortgage brokers and mortgage lenders of all aspects of a mortgage loan (other than a loan used to purchase the home or an open-end home equity line of credit).[649]

639 OCC Advisory Letter 2003-3, Avoiding Predatory and Abusive Lending Practices in Brokered and Purchased Loans (Feb. 21, 2003), available at www.occ.treas.gov/Advlst03.htm.

640 Nearly identical complaints were filed in each state. The Iowa complaint is available on the Iowa Attorney General's website, www.iowaattorneygeneral.org/latest_news/releases/dec_2002/hhpetition.pdf. Practitioners should consult their own state's complaint to determine whether it varies in any relevant ways from this description.

641 The Ohio settlement is available on Westlaw as State *ex rel.* Montgomery v. Household Int'l, Inc., 2002 WL 32391634 (Ohio Com. Pleas Dec. 16, 2002). Many other states have made their settlements available through a state website.

642 Pedwell v. First Union Nat'l Bank, 51 N.C. App. 236, 275 S.E.2d 565 (1981).

643 McClendon v. Metropolitan Mortgage Co., Clearinghouse No. 43,703G (Fla. Cir. Ct. Dade Cty. May 20, 1988).

644 Weatherman v. Gary-Wheaton Bank, 186 Ill. 2d 472, 713 N.E.2d 543 (1999); Stern v. Norwest Mortgage, Inc., 179 Ill. 2d 160, 688 N.E.2d 99 (1997).

645 First Texas Savings Ass'n v. Stiff Properties, 685 S.W.2d 703 (Tex. App. 1984).

646 Szczubelek v. Cendant Mortg. Corp., 215 F.R.D. 107 (D.N.J. 2003).

647 Letter by Minnesota Attorney General Humphrey to Minnesota Mortgage Lenders (Apr. 30, 1987); Missouri Attorney General Guidelines for Mortgage Banking Lenders; Attorney General of Texas Statement of Enforcement Policy to Texas Mortgage Lenders (June 26, 1986).

648 Lomas Mortgage USA, Inc., 5 Trade Reg. Rep. (CCH) ¶ 23,419 (F.T.C. C-3462 1993) (consent order).

649 Massachusetts Regulations Concerning Mortgage Brokers and

It is deceptive for a creditor to represent that it will provide a mortgage loan, but then back out of the deal.[650] However, a lender's preapproval letter stating that the loan was subject to final underwriting review and approval was found not to be deceptive.[651] It may be deceptive to offer one interest rate in a commitment letter, but then to unilaterally change the interest rates even where the commitment letter allows "renegotiation" of the interest rate.[652]

5.1.8.2 Promising Low-Cost Financing

It is deceptive to claim falsely that a home purchaser would be eligible for low-cost financing through a government benefit program.[653] It is a UDAP violation to advertise long-term mortgage loans, offer one year mortgage loans with a promise to automatically convert the short-term loan to a long-term loan, and then fail to do so.[654] Similarly, the FTC obtained an order for $2.4 million in redress from a company that sold shell homes with promises of construction loans that it claimed would be converted to thirty-year mortgages at rates as low as nine percent. The FTC alleged that the company violated these oral promises and refused to offer the promised long-term loans, or supplied mortgages at sharply higher rates than promised.[655]

5.1.8.3 Escrow Practices

A large mortgage banker agreed with the FTC to maintain procedures to insure the timely payment of all obligations payable from homeowners' escrow accounts.[656] The FTC had claimed that Lomas & Nettleton Financial Corporation had committed an unfair and deceptive practice by failing to pay hazard insurance premiums from homeowners' escrow accounts. A servicer's failure to make the appropriate payments from an escrow account also gives the consumer a private cause of action under the Real Estate Settlement Procedures Act (RESPA).[657]

5.1.8.4 Payoff of Mortgage

A bank engaged in unfair and deceptive practices by adding a bad check obligation to a mortgage, freezing a checking account without notice, unreasonably and unlawfully attempting to foreclose on the debtor's home and interfering with the debtor's attempt to refinance the obligation with another creditor.[658] A lender commits a UDAP violation by misrepresenting the payoff amount on a mortgage loan, thereby interfering with another lender's refinancing of the debt and leading to a foreclosure action.[659] Requiring the payment of unauthorized fees before a mortgage will be satisfied is a UDAP violation.[660] Merely adding such fees to a payoff statement, which gives the false impression that payment is required before the mortgage will be released, is a UDAP violation.[661] Violating a state statute requiring prompt recordation of the reconveyance of a deed of trust after payoff is also a UDAP violation.[662]

5.1.8.5 Equity Stripping

Predatory mortgage lenders seek to strip away a home's equity by luring the homeowner into an unaffordable loan that will result in foreclosure. Sometimes the lender structures the loan so that the payments appear to be affordable, but there is an unaffordable balloon payment, often almost as large as the original principal, after a number of years of payments.[663] Charging large non-refundable up-front fees is another method of stripping away a homeowner's equity.

Mortgage Lenders, Mass. Regs. Code tit. 940, §§ 8.02, 8.05.

650 Investors, Inc. v. Hadley, 738 S.W.2d 737 (Tex. App. 1987).

651 Honeycutt v. First Federal Bank, 278 F. Supp. 2d 893 (W.D. Tenn. 2003).

652 Madsen v. Western Am. Mortg. Co., 694 P.2d 1228 (Ariz. Ct. App. 1985).

653 Vaughn v. Consumer Home Mortg., Inc., 2003 WL 21241669 (E.D.N.Y. Mar. 23, 2003) (denial of motion to dismiss); Stephenson v. Capano Development, Inc., 462 A.2d 1069 (Del. 1983); Danny Darby Real Estate, Inc. v. Jacobs, 760 S.W.2d 711 (Tex. App. 1988).

654 FTC v. Nationwide Mortgage Co., 5 Trade Reg. Rep. (CCH) ¶ 22,540 (D.D.C. 1988) (consent order).

655 *See* Evans Products Co., 3 Trade Reg. Rep. (CCH) ¶ 22,372 (F.T.C. 812 3222 1986) (bankruptcy court approval of settlement).

656 Lomas & Nettleton Financial Corp., 102 F.T.C. 1356 (1983) (consent order). *But see* Seaway Nat'l Bank v. Cain, 629 N.E.2d 660 (Ill. App. Ct. 1994) (bank's failure to pay real estate taxes not a UDAP violation where contract supported bank and bank kept owner informed).

657 12 U.S.C. § 2605(f). *See* National Consumer Law Center, The Cost of Credit: Regulation and Legal Challenges § 11.3.1.3 (2d ed. 2000 and Supp.).

658 Morse v. Mutual Federal Savings & Loan Ass'n of Whitman, 536 F. Supp. 1271 (D. Mass. 1982).

659 Osbourne v. Capital City Mortgage Corp., 667 A.2d 1321 (D.C. App. 1995). *Accord In re* Jungkurth, 74 B.R. 323 (Bankr. E.D. Pa. 1987) (misrepresentation that check will pay off entire balance is UDAP violation).

660 Negrin v. Norwest Mortgage, Inc., 700 N.Y.S.2d 184 (App. Div. 1999).

661 Dwyer v. J.I. Kislak Mortgage Corp., 103 Wash. App. 542, 13 P.3d 240 (2000) (reversing summary judgment for lender). *But cf.* Lopez v. World Sav. & Loan Ass'n, 105 Cal. App. 4th 729, 130 Cal. Rptr. 42 (2003) (state statute that limited payoff fees was preempted by federal law); Stutman v. Chemical Bank, 95 N.Y.2d 24, 731 N.E.2d 608 (2000) (not deceptive to promise no prepayment charge but then charge fee for special closing arrangements); OTS Chief Counsel Letter P-2000-6 (Apr. 21, 2000) (federal law preempts state restrictions on payoff statement fees as applied to federal savings and loan associations); OTS Chief Counsel Letter P-99-3 (Mar. 10, 1999) (same); § 2.5.3, *supra*.

662 Bartold v. Glendale Fed. Bank, 81 Cal. App. 4th 816, 97 Cal. Rptr. 2d 226 (2000).

663 *See In re* Barker, 251 B.R. 250 (Bankr. E.D. Pa. 2000) (UDAP

Even if the homeowner refinances, the equity represented by those fees is gone. Usually the lender targets certain populations such as the elderly, minorities or residents of neighborhoods that do not have ready access to mainstream credit. An advisory letter to national banks issued by the Comptroller of the Currency identifies all of these practices as features of predatory lending.[664]

In *Associates Home Equity Services v. Troup*,[665] a New Jersey appellate court held that a UDAP claim should proceed to trial where a home improvement lender had signed borrowers to onerous terms. The elderly homeowner had been confused about the credit terms but the lender's representative had told her not to worry about them. This decision recognizes not only a UDAP cause of action, but also claims under state and federal discrimination laws for such predatory lending tactics. The FTC has proceeded against a number of lenders for predatory practices that violate the FTC Act and the Truth in Lending Act.[666]

Giving a loan based on the value of a home, without regard to the borrower's ability to repay, is a UDAP violation.[667] A lender's failure to disclose the disadvantageous cost or nature of a loan can lead to UDAP liability.[668] A lender who refinances an existing lower-rate mortgage may violate a state UDAP prohibition of knowing misrepresentation that a service is needed, i.e., the service of refinancing the loan.[669]

Borrowers who are victims of predatory lending should also investigate claims under the Truth in Lending Act,[670] the Real Estate Settlement Procedures Act (RESPA),[671] the Home Ownership and Equity Protection Act of 1994 (HOEPA),[672] federal and state fair housing and fair lending laws, and state usury laws.[673]

violation to sign naive debtor to balloon note without explaining it).

664 OCC Advisory Letter 2003-2, Guidelines for National Banks to Guard Against Predatory and Abusive Lending Practices (Feb. 21, 2003). See § 5.1.8.1, supra.

665 343 N.J. Super. 254, 778 A.2d 529 (App. Div. 2001).

666 *See* FTC v. Associates First Capital Corp., 5 Trade Reg. Rep. (CCH) ¶ 24,882 (complaint filed Mar. 6, 2001); FTC v. First Alliance Mortg. Co., 5 Trade Reg. Rep. (CCH) ¶ 14,810 (C.D. Cal., complaint filed Oct. 3, 2000); FirstPlus Financial Group, Inc., 5 Trade Reg. Rep. (CCH) ¶ 24,790 (consent order Nov. 28, 2000).

667 *See, e.g.*, Opportunity Mgmt. Co. v. Frost, 1999 Wash. App. LEXIS 336 (Feb. 16, 1999); Fidelity Fin. Servs. v. Hicks, 574 N.E.2d 15 (Ill. App. Ct. 1991) (allegations of deceptive practices used to make unaffordable loan in order to acquire equity in home stated a UDAP claim); *see also* OCC Advisory Letter 2003-2, *Guidelines for National Banks to Guard Against Predatory and Abusive Lending Practices* (Feb. 21, 2003); § 5.1.4, *supra*. *See generally* National Consumer Law Center, The Cost of Credit Ch. 11 (2d ed. 2000 and Supp.).

668 *In re* Barker, 251 B.R. 250 (Bankr. E.D. Pa. 2000); *In re* Milbourne, 108 B.R. 522 (Bankr. E.D. Pa. 1989). *See also* Besta v. Beneficial Loan Co., 855 F.2d 532 (8th Cir. 1988). *See* §§ 5.1.4, 5.1.6.2, 5.1.6.3, *supra*.

669 *See In re* Barker, 251 B.R. 250 (Bankr. E.D. Pa. 2000); *see also* OCC Advisory Letter 2003-2, *Guidelines for National Banks to Guard Against Predatory and Abusive Lending Practices* (Feb. 21, 2003) (even a single refinancing transaction can be abusive, unfair, and deceptive if it involves refinancing of a special subsidized mortgage).

5.1.9 Credit Cards and Related Services

5.1.9.1 Credit Card Marketing

The Office of the Comptroller of the Currency (OCC), which regulates national banks, has issued an advisory letter identifying a number of unfair and deceptive acts and practices in the marketing of credit cards.[674] The OCC letter characterizes as possibly unfair and deceptive the promotion of credit cards with credit limits "up to" a specified dollar amount if the "up to" amount is essentially illusory. Banks should not:

- Target consumers who have limited or poor credit histories with solicitations for credit cards with a maximum or "up to" credit limit that is far greater than most of these consumers are likely to receive;
- Provide most applicants with a "default credit line" that is significantly lower than the maximum amount advertised, without disclosing this possibility in the promotional materials; or
- Advertise the possible uses of a credit card when the initial available credit line is likely to be so limited that the advertised possible uses are substantially illusory.

Another potential unfair and deceptive practice pinpointed by the OCC letter is promotional rate offers that do not disclose material terms and limitations, such as time limits on the promotional rate, circumstances that could shorten the period the rate is in effect or cause the rate to increase, and limits on the types of charges or balances to which the rate will apply. It may also be unfair and deceptive not to disclose potential balance transfer fees or other fees or a policy of applying payments to promotional balances first. The OCC also considers it potentially unfair and deceptive not to disclose fully and prominently in promotional materials the circumstances under which the credit card agreement permits the bank to increase the consumer's APR or fees, or take other action to increase the cost of credit.

670 *See* National Consumer Law Center, Truth in Lending (5th ed. 2003 and Supp.).

671 *See* National Consumer Law Center, The Cost of Credit Ch. 11 (2d ed. 2000 and Supp.).

672 *See* National Consumer Law Center, Truth in Lending Ch. 9 (5th ed. 2003 and Supp.).

673 *See* National Consumer Law Center, The Cost of Credit (2d ed. 2000 and Supp.).

674 OCC Advisory Letter AL 2004-10 (Sept. 14, 2004), *available at* www.occ.treas.gov/Advslt04.htm.

5.1.9.2 Credit Card Finders

Credit card finders bombard consumers with offers to obtain credit cards for them. Often these offers are illusory. A 2004 FTC study estimated that, over a one-year period, more than 6.5 million people in the United States paid an advance fee to obtain a loan or credit card but never received it.[675]

Firms may not misrepresent their ability to obtain credit cards for consumers, claim that a full refund will be made if a card is not obtained, but then withhold a ten dollar processing fee, or misrepresent their relationship to creditors.[676] If the credit card finder markets its services over the telephone and promises a high likelihood of success in obtaining credit, the FTC's Telemarketing Rule prohibits requesting or receiving a fee or other consideration before the credit is obtained for the consumer.[677] The same rule's general prohibitions against deception and abusive tactics also apply to credit card finder services that are marketed by telephone, even if the seller does not promise easy credit.[678]

A common deceptive scheme is to promise that consumers who pay a membership fee will receive a credit card, without disclosing that the card can only be used for items in the telemarketer's catalog.[679] The FTC has also successfully challenged offers of credit cards that do not disclose that they require security in the form of real estate or cash on deposit.[680] But a Florida case held that it was not deceptive to fail to disclose that the credit card could only be used to order products from a particular catalog with a 50% down payment.[681] The court failed to give weight to the promoter's omission of many material facts, such as the down payment and requirements for converting to a more widely-accepted credit card, from both the postcard and the telemarketers' script. A later decision from the same court stresses that the first decision was in the context of a preliminary injunction and was not a determination on the merits.[682]

A related scam successfully challenged by the FTC is promising credit cards if one called a 900 number; the 900 number turned out to be a recorded message that promised an 800 number at the end of the message. In fact, many callers to the 800 number did not obtain a credit card and others were sold an unrelated lifetime membership in the

---

675 FTC, Consumer Fraud in the United States: An FTC Survey (2004) at 32.

676 FTC v. S&L Professional Credit Clinic, Inc., 5 Trade Reg. Rep. (CCH) ¶ 23,301 (N.D. Tex. 1992); FTC v. S&L Professional Credit Clinic, Inc., 5 Trade Reg. Rep. (CCH) ¶ 22,886 (N.D. Tex. 1990) (permanent injunction); FTC v. Credit Repair, Inc., 5 Trade Reg. Rep. (CCH) ¶ 22,807 (N.D. Ill. 1990) (consent decree); FTC v. Action Credit Sys., Inc., 3 Trade Reg. Rep. (CCH) ¶ 22,534 (N.D. Cal. 1988) (consent order); FTC v. Roberts, 3 Trade Reg. Rep. (CCH) ¶ 22,535 (D.N.J. 1988) (consent order); Universal Credit Network, 5 Trade Reg. Rep. (CCH) ¶ 22,812 (F.T.C. File No. 882 3085 1990) (consent order); NCS Credit Network, Inc., 5 Trade Reg. Rep. (CCH) ¶ 23,304 (F.T.C. File No. 892 3081 1992) (consent order); Steven M. Hull, 107 F.T.C. 477 (1986); George Tannus, 107 F.T.C. 488 (1986) (consent order); James R. Hernden, Jr., 107 F.T.C. 488 (1986) (consent order); John C. Anderson, 107 F.T.C. 437 (1986) (consent order); Service One Int'l Corp., 106 F.T.C. 528 (1985) (consent order). *See also* FTC v. SurecheK Sys., Inc., 5 Trade Reg. Rep. (CCH) ¶ 24,431 (N.D. Ga. 1998) (stipulated final judgment); FTC v. Hart, 5 Trade Reg. Rep. (CCH) ¶ 24,431 (N.D. Ga. 1998) (stipulated final judgment); FTC v. M.J.S. Financial Services, Inc., 5 Trade Reg. Rep. (CCH) ¶ 24,461 (N.D. Ga. 1998) (stipulated final judgment).

677 16 C.F.R. § 310.4(a)(4). *See* FTC v. 1263523 Ontario, Inc., 205 F. Supp. 2d 205 (S.D.N.Y. 2002) (issuing permanent injunction against seller that accepted fees before delivering credit cards and misrepresented refund policy); *In re* National Credit Mgmt. Group, 21 F. Supp. 2d 424 (D.N.J. 1998) (issuing preliminary injunction); People by Spitzer v. Telehublink, 756 N.Y.S.2d 285 (App. Div. 2003) (affirming permanent injunction against advance-fee credit card telemarketer).

678 16 C.F.R. §§ 310.3, 310.4; FTC v. Consumer Alliance, Inc., 2003 WL 22287364 (N.D. Ill. Sept. 30, 2003); FTC v. Mark Alan Conway, 5 Trade Reg. Rep. (CCH) ¶ 15149 (W.D. Cal. Aug. 27, 2001) (proposed consent decree; seller promised credit card but delivered a list of banks and a booklet); *In re* National Credit Mgmt. Group, 21 F. Supp. 2d 424 (D.N.J. 1998); New York v. Financial Services Network, 930 F. Supp. 865 (W.D.N.Y. 1996) (offered "pre-approved Resource Cards" but only provided application forms for credit cards from other institutions; advertised $30,000 line of credit but actually only offered finder's fee if consumer located mortgage investment for it). *See also* FTC v. OPCO Int'l Agency, Inc., 5 Trade Reg. Rep. (CCH) ¶ 24,879 (W.D. Mich. Feb. 21, 2001) (TRO against telemarketer that offered low-interest consolidation loan for a fee but delivered list of banks). *See generally* § 5.9.3.9, *infra*.

679 FTC v. Westcal Equipment, Inc., 5 Trade Reg. Rep. (CCH) ¶ 15388 (W.D. Wash. Mar. 26, 2003) (proposed consent decree against defendants who promised major credit card but delivered card that could only be used for merchandise in their catalog); FTC v. Consumer Money Markets, Inc., 5 Trade Reg. Rep. (CCH) ¶ 24,796 (D. Nev. Sept. 6, 2000) (consent decree); FTC v. Family Shoppers Union, Inc., 5 Trade Reg. Rep. (CCH) ¶ 23,368 (E.D. Va. 1993) (consent order); FTC v. M&H Assocs., 5 Trade Reg. Rep. (CCH) ¶ 23,245 (D. Md. 1992) (consent decree); FTC v. National Credit Savers, Inc., 5 Trade Reg. Rep. (CCH) ¶ 23,303 (M.D. Ala. 1992); FTC v. Timmerman, 5 Trade Reg. Rep. (CCH) ¶ 23,046 (D. Md. 1991) (consent order). *See also* FTC v. Andre, 5 Trade Reg. Rep. (CCH) ¶ 24,429 (N.D. Ill. 1998) (consent decree) (deceptive marketing of credit cards and credit repair involved initial fee and purchase requirements); FTC v. Consumer Credit Services, Inc., 5 Trade Reg. Rep. (CCH) ¶ 24,447 (D. Nev. 1998) (settlement).

680 *See, e.g.*, FTC v. Interactive Marketing Concepts, Inc., 5 Trade Reg. Rep. (CCH) ¶ 23,872 (D.N.J. 1995) (proposed consent decree) ("genuine" credit card marketed through 900 number required a minimum of $300 on deposit as security).

681 Millenium Communications & Fulfillment, Inc. v. Attorney General, 761 So. 2d 1256 (Fla. App. 2000). *Cf.* Consumer Money Markets, Inc., 5 Trade Reg. Rep. (CCH) ¶ 24,796 (D. Nev. Sept. 6, 2000) (consent decree) (telemarketer's failure to disclose limitation to catalog purchases and high cash advance fee was deceptive).

682 Millennium Communications & Fulfillment, Inc. v. Attorney General, 800 So. 2d 255 (Fla. App. 2001).

seller's services.[683] The FTC has also cracked down on other credit card finders that use 900 numbers so that the consumer pays for the call while he or she is being deceived over the phone.[684]

Some credit card finding operations are merely schemes to obtain the consumer's checking account number, and then to use electronic means to take money out of that account without the consumer's authorization. This abuse is detailed in § 5.1.10.3, *infra.*

Credit card finders may be liable under a number of statutes in addition to the state UDAP statute. Many states have a credit services organization act that applies to entities such as credit card finders who, for a fee, offer to obtain extensions of credit for consumers.[685] It may require licensure, disclosures, and a right to cancel. These statutes may contain their own civil liability provisions, plus a violation will probably be held to be a *per se* UDAP violation.[686] The state may also have a loan broker law that applies to credit card finders.[687] State and federal RICO liability should also be explored. Ohio includes operation of an unregistered credit services organization as a predicate offense under its state RICO statute, and the state supreme court upheld the conviction of a credit card finder under this statute.[688]

5.1.9.3 Unauthorized Credit Card Charges

Charging a consumer's credit card account without authorization is a UDAP violation.[689] It can be an unfair practice for a seller to request the consumer to sign a blank credit card slip for certain purposes, and then add charges to that blank slip for other purposes.[690]

Scams abound in which companies use deceptive means to get a consumer's credit card number and then make unauthorized charges to the consumer's account. The FTC has proceeded against a company that rented or sold consumers' credit card numbers to telemarketers, who would then charge the consumers for goods and services that had been promoted as free.[691] In another scam, a company defrauded consumers by mailing them certificates that said they had won prizes. When the consumers called the number on the mailer, telemarketers would request their credit card numbers and make unauthorized charges.[692]

The FTC has now amended its Telemarketing Sales Rule to prohibit the sale of unencrypted consumer account numbers.[693] The amended rule also prohibits unauthorized charges in telemarketing transactions.[694]

5.1.9.4 Credit Balances

The FTC has found it unfair or deceptive for a retailer:

- To fail to disclose to customers all material facts relating to its revolving credit balance practices (where an amount is owed to the customer in connection with the charge account);
- To fail to provide those having credit balances with periodic billing statements detailing the amounts of such balances, and with notices that they have a continuing right to request a refund of their credit balance; or
- To transfer out credit balances from charge customers' accounts without notice.[695]

It is also unfair for a creditor to fail to account to consumers for surpluses owed to them after collateral is sold.[696] A

683 FTC v. United States Sales Corp., 785 F. Supp. 737 (N.D. Ill. 1992).

684 *See* FTC v. Interactive Marketing Concepts, Inc., 5 Trade Reg. Rep. (CCH) ¶ 23,872 (D.N.J. 1995) (proposed consent decree); FTC v. M.D.M. Interests, Inc., 5 Trade Reg. Rep. (CCH) ¶ 23,262 (S.D. Tex. 1992) (consent order); FTC v. Timmerman, 5 Trade Reg. Rep. (CCH) ¶ 23,046 (D. Md. 1991) (consent order); FTC v. Interactive Communications Technology, Inc., 5 Trade Reg. Rep. (CCH) ¶ 23,212 (F.T.C. Dkt. C-3400 1992) (consent order).

685 *See* § 5.1.2.2.3, *supra*; National Consumer Law Center, Fair Credit Reporting Ch. 15 (5th ed. 2002 and Supp.).

686 *See* § 3.2.7, *supra.*

687 *See* People by Spitzer v. Telehublink, 756 N.Y.S.2d 285 (App. Div. 2003) (affirming permanent injunction against advance-fee credit card telemarketer). *See generally* § 5.1.3.1, *supra*; National Consumer Law Center, Fair Credit Reporting Ch. 15 (5th ed. 2002 and Supp.).

688 State v. Schlosser, 79 Ohio St. 3d 329, 681 N.E.2d 911 (1997). *See* § 9.3, *infra.*

689 FTC v. Vacation Travel Club, Inc., 5 Trade Reg. Rep. (CCH) ¶ 22,822 (M.D. Fla. 1990) (consent order); FTC v. Creative Advertising Specialty House, 5 Trade Reg. Rep. (CCH) ¶ 22,740 (E.D. Cal. Oct. 10, 1989) (consent order); FTC v. Amy Travel Services, Inc., 3 Trade Reg. Rep. (CCH) ¶ 22,546 (N.D. Ill. 1988).

690 Sprayfoam, Inc. v. Durant's Rental Centers, Inc., 39 Conn. Supp. 78, 468 A.2d 951 (Super. Ct. 1983).

691 FTC v. Capitol Club of N. Am., 5 Trade Reg. Rep. (CCH) ¶ 23,739 (D.N.J. 1994) (proposed consent decree). *See also* §§ 4.9.8, *supra*, 5.9.4.7.5, *infra.*

692 FTC v. Multinet Marketing, L.L.C., 5 Trade Reg. Rep. (CCH) ¶ 24,343 (N.D. Tex. 1998) (proposed final judgment and court order).

693 16 C.F.R. § 310.4(a)(5), *as amended by* 68 Fed. Reg. 2580 (Jan. 29, 2003). *See* § 5.9.3.7.5, *infra.*

694 16 C.F.R. § 310.4(a)(6). *See* § 5.9.3.8.1, *infra. See also* § 4.9.8, *supra* (deceptive billing practices).

695 Fred Meyer Inc., 96 F.T.C. 60 (1980) (consent order); Hertz Corp., 93 F.T.C. 980 (1978) (consent order); Genesco, Inc., 89 F.T.C. 451 (1977); Atlantic Ritchfield Co., 89 F.T.C. 330 (1977) (consent order); Carte Blanche Corp., 89 F.T.C. 305 (1977) (consent order); City Stores Inc., 89 F.T.C. 322 (1977) (consent order); Federated Dep't Stores, 89 F.T.C. 313 (1977) (consent order); Associated Dry Goods Corp., 85 F.T.C. 1096 (1975) (consent order); Gimbel Brothers, Inc., 85 F.T.C. 1102 (1975) (consent order); Carter Hawley Hale Stores Inc., 85 F.T.C. 1116 (1975) (consent order); McCrory Corp., 85 F.T.C. 1109 (1975) (consent order).

696 *See* § 5.1.1.5.4, *supra.*

lender may also commit a UDAP violation by misrepresenting the payoff amount on a loan.[697]

5.1.9.5 Credit Card Loss Protection and Reporting Services

A number of companies offer credit card loss protection. For example, they will, for a fee, to report to credit card issuers that a consumer has lost his or her credit cards. A 2004 FTC study estimated that, over a one-year period, more than 4.5 million people in the United States fell victim to a credit card protection scam.[698]

The FTC has ruled that it is deceptive for these companies not to disclose the limitations of the cardholder's maximum liability under the Consumer Credit Protection Act.[699] The FTC's Telemarketing Sales Rule, as amended effective March 31, 2003, now incorporates this disclosure requirement.[700] The rule applies to sales of credit card loss protection services made over the telephone, even when the buyer initiates the call in response to an advertisement, direct mail, fax, or e-mail solicitation.[701]

Sellers of credit card protection also often misrepresent that they are affiliated with legitimate credit card companies or the consumer's issuing bank.[702] Some of these sellers are branching out into selling bogus identity theft and telemarketing fraud prevention services.[703]

697 Osbourne v. Capital City Mortgage Corp., 667 A.2d 1321 (D.C. App. 1995).

698 FTC, Consumer Fraud in the United States: An FTC Survey (2004) at 32.

699 Credit Card Service Corp. v. FTC, 495 F.2d 1004 (D.C. Cir. 1974). *See also* FTC v. Farpoint Servs. Int'l, 5 Trade Reg. Rep. (CCH) ¶ 15307 (W.D. Wash. Aug. 30, 2002) (proposed consent decree); Source One Publications, Inc., 5 Trade Reg. Rep. (CCH) ¶ 15105 (D. Ariz. May 15, 2001) (banning defendant for life from credit card protection sales); FTC v. Liberty Direct, Inc., 5 Trade Reg. Rep. (CCH) ¶ 24,914 (D. Ariz. Apr. 20, 2001) (consent decree); FTC v. GEP LTD., 5 Trade Reg. Rep. (CCH) ¶ 24,758 (M.D. Fla. June 20, 2000) (consent decree); FTC v. Universal Marketing Servs., 5 Trade Reg. Rep. (CCH) ¶ 24,758 (W.D. Okla. June 20, 2000) (consent decree); FTC v. Tracker Corp. of Am., 5 Trade Reg. Rep. (CCH) ¶ 24,477 (N.D. Ga. 1998) (proposed consent decree).

700 16 C.F.R. § 310.3(a)(1)(vi), *as amended by* 68 Fed. Reg. 2580 (Jan. 29, 2003). *See* § 5.9.3.7.2, *infra*.

701 16 C.F.R. § 310.6(b)(5), (6), *as amended by* 68 Fed. Reg. 2580 (Jan. 29, 2003).

702 *See, e.g.*, FTC v. Consumer Alliance, Inc., 2003 WL 22287364 (N.D. Ill. Sept. 30, 2003).

703 *See* FTC v. Harvey Sloniker, 5 Trade Reg. Rep. (CCH) ¶ 15364 (D. Ariz. Feb. 6, 2003) (proposed consent decree); FTC v. R & R Consultants, Inc., 5 Trade Reg. Rep. (CCH) ¶ 15251 (N.D.N.Y. Apr. 25, 2002) (proposed consent decree against telemarketer who sold bogus ID theft protection and supposed advance fee low interest credit cards).

5.1.10 Bank Accounts, Checks, Other Payment Methods

5.1.10.1 Deposit Accounts

It is deceptive for a bank to fail to pay interest on an interest-bearing account and then refuse to pay back interest on the account when this practice is discovered.[704] A bank may also violate the UDAP statute by failing to inform a depositor that it has selected a savings account that will pay interest on only a portion of the deposits.[705]

5.1.10.2 Check Cashing

Check cashing outlets are common in low-income urban areas. They may also be fronts for illegal payday loan operations. Some states have special laws regulating the fees that these businesses can charge.[706] Even before Pennsylvania adopted such a statute, a court held that a check-cashing service engaged in a UDAP violation by charging $1156 to cash a $11,171 Social Security check.[707]

A bank's selective and wrongful dishonoring of checks is deceptive and unconscionable.[708] An appellate court has found a UDAP claim stated where the consumer alleged that a bank, without notice and authority, imposed a monthly charge for checking accounts with low balances.[709] Excessive bank fees may be unconscionable.[710] Lenders and banks committed UDAP violations by having consumers sign

704 Ashlock v. Sunwest Bank of Roswell, 107 N.M. 100, 753 P.2d 346 (1988).

705 Oswego Laborers' Local 214 Pension Fund v. Marine Midland Bank, 85 N.Y.2d 20, 647 N.E.2d 741 (1995).

706 *See* National Consumer Law Center, The Cost of Credit: Regulation and Legal Challenges Appx. A (2d ed. 2000 and Supp.).

707 *In re* Wernly, 91 B.R. 702 (Bankr. E.D. Pa. 1988). *But cf.* Hayes v. First Commerce Corp., 763 So. 2d 733 (La. App. 2000) (no UDAP violation for drawee bank to charge non-depositor $2 to cash check, even though U.C.C. Art. 3 defines a check as an unconditional promise to pay).

708 Farmers & Merchants State Bank of Krum v. Ferguson, 605 S.W.2d 320 (Tex. Civ. App. 1980), *modified on other grounds*, 617 S.W.2d 918 (Tex. 1981). *But cf.* Hill v. St. Paul Fed. Bank, 329 Ill. App. 3d 705, 768 N.E.2d 322 (2002) (posting method for overdrawn checks, which maximized overdraft fees, was not UDAP violation where bank disclosed the fees in accord with federal law); Framingham Auto Sales, Inc. v. Workers' Credit Union, 41 Mass. App. Ct. 416, 671 N.E.2d 963 (1996) (bank's wrongful dishonor of cashier's check in commercial transaction not a UDAP violation).

709 Littlefield v. Goldome Bank, 142 A.D.2d 978, 530 N.Y.S.2d 401 (1988).

710 *See, e.g.*, Perdue v. Crocker Nat'l Bank, 38 Cal. 3d 913, 702 P.2d 503, 216 Cal. Rptr. 345 (1985), *appeal dismissed*, 475 U.S. 1001 (1986). *But see* Consumer Action v. Wells Fargo Bank, 2002 Cal. App. Unpub. LEXIS 588 (Apr. 30, 2002) (unpublished, citation limited) (courts should not evaluate justification for fees); Saunders v. Michigan Avenue Nat'l Bank, 662 N.E.2d 602 (Ill. App. Ct. 1996) (no UDAP violation where bank

forms authorizing electronic fund transfers that falsely stated, contrary to the Electronic Fund Transfers Act, that they could not revoke the authorizations.[711] Banking and check cashing practices are discussed in detail in National Consumer Law Center, *Consumer Banking and Payments Law* (2d ed 2002 and Supp.).

5.1.10.3 "Telechecks" and Unauthorized Electronic Fund Transfers

5.1.10.3.1 Introduction

Consumer banking is undergoing dramatic changes as paper checks are being replaced by electronic images of checks and by electronic fund transfers. Unscrupulous merchants and collectors can take advantage of these changes to steal money from consumer checking accounts. The consumer's response is complicated by the fact that two entirely different sets of laws will apply to the transaction, depending on whether the unauthorized transfer originated on paper or electronically.

This subsection briefly summarizes these two different sets of consumer rights to contest unauthorized transfers from the consumer's account. These rights are examined in more detail in another NCLC manual, *Consumer Banking and Payments Law* (2d ed. 2002 and Supp.). This subsection also examines UDAP challenges to such transfers.

5.1.10.3.2 Telechecks or preauthorized drafts

Scam artists today take money out of consumer accounts in at least two different ways. One way involves "telechecks," "preauthorized drafts" or "demand drafts." The technique can be perfectly legitimate—a party (the "payee") obtains the consumer's advance permission to have money taken from the consumer's checking account to pay an obligation to that payee. Instead of a signed check, the payee presents to the bank an unsigned draft. The draft may look like a check, but, instead of a signature, has a notice stating "authorized by drawer," "debiting of account authorized by customer" or similar language.

The bank treats the draft like a signed check. This may be a convenient device where a consumer must make periodic payments to a lender, insurer, or merchant, because it allows for the automatic withdrawal of the amount due from the consumer's bank account without the consumer having to sign and mail each check.

The abuse occurs when a scam operator obtains the consumer's account number and bank's routing number (the "MICR" numbers on the bottom of the check) and presents a draft to the bank without the consumer's authorization. Once the scam operator obtains the relevant information, it can use desktop publishing technology to produce a check with the account information encoded on the bottom just as though it were the customer's own check. As a practical matter, neither the scam operator's bank nor the consumer's bank will review the signature block, but only the account information encoded on the bottom of the check.

5.1.10.3.3 Unauthorized electronic funds transfers

Similar to a telecheck is an unauthorized electronic transfer. Instead of presenting an unsigned check to the merchant's bank for payment, the merchant requests its bank to initiate an electronic transfer from the consumer's account to the merchant's account. Again, the merchant needs the consumer's account number and the consumer bank's routing number.

5.1.10.3.4 How the scam operator obtains the account numbers

The scam operator may obtain the account information in a number of different ways. The merchant may tell the consumer that the account number is needed to deposit a prize the consumer has won.[712] Some credit card finders use their service to discover the consumer's checking account number, and then electronically take money out of that account.[713] The same is the case with credit repair organizations,[714] and companies that promise, for a fee, to find the consumer unused scholarships and grants.[715]

Other scam operators ask for a checking account number, to be used only when specified services have been provided, but then take money out of the account before providing the services and without authorization.[716] Or the consumer can authorize a demand draft in a small amount, and then the merchant or debt collector can use the account number to withdraw larger or additional amounts beyond those authorized. The Internet also opens up many new opportunities for the deceptive identification of a consumer's bank account number.

---

charged $20 a day for overdrafts, where the charge had been expressly disclosed).

711 Cobb v. Monarch Fin. Co., 913 F. Supp. 1164 (N.D. Ill. 1995) (ruling on motion to dismiss).

712 FTC v. Windward Marketing, Ltd., 5 Trade Reg. Rep. (CCH) ¶ 24,223 (N.D. Ga. 1997) (proposed consent decree); Windward Marketing, Inc., 5 Trade Reg. Rep. (CCH) ¶ 24,060 (F.T.C. File No. X96 0026 June 21, 1996) (consent order).

713 *See* FTC v. Mandy Enterprises, Inc., 5 Trade Reg. Rep. (CCH) ¶ 23,181 (D.S.C. 1992).

714 FTC v. Ellis, 5 Trade Reg. Rep. (CCH) ¶ 24,179 (C.D. Cal. 1996) (proposed consent decree).

715 FTC v. Student Aid Inc., 5 Trade Reg. Rep. (CCH) ¶ 24,312 (S.D.N.Y. 1997) (proposed consent decree).

716 FTC v. Regency Services, Inc., 5 Trade Reg. Rep. (CCH) ¶ 24,219 (M.D. Fla. 1997) (proposed consent decree).

5.1.10.3.5 UCC determines consumer rights concerning unauthorized telechecks

When an unauthorized transfer is initiated using a paper telecheck, the consumer's rights are defined by Articles 3 and 4 of the UCC. Whenever amounts are taken out of the consumer's account without authorization, the consumer should *promptly* upon receipt of a monthly statement challenge the transaction with the consumer's own bank.[717] The consumer's challenge is not that the check was unsigned. The UCC has a loose definition of signature, and consumers can orally authorize others to sign for them as their agents.[718] The draft is thus "properly payable" by the consumer's bank if the consumer authorized the withdrawal.

The consumer's challenge on the withdrawal instead should be based on the fact that the consumer did not provide authorization for the merchant to debit the consumer's account.

Banks often operate on the presumption that someone with the consumer's account number has authorization to withdraw money from that account, so that the consumer may have difficulty persuading the bank that the withdrawal was without authorization.[719] The UCC sets no standards as to what types of documentation the merchant has to have to show the consumer's authorization. Nor does it explicitly provide for attorney fees for the consumer in actions to recover amounts taken out of the banking account without authorization.

The consumer's burden of showing that the check was unauthorized is further complicated because the scam operator may have notes or other documentation that purport to show that the consumer has in fact authorized the withdrawal. Then the consumer's claim may have to be that the records are self-serving and not accurate, or that the consumer did not realize he or she was authorizing the withdrawal, or that the consumer was authorizing a different amount to be withdrawn. The bank may also claim the consumer was negligent in facilitating the fraud.[720]

This difficulty of proving that the telecheck was unauthorized is exacerbated by the self-interest of the consumer's own bank. Where the merchant has skipped town, under the version of the UCC enacted in most states, it is the consumer's bank (not the merchant's bank) that bears the eventual loss if the consumer does not.[721] The 2002 Revision to UCC Articles 3 and 4, only adopted to date in Minnesota, and non-uniform amendments to Articles 3 and 4 in a number of states, more sensibly shift the burden of loss from the consumer's bank to the merchant's bank.[722] In these few states, the consumer's bank may be more willing to accept the consumer's claim that the check was unauthorized, but, even so, the merchant's bank may not, so that the consumer's bank will want evidence to present to the merchant's bank.

5.1.10.3.6 The EFTA and NACHA rules determine consumer rights concerning unauthorized electronic funds transfers

Where the unauthorized transfer from the consumer's account originates electronically, instead of by presentment of an unsigned paper check, an entirely different set of laws apply. The Electronic Funds Transfer Act (EFTA) and FRB Regulation E establish stronger legal protections than those available under the UCC.[723] The consumer has no liability for unauthorized transfers, even if not timely reported, and even if the consumer is negligent (although the consumer may be liable for future unauthorized transfers if the consumer fails to report past unauthorized transfers).[724] The EFTA also sets out an error resolution procedure. Some EFTA violations authorize treble or statutory damages, and attorney fees are generally available to prevailing consumers.

Additional protections concerning unauthorized electronic funds transfers are found in the rules of the National Automated Clearing House Association (NACHA) that operates the Automated Clearing House (ACH) network, the predominant network that facilitates electronic funds transfers between banks and other institutions. An electronic funds transfer initiated over the telephone requires the consumer's written or electronic signed authorization, unless the consumer initiates the call or there is a pre-existing relationship between the parties. In that case, the authorization must either be tape-recorded or followed up by a written

717 *See* U.C.C. §§ 3-406, 4-401, 4-406. The consumer must report the problem within a reasonable period of time after receiving the monthly statement. Problems arise where the consumer's returned checks are "truncated," meaning that the bank does not send the cancelled checks to the consumer as part of the monthly statement. (For example, all credit union share drafts are truncated.) Then the consumer may not notice the unauthorized check for some time. For a detailed description of consumer liability for unauthorized signatures, see National Consumer Law Center, Consumer Banking and Payments Law § 1.2 (2d ed. 2002 and Supp.).

718 U.C.C. § 1-201(39) defines signature broadly and probably includes a consumer authorizing the merchant to place a notice on the check saying that the account debit is authorized.

719 *See* U.C.C. § 3-308.

720 U.C.C. § 3-406.

721 *See* U.C.C. §§ 3-418, 4-208(a)(3). This placement of the loss on the consumer's bank instead of the merchant's bank has been changed in a recently revised version of U.C.C. Articles 3 and 4, only adopted to date in Minnesota.

722 *E.g.*, California, Ch. 316 of 1996 statutes, amending various sections of the U.C.C. to shift the risk of loss for fraudulent demand drafts from the drawee to the depositary bank. *See also* Gino A. Chilleri, *An Exception to Price v. Neay: California's Presentment and Transfer Warranties With Respect to Fraudulent Telemarketing Drafts*, 30 U.C.C. L. J. 44 (1997).

723 15 U.S.C. § 1693; 12 C.F.R. § 205.

724 *See* National Consumer Law Center, Consumer Banking and Payments Law § 4.5 (2d ed. 2002 and Supp.).

confirmation prior to the settlement date.[725] Additional protections are specified for transfers initiated over the Internet.

5.1.10.3.7 Distinguishing telechecks from electronic transfers

Although very different laws apply, telechecks and electronic transfers may appear virtually the same to a consumer reading a bank statement. Starting in late 2004, consumers no longer receive the original canceled paper check with their monthly statement, because the paper check, when deposited at the merchant's bank, will be converted to an electronic item. The most that the consumer will see in a monthly bank statement will be a copy of an electronic image of the original check. Many monthly bank statements will only provide the consumer with a description of the check, such as the date, amount, and the name of the payee. This description will not differ significantly from the description of an electronic funds transfer in the monthly statement, so many consumers will confuse the two.

The safest course is not to assume that a debit from a consumer's account was initiated by telecheck or by electronic funds transfer, and instead inquire specifically of the consumer's bank. The question is not whether the bank received an electronic debit or a paper one. The bank certainly will have received an electronic one. The question is what originated the chain of transfer requests from bank to bank: was it originated by a request for an electronic transfer or was it initiated by a paper telecheck.

5.1.10.3.8 FTC Telemarketing Rule and state statutes apply to both telechecks and electronic funds transfers

The FTC Telemarketing Rule prohibits any seller or telemarketer from submitting billing information for payment or collecting payment for goods or services or a charitable contribution, without the consumer's express verifiable authorization.[726] These requirements apply to both telechecks and electronic funds transfers.

The FTC Telemarketing Rule requires the merchant to obtain the consumer's express verifiable authorization, defined as one of the following three forms of verification:

- The consumer's express written and signed authorization;
- Tape-recorded express oral authorization, which must be made available on request to the consumer and the consumer's bank; or
- Written confirmation of the transaction sent to the consumer prior to submission of payment to the customer's bank.[727]

The tape recorded oral authorization must include not only the consumer's authorization, but also evidence of the consumer's receipt of the following information: the number of debits, charges, or payments (if more than one); the submission dates and amounts; the consumer's name; a telephone number for consumer inquiries; and the date of the oral authorization.[728] The written confirmation to the consumer must contain the same information and the procedures for the customer to receive a refund from the seller if the confirmation is inaccurate.[729] Written confirmation can not be used in transactions that involve a free trial period that converts to pay status unless the consumer affirmatively cancels, where the telemarketer already had the consumer's billing information before making the call.[730] An FTC Telemarketing Rule violation is a *per se* UDAP violation in many states.[731]

Vermont's telemarketing statute goes beyond the FTC rule and prohibits a telemarketer from using telechecks without the consumer's express written authorization. The Act also prohibits the telemarketer's bank from assisting in violating this provision. A telemarketer for purposes of the Vermont statute is a person who initiates or receives telephone calls from a consumer in connection with a program to market goods and services.[732]

Oklahoma's UDAP statute prohibits knowingly causing a charge to be made by any billing method to a consumer for products or services which the person knows are not authorized in advance by the consumer.[733] In addition, certain state identity theft statutes may have application where they prohibit obtaining bank account and other information about an individual without authorization.[734]

5.1.10.3.9 Lack of adequate verification as a UDAP violation

A seller who debits a consumer's account without proper authorization, or after the consumer has revoked authorization, commits a UDAP violation.[735] The more difficult issue

725 *See id.* § 4.14.

726 16 C.F.R. § 310.3(a)(3), *as amended by* 68 Fed. Reg. 2580 (Jan. 29, 2003), *reprinted at* Appx. D.2.1, *infra. See In re* National Credit Mgmt. Group, 21 F. Supp. 2d 424 (D.N.J. 1998) (credit repair telemarketer debited accounts without proper documentation of authorization and without informing consumers of its refund policy, which was illusory in any event). *See generally* § 5.9.2.3.7, *infra.*

727 *Id.*

728 *Id.*

729 *Id.*

730 *Id.*

731 *See* §§ 3.2.7, *supra*, 5.9.4.9.2, *infra.*

732 Vt. Stat. Ann. tit. 9, § 2464.

733 Okla Stat. Ann. tit. 15, § 753(25, (26).

734 *See, e.g.*, Ala. Code § 13A-8-192; Ark Code § 5-37-227.

735 *In re* National Credit Mgmt. Group, 21 F. Supp. 2d 424 (D.N.J. 1998).

is where there is a dispute over whether authorization has been given.

Rather than a factual dispute over the existence of authorization, it may be preferable to argue that the company has a responsibility to obtain verification of that authorization, and that a pattern of inadequate verification is an unfair or deceptive practice.

FTC Telemarketing Rule standards for verification may be useful to consumers in dealing with collectors or merchants not covered by the rule. If the company can not produce any of the three forms of verifiable authorization, the consumer can argue that the company has engaged in an unfair practice—that it is unfair to engage in the practice of soliciting telechecks while placing the burden on consumers to prove lack of authorization. The FTC Telemarketing Rule standards should serve as a guide as to the types of verification the company must obtain.

Moreover, scam operators will often use intermediaries to facilitate their fraud. Anyone knowingly assisting such a fraud, including assisting the seller to violate the FTC Telemarketing Rule or NACHA rules, can also be subject to a UDAP claim. A good example is an FTC complaint in federal court charging a payment processor with assisting telemarketers they knew (or consciously avoided knowing) were engaged in deceptive and abusive telemarketing practices. The FTC also alleged that the defendant engaged in an unfair practice by systematically breaching its contractual promise to financial institutions to adhere to NACHA rules governing telephone initiated electronic funds transfers.

The federal court has entered a stipulated preliminary injunction order prohibiting the defendants from processing ACH debits for entities engaged in the telemarketing of credit-related goods or services; processing telephone-initiated ACH debits for entities that engage in "cold-call" outbound telemarketing; and violating the Telemarketing Sales Rule.[736] The FTC is seeking redress for consumers and disgorgement of fees unlawfully earned through processing for fraudulent telemarketers.

5.2 Contracts, Warranties and Legal Rights

5.2.1 Contract Language for Non-English Speaking Consumers

5.2.1.1 Introduction

New immigrants are often new to the English language as well. Many rip-off artists prey on this vulnerability, coercing non-English speaking consumers to sign contracts or other documents that they do not understand. There are a number of ways to challenge contract transactions based language barriers, including state UDAP laws, contract claims and defenses, and affirmative fraud claims.

5.2.1.2 UDAP Claims

It may be unfair or deceptive not to translate important information into the same language as principally used in the transaction.[737] There are two prongs to the argument that it is a UDAP violation to fail to make non-English disclosures. A consumer is obviously confused and deceived if required disclosures are made in a manner the consumer can not understand. Several statutes explicitly require that retailers not take advantage of a consumer's inability to understand the language of an agreement.[738] Certainly not understanding the language in which the agreement is negotiated or written would meet this requirement. Second, non-English disclosure falls nicely into the FTC's unfairness approach.[739] A non-English speaking consumer can not reasonably avoid the fact that he or she can not understand English disclosures. The confusion can lead to substantial injury.

In a situation where a seller has a large number of non-English speaking customers, it would not be costly to add disclosures in a second language.[740] However, one case had held that a non-English speaker had to show affirmatively that release language written in English was not conspicuous.[741]

In Massachusetts, door-to-door sellers can not induce purchasers to sign documents if the seller has reason to know the buyer can not read or write or understand the terms of the agreement.[742] Wisconsin UDAP regulations require that all documents pertaining to door-to-door sales must be in English and the language principally used in the sale.[743] Violations of these and other state laws requiring translation of documents into the languages other than English will be

736 FTC v. First Am. Payment Processing, Inc., F.T.C. File No. 032 3261, Civil Action No. CV 04-0074 PHX SRB (D. Ariz. Jan. 20, 2004).

737 Kelcor Corp., 93 F.T.C. 9 (1979) (consent order); *See also* Cantu v. Butron, 921 S.W.2d 344 (Tex. App. 1996).

738 Kan. Stat. § 50-627(b)(1); Mich. Comp. Laws Ann. § 445.903 (1)(x); Ohio Rev. Code § 1345.03(B)(1) (factor in determining if unconscionable under UDAP statute); Wis. Stat. Ann. § 427.108.

739 *See* § 4.3.2, *supra*.

740 See generally Steven W. Bender, Consumer Protection for Latinos: Overcoming Language Fraud and English-Only In the Marketplace, 45 Am. U.L. Rev. 1027 (1996).

741 Vera v. North Star Dodge Sales, Inc., 989 S.W.2d 13 (Tex. App. 1998).

742 Massachusetts Consumer Protection Regulations, Mass. Regs. Code tit. 940, § 3.09, Door-to-Door Sales and Home Improvement Transactions.

743 Wisconsin Dep't of Agriculture, Trade and Consumer Protection Rules Wis. Admin. Code ch. ATCP 127, Home Solicitation Selling.

a *per se* UDAP violation in many states.[744]

The FTC has accepted numerous consent agreements requiring that consumers be provided with contracts, other pertinent documents, and written disclosures in the same language as used in the sales presentation.[745] These documents must be provided in a timely manner.[746]

The FTC also requires in its rule concerning door-to-door sales that disclosure be in the same language as the oral sales presentation.[747] The FTC's Used Car Rule has a similar requirement[748] There is no private right of action under the FTC Used Car Rule, but a violation of the rule may be actionable under a state UDAP statute.[749] Since the Used Car Rule was in part promulgated under the federal Magnuson-Moss Act, a good argument can also be made that it is a violation of the Magnuson-Moss Act to violate the Used Car Rule.[750]

UDAP claims are preferable to contract law claims because the general presumption in contract law is that a consumer has a duty to read a document or contract that she signs. This "duty to read" applies even if the consumer is illiterate (including illiterate in the language of the contract or generally illiterate in all languages). In cases of illiteracy or in cases where there is a language barrier, courts have found that consumers have an obligation to find someone to help them.[751] The theory is that the failure of a party to obtain a reading and explanation (or translation) is negligence, which will estop the complaining party from avoiding the contract on the grounds that they were ignorant of the contract's provisions. This theory has been adhered to, even in contracts of adhesion, in decisions throughout the 1980s and 1990s, including two Supreme Court decisions.[752]

5.2.1.3 Other Statutory Requirements

The Truth in Lending Act allows but does not compel translation of the required disclosures.[753] Claims may be available under the federal civil rights acts, 42 U.S.C. §§ 1981 and 1982 and/or the Fair Housing Act and Equal Credit Opportunity Act, particularly if there is a pattern that disproportionately impacts a particular racial minority or other protected group.[754]

Uniform Commercial Code and other unconscionability concepts also provide a basis to claim that disclosures should be made in the same language as the transaction. It would be unconscionable for a seller to use the buyer's inability to understand contract provisions to include oppressive terms in the agreement.[755]

Several states have addressed the problem of immigrant fraud by passing statutes and regulations that specifically

744 *See* § 3.2.7, *supra*.

745 U.S. v. United Recovery Sys., Inc., Civil Action No.: H-02-1410 (sl) (S.D. Tex. 2002) (consent decree), *available at* www.ftc.gov/os/2002/04/unitedconsent.pdf; Cavanaugh Communities, 93 F.T.C. 559 (1979) (consent order); Hiken Furniture Co., 91 F.T.C. 1115 (1978) (consent order); Insilco Corp., 91 F.T.C. 706 (1978) (consent order); Hallcraft Jewelers, Inc., 89 F.T.C. 415 (1977) (consent order); Almacenes Hernandez Corp., 87 F.T.C. 400 (1976) (consent order); Buch's Jewelry Co., 87 F.T.C. 394 (1976) (consent order); Carl Stepp, 88 F.T.C. 409 (1976) (consent order); Lafayette United Corp., 88 F.T.C. 683 (1976); Daby's Furniture Corp., 87 F.T.C. 389 (1976); J&J Furniture Corp., 87 F.T.C. 383 (1976) (consent order); J. Kurtz & Sons, Inc., 87 F.T.C. 1300 (1976); Mutual Home Equip. Co., 87 F.T.C. 606 (1976) (consent order); Weilt Co., 87 F.T.C. 406 (1976) (consent order); Atlantic Indus., 85 F.T.C. 903 (1975) (consent order); Library Marketing Service Inc., 85 F.T.C. 957 (1975) (consent order).

746 Grand Spaulding Dodge, Inc., 90 F.T.C. 406 (1977) (consent order).

747 16 C.F.R. § 429.1(a).

748 *See* the discussion at § 5.4.6.2, *infra*; Martinez v. Rick Case Cars, Inc., 278 F. Supp. 2d 1371 (S.D. Fla. 2003) (a violation of FTC rule requiring buyers guide and window sticker to be in Spanish is a violation of Florida's UDAP statute).

749 Martinez v. Rick Case Cars, Inc., 278 F. Supp. 2d 1371 (S.D. Fla. 2003) (it can be inferred that the alleged failure to provide Spanish-language Buyer's Guide contributed to consumer not receiving the necessary terms of the contract and subsequent financial loss).

750 *See* Currier v. Spencer, 299 Ark. 182, 772 S.W.2d 309 (1989) (upholding trial court's award of Magnuson-Moss attorney fees for violation of FTC Used Car Rule); § 5.4.6.2.3, *infra*.

751 See generally Steven W. Bender, Consumer Protection for Latinos: Overcoming Language and English-Only in the Marketplace, 45 Am. U. L. Rev. 1027 (1996).

752 Green Tree Fin. Corp.-Ala. v. Randolph, 531 U.S. 79 (2000) (regarding mandatory arbitration clause in a consumer loan); Carnival Cruise Lines v. Shute, 499 U.S. 585, 593 (1991) (regarding a forum selection clause in a cruise ticket). *See generally* Alan M. White and Cathy Lesser Mansfield, *Literacy and Contract*, 13.2 Stan. Law. & Pol. Rev. 233 (2002).

753 12 C.F.R. § 226.27; FRB Official Staff Commentary § 226.27. *See* Nevarez v. O'Connor Chevrolet, Inc., 303 F. Supp. 2d 927 (N.D. Ill. 2004) (car dealer not required to provide consumer with a Spanish copy of the retail installment contract under TILA, even if Ill. law has such a requirement); County Trust Co. v. Mora, 383 N.Y.S.2d 468, 470 (1975) (explaining that TILA does not require disclosures in Spanish even when consumers can not understand English): Equicredit Corp. v. Turcios, 752 N.Y.S.2d 684 (N.Y. App. Div. 2002) (while TILA disclosures "may" be made in a language other than English (12 C.F.R. § 226.27), there is no basis in law for requiring that TILA disclosures under 15 U.S.C. § 1638 made to borrowers who read, write and speak only Spanish, should be made in Spanish, to insure that disclosures are meaningful). On the other hand, a defective disclosure statement in English that a Spanish-only speaking consumer could not understand was no defense to liability. Zamarippa v. Cy's Car Sales, Inc., 674 F.2d 877, 879 (11th Cir. 1982).

754 *See* National Consumer Law Center, Credit Discrimination (3d ed. 2002 and Supp.).

755 Prevot v. Phillips Petroleum, Inc., 133 F. Supp. 2d 937 (S.D. Tex. 2001) (arbitration agreements signed by Spanish-speaking employees who did not understand English were unconscionable and unenforceable.). *See* § 4.4, *supra*. *See especially* § 4.4.4, *supra*. *See generally* Steven W. Bender, *Consumer Protection for Latinos: Overcoming Language Fraud and English-Only in the Marketplace*, 45 Am. U.L. Rev. 1027, 1040 (1996).

require translations of contracts for certain transactions or under certain circumstances. The provisions vary by state. In some states, the statute applies only to specific types of transactions like rent-to-own or door-to-door sales.[756] Translations may be required in any language in which the negotiations occurred or only in a specific language such as Spanish.[757] In Nevada, the Commissioner for Financial Institutions is required to prescribe forms for the application of credit and contracts to be used in the sale of vehicles and translate them into Spanish.[758]

California law requires written translations of certain loan documents, residential leases, and other consumer contracts that are negotiated primarily in Spanish, Chinese, Tagalog, Korean, and Vietnamese.[759] That statute provides for rescission of the transaction, where the language translation requirement is not met. Some businesses in California, especially car dealerships, have tried to circumvent the Spanish language contract requirements by providing consumers with only a blank copy of the contract in Spanish, leaving the only completed version of the contract in English.[760] This practice has led to several lawsuits, but no court has yet to rule on the legality of this practice.

Illinois law formerly required sellers to provide a translated written contract if a retail transaction was negotiated in a language other than English but, based on a 2001 amendment, the seller need only have the buyer sign a form in the language of negotiation stating that the seller explained the contract in that language.[761] Oregon law requires that statutory disclosures in lease-purchase agreements be provided in languages other than English.[762]

5.2.1.4 Relevance of "English-Only" Laws

A couple of states have passed "English-only" laws,[763] which might trump state laws requiring certain documents to be translated,[764] or even prevent courts from ordering documents to be translated as a matter of case law.[765] A California car dealer has even argued unsuccessfully that the California's Constitution that makes English the official language of the state, conflicts with the translation requirement. The court disagreed and found no conflict.[766] The constitutionality of such "English-only" laws is questionable.[767] Moreover, the much more prevalent state laws which declare English to be the "official language" of the

756 Ariz. Rev. Stat. §§ 44-1797.05 (applies to discount buying services), 44-5004 (door-to-door sales); Cal. Civ. Code §§ 1632 (Spanish, Chinese, Tagalog, Vietnameses, and Korean), 1689.21 (solicited seminar sales contracts); Del. Code Ann. tit. 6, § 4404 (door-to-door sales); D.C. Code § 28-3904(r)(5); Fla. Stat. Ann. §§ 636.015 (prepaid limited health services organizations), 641.305 (health maintenance organization), 641.421 (prepaid health clinics); 815 Ill. Comp. Stat. §§ 505/2B (home solicitation sales), 505/2N (all retail transactions, except for purchases made with credit card), 655/2 (rent-to-own); Ind. Code § 24-4.5-6-111(3)(3) (factor in unconscionability finding for credit transactions); Iowa Code § 537.5108(4)(e) (same); Kan. Stat. § 50-640 (door-to-door sales); Neb. Rev. Stat. § 69-1604 (door-to-door sales); N.J. Stat. Ann. § 17.16C-61.6 and 100 (retail installment sales); N.M. Stat. Ann. § 57-26-4 (rent-to-own advertisements in languages other than English require companies to have purchase agreements in the same languages as the advertisements and make the agreements available to consumers); N.Y. Pers. Prop. Law art. 10-A, § 428 (door-to-door); N.Y. Gen. Bus. §§ 391-1 (personal emergency response systems); N.Y. Gen. Bus. Law art. 24-A, § 369ee (cancellation notices for prize awards); N.Y. Gen. Bus. Law § 394-c(7)(b) (dating services); N.C. Gen. Stat. § 14.401.13 (cancellation notice); Or. Rev. Stat. § 646.249 (lease-purchase agreements); Pa. Stat. Ann. tit. 73, § 201-7 (door-to-door); 20 P.R. Laws Ann. § 3055; 17 P.R. Laws. Ann. § 510 (certain property sales); 10 P.R. Laws. Ann. § 741 (retail installment contracts); S.C. Code Ann. § 37-5-108(4)(e) (inability to understand language of agreement is factor in determining if creditor remedy is unconscionable); Tex. Bus. & Comm. Code Ann. §§ 35.72 (rent-to-own), 39.004(b) (home solicitation sales); Tex. Fin. Code § 348.006(d) (documentary fees in motor vehicle sales); Vt. Stat. Ann. tit. 9, § 2454 (door-to-door); Wis. Admin. Code ch. ATCP 127 (door-to-door); Wis. Stat. § 423.203 (notice of cancellation); Wyo. Stat. Ann. § 40-19-106 (rent-to-own).

757 *See* Cal. Civ. Code § 1632 (requiring translations of contracts into Spanish and conspicuous display of notice that business is required to provide an unsigned Spanish-language contract or agreement); Gutierrez v. PCH Roulette, Inc., 2003 WL 22422431 (Cal. App. Oct. 24, 2003) (unpublished, citation limited) (auto dealer who negotiated primarily in Spanish required to translate contract into Spanish).

758 Nev. Rev. Stat. § 97.299.

759 Cal. Civ. Code § 1632 (West). Prior to July 1, 2004, in California the translation requirement only applied to contracts negotiated primarily in Spanish. *See* Reyes v. Superior Court of Imperial County, 118 Cal. App. 3d 159, 173 Cal. Rptr. 267 (1981) (directing that deficiency judgment on an automobile loan in favor of finance company be reversed; Spanish-speaking buyer, who spoke no English, had not received translation of purchase and loan documents negotiated primarily in Spanish, but written in English).

760 *See* Edwin Garcia, *Car Contracts Criticized for Language Gap*, San Jose Mercury News, Feb. 17, 2003.

761 815 Ill. Comp. Stat. Ann. § 505/2N (*as amended* eff. Aug. 23, 2001).

762 Or. Rev. Stat. § 646.249. Both the California and Oregon statutes do not apply if consumers supply their own interpreters to conduct negotiations.

763 *See, e.g.*, Ariz. Const. art. 28, § 3; S.C. Code Ann. § 1-1-697.

764 See Steven W. Bender, Consumer Protection for Latinos: Overcoming Language Fraud and English-Only in the Marketplace, 45 Am. U.L. Rev. 1027, 1046 (1996).

765 *See id.* at 1053, n.143.

766 Gutierrez v. PCH Roulette, Inc., 2003 WL 22422431 (Cal. App. Oct. 24, 2003) (unpublished).

767 *See* Yniguez v. Arizonans for Official Language, 69 F.3d 920 (9th Cir. 1995) (declaring law unconstitutional), *vacated and remanded*, 520 U.S. 43 (1997), *on remand*, 118 F.3d 667 (9th Cir. 1997) (remanding to district court with instructions to dismiss case on procedural grounds); *In re* Initiative Petition No. 366, 46 P.3d 123 (Okla. 2002) (English-only provisions on ballot initiative would infringe on state constitutional rights to freedom of speech and right to petition government for redress of grievances).

state are unlikely to have any substantive impact on consumer protections.[768]

5.2.2 Plain English Contract Language

The landmark case of *Commonwealth v. Monumental Properties, Inc.* holds that the use of residential lease forms with "archaic and technical language beyond the easy comprehension of the consumer of average intelligence" may state a UDAP cause of action.[769] In addition, a number of states have enacted plain language laws[770] that apply broadly to many types of transactions.[771] Other states have plain language requirements included in lists of enumerated UDAP violations, rent-to-own (RTO) statutes, insurance codes, consumer credit statutes, and hearing aid sale provisions.[772]

These statutes typically require that contracts be written in a clear and coherent manner using words with common and everyday meanings, and appropriately divided and captioned by its various sections. Some statutes also require type of a readable size and ink that contrasts with the paper.[773]

Some statutes specify the consumer can recover actual damages or small statutory damages (e.g., $50 in an individual action and $10,000 in a class) for violations,[774] but some statutes specifically state that a violation does not make the contract void or provide a defense for a breach of contract action. Certain statutes also limit enforcement to a state agency or provide no explicit remedy. Minnesota's plain language statute allows a seller, creditor or lessor to submit proposed contracts to the attorney general for review to determine whether the contract complies with the plain language requirements.[775] Plain language determinations by the attorney general are not appealable.[776]

---

768 See Steven W. Bender, Consumer Protection for Latinos: Overcoming Language Fraud and English-Only in the Marketplace, 45 Am. U.L. Rev. 1027, 1049, n.124 (1996).

769 459 Pa. 450, 329 A.2d 812 (1974). *See also* Kan. Stat. Ann. § 50-627(b)(1); Oldendorf v. Gen. Motors Corp., 322 Ill. App. 3d 825, 751 N.E.2d 214, 256 Ill. Dec. 161 (2001) (deliberate obfuscation of warranty's coverage through use of vague, misleading, and contradictory language may be UDAP violation). *But see* Gonsalves v. First Ins. Co., 55 Haw. 155, 516 P.2d 720 (1975); Commonwealth v. Monumental Properties, Inc., 26 Pa. Commw. Ct. 399, 365 A.2d 442 (1976).

770 Conn. Gen. Stat. §§ 42-151 to -158 (consumer loans or credit, purchase or lease of consumer goods up to $25,000, residential leases); Haw. Rev. Stat. §§ 487A-1 to -4 (consumer loans or credit, purchase or lease of consumer goods up to $25,000, residential leases); Me. Rev. Stat. Ann. tit. 10, §§ 1121 to 1126 (consumer loans and leases up to $100,000); Minn. Stat. §§ 325G.29 to .37 (consumer sales, leases, loans, credit, residential leases, up to $50,000 but not purchases of realty); Mont. Code Ann. §§ 30-14-1101 to -1113 (consumer sales, leases, loans, under $50,000, but not insurance, transfers of real estate); N.Y. Gen. Bus. Law § 771 (home improvement contracts); Or. Rev. Stat. §§ 180.540 to .555 (consumer sales, credit, loans, up to $50,000, insurance; real estate specifically included); 73 Pa. Stat. Ann. §§ 2201 to 2212 (consumer sales, credit, loans, up to $50,000, not insurance); W. Va. Code § 46A-6-109 (consumer sales or leases, residential leases).

771 *But see* Schwab v. Sears, Roebuck & Co. (*In re* Dirienzo), 254 B.R. 334 (Bankr. M.D. Pa. 2000) (retailer's captive national bank falls within exemption in Plain Language Law for financial institutions; monthly bill statements are also not covered).

772 *See, e.g.*, Alaska Stat. § 45.50.471(b)(13) (consumer installment sales); Ark. Stat. Ann. § 4-88-107(a)(8) (UDAP); Cal. Civ. Code § 1793.1 (express warranties); Colo. Rev. Stat. § 6-1-105(1)(m) (UDAP); Conn. Gen. Stat. §§ 38a-295 to -300 (insurance policies); Conn. Gen. Stat. § 42-241 (rent-to-own); Del. Code Ann. tit. 6, § 2732 (consumer contracts); D.C. Code Ann. § 28-3904(r)(5) (UDAP); Fla. Stat. ch. 627.4145 (insurance policies); Fla. Stat. Ann. § 636.016 (prepaid limited health centers); Ga. Code Ann. § 33-3-25 (insurance policies); Haw. Rev. Stat. §§ 431:10-104 to -108 (insurance policies); 815 Ill. Comp. Stat. 655/2 (rent-to-own); Ind. Code § 27-1-26-3 (insurance policies); Ind. Code Ann. § 24-4.5-6-111(3)(e) (consumer credit code); Ind. Code Ann. § 24-7-3-4 (RTO); Iowa Code Ann. § 537.5108(4)(e) (factor listed for consideration in regard to unconscionability in actions by state administrator/consumer credit code); Iowa Code Ann. § 537-3606(1) (RTO); Kan. Stat. Ann. § 16a-6-111(3)(e) (factor listed for consideration in regard to unconscionability in actions by state administrator/consumer credit code); Kan. Stat. Ann. § 50-627(b)(1) (RTO); Ky. Rev. Stat. Ann. § 367.978(3), (6) (RTO); Mass. Gen. Laws ch. 175, § 2B (insurance policies); Mich. Comp. Laws § 500.2236(3) (insurance); Mich. Comp. Laws § 445.903(1)(x) (UDAP); Minn. Stat. § 153A.19 (hearing aids); Minn. Stat. § 72C.01-.13 (insurance policies); Miss. Code Ann. § 83-65-111 (motor vehicle service); Mo. Ann. Stat. § 346.020 (hearing aids); Mont. Code Ann. §§ 33-15-321 to -329 (insurance policies); Neb. Rev. Stat. § 69-2105(3), (6) (RTO); Nev. Rev. Stat. Ann. §§ 687B.122 to .128 (insurance policies); N.J. Rev. Stat. §§ 56:12-1 to -13; N.M. Stat. Ann. §§ 59A-19-1 to 59A-19-7 (insurance policies); N.Y. Gen. Obl. Law § 5-702 (consumer sales, lease, loan or credit, and residential leases); N.C. Gen. Stat. §§ 58-38-1 to -40 (insurance policies); N.D. Cent. Code §§ 26.1-36-13 to -16, 26.1-37-09 to -12 (insurance); Ohio Rev. Code Ann. §§ 3902.01 to .08 (insurance); Ohio Rev. Code Ann. § 1345.03 (UDAP); Okla. Stat. tit. 14A, § 6-111(3)(e) (factor listed for consideration in regard to unconscionability in actions by state administrator/consumer credit code); Okla. Stat. tit. 36, §§ 3641–49 (insurance policies); Or. Rev. Stat. §§ 743.100 to .109 (insurance policies); S.C. Code Ann. §§ 38-61-20 to -50 (insurance); S.C. Code Ann. § 37-5-108(4)(a) (inability to understand language of agreement is factor in determining if creditor remedy is unconscionable); S.D. Codified Laws Ann. §§ 58-11A-1 to 58-11A-9 (insurance policies); Tenn. Code Ann. §§ 56-7-1601 to -1609 (insurance policies); Tex. Bus. & Com. Code Ann. § 35.72 (rent-to-own); Tex. Ins. Code Ann. § 5.06 (automobile insurance policies); Tex. Ins. Code Ann. § 5.35 (fire and homeowners insurance policies); Tex. Ins. Code Ann. § 9.07A (homeowners title insurance policies); Tex. Ins. Code Ann. § 26.43 (health insurance policies); Va. Code Ann. § 38.2-3735 (credit insurance policies); W. Va. Code §§ 33-29-1 to -9 (life, accident and health insurance); Wis. Stat. Ann. § 426.108 (UDAP).

773 *See* Conn. Gen. Stat. § 42-152(b); Mont. Code. § 30-14-1103; 73 Pa. Stat. Ann. § 2205; W. Va. Code § 46A-6-109.

774 Haw. Rev. Stat. § 47A-1(b).

775 Minn. Stat. § 325G.35, subdiv. 1.

776 Minn. Stat. § 325G.35, subdiv. 2.

A violation of a plain language statute may be a *per se* UDAP violation.[777] UCC unconscionability concepts may also be helpful here.[778] Consumers and certainly a state attorney general office should be in a position to obtain an injunction against continued use of contracts violating a plain language statute.

5.2.3 Unfair and Unenforceable Adhesion Contract Terms

5.2.3.1 FTC Credit Practices Rule Sets Out Theory for Unfair Standard Form Contract Terms

A developed body of UDAP precedent finds certain adhesion contract provisions to be unfair or unconscionable. The best statement of when an adhesive contract term is unfair is found in the Statement of Basis and Purpose of the FTC's Credit Practices Rule.[779] The FTC defines an unfair practice as one that (1) causes substantial injury; (2) is not outweighed by any countervailing benefits to consumers or competition; and (3) that consumers themselves could not reasonably have avoided.[780] The Statement of Basis and Purpose then details how this three-part test applies to adhesion consumer credit contracts.

Taking the third element first, the FTC concludes that consumers can not reasonably avoid creditor remedies found in standard form credit agreements:

> The economic exigencies of extending credit to large numbers of consumers each day make standardization a necessity. . . .
>
> Consumers have limited incentives to search out better remedial provisions in credit contracts. The substantive similarities of contracts from different creditors mean that a search is less likely to reveal a different alternative. Because remedies are relevant only in the event of default, and default is relatively infrequent, consumers reasonably concentrate their search on such factors as interest rates and payment terms. Searching for credit contracts is also difficult, because contracts are written in obscure technical language, do not use standardized terminology, and may not be provided before the transaction is consummated. Individual creditors have little incentive to provide better terms and explain their benefits to consumers, because a costly education effort would be required with all creditors sharing the benefits. Moreover, such a campaign might differentially attract relatively high risk borrowers.
>
> For these reasons, the Commission concludes that consumers can not reasonably avoid the remedial provisions themselves. Nor can consumers, having signed a contract, avoid the harsh consequences of remedies by avoiding default. When default occurs, it is most often a response to events such as unemployment or illness that are not within the borrower's control. Thus consumers can not reasonably avoid the substantial injury these creditor remedies may inflict.[781]

Having thus concluded that consumers can not avoid collateral terms in standard form contracts, the FTC's three-part unfairness test is met if the adhesive credit contract provision causes substantial injury not outweighed by countervailing benefits.

The Statement of Basis and Purpose gives useful examples of how certain contract provisions cause substantial injury, both economic and emotional. The Statement also notes that all debtors, and not just defaulting consumers, suffer harm for harsh creditor remedies because even non-defaulting debtors live under the threat of the severe remedies. The ban on a creditor remedy protects these consumers in the same way as an insurance policy.[782]

In considering the countervailing benefits of these contract provisions, the Statement points out that one must consider the marginal benefit of a particular provision to the creditor. What is the extra benefit to consumers and competition of a particular provision assuming the creditor still has a varied arsenal of other remedies to choose from? For example, what is the marginal benefit of *cognovit* judgments where creditors can still utilize repossession, suit, garnishment, acceleration, and direct collection contacts.[783]

This analysis is further bolstered by the D.C. Circuit opinion upholding the rule.[784] The D.C. Circuit specifically approved of the FTC's three-part unfairness test, describing this standard as "the most precise definition of unfairness articulated by either the Commission or Congress," and finding that the FTC had properly applied this standard in its Credit Practices Rule.

The D.C. Circuit rejected creditor arguments that "unfairness" is limited to situations of seller misconduct or overreaching, such as practices involving seller deception, coercion, or withholding of material information. The court pointed to the FTC's Holder Rule[785] as precedent for the FTC's authority to correct allocations of post-purchase remedies. Even where the seller does nothing wrong, a practice can be unfair "where the seller takes advantage of an existing obstacle which prevents free consumer choice from

777 *See* § 3.2.7, *supra*. *See also* 73 Pa. Stat. Ann. § 2207(b).

778 *See* § 4.4, *supra*.

779 49 Fed. Reg. 7740 (Mar. 1, 1984).

780 *See* § 4.3.2, *supra*.

781 Statement of Basis and Purpose, 49 Fed. Reg. 7740 (Mar. 1, 1984) (footnotes omitted).

782 *Id.*

783 *Id.*

784 American Financial Services Ass'n v. FTC, 767 F.2d 957 (D.C. Cir. 1985), *cert. denied*, 475 U.S. 1011 (1986).

785 16 C.F.R. § 433 [*reprinted at* Appx. B.1, *infra*].

effectuating a self-correcting market."

The D.C. Circuit found such an imperfect market in the extension of consumer credit because consumers can not bargain over the contractors' creditor remedies and because creditors have no incentive to compete on the basis of the creditor remedies offered. A creditor remedy can thus be unfair even if it does not result from the creditor's deception, coercion, or non-disclosure, as long as it causes substantial consumer injury, not outweighed by countervailing benefits to competition.

Consider a specific example of how powerful this FTC analysis can be in challenging adhesion contract terms. Consumer credit contracts typically waive the debtor's right to notice that the note has been accelerated. The FTC has ruled that debtors can not avoid this or other adhesive contract terms. Consequently, the sole issue before the court in determining this practice's unfairness under a state UDAP statute is whether the resulting economic and emotional consequences of unexpected (and sometimes mistaken) acceleration and repossession are outweighed by the benefits of not having to notify the debtor of the acceleration.

5.2.3.2 Other FTC Precedent

Another important source of precedent as to when standard form contract provisions are UDAP violations is the Statement of Basis and Purpose of the FTC Trade Regulation Rule Concerning the Preservation of Consumer's Claims and Defenses (FTC Holder Rule):[786] "Where one party to a transaction enjoys a substantial advantage with respect to the consumers with whom he deals, it is appropriate for the Commission to determine whether the dominant party is using an overabundance of market power or commercial advantage in an inequitable manner."[787] Having concluded that this was the case where assignees and creditors insulate themselves from the consumer's claims and defenses against the seller, the FTC adopted the FTC Holder Rule.

Two FTC land sale cases are also important precedents for finding adhesion contract provisions to be unfair.[788] The Commission defined an adhesion contract as one that is preprinted, with standard boilerplate language, and presented with no bargaining, and where the two parties have unequal bargaining positions. An adhesion contract need not pertain to the necessities of life or involve a product unobtainable elsewhere. Once the FTC decides a contract is adhesive (thus preventing consumers from avoiding the injurious terms), the FTC will give careful scrutiny to the contract to determine if any terms are unfair, that is whether they cause substantial consumer injury without sufficient countervailing benefits.

In these two cases, the Commission found not only the enforcement but also the inclusion of a clause whereby the consumer forfeited all payments upon cancellation to be unfair. Also unfair was a provision requiring payment of interest on the purchase price, even though the consumer does not receive possession of the land until the last payment is made. There was insufficient evidence, however, to find substantial consumer injury in an integration clause that excluded oral representations from a written contract.

The FTC staff has also stated that it is unfair and deceptive to try to avoid the FTC Credit Practices Rule (which prohibits non-purchase money security interests in household goods) by taking a prohibited security interest in household goods and then later disclaiming that interest in the contract. The creditor listed as security various non-purchase money interests in household goods. Elsewhere, the contract stated that the contract did not take a security interest in any non-purchase money security interests in household goods if the loan was for personal, family or household purposes. The FTC staff said this should be regarded as an attempt to evade the rule and, as such, is unfair and deceptive.[789] An FTC consent agreement has also prohibited certain disclaimers of implied warranties that are unenforceable under state law.[790]

5.2.3.3 State Precedent Concerning Unenforceable Contract Terms

The California and Massachusetts Supreme Courts have ruled that a landlord commits an unfair and deceptive practice by including illegal and unenforceable terms in a lease agreement even if the terms are not enforced.[791] Tenants are likely to believe the lessor has authority to enforce the contract, so it deceives the tenants. A clause stating the creditor has the right to accelerate a note upon default is deceptive where state law limits the right to accelerate.[792]

The West Virginia Supreme Court has ruled that it is deceptive to include an unenforceable provision in a credit contract. The case had an added wrinkle that the unenforce-

786 The rule, but not the Statement of Basis and Purpose, is found at 16 C.F.R. § 433 [*reprinted at* Appx. B.1, *infra*].

787 40 Fed. Reg. 55,524 (Nov. 18, 1975).

788 AMREP Corp., 102 F.T.C. 1362 (1983), *aff'd*, 768 F.2d 1171 (10th Cir. 1985); Horizon Corp., 97 F.T.C. 464 (1981).

789 FTC Informal Staff Letter of Sandra Wilmore to the Legal Aid Society of Northwest North Carolina (Sept. 27, 1988).

790 Lindal Cedar Homes Inc., 87 F.T.C. 8 (1976). *See also* Baierl v. McTaggart, 245 Wis. 2d 632, 629 N.W.2d 277 (2001) (discussed in § 5.2.3.3, *infra*). *But see* Commonwealth v. Monumental Properties, Inc., 459 Pa. 450, 329 A.2d 812 (1974) (unenforceable provisions not *per se* unfair where provisions were enforceable in certain circumstances).

791 People v. McKale, 25 Cal. 3d 626, 602 P.2d 731, 159 Cal. Rptr. 811 (1980); Leardi v. Brown, 394 Mass. 151, 474 N.E.2d 1094 (1985). *But see* Perry v. Island Sav. & Loan Ass'n, 101 Wash. 2d 795, 684 P.2d 1281 (1984) (good faith enforcement of arguably valid due-on-sale clause not unfair).

792 Levine v. Baldwin, 23 Ohio Op. 3d 436 (C.P. Hamilton Cty. 1981).

able provision waived the consumer's exemption rights "to the extent permitted by law," and a statute made waivers of exemptions unenforceable. The waiver was thus not "permitted by law," so was a nullity. Nonetheless, the court found the provision misleading and confusing and thus a UDAP violation.[793]

The Wisconsin Supreme Court reached the same conclusion in ruling that inclusion of a prohibited clause in a residential lease renders the entire lease unenforceable.[794] The court noted that severing the illegal clause and allowing the remainder of the lease to be enforced would mean that landlords would suffer no consequences for including an illegal clause, and they would reap the benefits of the clause's *in terroram* effect on tenants.

Where a contract is unenforceable under state law or against public policy, the contract is also an unfair practice.[795] Thus, where a promise to pay to forestall criminal prosecution is found unenforceable under state law, the very agreement is an unfair trade practice.[796]

5.2.3.4 Other State Precedent on Adhesion Contracts

A state court in a UDAP case found an adhesion contract to be unfair where a condition to admittance to a hospital was an agreement that the consumer would pay all collection costs.[797] Massachusetts UDAP regulations prohibit, for home improvement or door-to-door sale contracts, confession of judgment clauses or other waivers of statutory or regulatory rights.[798] It is unfair for a landlord to insist that tenants sign a lease waiving their rights under the state's lead paint removal law.[799] A contract is deceptive if it promises performance in one clause but then adds another clause that makes the promise illusory.[800]

However, a New Jersey court held that a manufacturer's policy not to replace a product unless it was more than seventy percent defective was not unfair or unconscionable.[801] Similarly, courts are less likely to find contract provisions unfair where the contract relates to a commercial, not a consumer, transaction.[802] Finally, UCC unconscionability concepts are important sources for any argument that adhesion contracts violate UDAP statutes. These are summarized in § 4.4, *supra*.

5.2.3.5 Arbitration Clauses as Unfair or Unconscionable

A common standard form contract provision is a requirement that consumers submit their disputes to binding arbitration. Another NCLC manual, *Consumer Arbitration Agreements* (4th ed. 2004) examines whether these clauses are enforceable. The most common procedural context in which to examine the enforceability of an arbitration clause occurs where a consumer brings an action in court, and the court decides whether the action must be dismissed or stayed pending arbitration of the dispute. The court may find the arbitration clause unenforceable for any number of reasons, including that it is unconscionable.

Another approach is to bring an affirmative UDAP claim against the merchant for including an unfair, deceptive or unconscionable clause in its standard form contracts. An excellent example of this approach is *Ting v. AT&T*,[803] in which a federal magistrate approved a request for injunctive and declaratory relief under California's UDAP statute, stopping AT&T from utilizing its standard form arbitration clause. Procedural unconscionability was found in the use of a standard form contract designed so that most of AT&T customers would not read the arbitration clause. Substantive unconscionability was found in the fact that the clause limited the right to punitive damages and class actions, limited consumers' right to publicize the findings of the arbitration, shortened the limitations period, and created high fees and costs for consumers.

The Ninth Circuit upheld the trial court decision in most, but not all respects.[804] It upheld the ruling that many aspects of the arbitration clause were unconscionable and could be enjoined. But it rejected claims that the arbitration clause violated an anti-waiver provision of a California UDAP statute, finding that California provision preempted by the Federal Arbitration Act.

Even if the arbitration clause is found unenforceable on grounds other than unconscionability, the use of the clause may still be a UDAP violation. It is certainly unfair and deceptive to include in a standard form contract an unenforceable provision.[805]

793 Orlando v. Finance One, 369 S.E.2d 882 (W. Va. 1988). *But see* Sanghavi v. Paul Revere Life Ins. Co., 214 Conn. 303, 572 A.2d 307 (1990) (inclusion of invalid, unenforceable limit on benefit increase in insurance contract not a UDAP violation).

794 Baierl v. McTaggart, 245 Wis. 2d 632, 629 N.W.2d 277 (2001).

795 Adams v. Jones, 114 N.C. App. 256, 441 S.E.2d 699 (1994).

796 *Id.*

797 Bondanza v. Peninsula Hosp. & Medical Center, 23 Cal. 3d 260, 590 P.2d 22, 152 Cal. Rptr. 446 (1979).

798 Massachusetts Consumer Protection Regulations, Mass. Regs. Code tit. 940, § 3.09(9), Door-to-Door Sales and Home Improvement Transactions.

799 Manzaro v. McCann, 401 Mass. 880, 519 N.E.2d 1337 (1988).

800 Fendrich v. RBF, L.L.C., 842 So. 2d 1076 (Fla. Dist. Ct. App. 2003).

801 Palmucci v. Brunswick Corp., 311 N.J. Super. 607, 710 A.2d 1045 (App. Div. 1998).

802 *Cf.* Edart Truck Rental v. B. Swirsky & Co., 23 Conn. App. 137, 579 A.2d 133 (1990) (fine print clause in commercial lease not a UDAP violation where lessee had opportunity to but failed to read it); Seattle-First Nat'l Bank v. West Coast Rubber, Inc., 41 Wash. App. 604, 705 P.2d 800 (1985) (waiver of surety defenses in commercial transaction not unfair).

803 182 F. Supp. 2d 902 (N.D. Cal. 2002).

804 Ting v. AT&T, 319 F.3d 1126 (9th Cir. 2003).

805 *See* § 5.2.8, *infra*.

5.2.4 Contractual Misrepresentations

5.2.4.1 Deception Concerning the Nature of the Document Being Signed

It is deceptive to misrepresent the nature of documents the buyer is requested to sign or to conceal contract provisions from the consumer,[806] to misrepresent that contracts are not binding until some future event occurs,[807] to misrepresent that contracts are sold subject to cancellation,[808] or to procure consumers' signatures on blank or partially blank contracts.[809] It is deceptive for a sales representative to falsely claim he has authority to bind a contract and to claim that the contract is binding on the seller when it is not.[810]

The following have also been found to be UDAP violations: back dating a contract,[811] concealing a document among other forms to be signed, falsely notarizing a document,[812] or forging a consumer's signature on a contract or otherwise fabricating a contract.[813] It is also unfair for a merchant to remove an essential term from a contract or change other aspects of a contract without the consumer's consent.[814] It is deceptive to induce a consumer's spouse to sign a new contract less advantageous to the consumer by telling the spouse that an error had been made and the change was a mere formality.[815] For example, in one case a car dealer substituted a credit agreement with a new agreement raising the interest rate and deleting credit insurance. The debtor was out of town and the dealer asked the wife to sign the new agreement because it was a "mere formality."[816]

Some UDAP statutes and regulations affirmatively require that a written contract be prepared for some types of transactions.[817] Where the consumer's almost immediate cancellation of the deal is the reason no contract was prepared, however, there may not be a UDAP violation.[818] Idaho's UDAP statute prohibits obtaining a buyer's signature on a contract that contains blank spaces to be filled in after it is signed.[819]

806 Lifetime Inc., 59 F.T.C. 1231 (1961); H.L. Robinson Co., 38 F.T.C. 422 (1943); Idaho Admin. Code 04.02.01.032 (Contradictory Representations); Brooks v. Creech, 2003 WL 174805 (Tenn. Ct. App. Jan. 28, 2003) (misrepresentation that quitclaim deed was deed of trust); Baggett v. Crown Automotive Group, Inc., Clearinghouse No. 49,159 (Tenn. Ct. App. 1992); Coronado Products, Inc. v. Stewart, 1988 Tenn. LEXIS 672 (Tenn. Ct. App. Nov. 2, 1988) (misrepresenting binding contract as estimate and authorization for credit check); Sign-O-Life Signs, Inc. v. Delauventi Florists, Inc., 825 P.2d 714 (Wash. Ct. App. 1992); Wisconsin Dep't of Agriculture, Trade and Consumer Protection Rules Wis. Admin. Code R. ATCP 127.4, 127.44, 127.72, Direct Marketing. *See also* Rood v. Midwest Matrix Mart, 87 N.W.2d 186 (Mich. 1957) (misrepresentation of content and meaning of document states claim for fraud).

807 Pulphus v. Sullivan, 2003 WL 1964333, *18 (N.D. Ill. Apr. 28, 2003) (misrepresentation by mortgage broker that plaintiff was singing a loan application when in fact she was executing a mortgage stated claim for common law fraud); Eastern Detective Academy, Inc., 78 F.T.C. 1428 (1971) (detective school ordered to cease falsely representing that installment contracts are non-binding enrollment agreements, or that contracts are cancelable at the discretion of the customers, or otherwise misrepresenting the true nature and effect of the contract); Ezell, 76 F.T.C. 464 (1969) (consent order) (obtaining potential students' signatures on installment payment contracts by falsely representing that the contracts were non-binding enrollment applications or that students could cancel their enrollment at any time was unfair and deceptive; when prospective students failed to attend the course and make payments under the contract, school systematically filed collection actions and obtained judgments against students or assigned the contracts to collection agency); Key Learning Sys., Inc., 81 F.T.C. 296 (1972) (consent order) (franchisor of home instruction courses ordered to cease representing that contracts executed by purchasers will not be effective, binding or accepted by them until down payment received in full, or misrepresenting the nature and legal characteristics of any enrollment contract); Bates v. William Chevrolet/Geo, Inc., 785 N.E.2d 53, 60, 337 Ill. App. 3d 151, 159 (2003) (common law fraud and violation of Illinois Consumer Fraud Act established where defendant falsely represented to purchaser of automobile that retail installment contract was not binding without specification of the financing company and that the signing of the contract was a formality to get the car off the lot and satisfy a police officer in the event of a stop).

808 Kugler v. Romain, 58 N.J. 522, 279 A.2d 640 (1971); Mapp v. Toyota World, Inc., 344 S.E.2d 297 (N.C. Ct. App. 1986); Our Fair Lady Health Resort v. Miller, 564 S.W.2d 410 (Tex. Civ. App. 1978).

809 *In re* Wiggins, 273 B.R. 839, 858 (Bankr. D. Idaho 2001) (obtaining signature on notarized documents that contained blank spaces is UDAP violation); Empeco Corp., 71 F.T.C. 158 (1967); Fred Astaire Dance Studios, 63 F.T.C. 2210 (1963).

810 George Pharis Chevrolet v. Polk, 661 S.W.2d 314 (Tex. App. 1983); *see also* Wilder v. Squires, 315 S.E.2d 63 (N.C. Ct. App. 1984).

811 Bramley's Water Conditioning v. Hagen, 27 Ohio App. 3d 300, 501 N.E.2d 39 (1985).

812 Northwestern Bank v. Roseman, 344 S.E.2d 120 (N.C. Ct. App. 1986); *see also In re* Wiggins, 273 B.R. 839, 858 (Bankr. D. Idaho 2001) (obtaining signature on notarized documents that contained blank spaces is UDAP violation).

813 Page & Wirtz Constr. Co. v. Solomon, 110 N.M. 206, 794 P.2d 349 (1990).

814 Baggett v. Crown Automotive Group, Inc., 1992 WL 108710 (Tenn. Ct. App. May 22, 1992).

815 *Id.*

816 *Id.*

817 *See* D.C. Code § 28-3904(q); 37 Pa. Code § 301.4(a)(1) (written contract required in motor vehicle sales).

818 Banks v. Department of Consumer & Regulatory Affairs, 634 A.2d 433 (D.C. 1993).

819 Idaho Code § 48-603(12). *See In re* Wiggins, 273 B.R. 839, 858 (Bankr. D. Idaho 2001).

5.2.4.2 Oral Representations Inconsistent with the Contract

Oral representations inconsistent with written representations or contract provisions are deceptive.[820] A UDAP claim need not be based on breach of contract, but can rest solely on oral representations contrary to the seller performance. Ohio courts hold that it is a UDAP violation to fail to include oral representations in the written contract.[821]

Oral representations inconsistent with contract provisions are actionable even if the contract states that inconsistent oral statements are not part of the contract, or that agreements between a salesman and the consumer are not binding on the company.[822] Contractual waivers of the consumer's remedies are similarly ineffective.[823] The parol evidence rule does not prevent evidence of oral misrepresentations from being introduced at a UDAP trial.[824]

5.2.5 Breaches of Contract

5.2.5.1 Mere Breach of Contract May Not Be UDAP Violation

A mere breach of contract without anything else unfair or deceptive does not necessarily lead to a UDAP violation.[825] Courts generally require a pattern, deception, or some other

820 Idaho Admin. Code 04.02.01.032 (Contradictory Representations); McEvoy Travel Bureau, Inc. v. Norton Co., 408 Mass. 704, 563 N.E.2d 188 (1990) (seller's representation that contract clause was meaningless and that it did not intend to enforce it violated UDAP statute); Smalley v. Spitzer Ford, Inc., 1986 WL 14944 (Ohio Ct. App. Dec. 31, 1986) (failure to integrate all material statements and promises into written sales contract violated UDAP regulation, but judgment for consumer remanded for new trial on other grounds); Automobile Trader v. Simmons, 22 Ohio Op. 3d 149 (Ct. App. 1981) (statements at variance with contract's "as is" clause are UDAP violations); Tri-West Constr. v. Hernandez, 43 Or. App. 961, 607 P.2d 1375 (1979); Myers v. Ginsburg, 735 S.W.2d 600 (Tex. App. 1987); Wagner v. Morris, 658 S.W.2d 230 (Tex. App. 1983); Wisconsin Dep't of Agriculture, Trade and Consumer Protection Rules Wis. Admin. Code R. ATCP 127.14, 127.44, 172.72, Direct Marketing. *See also* Glazewski v. Allstate Ins. Co., 108 Ill. 2d 243, 483 N.E.2d 1263 (1985) (plaintiffs stated fraud claim where insurance policy was at variance with oral representations, but UDTPA claim could not be maintained since plaintiffs did not have grounds for injunctive relief). *But see* a line of Georgia cases to the contrary, discussed in § 4.2.17.3, *supra*. *But cf.* St. Paul Oil & Gas Corp. v. Trijon Exploration, Inc., 872 S.W.2d 27 (Tex. App. 1994) (where there is no contract, but only an invitation to bid, there can be no violation of UDAP statute's prohibition against misrepresenting contractual rights).

821 Lump v. Best Door & Window, Inc., 2002 Ohio App. LEXIS 1381 (Mar. 27, 2002).

822 *See* § 4.2.15, *supra*.

823 *Id.*

824 *Id.*

825 Randazzo v. Harris Bank Palatine, 262 F.3d 663 (7th Cir. 2001) (banker's demand for additional collateral not required by contract was simple breach of contract, not a UDAP violation); Commercial Union Ins. Co. v. Seven Provinces Ins. Co., 217 F.3d 33 (1st Cir. 2000) (not UDAP violation unless breach amounts to commercial extortion or involves similarly culpable conduct), *cert. denied*, 148 L. Ed. 2d 959 (2001); Bay Colony, Ltd. v. Trendmaker, Inc., 121 F.3d 998 (5th Cir. 1997) (no UDAP claim for a failed promise, unless there was no intent to fulfill promise at time it was made); Boulevard Assocs. v. Sovereign Hotels, Inc., 72 F.3d 1029 (2d Cir. 1995); Duro-Wood Treating Co. v. Century Forest Indus., 675 F.2d 745 (5th Cir. 1982) (Texas law) (simple breach of contract without anything else unfair is not UDAP violation); United Roasters Inc. v. Colgate Palmolive Co., 649 F.2d 985 (4th Cir. 1981) (North Carolina law) (intentional breach of contract between two businesses not necessarily unfair); Bruce v. Home Depot, USA, Inc., 308 F. Supp. 2d 72 (D. Conn. 2004); Texas Taco Cabana, L.P. v. Taco Cabana of New Mexico, Inc., 304 F. Supp. 2d 903 (W.D. Tex. 2003); Chicago Messenger Serv., Inc. v. Nextel Communications, Inc., 2003 WL 22225619 (N.D. Ill. Sept. 24, 2003); Ashlar Financial Services Corp. v. Sterling Fin. Co., 2002 WL 206439 (N.D. Tex. Feb. 8, 2002); Landreneau v. Fleet Fin. Group, 197 F. Supp. 2d 551 (M.D. La. 2002); Boston Pilots v. M/V Midnight Gambler, 2002 U.S. Dist. LEXIS 1290 (D. Mass. Jan. 17, 2002) (nonpayment of a bill, without more, is not a UDAP violation); Luckett v. Alpha Constr. & Development, Inc., 2001 U.S. Dist. LEXIS 17623 (N.D. Ill. Oct. 22, 2001) (promising to do something in the future and then failing to do it is not a UDAP violation); Callahan v. Harvest Bd. Int'l, Inc., 138 F. Supp. 2d 147 (D. Mass. 2001) (contract breach must involve wrongful purpose or have extortionate quality to be UDAP violation); Seacoast Mental Health Ctr. v. Sheakley Pension Admin., 2001 U.S. Dist. LEXIS 1026 (D.N.H. Jan. 5, 2001) (ordinary breach of contract not UDAP violation but may be if there is fiduciary duty); Norman v. Loomis Fargo & Co., 123 F. Supp. 2d 985 (W.D.N.C. 2000) (breach of unilateral contract that promised reward was not UDAP violation); Stern v. Great Western Bank, 959 F. Supp. 478 (N.D. Ill. 1997); Central Diversey M.R.I. v. Medical Mgmt., 952 F. Supp. 575 (N.D. Ill. 1996) (UDAP claim for breach of contract needs a consumer nexus); Canal Electric Co. v. Westinghouse Electric Corp., 756 F. Supp. 620 (D. Mass. 1990); Rhino Linings USA, Inc. v. Rocky Mountain Rhino Lining, Inc., 62 P.3d 142 (Colo. 2003); Hudson United Bank v. Cinnamon Ridge Corp., 81 Conn. App. 557, 845 A.2d 417 (Conn. App. Ct. 2004) (jury could reasonably conclude that breach of handwritten agreement and implied covenant of good faith and fair dealing did not rise to level of UDAP violation); PNR, Inc. v. Beacon Property Mgmt., Inc., 842 So. 2d 773, 777 n.2 (Fla. 2003); Gross v. Ideal Pool Corp., 181 Ga. App. 483, 352 S.E.2d 806 (1987); Bankier v. First Federal Savings & Loan Ass'n, 588 N.E.2d 391 (Ill. App. Ct. 1992); IK Corp. v. One Financial Place P'ship, 200 Ill. App. 3d 802, 558 N.E.2d 161 (1990) (commercial case); Exchange Nat'l Bank v. Farm Bureau Life Ins. Co., 108 Ill. App. 3d 212, 438 N.E.2d 1247 (1982) (not every breach of contract is a UDAP violation); Capitol Cadillac Olds, Inc. v. Roberts, 813 S.W.2d 287, 291 (Ky. 1991); Miles v. Shauntee, 664 S.W.2d 512 (Ky. 1984); Sparks v. Re/Max Allstar Realty, Inc., 55 S.W.3d 343 (Ky. App. 2000) (breach must be intentional or grossly negligent); Atkinson v. Rosenthal, 33 Mass. App. Ct. 219, 598 N.E.2d 666 (1992) (breach of contract must be a pattern to constitute a UDAP violation); Madan v. Royal Indemnity Co., 26 Mass. App. Ct. 756, 532 N.E.2d 1214 (1989) (mere breach of contract, without more, is not a UDAP violation, especially where the contract is oral and for the sale of

aggravating circumstances to make a breach of contract a UDAP violation.[826]

land); Sather v. State Farm Fire & Cas. Ins. Co., 2002 Minn. App. LEXIS 277 (Mar. 12, 2002) (unpublished, citation limited); Barry v. N.J. State Highway Authority, 245 N.J. Super. 302, 585 A.2d 420 (1990); Mitchell v. Linville, 557 S.E.2d 620 (N.C. App. 2001); Sessler v. Marsh, 551 S.E.2d 160 (N.C. App. 2001) (breach of contract caused by funding delays not UDAP violation); Gray v. North Carolina Ins. Underwriting Ass'n, 510 S.E.2d 396 (N.C. App. 1999), *rev'd on other grounds*, 352 N.C. 61, 529 S.E.2d 676 (2000) (must be substantial aggravating circumstances); Wachovia Bank & Trust v. Carrington Dev. Assocs., 459 S.E.2d 17 (N.C. Ct. App. 1995); Johnson v. North Carolina Dep't of Transp., 107 N.C. App. 63, 418 S.E.2d 700 (1992); Mosley & Mosley Builders v. Landin Ltd., 389 S.E.2d 576 (N.C. Ct. App. 1990); Chatham Racquet Club v. State *ex rel.* Zimmerman, 121 Pa. Commw. 642, 561 A.2d 354 (Pa. Commw. Ct. 1989) (no UDAP violation where defendant's interpretation of its obligations was reasonable); Columbia E. Assoc. v. Bi-Lo, Inc., 386 S.E.2d 259 (S.C. Ct. App. 1989) (intentional breach of contract, but both parties commercial entities); Gathings v. Robertson Brokerage Co., 367 S.E.2d 423 (S.C. Ct. App. 1988); Key Co. v. Fameco Distributors, 357 S.E.2d 476 (S.C. Ct. App. 1987) (contract between two businesses); Hamer v. Harris, 2002 WL 31469213 (Tenn. App. Nov. 6, 2002) (unpublished, citation limited); Crawford v. Ace Sign, Inc., 917 S.W.2d 12 (Tex. 1996) (breach of contract to publish Yellow Pages ad); Ashford Dev., Inc. v. U.S. Life Real Estate Services Corp., 661 S.W.2d 933 (Tex. 1984); Continental Dredging, Inc. v. De-Kaizered, Inc., 120 S.W.3d 380 (Tex. App. Sept. 26, 2003); Labrie v. Kenney, 95 S.W.3d 722 (Tex. App. 2003); Dickey v. Club Corp. of Am., 12 S.W.3d 172 (Tex. App. 2000); Guest v. Cochran, 993 S.W.2d 397 (Tex. App. 1999); Ken Petroleum Corp. v. Questor Drilling Corp., 976 S.W.2d 283 (Tex. App. 1998) (misrepresenting contractual rights is more than breach, especially where no breach of contract claim exists), *rev'd in part on other grounds*, 24 S.W.3d 344 (Tex. 2000); Basse Truck Line, Inc. v. First State Bank, 949 S.W.2d 17 (Tex. App. 1997) (bank's failure to pay check as promised); Bekins Moving & Storage Co. v. Williams, 947 S.W.2d 568 (Tex. App. 1997); Polley v. Odom, 957 S.W.2d 932 (Tex. App. 1997) (differing interpretation of contract is not a UDAP violation), *vacated pursuant to settlement agreement*, 963 S.W.2d 917 (Tex. App. 1998); Humble Nat'l Bank v. DCV, Inc., 933 S.W.2d 224 (Tex. App. 1996) (bank's failure to disburse funds in accordance with customer's instructions); Chilton Ins. Co. v. Pate & Pate Enterprises, Inc., 930 S.W.2d 877 (Tex. App. 1996) (surety's failure to complete public works project after subcontractor's default); Kuehnhoefer v. Welch, 893 S.W.2d 689 (Tex. App. 1995); Enterprise-Laredo v. Hachar's, 839 S.W.2d 822 (Tex. App. 1992); Quitta v. Fossati, 808 S.W.2d 636 (Tex. App. 1991); Heritage Housing Corp. v. Ferguson, 674 S.W.2d 363 (Tex. App. 1984); Keriotis v. Lombardo Rental Trust, 607 S.W.2d 44 (Tex. Civ. 1980) (not necessarily deceptive to breach an unenforceable contract); *see also* Rathgeber v. James Hemenway, Inc., 69 P.3d 710 (Or. 2003) (even if real estate agent made implied representation that he was competent, mere negligence in this particular transaction would not be UDAP violation). *But see* Brace v. Titcomb, 2002 WL 1335871 (Me. Super. May 17, 2002) (home improvement contractor's defective performance and contract breach are UDAP violations); Lump v. Best Door & Window, Inc., 2002 Ohio App. LEXIS 1381 (Mar. 27, 2002) (knowing breach of contract may be UDAP violation); Cardwell v. Tom Harrigan Oldsmobile, Inc., 1984 WL 5351 (Ohio Ct. App. June 27, 1984) (automobile dealer's refusal to abide by sales contract because of arithmetical error held a UDAP violation).

A Texas court viewed the "totality of the circumstances" in deciding whether a practice was more than a mere contract breach and therefore actionable under UDAP. Relevant factors to be considered included:

- Whether the representation was clearly factual, clearly interpretative, or a combination;
- Whether the relevant contractual language was ambiguous;
- Whether the parties were in substantially equal positions of knowledge;
- Whether there was evidence of overreaching;
- Whether there was evidence of unconscionable conduct;
- Whether there was a confidential or fiduciary relationship.[827]

5.2.5.2 Systematic Breach of Many Consumer Contracts as UDAP Violation

The FTC issued an important opinion in *Orkin Exterminating Co.* finding a company's systematic breach of its standard form contracts to be unfair, and the Eleventh Circuit affirmed that decision.[828] Orkin, the largest termite and pest-control company in the world, promised a fixed annual renewal fee in its annual inspection contracts. Nevertheless, Orkin unilaterally decided to raise this fee for approximately 200,000 customers.

Applying the FTC's three-part unfairness standard, the Commission had little difficulty finding Orkin's breach of contract to cause substantial harm, with no countervailing benefits to consumers or competition, and that consumers could not reasonably avoid or mitigate the breach. Consequently, the FTC ruled that, as a matter of law, this breach was an unfair trade practice, even though no deception or bad faith was involved. No evidence of materiality was needed; any breach of a provision in a standard form contract is a material unfair practice. The Eleventh Circuit

826 *See, e.g.*, Tubos de Acero v. Am. Int'l Investment Corp., 292 F.3d 471 (5th Cir. 2002); Sorenson v. H & R Block, Inc., 2002 WL 31194868 (D. Mass. Aug. 27, 2002); Becker v. Graber Builders, Inc., 149 N.C. App. 787, 561 S.E.2d 905 (2002).

827 West Anderson Plaza v. Exxon Mehdi Feyznia, 876 S.W.2d 528 (Tex. App. 1994). *Accord* Adler Paper Stock, Inc. v. Houston Refuse Disposal, Inc., 930 S.W.2d 761 (Tex. App. 1996). *See also* Petri v. Gatlin, 997 F. Supp. 956 (N.D. Ill. 1997); Munawar v. Cadle Co., 2 S.W.3d 12 (Tex. App. 1999) (draws distinction between non-actionable nonperformance and actionable failure to disclose facts).

828 108 F.T.C. 263 (1986), *aff'd*, 849 F.2d 1354 (11th Cir. 1988), *cert. denied*, 484 U.S. 1041 (1989); *see also* State *ex rel.* Guste v. Orkin Exterminating Co., 528 So. 2d 198 (La. Ct. App. 1988); *cf.* Allied Grape Growers v. Bronco Wine Co., 203 Cal. App. 3d 432, 249 Cal. Rptr. 872 (1988) (buyer engaged in unfair practice in refusing to purchase grape harvest as required to by contract).

not only affirmed the decision, but approved the specific unfairness analysis.[829]

Similarly, an assignee consistently enforced a contractual late charge in a manner consistent with industry practice, but at variance with the specific language of the credit agreement. The court found this practice to be a UDAP violation.[830] It has been found to be unfair for a campground to unilaterally change the membership agreements to the members' disadvantage where the major justification for the change was to increase campground profits.[831]

Massachusetts' highest court has ruled that conduct in disregard of known contractual arrangements intended to secure benefits for the breaching party is a UDAP violation.[832] An intermediate Massachusetts appellate court has interpreted this ruling to require, as in *Orkin*, a pattern of breach of contract.[833] Ohio courts hold that a pattern of inefficiency, incompetence, or continual stalling and evasion of legal obligations is a UDAP violation.[834]

5.2.5.3 Entering into Contract with No Intention to Fulfill Obligations

It can be deceptive to enter into an agreement with no intention of complying with the contract[835] or knowing that the contract could not or would not be fulfilled.[836] Sufficient deception may also be found in the defendant's actions in inducing the plaintiff to enter into the contract.[837] Kentucky decisions hold that either intent or gross negligence makes breach of a contract a UDAP violation.[838] A promise that fails is not within the Texas UDAP statute unless there was no intent to comply with that promise at the time it was made.[839]

5.2.5.4 Deception Accompanying the Contract Breach

North Carolina courts find that aggravating circumstances can make a mere breach of contract a UDAP violation. Thus deception accompanying the breach is sufficient to find a violation.[840] New Mexico courts allow UDAP recovery if a breach of contract is accompanied by a knowing misrepresentation.[841] Other courts agree that misrepresentations or omissions are sufficient.[842]

829 Orkin Exterminating Co. v. FTC, 849 F.2d 1354 (11th Cir. 1988), *cert. denied*, 484 U.S. 1041 (1989).

830 Andrews v. Fleet Real Estate Funding Corp., 78 B.R. 78 (Bankr. E.D. Pa. 1987).

831 Lester v. Resort Camplands Int'l Inc., 27 Conn. App. 59, 605 A.2d 550 (1992).

832 Anthony's Pier Four v. HBC Assocs., 411 Mass. 451, 583 N.E.2d 806 (1991). *Accord* Commercial Union Ins. Co. v. Seven Provinces Ins. Co., 217 F.3d 33 (1st Cir. 2000) (company committed UDAP violation by refusing to perform under its contract in order to force other company to compromise a valid claim); Nasco, Inc. v. Public Storage, Inc., 29 F.3d 28 (1st Cir. 1994); Massachusetts Employers Ins. Exchange v. PropacMass, 420 Mass. 39, 648 N.E.2d 435 (1995); Graves v. R.M. Packer Co., 45 Mass. App. Ct. 760, 702 N.E.2d 21 (1997). *See also* Ahern v. Scholz, 85 F.3d 774 (1st Cir. 1996) (discussing test); Community Builders v. Indian Motorcycle Associates, 692 N.E.2d 964 (Mass. App. Ct. 1998) (breach of contract was UDAP violation because of its extortionate quality).

833 Atkinson v. Rosenthal, 33 Mass. App. Ct. 219, 598 N.E.2d 666 (1992). *Accord* Golembiewski v. Hallberg Ins. Agency, Inc., 635 N.E.2d 452 (Ill. App. Ct. 1994) (pattern of breach of contract must be shown); Cetkovic v. Boch, Inc., 2003 WL 139779 (Mass. App. Jan. 13, 2003). *Cf.* Commercial Union Ins. Co. v. Seven Provinces Ins. Co., 9 F. Supp. 2d 49 (D. Mass. 1998) (finding UDAP violation in breach of contract without finding pattern), *aff'd*, 217 F.3d 33 (1st Cir. 2000).

834 Lump v. Best Door & Window, Inc., 2002 Ohio App. LEXIS 1381 (Mar. 27, 2002); Brown v. Lyons, 43 Ohio Misc. 14, 332 N.E.2d 380 (C.P. 1974).

835 *See* Krisa v. Equitable Life Assurance Soc., 113 F. Supp. 2d 694 (M.D. Pa. 2000) (insurance contract); Rhino Linings USA, Inc. v. Rocky Mountain Rhino Lining, Inc., 62 P.3d 142 (Colo. 2003); Morgan Servs., Inc. v. Episcopal Church Home & Affiliates Life Care Community, Inc., 305 A.D.2d 1105, 757 N.Y.S.2d 917 (2003) (reversing dismissal of UDAP claim that seller entered into contracts while knowing it would supply non-conforming goods, and threatened dissatisfied customers with enforcement of liquidated damages clause); Custom Molders, Inc. v. Roper Corp., 101 N.C. App. 606, 401 S.E.2d 96 (1991); Rathgeber v. Hemenway, Inc., 69 P.3d 710, 715 (Or. 2003) (statutory requirement of willfulness would have been met if defendant knew or had reason to know that he would not fulfill promised duties). *But cf.* Luckett v. Alpha Constr. & Development, Inc., 2001 U.S. Dist. LEXIS 17623 (N.D. Ill. Oct. 22, 2001).

836 Barry v. N.J. State Highway Authority, 245 N.J. Super. 302, 585 A.2d 420 (1990); State *ex rel.* Fisher v. Warren Star Theater, 84 Ohio App. 3d 435, 616 N.E.2d 1192 (1992) (sale of tickets for performance that had already been canceled).

837 Bradley v. Dean Witter Realty Inc., 967 F. Supp. 19 (D. Mass. 1997).

838 Sparks v. Re/Max Allstar Realty, 55 S.W.3d 343 (Ky. App. 2000); *see also* Capitol Cadillac Olds v. Roberts, 813 S.W.2d 287 (Ky. 1991) (no UDAP violation unless there is some element of intentional or grossly negligent conduct).

839 Bay Colony, Ltd. v. Trendmaker, Inc., 121 F.3d 998 (5th Cir. 1997); Consortium Information Services, Inc. v. National Information Services, Inc., 2001 U.S. Dist. LEXIS 19390 (N.D. Tex. Nov. 27, 2001).

840 Tubos de Acero v. Am. Int'l Investment Corp., 292 F.3d 471 (5th Cir. 2002); Edmondson v. American Motorcycle Ass'n, 2001 U.S. App. LEXIS 1506 (4th Cir. Feb. 2, 2001) (unpublished, citation limited) (N.C. law); Becker v. Graber Builders, Inc., 149 N.C. App. 787, 561 S.E.2d 905 (2002); Garlock v. Henson, 112 N.C. App. 243, 435 S.E.2d 114 (1993). *See also* Petri v. Gatlin, 997 F. Supp. 956 (N.D. Ill. 1997).

841 Diversey Corp. v. Chem-Source Corp., 965 P.2d 332 (N.M. App. Ct. 1998).

842 Texas Taco Cabana, L.P. v. Taco Cabana of New Mexico, Inc., 304 F. Supp. 2d 903 (W.D. Tex. 2003); National Center for Policy Analysis v. Fiscal Associates, Inc. 2002 WL 433038 (N.D. Tex. Mar. 15, 2002) (misrepresentations occurring after contract formation can be UDAP violations if they cause additional damage, *e.g.*, by inducing buyer to continue contractual relationship and pay for additional services); Naporano Iron &

A dealer's attempts to avoid the consequences of a breach of contract may bring it within the UDAP statute even if the breach, standing alone, would not. For example, in a Louisiana case, a seller delivered a custom-built mobile home that did not conform to the buyers' specifications. The seller's refusal to acknowledge the defects, refusal to refund the buyers' deposit, and delays in offering to correct the defects were UDAP violations.[843] It can be a UDAP violation to conceal a breach of contract.[844]

5.2.5.5 Unequal Relationship of the Parties

Conduct that manifests an inequitable assertion of power or position converts a breach of contract into a UDAP violation.[845] Even without misrepresentation or concealment, a home builder may face UDAP liability for faulty construction of a home, according to an Illinois appellate court.[846] The court cited the magnitude of the buyer's investment, the difficulty of inspecting the home during construction, the disparity of knowledge between the buyer and builder, and the potential for latent defects as factors distinguishing the case from those holding breaches of contract not to be UDAP violations. Courts will apply different standards if a UDAP claim involves a breach of contract dispute between two businesses, however.[847]

5.2.6 *Refunds and Cancellation Rights*

Several state UDAP regulations require that, absent a disclosed alternative policy, purchasers receive full refunds even for nondefective goods returned to a store, except for perishables and certain other enumerated exceptions.[848] It is also deceptive to disclose a "no cash refund" policy that is at variance with a consumer's warranty law rights.[849] For example, if a product is defective, and there is either an express or implied warranty, then the consumer may have the right to revoke acceptance and receive a full cash refund.[850] Statements or signs that there are no cash refunds, without disclosing an exception for defective merchandise, are thus deceptive because they misrepresent the consumer's legal rights.

The same can be said for store refund policies that do not make exceptions where a sale involves misrepresentations about the goods, their performance, or other characteristics. Such misrepresentation is also a basis to seek a full cash refund, and policies that do not explicitly allow for this are deceptive. Special cancellation standards for door-to-door sales, layaway plans, and deposits have been detailed elsewhere.[851]

It is deceptive to misrepresent refund and cancellation policies and rights,[852] and sellers must disclose their cancellation policies.[853] Oral misrepresentations as to cancella-

---

Metal Co. v. American Crane Corp., 79 F. Supp. 2d 494 (D.N.J. 1999); Continental Dredging, Inc. v. De-Kaizered, Inc., 120 S.W.3d 380 (Tex. App. Sept. 26, 2003); Royal Maccabees Life Ins. Co. v. James, 2003 WL 1848601 (Tex. App. Apr. 10, 2003).

843 Laurents v. Louisiana Mobile Homes, Inc., 689 So. 2d 536 (La. Ct. App. 1997); *see also* Lump v. Best Door & Window, Inc., 2002 Ohio App. LEXIS 1381 (Mar. 27, 2002).

844 State Street Bank & Trust Co. v. Mutual Life Ins. Co. of New York, 811 F. Supp. 915 (S.D.N.Y. 1993); Lump v. Best Door & Window, Inc., 2002 Ohio App. LEXIS 1381 (Mar. 27, 2002); Brown v. Lyons, 43 Ohio Misc. 14, 332 N.E.2d 380 (C.P. 1974).

845 Edmondson v. American Motorcycle Ass'n, 2001 U.S. App. LEXIS 1506 (4th Cir. Feb. 2, 2001) (unpublished, citation limited) (N.C. law); Lake Mary Ltd. P'ship v. Johnston, 551 S.E.2d 546 (N.C. App. 2001).

846 Falcon Associates, Inc. v. Cox, 699 N.E.2d 203 (Ill. App. Ct. 1998).

847 Lake County Grading Co. v. Advance Mechanical Contractors, 654 N.E.2d 1109 (Ill. App. Ct. 1995) (while proof of public injury, a pattern, or an effect on consumers generally is usually not required in a UDAP case, it is necessary in a breach of contract dispute between businesses). *Cf.* Petri v. Gatlin, 997 F. Supp. 956 (N.D. Ill. 1997) (this does not apply where one of the businesses purchases goods as a consumer, and not as a re-seller). *But see* Brody v. Finch University of Health Sciences, 698 N.E.2d 257 (Ill. App. Ct. 1998) (applying same doctrine in consumer context).

848 Connecticut Regulations for the Dep't of Consumer Protection, Conn. Agencies Regs., §§ 42-110b-16, -17, Disclosure of Refunded Exchange Policies; Rules for Utah Consumer Sales Practices Act, Utah Admin. Code R. 152-11-10(B), Deposits and Refunds; Vermont Consumer Fraud Rules, Code Vt. Rules 06 031 006, Disclosure of Refund Policy.

849 Baker v. Burlington Coat Factory Warehouse, 673 N.Y.S.2d 281, 34 U.C.C. Rep. 2d 1052 (N.Y. City Ct. 1998).

850 *See* National Consumer Law Center, Consumer Warranty Law (2d ed. 2001 and Supp.).

851 *See* § 4.9.1, *supra* and § 5.8.2, *infra.*

852 *In re* National Credit Mgmt. Group, 21 F. Supp. 2d 424 (D.N.J. 1998) (illusory refund policy was UDAP violation); United States v. Star Crest Products of California, Inc., Trade Reg. Rep. (CCH) ¶ 21,923 (C.D. Cal. 1982) (consent order); Ujena, Inc., 111 F.T.C. 699 (1989) (consent order); Little v. Paco Collection Services, 156 Ga. App. 175, 274 S.E.2d 147 (1980); State v. Kay, 115 N.H. 696, 350 A.2d 336 (1975); Swiss v. Williams, 184 N.J. Super. 243, 445 A.2d 486 (Dist. Cty. Mercer Cty. 1982); Mapp v. Toyota World, Inc., 344 S.E.2d 297 (N.C. Ct. App. 1986); Wilder v. Squires, 315 S.E.2d 63 (N.C. Ct. App. 1984); Brown v. Banks, Clearinghouse No. 27,065 (Ohio C.P. Cuyahoga Cty. 1976); Riley v. Enterprise Furniture Co., 54 Ohio Misc. 1, 375 N.E.2d 821 (Mun. Ct. 1977); Commonwealth v. Flick, 382 A.2d 762 (Pa. Commw. Ct. 1978); Commonwealth *ex rel.* Zimmerman v. Nickel, 26 Pa. D. & C.3d 115 (C.P. Mercer Cty. 1983); Commonwealth v. Programmed Learning Sys. Inc., Clearinghouse No. 26,019 (Pa. C.P. Allegheny Cty. 1975); State v. Western Capital Corp., 290 N.W.2d 467 (S.D. 1980); Dixon v. Brooks, 604 S.W.2d 330 (Tex. Civ. App. 1980); Charping v. Light, 578 S.W.2d 462 (Tex. Civ. App. 1979); Our Fair Lady Health Resort v. Miller, 564 S.W.2d 410 (Tex. Civ. App. 1978).

853 Kustom Enterprises Inc., 85 F.T.C. 840 (1975) (consent order); Little v. Paco Collection Services, 156 Ga. App. 175, 274 S.E.2d 147 (1980); Maryland Regulations of the Consumer Protection Division, Md. Regs. Code tit. 2, ch. 05, Refund Policy of Retailers; Massachusetts Consumer Protection Regulations, Mass. Regs. Code tit. 940, § 3.13B, Refunds, Return and Cancellation Privileges; Swiss v. Williams, 184 N.J. Super. 243, 445

tion policies are not cured by subsequent written disclosure,[854] nor can sellers excessively delay or fail to make legally required refunds.[855]

Liquidated damage clauses that do not reasonably forecast just compensation are penalty clauses and are thus unfair under a UDAP statute.[856] Forfeiture of the complete contract amount where the seller's damages upon cancellation are less than the full contract amount is an unenforceable penalty clause. A seller who represents that the contract can not be canceled—that is, that the liquidated damages upon cancellation is the full contract amount—is actually claiming that courts will enforce a penalty clause, and the seller's representation is thus deceptive.[857]

Statements in the contract or a subsequent oral claim by the seller that a contract can not be canceled should also be deceptive because this is a misrepresentation of basic contract law.[858] Any contract can be canceled with the consumer liable only for the seller's damages. A liquidated damages clause is enforceable, but only if it is for a reasonable amount in relation to the seller's anticipated damages.

It is deceptive to claim a consumer is bound by a contract where changed terms make the contract no longer binding.[859] It is also deceptive to misrepresent one's intent to carry through with an oral understanding about a business deal, in order to induce the other party to delay in exercising rights until those rights expire.[860]

It may be unconscionable to unreasonably refuse to allow a consumer to revoke acceptance of defective goods.[861] It is also deceptive to claim that a contract can not be canceled while having a "silent" cancellation policy that allows certain purchasers to cancel.[862] In fact, the failure to disclose that silent cancellation policy is deceptive.[863]

It is deceptive to try to entice a sale by making it seemingly easy to back out of, and then do everything possible to make sure the consumer can not cancel. Thus it is deceptive to take a deposit check with the promise not to negotiate it, and then immediately try to cash it, to immediately sell the consumer's trade-in so the consumer can not then cancel, and to tell the consumer he can back out of the deal and then claim later it is noncancellable.[864] It is an unfair practice to retain an item a consumer sought to return, and refuse to make a refund, because of a mistaken suspicion that the consumer is a shoplifter.[865]

A.2d 486 (Dist. Ct. Mercer Cty. 1982); Martinez v. Decorators Warehouse, 1983 WL 2896 (Ohio Ct. App. Dec. 15, 1983); Snyder v. Van's Camera, Inc., 1981 WL 6338 (Ohio Ct. App. June 24, 1981) (refusal to make refund unconscionable under Ohio statute where dealer did not post refund policy); Gibson v. Stillpass Brothers, Inc., 1980 WL 131230 (Ohio Ct. App. May 28, 1980); Robinson v. Valiton Motors, Inc., 1979 WL 52523 (Ohio Ct. Dec. 7, App. 1979). *But see* Kaplan v. Cablevision, Inc., 671 A.2d 716 (Pa. Super. 1996) (cable TV company did not violate UDAP statute by giving refunds only to consumers who complained about interrupted service).

854 Tri-West Constr. v. Hernandez, 43 Or. App. 961, 607 P.2d 1375 (1979).

855 Goodman v. FTC, 244 F.2d 584 (9th Cir. 1957); Jay Norris Inc., 91 F.T.C. 751 (1978), *modified*, 598 F.2d 1244 (2d Cir., 1979); United States v. Star Crest Products of California, Inc., Trade Reg. Rep. (CCH) ¶ 21,923 (C.D. Cal 1982) (consent order); International Masters Publishers, Inc., 109 F.T.C. 9 (1987) (consent order); Market Dev. Corp., 95 F.T.C. 100 (1980); Kustom Enterprises Inc., 85 F.T.C. 840 (1975) (consent order); Ford Motor Co. v. Mayes, 575 S.W.2d 480 (Ky. Ct. App. 1978); Patry v. Liberty Mobilhome Sales, Inc., 15 Mass. App. Ct. 701, 448 N.E.2d 405 (1983), *aff'd*, 475 N.E.2d 392 (Mass. 1985); State *ex rel.* Lefkowitz v. Bevis Indus. Inc., 63 Misc. 2d 1088, 314 N.Y.S.2d 60 (Sup. Ct. 1970); Wilder v. Squires, 315 S.E.2d 63 (N.C. Ct. App. 1984); Martinez v. Decorators Warehouse, 1983 WL 2896 (Ohio Ct. App. Dec. 15, 1983); Snyder v. Van's Camera, Inc., 1981 WL 6338 (Ohio Ct. App. June 24, 1981); Gibson v. Stillpass Brothers, Inc., 1980 WL 131230 (Ohio Ct. App. May 28, 1980); Robinson v. Valiton Motors, Inc., 1979 WL 52523 (Ohio Ct. App. Dec. 7, 1979); Brown v. Bredenbeck, 2 Ohio Op. 3d 286 (C.P. Franklin Cty. 1975); Brown v. Lyons, 43 Ohio Misc. 14, 332 N.E.2d 380 (C.P. Hamilton Cty. 1974); Commonwealth v. Flick, 382 A.2d 762 (Pa. Commw. Ct. 1978); Charping v. Light, 578 S.W.2d 462 (Tex. Civ. App. 1979); Our Fair Lady Health Resort v. Miller, 564 S.W.2d 410 (Tex. Civ. App. 1978); State v. Ralph Williams' N.W. Chrysler Plymouth, Inc., 82 Wash. 2d 265, 510 P.2d 233 (1973); Paulik v. Coombs, 120 Wis. 2d 431, 355 N.W.2d 357 (Ct. App. 1984).

856 AMREP Corp., 102 F.T.C. 1362 (1983), *aff'd*, 768 F.2d 1171 (10th Cir. 1985); Horizon Corp., 97 F.T.C. 464 (1981); Capitol Builders Inc., 92 F.T.C. 274 (1978) (consent order); United Builders Inc., 92 F.T.C. 291 (1978) (consent order).

857 Swiss v. Williams, 184 N.J. Super. 243, 445 A.2d 486 (Dist. Ct. Mercer Cty. 1982).

858 BNI New York Ltd. v. DeSanto, 177 Misc. 2d 9, 675 N.Y.S.2d 752 (City Ct. 1998).

859 FTC v. S.J.A. Society, Inc., 5 Trade Reg. Rep. (CCH) ¶ 24,321 (E.D. Va. 1997) (proposed consent decree) (seller tried to raise the agreed-upon price of subscription and then harassed and threatened consumers with lawsuits when they attempted to cancel the subscriptions); Teague Motor Co. v. Rowton, 84 Or. App. 72, 733 P.2d 93 (1987).

860 Chamberlayne School v. Banker, 30 Mass. App. Ct. 346, 568 N.E.2d 642 (1991).

861 Ford Motor Co. v. Mayes, 575 S.W.2d 480 (Ky. Ct. App. 1978); Laurents v. Louisiana Mobile Homes, Inc., 689 So. 2d 536 (La. Ct. App. 1997) (failure to refund deposit when seller knew goods were defective was UDAP violation). *See also* Jaramillo v. Gonzales, 50 P.3d 554 (N.M. App. 2002) (UDAP violation to refuse to acknowledge liability under FTC Holder Rule after consumer revokes acceptance); Baker v. Burlington Coat Factory Warehouse, 673 N.Y.S.2d 281, 34 U.C.C. Rep. 2d 1052 (N.Y. City Ct. 1998).

862 Commonwealth *ex rel.* Zimmerman v. Nickel, 26 Pa. D. & C.3d 115 (C.P. Mercer Cty. 1983).

863 *Id.*

864 Mapp v. Toyota World, Inc., 344 S.E.2d 297 (N.C. Ct. App. 1986).

865 Thomas v. Busby, 670 So. 2d 603 (La. App. 1996).

5.2.7 Guarantees, Warranties, and Service Contracts

5.2.7.1 Breach of Warranties as UDAP Violations

5.2.7.1.1 Introduction

While the Uniform Commercial Code and other state and federal law provide consumers with a remedy for breach of warranty,[866] consumers may wish to remedy a breach of warranty with UDAP remedies. UDAP statutes often award attorney fees and minimum or multiple damages, offering a stronger remedy than the UCC. But, for this very reason, courts may be hesitant to award attorney fees or multiple damages in a case that involves a simple, unintentional breach of warranty.

A UDAP action challenging a pattern of intentionally selling shoddy goods, where the seller refuses to respond reasonably to breach of warranty claims, will thus be a safer case to challenge warranty breaches as UDAP violations. Additional counts concerning misrepresentations of the express warranty will also give the case a stronger UDAP flavor. Advocates should allege both UDAP and UCC counts; UCC and UDAP remedies may be cumulative.[867]

5.2.7.1.2 UDAP statute may apply where breach of warranty claim is unavailable

A UDAP claim may be particularly useful where consumers are unable to show that they have met the UCC's requirements for creation or enforcement of a warranty. For example, an Illinois court affirmed the dismissal of class action warranty claims because the consumers were unable to show that they had given notice of the breach of warranty to the manufacturer.[868] The consumers had also, however, pleaded that the manufacturer knew of, but failed to disclose, the safety problems from which this model suffered. The court held that these allegations properly stated a UDAP claim, and allowed the class action to proceed.

Likewise, another court allowed a class action to proceed on a UDAP claim that a builder had failed to disclose defects in the exterior finish it used, even though warranty claims were time-barred and negligent misrepresentation claims were barred by the economic loss rule.[869] Because privity is not required under UDAP laws,[870] it may be possible to assert a breach of warranty under a state UDAP statute where traditional contract principles would not allow it.[871]

5.2.7.1.3 Warranty breach as per se *UDAP violation*

A majority of courts find it is a state UDAP violation to fail to comply with offered or implied warranties.[872] In

866 *See* National Consumer Law Center, Consumer Warranty Law (2d ed. 2001 and Supp.).

867 Jackson v. H. Frank Olds Inc., 65 Ill. App. 3d 591, 22 Ill. Dec. 230, 382 N.E.2d 550, 25 U.C.C. Rep. 125 (Ill. App. Ct. 1978); MacCormack v. Robins Constr., 11 Wash. App. 80, 521 P.2d 761 (1974). *See also* Chilton Ins. Co. v. Pate & Pate Enterprises, Inc., 930 S.W.2d 877 (Tex. App. 1996) (breach of warranty can be actionable under UDAP even if there is no separate deception-based UDAP claim). *See generally* §§ 8.3.9, 8.4.2.6, 8.4.3.8, *infra*.

868 Perona v. Volkswagen of Am., Inc., 684 N.E.2d 859 (Ill. App. Ct. 1997).

869 Griffith v. Centex Real Estate Corp., 93 Wash. App. 202, 969 P.2d 486 (1998).

870 Edwards v. Schuh, 5 S.W.3d 829 (Tex. App. 1999) (breach of express warranty claim allowed despite lack of privity between consumer and builder).

871 *Id.*

872 Watson v. Damon Corp., 2002 WL 32059736 (W.D. Mich. Dec. 17, 2002) (denying seller's motion for summary judgment); W.R. Constr. & Consulting, Inc. v. Jeld-Wen, Inc., 2002 WL 31194870 (D. Mass. Sept. 20, 2002); *In re* Ford Motor Co. Ignition Switch Prods. Liability Litig., 1999 WL 33495352 (D.N.J. July 27, 1999), *as modified on reconsideration*, (July 27, 1999) (breach of implied warranty of merchantability may be violation of Mass., Neb., Okla., and Pa. UDAP statutes); Canal Electric Co. v. Westinghouse Electric Corp., 756 F. Supp. 620 (D. Mass. 1990); Wood v. General Motors Corp., 673 F. Supp. 1108 (D. Mass. 1987) (breach of implied warranty *per se* UDAP violation); Korman Corp., 105 F.T.C. 347 (1985) (consent order); Sun Refining & Mfg. Co., 104 F.T.C. 578 (1984) (consent order) (failure to honor lifetime warranties); People v. Conway, 42 Cal. App. 3d 875, 117 Cal. Rptr. 251 (1974); Pape v. Goldbach, 1999 Conn. Super. LEXIS 3488 (Dec. 28, 1999) (breach of warranties in home construction contract may be UDAP violation); Krawiec v. Blake Manor Dev. Co., 26 Conn. App. 601, 602 A.2d 1062 (1992) (breach of warranty by builder that home would be constructed in workmanlike manner); Bert Smith Oldsmobile Inc. v. Franklin, 400 So. 2d 1235 (Fla. Dist. Ct. App. 1981); Ford Motor Co. v. Mayes, 575 S.W.2d 480 (Ky. Ct. App. 1978); Courtney v. Bassano, 1999 ME 101, 733 A.2d 973 (Me. 1999) (seller committed UDAP violation by breaching warranty of complete satisfaction and refusing to refund purchase price); Kyle v. Philip Morris Inc., 408 Mass. 162, 556 N.E.2d 1025 (1990) (breach of implied warranty that cigarettes are safe may state a UDAP claim); Maillet v. ATF-Davidson Co., 552 N.E.2d 95 (Mass. 1990) (negligent breach of warranty is UDAP violation); Calimlim v. Foreign Car Center, Inc., 392 Mass. 228, 467 N.E.2d 443 (1984); Burnham v. Mark IV Homes, Inc., 387 Mass. 575, 441 N.E.2d 1027 (1982); Slaney v. Westwood Auto, Inc., 366 Mass. 688, 322 N.E.2d 768 (1975); Herb Chambers of Auburn, Inc. v. Director of Office of Consumer Affairs and Bus. Reg., 60 Mass. App. Ct. 1123, 805 N.E.2d 532 (Mass. App. Ct. 2004) (violation of state lemon law requirements is UDAP violation); Alcan Aluminum Corp. v. Carlton Aluminum, Inc., 35 Mass. App. Ct. 161, 617 N.E.2d 1005 (1993); Mikos v. Chrysler Corp., 158 Mich. App. 781, 404 N.W.2d 783 (1987) (breach of implied warranty is *per se* UDAP); State *ex rel.* Webster v. Milbourn, 759 S.W.2d 862 (Mo. Ct. App. 1988); Neveroski v. Blair, 141 N.J. Super. 365, 358 A.2d 473 (Ch. Div. 1976); People v. Empyre Inground Pools, 642 N.Y.S.2d 344 (App. Div. 1996) (repeated failure to fulfill warranties by correcting defects is UDAP violation); People v.

particular, it is unconscionable to unreasonably refuse to allow a consumer to revoke acceptance of defective goods.[873] A significant minority of cases, however, hold that a breach of warranty is not automatically an unfair or deceptive practice,[874] and findings in other states that a warranty violation is an automatic UDAP violation may depend on the language of that state's UDAP statute.[875] Unless the UDAP statute creates a warranty, the warranty claim must exist independent of the UDAP statute.[876]

A federal court in a nationwide UDAP class action examined the warranties offered by a new car manufacturer, to see if these involved representations that the car was defect-free.[877] It found that the written warranty to repair any

---

Empyre Inground Pools, Inc., 642 N.Y.S.2d 344 (App. Div. 1996); Schroders, Inc. v. Hogan Sys., Inc., 137 Misc. 2d 738, 522 N.Y.S.2d 404 (Sup. Ct. 1987); Boyle v. Daimler Chrysler Corp., 2002 WL 1881157 (Ohio App. Aug. 16, 2002) (unpublished, citation limited); Lump v. Best Door & Window, Inc., 2002 Ohio App. LEXIS 1381 (Mar. 27, 2002); Boyle v. Daimler Chrysler Corp., 2002 WL 1881157 (Ohio App. Aug. 16, 2002) (unpublished, citation limited); Budner v. Lake Erie Homes, 2001 Ohio App. LEXIS 4446 (Sept. 28, 2001) (defendant's performance in building a pre-manufactured home on a foundation was so egregious that it was a UDAP violation); Miner v. Jayco, Inc., 1999 Ohio App. LEXIS 3944 (Aug. 27, 1999) (failure to repair); Brown v. Lyons, 43 Ohio Misc. 14, 332 N.E.2d 380 (C.P. Hamilton Cty. 1974); Keller v. Volkswagen of Am., Inc., 733 A.2d 642 (Pa. Super. 1999) (defendant's inability to repair vehicle shows breach of warranty or initial misrepresentation of vehicle's quality, either of which would be UDAP violations); Parkway Co. v. Woodruff, 901 S.W.2d 434 (Tex. 1995) (confirms that breach of implied warranty is UDAP violation, but holds that there is no implied warranty to perform future land development services in a good and workmanlike manner); Gupta v. Ritter Homes, Inc., 646 S.W.2d 168 (Tex. 1983) (implied warranty from original builder in sale of used home); LaBella v. Charlie Thomas, Inc., 942 S.W.2d 127 (Tex. App. 1997) (breach of implied warranty of repairs in a good and workmanlike manner); Sipes v. General Motors Corp., 946 S.W.2d 143 (Tex. App. 1997) (breach of U.C.C. warranty); Chilton Ins. Co. v. Pate & Pate Enterprises, Inc., 930 S.W.2d 877 (Tex. App. 1996); Parkway Co. v. Woodruff, 857 S.W.2d 903 (Tex. App. 1993) (breach of implied warranty is a UDAP violation if developers fail to develop property in a good and workmanlike matter, even as to consumers who ultimately buy the property from a separate builder); Green Tree Acceptance, Inc. v. Pierce, 768 S.W.2d 416 (Tex. App. 1989) (violation of implied warranties); McCrea v. Cubilla Condominium Corp., 769 S.W.2d 261 (Tex. App. 1988) (implied warranty in service transaction); Precision Homes, Inc. v. Cooper, 671 S.W.2d 924 (Tex. App. 1984); Massachusetts Consumer Protection Regulations, Mass. Regs. Code tit. 940, § 3.08(2), (3), Warranties, Service Contracts. *See also* Glyptal, Inc. v. Engelhard Corp., 801 F. Supp. 887 (D. Mass. 1992). *Cf.* People *ex rel.* Hartigan v. All Am. Aluminum & Constr. Co., 171 Ill. App. 3d 27, 524 N.E.2d 1067 (1988) (failure to honor warranties could be UDAP violation). *But cf.* State *ex rel.* Brady v. Gardiner, 2000 Del. Super. LEXIS 208 (June 5, 2000) (depleting trust fund set aside for warranty work not a UDAP violation as long as warranty work continues to be performed).

873 Ford Motor Co. v. Mayes, 575 S.W.2d 480 (Ky. Ct. App. 1978); Guiggey v. Bombardier, 615 A.2d 1169 (Me. 1992) (breach of warranty may be UDAP violation if seller's conduct is unfair or deceptive); Jones v. Swad Chevrolet, Clearinghouse No. 41,256 (Ohio C.P. Franklin Cty. 1985); Town East Ford Sales, Inc. v. Gray, 730 S.W.2d 796 (Tex. App. 1987). *See also* Jaramillo v. Gonzales, 50 P.3d 554 (N.M. App. 2002) (UDAP violation to refuse to acknowledge liability under FTC Holder Rule after consumer revokes acceptance).

874 Cipollone v. Liggett Group, Inc., 693 F. Supp. 208 (D.N.J. 1988), *aff'd in relevant part, rev'd in part on other grounds*, 893 F.3d 541, *rev'd in part, aff'd in part, remanded on other grounds*, 505 U.S. 504, 112 S. Ct. 2608, 120 L. Ed. 2d 407 (1992) (ruling on preemption issues); Associates Capital Services Corp. v. Fairway Private Cars, Inc., 590 F. Supp. 10 (E.D.N.Y. 1982) (must be more than just mere breach of warranty to be unfair); Gibbs v. Mase, 11 Conn. App. 289, 526 A.2d 7 (1987); Sharpe v. General Motors Corp., 401 S.E.2d 328 (Ga. App. Ct. 1991); DeLoach v. General Motors, 187 Ga. App. 159, 369 S.E.2d 484 (1988); Kleczek v. Jorgensen, 328 Ill. App. 3d 1012, 767 N.E.2d 913, 263 Ill. Dec. 187 (2002); Suminski v. Maine Appliance Warehouse, 602 A.2d 1173 (Me. 1992) (breach of statutory warranty may, given proper circumstances such as continual evasion of responsibility, violate UDAP statute); Inniss v. Methot Buick-Opel, Inc., 506 A.2d 212 (Me. 1986); Banville v. Huckins, 407 A.2d 294 (Me. 1979); Welch v. Fitzgerald-Hicks Dodge Inc., 121 N.H. 358, 430 A.2d 147 (1981) (good faith attempt to comply no violation); Coastal Group, Inc. v. Dryvit Sys., Inc., 274 N.J. Super. 171, 643 A.2d 649 (1994); DiNicola v. Watchung Furniture's Country Manor, 232 N.J. Super. 69, 556 A.2d 367 (1989); Palmucci v. Brunswick Corp., 311 N.J. Super. 607, 710 A.2d 1045 (App. Div. 1998); D'Ercole Sales, Inc. v. Fruehauf Corp., 206 N.J. Super. 11, 501 A.2d 990 (App. Div. 1985) (in commercial case, court finds failure to honor warranty and shoddy behavior not UDAP violation in facts of this particular case); Mehovic v. Ken Wilson Ford, Inc., 439 S.E.2d 184 (N.C. Ct. App. 1994); Morris v. Bailey, 358 S.E.2d 120 (N.C. Ct. App. 1987); Coble v. Richardson Corp. of Greensboro, 322 S.E.2d 817 (N.C. Ct. App. 1984); Warren v. Guttanit, Inc., 317 S.E.2d 5 (N.C. Ct. App. 1984); Wachovia Bank & Trust Co. v. Smith, 44 N.C. App. 685, 262 S.E.2d 646 (1980); Stone v. Paradise Park Homes, Inc., 37 N.C. App. 97, 245 S.E.2d 801 (1978); Hershenson v. Lake Champlain Motors Inc., 139 Vt. 219, 424 A.2d 1075 (1981); Christie v. Dalmig, 136 Vt. 597, 396 A.2d 1385 (1979) (limiting a Vermont UDAP regulation that rules that failure to comply with a warranty is a UDAP violation); Lidstrand v. Silvercrest Indus., 28 Wash. App. 359, 623 P.2d 710 (1981).

875 *See* Kaplan v. Cablevision, Inc., 671 A.2d 716 (Pa. Super. 1996) (Pennsylvania UDAP statute only prohibits failure to comply with written warranty); Tex. Bus. & Com. Code Ann. tit. 2, § 17.50(a)(2) (Vernon). *See also* Gateway 2000, Inc., 5 Trade Reg. Rep. (CCH) ¶ 24,467 (F.T.C. Dkt. No. C-3844 1998) (consent order).

876 Rocky Mountain Helicopters, Inc. v. Lubbock County Hosp. Dist., 987 S.W.2d 50 (Tex. 1998) (standard for court creation of an implied warranty for services); Anthony Equipment Corp. v. Irwin Steel Erectors, Inc., 115 S.W.3d 191 (Tex. App. 2003); Raymond v. Rahme, 78 S.W.3d 552 (Tex. App. 2002); Drury v. Baptist Memorial Hosp. Sys., 933 S.W.2d 668 (Tex. App. 1996); Humble Nat'l Bank v. DCV, Inc., 933 S.W.2d 224 (Tex. App. 1996). *Cf.* Murphy v. Campbell, 964 S.W.2d 265 (Tex. 1997) (no cause of action for breach of implied warranty of professional services). *See generally* National Consumer Law Center, Consumer Warranty Law (2d ed. 2001 and Supp.).

877 Snodgrass v. Ford Motor Co., 1999 WL 33495352 (D.N.J. May 14, 1999).

defects was not a warranty that the vehicle was defect-free, but actually acknowledged that the vehicle may have defects. The representation was that the manufacturer would fix any defects.[878]

On the other hand, the court found that the class could go forward based on a UDAP false representation claim, where those representations are found in the implied warranties that accompanied the vehicle as a matter of law. The implied warranty and thus the implied representation is that the vehicle is merchantable.[879]

5.2.7.1.4 *Aggravating circumstances can turn breach of warranty into UDAP violation*

Even in jurisdictions that do not follow a general rule that a breach of warranty is a UDAP violation, substantial aggravating circumstance can turn a breach of warranty into a UDAP claim.[880] For example, a warrantor engaged in unconscionable conduct when it used its superior knowledge of the homeowner's warranty to lull a consumer into inaction concerning the repairs by promising to do certain work, then claiming that the work was not covered by the warranty and refusing to do it.[881]

Similarly, it is unconscionable to deny warranty coverage for a stated reason and then continue searching for alternative grounds for denial as each attempted ground for denial becomes untenable.[882] Of course, even if a warranty violation is not an automatic UDAP violation, oral misrepresentations and other deceptive conduct related to a warranty breach are certainly actionable.[883]

5.2.7.1.5 *Magnuson-Moss breach of warranty violation as a* per se *UDAP violation*

Another important private warranty remedy is provided by the Magnuson-Moss Warranty Act.[884] The Act specifies substantive standards for certain express warranties and directs that sellers disclose the type of express warranty being offered.[885] The Act provides a private remedy and delegates enforcement of violations to the FTC as unfair or deceptive practices. Several courts have held that violations of the Magnuson-Moss warranty standards constitute unfair or deceptive practices, making UDAP remedies available as well as those provided by the Act.[886]

5.2.7.2 Service Contracts

5.2.7.2.1 *Duplication of warranty rights*

A growing area of consumer concern is the proliferation of marketing for service contracts. These contracts may duplicate existing warranties and may have so many exclusions as to be almost illusory. Sale techniques may also involve deception. Disclaiming implied warranties contrary to state law as a means of making it more likely that consumers will buy service contracts is a UDAP violation.[887] (Note that the Magnuson-Moss Act also limits disclaimer of implied warranties when a supplier enters into a service contract with the consumer.[888])

Maine has adopted UDAP regulations dealing with the sale of service contracts or extended warranties on automobiles. The regulations require the dealer to disclose if the manufacturer's express warranty, that automatically comes with the car, offers similar protection to an offered service contract which must be separately purchased. The dealer must also disclose to the consumer that, even without purchasing the service contract, the consumer is protected by an implied warranty that in Maine can not be waived.[889]

5.2.7.2.2 *Deceptive marketing techniques*

A Maine trial court has also considered whether maintenance agreements sold by Sears Roebuck on household appliances were marketed in an unfair or deceptive manner. The court ruled that Maine's implied warranty protections did not provide the same protection as the maintenance

878 *Id. But see In re* Ford Motor Co. Ignition Switch Prods. Liab. L.T., 194 F.R.D. 484 (D.N.J. 2000) (plaintiff's renewed petition for class certification denied).

879 Snodgrass v. Ford Motor Co., 1999 WL 33495352 (D.N.J. May 14, 1999).

880 Suber v. Chrysler Corp., 104 F.3d 578 (3d Cir. 1997) (New Jersey law).

881 HOW, Ins. v. Patriot Fin. Services, 786 S.W.2d 533 (Tex. App. 1990).

882 *Id. See also* State *ex rel.* Brady v. Gardiner, 2000 Del. Super. LEXIS 208 (June 5, 2000) (giving buyers a run-around on warranty work is a UDAP violation).

883 *See* Laurents v. Louisiana Mobile Homes, Inc., 689 So. 2d 536 (La. Ct. App. 1997) (seller's delays and denials were UDAP violations); Mehovic v. Ken Wilson Ford, Inc., 439 S.E.2d 184 (N.C. Ct. App. 1994).

884 15 U.S.C. § 2301–2312.

885 This Act is described in more detail in National Consumer Law Center, Consumer Warranty Law Ch. 2 (2d ed. 2001 and Supp.).

886 Skelton v. Gen. Motors Corp., 660 F.2d 311, 311 (7th Cir. 1981) (Magnuson-Moss designed to protect consumers "from deceptive warranty practices"); Cunningham v. Fleetwood Homes, 253 F.3d 611, 620-22 (11th Cir. 2001) (failure to disclose warranty exclusions constitutes an unfair or deceptive act or practice under Magnuson-Moss and FTC Act); Katharine Gibbs School v. FTC, 612 F.2d 658, 662 (2d Cir. 1979); FTC v. Va. Homes Mfg. Corp., 509 F. Supp. 51, 58 n.5 (D. Md. 1981) (violations of Magnuson-Moss Act are likewise unfair or deceptive under FTC Act).

887 Green v. Kansas City Power & Light Co. (*In re* Green), 281 B.R. 699 (D. Kan. 2002).

888 15 U.S.C. § 2308(a). *See* National Consumer Law Center, Consumer Warranty Law § 2.3.2 (2d ed. 2001 and Supp.).

889 Maine Unfair Trade Practices Regulations, Code Me. R. § 26-239 ch. 105 § 5, Sale of New Motor Vehicles.

agreements, and thus the sale of the agreements could not be challenged as merely duplicative of protection that state law required to be provided free of charge.[890]

The Maine trial court was also not concerned with oral statements by Sears employees at the point of sale downgrading the reliability record of Sears products, since consumers could always switch to a competitive appliance instead of buying a Sears maintenance product. But the court did find a UDAP violation where, after the sale was made, Sears employees called up consumers and falsely downgraded the products' reliability, thus attempting to sell maintenance agreements.[891] Evidence in the case showed most consumer appliances require little or no service.

The FTC and Montgomery Ward have reached a consent agreement whereby Montgomery Ward will not misrepresent service contract coverage or a product's need for maintenance, adjustment, or services.[892] The FTC had alleged that Montgomery Ward had falsely claimed certain products needed routine maintenance and adjustments, such as televisions, washing machines, dryers, and refrigerators. In fact, the service contract did not even cover all routine maintenance and adjustments. Montgomery Ward allegedly also stated that *Consumer Reports* recommends service contracts on appliances when this was not the case.

In another service contract case involving somewhat different facts, a challenge to a telephone company's sales techniques for its inside wiring maintenance contracts survived a motion to dismiss. The court found it could be a UDAP violation for the telephone company not to disclose that the maintenance contract is not regulated by the utility commission, that the customer can hire another company to repair inside wires, that the customer may not be responsible for repairing inside wires, and that inside wires only have to be repaired about every fourteen years. The phone company's misleading new customers into thinking they were receiving an unbiased, objective assessment of their telephone needs could also be a UDAP violation.[893]

Deceptive marketing of service contracts for automobiles involves some novel techniques. These are examined at § 5.4.3.6, *infra*.

5.2.7.2.3 Failure to pay consumer claims under the service contract

Another NCLC manual examines in detail consumer remedies where the service contract does not pay out on promised coverage. See NCLC's *Consumer Warranty Law* Ch. 18 (2d ed. 2001 and Supp.). The practice can also be a UDAP violation.

A court has also found a UDAP violation where a dealer refused to pay benefits under the service contract, while attempting to shift blame to the service contract administrator. The court pointed to the language of the service contact whereby the dealer and the administrator both made certain promises.[894]

5.2.7.2.4 Pricing practices

A major problem area with service contracts is the pricing structure and its relationship to the seller of the goods being protected by the contract. For example, there are allegations that automobile dealers sell service contracts for whatever price they can get, and pocket the difference between the purchase price and the set price the service contract company charges for the contract. A number of cases have considered this as a Truth in Lending issue (the amount the dealer retains potentially being a finance charge),[895] but the same facts can lead to UDAP issues as well. As the Seventh Circuit has stated:

> The consumer would have a greater incentive to shop around for an extended warranty, rather than take the one offered by the dealer, if he realized that the dealer was charging what the defendants' lawyer described as a "commission," and apparently a very sizeable one, for its efforts in procuring the warranty from a third party. Or the consumer might be more prone to haggle than if he thought that the entire fee had been levied by a third party and so was outside the dealer's direct control. Or he might go to another dealer in search of lower mark-ups on third-party charges.[896]

A good argument can be made that the representation of a price for a service contract or extended warranty is deceptive where that is not the price at all, but the total of the contract price and the dealer's markup. Certainly deceptive is any representation that the service contract is a good deal, a good price, or the like, or that the entire fee is paid to the service contract provider. Moreover, it may also be deceptive to fail to disclose the pricing arrangement. Deceptive pricing of automobile service contracts is examined in more detail at § 5.4.3.6, *infra*.

890 State v. Sears Roebuck & Co., Clearinghouse No. 40,629 (Me. Super. Ct. Aug. 1985).

891 *Id.*

892 Montgomery Ward & Co., 111 F.T.C. 364 (1988) (consent order).

893 Commonwealth *ex rel.* Zimmerman v. Bell Tel. Co., 551 A.2d 602 (Pa. Commw. Ct. 1988).

894 Ron Craft Chevrolet, Inc. v. Davis, 836 S.W.2d 672 (Tex. App. 1992).

895 Gibson v. Bob Watson Chevrolet-GEO, Inc., 112 F.3d 283 (7th Cir. 1997). *See* National Consumer Law Center, Truth in Lending § 4.7.3.4 (5th ed. 2003 and Supp.).

896 Gibson v. Bob Watson Chevrolet-GEO, Inc., 112 F.3d 283, 286 (7th Cir. 1997).

5.2.7.3 Misrepresentations Concerning the Status of a Guarantee

5.2.7.3.1 General

Various misrepresentations concerning the status of guarantees have been prohibited by state or FTC precedent. It is a UDAP violation:

- To advertise guarantees without disclosing the nature and extent of the guarantee, the manner in which the guarantor will perform, and the identity of the guarantor;[897]
- To fail to disclose the method of calculating the amount that will be paid under the guarantee, where the amount payable depends on, for example, how long the product has been in use;[898]
- To represent that a guarantee assures "satisfaction or your money back" or a "lifetime" guarantee without disclosing any limits or clarifying whose life is referenced;[899]
- To guarantee savings on purchases without disclosing what the guarantor will do if the savings are not realized, with any time limitations, for example, "if you can find this television cheaper anywhere in town within two weeks of purchase, I will refund you the difference";[900]
- To advertise guarantees if the guarantor can not or does not perform;[901]
- To use vague, misleading, and contradictory language and concealed clauses that deliberately obfuscate the warranty's coverage;[902]
- To fail to assume responsibility for the truth of a representation made in a guarantee that can be taken as a representation of fact;[903]
- To advertise a product as guaranteed, but deliver the product with a guarantee that is at variance with such promise;[904]
- To make certain express warranties in advertising, and

897 Brooks v. Midas-Int'l Corp., 47 Ill. App. 3d 266, 361 N.E.2d 815 (1977); Connecticut Regulations for the Dep't of Consumer Protection, Conn. Agencies Regs. §§ 42-110b-1 to -8, Representations of Guarantees; Massachusetts Consumer Protection Regulation, Mass. Regs. Code tit. 940, § 3.03, Deceptive Advertising of Guarantees.

But the FTC has revised its Guides Against Deceptive Advertising of Guarantees, 16 C.F.R. § 239 which had previously also required these disclosures. The Guides now state advertisers must only disclose that a warranty document, as specified in the FTC's Presale Availability Rule (16 C.F.R. § 702), is available for examination prior to purchase of the warranted product. *See* 50 Fed. Reg. 18466 (May 1, 1985).

898 *See* Connecticut Regulations for the Dep't of Consumer Protection, Conn. Agencies Regs. § 42-110b-3, Representations of Guarantees; Massachusetts Consumer Protection Regulations, Mass. Regs. Code tit. 940, § 3.03(2), Deceptive Advertising of Guarantees.

899 16 C.F.R. §§ 239.3, 239.4; Capp Homes v. Duarte, 617 F.2d 900 (1st Cir. 1980) (interpreting Massachusetts law); Benham v. Wallingford Auto Park, Inc., 2003 WL 22905163 (Conn. Super. Nov. 26, 2003); Courtney v. Bassano, 1999 ME 101, 733 A.2d 973 (Me. 1999) (seller committed UDAP violation by breaching warranty of complete satisfaction and refusing to refund purchase price); *see also* Connecticut Regulations for the Dep't of Consumer Protection, Conn. Agencies Regs. §§ 42-110b-5, -7, Representations of Guarantees; Massachusetts Consumer Protection Regulations, Mass. Regs. Code tit. 940, § 3.03(3), (4), Deceptive Advertising of Guarantees (seller must disclose which life guarantee refers to).

900 Jay Norris Inc., 91 F.T.C. 751 (1978), *modified*, 598 F.2d 1244 (2d Cir. 1979); Commodore Corp., 85 F.T.C. 472 (1975) (consent order); Fleetwood Enterprises, 85 F.T.C. 414 (1975) (consent order); Redman Indus. Inc., 85 F.T.C. 309 (1975) (consent order); Skyline Corp., 85 F.T.C. 444 (1975) (consent order); Capitol Mfg. Co., 73 F.T.C. 872 (1965); Connecticut Regulations for the Dep't of Consumer Protection, Conn. Agencies Regs. §§ 42-110b-1 to -6, Representations of Guarantees; Massachusetts Consumer Protection Regulations, Mass. Regs. Code tit. 940, § 3.03(5), Deceptive Advertising of Guarantees.

The practice was also prohibited by the FTC Guides Against Deceptive Advertising of Guarantees, 16 C.F.R. § 239. The FTC has now deleted this guide section because the section does not pertain to the same subject matter as the rest of the guarantee guides, which deal with defect warranties and satisfaction warranties. 50 Fed. Reg. 18469 (May 1, 1985).

901 16 C.F.R. § 239.5; Connecticut Regulations for the Dep't of Consumer Protection, Conn. Agencies Regs. §§ 42-110b-7, Representations of Guarantees; Massachusetts Consumer Protection Regulations, Mass. Regs. Code tit. 940, § 3.03(6), Deceptive Advertising of Guarantees; David v. Mast, 1999 Del. Ch. LEXIS 34 (Mar. 2, 1999) (advertising 10-year guarantee for roofing work when company was deeply in debt, had no assets, and was winding down was UDAP violation).

902 Oldendorf v. Gen. Motors Corp., 322 Ill. App. 3d 825, 751 N.E.2d 214, 256 Ill. Dec. 161 (2001). *See also* Household Retail Servs. v. State, 2001 Tex. App. LEXIS 5893 (Aug. 29, 2001) (affirmance of temporary injunction prohibiting misleading letters to consumers regarding their warranty rights).

903 Universal Carpet Distributing Co., 57 F.T.C. 609 (1959); Connecticut Regulations for the Dep't of Consumer Protection, Conn. Agencies Regs. §§ 42-110b—8, Representations of Guarantees; Attaway v. Tom's Auto Sales, Inc., 144 Ga. App. 813, 242 S.E.2d 740 (1978); Massachusetts Consumer Protection Regulations, Mass. Regs. Code tit. 940, § 3.03(7), Deceptive Advertising of Guarantees; Woods v. Littleton, 554 S.W.2d 662 (Tex. 1977).

This practice was also prohibited by the FTC Guides Against Deceptive Advertising of Guarantees, 16 C.F.R. § 239. The FTC has now deleted this provision from its guides, but has stated "the existing provision is an accurate statement of commission law. . . ." 50 Fed. Reg. 18469 (May 1, 1985).

904 Montgomery Ward Co. v. FTC, 379 F.2d 666 (7th Cir. 1967); Coro, Inc. v. FTC, 338 F.2d 149 (1st Cir. 1964), *cert. denied*, 380 U.S. 954 (1965); Western Radio Corp., 339 F.2d 937 (7th Cir. 1964); Baldwin Bracelet Corp. v. FTC, 325 F.2d 1012 (D.C. Cir. 1963), *cert. denied*, 377 U.S. 923 (1964); Clinton Watch Co. v. FTC, 291 F.2d 838 (7th Cir. 1961), *cert. denied*, 368 U.S. 952 (1962); Better Living, Inc. v. FTC, 259 F.2d 271 (3d Cir. 1958); Pati-Port Inc., 60 F.T.C. 35 (1962), *aff'd*, Pati-Port Inc. v. FTC, 313 F.2d 103 (4th Cir. 1963).

then to limit those warranties in the written warranty;[905]

- To improperly refuse to honor warranties on sales originating from non-exclusive distributors, or to fail to disclose that consumers have to return large products (e.g., a Craftmatic bed) to the factory at the owner's own expense to obtain the offered warranty work;[906]
- To misrepresent an express warranty, such as claiming a warranty is unconditional when there are conditions specified;[907]
- To subsequently disclaim an oral warranty with an "as is" contract,[908] or to disclaim implied warranties if this disclaimer is prohibited by law;[909]
- To fail to disclose that a product contains no warranty;[910]
- To disclaim implied warranties contrary to state law and then sell a service contract that covers what the implied warranty would have covered;[911]
- To represent that a product is covered by a warranty, but then to disavow coverage once major irreparable defects become apparent;[912]
- To fail to place a product under a warranty, as promised, even if the seller's failure to do so arises from a contract dispute between the seller and consumer;[913]
- To state that a product or device is warranted, while at the same time limiting the warranty so much that it is illusory;[914]
- To fail to reveal an upcharge on an extended warranty;[915]
- To represent that a product comes with a warranty when it does not.[916]

5.2.7.3.2 Thirty day, "50-50" warranties

Thirty-day "50-50" and similar warranties are common in low-end used-car sales. The dealer promises to repair the product for the first thirty days, with the consumer paying half the cost of parts and labor and the dealer paying the rest. The warranty requires that the consumer take the car to the dealer to be serviced.

These warranties can be illusory. The dealer can just double or triple the repair cost, and require the consumer to pay half that inflated amount. While the FTC has stated that a 50-50 warranty is not a *per se* violation of the federal Magnuson-Moss Warranty Act, it stressed that it would be deceptive for the warrantor to jack up the price of warranty repairs as a way of artificially increasing the consumer's share.[917]

Where a dealer provides a 50-50 or other written warranty, Magnuson-Moss prohibits the dealer from disclaiming implied warranties during the term of the written warranty.[918] Consequently, while the consumer must pay fifty percent of a repair under the written warranty, the consumer may be entitled to a warranty repair at no charge under the implied warranty of merchantability. It may thus be a UDAP violation for the dealer to seek fifty percent payment from the consumer.

---

905 State v. GAF Corp., 760 P.2d 310 (Utah 1988).

906 Craftmatic/Contour Org., Inc., 105 F.T.C. 366 (1985) (consent order); *see also* Korman Corp., 105 F.T.C. 347 (1985) (delays in home warranty repairs).

907 Benrus Watch Co. v. FTC, 352 F.2d 313 (8th Cir. 1965), *cert. denied*, 384 U.S. 939 (1966); Coro Inc. v. FTC, 338 F.2d 149 (1st Cir. 1964), *cert. denied*, 380 U.S. 954 (1965); American Aluminum Corp., 84 F.T.C. 48 (1974), *aff'd*, 522 F.2d 1278 (5th Cir. 1975), *cert. denied*, 426 U.S. 906 (1976); Tri-State Carpets Inc., 84 F.T.C. 1078 (1974); Wilbanks Carpet Specialists Inc., 84 F.T.C. 510 (1974); Southern States Distributing Co., 83 F.T.C. 1126 (1973); Interstate Builders Inc., 72 F.T.C. 370 (1967); Royal Constr. Co., 71 F.T.C. 762 (1967); Montgomery Ward & Co., 70 F.T.C. 52 (1966), *aff'd*, 379 F.2d 666 (7th Cir. 1967); John A. Guziak, 67 F.T.C. 1270 (1965), *aff'd*, 361 F.2d 700 (1966), *cert. denied*, 385 U.S. 1007 (1967); Luxury Indus., 59 F.T.C. 442 (1961); Fletcher v. Don Foss of Cleveland, Inc., 90 Ohio App. 3d 82, 628 N.E.2d 60 (1993). *But see* Smaldino v. Larsick, 90 Ohio App. 3d 691, 630 N.E.2d 408 (1993) (supplier's failure to fill in model number on warranty card is not a false representation).

908 Clayton v. McCary, 426 F. Supp. 248 (N.D. Ohio 1976); Attaway v. Tom's Auto Sales, Inc., 144 Ga. App. 813, 242 S.E.2d 742 (1978).

909 Mass. Regs. Code tit. 940, § 6.12.

910 Aubrey's R.V. Center, Inc. v. Tandy Corp., 46 Wash. App. 595, 731 P.2d 1124 (1987).

911 Green v. Kansas City Power & Light Co. (*In re* Green), 281 B.R. 699 (D. Kan. 2002).

912 Barbee v. Atlantic Marine Sales & Service, 115 N.C. App. 641, 446 S.E.2d 117 (1994).

913 Sunset Pools v. Schaefer, 869 S.W.2d 883 (Mo. Ct. App. 1994); Love v. Keith, 383 S.E.2d 674 (N.C. Ct. App. 1989).

914 Roelle v. Orkin Exterminating Co., 2000 Ohio App. LEXIS 5141 (Nov. 7, 2000); Fletcher v. Don Foss of Cleveland, Inc., 90 Ohio App. 3d 82, 628 N.E.2d 60 (1993); State *ex rel.* Celebrezze v. Ferraro, 63 Ohio App. 3d 168, 578 N.E.2d 492 (1989). *See also* Fendrich v. RBF, L.L.C., 842 So. 2d 1076 (Fla. Dist. Ct. App. 2003) (deceptive to promise performance in one clause but add another clause making the promise illusory).

915 Cannon v. Cherry Hill Toyota, Inc., 161 F. Supp. 2d 362 (D.N.J. 2001) (violates New Jersey UDAP requirement of disclosure of terms of any warranty or service contract offered by dealer).

916 Rose v. Ford, 2003 WL 21495081 (Cal. App. June 30, 2003) (unpublished, citation limited) (misrepresentation that vehicle was still under manufacturer's warranty); Ciampi v. Ogden Chrysler Plymouth, Inc., 634 N.E.2d 448 (Ill. App. Ct. 1994) (representation that vehicle had new car warranty was false because it had expired due to mileage); Knox v. Ludwick, 2001 Ohio App. LEXIS 4747 (Sept. 25, 2001) (affirming damage award for misrepresenting that RV came with 5-year warranty, which trial court held to be a UDAP violation).

917 FTC, Letter to Keith E. Whann, Esq. (Dec. 31, 2002), *available at* www.ftc.gov/os/2003/niadaresponseletter.htm. *See* National Consumer Law Center, Consumer Warranty Law § 2.4.1 (2d ed. 2001 and Supp.).

918 *See* National Consumer Law Center, Consumer Warranty Law § 2.3.2 (2d ed. 2001 and Supp.).

5.2.8 Other Misrepresentations of Legal Rights and Requirements; Misrepresentation of Law vs. Fact

It is deceptive to misrepresent the existence or nature of legal requirements or to misrepresent a product's conformity to legal or official standards.[919] It is also deceptive for a company to falsely claim that an agent has no authority to bind the company and that the company is thus not bound by a sales agreement.[920]

It is deceptive to use an oral sales presentation to obscure the meaning of legal disclosures given the consumer in writing.[921] A contract clause stating the creditor has the right to accelerate upon default is deceptive where state law limits the creditor's right to accelerate.[922] A landlord's inclusion of illegal and unenforceable terms in a lease agreement is a UDAP violation.[923]

It is deceptive for a collector to notify the debtor concerning the debtor's probable liability for the creditor's attorney fees where such attorney fees violate state law.[924] It is also a UDAP violation to try to collect attorney fees where those are prohibited by law.[925] Failure to disclose that a vehicle is a "gray market" vehicle, manufactured for sale outside the United States, is a UDAP violation.[926]

In one contract, a provision waiving the consumer's exemption rights "to the extent permitted by law" technically had no effect because state law prohibited the waiver. Nonetheless, the West Virginia Supreme Court ruled that the provision was still misleading and created a likelihood of confusion or misunderstanding.[927] Similarly, a Michigan court has held that it may be unfair and deceptive to cause consumers to rely on a confusing, ambiguous and misleading contract clause.[928]

A UDAP cause of action is available for a seller's oral misrepresentations of applicable law or the buyer's legal rights.[929] Moreover, in certain situations, one could argue that it is unfair or deceptive for the merchant to fail to disclose to the consumer applicable legal rights and obligations of both parties.[930]

But some courts may refuse to find a UDAP violation where the seller's misrepresentation is one of law, not of fact.[931] Since the justification for this approach is that both parties are presumed to be equally capable of knowing and interpreting the law,[932] this view should not be applicable to a merchant-consumer transaction.

Thus, a court has held that, although ordinarily a misrepresentation of a point of law may not serve as the basis for a UDAP claim, the consumer will have a UDAP claim where the defendant takes advantage of its superior knowledge of the law, where the circumstances are such that it is the same as a misrepresentation of fact, or where there is a fiduciary or confidential relationship.[933]

Other courts distinguish statements of law offered as opinion from statements of law offered as fact.[934] Thus an incorrect factual statement about energy tax credit is deceptive, even if the law is subsequently changed so that it conforms to the initial representation.[935]

---

919 *See* 3 Trade Reg. Rep. (CCH) ¶ 7,771 for FTC cases; *see also* Texas v. American Blastfax, Inc., 164 F. Supp. 2d 892 (W.D. Tex. 2001) (misrepresentation of scope of junk-fax law); C&D Electronics, Inc., 109 F.T.C. 72 (1987) (consent order); People v. Lyman, 253 Cal. App. 2d 959, 61 Cal. Rptr. 800 (1967); Leardi v. Brown, 394 Mass. 151, 474 N.E.2d 1094 (1985); Kugler v. Haitian Tours, Inc., 120 N.J. Super. 260, 293 A.2d 706 (Ch. Div. 1972); Commonwealth v. Foster, Clearinghouse No. 26,031 (Pa. C.P. Allegheny Cty. 1974). *But see* McCaskey v. Continental Airlines, Inc., 159 F. Supp. 2d 562 (E.D. Tex. 2001) (sending a release that is less than amount required by law not *per se* UDAP).

920 Williams v. Loftice, 576 S.W.2d 455 (Tex. Civ. App. 1978). *See also* § 4.2.15.4, *supra*.

921 Horizon Corp., 97 F.T.C. 464 (1981).

922 Levine v. Baldwin, 23 Ohio Op. 3d 436 (Hamilton Cty. 1981).

923 People v. McKale, 25 Cal. 3d 626, 602 P.2d 731, 159 Cal. Rptr. 811 (1980); Leardi v. Brown, 394 Mass. 151, 474 N.E.2d 1094 (1985). *But see* Perry v. Island Sav. & Loan Ass'n, 101 Wash. 2d 795, 684 P.2d 1281 (1984) (good faith enforcement of arguably valid due-on-sale clause not unfair). *See generally* § 5.2.3.3, *supra*.

924 Wiginton v. Pacific Credit Corp., 2 Haw. App. 435, 634 P.2d 111 (1981).

925 Elsea, Inc. v. Stapleton, 1998 Ohio App. LEXIS 3165 (Ohio Ct. App. July 2, 1998).

926 *In re* Edwards, 233 B.R. 461 (Bankr. D. Idaho 1999) (sale of tractor). *See* National Consumer Law Center, Consumer Warranty Law Ch. 13 (2d ed. 2001 and Supp.) for further discussion of gray market vehicles.

927 Orlando v. Finance One, 369 S.E.2d 882 (W. Va. 1988).

928 Michaels v. Amway Corp., 206 Mich. App. 644, 522 N.W.2d 703 (1994).

929 Preston v. Kelsey, 1986 WL 5376 (Ohio Ct. App. May 9, 1986) (oral misrepresentation of consumer's rights under auto sale contract violates UDAP statute).

930 Swiss v. Williams, 184 N.J. Super. 243, 445 A.2d 486 (Dist. Ct. Mercer Cty. 1982) (failure to disclose consumer's rescission rights); Wilder v. Squires, 315 S.E.2d 63 (N.C. Ct. App. 1984). *But see* Pleasants v. Home Federal Savings & Loan Ass'n, 116 Ariz. 319, 569 P.2d 261 (Ariz. Ct. App. 1977) (failure to disclose holding under pertinent case law found not actionable).

931 Aurora v. Green, 126 Ill. App. 3d 684, 468 N.E.2d 610 (1984). *But see* State *ex rel.* Corbin v. United Energy Corp., 151 Ariz. 45, 725 P.2d 752 (Ct. App. 1986); E.F. Hutton & Co. v. Youngblood, 708 S.W.2d 865 (Tex. App. 1986), *rev'd in part on other grounds*, 741 S.W.2d 363 (Tex. 1987) (attorney fee award reversed); Winton v. Johnson & Dix Fuel Corp., 515 A.2d 371 (Vt. 1986).

932 Aurora v. Green, 126 Ill. App. 3d 684, 467 N.E.2d 610 (1984).

933 Fidelity & Guar. Ins. Underwriters, Inc. v. Saenz, 865 S.W.2d 103 (Tex. App. 1993) (adjuster misrepresented future policy benefits), *rev'd on other grounds*, 925 S.W.2d 607 (Tex. 1996) (no actual damages shown, so plaintiff can not recover).

934 Winton v. Johnson & Dix Fuel Corp., 515 A.2d 371 (Vt. 1986).

935 *Id.*

5.2.9 Merchant's Slow Payment on Judgment Owed Consumer

There is nothing unfair about someone who can not afford to pay an obligation not paying that obligation. But merchants, creditors, and others may refuse to pay judgments owed consumers, or may pay very slowly, based on a calculated decision that the consumer can not force them to pay. Where a judgment is relatively small, a merchant may believe that the cost to the consumer of trying to collect the judgment will outweigh the amount that will be recovered.

In this situation, one response for the consumer, instead of just collecting on the old judgment, is to bring a new UDAP case seeking treble, punitive, and/or statutory damages, plus attorney fees for the merchant's failure to pay the old judgment. The availability of UDAP attorney fees may be particularly attractive where the consumer can not recover fees for efforts to collect the underlying judgment. The UDAP action can also be brought as a class action on behalf of all consumers whose judgments the merchant has not satisfied, or where the merchant was slow in making payment.

Another situation where a UDAP claim may make sense is where a merchant is avoiding paying a large judgment by keeping all its assets in sister corporations or in the names of individuals, while continuing to do business in the state. In this situation, a UDAP claim can be brought against the sister corporations and individuals, based on their participation with the merchant in evading the consumer judgment. In some states, the consumer can seek UDAP multiple damages, attorney fees, and an injunction against these entities conducting business in the state until the judgment is satisfied.

Thus in one case, a court has decided that it is a UDAP violation for a merchant to fail to satisfy a judgment in favor of a consumer while the merchant continues to engage in consumer transactions in Ohio.[936] A consumer's UDAP claim can proceed against sister corporations and a related individual for treble the amount of the $250,000 (i.e., $750,000), plus attorney fees. The court's decision that the UDAP claim could be pursued quickly led to a settlement in excess of the original $250,000 judgment, but less than the full $750,000 in treble damages that were sought.

In a similar case between two merchants, a corporation has been found to have engaged in a UDAP violation where it failed to pay an amount owed another corporation. The unfair practice was not the mere nonpayment, but that the nonpayment was based on the business judgment that it would cost the other corporation too much to collect the full amount, and that this would force a settlement for a lesser amount.[937] Likewise, an automobile dealer that engages in dilatory, obstructive and inconsistent actions and refuses to abide by an order under the state lemon law violates the state's UDAP statute.[938]

5.3 Insurance

5.3.1 Introduction

UDAP application to insurance practices is both complicated and of special practical importance. A frequent and substantial consumer problem is insurer nonpayment or delay in making claims payments. Related to this, an insurance policy's coverage may be less than promised. Insurers have used "twisting" and other unfair schemes to sell insurance that was not needed by the consumer or not in the consumer's best interests. Insurance policies may be overpriced. Special problems arise in the sale of credit insurance, lender force-placed insurance, and insurance "packed" with credit products.

The complexity of UDAP application to insurance practices stems in a large degree from state unfair insurance practices legislation that exists side by side with the UDAP statute. Does the state insurance legislation displace the UDAP statute or does it offer a guide to using the UDAP statute to challenge insurance practices?

Another complexity with insurance practices involves the number of potential parties involved. The consumer can be the individual who purchased the insurance, or can be an accident victim who wants to collect under the policy. Agents and brokers, claims adjusters and multiple insurers can further add to the cast of players.

This section first addresses the interrelationship of UDAP and state unfair insurance practices statutes. Then it examines UDAP principles of general applicability to insurance practices, and finally it presents four special cases of credit insurance, force-placed insurance, and non-credit insurance packed with a credit transaction, and mortgage insurance. This section must also be read in conjunction with § 2.3.1, *supra*, examining the scope of state UDAP statutes in relation to insurance practices.

936 George J. Goudreau, Jr., Trust v. North Shore Investment Co., 1998 WL 1284135 (Ohio C. P. Sept. 22, 1998). *See also* State *ex rel.* Celebrezze v. AAA Building Services, Inc., Case No. 89-CV-01-144 (Ohio C.P. Franklin Cty. 1990); State *ex rel.* Celebrezze v. Hall, Case No. 82-2664 (Ohio C.P. Lucas Cty. 1983).

937 Arthur D. Little, Inc. v. Dooyang Corp., 147 F.3d 47 (1st Cir. 1998) (Mass. law).

938 Herb Chambers of Auburn, Inc. v. Director of Office of Consumer Affairs and Bus. Reg., 60 Mass. App. Ct. 1123, 805 N.E.2d 532 (Mass. App. Ct. 2004).

5.3.2 Relation of UDAP to State Unfair Insurance Practices Act (UNIP) Legislation

5.3.2.1 UNIP Legislation Described

Every state has adopted legislation defining and prohibiting unfair methods of competition and unfair or deceptive acts and practices in the business of insurance.[939] This "unfair insurance practices" (UNIP) legislation applies broadly to all lines of insurance and is patterned after a model statute promulgated by the National Association of Insurance Commissioners (NAIC).[940]

The UNIP legislation, largely passed in order to avoid FTC and other federal regulatory authority over the insurance industry,[941] is nevertheless important to the presentation of UDAP claims against insurers and their agents. The UNIP statute applies to both insurers and insurance agents.[942] One court has ruled, however, that it does not apply to entities that are self-insured.[943] Similarly, a state's UNIP statute may not apply to a nonprofit joint underwriting association created by the state legislature to assure the availability of malpractice insurance.[944]

The typical UNIP statute lists specific practices that are considered unfair. Louisiana holds its statute's list to be exclusive rather than illustrative,[945] but this question will depend on the rules of construction and legislative history in each state. UNIP statutes are constitutional even though they impose duties on insurers that are not imposed on insureds and typically exclude workers' compensation insurance.[946]

Most UNIP legislation allows the insurance commissioner to promulgate regulations specifying in more detail what practices are unfair or deceptive.[947] Consequently, UDAP practitioners should always analyze any applicable insurance department regulations before utilizing a specific UNIP prohibition.[948] It may also be worth discovering if the state insurance commissioner has issued written decisions in administrative proceedings under the UNIP statute clarifying what practices are unfair and deceptive. Finally, there is a good argument that practices found unfair and deceptive in the NAIC model bill are UDAP violations even if the state UNIP statute does not include such an itemized prohibition. The NAIC model is updated more frequently than most state UNIP statutes.

---

939 Ala. Code §§ 27-12-1 to 27-12-24; Alaska Stat. §§ 21.36.010 to 21.36.460; Ariz. Rev. Stat. Ann. §§ 20-441 to 20-476; Ark. Stat. Ann. §§ 23-66-201 to 23-66-215, 23-66-601 to 23-66-610; Cal. Ins. Code §§ 790.01 to 790.10; Colo. Rev. Stat. §§ 10-3-1101 to 10-3-1114, 10-4-401 to 10-4-421; Conn. Gen. Stat. §§ 38a-815 to 38a-832; Del. Code Ann. tit. 18, §§ 2301 to 2318; Fla. Stat. §§ 626.951 to 626.99295; Ga. Code §§ 33-6-1 to 33-6-37; Haw. Rev. Stat. §§ 431:13-101 to 431:13-204; Idaho Code Ann. §§ 41-1301 to 41-1337; 215 Ill. Comp. Stat. Ann. §§ 5/421 to 5/434; Ind. Code §§ 27-4-1-1 to 27-4-1-19; Iowa Code §§ 507B.1 to 507B.14; Kan. Stat. Ann. §§ 40-2401 to 40-2421; Ky. Stat. Ann. §§ 304.12-010 to 304.12-270; La. Rev. Stat. Ann. §§ 22:1201 to 22:1214, 22:652 to 22.652.4; Me. Rev. Stat. Ann. tit. 24A, §§ 2151 to 2187; Md. Ins. Code Ann. §§ 27-101 to 913; Mass. Gen. Laws ch. 176D, §§ 1-14; Mich. Comp. Laws §§ 500.2001 to 2093; Minn. Stat. §§ 72A.17 to 72A.327; Miss. Code Ann. §§ 83-5-29 to 83-5-51; Mo. Rev. Stat. §§ 375.930 to 375.948; Mont. Code Ann. §§ 33-18-101 to 33-18-1006; Neb. Rev. Stat. §§ 44-1521 to 44-1544; Nev. Rev. Stat. §§ 686A.010 to 686A.280; N.H. Rev. Stat. Ann. §§ 417:1 to 417:30; N.J. Rev. Stat. §§ 17:29B-1 to 17:29B-19, 17B:30-1 to 17B:30-22; N.M. Stat. Ann. §§ 59A-16-1 to 59A-16-30; N.Y. Ins. Law §§ 2123, 2401-2613, 4224; N.C. Gen. Stat. § 58-63-1 to 58-63-65; N.D. Cent. Code §§ 26.1-04-01 to 26.1-04-19; Ohio Rev. Code Ann. §§ 3901.19 to 3901.221; Okla. Stat. tit. 36, §§ 1201 to 1219; Or. Rev. Stat. §§ 746.005 to 746.270; Pa. Stat. Ann. tit. 40, §§ 1171.1 to 1171.15; R.I. Gen. Laws §§ 27-29-1 to 27-29-17.4; S.C. Code Ann. §§ 38-57-10 to 38-57-320; S.D. Codified Laws Ann. §§ 58-33-1 to 58-33-89; Tenn. Code Ann. §§ 56-8-101 to 56-8-306; Tex. Ins. Code Ann. §§ 541.001 to 541.454; Utah Code Ann. §§ 31A-23a-402 to 31A-23-302; Vt. Stat. Ann. tit. 8, §§ 4721 to 4726; Va. Code Ann. §§ 38.2-500 to 38.2-517; Wash. Rev. Code §§ 48.30.005 to 48.30.330; W. Va. Code Ann. §§ 33-11-1 to 33-11-10, 33-11A-1 to 16; Wis. Stat. §§ 628.31 to 628.49; Wyo. Stat. §§ 26-13-101 to 26-13-124.

940 National Association of Ins. Commissioners, Model Regulation Service, 900-1 (NIARS Corp. 1984).

941 The McCarran-Ferguson Act, 15 U.S.C. §§ 1011–1015 (enacted in 1945) provides that federal antitrust law and the Federal Trade Commission Act "shall be applicable to the business of insurance to the extent such business is not regulated by State law." 15 U.S.C. § 1012(b). Federal courts interpret § 1012 as allowing state regulatory law to preempt the federal law described in § 1012(b), even though the state law is not effectively enforced or does not allow private litigants a right of recovery. 11 Holmes, Appleman on Insurance 2d, §§ 75.2 and 75.4 (1999 with supplements).

942 Fillinger v. Northwestern Agency, Inc., 938 P.2d 1347 (Mont. 1997).

943 Davidson v. American Freightways, Inc., 25 S.W.3d 94 (Ky. 2000).

944 Poznik v. Massachusetts Medical Professional Ins. Ass'n, 417 Mass. 48, 628 N.E.2d 1 (1994). *Cf.* Morrison v. Toys R Us, Inc., 441 Mass. 451, 806 N.E.2d 388 (Mass. 2004) (noting plaintiff's concession that self-insured retailer was not engaged in business of insurance so was not covered by UNIP statute).

945 Theriot v. Midland Risk Ins. Co., 694 So. 2d 184 (La. 1997).

946 Farmland Mut. Ins. Co. v. Johnson, 36 S.W.3d 368 (Ky. App. 2000).

947 Associated Agents, Inc. v. Department of Ins. & Fin., 107 Or. App. 654, 813 P.2d 1089 (1991) (upholding regulations limiting commissions for sale of Medigap policies); Federated Am. Ins. Co. v. Marquardt, 108 Wash. 2d 651, 741 P.2d 18 (1987) (upholding regulations establishing no-fault PIP minimum coverage); Escalante v. Sentry Ins., 49 Wash. App. 375, 743 P.2d 832 (1987) (violation of UNIP regulations *per se* UDAP violation).

948 *See* American Community Mut. Ins. Co. v. Commissioner of Ins., 195 Mich. App. 351, 491 N.W.2d 597 (1992).

5.3.2.2 Effect of UNIP Statute in a UDAP Action

5.3.2.2.1 UNIP standards as guides for determining UDAP violations

In most jurisdictions, a UNIP violation will be a *per se* UDAP violation since the UNIP statute is a legislative determination of what insurance practices are unfair or deceptive.[949] The same holds for violations of state insurance department regulations interpreting these standards.[950] In any event, if a UNIP statute prohibits a practice, consumer attorneys should certainly point this out to the court in arguing that the practice is unfair or deceptive under a UDAP statute.

On the other hand, where a UNIP statute defines certain practices as unfair, this does not mean that practices not enumerated in the UNIP statute can not be UDAP violations.[951] Similarly, where a practice is not a UNIP violation because no pattern of misconduct is shown, the practice can

949 Continental Ins. Co. v. Bahnan, 216 F.3d 150 (1st Cir. 2000) (Massachusetts UNIP violation can be basis for UDAP claim by consumer but not by business under § 11); Hipsky v. Allstate Ins. Co., 304 F. Supp. 2d 284 (D. Conn. 2004); Central Carolina Bank and Trust Co. v. Security Life of Denver Ins. Co., 247 F. Supp. 2d 791 (M.D.N.C. 2003); Hangarter v. Paul Revere Life Ins. Co., 236 F. Supp. 2d 1069 (N.D. Cal. 2002); Martin v. Am. Equity Ins. Co., 185 F. Supp. 2d 162 (D. Conn. 2002); Riordan v. Nationwide Mut. Fire Ins. Co., 756 F. Supp. 732 (S.D.N.Y. 1990); Stevens v. Superior Court, 89 Cal. Rptr. 2d 370 (Ct. App. 1999) (Unfair Competition Act allows private cause of action for performing unlicensed insurance transactions even though UNIP bars private cause of action for other unlawful insurance business practices); Macomber v. Travelers Prop. & Cas. Corp., 261 Conn. 620, 804 A.2d 180 (2002); Hopkins v. Liberty Mut. Ins. Co., 750 N.E.2d 943 (Mass. 2001); Smith v. Globe Life Ins., 597 N.W.2d 28 (Mich. 1999) (consumer may bring UDAP suit for UNIP violation; insurance department's regulation of insurance does not displace UDAP claim. Note that the legislature has now amended the UDAP statute to exclude insurers.); Gray v. North Carolina Ins. Underwriting Ass'n, 352 N.C. 61, 529 S.E.2d 676 (2000) (violations of not only UNIP prohibition of false advertising, but also prohibition against unfair claim settlement procedures, is UDAP violation); Pearce v. American Defender Life Ins. Co., 343 S.E.2d 174 (N.C. 1986); Murray v. Nationwide Mut. Ins. Co., 472 S.E.2d 358 (N.C. App. 1996); Miller v. Nationwide Mut. Ins. Co., 112 N.C. App. 295, 435 S.E.2d 537 (1993); Kron Medical Corp. v. Collier Cobb & Assoc., 107 N.C. App. 331, 420 S.E.2d 192 (1992); Vail v. Texas Farm Bureau Mut. Ins. Co., 754 S.W.2d 129 (Tex. 1988); Stewart Title Guaranty Co. v. Sterling, 772 S.W.2d 242 (Tex. App. 1989), *rev'd in part on other grounds*, 822 S.W.2d 1 (Tex. 1991); Indus. Indemnity Co. v. Kallevig, 114 Wash. 2d 907, 792 P.2d 520 (1990); Salois v. Mutual of Omaha Ins. Co., 90 Wash. 2d 355, 581 P.2d 1349 (1978); Levy v. North Am. Co. for Life & Health Ins., 90 Wash. 2d 846, 586 P.2d 845 (1978); Keller v. Allstate Ins. Co., 915 P.2d 1140 (Wash. App. 1996); Urban v. Mid-Century Ins., 905 P.2d 404 (Wash. App. 1995); Estate of Hall v. HAPO Federal Credit Union, 73 Wash. App. 359, 869 P.2d 116 (1994). *See also* Guinn v. American Integrity Ins. Co., 568 So. 2d 760 (Ala. 1990) (violation of UNIP statute given consideration in action for fraud); Miller v. Risk Mgmt. Foundation, 36 Mass. App. Ct. 411, 632 N.E.2d 841 (1994) (trial court appropriately looked to UNIP standards for aid in interpreting UDAP statute); MacGillivary v. W. Dana Bartlett Ins. Agency, 14 Mass. App. Ct. 52, 436 N.E.2d 964 (1982); Walts v. First Union Mortgage Corp., 686 N.Y.S.2d 428 (App. Div. 1999) (state mortgage insurance law can be enforced via UDAP action even though it does not create its own private cause of action); McKinnon v. International Fidelity Ins. Co., 704 N.Y.S.2d 774, 182 Misc. 2d 517 (N.Y. Sup. Ct. 1999) (bail bond statute can be enforced through UDAP action even though it does not create its own private cause of action); Luckenbill v. Hamilton Mut. Ins. Co., 2001 Ohio App. LEXIS 3856 (Aug. 31, 2001) (courts can consider UNIP standards within the context of another cause of action); Seattle Pump Co. v. Traders & General Ins. Co., 970 P.2d 361 (Wash. App. 1999) (violation of statutory duty of good faith can be UDAP violation). *Cf.* Lites v. Great Am. Ins. Co., 2000 U.S. Dist. LEXIS 9036 (E.D. Pa. June 23, 2000) (can not base UDAP claim on UNIP violation, but can base it on facts that would also show a UNIP violation); John Beaudette, Inc. v. Sentry Ins., 94 F. Supp. 2d 77 (D. Mass. 1999) (UNIP violation is UDAP violation only in suits brought by consumers, not business plaintiffs); AICCO, Inc. v. Insurance Co. of N. Am., 90 Cal. App. 4th 579, 109 Cal. Rptr. 2d 359 (2001) (even where can not base UDAP claim on UNIP violation, practices in addition to UNIP violation make the UDAP claim actionable). *But see* Smith v. Nationwide Mut. Fire Ins. Co., 935 F. Supp. 616 (W.D. Pa. 1996) (UDAP claim can not be based on UNIP violation); Kiewit Constr. Co. v. Westchester Fire Ins. Co., 878 F. Supp. 298 (D. Mass. 1995) (commercial plaintiff can not sue under § 11 of Massachusetts' UDAP statute for a UNIP violation); Coors v. Security Life of Denver Ins. Co., 2003 WL 22019815 (Colo. App. Aug. 28, 2003); Gordon v. Pennsylvania Blue Shield, 548 A.2d 600 (Pa. Super. Ct. 1988) (no private UNIP, so no UNIP violation to trigger *per se* UDAP violation); Griffin v. Allstate Ins. Co., 44 Pa. D. & C.4th 261, 1999 Phila. Cty. Rptr. LEXIS 22 (C.P. 1999) (no UDAP claim for violation of requirement of motor vehicle insurance statute that did not itself provide a remedy). *But cf.* Continental Western Ins. Co. v. Heritage Estates Mut. Housing Ass'n, 77 P.3d 911 (Colo. App. 2003) (UDAP remedies not available for UNIP violation; plaintiff did not assert a UDAP claim in any event).

950 Industrial Indemnity Co. v. Kallevig, 114 Wash. 2d 907, 792 P.2d 520 (1990); Anderson v. State Farm Mut. Ins. Co., 2 P.3d 1029 (Wash. App. 2000); *see also* Vail v. Texas Farm Bureau Mut. Ins. Co., 754 S.W.2d 129 (Tex. 1988); Strother v. Capital Bankers Life Ins. Co., 68 Wash. App. 224, 842 P.2d 504 (1992), *rev'd on other grounds*, 124 Wash. 2d 1, 873 P.2d 1185 (1994); *cf.* Dimarzo v. American Mut. Ins. Co., 389 Mass. 85, 449 N.E.2d 1189 (1983). *But cf.* Underwriters at Lloyds v. Denali Seafoods, Inc., 729 F. Supp. 721 (W.D. Wash. 1990) (where regulation itself requires that standards be violated with such frequency as to indicate general business practice, private action based on regulation violation must prove that insurer violated standards with such frequency).

951 M. DeMatteo Constr. Co. v. Century Indemnity Co., 182 F. Supp. 2d 146 (D. Mass. 2001); United States Fire Ins. Co. v. Nationwide Mut. Ins. Co., 735 F. Supp. 1320 (E.D.N.C. 1990). *But see* Lees v. Middlesex Ins. Co., 229 Conn. 842, 643 A.2d 1282 (1994) (where UDAP claim is based on same alleged practice as UNIP claim, proof of all the elements of the UNIP violation is required for the UDAP claim); Mead v. Burns, 199 Conn. 651, 509 A.2d 11 (1986) (UDAP claim only available if plaintiff shows UNIP violation).

still be a UDAP violation.[952] However, a UDAP claim predicated on bad faith will fail if an identical UNIP claim fails.[953]

5.3.2.2.2 UNIP action should not displace UDAP remedy

UDAP practitioners will still have to deal with questions as to whether insurance practices are within the UDAP statute's scope, such as where a UDAP statute exempts practices regulated by state agencies.[954] While some courts find a UNIP statute preempts a UDAP claim, most courts find otherwise.[955]

5.3.2.2.3 Exhaustion of UNIP administrative remedies as precondition to UDAP action

Another issue raised by the existence of the UNIP statute is whether a UDAP claimant must first exhaust UNIP remedies, that is whether the consumer must seek administrative relief before pursuing a UDAP action. State court decisions normally decline to invoke exhaustion if the remedy provided by an administrative proceeding would be inadequate to redress the claimant's injury.[956]

Most UNIP statutes only allow an administrative proceeding if it is in the public interest, implying that the insurance commissioner should not conduct an administrative proceeding to resolve uniquely individual complaints. If the commissioner refuses to hold a hearing or does not allow the consumer to intervene, the exhaustion requirement should not apply. General administrative law recognizes that a court should not stay an action in favor of an administrative determination if the administrative agency declines to resolve the issues presented by the claim.[957] Nor should a consumer who asserts a civil conspiracy claim based in part on violation of a UNIP statute, rather than an implied cause of action under the UNIP statute itself, be required to exhaust administrative remedies.[958]

Even if a court is the appropriate forum to hear an insurance challenge, the insurer may still raise the primary jurisdiction doctrine, particularly where the insurance department is investigating the same matter.[959] The doctrine comes into play whenever enforcement of a claim requires resolution of issues within the special competence of a regulatory agency. The action is suspended awaiting receipt of the views from the administrative agency; the action should not be dismissed.[960] And every insurance matter is not one within the special expertise of the insurance department where the doctrine should be imposed.[961]

5.3.2.3 Private UNIP Actions as Alternative to UDAP Action

5.3.2.3.1 Utility of a private UNIP claim

UNIP statutes generally do not have explicit private causes of action, and consequently do not offer attorney fees, statutory or multiple damages. Nevertheless, there are situations where a UNIP claim is advisable.

In some states, consumers may be able to recover consequential damages,[962] punitive damages,[963] or attorney fees[964] as a UNIP remedy. In addition, in certain states, insurance practices will be exempt from the UDAP statute, or the UNIP statute will be seen as displacing UDAP coverage.[965] Alternatively, the UDAP statute of limitations

952 High Country Arts & Craft v. Hartford Fire Ins. Co., 126 F.3d 629 (4th Cir. 1997) (North Carolina).

953 Greil v. Geico, 184 F. Supp. 2d 541 (N.D. Tex. 2002).

954 *See* §§ 2.3.1, 2.3.3, *supra.*

955 *See* § 2.3.1.3, *supra.*

956 *See* §§ 2.3.1, 2.3.3.6, *supra*; Mead v. Burns, 199 Conn. 651, 509 A.2d 11 (1986) (exhaustion of administrative remedies unnecessary); Escajeda v. Cigna Ins. Co., 934 S.W.2d 402 (Tex. App. 1996) (exhaustion of workers' compensation remedies not required as to claims not within workers' compensation act); Montgomery v. Blue Cross & Blue Shield of Texas, Inc., 923 S.W.2d 147 (Tex. App. 1996) (no exhaustion of administrative remedies if agency did not have authority or jurisdiction to handle extracontractual claims). *But see* Karlin v. Zalta, 154 Cal. App. 3d 953, 201 Cal. Rptr. 379 (1984); Greenberg v. Equitable Life Ins. Society of the United States, 110 Cal. Rptr. 470, 34 Cal. App. 1001 (1973); Liability Investigative Fund Effort, Inc. v. Medical Malpractice Joint Underwriting Ass'n, 409 Mass. 734, 569 N.E.2d 797 (1991) (plaintiff must file administrative complaint first since Insurance Commissioner has primary jurisdiction); Nelson v. Blue Shield of Massachusetts, Inc., 387 N.E.2d 589 (Mass. 1979) (the UDAP statute has since been amended to eliminate this requirement); Ambassador Ins. Co. v. Feldman, 598 P.2d 630 (Nev. 1979); Moy v. Schreiber Deed Security Co., 572 A.2d 758 (Pa. Super. Ct. 1990) (UDAP plaintiff must exhaust insurance department remedies where UDAP claim is based on violation of insurance laws); Producers Assistance Corp. v. Employers Ins. of Wausau, 934 S.W.2d 796 (Tex. App. 1996) (requiring exhaustion of remedies in a workers' compensation case even if agency can not provide all relief sought).

957 Mezines, Stern & Gauff, Administrative Law ¶ 47.03[1] (1984).

958 Alexander & Alexander v. Evander, 596 A.2d 687 (Md. Ct. Spec. App. 1991).

959 *See* Irvin v. Liberty Life Ins. Co., 2001 U.S. Dist. LEXIS 2935 (E.D. La. Mar. 12, 2001).

960 *See* AICCO, Inc. v. Insurance Co. of N. Am., 90 Cal. App. 4th 579, 109 Cal. Rptr. 2d 359 (2001).

961 *Id. See also* Chabner v. United of Omaha Life Ins. Co., 225 F.3d 1042 (9th Cir. 2000) (Cal. law).

962 *See* Princess Boat Rental, Inc. v. McGriff, Seibels & Williams, Inc., 1999 U.S. Dist. LEXIS 16134 (E.D. La. Oct. 14, 1999); State Farm Fire & Cas. Ins. Co. v. Vandiver, 970 S.W.2d 731 (Tex. App. 1998) (mental anguish damages require showing that insurer acted knowingly).

963 Poling v. Motorists Mut. Ins. Co., 192 W. Va. 46, 450 S.E.2d 635 (1994).

964 *See* Dunn v. Southern Farm Bureau Cas. Ins. Co., 991 S.W.2d 467 (Tex. App. 1998).

965 *See* § 2.3.1, *supra.*

or restrictions on the type of consumers or transactions can also limit the UDAP statute's applicability. In these situations, a private UNIP remedy may be helpful.

The best practice is usually to allege both UDAP and UNIP violations. However, care should be taken to distinguish between the two at trial, so that the verdict or judgment is clear as to which theory serves as the basis for a damage award.[966]

Where a jurisdiction does not recognize a private right of action under the UNIP statute,[967] another alternative is to base a bad faith claim on an insurer's violation of UNIP standards.[968] In fact, because punitive damages are a potential remedy under a bad faith claim, it may make sense to bring a bad faith claim even in jurisdictions that allow private UNIP causes of action. (In some states, a bad faith claim alone may not support punitive damages, but may support additional damages under the UDAP statute.[969])

Some courts allow UNIP and bad faith actions because the public policy supporting each is different.[970] Nevertheless, some courts find the UNIP cause of action has preempted the tort claim,[971] or has provided grounds not to adopt the bad faith theory.[972] Similarly, a minority of courts hold that certain UNIP prohibitions designed chiefly to insure the financial stability of an insurer and the insurer's compliance with its commission-approved rate structure preempt an insured's claim under a contract theory.[973]

5.3.2.3.2 Implying a private UNIP remedy

A number of state UNIP statutes have an explicit private remedy, but these are often limited in some regard. The Texas legislation provides a private right of action for unfair and deceptive acts,[974] but not for unfair claim settlement practices.[975] The Maine statute provides a private cause of action for certain specified violations.[976] Other statutes may only apply to claims settlement practices or only provide a private right of action through an administrative proceeding.[977]

---

966 Johnson & Higgins of Texas, Inc. v. Kenneco Energy, Inc., 962 S.W.2d 507 (Tex. 1998).

967 *See* § 5.3.2.3.2, *infra*.

968 Lewis v. Aetna U.S. Healthcare, Inc., 78 F. Supp. 2d 1202 (N.D. Okla. 1999) (Oklahoma refers to UNIP standards in determining bad faith claims); Wailua Assocs. v. Aetna Cas. & Sur. Co., 183 F.R.D. 550 (D. Haw. 1998) (plaintiff allowed to plead UNIP violations as evidence of bad faith); Hightower v. Farmers Ins. Exchange, 38 Cal. App. 4th 853, 45 Cal. Rptr. 348 (1995); Transamerica Premier Ins. Co. v. Brighton School District 27J, 940 P.2d 348 (Colo. 1997); Ingalls v. Paul Revere Life Ins. Group. 1997 N.D. 43, 561 N.W.2d 273 (N.D. 1997); Romano v. Nationwide Mut. Ins. Co., 646 A.2d 1228 (Pa. Super. 1994); Hollock v. Erie Ins. Exchange, 54 Pa. D. & C.4th 449 (C.P. 2002). *See also* Cary v. United of Omaha Life Ins. Co., 68 P.3d 462 (Colo. 2003) (referring to UNIP standards as supporting bad faith claim).

969 State Farm Fire & Cas. Co. v. Simmons, 963 S.W.2d 42 (Tex. 1998).

970 Correa v. Pennsylvania Manufacturers Ass'n Ins. Co., 618 F. Supp. 915 (D. Del. 1985); Aetna Casualty & Surety Co. v. Broadway Arms Corp., 281 Ark. 128, 664 S.W.2d 463 (1984); Employers Equitable Life Ins. Co. v. Williams, 282 Ark. 29, 665 S.W.2d 873 (1984); *see also* Appel v. Sentry Life Ins. Co., 701 P.2d 634 (Colo. Ct. App. 1985) (UNIP action does not preempt fraud count).

971 Glazewski v. Allstate Ins. Co., 81 Ill. Dec. 349, 126 Ill. App. 3d 401, 466 N.E.2d 1151 (1984), *rev'd in part on other grounds*, 108 Ill. 2d 243, 483 N.E.2d 1263 (1985) (holding that a plaintiff stated a claim for fraud but not for UDAP violation because did not have claim for injunctive relief); Vicente v. Prudential Ins. Co., 105 Md. App. 13, 658 A.2d 1106 (1995) (UNIP statute provides exclusive remedy and preempts tort claims); Lawton v. Great Southwest Fire Ins. Co., 392 A.2d 576 (N.H. 1978); Farris v. United States Fidelity & Guaranty Co., 587 P.2d 1015 (Or. 1978). *But see* Zappone v. Liberty Life Ins. Co., 349 Md. 45, 706 A.2d 1060 (1998).

972 Spencer v. Aetna Life & Casualty Ins. Co., 611 P.2d 149 (Kan. 1980); D'Ambrosio v. Pennsylvania Nat'l Mut. Casualty Ins. Co., 431 A.2d 966 (Pa. 1981); Herzon v. Blue Cross of Lehigh Valley 17 Pa. D. & C. 80 (Pa. C.P. 1980).

973 Homestead Supplies, Inc. v. Executive Life Ins. Co., 81 Cal. App. 3d 978, 147 Cal. Rptr. 22 (1978); Hyde Ins. Agency, Inc. v. Dixie Leasing Corp., 26 N.C. App. 138, 215 S.E.2d 162 (1975). *But see* Key Sys. Transit Lines v. Pacific Employers Ins. Co., 345 P.2d 257 (Cal. 1959); Contractor's Safety Ass'n v. California Compensation Ins. Co., 307 P.2d 626 (Cal. 1957). Some cases have held that although recovery of a rebate or promised inducement is precluded by the UNIP statutory prohibition, rescission by the insured under a theory of fraud is still possible. *See* Jamision v. Southern States Life Ins. Co., 3 Ariz. App. 131, 412 P.2d 306 (1966); R. D. Reeder Lathing Co. v. Cypress Ins. Co., 3 Cal. App. 998, 84 Cal. Rptr. 98 (1970).

974 Tex. Ins. Code Ann. §§ 541.151 to 541.162 (individual and class actions, including treble damages and attorney fees, for violation of ch. 541 prohibitions); Austin v. Servac Shipping Line, Ltd., 610 F. Supp. 229 (E.D. Tex. 1985), *rev'd in part on other grounds*, 794 F.2d 941 (5th Cir. 1986) (damages); Raincy-Mapes v. Queen Charters, Inc., 729 S.W.2d 907 (Tex. App. 1987) (treble damages mandatory); Aetna Casualty & Surety Co. v. Martin Surgical Supply Co., 689 S.W.2d 263 (Tex. App. 1985).

975 McKnight v. Ideal Mut. Ins. Co., 534 F. Supp. 362 (N.D. Tex. 1982) (no private right of action for unfair claim settlement cases); Maryland Ins. Co. v. Head Indus. Coatings & Services, Inc., 906 S.W.2d 218 (Tex. App. 1995) (no private right of action exists under section of Insurance Code specifically regulating claims settlement practices; however a private right does exist for those same practices under Insurance Code section prohibiting unfair and deceptive practices generally); *rev'd on other grounds*, 938 S.W.2d 27 (Tex. 1996) (insurer does not owe insured a duty of good faith and fair dealing to investigate and defend claims by a third party against the insured); Vail v. Texas Farm Bureau Mut. Ins. Co., 754 S.W.2d 129 (Tex. App. 1988) (same); Lone Star Life Ins. Co. v. Griffin, 574 S.W.2d 576 (Tex. Civ. App. 1978) (same).

976 24-A Me. Rev. Stat. § 2436-A(1). *See* Curtis v. Allstate Ins. Co., 787 A.2d 760 (Me. 2002).

977 *See* Fla. Stat. §§ 624.155 (damages, attorney fees, and, in certain situations, punitive damages); Kan. Stat. Ann. §§ 40-2407(3), 40-2411(c); La. Rev. Stat. § 22:1220 (private cause of action with awards of up to double damages or five thousand dollars, whichever is greater); Mass. Gen. Laws ch. 176D, § 7 (a court

Courts in thirty-one states have not implied a private right of action under the UNIP statute,[978] courts in five states have

may award punitive damages to an individual based on the commissioner's findings of a UNIP); Mont. Code Ann. § 33-18-242 (private cause of action for designated violation; punitive damages available); N.H. Rev. Stat. Ann. §§ 417:19-417:22 (finding of insurance commissioner is *prima facie* evidence in consumer's statutory proceeding to obtain damages resulting from UNIP violation); N.M. Stat. Ann. §§ 59A-16-14, 59A-16-30 (private remedy for UNIP violations, including debtor coercion); N.C. Gen. Stat. § 75-1.1 (state UDAP statute covers all UNIP violations); S.D. Codified Laws Ann. § 58-33-46.1 (explicit private right of action for damages and attorneys fees); *see also* Fla. Stat. § 624.155(2)(a); Blue Cross & Blue Shield v. Halifax Ins. Plan, 961 F. Supp. 271 (M.D. Fla. 1997) (plaintiff filed suit under Florida UNIP statute without first providing written notice to state insurance department; court dismissed case without prejudice and granted motion for leave to amend complaint); Peris v. Safeco Ins. Co., 916 P.2d 780 (Mont. 1996) (discussing requirements for suit by insured); O'Fallon v. Farmers Ins. Exchange, 859 P.2d 1008 (Mont. 1993); Dees v. American Nat'l Fire Ins. Co., 861 P.2d 141 (Mont. 1993); Quality Auto Parts v. Bluff City Buick, 876 S.W.2d 818 (Tenn. 1994) (private suit for UNIP violation); *Cf.* 42 Penn. Consol. Stat. § 8371 (actual and punitive damages for bad faith claim settlement policies); Henry v. State Farm Ins. Co., 788 F. Supp. 241 (E.D. Pa. 1992).

978 *Alabama*: Farlow v. Union Central Life Ins. Co., 874 F.2d 791 (11th Cir. 1989) (Alabama law); Allen v. State Farm Fire & Cas. Co., 59 F. Supp. 2d 1217 (S.D. Ala. 1999).

Alaska: Peter v. Schumacher Enterprises, Inc., 22 P.3d 481 (Alaska 2001) (but a private cause of action is available for violation of insurance law that requires insurer to offer uninsured and underinsured motorist coverage); O.K. Lumber Co. v. Providence Washington Ins. Co., 759 P.2d 523 (Alaska 1988) (no private UNIP cause of action, particularly where third-party claimant).

Colorado: Transamerica Premier Ins. Co. v. Brighton School District 27J, 923 P.2d 328 (Colo. Ct. App. 1997); Schnacker v. State Farm Mut. Auto Ins., 843 P.2d 102 (Colo. Ct. App. 1992); Farmers Group, Inc. v. Trimble, 658 P.2d 1370 (Colo. Ct. App. 1982).

Delaware: Brown v. Liberty Mut. Ins. Co., 1999 Del. Super. LEXIS 525 (Super. Ct. Aug. 20, 1999); Mentis v. Delaware Am. Life Ins. Co., 1999 Del. Super. LEXIS 419 (July 28, 1999); Yardley v. U. S. Healthcare, Inc., 698 A.2d 979 (Del. Super. Ct. 1996), *aff'd without op.*, 693 A.2d 1083 (Del. 1997).

Florida: Keehn v. Carolina Casualty Ins. Co., 758 F.2d 1522 (11th Cir. 1985) (Florida law).

Hawaii: Genovia v. Jackson Nat'l Life Ins. Co., 795 F. Supp. 1036 (D. Haw. 1992); Hough v. Pacific Ins. Co., 927 P.2d 858 (Haw. 1996); Hunt v. First Ins. Co., 922 P.2d 976 (Haw. Ct. App. 1996).

Idaho: State v. Bunker Hill Co., 647 F. Supp. 1064 (D. Idaho 1986); White v. Uniguard Mut. Ins. Co., 112 Idaho 94, 730 P.2d 1014 (1986); Greene v. Truck Ins. Exchange, 753 P.2d 274 (Idaho Ct. App. 1988).

Illinois: Impex Shrimp & Fish Co. v. Aetna Cas. & Sur. Co., 686 F. Supp. 183 (N.D. Ill. 1985); Elrad v. United Life & Acc. Ins. Co., 624 F. Supp. 742 (N.D. Ill. 1985); Scroggins v. Allstate Ins. Co., 30 Ill. Dec. 682, 74 Ill. App. 3d 1027, 393 N.E.2d 718 (1979).

Iowa: Terra Indus. v. Commonwealth Ins. Co. of Am., 990 F. Supp. 679 (N.D. Iowa 1997); Bates v. Allied Mut. Ins. Co., 467 N.W.2d 255 (Iowa 1991).

Kansas: Bonnell v. Bank of America, 284 F. Supp. 2d 1284 (D. Kan. 2003); Earth Scientists v. United States Fidelity & Guaranty Co., 619 F. Supp. 1465 (D. Kan. 1985); Spencer v. Aetna Life & Casualty Ins. Co., 611 P.2d 149 (Kan. 1980).

Louisiana: Clausen v. Fidelity & Deposit Co., 660 So. 2d 83 (La. Ct. App. 1995).

Maryland: Magan v. Medical Mut. Liability Ins. Soc., 81 Md. App. 301, 567 A.2d 503 (1989) (consumer has statutory appeal to court from administrative proceedings, but no common law cause of action); *cf.* Alexander & Alexander v. Evander, 596 A.2d 687, 700 n.8 (Md. Ct. Spec. App. 1991) (court assumes, without deciding, that there is no private cause of action, but allows consumers to assert civil conspiracy claim based in part on violation of the statute).

Massachusetts: Thorpe v. Mutual of Omaha Ins. Co., 984 F.2d 541 (1st Cir. 1993); Pariseau v. Albany Int'l Corp., 822 F. Supp. 843 (D. Mass. 1993).

Michigan: Board of Trustees of Michigan State Univ. v. Continental Cas. Co., 730 F. Supp. 1408 (W.D. Mich. 1990); Bell v. League Life Ins. Co., 149 Mich. App. 481, 387 N.W.2d 154 (1986); Crossley v. Allstate Ins. Co., 155 Mich. App. 694, 400 N.W.2d 625 (1986); Safie Enterprises v. Nationwide Mut. Fire Ins. Co., 146 Mich. App. 483, 747 (1985).

Minnesota: Morris v. American Family Mut. Ins. Co. 386 N.W.2d 233 (Minn. 1986); O'Reilly v. Allstate Ins. Co., 474 N.W.2d 221 (Minn. Ct. App. 1991).

Mississippi: Davenport v. St. Paul Fire & Marine Ins. Co., 978 F.2d 927 (5th Cir. 1992); Chain v. General Am. Life Ins. Co., 1996 U.S. Dist. LEXIS 21505 (N.D. Miss. Sept. 25, 1996) (vanishing premium case); Cunningham v. Massachusetts Mut. Life Ins. Co., 1996 U.S. Dist. LEXIS 21408 (N.D. Miss. July 3, 1996) (vanishing premium case); Protective Service Life Ins. Co. v. Carter, 445 So. 2d 215 (Miss. 1983).

Missouri: Dierkes v. Blue Cross & Blue Shield, 991 S.W.2d 662 (Mo. 1999); Wenthe v. Willis Corroon Corp., 932 S.W.2d 791 (Mo. App. 1996).

New Hampshire: Shaheen v. Preferred Mut. Ins. Co., 668 F. Supp. 716 (D.N.H. 1987); Lawton v. Great Southwest Fire Ins. Co., 392 A.2d 576 (N.H. 1978).

New Jersey: Pierzga v. Ohio Casualty Group of Ins. Co., 208 N.J. Super. 40, 504 A.2d 1200 (1986).

New York: Riordan v. Nationwide Mut. Fire Ins. Co., 756 F. Supp. 732 (S.D.N.Y. 1990); New York University v. Continental Ins. Co., 87 N.Y.2d 308, 662 N.E.2d 763 (1995) (no tort cause of action for violation of UNIP duty); Rocanova v. Equitable Life Assurance Soc., 83 N.Y.2d 603, 634 N.E.2d 940 (1994).

North Carolina: First Financial Sav. Bank, Inc. v. American Bankers Ins. Co., 783 F. Supp. 963 (E.D.N.C. 1991).

Ohio: Luckenbill v. Hamilton Mut. Ins. Co., 2001 Ohio App. LEXIS 3856 (Aug. 31, 2001); Elwert v. Pilot Life Ins. Co., 77 Ohio App. 3d 529, 602 N.E.2d 1219 (1991); Strack v. Westfield Cos., 33 Ohio App. 3d 336, 515 N.E.2d 1005 (1986); State *ex rel.* Blue Cross & Blue Shield v. Carroll, 21 Ohio App. 3d 263, 487 N.E.2d 576 (1985).

Oklahoma: Lewis v. Aetna U.S. Healthcare, Inc., 78 F. Supp. 2d 1202 (N.D. Okla. 1999).

Pennsylvania: Caplan v. Fellheimer Eichen, Braverman & Kaskey, 5 F. Supp. 2d 299 (E.D. Pa. 1998); Smith v. Nationwide Mut. Fire Ins. Co., 935 F. Supp. 616 (W.D. Pa. 1996); D'Ambrosio v. Pennsylvania Nat'l Mut. Casualty Ins. Co., 431 A.2d 966 (Pa. 1981); Strutz v. State Farm Mut. Ins. Co., 609

implied such a cause of action,[979] the cases in Connecticut[980] Indiana,[981] and North Dakota[982] are mixed, and California courts, while finding no private right of action for an unfair claim settlement,[983] find such a private cause of action for violation of a California UNIP provision dealing with twisting.[984] Even if a court does not find an implied private cause of action, it might find that a statute or regulation bars an insurance company from invoking a defense.[985]

In general, if a court implies a private right of action under the UNIP statute, then third party claimants (e.g., accident victims) can take advantage of the UNIP remedy as well.[986] The same is true for statutes that provide some kind of explicit private right of action.[987]

A.2d 569 (Pa. Super. Ct. 1992); Moy v. Schreiber Deed Security Co., 572 A.2d 758 (Pa. Super. Ct. 1990).

Rhode Island: Cowdell v. Cambridge Mut. Ins. Co., 808 F.2d 160 (1st Cir. 1986).

South Carolina: Gaskins v. Southern Farm Bur. Cas. Ins. Co., 343 S.C. 666, 541 S.E.2d 269 (App. 2000), *aff'd on other grounds*, 581 S.E.2d 169 (S.C. 2003).

Tennessee: Lindsey v. Allstate Ins. Co., 34 F. Supp. 2d 636 (W.D. Tenn. 1999); Myint v. Allstate Ins. Co., 970 S.W.2d 920 (Tenn. 1998). *But see* Isaac v. Life Investors Ins. Co. of Am., 749 F. Supp. 855 (E.D. Tenn. 1990).

Vermont: Wilder v. Aetna Life & Casualty Ins. Co., 433 A.2d 309 (Vt. 1981).

Virginia: A&E Supply Co. v. Nationwide Mut. Fire Ins. Co., 798 F.2d 669 (4th Cir. 1986).

Wisconsin: N.A.A.C.P. v. American Family Mut. Ins. Co., 978 F.2d 287 (7th Cir. 1992); Kranzush v. Badger State Mut. Casualty Co., 307 N.W.2d 256 (Wis. 1981).

Wyoming: Wilson v. State Farm Mut. Auto Ins. Co., 795 F. Supp. 1077 (D. Wyo. 1992); Herrig v. Herrig, 844 P.2d 487 (Wyo. 1992).

979 *Arizona*: Sparks v. Republic Nat'l Life Ins. Co., 132 Ariz. 529, 647 P.2d 1127 (1982); *see also* Williamson v. Allstate Ins. Co., 204 F.R.D. 641 (D. Ariz. 2001) (private cause of action is available for violation of UNIP prohibition of false advertising, but not for other violations).

Kentucky: State Farm Mut. Auto Ins. Co. v. Reeder, 763 S.W.2d 116 (Ky. 1988); Reker v. The Traveler's Indemnity Co., 2000 Ky. App. LEXIS 67 (Ky. Ct. App. June 23, 2000).

Montana: Fode v. Farmers Ins. Exchange, 719 P.2d 414 (Mont. 1986); Klaudt v. Fink, 658 P.2d 1065 (Mont. 1983); *but see* Shupak v. New York Life Ins. Co., 780 F. Supp. 1328 (D. Mont. 1991).

Nevada: Albert H. Wohlers & Co. v. Bartgis, 969 P.2d 949 (Nev. 1998) (affirming UNIP damage award against insurer without discussion of question of existence of private cause of action).

West Virginia: Weese v. Nationwide Ins. Co., 879 F.2d 115 (4th Cir. 1989); Morgan v. American Family Life Assurance Co., 559 F. Supp. 477 (W.D. Va. 1983); Taylor v. Nationwide Mut. Ins. Co., 2003 WL 22762025 (W. Va. Nov. 21, 2003); Morton v. Amos-Lee Securities, Inc., 195 W. Va. 691, 466 S.E.2d 542 (1995); Russell v. Amerisure Ins. Co., 189 W. Va. 594, 433 S.E.2d 532 (1993); Jenkins v. J. C. Penney Casualty Ins. Co., 280 S.E.2d 252 (W. Va. 1981).

980 Hipsky v. Allstate Ins. Co., 304 F. Supp. 2d 284 (D. Conn. 2004); Glynn v. Bankers Life and Casualty Co., 297 F. Supp. 2d 424 (D. Conn. 2003) (UIPA does not provide for a private cause of action); Martin v. Am. Equity Ins. Co., 185 F. Supp. 2d 162 (D. Conn. 2002) (no private right of action, but UNIP violations are actionable as UDAP violations); Peck v. Public Service Mut. Ins. Co., 114 F. Supp. 2d 51 (D. Conn. 2000) (interpreting Connecticut's direct action statute to allow third party to assert UDAP and UNIP claims against tortfeasor's insurance company after winning judgment against tortfeasor); Baroni v. Western Reserve Life Assurance Co., 1999 Conn. Super. LEXIS 2641 (Conn. Super. Sept. 29, 1999) (concluding that Connecticut superior courts are currently split regarding the availability of private right of action); *see also* D'Alessandro v. Clare, 1999 Conn. Super. LEXIS 864 (Super. Ct. Apr. 1, 1999) (UNIP statute does not give rights to third party claimants, at least until judgment is entered); *cf.* Macomber v. Travelers Prop. & Cas. Corp., 261 Conn. 620, 804 A.2d 180 (2002) (declining to reach issue). *But see* Heyman Assoc. v. Insurance Co., 231 Conn. 756, 653 A.2d 122 (1995) (ruling on private causes of action for UNIP and UDAP violations); Griswold v. Union Labor Life Ins. Co., 186 Conn. 507, 442 A.2d 920 (1982) (private right of action exists for UNIP violation); Perrelli v. Strathmore Farms, 2000 Conn. Super. LEXIS 539 (Super. Ct. Mar. 2, 2000) (no private right of action).

981 Dietrich v. Liberty Mut. Ins. Co., 759 F. Supp. 467 (N.D. Ind. 1991) (no private right of action); Dryden v. SunLife Assurance Co. of Canada, 737 F. Supp. 1058 (S.D. Ind. 1989) (private right of action).

982 Farmer's Union Central Exchange, Inc. v. Reliance Ins. Co., 675 F. Supp. 1534 (D.N.D. 1987) (no private right of action); Farmer's Union Central Exchange v. Reliance Ins., 626 F. Supp. 583 (D.N.D. 1985) (private right of action).

983 Chabner v. United of Omaha Life Ins. Co., 225 F.3d 1042 (9th Cir. 2000); Cates Constr, Inc. v. Talbot Partners, 980 P.2d 407 (Cal. 1999); Hadland v. N.N. Investors Life Ins. Co., 24 Cal. App. 4th 1578, 30 Cal. Rptr. 2d 88 (1994); Moradi-Shalal v. Fireman's Fund Ins., 46 Cal. 3d 287, 250 Cal. Rptr. 116, 758 P.2d 58 (1988); *see also* Textron Fin. Corp. v. Nat'l Union Fire Ins. Co., 2002 Cal. App. Unpub. LEXIS 6131 (June 28, 2002) (unpublished, citation limited) (plaintiff can not replead UNIP claim as UDAP claim).

984 Kentucky Central Life Ins. Co. v. LeDuc, 814 F. Supp. 832 (N.D. Cal. 1992).

985 *See* Spray, Gould & Bowers v. Associated Int'l Ins. Co., 71 Cal. App. 4th 1260, 84 Cal. Rptr. 2d 552 (1999) (California insurance regulation may only be affirmatively enforced by insurance commissioner, but it can be used to bar defendant insurance company from raising statute of limitation defense).

986 Weese v. Nationwide Ins. Co., 879 F.2d 115 (4th Cir. 1989); Gallagher v. Allstate Ins. Co., 74 F. Supp. 2d 652 (N.D. W. Va. 1999); State Farm Mut. Auto Ins. Co. v. Reeder, 763 S.W.2d 116 (Ky. 1988); Brewington v. Employers Fire Ins. Co., 992 P.2d 237 (Mont. 1999); K-W Indus. v. National Surety Corp., 754 P.2d 502 (Mont. 1988); Klettner v. State Farm Mut. Auto. Ins. Co., 205 W. Va. 587, 519 S.E.2d 870 (1999); Elmore v. State Farm Mut. Automobile Ins. Co., 504 S.E.2d 893 (W. Va. 1998); Jenkins v. J.C. Penney Casualty Ins. Co., 167 W. Va. 597, 280 S.E.2d 252 (1981). *But see* Hart-Anderson v. Hauck, 748 P.2d 937 (Mont. 1988) (only some parts of Unfair Claims Settlement Practice Act extends protections to third parties). *But cf.* Hipsky v. Allstate Ins. Co., 304 F. Supp. 2d 284 (D. Conn. 2004).

987 *See* Conquest v. Auto-Owners Ins. Co., 637 So. 2d 40 (Fla. Dist. Ct. App. 1994) (third parties can sue for violations of UNIP claims settlement standards); Theriot v. Midland Risk Ins. Co., 694 So. 2d 184 (La. 1997); Woodruff v. State Farm Ins. Co., 767 So. 2d 785 (La. App. 2000) (third party claimants can seek penalties under UNIP statute, but can not base claim on prohi-

Courts that refuse to imply a private UNIP remedy usually rely on their finding that the UNIP statute provides an adequate remedial scheme to protect insureds.[988] Consequently, consumer litigants should take special care in showing the court how limited is the administrative UNIP remedy.

UNIP legislation typically empowers the insurance commissioner to conduct administrative proceedings leading to cease and desist orders and other civil sanctions against an insurer, but does not authorize restitution or other relief in favor of an insured or claimant. Only a few courts have allowed a class action brought by a commissioner on behalf of injured insureds.[989]

Most UNIP administrative enforcement provisions allow proceedings only when they are in the public interest.[990] Arguably, this means that the insurance commissioner should not institute a proceeding in response to a uniquely individual consumer claim.

5.3.3 Unreasonable Refusal or Delay in Paying Claim as a UDAP Violation

5.3.3.1 Refusal to Pay

The most commonly litigated UDAP insurance case involves an insurer's failure to pay on a claim. Although the consumer would have an action for breach of contract, the UDAP claim may allow attorney fees and minimum, multiple, or punitive damages.

It is unfair for an insurance company to unreasonably refuse to pay policy benefits or to attempt to persuade policyholders to settle for less than they are entitled to.[991] It

---

bitions that only apply to insureds). *But see* Transport Ins. Co. v. Faircloth, 1995 Tex. LEXIS 32 (Tex. 1995); Allstate Ins. Co. v. Watson, 876 S.W.2d 145 (Tex. 1994); *In re* Valetutto, 976 S.W.2d 893 (Tex. App. 1998); Rocor Int'l, Inc. v. National Union Fire Ins., 966 S.W.2d 559 (Tex. App. 1998); First Am. Title Ins. Co. v. Willard, 949 S.W.2d 342 (Tex. App. 1997).

988 Earth Scientists v. United States Fidelity & Guaranty Co., 619 F. Supp. 1465 (D. Kan. 1985); Farmers Group, Inc. v. Trimble, 658 P.2d 1370 (Colo. Ct. App. 1982); Hoffman v. Allstate Ins. Co., 85 Ill. App. 3d 631, 407 N.E.2d 156 (1980); Hamilton v. Safeway Ins. Co., 432 N.E.2d 996, 998–99 (Ill. Ct. App. 1982); Seeman v. Liberty Mut. Ins. Co., 322 N.W.2d 35 (Iowa 1982); Spencer v. Aetna Life & Casualty Ins. Co., 611 P.2d 149 (Kan. 1980); Bell v. League Life Ins. Co., 149 Mich. App. 481, 387 N.W.2d 154 (1986); Morris v. American Family Mut. Ins. Co., 386 N.W.2d 233 (Minn. 1986); Lawton v. Great Southwest Fire Ins. Co., 392 A.2d 576 (N.H. 1978); D'Ambrosio v. Pennsylvania Nat'l Mut. Casualty Ins. Co., 431 A.2d 966 (Pa. 1981).

989 Tricor California, Inc. v. Superior Court (State Compensation Ins. Fund), 220 Cal. App. 3d 880, 269 Cal. Rptr. 642 (1990); Sheeran v. Progressive Life Ins. Co., 182 N.J. Super. 237, 440 A.2d 469 (1981).

990 NAIC model statute § 6; most states include this requirement for all proceedings by the insurance commissioner. *See* Ala. Code § 27-12-21; Ark. Stat. Ann. § 23-66-209(a); Colo. Rev. Stat. § 10-3-1107; Conn. Gen. Stat. § 38a-817(a); Del. Code Ann. tit 18, § 2307(a); Fla. Stat. § 626.9571; Ga. Code § 33-6-7(a); Haw. Rev. Stat. § 431:13-106(a); 215 Ill. Comp. Stat. Ann. § 5/426; Ind. Code §§ 27-4-1-5, 27-4-1-8; Iowa Code § 507B.6(1); Kan. Stat. Ann. § 40-2406(a); Mass. Gen. Laws ch. 176D, § 6; Mich. Comp. Laws § 500.2029; Minn. Stat. §§ 72A.22(1), 72A.25(1); Miss. Code Ann. §§ 83-5-39, 83-5-45; Mo. Rev. Stat. § 375.940(1); Neb. Rev. Stat. § 44-1528; Nev. Rev. Stat. §§ 686A.160, 686.170; N.H. Rev. Stat. Ann. §§ 417:6, 417:12; N.J. Rev. Stat. §§ 17B:30-17, 17B:30-18; N.Y. Ins. Law § 2405(a); N.C. Gen. Stat. §§ 58-63-25(a), 58-63-40(a); N.D. Cent. Code § 26.1-04-12; Okla. Stat. tit. 36, §§ 1206, 1209; R.I. Gen. Laws §§ 27-29-5, 27-29-8; Tenn. Code Ann. § 56-8-108(a); Tex. Ins. Code Ann. § 541.102.

A minority of states only impose the public interest requirements for proceedings with respect to practices not specifically prohibited by the UNIP law. *See* Alaska Stat. § 21.36.150; Cal. Ins. Code § 790.06; Ky. Stat. Ann. § 304.12-130(1); Md. Ins. Code Ann. § 27-104; Mont. Code Ann. § 33-18-1003(1); N.M. Stat. Ann. § 59A-16-28(A); S.D. Cod. Law § 58-33-38; Wyo. Stat. § 26-13-116(a).

991 Hamburger v. State Farm Mut. Automobile Ins. Co., 361 F.3d 875 (5th Cir. 2004); Riordan v. Nationwide Mut. Fire Ins. Co., 977 F.2d 47 (2d Cir. 1992) (New York law); Equitable Life Assurance Co. v. Porter-Englehart, 867 F.2d 79 (1st Cir. 1989) (Massachusetts law) (UDAP violation for insurer to file interpleader action rather than pay claim, where it was clear that beneficiary was entitled to at least part of the proceeds); Gulf Ins. Co. v. Jones, 2003 WL 22208551 (N.D. Tex. Sept. 24, 2003); Coury v. Allstate Texas Lloyds, 2003 WL 23204647 (S.D. Tex. July 1, 2003); Altimari v. John Hancock Variable Life Ins. Co., 247 F. Supp. 2d 637 (E.D. Pa. 2003) (insurer's nonfeasance insufficient); Hangarter v. Paul Revere Life Ins. Co., 236 F. Supp. 2d 1069 (N.D. Cal. 2002) (targeting certain claims for termination regardless of merit, sending claimants to biased medical examiners, shredding documents); Sparks v. Allstate Ins. Co., 98 F. Supp. 2d 933 (W.D. Tenn. 2000) (Tennessee UDAP statute covers unfair claims settlement practices, not just unfair sales practices); Ruch v. State Farm Fire & Cas. Co., 1998 U.S. Dist. LEXIS 19853 (N.D. Tex. Dec. 14, 1998); Lawson v. Potomac Ins. Co., 1998 U.S. Dist. LEXIS 14769 (N.D. Tex. Sept. 14, 1998); Grunbaum v. American Express Assur. Co., 1998 U.S. Dist. LEXIS 17627 (N.D. Tex. Nov. 2, 1998); Brownell v. State Farm Mut. Ins. Co., 757 F. Supp. 526 (E.D. Pa. 1991) (rejection of claims after misrepresentation that coverage was available violates UDAP statute); Riordan v. Nationwide Mut. Fire Ins. Co., 756 F. Supp. 732 (S.D.N.Y. 1990); Wolf Bros. Oil Co. v. International Surplus Lines Ins. Co., 718 F. Supp. 839 (W.D. Wash. 1989); WVG v. Pacific Ins. Co., 707 F. Supp. 70 (D.N.H. 1986); Carpentino v. Transport Ins. Co., 609 F. Supp. 556 (D. Conn. 1985); Shapiro v. American Home Assur. Co., 616 F. Supp. 906 (D. Miss. 1985); Barr Co. v. Safeco Ins. Co., 583 F. Supp. 248 (N.D. Ill. 1984) (misrepresentations that insurer would pay out on claims are actionable); Layton v. Liberty Mut. Fire Ins. Co., 530 F. Supp. 285 (E.D. Penn. 1981); Clegg v. Butler, 424 Mass. 413, 676 N.E.2d 1134 (1997) (unreasonable settlement offers to auto accident victim); Dimarzo v. American Mut. Ins. Co., 389 Mass. 85, 449 N.E.2d 1189 (1983) (over $400,000 in multiple damages and attorney fees); Bonofiglio v. Commercial Union Ins. Co., 411 Mass. 31, 576 N.E.2d 680 (1991) (double damages awarded); Jet Line Services v. American Employers Ins. Co., 404 Mass. 706, 537 N.E.2d 107 (1989) (insurer's late disclaimer of coverage violated UDAP statute); Van Dyke v. St. Paul Fire

is a UDAP violation to deny payment when the insurer knew or should have known that its liability was reasonably clear.[992] A related claim, discussed in another section, *infra*, is that the insurer misrepresented in advertising or elsewhere that it was generous in its settlements, when in practice it is not.[993]

On the other hand, a refusal to pay a claim that is based on a good faith judgment by the insurance company is not a UDAP violation.[994] Similarly, a consumer's action can not

& Marine Ins. Co., 388 Mass. 671, 448 N.E.2d 357 (1983) (factual question whether insurer undertook reasonable investigation before denying claim); Trempe v. Aetna Casualty & Surety Co., 20 Mass. App. Ct. 448, 480 N.E.2d 670 (1985) (insurer's delay and failure to give reasonable explanation for claim refusal does not display candor or fairness and thus UDAP violation); Hatch v. Am. Family Mut. Ins. Co., Clearinghouse No. 53,566 (Minn. Dist. Ct. Oct. 12, 2000) (when matching materials were unavailable, insurer violated specific UNIP provision by paying only for replacement of storm-damaged portions of homes with non-matching materials); People by Abrams v. American Motor Club, Inc., 179 A.D.2d 277, 852 N.Y.S.2d 688 (1992); Sulner v. General Accident Fire & Life Ins. Co., 471 N.Y.S.2d 794 (Sup. Ct. 1984); Miller v. Nationwide Mut. Ins. Co., 112 N.C. App. 295, 435 S.E.2d 537 (1993); Deetz v. Nationwide Mut. Ins. Co., 20 Pa. D. & C.3d 499 (C.P. Dauphin Cty. 1981); Pemberton v. Amoco Life Ins. Co., 2002 WL 32059028 (Tenn. Ct. App. Feb. 15, 2002); Provident Am. Ins. Co. v. Castaneda, 988 S.W.2d 189 (Tex. 1998); State Farm Fire & Cas. Co. v. Simmons, 963 S.W.2d 42 (Tex. 1998); Vail v. Texas Farm Bureau Mut. Life Ins. Co., 754 S.W.2d 129 (Tex. 1988); Provident Am. Ins. Co. v. Castaneda, 914 S.W.2d 273 (Tex. App. 1996); Aetna Cas. & Sur. Co. v. Garza, 906 S.W.2d 543 (Tex. App. 1995); Maryland Ins. Co. v. Head Indus. Coatings & Services, Inc., 906 S.W.2d 218 (Tex. App. 1995) (insurer's duty does not depend on the nature of coverage in the policy); GAB Bus. Services, Inc. v. Moore, 829 S.W.2d 345 (Tex. App. 1992); Fidelity & Cas. Co. v. Underwood, 791 S.W.2d 635 (Tex. App. 1990); Allied General Agency, Inc. v. Moody, 788 S.W.2d 601 (Tex. App. 1990); Levy v. North Am. Co. for Life & Health Ins., 90 Wash. 2d 846, 586 P.2d 845 (1978); Salois v. Mut. of Omaha Ins. Co., 90 Wash. 2d 355, 581 P.2d 1349 (1978); Industrial Indemnity Co. v. Kallevig, 54 Wash. App. 558, 774 P.2d 1230 (1989); Nguyen v. Glendale Constr. Co., 56 Wash. App. 196, 782 P.2d 1110 (1989); Nyby v. Allied Fidelity Ins. Co., 42 Wash. App. 543, 712 P.2d 861 (1986); Gould v. Mutual Life Ins. Co. of New York, 37 Wash. App. 756, 683 P.2d 207 (1984); Safeco Ins. Co. of Am. v. JMG Restaurants, Inc., 37 Wash. App. 1, 680 P.2d 409 (1984) (UDAP violation for insurer to act without reasonable justification; no need to show bad faith or fraud); Whistman v. West Am. of Ohio Cas. Group, 38 Wash. App. 580, 686 P.2d 1086 (1984); Rounds v. Union Bankers Ins. Co., 22 Wash. App. 613, 590 P.2d 1286 (1979). *See also* United States Fire Ins. Co. v. Nationwide Mut. Ins. Co., 735 F. Supp. 1320 (E.D.N.C. 1990); W.E. O'Neil Constr. Co. v. National Union Fire Ins. Co., 721 F. Supp. 984 (N.D. Ill. 1989) (pattern of failing to pay claims promptly satisfies any public injury requirement of Illinois UDAP statute). *Cf.* Simon v. UnumProvident Corp., 2002 U.S. Dist. LEXIS 9331 (E.D. Pa. May 23, 2002) (nonfeasance alone insufficient, but allegation that insured's doctor redacted a statement after adjuster called him is malfeasance); Gringeri v. Maryland Cas. Co., 1998 U.S. Dist. LEXIS 5931 (E.D. Pa. Apr. 28, 1998) (promise to pay benefits it has no intention of paying is UDAP violation, but mere failure to pay is not). *But see* Horowitz v. Federal Kemper Life Assurance Co., 57 F.3d 300 (3d Cir. 1995) (insurer's nonfeasance alone is insufficient to state Pennsylvania UDAP claim); Smith v. Am. Equity Ins. Co., 235 F. Supp. 2d 410 (E.D. Pa. 2002) (insurer's mere failure to pay claim is not UDAP violation); Parasco v. Pacific Indemnity Co., 920 F. Supp. 647 (E.D. Pa. 1996) (insurer's nonfeasance alone is insufficient to state Pennsylvania UDAP claim); Smith v. Nationwide Mut. Fire Ins. Co., 935 F. Supp. 616 (W.D. Pa. 1996) (nonfeasance alone will not support UDAP claim; plaintiff's allegation of improper post-loss investigation is sufficient); Klinger v. State Farm Mut. Auto Ins. Co., 895 F. Supp. 709 (Md. Pa. 1995) (insurer's nonfeasance alone is insufficient to state Pennsylvania UDAP claim); Aetna Casualty & Surety Co. v. Ericksen, 903 F. Supp. 836 (M.D. Pa. 1995) (same); Lombardo v. State Farm Mut. Auto Ins. Co., 800 F. Supp. 208 (E.D. Pa. 1992). *Cf.* Sichel v. Unum Provident Corp., 230 F. Supp. 2d 325 (S.D.N.Y. 2002) (procuring false medical reports in order to deny claims not deceptive because no members of public relied on the reports).

992 Parkans Intern. L.L.C. v. Zurich Ins. Co., 299 F.3d 514 (5th Cir. 2002); Dougherty v. State Farm Lloyds, 2002 WL 1285569 (N.D. Tex. June 5, 2002); Carper v. State Farm Lloyds, 2002 WL 31086074 (N.D. Tex. Sept. 13, 2002).

993 *See* § 5.3.4, *infra*.

994 Ferrara & DiMercurio, Inc. v. St. Paul Mercury Ins. Co., 169 F.3d 43 (1st Cir. 1999) (insurer's reliance on expert's report to deny claim was reasonable); Van Holt v. Liberty Mut. Fire Ins. Co., 163 F.3d 161 (3d Cir. 1998) (mere denial of insurance claim which claimant believes is proper is not UDAP violation); Gould v. Mutual Life Ins. Co., 735 F.2d 1165 (9th Cir. 1984) (Washington law) (mere denial of benefits based on a debatable question of coverage does not create bad faith refusal that would violate UDAP statute); Central Carolina Bank and Trust Co. v. Security Life of Denver Ins. Co., 247 F. Supp. 2d 791 (M.D.N.C. 2003); Acceptance Ins. Co. v. Newport Classic Homes, Inc., 2001 U.S. Dist. LEXIS 18997 (N.D. Tex. Nov. 19, 2001) (no UNIP or UDAP claim where the insurer had reasonable basis for denial); Behn v. Legion Ins. Co., 173 F. Supp. 2d 105 (D. Mass. 2001) (insurer's refusal to settle tort plaintiff's claim against the insured was not UDAP violation because liability was never reasonably clear); Willcox v. American Home Assur. Co., 900 F. Supp. 850 (S.D. Tex. 1995) (mere failure to defend insured in lawsuit is insufficient); National Grange Mut. Ins. v. Continental Casualty Ins., 650 F. Supp. 1404 (S.D.N.Y. 1986); Anderson v. National Security Fire & Casualty Co., 870 S.W.2d 432 (Ky. Ct. App. 1994); State Farm Fire & Cas. Ins. Co. v. Aulick, 781 S.W.2d 531 (Ky. Ct. App. 1989); Bobick v. United States Fidelity & Guaranty Ins. Co., 790 N.E.2d 653 (Mass. 2003) (insurer's offer was reasonable where jury ultimately made award in same range); Lumbermens Mut. Casualty Co. v. Offices Unlimited, Inc., 419 Mass. 462, 645 N.E.2d 1165 (1995) (denial of claim based on plausible interpretation of policy is not UDAP violation); Polaroid Corp. v. Travelers Indemnity Co., 414 Mass. 747, 610 N.E.2d 912 (1993) (no UDAP violation in refusal to defend insured where insurer reasonably concluded there was no coverage); Boston Symphony Orchestra, Inc. v. Commercial Union Ins. Co., 406 Mass. 7, 545 N.E.2d 1156 (1989) (no violation where insurer relied in good faith on plausible, although ultimately incorrect, interpretation of its policy); Swanson v. Bankers Life Co., 389 Mass. 345, 450 N.E.2d 577 (1983) (no unfairness in slow payment where insured's own lack of cooperation slowed insurance company's investigation); Johnson v. Hingham Mut. Fire Ins. Co., 59 Mass. App. Ct. 1104, 796 N.E.2d 465 (Mass. App. Ct.

be based on the unfair refusal to pay a valid claim where the policy clearly states that a risk is not covered by the policy.[995] If an insurer's failure to pay was simply negligent, it may not be subject to a UDAP or UNIP claim, although it still may be sued for breach of contract. In addition, as discussed at § 5.3.4, *infra*, the consumer may have a UDAP claim against the insurer if the company or its agent misrepresented at the time the policy was sold that such a risk would be covered.

When a refusal to pay claim is joined with an underlying claim of insurance coverage, the insurer may seek to bifurcate the claims. Some courts will stay the refusal to pay claim pending the outcome on the underlying coverage claim.[996] One rationale for bifurcating the claims is that granting discovery in the refusal to pay claim may reveal the insurer's impressions, legal theories and privileged communications.[997] Whether the consumer must prevail on the underlying claim for insurance benefits before pressing a failure to pay suit may vary depending on whether the suit is framed as a UNIP, UDAP, or bad faith claim.[998]

Certain special issues concerning the unfair refusal to pay a claim are presented in the credit insurance context. These are examined at § 5.3.10.6, *infra*.

5.3.3.2 Parties Liable for Unfair Claims Settlement Practices

Depending on the state, the consumer may have three different claims (in addition to breach of contract) for unfair claims settlement practices—UDAP, UNIP, and bad faith. In addition, depending on the state, these three claims may apply to different parties. Consequently, where more than one theory is available in a state, consider their differing scope.

For example, in a state where insurance is outside the scope of a UDAP statute, then UNIP or bad faith is the obvious choice. In Texas, in the absence of privity, a reinsurer may not have a duty of good faith and fair dealing with respect to the insured.[999] The insured, however, may sue the reinsurer under general UDAP or UNIP provisions.[1000] The insured may also sue the agent under general UDAP and UNIP theories.[1001] In Connecticut, the state UNIP statute has also been applied to reinsurance agreements between two insurers.[1002]

2003) (unpublished, text available at 2003 WL 22175936) (insurer may rely on claim adjuster's and counsel's advice to deny a claim if there is a legitimate dispute as to fault and damages); Parker v. D'Avolio, 664 N.E.2d 858 (Mass. App. Ct. 1996) (finding of bad faith refusal to settle is reserved for rare and exceptionally egregious cases); Bartlett v. Allstate Ins. Co., 929 P.2d 227 (Mont. 1996); Gelinas v. Metropolitan Property & Liability Ins. Co., 551 A.2d 962 (N.H. 1988); DeSimone v. Nationwide Mut. Ins. Co., 149 N.J. Super. 376, 373 A.2d 1025 (Law Div. 1977); Burgess v. Insurance Co., 44 N.C. App. 441, 261 S.E.2d 234 (1980); Myint v. Allstate Ins. Co., 970 S.W.2d 920 (Tenn. 1998) (reasonable denial of insurance claim is not UDAP violation); Stooksbury v. American National Property and Casualty Co., 126 S.W.3d 505 (Tenn. Ct. App. 2004) (no bad faith where defendant had legal grounds supporting its position that insurance coverage had been cancelled prior to the date of loss); Amer. Motorists Ins. Co. v. Fodge, 63 S.W.3d 801 (Tex. 2001) (no claim for refusing to pay for drugs if not entitled to medical treatment); Republic Ins. Co. v. Stoker, 903 S.W.2d 338 (Tex. 1995) (no claim if insurer denies claim for an invalid reason, but later discovers a valid reason for denial); Allstate Texas Lloyds v. Mason, 123 S.W.3d 690 (Tex. App. 2003); Allison v. Fire Ins. Exchange, 98 S.W.3d 227 (Tex. App. 2002); Saunders v. Commonwealth Lloyd's Ins. Co., 928 S.W.2d 322 (Tex. App. 1996); Two Pesos, Inc. v. Gulf Ins. Co., 901 S.W.2d 495 (Tex. App. 1995) (liability depends on proving that insurer knew or should have known that it had no reasonable basis for denying or delaying payment on a claim); Overton v. Consolidated Ins. Co., 38 P.3d 322 (Wash. 2002) (when insurer acts reasonably in denying coverage for a third-party suit against the insured, not a UDAP violation or bad faith); Leingang v. Pierce County Medical Bureau, 930 P.2d 288 (Wash. 1997); Transcontinental Ins. v. Washington Pub. Utl. Dist.'s Util. Sys., 111 Wash. 2d 452, 760 P.2d 337 (1988); Villella v. Public Employees Mut. Ins., Co., 106 Wash. 2d 806, 725 P.2d 957 (1986); Phil Shroeder v. Royal Globe Ins. Co., 99 Wash. 2d 65, 659 P.2d 509 (1983) (no bad faith refusal where insurer had case authority for position); Tornetta v. Allstate Ins. Co., 973 P.2d 8 (Wash. App. 1999) (fraud by insured bars UDAP recovery); Seattle Pump Co. v. Traders & General Ins. Co., 970 P.2d 361 (Wash. App. 1999) (reasonable denial of insurance coverage is not UDAP violation); Dombrosky v. Farmers Ins. Co., 928 P.2d 1127 (Wash. App. 1996); Keller v. Allstate Ins. Co., 915 P.2d 1140 (Wash. App. 1996); Wickswat v. Safeco Ins. Co., 78 Wash. App. 958, 904 P.2d 767 (1995) (consumer's intentional misrepresentations during the claims process justified insurer's failure to pay the claim); *see also* MacFarland v. United States Fidelity & Guarantee Co., 818 F. Supp. 108 (E.D. Pa. 1993) (mere refusal to pay is not deceptive); Gordon v. Pennsylvania Blue Shield, 548 A.2d 600 (Pa. Super. Ct. 1988).

995 Ruch v. State Farm Fire & Cas. Co., 1998 U.S. Dist. LEXIS 19853 (N.D. Tex. Dec. 14, 1998); *see also* Exeter v. GEICO Gen. Ins. Co., 2001 Wash. App. LEXIS 2630 (Dec. 3, 2001) (not unfair or deceptive for insurer to use cost of non-original equipment manufacturer parts as basis for settlement of claims where this was openly disclosed in the policy).

996 Sanchez v. Witham, 2003 WL 1880131 (Mass. App. Ct. Mar. 31, 2003) (discussing factors favoring bifurcation but affirming trial court's discretion not to bifurcate).

997 *Id.*

998 Jordache Enterprises, Inc. v. National Union Fire Ins. Co., 513 S.E.2d 692 (W. Va. 1998) (in contrast to bad faith claim, UNIP plaintiff need not have won suit on underlying contract).

999 Keightley v. Republic Ins. Co., 946 S.W.2d 124 (Tex. App. 1997), *op. withdrawn on joint motion due to settlement*, 1997 Tex. App. LEXIS 3950 (July 24, 1997). *See also* Nast v. State Farm Fire and Cas. Co., 82 S.W.3d 114 (Tex. App. 2002) (insurer has no duty of good faith and fair dealing to consumer who, because of agent's misrepresentations, never bought insurance from it).

1000 *Id.*; Maintenance v. ITT Hartford Group, 895 S.W.2d 816 (Tex. App. 1995) (reinsurer can be liable to consumer under UDAP statute even though duty of good faith does not apply to it).

1001 Brooks v. American Home Ins. Co., 1997 WL 538727 (N.D. Tex. 1997).

1002 Security Ins. Co. of Hartford v. Trustmark Ins. Co., 2002 WL

Although an insurer's agent under some state UDAP statutes may not be a "consumer" and therefore can not bring a UDAP claim, the agent may still be able to sue the insurer under the UNIP statute if its practices fall within that statute.[1003] Similarly, a firm hired by the insurer to investigate an insurance claim may not be covered by a UNIP statute,[1004] but that firm may be covered by a UDAP statute. Nevertheless, a North Carolina court has found that, where a private UNIP right of action is not available for a third party to bring an action against an insured, the UDAP claim should not be available either.[1005] The Massachusetts highest court has found that retailers which self-insure are not engaged in trade or commerce when they settle customers' personal injury claims, so are not subject to the UDAP statute for their claims settlement practices.[1006]

Nevada holds that the administrator of a medical insurance policy is not subject to UNIP claims.[1007] But in West Virginia, UNIP claims can be asserted not only against the insurance company but also against its claims adjuster employee.[1008]

5.3.3.3 Misuse of Superior Power as UDAP Violation

An unfair breach of the duty of good faith in settling an insurance claim constitutes a UDAP violation and may be established without a showing of misrepresentation, deceit or fraud.[1009] Actions without reasonable justification are enough,[1010] when an insurance company's conduct manifests an inequitable assertion of power or position.[1011] When the insured suffers a loss, the insurer's bargaining power increases in direct proportion to the size of the loss.[1012] Unfair claims settlement practices are an abuse of this power.

5.3.3.4 Excessive Delay and Evasiveness as a UDAP Violation

Excessive delay in responding to a claim may also be a UDAP violation.[1013] It is unfair to be dilatory in offering a settlement after insurer liability has become reasonably clear,[1014] or to proceed too slowly with an

---

32500873 (D. Conn. Aug. 22, 2002).

1003 Tweedell v. Hochheim Prairie Farm Mut. Ins. Ass'n, 962 S.W.2d 685 (Tex. App. 1998), *vacated on other grounds*, 997 S.W.2d 277 (Tex. 1999), *on remand*, 1 S.W.3d 304 (Tex. App. 1999).

1004 Dagley v. Haag Engineering Co., 18 S.W.3d 787 (Tex. App. 2000). *Contra* Vargas v. State Farm Lloyds, 216 F. Supp. 2d 643 (S.D. Tex. 2002).

1005 Lee v. Mutual Community Savings Bank, SSB, 525 S.E.2d 854 (N.C. Ct. App. 2000).

1006 Morrison v. Toys R Us, Inc., 441 Mass. 51, 806 N.E.2d 388 (Mass. 2004).

1007 Albert H. Wohlers & Co. v. Bartgis, 969 P.2d 949 (Nev. 1998).

1008 Taylor v. Nationwide Mut. Ins. Co., 2003 WL 22762025 (W. Va. Nov. 21, 2003). *But cf.* Stafford v. J.B. Hunt Transport, Inc., 270 F. Supp. 2d 773 (S.D. W. Va. 2003) (independent adjuster retained by self-insured company not subject to UNIP).

1009 Whistman v. West Am. of Ohio Cas. Group, 38 Wash. App. 580, 686 P.2d 1086 (1984). *See also* Union Bankers Ins. Co. v. Shelton, 889 S.W.2d 278 (Tex. 1994) (insurance company's duty of good faith and fair dealing extends to policy cancellation). *But see* Great Amer. Ins. Co. v. North Austin Mun. Util. Dist. No. 1, 908 S.W.2d 415 (Tex. 1995) (no duty of good faith and fair dealing between a surety and a bond obligee); Natividad v. Alexsis, Inc., 875 S.W.2d 695 (Tex. 1994) (adjuster has no duty of good faith and fair dealing separate from the insurer).

1010 Industrial Indemnity Co. v. Kallevig, 54 Wash. App. 558, 774 P.2d 1230 (1989); Safeco Ins. Co. v. JMG Restaurants, Inc., 37 Wash. App. 1, 680 P.2d 409 (1984); Whistman v. West Am. of Ohio Cas. Group, 38 Wash. App. 580, 686 P.2d 1086 (1984).

1011 Murray v. Nationwide Mut. Ins. Co., 472 S.E.2d 358 (N.C. App. 1996).

1012 *Id.*

1013 Kennedy v. Sphere Drake Ins. P.L.C., 2002 U.S. App. LEXIS 6054 (9th Cir. Apr. 2, 2002) (unpublished, citation limited) (Wash. law); Riordan v. Nationwide Mut. Fire Ins. Co., 977 F.2d 47 (2d Cir. 1992) (New York law); Travelers Ins. Co. v. Waltham Indus. Laboratories, 722 F. Supp. 814 (D. Mass. 1988) (delays while insurer investigated claims not unreasonable, so did not violate Massachusetts UDAP statute), *rev'd in part on other grounds*, 883 F.2d 1092 (1st Cir. 1989); Doe v. Liberty Mut. Ins. Co., 423 Mass. 366, 667 N.E.2d 1149 (1996) (delay due to loss of plaintiff's original claim letter, which caused plaintiff no prejudice, not a UDAP violation); People by Abrams v. American Motor Club, Inc., 179 A.D.2d 277, 852 N.Y.S.2d 688 (1992); Allstate Ins. Co. v. Bonner, 51 S.W.3d 289 (Tex. 2001) (liability under a prompt pay provision exists only if insurer is liable to pay the underlying claim); Provident Am. Ins. Co. v. Castaneda, 914 S.W.2d 273 (Tex. App. 1996); Anderson v. State Farm Mut. Ins. Co., 2 P.3d 1029 (Wash. App. 2000) (insured may recover damages caused by delay, e.g., interest, attorney fees, late charges on bills, even if insurer ultimately pays claim); Foltz v. Crum & Forster Personal Ins., 100 Wash. App. 1038, 2000 Wash. App. LEXIS 1109 (2000) (unpublished, citation limited) (delay is UNIP violation); Miller v. Fluharty, 500 S.E.2d 310 (W. Va. 1997) (insurer has duty to conduct prompt investigation of claim). *See also* Wellisch v. United Services Auto. Ass'n, 75 S.W.3d 53 (Tex. App. 2002) (delay in payment may be excused if insurer explains its reasons for denial and if its liability to pay did not exist at the time of the denial, such as in a claim for uninsured motorist coverage); Saunders v. Commonwealth Lloyd's Ins. Co., 928 S.W.2d 322 (Tex. App. 1996) (insurer can show reasonable causes for delay to avoid bad faith claim).

1014 St. Paul Reinsurance Co. v. Greenberg, 134 F.3d 1250 (5th Cir. 1998) (holding delay in payment actionable even if insurer had a reasonable justification for denial, as long as insurer is actually liable); Shannon R. Ginn Constr. Co. v. Reliance Ins. Co., 51 F. Supp. 2d 1347 (S.D. Fla. 1999); Tucker v. State Farm Fire & Cas. Co., 981 F. Supp. 461 (S.D. Tex. 1997); Hopkins v. Liberty Mut. Ins. Co., 750 N.E.2d 943 (Mass. 2001); Universe Life Ins. Co. v. Giles, 950 S.W.2d 48 (Tex. 1997); Dunn v. Southern Farm Bureau Cas. Ins. Co., 991 S.W.2d 467 (Tex. App. 1998); Poling v. Motorists Mut. Ins. Co., 192 W. Va. 46, 450 S.E.2d 635 (1994). *See also* Wailua Assocs. v. Aetna Cas. & Sur. Co., 27 F. Supp. 2d 1211 (D. Haw. 1998) (insurer who pays a claim after unreasonable delay may be held liable for bad faith).

investigation.[1015] Similarly, it is unfair for an insurer to systematically pay creditors promptly, but not consumers.[1016] The plaintiff may recover damages caused by the delay even if the insurer ultimately pays the claim.[1017] An insurer is liable for failure to make a prompt and fair settlement offer even if the evidence shows that the plaintiff would not have accepted the offer.[1018]

Also unfair is delaying the process by failing to acknowledge or to respond adequately to claims or refusing to settle a claim under one portion of a policy to influence settlement on another portion.[1019] A pattern of evasiveness, with constantly changing reasons for claim denial, intended to force the insured into settlement, is a UDAP violation.[1020]

1015 Luxury Living, Inc. v. Mid-Continent Cas. Co., 2003 WL 22116202 (S.D. Tex. Sept. 10, 2003) (contains good discussion of prompt payment law); Foltz v. Crum & Forster Personal Ins., 100 Wash. App. 1038 (2000).

1016 Garner v. Foundation Life Ins. Co., 17 Ark. App. 13, 702 S.W.2d 417 (1986).

1017 Anderson v. State Farm Mut. Ins. Co., 2 P.3d 1029 (Wash. App. 2000).

1018 Bobick v. United States Fidelity & Guaranty Ins. Co., 790 N.E.2d 653, 662–63 (Mass. 2003).

1019 NAIC model statute § 4(9); statutes cited at § 5.3.2.1, *supra*. *See also* Wells v. State Farm Fire & Cas. Co., 993 F.2d 510 (5th Cir. 1993); Columbia Mut. Ins. Co. v. Fiesta Mart, Inc., 987 F.2d 1124 (5th Cir. 1993); Peckham v. Continental Casualty Ins. Co., 895 F.2d 830 (1st Cir. 1990) (failure to keep insured informed of facts relating to coverage and settlement violates Massachusetts insurance law and UDAP statute); Standard Fire Ins. Co. v. Rominger, 827 F. Supp. 1277 (S.D. Tex. 1993); Brandt v. State Farm Mut. Automobile Ins. Co., 693 F. Supp. 877 (E.D. Cal. 1988) (upholding constitutionality of statute); Kanne v. Connecticut General Life Ins. Co., 607 F. Supp. 899 (C.D. Cal. 1985), *rev'd*, 819 F.2d 204 (9th Cir. 1987) (state law claims preempted by ERISA), *vacated*, 867 F.2d 489 (9th Cir. 1988), *cert. denied*, 492 U.S. 906 (1989); Thaler v. American Ins. Co., 34 Mass. App. Ct. 639, 614 N.E.2d 1021 (1993) (insurer's insistence on full release of its insured as condition of payment of policy limits unfair where liability of insured was clear and claim exceeded policy limits); Trempe v. Aetna Casualty & Surety Co., 20 Mass. App. Ct. 448, 480 N.E.2d 670 (1985); Dees v. American Nat'l Fire Ins. Co., 861 P.2d 141 (Mont. 1993); Walker v. St. Paul Fire & Marine Ins. Co., 786 P.2d 1157 (Mont. 1990); Miller v. Nationwide Mut. Ins. Co., 112 N.C. App. 295, 435 S.E.2d 537 (1993); Love of God Holiness Temple Church v. Union Standard Ins. Co., 860 S.W.2d 179 (Tex. App. 1993); State Farm Fire & Cas. Co. v. Simmons, 857 S.W.2d 126 (Tex. App. 1993); Commonwealth Lloyds Ins. Co. v. Downs, 853 S.W.2d 104 (Tex. App. 1993), *rev'd in part on other grounds*, 963 S.W.2d 42 (Tex. 1998) (punitive damages); Lee v. Safemate Life Ins. Co., 737 S.W.2d 84 (Tex. App. 1987); Urban v. Mid-Century Ins., 905 P.2d 404 (Wash. App. 1995) (adjuster's failure to make disclosures about insurance coverage to injured claimant voided settlement and violated UNIP and UDAP statutes).

1020 Commercial Union Ins. Co. v. Seven Provinces Ins. Co., 217 F.3d 33 (1st Cir. 2000), *cert. denied*, 148 L. Ed. 2d 959 (2001). *Accord* Foltz v. Crum & Forster Personal Ins., 100 Wash. App. 1038, 2000 Wash. App. LEXIS 1109 (2000) (unpublished, citation limited) (unreasonable failure to list all grounds for denial could be a UNIP violation).

An insurer can not avoid UDAP or UNIP liability by refusing to settle until the jury rules for the plaintiff on the underlying claim, and then stipulating to payment of the judgment amount.[1021] The consumer still suffers actual damages and can elect between recovering on the contract claim and accepting the damage award, or recovering potentially trebled damages on the UDAP claim.[1022] Any other rule would encourage insurers to avoid and delay settlement.

5.3.3.5 Excessive Paperwork Requirements as UDAP Violation

The Second Circuit has upheld a UDAP claim against an insurer where the insurer failed to acknowledge correspondence, required unnecessary paperwork, refused information because it was not on the insurer's own forms, and made unreasonable demands as to when different aspects of a claim would be settled.[1023]

5.3.3.6 Denial Must Be Based on Unambiguous Contract Exclusion, Not on a Business Judgment

If an insurance policy is ambiguous, a court will adopt the construction favoring coverage.[1024] It is a UDAP violation to fail to pay out on a policy based on a policy exclusion that the court found too vague to be enforceable.[1025] Exaggerating the scope of a policy exclusion in order to avoid paying a claim is a UDAP violation.[1026]

In determining whether liability has become "reasonably clear," the insurer must make an objective inquiry into the facts and the law. The cost of defending the claim, the size of the injured party's demand, and the insurer's business judgment are all *irrelevant* to the likelihood of liability.[1027]

1021 Hamburger v. State Farm Mut. Automobile Ins. Co., 361 F.3d 875 (5th Cir. 2004).

1022 Vazquez v. Allstate Ins. Co., 137 N.C. App. 741, 529 S.E.2d 480 (2000).

1023 Riordan v. Nationwide Mut. Fire Ins. Co., 977 F.2d 47 (2d Cir. 1992) (New York law).

1024 Jones v. Ray Ins. Agency, 59 S.W.3d 739 (Tex. App. 2001); Amarco Petroleum, Inc. v. Texas Pac. Indem. Co., 889 S.W.2d 695 (Tex. App. 1994).

1025 Norgan v. American Way Life Ins. Co., 188 Mich. App. 158, 469 N.W.2d 23 (1991) (to be eligible for the policy, the consumer, at the time of application, had to be "able to perform the normal duties" for a person of that age). *See also* Shannon R. Ginn Constr. Co. v. Reliance Ins. Co., 51 F. Supp. 2d 1347 (S.D. Fla. 1999).

1026 Nesbitt v. American Community Mut. Ins. Co., 236 Mich. App. 215, 600 N.W.2d 427 (1999).

1027 Demeo v. State Farm Mut. Automobile Ins. Co., 38 Mass. App. Ct. 955, 649 N.E.2d 803 (1995).

5.3.3.7 Failure to Conduct an Adequate Investigation as UDAP Violation

Mere denial of benefits due to a debatable question of coverage is not bad faith,[1028] but it is bad faith for an insurer to deny coverage based upon suspicion and conjecture; the insurer must make a good faith investigation of the facts before denying coverage.[1029] Even if, in fact, the claim is not covered by the policy, the insurer owes the insured a duty to perform a good faith investigation, and the expenses the insured incurs because of the insurer's breach of that duty can be compensated in a UDAP suit.[1030] Targeting certain claims for termination regardless of their merit, sending claimants to biased medical examiners, and taking steps such as shredding documents that fall below the insurance industry's general standards violate the state UDAP statute.[1031] It is an unfair practice to deny a claim, otherwise proper on its face, solely because of the results of a polygraph test upon the insured.[1032]

5.3.3.8 Insurer's Failure to Disclose and Deception in the Claims Settlement Process

An agent's concealment of the insurer's breach of its duties under the policy is actionable.[1033] The failure of an agent to notify or inform the insured that settlement with an uninsured carrier would prohibit the insured from collecting under her own policy can be a UDAP violation.[1034] Alteration of a form signed by the plaintiff, and misrepresentation of the plaintiff's duties to her physician, are UDAP violations.[1035] It is deceptive for the tortfeasor's insurance company to send mailings to injured parties that encourage them to settle their claims without attorneys by falsely implying that the insurance company will act as the injured party's representative.[1036] But another court held that an insurance company did not commit a UDAP violation by failing to advise the insured to get his own attorney before it took a statement from him that established non-coverage.[1037]

1028 Carper v. State Farm Lloyds, 2002 WL 31086074 (N.D. Tex. Sept. 13, 2002); Travelers Ins. Co. v. Waltham Indus. Laboratories, 722 F. Supp. 814 (D. Mass. 1988) (insurer's decision not to defend suit against insured did not violate Massachusetts UDAP statute), *rev'd in part on other grounds*, 883 F.2d 1092 (1st Cir. 1989); Brandt v. Time Ins. Co., 704 N.E.2d 843 (Ill. App. Ct. 1998) (insurer did not violate UDAP statute by investigating truthfulness of plaintiff's application only after she submitted claim); Guity v. Commerce Ins. Co., 631 N.E.2d 75 (Mass. App. Ct. 1994); U.S. Fire Ins. Co. v. Williams, 955 S.W.2d 267 (Tex. 1997); Transcontinental Ins. v. Washington Pub. Util. Dist.'s Util. Sys., 111 Wash. 2d 452, 760 P.2d 337 (1988); Shroeder v. Royal Globe Ins. Co., 99 Wash. 2d 65, 659 P.2d 509 (1983); Whistman v. West Am. of Ohio Cas. Group, 38 Wash. App. 580, 686 P.2d 1086 (1984); *see also* Hyde Athletic Indus. v. Continental Cas. Co., 969 F. Supp. 289 (E.D. Pa. 1997) (court considered standards in UNIP law when determining whether insurers violated state bad faith statute; summary judgment granted where no evidence that insurers acted with recklessness or ill will in dealing with plaintiffs' claims); Gulezian v. Lincoln Ins. Co., 399 Mass. 606, 506 N.E.2d 123 (1987).

1029 Fiess v. State Farm Lloyds, 2003 WL 21659408 (S.D. Tex. June 4, 2003); Walch v. United Services Auto. Ass'n Property Cas. Ins. Co., 2002 WL 31628179 (Tex. App. Nov. 21, 2002), *opinion withdrawn and case dismissed on joint motion of parties*, 2003 WL 302220 (Tex. App. Feb. 13, 2003); Industrial Indemnity Co. v. Kallevig, 114 Wash. 2d 907, 792 P.2d 520 (1990). *See also* Shannon R. Ginn Constr. Co. v. Reliance Ins. Co., 51 F. Supp. 2d 1347 (S.D. Fla. 1999). *But cf.* Betco Scaffolds Co. v. Houston United Cas. Ins. Co., 29 S.W.3d 341 (Tex. App. 2000) (if insured is not entitled to benefits under insurance contract, insurer would only be liable for DTPA claim if its conduct is extreme).

1030 Commercial Union Ins. Co. v. Seven Provinces Ins. Co., 217 F.3d 33 (1st Cir. 2000) (even if insurer has plausible defenses to claim, it must clearly articulate the defense and assert it in good faith), *cert. denied*, 148 L. Ed. 2d 959 (2001); Farmland Mut. Ins. Co. v. Johnson, 36 S.W.3d 368 (Ky. App. 2000) (insured may have UNIP claim even if insurance claim is debatable, as insurer has duty to investigate, negotiate, and attempt to reach a fair settlement of debatable as well as clear claims); Stumph v. Dallas Fire Ins. Co., 34 S.W.3d 722 (Tex. App. Dec. 21, 2000); Coventry Associates v. American States Ins. Co., 961 P.2d 933 (Wash. 1998). *See also* Bobick v. United States Fidelity & Guaranty Ins. Co., 790 N.E.2d 653, 662–63 (Mass. 2003) (duty to make prompt settlement offer or conduct a reasonable investigation before refusing to pay claims is not dependent upon the willingness of a claimant to accept such an offer); G & G Servs. v. Agora Syndicate, Inc., 993 P.2d 751 (N.M. Ct. App. 1999) (failing to establish and use reasonable standards for promptly investigating and processing claims is an unfair insurance practice; case applies this rule to insured's demand for defense); *cf.* Schaeffer v. Farmers Ins. Exchange, 2002 Wash. App. LEXIS 721 (Apr. 22, 2002) (unpublished, citation limited) (unreasonable investigation is UDAP violation only if insured shows harm).

1031 Hangarter v. Paul Revere Life Ins. Co., 236 F. Supp. 2d 1069 (N.D. Cal. 2002).

1032 Elder v. Coronet Ins. Co., 201 Ill. App. 3d 733, 558 N.E.2d 1312 (1990).

1033 Reyna v. Safeway Managing General Agency for State and County Mut. Fire Ins. Co., 27 S.W.3d 7 (Tex. App. 2000). *But cf.* Mauskar v. Hardgrove, 2003 WL 21403464 n.10 (Tex. App. June 19, 2003), which notes that the duty of good faith and fair dealing has not been extended to the agent of the insurer. Despite that dictum, the general rule is that an insurer is always responsible for the acts of its agent. Indeed, as another court noted, to recover under UNIP, a plaintiff does not even have to prove that the insurer's employee had either actual or apparent authority to bind the defendant, but only that defendant committed a UDAP violation. West v. Mendota Ins. Co., 2003 WL 21321066 (N.D. Tex. May 15, 2003). Under many UNIP and UDAP laws, an agent is individually responsible for his or her own misrepresentations, as well. *See* § 6.2, *infra*.

1034 Gaston v. Tennessee Farmers Mut. Ins. Co., 120 S.W.3d 815 (Tenn. 2004).

1035 Johnson v. First Union Corp., 496 S.E.2d 1 (N.C. App. 1998), *substituted decision issued reaching opposite result on other grounds*, 504 S.E.2d 808 (N.C. App. 1998) (workers' compensation statutes displace UDAP remedy).

1036 Commonwealth *ex rel.* Fisher v. Allstate Ins. Co., Clearinghouse No. 53,561 (Pa. Commw. Ct. Jan. 18, 2001).

1037 Tex. Farmers Ins. Co. v. McGuire, 744 S.W.2d 601 (Tex. 1998).

The Connecticut Supreme Court has held that it is deceptive for an insurance company to represent that it is purchasing an annuity of a certain value and cost for a tort victim, when actually its cost is less because it receives a secret rebate from the annuity company.[1038]

One remarkable case involves a major insurer attempting to avoid significant liability on potential claims by transferring its policies to another affiliated company that was undercapitalized. California's Court of Appeals found this to be deceptive where the policyholders were not fully informed of the nature of the transfer.[1039]

Violating a UNIP regulation by failing to disclose the existence of underinsured motorist coverage that might cover an insured's loss is a UDAP violation.[1040] Note the individual agent,[1041] or a non-agent employee of an insurer,[1042] can be held liable for his or her own misrepresentations.

5.3.3.9 Requiring Consumer to Sign Waiver as UDAP Violation

A court found unfair coercion where an insurer refused to pay an insurance settlement rightfully owed the consumer unless the consumer signed a waiver.[1043] It is also unfair to obtain a release where the consumer can not read, reason, or investigate the claim independently.[1044] Using misleading statements to obtain the injured party's signature on a medical release is deceptive.[1045] But an insurer did not commit a UDAP violation when the partial settlement check it sent inadvertently included language that would have released it from the rest of the insured's claim.[1046]

A third party, as opposed to the insured, can not complain that the tortfeasor's insurance company required a release before it would settle a claim, because the insurer's duty is to protect its insured.[1047] The insurer's duty of good faith and fair dealing may terminate, however, once a judgment is entered against it and it becomes a mere judgment debtor.[1048] On the other hand, if the claims adjuster who is working for the tortfeasor's insurance company develops a non-adversarial relationship with a victim, presents documents such as releases, and advises the victim to sign, this may amount to the practice of law and bring with it the duties imposed upon attorneys.[1049]

5.3.3.10 Third-Party Settlement Practices

An insured may have a UDAP cause of action against his or her insurer where a claim is made by a third party against the insured. It may be unfair or deceptive for an insurer to unreasonably refuse to settle the claim within the policy limits or to fail to inform the insured of such a claimant's settlement offer, if the result is that the litigated claim results in a judgment against the insured for an amount exceeding the policy limits.[1050]

Similarly, it can be a UDAP violation for an insurer to hide from its insured the insurer's intent to fully protect the insured, requiring the insured to obtain independent counsel to represent the insured's interests.[1051] In other words, the insurance company's bad faith failure to settle the claim within the policy limits may result in the insured being personally liable for the amount that a judgment exceeds the policy limits. If the insurer acts unreasonably, it can be liable to its insured for this extra liability suffered by the insured.

Another related practice is an insurer's refusal to defend a claim on behalf of the insured. For this to be a UDAP violation, one court has required there to be bad faith or deception on behalf of the insurer.[1052] Even if an insurer's refusal to defend is ultimately found incorrect, there may not

1038 Macomber v. Travelers Prop. & Cas. Corp., 261 Conn. 620, 804 A.2d 180 (2002).

1039 *See* AICCO, Inc. v. Insurance Co. of N. Am., 90 Cal. App. 4th 579, 109 Cal. Rptr. 2d 359 (2001).

1040 Anderson v. State Farm Mut. Ins. Co., 2 P.3d 1029 (Wash. App. 2000).

1041 Thomas v. Ohio Cas. Group of Ins. Companies, 3 F. Supp. 2d 764 (S.D. Tex. 1998).

1042 Liberty Mut. Ins. Co. v. Garrison Contractors, Inc., 966 S.W.2d 482 (Tex. 1998).

1043 Bertassi v. Allstate Ins. Co., 402 Mass. 366, 522 N.E.2d 949 (1988). *But see* Lazaris v. Metropolitan Property and Casualty Ins. Co., 703 N.E.2d 205 (Mass. 1998).

1044 Cravey v. Johnson, 493 S.E.2d 536 (Ga. App. Ct. 1997).

1045 Commonwealth *ex rel.* Fisher v. Allstate Ins. Co., Clearinghouse No. 53,561 (Pa. Commw. Ct. Jan. 18, 2001).

1046 Central Carolina Bank and Trust Co. v. Security Life of Denver Ins. Co., 247 F. Supp. 2d 791 (M.D. N.C. 2003).

1047 Gallagher v. Allstate Ins. Co., 74 F. Supp. 2d 652 (N.D. W. Va. 1999); *see also* Lazaris v. Metropolitan Property & Cas. Ins. Co., 428 Mass. 502, 703 N.E.2d 205 (1998).

1048 Mid-Century Ins. Co. v. Boyte, 80 S.W.3d 546 (Tex. 2002) (duty of good faith under common law and UDAP and UNIP statutes did not extend to period after entry of money judgment against insurer); Stewart Title Guar. Co. v. Aiello, 941 S.W.2d 68 (Tex. 1997).

1049 Jones v. Allstate Ins. Co., 45 P.3d 1068 (Wash. 2002).

1050 Dimarzo v. American Mut. Ins. Co., 389 Mass. 85, 449 N.E.2d 1189 (1983); Allstate Ins. Co. v. Kelly, 680 S.W.2d 595 (Tex. App. 1984). *But see* Travelers Indemnity Co. v. Citgo Petroleum Corp., 166 F.3d 761 (5th Cir. 1999).

1051 Nationwide Mut. Ins. Co. v. Holmes, 842 S.W.2d 335 (Tex. App. 1992). An insurer is not, however, liable for malpractice by an independent attorney it hires to represent and defend an insured. State Farm Mut. Auto. Ins. Co. v. Traver, 980 S.W.2d 625 (Tex. 1998).

1052 DeWitt Constr. Inc. v. Charter Oak Fire Ins. Co., 307 F.3d 1127 (9th Cir. 2002); Travelers Ins. Co. v. Waltham Indus. Laboratories, 722 F. Supp. 814 (D. Mass. 1988) (no violation of UDAP statute where decision not to defend suit was reasonable and based on advice and investigation of experienced attorney), *rev'd in part on other grounds*, 883 F.2d 1092 (1st Cir. 1989); National Grange Mut. Ins. Co. v. Continental Casualty Ins. Co., 650 F. Supp. 1404 (S.D.N.Y. 1986).

be UDAP liability if its interpretation of the policy was plausible.[1053]

In Texas, there is a separate court-made duty requiring an insurance company to defend third-party claims against the insured, called the *Stowers* doctrine after the case that established it.[1054] The *Stowers* doctrine is the sole remedy for an insurer's failure to settle third-party claims.[1055] However, if there are misrepresentations by the insurer that go beyond refusal to defend, there may be a bad-faith claim.[1056]

Whether a third-party claimant can pursue UNIP or UDAP claims regarding an insurer's settlement practices is discussed in other sections of this book.[1057]

5.3.3.11 Is a Pattern of Unfair Claims Payments a Precondition to a UDAP Action?

It is usually safest to allege that claim settlement practices violate the UDAP statute directly, and not that they violate the UNIP statute, and hence the UDAP statute. This is because most state UNIP statutes prohibit unfair claim settlement practices only when the practices are committed "with such frequency as to indicate a general business practice,"[1058] which may complicate the consumer's proof requirements. Such language may require the individual consumer plaintiff, when raising a private UNIP claim or a UDAP claim based on the UNIP statute, to show that the unfair claim settlement practice was a general business practice, not an isolated case.[1059] But a UDAP claim, not based on the UNIP violation, may not need to show frequency because that is not an element to a UDAP action.[1060]

If a consumer does present proof of a pattern of unfair claims payment practices, such proof may include evidence of various instances of unfair claim settlement practices or

---

1053 Timpson v. Transamerica Ins. Co., 41 Mass. App. Ct. 344, 669 N.E.2d 1092 (1996), *review denied*, 423 Mass. 1114, 674 N.E.2d 246 (1996).

1054 Stowers Furniture Co. v. American Indem. Co., 15 S.W.2d 544 (Tex. Comm'n App. 1929).

1055 Travelers Indemnity Co. v. Citgo Petroleum Corp., 166 F.3d 761 (5th Cir. 1999); HVAW v. American Motorists Ins. Co., 968 F. Supp. 1178 (N.D. Tex. 1997); Storebrand Ins. Co. U.K., Ltd. v. Employers Ins. of Wausau, 139 F.3d 1052 (5th Cir. 1998); Maryland Ins. Co. v. Head Indus. Coatings & Services, Inc., 938 S.W.2d 27 (Tex. 1996); Southstar Corp. v. St. Paul Surplus Lines Ins. Co., 42 S.W.3d 187 (Tex. App. 2001); Traver v. State Farm Mut. Auto. Ins. Co., 930 S.W.2d 862 (Tex. App. 1996), *rev'd on other grounds*, 980 S.W.2d 625 (Tex. 1998) (vicarious liability of insurer for malpractice of independent attorney). However, one intermediate Texas appellate court has held that an insured employer may bring a UNIP claim for the insurer's failure to settle claims made against its employee. Rocor Int'l, Inc. v. National Union Fire Ins. Co., 995 S.W.2d 804 (Tex. App. 1999) (en banc), *aff'd in part, rev'd in part*, 77 S.W.3d 253 (Tex. 2002) (claim available under UNIP statute, but not made out here, because no showing of proper offer of settlement by third party claimant).

1056 Ecotech Int'l, Inc. v. Griggs & Harrison, 928 S.W.2d 644 (Tex. App. 1996).

1057 *See* §§ 2.4.1.2, 5.3.2.3.2, *supra*.

1058 NAIC model statute § 4(9). For a listing of state UNIP statutes, see § 5.3.2.1, *supra*. A few UNIP statutes use different language. *See* Colo. Rev. Stat. § 10-3-1104(h) ("committing or performing, either in willful violation of this part . . . or with such frequency as to indicate a tendency to engage in a general business practice"); Mont. Code Ann. § 33-18-242 (proof of frequent violations is not necessary in suit by insured or third-party claimant); Mass. Gen. Laws ch. 176D, § 3(9) ("any of the following acts or omissions"); N.M. Stat. Ann. § 59A-16-20 ("knowingly committed or performed with such frequency as to indicate a general business practice"); Or. Rev. Stat. § 746.230(1) (no qualifying language). *See* Hopkins v. Liberty Mut. Ins. Co., 434 Mass. 556, 750 N.E.2d 943 (2001) (failure to make prompt settlement is a UNIP violation even if just a single incident).

1059 Maher v. Continental Casualty Co., 76 F.3d 535 (4th Cir. 1996); Martin v. Am. Equity Ins. Co., 185 F. Supp. 2d 162 (D. Conn. 2002); Volpe v. Paul Revere Life Ins. Co., 2001 U.S. Dist. LEXIS 14368 (D. Conn. Aug. 29, 2001); Benton v. Allstate Ins. Co., 2001 U.S. Dist. LEXIS 9448 (C.D. Cal. Feb. 26, 2001); United Technologies Corp. v. American Home Assurance Co., 989 F. Supp. 128 (D. Conn. 1997); Cook v. Principal Mut. Life Ins. Co., 784 F. Supp. 1513 (D. Mont. 1990); Safeco Ins. Co. of Am. v. McAllister, 785 F. Supp. 119 (D. Mont. 1990); Lees v. Middlesex Ins. Co., 229 Conn. 842, 643 A.2d 1282 (1994) (proof of frequent practice, involving more than one claim, required); Fode v. Farmers Ins. Exchange, 719 P.2d 414 (Mont. 1986); Klaudt v. Fink, 658 P.2d 1065 (Mont. 1983); Piduch v. Lumbermens Mut. Casualty Co., 124 A.D. 2d 999 (N.Y. 1986); Cash v. State Farm Mut. Auto. Ins. Co., 137 N.C. App. 192, 528 S.E.2d 372 (2000) (plaintiff must allege general business practice); Gray v. North Carolina Ins. Underwriting Ass'n, 510 S.E.2d 396 (N.C. App. 1999), *rev'd in part on other grounds*, 352 N.C. 61, 529 S.E.2d 676 (2000); Wake County Hosp. Sys. v. Safety Nat'l Casualty Corp., 487 S.E.2d 789 (N.C. Ct. App. 1997) (UNIP claim dismissed for failure to plead that violation was general business practice), *review denied*, 347 N.C. 410, 494 S.E.2d 600 (1997); Murray v. Nationwide Mut. Ins. Co., 472 S.E.2d 358 (N.C. App. 1996); Belmont Land & Inv. Co. v. Standard Fire Ins. Co., 403 S.E.2d 924 (N.C. Ct. App. 1991); Mocassin v. State Farm Mut. Automobile Ins. Co., 625 N.W.2d 264 (N.D. 2001); Ingalls v. Paul Revere Life Ins. Group. 1997 N.D. 43, 561 N.W.2d 273 (N.D. 1997); Volk v. Wisconsin Mortgage Assurance Co., 474 N.W.2d 40 (N.D. 1991); McCormick v. Allstate Ins. Co., 475 S.E.2d 507 (W. Va. 1996); Russell v. Amerisure Ins. Co., 189 W. Va. 594, 433 S.E.2d 532 (1993). *See* Martin v. Reliance Ins. Co., 954 F. Supp. 476 (D. Conn. 1997) (sufficient for complaint to allege that insurer committed similar misconduct with other insureds, therefore motion to dismiss was denied; unnecessary to include specific names or facts relating to other claims). *But see* Vail v. Texas Farm Bureau Mut. Ins. Co., 754 S.W.2d 129 (Tex. 1988) (need not show general business practice); Industrial Indemnity Co. v. Kallevig, 114 Wash. 2d 907, 792 P.2d 520 (1990) (although insurance regulation requires general business practice, state unfair insurance practices statute finds even one violation of regulation to violate statute and any statutory violation is *per se* UDAP violations).

1060 Gray v. North Carolina Ins. Underwriting Ass'n, 352 N.C. 61, 529 S.E.2d 676 (2000). *But see* Hilton v. Town of Wallingford, 1998 Conn. Super. LEXIS 1047 (Super. Ct. Apr. 14, 1998) (since isolated instance of unfair claims settlement does not violate UNIP statute, it can not be UDAP violation).

testimony by attorneys, adjusters, or others knowledgeable about a company's practices.[1061] Frequency can be proved not only by multiple instances of the same violation, but by the occurrence of different violations.[1062] It may be possible to satisfy the standard simply by showing that the insurer repeatedly denied the plaintiff's claim.[1063]

Advocates should also check their UNIP statute to see if another prohibition that does not require proof of a pattern is applicable. For example, while Connecticut's general prohibition of unfair claims settlement practices requires proof of a pattern,[1064] a separate subsection that forbids delays in payment of accident and health claims has no such requirement.[1065]

5.3.3.12 UDAP Claim Distinguished from Claim Based on Insurer's Breach of Contract

A UDAP claim based on unfair insurance claims practices is a separate and distinct claim from a contract claim that the claims payment has not been made. A UDAP suit alleging unreasonable refusal to pay a claim is based on factual inquiries and sources of duty that are separate and distinct from an action on the policy.[1066] In fact, a UDAP claim may exist even if there is not a breach of contract.[1067]

Even where the insurance company ultimately pays the insured's claim, the insurer may be found liable for unfair claim settlement procedures, such as failing to keep the insured informed.[1068] The insurer's violations of the state UNIP statute may be taken into account in determining whether it is liable for enhanced damages and attorney fees on the contract.[1069] On the other extreme, a UDAP claim may be available even where a claim is not covered by a policy if the insurer's claims adjusting or settling practices are so extreme that independent injury occurs.[1070] However, voluntary surrender of the policy may preclude a UNIP claim.[1071]

5.3.3.13 Litigating the Bad Faith Refusal as a UDAP Claim

The burden of proof of bad faith is on the consumer. This may well require the consumer to prove the absence of any reasonable basis for denial, and that the insurer knew, or should have known, that there was no reasonable basis.[1072] The mere failure to comply with a separate statute setting time limits for responding to a claim may not establish liability.[1073] Expert testimony may be admissible on the question of whether an insurance company's claim settlement practices are unfair.[1074]

In Texas, the elements for a UNIP or UDAP suit based on denial of a claim are the same as the elements necessary to show a breach of the common law duty of good faith and fair dealing.[1075] Thus, the defenses available to the common law duty may also be available to an UNIP or UDAP claim.[1076] If a UDAP action is based on a contractual bad faith claim, loss on the contract claim may require loss on the UDAP claim.[1077]

The statute of limitations for an action based on unfair refusal to pay a claim runs from the date of refusal of

1061 Fode v. Farmers Ins. Exchange, 719 P.2d 414 (Mont. 1986); Dodrill v. Nationwide Mut. Ins. Co., 201 W. Va. 1, 491 S.E.2d 1 (1996). *But see* Shannon R. Ginn Constr. Co. v. Reliance Ins. Co., 51 F. Supp. 2d 1347 (S.D. Fla. 1999) (neither unsworn complaints filed in other cases nor affidavit that did not offer evidence as to whether other claims denials were inappropriate were sufficient to defeat insurer's motion for summary judgment).

1062 Weese v. Nationwide Ins. Co., 879 F.2d 115 (4th Cir. 1989) (West Virginia law); Jenkins v. J.C. Penney Casualty Ins. Co., 167 W. Va. 597, 280 S.E.2d 252 (1981).

1063 Murray v. Nationwide Mut. Ins. Co., 472 S.E.2d 358 (N.C. App. 1996).

1064 Conn. Gen. Stat. § 38a-816(6).

1065 Conn. Gen. Stat. § 38a-816(15). *See* Pierce v. Aetna Life Ins. Co., 1998 Conn. Super. LEXIS 870 (Mar. 24, 1998) (frequency requirement does not apply to claim under § 816(15)).

1066 Lees v. Middlesex Ins. Co., 219 Conn. 644, 594 A.2d 952 (1991); Slider v. State Farm Mut. Auto. Ins. Co., 210 W. Va. 476, 557 S.E.2d 883 (2001) (UNIP and bad faith claims not barred by prior unsuccessful motion to have attorney fees awarded in underlying suit under policy).

1067 Northwinds Abatement, Inc. v. Employers Ins. of Wausau, 258 F.3d 345 (5th Cir. 2001) (Texas law).

1068 Peckham v. Continental Casualty Ins. Co., 895 F.2d 830 (1st Cir. 1990) (Massachusetts law).

1069 Miller v. Fluharty, 500 S.E.2d 310 (W. Va. 1997).

1070 West v. Mendota Ins. Co., 2003 WL 21321066 (N.D. Tex. May 15, 2003); Royal Maccabees Life Ins. Co. v. James, 2003 WL 1848601 (Tex. App. Apr. 10, 2003); Betco Scaffolds Co. v. Houston United Cas. Ins. Co., 29 S.W.3d 341 (Tex. App. 2000); Tivoli Corp. v. Jewelers Mut. Ins. Co., 932 S.W.2d 704 (Tex. App. 1996).

1071 Benbow v. All Am. Life Ins. Co., 1999 U.S. Dist. LEXIS 467 (N.D. Tex. Jan. 14, 1999).

1072 Higginbotham v. State Farm Mut. Auto. Ins. Co., 103 F.3d 456 (5th Cir. 1997); Universe Life Ins. Co. v. Giles, 950 S.W.2d 48 (Tex. 1997); Stewart Title Guar. Co. v. Aiello, 941 S.W.2d 68 (Tex. 1997); Gonzales v. Texas Workers' Compensation Fund, 950 S.W.2d 380 (Tex. App. 1997).

1073 Bekins Moving & Storage Co. v. Williams, 947 S.W.2d 568 (Tex. App. 1997).

1074 Pieffer v. State Farm Mut. Automobile Ins. Co., 940 P.2d 967 (Colo. Ct. App. 1996), *aff'd on other grounds*, 955 P.2d 1008 (Colo. 1998).

1075 Coury v. Allstate Texas Lloyds, 2003 WL 23204647 (S.D. Tex. July 1, 2003); Gulf Ins. Co. v. Jones, 2003 WL 22208551 (N.D. Tex. Sept. 24, 2003); Douglas v. State Farm Lloyds, 37 F. Supp. 2d 532 (S.D. Tex. 1999); Watson v. State Farm Lloyds, 56 F. Supp. 2d 734 (N.D. Tex. 1999); Batte v. Twin City Fire Ins. Co., 1999 U.S. Dist. LEXIS 18658 (N.D. Tex. Nov. 24, 1999), *aff'd without op.*, 234 F.3d 29 (5th Cir. 2000); Lane v. State Farm Mut. Auto. Ins. Co., 992 S.W.2d 545 (Tex. App. 1999).

1076 Lane v. State Farm Mut. Auto. Ins. Co., 992 S.W.2d 545 (Tex. App. 1999).

1077 Fiess v. State Farm Lloyds, 2003 WL 21659408 (S.D. Tex. June 4, 2003); Carter v. State Farm Mut. Auto. Ins. Co., 33 S.W.3d 369 (Tex. App. 2000).

coverage in Texas.[1078] The final refusal by the insurer, and not the initial refusal, is the determinative date.[1079]

5.3.4 Misrepresentations Concerning Policy Coverage

Even where an insurer's refusal to pay a claim is justified by the insurance policy language, UDAP statutes can challenge misrepresentations about the scope of policy coverage the insurer or its agent made at the time the policy was written. Thus UDAP statutes have successfully challenged misrepresentations of the coverages and benefits provided,[1080] the duration of the policy,[1081] the consumer's eligibility,[1082] and indemnification provisions.[1083] State UNIP legislation also prohibits misrepresentation by an insurer, agent, broker or adjuster of the terms, conditions, and the extent of insurance policy coverage,[1084] or the nature of the policy.[1085]

However, absent a specific misrepresentation of the terms, a consumer may have difficulty alleging that the insurer failed to disclose the lack of specific coverage.[1086] In one case, a court held that a representation that a policy covered "all risks" was not actionable, even though the policy excluded the type of harm (damage to house foundation due to earth movement) that ultimately incurred.[1087] Similarly, pre-approval of surgery will not serve as the basis for an action based on subsequent refusal to pay for the surgery, unless the consumer shows she would not have had the surgery without the pre-approval.[1088]

An agent's mere failure to increase the level of policy coverage is not actionable, absent an actual misrepresentation about the scope of availability of coverage.[1089] The

1078 Provident Am. Ins. Co. v. Castaneda, 988 S.W.2d 189 (Tex. 1998).

1079 Pena v. State Farm Lloyds, 980 S.W.2d 949 (Tex. App. 1998).

1080 Piper v. American Nat'l Life Ins. Co., 228 F. Supp. 2d 553 (M.D. Pa. 2002); Krisa v. Equitable Life Assurance Soc., 113 F. Supp. 2d 694 (M.D. Pa. 2000) (denying insurer's motion for summary judgment where allegations amounted to fraudulent inducement); Brownwell v. State Farm Mut. Ins. Co., 757 F. Supp. 526 (E.D. Pa. 1991) (insurer violated UDAP by misrepresenting that medical coverage was available while denying coverage for soft tissue injuries); National Health & Life Ins. Co., 70 F.T.C. 1033 (1966) (consent order); Commercial Travelers Ins. Co., 51 F.T.C. 682 (1955) (consent order); Illinois Commercial Men's Ass'n, 52 F.T.C. 351 (1955) (consent order); Southern Nat'l Ins. Co., 51 F.T.C. 894 (1955) (consent order); Lang v. Consumers Ins. Service, Inc., 583 N.E.2d 1147 (Ill. App. Ct. 1991) (UDAP violation to misrepresent existing insurance would cover a new vehicle); Glazewski v. Allstate Ins. Co., 126 Ill. App. 3d 401, 466 N.E.2d 1151 (1984) (deceptive to fail to disclose limited nature of insurance coverage), *rev'd in part*, 108 Ill. 2d 243, 483 N.E.2d 1263 (1985) (plaintiff stated a claim for fraud but not for violation because did not show basis for injunctive relief); Card v. Chase Manhattan Bank, 175 Misc. 2d 389, 669 N.Y.S.2d 117 (Civ. Ct. 1996) (consumers reasonably construed creditor's statements as indicating that credit life insurance included unemployment coverage); Solomon v. Hager, 2001 Tenn. App. LEXIS 929 (Dec. 27, 2001); Aetna Casualty & Surety Co. v. Marshall, 724 S.W.2d 770 (Tex. 1987); Royal Globe Ins. Co. v. Bar Consultants, Inc., 577 S.W.2d 688 (Tex. 1979); Royal Maccabees Life Ins. Co. v. James, 2003 WL 1848601 (Tex. App. Apr. 10, 2003); First Am. Title Ins. Co. v. Willard, 949 S.W.2d 342 (Tex. App. 1997); Maccabees Mut. Life Ins. Co. v. McNiel, 836 S.W.2d 229 (Tex. App. 1992); Frank B. Hall & Co. v. Beach, Inc., 733 S.W.2d 251 (Tex. App. 1987); Group Hosp. Services, Inc. v. Daniel, 704 S.W.2d 870 (Tex. App. 1985). *But see* Sanghavi v. Paul Revere Life Ins. Co., 214 Conn. 303, 572 A.2d 307 (1990) (insurer did not violate UDAP statute by including in its contract a limitation on benefit increases that violated state law and was unenforceable); Jones v. Universal Casualty Co., 630 N.E.2d 94 (Ill. App. Ct. 1994) (every ambiguity in an insurance contract that is resolved against the insurer does not amount to a UDAP violation); Charles Hester Enterprises, Inc. v. Illinois Founders Ins. Co., 114 Ill. 2d 278, 499 N.E.2d 1319 (1986); Robacki v. Allstate Ins. Co., 127 Ill. App. 3d 294, 468 N.E.2d 1251 (1984); Employers Casualty Co. v. Fambro, 694 S.W.2d 449 (Tex. App. 1985); McNeill v. McDavid Ins. Agency, 594 S.W.2d 198 (Tex. Civ. App. 1980). *But cf.* Foisy v. Royal Maccabees Life Ins. Co., 241 F. Supp. 2d 65 (D. Mass. 2002) (negligent misrepresentation of terms of annuity contract was not deceptive or a violation of state UDAP statute); Haisch v. Allstate Ins. Co., 197 Ariz. 606, 5 P.3d 940 (App. 2000) (not UNIP violation for insurer to fail to advise insured that it would not pay her for medical charges that her HMO covered).

1081 Beneficial Standard Life Ins. Co., 52 F.T.C. 342 (1955) (consent order); The Service Life Ins. Co., 52 F.T.C. 590 (1955) (consent order); Southern Nat'l Ins. Co., 51 F.T.C. 894 (1955) (consent order).

1082 Nast v. State Farm Fire and Cas. Co., 82 S.W.3d 114 (Tex. App. 2002).

1083 Illinois Commercial Men's Ass'n, 52 F.T.C. 351 (1955) (consent order); Southern Nat'l Ins. Co., 51 F.T.C. 894 (1955) (consent order).

1084 NAIC model statute § 4(1)(a); statutes cited at § 5.3.2.1, *supra*. *See also* Life Investors Ins. Co. v. Smith, 833 P.2d 864 (Colo. Ct. App. 1992); Aetna Casualty & Surety Co. v. Marshall, 724 S.W.2d 770 (Tex. 1987).

1085 NAIC model statute § 4(1)(e); statutes cited at § 5.3.2.1, *supra*. *See also* Kron Medical Corp. v. Collier Cobb & Assoc., 107 N.C. App. 331, 420 S.E.2d 192 (1992); Celtic Life Ins. Co. v. Coats, 885 S.W.2d 96 (Tex. 1994). *But see* HVAW Ltd. P'ship v. American Motorists Ins. Co., 968 F. Supp. 1178 (N.D. Tex. 1997) (erroneously holding that misrepresentations are only actionable if "material"). *But cf.* Cash v. State Farm Mut. Auto. Ins. Co., 137 N.C. App. 192, 528 S.E.2d 372 (2000) (insurer's payment of third party's phony claim, which caused insured's rates to increase, was not contrary to its representation that it did not want to pay false claims).

1086 Moore v. Whitney-Vaky Ins. Agency, 966 S.W.2d 690 (Tex. App. 1998).

1087 Muniz v. State Farm Lloyds, 974 S.W.2d 229 (Tex. App. 1998).

1088 Provident Am. Ins. Co. v. Castaneda, 988 S.W.2d 189 (Tex. 1998). *But cf.* Van Noy v. State Farm Mut. Automobile Ins. Co., 98 Wash. App. 487, 983 P.2d 1129 (1999) (insurer's delay in disapproving coverage can cause compensable damage if insured is left personally liable for treatment that he or she might have chosen to forgo), *aff'd on other grounds*, 142 Wash. 2d 784, 16 P.3d 574 (2001).

1089 Frazer v. Texas Farm Bureau Mut. Ins. Co., 4 S.W.3d 819 (Tex. App. 1999).

guarantee of good title in a title policy is not actionable, because it is actually merely a contract of indemnity and not an actual misrepresentation.[1090] However an affirmative misrepresentation in a title policy is actionable.[1091]

If an insurer misrepresented the scope of a policy's coverage, then the consumer's actual damages may equal the amount of the consumer's claim that was denied. It is as much insurer bad faith to refuse to pay a claim that the insurer misrepresented would be covered by the policy as it is to refuse to pay a claim that the policy language explicitly covers.[1092] The fact that the oral misrepresentation was later corrected by the policy language does not prevent the misrepresentation from being a UDAP violation.[1093] Refusing to tell an insured what portion of the cost of a medical procedure will be covered by insurance is also a UDAP violation.[1094]

Attempting to deny that coverage exists, in order to avoid a potential claim, is a UDAP violation.[1095] This principle applies even when the insurer attempts to deny a claim based on a misrepresentation in the consumer's application, where the insurance agent was responsible for that misrepresentation. For example, in one case an industrial life insurance salesman badgered a couple to take out a policy, and filled out the form for the couple who spoke no English. When the insurer tried to use misrepresentations in the application as grounds for refusing to pay a claim, the consumer successfully claimed the agent wrote down different answers on the application than those given to the agent by the consumer, and that such activity was unconscionable. The consumer thus prevailed not on the policy, but on a UDAP count based on deceptive conduct.[1096]

The UDAP claim can also be based not only on oral misrepresentation of coverage, but also the failure to clearly disclose policy limitations. Thus it is deceptive for an insurer to know that a policy would not cover the risks at issue and still sell the policy without disclosing this fact to the insured.[1097] Contract defenses are irrelevant to such an action.

It is important to pay attention to the statute of limitations when considering a UNIP misrepresentation claim. The claim may mature on the date the insured receives the insurance policy, because many courts impose a duty on the insured to read the policy, at which time any mispresentations as to coverage might be apparent.[1098]

5.3.5 Misrepresentations Concerning Insurer Claims Settlement Policies

An actionable UDAP violation may involve misrepresentations as to how generous the insurer will be in settling claims. Most UNIP statutes prohibit settlement offers that are unreasonable when compared to the insurer's claims in advertising or sales presentations concerning its generous claims payment policy.[1099] It has similarly been held deceptive to sell insurance without disclosing the insurance company's harsh and unfair claims settlement practices.[1100] But an insurer does not have a duty to advise an insured about every possible type of coverage available,[1101] or about all the contingencies that might affect claims under various state laws.[1102]

5.3.6 Twisting; Sale of Unnecessary Insurance; Other Unfair or Deceptive Sales Schemes

Insurance by its very nature is intangible, and leads to numerous schemes to market coverage that is unnecessary or not especially sensible for the consumer. Sections 5.3.10 (credit insurance), 5.3.11 (creditor force-placed insurance), and 5.3.12 (creditor packing of insurance), *infra*, discuss three such marketing schemes involving creditors selling insurance. This section describes precedent finding other schemes to be UDAP violations. But any unfair or deceptive scheme to market insurance is a UDAP violation.

A classic scheme to sell unnecessary insurance is called "twisting"—using various misrepresentations to get the

1090 Chicago Title Ins. Co. v. Alford, 3 S.W.3d 164 (Tex. App. 1999).

1091 *Id.*

1092 *See, e.g.*, Canutillo Independent School Dist. v. National Union Fire Ins. Co., 99 F.3d 695 (5th Cir. 1996); Sledge v. Mullin, 927 S.W.2d 89 (Tex. App. 1996).

1093 *See* § 4.2.17.1, *supra*.

1094 Green v. Blue Cross & Blue Shield, 47 Mass. App. Ct. 443, 713 N.E.2d 992 (1999).

1095 Cullen v. Valley Forge Life Ins. Co., 589 S.E.2d 423 (N.C. Ct. App. 2003).

1096 Southern Life & Health Ins. Co. v. Medrano, 698 S.W.2d 457 (Tex. App. 1985); *see also* Grunbaum v. American Express Assur. Co., 1998 U.S. Dist. LEXIS 17627 (N.D. Tex. Nov. 2, 1998); Stewart Title Guaranty Co. v. Sterling, 772 S.W.2d 242 (Tex. App. 1989), *rev'd in part on other grounds*, 822 S.W.2d 1 (Tex. 1991); Group Hosp. Services, Inc. v. Daniel, 704 S.W.2d 870 (Tex. App. 1985) (oral misrepresentations as to coverage are actionable).

1097 *See* Stewart Title Guaranty Co. v. Sterling, 772 S.W.2d 242 (Tex. App. 1989). *See also* Mass. Regs. Code tit. 940, § 9.04 (UDAP violation for group health insurer to terminate coverage for group's nonpayment without first disclosing the termination to individual group members).

1098 Hunton v. Guardian Life Ins. Co. of Am., 243 F. Supp. 2d 686 (S.D. Tex. 2002), *aff'd without op.*, 2003 WL 21418107 (5th Cir. June 10, 2003).

1099 NAIC model statute § 4(9)(h). *See* § 5.3.2.1, *supra* for a listing of state UNIP statutes.

1100 Elder v. Coronet Ins. Co., 201 Ill. App. 3d 733, 558 N.E.2d 1312 (1990).

1101 Mullins v. Commonwealth Life Ins. Co., 839 S.W.2d 245 (Ky. 1992).

1102 Fay v. Erie Ins. Group, 723 A.2d 712 (Pa. Super. 1999) (not a UDAP violation to sell policies that included a duplicate benefit that could not be collected); Treski v. Kemper Nat'l Ins. Companies, 674 A.2d 1106 (Pa. Super. 1996).

consumer to switch from one company to another. Twisting may be accomplished by using the cash-surrender value of the old policy to buy the new one or by making the old policy lapse. UNIP statutes prohibit "twisting"[1103] and the practice should be a UDAP violation as well. So should any misrepresentations for the purpose of inducing a lapse in coverage.[1104] The sale of new medigap insurance to replace a less expensive policy where the new policy provides no greater coverage should be found to be a UDAP violation.[1105] The highest court in New York has held that plaintiffs stated a UDAP claim in their allegation that an insurance company marketed life insurance by promoting a "vanishing premium" program that was based on interest rate projections it knew to be unrealistic.[1106]

One way to engage in twisting is to derogate the other insurance company. State UNIP legislation specifically prohibits misrepresentations about an insurer's financial condition.[1107] This should apply as much to misrepresentations about the poor financial condition of other insurers as it does to overly rosy descriptions of the company trying to sell the policy to the consumer. Nor can agents or the company misrepresent the consumer's cancellation rights[1108] or the requirements for a consumer to renew a policy.[1109]

1103 NAIC model statute §§ 4(1)(f),(g); statutes cited in § 5.3.2.1, *supra*. *See also* Strother v. Capital Bankers Life Ins. Co., 68 Wash. App. 224, 842 P.2d 504 (1992) (it could be a UDAP violation for a second insurer to fail to notify first insurer of switch in policy, as required by state insurance regulations), *rev'd on other grounds*, 124 Wash. 2d. 1, 873 P.2d 1185 (1994). *Cf.* HealthAmerica v. Menton, 551 So. 2d 235 (Ala. 1989).

1104 *Cf.* Heyman Assoc. v. Insurance Co., 231 Conn. 756, 653 A.2d 122 (1995) (finding no purposeful misrepresentations).

1105 *See* Guinn v. American Integrity Ins. Co., 568 So. 2d 760 (Ala. 1990) (trial court improperly dismissed action for fraud based on similar facts). *But see* Obenland v. Economy Fire & Casualty Co., 599 N.E.2d 999 (Ill. App. Ct. 1992) (sale of uninsured motorist coverage that duplicated existing coverage did not violate UDAP statute).

1106 Gaidon v. Guardian Life Ins. Co., 704 N.Y.S.2d 177, 725 N.E.2d 598 (N.Y. 1999) (reversing grant of motions to dismiss and for summary judgment), *aff'd on other grounds*, 96 N.Y.2d 201, 750 N.E.2d 1058 (2001). *Accord* Mentis v. Delaware Am. Life Ins. Co., 1999 Del. Super. LEXIS 419 (July 28, 1999) (denying motion to dismiss). *See also* Chain v. General Am. Life Ins. Co., 1996 U.S. Dist. LEXIS 221505 (N.D. Miss. Sept. 25, 1996) (dismissing UNIP claims but allowing fraud and misrepresentation claims to proceed); Cunningham v. Massachusetts Mut. Life. Ins. Co., 1996 U.S. Dist. LEXIS 21408 (N.D. Miss. 1996) (same); Varacallo v. Massachusetts Mut. Life Ins. Co., 332 N.J. Super. 31, 752 A.2d 807 (App. Div. 2000) (certifying class; since agents were not told the true facts, no individual issues exist regarding whether they told true facts to buyers). *But cf.* Parkhill v. Minnesota Mut. Life Ins. Co., 188 F.R.D. 332 (D. Minn. 1999) (denying class certification because of factual questions regarding reliance and oral sales pitches).

1107 NAIC model statute § 4(1)(d); statutes cited at § 5.3.2.1, *supra*.

1108 Illinois Commercial Men's Ass'n, 52 F.T.C. 351 (1955) (consent order).

1109 Ginocchio v. American Bankers Life Assur. Co., 889 F. Supp. 1078 (N.D. Ill. 1995).

One insurance scam aimed at low-income families preyed on recipients of the Earned Income Tax Credit (EITC) and the Health Insurance Credit. Three insurance companies and an agency allegedly misled about 1500 low-income workers into spending their EITC on questionable insurance policies.[1110] The insurance agent allegedly misrepresented to both employers and employees that employees could only receive the EITC if they enrolled in a special package of life and supplemental health insurance. The scam also allegedly promised benefits from the Federal Health Insurance Credit, which is available to EITC-eligible taxpayers who purchase health insurance that includes coverage for a child. The credit does not apply to supplemental health policies of the type being sold by the agent.

Other unfair insurance practices involve selling insurance to a consumer without the consumer's consent or understanding that insurance is being purchased, or forcing the consumer to purchase insurance as a condition of credit. The FTC has also prohibited issuing insurance without the insured's consent in another context.[1111]

Selling insurance without the required license is also a UDAP violation.[1112] Misrepresenting to a consumer that he is not eligible for insurance is also a UDAP violation.[1113] These practices are examined in more detail in §§ 5.3.10–5.3.13, *infra*, as they apply to credit insurance, force-placed insurance, non-credit insurance packed with a credit transaction, and mortgage insurance.

5.3.7 Unfair Discrimination

Insurance companies often charge different consumers varying premium levels for the same insurance or distinguish between consumers as to the granting, renewal, or cancellation of insurance. Consumers are often concerned that this may be discriminatory. On the other hand, making distinctions on the basis of risk is the essence of insurance.

A good first place to look for what types of insurance discrimination may be UDAP violations is the state UNIP statute. With wide variations, state UNIP legislation prohibits unfair discrimination in the issuance, renewal or extent of coverage, rates charged, or other terms or conditions of certain types of insurance. A number of UNIP statutes prohibit unfair discrimination in the terms or conditions of

1110 *See* "Morales Settles Lawsuit In Tax Credit Case," Press Release from the Texas Attorney General (Dec. 8, 1993) concerning EIC Benefits Inc, (including Gene E. Coulter individually), Massachusetts General Life Ins. Benefits Co., American Heritage Life Ins. Co., and the American Fidelity Assurance Co.

1111 Western Union Assurance Co., 74 F.T.C. 1250 (1968).

1112 Stevens v. Superior Court, 75 Cal. App. 4th 594, 89 Cal. Rptr. 2d 370 (1999).

1113 Morton v. Bank of the Bluegrass, 18 S.W.3d 353 (Ky. App. 1999).

insurance[1114] or prohibit unfair insurance discrimination more generally.[1115]

Selected UNIP statutes prohibit casualty insurers from discriminating with respect to geographic location of the property to be insured ("redlining"),[1116] or with respect to the age of residential property.[1117] Four UNIP statutes also prohibit casualty insurers from canceling, or refusing to issue or renew coverage because of physical or mental disability of the insured.[1118]

Forty-two UNIP statutes and regulations specifically prohibit, for all types of insurance, discrimination based on certain of the following grounds (the exact grounds varying by statute): race, creed, color, gender, marital status, mental or physical impairments, age, occupation, religion or national origin, domestic abuse.[1119] The federal civil rights

1114 Ala. Code § 27-12-11; Alaska Stat. § 21-36.090(a), (b); Ariz. Rev. Stat. Ann. § 20-448; Ark. Code Ann. § 23-66-206(14); Colo. Rev. Stat. § 10-3-1104(1) (prohibition applies to any insurance contract); Del. Code Ann. tit. 18, § 2304(13), (15); Fla. Stat. § 626.9541(1)(g); Ga. Code § 33-6-4(b)(8)(A)(i), (ii); Haw. Rev. Stat. § 431:13-103(a)(7)(A), (B) (prohibition applies to any insurance contract); Idaho Code § 41-1313(1), (2); 215 Ill. Comp. Stat. Ann. §§ 5/236, 5/364; Ind. Code § 27-4-1-4(7)(A), (B), (C); Iowa Code § 507B.4(7)(a), (b); Kan. Stat. Ann. § 40-2404(7); Ky. Stat. Ann. § 304.12-080; La. Rev. Stat. Ann. § 22:1214(7); Me. Rev. Stat. Ann. tit. 24A, § 2159(1), (2); Md. Ins. Code Ann. §§ 27-208(b), 27-212; Mass. Gen. Laws ch. 176D, § 3(7)(a), (b); Mich. Comp. Laws §§ 500.2019, 500.2020; Minn. Stat. § 72A.20(8), (9) (accident and health); Miss. Code Ann. § 83-5-35(g)(1), (2); Mo. Rev. Stat. § 375.936(11)(a), (b); Mont. Code Ann. § 33-18-206(1), (2), 33-18-210(3); Neb. Rev. Stat. § 44-1525(7); Nev. Rev. Stat. §§ 686A.100(1), (2), 686A.130; N.H. Rev. Stat. Ann. § 417:4(VIII) (any insurance); N.J. Rev. Stat. § 17B:30-12(a-b); N.M. Stat. Ann. § 59A-16-11(A), (B); N.Y. Ins. Law § 4224(a), (b); N.C. Gen. Stat. § 58-63-15(7); N.D. Cent. Code § 26.1-04-05; Ohio Rev. Code Ann. § 3901.21(F), (M); Okla. Stat. tit. 36, § 1204(7); Or. Rev. Stat. § 746.015(1); Pa. Stat. Ann. tit. 40, § 1171.5(a)(7); R.I. Gen. Laws § 27-29-4(7); S.C. Code Ann. § 38-57-120; S.D. Codified Laws Ann. §§ 58-33-12, 58-33-13, 58-33-26; Tenn. Code Ann. § 56-8-104(6); Vt. Stat. Ann. tit. 8, § 4724(7)(A) (prohibition applies to any insurance contract); Va. Code Ann. § 38.2-508(1), (2); W. Va. Code Ann. § 33-11-4(7); Wyo. Stat. §§ 26-13-109(a), 26-13-112(c); *see also* Chabner v. United of Omaha Life Ins. Co., 225 F.3d 1042 (9th Cir. 2000) (Cal. law) (discrimination on the basis of disability); Lans v. Mut. Life Ins. Co. of New York, 145 Ariz. 68, 699 P.2d 1299 (Ct. App. 1984) (factual question whether sex discrimination actionable under provision prohibiting discrimination generally); Otero v. Midland Life Ins. Co., 753 So. 2d 579 (Fla. Dist. Ct. App. 1999); Klinginsmith v. Missouri Dep't of Consumer Affairs, 693 S.W.2d 226 (Mo. Ct. App. 1985).

1115 Alaska Stat. § 21-36-090(b); Ariz. Rev. Stat. Ann. § 20-448; Ark. Code Ann. § 23-66-206(7)(B); Ala. Code § 27-12-11; Colo. Rev. Stat. § 10-3-1104; Del. Code Ann. tit. 18, § 2304(13), (15); Fla. Stat. § 6.9541(1)(g); Ga. Code § 33-6-4-(b)(8)(A)(ii); Idaho Code § 41-1313(2); 215 Ill. Comp. Stat. Ann. § 5/364; Ind. Code § 27-4-1-4(7)(B); Iowa Code § 507B.4(7)(b); Kan. Stat. Ann. § 40-2404(7)(b); Ky. Stat. Ann. § 304-12-080(3); La. Rev. Stat. Ann. § 22-1214(7)(b); Me. Rev. Stat. Ann. tit. 24A, § 2159(2); Mass. Gen. Laws ch. 176D, § 3(7)(b); Mich. Comp. Laws § 500.2020; Minn. Stat. § 72A-20(9); Miss. Code Ann. § 83-5-35(g)(2); Mo. Rev. Stat. § 375.936(11)(b); Mont. Code Ann. § 33-18-0206(2); Neb. Rev. Stat. § 44-1525(7)(b), (c); Nev. Rev. Stat. § 686A.100(2); N.H. Rev. Stat. Ann. § 417.4(VIII); N.J. Rev. Stat. § 17B:30-12(d) (health insurance only); N.M. Stat. Ann. § 59A-16-11(B); N.Y. Ins. Law § 4224(b); N.C. Gen. Stat. § 58-63-15(7)(b); Ohio Rev. Code. Ann. § 3901.21(M); Okla. Stat. tit. 36, § 1204(7)(b); Or. Rev. Stat. § 746.015(1); Pa. Stat. Ann. tit. 40, § 1171.5(a)(7)(ii); R.I. Gen. Laws § 27-29-4(7)(ii); S.C. Code Ann. § 38-57-120(2); S.D. Codified Laws Ann. § 58-33-13 (health insurance only); Tenn. Code Ann. § 56-8-104(6)(B); Va. Code Ann. § 38.2-508(2); W. Va. Code Ann. § 33-11-41(7)(b); Wyo. Stat. § 26-13-109(a)(ii) (disability insurance only).

1116 Alaska Stat. § 21.36.120; Ark. Code Ann. § 23-66-206(7)(C); Colo. Rev. Stat. § 10-3-1104(1)(f) (1987); Conn. Gen. Stat. Ann. § 38a-824 (see Conn. Agencies Reg. § 38a-824-3(a)(1)); Ga. Code Ann. § 33-6-4(b)(8)(A)(iii); Haw. Rev. Stat. § 431:13-103(7)(C); Ill. Comp. Stat. Ann. § 5/155.22; Ind. Code § 27-2-17-5(b)(2); Ky. Rev. Stat. § 304.20-340(3); La. Rev. Stat. Ann. 22 § 652(4)(A), 22:1214(7)(d); Mich. Comp. Law § 500.2027 (a)(iii) (1992); Minn. Stat. § 72A.20(13)(a); Mo. Rev. Stat. § 375.936(11)(c) (1991); Mont. Code Ann. § 33-18-210(5); Neb. Rev. Stat. § 44-1525(7)(c); N.C. Gen. Stat. § 58-63-15(7)(c); N.D. Cent. Code §§ 26.1-39-17(3), 26.1-04-03(8)(d); Or. Rev. Stat. § 746.018(2); R.I. Gen. Laws § 27-29-4(7)(iii); Va. Code § 38.2-508(4).

1117 Ark. Stat. Ann. § 23-66-206(14)(D); Conn. Gen. Stat. Ann. § 38a-824 (see Conn. Agencies Regs. § 38a-824-3(a)(5)); Ga. Code Ann. § 33-6-4(b)(8)(A)(iii) (1992); Haw. Rev. Stat. § 431:13-103(7)(D); Ky. Rev. Stat. § 304.20-340(3); La. Rev. Stat. Ann. 22 § 1214(7)(e); Minn. Stat. § 72A.20(13)(b); Mo. Rev. Stat. § 375-936(11)(d) (1991); Mont. Code Ann. § 33-18-210(6); Neb. Rev. Stat. § 44-1525(7)(d); N.C. Gen. Stat. § 58-63-15(7)(d); N.D. Cent. Code § 26.1-39-17(3); R.I. Gen. Laws § 27-29-4(7)(iv) (1993); Va. Code § 38.2-508(5).

1118 Ga. Code § 33-6-5(8); Haw. Rev. Stat. § 431:13-103(a)(7)(F); La. Rev. Stat. Ann. § 22:1214(7)(g); Mont. Code Ann. § 33-18-210(8).

1119 Ark. Stat. Ann. § 23-66-206(14)(G) (marital status, mental or physical impairment or race, color, creed or gender, national origin, citizenship); Ariz. Rev. Stat. Ann. § 20-448 (physical or mental impairment); Cal. Ins. Code § 790.03; Col. Rev. Stat. Ann. § 10-3-1104 (marital status, sex, blindness, partial blindness, physical disability, HIV, genetic information, domestic abuse); Conn. Gen. Stat. Ann. § 38a-816(12),(13) (physical disability, blindness or partial blindness, mental retardation); Del. Code Ann. tit. 18, § 2304(22) (race, color, religion, national origin); Fla. Stat. § 626.9541(1)(x) (refusal to insure or to continue to insure: race, color, creed, sex, marital status, national origin, residence, lawful occupation, age or placement of collateral business with insurer), § 626.9541(g)(3) (domestic abuse); Ga. Code Ann. § 33-6-4(b)(8), (15) (domestic abuse); Haw. Rev. Stat. § 431:13-103(7)(E) to (H) (gender, marital status, mentally or physically impaired); 215 Ill. Comp. Stat. 5/424 (3) & (4) (race, color, religion, national origin); 215 Ill. Comp. Stat. Ann. 5/155.22a (domestic abuse); Iowa Code § 507B.4(7)(c) (domestic abuse); Ind. Code § 27-4-1-4(15) (blindness); Kan. Stat. Ann. § 40-2404(7)(c) (blindness or partial blindness, domestic abuse); Ky. Stat. Ann. §§ 304.12-085, 304.20.340(1) (refusal to insure or to continue to insure: race, color, religion, national origin or gender); La. Rev. Stat. Ann. §§ 22.652.4(A), 22:1214(7)(f) (race, gender, marital status, religion, or national origin); Me. Rev. Stat. Ann. tit. 24-A, § 2159-A (refusal to insure or to continue to insure: blindness,

statutes[1120] and the Americans with Disabilities Act[1121] may also provide a private cause of action for discrimination on the basis of a prohibited characteristic.

5.3.8 *Third Party's Failure to Purchase Insurance for the Consumer*

An insurance claim where actual damages may be significant involves the situation where the consumer has a claim under a policy, but where an insurance agent, escrow holder, employer, or other third party failed to purchase the insurance. The consumer's actual damages equal at least the size of the claim, and it would be helpful to raise the claim as a UDAP violation, leading to attorney fees and possibly multiple or punitive damages. Even if the consumer does not yet have a claim that would have been covered under policy, so has not yet suffered actual damages, the failure to procure insurance is actionable.[1122]

It is a deceptive practice for an insurance agent to claim it had arranged for insurance coverage when the agent had not,[1123] or for an employer to accept premium payments from an employee, but not to forward the premiums to the insurer, resulting in the policy being canceled.[1124] An insurance broker's negligence in arranging for insurance through an unlicensed company in violation of state law is a *per se* UDAP violation, even though it was mere negligence.[1125] Also deceptive is an organization's attempt to pass itself off as an insurance company, representing its employees as insurance agents and its contracts as insurance contracts and failing to disclose that payment on claims is not guaranteed and that continued membership requires further donations.[1126]

5.3.9 *Excessive Premiums as a UDAP Violation*

Rates for a number of lines of insurance are approved by the state insurance commissioner or, in some cases, even set

physical or mental handicap), § 2159 (HIV), § 2159-B (domestic abuse), § 2159-C (genetic information); Md. Ins. Code Ann. §§ 27-208, 212, 501, 502, 504, 909 (race, creed, color, gender, religion, national origin, residence, blindness, or physical or mental disability, genetic information, domestic abuse); Mass Gen. Laws ch 176D § 3(7); Mich. Comp. Laws § 500.2027 (race, color, creed, marital status, gender, national origin, residence, age, handicap or lawful occupation); Minn. Stat. §§ 72A.20(8), (9), (16), (29) (accident, disability or health insurance: "on the basis of a disability," HIV, gender, marital status); Miss. Code Ann. § 83-5-35; Mo. Rev. Stat §§ 375.936(11)(e), (g), (h) (race, gender, color, creed, national origin, ancestry, gender, marital status, mental and physical impairments); Mont. Code Ann. § 33-18-210 (terms or conditions: race, color, creed, religion or national origin, gender, marital status), § 33-18-216 (domestic abuse), §§ 33-18-901 to 904 (genetic information); Neb. Rev. Stat. § 44-1525(7) (sex, marital status, physical or mental impairment); Nev. Rev. Stat. § 686A.130; N.H. Rev. Stat. Ann § 417:4 (VIII), (XIX) (on basis of age, residence, race, color, creed, national origin, ancestry, marital status, or lawful occupation, domestic abuse, HIV, area of residence); N.J. Rev. Stat. § 17B:30-12 (race, creed, color, national origin, ancestry, genetic information); N.M. Stat. Ann. §§ 59A-16-12 to 59A-16-13.2 (gender, race, color religion or national origin, blindness, poor health); N.Y. Ins. Law §§ 2606–2613 (race, color, creed, national origin, disability and can not refuse to issue or cancel policy on grounds of gender or marital status or mental disability, HIV, domestic abuse, genetic information); N.C. Gen. Stat. § 58-3-120 (any discrimination), § 58-3-215 (genetic information); N.D. Cent. Code § 26.1-04-05.1 (accident, health or disability insurance: visual acuity), § 26.1-39-24 (domestic abuse regarding property or casualty insurance); Ohio Rev. Code Ann. § 3901.21(L) (refusal to issue or renew, or cancellation: gender or marital status, blindness, disability, health status, genetic information, domestic abuse); Okla. Stat. tit 36 § 1204(7); Or. Rev. Stat. § 746.015 (physical handicaps, domestic abuse, age), § 746.135 (genetic information); 40 Pa. Cons. Stat. § 1171.5(7) (race, religion, nationality, ethnic group, age, gender, family size, occupation, residence or marital status), § 1171.5(14) (domestic abuse); R.I. Gen. Laws § 27-29-4(7) (gender, marital status, mental or physical impairments); S.C. Code Ann. § 38-55-50; S.D. Codified Laws Ann. § 55-33-12.1 (refusal to issue or renew, or cancellation: blindness), 58-33-13.1 (gender or marital status); Tenn. Code Ann. § 56-8-104(6), §§ 56-8-301 to 306 (domestic abuse); Vt. Stat. Ann. tit. 8, § 4724(7) (gender or marital status, sexual orientation/civil unions, genetic information, HIV); Va. Code Ann. §§ 38.2-508.1 to .4 (race, religion, national origin, gender, genetic information); Wash. Rev. Code §§ 48.18.480, 48.30.300 (gender, marital status, or sensory, mental or physical handicap); W. Va. Code § 33-11-4(7); Wis. Stat. Ann. § 628.34(3)(b) (mental or physical disability); Wyo. Stat. § 26-13-112. *See* Chabner v. United of Omaha Life Ins. Co., 225 F.3d 1042 (9th Cir. 2000) (Cal. law) (allowing UDAP claim for discriminating in life insurance rates without actuarial support); Otero v. Midland Mut. Life Ins. Co., 753 So. 2d 579 (Fla. App. 1999) (damages for bad faith refusal to insure based on national origin are the increased premium). *But see* Telles v. Commissioner of Ins., 410 Mass. 560, 574 N.E.2d 359 (1991) (rejecting claim that sale differential based on sex of insured is unfair discrimination).

1120 Moore v. Liberty Nat'l Ins. Co., 267 F.3d 1209 (11th Cir. 2001) (allowing §§ 1981 and 1982 claims to proceed against insurer for racial discrimination; not barred by McCarran-Ferguson Act). *See generally* National Consumer Law Center, Credit Discrimination § 7.3 (3d ed. 2002 and Supp.).

1121 *See, e.g.*, Pallozzi v. Allstate Life Ins. Co., 198 F.3d 28 (2d Cir. 1999); Doukas v. Metropolitan Life Ins. Co., 950 F. Supp. 422 (D.N.H. 1996). *See generally* National Consumer Law Center, Credit Discrimination § 3.5.2 (3d ed. 2002 and Supp.).

1122 Enyart v. Transamerica Ins. Co., 985 P.2d 556 (Ariz. Ct. App. 1998).

1123 McCrann v. Klaneckey, 667 S.W.2d 924 (Tex. App. 1984).

1124 Oil Country Haulers, Inc. v. Griffin, 668 S.W.2d 903 (Tex. App. 1984).

1125 MacGillivary v. W. Dana Bartlett Ins. Agency, 14 Mass. App. Ct. 52, 436 N.E.2d 964 (1982).

1126 American Security Benevolent Ass'n Inc. v. District Court, 147 N.W.2d 55 (Iowa 1966). *But cf.* Krueger v. State Farm Fire & Casualty Co., 510 N.W.2d 204 (Minn. Ct. App. 1993) (insufficient evidence that confusion of which division of insurance company was offering policy caused injury to consumer).

by the commissioner.[1127] Charging rates in excess of those approved by the state should certainly be a UDAP violation.[1128] In addition, an insurer may not increase policy premiums during the policy term without the insured's authority.[1129] Any misrepresentation to the consumer about the rates charged is also actionable.[1130] This also applies to future dividends or rebates. Thus state UNIP legislation prohibits misrepresentation by an insurer, agent, broker or adjuster concerning dividends or other surplus payable to insureds.[1131]

But it may be difficult to argue that rates approved by the state are UDAP violations. Under the "filed rate" doctrine, rates that are approved by the insurance department are *per se* reasonable and unassailable, so the policyholders can not challenge the rates themselves under a UDAP statute.[1132] Challenging the policy as providing illusory coverage may be a better approach.[1133]

1127 The actual approval process and which lines of insurance are covered by the process varies significantly from state to state. In general, though, residential homeowners, private passenger automobile, credit insurance, and vendor single interest insurance rates receive greater state scrutiny than life or health insurance rates.

1128 McKinnon v. International Fidelity Ins. Co., 704 N.Y.S.2d 774 (Sup. Ct. 1999) (charging more for bail bond than statute allows states UDAP claim); Walts v. First Union Mortgage Corp., 686 N.Y.S.2d 428 (App. Div. 1999) (same). *But cf.* Griffin v. Universal Casualty Co., 654 N.E.2d 694 (Ill. App. Ct. 1995) (selling a higher-priced policy because the value of the consumer's vehicle was inflated is not a UDAP violation unless the insurance company is responsible for inflating the value).

1129 St. Paul Fire & Marine Ins. Co. v. Updegrave, 656 P.2d 1130 (Wash. Ct. App. 1983).

1130 *See* § 5.3.4, *supra*. Where a consumer seeks reformation of an insurance contract (instead of just actual damages) based on pricing misrepresentations, insurers may object that such reformation would cause them to violate a state anti-discrimination statute, by requiring them to offer a lower rate to the plaintiff but not to other individuals in the same circumstances. Courts have differed in their response to this objection. *See* Kuebler v. Equitable Life, 555 N.W.2d 496 (Mich. App. 1996) and cases cited therein.

1131 NAIC model statute §§ 4(1) (b),(c),(h); statutes cited at § 5.3.2.1, *supra*. *See also* "vanishing premium" cases cited in § 5.3.6, *supra*.

1132 *See, e.g.*, Allen v. State Farm Fire & Cas. Co., 59 F. Supp. 2d 1217 (S.D. Ala. 1999); *In re* Empire Blue Cross & Blue Shield Customer Litigation, 622 N.Y.S.2d 843 (Sup. Ct. 1994) (plaintiffs UDAP, contract, and fraud claims are barred, but plaintiff could proceed with an individual action under a state insurance statute that made an insurer liable for the amount of the premium if it misrepresented its financial condition); N.C. Steel, Inc. v. National Council on Compensation Ins., 496 S.E.2d 369 (N.C. 1998) (claims under UNIP and UDAP statutes that insurers withheld information from Insurance Commissioner in rate-setting proceedings is barred by filed rate doctrine). *See also In re* Insurance Stacking Litigation, 754 A.2d 702 (Pa. Super. 2000) (questions involving rates are for insurance commissioner or legislature, not courts).

1133 *See* Vincent v. Safeco Ins. Co., 29 P.3d 943 (Idaho 2001); *see also* § 5.3.10.3, *infra*.

Where the state does not approve of insurance rates, it may be possible to challenge excessive rates as unfair or deceptive.[1134] Particularly for a private action based on the level of rates, it may be best to find some special aspect of the rate level that makes it unfair or deceptive.

A good example of this is a Washington UNIP regulation that finds certain rates charged for burial insurance and other low-face value life insurance policies to be unfair.[1135] The special circumstances in that case were that the insurance was offered without health questionnaires or other medical screening to the elderly, but instead, used "graded" death benefits, whereby the payable death benefit increases over time and does not reach the full face value of the policy for a number of years. Payment of these "graded" death benefits, combined with premiums which are expensive relative to the face value, resulted in premiums that almost equaled the death benefit. As a result, there was no real insurance function served by the policy. For example, in one policy with a $956 annual premium, the death benefit in the first year was $1000, and did not reach $2000 until year ten, at which point the consumer would have paid $9560 in premiums.[1136]

The resulting UNIP regulation defines as an unfair practice the sale of whole life insurance policies with a face value under $25,000 where benefits do not exceed a certain multiple of premiums, the multiple varying with the type of insurance sold. This regulation has widespread national significance, suggesting that it is a state UDAP violation to sell certain egregious kinds of industrial insurance,[1137] burial insurance, medigap insurance, or other forms of insurance where premiums are very high relative to potential benefits. The UDAP violation can be based on rates for a line of insurance, where rates are not approved by the state and where the relationship between paid-in premiums and benefits is unfair.

5.3.10 Credit Insurance

5.3.10.1 Introduction

Credit insurance is a frequent area of consumer abuse. Credit insurance is insurance protecting the creditor's inter-

1134 *See* Morgan v. Blue Cross & Blue Shield, 794 S.W.2d 629 (Ky. 1990) (insurance commissioner could challenge excessive health insurance rates as unfair under state UNIP statute); Omega Nat'l Ins. Co. v. Marquardt, 115 Wash. 2d 416, 799 P.2d 235 (1990) (upholding Wash. Admin. Code § 284-23-550, that prohibits certain life insurance rates as unfair).

1135 Wash. Admin. Code § 284-23-550, upheld in Omega Nat'l Ins. Co. v. Marquardt, 115 Wash. 2d 416, 799 P.2d 235 (1990).

1136 Source is Omega Nat'l Ins. Co. v. Marquardt, Second Affidavit of David Rogers, Chief Deputy Insurance Commissioner for the State of Washington (May 1, 1989).

1137 Industrial or debit insurance is low face value insurance for which premiums are usually collected door-to-door on a monthly or weekly basis.

est in repayment of a consumer debt. For example, credit life insurance pays off the outstanding balance on a loan if the debtor dies. Credit accident and health coverage makes installment payments when the debtor can not work because of a disability. Credit property insurance protects the collateral on a loan. Credit unemployment insurance pays installments when the consumer is unemployed.

Credit insurance is frequently sold at exorbitant prices that allow the creditor to obtain large profits from commissions. Because of those high commissions, creditors sometimes use deceptive and high-pressure sales tactics to sell the insurance.[1138]

Most states have, as part of their insurance code, a set of laws specifically regulating credit insurance.[1139] In addition, the state's general insurance laws will usually apply to credit insurance.[1140]

Some creditors sell "voluntary" credit insurance to nearly all their customers. While the UDAP insurance principles set out in the prior eight subsections generally apply to credit insurance, as well as to other lines of insurance, this subsection will discuss UDAP violations as they specifically relate to credit insurance.

5.3.10.2 Failure to Disclose Excessive Cost or Kickbacks

It is a UDAP violation to sell credit insurance at inflated prices and to fail to disclose that fact while in a fiduciary relationship to the borrower.[1141] An example of such a fiduciary relationship is based on the obligations of a bank holding company engaging in the sale of credit insurance, as specified by former Federal Reserve Board Regulation Y.[1142] This fiduciary relationship can also be found in the principal-agent relationship. For example, an insurance broker (even if that broker is a creditor) may be acting as an agent for the consumer in the purchase of insurance.[1143]

The lender's concealment of the benefits it derives from the sale of credit insurance, in the form of commissions, other consideration, and sometimes profits to a captive credit insurance company, may be another basis for UDAP liability.[1144] But one court has found where a debtor admits the creditor is not his agent in the sale of credit insurance, and where credit insurance was not required but the debtor requested the insurance, the creditor did not have to disclose that it received a 32% commission.[1145]

If a credit insurance sale is particularly disadvantageous to the consumer, it will be deceptive to fail to disclose this even if the creditor does not have a fiduciary relationship to the consumer.[1146] A court has thus held that creditors may not sell individual credit insurance policies to cosigners without informing them of the availability of lower-priced joint policies.[1147]

A related approach to attacking high credit insurance rates is to challenge the relationship between the creditor or agent and the insurance company. For example, submitting false invoices to consumers to conceal kickbacks by a title insurance company to a creditor is a UDAP violation.[1148] More on challenging high credit insurance rates is found in another NCLC manual, *The Cost of Credit: Regulation and Legal Challenges* Ch. 8 (2d ed. 2000 and Supp.).

5.3.10.3 Marketing Deception, Illusory Coverage

It is a factual issue whether advertising of free credit life insurance is deceptive where eligibility depends on the

1138 *See* National Consumer Law Center, The Cost of Credit: Regulation and Legal Challenges Ch 8 (2d ed. 2000 and Supp.) for a detailed discussion of credit insurance abuses).

1139 *See id.* § 8.4.

1140 *See, e.g.*, Morton v. Bank of the Bluegrass, 18 S.W.3d 353 (Ky. App. 1999).

1141 *In re* Dickson, 432 F. Supp. 752 (W.D.N.C. 1977); *see also In re* Milbourne, 108 B.R. 522 (Bankr. E.D. Pa. 1989) (lender's misrepresentation that credit insurance is required would violate UDAP statute even if written disclosures correctly describe insurance as voluntary); Browder v. Hanley Dawson Cadillac Co., 62 Ill. App. 3d 623, 379 N.E.2d 1206 (1978); State v. Ralph Williams' N.W. Chrysler Plymouth, Inc., 87 Wash. 2d 298, 553 P.2d 423 (1976). *Cf.* National Consumer Law Center, The Cost of Credit: Regulation and Legal Challenges § 8.5.2 (2d ed. 2000 and Supp.) for a discussion of voluntariness in the sale of credit insurance. *But see* Green v. Paradise Pontiac, 19 Ohio App. 3d 219, 483 N.E.2d 1213 (1984) (where no fiduciary duty between parties, no deception, where credit insurance is not required, and where consumer could purchase insurance on his own, no requirement that creditor disclose 32.5% commission).

1142 12 C.F.R. § 225 (now repealed). *See In re* Dickson, 432 F. Supp. 752 (W.D.N.C. 1977).

1143 *See* Budnitz, *The Sale of Credit Life Insurance: The Bank v. Fiduciary*, 62 N.C. L. Rev. 295 (1984); *see also* Starling v. Sproles, 311 S.E.2d 688 (N.C. Ct. App. 1984) (realty broker has fiduciary relationship to seller it represents).

1144 Sutton v. Viking Oldsmobile Nissan, Inc., 611 N.W.2d 60 (Minn. App. 2000) (reversing award of summary judgment to dealer on UDAP and fraud counts), *vacated and remanded for reconsideration on other grounds*, 623 N.W.2d 247 (Minn. 2001), *opinion on remand*, 2001 Minn. App. LEXIS 866 (July 31, 2001) (reversing summary judgment for seller on UDAP claim where buyer testified that he would have bargained for lower price or declined to buy service contract if seller had not misrepresented that charge was paid to others), *later op. at* 2004 WL 26595 (Minn. App. Jan. 6, 2004) (affirming jury verdict for dealer on service contract claim); Lemelledo v. Beneficial Mgmt. Corp., 289 N.J. Super. 489, 674 A.2d 582 (App. 1996), *aff'd*, 150 N.J. 255, 696 A.2d 546 (1997).

1145 Green v. Paradise Pontiac Inc., 19 Ohio App. 3d 219, 483 N.E.2d 1213 (1984).

1146 *See* Besta v. Beneficial Loan Co., 855 F.2d 532 (8th Cir. 1988) (unconscionable to fail to disclose that 6-year loan is less advantageous than a 3-year loan because of added cost of credit insurance and closing fees); *see also* § 4.2.14, *supra*.

1147 State v. Ralph Williams' N.W. Chrysler Plymouth Inc., 87 Wash. 2d 298, 553 P.2d 423 (1976).

1148 Fitzgerald v. Chicago Trade & Trust Co., 72 Ill. 2d 179, 380 N.E.2d 790 (1978).

debtor meeting certain physical pre-conditions.[1149] A creditor commits a UDAP violation by switching a credit disability policy mid-term to a different company with less generous benefits, particularly where any financial benefit from the switch goes to the creditor and not the consumer.[1150] This practice is an intentional UDAP violation that can result in multiple damages.[1151] However, an auto dealer was held not liable for failing to inform a consumer that a credit disability insurance policy would not cover her preexisting condition, where the dealer had no knowledge of her condition.[1152]

Credit insurance is generally decreasing term, meaning benefits decrease over time as the loan amount is repaid. Because of large prepayment penalties through use of the rule of 78, there can be a sizeable gap between a loan's pay-off amount and the amount paid under a decreasing term policy. Even though the Rule of 78 and the decreasing term policies are both legal, it may still be a UDAP violation to sell such a policy without disclosing the potential inadequacy of the coverage.[1153] It can be a UDAP violation for a creditor to misrepresent that credit insurance will pay off the full loan, even if the insurer later decides voluntarily to do just that.[1154]

It is also unfair or deceptive for a creditor knowingly to sell credit insurance to persons for whom the benefits are illusory.[1155] For example, people who are not employed at least thirty hours a week are commonly ineligible for disability benefits. Thus credit disability insurance is unlikely to offer any benefits to Social Security recipients, welfare recipients, or the unemployed, and the sale to those groups should be considered an unfair or deceptive practice.[1156]

5.3.10.4 Coercion in Selling Credit Insurance

5.3.10.4.1 Truth in Lending requirements

Under the federal Truth in Lending law, if creditors require the purchase of credit life, accident and health insurance, or unemployment insurance (but not credit property insurance), they must disclose this as part of the finance charge.[1157] Since almost all creditors disclose the premium as part of the amount financed rather than as part of the finance charge, they are prohibited from requiring the purchase of these lines of credit insurance. Instead, the consumer's purchase of this insurance through the creditor must be voluntary.

5.3.10.4.2 State insurance laws

The creditor coercion provisions of most state UNIP legislation, following the NAIC model, do not apply to credit insurance, except to the extent of forbidding creditors from requiring that insurance be purchased from particular insurers or agents.[1158] Another NAIC model statute regulates credit life, accident and disability insurance,[1159] and most states have adopted the NAIC model.[1160] But the NAIC model credit insurance statute provides only minimal restrictions on debtor coercion. A debtor must be free to purchase credit life, accident or disability insurance of the debtor's own choosing. The NAIC model also prohibits a creditor from charging amounts for credit insurance in excess of policy premiums.

The NAIC model UNIP statute and most state UNIP legislation prohibit practices intended to coerce or cause a

---

1149 Swanston v. McConnell Air Force Base Federal Credit Union, 8 Kan. App. 2d 538, 661 P.2d 826 (1983).

1150 Fort Worth Mortgage Corp. v. Abercrombie, 835 S.W.2d 262 (Tex. App. 1992).

1151 *Id.*

1152 Mackinac v. Arcadia Nat'l Life Ins. Co., 648 N.E.2d 237 (Ill. Ct. App. 1995).

1153 Marshall v. Citicorp Mortgage Inc., 601 So. 2d 669 (La. Ct. App. 1992).

1154 Juarez v. Bank of Austin, 659 S.W.2d 139 (Tex. App. 1983).

1155 *See* California v. ITT Financial Services, No. 656038-0, Clearinghouse No. 44,801S (Cal. Super. Ct., Alameda Cty., settlement filed Sept. 21, 1989); *see also* Clearinghouse No. 44,801S (complaint); Vincent v. Safeco Ins. Co., 29 P.3d 943 (Idaho 2001) (insurance policy that provides no or extremely minimal coverage is illusory and void).

1156 *See* National Consumer Law Center, The Cost of Credit: Regulation and Legal Challenges § 8.5.5 (2d ed. 2000 and Supp.) for a more detailed discussion of this issue.

1157 *See* National Consumer Law Center, Truth in Lending § 3.9.4.5.2 (5th ed. 2003 and Supp.).

1158 NAIC model statute § 5; *see* § 5.3.2.1, *supra*, for a listing of state UNIP statutes.

1159 Model Bill to Provide for the Regulation of Credit Life Insurance and Credit Accident and Health Insurance, National Association of Insurance Commissioners, Model Regulatory Service, 360-1, 370-1, and 375-1 (NIARS Corp., 1984).

1160 Alaska Stat. §§ 21.57.010 to 21.57.160; Ariz. Rev. Stat. Ann. §§ 20-1602 to 20-1616.1; Ark. Stat. Ann. §§ 23-87-101 to 23-87-119; Cal. Ins. Code §§ 779.1 to 779.36; Colo. Rev. Stat. §§ 10-10-101 to 10-10-119; Conn. Gen. Stat. §§ 38a-645 to 38a-658; Del. Code Ann. tit 18, §§ 3701 to 3713; Ga. Code §§ 33-31-1 to 33-31-12; Haw. Rev. Stat. §§ 431:10B-101 to 431:10B-114; Idaho Code §§ 41-2301 to 41-2316; 215 Ill. Comp. Stat. Ann. §§ 5/155.51 to 155.65; Ind. Code §§ 27-8-4-1 to 27-8-4-14; Ky. Rev. Stat. §§ 304.19-010 to 304.19-140; Me. Rev. Stat. Ann. tit. 24-A, §§ 2851 to 2864; Md. Ins. Code Ann. §§ 13-101 to 13-117; Mich. Comp. Laws §§ 550.601 to 550.624; Minn. Stat. §§ 62B.01 to 62B.14; Mo. Rev. Stat. §§ 385.010 to 385.080; Mont. Code Ann. § 33-21-101 to 33-21-207; Neb. Rev. Stat. §§ 44-1701 to 44-1713; Nev. Rev. Stat. §§ 690A.010 to 690A.140; N.H. Rev. Stat. Ann. §§ 408-A:1 to 408-A:15; N.J. Stat. Ann. §§ 17B:29-1 to 17B:29-13; N.M. Stat. Ann. §§ 59A-25-1 to 59A-25-14; N.C. Gen. Stat. § 58-57-1 to 58-57-80; N.D. Cent. Code §§ 26.1-37-01 to 26.1-37-16; Ohio Rev. Code Ann. §§ 3918.01 to 3918.99; Or. Rev. Stat. §§ 743.371 to 743.380; Pa. Stat. Ann. tit. 40, §§ 1007.1 to 1007.15; Tex. Ins. Code Ann. §§ 1153.001 to 1153.703; Utah Code Ann. §§ 31A-22-801 to 31A-22-809; Vt. Stat. Ann. tit. 8, §§ 4101 to 4115; Va. Code Ann. §§ 38.2-3717 to 38.2-3738; Wash. Rev. Code §§ 48.34.010 to 48.34.910; Wyo. Stat. §§ 26-21-101 to 26-21-114. *See also* N.Y. Ins. Law § 3201.

debtor to purchase insurance on property securing a loan, or insurance securing a loan, from the lender or from a particular insurer or group of insurers. This prohibition prevents a creditor from designating a particular insurer or agent as unacceptable or exclusively acceptable;[1161] soliciting insurance from the debtor prior to making a loan commitment on real estate;[1162] placing unreasonable restrictions on debtor-furnished credit insurance;[1163] and levying unreasonable charges for accepting debtor-supplied insurance.[1164]

5.3.10.4.3 State credit statutes

Generally of more importance to consumers than this state insurance legislation are state credit laws and regulations that require the lender to explain the benefits and limitations of credit insurance policies, or that prohibit making credit insurance mandatory. Violation of such laws would be evidence of a UDAP violation.[1165]

5.3.10.4.4 UDAP challenges

Where a creditor makes a credit insurance purchase voluntary in order to comply with the Truth in Lending Act, it is also a UDAP violation to misrepresent that credit insurance is required.[1166] Even if the consumer initials a provision stating that the consumer is purchasing the insurance voluntarily, it can be actionable if the consumer is not in fact doing so. The FTC has elaborated on this concept:

> Respondents argue that the contracts which consumers signed indicated that credit life insurance was not required for financing and this disclosure obviated the possibility of any deception. We disagree. It is clear from consumer testimony that oral deception was employed in some instances to cause consumers to ignore the warning on their sales agreement and accept credit insurance, despite a preference to avoid it. The fact that in certain instances consumers were able, after considerable exertion, to obtain deletion of the credit life requirement is also not a defense to the prior deception and high pressure selling which occurred and which led to the necessity for a battle in the first place.[1167]

It is also deceptive for a creditor to include credit insurance in the amount financed prior to presenting the contract to the consumer, with the creditor checking off without the consumer's authorization that the consumer wishes credit insurance and then asking for the consumer's signature without explaining that the consumer is purchasing credit insurance.[1168]

An interesting discussion of potential coercion by a creditor in the sale of insurance is found in a Michigan decision concerning whether a creditor's subsidiary would be licensed as an insurance agency.[1169] The court affirmed the Commissioner's finding that the potential for coercion in the sale of related insurance was too great to allow licensure. The court quoted the state insurance commissioner:

> We were concerned about the potential for coercion which is inherent in a financial institution's relationship with an application for a loan for a continuing customer who needs to go to that institution for occasional increases or refinancing or cyclical type of refinancing arrangement. . . .[1170]

The court agreed that, even if a consumer's signature attests that an insurance purchase is voluntary, that signature is insufficient evidence because the tie-in is structural. "People think that they will enhance the likelihood that they are going to get the credit by buying this other product."[1171] Creditors have strong incentives to use whatever techniques are available to increase profits; applicants are unlikely to complain, fearing that a complaint would jeopardize their access to credit.[1172]

One court has articulated its test for establishing allegations of coerced insurance as a UDAP claim: (1) the lender

1161 NAIC model statute § 5(a); *see* § 5.3.2.1, *supra* for a listing of state UNIP statutes.

1162 NAIC model statute § 5(b)(i); Mich. Comp. Laws § 500.2077; Mont. Code Ann. § 33-18-501(2)(a); N.H. Rev. Stat. Ann. § 417:4(XVI); Or. Rev. Stat. § 746.195(1) (applies to personal property as well); Tenn. Code Ann. § 56-8-106(2) (all insurance except automobile physical damage insurance).

1163 NAIC model statute § 5(b)(ii); *see* § 5.3.2.1, *supra* for a listing of state UNIP statutes.

1164 NAIC model statute § 5(b)(iii); *see* § 5.3.2.1, *supra* for a listing of state UNIP statutes.

1165 Lemelledo v. Beneficial Mgmt. Corp., 289 N.J. Super. 489, 674 A.2d 582 (App. 1996), *aff'd*, 150 N.J. 255, 696 A.2d 546 (1997).

1166 Hager v. American General Fin., Inc., 37 F. Supp. 2d 778 (S.D. W. Va. 1999); Peacock Buick Inc., 86 F.T.C. 1532 (1975); Jones v. Swad Chevrolet, Inc., Clearinghouse No. 41,256 (Ohio C.P. Franklin Cty. 1985); State v. Ralph Williams' N.W. Chrysler Plymouth, Inc., 87 Wash. 2d 298, 553 P.2d 423 (1976). *But see* Credithrift of Am., Inc. v. Whitley, 190 Ga. App. 833, 380 S.E.2d 489 (1989).

1167 Peacock Buick Inc., 86 F.T.C. 1532, 1558–59 (1975). *See also* Hager v. American General Fin., Inc., 37 F. Supp. 2d 778 (S.D. W. Va. 1999); Money Tree, Inc., 123 F.T.C. 1187 (1997) (complaint and consent order against lender that required borrowers to pay for credit insurance and to sign statement that it was voluntary); Tower Loan of Miss., Inc., 115 F.T.C. 140 (1992) (same). *But see* Strong v. First Family Fin. Servs., Inc., 202 F. Supp. 2d 536, 543–44 (S.D. Miss. 2002) (misrepresentation claim fails where consumers signed disclosure that credit insurance was not required).

1168 W.T. Grant Co., 83 F.T.C. 1328 (1974) (consent order).

1169 THM, Ltd. v. Comm'n of Ins., 176 Mich. App. 772, 440 N.W.2d 85 (1989).

1170 *Id.* at 176 Mich. App. at 782, 440 N.W.2d 90 (quoting the acting deputy commissioner of insurance).

1171 *Id.* (quoting Emmeth Vaughn, an insurance economist).

1172 *Id.*

affirmatively represented, by words or conduct, that insurance was in fact required and (2) the borrower purchased insurance as a result of the lender's action which he or she otherwise would not have. The borrower should be permitted to introduce evidence to prove those elements even if there is a signed voluntariness statement which the creditor obtained pursuant to Truth in Lending or a similar state law.[1173]

5.3.10.4.5 Coercion in connection with store credit cards

One area particularly susceptible for abuse in the sale of credit insurance is store credit cards. It is quite easy for a store to slip into the card application the consumer's acceptance of credit life, accident and health, property, and unemployment insurance. The consumer can be asked to sign the application twice, one of the signatures being just below small print requesting this insurance. Or the store could just sign the consumer up without the consumer's authorization. Then when items are purchased from the store, subsequent statements will include charges for this insurance.

A good example of this type of abuse was alleged against Levitz Furniture, American Bankers Insurance, and GE Capital Corporation.[1174] The allegation was that GE Capital Corporation, in conjunction with American Bankers Insurance, would reward or penalize Levitz and its employees depending on the credit insurance penetration rate. If Levitz's penetration rate exceeded 60% for a package of credit life insurance, credit disability insurance, credit unemployment insurance, and credit property insurance, then the applicable Levitz employee received at least $1 per policy sold and Levitz received $1.50. If the penetration rate fell below 50%, Levitz was penalized.

The complaint alleges that the penetration rate from 1993 to 1997 at Levitz was 75%. Premiums for these policies sold exceeded $20 million, but claim payouts were less than $2.5 million. The complaint also alleged that Levitz had engaged in various UDAP violations in the sale of the credit insurance. Levitz had consumers sign credit card applications twice without realizing that one of the signatures was assent for the credit insurance. Levitz did not give the consumers copies of the application. Levitz also would claim the insurance was free or was needed in case furniture fell off the truck when it was delivered. Levitz failed to disclose that insurance was being purchased. Much of this evidence forming the basis of the complaint apparently was gathered by test shoppers.

The case was settled when the defendants agreed to several million dollars in restitution and also two million dollars in civil penalties. Of special note, the injunction against future misconduct only reached to Levitz and to GE Capital and American Bankers in their dealings with Levitz. In other words, the settlement injunction had no effect on GE Capital and American Bankers' dealings with other retailers or other creditors.

5.3.10.4.6 Other resources concerning coercion

A more general discussion of creditor coercion in the sale of credit insurance is found at National Consumer Law Center, *The Cost of Credit: Regulation and Legal Challenges* Ch. 8 (2d ed. 2000 and Supp.). That discussion considers how to prove coercion and what legal theories the consumer can use to attack coercion—UDAP, Truth in Lending, state usury, and antitrust claims.

5.3.10.5 Purchase of Excessive Credit Property Insurance

A common creditor practice is to require the purchase of credit property insurance as part of a loan. While this may be legitimate, it is not proper to purchase insurance far in excess of the value of the loan collateral, to take collateral solely for the purpose of selling overpriced credit property insurance on that collateral, or to sell credit property insurance on property that is not collateral. UNIP statutes may prohibit the sale of credit insurance in amounts greater than necessary to cover the loan or the collateral.[1175]

In one contract reviewed by NCLC, the value of the collateral was listed at $1800, but the coverage sold was for $20,000 of household goods! As a result, the property insurance premium alone was nearly one-half of the amount financed ($720 premium out of $1525 amount financed).

It should be a UDAP violation to sell insurance where the creditor has no legal authority to sell such insurance (which may be the case if the property is not collateral), or to require insurance in excess of what is necessary to protect the lender's interest. Similarly unfair is a scheme to require collateral solely as a pretext for selling credit property insurance with a large commission to the creditor.[1176] Another unfair practice is failure to cancel the credit property insurance and rebate unearned insurance premiums when the loan is prepaid or the property repossessed.[1177] These

1173 *In re* Milbourne, 108 B.R. 522 (Bankr. E.D. Pa. 1988).

1174 People v. Levitz Furniture Corp., Clearinghouse No. 52,045 (Cal. Super. Ct. Aug. 18, 1997) (complaint and stipulation for entry of final judgment). *But cf.* Hayes v. Osterman Jewelers, Inc., 2002 Ohio App. LEXIS 1868 (Apr. 19, 2002) (no UDAP violation in construing ambiguous statement as request for credit insurance where charges were clearly disclosed on consumer's monthly bill).

1175 *See, e.g.*, N.C. Gen. Stat. § 58-63-15(13).

1176 California v. ITT Financial Services, No. 656038-0, Clearinghouse No. 44,801S (Cal. Super. Ct., Alameda Cty., settlement filed Sept. 21, 1989); *see also* Clearinghouse No. 44,801S (complaint). *See generally* National Consumer Law Center, The Cost of Credit: Regulation and Legal Challenges § 8.5.4.4 (2d ed. 2000 and Supp.).

1177 *See* California v. ITT Financial Services, No. 656038-0, Clearinghouse No. 44,801S (Cal. Super. Ct., Alameda Cty., settle-

credit property insurance practices are examined in three other NCLC manuals: *The Cost of Credit: Regulation and Legal Challenges* § 8.3.5 (2d ed. 2000 and Supp.); National Consumer Law Center, *Repossessions and Foreclosures* § 3.10 (5th ed. 2002); and *Truth in Lending* § 3.9.4.6 (5th ed. 2003 and Supp.).

5.3.10.6 Failure to Pay Credit Insurance Claims

The more general issue of unfair insurance claims practices as UDAP violations is examined at § 5.3.2, *supra*. This discussion focuses on special issues of an insurer's failure to pay off on a credit insurance policy.

A common credit insurance abuse that may be subject to a UDAP challenge is the refusal to pay an insurance claim because of a preexisting illness excluded by the current policy. Where the consumer had previous continuous credit insurance coverage through that creditor through a series of refinancings, denial of coverage may be deceptive or unfair. The creditor at least should have disclosed that the insurance claim should be made on a preceding policy or that the refinancing would cut off insurance rights on the prior policy.[1178] It may be unfair to deny coverage when insurance was in continuous effect before the illness was manifest. It is likewise a UDAP violation to misrepresent that a person is ineligible for coverage because of illness.[1179] The creditor itself may be liable if it has misrepresented the coverage of the insurance it sold or has failed to assist the consumer in presenting a claim.[1180]

An insurer may also commit a UDAP violation by using ambiguous policy provisions to terminate credit disability insurance coverage when its agent had told the consumer that the insurance would be automatically renewed without further premiums if the consumer became disabled.[1181] A state insurance commissioner has been upheld in a finding that a credit life insurance company had a practice of paying creditors promptly, but not beneficiaries, and that this practice was unfair.[1182]

ment filed Sept. 21, 1989); *see also* Clearinghouse No. 44,801S (complaint). This may be strictly illegal, thus resulting in other claims, as well. *See generally* National Consumer Law Center, The Cost of Credit: Regulation and Legal Challenges § 8.6 (2d ed. 2000 and Supp.).

1178 *Cf.* Suburban State Bank v. Squires, 145 Wis. 2d 445, 427 N.W.2d 393 (Ct. App. 1988) (where borrower had heart attack and collected on disability insurance and loan was refinanced, court upheld finding that creditor was negligent in not advising borrower that new disability policy would bar recovery if borrower had another heart attack).

1179 Morton v. Bank of the Bluegrass, 18 S.W.3d 353 (Ky. App. 1999).

1180 Card v. Chase Manhattan Bank, 175 Misc. 2d 389, 669 N.Y.S.2d 117 (Civ. Ct. 1996).

1181 Ginocchio v. American Bankers Life Assur. Co., 889 F. Supp. 1078 (N.D. Ill. 1995).

1182 Garner v. Foundation Life Ins. Co. of Arkansas, 17 Ark. App. 13, 702 S.W.2d 417 (1986).

5.3.11 Force-Placed Automobile Insurance

5.3.11.1 General

Automobile creditors typically require consumers to purchase collision and theft coverage to protect the creditor's interest in the automobile. The credit contract will authorize the creditor to purchase such insurance on behalf of the consumer if the consumer does not present evidence of continuous coverage or if the coverage ever lapses during the term of the loan. This coverage purchased by the creditor is often called "force-placed," "creditor-placed," or "collateral protection" insurance.

Force-placed homeowners', mobile home, boat, and other forms of property insurance are also sold in conjunction with loans taking that property as collateral. While the principles are similar no matter the nature of the collateral, this section will focus on the most common form of force-placed insurance, automobile insurance purchased for the consumer when the consumer fails to do so, where this is a requirement of a car loan.

The creditor pays the insurer under the master policy, and then seeks reimbursement from the consumer. Force-placed insurance premiums are generally added to the consumer's outstanding loan balance, and financed over the term of the loan at the same interest rate as the loan. Often the monthly payments remain unchanged, and the premium amount and accrued interest relating to that premium are charged as a balloon payment at the end of the loan. The creditor will not release its lien on the car until this full amount is paid, and may repossess the car solely on default of this insurance premium payment.

Another way to keep the monthly loan payments unchanged is to extend the length of the loan. Thus the balloon amount is paid out over a series of months past the scheduled end of the loan. A final approach to pay for the force-placed insurance premium is to increase the monthly payment. The premium and loan are both paid off by the originally scheduled last loan installment payment.

No matter how the force-placed coverage is financed, this type of insurance offers extraordinary potential for abuse because the lender is selecting the insurance but the consumer is being forced to pay for it. Often the lender will select extremely expensive insurance that will provide the consumer with little coverage, but which will have large kickbacks for the creditor. This type of insurance is a classic example of reverse competition, where the lender will purchase the most expensive coverage possible because this higher price allows higher kickbacks for the creditor. More detail on the nature and abuses concerning force-placed insurance can be found in Sheldon, *Force-Placed Automobile Insurance, Consumer Protection Problems and Potential Solutions* (AARP Public Policy Institute August, 1996).[1183]

1183 Available from the Public Policy Institute, AARP, 601 E Street, N.W., Washington, D.C. 20049.

Class actions and individual actions seeking large punitive damages have been quite successful in this area, as described below. The main focus of this subsection will be on listing a series of abuses that consumers can challenge in a simple individual action. These same abuses can also be the subject of a larger lawsuit.

5.3.11.2 Uncovering Force-Placed Insurance Problems

The most difficult aspect of investigating a force-placed insurance problem is discovering that the client has been sold this insurance. Occasionally the client will complain of the balloon payment or the extension of the loan agreement. Usually, however, the client will come to the attorney complaining about a threatened deficiency action on a repossession; the consumer will not realize that a large part of the owed deficiency may be related to the force-placed insurance premium.

The creditor's explanation of the amount owed for the deficiency will usually not identify the amount related to the force-placed insurance. Instead, this amount may be hidden as part of the outstanding loan obligation. So it is important to check the creditor's calculation of the outstanding loan obligation based on the original loan terms. Since force-placed insurance can be as much as $1000 a year (or more), it is usually not hard to spot a discrepancy indicating the presence of force-placed coverage. Alternatively, the consumer's attorney can ask in discovery whether the creditor has purchased physical damage insurance for the consumer. Even outside of litigation, Article 9 of the Uniform Commercial Code requires a creditor to respond within fourteen days to a request for an accounting.[1184] The accounting must identify the components of the amount due "in reasonable detail."[1185] In addition, if the creditor is claiming that the consumer is liable for a deficiency, the consumer is entitled to a broad-brush explanation of the calculation of the deficiency that may provide a clue about whether insurance was ever force-placed.[1186]

Only about one percent of automobile loans involve force-placed insurance, but a much higher percentage of repossessions involve such insurance, as well as a higher percentage of loans involving low-income borrowers. So it is generally a good idea to be alert for any evidence of the sale of this coverage when handling a repossession deficiency action.

Once the coverage is identified, there is a host of arguably unfair, deceptive, and illegal practices related to this coverage. The remaining subsections describe these in some detail.

1184 U.C.C. § 9-210(b).

1185 U.C.C. § 9-102(a)(4).

1186 U.C.C. § 9-616.

5.3.11.3 Failure to Disclose Severe Limits on Single Interest Coverage

When the lender purchases insurance for the consumer, it can select two different types of coverage. One type, often called vendor single interest, only pays on claims if the vehicle is repossessed or stolen.[1187] In other words, if the consumer retains possession of the vehicle, the insurance will make no payment after an accident and will not reduce the outstanding indebtedness. The only way the consumer can receive any benefit from the coverage is to surrender the vehicle to the creditor voluntarily.

Other creditors select what is often called limited dual interest coverage, which will pay off on claims even if the consumer retains possession of the vehicle. Even this coverage though will only pay out an amount not to exceed the outstanding balance on the loan.

Many consumers force placed with single interest coverage are stunned to realize that the insurance for which they are paying as much as $1000 a year will not pay out on any claims unless the car has first been repossessed. The UDAP issue here is whether various lender notices and the insurance certificate misrepresented or failed to disclose the limited nature of the coverage. The UDAP standard is not one of literal truthfulness (that an insurance expert would understand the limited nature of the coverage), but whether the typical consumer is confused.[1188] If so, then the consumer's actual damages are the full amount of the consumer's claim that is not covered.

In some states, the lender does not have authority to purchase single interest coverage to be paid by the consumer.[1189] Violating that state law may subject the lender not only to remedies under that law, but also to a state UDAP claim.

5.3.11.4 Charging the Consumer for Extra Coverages Not Authorized by the Credit Agreement

The credit agreement will specify the type of coverage the consumer should purchase to protect the lender's interest—usually collision and comprehensive coverage with stated deductibles. The contract allows the creditor to purchase this coverage for the consumer if the consumer does not.

There is a widespread practice of lenders instead purchasing additional coverages when the consumer's coverage lapses, and passing on the cost of such extra coverages to the consumer. This practice of charging the consumer for cov-

1187 *See, e.g.*, Am. Bankers' Ins. Co. v. Wells, 819 So. 2d 1196 (Miss. 2001).

1188 *See* § 4.2, *supra*.

1189 *But see* Ortiz v. GMAC, Clearinghouse No. 47,936A (Ill. Cir. Ct. Oct. 28, 1992) (state law does not prohibit sale of such coverage), *aff'd*, 283 Ill. App. 3d 242, 673 N.E.2d 424 (1996).

erages in addition to those authorized by the credit agreement should be an unfair and deceptive practice and a breach of contract.[1190] Examples of such extra coverages are coverages for repossession costs, skip, confiscation and conversion, payment of mechanics or other liens, and for a resulting deficiency. In addition, single interest insurance may have no or small deductibles, where the consumer, under the credit agreement, could have purchased coverage with a $500 or even higher deductible.[1191] (The lower force-placed deductible is a form of extra coverage; where single interest coverage is purchased, this lower deductible only protects the creditor.)

Since many of these coverages only benefit the creditor, actual damages should be easy to prove. If the insurance protects the creditor against the consumer's default, the consumer may have a Truth-in-Lending claim that the premium should have been included in the finance charge rather than in the amount financed.[1192]

There are several ways in which the consumer can be forced to pay for these extra coverages. One way is if the master policy between the lender and the insurer contains extra coverages beyond those specified in the credit agreement, and the master policy is paid for solely by force-placed insureds. In discovery, obtain the master policy, and not just the certificate of insurance received by the consumer.

Alternatively, the insurer can provide these extra coverages for free if the lender's loss experience is below certain levels. This should be treated as a subterfuge, little different than providing such coverages as part of the master policy paid by the consumer. Obtain through discovery all agreements or documents relating to experience-rated rebates, dividends, or other benefits going to the lender based on the loss experience of its customers.

Other times the lender will pay for extra coverages, but the price for these coverages will be far below the amount the lender receives in claim payments from the insurer. The consumer's excessively priced force-placed premium is subsidizing the below-cost additional coverages. The best way to check for this is to obtain through discovery the premium the lender paid for these extra coverages over the last several years and the payments that the insurer made to the lender on these coverages during those years.

5.3.11.5 Failure to Notify Consumers of Force-Placed Coverage

Consumers often do not realize that force-placed coverage has been placed on their vehicle. They only discover this at the end of the loan when they are told that a large balloon payment is due to pay for the premium and related financing costs. Typically, the insurer or lender claims to send two notices before force placing coverage, and then sends an insurance certificate evidencing the placement of force-placed coverage. Notification prior to placement of coverage or at least delivery of the certificate may be required by state law.

Nevertheless, there are widespread reports of insurers failing to send these notices or certificates. When the lender's or insurer's failure violates state law, that should certainly be actionable. It may also be a state UDAP violation to force place insurance without first warning the consumer of that fact.[1193]

5.3.11.6 Lenders Pocketing Experience-Related Refunds and Dividends

Insurers often provide lenders with refunds or dividends (as high as 50% of the premium) based on the fact that the insurer's force-placed claims payments to that lender are lower than expected. Lenders never pass these refunds or dividends on to the consumer, even though it was the consumer who paid the premium. This is most aggravated where the force-placed premium has been financed, and the consumer is still paying interest and principal on part of the premium that has already been returned by the insurer to the lender. While the lender's failure to pass on rebates to the force-placed insured appears to be standard practice in the industry, the practice could lead to claims for UDAP damages or even punitive damages based on a fraud, theft, or conversion claim.[1194]

5.3.11.7 Kickbacks to Lenders

Because the lender makes the decision about which insurer to use, and since the lender does not eventually have to pay for the premium, there is a built-in incentive for the lender to select the insurer that pays the lender the most in

1190 Hogan v. Valley Nat'l Financial Services Co., Clearinghouse No. 50,428 (D. Colo. Feb. 1, 1995) (ruling on motion to dismiss); Moore v. Fidelity Financial Services, 869 F. Supp. 557 (N.D. Ill. 1994); Clingerman v. Ford Motor Credit Co., Clearinghouse No. 50,427 (Ariz. Super. Ct. Nov. 1, 1994) (ruling on motion to dismiss); Kenty v. Transamerica Premium Ins. Co., 72 Ohio St. 3d 415, 650 N.E.2d 863 (1995). *But see* Kenty v. Bank One, N.A., 67 F.3d 1257 (6th Cir. 1995) (not finding a RICO violation).

1191 *But see* Acree v. General Motors Acceptance Corp., No. 531927, Clearinghouse No. 51,297 (Cal. Super. Ct. Apr. 26, 1996) (no UDAP violation where lender purchased force-placed coverage with a lower deductible than required under the contract).

1192 Hogan v. Valley Nat'l Financial Services Co., Clearinghouse No. 50,428 (D. Colo. Feb. 1, 1995) (ruling on motion to dismiss).

1193 *But see* Ortiz v. GMAC, Clearinghouse No. 47,936A (Ill. Cir. Ct. Oct. 28, 1992), *aff'd*, 285 Ill. App. 3d 242, 673 N.E.2d 424 (1996).

1194 *See* Kenty v. Bank One, N.A., 67 F.3d 1257 (6th Cir. 1995) (practice may violate RICO statute).

the form of kickbacks or other compensation. Because the more overpriced an insurance premium is, the more room there is for kickbacks to the lender, the result often is for the lender to select the most expensive insurance carrier, not the carrier offering the best deal for the consumer.

The practice of a lender selecting the most expensive possible coverage, representing the premium amount as the gross amount the insurer charges before deducting insurer payments to the lender, and then failing to disclose kickbacks and other compensation is arguably a UDAP violation.[1195] So is the practice of receiving commissions for the force-placed insurance where the creditor is not licensed to act as an agent for those coverages.[1196] In discovery, consumer attorneys can seek all forms of commission, compensation, expense reimbursement, and other payments from the insurer to the lender.

This investigation is complicated because commissions may go to agents who are related to the lender, the lender and insurer may be owned by the same company, or there may be other interrelationships used to funnel kickbacks. It still should be a UDAP violation to use a captive insurance company and charge higher than normal premiums without disclosing this to the consumer.

5.3.11.8 Forcing the Consumer to Pay for Tracking and Notification Costs for *Other* Consumers

The credit agreement requires the consumer to carry physical damage coverage or the lender will purchase such coverage for the consumer. The agreement does not authorize the lender to purchase insurance for the consumer whose premium also goes to pay for the insurer's and lender's expenses to track and notify *other* customers who are not force placed.

The insurer obtains the lender's business by agreeing to take on for no extra charge the lender's normal business expenses to track all its customers to see if insurance is in place and to deal with them if it is not. The insurer can do this because it passes all of these expenses onto those who are force placed in the form of higher premiums.

It is arguably a UDAP violation for a lender to select insurance whose premium is based on the force-placed insured paying for everyone else's tracking and notification expenses.

5.3.11.9 Inflating Financing Costs

Lenders often, without the consumer's permission, purchase force-placed insurance for the remainder of the car loan—for a term as long as five years—through one up-front premium payment. The lender then finances this payment for the full term of the loan, often requiring no payment on principal during that time. That way interest is accruing on the highest possible force-placed premium for the longest possible time. At the end of the loan term, a huge balloon is due equaling the insurance premium and financing costs.

Such practices of maximizing the financing costs to the consumer without the consumer's permission should be an unfair practice.[1197] For example, the borrower would pay far less over the life of the loan if one-year insurance policies were purchased each year and those policy premiums were repaid during that year.

5.3.11.10 Selecting Legal Claims

In addition to the UDAP and breach of contract claims described above, force-placed insurance abuses may be challenged under a number of other possible theories. In general, it is easier to make out a case against the lender than the insurer. The consumer's relationship to the insurer is more indirect, and the court may not find the requisite privity or duty in a lawsuit against the insurer,[1198] where it might in a claim against the lender. National Consumer Law Center, *Consumer Law Pleadings*, No. 1 (Cumulative CD-Rom and Index Guide) includes a complaint and other documents in a case raising a variety of claims regarding force-placed insurance, also found on the CD-Rom accompanying this volume.[1199]

The Mississippi Supreme Court has allowed a claim based on breach of fiduciary duty against the lender and insurer to proceed, despite various defenses including the filed rate doctrine (the rates had been filed with the state).[1200] A second Mississippi Supreme Court decision, issued on a fuller factual record, holds that the filed rate

1195 *See* Kenty v. Bank One, N.A., 67 F.3d 1257 (6th Cir. 1995) (practice may violate RICO statute); Clingerman v. Ford Motor Credit Co., Clearinghouse No. 50,427 (Ariz. Super. Ct. Nov. 1, 1994) (ruling on motion to dismiss). *See also* Norwest Mortgage, Inc. v. Superior Court, 72 Cal. App. 4th 214, 85 Cal. Rptr. 2d 18 (1999) (reversing certification of nationwide class on UDAP claim challenging force-placed insurance kickbacks, but directing consideration of narrower class).

1196 Clingerman v. Ford Motor Credit Co., Clearinghouse No. 50,427 (Ariz. Super. Ct. Nov. 1, 1994) (allegation of secret commissions states claim).

1197 *See* Acree v. General Motors Acceptance Corp., No. 531,927, Clearinghouse No. 51,297 (Cal. Super. Ct. Apr. 26, 1996).

1198 *See* Surrett v. TIG Premier Ins. Co., 869 F. Supp. 919 (M.D. Ala. 1994).

1199 National Consumer Law Center, Consumer Law Pleadings, No. 1, Ch. 2 (CD-Rom and Index Guide), also found on the CD-Rom accompanying this volume. *See also* National Consumer Law Center, Consumer Class Actions: A Practical Litigation Guide Appxs. D.8, E.3, K.4, L.6, and M.4 (5th ed. 2002 and Supp.) for a sample complaint, discovery, motions, and briefs regarding force-placed insurance, also found on the CD-Rom accompanying this volume.

1200 American Bankers Ins. Co. v. Alexander, 534 U.S. 944, 122 S. Ct. 324, 151 L. Ed. 2d 242 (2001).

doctrine bars claims that force-placed insurance rates are excessive but not claims involving (1) illegally backdating worthless insurance coverage for the sole purpose of garnering extra unearned premiums; (2) charging force-placed insurance premiums based upon the gross amount of the loan as opposed to the net payoff or the actual cash value of the vehicle; (3) requiring that the consumer's vehicle be repossessed before it could be repaired or a claim made; (4) exceeding the filed rates.[1201] The court held that neither the creditor nor the insurance company had a fiduciary duty to consumers and that the consumers could not show fraud because the defendants did not make any affirmative misrepresentations, but the consumers' claim of breach of the duty of good faith and fair dealer was viable against the creditor.

RICO is a viable claim against the lender.[1202] The National Bank Act[1203] provides another possible federal claim against national banks, if the bank's practice can be viewed as charging excessive interest.[1204] However, since national banks are permitted to charge up to the rate allowed by state laws for the most-favored state-chartered banks, the viability of this claim will depend on the nature of state usury laws affecting state-chartered banks.[1205]

Another federal claim that has met with even less success is an anti-tying claim under the National Bank Holding Company Act.[1206] On the other hand, the Truth in Lending Act may require the lender to provide new disclosures when it force places insurance that includes additional coverage or coverage beyond that authorized by the contract.[1207] The failure to disclose the balloon payment created by the force-placed insurance premium repayment arrangement may also violate state credit statutes.[1208]

In general, state insurance law is not effective in this area, and provides minimal assistance to a private litigant. One exception may be a regulation adopted by the New Mexico insurance department, Creditor-Placed Credit Property Insurance.[1209] This is the first state to take a hard look at current force-placed insurance practices and then respond to those with a specific insurance regulation or statute.

5.3.11.11 Settlements and Other Consumer Recoveries

Where cases are properly framed, lawsuits in this area are being settled favorably for consumers. A Ford Motor Credit Company subsidiary settled a force-placed insurance case in 1993 for $58.3 million; Barnett Banks settled for $19 million in the same year; First Interstate Bancorp settled for $16 million in 1992; and Mellon Bank Corp. settled for $6 million in 1990.

While class actions have been the major approach to challenging force-placed insurance abuses, an individual action seeking punitive damages is another risk that lenders and insurers take when they overreach. A Mississippi jury awarded an individual $38 million in punitive damages to be paid by Trust Mart National Bank and a general insurance agent.[1210]

5.3.12 "Packing" Non-Credit Insurance in Conjunction with Credit Sale

5.3.12.1 Insurance Packing Described

A common, but unfair creditor practice is "packing" or folding in various insurance products with the extension of a loan. The consumer is often unaware that part of the loan documents include purchase of various forms of insurance *in addition to* the standard credit insurance traditionally sold with a loan. Optional insurance premiums are added to a loan amount without the customer's request, and at the closing the lender presents the customer with pre-prepared loan documents that include such insurance charges. The industry leaders at one time in insurance packing were various ITT subsidiaries—Aetna Finance Co., Thorp Finance and ITT Consumer Financial Corp.[1211]

1201 Am. Bankers' Ins. Co. v. Wells, 819 So. 2d 1196 (Miss. 2001).

1202 *See* Bermudez v. First of Am. Bank Champion, 860 F. Supp. 580 (N.D. Ill. 1994), *op. withdrawn pursuant to settlement*, 886 F. Supp. 643 (N.D. Ill. 1995). *But cf.* Kenty v. Bank One, N.A., 92 F.3d 384 (6th Cir. 1996) (bank's notices about type of insurance purchased too general to constitute mail fraud, so no RICO claim).

1203 12 U.S.C. § 38.

1204 *But see* Doe v. Norwest Bank Minnesota, N.A., 107 F.3d 1297 (8th Cir. 1997) (insurance charges are not interest under the National Bank Act).

1205 *See* Kenty v. Bank One, N.A., 67 F.3d 1257 (6th Cir. 1995). *See also* National Consumer Law Center, The Cost of Credit: Regulation and Legal Challenges §§ 3.4, 3.5 (2d ed. 2000 and Supp.).

1206 *See* Doe v. Norwest Bank Minnesota, N.A., 107 F.3d 1297 (8th Cir. 1997); McClain v. South Carolina Nat'l Bank, 105 F.3d 898 (4th Cir. 1997); Kenty v. Bank One, N.A., 67 F.3d 1257 (6th Cir. 1995) (dismissing claim under 12 U.S.C. § 1972).

1207 *See* Hogan v. Valley Nat'l Financial Services Co., Clearinghouse No. 50,428 (D. Colo. Feb. 1, 1995) (ruling on motion to dismiss); Moore v. Fidelity Financial Services, 869 F. Supp. 557 (N.D. Ill. 1994). *See generally* National Consumer Law Center, Truth in Lending § 3.9.4.4.2 (5th ed. 2003 and Supp.).

1208 *See* Bank of Oklahoma N.A. v. Portis, 942 P.2d 249 (Okla. Civ. App. 1997) (UCCC violation for failure to disclose balloon).

1209 N.M. Admin. Code § 13.18.3. *See In the Matter of* the Adoption of 13 NMAC 18.3, Force-Placed Credit Property Ins., Order Adopting New Rule, Dkt. 98-364-IN, Clearinghouse No. 52,123 (Dec. 11, 1998). *See also* The David Cox Co., Report to the New Mexico Dep't of Ins. Regarding Force Placed Ins., Clearinghouse No. 52,124 (Nov. 1, 1998).

1210 The judge remitted the punitive damages to $5 million. Smith v. Trustmark Nat'l Bank, Clearinghouse No. 51,298 (Miss. Cir. Ct. Aug. 4, 1995) (opinion and order).

1211 *See* Samorano v. Aetna Fin. Co., No. 213316 (Ariz. Super. Ct. Pima Cty. filed Dec. 8, 1983); Urbina v. Aetna Fin. Co., Civ.

A good statement of the scheme is found in the early litigation involving the Wisconsin Attorney General's office. The Wisconsin Attorney General had alleged that Aetna, usually unbeknownst to its customers, "packed" or loaded onto consumer loans various types of expensive optional insurance. Typically the debtor would request a loan in a specified amount. The lender would telephone back that the loan plus optional insurance had been approved with a stated monthly payment, never mentioning the total loan amount. When the debtor arrived at the lender's offices for the closing, all loan and insurance documents had been typed and intermingled, making them look like one transaction.

Actually, what many Aetna customers had purchased in addition to the loan was some combination of the following:

- Credit life insurance and credit accident and health insurance.
- "Unipay," a single premium policy covering certain types of accidental death and dismemberment until age 65. This policy is not credit insurance, and is unrelated to the credit life and A&H policies purchased. Because one premium payment keeps the policy in force until age 65, premiums cost as much as $475. Sometimes Aetna sold separate policies to the husband and the wife.
- "SPT-5," a five-year term, single premium life insurance policy, again totally unrelated to the credit life policy. The single premium payment could cost as much as $523.
- "ITT Thrift Club" costing $24.50 that gives the debtor the opportunity of discounts on hotels, rental cars, and other purchases.
- Credit property insurance on household goods taken as collateral for the personal loan, even if the debtor already had property insurance on those goods, and often when the consumer had no idea that household goods would be required as collateral on the loan.

83-452 TUC-ACM (D. Ariz. filed June 30, 1983); Memorandum of Agreement between Colorado Attorney General and Aetna Fin. Co., Clearinghouse No. 38,916 (Apr. 16, 1985); Settlement Agreement between Iowa Attorney General and Thorp Credit announced June 6, 1984; Assurance and Order between the Minnesota Attorney General and ITT Consumer Financial Corp., Clearinghouse No. 41,253 (June 10, 1985); State v. Aetna Fin. Co., Case No. 84 CV0103 (Wis. Cir. Ct. Dane Cty. 1984) (preliminary injunction and settlement); California v. ITT Consumer Financial Corp., No. 656038-0 (Cal. Super. Ct., Alameda Cty, settlement filed Sept. 21, 1989); Hawkins v. Thorp Loan & Thrift, No. 85-6074, Clearinghouse No. 44,801V, W (Minn. Dist. Ct. Hennepin Cty., settlement filed July 10, 1991). *See also* The Wall Street Journal, Feb. 26, 1985 at p. 1; Sept. 22, 1989 at A3.

Several pleadings and settlement documents are available in an insurance packing document bank as Clearinghouse No. 44,801. As the material is voluminous, you may wish to review an index of the documents in National Consumer Law Center, The Cost of Credit: Regulation and Legal Challenges § 8.7.4, n.645 (2d ed. 2000 and Supp.).

The prices for most of this insurance are unregulated; one issue in the Wisconsin Aetna litigation was whether the insurance premiums were unconscionably high. Not only were Aetna's customers purchasing large amounts of "optional insurance," but they were also financing these insurance payments at high small-loan interest rates—23% APR in Wisconsin. (One would expect insurance premium financing to be offered at lower interest rates than personal loans because of the risk-free nature of the premium loan. The lender can cancel the insurance upon the debtor's default with only the slightest possibility of a small loss.)

The Wisconsin Attorney General's office, as was the case in other actions, alleged that many debtors never realized that they were purchasing any insurance. Other debtors believed that they were buying just credit insurance, thought the insurance was required because the papers were already made out, or thought that the ancillary products were free.

Loan officers faced with heavy insurance sales quotas used various techniques to persuade hesitant customers to sign up for insurance.[1212] For example, where debtors needed cash right away, loan officers might claim that retyping the papers would take three or four days, or that the loan would have to be resubmitted for approval.

5.3.12.2 Insurance Packing as a UDAP Violation

UDAP statutes are particularly appropriate to challenge "packing" schemes. Credit and insurance documents may show no irregularities, with the consumer's signature next to disclaimers that the consumer knows that the insurance is optional, that the insurance has a specific purpose and price, that the consumer is purchasing the insurance voluntarily, that the company is not bound by oral statements of its agents, etc. But none of this hinders a successful UDAP claim for oral misrepresentations or high-pressure sales. Subsequent written clarifications or disclaimers are no defense to a deception claim.[1213]

It is a UDAP violation to fail to disclose important information about the optional insurance to the consumer before the closing, that is, during the application and approval process.[1214] This duty to clearly inform the consumer

1212 At least two ITT Financial affiliates' employees brought wrongful discharge cases against their companies, alleging they were fired because they did not pack their customers' loans or meet sales quotas. Laws v. Aetna Fin., 667 F. Supp. 342 (N.D. Miss. 1987); Zimmer v. Thorp Credit, Civ. No. 33,073 (Iowa Dist. Ct., Marion Cty., filed Dec., 1984) (case dismissed upon negotiated settlement).

1213 *See* § 4.2.17, *supra*.

1214 *See* Fox v. Industrial Cas. Ins. Co., 98 Ill. App. 3d 543, 424 N.E.2d 839 (1981) (reversing dismissal of claim that insurance company violated UDAP statute when its car dealer agent included overpriced accidental death insurance, which overlapped with auto insurance, in car sale contract without disclosure); Lemelledo v. Beneficial Mgmt. Corp., 289 N.J. Super. 489, 674 A.2d 582 (App. 1996), *aff'd* 150 N.J. 255, 696 A.2d

of all relevant aspects of the insurance sale is even stronger if the finance company has a fiduciary duty to the customer. One commentator argues that a creditor selling insurance acts as the customer's agent, and thus has a fiduciary duty to that customer.[1215] The agent then has a duty to provide information the principal would desire to have and to advise the client as to the benefits and drawbacks of the purchase. The failure to fulfill this fiduciary duty may be a UDAP violation.[1216]

The lender's concealment of the benefits it derives from the sale of credit insurance, in the form of commissions, other consideration, and sometimes profits to a captive credit insurance company, may be another basis for UDAP liability.[1217] Violation of state credit laws and regulations that require the lender to explain the benefits and limitations of credit insurance policies, and that prohibit making credit insurance mandatory, is evidence of a UDAP violation.[1218] In some states, it may simply be illegal for lenders to sell non-credit insurance at all.[1219] To sell consumers insurance without the legal right to do so should also be a UDAP violation.

It is not surprising then that numerous UDAP claims involving insurance packing have been settled.[1220] In addition, a Wisconsin court found sufficient grounds under the state UDAP statute to order Aetna Finance to inform customers:

- If collateral is required, property insurance is required, and that, in lieu of new property insurance, Aetna customers can obtain a loss payable binder for the customer's preexisting property insurance, or that they can purchase such insurance elsewhere;
- The specific costs, amounts, benefits and coverages of Aetna's insurance, obtaining the customer's separate consent for that insurance, including separate oral disclosures of the monthly payments with and without the optional insurance;
- That the purchase of Unipay, SPT-5, household contents insurance, or ITT Consumer Thrift Club has no bearing on whether the customer receives a loan.

Aetna must also:

- Inquire whether insurance is suitable for a particular customer;
- Inquire whether the customer wishes to pay cash or finance the insurance; and
- Immediately rewrite the consumer loan if the customer objects to the insurance.[1221]

5.3.13 Mortgage Insurance

One current issue is whether lenders have a responsibility to inform borrowers that they can cancel their mortgage insurance once their equity in their home exceeds a certain amount. For example, Freddie Mac or Fannie Mae may establish standards whereby consumers must purchase mortgage insurance (protecting the lender from the borrower's default) if the loan amount exceeds 80% of the property's value.

Over time the consumer's payments will decrease the amount of the loan and improvements or market conditions may increase the home's value. When the amount of the loan falls below 80% of the home's value, can the consumer cancel the insurance? If the consumer can, must the servicing lender so inform the consumer? One case found no such responsibility for disclosure under a UDAP statute where the loan agreement stated the consumer must make payments "until such time as the requirement for the insurance

546 (1997). *See also* § 4.2.14, *supra.*

1215 Budnitz, *The Sale of Credit Life Insurance: The Bank as Fiduciary*, 62 N.C.L. Rev. 295 (1984). *See also* National Consumer Law Center, The Cost of Credit: Regulation and Legal Challenges § 8.7.2 (2d ed. 2000 and Supp.).

1216 *See In re* Dickson, 432 F. Supp. 752 (W.D.N.C. 1977); Browder v. Hanley Dawson Cadillac Co., 62 Ill. App. 3d 623, 379 N.E.2d 1206 (1978); State v. Ralph Williams' N.W. Chrysler Plymouth, Inc., 87 Wash. 2d 298, 553 P.2d 423 (1976). *See also* Tomaszewski v. McKeon Ford, Inc., 240 N.J. Super. 404, 573 A.2d 501 (App. Div. 1990).

There may also be a separate common law duty to disclose. Restatement (Second) of Torts § 551(2) (1977). *See* Bair v. Public Services Employees Credit Union, 709 P.2d 961 (Colo. Ct. App. 1985); National Consumer Law Center, The Cost of Credit: Regulation and Legal Challenges § 8.7.3 (2d ed. 2000 and Supp.). *Cf.* Suburban State Bank v. Squires, 145 Wis. 2d 445, 427 N.W.2d 393 (Ct. App. 1988).

1217 Lemelledo v. Beneficial Mgmt. Corp., 150 N.J. 255, 696 A.2d 546 (1997), *aff'g* 289 N.J. Super. 489, 674 A.2d 582 (App. 1996).

1218 *Id.*

1219 *See, e.g.*, Hawkins v. Thorp Credit & Thrift Co., 441 N.W.2d 470 (Minn. 1989); National Consumer Law Center, The Cost of Credit: Regulation and Legal Challenges § 8.5.4.3 (2d ed. 2000 and Supp.).

1220 *See* Samorano v. Aetna Fin. Co., No. 213316 (Ariz. Super. Ct. Pima Cty. filed Dec. 8, 1983) ($2.6 million); Urbina v. Aetna Fin. Co., Civ. 83-452 TUC-ACM (D. Ariz. filed June 30, 1983); California v. ITT Financial Services, No. 656038-0, Clearinghouse No. 44,801S (Cal. Super. Ct., Alameda Cty., settlement filed Sept. 21, 1989) (approximately $50 million); Memorandum of Agreement between Colorado Attorney General and Aetna Fin. Co., Clearinghouse No. 38,916 (Apr. 16, 1985); Hawkins v. Thorp Credit & Thrift Co., 441 N.W.2d 470 (Minn. 1989), *order preliminarily approving settlement and certifying settlement classes*, Clearinghouse No. 44,801W (Minn. Dist. Ct, Hennepin Cty. July 10, 1991); Assurance and Order between the Minnesota Attorney General and ITT Consumer Financial Corp., Clearinghouse No. 41,253 (June 10, 1985).

1221 State v. Aetna Fin., Clearinghouse No. 44,801 (Wis. Cir. Ct., Dane Cty. 1984); *see also* Clearinghouse No. 44,801P (complaint), 44,801Q (plaintiff's proposed findings of fact, conclusions of law and order for temporary injunction), 44,801R (stipulation and consent order).

terminates in accordance with [an agreement] or applicable law."[1222]

A New York court has, however, recognized the viability of UDAP claims where the mortgage company continued to bill the homeowners for mortgage insurance after the loan amount fell below the percentage of appraised value set by a state statute.[1223] The homeowners alleged that, by continuing to bill them, the mortgage companies induced them to believe that the payments were still required. The court also recognized a contract claim on the basis that the mortgage contracts incorporated the terms of the mortgage insurance law,[1224] but held that the state mortgage insurance law did not create a private cause of action. For mortgage loans made after July 1, 1999, the Federal Homeowner's Protection Act of 1998 creates a right to cancel mortgage insurance in some circumstances at 80% loan-to-value ratio, requires automatic termination at 78%, and requires annual disclosures.[1225]

5.4 Automobiles, Mobile Homes, Travel

5.4.1 Automobile Repairs and Towing

5.4.1.1 Introduction

Automobile repair and towing problems are major areas of consumer abuse. Another NCLC manual discusses automobile warranty and automobile repair warranties in depth;[1226] this section analyzes UDAP approaches to automobile repair problems, and § 5.4.1.8, *infra* analyzes UDAP precedent dealing with automobile towing. UDAP precedent dealing with repair issues more generally is analyzed in § 4.9.7, *supra*.

In litigating automobile repair cases, the consumer's attorney should take care to prove ownership of the vehicle through the certificate of title. Nevertheless, one court has held such formal proof unnecessary in the absence of competing claims to ownership.[1227]

1222 Deerman v. Federal Home Loan Mortg. Corp., 955 F. Supp. 1393 (N.D. Ala. 1997), *aff'd without op.*, 140 F.3d 1043 (11th Cir. 1998). *Accord* Perez v. Citicorp Mortgage, Inc., 703 N.E.2d 518 (Ill. App. Ct. 1998) (also holding that new state law requiring disclosure when mortgage insurance could be cancelled did not apply to loans in question).

1223 Walts v. First Union Mortgage Corp., 686 N.Y.S.2d 428 (App. Div. 1999) (upholding denial of motions to dismiss and for summary judgment).

1224 *Id.*

1225 12 U.S.C. § 4901 *et seq. See* National Consumer Law Center, The Cost of Credit: Regulation and Legal Challenges § 11.5 (2d ed. 2000 and Supp.) for further discussion of state and federal challenges to mortgage insurance abuses.

1226 *See* National Consumer Law Center, Consumer Warranty Law Ch. 17 (2d ed. 2001 and Supp.).

1227 Calderone v. Jim's Body Shop, 75 Ohio App. 3d 506, 599 N.E.2d 848 (1991).

5.4.1.2 Estimates, Repair Orders

State UDAP regulations and cases often require automobile repair shops to provide consumers with written price estimates and repair orders.[1228] Backdating these documents or creating false ones is a UDAP violation.[1229] New Mexico UDAP regulations find it deceptive for a repair shop to fail to post the current method by which labor charges are calculated.[1230] Repair shops may only perform repairs beyond the estimated price with the buyer's consent[1231] and

1228 Massachusetts Consumer Protection Regulations, Mass. Regs. Code tit. 940, § 5.05, Motor Vehicle Repairs and Services; Mont. Admin. R. Ch. 2.61.203; Scibek v. Longette, 339 N.J. Super. 72, 770 A.2d 1242 (App. Div. 2001) (violation actionable even where consumer was sophisticated and may not have been prejudiced by the violation); Jiries v. BP Oil, 682 A.2d 1241 (N.J. Super. Law Div. 1996); Huffmaster v. Robinson, 221 N.J. Super. 315, 534 A.2d 435 (Law Div. 1986); N.J. Admin. Code ch. 13:45A.26C.2, Automotive Repairs; N.M. Admin Code § 12.2.6.10, Requirements of Repair of Vehicles; Weaver v. Armando's, Inc., 2003 WL 22071470 (Ohio App. Sept. 3, 2003) (unpublished, citation limited) (facts did not show violation); Crye v. Smolak, 110 Ohio App. 3d 504, 674 N.E.2d 779 (1996); Snider v. Conley's Serv., 2000 Ohio App. LEXIS 2601 (June 12, 2000) (remanding for award of treble damages); Funk v. Montgomery AMC/Jeep/Renault, 66 Ohio App. 3d 815, 586 N.E.2d 1113 (1990) (repair orders not required under Ohio Rule where dealer absorbed cost of repairs); Crenshaw v. Simione, Clearinghouse No. 47,840, 1988 Ohio App. LEXIS 1953 (Ohio Ct. App. 1988); Brown v. Deacon's Chrysler Plymouth, Inc., 14 Ohio Op. 3d 436 (Ct. App. 1979); Brown v. Spitzer Ford, Inc., 11 Ohio Op. 3d 84 (Ct. App. 1978); Ohio Admin. Code § 109:4-3-13, Motor Vehicle Repairs or Services; Pennsylvania Regulations of the Bureau of Consumer Protection, 37 Pa. Code § 301.5, Automobile Industry Trade Practices; Wisconsin Department of Agriculture, Trade, and Consumer Protection Rules, Wis. Admin. Code ch. ATCP 132. *See also* Testan v. Carlsen Motor Cars, Inc., 2002 Cal. App. LEXIS 1837 (Feb. 19, 2002) (unpublished, citation limited) (not deceptive to base repair charges on a flat rate for the type of job, rather than an hourly rate); Nev. Rev. Stat. § 597.490 *et seq.*

1229 Smith v. Stacy, 2001 Ohio App. LEXIS 3202 (June 19, 2001).

1230 N.M. Admin. Code § 12.2.6.9, Requirements of Repair of Vehicles.

1231 General Transmissions Corp. of Washington, 73 F.T.C. 399 (1968); Massachusetts Consumer Protection Regulations, Mass. Regs. Code tit. 940, § 5.05 Motor Vehicle Repairs and Services; Code Miss. Rules § 24-000-002-43; Mont. Admin. R. Ch. 2.61.203; Skeer v. EMK Motors, 187 N.J. Super. 465, 455 A.2d 508 (App. Div. 1982); Levin v. Lewis, 179 N.J. Super. 193, 431 A.2d 157 (App. Div. 1981) (applies also to restorers of antique automobiles); Huffmaster v. Robinson, 221 N.J. Super. 315, 534 A.2d 435 (Law Div. 1986); N.J. Admin. Code ch. 13:45A.26C.2, Automotive Repairs; N.M. Admin. Code § 12.2.6.10, Requirements of Repair of Vehicles; Crenshaw v. Simione, C.A. No. 13273, Clearinghouse No. 47,840, 1988 Ohio App. LEXIS 1953 (Ohio Ct. App. 1988) (enforces rule that customer must consult if repair cost is more than 10% higher than estimate); Creeger v. Betz, 1974 Ohio App. LEXIS 3458 (Dec. 27, 1974); Ohio Admin. Code § 109:4-3-13, Motor Vehicle Repairs or Services; Riviera Motors Inc. v. Higbee, 45 Or. App. 545, 609 P.2d 369 (1980); Pennsylvania Regulations of the

must disclose in advance any separate charge for making estimates.[1232]

A Maryland court has held that diagnosis of a car's problem is distinct from vehicle repair, and not covered by the state's UDAP repair rule requiring price estimates in advance.[1233] Of course, unfair or deceptive diagnostic practices are UDAP violations, such as the failure to disclose a substantial charge to diagnose a problem, but they are not covered by Maryland's repair rule.

A Wisconsin case has analyzed the appropriate remedy where a repair shop violates a UDAP regulation prohibiting the shop from collecting for repairs without a written repair order.[1234] The regulation states that all initial repair contracts must be in writing, and oral repair authorizations are permissible only for subsequent changes. Where the initial contract is not in writing, the shop can not collect at all for unauthorized repairs, the repair contract becomes invalid as a matter of law, and the shop may collect only through *quantum meruit* for other repairs orally authorized.[1235]

A similar New Jersey case where work was done without a written estimate or authorization also resulted in the court ruling that the repair contract was unenforceable. The New Jersey court utilized three different theories—the repair contract was void against public policy; the repair shop may not enforce an illegal contract; and no contract was consummated because the regulation stated that a contract may not be entered into without written authorization.[1236] Where a repair shop performs repairs without giving an estimate and without the consumer's authorization, and the consumer pays the bill in order to get the vehicle, but then stops payment on the check, the consumer may be able to raise the shop's violation of UDAP regulations as a defense to a larceny prosecution.[1237]

It is unfair for a body shop to give an insurance company and the consumer an estimate of repair costs, and then notify only the insurance company and obtain its authorization for a higher price when the accident damage was greater than anticipated. Even though the consumer did not have to pay for the increased bill, the consumer should still have been notified. The consumer might have decided not to go forward with the repairs, but instead might have agreed to treat the car as totaled, turning the car into the insurer for a larger insurance payment directly to the consumer.[1238]

It is deceptive to withhold diagnostic information after external inspection of a car, as a means of inducing the consumer to agree to a more expensive internal inspection.[1239] Once the repair firm has diagnosed the vehicle's problems to the point where it can project the costs of repairs that are certainly needed and the possible costs of repairs that are likely to be required, it must give the consumer this information.[1240]

5.4.1.3 Replaced Parts and Invoices

Consumers must be told that they have the right in most cases to keep, and in other cases to inspect, replaced parts.[1241] UDAP regulations and decisions in a number of states also indicate that automobile repair shops must pro-

---

Bureau of Consumer Protection, 37 Pa. Code ch. 301.5, Automobile Industry Trade Practices; Hyder-Ingram Chevrolet Inc. v. Kutach, 612 S.W.2d 687 (Tex. Civ. App. 1981); Wisconsin Department of Agriculture, Trade, and Consumer Protection Rules, Wis. Admin. Code ch. ATCP 132.06.

1232 Massachusetts Consumer Protection Regulations, Mass. Regs. Code tit. 940, § 5.05, Motor Vehicle Repairs and Services; N.M. Admin. Code § 12.2.6.11, Requirements of Repair of Vehicles; Ohio Admin. Code § 109:4-3-13, Motor Vehicle Repairs or Services; Pennsylvania Regulations of the Bureau of Consumer Protection, 37 Pa. Code ch. 301.5, Automobile Industry Trade Practices (1978); Wisconsin Department of Agriculture, Trade, and Consumer Protection Rules, Wis. Admin. Code ch. ATCP 132, Motor Vehicle Repair § 132.09.

1233 State v. Cottman Transmissions Sys., Inc., 86 Md. App. 714, 587 A.2d 1190 (1991).

1234 Huff & Morse, Inc. v. Riordon, 345 N.W.2d 504 (Wis. Ct. App. 1981).

1235 *Id.*

1236 Huffmaster v. Robinson, 221 N.J. Super. 315, 534 A.2d 435 (Law Div. 1986).

1237 Commonwealth v. Swan, 38 Mass. App. Ct. 539, 649 N.E.2d 795 (1995).

1238 Young v. Century Lincoln-Mercury, Inc., 396 S.E.2d 105 (S.C. Ct. App. 1990), *aff'd in relevant part, rev'd in part on other grounds*, 309 S.C. 263, 422 S.E.2d 103 (1992).

1239 State v. Cottman Transmissions Sys., Inc., 86 Md. App. 714, 587 A.2d 1190 (1991).

1240 *Id.*

1241 People v. Regan, 95 Cal. App. 3d Supp. 1, 157 Cal. Rptr. 62 (1979); Idaho Consumer Protection Regulations, Idaho Admin. Code 04.02.01.132, Repairs and Improvements; Massachusetts Consumer Protection Regulations, Mass. Regs. Code tit. 940, § 5.05, Motor Vehicle Repairs and Services; Code of Mississippi Rules 24-000-002, Rule 47; Mont. Admin. R. 2.61.203; N.J. Admin. Code ch. 13:45A-26C.2, Automotive Repairs; Vannoy v. Capital Lincoln-Mercury Sales, Inc., 88 Ohio App. 3d 138, 623 N.E.2d 177 (1993) (rule applies to all repairs, not just those exceeding $25; posting a sign that parts are available upon request is not "tendering"; need to "save" parts in case warranty company wants them does not excuse violation); Brown v. Bob Kay, 14 Ohio Op. 3d 329 (Ct. App. 1979); Brown v. Deacon's Chrysler Plymouth, 14 Ohio Op. 3d 436 (Ct. App. 1979); Brown v. Spitzer Ford, Inc., 11 Ohio Op. 3d 84 (Ct. App. 1978); Brown v. Joe Schott Chevrolet Inc., Clearinghouse No. 27,051 (Ohio C.P. Hamilton Cty. 1976); Ohio Admin. Code § 109:4-3-13, Motor Vehicle Repairs or Services; Pennsylvania Regulations of the Bureau of Consumer Protection, 37 Pa. Code § 301.5, Automobile Industry Trade Practices; Wisconsin Department of Agriculture, Trade, and Consumer Protection Rules, Wis. Admin. Code ch. ATCP 132.07. *But cf.* Scanlon v. Fox, 2001 Ohio App. LEXIS 3983 (Sept. 6, 2001) (putting a checkbox on estimate form that consumer can check if consumer wants parts back constitutes a tender and satisfies rule; tender complies with rule even if shop retains part for period of time to test it); Funk v. Montgomery AMC/Jeep/Renault, 66 Ohio App. 3d 815, 586 N.E.2d 1113 (1990) (rule does not apply where dealer absorbs cost of repairs).

vide invoices detailing all parts and labor supplied,[1242] identifying warranty work performed,[1243] disclosing the nature of the guarantee,[1244] and stating if used or rebuilt parts are utilized.[1245] Failure to give an invoice may be a UDAP violation even in the absence of a requirement in a UDAP regulation.[1246] Evidence about the requirements of the state's lemon law may be admissible to establish the standard in the industry regarding provision of invoices, even if the lemon law is not applicable to the particular case.[1247] Padding bills for automobile repair work not performed or parts not used is a UDAP violation.[1248]

5.4.1.4 Misrepresentation That Work Is Required or of Type of Work Performed; Shoddy Work

It is deceptive to misrepresent which repairs and parts are covered by warranty or to claim falsely that repairs are necessary, that work has been done, or that a car is in a dangerous condition.[1249] Shops may not charge for unauthorized, unnecessary, or unperformed repairs,[1250] or alter vehicles so that additional repairs are required.[1251] A repair shop can not take an engine apart without authorization, and then demand payment to return the engine to normal.[1252]

In one case, a repair shop employee claimed he was terminated because he would not "upsell" a fuel injector flush on every vehicle he serviced. Experts in the case testified that the service was unnecessary on many cars. The appellate court ruled that this practice could be a UDAP violation, and that the termination could be found to be wrongful.[1253]

Repairs must be performed as represented.[1254] For example, repair shops must replace all parts they promise to

1242 Brunswick Exchange Inc., 74 F.T.C. 894 (1968) (consent order); Idaho Consumer Protection Regulations, Idaho Admin. Code 04.02.01.131, Repairs and Improvements; Massachusetts Consumer Protection Regulations, Mass. Regs. Code tit. 940, § 5.05, Motor Vehicle Repairs and Services; Code Mississippi Rules 24-000-002, Rule 46; N.J. Admin. Code ch. 13:45A-26C.2, Automotive Repairs; N.M. Admin. Code § 12.2.6.10, Requirements of Repair of Vehicles; Weaver v. Armando's, Inc., 2003 WL 22071470 (Ohio App. Sept. 3, 2003) (unpublished, citation limited) (no violation where consumer had not picked up car at time of trial); Dantzig v. Sloe, 115 Ohio App. 3d 64, 684 N.E.2d 715 (1996) (failure to provide itemized list of repairs performed violates Ohio UDAP regulation); Funk v. Montgomery AMC/Jeep/Renault, 66 Ohio App. 3d 815, 586 N.E.2d 1113 (1990) (invoices not required under Ohio rule where dealer absorbed cost of repairs); Brown v. Joe Schott Chevrolet Inc., Clearinghouse No. 27,051 (C.P. Hamilton Cty., Ohio 1976); Ohio Admin. Code § 109:4-3-13, Motor Vehicle Repairs or Services; Pennsylvania Regulations of the Bureau of Consumer Protection, 37 Pa. Code § 301.5, Automobile Industry Trade Practices; Wisconsin Department of Agriculture, Trade, and Consumer Protection Rules, Wis. Admin. Code ch. ATCP 132, Motor Vehicle Repair § 132.08.

1243 Wisconsin Department of Agriculture, Trade, and Consumer Protection Rules, Wis. Admin. Code ch. ATCP 132, Motor Vehicle Repair § 132.08.

1244 N.J. Admin. Code § 13:45A-26C(2), Automotive Repairs.

1245 Maurice Lenett, 49 F.T.C. 914 (1953); M&M Spring Co., 50 F.T.C. 207 (1953); FTC Guides For The Rebuilt Reconditioned and Other Used Automobile Parts Industry, 16 C.F.R. Part 20; N.J. Admin. Code ch. 13:45A, subch. 26C, Automotive Repairs; N.M. Admin. Code § 12.2.6.10, Requirements of Repair of Vehicles; Brown v. Spitzer Ford, Inc., 11 Ohio Op. 3d 84 (Ct. App. 1978); Pennsylvania Regulations of the Bureau of Consumer Protection, 37 Pa. Code § 301.5; Automobile Industry Trade Practices; Wisconsin Department of Agriculture, Trade, and Consumer Protection Rules, Wis. Admin. Code ch. ATCP 132.08, Motor Vehicle Repair.

1246 Johnson v. Hyundai Motor Am., 698 A.2d 631 (Pa. Super. Ct. 1997), *appeal denied*, 551 Pa. 704, 712 A.2d 286 (1998).

1247 *Id.*

1248 State v. Fallon, 1998 Del. Super. LEXIS 186 (Feb. 27, 1998); Barnes v. Jones Chevrolet Co., 358 S.E.2d 156 (S.C. Ct. App. 1987).

1249 State *ex rel.* Brady v. Fallon, 1998 Del. Super. LEXIS 186 (Feb. 27, 1998); Perkins v. Stapleton Buick-GMC Truck, Inc., 2001 Ohio App. LEXIS 2651 (June 15, 2001) (repeatedly representing that repairs had been made when they had not been successful would be UDAP violation); Brown v. Joe Schott Chevrolet Inc., Clearinghouse No. 27,051 (Ohio C.P. Hamilton Cty., 1976); Idaho Consumer Protection Regulations, Idaho Admin. Code 04.02.01.130, Repairs and Improvements; Massachusetts Consumer Protection Regulations, Mass. Regs. Code tit. 940, § 5.05, Motor Vehicle Repairs and Services; Mont. Admin. R. Ch. 2.61.203; Ohio Admin. Code § 109:4-3-13, Motor Vehicle Repairs or Services; Pennsylvania Regulations of the Bureau of Consumer Protection, 37 Pa. Code § 301.5, Automobile Industry Trade Practices; Wisconsin Department of Agriculture, Trade, and Consumer Protection Rules, Wis. Admin. Code ch. ATCP 132, Motor Vehicle Repair § 132.09.

1250 Crown Buick, Inc. v. Bercier, 483 So. 2d 1310 (La. Ct. App. 1986); Brown v. Deacon's Chrysler Plymouth, Inc., 14 Ohio Op. 3d 436 (Ct. App. 1979); Brown v. Spitzer Ford, Inc., 11 Ohio Op. 3d 84 (Ct. App. 1978); Brown v. Joe Schott Chevrolet, Inc., Clearinghouse No. 27,051 (Ohio C.P. Hamilton Cty. 1976); Idaho Consumer Protection Regulations, Idaho Admin. Code 04.02.01.130, Repairs and Improvements; Massachusetts Consumer Protection Regulations, Mass. Regs. Code tit. 940, § 5.05, Motor Vehicle Repairs and Services; Code of Miss. Rules § 24-000-002, Rule 45; Mont. Admin. R. § 2.61.203; N.J. Admin. Code § 13:45A-26C.2, Automotive Repairs; Ohio Admin. Code § 109:4-3-13 Motor Vehicle Repairs or Services; Pennsylvania Regulations of the Bureau of Consumer Protection, 37 Pa. Code § 301.5, Automobile Industry Trade Practices (1978); Wisconsin Department of Agriculture, Trade, and Consumer Protection Rules, Wis. Admin. Code ch. ATCP 132, Motor Vehicle Repair § 132.09.

1251 Wisconsin Department of Agriculture, Trade, and Consumer Protection Rules, Wis. Admin. Code ch. ATCP 132, Motor Vehicle Repair § 132.09.

1252 Crown Buick Inc. v. Bercier, 483 So. 2d 1310 (La. Ct. App. 1986). *See also* Crye v. Smolak, 110 Ohio App. 3d 504, 674 N.E.2d 779 (1996).

1253 Jones v. Stevinson's Golden Ford, 36 P.3d 129 (Colo. App. 2001).

1254 General Transmissions Corp. of Washington, 73 F.T.C. 399 (1968). *See also* Baker v. Tri-County Harley Davidson, Inc., 1999 Ohio App. LEXIS 5353 (Nov. 15, 1999) (repair shop violated Ohio UDAP rule by falsely representing that repairs had been completed); Crye v. Smolak, 110 Ohio App. 3d 504, 674 N.E.2d 779 (1996) (misrepresentation of the status of repairs).

replace.[1255] Shops can not depart from trade standards of workmanlike repair.[1256] Of course, not every repair that does not meet a consumer's expectations is a deceptive practice.[1257] But Ohio courts have held that a repair shop's pattern of inefficiency, incompetence, or evasion of legal obligations may be a UDAP violation.[1258]

5.4.1.5 Timeliness of Repairs; Unauthorized Use of Car

If a repair shop promises to complete repairs within a certain time, it is a UDAP violation not to.[1259] Several states have UDAP regulations requiring that repairs be performed within twenty-four hours unless otherwise agreed upon.[1260] Even without an agreement as to the completion date, lengthy delay is a UDAP violation.[1261] When a repair shop changes ownership, the new owners can not hide behind the sale agreement in failing to repair cars already at the shop.[1262] Shops can not use the customer's car for purposes other than test drives or delivery to the customer.[1263]

5.4.1.6 Failure to Correct Inadequate Repairs

Unless the repair shop discloses that it does not guarantee its work, if the shop returns the car as fixed, and in fact the problem has not been corrected, the shop must make additional repairs at no cost to the consumer.[1264] It is deceptive to perform the wrong repair job, thus failing to correct a problem, and then insist that the job was done correctly and that there will be an additional charge to perform additional repairs.[1265] New Mexico UDAP regulations find it deceptive for a repair shop to fail to post the major provisions of their warranty policy and to either fail to provide consumers with a written warranty or a statement that there is no warranty.[1266] The shop must also provide the details of its warranty upon request.[1267]

5.4.1.7 Bill Collecting Practices

Shops must return the buyer's car if the buyer pays for all repairs the buyer authorized to be performed.[1268] Merchants may not wrongfully permit a lien to be filed against a car.[1269] Holding the car pursuant to a common law possessory mechanic's lien after violating UDAP regulations is a deceptive and unfair practice.[1270] Selling the consumer a warranty on repair work, but then refusing to fulfill it unless the consumer pays for additional work on the vehicle, is deceptive.[1271]

5.4.1.8 Towing Practices

It is unfair or deceptive for a towing company to commit the following practices: to refuse to allow the owner access to the car or to personal property within the car;[1272] to impose storage charges after demand by the owner for release of the vehicle, when the owner did not consent to the tow;[1273] to tow away cars without sufficient warning; to

---

1255 *See* Hugh Wood Ford, Inc. v. Galloway, 830 S.W.2d 296 (Tex. App. 1992).

1256 Claude Nolan Cadillac, Inc. v. Griffin, 610 So. 2d 725 (Fla. Dist. Ct. App. 1992); Snider v. Conley's Serv., 2000 Ohio App. LEXIS 2601 (June 12, 2000) (remanding for award of treble damages). *See also* Check v. Clifford Chrysler-Plymouth, 794 N.E.2d 829 (Ill. App. 2003) (dealer violated UDAP statute by having shoddy repairs done to vehicle and then selling it as new).

1257 Capitol Cadillac Olds, Inc. v. Roberts, 813 S.W.2d 287 (Ky. 1991).

1258 Perkins v. Stapleton Buick-GMC Truck, Inc., 2001 Ohio App. LEXIS 2651 (June 15, 2001); Pearson v. Tom Harrigan Oldsmobile-Nissan, Inc. 1991 Ohio App. LEXIS 4425 (Sept. 16, 1991); Brown v. Lyons, 43 Ohio Misc. 14, 332 N.E.2d 380 (C.P. 1974).

1259 Baker v. Tri-County Harley Davidson, Inc., 1999 Ohio App. LEXIS 5353 (Nov. 15, 1999).

1260 Massachusetts Consumer Protection Regulations, Mass. Regs. Code tit. 940, § 5.05, Motor Vehicle Repairs and Services; Pennsylvania Regulations of the Bureau of Consumer Protection, 37 Pa. Code § 301.5, Automobile Industry Trade Practices.

1261 Croskey v. Leach, 2002 WL 31323243 (Ohio App. Oct. 18, 2002) (unpublished, citation limited).

1262 Brown v. Galleria Area Ford, Inc., 752 S.W.2d 114 (Tex. 1988).

1263 Massachusetts Consumer Protection Regulations, Mass. Regs. Code tit. 940, § 5.05, Motor Vehicle Repairs and Services; Pennsylvania Regulations of the Bureau of Consumer Protection, 37 Pa. Code § 301.5, Automobile Industry Trade Practices; Ramey v. Kingsport Motors Inc., 1992 Tenn. App. LEXIS 316, Clearinghouse No. 51,280 (Tenn. App. 1991).

1264 Massachusetts Consumer Protection Regulations, Mass. Regs. Code tit. 940, § 5.05, Motor Vehicle Repairs and Services; Pennsylvania Regulations of the Bureau of Consumer Protection, 37 Pa. Code § 301.5, Automobile Industry Trade Practices; Padgett v. Bert Ogden Motor's, Inc., 869 S.W.2d 532 (Tex. App. 1993).

1265 Joseph v. Hendrix, 536 So. 2d 448 (La. Ct. App. 1988).

1266 N.M. Admin. Code § 12.2.6.9, Requirements of Repair of Vehicles.

1267 *Id.*

1268 Idaho Consumer Protection Regulations, Idaho Admin. Code 04.02.01.130, Repairs and Improvements; Frank J. Linhares Co. v. Reliance Ins., 4 Mass. App. Ct. 617, 357 N.E.2d 313 (1976); Huffmaster v. Robinson, 221 N.J. Super. 315, 534 A.2d 435 (Law Div. 1986); Wisconsin Department of Agriculture, Trade, and Consumer Protection Rules, Wis. Admin. Code ch. ATCP 132, Motor Vehicle Repair § 132.09. *But see* Meyer v. Diesel Equip. Co., 1 Kan. App. 2d 574, 570 P.2d 1374 (1977).

1269 Idaho Consumer Protection Regulations, Idaho Admin. Code 04.02.01.130, Repairs and Improvements; N.M. Admin. Code § 12.2.6.10(D), Requirements of Repair of Vehicles.

1270 Smith v. Stacy, 2001 Ohio App. LEXIS 3202 (June 19, 2001).

1271 Giarratano v. Midas Muffler, 630 N.Y.S.2d 656, 27 U.C.C. Rep. 2d 87 (City Ct. 1995).

1272 Halloran's v. Spillane's Servicecenter, Inc., 41 Conn. Supp. 484, 587 A.2d 176 (1990).

1273 *Id.*

charge "let-down" fees when owners return to cars while they are being hoisted; or to coerce the consumer into paying through use of physical intimidation or misrepresentations concerning the towing company's legal rights.[1274] It is also deceptive and unconscionable to demand payment for a tow even though the car was legally parked, and should not have been towed.[1275] Also unfair is the towing company charging unconscionable fees and forcing consumers to waive their right to bring a damage claim.[1276] A UDAP violation also occurs when a towing company uses a statutory lien to compel payment of inappropriate and excessive fees.[1277]

It is also a UDAP violation for a towing company to never tell a car owner that it has towed the owner's car and to allow property to be missing from the car when the owner recovers the vehicle.[1278] A towing company that does not have a lien under state law on the towed vehicle, but still refuses to release the car within a reasonable time after demand by the owner, unless the owner pays the towing and storage charges, commits conversion and a UDAP violation.[1279] It likewise violates the UDAP statute for a towing company to refuse to release vehicles except during weekday business hours, when it tows vehicles twenty-four hours a day, seven days a week.[1280] A UDAP plaintiff has also recovered damages for damage done to a towed car while in the towing company's possession.[1281]

On the other hand, where a consumer is given clear notice not to park in a certain location, the property owner has not committed a UDAP violation when it tows the consumer's vehicle.[1282] The property owner may not be liable for the practices of an independent towing company without showing some type of participation by the property owner.[1283]

1274 People v. James, 122 Cal. App. 3d 25, 177 Cal. Rptr. 110 (1981).

1275 Allied Towing Serv. v. Mitchell, 833 S.W.2d 577 (Tex. App. 1992).

1276 Demeo v. State Farm Mut. Automobile Ins. Co., 38 Mass. App. Ct. 955, 649 N.E.2d 803 (1995).

1277 Commonwealth Mut. Ins. Co. v. Vigorito, 2003 WL 328854 (Mass. App. Div. Feb. 7, 2003).

1278 Waters v. Hollie, 642 S.W.2d 90 (Tex. App. 1982).

1279 Halloran's v. Spillane's Servicecenter, Inc., 41 Conn. Supp. 484, 587 A.2d 176 (1990). *Cf.* Lawson v. Whitey's Frame Shop, 241 Conn. 678, 697 A.2d 1137 (1997) (disposing of towed vehicles did not violate UDAP statute where city ordinance and towing company's contract with city authorized disposal); Estep v. Johnson, 123 Ohio App. 3d 307, 704 N.E.2d 58 (1998) (wrongful sale of towed vehicle was conversion but not UDAP violation).

1280 Halloran's v. Spillane's Servicecenter, Inc., 41 Conn. Supp. 484, 587 A.2d 176 (1990).

1281 Allied Towing Serv. v. Mitchell, 833 S.W.2d 577 (Tex. App. 1992).

1282 *See* Ames v. Oceanside Welding & Towing Co., 767 A.2d 677 (R.I. 2001).

1283 *Id.*

5.4.2 Discovery in Automobile Sales Cases

5.4.2.1 Introduction

This section discusses what documentary records are available from a car dealer that can help prove the unfair and deceptive practices discussed in the later sections. The section also examines other sources of information.

Many view an automobile UDAP case as a swearing contest between the consumer and dealer. Added to the fact that many juries may trust a consumer over a car salesman, the consumer also has access to the dealer's detailed records of each and every transaction, and these records can not only reveal the deception, but point to systematic illegal schemes by the dealership. This is particularly the case when all the documents pertaining to a transaction are compared and analyzed, and then supplemented with documents from other sources.

Discovery should begin immediately upon filing suit, particularly requests for admissions, interrogatories and requests for documents. The request for production of documents should define "document" broadly, to include all original drafts, copies, and electronically stored data in every medium. Much of the key information may not be found in paper documents. In addition, training videos and similar media may prove extremely instructive.

One technique for obtaining the maximum amount of information is to follow up document demands with depositions where the dealer employee is asked to bring the *original* deal file. While the deposition is being conducted, the original deal file is copied; then, compare this deal file with the file produced in response to the document request. Because of the growing use and sophistication of dealer computer systems to record customer data, it is often helpful to discover the name and depose the individual technician who runs the dealership's computer system.

Dealers have so much paper on their sales that document management can become an issue in class actions or other investigations of a number of purchases from a dealership. Coding is one such technique to manage files—assigning a unique number to each document, perhaps numbering them as the documents are copied. Then index each document with a brief description, including dates, names, and subjects, and code the documents by issue. A good coding form will identify each element of each cause of action. It will also have significant other headings, such as assets, witnesses, and damages. Each document should also be coded as to its evidentiary value, indicating both the relevant issue and the weight of its value.

Seek copies of the installment sales agreement and other paperwork both from the dealer and from the finance company and compare this with the agreement retained by the consumer. Practitioners report an amazing amount of forgeries and alterations. For example, after the deal is finalized, the dealer may discover that its finance company refuses to purchase the paper, where there is too much paid for various add-ons or where the deposit is inadequate. The solution may be that the dealer juggles the numbers from the first contract to keep the monthly payments the same, but rearrange the components to meet the finance company requirements. This will require alterations of the original contract or a new contract with a forged signature.

Similarly, compare the options the dealer tells the finance company are installed with the vehicle with the options that are in fact present. One way that dealers justify to financers for inflated cash prices is that the car comes equipped with special options. In other words, the consumer does not know enough to question a deal, but the finance company does because it wants its collateral value to bear a certain relationship to the loan amount. Of course, the consumer may have a claim if the paperwork represents that certain options are installed where they are not.

5.4.2.2 Deal Files and File Jackets

The major filing system maintained by motor vehicle dealers contains "deal files." A deal file is the complete record of a single vehicle transaction. While dealers have differing filing systems, most deal files are grouped by new or used vehicle, sorted by year, and are filed alphabetically by buyer's last name. The transaction documents are kept together in a "jacket."

The file jacket itself is an important document, as it lists significant identification and sales information that summarizes the entire transaction. Always copy the file jacket when pulling deal files.

If the vehicle is used, the deal jacket will identify where the dealer obtained the vehicle—at auction, from a wholesaler, or by trade-in. The dealer's purchase price, appraised value (known generally as actual cash value, or ACV), and selling price may also be listed. A comparison of these three figures alone reveals a lot about the transaction. The dates of acquisition and resale are also usually included, revealing how long the vehicle was in stock.

However, it is important to remember that most of the information on the jacket is only a summary of information contained on original documents inside the file, and that errors in recording do occur. Make sure to work from the original documents in preparing evidence for trial.

5.4.2.3 The Worksheet, Purchase Order, and Retail Installment Sales Contract

The worksheet is one of the most important pieces of paper in the deal file. The form is sometimes called a "four-square" worksheet, because it usually deals exclusively with the four primary aspects of a deal, at least from the dealer's viewpoint. Those four aspects are purchase price, trade-in allowance, cash down payment, and monthly payment. In many high-pressure selling systems, the four-square is used to confuse and pressure consumers into accepting purchase terms that are less than equitable.

The document is important because it reflects the course of the negotiation. As terms are negotiated, offers, rejections, and counter offers are recorded on the four-square. Carefully reviewing the four-square will help determine both the extent of negotiations and the final terms that were agreed to by the parties, which are usually circled and initialed.

The purchase order (sometimes Buyer's Order) reflects the final terms of sale between the selling dealer and the buyer. This document is usually printed in the business manager's office, and should reflect the final terms negotiated between the buyer and the salesperson, plus any additional products or services sold by the business manager. However, even if all the terms are correctly carried forward from the negotiation worksheet, there are still a number of potential problems with this form.

First, check that the form contains all required disclosures under state and federal motor vehicle laws. Some states require specific language in purchase orders, particularly concerning trade-in allowances and as-is sales. The nature of the car's warranty should be disclosed, even for used cars (as required by the FTC's Used Car Rule). If the sale is contingent on financing, that contingency should be clearly stated. The vehicle sold should conform to the description of the vehicle on the form. Check that the odometer statement matches that provided on the federally required odometer form.

The retail installment sales contract document should reflect the terms printed on the purchase order and negotiated on the four-square worksheet. Make sure the form used complies with TIL requirements, particularly as to credit insurance disclosures. Most dealers use computer programs to calculate charges and print these forms.

5.4.2.4 Odometer Statements and Title Documents

There should be in every deal file two sets of documents evidencing a transfer of ownership (copies of titles, reassignment forms, powers of attorney, and/or odometer statements): one set that was filled out when the dealer acquired the vehicle and one that was filled out by the dealer during the sale of the vehicle. There are a number of things to check for when comparing these forms: that the VINs match; that the dates are correct; and that the mileage increases over time. Pay particular attention to which of three boxes are checked on the form: if the "mileage exceeds mechanical limitations" box is checked, it means there are 100,000 miles on the vehicle, *plus* whatever mileage is indicated. Unfortunately, a mileage reading of 145,000 needs only be recorded as 45,000 miles, with the correct box checked.

Titles and reassignment forms can also show prior owners, salvage history, and other aspects of a vehicle's history. Names and addresses of prior owners may prove useful in conducting an investigation. The documents may also involve forgeries and other alterations. More on title transfer documents is found in NCLC's *Automobile Fraud* (2d ed. 2003 and Supp.).

Title clerks at dealerships have extensive training and experience with these documents. If a case involves a lot of title work, consider deposing the title clerk at the dealership for preliminary background information.

5.4.2.5 Recap Sheets and Charge Backs

Depending on the computer system used by the dealer, most dealers will print a "recap" of the deal and place it in the deal file. This document details the profit on the transaction by department, the salespeople commissioned on the deal, their pay, the house share, and the dealer's net profit. This document can be quite useful. If a recap sheet is not in the deal file, the dealer probably has them stored in some other filing system.

When any profit on a transaction is lost after the deal is done, the loss is "charged back" against any person who received a commission on that profit. For example, if a repair results in a come-back, the service writer may have a "charge back" on her payroll. If a service contract or credit insurance policy is cancelled, the business manager will have a charge back. If an entire deal is unwound, the salespeople involved in the transaction will have a charge back. A second recap sheet will be printed out after the cancellation that will list "charge backs."

Charge back documents are important because they point to potentially dissatisfied customers. The poorly done service work is obviously going to involve a dissatisfied customer. Service contract and credit insurance charge backs may indicate the consumer was unaware that the product was included in the transaction, a disclosure issue in packing cases. A charge back for financing (where the customer refinanced with another lender shortly after purchase) may indicate the APR and/or the finance reserve was too high. A complete unwind of a deal raises all sorts of possibilities, but will almost always involve a very dissatisfied customer.

5.4.2.6 Finance Facsimiles, Finance Reserves, and the Credit Application

There is no particular name for finance facsimiles in the industry, but they are usually in the deal file. These documents are generated by lenders in response to the business manager's attempt to sell the paper to a lending institution. Typically the dealer sends a copy of the purchase order and credit application to the lender by facsimile. The lender then responds, by facsimile, with a yes, no, or maybe. (There is a growing trend to replace facsimiles with e-mail and other Internet-based communications. These may or may not be included in a printed form in the deal file, but may be stored at the dealer and finance company in electronic form.)

Whether the finance company responds by fax or e-mail, it is the "maybes" that are most interesting, because dealers generally misrepresent this response to the consumer. Dealers often tell the consumer that the loan was approved, but that they need more money down, or a cosigner, or a higher rate. If the consumer objects, the dealer claims the trade-in has been sold (illegal as the deal was contingent, so title could not transfer until the contingency was met), or that the consumer is bound by the contract (which is a misrepresentation, because once the contingency fails, or the dealer makes a counter offer, the deal is dead, and must be unwound *before* further negotiations with the consumer).

These documents are crucial to show the *date and time* of acceptance/rejection/conditional acceptance by each lending institution contacted by the dealer. In a case where the consumer has been kept on the hook for some time (some states require acceptance or rejection of contingent paper within a set period of time), these documents can be evidence of violations.

The facsimile evidencing the purchase of the note will disclose the APR the financial institution will pay the dealer for the note, known as their "buy rate." The facsimile may also disclose the permissible APR the dealer can charge the consumer, that is, the APR actually entered on the retail installment sales contract in the TIL boxes. The difference between the buy rate and the rate charged the consumer is the "finance reserve," a source of considerable profit to the dealership. Financial institutions regulate the amount of finance reserve a dealer can charge a consumer, and some institutions, particularly credit unions, prohibit finance reserves at all.

Though the documents may not reflect the rates offered, be sure to inquire as to what the clients were told about the rate they received. Representations that the rate is the "best" or "lowest," or words to that effect, may be deceptive where the dealer has taken a finance reserve. Compare the figures on the facsimile with the retail installment contract and the recap sheet to make sure all the numbers are consistent. The dealer will also have agreements with financial institutions that spell out the dealer's obligations when it arranges financing for a deal, including the kickbacks it will receive.

Another document is the business manager's summary. There is no standard name for this document, but it is a summary of the conversations the business manager had with the lending institutions and the consumer in an effort to get a deal bought. Business managers work very hard to get their paper bought, and generally keep accurate records of their efforts. If the paper was conditionally accepted by the lender, and the dealer attempted to extract an additional down payment from the consumer to get the deal bought, that conversation may have been recorded on this form.

The consumer usually fills out a credit application by hand; the dealer may type the form for submission to the lender. Errors, especially those that present the consumer in a more favorable light, may indicate illegal activity by the dealer, especially if the consumer has marginal credit.[1284]

If a consumer is a cash buyer, however, the presence of a credit application in a file may be evidence of a different kind of practice. Some cash buyers do not want the dealer to run a credit report at all, and so refuse to authorize a report. Dealers, however, want that financial information so they can ascertain the buying power of the consumer (which can be used to upsell products). Nevertheless, this is not a permissible use of a credit report under the Fair Credit Reporting Act.[1285] If there is a credit report, determine if the consumer refused to authorize a credit check, or if the consumer only agreed to the check after the dealer misrepresented its necessity.

5.4.2.7 Log Books, Cash Draw Files, and Business Manager's Penetration and Performance Reports

There is generally at least one daily log or ledger maintained by dealerships. The daily ledger is usually maintained by the business manager, though the sales manager may maintain it, or keep a separate record. These books generally record every transaction entered into during a day, in chronological order. The log will contain the consumer's name, vehicle, salespeople's names, and the financial aspects of the transaction.

The business manager's log book may be particularly valuable for investigations into whether dealers are using questionable means to add-on credit insurance, service contracts and other charges onto the sale (sometimes called "packing"). The log books record which products were sold by the business manager, and can be used to quickly determine the penetration of finance and insurance products at the dealership. The log book may record the payment-in, payment-out information that is essential to tracking the effectiveness of packing.

Dealers may provide their employees with incentives to pack consumers, by providing those employees a small cash bonus, called a "spiff," that is usually paid on the spot by the business or sales manager. In this case, it is called a "packed payment spiff."

Business managers sometimes use the log book to keep track of payments quoted by salespeople. The "payment in" column lists the payment the customer was closed on by the desk manager working with the salesperson. For example, the four square document may have "$350/mo" circled in the payment square, indicating agreement at that amount. That amount would be recorded on the business manager's log, along with an indication as to whether the payment was packed, and if so, by how much and which salesperson was due a spiff.

Spiffs can also vary depending on the amount of pack: a $10 a month pack may generate a $10 spiff; $20 pack gets a $20 spiff. Both the business manager and the sales manager have to take cash draws to pay spiffs. Consequently, cash draw files are relevant documents to discover. The account records may show what types of sales incentives were being offered during specific periods of time.

The log book will also record the "payment out." Payment out is simply the final payment agreed to by the consumer after finalizing the transaction with the business manager. The difference between the payment in and the payment out is the "bump." The business manager's commission structure may be based, in part, on his or her "bump" over the packed payment.

This commission may be specified in the dealer's pay and commission policies. Some dealers also have forms targeted exclusively to keep track of packed payments, called, appropriately, pack tracking forms.

In addition to the log book, business managers are required to keep detailed, monthly summaries of their performance. The commission structure for business managers is usually relatively complicated, so dealers insist on excellent records. Third-party providers of the credit insurance and other products also monitor their performance.

5.4.2.8 Payroll Records, Policy and Procedure Manuals, Training Manuals, Advertising

Payroll records contain a wealth of information. In addition to the income of various employees, chargebacks, spiffs, and payroll notations reveal the sales culture at the dealership. A significant number of chargebacks associated with one salesperson, or a certain sales crew may provide evidence of deceptive sales practices.

Most dealerships have extensive policy and procedure manuals, covering everything from employee parking to retirement benefits. Included in these materials may be commission and pricing policies that point to hidden finance charges; advertising programs that support deceptive advertising allegations; and service department policies that indicate the service writers have financial incentives to discover problems with customer vehicles. Dealerships have extensive sales meetings, and agendas and notes from sales meetings for a specified period of time may be relevant.

Advertising violations are quite common. Always ask for and review the dealer's advertising files, especially copies of radio and television advertising, and compare the advertis-

1284 *See* Pretzer v. Motor Vehicle Bd., 2004 WL 422623 (Tex. Mar. 5, 2004) (documenting dealer's widespread falsification of credit applications).

1285 *See* § 5.4.4.2, *infra*.

ing to state and federal regulations. Drafts of advertising can be very helpful as well.

Training manuals are another fruitful area of inquiry. Consumers (and attorneys) frequently underestimate the quality and characteristics of the salesforce employed by dealerships. It is a highly competitive, potentially lucrative position. Salespeople have continuing sales education that exceeds anything required of licensed professionals; they either sell or they starve. As a result, there is a significant industry that provides sales training to dealerships, and many of the techniques they teach are deceptive.

Always ask for sales training materials, particularly those provided by third-party providers, and review them carefully. (Much of the manufacturer training materials will be about the vehicles themselves; focus only on sales training provided by manufacturers, not product presentation.) If third-party providers, including manufacturers, provide training at the dealership, consider naming them as defendants and serve them a full set of discovery requests at the same time the dealership is served.

An example of the type of scheme that may be explicitly taught through training materials is the "high penny roll," which instructs dealers to simply inflate monthly payments to a set amount, say from $350.15 to $350.89. The .74 bump individually has no significance; however, to a dealer selling more than 100 cars a month, with a 70% financed penetration rate, the total amount is significant.

A "conversion" is an attempt by the business manager to convert a cash buyer into a finance buyer (the "cash" conversion), and a retail buyer into a lessee (the "lease" conversion). Both of these "conversions" are taught by private third-party sales and promotion experts, who sell their services to dealers, promising big returns in profits. Training manuals provided by these firms contain a wealth of background information concerning theories and tactics in automotive sales, including conversion examples, and should always be reviewed very carefully. The same is true of training materials provided by credit insurers and service contract providers.

5.4.2.9 Dealer Contracts with Third Parties; Association Files

The dealership will have contractual relationships with a number of suppliers. For example, the dealer will be an agent of the provider of the credit insurance and service contract policies sold by the dealership. This contract, particularly as it reflects the financial incentives to the dealer to move policies, may be of significant value.

Some service contract and credit insurance providers encourage dealers to establish off-shore reinsurance companies to carry the policies. On a $1000 credit insurance policy, for example, the dealer gets the commission, say $400, and sends the balance to the issuing insurance company. That company takes a "seating fee," say $250, and sends the balance to the dealer's off-shore reinsurance company. The dealer gets the money to invest, gets the interest off the investment, and when the policy expires, gets the principal as well. With both service contracts and credit insurance there is some concern that the dealer's interest in keeping claims against the policies low leads to bad faith dealings with consumers seeking coverage.

Dealers frequently belong to trade associations, and trade association meeting minutes contain valuable information on industry business practices. Depending on the scope of a case, consider reviewing the dealer's association file.

5.4.2.10 The Title Chain

An examination of a vehicle's title chain is critical in any case involving a dispute about the vehicle's history or a "yo-yo" sale, and can be surprisingly important in other contexts as well. A vehicle's title history will require obtaining a series of titles from one or more state departments of motor vehicle. Summary information can be obtained quickly and cheaply over the Internet (e.g., www.carfax.com), but this information is often incomplete and even inaccurate.

A detailed analysis of how to conduct a title search and information about summary title searches is found in NCLC's *Automobile Fraud* (2d ed. 2003 and Supp.). That volume explains not only how to obtain the information, but also how to use it in an automobile investigation.

5.4.2.11 Other Sources of Information

5.4.2.11.1 Inspection of the vehicle and accompanying documentation

In many car cases it is important to have an expert examine the vehicle. Even a cursory examination by the attorney is often helpful. Inspect not only the vehicle itself, but information found in and on the vehicle—the vehicle identification number (VIN), stickers on the driver's door and under the hood, documentation found in the glove box are only some examples. More information about what documentation to review, and why, and also information about a physical inspection of the vehicle can be found in NCLC's *Automobile Fraud* Ch. 2 (2d ed. 2003 and Supp.).

5.4.2.11.2 Licensing agencies and the state insurance department

In most states, automobile dealerships are licensed and strictly regulated. This has two implications. One is that a consumer's attorney may be able to prevail upon an investigator for that agency or other state official with investigatory authority to make an unannounced visit to the dealership. The investigator can then pull the consumer's file before the dealership has a chance to sanitize it during the course of a private litigation.

This approach is particularly important where the consumer claims never to have received copies of key documents. It may be that the investigator will still see the client's carbon copy of the document still in the file.

In addition, one of the best sources of information about a dealer and its business practices will be public records at the licensing agency. Ask for original and current applications, yearly updates, change of ownership files, manufacturer warranty agreements, lists of third-party suppliers, bonding information, financial statements, corporate status, identification of owners, employee lists, and management and organizational charts.

The agency may also serve a law enforcement or regulatory role. One can ask for all complaints, preliminary investigations, completed investigative reports, citations and fines, regulatory and administrative actions, injunctions, judgments, and license suspension or revocation actions. The agency may try and claim investigative files are not subject to public disclosure; closed cases are almost always subject to full disclosure.

In most states, dealerships are also licensed to sell insurance, particularly credit life and disability insurance. Because of this, the dealership will have to provide significant financial and organizational information to the insurance department. Consider examining applications, agency relationships, individual licensees, and, most importantly, former licensees. Also look for complaints, investigative reports, regulatory and administrative action, and the presence of existing or pending injunctions.

5.4.2.11.3 Law enforcement and consumer complaint agencies; revenue agencies

Automobile dealerships consistently generate the largest volume of consumer complaints of any industry, nationwide, for as long as complaints have been tabulated. Accordingly, every law enforcement and consumer agency in a state may have records concerning a dealership—complaints, investigative files, advertising enforcement files, sales practices enforcement files, correspondence with state automotive dealers' associations, both new and used, all monthly investigative updates that mention investigations of the dealership, and correspondence between the agency and the dealership.

Any tax record that is subject to public disclosure should be examined. A phone call to the local taxing authorities will determine what, if anything, is available. If information is available, a request for public disclosure can be filed.

5.4.2.11.4 Court files and former employees

Court files are an excellent source of information. Check every court, including small claims court, for cases involving the dealer, the principal, and even high-level managers. Review the cases for patterns of deceptive practices, upset consumers, and disgruntled former employees. Any one of the them, particularly the former employees, may have relevant information.

Throughout an investigation, keep an eye out for former employees. Check that list against court records for wage and labor disputes. Turnover at dealerships is high, and finding the right former employee can make a world of difference in a case.

Another important source of disgruntled former employees may be a labor law or employment discrimination law firm that is representing the former employee in a dispute against a dealership. The state employment department may also have records of disputes between dealers and their employees.

Note that state rules of professional conduct may differ as to whether *ex parte* contact of former employees is permitted. The answer may depend on whether the suit has been filed, and whether, for filed suits, the ex-employee can be considered an agent of the dealership.

5.4.2.11.5 Competitors and trade associations

Not surprisingly, competitors know what is going on in the industry. While some dealers will not cooperate, experts report in a surprising number of cases that dealers are willing to help explain industry practices. Don't mention any names, just ask if they have heard of the practice before, how does it work, where does it happen, and, most importantly, what tracks does it leave in the dealership. Often a competitor will not talk about individual dealerships, but there are exceptions even to this rule.

Dealers' trade associations can be a great source of information, if they will cooperate. The associations know the deceptive practices, they know the bad apples in the industry, and they want to avoid any bad press. Ask them about the practice at issue, its history, how it is done, what happens to consumers, and how the practice can be stopped. Ask them for information on statutes, regulations, and practice guidelines. Ask them about enforcement, proposed legislation, and consumer education on the issue.

5.4.2.11.6 Prior owners, the manufacturer's warranty records, dealer repair records, auction records

Prior owners often are wonderful witnesses about a vehicle's mechanical or wreck history. The manufacturer will often keep detailed records of all warranty work on a vehicle, and a franchise dealership should have access to this information. The dealers who have worked on a vehicle will also keep repair records, and even vehicle auctions keep records of used cars going through their doors. More discussion on these sources of information can be found in NCLC's *Automobile Fraud* Ch. 2 (2d ed. 2003 and Supp.).

5.4.2.11.7 Taperecording conversations between dealer and consumer

Often a dealer's oral statements are key to the case, but the dealer denies making them. Tape recording a conversation between the consumer and the dealer is a way to substantiate the consumer's version of the events.

In a majority of states it is legal for one party to a phone conversation to tape the conversation secretly.[1286] Even in those states, however, an attorney should not secretly tape record a conversation, and in some states there are ethical issues about whether an attorney can advise a client to do so. The jurisdiction's rulings on these issues should be researched thoroughly before suggesting that a client record a conversation with the dealer.

Assuming that there are no legal or ethical impediments, the best occasion for recording a telephone conversation is when the dealer is trying to save the deal and wants the consumer to cooperate. If the consumer asks the dealer to explain the same thing several times—for example, why the car is listed on the contract as having features it does not have—the dealer will usually assume the consumer is stupid and will explain it in very simple, direct language.

5.4.2.11.8 The Internet

Practitioners are reporting more and more useful information found on the Internet. For mechanical information, they report:

- www.autopedia.com
- www.cartalk.msn.com
- www.essential.org/cas
- www.nhtsa.dot.gov

For service bulletins, try:

- www.alldata.com/consumer/TSB/yr.html

For Kelly Blue Book:

- www.carfaxreport.comwww.kbb.com

5.4.2.11.9 The NADA Code of Ethics

The National Automobile Dealers Association (NADA) publishes a code of ethics at its website, www.nada.org. Practitioners have reported success asking dealers if they subscribe to the NADA Code. Some dealers state no, and this has an impact on the jury. If they state yes, then the question is whether the conduct complies with that code.

The Code actually comes in two parts. First there is what NADA calls a poster:

> As a member of the National Automobile Dealers Association, this dealership subscribes to the following principles and standards. Implicit in this Code is the requirement that NADA members comply fully with all federal, state, and local laws governing their businesses.
>
> We pledge to:
>
> - Operate this business in accord with the highest standards of ethical conduct.
> - Treat each customer in a fair, open, and honest manner, and fully comply with all laws that prohibit discrimination.
> - Meet the transportation needs of our customers in a knowledgeable and professional manner.
> - Represent our products clearly and factually, standing fully behind our warranties, direct and implied, and in all other ways justifying the customer's respect and confidence.
> - Advertise our products in a positive, factual, and informative manner.
> - Detail charges to assist our customers in understanding repair work and provide written estimates of any service work to be performed, upon request, or as required by law.
> - Resolve customer concerns promptly and courteously.
> - Put our promises in writing and stand behind them.

In addition to the poster, there is an ethics guide, that NADA states "focuses on four key areas of dealership operations: sales, service, financial services and advertising." The ethics guide states:

> 1. ADVERTISING
> This dealership is committed to advertising its products and services in a clear, conspicuous and accurate manner that fully complies with applicable legal requirements. This includes disclosing credit terms in accordance with the federal Truth in Lending Act and consistent with state and local law.
> 2. FINANCIAL SERVICES
> Implicit in these standards is the requirement that NADA members comply fully with all federal, state, and local laws governing their businesses. At this dealership, the finance and insurance professionals will at all times
>
> - Disclose fully to customers the costs, terms, and contractual obligations of credit and lease transactions. Documents will be written in a simple, plain, and unambiguous manner to

1286 *See* National Consumer Law Center, Fair Debt Collection § 2.2.4 (5th ed. 2004 and Supp.).

the extent permitted by federal and state law.

- Offer optional insurance or other optional products in a clear and informative manner. Any purchase of such a product must reflect a voluntary choice by the consumer.
- Advertise financial services products in a clear and non-deceptive manner.

3. SALES
Implicit in these standards is the requirement that NADA members comply fully with all federal, state, and local laws governing their businesses. At this dealership, the sales professionals will at all times

- Embrace the spirit and the letter of the law governing the retail sales of new and used vehicles.
- Be honest and truthful when dealing with customers.
- Have a thorough knowledge of the product and be able to apply that knowledge to help satisfy the transportation needs of the customers.
- Provide each customer with a thorough and clear explanation of the steps involved in the purchase or lease of a vehicle and follow those steps diligently.
- Always treat each customer in a professional manner.
- Be responsible for the prompt performance of post-sale administrative and delivery procedures.
- Represent the dealership and the automobile industry in a professional manner.

4. SERVICE
Implicit in these standards is the requirement that NADA members comply fully with all federal, state, and local laws governing their businesses. At this dealership, the service professionals will at all times

- Perform high quality repair service at a fair and competitive price.
- Employ trained and skilled technicians.
- Furnish an itemized invoice for parts and services that clearly identifies any used or remanufactured parts. Replaced parts may be inspected upon request.
- Have a sense of personal obligation to each customer.
- When appropriate, recommend corrective and maintenance services, explaining to the customer which of these are required to correct existing problems and which are for preventive maintenance.
- Provide each customer a price estimate for work to be performed, upon request, or as required by law.
- Make available copies of any warranties covering parts or services.
- Obtain prior authorization for all work done.
- Notify the customer if appointments or completion promises can not be kept.
- Maintain customer service records as required by law.
- Exercise reasonable care for the customer's property while in the dealership's possession.
- Maintain a system to provide for a prompt response to all customer complaints.
- Uphold the highest standards of service in our profession.

5.4.2.12 Uncovering Hidden Dealer Assets

Often used car dealers that most flagrantly violate consumer rights appear to have few assets, discouraging attorneys from litigating against them. But behind the shabby exterior there may be valuable assets that can pay a judgment.

A visit to the premises may reveal:

- Tool boxes, tools, or auto repair equipment. A professional toolbox with tools can be worth up to $50,000.
- A tow truck parked nearby. State title records will show the vehicle's owner and any liens.
- The owner's fancy car, boat, or RV. Car dealers like cars. Look for a high-priced vehicle at the back of the lot, and request the state DMV to identify all cars, trucks, RVs, boats, and airplanes listed in the name of the dealership, the owner, and the owner's family.
- Expensive or high-line inventory. Note license numbers, VINs, or in-house inventory numbers found on vehicles at the dealer's lot. Dealerships that assign stock numbers to vehicles have an in-house tracking system that will help you track sales and assets.
- Indication of who owns the property where the dealership is located. There may be a notice posted about who to call in an emergency. Ownership is important where the real estate owner turns out to be the dealer's alter ego. Even if not related to the dealer, the landlord may have information that will lead to concealed bank accounts. The security deposit check for the premises may have been written on a separate bank account that predates the official account the dealership established once it opened at the site.

Also look for signs or advertisements offering in-house financing. There may be a separate but related—and collectable—corporation that handles this aspect of transactions.

The dealer's former and current employees are key sources about both the dealer's practices and its assets. Dealers may conceal the identity of its employees by "forgetting" some of them. As a rule of thumb, a dealership that sells:

- 1 to 10 cars a month needs 1 dealer and 1 "helper";
- 10 to 30 cars a month needs 1 dealer and 2 employees;
- 30 to 50 cars a month needs 1 dealer and 3 employees;

- 50 to 75 cars a month needs 1 dealer and 4 employees;
- 75 or more cars a month needs 1 dealer and 5 employees.

Sources for identifying the dealership's employees include the dealership's file at the state licensing office; state licensing records for salespersons; records of the state unemployment compensation agency (these may be protected from discovery by state law, however); and the dealer's own records. Ask the dealer to identify not just employees, but also all persons who locate or buy vehicles for compensation, all people and notaries who handle titling and other documents; and the dealership's bookkeeper. The notary may have a logbook that identifies all parties that have appeared before him.

The porter, mechanic, or detail person who picks up, delivers, and works on vehicles can be a terrific source of information. These individuals often work on the owner's vehicles, or deliver vehicles to and from the owner's home, so an provide invaluable information about the owner's personal assets.

Information filed with public agencies also may help uncover dealer assets. Agencies to check include the corporations division of the Secretary of State's office, the dealer's licensing board, and any salesperson's licensing agency. These agencies will not only have records relating to the dealership, but also may have records of the bank accounts on which checks for annual fees were drawn.

NCLC's *Automobile Fraud* § 9.13 (2d ed 2003 and Supp.) examines this subject in more detail. That discussion includes how to locate the dealer's bank accounts and debts owed to the dealer that can be garnished, and how to evaluate the dealer's insurance policy and any state-mandated bond.

5.4.3 "Back End" Sales: Rust-Proofing, Financing, Insurance, Service Contracts, Documentary Charges, and Other Add-Ons

5.4.3.1 Back-End Sales Explained

The negotiation of a sales price on a vehicle is often called the front-end of a transaction. As much as ninety percent of dealer profits come from the back-end. The consumer typically is led from the salesman who has negotiated the deal to a finance and insurance (F & I) sales manager, sometimes known as the Business Manager, who is responsible for closing the transaction, arranging financing, and selling after-market items and supplemental products and services. Examples include: the "chemicals," such as rustproofing, undercoating, paint sealant, fabric protectant, and vinyl protectant; optional items such as floor mats, bras, and spoilers; financing or leasing; service contracts; credit insurance; and, in some states, gap insurance.

The essence of a dealer add-on is that it is usually discussed after a final price for the car is negotiated, and is a charge to the consumer in addition to the negotiated price for the car, increasing both the consumer's total cost and the dealer's profit. In practical terms, a dealer add-on is usually listed in the sales agreement on a line below the negotiated price for the car, and may even be pre-printed on the form next to taxes to give the impression that it is standard with every purchase.

5.4.3.2 "Packing" of Back-End Charges

A number of state UDAP regulations find it unfair or deceptive for a dealer to negotiate the terms of the sale of a car and thereafter add the cost of certain items, such as extended warranties, credit life, dealer preparation, or undercoating, to the contract without the consumer's knowledge and consent.[1287]

The dealer can add these costs in one of two principal ways. The more obvious approach is to add these costs onto the negotiated price for the car, and present the consumer with a final contract with these extras included.

One of the more prevalent and surprising techniques dealers use to sell back-end charges does the exact opposite, through the technique of "packing." Consumer sales resistance to these extra charges is eliminated because the consumer does not even know these charges are being assessed.

Instead of adding these charges onto a negotiated price, the dealer inflates the monthly payment from that which should be derived mathematically from the negotiated interest rate and negotiated sales price, providing "room" for the dealer to add in other charges to make the numbers come out right.

Third-party providers of credit insurance and other back-end products aggressively compete for dealership accounts, and will provide significant financial incentives, training, and marketing assistance to dealers to get business. One of the principle techniques they teach is the "pack," and, as a result, this practice has become widespread in the automobile dealership industry.

Packing in motor vehicle cases is the intentional misquoting of a monthly payment necessary to retire the debt on a motor vehicle. By adding money to the monthly payment (called "packing" or "loading" the payment) when it is initially quoted to the consumer, the dealer creates "room"

1287 Idaho Consumer Protection Regulations, Idaho Admin. Code 04.02.01.234, Other Advertising Practices; Ill. Admin. Code tit. 14, § 475.580, Motor Vehicle Advertising; N.M. Admin. Code § 12.2.4.24, Advertising and Sale of Motor Vehicles; N.J. Admin. Code § 13:45A-26B.2 (add-ons must be individually itemized, showing price for each); Delaney v. Garden State Auto Park, 318 N.J. Super. 15, 722 A.2d 967 (App. Div. 1999) (awarding treble damages for failure to itemize add-ons).

into which other products or services can be sold. Because these additional items are "provided" at no increase in monthly payment, consumers are mislead into believing there is no charge for the items.

In the normal course of a vehicle purchase, the consumer settles on a particular vehicle and enters into negotiations with a salesperson. The consumer indicates a desired purchase price, cash down amount, trade-in allowance, and occasionally even specifies finance terms. The salesperson takes this information to the sales manager, who inputs the information into the dealership's computer. The computer then calculates a monthly payment, based on either the customer's offer or the dealer's counter offer. This monthly payment is then given to the consumer.

In some cases this payment is a legitimate "stripped" or "bare" payment, in that it will only cover the cost of the car. In many cases, however, the payment will be packed. The desk manager obtains the packed payment by one of three principle methods: (1) adding a flat dollar amount, say $30, to every payment; (2) setting the defaults on the computer program to include a charge for credit insurance or other back-end items; or (3) setting the defaults on the computer program to calculate the payment with an unreasonably short term and/or an unreasonably high APR.

Assuming the consumer agrees to purchase the motor vehicle at the packed payment amount, the salesperson introduces the consumer to the business manager. The business manager prepares the loan papers, which include the charges for the back-end items. The business manager uses an "assumptive" closing technique, indicating that these services "are provided in the monthly payment as part of our optional payment protection plan." Only later (or never) does the consumer discover that the transaction included thousands of dollars of back-end charges.

Originally, the packed payment was used to sell credit insurance or increase financing costs. It can also be used to sell service contracts, vehicle options, or almost anything the dealer can devise. Often whatever service the dealer can make the largest profit on will be the product being "packed."

One of the most significant investigations into automotive payment packing has resulted in a consent decree between the State of Washington and Resource Dealer Group, Inc. (RDG). RDG was alleged to be a leader in training car dealerships in how to engage in packing. RDG benefits because the dealers pack RDG's products into the monthly charges, and the dealers benefit because RDG shares the profits with the dealers.

RDG signed a consent agreement with the Washington State Attorney General whereby it agreed in the state of Washington not to teach, train, track, or aid and abet others to misrepresent the amount of a monthly automobile payment, the voluntary and optional nature of RDG's products, or the price of credit insurance or service contracts. It also agreed not to teach, train, track, or aid and abet others to deceptively adjust higher monthly payment amounts. Restitution for certain customers was also specified, and fines and attorney fees were levied.

5.4.3.3 Rustproofing and Other Dealer-Installed Add-Ons

5.4.3.3.1 General

An important car dealer profit-center (and source of UDAP violations) involves dealer installed add-ons, such as rustproofing, alarms, gas and glaze packages,[1288] and undercoating. While rustproofing was the dealer add-on of choice in the 1980s, it continues to prove profitable under different names, such as an "environmental protection package." Such a package may include rustproofing, glazing, and undercoating, and may cost over $1000. The cost to the dealer of this add-on may be in the range of $100.[1289] It is not surprising then that the dealer will aggressively sell the package.

Many dealer-installed add-ons may not be of any real value to the consumer. Rustproofing may even be harmful. Most new cars today come with factory rustproofing and an extensive rustproofing warranty, sometimes even a life-time warranty. Manufacturer warranty books, owner's manuals and sales brochures may specifically state that after-market rustproofing is not necessary. Dealer rustproofing may even void the manufacturer's warranty.

Improperly installed, after-market rustproofing can increase the likelihood of corrosion or rust. The treatment can clog drain holes designed into the automobile, trapping moisture inside. New holes drilled for rustproofing's installation can be the starting points for early onset of rust. These treatments have also been known to cause damage to electrical and mechanical systems and to interfere with seat belt operation during an accident. Damage caused by after-market rustproofing is not covered by the manufacturer's new car warranty.

Consequently, dealer representations about rustproofing are often deceptive or fail to disclose important information. For example, it is deceptive to claim that rustproofing is necessary or desirable where the manufacturer has already rustproofed the vehicle. In addition, dealers may not be disclosing before the sale of rustproofing that the owner's manual and other documents state that after-market rustproofing is not necessary. Automobile buyers generally do not have any opportunity to see a copy of the warranty books and owner's manuals until after delivery of the vehicle, much less before the purchase order is written up.

1288 Charges in the $595 range for about $30 worth of gasoline and waxing.

1289 Delaney v. Garden State Auto Park, 318 N.J. Super. 15, 722 A.2d 967 (App. Div. 1999) (buyer charged $2200 for rustproofing, undercoating, paint sealer and fabric guard for which dealer paid $85).

Rustproofing is often sold in conjunction with undercoating. Undercoating may also provide little value to the consumer, but may hide any prior damage to the car that would have been revealed by an inspection of the car's underside. "Glazing" may also provide little real benefit to the consumer.

Glass etching has value in identifying the car and the window, thus preventing thefts and in recovering cars that are stolen. But dealers may aggressively overcharge for this service, for example charging $595 for something that can be done for one-tenth the charge elsewhere. Other dealers sell a lower priced glass etching in the $150 range, that includes an insurance policy if the car is stolen, and the paperwork resembles an official state document. Consumers often do not realize they have purchased the item and so do not make claims on the insurance policy if their vehicle is stolen.

5.4.3.3.2 UDAP precedent concerning rustproofing

Most of the case law on dealer installed options relate to rustproofing. Nevertheless, these principles may be applicable to other options as well. A Maine UDAP regulation finds it deceptive for a dealer to fail to apply rustproofing to the whole vehicle.[1290] An Ohio UDAP regulation prohibits misrepresentations concerning rust-inhibitors, requires that dealers offer guarantees with rust inhibitor sales, and requires dealers to live up to this guarantee, specifically disallowing a number of common dealer excuses for not repairing rust damage.[1291]

Similarly, the Maine Supreme Judicial Court has found the following rustproofing practices to be UDAP violations: failure to rustproof vehicles adequately, failure to train rustproofing personnel adequately, failure to provide adequate tools and manuals necessary for proper rustproofing, failure to supervise rustproofing operations properly, failure to establish quality-control procedures, and failure to conduct adequate follow-up rustproofing inspections.[1292] Illusory rustproofing guarantees are also deceptive.[1293]

A Florida court awarded an individual consumer $1250 actual damages and $5.1 million punitive damages for a Toyota distributor's fraudulent rustproofing practices.[1294] According to the consumer, the distributors had never injected rustproofing into the car, and in fact engaged in a pattern of not rustproofing cars as requested.

In another case, consumers alleged that an auto dealer sold them worthless, unnecessary rustproofing that in fact was never applied to the car. The dealer owned the rustproofing company and used its position to sell rustproofing, preprinting this add-on on contract forms. The dealer also sold an extended warranty against paint deterioration that had such vague and broad exclusions as to be worthless. The court held that, on these facts, the buyers had stated a UDAP claim.[1295]

5.4.3.4 Dealer Kickbacks on Financing

5.4.3.4.1 The Practice Explained

Traditionally, when a merchant assigns a consumer obligation to a financer, the financer pays the merchant less than the face value of the note—it is discounted because the stated interest rate is insufficient to cover the financer's risk. A practice now in widespread use in the automobile industry is the exact opposite—the financer provides the dealer with a kickback for assigning it the note at face value. That is, the financer pays the dealer more than the face value of the note.

The way this works is that the dealer and lender enter into a motor vehicle dealer agreement whereby the lender agrees to purchase car loans from the dealer at specified interest rates (called "buy rates") depending on the consumer's risk. The dealer, as the credit seller, sets whatever interest rate it wants for the car loan, within a range specified by the lender. The bottom of that range is the "buy rate," and the lender may also specify a maximum allowable rate. If the loan is made at the buy rate, there is no kickback to the dealer, or only a small fixed payment.

On the other hand, if the dealer convinces the consumer to accept financing at a rate higher than the "buy rate," this difference between the actual rate and the buy rate is called the "yield spread premium." This premium is split between the dealer and lender pursuant to the written agreement. One typical example is where the lender keeps 25% of the difference and kicks back 75% to the dealer. In some cases, 100% of the yield-spread is kicked back to the dealer.

For example, consider a car purchased for $21,456.17 for a term of 72 months. If the lender is willing to purchase the loan at a 10.5% buy rate, but the dealer convinces the consumer to sign up for 16.5% financing, there is a $4926.65 yield spread premium. If the dealer agreement calls for a 75%/25% split, then the dealer would keep $3694.99 as its kickback and the lender gets an extra $1231.66 in interest over and above what would occur at a loan written at the buy rate.

The "buy rate" is never disclosed to the consumer, nor the fact that the dealer is making a profit on the financing. Quite the opposite is true—the dealer gives the impression that the interest rate it quotes and that is specified on the retail installment contract is mandated by the lender, that the

1290 Code of Me. Rules 26-239-105.6, Sale of New Motor Vehicles.

1291 Ohio Admin. Code § 109:4-3-15, Motor Vehicle Rust Inhibitors (1980).

1292 State v. Bob Chambers Ford, 522 A.2d 362 (Me. 1987).

1293 *Id.*

1294 Drucker v. Oakland Toyota, Inc., Case No. 83-04569 "CR" (Fla. Cir. Ct. Broward Cty. Dec. 1984).

1295 Taylor v. Bob O'Connor Ford, Inc., 2000 U.S. Dist. LEXIS 11486 (N.D. Ill. June 26, 2000).

consumer's full monthly payment will go to the lender. The consumer is unaware that the dealer is quoting an interest rate that will maximize profit for the dealer, and is not the lowest rate that the lender is willing to offer to that consumer.

5.4.3.4.2 ECOA challenges

The most successful approach to date to challenge such dealer kickbacks is to bring claims under the Equal Credit Opportunity Act (ECOA) against automotive financers, and not the dealers.[1296] These cases are described in detail in another NCLC manual.[1297] In a nutshell, investigations have found that the finance companies' practice of allowing discretion to dealers as to how much they mark up the finance charge among those with the same risk (i.e., the same buy rate) has the *effect* of charging African-Americans and other minorities higher interest rates than Whites of the same risk.[1298] In cases involving Nissan and GMAC, the plaintiffs have alleged that African-Americans were over 200% more likely to be charged a marked-up interest rate than similarly situated whites, and thus disproportionately impacted by the practice. Furthermore, African-Americans were allegedly charged more per markup—an average of about $950 per markup, compared with an average markup for whites of, respectively, $500 (NMAC) and $650 (GMAC).[1299]

The allegation is that the credit system created by the financer thus has the effect of discriminating, even if there is no intent by the financer. Credit systems that have such an effect may violate the ECOA.[1300] To date, ECOA challenges have been brought against GMAC, Nissan, Ford, Chrysler, Toyota and other major auto financers, with settlements being reached in both the GMAC and Nissan class actions.[1301] An unreported federal court decision on class certification in the GMAC case provides a good overview of the issues in these cases, and is found on the companion CD-Rom.

5.4.3.4.3 TIL and state law challenges

Truth in Lending is not a productive approach to challenging yield spread premiums because the interest rate disclosed to the consumer is the rate the consumer pays. In addition, consumers have lost cases based on technical violations of certain state credit statutes.[1302]

On the other hand, Louisiana law now requires dealers to disclose in writing that they may be participating in the finance charges, and the difference between the buy rate and contract rate are capped at 3%.[1303] Proposed legislation has also been considered in other states, at least in California, Illinois, and New York.

5.4.3.4.4 UDAP challenges

UDAP claims against dealers are another way to challenge kickbacks of a yield spread premium. This is certainly the case for any oral misrepresentation. For example, any dealer representation that the financer would not accept anything less than 16.5% is clearly false where the buy rate in fact was 14%. If a consumer asks the dealer whether the lender will accept a lower interest rate, the dealer's answer may also be deceptive.[1304]

In addition, it may also be deceptive for the dealer to fail to disclose its kickback from the assignee.[1305] In other

---

1296 Of course, dealers that engage in intentional discrimination in their finance charge mark-up practices violate federal anti-discrimination statutes and are liable for actual and punitive damages and attorneys fees. Bringing class actions against finance companies to date has proven the more favored approach.

1297 *See* National Consumer Law Center, Credit Discrimination (3d ed. 2002 and Supp.).

1298 Internet links to a series of expert reports supporting this conclusion are found on the companion CD-Rom, relating both to Nissan Acceptance and General Motors Acceptance.

1299 Cason v. Nissan Motor Acceptance Corp. (M.D. Tenn. Feb. 18, 2003) (eighth amended complaint); Coleman v. Gen. Motors Acceptance Corp. (M.D. Tenn. Aug. 2002) (seventh amended complaint). Internet links to both complaints are found on the companion CD-Rom.

1300 Perhaps the best discussion supporting this theory is found in a federal court's decision upholding class certification in Coleman v. Gen. Motors Acceptance Corp. (M.D. Tenn. Jan. 14 2004), *reprinted on* the companion CD-Rom.

1301 The settlements are found at www.consumerlaw.org.

1302 *See* Kunert v. Ford, 2001 WL 1711308 (Cal. Super. Oct. 9, 2001); Kunert v. Bank of America National Trust and Savings Assoc., 2001 WL 1715929 (Cal. Super. Aug. 3, 2001).

1303 La. Rev. Stat. § 32:1254(N)(3)(k).

1304 *But cf.* Bramlett v. Adamson Ford, Inc. (*Ex parte* Ford Motor Credit Co.), 717 So. 2d 781 (Ala. 1997) finds that a common law fraud claim is not available where the consumer merely asked why the interest rate was so high. This same conduct though may state a claim under a state UDAP violation, which is a broader standard than common law fraud.

1305 *See* Taylor v. Bob O'Connor Ford, Inc., 1998 U.S. Dist. LEXIS 5095 (N.D. Ill. Apr. 10, 1998) (UDAP violation to fail to disclose kickback where dealer has an agency relationship with the consumer), *later op. at* 2000 U.S. Dist. LEXIS 11486 (N.D. Ill. June 26, 2000) (nondisclosure of yield spread premium could be UDAP violation if buyers allege that dealer acted as their agent); *see also* Sutton v. Viking Oldsmobile Nissan, Inc., 611 N.W.2d 60 (Minn. App. 2000) (reversing dismissal of claim that dealer violated UDAP statute by falsely stating in contract that charge for extended warranty was "paid to others"), *vacated*, 623 N.W.2d 247 (Minn. 2001) (vacating and remanding for reconsideration in light of Group Health Plan, Inc. v. Philip Morris, Inc., 621 N.W.2d 2 (Minn. 2001)), *opinion on remand*, 2001 Minn. App. LEXIS 866 (July 31, 2001) (reversing summary judgment for seller on UDAP claim where buyer testified that he would have bargained for lower price or declined to buy service contract if seller had not misrepresented that charge was paid to others); Smith v. Precision Chevrolet Oldsmobile, Clearinghouse No. 52,495 (N.J. Super. Ct. Law Div. July 29, 1999);

words, it is deceptive for the dealer to fail to disclose that the dealer is setting the interest rate, not the lender, and that the dealer receives a kickback.

The dealer has presented an overall impression that the lender is setting the interest rate. The loan papers have the lender's name on it; the dealer indicates it has to obtain approval from the lender; all indicia presented to the consumer are that the car is being financed with the lender. The dealer does not correct the false impression that the lender is setting the interest rate and this failure to disclose is deceptive.

Where a yield spread premium is involved in a "yo-yo" or "spot delivery" sale,[1306] the dealer's position can be even less tenable. Consider where the dealer informs the consumer that it is canceling the deal because the assignee will not accept the stated interest rate. But the deal is unacceptable to the dealer because there is no room for a kickback of the size it seeks.

5.4.3.5 Dealer's Altering of Consumer's Credit Application, Fictitious Down Payments, and Other Frauds on the Financer

A common practice is for a dealer, intent on making a sale and obtaining financing approval, to falsify the consumer's creditworthiness. The dealer will be selling the installment loan to a lender without recourse, meaning that the lender, not the dealer, bears the loss if the consumer can not afford the payments, and defaults. Meanwhile, the dealer has made a profit on the car sale and has obtained a kickback from the lender on the financing.[1307]

One way for a dealer to make a consumer look more creditworthy to the lender is for the dealer to alter the consumer's credit application.[1308] Another way is to include a down payment on the loan documents, but never recover this down payment from the consumer,[1309] or to make a side loan to the consumer to pay for the down payment. The dealer can recover the lost down payment by jacking up the vehicle's sale price. A $8000 loan looks less risky to a lender if it is based on a $10,000 cash price with a $2000 down payment than a $8000 cash price with no down payment. Another dealer practice is to inflate the features found on the car being purchased, so that the financer believes the collateral is worth more than it is.

Of course, such dealer practices are clearly wrongful. Consumer claims under UDAP and other statutes are examined at § 5.1.4.5, *supra*. Also discussed in that section are approaches to proving the consumer's damages and a warning that the consumer's possible participation in the misrepresentation must be carefully reviewed.

5.4.3.6 Service Contracts, Extended Warranties

5.4.3.6.1 Undisclosed dealer profit on sale of contract

There is evidence today that dealers price service contracts, not based on the service contract provider's suggested retail price, but upon the maximum amount that the finance company will allow. In other words, lenders buying dealer paper will set maximum amounts of back-end charges (such as credit insurance and service contracts) that the lender will accept on a deal. For example, a lender may allow $1300 in back-end fees. The dealer will price the service contract for $1300, because the dealer will make more that way than selling $400 of credit insurance and a $900 service contract.

Some practitioners report that service contract prices range from $1200 to $1900, with dealers keeping far more than 50% of that charge. Another reports prices as high as $3800, where such high premiums are generally assessed against Native Americans. One dealer even charged a consumer $995 for a contract whose maximum payout was $1200. *Automobile News* reports that the average gross profit on a used-car service contract is $455, totaling almost $2 billion in gross profit for dealers.

While it may require discovery to determine what portion of the service contract the dealer retains itself, an idea of a fair price can be approximated by finding the price of a service contract offered to the general public and not sold through dealerships.[1310] Another tip may be if sales tax is charged on part, but not the full service contract amount. This may indicate that the dealer is paying sales tax on the charge from the provider, but not on the dealer's own mark-up of that service contract price.

There are several ways for a consumer to bring a UDAP challenge against such price gouging. The practice can be found deceptive where the sales agreement describes the service contract price as the "amounts paid to others on your behalf." This is not the amount paid on the consumer's behalf. The actual cost to the dealer is the amount paid on the consumer's behalf, and the dealer keeps the difference.[1311]

Harvey v. Ford Motor Credit Co., 8 S.W.3d 273 (Tenn. Ct. App. 1999); Adkinson v. Harpeth Ford-Mercury, Inc., 1991 WL 17177 (Tenn. Ct. App. 1991). *But see* Baldwin v. Laurel Ford Lincoln Mercury, Inc., 32 F. Supp. 2d 894 (S.D. Miss. 1998); Kunert v. Mission Fin. Serv. Corp., 110 Cal. App. 4th 424 (2003); Geller v. Onyx Acceptance Corp., 2001 WL 1711313 (Cal. Super. Ct. Nov. 13, 2001). *But cf.* Bramlett v. Adamson Ford, Inc., 717 So. 2d 781 (Ala. 1997) (common law fraud claim is not available for the dealer's failure to disclose this kickback. Note that this same conduct though may state a UDAP claim because the elements of UDAP failure to disclose are different than a fraudulent failure to disclose).

1306 *See* § 5.4.5, *infra*.

1307 *See* § 5.4.3.4, *supra*.

1308 *See* Knapp v. Americredit Fin. Servs., Inc., 245 F. Supp. 2d 841 (S.D. W. Va. 2003).

1309 *Id.*

1310 See, for example, www.warrantydirect.com, which offers extended warranties by Warranty Direct.

1311 *See* Cirone-Shadow v. Union Nissan of Waukegan, 955 F. Supp.

The Seventh Circuit, in an important opinion, has described why the undisclosed mark-ups of service contracts is abusive:

> The consumer would have a greater incentive to shop around for an extended warranty, rather than take the one offered by the dealer, if he realized that the dealer was charging what the defendants' lawyer described as a "commission," and apparently a very sizeable one, for its efforts in procuring the warranty from a third party. Or the consumer might be more prone to haggle than if he thought that the entire fee had been levied by a third party and so was outside the dealer's direct control. Or he might go to another dealer in search of lower mark-ups on third-party charges.[1312]

A good argument can be made that the representation of a price for a service contract or extended warranty is deceptive where that is not the price at all, but the total of the contract price and the dealer's markup.[1313] Certainly deceptive is any representation that the service contract is a good deal, a good price, or the like. In addition, it is deceptive for a dealer to misrepresent that it had no authority to negotiate the sale price of a service contract, that the price is fixed by the manufacturer.[1314]

Moreover, it may also be deceptive to fail to disclose the pricing arrangement. It may be that not only the dealer, but also the service contract provider can be found liable for participating in the scheme to deceive the consumer.[1315]

5.4.3.6.2 Where dealer is actually the service contract provider

Keeping large portions of the service contract price is only one method dealers use to profit from such contracts. Since so little is ever paid out under these contracts in relation to their price, the service contract provider itself will make a large profit even on the portion of the premium that is not kept by the dealer. Dealers thus have an incentive to not only sell the policy, but to become the service contract provider, so that they can keep all the profit derived from the contract's sale. Particularly where the service contract provider is not the car's manufacturer, the contract provider could be owned by the dealer or a close relation of the dealer's, or that an offshore company owned by the dealer owns the service contract provider.

If the dealer owns the service contract company, the dealer may set up a relationship with a fulfillment house, which will actually provide the warranty coverage. The fulfillment house may charge the dealer only $50 or $75 dollars a policy; the rest of the profit is split between the dealer personally (the owner of the service contract company) and the dealership. In such a relationship, it is questionable whether the dealer can state that the service contract fee is an amount paid to others, where it is actually being kept by the dealer and dealership. Another consideration where the dealer or a family member owns the service contract company is whether this ownership is allowed under state law—some states prohibit dealers from owning service contract companies.

5.4.3.6.3 Does the contract provide meaningful benefits?

A Maine UDAP regulation deals with the sale of service contracts or extended warranties. The dealer must disclose if the manufacturer's express warranty that comes with a car offers similar protection to a service contract which must be separately purchased. The dealer must also disclose that under Maine law the consumer has the protection of an implied warranty (that can not be waived) even if the consumer does not purchase a service contract.[1316] There also is substantial precedent in the insurance context that sale of illusory coverage is deceptive.[1317]

---

938 (N.D. Ill. 1997) (denying defendant's summary judgment motion relating to UDAP class claim); Cemail v. Viking Dodge, Inc., 982 F. Supp. 1296 (N.D. Ill. 1997) (same); Lindsey v. Ed Johnson Oldsmobile, Inc., 1996 U.S. Dist. LEXIS 10236 (N.D. Ill. July 18, 1996) (same); Shields v. Lefta, Inc., 888 F. Supp. 894 (N.D. Ill. 1995) (same); Bernhauser v. Glen Ellyn Dodge, Inc., 288 Ill. App. 3d 984, 683 N.E.2d 1194 (1997) (it can be deceptive to misrepresent that all the service contract premium would be paid to others; the service contract provider could also be found liable under a civil conspiracy theory); Grimaldi v. Webb, 668 N.E.2d 39 (Ill. App. Ct. 1996) (same), *appeal denied*, 169 Ill. 2d 566, 675 N.E.2d 632 (1996); Cannon v. Cherry Hill Toyota, 184 F.R.D. 540 (D.N.J. 1999) (certifying class in UDAP challenge to dealer's false statement that price for service contract was "paid to others"). A number of cases have considered this as a Truth in Lending issue, the amount the dealer retains potentially being a finance charge. *See, e.g.*, Gibson v. Bob Watson Chevrolet-Geo, Inc., 112 F.3d 283 (7th Cir. 1997). *But cf.* Groth v. Rohr-Ville Motors, Inc., 1997 U.S. Dist. LEXIS 15274 (N.D. Ill. Sept. 29, 1997) (disclosing $1000 as being paid to others was deceptive where only $468 was paid to others, the balance of $532 being kept by the dealer; nevertheless, the consumer did not show that this misrepresentation caused any injury; the consumer admitted to not even realizing that the service contract had been purchased).

1312 Gibson v. Bob Watson Chevrolet-GEO, Inc., 112 F.3d 283 (7th Cir. 1997).

1313 Cannon v. Cherry Hill Toyota, Inc., 161 F. Supp. 2d 362 (D.N.J. 2001) (failure to disclose upcharge is violation of New Jersey UDAP requirement of disclosure of terms of any warranty or service contract offered by dealer).

1314 *See* Grimaldi v. Webb, 668 N.E.2d 39 (Ill. App. Ct. 1996).

1315 Bernhauser v. Glen Ellyn Dodge, Inc., 288 Ill. App. 3d 984, 683 N.E.2d 1194 (1997) (civil conspiracy claim against Chrysler can proceed to trial).

1316 Maine Unfair Trade Practices Regulations, Sale of New Motor Vehicles, Code Me. Rules 26-239-105 § 5.

1317 Glazewski v. Coronet Ins. Co., 108 Ill. 2d 243, 483 N.E.2d 1263 (1985) (sale of illusory insurance coverage is fraud). *See also* Roche v. Fireside Chrysler-Plymouth Mazda, Inc., 600 N.E.2d 1218 (Ill. App. Ct. 1992) (sale of illusory extended warranty

The FTC has also issued an order against an automobile service contract company, finding that there were hidden limitations on the contract, that it was difficult to obtain the company's authorization for repairs, and that the company unilaterally canceled policies where the consumer filed too many claims.[1318] The Commission also found no preemption by the McCarran-Ferguson Act, even if the contract was an insurance policy, because state insurance departments were not regulating the company.[1319] (The McCarran-Ferguson issue is not relevant to an action under a *state* UDAP statute.)

Some companies, such as Wynn, do not offer a traditional service contract. Instead, if a consumer purchases their oil, they warrant a certain performance level for the car in general. The exact nature of this warranty may be misrepresented to the consumer. In addition, some of these warranties do not begin for fifteen days after the contract is signed, and so offer no protection to the consumer during that period—a fact that is rarely disclosed.

5.4.3.6.4 *Undisclosed inspection fees*

Another service contract scam has been the subject of UDAP litigation. A dealer sells a service contract without disclosing any additional fees that will be imposed if the consumer makes a claim under the contract. Then, when the consumer returns to that dealer for repairs under the service contract, the dealer charges an inspection fee to determine if the repairs are covered under the contract. In one case the fees were $695. A federal court has held that these facts state a UDAP claim.[1320]

5.4.3.6.5 *Who must provide benefits on the service contract*

A court has found a UDAP violation where a dealer refused to pay benefits under the service contract, even while the dealer attempted to shift blame to the service contract administrator. The court pointed to the language of the service contact whereby the dealer and the administrator both made certain promises.[1321]

Other times the administrator and the insurance company with whom the dealer contracts have no direct contractual relationship with the consumer. In that situation, it is important to always include the dealer in any UDAP claim on the service contract.[1322]

The Texas Attorney General has issued an important advisory concerning service contracts. Where a contract administrator administers a service contract between dealer and consumer, and the administrator becomes insolvent, this does not relieve the duty of the dealer to fulfill its obligations under the contract.[1323] Where the dealer acts as an agent selling the contract for a third party who is responsible for repairs, the dealer is responsible if that third party becomes insolvent. This is because typically the dealer will not be a licensed insurance agent nor the third party a licensed insurer. Where an unauthorized insurer fails to pay a valid claim, any person who assisted in the procurement of such insurance is liable for the full amount of the unpaid claim.[1324] More on consumer claims under a service contract can be found in NCLC's *Consumer Warranty Law* Ch. 18 (2d ed. 2001 and Supp.).

5.4.3.7 Credit Insurance and Other Insurance Products

Very profitable back-end charges for auto dealers are credit insurance, gap insurance, and other insurance products. Insurers compete with each other to provide insurance products that offer the dealer the highest commission, and dealers work for a high "penetration rate" (percentage of customers who purchase this voluntary insurance). UDAP precedent concerning credit and other insurance products is found at § 5.3, *supra*. See also NCLC's *The Cost of Credit: Regulation and Legal Challenges* Ch. 8 (2d ed. 2000 and Supp.).

5.4.3.8 Documentary Fees and Other "Paper" Charges

5.4.3.8.1 *Introduction*

Most car sales today include extra essentially illusory fees added to the final purchase price: documentary (doc) fees, conveyance or transfer fees,[1325] NADW, or other coupon books,[1326]

coverage held to be UDAP violation by trial court; appellate court holds no UDAP violation because no damages proven).

1318 Griffin Sys., 5 Trade Reg. Rep. (CCH) ¶ 23,603 (F.T.C. Dkt. 9249 1994) (final decision).

1319 *Id.*

1320 Williams v. Ford Motor Co., 990 F. Supp. 551 (N.D. Ill. 1997).

1321 Ron Craft Chevrolet, Inc. v. Davis, 836 S.W.2d 672 (Tex. App. 1992).

1322 *See* Harman v. MIA Serv. Contracts, 858 P.2d 19 (Mont. 1993).

1323 Texas Attorney General's Business Advisory Regulating Extended Serv. Warranties, Clearinghouse No. 47,929 (Oct. 14, 1991).

1324 *Id.*

1325 A documentary or conveyance fee, ranging from $50 to even $400, is usually explained as the cost of the service that the dealer's runner, not the consumer, stands in line at the department of motor vehicles. But in some states the consumer still has to wait in line even after paying the doc fee. In others, the consumer's insurance agent will arrange the transfer or the dealer can register on line in a matter of seconds.

1326 For example, dealers are charging around $275 for a book that contains coupons for free oil changes and discounts on car rentals and hotel stays. The value of the book to the consumer is far less than $275. Some coupon books may even appear to have a value close to their cost, but in many cases the consumer

inventory tax,[1327] advertising fees,[1328] dealer services, emergency road-side assistance, consumer packages, consumer services, and the like.[1329] Often preprinted on the final sales agreement near government fees and taxes, they are intended to appear as if they are required by a government agency, where they are really simply extra profit to the dealer and provide little or no benefit to the consumer. A good example is a $295 charge for "advertising" that is preprinted next to the taxes line. In fact, all that has happened is that the sales price has been increased after a negotiated price had been reached.

5.4.3.8.2 UDAP challenges

UDAP claims can successfully challenge many fees. If a fee is optional, not disclosing this option is deceptive, especially while making it appear that the fee is required, such as by pre-printing the charge on the sales agreement.[1330] A state court has ruled deceptive the practice of using preprinted sales forms already having printed on them a $97.50 charge for the "NADW coupon packet" without explaining the charge or informing the consumer it is optional.[1331] Similarly, it is a UDAP violation to preprint a "delivery and handling" fee on the order form, implying that the fee is non-negotiable, and to print a list of services the fee covers that includes many that the dealer does not actually provide.[1332]

It can also be deceptive to label a charge as being official fees, where only a portion of that charge actually goes to government fees.[1333] In addition, the dealer's oral explanation of the fee often will be deceptive. Note how the charge is described in the Truth in Lending and other documentation. Similar to the parallel issue with service contracts,[1334] if the charge is described as an amount paid to others, this may be deceptive where the dealer keeps most of the charge as profit.

It is also a UDAP violation to add a fee after the final price has been negotiated. This is a unilateral repudiation of an agreement, and done without the consumer's knowledge or knowing authorization.[1335] In addition, if the doc fee is just to provide the consumer with good title to the car purchased, isn't good title implicit in a purchase of a car? Charging extra for arranging the title is akin to charging separately for the steering wheel after a final price has been arrived at.

Where a charge is not optional, but required, it is a UDAP violation not to disclose that charge as part of any disclosure of the vehicle's price: in advertising, in a window sticker, as part of the negotiated price, as indicated on the deal sheet, and on subsequent documents. Where the dealer defends that the charge was really optional, discover if anyone actually purchased a car without the charge. In the case of window etching (a $199 charge for a minimal job of etching a number into glass), one dealer has stated in deposition that 100% of its new cars are etched at the time they are brought into inventory, meaning that this is not an option at all.

Make sure the service or product related to the charge was also delivered; the dealer's failure to perform is a UDAP violation.[1336] Did the consumer receive the $300 worth of NADW coupons? Did the dealer actually perform handling and prep services, has the manufacturer already reimbursed

---

will not own the car for enough years for the book to really be worth it.

1327 Inventory tax or *ad valorem* charges are for taxes the dealer must pay, not the consumer.

1328 Advertising fees are also dealer expenses, not services provided to the consumer.

1329 One dealer has a CRA fee which is for "customer retention appreciation."

1330 Motzer Dodge Jeep Eagle, Inc. v. Ohio Attorney General, 642 N.E.2d 20 (Ohio Ct. App. 1994); Charlie's Dodge, Inc. v. Celebrezze, 596 N.E.2d 486 (Ohio Ct. App. 1991); Jones v. Swad Chevrolet, Inc, Clearinghouse No. 41,256A (Ohio C.P. 1985), *aff'd on other grounds*, 1986 Ohio App. LEXIS 6904 (May 22, 1986). *But cf.* Nigh v. Koons Buick Pontiac GMC, Inc. 143 F. Supp. 2d 535 (E.D. Va. 2001), *aff'd on other grounds*, 319 F.3d 119 (4th Cir. 2003), *cert. granted on other issues*, 124 S. Ct. 1144 (2004) (no UDAP violation where fee mandatory for all customers and no representation that it was a government fee).

1331 Jones v. Swad Chevrolet, Clearinghouse No. 41,256 (Ohio C.P. Franklin Cty. 1985), *aff'd on other grounds*, 1986 Ohio App. LEXIS 6904 (May 22, 1986).

1332 Motzer Jeep Eagle, Inc. v. Ohio Attorney General, 95 Ohio App. 3d 183, 642 N.E.2d 20 (1994).

1333 *See* Fielder v. Credit Acceptance Corp., 19 F. Supp. 2d 966 (W.D. Mo. 1998), *vacated and remanded on other grounds*, 188 F.3d 1031 (8th Cir. 1999). *But see* Nigh v. Koons Buick Pontiac GMC, Inc., 143 F. Supp. 2d 535 (E.D. Va. 2001) (no UDAP violation where consumer misunderstood a "mandatory" processing fee as being required by state law, where it was only required by the dealer), *aff'd on other grounds*, 319 F.3d 119 (4th Cir. 2003), *cert. granted on other issues*, 124 S. Ct. 1144 (2004).

1334 *See* § 5.4.3.6.1, *supra*.

1335 People v. Conway, 42 Cal. App. 3d 875, 117 Cal. Rptr. 251 (1974); Massachusetts Consumer Protection Regulations, Mass. Regs. Code tit. 940, § 5.04, Motor Vehicle Regulations; Jones v. Swad Chevrolet, Inc, Clearinghouse No. 41,256A (Ohio C.P. 1985), *aff'd on other grounds*, 1986 Ohio App. LEXIS 6904 (May 22, 1986); Richardson v. Car Lot Co., 10 Ohio Misc. 2d 32 (Akron Mun. Ct. 1983) (raising price $325 for "delivery, get ready, and handling"); Ohio Admin. Code § 109:4-3-16, Advertisement and Sale of Motor Vehicles; Sanders v. Francis, 277 Or. 593, 561 P.2d 1003 (1977); Pennsylvania Regulations of the Bureau of Consumer Protection, 37 Pa. Code ch. 301.4(7), Automobile Industry Trade Practices; Northview Motors, Inc. v. Commonwealth, 562 A.2d 977 (Pa. Commw. Ct. 1989); Crawford Chevrolet Inc. v. McLarty, 519 S.W.2d 656 (Tex. Civ. App. 1975).

1336 Motzer Dodge Jeep Eagle, Inc. v. Ohio Attorney General, 642 N.E.2d 20 (Ohio Ct. App. 1994); Jones v. Swad Chevrolet, Inc., Clearinghouse No. 41,256A (Ohio C.P. 1985), *aff'd on other grounds*, 1986 Ohio App. LEXIS 6904 (May 22, 1986).

the dealer for these services, and do these services even apply to a used vehicle?[1337]

If the consumer pays a sales tax on the dealer fee, discover what that implies under state law concerning the fee. If sales tax is only assessed on goods, not services, sales tax on a "doc fee" shows that no service is offered, it is just a disguised add-on to the car's price.

In addition, a number of states have UDAP car sales regulations that specify in detail permissible dealer charges.[1338] A court may also find the mark-up implicit in the fee to be so excessive as to be unfair or unconscionable, particularly where a UDAP statute specifies excess price as one type of unfair or unconscionable practice. That is charging two hundred dollars for a two dollar service may be viewed as a UDAP violation.

5.4.3.8.3 Truth in Lending challenges

If the fee is considered optional, determine if it is required of all credit customers. If a fee is optional for cash customers, but required of credit customers, then the fee is a finance charge and should be disclosed as such. Dealers violate the federal Truth in Lending law (TIL) if they disclose such fees in the amount financed, instead of in the finance charge.[1339] An example is doc fees required for credit purchasers (the dealer will want to make sure its lien is properly recorded on the title), but in theory are optional for cash customers, who can do this service themselves.[1340]

A way to show that a fee is not required of cash customers is to demonstrate that the fee is not included in the buyer's order or other document reflecting the final cash price. The fee instead only shows up later on the credit agreement, and is thus linked to credit and should be treated as a finance charge.

5.4.3.8.4 Anti-trust claims

Consumers have anti-trust claims (for treble damages and attorney fees) if car dealers, through their association or otherwise, get together to establish standard types of extra fees. For example, an action has successfully alleged that the Louisiana dealership association colluded with the state's dealers, in violation of the Federal Clayton Act, to create a separate charge to reimburse dealers for the inventory tax dealers must pay the state. The allegation was not that the dealers had fixed prices, but that they had engaged in concerted action that had an impact on prices.

The federal court certified a plaintiff class of all Louisiana car purchasers over a ten-year period and a defendant class of all Louisiana car dealers, and rejected the defendants' summary judgment motions. A settlement has been reached valued at several hundred million dollars. Key documents in the case are available as Clearinghouse No. 52,030.[1341]

5.4.3.8.5 State statutory restrictions

States also have explicit restrictions on certain dealer charges. Virginia requires all charges to be disclosed on the buyer's order. Connecticut requires doc fee charges to be included in advertised prices. New York and Rhode Island regulate the amount of documentary fees. Indiana's documentary fee statute requires that the fees reflect expenses actually incurred to prepare documents that are not incidental to the extension of credit, that the fee be both disclosed and negotiated, and that it not be preprinted on the sales documents.[1342] Louisiana's statute allows a $35 documentary fee.[1343] Illinois's statute provides for a $40 fee, adjusted annually for inflation that need not be included in the advertised price, but whose nature must be disclosed to the consumer.[1344] Texas allows a voluntary fee up to $50.[1345] California provides for a $45 limit on document fees.[1346] Ohio law limits documentary fees to $100.[1347]

5.4.4 Unfair Dealer Negotiation Practices

5.4.4.1 The Turnover System

One of the most oppressive typical sales techniques that car dealerships employ is the "TO" or turnover system, where a series of sales personnel are used to wear down a consumer. The first salesperson the consumer meets is a "liner" or "greeter" who qualifies the consumer—that is sizes up how vulnerable the consumer is and how much the dealer can take advantage of the consumer. When the consumer settles upon a car, the parties go inside, where the salesperson obtains a driver's license, keys to the trade-in, or deposit, which is given to the "desk." This prevents the consumer from leaving prematurely.

At some point early in the negotiation, the consumer may

1337 *See* Motzer Dodge Jeep Eagle, Inc. v. Ohio Attorney General, 642 N.E.2d 20 (Ohio Ct. App. 1994).

1338 *See* § 5.4.3.8.5, *infra*.

1339 Compton v. Altavista Motors, Inc., 121 F. Supp. 2d 932 (W.D. Va. 2000); *see* National Consumer Law Center, Truth in Lending §§ 3.6, 3.10 (5th ed. 2003 and Supp.).

1340 *See* Compton v. Altavista Motors, Inc., 121 F. Supp. 2d 932 (W.D. Va. 2000).

1341 Cook v. Powell Buick, Inc. (W.D. La. complaint filed 1994). Documents available through the Clearinghouse number include the First Amended Complaint, Findings and Recommendation (concerning class certification and defendants' motion for partial summary judgment), The Proposed Settlement Agreement, and The Notice of Settlement.

1342 Ind. Code § 9-23-3-6.5.

1343 La. Rev. Stat. 6:960.

1344 *See* 815 Ill. Comp. Stat. 375/11.1; 14 Ill. Admin. Code 475.

1345 Tex. Fin. Code § 348.006.

1346 Cal. Veh. Code § 11713.1(b) (sales); Cal. Civ. Code § 1985.8(c)(5) (leases).

1347 Ohio Rev. Code § 1317.07; Ohio Admin. Code 109:4-3-16(21).

be passed on to another salesperson, often called the "closer" who is specially trained to negotiate. But even the closer does not have authority to make a deal. Instead, offers are shuttled between the consumer and the "desk" for approval. The closer may not even take an offer to the desk, but just pretend to do so as part of the technique.

When a price is negotiated, then the consumer is moved to the highest paid salesman—the finance and insurance manager. It is this person who will sell many of the extras—service contracts, credit insurance, and other options, switch the consumer to a lease or finalize the financing.

The most abusive form of the turnover system involves the virtual imprisonment of the consumer, as teams of dealer employees relentlessly pressure the consumer for hours. The consumer is not allowed to leave the premises, and the dealer even refuses to give the consumer back the car keys the consumer used to drive to the lot. There are even horrific examples of elderly or diabetic consumers being kept at dealerships for more than eight hours, or parents being prevented from meeting their retarded son when the school bus was dropping off the son at a busy intersection.

In such cases, in addition to UDAP claims, the consumer's attorney should consider tort claims for false imprisonment, duress, and even breach of fiduciary duty. Taking possession of someone's car keys is a bailment, with specific fiduciary obligations.

5.4.4.2 Dealer's Illegal Use of Consumer Credit Reports

In an apparently standard automobile sales technique, many car dealers pull a consumer's credit report almost as soon as the consumer walks into the showroom. The dealer requires the consumer's driver license to test drive a car, to enter a contest, or just as a precondition for meeting with a salesperson. With the license or similar information, the dealer pulls the consumer's credit report without the consumer's knowledge. This provides key information to the salesperson in sizing up the consumer, information that will be used to the dealer's best advantage in any negotiations.

The FTC has found this practice to be illegal,[1348] because the Fair Credit Reporting Act (FCRA) only allows release of a consumer's credit report for specified permissible purposes.[1349] To size up a potential customer before the consumer has even applied for credit is not such a permissible purpose. While the dealer can seek a credit report if the consumer applies for credit or pays by personal check, the dealer has no permissible purpose when the consumer is only comparison shopping, test driving the vehicle, or negotiating the purchase price.

Pulling a consumer's credit report illegally causes the consumer two types of harm. One is to put the consumer at a disadvantage to the dealer in the sales negotiation. The other is that user requests for a consumer's credit report are themselves recorded in the consumer's credit reporting file. Many creditors view adversely consumer credit reports that contain too many creditor requests for the consumer's report. In other words, the dealer practice of immediately pulling a consumer's credit report can seriously injure a consumer's credit rating when the consumer does nothing other than visit five or so dealers over a weekend.

Proving this illegal use of a credit report may not be too difficult, even if the consumer later applies for credit from the dealer or gives the dealer a personal check. Credit reporting agencies should have the time the dealer ordered the report, and most dealerships "clock in" a customer when they arrive at the dealership.[1350] Look for cases where the report was pulled within minutes of the consumer walking in the door. Also where more than one adult is shopping for a vehicle, look to see if a credit report was pulled on an individual who is not seeking credit.[1351]

When a consumer wants to bring a UDAP challenge to a car dealer's sales practices, there are certain advantages to adding a claim based on the illegal use of the consumer's credit report. If the consumer wants to be in federal court, this FCRA violation will provide a basis for such jurisdiction. (If the consumer wishes to stay in state court, the same claim can be made under the UDAP statute or a state credit reporting statute.[1352]) A FCRA violation also leads to consumer attorney fees, if there is any doubt about such fees under a particular state's UDAP statute, or if there is any doubt about the consumer prevailing on other claims. The FCRA violation can also lead to punitive damages if the violation is willful and knowing.

5.4.4.3 "Unhorsing" and Selling the Consumer's Trade-In Prematurely

The car industry uses the term "unhorsing" for its established practice of stripping consumers of their existing vehicles so that the consumer has no choice but to purchase another vehicle. Dealers may do whatever it takes to unhorse the consumer, even to the point of simply refusing to return a consumer's car keys when requested or laughing at the consumer and throwing the keys on the roof. If the consumer

1348 *See* Letter from David Medine to Karen Coffey, Texas Automobile Dealers Association (Feb. 11, 1998), *found on* the companion CD-Rom; *see also* Castro v. Union Nissan, Inc., 2002 WL 1466810 (N.D. Ill. July 8, 2002).

1349 *See* National Consumer Law Center, Fair Credit Reporting Ch. 5 (5th ed. 2002 and Supp.).

1350 Records indicating this clock time will often be found in documents held at the sales desk tower or in the manager's deal log. Larger dealerships will have the time entered into their computer system.

1351 *See* Castro v. Union Nissan, Inc., 2002 WL 1466810 (N.D. Ill. July 8, 2002).

1352 *See* National Consumer Law Center, Fair Credit Reporting § 10.4 (5th ed. 2002 and Supp.).

takes a new vehicle home for a test drive, and returns to get his old vehicle the next day, the dealer may claim that the trade-in has already been sold.

The failure to return a trade-in can take place at a number of different times, but is perhaps best summarized by the South Carolina Court of Appeals: "In the final analysis, [the consumer] was riding when he went to the dealership and ended up walking."[1353] It is a UDAP violation for a dealer to refuse to return a car it is appraising for its trade-in value.[1354] Selling a trade-in immediately so that the consumer can not back out of the sale has also been found to be a UDAP violation.[1355] (Of course, refusing to return a consumer's property may also lead to various tort claims as well. For example, in Indiana, such an action has been found to fit under the state's criminal conversion statute, and the Indiana Crime Victim's Relief Act provides for treble damages and attorney fees for such conversion.[1356] Punitive damages may be available under other theories as well.)

The most common situation where a dealer refuses to return a trade-in is where the dealer cancels a sale because the financing falls through, and then refuses to return the consumer's trade-in, thus putting pressure on the consumer to renegotiate the original deal at a higher financing rate. The dealer may claim the consumer's trade-in vehicle has already been sold, leaving the consumer with no car to drive.[1357] If the dealer claims that the sales is not final until financing goes through, then the dealer has no right to sell the consumer's trade-in until financing is finalized. The trade-in (by its very nature) is part of the sale transaction and does not revert to the dealer until the sale is final.

Arizona, Colorado and Louisiana statutes declare that the trade-in can not be sold until the deal is complete, and the Colorado, New Hampshire, Virginia and Washington statutes require that the trade-in be returned to the consumer if the sale is cancelled.[1358] Virginia requires dealers to disclose that down-payments and trade-ins must be returned if the dealer cancels the sale because financing has fallen through.[1359] Massachusetts regulations find it to be UDAP violation to fail to refund the full amount of a deposit where financing falls through.[1360] California has a statute protecting the consumer's trade-in where the dealer assists the consumer in obtaining a loan from a third party lender to pay for the vehicle purchase. If the consumer does not obtain the loan, the agreement is rescinded and all consideration must be returned to the consumer without demand.[1361]

Utah requires the return of any deposit or trade-in, but allows the dealer a reimbursement based on the current IRS mileage allowance times the number of miles driven in any vehicle the consumer must return where financing has fallen through. In addition, if the trade-in is no longer available, the dealer must reimburse the consumer for its value, based on the trade-in allowance specified in the contract.[1362] In Oregon, any deposit or trade-in must be returned, and the trade-in can not be sold, but the dealer can recover a mileage allowance for miles driven on the vehicle whose sale is cancelled.[1363]

The Maryland Motor Vehicle Administration states that all personnel who handle trade-ins must be aware of the importance of ascertaining whether the sale has been finalized before disposing of the traded-in vehicle.[1364] Idaho UDAP regulations require either return of the vehicle or payment of the trade-in allowance within one business day.[1365] Under the Illinois UDAP statute, a dealer must return the trade-in and down payment if a sale falls through because the seller finds the consumer's credit rating unsatisfactory.[1366] The violation under the Illinois statutes is if the dealer fails to return the down payment or trade-in, not that the dealer refuses to return the down payment or trade-in. Consequently, the consumer need not show that the consumer requested the return and the dealer refused the request.[1367]

Nor can a dealer refuse to return a trade-in until the consumer reimburses the dealer for the amount the dealer paid off the consumer's lender on the trade-in. The dealer paid off the lien at its own risk where a vehicle sale was contingent on financing being approved, and its paying off

1353 Kucharski v. Rick Hendrick Chevrolet Ltd. P'ship, 2002 WL 31386090 (S.C. Ct. App. Sept. 18, 2002).

1354 State v. Ralph Williams N.W. Chrysler Plymouth, Inc., 87 Wash. 2d 298, 553 P.2d 423 (1976). *See also* Apple Imports, Inc. v. Koole, 945 S.W.2d 895 (Tex. App. 1997).

1355 Mapp v. Toyota World, Inc., 344 S.E.2d 297 (N.C. Ct. App. 1986); Apple Imports, Inc. v. Koole, 945 S.W.2d 895 (Tex. App. 1997).

1356 Palmer Dodge, Inc. v. Long, 791 N.E.2d 788 (Ind. Ct. App. 2003). A violation of Ind. Code § 35-43-4-3 (criminal conversion) can be civilly remedied under Ind. Code § 34-24-3-1.

1357 *See* Kucharski v. Rick Hendrick Chevrolet Ltd. P'ship, 2002 WL 31386090 (S.C. Ct. App. Sept. 18, 2002).

1358 Ariz. Rev. Stat. § 44-1371; Colo. Rev. Stat. 6-1-708; La. Rev. Stat. § 32:1254(N)(3)(f); N.H. Stat. § 361-A:10-b (effective July 23, 2004); Va. Code § 46.2-1530; Wash Rev. Code § 46.70.180(4).

1359 Va. Code § 46.2-1531.

1360 Mass. Regs. Code tit. 940, § 5.04(9)(b).

1361 Cal. Civ. Code § 2982.5(d)(5). California also has a statute that applies "in the event of breach by the seller" that requires the seller to pay within five days the greater of the trade-in's stated value in the contract or its fair market value. Cal. Civ. Code § 2982.7(b). Particularly where the dealer has no legal right to cancel the sale, the seller has certainly breached the agreement.

1362 Utah Stat. § 41-3-401.

1363 Or. Stat. § 646.877.

1364 Maryland Motor Vehicle Administration, *"Spot Delivery"-"Fronting"-"MacArthur Statement" etc*, Bulletin D-11 98-01, Clearinghouse No. 52,142 (Nov. 30, 1998).

1365 Idaho Admin. Code 04.02.01.237.

1366 Bates v. William Chevrolet/Geo, Inc., 785 N.E.2d 53 (Ill. App. Ct. 2003); Jones v. William Buick, Inc., 785 N.E.2d 910 (Ill. App. Ct. 2003); Roche v. Fireside Chrysler-Plymouth, 600 N.E.2d 1218 (Ill. App. Ct. 1992). *See also* Apple Imports, Inc. v. Koole, 945 S.W.2d 895 (Tex. App. 1997).

1367 Fox v. The Montell Corp., 2001 WL 293632 (N.D. Ill. Mar. 19, 2001).

the lien did not provide a basis to retain possession of the trade-in.[1368]

Where a dealer fails to return the down payment for ten days, and then returns that payment only after receiving a letter from the consumer's attorney alleging fraud, the consumer has a cause of action for damages caused by the delay in receiving the refund.[1369] It may also be a UDAP violation to fail to disclose a dealer policy of not returning down payments, and this UDAP violation can then lead to an attorney fee award, even where damages are minimal because the deposit is returned after litigation is threatened.[1370]

In addition, never take a dealer's word that it has already sold the consumer's vehicle, since the representation is usually false.[1371] This can easily be uncovered by examining the vehicle's title and the dates of all transfers. The dealer can not sell the consumer's vehicle until the consumer has signed over the title to the dealer, and the dealer's disposition of the vehicle is not final until it signs the title over to the buyer. Copies of the title should be available both from the dealer and the state department of motor vehicles.

Check also to see when the dealer assigned the car a stock number, because dealers do not sell cars without such numbers. Be wary of dealer sales of trade-ins to dealer employees or related companies. Similarly, a sale of the trade-in the same day the dealer notifies the consumer that the deal is off may be proof of the dealer's intent to force the consumer into another, less advantageous deal. Dealers also maintain detailed inventory records of vehicles on the lot or still owned by the dealer. These inventories are kept current at least once a month, and often more frequently. The consumer's attorney can thus ascertain whether a particular vehicle was still on the lot as of a given date from the dealer's own records.

5.4.4.4 Dealers Hiding Trade-Ins' Negative Equity

In a surprising number of credit and lease transactions, the vehicle the consumer wishes to trade-in has negative equity. That is, the vehicle is worth less than the outstanding loan on that vehicle, or the early termination of a lease on that vehicle will create a sizeable early termination charge.

There are a number of reasons that dealers do not want to write up a transaction disclosing the fact that the consumer's obligation will go up because of the trade-in, not down. Most obviously, many consumers would react by backing out of the deal, at least until they had made significantly more payments on their existing car loan or reached the scheduled termination of the lease. In addition, dealers like to avoid negative trade-ins because lenders do not like to purchase car paper with such trade-ins and because dealers may not be licensed under state law to loan a consumer money to pay off a prior loan.

The solution for many dealers is to re-write the transaction so that the negative equity in the trade-in is hidden from the consumer. This is done various ways, but they generally all have in common that the price of the new car goes up to offset the fact that the dealer inflates the value of the trade-in.

For example, a trade-in worth $1000, but with $2000 owing on its car loan, will be listed on the sales document as being bought by the dealer for $3000, less the $2000 car loan, or a net value of $1000. Since the vehicle is really worth $2000 less than this, the dealer inflates the cash price of the new car by at least $2000. The consumer is particularly pleased because he got a higher price for the trade-in than he thought, but fails to discover in the paperwork that the cash price of the new car has been raised. Dealers are adept at writing up transactions as to be incomprehensible to many consumers.

This practice of hiding negative equity is deceptive because the dealer has misrepresented the true nature of the transaction.[1372] Dealers often argue that there is no damage, because the car's cash price has been inflated no more than the trade-in. This misses the point that if the consumer understood what was really happening, the consumer would not have gone through with the deal.

This practice may violate a state UDAP regulation or motor vehicle finance statute that requires the "cash price" of the new vehicle to be listed in the sales documents.[1373] It may also run afoul of a prohibition, established by case law or UDAP regulations, against increasing the sales price over the figure advertised.[1374]

The consumer also suffers actual damages in those states where the consumer pays a sales tax on the new car's cash price. Inflating that price inflates the sales tax. Not only is this actual damages, but the failure to disclose this amount as a finance charge may also violate Truth in Lending.[1375] Nevertheless, this form of actual damages is not present in

1368 Palmer Dodge, Inc. v. Long, 791 N.E.2d 788 (Ind. Ct. App. 2003).

1369 Jones v. William Buick, Inc., 785 N.E.2d 910 (Ill. App. Ct. 2003).

1370 *Id.*

1371 *See, e.g.*, Brown v. North Jackson Nissan, Inc., 856 So. 2d 692 (Miss. Ct. App. 2003); Wyman v. Terry Schulte Chevrolet, Inc., 584 N.W.2d 103 (N.D. 1998). *But cf.* Buie v. Palm Springs Motors, Inc., 2001 U.S. Dist. LEXIS 13756 (C.D. Cal. May 14, 2001) (no proof that representation was false), *aff'd*, 2002 U.S. App. LEXIS 11046 (C.D. Cal. June 5, 2002).

1372 White v. Kent, 47 Ohio App. 3d 105, 547 N.E.2d 386 (1988) (deceptive to increase sales price of car by amount allowed on trade-in). *See also* Northview Motors, Inc. v. Commonwealth, 562 A.2d 977 (Pa. Commw. Ct. 1989) (deceptive to recoup high advertised trade-in price by increasing normal selling price).

1373 *See* § 5.4.7.2, *infra*.

1374 The Truth in Lending Act also includes specific disclosure requirements for trade-ins. *See* National Consumer Law Center, Truth in Lending § 4.6.2 (5th ed. 2003 and Supp.).

1375 Person v. Courtesy Motors, Inc., 2001 WL 34072209 (W.D. Mich. Apr. 6, 2001).

those states whose sales tax is computed on the net difference between the new car's price and the trade-in allowance. Inflating both an equal amount does not change the tax bill in such states.

Dealers that inflate trade-in values are also violating federal law where they assign the note to a federally-insured institution. Anyone knowingly making a false statement or overvaluing security for the purpose of influencing an action of a federally insured financial institution shall be fined not more than $1 million or imprisoned not more than thirty years, or both.[1376]

5.4.4.5 Dealer Failing to Payoff the Lien on the Consumer's Trade-In

A surprisingly common abuse is for a dealer to take a vehicle in trade, but not to pay off the amount owed the consumer's lender on the trade-in's car loan. This can also happen when the consumer turns in a lease, and expects any early termination charge to be paid by the dealer as part of the purchase price of another vehicle. In both these cases, where the dealer fails to make the owed payments, the consumer's lender comes after the consumer for repayment. This practice by the dealer can be a UDAP violation.[1377]

The dealer may fail to pay off the trade-in vehicle because of a generally shaky financial situation or as part of a scheme to take advantage of the "float" after the time it gets the money for the new car. In a yo-yo sales scheme, the dealer may wait to pay off the trade-in vehicle until it has found financing for the new buyer. Sometimes the dealer actually sells the trade-in vehicle to someone else before paying off the debt, planning to conceal the existence of the lien by delaying in providing the title.

5.4.4.6 Lowering the Trade-In's Agreed-Upon Price

Another common dealer technique is to negotiate a final deal with the consumer as to price of a new car and the value for a trade-in, and then at a later time reduce the trade-in value. Dealers will have various rationales for doing this, but the bottom line is that the consumer pays a higher net price than agreed upon for the new vehicle.

This abuse has special application to recreational vehicle (RV) sales, because RV sales are for more money than the typical car sale and require extensive negotiations as to options. Generally, the trade-in RV is not delivered to the selling dealer until *after* negotiations are concluded. Dealers may attempt to renegotiate the deal late in the game, claiming they made a "mistake" in valuing the consumer's trade-in vehicle.

Whether involving a passenger vehicle or RV, the practice has widely been found to be a UDAP violation.[1378] This applies not just to a dealer lowering a trade-in value after individual negotiation, but also reneging on advertising that offers a minimum amount for any trade-in.[1379]

5.4.4.7 Playing Fast and Loose with the Paperwork

Contracts must reflect the agreement reached and may not have blank spaces.[1380] The seller must give the consumer a

1376 18 U.S.C. § 1014.

1377 *See* Castro v. Union Nissan, Inc., 2002 WL 1466810 (N.D. Ill. July 8, 2002). *Cf.* Tresh v. Mid-Ohio Ford AMC-Jeep-Renault, Inc., 1989 Ohio App. LEXIS 1102 (Mar. 21, 1989) (dealer's failure to pay off debt on trade-in vehicle was contract violation even though it was result of employee's mistaken recordation of payoff amount). *But see* Nigh v. Koons Buick Pontiac GMC, Inc., 143 F. Supp. 2d 535 (E.D. Va. 2001) (no UDAP violation where under Virginia law mere failure to perform a promise is not a misrepresentation), *aff'd on other grounds*, 319 F.2d 119 (4th Cir. 2003), *cert. granted on other issues*, 124 S. Ct. 1144 (2004).

1378 Standards for Advertising and Selling Motor Vehicles, Conn. Agencies Regs. § 42-110b-28; Suris v. Gilmore Liquidating, Inc., 651 So. 2d 1283 (Fla. Dist. Ct. App. 1995) (lowering trade-in allowance after showing buyer worksheets with a higher allowance may violate UDAP statute); Md. Admin. Code 11.12.01.14; Massachusetts Consumer Protection Regulations, Mass. Regs. Code tit. 940, §§ 5.02, 5.04, Motor Vehicle Regulations; N.J. Admin. Code ch. 13:45A-26A.7, Motor Vehicle Advertising Practices; N.M. Admin. Code § 12.2.4.15, Advertising and Sale of Motor Vehicles; Ohio Admin. Code § 109:4-3-16, Advertisement and Sale of Motor Vehicles; McDonald v. Bedford Datsun, 59 Ohio App. 3d 38 (1989) (unjustified lowering of agreed upon trade-in price is UDAP violation even though contract allowed reappraisal of trade-in at time new automobile was delivered); Smalley v. Spitzer Ford, Inc., 1986 Ohio App. LEXIS 9585 (Dec. 31, 1986) (raising purchase price and lowering trade-in allowances violated UDAP regulations); Freitag v. Bill Swad Datsun, 3 Ohio App. 3d 83, 443 N.E.2d 988 (1981) (lowering agreed trade-in allowance when new car delivered); Richardson v. Car Lot Co., 10 Ohio Misc. 2d 32, 462 N.E.2d 459 (Akron Mun. Ct. 1983) (failure to include trade-in value in sales contract); State *ex rel.* Redden v. Willamette Recreation Inc., 54 Or. App. 156, 634 P.2d 286 (1981) (lowering trade-in allowance from original agreement); Pennsylvania Regulations of the Bureau of Consumer Protection, 37 Pa. Code §§ 301.2, 301.4, Automobile Industry Trade Practices; *see also* Wash. Rev. Code § 46.70.180(4)(b) (prohibiting the practice except for certain narrow exceptions); *cf.* Davis v. Wholesale Motors, Inc., 949 P.2d 1026 (Haw. App. 1997) (dealer's misrepresentation of wholesale value of trade-in vehicle would have been a UDAP violation if proven); Robinson v. McDougal, 62 Ohio App. 3d 253, 575 N.E.2d 469 (1988) (receipts for down payments must conform to state UDAP regulations on the subject).

1379 Izadi v. Machado (Gus) Ford, Inc., 550 So. 2d 1135 (Fla. Dist. Ct. App. 1989) (UDAP claim properly pleaded where advertised $3000 minimum trade-in only applied to purchase of specified cars and where limitation only described in small print).

1380 Robinson v. McDougal, 62 Ohio App. 3d 253, 575 N.E.2d 469 (1988); Gaylan v. Dave Towell Cadillac, Inc., 15 Ohio Misc. 2d 1, 473 N.E.2d 64 (Mun. Ct. 1984).

copy of the sales contract when executed,[1381] and copies of all other pertinent documents which place an obligation upon the consumer.[1382]

Sellers may not interfere with the buyer's right to read the contract before signing,[1383] or misrepresent the nature or import of documents being signed.[1384] Material oral representations must be integrated into the contract.[1385] Sales personnel may not misrepresent that they have authority to bind a contract, where the contract in fact was not binding.[1386] Refusing to transfer title unless the consumer pays charges beyond those required by the contract is a UDAP violation.[1387]

It may be a UDAP violation to induce a cosigner to sign as a co-buyer as a means of denying him or her the benefits as a cosigner of a state law that limits a cosigner's obligation to that of a guarantor.[1388] Inducing a person to act as a "straw buyer" for a friend or relative, without disclosing that the straw buyer will be the sole legal obligor and will also have title to the car is similarly deceptive. Straw purchases also usually violate the dealer's agreement with the creditor and the warranties the dealer makes when it assigns the installment contract to the creditor. A seller who structures a deal to conceal the identity of the real purchaser may violate the federal Credit Repair Organizations Act or a similar state law.[1389] The fact that the dealer knew that the friend or relative was the real buyer can often be established by showing that the dealer checked that person's credit first. Misrepresentations about credit terms are detailed elsewhere in this manual.[1390]

5.4.4.8 Misrepresentations as to Consumer's Cancellation Rights; Three-Day Cooling-Off Period Under Credit Repair Laws

Penalties for canceling sales and the handling of deposits and cancellation rights must be disclosed.[1391] A dealer can not promise consumers they may back out of a deal, when this is not the case.[1392] Penalty clauses in sales contracts may be unenforceable if they provide for unreasonable liquidated damages, as a matter of contract law.

While the existence of a three-day cooling-off period for car sales is a widespread misconception, in an odd twist, consumers may now have such a cancellation right, at least for certain types of car sales or in certain states. Federal or state credit repair legislation may treat car dealers as credit repair organizations, and, as such, they must provide a three-day cooling off period and meet other statutory requirements. Failure to comply can lead to voiding of the transaction. This potentially significant development is examined in detail at § 5.1.2.2.6, *supra*.

5.4.5 Yo-Yo (Spot-Delivery) Abuses

5.4.5.1 Successful Consumer Litigation Challenges

5.4.5.1.1 The yo-yo explained

Yo-yo transactions, also referred to as spot-delivery, take-back, MacArthur ("I shall return") or gimme-back, are one of the most widespread automobile dealer abuses today, applying to new and used car sales and automotive leases. The yo-yo sale is standard operating procedure at many dealerships.

The consumer believes a vehicle's installment sale or lease is final and the dealer gives the consumer possession of the car "on the spot." The dealer later tells the consumer to return the car because financing has fallen through.[1393] If the consumer does not return the vehicle or agree to rewrite

1381 Massachusetts Consumer Protection Regulations, Mass. Regs. Code tit. 940, § 5.04, Motor Vehicle Regulations.

1382 Pennsylvania Regulations of the Bureau of Consumer Protection, 37 Pa. Code § 301.4(a)(1), (3); Northview Motors, Inc. v. Commonwealth, 562 A.2d 977 (Pa. Commw. Ct. 1989).

1383 State v. Ralph Williams' N.W. Chrysler Plymouth, Inc., 87 Wash. 2d 298, 553 P.2d 423 (1976).

1384 Baggett v. Crown Automotive Group, Inc., 1992 WL 108710 (Tenn. Ct. App. May 22, 1992).

1385 Renner v. Derin Acquisition Corp., 111 Ohio App. 3d 326, 676 N.E.2d 151 (1996); Smalley v. Spitzer Ford, Inc., 1986 Ohio App. LEXIS 9585 (Dec. 31, 1986); Richardson v. Car Lot Co., 10 Ohio Misc. 2d 32, 462 N.E.2d 459 (Akron Mun. Ct. 1983) (failure to include promised warranty and trade-in value in sales contract); Ohio Admin. Code § 109:4-3-16, Advertisement and Sale of Motor Vehicles.

1386 IFG Leasing Co. v. Ellis, 748 S.W.2d 564 (Tex. App. 1988); George Pharis Chevrolet v. Polk, 661 S.W.2d 314 (Tex. App. 1983).

1387 Cardwell v. Tom Harrigan Oldsmobile, Inc., 1984 Ohio App. LEXIS 10104 (June 27, 1984).

1388 Lee v. Nationwide Cassel, L.P., 660 N.E.2d 94 (Ill. App. Ct. 1995), *rev'd*, 174 Ill. 2d 540, 675 N.E.2d 599, 221 Ill. Dec. 404 (1996) (no UDAP liability because co-signor statute's interpretation was unsettled).

1389 15 U.S.C. § 1679b(a)(1), (2). *See* Lacey v. William Chrysler Plymouth Inc., 2004 U.S. Dist. LEXIS 2479 (N.D. Ill. Feb. 20, 2004) (creditor who instructs customer to misrepresent income may be liable under CROA even if it does not meet definition of credit repair organization). *See also* § 5.1.2.2, *supra*; National Consumer Law Center, Fair Credit Reporting Ch. 15 (5th ed. 2002 and Supp.).

1390 *See* § 5.1.7, *supra*. *See also* N.M. Admin. Code § 12.2.4.18, Advertising and Sale of Motor Vehicles.

1391 Massachusetts Consumer Protection Regulations, Mass. Regs. Code tit. 940, § 5.04, Motor Vehicle Regulations; Pennsylvania Reg. of the Bureau of Consumer Protection, 37 Pa. Code § 301.4, Automobile Industry Trade Practices (1978). *Cf.* Jones v. Wide World of Cars, Inc., 820 F. Supp. 132 (S.D.N.Y. 1993).

1392 Mapp v. Toyota World, Inc., 344 S.E.2d 297 (N.C. Ct. App. 1986).

1393 *See, e.g.*, Barnes v. Rosenthal Toyota, Inc., 126 Md. App. 97, 727 A.2d 431 (Spec. App. 1999).

the transaction on less favorable terms, the dealer repossesses the vehicle, and in some extreme cases has the consumer arrested.

Yo-yo sales are one-sided. The dealer insists that the consumer is bound by the agreement, but the dealer feels free to back out of the deal. Although the true motivation for the dealer backing out can be one of any number of things, the stated justification usually is that the financing fell through.[1394]

Even if this stated justification is in fact the real one, it is still misleading in two ways. First, it implies that the dealer is simply arranging financing with a third party lender. In fact, the dealer is the originating creditor extending the installment loan to the consumer. The dealer is then seeking to sell that installment sales contract to a lender. Second, in our credit market, the dealer can always find a buyer for the installment loan. The only question is whether the dealer will have to sell the loan at a loss, will break even, or whether it can make a profit selling the loan. Because dealers often make a profit selling the paper,[1395] another way to re-phrase the dealer's justification for canceling the sale is that the dealer could not sell the loan paper at a profit, and thus wants to back out of the deal.

In its most insidious form, a yo-yo is a premeditated sales tactic to squeeze more money out of the consumer by canceling the first contract in the hopes of reworking the terms. The dealer decides it will have more leverage pretending to agree to one loan package, but then bringing the consumer back to the dealership a second, third or even fourth time, to keep re-negotiating the deal. The consumer must either return the vehicle or agree to substantially higher monthly payments, a higher down payment, a longer term loan, or a different (worse) car.

The dealer's leverage on the typical consumer in this situation is crushing: after showing off the car to family and friends, consumers must either rewrite the deal or admit to their family and friends that their credit record is so bad the car had to be returned. Moreover, dealers often pressure consumers into re-writing the deal by claiming that the trade-in has already been sold, or that the consumer will not get back any of the down payment if the deal dissolves.

Whether the yo-yo sale is part of a scheme from the beginning to bump up the financing costs, or the dealer just thinks better of the transaction after it communicates with lenders, the yo-yo sale is a classic one-sided transaction. On the one hand, once the consumer drives the car off the lot, the consumer is locked into the sale. The dealer does not want the consumer to think about the deal overnight—it wants the deal closed on the spot. As described in § 5.4.4.1, *supra*, the dealer has just put a full court press on the consumer, perhaps sending in sales personnel in relays. The last thing the dealer wants is for the consumer to go home and think things over, with the opportunity to back out of the deal.

On the other hand, the dealer wants to retain its options when the consumer drives off the lot with the car. It does not want to be rushed into a hasty deal. It wants time for its personnel to determine how much profit can really be made out of the deal selling the loan paper, and whether the lender will agree to the many add-on charges the dealer has packed into the deal. The dealer may also want time to reflect on whether it can squeeze more out of the consumer, or, if not, whether it is better off selling the vehicle to someone else.

Usually, the dealer will want to hide this one-sided nature of the transaction. It does not want consumers to think that they can get out of a deal just because the dealer can. So the dealer will not disclose that the deal, from the dealer's point of view, is not final.[1396]

5.4.5.1.2 Litigation approaches and the organization of this section

While yo-yo sales have been widespread at dealerships for years, consumer lawyers only recently have began to aggressively challenge the practice. It has taken some time for consumer attorneys to unravel these transactions, and to realize that the typical yo-yo involves numerous law violations.

There have been some false starts in litigation, resulting in some adverse rulings, but as attorneys hone in on the crux of the illegality, results have been much better. A number of attorneys are reporting settlements in individual yo-yos in excess of $100,000. Other attorneys are reporting routine yo-yo settlements in the $20,000 to $40,000 range. On the other hand, yo-yo transactions are complex, each individual case may have unique facts, and courts often are confused about the applicable law, particularly where the consumer's attorney does not present the case in sufficient detail. Some yo-yo challenges thus are dismissed.[1397]

This subsection (§ 5.4.5) examines various approaches consumers can use to challenge yo-yo sales. To oversimplify, there are two major strategies in a yo-yo case, although a litigant may wish to explore both. One is a fact-intensive demonstration that the dealer has engaged in UDAP, fraud,

1394 *Cf.* Janikowski v. Lynch Ford Inc., 210 F.3d 765 (7th Cir. 2000) (no UDAP violation where consumer came into dealership just before closing, dealer told consumer that consumer might not qualify for 5.9% financing on note with financing contingency, dealer let the consumer drive the car home that night without the consumer yet bringing in the trade-in, and the contract was re-written the next day at 11.9% after lender downgraded consumer's credit rating to a "4" from the "2" estimated by the dealership, the consumer failed to show dealer acted with knowledge or intent).

1395 *See* § 5.4.3.4, *supra*.

1396 *But cf.* Janikowski v. Lynch Ford Inc., 210 F.3d 765 (7th Cir. 2000) (no UDAP violation where dealer clearly warned consumer that deal was not final, and dealer on the facts of that case, was taking a greater risk than the consumer if deal fell through).

1397 *See* Geller v. Onyx Acceptance Corp., 2001 WL 1711313 (Cal. Super. Ct. Nov. 13, 2001).

conversion, or other law violations, and the consumer seeks actual and perhaps multiple or punitive damages. The other focuses on the paperwork that dealers and lenders are required to provide in yo-yo transactions. Their frequent non-compliance violates Truth in Lending (TIL), Equal Credit Opportunity Act (ECOA), or Fair Credit Reporting Act (FCRA) disclosure and notice requirements, leading to claims for actual, statutory, and punitive damages, plus attorney fees. The first strategy will likely land the litigants in state court, but the second strategy or a combination of the two will meet federal court jurisdictional requirements.

Section 5.4.5.2 examines whether a dealer's cancellation of an automotive sale or lease is legal and whether the transaction leading to that cancellation involved UDAP violations. The next two subsections summarize common ECOA, FCRA and TIL disclosure and notice violations in yo-yo transactions.[1398] Section 5.4.5.5 then details why dealers, even if they can cancel the transaction, almost always improperly structure the yo-yo transaction, leading to further law violations.

The next two subsections explore UDAP and other yo-yo violations occurring after the deal is canceled, involving return of the consumer's trade-in or deposit and involving the dealer's attempts to switch the consumer to a less favorable, second transaction.[1399] The last two subsections provide litigation practice pointers—whether an arbitration clause in a yo-yo transaction is binding on the consumer and types of discovery that should be sought in yo-yo litigation.[1400]

At present there are significant variations in state law treatment of yo-yo transactions, so that it is also important to stay current with a particular jurisdiction's statutory law in this area and any administrative rulings from the state dealer licensing board, the department of motor vehicle, the attorney general's office, or other state agency. Arizona, Colorado, Illinois, Louisiana, Virginia, Utah, and Washington have enacted yo-yo statutes,[1401] and a North Carolina statute has some relevance to yo-yos.[1402] Arizona, Maine, Maryland, and Michigan have issued important administrative interpretations to dealers on the subject,[1403] and Idaho and Ohio UDAP regulations provide certain minimal protections.[1404] In addition, many statutes regulate portions of the yo-yo transaction, and these will be described *infra*. For example, a number of states limit a dealer's ability to resell the consumer's trade-in before the deal is final.

5.4.5.2 Dealer's Right to Cancel the Yo-Yo Transaction

5.4.5.2.1 Absent valid contingency clause, no right to cancel

In the most egregious case, the dealer attempts a yo-yo sale with no written document or other basis for making the sale contingent on financing. Instead, the dealer preys on the consumer's ignorance (and some courts' confusion) as to the relationship of the dealer and the bank or finance company. In the typical motor vehicle installment sales agreement, it is the dealer that originally extends credit. Its name is on the note as the creditor and it is bound to the credit contract by signing it or by offering it to the consumer.

The bank or finance company, who most people assume is the lender, is actually just an assignee from the dealer. If the finance company declines the assignment, there is still a binding credit agreement between the consumer and dealer. Even though the dealer may not think of itself as extending credit and may even orally state that it does not do financing, as a matter of law, by entering into the credit agreement, it has extended credit, even if it routinely assigns the contract to a finance company. The consumer's obligation to pay for the car, pursuant to the purchase agreement, has been met by the retail installment sales agreement that replaces the obligation to pay cash with the obligation to pay the dealer on a monthly basis. The consumer is not in default of that agreement simply because the dealer fails to assign the agreement to a third party.[1405]

The mistaken belief that the bank or finance company is the originating lender is fostered in part by the loan paper itself, which will be a form provided by the assignee, with the assignee's name typeset in large letters at the top of the form. But, if one examines the loan paper, the dealer will

1398 *See* §§ 5.4.5.3, 5.4.5.4, *infra.*

1399 *See* §§ 5.4.5.6, 5.4.5.7, *infra.*

1400 *See* §§ 5.4.5.8, 5.4.5.9, *infra.*

1401 Ariz. Rev. Stat. § 44-1371; Colo. Rev. Stat. § 6-1-708; 815 Ill. Comp. Stat. § 505/2C; La. Rev. Stat. § 32:1254(N)(3)(f); Utah Stat. § 41-3-401; Va. Code § 46.2-1530; Wash. Rev. Code § 46.70.180(4).

1402 N.C. Gen. Stat. § 20-75.1.

1403 The Arizona Attorney General's Automobile Advertising Guidelines (1993); Office of Consumer Credit Regulation, *Maine Creditor Update* p.8 (Issue #38, Oct./Nov. 1999), Clearinghouse No. 52,522; Maine Office of Consumer Credit Regulation, Examination of Cens Auto Group, Inc., Clearinghouse No. 52,521 (Oct. 29, 1999); Maryland Motor Vehicle Administration, *"Spot Delivery"-"Fronting"-"MacArthur Statement" etc.*, Bulletin D-11 98-01, Clearinghouse No. 52,142 (Nov. 30, 1998); Letter from Murray Brown, Deputy Commissioner, Michigan Department of Commerce to [the licensee addressed], Clearinghouse No. 52,029 (May 22, 1989); Michigan Automobile Dealers Association, Dealer Advisory, "Spot Deliveries," Clearinghouse No. 52,519 (Oct. 24, 1997).

1404 Idaho Admin. Code 04.02.01.237; Ohio Admin. Code 109:4-3-16(A)(30); *see* Braucher v. Mariemont Auto, 2002 WL 1393570 (Ohio App. June 28, 2002) (yo-yo seller violated regulation by not having written contingency agreement).

1405 *See* Walker Mobile Home Sales v. Walker, 965 S.W.2d 271 (Mo. Ct. App. 1998) (consumer not liable to dealer where consumer offered to make installment payments to dealer, but dealer refused to accept payments where prospective assignee refused to take assignment); Ohio Admin. Code 109:4-3-16(A)(30) (requiring any contingency on the sale to be in writing stating the parties' obligations if financing is not obtained).

have signed it as the original creditor, and then assigned that paper to the bank or finance company.

5.4.5.2.2 *Contingency must be in writing*

To make a transaction contingent on the dealer obtaining financing, the parties must explicitly agree to such a condition. A financing contingency that is only orally conveyed to the consumer is not effective. State motor vehicle and retail installment sales statutes require that all the terms be included in the installment loan agreement. Such oral statements also run afoul of the parole evidence rule and the statute of frauds. Moreover, the installment sales agreement itself often states that its terms supersede any other agreements, and may even state that the dealership is not bound by the statements of its employees. A number of states have also explicitly required yo-yo contingency clauses to be in writing, either by statute[1406] or pursuant to a UDAP regulation.[1407]

One word of warning: do not accept a client's belief that there was no contingency agreement. Instead, ask the dealer in writing for a copy of whatever it claims entitles it to undo the deal. Car dealerships often hand consumers a stack of documents to sign, and hurry the consumer through the process without consumers knowing what they had just agreed to and without giving the consumer copies of the documents they have just signed.

5.4.5.2.3 *Cancellation allegedly based on credit application misstatements*

The dealer may claim it is canceling the deal because the consumer lied on the credit application, and that this triggers a default or allows the dealer to cancel on the basis of the consumer's material fraudulent misrepresentation. Instead, experience shows that the dealer is usually most at fault for misstatements on a credit application. To make the sale, the dealer may either insert false information in the credit application without the consumer's knowledge, or direct the consumer to make specified misstatements with oral assurances that it is all right.[1408]

To avoid such dealer defenses, the consumer's attorney, immediately upon filing suit, even before the dealer responds, should send discovery to the financer, asking for all information about when purchase of the paper was initially approved and why the financer subsequently refused to purchase the paper. Finance companies are unlikely to back up the dealer that the later denial was caused by misstatements in the credit application.

To act as a ground for default, justifying repossession of the vehicle, the installment sales agreement must explicitly state either that such misstatements or the lender's insecurity is a ground for default, and state law must allow such a grounds for default.[1409] In addition, even if the creditor can legally declare a default for this reason, a default is only valid if this is the real reason for declaring the default. If the dealer declares a default, the dealer's recovery of the car must comply with UCC Article 9 and other state repossession law, as set out briefly at § 5.4.5.5.7, *infra,* and in much more detail in NCLC's *Repossessions and Foreclosures* (5th ed. 2002 and Supp.).

5.4.5.2.4 *Absence of dealer signature does not create a valid contingency*

Some dealers do not sign the loan agreement, and then argue that the financing agreement is not final for this reason. Nevertheless, the filled-in contract should be viewed as the dealer's offer, and the consumer's signature is acceptance, so the contract is binding.[1410] The dealer's failure to sign the installment sales agreement may also violate the state installment sales act.[1411]

In addition, the dealer's notations on the contract may be sufficient to show a signature. In particular, check to see if the dealer's name is typed below the signature line. The Uniform Commercial Code section 1-201(39) defines "signed" as "any symbol executed or adopted by a party with present intention to authenticate a writing." The Official Comment notes that the signature may be printed, stamped, or written, and may even be found in the letterhead.[1412]

Finally, dealers may want to think twice before they establish a rule of law that an installment sales agreement is not binding until the dealer signs the document. In that case, consumers may be able to back out of car deals even if they

1406 La. Rev. Stat. § 32:1254(N)(3)(f), *as amended by* Act 670 (2004); N.H. Stat. § 361-A:10-b (effective July 23, 2004); Utah Stat. § 41-3-401; Va. Code § 46.2-1530.

1407 Idaho Admin. Code 04.02.01.237; Ohio Admin. Code 109:4-3-16(A)(30). *See also* Braucher v. Mariemont Auto, 2002 WL 1393570 (Ohio Ct. App. June 28, 2002); Renner v. Derin Acquisition Corp., 111 Ohio App. 3d 326, 676 N.E.2d 151 (1996).

1408 *See* Knapp v. Americredit Fin. Servs., Inc., 245 F. Supp. 2d 841 (S.D. W. Va. 2003); Gelco Corp. v. Major Chevrolet, Inc., 2002 WL 31427027 (N.D. Ill. Oct. 30, 2002).

1409 *See* National Consumer Law Center, Repossessions and Foreclosures § 4.2 (5th ed. 2002 and Supp.).

1410 *See* Cannon v. Metro Ford, Inc., 242 F. Supp. 2d 1322 (S.D. Fla. 2002) (consumer's signature consummates the transaction even if dealer does not sign agreement). *But see* Dauti v. Hartford Auto Plaza, Ltd., 213 F. Supp. 2d 116 (D. Conn. 2002).

1411 *See* Cannon v. Metro Ford, Inc., 242 F. Supp. 2d 1322 (S.D. Fla. 2002); *cf.* Miranda v. Autonation USA, Corp., Clearinghouse No. 53558 (Fla. Cir. Ct. Oct. 31, 2000) (certifying class on claim that seller failed to make timely delivery to buyer of copy of retail installment contract signed by buyer and seller), *aff'd in relevant part, rev'd in part on other grounds*, 789 So. 2d 1188 (Fla. App. 2001). *But see* Scott v. Forest Lake Chrysler-Plymouth-Dodge, 611 N.W.2d 346 (Minn. 2000).

1412 *See* Official Comment 39 to U.C.C. § 1-201.

take the vehicle home, as long as they cancel before the dealer affixes its signature to the agreement.

5.4.5.2.5 Does contingency clause comply with state law?

Any contingency clause must comport with state law. In some states, a contingency clause is illegal.[1413] For example, the Maryland Motor Vehicle Administration states that dealers are not to use contingent or supplemental contracts.[1414] A letter from the Michigan Department of Commerce finds such a contingency to violate the Michigan Motor Vehicle Sales Finance Act. The Act prohibits any waivers in the agreement of the consumer's rights under the Act.[1415] That the Act prohibits contingency clauses is also implicit in the fact that the form of binding agreement specified by the Act does not include such a contingency. The letter also finds the contingency clauses to be coercive and unconscionable.

The Michigan logic applies to other motor vehicle installment sales acts. In addition, some retail installment sales acts require that the installment sales agreement contains "final" terms. This requirement is not met where an agreement is contingent on a subsequent event.

Some state statutes limit the scope of a contingency clause. A Washington statute outlaws contingent sales unless the dealer either accepts or cancels the sale within three business days.[1416] Utah law only accepts contingency clauses that give the dealer seven days to cancel,[1417] and Louisiana law requires the contingency to allow the dealer only twenty-five days.[1418]

On the other hand, state-mandated disclosure of the existence of a contingency clause must not be confused with the contingency clause itself. For example, in Virginia, state law specifies a notice that must be placed in the buyer's order stating that *if* a contingency clause is included, then the consumer has certain rights.[1419] This state-mandated notice is *not* a contingency clause and can not act as one, even though dealers often act as if it does.

5.4.5.2.6 Where contingency placed in a separate document or conflicts with other loan terms

Contingency "riders" found outside the retail installment sales agreement are subject to challenge. A Pennsylvania Attorney General complaint resulting in a consent order argues that any condition on a motor vehicle installment sales agreement must be found in the agreement itself, and not placed in a separate rider.[1420] If the rider is a separate document, the failure to provide the rider to the consumer at the time of the transaction will also violate state motor vehicle finance laws that require that consumers receive copies of the contract. In addition, if the main contract specifies that it is the complete understanding between the parties, and other documents are not to be incorporated, then the rider should not be effective under basic contract principles. Moreover, a number of state motor vehicle financings and leasing acts explicitly state that all terms of the agreement must be in a single document—sometimes called the single document rule.[1421]

A rider should not conflict with the main document either. For example, where an installment sales agreement states that the dealer has sold the vehicle to the consumer, and that the transaction is final, then a separate document should not indicate that the transaction is *not* final. For a rider to be effective laying out a bailment agreement until financing is complete, the installment sales agreement must clearly state that it is a condition precedent agreement, that it is not a final one. Then a rider can lay out the terms of the bailment until the condition is met and the car is actually sold to the consumer.

There are other reasons why a contingency clause may not be effective if placed in only certain of the deal documents. For example, consider where the clause is found only in a buyer's order, but not in the final installment sales agreement. The buyer's order makes the transaction conditional on financing being obtained. That financing is obtained in the installment sales agreement. The fact that the dealer can not subsequently sell that note is irrelevant to the fact that the condition in the buyer's order has been met, that financing has been obtained. Moreover, the terms of the original buyer's order are replaced by the subsequent installment sales agreement which is the final understanding of the parties.

Carefully examine the documents to see if handwritten or typed provisions conflict with and override the contingency clause. For example, in one mobile home sale, a court found

1413 *But see* Ed Bozarth Chevrolet, Inc. v. Black, 77 P.3d 1009 (Kan. Ct. App. 2003) (generally upholding a contingency clause against various challenges).

1414 Maryland Motor Vehicle Administration, *"Spot Delivery"-"Fronting"-"MacArthur Statement" etc*, Bulletin D-11 98-01, Clearinghouse No. 52,142 (Nov. 30, 1998).

1415 Letter from Murray Brown, Deputy Commissioner, Michigan Department of Commerce to [the licensee addressed], Clearinghouse No. 52,029 (May 22, 1989).

1416 Wash. Rev. Code § 46.70.180(4).

1417 Utah Stat. § 41-3-401.

1418 La. Rev. Stat. 32:1254(N)(3)(f), *as amended by* Act 670 (2004).

1419 Va. Code § 46.2-1530(A)(12).

1420 Commonwealth v. Metro Chrysler-Plymouth Jeep-Eagle, Inc., Clearinghouse No. 52,028 (Pa. Commw. Ct. 1997). *But see* Scott v. Lake Chrysler-Plymouth-Dodge, 611 N.W.2d 346 (Minn. 2000).

1421 *See, e.g.*, Cal. Civ. Code § 2985.8 (leasing); Kroupa v. Sunrise Ford, 77 Cal. App. 4th 835, 92 Cal. Rptr. 2d 42 (Cal. App. 1999); Wash. Rev. Code § 63.14.020; Kenworthy v. Bolin, 17 Wash. App. 650, 564 P.2d 835 (1977). *See also* Ohio Rev. Code § 1317.02. *But see* Sharlow v. Wally McCarthy Pontiac-GMC Trucks-Hyundai, Inc., 2000 U.S. App. LEXIS 15627 (8th Cir. July 6, 2000) (unpublished, citation limited) (following *Scott*); Scott v. Forest Lake Chrysler-Plymouth-Dodge, 611 N.W.2d 346 (Minn. 2000) (contingency clause need not be included in retail installment contract despite single document rule).

the existence of typed language setting out the payment terms and interest rate to override a preprinted contingency clause.[1422]

Certain contingency clauses may be drafted so poorly or are so one-sided as to raise special issues. For example, one dealer used a contingency clause that required the consumer to agree in advance to an unspecified higher interest rate if the contract at the stated rate could not be assigned to a financer. The court overruled the dealer's objections and allowed the case to go forward to determine if this clause violated the installment sales statute. That statute requires the terms to be in writing, that the finance charge be disclosed, and that no blank spaces be included in the contract to be filled in later.[1423] The case also went forward on the claim that the contingency is so one-sided that a court could find it to be unenforceable.[1424]

5.4.5.2.7 Have the exact conditions allowing cancellation occurred?

That the agreement includes a valid contingency clause does not give the dealer the right to cancel the transaction. Events must occur that are stated in the contingency clause to be grounds to cancel the agreement. Do not assume that the lender refused to purchase the paper just because the dealer so alleges, and do not assume that the dealer even sought out lenders to purchase the note.[1425] Discovery of the faxes or electronic messages back and forth between the dealer and various financers will show whether the dealer ever requested financing at the agreed amount and whether the offer was accepted. In addition, as explained in § 5.4.5.3, *infra*, lenders must provide written notice of any adverse action on the consumer's credit application, and the lender must retain for twenty-five months all documents evidencing this denial of credit.

Also consider carefully the language of the dealer contingency clause. Is the deal contingent on the originating lender's approval (i.e., the dealer's) or on the lender's ability to sell the paper to another party? If it is contingent on the originating lender's approval, that has already been granted. The dealer, who is the originating lender, has already taken the credit information and offered financing at a given rate.

Automobile paper is often sold with a yield spread premium, being the difference between what the finance company will accept (the buy rate) and the rate at which the dealer writes up the loan. The dealer pockets most or all of the yield spread as a kickback.[1426] Consider whether financing really fell through where the rate specified in the installment sales agreement is 15%, but the loan is offered to the assignee not at that rate, but at a buy rate of 11%.

Has the dealer made a good faith effort to finance the 15% paper when it is only offering it to other lenders at 11%? Before canceling the sale, must the dealer instead seek a buyer for the paper at 15%? The contingency clause does not specify that the dealer can cancel if it can not find a lender to purchase the paper at a significant profit to the dealer. In any event, it is surely deceptive to state that financing can not be arranged for a 15% loan where the dealer never sought a lender out to purchase the loan at 15%. And it surely should be a UDAP violation to fail to disclose, when selling a vehicle pursuant to a contingency clause, that the sale is not contingent on a lender purchasing the paper at 15%, but instead at 11%.

A New Hampshire statute references cancellation where "approval of the terms of the retail installment contract can not be obtained."[1427] This would seem to allow cancellation only if the dealer can not obtain financing at the rate described in the contract, not at some lower interest rate selected by the dealer.

Other contingency clauses may be so poorly drafted so that it is difficult to determine if the contingency has occurred. For example, a number of clauses state that the contract can be cancelled if financing is not obtained within ten days.[1428] This should be interpreted as saying the dealer has the option of canceling the sale within days, if it can not obtain financing. Failure to notify the consumer within ten days ends the dealer's right to cancel. The opposite conclusion would be nonsensical, that the dealer can wait as long as it wants to cancel the sale, if it did not obtain financing in the first ten days.

5.4.5.2.8 Where dealer knows in advance that contingency will not be met

Check to see if the faxes or e-mails between the dealer and the finance company show a denial even before the consumer left with the car, or whether the underwriting standards that lenders provide the dealer demonstrate that the dealer knew in advance that the financing would fail. A yo-yo sale is a UDAP violation where the dealer knows in advance with a high degree of certainty that a consumer will not qualify for financing, but still writes up a sale as if the consumer will receive that financing.[1429] Instead, the dealer should have disclosed at that point the cost of the financing

1422 Smith v. Homes Today, Inc., 296 B.R. 46 (Bankr. M.D. Ala. 2003).

1423 Couture v. G.W.M., Inc., 2002 WL 31962752 (N.H. Super. Ct. Dec. 3, 2002).

1424 *Id.*

1425 *Cf.* Peak v. Ted Russell Enterprises, Inc., 2000 Tenn. App. LEXIS 120 (Feb. 28, 2000) (no UDAP violation where undisputed evidence showed that dealer attempted unsuccessfully to find financing).

1426 *See* § 5.4.3.4, *supra.*

1427 N.H. Stat. § 361-A:10-b (effective July 23, 2004).

1428 *See* Fox v. The Montell Corp., 2001 WL 293632 (N.D. Ill. Mar. 19, 2001); Williams v. Thomas Pontiac-GMC-Nissan-Hyundai, 1999 U.S. Dist. LEXIS 15045 (N.D. Ill. Sept. 22, 1999).

1429 Grimaldi v. Webb, 668 N.E.2d 39 (Ill. App. Ct. 1996).

for which the consumer would eventually qualify. A dealer knowing that financing will fall through also indicates that the yo-yo is a premeditated, unfair sales tactic to bump up the consumer to a higher financing level, by stripping the consumer of the trade-in and allowing the consumer to show off the vehicle to family and friends.

5.4.5.2.9 *Misrepresentations that the sale is final*

Dealer representations that the sale is final, when in fact it is still contingent on financing being approved, are actionable. If the dealer assures the consumer that the financing has gone through, and the consumer takes actions relying on that statement, this leads both to consumer claims of a UDAP violation and that the dealer is estopped from canceling the original credit sale agreement.[1430] Some courts find oral misrepresentations not actionable if they are corrected by the written terms of the sale. But an oral misrepresentation that financing has been approved is not corrected by a contract that states that the contract can be cancelled if financing is not approved. The two representations are entirely consistent with each other—a deal can be contingent on financing being approved and the financing can also be approved.[1431]

In addition, a false claim that financing has been approved is an ECOA violation. The ECOA requires oral or written notice when financing has been approved.[1432] An oral notification that is inaccurate violates this notice requirement. ECOA violations lead to federal court jurisdiction and claims for actual and punitive damages, as well as attorney fees.

5.4.5.2.10 *Consumer remedies where cancellation not valid*

Where the dealer does not have the right to cancel the agreement, the dealer's attempt to undo a binding credit agreement is unfair, deceptive, and wrongful, leading to potential UDAP, fraud, and breach of contract claims.[1433] Clearly seizing the vehicle when the dealer has no legal basis for the seizure is conversion or a related tort.[1434] It is also a UDAP violation for the dealer to misrepresent to the consumer its legal right to recover the vehicle. A dealership commits a UDAP violation by trying to coerce the consumer into accepting less favorable contract terms after committing itself to the original terms.[1435] Where payments go up or the consumer is switched to a less valuable vehicle, another theory is unjust enrichment.

5.4.5.3 Importance of ECOA and FCRA Claims

5.4.5.3.1 *Introduction*

Equal Credit Opportunity Act (ECOA) and/or Fair Credit Reporting Act (FCRA) notice claims are often an integral part of a yo-yo litigation, for at least two reasons. First, these

1430 Mayberry v. Ememessay, Inc., 201 F. Supp. 2d 687 (W.D. Va. 2002) (if facts so indicate, representations can be found to be deceptive); Jafri v. Lynch Ford, 2000 U.S. Dist. LEXIS 20736 (N.D. Ill. Aug. 25, 2000); Heltzel v. Mecham Pontiac, 730 P.2d 235 (Ariz. 1986); Singleton v. Stokes Motors, Inc., 2004 WL 764941 (S.C. 2004). *See also* Colo. Rev. Stat. § 6-1-708(1)(a)(I). *But cf.* Castellana v. Conyers Toyota, Inc. 407 S.E.2d 64 (Ga. Ct. App. 1991) (no UDAP violation because under Georgia's unusual UDAP interpretations, not followed by any other state, no UDAP violation if oral misrepresentations are corrected in the written agreement).

1431 Mayberry v. Ememessay, Inc., 201 F. Supp. 2d 687 (W.D. Va. 2002).

1432 *See* § 5.4.5.3, *infra*; *see generally* National Consumer Law Center, Credit Discrimination Ch. 10 (3d ed. 2002 and Supp.).

1433 *See* Daenzer v. Wayland Ford, Inc., 2002 WL 1050209 (E.D. Mich. May 7, 2002); Pescia v. Auburn Ford-Lincoln Mercury, 68 F. Supp. 2d 1269 (M.D. Ala. 1999) (dealer had duty to disclose that the sale was not final, was subject to financing approval, and that the terms and conditions of the final contract may be different from the contract that the consumer signed); Duty v. Ricart Properties, Inc., 2003 WL 21470368 (Ohio Ct. App. June 26, 2003); Braucher v. Mariemont Auto, 2002 WL 1393570 (Ohio Ct. App. June 28, 2002) (deceptive to fail to disclose financing contingency); Cardwell v. Tom Harrigan Oldsmobile, Inc., 1984 Ohio App. LEXIS 10104 (June 27, 1984) (dealer violated UDAP statute by refusing to transfer title unless buyer paid charges beyond those required by contract). *See also* Rayburn v. Car Credit Center Corp., 2000 U.S. Dist. LEXIS 14944 (N.D. Ill. Oct. 6, 2000) (misrepresentation that financing had been obtained would be UDAP violation); Williams v. First Government Mortgage & Investors Corp., 974 F. Supp. 17 (D.D.C. 1997), *aff'd*, 176 F.3d 497 (D.C. Cir. 1999) (UDAP claim survives motion to dismiss); Office of Consumer Credit Regulation, *Maine Creditor Update* p.8 (Issue #38, Oct./Nov. 1999), Clearinghouse No. 52,522 (practice is unconscionable); Maine Office of Consumer Credit Regulation, Examination of Cens Auto Group, Inc., Clearinghouse No. 52,521 (Oct. 29, 1999) (same). *But see* Janikowski v. Lynch Ford Inc., 210 F.3d 765 (7th Cir. 2000) (no UDAP violation where consumer came into dealership just before closing, dealer told consumer that consumer might not qualify for 5.9% financing and that the note had a financing contingency, dealer let the consumer drive the car home that night without the consumer yet bringing in the trade-in, and the contract was re-written the next day at 11.9% after lender downgraded consumer's credit rating to a "4" from the "2" estimated by the dealership, the consumer failed to show dealer acted with knowledge or intent); Williams v. Thomas Pontiac-GMC-Nissan-Hyundai, 1999 U.S. Dist. LEXIS 15045 (N.D. Ill. Sept. 22, 1999) (allegation of facts that dealer misrepresented willingness to sell automobile at terms set forth in retail installment contract sufficient to defeat motion to dismiss). *Cf.* Williams v. Rizza Chevrolet-Geo, Inc., 2000 U.S. Dist. LEXIS 2695 (N.D. Ill. Mar. 1, 2000) (class not certified where common issues did not predominate).

1434 *See* NCLC's Repossessions and Foreclosures § 13.6.2 (5th ed. 2002 and Supp.). *See also* Williams v. Thomas Pontiac-GMC-Nissan-Hyundai, 1999 U.S. Dist. LEXIS 15045 (N.D. Ill. Sept. 22, 1999).

1435 Roche v. Fireside Chrysler-Plymouth, 600 N.E.2d 1218 (Ill. App. Ct. 1992).

claims offer an opportunity to discover evidence related to the dealer's claim that "financing fell through." Written notice must be provided the consumer as to the grounds for any credit denial and lenders must keep records of credit denials for twenty-five months.[1436]

Second, practitioners report that yo-yo transactions frequently violate ECOA and FCRA notice requirements. Not only are notices not sent, but, even if the lender can provide evidence that the notice was sent, the notice is often incomplete or inaccurate. Such violations lead to federal court jurisdiction, actual and punitive damages and attorney fees. Because multiple lenders may be violating notice requirements, the consumer may even be able to recover punitive damages awards from a number of different defendants. ECOA and FCRA claims are available in any type of yo-yo transaction, whether the deal was renegotiated on less favorable terms, falls through, or even when the dealer never cancels the original agreement.

While this subsection outlines the applicability of the ECOA and FCRA to yo-yo transactions, a more detailed analysis is found in two other NCLC manuals, *Credit Discrimination* and *Fair Credit Reporting*. Those manuals also contain sample pleadings and reprint relevant primary source material in their appendices and on their companion CD-Roms.

5.4.5.3.2 Notice requirements

In the typical yo-yo transaction, the dealer uses the consumer's credit application and credit report to perform an initial evaluation on the consumer's credit. This initial evaluation will be a factor in the interest rate set by the dealer in the installment sales agreement, and will also determine which lenders (if any) that the dealer will forward the agreement for approval. The dealer will ask those lenders if they will purchase the installment sales agreement, and at what price. If financing has really fallen through, one or more of these lenders will reject the agreement on the terms set by the dealer.

Whenever any of these lenders or the dealer takes an adverse action, various notice requirements are triggered under both the ECOA and FCRA. It is important to keep track of both statutes, because dealers and lenders will show great imagination in their attempts to show that one or the other of these statutes does not apply. Typically though, even if there is an argument that the ECOA is not applicable because of the fact pattern the lender alleges, the FCRA requirements will still apply under those facts, or vice versa.

The ECOA requires creditors and assignees to provide a written notice of the reasons for any adverse action on the consumer's credit application.[1437] If an application is not acted upon because it is incomplete, written notice of that is also required. If a counter-offer is made instead, other notice requirements apply. The FCRA, on the other hand, requires written notice whenever a "user" of a credit report takes adverse action based at least in part on information from a credit report.[1438] The notice must include the name of the reporting agency supplying the information.

The creditor can use one combined notice that contains the information required by the ECOA and FCRA notice requirements. On the other hand, parties must still comply with the FCRA notice, if applicable, even if the ECOA notice does not apply in a particular case, and vice versa.

As a result, the following notices should be sent:

- The dealer should send an FCRA notice whenever it uses the consumer's credit report and takes any adverse action based on that report—such as increasing the interest rate, not forwarding the application to any lender or only forwarding the application to certain sub-prime lenders.
- *Each* lender that turns down a credit application based in part on a credit report must send the FCRA notice. Because each lender may use a different reporting agency, each lender must send a separate notice, indicating which agency's report was used.
- Dealers are creditors (as discussed in § 5.4.5.3.3, *infra*), and thus must send an ECOA notice whenever they take an adverse action on the consumer's credit application.
- Where a potential assignee turns the installment sales agreement down, it should also send an ECOA notice, including the reasons for the adverse action. The ECOA (unlike the FCRA) only requires one party to provide the notice of adverse action. If one lender provides that notice, the dealer and other lenders need not do so as well.[1439]

5.4.5.3.3 Is the dealer a covered creditor?

Dealers will often argue that they are not a creditor under

1436 12 C.F.R. § 202.12(b).

1437 *See* 12 C.F.R. § 202.9; *see also* Cannon v. Metro Ford, Inc., 242 F. Supp. 2d 1322 (S.D. Fla. 2002); Davis v. Regional Acceptance Corp., 2002 U.S. Dist. LEXIS 16775 (E.D. Va. Sept. 5, 2002); Fox v. The Montell Corp., 2001 WL 293632 (N.D. Ill. Mar. 19, 2001); Williams v. Thomas Pontiac, 1999 U.S. Dist. LEXIS 15045 (N.D. Ill. Sept. 22, 1999) (yo-yo sale); Williams v. First Government Mortgage & Investors Corp., 974 F. Supp. 17 (D.D.C. 1997), *aff'd*, 225 F.3d 738 (D.C. Cir. 2000) (ECOA claim survives motion to dismiss). *Cf.* Johnson v. Grossinger Motorcorp, Inc., 324 Ill. App. 3d 354, 753 N.E.2d 431 (2001) (no ECOA violation where credit provisionally approved pending completion of paperwork, and paperwork never completed by consumer). *But see* 12 C.F.R. § 202.9(d) (oral notification sufficient if lender act on less than 150 applications a year).

1438 Nevertheless, it is important to show that a credit report was used in the adverse action, or the FCRA claim will fail. *See* Castro v. Union Nissan, Inc., 2002 WL 1466810 (N.D. Ill. July 8, 2002).

1439 *See* Leguillou v. Lynch Ford, Inc., 2000 U.S. Dist. LEXIS 1668 (N.D. Ill. Feb. 10, 2000).

the ECOA and are thus not liable for ECOA violations. For starters, this is no defense to an FCRA violation, because the FCRA applies to anyone who uses a credit report. In addition, a close analysis of the scope of the ECOA clearly demonstrates that dealers originating installment sales agreements are covered by the ECOA.[1440] Nor can the dealer avoid liability by claiming it was the responsibility of the assignee to provide the notice.[1441]

The ECOA defines creditor as someone who "in the ordinary course of business, regularly participates in the credit decision, including setting the terms of the credit. The term creditor includes a creditor's assignee, transferee, or subrogee who so participates."[1442] Both the dealer and assignee lender clearly meet this definition.

Dealers sometimes argue that they are not creditors either because they are or because they are not arrangers of credit, defined for purposes of the ECOA as "a person who, in the ordinary course of business, regularly refers applicants or prospective applicants to creditors, or selects or offers to select creditors to whom requests for credit may be made."[1443]

Some dealer argue that they are arrangers of credit and arrangers need not comply with the notice requirement. But the dealer then both meets the definition of creditor and the definition of arranger, and is thus both. The regulation to which the dealers point clearly states that "the term creditor also includes" arrangers, so that someone can clearly be both.[1444] The dealer then must send notice based on its status as a creditor, even if it need not do so as an arranger.

In an even stranger argument, some dealers argue that they are not arrangers, and because they are not arrangers, then they are not creditors. But one can be a creditor even if one is not an arranger. "The term creditor also includes" arrangers, so that some creditors are not arrangers.

Nevertheless, courts are often confused about whose responsibility it is to provide the notice of adverse action—the dealer who is the originating creditor and who cancels the loan agreement, or a finance company who refuses to purchase the agreement.[1445] The dealer will argue that it has not taken the adverse action, that the potential financers have. The financers will claim they have merely declined to invest in the completed installment sale between the dealer and consumer. Thus it is strongly advised that, until these issues are clarified, that the consumer allege in the alternative that both parties are liable for the ECOA violation.

5.4.5.3.4 The counter-offer defense

Dealers may argue that, after canceling a sale, they have made a counter-offer, and thus have not denied credit. The ECOA requires notice of such a counter-offer within thirty days.[1446] In addition, in many yo-yos, no counter-offer is made, or an offer is made only some days after an unconditional denial. Query also whether even an immediate offer of lease terms can be considered a counter-offer to a credit application. Moreover, a counter-offer would have to be a firm one; dealers sometimes back out of second deals as readily as first deals. Any rider that gives the dealer the right to back out of a second offer if financing does not come through is not a true counter-offer.

In a yo-yo sale, the originating creditor (i.e., the dealer) has already agreed to finance the purchase. It is the assignee who allegedly refuses to purchase the loan. Consequently, this is really an adverse action on an existing account for which the ECOA requires written notice within thirty days, whether or not there is a counter-offer.[1447]

Moreover, the adverse action will almost certainly involve the use of the consumer's credit report. The Fair Credit Reporting Act (FCRA) has its own notice requirements where a user of a credit report takes adverse action on the basis of information contained in a credit report—the creditor must identify the name, address, and phone number of the consumer reporting agency making the report to the creditor, must disclose the consumer's right to a free credit report, and to dispute the contents of the report.[1448] There is no exception to this notice requirement where the creditor makes a counter-offer, because the purpose of the notice is

1440 Treadway v. Gateway Chevrolet Oldsmobile, Inc., 362 F.3d 971 (7th Cir. 2004); Payne v. Ken Diepholz Ford Lincoln Mercury, Inc., 2004 WL 40631 (N.D. Ill. Jan. 5, 2004); Bayard v. Behlmann Automotive Servs., Inc., 292 F. Supp. 2d 1181 (E.D. Mo. 2003); Gallegos v. Rizza Chevrolet, Inc., 2003 WL 22326523 (N.D. Ill. Oct. 9, 2003); Najieb v. Chrysler-Plymouth, 2002 WL 31906466 (N.D. Ill. Dec. 31, 2002); *see also* Nevarez v. O'Connnor Chevrolet, Inc., 303 F. Supp. 2d 927 (N.D. Ill. 2004).

1441 Najieb v. Chrysler-Plymouth, 2002 WL 31906466 (N.D. Ill. Dec. 31, 2002).

1442 12 C.F.R. § 202.1(*l*).

1443 *Id.*

1444 *Id.*

1445 *See* Castro v. Union Nissan, Inc., 2002 WL 1466810 (N.D. Ill. July 8, 2002); Fox v. The Montell Corp., 2001 WL 293632 (N.D. Ill. Mar. 19, 2001).

1446 12 C.F.R. § 202.9(a)(1)(i). *See also* National Consumer Law Center, Credit Discrimination (3d ed. 2002 and Supp.).

1447 12 C.F.R. §§ 202.9(a)(1)(iii), 202.2(c)(1)(ii). *See also* National Consumer Law Center, Credit Discrimination (3d ed. 2002 and Supp.).

1448 *See* 15 U.S.C. § 1681m; National Consumer Law Center, Fair Credit Reporting § 6.4 (5th ed. 2002 and Supp.); *see also* Treadway v. Gateway Chevrolet Oldsmobile, Inc., 362 F.3d 971 (7th Cir. 2004); Davis v. Regional Acceptance Corp., 2002 U.S. Dist. LEXIS 16775 (E.D. Va. Sept. 5, 2002); *cf.* Sapia v. Regency Motors, 276 F.3d 747 (5th Cir. 2002) (no FCRA liability for failure to send adverse action notice in yo-yo sale where consumer suffered no damage and did not prove willfulness); Cannon v. Metro Ford, Inc., 242 F. Supp. 2d 1322 (S.D. Fla. 2002). *But see* Najieb v. Chrysler-Plymouth, 2002 WL 31906466 (N.D. Ill. Dec. 31, 2002) (no adverse use of credit report by dealer shown); Mayberry v. Ememessay, Inc., 201 F. Supp. 2d 687 (W.D. Va. 2002) (no use of credit report shown and no adverse action where consumer offered identical financing with another creditor).

to let the consumer know that the terms of the loan they requested have been made more onerous because of the credit report, and that they can check that credit report to make sure it is accurate.

5.4.5.3.5 *Other dealer defenses*

Another possible dealer defense is that the consumer did not supply all the required information for the credit application. But the ECOA clearly states that a written adverse action notice is still required even where the consumer has not provided all the requested credit information.[1449]

Similarly, it is no defense that the dealer refused to forward the credit application to other lenders, because of the consumer's credit record. This refusal by the dealer is an adverse action, requiring written notice from the dealer to the consumer,[1450] and would also require notice under the FCRA if a credit report was used in taking this adverse action.[1451] The fact that the dealer can not extend credit is irrelevant to the question whether the dealer took an adverse action concerning the credit application,[1452] and the fact that no application was forwarded to a creditor is also irrelevant, because the consumer made such an application.[1453] Of course, the dealer admitting that it did not even try to obtain financing bears on the question as to whether the dealer can legitimately cancel the transaction based on a financing contingency.

Similarly, dealers may argue that they do not have to provide a notice under the FCRA, because the dealer has not taken an adverse action based on a credit report. Instead, it has just forwarded the application to creditors, who may look at the consumer's credit report. But typically the dealer will review the consumer's credit report, and, on that basis, may require a co-signer or may submit the application to a subprime lender. Such actions are adverse actions, requiring the dealer to notify the consumer that a credit report has led to such actions.[1454]

5.4.5.3.6 *ECOA and FCRA remedies*

ECOA and FCRA notice violations lead to significant consumer recoveries. For willful FCRA violations, the consumer can recover actual damages or statutory damages not less than $100 or not more than $1000, plus such amount of punitive damages as the court may allow, plus attorney fees.[1455] For any ECOA violation, the consumer can recover actual damages plus punitive damages not greater than $10,000, plus attorney fees. In a class action, maximum punitive damages can not exceed the lesser of $500,000 or 1% of the dealer's net worth.[1456] In addition, these federal claims provide for federal court jurisdiction.

5.4.5.4 Where Consumer Goes Home with a Car, But No Credit Disclosures

A common dealer practice in any yo-yo transaction is to have the consumer sign an installment sales agreement with TIL and state installment sales act disclosures, and then to send the consumer home with the car, but not the paperwork.[1457] If the deal is later re-written with a new contract, the dealer does not want the consumer to have more than one set of disclosures. For one thing, this would allow the consumer to see precisely how much worse the second deal is than the first. Moreover, consumers may attempt to enforce the first agreement if they have a copy of it.[1458] Dealers have also been known to tinker with a car sale's terms even after the consumer signs the installment sales agreement, to make the transaction meet the lender's criteria or to increase the dealer's profit. For example, in one class action, the plaintiffs alleged that, even when consumers requested a copy of the installment agreement, the dealer refused to hand it over until the "loan had been funded."[1459]

Failing to provide the consumer with a copy of TIL disclosures at the time the consumer becomes obligated is a TIL violation.[1460] The Federal Reserve Board in 2002 amended its Commentary to state explicitly (and with retroactive application[1461]) that "the consumer receives a copy to keep at the time the consumer becomes obligated."[1462]

1449 Payne v. Ken Diepholz Ford Lincoln Mercury, Inc., 2004 WL 40631 (N.D. Ill. Jan. 5, 2004).

1450 Treadway v. Gateway Chevrolet Oldsmobile, Inc., 362 F.3d 971 (7th Cir. 2004); Lacey v. William Chrysler Plymouth Inc., 2004 WL 415972 (N.D. Ill. Feb. 23, 2004).

1451 Treadway v. Gateway Chevrolet Oldsmobile, Inc., 362 F.3d 971 (7th Cir. 2004).

1452 *Id.*

1453 *Id.*

1454 Payne v. Ken Diepholz Ford Lincoln Mercury, Inc., 2004 WL 40631 (N.D. Ill. Jan. 5, 2004).

1455 15 U.S.C. § 1681n.

1456 15 U.S.C. § 1691e.

1457 Another variant is to have the consumer sign documents in blank, retained by the dealer. Such a practice is a clear TIL and installment sales act violation. *See* Lacey v. William Chrysler Plymouth Inc., 2004 WL 415972 (N.D. Ill. Feb. 23, 2004).

1458 *See* Daenzer v. Wayland Ford, Inc., 2002 WL 1050209 (E.D. Mich. May 7, 2002).

1459 Daenzer v. Wayland Ford, Inc., 193 F. Supp. 2d 1030 (W.D. Mich. 2002), *later opinion at* 2002 WL 1050209 (E.D. Mich. May 7, 2002). *See also* Knapp v. Americredit Fin. Servs., Inc., 245 F. Supp. 2d 841 (S.D. W. Va. 2003).

1460 *See* Knapp v. Americredit Fin. Servs., Inc., 245 F. Supp. 2d 841 (S.D. W. Va. 2003); Buie v. Palm Springs Motors, Inc., 2001 U.S. Dist. LEXIS 13756 (C.D. Cal. May 14, 2001), *aff'd*, 2002 U.S. App. LEXIS 11046 (C.D. Cal. June 5, 2002).

1461 The FRB stated that this commentary provision does not involve new requirements on creditors, and thus its application is not just prospective. 67 Fed. Reg. 16982 (Apr. 9, 2002) (background).

1462 Official Staff Commentary to Regulation Z, 12 C.F.R. § 226.17(b)-3, 67 Fed. Reg. 16982 (Apr. 9, 2002).

The FRB's explanation of this requirement is even more enlightening:

> Some industry commenters . . . suggest that creditors are required only to give consumers a copy to keep within a reasonable time after consummation. The Board believes such a result would be inconsistent with the regulation's requirement that consumers receive a copy, in a form they may keep, before consummation. Under the final comment as adopted, consumers must receive a copy to keep at the time they become obligated."[1463]

Dealers will argue that disclosures need not be handed over when the consumer takes the car home because the yo-yo sale is conditional, and thus has not been consummated. As such, they argue, disclosures need not be provided the consumer until the financing goes through. But the question is not whether the dealer can still back out of the deal, but whether the consumer is obligated. TIL looks at the transaction from the consumer's perspective.[1464] Since the consumer has become obligated, subject to the dealer canceling, the consumer must receive the disclosures.[1465]

While dealers thus frequently violate TILA, courts are divided as to whether statutory damages are available for a TIL violation involving the failure to provide the consumer with a copy of the disclosures at the time of consummation, and what standards must be met to obtain actual damages. For more on these issues, see NCLC's *Truth in Lending* manual.[1466]

Even where TIL damages prove difficult to obtain, statutory or actual damages may be available under a state installment sales act or UDAP statute. Installment sales acts often require the dealer to provide the consumer with a copy of the credit agreement.[1467] In addition, it should be a UDAP violation to violate TIL and fail to hand over material disclosures to the consumer.[1468]

5.4.5.5 Dealers Almost Always Improperly Structure the Yo-Yo

5.4.5.5.1 How dealers improperly mix and match two different types of transactions

Dealers not satisfied with a one-sided transaction where they can cancel a deal, but the consumer can not, then proceed to structure the yo-yo so that every aspect of the transaction benefits the dealer and not the consumer. In their eagerness to do so, dealers violate various federal and state laws.

When a consumer drives off the lot with the vehicle, conceptually either one of two transactions has occurred. One type of transaction (a condition precedent contract) has the consumer driving off the lot with a vehicle still owned by the dealer (a bailment), and ownership will be transferred when the dealer determines that the conditions precedent to the transaction have been met.[1469] In the other possible type of transaction, vehicle ownership is transferred to the consumer, but this sale (a condition subsequent contract) can be cancelled if a particular condition is not met—if the financing is not approved.

In other words, when the consumer drives off the lot, ownership has to rest either with the dealer or the consumer—ownership can not be in a legal limbo. Dealers, on the other hand, structure yo-yos to fully comply with neither of these scenarios. Instead, they create a legal mish-mash providing the most benefits to themselves. Dealers intermingle and intentionally confuse two very distinct transactions—a condition precedent and a condition subsequent sale.[1470] The confusion optimizes profits and convenience for the dealer, but it also leads to a number of law violations.

1463 67 Fed. Reg. 16982 (Apr. 9, 2002) (Proposed Revisions Section 226.17(b) Time of Disclosures). *See also* Knapp v. Americredit Fin. Servs., Inc., 245 F. Supp. 2d 841 (S.D. W. Va. 2003); Daenzer v. Wayland Ford, Inc., 2002 WL 1050209 (E.D. Mich. May 7, 2002). *Cf.* Castro v. Union Nissan, Inc., 2002 WL 1466810 (N.D. Ill. July 8, 2002); Daenzer v. Wayland Ford, Inc., 193 F. Supp. 2d 1030 (W.D. Mich. 2002).

1464 *See* Nigh v. Koons Buick Pontiac GMC, Inc., 319 F.3d 119 (4th Cir. 2003), *cert. granted on other issues*, 124 S. Ct. 1144 (2004); Fairley v. Turan-Foley Imports, Inc., 65 F.3d 475 (5th Cir. 1995); Cody v. Community Loan Corp., 606 F.2d 499 (5th Cir. 1979). *See also* Buie v. Palm Springs Motors, Inc., 2001 U.S. Dist. LEXIS 13756 (C.D. Cal. May 14, 2001).

1465 *See* Bragg v. Bill Heard Chevrolet, Inc., 374 F.3d 1060 (11th Cir. 2004); Nigh v. Koons Buck Pontiac GMC, Inc., 319 F.3d 119 (4th Cir. 2003), *cert. granted on other issues*, 124 S. Ct. 1144 (2004).

1466 National Consumer Law Center, Truth in Lending §§ 4.3.6, 8.5, 8.6.2.3, 8.6.5.3.4 (5th ed. 2003 and Supp.). *See also* Daenzer v. Wayland Ford, Inc., 193 F. Supp. 2d 1030 (W.D. Mich. 2002); Wojcik v. Courtesy Auto Sales, Inc., 2002 WL 31663298 (D. Neb. Nov. 25, 2002); Graham v. RRR, L.L.C., 202 F. Supp. 2d 483 (E.D. Va. 2002), *aff'd*, 2003 WL 139432 (4th Cir. Jan. 21, 2003) (unpublished, citation limited).

1467 *See* Mich. Comp. Laws § 566.302. *See also* Daenzer v. Wayland Ford, Inc., 2002 WL 1050209 (E.D. Mich. May 7, 2002), *earlier opinion at* 193 F. Supp. 2d 1030 (W.D. Mich. 2002).

1468 *See* Daenzer v. Wayland Ford, Inc., 2002 WL 1050209 (E.D. Mich. May 7, 2002), *earlier op. at* 193 F. Supp. 2d 1030 (W.D. Mich. 2002).

1469 Peak v. Ted Russell Enterprises, Inc., 2000 Tenn. App. LEXIS 120 (Feb. 28, 2000).

1470 *See* Jasper v. New Rogers Pontiac, Inc., 1999 U.S. Dist. LEXIS 17578 (N.D. Ill. Nov. 4, 1999) (discussing the two types of conditions in a spot delivery case). *Cf.* Allen v. Lynn Hickey Dodge, Inc., 39 P.3d 781 (Okla. 2001) (court can not decide on summary judgment whether ownership remained in the dealer or had been transferred to the consumer).

5.4.5.5.2 *Is it an illegal condition precedent or an illegal condition subsequent yo-yo?*

In challenging a yo-yo sale, it is imperative to allege all possible law violations, without assuming whether the condition is either precedent or subsequent. To allege that the dealer's conduct in a condition precedent transaction violates certain laws relating to such a transaction invites the dealer to argue that the transaction is a condition subsequent one, where such conduct is allowed.[1471] Instead, the consumer should make allegations in the alternative. If the court finds that a transaction is not a condition precedent, allege the dealer violated laws related to condition subsequent transactions, and *vice versa.*

Nevertheless, it is usually prudent to have some kind of idea whether a transaction is really a condition subsequent yo-yo with features of a condition precedent yo-yo, or vice versa. For example, where a court rules definitively that the transaction is a condition subsequent, this simplifies the consumer's proof problems, having only to show that the transaction does not comply with that form of transfer.

Some contingency clauses are drafted in such a way to be clearly a condition subsequent or precedent agreement. For example, a clause that provides that the dealer can elect to rescind a contract if the seller is unable to assign the note clearly states that there is a contact, and that one party, but not the other has the option of rescinding the contract if a certain event occurs.[1472] On the other hand, a clause that states that the contract becomes effective only when an event occurs would be a condition precedent agreement.

Another factor will be whether ownership has passed to the consumer, making it a condition subsequent transaction. Where it is ambiguous whether title has passed to the consumer, courts will generally find that title has passed.[1473] This is reinforced by UCC § 2-401(1): "Any retention or reservation by the seller of title (property) in goods shipped or delivered to the buyer is limited in effect to a reservation of a security interest." Similarly, UCC § 1-201(37) states: "The retention or reservation of title by a seller of goods notwithstanding shipment or delivery to the buyer is limited in effect to a reservation of a 'security interest.' "

But this UCC language is not definitive. Obviously, where a dealer lets a consumer take a test drive, it has not delivered the vehicle to a buyer, and title has not passed. Moreover, UCC § 2-401(2) seems to allow the parties to explicitly agree when title passes to the buyer. But the presumption under the UCC is that delivery of the vehicle to a buyer leaves the seller only with a security interest, and that title passing is not contingent on subsequent events. Because title has passed, the transaction is a condition subsequent transaction. But a number of states have an opposite rule, that ownership does not pass on to the consumer until the actual title document is signed over to the consumer.[1474] In that case, the transaction would be a condition precedent one unless the title is actually signed over.

A third criterion will be whether the dealer's conduct is more consistent with a condition subsequent or precedent agreement. For example, a transaction is more like a condition subsequent one where, as of the day the consumer takes the car home, interest begins accruing, insurance and service contract polices begin operating, and the dealer sells the consumer's trade-in.

5.4.5.5.3 *Dealer practices inconsistent with a condition precedent transaction*

In a condition precedent sale, the dealer is the owner and, until the sale is finalized, the consumer's rights and obligations as to the vehicle are those of a bailee. Dealers often engage in the following practices inconsistent with this relationship:

1. *Earning interest before the loan is extended.* Check to see when the loan documents state that interest charges began accruing. In a condition precedent sale, until the assignee agrees to purchase the paper, no sale has occurred. The consumer does not have title in the car, and the consumer has not yet borrowed any money. The dealer still owns the car. Consequently, the finance charges on the loan should not be accruing. No loan proceeds have been disbursed, so no interest should be charged on those proceeds. To do so may be usurious under state law and should certainly be a UDAP violation.

2. *Disclosure of loan term and APR.* Not only can the dealer not charge interest on a loan before the loan proceeds are disbursed, but it can not disclose the loan terms as if the loan had been disbursed as of the date the consumer drives away with the car, when that is not the case. Instead TIL disclosures should be labeled estimates because the loan's starting date has not been determined and the precise APR can not yet be computed.[1475] This is because the first

1471 Leguillou v. Lynch Ford, Inc., 2000 U.S. Dist. LEXIS 1668 (N.D. Ill. Feb. 10, 2000); Jasper v. New Rogers Pontiac, Inc., 1999 U.S. Dist. LEXIS 17578 (N.D. Ill. Nov. 4, 1999).

1472 Buie v. Palm Springs Motors, Inc., 2001 U.S. Dist. LEXIS 13756 (C.D. Cal. 2001), *aff'd*, 2002 U.S. App. LEXIS 11046 (C.D. Cal. June 5, 2002).

1473 *See* McCarthy v. Imported Cars of Maryland, Inc., 230 B.R. 466 (Bankr. D.D.C. 1999); American States Ins. Co. v. Farmers Alliance Mut. Ins. Co., 20 P.3d 743 (Kan. Ct. App. 2001) (looking to the parties' intent); *see also* Medico Leasing Co. v. Smith, 457 P.2d 548 (Okla. 1969) (ownership can pass even where title documents not completed).

1474 Ohio Rev. Code § 4505.04(A); Tex. Transp. Code § 501.073; *see also* Brockman v. Regency Fin. Corp., 124 S.W.3d 43 (Mo. Ct. App. 2004); Saturn of Kings Automall, Inc. v. Mike Albert Leasing, Inc., 751 N.E.2d 1019 (Ohio 2001); Braucher v. Mariemont Auto, 2002 WL 1393570 (Ohio Ct. App. June 28, 2002); Morey v. Page, 802 S.W.2d 779 (Tex. App. 1990).

1475 *See* National Consumer Law Center, Truth in Lending § 4.4 (5th ed. 2003 and Supp.); *see also* Davis v. Regional Acceptance Corp., 2002 U.S. Dist. LEXIS 16775 (E.D. Va. Sept. 5, 2002);

payment period is now shorter than originally assumed. Since the finance charges stay constant and the length of the loan has decreased, the APR increases from the rate initially disclosed.[1476] This is perhaps easiest to see where the original loan is not approved and the consumer and dealer agree to a new loan two weeks later. The new loan should be written based on being consummated two weeks later, and the payment schedule and computation of the APR all should assume the finance charges start accruing on that later date.

3. *Shortening of a service contract's term and excessive finance charges relating to that contract.* Service contracts purchased by consumers will be for a fixed time period, and that period will begin when the contract is signed. But, if the consumer does not own the vehicle, and there is no bailment agreement requiring consumers to repair the vehicle, the service contract term should not begin until the consumer actually owns the vehicle. In addition, the consumer will be paying finance charges on the prepaid service contract before the service contract should actually take effect.

4. *Excess insurance premiums and related finance charges.* Dealers will also start the term of various insurance policies from the date the consumer drives off with the car, instead of the date the consumer is the owner—such as GAP, credit, and physical damage insurance. The dealer may even force place insurance before the consumer actually owns the car. Any insurance sold in conjunction with the sale should have a start date, not as of the date the car is delivered to the consumer, but as of the date the condition is met and the consumer becomes the vehicle's owner. Premiums should be calculated based on the date title is transferred, not the date the car is delivered. The consumer's policy should not cover damage to a vehicle where the dealer still owns the vehicle, and the consumer should not pay credit or GAP insurance for periods before the loan is even disbursed. The dealer will have its own insurance policy, and that policy will cover claims made until actual ownership is transferred to the consumer.[1477] Such excessive insurance premiums have both UDAP and TIL consequences,[1478] and may also violate state insurance or credit law. And of course, the consumer should not pay for finance charges to purchase this insurance before the insurance goes into effect.

5. *Improper treatment of consumer trade-in.* If a sale is truly a condition precedent transaction, then the dealer has no right to sell the consumer's trade-in until the sale of the new car has been finalized. The trade-in is provided to the dealer on the condition the sale goes through. The consumer has not separately sold the consumer's existing vehicle to the dealer; the sale is part of the purchase of the new vehicle. To sell the trade-in before the sale of the new car has been finalized would be conversion, and also a UDAP violation.[1479]

6. *Improper use of temporary tags.* Dealers putting temporary tags on a vehicle in the consumer's name or giving the consumer a temporary registration or title creates the false impression that the consumer has purchased the vehicle, preventing the consumer from trying to back out of the sale. Such practices may also be illegal. Temporary plates under state law are usually only available where title has been transferred, which is not the case in a condition precedent sale. For example, the Maryland Motor Vehicle Administration authorizes dealers to issue temporary tags only to bona fide purchasers—those for whom all aspects of the deal are complete.[1480] In Virginia, a temporary certificate can be issued if the dealer is unable to deliver a certificate of title for reasons beyond the dealer's control. But a federal court has ruled that not wanting to turn over title because of the yo-yo sale is not such a reason beyond the dealer's control.[1481] More importantly, the Virginia Code states that issuance of a temporary certificate of ownership shall have

---

cf. Payne v. Ken Diepholz Ford Lincoln Mercury, Inc., 2004 WL 40631 (N.D. Ill. Jan. 5, 2004); Williams v. Rizza Chevrolet-Geo, Inc., 2000 U.S. Dist. LEXIS 2695 (N.D. Ill. Mar. 1, 2000) (Truth in Lending class action certified in spot delivery case); Williams v. First Government Mortgage & Investors Corp., 974 F. Supp. 17 (D.D.C. 1997), *aff'd*, 225 F.3d 738 (D.C. Cir. 2000) (TIL claim survives motion to dismiss). *But cf.* Janikowski v. Lynch Ford Inc., 210 F.3d 765 (7th Cir. 2000) (no TIL violation where consumer entered into two contracts on succeeding days and each disclosure was accurate); Graham v. RRR, L.L.C., 202 F. Supp. 2d 483 (E.D. Va. 2002) (court may be treating transaction as a condition subsequent sale), *aff'd*, 2003 WL 139432 (4th Cir. Jan. 21, 2003) (unpublished, citation limited); Nigh v. Koons Buick Pontiac GMC, Inc., 143 F. Supp. 2d 535 (E.D. Va. 2001) (court does not require disclosures be marked as estimates, but does not find whether transaction is condition precedent or subsequent sale), *aff'd on other grounds*, 319 F.3d 119 (4th Cir. 2003), *cert. granted on other issues*, 124 S. Ct. 1144 (2004).

1476 *See* National Consumer Law Center, Truth in Lending § 4.6.4.6 (5th ed. 2003 and Supp.). Whether this is a TIL violation will depend on whether the difference in the APR is within TIL's tolerances and whether the irregular first period can be disregarded under TIL rules in calculation of the APR.

1477 *See* N.C. Gen. Stat. § 20-75.1 (where sale contingent on financing, and title will transfer after financing is approved, dealer's insurance policy covers the vehicle; consumer's insurance policy is only effective with the transfer of title); *cf.* Tyler Car & Truck Center v. Empire Fire & Marine Ins. Co., 2 S.W.3d 482 (Tex. App. 1999) (ownership had transferred, so dealer's insurer no longer liable).

1478 *See* National Consumer Law Center, Truth in Lending § 4.4.6.5 (5th ed. 2003 and Supp.); *cf.* Compton v. Altavista Motors, Inc., 121 F. Supp. 2d 932 (W.D. Va. 2000).

1479 *See* Samuels v. King Motor Co., 782 So. 2d 489 (Fla. Dist. Ct. App. 2001); Hensley v. Paul Miller Ford, 508 S.W.2d 759 (Ky. 1974). *But cf.* Johnson v. Grossinger Motorcorp, Inc., 324 Ill. App. 3d 354, 753 N.E.2d 431 (2001) (where trade-in was part of valid condition subsequent sale, and dealer rightfully cancelled the sale, dealer did not commit conversion by selling trade-in before condition subsequent occurred).

1480 Maryland Motor Vehicle Administration, "*Spot Delivery*"-"*Fronting*"-"*MacArthur Statement*" *etc*, Bulletin D-11 98-01, Clearinghouse No. 52,142 (Nov. 30, 1998).

1481 *In re* Field, 219 B.R. 115 (E.D. Va. 1998), *aff'd without op.*, 173 F.3d 424 (4th Cir. 1999).

the effect of vesting ownership in the consumer.[1482] If the consumer owns the vehicle, then the sale is not a condition precedent, but a condition subsequent transaction. Also look at any paperwork related to the temporary tag. In many states, the dealer must specify the date of sale. If the vehicle has been sold, the dealer can not claim the sale is not finalized pending the condition precedent.

7. *Improper use of dealer plates.* In some states, dealers can not allow consumers to use the dealer's plates on a vehicle for a lengthy period of time. For example, Maryland allows a such use of dealer plates only for a period of ten days from the date of delivery.[1483]

8. *Dealer misrepresentation as to consumer's cancellation rights.* Massachusetts UDAP regulations require that, in any condition precedent sale, notice be provided to the consumer that the consumer can cancel the contract and receive a full refund until the dealer accepts the contract.[1484] Failure to make the notice or abide by its terms would be a UDAP violation. Even where state law does not explicitly state that the consumer can cancel a condition precedent sale, the dealer can not misrepresent the consumer's rights to cancel. For example, the dealer can not say the consumer now owns the car and thus can not back out of the deal. The consumer does not own the car. Instead, the consumer, at most has promised to purchase the car. Breach of such a promise at best gives the dealer the right to sue for damages, but the consumer has every right to return the car. No title has transferred.

5.4.5.5.4 UDAP violations in condition precedent transactions

As set out in § 5.4.5.5.3, *supra*, there are many possible law violations in a condition precedent yo-yo, and many of these involve UDAP claims. Dealers may argue that a cancelled condition precedent yo-yo sale means there has been no sale, and the consumer can not thus bring a UDAP claim against the dealer. The consumer's response to this defense will vary with the language of the relevant state UDAP statute. The defense is clearly groundless where the UDAP statute applies to practices in trade or commerce, or to "solicitations to supply products" or where the consumer "seeks" to purchase goods.[1485] For example, Ohio's UDAP statute applies to a "sale, lease, . . . or other transfer of an item of goods," and an appellate court has found a cancelled yo-yo to be an "other transfer" even though ownership never passed to the consumer.[1486]

Even if a state UDAP statute's literal language only applies to where a sale has occurred, the UDAP statute should still apply. This is because courts are liberal in their interpretations of a UDAP statute's scope, and find that the statute interpreted as a whole, can be extended to cover non-sale transactions.[1487] In addition, as set out in § 5.4.5.5.3, *supra*, the supposedly condition precedent transaction has many of the features of a sale. In any event, a common law fraud and other claims are generally still available.[1488]

5.4.5.5.5 Condition subsequent sales often violate federal and state titling requirements

In condition subsequent yo-yos, dealers play fast and loose with federal and state titling requirements, because it is inconvenient for them to follow the law. In a condition subsequent sale, by definition, ownership passes to the consumer. If the transaction is legally canceled, ownership transfers back to the dealer. Each of these transfers must be evidenced by signatures on a title document, so that these transfers become a permanent part of the vehicle's title chain. Dealers flouting these legal requirements are then whipsawed. The court will either treat the transaction as a condition precedent sale (which will lead to a finding of various law violations set out in § 5.4.5.5.3), or find that the dealer has violated federal and state titling requirements.

These titling requirements are different for new and used vehicles. For a new vehicle, the dealer only signs over the Manufacturer's Statement of Origin (MSO) to the consumer, because there is as yet no title issued for the vehicle. Federal law does set out requirements as to MSO assignment, so state law will determine if the dealer's failure to physically sign over the MSO to the consumer is a violation. It is no excuse for failing to assign over the MSO that ownership later transfers back to the dealer.

Also examine the subsequent history of a new vehicle. A title search will indicate the name and address of a subsequent purchaser, and contacting that purchaser will determine whether the vehicle subsequently was sold as used, or whether the dealer violated the UDAP statute by selling it as new.[1489] Also explore the paperwork of that subsequent sale to see if the dealer used an MSO to transfer title. If so, it never assigned the MSO to the first consumer or it illegally acquired a second MSO for the same vehicle.[1490]

The dealer gets into even more trouble when it fails to

1482 Va. Code Ann. § 46.2-1542.

1483 Maryland Motor Vehicle Administration, *"Spot Delivery"-"Fronting"-"MacArthur Statement" etc*, Bulletin D-11 98-01, Clearinghouse No. 52,142 (Nov. 30, 1998).

1484 940 Code Mass. Regs. § 5.04(2)(e).

1485 *See* § 2.2.3.1, *supra*.

1486 Braucher v. Mariemont Auto, 2002 WL 1393570 (Ohio Ct. App. June 28, 2002), *review denied*, 777 N.E.2d 278 (Ohio 2002).

1487 *See* Ch. 2, note 368, *supra*.

1488 Bates v. William Chevrolet/Geo, Inc., 785 N.E.2d 53 (Ill. App. Ct. 2003).

1489 *See* § 5.4.6.3, *infra*.

1490 Dealers may tell manufacturers that they have lost the original MSO and need a duplicate. Such a practice to hide the first MSO is clearly fraudulent. Nevertheless, it is probably more common for a dealer never to sign over the MSO to the first consumer, anticipating the possible yo-yo.

follow titling requirements for a used vehicle. Federal law requires that, whenever ownership of a used vehicle is transferred, that certain disclosures be made in writing on a title document, signed by both the transferor and the transferee.[1491] That transfer then permanently becomes part of the vehicle's official chain of title. Federal law does not specify the time period within which the title document must be signed over, but there are no exceptions to the requirement that it must be signed over whenever ownership transfers.

Consequently, in a condition subsequent used car sale, the dealer must sign over title documents to the consumer. When the dealer cancels the sale, it must either obtain the consumer's signature on title documents transferring ownership back to the dealer or obtain a repossession title from the state. Even if the dealer seizes the vehicle almost immediately, the dealer can not "skip" the consumer's ownership in the title chain. It must still evidence the transaction on the title documents as one where title went from the dealer to consumer to dealer.

Whether the dealer complied can be easily checked by a title search on the vehicle. Where the title does not show both transfers, the dealer could have resorted to any number of tricks. One approach is to delay transfer of the title document to the consumer until the dealer decides the sale is final, and then bring the consumer back in to sign the title document at that later date. If the sale is canceled, the dealer never assigns over the title.

But this approach is risky for the dealer, because bringing the consumer back to sign the title transfer documents risks the consumer viewing this as an opportunity to back out of a bad deal. One solution for the dealer is to simply forge the consumer's signature when it decides to transfer title to the consumer. Some dealers use a more sophisticated scam. When they hand the consumer the car keys, they have the consumer sign a power of attorney or reassignment form, instead of the actual title. The dealer physically retains this document (allegedly to handle application of a new title for the consumer), and then destroys the document if the deal is canceled. If the deal goes through, the dealer uses this document to transfer title. This approach may involve two different law violations: dealers may violate strict requirements about when and how such powers of attorney or reassignment forms can be used in lieu of the actual title,[1492] and destruction of the document is clearly improper.

Failure to properly evidence the changes of ownership on title documents violates the federal Motor Vehicle Information and Cost Savings Act (MVICSA), resulting in treble damages or $1500 minimum damages, attorney fees, and federal court jurisdiction.[1493] MVICSA violations require intent to defraud, and such intent can be shown from the knowing MVICSA violation in aid of the yo-yo scheme. Nevertheless, courts are split as to whether the intent to defraud must relate to mileage misrepresentations.[1494] But even where a court requires such a nexus, the consumer can argue that the title skipping scheme is directly related to odometer misrepresentations. By skipping title, the dealer hides the fact from subsequent purchasers and government enforcement officials that the first consumer purchaser never certified to the dealer that the odometer mileage was accurate, and so the dealer does not know whether that consumer turned back the odometer.[1495]

The MVICSA violation should also be a UDAP violation, with or without proof of intent. In addition, the dealer, by keeping the consumer's ownership hidden in either a new or used car yo-yo, will be misrepresenting to subsequent purchasers the number of prior owners, which is a UDAP violation and fraudulent.[1496]

State law may provide additional requirements beyond those found in the MVICSA. For example, it may specify when title must be signed over when vehicle ownership is transferred.[1497] In some states, a transfer without a simultaneous signing over of the title or manufacturer's statement of origin is not effective, so that ownership is not transferred until that event.[1498] In that case, a yo-yo transaction should be viewed as a condition precedent. Otherwise, the dealer's

1491 *See* 49 C.F.R. § 580.5; National Consumer Law Center, Automobile Fraud Ch. 3 (2d ed. 2003 and Supp.).

1492 *See* National Consumer Law Center, Automobile Fraud Ch. 3 (2d ed. 2003 and Supp.).

1493 *Id.* at Ch. 5. Both the first consumer and a subsequent purchaser would have claims for at least $1500 and attorney fees, based on this MVICSA violation, because the MVICSA has a very liberal standing requirement. *Id.* § 5.2.1.

1494 *Id.* at Ch. 3.

1495 *See* Tuckish v. Pompano Motor Co., 2004 WL 2203769 (S.D. Fla. Sept. 23, 2004) (discussing intent to defraud where not related to odometer disclosure and then discussing how allegation of Canadian origin relates to conversion of miles to kilometers on the odometer).

1496 § 5.4.6.4, *infra.*

1497 *See* Conn. Gen. Stat. § 14-179 (at the time of delivery, seller must execute an assignment and warranty of title to transferee); American States Ins. Co. v. Farmers Alliance Mut. Ins. Co., 20 P.3d 743 (Kan. Ct. App. 2001) (Kansas law requires title to be transferred within 30 days of sale); National Consumer Law Center, Automobile Fraud Appx. C (2d ed. 2003 and Supp.). *See also* Ed Bozarth Chevrolet, Inc., 77 P.3d 1009 (Kan. Ct. App. 2003) (where Kansas law allows seller 30 days to transfer title, where parties so agree, yo-yo sale can be found consistent with that requirement where sale canceled before 30 day period expired). In Virginia, if for reasons beyond the dealer's control, the dealer can not produce the title when the vehicle is sold and turned over to the consumer, then the dealer shall execute a temporary certificate of ownership, and a copy shall be in the consumer's possession at all times when the consumer operates the vehicle. If a title is not produced within 30 days, the consumer can cancel the transaction. Va. Code Ann. § 46.2-1542. *See* Nigh v. Koons Buick Pontiac GMC, Inc., 319 F.3d 119 (4th Cir. 2003) (30 days had not expired, so consumer could not rescind), *aff'd on other grounds*, 319 F.3d 119 (4th Cir. 2003), *cert. granted on other issues*, 124 S. Ct. 1144 (2004).

1498 *See* Ohio Rev. Code § 4505.04(A). *See also* Braucher v. Mariemont Auto, 2002 WL 1393570 (Ohio Ct. App. June 28, 2002).

failure to transfer title when legally required is common law fraud and a UDAP violation.[1499]

Do not confuse state law that requires title to be transferred at the time of sale with state law that provides a certain number of days after the sale for the consumer to apply for a new title or to register the vehicle. The signing over of the old title must be done within one period. At a later date, the old title, now in the consumer's name, must be turned in for a new title, also in the consumer's name.

It is also helpful to check whether the dealer has complied with state law relating to temporary tags and the like. In Virginia, a temporary certificate can be issued if the dealer is unable to deliver a certificate of title for reasons beyond the dealer's control. But a federal court has ruled that not wanting to turn over title because of the yo-yo sale is not such a reason beyond the dealer's control.[1500]

5.4.5.5.6 *Where dealer seeks a repossession title after recovering a yo-yo vehicle*

Where dealers sign over the actual title to a consumer and then decides to cancel the deal, the dealer needs not only to recover the vehicle, but also legal title to the vehicle. It often does so through a repossession title. But this is complicated because, when transferring title to the consumer, dealers usually will have placed a lien on the car's title not in their own name, but in the name of the expected assignee. The dealer, when it repossesses the car, will try to obtain a repossession title in its own name, instead of in the name listed on the title as the lienholder. The dealer may even resort to forging or falsifying the lienholder's signature on documents to get a repossession title in the dealer's own name.

A good indicator of such hanky-panky is a repossession title application that asks that the title be sent to the dealer's address where the lender is listed as the lienholder. Also check whether the individual specified in the application actually works for the lender or is a dealer employee. Try to determine if the "transfer" of the repossession title from the lender to the dealer was in fact forged by the dealer. This type of misconduct may result in revocation of the dealer's license, and will certainly sour the lender's view of the dealer.

1499 *In re* Jenkins, 249 B.R. 532 (Bankr. W.D. Mo. 2000); Renner v. Derin Acquisition Corp., 111 Ohio App. 3d 326, 676 N.E.2d 151 (1996). *See also* Griffin v. Security Pacific Auto. Fin. Servs. Corp., 33 F. Supp. 2d 926 (D. Kan. 1998) (plaintiffs had UDAP claim against seller despite fact that sale was void because of failure to deliver title); Antle v. Reynolds, 15 S.W.3d 762 (Mo. App. 2000) (same); Mont. Admin. R. § 2.61.204(14); Blevins v. Wright's Fin. Servs., Inc., No. 95-CVH-2435 (Ohio Mun. Ct. 1996); Franklin v. State, 631 S.W.2d 519 (Tex. App. 1982).

1500 *In re* Field, 219 B.R. 115 (E.D. Va. 1998), *aff'd without op.*, 173 F.3d 424 (4th Cir. 1999).

5.4.5.5.7 *Condition subsequent sales must comply with UCC Article 9*

In a condition subsequent sale, the dealer's rights in recovering the vehicle are specified by UCC Article 9. This is the case whether the consumer returns the vehicle voluntarily or the dealer repossesses the vehicle. The consumer, by definition, is the owner, and the dealer is, at best, a secured creditor.[1501] Even if the dealer states that it is repossessing pursuant to the contingency clause and not the security interest, this makes no difference for purposes of Article 9. Article 9 applies whenever a creditor attempts to reserve rights in collateral owned by a consumer, no matter the form or substance of that reservation of rights.[1502]

UCC Article 9 requirements as to recovery of the vehicle are set out in detail in NCLC's *Repossessions and Foreclosures* (5th ed. 2002 and Supp.). In a nutshell, any repossession can not breach the peace, which means that it can not be accomplished over the consumer's objections. In some states, right to cure laws require as much as a thirty-day notice before the dealer can repossess the vehicle. After recovering the vehicle, the dealer must send the consumer notice of sale, and conduct any sale in a commercially reasonable manner. The dealer can not sell the vehicle to itself, and any subsequent sale of the vehicle for a higher price than that paid by the consumer may require the dealer to pay the consumer a surplus. Article 9 violations lead to statutory damages of the initial finance charge plus 10% of the amount financed, as set out in the original contract that the dealer cancels.

5.4.5.5.8 *Truth in Lending violations in a condition subsequent sales*

Unlike a condition precedent sale, in a condition subsequent sale, the TIL disclosure is not an estimate, and thus is not disclosed with an "e."[1503] It is the transaction as described in the disclosure form—the finance charge begins accruing on the date of the sale, because the consumer

1501 *Cf.* Williams v. First Government Mortgage & Investors Corp., 974 F. Supp. 17 (D.D.C. 1997), *aff'd*, 225 F.3d 738 (D.C. Cir. 2000) (wrongful repossession claim survives motion to dismiss). *But see* Leguillou v. Lynch Ford, Inc., 2000 U.S. Dist. LEXIS 1668 (N.D. Ill. Feb. 10, 2000) (where consumer never alleged that consumer was the vehicle's owner under a condition subsequent contract, court found the consumer never owned the vehicle, and thus no security interest created).

1502 *See* National Consumer Law Center, Repossessions and Foreclosures § 2.1.2 (5th ed. 2002 and Supp.). *See also* McCarthy v. Imported Cars of Maryland, Inc. (*In re* Johnson), 230 B.R. 466 (Bankr. D.D.C. 1999) (citing U.C.C. § 2-401(2), the seller, at best, retains a security interest in the vehicle. Since the dealer had not perfected its security interest, it lost its priority when the consumer filed for bankruptcy).

1503 *See* Leguillou v. Lynch Ford, Inc., 2000 U.S. Dist. LEXIS 1668 (N.D. Ill. Feb. 10, 2000); Jasper v. New Rogers Pontiac, Inc., 1999 U.S. Dist. LEXIS 17578 (N.D. Ill. Nov. 4, 1999).

obtains title on that date.[1504] Of course, if the agreement specifies that the dealer can unilaterally require an additional down payment or otherwise change the credit terms in its attempt to obtain financing, with the consumer not retaining the right to cancel the agreement based on those changed terms, then the disclosures must be marked with an "e."[1505]

Of more significance, dealers frequently fail to provide the consumer copies of the Truth in Lending disclosures when the consumer leaves with the vehicle. As set out in § 5.4.5.4, *supra*, whether a sale involves a condition subsequent or precedent, this practice violates TIL and state installment sales statutes. But there is even less of a defense if it is a condition subsequent sale.

5.4.5.6 Trade-Ins and Deposits

When the dealer cancels a sale, it will often try to force the consumer to keep the purchased vehicle, but at a higher financing rate. One of its most effective tactics will be to refuse to return the consumer's trade-in, leaving the consumer without a vehicle. As described earlier, it is illegal to sell a trade-in where a transaction involves a condition precedent.[1506] In addition, a number of state statutes explicitly state that in *any* contingent sale, the dealer can not sell the trade-in until the deal is finalized.[1507] Moreover, the representation that the trade-in has been sold is usually false, and it is certainly a UDAP violation to misrepresent that a vehicle has already been sold where it has not. Techniques for determining if the vehicle has actually been sold are described in an earlier subsection.[1508]

Nor can a dealer refuse to return a trade-in until the consumer reimburses the dealer for the amount the dealer paid off the consumer's lender on the trade-in. The dealer paid off the lien at its own risk where a vehicle sale was contingent on financing being approved, and its paying off the lien did not provide a basis to retain possession of the trade-in.[1509] At best, the dealer might have a *quantum meruit* claim against the consumer, but the possibility of such a claim does not justify retention of the consumer's property. Note that retention of the consumer's property is not only a UDAP violation, but should lead to various tort claims as well. For example, in Indiana, such an action has been found to fit under the state's criminal conversion statute, and the Indiana Crime Victim's Relief Act provides for treble damages and attorney fees for such conversion.[1510] Punitive damages should also be available under tort theories in many states.

Dealers sometimes seek to keep the down payment or trade-in as "damages" for the failed yo-yo transaction. State law may either prohibit or limit this, declaring that the consumer can not be charged if the deal falls through and all deposits must be refunded.[1511] These state statutes and interpretations prevent the seller from retaining a portion of the down payment as liquidated damages or rent for the consumer's use of the vehicle.[1512]

Even without such statutory restriction, it is hard to see how dealers can justify penalizing the consumer because the dealer has failed to find a buyer for its own paper.[1513] The Fifth Circuit has upheld $150,000 of a $700,000 punitive damages verdict against a mobile home dealer who took a $4000 deposit from a consumer, telling her it would be refunded if financing could not be arranged, but then refused to return it.[1514]

In another case, the dealer complained that the consumer was getting a "free ride" for the time the vehicle was in the consumer's possession. The court noted that the dealer could have included in the agreement a rental fee for those days the vehicle was used by the consumer, if the transaction was subsequently cancelled. Moreover, the dealer did not demand the vehicle's return as soon as financing fell through, but attempted to negotiate a new deal while the consumer retained possession.[1515] Utah and Oregon that allows the dealer reimbursement based on an allowance per mile times the number of miles driven.[1516]

1504 *Id.*

1505 Cardenas v. Classic Chevrolet, Inc., 2000 U.S. Dist. LEXIS 16873 (N.D. Ill. Nov. 3, 2000); *cf.* Williams v. Thomas Pontiac-GMC-Nissan-Hyundai, 1999 U.S. Dist. LEXIS 15045 (N.D. Ill. Sept. 22, 1999).

1506 *See* § 5.4.4.3, *supra.*

1507 *See id.*

1508 *See* § 5.4.4.4.3, *supra.*

1509 Palmer Dodge, Inc. v. Long, 791 N.E.2d 788 (Ind. Ct. App. 2003).

1510 Palmer Dodge, Inc. v. Long, 791 N.E.2d 788 (Ind. Ct. App. 2003). A violation of Ind. Code § 35-43-4-3 (criminal conversion) can be civilly remedied under Ind. Code § 34-24-3-1.

1511 *See, e.g.,* The Arizona Attorney General's Automobile Advertising Guidelines; Colo. Rev. Stat. § 6-1-708; 815 Ill. Comp. Stat. § 505/2C; La. Rev. Stat. § 32:1254(N)(3)(f); Maryland Motor Vehicle Administration, "*Spot Delivery*"-"*Fronting*"-"*MacArthur Statement*" *etc*, Bulletin D-11 98-01, Clearinghouse No. 52,142 (Nov. 30, 1998); Or. Stat. § 646.877; Utah Stat. § 41-3-401; Va. Code § 46.2-1530(12); Wash Rev. Code § 46.70.180(4).

1512 *See* Castro v. Union Nissan, Inc., 2002 WL 1466810 (N.D. Ill. July 8, 2002). But see the discussion at the end of this subsection of the Oregon and Utah statutes that provide the dealer with an amount based on the number of miles driven.

1513 Violette v. P.A. Days, Inc., 2002 U.S. Dist. LEXIS 23246 (S.D. Ohio Oct. 18, 2002); Bates v. William Chevrolet/Geo, Inc., 785 N.E.2d 53 (Ill. App. Ct. 2003) (deceptive to refuse to return the trade-in); *see* Samuels v. King Motor Co., 782 So. 2d 489 (Fla. Dist. Ct. App. 2001) (UDAP violation to state purchase contingent on financing, but then to dispose of vehicle before contingency resolved, and to refuse to compensate consumer for trade-in).

1514 Watson v. Johnson Mobile Homes, 284 F.3d 568 (5th Cir. 2002).

1515 Rucker v. Sheehy Alexandria, Inc., 244 F. Supp. 2d 618 (E.D. Va. 2003).

1516 Or. Stat. § 646.877; Utah Stat. § 41-3-401.

5.4.5.7 Misrepresentations After Yo-Yo Cancellation

5.4.5.7.1 Re-negotiation misrepresentations

In the subsequent negotiation over new terms for the vehicle sale, after the original credit sale has been cancelled, the dealer can engage in all kinds of misrepresentations. It can certainly be found deceptive for a dealer to represent that if a consumer does not sign another installment agreement, that the vehicle would be considered stolen.[1517] Conversely, the dealer may represent that the consumer has no choice but to sign another, less advantageous deal. On the contrary, the consumer has every right at that point instead to walk away from the deal.[1518]

It should also be deceptive for a dealer to represent that a certain replacement financing is the best the dealer could find where the consumer could in fact qualify for less expensive financing through that dealer. A dealer's attempt to increase the purchase price as part of the new financing or to eliminate a promised rebate should be a UDAP violation, since the sale price has already been finalized and what is only at issue is the financing.[1519] This increase in the cash price could also be viewed as a hidden finance charge, that must be disclosed as a finance charge in the TIL disclosure and reflected in the APR.

5.4.5.7.2 Backdating documentation of a subsequent sale

In many cancelled yo-yo sales, the dealer re-writes the transaction at a higher interest rate or a higher down payment, or may even switch the vehicle itself. Any such subsequent transaction occurs on the date of that subsequent transaction, and is not retroactively effective from the date of the first transaction that has now been cancelled.

Dealers, on the other hand, may want to backdate documents for any number of reasons. In fact, the dealer in one federal case argued that it is standard industry practice for car dealers to backdate contracts. Even though the agreement is re-written several times over a period of weeks, the subsequent contracts will all be backdated to the date of the first contract. The dealer even alleged that banks will only accept contracts that have been backdated to the date of the vehicle's delivery.[1520]

1517 *See* Nigh v. Koons Buick Pontiac GMC, 143 F. Supp. 2d 535 (E.D Va. 2001), *aff'd on this ground* 319 F.3d 119 (4th Cir. 2003), *cert. granted on other issues*, 124 S. Ct. 1144 (2004).

1518 *See* Violette v. P.A. Days, Inc., 2002 U.S. Dist. LEXIS 23246 (S.D. Ohio Oct. 18, 2002).

1519 *See* Ohio Admin. Code § 109:4-3-16(B)(17). *See also* § 5.4.7.2, *infra*.

1520 *See* Rucker v. Sheehy Alexandria, Inc., 228 F. Supp. 2d 711 (E.D. Va. 2002), *reconsideration denied* 244 F. Supp. 2d 618 (E.D. Va. 2003).

Where the dealer writes a new lease or credit sale and backdates the disclosure form to the original date, this should be a Truth in Lending or Consumer Leasing Act violation,[1521] as well as violation of other state law (such as an installment sales act). Regulation Z specifies that the term of a transaction begins at consummation (or later in certain situations).[1522] Consummation occurs not when the consumer takes possession of the vehicle, but at the time the consumer becomes contractually obligated on a credit transaction.[1523] That occurs when the consumer agrees to the second contract. According to one federal court, the key TIL issue when a contract is back-dated is that use of that earlier date in the computation of the APR results in the disclosure of an inaccurate APR.[1524]

5.4.5.8 Must the Consumer Arbitrate Yo-Yo Sale Claims?

Ways to defeat a binding arbitration requirement are summarized at § 7.6.7, *infra*, and detailed in another NCLC manual, *Consumer Arbitration Agreements* (4th ed. 2004). This subsection examines an additional way to challenge such a requirement—that the very nature of the yo-yo makes the clause unenforceable. In a contingent precedent yo-yo, if the sale is not finalized, then the contract never takes effect, and the dealer can not rely on the arbitration clause in that contract.[1525] Similarly, if the dealer has cancelled a condition subsequent agreement, the terms of that agreement should longer apply, including the arbitration clause. Even if a court were to disagree and find arbitration clauses unenforceable only in a condition precedent and not a condition subsequent agreement, the consumer can allege that the

1521 *See* Jafri v. Lynch Ford, Clearinghouse No. 53,536 (N.D. Ill. Aug. 25, 2000). *But cf.* Nigh v. Koons Buick Pontiac GMC, Inc., 319 F.3d 119 (4th Cir. 2003) (while declining to rule on the issue raised in *Rucker*, the decision indicates that accurately stating the contractual obligation is no TIL violation; court does not address whether obligation that charges for interest for period before credit agreement was consummated violates other state law or whether this violates TIL's APR calculation rules), *cert. granted on other issues*, 124 S. Ct. 1144 (2004).

1522 12 C.F.R. § 226 App. J(b).

1523 12 C.F.R. § 226.2(a)(13).

1524 Rucker v. Sheehy Alexandria, Inc., 228 F. Supp. 2d 711 (E.D. Va. 2002), *reconsideration denied* 244 F. Supp. 2d 618 (E.D. Va. 2003). Although use of the backdate should result in an inaccurate APR, not every inaccurate APR disclosure is a TIL violation. As with any APR mis-disclosure, there will be no TIL violation if the APR understatement is within TIL's disclosures or where TIL tolerances allow the irregularity of the first period to be disregarded for purposes of the APR calculation.

1525 Eady v. Bill Heard Chevrolet, Co., 274 F. Supp. 2d 1284 (M.D. Ala. 2003); *Ex parte* Payne, 741 So. 2d 398 (Ala. 1999). *See also Ex parte* Horton Family Housing, Inc., 2003 WL 22753458 (Ala. Nov. 21, 2003). *But see* Jacobsen v. J.K. Pontiac GMC Truck, Inc., 2001 U.S. Dist. LEXIS 20393 (N.D. Ill. Dec. 10, 2001).

yo-yo was a condition precedent one because no title ever changed hands.

5.4.5.9 Discovery in Yo-Yo Sale Cases

The following are documents that should be requested from the dealer in a yo-yo case:

- All documents signed by the consumer.
- Each temporary tag and temporary registration, and documents sent to the DMV pertaining to such temporary tags or registration.
- Each application for permanent registration or tags and every document received concerning transfer of tags.
- All of the consumer's statements or other application for financing, every credit report of the consumer and any other document pertaining to the consumer's expenses, income, liabilities, creditworthiness, integrity, employment, relatives, references, residence, credit score or any other document that the dealer relied on in assuming the consumer would obtain financing. The dealer should specify if any of these documents were provided to a lender in conjunction with a financing application.
- The deal file including all its contents, for five transactions the dealer contends supports its belief that a lender would accept the consumer's installment contract for financing.
- Every document the dealer received from any lender in connection with the consumer's application, including each call back sheet, credit decision, fax or other document pertaining to the application.
- The file jacket itself (much information is found on the jacket, not in it). Look for the credit score; see if the dealer was reasonable in its choice of lenders or whether the dealer knew the lender would reject a credit score as listed. Also is there evidence in the deal jacket that the dealer tried to seek approval of the loan even after the initial rejection, or did it have no intent to obtain the financing? Also look on the jacket for a date of sale, a date before which the title should not be mailed and the date the title is mailed.
- All notes and other documents from the dealer which refer to the financing or attempted financing, all payments received from the consumer, every promissory note signed by the consumer, each document by which the dealer asserts a security interest, including any document referring to contingencies on the sale of the vehicle or on the financing.
- Each title to the vehicle, documents received from a government agency as to when dealers may issue temporary tags or registration, and the underwriting guidelines or program information that the dealer possesses concerning any lender with which it does business.
- All documents pertaining to the consumer's trade-in, the stock and inventory cards or similar recoveries for the consumer's trade-in and the vehicle the consumer purchased, and the daily cash receipt journal or ledger that reflects any of the consumer's payments.
- All documents relating to bonuses, spiffs, or other incentives concerning the purchase of the vehicle, all documents concerning commissions to each dealer employee in connection to the purchased vehicle or trade-in, including sales personnel, the F & I officer, sales manager, and including all hard copies or any computer entry.
- All wash out sheets, internal worksheets, reconciliations, or other documents that refer to front end or back end of the deal, including reserves set or profits made, all internal invoices, controls or accounting documents referring to the vehicle's price, all documents relating to the dealer's pack or gross, net, or other profits earned by the dealer or its personnel in connection to the deal.
- All internal memos or other documents providing directions to the dealer's title clerks, registration clerks, tag clerks, accounting personnel, sales or other staff in connection with the consumer's deal, its financing, temporary tags or registration.
- All documents used to train the dealer's personnel in connection with issuing temporary tags, temporary registrations, or spot deliveries.

In addition, possible areas for interrogatories to explore (or questions to ask in depositions) include the following areas:

- The names and actions of each person involved in obtaining financing approval from another lender for the deal.
- A detailed statement of all factors that were an obstacle to the consumer's obtaining credit approval.
- A detailed statement of why the dealer thought financing would be obtained for this particular borrower.
- A description of all procedures a dealer uses in delivering the vehicle to the consumer prior to obtaining outside financing, including paperwork to be signed by the consumer, oral disclosures to be given the consumer, and when and under what circumstances temporary tags and registrations are issued.
- Identify each customer who in the last year was spot delivered a vehicle and for whom financing did not go through or went through at a higher rate.
- Identify any misrepresentation or errors that the dealer believes the consumer made in the purchase or credit application, and all facts upon which the dealer relied in making this judgment.

Also very helpful are copies of any handbooks from the state motor vehicle department or even the state dealer trade association that explain how a dealer is to transfer titles and otherwise complete the necessary paperwork in a vehicle sale. For example, in California there is a *Handbook for Dealers and Registration Services*. In Virginia it is called the *Virginia Motor Vehicle Dealer Manual*. Why a dealer handled the paperwork in a particular way may only make sense when one can determine the way the dealer was supposed to handle the documents. One can also depose the dealer to find out why the approved procedures were ignored in the consumer's case.

5.4.6 Used Car Sales

5.4.6.1 Introduction

Used car sales are an important area of consumer abuse. This subsection covers both sale of cars that are offered as used and also cars sold as new when they are really used. The next subsection examines UDAP precedent dealing with new car sales. In handling a used car case, it is important to examine §§ 5.4.2 through 5.4.5, *supra*, as well.

5.4.6.2 FTC Used Car Rule

5.4.6.2.1 The rule's scope

The FTC's Trade Regulation Rule on the Sale of Used Motor Vehicles (Used Car Rule)[1526] applies to motor vehicles, defined as any motorized vehicle, other than a motorcycle, with a gross vehicle weight rating under 8500 pounds, a curb weight less than 6000 pounds, and a frontal area less than 46 square feet.[1527] The rule applies to any used vehicle, defined as one driven more than the limited use necessary in moving or road testing a new vehicle prior to delivery to a consumer.[1528] Since this definition applies even to vehicles where title has never been transferred to a retail purchaser, the rule applies to demonstrators, executive vehicles, and any other car with even minimal mileage already registered on the odometer.[1529]

The rule's obligations apply to any dealer, defined as a business that sells five or more used vehicles in the prior 12 months, but does not apply to a bank[1530] or financial institution, a business selling a used vehicle to an employee of that business, or a lessor selling a leased vehicle to the lessee.[1531] The rule protects a wide class of consumers, including those who buy a car for business purposes.[1532]

The rule generally applies whenever a dealer *offers* a used vehicle for sale. Thus, even if a vehicle is eventually leased, and not sold to a consumer, the dealer still must comply with most rule provisions when it first offers the vehicle to the public for sale.

5.4.6.2.2 Rule requirements

The Used Car Rule has three main requirements:

- A window sticker must be affixed to the vehicle, containing specified information;
- A copy of the window sticker must be provided to the consumer, the information from that sticker must be incorporated into the sales agreement, and no statements can be made to the consumer contradicting information on the sticker;
- A series of misrepresentations are prohibited and certain warranty information must be disclosed.

The window sticker must be exactly as set out in the rule, reprinted at Appendix B.6, *infra,* with the same wording, heading, punctuation, types styles, sizes and format indicated.[1533] The sticker must be displayed prominently on a location on the vehicle in a fashion so that both sides are readily readable. While it can be taken down during a test drive, it must be returned as soon as the test drive is over.[1534]

When a sale is conducted in Spanish, the window sticker and the contract language disclosures must be available in both Spanish and English.[1535] The Spanish version of the

1526 16 C.F.R. § 455 [*reprinted at* Appx. B.6, *infra*]; *see also* Staff Compliance Guidelines, 53 Fed. Reg. 17658 (May 17, 1988). This is not the same rule that was promulgated on August 18, 1981. *See* 46 Fed. Reg. 41328 (1981). Congress, in May, 1982, vetoed the 1981 rule, but the congressional veto was overturned on constitutional grounds. Consumers Union v. FTC, 691 F.2d 575 (D.C. Cir. 1982), *aff'd*, U.S. Senate v. FTC and U.S. House of Representatives v. FTC, 463 U.S. 1216 (1983). The FTC then reconsidered the 1981 rule, and finally adopted a more limited rule by deleting the "known defects" requirement of the 1981 rule. Consequently, while the 1985 rule requires certain dealer disclosures, it does not require dealers to disclose known defects in the cars they are selling. In 1994, as part of its periodic review under the Regulatory Flexibility Act, the FTC solicited comments on whether changes were warranted to the Used Car Rule. After reviewing the rule, the FTC concluded that it was working and achieving its objectives at minimal cost to dealers. The FTC retained the rule, with several non-substantive amendments. 60 Fed. Reg. 62195 (Dec. 5, 1995).

1527 16 C.F.R. § 455.1(d)(1).

1528 16 C.F.R. § 455.1(d)(2).

1529 *See also* Regulatory Flexibility Act and Periodic Review of Used Motor Vehicle Trade Regulation Rule, 60 Fed. Reg. 62195, 62197 (Dec. 5, 1995) (re-affirming that demonstrators are covered even if the original certificate of origin has never been transferred).

1530 The FTC does not have jurisdiction over banks. Instead, Congress left to the Federal Reserve Board (FRB) the authority to enact a substantially similar rule that applies to banks. But the FRB has decided not to adopt such a rule because banks do not sell used cars at retail sales. 50 Fed. Reg. 11945 (Mar. 26, 1985).

1531 16 C.F.R. § 455.1(d)(3).

1532 16 C.F.R. § 455.1(d)(4).

1533 16 C.F.R. § 455.2(a)(2).

1534 16 C.F.R. § 455.2(a)(1).

1535 16 C.F.R. § 455.5.

window sticker is also reprinted in the rule.

The dealer checks the box describing the type of warranty being offered—no warranty, full warranty, limited warranty, and whether the dealer pays only a percentage of labor and parts. Systems covered and the duration of each warranty must be listed. The dealer also checks if a service contract is available.[1536]

The window sticker (sometimes called the Buyers Guide) must be amended if negotiations alter the warranty coverage,[1537] must be given to the consumer upon sale,[1538] and must be incorporated by reference into the contract, overriding any contrary provisions in the contract.[1539]

For example, if a service contract is sold after the initial accepted offer, and the car can no longer be sold "as is,"[1540] the dealer must amend the Buyers Guide to delete the "as is" disclosure. Moreover, the sales agreement must be changed so that it also does not state that the car is sold "as is." Sometimes, after selling a service contract, the dealer will stamp the sales agreement with language overriding the "as is" disclaimer, but elsewhere in the same contract will be language stating that the vehicle is sold "as is." Not only is this inadequate, but the Buyers Guide must be amended as well.

Similarly, state law may prohibit disclaimers of implied warranties or create certain minimum standards as to a used car warranty.[1541] In that case, the dealer can not check the "as is" box on the Buyers Guide, and nothing in the contract should indicate the sale is "as is."

The rule also specifies that it is deceptive for a used car dealer to:

- Misrepresent the mechanical condition of a used vehicle;
- Misrepresent the terms of any warranty offered in connection with the sale of a used vehicle; or
- Represent that a used vehicle is sold with a warranty when the vehicle is sold without a warranty.[1542]

The rule also makes it an unfair practice for any used car dealer to:

- Fail to disclose, prior to sale, that a used vehicle is sold without any warranty; or
- Fail to make available, prior to sale, the terms of any written warranty offered in connection with the sale of a used vehicle.[1543]

5.4.6.2.3 Common rule violations

FTC enforcement of the Used Car Rule has found widespread violations.[1544] Consumer attorneys thus should be alert for potential violations of the FTC Used Car Rule and should ensure that dealers:

- Post a *completed* guide on their cars, and leave them there except during test drives;[1545]
- Replace the guide after its removal for a test drive;
- Follow the type, size, production, capitalization, color, and wording requirements, with no extraneous information included;
- Complete the guide properly, particularly in checking the correct warranty disclosure boxes; an implied warranty only box should be included in the form and checked where appropriate, particularly in states not allowing the waiver of implied warranties;
- Make sure the warranty disclosed on the guide matches the warranty provided for in the written agreement;
- Use the Spanish language Buyers Guide where required;
- Include the required language in the contract;
- Give the buyer the Guide or a copy;
- If a service contract is sold, the service contract box must be checked, as well as either the warranty box or the implied warranty box.

5.4.6.2.4 Remedies for rule violations

Violations of the Used Car Rule violate the FTC Act, and the FTC has brought enforcement actions for Used Car Rule violations.[1546] As with any FTC rule, there is no private right

1536 16 C.F.R. § 455.2.

1537 16 C.F.R. § 455.2(b)(2).

1538 16 C.F.R. § 455.3(a).

1539 16 C.F.R. § 455.3(b).

1540 The Magnuson-Moss Warranty Act prohibits disclaimers of implied warranties where a service contract is sold in conjunction with the goods.

1541 *See* National Consumer Law Center, Consumer Warranty Law Ch. 14 (2d ed. 2001 and Supp.).

1542 16 C.F.R. § 455.1.

1543 *Id.*

1544 *See* § 5.4.6.2.4, *infra.*

1545 *See* Buskirk v. Harrell, 2000 Ohio App. LEXIS 3100 (Ohio Ct. App. June 28, 2000) (in consumer's case alleging dealer failed to provide a window sticker, court gives credence to consumer's photographs of dealer's lot that show cars without window stickers).

1546 *See, e.g.*, FTC v. Americlean Ltd., 5 Trade Reg. Rep. (CCH) ¶ 23,369 (E.D. Va. 1993) (consent decree); United States v. Payless Auto Sales, Inc., 5 Trade Reg. Rep. (CCH) ¶ 23,371 (E.D. Va. 1993) (consent decree); United States v. American Sys., Inc., 5 Trade Reg. Rep. (CCH) ¶ 23,389 (M.D. Fla. 1993); FTC v. John Michael Auto Sales, Inc., 5 Trade Reg. Rep. (CCH) ¶ 23,216 (D. Md. 1992) (consent decree); United States v. Hern Oldsmobile-GMC Truck, Inc., 5 Trade Reg. Rep. (CCH) ¶ 23,220 (N.D. Ohio 1992) (consent judgment); FTC v. M.A.S.H. Motors, Inc., 5 Trade Reg. Rep. (CCH) ¶ 23,226 (D. Okla. 1992) (consent decree); FTC v. Quality Motor Co., 5 Trade Reg. Rep. (CCH) ¶ 23,229 (W.D. Okla. 1992) (consent decree); Snyder's Used Cars, Inc., 5 Trade Reg. Rep. (CCH) ¶ 23,242 (F.T.C. File No. 912 3223 1992) (consent decree); United States v. McNevin

of action under the FTC Act for rule violations. Nevertheless, a rule violation should be actionable under a state UDAP statute, since an FTC rule should guide courts in interpreting state UDAP statutes.[1547] Since the FTC Used Car Rule was in part promulgated under the federal Magnuson-Moss Act,[1548] a good argument can be made that it is a Magnuson-Moss Act violation to violate the Used Car Rule.[1549]

5.4.6.2.5 Where Buyers Guide warranty disclosure conflicts with warranty provided in the sales agreement

The rule states clearly that the dealer may not make any statements, oral or written, that contradict the disclosures in the Buyers Guide. The dealer can negotiate the warranty coverage so that the final sale has different terms than that first disclosed on the Buyers Guide, but then the final warranty terms have to be identified in the contract of sale and summarized on the copy of the Buyers Guide that is provided to the consumer.[1550]

Cadillac, 5 Trade Reg. Rep. (CCH) ¶ 23,246 (N.D. Cal. 1992) (consent decree); FTC v. Montoya, 5 Trade Reg. Rep. (CCH) ¶ 23,254 (D.N.M. 1992) (consent decree); FTC v. Tom's Motors, Inc., 5 Trade Reg. Rep. (CCH) ¶ 23,255 (D.N.M. 1992) (consent decree); United States v. Car City, Inc., 5 Trade Reg. Rep. (CCH) ¶ 23,274 (S.D. Iowa 1992) (consent decree); United States v. Liberty Motors, Inc., 5 Trade Reg. Rep. (CCH) ¶ 23,275 (E.D. Va. 1992) (consent decree); United States v. TJ Motors, Inc. 5 Trade Reg. Rep. (CCH) ¶ 23,294 (N.D. Ill. 1992) (consent decree); United States v. Credit Car Connection, 5 Trade Reg. Rep. (CCH) ¶ 23,148 (M.D. Fla. 1992) (consent order); United States v. Ghoregan, 5 Trade Reg. Rep. (CCH) ¶ 23,170 (W.D. Okla. 1992) (consent order).

1547 *See* Milton v. Riverside Auto Exchange, Clearinghouse No. 55453 (Montgomery County Court, Ohio, Aug. 27, 1991) (UDAP statute allows rescission of used car sale where seller did not post Buyer's Guide); §§ 3.2.6, 3.2.7 3.5.5, *supra*. *See also* Consumer Protection Division Enforcement Statements Concerning Motor Vehicle Advertising & Sales Practices, Iowa Dept. of Transportation, Dealer Operating Manual VII-2, Clearinghouse No. 49,156; Buskirk v. Harrell, 2000 Ohio App. LEXIS 3100 (Ohio Ct. App. June 28, 2000); Cummins v. Dave Fillmore Car Co., 1987 WL 19186 (Ohio App. Oct. 27, 1987) (omission of statement that information on Buyers Guide was part of contract was UDAP violation, but no actual damages shown and buyer not entitled to rescission); Rubin v. Gallery Auto Sales, 1997 WL 1068459 (Ohio C.P. June 9, 1997) (failure to display Buyers Guide and to fill it in properly are UDAP violations). *But see In re* Lake Auto, Inc., 1989 Minn. App. LEXIS 178 (Feb. 10, 1989) (unpublished opinion) (failure to post buyer's guide not state UDAP violation).

1548 *See* 15 U.S.C. § 2309(b); 16 C.F.R. § 455 (Authority). *See also* National Consumer Law Center, Consumer Warranty Law Ch. 2 (2d ed. 2001 and Supp.) for a discussion of the Magnuson-Moss Warranty Act.

1549 *See* Currier v. Spencer, 299 Ark. 182, 772 S.W.2d 309 (1989) (upholding trial court's award of Magnuson-Moss attorney fees for violation of FTC Used Car Rule).

1550 16 C.F.R. § 455.4.

Consequently, if the Buyers Guide provided to the consumer indicates that any implied or express warranties are given with the sale, then the sales agreement can not identify the transaction as "as is" or without warranties. The same is true if the agreement provides for warranties, but the Guide discloses the sale "as is." These sales agreement provisions would directly contradict the disclosures in the Buyers Guide. This rule violation should also be a state UDAP violation.[1551]

The same should be true if the contract is silent on warranties and the Buyers Guide states the sale is "as is." Silence means that implied warranties are not disclaimed. If the contract provides for implied warranties, this is inconsistent with a Buyers Guide that states the sale is "as is."

5.4.6.2.6 FTC Used Car Rule does not insulate sellers from UDAP liability

Seller compliance with the FTC Used Car Rule does not insulate the seller from UDAP liability. For example, although the FTC considered and rejected a rule requirement that dealers disclose known defects, compliance with the rule does not prevent a state UDAP action alleging the dealer failed to disclose known defects.[1552]

5.4.6.3 Sale of Used Cars as New; Demonstrators and Program Cars

It is deceptive to sell a used car as new or to fail to disclose that a car is used.[1553] Similarly, it is deceptive to fail to disclose that a car had a prior owner.[1554] The bigger issue in these cases is when does a vehicle cease to be new and similarly when does it have a prior owner.

1551 Lawhorn v. Joseph Toyota, Inc., 141 Ohio App. 3d 153, 750 N.E.2d 610 (2001).

1552 Hinds v. Paul's Auto Werkstatt, Inc., 107 Or. App. 63, 810 P.2d 874 (1991). *Accord* Totz v. Continental DuPage Acura, 602 N.E.2d 1374 (Ill. App. Ct. 1992).

1553 *See* Peacock Buick Inc., 86 F.T.C. 1532 (1975); Lustine Chevrolet, 86 F.T.C. 1197 (1975) (consent order); Rosenthal Chevrolet, 86 F.T.C. 777 (1975) (consent order); Logan Ford Co., 84 F.T.C. 505 (1974) (consent order); Ted Britt Ford Sales, Inc., 84 F.T.C. 499 (1974) (consent order); People v. Conway, 42 Cal. App. 3d 875, 117 Cal. Rptr. 251 (1974); Searcy v. Bend Garage Co., 286 Or. 11, 592 P.2d 558 (1979); Stokes v. Gary Barbera Enterprises, Inc., 783 A.2d 296 (Pa. Super. 2001); Ancira GMC Trucks and Motor Homes, Inc. v. Motor Vehicle Board, 1999 Tex. App. LEXIS 6908 (Tex. App. Sept. 10, 1999); Pontiac v. Elliot, 775 S.W.2d 395 (Tex. App. 1989); Jack Roach Ford v. De Urdanavia, 659 S.W.2d 725 (Tex. App. 1983); Idaho Consumer Protection Regulations, Idaho Admin. Code 04.02.01.234, Other Advertising Practices; Code Miss. Rules § 24 000 002, Rule 49; N.M. Admin. Code § 12.2.4.8, Regulations for the Advertising and Sale of Motor Vehicles. *See also* § 4.9.4, *supra*.

1554 *See* Buechin v. Ogden Chrysler-Plymouth, Inc., 159 Ill. App. 3d 237, 511 N.W.2d 1330 (1987); Lee v. Payton, 313 S.E.2d 247 (N.C. Ct. App. 1984) (demonstrator had in fact prior owner).

A car that has been sold or leased at retail is certainly used.[1555] In general, this means that any car with a title is used. When a car is new, it just is accompanied by the manufacturer's statement of origin (MSO). There is no title. When that vehicle is sold at retail, the MSO is assigned to the retail purchaser, who then applies for a title. A title will only appear in the name of a retail purchaser. If a title is assigned to a consumer when buying a vehicle, that vehicle is used.

But the lack of a title does not make a vehicle new. A consumer being assigned a "clean" MSO (no assignment on the MSO) does not make the vehicle new, for a number of reasons. First, dealers have been known to sell a vehicle for retail use, assign the MSO to the retail purchaser, take the car back, and then destroy the MSO indicating the transfer. The dealer then requests a clean, duplicate MSO from the manufacturer, claiming the old one was lost or destroyed. More commonly, a car will be returned after extensive use, but before the MSO is signed over to a retail purchaser.

While a test drive does not make a vehicle used, more extensive use does. Where a consumer returns a new car the day after purchase because it was not operating correctly, and the dealer repairs the vehicle and sells the car to a second consumer, the second vehicle sale involves a "used" car, and the seller should have disclosed the car was used, not new.[1556] Even though prior use was minimal and the car is like new, sale of the car as new is deceptive: "if an automobile has been physically used by anyone for purposes beyond the uses incidental to the sales process, that fact must be disclosed."[1557]

A Maryland Attorney General Opinion goes into some detail as to when a car loses its status as new.[1558] A car being driven a few miles incidental to the sale process does not deprive a vehicle of its "newness." But whenever a dealer releases a vehicle to be driven by the buyer as he or she pleases, the vehicle's status as new is jeopardized. If the buyer then drives the vehicle more than an insignificant number of miles, damages it, alters it, or subjects it to unusual driving conditions—such as racing—the vehicle is no longer new.[1559]

As described in more detail in § 5.4.5, *infra*, a common sales tactic today is the "yo-yo" sale or spot delivery. The consumer drives the car home assuming the sale is final, but the dealer calls the consumer back saying financing has fallen through and the deal must be reworked on less favorable terms. Such vehicles are often recovered weeks later, sometimes after a repossession. Even where a MSO has never been signed over to the consumer, such a vehicle should be considered used.

In one case the dealer had spot delivered a motor home, and when the financing fell through obtained a court order stopping the titling of the vehicle to the new owner, and then recovered the vehicle after it had been driven several hundred miles. Despite a court determination that the vehicle was not to be titled in the name of the first purchaser, it was deceptive to sell the motor home subsequently as new.[1560]

Another issue whether a vehicle is used relates to damage even before it arrives at a dealership. A number of courts have found that a new car damaged in transit to the dealership and subsequently repaired could be found to be "used."[1561] The Alabama Supreme Court has articulated a "reasonable expectation" test for determining whether a vehicle that has been damaged is new or used.[1562] Whether damage to a vehicle is significant enough to make it "used" is a question of fact for the jury.[1563] A car in a deteriorated condition can not be represented as new even when it has been driven only a few hundred miles.[1564]

More commonly, UDAP cases do not focus on whether the damaged vehicle is new or used, but on the dealer's failure to disclose that a supposedly new car has been damaged and then repaired. That is, whether the car is deemed still new or used, the repairs should be disclosed. A number of states have statutes directly on point. These statutes and the failure to disclose repairs in supposedly new vehicles are examined at § 5.4.7.4, *infra*.

Another way a car with substantial use can remain untitled involves demonstrators or program cars. A car can be driven thousands of miles before it is sold to its first retail buyer when it is used as a demonstrator at the dealership, or driven by a manufacturer or dealer executive or official. An Illinois jury found that a car used as a "demo," with 13,000 miles on it, was not new even though it had never been titled.[1565] In addition, dealers may represent a vehicle as a

---

1555 Kondo v. Marietta Toyota, Inc., 224 Ga. App. 490, 480 S.E.2d 851 (1997); Texas Attorney General's Business Advisory Regulating "Program" Vehicle Advertising, Clearinghouse No. 47,930 (Apr. 30, 1991).

1556 Pontiac v. Elliot, 775 S.W.2d 395 (Tex. App. 1989).

1557 Weigel v. Ron Tonkin Chevrolet, Co., 298 Or. 127, 690 P.2d 488 (1984).

1558 84 Opinions of the Maryland Attorney General, Opinion No. 89-048 (Dec. 22, 1989). *See also* N.M. Admin. Code § 12.2.4.8, Regulations for the Advertising and Sale of Motor Vehicles.

1559 84 Opinions of the Maryland Attorney General, Opinion No. 89-048 (Dec. 22, 1989). *But see* Kondo v. Marietta Toyota, Inc., 224 Ga. App. 490, 480 S.E.2d 851 (1997).

1560 Ancira GMC Trucks and Motor Homes, Inc. v. Motor Vehicle Board, 1999 Tex. App. LEXIS 6908 (Tex. App. Sept. 10, 1999).

1561 Chrysler Corp. v. Schiffer, 736 So. 2d 538 (Ala. 1999) (affirming jury finding that damage and repair to vehicle rendered it used); Brooks v. Hurst Buick Pontiac-Olds-GMC, Inc., 23 Ohio App. 3d 85, 491 N.E.2d 345 (1985). *See also* Vercher v. Ford Motor Co., 527 So. 2d 995 (La. Ct. App. 1988) (deceptive to fail to disclose that new car had damage that was repaired); Pirozzi v. Penske-Olds-Cadillac-GMS, 605 A.2d 373 (Pa. Super. Ct. 1992). *But see* Kondo v. Marietta Toyota, Inc., 224 Ga. App. 490, 480 S.E.2d 851 (1997).

1562 Chrysler Corp. v. Schiffer, 736 So. 2d 538 (Ala. 1999).

1563 *Id.*

1564 Jack Roach Ford v. De Urdanavia, 659 S.W.2d 725 (Tex. App. 1983).

1565 Ciampi v. Ogden Chrysler Plymouth, Inc., 634 N.E.2d 448 (Ill. App. Ct. 1994).

"demo" or executive car when its actual use was quite different. Some states have regulations that define when a car is considered a "demo."[1566]

It is also deceptive to fail to disclose that a new car was actually a demonstrator.[1567] Whether a demonstrator or executive car is treated as new or used,[1568] the exact nature of the prior use should be disclosed.[1569]

The Texas Attorney General has issued a business advisory on the sale of "program" cars.[1570] Advertising for *new* cars (never having been subject to a retail sale or lease) must disclose if the car is a demonstrator, executive car, or official car. Advertising for any car that is *used* (i.e., one that has been sold or leased at retail) must clearly disclose the vehicle as used if the dealer implies that it obtained the car from the manufacturer, such as a "program car," "factory auction car" or "special factory purchase."

5.4.6.4 Nature of Prior Use

Subsequent subsections will describe when it is deceptive to sell a vehicle without describing a history of damage, mechanical repairs, or odometer tampering. The prior subsection explored when a car sold as new is really used. In addition, it is deceptive to misrepresent or fail to disclose the nature of a car's prior use, such as where the vehicle has been repossessed or was used as a taxicab, police car, driver's education car, or rental vehicle.[1571]

1566 *See, e.g.*, Ohio Admin. Code § 109:4-3-16(A)(8).

1567 Motzer Dodge Jeep Eagle, Inc. v. Ohio Attorney General, 95 Ohio App. 3d 183, 642 N.E.2d 20 (1994) (even though oral disclosure made, failure to make written disclosures of prior use as demonstrator violated state UDAP regulation); Searcy v. Bend Garage Co., 286 Or. 11, 592 P.2d 558 (1979). *But see* McGraw v. Loyola Ford, Inc., 124 Md. App. 560, 723 A.2d 502 (1999) (erroneous description of vehicle as new rather than demonstrator on order form not a UDAP violation where buyer was orally informed of the true prior use and was not misled); *cf.* Hodges v. Koons Buick Pontiac GMC, Inc., 180 F. Supp. 2d 786 (E.D. Va. 2001) (describing demonstrator car as new was not UDAP violation when seller told buyer it was a demo, buyer signed odometer statement showing mileage, and buyer knew it was a demo).

1568 *Cf.* Bennett v. D.L. Claborn Buick, Inc., 414 S.E.2d 12 (Ga. App. Ct. 1991) (jury question whether representation of demonstrator as new car was deceptive, even though state allowed it to be titled as new).

1569 *See* Catrett v. Landmark Dodge, Inc., 253 Ga. App. 639, 560 S.E.2d 101 (2002) (describing car as demonstrator when it had been previously owned and wrecked violates used-for-new rule); Hale v. Basin Motor Co., 110 N.M. 314, 795 P.2d 1006 (1990) (while sale of a demonstrator that has been in an accident is not the sale of "used for new," it may still be deceptive and is certainly a violation of a special UDAP requirement in that state that dealers disclose whether there has been "alteration" to a car); Inman v. Ken Hyatt Chrysler Plymouth, Inc., 294 S.C. 240, 363 S.E.2d 691 (1988) (misrepresented prior use as demonstrator when it had been returned for repair problems); Paty v. Herb Adcox Chevrolet Co., 756 S.W.2d 697 (Tex. App. 1988) (failed to disclose demonstrator had been in an accident); Code Vt. Rule §§ 06-031-018, Rule CF 118.04, Automobile Advertising (executive cars, factory cars, and "new" cars).

1570 Texas Attorney General's Business Advisory Regulating "Program" Vehicle Advertising, Clearinghouse No. 47,930 (Apr. 30, 1991).

1571 Salmeron v. Highlands Ford Sales, Inc., 271 F. Supp. 2d 1314 (D.N.M. 2003) (misrepresentation that vehicle was demonstrator, and failure to disclose that it had been a rental car and in an accident); Peacock Buick Inc., 86 F.T.C. 1532 (1975); Hertz Corp., 88 F.T.C. 238 (1976) (consent order); Lustine Chevrolet, 86 F.T.C. 1197 (1975) (consent order); Rosenthal Chevrolet, 86 F.T.C. 777 (1975) (consent order); Logan Ford Co., 84 F.T.C. 505 (1974) (consent order); Ted Britt Ford Sales, Inc., 84 F.T.C. 499 (1974) (consent order); Standards for Advertising and Selling Motor Vehicles, Conn. Agencies Regs. § 42-110b-28; Idaho Consumer Protection Regulations, Idaho Admin. Code 04.02.01.234, Other Advertising Practices; Ill. Admin. Code tit. 14, §§ 475.510, .520, Motor Vehicle Advertising; Consumer Protection Division Enforcement Statements Concerning Motor Vehicle Advertising & Sales Practices, Iowa Dept. of Transportation, Dealer Operating Manual VII-2, Clearinghouse No. 49,156; Massachusetts Consumer Protection Regulations, Mass. Regs. Code tit. 940, § 5.04, Motor Vehicle Regulations; Mont. Admin. R. § 2.61.204; N.J. Admin. Code § 13:45A-26A.5 to .7, Motor Vehicle Advertising Practices; N.M. Admin. Code § 12.2.4.8, Regulations for the Advertising and Sale of Motor Vehicles; N.Y. Veh. & Traffic Law § 417-a; Ohio Admin. Code § 109:4-3-16(B)(15), Motor Vehicle Repairs or Services; Ohio Admin. Code § 109:4-3-08; New For Used; Pennsylvania Regulations of the Bureau of Consumer Protection, 37 Pa. Code § 301.2, Automobile Industry Trade Practices (1978); Code Vt. Rules §§ 06-031-0007, Rule CF 108, Odometers, and Rule CF 118.04, Automobile Advertising (executive cars, factory cars, and "new" cars); Phillips v. David McDermott Chevrolet, Inc., 1992 Conn. Super. LEXIS 888 (Mar. 24, 1992) (rental vehicle), *aff'd per curiam*, 30 Conn. App. 906, 618 A.2d 594 (1993); Miller v. William Chevrolet/Geo, Inc., 326 Ill. App. 3d 642, 762 N.E.2d 1 (2001) (description of former rental car as "executive driven" was false statement of material fact for both fraud and UDAP claims); State *ex rel.* Danforth v. Independence Dodge, Inc., 494 S.W.2d 362 (Mo. Ct. App. 1973) (damaged rental car purchased at auction can not be represented as driven only by dealer's general manager); Kopischke v. First Continental Corp., 610 P.2d 668 (Mont. 1980) (Montana UDAP regulation prohibiting misrepresentation of prior usage is within state's authority; prior history of a repossession); State *ex rel.* Fisher v. Rose Chevrolet, Inc., 82 Ohio App. 3d 520, 612 N.E.2d 782 (1992) (partially true but misleading answer to consumer's question was deceptive where it concealed prior use as a rental car); Hardy v. Toler, 288 N.C. 303, 218 S.E.2d 342 (1975) (misrepresentation of number of prior owners); Gonzalez v. Global Truck & Equip. Inc., 625 S.W.2d 348 (Tex. Civ. App. 1981) (oral representations concerning age even where subsequently corrected in written documents). *Cf.* Toirkens v. Willett Toyota, Inc., 192 Ga. App. 109, 384 S.E.2d 218 (1989) (no violation where car disclosed as used demonstrator and extent of prior use, if not identity of prior holder of title, disclosed). *But see In re* Crown Auto Dealerships, Inc., 187 B.R. 1009 (Bankr. M.D. Fla. 1995) (failure to disclose that a vehicle had been stolen and recovered may not be a UDAP violation if no damage to the vehicle resulted); Kenney v. Healey Ford-Lincoln-Mercury, 53 Conn. App. 327, 730 A.2d 115 (1999) (no duty to disclose vehicle's rental fleet and collision history, where disclosure would not have made a difference in decision to purchase).

A dealer's representation that a car was a "demo," when it had actually been an airport rental car or had another prior use, is a UDAP violation.[1572] Representing a car as belonging to a factory official is deceptive where it was used in a driver's education program.[1573] It is similarly deceptive to represent that a damaged rental sold at auction was driven only by the dealer's general manager.[1574] Selling a used car as having been leased as part of a fleet is deceptive where the dealer had actually rented out the vehicle on a daily basis, as a "dealer rent-a-car" or "DRAC."[1575]

Often a vehicle's prior use can be determined by performing a search of the vehicle's title. This will require a search that produces copies of the actual title documents over time, not a Carfax or similar computer search, which does not list prior owners' names. Examining the names of each owner can often provide information contrary to the dealer's representations, and it certainly determines the number of prior owners, which may be contrary to the dealer's sales pitch. If a prior owner's name does not indicate prior use, the title can still be used to contact that prior owner, since the entity's address must be listed on the title. For more discussion of title searches, investigating prior use, and caselaw concerning prior use misrepresentations, see NCLC's *Automobile Fraud* (2d ed. 2003 and Supp.).

5.4.6.5 Odometer Rollbacks and Mileage Misrepresentations

5.4.6.5.1 UDAP precedent

Tampering with odometers, failing to disclose accurate odometer readings, and misrepresenting a car's mileage are also deceptive.[1576] Even a dealer's innocent misrepresentation of a vehicle's odometer reading, due to a rollback by a previous owner, is a UDAP violation, since scienter and intent are not elements of UDAP claims.[1577] Techniques to investigate and prove odometer misrepresentations are examined in detail in another NCLC manual, *Automobile Fraud* (2d ed. 2003 and Supp.).

5.4.6.5.2 Federal Odometer Act prohibits oral misrepresentations

In cases of odometer tampering and mileage misrepresentations, it is also important to consider actions under the federal or a state odometer law. The federal odometer law provides for federal court jurisdiction, mandatory treble actual damages or $1500, whichever is greater, plus attorney

1572 Salmeron v. Highlands Ford Sales, Inc., 271 F. Supp. 2d 1314 (D.N.M. 2003); Peacock Buick Inc., 86 F.T.C. 1532 (1975); Lustine Chevrolet, 86 F.T.C. 1197 (1975) (consent order); Rosenthal Chevrolet, 86 F.T.C. 777 (1975) (consent order) (used in driver education courses); Catrett v. Landmark Dodge, Inc., 253 Ga. App. 639, 560 S.E.2d 101 (2002) (car represented as demonstrator had been previously owned and wrecked); Duran v. Leslie Oldsmobile, 594 N.E.2d 1355 (Ill. App. Ct. 1992); Lee v. Payton, 313 S.E.2d 247 (N.C. Ct. App. 1984) (car had prior owner); River Oaks L-M, Inc. v. Whalen, 1998 Tex. App. LEXIS 5687 (Tex. App. Sept. 3, 1998) (car represented as demonstrator was actually a rental vehicle); *see also* Consumer Protection Division Enforcement Statements Concerning Motor Vehicle Advertising & Sales Practices, Iowa Dept. of Transportation, Dealer Operating Manual VII-2, Clearinghouse No. 49,156.

1573 Peacock Buick Inc., 86 F.T.C. 1532 (1975). *See also* Ill. Admin. Code tit. 14, part 475.510, Motor Vehicle Advertising.

1574 State *ex rel.* Danforth v. Independence Dodge, Inc., 494 S.W.2d 362 (Mo. Ct. App. 1973).

1575 Dowd v. Imperial Chrysler-Plymouth, Inc., 381 S.E.2d 212 (S.C. Ct. App. 1989).

1576 Boudreaux v. Puckett, 611 F.2d 1028 (5th Cir. 1980) (interpreting the Louisiana UDAP statute); Sandi v. Dependable Auto Center, Inc., 2000 U.S. Dist. LEXIS 19807 (E.D.N.Y. Dec. 27, 2000); Roberts v. Rohrman, 909 F. Supp. 545 (N.D. Ill. 1995) (dealer may violate UDAP statute by unknowingly making inaccurate odometer disclosure); Attorney General v. Dickson, 717 F. Supp. 1090 (D. Md. 1989); German Auto Agency, 79 F.T.C. 504 (1971) (consent order); Arlington Imports Inc., 77 F.T.C. 1109 (1970) (consent order); Standards for Advertising and Selling Motor Vehicles, Conn. Agencies Regs. § 42-110b-28; *In re* Brandywine Volkswagen, Ltd., 312 A.2d 632 (Del. 1973); Gordon v. Stickney, 2000 Del. Super. LEXIS 209 (Del. Super. Ct. May 11, 2000); Hauser Motor Co. v. Byrd, 377 So. 2d 773 (Fla. Dist. Ct. App. 1980); Burke v. Atamian Porsche Audi Inc., Clearinghouse No. 25,841 (Mass. Super. Ct. 1978); State *ex rel.* Danforth v. Independence Dodge, 494 S.W.2d 362 (Mo. Ct. App. 1973); Mont. Admin. R. Ch. 8.78.204; Fenwick v. Kay Am. Jeep, Inc., 72 N.J. 372, 371 A.2d 13 (1977); Wildstein v. Tru Motors, Inc., 227 N.J. Super. 331, 547 A.2d 340 (Law Div. 1988) (intentional resetting of odometer is unconscionable); *In re* People *ex rel.* Spitzer v. Condor Pontiac, Cadillac, Buick & GMC Trucks, Inc., 2003 WL 21649689 (N.Y. Sup. Ct. July 2, 2003); Washburn v. Vandiver, 379 S.E.2d 65 (N.C. Ct. App. 1989); Brown v. Flag Motor Car Co., 1977 Ohio App. LEXIS 7589 (Sept. 27, 1977); Brown v. Town & Country Auto Sales, Inc., 43 Ohio App. 2d 119, 334 N.E.2d 488 (1974); Brown v. Bill Garlic Motors Inc., Clearinghouse 16,058 (Ohio C.P. Huron Cty. 1976); Brown v. Lancaster Chrysler-Plymouth, Inc., Clearinghouse No. 27,061 (Ohio C.P. Greene Cty. 1976); Brown v. Waddell, 3 Ohio Op. 3d 357 (C.P. Greene Cty. 1976); Commonwealth v. Lenny Levy's Chrysler-Plymouth, Clearinghouse No. 26,023 (Pa. C.P. Allegheny Cty. 1971); Tilson v. Buchanan, 1991 Tenn. App. LEXIS 99, Clearinghouse No. 51,281 (Tenn. App. 1991); Green Tree Acceptance, Inc. v. Holmes, 803 S.W.2d 458 (Tex. App. 1991); Houston v. Mike Black Auto Sales, Inc., 788 S.W.2d 696 (Tex. App. 1990); N.J. Admin. Code § 13:45A-26A.5 and .6, Motor Vehicle Advertising Practices; Pennsylvania Regulations of the Bureau of Consumer Protection, 37 Pa. Code § 301.4, Automobile Industry Trade Practices (1978); Code Vt. Rules § 06-031-007, Rule CF 108, Odometers.

1577 Roberts v. Rohrman, 909 F. Supp. 545 (N.D. Ill. 1995) (dealer may violate UDAP statute by unknowingly making inaccurate odometer disclosure); Prishwalko v. Bob Thomas Ford, Inc., 33 Conn. App. 575, 636 A.2d 1383 (1994); Crown Ford, Inc. v. Crawford, 473 S.E.2d 554 (Ga. App. Ct. 1996) (odometer had been replaced before dealer acquired the car). *See also* Kopischke v. First Continental Corp., 610 P.2d 668 (Mont. 1980).

fees for prevailing consumers. Both federal and state odometer laws are considered in detail in National Consumer Law Center, *Automobile Fraud* (2d ed. 2003 and Supp.). In addition, the more egregious odometer tampering cases should also be handled with a common law deceit count seeking punitive damages, also examined in that volume.

Often it is best to plead a number of different theories. For example, see National Consumer Law Center, *Consumer Law Pleadings,* No. 1, § 3.1 (CD-Rom and Index Guide), also found on the CD-Rom accompanying this volume, for a complaint regarding odometer rollbacks that combines UDAP, odometer law, and warranty claims.[1578]

This subsection focuses on one special application of the Federal Odometer Act that is often overlooked. The Act requires dealers to provide buyers with an odometer disclosure statement as specified by National Highway Transportation Safety Administration (NHTSA) regulations, and prohibits the dealer from giving "a false statement to the transferee in making the disclosure required by such regulation."[1579]

Both the Fourth and Eighth Circuits have interpreted this provision as providing an Odometer Act cause of action not just for errors in the odometer disclosure statement, but also for oral misrepresentations or for written misrepresentations found elsewhere in the transfer documents.[1580] That is, a dealer's oral misrepresentation of the mileage or a misrepresentation found in a sales document not only is a UDAP violation, but also a federal Odometer Act violation, providing statutory and treble damages and federal court jurisdiction.

One important limitation on this use or any other use of the Federal Odometer Act is that the consumer must show the dealer's intent to defraud. Odometer Act cases have inferred intent to defraud where the dealer recklessly or carelessly disregarded indications of a mileage representation's falseness, or reasonably should have known that the mileage was inaccurate.[1581] Dealers have a special duty to inspect a vehicle for indications of mileage alterations.[1582]

Another possible limitation on use of the Odometer Act to challenge mileage misrepresentations applies to cars over ten years old. The National Highway Transportation Safety Administration has exempted from the disclosure requirements a transfer of a vehicle over ten years old.[1583] Since the Act prohibits the dealer from giving a false statement to the transferee "in making the disclosure required by such regulation," the exemption arguably also takes cars over ten years old outside the protection of the provision prohibiting the giving of a false statement.[1584] Nevertheless, there is a strong argument that a dealer that voluntarily provides a disclosure statement for a car over ten years old has waived the NHTSA exemption.[1585] Then the prohibition against false mileage statements should apply as well.

5.4.6.6 Sale of Salvage and Flood-Damaged Cars and Undisclosed Body Damage

5.4.6.6.1 Nature of the problem

Experts estimate that perhaps half a million of the fifteen million used cars sold each year in this country were actually declared "total" losses because of wreck damage, were then rebuilt, and ultimately were resold to unsuspecting consumers. Millions more are sold that were in a serious wreck, but were never declared to be total losses. Each time a major flood hits an area, thousands of cars suffer flood damage, but many of these cars are re-sold to consumers unaware of that flood history.

Wrecked or flood-damaged cars are termed "total" losses because insurance companies conclude that they would cost more to repair than they are worth. How then can rebuilders be part of a thriving industry that buys these salvage vehicles, rebuilds them and resells them at a profit?

The answer is generally that the repairs on the cars are woefully inadequate, ignoring the complicated measures necessary to make today's more sophisticated cars meet their designed safety standards. Rebuilders of salvaged cars are basically unregulated, located in backyard shops across the nation, and not even saddled with the most basic labeling requirements for these remanufactured goods.

These vehicles not only have less actual value than as represented by the dealer, but often have major safety defects. Today's complex vehicles were not designed to be totally wrecked and then quickly and inexpensively salvaged by unauthorized repair shops.

For example, CBS's *60 Minutes* aired footage of the back half of one car being welded to the front half of another car. The show followed another salvaged vehicle that was still

1578 That chapter also contains interrogatories, class memoranda, summary judgment pleadings, and settlement documents concerning a dealer's odometer tampering.

1579 49 U.S.C. § 32705(a)(2). This was originally codified at 15 U.S.C. § 1988. The recodification, Pub. L. No. 103-429 (Oct. 31, 1994), mistakenly changed the meaning of this provision. This error was corrected by Pub. L. No. 104-287 § 5 (Oct. 11, 1996).

1580 Hughes v. Box, 814 F.2d 498 (8th Cir. 1987); Ryan v. Edwards, 592 F.2d 756 (4th Cir. 1979). *Cf.* Lee v. Gallup Auto Sales, Inc., 135 F.3d 1359 (10th Cir. 1998) (mentioning this precedent, but not ruling on the issue).

1581 *See* National Consumer Law Center, Automobile Fraud § 3.8 (2d ed. 2003 and Supp.).

1582 *Id.*

1583 49 C.F.R. § 580.5; *see also* 49 U.S.C. § 32705(a). There is uncertainty whether this applies to transactions before June 9, 1998, and probably does not apply to transactions before November 15, 1995. For more details, see National Consumer Law Center, Automobile Fraud § 3.6.4 (2d ed. 2003 and Supp.).

1584 The NHTSA exemption for cars over ten years old only applies to the Act's *disclosure* requirement, so that the Act still prohibits odometer tampering of such cars.

1585 Smith v. Walt Bennett Ford, Inc., 864 S.W.2d 817 (Ark. 1993).

unsafe but sold without disclosure of its history to another consumer, who within two weeks wrecked the car again and almost died.

Similarly, after major flooding, one can expect thousands of vehicles with severe flood damage to be re-sold without disclosure of this history, even though the flood damage can be serious, if difficult to detect for a consumer. Finally, millions of vehicles that were in significant collisions, but not declared salvage, are resold each year without disclosure of this history.

5.4.6.6.2 Discovering a salvage or wreck history

This subsection provides a brief overview of how to discover a vehicle's salvage, flood, or wreck history. Far more detail is found in NCLC's *Automobile Fraud* (2d ed. 2003 and Supp.).

While laws in many states require salvage vehicles to have their title branded, this requirement often provides little assistance to the consumer. With surprising ease, titles to junk cars that have been branded "salvage" can be exchanged for titles that provide no indication to a consumer being transferred that title that the vehicle has been salvaged. In many states, for example, it is perfectly legal for a dealer to buy a wrecked vehicle that has a salvage title, rebuild the vehicle, and then apply for and obtain a new title that has no indication whatsoever that the vehicle was salvage.

One way to discover whether a car has a prior salvage title is to run a title history with the state registry of motor vehicles. If a car came in from out-of-state, it will also be necessary to run a title history in that other state. Detailed guidance on running title history and other techniques to determine a car's history are found in another NCLC manual, *Automobile Fraud* (2d ed. 2003 and Supp.).

Running a title history is not a sure-fire method of determining a car was previously wrecked, only whether there was a "salvage" title in the car's history. Seven states still do not require notation on a car's title that it has been totally wrecked. In addition, many insurance companies play a major supporting role in this problem by failing to obtain titles that show "salvage" for wrecked cars, even when state statutes require them to do so. Insurance companies reap large benefits from selling salvaged vehicles with "clean" titles because the salvage can be resold to rebuilders at inflated prices (because, in turn, this helps the rebuilders conceal the wreck histories of the vehicles). In addition, partial wrecks retained by the owner and repaired will have no indication on the chain of title of that accident history.

The best way to uncover evidence of a prior wreck or flood damage is to have an expert give the vehicle a careful physical examination.[1586] An expert can almost always determine the extent of the original damage and the quality of the repair job.

5.4.6.6.3 Undisclosed salvage or wreck history as a UDAP violation

It is legal in many states for rebuilders to obtain titles that eliminate the "salvage" labels. Nevertheless, it is a state UDAP violation to sell a wrecked vehicle without disclosing this history.[1587] Similarly, it is deceptive to fail to disclose

---

1586 *See* National Consumer Law Center, Automobile Fraud § 2.2.9 (2d ed. 2003 and Supp.).

1587 Locascio v. Imports Unlimited, Inc., 309 F. Supp. 2d 267 (D. Conn. 2004) (telling buyer that vehicle had only 5% chance of having rebuilt title, and concealing vehicle title from her, was UDAP violation); Salmeron v. Highlands Ford Sales, Inc., 271 F. Supp. 2d 1314 (D.N.M. 2003); Go For It, Inc. v. Aircraft Sales Corp., 2003 WL 21504600 (N.D. Ill. June 27, 2003) (failure to disclose airplane's damage history). *See, e.g.*, Szwebel v. Pap's Auto Sales, Inc., 2003 WL 21750841 (N.D. Ill. July 29, 2003) (magistrate's report and recommendation); *In re* Russell, 181 B.R. 616 (M.D. Ala. 1995); Richie v. Bank of Am. Auto Fin. Corp., 2002 Cal. App. Unpub. LEXIS 6077 (June 28, 2002) (unpublished, citation limited) (allowing car buyer to assert UDAP claim against prior owner who auctioned car to selling dealer without disclosing known frame damage); Plaza Pontiac v. Shaw, 158 Ga. App. 799, 282 S.E.2d 383 (1981) (damaged and reconditioned); Totz v. Continental DuPage Acura, 602 N.E.2d 1374 (Ill. App. Ct. 1992); Crowder v. Bob Oberling Enterprises, Inc., 148 Ill. App. 3d 313, 499 N.E.2d 115 (1986) (failure to disclose salvage history); Singleton v. River Oaks Toyota, Inc., Clearinghouse No. 54581A (Ill. Cir. Ct. Oct. 10, 2000); Ross v. Bob Saks Toyota, Inc., Clearinghouse No. 54,543 (Mich. Cir. Ct. Aug. 1, 2001); Hardy v. Toler, 288 N.C. 303, 218 S.E.2d 342 (1975); Torrance v. AS & L Motors, 459 S.E.2d 67 (N.C. Ct. App. 1995) (salesman's statement that vehicle had not been wrecked was a UDAP violation); Ford v. Brewer, 1986 Ohio App. LEXIS 9790 (Dec. 9, 1986) (failure to disclose that vehicle had been in serious wreck); Fate v. Dick Callendar Buick, 1986 Ohio App. LEXIS 6878 (May 23, 1986) (failure to disclose previous accident); Parrott v. Carr Chevrolet, Inc., 331 Or. 537, 17 P.3d 473 (2001) (reinstating jury award of $1 million in punitive damages); Smith v. Scott Lewis Chevrolet, Inc., 843 S.W.2d 9 (Tenn. Ct. App. 1992); Lorentz v. Deardan, 834 S.W.2d 316 (Tenn. Ct. App. 1992); River Oaks L-M, Inc. v. Whalen, 1998 Tex. App. LEXIS 5687 (Tex. App. Sept. 3, 1998) (car represented as having been in a minor accident was actually in a major collision); Paty v. Herb Adcox Chevrolet Co., 756 S.W.2d 697 (Tex. App. 1988) (failed to disclose demonstrator had been in an accident); 61 Iowa Admin. Code 27.1(714); Consumer Protection Division Enforcement Statements Concerning Motor Vehicle Advertising & Sales Practices, Iowa Dept. of Transportation, Dealer Operating Manual VII-2, Clearinghouse No. 49,156; Ohio Admin. Code 109:4-3-16(B)(14); Opinion of Virginia Attorney General, William Broaddus to the Honorable George Heilig, Jr., Member, House of Delegates, Clearinghouse No. 40,631 (Aug. 21, 1985) (must disclose prior wreck, the extent of repairs, and how repairs affect the warranty). *See also* Tandy v. Marti, 213 F. Supp. 2d 935, 938 n.1 (N.D. Ill. 2002) (denying motion to dismiss consumer's claims against wholesaler who sold vehicle

flood damage to a car.[1588] In addition, most states have enacted disclosure laws concerning salvaged vehicles,[1589] and it may be a *per se* UDAP violation to fail to comply with these statutes.

It is also a UDAP violation to engage in a title laundering scheme to avoid the disclosure of a salvage brand in the chain of title.[1590] This commonly occurs where insurance companies take cars as salvage but do not obtain a salvage title or ship the vehicle out of state where there is not a strict salvage brand requirement.

Insurance companies may also want to keep their name off the title chain, because this is a dead give-away that the vehicle has been transferred to the insurance company after a total loss. One technique is title skipping, whereby the consumer signs over title not to the insurance company, but to an entity that is purchasing the vehicle from the insurance company. Such title skipping violates state titling laws and should be deceptive and even fraudulent. A UDAP action may also proceed against a wholesaler who sold a wrecked car to a retailer, knowing the vehicle was unsafe and that the retailer was likely to sell it to the public.[1591]

Salvage fraud is such a serious safety hazard as well as the obvious pecuniary loss that consumers should consider claims for punitive damages. Where a UDAP statute does not authorize such damages, a common law fraud count can be appended to the UDAP claim. Even if the dealer never states affirmatively that the vehicle has not been wrecked, expert testimony almost always will show that existing wreck damage was so obvious that the dealer had to know that the vehicle had been wrecked. Of course, if the dealer affirmatively represents that the vehicle has not been wrecked, or represents (as often occurs) that the vehicle has had only minor damage, this constitutes fraud even if the dealer did not know that the vehicle had been wrecked. Detailed sample pleadings, as well as detailed analysis concerning common law fraud claims for salvage fraud is found in NCLC's *Automobile Fraud* (2d ed. 2003 and Supp.).

to retailer without revealing damage); Campbell v. Beak, 568 S.E.2d 801 (Ga. App. 2002) (misrepresentation that car had not been wrecked was UDAP violation); Ramirez v. C.L.A.S., Inc., 2000 Mass. App. Div. LEXIS 6 (Jan. 13, 2002) (failure to disclose that repaired salvage vehicle lacked visible VIN so could not be legally driven until state provided replacement VIN was UDAP violation); Morris v. Mack's Used Cars, 824 S.W.2d 538 (Tenn. 1992) (implicit holding is that failure to disclose salvage history is UDAP violation). *But see* Nigh v. Koons Buick Pontiac GMC, Inc., 143 F. Supp. 2d 535 (E.D. Va. 2001) (no UDAP violation where state law requires misrepresentation to be knowing and no evidence that misrepresentation was knowing), *aff'd on other grounds*, 319 F.3d 119 (4th Cir. 2003), *cert. granted on other issues*, 124 S. Ct. 1144 (2004). *See also* Freeman v. A & J Auto MN, Inc., 2003 WL 22136807 (Minn. App. Sept. 16, 2003) (unpublished, citation limited) (representing that vehicle had been stolen and recovered, when in fact it had been wrecked, would be deceptive). *Cf.* Ramsey v. Keever's Used Cars, 92 N.C. App. 187, 374 S.E.2d 135 (1988) (no deception found where seller unaware of prior damage); Hubbard v. Bob McDorman Chevrolet, 104 Ohio App. 3d 621, 662 N.E.2d 1102 (1995) (no UDAP violation where buyer did not prove seller knew vehicle was salvaged).

1588 Letter of Iowa Attorney General William Brouch to General Counsel of Iowa Automobile Dealers Ass'n, Clearinghouse No. 50,411 (Aug. 24, 1993); 37 Pa. Code § 301.2(5); Commonwealth v. Luther Ford Sales Inc., 60 Pa. Commw. 123, 430 A.2d 1053 (1981) (non-disclosure of flood damage even though transaction carried out fairly).

1589 *See* National Consumer Law Center, Automobile Fraud Appx. C (2d ed. 2003 and Supp.) for a state-by-state analysis of these laws.

1590 Conatzer v. American Mercury Ins. Co., 15 P.3d 1252 (Okla. Civ. App. 2000).

1591 Tandy v. Marti, Clearinghouse No. 54557 (S.D. Ill. Apr. 29, 2002).

5.4.6.7 "Lemon Laundering" (Undisclosed Sale of Car Previously Returned as a Lemon)

5.4.6.7.1 Introduction

A current problem with the sale of many low-mileage, recently manufactured used cars is the sellers' failure to disclose that the car had previously been returned to the manufacturer pursuant to a state lemon law. Cars returned as lemons have to go somewhere, and that somewhere is often used car lots where these cars are then sold to unsuspecting consumers. Manufacturers and dealers have obvious incentives to engage in this kind of fraud. They are stuck with thousands of defective cars, and can resell them for more money if they cover up those defects.

This subsection provides a brief overview of lemon laundering and examines UDAP precedent. A more detailed discussion is found in another NCLC manual, *Automobile Fraud* (2d ed. 2003 and Supp.). Sample complaints, interrogatories and document requests in a lemon laundering case are found on the CD-Rom accompanying this volume.

Of course, dealers can be liable under a UDAP claim for failure to disclose the past repair history or defects for a used vehicle. This is examined at § 5.4.6.8.1, *infra*. This subsection focuses on non-disclosure of fairly new vehicles that have been turned into the manufacturer or that have been returned to the dealer pursuant to an arrangement involving the manufacturer.

What is unique about lemon laundering is that the alleged fraud can be conducted not by individual dealers on a case-by-case basis, but by manufacturers on a wholesale basis. For example, the New York Attorney General reached a state-wide settlement with Chrysler, resulting in $2 million in refunds to 400 car owners.[1592] General Motors reached a settlement with the California Department of Motor Vehicles for lemon buybacks in that state, and a similar action involved California and Chrysler.[1593]

1592 *In re* Chrysler Motors Corp. Assurance of Discontinuance (Sept. 8, 1988).

1593 *In re* Chrysler Motors Corp., filed by California Department of Motor Vehicles, Case No. M-605, OAH No. N-940794 (filed Aug. 17, 1994).

Another unique aspect of lemon laundering is that a number of states have enacted statutes regulating the practice, imposing obligations often both on the manufacturer and dealer. A manufacturer's systematic violation of a lemon laundering statute should make class action treatment particularly appropriate, the defendants are deep pockets, individual damages are significant, and the violation is common to a large class of consumers.

5.4.6.7.2 Lemon laundering abuses

When a manufacturer receives a lemon buyback, it rarely scraps the car, but instead resells it. Before selling it, it may ask a local dealer to repair the defect, and state law may require the manufacturer to repair the vehicle. Even when repairs are initiated, however, the question arises as to whether all needed repairs are performed. Manufacturers may repair only one of multiple defects, claiming that the buyback was pursuant to only the one problem.

Alternatively, the manufacturer can sell the vehicle to the dealer taking redelivery from the consumer or to the repairing dealer. In either of these cases, the dealer has actual knowledge of the lemon history. The dealer in this scenario engages in intentional deception where it fails to disclose this knowledge to the consumer buyer.

The most common method of selling a lemon buyback is through an automobile auction. The manufacturer may submit to the auction a memorandum of sale with only a brief description of the vehicle's lemon history. In assessing a manufacturer's liability in a lemon laundering case, carefully assess this description, because all subsequent buyers will rely at best on this description in the memorandum of sale.

5.4.6.7.3 How to discover if a vehicle is a laundered lemon

Examining a vehicle's title history can help uncover lemon laundering. In almost half the states, the fact that a vehicle has been repurchased pursuant to a lemon statute must be branded on the title.[1594] Manufacturers can avoid this requirement by moving the lemon car to a state without a branding requirement or, at least in some states, by settling a buyback case prior to a final order, and then describing the vehicle as a voluntary or "goodwill" buyback not covered by the branding requirement.

Consequently, it is important to examine other aspects of the title history to uncover anything suspicious. A car returned to the manufacturer, particularly during the 12,000-mile warranty period is usually a lemon, unless it was used as a short-term lease vehicle or daily rental (most short-term leases and daily rentals will have a prior owner who was a business, not an individual).

Similarly, be alert for the possibility of a resold lemon whenever a car, in its first year, is sold by the original owner to a dealer representing the manufacturer, particularly to the car's original dealer. Although this may just be a trade-in, consumers usually keep new cars for several years before trading them in.

The title may have to be traced back several sales. The manufacturer may have sold the car to dealer "A" who sold it to dealer "B" who sold it to dealer "C" who then sold the vehicle to the consumer. In the process, the car may have been moved around between several different states. Such movement should always be viewed with suspicion. Details on searching a title history is found in another NCLC volume.[1595]

The most direct and persuasive evidence of a car's lemon history often comes from the vehicle's previous consumer owner. Owning a lemon is an experience few consumers forget. A few states require a dealer to provide the name of the previous owner to prospective buyers. A title search may provide this information as well.

Manufacturers keep excellent records of all their cars to keep track of the warranty period, warranty work performed, and to issue recall notices. Interrogatories and requests for documents from a manufacture in a lemon laundering case are provided in another NCLC manual.[1596]

The dealer is another good source of information. A number of dealers can be involved in a transaction—most particularly the dealer who serviced the car before the buyback and the dealer selling the laundered lemon to the consumer. The dealer servicing the vehicle before the buyback should have records of all repair work, which may also include correspondence with the prior owner. Actual interviews with dealer personnel may also prove helpful. Interrogatories and requests for documents from a servicing dealer in a lemon laundering case are provided in hard copy and on a CD-Rom in NCLC's *Automobile Fraud* (2d ed. 2003 and Supp.)

It is also useful to find out as much from the selling dealer as possible, including the chain of ownership back to the manufacturer and what each person in the chain told the next dealer concerning the car's repair history. A selling dealer's knowledge of the lemon history may raise liability issues for that dealer. Conversely, if that dealer was not told the lemon history, someone in the chain of ownership hid this information.

1594 *See* National Consumer Law Center, Automobile Fraud Appx. C (2d ed. 2003 and Supp.) for a state-by-state analysis of these laws.

1595 *See* National Consumer Law Center, Automobile Fraud Ch. 2 (2d ed. 2003 and Supp.). *See also id.* at Appx. D for a listing of state sources on title history.

1596 *See* the companion CD-Rom to National Consumer Law Center, Automobile Fraud (2d ed. 2003 and Supp.); *see also* Consumer Law Pleadings, No.2, § 6.1 (CD-Rom and Index Guide), also found on the CD-Rom accompanying this volume.

Another possibility is to ask the selling dealer or some other repair or body shop to examine the vehicle to discover a lemon history. Prior repair work may be visible. The repair shop may also have access to technical service bulletins that discuss known defects and suggested repairs.

Certain states allow the manufacturer who provides a buyback the right to recoup fees and registration paid to the state.[1597] In those states, the manufacturer's request for reimbursement from the state is direct evidence that the vehicle was in fact repurchased pursuant to the lemon law.

5.4.6.7.4 Lemon laundering as a UDAP violation

While there is little UDAP precedent dealing with lemon laundering, there also should be little question that the undisclosed sale of a vehicle with a lemon buyback history is a state UDAP violation, since any misrepresentation or failure to disclose a vehicle's prior use is a UDAP violation.[1598] The consumer should be able to bring such a claim against both the selling dealer and the manufacturer. The lack of privity between the manufacturer and consumer is no defense for the manufacturer in a UDAP action.[1599] A dealer's ignorance of the manufacturer's lemon laundering is also no defense for the dealer: knowledge and intent are not elements of a UDAP claim.[1600]

New Mexico UDAP regulations provide that it is an unfair or deceptive trade practice for a dealer or manufacturer to sell a vehicle knowing that it has a lemon buyback history unless prior to the sale the dealer or manufacturer clearly and conspicuously discloses in writing to any prospective purchaser that the vehicle was returned due to one or more defects under the lemon law of New Mexico or any other state.[1601] The dealer or manufacturer must also disclose the nature of the defects, if known.[1602]

In addition, § 5.4.6.7.5, *infra* indicates that a number of states have enacted state lemon laundering legislation. A violation of such a statute may be a UDAP violation, either by the terms of the statute itself, or because violation of a statute protecting the public is an unfair practice.[1603]

1597 *See, e.g.*, Cal. Civ. Code § 1793.25.

1598 *See* § 5.4.3.4, *supra*. *See also* Alexander v. DaimlerChrysler Corp., 2004 WL 179369 (N.C. Super. Jan. 30, 2004) (dealer's violation of lemon laundering law is UDAP violation if proven); Inman v. Ken Hyatt Chrysler Plymouth, Inc., 294 S.C. 240, 363 S.E.2d 691 (1988) (misrepresented prior use as demonstrator when it had been returned for repair problems).

1599 § 4.2.15, *supra*.

1600 §§ 4.2.4, 4.2.5, *supra*.

1601 New Mexico Office of the Attorney General Regulations for the Advertising and Sale of Motor Vehicles, N.M. Admin. Code § 12.2.4.28.

1602 *Id.*

1603 *See* § 3.2.7, *supra*.

5.4.6.7.5 State lemon laundering statutes

Forty states and the District of Columbia have enacted lemon laundering laws.[1604] (Another NCLC manual examines these statutes in detail;[1605] this discussion will only summarize that analysis.) These statutes are useful supplements to a UDAP claim. A violation of the standards set out in the state lemon laundering statute may be a UDAP violation. The lemon laundering laws also establish title identification requirements that are useful in discovery in a UDAP case. In addition, a lemon laundering statutory claim may be the best approach to a class action against the manufacturer, since it may be relatively straight-forward to show a manufacturer's widespread violation of the specific requirements of a state lemon laundering statute.[1606]

Lemon laundering statutes vary significantly from state to state. In general, when a manufacturer buys back a car, the lemon laundering law usually requires the manufacturer to disclose that the car was a buyback and in a number of states must brand the title with a lemon law warning prior to resale,[1607] using such terms as "manufacturer buyback,"

1604 Ala. Stat. §§ 8-20A-3, 8-20A-4, 8-20A-5; Alaska Stat. § 45.45.335; Ariz. Rev. Stat. Ann. § 44-1266; Ark. Code. Ann. § 4-90-412; Cal. Civ. Code §§ 1793.23, 1793.24; Colo. Rev. Stat. § 6-1-708(1)(b); Conn. Gen. Stat. Ann. §§ 42-179(g), 42-179(i); D.C. Code Ann. § 50-502(g)(3); Fla. Stat. Ann. §§ 681.111, 681.112, 681.114(2), 319.14; Ga. Code. Ann. § 10-1-785; Haw. Rev. Stat. §§ 481I-3(k), (l), 481I-3(k)(3), 481J-4, 481J-7; Idaho Code § 48-905; 625 Ill. Comp. Stat. § 5/5-104.2; Ind. Code §§ 24-5-13.5-10, 24-5-13.15-11, 24-5-13.5-13; Iowa Code Ann. §§ 322G.11, 322G.12; Kan. Stat. Ann. §§ 50-645, 50-659; La. Rev. Stat. Ann. §§ 51:1945.1, 51:1946; Me. Rev. Stat. Ann. tit. 10, §§ 1167, 1163(7); Md. Code Ann. Com. Law § 14-1502; Mass. Gen. Law. ch. 90, § 7N1/2(5); Minn. Stat. Ann. §§ 325F.655(5)(a), 325F.665(5), 325.665(9); Mont. Code Ann. § 61-4-525; N.J. Stat. Ann. § 56:12-35; N.M. Stat. Ann. § 57-16A-7; N.Y. Veh. & Traf. Law § 417-a(2); N.C. Gen. Stat. § 20-351.3(d); N.D. Cent. Code. § 51-07-22; Ohio Rev. Code Ann. § 1345.76; Pa. Stat. Ann. tit. 73, §§ 1960(a) and (b), 1961, and 1962; R.I. Gen. Laws. §§ 31-5.2-9, 31-5.2-10. 31-5.2-11; S.C. Code Ann. §§ 56-28-50, 56-28-100, 56-28-110; S.D. Codified Laws Ann. § 32-6D-9; Tex. Occupations Code § 2301.610; Utah Code Ann. §§ 41-3-406 to 41-3-414, 41-1a-522; Vt. Stat. Ann. tit. 9, §§ 4179, 4181; Va. Code §§ 18.2-11, 59.1-207.15, 59.1-207.16:1; Wash. Rev. Code. Ann. § 19.118.061; W. Va. Code §§ 46A-6A-7, 46A-6A-9; Wis. Stat. Ann § 218.0171(2)(d). See National Consumer Law Center, Automobile Fraud Appx. C (2d ed. 2003 and Supp.) for a summary of each of these statutes.

1605 *See* National Consumer Law Center, Automobile Fraud (2d ed 2003 and Supp.).

1606 *See, e.g.*, *In re* Chrysler Motors Corp. Assurance of Discontinuance (Sept. 8, 1988). Chrysler apparently violated N.Y. Vehicle and Traffic Law § 417-a(2) and Gen. Bus. Law § 198-a(c).

1607 Ala. Stat. § 8-20A-4 (Michie); Cal. Civ. Code §§ 1793.23, 1793.24 (West); Conn. Gen. Stat. Ann. §§ 42-179(g); 42-179(i) (West); D.C. Code Ann. § 50-502(g)(3) (Michie); Fla. Stat. Ann. §§ 681.114(2), 319.14 (West); Ind. Code §§ 24-5-13.5-10, 24-5-13.15-11, 24-5-13.5-12 (Michie); Iowa Code Ann. § 322G.12 (West); La. Rev. Stat. Ann. § 51:1945.1 (West); Md.

"lemon law buyback," or "did not conform to its warranty." If the car has a dangerous defect, some states prohibit resale within the state.[1608]

Statutes differ as to whether there must be an additional disclosure about the nature of the repair problem and the repairs performed to correct the problem. In some states, this disclosure is to the dealer buying the vehicle from the manufacturer and in others to the consumer.

The application of a state lemon laundering statute may be affected by the exact nature of the manufacturer's buyback of the vehicle in question. Manufacturers will allege that they have not violated a state lemon laundering statute because the vehicle technically was never a lemon, that the manufacturer repurchased the car as a goodwill gesture and not pursuant to a state lemon law. The resolution of this defense will generally turn on the exact language of the state lemon laundering statute and on the precise facts of the case. Of course, even if the lemon laundering statute is not technically violated, it is still a UDAP violation for the manufacturer and dealer to fail to disclose the major repair history of a vehicle.

When a consumer sues a manufacturer for failing to comply with the state lemon laundering statute, the manufacturer is likely to raise privity as a defense—that the consumer purchased the car from a dealer, and not from the manufacturer. Nevertheless, lack of privity is not a defense to a state UDAP claim.[1609] It should not be a defense under a state lemon laundering statute either. The statutes place the obligation on the manufacturer to disclose, not on the dealer. It is unlikely that the legislative intent was that there would be no remedy for the manufacturer failing in that duty.

5.4.6.7.6 Other causes of action

A manufacturer or dealer's knowing and intentional misrepresentation about a vehicle's history should also be sufficient to prove common law fraud or deceit, which can lead to a punitive damages award. The same facts may also be sufficient for a federal or state RICO claim that can lead to treble damages and attorney fees. Even an unintentional misrepresentation about a lemon history may allow rescission of the sales agreement.

Breach of express and implied warranties and Magnuson-Moss Act violations would also be available where an automobile's defects are at variance with the vehicle's warranties. Usually in a used car sale, the dealer offers the warranty, but some state lemon laundering statutes require that the manufacturer provide the consumer with a warranty as well. The statutory buyback claim may also overlap with the manufacturer's continuing responsibility under the original new vehicle warranty.

In fact, in states with lemon laws expressly covering resale of low-mileage vehicles sold with the remainder of the original factory warranty, the consumer may be able to take advantage of a state lemon law to return the vehicle to the manufacturer.[1610] In that case, the vehicle will be returned to the manufacturer for major repair problems by two different consumers!

5.4.6.8 Non-disclosure or Misrepresentation of Vehicle Defects

5.4.6.8.1 General

Many vehicles have defects, but were never returned as lemons to the manufacturer. Sale of used cars without disclosing serious defects should be a UDAP violation.[1611] Even though the FTC considered and rejected a version of the FTC Used Car Rule that would have required dealer disclosure of mechanical defects, the fact that the FTC failed to do so does not prevent it from being a UDAP violation to fail to disclose such defects.[1612]

A car dealer was found subject to treble the consumer's personal injuries where it failed to disclose a car was sold with defective brakes.[1613] Similarly, it can be unconscionable to fail to give a car purchaser a refund by stalling and not disclosing that a defect is permanent.[1614] State inspection statutes also provide protections for used car buyers. A dealer's violation of an inspection statute may be a *per se* UDAP violation.[1615]

Code Ann. Com. Law § 14-1502 (Michie); N.J. Stat. Ann. § 56:12-35 (West); N.Y. Veh. & Traf. Law § 417-a(2); Ohio Rev. Code Ann. § 1345.76; Pa. Stat. Ann. tit. 73, §§ 1960(a) and (b), 1961, and 1962; S.D. Codified Laws Ann. § 32-6D-9 (Michie); Utah Code Ann. §§ 41-3-409, 41-1a-522 (Michie); Vt. Stat. Ann. tit. 9, § 4181 (Michie); Wash Rev. Code. Ann. § 19.118.061 (West).

1608 *See, e.g.*, N.H. Rev. Stat. § 357-D:12; Pearn v. Daimlerchrysler Corp., 148 Ohio App. 3d 228, 772 N.E.2d 712 (2002) (restrictions on resale place non-delegable duty upon manufacturer); Vt. Stat. Ann. tit. 9, § 4181.

1609 *See* § 4.2.15.3, *supra.*

1610 *See* Jensen v. BMW of N. Am., 35 Cal. App. 4th 112, 41 Cal. Rptr. 2d 295 (1995).

1611 Check v. Clifford Chrysler-Plymouth, 794 N.E.2d 829 (Ill. App. 2003) (UDAP violation to sell vehicle with substantially defective paint job as new); Calimlim v. Foreign Car Center, Inc., 392 Mass. 228, 467 N.E.2d 443 (1984); Mackesy v. Fotopoulos, 2002 WL 971812 (Mass. App. May 7, 2002). *See also* Kopischke v. First Continental Corp., 610 P.2d 668 (Mont. 1980). *But see* Walker v. Cadillac Motor Car Div., 63 Ohio App. 3d 220, 578 N.E.2d 524 (1989) (representation that car was in "A-1" condition not deceptive where buyer did not believe it and car performed adequately given its age and mileage).

1612 *See* Totz v. Continental DuPage Acura, 602 N.E.2d 1374 (Ill. App. Ct. 1992); Hinds v. Paul's Auto Werkstett, Inc., 107 Or. App. 63, 810 P.2d 874 (1991).

1613 Mahan Volkswagen, Inc. v. Hall, 648 S.W.2d 324 (Tex. App. 1982).

1614 North Star Dodge Sales, Inc. v. Luna, 653 S.W.2d 892 (Tex. App. 1983), *aff'd in part, rev'd in part on other grounds*, 667 S.W.2d 115 (Tex. 1984).

1615 Ritchie v. Empire Ford Sales Inc. (N.Y. City Ct. Nov. 7, 1996).

Of course, it is clear that used car dealers can not misrepresent that a car is defect-free.[1616] For example, it is deceptive to misrepresent that a vehicle does not have carburetor problems, and to claim subsequently that any carburetor problems have been repaired.[1617] Dealers also can not misrepresent that a car had passed a state safety inspection.[1618] A complaint and discovery requests in a case involving dealer misrepresentation of a used car's condition are found on the CD-Rom accompanying this volume.

5.4.6.8.2 The special case of a demonstrator with a repair history

A vehicle that is a true demonstrator, program car, executive vehicle, or the like has never been titled, and still retains its status under many state laws as a new vehicle. This has an interesting application where, as is the case in many states, a state law requires disclosure of damage to new vehicles if that damage is over a certain dollar amount.[1619] Unless specifically excluded by state law, demonstrators should be covered by these new car damage disclosure laws. As a result, dealers will have to provide detailed disclosures of prior repairs for such vehicles that exceed the statute's dollar threshold. The failure should be a violation of these statutes and a UDAP violation.[1620]

5.4.6.8.3 Dealer re-sale of the same junk used RV or car to lure consumers into more costly deals

Apparently, some used vehicle dealers, particularly recreational vehicle dealers, are engaging in a churning scheme whereby they seek out defective vehicles to be re-sold to multiple consumers. These junkers are advertised at very low prices, bringing customers onto the lot. The consumer is either switched to another vehicle or sold the defective vehicle. When it soon breaks down, the consumer brings the vehicle back and is switched into another vehicle. The consumer often does not realize that the trade-in for the junk vehicle is lower than what the consumer paid for it originally. The consumer is switched to a more expensive vehicle and the dealership has made a profit on the sale of the junk vehicle on top of its profit selling the second vehicle. Apparently training tapes actually teach this technique. One attorney reports that one junk recreational vehicle was sold five times by one dealer.

5.4.6.9 Misrepresentations Concerning Clear Title

When a car dealer represents that it can sell a car, it represents that it has good title to the car.[1621] It is a UDAP violation for even an innocent car dealer relying on a seemingly valid certificate of title to sell a car that later turns out to be stolen.[1622] It is also a UDAP violation to sell an automobile without a certificate of title in violation of the state certificate of title law.[1623] The dealer must properly handle any lien on the car.[1624]

1616 FTC Used Car Rule, 16 C.F.R. § 455.1 [*reprinted at* Appx. B.6, *infra*]; Rose v. Ford, 2003 WL 21495081 (Cal. App. June 30, 2003) (unpublished, citation limited); Briggs v. Carol Cars, Inc., 407 Mass. 391, 553 N.E.2d 930 (1990) (misrepresentation that car was in good condition, had only one owner, had low mileage and had certain repairs violated UDAP statute); Mackesy v. Fotopoulos, 2002 WL 971812 (Mass. App. May 7, 2002); Morris v. Bailey, 358 S.E.2d 120 (N.C. Ct. App. 1987); Lee v. Payton, 313 S.E.2d 247 (N.C. Ct. App. 1984); Howard v. Norman's Auto Sales, 2003 WL 21267261 (Ohio App. June 3, 2003) (unpublished, citation limited) (dealer violated UDAP statute by representing that car was in good condition and that it would not need repairs for 6–8 months); Murray v. D&J Motor Co., 958 P.2d 823 (Okla. App. 1998) (false representations that car had been inspected, was fine and reliable, and that nothing was wrong with engine, created jury question as to UDAP violation); Harris v. Chalet Car Co., 280 Or. 679, 572 P.2d 623 (1977); Wolverton v. Stanwood, 278 Or. 341, 563 P.2d 1203 (1977); Pennsylvania Regulations of the Bureau of Consumer Protection, 37 Pa. Code § 301.2(5), Automobile Industry Trade Practices (1978); Dillan v. Troublefield, 601 S.W.2d 141 (Tex. Civ. App. 1980) (misrepresentation concerning the need for new parts and repairs); Valley Datsun v. Martinez, 578 S.W.2d 485 (Tex. Civ. App. 1979); State v. Ralph Williams' N.W. Chrysler Plymouth, Inc., 87 Wash. 2d 298, 553 P.2d 423 (1976); Testo v. Russ Dunmire Oldsmobile, Inc., 16 Wash. App. 39, 554 P.2d 349 (1976). *See also* People v. Conway, 42 Cal. App. 3d 875, 117 Cal. Rptr. 251 (1974); Gent v. Collinsville Volkswagen, 116 Ill. App. 3d 496, 451 N.E.2d 1386 (1983); Bernard v. Central Carolina Truck Sales, 314 S.E.2d 582 (N.C. Ct. App. 1984).

1617 Town East Ford Sales, Inc. v. Gray, 730 S.W.2d 796 (Tex. App. 1987).

1618 Viene v. Concours Auto Sales, Inc., 787 S.W.2d 814 (Mo. Ct. App. 1990).

1619 *See* § 5.4.7.4, *supra.*

1620 *See* Neal Pope, Inc. v. Garlington, 537 S.E.2d 179 (Ga. Ct. App. 2000).

1621 Lone Star Ford, Inc. v. McGlashan, 681 S.W.2d 720 (Tex. App. 1984).

1622 Regency Nissan, Inc. v. Taylor, 194 Ga. App. 645, 395 S.E.2d 665 (1990) (where seller has notice of potential title problem, must take reasonable response to ascertain true facts); Keller v. Judd, 671 S.W.2d 604 (Tex. App. 1984).

1623 Mont. Admin. R. § 2.61.204(14); *In re* Jenkins, 249 B.R. 532 (Bankr. W.D. Mo. 2000) (failure to deliver title is common law fraud); Blevins v. Wright's Fin. Servs., Inc., No. 95-CVH-2435 (Ohio Mun. Ct. 1996); Franklin v. State, 631 S.W.2d 519 (Tex. App. 1982); *see also* Griffin v. Security Pacific Auto. Fin. Servs. Corp., 33 F. Supp. 2d 926 (D. Kan. 1998) (plaintiffs had UDAP claim against seller despite fact that sale was void because of failure to deliver title); Antle v. Reynolds, 15 S.W.3d 762 (Mo. App. 2000); Renner v. Derin Acquisition Corp., 111 Ohio App. 3d 326, 676 N.E.2d 151 (1996); Dan Boone Mitsubishi, Inc. v. Ebrom, 830 S.W.2d 334 (Tex. App. 1992).

1624 Gill v. Petrazzuoli Brothers, Inc., 10 Conn. App. 22, 521 A.2d 212 (1987).

5.4.6.10 Misrepresentations of Vehicle Characteristics

Used car dealers can not misrepresent a car's characteristics, such as the number of cylinders that a vehicle contains.[1625] It is also deceptive to fail to disclose that the engine in the vehicle is not the type designed for that vehicle.[1626] A dealer engages in a deceptive practice where it sells an engine different than represented, and which was not in as good working order as represented.[1627] Misrepresenting the model of a vehicle is a UDAP violation.[1628]

5.4.6.11 Misrepresentations as to Vehicle Warranty

Dealers can not misrepresent the extent of the warranty,[1629] or represent that a vehicle is sold with a warranty, when it is not.[1630] Dealers must also disclose, prior to sale, that a used vehicle is sold without any warranty,[1631] or if it contains a warranty, the terms of any written warranty offered in connection with the sale of a used vehicle.[1632]

5.4.6.12 Excessive Price

Used car dealers are notorious for price gouging. There is a growing body of evidence that dealers discriminate on the basis of price based on race, gender, and other invidious categories. Such price discrimination may violate federal and state discrimination statutes.[1633] Where excessive used car prices are hidden in a finance charge, this may also lead to Truth in Lending violations.[1634]

The UDAP issue will be whether excessively high prices are unfair or deceptive. There should be no question that it is deceptive to make affirmative misrepresentations that a sale price is low, competitive, at book value, or the like.[1635] Similarly deceptive is the practice of raising the price in the sales agreement to a level higher than agreed upon.[1636] It can also be deceptive to sell a vehicle for a price higher than it advertised.[1637] The more difficult question is whether evidence of a high price by itself is unfair or deceptive. At least one case has found selling cars at unreasonably high prices to be a UDAP violation.[1638] It may also be deceptive to fail to disclose that a price is higher than the MSRP or higher than normal.

The consumer has an interesting claim relating to the sale of overpriced used cars where the dealer also sells the consumer gap insurance. This insurance pays off any remaining amount the consumer may owe after the consumer's car insurance pays off a total loss. For example, the consumer's pay-off on a loan may exceed the car's fair market value as determined by the insurance company, and the automobile insurance policy will pay out no more than that amount. Gap insurance covers this difference between the amount owed on the loan and the insurance payment.

However, the gap insurance policy may exclude any car purchased if the amount financed exceeds 115% or some other percentage of the retail value of such a vehicle as specified in a car value guidebook issued by the National Automobile Dealers Association or similar entity. Thus, a dealer who charges the consumer far in excess of the retail value for the car has actual knowledge that the gap insurance it sells on the vehicle is totally worthless.[1639]

5.4.6.13 Buy Here—Pay Here Dealerships

5.4.6.13.1 General

In recent years there has been an explosive growth of "buy here—pay here" dealerships. These used car dealers concentrate on those who perceive themselves as high credit risks who would have difficulty finding automobile financing elsewhere. Targeted-advertising offers financing for all comers, which is not difficult for the dealer because the price of the vehicle may be fantastically overpriced, and the dealer may demand a large down payment that exceeds the vehicle's value. (It is a UDAP violation to advertise financing for

1625 Duncan v. Luke Johnson Ford Inc., 603 S.W.2d 777 (Tex. 1980).

1626 Merza v. Stephen's World of Wheels, Clearinghouse No. 40,633 (Conn. Super. Ct. 1985).

1627 Wolverton v. Stanwood, 278 Or. 341, 563 P.2d 1203 (1977). *See also* Givens v. Bourrie, 190 Ga. App. 425, 379 S.E.2d 223 (1989) (seller misrepresented size of rebuilt engine to be inserted into vehicle).

1628 Fribourg v. Vandemark, 1999 Ohio App. LEXIS 3424 (July 26, 1999) (dealer misrepresented Beretta as Beretta GT).

1629 FTC Used Car Rule, 16 C.F.R. § 455.1; Ciampi v. Ogden Chrysler Plymouth, Inc., 634 N.E.2d 448 (Ill. App. Ct. 1994).

1630 FTC Used Car Rule, 16 C.F.R. § 455.1; Hardy v. Toler, 288 N.C. 303, 218 S.E.2d 342 (1975).

1631 FTC Used Car Rule, 16 C.F.R. § 455.1.

1632 *Id.*

1633 *See, e.g.*, 15 U.S.C. § 1691 (Equal Credit Opportunity Act), 42 U.S.C. §§ 1981, 1982, 1988 (Civil Rights Acts). *See generally* National Consumer Law Center, Credit Discrimination (3d ed. 2002 and Supp.).

1634 *See* National Consumer Law Center, Truth in Lending § 3.10 (5th ed. 2003 and Supp.).

1635 Davis v. Wholesale Motors, Inc., 949 P.2d 1026 (Haw. App. 1997) (misrepresentation of vehicle's list price was UDAP violation).

1636 People v. Conway, 42 Cal. App. 3d 875, 117 Cal. Rptr. 251 (1974).

1637 *See* Castro v. Union Nissan, Inc., 2002 WL 1466810 (N.D. Ill. July 8, 2002).

1638 State v. Ralph Williams N.W. Chrysler Plymouth, Inc., 87 Wash. 2d 298, 553 P.2d 43 (1976). *See also* Bruner v. Credit Motors, Inc., Clearinghouse No. 55602 (Toledo Mun. Ct., Lucas County, Ohio, Mar. 22, 1991).

1639 *See* Johnson v. Rohr-Ville Motors, Inc., 1996 U.S. Dist. LEXIS 11089 (N.D. Ill. Aug. 2, 1996).

all comers, and then to turn a consumer down for financing.[1640])

"Buy here, pay here" dealerships often require the consumer to stop by the dealership every pay day, so that payment may be required twice a month or even weekly. Missing just one weekly payment can lead to repossession.

Some "buy here, pay here" dealerships may even use starter-interruption devices. If a consumer does not go to the dealership to make a payment, the dealership does not provide a new code. Without the new code, the vehicle will not start.

One survey found the average "buy here, pay here" dealership sold 588 cars a year, at an average net profit of $1226 per car (compared to $230 net profits for a new vehicle at a new car dealership, including finance and insurance income). It estimates that there are 10,000 "buy here, pay here" dealerships around the country, almost all of which are independent used car dealerships.[1641]

An important characteristic of a "buy here—pay here" dealership is that the consumer is rarely told the vehicle's price. Its price is not disclosed in advertising, is not posted on the vehicle or elsewhere on the lot, and is not disclosed during sales negotiations. Consumer questions concerning price are defeated with a reference to the consumer's poor credit, and the opportunity to restore that credit through a purchase. The dealer instead concentrates on the consumer's ability to leave the lot with a car and the monthly payment.

The car is usually sold based on a fixed formula, commonly a multiple of the car's actual cash value. Typical formulas result in prices at least two times actual cash value. The dealer will then seek a down payment exceeding the car's cost to the dealer and even exceeding the car's actual cash value. With a large enough down payment, the dealer profits even if the consumer never makes a payment. The importance of the down payment in this scheme is evidenced by the fact that the salesperson's commission may be based not on the car's selling price, but on the size of the down payment.

While stated interest rates will be high, the actual rate will be much higher because part of the financing costs will be hidden in the high sales price. A company, for example, may sell virtually the same car at another of its dealerships across town at a very different price. Pay special attention to who owns a "buy here—pay here" dealership. Is the lot just a department of a larger dealership? Does the owner also own other dealerships? There may even be special salespeople that just sell "buy here—pay here" at the same location that other consumers pay more standard prices.

Evidence that the same person sells similar cars at very different prices is evidence of hidden finance charges. The difference in cash prices is really based on the risk of financing, and this risk is a finance charge under Truth in Lending. Disclosing this portion of the cash price in the amount financed instead of as a finance charge should violate Truth in Lending. The practice may also be deceptive, because the dealer is misrepresenting the actual terms of sale and financing and because the dealer hides the true cost of financing and the fact that the same car can be purchased from another subsidiary for a very different price.[1642]

Pay special attention at "buy here—pay here" dealerships to representations that certain add-ons are required because the consumer is such a bad credit risk. For example, the dealer may state that credit life, accident and health, or unemployment insurance are required, when the actual Truth in Lending disclosure statement indicates they are optional. If an option is required because of the credit transaction, then the option is likely to be viewed as a finance charge, again leading to a Truth in Lending violation, because the charge almost certainly will be included instead in the amount financed.

5.4.6.13.2 *Credit repair laws may apply to "buy here—pay here" dealerships*

An integral part of most "buy here—pay here" dealerships is that they offer to improve the consumer's credit rating, presumably by providing financing that allows the consumer to build a credit history. As examined in another section, *supra*, such representations may bring the dealership within the scope of the federal or a state credit repair statute.[1643] If that is the case, the dealership has to offer a three-day cooling-off period, the transaction can be voided if the law is violated, and other significant consumer rights are provided.[1644]

5.4.6.13.3 *Revolving repossession practices*

"Buy here—pay here" dealerships aggressively repossess cars if the consumer is behind in monthly or weekly payments. This can quickly lead to a "revolving repossession" scheme because the cars have such low cash value and because the dealership can turn around and sell the same car for so much. That is, there is a tendency for "buy here—pay here" dealerships to purchase the car back themselves and

1640 Vermont Consumer Fraud Rules, Rule CF 118, Automobile Advertising. *See also* § 5.1.7.1, *supra*.

1641 Leedom and Assocs. L.L.C., Sarasota, Florida, *as reported at* www.autonews.com/article.cms?articleId=41507.

1642 State *ex rel.* Brady v. 3-D Auto World, 2000 Del. Super. LEXIS 17 (Jan. 19, 2000) (increasing the price of the car for credit customers while advertising "0% financing" may be a UDAP violation if it deceives buyers); Vermont Consumer Fraud Rules, Code Vt Rules 06 031 018, Rule CF 118.06(c), Automobile Advertising (if the dealer will increase the car's cash price to finance a particular individual, the dealer must disclose this fact).

1643 *See* § 5.1.2.2, *supra*. *But see* Wojcik v. Courtesy Auto Sales, Inc., 2002 WL 31663298 (D. Neb. Nov. 25, 2002).

1644 *Id.*

resell the car to another consumer. For example, the dealer may initially purchase a car for $500, sell it to a consumer for $4000, a month or two later repossess the car and buy it at its own repossession sale for $400, and then resell the car to a second consumer for $4500. The dealer may also seek thousands of dollars in a deficiency claim from the first buyer.

Revolving repossession schemes typically violate Uniform Commercial Code Article 9 standards, making the dealer liable for substantial statutory penalties and actual damages. These same violations may also lead to UDAP violations. See in particular NCLC's *Repossessions and Foreclosures* § 10.9.4 (5th ed. 2002 and Supp.).

5.4.6.13.4 Information to obtain in discovery

Finance companies and others aggressively promote "buy here—pay here" programs and provide extensive training and advice on how to set up and maintain such a program. Consequently, discovery requests may produce graphic material explaining how the dealership operates. In addition to deposing sales and management personnel involved in the program, request all documents dealing with the program, particularly sales and training manuals. Manuals provided by third-party finance companies should especially be sought.

Also seek representative deal files of both "buy here—pay here" and regular retail sales. Key documents to rely on in a deal file include the dealer's purchase or appraisal documents, which will indicate the dealer's actual cash value for the vehicle; the dealer's "stock card," which may list the actual cash value and asking price; and the sales documents, which will list the selling price. Remember to ask for electronically stored data, as most dealers now use computers.

5.4.6.14 Private Sellers and Curbstoners

Sometimes a consumer buys a vehicle through a want ad from someone who appears to be a private seller. If the vehicle turns out to be a problem vehicle—a rebuilt wreck, for example—the buyer should always investigate whether the seller really is just an individual selling his or her own car. A subpoena to the newspaper where the car was advertised may reveal that the seller has advertised many cars, suggesting that selling cars is actually a side business. Depending on the volume of business, the seller may have been required to obtain a dealer's license from the state. Operating without a license is not only a UDAP violation,[1645] but also gives the buyer a common law right to cancel the sale.[1646]

1645 *See* § 4.7.7.2, *supra.*
1646 *See* § 9.5.8, *infra.*

The FTC's Used Car Rule applies to any person or organization that sold five or more vehicles in the previous twelve months.[1647] If the seller meets this standard but has not complied with the Used Car Rule, most courts will find a UDAP violation.[1648]

Curbstoners are vehicle sellers who do business on street corners or other public places. The FTC's rule requiring a three-day right to cancel for door-to-door and other off-premises sales exempts curbstoners, but only if they have a permanent place of business.[1649] If a curbstoner has a high enough volume to be considered "engaged in" off-premises sales,[1650] and does not have a permanent place of business, then the consumer may have a continuing right to cancel.[1651]

5.4.7 New Car Sales

5.4.7.1 Introduction

New car sales pose a number of issues, covered in various places in NCLC manuals:

- Warranty coverage, breach of warranties, revocation of acceptance, lemon law protections, compliance with service contracts, and automobile repair warranties are covered in NCLC's *Consumer Warranty Law* (2d ed. 2001 and Supp.).
- The credit and lease aspects of new car sales are examined in some depth at NCLC's *Truth in Lending* (5th ed. 2003 and Supp.) and also in NCLC's *The Cost of Credit: Regulation and Legal Challenges* (2d ed. 2000 and Supp.).
- Repossessions is covered in NCLC's *Repossessions and Foreclosures* (5th ed. 2002 and Supp.).
- Discovery in new car cases is examined at § 5.4.2, *supra.*
- Sale of add-ons and other back-end charges is analyzed at § 5.4.3, *supra.*
- Unfair dealer negotiation tactics are reviewed at § 5.4.4, *supra.*
- Yo-yo or spot deliveries are examined at § 5.4.5, *supra.*
- Automobile leasing deception is reviewed at § 5.4.8, *infra.*
- Deceptive representations concerning demonstrators is found at § 5.4.6.3, *supra.*

This subsection focuses on pricing misrepresentations, Monroney stickers, undisclosed damage to new vehicles before they are sold, misrepresentations as to the vehicle's identity, stealing manufacturer rebates, failure to disclose

1647 16 C.F.R. § 455.1(d)(3), *reproduced in* Appx. B.6, *infra.*
1648 *See* § 5.4.6.2, *supra.*
1649 16 C.F.R. § 429.3(a). *See* § 5.8.2.4.1, *infra.*
1650 16 C.F.R. § 429.0(c) (definition of "seller"), (a) (definition of "door-to-door sale" as including any off-premises sale).
1651 *See* § 5.8.2.6.3, *infra.*

vehicle defects, warranty misrepresentations, destination charges, and slow delivery of ordered vehicles.

5.4.7.2 Pricing Misrepresentations

State UDAP statutes prohibit assorted deceptive pricing representations concerning discount and special bargains,[1652] bait and switch, and the advertising of unavailable cars.[1653] Price representations must clearly disclose what the purchase price includes and other additional costs must be disclosed.[1654] An advertisement offering $99 a month, no money down is deceptive where the dealer only is offering the car at $99 a month or no money down, but not both.[1655] Advertising that buyers could just "sign and drive" without stating that they would have to pass a credit check is deceptive.[1656]

A seller can not conceal a car's advertised price or the manufacturer's suggested list price from a walk-in customer, and negotiate a higher price with that customer.[1657] In addition to violating general UDAP prohibitions of deception and non-disclosure, this practice amounts to advertising goods with the intent not to sell them as advertised, a common prohibition in many state UDAP statutes.[1658] Misrepresenting a vehicle's list price is a UDAP violation.[1659] Sellers can not subsequently inflate prices already agreed upon.[1660]

A seller can not agree to one price in the purchase agreement, and then raise the cash price in the credit documents. Such an increase in price for a financed sale is really a finance charge, and is misrepresented as part of the cash price.[1661]

In analyzing dealer new car pricing representations, it is useful to understand the following terms, listed in order of increasing price:

1652 Haleakala Motors Ltd., 88 F.T.C. 753 (1976) (consent order); Standards for Advertising and Selling Motor Vehicles, Conn. Agencies Regs. § 42-110b-28; Florida Attorney General Opinion 88-58, Clearinghouse No. 44,811 (Dec. 23, 1988); Ill. Admin. Code tit. 14, § 475.310 to .420, Motor Vehicle Advertising; Massachusetts Consumer Protection Regulations, Mass. Regs. Code tit. 940, § 5.02 Motor Vehicle Regulations; N.J. Admin. Code ch. 13:45A-26A.4 to .7, Motor Vehicle Advertising Practices; N.M. Admin. Code § 12.24.10 to .23, Advertising and Sale of Motor Vehicles; Ohio Admin. Code § 109:4-3-16, Advertisement and Sale of Motor Vehicles; Oregon Administrative Rules, 137-020-0020, Motor Vehicles Price Disclosure; Pennsylvania Regulations of the Bureau of Consumer Protection, 37 Pa. Code §§ 301.2, 301.4, Automobile Industry Trade Practices; State v. Ralph Williams' N.W. Chrysler Plymouth, Inc., 87 Wash. 2d 298, 553 P.2d 423 (1976). *See* Conley v. Lindsay Acura, 123 Ohio App. 3d 570, 704 N.E.2d 1246 (1997) (not a UDAP violation to fail to state in advertisement that customer could use only one discount coupon per purchase, since omission would not mislead a reasonable consumer).

1653 People v. Conway, 42 Cal. App. 3d 875, 117 Cal. Rptr. 251 (1974); Greenbrier Dodge v. May, 155 Ga. App. 892, 273 S.E.2d 186 (1980); State v. Ralph Williams' N.W. Chrysler Plymouth, Inc., 87 Wash. 2d 298, 553 P.2d 423 (1976); Standards for Advertising and Selling Motor Vehicles, Conn. Agencies Regs. § 42-110b-28; Code Me. Rules 26-239, ch. 105, Sale of New Motor Vehicles; New Jersey Administrative Rules of the Div. of Consumer Affairs, N.J. Admin. Code ch. 13:45A-26A.4, Motor Vehicle Advertising Practices; N.M. Admin Code §§ 12.2.4.10 to .23, Advertising and Sale of Motor Vehicles; Ohio Admin. Code § 109:4-3-16, Advertisement and sale of motor vehicles; Pennsylvania Regulations of the Bureau of Consumer Protection, 37 Pa. Code §§ 301.2, 301.4, Automobile Industry Trade Practices; *see also* Gaylan v. Dave Towell Cadillac, Inc., 15 Ohio Misc. 2d 1, 473 N.E.2d 64 (Mun. Ct. 1984) (deceptive to sell car at price higher than advertised).

1654 Peacock Buick, Inc., 86 F.T.C. 1532 (1975); Haleakala Motors Ltd., 88 F.T.C. 753 (1976) (consent order); Standards for Advertising and Selling Motor Vehicles, Conn. Agencies Regs. § 42-110b-28; Code Me. Rules § 26-239, ch. 105, Sale of New Motor Vehicles; Massachusetts Consumer Protection Regulations, Mass. Regs. Code tit. 940, § 5.02, Motor Vehicle Regulations; New Jersey Administrative Rules of the Div. of Consumer Affairs, N.J. Admin. Code ch. 13:45A-.5 to .7, Motor Vehicle Advertising Practices; Ohio Admin. Code § 109:4-3-16, Advertisement and sale of motor vehicles; Pennsylvania Regulations of the Bureau of Consumer Protection, 37 Pa. Code §§ 301.2, 301.4, Automobile Industry Trade Practices.

1655 State v. Terry Buick, Inc., 520 N.Y.S.2d 497 (Sup. Ct. 1987).

1656 Feinberg v. Red Bank Volvo, Inc., 331 N.J. Super. 506, 752 A.2d 720 (App. Div. 2000) (dealer's acts violated regulation requiring that all limitations be disclosed along with offer).

1657 Castro v. Union Nissan, Inc., 2002 WL 1466810 (N.D. Ill. July 8, 2002); Valencia v. Crabtree Imports, Inc., 2004 WL 424499 (Conn. Super. Feb. 24, 2004) (unpublished, citation limited) (denying motion to strike complaint); Suris v. Gilmore Liquidating, Inc., 651 So. 2d 1283 (Fla. Dist. Ct. App. 1995); Ciampi v. Ogden Chrysler Plymouth, Inc., 634 N.E.2d 448 (Ill. App. Ct. 1994); Affrunti v. Village Ford Sales, Inc., 232 Ill. App. 3d 704, 597 N.E.2d 1242 (1992); Motzer Jeep Eagle, Inc. v. Ohio Attorney General, 95 Ohio App. 3d 183, 642 N.E.2d 20 (1994) (interpreting Ohio UDAP regulation); Hamilton v. Davis Buick Co., Clearinghouse No. 53,569 (Ohio C.P. Ct. June 24, 1980). *See also* Collins v. Fred Haas Toyota, 21 S.W.3d 606 (Tex. App. 2000) (similar ruling under Tex. Finance Code).

1658 Castro v. Union Nissan, Inc., 2002 WL 1466810 (N.D. Ill. July 8, 2002).

1659 Davis v. Wholesale Motors, Inc., 949 P.2d 1026 (Haw. App. 1997).

1660 People v. Conway, 42 Cal. App. 3d 875, 117 Cal. Rptr. 251 (1974); Renner v. Derin Acquisition Corp., 111 Ohio App. 3d 326, 676 N.E.2d 151 (1996), *appeal denied*, 77 Ohio St. 3d 1980, 673 N.E.2d 142 (1996) (enforcing Ohio UDAP regulation that prohibits dealer from demanding more than contract price); Richardson v. Car Lot Co., 10 Ohio Misc. 2d 32, (Akron Mun. Ct. 1983) (raising price $325 for "delivery, get ready, and handling"); Sanders v. Francis, 277 Or. 593, 561 P.2d 1003 (1971); Northview Motors, Inc. v. Commonwealth, 562 A.2d 977 (Pa. Commw. Ct. 1989); Crawford Chevrolet Inc. v. McLarty, 519 S.W.2d 656 (Tex. Civ. App. 1975); Massachusetts Consumer Protection Regulations, Mass. Regs. Code tit. 940, § 5.04, Motor Vehicle Regulations; Ohio Admin. Code § 109:4-3-16, Advertisement and Sale of Motor Vehicles; Pennsylvania Regulations of the Bureau of Consumer Protection, 37 Pa. Code § 301.4, Automobile Industry Trade Practices.

1661 Taylor v. Bob O'Connor Ford, Inc., 1998 U.S. Dist. LEXIS 5095 (N.D. Ill. Apr. 10, 1998).

- *Invoice Price* is the manufacturer's initial charge to the dealer. This is usually higher than the dealer's final cost because dealers often receive rebates, allowances, discounts, and incentive awards. The invoice price always includes freight (also known as destination and delivery). If a car price is based on the invoice price (for example, "at invoice," "$100 below invoice," "two percent above invoice"), be sure freight is not later added to the sales contract.
- *Base Price* is the retail price of the car without options, but includes standard equipment, factory warranty, and freight. This price is printed on the Monroney sticker (see below).
- *Monroney Sticker Price*, which appears on a label required by federal law, indicates the base price, the manufacturer's installed options with the manufacturer's suggested retail price of these options, and the manufacturer's transportation charge.[1662] NADA Guides list the manufacturer's suggested retail price (MSRP) for vehicles. MSRPs can also be found online.[1663] Monroney stickers are not required on recreational vehicle (RV) sales. Consequently, dealers often show manufacturer's invoice prices, but the dealer may alter these invoices with white-out and copy machines so that the disclosed invoice price is far higher than what the dealer actually pays the manufacturer.
- *Dealer Sticker Price*, usually on a supplemental sticker, is the Monroney sticker price plus the suggested retail price of dealer-installed options, such as additional dealer mark-up (ADM) or additional dealer profit (ADP), dealer preparation, and undercoating. Most cars are sold for less than the sticker price because of negotiations between the seller and buyer.

Idaho,[1664] Illinois,[1665] New Jersey,[1666] New Mexico,[1667] and Oregon[1668] UDAP regulations on new car advertising prohibit in great detail various pricing deceptions, and the New York Attorney General has issued similar automobile advertising guidelines.[1669] A New Jersey regulation prohibits any price comparison to dealer cost or inventory price.[1670] The New Jersey Supreme Court has upheld this regulation and expansively interpreted it after a lengthy discussion of how dealer invoice price and dealer cost are terms susceptible to numerous meanings.[1671]

A Missouri Supreme Court decision also upholds a regulation prohibiting references to "invoice" price in advertisements.[1672] Massachusetts UDAP regulations prohibit the use of the term "invoice price" in motor vehicle advertisements except under strict disclosure requirements.[1673] The term is inherently deceptive because it has a specialized, unique meaning in the automobile industry and is subject to manipulation by undisclosed dealer rebates, allowances, and incentives. Vermont now also has automobile advertising regulations that set out various prohibited pricing practices.[1674]

The Wisconsin UDAP statute prohibits comparisons to the manufacturer's suggested retail price without disclosures about the meaning of that price.[1675] The Arizona Attorney General has issued an opinion letter that the use of the Manufacturer's Suggested Retail Price in comparison advertising is deceptive when neither the advertiser nor its competitors have made substantial or regular sales at that price.[1676] This opinion relies heavily on an FTC guide that sets forth the same principle.[1677]

Another misleading advertising ploy is to offer to match competitors' prices, without disclosing the terms and conditions of such an offer. The Missouri Supreme Court upheld sanctions imposed by the state agency against a dealer for violating Missouri's prohibition of such advertisements.[1678] One of the undisclosed conditions there was a requirement for the consumer to have paid a deposit on a vehicle at another dealership. The court held that such conditions can make the "we'll match any price" guarantee illusory, and rejected the dealer's constitutional challenge to the rule.

The Maryland Attorney General has listed seventeen common UDAP violations found in automobile price advertising:

1. Advertising, by use of terms such as "direct factory outlet" or "factory sale," that a special relationship

---

1662 *See* § 5.4.7.3, *infra.*

1663 *See* www.carsdirect.com and www.theautochannel.com.

1664 Idaho Admin. Code § 04.02.01.233. *See also* Office of the Idaho Attorney General, Guidelines for Motor Vehicle Advertising in Idaho (May 29, 1992).

1665 Ill. Admin. Code tit. 14, §§ 475.310 to .420, Motor Vehicle Advertising.

1666 N.J. Admin. Code ch. 13:45A-26A.4 to .8, Motor Vehicle Advertising Practices.

1667 N.M. Admin. Code §§ 12.2.4.10 to .23, Advertising and Sale of Motor Vehicles.

1668 Oregon Administrative Regulations 137-020-0050, Motor Vehicle Advertising; *see also* Oregon Attorney General's Trade Practice Guidelines 87-10, Motor Vehicle Advertising Limitations, 87-3, Invoice Pricing, 87-4, "Full" Cash Price, 87-1, Below Market Financing.

1669 New York Attorney General Automobile Advertising Guidelines (Nov. 1988).

1670 *See* N.J. Admin. Code 13:45A-26A.7(a)(10).

1671 Barry v. Arrow Pontiac, Inc., 100 N.J. 57, 494 A.2d 804 (1985).

1672 Adams Ford Belton, Inc. v. Missouri Motor Vehicle Comm'n, 946 S.W.2d 199 (Mo. 1997), *cert. denied*, 522 U.S. 952 (1997).

1673 Mass. Regs. Code tit. 940, § 5.02(5); Commonwealth v. Fall River Motor Sales, Inc., 409 Mass. 302, 565 N.E.2d 1205 (1991) (enforcing the regulation); *see also* Idaho Consumer Protection Regulations, Idaho Admin. Code 04.02.01.233, Price Advertising; Ill. Admin. Code tit. 14, § 475.410, Motor Vehicle Advertising.

1674 Code Vt. Rules 06-031-018, CF 118, Automobile Advertising.

1675 Wis. Stat. Ann. §§ 100.18, 100.20.

1676 Arizona Attorney General Opinion I95-16 (R95-33), Clearinghouse No. 51.269 (12-12-95).

1677 16 C.F.R. § 233.3(f).

1678 Adams Ford Belton, Inc. v. Missouri Motor Vehicle Comm'n, 946 S.W.2d 199 (Mo. 1997), *cert. denied*, 522 U.S. 952 (1997).

exists between an automobile manufacturer and a particular dealer, when, in fact, no special relationship exists;

2. Advertising that vehicles in stock at a particular location are being "liquidated" or otherwise disposed of by the manufacturer when, in fact, the vehicles are simply being sold by a dealer;
3. Advertising that savings are available because of the volume of vehicles purchased by the dealer when, in fact, the wholesale cost of the vehicle is the same to each dealer regardless of the volume of vehicles purchased;
4. Advertising that vehicles are available for sale at prices under cost, at cost, or slightly above cost when, in fact, the vehicles are being offered at prices that still include significant profit to the dealer,

   or, will result in significant profit when additional funds, held back from the dealer at the time of the transaction, are received;

5. Advertising that a vehicle may be purchased for "no money down" when, in fact, any initial costs such as taxes, tags or freight charges must be paid by the consumer at the time the contract is consummated;
6. Advertising that below-market interest rates are available without prominently disclosing any conditions, other than creditworthiness, that must be satisfied to qualify for such rates;
7. Advertising that a particular vehicle is available at a particular price when, in fact, the vehicle is not available;
8. Advertising that fails to disclose precisely the options and special equipment that are included with a vehicle at the advertised price;
9. Failing to disclose that only a limited number of vehicles are available at an advertised price, when such is the case. Simply stating a vehicle stock number in the advertisement does not adequately disclose this fact;
10. Advertising guaranteed minimum trade-ins when, in fact, the lowest price at which the dealer is prepared to sell a vehicle will be increased to compensate the dealer for the loss it will incur for accepting a trade-in worth less than the guaranteed minimum;
11. Selling a vehicle for more than the current advertised price, even if the advertised price has not been communicated to the purchaser;
12. Advertising financial incentives, such as rebates or below-market interest rates when, in fact, the lowest price at which the dealer is prepared to sell a vehicle is being increased to compensate the dealer for the cost of the incentive. A dealer may advertise such financial incentives if it prominently and clearly discloses the relationship between the financial incentive and the lowest price at which the vehicle will be sold;
13. Advertising that fails to distinguish adequately between the offer of a vehicle for sale and the offer of a vehicle for lease;
14. Advertising that fails to include all the disclosures required under the federal Truth in Lending Act or the federal Consumer Leasing Act;
15. Advertising that lists in small print important disclosures that attempt to modify the message of more prominent portions of the advertisements;
16. Allowing a consumer to accept delivery of a motor vehicle prior to all terms being finalized, including all financial terms, unless the consumer is clearly informed in a separate, prominent notice that a binding contract does not exist and that the motor vehicle can be returned if the consumer is in any way dissatisfied with the proposed deal. Once a contract binding both parties is created, the consumer's right to return the motor vehicle, unless otherwise authorized, is extinguished; and
17. Disposing of a customer's trade-in vehicle before the motor vehicle transaction for which the trade-in was supplied has been consummated.[1679]

The FTC has also challenged the following practices that new car dealers utilize to charge the consumer more than the sticker price: making a profit on "freight" charges by requiring buyers to purchase expensive options or misrepresenting that the dealer can not sell the car without options.[1680]

The Iowa Attorney General's office has stated in enforcement guidelines that it is deceptive to offer accessory merchandise or services as "free" where the motor vehicle itself is sold subject to bargaining.[1681] The FTC has accepted a consent order from a car manufacturer concerning undisclosed conditions put on a $100 offer to test drive one of its cars.[1682] An Ohio court, interpreting a state regulation, has required that a price offer contained in an advertisement must continue in effect for ninety days unless the offer relates to a specific vehicle that is sold or the advertisement states a termination date.[1683]

1679 Letter by Joseph Curran, Jr., Maryland Attorney General, to every licensed auto dealer in Maryland.

1680 Bill Crouch Imports Inc., 96 F.T.C. 111 (1980) (consent order); *see also* Code Me. Rules 26-239, ch. 105 §§ 4, 5, Maine Unfair Trade Practice Regulations, Sale of New Motor Vehicles (dealer must disclose extra options and that purchase of options can not be sale condition).

1681 Consumer Protection Division Enforcement Statements Concerning Motor Vehicle Advertising & Sales Practices, Iowa Dept. of Transportation, Dealer Operating Manual VII-2, Clearinghouse No. 49,156. *See also* Ill. Admin. Code tit. 14, § 475.590, Motor Vehicle Advertising.

1682 Nissan Motor Corp. in USA, 5 Trade Reg. Rep. (CCH) ¶ 23,569 (F.T.C. C-3502 1994) (consent order).

1683 Motzer Jeep Eagle, Inc. v. Ohio Attorney General, 95 Ohio App. 3d 183, 642 N.E.2d 20 (1994).

5.4.7.3 The Monroney Sticker

The manufacturer, prior to delivery of a new vehicle to a dealer, must affix a sticker to the windshield or side window. The sticker must be clear, distinct and correct, and must include the make, model, and vehicle identification number, the final assembly point, the name and place of business of the intended dealer, and how the vehicle is to be transported to that address.[1684]

The sticker also lists the manufacturer's suggested retail price, the suggested retail price of each accessory or option that is physically attached to the vehicle at the time of delivery to the dealer and that is not included in the suggested retail price.[1685] Finally, the sticker shows the amount charged to the dealer for transportation of the vehicle to the location at which it is delivered to the dealer, plus the sum of the vehicle's suggested retail price, options, and delivery charges.[1686]

Any manufacturer who willfully fails to affix such a label or fails to endorse the label or makes any false endorsement will be fined not more than $1000. Such failure with respect to each vehicle constitutes a separate offense.[1687] Anyone who willfully removes, alters, or renders illegible any label or endorsement before the vehicle is delivered to the actual possession of the ultimate purchaser shall be fined not more than $1000 or imprisoned not more than one year, or both. Such removal or alternation respect to each vehicle shall constitute a separate offense.[1688] At least one court has found no private right of action under this federal statute,[1689] but a violation should be a state UDAP violation.

The Monroney sticker price is a suggested retail price. Consequently, a dealer is free to charge more or less than that price for the vehicle. On the other hand, the dealer is not free to advertise a sticker price and then sell the vehicle for more than the advertised price.[1690]

Selling above sticker price is particularly common in situations where the dealer inflates a trade-in value, and then compensates for this by increasing the new vehicle's selling price. Dealers can not accomplish this sleight of hand by concealing or misrepresenting the vehicle's sticker price, or by inflating the price already negotiated.[1691] It can also be deceptive to fail to attach the Monroney sticker price to a vehicle, and then sell the vehicle for more than the sticker price.[1692] An FTC consent order requires a dealer to disclose if the purchase price exceeds the sticker price.[1693]

1684 15 U.S.C. § 1232.

1685 *Id.*

1686 *Id.*

1687 15 U.S.C. § 1233(a), (b).

1688 15 U.S.C. § 1233(c).

1689 Reiff v. Don Rosen Cadillac-BMW, Inc., 501 F. Supp. 77 (E.D. Pa. 1980).

1690 *See* § 5.4.7.2, *supra*; *see also* Reg. Conn. State Agencies 42-110b-28.

1691 *See* § 5.4.7.2, notes 1657–1660, *supra.*

1692 *See* Pappas v. Southwest Partners, Inc., 2002 WL 1334875 (N.D. Ill. June 17, 2002).

5.4.7.4 Undisclosed Damage Before a New Car Is Sold

New automobiles may be damaged in transit to the dealership or may be damaged at the dealership before the consumer takes over ownership. Manufacturers and dealers prefer to fix and repaint these vehicles and pass them off as new. The practice has become so common that about half the states have enacted laws regulating the practice, requiring disclosure of any damage to the vehicle.

Usually, the disclosure need be made only if the damage is over a certain dollar amount.[1694] For example, Alabama

1693 *See In re* Bill Crouch Foreign, Inc., 96 F.T.C. 111 (1980).

1694 Ala. Code § 8-19-5(22)(c) (disclosure when the cost of repairs exceeds 3% or $500, whichever is greater); Ariz. Rev. Stat. Ann. § 28-4411 (disclosure of vehicle repairs costing more than 3% of suggested retail price); Ark. Code Ann. § 23-112-705 (disclosure of damage costing more than 6% of retail value to repair); Cal. Veh. Code Ann. § 9990-9994 (West Supp.) (disclosure when the cost of repairs exceeds 3% or $500, whichever is greater); Fla. Stat. §§ 501.975, 501.976(19) (dealers disclose paint repair costing more than $100 of which they have actual knowledge); Ga. Code Ann. § 40-1-5(b)-(e) (disclosure of paint damage that costs more than $500 to repair or damage that costs more than 5% of the MSRP); Idaho Code § 49-1624 (disclosure of damage costing more than 6% of retail value to repair); 815 Ill. Comp. Stat. § 710/5 (disclosure of damage costing more than 6% of retail value to repair); Ind. Code §§ 9-23-4-4, 9-23-4-5 (4% disclosure threshold); Ky. Rev. Stat. Ann. § 190.0491(5) (Baldwin) (disclosure of damage costing more than 6% of retail value to repair); La. Rev. Stat. Ann. § 32:1260 (disclosure of damage costing more than 6% of retail value to repair); Code of Miss. Rules 50 014 003, Miss. Motor Vehicle Comm'n, Regulation No. 1 (disclosure of damage costing more than 6% of retail value to repair); Minn. Stat. § 325F.664 (disclosure of repairs costing more than 4% of suggested retail price or $500, whichever is greater); N.H. Rev. Stat. Ann. § 357-C:5(III)(d) (disclosure of damage costing more than 6% of retail value to repair); N.Y. Gen. Bus. Law 396-p(5)(a), (d) (McKinney Supp.) (disclosure when the cost of repairs exceeds 5% of suggested retail price); N.C. Gen. Stat. § 20-305.1(d)(5a) and (5l) (disclosure of vehicle repairs costing more than 3% of suggested retail price); N.D. Admin. Code § 37-09-01-01 to -03 (disclosure of repairs costing $3,000 or more); Ohio Rev. Code Ann. § 4517.61 (disclosure of damage costing more than 6% of retail value to repair); Okla. Stat. tit. 47, 1112.1 (disclosure when the cost of repairs exceeds 3% or $500, whichever is greater); Or. Rev. Stat. § 650.155 (manufacturers must disclose all "post-manufacturing" damage and repairs); R.I. Gen. Laws § 31-5.1-18(d), (f) (disclosure of damage costing more than 6% of retail value to repair); S.C. Code § 56-32-20 (disclosure of vehicle repairs costing more than 3% of suggested retail price); Va. Code Ann. § 46.2-1571(D), (E) (disclosure of vehicle repairs costing more than 3% of suggested retail price); Vt. Stat. Ann. tit. 9, 4087(d) (5% disclosure threshold for the first $10,000 in repair costs and 2% thereafter); Wyo. Stat. § 31-16-115 (disclosure of damage costing more than 6% of retail value to repair). *Cf.* Wis. Stat. § 218.0422 (manufacturer must make disclosure to dealer).

requires disclosure of damage where the repair cost exceeds the greater of $500 or 3% of the manufacturer's suggested list price.[1695] New Jersey requires disclosure of vehicle repairs or body work having a retail value of $1000 or more.[1696]

Ohio UDAP rules, like some state statutes, require sellers to disclose the extent of any previous damage to a new car, where the repair cost for the previous damage exceeded six percent of the manufacturer's suggested retail price.[1697] Thus, a seller's failure to disclose that a new car had required $3900 in repairs was a UDAP violation entitling the buyer to rescind the purchase.[1698]

Nevertheless, a large amount of damage can often be incurred without such disclosure, because such statutes typically exclude from the dollar amount bumpers, tires, glass, and other replacement parts that are easily removed and replaced. So for example, the dealer may have to make no disclosure where all a car's windows were broken out, the fenders and hood smashed, all tires slashed, and the lights broken. On the other hand, an appellate court in Kentucky has ruled that its statute applies not just to body damage, but also to mechanical problems that manifest themselves and are repaired prior to sale.[1699]

Some of these statutes will define "new" cars as including demonstrators. In that case, the dealer will have to disclose any damage to the vehicle, even if occurred months after delivery to the dealer and only after thousands of miles of driving.[1700] A more detailed discussion of new car damage disclosure statutes is found in another NCLC manual, *Automobile Fraud* § 6.2.2 (2d ed. 2003 and Supp.).

Even where a state has not enacted a specific statute covering undisclosed damage to new car, or where the damage is under the statute's threshold, the practice can be a state UDAP violation.[1701] Thus it can be deceptive to perform body work on a car, and then repaint it and not disclose the damage.[1702] It is similarly deceptive to fail to disclose paint variations, when in fact the car had been damaged by hail, had to be repainted, and would experience severe repair problems.[1703]

On the other hand, some state statutes that find a violation if the undisclosed damage is over a certain threshold specify that there is no UDAP violation or potential fraud claim if the damage is under the threshold amount. These statutes thus can act as a shield for the manufacturers and dealers, and not just a sword for the consumer.

5.4.7.5 Misrepresentation of Vehicle Identity, Characteristics

Sellers can not switch a different car for the one the consumer believes he or she is buying.[1704] Similarly it may be deceptive for a dealer to negotiate a selling price for a car, and then deliver a substitute car for the same price, but containing fewer options or features.[1705]

A dealer commits a UDAP violation by misrepresenting that a new car is identical to an earlier model.[1706] Dealers can not sell an Oldsmobile with a Chevrolet engine.[1707] Sellers must disclose a vehicle's correct year and make.[1708]

Many, but not all, of the statutes exclude from the computation of repair cost the value of certain components—typically items such as glass, tires, wheels and bumpers—when they are replaced with identical manufacturer's original equipment. *E.g.*, Cal. Veh. Code Ann. § 9990-9994 (West Supp.); Ga. Code Ann. § 40-1-5(b)-(e); 815 Ill. Comp. Stat. § 710/5; Ky. Rev. Stat. Ann. § 190.0491(5) (Baldwin); Okla. Stat. tit. 47, 1112.1; Va. Code Ann. § 46.2-1571(D) (Supp.); Vt. Stat. Ann. tit. 9, 4087(d).

1695 Ala. Code § 8-19-5. *See also* Hines v. Riverside Chevrolet-Olds, Inc., 655 So. 2d 909 (Ala. 1994) (consumer has option of fraud claim for smaller amount of damage even after adoption of regulation); BMW of N. Am. v. Gore, 646 So. 2d 619 (Ala. 1994) (nondisclosure of smaller amount of damage was fraud prior to statute's enactment), *punitive damages award rev'd*, 116 S. Ct. 1589 (1996).

1696 N.J. Admin. Code 13:45A-26A.7(a)7.

1697 Ohio Admin. Code 109:4-3-16(B)(14); Andrews v. Scott Pontiac Cadillac GMC, Inc., 71 Ohio App. 3d 613, 594 N.E.2d 1127 (1991).

1698 Andrews v. Scott Pontiac Cadillac GMC, Inc., 71 Ohio App. 3d 613, 594 N.E.2d 1127 (1991).

1699 Smith v. General Motors Corp., 979 S.W.2d 127 (Ky. App. Ct. 1998).

1700 *See* § 5.4.6.3, *supra*.

1701 Smith v. General Motors Corp., 979 S.W.2d 127 (Ky. App. Ct. 1998) (sale of van as new without disclosure of pre-sale mechanical repairs could be UDAP violation).

1702 Nemore, Nemore & Silverman v. W.A. Austin Chevrolet, D.N.C.V. 81 0054979S (Conn. Super. Ct. 1982); Check v. Clifford Chrysler-Plymouth, 794 N.E.2d 829 (Ill. App. 2003) (UDAP violation to sell vehicle as new after defective paint job to repair pre-sale damage); Watkins v. Roach Cadillac Inc., 7 Kan. App. 2d 8, 637 P.2d 458 (1981); Bell v. Kent-Brown Chevrolet Co., 1 Kan. App. 131, 561 P.2d 907 (1977).

1703 Vercher v. Ford Motor Co., 527 So. 2d 995 (La. Ct. App. 1988).

1704 People v. Conway, 42 Cal. App. 3d 875, 117 Cal. Rptr. 251 (1974); Kohl v. Silver Lake Motors, Inc., 369 Mass. 795, 343 N.E.2d 375 (1976); Tallmadge v. Aurora Chrysler Plymouth, 25 Wash. App. 90, 605 P.2d 1275 (1979). *See also* Dennis Weaver Chevrolet, Inc. v. Chadwick, 575 S.W.2d 619 (Tex. Civ. App. 1979) (switching carburetors).

1705 David McDavid Pontiac, Inc. v. Nix, 681 S.W.2d 831 (Tex. App. 1984). *See also* Ohio Admin. Code § 109:4-3-13, Motor Vehicle Repairs or Services.

1706 Mercedes-Benz of N. Am., Inc. v. Garten, 94 Md. App. 547, 618 A.2d 233 (1993).

1707 Gour v. Daray Motor Co., 373 So. 2d 571 (La. Ct. App. 1979). *See also* Oster v. Swad Chevrolet, 1982 Ohio App. LEXIS 15049 (June 17, 1982) (sale of car with V8 engine where it was represented to have V6 engine).

1708 Burke v. Atamian Porsche Audi Inc., Clearinghouse No. 25,841 (Mass. Super. Ct. 1978); Myers v. Liberty Lincoln-Mercury, Inc., 89 N.C. App. 335, 365 S.E.2d 663 (N.C. Ct. App. 1988); Bernard v. Central Carolina Truck Sales, 314 S.E.2d 582 (N.C. Ct. App. 1984); Standards for Advertising and Selling Motor Vehicles, Conn. Agencies Regs. § 42-110b-28; Code Me. Rules § 26-239, ch. 105 § 7, Sale of New Motor Vehicles; N.J. Admin. Code §§ 13:45A-26A.5, .6, Motor Vehicle Advertising Prac-

A manufacturer may not redesignate the "years" of unsold vehicles.[1709] Sellers are responsible for verifying the accuracy of the advertisements they place, and the buyer does not have a duty to investigate the truth of the statements in the advertisement.[1710]

It is a UDAP violation to recommend a particular model car as able to pull a trailer, and then fail to rectify the situation when the model can not fulfill that purpose.[1711] Another case found actionable various misrepresentations involving the installation of "after-market" air conditioning (i.e., not "factory air").[1712] Claims about automobile fuel consumption must be based on statistically valid tests, and the test results must be at the place of sale in understandable language.[1713] Gas mileage claims must be based on normal vehicle use.[1714] Actionable misrepresentations include a vehicle's structural strength, quickness, or performance.[1715]

tices; Ohio Admin. Code § 109:4-3-16, Advertisement and Sale of Motor Vehicles; Or. Admin. R. § 137-20-0030; Pennsylvania Regulations of the Bureau of Consumer Protection, 37 Pa. Code § 301.4, Automobile Industry Trade Practices. *But cf.* Davis v. Axelrod Chrysler Plymouth, Inc., 2003 WL 194888 (Ohio App. Jan. 30, 2003) (model name on spare tire cover was not misrepresentation of vehicle model where all other documentation identified correct model).

1709 Chrysler Corp., 94 F.T.C. 245 (1979) (consent order); Ford Motor Co., 94 F.T.C. 236 (1979) (consent order); International Harvester Co., 94 F.T.C. 281 (1979) (consent order); Mack Trucks Inc., 94 F.T.C. 236 (1979) (consent order); Paccar Inc., 94 F.T.C. 263 (1979) (consent order); White Motor Corp., 94 F.T.C. 272 (1979) (consent order).

1710 Sauvey v. Ford, 2003 WL 21386282 (Ohio App. June 13, 2003) (unpublished, citation limited).

1711 Jeep Eagle Sales Corp. v. Mack Massey Motors, Inc., 814 S.W.2d 167 (Tex. App. 1991).

1712 *See* Couto v. Gibson, Inc., 1992 Ohio App. LEXIS 756, Clearinghouse No. 46,799 (Feb. 26, 1992).

1713 Ford Motor Co., 93 F.T.C. 873 (1979) (consent order); Chrysler Corp., 87 F.T.C. 719 (1976), *aff'd*, 561 F.2d 357 (D.C. Cir. 1977); Camp Chevrolet Inc., 84 F.T.C. 648 (1974) (consent order); General Motors Corp., 84 F.T.C. 653 (1974) (consent order); McCallum Ford Sales, Inc., 84 F.T.C. 643 (1974) (consent order); *see also* State *ex rel.* Corbin v. Tucson Public Auction, 147 Ariz. 213, 709 P.2d 570 (Ct. App. 1985).

1714 Ford Motor Co., 87 F.T.C. 756 (1976).

1715 Lilly v. Ford Motor Co., 2002 U.S. Dist. LEXIS 910 (N.D. Ill. Jan. 17, 2002) (deceptive public statements regarding stalling problem); Tufts v. Newmar Corp., 53 F. Supp. 2d 1171 (D. Kan. 1999) (false statement regarding weight of recreational vehicle); Scali, McCabe, Sloves, Inc., 115 F.T.C. 96 (1992) (consent order) (advertising agency ordered to pay $100,000 for creating advertisement that misrepresented crashworthiness of vehicle); Ford Motor Co., 93 F.T.C. 873 (1979) (consent order); Chrysler Corp., 87 F.T.C. 719 (1976), *aff'd*, 561 F.2d 357 (D.C. Cir. 1977); General Motors Corp., 85 F.T.C. 27 (1975) (consent order); Ford Motor Co., 84 F.T.C. 729 (1974) (consent order); State *ex rel.* Corbin v. Tucson Public Auction, 147 Ariz. 213, 709 P.2d 570 (Ct. App. 1985) (misrepresentations about ability to tow cars and fuel economy); Bernard v. Central Carolina Truck Sales, 314 S.E.2d 582 (N.C. Ct. App. 1984).

5.4.7.6 Stealing Manufacturer Rebates

There are widespread allegations of dealers stealing rebates that manufacturers provide the consumer. Obviously this practice is a UDAP violation,[1716] in addition to a tort, and the more difficult issue is how to discover and prove that the theft took place.

One pattern is for the consumer to be unaware of the rebate, and the dealer just keeps it. Manufacturers may provide blank rebate checks to dealers by the pad, with instructions for the dealer to write the check out to the consumer at the point of sale. The dealer fills in the consumer's name as payee and sends a duplicate off to the manufacturer. Supposedly, the consumer endorses the check over to the dealer as a down payment, or receives cash for the rebate check.

A subpoena of the dealer's bank records can produce copies of every rebate check, front and *back*, that the dealer deposited into its account. If the consumer to whom the check is made out does not remember any rebate check, then it is possible that the consumer's indorsement of the rebate check back to the dealer has been forged. If there has been forgery, it may prove fruitful to investigate other rebate checks supposedly indorsed to the same dealer.

The other type of rebate theft involves giving the rebate with one hand and taking it away with the other. For example, a dealer may say "you have to pay tax on the rebate amount. So we'll just add the rebate to the car's sale price and deduct it at the bottom." This is only one way by which the dealer raises the car's price by the amount of the rebate, deducts the rebate, and the consumer has received no benefit from the rebate at all—it has been swallowed.

5.4.7.7 Destination Charges

One interesting and unresolved question is whether it is a UDAP violation for automobile manufacturers to include in a new car sticker price a "destination charge" that is not based on actual transportation costs. Some manufacturers use a "destination charge" that is an average charge for all cars shipped that year, and not the actual charge to ship a particular car from the manufacturer to a particular destination. Lawsuits challenging this practice have been settled, but the terms are confidential.

5.4.7.8 Slow and Non-Delivery of Ordered Cars

A few state UDAP regulations establish standards concerning slow delivery of ordered cars.[1717] More generally, it may

1716 Grimaldi v. Webb, 668 N.E.2d 39 (Ill. App. Ct. 1996).

1717 Massachusetts Consumer Protection Regulations, Mass. Regs. Code tit. 940, § 5.04, Motor Vehicle Regulations; Pennsylvania Regulations of the Bureau of Consumer Protection, 37 Pa. Code § 301.4, Automobile Industry Trade Practices.

be a UDAP violation to continually stall a consumer and mislead the consumer into believing a car will be delivered when the dealer has no basis for this claim.[1718] Dealers can not misrepresent that delivery will be soon when they know this will not happen.[1719] Nor can a dealer fail to order a model as promised, and then later try to switch the consumer to a more expensive car.[1720] Ohio UDAP regulations require a dealer to return the consumer's deposit within eight weeks if the consumer's order can not be filled.[1721]

The responsibility to provide accurate information about a car's delivery date is not limited to the dealer. It is deceptive for a car distributor to fail to disclose to a consumer that the automobile dealer the consumer is working with is in financial difficulty and that payment for the car may never be forwarded to the distributor, leaving the consumer with no money and no car.[1722]

5.4.7.9 Misrepresentation of Warranties Offered

Warranties on purchased cars must be disclosed and may not be misrepresented,[1723] and dealers may not misrepresent the characteristics of their own business.[1724] Dealers must comply with warranties, guarantees, and promises.[1725]

One unfair warranty practice is called "burning" a vehicle, whereby a dealer marks a vehicle as sold prior to it actually being sold, allowing the dealer to obtain new allotments of vehicles from the manufacturer because it has already "sold" the vehicles on its lot, and allows the dealer and manufacturer to show investors and others positive sale numbers.

At least certain dealers, when the car is really sold, then fill out a form called a "change of owner name and/or owner's address form." The problem is that the new car warranty begins when the vehicle was burned, rather the actual date the vehicle was sold, cutting down the available warranty coverage.

5.4.7.10 Manufacturer and Dealer Handling of New Car Defects

5.4.7.10.1 Obligation to disclose known defects

Safety and other material defects in a car must be disclosed before purchase.[1726] Failure to disclose defects known at the time of sale is a UDAP violation despite the dealer's later compliance with federal automobile recall notice regulations.[1727] A manufacturer and dealer engage in a deceptive practice when they conceal knowledge concerning a car's defects and misrepresent to a consumer the cause of a car's problems.[1728] Similarly, it is deceptive not to repair defects after assuring the consumer that problems would be fixed.[1729]

1718 Wilman v. Ewen, 230 Kan. 262, 634 P.2d 1061 (1981).

1719 *Id.*; *see also* Foley v. L&L Int'l, Inc., 88 N.C. App. 710, 364 S.E.2d 733 (N.C. Ct. App. 1988); Bob Robertson, Inc. v. Webster, 679 S.W.2d 683 (Tex. App. 1984); Standards for Advertising and Selling Motor Vehicles, Conn. Agencies Regs. § 42-110b-28; Ohio Admin. Code § 109:4-3-16(B)(6), (7), (8), Advertisement and sale of motor vehicles.

1720 Miles Rich Chrysler-Plymouth, Inc. v. Mass, 201 Ga. App. 693, 411 S.E.2d 901 (1991).

1721 Ohio Admin. Code 109:4-3-09; *see also* McCalley v. Ganley Dodge, Inc., Clearinghouse No. 47,846, 1988 Ohio App. LEXIS 375 (Ohio Ct. App. 1988); Hirsch v. Astley Lincoln-Mercury, 1983 Ohio App. LEXIS 13524 (June 30, 1983).

1722 Temborius v. Slatkin, 157 Mich. App. 587, 403 N.W.2d 821 (1986).

1723 Duran v. Leslie Oldsmobile, 594 N.E.2d 1355 (Ill. App. Ct. 1992) (misrepresentation of duration of warranty); State v. Ralph Williams' N.W. Chrysler Plymouth, Inc., 87 Wash. 2d 298, 553 P.2d 423 (1976); N.M. Admin. Code § 12.2.4.25, Advertising and Sale of Motor Vehicles; Pennsylvania Regulations of the Bureau of Consumer Protection, 37 Pa. Code § 301.2, .4, Automobile Industry Trade Practices (1978).

1724 N.J. Admin. Code ch. 13:45A-26A.5, Motor Vehicle Advertising Practices; Pennsylvania Regulations of the Bureau of Consumer Protection, 37 Pa. Code § 301.2, .4, Automobile Industry Trade Practices.

1725 People v. Conway, 42 Cal. App. 3d 875, 117 Cal. Rptr. 251 (1974); Ford Motor Co. v. Mayes, 575 S.W.2d 480 (Ky. Ct. App. 1978); Slaney v. Westwood Auto, Inc., 366 Mass. 688, 322 N.E.2d 768 (1975); Allen v. Parsons, 555 S.W.2d 522 (Tex. Civ. App. 1977); Volkswagen of Am., Inc. v. Licht, 544 S.W.2d 442 (Tex. Civ. App. 1976); Massachusetts Consumer Protection Regulations, Mass. Regs. Code tit. 940, § 5.04, Motor Vehicle Regulations; Pennsylvania Regulations of the Bureau of Consumer Protection, 37 Pa. Code § 301.4, Automobile Industry Trade Practices (1978).

1726 American Motors Corp., 100 F.T.C. 229 (1982) (consent order) (must disclose that sharp turn in jeep may cause driver to lose control); Outboard Marine Corp. v. Superior Court (Howarth), 52 Cal. App. 3d 30, 124 Cal. Rptr. 852 (1975) (failure to disclose defective design in off-road vehicle); Paces Ferry Dodge, Inc. v. Thomas, 174 Ga. App. 642, 331 S.E.2d 4 (1985); Connick v. Suzuki Motor Co., 174 Ill. 2d 482, 675 N.E.2d 584 (1996) (Suzuki Samurai's potential for roll-overs); Perona v. Volkswagen of Am., Inc., 292 Ill. App. 3d 59, 684 N.E.2d 859 (1997) (sudden acceleration by Audi 5000s); Perona v. Volkswagen of Am., Inc., 684 N.E.2d 859 (Ill. App. Ct. 1997) (failure to disclose defect that could cause unintended acceleration); Slaney v. Westwood Auto, Inc., 366 Mass. 688, 322 N.E.2d 768 (1975); Northview Motors, Inc. v. Commonwealth, 562 A.2d 977 (Pa. Commw. Ct. 1989); Massachusetts Consumer Protection Regulations, Mass. Regs. Code tit. 940, §§ 5.02, 5.04, Motor Vehicle Regulations; Pennsylvania Regulations of the Bureau of Consumer Protection, 37 Pa. Code § 301.4, Automobile Industry Trade Practices. *But see* Norman Gershman's Things to Wear, Inc. v. Mercedez-Benz of N. Am., 558 A.2d 1066 (Del. Super. Ct. 1989) (no violation where it would have been impossible for dealer to discover the defect before sale), *aff'd on other grounds*, 596 A.2d 1358 (Del. 1991).

1727 DeMarco v. Bay Ridge Car World, 169 A.D.2d 808, 565 N.Y.S.2d 176 (1991).

1728 Farrell v. General Motors Corp., 249 Kan. 231, 845 P.2d 5381 (1991). *See also* Connick v. Suzuki Motor Co., 174 Ill. 2d 482, 675 N.E.2d 584 (1996).

1729 Vista Chevrolet, Inc. v. Lewis, 704 S.W.2d 363 (Tex. App. 1985), *aff'd in part, rev'd in part*, 709 S.W.2d 176 (Tex. 1986) (plaintiff will not be given second opportunity to prove damages).

A number of major automobile makers have signed FTC consent agreements requiring them to disclose major defects in cars and to disclose which defects the company will remedy.[1730] Seven state attorneys general also reached agreement with Suzuki Motor Corporation concerning undisclosed roll-over hazards of the Suzuki Samurai.[1731] The Center for Automobile Safety in Washington, D.C., a public interest advocacy organization, maintains a clearinghouse of information on automobile and mobile home defects.

5.4.7.10.2 Secret warranties

Secret warranties have been an automobile industry practice for many years. After the automobile's written warranty expires, manufacturers often establish a policy to pay for repairs for certain widespread defects rather than deal with customer complaints on a case-by-case basis. Because these policies are communicated only to the company's regional offices and sometimes to the dealers, but never to consumers, they are called "secret warranties."

Secret warranties are difficult to document and discover. Generally the manufacturer issues a bulletin to regional offices, and sometimes to dealers, stating that it will pay to have a particular problem fixed, usually only for a predetermined period of time and/or mileage on the vehicle. In fact, these secret warranties benefit only those consumers who complain loudly and persistently enough, and to the right party. Those who are less aggressive never find out about them and generally end up paying for the cost of the repair or foregoing it. Manufacturers, moreover, will often deny the existence of these secret warranties or describe them as merely "goodwill" or "customer relations" gestures.

Even when a consumer is reimbursed or a repair is made at the manufacturer's expense, the only expense covered is the cost of the repair. Consequential damages resulting from the defect or costs for attempted repairs of misdiagnosed problems are not compensated.

There is currently no explicit federal requirement that manufacturers publicize these policies or communicate them directly to the consumer. Ford and Chrysler have agreed not to have a "secret" extension of the warranty only for consumers who persistently complain.[1732]

A strong argument can be made that the practice of secret warranties is a UDAP violation. The manufacturer has, by its policy to repair the problem in certain cases, implicitly admitted that there is a defect for which it should be responsible, but has not disclosed this defect or that it will repair the defect. Most likely, the manufacturer will argue that repairs have been authorized merely for "goodwill" or "customer relations." The consumer, however, can assert a distinction between "goodwill" gestures and this kind of widespread repair reimbursement authorized in advance for anticipated failures. The secrecy of the policy, its availability only to those who are aggressive in pursuing their complaints to a party informed of the policy, and the denial of compensation after the cutoff when timely complaints were made also make the policy unfair and deceptive.

Additionally, the consumer may have a claim for breach of the implied warranty of merchantability. The secret warranty itself should be sufficient admission of the existence of a defect. Although the manufacturer's express warranty has already expired, the implied warranty of merchantability may continue. Since the only defects covered by secret warranties are those widespread defects built into the vehicle for which the manufacturer has acknowledged responsibility, it is easy to prove that the defect existed at the time the car left the manufacturer.

Consumers who encounter a defect after expiration of the written warranty should first contact the regional office[1733] of the manufacturer and aggressively pursue coverage or reimbursement for repair costs. At the same time they should contact the Center for Auto Safety, 1825 Connecticut Ave, NW, Suite 330, Washington, DC 20009-5708, (202) 328-7700, www.autosafety.org, which has specific information on the secret warranties of various automobile manufacturers A listing of service bulletins is also found at ww.alldata.com/consumer/TSB/yr.html.

An aggressive and persistent approach directly with the regional office is necessary because repairs or refunds are not authorized in every case. It may be necessary to create the kind of "nuisance" complaint for which these policies were formulated. The involvement of an attorney on behalf of the consumer at this point, with its implicit threat of potential litigation, could make a difference in the manufacturer's response.

1730 Volkswagen of Am., Inc., 110 F.T.C. 392 (1988) (consent order) (oil consumption problems; Volkswagen set up Better Business Bureau arbitration programs); Saab-Scandia of Am., Inc., 107 F.T.C. 410 (1986) (consent order) (defective points); General Motors Corp., 102 F.T.C. 1741 (1983) (consent order) (defects with transmissions, camshafts, and fuel injection pumps; GM agreed to set up a nationwide arbitration program); American Honda Motor Co., 99 F.T.C. 305 (1982) (consent order) (premature rust); Chrysler Corp., 99 F.T.C. 347 (1982) (consent order) (likely to leak oil unless follow revised instructions only given to dealers, not car owners); Volkswagen of Am., Inc., 99 F.T.C. 446 (1982) (consent order) (same).

1731 *See* New York Dep't of Law, News from Attorney General Robert Abrams (Mar. 23, 1989). The seven states are California, Massachusetts, Minnesota, Missouri, New York, Texas and Washington. *See also* Connick v. Suzuki Motor Co., 174 Ill. 2d 482, 675 N.E.2d 584 (1996).

1732 Chrysler Corp., 96 F.T.C. 134 (1980) (consent order); Ford Motor Co., 96 F.T.C. 362 (1980) (consent order).

1733 Consumers should contact the manufacturer's regional office because the secret warranties are always communicated to the regional offices, but may not be communicated to all dealers. Moreover, it is more likely that someone at the regional office will be in a position to authorize secret warranty repairs.

If consumers are dissatisfied with the regional office's offer they should consider bringing UDAP and breach of implied warranty claims against the manufacturer. If a matter is already in litigation on issues related to the car defects, the consumer should try to find out whether any secret warranties apply to the defect in order to aid in proof of the consumer's claims.

5.4.7.10.3 Breach of written and implied warranties as UDAP violations

The failure of a manufacturer to make reasonable efforts to meet its warranty obligations should be a UDAP violation. Repeated unsuccessful attempts to repair a vehicle can be found to be a UDAP violation.[1734] The FTC has accepted a consent order from Jeep Eagle Corporation concerning the automobile manufacturer's failure to perform warranty service promptly and its failure to successfully fix cars.[1735]

A closer question is whether the mere breach of warranty is a *per se* UDAP violation. This issue is examined in some detail at § 5.2.7.1, *supra*. That is, a UDAP claim may be stated against a manufacturer not just for failing to disclose known defects, but for breach of an implied warranty because the implied warranty implicitly represents the vehicle is defect-free.

Thus, a federal court in a nation-wide UDAP class action examined the warranties offered by a new car manufacturer, to see if these involved representations that the car was defect-free.[1736] It found that the written warranty to repair any defects was not a warranty that the vehicle was defect-free, but actually acknowledged that the vehicle may have defects. The representation was that the manufacturer would fix any defects.[1737]

On the other hand, the court found that the class could go forward based on a UDAP false representation claim, where those representations are found in the implied warranties that accompanied the vehicle as a matter of law. The implied warranty and thus the implied representation is that the vehicle is merchantable.[1738] Of course, if under applicable warranty law, if no implied warranty from the manufacturer accompanies the vehicle, then there is no implicit representation emanating from the implied warranty.[1739]

1734 Keller v. Volkswagen of Am., Inc., 733 A.2d 642 (Pa. Super. Ct. 1999).

1735 Jeep Eagle Corp., F.T.C. File No. 842 3113, 5 Trade Reg. Rep. (CCH) ¶ 22,765 (F.T.C. Nov. 20, 1989) (consent order).

1736 Snodgrass v. Ford Motor Co., Clearinghouse No. 52520 (D.N.J. May 14, 1999).

1737 *Id.*

1738 *Id.*

1739 *Id.*

5.4.8 Automobile Leases

5.4.8.1 Applicability of UDAP to Automobile Leases

There should be little question that automobile lease practices are within a UDAP statute's scope—UDAP statutes invariably apply to consumer transactions, to practices within trade or commerce, or to sales or leases.[1740] Nor will there be issues of specific statutory exemptions for automobile dealers or lessors.[1741]

Consequently, UDAP statutes are well suited to challenge automobile lease practices. Perhaps the only issue presented (besides whether the practice is unfair or deceptive) will be whether the lessor is liable for the dealer's UDAP violations. It is often more practical to defend the lessor's collection action with such UDAP claims than it is to bring an affirmative UDAP action against the dealer.

Typically, the dealer will be the original lessor and the leasing company will be the dealer's assignee. In that case, the consumer can raise all UDAP claims against the dealer as defenses to payment to the assignee leasing company. Where the dealer arranges a lease directly with the leasing company, the consumer will have to consider a different approach to raising dealer-related claims as a defense on the lease. Such issues are detailed at Chapter 6, *infra*.

5.4.8.2 Deceptive Inducements and Misrepresentations About the Nature of the Lease

While not every lease involves a UDAP violation,[1742] many dealer representations and failure to disclose important terms concerning car leases are UDAP violations. These include the following practices:

- Misrepresentations to consumers that they are buying a car when they are only leasing it;[1743]
- Misrepresentations about the size of a down payment (e.g., claiming no down payment where consumer still

1740 *See* Appx. A, *infra*.

1741 *Id.*

1742 Hageman v. Twin City Chrysler-Plymouth, 681 F. Supp. 303 (M.D.N.C. 1988); Blum v. General Motors Acceptance Corp., 185 Ga. App. 714, 365 S.E.2d 474 (1988) (no UDAP violation where lessor did not mislead consumer); Delta Chevrolet, Inc. v. Wells, 187 Ga. App. 694, 371 S.E.2d 250 (1988); Kelley v. Ford Motor Credit Co., 137 Ohio App. 3d 12, 738 N.E.2d 9 (2000) (failure to itemize lease fees not a UDAP violation where neither monthly payment nor total cost of lease was misrepresented).

1743 Cummings v. Warren Henry Motors, Inc., 648 So. 2d 1230 (Fla. Dist. Ct. App. 1995). *See also* Nat'l City Bank v. Hayden, 2003 WL 193510 (Mich. App. Jan. 28, 2003) (misrepresentation that sales contract was a lease would be a UDAP violation).

has to make payments at lease consummation);[1744]

- Failure to disclose that a lease is based on a purchase price higher than that agreed-upon or higher than the car's sticker price;[1745]
- Misrepresentations that the consumer is building up equity in the car;[1746]
- Misrepresentations that the consumer has an option to purchase a leased vehicle when such option is not in the lease agreement,[1747] or other misrepresentations about the nature of the purchase option;[1748]
- Misrepresentations about the consumer's rights and responsibilities;[1749]
- Misrepresentation about whether the consumer will be liable for a charge upon early termination of the lease;[1750]
- Misrepresentations as to how the consumer's trade-in is reflected in the transaction and failure to fully credit the consumer for the agreed value of the trade-in;[1751]
- Failure to explain fully how a trade-in of one leased car for another lease resulted in significant loss to the consumer;[1752]
- Failure to return a security deposit when a lease is converted to a credit sale;[1753]
- Miscalculation of the amount owed when "flipping over" a lease into a credit sale;[1754]
- Misrepresenting service contracts or extended warranties as free where they are hidden in the capitalized cost and increase the monthly lease payment;
- Misrepresentations about the lease rate, such as quoting money factors that are not comparable to an APR or claiming there is no interest charged (where there is a lease rate).

New Jersey has also enacted detailed regulations specifying terms that must be disclosed in automobile lease advertising.[1755] Hawaii has adopted similar requirements as part of a consumer leasing statute.[1756] Ohio's regulations that prohibit attempts to raise the purchase price of a vehicle[1757] also apply to attempts to increase the consumer's obligation for a leased vehicle.[1758] The FTC has also accepted a number of consent orders dealing with lessors misrepresenting lease terms in advertisements: omitting or burying in small print key cost information, and misrepresenting the nature of the transaction and of model availability.[1759]

A New Jersey consumer leasing statute also requires that consumers have a twenty-four hour business day to review any lease disclosures before the lease is binding.[1760] This legislation, though, has largely been made irrelevant by an administrative regulation allowing consumers to waive this right as long as the waiver is in the lease agreement in twelve point type.[1761]

A court has considered whether GMAC should be held liable for a consumer being switched from a credit sale to a lease of a vehicle because GMAC conducted training sessions for employees at the auto dealership. At the training sessions the employees were allegedly taught the bait-and-switch procedure used on the consumer and explained how the use of a lease agreement could lead to deceiving the consumer about the transaction's true cost. The court found

1744 For example, fifteen state attorneys general have brought a UDAP action against Mazda on this issue. *See* Office of the Attorney General Grant Woods, News Release, Attorney General Woods Sues Mazda Over Deceptive Lease Ads (Oct. 28, 1996).

1745 Kinerd v. Colonial Leasing Co., 800 S.W.2d 187 (Tex. 1990) (unconscionable practice in violation of UDAP statute where lease based on excessive amount lessor paid dealer for equipment, and lessor then passed that price on to the lessee).

1746 *See* Couto v. Gibson, Inc., 1992 Ohio App. LEXIS 756, Clearinghouse No. 46,799 (Feb. 26, 1992).

1747 *See* Edwards v. William H. Porter, Inc., 1991 Del. Super. LEXIS 315 (Dec. 3, 1991), *aff'd on other grounds*, 616 A.2d 838 (Del. 1992).

1748 *See* A.V.I., Inc. v. Heathington, 842 S.W.2d 712 (Tex. App. 1992) (farm lease).

1749 Highsmith v. Chrysler Credit Corp., 18 F.3d 434 (7th Cir. 1994).

1750 Clement v. St. Charles Nissan, Inc., 103 S.W.3d 898 (Mo. App. 2003). *See* § 5.4.8.3, *infra*.

1751 Taylor v. United Mgmt., Inc., 51 F. Supp. 2d 1212 (D.N.M. 1999) (deceptive to represent trade-in as a cash down payment and to credit buyer with less than the full amount). *See* Adkinson v. Harpeth Ford-Mercury, Inc., 1991 Tenn. App. LEXIS 114 (Feb. 15, 1991) (lessor added trade-in value to initial cost of leased car instead of subtracting value from initial cost).

There are at least three ways to steal a consumer's trade-in, down payment, or rebate. The lessor can increase the car's capitalized cost to offset all or part of the value of the consumer's credit. Second, the dealer can fail to adjust the capitalized cost for all or some of the consumer's credit. Or alternatively, as in Myers v. Hexagon Co., 54 F. Supp. 2d 742 (E.D. Tenn. 1998), the dealer can just ignore the promised credit and mark on the lease "n/a" on the trade-in and capitalized cost reduction lines.

1752 Waterloo Leasing Co. v. McNatt, 620 S.W.2d 194 (Tex. App. 1981).

1753 *See* Adkinson v. Harpeth Ford-Mercury, Inc., 1991 Tenn. App. LEXIS 114 (Feb. 15, 1991).

1754 *Id.*

1755 N.J. Admin. Code § 13:45A-26A.6, Motor Vehicle Advertising Practices, Mandatory Disclosure in Advertisements for Lease of a New or Used Motor Vehicle. *See also* N.M. Admin. Code § 12.2.4.19, Advertising and Sale of Motor Vehicles.

1756 Haw. Rev. Stat. § 481L-2.

1757 Ohio Admin. Code § 109:4-3-16, Advertisement and Sale of Motor Vehicles.

1758 Frey v. Vin Devers, Inc., 80 Ohio App. 3d 1, 608 N.E.2d 796 (1992).

1759 Toyota Motor Sales U.S.A., 5 Trade Reg. Rep. (CCH) ¶ 24,337 (F.T.C. Dkt. C-3776 1998) (consent order); Chrysler Corp., 5 Trade Reg. Rep. (CCH) ¶ 24,518 (F.T.C. Dkts. C-3845 to 3847 1998) (consent orders); Dunphy Nissan, Inc, 5 Trade Reg. Rep. (CCH) ¶ 24,518 (F.T.C. Dkt. C-3924 1998) (consent order); Foote, Cone & Belding Advertising, Inc., 5 Trade Reg. Rep. ¶ 24,373 (F.T.C. Dkts. C-3792 to 3794 1998) (consent orders) (deceptive "zero down" and "penny down" advertisements, deceptive use of "triggering" terms, information presented in unreadable formats, use of balloon payments).

1760 N.J. Rev. Code § 56:12-67.

1761 N.J. Admin. Code 13:45A-28.8.

this to clearly be a UDAP violation by GMAC if proved, but the consumer had failed to show any connection between the training sessions and the harm caused to the consumer.[1762]

5.4.8.3 Early Termination and Default

A major area of consumer concern involves penalties that consumers are charged when they terminate an automobile lease early or default. The UDAP issues are three-fold: misrepresentations and failures to disclose the true nature of early termination liability; lessor misapplication of its own early termination formula; and formulas that produce excessive charges and unreasonable results.

UDAP statutes should be able to challenge the following lessor practices:

- Misrepresentations about the consumer's liability at early termination or the nature of the early termination or default formula;[1763]
- Misrepresentations that consumers may cancel at any time with no further obligation or that the consumer can cancel for any reason for the next three days;[1764]
- Applying a different formula to compute early termination liability than that disclosed in the lease;[1765]
- Inflating the payoff figure when the consumer terminates early. An early warning sign of an inflated payoff amount is if the leasing company requires the consumer to obtain the payoff number from the originating dealer, instead of the lessor. There is obviously no reason why the lessor can not provide this number, and its refusal to do so may indicate an arrangement whereby the lessor allows the dealer: to quote an inflated number, to discourage the consumer from terminating early, to switch the consumer into another lease, or some combination of the three. It may be fruitful to discover the financial incentives whereby the lessor forces the consumer to contact the dealer, and determine if the lessor should be held jointly liable with the dealer for any fraud.

Another common misrepresentation involves a dealer taking a leased vehicle back "in trade" for a new vehicle. The dealer may lead the consumer to believe that the dealer can speak for the lessor as to the amount of the early termination penalty. After the deal is completed, the consumer is surprised by a demand for a higher early termination charge from the lessor. Or the consumer may have been led to believe that there would be no early termination charge assessed, that this was all included in the price of the new vehicle. Such misrepresentations should be UDAP violations. The dealer not only misrepresents the nature of a transaction, but will often misrepresent the dealer's status is relationship to the lessor.

In addition, charging an amount that is unreasonable or unconscionable should also be a UDAP violation. For example, in one case a default formula failed to give the consumer a rebate for unearned lease charges and the court found the formula unconscionable.[1766]

One court came to the incorrect conclusion that a lease provision prohibiting early termination was not a UDAP violation.[1767] It is a basic contract law principle that any party can breach a contract and only be liable for the other party's damages. By inserting a provision prohibiting early termination, this misrepresents the consumer's fundamental contract rights. The provision instead should have said that any early termination will be treated as a default and the consumer's liability will be as specified in the lease.

When an early termination formula is excessive and unreasonable is detailed in two other NCLC manuals—National Consumer Law Center, *Truth in Lending* Ch. 10 (5th ed. 2003 and Supp.) and National Consumer Law Center, *Repossessions and Foreclosures* § 14.2 (5th ed. 2002 and Supp.). While such unreasonable charges may violate the Consumer Leasing Act and be unenforceable as penalty clauses, another approach is to challenge them as unfair under a state UDAP statute.

Two other NCLC manuals provide sample pleadings concerning automobile leases. National Consumer Law Center, *Consumer Law Pleadings,* No. 1, Ch. 9 (CD-Rom and Index Guide) contains a sample complaint, discovery requests, and class action papers in a case asserting that the use of an incomprehensible termination penalty clause, coupled with a clause that requires the consumer to make payments irrespective of the condition of the vehicle, is a UDAP violation. National Consumer Law Center, *Consumer Class Actions* (5th ed. 2002 and Supp.) at Appendices D.5, E.2, L.6, M.5, O.3, and P.2 contains pleadings, discovery requests, motions, and briefs in class action litigation challenging early termination penalties and Consumer Leasing Act disclosures.

1762 General Motors Acceptance Corp. v. Laesser, 718 So. 2d 276 (Fla. Dist. Ct. App. 1998).

1763 *See* Highsmith v. Chrylser Credit Corp., 18 F.3d 434 (7th Cir. 1994); Clement v. St. Charles Nissan, Inc., 103 S.W.3d 898 (Mo. App. 2003).

1764 Waterloo Leasing Co. v. McNatt, 620 S.W.2d 194 (Tex. App. 1981).

1765 *See* Highsmith v. Chrylser Credit Corp., 18 F.3d 434 (7th Cir. 1994).

1766 John Deere Leasing Co. v. Blubaugh, 636 F. Supp. 1569 (D. Kan. 1986).

1767 *See* Robinson v. Toyota Motor Credit Corp., 735 N.E.2d 724 (Ill. App. Ct. 2000), *aff'd in part, rev'd in part on other grounds,* 775 N.E.2d 951 (Ill. 2002).

5.4.8.4 UDAP Violations at Scheduled Termination, Including Charges for Excess Mileage and Wear

Virtually all consumer automobile leases today are closed-end, meaning that the consumer at lease termination has no liability for the fact that the vehicle has depreciated more than originally anticipated. It is thus a UDAP violation to misrepresent that the consumer would owe a large penalty at scheduled termination (to encourage the consumer to "flip-over" the lease to a purchase).[1768]

At scheduled termination, the consumer is liable for mileage in excess of that authorized by the lease and for unusual wear and tear. The federal Consumer Leasing Act requires that charges for excess mileage or wear be clearly disclosed in the lease.[1769]

Nevertheless, in part because lessors typically lose money if the consumer turns in a leased vehicle instead of exercising a purchase option, there are widespread reports of deceptive practices at lease scheduled termination in assessing charges for excess wear and tear. Examples of possible deceptive practices include:

- Claiming that the car had options it never had, and then charging the consumer at termination because the consumer allegedly removed these options from the car.
- Orally complimenting the consumer at termination for the car's pristine condition, and several months later assessing charges for excess wear when it is too late for the consumer to inspect the wear being alleged.
- Changing the mileage limitation through trickery, and then assessing a high excess mileage charge because the consumer has exceeded the now lower mileage limit. For example, the lessor may ask the consumer to sign a replacement lease "due to inadvertent error in the paperwork" which the consumer does because the monthly payment is unchanged. The consumer never notices the change in the mileage limitation.
- Inflating the amount of damage or the amount that the damage decreases the vehicle's market value, and not repairing damage under the vehicle's warranty or service contract.

5.4.8.5 UCC Article 2A Unconscionability as Alternative to UDAP Claim

While UDAP statutes are well-suited to challenge automobile leases, another theory should also be considered—that the dealer or lessor has engaged in unconscionable conduct in violation of UCC § 2A. Every state except Louisiana has now enacted Uniform Commercial Code Article 2A on Leases.

UCC § 2A-108, "Unconscionability," incorporates the same protections found in UCC § 2-302 dealing with unconscionability in sales transactions, and then adds two important provisions not found in Article 2 on Sales. Both UCC §§ 2-302 and 2A-108 allow courts to refuse to enforce unconscionable provisions in the lease or sales agreement. However, Article 2A also authorizes a court to grant appropriate relief where a lease is *induced* by unconscionable conduct or where unconscionable conduct has occurred in the lessor's *collection* activities.

Second, UCC § 2A-108 requires that a court must award consumers their attorney fees if they prevail under an unconscionability claim. Fees are available to a prevailing lessor only if the lessee knew the action was groundless. The size of the consumer's recovery does not control the size of the consumer's attorney fee award.

UCC § 2A-108 will apply to many automobile lease transactions. Not only can consumers challenge the lease terms as unconscionable, but they can also challenge as unconscionable oral sales representations, attempts to collect a deficiency, or repossession tactics.

Use of UCC § 2A-108 will have the following advantages over a UDAP claim:

- *Post-Sale Transactions*. Some UDAP statutes do not apply to practices occurring after the transaction has been finalized, such as collection tactics. UCC § 2A-108 specifically applies to those transactions.
- *Non-Deceptive Abuses*. Most UDAP statutes prohibit unfair or unconscionable practices, but some state statutes only prohibit deceptive practices or a specific laundry list of deceptive practices. In those states, UCC § 2A-108's unconscionability standard is superior where the lessor's practice is abusive but not deceptive.
- *Statute of Limitations*. Some UDAP statutes have a short limitations period. UCC § 2A-506 specifies a four-year period for actions for default under a lease contract.
- *Equitable Relief*. Not all UDAP statutes authorize equitable relief (and a few may not even authorize a damage recovery). UCC § 2A-108 authorizes a court to grant "appropriate relief."
- *Attorney Fees*. Some UDAP statutes do not authorize attorney fees, many do not mandate fees for consumers, while a few authorize fees for either party. UCC § 2A-108 mandates fees for a consumer, but authorizes fees for the lessor only if the consumer knew the action was groundless.

1768 Adkinson v. Harpeth Ford-Mercury, Inc., 1991 Tenn. App. LEXIS 114 (Feb. 15, 1991).

1769 *See* National Consumer Law Center, Truth in Lending Ch. 10 (5th ed. 2003 and Supp.).

5.4.9 Daily Rental Car Practices

5.4.9.1 Introduction

While a car lease is usually for a period of years, car rentals are generally daily or weekly. UDAP issues dealing with car rentals usually involve one of three issues: deceptive sales of collision damage waivers and insurance products, misrepresentations about the cost or nature of a rental or related charges, and excess charges to repair damage to the vehicle.

5.4.9.2 Collision Damage Waivers and Insurance

One of the most confusing areas for consumers involves the advisability to purchase insurance or collision damage waivers on car rentals. The very term collision damage waiver may be confusing. A major car rental company has been found liable for misrepresenting that "Collision Damage Waiver" (CDW) was insurance, additional coverage, and protection against negligence which would protect the renter against liability in the event of an accident. In fact, even with the CDW, the consumer could be liable for damages if the consumer was considered negligent. All CDW did was eliminate the consumer's already limited liability (ranging from $500 to $2500) when the consumer was *not* at fault.[1770]

Another court has allowed the consumer to proceed with a claim that the rental company violated the UDAP statute by misrepresenting the uses, characteristics, and advantages of CDW and by concealing material information.[1771] Another case dealing with CDW, however, found that the rental company did not commit any UDAP violations.[1772] In that case, the rental company disclosed that "CDW is not insurance," and the court held that this was proper. The court also held that the company was not required to disclose to the consumer that CDW might duplicate other insurance coverage.[1773]

To the extent to which a rental car company does sell an insurance product, it is important to determine if the company is licensed under state law to sell that insurance. Where a license is required, the sale of such insurance without a license is a UDAP violation.[1774] But one court has ruled that since the state had not definitely ruled whether CDW was insurance, a company could not be subjected to liability for selling it without a license.[1775]

UDAP precedent in this area includes the Car Rental Practices Guidelines issued by the National Association of Attorneys General Task Force on the Car Rental Industry Advertising and Practices, and found on the CD-Rom accompanying this volume. The Guidelines set out standards for the sale of CDW.[1776] Advocates should also check whether their state has a special statute regulating collision damage waivers.

5.4.9.3 Undisclosed Charges and Switching of Car Models

Car rental companies will often assess charges in addition to advertised rental rates. The failure to disclose these charges can be deceptive. Thus the FTC has accepted consent agreements in cases dealing with the failure to disclose airport surcharges, mandatory fuel charges, and other charges or limitations to advertised prices.[1777] Charging the consumer for not returning the car to the location where it was rented, without having notified the consumer in advance of this requirement, is deceptive.[1778] On the other hand, one court has found that offering the option of Personal Accident Insurance and imposing an hourly late return charge are not deceptive where there is full disclosure and no evidence of high-pressure sales tactics.[1779]

The National Association of Attorneys General Task Force on the Car Rental Industry Advertising and Practices has issued Car Rental Practices Guidelines, reprinted on the CD-Rom accompanying this volume.[1780] The Guidelines deal with the nondisclosure of additional costs, such as mileage charges, geographical limitations, drop-off charges, advance reservation requirements, penalties for early or late returns, additional driver fees, and prices for collision damage waivers (CDW).

Disclosing high per-gallon charges for returning the vehicle with less than a full tank of gas in an obscure, confusing way, so that consumers do not know to avoid the charge, is a UDAP violation.[1781] Challenges to the amount of the charge, however, have been unsuccessful where a

1770 People v. Dollar Rent-a-Car Sys., 211 Cal. App. 3d 119, 259 Cal. Rptr. 191 (1989).

1771 Mangone v. U-Haul Int'l, Inc., 7 P.3d 189 (Colo. App. 1999).

1772 Chabraja v. Avis Rent-A-Car Sys., Inc., 549 N.E.2d 872 (Ill. App. Ct. 1989).

1773 *Accord* Lewis v. Hertz Corp., 581 N.Y.S.2d 305 (App. Div. 1992) (no UDAP violation in light of full disclosure); Super Glue Corp. v. Avis Rent-A-Car Sys., Inc., 159 A.D.2d 68, 557 N.Y.S.2d 959 (1990).

1774 Newland v. Budget Rent-a-Car Sys., Inc., 319 Ill. App. 3d 453, 744 N.E.2d 902, 253 Ill. Dec. 169 (2001).

1775 Mangone v. U-Haul Int'l, Inc., 7 P.3d 189 (Colo. App. 1999).

1776 Reprinted at 56 Antitrust & Trade Reg. Report (BNA) S-1 (Mar. 16, 1989).

1777 Value Rent-A-Car, 5 Trade Reg. Rep. (CCH) ¶ 23,249 (F.T.C. Dkt. C-3420 1993) (consent order); General Rent-A-Car Sys., Inc., 111 F.T.C. 694 (1989) (consent order); Alamo Rent-A-Car, Inc., 111 F.T.C. 644 (1989) (consent order).

1778 Garcia v. L&R Realty, Inc., 790 A.2d 936 (N.J. Super. Ct. App. Div. 2002) (Mass. law).

1779 Lewis v. Hertz Corp., 581 N.Y.S.2d 305 (App. Div. 1992).

1780 Reprinted at 56 Antitrust & Trade Reg. Report (BNA) S-1 (Mar. 16, 1989).

1781 Schnall v. Hertz Corp., 78 Cal. App. 4th 1144, 93 Cal. Rptr. 2d 439 (2000). *But cf.* Shvarts v. Budget Group, Inc., 81 Cal. App. 4th 1153, 97 Cal. Rptr. 2d 722 (2000) (finding disclosure clear).

state statute specifically authorized the charge.[1782] For example, two New York courts have held that a rental car company's charges and procedures for refueling returned rental cars did not violate state gasoline price disclosure laws and were not deceptive,[1783] but one of the cases holds that these practices may have violated the company's contract with the consumer.[1784]

A related practice to charging a consumer more for a given model than the advertised rate is to provide the consumer a less valuable car than advertised. Thus the FTC has accepted consent orders against companies for switching consumers to different car models than reserved.[1785] Similarly, the NAAG guidelines cover problems of car rental companies not disclosing restrictions on availability and use of rental cars in their advertising material.[1786] Another deceptive rental practice is failing to disclose to prospective renters that the rental company does not make necessary repairs in response to a manufacturer's recall notices.[1787]

5.4.9.4 Excess Charges to Repair Damage

When a rental car is damaged and the consumer is liable for the damage, the consumer is often at the rental company's mercy as to how that liability is computed. A number of UDAP actions have challenged rental car company computation of repair charges that consumers must pay.

The attorneys general of Iowa, Kansas, Massachusetts, Missouri, New York and Texas sued the Hertz Corporation, alleging UDAP violations involving Hertz asserting and collecting claims from customers for physical damage to its vehicles in excess of the actual cost to repair the vehicles, with disclosure on claims documentation that claims were being assessed at "prevailing retail prices." Hertz claimed that the "prevailing retail prices" disclosure allowed it to charge customers in excess of its actual costs.

Nevertheless, Hertz agreed to a settlement whereby it would cease charging customers in excess of its actual cost and would refund to customers any amount Hertz received in excess of that cost. Hertz also agreed that the settlement would be effective in other states where the state attorney general opted to join the settlement. Most state attorneys general have done so.[1788]

The California Attorney General has also successfully brought a similar suit against Dollar Rent-a-Car, that charged the consumer based on a "retail" rate to repair cars, which was higher than the rental agency's actual cost. The company also charged the consumer a "retail rental rate" for the time the car was out of service, which was higher than the actual rental rates customers were in fact charged for the car.[1789]

5.4.10 *Automobile Sub-Lease Scams, Brokers, and Car Finders*

5.4.10.1 Automobile Sub-Leases

5.4.10.1.1 Described

The automobile sub-lease scam involves a firm taking over, without the lessor's or creditor's permission, an automobile lease or car loan from a consumer who wants to get out of the lease or loan. The firm then subleases the car to another consumer.

This scheme preys upon a consumer's difficulty in getting out of the lease or car loan because early termination will lead to a huge penalty or deficiency, a debtor's fear of repossession, and the sublessee's perceived inability to obtain a car through more traditional channels. The mechanics of this scam can be seen by examining the scam operator's (broker's) relationship to the three other parties in the deal:

- *The lessor* or creditor prohibits in its lease or credit contract the sale or sublease of the vehicle without the creditor or lessor's permission. In arranging for the car's sublease, the broker never informs the lessor or creditor and the lessor or creditor thus loses track of the car's whereabouts and no longer knows whether the car is insured. The broker may or may not pass on lease payments to the lessor or creditor.
- *When a consumer debtor or lessee* can not afford to continue to make lease or car payments, an attractive alternative to turning the car in and paying a huge penalty or deficiency is subleasing the car to another, who presumably will keep up the car payments. The consumer will usually pay the broker a fee for the broker's taking the car off the consumer's hands. What the consumer does not understand is that the sublease is not effective, because the broker has never obtained

1782 Schnall v. Hertz Corp., 78 Cal. App. 4th 1144, 93 Cal. Rptr. 2d 439 (2000); Shvarts v. Budget Group, Inc., 81 Cal. App. 4th 1153, 97 Cal. Rptr. 2d 722 (2000) (finding disclosure clear).

1783 Lewis v. Hertz Corp., 181 A.D.2d 493, 581 N.Y.S.2d 305 (1992); Super Glue Corp. v. Avis Rent-A-Car Sys., Inc., 159 A.D.2d 68, 557 N.Y.S.2d 959 (1990).

1784 Super Glue Corp. v. Avis Rent-A-Car Sys., Inc., 159 A.D.2d 68, 557 N.Y.S.2d 959 (1990).

1785 General Rent-A-Car Sys., Inc., 111 F.T.C. 694 (1989) (consent order); Alamo Rent-A-Car, Inc., 111 F.T.C. 644 (1989) (consent order).

1786 National Association of Attorneys General Task Force on The Car Rental Industry Advertising and Practices, Car Rental Practices Guidelines, reprinted at 56 Antitrust & Trade Reg. Report (BNA) S-1 (Mar. 16, 1989).

1787 Budget Rent-A-Car Corp., F.T.C. No. 882 3235, 5 Trade Reg. Rep. (CCH) ¶ 22,632 (F.T.C. 1988) (consent order).

1788 Abrams v. Hertz Corp., Clearinghouse No. 43,081 (N.Y. Sup. Ct. Aug. 5, 1988) (consent judgment).

1789 People v. Dollar Rent-a-Car Sys., 211 Cal. App. 3d 119, 259 Cal. Rptr. 191 (1989).

permission from the creditor or lessor for another party to assume the obligation. The consumer remains liable under the lease, and may even be liable for any accident involving the vehicle. The original owner thus effectively loses control over the car (which can easily disappear without a trace, especially in another state), while still being legally obligated to the creditor or lessor for the full contractual obligation.

- *The sublessee* leases the car from the broker. The sublessee typically makes a large initial payment to the broker and then makes monthly payments to the broker on the lease and the automobile insurance. The broker usually keeps the large initial payment. It is supposed to, but may not, pass the monthly payments on to the lessor or creditor and insurer. The broker typically will not register the change in the car's ownership with the department of motor vehicles because this will alert the lender or lessor. Failure to register the car in the sublessee's name and the no-sublease clause in the original loan or lease means the sublessee has virtually no legal right to the car. This contrasts with representations the broker may make that the sublease will be able to keep the car after the lease term. The sublessee may also be surprised to discover he or she is driving an uninsured vehicle or that the vehicle will be insured by agencies operating fraudulently in collusion with the automobile broker.

The typical way to discover whether such brokers are operating in an area is to look for their advertisements in newspaper classified sections, buy-sell publications, and automobile shopper-type publications. Brokers generally place two types of ads. One type offers consumers cars in exchange for a broker fee and assumption of the existing loan or lease. The second type of ad offers to assume an existing car owner's car or lease payments to relieve the car owner of financial burdens.

5.4.10.1.2 Consumer remedies

A good example of an autobroker scam is found in *Omari v. National Security Financial Services, Inc.*,[1790] where the California Director of Consumer Affairs succeeded in proving that National Security, an automobile subleasing business, failed to obtain lessors' approval prior to subleasing vehicles, failed to notify the Department of Motor Vehicles of the transfers, failed to disclose to lessees that they were still liable on the lease, and misrepresented to sublessees that they had an interest in the lease. The court found these to be UDAP violations.

Almost half the states have enacted legislation defining and prohibiting unlawful subleasing of a motor vehicle.[1791] Several of the state attorney general offices in these states report that all automobile brokers closed down operation in their state in response to the legislation.

The federal Consumer Leasing Act (CLA)[1792] provides another innovative remedy for sublessees victimized by automobile broker fraud. The CLA places requirements on those "arranging to lease,"[1793] which means offering to provide a lease which will be extended by another whereby the arranger receives a fee or other consideration or participates in the preparation of lease documents.[1794] As a result, the CLA requires that automobile brokers provide sublessees with detailed CLA disclosures, as if they were the lessor. Experience has shown that brokers do not comply with these CLA requirements.

Before pursuing a CLA claim, make sure the sublease is not terminable within the first four months, since the CLA would not apply.[1795] In the typical automobile broker-arranged sublease, this is not a problem—the term will be for four months or more.

The automobile broker's CLA violation gives the sublessee a federal claim, in federal court if desired, for large statutory damages *plus* actual damages *plus* attorney fees.[1796] Federal court jurisdiction is a particular advantage where federal court service of process or other aspects of the federal system are preferable to state court—such as federal class action procedure. The CLA is analyzed in more detail in another NCLC manual.[1797]

1790 Clearinghouse No. 43,082 (Cal. Super. Ct. 1988) (summary judgment order); 440 S.E.2d 670 (1994). *See also* Thompson v. State, 211 Ga. App. 887 (upholding state RICO conviction); People v. Interstate Automobile Mgmt., Inc., Clearinghouse No. 49,149 (N.Y. Sup. Ct. Westchester Cty. Dec. 14, 1992).

1791 Ariz. Rev. Stat. Ann. §§ 13-3717, 12-632; Ark. Code Ann. §§ 4-100-101 to 103; Cal. Civ. Code § 3343.5; Cal. Penal Code §§ 570 to 574; Colo. Rev. Stat. Ann. §§ 18-5-801, 803; Fla. Stat. Ann. § 817.5621; Ga. Code Ann. §§ 10-1-39 to -41; Ind. Code §§ 24-5-16-1 to -19; 625 Ill. Comp. Stat. § 5/6-305.1; Md. Crim. Law § 8-408; Mich. Comp. Laws Ann. § 750.417a; Minn. Stat. § 325F.666; Mo. Rev. Stat. §§ 407.738 to .748; N.J. Stat. Ann. §§ 56:12-71 to -74; N.Y. Gen. Bus. Law § 890; N.C. Gen. Stat. § 20-106.2; Or. Rev. Stat. Ann. § 822.090; S.C. Code §§ 37-13-10 to 37-13-90; Tenn. Code Ann. § 39-14-147; Tex. Penal Code Ann. 32.34 (Vernon); Utah Code Ann. § 76-6-522; Va. Code Ann. § 18.2-115.1; Wash. Rev. Code. Ann. § 19.116.005 to .900. *See also* People v. Carter, 37 Cal. Rptr. 2d 59 (Cal. App. 1994) (California statute's constitutionality upheld; statute properly applied to defendant who solicited prospective sublessors and sublessees, provided the paperwork, and pocketed a hefty "transaction fee" for each transfer, even though party did not effect actual transfer); Consumer Protection Division Enforcement Statements Concerning Motor Vehicle Advertising & Sales Practices, Iowa Dept. of Transportation, Dealer Operating Manual VII-2, Clearinghouse No. 49,156.

1792 15 U.S.C. § 1667.

1793 15 U.S.C. § 1667(3).

1794 12 C.F.R. § 213.2(h).

1795 15 U.S.C. § 1667(1).

1796 15 U.S.C. § 1640.

1797 National Consumer Law Center, Truth in Lending Ch. 10 (5th ed. 2003 and Supp.).

5.4.10.2 Dealers Assisting Consumer in Renting Their RV

A related problem area is a dealer assisting a recreational vehicle owner in renting the vehicle to others. When a consumer could not afford the cost of operating his recreational vehicle, he agreed with a dealership to split the revenues resulting from the dealer renting out the vehicle. A court awarded $5000 actual damages and $25,000 punitive damages where the dealer never explained or compensated the consumer for unusual deterioration to the vehicle, charged the consumer for repairs that should have been charged against the renter's security deposit, charged the consumer for repairs never done, and understated the mileage the vehicle was driven by renters.[1798]

5.4.10.3 Automobile Finding Services

The FTC has successfully sued a company's practice of offering information on "Hot Cars" via a 900 telephone number.[1799] Advertising showed fancy cars in excellent condition and indicated that cars that had been repossessed or seized in drug arrests could be purchased at auction for as little as $100. Prerecorded information indicated that an 800-telephone number for more specific information would be given at the end of the tape, but after twenty dollars of 900 charges, the 800 number provided was used chiefly to sell callers a lifetime membership.[1800] In fact, it is virtually impossible to find good cars at an automobile auction for as little as $100.[1801]

5.4.11 Sale of Automobile Accessories

An FTC administrative law judge has issued an opinion finding various deceptive practices engaged by a company selling the "rust evader" or "rust buster" that was purported to be an electronic corrosion control device for automobiles.[1802] The FTC has also issued orders against companies that had no basis to advertise that an add-on braking system performs as effectively as a factory-installed system.[1803] The FTC has settled a complaint alleging misrepresentations concerning a lighter-to-lighter automobile battery charger.[1804] FTC consent orders deal with claims concerning motor oil and fuel additives.[1805]

Representations concerning devices allegedly improving cars' fuel efficiency are analyzed in § 5.6.6, *infra*. The FTC has reached a consent agreement with a company allegedly misrepresenting the characteristics of mobile telephones.[1806] Another FTC consent order involves oil, anti-freeze, and transmission fluid misrepresentations.[1807] Other FTC consent orders relate to spark plugs that promise a certain level of efficiency and effectiveness.[1808] New Jersey has UDAP regulations dealing with disclosure of tire identification numbers.[1809]

5.4.12 Mobile Home Sales

5.4.12.1 Introduction

A number of different federal and state laws offer protections to buyers of mobile homes, relating to manufacturing, sales, financing, transportation, warranties, health and safety, and mobile home parks and tenants. These statutes are analyzed in other volumes.[1810] UDAP statutes can provide additional remedies for violations of these other statutes and can also be used to define additional unfair or deceptive mobile home practices.[1811]

This section analyzes mobile home sales and the related practice of selling land-home packages, whereby the consumer in the same or closely related transactions purchases a home and purchases a lot to place the home. Scction 5.5.1, *infra* examines mobile home park issues, where a consumer owns the home but leases a lot in a park site.

1798 Schmidt v. American Leasco, 139 Ariz. 509, 679 P.2d 533 (Ct. App. 1984).

1799 *See* FTC v. United States Sales Corp., 785 F. Supp. 737 (N.D. Ill. 1992).

1800 *Id.*

1801 *Id.*

1802 RustEvader Corp., 5 Trade Reg. Rep. 24045 (F.T.C. Dkt. 9274 June 7, 1996) (initial decision).

1803 Brake Guard Products, Inc., 5 Trade Reg. Rep. (CCH) ¶ 24,380 (F.T.C. Dkt. 9277 1998) (final order); Automotive Breakthrough Sciences, Inc., 5 Trade Reg. Rep. (CCH) ¶ 24,508 (F.T.C. Dkt. 9275 1998) (final order).

1804 Cooper Rand Corp., 111 F.T.C. 604 (1989) (consent order); Plas-Tix USA, Inc., 109 F.T.C. 149 (1987) (consent order).

1805 Prolong Super Lubricants, 5 Trade Reg. Rep. (CCH) ¶ 24,644 (F.T.C. Dkt. C-3906 1999) (consent order) (misrepresentation as to motor oil additive); Castrol N. Am., Inc., 5 Trade Reg. Rep. (CCH) ¶ 24,651 (F.T.C. Dkt. C-3910 1999) (consent order) (misrepresentation, fuel additives); Shell Oil Co., 5 Trade Reg. Rep. (CCH) ¶ 24,652 (F.T.C. Dkt. C-3912 1999) (consent order) (same).

1806 GCS Electronics, 108 F.T.C. 158 (1986) (consent order).

1807 Pittsburg Penn Oil Co., 108 F.T.C. 123 (1986) (consent order).

1808 SpitFire Inc., 5 Trade Reg. Rep. (CCH) ¶ 24,206 (F.T.C. Dkt. C-3737 1997) (consent order).

1809 New Jersey Administrative Rules of the Div. of Consumer Affairs, N.J. Admin. Code ch. 13:45A, subch. 8, Tire Distributors and Dealers.

1810 *See, e.g.*, National Consumer Law Center, Consumer Warranty Law (2d ed. 2001 and Supp.); The American Association of Retired Persons, Manufactured Housing Community Tenants: Shifting the Balance of Power (2004).

1811 *See* National Consumer Law Center, Consumer Law Pleadings, No. 2, § 4.1 (CD-Rom and Index Guide), *also found on* the CD-Rom accompanying this volume, for a complaint alleging UDAP and other claims concerning a fraudulent mobile home sale.

5.4.12.2 Federal Actions

The FTC proposed, but then terminated a rulemaking proceeding concerning mobile home sales and service.[1812] The rule would have required mobile home manufacturers and dealers who offer written warranties to provide full and timely service for all covered defects. Although there is no FTC rule, the FTC Staff Report to the Commission recommending a final rule provides useful factual and legal background in this area.[1813]

The Commission has brought a number of individual actions resulting in consent agreements under which mobile home dealers have agreed to maintain an adequate warranty system so that each mobile home sold receives full service and repair of any defects covered by the warranty within a reasonable time. The dealers must also inform purchasers of the extent of the warranty protection.[1814]

In 1988, the U.S. Department of Housing and Urban Development (HUD) charged that there were serious design and safety defects in thousands of mobile homes produced by the nation's largest mobile home manufacturer. A lawsuit filed in the Delaware Federal District Court in 1988 alleged that 20,000 Fleetwood homes built in 1983 and 1984 failed to meet federal construction and safety standards. Similar problems may also exist in certain Fleetwood models built as early as 1976.[1815]

HUD charged that Fleetwood Enterprises, Inc. constructed mobile homes with support walls failing to meet HUD construction and safety standards. In addition, HUD alleged that thousands of homes had faulty metal straps which failed to hold roofs down as required by HUD standards.

5.4.12.3 State UDAP Precedent

It is deceptive to sell a defective mobile home not fit for winter habitation,[1816] to substitute a different mobile home from that ordered before delivery,[1817] or to misrepresent a home's prior use,[1818] energy consumption,[1819] or the cost to move the home.[1820] Sellers may not misrepresent the selling price, the seller's mark-up on wholesale costs, or the existence of free products, and dealers must disclose additional charges beyond advertised prices.[1821]

It is deceptive to misrepresent that a home is well-insulated and that the seller will cure any defects.[1822] Setting the home up improperly, and then failing to correct the defects, is a UDAP violation.[1823] One court has held that a seller may avoid UDAP liability, however, by promptly remedying defects that exist in the mobile home.[1824] It is also deceptive to misrepresent the quality or standard of a mobile home.[1825]

It is also a UDAP violation to fail to disclose to a mobile home purchaser that the lot the purchaser plans to install the home on is not zoned for mobile homes,[1826] or to fail to disclose the buyer's inability to keep the mobile home in the park in which it is presently situated.[1827] It is deceptive for a mobile home dealer to falsely inform a consumer in the military that the military would pay the costs of moving the

---

1812 The rule was proposed at 40 Fed. Reg. 104 (May 29, 1975); the termination of the rulemaking proceeding is referenced at 52 Fed. Reg. 15185 (Apr. 27, 1987).

1813 Bureau of Consumer Protection Mobile Home Sales and Services, Final Staff Report to the Federal Trade Commission and Proposed Trade Regulation Rule, Clearinghouse No. 31,040 (Aug. 1980).

1814 Centurion Int'l, 103 F.T.C. 84 (1984) (consent order); Commodore Corp., 85 F.T.C. 472 (1975) (consent order); Redman Indus. Inc., 85 F.T.C. 309 (1975) (consent order); Skyline Corp., 85 F.T.C. 444 (1975) (consent order).

1815 *See* United States v. Fleetwood Enterprises, 689 F. Supp. 389 (D. Del. 1988) (order dealing with motions to strike and requests for protective orders); *see also* U.S. Dept. of Housing and Urban Development, News Release (Feb. 10, 1988); *cf.* United States v. Fleetwood Enterprises, Inc., 702 F. Supp. 1082 (D. Del. 1988) (procedural issues).

1816 Potter v. Dangler Mobile Homes, 61 Ohio Misc. 14 (C.P. Paulding Cty., 1977); *see also* Manufactured Housing Mgmt. v. Tubb, 643 S.W.2d 483 (Tex. App. 1982) (misrepresenting a mobile home as defect free).

1817 State v. Packard, Clearinghouse No. 27,066 (Vt. Super. Ct. 1977); *see also* Chavarria v. Fleetwood Retail Corp., Clearinghouse No. 54576 (N.M. Dist. Ct. Aug. 29, 2002) (dealer's misrepresentation that lender would not approve larger home, which enabled it to sell smaller home at the same price, was UDAP violation); Estate of Cattano v. High Touch Homes, Inc., 2002 WL 1290411 (Ohio App. May 24, 2002) (unpublished, citation limited) (modular home did not conform to model consumer was shown).

1818 *Id.*

1819 Recreational Vehicle Institute, 84 F.T.C. 720 (1974) (consent order); Trailer Coach Ass'n, 84 F.T.C. 713 (1974) (consent order).

1820 Allen v. Morgan Drive Away, Inc., 273 Or. 614, 542 P.2d 896 (1975).

1821 Taylor Mobile Homes Inc., 82 F.T.C. 1145 (1973) (consent order); Chavarria v. Fleetwood Retail Corp., Clearinghouse No. 54576 (N.M. Dist. Ct. Aug. 29, 2002) (misrepresentations about features and financing were UDAP violations).

1822 Dunlap v. Jimmy GMC Tucson, Inc., 136 Ariz. 338, 666 P.2d 83 (Ct. App. 1983) (recreational vehicle purchased for year-round living).

1823 Chavarria v. Fleetwood Retail Corp., Clearinghouse No. 54576 (N.M. Dist. Ct. Aug. 29, 2002).

1824 Wenzel v. Brault's Mobile Homes, Inc., 566 A.2d 993 (Vt. 1989).

1825 Burton v. Elsea, Inc., 1999 Ohio App. LEXIS 6401 (Dec. 27, 1999) (statement that mobile home was in A-1 condition and that roof leak had been fixed was UDAP violation); Etheridge v. Oak Creek Mobile Homes, 989 S.W.2d 412 (Tex. App. 1999) (UDAP liability shown when home did not conform to glowing description in brochure); Chrysler Corp. v. Schuenemann, 618 S.W.2d 799 (Tex. Civ. App. 1981).

1826 Patry v. Liberty Mobilehome Sales, Inc., 15 Mass. App. Ct. 701, 448 N.E.2d 405 (1983), *aff'd*, 475 N.E.2d 392 (Mass. 1985).

1827 Caldwell v. Pop's Homes Inc., 54 Or. App. 104, 634 P.2d 471 (1981).

home if the consumer were later transferred.[1828] It has also been found to be a UDAP violation to fail to acknowledge liability under the FTC Holder Rule.[1829]

A Washington case gives a good example of the use of a UDAP statute in a typical convoluted mobile home sale situation. A dealer arranged for the consumer to obtain financing from a mortgage company. The financing company charged $800 to supervise the preparation of the lot by yet another company. When the lot preparation company failed to perform adequately, the finance company paid the preparation company over the consumers' objections, but otherwise failed to supervise the preparation. The dealer then delivered to the consumer a home different than the one purchased, and both the dealer and mortgage company ignored the consumer's requests to rescind the transaction. A UDAP claim eventually resulted in treble damages and attorney fees.[1830]

Other problems relate to the linkage of a mobile home park space to the consumer purchasing a home from a particular dealer.[1831] A related problem is the dealer promising the buyer a specific lot to place the home, but after the sale is complete, reneging on that promise.

There have been extensive allegations that dealers inflate both the value of a home and a consumer's creditworthiness to finalize home sales where the dealer knows the consumer can not afford the purchase, and will likely default. Variants include mobile home purchases with low interest rates the first year, that quickly escalate for the remaining twenty-nine years of the loan. Dealers may also subsidize park rentals the first year or take other actions to make the first year's payments affordable. When consumers question their ability to make future years' installments, the dealer tells them that their appreciating equity will make refinancing easy that will maintain the low payments. Refinancing of course never materializes. The appreciating equity is also often fictional, as mobile homes depreciate rapidly. Particularly if the buyer has long-term financing, the value of the home usually goes down faster than the debt principal. Some dealers also use various deceptions to induce the lender to loan more than the home is worth, so the consumer ends up overloaded with debt and with little to show for it.[1832] See the discussion at § 5.1.4, *supra*, regarding the improvident extension of credit.

1828 Strickland v. A&C Mobile Homes, 321 S.E.2d 16 (N.C. Ct. App. 1984).

1829 *See* Jaramillo v. Gonzales, 50 P.3d 554 (N.M. Ct. App. 2002) (bank's refusal to acknowledge its liability under the FTC Holder Rule was tantamount to an incorrect and misleading assertion that no claims could be brought against it was a violation of Unfair Practices Act.); § 6.6.1, *infra*.

1830 *See* Mason v. Mortgage America, Inc., 114 Wash. 2d 842, 792 P.2d 142 (1990); *see also* Chavarria v. Fleetwood Retail Corp., Clearinghouse No. 54576 (N.M. Dist. Ct. Aug. 29, 2002) (awarding UDAP treble damages for deception in sale of home, financing, and setup).

1831 *See* § 5.5.1.2, *infra*.

1832 *See, e.g.*, Chavarria v. Fleetwood Retail Corp., Clearinghouse No. 54576 (N.M. Dist. Ct. Aug. 29, 2002).

5.4.12.4 Brokers Selling Mobile Homes for Consumers

Oregon has enacted UDAP regulations to protect consumers who contract with brokers to sell their mobile home.[1833] Brokers must provide a written agreement specifying the terms, the selling price, the expenses to be deducted from that price, the broker's commission, and whether the broker must approve of the purchasers. Any signed purchase and sale agreement must be provided immediately.

5.4.12.5 Land-Home Packages

A number of abuses relate to the sale of a mobile home and a lot to install the home in the same or closely related transactions—called "land-home packages." In some parts of the country, this is more common than purchases of homes to be placed into mobile home parks. Usually the lot owner is a separate entity than the home dealer. The lot owner will subdivide land into lots approximately one-quarter acre in size, and establish a business arrangement with a mobile home dealer. The consumer effectively engages in two transactions, a home purchase and a real estate closing, although the consumer may view these as the identical transaction.

A third party may be the one actually installing the home on the lot. Installation problems are far more rampant in such land-home packages than where the home is sited in a mobile home park because these lots have never been used to install a home, because a park operator is not present to supervise the installation, because some installers require that the consumer *not* be present for the installation, and because the installers are often paid minimal amounts and may have minimal expertise. Once the home is dumped on the lot, everyone attempts to wash their hands of the transaction and point the finger at someone else—the manufacturer, the dealer, the installer, or even the lot seller.

Even worse, the lot may be unsuitable for a home. Water seepage into or under the home is a common occurrence. The developer also may fail to build the promised features of the development, such as parks, driveways, and lighted streets.

One UDAP scope issue in these transactions is whether the UDAP statute applies to real estate sales. If it does not, home dealers may argue that not only is the lot transaction not covered, but neither is the home sale. The dealer may claim that the home comes permanently affixed to the land. This is rarely the case, but instead the mobile home is installed as any

1833 Or. Admin. R. 137-20-0025, Mobile Home Consignment.

mobile home would be, and the home transaction in any event is separate from the land transaction.

There is little case law or regulations dealing specifically with land-home packages. If a transaction involves a HUD-insured loan, then certain requirements are placed on the dealer. The dealer must inspect the home as installed on the homesite for structural damage or other defects resulting from the transportation and installation.[1834] The site shall comply with certain standards as to water and sewage systems, zoning ordinances, standards as to vehicular access, and other local standards.[1835]

5.4.13 Travel

5.4.13.1 Air Travel

In 1987, the National Association of Attorneys General enacted guidelines for the air travel industry.[1836] The guidelines dealt with nondisclosure of restrictions and limitations of advertised fares, the unavailability of flights at advertised fares, nondisclosure of fuel, tax, and other surcharges in advertised fares, one-way fare prices requiring round-trip tickets, airlines making changes in frequent flier programs that would reduce benefits already accrued, and the failure to make disclosures concerning restrictions on compensation for voluntarily bumped passengers. In 1992, however, the United States Supreme Court[1837] ruled that enforcement of the guidelines relating to fare advertising was preempted by the Airline Deregulation Act.[1838] Three years later, the Court ruled that the federal statute also preempted the guidelines relating to the operation of airlines' frequent flyer programs.[1839]

5.4.13.2 Cruises

A Florida court has held that a cruise line's description of a charge as a "port charges" was an implicit representation that it was a pass-through charge. The court allowed a class action to go forward challenging the cruise line's retention of a portion of the charge.[1840] The consumers sufficiently alleged reliance and damages simply by showing that they paid the charge, even if they paid no attention to that term of the bill, and paid the bill willingly.[1841]

5.4.13.3 Travel Packages and Certificates

States and the FTC have adopted a variety of approaches to fraud in the sale of travel packages. Georgia's UDAP statute prohibits various misrepresentations in connection with vacation promotions.[1842] Promoters must specifically describe any meals, transportation or lodging that are not covered and must disclose if a deposit is required to secure a reservation.

Vermont UDAP regulations also concern the sale of vacation packages where it appears the consumer is being offered a free trip.[1843] The seller must disclose that a purchase is required, that the package may involve a sales presentation, if that is the case, and must also disclose whether transportation is included and a description of the accommodations.

Massachusetts UDAP regulations detail deceptive practices in the sale of travel services and require disclosures about the price, the identity of the provider, the substitute and cancellation policies, and the terms of any trip cancellation insurance that is offered or provided.[1844] Consumers are given the right to cancel the deal if the disclosures are not made. The regulations also prohibit misrepresentations, require prompt delivery of tickets, require sellers to document that they have transmitted the consumer's payment to the provider, and require refunds in some circumstances when the seller fails to provide the promised services. A number of other states have specific statutes that deal with deceptive practices in the travel industry.[1845]

The FTC has proceeded against sellers who misrepresented the value and characteristics of vacation certificates.[1846] The FTC has also proceeded against a travel scam

1834 24 C.F.R. § 201.21(c)(4).

1835 24 C.F.R. § 201.21(e)(4).

1836 National Association of Attorneys General, Guidelines for Air Travel Advertising, Adopted December 12, 1987, 53 AntiTrust & Trade Reg. Report S-1 (Dec. 17, 1987).

1837 Morales v. Trans World Airlines, Inc., 504 U.S. 374, 112 S. Ct. 2031, 119 L. Ed. 2d 157 (1992).

1838 49 U.S.C. § 41713(b)(1).

1839 American Airlines, Inc. v. Wolens, 513 U.S. 219, 115 S. Ct. 817, 130 L. Ed. 2d 715 (1995). *See* § 2.5.5, *supra*.

1840 Latman v. Costa Cruise Lines, 758 So. 2d 699 (Fla. App. 2000). *See also* Pickett v. Holland Am. Line-Westours, Inc., 6 P.3d 63 (Wash. App. 2000), *rev'd on other grounds*, 35 P.3d 351 (Wash. 2001).

1841 Latman v. Costa Cruise Lines, 758 So. 2d 699 (Fla. App. 2000).

1842 Ga. Code Ann. § 10-1-393(b)(22).

1843 Code of Vermont Rules 06 031 017, Vermont Consumer Fraud Rules, Rule CF 116, Sale of Vacation Packages.

1844 Mass. Regs. Code tit. 940, § 15.00.

1845 *See, e.g.*, Cal. Bus. & Prof. Code §§ 17550.10 to 17556.5; Fla. Stat. Ann. § 559.926 to .939.

1846 Holiday Plus Travel, L.L.C., 5 Trade Reg. Rep. (CCH) ¶ 15107 (C.D. Cal. May 29, 2001) (proposed consent decree against company that misrepresented refund policies and that consumers won free vacations); FTC v. Discovery Rental, Inc., 5 Trade Reg. Rep. (CCH) ¶ 15110 (M.D. Fla. June 4, 2001) (proposed consent decree); FTC v. Resorts Exchange Int'l, 5 Trade Reg. Rep. (CCH) ¶ 15141 (M.D. Fla. Aug. 8, 2001) (stipulated final judgment against travel package seller who used unsolicited faxes and misrepresented costs); FTC v. Med Resorts Int'l, Inc., 5 Trade Reg. Rep. (CCH) ¶ 15174 (N.D. Ill. Nov. 1, 2001) (proposed consent decree against seller that misrepresented costs and features of travel club); FTC v. Passport International(e), Inc., 5 Trade Reg. Rep. (CCH) ¶ 23,406 (M.D. Fla. 1993) (consent order), FTC v. Travel World Int'l, 5 Trade Reg. Rep. (CCH) ¶ 22,757 (M.D. Fla. Nov. 2, 1989) (stipulated injunc-

that targeted immigrants and repeatedly failed to deliver pre-paid airline tickets, and promised but failed to make refunds to the consumers.[1847] It has also challenged the practice of misrepresenting the sponsorship of select hotels, and refusing to refund payments when the vacation was not as described.[1848] Another deceptive scheme challenged by the FTC is offering vacations as a sweepstakes prize, but where the consumer must purchase an airline ticket as an entry fee.[1849] Fraudulent travel package promoters often use unsolicited faxes to lure customers.[1850]

The highest court in Maryland held a prize promotion deceptive that involved purportedly free airline tickets.[1851] The seller did not disclose the fifteen dollar per person non-refundable registration fee, the seven to twelve day minimum hotel stay that the winner had to pay for, and a number of other fees.

5.4.13.4 Travel Agents

Travel agents hold themselves out as travel experts on which consumers can rely.[1852] Their role is analogous to that of a fiduciary in whom clients place their trust.[1853] Travel agents have the duty to investigate destinations, suppliers, and tour operators, and to verify that travel packages with the represented features are actually available. They must disclose conflicts of interest and can not push clients into trips against their interests.[1854] A representation that tickets are refundable when they are not is a UDAP violation, and may give rise to liability for breach of contract, negligence, misrepresentation, and breach of fiduciary duty as well.[1855] A travel agent may commit a UDAP violation by failing to disclose physical safety risks of tours it markets.[1856]

tion). *See also* FTC v. Roger S. Dolgin, 5 Trade Reg. Rep. (CCH) ¶ 24,492 (N.D. Cal. 1998) (consent decree); FTC v. World Travel Vacation Brokers, Inc., 5 Trade Reg. Rep. (CCH) ¶ 23,130 (N.D. Ill. 1992) (consent order).

1847 FTC v. Your Travels & Tours, Inc., 5 Trade Reg. Rep. (CCH) ¶ 24,499 (D. Mass. 1998) (consent decree).

1848 FTC v. Travel Bahamas Tours, Inc., 5 Trade Reg. Rep. (CCH) ¶ 24,456 (S.D. Fla. 1998) (proposed consent decree).

1849 FTC v. Lubell, 5 Trade Reg. Rep. (CCH) ¶ 24,274 (S.D. Iowa 1997) (proposed consent decree).

1850 *See* FTC v. Epic Resorts, L.L.C., 5 Trade Reg. Rep. (CCH) ¶ 15150 (M.D. Fla. Sept. 5, 2001). *See also* § 5.9.3.3, *infra* (federal junk fax prohibition).

1851 Luskin's, Inc. v. Consumer Protection Div., 353 Md. 335, 726 A.2d 702 (1999).

1852 Pellegrini v. Landmark Travel Group, 628 N.Y.S.2d 1003 (City Ct. 1995).

1853 *Id.*, quoting from C.A.B. Order 70-12-165 (Dec. 31, 1970); Krautsack v. Anderson, 329 Ill. App. 3d 666, 768 N.E.2d 133, 263 Ill. Dec. 373 (2002).

1854 Krautsack v. Anderson, 329 Ill. App. 3d 666, 768 N.E.2d 133, 263 Ill. Dec. 373 (2002).

1855 Pellegrini v. Landmark Travel Group, 628 N.Y.S.2d 1003 (City Ct. 1995).

1856 Maurer v. Cerkvenik-Anderson Travel, Inc., 181 Ariz. 294, 890 P.2d 69 (App. 1994).

5.5 Apartment Rentals, Mobile Home Parks, Migrant Camps, Real Estate Sales, and Storage

5.5.1 *Mobile Home Parks*

5.5.1.1 Preliminary Issues

Mobile home park abuses are within the scope of most state UDAP statutes, but in a few jurisdictions mobile home park and other real estate rentals may be outside the UDAP statute's coverage. This issue is analyzed in § 2.2.6, *supra*.

Another preliminary point is that UDAP precedent defining unfair or deceptive landlord-tenant practices may also be applicable to mobile home parks. Consumer litigants should not only analyze the mobile home park cases and regulations detailed in this section, but should also refer to § 5.5.2, *infra*, which analyzes landlord-tenant UDAP precedent.

A few states have UDAP regulations that forbid specific unfair and deceptive practices by mobile home parks. Many other states address these same concerns through a separate statute that deals solely with mobile home parks.[1857] These statutes often include their own remedies, but, in most states, a violation will also constitute a UDAP violation.[1858]

5.5.1.2 Park Rental Agreements, Rules, and Fees; Performance of Park Obligations; Sale of Utilities

Wisconsin UDAP regulations require mobile home parks to disclose all park rules, entrance and exit charges and other separate fees, and a park's arrangements for the sale of electricity, gas, and other items.[1859] Some states prohibit separate charges for entrance into and exit from the park or making a profit on certain required purchases.[1860] Requiring a mobile home park resident to buy utility service or other goods or services from a specified supplier may run afoul of state mobile home park law, the state UDAP statute, and antitrust law.[1861]

1857 *See* § 5.5.1.5.2, *infra*.

1858 *See* § 3.2.7, *supra*.

1859 Wisconsin Dep't of Agriculture, Trade and Consumer Protection Rules, Wis. Admin. Code ch. ATCP 125, Mobile Home Parks § 125.03.

1860 *Id.*; *see also* Macleod Mobile Homes Inc., 94 F.T.C. 144 (1979) (consent order) (requiring purchase of fuel from designated sellers). *But see* Vermont Mobile Home Owners' Ass'n, Inc. v. Lapierre, 131 F. Supp. 2d 553 (D. Vt. 2001) (where consumers alleged that entrance fee hidden in tied purchase of mobile home, claim failed where no evidence that paid more than market value for mobile home).

1861 *See* National Consumer Law Center, Consumer Law Pleadings, No. 2, § 2.2 (CD-Rom and Index Guide), also found on the CD-Rom accompanying this volume, for sample pleadings and

Conditioning the lease of a mobile home site upon purchase of a mobile home from the park owner is an antitrust and UDAP violation.[1862] Wisconsin's UDAP regulation on mobile home parks[1863] prohibits conditioning rental of a site on the purchase of a mobile home from the park operator or otherwise discriminating against those not buying a home from the operator.[1864] Mobile home park operators must also fulfill all representations, including providing all promised facilities and services[1865] and maintaining the park in a habitable condition.[1866] Operating a mobile home park without a license required by the state is a UDAP violation.[1867]

Wisconsin's UDAP regulation requires that rental agreements be for at least a year and specify the rent, the services not included in the rent, and the nature of the tenant's duty to remove the home upon the lease's termination.[1868] The Wisconsin regulations also state that rent may not be increased during the tenancy, that rule changes must be disclosed in advance, and that tenants will not have to relocate their site within the park. Park operators in Wisconsin can not require tenants to make permanent improvements, restrict the choice of vendors in the park, or enter a tenant's home without permission except under certain enumerated circumstances.

briefs raising these claims. *But see* Northern States Power Co. v. National Gas Co., 606 N.W.2d 613 (Wis. App. 1999) (upholding Wis. Admin. Code § ATCP 125.04(2) & (3), which allows mobile home park to mandate that tenants use a particular vendor for utility service provided through the park's facilities).

1862 Russell v. Atkins, 679 A.2d 333 (Vt. 1996). *But see* Vermont Mobile Home Owners' Ass'n, Inc. v. Lapierre, 131 F. Supp. 2d 553 (D. Vt. 2001) (no federal antitrust violation where consumers failed to show economic power in the tying product market and failed to show injury from tying arrangement; no UDAP claim where no actual damages shown and claim for injunctive relief is moot).

1863 Wisconsin Dep't of Agriculture, Trade and Consumer Protection Rules, Wis. Admin. Code ch. ATCP 125, Mobile Home Parks § 125.02.

1864 *See also* Macleod Mobile Homes Inc., 94 F.T.C. 144 (1979) (consent order); Mobile Homes Multiplex Corp., 94 F.T.C. 151 (1979) (consent order); Taylor Mobile Homes, Inc., 82 F.T.C. 1145 (1973) (consent order) (concerning discrimination against park applicants who do not purchase mobile homes from the park operator).

1865 Hallmark Group Cos. Inc., 84 F.T.C. 1 (1974) (consent order); Fulkerson v. MHC Operating Ltd., 2002 WL 32067510 (Del. Super. Sept. 24, 2002) (unpublished, citation limited) (inducing lot rentals by stating that lot rent included water, while negotiating sale of water system to private entity, could be UDAP violation).

1866 Danusis v. Longo, 48 Mass. App. Ct. 254, 720 N.E.2d 470 (1999) (failure to maintain mobile home park is actionable under UDAP statute). *See* National Consumer Law Center, Consumer Law Pleadings, No. 2, Ch. 2 (CD-Rom and Index Guide), also found on the CD-Rom accompanying this volume, for a complaint, motions, discovery requests, and briefs concerning uninhabitable mobile home park conditions.

1867 Danusis v. Longo, 48 Mass. App. Ct. 254, 720 N.E.2d 470 (1999).

1868 Wisconsin Dep't of Agriculture, Trade and Consumer Protection Rules, Wis. Admin. Code ch. ATCP 125, Mobile Home Parks § 125.03.

In many of the states that do not have a UDAP regulation dealing with mobile home park practices, there is a separate mobile home park statute that addresses similar issues.[1869] Violations of these statutes will usually constitute UDAP violations. But the Vermont Supreme Court ruled that a park owner's demand for a rental amount that had been disapproved under the mobile home park statute's former rent control provision was not a UDAP violation where an appeal of the disapproval was pending and there was no evidence of retaliation, unfounded or oppressive legal tactics, or other unconscionable conduct.[1870]

Other UDAP case law prohibits mobile home parks from requiring tenants to sign leases that include illegal and unenforceable clauses, even though the park does not enforce these clauses.[1871] Also deceptive are false claims that a park is for "adults only."[1872]

In a decision expanding the scope of the UDAP statute to include civil rights violations, a California court has held that running a mobile home park in a discriminatory manner qualifies as a violation of California's UDAP statute, as a matter of law, and requires no special jury finding on the issue.[1873] Under this decision, discriminatory practices, like other forms of unscrupulous business practices, give rise to UDAP claims, which may provide for supplemental or alternative relief to traditional civil rights claims.

5.5.1.3 Unfair Restriction on Tenant's Sale of the Home

A park may engage in unfair practices where it assesses charges or places other restrictions on a tenant's sale of the tenant's own mobile home.[1874] It is not unfair, however, for a mobile home park to offer a low price for a home when other buyers were available to the consumer.[1875]

1869 *See* § 5.5.1.5.2, *infra.*

1870 Lalande Air & Water Corp. v. Pratt, 795 A.2d 1233 (Vt. 2002).

1871 People v. McKale, 25 Cal. 3d 626, 602 P.2d 731, 159 Cal. Rptr. 811 (1980).

1872 *Id.*

1873 Fernwood v. Almeyda, 2002 WL 31862850 (Cal. App. Dec. 20, 2002) (unpublished, citation limited) (upholding permanent injunction under § 17200 prohibiting mobile home park owner from discriminating on the basis of familial status).

1874 Wisconsin Dep't of Agriculture, Trade and Consumer Protection Rules, Wis. Admin. Code ch. ATCP 125.06, Mobile Home Parks; Benkoski v. Flood, 229 Wis. 2d 377, 599 N.W.2d 885 (App. 1999) (interpreting Wis. Admin. Code § ATCP 125.06(1)(a) to forbid a park from requiring a mobile home to be removed from the park upon resale); *see also* Macleod Mobile Homes Inc., 94 F.T.C. 144 (1979) (consent order); Commonwealth v. DeCotis, 366 Mass. 234, 316 N.E.2d 748 (1974); Benkoski v. Flood, 242 Wis. 2d 652, 626 N.W.2d 851 (App. 2001) (affirming damage award for violation of Wisconsin rule prohibiting unreasonable restrictions on sale of home); State v. Fonk's Mobile Home Park, 133 Wis. 2d 287, 395 N.W.2d 786 (Ct. App. 1986).

1875 Daddona v. Liberty Mobile Home Sales, 209 Conn. 243, 550 A.2d 1061 (1988).

Illinois courts have struck down several related practices. It is unfair to require tenants to sell their mobile homes directly to the park owner at low prices, and to prohibit tenants from leasing their homes to other parties, particularly where this policy was not disclosed before the consumers moved into the park.[1876] It is unfair to charge tenants a $1500 commission when they sell their homes unless this commission accurately reflects the park's actual expenses, and unless the park discloses this charge before the tenant moves into the park.[1877]

5.5.1.4 Park Eviction Practices

Mobile home park owners' eviction practices may also run afoul of UDAP statutes. Wisconsin UDAP regulations require mobile home parks to disclose grounds for eviction.[1878] It is a UDAP violation to mislead mobile home park tenants about their rights or wrongfully cause them to submit to an eviction.[1879] Operators can not terminate or refuse to renew leases in retaliation for the tenant joining an association or because operators want the site for another buyer purchasing a mobile home from the operator.[1880] A trial court has awarded damages against a park on various theories, including UDAP, for a park's failure to provide sanitary conditions and other services and for threatening to evict those who complained of the conditions.[1881] It is unfair to evict tenants by dismantling their mobile home.[1882]

5.5.1.5 Other Approaches to Protecting Mobile Home Park Tenants

5.5.1.5.1 Tenant ownership of the park

These UDAP cases and regulations present a piecemeal approach to a fundamental problem. Mobile home park tenants, who own mobile homes that are installed on a rented site, are extremely vulnerable to park operator overreaching. "Mobile homes" are not really very mobile; they cost thousands of dollars to move, not counting the potential for serious structural damage to the home. Moreover, there may be no other place to go. In many areas *no* park space is available for someone wishing to move in a used home.

Park operators can take advantage of their extraordinary leverage through astronomical rent hikes, unreasonable fees and charges, and a failure to maintain the park. When a tenant tries to sell the home, the park may require a large commission or, even worse, by refusing to accept potential buyers, force the tenant to sell the home to the park at a fraction of its value. The most serious problem is where a park decides to close down, for example, to sell out to a shopping center developer.

The core problem is that tenants are mixing home ownership with short-term rental of the park site.[1883] In response, a growing trend is to convert mobile home parks to cooperatives or condominiums.[1884] The residents then set all fees and rules and are responsible for maintaining the park. Further, the threat of an unwanted change in land use is eliminated.

A number of states have adopted statutes giving tenants a right of first refusal when a mobile home park is sold or converted to another use.[1885] These statutes typically allow a tenants' organization, if it represents a certain percentage of park residents, to match any offer within a certain number of days.

5.5.1.5.2 Comprehensive mobile home park legislation

Thirty-six states have enacted comprehensive legislation dealing with mobile home parks.[1886] Many of these statutes

1876 People *ex rel.* Fahner v. Testa, 112 Ill. App. 3d 834, 445 N.E.2d 1249 (1983).

1877 People *ex rel.* Fahner v. Hedrich, 108 Ill. App. 3d 83, 438 N.E.2d 924 (1982).

1878 Wisconsin Dep't of Agriculture, Trade and Consumer Protection Rules, Wis. Admin. Code ch. ATCP 125.08, Mobile Home Parks.

1879 Gibbs v. Southeastern Investment Corp., 705 F. Supp. 738 (D. Conn. 1989).

1880 Wisconsin Dep't of Agriculture, Trade and Consumer Protection Rules, Wis. Admin. Code ch. ATCP 125.08, Mobile Home Parks.

1881 Wiley v. Cutler, Clearinghouse No. 44,066 (Mont. Dist. Ct. Ravalli Cty. Apr. 27, 1988).

1882 Daddona v. Liberty Mobile Home Sales, 209 Conn. 243, 550 A.2d 1061 (1988); *see also* Sweet v. Roy, 801 A.2d 694 (Vt. 2002) (affirming judgment against mobile home park owner for use of strong-arm tactics to evict resident).

1883 This problem obviously does not occur where the tenant rents both the home and the site—in that case tenants can more readily refuse to comply with overreaching landlord behavior.

1884 In Florida hundreds of parks have converted.

1885 Conn. Gen. Stat. § 21-70(f)(2)–(4); Del. Code Ann. tit. 25, § 7108 (applies only to condominium or cooperative conversion); Fla. Stat. § 723.071; Mass. Gen. Laws, ch. 140, § 32R; N.H. Rev. Stat. Ann. § 205-A:21; Vt. Stat. Ann. tit. 10, § 6242; Wash. Rev. Code § 59.23. *But see* Manufactured Housing Communities of Washington v. State, 142 Wash. 2d 347, 13 P.3d 183 (2000) (statute invalidated as unconstitutional).

1886 Alaska Stat. §§ 34.03.225, 45.30.070 (limited statutes dealing with tie-ins and park's right to terminate tenancy); Ariz. Rev. Stat. Ann. §§ 33-1401 to -1491 (comprehensive statute); Cal. Civ. Code § 798 (comprehensive statute) (California has numerous provisions relating to mobile homes; this is only one of them); Colo. Rev. Stat. §§ 38-12-200.1 to -217 (limited statute prohibiting tie-ins, requires court procedures for evictions and fee disclosures in lease); Conn. Gen. Stat. §§ 21-64 to -84a (comprehensive statute); Del. Code Ann. tit. 25, §§ 7001 to 7037, 7101 to 7114; Fla. Stat. §§ 723.001 to .0861 (comprehensive statute); Idaho Code §§ 55-2001 to -2019; 765 Ill. Comp. Stat. Ann. § 745/1 to 26 (comprehensive statute); Ind.

require a written lease, good cause for eviction, disclosure of fees, and notification to residents of changed land use. Typical statutes prohibit unreasonable rules, waiver of statutory rights, retaliatory evictions, and restrictions on a resident's choice of vendors. In most states it will be clear that violation of these standards is a UDAP violation.[1887]

The majority of these statutes give residents the right to cure defaults and allow the residents to sell their own homes, but still give the park owners a veto over new purchasers. A few of these statutes offer more significant protections—such as prohibiting tie-ins between selling a home and renting a park site, prohibiting entrance and exit fees, or providing residents with a right of first refusal,[1888] a warranty of habitability, or a buy-out of their home at fair market value when the park closes down.

The American Association of Retired Persons has also proposed a model home park statute.[1889] In addition to analyzing existing state legislation and areas of weakness, the proposal suggests a two-year lease term, renewable indefinitely, and tenant protections where there is a changed land use of the park site.

Code Ann. §§ 16-41-27-1 to -34; Iowa Code § 562B.1 to .32; Kan. Stat. Ann. §§ 58-25,100 to 25,126; Ky. Rev. Stat. Ann. § 219.310 (authorizing state agency to establish a comprehensive regulation); Me. Rev. Stat. Ann. tit. 10, §§ 9091 to 9100; Md. Real Prop. Code tit. 8A, §§ 101 to 1803 (comprehensive statute); Mass. Gen. Laws ch. 140, §§ 32A to 32S (comprehensive statute); Mass. Regs. Code 940, § 10.00 *et seq.*; Mich. Comp. Laws §§ 125.2301 to .2350, 600.5771 to .5785; Minn. Stat. §§ 327C.01 to .15; Mont. Code Ann. §§ 70-24-313 to -315, 70-24-436 (dealing with park's right to terminate tenancy, unreasonable rules, park owner's maintenance obligations); Neb. Rev. Stat. §§ 76-1450 to -14,111; Nev. Rev. Stat. §§ 118B.010 to .260; N.H. Rev. Stat. Ann. ch. 205-A; N.J. Stat. §§ 46:86-2 to -21; N.J. Admin. Code § 5:24-1.1 to -2.11; N.M. Stat. Ann. §§ 47-10-1 to -23; N.Y. Real Prop. Law §§ 233, 735; N.D. Cent. Code §§ 23-10-01 to -12; Ohio Rev. Code §§ 3733.01 to .20; Or. Rev. Stat. Ann. §§ 90.505 to .840; 68 Pa. Cons. Stat. §§ 398.1 to .16; R.I. Gen. Laws §§ 31-44-1 to -21, 31-44.1-1 to 31-44.1-3; S.C. Code Ann. §§ 27-47-10 to -620; Utah Code Ann. §§ 57-16-1 to -16; Vt. Stat. Ann. tit. 10, §§ 6201 to 6266; Va. Code Ann. §§ 55-248.41 to .52; Wash. Rev. Code §§ 59.20.010 to .901; W. Va. Code §§ 37-15-1 to -8; Wis. Stat. § 710.15; Wis. Admin. Code §§ 125.01 to .08.

1887 Massachusetts v. Bumila, Clearinghouse No. 51,267 (Mass. Housing Ct. Mar. 27, 1996) (ordering UDAP remedies for park's requirement that mobile home residents purchase propane from it). *See* § 3.2.7, *supra*, for a general discussion of violations of other statutes being UDAP violations.

1888 *See* Greenfield Country Estates Tenants Ass'n v. Deep, 1995 Mass. Super. LEXIS 650 (Feb. 15, 1995) (enforcing tenants' right to be afforded opportunity to buy park when it is to be sold), *aff'd*, 423 Mass. 81, 666 N.E.2d 988 (1996).

1889 American Association of Retired Persons, Manufactured Housing Community Tenants: Shifting the Balance of Power (2004 AARP).

5.5.1.5.3 Mobile home park tenant associations, creative use of UDAP statutes, and other legal theories

Where it is not practical for an attorney to represent a tenant, one option is to refer the tenant to a local or state-wide mobile home park tenant association or manufactured-housing owner association. Associations use lay advocates to assist the resident without the expense of hiring an attorney, or enable a number of residents with similar problems to obtain joint legal representation.

UDAP statutes usually can provide victimized mobile home park residents with relief. A park operator's failure to disclose important information and oral misrepresentations—e.g., that the operator had no plans to close down the park, that rent increases will be moderate, that there will be no problem selling the resident's home to a new buyer—are actionable under UDAP statutes no matter what the lease agreement states. Where state mobile home park or landlord-tenant legislation exists but does not provide adequate private remedies, violation of these statutes also may be UDAP violations.

Other potential avenues for park residents' redress include state landlord-tenant legislation, local mobile home park ordinances, and, particularly in California, local rent control ordinances. Finally, fraud or other tort theories are useful because of the availability of punitive damages.

5.5.2 Landlord-Tenant Practices

5.5.2.1 Introduction

UDAP statutes can be used to challenge landlord-tenant practices except in those states where leases of real property have been interpreted to be outside the statute's scope.[1890] A few states have developed extensive UDAP requirements for landlords. Whether a tenant can assert UDAP counterclaims in an eviction case depends on the state eviction law.[1891]

The most fertile source of UDAP precedent in the landlord-tenant area is a state's landlord-tenant law, particularly if a court rules that a violation of that law is a *per se* UDAP violation. Then landlord-tenant code violations become au-

1890 *See* § 2.2.6, *supra*.

1891 Hoffer v. Szumski, 129 Or. App. 7, 877 P.2d 128 (1994) (UDAP counterclaim may be asserted where landlord seeks back rent as well as eviction). *See* National Consumer Law Center, Consumer Law Pleadings, No. 2, § 1.1 (CD-Rom and Index Guide), also found on the CD-Rom accompanying this volume, for a UDAP answer and counterclaim to a landlord's claim for back rent, alleging that lease terms are void, unenforceable, and illegal penalties, and § 1.2 for a UDAP answer and counterclaim to an eviction action, based on uninhabitable conditions, along with proposed findings of facts and conclusions of law and two appellate briefs, both also found on the CD-Rom accompanying this volume.

tomatic UDAP violations.[1892] It may be possible to raise claims of housing discrimination as UDAP claims.[1893]

5.5.2.2 Security Deposits and Calculation of Rents

UDAP regulations require landlords to disclose all terms and all tenants' rights pertaining to security deposits and to itemize any claims against the deposit.[1894] Landlords may not withhold excessive amounts from the security deposit.[1895]

Many states have provisions in their UDAP statute or regulations that prohibit misrepresentations about the need for repairs. A landlord who misrepresents that a security deposit was withheld because repairs were necessary may violate this specific prohibition.[1896]

It is unfair to collect rent the landlord is not entitled to or to deduct rental payments from the security deposit.[1897] It is also a UDAP violation for a landlord to selectively understand the rent control ordinance, and thus charge more than the allowed maximum rent.[1898]

5.5.2.3 Rental Agreements

Rental agreements must be readable[1899] and may not contain illegal or unenforceable terms.[1900] Rents may only be escalated during the lease term if agreed upon and disclosed in advance.[1901] Obtaining the tenants' signatures on a lease by taking advantage of their inability to speak or read English may be a UDAP violation.[1902] A lease is void where the landlord violated a UDAP regulation requiring the tenant to be given a copy of the rental agreement before paying any earnest money or security deposit.[1903] While a landlord's failure to inform a tenant that she would be potentially liable for the upstairs tenants' electric usage, which was on her meter, was a deceptive trade practice, the tenant was denied a UDAP recovery where she freely agreed to the billing arrangement once she learned of it.[1904]

It is unfair to convince a tenant to sign lease documents in blank.[1905] Accepting a tenant's security deposit, then

1892 *See* § 3.2.3, *supra*. *See also* Hernandez v. Stabach, 145 Cal. App. 3d 309, 193 Cal. Rptr. 350 (1983), *modified* 146 Cal. App. 3d 199b (1983) (California UDAP statute explicitly prohibits business practices forbidden by law; retaliatory eviction in violation of state law is a UDAP violation); Conaway v. Prestia, 191 Conn. 484, 464 A.2d 847 (1983); Connelly v. New Haven Housing Authority, 8 Conn. L. Trib. No. 31 (Super. Ct. 1982) (health and safety code violation in public housing may constitute UDAP violation), *rev'd on other grounds*, 213 Conn. 354, 567 A.2d 1212 (1990) (UDAP does not apply to municipal housing authority); Montanez v. Bagg, 24 Mass. App. Ct. 954, 510 N.E.2d 298 (1987); Dannenmaier v. Harold Brown, Clearinghouse No. 35,755 (Mass. Boston Housing Ct. Dec. 19, 1983) (discrimination against prospective law student tenants *per se* violation based on state law prohibiting housing discrimination). *But see* Miles v. Shauntee, 664 S.W.2d 512 (Ky. 1984) (housing code violation not *per se* UDAP violation where no private right of action for housing code violations); State v. Schwab, 693 P.2d 108 (Wash. 1985) (state housing legislation violation preempts UDAP action instead of creating *per se* action).

1893 King v. First, 46 Mass. App. Ct. 372, 705 N.E.2d 1172 (1999) (requiring plaintiff to pursue state administrative remedies before bringing UDAP claim alleging racial discrimination in housing).

1894 Massachusetts Consumer Protection Regulations, Mass. Regs. Code tit. 940, § 3.17(3)(b)(3), Landlord-Tenant; Wis. Admin. Code ch. ATCP 134.06(2); *see also* Three & One Co. v. Geilfuss, 178 Wis. 2d 400, 504 N.W.2d 393 (1993) (interpreting Wisconsin regulation); Harris, Luck, Rubin v. Turenske, 1996 Wisc. App. LEXIS 1424 (Nov. 12, 1996) (awarding double damages for violation of UDAP rule regarding itemization of claims); Moonlight v. Boyce, 125 Wis. 2d 298, 372 N.W.2d 479 (Ct. App. 1985).

1895 Goes v. Feldman, 8 Mass. App. Ct. 84, 391 N.E.2d 943 (1979); Smolen v. Dahlman Apartments, Ltd., 338 N.W.2d 892 (Mich. Ct. App. 1983); Commonwealth v. National Apartment Leasing Co., 529 A.2d 1157 (Pa. Commw. Ct. 1987); Armour v. Klecker, 169 Wis. 2d 692, 486 N.W.2d 563 (Ct. App. 1992); Pierce v. Norwick, 550 N.W.2d 451 (Wis. App. 1996) (if landlord sends the required itemized statement, double damage award is limited to net amount owed to tenant); Weller v. Dept. of Agriculture, Trade and Consumer Protection, No. 78-813 (Wis. Ct. App. 1980), *aff'd*, 109 Wis. 2d 665, 327 N.W.2d 178 (1982); *see also* Paulik v. Coombs, 120 Wis. 2d 431, 355 N.W.2d 357 (Ct. App. 1984); *cf.* Tarka v. Filipovic, 45 Conn. App. 46, 694 A.2d 824 (1997) (landlord's unknowing violation of law requiring security deposits to be placed in interest-bearing account not a UDAP violation).

1896 Wallace v. Pastore, 742 A.2d 1090 (Pa. Super. 1999).

1897 McGrath v. Mishara, 386 Mass. 74, 434 N.E.2d 1215 (1982); Armour v. Klecker, 169 Wis. 2d 692, 486 N.W.2d 563 (Ct. App. 1992); *see also* Rita v. Corella, 394 Mass. 822, 477 N.E.2d 1016 (1985); Commonwealth v. Chatham Development Co., 49 Mass. App. Ct. 525, 731 N.E.2d 89 (2000) (unfair to collect late fee contrary to UDAP regulation). *But cf.* Lalande Air & Water Corp. v. Pratt, 795 A.2d 1233 (Vt. 2002) (mobile home park's demand for rental amount disapproved by rent control commission not unfair where appeal of disapproval was pending and no evidence of retaliation, oppression, etc.).

1898 Cohen v. De La Cruz, 106 F.3d 52 (3d Cir. 1997) (New Jersey law), *aff'd on other grounds*, 523 U.S. 213, 118 S. Ct. 1212, 130 L. Ed. 2d 341 (1998). *See also* Commonwealth v. Chatham Development Co., 49 Mass. App. Ct. 525, 731 N.E.2d 89 (2000) (unfair to collect late fee contrary to UDAP regulation).

1899 Commonwealth v. Monumental Properties, Inc., 459 Pa. 450, 329 A.2d 812 (1974).

1900 People v. McKale, 25 Cal. 3d 626, 602 P.2d 731, 159 Cal. Rptr. 811 (1980); Leardi v. Brown, 394 Mass. 151, 474 N.E.2d 1094 (1985); 316 49 St. Assocs. Ltd. v. Galvez, 269 N.J. Super. 481, 635 A.2d 1013 (1994) (inclusion of inapplicable, misleading disclosure, and use of phony lease-purchase option to evade rent control ordinance may be UDAP violations).

1901 Massachusetts Consumer Protection Regulations, Mass. Regs. Code tit. 940, § 3.17(2), (3), Landlord-Tenant.

1902 316 49 St. Assocs. Ltd. v. Galvez, 269 N.J. Super. 481, 635 A.2d 1013 (1994).

1903 Harris, Luck, Rubin v. Turenske, 1996 Wisc. App. LEXIS 1424 (Nov. 12, 1996).

1904 Legg v. Castruccio, 100 Md. App. 748, 642 A.2d 906 (1994).

1905 Bissonette v. American Heritage Agency, 1985 Conn. Super. LEXIS 262 (Housing Div. Feb. 7, 1985).

refusing to rent out the apartment and refusing to return the deposit, is a UDAP violation.[1906] It is a UDAP violation to have a tenant pay for heat and hot water without a written agreement, contrary to a state health regulation.[1907] In some jurisdictions, landlords must designate an agent who will accept all legal notices.[1908]

5.5.2.4 Substandard Housing

Rental units may not contain illegal hazards that endanger the occupant's well-being or that make the unit unfit for habitation. A landlord who rents out an apartment impliedly represents that it is in compliance with applicable health and safety codes; if it is not, the landlord has committed a UDAP violation.[1909] Other UDAP violations include renting out residential premises in which there is lead paint that exceeds statutory limits[1910] and collection of the full amount of rent while the unit is in violation of the housing code or where the unit had material defects rendering it unsafe or unfit.[1911] Massachusetts' highest court has affirmed a $61,475 treble damages judgment against a landlord who rented an uninhabitable apartment to a tenant, refused to repair it, and was abusive and threatening to the tenant.[1912] A North Carolina court holds that the measure of damages for substandard housing conditions is the difference between the fair rental value of the property in the warranted condition and its actual fair rental value, but damages can not exceed the total amount of rent paid by the tenant.[1913]

A landlord's continuous and systematic breach of the implied warranty of habitability has been found to be unfair. Although not every breach of warranty would be a violation, either an egregious or a continuous one would be, as where the landlord continuously failed to remedy defects despite notices and judicial proceedings.[1914]

The landlord must disclose all violations of law in the unit, and must correct or pay to correct all such violations.[1915] Even if a landlord rents a unit not knowing about

1906 Collard v. Reagan, 2002 WL 1357052 (Wash. App. June 21, 2002) (unpublished, citation limited).

1907 Poncz v. Loftin, 607 N.E.2d 765 (Mass. App. Ct. 1993).

1908 *See, e.g.*, Massachusetts Consumer Protection Regulations, Mass. Regs. Code tit. 940, § 3.17(3)(b)(2), Landlord-Tenant.

1909 Simms v. Candela, 45 Conn. Supp. 267, 711 A.2d 778 (1998) (tenant's personal injury due to landlord's failure to maintain gutters in compliance with housing standards is actionable under UDAP statute); Benik v. Hatcher, 358 Md. 507, 750 A.2d 10 (2000); Jablonski v. Clemons, 60 Mass. App. Ct. 473, 803 N.E.2d 730 (Mass. App. Ct. 2004); Grundberg v. Gill, 56 Mass. App. Ct. 1116, 780 N.E.2d 158 (Mass. App. Ct. 2002) (unpublished); L'Esperance v. Benware, 830 A.2d 675 (Vt. 2003) (renting out house that did not comply with health and safety codes was UDAP violation); Bisson v. Ward, 628 A.2d 1256 (Vt. 1993) (remanding for consideration of exemplary damages). *But cf.* Beacon Property Mgmt., Inc. v. PNR, Inc., 785 So. 2d 564 (Fla. App. 2001) (tenants can only bring UDAP claim for substandard conditions against landlord, not company landlord hired to maintain premises), *rev'd on other grounds*, 842 So. 2d 773 (Fla. 2003).

1910 Hardy v. Griffin, 41 Conn. Supp. 283, 569 A.2d 49 (1989); Forrest v. P&L Real Estate Investment Co., 134 Md. App. 371, 759 A.2d 1187 (2000) (landlord can be liable even if unaware of lead paint if landlord's knowledge of likelihood exceeds tenant's). *See also* Berg v. Byrd, 124 Md. App. 208, 720 A.2d 1283 (1998) (renting out premises without disclosing that they contain chipping paint is a UDAP violation); Davis v. Goodman, 700 A.2d 798 (Md. Ct. Spec. App. 1997) (failure to inform tenant of lead paint and its dangers). *Cf.* Williams-Ward v. Lorenzo Pitts, Inc., 908 F. Supp. 48 (D. Mass. 1995) (no UDAP liability for failure to disclose lead paint of which landlord was unaware); Hayes v. Hambruch, 841 F. Supp. 706 (D. Md. 1994) (no UDAP violation where landlord unaware of lead), *aff'd without op.*, 64 F.3d 657 (4th Cir. 1995); Benik v. Hatcher, 358 Md. 507, 750 A.2d 10 (2000); Richwind v. Brunson, 335 Md. 661, 645 A.2d 1147 (1994) (no UDAP violation where tenants lived in premises for two years before defendant bought it, so were not induced to enter into lease by any acts of defendants); Scroggins v. Dahne, 335 Md. 688, 645 A.2d 1160 (1994) (no UDAP liability for lead paint problem that arose during term, rather than at inception, of lease); Underwood v. Risman, 414 Mass. 96, 605 N.E.2d 832 (1993) (no duty to disclose lead paint hazard of which landlord was unaware).

1911 Conaway v. Prestia, 191 Conn. 484, 464 A.2d 847 (1983) (UDAP violation to collect rent for apartments that were in substandard condition and lacked certificate of occupancy); Spaulding v. Young, 32 Mass. App. Ct. 624, 592 N.E.2d 1348 (1992) (landlord is liable under UDAP statute if conditions seriously or materially impair the health or safety and well being of an occupant, whether or not the conditions violate the Sanitary or Housing Code); Pierce v. Reichard, 593 S. E. 2d 787 (N.C. Ct. App. 2004) (landlord is liable for UDAP violation and treble damages for failing, despite tenant's complaints, to repair leaking roof or remove rotten tree that later fell on tenant's car); Cardwell v. Henry, 549 S.E.2d 587 (N.C. App. 2001); Allen v. Simmons, 99 N.C. App. 636, 394 S.E.2d 478 (1990) (unfair to collect rent on an apartment containing numerous defects making it unfit and uninhabitable, where the landlord had notice of those defects and did not correct them); Cotton v. Stanley, 86 N.C. App. 534, 358 S.E.2d 692, *cert. denied*, 321 N.C. 296, 362 S.E.2d 779 (1987). *Cf.* Lynch v. James, 692 N.E.2d 81 (Mass. App. Ct. 1998) (failure to install window stops or guards not UDAP violation since housing code did not require them and they were not vital to use of apartment), *review denied*, 427 Mass. 1106, 699 N.E.2d 850 (1998).

1912 Haddad v. Gonzalez, 410 Mass. 855, 576 N.E.2d 658 (1991). *See also* Grundberg v. Gill, 56 Mass. App. Ct. 1116, 780 N.E.2d 158 (Mass. App. Ct. 2002) (unpublished) (affirming UDAP treble damages where landlord knew or should have known that failure to correct septic system would result in severe emotional distress and breach of warranty).

1913 Cardwell v. Henry, 549 S.E.2d 587 (N.C. App. 2001).

1914 *In re* Clark, 96 B.R. 569 (Bankr. E.D. Pa. 1989). Cruz Mgmt. Co. v. Thomas, 417 Mass. 782, 633 N.E.2d 390 (1994) (substantial and material breach of implied warranty of habitability is a UDAP violation, even if negligent); Creekside Apartments v. Poteat, 446 S.E.2d 826 (N.C. Ct. App. 1994). *But cf.* Brightful v. Gregory (*In re* Brightful), 1999 Bankr. LEXIS 1278 (Bankr. E.D. Pa. Oct. 8, 1999) (violations of implied warranty of habitability that were not egregious or continuous were not UDAP violations); Sam v. Beaird, 685 So. 2d 742 (Ala. Civ. App. 1996) (no UDAP violation where landlord took steps to correct problems once he learned of them).

1915 Nielsen v. Wisniewski, 32 Conn. App. 133, 628 A.2d 25 (1993)

serious housing violations, it is unconscionable for the landlord to fail to remedy the violations.[1916] The tenant is in an untenable position of having to move out or live with substandard conditions.

5.5.2.5 Failure to Obtain Occupancy Certificates

It is a *per se* UDAP violation to rent property and accept rents when the landlord has failed to obtain a certificate of occupancy required by state law.[1917] Since the licensing requirement is meant to protect the public, the landlord may not be permitted to collect rents, even under a *quantum meruit* theory.[1918] The mere collection of such rent may be a UDAP violation.[1919]

It is a UDAP violation for a landlord to misrepresent that an apartment has a proper certificate of occupancy.[1920] It is likewise a UDAP violation to misrepresent one's authority under the rules of a cooperative apartment building to rent a unit to a prospective subtenant.[1921]

5.5.2.6 Safety-Related Violations

A landlord who represents that an apartment building has various safety features may be liable under UDAP for an assault upon a tenant, if the criminal act was reasonably foreseeable and a direct and proximate result of the deception.[1922] A landlord's misrepresentation of the tenant's right to have additional locks put on her door is actionable pursuant to a UDAP statute, when the tenant was sexually assaulted by a person who obtained a key to her apartment through the landlord's negligence.[1923]

5.5.2.7 Utilities

If the landlord agrees to do so, the landlord must provide utility services and may not cause the services' termination.[1924] Violation of the state's utility service laws and regulations may be a UDAP violation where the tenant's dispute involves utility service, equipment, or meters.[1925] Nonetheless, a Maryland court has held that a landlord did not violate the state UDAP statute by requiring a tenant to contract for utility service on a single meter, and split the bill with the upstairs tenants.[1926] The court held that the tenant could have avoided the injury by moving out early in the tenancy, and that the single meter did not violate Maryland public policy as expressed in its utility service laws.

5.5.2.8 The Tenant's Early Termination

A "termination fee" in a lease, under which the tenant who terminated the lease early was charged one and one-half months' rent even if the landlord re-rented the unit immediately, was an unenforceable penalty.[1927] But the evidence

---

(landlord's unlawful utility terminations and breach of promises to repair unit violated UDAP); Dorgan v. Loukas, 473 N.E.2d 1151 (Mass. App. Ct. 1985); Weller v. Dep't of Agriculture, Trade and Consumer Protection, No. 78-813 (Wis. Ct. App. 1980), *aff'd*, 109 Wis. 2d 665, 327 N.W.2d 178 (1982); Massachusetts Consumer Protection Regulations, Mass. Regs. Code tit. 940, § 3.17(1), Landlord-Tenant. *But see* Richwind v. Brunson, 335 Md. 661, 645 A.2d 1147 (1994) (UDAP statute does not apply to lead paint problem that arose during term, rather than at inception, of lease); Scroggins v. Dahne, 335 Md. 688, 645 A.2d 1160 (1994) (UDAP statute does not apply to lead paint problem that arose during term, rather than at inception of lease); Underwood v. Risman, 414 Mass. 96, 605 N.E.2d 832 (1993) (landlord is responsible only for disclosing hazards of which he has actual knowledge).

1916 Wade v. Jobe, 818 P.2d 1006 (Utah 1991). *See also* Benik v. Hatcher, 358 Md. 507, 750 A.2d 10 (2000) (landlord liable for nondisclosure of lead paint hazard even if unaware of it).

1917 Conaway v. Prestia, 191 Conn. 484, 464 A.2d 847 (1983); Golt v. Phillips, 308 Md. 1, 517 A.2d 328 (1986); *see also* Cybal v. Atrium Palace Syndicate, 272 N.J. Super. 330, 639 A.2d 1146 (1994) (condominium seller committed UDAP violation by refusing to return buyers' deposits when it had not obtained certificates of occupancy by closing date); Borders v. Newton, 315 S.E.2d 731 (N.C. Ct. App. 1984).

1918 Golt v. Phillips, 308 Md. 1, 517 A.2d 328 (1986).

1919 *Id.*

1920 Bartolomeo v. Runco, 162 N.Y. Misc. 2d 485, 616 N.Y.S.2d 695 (City Ct. 1994).

1921 Yochim v. McGrath, 165 Misc. 2d 10, 626 N.Y.S.2d 685 (Yonkers City Ct. 1995).

1922 Miller v. Charles E. Smith Mgmt., Inc., 1999 U.S. App. LEXIS 1013 (4th Cir. Jan. 26, 1999) (allegations that landlord misrepresented security features of apartment states UDAP claim where tenant relied on them and was murdered), *later appeal*, 2001 WL 459070 (4th Cir. May 2, 2001) (unpublished, citation limited) (affirming judgment after trial against plaintiff's fraud claim because causal connection was too remote; UDAP claim was dismissed by trial court on other grounds). *See* Shea v. Preservation Chicago, Inc., 206 Ill. App. 3d 657, 565 N.E.2d 20 (1990) (landlord did not violate UDAP statute by misrepresenting that security door and lock would be repaired before tenancy began, where landlord was not alleged to have known at the time that this representation would not be fulfilled); Petrauskas v. Wexenthaller Realty Mgmt., Inc., 186 Ill. App. 3d 820, 542 N.E.2d 902 (1989) (no UDAP liability because criminal act not reasonably foreseeable); Fitzpatrick v. ACF Properties Group, 595 N.E.2d 1327 (Ill. App. Ct. 1992) (no UDAP violation where assault victim's injuries were not proximately caused by landlord's statements regarding safety of apartment complex).

1923 Berry Property Mgmt., Inc. v. Bliskey, 850 S.W.2d 644 (Tex. App. 1993).

1924 Nielsen v. Wisniewski, 32 Conn. App. 133, 628 A.2d 25 (1993) (cutting off tenant's utility service violated UDAP); Bissonette v. American Heritage Agency, 1985 Conn. Super. LEXIS 262 (Housing Div. Feb. 7, 1985). *Cf.* Tarka v. Filipovic, 45 Conn. App. 46, 694 A.2d 824 (1997) (temporary interruption of electric service, quickly remedied, not a UDAP violation).

1925 Legg v. Castruccio, 100 Md. App. 748, 642 A.2d 906 (1994).

1926 *Id.*

1927 Woodhaven Apartments v. Washington, 942 P.2d 918 (Utah 1997).

was insufficient to establish a violation of the UDAP statute's unconscionability standard because the tenant did not introduce evidence of the actual costs to the landlord of early termination.

Damages for a tenant's breach of the lease are limited to those specified by state law. The landlord may not require rent for periods when the tenant was not obligated to occupy and did not in fact occupy the unit.[1928] A landlord's attempt to convert a tenant's breach of the lease into a UDAP violation, where there was no showing of a pattern of breaches of contract by the tenant, has been rejected.[1929]

5.5.2.9 Deceptive Notices to Quit

It can be a UDAP violation where a landlord's form notice to quit does not clearly indicate the tenant's legal rights. A housing court has found deceptive the image of a uniformed police officer on the notice; wording that implied, at least to unsophisticated tenants, that the landlord will resort to self-help eviction; and the failure to disclose the tenant's right to judicial process to contest the eviction.[1930] The court seemed persuaded by testimony from the tenant's readability expert that the "language of the notice is highly unreadable because of its unnecessary use of legalese and archaic vocabulary, long sentences, and poor syntax."[1931] The tenant's brief[1932] also cited to a far clearer and more accurate sample notice to quit set forth in the state's practice series.

In granting summary judgment, the court found that these UDAP violations rendered the notice ineffective to terminate a tenancy and dismissed the landlord's claims for rent and possession. Because this was a UDAP action, the court did not require proof that the tenant was actually deceived. The court also issued a permanent injunction prohibiting use of similar notices.

1928 Massachusetts Consumer Protection Regulations, Mass. Regs. Code tit. 940, § 3.17(b)(d), Landlord-Tenant.

1929 Atkinson v. Rosenthal, 33 Mass. App. Ct. 219, 598 N.E.2d 666 (1992).

1930 *Id.* The consumer's attorney was prepared to use witnesses who would testify that numerous tenants in the area do not understand that they have a right to judicial process before eviction. Potential witnesses were tenant agency employees who regularly advise tenants.

1931 The expert was the chair of a local college English department. He produced an affidavit stating that the notice was at the fifteenth grade reading level and was ambiguous even to those who read at that high level. Affidavit of Paul LeBlanc, Clearinghouse No. 45,950B (May 13, 1991). The consumer's attorney then contrasted this with census data showing low educational levels for many of those in the surrounding low-income communities.

1932 Memorandum in Support of Defendant's Motion for Partial Summary Judgment, Clearinghouse No. 45,950C (May 13, 1991).

5.5.2.10 Evictions and Related Practices

A number of different UDAP precedents agree that a landlord engages in a UDAP violation when it evicts a tenant in retaliation for the tenant complaining to the landlord or legal authorities or for joining a tenant's organization.[1933] It is a UDAP violation to violate a bankruptcy court's automatic stay and to try to force a consumer-in-bankruptcy out of an apartment.[1934]

It is also a UDAP violation to try to force tenants out of an apartment (to allow condominium conversion or to avoid rent control laws) by allowing the building to deteriorate seriously and by illegally raising rents.[1935] It is unconscionable for a landlord to allow a serious housing code violation to persist so that the unit is condemned and the tenant is forced out.[1936] A federal court has also found potentially deceptive a landlord's filing of a complaint for possession without proper notice to the tenant that the landlord was terminating her lease and the basis for the eviction.[1937]

A landlord may commit a UDAP violation by misleading a tenant as to her rights and wrongfully causing her to submit to an eviction.[1938] It is a UDAP violation for a landlord to illegally enter a leased premise and forcibly evict the tenant.[1939] It is also a UDAP violation to lock a tenant out of his apartment and confiscate his personal property,[1940] or to cut off water and electricity in an attempt to evict a tenant, leaving the property in an unsafe condition.[1941] In an

1933 Hernandez v. Stabach, 145 Cal. App. 3d 309, 193 Cal. Rptr. 350 (1983), *modified* 146 Cal. App. 3d 199b (1983) (UDAP statute prohibits business practices forbidden by law, and state law prohibits retaliatory evictions); Kendig v. Kendall Constr. Co., 317 So. 2d 138 (Fla. Dist. Ct. App. 1975); Massachusetts Consumer Protection Regulations, Mass. Regs. Code tit. 940, § 3.17(b)(b), Landlord-Tenant.

1934 Aponte v. Aungst, 82 B.R. 738 (Bankr. E.D. Pa. 1988).

1935 49 Prospect Street v. Sheva Gardens, 227 N.J. Super. 449, 547 A.2d 1134 (App. Div. 1988).

1936 Wade v. Jobe, 818 P.2d 1006 (Utah 1991). *But see* Carlie v. Morgan, 922 P.2d 1 (Utah 1996) (holding that Utah's Fit Premises Act has displaced UDAP statute for uninhabitability claims).

1937 Anast v. Commonwealth Apartments, 956 F. Supp. 792 (N.D. Ill. 1997).

1938 Gibbs v. Southeastern Investment Corp., 705 F. Supp. 738 (D. Conn. 1989) (mobile home lot eviction).

1939 Mosley & Mosley Builders v. Landin Ltd., 389 S.E.2d 576 (N.C. Ct. App. 1990); *see also* Sweet v. Roy, 801 A.2d 694 (Vt. 2002) (affirming judgment against mobile home park owner for use of strong-arm tactics to evict resident).

1940 Prestien v. Roets, 477 N.W.2d 363 (Wis. Ct. Ct. App. 1991) unpublished, limited precedent opinion, text available at 1991 Wisc. App. LEXIS 1296). *But see* Levin v. Lynn, 310 N.J. Super. 177, 708 A.2d 454 (App. Div. 1998) (not a UDAP violation for rental agent to authorize new tenants to move existing tenants' property out of the unit).

1941 Stanley v. Moore, 439 S.E.2d 250 (N.C. Ct. App. 1994). The North Carolina Supreme Court reversed the court of appeals' denial of treble damages and attorney fees in 454 S.E.2d 225 (N.C. 1995). *See* National Consumer Law Center, Consumer

early decision, the North Carolina Supreme Court held that a landlord did not violate the UDAP statute by padlocking the apartment when the tenant failed to pay rent.[1942] Shortly thereafter, the legislature adopted a landlord-tenant law that prohibited self-help eviction, and the court then held that a violation of this law *was* a UDAP violation.[1943] Such conduct is also likely to be treated as tortious in many jurisdictions.

It is unfair and deceptive to sue tenants for damage to property and cleaning costs before the tenant has vacated, or to falsely claim in a suit that attorney fees are due and owing.[1944] It is also unfair for a landlord to charge excessive late payment penalties or institute unnecessary summary ejectment proceedings.[1945]

Massachusetts UDAP regulations require that landlords follow the eviction provisions of state law and prohibit landlords from penalizing payments less than thirty days late.[1946] It is a UDAP violation in Massachusetts for a landlord to include in its lease agreement authorization to charge $20 for each fourteen-day notice to quit sent to the tenant, because state law prohibits late charges during the statutory 30-day grace period for payment of rent.[1947] While it is common practice, and apparently legal, to send the fourteen-day notice to quit during the thirty-day grace period, late charges can not be imposed for such a notice.

In analyzing a landlord's liability for a lockout, utility shutoff, or other abusive steps to remove the tenant, remember that the landlord is often taking these steps as a means to enforce a rent debt. The state's debt collection practices statute or regulation may give the tenant additional causes of action.[1948] If an independent party other than the property owner is involved, the tenant may also be able to sue under the Fair Debt Collection Practices Act.[1949] A landlord's unreasonable entry onto a tenant's premises may be a UDAP violation.[1950]

5.5.2.11 Landlord Seizure of the Tenant's Possessions

A moving and storage company engaged in UDAP violations where it negligently held a tenant's property after a sheriff contracted with the moving and storage company to move the contents of the tenant's apartment.[1951] Among its deceptive practices were selling the collateral before the time specified in a notice to the tenant and allowing items to be broken and stolen.[1952] Similarly a landlord commits a UDAP violation by selling a tenant's property without a valid lien.[1953]

5.5.3 Home Finders

Fraudulent home finders promise, for a fee, to find housing for low-income people to purchase or rent. In areas where housing is scarce or substandard, or where segregated housing patterns lock people out of large portions of the housing market, home finders have considerable appeal. False and exaggerated claims by home finders are appropriate subjects for UDAP claims.[1954]

Law Pleadings, No. 2, § 1.3 (CD-Rom and Index Guide), also found on the CD-Rom accompanying this volume, for a sample UDAP complaint, along with motions for injunctive relief, a proposed TRO, and a trial brief concerning constructive eviction through a utility shut-off.

1942 Spinks v. Taylor & Richardson, 303 N.C. 256, 278 S.E.2d 501 (1981). *But see* Freeman v. Alamo Mgmt. Co., 24 Conn. App. 124, 586 A.2d 619 (1991) (self-help eviction of holdover tenant violates UDAP statute), *rev'd in part on other grounds*, 221 Conn. 674, 607 A.2d 370 (1992) (reinstating multiple damage award).

1943 Stanley v. Moore, 454 S.E.2d 225 (N.C. 1995).

1944 Love v. Amsler, Clearinghouse No. 44,805 (Minn. Dist. Ct. Hennepin Cty. July 15, 1988), *aff'd*, 441 N.W.2d 555 (Minn. Ct. App. 1989).

1945 Travieso v. Gutman, Mintz, Baker & Sonnenfeldt, P.C., 1995 U.S. Dist. LEXIS 17804 (E.D.N.Y. Nov. 16, 1995) (denying motion to dismiss FDCPA and UDAP claims challenging routine filing of groundless evictions as a means of collecting debts not owed); Cotton v. Stanley, 86 N.C. App. 534, 358 S.E.2d 692, *cert. denied*, 321 N.C. 296, 362 S.E.2d 779 (1987). *See also* Friday v. United Dominion Realty Trust, Inc., 155 N.C. App. 671, 575 S.E.2d 532 (N.C. Ct. App. 2003) (charging late fee in excess of amount allowed by state law and administrative fee in excess of that allowed by lease violates state debt collection law, which is part of UDAP statute).

1946 Massachusetts Consumer Protection Regulations, Mass. Regs. Code tit. 940, § 3.17(5)(a), (6)(a), Landlord-Tenant. *See* Commonwealth v. Chatham Development Co., 49 Mass. App. Ct. 525, 731 N.E.2d 89 (2000) (affirming injunction, civil penalties, and attorney fees for charging constable service fee in violation of regulation).

1947 Copley Mgmt. & Dev. Corp. v. Andersen, SC 08517, Clearinghouse No. 45,926 (Mass. Housing Ct., Boston, Nov. 2, 1990).

1948 Daniels v. Baritz, 2003 WL 21027238 (E.D. Pa. Apr. 30, 2003); Clarkson v. DeCaceres, 105 B.R. 266 (Bankr. E.D. Pa. 1989); Aponte v. Aungst, 82 B.R. 738 (Bankr. E.D. Pa. 1988) (application of former UDAP debt collection rule (now replaced by statute) to illegal eviction). *See also* Freeman v. Alamo Mgmt. Co., 24 Conn. App. 124, 586 A.2d 619 (1991) (self-help eviction of holdover tenant violates UDAP statute).

1949 *See, e.g.*, Travieso v. Gutman, Mintz, Baker & Sonnenfeldt, P.C., 1995 U.S. Dist. LEXIS 17804 (E.D.N.Y. Nov. 16, 1995). *See* National Consumer Law Center, Fair Debt Collection (5th ed. 2004) for a full analysis of the application of the FDCPA to landlord-tenant matters.

1950 Love v. Presley, 34 N.C. App. 503, 239 S.E.2d 574 (1977); Massachusetts Consumer Protection Regulations, Mass. Regs. Code tit. 940, § 3.17(6), Landlord-Tenant.

1951 Nelson v. Schanzer, 788 S.W.2d 81 (Tex. App. 1990).

1952 *Id.*

1953 Clarkson v. DeCaceres, 105 B.R. 266 (Bankr. E.D. Pa. 1989). *See also* Freeman v. Alamo Mgmt. Co., 24 Conn. App. 124, 586 A.2d 619 (1991) (landlord violates UDAP by taking and disposing of tenant's property as part of self-help eviction).

1954 *See* National Consumer Law Center, Consumer Law Pleadings, No. 2, § 4.2 (CD-Rom and Index Guide) for an example of a complaint and class certification papers in a case involving

General UDAP principles regarding deception, nondisclosure, bait and switch tactics, and deposits may be helpful in dealing with home finders.[1955] If any aspect of the deal involves improving the consumer's credit record or obtaining extensions of credit for the consumer, advocates should investigate the possibility of claims under state and federal credit repair laws.[1956]

Some states have separate statutes regarding housing referral services, violation of which may trigger a variety of remedies, including UDAP remedies. For example, Ohio's real estate broker law covers people who collect rental information for purposes of referring prospective tenants to rental units for a fee.[1957] The statute requires that these housing referral services be licensed and that they offer consumers a refund if the consumer is unable to obtain suitable housing through the service. Florida[1958] and California[1959] have similar statutes.

A final fact to check is whether any of the principals are licensed real estate agents. If they are, there may be a state real estate recovery fund out of which the consumer's losses can be paid.[1960]

5.5.4 Migrant Farmworker Camps

Rodriguez v. Berrybrook Farms, Inc.[1961] used a state UDAP statute to bring a class action challenge to numerous practices by an employer of migrant farm workers. In Michigan, the UDAP statute applies to landlord-tenant practices. The court in *Berrybrook Farms* agreed with the migrant farm workers that owners of migrant camps are landlords and those who live in the camps are tenants, even where no money for rent actually changes hands. A portion of the migrant's compensation for work is free housing.

The UDAP statute applies to the provision of goods or services for personal, family, or household purposes. Migrant farmers' housing is within the scope of this definition even though the employer is only incidentally involved in providing housing, and is primarily engaged in agribusiness. The housing itself is used for personal, family, or household purposes. It is irrelevant that there is no written lease for UDAP purposes, because oral representations are actionable under a UDAP theory.

Consequently, the *Berrybrook Farms* court allowed a class of migrant workers to go to trial to prove their UDAP claims concerning oral misrepresentations as to the condition of living quarters. (The court did dismiss certain UDAP claims pertaining to sections of the Michigan UDAP statute not applying to landlord-tenant transactions.)

The migrant workers in *Berrybrook Farms* alleged that they were housed in rural shacks which were declared uninhabitable and which were refused occupancy permits by the Michigan Department of Health. Rent payments were also subtracted from paychecks, while at the time of recruitment the workers thought the housing was free. In addition, the farm employer was not licensed by the U.S. Department of Labor to house migrant workers.

The migrants' federal claims in *Berrybrook Farms* were brought pursuant to the Migrant and Seasonal Agricultural Worker Protection Act.[1962] But the migrant workers added a UDAP cause of action as a pendent state claim to their federal court action. There are several reasons for migrant workers to add UDAP claims to their Federal Agricultural Worker Protection Act claims:

- UDAP statutes usually authorize attorney fees, while the federal act does not;
- UDAP statutes often authorize multiple or punitive damages, while the federal act only authorizes actual damages;
- The federal statute authorizes statutory damages up to $500 per plaintiff per violation; a state UDAP statute will not offer better statutory damages, but it is possible to argue for recovery of statutory damages under the federal act and treble damages under the UDAP statute;
- The UDAP statute violation may be easier to prove in certain circumstances;
- If the precedent is established that migrant workers' relations with their employer are in the nature of a landlord and a tenant for purposes of a UDAP statute, this may lead to courts recognizing that state landlord-tenant legislation also applies to migrants. Such a recognition would lead to the creation of numerous substantive rights for migrant tenants.

5.5.5 Real Estate Sales

5.5.5.1 Inapplicability of Seller Defenses

In general, material misrepresentations in a home sale are actionable under a UDAP statute.[1963] An "as-is" clause is

fraud by a home finder, also found on the CD-Rom accompanying this volume.

1955 *See* §§ 4.2, 4.2.14, 4.6.1, 4.9.1, *supra.*

1956 *See* National Consumer Law Center, Fair Credit Reporting Ch. 15 (5th ed. 2002 and Supp.).

1957 Ohio Rev. Code Ann. § 4735.01 *et seq.*

1958 Fla. Stat. Ann. § 475.453(1).

1959 Cal. Bus. & Prof. Code § 10167.9.

1960 *See, e.g.,* Fla. Stat. Ann. § 475.483; Ohio Rev. Code §§ 4735.12, 4735.01(9) (specifically authorizes recovery from real estate recovery fund for losses caused by housing referral services); 63 Pa. Stat. § 455.801 *et seq.* (general real estate recovery fund statute).

1961 672 F. Supp. 1009 (W.D. Mich. 1987).

1962 29 U.S.C. § 1801 *et seq.*

1963 Banks v. Consumer Home Mortg., Inc., 2003 WL 21251584 (E.D.N.Y. Mar. 28, 2003) (allegations that home sellers misrepresented home's fair market value, that repairs would be made, that only cosmetic repairs were necessary, and that buyers could rely on sellers and sellers' colleagues, sufficient to withstand motion to dismiss); Sherrod v. Holzshuh, 274 Or. 327, 546 P.2d

no defense to such practices by the broker.[1964] Even a negligent misrepresentation may be a UDAP violation.[1965]

Buyers who have been induced by misrepresentations to enter into a contract to buy a home may maintain a UDAP action even if, after learning the truth, they proceed with the closing. The buyers would no longer have the option of rescinding the contract, but can sue for damages for fraud or UDAP violations.[1966] Nor is it a defense to a UDAP misrepresentation and nondisclosure claim that the buyers would have learned of the home's true condition if they had the home competently inspected.[1967]

5.5.5.2 Deception Concerning the Nature of the Home

Real estate brokers and sellers must disclose material defects in houses offered for sale. Courts have held that the state's UDAP statute requires disclosure of the following conditions:

- Drainage or water problems;[1968]
- A bad foundation;[1969]
- The existence of a nearby detraction, such as a closed toxic landfill, that affects the safety and value of a home;[1970]
- That the former occupant of the home had committed sex crimes there;[1971]
- That the mortgage is in default;[1972]
- The risk of high winds;[1973]
- That the property is scheduled to be demolished by the city;[1974]
- Defects or problems with a building lot.[1975]

Some states have real estate disclosure laws that require the seller to give the buyer a form that states whether certain defects exist. False statements on such a form are UDAP violations.[1976]

UDAP violations include misrepresentations concerning a home's square footage,[1977] the existence of insect infestation,[1978] the condition of the heating system,[1979] the state of the septic system,[1980] the location of the property line,[1981] that the adjoining lot will be conservation land,[1982] or other

470 (1976); Allen v. American Land Research, 95 Wash. 2d 841, 631 P.2d 930 (1981) ("investment counselors" fail to disclose material facts concerning realty). *But see* Sohaey v. Van Cura, 607 N.E.2d 253 (Ill. App. Ct. 1992) (mere statements of opinion by broker with respect to future events not a UDAP violation), *aff'd on other grounds, remanded*, 158 Ill. 2d 375, 634 N.E.2d 707, 199 Ill. Dec. 654 (1994); Koagel v. Ryan Homes, Inc., 167 A.D.2d 822, 562 N.Y.S.2d 312 (1990) (real estate agent's inaccurate projection of future real estate taxes not actionable under UDAP statute).

1964 Sherrod v. Holzshuh, 274 Or. 327, 546 P.2d 470 (1976).

1965 Reed v. Wally Conard Constr., Inc., 1999 Tenn. App. LEXIS 681 (Oct. 13, 1999) (builder's negligent misrepresentation regarding placement of house on lot violated UDAP statute).

1966 Sonnenberg v. Security Mgmt., 325 Md. 117, 599 A.2d 820 (1992). *Accord* Gennari v. Weichert Co. Realtors, 288 N.J. Super. 504, 672 A.2d 1190 (App. 1996) (buyers could have rescinded contracts only to their severe detriment), *aff'd, modified*, 148 N.J. 582, 691 A.2d 350 (1997).

1967 Smith v. Levine, 911 S.W.2d 427 (Tex. App. 1995).

1968 Young v. Joyce, 351 A.2d 857 (Del. 1975); Riley v. Fair & Co. Realtors, 150 Ill. App. 3d 597, 502 N.E.2d 45 (1986); Heller v. Silverbranch Constr. Corp., 376 Mass. 621, 382 N.E.2d 1065 (1978); Marshall v. Beaulieu, 61 Mass. App. Ct. 1102, 807 N.E.2d 252 (Mass. App. Ct. 2002) (unpublished, text available at 2004 WL 936591) (failure to mention occasional seepage problem was a UDAP violation, but not serious enough to warrant doubling or tripling damages); Stone v. Homes, Inc., 37 N.C. App. 97, 245 S.E.2d 801 (1978); McRae v. Bolstad, 101 Wash. 2d 161, 676 P.2d 496 (1984) (failure to disclose sewage problems); Edmonds v. John L. Scott Real Estate, Inc., 942 P.2d 1072 (Wash. Ct. App. 1997) (failure to disclose basement water problem); Luxon v. Caviezel, 42 Wash. App. 261, 710 P.2d 809 (1985). *See also* Cameron v. Martin Marietta Corp., 729 F. Supp. 1529 (E.D.N.C. 1990) (failure to disclose contamination could be UDAP violation); Svendsen v. Stock, 23 P.3d 455 (Wash. 2001).

1969 Smith v. Levine, 911 S.W.2d 427 (Tex. App. 1995).

1970 Tanpiengco v. Tasto, 72 Conn. App. 817, 806 A.2d 1080 (2002) (affirming award of $20,000 punitive damages); Strawn v. Canuso, 140 N.J. 43, 657 A.2d 420 (1995); *cf.* Nobrega v. Edison Glen Assocs., 772 A.2d 368 (N.J. 2001) (non-disclosure of nearby contaminated sites). *But cf.* Levine v. Kramer Group, 354 N.J. Super. 397, 807 A.2d 264 (App. Div. 2002) (UDAP statute does not require disclosure of transient social conditions, here an unbalanced neighbor, that might affect value of property).

1971 Sanchez v. Guerrero, 885 S.W.2d 487 (Tex. App. 1994).

1972 Nash v. Hoopes, 332 A.2d 411 (Del. Super. Ct. 1975).

1973 Carter v. Gugliuzzi, 716 A.2d 17 (Vt. 1998).

1974 Ojeda de Toca v. Wise, 748 S.W.2d 449 (Tex. 1988).

1975 Guest v. Phillips Petroleum Co., 981 F.2d 218 (5th Cir. 1993) (Texas law) (uncapped abandoned oil well on building lot); Sherrard v. Dickson, 1997 Tenn. App. LEXIS 638 (Sept. 23, 1997) (extent and construction implications of brush on the property).

1976 Edmonds v. John L. Scott Real Estate, Inc., 942 P.2d 1072 (Wash. App. 1997).

1977 Cameron v. Terrell & Garrett Inc., 618 S.W.2d 535 (Tex. 1981); George D. Thomas Builder, Inc. v. Timmons, 658 S.W.2d 194 (Tex. App. 1983).

1978 Byrne v. Weichert Realtors, 290 N.J. Super. 126, 675 A.2d 235 (1996) (misrepresentation of extent of termite damage); Robertson v. Boyd, 88 N.C. App. 437, 363 S.E.2d 672 (1988) (failed to disclose termite damage and actively engaged in attempt to prevent consumers from learning of damage); Raudebaugh v. Action Pest Control, Inc., 59 Or. App. 166, 650 P.2d 1006 (1982).

1979 Glickman v. Brown, 21 Mass. App. Ct. 229, 486 N.E.2d 737 (1985).

1980 Snierson v. Scruton, 145 N.H. 73, 761 A.2d 1046 (2000).

1981 Reed v. Wally Conard Constr., Inc., 1999 Tenn. App. LEXIS 681 (Oct. 13, 1999) (placement of house on lot); Stringer v. Perales, 2003 WL 1848594 (Tex. App. Apr. 10, 2003) (unpublished, citation limited).

1982 Brandt v. Olympic Constr., Inc., 16 Mass. App. Ct. 913, 449 N.E.2d 1231 (1983).

features of the home.[1983] A seller commits a UDAP violation by promoting overpriced, poorly rehabilitated homes, promising but failing to make repairs, steering buyers to affiliated mortgage bankers and attorneys who will not caution or protect them, threatening to withhold the deposit of buyers who complain, and falsely portraying FHA involvement.[1984] Falsely representing that repairs will be made is a UDAP violation.[1985] Brokers can not misrepresent the nature of the builder or the quality of a home.[1986]

House inspectors have been found liable for UDAP damages for faulty reports on a house's foundation[1987] and the existence of a water intrusion problem in a house's basement.[1988] A particularly interesting case exposed a home inspection company's conflict of interest, which led it to soft-pedal defects in order to avoid killing the sale of the home and antagonizing the realtors on whom it relied for referrals.[1989]

Brokers can be liable for misrepresentation concerning zoning and the number of structures that can be built on a lot.[1990] But a seller's failure to disclose that its statement of the size of a lot included land over which public roads ran was not a UDAP violation where the statement was explicitly an estimate and the buyer took the land "as is."[1991] Nor is it a UDAP violation to sell a home "as is."[1992]

5.5.5.3 UDAP Violations Concerning Title, Financing, and the Homeowner's Legal Rights

It is deceptive for a broker to misrepresent the interest rate of an assumable mortgage,[1993] or to fail to disclose that low-cost financing is subject to conditions and restrictions that will make it difficult for the home buyer to qualify.[1994] A complaint stated a UDAP claim against sellers, a mortgage lender, attorneys, and an appraiser who were all involved in a scheme to sell substandard homes at inflated prices.[1995] It is deceptive for a seller to lead a buyer into believing that an extension of the closing date had been agreed to, and then to refuse to go through with the deal because the original closing date had passed.[1996]

It can also be deceptive for a seller to state that it will arrange a title search and title insurance and fail to do so, leading to damage to the purchaser where the title is not clear.[1997] It can be deceptive for a broker to misrepresent to a home buyer that it is the seller's responsibility to repair any substantial defects in the property,[1998] or to misrepresent that a purchase agreement gives the buyer rights to the property the agreement can not give.[1999] Representations that defects will be repaired must be honored.[2000] It is deceptive for a title insurance company to fail to disclose liens on property to be purchased.[2001] Giving the buyer a warranty deed stating that the buyer is acquiring title free and clear of liens,

---

1983 Ricco v. Riva, 669 N.W.2d 193 (Wis. App. 2003) (misrepresentation that there were living quarters in an outbuilding).

1984 Banks v. Consumer Home Mortg., Inc., 2003 WL 21251584 (E.D.N.Y. Mar. 28, 2003); Vaughn v. Consumer Home Mortg., Inc., 2003 WL 21241669 (E.D.N.Y. Mar. 23, 2003); Polonetsky v. Better Homes Depot, 97 N.Y.2d 46, 760 N.E.2d 1274, 735 N.Y.S.2d 479 (2001) (interpretation of city UDAP ordinance).

1985 Vaughn v. Consumer Home Mortg., Inc., 2003 WL 21241669 (E.D.N.Y. Mar. 23, 2003) (denial of motion to dismiss).

1986 Gennari v. Weichert Co. Realtors, 148 N.J. 582, 691 A.2d 350 (1997).

1987 Guilbeau v. Anderson, 841 S.W.2d 517 (Tex. App. 1992).

1988 Ricciardi v. Frank, 620 N.Y.S.2d 918 (City Court 1994), *aff'd as modified*, 170 Misc. 2d 777, 655 N.Y.S.2d 242 (App. Term 1996); Lee v. C.D.E. Home Inspection Co., 2002 WL 1938248 (Ohio App. Aug. 22, 2002) (report that no significant defects were found in crawlspace not deceptive where it disclosed that inspector had only made inspection from entrance). *See also* Banks v. Consumer Home Mortg., Inc., 2003 WL 21251584 (E.D.N.Y. Mar. 28, 2003) (allegations that home inspector made misleading statements about condition of property and falsely certified that work was completed state UDAP claim).

1989 Herner v. HouseMaster of Am., Inc., 349 N.J. Super. 89, 793 A.2d 55 (App. Div. 2002).

1990 Price v. Long Realty, Inc., 199 Mich. App. 461, 502 N.W.2d 337 (1993).

1991 Karlsson v. Federal Deposit Ins. Corp., 942 F. Supp. 1022 (E.D. Pa. 1996), *aff'd without op.*, 107 F.3d 862 (3d Cir. 1997). *See also* Lopata v. Miller, 122 Md. App. 76, 712 A.2d 24 (Spec. App. 1998) (realtor's innocent misrepresentation of lot size not tortious); Prudential Ins. Co. v. Jefferson, 896 S.W.2d 156 (Tex. 1995) (no duty to disclose possibility of asbestos where buyer and seller had equal knowledge and buyer bought building as is). *But cf.* Capiccioni v. Brennan Naperville, Inc., 339 Ill. App. 3d 927, 791 N.E.2d 553 (2003) (real estate agent generally not liable for misstatements of law, but may be liable for misstatement about which school district home was in, where buyers had no reliable way to check this information); Discover Realty Corp. v. David, 49 Mass. App. Ct. 535, 731 N.E.2d 79 (2000) (broker has claim against seller for misrepresenting status of "paper street" running through back yard).

1992 Dixon v. ERA Twin County Realty, Inc., 2002 WL 31630854 (Wash. App. Nov. 22, 2002) (unpublished, citation limited).

1993 Beard v. Gress, 90 Ill. App. 3d 622, 413 N.E.2d 448 (1980); Wagner v. Morris, 658 S.W.2d 230 (Tex. App. 1983).

1994 Stephenson v. Capano Dev., Inc., 462 A.2d 1069 (Del. 1983); Danny Darby Real Estate, Inc. v. Jacobs, 760 S.W.2d 711 (Tex. App. 1988).

1995 Vaughn v. Consumer Home Mortg., Inc., 2003 WL 21241669 (E.D.N.Y. Mar. 23, 2003); Banks v. Consumer Home Mortg., Inc., 2003 WL 21251584 (E.D.N.Y. Mar. 28, 2003) (companion case with similar facts). *See* § 5.5.5.6, *infra*.

1996 Rex Lumber Co. v. Acton Block Co., 29 Mass. App. Ct. 510, 562 N.E.2d 845 (1990).

1997 *See* Menuskin v. Williams, 145 F.3d 755 (6th Cir. 1998) (Tennessee law).

1998 Buzzard v. Bolger, 117 Ill. App. 3d 887, 453 N.E.2d 1132 (1983).

1999 Citizens State Bank of Dickinson v. Bowles, 663 S.W.2d 845 (Tex. App. 1983).

2000 Vaughn v. Consumer Home Mortg., Inc., 2003 WL 21241669 (E.D.N.Y. Mar. 23, 2003) (denial of motion to dismiss); MacDonald v. Mobley, 555 S.W.2d 916 (Tex. Civ. App. 1977).

2001 Gibbs v. Main Bank of Houston, 666 S.W.2d 554 (Tex. App 1984); *see also* Milbrant v. Huber, 149 Wis. 2d 275, 440 N.W.2d 807 (Ct. App. 1989).

while knowing that liens exist, is deceptive.[2002] It is a UDAP violation to mislead a consumer and delay his seeking legal redress concerning the property's defective title.[2003] It may be a UDAP violation to alter a land sales agreement and record it, provided that the other criteria for a UDAP violation are met.[2004]

A real estate appraiser who makes a good faith error in giving an opinion about the value of a home may not be liable, but a knowing misrepresentation may be actionable.[2005] An appraiser for a bank who performs a negligent pre-sale inspection of a home may be liable to the buyers if their reliance and injury are reasonably foreseeable.[2006]

5.5.5.4 Property Flipping

In property flipping schemes, a speculator buys dilapidated residential properties at low prices and resells them to unsophisticated first-time home buyers at huge markups. Often the speculator makes cosmetic repairs to the property, or promises the buyer that repairs will be made after closing. Typically the speculator works with loan officers, closing agents, attorneys, building inspectors, and appraisers[2007] who aid in securing financing and keeping the buyer in the dark. Adding these players as parties to a lawsuit is often important, because the scam artist may be long gone or without assets by the time the consumer becomes aware of the fraud.

A Maryland decision, now on appeal to the state supreme court, holds both an appraiser and a loan officer liable to the home buyers in such a scheme.[2008] The loan officer had met with the speculator at the beginning of the scheme, advised him about how to secure FHA loans for the home buyers, and gave him paperwork to use to falsify the source of down payments and closing costs. The loan officer then worked with the speculator to generate inflated sales prices. At closings, the loan officer's conduct helped confirm the buyers' impression that the speculator was working for them. The appraiser's role was to issue inflated appraisals, sometimes basing them on information provided by the speculator. Some of the appraisals were worded in a way that concealed that they were based on non-comparable properties or out-of-date sales prices.

These acts established that the loan officer and appraiser were liable for fraud and UDAP violations, and that they had participated in a civil conspiracy to defraud the buyers. The court was not troubled by the fact that the appraisals were not communicated directly to the home buyers. The appraiser's misrepresentations about the values of the properties were communicated to the buyers indirectly by the mere availability of financing to complete the transaction, and the scheme would have fallen through without the appraisals. Nor did it matter that the home buyers had not entered into a transaction with the appraiser. The appraiser's deception so infected the transaction that it would be deemed to have been committed in the sale. The court not only upheld substantial compensatory damage awards, but also reversed the trial court's refusal to allow the jury to consider punitive damages against the loan officer and the appraiser.

Another court, in a property flipping suit brought by the state attorney general, held that an appraiser could be subject to the UDAP statute's prohibition against causing a likelihood of confusion or misunderstanding regarding the source, sponsorship or certification of goods or services.[2009] The court held that the appraisals, which were based on incomplete and inaccurate information provided by the speculators and without visits to the homes, could amount to a certification that the homes were actually worth the selling price.

In another case, New York's highest court held that a complaint stated a claim by alleging that the speculator misrepresented that the contractors and closing attorneys to whom the buyers were steered were FHA-approved.[2010] This violated a UDAP prohibition against representing that goods or services have sponsorship or approval that they do not have. Similar prohibitions are found in many states' UDAP statutes. The court also held that the principal's participation in the scheme, and his false promises that repairs would be made, were sufficient to state a UDAP claim against him in his personal capacity.[2011]

Two other New York cases hold a host of parties potentially liable on UDAP, fraud, and conspiracy counts in a property flipping scheme. In one case,[2012] the company and

---

2002 Gemignani v. Pete, 71 P.3d 87 (Or. App. 2003).

2003 Egudin v. Carriage Court Condominium, 528 So. 2d 1043 (La. Ct. App. 1988).

2004 Francoline v. Klatt, 26 Conn. App. 203, 600 A.2d 8 (1991).

2005 Advanced Fin. Servs., Inc. v. Associated Appraisal Servs., Inc., 79 Conn. App. 22, 830 A.2d 240 (Conn. App. Ct. 2003) (finding appraiser and independent contractor liable to lender on UDAP claim where they made false and misleading appraisal and certification that work was completed, and failed disclose that property had been vandalized); Sampen v. Dabrowski, 584 N.E.2d 493 (Ill. App. Ct. 1991). *See also* Macoviak v. Chase Home Mortgage Corp., 40 Mass. App. Ct. 755, 667 N.E.2d 900 (1996) (negligent over-appraisal not actionable).

2006 Tackling v. Shinerman, 42 Conn. Supp. 517, 630 A.2d 1381 (1993).

2007 *See also* § 5.5.5.6, *infra* (special issues concerning liability of appraisers).

2008 Hoffman v. Stamper, 843 A.2d 153 (Md. Spec. App. 2004), *review granted*, 851 A.2d 593 (Md. 2004).

2009 Commonwealth v. Percudani, 844 A.2d 35 (Pa. Commw. Ct. 2004) (but rejecting argument that appraisal violated another section of UDAP statute, limiting it to advertisements).

2010 Polonetsky v. Better Homes Depot, Inc., 97 N.Y.2d 46, 735 N.Y.S.2d 479, 760 N.E.2d 1274 (2001).

2011 *But cf.* Honorable v. Easy Life Real Estate Sys., Inc., 182 F.R.D. 553 (N.D. Ill. 1998) (descriptions of properties as "newly rehabbed" too general to support UDAP claim; promises of repairs made after sale not UDAP violation because did not induce the sale).

2012 Banks v. Consumer Home Mortg., Inc., 2003 WL 21252584, at *5 (E.D.N.Y. Mar. 28, 2003).

individuals that dealt directly with the consumers in reselling the property were potentially liable for fraud and UDAP violations because of, *inter alia*, their false statements about the property's value and their steering of the consumers toward other members of the conspiracy. The principals of the company that originally bought the properties were also potentially liable because of their knowledge of and involvement in the fraud, even though they did not personally interact with the consumers. The court also denied motions to dismiss by a variety of individuals whose acts enabled the fraud to succeed: the attorneys who handled the closing for the lender and the seller but did not reveal problems and discrepancies; an individual who attended the closing in place of one of the principals as a means of concealing the principal's relationship with another conspirator; the principal and agent for the lender that financed the sale; and the inspector who did not reveal the property's defects. The second case makes a similar analysis as to a similar array of participants.[2013]

Civil conspiracy claims are especially worth investigating in property flipping cases as ways of reaching people who enabled the scheme to succeed but did not deal directly with the buyer.[2014] Discrimination claims may also be appropriate if the speculator targets a minority group or other protected class.[2015] Claims under the federal Credit Repair Organizations Act,[2016] a state credit repair law,[2017] or a federal or state RICO statute[2018] are also possible and may offer enhanced remedies and procedural advantages. A court dismissed a RICO claim based on the speculator's submission of false information to banks, however, on the theory that the buyers were not the victims of that crime.[2019]

The consumer's attorney should also examine the lender's compliance with recent FHA property flipping guidelines, effective for applications for FHA-insured loans signed on or after June 2, 2003:[2020]

- The seller must be the owner of record, and the lender must submit to HUD documentation showing this to be the case. A speculator can not sell or assign to the consumer the sales contract by which the seller had purchased the property.
- A sales contract can not be executed with a consumer within 90 days of the settlement date by which the seller acquired the property. The lender must submit appropriate documentation to show this requirement has been met.
- For sales contracts signed between 91 and 180 days after the seller's settlement date, where the re-sale price is 100% over the purchase price, the lender must have a second appraisal.[2021]

Making FHA-insured loans in violation of these guidelines should be a *per se* UDAP violation and evidence of a conspiracy to defraud the consumer. Phony documentation or other attempts by the lender to evade these requirements should also be a UDAP violation.

5.5.5.5 Special Issues Concerning Real Estate Agents and Brokers

Since scienter and intent are generally not elements of a UDAP claim,[2022] a real estate broker may even be liable for unintentional misrepresentations.[2023] A few UDAP statutes protect real estate agents by subjecting them to UDAP actions only if they know that their claims are false or misleading.[2024]

Brokers must disclose any financial interest they have in a sale.[2025] Misrepresentation about the source and method of

2013 Vaughn v. Consumer Home Mortg., Inc., 2003 WL 21241669, at *6 (E.D.N.Y. Mar. 23, 2003).

2014 *See* § 6.5.2.3, *infra.*

2015 *See* Honorable v. Easy Life Real Estate Sys., Inc., 100 F. Supp. 2d 885 (N.D. Ill. 2000) (denying defendants' motion for summary judgment on § 1981 and Fair Housing Act claims). *See* National Consumer Law Center, Credit Discrimination (3d ed. 2002 and Supp.).

2016 *See* § 5.1.2.2.2, *supra.*

2017 *See* § 5.1.2.2.3, *supra.*

2018 *See* § 9.2, 9.3, *infra.*

2019 Honorable v. Easy Life Real Estate Sys., Inc., 182 F.R.D. 553 (N.D. Ill. 1998). *See* § 9.2.3.6.2, *infra* (standing issues in RICO claims).

2020 HUD Mortgagee Letter 2003-07 (May 22, 2003), *available at* www.hud.gov.

2021 24 C.F.R. § 203.37a.

2022 *See* §§ 4.2.4, 4.2.5, *supra. But cf.* Siudyla v. Chemexec Relocation Sys., Inc., 23 Conn. App. 180, 579 A.2d 578 (1990) (relocation company did not commit a UDAP violation by failing to disclose problems with a well, where the company made it clear to the buyers that it was not in a position to make any representations about the property).

2023 Ji v. Palmer, 333 N.J. Super. 451, 755 A.2d 1221 (App. Div. 2000) (broker's statement that document provided at closing looked acceptable could be UDAP violation); Gennari v. Weichert Co. Realtors, 288 N.J. Super. 504, 672 A.2d 1190 (App. 1996), *aff'd, modified*, 148 N.J. 582, 691 A.2d 350 (1997).

2024 815 Ill. Comp. Stat. § 505/10b(4); Wis. Stat. § 100.18(12)(b); Capiccioni v. Brennan Naperville, Inc., 339 Ill. App. 3d 927, 791 N.E.2d 553 (2003) (defense is unavailable to realtor unless source of the misinformation was the owner of the home); Sohaey v. Van Cura, 607 N.E.2d 253 (Ill. App. Ct. 1992) (broker must know of falsity or have been able to discover it by the exercise of ordinary care), *aff'd on other issues, remanded*, 158 Ill. 2d 375, 634 N.E.2d 707, 199 Ill. Dec. 654 (1994). *See also* Kleczek v. Jorgensen, 328 Ill. App. 3d 1012, 767 N.E.2d 913, 263 Ill. Dec. 187 (2002) (exemption does not apply to builder who does not have real estate license); Harkala v. Wildwood Realty, Inc., 200 Ill. App. 3d 447, 558 N.E.2d 195 (1990); Connor v. Merrill Lynch Realty, Inc., 581 N.E.2d 196 (Ill. App. Ct. 1991); Julian v. Spiegel, 135 Ill. App. 3d 458, 481 N.E.2d 903 (1985); *Cf.* Ricco v. Riva, 669 N.W.2d 193 (Wis. App. 2003) (sellers can be liable for misrepresentations even though they were made through a real estate agent who is not liable).

2025 Seligman v. First Nat'l Investments, Inc., 184 Ill. App. 3d 1053, 540 N.E.2d 1057 (1989) (broker was trying to buy the same

calculating the sales commission is a UDAP violation.[2026] But mere nondisclosure that the broker was operating on the standard commission is not deceptive.[2027] While providing a disclosure form required by statute can not be a UDAP violation, a real estate agent's failure to perform the duties disclosed on the form may be.[2028]

A real estate agency committed a UDAP violation when it made a unilateral decision that the buyer's earnest money would be forfeited, without conducting any investigation about whether the seller had breached the agreement by failing to make repairs.[2029] But a court has found that a disappointed bidder could not recover from a broker who showed the bid to a competing buyer, who used it to craft a better offer, since the broker's duty was to the seller.[2030]

It is unfair for a real estate agent who is also a local public official to misuse his public authority to effectuate a sale to the consumer's detriment.[2031] An escrow agent's engaging in the unauthorized practice of law in handling real estate closing documents is a deceptive practice.[2032]

Sellers as well as buyers of real estate can be victimized by broker fraud. The FTC has brought suit against a company that masterminded a scheme in which telemarketers falsely claimed that they had been contacted by buyers interested in purchasing the owner's land, and that the owner, for a fee, could sell the home that day.[2033] The FTC also has obtained a consent order from the operator of Better Homes and Gardens Real Estate Service whereby the realty service will not misrepresent the extent to which all its franchisees offer certain services or the extent of the training, knowledge or success of its realtors.[2034]

Brokers can not misrepresent that the broker's homes are sold within several days when that is not the case.[2035] Because of the special relationship between a seller and the real estate broker representing the seller, it is deceptive for the broker to purchase the property it is brokering without fully disclosing all material facts to the seller, including all other purchase offers.[2036]

UDAP claims against real estate agents and brokers must be distinguished from claims of professional negligence. The latter claim can be asserted only where the agent or broker represented the aggrieved party, and expert testimony may be required to establish the standard of care. A UDAP claim for misrepresentation can, however, be asserted regardless of the relationship between the parties. Expert testimony is unnecessary to establish that a representation is false.[2037]

Advocates dealing with home sale fraud should investigate whether their state has a real estate recovery fund to compensate victims of fraud by realtors.[2038] Such a fund may enable consumers to recover against a defendant who would otherwise be judgment-proof.

5.5.5.6 Special Issues Concerning Appraisers

An inflated appraisal is the linchpin of a property flipping scheme.[2039] It is also a key part of many predatory loan schemes. Loan brokers secure inflated appraisals to persuade lenders to extend loans larger than the borrower's income and assets justify.[2040] In either case, the appraisal is essential to the scam artist's ultimate goal of bleeding away money from a loan secured by the victim's property.

Since the consumer usually has limited contact with the appraiser, the appraiser's involvement in the fraud may not be obvious. Nonetheless, the appraiser may be liable for fraud, civil conspiracy, UDAP violations, violation of state appraiser licensing laws, and even RICO violations. Investigating the facts surrounding the appraisal may also reveal how others—those who arranged for or used the appraisal—are tied into the fraud.

There can be little question that a falsified appraisal meets the standard of deception in a UDAP statute[2041] and is a

---

property); Wilkinson v. Smith, 31 Wash. App. 1, 639 P.2d 768 (1982).

2026 York v. InTrust Bank, N.A., 265 Kan. 271, 962 P.2d 405 (1998).

2027 Abernathy v. Squires Realty Co., 55 N.C. App. 354, 285 S.E.2d 325 (1982).

2028 Rathgeber v. Hemenway, Inc., 69 P.3d 710, 715 (Or. 2003) (ruling for defendant on other grounds).

2029 Edmonds v. John L. Scott Real Estate, Inc., 942 P.2d 1072 (Wash. Ct. App. 1997).

2030 Sing v. John L. Scott, Inc., 134 Wash. 2d 24, 948 P.2d 816 (1997).

2031 Piccuirro v. Gaitenby, 20 Mass. App. Ct. 286, 480 N.E.2d 30 (1985).

2032 Bowers v. Transamerican Title Ins. Co., 675 P.2d 193 (Wash. 1983).

2033 FTC v. Marketing Response Group, 5 Trade Reg. Rep. (CCH) ¶ 23,958 (M.D. Fla. 1996) (filing of complaint).

2034 Meredith Corp., 101 F.T.C. 390 (1983) (consent order).

2035 People v. Forest E. Olson, Inc., 137 Cal. App. 3d 137, 186 Cal. Rptr. 806 (1982).

2036 Kirkruff v. Wisegarver, 697 N.E.2d 406 (Ill. App. Ct. 1998); Starling v. Sproles, 311 S.E.2d 688 (N.C. Ct. App. 1984).

2037 Durbin v. Ross, 916 P.2d 758 (Mont. 1996).

2038 *See, e.g.*, 63 Pa. Stat. § 455.801 to .803.

2039 Vaughn v. Consumer Home Mortg., Inc., 2003 WL 21241669, at *6 (E.D.N.Y. Mar. 23, 2003) (inflated appraisal "supported the allegedly inflated price plaintiffs paid for the property, and made possible the acquisition of FHA mortgage insurance, without which the defendants could not have hoped to profit from their alleged scheme"). *See* § 5.5.5.4, *supra*.

2040 *See, e.g.*, Hill v. Meritech Mortg. Servs., Inc. (*In re* Hill), No. 01-30171SR, Adv. No. 01-848 (Bankr. E.D. Pa. Sept. 27, 2002).

2041 Vaughn v. Consumer Home Mortg., Inc., 2003 WL 21241669, at *6 (E.D.N.Y. Mar. 23, 2003); Banks v. Consumer Home Mortg., Inc., 2003 WL 21252584, at *5 (E.D.N.Y. Mar. 28, 2003); Tackling v. Shinerman, 630 A.2d 1381 (Conn. Super. 1993) (rejecting appraiser's motion for summary judgment on claim that failure to detect lead paint was UDAP violation); Commonwealth v. Percudani, 844 A.2d 35 (Pa. Commw. Ct. 2004). *See also* Advanced Fin. Servs., Inc. v. Associated Appraisal Servs., Inc., 830 A.2d 240 (Conn. App. 2003) (affirming

misrepresentation that will support a fraud claim.[2042] UDAP claims are particularly flexible since in most states the consumer does not have to show reliance,[2043] privity of contract is unnecessary,[2044] and non-disclosure is just as actionable as affirmative deception.[2045] As to fraud, the general rule is that a party whose misrepresentation reaches third parties indirectly is liable as long as there was reason to expect that the third parties would learn of and rely on it.[2046]

Submission of a falsified appraisal to a financial institution may also constitute bank fraud,[2047] a predicate act under the federal RICO statute. Consumers bringing a RICO suit on this basis may, however, have to convince the court that they, in addition to the bank, are victims of this fraud.[2048]

Common law fraud requires proof that the consumers relied to their detriment on the misrepresentation, a showing that can be problematic if the consumer was not given the appraisal before consummation of the transaction. But an appraiser can be liable for aiding and abetting the other defendants' fraud even if the consumer never heard or relied on the appraiser's own misrepresentation.[2049] Most courts use similar principles to determine UDAP liability as well.[2050]

An appraiser can also be liable for the tort of civil conspiracy if its appraisal enabled others to defraud the consumer. The elements of a cause of action for civil conspiracy are generally an agreement by two or more persons to perform an overt act or acts in furtherance of the agreement to accomplish an unlawful purpose (or a lawful purpose by unlawful means), causing injury to another.[2051] Every participant in the conspiracy is liable for the acts of all the other participants.[2052] Thus, an appraiser whose falsified appraisal enabled the scam artist's fraud to succeed was liable for the entire fraud, and possibly for punitive damages, even though the consumers never read the appraisal.[2053]

Finally, even a consumer who never read the appraisal may have relied on it in some way. A Maryland court held that an appraiser's representation about the value of a home was communicated to the buyer, indirectly, by the mere availability of financing to complete the transaction.[2054] Another court held that, by giving the appraiser access to his home to perform the appraisal, the homeowner may have implicitly relied on him to perform the appraisal without deception.[2055]

A negligence claim against the appraiser should also be investigated, particularly since appraisers often carry insurance that applies to negligent acts. One issue will be whether an appraiser hired by the lender owed a duty of care to the buyer. A Connecticut court held that an appraiser would have a duty to the buyer if a reasonable person, knowing what the appraiser knew or should have known, would anticipate that

---

UDAP judgment for actual and punitive damages for lender that made loan in reliance on falsified appraisal). *But see* Sampen v. Dabrowski, 222 Ill. App. 3d 918, 584 N.E.2d 493 (1991) (no UDAP violation where erroneous appraisal of commercial property was clearly identified as opinion only); Sparks v. Re/MAX Allstar Realty, Inc., 55 S.W.3d 343 (Ky. App. 2000) (denying UDAP claim where consumers signed agreement that appraisal was solely for use of bank and they should not rely on it; case involved negligent rather than fraudulent appraisal). *But cf.* Nei v. Boston Survey Consultants, Inc., 388 Mass. 320, 446 N.E.2d 681 (1983) (appraiser hired by owner has no duty under UDAP statute to explain significance of accurate report to buyer).

2042 Vaughn v. Consumer Home Mortg., Inc., 2003 WL 21241669 (E.D.N.Y. Mar. 23, 2003); Banks v. Consumer Home Mortg., Inc., 2003 WL 21252584 (E.D.N.Y. Mar. 28, 2003); Hoffman v. Stamper, 843 A.2d 153, 190 (Md. Ct. Spec. App. 2004), *review granted*, 851 A.2d 593 (Md. 2004); Moore v. Mortgagestar, Inc., Civ. Action No. 2:01-0226, Clearinghouse No. 55606 (S.D. W. Va. Dec. 18, 2002). *But see* Sampen v. Dabrowski, 584 N.E.2d 493 (Ill. App. 1991) (home buyer could not base UDAP claim on appraisal that was clearly identified as an opinion, where no fraud or concealment was shown); Macoviak v. Chase Home Mortg. Corp., 667 N.E.2d 900 (Mass. App. 1996) (mere negligence in over-appraisal not UDAP violation).

2043 *See* § 4.2.12, *supra*. *But cf.* Commonwealth v. Percudani, 844 A.2d 35, 48 (Pa. Commw. Ct. 2004) (reliance unnecessary in AG suit, but stating in dictum that for private UDAP action home buyer must show reliance on falsified appraisal).

2044 *See* § 4.2.15.3, *supra*.

2045 *See* § 4.2.14, *supra*.

2046 Restatement (2d) of Torts § 533; National Consumer Law Center Automobile Fraud § 7.5.2 (2d ed. 2003 and Supp.).

2047 18 U.S.C. § 1344. The bank may or may not be an innocent victim. Sometimes a bank officer whose compensation depends on bringing business into a bank is complicit in falsification, or the bank may be relying on passing the loan on to the secondary market or recovering from mortgage insurance.

2048 *Compare* Matthews v. New Century Mortg. Corp., 185 F. Supp. 2d 874 (S.D. Ohio 2002) (denying motion to dismiss RICO claim where broker submitted false information to lender) *with* Honorable v. Easy Life Real Estate Sys., Inc., 182 F.R.D. 553 (N.D. Ill. 1998) (granting motion to dismiss RICO claim on ground that banks, not consumers, were victims of realtors' falsification).

2049 *See, e.g.*, Banks v. Consumer Home Mortg., Inc., 2003 WL 21252584, at *5 (E.D.N.Y. Mar. 28, 2003) (describing aiding and abetting standards); Restatement (2d) of Torts § 876(b).

2050 Banks v. Consumer Home Mortg., Inc., 2003 WL 21252584, at *5 (E.D.N.Y. Mar. 28, 2003). *See generally* § 6.5.2.2, *infra*.

2051 Adcock v. Brakegate, Ltd., 164 Ill. 2d 54, 645 N.E.2d 888 (1994). *See also* Banks v. Consumer Home Mortg., Inc., 2003 WL 21252584, at *5 (E.D.N.Y. Mar. 28, 2003) (home flipping case involving inflated appraisals); Moore v. Mortgagestar, Inc., Civ. Action No. 2:01-0226, Clearinghouse No. 55606 (S.D. W. Va. Dec. 18, 2002) (denying motion to dismiss conspiracy claim against appraiser in predatory lending scheme). *See generally* § 6.5.2.3, *infra*.

2052 Matthews v. New Century Mortg. Corp., 185 F. Supp. 2d 874, 889 (S.D. Ohio 2002) (predatory loan with falsified income statement).

2053 Hoffman v. Stamper, 843 A.2d 153, 184–87 (Md. Ct. Spec. App. 2004) (appraiser liable to home buyers on conspiracy count and for aiding and abetting fraud even though they never read the appraisal), *review granted*, 851 A.2d 593 (Md. 2004).

2054 *Id.*

2055 Hill v. Meritech Mortg. Servs., Inc. (*In re* Hill), No. 01-30171SR, Adv. No. 01-848 (Bankr. E.D. Pa. Sept. 27, 2002).

harm of the general nature the buyer suffered was likely to result from the appraiser's act or failure to act.[2056]

5.5.5.7 Special Issues Concerning Home Builders

5.5.5.7.1 Misrepresentations concerning the home or work to be performed

It is deceptive to misrepresent that homes are built in accordance with good construction practices, that they meet HUD minimum standards, that they are free of structural defects, that there are no drainage or water problems, that parks and public transportation will soon be built nearby, or that the homes are ready for immediate occupancy.[2057] Charging extra money for rooms included in the advertised description and selling "bedrooms" with inadequate insulation and waterproofing to serve as bedrooms are also deceptive practices.[2058]

State cases have found it deceptive to misrepresent the amount of water in the crawl space and the level of insulation of the garage;[2059] that a home would be built in a good and workmanlike manner; that the house would conform to specifications or to a model home;[2060] that electrical wire would be installed according to local codes; that extra charges were necessary to comply with local codes; or other aspects concerning building codes.[2061] Even without any misrepresentations, it is a UDAP violation to fail to comply with a building code.[2062]

It is of course deceptive to sell a lot that the seller does not own.[2063] It is also a UDAP violation for a home builder to make a practice of quoting unrealistically low estimates to construct homes and then involve consumers "in a painful morass of cost overruns and unexpectedly high cash outlays."[2064] A home builder disclosing a "small water problem" does not avoid UDAP liability where the builder fails to fix the problem as promised and the problem is significant.[2065]

The duty to disclose is strong. A seller's failure to disclose known severe plumbing problems was not excused because the buyers hired a home inspector, who did not discover the plumbing problems.[2066] It can be a UDAP violation to fail to fix disclosed defects, not disclose other defects, and understate the extent of existing problems when the consumer purchases a home.[2067]

It is deceptive for an individual to falsely represent that he had a contractor's license and would supervise the construction.[2068] Relocating an access roadway after the home is sold may be a UDAP violation where the buyers reasonably relied on the assumption that the roadway would not be moved.[2069]

5.5.5.7.2 Performance problems, warranties

A home builder commits an unfair and deceptive practice by taking a deposit, never starting the work, and refusing to return the deposit.[2070] A Maine builder violated the UDAP statute by failing to provide a written contract, as required by the state Home Construction Contracts Act.[2071] But a UDAP claim against a Maryland builder for violation of the contract requirements of a similar statute was denied be-

---

2056 *See* Tackling v. Shinerman, 630 A.2d 1381 (Conn. Super. 1993) (denying appraiser's motion for summary judgment on buyers' claim that appraiser was negligent in failing to detect lead pain).

2057 Kaufman & Broad, Inc., 93 F.T.C. 253 (1979) (consent order).

2058 *Id.*

2059 Hoke v. Beck, 587 N.E.2d 4 (Ill. App. Ct. 1992). *Accord* Brandon v. Winnett, 1995 Tenn. App. LEXIS 508, Clearinghouse No. 51,279 (Tenn. App. 1995) (negligent misrepresentation regarding cause of water in basement was UDAP violation).

2060 Siegel v. Levy Organization Dev. Co., 153 Ill. 2d 534, 607 N.E.2d 194 (1992) (condominium's terrace did not conform to model); Hartford Accident & Indemnity Co. v. Scarlett Harbor Assocs., 109 Md. App. 217, 674 A.2d 106 (1996) (misrepresentation that condominium would conform to specifications), *aff'd on other grounds*, 346 Md. 122, 695 A.2d 153 (1997); Forton v. Laszar, 239 Mich. App. 711, 609 N.W.2d 850 (2000) (deviation from blueprints, resulting in defects in home, was UDAP violation).

2061 Jim Walter Homes, Inc. v. Valencia, 679 S.W.2d 239 (Tex. App. 1984), *aff'd as modified*, 690 S.W.2d 239 (Tex. 1985); Jim Walter Homes Inc. v. Chapa, 614 S.W.2d 838 (Tex. Civ. App. 1981); Jim Walter Homes Inc. v. Castillo, 616 S.W.2d 630 (Tex. Civ. App. 1981); Jim Walter Homes Inc. v. Geffert, 614 S.W.2d 843 (Tex. Civ. App. 1981); Jim Walter Homes Inc. v. Mora, 622 S.W.2d 878 (Tex. Civ. App. 1981); Norwood Builders Inc. v. Toler, 609 S.W.2d 861 (Tex. Civ. App. 1981); Ridco Inc. v. Sexton, 623 S.W.2d 792 (Tex. Civ. App. 1981); Bynum v. Klentak, 1999 Wash. App. LEXIS 76 (Jan. 19, 1999) (builder violated UDAP statute by intentionally or negligently ignoring building code requirements and falsely stating that he did not know if the property contained any fill material); Keyes v. Bollinger, 27 Wash. App. 755, 621 P.2d 168 (1981).

2062 Becker v. Graber Builders, Inc., 149 N.C. App. 787, 561 S.E.2d 905 (2002).

2063 Dailey v. Sundance Ranches, Inc., 59 Or. App. 142, 650 P.2d 994 (1982).

2064 Quate v. Caudle, 381 S.E.2d 842 (N.C. Ct. App. 1989).

2065 *See* Hoke v. Beck, 587 N.E.2d 4 (Ill. App. Ct. 1992) (misrepresentation regarding amount of water in home's crawl space); Rucker v. Huffman, 99 N.C. App. 137, 392 S.E.2d 419 (1990). *Accord* Grove v. Huffman, 634 N.E.2d 1184 (Ill. App. Ct. 1994) (builder's misrepresentations that he would design or build house so that it would not have water problems violated UDAP statute).

2066 Blackstock v. Dudley, 12 S.W.3d 131 (Tex. App. 1999).

2067 Masure v. Donnelly, 962 F.2d 128 (1st Cir. 1992) (Maine law).

2068 Anden v. Litinsky, 472 So. 2d 825 (Fla. Dist. Ct. App. 1985).

2069 Conway v. American Excavating, Inc., 41 Conn. App. 437, 676 A.2d 881 (1996). *Cf.* Karlsson v. Federal Deposit Ins. Corp., 942 F. Supp. 1022 (E.D. Pa. 1996) (no UDAP violation where seller had not represented that estimate of lot size was precise).

2070 R.S. Assocs. General Building Contractors Inc. v. Devona, 610 S.W.2d 190 (Tex. Civ. App. 1980).

2071 VanVoorhees v. Dodge, 679 A.2d 1077 (Me. 1996); Dudley v. Wyler, 647 A.2d 90 (Me. 1994).

cause of the failure to show that the violation caused damage.[2072]

It is a UDAP violation for a home builder to fail to complete the work promised or to substitute inferior materials for those authorized.[2073] Failure to build a home as promised to meet Veterans Administration approval is deceptive since the contract doctrine of substantial performance does not apply to a UDAP action.[2074]

A builder who breaches warranties that a home will be constructed on a lot in a workmanlike manner violates the UDAP statute where improper grading of the lot leads to flooding and erosion.[2075] Egregiously bad construction work may be a UDAP violation in and of itself.[2076] A homeowner may also have warranty or UDAP claims against the suppliers of component parts.[2077] Also deceptive are a home builder's long delays and failure to correct defects covered by an express warranty.[2078] It is unconscionable to lull a consumer into thinking repairs will be covered by a home warranty (in this case a "HOW" warranty) and then use a series of spurious reasons to deny warranty coverage.[2079] A buyer of a used home may be able to bring a UDAP action against the original builder for a breach of implied warranty.[2080] A UDAP claim may succeed where a warranty claim is precluded because of the statute of limitations or other problems.[2081]

Many home builder issues have involved the Homeowners Warranty Insurance Co. (HOWIC) and Home Owners Warranty Corporation (HOW). Both HOWIC and HOW are subsidiaries of the Home Warranty Corporation, which is owned by thousands of builders around the country. HOW administered builders' limited warranties, while HOWIC provided coverage after default by a builder. All three companies were placed in receivership in 1994.[2082]

HOWIC has argued that it is exempt from state UDAP statutes because it is a "risk retention group" and the Federal Product Liability Risk Retention Act[2083] exempts such groups from state regulation. Whatever the scope of this exemption in the Federal Product Liability Risk Retention Act, courts usually resolve the issue by holding HOWIC is not a risk-retention group.[2084]

It is deceptive to represent that one is a "HOW" builder and not place a home in the HOW warranty program because all HOW builders must place their homes under the HOW warranty program.[2085] Moreover, a builder who promises to place a home in a warranty program commits a deceptive practice where it refuses to do so because of a contract dispute with the consumer.[2086]

5.5.5.8 Precut Housing

The FTC has accepted consent agreements to resolve challenges against practices in the sale of precut housing, such as misrepresentations as to the ease of assembling the housing without outside help, that all parts will be exactly precut, that instructions will be useful to a particular house, that all necessary parts will be supplied in adequate quantity and in a timely fashion, and that everything is included in the advertised price.[2087] General UDAP principles regarding deception, nondisclosure, and bait and switch are helpful in such cases.[2088]

5.5.5.9 Land Fraud Schemes

The FTC has been active against land fraud schemes for not disclosing the risks involved in land investments,[2089] such as that property is in flood areas and that water and

2072 DeReggi Constr. Co. v. Mate, 130 Md. App. 648, 747 A.2d 743 (2000). *See* § 5.6.1, *supra*, for a discussion of similar issues under state home improvement statutes. *See generally* National Consumer Law Center, Consumer Warranty Law Ch. 16 (2d ed. 2001 and Supp.) (discussion of state new home warranty and construction laws).

2073 Ybarra v. Saldona, 624 S.W.2d 948 (Tex. Civ. App. 1981); Eastlake Constr. Co. v. Hess, 686 P.2d 465 (Wash. 1984).

2074 Smith v. Baldwin, 611 S.W.2d 611 (Tex. 1981).

2075 Krawiec v. Blake Manor Dev. Co., 26 Conn. App. 601, 602 A.2d 1062 (1992). *But cf.* Griffith v. Centex Real Estate Corp., 93 Wash. App. 202, 969 P.2d 486 (1998) (failure to comply with industry standards is not by itself a UDAP violation, but may be evidence of a UDAP violation).

2076 Budner v. Lake Erie Homes, 2001 Ohio App. LEXIS 4446 (Sept. 28, 2001).

2077 DiIorio v. Structural Stone & Brick Co., 368 N.J. Super. 134, 845 A.2d 658 (App. Div. 2004). *See* National Consumer Law Center, Consumer Warranty Law (2d ed. 2001 and Supp.).

2078 The Korman Corp., 105 F.T.C. 347 (1985) (consent order); Ward Corp., 105 F.T.C. 250 (1985) (consent order); Great Am. Housebuilders, Inc. v. Gerhart, 798 S.W.2d 8 (Tex. App. 1986).

2079 HOW, Ins. v. Patriot Fin. Servs., 786 S.W.2d 533 (Tex. App. 1990).

2080 Gupta v. Ritter Homes, Inc., 646 S.W.2d 168 (Tex. 1983). *But see* Reynolds v. Ryland Group, Inc., 340 S.C. 331, 531 S.E.2d 917 (2000) (subsequent purchasers can not assert UDAP claim against builder).

2081 Griffith v. Centex Real Estate FCorp., 93 Wash. App. 202, 969 P.2d 486 (1998) (UDAP claim that builder failed to disclose defects in exterior finish allowed to proceed even though warranty claim was time-barred and negligent misrepresentation claim was barred by economic loss rule).

2082 *See* www.howcorp.com.

2083 15 U.S.C. § 3901.

2084 *See* Home Warranty Corp. v. Caldwell, 777 F.2d 1455 (11th Cir. 1985); Nguyen v. Glendale Constr. Co., 56 Wash. App. 196, 782 P.2d 1110 (1989).

2085 Love v. Keith, 383 S.E.2d 674 (N.C. Ct. App. 1989).

2086 *Id.*

2087 Insilco Corp., 91 F.T.C. 706 (1978) (consent order); Lindal Cedar Homes Inc., 87 F.T.C. 8 (1976) (consent order).

2088 *See* §§ 4.2, 4.2.14, 4.6.1, *supra.*

2089 Southwest Sunsites, Inc., 105 F.T.C. 7 (1985), *aff'd*, 785 F.2d 1431 (9th Cir. 1986); Cavanaugh Communities Corp., 93 F.T.C. 559 (1979) (consent order); Flagg Indus., Inc., 90 F.T.C. 226 (1977) (consent order); Las Animas Ranch Inc., 89 F.T.C. 255 (1977) (consent order); ITT Corp., 88 F.T.C. 933 (1976) (consent order).

sewage is unavailable.[2090] The FTC has displayed similar concern for sellers misrepresenting the availability of utilities,[2091] the location of lots,[2092] the quality of land,[2093] the condition of planned development,[2094] whether land has been subdivided,[2095] the availability of employment opportunities, urban growth, or the advent of industry in the area,[2096] and the structures or improvements on the land.[2097]

Also deceptive are misrepresentations concerning the future irrigation of farm land,[2098] height restrictions of neighboring houses in a development,[2099] the climate,[2100] the accessibility or number of lots available,[2101] or cancellation rights and the seller's refund policy.[2102] It is deceptive to enter into a land sale contract while knowing that title is not clear, and then to repudiate the contract on a pretense, sell the land to someone else, and keep the original buyer's earnest money.[2103]

While these misrepresentations are common in land fraud schemes, the key deception involves misrepresentation of resale opportunities or potential profits[2104] and the use of high pressure and deceptive sales techniques to sell lots at many times their true value.[2105] The FTC has ruled that it is unfair to induce and retain payments on land of little or no value for the intended purposes, as where land is worth about $50 an acre and sold for from $600 to $1200 an acre.[2106]

It is unfair to draft land sale contracts whereby defaulting purchasers forfeit more than the seller's reasonable damages, or whereby the buyer does not obtain title until the buyer has paid in full.[2107] Nor can sellers refuse to sell property as advertised.[2108]

The Interstate Land Sales Full Disclosure Act[2109] also provides important protections for consumers in land sale schemes. It requires persons engaged in certain interstate sales or leases of land to register the offering with HUD.[2110] Developers must furnish prospective purchasers and lessees with a property report containing information required by the Secretary of HUD.[2111] The statute also prohibits fraudu-

2090 Southwest Sunsites, Inc., 105 F.T.C. 7 (1985), *aff'd*, 785 F.2d 1431 (9th Cir. 1986); Cavanaugh Communities Corp., 93 F.T.C. 559 (1979) (consent order). *See also* Steed Realty v. Oveisi, 823 S.W.2d 195 (Tenn. Ct. App. 1991). *Accord* Schwartz v. Rose, 418 Mass. 41, 634 N.E.2d 105 (1994) (failure to disclose conservation commission's letter that asserted that lots contained wetlands).

2091 Southwest Sunsites, Inc., 105 F.T.C. 7 (1985), *aff'd*, 785 F.2d 1431 (9th Cir. 1986); Horizon Corp., 97 F.T.C. 464 (1981); Banker's Life & Casualty Co., 94 F.T.C. 363 (1979) (consent order); Cavanaugh Communities, 93 F.T.C. 559 (1979) (consent order); Las Animas Ranch Inc., 89 F.T.C. 255 (1977) (consent order).

2092 Las Animas Ranch Inc., 89 F.T.C. 255 (1977) (consent order); Arizona Valley Dev. Co., 66 F.T.C. 902 (1964) (consent order). *See also* Hofstad v. Fairfield Communities, Inc., 595 S.E.2d 813 (N.C. Ct. App. 2004).

2093 Southwest Sunsites, Inc., 105 F.T.C. 7 (1985), *aff'd*, 785 F.2d 1431 (9th Cir. 1986); Horizon Corp., 97 F.T.C. 464 (1981); Bankers Life & Casualty Co., 94 F.T.C. 363 (1979) (consent order); Las Animas Ranch Inc., 89 F.T.C. 255 (1977) (consent order). *See also* Canady v. Mann, 107 N.C. App. 252, 419 S.E.2d 597 (1992).

2094 Horizon Corp., 97 F.T.C. 464 (1981); ITT Corp., 88 F.T.C. 933 (1976) (consent order); GAC Corp., 84 F.T.C. 163 (1974) (consent order); Grand Western United Corp., 81 F.T.C. 661 (1972) (consent order); Appel v. Presley Companies, 806 P.2d 1054 (N.M. 1991) (factual issue whether seller misrepresented that certain building lots would remain undeveloped and that restrictive covenants in property deeds would maintain intended character of the development). *See also* Canady v. Mann, 107 N.C. App. 252, 419 S.E.2d 597 (1992); Steed Realty v. Oveisi, 823 S.W.2d 195 (Tenn. Ct. App. 1991).

2095 Beltz v. Dings, 27 Kan. App. 2d 507, 6 P.3d 424 (2000).

2096 Southwest Sunsites, Inc., 105 F.T.C. 7 (1985) *aff'd*, 785 F.2d 1431 (9th Cir. 1986); AMREP Corp., 102 F.T.C. 1362 (1983), *aff'd*, 768 F.2d 1171 (10th Cir. 1985); Horizon Corp., 97 F.T.C. 464 (1981); Flagg Indus., Inc., 90 F.T.C. 226 (1976) (consent order); Arizona Valley Dev. Co., 66 F.T.C. 902 (1964) (consent order).

2097 Urban Redevelopment Inc., 93 F.T.C. 692 (1973) (consent order). *See also* Schafer v. Conner, 805 S.W.2d 554 (Tex. App. 1991).

2098 Correa v. Pecos Valley Dev. Corp., 126 Ariz. 601, 617 P.2d 767 (Ct. App. 1980).

2099 Mabin v. Tualatin Dev. Co., 48 Or. App. 271, 616 P.2d 1196 (1980).

2100 Arizona Valley Dev. Co., 66 F.T.C. 902 (1964) (consent order).

2101 Arizona Valley Dev. Co., 66 F.T.C. 902 (1964) (consent order); Walter v. Hall, 940 P.2d 991 (Colo. Ct. App. 1996) (misrepresentation that an easement gave access to the land).

2102 Horizon Corp., 97 F.T.C. 464 (1981); Bankers Life & Casualty Co., 94 F.T.C. 363 (1979) (consent order); Flagg Indus., Inc., 90 F.T.C. 226 (1976) (consent order); Arizona Valley Dev. Co., 66 F.T.C. 902 (1964) (consent order).

2103 Poor v. Hill, 138 N.C. App. 19, 530 S.E.2d 838 (2000).

2104 Southwest Sunsites, Inc., 105 F.T.C. 7 (1985), *aff'd*, 785 F.2d 1431 (9th Cir. 1986); AMREP Corp., 102 F.T.C. 1362 (1983), *aff'd*, 768 F.2d 1171 (10th Cir. 1985); Horizon Corp., 97 F.T.C. 464 (1981); Bankers Life & Casualty Co., 94 F.T.C. 363 (1979) (consent order); Flagg Indus., Inc., 90 F.T.C. 226 (1976) (consent order). *See also* Canady v. Mann, 107 N.C. App. 252, 419 S.E.2d 597 (1992).

2105 AMREP Corp., 102 F.T.C. 1362 (1983), *aff'd*, 768 F.2d 1171 (10th Cir. 1985); Horizon Corp., 97 F.T.C. 464 (1981).

2106 Southwest Sunsites, Inc., 105 F.T.C. 7 (1985), *aff'd*, 785 F.2d 1431 (9th Cir. 1986).

2107 AMREP Corp., 102 F.T.C. 1362 (1983), *aff'd*, 768 F.2d 1171 (10th Cir. 1985); Horizon Corp., 97 F.T.C. 464 (1981); Bankers Life & Casualty Co., 94 F.T.C. 363 (1979) (consent order). *See also* Stringer v. Perales, 2003 WL 1848594 (Tex. App. Apr. 10, 2003) (unpublished, citation limited) (affirming award of damages for wrongful removal of land contract buyer from home).

2108 Turkey Mountain Estates Inc., 84 F.T.C. 698 (1974) (consent order).

2109 15 U.S.C. § 1701 *et seq. See also* 24 C.F.R. Part 1710.

2110 15 U.S.C. §§ 1703(a)(1)(A), 1704, 1707. For a particularly egregious example of a non-complying defendant, see HUD v. Cost Control Marketing & Sales Mgmt. of Virginia, Inc., 64 F.3d 920 (4th Cir. 1995). Failure to furnish a property report may warrant an order compelling compliance or permitting revocation by plaintiffs. Moscony v. Quaker Farms, L.P., 2000 U.S. Dist. LEXIS 17772 (E.D. Pa. Dec. 8, 2000).

2111 15 U.S.C. § 1707.

lent or deceitful practices, untrue statements, and omissions of material facts.[2112] Consumers have the right to bring a private cause of action for damages, specific performance, interest, court costs, attorney fees, independent-appraiser fees, and travel to and from the subject lot.[2113] State law may have similar registration requirements, violation of which should be considered a UDAP violation.[2114]

5.5.5.10 Condominiums and Timeshares

New Mexico has UDAP regulations dealing with contest promotions for the sale of subdivided land, timeshares, condominiums, and membership campgrounds.[2115] A Missouri regulation deals with promotions of timeshare plans.[2116] Vermont UDAP regulations relate to offers of supposedly free travel packages used in timeshare marketing.[2117] Other states have separate statutes regulating this area.[2118]

The FTC has settled charges involving various misrepresentations as to ownership, location, number of timeshares available, and exchangeability.[2119] The FTC has also succeeded in obtaining a stipulated injunction against a company allegedly misrepresenting its services in reselling timeshares, making unsubstantiated statements about re-sale success rates, misrepresenting its affiliations, and falsely guaranteeing that timeshares would be sold.[2120] A New Jersey condominium developer violated the state's UDAP statute by refusing to return buyers' deposits when it had not obtained the required certificates of occupancy by the closing date.[2121] A Wisconsin court ordered rescission and double damages against a timeshare seller that used an illegal referral sales scheme to induce purchases.[2122] There are similar problems in the sale of campground resort memberships as with timeshare sales, and practitioners with timeshare cases should also refer to § 5.10.5, *infra* about campground resort memberships.

5.5.6 Storage of Goods

Article 7 of the Uniform Commercial Code governs the creation and enforcement of liens by persons engaged in the business of storing goods for hire. Other entities that store property, such as automobile towing companies, may have a common law or statutory lien.[2123] A company that retains or sells a consumer's property without a valid lien violates the state UDAP statute.[2124] A storage facility's failure to live up to its explicit and implicit representations can be actionable under a UDAP statute.[2125]

Illegal retention or sale of property as a means of collecting a debt may also run afoul of the state debt collection statute or regulation.[2126] There may also be a UDAP regulation governing the particular type of actor, as, for example, when an automobile repair shop is storing a vehicle. State UDAP regulations and general principles regarding deposits, disclosures, and deception may also be helpful.[2127]

5.6 Home Improvements and Related Services, Utilities and Telecommunications

5.6.1 Home Improvement Sales

5.6.1.1 Introduction

Home improvement sales, such as residential siding, roofing, storm windows, and basement waterproofing, may display a wide array of UDAP violations—some consider home improvement scams the classic form of consumer abuse. Because so many different types of UDAP violations may be involved, reference should be made to other sections of Chapters 4 and 5, such as those dealing with door-to-door

---

2112 15 U.S.C. § 1703(a).

2113 15 U.S.C. § 1709.

2114 Walter v. Hall, 940 P.2d 991 (Colo. Ct. App. 1996). *See* § 3.2.7, *supra*. *See also* 24 C.F.R. § 1710.500 (if HUD determines that a state program provides equal protection to the federal program, HUD registration requirements satisfied if state instead of HUD forms submitted to HUD). *Cf.* N.J. Admin. Code tit. 11, § 11:5-9.3.

2115 N.M. Admin. Code § 12.2.3, Requirements for the Promotion and Advertising of Subdivided Land, Time Share Interests, Condominiums and Membership Campgrounds.

2116 Mo. Code Regs. tit. 15, § 60-4.010 *et seq.*, Time Share Regulations.

2117 Code of Vt Rules § 06 031 17 Rule CF 116, Sale of Vacation Packages.

2118 *See, e.g.*, 63 Pa. Stat. § 455.609.

2119 James R. Quincy, 5 Trade Reg. Rep. (CCH) ¶ 22,569 (W.D. Wash. July 21, 1988) (stipulated final judgment).

2120 FTC v. Timeshare Owners Foundation, Inc., 5 Trade Reg. Rep. (CCH) ¶ 22,850 (M.D. Fla. 1990) (stipulated permanent injunction). *See also* FTC v. PM Marketing Masters, Inc., 5 Trade Reg. Rep. (CCH) ¶ 23,136 (M.D. Fla. 1992) (permanent injunction); FTC v. Turcal, Inc., 5 Trade Reg. Rep. (CCH) ¶ 23,800 (C.D. Cal. 1995) (proposed consent decree).

2121 Cybal v. Atrium Palace Syndicate, 272 N.J. Super. 330, 639 A.2d 1146 (1994).

2122 Pliss v. Peppertree Resort Villas, Inc., 663 N.W.2d 851 (Wis. App. 2003).

2123 *See* National Consumer Law Center, Repossessions and Foreclosures Ch. 15 (5th ed. 2002 and Supp.).

2124 Hammer v. Nikol, 659 A.2d 617 (Pa. Commw. 1995). *See also* Clarkson v. DeCaceres, 105 B.R. 266 (Bankr. E.D. Pa. 1989) (landlord-tenant); Freeman v. Alamo Mgmt. Co., 24 Conn. App. 124, 586 A.2d 619 (1991) (landlord violates UDAP by taking and disposing of tenant's property as part of self-help eviction); Nelson v. Schanzer, 788 S.W.2d 81 (Tex. App. 1990).

2125 Eifler v. Shurgard Capital Mgmt. Corp., 71 Wash. App. 684, 861 P.2d 1071 (1993).

2126 *See* § 5.1.1.1, *supra*.

2127 *See* §§ 4.9.1, 4.2.14, 4.2, *supra*.

sales, high pressure sales, energy savings claims, repair practices, misrepresentations of product characteristics, deceptive pricing, and bait and switch. This section will detail precedent involving home improvement sales, but rulings involving similar practices in other industries are also good precedent.

Consumers who have been cheated by home improvement contractors may also have claims under the Truth in Lending Act[2128] and state home improvement laws.[2129] Violations of state home improvement laws may constitute UDAP violations as well.[2130] A number of states have adopted home improvement regulations under their UDAP statutes.[2131] Wisconsin has enacted a UDAP regulation dealing specifically with problems in basement waterproofing.[2132]

5.6.1.2 Marketing Misrepresentations

Bait and switch practices in home repair sales are deceptive.[2133] Similarly deceptive are misrepresentations involving reduced prices,[2134] "free gifts,"[2135] the seller's relationship with a manufacturer,[2136] the qualifications of workers,[2137] a product's durability or maintenance characteristics,[2138] its composition[2139] or brand,[2140] its insulating or energy savings value,[2141] or claims that the buyers are receiving a discount because their home will be used as a "model."[2142] It is deceptive to misrepresent that the consumer is specially selected[2143] or that an offer is for a limited

2128 *See* National Consumer Law Center, Truth in Lending (5th ed. 2003 and Supp.).

2129 *See, e.g.*, Rizzo Pool Co. v. Del Grosso, 232 Conn. 666, 657 A.2d 1087 (1995) (claims under state Home Improvement Act); A. Secondino & Son, Inc. v. LoRicco, 215 Conn. 336, 576 A.2d 464 (1990) (same); People v. Watts, 181 Ill. 2d 133, 692 N.E.2d 315 (1998) (presumption of intent makes criminal home repair fraud statute unconstitutional). *See generally* National Consumer Law Center, Consumer Warranty Law Ch. 17 (2d ed. 2001 and Supp.).

2130 Woronecki v. Trappe, 228 Conn. 574, 637 A.2d 783 (1994).

2131 *See* Appx. A, *infra*.

2132 Wisconsin Dep't of Agriculture, Trade and Consumer Protection Rules, Wis. Admin. Code ch. ATCP 111, Basement Waterproofing Unfair Trade Practices. *See also* Everseal Waterproofing Corp., 89 F.T.C. 110 (1977) (consent order); National Meridian Servs., 89 F.T.C. 192 (1977) (consent order); Northerlin Co., 88 F.T.C. 38 (1976) (consent order).

2133 Mutual Constr. Co., 87 F.T.C. 621 (1976); American Aluminum Corp., 84 F.T.C. 48 (1974), *aff'd*, 522 F.2d 1278 (5th Cir. 1975), *cert. denied*, 426 U.S. 906 (1976); Southern States Distributing Co., 83 F.T.C. 1126 (1973); All-State Indus. of North Carolina Inc., 75 F.T.C. 465 (1969), *aff'd*, 423 F.2d 423 (4th Cir. 1969), *cert. denied*, 400 U.S. 828 (1970); Royal Constr. Co., 71 F.T.C. 762 (1967); Aluminum Indus. Inc., 67 F.T.C. 1 (1965); Better Living Inc., 54 F.T.C. 648, *aff'd*, 259 F.2d 271 (3d Cir. 1958); Wisconsin Dep't of Agriculture, Trade and Consumer Protection Rules, Wis. Admin. Code ch. ATCP 110.02(3), Home Improvement Trade Practices.

2134 American Aluminum Corp., 84 F.T.C. 48 (1974), *aff'd*, 522 F.2d 1278 (5th Cir. 1975), *cert. denied*, 426 U.S. 906 (1976); Certified Building Products, 83 F.T.C. 1004 (1973), *aff'd sub nom.* Thiret v. FTC, 512 F.2d 176 (10th Cir. 1975); Bruce v. Home Depot, USA, Inc., 308 F. Supp. 2d 72 (D. Conn. 2004) (UDAP claim is actionable against contractor who lacks the capacity to provide promised kitchen components at the contract price); FTC v. AAA Electric Inc., 5 Trade Reg. Rep. (CCH) ¶ 23,795 (C.D. Cal. 1995) (proposed consent decree); All-State Indus. of North Carolina Inc., 75 F.T.C. 465 (1969), *aff'd*, 423 F.2d 423 (4th Cir. 1969); *cert. denied*, 400 U.S. 828 (1970); Royal Constr. Co., 71 F.T.C. 762 (1967); Wisconsin Dep't of Agriculture, Trade and Consumer Protection Rules, Wis. Admin. Code ch. ATCP 110.02(6), Home Improvement Trade Practices.

2135 American Aluminum Corp., 84 F.T.C. 48 (1974), *aff'd*, 522 F.2d 1278 (5th Cir. 1975), *cert. denied*, 426 U.S. 906 (1976); Royal Constr. Co., 71 F.T.C. 762 (1967); Wisconsin Dep't of Agriculture, Trade and Consumer Protection Rules, Wis. Admin. Code, ch. ATCP 110.02(5), Home Improvement Trade Practices.

2136 Certified Building Products, 83 F.T.C. 1004 (1973), *aff'd sub nom.* Thiret v. FTC, 512 F.2d 176 (10th Cir. 1975); Southern States Distributing Co., 83 F.T.C. 1126 (1973); All-State Indus. of North Carolina Inc., 75 F.T.C. 465 (1969), *aff'd*, 423 F.2d 423 (4th Cir. 1969), *cert. denied*, 400 U.S. 828 (1970); Wisconsin Dep't of Agriculture, Trade and Consumer Protection Rules, Wis. Admin. Code ch. ATCP 110.02(4), Home Improvement Trade Practices.

2137 FTC v. AAA Electric Inc., 5 Trade Reg. Rep. (CCH) ¶ 23,795 (C.D. Cal. 1995) (proposed consent decree) (false claim that electrician was certified by trade association).

2138 Mutual Constr. Co., 87 F.T.C. 621 (1976); American Aluminum Corp., 84 F.T.C. 48 (1974), *aff'd per curiam* 522 F.2d 1278 (5th Cir. 1975), *cert. denied*, 426 U.S. 906 (1976); Certified Building Products, 83 F.T.C. 1004 (1973), *aff'd sub nom.* Thiret v. FTC, 512 F.2d 176 (10th Cir. 1975); Southern States Distributing Co., 83 F.T.C. 1126 (1973); Better Living Inc., 54 F.T.C. 648, *aff'd*, 259 F.2d 271 (3d Cir. 1958); Wisconsin Dep't of Agriculture, Trade, and Consumer Protection Rules, Wis. Admin. Code ch. ATCP 110.02(2), Home Improvement Trade Practices. *But cf.* Anunziatta v. Orkin Exterminating Co., 180 F. Supp. 2d 353 (N.D.N.Y. 2001) (ads were not specific enough to be deceptive).

2139 Southern States Distributing Co., 83 F.T.C. 1126 (1973).

2140 Wiseman v. Kirkman, 2002 WL 31243522 (Ohio App. Oct. 4, 2002) (unpublished, citation limited) (contracting to install one brand of appliance but installing another and keeping the savings is a UDAP violation).

2141 *See* § 5.6.7, *infra*.

2142 Mutual Constr. Co., 87 F.T.C. 621 (1976); American Aluminum Corp., 84 F.T.C. 48 (1974), *aff'd per curiam* 522 F.2d 1278 (5th Cir. 1975), *cert. denied*, 426 U.S. 906 (1976); All-State Indus. of North Carolina Inc., 75 F.T.C. 465 (1969), *aff'd*, 423 F.2d 423 (4th Cir. 1969), *cert. denied*, 400 U.S. 828 (1970); Gulf Coast Aluminum Co., 71 F.T.C. 339 (1967); Interstate Builders Inc., 72 F.T.C. 370 (1967); Royal Constr. Co., 71 F.T.C. 762 (1967); John A. Guziak, 67 F.T.C. 1270 (1965), *aff'd*, 361 F.2d 700 (8th Cir. 1966), *cert. denied*, 385 U.S. 1007 (1967); Luxury Indus. Inc., 59 F.T.C. 442 (1961); Idaho Consumer Protection Regulations, Idaho Admin. Code § 04.02.01.130(05), Repairs and Improvements; Massachusetts Consumer Protection Regulations, Mass. Regs. Code tit. 940, § 3.09(3), Door-to-Door Sales and Home Improvement Transactions; W. Va. Code St. R. tit. 142, § 142-5-3; Wisconsin Dep't of Agriculture, Trade and Consumer Protection Rules, Wis. Admin. Code ch. ATCP 110.02(1), Home Improvement Trade Practices.

2143 Mutual Constr. Co., 87 F.T.C. 621 (1976); American Aluminum Corp., 84 F.T.C. 48 (1974), *aff'd*, 522 F.2d 1278 (5th Cir. 1975), *cert. denied*, 426 U.S. 906 (1976); Aluminum Indus. Inc., 67

time only.[2144] In West Virginia, a UDAP regulation prohibits misrepresentations and false inducements.[2145] Ohio UDAP regulations require an estimate before work is started.[2146]

It is deceptive to gain entry to the buyer's home by misrepresenting the seller's right to conduct an inspection, the seller's relation with manufacturers, or the seller's status.[2147] Another deceptive practice is to enter a home in the guise of performing a pest control inspection, for the real purpose of selling unnecessary foundation or other home repairs.[2148] A home improvement contractor has been found to violate a UDAP statute for soliciting repairs to fire-damaged residences while the cinders were still smoldering, when consumers were confused or frightened.[2149] Contractors may not misrepresent that repairs are necessary or that a home is in a dangerous condition.[2150]

5.6.1.3 The Home Improvement Contract and Warranties

In many states, a UDAP or home improvement statute or regulation requires that contracts must have all blanks filled in and must disclose the full price, all charges and fees, the completion date, the work to be done, and any applicable warranties.[2151] Maine's Home Construction Contracts Act and a West Virginia regulation require all home improvement contracts for more than a certain amount ($3000 in Maine and $250 in West Virginia) to be in writing,[2152] and West Virginia requires the contractor to give the consumer a completion date.[2153] Indiana's home improvement contract statute has similar requirements and provides that a violation constitutes a UDAP violation.[2154] New Jersey has a similar regulation under its UDAP statute, but it does not apply to reconstruction of a totally gutted house.[2155] Nor does it apply to a subcontractor who dealt only with the general

F.T.C. 1 (1965); Frieston Products Inc., 64 F.T.C. 1416 (1964); Luxury Indus. Inc., 59 F.T.C. 442 (1961).

2144 American Aluminum Corp., 84 F.T.C. 48 (1974), *aff'd*, 522 F.2d 1278 (5th Cir. 1975), *cert. denied*, 426 U.S. 906 (1976); Certified Building Products, 83 F.T.C. 1004 (1973), *aff'd sub nom.* Thiret v. FTC, 512 F.2d 176 (10th Cir. 1975); Southern States Distributing Co., 83 F.T.C. 1126 (1973); All-State Indus. of North Carolina Inc., 75 F.T.C. 465 (1969), *aff'd*, 423 F.2d 423 (4th Cir. 1969), *cert. denied*, 400 U.S. 828 (1970); Royal Constr. Co., 71 F.T.C. 762 (1967).

2145 W. Va. Code St. R. § 142-5-3.

2146 Erie Shore Builders v. Leimbach, 2001 Ohio App. LEXIS 3158 (July 13, 2001).

2147 Holland Furnace Co. v. FTC, 295 F.2d 302 (7th Cir. 1961); FTC v. AAA Electric Inc., 5 Trade Reg. Rep. (CCH) ¶ 23,795 (C.D. Cal. 1995) (proposed consent decree); Massachusetts Consumer Protection Regulations, Mass. Regs. Code tit. 940, § 3.09(1), Door-to-Door Sales and Home Improvement Transactions; Wisconsin Dep't of Agriculture, Trade and Consumer Protection Rules, Wis. Admin. Code ch. ATCP 110.02(4), Home Improvement Trade Practices.

2148 *See* State v. Shaw, 847 S.W.2d 768 (Mo. 1993).

2149 Brown v. Banks, Clearinghouse No. 27,065 (Ohio C.P. Cuyahoga Cty. 1976).

2150 FTC v. AAA Electric Inc., 5 Trade Reg. Rep. (CCH) ¶ 23,795 (C.D. Cal. 1995) (proposed consent decree); Wiseman v. Kirkman, 2002 WL 31243522 (Ohio App. Oct. 4, 2002) (unpublished, citation limited) (rerouting plumbing in mistaken belief that it violated state law was UDAP violation); Idaho Consumer Protection Regulations, Idaho Admin. Code § 04.02.01.130, Repairs and Improvements; Code Miss. Rules § 24-000-002, Rule 45; W. Va. Code St. R. tit. 142, § 142-5-3.1.20; Wisconsin Dep't of Agriculture, Trade and Consumer Protection Rules, Wis. Admin. Code ch. ATCP 110.02(9), Home Improvement Trade Practices; *see also* State v. Shaw, 847 S.W.2d 768 (Mo. 1993); Jefferies v. Phillips, 451 S.E.2d 21 (S.C. Ct. App. 1994) ("padding" estimate by exaggerating the amount of work that was necessary would have been a UDAP violation).

2151 Brace v. Titcomb, 2002 WL 1335871 (Me. Super. May 17, 2002); W. Va. Code St. R. tit. 142, § 142-5-3; Wisconsin Dep't of Agriculture, Trade and Consumer Protection Rules, Wis. Admin. Code ch. ATCP 110.05, Home Improvement Trade Practices. *See also* Rizzo Pool Co. v. Del Grosso, 232 Conn. 666, 657 A.2d 1087 (1995) (under state Home Improvement Act, contract that fails to state commencement and completion dates is unenforceable unless consumer acts in bad faith); A. Secondino & Son, Inc. v. LoRicco, 215 Conn. 336, 576 A.2d 464 (1990) (contractor who failed to comply with state Home Improvement Act requirement of written contract can not recover in quasi contract unless consumer acted in bad faith); Scott v. Mayflower Home Improvement Corp., 363 N.J. Super. 145, 831 A.2d 564 (App. Div. 2001); Branigan v. Level on the Level, Inc., 326 N.J. Super. 24, 740 A.2d 643 (App. Div. 1999) (failure to state starting date and completion date in contract violated UDAP regulation); People v. Empyre Inground Pools Inc., 642 N.Y.S.2d 344 (App. Div. 1996) (enjoining defendant from engaging in home improvement business because of violations of New York's home improvement contract law); Snyder v. Badgerland Mobile Homes, Inc., 659 N.W.2d 887 (Wis. App. 2003) (salesperson's address need not be separately stated on contract if it is same as seller's; omission of starting and completion dates at buyer's request not grounds to cancel). *But cf.* Wowaka & Sons, Inc. v. Pardell, 242 A.D.2d 1, 672 N.Y.S.2d 358 (1998) (failure of home improvement contract to contain all the information required by statute does not render it unenforceable).

2152 William Mushero, Inc. v. Hull, 667 A.2d 853 (Me. 1995) (awarding homeowner damages for contractor's failure to perform according to specifications, where contract had not been reduced to writing); Snyder v. Badgerland Mobile Homes, Inc., 659 N.W.2d 887 (Wis. App. 2003) (no UDAP claim where seller's omission of starting and completion dates from contract, at consumer's request, caused consumers no loss); Me. Rev. Stat. Ann. tit. 10, § 1487; W. Va. Code St. R. tit. 142, §§ 142-5-3.1.1, 142-5-3.3.3. *See also* A. Secondino & Son, Inc. v. LoRicco, 215 Conn. 336, 576 A.2d 464 (1990) (contractor can not recover where home improvement contract not reduced to writing, in violation of Connecticut's Home Improvement Act); Marascio v. Campanella, 298 N.J. Super. 491, 689 A.2d 852 (App. Div. 1997) (New Jersey home improvement contracts over $200 must be in writing; an oral contract is unenforceable); § 8.3.5, *infra*. *Cf.* Jakubowski v. Rock Valley Builders, 588 N.W.2d 928 (Wis. App. 1998) (unpublished limited precedent opinion, text available at 1998 Wisc. App. LEXIS 1363) (contractor's failure to provide clear written contract violated UDAP statute, but did not cause the consumers' damages).

2153 W. Va. Code St. R. § 142-5-3.1.2.

2154 Mullis v. Brennan, 716 N.E.2d 58 (Ind. App. 1999).

2155 Messeka Sheet Metal Co. v. Hodder, 368 N.J. Super. 116, 845 A.2d 646 (App. Div. 2004).

contractor, not the homeowner.[2156] Home improvement contracts that are highly one-sided may violate a UDAP statute's prohibition of unfairness or unconscionability.[2157]

Proving that damages are proximately caused by violations of the formal requirements of home improvement contract statutes can be tricky, but plaintiffs have succeeded when they were able to tie the violation to some particular aspect of the work.[2158] For example, the lack of a written contract, or its failure to set forth the specifications in the detail required by the statute, may be portrayed as one of the causes of a dispute over what work was agreed to. Some home improvement contract laws or UDAP statutes allow cancellation or rescission in some circumstances.[2159]

State UDAP regulations require that if a language other than English is used in negotiations, the contract must also be in that language; certain disabled buyers must have the contract read to them; and sellers can not induce signatures from those who can not read or understand the contract.[2160] It is deceptive to begin work or to use other tactics to pressure buyers into being bound to an agreement when no binding contract exists[2161] or to misrepresent a buyer's cancellation rights.[2162] Full payment can not be demanded until the work is completed, and the seller can not misrepresent the effect of signing documents.[2163] New Jersey requires all changes in home improvement contracts to be in writing or signed.[2164] A contractor who performs "extras" without a signed contract risks nonpayment.[2165]

Sellers can not misrepresent guarantees[2166] and must disclose the extent and nature of the guarantee.[2167] West Virginia's UDAP regulation prohibits disclaimers of warranties.[2168]

5.6.1.4 Building Permits and Construction Standards

A home improvement contractor's representation that it would obtain approval of the appropriate government authority is an implicit promise to comply with government standards. Failure to procure a required building permit is a UDAP violation.[2169] Nor may a repairman charge for fictitious government fees that are not turned over to a third party.[2170]

5.6.1.5 High Prices and Changes in the Agreed-Upon Price

Unconscionable prices may be a UDAP violation where little or no services are actually provided and the consumer is given no real alternative, or where the dealer has advertised that it charges low prices.[2171] The seller may not change the price or the nature of the work to be done without the buyer's authorization.[2172] Nor may contractors represent

---

2156 *Id.*

2157 *Cf.* Matthews v. New Century Mortg. Corp., 185 F. Supp. 2d 874 (S.D. Ohio 2002) (upholding common law unconscionability claim against motion to dismiss).

2158 Mullis v. Brennan, 716 N.E.2d 58 (Ind. App. 1999) (causation shown between lack of detail in contract and contractor's failure to cure deficiencies in work). *See also* Scott v. Mayflower Home Improvement Corp., 363 N.J. Super. 145, 831 A.2d 564 (Law Div. 2001) (consumers may have suffered ascertainable loss where home improvement contractor used unlicensed salespersons, violated state requirements for specification of costs, finance charges, and the work to be done, charged unconscionably high prices, and performed shoddy work).

2159 *Cf.* Snyder v. Badgerland Mobile Homes, Inc., 659 N.W.2d 887 (Wis. App. 2003) (buyer would have had right to cancel if seller had omitted completion deadline and seller had not done work in timely manner).

2160 Massachusetts Consumer Protection Regulations, Mass. Regs. Code tit. 940, § 3.09(6), Door-to-Door Sales and Home Improvement Transactions; Wisconsin Dep't of Agriculture, Trade and Consumer Protection Rules, Wis. Admin. Code ch. ATCP 110.5(6), Home Improvement Trade Practices.

2161 Wisconsin Dep't of Agriculture, Trade and Consumer Protection Rules, Wis. Admin. Code ch. ATCP 110.02(7), Home Improvement Trade Practices.

2162 Brown v. Banks, Clearinghouse No. 27,065 (Ohio C.P. Cuyahoga Cty. 1976). *See also* W. Va. Code St. R. tit. 142, § 142-5-3.3.2.

2163 Perma-Stone Corp. v. Merkel, 255 Wis. 565, 39 N.W.2d 730 (1949); W. Va. Code St. R. tit. 142, § 142-5-3; Wisconsin Dep't of Agriculture, Trade and Consumer Protection Rules, Wis. Admin. Code ch. ATCP 110.02(6), Home Improvement Trade Practices.

2164 Blake Constr. v. Pavlik, 236 N.J. Super. 73, 564 A.2d 130 (1989).

2165 *Id.*

2166 American Aluminum Corp., 84 F.T.C. 48 (1974), *aff'd*, 522 F.2d 1278 (5th Cir. 1975), *cert. denied*, 426 U.S. 906 (1976); Southern States Distributing Co., 83 F.T.C. 1126 (1973); Inter-State Builders Inc., 72 F.T.C. 370 (1967); Royal Constr. Co., 71 F.T.C. 762 (1967); John A. Guziak, 67 F.T.C. 1270 (1965), *aff'd*, 361 F.2d 700 (8th Cir. 1966), *cert. denied*, 385 U.S. 1007 (1967); Luxury Indus., 59 F.T.C. 442 (1961); Better Living Inc., 54 F.T.C. 648, *aff'd*, 259 F.2d 271 (3d Cir. 1958).

2167 Tri-State Home Improvement Co., 78 F.T.C. 484 (1971) (consent order); Harry Stroiman, 78 F.T.C. 570 (1971) (consent order); Eugene Miller, 78 F.T.C. 1016 (1971) (consent order).

2168 W. Va. Code St. R. tit. 142, § 142-5-3.

2169 Becker v. Graber Builders, Inc., 149 N.C. App. 787, 561 S.E.2d 905 (2002); Hurst v. Sears, Roebuck & Co., 647 S.W.2d 249 (Tex. 1983) (failure to get building permit and get city to inspect repairs is UDAP violation even where it was impossible to get permit). *See also* Cox v. Sears, Roebuck & Co., 138 N.J. 2, 647 A.2d 454 (1994) (contractor committed UDAP violation by failing to obtain required permits). *See also* § 5.5.5.7.1, *supra*.

2170 Jim Walter Homes Inc. v. White, 617 S.W.2d 767 (Tex. Civ. App. 1981).

2171 People *ex rel.* Hartigan v. Knecht Servs., 216 Ill. App. 3d 843, 575 N.E.2d 1378 (1991).

2172 Idaho Consumer Regulations, Idaho Admin. Code § 04.02.01.121, Estimates; Ohio Admin. Code § 109:4-3-05(D)(3). *Cf.* Finn v. Krumroy Constr. Co., 68 Ohio App. 3d 480, 589 N.E.2d 58 (1990) (no UDAP violation because buyers authorized additional work).

that a house can be repaired within the limits of an insurance policy when it can not.[2173]

5.6.1.6 Failure to Perform Work Properly and as Scheduled

Work must be performed when promised unless delayed by factors outside the seller's control.[2174] Even though circumstances justify a delay, a contractor does not provide a completion date to be helpful, but so consumers can rely on it. A contractor should have been able to foresee ordinary reasons for delay and adjust for them since the delays were within the contractor's, not the consumer's control.[2175] Even if a delay is excusable, the contractor must promptly notify the consumer of the delay.[2176] A delay of almost one year in installing windows is unconscionable.[2177]

Sellers may not misrepresent that work has been performed,[2178] and work must be as warranted.[2179] Misrepresentations about the nature and extent of the work are also unlawful.[2180] It is an unfair and deceptive practice to employ repair workers guilty of shoddy workmanship and persons with inadequate training or supervision to perform the assigned work.[2181] Courts have had little trouble finding a UDAP violation where a contractor fails to commence or complete work for which it has accepted payment, fails to do work in a workmanlike manner, or fails to remedy defective work or issue refunds.[2182] It is a UDAP violation for a contractor to specify the nature of work to be performed in brochures, blueprints, and oral representations, and then to perform different work than promised.[2183]

5.6.1.7 Credit-Related Practices and Lender Liability

Two state UDAP regulations, as well as an FTC rule, limit holder-in-due-course status for home repair contracts,[2184] and another regulation proscribes wrongful liens on the buyer's house.[2185] In connection with a credit transaction in which a security interest is acquired in the customer's principal residence, it is unfair or deceptive:

- To violate Federal Reserve Board Regulation Z by failing to provide copies of the notice of the opportunity to rescind and the notice of the effect of rescission;[2186]
- To make physical changes in a customer's property, perform any work, or make any deliveries within the three-day recession period;[2187]

2173 Captain & Co. v. Stenberg, 505 N.E.2d 88 (Ind. Ct. App. 1987).

2174 Bruce v. Home Depot, USA, Inc., 308 F. Supp. 2d 72 (D. Conn. 2004); Leduc v. Rotar, 2004 WL 298979 (Mich. App. Feb. 17, 2004) (unpublished, citation limited) (failing to acquire or install furnace and failing to return consumer's money); Commonwealth of Pennsylvania Diversified Chemicals, Inc., Clearinghouse No. 50,440 (Pa. C.P. Oct. 6, 1994) (pattern of nondelivery is a UDAP violation); W. Va. Code St. R. tit. 142, § 142-5-3; Wisconsin Dep't of Agriculture, Trade and Consumer Protection Rules, Wis. Admin. Code ch. ATCP 110.07, Home Improvement Trade Practices.

2175 Keyes v. Bollinger, 31 Wash. App. 286, 640 P.2d 1077 (1982).

2176 State v. Clausen, 105 Wis. 2d 231, 313 N.W.2d 819 (1982).

2177 Sinkfield v. Strong, 34 Ohio Misc. 2d 19, 517 N.E.2d 1051 (Mun. Ct. 1987).

2178 Idaho Consumer Protection Regulations, Idaho Admin. Code § 04.02.01.130, Repairs and Improvements (1970); *see also* State v. Shaw, 847 S.W.2d 768 (Mo. 1993); Orkin Exterminating Co. v. Lesassier, 688 S.W.2d 651 (Tex. App. 1985); Small v. Baker, 605 S.W.2d 401 (Tex. Civ. App. 1980).

2179 Haag v. Dry Basement, Inc., 11 Kan. App. 2d 649, 732 P.2d 392 (1987); Brown v. Banks, Clearinghouse No. 27,065 (Ohio C.P. Cuyahoga Cty. 1976); Commonwealth v. Burns, 663 A.2d 308 (Pa. Commw. 1995) (home improvement contractor violated UDAP statute by performing repairs below the standard of workmanship agreed to in writing); Commonwealth v. Premier Basement Waterproofing Co., Clearinghouse No. 26,020 (Pa. C.P. Erie Cty. 1973). *But see* Brooks v. Ibsen, 2001 Tenn. App. LEXIS 630 (Aug. 24, 2001) (vacating judgment that awarded UDAP remedies for improper construction of swimming pool).

2180 Anunziatta v. Orkin Exterminating Co., 180 F. Supp. 2d 353 (N.D.N.Y. 2001).

2181 People *ex rel.* Hartigan v. Knecht Servs., 216 Ill. App. 3d 843, 575 N.E.2d 1378 (1991).

2182 Wirt v. Matthews, 2002 WL 31999339 (Del. Com. Pleas Apr. 9, 2002), *disposing of motion for reargument of* 2002 WL 31999360 (Del. Com. Pleas Feb. 7, 2002) (unpublished, citation limited); Brace v. Titcomb, 2002 WL 1335871 (Me. Super. May 17, 2002); Cox v. Sears, Roebuck & Co., 138 N.J. 2, 647 A.2d 454 (1994) (failure to comply with UDAP regulations, which resulted in defective work, was a UDAP violation even though defective performance itself was not unconscionable); Becker v. Graber Builders, Inc., 149 N.C. App. 787, 561 S.E.2d 905 (2002) (home construction contract); People v. Etling, Clearinghouse No. 43,084 (N.Y. Sup. Ct. 1987); Erie Shore Builders v. Leimbach, 2001 Ohio App. LEXIS 3158 (July 13, 2001); Fit 'N' Fun Pools, Inc. v. Shelly, 2001 Ohio App. LEXIS 3 (Ohio Ct. App. Jan. 3, 2001) (failure to perform in a workmanlike manner is a UDAP violation); *cf.* Gatrell v. Kilgore, 1999 Ohio App. LEXIS 6170 (Dec. 22, 1999) (inadequate installation of septic system was not a UDAP violation). *But see* Sparks v. Re/Max Allstar Realty, Inc., 55 S.W.3d 343 (Ky. App. 2000) (inadequate performance of termite inspection and treatment not a UDAP violation unless intentional or grossly negligent); Sampson v. Winnie, 2001 Tenn. App. LEXIS 894 (Dec. 11, 2001) (performing home improvements in deficient manner is not UDAP violation).

2183 Lapierre v. Samco Dev. Co., 103 N.C. App. 551, 406 S.E.2d 646 (1991).

2184 Massachusetts Consumer Protection Regulations, Mass. Regs. Code tit. 940, § 3.09(9), (10), Door-to-Door Sales and Home Improvement Transactions; Wisconsin Dep't of Agriculture, Trade and Consumer Protection Rules, Wis. Admin. Code ch. ATCP 110.06, Home Improvement Trade Practices. The FTC rule is discussed at § 6.6, *infra*.

2185 Idaho Consumer Protection Regulations, Idaho Admin. Code § 04.02.01.130, Repairs and Improvements.

2186 Certified Building Products, 83 F.T.C. 1004 (1973), *aff'd sub nom.* Thiret v. FTC, 512 F.2d 176 (10th Cir. 1975); Fabbis Inc., 81 F.T.C. 678 (1972).

2187 Fabbis Inc., 81 F.T.C. 678 (1972).

- To represent that customers are liable for damages in the event they rescind.[2188]

The Truth in Lending Act makes most home improvement contracts cancelable by the consumer for three business days and rescindable for up to three years if material disclosures are not provided or work is commenced during the three-day cancellation period.[2189] For certain high-rate home improvement transactions that involve a security interest in the consumer's home, the Home Ownership and Equity Protection Act (HOEPA) prohibits certain abusive credit terms.[2190] It also prohibits engaging in a pattern or practice of extending credit without regard to the consumer's repayment ability, and requires the check for the proceeds to be made out to the consumer or jointly to the consumer and the contractor, or, at the election of the consumer, through an escrow agent.[2191]

One notable trend involving home improvement contractors is for the defrauded consumer to sue the participating finance company for punitive damages. A number of Alabama juries have awarded damages in the millions of dollars for each homeowner.[2192]

5.6.2 Alarm and Emergency Response Systems, Other Emergency Devices

A burglar alarm installer engages in a deceptive practice by falsely claiming that a burglar cutting the system wires would still trigger an alarm, that the police would arrive in only a few minutes, and that a panic button would work even with the wires cut.[2193] Advertising by a heat detector manufacturer is deceptive where dangerous amounts of smoke and carbon monoxide can accumulate before the alarm goes off.[2194] The FTC has also successfully challenged misrepresentations by manufacturers of descent, rescue and escape systems,[2195] fire and smoke protection masks,[2196] and survival suits.[2197]

Another area of potential deception involves the marketing of emergency response systems, often targeting elderly and handicapped people. There may be misrepresentations about the company's relationship with local emergency services and 911, deceptive pricing schemes, and misrepresentations about cancellation rights and whether a transaction is a lease or purchase.[2198] Sales may also be accompanied by unfair high pressure sales techniques, such as installing the equipment before the consumer gives authorization and by humiliating techniques such as the seller calling the consumer's friends and relatives to obtain the initial installment.[2199]

5.6.3 Pest Control Services

A termite control service engages in a deceptive practice when it fails to live up to its promise to prevent termite infestation.[2200] It is deceptive to misrepresent that there is termite infestation, or to use scare tactics to sell a termite prevention service.[2201] A termite service engages in a deceptive practice when it fails to disclose in a report the full extent of a termite problem it knows to exist.[2202] It is deceptive and unconscionable to disclose that the pest control service is guaranteed, while at the same time limiting the warranty so drastically that the guarantee is illusory.[2203]

The FTC has also ruled it unfair for an exterminating company to promise annual inspections at a fixed annual fee that would never increase, and then raise the prices of those annual inspections.[2204] The FTC also has accepted consent orders from firms selling ultrasonic pest control devices.[2205]

2188 American Aluminum Corp., 84 F.T.C. 48 (1974), *aff'd*, 522 F.2d 1278 (5th Cir. 1975), *cert. denied*, 426 U.S. 906 (1976); Certified Building Products, 83 F.T.C. 1004 (1973), *aff'd sub nom.* Thiret v. FTC, 512 F.2d 176 (10th Cir. 1975).

2189 *See* National Consumer Law Center, Truth in Lending Ch. 6 (5th ed. 2003 and Supp.).

2190 15 U.S.C. §§ 1602(aa), 1639.

2191 *Id. See* National Consumer Law Center, Truth in Lending Ch. 9 (5th ed. 2003 and Supp.).

2192 *See* Union Mortgage Co. v. Barlow, 595 So. 2d 1335 (Ala. 1992) ($6 million in punitive damages). It has also been reported that a jury in July, 1991 in Barbour County, Alabama, awarded five families $9 million each in a similar case against Union Mortgage. A May, 1992 Barbour county jury awarded $2.1 million in the case of Holiday v. Chrysler Fin. Servs.

2193 Pope v. Rollins Protective Servs. Co., 703 F.2d 197 (5th Cir. 1983) ($150,000 damages for pain and suffering resulting from burglary trebled under UDAP statute); *see also* Gill v. Rollins Protective Servs. Co., 836 F.2d 194 (4th Cir. 1987) (Virginia law); FTC v. GPT Marketing, Inc., 5 Trade Reg. Rep. (CCH) ¶ 22,808 (N.D. Tex. 1990) (preliminary injunction); Rollins, Inc. v. Heller, 454 So. 2d 580 (Fla. Dist. Ct. App. 1984).

2194 Figgie Int'l, Inc., 107 F.T.C. 313 (1986).

2195 Descent Control, Inc., 105 F.T.C. 280 (1985).

2196 Puritan-Bennett Areo Sys. Co., 110 F.T.C. 86 (1987) (consent order).

2197 Aquanatics Corp., 3 Trade Reg. Rep. (CCH) ¶ 22,411 (F.T.C. Dkt. C-3207 1987) (consent order).

2198 State v. The Emergency Response People, Clearinghouse No. 50,413 (Ark. Ch. Ct. Pulaski Cty. Dec. 22, 1993) (consent order).

2199 *Id.*

2200 Orkin Exterminating Co. v. Lesassier, 688 S.W.2d 651 (Tex. App. 1985); Hill & Hill Exterminators v. McKnight, 678 S.W.2d 515 (Tex. App. 1984) (but homeowners entitled to no relief because of failure to prove when termite problems arose), *aff'd*, 689 S.W.2d 206 (Tex. 1985). *But see* Clarken v. Orkin Exterminating Co., 761 F.2d 189 (4th Cir. 1985) (South Carolina law) (incompetence does not make termite extermination deceptive).

2201 Bandura v. Orkin Exterminating Co., 664 F. Supp. 1218 (N.D. Ill. 1987), *aff'd*, 865 F.2d 816 (7th Cir. 1988) (Illinois law).

2202 Warren v. LeMay, 142 Ill. App. 3d 550, 491 N.E.2d 464 (1986).

2203 State *ex rel.* Celebrezze v. Ferraro, 63 Ohio App. 3d 168, 578 N.E.2d 492 (1989).

2204 Orkin Exterminating Co., 108 F.T.C. 263 (1986), *aff'd*, 849 F.2d 1354 (11th Cir. 1988), *cert. denied*, 484 U.S. 865 (1989); *see also* State *ex rel.* Guste v. Orkin Exterminating Co., 528 So. 2d 198 (La. Ct. App. 1988). *See generally* § 5.2.5.2, *supra*.

2205 Saga Int'l, Inc., 108 F.T.C. 62 (1986) (consent order); Wein Products, Inc., 106 F.T.C. 51 (1985) (consent order); Sentronic Controls Corp., 105 F.T.C. 197 (1984) (consent order).

5.6.4 Household Goods Movers

Whether a UDAP approach is viable against household goods moving companies depends on whether the claim is preempted by federal transportation law. The Carmack amendment preempts many state claims against interstate freight carriers.[2206] UDAP claims may be viable, however, for transportation that does not cross a state line.

If a UDAP claim is preempted, federal transportation laws create a private cause of action in a number of circumstances.[2207] Federal regulations set substantive standards for the transportation of household goods in interstate or foreign commerce.[2208]

5.6.5 Water Quality Improvement Systems

As concerns about the safety of drinking water increase, especially after natural disasters or news stories about water contaminants, law enforcement, state and local agencies and consumer advocates should be concerned about deceptive schemes concerning home water filtration and treatment systems.[2209]

Delaware has a law that specifically addresses residential water treatment sales scams.[2210] It may provide a useful catalog of deceptive acts in other states as well. The purpose of the act is to "safeguard the public against deceit and misrepresentation and to ensure, foster and encourage truthful practices and disclosures in the door-to-door sale of residential water treatment systems."[2211] The act makes a distinction between health-related tests for contaminants (regulated by the U.S. Environmental Protection Agency or the Delaware Office of Drinking Water) and aesthetic tests of water which are not related to health.[2212] The act requires all health-related tests to be performed by a state certified laboratory that is not affiliated with the seller of the home treatment system.[2213] Performance or display of precipitation tests or heavy metal tests, frequently used in water treatment scams, is unlawful.[2214]

The act[2215] makes it an unlawful practice for door-to-door sellers of residential water treatment systems:

- To fail to display an identification badge;
- To fail to furnish a written disclosure to each buyer listing the name, address and phone number of the seller and salesperson;
- To perform or display during a visit to the buyer's home a precipitation test or heavy metals test;
- To fail to furnish a document for in-home aesthetic tests that conspicuously discloses the test results and that aesthetic tests are related to matters of personal taste, not health;
- To fail to use a certified laboratory for health-related tests, and
- To fail to furnish a copy of any report from a certified laboratory that pertains to the buyer's home.

The FTC has accepted a number of consent orders dealing with countertop water distillers,[2216] other home water-purification devices,[2217] and the use of unreliable tests that allegedly showed that the consumer's water was contaminated.[2218] The FTC has also affirmed an administrative law judge's findings that a company advertised that its product would make tap water clean when the company knew the product actually added a potentially hazardous chemical, a suspected carcinogen, to the water.[2219]

2206 49 U.S.C. § 14706 (formerly 49 U.S.C. § 20). *See* § 2.5.5, *supra*.

2207 49 U.S.C. §§ 14704–14706.

2208 49 C.F.R. Part 375.

2209 See, e.g., Ashley Cook, City officials warn citizens of possible water scam, Lufkin Daily News/Cox News, Feb. 27, 2004; Health Department warns of filter scam, Ark. Democrat Gazette, Aug. 16, 2003; Police probing possible water treatment firm scam, Palm Beach Post, July 4, 2002; Nancy Paradis, Home water tests prove costly, St. Petersburg Times, May 5, 2002; Jenifer Ragland, The Region 3 on Trial in Scam Aimed at Latinos, L.A. Times, Aug. 9, 2001.

2210 Delaware Residential Water Treatment System Sales Act, Del. Code tit. 6, § 2501B.

2211 Del. Code tit. 6, § 2502B.

2212 Del. Code tit. 6, §§ 2503B(a), (e), 2504B(3) and 2505B.

2213 Del. Code tit. 6, §§ 2503B(c), 2504B(3) and 2505B(a).

2214 Del. Code tit. 6, § 2504B(3). For an example of the misuse of these tests see, People v. Saenz, 2003 WL 1489274 (Cal. App. Mar. 25, 2003) (buyer told home water tests showed that there were feces, dead animals and other contaminants in her tap water and that diseases from the water had killed children).

2215 Del. Code tit. 6, §§ 2504B–2505B.

2216 FTC v. C&L Indus., Inc., 5 Trade Reg. Rep. (CCH) ¶ 23,198 (N.D. Tex. 1992) (consent judgment); FTC v. GPT Marketing, Inc., 5 Trade Reg. Rep. (CCH) ¶ 22,808 (N.D. Tex. 1990) (preliminary injunction); FTC v. U.S. Consumer Products, Inc., 5 Trade Reg. Rep. (CCH) ¶ 22,950 (S.D. Fla. 1990) (stipulated order for permanent injunction) (misrepresentation that water purifier registered with the EPA); Associated Mills, Inc., 111 F.T.C. 623 (1989) (consent order); New Medical Techniques, Inc., 110 F.T.C. 125 (1987) (consent order); *see also* FTC v. U.S. Consumer Promotions, 5 Trade Reg. Rep. (CCH) ¶ 22,711 (S.D. Fla. July 29, 1989) (temporary restraining order) (misrepresentations concerning water purifiers' performance, EPA approval, company's return policies, and warranty).

2217 FTC v. Water Resources Int'l, Inc., 5 Trade Reg. Rep. (CCH) ¶ 23,886 (C.D. Cal. 1995) (proposed consent decree); *see also* Hazelhurst v. Brita Products Co., 295 A.D.2d 240, 744 N.Y.S.2d 31 (2002) (appellate court decertifies class in suit alleging misrepresentations about water filters because showing of injury would require individual determinations and reliance on alleged misrepresentations varied among individuals).

2218 *Id.*

2219 North Am. Philips Corp., 111 F.T.C. 139 (1988).

5.6.6 Radon Testing

Radon testing carries the potential for scare tactics, misrepresentation of the accuracy, results, and implications of tests, and exaggeration of the qualifications of the technician performing the test. The general principles applicable to home improvement contracts are applicable to radon testing as well.[2220] The Illinois UDAP statute includes specific requirements for radon testing. The statute prohibits misrepresenting the capabilities of a device for detecting or measuring radon, or the results of a test.[2221] Many other states have non-UDAP statutes regulating radon testing, and courts are likely to find that a violation is a *per se* UDAP violation.[2222] The FTC has successfully challenged false claims made by a radon removal service.[2223]

5.6.7 Energy Savings Claims

The FTC has enacted a Trade Regulation Rule on Labeling and Advertising of Home Insulation,[2224] requiring the testing and disclosure of R-values, a standard measure of insulating effectiveness, and related information concerning home insulation products. It is unfair or deceptive to misrepresent the energy efficiency of insulating materials or to misrepresent that a material is an effective insulator.[2225]

The FTC revises its Appliance Labeling Rule periodically on the basis of updated information from the Department of Energy.[2226] The Appliance Labeling Rule, as required by the Energy Policy and Conservation Act,[2227] requires the disclosure of energy efficiency, consumption, or cost information on labels and retail sales catalogs for eight categories of appliances, including air conditioners, furnaces and water heaters.[2228] The Eleventh Circuit applied a five-year statute of limitations to a suit seeking a civil fine for alleged violations of efficiency standards for a heating and air conditioning system under that statute.[2229]

Similarly prohibited are deceptive energy-saving claims for aluminum siding,[2230] misrepresentations that insulation is nonflammable or nontoxic,[2231] and misrepresentations as to the extent to which various devices conserve fuel.[2232] Also deceptive are representations that a consumer's purchase will qualify the consumer for state energy tax credits, unless the seller discloses limitations on the availability of these credits.[2233]

FTC consent agreements have also dealt with deceptive energy savings and performance claims for quartz heaters,[2234] light bulbs,[2235] "transient voltage surge suppressors,"[2236] and solar furnaces.[2237] State cases have prohibited

2220 *See* § 5.6.1, *supra.*

2221 815 Ill. Comp. Stat. Ann. §§ 505/2U, 505/2V, 505/2W.

2222 *See* § 3.2.7, *supra.*

2223 Ion Sys., Inc., 5 Trade Reg. Rep. (CCH) ¶ 23,386 (F.T.C. Dkt. C-3451) (consent order).

2224 16 C.F.R. Part 460. *See* 45 Fed. Reg. 54,702 (1980); 45 Fed. Reg. 68,920 (1980); 45 Fed. Reg. 68,927 (1980); 44 Fed. Reg. 50,218 (1979). *See also* United States v. Channell Home Centers, 5 Trade Reg. Rep. (CCH) ¶ 23,318 (E.D. Va. 1993) (consent order).

2225 Certified Building Products Inc., *aff'd sub nom.* Thiret v. FTC, 512 F.2d 176 (10th Cir. 1975); Kryton Coatings Int'l, Inc., Dkt. C-4052, www.ftc.gov/os/2002/06/krytondo.htm (June 14, 2002) (consent order); Heatcool Inc., 101 F.T.C. 24 (1983) (consent order) (storm windows); Plaskolite, Inc., 101 F.T.C. 344 (1983) (consent order) (storm windows); Owens-Corning Fiberglass Corp., 88 F.T.C. 465 (1976) (consent order); Denny Corp., 66 F.T.C. 573 (1964); Insul-Seal Products Inc., 66 F.T.C. (1964).

2226 67 Fed. Reg. 39269 (June 7, 2002).

2227 42 U.S.C. § 6201.

2228 16 C.F.R. Part 305.

2229 Trawinski v. United Technologies, 313 F.3d 1295 (11th Cir. 2002).

2230 Mastic Corp., 99 F.T.C. 405 (1982) (consent order); Vinyl Improvement Products Co., 99 F.T.C. 415 (1982) (consent order); American Co. of Am., 93 F.T.C. 743 (1976) (consent order).

2231 Kettle Moraine Electric Inc., Trade Reg. Rep. (CCH) ¶ 21,658 (F.T.C. Docket No. C-3016 (1980)) (consent order); Brelike Enterprises, 89 F.T.C. 77 (1977) (consent order); Rapperswill Corp., 89 F.T.C. 71 (1977) (consent order).

2232 FTC v. Amerdream Corp., 5 Trade Reg. Rep. (CCH) ¶ 23,234 (D. Ariz. 1992) (stipulated final judgment); Sun Co., 115 F.T.C. 560 (1992) (consent order) (forbidding representations regarding superiority of ultra octane gasoline without substantiation); Haverhills, Inc., 114 F.T.C. 17 (1991) (consent order) (claims regarding fuel economy produced by "Fuel Magnetizer"); Cliffdale Assocs., 103 F.T.C. 110 (1984); TK-7 Corp., 5 Trade Reg. Rep. (CCH) ¶ 22,948 (F.T.C. Dkt. 9224 1991) (consent order); Nutronics Corp., 113 F.T.C. 97 (1990); Electronic Sys. Int'l, Inc., 108 F.T.C. 148 (1986) (consent order); Electro Tech Mfg., Inc., 108 F.T.C. 6 (1986) (consent order); National Energy Assoc., 107 F.T.C. 39 (1986) (consent order); John Trendwell, 106 F.T.C. 163 (1985); California-Texas Oil Co., 104 F.T.C. 268 (1984) (consent order); Cynex Mfg. Corp., 3 Trade Reg. Rep. (CCH) ¶ 22,152 (F.T.C. File No. 8223122, May 18, 1984) (consent order); Ball-Matic Corp., 98 F.T.C. 836 (1981) (consent order); Great N. Am. Indus. Inc., 98 F.T.C. 817 (1981) (consent order); Mobil Oil Corp., 97 F.T.C. 129 (1981) (consent order); Mid-City Chevrolet, Inc., 95 F.T.C. 371 (1980) (consent order); Intermatic Inc., 93 F.T.C. 537 (1979) (consent order); Admarketing Inc., 94 F.T.C. 664 (1979) (consent order); American Consumer Inc., 94 F.T.C. 648 (1979) (consent order); C.I. Energy Dev. Inc., 94 F.T.C. 1337 (1979) (consent order); Leroy Gordon Cooper, Jr., 94 F.T.C. 674 (1979) (consent order); R.R. Int'l Inc., 94 F.T.C. 1312 (1979) (consent order); Albano Enterprises, 89 F.T.C. 523 (1977) (consent order).

2233 Winton v. Johnson & Dix Fuel Corp., 515 A.2d 371 (Vt. 1986).

2234 Boekamp Inc., 97 F.T.C. 291 (1981) (consent order); Energy Efficient Sys. Inc., 97 F.T.C. 265 (1981) (consent order).

2235 Osran Sylvania, Inc., 5 Trade Reg. Rep. (CCH) ¶ 23,448 (F.T.C. C-3471 1994) (consent order); General Electric Co., 5 Trade Reg. Rep. (CCH) ¶ 23,279 (F.T.C. Dkt. C-3414 1993) (consent order).

2236 FTC v. Solar Sales, Inc., 5 Trade Reg. Rep. (CCH) ¶ 23,322 (S.D. Fla. 1993) (consent decree).

2237 Solar Am., Inc., 3 Trade Reg. Rep. (CCH) ¶ 22,520 (F.T.C. File #852 3014 1988) (consent order); Solar Age Indus., 109 F.T.C. 23 (1987) (consent order); Champion Home Builders Co., 101 F.T.C. 316 (1983) (consent order).

false claims as to the effectiveness of solar hot water heaters[2238] and devices to conserve home electricity usage.[2239] It may also be deceptive to fail to disclose air conditioners' and heating pumps' capacity and efficiency.[2240]

Ohio UDAP regulations require disclosures regarding home insulation similar to those required by the FTC rule.[2241] A company that violated the regulation was held liable for $69,000 in treble damages.[2242] Maine has enacted another UDAP regulation requiring a health and safety warning for formaldehyde foam insulation, disclosing that the insulation is not recommended for specified uses.[2243]

5.6.8 Unregulated Heating Fuel and Gasoline

5.6.8.1 Problems Facing Users of Oil, Propane, Kerosene, and Wood

Practitioners often encounter clients with home heating problems. State law, public utility commission regulations and constitutional due process requirements will offer some protection to users of natural gas or electric heat.[2244] But there is little or no regulation of the sale of such heating fuels as oil, propane, kerosene, and wood. At the same time, many consumers of unregulated fuels—such as mobile home residents, those living in rural areas, and tenants in older northeastern housing—strongly need legal protection. Practitioners may find state UDAP statutes their only remedy to deal with abuses in the sale of these unregulated fuels.

Users of oil, propane, kerosene, and wood may encounter various problems with fuel dealers' minimum purchase requirements and credit terms:

- High minimum purchase requirements, forcing consumers to pay for more fuel than they can store;
- Nondisclosure of minimum purchase requirements;
- Requirements that consumers rent large, expensive tanks from fuel suppliers;
- Removal of the regulator from tanks when consumers are delinquent in payments, preventing consumers not only from using fuel unpaid for, but also fuel already purchased;
- Removal of rented tanks when customers are delinquent in payments;
- Refusal to sell new fuel even on a cash basis when a consumer is delinquent in making payments;
- Cash prepayment requirements, even in emergencies, and even when large minimum use requirements make this impossible for many users;
- Arbitrary discrimination in deciding which customers to treat on a cash versus credit basis;
- Fuel suppliers' refusal to make emergency repairs on heating systems when consumers are delinquent in their fuel bills; and
- Fuel suppliers suddenly terminating their service of making emergency repairs.

Other major problems involve billing practices, misrepresentation of the quantity or nature of the product being sold, and service problems. Unscrupulous dealer practices include the following:

- False guarantees of fixed prices;[2245]
- Unauthorized price increases;
- Failure to honor the quoted price;
- Undisclosed fees (e.g., under-utilization fee, pump-out fee, tank removal fee, termination fee, environmental fee, hazardous materials fee);
- Lowering the BTU content of propane, by diluting it with air;
- Not disclosing that the kerosene being sold is low quality and that it will be dangerous to use with certain kerosene heaters;
- Selling a "cord" of wood that is not a standard measured cord;
- Selling soft wood as hard wood;
- Selling unseasoned wood as seasoned wood;
- Failure to deliver fuel under a pre-paid contract; and
- Failure to refund for fuel pumped out of the tank at the end of service.

Another problem is that mobile home parks sometimes require tenants in mobile home parks to purchase their fuel from the park owner, often on extremely unfavorable terms.[2246] During times of petroleum shortages, prices for gasoline and oil can skyrocket to rates that are unaffordable for many consumers.

2238 State *ex rel.* Corbin v. United Energy Corp., 151 Ariz. 45, 725 P.2d 752 (Ct. App. 1986); Rosa v. Johnson, 651 P.2d 1228 (Haw. Ct. App. 1982).

2239 State *ex rel.* McLeod v. Whiteside, Clearinghouse No. 38,907 (S.C. C.P. 1981).

2240 *See* Fedders Corp. v. FTC, 529 F.2d 1398 (2d Cir. 1976).

2241 Ohio Admin. Code § 109:4-3-14.

2242 Green v. USA Energy Consultants, 1986 Ohio App. LEXIS 8309 (Sept. 18, 1986).

2243 Code Me. Rules § 26-239 ch. 102, Dept. of Att'y Gen., Trade practices in the Sale of Urea Formaldehyde Foam Insulation.

2244 *See generally* National Consumer Law Center, Access to Utility Service (3d ed. 2004). *See also* § 5.6.9, *infra*.

2245 Mick v. Level Propane Gases, Inc., 168 F. Supp. 2d 804 (S.D. Ohio 2001) (issuing preliminary injunction); People v. Wilco, 284 A.D.2d 469, 728 N.Y.S.2d 471 (N.Y. App. Div. 2001).

2246 *See* § 5.5.1.2, *supra*.

5.6.8.2 Applicability of the UDAP Statute

Because of the lack of alternative regulation of any of these potential sales abuses, a state's UDAP statute is the obvious place for a practitioner to turn. The UDAP statute's general applicability will give the practitioner at least an opportunity to show that these practices are deceptive or unfair. Scope questions will not usually be a problem, nor will there likely be an issue as to whether any state regulation preempts the UDAP statute, since these fuels are largely unregulated.

In Ohio, an intermediate appellate court held that a propane dealer fell within the UDAP statute's exemption for natural gas companies.[2247] Three years later, however, the state supreme court, interpreting the same statutory language, held that a propane dealer was not a natural gas company,[2248] so the earlier decision should have no precedential value. Indeed, soon after the state supreme court's decision a federal court in Ohio issued an injunction under the UDAP statute against a propane supplier.[2249] Since scope issues are unlikely, the significant issue in a UDAP challenge to these heating fuel sales practices is whether the consumer's attorney can provide enough facts to show that the particular conduct is deceptive, unfair, or unconscionable.

5.6.8.3 UDAP Case Law

There is very little UDAP case law in this area. In *Mick v. Level Propane*,[2250] the district court, in deciding whether to grant injunctive relief to customers of propane company found that the customers had demonstrated substantial likelihood that the companies' practices were either deceptive or unconscionable.[2251] The plaintiffs had presented evidence that they were overcharged; had difficulty receiving propane services due to good faith billing disputes; relied on guarantees on price to their detriment; were not given any notice that the company would not honor their guaranteed prices or that the low price was contingent on the company securing low price supply contracts; and were not notified that there was a time limit for use of pre-purchased propane.[2252]

One not very favorable case is *McFoy v. Amerigas, Inc.*[2253] The lower court[2254] had granted summary judgment to the consumer class, ruling that it was deceptive for a propane dealer to assess a minimum charge where this was only disclosed in the service application as "the schedule of rates and minimum usage requirements applicable hereunder shall be those prevailing at the time of the sale within the price territory established by the company in which the installation is located." The lower court also found abusive the seller's practice of pulling regulators from fuel tanks with little or no notice, depriving customers of gas they had already purchased. For example, one customer owed only $20 but lost use of a tank 40% full. The lower court reasoned "the nature of the business involved magnifies the potential for abuse with regulator pulling. Gas for heat is conceivably a matter of life and death in the winter. There is much more at stake than mere inconvenience as when your car or stereo is repossessed."

The West Virginia Supreme Court reversed the summary judgment in favor of the consumers, ruling that it was a jury question whether the minimum usage charge had been reasonably disclosed. Factual issues also prevented summary judgment on the issue of pulling the gas regulator because the consumer had told the fuel dealer to stop all future service. Nevertheless, the court did indicate it may be unfair to prevent a customer from using gas already purchased.

5.6.8.4 UDAP Regulations

More helpful for consumer attorneys may be a number of states' UDAP regulations. Vermont amended its UDAP statute to require the attorney general to adopt propane (liquefied petroleum) gas UDAP regulations dealing with notice prior to disconnection, repayment agreements, minimum delivery, discrimination, security deposits and the assessment of fees and charges.[2255] The Vermont Attorney General has issued regulations complying with this legislative mandate.[2256] For example, these rules make it an unfair and deceptive trade practice for a propane company to disconnect in certain circumstances where propane is the primary source of heat or there is an imminent and serious health hazard or to disconnect before offering the consumer the opportunity to enter into a reasonable payment plan.[2257] Propane companies must provide written notice of disconnection, are restricted as to when they can disconnect, and must be able to reconnect within 24 hours.[2258] The rules also cover minimum deliveries, cash payments, security deposits and refunds, delivery fees, credit practices, third party payments and discrimination.[2259]

2247 Haning v. Rutland Furniture, 115 Ohio App. 3d 61, 684 N.E.2d 713 (1996).

2248 Haning v. Public Utilities Commission of Ohio, 86 Ohio St. 3d 121, 712 N.E.2d 707 (1999) (issue was whether PUC's jurisdiction extends to propane dealers).

2249 Mick v. Level Propane Gases, Inc., 168 F. Supp. 2d 804 (S.D. Ohio 2001).

2250 168 F. Supp. 2d 804 (2001).

2251 *Id.* at 813.

2252 *Id.*

2253 295 S.E.2d 16 (W. Va. 1982).

2254 Civ. Act. No 78-C-658 (W. Va. Cir. Ct. 1980).

2255 Vt. Stat. Ann. tit. 9, § 2461(b).

2256 Vt. Code R. 06 031 011.

2257 Vt. Code R. 06 031 011 Rule CF 111.03.

2258 Vt. Code R. 06 031 011 Rule CF 111.04-.08.

2259 Vt. Code R. 06 031 011 Rule CF 111.09-.14.

Maine's unfair trade practices regulations on the "Sale of Residential Heating Oil" apply to residential home heating oil sales from October 15 through April 30 each year. Dealers must sell fuel within their service areas to anyone who pays cash even if the consumer has not paid for a previous delivery, or is not an established customer. Similarly, fuel must be delivered if a government community action agency guarantees payment. A dealer may not unfairly discriminate among its customers concerning requests for immediate service, unscheduled deliveries of twenty gallons or more, or charge more than five dollars extra for small deliveries. Surcharges for unscheduled deliveries may only equal the dealer's actual additional costs. The dealer may not violate federal and state credit discrimination statutes. The dealer must deliver oil at the quoted price unless the dealer has specifically stated that the price is determined on the day of delivery or that the price on delivery may be higher than the quoted price.[2260]

Connecticut regulations cover the sale of home heating oil, propane, kerosene, coal, wood, and other residential heating fuels. Sellers must sell their products within a seller's delivery area to all cash buyers, irrespective of the buyer's credit history or lack of history with the seller. The sale must be on the same terms as other cash buyers. Nor can sellers enter into arrangements with property owners that would result in that owner's tenants having to purchase products from the seller.[2261]

These regulations show that state UDAP regulations can be an effective way of preventing unregulated fuel sales abuses. Once rules have been issued, a consumer can just allege a rule violation rather than try to convince a court as a matter of first impression that a particular practice is unfair or deceptive.

5.6.8.5 Price Gouging on Petroleum Products

The Connecticut, Massachusetts and Iowa Attorneys General have enacted UDAP regulations[2262] pursuant to their statutory authority to prevent "unfair or deceptive acts or practices"[2263] that prohibit "unconscionably excessive" prices for petroleum products (including home heating oil and propane) or utilities during market disruptions or disasters. "Unconscionably excessive" is defined as prices substantially higher than petroleum prices immediately prior to the onset of the market disruption, unless the increase is justified by higher costs.

A New York statute prohibits unconscionably excessive prices during market disruptions. The New York statute applies this prohibition not just to petroleum products, but to any "consumer goods and services vital and necessary for the health, safety and welfare of consumers."[2264] The New York statute has survived constitutional challenge[2265] and has been successfully applied to the sale of electric generators following a hurricane, where the generators were priced generally 5% to 30% above retail, with a few sales 60% above retail.[2266]

Several other states have statutes that expressly prohibit unconscionably excessive prices for petroleum products and fuel during an declared state of emergency or disaster.[2267] Other states have statutes that prohibit price-gouging during emergencies or disasters that cover essential goods and services.[2268]

5.6.8.6 UDAP Principles Applicable to the Sale of Unregulated Fuels

Even when there is no UDAP case law right on point, established UDAP principles should apply to unregulated fuel sales abuses. The failure to disclose is certainly deceptive.[2269] Consequently, a practice may be deceptive just because the dealer springs it on the customer as a surprise, such as the minimum usage requirement in *McFoy v. Amerigas*.[2270]

Similarly, cases dealing with adulterating propane, selling unsafe kerosene, or short-quantities for wood may be handled like cases that deal with misrepresentations of other products' quantity, quality, safety composition, and characteristics.[2271] Precedent dealing with deceptive debt collection practices or misrepresentations as to price and credit terms may also be applicable to related unregulated fuel abuses.[2272]

2260 Code Me. R. 26-239 ch. 100.

2261 Conn. Agencies Regs. § 42-110b-31.

2262 Conn. Agencies Regs. § 42-110b-29; Mass. Regs. Code tit. 940, § 3.18; Iowa Admin. Code r. 61-31.1(714). *Cf.* Mo. Code Regs. Ann. tit. 15, § 60-8.030 (charging an excessive price for a "necessity" within a disaster area is an unfair practice).

2263 *See* Conn. Gen. Stat. § 42-110a; Mass. Gen. Laws ch. 93A; Iowa Code § 714.16(2)a.

2264 N.Y. Gen. Bus. Law § 396-r.

2265 People v. Two Wheel Corp., 128 A.D.2d 507, 512 N.Y.S.2d 439 (1987), *aff'd on other grounds* 71 N.Y.2d 693, 530 N.Y.S.2d 46, 525 N.E.2d 692 (1988) (statute not overly vague). *Cf.* State v. Strong Oil Co., 87 A.D. 374, 451 N.Y.S.2d 437 (1982) (Federal Emergency Petroleum Allocation Act, 15 U.S.C. § 751 [since rescinded] preempts application of New York statute to petroleum prices). *See* § 4.3.11, *supra*.

2266 People v. Two Wheel Corp., 71 N.Y.2d 693, 530 N.Y.S.2d 46, 525 N.E.2d 692 (1988). *See also* Vacco v. Chazy Hardware, Inc., 176 Misc. 2d 960, 675 N.Y.S.2d 770 (1998) (markups on generators rose 59% to 93% after power outages from an ice storm are unconscionably excessive).

2267 *See, e.g.*, Ark. Code Ann. § 4-88-303; Cal. Penal Code § 396; Fla. Stat. § 501.160; Ind. Code § 4-6-9.1; S.C. Code Ann. § 39-5-145; Tex. Bus. & Comm. Code § 17.46(27); Va. Code § 59.1-525 *et seq.*; W. Va. Code § 46a-6J-3. *See generally* § 4.3.11, *supra*.

2268 La. Rev. Stat. Ann. § 29:732; Tenn. Code Ann. § 47-18-5101.

2269 *See* § 4.2.14, *supra*.

2270 170 W. Va. 526, 295 S.E.2d 16 (1982) (reasonableness of notice at issue).

2271 *See* §§ 4.6.1, 4.6.3, 4.6.4, 4.6.5, *supra*.

2272 *See, e.g.*, People v. Wilco Energy Corp., 284 A.D.2d 469, 728

Perhaps most importantly, a practice can be unfair or deceptive even if it has never been challenged before.[2273] Thus look for any aspect of the sales transaction that has the capacity to deceive even if only the most gullible consumers would be deceived.

In states that prohibit unfair or unconscionable practices, the court may find a practice unfair if it causes substantial consumer injury, not outweighed by countervailing benefits, where the consumer could not reasonably be expected to avoid the injury.[2274] Take particular note of situations where a community has only one fuel dealer and the consumer has no real choice about selecting an alternative fuel supplier.

Where the consumer thus can not avoid the dealer's practices, courts in determining a practice's unfairness will have to balance consumer injury with countervailing business benefits. This is essentially a factual issue, and much will turn on the extent of the consumer injury and a showing that the fuel supplier will not be seriously harmed by an alternative means of doing business. A good demonstration that the consumer injury outweighs business benefits is if state law or public utility regulations prohibit the analogous practice for regulated fuels.

Finally, note that in many situations injunctive relief (including a temporary restraining order) may be the appropriate remedy, bringing the consumer quick relief during winter months, while not penalizing the merchant for past business practices. Courts may be more likely to tell a dealer to stop a previously unchallenged practice than to award money damages. UDAP injunctive relief is discussed in more detail in other sections.[2275]

5.6.9 Gas and Electric Service

5.6.9.1 Abuses Relating to Utility De-Regulation

5.6.9.1.1 Effects of deregulation on consumers

The recent trend to restructure the electric and gas industries appears to have lost its steam, in part due to the market manipulation debacle in California.[2276] In the states that have restructured, the distribution company that services the wires and gas pipeline entering the consumer's home is typically still regulated.[2277] Municipal utilities and rural electric cooperatives remain unregulated. In general, under the Federal Power Act,[2278] the Federal Energy Regulatory Commission (FERC) has "exclusive" authority to regulate the transmission and sale of electric energy in interstate commerce. Under the Natural Gas Act,[2279] the FERC has regulatory jurisdiction over wholesale transactions and the interstate pipelines. States exercise jurisdiction over retail sales of electricity and natural gas.

Retail competition under restructuring occurs when consumers can choose the company that furnishes the gas or electricity to their distribution company. In limited circumstances some customers have the ability to purchase power directly from a competitive supplier or marketer. These competitive sellers and marketers will, in many cases, be subject only to minimal licensure requirements and some consumer protection such as rules governing information disclosure and slamming.[2280] Deregulated long-distance telephone service has created a number of serious marketing abuses,[2281] and the same potential exists for the marketing of gas or electricity in a newly deregulated environment.[2282]

UDAP claims for wholesale energy market abuses have been thwarted by federal preemption and the filed rate doctrine. In a few very limited cases, UDAP claims for wholesale market abuses have successfully avoided being removed to federal court.[2283]

5.6.9.1.2 Retail energy market abuses

An example of retail marketing abuse is found in a federal court action concerning a company's offer of natural gas to owners of apartment buildings at significant discounts compared to prices provided by the local gas distribution companies (LDCs). Commercial customers are provided the option of either purchasing gas and gas distribution services from the LDC or purchasing the gas from another company and the distribution service from the LDC. In this federal action, the consumers alleged that the company promised prices cheaper than the LDC, but did not deliver on those promises.[2284]

N.Y.S.2d 471 (N.Y. App. Div. 2001) (deceptive to promise long-term fixed price for heating oil and then raise price); *cf.* McFoy v. Amerigas, Inc., 170 W. Va 526, 295 S.E.2d 16 (W. Va. 1982) (vendor's removal of regulators from tanks states valid claim of unlawful debt collection practices if it denies customers use of gas for which they already paid). *See* § 5.1, *supra.*

2273 *See* § 3.3.4.3, *supra.*

2274 *See* § 4.3.2, *supra.*

2275 *See* §§ 8.6, 10.7.1, *infra.*

2276 *See generally* National Consumer Law Center, Access to Utility Service (3d ed. 2004). The California Attorney General initiated over a dozen lawsuits against electricity wholesalers alleging unfair business prices. *See* California *ex rel.* Lockyer v. Mirant Corp., 2002 WL 1897669 (N.D. Cal. Aug. 6, 2002), *aff'd,* 375 F.3d 831 (9th Cir. 2004) for a summary of the lawsuits.

2277 *See* National Consumer Law Center, Access to Utility Service Ch. 1 (3d ed. 2004).

2278 16 U.S.C. § 824 *et seq.*

2279 15 U.S.C. § 717 *et seq.*

2280 *See* National Consumer Law Center, Access to Utility Service Ch. 1 (3d ed. 2004).

2281 *See* § 5.6.10, *infra.*

2282 See, e.g., Energy Company Sued for Deceptive Practices: Company Accused of "Slamming" and Door-to-Door Sales Violations, New York State Attorney General Press Release, April 19, 2002.

2283 *See* § 5.6.9.1.3, *infra.*

2284 Petri v. Gatlin, 997 F. Supp. 956 (N.D. Ill. 1997); *cf.* Mid-Atlantic Power Supply Ass'n v. Pennsylvania Public Utility

The court found that misrepresentations in marketing material concerning the price discounts available are UDAP violations.[2285] Claims of potential savings of 15% to 35% are not mere puffing, but are statements of fact, and are deceptive where there was never even a potential for such savings.[2286] In Pennsylvania, however, class certification was denied in a suit against an electric supplier for false advertising of the cost of electricity because the state's Unfair Trade Practices and Consumer Protection Law requires that each plaintiff must allege reliance on the false advertisements.[2287]

As consumers are given a choice of electric power providers, expect to see practices similar to slamming by long-distance telephone carriers, where consumers are switched without the consumer's permission.[2288] Illinois has already enacted a statute dealing with the problem.[2289]

Illinois's statute also deals with electric service advertising in a deregulated market,[2290] and billing and collection practices of providers of electricity to the distribution companies.[2291] The statutes also provide for enhanced penalties against the electric service provider if any of these statutes are violated and an elderly or disabled person is victimized.[2292]

5.6.9.1.3 Wholesale energy market abuses

The Ninth Circuit recently held that several lawsuits brought by the California Attorney General alleging UDAP violations by wholesale electricity suppliers were appropriately removed to federal court and that the UDAP claims were preempted by federal law.[2293] The state alleged that the energy producers fraudulently double-sold their reserve generation capacity (which they were paid under contract to hold in reserve) by selling that same reserve on the spot market. This limitation of supply destabilized the state's electricity grid which requires a balance of supply and demand and left the electricity system vulnerable to blackouts and other disruptions. In this case the Ninth Circuit found that the UDAP claims were basically an attempt to enforce FERC-filed tariffs which fall under the exclusive jurisdiction of the district court.[2294] The court also held that the UDAP claims were preempted by FERC's exclusive jurisdiction over the tariffs and barred by the filed rate doctrine.[2295]

There have been different outcomes in prior lower court cases where there was an independent state law basis for the UDAP claim and the state claim did not necessarily entail the application of federal law. In one case,[2296] the underlying UDAP claim against energy companies was based on alleged anticompetitive activities in violation of the state's antitrust laws. Electric consumers alleged that power marketers artificially inflated the wholesale and retail electricity prices in California by their anticompetitive activities in the energy market. The district court, in granting the consumers' motion to remand, held that the Federal Power Act did not completely preempt consumers' state law claims and the state law claims did not require interpretation or application of federal law.[2297] However, another court held that the filed

Commission, 755 A.2d 723 (Pa. Commw. Ct. 2000) (upholding PUC's jurisdiction under PA Customer Choice Act over company's deceptive marketing of provider of last resort service, and affirming order prohibiting further deceptive marketing practices).

2285 Petri v. Gatlin, 997 F. Supp. 956 (N.D. Ill. 1997); *cf.* Mid-Atlantic Power Supply Ass'n v. Pennsylvania Public Utility Commission, 755 A.2d 723 (Pa. Commw. Ct. 2000) (upholding PUC's jurisdiction under PA Customer Choice Act over company's deceptive marketing of provider of last resort service, and affirming order prohibiting further deceptive marketing practices).

2286 Petri v. Gatlin, 997 F. Supp. 956 (N.D. Ill. 1997).

2287 Aronson v. Greenmountain.com, 809 A.2d 399 (Pa. Super. 2002).

2288 As reported in *Texas Retail Electric Scorecard 2002 Year End Review*, by Regulatory Compliance Servs., in the first full year of electric competition in Texas, slamming complaints received by the Public Utility Commission of Texas rose from 145 in 2001 to 1441 in 2002 and cramming rose from 2 complaints to 355 in the same time period. *See* § 5.6.10.3, *infra* for a discussion of telephone long-distance carrier slamming.

2289 815 Ill. Comp. Stat. 505/2EE.

2290 815 Ill. Comp. Stat. 505/2GG.

2291 815 Ill. Comp. Stat. 505/2HH.

2292 815 Ill. Comp. Stat. 505/2FF.

2293 People of State of Cal. *ex rel.* Lockyer v. Dynagy, 375 F.3d 831 (9th Cir. 2004).

2294 *Id. See also* T & E Pastorino Nursery v. Duke Energy Trading and Marketing, 268 F. Supp. 2d 1240 (S.D. Cal. 2003) (federal courts have exclusive jurisdiction of claims, that while premised as UDAP violations, are founded to some degree on conduct governed by FERC-filed tariffs) and T & E Pastorino Nursery v. Duke Energy Trading and Marketing, 2003 WL 22110491 (S.D. Cal. Aug. 27, 2003)) (court dismisses UDAP case because claims alleging companies overcharged for wholesale electricity through gaming of the power market is both field and conflict preempted by the Fed. Power Act and claims are also barred by the filed rate doctrine); *In re* California Wholesale Electricity Antitrust Litigation, 244 F. Supp. 2d 1072 (S.D. Cal. 2003) (filed rate doctrine precluded antitrust and UDAP suit because it would involve review of FERC-filed rates and federal field preemption of wholesale electricity pricing).

2295 For more discussion of the filed rate doctrine, see § 5.6.10.1, *infra*.

2296 Hendricks v. Dynegy Power Marketing, Inc., 160 F. Supp. 2d 1155 (S.D. Cal. 2001).

2297 160 F. Supp. 2d 1155 (S.D. Cal. 2001). *See also In re* California Retail Natural Gas and Electricity Antitrust Litig., 170 F. Supp. 2d 1052 (D. Nev. 2001) (remanding cases against energy providers to state court; no Federal Power Act and Natural Gas Policy Act do not preempt Cal. antitrust and UDAP statutes; federal tariffs did not regulate conduct at issue (conspiring to inflate energy prices on spot market); Natural Gas Anti-Trust Cases, 2002 WL 31570296 (Cal. Super. Oct. 16, 2002) (taking judicial notice that California UDAP claims based on violations of the state's antitrust laws were not barred by the Supremacy

rate doctrine precluded state antitrust and UDAP actions because they would involve review of FERC-filed rates.[2298]

5.6.9.2 Illegal Shut-Offs

Increasingly, UDAP remedies are being used where a gas or electric utility illegally shuts off a client's utility service.[2299] (For more detail on this subject, see NCLC's *Access to Utility Service* (3d ed. 2004).) Re-connecting a client's utility service does not fully remedy the illegal shutoff. While the service is shut off, the consumer invariably suffers various injuries—food spoilage, frozen pipes, lost use of the housing unit, the cost of alternative housing, pain and suffering. Since state utility commissions usually do not redress these injuries, a private tort action may be the best approach.[2300]

Practitioners should consider adding to their tort claim a UDAP count.[2301] Unlike a tort claim, UDAP recoveries in most states include an attorney fee award and may provide minimum statutory damages, even if actual damages can not be proven. Since the tort and UDAP claims will also have different standards—breach of a duty of care, compared with unfair or deceptive practices—pleading two different theories increases the chances of recovery on at least one.[2302]

There are two important reasons why unlawful shutoffs should always be pleaded not only as UDAP violations, but also as torts. Most UDAP statutes will not authorize punitive damages, while the tort claim will, where there is reckless disregard of societal interests. UDAP statutes often will authorize treble damages, and a court reluctant to award large punitive damages may award UDAP treble damages. Nevertheless, even in those situations, it is best to give the court a choice between awarding large punitive damages or treble damages.

The second reason for including the tort claim is that the court may find the practice outside the UDAP statute's scope, while tort claims will have few limitations on their scope.[2303] Certain UDAP statutes specifically exempt utilities or practices regulated by state agencies, and questions arise as to whether a UDAP statute can be used against a *public* utility.[2304] More detailed discussion of UDAP statutes' applicability to utility cases is found in earlier sections.[2305]

5.6.10 Telephone, Telecommunications, and Internet Services

5.6.10.1 The Filed Rate Doctrine

5.6.10.1.1 Described

The "filed rate doctrine" bars suits against regulated utilities that seek to vary the terms of the applicable tariff.[2306] Claims that a utility's rates and terms are unreasonable, wherever such rates have been "approved" through the filing of tariffs with federal or state regulatory authorities, have been barred by this doctrine.[2307] Thus, challenges to the rates charged by providers of telephone and other utility services will not be successful where those rates have been filed in tariffs with regulatory authorities.[2308] Even

Clause nor the filed rate doctrine and state antitrust laws and the state antitrust and unfair competition causes of action do not conflict with federal law).

2298 *In re* California Wholesale Electricity Antitrust Litigation, 244 F. Supp. 2d 1072 (S.D. Cal. 2003).

2299 Bailey v. Gulf States Utils. Co., 27 S.W.3d 713 (Tex. App. 2000) (electricity is a product in a Tex. Deceptive Trade Practices Act analysis); *see also* Stanley v. Moore, 339 N.C. 717, 454 S.E.2d 225 (1995) (landlord subject to treble damages under state UDAP for severing electric wires and shutting off water supply).

2300 *See* National Consumer Law Center, Access to Utility Service (3d ed. 2004) for a full discussion of utility shut-off issues.

2301 Stanley v. Moore, 339 N.C. 717, 454 S.E.2d 225 (1995) ("party may plead alternative theories of recovery based on the same conduct or transaction and then make an election of remedies"). *See* National Consumer Law Center, Access to Utility Service (3d ed. 2004) for a full discussion of UDAP statutes' application to utility shutoffs.

2302 *Cf.* Gulf States Utilities Co. v. Low, 79 S.W.3d 561 (Tex. 2002) (no damages for mental anguish under the state's Deceptive Trade Practices Act for termination of resident's electricity service because there was no finding that the utility knowingly engaged in unconscionable conduct; actual damages for food spoilage under the DTPA reversed because no evidence of the food's value was provided, but $12,000 in damages allowed under a negligence theory).

2303 *See, e.g.*, Gulf States Utilities Co. v. Low, 79 S.W.3d 561 (Tex. 2002) (state supreme court allows recovery for wrongful termination under negligence cause of action instead of UDAP).

2304 *See, e.g.*, Canterbury v. Columbia Gas of Ohio, 2001 WL 1681132 (S.D. Ohio 2001) (utility's disconnection of service to collect a time-barred debt not subject to UDAP statute because provision of natural gas is excluded from definition of "consumer transaction"). *But see* Andrade v. Johnson, 345 S.C. 216, 546 S.E.2d 665 (2001) (utility commission's rate increase order which merely mentioned the program at issue but did not provide any regulatory control over the programs creation or implementation did not exempt utility under the UDAP act), *rev'd on other grounds*, 356 S.C. 238, 588 S.E.2d 588 (2003).

2305 §§ 2.3.2, 2.3.3, 2.3.5, 2.3.6, *supra*.

2306 AT&T Corp. v. Central Office Tel. Inc., 524 U.S. 214 (1998); Adamson v. Worldcom Communications, Inc., 190 Or. App. 215, 78 P.3d 577 (2003).

2307 *See* Square D Co. v. Niagara Frontier Tariff Bureau, 476 U.S. 409, 106 S. Ct. 1922, 90 L. Ed. 2d 413 (1986); Arkansas Louisiana Gas Co. v. Hall, 453 U.S. 571, 101 S. Ct. 2925, 69 L. Ed. 2d 856 (1981); Keogh v. Chicago & Northwestern Railway Co., 260 U.S. 156, 43 S. Ct. 47, 67 L. Ed. 2d 183 (1922). *See also* § 2.5.6, *supra*.

2308 *See* AT&T Corp. v. Central Office Tel. Inc., 524 U.S. 214 (1998) (filed rate doctrine bars the judicial challenge to the validity of a filed tariff); Wegoland, Ltd. v. NYNEX Corp., 27 F.3d 17 (2d Cir. 1994); H.J., Inc. v. Northwestern Bell Tel. Co., 954 F.2d 485 (8th Cir. 1992); Young Soon Oh v. AT&T Corp., 76 F. Supp. 2d 551 (D.N.J. 1999) (challenges to approved rates are barred;

claims that regulators have been defrauded in the rate setting process will not be permitted.[2309]

Pursuant to the filed rate doctrine, claims against providers of telephone services have been unsuccessful, whether based on UDAP, false advertising or common law fraud theories, where consumers have alleged that telephone rates were either misrepresented to them directly, or were misrepresented in advertisements.[2310] As long as the customer was charged the filed rate, which is deemed to be reasonable *per se*, courts will find that the customer suffered no damages as a result of any allegedly wrongful conduct by the provider of telephone services.[2311]

Cases have survived the filed rate doctrine where the claims have not sought to vary the terms of the tariff. A California case avoided the filed rate doctrine in a challenge to a utility company's inclusion of a charge in its filed rates for upgrading its equipment which is located at the consumer's home or business. The utility subsequently scaled back the equipment upgrade, but continued to charge the higher rates. The court allowed UDAP claims to proceed, reasoning that the suit was not a challenge to the rates themselves but to the company's failure to deliver the services for which it had charged.[2312] The filed rate doctrine may also be inapplicable to claims for injunctive relief.[2313]

5.6.10.1.2 Telephone services not covered by the doctrine

The Federal Communications Commission (FCC) required interstate long-distance providers to "detariff" by July 31, 2001,[2314] meaning that rates and conditions will be

court declines to decide whether UDAP claim seeking to enforce tariff is barred); Hardy v. Claircom Communications Group, Inc., 88 Wash. App. 488, 937 P.2d 1128 (1997); Concord Assoc. v. Public Serv. Commission of State of NY, 301 A.D.2d 828, 754 N.Y.S.2d 93 (App. Div. 3d Dept. 2003) (filed rate doctrine bars challenge to water rates); *cf.* CenturyTel of Midwest-Kendall, Inc. v. Public Serv. Commission, 257 Wis. 2d 837, 653 N.W.2d 130 (Wis. App. 2002) (utility that raised rates without a hearing and commission approval violated the state's filed rate statute and consumers were entitled to a refund). *See also* § 5.6.9, *infra* for challenges to natural gas and electric rates.

2309 Wegoland, Ltd. v. NYNEX Corp., 27 F.3d 17 (2d Cir. 1994); Hardy v. Clairdom Communications Group, Inc., 88 Wash. App. 488, 937 P.2d 1128 (Wash. Ct. App. 1997). *See also* N.C. Steel, Inc. v. National Council on Compensation Ins., 347 N.C. 627, 496 S.E.2d 369 (1998) (context of insurance rates).

2310 *See* Evanns v. AT&T Corp., 229 F.3d 837 (9th Cir. 2000) (challenge to company's characterization of the universal service fund charge barred by the filed rate doctrine because it was beyond the company's obligation to customer set out in the filed tariff); Cahnmann v. Sprint Corp., 133 F.3d 484 (7th Cir. 1998) (barring UDAP claim that alleged that carrier promised special rates but did not provide them); Marco Supply Co. v. AT&T Communications, Inc., 875 F.2d 434 (4th Cir. 1989); *In re* Universal Serv. Fund Tel. Billing Practices Litigation, 300 F. Supp. 2d 1107 (D. Kan. 2003) (pre-detariffing UDAP claim regarding misrepresentation of universal service charge barred by the filed rate doctrine); Trodent Dev. Corp. v. MCI Worldcom Communications, Inc., 2002 WL 531358 (N.D. Ill. Apr. 9, 2002); Stein v. Sprint Corp., 22 F. Supp. 2d 1210 (D. Kan. 1998) (because of filed rate doctrine, plaintiff can not have relied on advertisements regarding rates, so UDAP claim is dismissed); Katz v. MCI Telecommunications Corp., 14 F. Supp. 2d 271 (E.D.N.Y. 1998) (filed rate doctrine precludes claim that telephone company misrepresented its rates); Marcus v. AT&T Corp., 938 F. Supp. 1158 (S.D.N.Y. 1996), *aff'd*, 138 F.3d 46 (2d Cir. 1998) (filed rate doctrine bars fraud claim and precludes UDAP damages); Guglielmo v. Worldcom, Inc., 148 N.H. 309, 808 A.2d 65 (2002); Weinberg v. Sprint Corp., 173 N.J. 233, 801 A.2d 281 (2002) (doctrine bars damages on UDAP or contract claims that seek to enforce a rate other than the filed rate); Valdez v. State, 132 N.M. 667, 54 P.3d 71 (2002); Doyle v. AT&T, 304 A.D.2d 521, 760 N.Y.S.2d 503 (App. Div. 2003); Porr v. Nynex Corp., 230 A.D.2d 564, 660 N.Y.S.2d 440 (App. Div. 1997); Hardy v. Claircom Communications Group, Inc., 86 Wash. App. 488, 937 P.2d 1128 (1997). *But cf.* Atilano v. Zero Plus Dialing, Inc., 2002 WL 185455 (N.D. Ill. Feb. 4, 2002) (filed rate doctrine does not bar claim regarding deception in inducing plaintiff to accept collect calls, which does not relate to rates).

2311 *See* Transportation Data Interchange v. AT&T Corp., 920 F. Supp. 86 (D. Md. 1996); Gugliemo v. Worldcom, 148 N.H. 309, 808 A.2d 65 (2002) (antitrust and consumer protection act claims brought by recipients of interstate collect calls from inmates was barred by the filed rate doctrine); Weinberg v. Sprint Corp., 173 N.J. 233, 801 A.2d 281 (2002) (filed rate doctrine barred challenge to phone company's practice of rounding-up to the nearest minute in calculation of charge); Valdez v. State of New Mexico, 132 N.M. 667, 54 P.3d 71 (2002) (claims by recipients of collect calls from inmates challenging high rates was barred by the filed rate doctrine and primary jurisdiction doctrine along with other grounds).

2312 Wise v. Pacific Gas & Electric Co., 77 Cal. App. 4th 287, 91 Cal. Rptr. 2d 479 (1999). *See also* Brown v. MCI Worldcom Network Servs., Inc., 277 F.3d 1166 (9th Cir. 2002) (suit to enforce an existing tariff is not barred by the filed rate doctrine); Atilano v. Zero Plus Dialing, 2002 WL 185455 (N.D. Ill. Feb. 1, 2002) (filed rate doctrine was not a bar to a claim alleging phone company operators fraudulently induced customers to accept international calls by falsely claiming the calls were from relatives or other known individuals); Adamson v. Worldcom, Inc., 190 Or. App. 215 (2003) (filed rate doctrine not a bar to a claim that company willfully misled customer about having long-distance service).

2313 Guglielmo v. Worldcom, Inc., 148 N.H. 309, 808 A.2d 65 (2002); Weinberg v. Sprint Corp., 173 N.J. 233, 801 A.2d 281 (2002) (denying injunctive relief on other grounds). *See also* Valdez v. State, 132 N.M. 667, 54 P.3d 71 (2002) (suggesting that injunctive relief is not barred, but denying it on other grounds). *Cf.* Hill v. Bellsouth Telecom, Inc., 364 F.3d 1308 (11th Cir. 2004) (UDAP claim seeking only monetary relief, if successful, would result in customer getting a discounted rate contra the tariff and would be a retroactive determination that the filed rates were unreasonable).

2314 47 U.S.C. § 160 (forbearance authority granted in § 10 of the Telecommunications Act of 1996). *See* Policy and Rules Concerning the Interstate, Interexchange Marketplace, Implementatino of 254(g) of the Communications Act of 1934, 61 Fed. Reg. 59340, 59352 (Nov. 22, 1996), for a discussion of the statutory authority for detariffing.

set by contract with the consumer and no longer by a tariff submitted to a utility regulator. Because of this change, the filed rate doctrine will no longer protect long-distance companies.[2315]

The FCC stated that in the absence of tariffs, consumers would "not only have our complaint process, but will also be able to pursue remedies under state consumer protection and contract laws."[2316] A recent Ninth Circuit case, *Ting v. AT&T,* rejected the industry's argument that the Federal Communications Act as amended in 1996 preempts state consumer protection and contract law.[2317] The Ninth Circuit affirmed a lower court's finding that a long-distance company's customer service contract that prohibited class actions and required arbitration was unconscionable under state law. However, a Seventh Circuit case (which was criticized in *Ting*) held that the Federal Communications Act preempts state law challenges regarding the unconscionability of an arbitration clause in a long-distance phone service contract.[2318]

The long-distance companies' practice of recouping universal service fund contributions has also been challenged in several lawsuits. Suits alleging long-distance companies misrepresented their practice of recouping universal service fund contributions were allowed to proceed in state court.[2319]

Cellular telephone service providers have never been required to file their rates with the FCC, so can not claim the shield of the filed rate doctrine.[2320] A reseller of telephone services through pre-paid calling cards is also not protected by the doctrine.[2321] Nevertheless, the doctrine is relevant for long-distance practices before a company detariffed and for other telephone services subject to a tariff.

Even where filed tariffs are not a bar to a UDAP claim, another potential barrier is the question whether the FCC or a state public utility commission has exclusive jurisdiction over the issue. The FCC unbundled the sale of telephone equipment from telephone service in the 1980s and this segment of the market is unregulated, and as a result the FCC does not regulate equipment sale practices. Consequently, in an action against Lucent and AT&T concerning the sale of equipment with residential phone service, the court allowed a UDAP claim to proceed despite claims that the matter was more properly brought before the FCC.[2322] Recently, a state appellate court held that the state utility commission did not have exclusive jurisdiction over UDAP claims against a competitive local phone company alleging excessive charges.[2323]

5.6.10.2 Marketing and Billing for Telecommunications Services

The FCC and the FTC have issued a joint policy statement on deceptive advertising for long-distance telephone service.[2324] Among other things, this policy statement requires all claims to be truthful, non-misleading and substantiated; all costs to be disclosed, including per-call charges, monthly fees, and universal service charges; and all disclosures to be clear and conspicuous without distractions.[2325]

2315 *But cf.* Trodent Dev. Corp. v. MCI Worldcom Communications, Inc., 2002 WL 531358 (N.D. Ill. Apr. 9, 2002) (filed rate doctrine applied where contract was signed while tariff was in effect, even though detariffing occurred during contract term).

2316 FCC, Second Report and Order, 11 F.C.C.R. 20,730 at ¶ 42.

2317 Ting v. AT&T, 319 F.3d 1126 (9th Cir. 2003). *See also In re* Universal Serv. Fund Tel. Billing Practices Litigation, 300 F. Supp. 2d 1107 (D. Kan. 2003) (Federal Communications Act preempts plaintiffs' challenge to the terms of the contract as substantively unconscionable, but not their procedural unconscionability challenge involving the manner of contract formation).

2318 Boomer v. AT&T, 309 F.3d 404 (7th Cir. 2002).

2319 *In re* Universal Serv. Fund Tel. Billing Practices Litigation, 300 F. Supp. 2d 1107 (D. Kan. 2003) (post-detariffing Kan. UDAP claim alleging misrepresentation of universal service fund charges not barred by the filed rate doctrine and not preempted by Federal Communications Act).

2320 Tenore v. AT&T Wireless Servs., 136 Wash. 2d 322, 962 P.2d 104 (1998) (also rejecting arguments that plaintiffs' claims of deceptive advertising are preempted by the Federal Communications Act and that the FCC has primary jurisdiction); *see also* Gilmore v. Southwestern Bell Mobile Sys., 210 F.R.D. 212 (N.D. Ill. 2001) (declining to refer complaint regarding cellular phone service to FCC under primary jurisdiction doctrine; federal court can also hear plaintiff's contract and fraud-type claims), *dismissed without prejudice*, 224 F. Supp. 2d 1172 (N.D. Ill. 2002) (dismissing claim without prejudice and referring it to FCC under primary jurisdiction doctrine after complaint amended to challenged the reasonableness of the rate); Union Ink Co. v. AT&T Corp., 352 N.J. Super. 617, 801 A.2d 361 (App. Div. 2002). Note that, even if the filed rate doctrine is inapplicable, preemption issues may protect wireless carriers from some UDAP suits. Naevus Int'l, Inc. v. AT&T Corp., 185 Misc. 2d 655, 713 N.Y.S.2d 642 (Sup. Ct. 2000) (complaint that wireless service quality is poor is an attack on rates so is preempted under 47 U.S.C. § 322, but UDAP and fraud claims relating to unlawful acts and false advertising are not), *modified in part on other grounds and aff'd*, 283 A.D.2d 171, 724 N.Y.S.2d 721 (2001).

2321 Smith v. SBC Communications Inc., 178 N.J. 265, 839 A.2d 850 (2004).

2322 *See, e.g.*, Qwest v. Kelly, 204 Ariz. 25, 59 P.3d 789 (2002) (residential tenants' suit against phone company for selling inside wire maintenance service through fraudulent and deceptive practices and misrepresentations of fact was not barred by the filed rate doctrine and did not fall within the state utility commission's exclusive jurisdiction); Cundiff v. GTE California, Inc., 101 Cal. App. 4th 1395 (2002); Crain v. Lucent Technologies, 317 Ill. App. 3d 486, 739 N.E.2d 639 (2000).

2323 Wernikoff v. RCN Telecom Servs. of Illinois, Inc., 341 Ill. App. 3d 89, 791 N.E.2d 1195 (2003).

2324 *In the Matter of* Joint FCC/FTC Policy Statement for Advertising of Dial-Around and Other Long-Distance Servs. to Consumers, File No. 00-EB-TCD-1(PS) (Mar. 1, 2000), available on the FCC's website at www.fcc.gov/Bureaus/Miscellaneous/News_Releases/2000/nrmc0009.html.

2325 FCC Press Release, *FCC Proposes $1,000,000 in total fines against two carriers for deceptive marketing practices*, April 2,

Time limits on advertised rates, e.g., that they are available only between 7:00 P.M. and 7:00 A.M., must be clearly and conspicuously disclosed. Making information about limitations available only by calling a toll-free telephone number or visiting a website is insufficient. Providers must have a reasonable basis and must use recent data for comparative price claims. While this statement is not enforceable as a regulation, it should be very persuasive to courts or agencies interpreting statutes and regulations that prohibit unfair or deceptive practices.

The National Association of State Utility Consumer Advocates (NASUCA) petitioned the Federal Communications Commission for a declaratory ruling that long-distance and wireless companies' practice of over-recovering their operating costs through misleading line-item charges on consumer phone bills is unreasonable, unjust and unlawful. In addition to other relief, NASUCA is seeking to have the FCC prohibit carriers from imposing surcharges or line-item fees unless they are mandated by federal, state, or local law and the amount of the charge conforms to the amount expressly authorized.[2326]

A Wisconsin statute prohibits misrepresentations in the marketing of telecommunications service and regulates billing and collection practices.[2327] Wisconsin UDAP rules[2328] adopted pursuant to this statute require disclosures about services and prices, restrict price increases without twenty-five to ninety days advance notice, prohibit negative-option billing,[2329] limit automatic renewal clauses, require free cancellation of service at the consumer's request, restrict prize promotions, and prohibit various misrepresentations.

In a recent state supreme court case, purchasers of prepaid calling cards were allowed to proceed with their consumer fraud and breach of contract claims against the retailer of the cards for false advertisement of the rates.[2330] A local phone company recently settled a class action suit alleging the company misled customers who purchased voice mail service by failing to disclose that, in addition to the monthly fee there was a per-message charge of five cents.[2331]

2001 (two long-distance companies failed to disclose that the advertised cents-per-minute rate was limited to a two-month promotional period and that the regular rate was actually double the promotional rate).

2326 *In the Matter of* Truth-In-Billing and Billing Format, NASUCA's Petition For Declaratory Ruling Regarding Monthly Line Items And Surcharges Imposed By Telecom Carriers, CC Dkt No. 98-170, March 30 2004. *See also* 69 Fed. Reg. 33021, June 14, 2004 (FCC's notice for comments on NASUCA's petition).

2327 Wis. Stat. Ann. § 100.207.

2328 Wis. Admin. Code ch. ATCP 123.

2329 *See* § 5.8.5, *infra* for further discussion of negative option billing.

2330 Smith v. SBC Communications Inc, 178 N.J. 265, 839 A.2d 850 (2004).

2331 SBC to Give Voice Mail Customers Compensation for Misleading Marketing Under Class Action Settlement Negotiated by CUB—Group, Dow Jones Newswires, Wall Street Journal, March 26, 2004.

Consumers were unsuccessful in their attempt to have the state utility commission adjudicate claims that a local phone company had violated the state's unfair practices act and false advertising act in the marketing of optional phone services.[2332] The California Public Utilities Commission had found that certain phone company's practices were unlawful but declined to hear the claims based on the state's unfair competition law and the court of appeals ruled that the Commission had no jurisdiction over the unfair practices act and false advertising act claims.[2333]

5.6.10.3 Slamming (Changing Long-Distance Carriers without the Consumer's Authorization)

A common problem is "slamming," the practice of changing a customer's long-distance carrier without the customer's consent. In a 2004 study, the FTC estimated that there had been over 17 million incidents of slamming in a one-year period.[2334]

The Telecommunications Act of 1996 requires the FCC to establish verification protocols, so that a company can determine whether a consumer's request to switch carriers is bona fide.[2335] The FCC in 1998 adopted new rules intended to eradicate the financial incentive for slamming.[2336] The new rules generally absolve consumers of all slammed charges for thirty days after an unauthorized change.[2337] The

2332 Greenlining Institute v. Public Utilities Commission, 103 Cal. App. 4th 1324 (2002).

2333 *Id.*

2334 Consumer Fraud in the United States: An FTC Survey at 32 (2004).

2335 47 U.S.C. § 258(a); Telecommunications Act of 1996, Pub. L. No. 104-104, 110 Stat. 56 (1996).

2336 47 C.F.R. § 64.1100 *et seq.*; Third Order on Reconsideration and Second Further Notice of Proposed Rule Making, 18 F.C.C. Rcd. 5099 (2003); Order, F.C.C. 03-116, (rel. May 23, 2003); First Order on Reconsideration, 15 F.C.C. Rcd. 8158 (2000), *stay lifted*, MCI Worldcom v. FCC, No 99-1125 (D.C. Cir. June 27, 2000); Third Report and Order and Second Order on Reconsideration, 15 F.C.C. Rcd. 15996 (2000), Order F.C.C. 01-67 (rel. Feb. 22, 2001); *In the Matter of* Implementation of the Subscriber Carrier Selection Change Provisions of the Telecommunications Act of 1996, CC Docket No. 94-129; Second Report & Order & Further Notice of Proposed Rulemaking (Dec. 17, 1998), stayed in part, MCI WorldCom v. FCC, No. 99-1125 (D.C. Cir. May 18, 1999).

2337 47 C.F.R. §§ 64.1140, 64.1160. This rule applies so long as the consumer has not yet paid the unauthorized carrier; where the consumer has paid the unauthorized carrier, the unauthorized carrier must pay 150% of the charges to the authorized carrier and then the authorized carrier must refund or credit 50% of the charges paid by the consumer. 47 C.F.R. §§ 64.1140, 64.1170. An authorized carrier must also reinstate the consumer in any premium program in which the consumer was previously enrolled, and restore any premiums the consumer lost due to the slamming if a consumer has paid the unauthorized carrier for the slamming charges. 47 C.F.R. § 64.1170. The FCC has also eliminated as a verification option the "welcome package": the

new rules also tighten up the procedures by which a consumer's request to switch carriers must be verified, and extend those verification requirements to all telecommunication carriers.[2338] A company that submits or executes an unauthorized switch is liable to the displaced carrier in the amount of 150% all charges paid to the new carrier by the consumer.[2339] A district court in Connecticut concluded that consumers have a private cause of action under this statute.[2340] Some states have also adopted statutes or regulations that deal with slamming.[2341]

The New York Attorney General's issuance of subpoenas to investigate fraudulent sale of long-distance service in a "slamming" scheme was upheld.[2342] The carrier allegedly sent consumers promotional checks containing fine print offers of service, and construed cashing the check as authorization to substitute itself as the consumer's long-distance carrier.

5.6.10.4 Prepaid Phone Cards

Another growing area of telephone abuse involves prepaid telephone cards. For example, the FTC has negotiated a consent decree with a prepaid telephone card company that targeted the Indian-American community by fraudulently promising low calling rates to India, but either never issued the calling cards or issued cards that did not function properly.[2343] Recently, the Supreme Court of New Jersey allowed a class action suit alleging UDAP violations against pre-paid calling card retailers for deceptive advertising of the rates to move forward.[2344] The court held that the filed rate doctrine was not an absolute bar to the consumer fraud and breach of contract claims. The court also noted that the facts of the case suggest that the retailer and the consumer entered into a contractual relationship for the prepaid phone card services that was completely separate from the terms offered under the filed tariff.

5.6.10.5 Unauthorized Charges

This subsection examines the UDAP implications of a telephone company's insistence on collection of unauthorized charges. Section 5.9.3, *infra*, reviews the related topics of pay-per-call or 900-number services, and the practice of "cramming" or submitting to a consumer's telephone bill charges that are only marginally related to telephone service.

It is a deceptive practice for a company to represent that telephone subscribers are legally obligated to pay for bills irrespective of whether they used or authorized use of the calls.[2345] It is even deceptive for a company to bill the subscriber, without further representation, where it knows there is a good chance the person initiating the call was not authorized to make the call.[2346]

Where a tariff and the filed rate doctrine does not apply to telephone services, then there is no legal basis to require that subscribers to a phone line pay for services they neither used nor authorized.[2347] To even charge such services to the line subscriber instead of the actual user is an unfair practice.[2348]

5.6.10.6 Inside Wiring Maintenance Contracts and Phone Rental

A UDAP case has challenged a telephone company's sales techniques for its inside wiring maintenance contracts. The court rejected the telephone company's motion to dismiss, finding it could be a UDAP violation for the telephone company not to disclose that the maintenance contract is not regulated by the utility commission, that the customer can hire another company to repair inside wires, that the customer may not be responsible for repairing inside wires, and that inside wires only have to be repaired about every

enclosure of a postcard that states that if the consumer does not return it service will be switched. 47 C.F.R. § 64.1130(g). The FCC also felt that consumers should not have to suffer an "affirmative burden," therefore all verifications must be one of: a written or electronically signed authorization from the consumer that meets the regulation's requirements, an electronic verification via a toll-free number used exclusively for confirming orders, or an independent third party verification. 47 C.F.R. §§ 64.1120, 64.1130. *See also* National Consumer Law Center, Access to Utility Service (3d ed. 2004).

2338 47 C.F.R. § 1120. *But see* AT&T Corp. v. FCC, 323 F.3d 1081 (D.C. Cir. 2003) (FCC exceeded its statutory authority by requiring that carrier not only comply with verification procedures but also have actual consumer authorization, which amounts to a requirement that carrier guarantee that each switch of carriers is authorized).

2339 47 U.S.C. § 258; 47 C.F.R. §§ 64.1140, 64.1170.

2340 Valdes v. Qwest Communications Int'l, 147 F. Supp. 2d 116 (D. Conn. 2001).

2341 *See, e.g.*, Idaho Code § 48-603D; 220 Ill. Comp. Stat. 5/13-902; 815 Ill. Comp. Stat. § 505/2DD; *see also* Sapp v. AT&T, 215 F. Supp. 2d 1273 (M.D. Ala. 2002) (remanding a slamming case to state court and finding the complete preemption and filed rate doctrines inapplicable); Doty v. Frontier Communications Inc., 272 Kan 880, 36 P.3d 250 (2001) (upholding and applying Kansas anti-slamming law).

2342 Oncor Communications v. State of New York, 218 A.D.2d 60, 636 N.Y.S.2d 176 (1996).

2343 FTC v. Trans-Asian Communications, Inc., 5 Trade Reg. Rep. (CCH) ¶ 24,403 (S.D.N.Y. 1998) (proposed consent decree).

2344 Smith v. SBC Communications Inc., 178 N.J. 265, 839 A.2d 850 (2004).

2345 FTC v. Ty Anderson, Inc., 5 Trade Reg. Rep. (CCH) ¶ 15147 (W.D. Wash. Aug. 21, 2001); FTC v. Verity Int'l, Ltd., 124 F. Supp. 2d 193 (S.D.N.Y. 2000).

2346 FTC v. Verity Int'l, Ltd., 124 F. Supp. 2d 193 (S.D.N.Y. 2000). *See also* Drizin v. Sprint Corp., 3 A.D.3d 388, 771 N.Y.S.2d 82 (2004) (complaint alleging long-distance companies' practice of misleading callers into using their toll-free long-distance service by replicating a competitor's toll-free long-distance calling service except for one digit ("fat fingers") supports a NY UDAP cause of action).

2347 FTC v. Verity Int'l, Ltd., 124 F. Supp. 2d 193 (S.D.N.Y. 2000).

2348 *Id.*

fourteen years. Additionally, misleading new customers into thinking they were receiving an unbiased, objective assessment of their telephone needs was a potential UDAP violation.[2349] Since UDAP claims are within a trial court's jurisdiction and evaluation of deceptive sales techniques does not require the specialized expertise of the public utility commission, the exhaustion of remedies rule and the primary jurisdiction doctrine should not prevent a state court from hearing a UDAP challenge to sales techniques for inside wiring maintenance contracts.[2350]

Until 1984, residential phone service customers had to rent phones from the telephone company. With the detariffing of customer premises equipment, customers could choose to own their phones and some local phone companies stopped their phone rental service. Some customers did not return the company's phone and some phone companies, like GTE, continued the phone rental program. GTE listed a monthly charge on the phone bill called "equipment rental" with no accompanying description. Customers of GTE were billed hundreds of dollars or more for unreturned or unaccounted for phones through this charge. Many of these customers were senior citizens who had held on to their rotary phones that were now worth less than $20. In *Cundiff v. GTE California Inc.*,[2351] customers sued the phone company, alleging the "equipment rental" charge was false and misleading. The lower court had originally held that the state utility commission had exclusive jurisdiction to hear the case, but the appellate court disagreed. The appellate court noted that the state public utility code explicitly authorized courts to hear claims against utilities and that this case did not interfere with the commission's regulation of utilities.[2352] The appellate court also noted that the topic of deception, the alleged intentional or negligent misrepresentation of the "equipment rental" charge, was a subject over which the state utility commission would not have more expertise than a trial court and that the commission lacked the authority to grant relief under the consumer protection statutes.[2353]

5.6.10.7 Internet Service Providers

A growing body of UDAP law is developing regarding Internet service providers as in other fields of commerce. In one case, subscribers sued America Online (AOL) under UDAP and other theories because AOL failed to disclose connection and disconnection times, rounded up billing times, used misleading advertising regarding its hourly rate, unfairly calculated its service charge, improperly charged for downloading, delays, and time in "free areas," failed to refund charges after cancellation, and made unauthorized withdrawals from checking accounts.[2354] The FTC won a consent order, requiring disclosure of fees and refund of charges, against a company that advertised Internet access as free when actually the subscriber had to pay long-distance charges or $3.95 an hour for use of the company's 800 number.[2355] Another consent order requires disclosures and refunds by an Internet service provider that promoted a free trial period but failed to disclose its restrictive cancellation procedures.[2356] It also misrepresented its terms, its prices, and the reasons it sought consumers' credit card and identification information. The FTC has also proceeded against fraudulent sellers of domain names.[2357]

Another lawsuit, dismissed on technical grounds, alleged that when AOL instituted its flat-fee program, AOL's network overloaded. Despite this, AOL continued with a flurry of advertising to continue enrolling new subscribers for the already overloaded network.[2358]

A 2004 FTC study estimated that, over a one-year period, there were almost two million incidents of Internet service providers charging consumers for service they had not authorized.[2359] The FTC has proceeded against Internet service providers that used deceptive means to enroll new members.[2360] It has also charged a number of Internet

2349 Commonwealth *ex rel.* Zimmerman v. Bell Tel. Co., 121 Pa. Commw. 642, 551 A.2d 602 (1988).

2350 State *ex rel.* Bell Atlantic-WV v. Ranson, 201 W. Va 402, 497 S.E.2d 755 (1997). This case also gives a brief summary of the history of deregulation of inside wiring maintenance charges. *See also* Qwest v. Kelly, 204 Ariz. 25, 59 P.3d 789 (2002) (residential tenants' suit against phone company for selling inside wire maintenance service through fraudulent and deceptive practices and misrepresentations of fact was not barred by the filed rate doctrine and did not fall within the state utility commission's exclusive jurisdiction).

2351 101 Cal. App. 4th 1395 (2002).

2352 *Id.* at 1405–1409.

2353 *Id.* at 1413–1414.

2354 *See* Hagen v. America Online, Inc. No. 971047 (Cal. Super. Ct. Mar. 18, 1997), *referenced in* Howard v. America Online, Inc., 208 F.3d 741 (9th Cir. 2000). *See also* FTC v. New Millennium Concepts, Inc., 5 Trade Reg. Rep. (CCH) ¶ 15180 (N.D. Ill. Nov. 20, 2001) (company induced consumers to pay fee and give personal information in return for free monthly Internet service; proposed consent decree requires information to be destroyed and $481,172.05 judgment against principal); U.S. v. Netpliance, Inc., 5 Trade Reg. Rep. (CCH) ¶ 15125 (W.D. Tex. July 2, 2001) (proposed consent decree) (misrepresentation of feature of service, nondisclosure of its limitations, unauthorized billing).

2355 Gateway, Inc., Dkt. C-4015, www.ftc.gov/os/2001/06/gatewaydo.htm (June 22, 2001) (consent order); *see also* Juno Online Servs., Inc., Dkt. C-4016 www.ftc.gov/opa/2001/06/fyi0137.htm (June 29, 2001) (consent order).

2356 Juno Online Servs., Inc., Dkt. C-4016, www.ftc.gov/opa/2001/06/fyi0137.htm (June 29, 2001) (consent order).

2357 FTC v. 1268957 Ontario Inc., 5 Trade Reg. Rep. (CCH) ¶ 15249 (N.D. Ga. Mar. 29, 2002) (consent decree) (seller misrepresented that third party had applied for identical domain name).

2358 *See* Howard v. America Online, Inc., 208 F.3d 741 (9th Cir. 2000).

2359 FTC, Consumer Fraud in the United States: An FTC Survey (2004) at 32.

2360 FTC v. Cyberspace.com, 2002 WL 32060289 (W.D. Wash. July 10, 2002) (partial summary judgment against company that sent $3.50 rebate checks to small businesses and consumers, and treated cashing of check as consent to provision of Internet

service providers with misrepresenting the cost of service or restrictions on cancellation.[2361]

5.6.11 Water and Sewer Service

5.6.11.1 Overview

UDAP actions against regulated privately-owned utilities and municipally-owned utilities have encountered numerous barriers due to exemptions in state UDAP statutes, available adequate administrative remedies before the state utility commission or because non-profit municipal utilities are not found to be "in trade or commerce."[2362] Even so, there are limited areas where UDAP actions have been permitted against water utilities. UDAP actions involving water and sewer service have encountered greater success where the entity is an unregulated utility or non-utility.

5.6.11.2 Water and Sewer Service by a regulated utility or municipality

Some courts have allowed UDAP claims against water utilities to move forward in limited instances. In *Hartwell Corp. v. Superior Court*, the California Supreme Court allowed a UDAP claim where a regulated water utility provided contaminated water to consumers over a period of years. The court held that "damage claims based on the theory that the water failed to meet federal and state drinking water standards are not preempted [by a state law restricting the superior court's jurisdiction over PUC matters] . . . A jury award based on a finding that a public water utility violated DHS standards would not interfere with the PUC regulatory policy requiring water utility compliance with those standards."[2363] The court reasoned that there was no interference because while the PUC could redress violations of the law or its orders in a number of ways, those remedies are essentially prospective in nature and the PUC can not provide relief for past violations.[2364] Another court allowed a UDAP claim to move forward where the water utility had placed improper amounts of a treatment chemical in the water causing a gelatin-like substance which damaged hot water-systems.[2365]

Regulation of utility rates ("just and reasonable rates") falls squarely within a state utility commission's authority. Claims involving rates are thus more likely than other claims to be found exempt from state UDAP laws.[2366] UDAP actions involving the water and sewer rates of municipal utilities have also been unsuccessful where rates for nonresidents are higher than for residents.[2367]

5.6.11.3 Water Quality and Service Provided by Non-regulated Entities

Where water is supplied by a non-regulated entity, there should be little question that the UDAP statute applies. The California Supreme Court has held that a state restriction on the superior court's jurisdiction in matters interfering with state utility commission activity did not apply to non-regulated water providers. For even if the court returned findings on water safety issues involving non-regulated water providers that conflicted with the state utility commission on same or similar issues, the rulings would not interfere with the commission's official regulatory duties.[2368] The court also noted that, "unlike the regulated water providers, the PUC has no jurisdiction to hear complaints or claims against any nonregulated entities. If claims against nonregulated entities were preempted [by a state law restricting the superior court's jurisdiction over PUC matters], they could not be heard in any forum."[2369]

In another case,[2370] tenants successfully sued their landlord under a UDAP claim where the landlord failed to provide safe and potable water. The landlord had violated the state's consumer fraud act by renting a house supplied with water from a nearby spring contaminated with E. coli.

There have been successful UDAP claims against developers involving water and sewer issues. A developer was found liable for UDAP violations because he sold lots which did not comply with septic and well water system conditions in the land use permit resulting in residents having little or

service). *See also* FTC v. Automated Transaction Corp., 5 Trade Reg. Rep. (CCH) ¶ 15206 (S.D. Fla. Jan. 24, 2002) (bogus bills for Internet service); FTC v. Mercury Marketing, 2003 WL 23277324 (E.D. Pa Dec. 29, 2003) (company violated stipulated final judgment and order with FTC by continuing to mislead customers into receiving Internet services by failing to disclose that consumers would be billed on their phone bills unless they affirmatively notified the company of the rejection of service).

2361 Gateway, Inc., 5 Trade Reg. Rep. (CCH) ¶ 15103 (Dkt C-4015, June 22, 2001) (proposed consent order); Juno Online Servs., Inc., 5 Trade Reg. Rep. (CCH) ¶ 15104 (Dkt C-4016, June 25, 2001) (proposed consent order); U.S. v. Netpliance, Inc., 5 Trade Reg. Rep. (CCH) ¶ 15125 (W.D. Tex. June 2, 2001) (consent decree).

2362 See §§ 2.3.2, 2.3.6, *supra* for more discussion about challenges to brining a UDAP claim against a regulated utility or municipality. *See also* NCLC's Access to Utility Service (3d ed. 2004) for more information on regulated and unregulated utility practices.

2363 27 Cal. 4th 256, 276, 38 P.3d 1098 (2002).

2364 *Id.* at 277.

2365 Sternberg v. N.Y. Water Serv. Corp., 548 N.Y.S.2d 247 (A.D. 1989).

2366 For more discussion on how service quality issues have frequently been doomed by recasting as rates issues see § 5.6.10.1, *infra* (filed rate doctrine).

2367 *See, e.g.*, Calcaterra v. City of Columbia, 432 S.E.2d 498 (S.C. App. 1993).

2368 Hartwell Corp. v. Superior Ct, 27 Cal. 4th 256, 280–81, 38 P.3d 1098 (2002).

2369 *Id.* at 282.

2370 L'Esperance v. Benware, 830 A.2d 675 (Vt. 2003).

no water pressure, sewage effluent surfacing and stagnating and water wells contaminated with fecal waste.[2371] In another case, a developer violated the state's deceptive trade practices act by failing to correctly install homeowners' sewer line per plat.[2372]

There have also been UDAP cases against water treatment system designers and distributors of plumbing components. A UDAP claim survived a summary judgment motion in a suit alleging that distributors of galvanized plumbing parts that discharged lead into drinking water violated the state's law regulating discharge of carcinogens and teratogens into drinking water and thus violated the state's unfair competition law.[2373]

A recent attempt to argue that a failed waste water removal system violated the state's clean water act and thus violated the state's UDAP law was unsuccessful. An appellate court held that the state's unfair and deceptive trade practices act could not be used to create a private right of action for a violation of the state's clean water act.[2374] Homeowners had sued the designers of a waste removal system that had failed causing the homeowners to pay to connect to the city water and sewer system. The appellate court found the state's clean water act contained a provision to regulate the deceptive behavior at issue in this case, thus providing the exclusive remedy. The state's clean water act provided for enforcement through civil, criminal and injunctive relief, but did not create a private right of action.[2375]

5.7 Household Products

5.7.1 Encyclopedias and Magazines

It is deceptive for encyclopedia salespersons to conceal their status or misrepresent their purpose in contacting the consumer.[2376] It is deceptive to misrepresent that consumers will receive discounts because they are specially selected or if they assist in the encyclopedia's promotion[2377] or that consumers will receive "free merchandise."[2378] Other deceptive acts are misrepresentations as to the time period over which the books can be paid for or the size of installments,[2379] that books are sold under a federal grant for use in "Head Start," or that they will lead to a high school equivalency diploma.[2380] Sellers may not misrepresent the relationship between the publisher and the source of educational material[2381] and must disclose if a volume is abridged.[2382]

Magazine sellers must be authorized to sell the magazines they offer.[2383] Magazines ordered, and not substitutes, must be delivered within ninety days, and refunds must be provided if the magazine order can not be fulfilled.[2384] Misrepresentations as to savings, cost, value, service, contract, or the purpose of the seller's call are proscribed.[2385] Sellers may not mail magazines unsolicited, and then misrepresent that nonpayment will adversely affect the consumer's credit rating or that accounts will be referred to a debt collection agency.[2386] For other principles that apply to magazine and

2371 State of Vermont v. Therrien, 161 Vt. 26 633 A.2d 272 (1993), *aff'd*, 830 A.2d 28 (Vt. 2003) (attorney's liability for drafting deeds).

2372 Dizdar v. Moreno, 2003 WL 22478606 (Tex. App. Oct. 30, 2003) (unpublished, citation limited).

2373 Mateel Environmental Justice Foundation v. Edmund A. Gray Co., 115 Cal. App. 4th 8, 9 Cal. Rptr. 3d 486 (2003).

2374 Brinkman v. Barrett Kays & Assocs., 155 N.C. App. 738, 575 S.E.2d 40 (2003).

2375 *Id.* at 44–45.

2376 Dixie Reader's Serv., Inc., 80 F.T.C. 215 (1972) (consent order); Publix Circulation Serv., Inc., 80 F.T.C. 187 (1972) (consent order); Subscription Bureau Ltd., 80 F.T.C. 201 (1972) (consent order); Crowell-Collier Publishing Co., 70 F.T.C. 977 (1966); Basic Books, 56 F.T.C. 69 (1959), *aff'd*, 276 F.2d 718 (7th Cir. 1960); State *ex rel.* Spannus v. Mecca Enterprises, Inc., 262 N.W.2d 152 (Minn. 1978).

2377 Consumer Products of Am., Inc., 72 F.T.C. 533 (1967), *aff'd*, 400 F.2d 930 (1968), *cert. denied*, 393 U.S. 1088 (1969); Crowell-Collier Publishing Co., 70 F.T.C. 977 (1966); Basic Books, 56 F.T.C. 69 (1959), *aff'd*, 276 F.2d 718 (7th Cir. 1960); Americana Corp., 45 F.T.C. 32 (1948), *aff'd*, No. 21109 (2d Cir. 1950).

2378 Encyclopedia Brittanica, Inc., 87 F.T.C. 421 (1976), *aff'd*, 605 F.2d 964 (1978); Consumer Products of Am., Inc., 72 F.T.C. 533 (1967), *aff'd*, 400 F.2d 930 (1968), *cert. denied*, 393 U.S. 1088 (1969); The Crowell-Collier Publishing Co., 70 F.T.C. 977 (1966); Basic Books, 56 F.T.C. 69 (1959), *aff'd*, 276 F.2d 718 (7th Cir. 1960); Book of the Month Club, Inc., 48 F.T.C. 1297 (1952), *aff'd*, 202 F.2d 486 (1953).

2379 Standard Educ., Inc., 79 F.T.C. 858 (1971); Basic Books, 56 F.T.C. 69 (1959), *aff'd*, 276 F.2d 718 (7th Cir. 1960).

2380 Kugler v. Romain, 58 N.J. 522, 279 A.2d 640 (1971); Massachusetts Consumer Protection Regulations, Mass. Regs. Code tit. 940, § 3.14, Subscription and Mail Orders. *See also* Commonwealth v. Programmed Learning Sys., Inc., Clearinghouse No. 26,019 (Pa. C.P. Allegheny Cty. 1975).

2381 Frank Marks, 39 F.T.C. 171 (1944); Park, Austin & Lipscomb, 34 F.T.C. 59 (1942), *aff'd*, 142 F.2d 437 (1943), *cert. denied*, 323 U.S. 753 (1944); J. Herbert Blackhurst, 32 F.T.C. 574 (1941).

2382 Belmont Productions, Inc., 66 F.T.C. 600 (1964); Bantam Books, Inc., 55 F.T.C. 779 (1958), *aff'd*, 275 F.2d 680 (1960).

2383 La. Admin. Code tit. 26, pt. III, § 505, Magazine and Periodical Subscription Service Sale Practices.

2384 Brown v. Cole, Clearinghouse No. 27,057 (Ohio C.P. Richland Cty. 1976); Brown v. Wonderful World Publishing Co., Clearinghouse No. 27,055 (Ohio C.P. Franklin Cty. 1976); Brown v. Bredenbeck, 2 Ohio Op. 3d 286 (C.P. Franklin Cty. 1975); La. Admin. Code tit. 16, pt. III, § 505, Magazine and Periodical Subscription Service Sale Practices; *see also* FTC v. Rocky Mountain Circulation, 3 Trade Reg. Rep. (CCH) ¶ 22,479 (D. Colo. 1987) (consent order); People v. Lipsitz, 174 Misc. 2d 571, 663 N.Y.S.2d 468 (Sup. Ct. 1997) (failure to deliver promised magazines).

2385 La. Admin. Code tit. 16, pt. III, § 505, Magazine and Periodical Subscription Service Sale Practices; Massachusetts Consumer Protection Regulations, Mass. Regs. Code tit. 940, § 3.14, Subscription and Mail Orders.

2386 CBS Inc., 90 F.T.C. 9 (1977) (consent order). *See also* § 5.8.4, *infra*.

book sales, consult previous sections of this manual dealing with bait and switch,[2387] negative option plans[2388] (such as book-of-the-month clubs), mail order sales,[2389] telemarketing,[2390] and unsolicited merchandise.[2391]

5.7.2 Freezer Meats

Freezer meat plans involve purchase of discount meat through quantity purchases. Low advertised prices may be an illegal bait and switch scheme, such as when advertised meat is not available or when unappealing meat is shown to consumers who inquire as to the advertised meat.[2392] It is deceptive to misrepresent the quality of meat offered for sale, the available price savings, or the number of pounds of meat in a bundle offered for sale.[2393]

Several states have enacted regulations dealing with use of meat's true name, correct use of USDA grading terms, other representations as to food cut, grade, brand, origin, and measure, and disclosure when non-beef additives have been added and when meat has been frozen.[2394] Sellers must disclose if advertised weight is hanging weight subject to weight loss[2395] and if weight estimates are before trimming and cutting.[2396] Sellers can not substitute meat for that ordered.[2397]

2387 *See* § 4.6.1, *supra.*

2388 *See* § 5.8.5, *infra.*

2389 *See* § 5.8.1, *infra.*

2390 *See* § 5.9, *infra.*

2391 *See* § 5.8.4, *infra.*

2392 Nevada Meats, Inc., 84 F.T.C. 493 (consent order); Seekonk Freezer Meats, Inc., 82 F.T.C. 1025 (1973); Supreme Freezer Meats, Inc., 73 F.T.C. 990 (1968); State v. Quality Meats of Concord, Inc., Clearinghouse No. 44,812 (Alaska Super. Ct. Dec. 28, 1988) (preliminary injunction); New Jersey Administrative Rules of the Division of Consumer Affairs, N.J. Admin. Code ch. 13:45A, subch. 3, Sale of Meat at Retail (1976); Wisconsin Dep't of Agriculture, Trade and Consumer Protection Rules, Wis. Admin. Code ch. ATCP 109, Freezer Meat and Food Service Plan Trade Practices.

2393 Seekonk Freezer Meats, 82 F.T.C. 1025 (1973); State v. Middleton Beef Co., 84 A.D.2d 834, 444 N.Y.S.2d 184 (1981); *see also* Vasquez v. Superior Court (Karp), 4 Cal. 3d 800, 484 P.2d 964, 94 Cal. Rep. 796 (1977); Wisconsin Dep't of Agriculture, Trade and Consumer Protection Rules, Wis. Admin. Code ch. ATCP 109, Freezer Meat and Food Service Plan Trade Practices.

2394 New Jersey Administrative Rules of the Division of Consumer Affairs, N.J. Admin. Code ch. 13:45A, subch. 3, Sale of Meat at Retail (1976); Wisconsin Dep't of Agriculture, Trade and Consumer Protection Rules, Wis. Admin. Code ch. ATCP 109, Freezer Meat and Food Service Plan Trade Practices § 109.02. *See also* Anglo Cofone, 79 F.T.C. 334 (1971) (consent order).

2395 Seekonk Freezer Meats, 82 F.T.C. 1025 (1973); Brown v. Just-Good Meats, Inc., Clearinghouse No. 27,053 (Ohio C.P. Trumbull Cty. 1974), *aff'd on other grounds*, 1975 Ohio App. LEXIS 6872 (Feb. 10, 1975).

2396 Nevada Meats, Inc., 84 F.T.C. 493 (1974) (consent order).

2397 Wisconsin Dep't of Agriculture, Trade and Consumer Protection Rules, Wis. Admin. Code ch. ATCP 109, Freezer Meat and Food Service Plan Trade Practices § 109.02(1)(b).

The benefits of joining a freezer meat plan and individuals' food requirements can not be misrepresented. Buyers must get current price lists, sellers must sell at those prices, and sellers must furnish itemized bills and comply with all guarantees and arrangements for exchanging food.[2398]

5.7.3 Furniture and Carpet Sales

Important principles dealing with furniture and carpet sales can be found in previous sections dealing with bait and switch,[2399] deceptive pricing,[2400] delay and nondelivery,[2401] damaged and defective goods,[2402] substitution of goods,[2403] layaway plans, security deposits, refund policies, and cancellation provisions,[2404] warranties,[2405] used as new,[2406] and disparagement.[2407] It is deceptive to advertise carpet prices in noncustomary units of measure (e.g., feet instead of yards).[2408]

2398 Wisconsin Dep't of Agriculture, Trade and Consumer Protection Rules, Wis. Admin. Code ch. ATCP 109, Freezer Meat and Food Service Plan Trade Practices §§ 109.02, 109.03.

2399 *See* § 4.6.1, *supra. See also* Carpets "R" Us, Inc., 87 F.T.C. 303 (1976); Maryland Carpet Outlet, Inc., 85 F.T.C. 754 (1975); Sir Carpet, Inc., 85 F.T.C. 190 (1975); C.D. Paige Co., 85 F.T.C. 1048 (1975); Wilbanks Carpet Specialists, Inc., 84 F.T.C. 510 (1974); Tri-State Carpets, Inc., 84 F.T.C. 1078 (1974); Williams v. Bruno Appliance & Furniture, 62 Ill. App. 3d 219, 379 N.E.2d 52 (1978); Commonwealth v. R&W Indus., Clearinghouse No. 26,021 (Pa. Commw. Ct. 1976).

2400 *See* § 4.6.3, *supra. See also* Carpets "R" Us, Inc., 87 F.T.C. 303 (1976); Hollywood Carpet, Inc., 86 F.T.C. 784 (1975); Fashion Floors, Inc., 85 F.T.C. 820 (1975); Maryland Carpet Outlet, Inc., 85 F.T.C. 754 (1975); C.D. Paige Co., 85 F.T.C. 1048 (1975); Williams v. Bruno Appliance & Furniture, 62 Ill. App. 3d 219, 379 N.E.2d 52 (1978); Commonwealth v. R&W Indus., Clearinghouse No. 26,021 (Pa. Commw. Ct. 1976).

2401 *See* § 4.9.2, *supra. See also* Walker-Thomas Furniture Co., 87 F.T.C. 26 (1976) (consent order); State v. Hudson Furniture Co., 165 N.J. Super. 516, 398 A.2d 900 (App. Div. 1979); New Jersey Administrative Rules of the Div. of Consumer Affairs, N.J. Admin. Code ch. 13:45A, subch. 5, Household Furniture and Furnishings.

2402 *See* § 4.9.3, *supra.*

2403 *See* § 4.9.5, *supra.*

2404 *See* §§ 4.9.1, 5.2.6, *supra. See also* Certified Leasing Co., 89 F.T.C. 222 (1977) (consent order); Furniture Corp. of America, 88 F.T.C. 726 (1976) (consent order); Riley v. Enterprise Furniture Co., 54 Ohio Misc. 1, 375 N.E.2d 821 (Mun. Ct. Sylvania, Ohio 1977).

2405 *See* § 5.2.7, *supra. See also* Tri-State Carpets, Inc., 84 F.T.C. 1078 (1974); Kaufman Carpet Co., 88 F.T.C. 379 (1976) (consent order); J. Kurtz & Sons, Inc., 87 F.T.C. 1300 (1976) (consent order); Levitz Furniture Corp., 88 F.T.C. 263 (1976) (consent order).

2406 *See* § 4.9.4, *supra. See also* Walker-Thomas Furniture Co., 87 F.T.C. 26 (1976) (consent order).

2407 *See* § 4.7.10, *supra. See also* Carpets "R" Us, Inc., 87 F.T.C. 303 (1976); Wilbanks Carpet Specialists, Inc., 84 F.T.C. 510 (1974).

2408 Carpets "R" Us, Inc., 87 F.T.C. 303 (1976); Sir Carpet, Inc., 85 F.T.C. 190 (1975).

The FTC formerly had a guide for the household furniture industry[2409] dealing with product composition, trade names, identity of woods, leather, other coverings, stuffing, origin, and style, and use of the words "floor sample" and "discontinued model." In 2002 it concluded that changes in manufacturing processes, materials usage, terminology, and consumer expectations had rendered the guide outmoded. The FTC therefore rescinded the guide,[2410] but at the same time it stressed its unfettered ability under the FTC Act's general prohibitions to pursue sellers and manufacturers for unfair and deceptive acts in the labeling, advertising, or sale of household furniture.

5.7.4 Rent-To-Own Sales

5.7.4.1 Importance of UDAP Approach

The rent-to-own (RTO) industry is a major source of sales, particularly of appliances, to the low-income community. The RTO industry aims its marketing efforts—which suggest no credit requirements, low payments, quick delivery, and no cancellation penalties—at low-income consumers by advertising in minority media, buses, and in public housing projects.

RTO practices generate a substantial number of consumer complaints, and consumer attorneys frequently are searching for claims to bring against RTO companies. The RTO industry, on the other hand, argues that it need not comply with nearly every consumer protection statute (e.g., Uniform Commercial Code Article 9, Truth-in-Lending, usury laws, door-to-door laws) which is applicable to other retailers and financers of consumer goods.

The legal position of the RTO industry is tied very closely to its standard form contract. The contract is styled as a short-term (usually weekly) agreement to rent an appliance to the consumer. Most RTO contracts[2411] also expressly provide that the contract is renewable and that ownership will pass to the consumer after a stated number of periodic payments, usually after one to two years. According to many consumer lawyers, RTO customers enter into the transaction with the expectation of buying an appliance and are not interested in the rental aspects of the RTO contract.[2412] However, by emphasizing the rental option and minimizing the purchase option in its form contracts, the RTO industry argues it is not subject to laws that apply to sales, longer term leases, or credit sales.

Other NCLC manuals analyze whether this is in fact the case. Discussions as to whether the federal Truth in Lending or Consumer Leasing Acts apply to RTO transactions are found in NCLC's *Truth in Lending* manual.[2413] Whether state credit legislation applies to an RTO transaction is examined in NCLC's *Cost of Credit* manual,[2414] and whether UCC Article 9 regulates RTO repossessions is analyzed in NCLC's *Repossessions and Foreclosures* manual.[2415] RTO warranty issues are discussed in NCLC's *Consumer Warranty Law* manual.[2416]

Virtually every state has enacted (generally at the request of the industry itself) legislation placing certain requirements on RTO transactions, usually relating to repossession practices. The best listing and discussion of these statutes is found in NCLC's *Repossessions and Foreclosures* manual.[2417] But these statutes offer few consumer protections.

This is why a UDAP statute is such an important tool in dealing with RTO abuses. Almost alone among consumer statutes with significant private remedies, a state UDAP statute will almost always apply to RTO sales and even repossession abuses.[2418] (Another fruitful approach is to bring a claim under UCC Article 2A's unconscionability provision, as described in § 5.7.4.7, *infra.*)

Whether oral or written statements were made and whether they were misleading to the consumer are factual questions not easily resolvable even by affidavits or documentary evidence. This is particularly important in a collection action instituted by an RTO company, because factual issues force the company to go to trial. If the consumer prevails on the UDAP claim, the RTO company will usually have to pay the consumer's attorney fees.

For a good example of a complaint, discovery requests, and a brief in an RTO case, see NCLC's *Consumer Law Pleadings*, No. 2, Ch. 8 (CD-Rom and Index Guide), also

2409 16 C.F.R. Part 250 (1973). *See also* Carpets "R" Us, Inc., 87 F.T.C. 303 (1976); Fashion Floors, Inc., 85 F.T.C. 820 (1975); Hollywood Carpet, Inc., 86 F.T.C. 784 (1975).

2410 97 Fed. Reg. 9923 (Mar. 5, 2002).

2411 Some RTO form contracts provide that a portion of some or all payments are applied to the purchase of the appliance, the price of which may be stated in the form. Other RTO form contracts provide that the purchase option may be exercised by paying a large (balloon) payment after a stated number of periodic payments. Still other RTO form contracts do not include a purchase option (although the option may be conveyed orally or set forth in a separate document). Also, there may be some firms that only lease and provide no purchase option.

2412 *See generally* D. Ramp, *Renting to Own in the United States*, 24 Clearinghouse Rev. 797 (Dec. 1990).

2413 National Consumer Law Center, Truth in Lending §§ 2.5.4, 10.2.1 (5th ed. 2003 and Supp.).

2414 National Consumer Law Center, The Cost of Credit: Regulation and Legal Challenges (2d ed. 2000 and Supp.).

2415 National Consumer Law Center, Repossessions and Foreclosures § 14.3.2 (5th ed. 2002 and Supp.).

2416 National Consumer Law Center, Consumer Warranty Law Ch. 19 (2d ed. 2001 and Supp.).

2417 National Consumer Law Center, Repossessions and Foreclosures §§ 14.1.3.3, 14.3 (5th ed. 2002 and Supp.).

2418 *E.g.*, Starks v. Rent-A-Center, Clearinghouse No. 45,215 (Minn. Dist. Ct. 1990) (motion denied to dismiss claims under Minnesota RISA, UDAP and RICO; TILA claim dismissed finding the RTO contract is terminable without penalty at any time; RISA claim has since been limited by Minn. Stat. Ann. § 325F.82 to .95 (eff. Aug. 1, 1990)).

found on the CD-Rom accompanying this volume. The case challenges the terms of a rent-to-own contract under UDAP, UCC Article 2A, and other state law grounds.

5.7.4.2 Applicability of UDAP Statutes to RTO Transactions

RTO practices are almost always within the scope of a state UDAP statute. Statutes that apply to practices in "trade or commerce" certainly apply even to straight leases.[2419] A UDAP statute applying to sales or leases of consumer goods also clearly applies to RTO transactions. Even if a statute's scope is explicitly limited to only the "sale" of goods, the liberal construction afforded this legislation means that straight leases are also covered.[2420] There is no reported case where a company has questioned whether a UDAP statute applies to RTO transactions.

Of course, whether a UDAP statute applies to RTO repossession and debt collection abuses will depend on whether the UDAP statute in general applies to such post-sale transactions.[2421] But UDAP statutes clearly apply to deceptive advertising, oral misrepresentations, unfair contract terms, failure to offer promised services or goods, and non-disclosure of material facts.

5.7.4.3 Deceptive RTO Inducements, Sales and Warranty Practices

UDAP claims are an effective approach for dealing with the following RTO abuses:

- Advertising low-priced appliances, and then switching the consumer to a higher priced alternative.[2422]
- Engaging in high-pressure door-to-door sales.[2423]
- Misrepresenting easy credit terms, low payments, or that there will be no credit checks.[2424]
- Misrepresenting prices as bargains or the extent of savings compared to the RTO retailer's previous prices or competitors' prices.[2425]
- Failing to disclose a cash retail price if there is a possibility that the goods will ever be sold.[2426]
- Failing to disclose the true purchase price over the total lease term.[2427]
- Charging a total of payments that is several times the regular retail price of an item, or charging an implicit interest rate far in excess of the comparable limits on an installment sale.[2428]
- Describing the transaction as a lease when it in fact is a contract for sale.[2429]
- Lowballing, i.e, adding previously undisclosed delivery, documentary or other extra charges after the price has been agreed upon.[2430]
- Renting used appliances as new, misrepresenting an appliance's prior use, or not disclosing that appliances are used.[2431]
- Misrepresenting that most RTO participants end up owning the appliance where this is not the case, particularly where the RTO company strictly enforces the contract clauses to discourage ownership.
- Misrepresenting the steps necessary to exercise the purchase option.
- Referral sales, i.e., promising consumers a rebate if friends or neighbors referred by the consumer also lease merchandise from the lessor.[2432]
- Violating the state retail installment sales act, Truth in

2419 *See* Conaway v. Prestia, 191 Conn. 484, 464 A.2d 847 (1983); People *ex rel.* Fahner v. Testa, 112 Ill. App. 3d 834, 445 N.E.2d 1249 (1983); Commonwealth v. DeCotis, 366 Mass. 234, 316 N.E.2d 748 (1974); Marshall v. Miller, 47 N.C. App. 530, 268 S.E.2d 97 (1980), *modified on other grounds*, 302 N.C. 539, 276 S.E.2d 397 (1981).

2420 *See* Commonwealth v. Monumental Properties, Inc., 459 Pa. 450, 329 A.2d 812 (1974).

2421 *See* § 2.2.2, *supra*.

2422 *See* § 4.6.1, *supra*.

2423 *See* §§ 4.8, *supra*, 5.8.2, *infra*.

2424 *See* § 5.1.7.1, *supra*.

2425 *See* § 4.6.3, *supra*.

2426 State v. Colortyme, Inc., Clearinghouse No. 50,404 (Wis. Cir. Ct. May 25, 1994) (consent judgment).

2427 *See* §§ 4.2.14, 5.1.7.1, *supra*. *See also* Murphy v. McNamara, 36 Conn. Supp. 183, 416 A.2d 170, 27 U.C.C. Rep. 911 (Super. Ct. 1979); Mass. Regs. Code tit. 940, § 6.11(2) (requires disclosure in advertising of the total dollar amount that must be paid to own a product).

2428 *See* Murphy v. McNamara, 36 Conn. Supp. 183, 416 A.2d 170 (Super. Ct. 1979); Green v. Continental Rentals, 292 N.J. Super. 241, 678 A.2d 759 (Law. Div. 1994), *later op. at* 1996 WL 394037 (N.J. Super. 1996); State v. Rentavision Corp. of Am., Clearinghouse No. 35,731 (Tenn. Ch. Ct. Davidson Cty. 1983). *See also* §§ 4.3, 4.4, 5.1.7, *supra*. *But see* Remco Enterprises v. Houston, 677 P.2d 567 (Kan. Ct. App. 1984) (refusing to overturn finding that price 108% higher than normal is not unconscionable where consumer receives additional benefits from rental).

It is safer not to limit the deceptive practices claim to one based solely on unconscionably high prices. Other stronger UDAP claims, such as deceptive advertising, misleading sales pitches, and abusive collection practices should be included when they are available.

2429 Green v. Kansas City Power & Light Co. (*In re* Green), 281 B.R. 699 (D. Kan. 2002); Barco Auto Leasing Corp. v. House, Clearinghouse No. 40,641 (Conn. Super. Ct. Oct. 26, 1983), *aff'd in part, rev'd in part on other grounds*, 202 Conn. 106, 520 A.2d 162 (1987).

2430 *See* § 4.6.5, *supra*.

2431 Mass. Regs. Code tit. 940, § 6.11(3) (requires disclosure in advertising if goods leased with an option to purchase are in fact used); Code Vt. Rules § 06 031 015, Rule CF 115, Rent-to-Own Disclosures (requires disclosure as to whether an RTO good is used and when it was purchased), *upheld in* Thorn, Americas, Inc. v. Vermont Attorney General, Clearinghouse No. 51,957 (Vt. Super. Ct. Mar. 7, 1997). *See also* § 4.9.4, *supra*. *But cf.* State v. Action TV Rentals, Inc., 297 Md. 531, 467 A.2d 1000 (1983).

2432 *See* § 5.8.3, *infra*.

Lending, or other state or federal credit legislation, if applicable.[2433]

- Delivering defective products, failing to repair as promised, or failing to live up to warranties.[2434]

5.7.4.4 Disclosure of RTO Transaction's Effective Annual Percentage Rate

A fundamental problem with RTO transactions is that the effective interest rate or annual percentage rate in the transaction is often 100%, 200% or more, but this number is never disclosed to consumers. In response to this problem, the Vermont legislature ordered that "[t]he attorney general shall adopt by rule standards for the full and conspicuous disclosure to consumers of the terms of rent-to-own agreements."[2435] The attorney general's rule, effective January 1, 1997, declares it a state UDAP violation for an RTO company to fail to make certain mandated disclosures, including the cash price of the rented item, and the effective annual percentage rate (EAPR) associated with the transaction.[2436]

The EAPR is computed the same way as a TIL APR computation. The amount financed is the disclosed cash price (which is the bona fide retail cash price for which the company would sell the item). The total of payments is the total of payments necessary to purchase the item. The finance charge is the difference between total of payments and cash price (with certain possible exceptions). The payment schedule is that disclosed in the transaction to purchase the item.[2437]

RTO companies in Vermont unsuccessfully sought a preliminary injunction preventing the rule from going into effect.[2438] The RTO companies did *not* appeal this decision.

While Vermont is unique in requiring the state attorney general to enact a rule dealing with RTO disclosures, the majority of state UDAP statutes give the state attorney general authority to enact regulations defining unfair and deceptive practices.[2439] The failure to disclose important information in an RTO transaction can certainly be such an unfair or deceptive practice.

5.7.4.5 Applicability of Three-Day Cooling-Off Period to RTO Transactions

An often overlooked way to challenge an RTO transaction is to argue that the RTO retailer should have complied with either the FTC rule concerning a "Cooling-Off Period for Door-to-Door Sales"[2440] or an analogous state statute. Such coverage should be investigated because some major RTO companies solicit customers door to door. Even when not solicited at the residence, door-to-door laws may still apply if the transaction was conducted by phone or otherwise consummated in the residence. This discussion concentrates on whether an RTO company must comply with the FTC rule, but state cooling-off period legislation may apply to RTO transactions even when the FTC rule does not. More on the scope of the FTC rule and state laws is found at § 5.8.2, *infra*.

RTO and other rental transactions are clearly covered by the FTC rule. A door-to-door transaction covered by the FTC rule is:

> A sale, *lease*, or *rental* of consumer goods or services with a purchase price of $25 or more, whether under single or *multiple contracts*, in which the seller or his representative personally solicits the sale, including those in response to or following an invitation by the buyer, and the buyer's agreement or offer to purchase is made at a place other than the place of business of the seller. (Emphasis added.)[2441]

The rule's Statement of Basis and Purpose explains that the rule was redrafted to make it clear that leases were covered so that door-to-door sellers could not escape the rule provisions by leasing their goods instead of selling them.[2442]

The purpose of the rule's exemption for sales under $25 is not to exclude major appliance leases, but only "sales by milkmen, laundrymen, and other route salesmen. . . ."[2443] Certain appliance leases are clearly covered by the rule where the initial deposit and first payment exceed $25. Some state door-to-door statutes have a minimum of only $10, not $25.

Nevertheless, there will be cases where courts will be asked to decide whether the $25 purchase price minimum refers to each installment payment or to the total of payments. Since the rule defines purchase price as "the total price paid or to be paid for the consumer goods,"[2444] this issue should be decided in favor of coverage. Moreover, the rule's $25 minimum also applies to the total of multiple contracts "to insure that the rule would apply to transactions in which the seller writes up a number of invoices or contracts none of which show a price of $10 or more, but when taken together the total price exceeds that amount."[2445]

2433 Barco Auto Leasing Corp. v. House, Clearinghouse No, 40,641 (Conn. Super. Ct. 1983); *see also* § 3.2.7 *supra*.

2434 *See* §§ 4.9.3, 4.9.7, 5.2.7, *supra*.

2435 9 Vt. Stat. Ann. § 41b(a).

2436 Code Vt. Rules 06 031 015, Rule CF 115.04, Clearinghouse No. 51,958 (effective Jan. 1, 1997).

2437 *Id.*

2438 Thorn, Americas, Inc. v. Vermont Attorney General, Clearinghouse No. 51,957 (Vt. Super. Ct. Mar. 7, 1997).

2439 *See* Appx. A, *infra*.

2440 16 C.F.R. Part 429 [*reprinted at* Appx. B.3, *infra*]; *see also* § 5.8.2, *infra*.

2441 16 C.F.R. § 429.0(a).

2442 *See* 37 Fed. Reg. 22945 (Oct. 26, 1972).

2443 *See id.* at 22945.

2444 16 C.F.R. § 429.0(e).

2445 Statement of Basis and Purpose, 37 Fed. Reg. 22945 (Oct. 26, 1982).

RTO companies may argue that the rule does not apply because the RTO agreement is made over the telephone or in the RTO store. Consumer practitioners should consider the following factors in determining whether the rule applies:

- The rule should apply if the original order was taken door to door, through hand-billing on the street, at a place of employment, or some place other than the lessor's store.
- The FTC rule does not apply if the transaction is "[c]onducted and consummated *entirely* by mail or telephone; and without *any* other contact between the buyer and the seller . . . prior to delivery of the goods. . . ."[2446]
- Even if the RTO firm filled out an order over the telephone, the *consummation* of the contract may still take place in the consumer's home. Determine what documents were signed or initialed, whether the delivery person had discretion not to leave the goods (as is the usual case), where the initial installment was paid, and what disclosures were presented for the first time in the consumer's home. This information should help determine where the buyer's "agreement" was made. The signing and disclosing of documents in the consumer's home also constitutes *contact* between the RTO firm and consumer prior to delivery, even if it is just minutes prior to delivery.
- Many RTO firms perform credit or character checks after taking orders, or refuse to deliver an order if the routeman does not like the looks of an apartment or does not receive the initial payment in cash. Arguably in those cases there is no mutual agreement at the time of the order, but only when the contract is signed.
- Were the original negotiations conducted at the RTO store? The FTC rule exempts transactions: "Made pursuant to prior negotiations in the course of a visit by the buyer to a retail business establishment. . . ."[2447]
- By the explicit terms of the FTC rule, if an RTO representative is in the consumer's home to repair an appliance, and rents that consumer another appliance, the transaction is covered by the rule.[2448]

If the RTO retailer is covered by the FTC rule or by an analogous state law, the consumer's rights and remedies are set out at § 5.8.2, *infra*.

5.7.4.6 Deceptive Repossession and Debt Collection Tactics

An important source of RTO customer complaints involves repossession tactics. These too can be UDAP violations:

- Threatening criminal or civil action that RTO employees have no intention of instituting (such as use of lease larceny statutes against customers for unreturned goods even if those statutes do not apply to RTO transactions).[2449]
- Misrepresenting RTO routemen as law enforcement officials to repossess appliances or collect debts.[2450]
- Upon the consumer's default, seeking or threatening to seek not just past due payments, but the total "unpaid balances" or other amounts that the lessor is not entitled to pursuant to the contract.[2451]
- Repossessing appliances by falsely claiming that RTO routemen will repair or replace the appliance with a newer or better working model (known as a "switch-out").[2452]
- Threats of repossession or suit when the RTO company knows the consumer disputes the RTO company's legal claim.[2453]
- Outrageous collection efforts, e.g., a campaign of harassing letters, phone calls and threats.[2454]
- Entering a consumer's home and taking away an RTO appliance without contemporaneous consent by the consumer.[2455]
- Using force or violence (or having that reputation) to repossess RTO appliances.[2456]
- Engaging in other harassing or deceptive collection practices.[2457]

2446 16 C.F.R. § 429.0(a)(4) (emphasis added).

2447 16 C.F.R. § 429.0(a)(1).

2448 16 C.F.R. § 429.0(a)(5).

2449 State v. Ell, 813 S.W.2d 26 (Mo. Ct. App. 1991).

2450 *See* §§ 5.1.1.1.3, 5.1.1.5.3, *supra*; *see also* State v. Action TV Rentals, Inc., 297 Md. 531, 467 A.2d 1000 (1983).

2451 *See* § 5.1.1.1.7, *supra*. *See also* State v. Rentavision Corp. of Am., Clearinghouse No. 35,731 (Tenn. Ch. Ct. Davidson Cty. 1983).

2452 *See* § 5.1.1.5.3, *supra*. *See also* State v. Action TV Rentals, 297 Md. 531, 467 A.2d 1000 (1983).

2453 *See* National Consumer Law Center, Fair Debt Collection §§ 5.6.6, 11.3.4 (5th ed. 2004); *see also* Murphy v. McNamara, 36 Conn. Supp. 183, 416 A.2d 170 (1979).

2454 National Consumer Law Center, Fair Debt Collection §§ 10.2, 11.2.4.2, 11.3.4 (5th ed. 2004).

2455 *See* Kimble v. Universal TV Rental, 417 N.E.2d 597, 65 Ohio Misc. 17, 19 Ohio Op. 3d 172, (Mun. Ct. 1980) (damages of $10 for trespass, $936.60 for conversion, and $4000 punitive awarded for RTO repossession where firm broke into locked, unoccupied apartment without consumer's consent). *See also* Mercer v. D.E.F., Inc., 48 B.R. 562 (Bankr. D. Minn. 1985) ($8000 actual and punitive damages for a frightening RTO repossession violating bankruptcy automatic stay); Taylor v. Action Household Rentals, Inc., 351 So. 2d 865 (La. Ct. App. 1977) ($600 trespass damages); Fassit v. United T.V. Rentals, Inc., 297 So. 2d 283 (La. Ct. App. 1974) ($500 trespass damages).

2456 *See* National Consumer Law Center, Fair Debt Collection §§ 11.2.4.2, 11.3.4 (5th ed. 2004).

2457 *See* § 5.1.1.1, *supra*; *see also* Murphy v. McNamara, 36 Conn. Supp. 183, 416 A.2d 170 (Super. Ct. 1979).

5.7.4.7 UCC Article 2A Unconscionability as Alternative to UDAP

Another viable legal theory for many of the same RTO practices that a UDAP statute can reach is an unconscionability claim under UCC Article 2A on Leases. UCC § 2A-108, "Unconscionability," allows courts to refuse to enforce unconscionable provisions in the RTO agreement, and also to grant appropriate relief where an RTO transaction is induced by unconscionable conduct or where unconscionable conduct has occurred in the RTO collection activities.[2458] The court must award prevailing consumers their attorney fees. Fees are available to a prevailing lessor only if the lessee knew the action was groundless.

A UCC § 2A-108 claim will have the following advantages over a UDAP claim:

- *Post-Sale Transactions.* Some UDAP statutes do not apply to practices occurring after the transaction has been finalized, such as collection tactics. UCC § 2A-108 specifically applies to those transactions.
- *Non-Deceptive Abuses.* Most UDAP statutes prohibit unfair or unconscionable practices, but some state statutes only prohibit deceptive practices or a specific laundry list of deceptive practices. In those states, UCC § 2A-108's unconscionability standard is superior where the lessor's practice is abusive but not deceptive.
- *Statute of Limitations.* Some UDAP statutes have a short limitations period. UCC Article 2A-506 specifies a four-year period for actions for default under a lease contract.
- *Equitable Relief.* Not all UDAP statutes authorize equitable relief (and Iowa's does not even authorize a damage recovery). UCC Article 2A-108 authorizes a court to grant "appropriate relief."
- *Attorney Fees.* Some UDAP statutes do not authorize attorney fees, many do not mandate fees for consumers, while a few authorize fees for either party. UCC § 2A-108 mandates fees for a consumer, but authorizes fees for the lessor only if the consumer knew the action was groundless.

5.7.5 *Household Cleaners and Purifiers*

FTC consent orders deal with misrepresentations concerning the effectiveness of air cleaners and deodorizers[2459] and carpet cleaners.[2460] The Minnesota Attorney General and the FTC have also successfully enjoined the practices of a company selling an air purifier that emits ozone into the air. The trial court found no positive health benefits and a significant safety hazard.[2461]

5.7.6 *Computers and Other Electronic Equipment*

The FTC obtained a consent order from a computer manufacturer concerning misrepresentations that certain optional equipment would be available in the near future, and about the equipment's ability to run certain software programs.[2462] Other FTC consent agreements involve misrepresentations concerning the memory capacity of a computer,[2463] and misrepresentations that a telephone has touch tone dialing.[2464] Other FTC consent orders deal with misrepresentations as to availability of computer products ordered by mail,[2465] warranty terms,[2466] protection from power failures,[2467] and computer lease terms.[2468]

2458 Cari Rentals v. Hall, Clearinghouse No. 49,940 (Iowa Dist. Ct. 1993). *See also* National Consumer Law Center, Consumer Law Pleadings, No. 2, Ch. 8 (CD-Rom and Index Guide) for a complaint, discovery requests, and brief in a case challenging the terms of a rent-to-own contract under Article 2A, UDAP, and other state law grounds, also found on the CD-Rom accompanying this volume. *But see In re* Allen, 174 B.R. 293 (Bankr. D. Or. 1994) (no unconscionability found in RTO transaction).

2459 Honeywell, Inc., 5 Trade Reg. Rep. (CCH) ¶ 24,358 (F.T.C. Dkt. No. C-3823 1998) (consent order); Pyraponic Indus. II, Inc., 115 F.T.C. 636, 5 Trade Reg. Rep. (CCH) ¶ 23,194 (1992) (consent order); Newtron Products Co., 115 F.T.C. 381, 5 Trade Reg. Rep. (CCH) ¶ 23,054 (1991) (consent order); North Am. Philips Corp., 107 F.T.C. 62 (1986) (consent order); Sunbeam Corp., 107 F.T.C. 226 (1986) (consent order); 133 Associated Mills, Inc., 106 F.T.C. 5 (1985); Russ-Hampton Indus., Inc., 3 Trade Reg. Rep. (CCH) ¶ 22,225 (F.T.C. Dkt. No. 9167 1985) (consent order); Young & Rubicon/Zemp, Inc., 105 F.T.C. 317 (1985).

2460 Blue Lustre Home Care Products, 108 F.T.C. 41 (1986) (consent order).

2461 State v. Alpine Air Products, Inc., 490 N.W.2d 888 (Minn. Ct. App. 1992), *aff'd*, 500 N.W.2d 788 (Minn. 1993) (excessive amounts of ozone in a room can be a health hazard); Live-Lee Productions, Inc., 5 Trade Reg. Rep. (CCH) ¶ 23,842 (F.T.C. Dkt. No. C-3620 1995) (consent order).

2462 Commodore Bus. Machines, Inc., 105 F.T.C. 230 (1985) (consent order). *See also* Coleco Indus., Inc., 111 F.T.C. 651 (1989) (consent order).

2463 NEC Home Electronics (U.S.A.), Inc., 110 F.T.C. 501 (1988) (consent order).

2464 Cosmo Communications Corp., 108 F.T.C. 255 (1986) (consent order).

2465 U.S. v. Dell Computer Corp., 5 Trade Reg. Rep. (CCH) ¶ 24,411 (W.D. Tex. 1998) (consent order) (FTC Mail Order Rule violated where computer software advertised as part of system package was unavailable for delivery).

2466 Apple Computer, Inc., 5 Trade Reg. Rep. (CCH) ¶ 24,557 (F.T.C. Dkt. C-3890 1999) (consent order) (fees charged for "free" access to technical support); Tiger Direct, Inc., 5 Trade Reg. Rep. ¶ 24,619 (F.T.C. Dkt. 3903 1999) (consent order); Gateway 2000, Inc., 5 Trade Reg. Rep. (CCH) ¶ 24,467 (F.T.C. Dkt. C-3844 1998) (consent order) (false advertising, "money-back" guarantees and "on-site service").

2467 Gen. Signal Power Sys., 5 Trade Reg. Rep. (CCH) ¶ 24,545 (F.T.C. Dkt. C-3860 1999) (consent order) ("uninterruptible power systems").

2468 Dell Computer Corp., 5 Trade Reg. Rep. (CCH) ¶ 24,602 (F.T.C. Dkts. C-3888, C-3887 1999) (consent orders).

The FTC has challenged selling cable decoders and descramblers to unauthorized users so that those users could avoid cable fees; such a practice was unfair to paying customers.[2469] Consumers who purchased a satellite television with an illegal descrambler, believing that the system was legal, have a UDAP deception claim against the seller.[2470]

5.7.7 Toys and Musical Instruments

A piano manufacturer has agreed to an FTC consent order concerning representations regarding its sound boards.[2471] The FTC has also accepted several consent orders dealing with various misrepresentations found in television commercials for children's toys.[2472]

5.7.8 Environmental Claims for Household Products

The FTC has issued Guides for the Use of Environmental Marketing Claims.[2473] The guides set out general principles, and have more specific standards about the use of terms such as biodegradable, recyclable, refillable, and ozone friendly.[2474] The guides apply to environmental claims included in labeling, advertising, promotional materials and all other forms of marketing, whether asserted directly or by implication through words, symbols, emblems, logos, depictions, product brand names, or any other means.[2475]

Specifically, the guides state that any party making an express or implied claim that presents an objective assertion about the environmental attribute of a product or packaging must, at the time the claim is made, possess and rely upon a reasonable basis substantiating the claim.[2476] A reasonable basis consists of competent and reliable evidence. In addition, an environmental marketing claim should be presented in a way that makes clear whether the environmental attribute or benefit being asserted refers to the product, the product's packaging, or to a portion or component of the product or package.[2477]

The guides also state that it is deceptive to misrepresent, directly or by implication, that a product or package offers a general environmental benefit, is degradable, biodegradable,[2478] photodegradable, compostable, recyclable,[2479] refillable, ozone "friendly,"[2480] or is low in weight, volume or toxicity.[2481] A product or package should not be marketed as recyclable unless it can be collected, separated or otherwise recovered from the solid waste stream for use in the form of raw materials, in the manufacture or assembly of a new package or product.[2482]

For products or packages that are made of both recyclable and non-recyclable components, the recyclable claim should be adequately qualified to avoid consumer deception about which portions or components of the product or package are recyclable.[2483] A recycled content claim may be made only for materials that have been recovered or otherwise diverted from the solid waste stream, either during the manufacturing process (pre-consumer) or after consumer use (post-consumer).[2484]

2469 C&D Electronics, Inc., 109 F.T.C. 72 (1987) (consent order).

2470 Karst v. Goldberg, 88 Ohio App. 3d 413, 623 N.E.2d 1348 (1993).

2471 Samick Music Corp., 5 Trade Reg. Rep. (CCH) ¶ 23,564 (F.T.C. C-3496 1994) (consent order).

2472 Azark-Hamway Int'l, Inc., 5 Trade Reg. Rep. (CCH) ¶ 23,977 (F.T.C. C-3653 1996); Hasbro Inc., 5 Trade Reg. Rep. (CCH) ¶ 23,374 (F.T.C. Dkt. C-3446 1993) (consent order); Lewis Galoob Toys, Inc., 114 F.T.C. 187 (1991) (consent order); Towne, Silverstein, Rotter, Inc., 114 F.T.C. 218 (1991) (consent order) (order against ad agency that created deceptive commercials).

2473 16 C.F.R. Part 260.

2474 *Id.*

2475 16 C.F.R. § 260.2.

2476 16 C.F.R. § 260.5; FTC v. One Source Worldwide Network, Inc., 5 Trade Reg. Rep. (CCH) ¶ 24,628 (D. Tex. 1999) (proposed consent decree) (misrepresentation as to effectiveness of laundry detergent substitute that changed water's molecular structure).

2477 16 C.F.R. § 260.6.

2478 The FTC has also accepted settlements concerning biodegradability claims for diapers, trash bags, and other plastic products. *See* LePage's Inc., 5 Trade Reg. Rep. (CCH) ¶ 23,589 (F.T.C. C-3506 1994); Oak Hill Indus. Corp., 5 Trade Reg. Rep. (CCH) ¶ 23,590 (F.T.C. C-3507 1994); AJM Packaging Corp., 5 Trade Reg. Rep. (CCH) ¶ 23,598 (F.T.C. C-3508 1994); Amoco Chemical Co., 5 Trade Reg. Rep. (CCH) ¶ 23,617 (F.T.C. C-3514 1994); Mobil Oil Corp., 5 Trade Reg. Rep. (CCH) ¶ 23,238 (F.T.C. Dkt. C-3415 1993); North Am. Plastics Corp., 5 Trade Reg. Rep. (CCH) ¶ 23,362 (F.T.C. File No. 902 3184 1993); BPI Environmental, Inc., 5 Trade Reg. Rep. (CCH) ¶ 23,363 (F.T.C. File No. 902 3235 1993); Archer Daniels Midland Co., 5 Trade Reg. Rep. (CCH) ¶ 23,311 (F.T.C. File No. 902 3283 1993); American Enviro Products, 115 F.T.C. 399, 5 Trade Reg. Rep. (CCH) ¶ 23,048 (1992); RMED Int'l, Inc., 115 F.T.C. 572, 5 Trade Reg. Rep. (CCH) ¶ 23,149 (1992); First Brands Corp., 5 Trade Reg. Rep. (CCH) ¶ 23,069 (F.T.C. C-3358 1992).

2479 FTC consent orders have also dealt with whether food containers and other products are recyclable. *See* White Castle Sys., Inc., 5 Trade Reg. Rep. (CCH) ¶ 23,474 (F.T.C. C-3477 1994); America's Favorite Chicken, 5 Trade Reg. Rep. (CCH) ¶ 23,579 (F.T.C. C-3504 1994).

2480 A number of FTC consent agreements have also dealt with claims that aerosol claims are ozone safe. Perfect Data Corp., 5 Trade Reg. Rep. (CCH) ¶ 23,316 (F.T.C. Dkt. C-3452 1993); Nationwide Indus., Inc., 5 Trade Reg. Rep. (CCH) ¶ 23,407 (F.T.C. File No. 902 3364 1993); Tech Spray, Inc., 115 F.T.C. 433, 5 Trade Reg. Rep. (CCH) ¶ 23,125 (1992); Zipatone, Inc., 114 F.T.C. 376, 5 Trade Reg. Rep. (CCH) ¶ 22,976 (1991) . *See also* Jerome Russell Cosmetics USA, Inc., 114 F.T.C. 514, 5 Trade Reg. Rep. (CCH) ¶ 23,001 (1991) (claim that cosmetics are ozone safe).

2481 16 C.F.R. § 260.7.

2482 *Id.*

2483 *Id.*

2484 *Id.*

FTC consent agreements have also dealt with claims of pesticide-free produce,[2485] whether a company's lawn care pesticides are safe,[2486] and whether coffee filters,[2487] anti-freeze,[2488] ice-melting products,[2489] soap,[2490] hair spray,[2491] and other products[2492] are as environmentally sound as advertised. New Mexico and Wisconsin have also enacted UDAP regulations dealing with environmental labeling of products, including degradability, recyclability and recycled contents representations.[2493] A similar California statute has been upheld against a First Amendment challenge.[2494]

5.7.9 Handguns

Massachusetts has enacted a UDAP regulation that prohibits violations of state gun control laws and the sale of handguns from inferior materials. It also requires tamper-resistant serial numbers, childproofing or safety devices, and safety warnings.[2495] The Massachusetts Supreme Judicial Court has upheld the majority of this regulation as within the attorney general's authority.[2496] The court's decision recognizes that sale of a dangerous and defective product is unfair and deceptive under the state UDAP statute, as it is under the FTC Act. The attorney general's authority to regulate the sale of handguns was reinforced while the challenge to the regulation was pending by the state legislature's adoption of a handgun control statute that incorporated most of the provisions of the regulation. The Connecticut Supreme Court held that a municipality did not have standing to sue gun manufacturers under the state UDAP statute for the victimization of its citizens and the increased cost of police, health care, and related services.[2497]

5.7.10 Miscellaneous Household Products

The sale of overpriced pots and pans, represented to help prevent heart disease and promote infant health, is a UDAP violation.[2498] The FTC has settled cases dealing with allegations that a photoprocessing package offered consumers was virtually worthless and an unacceptably bad bargain,[2499] and that a company misrepresented the performances of athletic shoes.[2500] Other FTC consent orders deal with misrepresentations dealing with ultrasonic flea collars,[2501] buzzers that eliminate rodents,[2502] and a mace spray for personal protection.[2503]

5.8 Door-to-Door, Mail Order, Referral, Unsolicited, Negative Option Sales

5.8.1 Mail-Order Sales

5.8.1.1 FTC Rule

The FTC's Mail or Telephone Order Merchandise Rule[2504] requires that mail-order sellers have a reasonable basis to expect to be able to deliver mail-order merchandise within the time specified in their advertising or within thirty days if no time is specified.[2505] The rule requires that all

2485 Redmond Products, Inc., 5 Trade Reg. Rep. (CCH) ¶ 23,487 (F.T.C. C-3479 1994) (consent order); The Texwipe Co., 5 Trade Reg. Rep. (CCH) ¶ 23,426 (F.T.C. C-3466 1993) (consent order); The Vons Companies, Inc., 5 Trade Reg. Rep. (CCH) ¶ 22,842 (F.T.C. Dkt. C-3302 1990) (consent order).

2486 Orkin Exterminating Co., 5 Trade Reg. Rep. (CCH) ¶ 23,619 (F.T.C. C-3495 1994) (consent order); Orkin Exterminating Co., 5 Trade Reg. Rep. (CCH) ¶ 23,349 (F.T.C. File No. 912 3237 1993) (consent order).

2487 Mr. Coffee, Inc., 5 Trade Reg. Rep. (CCH) ¶ 23,361 (F.T.C. File No. 912 3036 1993) (consent order).

2488 Safe Brands Corp., 5 Trade Reg. Rep. (CCH) ¶ 23,931 (F.T.C. C-3647 1996) (consent order).

2489 Chempharon Laboratory, Inc., 5 Trade Reg. Rep. (CCH) ¶ 23,666 (F.T.C. Dkt. C-3545 1994) (consent order).

2490 FTC v. Water Resources Int'l, Inc., 5 Trade Reg. Rep. (CCH) ¶ 23,886 (C.D. Cal. 1995) (proposed consent decree); Mattel Inc., 5 Trade Reg. Rep. (CCH) ¶ 23,792 (F.T.C. Dkt. No. C-3591) (consent order); Creative Aerosol Corp., 5 Trade Reg. Rep. (CCH) ¶ 23,691 (F.T.C. Dkt. C-3548 1995) (consent order).

2491 DeMert & Dougherty, Inc., 5 Trade Reg. Rep. (CCH) ¶ 23,364 (F.T.C. Dkt. C-3456 1993) (consent order).

2492 First Brands Corp., 115 F.T.C. 1 (1992) (consent order).

2493 N.M. Admin. Code § 12.2.5; Wis. Dep't of Agriculture, Trade & Consumer Protection Rules, Wis. Admin. Code ch. ATCP 137, Environmental Labeling of Products.

2494 Ass'n of Nat'l Advertisers, Inc. v. Lungren, 44 F.3d 726 (9th Cir. 1994).

2495 Massachusetts Consumer Protection Regulations, Mass. Reg. Code tit. 940, § 16, Handgun Sales.

2496 American Shooting Sports Council v. Attorney General, 429 Mass. 871, 711 N.E.2d 899 (1999).

2497 Ganim v. Smith and Wesson Corp., 258 Conn. 313, 780 A.2d 98 (2001).

2498 Rossi v. 21st Century Concepts, Inc., 162 N.Y. Misc. 2d 932 (Yonkers City Ct. 1994).

2499 FTC v. Traditional Indus., Inc., 5 Trade Reg. Rep. (CCH) ¶ 22,721 (W.D. Wash. Aug. 17, 1989) (consent order).

2500 Asics Tiger Corp., 114 F.T.C. 264, 5 Trade Reg. Rep. (CCH) ¶ 22,933 (1991) (court order).

2501 Elexis Corp., 115 F.T.C. 118, 5 Trade Reg. Rep. (CCH) ¶ 23,099 (1991) (consent order).

2502 Exhart Environmental Sys., Inc., 115 F.T.C. 613, 5 Trade Reg. Rep. (CCH) ¶ 23,164 (F.T.C. C-3384 1992) (consent order). *See also* Sonic Technology Products, Inc., 5 Trade Reg. Rep. (CCH) ¶ 23,550 (F.T.C. Dkt. 9252 1994) (consent order).

2503 MACE Security Int'l, 5 Trade Reg. Rep. (CCH) ¶ 23,525 (F.T.C. C-3487 1994) (consent order).

2504 16 C.F.R. § 435 [*reprinted at* Appx. B.4, *infra*]. *See also* United States v. DelMonte Corp., 3 Trade Reg. Rep. (CCH) ¶ 22,307 (N.D. Cal. Nov. 18, 1985) (consent order) (upholding FTC's authority to issue the rule).

2505 16 C.F.R. § 435.1(a)(1). The rule allows this period to be extended to 50 days where the order is accompanied by a request to establish credit with the merchant. *See also* FTC v. Staples, Inc., 5 Trade Reg. Rep. (CCH) ¶ 15411 (D. Mass. May

merchandise ordered by telephone or by mail be delivered within thirty days,[2506] unless the merchant at the time of sale provided for a longer delivery time or unless the buyer later opts to wait a longer period instead of receiving a full refund. If this deadline can not be met, the seller, as soon as it becomes aware of that fact, must give the consumer the option of canceling the order[2507] and receiving a full refund[2508] or consenting to a delay. The period begins to run from the buyer's order date.[2509] Posting information about the order on the seller's website is insufficient; the seller must contact the customer directly.[2510] The seller can not extend the delivery deadline by counting the thirty days as running from a later date when the seller actually charges the buyer's credit card.[2511]

The merchant does not comply with the rule by sending only part of what was ordered within thirty days. For example, if software is bundled with a computer, the merchant violates the Mail Order Rule by not shipping the software with the computer and not offering consumers the option of either consenting to a delay in shipping or canceling the order and receiving a full refund.[2512] Charging a cancellation fee is a violation because it is inconsistent with the requirement of a full refund.[2513]

The rule originally covered only mail-order sales, but the FTC expanded it, effective March 1, 1994, to apply to telephone sales as well.[2514] The revised rule is written broadly enough to apply to on-line sales and orders made by fax as well as traditional telephone and mail sales.[2515]

5.8.1.2 Other Precedent

Two states have incorporated the FTC rule into their UDAP regulations.[2516] Other state UDAP regulations are similar, but slightly weaker, for example by giving sellers six weeks instead of thirty days to make delivery or by giving sellers the additional option of delivering substitute goods of equivalent or superior value.[2517]

22, 2003) (proposed consent decree) (website claimed one-day delivery but did not disclose limitations); FTC v. Computers by Us, Inc., 5 Trade Reg. Rep. (CCH) ¶ 15148 (D. Md. Aug. 30, 2001) (web-based auction); Market Dev. Corp., 95 F.T.C. 100 (1980); Jay Norris Inc., 91 F.T.C. 751 (1978); Nursery Barn, 92 F.T.C. 924 (1978) (consent order); Baltimore Stereo Wholesalers, 86 F.T.C. 930 (1975) (consent order); Wards Co., 86 F.T.C. 938 (1975) (consent order); Auslander Decorator Furniture, 83 F.T.C. 1542 (1973).

2506 The rule allows this period to be extended to 50 days where the order is accompanied by a request to establish credit with the merchant.

2507 *See also* FTC v. Ralston Purina Co., 5 Trade Reg. Rep. (CCH) ¶ 23,210 (E.D. Mo. 1992) (consent decree); United States v. Mail Order Products, Inc., 5 Trade Reg. Rep. (CCH) ¶ 22,693 (D.N.J. May 22, 1989) (consent decree); Northeastern Software, Inc., F.T.C. File No. 872 3009, 5 Trade Reg. Rep. (CCH) ¶ 22,697 (F.T.C. July 10, 1989) (consent order); Jay Norris Inc., 91 F.T.C. 751 (1978) (sellers must disclose the right to cancel for slow delivery).

2508 *See also* FTC v. George L. Capell, 5 Trade Reg. Rep. (CCH) ¶ 15179 (E.D. Pa. Nov. 14, 2001) (proposed consent decree prohibiting seller of computers from violating mail order rule); FTC v. American Direct Marketing, Inc., 5 Trade Reg. Rep. (CCH) ¶ 23,979 (M.D. Tenn. 1996) (proposed consent decree); United States v. Telebrands Corp., 5 Trade Reg. Rep. (CCH) ¶ 24,107 (W.D. Va. 1996) (proposed consent decree); United States v. American Distribution, Inc., 5 Trade Reg. Rep. (CCH) ¶ 23,843 (E.D. Va. 1995) (proposed consent decree); FTC v. Haband Co., 5 Trade Reg. Rep. (CCH) ¶ 23,680 (D. N.J. Sept. 27, 1994) (proposed consent order prohibiting defendant from substituting materially different merchandise for unavailable products without customer approval); FTC v. Advance Watch Co., 5 Trade Reg. Rep. (CCH) ¶ 23,637 (E.D. Mich. July 15, 1994) (consent order); FTC v. Ralston Purina Co., 5 Trade Reg. Rep. (CCH) ¶ 23,210 (E.D. Mo. 1992) (consent decree); United States v. Lillian Vernon Corp., 5 Trade Reg. Rep. (CCH) ¶ 23,270 (S.D.N.Y. 1992) (consent decree) (failure to refund shipping and handling charges); United States v. Direct Marketing of Virginia, Inc., 5 Trade Reg. Rep. (CCH) ¶ 22,818 (S.D.N.Y. 1990) (consent decree); United States v. JS&A Group, Inc., 5 Trade Reg. Rep. (CCH) ¶ 22,918 (N.D. Ill. 1990) (consent decree); Northeastern Software, Inc., F.T.C. File No. 872 3009, 5 Trade Reg. Rep. (CCH) ¶ 22,697 (F.T.C. July 10, 1989) (consent order); United States v. Mail Order Products, Inc., 5 Trade Reg. Rep. (CCH) ¶ 22,693 (D.N.J. May 22, 1989) (consent decree); Sheldon Friedlisch Marketing, Inc., 3 Trade Reg. Rep. (CCH) ¶ 22,472 (F.T.C. File 832 3014 1987) (consent order); FTC v. Westbranch Ltd., Trade Reg. Rep. (CCH) ¶ 21,928 (D. Conn. 1982) (consent order); United States v. Star Crest Products of California Inc., Trade Reg. Rep. (CCH) ¶ 21,923 (C.D. Cal. 1982) (consent order); Baltimore Stereo Wholesalers, 86 F.T.C. 930 (1975) (consent order); Wards Co., 86 F.T.C. 938 (1975) (consent order); U.S. General Supply Co., 80 F.T.C. 857 (1972) (consent order).

2509 16 C.F.R. § 435.1(a)(1)(ii).

2510 U.S. v. Pet Express, Inc., 5 Trade Reg. Rep. (CCH) ¶ 15185 (E.D. Va. Dec. 10, 2001) (proposed consent decree).

2511 FTC, Supplementary Information for Amended Mail Order Rule, 58 Fed. Reg. 49096, 49113–14 (Sept. 21, 1993).

2512 FTC v. Dell Computer Corp., 5 Trade Reg. Rep. (CCH) ¶ 24,411 (W.D. Tex. 1998) (proposed consent decree).

2513 U.S. v. Dynamic Wheels & Tires, Inc., 5 Trade Reg. Rep. (CCH) ¶ 15308 (C.D. Cal. Sept. 30, 2002) (proposed consent decree against company that charged "restocking fee"); FTC v. Charles Smith, 5 Trade Reg. Rep. (CCH) ¶ 15194 (C.D. Cal. Dec. 20, 2001) (proposed consent decree).

2514 58 Fed. Reg. 49096 (Sept. 21, 1993), amending 16 C.F.R. 435 (effective Mar. 1, 1994), *reprinted at* Appx. B.4, *infra*.

2515 16 C.F.R. § 435.2(b). *See* FTC, Dot Com Disclosure § 14(A)(2) (2000) (providing guidance on how on-line sellers should comply with rule). *See also* FTC v. Bargains & Deals Magazine, 5 Trade Reg. Rep. (CCH) ¶ 15162 (W.D. Wash. Oct. 11, 2001) (complaint filed and TRO issued to enforce mail order rule to Internet sale).

2516 Georgia Office of Consumer Affairs Regulations, Ga. Comp. R. & Regs. r. 122; Idaho Consumer Protection Regulations, Idaho Admin. Code § 04.02.01.141, Time of Delivery or Performance, Mail Order Sales.

2517 New Jersey Administrative Rules of the Division of Consumer Affairs, N.J. Admin. Code § 13:45A-1.1, Deceptive Mail Order Practices (allows 6 weeks); Ohio Admin. Code § 109:4-3-09, Failure to Deliver/Substitution of Goods or Services (allows 8 weeks); Rules of Utah Consumer Sales Practices Act, Utah

Still other state UDAP regulations require mail-order sellers to disclose in all materials their legal name and address.[2518] It has been found deceptive for sellers to fail to disclose that not all items are kept in stock,[2519] to misrepresent that parcels are insured against loss,[2520] and to misrepresent that refunds or exchanges will be processed promptly.[2521]

Unsolicited merchandise received in the mail is dealt with elsewhere in this manual.[2522]

5.8.2 Door-to-Door and Off-Premises Sales

5.8.2.1 The FTC Cooling-Off Period Rule

Door-to-door sales have a history of high-pressure tactics, deception and other systematic consumer abuse.[2523] A three-day cooling-off period is a remedy designed to meet these problems by giving consumers an opportunity to reevaluate their purchase decisions away from the salesperson's hard sell. The remedy also lessens sellers' incentive to use high-pressure sales tactics because, when consumers cancel high-pressure sales, sellers are left with no profit for their investment of time and energy.

The FTC has promulgated a Trade Regulation Rule Concerning a Cooling-Off Period for Door-to-Door Sales.[2524] The rule is reprinted as Appx. B.3, *infra.* The companion CD-Rom to this volume includes not only the rule itself but also the FTC's Statement of Basis and Purpose when it adopted the rule, and three advisory opinion letters issued by the FTC.

The rule gives the consumer the right to cancel a home-solicitation transaction; requires that certain information and forms be given to the consumer at the time of the transaction; and provides rights, duties, and responsibilities of merchants, consumers, and other parties involved in such transactions. The rule applies not just to door-to-door transactions but other off-premises transactions, e.g., in motels or other temporary locations.

It is important to be familiar with all aspects of this rule. While many door-to-door sellers comply with the rule's basic requirements, sellers often neglect to comply with several less well-known requirements. For sales covered by the FTC rule, the seller must provide the consumer with a fully completed copy of the sales contract,[2525] attach to that contract two copies of a written notice of cancellation,[2526] and orally inform the consumer of his or her cancellation rights at the time the contract is signed.[2527] In immediate proximity to the space reserved in the contract for the buyer's signature must be a statement of the buyer's right to cancel.[2528] Both the contract and the notice of cancellation must be in the same language, e.g., Spanish, as the oral sales presentation.[2529]

Note that two copies of the notice of cancellation must be attached to the contract. Sellers may get into trouble by forgetting to include the second of these two notices.[2530] The seller has several options as to how to provide two copies of the notice, as long as one copy can be easily returned to the seller. One copy may be in the contract and one copy in a separate form, or the seller can give the consumer two copies of the contract with the form integrated into each copy. But when one copy of the form is returned, the consumer must be able to retain a completed copy of both the form and the contract. The contract itself must also notify consumers where to find these forms (e.g., back of the contract, in a separate form).[2531]

While the rule as originally drafted required sellers to include the exact notice language mandated by the rule, the rule now allows sellers to shorten the mandated notice language by omitting certain language which does not apply to a particular transaction, e.g., language relating to trade-ins where there is no trade-in, language relating to negotiable instruments where there is no negotiable instrument, or language about property delivered before expiration of the

Admin. Rules 152-11-8, Failure to Deliver/Substitution of Goods; Vermont Consumer Fraud Rules, Rule CF 105, Substitution of Products/Failure to Deliver. *See also* People v. Columbia Research Corp., 71 Cal. App. 3d 607, 139 Cal. Rptr. 517 (1977).

2518 Idaho Consumer Protection Regulations, Idaho Admin. Code § 04.02.01.163, Mail Order and Catalog Sales; New Jersey Administrative Rules of the Division of Consumer Affairs, N.J. Admin. Code § 13:45A-1.1, Deceptive Mail Order Practices.

2519 U.S. General Supply Co., 80 F.T.C. 857 (1972) (consent order).

2520 Jay Norris Inc., 91 F.T.C. 751 (1978).

2521 *Id.*

2522 *See* § 5.8.4, *infra.*

2523 *See* International Society for Krishna Consciousness v. Lee, 505 U.S. 672, 112 S. Ct. 2701, 2722, 120 L. Ed. 2d 541 (1992) (Kennedy, J., concurring).

2524 16 C.F.R. § 429 [reprinted at Appx. B.3, *infra*]. In 1995, after requesting public comment and reviewing the rule, the FTC continued the rule in effect with minor changes. 60 Fed. Reg. 54,180 (Oct. 20, 1995).

2525 16 C.F.R. § 429.1(a); *see* Paramount Builders, Inc. v. Commonwealth, 260 Va. 22, 530 S.E.2d 142 (2000) (ruling on civil investigative order) (failure to give copies violates state cooling-off statute). *Cf.* Consolidated Texas Fin. v. Shearer, 739 S.W.2d 477 (Tex. App. 1987).

2526 16 C.F.R. § 429.1(b); United States v. Mission Plans, Inc., 5 Trade Reg. Rep. (CCH) ¶ 23,660 (S.D. Tex. Sept. 2, 1994) (consent decree requiring pre-need funeral plan seller to give notice of right to cancel and cancellation forms); *see also* United States v. Dixie Readers' Serv., Inc., 3 Trade Reg. Rep. (CCH) ¶ 22,306 (S.D. Miss. Nov. 14, 1985) (consent order).

2527 16 C.F.R. § 429.1(e).

2528 16 C.F.R. § 429.1(a). *Cf.* Consolidated Texas Fin. v. Shearer, 739 S.W.2d 477 (Tex. App. 1987).

2529 16 C.F.R. § 429.1(a), (b).

2530 Eastern Roofing & Aluminum Co. v. Brock, 320 S.E.2d 22 (N.C. Ct. App. 1984); *see also* Op. Mich. Att'y Gen. No. 5792 (1980) (notice on reverse side of contract does not comply with Michigan law).

2531 16 C.F.R. § 429.1(a).

three-day period.[2532] This actually increases the likelihood of rule violations. Look for sellers to copy other sellers' notices, not realizing that the other seller has properly deleted language not applicable to that seller, but which is applicable to the copying seller, and which must be included in that seller's notice.

The rule also specifies that the seller may not misrepresent the buyer's right to cancel[2533] nor include in the contract any waiver of rights created by the FTC rule.[2534] It is no defense to the FTC rule that the seller offers a better cancellation policy than the FTC rule; the seller must disclose and comply with its own stated policy and also with the FTC rule.[2535]

The seller can not assign or sell the consumer's note for five business days[2536] and must make a full refund of all payments and cancel all indebtedness within ten business days of receipt of a buyer's cancellation notice.[2537] Obviously, it is improper for a seller to backdate the contract and cancellation notice to thwart the consumer's three-day cancellation right.[2538]

5.8.2.2 Interrelation of FTC Rule with State Law

Every state has enacted a three-day cooling-off period law analogous to the FTC rule.[2539] Such statutes are constitutional even though they single out door-to-door sales for special treatment.[2540]

Some of these statutes reiterate the FTC rule almost exactly or state that compliance with the FTC rule automatically satisfies the requirements of the state law. But other state cooling-off statutes set out requirements different than those specified in the FTC rule. The North Dakota cooling-off statute, for example, has been amended to provide those over sixty-five years of age with a fifteen-day cooling-off period or a thirty-day guarantee.[2541] Most of the differences between the state rules and the FTC rules are relatively minor, so interpretations of one are relevant to the other.

Compliance with the FTC rule does not exempt a seller from complying with state laws regulating door-to-door sales, except to the extent that the state law is directly inconsistent with the FTC rule. A state law is directly inconsistent with the FTC rule and is preempted by the FTC rule where it provides the consumer a right to cancel which is weaker than that provided by the FTC rule or which permits the imposition of any cancellation fee or penalty on the buyer.[2542] State law is also preempted if it does not require that the seller give the buyer notice of his or her right to cancel the transaction in substantially the same form and manner provided for in the FTC rule.[2543] But if there is no conflict, the seller will have to comply with both the FTC rule and state law.[2544]

The FTC has issued an advisory opinion clarifying the issue of preemption of state cooling-off statutes.[2545] A seller

2532 16 C.F.R. § 429.1(b).

2533 16 C.F.R. § 429.1(f).

2534 16 C.F.R. § 429.1(d). *See also* Tee Pee Fence & Railing Corp. v. Olah, 544 N.Y.S.2d 112 (N.Y. City Civ. Ct. 1989) (waiver of right to cancel is void even though on a separate sheet of paper); Paramount Builders, Inc. v. Commonwealth, 260 Va. 22, 530 S.E.2d 142 (2000) (ruling on civil investigative order) (having consumer sign waiver of right to cancel as condition of getting a discount violates state cooling-off statute even though waiver is void).

2535 State v. Sears Roebuck & Co., Clearinghouse No. 40,629 (Me. Super. Ct. Aug. 1985).

2536 16 C.F.R. § 429.1(h).

2537 16 C.F.R. § 429.1(g), (i); *see also* United States v. Dixie Readers' Serv., Inc., 3 Trade Reg. Rep. (CCH) ¶ 22,306 (S.D. Miss. Nov. 14, 1985) (consent order).

2538 *See* Consolidated Texas Fin. v. Shearer, 739 S.W.2d 477 (Tex. App. 1987).

2539 Ala. Code §§ 5-19-1(8), 5-19-12; Alaska Stat. §§ 45.02.350 (door-to-door sales; five-day period), 45.63.030 (telephonic solicitations; seven-day period); Ariz. Rev. Stat. Ann. §§ 44-5001 to 44-5008; Ark. Stat. Ann. §§ 4-89-101 to 4-89-110; Cal. Civ. Code §§ 1689.5 to 1689.14; Colo. Rev. Stat. §§ 5-3-401 to 5-3-405; Conn. Gen. Stat. Ann. §§ 42-134a to 42-143; Del. Code Ann. tit 6, §§ 4401 to 4405; D.C. Code Ann. § 28-3811; Fla. Stat. Ann. §§ 501.021 to 501.055; Ga. Code Ann. § 10-1-6; Haw. Rev. Stat. §§ 481C-1 to 481C-6; Idaho Code §§ 28-43-401 to 28-43-405; 815 Ill. Comp. Stat. Ann. § 505/2B; Ind. Code Ann. §§ 24-4.5-2-501 to 24-4.5-2-502, §§ 24-5-10-1 to 24-5-10-18; Iowa Code Ann. §§ 555A.1 to 555A.6; Kan. Stat. Ann. § 50-640; Ky. Rev. Stat. Ann. §§ 367.410 to 367.460; La. Rev. Stat. Ann. §§ 9:3538 to 9:3541; Me. Rev. Stat. Ann. tit. 32, §§ 4661 to 4670 and tit. 9-A, §§ 3-501 to 3-507; Md. Com. Law Code Ann. §§ 14-301 to 14-306; Mass. Gen. Laws Ann. ch. 93, § 48; Mich. Comp. Laws Ann. §§ 445.111 to 445.117; Minn. Stat. Ann. §§ 325G.06 to 325G.11; Miss. Code Ann. §§ 75-66-1 to 75-66-11; Mo. Rev. Stat. §§ 407.700 to 407.720; Mont. Code Ann. §§ 30-14-501 to 30-14-508; Neb. Rev. Stat. §§ 69-1601 to 69-1607; Nev. Rev. Stat. §§ 598.140 to 598.280 and 598.2801; N.H. Rev. Stat. Ann. §§ 361-B:1 to 361-B:3; N.J. Rev. Stat. Ann. §§ 17:16C-61.1 to 17:16C-61.9; N.M. Stat. Ann. § 57-12-21; N.Y. Pers. Prop. Law §§ 425 to 431; N.C. Gen. Stat. §§ 25A-38 to 25A-42; N.D. Cent. Code §§ 51-18-01 to 51-18-09; Ohio Rev. Code Ann. §§ 1345.21 to 1345.28; Okla. Stat. Ann. tit. 14A, §§ 2-501 to 2-505; Or. Rev. Stat. §§ 83.710 to 83.750; Pa. Stat. Ann. tit. 73, § 201-7; R.I. Gen. Laws §§ 6-28-1 to 6-28-8; S.C. Code Ann. §§ 37-2-501 to 37-2-506; S.D. Comp. Laws Ann. §§ 37-24-5.1 to 37-24-5.7; Tenn. Code Ann. §§ 47-18-701 to 47-18-708; Tex. Bus. & Com. Code Ann. §§ 39.001 to 39.009; Utah Code Ann. §§ 70C-5-101 to 70C-1-105; Vt. Stat. Ann. tit. 9, §§ 2451a, 2454; Va. Code Ann. §§ 59.1-21.1 to 59.1-21.7:1; Wash. Rev. Code Ann. §§ 63.14.040, 63.14.120, 63.14.150, 63.14.154; W. Va. Code §§ 46A-2-132 to 46A-2-135; Wis. Stat. Ann. §§ 423.201 to 423.205; Wyo. Stat. §§ 40-12-104, 40-14-251 to 40-14-255.

2540 State v. Direct Sellers Ass'n, 108 Ariz. 165, 494 P.2d 361 (1972).

2541 N.D. Cent. Code §§ 51-18-02 and -04, *as amended by* 1991 N.D. Laws 530, 531.

2542 16 C.F.R. § 429.2(b) [*reprinted at* Appx. B.3, *infra*].

2543 *Id.*

2544 *See* Bruntaeger v. Zeller, 515 A.2d 123 (Vt. 1986).

2545 FTC Advisory Opinion, Consumer Cred. Guide (CCH) ¶ 98,583 (July 1, 1975), *reproduced on* the companion CD-Rom to this volume.

can be required to give two incompatible cooling-off period notices—one mandated by the FTC rule and one by state law—

> as long as any language in the state or municipal notice directly inconsistent with the rule is stricken. Since the Commission's rule gives the consumer a unilateral right to cancel a transaction within three days, without penalty or fee, language in a state notice misinforming the buyer of the existence of a penalty or fee (i.e., "If you cancel, the seller may keep all or part of your cash down payment") is directly inconsistent with the rule and, if included in the sales contract or receipt, must be stricken. Moreover, since the buyer's right to cancel transactions covered by the rule is not limited to agreements solicited at or near the buyer's residence, does not require the buyer to furnish any reason for cancellation, and may be exercised by mail or delivery of any written notice or telegram, any language to the contrary in a state notice is similarly directly inconsistent with the rule.[2546]

The FTC has issued another advisory opinion that the cooling-off notice provided for in the Uniform Consumer Credit Code misinforms buyers as to their rights under the FTC rule and conflicts with the FTC notice because the FTC rule's coverage is broader than that of the UCCC, and the UCCC notice implies that the buyer must state a specific reason for canceling the transaction.[2547]

5.8.2.3 Interrelation of FTC Rule and State Law with Truth in Lending Rescission

Another source of consumer cancellation rights is the rescission notice required by the Truth in Lending Act where a creditor takes a security interest in the debtor's home.[2548] The FTC rule explicitly states that it does not apply in situations where the TIL rescission notice is required.[2549] In fact, mistakenly disclosing a right to cancel under the FTC rule or state law may violate the Truth in Lending Act by obscuring or contradicting the notice of the TIL rescission right.[2550]

While the FTC rule does not apply where TIL rescission rights are applicable, state cooling-off statutes *do* apply, unless they are inconsistent with the TIL requirements.[2551] For example, a federal court has ruled that Mississippi's state cooling-off law is not inconsistent with TIL even though the state law places extra requirements on the creditor, and that, consequently, the creditor must comply with both statutes.[2552] Some state laws include an exemption similar to the FTC rule's, however.[2553] Giving the consumer the Truth in Lending rescission notice does not constitute substantial compliance with a state law requirement that the consumer be given a notice of cancellation.[2554]

5.8.2.4 Scope of the FTC Rule

5.8.2.4.1 Sales outside the home are also covered

The FTC rule applies to the sale, lease, or rental of consumer goods purchased primarily for personal, family, or household purposes.[2555] For the rule to apply, the sale need not be consummated in the buyer's "home." The definition of "home-solicitation sales" extends to all sales where "the seller or his representative personally solicits the sale, including those in response to or following an invitation by the buyer, and the buyer's agreement or offer to purchase is made at a place other than the place of business of the seller."[2556]

Sales in locations outside the consumer's home but not at the seller's place of business are covered.[2557] The rule, as revised in 1995, lists sales "at facilities rented on a temporary or short-term basis, such as hotel or motel rooms, convention centers, fairgrounds and restaurants, or sales at the buyer's workplace or in dormitory lounges" as examples of sales that are covered.[2558] A company that persuades a

2546 *Id.*

2547 FTC Advisory Opinion, 87 F.T.C. 1444 (1976), *reproduced on* the companion CD-Rom to this volume.

2548 15 U.S.C. §§ 1602(u), 1635(a).

2549 16 C.F.R. § 429.0(a)(2); Letter No. 1054, Consumer Cred. Guide (CCH) ¶ 31,378 (June 1, 1976).

2550 *See* Williams v. Empire Funding Corp., 109 F. Supp. 2d 352 (E.D. Pa. 2000).

2551 *See* 12 C.F.R. § 226.28; *see also* Reynolds v. D&N Bank, 792 F. Supp. 1035 (E.D. Mich. 1992).

2552 Cole v. Lovett, 672 F. Supp. 947 (S.D. Miss. 1987). *See also* Reynolds v. D&N Bank, 792 F. Supp. 1035 (E.D. Mich. 1992).

2553 Hanlin v. Ohio Builders & Remodelers, Inc., 196 F. Supp. 2d 572 (S.D. Ohio 2001) (state home solicitation sales act does not give right to cancel contract with home improvement lender since TILA provides right to rescind).

2554 Gross v. Bildex, Inc., 647 N.E.2d 573 (Ohio Mun. 1994); Hines v. Thermal-Gard of Ohio, Inc., 46 Ohio Misc. 2d 11, 546 N.E.2d 487 (Mun. Ct. 1988).

2555 16 C.F.R. § 429.0(a), (b). *Cf.* Moore v. R.Z. Sims Chevrolet-Subaru, Inc., 241 Kan. 542, 738 P.2d 852 (1987) (state cooling off statute does not apply where truck not intended for personal, family or household purpose); Reagan Nat'l Advertising v. Lakeway 620 Partners, 2001 Tex. App. LEXIS 4375 (June 29, 2001) (unpublished, citation limited) (Texas statute only applies to consumer transactions, and successor to consumer's interest can not sue as consumer).

2556 16 C.F.R. § 429.0(a).

2557 *See* Louis Luskin & Sons, Inc. v. Samovitz, 166 Cal. App. 3d 533, 212 Cal. Rptr. 612 (1985); State *ex rel.* Abrams v. Kase, Clearinghouse No. 43,079 (N.Y. Sup. Ct. 1986). *See also* Brunteager v. Zeller, 515 A.2d 123 (Vt. 1986) (sale in hotel room within state cooling-off statute). *Cf.* Reusch v. Roob, 234 Wis. 2d 270, 610 N.W.2d 168 (App. 2000) (sale at one of seller's two places of business not covered by state cooling-off statute).

2558 16 C.F.R. § 429.0(a). This provision of the revised regulation adopts the position that the FTC has expressed in the past. *See*

sales prospect to set up and invite neighbors to an in-home sales meeting is also covered by the rule.[2559]

Sellers of automobiles, vans, trucks or other motor vehicles at auctions, tent sales or other temporary places of business are specifically exempted from the rule, as long as the seller is a seller of vehicles with a permanent place of business.[2560] This provision, which was added to the rule in 1995, expands upon an exemption the FTC adopted in 1988[2561] in that it exempts sellers of all motor vehicles rather than just automobiles. It also exempts "curbstone" sales as long as the seller has a permanent place of business.[2562] Sales of arts and crafts at fairs and similar places are also exempt.[2563]

5.8.2.4.2 Effect of prior negotiations, seller being invited to the home

If the sale is made in the consumer's home following prior negotiations at the seller's place of business, the sale is not covered on the theory that "while such sales are actually consummated in the home, the attributes of the typical door-to-door sale are not present—the consumer has not been duped or otherwise deceived as to the nature of the sales call."[2564] For example, where a loan transaction takes place at the creditor's place of business, and subsequently an appraiser visits the consumer's home, the rule does not apply.[2565] Nor does the rule apply where the consumers go to the seller's place of business and commit themselves there to the sale, even though the seller later visits their home to determine what materials will be needed and to calculate a firm price.[2566] In order for this exception to apply, the seller's place of business where the prior negotiations occurred must be a retail business establishment at a fixed permanent location where the goods are exhibited or the services are offered for sale on a continuing basis.[2567]

Similarly, the rule does not apply if the buyer asks the seller to visit the buyer's home for the purpose of repairing personal property.[2568] But if, in the course of that visit, the repairman sells the buyer additional goods (other than necessary replacement parts) or additional services, that additional sale must comply with the FTC rule. Similarly, after a product is sold in a store, the rule should apply to subsequent in-home solicitations to sell a maintenance agreement on that product.[2569] Sales based on a referral by neighbors should also be covered by the rule.[2570]

5.8.2.4.3 Emergency exception

There is also an emergency exception to the rule. For this to apply, the buyer must provide a statement in the buyer's handwriting describing the emergency and expressly waiving the three-day cancellation right.[2571] A seller must comply strictly with the requirements of the emergency exception, and courts will scrutinize alleged emergency waivers closely.[2572] A seller can not claim an emergency waiver where it did not start work until after the three-day cancellation period had passed.[2573]

5.8.2.4.4 Mail and telephone sales

Transactions conducted and consummated entirely by mail or telephone and without other contact between the

---

60 Fed. Reg. 54180 (Oct. 20, 1995), discussing the reasons for adding these examples to the rule; 53 Fed. Reg. 45455, 45458 (Nov. 10, 1988); FTC Advisory Opinion to "est, an educational corporation" (July 14, 1976), *reproduced on* the companion CD-Rom to this volume; Holloway, FTC Informal Staff Opinion Letter (May 11, 1990), Clearinghouse No. 45,909 (photo session and sale of prints in hotel room). *See also* FTC v. Screen Test USA, 5 Consumer Cred. Guide (CCH) ¶ 24,699 (E.D. Va. Aug. 31, 1999) (consent decree) (hotel room sales).

2559 U.S. v. Sanders, 5 Trade Reg. Rep. (CCH) ¶ 24,742 (D. Md. Apr. 2, 2000) (consent order).

2560 16 C.F.R. § 429.3(a).

2561 53 Fed. Reg. 45455 (Nov. 10, 1988).

2562 *See* 60 Fed. Reg. 54180, 54183 (Oct. 20, 1995).

2563 16 C.F.R. § 429.3(b). This exemption, added to the rule in 1995, merely codifies an exemption adopted by the FTC in 1988. 53 Fed. Reg. 45455 (Nov. 10, 1988).

2564 Statement of Basis and Purpose, 37 Fed. Reg. 22946 (Oct. 26, 1972); *see also* Moore v. R.Z. Sims Chevrolet-Subaru, Inc., 241 Kan. 542, 738 P.2d 852 (1987).

2565 Saler v. Hurvitz, 84 B.R. 45 (Bankr. E.D. Pa. 1988).

2566 Cooper v. Crow, 574 So. 2d 438 (La. App. 1991).

2567 16 C.F.R. § 429.0(a)(1). *See* Clemens v. Duwel, 100 Ohio App. 3d 423, 654 N.E.2d 171 (1995) (comparable state law exception did not apply because home improvement contractor's home, where he maintained his office, was not a retail business establishment).

2568 16 C.F.R. § 429.0(a)(5). *See* Bratka v. Smiley, 2003 WL 1065603 (Ohio App. Mar. 11, 2003) (unpublished, citation limited) (finding exception inapplicable); Smaldino v. Larsick, 90 Ohio App. 3d 691, 630 N.E.2d 408 (1993) (cooling-off period under comparable provision of state law does not apply where repairman sold new furnace instead of repairing broken one, where repair was not a realistic option). *See also* Brown v. Jacob, 476 N.W.2d 156 (Mich. 1991). *Cf.* Papp v. J&W Roofing & General Contracting, 1999 Ohio App. LEXIS 6042 (Dec. 17, 1999) (exception for repair of personal property under identical state statutory language applies to contract to replace roof).

2569 State v. Sears Roebuck & Co., Clearinghouse No. 40,629 (Me. Super. Ct. 1985).

2570 Cole v. Lovett, 672 F. Supp. 947 (S.D. Miss. 1987).

2571 16 C.F.R. § 429.0(a)(3) [reprinted at Appx. B.3, *infra*]. *See* Smaldino v. Larsick, 90 Ohio App. 3d 691, 630 N.E.2d 408 (1993) (even in undisputed emergency, cooling-off period applies unless buyer signs statement under comparable provision of state law). *See also* McClure v. Kline Roofing Siding & Insulation, Inc., 35 Pa. D. & C.3d 1 (C.P. Lancaster Cty. 1985) (seller's responsibility not consumer's to obtain the written waiver in emergency situations).

2572 Tee Pee Fence & Railing Corp. v. Olah, 544 N.Y.S.2d 112 (N.Y. City Civ. Ct. 1989).

2573 *Id.*

buyer and seller prior to delivery of goods or services are explicitly excluded from coverage under the FTC rule.[2574] If there is other contact with the buyer, however, this exception does not apply.[2575] Note that state telemarketing laws may provide buyers the right to cancel a telephone sale, even though the FTC rule does not.[2576]

5.8.2.4.5 Leases, rent-to-own transactions, transactions under $25

The rule explicitly applies to leases and rentals of consumer goods,[2577] and the rule's Statement of Basis and Purpose explains that the rule was redrafted to make it clear that leases were covered so that door-to-door sellers could not escape the rule by leasing their goods instead of selling them.[2578] The rule may thus provide an often overlooked way to challenge "rent-to-own" appliance transactions, particularly if the original order was not taken at the seller's place of business, or if the contract was consummated in the buyer's home (even if an order was taken over the telephone). "Rent-to-own" companies routinely do not supply the cancellation notice specified in the FTC rule.

The FTC rule does exempt sales under $25.[2579] Rent-to-own companies may argue that this exclusion for small sales also covers "rent-to-own" terminable leases where the initial deposit and weekly or monthly payments do not exceed $25. In other words, there is an issue whether the $25 minimum applies to each monthly or weekly lease payment or to the total of payments. But the purpose of the rule's exemption for sales under $25 is not to exclude such things as appliance leases, but only "sales by milkmen, laundrymen, and other route salesmen who customarily make sales which would otherwise fall within the scope of the Rule. . . ."[2580] The rule also defines purchase price as "the total price paid or *to be paid* for the consumer goods."[2581] The rule's $25 minimum also applies to the total of multiple contracts "to insure that the rule would apply to transactions in which the seller writes up a number of invoices or contracts none of which show a price of [$25] or more, but when taken together the total price exceeds that amount."[2582]

2574 16 C.F.R. § 429.0(a)(4).

2575 Smaldino v. Larsick, 90 Ohio App. 3d 691, 630 N.E.2d 408 (1993) (construing comparable language of state cooling-off period law).

2576 *See* § 5.9.5.3, Appx. E, *infra*.

2577 16 C.F.R. § 429.0(a) and (b).

2578 37 Fed. Reg. 22945 (Oct. 26, 1972).

2579 16 C.F.R. § 429.0(a).

2580 Statement of Basis and Purpose, 37 Fed. Reg. 22945 (Oct. 26, 1972).

2581 16 C.F.R. § 429.0(e).

2582 Statement of Basis and Purpose, 37 Fed. Reg. 22945 (Oct. 26, 1972). *Cf.* Holloway, FTC Informal Staff Opinion Letter (May 11, 1990) Clearinghouse No. 45,909 (test is whether two charges involve two separate transactions).

5.8.2.4.6 Sales of real property, home improvements, securities, and insurance

The rule explicitly exempts the sale or rental of real property, the sale of insurance, and the sale of securities.[2583] However, the rule may apply to transactions in which a consumer engages a real estate broker to sell his home or to rent and manage his residence during a temporary period of absence.[2584]

The exclusion for the sale or rental of real property has no effect on the coverage of home improvement transactions. The FTC has explicitly stated that transactions "such as the sale of driveway resurfacing, aluminum siding, roofing materials or treatment, landscaping, or repairs to the home or to other real property" are not excluded from the rule.[2585]

5.8.2.4.7 What sellers are covered

The FTC rule covers sellers who are "engaged in the door-to-door sale of consumer goods or services."[2586] On its face, this language does not require that the seller be regularly engaged in that type of transaction, so occasional door-to-door sales by a seller who usually sells from a regular business location should be covered. By contrast, a state court has interpreted its differently-worded cooling-off statute to apply only to sellers who are regularly engaged in door-to-door sales.[2587]

5.8.2.5 Scope of State Laws

5.8.2.5.1 Overview

If a sale is outside the scope of the FTC rule but covered by state law, the seller must still comply with the state law. If the FTC rule, but not the state statute, applies to a sale, the seller must comply with the FTC rule. If both the FTC rule and state law apply, the seller must comply with both to the extent that the state law does not conflict with the FTC rule.[2588]

The fact that the buyer may be a sophisticated consumer who initiated contact with the seller and who conducted lengthy negotiations over the purchase of a very expensive product does not make a state cooling-off law inapplicable.[2589] State cooling-off laws apply whether or not the

2583 16 C.F.R. § 429.0(a)(6).

2584 Statement of Basis and Purpose, 37 Fed. Reg. 22948 (Oct. 26, 1972).

2585 Statement of Basis and Purpose, 37 Fed. Reg. 22947 (Oct. 26, 1972). *See also* § 5.8.2.5.5, *infra*.

2586 16 C.F.R. § 429.0(c).

2587 Bradley v. North Country Auto and Marine, 999 P.2d 308 (2000).

2588 *See* § 5.8.2.2, *supra*.

2589 Burke v. Yingling, 666 A.2d 288 (Pa. Super. 1995).

consumer appears to need special protection.[2590] But a home improvement contract that was worked out because of the parties' prior personal relationship was not covered by the Pennsylvania cooling-off statute even though it was signed in the buyer's home.[2591] State home improvement laws generally protect buyers only, so a person who signs a contract in his or her home to sell something does not have the right to cancel it.[2592]

When a transaction has connections to more than one state, the court must decide which state's law to apply. In one case, a court applied the California home solicitation sales law where an heir-finder hired by the attorney for an estate in Texas entered into a contract with the heir in the heir's California home.[2593] In another case, a federal court in Illinois concluded at the summary judgment stage that because the seller was a New York corporation, the purchased good was in New York during the negotiations, and the buyer visited New York to view the good, New York law may be applied.[2594]

5.8.2.5.2 Coverage that is broader than the FTC rule

A number of states have enacted cooling-off legislation covering an even wider range of consumer transactions than the FTC rule. For example, some states exclude only sales under $10 or $15 instead of the FTC's $25. Some state cooling-off statutes apply to seller-initiated telephone sales, either by explicit statutory definition[2595] or by judicial interpretation.[2596] For statutes that cover telephone sales, it is the location where the call is received, not where it originates, that is decisive.[2597]

At least one state cooling-off statute explicitly applies to purchases of realty except when the purchaser is represented by a licensed attorney or when the transaction is negotiated by a licensed real estate broker.[2598] Ohio's statute implies that some sales or rentals of real property are covered, since it excludes sales and rentals by licensed real estate brokers or salespersons.[2599] Several states, while excluding the sale of insurance, do include the services of an insurance adjuster within the scope of the home solicitation statute.[2600] Unlike the FTC rule, the Pennsylvania statute does not have special exemptions for any types of transactions and is applicable to all buyer-initiated sales.[2601]

The FTC rule excludes home repairs where the buyer initiates the contact.[2602] Some state cooling-off statutes have similar exceptions.[2603] Sales based on referrals by neighbors are considered seller-initiated.[2604]

5.8.2.5.3 Narrower coverage than the FTC rule

Of course, state cooling-off legislation may have a narrower coverage than the FTC rule. Some state statutes require that "the seller or his representative personally solicit the sale." This has been interpreted to require an affirmative act on the part of the seller and no prior contact between the seller and buyer.[2605] Other courts do not look to

2590 *Id.*

2591 Lou Botti Constr. v. Harbulak, 760 A.2d 896 (Pa. Super. 2000).

2592 DeFazio v. Gregory, 836 A.2d 935 (Pa. Super. 2003).

2593 *In re* Estate of Rhymer, 969 S.W.2d 126 (Tex. App. 1998) ("very nature of home solicitation statutes argues strongly in favor of applying the law of the state where the solicitation occurred").

2594 Pritzker v. Krishna Gallery of Asian Arts Inc., 1996 U.S. Dist. LEXIS 14398 (N.D. Ill. 1996).

2595 Alaska Stat. § 45.02.350; Ark. Stat. Ann. § 4-89-102(4)(B)); Fla. Stat. Ann. § 501.021(1); La. Rev. Stat. Ann. § 9:3516(20); Me. Rev. Stat. Ann. tit. 32, § 4662; State v. Sears Roebuck & Co., Clearinghouse No. 40,629 (Me. Super. Ct. 1985); Mich. Comp. Laws Ann. § 445.111(a); Mont. Code Ann. § 30-14-502(2); N.D. Cent. Code § 51-18-01; Or. Rev. Stat. § 83.710(b)(3) (only for periodicals, magazines, and other reading material except for newspapers); Vt. Stat. Ann. tit. 9, § 2451a(d); Wis. Stat. Ann. § 423.201; Wyo. State § 40-12-104. *See also* State v. Roob, 2003 WL 22137896 (Wis. App. Sept. 17, 2003) (unpublished, citation limited) (interpreting Wis. Admin. Code § ATCP § 127.01 to cover sale that was solicited by telephone call to buyer's home and fax to her job).

2596 People v. Toomey, 157 Cal App. 3d 1, 203 Cal. Rptr. 642, 71 Cal. 3d 245 (1984) (telephone solicitations initiated from seller's offices are included within the scope of the statute where contract was made at buyer's home); Hollywood Decorators, Inc. v. Lancet, 118 Misc. 2d 1096 (N.Y. Sup. Ct. 1983) (statute applied where seller advertised by radio, buyer telephoned seller, and seller met with buyer at his home and executed contract); Brown v. Martinelli, 419 N.E.2d 1081 (Ohio 1981) (Ohio's home solicitation sales act includes telephone contacts initiated by the seller). *But see* United Consumers Club v. Griffin, 85 Ohio App. 3d 210, 619 N.E.2d 489 (1993) (sale initiated by seller's call to consumer's home not covered where contract signed at seller's fixed, permanent retail establishment).

2597 State v. Roob, 2003 WL 22137896 (Wis. App. Sept. 17, 2003) (unpublished, citation limited).

2598 Tex. Bus. & Comm. Code Ann. § 39.002(b)(4); McDaniel v. Pettigrew, 536 S.W.2d 611 (Tex. 1976).

2599 Ohio Rev. Code § 1345.21(F)(1).

2600 Williams v. Kapilow & Son, Inc., 105 Cal. App. 3d 156, 164 Cal. Rptr. 176 (1980); Culbreth v. Lawrence J. Miller, Inc., 328 Pa. Super. 374, 477 A.2d 491 (1984).

2601 Burke v. Yingling, 666 A.2d 288 (Pa. Super. 1995).

2602 16 C.F.R. § 429.0(a)(5).

2603 Bratka v. Smiley, 2003 WL 1065603 (Ohio App. Mar. 11, 2003) (unpublished, citation limited) (finding exception applicable). *See* Brown v. Jacob, 439 Mich. 862, 476 N.W.2d 156 (1991) (contract signed in home after buyer called seller's place of business and began negotiations over phone not covered), *rev'g* 183 Mich. App. 387, 454 N.W.2d 226 (1990). *But cf.* Williams v. Schroyer, 2000 Ohio App. LEXIS 5798 (Dec. 13, 2000) (home repair transaction covered where buyer called seller but then further negotiations took place at home).

2604 Cole v. Lovett, 672 F. Supp. 947 (S.D. Miss. 1987).

2605 All Am. Pools, Inc. v. Lato, 20 Conn. App. 625, 569 A.2d 562 (1990) (transaction not covered by state cooling-off law where initial contact took place at seller's place of business); Op. Att'y Gen. 075-31 (Florida Feb. 14, 1975) (if the sale is the result of a request for specific goods or services by the purchaser rather than as the result of personal persuasion or inducement on the

see whether the transaction was initiated by the seller or the buyer, but only consider whether the contract was made at the buyer's home.[2606] In some states, buyer-initiated sales are exempt if the seller maintains a business establishment in the state at a fixed location where the goods and services are offered or exhibited for sale.[2607] Some states also exclude certain categories of sellers completely.[2608] In addition, since a number of the state laws were patterned after the cooling-off period created by the Uniform Consumer Credit Code, some of these state laws only apply to credit sales.

5.8.2.5.4 Level of in-home contact required under state statutes

State statutes vary in the level of in-home contact with the consumer that they require. The Illinois statute at one time granted a right to cancel any sale that occurred "as a result of or in connection with a salesman's direct contact with or call on the consumer at his residence." An Illinois appellate court interpreted this language to cover a membership campground sale that was initiated by a written solicitation mailed to the consumer's home.[2609] The court distinguished between advertisements, which are aimed at the general public and would not constitute "contact" under the statute, and these solicitations, which were personally addressed to selected individuals and asked them to take specific steps. While the Illinois statute was subsequently amended to require the seller to be physically present at the buyer's residence,[2610] the decision is still persuasive precedent for interpretation of other states' statutes.

Similarly, while the Pennsylvania statute only applies to contacts or calls at the buyer's residence,[2611] its coverage goes beyond sales that are consummated at the consumer's home. The statute also covers sales that are finalized outside the home, as long as there was sufficient initial contact at the buyer's home.[2612] For example, a court refused to dismiss a claim under the Pennsylvania statute where the sales presentation was at the seller's place of business and the only in-home contact was that the seller wrote and telephoned the consumers at their home.[2613] Pennsylvania's statute has now been amended to make it clear that it covers sales that are

---

part of the seller, it is not subject to the right to cancel provision); Bramblewood Investors, Inc. v. C&G Assocs., 262 N.J. Super. 96, 619 A.2d 1332 (1992) (home solicitation sales act does not apply where buyer initiates contact and seller has fixed place of business in the state where the goods are offered for sale); State v. Stereo Importers, Inc., 114 Misc. 2d 864 (N.Y. Sup. Ct. 1982); Tambur's Inc. v. Hiltner, 55 Ohio App. 2d 90, 9 Ohio Op. 3d 239, 379 N.E.2d 231 (1977) (a transaction is not subject to the home solicitation sales act where the buyer initiates the contact by calling the seller and the seller subsequently sends a salesman to the buyer's home); Langston v. Brewer, 649 S.W.2d 827 (Tex. App. 1983) (home solicitation sales act does not apply where parties were involved in prior transaction, buyer contacted seller with regard to furnishing services, and after negotiations a contract entered into at home of buyer). *See also* Clemens v. Duwel, 100 Ohio App. 3d 423, 654 N.E.2d 171 (1995) (interpreting Ohio exception for some buyer-initiated sales, which, unlike the FTC rule, does not require that prior negotiations have occurred at the seller's place of business); R. Bauer & Sons Roofing & Siding, Inc. v. Kinderman, 83 Ohio App. 3d 53, 613 N.E.2d 1083 (1992) (Ohio statute's exclusion for buyer initiated contact where the seller has fixed locations that exhibit the goods or services is satisfied where consumer contacts seller and seller has sample of home improvement products at its store); Williams, Ohio Consumer Law § 3.6 (2002 ed.) for further discussion of the Ohio Home Solicitation Sales Act and *Tambur's*.

2606 Weatherall Aluminum Products Co. v. Scott, 71 Cal. App. 3d 245, 139 Cal. Rptr. 329 (1977) (contract entered into at the buyer's home fell within the purview of the statute even though the buyer initiated negotiations by telephoning the seller and expressing an interest in his product); *cf.* Von Lehn v. Astor Art Galleries, 86 Misc. 2d 1 (N.Y. 1976); Hollywood Decorators, Inc. v. Lancet, 118 Misc. 2d 1096 (N.Y. Sup. Ct. 1983) (contract for interior decoration solicited by means of radio advertisement and negotiated at a subsequent meeting between the parties at buyer's home is subject to the statute even where buyer first contacted seller by telephone); Cook v. Stevens, 44 Ohio App. 3d 135, 541 N.E.2d 628 (1988) (home improvement sale initiated by buyer not excluded under Ohio statute where seller did not have a fixed business location at which the goods and services were exhibited or offered); Hines v. Thermal-Gard of Ohio, Inc., 46 Ohio Misc. 2d 11, 546 N.E.2d 487 (Mun. Ct. 1988) (same); Opinion of the Virginia Attorney General William Broaddus to the Honorable George Heilig, Jr., Member, House of Delegates, Clearinghouse No. 40,630 (Jan. 29, 1985) ("prior negotiations" exception does not apply to brief telephone conversation nor to prior dealings between the parties concerning a different product).

2607 Bramblewood Investors, Inc. v. C&G Assocs., 262 N.J. Super. 96, 619 A.2d 1332 (1992); Gallagher v. O'Connor, 2003 WL 22220337 (Ohio App. Sept. 26, 2003) (unpublished, citation limited) (exemption did not apply where seller's home office did not have separate entrance, phone lines, or showroom, and was not made known to public); Bratka v. Smiley, 2003 WL 1065603 (Ohio App. Mar. 11, 2003) (unpublished, citation limited) (finding exception applicable); New Phila, Inc. v. Sagrilla, 2002 WL 1467771 (Ohio App. June 26, 2002) (unpublished, citation limited) (exemption does not have to be pleaded as an affirmative defense, but does not apply unless seller displays or offers the goods for sale at the fixed location); Patterson v. Stockert, 2000 Ohio App. LEXIS 6004 (Dec. 13, 2000); Chegan v. AAAA Continental Heating, 1999 Ohio App. LEXIS 5572 (Nov. 24, 1999) (finding that transaction fell within exception); Clemens v. Duwel, 100 Ohio App. 2d 423, 654 N.E.2d 171 (1995) (interpreting exception not to apply).

2608 *See, e.g.*, Ohio Rev. Code § 1345.21(F)(5) (excluding goods or services sold by licensed motor vehicle dealers).

2609 Warren v. Borger, 184 Ill. App. 3d 38, 539 N.E.2d 1284 (1989).

2610 *See* 815 Ill. Comp. Stat. Ann. 505/2B, *as amended by* Illinois Laws 86-898 § 2 (effective Jan. 1, 1990).

2611 73 Pa. Stat. § 201-7(a).

2612 Staub v. Outdoor World Corp., 70 Lanc. 412, Clearinghouse No. 45,940 (Pa. C.P. Lancaster Cty. 1987). *But cf.* Lewis v. Delta Funding Corp. (*In re* Lewis), 290 B.R. 541 (Bankr. E.D. Pa. 2003) (single call by buyer from her home to seller insufficient).

2613 Staub v. Outdoor World Corp., 70 Lanc. 412, Clearinghouse No. 45,940 (Pa. C.P. Lancaster Cty. 1987).

made in connection with a contact or call upon the buyer either in person or by telephone.[2614] On the other hand, New York's statute has been interpreted to apply only when the contract is actually signed in the consumer's home.[2615] Michigan's statute likewise requires that the agreement to purchase be given in the home.[2616] The same court also held that an order given by telephone fell outside of the statute where it occurred as part of the parties' ongoing relationship, not in response to a call or visit to the home. Whether state home solicitation sale laws cover sales made by telephone is discussed in more detail in §§ 5.9.5.3 and 5.9.5.4, *infra*.

5.8.2.5.5 *Particular interpretations of state law scope provisions*

Coverage of home-improvement contracts has been an issue under Ohio's Home Solicitation Sales Act. An older Ohio case[2617] holds that home-improvement transactions are not covered by its statute. Newer cases, citing the interpretation of the FTC rule, the prevalence of "flim-flam artists" in the home-improvement business, and the unlikelihood that the legislature would have intended to exclude these transactions, find that they are covered.[2618] If the buyer has initiated the sale by inviting the seller to the home and the seller has a business establishment at a fixed location in the state where the goods or services are offered to be exhibited for sale, however, the transaction is exempt.[2619] The Maryland Supreme Court, interpreting a virtually identical statute and relying on the FTC's statement of the basis and purpose for its rule, finds that home-improvement transactions are covered.[2620] Mortgage brokers are covered if the statute includes sellers of services.[2621]

2614 73 Pa. Stat. § 201-7(a), as amended effective February 2, 1997.

2615 Niemiec v. Kellmark Corp., 581 N.Y.S.2d 569 (City Ct. 1992).

2616 Patrick v. U.S. Tangible Investment Corp., 595 N.W.2d 162 (Mich. App. Ct. 1999) (court also found the statute inapplicable because the buyer sought out the seller in hopes of enhancing investments).

2617 Tambur's, Inc. v. Hiltner, 55 Ohio App. 2d 90, 9 Ohio Op. 3d 239, 379 N.E.2d 231 (1977).

2618 Rusk Indus. v. Alexander, 2002 Ohio App. LEXIS 2137 (May 3, 2002); Camardo v. Reeder, 2002 WL 1349083 (Ohio App. June 20, 2002) (unpublished, citation limited); Papp v. J&W Roofing & General Contracting, 1999 Ohio App. LEXIS 6042 (Dec. 17, 1999); R. Bauer & Sons Roofing & Siding, Inc. v. Kinderman, 83 Ohio App. 3d 53 (1992) and cases cited therein; Gross v. Bildex, Inc., 647 N.E.2d 573 (Ohio Mun. 1994); Hines v. Thermal-Gard of Ohio, Inc., 46 Ohio Misc. 2d 11, 546 N.E.2d 487 (Mun. Ct. 1988). *See also* Clemens v. Duwel, 100 Ohio App. 3d 423, 654 N.E.2d 171 (1995) (applying cooling-off statute to home improvement contract without discussion of *Tambur's*).

2619 Zolg v. Yeager, 122 Ohio App. 3d 269, 701 N.E.2d 723 (1997).

2620 Crystal v. West & Callahan, 328 Md. 318, 614 A.2d 560 (1992). *Accord* Domestic Bank v. Johnson (*In re* Johnson), 239 B.R. 255 (Bankr. D.R.I. 1999) (door-to-door solicitation of home improvement work, where contract is signed in home, is covered by home solicitation sales act).

2621 Bank of New York v. Kaiser, 2003 WL 23335972 (Ohio Com. Pleas Aug. 16, 2003).

The Kansas door-to-door sales statute applies to sales conducted in any location that is not the seller's place of business, whether or not it is the consumer's home.[2622] Since the statute is not restricted to consumer goods and applies to sole proprietors as well as individuals, it allowed a restaurant owner to cancel a contract for a jukebox entered into in the restaurant.[2623]

A Massachusetts court, relying merely on the "spirit" of its home-solicitation sales statute, has held that subsequent negotiations can remove a transaction from the scope of the state rule. It held that if a buyer asks the seller to visit his home and then enters into "a course of negotiation and an exchange of drafts" of the contract, the rule is no longer necessary to protect the buyer from undue pressure.[2624] Other courts have been more willing to follow the statutory language.[2625]

5.8.2.6 Consumers' Rights Under FTC Rule, State Statutes

5.8.2.6.1 *Mechanics of three-day cancellation right*

A consumer may cancel a covered home-solicitation sale under the FTC rule and the typical state statute without penalty or obligation within three business days from the day on which the contract was signed. To cancel the transaction, the consumer must mail or deliver either a signed and dated copy of the "Notice of Cancellation" or any other written notice of intent to cancel. The consumer may also cancel the transaction by telegram.[2626] Merely stopping payment on a check may be insufficient to serve as cancellation, however.[2627] An unreported Ohio case holds that, where the statute specifies that the cancellation notice must be sent to the seller's address stated in the contract, cancellation can not be accomplished through a pleading served on the seller's attorney.[2628] However, other courts may find that the attorney is the seller's agent for delivery of notices.

2622 Kan. Stat. Ann. § 50-640.

2623 Dealers Leasing, Inc. v. Allen, 994 P.2d 651 (Kan. App. 1999).

2624 Donaher v. Porcaro, 715 N.E.2d 464 (Mass. App. Ct. 1999).

2625 *See* Burke v. Yingling, 666 A.2d 288 (Pa. Super. 1995).

2626 16 C.F.R. § 429.1(b). Gulf Indus., Inc. v. Hahn, 156 Ariz. 153, 750 P.2d 911 (Ct. App. 1988) (buyer or buyer's agent placing notice into possession of seller, without intervention of a third party, is notice given "in person" within meaning of state cooling-off statute). *See also* American Buyer's Club, Inc. v. Shaffer, 46 Ill. App. 3d 266, 361 N.E.2d 1380 (1970) (oral or other notice reasonably calculated to inform seller is adequate under Illinois law). *But see* State v. Columbus Kirby Co., 37 Ohio Misc. 106 (C.P. 1974) (hand-delivered notice to cancel held ineffective where statute required certified mail).

2627 Williams v. Schroyer, 2000 Ohio App. LEXIS 5798 (Dec. 13, 2000).

2628 Camardo v. Reeder, 2002 WL 1349083 (Ohio App. June 20, 2002) (unpublished, citation limited).

If the consumer cancels, the seller must return any payments made and any property traded in within ten days after receiving the cancellation notice. The consumer then must either make available to the seller any goods delivered under the contract or comply with the instructions of the seller regarding the return shipment of the goods at the seller's risk and expense. If the seller does not pick up the goods within twenty days of the cancellation notice, the goods become the property of the buyer without further obligation.[2629] If the buyer fails to make the goods available to the seller, or fails to return the goods after agreeing to do so, the buyer remains liable for performance of all obligations under the contract.[2630]

5.8.2.6.2 No recovery for services performed prior to cancellation

The FTC interprets this cancellation right strictly against the seller, even when the seller has already performed the contracted-for services before the cancellation period has expired. In non-emergency situations, the seller bears the full risk of cancellation if it elects to perform before the three days have expired. If the buyer exercises his or her cancellation right, the buyer does not have to pay a penalty and is not liable on the basis of *quantum meruit* for services performed.[2631]

Thus if a home improvement contractor performed certain work on a house, and the consumer properly canceled, the consumer would owe nothing, although the contractor could take back any materials supplied. Where the materials are already attached to the house, the consumer's attorney should argue that the materials should only be removed where the contractor can provide adequate assurance the house will be returned to its original condition.[2632] In any event, it may be a UDAP violation for a seller to systematically perform services during the three-day period if this is used as a method of frustrating consumers' cancellation rights.[2633]

5.8.2.6.3 Continuing right to cancel if notice is defective

Another issue is whether the cooling-off period begins to run after a defective notice of the right to cancel. State cooling-off statutes have been interpreted as providing consumers with a continuing right to cancel where the seller has not provided the consumer with proper notice of the consumer's right to cancel. The seller's failure to orally explain the consumer's cancellation right, failure to attach the notice of cancellation to the contract or failure to provide a statement of the buyer's right to cancel in the contract in

2629 16 C.F.R. § 429.1(b). *See also* Cole v. Lovett, 672 F. Supp. 947 (S.D. Miss. 1987); Domestic Bank v. Johnson (*In re* Johnson), 239 B.R. 255 (Bankr. D.R.I. 1999) (goods become property of buyer if seller does not return money and demand return of goods).

2630 16 C.F.R. § 429.1(b).

2631 Statement of Basis and Purpose, 37 Fed Reg. 22,947 (Oct. 26, 1972); *see also* Cole v. Lovett, 672 F. Supp. 947 (S.D. Miss. 1987); Louis Luskin & Sons, Inc. v. Samovitz, 166 Cal. App. 3d 533, 212 Cal. Rptr. 612 (1985) (no *quantum merit* recovery); Brown v. Jacob, 183 Mich. App. 387, 454 N.W.2d 226 (1990) (Mich. Comp. Laws § 445.115(2) explicitly states seller not entitled to compensation for work before cancellation), *rev'd on other grounds*, 439 Mich. 862, 476 N.W.2d 156 (1991) (statute held inapplicable); Patterson v. Stockert, 2000 Ohio App. LEXIS 6004 (Dec. 13, 2000); Papp v. J&W Roofing & General Contracting, 1999 Ohio App. LEXIS 6042 (Dec. 17, 1999) (risk is on contractor who begins performance during cancellation period); Clemens v. Duwel, 100 Ohio App. 3d 423, 654 N.E.2d 171 (1995) (seller who does home improvement work before giving notice of right to cancel can not recover value of goods or services, and buyer need not return the goods that have already been installed in the home); R. Bauer & Sons Roofing & Siding, Inc. v. Kinderman, 83 Ohio App. 3d 53, 613 N.E.2d 1083 (1992) (home improvement contractor who begins performance prior to giving notice of right to cancel assumes the risk); Gross v. Bildex, Inc., 647 N.E.2d 573 (Ohio Mun. 1994) (builder can not complain of injustice where it began work before giving a notice of the right to cancel); Hines v. Thermal-Gard of Ohio, Inc., 46 Ohio Misc. 2d 11, 546 N.E.2d 487 (Mun. Ct. 1988) (seller who installed windows before giving notice of cancellation can not recover them after consumer cancels); American Quality Roofing, Inc. v. Ipock, 730 S.W.2d 470 (Tex. App. 1987) (failure to offer cancellation right apparently complete defense to action to collect on services rendered). *Cf.* Barrett Builders v. Miller, 576 A.2d 455 (Conn. 1990) (contractor could not recover in quasi contract for work performed where home improvement contract did not comply with statutory requirement that the written contract contain the entire agreement of the parties); Scibek v. Longette, 339 N.J. Super. 72, 770 A.2d 1242 (App. Div. 2001) (repair shop that violated UDAP rule requiring estimates and authorizations could not recover for work). *But see* Pelletier v. Johnson, 937 P.2d 668 (Ariz. Ct. App. 1996) (*quantum meruit* recovery allowed to builder where buyer knew of right to cancel and was not harmed by omission of contract language required by statute); Kidd v. Greenspan Co., 2003 WL 356870 (Cal. App. Feb. 19, 2003) (unpublished, citation limited) (possibility of *quantum meruit* recovery defeats class certification); Beley v. Ventura County Municipal Court, 100 Cal. App. 3d 5, 160 Cal. Rptr. 508 (1979) (contractor was entitled to recover on *quantum meruit* for reasonable value of improvements); Hurlbert v. Cottier, 56 Ill. App. 3d 893, 372 N.E.2d 734 (1978) (consumer could rescind a contract for siding already installed, but had to tender the siding's reasonable value if it could not be returned "in its original condition"); Precision Builders & Restoration Specialties, Inc. v. Shea, 195 Mass. App. Div. 103 (1995) (contractor's *quantum meruit* claim against homeowners who canceled renovation claim was not barred by cooling-off statute); Laymance v. Vaughn, 857 S.W.2d 36 (Tenn. Ct. App. 1993) (state statute specifies that seller entitled to fair market value of services performed prior to cancellation).

2632 Family Constr. v. Dist. of Columbia Dept. of Consumer & Regulatory Affairs, 484 A.2d 250 (D.C. App. 1984).

2633 State *ex rel.* Corbin v. United Energy Corp. of Am., 151 Ariz. 45, 725 P.2d 752 (Ct. App. 1986). *See also* Ky. Op. Att'y Gen. 92-41 (1992) (a seller's performance of work in order to discourage the buyer from exercising cancellation rights may be an unfair trade practice).

immediate proximity to the space reserved for the buyer's signature (rather than on the reverse side) enables the buyer to cancel the contract even well after the three-day period has expired.[2634] A laches argument will be unavailing where the consumer was not informed of the right to cancel.[2635] If the seller has performed before giving a proper notice of the right to cancel, the consumer has the right to cancel even if the goods or services can no longer be returned, as the seller acted at its own risk.[2636]

A New York case has also implied a continuing right for a consumer to cancel a contract where the FTC rule was not complied with, although the FTC rule and the New York UDAP law at the time did not provide a private right of action.[2637] The Illinois cooling-off statute provides the consumer with actual damages and "other relief," and this has been held to include a right to rescind where no cooling-off notice was provided.[2638]

5.8.2.6.4 Other consumer protections

The FTC rule includes several other protections for the buyer aside from the right to cancel. It prohibits confession of judgment clauses in door-to-door sales contracts,[2639] and prohibits sale or assignment of the note or contract to a third party prior to midnight of the fifth business day following the sale.[2640] These protections are duplicated in the typical

2634 Reynolds v. D&N Bank, 792 F. Supp. 1035 (E.D. Mich. 1992) (state cooling-off statute explicitly gives continuous right to cancel); Cole v. Lovett, 672 F. Supp. 947 (S.D. Miss.) (purchasers who had not received statutorily required notice of right to cancel properly and timely exercised their right to cancel by letter two years after contract signed), *aff'd without op.*, 833 F.2d 1008 (5th Cir. 1987); Domestic Bank v. Johnson (*In re* Johnson), 239 B.R. 255 (Bankr. D.R.I. 1999) (where contract does not conform to statute, buyer's right to cancel is not time-limited); Williams v. Kapilow & Son Inc., 105 Cal. App. 3d 156, 164 Cal. Rptr. 176 (1980) (consumer had cause of action for rescission where contract contained no notice of his right to cancel); Beley v. Ventura County Municipal Court, 100 Cal. App. 3d 5, 160 Cal. Rptr. 508 (1979); Pinnacle Energy v. Price, 2001 Del. C.P. LEXIS 28 (Mar. 21, 2001) (allowing continuing right to cancel where seller did not print cancellation notice in conspicuous different ink color and cancellation form was not attached to contract; even if cancellation within reasonable time were requirement, consumer met this criterion); Warren v. Borger, 184 Ill. App. 3d 38, 539 N.E.2d 1284 (1989) (where seller gave buyers no notice of right to cancel, buyers had continuing right to cancel); Crystal v. West & Callahan, Inc., 328 Md. 318, 614 A.2d 560 (1992) (where seller fails to give required disclosures, right to cancel continues for a reasonable length of time); Brown v. Jacob, 183 Mich. App. 387, 454 N.W.2d 226 (1990) (statute gives continuing right to cancel where no cancellation notice provided to the consumer), *rev'd on other grounds*, 439 Mich. 862, 476 N.W.2d 156 (1991); Swiss v. Williams, 184 N.J. Super. 243, 445 A.2d 486 (1982) (the three-day notification period for rescission does not begin to run against the buyer until a receipt informing buyer of rescission rights is received by buyer); Community Nat'l Bank & Trust Co. v. McClammy, 138 A.D.2d 339, 525 N.Y.S.2d 629 (1988); State *ex rel.* Abrams v. Kase, Clearinghouse No. 43,079 (N.Y. Sup. Ct. 1986); Hollywood Decorators, Inc. v. Lancet, 118 Misc. 2d 1096 (N.Y. Sup. Ct. 1983) (buyer's time to cancel did not begin to run until the seller's compliance with the act); Vom Lehn v. Astor Art Galleries, 86 Misc. 2d 1 (Sup. Ct. 1976) (to gain the benefit of the three-day time limitation, the seller was required to furnish the buyers with a perforated card specifically advising them of their right to cancel the sale within the three-day period); Rossi v. 21st Century Concepts, Inc., 162 Misc. 2d 932, 618 N.Y.S.2d 182 (Yonkers City Ct. 1994) (seller's failure to fill in name, address, date of transaction, and last day to cancel on notice gives consumer continuing right to cancel); Camardo v. Reeder, 2002 WL 1349083 (Ohio App. June 20, 2002) (unpublished, citation limited); Patterson v. Stockert, 2000 Ohio App. LEXIS 6004 (Dec. 13, 2000) (does not begin to run where seller did not give notice of right to cancel); Papp v. J&W Roofing & General Contracting, 1999 Ohio App. LEXIS 6042 (Dec. 17, 1999); Clemens v. Duwel, 100 Ohio App. 3d 423, 654 N.E.2d 171 (1995); Gross v. Bildex, Inc., 647 N.E.2d 573 (Ohio Mun. 1994) (the consumer's right to cancel never expired where the seller gave the consumer a notice of the Truth in Lending rescission right rather than a notice of the right to cancel under the Home Solicitation Sales Act); Hines v. Thermal-Gard of Ohio, Inc., 46 Ohio Misc. 2d 11, 546 N.E.2d 487 (Mun. Ct. 1988); American Quality Roofing, Inc. v. Ipock, 730 S.W.2d 470 (Tex. App. 1987) (failure to give notice gives consumer complete defense to seller's collection action); De La Fuente v. Home Savings Ass'n, 669 S.W.2d 137 (Tex. App. 1984) (sellers violated home solicitation sales act by assigning a note to a third party on the same day it was executed giving buyer cause of action for rescission); Gramatan Home Investors Corp. v. Starling, 470 A.2d 1157 (Vt. 1983); *see also* Oxford Fin. Cos. v. Velez, 807 S.W.2d 460 (Tex. App. 1991); Consolidated Texas Fin. v. Shearer, 739 S.W.2d 477 (Tex. App. 1987) (defective notice allows consumer to cancel foreclosure sale where seller enforced statutory lien on consumer's home); Letter from Virginia Attorney General Mary Terry to Judge J.R. Zepkin, Clearinghouse No. 44,810 (Feb. 24, 1989) (failure to include required contract term, such as cancellation right, makes contract void and unenforceable). *But see* Wright Bros. Builders, Inc. v. Dowling, 247 Conn. 218, 720 A.2d 235 (1998) (strict compliance but not perfect, ritualistic compliance is required; failure to include second copy of cancellation notice and to fill in transaction date and cancellation date did not give buyer continuing right to cancel); Crystal v. West & Callahan, 328 Md. 318, 614 A.2d 560 (1992) (right to cancel continues only for a reasonable time where notice is not given, since Maryland's statute deleted the provision that it runs until notice is given); Ochocinska v. National Fire Adjustment Co., 577 N.Y.S.2d 998 (App. Div. 1991) (error in specifying last day to cancel, where there was no consumer reliance, does not create continuing right to cancel).

2635 Domestic Bank v. Johnson (*In re* Johnson), 239 B.R. 255 (Bankr. D.R.I. 1999). *But cf.* Williams v. Schroyer, 2000 Ohio App. LEXIS 5798 (Dec. 13, 2000) (importing requirement from different statute that consumer cancel within reasonable time after discovering grounds).

2636 *See* § 5.8.2.6.2, *supra*.

2637 Donnelly v. Mustang Pools, Inc., 84 Misc. 2d 28, 374 N.Y.S.2d 967 (Sup. Ct. 1975).

2638 Guess v. Brophy, 164 Ill. App. 3d 75, 517 N.E.2d 693 (1987).

2639 16 C.F.R. § 429.1(d).

2640 16 C.F.R. § 429.1(h).

state home solicitation sale statute or regulation.[2641] Some state laws impose additional requirements such as particular disclosures.[2642]

5.8.2.7 Other Consumer Remedies Under Cooling-Off Rule, State Statutes

There is no direct right to bring a private damage action for violation of the FTC Door-to-Door Rule. Of course, if the seller includes the cancellation notice in the contract, the consumer should be able to enforce this contract right. Otherwise, the consumer should argue that a violation of the FTC rule is a *per se* UDAP violation.[2643] In fact, several states have enacted UDAP regulations that reiterate the FTC rule,[2644] so that a violation of the rule in these states is clearly a *per se* UDAP violation.

State cooling-off statutes often provide an explicit private remedy, either in the statute itself[2645] or by stating that a violation is an automatic UDAP violation.[2646] Even where a violation of the cooling-off statute is not explicitly defined as a violation of the state UDAP statute, a strong argument can still be made that a violation of that statute is a *per se* UDAP violation.[2647] Where the state cooling-off statute allows a private action for cancellation and states that a violation is a UDAP violation, the consumer may be required to elect one remedy or the other.[2648] Other possible theories for enforcing the right to cancel are that the right to cancel is an express or implied contract term;[2649] that the absence of the notice of the right to cancel makes the contract illegal and unenforceable;[2650] or that the consumer should be allowed to invoke the equitable remedy of cancellation. If the contract is subject to the FTC Holder Rule, an assignee is liable for cancellation to the same extent as the original contracting party, with monetary liability capped at the amount the consumer has paid.[2651]

5.8.3 Referral Sales

In a referral sales scheme, the seller offers the buyer a discount contingent upon the buyer supplying the seller with referrals of other consumers and usually contingent upon these consumers also purchasing the seller's product. Such offers are often accompanied by claims of eventual discounts that are either exaggerated or even mathematically impossible if made widely enough in particular sales area. Savings claims are contingent on future events. The seller often has no basis for the claim, and buyers often receive no discount at all.

A number of states make the use of a referral sale plan, no matter how reasonable the accompanying representations, a *per se* UDAP violation.[2652] Such a ruling that the scheme is

2641 *See, e.g.*, Idaho Rules of Consumer Prot., Idaho Admin. Code § 04.02.01.170.

2642 N.Y. Pers. Prop. Law § 428(4); Rusk Indus. v. Alexander, 2002 Ohio App. LEXIS 2137 (May 3, 2002) (nondisclosures violated home solicitation sales act but caused no damage so were not UDAP violations); *see also* Rossi v. 21st Century Concepts, Inc., 162 Misc. 2d 932, 618 N.Y.S.2d 182 (Yonkers City Ct. 1994).

2643 *See* §§ 3.2.6, 3.2.7, *supra*. *See also* Eastern Roofing & Aluminum Co. v. Brock, 320 S.E.2d 22 (N.C. Ct. App. 1984). *But see* State *ex rel.* Miller v. Santa Rosa Sales & Marketing, Inc., 475 N.W.2d 210 (Iowa 1991) (attorney general can not utilize UDAP remedies where cooling-off statute provides attorney general with different remedial scheme; statute has now been amended to correct this defect); Iowa *ex rel.* Campbell v. C-Pals Corp., Clearinghouse No. 50,444 (Iowa Dist. Ct. Dec. 19, 1994); Laymance v. Vaughn, 857 S.W.2d 36 (Tenn. Ct. App. 1992).

2644 *See* Georgia Office of Consumer Affairs Regulations, Ga. Comp. R. & Regs. § 122-3-.01; Idaho Consumer Protection Regulations, Idaho Admin. Code § 04.02.01.170, Cooling-Off Period for Door-to-Door Sales.

2645 Minn. Stat. Ann. § 325G.11. *See* Levitan Sons v. Francis, 88 Misc. 2d 125 (Sup. Ct. 1976); Vom Lehn v. Astor Art Galleries, 86 Misc. 2d 1 (Sup. Ct. 1976); Commonwealth v. Flick, 382 A.2d 762 (Pa. Commw. 1978); De La Fuente v. Home Savings Ass'n, 669 S.W.2d 137 (Tex. App. 1984).

2646 *See, e.g.*, Gross v. Bildex, Inc., 647 N.E.2d 573 (Ohio Mun. 1994) (failure to provide notice of cancellation, commencing performance prematurely, and failure to return deposit violated UDAP statute; treble damages awarded); Hines v. Thermal-Gard of Ohio, Inc., 46 Ohio Misc. 2d 11, 546 N.E.2d 487 (Mun. Ct. 1988) (commencing performance before giving notice of cancellation was a violation of state cooling-off statute and, therefore, violated state UDAP statute as well); Culbreth v. Lawrence J. Miller, Inc., 328 Pa. Super. 374, 447 A.2d 491 (1984).

2647 Rossi v. 21st Century Concepts, Inc., 162 Misc. 2d 932, 618 N.Y.S.2d 182 (Yonkers City Ct. 1994). *See* Bruntaeger v. Zeller, 515 A.2d 123 (Vt. 1986); *see also* § 3.2.7, *supra*.

2648 Clemens v. Duwel, 100 Ohio App. 3d 423, 654 N.E.2d 171 (1995).

2649 *See* §§ 6.6.2.1, 6.6.4.2, *infra*.

2650 *See* § 6.6.4.6, *infra*.

2651 Cole v. Lovett, 672 F. Supp. 947 (S.D. Miss. 1987), *aff'd without op.*, 833 F.2d 1008 (5th Cir. 1987). *See* § 6.6, *infra*.

2652 State *ex rel.* Miller v. American Professional Marketing, Inc., 382 N.W.2d 117 (Iowa 1986) (although referral sales are outlawed, sales scheme is not a referral sale); Brown v. Jacob, 476 N.W.2d 156 (Mich. 1991); Commonwealth v. Gold Bond Indus., Inc., Clearinghouse No. 26,028 (Pa. C.P. Allegheny Cty. 1973); Commonwealth v. Commercial Enterprises, Inc., Clearinghouse No. 26,036 (Pa. C.P. Erie Cty. 1972); Wesware Inc. v. State, 488 S.W.2d 844 (Tex. Civ. App. 1972); Pliss v. Peppertree Resort Villas, Inc., 663 N.W.2d 851 (Wis. App. 2003) (offering a benefit for referrals as a sale inducement violates UDAP regulation if benefit will not be conferred prior to completion of sale); Idaho Admin. Code 04.02.01.180 to .182, Referral Sale; Massachusetts Consumer Protection Regulations, Mass. Regs. Code tit. 940, § 3.06, Referral Schemes; Tennessee Attorney General Opinion No. 95-089, Clearinghouse No. 51,275 (Aug. 29, 1995) (cellular telephone referral sales brochure violates Tennessee law); Rules of the Utah Consumer Sales Practices Act, Utah Admin. Rules 152-11-11, Franchises, Distributorships, Referral Sales, and Pyramid Sales Marketing Schemes; Wisconsin Dept. of Agriculture, Trade and Consumer Protection

a *per se* violation has been upheld against constitutional challenges.[2653] Where a state does not prohibit referral sales *per se*, the plan can still be deceptive if claims are exaggerated or unsubstantiated.[2654]

5.8.4 Unsolicited Goods

Selling unsolicited goods involves the seller delivering goods which the consumer has never ordered and then charging the consumer for their price. The "seller" may threaten to turn over accounts to a debt collection agency or report the delinquency to a credit reporting agency. Consumers who refuse to accept unsolicited goods may also be threatened with liability for storage charges. Consumers, unsure of their legal rights, find it inconvenient and costly to mail the goods back and may pay the seller for them in the face of debt collection efforts.

The FTC has challenged many schemes involving unordered goods. In one telemarketing scheme, a seller allegedly promised free gifts to business employees in order to get their names, then placed their names on invoices for unordered merchandise as a means of leading the company to believe that the merchandise had been properly ordered.[2655] In a second scheme, consumers were induced to call a 900 number to claim packages that were being held after failed attempts at delivery. The packages contained unordered merchandise and were not being held by a postal carrier.[2656] Another telemarketer represented that it was the customer's usual supplier; it shipped unordered merchandise, sent bills, and used the name of a fictitious law firm when attempting to collect.[2657] Another scheme substituted more expensive items in place of durable medical equipment consumers ordered.[2658] The FTC has also negotiated a consent order with a company that fraudulently sent past-due and renewal invoices to organizations, including churches and nonprofit organizations, for unordered computer repair service contracts and provided an 800 number for unlimited maintenance and repair services but rarely provided these services.[2659] Another variant is to bill companies for advertising that they never requested.[2660]

Federal law prohibits the use of the mails to send unordered merchandise, with the exception of free gifts, and requires that a notice accompany the gift disclosing that the

Rules, Wis. Ad. Code, ACTP 121.02, Referral Selling Plans. Separate legislation prohibits referral sales in many states, *e.g.*, Ala. Code § 8-19-5(18); Alaska Stat. § 45.50.471(b)(19); Ariz. Rev. Stat. § 44-5003; Colo. Rev. Stat. § 5-3-209; Conn. Gen. Stat. § 42-140 (home solicitation sales); D.C. Code § 28-3810; Idaho Code § 28-43-308; 815 Ill. Comp. Stat. Ann. § 505/2A; Ind. Code Ann. § 24-4.5-2-411; Iowa Code § 714.16(2)(b); Kan. Stat. Ann. §§ 162-3-309, 50-626(b)(1)(E); La. Rev. Stat. § 9:3536; Me. Rev. Stat. tit. 9A, § 3-309, tit. 32, § 4669; Md. Comm. Law Code § 13-304; Minn. Stat. § 325F.69(2); Neb. Rev. Stat. § 87-302(a)(13); N.M. Stat. Ann. § 57-12-5; N.C. Gen. Stat. § 25A-37; N.D. Cent. Code §§ 51-16.1-01 to -05; Okla. Stat. tit. 14A, § 2-411; Or. Rev. Stat. § 646.608(l); 73 Pa. Stat. § 201-2(4)(xii) (part of UDAP statute); S.C. Code Ann. § 37-2-411; S.D. Codified Laws § 37-24-6(4); Tenn. Code Ann. § 47-18-104(b)(19); Tex. Bus. & Com. Code § 17.46(b)(18); Utah Code Ann. § 70C-2-207; Va. Code § 18.2-242.1; W. Va. Code Ann. §§ 46A-2-110, 46B-4-2; Wyo. Stat. §§ 40-3-103, 40-14-245.

2653 These challenges usually involve prohibitions of pyramid sales schemes or prohibitions of both referral and pyramid schemes. *See* State *ex rel.* Turner v. Koscot Interplanetary Inc., 191 N.W.2d 624 (Iowa 1971); State v. Koscot Interplanetary Inc., 212 Kan. 668, 512 P.2d 416 (1973); State v. Lambert, 68 Wis. 2d 523, 229 N.W.2d 622 (1975); HM Distributors of Milwaukee, Inc. v. Department of Agriculture, 55 Wis. 2d 261, 198 N.W.2d 598 (1972).

2654 Grolier, Inc., 91 F.T.C. 315 (1978), *vacated on other grounds*, 615 F.2d 1215 (9th Cir. 1980); Southern States Distributing Co., 83 F.T.C. 1126 (1973); Federal Constr. Co., 75 F.T.C. 319 (1969); Luxor Carpet Inc., 67 F.T.C. 1152 (1965); Herley Press Ironer of Central Am., 66 F.T.C. 522 (1964); Insul-Seal Products, 66 F.T.C. 36 (1964).

2655 FTC v. Gen. Supply Centers, Inc., 5 Trade Reg. Rep. (CCH) ¶ 15398 (S.D. Cal. Apr. 16, 2003) (proposed consent decree) (toner phoner scheme); FTC v. Pendleton Group, Inc., 5 Trade Reg. Rep. (CCH) ¶ 15313 (C.D. Cal. Sept. 27, 2002) (proposed consent decree) (toner phoner scheme); FTC v. Modern Concept Marketing, Inc., 5 Trade Reg. Rep. (CCH) ¶ 15243 (C.D. Cal. Apr. 19, 2002) (toner phoner scam); FTC v. Pacific Office Sys., Inc., 5 Trade Reg. Rep. (CCH) ¶ 15127 (C.D. Cal. July 3, 2001) (toner phoner scheme); FTC v. Central Supplies, Inc., 5 Trade Reg. Rep. (CCH) ¶ 23,870 (N.D. Ill. 1995) (proposed consent decree). *See also* FTC v. McGowan, 5 Trade Reg. Rep. (CCH) ¶ 24,248 (D.N.J. 1997) (proposed consent decree); FTC v. United Wholesalers, Inc., 5 Trade Reg. Rep. (CCH) ¶ 23,849 (S.D. Fla. 1995) (preliminary injunction) (similar scheme); FTC v. Crittenden, 5 Trade Reg. Rep. (CCH) ¶ 23,233 (C.D. Cal. 1992) (stipulated final judgment) (sending unordered office equipment under guise that someone in office had ordered it).

2656 FTC v. Interactive Marketing Concepts, Inc., 5 Trade Reg. Rep. (CCH) ¶ 23,872 (D.N.J. 1995) (proposed consent decree).

2657 FTC v. United Wholesalers, Inc., 5 Trade Reg. Rep. (CCH) ¶ 23,849 (S.D. Fla. 1995) (preliminary injunction), ¶ 23,965 (1996) (proposed consent order requiring transfer of $1.3 million assets and payment of $202,000); FTC v. North Am. Supply, Inc., 5 Trade Reg. Rep. (CCH) ¶ 23,925 (C.D. Cal. 1995) (proposed consent order) (pretending to be regular supplier).

2658 FTC v. Freedom Medical, Inc., 5 Trade Reg. Rep. (CCH) ¶ 23,964 (S.D. Ohio 1996) (consent decree); FTC v. Motion Medical, Inc., 5 Trade Reg. Rep. (CCH) ¶ 24,036 (S.D. Ohio 1996) (consent order).

2659 FTC v. AKOA, Inc., 5 Trade Reg. Rep. (CCH) ¶ 24,408 (C.D. Cal. 1998) (consent decree).

2660 Image Sales & Consultants, Inc., 5 Trade Reg. Rep. (CCH) ¶ 24,442 (N.D. Ill. 1998) (consent decree); The Century Group, 5 Trade Reg. Rep. (CCH) ¶ 24,442 (N.D. Ill. 1998) (consent decree); FTC v. Dean Thomas Corp., 5 Trade Reg. Rep. (CCH) ¶ 24,327 (N.D. Ind. 1997) (stipulated final judgment). *See also* FTC v. Sparta Chem. Inc., 5 Trade Reg. Rep. (CCH) ¶ 24,167 (D.N.J. 1996) (proposed consent decree); FTC v. Commercial Electrical Supply Inc., 5 Trade Reg. Rep. (CCH) ¶ 24,167 (D. Md. 1996) (proposed consent decree); FTC v. National Bus. Distributors Co., 5 Trade Reg. Rep. (CCH) ¶ 24,167 (C.D. Cal. 1996) (proposed consent decree).

consumer may treat unsolicited merchandise as a gift.[2661] Infractions are *per se* violations of the FTC Act.[2662] A private remedy has also been implied under the federal law.[2663] Thus a private litigant can bring an action under either the federal law[2664] or the state UDAP statute.[2665] It is also a state UDAP violation to send the consumer a document that looks like an invoice as part of an offer for services, in an attempt to lead the consumer to believe that the services have already been ordered.[2666]

It is deceptive to deliver products in quantities greater than ordered and then bill the consumer for all items delivered.[2667] The FTC has reached a consent order with a sweepstakes company that sent out sweepstakes applications which also contained a box where the consumer could subscribe to magazines. The company then sent out trial subscriptions to consumers whether or not they checked the box requesting the subscription.[2668]

5.8.5 Negative Option Plans

Negative option plans—a book-of-the-month club is a common example—require plan participants to make affirmative and timely rejection of a sale offer. Silence is treated as a binding contract. The FTC rule concerning use of negative option plans requires sellers to disclose plan terms, including the negative option, minimum purchase requirements, cancellation rights, postage charges, and refusal rights.[2669] Membership must be canceled upon request when minimum obligations have been met.

The seller must also give the consumer written notice of the nature of the goods before their arrival, including a form allowing the consumer to refuse the selection. The FTC has indicated that notification by e-mail may suffice if the seller gives the consumer clear notice, before enrolling in the plan, about how notices will be sent.[2670] In addition, the federal E-Sign statute[2671] requires the seller to make specific disclosures prior to obtaining the consumer's consent to receive electronic notification.[2672] E-Sign also requires the consumer to either give or confirm consent electronically, in a manner that "reasonably demonstrates" that the consumer can access information in the electronic form that the seller will use.[2673]

The FTC has ruled that it is deceptive to misrepresent that the buyer can reject each product upon receipt or that after cancellation the consumer will not receive anything.[2674] The FTC has accepted a consent order concerning a music library firm where its sales representatives misrepresented the purpose of their visit as a music survey and misrepresented the number and retail price of the tapes offered, and the company advertised the plan as a pay-as-you-go arrangement but then switched customers to longer term contracts.[2675] The FTC's telemarketing rule has additional restrictions and requirements for negative option plans sold

2661 39 U.S.C. § 3009.

2662 U.S. v. Creative Publishing Int'l, Inc., 5 Trade Reg. Rep. (CCH) ¶ 15108 (D. Minn. May 30, 2001) (proposed consent order requiring company to forfeit right to payment for books shipped); FTC v. Totu, 5 Trade Reg. Rep. (CCH) ¶ 23,765 (E.D. Cal. Aug. 23, 1994) (proposed stipulated final judgment) (elaborate scheme to lead businesses to believe that unordered merchandise had actually been ordered); FTC v. Hosiery Corp. of Am., Inc., 3 Trade Reg. Rep. (CCH) ¶ 22,187 (E.D. Pa. 1984); U.S. v. Random Stationers, Inc., 3 Trade Reg. Rep. (CCH) ¶ 22,179 (S.D. Fla. 1984); Golden Fifty Pharmaceutical Co., 77 F.T.C. 277 (1970); Commercial Lighting Products, Inc., 95 F.T.C. 750 (1980) (consent order); CBS Inc., 90 F.T.C. 9 (1977) (consent order); Sunshine Art Studios, Inc., 81 F.T.C. 836 (1972), *aff'd*, 481 F.2d 1171 (1st Cir. 1973); GBI Corp., 80 F.T.C. 155 (1972) (consent order). *See also* Consumer Home Equipment v. FTC, 164 F.2d 972 (6th Cir. 1947), *cert. denied*, 331 U.S. 860 (1947).

2663 Kipperman v. Academy Life Ins. Co., 554 F.2d 377 (9th Cir. 1977); Crosley v. Lens Express, Inc., 2001 WL 650728 (W.D. Tex. Feb. 12, 2001).

2664 39 U.S.C. § 3009.

2665 *See* Idaho Consumer Protection Regulations, Idaho Admin. Code § 04.02.01.220, Unordered Goods or Services; 15 Mo. Code Regs. 60-8.060.

2666 Telcom Directories, Inc. v. Commonwealth *ex rel.* Cowan, 833 S.W.2d 848 (Ky. Ct. App. 1992).

2667 Star Office Supply Co., 77 F.T.C. 383 (1970); Commercial Lighting Products, 95 F.T.C. 750 (1980) (consent order).

2668 McCall Publishing Co., 3 Trade Reg. Rep. (CCH) ¶ 22,491 (F.T.C. File #852 3119 1987) (consent order).

2669 16 C.F.R. Part 425. In 1998 the FTC completed a periodic review of the Negative Option Plan rule, retaining it in its existing form with minor technical changes. 63 Fed. Reg. 44555 (Aug. 20, 1998). *See* 62 Fed. Reg. 15135 (Mar. 31, 1997). *See also* U.S. v. Micro Star Software, Inc., 5 Trade Reg. Rep. (CCH) ¶ 15258 (S.D. Cal. May 22, 2002); U.S. v. Oxmoor House, 5 Trade Reg. Rep. (CCH) ¶ 15321 (N.D. Ala. Nov. 7, 2002) (proposed consent decree against telemarketer who failed to disclose that consumer who kept and paid for product beyond 30 day free trial period would be automatically enrolled in negative option book program); FTC v. Travel World Int'l, 5 Trade Reg. Rep. (CCH) ¶ 22,757 (M.D. Fla. Nov. 2, 1989) (stipulated injunction) (negative option billed without permission); Utah Admin. R. § 152-11-12, Negative Options.

2670 FTC, Dot Com Disclosures § IV(A)(2) (2000).

2671 15 U.S.C. § 7001 *et seq.* See National Consumer Law Center, Consumer Banking and Payments Law Ch. 9 (2d ed. 2002 and Supp.) for a more detailed discussion of this statute.

2672 15 U.S.C. § 7001(c)(1)(B), (C). See § 4.2.14.3.10, *supra*, for further discussion of E-Sign.

2673 15 U.S.C. § 7001(c)(1)(C)(ii).

2674 Grolier, Inc., 91 F.T.C. 315 (1978), *vacated on other grounds*, 615 F.2d 1215 (9th Cir. 1980); Marshall Cavandish Corp., 86 F.T.C. 86 (1975) (consent order); Greystone Corp., 86 F.T.C. 94 (1975) (consent order); Crowell-Collier & Macmillan, Inc., 82 F.T.C. 1292 (1973) (consent order).

2675 Music Library Assocs., Inc., 3 Trade Reg. Rep. (CCH) ¶ 22,334 (F.T.C. Feb. 24, 1986) (consent order). *See also* U.S. v. Creative Publishing Int'l, Inc., 5 Trade Reg. Rep. (CCH) ¶ 15108 (D. Minn. May 30, 2001) (proposed consent decree against company that enticed consumers to accept free trial book offers, then enrolled them in negative option book clubs without their consent).

through telemarketing.[2676] Georgia,[2677] Idaho,[2678] Missouri,[2679] New York,[2680] Oregon,[2681] Utah,[2682] and Wisconsin[2683] have their own negative option UDAP regulations, specifying disclosures required in such plans. The Federal Cable Television Consumer Protection and Competition Act prohibits negative option billing for cable TV services.[2684]

5.9 Telemarketing, 900 Numbers, On-Line Fraud, and Spam

5.9.1 Introduction

Telemarketing, 900-number, and Internet scams have grown rapidly in recent years, spurred by the advent of technology such as automatic dialing systems and 900 numbers. The scams cover a broad range of solicitations, including advance fee loans, business opportunities and investments, credit card protection plans, credit repair, charitable solicitations, employment opportunities and work-at-home schemes. Telemarketing and Internet scams are particularly frustrating areas for law enforcement officials since the principals can easily move across state lines or even international borders.[2685]

Many telemarketers specialize in "reloading," i.e., soliciting people who have demonstrated their vulnerability by succumbing to previous telemarketing pitches.[2686] A particularly poignant sub-industry is the "recovery room" scam. These are telemarketing fraud artists who prey on people who have already been victimized once by other telemarketers. The "recovery room" operator promises, for an advance fee, to get the victims refunds or the prizes or goods that were never delivered.[2687]

This section first examines telemarketing fraud and the remedies for it, then 900-number scams, on-line fraud, and spam. It also discusses a number of practical steps consumers can take to avoid paying charges caused by telemarketing or 900-number fraud, and to prevent future victimization.

5.9.2 Overview of State and Federal Telemarketing Statutes and Regulations

Telemarketing is covered by several different and sometimes overlapping federal and state statutes and regulations:

- The Telephone Consumer Protection Act,[2688] which is administered by the Federal Communications Commission and which offers a private cause of action in state court for violations. It focuses mostly on abusive methods of contacting the consumer, such as unsolicited faxes and prerecorded messages, but also restricts telephone solicitations at inconvenient hours, and includes a nationwide do-not-call rule.
- The Telemarketing and Consumer Fraud and Abuse Prevention Act,[2689] which is administered by the FTC. It offers a private cause of action, but only where the plaintiff's damages exceed $50,000. It, and the Telemarketing Sales Rule[2690] the FTC promulgated pursuant to it, focus on the content of telemarketing calls, forbidding various forms of deception and abuse. It overlaps with the Telephone Consumer Protection Act in its prohibition of calls at inconvenient hours, abandoned calls, and Caller ID blocking; its requirement of company-specific do-not-call lists; its nationwide do-not-call rule; and its requirement that callers identify the entity on whose behalf they are calling.

2676 *See* §§ 5.9.4.7.3, 5.9.4.7.5, *infra*.

2677 Ga. Comp. R. & Regs. r. 122-4-.01 (adopting FTC rule by reference).

2678 Idaho Admin. Code 04.02.01.020(34).

2679 15 Mo. Code Regs. § 60-8.060.

2680 9 N.Y.C.R.R. § 595.3 (cable TV).

2681 Or. Admin. R. § 137-020-0300 (Nov. 14, 1991).

2682 Utah Admin. Code R. 152-11-12.

2683 Wis. Admin. Code ATCP 123.06 (cable TV).

2684 47 U.S.C. § 543(f). See § 2.5, *infra*, for cases discussing the preemptive effect of federal statutes on state law.

2685 *See* National Consumers League, NCL Bulletin, Vol 59, No. 2 at 5; Congressional findings at 15 U.S.C. § 6101; FTC, Fraudbusters!, the Official Quarterly of the Telemarketing Complaint System (Apr. 1995); NCLC REPORTS, *Deceptive Practices & Warranties Ed.* at 15 (Jan./Feb. 1996).

2686 *See* United States v. Johnson, 297 F.3d 845 (9th Cir. 2002) (affirming wire fraud, mail fraud and money laundering convictions for telemarketing scheme that included reloading and targeting of elderly); United States v. Ciccone, 219 F.3d 1078 (9th Cir. 2000) (affirming wire fraud conviction of reloader).

2687 *See* description at 60 Fed. Reg. 8318 (Feb. 14, 1995) and United States v. Jackson, 95 F.3d 500 (7th Cir. 1996) (discussing vulnerability of those who have been victimized once). The FTC's rule implementing the Telemarketing and Consumer Fraud and Abuse Prevention Act originally proposed to ban telemarketers from selling their customer lists when they were under a federal court order for telemarketing fraud. 60 Fed. Reg. 8320, 8332. The FTC deleted this prohibition in its revised proposal, 60 Fed. Reg. 30420 (June 8, 1995), and it did not appear in the final rule or in the rule as amended in 2003. The final rule prohibits "recovery rooms" from receiving payment prior to restoring the money or property to the consumer. *See* 16 C.F.R. § 310.4(a)(3); § 5.9.4.7.4, *infra*. FTC orders against telemarketers also often prohibit them from selling their "customer" lists. *See* § 5.9.7.3, *infra*.

2688 47 U.S.C. § 227, *reproduced at* Appx. D.1.3, *infra*. *See* § 5.9.3, *infra*.

2689 15 U.S.C. §§ 6101 to 6108, *reproduced at* Appx. D.1.1, *infra*. *See* § 5.9.4, *infra*.

2690 16 C.F.R. Part 310. The rule is reprinted at Appx. D.2.1, *infra*. The Federal Register notices announcing the original rule, 60 Fed. Reg. 43842 (Aug. 23, 1995), and the 2003 amendments to it, 68 Fed. Reg. 4580 (Jan. 29, 2003), including the FTC's lengthy and detailed Statements of Basis and Purpose, are reproduced on the companion CD-Rom to this volume.

- The FTC's Mail or Telephone Merchandise Rule,[2691] which requires prompt delivery of merchandise. It does not create a private cause of action but in most states will be enforceable through the state UDAP statute.
- State telemarketing statutes, which typically overlap to at least some extent with the FTC rule and usually offer a private cause of action.[2692] These are summarized in Appx. D, *infra*.

These laws are examined in detail in the following subsections.

5.9.3 Telephone Consumer Protection Act

5.9.3.1 Scope

The federal Telephone Consumer Protection Act of 1991 (TCPA)[2693] provides certain protections against telemarketing calls. One of its provisions authorizes the FCC to adopt rules, and the FCC's rule[2694] includes a number of substantive provisions that go beyond the statute.

Since telephone lines are part of an aggregate interstate system even when used for intrastate calls, Congress has authority to regulate intrastate calls.[2695] Accordingly, the statute covers both interstate and intrastate calls,[2696] although it does not preempt state laws that impose more restrictive intrastate requirements.[2697] Calls by nonprofit organizations and to persons with whom the caller has an established business relationship[2698] are excluded from most protections.[2699] Certain protections only apply to calls to residential customers.[2700]

5.9.3.2 Challenges to Statute and Regulation

Challenges to the constitutionality of the TCPA on grounds that its restrictions on fax advertising violate the First Amendment have generally been unsuccessful. The statute is constitutional as a content-neutral restriction on the time, place and manner of protected speech,[2701] and does not violate the Equal Protection Clause.[2702] The restrictions on prerecorded telephone messages and junk faxes are not unconstitutionally vague and do not violate the First Amendment.[2703] The Commerce Clause does not prevent a state court from issuing a nationwide injunction against a junk faxer, as long as the injunction is tailored so that it does not prohibit legal faxes and only applies where the enjoined activity has an appro-

2691 16 C.F.R. § 435. *See* § 5.8.1, *infra*.

2692 *See* § 5.9.5.3, *infra*.

2693 47 U.S.C. § 227 [*reproduced at* Appx. D.1.3, *infra*]. *See* Kaufman v. ACS Sys., Inc., 110 Cal. App. 4th 886, 2 Cal. Rptr. 3d 296 (2003) (discussion of legislative history of TCPA). A good on-line resource on the statute is www.TCPALaw.com.

2694 47 C.F.R. § 64.1200. The FCC's report adopting the original version of this rule may be found at 7 F.C.C.R. 8752, 1992 WL 690928 (Oct. 16, 1992). The FCC also set out its interpretation of the rule in a consumer information sheet, *Telephone Solicitations, Autodialed and Artificial or Prerecorded Voice Message Telephone Calls, and the Use of Fax Machines*, 8 F.C.C.R. 480, 1993 WL 756669 (Jan. 11, 1993). The report adopting the 2003 amendments may be found at 2003 WL 21517853 (July 3, 2003).

2695 Texas v. American Blast Fax, Inc., 121 F. Supp. 2d 1085 (W.D. Tex. 2000). *See also* Hilary B. Miller and Robert R. Biggerstaff, Application of the Telephone Consumer Protection Act to Intrastate Telemarketing Calls and Faxes, 52 Fed. Comm. L.J. 667, 686 (2000).

2696 47 U.S.C. § 152(b); Manufacturers Auto Leasing, Inc. v. Autoflex Leasing, Inc., 2004 WL 966306 (Tex. App. May 6, 2004). *See* Texas v. American Blast Fax, Inc., 121 F. Supp. 2d 1085 (W.D. Tex. 2000); Omnibus Int'l v. AT&T, Inc., 111 S.W.3d 818 (Tex. App. 2003); Hooters of Augusta, Inc. v. Nicholson, 245 Ga. App. 363, 537 S.E.2d 468 (2000).

2697 47 U.S.C. § 226(e).

2698 "Established business relationship" is defined at 47 C.F.R. § 64.1200(f)(4). *See* Charvat v. Dispatch Consumer Servs., 95 Ohio St. 3d 505, 769 N.E.2d 829 (2002) (consumer's request not to receive any more calls terminated established business relationship exception).

2699 47 U.S.C. § 227(a)(3).

2700 47 C.F.R. § 64.1200(e) (restricting calls "to a residential telephone subscriber"). *See* Adamo v. AT&T, 2001 Ohio App. LEXIS 4989 (Nov. 8, 2001) (do-not-call list protections).

2701 Missouri *ex rel.* Nixon v. Am. Blast Fax, Inc., 323 F.3d 649 (8th Cir. 2003) (junk fax prohibition); Moser v. FCC, 46 F.3d 970 (9th Cir. 1995); Minn. *ex rel.* Hatch v. Sunbelt Communications & Mktg., 282 F. Supp. 2d 976 (D. Minn. 2002) (junk fax prohibition); Texas v. American Blast Fax, Inc., 121 F. Supp. 2d 1085 (W.D. Tex. 2000); Kenro, Inc. v. Fax Daily, Inc., 962 F. Supp. 1162 (S.D. Ind. 1997) (junk fax prohibition constitutional); *see also* Destination Ventures, Ltd. v. FCC, 46 F.3d 54 (9th Cir. 1995) (restriction on unsolicited fax transmissions directly advances substantial governmental interest in manner that is no more extensive than necessary), *aff'd*, 46 F.3d 54 (9th Cir. 1995); Kaufman v. ACS Sys., Inc., 110 Cal. App. 4th 886, 2 Cal. Rptr. 3d 296 (2003) (junk fax prohibition does not violate 1st Amendment and is not void for vagueness); Covington & Burling v. Int'l Marketing & Research, Inc., 2003 WL 21384825 (D.C. Super. Apr. 17, 2003) (junk fax prohibition does not violate 1st Amendment and is not void for vagueness); State *ex rel.* Humphrey v. Casino Marketing Group, Inc., 491 N.W.2d 882 (Minn. 1992) (Minnesota's statutory restriction on automatic dialing announcement devices upheld); Harjoe v. Herz Fin., 108 S.W.3d 653 (Mo. 2003) (junk fax prohibition does not violate 1st or 14th Amendment and is not unconstitutionally vague); Rudgayzer & Gratt v. Enine, Inc., 2004 WL 877852 (N.Y. App. Div. Apr. 14, 2004) (junk fax prohibition does not violate First Amendment); Jemiola v. XYZ Corp., 802 N.E.2d 745 (Ohio Com. Pl. 2003) (junk fax prohibition does not violate 1st or 14th Amendment). *See generally* § 7.10.2, *infra*.

2702 Texas v. American Blast Fax, Inc., 121 F. Supp. 2d 1085 (W.D. Tex. 2000).

2703 Moser v. FCC, 46 F.3d 970 (9th Cir. 1995) (prerecorded messages); Covington & Burling v. Int'l Marketing & Research, Inc., 2003 WL 21384825 (D.C. Super. Apr. 17, 2003) (junk fax prohibition not unconstitutionally vague); Harjoe v. Herz Fin., 108 S.W.3d 653 (Mo. 2003) (junk fax prohibition not unconstitutionally vague); Margulis v. P & M Consulting, Inc., 121 S.W.3d 246 (Mo. App. 2003) (prerecorded messages).

priate connection to the forum state.[2704] The distinction the FCC made between commercial and non-commercial telephone solicitations in its do-not-call rule does not unconstitutionally restrict speech based on content.[2705]

Courts have held that the FCC's regulations are within its authority and entitled to deference.[2706] They have also given deference to the FCC's interpretation of its rule.[2707] The TCPA is remedial legislation that is entitled to a liberal construction.[2708]

5.9.3.3 Junk Faxes

The statute and the FCC's regulation adopted under it prohibit the use of a telephone fax machine, a computer, or any other device to send an unsolicited advertisement to a telephone fax machine.[2709] This prohibition applies regardless of whether the message is sent to a fax server, which receives and stores the message for later printing, or to a fax machine that automatically prints each message.[2710] The recipient is under no obligation to contact the sender and request that no further faxes be sent.[2711]

In determining whether an unsolicited fax is an advertisement, the court must consider circumstances such as the sender's identity and motives, not just the four corners of the fax.[2712] A fax that pitches a product or service in the guise of providing information about it is an advertisement.[2713]

Faxing unsolicited advertisements is allowed if the consumer has given prior express invitation or permission,[2714] but the faxer has the burden of proving this exception.[2715] Publishing one's fax number in, for example, a professional association's directory, is not consent.[2716] This authorization can not be in the form of a negative option.[2717] Even before this amendment, courts held that consent could not be inferred.[2718] Effective January 1, 2005, the FCC requires such consent to be evidenced by a signed, written statement that includes the recipient's fax number and clearly indicates consent to receive fax advertisements.[2719]

"War dialing" (dialing numbers to determine whether they are fax or voice lines) is specifically prohibited.[2720] Tips on investigating junk faxes and profiles of junk faxers may be found at www.junkfax.org.

5.9.3.4 Restriction on Auto Dialers and Abandoned Calls

The TCPA prohibits using an automatic dialing system[2721] or an artificial or prerecorded voice to make any call

---

2704 National Notary Assn. v. U.S. Notary, 2002 WL 1265555 (Cal. App. June 7, 2002) (unpublished, citation limited).

2705 Mainstream Marketing Servs. v. FTC, 358 F.3d 1228 (10th Cir. 2004).

2706 *Id.* (established business relationship exception to FCC's do-not-call rule was within its authority); Charvat v. Dispatch Consumer Servs., 95 Ohio St. 3d 505, 769 N.E.2d 829 (2002) (giving deference to interpretation at 1992 WL 690928 (Oct. 16, 1992); Omnibus Int'l v. AT&T, Inc., 111 S.W.3d 818 (Tex. App. 2003) (giving deference to interpretation at 8 F.C.C.R. 480 (1993)).

2707 Margulis v. P & M Consulting, Inc., 121 S.W.3d 246 (Mo. App. 2003); Charvat v. Dispatch Consumer Servs., 95 Ohio St. 3d 505, 769 N.E.2d 829 (2002); Omnibus Int'l v. AT&T, Inc., 111 S.W.3d 818 (Tex. App. 2003).

2708 Jemiola v. XYZ Corp., 802 N.E.2d 745 (Ohio Com. Pl. 2003). *See also* Hooters of Augusta, Inc. v. Am. Global Ins. Co., 272 F. Supp. 2d 1365, 1375-6 (S.D. Ga. 2003) (TCPA is remedial statute).

2709 47 U.S.C. § 227(b)(1)(C); 47 C.F.R. § 64.1200(a)(3); Lary v. Flasch Bus. Consulting, 2003 WL 22463948 (Ala. Civ. App. Oct. 31, 2003) (reversing dismissal of junk fax claim); Grady v. OTC Investor's Edge, 2003 WL 22828294 (Ohio Com. Pl. Oct. 15, 2003) (awarding $1500 treble damages plus $200 UDAP statutory damages for junk fax). *See* Minn. *ex rel.* Hatch v. Sunbelt Communications and Mktg., 282 F. Supp. 2d 976 (D. Minn. 2002) (granting preliminary injunction against unsolicited faxes); National Notary Assn. v. U.S. Notary, 2002 WL 1265555 (Cal. App. June 7, 2002) (unpublished, citation limited) (upholding nationwide injunction under California UDAP statute, limiting a California company from sending unsolicited faxes). *See also* Kaufman v. ACS Sys., Inc., 110 Cal. App. 4th 886, 2 Cal. Rptr. 3d 296 (2003) (summarizing legislative history and testimony in favor of junk fax prohibition). Many states also have laws prohibiting unsolicited faxes. *See* Texas v. American Blast Fax, Inc., 159 F. Supp. 2d 936 (W.D. Tex. 2001), *judgment entered*, 164 F. Supp. 2d 892 (W.D. Tex. 2001).

2710 47 U.S.C. § 227(a)(2)(B) (defining telephone facsimile machine as one that has the *capacity* to transcribe text or images from an electronic signal onto paper); FCC Report and Order in the Matter of Rules and Regulations Implementing the Telephone Consumer Protection Act of 1991 at ¶¶ 198-202, 18 F.C.C.R. 14014, 2003 WL 21517853 (July 3, 2003); Covington & Burling v. Int'l Marketing & Research, Inc., 2003 WL 21384825 (D.C. Super. Apr. 17, 2003).

2711 Manufacturers Auto Leasing, Inc. v. Autoflex Leasing, Inc., 2004 WL 966306 (Tex. App. May 6, 2004) (citing FCC rulings).

2712 Rudgayzer & Gratt v. Enine, Inc., 2004 WL 877852 (N.Y. App. Div. Apr. 14, 2004).

2713 *Id.*

2714 47 U.S.C. § 227(a)(4); 47 C.F.R. § 64.1200(f)(7).

2715 Covington & Burling v. Int'l Marketing & Research, Inc., 2003 WL 21384825 (D.C. Super. Apr. 17, 2003); Jemiola v. XYZ Corp., 802 N.E.2d 745 (Ohio Com. Pl. 2003); Grady v. St. Cloud Mortg. Co., 2003 WL 21190993 (Ohio C.P. Mar. 7, 2003) (unpublished, citation limited).

2716 FCC Report and Order in the Matter of Rules and Regulations Implementing the Telephone Consumer Protection Act of 1991, at ¶ 193, 18 F.C.C.R. 14014, 2003 WL 21517853 (July 3, 2003).

2717 FCC Report and Order in the Matter of Rules and Regulations Implementing the Telephone Consumer Protection Act of 1991, at ¶ 191, 18 F.C.C.R. 14014, 2003 WL 21517853 (July 3, 2003).

2718 Jemiola v. XYZ Corp., 802 N.E.2d 745 (Ohio Com. Pl. 2003).

2719 47 C.F.R. § 64.1200(a)(3)(i). *See* 68 Fed. Reg. 50978 (Aug. 25, 2003) (establishing effective date).

2720 47 C.F.R. § 64.1200(a)(7); FCC Report and Order in the Matter of Rules and Regulations Implementing the Telephone Consumer Protection Act of 1991, at ¶ 135, 18 F.C.C.R. 14014, 2003 WL 21517853 (July 3, 2003). The effective date was announced at 68 Fed. Reg. 44144 (July 25, 2003).

2721 The term encompasses "predictive dialers." *See* FCC Report and Order in the Matter of Rules and Regulations Implementing

to an emergency telephone line, a patient or guest room at a nursing home, hospital, or similar health facility, or a pager, cellular phone, or other service in which the called party is charged for the call.[2722] The prohibition against autodialing of cellular phone numbers applies to both text and voice messages.[2723] Live telephone solicitations to wireless subscribers are not prohibited, but subscribers can place their cellular telephone numbers on the do-not-call list.[2724]

Another problem with automatic dialing systems is that they lead to abandoned calls, because the called party may answer the call at a time when all of the solicitors are still on other calls. The rule prohibits abandonment of more than 3% of all telemarketing calls that are answered by a live person.[2725] The FTC's telemarketing rule has a similar prohibition, but has a less generous way of measuring the 3% safe harbor.[2726] The rule also prohibits disconnection of unanswered telemarketing calls prior to at least 15 seconds or four rings.[2727]

5.9.3.5 Prerecorded Calls

The statute prohibits placing a call that uses an artificial or pre-recorded voice to a residence without the prior express consent of the called party.[2728] Listing one's number in the telephone directory does not constitute express consent.[2729] Nor does placing a call to a company that then captures the consumer's phone number.[2730] Obtaining consent during the call, e.g., by asking the consumer to press numbers on the telephone keypad to hear a message, is also insufficient.[2731]

Pre-recorded calls are allowed, however, if the caller is a tax-exempt nonprofit organization; the call is for emergency purposes; the caller has an established business relationship with the called party;[2732] the call is for non-commercial purposes; or the call is for commercial purposes but does not include any unsolicited advertisements and is not a "telephone solicitation."[2733] A call that contains free offers and information about goods and services that are commercially available does not fall into these exceptions, however.[2734] Nor does a purported survey that is preliminary to a sales call.[2735] Debt collection calls fall into this exemption because they do not transmit unsolicited advertisements and the collector has an established business relationship with the debtor.[2736]

All artificial or prerecorded messages must identify the entity responsible for initiating the call and provide a telephone number to which the consumer can make a do-not-call request.[2737] A prerecorded call that meets the FTC's definition of telemarketing is subject to the FTC's Telemarketing Sales Rule as well as the FCC rule.[2738]

---

the Telephone Consumer Protection Act of 1991, at ¶¶ 131-134, 18 F.C.C.R. 14014, 2003 WL 21517853 (July 3, 2003).

2722 47 U.S.C. § 227(b)(1)(A); 47 C.F.R. § 64.1200(a)(1). Many states also have statutes restricting autodialing, and the FCC has declined to preempt such laws. *See* FCC Report and Order in the Matter of Rules and Regulations Implementing the Telephone Consumer Protection Act of 1991, at ¶ 134, 18 F.C.C.R. 14014, 2003 WL 21517853 (July 3, 2003). *See also* Lary v. Flasch Bus. Consulting, 2003 WL 22463948 (Ala. Civ. App. Oct. 31, 2003) (reversing dismissal of claim that defendants used autodialer to call physician's emergency line).

2723 FCC Report and Order in the Matter of Rules and Regulations Implementing the Telephone Consumer Protection Act of 1991, at ¶ 165, 18 F.C.C.R. 14014, 2003 WL 21517853 (July 3, 2003).

2724 *Id.* at ¶ 166. *See* §§ 5.9.3.6, 5.9.4.6.3, *infra* (FCC and FTC do-not-call rules).

2725 47 C.F.R. § 64.1200(a)(6).

2726 *See* CC Report and Order in the Matter of Rules and Regulations Implementing the Telephone Consumer Protection Act of 1991, at ¶¶ 149, 152, 18 F.C.C.R. 14014, 2003 WL 21517853 (July 3, 2003); § 5.9.4.5.2, *infra.*

2727 47 C.F.R. § 64.1200(a)(5).

2728 47 U.S.C. § 227(b)(1)(B); 47 C.F.R. § 64.1200(a)(2). Many states also have laws restricting this practice.

2729 Kaplan v. First City Mortgage, 183 Misc. 2d 24, 701 N.Y.S.2d 859 (City Ct. 1999).

2730 7 F.C.C.R. 8752, 1992 WL 690928, ¶ 31 (Oct. 16, 1992).

2731 Margulis v. P & M Consulting, Inc., 121 S.W.3d 246 (Mo. App. 2003); FCC Report and Order in the Matter of Rules and Regulations Implementing the Telephone Consumer Protection Act of 1991, at ¶ 142, 18 F.C.C.R. 14014, 2003 WL 21517853 (July 3, 2003).

2732 "Established business relationship" is defined at 47 C.F.R. § 64.1200(f)(3). When it adopted the original rule, the FCC made it clear that the consumer's termination of the relationship terminates consent to receive these calls. 7 F.C.C.R. 8752, 1992 WL 690928, ¶ 35 (Oct. 16, 1992). Telling the business or entity not to call anymore also terminates the exception for established business relationships. *See* Schneider v. Susquehanna Radio Corp., 260 Ga. App. 296, 581 S.E.2d 603 (2003) (no violation where consumer was enrolled in discount club operated by caller, even though call transmitted an unsolicited advertisement); *Telephone Solicitations, Autodialed and Artificial or Prerecorded Voice Message Telephone Calls, and the Use of Fax Machines*, 8 F.C.C.R. 480, 1993 WL 756669 (Jan. 11, 1993). The FCC codified this position when it amended the rule in 2003. *See* 47 C.F.R. § 64.1200(f)(3)(i).

2733 47 C.F.R. § 64.1200(a)(2). *See* definition of "telephone solicitation" at 47 C.F.R. § 64.1200(f)(9); FCC Report and Order in the Matter of Rules and Regulations Implementing the Telephone Consumer Protection Act of 1991, at ¶ 141, 18 F.C.C.R. 14014, 2003 WL 21517853 (July 3, 2003) (rationale for addition of "telephone solicitation" to this portion of rule).

2734 Charvat v. Crawford, 799 N.E.2d 661 (Ohio App. 2003); FCC Report and Order in the Matter of Rules and Regulations Implementing the Telephone Consumer Protection Act of 1991, 18 F.C.C.R. 14014, ¶¶ 139–141, 2003 WL 21517853 (July 3, 2003).

2735 Margulis v. P & M Consulting, Inc., 121 S.W.3d 246 (Mo. App. 2003) (interpreting pre-2003 version of regulation, but citing FCC's 2003 amendments).

2736 47 C.F.R. § 64.1200(a)(2)(iii), (iv). *See* 7 F.C.C.R. 8752, 1992 WL 690928, ¶ 39 (Oct. 16, 1992).

2737 47 C.F.R. § 64.1200(b).

2738 68 Fed. Reg. 4580, 4587 (Jan. 29, 2003) (FTC's discussion of coverage of prerecorded sales messages).

5.9.3.6 General and Company-Specific Do-Not-Call Lists

In 2003, the FCC followed the lead of the FTC[2739] and adopted a nationwide do-not-call rule.[2740] Information about registering a telephone number on the list is found at § 5.9.4.6.3, *infra.*

A significant feature of the FCC's rule is its broad scope. The FCC's rule covers all entities engaged in telemarketing, even purely intrastate transactions.[2741] By contrast, the FTC's rule extends only to telemarketing that involves at least one interstate call,[2742] and it does not cover banks, credit unions, savings and loan associations, airlines, common carriers such as telephone companies, and insurance companies.[2743]

Both agencies exempt calls by or on behalf of tax-exempt non-profit organizations from the nationwide do-not-call list.[2744] The FTC's rule is broader than the FCC's in one respect, though—it requires for-profit solicitors for non-profit organizations to stop calling consumers who ask that their names be placed on a company-specific list.[2745] By contrast, the FCC's rule exempts solicitors for non-profit organizations from both the nationwide and the company-specific do-not-call rules.[2746]

The FTC's rule exempts calls to businesses,[2747] and the FCC's rule only applies to calls to residential telephone subscribers,[2748] so neither affects telemarketing calls to businesses. Both also exempt calls made to someone with whom the company has an "established business relationship."[2749] Such a relationship lasts only 18 months after the consumer's last purchase or transaction with the company, or 3 months after the consumer makes an inquiry or application regarding the company's products or services.[2750] Even within the 18- or 3-month window, the consumer can stop the calls by asking to be put on the company-specific do-not-call list.[2751]

Perhaps the most significant result of the FCC's adoption of a nationwide do-not-call rule is that consumers now have an explicit private cause of action if telemarketers continue to call them after they register on the do-not-call list.[2752]

The FCC also requires telemarketers to maintain company-specific do-not-call lists and to honor no-call requests for five years.[2753] Companies must also have a do-not-call list policy and make it available to consumers upon request.[2754] Callers must identify themselves and their company, and give a telephone number or address.[2755]

5.9.3.7 Restrictions on Calling Times

The FCC regulation prohibits telephone solicitations before 8:00 A.M. or after 9:00 P.M., local time (determined by the called party's location).[2756] Calls during the prohibited hours are violations even if the caller hangs up before the consumer answers.[2757] These restrictions apply to wireless telephones as well as land lines.[2758]

2739 *See* § 5.9.4.6.3, *infra.*

2740 47 C.F.R. § 64.1200(c)(2). *See* FCC Report and Order in the Matter of Rules and Regulations Implementing the Telephone Consumer Protection Act of 1991, 18 F.C.C.R. 14014, 2003 WL 21517853 (July 3, 2003).

2741 FCC Report and Order in the Matter of Rules and Regulations Implementing the Telephone Consumer Protection Act of 1991, 18 F.C.C.R. 14014, ¶¶ 212, 2003 WL 21517853 (July 3, 2003).

2742 15 U.S.C. § 6106(4); *see* 68 Fed. Reg. 4587 (Jan. 29, 2003) (Statement of Basis and Purpose for FTC rule); FCC Order at ¶ 212 124.

2743 FCC Order at ¶ 212; 68 Fed. Reg. 4568–67 (Jan. 29, 2003).

2744 16 C.F.R. § 310.6(a) (FTC rule); 47 C.F.R. § 64.1200(f)(9)(iii), (d)(7) (FCC rule). *See* FCC Order at ¶ 45; 68 Fed. Reg. 4585–87 (Jan. 29, 2003).

2745 16 C.F.R. § 310.2(cc).

2746 *Cf.* 47 C.F.R. § 64.1200(d)(7), (f)(9)(iii) (FCC rule) to 16 C.F.R. § 310.6(a) (FTC rule; exempting for-profit solicitors of charitable contributions only from nationwide do-not-call list).

2747 16 C.F.R. § 310.6(b)(7). This section provides, however, that "toner phoner" calls (calls to induce the retail sale of nondurable office or cleaning supplies to a business) are covered by the FTC rule except for the nationwide do-not-call list.

2748 47 C.F.R. § 64.1200(c)(2).

2749 47 C.F.R. 64.1200(f)(3), (9)(iii) (FCC rule); 16 C.F.R. § 310.4(b)(iii)(B)(ii) (FTC rule). *See* FCC Order at 29 ¶ 42. The FCC's rule also makes an exception for calls to persons with whom the telemarketer has a "personal relationship," 47 C.F.R. § 64.1200(c)(iii), while the FTC rule does not have this exception.

2750 47 C.F.R. § 64.1200(f)(3) (FCC rule); 16 C.F.R. § 310.2(n) (FTC rule).

2751 FCC Report and Order in the Matter of Rules and Regulations Implementing the Telephone Consumer Protection Act of 1991 at ¶ 124, 18 F.C.C.R. 14014, 2003 WL 21517853 (July 3, 2003). The FTC rule is the same: 68 Fed. Reg. 4580, 4634 (Jan. 29, 2003).

2752 *See* Worsham v. Nationwide Ins. Co., 138 Md. App. 487, 772 A.2d 868 (2001) (consumer has private cause of action if a repeat call is made after request to be placed on no-call list); Charvat v. Dispatch Consumer Servs., 95 Ohio St. 3d 505, 769 N.E.2d 829 (2002) (an existing customer can terminate an "established business relationship" for purposes of the TCPA by asking to be placed on company do-not-call list); Adamo v. AT&T, 2001 WL 1382757 (Ohio App. Nov. 8, 2001) (affirming award of treble damages for violation of requirement). *See generally* § 5.9.3.9, *infra.*

2753 47 C.F.R. § 64.1200(d) (note that former § 64.1200(e)(2) required companies to honor do-not-call requests for 10 years).

2754 47 C.F.R. § 64.1200(d)(1). *See* Adamo v. AT&T, 2001 WL 1382757 (Ohio App. Nov. 8, 2001) (affirming award of treble damages for violation of requirement).

2755 47 C.F.R. § 64.1200(d)(4).

2756 47 C.F.R. § 64.1200(c)(1). *See* Irvine v. Akron Beacon Journal, 147 Ohio App. 3d 428, 770 N.E.2d 1105 (Ohio Ct. App. 2002) (use of auto-dialer during prohibited hours a violation of TCPA).

2757 Irvine v. Akron Beacon Journal, 147 Ohio App. 3d 428, 770 N.E.2d 1105 (Ohio Ct. App. 2002).

2758 FCC Report and Order in the Matter of Rules and Regulations Implementing the Telephone Consumer Protection Act of 1991, at ¶ 167, 18 F.C.C.R. 14014, 2003 WL 21517853 (July 3, 2003).

5.9.3.8 Prohibition of Caller ID Blocking

The FCC also requires any person or entity that engages in telemarketing to transmit Caller ID information to the called party, and prohibits Caller ID blocking.[2759] This rule was effective on January 29, 2004,[2760] the same effective date as the parallel provisions of the FTC telemarketing rule.[2761]

5.9.3.9 Consumer Remedies

5.9.3.9.1 Creation of private cause of action

The Telephone Consumer Protection Act creates two private causes of action, both for actual damages or $500, whichever is greater, with the award trebled for willful or knowing violations.[2762] One allows suit for violation of the subsection restricting junk faxes, prerecorded telephone calls, and autodialers, and the regulations under that subsection.[2763] A single violation is sufficient to create liability.[2764]

The other private cause of action allows suit by a person who receives more than one telephone call within any 12-month period on behalf of the same entity in violation of the regulations adopted under the subsection of the statute that deals with telephone subscriber privacy rights.[2765] This gives the consumer a private cause of action for more than one call within a 12-month period that violates the nationwide or company-specific do-not-call rule. This cause of action is probably also available to enforce the restriction on calling times, the prohibition against blocking Caller ID, the restrictions against abandoned calls, and the requirement that telemarketers identify the entity on whose behalf they are calling, since these also relate to privacy.[2766] There is a four-year statute of limitations.[2767] There is no private cause of action, however, to enforce the technical and procedural standards for telecommunications equipment set forth in section 227(d).[2768] Consumers may also file complaints with the FCC.[2769]

5.9.3.9.2 Jurisdiction in state and federal court

The Act explicitly grants consumers the right to bring suit for violations in state court "if otherwise permitted by the laws or rules of court" of the state.[2770] The legislative history suggests that Congress intended to make it clear that the statute did not override state court rules about venue, jurisdictional amounts, and similar matters.[2771] Most courts have held that this language allows states to opt out of jurisdiction over these cases rather than requiring an affirmative act to opt in.[2772]

2759 47 C.F.R. § 64.1601(e).

2760 FCC Report and Order in the Matter of Rules and Regulations Implementing the Telephone Consumer Protection Act of 1991, at ¶ 184, 18 F.C.C.R. 14014, 2003 WL 21517853 (July 3, 2003).

2761 16 C.F.R. § 310.4(a)(7). *See* § 5.9.4.6.4, *infra*.

2762 47 U.S.C. § 227(b)(3), (c)(5). *See* Charvat v. Dispatch Consumer Servs., 95 Ohio St. 3d 505, 769 N.E.2d 829 (2002) (referring to private cause of action as "[t]he teeth of the Act").

2763 47 U.S.C. § 227(b); Margulis v. P & M Consulting, Inc., 121 S.W.3d 246 (Mo. App. 2003) (anyone in household to which call was made has standing to sue). *See also* Nat'l Notary Ass'n v. U.S. Notary, 2002 WL 1265555 (Cal. App. June 7, 2002) (unpublished, citation limited) (company that was harmed by its competitor's use of illegal junk faxes may bring UDAP suit even though it did not receive any faxes itself).

2764 Lary v. Tom Taylor Agency, 2003 WL 22463950 (Ala. Civ. App. Oct. 31, 2003).

2765 47 U.S.C. § 227(c)(5).

2766 47 U.S.C. § 227(c)(5) creates a private cause of action for any person who has received more than one telephone call in a 12-month period in violation of the FCC's regulation promulgated pursuant to the subscriber privacy provisions of the statute. The FCC adopted the restriction on calling times, 47 C.F.R. § 64.1200(e)(1) pursuant to this authority. 7 F.C.C.R. 8752, 1992 WL 690928 ¶ 26 (Oct. 16, 1992). It appears that the identification requirement, 47 C.F.R. § 64.1200(e)(2)(iv), is also a privacy protection regulation, promulgated pursuant to this authority, since it relates to telephone solicitations and is essential if a company-specific do-not-call list is to be enforceable. The same is true of the prohibition against blocking Caller ID. *See* FCC Report and Order in the Matter of Rules and Regulations Implementing the Telephone Consumer Protection Act of 1991 at ¶ 183, 18 F.C.C.R. 14014, 2003 WL 21517853 (July 3, 2003) (citing privacy concerns as reason for prohibition). The FCC also cited privacy concerns in adopting the restrictions on abandoned calls. *See Id.* ¶¶ 146–49.

2767 28 U.S.C. § 1658. *See* Jemiola v. XYZ Corp., 802 N.E.2d 745 (Ohio Com. Pl. 2003); Grady v. OTC Investor's Edge, 2003 WL 22828294 (Ohio Com. Pl. Oct. 15, 2003).

2768 Lary v. Flasch Bus. Consulting, 2003 WL 22463948 (Ala. Civ. App. Oct. 31, 2003).

2769 Complaints can be filed through the FCC's website, www.fcc.gov/ccb/enforce/index-complaints.html

2770 47 U.S.C. § 227(b)(3), (c)(5).

2771 *See* comments of Senator Hollings, 137 Cong. Rec. S16205–16206 (Nov. 7, 1991) ("the bill does not, because of constitutional constraints, dictate to the States which court in each State shall be the proper venue for such an action, as this is a matter for State legislators to determine"). *See also* Schulman v. Chase Manhattan Bank, 268 A.D.2d 174, 710 N.Y.S.2d 368 (2000) (relying on legislative history).

2772 Murphey v. Lanier, 204 F.3d 911 (9th Cir. 2000); Bigerstaff v. Voice Power Telecommunications, Inc., 221 F. Supp. 2d 652 (D.S.C. 2002); Lary v. Tom Taylor Agency, 2003 WL 22463950 (Ala. Civ. App. Oct. 31, 2003); Lary v. Flasch Bus. Consulting, 2003 WL 22463948 (Ala. Civ. App. Oct. 31, 2003); Kaufman v. ACS Sys., Inc., 110 Cal. App. 4th 886, 2 Cal. Rptr. 3d 296 (2003) (California's enactment and later repeal of law to ban junk faxes until TCPA took effect does not show intent to close state courts to TCPA suits); Condon v. Office Depot, Inc., 855 So. 2d 644 (Fla. Dist. Ct. App. 2003); Hooters of Augusta, Inc. v. Nicholson, 245 Ga. App. 363, 537 S.E.2d 468 (2000); R.A. Ponte Architects, Ltd. v. Investors' Alert, Inc., 2004 WL 1900381 (Md. Aug. 26, 2004); Worsham v. Nationwide Ins. Co., 138 Md. App. 487, 772 A.2d 868 (2001) (allowing private cause of action in state court for violation of company-specific do-not-call rule); Zelma v. Market U.S.A., 343 N.J. Super. 356,

Several courts have held that federal courts do not have jurisdiction over consumer suits to enforce the statute.[2773] The statute does authorize state attorneys general to seek injunctive relief in federal court, however.[2774] In addition, several courts have held that federal courts have original jurisdiction over TCPA suits if the amount in controversy exceeds $75,000 and there is diversity of citizenship among the parties.[2775] Damages in a TCPA suit will only exceed $75,000 if the plaintiff has suffered significant actual damages or the defendant has committed a large number of violations against the same person, creating liability for multiple statutory damage awards.

778 A.2d 591 (Law. Div. 2001); Schulman v. Chase Manhattan Bank, 268 A.D.2d 174, 710 N.Y.S.2d 368 (2000); Betor v. Quantalytics, Inc., 2003 WL 22407121 (Ohio Com. Pl. Oct. 3, 2003); Jemiola v. XYZ Corp., 802 N.E.2d 745 (Ohio Com. Pl. 2003); Aronson v. Fax.com Inc., 51 Pa. D & C.4th 421, 2001 WL 1202609 (C.P. 2001). *See* Reynolds v. Diamond Foods & Poultry, Inc., 79 S.W.3d 907 (Mo. 2002). *Cf.* Manufacturers Auto Leasing, Inc. v. Autoflex Leasing, Inc., 2004 WL 966306 (Tex. App. May 6, 2004) (noting that Texas statute specifically allows TCPA suits in state courts). *But see* Mulhern v. MacLeod, 2003 WL 22285515 (Mass. Super. July 16,. 2003) (states must opt in; since Mass. passed a junk fax law without including a private right of action under the TCPA, it did not opt in); Autoflex Leasing, Inc. v. Manufacturers Auto Leasing, 16 S.W.3d 815 (Tex. App. 2000) (states must pass laws or adopt rules consenting to TCPA suits).

2773 Murphey v. Lanier, 204 F.3d 911 (9th Cir. 2000); ErieNet, Inc. v. Velocity Net, Inc., 156 F.3d 513 (3d Cir. 1998); Nicholson v. Hooters of Augusta, Inc., 136 F.3d 1287 (11th Cir. 1998); Chair King, Inc. v. Houston Cellular Corp., 131 F.3d 507 (5th Cir. 1997); International Science & Technology Institute Inc. v. Inacom Communications Inc., 106 F.3d 1146 (4th Cir. 1997); Gold Seal Termite & Pest Control Co. v. DirecTV, Inc., 2003 WL 21508177 (S.D. Ind. June 10, 2003); Redefining Progress v. Fax.com, Inc., 2003 WL 926853 (N.D. Cal. Mar. 3, 2003) (no federal jurisdiction under 47 U.S.C. § 207 over TCPA action); Stonecrafters, Inc. v. CM Sys., Inc., 2003 WL 22415976 (N.D. Ill. Oct. 21, 2003); Biggerstaff v. Voice Power Tellecommunications, Inc., 221 F. Supp. 2d 652 (D.S.C. 2002); Brandt v. Welch, 2001 U.S. Dist. LEXIS 21367 (N.D. Tex. Dec. 21, 2001); Barry v. Dell Computer Corp., 2000 U.S. Dist. LEXIS 20630 (D. Minn. Oct. 18, 2000); Compoli v. AVT Corp., 116 F. Supp. 2d 926 (N.D. Ohio 2000); Foxhall Realty Law Offices, Inc. v. Telecommunications Premium Servs., Ltd., 975 F. Supp. 329 (S.D.N.Y. 1997), *aff'd*, 156 F.3d 432 (2d Cir. 1998); Hooters of Augusta, Inc. v. Nicholson, 245 Ga. App. 363, 537 S.E.2d 468 (2000). *Cf.* Kinder v. Citibank, 2000 WL 1409762 (S.D. Cal. Sept. 14, 2000) (federal courts do not have general federal jurisdiction, but may exercise diversity or supplement jurisdiction over TCPA claims). *But see* Kenro, Inc. v. Fax Daily, Inc., 962 F. Supp. 1162 (S.D. Ind. 1997) (federal courts have federal question jurisdiction over TCPA suits).

2774 47 U.S.C. § 227(f). *See* Texas v. American Blast Fax, Inc., 164 F. Supp. 2d 892 (W.D. Tex. 2001).

2775 Kopff v. World Research Group, L.L.C., 2003 WL 23147490 (D.D.C. Dec. 24, 2003) (allowing removal of suit to federal court); Accounting Outsourcing, L.L.C. v. Verizon Wireless Personal Communications, L.P., 294 F. Supp. 2d 834 (M.D. La. 2003) (allowing removal); Kenro, Inc. v. Fax Daily, Inc., 962 F. Supp. 1162 (S.D. Ind. 1997) (federal courts have federal question jurisdiction over TCPA suits). *Cf.* Gold Seal Termite & Pest Control Co. v. DirecTV, Inc., 2003 WL 21508177 (S.D. Ind. June 10, 2003) (entertaining possibility of diversity jurisdiction but finding amount in controversy not met; class members' claims can not be aggregated).

5.9.3.9.3 Relief

Consumers may seek an injunction or the greater of actual monetary loss or up to $500 for each violation.[2776] The court may treble the damages if it finds that the defendant's violation was willful or knowing.[2777] The federal statute does not provide for an attorney fee award, but the consumer may be able to assert a parallel claim under the state UDAP statute and win fees under that statute.[2778]

The statutory damage award is intended both as compensation and as deterrence, and is not so disproportionate to actual damages as to violate due process.[2779] The consumer need not prove any monetary loss or actual damages in order to recover the statutory penalty;[2780] because such losses are likely to be minimal, a statutory penalty is necessary to motivate consumers to enforce the statute.[2781]

2776 47 U.S.C. § 227(b)(3), (c)(5); Adamo v. AT&T, 2001 Ohio App. LEXIS 4989 (Ohio Ct. App. Nov. 8, 2001) (awarding treble damages for calls made after request to be placed on do-not-call list and for failure to provide written do-not-call policy on request).

2777 47 U.S.C. § 227(b)(3). *See* Irvine v. Akron Beacon Journal, 147 Ohio App. 3d 428, 770 N.E.2d 1105 (Ohio Ct. App. 2002) (under TCPA, the trial court has authority to award treble damages in lieu of statutory damages but not in addition to them); Adamo v. AT&T, 2001 WL 1382757 (Ohio App. Nov. 8, 2001); Grady v. OTC Investor's Edge, 2003 WL 22828294 (Ohio Com. Pl. Oct. 15, 2003) (awarding treble damages).

2778 Dubsky v. Advanced Cellular Communications, Inc., 2004 WL 503757 (Ohio Com. Pleas Feb. 24, 2004) (unpublished, citation limited); Jemiola v. XYZ Corp., 802 N.E.2d 745 (Ohio Com. Pl. 2003) (awarding fees under UDAP statute for junk faxes); Grady v. OTC Investor's Edge, 2003 WL 22828294 (Ohio Com. Pl. Oct. 15, 2003) (awarding statutory damages and attorney fees under state UDAP statute in addition to TCPA award). *See, e.g.*, Grady v. St. Cloud Mortg. Co., 2003 WL 21190993 (Ohio C.P. Mar. 7, 2003) (unpublished, citation limited).

2779 Texas v. American Blast Fax, Inc., 121 F. Supp. 2d 1085 (W.D. Tex. 2000); Kenro, Inc. v. Fax Daily, Inc., 962 F. Supp. 1162 (S.D. Ind. 1997); ESI Ergonomic Solutions v. United Artists Theatre Circuit, Inc., 50 P.3d 844 (Ariz. App. 2002); Kaufman v. ACS Sys., Inc., 110 Cal. App. 4th 886, 2 Cal. Rptr. 3d 296 (2003); Harjoe v. Herz Fin., 108 S.W.3d 653 (Mo. 2003). *See also* Worsham v. Nationwide Ins. Co., 138 Md. App. 487, 772 A.2d 868 (2001) ($500 is to be awarded per call, not per violation).

2780 Kaplan v. Democrat & Chronicle, 701 N.Y.S.2d 859 (App. Div. 1999) (reversing dismissal of complaint of consumer who sued after receiving three telephone calls soliciting newspaper subscriptions in violation of the TCPA but could not show any monetary loss); Kaplan v. First City Mortgage, 183 Misc. 2d 24, 710 N.Y.S.2d 859 (City Ct. 1999).

2781 Kaplan v. Democrat & Chronicle, 698 N.Y.S.2d 799, 801 (App. Div. 1999).

The Missouri Supreme Court has held that a two-page junk fax that contains a single advertisement is one, not two, violations.[2782] In many instances, however, it will be possible to characterize each page of a fax transmission as a separate ad.

For purposes of the treble damage provision, "willfully" means merely that the defendant acted voluntarily and under its own free will, regardless of whether the defendant knew it was acting in violation of the statute.[2783] One case has held that a person acts "knowingly" if the individual had reason to know or should have known that he or she engaged in acts which could constitute a violation of the statute.[2784]

Courts have differed about whether class certification is appropriate for unsolicited fax claims.[2785]

5.9.3.9.4 Who is liable

The fact that an independent contractor actually places the calls does not insulate the principal from liability.[2786] Contractors who sell the service of broadcasting unsolicited faxes on behalf of advertisers are subject to liability under the Act.[2787] The FCC's revised rule, effective August 25, 2003, provides that a fax broadcaster[2788] is liable for sending unsolicited faxes if it demonstrates a high degree of involvement in, or actual notice of, the unlawful activity and fails to take steps to prevent the fax transmission.[2789] A fax broadcaster meets this standard if it supplies the fax numbers or determines the content of the ads.[2790] If a fax broadcaster is highly involved in the sender's messages, it must be identified on the fax along with the sender.[2791] The advertiser and the fax broadcaster may be jointly liable if they both demonstrate a high degree of involvement.[2792] Officers of a company can also be held personally liable under TCPA if they actively engaged in the conduct that violated the TCPA or actively oversaw and directed such conduct.[2793]

5.9.4 FTC Telemarketing Sales Rule and Statute

5.9.4.1 Overview

After adopting the Telephone Consumer Protection Act (discussed in the previous section) in 1991, Congress revisited the area of telemarketing fraud in 1994 with the Telemarketing and Consumer Fraud and Abuse Prevention Act.[2794] The statute itself only contains broad guidelines, but it requires the FTC to issue regulations prohibiting deceptive and abusive telemarketing acts and practices.[2795]

The statute sets forth only a few requirements for the substance of the FTC's rule, specifying that it restrict late-night and early-morning calls, require disclosures, and prohibit coercive calls and calls that abuse the consumer's right to privacy.[2796] The FTC's rule goes well beyond these

2782 Harjoe v. Herz Fin., 108 S.W.3d 653 (Mo. 2003).

2783 Dubsky v. Advanced Cellular Communications, Inc., 2004 WL 503757 (Ohio Com. Pleas Feb. 24, 2004) (unpublished, citation limited); Grady v. OTC Investor's Edge, 2003 WL 22828294 (Ohio Com. Pl. Oct. 15, 2003); Jemiola v. XYZ Corp., 802 N.E.2d 745 (Ohio Com. Pl. 2003). *See also* 47 U.S.C. § 312(f)(1) (defining willfulness for purpose of FCC administrative sanctions). *Cf.* Covington & Burling v. Int'l Marketing & Research, Inc., 2003 WL 21384825 (D.C. Super. Apr. 17, 2003) (finding evidence of willfulness in fax broadcaster's failure to remove numbers from its database immediately upon request). *But see* Manufacturers Auto Leasing, Inc. v. Autoflex Leasing, Inc., 2004 WL 966306 (Tex. App. May 6, 2004) (TCPA is willfully or knowingly violated when defendant knows of TCPA's prohibitions, knows plaintiff has not given permission to send a fax ad, yet faxes the ad).

2784 Covington & Burling v. Int'l Marketing & Research, Inc., 2003 WL 21384825 (D.C. Super. Apr. 17, 2003).

2785 *Class certification appropriate:* ESI Ergonomic Solutions v. United Artists Theatre Circuit, Inc., 50 P.3d 844 (Ariz. App. 2002) (reversing denial of class certification); Kaufman v. ACS Sys., Inc., 110 Cal. App. 4th 886, 2 Cal. Rptr. 3d 296 (2003) (TCPA does not foreclose class actions; must be decided on case-by-case basis); Dubsky v. Advanced Cellular Communications, Inc., 2004 WL 503757 (Ohio Com. Pleas Feb. 24, 2004) (unpublished, citation limited) (granting class certification); Hooters of Augusta, Inc. v. Nicholson, 245 Ga. App. 363, 537 S.E.2d 468 (2000) (affirming class certification).

Not appropriate: Kenro, Inc. v. Fax Daily, Inc., 962 F. Supp. 1162 (S.D. Ind. 1997) (determination of class membership would inappropriately require addressing the merits of the claim, particularly, determining whether faxes were in fact, unsolicited); Forman v. Data Transfer, Inc., 164 F.R.D. 400 (E.D. Pa. 1995) (same); Livingston v. U.S. Bank, 58 P.3d 1088 (Colo. App. 2002) (same); Rudgayzer & Gratt v. LRS Communications, Inc., 2003 WL 22344990 (N.Y. Civ. Ct. Sept. 29, 2003) (barring TCPA class action on state law grounds). *Cf.* Kondos v. Lincoln Property Co., 110 S.W.3d 716 (Tex. App. 2003) (reversing class certification because of lack of rigorous analysis; plaintiffs may pursue certification again upon remand).

2786 Covington & Burling v. Int'l Marketing & Research, Inc., 2003 WL 21384825 (D.C. Super. Apr. 17, 2003); Hooters of Augusta, Inc. v. Nicholson, 245 Ga. App. 363, 537 S.E.2d 468 (2000); Worsham v. Nationwide Ins. Co., 138 Md. App. 487, 772 A.2d 868 (2001) (once consumer asks one insurance agent to place him on do not call list, no other agents for that company may call, even if they are independent contractors).

2787 Texas v. American Blast Fax, Inc., 121 F. Supp. 2d 1085 (W.D. Tex. 2000); Covington & Burling v. Int'l Marketing & Research, Inc., 2003 WL 21384825 (D.C. Super. Apr. 17, 2003).

2788 *See* definition at 47 C.F.R. § 64.1200(f)(4).

2789 47 C.F.R. § 64.1200(a)(3)(ii). The effective date was announced at 68 Fed. Reg. 44144 (July 25, 2003).

2790 FCC Report and Order in the Matter of Rules and Regulations Implementing the Telephone Consumer Protection Act of 1991, at § 195, 18 F.C.C.R. 14014, 2003 WL 21517853 (July 3, 2003).

2791 47 C.F.R. § 68.318(d).

2792 *Id.*

2793 Texas v. American Blast Fax, Inc., 164 F. Supp. 2d 892 (W.D. Tex. 2001); Covington & Burling v. Int'l Marketing & Research, Inc., 2003 WL 21384825 (D.C. Super. Apr. 17, 2003).

2794 15 U.S.C. §§ 6101 to 6108 [*reprinted in* Appx. D.1.1, *infra*].

2795 15 U.S.C. § 6102.

2796 15 U.S.C. § 6102(a).

mandated provisions.[2797] A number of stock exchanges and similar organizations have adopted similar regulations for telemarketing in the securities industry.[2798]

On January 29, 2003, the FTC adopted a number of amendments to the Telemarketing Sales Rule.[2799] The most notable amendments were a nationwide do-not-call list, a ban on blocking caller identification information, and a requirement that sellers or telemarketers who accept payment via novel payment methods obtain express verifiable authorization from the customer. Most of the amendments were effective March 31, 2003,[2800] but the nationwide do-not-call list went into effect in October of that year.

5.9.4.2 Scope of Statute and Rule

Telemarketing is broadly defined in the statute to include a plan, program, or campaign conducted to induce the purchase of goods or services, or a charitable contribution, donation, or gift of money or any other thing of value, by use of one or more telephones, that involves more than one interstate telephone call.[2801] The rule covers both seller-initiated calls and calls initiated by the customer in response to certain advertisements, direct mail solicitations, and e-mail solicitations.[2802] Not only telemarketers themselves, but also any person who provides substantial assistance or support to a telemarketer while knowing or consciously avoiding knowledge of the telemarketer's violations, is liable under the rule.[2803]

The statute excludes most sales (other than upsales)[2804] made to consumers who initiate a call without any solicitation[2805] or only after receiving a catalog, seeing an advertisement, or, in some cases, receiving a direct mail solicitation that contains certain disclosures.[2806] Notwithstanding these exceptions, however, the rule covers consumer-initiated calls in response to advertisements or mailings relating to investment opportunities, most business opportunities, credit card loss protection services, credit repair services, recovery of previous telemarketing losses, or easy-credit advance-fee loan scams, or in response to direct mail solicitations regarding prize promotions.[2807]

Retail sales to businesses of products other than nondurable office and cleaning supplies are exempt.[2808] In addition, due to general limitations on the FTC's jurisdiction, the rule does not apply to banks, federal credit unions, federal savings and loans, common carriers, and regulated insurers.[2809] A federal court found that the FTC has authority to enforce the Telemarketing Sales Rule against a subsidiary of a national bank, however.[2810] Furthermore, the FTC maintains that the rule covers non-bank entities that conduct telemarketing on behalf of banks.[2811] The same principle applies to other exempt entities such as common carriers: they are exempt if they do their own telemarketing, but the rule covers non-exempt entities they hire.[2812]

Three types of calls are exempt from most but not all of the rule's requirements. This partial exemption applies to:

- Calls where the sale is not completed and payment is not required until after a face-to-face sales presentation by the seller.[2813]
- Calls on behalf of 900-number providers regulated by another FTC rule.[2814]
- Calls selling franchises governed by the FTC's Franchise Rule.[2815]

These three types of calls are subject only to the rule's (1) prohibitions against abusive language, repeated calls, abandoned calls, sale of account information, and Caller ID blocking, (2) calling time restrictions, and (3) do-not-call list requirements.[2816]

2797 16 C.F.R. § 310, *as amended by* 68 Fed. Reg. 4580 (Jan. 29, 2003).

2798 *See* 60 Fed. Reg. 31527 (June 15, 1995) (NASD) and 60 Fed. Reg. 31337 (June 7, 1995) (NYSE). *See also* 15 U.S.C. § 6102(d).

2799 68 Fed. Reg. 4580 (Jan. 29, 2003), *amending* 16 C.F.R. Part 310.

2800 Full compliance with the new Caller ID transmission rules was required only as of January 29, 2004. 68 Fed. Reg. 4850, 4850 (Jan. 29, 2003).

2801 15 U.S.C. § 6106(4). The FTC's coverage definitions are found at 16 C.F.R. § 310.2. The FTC considered including on-line services in its definition, but decided not to. 60 Fed. Reg. 30411 (June 8, 1995). The FTC does assert jurisdiction over deceptive providers of on-line services under its general authority, however. *Id. See* § 5.9.9, *infra.*

2802 *See* 16 C.F.R. § 310.6(b)(5), (6). *See also* FTC, Dot Com Disclosures § IV(B) (2000), *available at* www.ftc.gov.

2803 16 C.F.R. § 310.3(b). *See* § 5.9.8, *infra.*

2804 *See* § 5.9.4.7.1, *infra.*

2805 16 C.F.R. § 310.6(d).

2806 15 U.S.C. § 6106(4); 16 C.F.R. § 310.6(e), (f). Direct mail includes faxes, e-mail, and other methods of delivery directed to specific addresses or persons. 16 C.F.R. § 310.6(b)(6). *See also* Distributel, Inc. v. State, 933 P.2d 1137 (Alaska 1997) (similar language in Alaska telemarketing law does not exclude sales made when the seller called the consumer after having sent a catalog).

2807 16 C.F.R. § 310.6(b)(5), (6).

2808 16 C.F.R. § 310.6(g). *See* FTC v. Corporate Supplies, inc., 5 Trade Reg. Rep. (CCH) ¶ 24,884 (N.D. Ga. Mar. 5, 2001) (stipulated final judgment barring telemarketer from future sales of office supplies).

2809 68 Fed. Reg. 4580, 4581 n.21 (Jan. 29, 2003); FTC, Complying with the Telemarketing Sales Rule at 7 (Apr. 1996).

2810 Minn. *ex rel.* Hatch v. Fleet Mortg. Corp., 181 F. Supp. 2d 995 (D. Minn. 2001).

2811 68 Fed. Reg. 4580, 4586, 4587 (Jan. 29, 2003).

2812 *Id.*

2813 16 C.F.R. § 310.6(b)(3).

2814 16 C.F.R. § 310.6(b)(1).

2815 16 C.F.R. § 310.6(b)(2). The FTC's Franchise Rule is found at 16 C.F.R. Part 436. *See* § 5.13.1.1, *infra* (discussion of FTC's Franchise Rule).

2816 68 Fed. Reg. 4580, 4656 (Jan. 29, 2003).

Prior to the 2003 amendments, the rule applied to telephone campaigns to solicit charitable contributions if the calls constituted a plan, program, or campaign to induce the purchase of goods or services. If the primary purpose of the calls was to elicit donations, and any goods or services provided had an actual or claimed value less than the donation, the rule did not apply.[2817] The USA PATRIOT Act of 2001 expanded the coverage of the Telemarketing and Consumer Fraud and Abuse Prevention Act to include charitable fund raising conducted by for-profit telemarketers for or on behalf of charitable organizations.[2818] In accordance with these changes, the FTC amended the Telemarketing Sales Rule, effective March 31, 2003, to include telemarketing which is conducted to induce a charitable contribution,[2819] while at the same time reiterating that non-profit organizations themselves fall outside its jurisdiction.[2820] One part of the rule—the national do-not-call list—does not apply to telemarketers who solicit charitable donations,[2821] but they are subject to the requirement of a company-specific do-not-call list.[2822]

5.9.4.3 Disclosures Required

5.9.4.3.1 General disclosure requirements

The Telemarketing Sales Rule includes several disclosure requirements, depending on the type of transaction involved. In general, disclosures must be truthful, clear and conspicuous.[2823] The rule requires telemarketers, at the outset of an outgoing call or an upsell[2824] to induce the purchase of goods or services, to make prompt oral disclosure of the identity of the seller, that the purpose of the call is to sell goods or services, and the nature of the goods or services.[2825] Callers seeking charitable donations must make prompt oral disclosure of the identity of the charitable organization on behalf of which the call is made and that the purpose of the call is to solicit a charitable donation.[2826] In response to suggestions to clarify that prompt disclosure means "at the onset of a call," the FTC stated that no clarification was necessary because prompt means "at once or without delay, and before any substantive information about a prize, product or service is conveyed to the consumer."[2827]

In addition, before the consumer pays for goods or services, the seller must make a number of disclosures. The rule does not require that these disclosures be oral, so they may be in a catalog or advertisement to which the consumer has responded.[2828] These disclosures are required in all telemarketing sales covered by the rule, including calls initiated by the consumer.[2829] The seller must disclose the total costs to purchase, receive, or use the goods or services;[2830] the quantity of goods or services being purchased; and all material restrictions, limitations, or conditions to purchase, receive, or use the goods or services.[2831] The illegality of the

2817 American Tel. Fundraisers Ass'n, Inc., 5 Trade Reg. Rep. (CCH) ¶ 23,951 (FTC advisory opinion 1995). See § 5.13.5, *infra*, for a discussion of the application of UDAP statutes to charitable solicitations.

2818 Uniting and Strengthening America by Providing Appropriate Tools Required to Intercept and Obstruct Terrorism Act of 2001, Pub. L. No. 107-56 (Oct. 25, 2001), *amending* 15 U.S.C. § 6102(a)(2)(3). *See* 68 Fed. Reg. 4585, 4586 (Jan. 29, 2003) (discussion of ambiguities in scope of these amendments).

2819 16 C.F.R. § 310.2(cc). "Charitable contribution" is defined at 16 C.F.R. § 310.2(f).

2820 68 Fed. Reg. 4580, 4585, 4586 (Jan. 29, 2003).

2821 16 C.F.R. § 310.6(a).

2822 68 Fed. Reg. 4580, 4629 (Jan. 29, 2003).

2823 16 C.F.R. §§ 310.3(a)(1), 310.4(d), (e), *as amended by* 68 Fed. Reg. 4670 (Jan. 29, 2003).

2824 *See* § 5.9.4.7.1, *infra* (discussion of upsells).

2825 16 C.F.R. § 310.4(d). *See* FTC v. Liberty Direct, Inc., 5 Trade Reg. Rep. (CCH) ¶ 24,914 (D. Ariz. Apr. 20, 2001) (consent decree) (complaint alleged that defendants sold credit card loss protection service without initial disclosure of purpose of call). The FCC rule, 47 C.F.R. § 64.1200(d)(4), also requires disclosure of the identity of the company on whose behalf the call is placed.

2826 16 C.F.R. § 310.4(e). *See* Pub. L. No. 107-56, § 1011(b)(2) (requiring prompt and clear disclosure that the purpose of the call is to solicit charitable contributions, donations, or gifts "and to make such other disclosures as the Commission considers appropriate, including the name and mailing address of the charitable organization. . . .").

2827 67 Fed. Reg. 4502, 4526–4527 (Jan. 30, 2002). *Accord* 68 Fed. Reg. 4580, 4648 (Jan. 29, 2003).

2828 FTC, *Complying With the Telemarketing Sales Rule*, *available at* www.ftc.gov/bcp/conline/pubs/buspubs/tsrcomp.htm.

2829 *See* § 5.9.4.2, *supra* (scope of rule).

2830 Although the FTC states that the best practice is to disclose the total of payments whenever possible, the telemarketer need only disclose the number of installment payments and the amount of each payment. 68 Fed. Reg. 4580, 4599, 4600 (Jan. 29, 2003). For offers of consumer credit products subject to the Truth in Lending Act (TILA), 15 U.S.C. § 1601, *et seq.*, and Regulation Z, 12 C.F.R. § 226, compliance with the disclosure requirements under TILA and Regulation Z constitutes compliance with the rule's cost disclosure requirements. 16 C.F.R. § 310.3 n.2.

2831 16 C.F.R. §§ 310.3(a)(1), 310.2(q) (definition of "material"). *See also* FTC v. First Impressions, Inc., 5 Trade Reg. Rep. (CCH) ¶ 24,774 (S.D. Fla. July 10, 2000) (consent decree against telemarketer who told consumers they had won free vacations without disclosing fees that were required); FTC v. Commonwealth Marketing Group, 5 Trade Reg. Rep. (CCH) ¶ 24,717 (W.D. Pa. Mar. 6, 2000) (consent order granting permanent injunction against telemarketer who represented that consumers had won vacations but disclosed various additional fees only later); FTC v. Arlington Press, Inc., No. 98-9260 (C.D. Cal. 1999) (stipulated order for permanent injunction for violation of the TCPA arising from auction and foreclosed home information packages that failed to disclose in a clear and conspicuous manner the total cost of products and refund policy); FTC v. Clarendon House, Inc., No. 98-9262 (C.D. Cal. 1999) (stipulated order for permanent injunction arising from deceptive information packages on seized cars, foreclosed homes, and job opportunity packages, ordering payment of nearly $4 million, less stipulated charge backs by customers); *In re* National Credit Mgmt. Group, 21 F. Supp. 2d 424 (D.N.J. 1998) (issuing injunction against telemarketer who disclosed only initial fee for

goods or services offered is a material restriction that must be disclosed.[2832]

If the seller has a policy of not making refunds, cancellations, exchanges, or repurchases, the telemarketer must inform the consumer that this is the seller's policy.[2833] Regardless of the nature of the policy, if the telemarketer makes any representation about a refund policy, the telemarketer must disclose all material terms and conditions of the policy.[2834]

5.9.4.3.2 Special disclosure requirements for prize promotions

For prize promotions, in addition to the standard oral disclosures at the outset of the call, the telemarketer must state that no purchase is necessary to enter, and that any purchase or payment will not increase the person's chances of winning.[2835] This disclosure is required in outgoing calls and upsells.

In addition, in all telemarketing transactions involving prize promotions, before the consumer pays, the telemarketer must disclose the odds of winning or, if the odds can not be calculated in advance, the factors used in calculating the odds; that no purchase is necessary; that any purchase or payment will not increase the person's chance of winning; how to make use of the no-purchase option or an address or local or toll-free telephone number from which this information can be obtained; and all material costs or conditions to receive the prize.[2836]

5.9.4.4 Prohibition Against Deception

5.9.4.4.1 General prohibition

The rule prohibits telemarketers from making any false or misleading statements to induce any person to pay for goods and services.[2837] In evaluating alleged violations of this prohibition, a federal court in New York looked beyond the seller's claim that its statements were literally true, and granted a preliminary injunction against advertisements that were designed to foster the impression that the seller was actually offering a credit card.[2838] Another federal court in New York issued a permanent injunction against an FCC license brokering company that made false or misleading statements regarding the profitability of FCC licenses and the difficulty of obtaining them.[2839]

The rule also prohibits telemarketers from misrepresenting, directly or by implication, the total cost and quantity of goods or services; material restrictions, limitations or conditions to purchase, receive or use the goods or services;[2840] any material aspect of the performance, efficacy, nature, or central characteristics of the goods or services; any material aspects of the seller's refund, cancellation, exchange, or repurchase policies; material aspects of prize promotions; material aspects of investment opportunities; or a seller's or telemarketer's affiliation with or endorsement by any government or third-party organization.[2841]

---

marketed program, without disclosing the total costs); New York v. Financial Servs. Network, 930 F. Supp. 865 (W.D.N.Y. 1996) (issuing preliminary injunction against telemarketer who revealed limitations on credit cards only after consumers paid fee); People *ex rel.* Spitzer v. Telehublink Corp., 301 A.D.2d 1006, 756 N.Y.S.2d 285 (2003) (affirming permanent injunction and restitution order against telemarketer that did not disclose that credit card could only be used to buy items from seller's catalog).

2832 68 Fed. Reg. 4580, 4600 (Jan. 29, 2003).

2833 16 C.F.R. § 310.3(a)(1)(iii).

2834 *Id.*

2835 16 C.F.R. § 310.4(d). *See* FTC v. Silver State Western Publishing, Inc., 5 Trade Reg. Rep. (CCH) ¶ 24,031 (D. Nev. 1996) (filing of complaint) (charging defendants with misrepresenting value of prize and failing to disclose that no purchase was necessary).

2836 16 C.F.R. § 310.3(a)(1)(iv), (v). Since telemarketers must disclose that no purchase or payment is required to win a prize or participate in a prize promotion, the FTC explained that the costs that must be disclosed are any incidental costs other than a purchase or payment. *See* 68 Fed. Reg. 4580, 4601 (Jan. 29, 2003).

2837 16 C.F.R. § 310.3(a)(4). *See also* FTC v. World Media Brokers, Inc., 2004 WL 432475 (N.D. Ill. Mar. 2, 2004) (telemarketer's misrepresentation of legality of sale of foreign lottery tickets); FTC v. Consumer Alliance, Inc., 2003 WL 22287364 (N.D. Ill. Sept. 30, 2003) (misrepresentation and unauthorized billing in sale of credit card protection and advance fee credit cards); FTC v. Growth Plus Int'l Marketing, Inc., 2001 U.S. Dist. LEXIS 1215 (N.D. Ill. Jan. 4, 2001) (granting preliminary injunction based on FTC's showing of deception); FTC v. Woofter Investment Corp., 5 Trade Reg. Rep. (CCH) ¶ 24,551 (D. Nev. 1998) (proposed consent decree); FTC v. Pacific Rims Pools Int'l, 5 Trade Reg. Rep. (CCH) ¶ 24,551 (W.D. Wash. 1998) (proposed consent decree); People *ex rel.* Spitzer v. Telehublink Corp., 301 A.D.2d 1006, 756 N.Y.S.2d 285 (2003) (affirming permanent injunction and restitution order against telemarketer that promised major credit card but delivered card for purchasing items from seller's catalog).

2838 New York v. Financial Servs. Network, 930 F. Supp. 865 (W.D.N.Y. 1996).

2839 Federal Trade Comm'n v. Micom Corp., 1997 U.S. Dist. LEXIS 3404, 1997-1 Trade Cas. (CCH) ¶ 71,753 (S.D.N.Y. Mar. 12, 1997).

2840 *See* People *ex rel.* Spitzer v. Telehublink Corp., 301 A.D.2d 1006, 756 N.Y.S.2d 285 (2003) (affirming permanent injunction and restitution order against telemarketer that did not disclose that credit card could only be used to buy items from seller's catalog).

2841 16 C.F.R. § 310.3(a)(2). *See also* FTC v. 1263523 Ontario, Inc., 205 F. Supp. 2d 205 (S.D.N.Y. 2002) (entering permanent injunction against advance fee credit card telemarketer that misrepresented its refund policy); FTC v. Growth Plus Int'l Mktg., Inc., 2001 U.S. Dist. LEXIS 1215 (N.D. Ill. Jan. 9, 2001)

5.9.4.4.2 Charitable contributions

For solicitations of charitable contributions, the 2003 amendments to the rule specifically prohibit misrepresentations of the following:[2842]

- The nature, purpose, or mission of any entity on behalf of which the charitable contribution is being requested;
- That any charitable contribution is tax deductible in whole or in part;
- The purpose for which the charitable contribution will be used;[2843]
- The amount that goes to the charitable organization or program after administrative costs are deducted;
- Material aspects of prize promotions, including that a charitable contribution is required to win a prize; or
- Affiliation, endorsements or sponsorship by any person or government.[2844]

5.9.4.4.3 Prize promotions and investment opportunities

The rule prohibits several specific deceptions in prize promotions and investment opportunities. For prize promotions, the rule prohibits misrepresenting any material aspect of the promotion, including odds of receiving the prize, the nature or value of the prize, or that a purchase or payment is required to win a prize.[2845] For investment opportunities, the rule prohibits misrepresentation of any material aspect of the opportunity, including the risk, liquidity, earnings potential or profitability.[2846]

5.9.4.5 Harassment and Abuse

5.9.4.5.1 General prohibition

The rule prohibits threats, intimidation, and the use of profane or obscene language.[2847] Harassment by repeated calls is prohibited, as are return calls to a person who has said that he or she does not want to receive calls from a particular seller.[2848]

5.9.4.5.2 Abandoned calls

The amended rule attempts to address dead air or hang-up calls that consumers receive from telemarketers.[2849] These calls result from telemarketers' use of automatic dialing equipment (predictive dialers) that call too many numbers for the employees of the telemarketing company to handle. Consumers rightfully complain that they rush to answer the phone, only to find no one at the other end of the call.[2850]

The amended rule prohibits telemarketers from abandoning outbound calls, but provides for a "safe harbor." An abandoned call occurs when a sales representative fails to connect with the consumer within two seconds after that consumer finishes saying hello or another greeting.[2851] Pursuant to the safe harbor, the FTC will refrain from bringing an enforcement action against a telemarketer if the telemarketer or seller (1) employs technology that ensures abandonment of no more than three percent of all calls answered by a consumer; (2) allows each telemarketing call placed to ring for at least fifteen seconds or four complete rings before disconnecting the unanswered call; (3) promptly plays a recorded message whenever a sales representative is not available to speak within two seconds of the completion of the consumer's greeting; and (4) retains records establishing compliance with these requirements.[2852] These restrictions on abandoned calls were effective on October 1, 2003, six months later than most of the rest of the amended rule.[2853] A federal court has held that these restrictions were within the FTC's statutory authority.[2854] The rule that the FCC adopted under the Telephone Consumer Protection Act, as amended effective October 1, 2003, also prohibits abandoned calls, but with a somewhat more generous safe harbor.[2855]

(granting preliminary injunction against defendants who misrepresented legality of selling Canadian lottery tickets in the U.S., their authorization by the Canadian government to sell these tickets, and the chances of winning); FTC v. Marketing Response Group, Inc., 5 Trade Reg. Rep. (CCH) ¶ 24,194 (M.D. Fla. 1997) (violated rule by luring consumers into purchasing materials or magazine subscriptions in exchange for valuable prizes or awards); FTC v. Silver State Western Publishing, Inc., 5 Trade Reg. Rep. (CCH) ¶ 24,166 (D. Nev. 1996) (proposed consent decree) (same).

2842 16 C.F.R. § 310.3(d). *See* 68 Fed. Reg. 4580, 4612, 4613 (Jan. 29, 2003) (discussion of rationale and details).

2843 The FTC interprets this prohibition to encompass misrepresentations that a charity or its services are local. 68 Fed. Reg. 4580, 4613 (Jan. 29, 2003).

2844 The FTC interprets this prohibition as extending to "sound-alikes," the use of a name similar or identical to that of a legitimate charity. 68 Fed. Reg. 4580, 4613 (Jan. 29, 2003).

2845 16 C.F.R. § 310.3(a)(2)(v).

2846 16 C.F.R. § 310.3(a)(2)(vi).

2847 16 C.F.R. § 310.4(a)(1).

2848 16 C.F.R. § 310.4(b).

2849 16 C.F.R. § 310.4(b)(1)(iv).

2850 68 Fed. Reg. 4580, 4641, 4645 (Jan. 29, 2003). *See* Irvine v. Akron Beacon Journal, 770 N.E.2d 1105 (Ohio App. 2002).

2851 16 C.F.R. § 310.4(b)(1)(iv).

2852 16 C.F.R. § 310.4(b)(4)(i)–(iv).

2853 FTC, Telemarketing Sales Rule, Stay of Compliance Date, 68 Fed. Reg. 16414 (Apr. 4, 2003).

2854 U.S. Security v. FTC, 282 F. Supp. 2d 1285 (W.D. Okla. 2003).

2855 47 C.F.R. § 64.1200(a)(6); 68 Fed. Reg. 44144 (July 25, 2003) (establishing effective date). *See* § 5.9.3.4, *supra*.

5.9.4.6 Privacy Issues: Calling Hours, Do-Not-Call Lists, and Caller ID Blocking

5.9.4.6.1 Calling hours

Like the FCC's rule under the Telephone Consumer Protection Act,[2856] the FTC's rule allows calls to be made only between 8:00 A.M. and 9:00 P.M.[2857] Calls at other times require the consumer's prior consent.[2858]

5.9.4.6.2 Company-specific do-not-call lists

The Telemarketing Sales Rule prohibits a seller or telemarketer from calling a person who has previously asked to be placed on the seller's do-not-call list.[2859] Each seller must maintain a company-specific do-not-call list. The 2003 amendments expand this requirement to include callers who solicit charitable donations.[2860]

Telemarketers are prohibited from denying or interfering in any way with a person's right to be placed on a do-not-call list.[2861] Hanging up on a person who starts to ask not to be called is a violation.[2862] Directing another person to deny or interfere with a person's right to be placed on a do-not-call list is a violation.[2863] The FCC's rule under the Telephone Consumer Protection Act also requires telemarketers to maintain and abide by company-specific do-not-call lists,[2864] but exempts solicitors for non-profit organizations.[2865]

5.9.4.6.3 Nationwide do-not-call list

In 2003, the FTC expanded the Telemarketing Sales Rule to establish a national do-not-call registry. Operation of the do-not-call list was made contingent on Congressional funding.[2866] Congress approved funding on March 11, 2003, at the same time directing the FCC to issue a final do-not-call rule that maximized consistency with the FTC's rule.[2867] The nationwide do-not-call list rule that the FCC subsequently adopted, which is similar but applies to a larger universe of telemarketers, is discussed in § 5.9.3.6, *supra*.

Litigation caused a slight delay in the launch of the do-not-call list. Shortly before it was to go into effect, a federal district court held that it exceeded the FTC's statutory authority.[2868] Congress responded by passing a new law within days that made the FTC's authority clearer.[2869] Then a second district court held the FTC's do-not-call rules unconstitutional because it treated commercial calls differently than non-commercial calls.[2870] The Tenth Circuit stayed the district court's order and the do-not-call rule went into effect a few days after the originally scheduled date of October 1, 2003.[2871] In early 2004, the Tenth Circuit reversed the district court and upheld the constitutionality of both the FTC's and the FCC's do-not-call rules.[2872]

The do-not-call registry is intended to enable consumers to stop most unwanted telemarketing calls.[2873] Individuals can register their telephone numbers on the do-not-call list by calling 1-888-382-1222 (TTY 1-866-290-4236). The call must be made from the telephone number that the consumer wishes to register. In the alternative, a consumer can register one or more numbers through the FTC's website, www.ftc.gov/donotcall. The do-not-call list includes cell phone numbers and pager numbers,[2874] so consumers should register these as well as land line numbers.

Consumers who continue to receive calls after registering for the do-not-call registry can file a complaint with the FTC, which can fine telemarketers up to $11,000 for each call.[2875] A consumer's number remains on the registry for five years or until the consumer takes the number off the registry or changes phone numbers. After five years, consumers can renew their registration with the FTC.[2876] Consumers who want to receive information from a specific company may give that company signed written permission to call, even though the consumer is on the national registry.[2877]

One major exemption in the rule allows telemarketers to call consumers with whom they have an established busi-

2856 *See* § 5.9.3.8, *supra*.
2857 16 C.F.R. § 310.4(c).
2858 *Id.*
2859 16 C.F.R. § 310.4(b)(1)(iii); FTC v. Epic Resorts, L.L.C., 5 Trade Reg. Rep. (CCH) ¶ 15150 (M.D. Fla. Sept. 5, 2001) (proposed consent decree enjoining violations of company-specific do-not-call rule).
2860 16 C.F.R. § 310.6(a). *See also* 68 Fed. Reg. 4580, 4636–37 (Jan. 29, 2003) (FTC's explanation of this provision).
2861 16 C.F.R. § 310.4(b)(ii).
2862 68 Fed. Reg. 4580, 4628 (Jan. 29, 2003).
2863 16 C.F.R. § 310.4(b)(1)(ii). *See* 68 Fed. Reg. 4580, 4628 (Jan. 29, 2003).
2864 47 C.F.R. § 64.1200(d). *See* § 5.9.3.6, *supra*.
2865 47 C.F.R. § 64.1200(d)(7), (f)(9)(iii). *See* § 5.9.3.7, *supra*.
2866 Statement of Basis and Purpose, 68 Fed. Reg. 4580, 4580 (Jan. 29, 2003).
2867 Do Not Call Implementation Act, Pub. L. No. 108-10, 117 Stat. 557 (Mar. 11, 2003).
2868 U.S. Security v. FTC, 282 F. Supp. 2d 1285 (W.D. Okla. 2003), *rev'd*, 358 F.3d 1228 (10th Cir. 2004).
2869 An Act to Ratify the Authority of the Federal Trade Commission to Establish a Do-Not-Call Registry, Pub. L. No. 108-82, 117 Stat. 1006 (2003). *See* Mainstream Marketing, Inc. v. FTC, 358 F.3d 1228 (10th Cir. 2004) (rule was within FTC's authority both before and after the new law).
2870 Mainstream Marketing, Inc. v. FTC, 283 F. Supp. 2d 1151 (D. Colo. 2003), *rev'd*, 358 F.3d 1228 (10th Cir. 2004).
2871 FTC v. Mainstream Marketing, Inc., 345 F.3d 850 (10th Cir. 2003).
2872 Mainstream Marketing, Inc. v. FTC, 358 F.3d 1228 (10th Cir. 2004).
2873 Q & A: The FTC's Changes to the Telemarketing Sales Rule, available at www.ftc.gov/bcp/conline/pubs/alerts/dncalrt.htm.
2874 68 Fed. Reg. 4580, 4632–33 (Jan. 29, 2003).
2875 *Id.*
2876 *Id.*
2877 68 Fed. Reg. 4580, 4634 (Jan. 29, 2003).

ness relationship.[2878] Such a relationship exists if the consumer has purchased, leased, or rented goods or services from the company within 18 months preceding the call, or if the consumer has submitted an application or made an inquiry to the company within three months preceding the call.[2879] However, even if an established business relationship exists, consumers may still make a specific request to the company not to call.[2880]

A second major exception is for calls seeking donations to non-profit organizations.[2881] These solicitors must still, however, place a consumer on an organization-specific do-not-call list if the consumer so requests.[2882] There is also an exception for business-to-business calls.[2883]

The FTC's do-not-call registry requirements are intended to be at least as stringent as most state laws.[2884] However, the FTC declined to preempt state laws,[2885] and states are able to continue to enforce their telemarketing laws, including their do-not-call lists, for intrastate telemarketing calls.[2886] The FTC has coordinated its do-not-call registry with many states' do-not-call lists so that consumers can register for both the federal and state list at the same time.[2887] Consumers in doubt about whether a single registration suffices should register for both the national do-not-call list and their respective state list.

Even the announcement of the do-not-call list attracted scam artists. The FTC proceeded against an individual who induced consumers to pay him to pre-register them for the do-not-call list. Part of his goal was to get personal information from the consumers. He also sold a service that would allegedly block telemarketing calls and junk mail and faxes.[2888]

5.9.4.6.4 Prohibition against Caller ID blocking

The amended Telemarketing Sales Rule prohibits telemarketers from blocking the transmission of information about the call to consumers' Caller ID services.[2889] The effective date for this provision was January 29, 2004.[2890] The telemarketer must transmit or cause to be transmitted either the telemarketer's name and telephone number or the name and telephone number (answered during regular business hours) of the business or organization on whose behalf the telemarketer is calling.[2891] The FTC has indicated that technical failures outside the telemarketer's control will not be considered violations as long as the telemarketer has taken all available steps to comply with the rule.[2892] An FCC rule, as amended effective January 29, 2004, also prohibits Caller ID blocking.[2893]

5.9.4.7 Special Rules for Particular Types of Telemarketing Solicitations

5.9.4.7.1 Upsells

The amended Telemarketing Sales Rule has special provisions for "upsells." An upsell is a solicitation for goods or services that follows an initial transaction of any sort in a single telephone call.[2894] For example, an upsell occurs if a consumer calls a company for technical support, and in the course of the call the company solicits the consumer to buy a new product or service. Or the consumer may call a seller in response to an advertisement for one item, and in the course of the call the seller tries to sell a different product. It is also an upsell if a telemarketer calls a consumer, makes a sale, and then starts another sales pitch or transfers the consumer to a different seller who makes a new sales pitch.[2895] Under the amended rule, the oral disclosures mandated by section 310.4(d) must be promptly made at the initiation of the upsell if any of the information differs from that disclosed in the initial transaction.[2896]

5.9.4.7.2 Credit card protection services

One particularly prevalent scam that often targets the elderly is the sale of unnecessary credit card protection plans.[2897] Unscrupulous telemarketers often misrepresent

2878 16 C.F.R. § 310.4(b)(iii)(B)(ii). *See* 68 Fed. Reg. 4580, 4633, 4634 (Jan. 29, 2003). The FCC's nationwide do-not-call rule has a similar exception. *See* 47 C.F.R. § 64.1200(f)(3), (9).

2879 16 C.F.R. § 310.2(n). *See* 68 Fed. Reg. 4580, 4591–94 (Jan. 29, 2003).

2880 68 Fed. Reg. 4634 (Jan. 29, 2003).

2881 16 C.F.R. § 310.6(a). *See* 68 Fed. Reg. 4580, 4629, 4634–37,4654 (Jan. 29, 2003).

2882 68 Fed. Reg. 4580, 4636, 4637 (Jan. 29, 2003).

2883 16 C.F.R. § 310.6(b)(7). *See* 68 Fed. Reg. 4580, 4632 (Jan. 29, 2003).

2884 Q & A: The FTC's Changes to the Telemarketing Sales Rule, available at www.ftc.gov/bcp/conline/pubs/alerts/dncalrt.htm

2885 68 Fed. Reg. 4580, 4638 (Jan. 29, 2003).

2886 *Id.*

2887 Fed. Reg. 4580, 4638, 4641 (Jan. 29, 2003).

2888 FTC v. Kevin Chase, 5 Trade Reg. Rep. (CCH) ¶ 15407 (N.D. Cal. May 6, 2003) (complaint).

2889 16 C.F.R. § 310.4(a)(7). *See* 68 Fed. Reg. 4580, 4623–28 (Jan. 29, 2003). "Caller identification service" is defined at 16 C.F.R. § 310.2(d).

2890 68 Fed. Reg. 4580, 4623 (Jan. 29, 2003).

2891 16 C.F.R. § 310.4(a)(7).

2892 68 Fed. Reg. 4580, 4626 (Jan. 29, 2003).

2893 47 C.F.R. § 64.1601(e); 68 Fed. Reg. 44144 (July 24, 2003) (establishing effective date). *See* § 5.9.3.8, *supra*.

2894 16 C.F.R. § 310.2(dd); *see* 68 Fed. Reg. 4580, 4656 (Jan. 29, 2003).

2895 68 Fed. Reg. 4580, 4596, 4597 (Jan. 29, 2003).

2896 16 C.F.R. § 310.4(d). *See* 68 Fed. Reg. 4580, 4648 (Jan. 29, 2003) (noting addition of words "or internal or external upsell" in § 310.4(d)'s prefatory language).

2897 *See* 68 Fed. Reg. 4580, 4601, 4602 (Jan. 29, 2003); 67 Fed. Reg. 4503 (Jan. 30, 2002) (National Consumers League reported fraudulent solicitation of credit card protection plans ranked 9th among the most numerous complaints to the National Fraud

that they are affiliated with the credit card issuer and that, without a credit card protection plan, the consumer has unlimited liability for the unauthorized use of his or her credit card.[2898] In fact, federal law limits such liability to no more than $50 in most situations.[2899] These types of misrepresentations are prohibited under the amended rule.[2900] The amended rule also requires affirmative disclosure of existing limits on cardholder liability for unauthorized use.[2901]

5.9.4.7.3 Negative-option sales

The amended Telemarketing Sales Rule places special disclosure requirements on any sale that has a "negative option" feature. A negative-option feature is any provision under which the consumer's silence or failure to take an affirmative action to reject goods or services or to cancel the agreement is interpreted by the seller as an acceptance of the offer.[2902] An example is a plan in which the consumer receives periodic announcements of selections that are sent automatically and billed to the consumer unless the consumer tells the company not to send the item.[2903] The FTC also has a separate rule governing negative option plans in general.[2904]

Whenever an offer includes a negative option feature, the rule requires disclosure of all its material terms and conditions.[2905] The disclosure must include the fact that the consumer's account will be charged unless the consumer takes an affirmative action to avoid the charge; the dates that charges will be submitted for payment, and the specific steps the consumer must take to avoid the charges.[2906] These disclosure must be made before the customer pays.[2907] The rule also prohibits misrepresentation regarding negative option features.[2908]

Additional restrictions are applicable to one type of negative-option feature—"free-to-pay" sales in which the consumer has a free trial for a period of time but then is charged unless he or she takes some affirmative step to reject the sale. These are discussed in § 5.9.4.7.5, *infra*.

5.9.4.7.4 Special restrictions for credit repair services, advance-fee credit offers, and recovery rooms

The rule includes special consumer protections for three particular areas of telemarketing fraud:

- Credit repair services,[2909] which promise to improve the consumer's credit record;
- Telemarketers who offer to arrange extensions of credit and represent a high likelihood of success; and
- "Recovery rooms," which promise, for a fee, to regain money or property lost in a previous telemarketing scam.

The rule prohibits telemarketers in all three of these areas from seeking payment from the consumer before improving the credit record,[2910] obtaining the credit,[2911] or recovering

---

Information Center in 1999 with over 71% of the victims over age 50). *See also* 67 Fed. Reg. 4503–4504, 4541 (Jan. 30, 2002) (discussion of proposed rule).

2898 *See* FTC v. Consumer Alliance, Inc., 2003 WL 22287364 (N.D. Ill. Sept. 30, 2003) (finding deception); FTC v. Millennium Indus., Inc., 5 Trade Reg. Rep. (CCH) ¶ 15261 (D. Ariz. May 29, 2002) (proposed consent decree); FTC v. Capital Card Servs., Inc., 5 Trade Reg. Rep. (CCH) ¶ 15134 (D. Ariz. July 25, 2001) (proposed consent decree against credit card protection seller); FTC and State of Illinois v. Membership Servs., Inc. and James M. Scwindt (S.D. Cal. Oct. 31, 2001) at www.ftc.gov/os/2001/10/msipi.pdf (stipulated preliminary injunction with asset freeze against a telemarketer who made false and misleading statements to induce consumers to buy credit card protection plans). *See also* FTC v. R & R Consultants, Inc., 5 Trade Reg. Rep. (CCH) ¶ 15251 (N.D.N.Y. Apr. 25, 2002) (proposed consent decree against telemarketer who sold bogus ID theft protection and advance fee credit cards); FTC v. Consumer Repair Svcs., Inc., No. 00-11218 (C.D. Cal. filed Oct. 23, 2000) at www.ftc.gov/os/2000/10/proconrepaircmp.pdf; FTC v. Forum Mktg Svs., Inc., No. 00 CV0905C (W.D.N.Y. filed Oct. 23, 2000) at www.ftc.gov/os/2000/10/forummarket.pdf; FTC v. 1306506 Ontario Ltd., No. CV0906A (SR) (W.D.N.Y filed Oct. 23, 2000) at www.ftc.gov/os/2000/10/ontariocomp.htm; FTC v. Capital Card Svcs., Inc., and Cory M. Harris, No. CIV 00 1993 PHX EHC (D. Ariz. filed Sept. 14, 1999) at www.ftc.gov/os/2001/07/capitalcardservicesstip.htm (stipulation for final entry and order filed in D. Ariz. July 2001).

2899 15 U.S.C. § 1643.

2900 16 C.F.R. § 310.3(a)(2)(vii) and (viii).

2901 16 C.F.R. § 310.3(a)(1)(vi).

2902 16 C.F.R. § 310.2(t). *See* 68 Fed. Reg. 4580, 4594 (Jan. 29, 2003) (explanation of definition).

2903 *See* 68 Fed. Reg. 4580, 4594 (Jan. 29, 2003).

2904 16 C.F.R. Part 425. *See* § 5.8.5, *supra*.

2905 16 C.F.R. § 310.3(a)(1)(vii). *See also* U.S. v. Oxmoor House, 5 Trade Reg. Rep. (CCH) ¶ 15321 (N.D. Ala. Nov. 7, 2002) (proposed consent decree in pre-amendment case against telemarketer who failed to disclose that consumer who kept and paid for product beyond 30-day free trial period would be automatically enrolled in negative option book program); U.S. v. Micro Star Software, Inc., 5 Trade Reg. Rep. (CCH) ¶ 15258 (S.D. Cal. May 22, 2002) (proposed consent decree in pre-amendment case).

2906 16 C.F.R. § 310.3(a)(1)(vii).

2907 *Id.*

2908 16 C.F.R. § 310.3(a)(2)(ix).

2909 This provision of the rule remains enforceable despite the subsequent passage of the more specific Credit Repair Organizations Act (15 U.S.C. §§ 1679–1679j). Tennessee v. Lexington Law Firms, 1997 U.S. Dist. LEXIS 7403, 1997-1 Trade Cas. (CCH) ¶ 71,8201 (M.D. Tenn. May 14, 1997).

2910 16 C.F.R. § 310.4(a)(2). *See* FTC v. Mehnet Akca, 5 Trade Reg. Rep. (CCH) ¶ 24,663 (D. Colo. Oct. 21, 1999) (consent decree); FTC v. Ellis, 5 Trade Reg. Rep. (CCH) ¶ 23,978 (C.D. Cal. 1996) (TRO).

2911 16 C.F.R. § 310.4(a)(4); People *ex rel.* Spitzer v. Telehublink Corp., 301 A.D.2d 1006, 756 N.Y.S.2d 285 (2003). *See* FTC v. Consumer Alliance, Inc., 2003 WL 22287364 (N.D. Ill. Sept. 30, 2003); FTC v. Bay Area Bus. Council, Inc., 2003 WL

the money or property.[2912] In the case of credit repair services, the telemarketer must wait for payment until six months after providing the consumer an improved credit report.[2913] A telemarketer that advertised pre-approved credit could not escape the prohibition against advance payment by arguing that it did not actually issue credit itself, or by characterizing its charges as "membership fees" for its investment and credit application services rather than as fees for credit.[2914] The rule applies to the telemarketing activities of attorneys offering credit repair services.[2915]

Credit repair services that accept advance fees also run afoul of the federal Credit Repair Organizations Act.[2916] That statute prohibits advance payment, although it does not require the credit repair organization to wait six months after providing the consumer an improved credit report. It also requires a three-day right to cancel and prohibits various deceptions. Unlike the Telemarketing Rule, the CROA explicitly grants consumers a private cause of action regardless of the amount of damage.[2917] Many states have similar statutes, often with broader coverage that includes loan brokers as well as credit repair organizations, and these statutes usually also provide for a private cause of action.[2918]

5.9.4.7.5 Preacquired account telemarketing

A recent and troublesome trend in telemarketing abuses is the seller's use of billing account information that is has

---

1220245 (N.D. Ill. Mar. 14, 2003) (denying motion to dismiss); FTC v. Efficient Telesales Servs., Inc., 5 Trade Reg. Rep. (CCH) ¶ 15418 (N.D. Ill. Feb. 5, 2003) (default judgment barring company from selling advance fee credit cards and requiring $1.3 million consumer redress); FTC v. Harvey Sloniker, 5 Trade Reg. Rep. (CCH) ¶ 15364 (D. Ariz. Feb. 6, 2003) (proposed consent decree); FTC v. Antoine Peissel, 5 Trade Reg. Rep. (CCH) ¶ 15338 (S.D. Tex. Dec. 6, 2002) (proposed consent decree) (telemarketer promised loan but just delivered loan application); FTC v. Tungsten Group, 5 Trade Reg. Rep. (CCH) ¶ 15283 (E.D. Va. July 30, 2002) (proposed consent decree); FTC v. R & R Consultants, Inc., 5 Trade Reg. Rep. (CCH) ¶ 15251 (N.D.N.Y. Apr. 25, 2002) (proposed consent decree); FTC v. Navestar D.M., Inc., 5 Trade Reg. Rep. (CCH) ¶ 15198 (W.D.N.Y. Jan. 3, 2002); FTC v. 1263523 Ontario, Inc., 205 F. Supp. 2d 205 (S.D.N.Y. 2002) (granting permanent injunction against advance fee credit card telemarketer); FTC v. Mark Alan Conway, 5 Trade Reg. Rep. (CCH) ¶ 15149 (W.D. Cal. Aug. 27, 2001); FTC v. Financial Servs., 5 Trade Reg. Rep. (CCH) ¶ 15173 (Oct. 31, 2001) (proposed consent decree); FTC v. First Fin. Solutions, Inc., 5 Trade Reg. Rep. (CCH) ¶ 15181 (N.D. Ill. Nov. 20, 2001) (TRO against advance fee credit card scam; seller provided a stored value card and literature regarding a membership benefits program rather than a credit card), ¶ 15311 (N.D. Ill. Sept. 26, 2002) (settlement); FTC v. First Credit Alliance, Inc., 5 Trade Reg. Rep. (CCH) ¶ 15189 (D. Conn. Dec. 12, 2001) (proposed consent decree); FTC v. Wilcox, 5 Trade Reg. Rep. (CCH) ¶ 24,827 (S.D. Tex. Apr. 20, 2001) (consent decree against advance fee credit card telemarketer); FTC v. Homelife Credit, No. CV00-06154 CM (Ex) (C.D. Cal. Aug. 24, 2001) at www.ftc.gov/os/2001/08/conwaystip.pdf (advance fee credit card scheme); FTC v. Credit Approval Svc, No. G-00-324 (S.D. Tex. Apr. 20, 2001) at www.ftc.gov/os/2001/04/bancaschurch.pdf (advance fee credit card scheme); FTC v. First Credit Alliance, No. 300 CV 1049 (D. Conn. Dec. 5, 2000) at www.ftc.gov/os/2001/12/fcastiporder.pdf (stipulated final judgment in advance fee credit card scheme); 5 Trade Reg. Rep. (CCH) ¶ 24,827 (S.D. Tex. Nov. 2, 2000) (order jailing telemarketer for violating injunction); FTC v. Wallace, 2000 U.S. Dist. LEXIS 10506 (N.D. Ga. May 25, 2000) (entering default judgment against telemarketer who solicited advance fees for credit cards); FTC v. Consumer Money Markets, Inc., 5 Trade Reg. Rptr. (CCH) ¶ 24,796 (D. Nev. Sept. 6, 2000) (consent decree); FTC v. Modern Credit Fin. Servs., Inc., 5 Trade Reg. Rptr. (CCH) ¶ 24,745 (N.D. Tex. May 4, 2000) (stipulated final judgment); *In re* National Credit Mgmt. Group, 21 F. Supp. 2d 424 (D.N.J. 1998) (offer of a pre-approved credit card promises a high likelihood of success in obtaining credit, therefore telemarketer's requesting and receiving funds in advance of delivering services violated rule); FTC v. Consumer Credit Servs., Inc., 5 Trade Reg. Rep. (CCH) ¶ 24,447 (D. Nev. 1998) (defendant issued its own credit card that could only be used to purchase items from its own catalog); FTC v. Pinnacle Fin. Servs., 5 Trade Reg. Rep. (CCH) ¶ 24,376 (D. Ariz. 1998) (complaints and proposed consent decrees); FTC v. Andre, 5 Trade Reg. Rep. (CCH) ¶ 24,379 (N.D. Ill. 1998) (complaint and preliminary injunction); FTC v. Dunn, 5 Trade Reg. Rep. (CCH) ¶ 24,088 (D.S.C. 1997) (consent decree); New York v. Financial Servs. Network, 930 F. Supp. 865 (W.D.N.Y. 1996) (granting preliminary injunction against advance fee credit telemarketer); *FTC, States and Canadian Provinces Launch Crackdown on Outfits Falsely Promising Credit Cards and Loans for an Advance Fee*, FTC Press Release, June 20, 2000.

2912 16 C.F.R. § 310.4(a)(3). A number of state telemarketing statutes also prohibit advance payment for recovery services. *See also* FTC v. FANS, Inc., 5 Trade Reg. Rep. ¶ 24,389 (CCH) (D. Nev. 1998) (consent decree) (misrepresented to victims of telemarketing scams that they could recover a substantial portion of the money they lost for an advance fee equivalent to a percentage of the consumers' previous losses); FTC v. Telecommunications Protection Agency, Inc., 5 Trade Reg. Rep. (CCH) ¶ 24,173 (E.D. Okla. 1998) (proposed consent decree) (same); FTC v. Meridian Capital Mgmt., Inc., 5 Trade Reg. Rep. (CCH) ¶ 24,164 (D. Nev. 1996) (proposed consent decree) (same). In the 2002 proposed amendments to the Telemarketing Sales Rule, the FTC stated that it would not prohibit the sale of "victim lists" in the rule because "combating the practice of targeting vulnerable groups is a challenge best left to the discretion of law enforcement agencies who may seek injunctions and other penalties on a case-by-case basis in individual law enforcement actions." 67 Fed. Reg. 4525–4526 (Jan. 30, 2002). The FTC reiterated this position when it adopted the final amendment to the rule. 68 Fed. Reg. 4580, 4653 (Jan. 29, 2003).

2913 16 C.F.R. § 310.4(a)(2)(ii).

2914 New York v. Financial Servs. Network, 930 F. Supp. 865 (W.D.N.Y. 1996).

2915 Tennessee v. Lexington Law Firms, 1997 U.S. Dist. LEXIS 7403, 1997-1 Trade Cas. (CCH) ¶ 71,8201 (M.D. Tenn. May 14, 1997) (rejecting arguments that application to attorneys was unconstitutional and beyond scope of statute).

2916 15 U.S.C. § 1679b(b).

2917 15 U.S.C. § 1679g. *See* National Consumer Law Center, Fair Credit Reporting Ch. 8 (5th ed. 2002 and Supp.).

2918 *See* National Consumer Law Center, Fair Credit Reporting Ch. 8 (5th ed. 2002 and Supp.).

before it calls the consumer.[2919] Before the telemarketer places a call, the telemarketer already has the information needed to bill the consumer through a credit card, debit card, checking account, utility bill, mortgage statement or some other payment method.[2920] The FTC terms this "preacquired account information."[2921] Consumers in this situation are at a grave disadvantage because they have lost the control in the transaction that comes from the ability to withhold the information necessary to effect payment.[2922]

In response to these problems, the FTC took several steps in its 2003 amendments. First, it amended the Telemarketing Sales Rule to prohibit sale of unencrypted account information, or any disclosure or receipt of such information for consideration.[2923] This prohibition is consistent with the Gramm-Leach-Bliley Act,[2924] under which financial institutions and third parties with which they do business may provide consumer account information to other third parties only in encrypted form for marketing purposes.[2925] The effect of the Telemarketing Sales Rule is to expand this limitation beyond financial institutions to telemarketers.

The prohibition against sale of account information does not, however, mean that a telemarketer will never have the consumer's account information before placing the call. For example, the telemarketer may already have the consumer's account information because the consumer previously made a purchase from that company. Or the telemarketer may not have the consumer's account information, but is involved in a joint marketing arrangement with a company that does.

The FTC considered, but decided against, prohibiting all use of preacquired account information in telemarketing. Instead, it added two specific requirements that apply just to preacquired account telemarketing. First, for any telemarketing transaction involving preacquired account information, the seller or telemarketer must: (a) at a minimum, identify the account to be charged with sufficient specificity for the customer or donor to understand what account will be charged; and (b) obtain the customer's or donor's express agreement to be charged for the goods or services and to be charged using the account number identified by the customer.[2926]

Second, the FTC adopted a special rule for telemarketing transactions that involve both preacquired account information and a "free-to-pay" conversion feature. These are transactions in which consumers receive products or services for free for an initial period but incur an obligation to pay if they fail to take affirmative action to cancel before that period ends.[2927] The FTC concluded that this combination posed the greatest risk of harm to consumers, as they are often presented as low-involvement marketing decisions in which consumers are simply previewing the product or service.[2928] For these telemarketing calls, the solicitor must (a) obtain from the customer, at a minimum, the last four digits of the account number to be charged; (b) obtain the customer's express agreement to be charged for the goods or services and to be charged using the account identified by the customer; and (c) make an audio recording of the entire transaction.[2929] These rules apply to both incoming and outgoing telephone calls.[2930]

A telemarketer who uses preacquired account information to charge a consumer's account without authorization will also violate the rule's general prohibition against unauthorized billing.[2931] The telemarketer may also be in violation of state identity theft statutes. For example, in Arkansas, "[a] person commits financial identity fraud if, with the intent to unlawfully appropriate financial resources of another person to his or her own use . . . , and without the authorization of that person, he or she (A) Obtains or records identifying information that would assist in accessing the financial resources of the other person; or (B) Accesses or

2919 67 Fed. Reg. 4495, 4512–4514 (Jan. 30, 2002) (FTC notes the increase in preacquired account telemarketing in the past five years).

2920 The FTC's Privacy Rule, 16 C.F.R. Part 313, as mandated by the Gramm-Leach-Bliley Act, 15 U.S.C. §§ 6801–6810, prohibits financial institutions from disclosing customer account numbers or other similar forms of access to non-affiliated third parties for use in marketing (includes telemarketing).

2921 16 C.F.R. § 310.2(w).

2922 *See* FTC v. J.K. Publications, Inc., 99 F. Supp. 2d 1176 (C.D. Cal. 2000) (non-telemarketing case in which the defendant purchased unencrypted lists of consumer account numbers and used the numbers to charge consumers' accounts without authorization).

2923 16 C.F.R. § 310.4(a)(5). *See* 68 Fed. Reg. 4580, 4615, 4616 (Jan. 29, 2003).

2924 15 U.S.C. §§ 6801–6810.

2925 *See* 68 Fed. Reg. 4580, 4616 (Jan. 29, 2003).

2926 16 C.F.R. § 310.4(a)(6). *See* 68 Fed. Reg. 4580, 4623 (Jan. 29, 2003).

2927 16 C.F.R. § 310.2(o). *See* 68 Fed. Reg. 4580, 4594 (Jan. 29, 2003).

2928 68 Fed. Reg. 4580, 4602 (Jan. 29, 2003); FTC v. Cross Media, 5 Trade Reg. Rep. (CCH) ¶ 15246 (N.D. Ga. June 9, 2003) (pre-amendment case); FTC v. Preferred Alliance, Inc., 5 Trade Reg. Rep. (CCH) ¶ 15365 (N.D. Ga. Feb. 12, 2003) (pre-amendment complaint against telemarketers who sold free trial offers that were actually negative option plans that would result in charges if consumer did not cancel); FTC v. Ira Smolev, 5 Trade Reg. Rep. (CCH) ¶ 15167 (S.D. Fla. Oct. 23, 2001) (proposed consent decree ordering $8.3 million in restitution against buyers club that misled consumers into accepting "free" trial memberships, then billed them unless they cancelled). *See, e.g.*, Minn. *ex rel.* Hatch v. Fleet Mortg. Corp., 158 F. Supp. 2d 962 (D. Minn. 2001), *motion to dismiss denied*, 181 F. Supp. 2d 995 (D. Minn. 2001) (promoting "free trial period" while obscuring fact that monthly charges will be assessed unless consumer cancels is deceptive); FTC v. Smoley, No. 01 8922CIV ZLOCH (S.D. Fla. 2001) (defendants lured consumers to call by offering inexpensive lighting product, obtaining account information from consumer in initial transaction, and then upsold free-to-pay conversion buyers club membership).

2929 16 C.F.R. § 310.4(a)(6)(i). *See* 68 Fed. Reg. 4580, 4621 (Jan. 29, 2003).

2930 68 Fed. Reg. 4580, 4621 (Jan. 29, 2003).

2931 16 C.F.R. § 310.4(a)(6).

attempts to access the financial resources of the other person through the use of the identifying information. . . ." The Arkansas statute defines "identifying information" to include SSNs, bank account numbers, credit and debit card numbers, digital signatures, and other identifiers.[2932]

A federal court has upheld the amended rule's restrictions on pre-acquired account telemarketing even though the restrictions in the final rule are broader than those in the proposed rule.[2933]

5.9.4.8 Protections Against Unauthorized Billing and Credit Card Laundering

5.9.4.8.1 Prohibition against unauthorized billing

In its 2003 amendments, the FTC added a prohibition of unauthorized billing. It is a violation of the rule to cause a billing information to be submitted for payment, directly or indirectly, without the express informed consent of the customer or donor.[2934] This prohibition applies to all telemarketing. The customer or donor must affirmatively and unambiguously articulate consent in order for it to be express.[2935] Neither silence nor an ambiguous response constitutes consent.[2936] Customers or donors must have received all required material disclosures under the rule in order for the consent to be informed.[2937] Even before the rule was amended, the FTC used general prohibitions against unfair and deceptive conduct to proceed against sellers who billed consumers without their authorization.[2938]

5.9.4.8.2 Requirement of "express verifiable authorization" when payment is made by certain methods

The Telemarketing Sales rule has an additional protection against unauthorized billing. When the telemarketer submits billing information to a payment device other than a standard credit or debit card, it must first obtain the consumer's "express verifiable authorization."[2939] The gist of this requirement is that the telemarketer must document or record the consumer's authorization before it can obtain payment.

2932 Ark. Code Ann. § 5-37-227; *see also* National Consumer Law Center, Fair Credit Reporting § 16.6.3 (5th ed. 2002 and Supp.).

2933 U.S. Security v. FTC, 2003 WL 22203719 (W.D. Okla. Sept. 23, 2003).

2934 16 C.F.R. §§ 310.4(a)(6), 310.2(b) (definition of billing information).

2935 68 Fed. Reg. 4580, 4620 (Jan. 29, 2003).

2936 *Id.*

2937 *Id.*

2938 FTC v. Consumer Alliance, Inc., 2003 WL 22287364 (N.D. Ill. Sept. 30, 2003). *See, e.g.,* FTC v. Cross Media, 5 Trade Reg. Rep. (CCH) ¶ 15246 (N.D. Ga. June 9, 2003) (proposed consent decree).

2939 16 C.F.R. § 310.3(a)(3).

"Express verifiable authorization" can occur in any of three ways: (1) express written authorization by the customer, including signature; (2) express oral authorization that is tape-recorded along with numerous disclosures[2940] and made available upon request to the customer's bank; or (3) written confirmation of the transaction, clearly and conspicuously labeled as such on the envelope, and sent to the customer before submission of the billing information for payment.[2941] (This third method of authorization is not allowed, however, for transactions that involve a free-to-pay conversion and pre-acquired account telemarketing.[2942]) Telemarketers must be prepared to offer proof of these authorizations, and written confirmations must contain all of the information required by the rule.[2943]

The two exceptions to this requirement are (1) credit cards that are subject to the protections of the Truth in Lending Act and Regulation Z,[2944] and (2) debit cards that are subject to the protections of the Electronic Fund Transfers Act (EFTA) and Regulation E.[2945] These statutes and regulations give consumers various protections that reduce the likelihood of unauthorized payment when they use credit and debit cards. By contrast, the FTC was concerned that telemarketers' use of novel payment methods that lacked these protections facilitated unauthorized billing. For example, telemarketers have developed ways to cram charges onto consumers' telephone bills or mortgage bills.[2946] Telemarketers have also often used "demand drafts," a way

2940 16 C.F.R. § 310.3(a)(3)(ii).

2941 16 C.F.R. § 310.3(a)(3).

2942 16 C.F.R. § 310.3(a)(3)(iii). *See* 68 Fed. Reg. 4580, 4611 (Jan. 29, 2003).

2943 *In re* National Credit Mgmt. Group, 21 F. Supp. 2d 424 (D.N.J. 1998) (finding telemarketer of credit monitoring and credit card services violated rule by debiting consumers' accounts without proper authorization and accepting customer certifications that oral authorization was not given where company could not provide tape-recorded verification; written confirmations that did not confirm the date of the oral authorization or inform consumers of how to obtain a refund were insufficient to comply with the rule). *See also* FTC v. Productive Marketing, Inc., 5 Trade Reg. Rep. (CCH) ¶ 24,851 (C.D. Cal. 2001) (consent decree against telemarketer who charged credit cards and checking accounts without authorization).

2944 16 C.F.R. § 310.3(a)(3). *See* 68 Fed. Reg. 4605–11 (Jan. 29, 2003).

2945 *Id.*

2946 *See* Minn. *ex rel.* Hatch v. Fleet Mortg. Corp., 158 F. Supp. 2d 962 (D. Minn. 2001), *motion to dismiss denied*, 181 F. Supp. 2d 995 (D. Minn. 2001) (mortgage company provided telemarketing firm with customer account information to sell membership programs for discount services such as car repair and health care). *See also* FTC v. Verity Int'l, Ltd., 5 Trade Reg. Rep. (CCH) ¶ 15330 (Nov. 21, 2002) (consent order barring billing aggregator from billing any charges based on electronic capture of consumer's telephone number; defendant waives $1.6 million in consumer payments); FTC v. RJB Telecom, Inc., 5 Trade Reg. Rep. (CCH) ¶ 15155 (D. Ariz. Sept. 26, 2001) (proposed consent decree against adult website company that billed credit cards and phone bills without authorization); § 4.9.8, *supra*.

of obtaining payment from a consumer's bank account without the consumer's signature on a check or other instrument.[2947] These payment methods typically lack the dispute resolution rights and protection against unlimited liability for unauthorized charges that TILA and EFTA provide.

If a telemarketer is found to have acted fraudulently, the FTC has gone even farther and required written authorization and written disclosures before the seller can debit any consumers' credit card accounts or checking accounts.[2948]

5.9.4.8.3 Credit card laundering

The rule restricts credit card laundering by limiting telemarketers' ability to process credit card charges through other merchants.[2949] In any telemarketing case, it is important to investigate credit card laundering, because it may lead to other entities that will be liable for the telemarketer's fraud.

Legitimate merchants who want to be able to accept credit card payments from customers establish a merchant account with a financial institution that is a member of a credit card system such as VISA or Mastercard.[2950] This financial institution is called the "merchant bank." When a customer pays the merchant by credit card, the merchant gives the charge slips to the merchant bank. The merchant bank then pays the amount of the charge, minus a fee, into the merchant's account and submits the charge slip through the credit card processing system to the customer's bank (the "issuing bank") for reimbursement. If, however, the customer returns the purchased item or disputes the charge, then the issuing bank re-credits the customer's account and gets a refund from the merchant bank, which then ask the merchant for a refund.

Because of the high rate of chargebacks and the fear that the telemarketer will not be around to pay refunds, banks do not like to let telemarketers open merchant accounts. Some banks, such as VISA-affiliated banks, prohibit telemarketers from directly depositing credit card transactions. These restrictions have led to the growth of credit card factoring services for telemarketers.

In credit card factoring, the telemarketer works out an agreement with a third party (the factoring merchant) to process credit card transactions through the third party's merchant account. The factoring merchant charges a fee for this service. The merchant bank may not be aware that charge slips for telemarketing transactions are being deposited in the account, although other signs such as a large number of chargebacks may become apparent to it.

The Telemarketing Rule prohibits credit card factoring except as expressly permitted by the credit card system.[2951] It is a violation for a telemarketer to obtain access to the credit card system through a business relationship or an affiliation with a merchant, unless such access is authorized under the terms of the merchant account and by the credit card system.[2952] Both the factoring merchant[2953] and the telemarketer[2954] violate the rule if the factoring merchant submits the telemarketer's charge slips for payment through its merchant account without authorization. Misrepresenting the nature of the account to the merchant bank may also constitute bank fraud[2955] and violate state criminal laws.[2956]

5.9.4.9 Public and Private Enforcement of the Rule

5.9.4.9.1 Public enforcement

The FTC has enforcement authority.[2957] State attorneys general and other state consumer protection authorities are also authorized to file suit in federal court for injunctive relief, damages, restitution and other relief if any person has engaged or is engaging in a pattern or practice of telemarketing that violates the rule.[2958] One federal court has held that because the rule's prohibitions against deceptive telemarketing acts and practices sound in fraud, Federal Rule of Civil Procedure 9(b)'s heightened pleading requirements for allegations of fraud apply to claims made pursuant

2947 *See* § 5.1.10.3, *supra*.

2948 FTC v. Liberty Direct, Inc., 5 Trade Reg. Rep. (CCH) ¶ 24,914 (D. Ariz. Apr. 2, 2001) (consent decree).

2949 16 C.F.R. § 310.3(c). *See, e.g.*, FTC v. Woofter Inc. Corp., No. CV-97-0515 (D. Nev. 1999) (stipulated order for permanent injunction and final judgment) (defendants allegedly assisted Canadian-based telemarketer in selling foreign lottery tickets and laundering credit cards); FTC v. Win USA Servs., Ltd., 5 Trade Reg. Rep. (CCH) ¶ 24,530 (W.D. Wash. 1998) (complaint) (international lottery scheme that targeted senior citizens).

2950 This summary is based on FTC, Complying with the Telemarketing Sales Rule at 22 (Apr. 1996) and U.S. v. Dabbs, 134 F.3d 1071 (11th Cir. 1998); Padilla v. State, 753 So. 2d 659 (Fla. App. 2000).

2951 16 C.F.R. § 310.3(c).

2952 16 C.F.R. § 310.3(c)(3).

2953 16 C.F.R. § 310.3(c)(1).

2954 16 C.F.R. § 310.3(c)(2).

2955 U.S. v. Dabbs, 134 F.3d 1071 (11th Cir. 1998).

2956 *See* Padilla v. State, 753 So. 2d 659 (Fla. App. 2000) (both seller and factoring merchant would violate law if seller knows that merchant account is a subterfuge; not shown here).

2957 15 U.S.C. §§ 6102(c), 6105. *See* Federal Trade Commission v. Micom Corp., 1997 U.S. Dist. LEXIS 3404, 1997-1 Trade Cas. (CCH) ¶ 71,753 (S.D.N.Y. Mar. 12, 1997).

2958 15 U.S.C. § 6103(a), (f). *See, e.g.*, Tennessee v. Lexington Law Firms, 1997 U.S. Dist. LEXIS 7403, 1997-1 Trade Cas. (CCH) ¶ 71,8201 (M.D. Tenn. May 14, 1997) (seeking a permanent injunction and other equitable relief); New York v. Financial Servs. Network, 930 F. Supp. 865 (W.D.N.Y. 1996) (granting preliminary injunction in suit brought by New York and North Carolina). *See also* Iowa Code Ann. § 714.16 (authorizing Iowa Attorney General to bring suit under the federal statute on behalf of Iowa residents).

to the rule.[2959] A state may rely on deceptive telemarketing acts and practices which took place outside of the state in satisfying the statute's requirement of alleging a pattern or practice of telemarketing which violates the rule.[2960] One court has held that the statute does not limit the time period within which the state can sue.[2961]

5.9.4.9.2 Private enforcement

The statute creates a private cause of action, but only where each plaintiff's damages exceed $50,000.[2962] Consumers can, however, bring suit under their state UDAP statute, since a violation of the FTC rule will be treated as a *per se* UDAP violation in most states.[2963]

Consumers can also proceed under the Telephone Consumer Protection Act,[2964] which is more generous in its grant of a private cause of action, for acts that violate both statutes. There are several instances in which this overlap occurs. First, both the Telephone Consumer Protection Act and the FTC Telemarketing Sales Rule prohibit calls to persons who have placed themselves on a company-specific or the nationwide do-not-call list. The Telephone Consumer Protection Act grants a private cause of action to a consumer who has received more than one call within a twelve-month period in violation of this prohibition.[2965]

Second, both the FTC and the FCC regulations prohibit calls at inconvenient times (earlier than 8:00 A.M. or after 9:00 P.M.). Third, both rules require telemarketers to identify the person or entity on whose behalf the call is made. In addition, both rules restrict abandoned calls and prohibit telemarketers from blocking Caller ID service. Since all of these requirements are found only in the FCC's rule, not in the Telephone Consumer Protection Act itself, it is less clear which of that Act's two private cause of action provisions[2966] applies to it.[2967]

2959 Tennessee v. Lexington Law Firms, 1997 U.S. Dist. LEXIS 7403, 1997-1 Trade Cas. (CCH) ¶ 71,8201 (M.D. Tenn. May 14, 1997).

2960 *Id. See also* Illinois v. Tri-Star Indus. Lighting, Inc., 2000 U.S. Dist. LEXIS 15376 (N.D. Ill. Oct. 5, 2000) (state can discover information about telemarketer's out-of-state sales because of its authority to protect legitimate in-state sellers from unlawful competition).

2961 Illinois v. Tri-Star Indus. Lighting, Inc., 2000 U.S. Dist. LEXIS 14948 (N.D. Ill. Oct. 11, 2000).

2962 15 U.S.C. § 6104(a).

2963 *See* §§ 2.3.7, 3.2.6, 3.4.5, *supra*.

2964 *See* § 5.9.3, *supra*.

2965 47 U.S.C. § 227(c)(5).

2966 17 U.S.C. § 227(b)(3), (c)(5).

2967 *See* § 5.9.3.9, *supra*.

5.9.5 Other State and Federal Law Applicable to Telemarketing

5.9.5.1 FTC Mail or Telephone Order Merchandise Rule

The FTC's Mail or Telephone Order Merchandise Rule[2968] requires that all merchandise ordered by telephone or by mail be delivered within thirty days,[2969] unless the merchant at the time of sale provided for a longer delivery time or unless the buyer later opts to wait a longer period instead of receiving a full refund.

While there is little that the FTC rule can do about a fly-by-night operation that takes telephone orders and disappears, the rule does give consumers a specific time frame within which to follow up a seller's failure to respond. If, within thirty days of a telephone order, the consumer neither receives the ordered merchandise nor receives some communication offering a full refund, there has been a violation. The thirty-day period begins to run from the buyer's order date. This should also be an early warning of a possible scam and indication that the merchandise may never be delivered. At that point, if not before, the consumer should actively pursue the matter with the proper authorities before the seller goes out of business. It may also not be too late for the consumer to withhold payment of a credit card bill for the purchase.[2970] Violation of the rule, or a comparable state regulation, can also be the basis for a UDAP claim.[2971]

5.9.5.2 State and Federal RICO Statutes

State and federal RICO statutes offer particularly promising approaches to telemarketing fraud.[2972] Nearly all cases will involve federal wire fraud, making liability possible if the other requirements of the federal RICO statute can be satisfied.[2973] A scheme to defraud may consist of failure to make disclosures required by the FTC's Telemarketing Sales Rule.[2974]

2968 16 C.F.R. § 435 [*reprinted in* Appx. B.4 *infra*]. The rule was expanded to apply to telephone sales effective March 1, 1994. *See* 58 Fed. Reg. 49096 (Sept. 21, 1993). *See also* § 5.8.1, *supra* (general discussion of rule).

2969 The rule allows this period to be extended to 50 days where the order is accompanied by a request to establish credit with the merchant.

2970 *See* § 5.9.7.1, *infra*.

2971 *See* §§ 3.2.7, 5.8.1.2, *supra*.

2972 *See, e.g.*, McClain v. Coverdell & Co., 272 F. Supp. 2d 631 (E.D. Mich. 2003) (refusing to dismiss federal RICO claims against telemarketer).

2973 U.S. v. Woods, 335 F.3d 993 (9th Cir. 2003) (affirming telemarketers' mail and wire fraud convictions); U.S. v. Manion, 339 F.3d 1153 (9th Cir. 2003) (affirming individual telemarketer's conviction for mail and wire fraud). *See, e.g.*, United States v. Ciccone, 219 F.3d 1078 (9th Cir. 2000) (affirming telemarketer's wire fraud conviction).

2974 U.S. v. Woods, 335 F.3d 993, 1001 (9th Cir. 2003) (affirming telemarketers' mail and wire fraud convictions).

Some state RICO statutes have less complex proof requirements than federal RICO, and many list federal wire fraud, or state offenses such as fraud, as predicate offenses.[2975] Ohio's RICO statute lists operation of an unregistered credit services organization as a predicate offense, and the state supreme court recently upheld under this statute the conviction of an individual who telemarketed credit cards.[2976] Interpreting the state RICO statute as a strict liability statute, the court held that no proof of culpable intent was required. While this decision relates to criminal rather than civil RICO liability, the principles should apply equally to civil cases. Fraudulent telemarketers may also be criminally prosecuted under state and federal wire fraud and RICO statutes.[2977]

5.9.5.3 State Telemarketing Fraud Statutes

Most states[2978] have enacted their own protections against telemarketing fraud. Regulation of telephone solicitation does not violate the First Amendment[2979] or equal protection and due process requirements.[2980] The Federal Telephone Consumer Protection Act does not preempt more restrictive state laws.[2981]

These statutes, which are summarized in Appendix E, *infra*, typically require registration and bonding, disclosures, and submission of sales scripts and information about prizes to the state enforcement agency. Some take steps to protect the public from annoyance and inconvenience by restricting the time of calls or requiring the salesperson to hang up as soon as the consumer indicates a lack of interest.[2982] Many prohibit telemarketers from calling people who have listed themselves on a statewide database or the nationwide do-not-call registry.[2983] A number of state telemarketing laws also prohibit telemarketers from blocking Caller ID

Many state telemarketing statutes give consumers the right to cancel the sale within a set time period.[2984] Some, such as North Dakota's,[2985] explicitly grant consumers a three-day or longer right to cancel. Others, like Alabama, accomplish the same purpose by requiring covered telephone sales to be confirmed by a signed written contract and prohibiting charges to the consumer's credit card until the signed contract is returned to the seller.[2986] A few states, such as Virginia, have simply expanded a door-to-door sales law, which includes a right to cancel, to cover telephone sales.[2987] Even without special amendments, some state home solicitation sales laws may be phrased broadly enough to cover telemarketing.[2988]

Idaho provides that minors can disaffirm telephone sales without liability and that parents are not liable for minors' purchases.[2989] A number of states restrict or prohibit courier

---

2975 *See* § 9.2, *infra*.

2976 State v. Schlosser, 79 Ohio St. 3d 329, 681 N.E.2d 911 (1997).

2977 *See, e.g.*, United States v. Jackson, 95 F.3d 500 (7th Cir. 1997); United States v. Harris, 920 F. Supp. 132 (D. Nev. 1996).

2978 State telemarketing laws are summarized in Appx. E, *infra*.

2979 Nat'l Fed. of the Blind v. Pryor, 258 F.3d 851 (8th Cir. 2001) (requirement that solicitor discontinue call upon request does not violate First Amendment even as applied to charitable solicitations); Fraternal Order of Police v. Stenehjem, 287 F. Supp. 2d 1023 (D.N.D. 2003) (statute's restrictions on commercial telemarketers does not violate 1st Amendment, but application of the law to outside solicitors of charitable contributions does); Desnick v. Department of Professional Regulation, 171 Ill. 2d 510, 665 N.E.2d 1346 (1996). *See also* Federal Trade Commission, Telemarketing Sales Rule, Final Rule, Statement of Basis and Purpose, 68 Fed. Reg. 4580, 4634–37 (Jan. 29, 2003) (discussing First Amendment considerations in do-not-call lists for commercial and non-profit telemarketers); Minnesota *ex rel.* Humphrey v. Casino Marketing Group Inc., 491 N.W.2d 882 (Minn. 1992) (lower court's temporary injunction under the state automatic dialing-announcing devices statutes does not violate the First Amendment of the U.S. Constitution or the Minnesota Constitution); Erwin v. State, 111 Nev. 1535, 908 P.2d 1367 (1995) (generally upholding statute against First Amendment challenge, but remanding case to determine if registration fees and bonding requirement are more onerous than necessary to cover the administrative and enforcement costs of the statute and to meet the statute's purposes).

2980 Nat'l Fed. of the Blind v. Pryor, 258 F.3d 851 (8th Cir. 2001) (equal protection); Erwin v. State, 111 Nev. 1535, 908 P.2d 1367 (1995).

2981 47 U.S.C. § 227(e). *See* Texas v. American Blast Fax, Inc., 121 F. Supp. 2d 1085 (W.D. Tex. 2000).

2982 *See, e.g.*, Fla. Stat. Ann. § 501.616(6); Haw. Rev. Stat. §§ 481P-3(7) (telemarketer must keep list); Idaho Code §§ 48-1003 to 48-1003A; Ky. Rev. Stat. § 367.46955; Miss. Code Ann. § 77-3-603; Or. Rev. Stat. § 646.563 (telemarketer must keep list); R.I. Gen. Laws §§ 5-61-2(9), 5-61-3.5 and 5-61-3.6.

2983 According to the FTC, 27 states have do-not-call laws—Alabama, Arkansas, California, Colorado, Connecticut, Florida, Georgia, Idaho, Illinois, Indiana, Kansas, Kentucky, Louisiana, Maine, Massachusetts, Minnesota, Missouri, New Jersey, New York, Oklahoma, Oregon, Pennsylvania, Tennessee, Texas, Vermont, Wisconsin, and Wyoming—and many other states are considering such legislation. 68 Fed. Reg. 4580, 4630 n.592 (Jan. 29, 2003).

2984 *See, e.g.*, Ala. Code § 8-19A-14; Okla. Stat. tit. 15, § 775A.4; Utah Code Ann. § 13-26-5; Wash. Rev. Code Ann. § 19.158.120.

2985 N.D. Cent. Code § 51-18-02.

2986 Ala. Code § 8-19A-14.

2987 Va. Code § 59.1-21.2.

2988 *See* Del. Code Ann. tit. 6, §§ 4401 to 4405 (door-to-door sales broadly defined in § 4403); Minn. Stat. Ann. §§ 325G.06 to 325G.11 (home solicitation sale defined at § 325G.06); Pa. Stat. tit. 73, § 201-7(a); Tenn. Code Ann. §§ 47-18-701 to 47-18-708 (home solicitation-credit sales); Tex. Bus. & Comm. Code §§ 39.001 to 39.009 (certain consumer transactions, coverage defined at § 39.002); Wis. Stat. Ann. §§ 423.201 to 423.205 (consumer approval transactions, defined at § 423.201); Wyo. Stat. §§ 40-14-251 to 40-14-255 (home solicitation—credit sales only). Four other jurisdictions require that a door to door sale involve a solicitation at a residence, but their broad definitions may still cover telemarketing calls made to the home: D.C. Code Ann. § 28-3811; Mo. Rev. Stat. §§ 407.700 to 407.720 (home solicitation credit sales); N.C. Gen. Stat. §§ 25A-38 to 25A-42; and S.C. Code Ann. §§ 37-2-501 to 37-2-507.

2989 Idaho Code § 48-1008.

pickups of the consumer's payment.[2990] Under Vermont's statute, any "telecheck" drawing on the consumer's bank account based on the consumer's oral approval must be accompanied by the consumer's authorization in writing.[2991]

Coverage under state telemarketing statutes varies. Some, such as one of Indiana's two telemarketing statutes, target just a few types of telemarketing sales, such as prize promotions and sales of precious metals, gemstones, and oil and gas rights.[2992] (Many states that originally had narrow telemarketing statutes have broadened them in recent years or have adopted a second, broader statute.) A second pattern, which covers much more, is to define telemarketing broadly and then list exceptions. Statutes that follow this pattern typically exclude sales that involve some face-to-face contact, sales to prior customers, sales by established businesses, catalog sales, and sales of specified items such as newspapers, magazines, cable TV service, and insurance. Many states have statutes that specifically cover pre-recorded solicitations made with the assistance of automated dialing systems.[2993] Most statutes allow a private cause of action or make violations *per se* UDAP violations.

5.9.5.4 UDAP, Fraud, and Other State Statutes

Claims based on general UDAP standards and common law fraud may be available against entities involved in telemarketing fraud.[2994] Advocates should also check their state's door-to-door sales law to see if it covers telephone solicitations. If it does, the consumer may have a right to cancel the sale that can still be exercised.[2995] Some retail sales laws also include provisions regarding such matters as the need for written contracts in telephone sales.[2996] If the fraud involved solicitations for phony charitable purposes, the state may have a charitable solicitations law that applies.

5.9.6 *Identifying All the Entities Liable for a Telemarketer's Fraud*

Fraudulent telemarketers are often fly-by-night outfits that can not be located or lack assets from which reimbursement to injured consumers can be exacted. Other entities may share liability with the telemarketer. Claims against other entities are particularly well-suited for class action treatment, since proof of the defendant's facilitation of the fraudulent scheme would probably establish its liability toward all victims. Both individuals and corporations can meet the definition of "telemarketer" and be liable for violating the FTC's rule.[2997]

The FTC's Telemarketing Sales Rule declares it a deceptive act for a person to provide substantial assistance to a telemarketer while knowing, or consciously avoiding knowledge, that the telemarketer was violating the rule.[2998] The FTC recognizes the following as examples of substantial assistance: providing lists of contacts to a seller or telemarketer that identify people who are over age fifty-five, have bad credit histories, or have been victimized previously by deceptive telemarketing or direct sales;[2999] providing certificates for travel-related services to be used as a sales promotion device; providing scripts, advertising, or other promotional material;[3000] or providing inflated appraisals or phony testimonials for goods or services sold through telemarketing.[3001] A bank that approved telemarketers'

2990 Kan. Stat. Ann. § 50-670(e) (courier pick-up); Ky. Rev. Stat. § 367.46955(5) and (6) (courier pick-up; verifiable authorization); Me. Rev. Stat. Ann. tit. 32, § 14716 (transient seller may not use courier pick-up); Mich. Comp. Laws Ann. §§ 445.111c(d) (verifiable authorization) and 445.112 (courier pick-up); Mo. Stat. Ann. § 407.1076 (8) and (9) (verifiable authorization; courier pick-up); Vt. Stat. Ann. tit. 9, § 2464.

2991 Vt. Stat. Ann. tit. 9, § 2464.

2992 Ind. Code Ann. § 24-5-12-8. *See also* Cal. Bus. & Prof. Code § 17511.1. Indiana's second telemarketing statute defines "telephone sales call" and "telephone solicitor" broadly and then lists exceptions. *See* Ind. Code Ann. §§ 24-4.7-1-1 to 24-4.7-5-6.

2993 *See, e.g.*, Ariz. Rev. Stat. Ann. § 13-2919; Colo. Rev. Stat. § 18-9-311; Minn. Stat. §§ 325E.26–.31; Mont. Code Ann. § 45-8-216. *See also* Minnesota *ex rel.* Humphrey v. Casino Marketing Group Inc., 491 N.W.2d 882 (Minn. 1992) (lower court's temporary injunction under the state automatic dialing-announcing devices statutes does not violate the First Amendment of the U.S. Constitution or the Minnesota Constitution).

2994 *See, e.g.*, FTC v. Think Achievement Corp., 144 F. Supp. 2d 993 (N.D. Ind. 2000) (applying FTC Act's general prohibition against deception to telemarketer), *later op. at* 144 F. Supp. 2d 1029 (N.D. Ind. 2000) (ordering disgorgement by non-wrongdoer who had possession of defendant's funds), *aff'd in part, rev'd in part on other grounds*, 312 F.3d 259 (7th Cir. 2002).

2995 *See, e.g.*, Ind. Code Ann. § 24-4.5-2-501; Mich. Comp. Laws Ann. § 445.111; Mont. Code Ann. § 30-14-502 (includes telephone sales with few exceptions); Or. Rev. Stat. § 83.710 (extends the state home solicitation sales law to seller-initiated telephone sales where there is no personal contact with the buyer). See §§ 5.8.2.4.4, 5.9.5.3 *supra*, for further discussion of coverage of telephone sales by state door-to-door sales laws.

2996 *See, e.g.*, La. Rev. Stat. § 45:831; Or. Rev. Stat. § 83.715.

2997 FTC v. Consumer Alliance, Inc., 2003 WL 22287364 (N.D. Ill. Sept. 30, 2003).

2998 16 C.F.R. § 310.3(b). The FTC rejected law enforcement and consumer advocates' recommendations to change the "conscious avoidance" standard to a "knew or should have known" standard. It stated that the conscious avoidance standard was more appropriate "when liability to pay redress or civil penalties rests on another person's violation of the Rule." 68 Fed. Reg. 4580, 4612 (Jan. 29, 2003).

2999 *See* FTC v. Consumer Money Markets, Inc., 5 Trade Reg. Rep. (CCH) ¶ 24,796 (D. Nev. Sept. 6, 2000) (consent decree requiring list broker to disgorge $150,000).

3000 FTC v. Consumer Alliance, Inc., 2003 WL 22287364 (N.D. Ill. Sept. 30, 2003) (defendants who wrote telemarketers' scripts are liable); FTC v. Bruce Turianski, 5 Trade Reg. Rep. (CCH) ¶ 15341 (S.D. Fla. Dec. 10, 2002) (proposed consent decree against individual who wrote telemarketers' scripts).

3001 Statement of Basis and Purpose, 60 Fed. Reg. 43852 (Aug. 23, 1995). The FTC gives cleaning a telemarketer's office or deliv-

scripts, allowed them to use its name, and benefited financially from the transactions can be held liable.[3002] Companies that supply software for creditors to process and submit "demand drafts" may be liable under this provision if they do not take steps to ensure that the telemarketer complies with the requirements of the rule for documenting the consumer's authorization.[3003] The FTC has filed suit against a company that masterminded real estate telemarketing schemes for various promoters by providing mailing lists, promotional mailings, and a printing and mailing service.[3004] It has also won consent decrees against a company that assisted Canadian telemarketers in laundering credit card transactions,[3005] a company that performed customer service and shipped goods for a telemarketer,[3006] and a company that submitted telemarketers' charges to telephone companies to appear on consumers' telephone bills.[3007]

Even without this rule, companies that facilitate telemarketing fraud are liable for it. Before the Telemarketing Rule was adopted, the FTC obtained an FTC consent order requiring a company to pay $9 million in consumer redress where it supplied the products that were sold, trained the telemarketers, and extended credit to the victims to buy the products.[3008]

A credit card issuer may also be liable for telemarketing fraud if it continues to process a telemarketer's card charges even after it knew or should have known of the fraud.[3009] In *Citicorp Credit Services, Inc.*,[3010] discussed in § 6.5.3, *infra*, the FTC claimed that Citicorp should have known of a fraud based on the large number of consumer complaints and a 25% chargeback rate that was about twenty times the industry average. ("Chargeback" is the rate at which the charge is removed from the consumer's account and charged back to the merchant.) While this was not a telemarketing case, it illustrates the types of evidence and arguments that may be effective. Any intermediary that processes or receives charges generated by a telemarketer should be liable under this standard if there is a high rate of chargebacks or other rejections.[3011]

There may also be an independent service organization (ISO)[3012] involved in a telemarketing fraud. ISOs are entities that assist merchants in establishing relationships with bank card issuers. The FTC has obtained a consent order against an ISO for doing business with telemarketers where it should have known the telemarketers were deceiving consumers.[3013] The consumer's attorney should also investigate whether the telemarketer posted a bond pursuant to a state telemarketing law.[3014]

Vermont's telemarketing statute also imposes liability upon a courier service or the telemarketer's financial institution that assists the telemarketer to violate the state telemarketing statute. That statute prohibits courier pickups of the consumer's payment or negotiable instruments drawn on the consumer's bank account without the consumer's authorization in writing.[3015]

The telemarketer's individual officers may also be personally liable for its wrongful activities.[3016] The FTC has also had some success in forcing uninvolved parties to disgorge profits that telemarketers had transferred to them.[3017]

---

ering lunches to the telemarketer's premises as examples of activities that would not constitute substantial assistance. FTC, Complying With the Telemarketing Sales Rule at 21 (Apr. 1996).

3002 Minnesota *ex rel.* Hatch v. Fleet Mortg. Corp., 158 F. Supp. 2d 962 (D. Minn. 2001).

3003 FTC, Complying with the Telemarketing Sales Rule at 21 (Apr. 1996). *See* FTC v. Cordeiro, 5 Trade Reg. Rep. (CCH) ¶ 24,870 (N.D. Cal. Feb. 5, 2001) (consent order against defendant who provided account debiting services to process demand drafts through U.S. banks for Canadian telemarketers; high rejection and return rates should have signaled that there were fundamental problems with the telemarketer's business). *See also* FTC v. Electronic Fin. Group, Inc., www.ftc.gov/opa/2003/07/efg.htm (W.D. Tex. July 7, 2003) (complaint and TRO against company that processed electronic payments on behalf of telemarketers in violation of rules of the National Automated Clearing House Ass'n).

3004 FTC v. Marketing Response Group, 5 Trade Reg. Rep. (CCH) ¶ 23,958 (M.D. Fla. 1996) (filing of complaint).

3005 FTC v. Woofter Investment Corp., 5 Trade Reg. Rep. (CCH) ¶ 24,437 (D. Nev. 1998) (consent decree).

3006 FTC v. Allstate Bus. Distribution Center, Inc., 5 Trade Reg. Rep. (CCH) ¶ 15130 (C.D. Cal. June 20, 2001) (proposed consent decree).

3007 FTC v. Hold Billing Servs., 5 Trade Reg. Rep. (CCH) ¶ 24,659 (W.D. Tex. Oct. 6, 1999) (consent decree). *See also* FTC v. New Century Equity Holdings Corp., Inc., 5 Trade Reg. Rep. (CCH) ¶ 15139 (D.D.C. Aug. 1, 2001).

3008 FTC v. Unimet Credit Corp., 5 Trade Reg. Rep. (CCH) ¶ 23,730 (C.D. Cal. Dec. 19, 1994).

3009 FTC v. Electronic Clearinghouse, Inc., 5 Trade Reg. Rep. (CCH) ¶ 23,517 (D. Nev. Dec. 21, 1993) (consent decree); Citicorp Credit Servs., Inc., 5 Trade Reg. Rep. (CCH) ¶ 23,280 (F.T.C. Dkt. C-3413 1993) (consent order).

3010 5 Trade Reg. Rep. (CCH) ¶ 23,280 (F.T.C. Dkt. C-3413 1993) (consent order).

3011 *See* FTC v. Cordeiro, 5 Trade Reg. Rep. (CCH) ¶ 24,870 (N.D. Cal. Feb. 5, 2001). *Cf.* FTC v. First Capital Consumer Membership Servs., Inc., 206 F.R.D. 358 (W.D.N.Y. 2001) (denying credit card intermediary's motion to intervene in FTC suit against telemarketer).

3012 The Electronic Clearing House, Inc. is an example of an ISO dealing with telemarketers.

3013 *See* FTC v. Electronic Clearinghouse, Inc., 5 Trade Reg. Rep. (CCH) ¶ 23,517 (D. Nev. Dec. 21, 1993) (consent decree); see § 6.5.1, *infra* for further description.

3014 *See* § 5.9.5.3, *supra.*

3015 Vt. Stat. Ann. tit. 9, § 2464.

3016 FTC v. Publishing Clearing House, Inc., 104 F.3d 1168 (9th Cir. 1997); Texas v. American Blast Fax, Inc., 164 F. Supp. 2d 892 (W.D. Tex. 2001) (officers of a company can also be held personally liable under TCPA if they actively engaged in the conduct that violated the TCPA or actively oversaw and directed such conduct). *See generally* § 6.4.2, *infra.*

3017 FTC v. Think Achievement Corp., 144 F. Supp. 2d 993 (N.D. Ind. 2000) (telemarketer transferred large sums to wife a few days before FTC named him as defendant), *aff'd in part, rev'd*

5.9.7 Practical Steps to Remedy or Prevent Telemarketing Fraud

5.9.7.1 Withholding Payment on Credit Card Bill for Fraudulent Telemarketing Sale

If the consumer used a credit card, federal law allows the consumer to refuse to pay for goods not delivered or delivered not as represented.[3018] The credit card issuer is subject to all claims (except tort claims) and defenses arising out of the sale, up to the amount of credit still owing for the sale. The only preconditions to this right are that the consumer first made a good faith effort to resolve the matter with the telemarketer, the amount at stake must exceed $50, and the transaction must have occurred in the same state (or within 100 miles) of the cardholder's current address. Consumers should take the position that the telephone transaction occurred in the consumer's home state, since that is where the telemarketer initiated the sale. The consumer should not pay the disputed charge before invoking this right, however, as payment waives the right to assert the claims about the telemarketer's deceptive or fraudulent conduct against the card issuer.[3019]

Where the amount at stake is less than $50, or the other requirements for withholding payment have not been met, the consumer has the option of notifying the card issuer under the Fair Credit Billing Act (FCBA) of a billing error.[3020] The Federal Reserve Board (FRB) has stated that the failure to provide purchased goods or services is a billing error.[3021] The credit card issuer must then initiate an investigation and reverse the charge if warranted.

5.9.7.2 Fraud Hotline

A simple step that consumers can take if they suspect telemarketing fraud is to telephone the National Fraud Information Center at 1-800-876-7060. This service was established by a coalition of groups battling telephone fraud and operates from the National Consumers League. Reports can also be made on-line or by mail.[3022] The line is open 9:00 A.M. to 5:00 P.M. eastern standard time and operators may be able to give guidance as to whether a telemarketing call appears fraudulent. If so, the center will file a complaint for the consumer with the FBI, the FTC, and the local police.

The FTC maintains a database called Consumer Sentinel. It is housed on a restricted-access secure website, that provides national, international, federal and local law enforcement agencies immediate access to Internet cons, telemarketing scams, and other consumer fraud-related complaints. The database contains fraud complaints made to the FTC and to the National Fraud Information Center and other federal, state, and local law enforcement agencies and private organizations. The public website, www.consumer.gov/sentinel, contains consumer tips and information about fraud trends.[3023]

Reporting telemarketing fraud to law enforcement authorities through the hotline may be particularly useful for consumers who, having paid by check or cash, can not withhold payment of a credit card bill. Reporting telemarketing fraud to the hotline is also important so that law enforcement authorities have information about the location and tactics of fraudulent telemarketers.

5.9.7.3 Stopping Future Consumer Victimization

Telemarketing fraud operators know that some of the best prospects for future sales are past victims, particularly the elderly. These individuals have shown a propensity to be duped by telephone pitches and are likely to be solicited again. For example, recovery room schemes offer (for a fee) to facilitate the delivery to the consumer of all those free prizes and gifts that were never delivered.[3024] In one scheme, callers promised to recover victims' investments for an advance fee of 10% plus 10% of the recovery. They also told victims that their company was on the verge of filing a class action on behalf of victims, and the consumer

---

in part on other grounds, 312 F.3d 259 (7th Cir. 2002). *But cf.* McGregor v. Chierico, 206 F.3d 1378 (11th Cir. 2000) (reversing contempt order requiring fraudulent telemarketer's wife to forfeit joint assets where she was not guilty of contempt).

3018 *See* 15 U.S.C. § 1666i; Reg. Z § 226.12(c). *See also* § 6.6.6, *infra;* National Consumer Law Center, Truth in Lending § 5.9.5 (5th ed. 2003 and Supp.).

3019 After payment, the claim could still be asserted as a billing error, however. *See* § 6.6.5.6.6, *infra.*

3020 *See* 15 U.S.C. § 1666; § 6.6.5.6.6, *infra*; *see also* National Consumer Law Center, Truth in Lending § 5.8 (5th ed. 2003 and Supp.).

3021 Official Staff Commentary § 226.13(a)(3).

3022 The web address for on-line reports is www.fraud.org.

3023 *See* 5 Trade Reg. Rep. (CCH) ¶ 23,941 (D. Nev. 1995), for a description of this database.

3024 FTC v. Desert Fin. Group, Inc., 5 Trade Reg. Rep. (CCH) ¶ 24,011 (D. Nev. 1996) (proposed consent decree), ¶ 23,941 (D. Nev. 1995) (filing of complaints), ¶ 23,762 (D. Nev. 1995) (complaint) (callers falsely represented that they were holding the prizes that had been promised, and that they would deliver them if the victim made a charitable contribution); FTC v. PFR, 5 Trade Reg. Rep. (CCH) ¶ 23,946 (proposed consent decree), ¶ 23,777 (complaint), ¶ 23,762 (complaint) (D. Nev. 1995) (callers falsely represented that they were holding the prizes that had been promised, and that they would deliver them if the victim made a charitable contribution); FTC v. Meridian Capital Mgmt., 5 Trade Reg. Rep. (CCH) ¶ 24,020 (D. Nev. 1996) (proposed final order); FTC v. Canicatti, 5 Trade Reg. Rep. (CCH) ¶ 23,835 (D. Nev. 1995) (proposed consent decree); FTC v. Thomas E. O'Day, 5 Trade Reg. Rep. (CCH) ¶ 23,815 (M.D. Fla. 1994), ¶ 23,905 (1995) (consent order) (defendants offered, for a fee, to sell gemstones consumers had bought from other telemarketers); FTC v. United Consumer Servs., Inc., 5 Trade Reg. Rep. (CCH) ¶ 23,724 (N.D. Ga. 1994) (complaint), ¶ 23,777 (proposed consent decree).

had to pay an advance fee immediately in order to participate in the suit.[3025] These operators often have all the trappings of a public agency or non-profit organization. One recovery room, for example, called itself "Senior Citizens Against Telemarketing" and allegedly claimed a special relationship with the FTC and state attorneys general that helped it get money back for victims of telemarketing fraud.[3026] To deter this recovery room fraud, some FTC orders prohibit the defendants from selling or transferring their customer lists.[3027]

One way to reduce such repeat fraud is to advise the consumer to register on the nationwide do-not-call list.[3028] The consumer should also register on any statewide list, since the state do-not-call statute or rule may have a broader scope or better remedies. Registering on the nationwide do-not-call list will not protect the consumer from callers who solicit charitable contributions or from calls on behalf of companies that have an "established business relationship" with the consumer.[3029] To stop these calls, the consumer should make a specific oral or written do-not-call request to each of them. These callers must then place the consumer on a company-specific do-not-call list.[3030]

5.9.8 900-Number Fraud

5.9.8.1 Nature of 900-Number Fraud

The use of 900 numbers (also known as "pay-per-call" or "information access" services) creates new horizons for telephone fraud.[3031] The provider's charges for deceiving the consumer appear on the consumer's telephone bill. For example, in one scam, consumers were invited to enter a prize contest by calling a 900 number. Even for those who won, the charges for the call generally exceeded the value of the prize.[3032] One of the FTC's cases involved a 900-number provider who promised information that would save consumers $4000 a year on grocery bills. Callers were charged $10 to $24 to hear a long spiel about how to redeem cents-off coupons.[3033] The same company also enticed people to call 900 numbers to get Visa and MasterCard credit cards for which it claimed anyone could qualify, and to get packages that were being held after failed delivery attempts but which turned out to contain only unsolicited merchandise. Another case involved a provider who promised credit cards to those who called its 900 number. The 900 number turned out to be a recorded message that promised an 800 number at the end. Many of those calling the 800 number did not get a credit card but were sold an unrelated lifetime membership in the seller's services.[3034]

The FTC has targeted "cramming," the practice of causing unauthorized charges for non-traditional telephone services to appear on a consumer's telephone bill.[3035] In one type of scheme, a crammer will advertise a "free" service reached through an 800 number. When the consumer calls the 800 number, the crammer picks up the number the consumer is calling from by using an automated number identification system, similar to Caller-ID. The crammer then charges the consumer for the call and submits the bills for those calls, sometimes at international collect-call rates, to the local exchange carrier to be included with the consumer's regular telephone bill.[3036]

3025 FTC v. Meridian Capital Mgmt., Inc., 5 Trade Reg. Rep. (CCH) ¶ 23,881 (D.D.C. 1995) (TRO).

3026 FTC v. USM Corp., 5 Trade Reg. Rep. (CCH) ¶ 23,862 (D. Nev. 1995) (complaint filed and TRO granted).

3027 *See, e.g.*, FTC v. United Wholesalers, Inc., 5 Trade Reg. Rep. (CCH) ¶ 23,849 (S.D. Fla. 1995) (preliminary injunction), ¶ 23,965 (1996) (proposed consent order). In the 2002 proposed amendments to the Telemarketing Sales Rule, the FTC stated that it would not adopt a blanket prohibition against the sale of "victim lists" in the rule because "combating the practice of targeting vulnerable groups is a challenge best left to the discretion of law enforcement agencies who may seek injunctions and other penalties on a case-by-case basis in individual law enforcement actions." 67 Fed. Reg. 4525–4526 (Jan. 30, 2002).

3028 *See* § 5.9.4.6.3, *supra.*

3029 *Id.*; *see also* § 5.9.4.6.2, *supra.*

3030 *See* § 5.9.4.6.2, *supra.*

3031 900-number fraud can victimize even the intended victimizers. The FTC has filed suit against a company that fraudulently sold 900 number operations to people as investment opportunities. Genesis One Corp., 5 Trade Reg. Rep. (CCH) ¶ 23,991 (C.D. Cal. 1996) (filing of complaints).

3032 Sikes v. American Teleline, Inc. 281 F.3d 1350 (11th Cir. 2002) (ruling on class certification). *See also* People v. Allied Marketing Group, Inc., 633 N.Y.S.2d 137 (App. Div. 1995) (affirming injunctive relief, restitution, and performance bond order against fraudulent sweepstakes scheme that used 800 and 900 numbers).

3033 FTC v. Interactive Marketing Concepts, Inc., 5 Trade Reg. Rep. (CCH) ¶ 23,872 (D.N.J. 1995) (proposed consent decree).

3034 FTC v. United States Sales Corp., 785 F. Supp. 737 (N.D. Ill. 1992). *See also* § 5.1.9.2, *supra.*

3035 *See, e.g.*, FTC v. Hold Billing Servs., Ltd., 5 Trade Reg. Rep. (CCH) ¶ 24,659, Civ. Action No. SA-98-CA-0629-FB (W.D. Tex. 1999) (stipulated final judgment) (defendants, including a for-profit veterans' association, agreed to pay $1.6 million to redress claims that their sweepstakes entry form did not adequately disclose that completion would order member services, charges for which would appear on the billing statement of the telephone number appearing on the form); FTC v. Allstate Communications, Inc, 5 Trade Reg. Rep. (CCH) ¶ 24,450 (C.D. Cal. 1998) (stipulated preliminary injunction) (charged customers on their phone bills or look-alike bills for services they had not purchased); FTC v. Interactive Audiotext Servs., Inc., 5 Trade Reg. Rep. (CCH) ¶ 24,542 (C.D. Cal. 1998) (complaint); FTC v. Communications Concepts & Invs., 5 Trade Reg. Rep. (CCH) ¶ 24,458 (S.D. Fla. 1998) (complaint) (targeting use of automatic number identification to bill calls made to consumers after consumer called 800 number); FTC v. Hold Billing Servs., Ltd., 5 Trade Reg. Rep. (CCH) ¶ 24,464 (N.D. Ga. 1998) (complaint and order) ("singles" service, charged $4/minute).

3036 *See* FTC v. Int'l Telemedia Assocs., Inc., 5 Trade Reg. Rep. (CCH) ¶ 15170 (N.D. Ga. Oct. 31, 2001); FTC v. American TelNet, 5 Trade Reg. Rep. (CCH) ¶ 24,618 (S.D. Fla. June 10,

In perhaps the most inventive example of a cramming fraud, consumers who visited the defendants' Internet site and downloaded a program had their computers unknowingly disconnected from their own local service providers and reconnected to a number in Moldova. The consumers then faced inflated charges to Moldova instead of local usage charges.[3037]

5.9.8.2 Federal 900-Number Regulation

The Telephone Disclosure and Dispute Resolution Act of 1992 regulates 900 numbers on the federal level. Some parts of this law apply to telephone companies and are enforceable by the FCC,[3038] while other provisions apply to 900-number providers and are enforceable by the FTC.[3039] One court has held that this law did not apply to dial-up Internet access calls that were fraudulently generated by adult websites to telephone numbers in distant Pacific island nations.[3040] Even though the consumers incurred significant charges for the calls, the calls were not to 900 numbers and the charges were just for transmission, not for services. The court found more merit in claims under the provisions of federal communications laws that require fair and reasonable rates and prohibit overcharges,[3041] but held that these claims were within the primary jurisdiction of the FCC.

One of the key protections of this statute is that it prohibits common carriers from disconnecting a subscriber's local or long-distance service because of unpaid charges for any pay-per-call service.[3042] Because of this protection, consumers whose telephone bills include charges for 900-number service that was fraudulent or that they did not authorize should be advised to refuse to pay. To alert consumers to the existence of 900-number charges on their bill, carriers are required to itemize these charges separately.[3043]

Carriers must establish a procedure for handling consumer complaints about 900-number charges but have discretion about the standards for forgiving charges.[3044] Carriers are, however, required to forgive the debt and refund any payment if the FTC, the FCC, or a court finds that the 900-number service violated the federal law or regulations.[3045] Providers may not misrepresent to line subscribers that they are legally obligated to pay for 900 number services.[3046]

The statute and regulations create a number of other consumer protections. Where technically feasible, telephone companies must offer consumers the option of blocking access from their telephone to pay-per-call services.[3047] Entities offering pay-per-call service must make disclosures regarding costs in advertisements and in a preamble when the consumer calls the number.[3048] The consumer can hang up during or within three seconds after the preamble without incurring any charges.[3049] For prize promotions, advertisers must disclose the chance of winning and an alternate, free way of entering any game of chance or sweepstakes.[3050]

Providers can not direct advertisements at children under age 12 except for bona fide educational products.[3051] Advertisements directed to children under age 18 are allowed but must include a warning that parental permission is necessary for any calls.[3052]

1999) (order requiring write-off of bills and $2 million in consumer redress).

3037 FTC v. Audiotex Connection, Inc., 5 Trade Reg. Rep. (CCH) ¶ 24,212 (E.D.N.Y. 1997) (temporary restraining order).

3038 47 U.S.C. § 228 [*reprinted in* Appx. D.1.4, *infra*]. The FCC's regulations are found at 47 C.F.R. Part 64 [*reprinted in* Appx. D.2.3, *infra*].

3039 15 U.S.C. § 5711 [*reprinted in* Appx. D.1.2, *infra*]. The FTC's regulations are found at 16 C.F.R. Part 308 [*reprinted in* Appx. D.2.2, *infra*]. The FTC's Statement of Basis and Purpose for this rule was published at 58 Fed. Reg. 42364 (Aug. 9, 1993). Under the terms of the rule, the FTC was required to initiate a review of the rule prior to November, 1997. Comments were requested at 62 Fed. Reg. 11750 (Mar. 12, 1997), and the comment period was extended to March 10, 1999. 64 Fed. Reg. 61 (Jan. 4, 1999). Although the FTC has held two public workshops on the rule, other mandated rulemaking has prevented it from concluding the proceeding, and it currently is expected a staff recommendation in early 2005. 69 Fed. Reg. 38599 (June 28, 2004).

3040 Niehaus v. AT&T Corp., 218 F. Supp. 2d 531 (S.D.N.Y. 2002).

3041 47 U.S.C. §§ 201(b), 203(c).

3042 47 U.S.C. § 228(c)(4); 47 C.F.R. § 64.1507; *see* also 16 C.F.R. § 308.7(g).

3043 47 U.S.C. § 228(d)(4).

3044 47 C.F.R. § 64.1511(a).

3045 47 U.S.C. § 228(f); 47 C.F.R. § 64.1511(2).

3046 FTC v. 800 Connect, Inc., 5 Trade Reg. Rep. (CCH) ¶ 15360 (S.D. Fla. Feb. 3, 2003) (proposed consent decree); FTC v. Alyon Technologies, Inc., 2003 WL 22319428 (N.D. Ga. July 10, 2003) (consent order).

3047 47 U.S.C. § 228(c)(5); 47 C.F.R. § 64.1508.

3048 15 U.S.C. § 5711(a)(1), (2); 16 C.F.R. §§ 308.3, 308.5. *See* FTC v. 800 Connect, Inc., 5 Trade Reg. Rep. (CCH) ¶ 15360 (S.D. Fla. Feb. 3, 2003) (proposed consent decree); FTC v. Access Resource Servs., 5 Trade Reg. Rep. (CCH) ¶ 15325 (S.D. Fla. Nov. 4, 2002) (proposed consent decree); Federal Trade Commission v. Career Information Servs., Inc., 1996 U.S. Dist. LEXIS 21207, 1996-2 Trade Cas. (CCH) ¶ 71,468 (N.D. Ga. June 21, 1996) (issuing preliminary injunction prohibiting pay-per-call service from failing to make required disclosures).

3049 15 U.S.C. § 5711 (a)(2)(B); 16 C.F.R. § 308.5(b).

3050 16 C.F.R. § 308.3(c).

3051 15 U.S.C. § 5711(a)(1)(D); 16 C.F.R. § 308.3(e). Even before the 900-number federal legislation, the FTC had accepted a series of consent orders dealing with companies pitching 900 numbers to children, offering free gifts and stories, without encouraging parental supervision. Fone Telecommunications, 5 Trade Reg. Rep. (CCH) ¶ 23,348 (F.T.C. Dkt. C-3432 1993) (consent order); Phone Programs, Inc., 115 F.T.C. 977, 5 Trade Reg. Rep. (CCH) ¶ 23,259 (1992) (consent order); Teleline, Inc., 114 F.T.C. 399 (1991) (consent order); Audio Communications, Inc., 114 F.T.C. 414 (1991) (consent order); Teleline, Inc., 5 Trade Reg. Rep. (CCH) ¶ 22,989 (F.T.C. File No. 892 3229 1991) (consent order).

3052 15 U.S.C. § 5711(a)(1)(E); 16 C.F.R. § 308.3(f). For examples of 900-number fraud directed at children, and the FTC's ap-

Providers can not switch consumers from an 800 number to a 900 number.[3053] Nor can they switch consumers from an 800 number to a collect call.[3054]

Telephone companies must require their subscribers to comply with the statute and must terminate them if they violate it.[3055] FCC regulations also forbid the telephone company from billing the consumer for pay-per-call services that it knows or has reason to know violate the regulations.[3056]

The FCC has recently opened a new proceeding to review the effectiveness of its rules regarding pay-per-call, 1-800 and audiotext services.[3057] The Commission is concerned that the exceptions and exemptions in the existing 1-900 rule along with changes in technology have allowed companies to circumvent the consumer protections in the rule. In the first six months of 2004, the Commission received almost 5000 consumer complaints that referenced toll-free numbers.[3058] The Commission is also exploring whether to extend protections to the phone-line subscriber (current rules protect the calling party)[3059] and how to protect consumers from new practices such as "modem highjacking" which switch customers over to higher cost service. Pay-per-call providers have also migrated away from 1-900 numbers to avoid regulation, using revenue sharing agreements and instant credit to mask the nature of their services.[3060] The Commission is also exploring whether it needs to modify the definitions of exempted directory services and data services.[3061]

The FTC, the FCC, and state consumer protection officials all have enforcement authority under the federal law.[3062] While the Act does not give consumers a private cause of action, it should be clear that its standards are enforceable through state UDAP laws.[3063]

5.9.8.3 State Laws Regulating 900 Numbers

A number of states have enacted statutes to protect consumers from abusive 900-number practices.[3064] In other states, the public utility commission allows regulated telephone companies to provide transmission services (a necessity for the 900-number provider) only if the provider complies with a detailed list of consumer protections.[3065] Other states simply require that 900-number charges be separately itemized and conspicuously identified on telephone bills, that consumers be advised that basic telephone service may not be refused or terminated, nor a deposit required, for nonpayment of 900-number bills, and that basic service must include options for blocking 900-number calls.[3066]

---

proach to the problem prior to the current regulations, see Phone Programs, Inc., 115 F.T.C. 977 (1992) (consent order), Teleline, Inc., 114 F.T.C. 399 (1991) (consent order), and Audio Communications, Inc., 114 F.T.C. 414 (1991) (consent order).

3053 47 U.S.C. § 228(c)(7); 15 U.S.C. § 5711(a)(2)(F); 47 C.F.R. § 64.1504; 16 C.F.R. § 308.5(i); FTC v. 800 Connect, Inc., 5 Trade Reg. Rep. (CCH) ¶ 15360 (S.D. Fla. Feb. 3, 2003) (proposed consent decree against company that charged consumers for re-routing misdialed calls to 800-numbers). The statute provides an exception where the calling party and the provider have a written agreement and the calling party must use a personal identification number. These protections were tightened up by the Telecommunications Act of 1996, Pub. Law No. 104-104, § 701. *See also* FTC v. Interactive Audiotext Servs., Inc., 5 Trade Reg. Rep. (CCH) ¶ 24,542 (C.D. Cal. 1998) (stipulated final judgment and order for permanent injunction).

3054 47 U.S.C. § 228(c)(7)(D); 47 C.F.R. § 64.1504(d); *In re* Tel. Publishing Corp. & Telemedia Network, Inc., 1997 FCC LEXIS 2070 (1997) (F.C.C. Apr., 18 1997) (notice of apparent liability for forfeiture). *See also* 16 C.F.R. § 308.5(i)(4) (prohibiting use of 800 number or other toll free number in a manner that results in a caller being called back collect for information or entertainment services). *See* FTC v. Automated Transaction Corp., Case No. 00-7599-CIV-Hurley/Lynch (S.D. Fla. Jan. 24, 2002) at www.ftc.gov/os/2002/01/ftcvatclipton.pdf (stipulated judgment and order for permanent injunction and other equitable relief); FTC v. International Telemedia Assoc., Inc., Civil No. 1:98-CV-1935 (N.D. Ga. 2001) at www.ftc.gov/os/2001/10/itastipfinaljdmt.pdf (stipulated final judgment and order enjoining company from using a 1-800 number that results in a caller being called back collect); United States v. American TelNet, Inc., 5 Trade Reg. Rep. (CCH) ¶ 23,723 (S.D. Fla. 1994) (proposed consent decree against service bureau that switched callers from an 800 number to a 900 number and did not make the required price disclosures).

3055 47 U.S.C. § 228(c)(3); 47 C.F.R. §§ 64.1502, 64.1503.

3056 47 U.S.C. § 228(d); 47 C.F.R. § 64.1510.

3057 Federal Communications Commission, "Policies and Rules Governing Interstate Pay-Per-Call and Other Information Services Pursuant to the Telecommunications Act of 1996" F.C.C. 04-162, CC Docket No. 96-146, CG Docket No. 04-244, CC Docket No. 98-170, RM-8783, ENF 95-20 (July 16, 2004).

3058 *Id.* at ¶ 11.

3059 *Id.* at ¶ 12.

3060 *Id.* at ¶¶ 19–90.

3061 *Id.* at ¶¶ 32–35.

3062 15 U.S.C. §§ 5712, 5713; 47 U.S.C. § 228.

3063 *See* §§ 3.2.6, 3.2.7, 3.4.5, *supra*.

3064 State laws on 900-number abuses include are summarized in Appx. E, *infra*. *See also* Colo. Rev. Stat. §§ 6-1-302 and 6-1-303 (references to pay per call in telemarketing statute); Del. Code tit. 6, § 2504A (extra recordkeeping requirements for prize promotions which invite consumer's call to a 900 number); Iowa Code § 535C.2 (regulated loan brokers' "advance fee" defined to include pay per call charges); Minn. Stat. § 237.66 (phone companies must advise residential customers of available 900 blocking options); N.H. Rev. Stat. § 358-O:4 (requirements for prize promotions); N.C. Stat. § 66-265 (telemarketing statute forbids prize promotions which include call to 900 number).

3065 3 Alaska Admin. Code § 53.500 et seq.; Fla. Admin. Code § 25-4.110; Ill. Admin. Code tit. 83, part 772 (implements pay per call statute); S.C. Code Regs. 103-632

3066 Code Maine Rules § 65-407-202; N.H. Admin. Rules Puc 1306.01 (basic telephone service must include 900 blocking option); N.J. Admin. Code § 14:3-7.17 (defines pay per call as non-basic; basic service may not be terminated or denied for nonpayment for non-basic); 4 N.C. Admin. Code 11.R17-2; Okla. Admin. Code Ann. 4901:1-5-25 Appx. B (billing and customer information); Or. Admin. Rules 860-021-0620 and

State statutes and regulations are important because the federal regulations only cover interstate 900-number services.[3067] However, the FCC has preempted state regulation where intrastate and interstate components of a service, such as 1-900 service blocking, are inseverable and state regulation would impede federal policies.[3068] Pay-per-call services reached through local exchanges such as 976 or 960 are also left to state regulation.[3069]

Like the federal statutes and regulations, almost all of the state laws require cost disclosures in advertisements and in a brief oral preamble after a customer places a call.[3070] The typical state statute also restricts prize promotions[3071] and prohibits various methods of switching a consumer from a free call to a pay-per-call call.[3072]

Louisiana's statute prohibits repetition of material and other gimmicks to prolong the call.[3073] It also departs from the typical statute by addressing the value of the information the 900 number provides, prohibiting untimely, out-of-date, or garbled information.[3074] Oklahoma's statute prohibits billing for 900-number calls that provide vulgar, violent, obscene, or racist information or false or misleading advertisements.[3075] California's statute explicitly includes transactions over the Internet.[3076]

A number of state statutes repeat the federal prohibition against disconnection of local or long-distance service because of nonpayment of 900-number charges, and the requirement that telephone bills itemize 900-number charges. Wisconsin requires telephone companies to disclose on the bill that telephone service can not be disconnected for failure to pay 900-number charges.[3077] Vermont and Oregon require full refunds upon request in several situations.[3078] California requires any broadcast or print advertisement or notice that has a 900 number to be written in the same language as the language used in a recorded message or by the live operator of the 900-number call.[3079]

Many state 900-number statutes declare that a violation is a UDAP violation, but a few set forth no private cause of action or list only criminal penalties. Even where the 900-number statute does not specify a remedy, a violation may be a *per se* violation of the state UDAP statute.[3080]

In addition to the laws directed specifically at 900 numbers, state laws regulating telephone sales in general may apply, depending on their coverage provisions.

860-034-0290 (utilities which provide billing and collection services for 900 number providers must advise consumers of their rights under 900 number statute); Admin. Rules S.D. 20:10:05:05, 20:10:09:03, 20:10:10:04, and 20:10:10:10; Tenn. Comp. R. and Regs. R.1220-4-2-.58 (must offer 900 number blocking); 16 Tex. Admin. Code 26.124; Wash. Admin. Code § 230-46-025 (forbids use of 900 number in promotional game of chance).

3067 See the FTC's Statement of Basis and Purpose for its 900-number rule, 58 Fed. Reg. 42364, 42367 (Aug. 9, 1993) for a discussion of this issue.

3068 *See* 10 F.C.C.R. 4153, "Memorandum Opinion and Order on Reconsideration In the Matter of Petition for an Expedited Declaratory Ruling Filed by National Association for Information Services, Audio Communications, Inc., and Ryder Communications, Inc." (Dec. 30, 1994) (Telephone Disclosure and Dispute Resolution Act preempts South Carolina's regulation providing automatic default blocking for intrastate 900 service).

3069 *See* 47 U.S.C. § 228(g)(4) ("Nothing in this section shall preclude any State from enacting and enforcing additional and complementary oversight and regulatory systems or procedures, or both, so long as such systems and procedures govern intrastate services and do not significantly impede the enforcement of this section or other Federal statutes").

3070 *See, e.g.*, Ariz. Rev. Stat. Ann. § 13-2920; Cal. Bus. & Prof. Code § 17539.5 (disclosures in solicitations); Idaho Code § 48-1103, 1104; 815 Ill. Comp. Stat. Ann. § 520.10; Iowa Code Ann. § 714A.2, .3; La. Rev. Stat. Ann. § 51:1731 (disclosures in ads); Or. Rev. Stat. § 759.705, 710; Vt. Stat. Ann. tit. 9, § 2501 *et seq.*; Va. Code § 59.1-430; Wash. Rev. Code Ann. § 19.162.030, .040.

3071 *See, e.g.*, Cal. Bus. & Prof. Code § 17539.5; 815 Ill. Comp. Stat. Ann. § 520/10(d); Vt. Stat. Ann. tit. 9, § 2507.

3072 *See, e.g.*, Ariz. Rev. Stat. Ann. § 13-2920; Cal. Bus. & Prof. Code § 17539.5; Vt. Stat. Ann. tit. 9, § 2513.

3073 La. Rev. Stat. Ann. § 51:1733. *See also* Wis. Stat. Ann. § 196.208 (prohibits charge for time caller is on hold).

3074 La. Rev. Stat. Ann. § 51:1733.

5.9.8.4 Other Entities Liable for a Provider's 900-Number Fraud

Nonpayment of 900-number charges is the simplest and most effective remedy for 900-number fraud. Some consumers may have already paid these charges, however, and may have difficulty recovering the money from fly-by-night 900-number providers. One thing to investigate in such a case is whether the provider posted a bond pursuant to the state's telemarketing law.[3081]

Other entities that provided services or technology that facilitated the 900-number fraud may be liable if they knew or should have known of the fraud. Several suits have sought to cast liability on telephone carriers that receive a portion of the profits from fraudulent 900-number schemes. For example, one case involved games of chance that people played by calling a 900 number. Even for those who won, the prize usually was worth less than the 900-number charges they incurred. The consumers alleged that AT&T provided the 900 numbers, billing services, and answering machines used in the scheme, received a substantial portion of the profits, and knew or should have known of its fraudulent nature. The

3075 Okla. Stat. Ann. tit. 17, § 140.2.

3076 Cal. Bus. & Prof. Code § 17539.5.

3077 Wis. Stat. Ann. § 196.208.

3078 Or. Rev. Stat. § 759.720 (charges made by children or mentally disabled individuals); Vt. Stat. Ann. tit. 9, §§ 2505 (credit cards and loans), 2507 (prize promotions), 2508 (use by children), 2509 (charitable donations).

3079 Cal. Bus. & Prof. Code § 17539.6.

3080 *See* § 3.2.7, *supra*.

3081 *See* discussion at § 5.9.5.3, *supra*.

district court initially certified the action as a class action,[3082] but the court of appeals reversed the class certification on the ground that consumers had to show damages and reliance individually.[3083] Nonetheless, many courts have accepted the underlying liability theory.[3084]

Entities known as "service bureaus" are also often involved in 900-number schemes. They act as intermediaries between the telephone company and pay-per-call providers, providing access to telephone service and voice storage for the providers.[3085] An FTC regulation makes them liable if they know or should know of violations of the FTC's pay-per-call rule by providers.[3086] The FTC won a consent order requiring a service bureau to pay $2 million in consumer redress due to its facilitation of a 900-number scam.[3087] A "billing aggregator" that acts as an intermediary to enable a service provider to cram a charge onto a consumer's telephone bill can also be held liable for the provider's violations.[3088]

Many 900-number laws have criminal as well as civil penalties, and many state attorney general offices have given priority to fighting 900-number fraud. Consumers should be encouraged to report 900-number fraud to law enforcement officials and state consumer protection authorities. Not only may the consumer benefit through a restitution order, but information about telephone fraud helps law enforcement authorities locate and prosecute fraudulent providers.

5.9.8.5 Practical Suggestions to Avoid 900-Number Fraud

Many consumers who have been hit once by 900-number fraud are vulnerable to repeat victimization. A household member or visitor who has run up 900-number charges once may be likely to do so again. Consumers can prevent 900-number calls from their telephones by having the telephone company block them.[3089] Consumers can also contact the nationwide telephone fraud hotline[3090] if they are concerned about a particular provider's legitimacy.

5.9.9 *On-Line Fraud*

Consumer fraud is abundant on the Internet. Credit repair services,[3091] miracle cures and weight loss products,[3092] pyramid schemes,[3093] off-site betting[3094] and bogus income opportunities[3095] are widely marketed over the Internet. In one scheme, the Internet was used not only to market products, but also to solicit the user to download a program that hijacked the user's computer modem so that all calls were routed through Moldova at great expense to the consumer. The operator of the scheme had an arrangement with the international telephone carrier to get a cut of the revenue generated by the calls.[3096] In another scheme, website op-

---

3082 Sikes v. American Tel. & Tel. Co., Clearinghouse No. 50,437 (S.D. Ga. May 13, 1994), *motion to decertify class denied, parties' motions for summary judgment denied*, 179 F.R.D. 342 (S.D. Ga. 1998).

3083 Sikes v. Teleline, Inc., 281 F.3d 1350 (11th Cir. 2002). *See also* Andrews v. American Tel. & Tel. Co., 95 F.3d 1014 (11th Cir. 1996) (declining to certify a nationwide class action relating to hundreds of 900-number telemarketing programs).

3084 *See* § 6.5, *infra*. *But see* Zekman v. Direct Am. Marketers, 182 Ill. 2d 359, 695 N.E.2d 853 (1998) (declining to import common law fraud concepts into UDAP statute, so AT&T not liable for another company's 900-number fraud even if it knowingly received the benefits).

3085 *See* definition of service bureau at 16 C.F.R. § 308.2(d)(i) and description at United States v. American TelNet, Inc., 5 Trade Reg. Rep. (CCH) ¶ 23,723 (C.D. Cal. 1994) (consent order).

3086 16 C.F.R. § 308.5(l).

3087 United States v. American TelNet, Inc., 5 Trade Reg. Rep. (CCH) ¶ 23,723 (C.D. Cal. 1994) (consent order).

3088 FTC v. New Century Equity Holdings Corp., Inc., 5 Trade Reg. Rep. (CCH) ¶ 15139 (D.D.C. Aug. 1, 2001) (failure to investigate charges after consumer complained was violation); U.S. v. Enhanced Servs. Billing, Inc., Civ. No. 01 1660 (D.C. filed Aug. 1, 2001) at www.ftc.gov/os/2001/08/enhancedbillingstip.pdf (billing aggregator failed to perform a reasonable investigation into disputed 1-900 charges); Saltzman v. Enhanced Servs. Billing, Inc., 2003 WL 21750606 (Ill. App. July 29, 2003). *See* FTC v. International Telemedia Assoc., Inc., Civil No. 1:98-CV-1935 (N.D. Ga. 2001) at www.ftc.gov/os/2001/10/itastipfinaljdmt.pdf (stipulated final judgment and order); FTC v. Hold Billing Servs., Ltd., 5 Trade Reg. Rep. (CCH) ¶ 24,464 (N.D. Ga. 1998) (complaint and order); FTC press release at www.ftc.gov/opa/2001/10/ita7.htm.

3089 47 U.S.C. § 228(c)(5); 47 C.F.R. § 64.1508. Some state 900 number statutes also require blocking, and may specify the charges that the telephone company can impose for this service.

3090 *See* § 5.9.3.8.2, *supra*.

3091 U.S. v. Black, 5 Trade Reg. Rep. (CCH) ¶ 24,769 (M.D. Fla. June 6, 2000) (stipulated final judgment); FTC v. Consumer Credit Advocates, P.C., 5 Trade Reg. Rep. (CCH) ¶ 24,003 (S.D.N.Y. 1996) (proposed consent decree).

3092 FTC v. Enforma Natural Products, 5 Trade Reg. Rep. (CCH) ¶ 24,734 (C.D. Cal. Apr. 25, 2000) (stipulated final order) (false weight loss claims); FTC v. CMO Distribution Centers, 2000 FTC LEXIS 71 (May 16, 2000) (complaint and consent order) (website touted products as cures for cancer, AIDS, diabetes). *See also* State *ex rel.* Stovall v. Confirmed.com, 38 P.3d 707 (Kan. 2002) (finding sale of Viagra over Internet without medical exam not a UDAP violation, although it was enjoined on other grounds).

3093 FTC's Press Release, *FTC Launches Crackdown on Deceptive Junk E-Mail* (Feb. 12, 2002), *complaints and final judgments available at* www.ftc.gov/opa/2002/02/eileenspam1.htm) (sting operation against deceptive chain-letter scheme); FTC v. Silver State Western Publishing, Inc., 5 Trade Reg. Rep. (CCH) ¶ 24,031 (D. Nev. 1996) (filing of complaint).

3094 National Consumers League, NCL Bulletin, Vol 59, No. 2 at 5.

3095 FTC v. iMall, Inc., F.T.C. File No. 972-3224 (C.D. Cal. Apr. 15, 1999) (stipulated final judgment against Internet company that made false earnings claims for Internet-based businesses it promoted); FTC v. Fortuna Alliance, L.L.C., 5 Trade Reg. Rep. (CCH) ¶ 24,039 (W.D. Wash. 1996) (TRO).

3096 National Consumers League, NCL Bulletin, Vol 59, No. 2 at 7. *See, e.g.*, FTC v. Hillary Sheinkin, 5 Trade Reg. Rep. (CCH) ¶ 15146 (D.S.C. Aug. 15, 2001) (settlement regarding adult website that surreptitiously downloaded dialer program onto users' computers, routing calls through Madagascar); FTC v. Hillary

erators claimed that credit card numbers were needed only to verify that consumers were of legal age to view "free" adult websites, and then submitted charges to the user's credit card. The owners and operators of the sites were required to pay $30 million to settle the suit brought by the FTC and the New York Attorney General.[3097] The FTC also won an injunctive order and $1,800,000 in consumer redress against an individual who owned websites similar in name to well-known sites. Consumers who reached the wrong site by mistake were bombarded with pop-up ads. Clicking "close" or "back" only launched more ads.[3098]

While the FTC's Telemarketing Rule does not apply to on-line services,[3099] the FTC can proceed against deceptive on-line service providers under its general authority. It has done so in several cases[3100] and it has announced that it intends to monitor the Internet vigorously for fraud.[3101]

The FTC's Mail or Telephone Order Merchandise Rule[3102] provides a remedy for on-line fraud where the problem is failure to deliver, or delay in delivering merchandise. The rule broadly provides that it covers sales made by "any direct or indirect use of the telephone to order merchandise, regardless of whether the telephone is activated by, or the language used is that of human beings, machines, or both."[3103] This language clearly includes sales conducted on-line.[3104]

The FTC's Trade Regulation Rule on Franchising and Business Opportunities[3105] requires certain disclosures in connection with the advertisement and sale of franchises and business opportunities, and applies to transactions over the Internet. Failure to comply with this rule is a *per se* violation of most UDAP statutes.

Another practice targeted by the FTC involves credit card "cramming" by Internet businesses. A number of cases have been brought against businesses that billed consumers' credit cards for "free" website services or for unauthorized purchases, often obtaining credit card information by asking for a credit card number to verify that the user is over eighteen.[3106] The Truth in Lending Act subjects the credit card issuer to the consumer's claims and defenses against the merchant, provided certain conditions are met,[3107] and also provides a procedure for consumers to dispute charges.[3108]

The FTC has issued a policy statement about how its consumer protection rules apply to advertising and marketing on electronic media.[3109] FTC rules and guides that apply to written or printed advertisements also apply to on-line advertisements. Disclosures that are necessary to prevent an advertisement from being misleading must be clear and conspicuous in on-line ads. In determining whether a disclosure meets this standard, the FTC looks at the placement of the advertisement, whether other parts of it distract attention from the disclosure, the duration of visual disclo-

---

Sheinkin, No. 2-00-3636-18 (D.S.C. filed Nov. 18, 2000) at www.ftc.gov/os/2001/08/sheinkin.pdf; FTC v. Ty Anderson, No. C00-1843P (W.D. Wash. filed Oct. 27, 2000) at www.ftc.gov/os/2001/08/pornopicorder.htm. *See* FTC v. Audiotext Connection, Inc., 5 Trade Reg. Rep. (CCH) ¶ 24,345 (E.D.N.Y. 1998) (complaint and consent decree). *See also* FTC v. Verity Int'l, Ltd., 194 F. Supp. 2d 270 (S.D.N.Y. 2002) (issuing preliminary injunction in scheme that purportedly routed Internet access through Madagascar and billed for international call); FTC Staff Opinion, response to letter from Roy Ellyatt, International Telemedia Assoc. (Sept. 29, 1999) at www.ftc.gov/bcp/adcon/900rule/ellyatt.htm (proposed disclaimer screens before consumers accessed toll-billed entertainment program are most likely inadequate to withstand challenge under § 5 of the FTC Act).

3097 FTC v. Crescent Publishing Group, Inc. (S.D.N.Y filed 2001) at www.ftc.gov/os/2001/11/crescentstip.pdf (stipulated final judgment and order). *See also* FTC v. RJB Telecom, Inc., 5 Trade Reg. Rep. (CCH) ¶ 15155 (D. Ariz. Sept. 26, 2001).

3098 FTC v. John Zuccarini, 5 Trade Reg. Rep. (CCH) ¶ 15259 (E.D. Pa. May 24, 2002).

3099 *See* the Statement of Basis and Purpose for the FTC's Telemarketing Rule at the Proposal Stage, 60 Fed. Reg. 30411 (June 8, 1995).

3100 FTC v. Zuccarini, 2002 WL 1378421 (E.D. Pa. Apr. 9, 2002) (entering permanent injunction against individual who redirected consumers from their intended destinations to his own webpages and then obstructed them from exiting those pages); FTC v. Consumer Credit Advocates, P.C., 5 Trade Reg. Rep. (CCH) ¶ 24,003 (S.D.N.Y. 1996) (proposed consent decree); FTC v. Brandzel, 5 Trade Reg. Rep. (CCH) ¶ 23,999 (N.D. Ill. 1996) (filing of complaint); FTC v. Fortuna Alliance, L.L.C., 5 Trade Reg. Rep. (CCH) ¶ 24,039 (W.D. Wash. 1996) (TRO). *See also* § 5.6.9.10, *supra.*

3101 FTC v. Research Awards Center, Inc., 5 Trade Reg. Rep. (CCH) ¶ 23,990 (D. Md. 1996) (proposed consent decree). The FTC refused to broaden the scope of the Telemarketing Sales Rule to cover on-line services in its 2002 proposed amendments to the rule. Instead, the Commission has chosen to rely on the growing body of Internet fraud and deception case law and the Commission's education materials for on-line advertising disclosures to provide guidance for promoting and marketing on the Internet. 67 Fed. Reg. 4497–4498 (Jan. 30, 2002).

3102 16 C.F.R. § 435. *See* § 5.8.1, *supra.*

3103 16 C.F.R. § 435.2(b).

3104 *See* FTC v. Auctionsaver, 5 Trade Reg. Rep. (CCH) ¶ 15252 (S.D. Cal. Apr. 22, 2002) (consent decree against Internet-based computer seller that violated mail order rule); FTC v. Computers by Us, Inc., 5 Trade Reg. Rep. (CCH) ¶ 15148 (D. Md. Aug. 30, 2001) (proposed consent decree against web-based auction that made slow delivery and did not honor cancellation requests; also bars misrepresentation that auction owns the items it is auctioning); FTC v. Bargains & Deals Magazine, L.L.C. (W.D. Wash. Oct. 11, 2001) at www.ftc.gov/os/2001/10/bdmcmp.htm (complaint for permanent injunction and other equitable relief); FTC v. Brandzel, 5 Trade Reg. Rep. (CCH) ¶ 23,999 (N.D. Ill. 1996) (filing of complaint).

3105 16 C.F.R. Part 436. *See* § 5.13.1, *infra.*

3106 *See* FTC v. J.K. Publications, Inc., 99 F. Supp. 2d 1176 (C.D. Cal. 2001); FTC v. Crescent Publishing Group, Inc., 129 F. Supp. 2d 311 (S.D.N.Y. 2001) (adult website offered free tour but did not clearly disclose when tour became not free, and in fact crafted disclosure to deceive consumers about charges; seller processed credit card charges through VISA in Guatemala in order to evade VISA's chargeback monitoring program).

3107 15 U.S.C. § 1666i. *See* § 6.6.5.6.1–6.6.5.6.5, *infra.*

3108 15 U.S.C. § 1666. *See* § 6.6.5.6.6, *infra.*

3109 FTC, Dot Com Disclosures (2000), *available at* www.ftc.gov.

sures and the volume and cadence of audio disclosures, whether the language is understandable, and whether the advertisement is so lengthy that the disclosure needs to be repeated.

Whether state telephone sales laws apply to on-line sales will depend on their language. Georgia's telemarketing law explicitly applies to theft offenses committed "while engaging in any activity on the Internet or any similar computerized system which individuals connect to by use of a computer and a modem."[3110] Virginia's home solicitation sales law covers sales conducted by telephone "or other electronic means."[3111] If an e-mail message invites consumers to call the sender to purchase goods or services, the FTC's Telemarketing Sales Rule applies to the telephone call and the sale.[3112]

There should be no room for dispute that general UDAP prohibitions apply to on-line fraud. Some states are, however, amending their UDAP statutes to make it clear that advertising, offers, and publications that are transmitted electronically or over the Internet fall within the statute.[3113]

Fraudulent promoters who use the Internet may argue that only their home state, and not the consumer's home state, has jurisdiction over them. Courts have rejected this argument, analogizing a posting on the Internet to the placement of an advertisement in a national publication, both of which are purposeful attempts to reach consumers in distant states.[3114] Conversely, a New York business which sold magazine subscriptions over the Internet to consumers in other states and countries, but then failed to deliver the magazines, was subject to New York jurisdiction because of its physical presence in the state.[3115]

5.9.10 Unsolicited Bulk Commercial E-mail

5.9.10.1 Why Unsolicited Bulk Commercial E-mail Is a Problem for Consumers

Unsolicited bulk commercial e-mail, commonly known as "spam,"[3116] is a problem for consumers for a number of reasons. First, its low cost and anonymity attract fraudulent sellers. Pyramid schemes, miracle cures, pornography, and a host of bogus products are marketed by spam. Spam can contain viruses. Any response to spam, even to request that no further solicitations be sent, gives information to the entity that sent the spam and can undermine the consumer's privacy.

Spam increases costs for Internet Service Providers (ISPs), which have to add increased capacity to deal with spam, which makes up a substantial percentage of e-mail traffic. Since customers complain about receiving spam, ISPs have to add customer service staff. Many also purchase programs to filter out spam. All of these costs are ultimately passed on to consumers in the form of increased prices.

Spam also increases direct costs for individual consumers. The time spent receiving spam ties up the consumer's telephone line. If the consumer pays for Internet access by the hour instead of a flat monthly fee, receiving spam increases the charges. Receipt of spam also occupies the resources of the consumer's computer system.

Perhaps the worst problem caused by spam is that it undermines legitimate use of e-mail. When Congress passed the federal E-Sign statute in 2000,[3117] it imagined that e-mail would be an efficient, cost-effective way for companies to communicate with consumers. Spam undermines this goal. A consumer who is flooded by an ocean of spam is

3110 Ga. Code Ann. § 10-1-393.5(b).

3111 Va. Code § 59.1-21.2.

3112 16 C.F.R. § 310.6(b)(6).

3113 *See, e.g.*, Cal. Bus. & Prof. Code § 17538. *See also* Specht v. Netscape Communications Corp., 306 F.3d 17, 34 n.17 (2d Cir. 2002) (discussing Cal. statute and other standards for on-line disclosures).

3114 *See, e.g.*, Inset Sys., Inc. v. Instruction Set, Inc., 937 F. Supp. 161 (D. Conn. 1996) (Connecticut court had personal jurisdiction under state long arm statute over Massachusetts corporation which repeatedly solicited business in Connecticut by advertising on the Internet and having a toll-free telephone number); State v. Granite Gate Resorts, Inc., 568 N.W.2d 715 (Minn. App. 1997), *aff'd by equally divided court*, 576 N.W.2d 747 (Minn. 1998). *But cf.* Bailey v. Turbine Design, Inc., 86 F. Supp. 2d 790 (W.D. Tenn. 2000) (general posting on Internet not sufficient to establish minimum contacts, but personal jurisdiction may be appropriate where there is something more to indicate that defendant purposefully directed activities to the forum state); *but see* Loudon Plastics, Inc. v. Brenner Tool & Die, Inc., 74 F. Supp. 2d 182 (N.D.N.Y. 1999) (accessibility of nonresident manufacturer's passive Internet website to New York residents did not provide sufficient minimum contacts for state to exercise personal jurisdiction over manufacturer in breach of contract action). *See generally* § 7.6.1, *infra*.

3115 People by Vacco v. Lipsitz, 174 Misc. 2d 571, 663 N.Y.S.2d 468 (Sup. Ct. 1997). *See also* CompuServ, Inc. v. Patterson, 89 F.3d 1257 (6th Cir. 1996).

3116 "SPAM" is a trademark of the Hormel Food Co., but that company states on its website that it does not object to the use of the term to mean unsolicited bulk commercial e-mail as long as the term is printed in lower case letters. For discussions of issues regarding spam, *see* David E. Sorkin, *Technical and Legal Approaches to Unsolicited Electronic Mail*, 35 U.S.F.L. Rev. 325 (Winter 2001), posted at www.spamlaws.com; David E. Sorkin, *Unsolicited Commercial E-Mail and the Telephone Consumer Protection Act of 1991*, 45 Buffalo L. Rev. 1001 (1997), posted at www.spamlaws.com; Sabra-Anne Kalin, *Note*, 16 Berkeley Tech. L.J. 435 (2001); Gary S. Moorefield, *Note: SPAM: It's Not Just for Breakfast Anymore: Federal Legislation and the Fight to Free the Internet from Unsolicited Commercial E-Mail*, 5 B.R. J. Sci. & Tech. L. 10 (Spring 1999); Max. P. Ochoa, *Case Note: Legislative Note: Recent State Laws Regulating Unsolicited Electronic Mail*, 16 Computer & High Tech L.J. 459 (May 2000).

3117 15 U.S.C. § 7001 *et seq. See* National Consumer Law Center, Consumer Banking and Payments Law (2d ed. 2002 and Supp.).

likely to overlook important legitimate e-mail messages. Spam can fill up the consumer's e-mail storage capacity and prevent the consumer from receiving legitimate messages. Worse yet, the consumer or the consumer's ISP may use a spam filtering program that over-screens, blocking legitimate messages along with the spam. There is particular danger if E-Sign or other statutes are interpreted to allow notices to be considered sent without proof that the consumer actually received and opened the message.

There is debate within the Internet community about whether spam ought to be regulated, and some favor technological solutions. These solutions are imperfect, however. Filtering programs can overscreen or underscreen, and spam senders usually devise ways to evade filtering systems. Technological solutions also carry costs that are passed on to consumers.

On January 1, 2004, the Controlling the Assault of Non-Solicited Pornography and Marketing Act of 2003 (CAN-SPAM) became effective.[3118] This federal legislation has been criticized by some for preempting more aggressive state laws that combat spam.[3119] CAN-SPAM prohibits misleading spam and requires that subject headings not be misleading to a reasonable recipient.[3120] In addition, spam must provide the valid postal address and actual e-mail address of the sender and spammers must honor recipients' requests not to receive further communications.[3121] Unfortunately, these requirements are widely ignored and are ill-considered in any event since a consumer must open, read, and respond to spam in order to opt out.

Despite the passage of CAN-SPAM, there has been no decrease in spam.[3122] Spammers continue to hide their identities and locations, and spam is increasingly originated overseas, thereby creating further enforcement problems.[3123] The FCC has rejected the idea of a do-not-spam list out of fear that the list itself would become a source of e-mail addresses that spammers could exploit.[3124] Enforcement of CAN-SPAM is made even more difficult by the fact that the statute does not permit an individual right of action. Instead, the statute must be enforced by various state and federal agencies or ISPs.[3125] The provisions of CAN-SPAM and other legal theories for suing spam senders are discussed below.

5.9.10.2 Legal Theories for Suing Spam Senders

5.9.10.2.1 Federal CAN-SPAM Act provides no private cause of action

CAN-SPAM, the federal response to the problem of spam, contains six important requirements concerning the content of unsolicited commercial e-mail. First, the use of false or misleading "header information" is prohibited.[3126] The use of deceptive subject headings is similarly prohibited.[3127] The third requirement CAN-SPAM imposes is that each message must contain a working electronic return address conspicuously displayed so that recipients can opt out of receiving further spam.[3128] This link must operate for 30 days from the transmission of the message. Fourth, it is unlawful for a spammer to continue sending unsolicited commercial e-mail to the recipient after ten days of receiving an opt-out request.[3129] Also, each message must provide the "valid physical postal address of the sender" and include a clear statement that it is an advertisement or solicitation and that the recipient has a right to not receive further spam from the sender.[3130] Lastly, CAN-SPAM requires that pornographic e-mails be identified as such in their subject headings if they are being sent without the prior consent of the recipient. Failure to provide this notice could result in up to five years imprisonment.[3131] The FTC has proposed rules to implement this provision and to define when a message is spam.[3132]

CAN-SPAM also seeks to outlaw the techniques used by spammers to saturate e-mail accounts. Section 7704(b)(1) makes it unlawful for spammers to harvest e-mail addresses with an automatic address finding program and to generate e-mail addresses alphabetically in what is known as a dictionary attack.[3133] That section also prohibits the creation of multiple e-mail accounts through automated means in order to transmit spam that is unlawful under section 7704(a).[3134]

Section 7705 is meant to aid the enforcement of CAN-SPAM. Instead of requiring that the originator of each

3118 15 U.S.C. § 7701, *et seq.*

3119 *See* Elizabeth A. Alongi, Note, *Has the U.S. Canned Spam?*, 46 Ariz. L. Rev. 263, 287–89 (2004); Andre R. Jaglom, *Internet, Distribution, E-Commerce and Other Computer Related Issues*, SJ075 ALI-ABA 505, 517–20 (2004). *But See* Glenn B. Manishin & Stephanie A. Joyce, *Overview of Current Spam Law and Policy*, 784 PLI/Pat 9, 15–16 (2004) (stating that far reaching federal preemption is an achievement of CAN-SPAM).

3120 15 U.S.C. § 7704(a)(1), (2).

3121 15 U.S.C. § 7704(a)(3)–(5).

3122 Elizabeth A. Alongi, Note, *Has the U.S. Canned Spam?*, 46 Ariz. L. Rev. 263, 288 (2004).

3123 *Id.*

3124 *Id. See also* Mary Kissel, FTC Says "Do Not E-mail List" Isn't Feasible, Wall St. J., June 16, 2004, at D12.

3125 15 U.S.C. § 7706. *See* Adam Zitter, Note, *Good Laws for Junk Fax? Government Regulation of Unsolicited Solicitations*, 72 Fordham L. Rev. 2767, 2789 (2004).

3126 15 U.S.C. § 7704(a)(1). Header information is defined by 15 U.S.C. § 7702 as the source, destination and routing information of an e-mail.

3127 15 U.S.C. § 7704(a)(2).

3128 15 U.S.C. § 7704(a)(3).

3129 15 U.S.C. § 7704(a)(4).

3130 15 U.S.C. § 7704(a)(5).

3131 15 U.S.C. § 7704(d).

3132 69 Fed. Reg. 50091 (Aug. 13, 2004).

3133 15 U.S.C. § 7704(b). *See* S. Rep. 108-102, 2004 U.S.C.C.A.N. 2348, 2363 (July 16, 2003).

3134 *Id.*

offending e-mail be found, companies who knowingly promote their business through prohibited spam are subject to the available remedies under the CAN-SPAM.[3135] This obviates the need to seek out the often hard to find spammer and allows those enforcing the act to "follow the money" to the company that is knowingly benefiting from spam.[3136]

CAN-SPAM is generally enforced by the FTC, but other agencies are responsible for enforcing its terms against organizations that fall under their jurisdiction.[3137] For example, violation of the by a securities broker would give the SEC the ability to bring an enforcement action.[3138] State attorneys general can also bring enforcement actions if they believe that a violation has caused harm to citizens of the state.[3139] ISPs are authorized to enforce CAN-SPAM by demonstrating that they have been "adversely affected" by a violation.[3140] There is no consumer right of action under CAN-SPAM.[3141]

In actions by states or ISPs, damages are generally limited to $1,000,000, but may be increased if a knowing or willful violation of CAN-SPAM is demonstrated.[3142] In addition, the prevailing party in a CAN-SPAM action may be awarded attorney fees at the court's discretion.[3143] In enforcement actions by the FTC or other commissions, the enforcement powers are described by the statute which governs that commission.[3144]

5.9.10.2.2 Telephone Consumer Protection Act

The Telephone Consumer Protection Act prohibits sending of unsolicited advertisements to a "telephone facsimile machine."[3145] "Telephone facsimile machine" is defined as "equipment which has the capacity . . . (B) to transcribe text or images (or both) from an electronic signal received over a regular telephone line onto paper."[3146] On its face, this definition appears to include e-mail messages that are transmitted over a telephone line to a computer that has the capacity to print the message. It might also include a computer that was not attached to a printer if it was able to save the message to disk for later printing.[3147] At least one court, however, has held that the Telephone Consumer Protection Act does not apply to unsolicited bulk e-mail.[3148]

If the Telephone Consumer Protection Act were interpreted to apply to spam, it would provide an attractive private cause of action for consumers. It provides for a private cause of action for $500, which is to be trebled if the violation was willful or knowing.[3149] There is no explicit requirement that the consumer show actual damages. At least one court has certified a class action under this statute.[3150] There are no reported cases dealing with the application of the Telephone Consumer Protection Act to unsolicited commercial e-mail.

5.9.10.2.3 Other federal laws

Some ISPs and commercial websites have successfully sued spam senders under two provisions of the federal criminal code: 18 U.S.C. § 2701, which prohibits unlawful access to stored communications, and 18 U.S.C. § 1030, which includes a prohibition against hacking into a computer.[3151] These cases involved spammers who harvested consumers' e-mail addresses from websites, contrary to the website's posted policy, or sent spam with a forged return address so that replies and bounced-back messages went to the ISP. These statutes are unlikely to apply in a consumer context. ISPs have also won trademark claims where spammers used the ISP's name in a counterfeit return address.[3152]

3135 15 U.S.C. § 7705. *See* S. Rep. 108-102, 2004 U.S.C.C.A.N. 2348, 2363.

3136 *See* S. Rep. 108-102, 2004 U.S.C.C.A.N. 2348, 2363.

3137 15 U.S.C. § 7706(a).

3138 15 U.S.C. § 7706(b)(3).

3139 15 U.S.C. § 7706(f).

3140 15 U.S.C. § 7706(g).

3141 *See* Elizabeth A. Alongi, Note, *Has the U.S. Canned Spam?*, 46 Ariz. L. Rev. 263, 288 (2004) (criticizing CAN-SPAM for pre-empting state laws which did include a private right of action).

3142 15 U.S.C. § 7706(f)(3)(B)–(C), (g)(3)(B)–(C).

3143 15 U.S.C. § 7706(f)(4), (g)(4).

3144 15 U.S.C. § 7706(c).

3145 47 U.S.C. § 227(b)(1)(C).

3146 47 U.S.C. § 227(a)(2).

3147 *See* David E. Sorkin, *Unsolicited Commercial E-Mail and the Telephone Consumer Protection Act of 1991*, 45 Buffalo L. Rev. 1001 (1997), posted at www.spamlaws.com (detailed analysis of statutory construction issues).

3148 Aronson v. Bright-Teeth Now, L.L.C., 824 A.2d 320 (Pa. Super. 2003) (unsolicited bulk e-mail does not place the same burdens on recipient as faxes; legislative history does not indicate that statute was intended to cover e-mail).

3149 47 U.S.C. § 227(b)(3).

3150 Hooters of Augusta, Inc. v. Nicholson, 245 Ga. App. 363, 537 S.E.2d 468 (2000). *But cf.* Kenro, Inc. v. Fax Daily, Inc., 962 F. Supp. 1162 (S.D. Ind. 1997) (determination of class membership would inappropriately require addressing the merits of the claim, particularly determining whether faxes were in fact unsolicited); Forman v. Data Transfer, Inc., 164 F.R.D. 400 (E.D. Pa. 1995) (same); Livingston v. U.S. Bank, N.A., 58 P.3d 1088 (Colo. App. 2002) (class certification denied because class not properly identified and individual issues predominate over common issues).

3151 *See* America Online v. LCGM, 46 F. Supp. 2d 444 (E.D. Va. 1998); Hotmail Corp. v. Van Money Pie Inc., 1998 U.S. Dist. LEXIS 10729 (N.D. Cal. Apr. 16, 1998) (granting preliminary injunction).

3152 Classified Ventures v. Softcell Marketing, Inc., 109 F. Supp. 2d 898 (N.D. Ill. 2000) (stipulated judgment); America Online, Inc. v. IMS, 24 F. Supp. 2d 548 (E.D. Va. 1998); America Online v. LCGM, 46 F. Supp. 2d 444 (E.D. Va. 1998); Hotmail Corp. v. Van Money Pie Inc., 1998 U.S. Dist. LEXIS 10729 (N.D. Cal. Apr. 16, 1998) (granting preliminary injunction).

5.9.10.2.4 State anti-spam laws

About thirty-six states have anti-spam laws.[3153] The substantive provisions of these laws vary. Some prohibit deception in headers—the routing information that accompanies an e-mail message—or subject lines. A few require the message to include a specific marker, such as "ADV," in the subject line, so that recipients can identify and screen out unsolicited commercial messages if they choose.

State anti-spam statutes have been upheld against challenges that they impermissibly regulate interstate commerce. In *State v. Heckel*, the Washington Supreme Court upheld the constitutionality of an anti-spam statute that prohibited deception in headers and subject lines.[3154] A California appellate decision upheld a similar prohibition against deception in spam.[3155] The court was particularly persuaded by the fact that the California statute applied only to spam that was delivered to California residents via an ISP's service or equipment located in the state.

Effective January 1, 2004, a federal law, the Controlling the Assault of Non-Solicited Pornography and Marketing Act of 2003 (CAN-SPAM), preempts much of the state law governing spam.[3156] CAN-SPAM preempts state law "that expressly regulates the use of electronic mail to send commercial messages," but does not supersede state laws which prohibit "falsity or deception in any portion of a commercial electronic mail message."[3157] Any state law requiring certain information to be incorporated into spam is now preempted.[3158] State laws requiring spammers to refrain from e-mailing users who have opted not to receive spam (opt-out laws) and/or to refrain from spamming until an e-mail user has opted to receive spam (opt-in laws) are superseded by CAN-SPAM.[3159] Also, CAN-SPAM preempts requirements that spammers place abbreviations such as "ADV" in subject headings to identify an e-mail as spam.[3160]

3153 *See* www.spamlaws.com (summary of state anti-spam laws and the new federal law).

3154 State v. Heckel, 24 P.3d 404 (Wash. 2001). There have been several successful small claims suits in Washington against companies sending deceptive spam. *See* http://news.com.com/2100-0123-868332.html.

3155 Ferguson v. Friendfinders, Inc., 94 Cal. App. 4th 1255, 115 Cal. Rptr. 2d 258 (2002).

3156 15 U.S.C. § 7707(b); 150 Cong. Rec. E72-02, E 73 (2004) (remarks of Rep. Dingell). *See* Andre R. Jalgom, *Internet, Distribution, E-Commerce and Other Computer Related Issues*, SJ075 ALI-ABA 505, 517–18 (2004).

3157 15 U.S.C. § 7707(b); 150 Cong. Rec. E72-02, E 73 (2004) (remarks of Rep. Dingell). *See* Andre R. Jaglom, *Internet, Distribution, E-Commerce and Other Computer Related Issues*, SJ075 ALI-ABA 505, 517–18 (2004) (explaining that laws such as Virginia's which criminalize the falsifying of header information in violation of an ISP's policy are undisturbed by CAN-SPAM).

3158 *Id.*

3159 *See* 150 Cong. Rec. E72-02, E73 (2004) (remarks of Rep. Dingell); Andre R. Jaglom, *Internet, Distribution, E-Commerce and Other Computer Related Issues*, SJ075 ALI-ABA 505, 517–18 (2004).

3160 *Id.*

The majority of anti-spam laws provide a special private cause of action, often including statutory damages such as $10 per message or a flat award of $500. Many of these also allow a prevailing plaintiff to recover costs and attorney fees. While these amounts are small, they could be very significant in a class action. Even in an individual action, many people will have received so many e-mail messages that the cumulative statutory damages could be significant. Although no court has decided the issue the private right of action provided by many state anti-spam laws may have survived CAN-SPAM to the extent that the substantive provision is not preempted.

Instead of creating a special cause of action, some anti-spam laws are amendments to the state UDAP statute, so a violation could be redressed under that statute.[3161] A few provide only criminal penalties, but a UDAP cause of action may still be available for violations, as in most states a violation of a consumer protection law is a *per se* UDAP violation.[3162] However, a state can not regulate the manner of sending commercial e-mail (as opposed to the deceptive content) simply by calling the regulation an anti-fraud law.[3163]

One significant potential problem is the question whether a recipient of spam must show an actual injury in order to recover statutory damages. Some anti-spam statutes, such as Colorado's and Nevada's, do not have an explicit requirement of actual damage, but others provide a private cause of action only for actual damages or only for a person who has been injured. Most UDAP statutes also require a showing of actual damage, and some specify an "ascertainable loss of money or property."[3164]

There should be no question that a person who falls for a fraudulent spam advertisement and pays out money has satisfied any injury requirement. A harder question is whether the simple receipt of spam is sufficient to support a claim. An FTC decision has held, over two dissents, that receipt of deceptive spam contrary to the privacy policy of the website from which addresses were harvested amounts to substantial consumer injury as required by the FTC's definition of unfairness.[3165] Consumers might also be able to draw some support from decisions holding that spammers committed trespass to chattels when their e-mails occupied an ISP's capacity due to the receipt of unwanted e-mail. These decisions recognize that there is some injury just from

3161 *See* Ferguson v. Friendfinders, Inc., 94 Cal. App. 4th 1255, 115 Cal. Rptr. 2d 258 (2002) (reversing dismissal of consumer's claims against spammer under state UDAP statutes).

3162 *See* § 3.2.7, *supra*.

3163 150 Cong. Rec. E72-02, E73 (2004) (remarks of Rep. Dingell).

3164 *See* § 7.5.2, *infra*.

3165 Register.com, Inc. v. Verio, Inc., 126 F. Supp. 2d 238 (S.D.N.Y. 2000); FTC v. Reverseauction.com, Inc., 5 Trade Reg. Rptr. (CCH) ¶ 24,688 (D.D.C. Jan. 6, 2000) (decision to accept consent decree).

the temporary reduction in a computer's capacity due to the receipt of unwanted e-mail. A consumer who pays for Internet access by the hour rather than on a flat monthly rate will probably be able to show some monetary loss due to receipt of spam. Businesses might also be able to show damage in the form of wages paid to employees whose time was wasted receiving and deleting unwanted e-mail messages.

The consumer who receives the unsolicited e-mail is not the only one injured by spam. If the spammer forges the return address or "header," an innocent third party may be inundated by bounce back messages and protest e-mails. The FTC's proceedings against spammers in these circumstances are authority that these acts are unfair and deceptive.[3166]

5.9.10.2.5 Other state law claims

ISPs have successfully asserted the ancient common law claim of trespass to chattels against spammers.[3167] Trespass to chattels is the use of a chattel without the consent or exceeding the consent of the owner, impairing use, value, or condition of the chattel.[3168] These cases have held that a spammer who temporarily intrudes on a computer electronically to harvest e-mail addresses, or temporarily takes up a part of the computer's capacity with spam messages, sufficiently impairs the chattel to support the cause of action. It is conceivable that a consumer could assert a trespass to chattels claim based on the temporary reduction in the computer's capacity due to receipt of spam. CAN-SPAM does not preempt state laws of general application that could be used to attack spammers, such as computer fraud laws, general purpose deceptive trade practices laws, or common law theories arising under trespass, contract or tort.[3169]

5.9.10.3 Practical Problems in Suing Spammers

The first practical problem in suing a spammer is finding the perpetrator. Spammers take great pains to conceal their actual identities and locations. Some people in the Internet community may have the ability to track down spammers.[3170] Established companies may also sometimes violate state anti-spam laws.

Collectability is also likely to be a problem in suits against spammers. But usually there are others involved in sending out the spam—software developers, credit card factors (intermediaries who help the spammer obtain credit card payments), address harvesters, spam-friendly ISPs. Some of these entities may be more collectable. A few state anti-spam statutes, such as Tennessee's and Rhode Island's, explicitly deal with certain aiders and abetters.[3171] In other states, the UDAP statute or standard tort law may extend liability to other entities that are involved in sending spam.[3172]

5.10 Future-Service Contracts: Health Spas, Dance Studios, Membership Campgrounds, Buying Clubs, and Trade Schools

5.10.1 Introduction

A future-service contract is an agreement by which a consumer commits to pay for services to be rendered over a period of time. Differing forms of future-service contracts may appear at first to have little to do with each other, e.g., vocational schools, buying clubs, health spas, and camp-

3166 Jessica Farrah Drees, File Nos. 022-3234 to -3237, -3077, -3302, 5 Trade Reg. Rep. (CCH) ¶ 15323 (Nov. 13, 2002).

3167 Register.com, Inc. v. Verio, Inc., 126 F. Supp. 2d 238 (S.D.N.Y. 2000) (intruding electronically into business's database to harvest e-mail addresses, without authorization, causes harm by reducing the system's capacity); America Online v. Nat'l Health Care Discount, Inc., 121 F. Supp. 2d 1255 (N.D. Iowa 2000); America Online, Inc. v. LCGM, Inc., 46 F. Supp. 2d 444 (E.D. Va. 1998); Hotmail Corp. v. Van Money Pie, Inc., 1998 U.S. Dist. LEXIS 10729 (N.D. Cal. Apr. 16, 1998); America Online, Inc. v. IMS, 24 F. Supp. 2d 548 (E.D. Va. 1998) (granting summary judgment against spammer on trespass to chattels and other claims); CompuServe, Inc. v. CyberPromotions, Inc., 962 F. Supp. 1015, 1022 (S.D. Ohio 1997) (issuing a preliminary injunction against spammer on theory of trespass to chattels). *See also* Verizon Online Servs., Inc. v. Ralsky, 203 F. Supp. 2d 601 (E.D. Va. 2002) (in trespass to chattel case, transmission of unsolicited bulk e-mail through plaintiff ISP by out-of-state defendant is sufficient minimum contacts to satisfy due process personal jurisdiction requirements); Internet Doorway, Inc. v. Parks, 138 F. Supp. 2d 773 (S.D. Miss. 2001) (in suit by ISP for trespass to chattel, personal jurisdiction proper over defendant who sent e-mail to state resident; active nature of e-mail satisfies minimum contact with state; tort occurred when state resident opened e-mail). *But see* Intel Corp. v. Hamidi 71 P.3d 296, 303–04 (Cal. 2003) (rejecting plaintiff's claim that defendant's spamming of its computer system constituted a trespass to chattels).

3168 Intel Corp. v. Hamidi, 94 Cal. App. 4th 325, 114 Cal. Rptr. 2d 244 (2001), *review granted, depublished*, 43 P.3d 587 (Cal. 2002).

3169 15 U.S.C. § 7707(b)(2); *See* 150 Cong. Rec. E72-02, E73 (2004) (remarks of Rep. Dingell); S. Rep. 108-102, 2004 U.S.C.C.A.N. 2348, 2365 (July 16, 2003).

3170 *See* "bounty hunter" suggestion at www.spamcon.org/articles/finances.

3171 *See* America Online Inc. v. Nat'l Health Care Discount, Inc., 121 F. Supp. 2d 1255 (N.D. Iowa 2000) (declining to grant summary judgment on issue whether merchant was liable for acts of spammer it hired). *But see* Seidl v. Greentree Mortg. Co., 30 F. Supp. 2d 1292 (D. Colo. 1998) (spammer was seller's independent contractor, so seller was not liable for harm caused by spammer's forged use of plaintiff's return address).

3172 *See* Ch. 6, *infra*.

ground resorts. But it is striking how similar the UDAP issues are in each of these contracts.

Unscrupulous future-service contract sellers develop a sophisticated and expensive sales presentation, involving commissioned salespersons, often working in relays, who exert extraordinary pressure to obtain the consumer's signature on a series of legal documents. Key to the sales pitch is the attempt to convince a consumer with limited resources to unalterably commit in advance *today* to a large payment for services stretching out into the future, services that the consumer does not presently even utilize.

Once the consumer signs, an unscrupulous future-service contract seller then makes it as difficult as possible for the consumer to cancel. The actual services may not be as represented, may be of little value, or may be of no benefit to the consumer. The seller, having devoted its resources to making the sale and making it difficult for the consumer to cancel, has little incentive to worry about the worth of its services.

This section organizes existing UDAP precedent concerning future-service contracts based upon specific types of services—health spas, dance studios, campground resort memberships, buying clubs, and trade schools. Nevertheless, much of the analysis for one type will apply to the others. The following common issues apply to most future-service contracts:

- Deceptive techniques to identify potential customers and to get the salesperson's foot in the door or attract the consumer to the seller's place of business.[3173]
- High-pressure or sophisticated sales techniques, almost forcing the consumer to sign up the day of the sales presentation.
- Misrepresentations as to the quality, worth, or nature of the service.
- Misrepresentations as to the consumer's cancellation rights.
- Deceptive techniques used to frustrate the consumer's legal right to cancel under state law and to discourage the consumer from formally canceling the contract.
- Huge penalties when the consumer tries to cancel, even if the cancellation is based on the consumer's health, inability to benefit from the service, or relocation.
- Problems when the future-service seller closes its business without refunding payments to consumers.

One remarkable feature of future-service companies is that unscrupulous sellers are always on the lookout for new types of future-service schemes—ones where consumers can be pressured into committing large sums of money for a service they have never previously needed and do not fully understand, but which they will not feel able to cancel once the deception becomes apparent. Early FTC activity focused on dance studios, then turned to vocational school issues in the 1970s. Health spa problems appeared somewhat later, then problems with campground membership resorts. Whatever type of future-service scheme that unscrupulous sellers turn to next, UDAP attorneys should rely on precedent dealing with prior forms of future-service contract abuse.

Many states have statutes that provide consumer protections for specific types of future-service contracts. Ohio is one of the few states to deal systematically with all future-service contracts. The Ohio Prepaid Entertainment Contract Act applies broadly to dance studios, dating services, martial arts training, health spas, and weight reduction clinics.[3174] A Florida UDAP regulation applies generally to contracts for future consumer services and creates a three-day right to cancel.[3175]

5.10.2 Cancellation of Future-Service Contracts

5.10.2.1 The Seller's Contract Provision

Critical to any future-service contract scam is making it difficult for a consumer to obtain a refund after canceling. The investment in expensive selling techniques will not pay off if consumers can rethink the transaction in the quiet of their own homes and then back out of the deal. Consequently, any future-service scheme will have an elaborate system whereby the consumer forfeits all or much of the contract obligation even if the consumer cancels before few, if any, services are provided.

A multi-step analysis is necessary to evaluate a consumer's right to cancel a future-service contract and receive a full or significant refund. The first step is to determine the consumer's contractual rights to cancel. The contract may specify a particular method of cancellation, and the consumer should usually follow that procedure carefully, making sure documentation is retained as to the date of the consumer's cancellation. (If the consumer is also claiming a statutory right to cancel the contract, as discussed in the following section, the cancellation letter should make it clear that the consumer is exercising both rights in the alternative.) The contract will also specify a formula to calculate the consumer's refund or the contract may specify that the contract is not cancelable. The contract may also specify a three-day or other cancellation period.

3173 See the detailed description of these techniques in the context of membership campground sales at § 5.10.5, *infra*.

3174 Ohio Rev. Code § 1345.41 *et seq. See* Williams, Ohio Consumer Law, Ch. 4 (2002 ed.) for an analysis of this law; *see also* Widlar v. Matchmaker Int'l, 2002 WL 1303218 (Ohio App. June 7, 2002) (interpreting cancellation deadline).

3175 Fla. Admin. Code R. 2-18.002.

5.10.2.2 State Statutes May Override Contractual Cancellation Provision

The next step is to determine if the contractual cancellation provision complies with state law. Many states have enacted legislation covering health spas, vocational schools, or other future services. These state laws will specify minimum refund formulas or cooling-off periods. A three-day cooling-off period will generally also apply if the sale was not at the seller's principal place of business.[3176] If the contract was sold through telephone solicitation, the consumer's advocate should also check whether a state telemarketing law provides a right to cancel.[3177]

If there is a three-day cooling-off period, pay special attention to attempts to obfuscate or defeat this right, such as misdating or leaving blanks in contracts or cancellation right notices or orally misrepresenting a consumer's right to cancel within three days. There may be a resulting continual right to cancel.[3178]

5.10.2.3 Contract Law Defenses May Provide Additional Protections

The next step is to determine as a matter of state contract law what the consumer's rights and obligations are if the consumer stops paying the note, effectively breaching the contract. There are several contract law issues as to whether the seller may sue on the note for the full amount (in the case of a non-cancelable contract) or for some lesser amount specified by the contract (in the contract's refund provision). One of the contract law issues is whether the seller's cancellation provision is an enforceable liquidated damages clause or an unenforceable penalty clause. Generally, a court will enforce a liquidated damages clause only if it is in an amount that is a reasonable estimate, as of the time the contract is entered into, of the seller's anticipated damages from the breach.[3179] At least in some jurisdictions, a liquidated damages clause is also only enforceable if the amount of actual damages is difficult to ascertain.[3180] Another contract issue is whether the seller has a duty to mitigate its damages by reselling the membership or otherwise arranging its program to minimize its losses due to the consumer's cancellation.

A seller's actual damages upon a consumer's cancellation of a future-service contract can be quite complicated, depending on whether a limited amount of memberships are available, whether there is a strict time schedule for the provision of the services, whether there are marginal costs to the seller each time the consumer uses the services, and how easy it is to resell the consumer's membership. Consumers should structure the litigation so that the burden is on the seller to prove its damages.

Another potential contract law defense in future-service contract cases is whether there is an anticipatory breach of the contract by the seller. That is, the future-service company may be run so that its demise is imminent. The future-service company fails to build up the reserves of capital necessary to fulfill the promise of future services. Often a future-service contract scheme resembles a pyramid sale or Ponzi scheme where each new member's payment goes to expensive current marketing activities and to supply promised services to existing members. At some point, the whole company will fall like a house of cards because it reaches the capacity of its membership or market and can not obtain additional new contract payments to fulfill past obligations.[3181] Where consumers use this anticipatory breach theory and have alleged that the future-service seller is so financially insecure as to soon be out of business, consumers' attorneys report excellent settlement results. Future-service contract companies tend to avoid trials in order to maintain the secrecy that surrounds their financial information. Additional contract law approaches involve allegations of fraud, misrepresentation, mistake, impossibility, and duress as grounds to rescind the contract or as defenses to a contract action.[3182]

5.10.2.4 UDAP Approaches

Another approach in a future-service contract cancellation case is to argue that UDAP principles allow the consumer's cancellation with a full or large refund since the seller should be limited to no more than actual lost profits as damages. There is little case law in this area, but FTC cases find unfair the mere inclusion of forfeiture clauses in adhesion contracts. In particular, it is unfair to utilize a contract provision whereby, upon default, the consumer forfeits all payments made in a land sale, and receives no title to the land.[3183]

In addition, these facts fit nicely into the FTC's three-part unfairness analysis.[3184] The FTC's Statement of Basis and Purpose for its Credit Practices Rule is excellent authority for the fact that consumers can not reasonably avoid provisions in standard form contracts dealing with the seller's default remedies. One part of the FTC's unfairness test has thus been met. The second part is also met because harsh cancellation provisions cause consumers significant injury, not only the loss of money to those who cancel, but also to others who would cancel with a different refund formula.[3185]

3176 *See* § 5.8.2.3, *supra*.

3177 *See* § 5.9.2.5, *supra*.

3178 *See* § 5.8.2.6.3, *supra*.

3179 11 Corbin on Contracts § 1059 (interim ed. 2002).

3180 *Id.* at § 1060.

3181 *See* § 5.10.3.3, *infra*.

3182 *See* § 9.5, *infra*.

3183 *See* § 5.2.3, *supra*.

3184 *See* § 4.3.2, *supra*.

3185 The FTC made this argument in the Statement of Basis and

Consequently, the determination that a non-cancelable future-service contract is unfair depends on the third part of the FTC's unfairness test, whether the injury to consumers is outweighed by the benefits to consumers and competition. This is a factual question that will depend on the nature of each type of future-service contract and cancellation formula.

Many state UDAP statutes also prohibit unconscionability.[3186] There is substantial authority that penalty clauses and excessive liquidated damage clauses are unconscionable.[3187]

If the seller has assigned the note or arranged financing through a separate creditor, the consumer should still be able to raise UDAP and other law violations both affirmatively and defensively against the creditor. This issue is discussed in another section.[3188]

5.10.3 Health Spas

5.10.3.1 FTC Rulemaking Proceeding, State Statutes

Health spas appeal to consumers' desires for physical fitness and attractive bodies. Some use free trials and exaggerated claims to lure consumers into high-pressure sales presentations. Consumers are often signed under intense sales pressure before they can reflect upon the appropriateness of the program for them or their ability to make the necessary financial, time, and physical commitment.

The FTC proposed a Trade Regulation Rule Concerning Health Spas[3189] but, in 1986, terminated the rule proceeding[3190] based on a staff finding that the rulemaking record was stale (the presiding officer had issued his report in 1979) and that there was insufficient evidence that the reported abuses were prevalent throughout the industry. The report singled out the chain of European Health Spas as the cause of a substantial number of the complaints on the record.[3191] Nevertheless, the rulemaking proceeding did result in two reports—a presiding officer's report[3192] and a staff report[3193]—that practitioners may find helpful in health spa cases.

State health spa laws take on new importance in light of the termination of the FTC proceeding. A majority of states have enacted such legislation.[3194] These laws uniformly provide for a cooling-off period. Most of these laws also require health spas to be bonded[3195] or to escrow certain receipts and limit the length of health spa contracts (usually to three years).[3196] Several statutes also make the health club contract unenforceable against the consumer where an op-

Purpose of the Credit Practices Rule that harsh creditor remedies affect not only those victimized by the remedy but those who do not default. *See* 49 Fed. Reg. 7744 (Mar. 1, 1984).

3186 *See* § 4.4, *supra*.

3187 *See* § 4.4.9.2, *supra*.

3188 *See* § 6.6, *infra*.

3189 F.T.C. Pub. Rcd. No. 215-50.

3190 51 Fed. Reg. 14856 (Apr. 21, 1986).

3191 FTC Bureau of Consumer Protection, Health Spas Final Staff Report, Clearinghouse No. 38,915 (Dec. 1984).

3192 Clearinghouse No. 31,042A.

3193 Clearinghouse No. 31,042B.

3194 Ala. Code §§ 8-23-1 to 8-23-13; Ariz. Rev. Stat. §§ 44-1791 to 44-1796; Ark. Code Ann. §§ 4-94-101 to 4-94-109; Cal. Civ. Code §§ 1812.80 to 1812.95; Colo. Rev. Stat. § 6-1-704; Conn. Gen. Stat. §§ 21a-216 to 21a-227; D.C. Code § 28-3817; Del. Code Ann. tit. 6, §§ 4201 to 4222; Fla. Stat. §§ 501.012 to 501.019; Ga. Code Ann. § 10-1-393.2; Haw. Rev. Stat. ch. 486N-1 to 486N-11; 815 Ill. Comp. Stat. §§ 645/1 to 645/14; Ind. Code §§ 24-5-7-1 to 24-5-7-18; Iowa Code §§ 552.1 to 552.22; Ky. Rev. Stat. Ann. §§ 367.900 to 367.930; La. Rev. Stat. Ann. §§ 51:1575 to 51:1582; Mass. Gen. Laws ch. 93, §§ 78 to 88; Md. Com. Law. Code Ann. §§ 14-12B-01 to 14-12B-08; Minn. Stat. §§ 325G.23 to 325G.28; Miss. Code Ann. §§ 75-83-1 to 75-83-15; Mo. Rev. Stat. §§ 407.325 to 407.340; Mo. Code of State Rules 60-6; Nev. Rev. Stat. §§ 598.940 to 598.966; N.H. Rev. Stat. Ann. §§ 358-I:1 to 358-I:10; N.J. Rev. Stat. §§ 56:8-39 to 56:8-48; N.Y. Gen Bus. Law §§ 620 to 631; N.C. Gen. Stat. §§ 66-118 to 66-125 (applies to all "prepaid entertainment contracts"); Ohio Rev. Code Ann. §§ 1345.41 to 1345.50 (applies to all "prepaid entertainment contracts"); Okla. Stat. tit. 59, §§ 2000 to 2012; Or. Rev. Stat. §§ 646.661 to 646.691; 73 Pa. Cons. Stat. §§ 2161 to 2177; R.I. Gen. Laws §§ 5-50-1 to 5-50-11; S.C. Code Ann. §§ 44-79-10 to 44-79-120; S.D. Codified Laws §§ 37-26-1 to 37-26-11 (broadly defining "buying club" such that it may include health spas); Tenn. Code Ann. §§ 47-18-301 to 47-18-320; Tex. Occupations Code §§ 702.001 to .558; Utah Code Ann. §§ 13-23-1 to 13-23-7; Va. Code Ann. §§ 59.1-294 to 59.1-310; Wash. Rev. Code §§ 19.142.010 to 19.142.901; 142 Code of W. Va. Regs. § 13, Health Spas; Wis. Stat. §§ 100.177 and .178.

See Consumer Law-Health Spa Services Act, 17 Ind. L. Rev. 422 (1984) for a discussion of the Indiana Law; Williams, Ohio Consumer Law, Ch. 4 (2002 ed.) for an analysis of Ohio's law; legal memorandum from Tennessee Attorney General to John Neff, Commissioner of Tennessee Dep't of Commerce and Ins., regarding administration of health club statute, Clearinghouse No. 38,914 (Jan. 15, 1985); *Health Club Liability*, 79 A.L.R.4th 127. *See also* Melino v. Equinox Fitness Club, 2004 WL 635793 (N.Y. App. Div. Apr. 1, 2004) (consumer who never sought to cancel does not have standing to challenge contract's failure to include cancellation rights mandated by statute); DeRiso v. Synergy USA, 773 N.Y.S.2d 563 (App. Div. 2004) (same); Sokoloff v. Town Sports Int'l, Inc., 2004 WL 636253 (N.Y. App. Div. Apr. 1, 2004) (clauses prohibited by statute do not give rise to private cause of action unless plaintiff suffered injury); People v. 21st Century Leisure Spa, 153 Misc. 2d 938, 583 N.Y.S.2d 726 (Sup. Ct. 1991) (bonding and refund requirements applied to defunct corporation and its president).

3195 Where deceptive practices have been shown, the FTC has also issued orders requiring health spas to obtain performance bonds before accepting advance payments. *See* Lady Venus Centers, Inc., 3 Trade Reg. Rep. (CCH) ¶ 22,126 (F.T.C. File No. 812 3134 Feb. 23, 1984) (consent order).

3196 *See* Nadoff v. Club Central, 2003 WL 21537405 (N.Y. Dist. Ct. June 27, 2003) (one-year health spa contract violated prohibition against contracts longer than three years where it ran for 38 months because of automatic month-to-month renewal clause).

erator fails to comply with the health spa statute or uses misleading information to induce the consumer to sign the agreement.[3197] The Tennessee Supreme Court and a Minnesota appellate court have upheld the constitutionality of their state health spa statutes.[3198]

The scope of state health spa statutes varies from state to state. Advocates dealing with such enterprises as weight loss clinics, martial arts studios, tanning salons, and racquet clubs should analyze their state health spa statute carefully to determine whether it might afford a right to cancel or other protections.[3199] Nevertheless, an Ohio court rejected a buyer's argument that the health spa cooling-off period should apply to a contract for membership in a campground that made health club facilities available.[3200]

5.10.3.2 UDAP Precedent

UDAP statutes are also well-suited to handling health spa issues. The following spa practices may be unfair or deceptive:

- Claiming that a contract can not be canceled or can only be canceled after paying an unreasonably high penalty;[3201]
- Refusing to honor the consumer's cancellation pursuant to the health spa's cooling-off period[3202] or failing to disclose the consumer's right to cancel;[3203]
- Selling a membership to a consumer not physically qualified to participate in the spa's activities;
- Misrepresenting the nature and extent of a binding contract, such as misrepresenting a binding contract as a membership application or a guest register;
- Closing or not offering the full range of facilities and services promised without offering a refund;[3204]
- Using coercive sales tactics, including obscenities, humiliation, fear, and even force to enroll a consumer;[3205]
- Charging some health spa customers significantly more than the normal membership fee;[3206]
- Advertising "two memberships for the price of one" without conspicuously disclosing the terms and conditions of the offer;[3207]
- Misrepresenting the results possible from participation in spa programs, in particular concerning weight reduction or figure-shaping,[3208] health improvement,[3209] or other benefits from the program.[3210]

Violation of the specific requirements of a state health spa statute may also be a UDAP violation.[3211]

The FTC has accepted a number of consent orders against health spas that misrepresent special membership prices,[3212]

3197 Del. Code Ann. tit. 6, §§ 4211 and 4212; Ga. Code § 10-1-393.2; Iowa Code § 552.3; Mass. Gen. Laws ch. 93, § 85; Tenn. Code Ann. § 47-18-303. *See* Georgia Receivables, Inc. v. Welch, 242 Ga. App. 146, 529 S.E.2d 164 (2000) (contract void and unenforceable because cancellation notice was not in three separate paragraphs, was sandwiched in between other unrelated sentences, did not have last date for cancellation filled in, and misstated cancellation period); Georgia Receivables, Inc. v. Kirk, 242 Ga. App. 801, 531 S.E.2d 393 (2000) (noncomplying contract void); Georgia Receivables, Inc. v. Te, 240 Ga. App. 292, 523 S.E.2d 352 (1999) (non-complying health spa contracts are unenforceable even if defendant does not raise this defense); Nadoff v. Club Central, 2003 WL 21537405 (N.Y. Dist. Ct. June 27, 2003) (granting restitution of fees paid where health spa statute made contract void and unenforceable). *But cf.* State v. Thompson, 2003 WL 1442414 (Tenn. Ct. App. Mar. 20, 2003) (unpublished, citation limited) (affirming denial of AG's request for restitution for period health club was unlicensed, because no consumers claimed any ascertainable loss).

3198 State *ex rel.* Humphrey v. Ri-Mel, Inc., 417 N.W.2d 102 (Minn. Ct. App. 1987); State v. Southern Fitness and Health, Inc., 743 S.W.2d 160 (Tenn. 1987).

3199 *See, e.g.*, Brownridge Institute of Karate, Inc. v. Dorris, 162 Ill. App. 3d 483, 515 N.E.2d 373 (1987) (Illinois Physical Fitness Services Act applies to karate school). *But see* Louisiana Op. Att'y Gen. 95-353 (1995) (a martial arts school which provides structured instructional classes is not a Physical Fitness Center as defined by the Physical Fitness Services Act); Commonwealth by Fisher v. Tiger Schulmann's Karate Centers, 812 A.2d 614 (Pa. 2002) (karate center is not a "physical culture service enterprise" governed by state health spa law).

3200 Kovach v. Erie Islands Resort & Marina, Inc., 93 Ohio App. 3d 11, 637 N.E.2d 382 (1994).

3201 Contract clauses that require the consumer to forfeit more than the spa's reasonable damages are unenforceable penalty clauses. *See* § 5.10.2.3, *supra*.

3202 Silhouette Nat'l Health Spas, Inc., 84 F.T.C. 323 (1974) (consent order); Our Fair Lady Health Resort v. Miller, 564 S.W.2d 410 (Tex. Civ. App. 1970).

3203 Universal Figure Form of Youngstown, Inc., 81 F.T.C. 785 (1972) (consent order); Holiday Universal, Inc., 78 F.T.C. 187 (1971) (consent order); Little v. Paco Collection Servs., 156 Ga. App. 175, 274 S.E.2d 147 (1980).

3204 *See, e.g.*, Lady Venus Centers, Inc., 3 Trade Reg. Rep. (CCH) ¶ 22,126 (F.T.C. File No. 812 3134 Feb. 23, 1984) (consent order).

3205 *See* W. Va. Code St. Regs. § 142-13-7.1, Health Spas.

3206 See id.

3207 Mid-America Acceptance Co. v. Lightle, 63 Ohio App. 3d 590, 579 N.E.2d 721 (1989).

3208 Ronnie Ray, 84 F.T.C. 1238 (1974) (consent order); Silhouette Nat'l Health Spas, Inc., 84 F.T.C. 323 (1974) (consent order); Holiday Universal, Inc., 78 F.T.C. 187 (1971).

3209 Plaza Club, Inc., 80 F.T.C. 62 (1972) (consent order); Holiday Universal, Inc., 78 F.T.C. 187 (1971) (consent order).

3210 Nutritone, Inc., 112 F.T.C. 179 (1989) (consent order); Gloria Stevens, Inc., 84 F.T.C. 438 (1974) (consent order); Jack LaLanne Mgmt. Corp., 84 F.T.C. 1139 (1974) (consent order); Holiday Universal, Inc., 78 F.T.C. 187 (1971) (consent order).

3211 Mid-America Acceptance Co. v. Lightle, 63 Ohio App. 3d 590, 579 N.E.2d 721 (1989); *see also* § 3.2.7, *supra*.

3212 Gloria Stevens, Inc., 84 F.T.C. 438 (1974) (consent order); Jack LaLanne Mgmt. Corp., 84 F.T.C. 1139 (1974) (consent order); Plaza Club, Inc., 80 F.T.C. 62 (1972) (consent order); Universal Figure Form of Youngstown, Inc., 81 F.T.C. 785 (1972) (consent order); Holiday Universal, Inc., 78 F.T.C. 187 (1971) (consent order).

the nature of limited memberships,[3213] or the availability of facilities.[3214] Spas must allow applicants to consult with a physician before joining[3215] and must disclose health hazards of treatment.[3216] Spas can not use deceptive before-and-after photographs.[3217]

5.10.3.3 When a Spa Closes Down

An earlier subsection[3218] detailed state laws that create bonding and escrow requirements for health spas. These protections will provide at least minimum protection when a spa closes.

A decision by a bankruptcy court is of special interest to consumers who purchase health spa memberships shortly before a health spa goes into bankruptcy. The court ruled that it was deceptive and fraudulent for a spa to continue selling memberships after it was insolvent.[3219] Those memberships were sold based on the false "implied representation that the spa intended to and had the financial ability to provide the benefits of membership throughout the term of the agreements."[3220] This reckless disregard by the spa was found to constitute fraud within the meaning of the Bankruptcy Act, preventing the consumers' claims from being discharged in bankruptcy. Furthermore, because the corporate veil was pierced, the individual owner was personably liable for these nondischargeable debts. If a spa closes down and has not escrowed the money necessary for refunds, it may also be helpful to determine if there is a licensor or parent corporation that may be liable.[3221]

A Maryland case found it a UDAP violation for a spa to close without providing members with refunds and ordered refunds for all members.[3222] New York courts have also found fraudulent a health spa's closing without notice, not allowing members to recover their possessions, not paying owed refunds, and continuing to solicit business even though the spa knew it would close.[3223] A court has found, however, that a company that bought a health spa's assets, subject to existing memberships, at a bankruptcy sale, did not violate the state's UDAP statute by increasing the fees for existing members.[3224]

5.10.4 Dance Studios

Dance studios have been challenged for engaging in unusually abusive sales practices, such as using high-pressure sales, flattery, and sham tests to sign up an elderly widow for a $18,000 dance lesson contract, then trying to switch her to a $49,000 contract, and, upon failing, discouraging her from attending the remaining lessons.[3225] Other high-pressure sales have also been found unfair or deceptive.[3226] Also deceptive are misrepresentations that lessons are free or at reduced prices,[3227] misrepresentations concerning terms and conditions,[3228] and encouraging applicants to sign incomplete contracts.[3229]

5.10.5 Campground Resort Memberships[3230]

5.10.5.1 A Case Study of Abusive Sales Techniques

Too often in the campground membership resort business, consumers are subjected to two-hour sales pitches and are pressured into making—and financing—a major purchase in the course of one afternoon. They later discover that their memberships offer them little of what was promised and that the resort has developed sophisticated techniques to discourage cancellation. This subsection describes the type of problems reported by attorneys representing consumers in

3213 International Servs. Indus., 84 F.T.C. 408 (1974) (consent order); Universal Figure Form of Youngstown, Inc., 81 F.T.C. 785 (1972) (consent order).

3214 Lady Venus Centers, Inc., 3 Trade Reg. Rep. (CCH) ¶ 22,126 (F.T.C. File No. 812 3134 Feb. 23, 1984) (consent order); Jack LaLanne Mgmt. Corp., 84 F.T.C. 1139 (1974) (consent order); Silhouette Nat'l Health Spas, Inc., 84 F.T.C. 323 (1974) (consent order); Plaza Club, Inc., 80 F.T.C. 62 (1972) (consent order); Holiday Universal, Inc., 78 F.T.C. 187 (1971) (consent order).

3215 Gloria Stevens, Inc., 84 F.T.C. 438 (1974) (consent order).

3216 Baton Rouge Athletic Club & Health Spa, Inc., 83 F.T.C. 1316 (1974) (consent order).

3217 Universal Figure Form of Youngstown, Inc., 81 F.T.C. 785 (1972) (consent order); Holiday Universal, Inc., 78 F.T.C. 187 (1971) (consent order).

3218 § 5.10.3.1 *supra*.

3219 Kelley v. Sclater (*In re* Sclater), 40 B.R. 594 (E.D. Mich. 1984). *Accord* Lady Venus Centers, Inc., 3 Trade Reg. Rep. (CCH) ¶ 22,126 (F.T.C. File No. 812 3134 Feb. 23, 1984) (consent order).

3220 Kelley v. Sclater (*In re* Sclater), 40 B.R. 594, 601 (E.D. Mich. 1984).

3221 *See, e.g.*, Stuppy v. World Gym Int'l, Inc., 2003 WL 886724 (Cal. App. Mar. 7, 2003) (unpublished, citation limited).

3222 State v. Andrews, 73 Md. App. 80, 533 A.3d 282 (1987).

3223 People *ex rel.* Abrams v. Apple Health & Sports Clubs, Ltd., 206 A.D.2d 266, 613 N.Y.S.2d 868 (1994); People v. 21st Century Leisure Spa, 153 Misc. 2d 938, 583 N.Y.S.2d 726 (Sup. Ct. 1991); Lady Venus Centers, Inc., 3 Trade Reg. Rep. (CCH) ¶ 22,126 (F.T.C. File No. 812 3134 Feb. 23, 1984) (consent order).

3224 Chatham Racquet Club v. Commonwealth *ex rel.* Zimmerman, 561 A.2d 354 (Pa. Commw. Ct. 1989).

3225 Bennett v. Bailey, 597 S.W.2d 532 (Tex. Civ. App. 1980). *See also* Brown v. Silzar, 1981 Ohio App. LEXIS 13616 (Feb. 28, 1981) (bait and switch tactics, concealment of right to cancel).

3226 Arthur Murray Studio, 78 F.T.C. 401 (1971).

3227 Arthur Murray Studio, 78 F.T.C. 401 (1971); Fred Astaire Dance Studio, 64 F.T.C. 1295 (1964).

3228 Dance World, Inc., 83 F.T.C. 1430 (1974) (consent order).

3229 Fred Astaire Dance Studio, 64 F.T.C. 1295 (1964).

3230 Much of this subsection is based on materials submitted by Helen Kendrick, a private attorney in Bucyrus, Ohio.

this area. Although some details are unique to campground sales, the general approach is common to many high-pressure sellers.

Typically, resorts solicit buyers through letters that promise that the consumer has been specially selected to win a prize from a group of prizes including at least one high-priced item, such as an automobile. The letter further informs the consumer that receipt of the prize is conditioned on various "company eligibility rules" and that, in order to claim their prize, husband and wife must telephone to schedule an appointment at the resort. The resort does not divulge the price over the telephone but just gathers employment, credit and other information, and schedules an appointment at the resort.

When the couple arrives at the resort, a receptionist requests that they show their driver's licenses and a major bank credit card to prove their identities entitling them to their prize. They are directed to a waiting area decorated with photographs of resort members and other resorts around the country, industry awards given to the resort management, and renderings of future improvements to be made at the resort.

Shortly thereafter, a "tour guide" greets the couple and congratulates them on their being selected for a prize, and tells them that he or she is able to give them a "lifetime of vacations," for a reduced price, but only on that day. Removing a preprinted form from a folder, he or she asks the couple about their hobbies, commenting about how the resort could meet their interests. The tour guide then takes the couple in his or her car on a tour of the resort.

The tour is not limited to existing facilities. Locations of future improvements, such as indoor swimming pools and community rooms, are also pointed out. The threesome then returns to the resort office, where the tour guide shows them photographs of affiliated resorts, with emphasis given to those located near major tourist attractions, such as Disney World, and tells them that their membership privileges allow them to camp at any of these resorts for a mere $1.00 per night.

Once the couple shows interest in the facilities, the tour guide addresses the issue of cost by making comparisons with the cost of other forms of vacations, asking the couple to suggest alternative vacation approaches. On a preprinted form, which is divided into several sections, the tour guide writes down costs of the different vacation options selected, such as ownership of a vacation house (complete with utility costs, insurance, and tax assessments); timesharing (with the usual understanding that such arrangements are seldom available when needed); or ten years of two-week vacations during which the family stays at motels and eats all meals at restaurants. These options are contrasted against the benefits and costs of the resort membership being offered to the consumers—this one day only. Typically, the consumers are then asked what they believe a resort membership, with all the benefits shown and promised, would cost. The couple then looks at the total costs of the other options which they themselves suggested, costs which usually range from ten to fifty thousand dollars. When they demur, the tour guide then launches into an explanation of the various types of memberships available to them that day only.

The "basic" rate, he or she explains, is (for example) only $4995. A basic membership can not be transferred by the original purchaser, nor can it be "willed" to the purchaser's children. It does not include membership in the nationwide network (which is an additional $295). The basic membership is available to people who have not been specifically selected, or who have failed to purchase a membership on their first visit.

However, the tour guide informs the lucky couple, because they were specially selected, they are eligible for the "preferred," "founders," or "charter" membership, which has many more benefits than the basic and costs substantially less. This type of membership, which includes automatic free membership in the nationwide network, can be transferred three times *upon approval by resort management* and can be "willed" for additional generations. What a splendid gift for their children, the couple is told. Besides, when the resort began to sell memberships one year ago, the basic membership price was only $2995, but with the improvements which have been and will soon be made, the costs of new memberships will increase, the next increase in just a few weeks. And if the couple decides to sell their preferred membership, the resort has people ready to help them, for a small fee. The couple is told that they must make their decision today and that once they leave the resort grounds, the charter membership rates are no longer available to them.

If the couple agrees to purchase a membership at this point, the tour guide brings out several papers from his or her notebook. Among those papers is an agreement to purchase the preferred membership, which the couple then signs. The tour guide announces the sale to the others in the sales room, with resulting fanfare, such as the ringing of bells and the taking of a Polaroid photo of the consumers, which is posted in the sales room.

Then the couple is told to sign a preprinted form containing various declarations, usually including statements that they were not high-pressured into purchasing the membership, that they agree that the purchase contract can not be canceled, that they agree that there is no "cooling-off period," that they agree they were not told that a membership was an investment, and that they agree to abide by the rules and regulations of the resort, both present and future. Other resort officials witness the consumers' initialing of this document. By the time the couple signs this form, they have received nothing which tells them, in writing, the actual benefits provided by the membership.

The tour guide then disappears into the office, from which he and another individual emerge, clutching at least a dozen additional documents. This second individual, identified as the couple's "financial advisor," but referred to in the business as a "T.O." for take-over, assumes responsibility for the remainder of the sale. Only at this point are the couple's actual finances and ability to pay discussed with them. An arrangement can be worked out for anyone who wants a membership, the couple is told. Even down payments can be deferred or they might qualify for certain discounts offered to a limited number of individuals. And the total membership price, or even a down payment, can be charged on their bank credit card. Counter checks and promissory notes are available for those purchasers who left their wallets or checkbooks at home.

The couple soon agrees to make a particular down payment and further agrees to make monthly installment payments of an amount negotiated by their financial advisor. The resort is affiliated with a local bank or a chain of resorts, explains the T.O., who has agreed to allow the members to finance their purchase by filling out the forms at the resort that very day. However, just in case the bank rejects their application for a loan, the resort tells the consumers that they will not be denied their membership; the resort will finance it. In order to accomplish all this, without requiring the couple to make a return visit, the T.O. has them sign a credit application for the bank as well as two installment notes, each for the entire sale price, with one note identifying the creditor as the bank, the other identifying the creditor as the resort.

The T.O. then presents the couple with a certificate of membership in the resort, past issues of the resort newsletter, a membership agreement, the resort rule book, the application for membership in the nationwide program, terms and conditions of membership, a security agreement listing the membership as collateral, the trailer rental program rules, a list of coming events for the next month, a temporary membership card and a decal. The T.O. points to several places on some of the documents which require the members' signatures. After signing where they are told, the new members are congratulated on their wise purchase and are escorted to the prize room where the clerk, after reading the numbers on the solicitation letter, hands them their prize, congratulating them on their good fortune. The couple leaves the resort after a three-hour stay.

On the way home from the resort, the new members for the first time begin to read the papers they signed at the resort. They are shocked to discover that the papers they signed do not say what the tour guide told them. When they arrive home, they telephone the resort, only to be told that they have signed a legal contract, that if they read the rules, they would see that their down payment is nonrefundable, and that if they try to stop payment on their check, they will be committing a crime.

The couple, feeling ashamed and foolish, allow their check to clear and make a few monthly payments. They soon become very angry over the situation, particularly since they have not attempted to use the resort facilities. They write a letter to the resort to cancel the membership and then stop making payments. The resort sends them a few form letters requesting payment, threatening legal action such as garnishment of wages, and directing the consumers to read their contracts, which they signed admitting they had not been pressured into joining. After ignoring these letters, the consumers get a letter from an attorney's office, telling them they owe the resort the entire balance of the installment note. Their next stop is your office.

At the initial interview, the attorney must recognize that the consumers view themselves as stupid, gullible individuals. They may be reluctant to review their visit to the resort. Knowing the probable sales scenario may make it easier to obtain the necessary information from them.

5.10.5.2 Potential Campground Membership Resort UDAP Violations

Campground membership clients typically arrive at the lawyer's office with a manila envelope full of documents that on their face contain numerous UDAP and other law violations. The first document to review is the campground's mail solicitation, which may contain several common UDAP violations.

- Prize offers often fail to comply with UDAP rules concerning such solicitations.[3231] These solicitations are often deceitful, incomplete and manipulative. Consumers are not informed of the value of the prize and the chances of winning it,[3232] the identity of the party who mass mailed the solicitations[3233] or the fact that they were not "specially selected" as the solicitation indicates.[3234]

3231 Consumer Protection Div. v. Outdoor World Corp., 91 Md. App. 275, 603 A.2d 1376 (1992).

3232 Outdoor World Corp., F.T.C. Dkt. No. 9229, 5 Trade Reg. Rep. (CCH) ¶ 22,780 (F.T.C. 1990) (consent order); Commonwealth v. Resort Developers, Inc., Clearinghouse No. 44,815 (Ky. Commw. Ct. Nov. 23, 1988) (restraining order); Consumer Protection Div. v. Outdoor World Corp., 91 Md. App. 275, 603 A.2d 1376 (1992); State *ex rel.* Webster v. Areaco Inv. Co., 756 S.W.2d 633 (Mo. Ct. App. 1988) (prizes were not as represented, e.g., "two man boat" was child's plastic raft); State *ex rel.* Webster v. Thousand Trails, Inc., Clearinghouse No. 41,273 (Mo. Cir. Ct. St. Louis Cty. 1986); *see also* State *ex rel.* Webster v. Missouri Trails Resort Corp., 627 F. Supp. 86 (E.D. Mo. 1985); State *ex rel.* Thornburg v. Holiday Resort Development, Inc., Clearinghouse No. 43,083 (N.C. Super. Ct. 1988); N.M. Admin. Code tit. 12, § 2.3.9; State v. Peppertree Resort Villas, Inc., 651 N.W.2d 345 (Wis. App. 2002) (upholding trial court's refusal to modify consent order requiring restitution for prize violations).

3233 Consumer Protection Div. v. Outdoor World Corp., 91 Md. App. 275, 603 A.2d 1376 (1992).

3234 N.M. Admin. Code tit. 12, § 2.3.9 (general ban on false or misleading statements in promotions of sales of subdivided land, time shares, condos, and membership campgrounds); Con-

- Consumers are not informed of the conditions that must be met in order to receive the promised reward.[3235] Consumers who are lured to campgrounds by prize offers are surprised to find that they must endure a lengthy high-pressure sales pitch in order to collect the prize.[3236] The prizes are often not the valuable gifts initially described,[3237] but instead are of negligible value or sometimes nonexistent.[3238]

The next document to review is the purchase contract, which may have the following UDAP violations:

- Failure to disclose total costs of membership to the consumer;
- Omissions and misrepresentations concerning consumers' rights of cancellation and rescission;[3239]
- Acceleration rights and collection costs for the campground that are prohibited by state law;
- Misstatement of the nature of the interest in the campground being sold, such as use of the terms "mortgage" and "lease," where the consumer was buying an undivided leasehold interest in the entire park, with no right to use a particular space at a particular time;[3240]
- Forfeiture clauses and collateral agreements whereby the consumer loses all payments made and the membership in the event of even minor defaults; and
- A disclaimer of all liability for any injuries occurring on the resort, with the member agreeing to indemnify the resort if such injuries occur.

The next step is to review with the clients the sales presentation itself. These presentations are sometimes rife with UDAP violations.

- "Special" discounts are promised, but are actually being offered to every buyer.[3241] Fictitious discounts are offered to those who purchase memberships immediately without taking time to consider the decision.[3242] Campground operators create misleading price comparisons with other types of vacations to convince consumers to purchase a membership.[3243]
- Consumers are sometimes misled with respect to the resale market for their memberships. The likely value, the ease of resale, and resale assistance from the campground may all be overstated.[3244]
- Consumers must endure high-pressure sales pitches[3245] in which the campground salesman misconstrues or even contradicts the actual terms of the contract that purchasers must sign. Salesmen also misrepresent the number of memberships still available,[3246] the consumer's cancellation rights,[3247] the cost of dues, whether there are other costs, the amenities offered and to be built, the consumer's ability to use other campgrounds or parks,[3248] the availability of campsites, the extent of security and exclusivity at the campground, and the extent of government regulation concerning the campground.[3249] Consumers are often misled to believe that they must purchase a membership in order to buy a lot on the grounds.[3250]
- Agreements utilize integration clauses to incorporate into the membership unfavorable terms which the consumers have not seen.[3251] Consumers' rights under the

sumer Protection Div. v. Outdoor World Corp., 91 Md. App. 275, 603 A.2d 1376 (1992).

3235 State *ex rel.* Webster v. Areaco Inv. Co., 756 S.W.2d 633 (Mo. Ct. App. 1988). *See also* N.M. Admin. Code tit. 12, § 2.3.9.

3236 Consumer Protection Div. v. Outdoor World Corp., 91 Md. App. 275, 603 A.2d 1376 (1992).

3237 State *ex rel.* Webster v. Thousand Trails, Inc., Clearinghouse No. 41,273 (Mo. Cir. Ct. St. Louis Cty. 1986); *see also* State *ex rel.* Webster v. Missouri Trails Resort Corp., 627 F. Supp. 86 (E.D. Mo. 1985).

3238 State *ex rel.* Thornburg v. Holiday Resort Development, Inc., Clearinghouse No. 43,085 (N.C. Super. 1988). *See* §§ 4.6.6, *supra*, 5.13.4, *infra*.

3239 State *ex rel.* Webster v. Thousand Trails, Inc., Clearinghouse No. 41,273 (Mo. Cir. Ct. St. Louis Cty. 1986); *see also* State *ex rel.* Webster v. Missouri Trails Resort Corp., 627 F. Supp. 86 (E.D. Mo. 1985).

3240 *Id.*; Commonwealth *ex rel.* Zimmerman v. Nickel, 26 Pa. D. & C.3d 115 (C.P. Mercer Cty. 1983).

3241 Consumer Protection Div. v. Outdoor World Corp., 91 Md. App. 275, 603 A.2d 1376 (1992).

3242 State *ex rel.* Thornburg v. Holiday Resort Development, Inc., Clearinghouse No. 43,085 (N.C. Super. Ct. 1988). *See also* Consumer Protection Div. v. Outdoor World Corp., 91 Md. App. 275, 603 A.2d 1376 (1992).

3243 Consumer Protection Div. v. Outdoor World Corp., 91 Md. App. 275, 603 A.2d 1376 (1992).

3244 Commonwealth v. Resort Developers, Inc., Clearinghouse No. 44,815 (Ky. Commw. Ct. Nov. 23, 1988) (restraining order); Consumer Protection Div. v. Outdoor World Corp., 91 Md. App. 275, 603 A.2d 1376 (1992) (misrepresentations of assignability or transferability of membership violated UDAP statute); State *ex rel.* Webster v. Areaco Inv. Co., 756 S.W.2d 633 (Mo. Ct. App. 1988); Commonwealth *ex rel.* Zimmerman v. Nickel, 26 Pa. D. & C.3d 115 (C.P. Mercer Cty. 1983).

3245 Consumer Protection Div. v. Outdoor World Corp., 91 Md. App. 275, 603 A.2d 1376 (1992) (sales pitches lasting up to 9 hours, with the consumer not being allowed to communicate with others).

3246 *Id.*

3247 State *ex rel.* Webster v. Thousand Trails, Inc., Clearinghouse No. 41,273 (Mo. Cir. Ct. St. Louis Cty. 1986); *see also* State *ex rel.* Webster v. Missouri Trails Resort Corp., 627 F. Supp. 86 (E.D. Mo. 1985).

3248 Commonwealth v. Resort Developers, Inc., Clearinghouse No. 44,815 (Ky. Commw. Ct. Nov. 23, 1988) (restraining order); State *ex rel.* Webster v. Areaco Inv. Co., 756 S.W.2d 633 (Mo. Ct. App. 1988).

3249 Consumer Protection Div. v. Outdoor World Corp., 91 Md. App. 275, 603 A.2d 1376 (1992); State *ex rel.* Webster v. Thousand Trails, Inc., Clearinghouse No. 41,273 (Mo. Cir. Ct. St. Louis Cty. 1986); *see also* State *ex rel.* Webster v. Missouri Trails Resort Corp., 627 F. Supp. 86 (E.D. Mo. 1985).

3250 State *ex rel.* Webster v. Areaco Inv. Co., 756 S.W.2d 633 (Mo. Ct. App. 1988).

3251 Commonwealth v. Resort Developers, Inc., Clearinghouse No.

contract and the nature of the interest purchased are often not disclosed until the agreement incorporating these terms has been signed.[3252] Consumers who refuse to assent to the terms of the incorporated agreements are told that they have breached the initial contract to purchase.

- The salesmen will sometimes solicit and/or accept post-dated checks and credit card charges despite the knowledge that the consumer will not be able to afford a membership or even the down payment.[3253] Credit card charges may be applied in a manner not authorized by the consumer. Consumers who seek refunds are stymied because the campground's slow and restrictive refund policy was not disclosed.
- Unconscionable contract terms grant the campground exclusive authority to terminate memberships. Campgrounds also retain the right to unilaterally alter the consumers' obligations under the membership agreements.

Resorts may also be guilty of another invidious practice, having a policy against selling to non-whites, who are called "walks," as they are merely walked through the sales room to the prize room and hurried off the resort. Telephone receptionists may be monitored to insure that they tell callers who "sound black" that no appointments are available. Yet most resorts prominently display Fair Housing decals in their lobbies. These practices may violate civil rights legislation and the Equal Credit Opportunity Act.

Since membership campgrounds often lure consumers to the site with an unsolicited invitation mailed to the consumer's home, advocates should investigate the applicability of the state statute granting a right to cancel home solicitation sales. At least one court has ruled that consumers do have the right to cancel membership campground contracts under the state cooling-off law.[3254]

It is unfair for a campground to unilaterally change the terms of the membership agreement to consumers' disadvantage where the major justification was to increase campground profits.[3255] A court has also awarded multiple UDAP damages and punitive damages in a case involving a "beach club" where consumers had purchased the right to use a beach resort for annual dues which could not be increased beyond the rate of inflation. A company acquiring the club jacked up fees 50% and then terminated memberships on fictitious grounds.[3256]

5.10.5.3 Special Membership Campground Statutes

In response to these abuses, a number of states have enacted statutes regulating the sale of campground memberships, or, more generally, vacation timeshares.[3257] Sales which transfer an interest in land may be regulated under the statute covering timeshare condos.[3258]

Many of these statutes require a campground operator to register with a state agency and provide detailed information about its financial condition, prior experience, whether any of its principals have been criminally convicted or subject to administrative penalties for actions involving fraud or deceit, a description of the facilities provided, sometimes including the ratio of memberships sold to campsites available, copies of contracts, promotional materials and copies of scripts for sales presentations. Operators may also be

44,815 (Ky. Commw. Ct. Nov. 23, 1988) (restraining order); State *ex rel.* Webster v. Areaco Inv. Co., 756 S.W.2d 633 (Mo. Ct. App. 1988).

3252 *Id.*; Commonwealth *ex rel.* Zimmerman v. Nickel, 26 Pa. D. & C.3d 115 (C.P. Mercer Cty. 1983).

3253 State *ex rel.* Thornburg v. Holiday Resort Development, Inc., Clearinghouse No. 43,085 (N.C. Super. Ct. 1988).

3254 Warren v. Borger, 184 Ill. App. 3d 38, 539 N.E.2d 1284 (1989). *See also* Staub v. Outdoor World Corp., 70 Lanc. 412, Clearinghouse No. 45,940 (Pa. C.P. Lancaster Cty. 1987) (denying resort's motion for summary judgment). *But see* State *ex rel.* Zimmerman v. Nickel, 26 Pa. D. & C.3d 115 (C.P. Mercer Cty. 1983). For a discussion of the scope of state home solicitation cancellation statutes, see § 5.8.2.5, *supra*.

3255 Lester v. Resort Camplands Int'l, Inc., 27 Conn. App. 59, 605 A.2d 550 (1992).

3256 *See* Baker v. Chavis, 410 S.E.2d 600 (S.C. Ct. App. 1991).

3257 Ala. Code §§ 34-27-50 through -70 (vacation timeshares, defined to include membership camping); Ariz. Rev. Stats. §§ 32-2198.01 through .14; Cal. Civ. Code §§ 1812.300 to .315; Colo. Rev. Stat. §§ 6-1-101 to 6-1-115 (including campground memberships in the definition of timeshare); Del. Code tit. 6, §§ 2801 to 2809; Fla. Stats. §§ 509.502 to .512; Ga. Code Ann. §§ 10-1-390 to 10-1-407; 815 Ill. Comp. Stat. 635/1 to /5; Iowa Code ch. 557B; La. Rev. Stat. Ann. §§ 9:1131.10.1 to 9:1131.30 (applying to timeshares); Maine Rev. Stat. tit. 33, §§ 589 to 589-C; Md. Comm. §§ 14-2401 to -2403 (vacation clubs); Mass. Gen. Laws ch. 93, § 48A (real estate time shares regulated under Mass. Gen. Laws ch. 183B); Minn. Stat. §§ 82A.01 to .26; Mo. Rev. Stat. §§ 407.600 to 407.630 (applying to timeshares); Mont. Code Ann. §§ 37-53-101 to 37-53-506 (including campgrounds in the definition of timeshare); Neb. Rev. Stat. §§ 76-2101 to 2121; Nev. Rev. Stat. Ann. §§ 119B.070 to .430; N.Y. Gen. Bus. §§ 651 to 660; N.C. Gen. Stat. §§ 66-230 to 66-247; Ohio Rev. Code Ann. §§ 4719.01 to 4719.99 (regulating telemarketing of products and services including campground memberships); Or. Rev. Stat. 94.953 to .989; 63 Penn. Stat. §§ 455.581, 604(5) and .604(18) and .609; S.C. Code Ann. § 27-32-10 to -250; Tenn. Code Ann. §§ 66-32-301 to -312; Tex. Prop. Code §§ 222.001 to .013; Va. Code §§ 59.1-311 to .335; Wash. Rev. Code §§ 19.105.300 to .930; W. Va. Code §§ 46A-6F-104 to 46A-6F-703 (regulating telemarketing of products and services including campground memberships). *See* Colbert v. Bank America, Inc., 295 A.D.2d 300, 743 N.Y.S.2d 150 (2002) (upholding trial court's denial of summary judgment against consumers on claim under Membership Campground Act); *see also* Comments on Vt. Stat. Ann. tit. 27A, § 1-103 (certain membership camping transactions regulated under condo statute).

3258 *See e.g.*, Mass. Gen. Laws ch. 93, § 48A (real estate time shares regulated under Mass. Gen. Laws ch. 183B); Official Comment 22 to 27A Vt. Stat. Ann. § 1-103 (certain membership camping transactions regulated under condo statute).

required to post a bond or other form of security and to place certain funds in escrow. Licensing of brokers and salespeople is commonly required and licenses may be revoked for fraudulent or misleading conduct. If the campground land is encumbered, the owner must have a "nondisturbance agreement" in which the creditor agrees that its rights are subordinate to those of the campground members.

Most statutes mandate provision of a disclosure statement before signing, and require the inclusion of certain terms in the contract, including a cooling-off period of three to seven days. A longer cooling-off period may be required if the purchaser signs before having inspected the campground. (In Texas, a cooling-off period is allowed only if the purchaser signs before inspecting.[3259]) Consumers may also be given cancellation rights if facilities are no longer available as promised.

Promotions involving gifts and prizes may be strictly regulated. Florida forbids such promotions.[3260] A few states require operators to obtain a permit or post bond before conducting a game of chance.[3261] A number of other states require detailed disclosure of the value of the gift, the approximate odds, the sales purpose of the promotion, and any conditions and limitations. Many state statutes provide that a violation is a UDAP violation, while others provide private remedies or administrative enforcement.

5.10.5.4 Practice Tips

The first step in a membership campground case is to determine if the state has adopted a specific consumer protection statute or regulation dealing with this industry. These statutes, which are described in the previous subsection, typically offer significant protections.

Even if the state has not adopted a membership campground statute or regulation, other consumer protection laws may apply. An Ohio court rejected a buyer's attempts to extend the state's health spa law to a campground membership resort that made health club facilities available to members,[3262] but this approach might work in other states.

Some resorts convert their "memberships" into "landshares" wherein the purchaser is entitled to receive a quitclaim deed to a minuscule co-tenancy, e.g., a one four-thousandth share, of the actual resort real estate upon completion of the payments. Characterizing the transaction as a real estate sale may exclude the transaction in some states from the scope of the UDAP statute and will also complicate the question of the consumer's cancellation rights. However, it can be argued that the selling of landshares is purely a subterfuge and that courts must look to what is actually being transferred, i.e., the use of the resort facilities, not the form of the transfer. In addition, most landshares do not conform to the state requirements for real estate transfers.

Proving that a campground membership is worthless as an investment will support UDAP claims concerning misrepresentations of a membership's profit potential. It will also help establish the consumer's damages. One approach to proving the membership value is to bring in an expert to testify that one four-thousandth share of seventy acres of real estate has no practical value. Another argument is that upon default neither the creditor nor the resort tries to resell the membership, which would be the case if it had any value. There is certainly a duty imposed upon a resort or creditor suing for a breach of contract to sell the membership to mitigate damages when it declares the membership forfeited.

Typically, a financial institution and not the resort is the creditor. The resort will have arranged the loan and the FTC holder-in-due-course language should be included, making the creditor subject to all claims against the resort. The resort may argue that this is a real estate transaction, which means the FTC Holder Rule does not apply.[3263] But this characterization of the sale as one involving real estate should be challenged. Assuming the FTC Holder Rule applies, the failure to include the notice is probably a state UDAP violation. It may also be useful to find the creditor independently responsible for UDAP violations in which it participated along with the resort.

The attorney should obtain any and all agreements between the resort and the financial institution. Most arrangements establish a reserve account for the resort at the bank through which the bank pays the resort some of the profit from the financing. The financial institution usually maintains veto power over all financing forms used by the resort and reserves the right to operate the resort, or even select its management, at the bank's sole discretion. Sales staff frequently are trained by the bank, and the agreements state that two installment notes, one in favor of the bank and one in favor of the resort, be executed by the prospective member. Rarely, if ever, is either note returned to the member.

In addition, the bank provides credit applications to be completed at the resort. If the bank rejects a credit application due to lack of creditworthiness, the resort finances the membership. In litigation, the consumer can use this credit rejection against the resort as proof that the resort knew there was little probability that the consumer would be able to make the payments.

3259 Tex. Prop. Code § 222.008.

3260 Fla. Stat. § 509.508.

3261 *See, e.g.*, Ariz. Rev. Stat. § 32-2198.10.

3262 Kovach v. Erie Islands Resort & Marina, Inc., 93 Ohio App. 3d 11, 637 N.E.2d 382 (1994).

3263 *See* § 6.6.2.2, *infra*. *See* National Consumer Law Center, Consumer Law Pleadings, No. 1, Ch. 6 (CD-Rom and Index Guide) for a complaint, discovery materials, and briefs in a class action against a bank that accepted campground membership loans without the FTC Holder Notice. These materials are also found on the CD-Rom accompanying this volume.

The client has probably paid a fee of about $25 to a nationwide campground network, such as Coast-to-Coast, to obtain reciprocal privileges with other campgrounds around the country. Contact the nationwide campground network, whose personnel will usually make an immediate refund.

Write the resort demanding cancellation and return of both the deposit and installment notes. Some resorts will agree to cancel a membership because they "do not want dissatisfied members," but your client should be prepared for litigation. Copies of all letters sent to the resort should also be sent to the institution which financed the transaction and to the state attorney general.

Discover any connection owners may have, or have had, with other resorts, including those in other states. This is particularly important when dealing with a parent company which controls or owns resorts in other states, as it may have been successfully sued for the same practices in other jurisdictions. If the parent company or other related entities were involved in the fraud, or ratified it or knowingly accepted its benefits, they should be liable.[3264]

Get the resort's list of membership purchasers and compare this with the roster of those still entitled to access to the resort. The fact that most who have signed up no longer have access may help a jury reach the conclusion that the resort is fast-talking a large number of consumers into a worthless purchase.

Consider naming individual owners or officers as parties to the suit. Owners may plead ignorance of the daily sales practices at the resort, trying to shift blame to the marketing company the owner has hired to sell memberships. But resort owners are very much aware of the practices of their marketing companies. In addition, many resorts use marketing companies whose techniques have been found to be unfair, deceptive or unconscionable in other jurisdictions. Resort owners know exactly what they are doing.

Most resorts maintain a complete file on all visitors, which contains everything from the solicitation letter to the installment notes. However, most will deny the existence of any canned sales pitch. Fortunately for the consumer, resorts select their cadre of tour guides from the ranks of recent high school graduates or displaced homemakers and pay them on a strictly commission basis. Few tour guides last more than a few months on the job. The name of the tour guide who has sold the membership to your client appears on some of the documents in your client's possession, so the tour guide can be traced. A former tour guide can be a powerful witness against the resort, with testimony about training, management's control of the sales pitch, and canned responses to certain consumer questions.

Asking a former tour guide to explain some of the fine print or "legalese" on a document can be particularly effective, as most can not explain the terms. Instead they stumble through the canned answers aimed at diverting the consumer's attention. A tour guide can also tell you about the numerous complaints received from members dissatisfied with their purchase and can give you a rough estimate of the percentage of sales which default relatively soon after purchase.

Search for all assets of the owners. Resorts attempt to minimize assets, preparing for the almost inevitable litigation. Consequently, several dummy corporations are set up by management. For example, one may own the R.V.'s and equipment located at the resort and then lease them back to the resort. Or the real estate may be owned by one dummy corporation to which the resort itself has granted a mortgage.

Take a tour yourself. You will be surprised at how desirable a membership appears, and how kind and understanding your tour guide and financial advisor are; after all, they have chosen you for the special privilege of membership at a ridiculously low price.

An important tip is to consider suing the financial institution, particularly when the campground is bankrupt or without significant assets. A financial institution is liable if it knows of the campground's fraud yet furthers the scheme by continuing to advance funds.[3265] In one class action against a bank, it was alleged that the bank aided and abetted various campground frauds, that the bank was engaged in RICO violations involving the campground, and that the bank was liable under the FTC Holder Notice for claims against the campground. The bank settled for over $4 million.[3266]

5.10.6 Buying Clubs; Discount Coupons

A buying club offers members alleged discounts on merchandise in return for payment of a membership fee. A 2004 FTC survey showed that, over a two-year period, four million U.S. adults were billed for buying club memberships or buyers' guides that they had not agreed to purchase.[3267] It is deceptive for a buying club to fail to disclose clearly if merchandise can only be bought through catalogs, with no samples available, since the operation of a buying club is unfamiliar to consumers.[3268] Nor can a club falsely represent

3264 *See, e.g.*, Meachum v. Outdoor World Corp., 235 A.D.2d 462, 652 N.Y.S.2d 749 (1997).

3265 Weiss v. Finova, 1995 U.S. Dist. LEXIS 18713 (N.D. Ill. Dec. 13, 1995). *See* §§ 6.4 to 6.6, *infra*.

3266 Conley v. Bank One, Youngstown, N.A., Clearinghouse No. 49,152 (N.D. Ohio July 16, 1993) (stipulation of settlement). *See* National Consumer Law Center, Consumer Law Pleadings, No. 1, § 6.1 (CD-Rom and Index Guide) for an example of a complaint asserting RICO, breach of contract and other claims against a lender in a case arising out of abusive sales of campground memberships. This complaint is also found on the CD-Rom accompanying this volume.

3267 FTC, Consumer Fraud in the United Sates: An FTC Survey (Aug. 2004), at ES-2, 26.

3268 American Buyers Club of Mt. Vernon v. Hayes, 46 Ill. App. 3d 270, 361 N.E.2d 1383 (1977).

its merchandise as being at a discount.[3269] The sale of lifetime memberships has been found deceptive where a club's longest contract with a participating merchant was for ten years.[3270] Clubs may not misrepresent membership as free[3271] or that goods can be purchased on approval,[3272] falsely claim goods will be delivered within three days,[3273] misrepresent the size and true nature of the club and the savings experienced by members,[3274] or fail to disclose relevant information regarding benefits and service assistance.[3275]

Advocates dealing with buying clubs should analyze carefully whether the consumer has a right to cancel under the FTC rule regarding door-to-door sales or a state equivalent, since the sale often begins with a contact or call to the buyer's home.[3276] Another approach is price unconscionability, which one court has used to void a buyer's club contract.[3277] Buying clubs which offer commissions for recruiting new members may also run afoul of state and federal securities laws and state laws regarding referral sales and pyramid sales.[3278]

Illinois has adopted UDAP regulations that extensively regulate buying clubs.[3279] These regulations require disclosure of club policies and features, prohibit referral sales and certain misrepresentations, require a three-day cooling-off period, limit contracts to five years, require a bond, and require various protections against club closure or misappropriate of funds. Many states have special statutes that impose similar requirements.[3280]

Another problem area related to buying clubs is the sale of discount coupons. Abuses may involve situations where the coupons are redeemable at stores which are not still operating, where stores require coupon holders to submit to long waiting periods, or where stores offer the same discounts to non-coupon holders. These three practices have been held to be unfair and deceptive.[3281]

5.10.7 Trade School Abuses

5.10.7.1 Nature and History of Trade School Abuses

Unfair and deceptive vocational and correspondence school practices are a tremendous source of financial loss and loss of opportunity for consumers, particularly low-income consumers hoping to break out of poverty. Attracted by the financing provided by government student loan and grant programs, many vocational school scams and ill-conceived schools have exploited federally funded student assistance programs.

Abuses were particularly widespread during the 1980s and early 1990s when student financial assistance became more widely available for non-high-school graduates and for vocational training. Schools were able to pressure vulnerable and low-income consumers into signing documents obligating them to thousands of dollars in federally-insured student loans. The schools then took the money, delivered worthless services, and, in many cases, disappeared, often closing in the middle of a student's course of study.

The situation has improved significantly since the early 1990s, as over a thousand schools have been barred from federal loan programs due to their high loan default rates.[3282] Nonetheless, trade school abuses persist and new trade school abuses are likely as welfare reform programs with school-based educational components offer new sources of government education money. Further, students victimized by earlier abuses may still be facing collection of those student loans, even decades later.

3269 Compact Electra Corp., 83 F.T.C. 547 (1973) (consent order); Compact Vacuum Centers, Inc., 79 F.T.C. 518 (1971) (consent order); American Buyers Club of Mt. Vernon v. Honecker, 46 Ill. App. 3d 252, 361 N.E.2d 1370 (1977).

3270 Hyland v. Aquarian Age 2000, Inc., 148 N.J. Super. 186, 372 A.2d 370 (Ch. Div. 1977).

3271 FTC v. Ira Smolev, 5 Trade Reg. Rep. (CCH) ¶ 15167 (S.D. Fla. Oct. 23, 2001) (proposed consent decree ordering $8.3 million in restitution against buyers club that misled consumers into accepting "free" trial memberships, then billed them unless they cancelled).

3272 Compact Electra Corp., 83 F.T.C. 547 (1973) (consent order).

3273 Compact Vacuum Centers, Inc., 79 F.T.C. 518 (1971) (consent order).

3274 American Consumer Serv., Inc., 89 F.T.C. 492 (1977) (consent order).

3275 *Id.*

3276 *See* § 5.8.2, *supra*. *Cf.* Niemiec v. Kellmark Corp., 581 N.Y.S.2d 569 (City Ct. 1992) (rejecting application of New York's Door-to-Door Sale Protection Act).

3277 Niemiec v. Kellmark Corp., 581 N.Y.S.2d 569 (City Ct. 1992).

3278 *See, e.g.*, Rhodes v. Consumers' Buyline, Inc., 868 F. Supp. 368 (D. Mass. 1993) (ruling on motion to dismiss).

3279 Illinois Attorney General Buyers Club Rules, 14 Ill. Admin. Code § 460; *see also* People *ex rel.* Fahner v. American Buyer's Club, 115 Ill. App. 3d 759, 450 N.E.2d 905 (1983); United Consumers Club, Inc. v. Attorney General, 119 Ill. App. 3d 701, 456 N.E.2d 856 (1983).

3280 *See, e.g.*, Ariz. Rev. Stat. §§ 44-1797 to 44-1797.20; Cal. Civ. Code §§ 1812.100 to 1812.129; Colo. Rev. Stat. § 6-1-706; Conn. Gen. Stat. § 42-310; Fla. Stat. Ann. § 559.3901; Ga. Code Ann. § 10-1-591; Haw. Rev. Stat. § 481B-1.5 (concerning mail order buying clubs); Iowa Code §§ 522A.1 to 522A.5; Ky. Rev. Stat. § 367.395; Minn. Stat. Ann. § 325G.27; Mo. Rev. Stat. § 407.670; Nev. Rev. Stat. § 598.942; N.H. Rev. Stat. Ann. § 358-J:1; N.C. Gen. Stat. § 66-131; S.C. Code Ann. §§ 39-61-10 to 39-61-200 (broadly defining motor clubs to include clubs which offer discounts on services and merchandise); S.D. Codified Laws Ann. § 37-26-1; Tenn. Code Ann. § 47-18-501; Wis. Stat. Ann. § 136.01.

3281 People v. Toomey, 157 Cal. App. 3d 1, 203 Cal. Rptr. 642 (1984).

3282 See Stephen Burd, Default Rate on Student Loans Drops for Sixth Consecutive Year, Chron. of Higher Educ., Nov. 8, 1998; U.S. Department of Education, Accountability for Results Works: College Loan Default Rates Continue to Decline, Press Release (Sept. 19, 2001). Individual school default rates are posted on the Department of Education website at www.ed.gov/offices/OSFAP/defaultmanagement/cdr.html.

Despite these improvements, trade school fraud is still a significant problem. Unfortunately, the situation has worsened as the for-profit education sector has grown.[3283] An additional factor fueling new abuses is the rise of private student loan products.[3284]

This section outlines UDAP and other theories to seek a remedy for students who have been victimized by trade school fraud. Another NCLC volume, *Student Loan Law* (2d ed. 2002 and Supp.), explores litigation against trade schools and alternatives for students saddled with student loan debt in greater detail.

5.10.7.2 FTC Guides

The FTC has issued guides concerning unfair and deceptive private vocational school practices.[3285] The guides specify that schools can not misrepresent, through their name or otherwise that they are connected with government agencies or civil service commissions or that they are an employment agency or employer.[3286]

Among other provisions, the FTC Guides require that schools disclose if the course is offered through correspondence.[3287] It is deceptive for a school to misrepresent the nature of its approval or accreditation or the extent to which former students, employers, or counselors recommend a course.[3288]

It is deceptive for a school to misrepresent the availability of employment after graduation from a course, the success that graduates have realized in obtaining such employment or the salary that graduates will receive in such employment.[3289] It is also deceptive for a school to misrepresent that the lack of a high school education or prior training is not an impediment to successful completion of a course or obtaining employment.[3290]

5.10.7.3 UDAP Precedent

Courts interpreting state UDAP statutes and the FTC Act's general prohibition against unfairness and deception have identified a number of other trade school practices not enumerated in the FTC Guides as unfair or deceptive. These decisions provide important additional principles concerning job and earnings claims, student loans, and refund policies.

Schools may not deceive students with respect to the nature, terms or conditions of contractual obligations, veterans' educational benefits, and federally insured student loans.[3291] A school may not misrepresent its refund policy or deceive students into attending additional classes before dropping out with the result that their contractual obligation is significantly increased under the refund formula.[3292] Schools must also pay all owed refunds.[3293]

3283 *See generally* National Consumer Law Center, Student Loan Law § 9.1.3.1 (2d ed 2002 and Supp.).

3284 *See id.* § 1.9.

3285 Guides for Private Vocational and Distance Education Schools, 16 C.F.R. § 254 *et. seq.* In 1978, the FTC also promulgated a rule related to private trade school activities. Trade Regulation Rule Concerning Proprietary Vocational and Home-Study Schools, 43 Fed. Reg. 60,795 (Dec. 18, 1978). The Commission withdrew the Vocational School Rule's effective date pending further Commission action, and in 1988 finally terminated the rule. 53 Fed. Reg. 29,482 (Aug. 5, 1988). Nevertheless, the rule's Statement of Basis and Purpose, 43 Fed. Reg. 60,791 (Dec. 18, 1978), and the FTC staff report recommending the rule still provide a useful factual and legal background to vocational school issues. Bureau of Consumer Protection, Proprietary Vocational and Home-Study Schools, Final Report and Proposed Trade Regulation Rule, Clearinghouse No. 31,041 (1976).

3286 16 C.F.R. § 254.2. *See also* FTC v. Couture School of Modeling, 5 Trade Reg. Rep. (CCH) ¶ 22,815 (D. Md. 1990) (injunction); United States v. Eyler, 5 Trade Reg. Rep. (CCH) ¶ 22,891 (M.D. Fla. 1990) (consent decree); People v. Wilshire Computer College, Clearinghouse No. 46,309B (Cal. Super. Ct. 1991) (preliminary injunction pursuant to stipulation).

3287 16 C.F.R. § 254.2(c).

3288 16 C.F.R. § 254.3. *See also* Malone v. Academy of Court Reporting, 64 Ohio App. 3d 588, 582 N.E.2d 54 (1990) (concealment of fact that school was not certified or accredited to issue promised associate degree violates UDAP statute); Cavaliere v. Duff's Bus. Institute, 605 A.2d 397 (Pa. Super. Ct. 1992); Webster College v. Speier, 605 S.W.2d 712 (Tex. Civ. App. 1980). *But see* Lidecker v. Kendall College, 550 N.E.2d 1121 (Ill. App. Ct. 1990) (failure to inform prospective students of nursing school's lack of accreditation not a UDAP violation where school did not intend that students rely on the omission, and the lack of accreditation did not cause the student harm); *cf.* Ambrose v. New England Ass'n of Schools and Colleges, 252 F.3d 488 (1st Cir. 2001) (accrediting organization not liable for negligent accreditation). For a discussion of possible claims against accreditation agencies, see National Consumer Law Center, Student Loan Law § 9.4.1.2 (2d ed. 2002 and Supp.).

3289 16 C.F.R. § 254.4(d).

3290 16 C.F.R. § 254.5.

3291 Bell & Howell Co., 95 F.T.C. 761 (1980) (consent order); People v. Wilshire Computer College, Clearinghouse No. 46,309B (Cal. Super. Ct. 1991) (preliminary injunction pursuant to stipulation); Manley v. Wichita Bus. College, 237 Kan. 427, 701 P.2d 893 (1985). *But see* Finstad v. Wasburn University of Topeka, 845 P.2d 685 (Kan. 1993) (overruling the holding in *Manley* that actual damages are not required in Kansas UDAP cases); Gamble v. University Sys. of New Hampshire, 610 A.2d 357 (N.H. 1992) (university's imposition of mid-semester tuition increase due to fiscal crisis not a UDAP violation where it notified almost all affected students of possible increase in letter accompanying initial billing for semester).

3292 People v. Wilshire Computer College, Clearinghouse No. 46,309B (Cal. Super. Ct. 1991) (preliminary injunction pursuant to stipulation); Manley v. Wichita Bus. College, 237 Kan. 427, 701 P.2d 893 (1985); Reynolds v. Sterling College, Inc., 750 A.2d 1020 (Vt. 2000) (summary judgment awarded to student on contractual claim, consumer fraud claim remanded; change in refund policy after substantial tuition payments had been made found to be a unilateral modification of specific contractual term for which no consideration had been received). *But see* Finstad v. Wasburn University of Topeka, 845 P.2d 685 (Kan. 1993) (overruling the holding in *Manley* that actual damages are not required in Kansas UDAP cases).

3293 United States v. Eyler, 5 Trade Reg. Rep. (CCH) ¶ 22,891 (M.D.

It is deceptive to misrepresent the amount of personalized instruction available in a correspondence course, or the difficulty of the correspondence courses themselves.[3294] Schools can not misrepresent students' ability to benefit from a course or fail to meet state entrance standards.[3295] Nor can schools encourage students to falsify their identity or immigration status.[3296]

Also deceptive are misrepresentations concerning the nature of school placement services.[3297] For example, in one UDAP case, consumer recovery was based on the school's "admissions officers" (who worked on commission and made as much as $56,000 a year) promising 90% to 95% job placement when in fact the school was reporting to its accrediting agency job placement rates averaging only 47%. The school's higher 90% to 95% figure was derived only from students who kept in touch with the school's placement office, not the total number of the school's graduates.[3298]

Another source of precedent on unfair or deceptive trade school practices may be found in a state's education statutes, such as California's Maxine Waters Student Protection Act.[3299] In some cases, these statutes will provide for a private right of action. If not, a violation of these standards may be actionable under a state UDAP statute.

Despite the existence of federal regulation of the student financial assistance programs, the Higher Education Act should only preempt state claims, including UDAP claims, that conflict with the purposes or provisions of the HEA.[3300]

5.10.7.4 Other Claims

In some states, a state RICO claim may provide superior remedies to a UDAP claim, or the two together may provide more relief than just a UDAP claim.[3301] Federal RICO claims are also a possibility.[3302] Common law fraud claims should be considered, as well, because of the possibility of punitive damages.[3303]

Courts have found a variety of legal theories sufficient to rescind enrollment agreements and have directed schools to reimburse students for their tuition payments or student loan debts.[3304] While courts will not allow a claim for educational

---

Fla. 1990) (consent decree); People v. Wilshire Computer College, Clearinghouse No. 46,309B (Cal. Super. Ct. 1991) (preliminary injunction pursuant to stipulation). In addition, there is now a federal discharge program to reimburse students for unpaid refunds. *See* National Consumer Law Center, Student Loan Law § 6.4 (2d ed. 2002 and Supp.).

3294 Bell & Howell Co., 95 F.T.C. 761 (1980) (consent order).

3295 People v. Wilshire Computer College, Clearinghouse No. 46,309B (Cal. Super. Ct. 1991) (preliminary injunction pursuant to stipulation).

3296 *Id.*

3297 Control Data Corp., 97 F.T.C. 84 (1981) (consent order); Bell & Howell Co., 95 F.T.C. 761 (1980) (consent order); Universal Training Serv. Inc., 94 F.T.C. 167 (1979) (consent order); Art Instruction Schools Inc., 93 F.T.C. 32 (1979) (consent order); Driver Training Institute Inc., 92 F.T.C. 235 (1978) (consent order); Commercial Programming Unlimited Inc., 88 F.T.C. 913 (1976) (consent order); Lafayette United Corp., 88 F.T.C. 683 (1976) (consent order); Lear Siegler Inc., 86 F.T.C. 860 (1975) (consent order); Weaver Airline Personnel School, 85 F.T.C. 237 (1975) (consent order); Eastern Detective Academy Inc., 78 F.T.C. 1428 (1971); Missouri College of Automation, 67 F.T.C. 258 (1965) (consent order); People *ex rel.* Abrams v. New York Vocational School, Inc., Clearinghouse No. 43,088 (N.Y. Sup. Ct. 1987); *see also* Collins v. Minn. School of Bus., 655 N.W.2d 320 (Minn. 2003) (misrepresentation of career opportunities is UDAP violation).

3298 Beckett v. Computer Career Institute, Inc. (Or. Cir. Ct. July 2, 1990), *aff'd in part and rev'd in part*, 120 Or. App. 143, 852 P.2d 840 (1993).

3299 Cal. Civ. Code § 94840 (formerly § 94316). Most of the provisions in the California Student Protection Act apply only to violations that occurred after January 1, 1990. For some provisions, the effective date is January 1, 1991. There are some, more limited protections in the California Code for pre-1990 violations. *See, e.g.*, former Cal. Educ. Code § 94321. The act is scheduled to be repealed as of January 1, 2005, but the legislature may act during 2004 to extend the law.

3300 *See* Cliff v. Payco General Am. Credits, 363 F.3d 1113 (11th Cir. 2004) (HEA does not occupy the field of student loan debt collection and state fair debt collection claims not preempted); Morgan v. Markerdowne Corp., 976 F. Supp. 301 (D.N.J. 1997), *class cert. denied*, 201 F.R.D. 341 (D.N.J. 2001) (although HEA does not preempt all state law, it does preempt any state law which conflicts with it; HEA impliedly preempted borrower's state law claims to the extent they would hold the lender and guaranty agency liable for the alleged school misrepresentations). *See generally* National Consumer Law Center, Student Loan Law § 9.3.2.1 (2d ed. 2002 and Supp.).

3301 *See* Beckett v. Computer Career Institute, Inc. (Or. Cir. Ct. July 2, 1990) (awarding multiple and punitive damages on RICO and UDAP claims), *aff'd in part and rev'd in part*, 120 Or. App. 143, 852 P.2d 840 (1993) (reversing state RICO recovery on technical grounds, but affirming UDAP actual and punitive damages).

3302 *See* Rosario v. Livaditis, 963 F.2d 1013 (7th Cir. 1992), *cert. denied*, 506 U.S. 1051 (1993) (Illinois law); Rodriguez v. McKinney, 878 F. Supp. 744 (E.D. Pa. 1995); Moy v. Adelphi Institute, Inc., 866 F. Supp. 696 (E.D.N.Y. 1994); Gonzalez v. North Am. College, 700 F. Supp. 362 (S.D. Tex. 1988) (students sufficiently alleged RICO claim). *But see* Johnson v. Midland Career Institute, 1996 U.S. Dist. LEXIS 1308 (N.D. Ill. 1996).

3303 *See* Moy v. Adelphi Institute, Inc., 866 F. Supp. 696 (E.D.N.Y. 1994) (misrepresentation and fraud claims survived motion to dismiss, but not claim for negligent misrepresentation or breach of fiduciary duty); Phillips College of Alabama, Inc. v. Lester, 622 So. 2d 308 (Ala. 1993) (a valid fraud claim asserted against school that had promised in written materials but failed to provide a specific number of hours of practical training); Craig v. Forest Institute of Professional Psychology, 713 So. 2d 967 (Ala. Civ. App. 1997); Hellvig v. City of New York, 662 N.Y.S.2d 316 (App. Div. 1995) (while educational malpractice is not actionable, causes of action are recognized for fraud and other intentional torts if properly pleaded); Carol Crocca, *Liability of Private Vocational or Trade School for Fraud or Misrepresentation Including Student to Enroll or Pay Fees*, 85 A.L.R.4th 1079 (1991 and Supp.).

3304 Andrē v. Pace University, 170 Misc. 2d 893, 655 N.Y.S.2d 777 (1996), *rev'g* 161 Misc. 2d 613, 618 N.Y.S.2d 975 (1994)

malpractice, they may allow a contract claim based on failure to provide any instruction or failure to provide a specific service.[3305] Students may also have contract claims against the school. School catalogs, bulletins, and regulations should be considered part of the contract between the school and its students.[3306] The more limited the claim (for example, based on a school's failure to offer a particular promised course) and the more it is tied to written promises, the more likely it is that a court will treat it as a contract claim rather than an educational malpractice claim.[3307] Some courts have also allowed an implied contract theory.[3308]

In one case, a court found failure of consideration where the school accepted the student's tuition and failed to provide the promised educational services.[3309] In another case, the court awarded summary judgment to a student, agreeing that a change in the school's refund policy after substantial tuition payments had been made was a unilateral modification of a specific contractual term for which no consideration had been received.[3310]

Most courts find that there is no implied private right of action under the federal Higher Education Act (HEA).[3311]

(school's complete failure to provide course at promised level allows damages and rescission); Brown v. Hambric, 638 N.Y.S.2d 873, 168 Misc. 2d 502 (1995) (travel agent school found to be a deceptive pyramid scheme; rescission of contract warranted and failure to deliver the promised support and training was unconscionable and deceptive business practice); James v. SCS Bus. & Technical Institute, 595 N.Y.S.2d 885 (Civ. Ct. Cty. of New York 1992) (unconscionability and lack of consideration); Cavaliere v. Duff's Bus. Institute, 605 A.2d 397 (Pa. Super. Ct. 1992) (general claim of lack of quality education not actionable, but misrepresentation or breach of contract would be).

3305 Ambrose v. New England Ass'n of Schools and Colleges, Inc., 252 F.3d 488 (1st Cir. 2001) (claim regarding falsity of general statements about accreditation was really a claim for negligent accreditation and could not be maintained); Johnson v. Schmitz, 119 F. Supp. 2d 90 (D. Conn. 2000); Whayne v. United States Department of Educ., 915 F. Supp. 1143 (D. Kan. 1996) (allegation that education simply was not good enough insufficient to state a claim for breach of contract; educational malpractice claim rejected as a matter of state law); Cencor Inc. v. Tolman, 868 P.2d 396 (Colo. 1994) (although no claim for educational malpractice, plaintiff may have a claim for failure to provide a specific service); Page v. Klein Tools, Inc., 610 N.W.2d 900 (Mich. 2000) (explains policy considerations underlying various courts' rejection of educational malpractice claims); Alsides v. Brown Institute, 592 N.W.2d 468 (Minn. App. Ct. 1999) (courts may consider contract, fraud, and misrepresentation claims only if they do not require inquiry into the nuances of educational processes and theories); Andre v. Pace University, 170 Misc. 2d 893, 655 N.Y.S.2d 777 (1996), *rev'g* 161 Misc. 2d 613, 618 N.Y.S.2d 975 (1994); Cavaliere v. Duff's Bus. Institute, 413 Pa. Super. 357, 605 A.2d 397 (1992) (if the contract with the school were to provide for certain specified services such as, for example, a designated number of hours of instruction and the school failed to meet its obligation, then a contract action with appropriate consequential damages might be viable). *See generally* National Consumer Law Center, Student Loan Law § 9.3.4.2 (2d ed. 2002 and Supp.).

3306 Ross v. Creighton University, 957 F.2d 410 (7th Cir. 1992) (basic legal relationship between student and school is contractual in nature). *See also* Gally v. Columbia University, 22 F. Supp. 2d 199 (S.D.N.Y. 1998) (implied contract between students and school required university to act in good faith and students to satisfy academic requirements and comply with school procedures); Zumbrun v. University of So. Cal., 25 Cal. App. 3d 1, 101 Cal. Rptr. 499 (1972); Wickstrom v. North Idaho College, 725 P.2d 155 (Idaho 1986).

3307 Johnson v. Schmitz, 119 F. Supp. 2d 90 (D. Conn. 2000) (claim that faculty member misappropriated student's ideas and research is not an educational malpractice claim so can be basis of breach of contract); Dillon v. Ultrasound Diagnostic Schools, 1997 U.S. Dist. LEXIS 20795 (E.D. Pa. 1997) (plaintiff's complaints identified specific alleged benefits and services which defendants promised and failed to provide so as to state a claim for breach of educational contract); Grundlach v. Reinstein, 924 F. Supp. 684 (E.D. Pa. 1996), *aff'd*, 114 F.3d 1172 (3d Cir. 1997) (no written contact between law school and student, student failed to identify specific manner in which school breached contract); Cencor Inc. v. Tolman, 868 P.2d 396 (Colo. 1994) (court agreed that enrollment agreement and school catalog constituted the express terms of the contract and that students showed specific services which had not been provided; also found failure to provide qualified teacher); Wickstrom v. North Idaho College, 725 P.2d 155 (Idaho 1986); Alsides v. Brown Institute, 592 N.W.2d 468 (Minn. App. Ct. 1999) (allowing students to proceed with claims involving a computer school's promises to provide instruction on a particular software program and particular types of computers; frequent absences or tardiness of instructors; insufficient operable computers; outdated hardware and software; and failure to deliver the number of hours of instruction promised); Squires v. Sierra Nevada Ed. Foundation, 823 P.2d 256 (Nev. 1991); Brown v. Hambric, 638 N.Y.S.2d 873, 168 Misc. 2d 502 (1995); Ryan v. University of N.C. Hosps., 494 S.E.2d 789 (N.C. App. 1998) (court upheld claim for breach of contract); Britt v. Chestnut Hill College, 429 Pa. Super. 263, 632 A.2d 557 (Pa. Super. 1993); Thomas v. French, 30 Wash. App. 811, 638 P.2d 613 (1981), *rev'd on other grounds*, 99 Wash. 2d 95, 659 P.2d 1097 (1983) (viable contract claim where private cosmetology school's contract expressly required the school to prepare the students to take a state cosmetology exam).

3308 Gally v. Columbia University, 22 F. Supp. 2d 199 (S.D.N.Y. 1998); Gupta v. New Britain Gen. Hosp., 687 A.2d 111 (Conn. 1996) (residency contract is an educational contract carrying an implied covenant of good faith and fair dealing, but resident failed to produce any evidence showing hospital showed bad faith or arbitrary manner in its dismissal of resident); Wickstrom v. North Idaho College, 725 P.2d 155 (Idaho 1986) (valid cause of action based on breach of implied contract where school failed to satisfy "objective criteria" such as number of hours). *But see* Harris v. Adler School of Professional Psychology, 723 N.E.2d 717 (Ill. App. Ct. 1999) (no cause of action in Illinois for breach of implied provision of good faith; students dismissed from doctoral program on basis of failed exam had alleged school breached implied term in failing to have objective and articulable criteria for grading exams).

3309 James v. SCS Bus. & Technical Institute, 59 N.Y.S.2d 885 (Civ. Ct. Cty. of New York 1992).

3310 Reynolds v. Sterling College, Inc., 750 A.2d 1020 (Vt. 2000).

3311 *See* Christopher v. U.S., 64 Fed. Appx. 132, 2003 WL 1904785 (10th Cir. 2003); McCulloch v. PNC Bank, Inc., 298 F.3d 1217 (11th Cir. 2002) (in enacting the HEA, Congress expressly

The HEA also explicitly states that failure to comply with its loan disclosure requirements does *not* provide a basis for a claim for civil damages.[3312]

5.10.7.5 Advising Trade School Clients

There are several significant obstacles to litigation regarding trade school abuses. First, in many cases, the school will already be closed by the time the client seeks assistance. It is also very common for schools to close during the course of litigation. In either event, collection of a judgment from the school will be difficult or impossible.

Statutes of limitation can also be an obstacle. Clients often seek legal help for student loans long after they have left the school, at a point when the government is attempting to collect a defaulted student loan. Since there is no statute of limitations for most student loan debts, collection efforts can go on indefinitely.[3313] But there are statutes of limitations for UDAP and other affirmative claims that may prevent an affirmative suit. In addition, the client may already be facing a collection lawsuit for the loan. In these circumstances, the borrower will be forced to raise the school-related claim by way of recoupment to an action to collect on the debt, or as a declaratory action that the debt is not owed.[3314] Unfortunately, for pre-1994 Federal Family Education Loans (FFELs), some courts refuse to allow borrowers to raise school-related claims defensively.[3315]

If the client's major concern is a student loan obligation, there are other avenues of relief. The Department of Education will discharge the obligation if the school closed while the student attended or within ninety days after the student withdrew; if the school falsely certified that the student had the ability to benefit from a course of study; or if the student withdrew but the school failed to refund the portion of the tuition that was required by the contract. The Department of Education will consider requests to discharge whole groups of students who were affected by the same practice. Discharges are also available if the student is now permanently and totally disabled, and there are also a variety of repayment and consolidation loan programs that can ease the student's financial burden. All of these alternatives are discussed in detail in NCLC's *Student Loan Law* (2d ed. 2002 and Supp.).

5.11 Health, Nutrition, and Funerals

5.11.1 Hearing Aids

The FTC proposed in 1978 a Trade Regulation Rule Concerning Hearing Aids, but this proceeding was terminated.[3316] The proceeding did produce a useful FTC staff report.[3317] The FTC has also challenged hearing-aid sales practices in a number of individual cases. It is unfair or deceptive to misrepresent a hearing aid's benefits, performance, or efficacy.[3318] Such misrepresentations include

---

provided a detailed regulatory scheme which confers on the Secretary of Education the exclusive authority to monitor and enforce the provisions of the HEA); Labickas v. Arkansas State University, 78 F.3d 333 (8th Cir. 1996), *cert. denied*, 117 S. Ct. 395, 136 L. Ed. 2d. 310 (1997); White v. The Apollo Group, 241 F. Supp. 2d 710 (W.D. Tex. 2003); Robinett v. Delgado Comm. College, 2000 WL 798407 (E.D. La June 19, 2000); Waugh v. Conn. Student Loan Foundation, 966 F. Supp. 141 (D. Conn. 1997). Morgan v. Markerdowne Corp., 976 F. Supp. 301 (D.N.J. 1997); Bartels v. Alabama Commercial College, 918 F. Supp. 1565 (S.D. Ga. 1995), *aff'd without published op.*, 189 F.3d 483 (11th Cir. 1999), *cert. denied*, 528 U.S. 1074 (2000); Moy v. Adelphi Institute, Inc., 866 F. Supp. 696 (E.D.N.Y. 1994); Spinner v. Chesapeake Bus. Institute of Virginia, Clearinghouse No. 49,131A (E.D. Va. Feb. 5, 1993); Jackson v. Culinary School of Washington, 811 F. Supp. 714 (D.D.C. 1993) (claim dismissed based on summary judgment motion that students had not presented evidence of origination relationship), *aff'd on other grounds*, 27 F.3d 573 (D.C. Cir. 1994) (origination theory not enforceable against the Secretary), *vacated on other grounds*, 115 S. Ct. 2573 (1995) (appellate court used *de novo* instead of abuse of discretion standard to review district court's decision to decide state law issues in declaratory judgment action), *remanded to district court on state law claims, but affirming own ruling on origination*, 59 F.3d 254 (D.C. Cir. 1995) (to determine on what basis federal court decided to rule on state law issues), *motion dismissed*, 1995 U.S. App. LEXIS 22304 (D.C. Cir. 1995); Keams v. Tempe Technical Institute, 807 F. Supp. 569 (D. Ariz. 1992); Shorter v. Alexander, Clearinghouse No. 47,950 (N.D. Ga. Dec. 8, 1992); Graham v. Security Sav. & Loan, 125 F.R.D. 687 (N.D. Ind. 1989). *But see* Tipton v. Northeastern Bus. College, Clearinghouse No. 44,339 (S.D. W. Va. Jan. 8, 1988) (private right of action); Chavez v. LTV Aerospace Corp., 412 F. Supp. 4 (N.D. Tex. 1976) (private cause of action where school allegedly imposed illegal charges on students).

3312 20 U.S.C. § 1083(c).

3313 20 U.S.C. § 1091a. *See* National Consumer Law Center, Student Loan Law § 3.2 (2d ed. 2002 and Supp.).

3314 *See* National Consumer Law Center, Student Loan Law § 9.5 (2d ed. 2002 and Supp.).

3315 This issue is discussed in detail in National Consumer Law Center, Student Loan Law § 9.5.3 (2d ed. 2002 and Supp.).

3316 F.T.C. Pub. Rcd. No. 215-44. The FTC, after terminating the rule, requested additional staff investigation at 50 Fed. Reg. 18120 (Apr. 29, 1985).

3317 Staff Report on Trade Regulation Rule Concerning Hearing Aids, Clearinghouse No. 31,043 (Nov. 1978).

3318 *In re* Dahlberg and the FTC, 5 Trade Reg. Rep. (CCH) ¶ 23,928 (D. Minn. 1995); FTC v. Beltone Electronics Corp., 5 Trade Reg. Rep. (CCH) ¶ 23,731 (N.D. Ill. 1994) (proposed consent decree) (unsubstantiated claim that hearing aid resolved background noise problems); Dahlberg Electronics, Inc., 88 F.T.C. 319 (1976) (consent order); Maico Hearing Instruments, Inc., 88 F.T.C. 298 (1976) (consent order); Qualitone, Inc., 88 F.T.C. 287 (1976) (consent order); Radioear Corp., 88 F.T.C. 308 (1976) (consent order); Sonotone Corp., 88 F.T.C. 368 (1976) (consent order); Mather Hearing Aid Distributors, Inc., 78 F.T.C. 709 (1971); Commonwealth v. Hush-Tone Indus., Inc., 4 Pa. Comm. 1, 1971 Pa. Commw. LEXIS 290 (1971).

falsely claiming that the hearing aid is a new invention,[3319] is helpful regardless of the hearing disability,[3320] will return hearing to normal,[3321] or will prevent hearing deterioration.[3322]

Other actionable misrepresentations involve claims that hearing aids in both ears will perform better,[3323] that there is a permanent source of power,[3324] or that the aid is invisible when worn.[3325] It is deceptive to misrepresent government approval,[3326] indicate medical training for sales personnel,[3327] or misrepresent the guarantee.[3328] The FTC has also obtained consent orders against a series of hearing-aid sellers who falsely claimed (in the yellow pages) that Medicare helps cover the cost of hearing aids or hearing tests.[3329]

Hearing-aid abuses affect those with loss of hearing, often the elderly. As such, these practices are targeted at consumers who are especially vulnerable. Representations that may not deceive most consumers may still be actionable when those with hearing loss are recipients of sales presentations.[3330] Complaints should thus emphasize the vulnerable nature of the consumer.

States commonly require hearing-aid sellers to be licensed. A number of cases have held that violation of a state licensing statute is a UDAP violation.[3331]

3319 FTC v. Beltone Electronics Corp., 5 Trade Reg. Rep. (CCH) ¶ 23,731 (N.D. Ill. 1994) (proposed consent decree); Mather Hearing Center, Inc., 78 F.T.C. 1265 (1971) (consent order); Telex Corp., 79 F.T.C. 61 (1971) (consent order).

3320 Mather Hearing Aid Distributors, Inc., 78 F.T.C. 709 (1971); Community Hearing Center, Inc., 78 F.T.C. 1265 (1971) (consent order); Telex Corp., 79 F.T.C. 61 (1971) (consent order); Commonwealth v. Hush-Tone Indus., Inc., 4 Pa. Comm. 1, 1971 Pa. Commw. LEXIS 290 (1971).

3321 Mountain States Hearing Serv., 77 F.T.C. 640 (1970) (consent order); Regal Audio Instruments, 66 F.T.C. 989 (1964) (consent order).

3322 Mountain States Hearing Serv., 77 F.T.C. 640 (1970) (consent order).

3323 Mather Hearing Aid Distributors, Inc., 78 F.T.C. 709 (1971).

3324 Regal Audio Instruments, 66 F.T.C. 989 (1964) (consent order).

3325 Mather Hearing Aid Distributors, Inc., 78 F.T.C. 709 (1971); Audivox, Inc., 56 F.T.C. 215 (1959), *aff'd*, 275 F.2d 685 (1st Cir. 1960); Beltone Hearing Aid Co., 56 F.T.C. 387 (1959) (consent order); Qualiton Hearing Aid Co., 55 F.T.C. 120 (1958) (consent order); Otarion Inc., 54 F.T.C. 382 (1957) (consent order); Dahlberg Co., 50 F.T.C. 938 (1954) (consent order).

3326 Dictograph Products, Inc., 50 F.T.C. 179 (1953) (consent order).

3327 Mather Hearing Aid Distributors, Inc., 78 F.T.C. 709 (1971).

3328 Community Hearing Center, Inc., 78 F.T.C. 1265 (1971) (consent order); Regal Audio Instruments, 66 F.T.C. 989 (1964).

3329 *See* Brooklyn Audiology Assocs., 5 Trade Reg. Rep. (CCH) ¶ 23,353 (F.T.C. Dkt. C-3433 1993) (consent order).

3330 *See for example* Belmont Laboratories, Inc. v. FTC, 103 F.2d 538 (3d Cir. 1939); Commonwealth v. Hush-Tone Indus., Inc., 4 Pa. Commw. 1, 1971 Pa. Commw. LEXIS 290 (1971). *See also* § 4.2.11, *supra*.

3331 *See* § 4.7.7.2, *supra*.

5.11.2 *Other Medical Cures, Food Advertising*

Every year, the FTC brings proceedings against purveyors of dozens if not hundreds of unsubstantiated medical cures, diet products, nutritional supplements, and the like. It is deceptive to make false or unsubstantiated claims about the risks, effectiveness, or features of medications[3332] or medi-

3332 *Aspirin substitutes*: Walgreen Co., 109 F.T.C. 156 (1987) (consent order); Thompson Medical Co., 104 F.T.C. 648 (1984), *aff'd*, 791 F.2d 189 (D.C. Cir. 1986); Bristol-Myers Co., 102 F.T.C. 21 (1983); Sterling Drug, Inc., 102 F.T.C. 395 (1983); American Home Products Corp., 98 F.T.C. 136 (1981), *aff'd*, 695 F.2d 681 (3d Cir. 1981). *Side effects*: Adria Laboratories, Inc., 103 F.T.C. 512 (1984) (consent order regarding claim that product did not have aspirin side effects). *Cold and allergy treatments*: Quigley Corp., 5 Trade Reg. Rep. (CCH) ¶ 24,674 (F.T.C. Dkt. C-3926 2000) (consent order) (lozenges for colds and allergies); QVC, Inc., 5 Trade Reg. Rep. (CCH) ¶ 24,673 (F.T.C. Dkt. No. C-3954, June 14, 2000) (consent order) (lozenges); Viral Response Sys., 115 F.T.C. 676, 5 Trade Reg. Rep. (CCH) ¶ 23,135 (1992) (consent order). *Acne treatments*: A.H.C. Pharmacal Inc., 95 F.T.C. 528 (1980) (consent order); Harvey Glass M.D., 95 F.T.C. 247 (1980) (consent order); Hayoun Cosmetique Inc., 95 F.T.C. 794 (1980) (consent order); San-Mar Laboratories Inc., 95 F.T.C. 236 (1980) (consent order); Karr Preventative Medical Products Inc., 94 F.T.C. 1080 (1979) (consent order); National Media Group, Inc., 94 F.T.C. 1098 (1979) (consent order). *Treatments for arthritis and muscle strain*: SmartSource Science Laboratories, Inc., 5 Trade Reg. Rep. (CCH) ¶ 24,788 (F.T.C. Dkt. No. C-3980, Nov. 20, 2000) (consent order regarding skin cream that allegedly cured joint pain); CMO Distrib. Centers, 5 Trade Reg. Rep. (CCH) 24,722 (F.T.C. Dkt. No. C-3942, May 16, 2000) (consent order); EHP Prods., Inc., 5 Trade Reg. Rep. (CCH) ¶ 24,723 (F.T.C. Dkt. No. C-3940, May 16, 2000); Melinda Sneed, 5 Trade Reg. Rep. (CCH) ¶ 24,623 (F.T.C. Dkt. No. C-3896, Sept. 7, 1999) (consent order); Olsen Laboratories, Inc., 5 Trade Reg. Rep. (CCH) ¶ 23,717 (F.T.C. C-3556 1995); Numex Corp., 5 Trade Reg. Rep. (CCH) ¶ 23,402 (F.T.C. File No. 912 3280 1993) (consent order regarding hand-held roller device to cure arthritis); Biopractic Group, Inc., 104 F.T.C. 845 (1984) (consent order). *Pain relief*: FTC v. Blue Stuff, Inc., 5 Trade Reg. Rep. (CCH) ¶ 15327 (W.D. Okla. Nov. 18, 2002) (proposed consent decree); Novartis Corp., 5 Trade Reg. Rep. (CCH) ¶ 24,614 (F.T.C. Dkt. 9279 1999) (final decision) (false advertising, analgesic for back pain), *aff'd*, 223 F.3d 783 (D.C. Cir. 2000); Body Sys. Technology, Inc., 5 Trade Reg. Rep. (CCH) ¶ 24,622 (F.T.C. Dkt. C-3895 1999) (consent order) (false advertising, analgesic for back pain); Natural Innovations, Inc., 5 Trade Reg. Rep. (CCH) ¶ 24,170 (F.T.C. Dkt. No. C-3718 1997) (consent order); World Media TV, Inc., 5 Trade Reg. Rep. (CCH) ¶ 24,170 (F.T.C. Dkt. No. C-3717 1997) (consent order). *Cholesterol reduction*: Body Wise Int'l, Inc., 5 Trade Reg. Rep. (CCH) ¶ 23,831 (F.T.C. Dkt. No. C-3617 1995) (consent order); Gracewood Fruit Co., 5 Trade Reg. Rep. (CCH) ¶ 23,359 (F.T.C. File No. 922 3056 1993) (consent order); CPC Int'l, Inc., 114 F.T.C. 1, 1991 FTC LEXIS 10, 5 Trade Reg. Rep. (CCH) ¶ 22,841 (1991) (consent order); Pacific Rice Products, Inc., 115 F.T.C. 763, 1992 FTC LEXIS 220, 5 Trade Reg. Rep. (CCH) ¶ 23,053 (1991) (consent order); Bertolli USA, Inc., 115 F.T.C. 774, 1992 FTC LEXIS 218, 5 Trade Reg. Rep. (CCH) ¶ 20,052 (1991) (consent order). *Cancer-fighting products*: FTC v. David J. Walker, 5 Trade Reg. Rep. (CCH) ¶ 15318 (W.D.

cal or surgical procedures.[3333] The very name "Aspercreme" is misleading if a product does not contain aspirin.[3334] Marketing health products without disclosing their side effects is unfair and deceptive.[3335]

It is deceptive to market an in-the-home AIDS test that misrepresents FDA approval and is only a lifestyle questionnaire.[3336] Similarly deceptive is the sale of an "HIV Negative Card" that can not guarantee that the holder is HIV negative.[3337] The making of unsubstantiated claims regarding purported AIDS cures and prevention products is also deceptive.[3338]

False or unsubstantiated claims about diet products,[3339]

Wash. Oct. 28, 2002); FTC v. BioPulse Int'l, Inc., 5 Trade Reg. Rep. (CCH) ¶ 15277 (N.D. Cal. July 23, 2002) (proposed consent decree) (insulin-induced hypoglycemic sleep therapy and acoustic lightwave therapy); FTC v. Western Dietary Prods., 5 Trade Reg. Rep. (CCH) ¶ 15114 (complaint), ¶ 15197 (proposed consent decree); FTC v. Lane Labs-USA, Inc., 5 Trade Reg. Rep. (CCH) ¶ 24,768 (D.N.J. June 28, 2000) (stipulated final order). *Liver disease*: FTC v. Liverite Prods., Inc., 5 Trade Reg. Rep. (CCH) ¶ 15143 (C.D. Cal. Aug. 21, 2001). *Other health benefits:* FTC v. Christopher Enters., Inc., 5 Trade Reg. Rep. (CCH) ¶ 15126 (D. Utah July 3, 2001) (proposed consent decree) (herbal cures); FTC v. Western Botanicals, Inc., 5 Trade Reg. Rep. (CCH) ¶ 15131 (E.D. Cal. July 11, 2001) (stipulation to final order) (herbal cures); FTC v. Bayer Corp., 5 Trade Reg. Rep. (CCH) ¶ 24,692 (D.D.C. 2000) (consent order against unsubstantiated claims regarding aspirin therapy to prevent heart attacks and stroke); Med Gen, Inc., Dkt. C-4061, www.ftc.gov/opa/2002/07/fyi0240.htm (July 19, 2002) (consent order) (throat spray that prevented snoring and sleep apnea); ForMor, Inc., Dkt. C-4021, www.ftc.gov/opa/2001/08/fyi0142.htm (Aug. 3, 2001) (shark cartilage, St. John's wort, colloidal silver) (consent order); Michael Forrest, Dkt C-4020, www.ftc.gov/opa/2001/08/fyi0142.htm (Aug. 3, 2001) (herbs and pulsing magnetic box) (consent order); Aaron Co., www.ftc.gov/opa/2001/08/fyi0142.htm (Aug. 3, 2001) (consent order) (colloidal silver and dietary supplements); Conopco, Inc., 5 Trade Reg. Rep. (CCH) ¶ 24,650 (F.T.C. Dkt. No. C-3914, Dec. 22, 1999) (illness-fighting hand lotion); Pain Stops Here!, Inc., 5 Trade Reg. Rep. (CCH) ¶ 24,624 (F.T.C. Dkt. C-3898 1999) (consent order) (magnetic devices curing various ailments); Magnetic Therapeutic Technologies, Inc., 5 Trade Reg. Rep. (CCH) ¶ 24,625 (F.T.C. Dkt. C-3897 1999) (consent order) (same); Nutrivida, Inc., 5 Trade Reg. Rep. (CCH) ¶ 24,459 (F.T.C. Dkt. C-3826, 1998) (consent order) (various benefits claimed for shark cartilage capsules); Care Technologies, Inc., 5 Trade Reg. Rep. (CCH) ¶ 24,502 (F.T.C. Dkt. C-3840 1998) (consent orders) (head lice treatments); FTC v. Trudeau, 5 Trade Reg. Rep. (CCH) ¶ 24,368 (N.D. Ill. 1998) (consent order); FTC v. Wright, 5 Trade Reg. Rep. (CCH) ¶ 24,368 (N.D. Ill. 1998) (consent order); Roger J. Callahan, 5 Trade Reg. Rep. (CCH) ¶ 24,368 (F.T.C. Dkt. No. C-3797 1998) (consent order); Tru-Vantage Int'l L.L.C., 5 Trade Reg. Rep. (CCH) ¶ 24,368 (F.T.C. Dkt. No. C-3798 1998) (consent order); JeanieEller, 5 Trade Reg. Rep. (CCH) ¶ 24,368 (F.T.C. Dkt. No. C-3799 1998) (consent order); Mega Sys. Int'l Inc., 5 Trade Reg. Rep. (CCH) ¶ 24,368 (F.T.C. Dkt. No. C-3811 1998) (consent order); Howard Berg, 5 Trade Reg. Rep. (CCH) ¶ 24,368 (F.T.C. Dkt. No. C-3812 1998) (consent order).

3333 FTC v. Wellquest Int'l, Inc., 5 Trade Reg. Rep. (CCH) ¶ 15440 (C.D. Cal. July 10, 2003) (proposed consent order requiring doctor who endorsed product to have substantiation and make disclosure about sleep apnea); Snore Formula, Inc., File No. 022-3247, www.ftc.gov/opa/2003/07/fyi0347.htm (July 29, 2003) (consent order) (defendants must have substantiation and disclose warning about sleep apnea); David Green, M.D., 5 Trade Reg. Rep. (CCH) ¶ 23,794 (F.T.C. Dkt. No. C-3589 1995) (consent order) (varicose vein treatment); Vein Clinics of Am., Inc., 5 Trade Reg. Rep. (CCH) ¶ 23,534 (F.T.C. C-3501 1994) (consent order) (same); Dr. Scott M. Ross, 115 F.T.C. 54, 1992 FTC LEXIS 28, 5 Trade Reg. Rep. (CCH) ¶ 23,079 (1992) (consent order) (claims about risks and benefits of liposuction); NME Hosps. Inc., 115 F.T.C. 798, 1992 FTC LEXIS 223, 5 Trade Reg. Rep. (CCH) ¶ 23,206 (1992) (consent order); BelAge Plastic Surgery Center, 115 F.T.C. 871, 1992 FTC LEXIS 230, 5 Trade Reg. Rep. (CCH) ¶ 23,219 (1992) (consent order) (claims by surgical centers regarding breast implants).

3334 Thompson Medical Co., 104 F.T.C. 648 (1984), *aff'd*, 791 F.2d 189 (D.C. Cir. 1986).

3335 Panda Herbal Int'l, Dkt C-4018, www.ftc.gov/opa/2001/08/fyi0142.htm (Aug. 3, 2001) (consent order); Aaron Co., www.ftc.gov/opa/2001/08/fyi0142.htm (Aug. 3, 2001) (consent order). *See also* Laser Vision Institute, L.L.C., File No. 022-3053, and LCA-Vision, Inc., File No. 022-3098, www.ftc.gov/opa/2003/07/fyi0343.htm (July 11, 2003) (consent orders against laser surgery clinics that advertised free consultations but required non-refundable $300 deposit before advising consumer about risks and limitations).

3336 FTC v. Feiler, 5 Trade Reg. Rep. (CCH) ¶ 22,739 (D. Nev. Oct. 3, 1989) (consent judgment). *See also* FTC v. Medimax, Inc., 5 Trade Reg. Rep. (CCH) ¶ 24,720 (M.D. Fla. 2000) (permanent injunction against marketer of faulty AIDS test); FTC v. Cyberlinx Market, Inc., 5 Trade Reg. Rep. (CCH) ¶ 24,676 (D. Nev. Nov. 17, 1999) (consent decree against seller of faulty AIDS test kits).

3337 People v. Overs Enterprises, Inc., Clearinghouse No. 49,151 (N.Y. Sup. Ct. Westchester Cty. Jan. 6, 1992).

3338 FTC v. Alfa Scientific Designs, Inc., 5 Trade Reg. Rep. (CCH) ¶ 24,695 (S.D. Cal. 2000) (consent order) (HIV home test kits); FTC v. Medimax, Inc., 5 Trade Reg. Rep. ¶ 24,720 (M.D. Fla. 2000) (consent order) (same); FTC v. Cyberlinx Marketing, Inc., 5 Trade Reg. Rep. (CCH) ¶ 24,676 (D. Nev. 1999) (consent order) (same); FTC v. Redhead, 5 Trade Reg. Rep. (CCH) ¶ 23,664 (D. Or. Sept. 9, 1994) (proposed consent decree); Johnson & Johnson Consumer Products, Inc., 5 Trade Reg. Rep. (CCH) ¶ 23,909 (F.T.C. C-3636 1996) (consent order).

3339 U.S. v. Lifestyle Fascination, Inc., 5 Trade Reg. Rep. (CCH) ¶ 15439 (D.N.J. July 9, 2003) (fat-burning drink); FTC v. Rexall Sundown, Inc., 5 Trade Reg. Rep. (CCH) ¶ 15374 (S.D. Fla. Mar. 22, 2003) (cellulite treatment product); FTC v. No. 9068-8425 Quebec, Inc., 2003 WL 31082950 (N.D.N.Y. Sept. 6, 2002) (TRO); FTC v. No. 9068-8425 Quebec, Inc., 2003 WL 31082950 (N.D.N.Y. Sept. 6, 2002) (TRO); FTC v. Garvey, 5 Trade Reg. Rep. (CCH) ¶ 24,795 (C.D. Cal. Aug. 31, 2000) (stipulated final order); FTC v. Enforma Natural Prods., Inc., 5 Trade Reg. Rep. (CCH) ¶ 24,734 (C.D. Cal. Apr. 25, 2000) (stipulated final order); FTC v. Slim Am., Inc., 5 Trade Reg. Rep. 24,630 (S.D. Fla. 1999); FTC v. Silueta Distributors, Inc., 5 Trade Reg. Rep. (CCH) ¶ 23,641 (N.D. Cal. July 11, 1994) (preliminary injunction) ¶ 23,782 (summary judgment) (claims that skin cream breaks down cellulite or fat); FTC v. Allied Int'l Corp., 5 Trade Reg. Rep. (CCH) ¶ 22,972 (C.D. Cal. 1991) (consent order regarding "fat magnets"); ValueVision Int'l, Inc., www.ftc.gov/opa/2001/08/fyi0145.htm (Aug. 24, 2001) (consent order); Weider Nutrition Int'l, 5 Trade Reg. Rep. (CCH) ¶ 24,817 (F.T.C. Dkt. No. C-3983, 2000) (consent order); Herbal Worldwide Holdings Corp., 5

diet pills,[3340] diet schemes,[3341] and weight-loss clinics[3342] are deceptive. A number of FTC orders likewise prohibit deceptive claims by "stop smoking" clinics and products.[3343] Unsubstantiated claims that a product detects health hazards such as anthrax spores are deceptive.[3344]

A seller may not misrepresent the safety of hair implants or fail to disclose that hair implants are unsafe.[3345] Also deceptive are false or unsubstantiated claims concerning baldness preventatives and remedies,[3346] hair-removal devices,[3347] anti-wrinkle treatments,[3348] sunglasses that protect

---

Trade Reg. Rep. (CCH) ¶ 24,458 (F.T.C. Dkt. C-3827 1998) (consent order) (weight reduction advertisement); TrendMark Int'l, Inc., 5 Trade Reg. Rep. (CCH) ¶ 24,448 (F.T.C. Dkt. No. C-3829 1998) (consent order); Richard Crew, 114 F.T.C. 230, 1991 FTC LEXIS 81 (1991) (consent order); (diet patch); Robert Francis, 114 F.T.C. 240, 1991 FTC LEXIS 82 (1991) (consent order) (diet patch); Thomas A. Dardas, 3 Trade Reg. Rep. (CCH) ¶ 22,172 (F.T.C. C-3144 1984) (consent order regarding claims about effectiveness of acu-form ear mold as a diet product). *See also* Delahunt v. Cytodyne Technologies, 241 F. Supp. 2d 827 (S.D. Ohio 2003) (declining to dismiss class action alleging mislabeling of components of diet product); Consumer Justice Center v. Olympian Labs, Inc., 99 Cal. App. 4th 1056, 121 Cal. Rptr. 2d 749 (2002) (suit regarding false advertising of weight-loss supplement not preempted by federal law).

3340 Porter & Dietsch Inc. v. FTC, 605 F.2d 294 (7th Cir. 1979); FTC v. Slim Am., Inc., 5 Trade Reg. Rep. (CCH) ¶ 24,630 (S.D. Fla. 1999) (final judgment) (weight loss pills); FTC v. Allied Int'l Corp., 5 Trade Reg. Rep. (CCH) ¶ 22,972 (C.D. Cal. 1991) (consent order); FTC v. Kingsbridge Media & Marketing, Inc., 3 Trade Reg. Rep. (CCH) ¶ 22,547 (D. Ariz. 1988) (consent order); Twin Star Productions, Inc., 5 Trade Reg. Rep. (CCH) ¶ 22,821 (F.T.C. C-3307 1990) (consent order); Buckingham Productions, Inc., 110 F.T.C. 37 (1987) (consent order); Dr. Barry Bricklin, 106 F.T.C. 115 (1985) (consent order).

3341 *See, e.g.*, FTC v. Pacific Medical Clinics Mgmt., Inc., 5 Trade Reg. Rep. (CCH) ¶ 23,173 (S.D. Cal. 1992); Weight Watchers Int'l, Inc., 5 Trade Reg. Rep. (CCH) ¶ 24,333 (F.T.C. Dkt. No. 9261 1997) (consent order); WLAR Co., 5 Trade Reg. Rep. (CCH) ¶ 23,829 (F.T.C. Dkt. No. C-3641 1996) (consent order) (unsubstantiated claims for diet plan and failure to disclose that diet product was merely a booklet); Body Wise Int'l, Inc., 5 Trade Reg. Rep. (CCH) ¶ 23,831 (F.T.C. Dkt. No. C-3617 1995) (consent order); J. Walter Thompson USA, Inc., 5 Trade Reg. Rep. (CCH) ¶ 23,861 (F.T.C. C-3622 1995) (consent order) (misrepresentation of survey results); Gorayeb Seminars, Inc., 5 Trade Reg. Rep. (CCH) ¶ 23,639 (F.T.C. Dkt. C-3561 1995) (consent order) (group hypnosis seminar); American Institute of Smoking Cessation, Inc., 5 Trade Reg. Rep. (CCH) ¶ 23,640 (F.T.C. Dkt. C-3560 1995) (consent order) (group hypnosis seminar); Formu-3 Int'l, Inc., 5 Trade Reg. Rep. (CCH) ¶ 23,751 (F.T.C. Dkt. C-3568 1995) (consent order); Ninzu, Inc., 5 Trade Reg. Rep. (CCH) ¶ 23,752 (F.T.C. Dkt. C-3566 1995) (consent order) (clip placed on ear to suppress appetite); Taleigh Corp., 5 Trade Reg. Rep. (CCH) ¶ 23,783 (F.T.C. Dkt. C-3587 1995) (consent order); Original Marketing Inc, 5 Trade Reg. Rep. (CCH) ¶ 23,816 (F.T.C. Dkt. No. C-3596 1995) (consent order) (appetite controls through acupressure device inserted in ear); Schering Corp., 5 Trade Reg. Rep. (CCH) ¶ 23,646 (F.T.C. Dkt. 9232 1994) (consent order); L&S Research Corp., 5 Trade Reg. Rep. (CCH) ¶ 23,633 (F.T.C. Dkt. C-3534 1994) (consent order); Nature's Cleaners, Inc., 5 Trade Reg. Rep. (CCH) ¶ 23,379 (F.T.C. Dkt. C-3450 1993); Nu-Day Enterprises, Inc., 115 F.T.C. 479, 1992 FTC LEXIS 105, 5 Trade Reg. Rep. (CCH) ¶ 23,089 (1992) (consent order); Slender You, Inc., 115 F.T.C. 592, 1992 FTC LEXIS 142, 5 Trade Reg. Rep. (CCH) ¶ 23,108 (1992) (consent order); Jason Pharmaceutical, Inc., 115 F.T.C. 899, 1992 FTC LEXIS 237 (1992) (consent order); National Center for Nutrition, Inc., 115 F.T.C. 676 (1992) (consent order) (misrepresentations about efficacy of low-calorie diet and failure to disclose health risks); Sandoz Nutrition Corp., 115 F.T.C. 741, 1992 FTC LEXIS 236, 5 Trade Reg. Rep. (CCH) ¶ 23,073 (1991) (consent order); Spanish Telemarketing Indus., Inc., 114 F.T.C. 754, 1991 FTC LEXIS 520, 5 Trade Reg. Rep. (CCH) ¶ 23,070 (F.T.C. C-3353 1991) (consent order).

3342 Beverly Hills Weight Loss Clinics Int'l, 5 Trade Reg. Rep. (CCH) ¶ 23,611 (F.T.C. C-3515 1994) (consent order); Diet Center, Inc., 5 Trade Reg. Rep. (CCH) ¶ 23,466 (F.T.C. C-3474 1993) (consent order).

3343 Live-Lee Productions, Inc., 5 Trade Reg. Rep. (CCH) ¶ 23,842 (F.T.C. Dkt. No. C-3620 1995) (consent order) (vitamin spray); Gorayeb Seminars, Inc., 5 Trade Reg. Rep. (CCH) ¶ 23,639 (F.T.C. Dkt. C-3561 1995) (consent order) (group hypnosis seminar); American Institute of Smoking Cessation, Inc., 5 Trade Reg. Rep. (CCH) ¶ 23,640 (F.T.C. Dkt. C-3560 1995) (consent order) (group hypnosis seminar); Taleigh Corp., 5 Trade Reg. Rep. (CCH) ¶ 23,783 (F.T.C. Dkt. C-3587 1995) (consent order) (non-prescription stop-smoking patch); Alan v. Phan, 5 Trade Reg. Rep. (CCH) ¶ 23,297 (F.T.C. Dkt. C-3417 1993) (consent order regarding claim that non-tobacco product helped people quit smoking). *See also* Alternative Cigarettes, Inc., 5 Trade Reg. Rep. (CCH) ¶ 24,736 (June 14, 2000) (consent order regarding claim that company's cigarettes were less hazardous); Santa Fe Natural Tobacco Co., 5 Trade Reg. Rep. (CCH) ¶ 24,736 (F.T.C. Dkt. No. C-3952, June 12, 2000) (same).

3344 FTC v. Sani-Pure Laboratories, 5 Trade Reg. Rep. (CCH) ¶ 15317 (D.N.J. Oct. 4, 2002); FTC v. Vital Living Prods., Inc., 5 Trade Reg. Rep. (CCH) ¶ 15223 (W.D.N.C. Feb. 22, 2002) (proposed consent order).

3345 Hair Extension of Beverly Hills, Inc., 95 F.T.C. 361 (1980) (consent order); Terrance D. Lesko, M.D., 96 F.T.C. 73 (1980) (consent order).

3346 FTC v. Pantron I Corp., 33 F.3d 1088 (9th Cir. 1994); FTC v. Pantron I. Corp., 5 Trade Reg. Rep. (CCH) ¶ 24,208 (C.D. Cal. 1997) (proposed consent decree); FTC v. California Pacific Research, Inc., 5 Trade Reg. Rep. (CCH) ¶ 23,217 (D. Nev. 1992) (consent judgment); FTC v. California Pacific Research, Inc., 5 Trade Reg. Rep. (CCH) ¶ 22,669 (D. Nev. Apr. 10, 1989); Jacqueline Sabal, 5 Trade Reg. Rep. (CCH) ¶ 24,525 (File No. X98 0012, Nov. 12, 1998) (stipulated final judgment); Synchronal Corp., 5 Trade Reg. Rep. (CCH) ¶ 23,404 (F.T.C. Dkt. 9251 1993) (consent order); Patricia Wexler, M.D., 115 F.T.C. 849, 1992 FTC LEXIS 225, 5 Trade Reg. Rep. (CCH) ¶ 23,213 (1992) (consent order); FTC v. California Pacific Research, 5 Trade Reg. Rep. (CCH) ¶ 23,059 (D. Nev. 1991) (consent order).

3347 Removatron Int'l Corp., 111 F.T.C. 206 (1988), *aff'd*, 884 F.2d 1489 (11th Cir. 1989). *See also* Removatron Int'l Corp., 114 F.T.C. 715 (1991) (modification of original order).

3348 Conair Corp., 5 Trade Reg. Rep. (CCH) ¶ 23,352 (F.T.C. Dkt. C-3431 1993) (consent order); Medical Marketing Servs., 5 Trade Reg. Rep. (CCH) ¶ 23,271 (F.T.C. Dkt. C-3409 1993) (consent order regarding chemical face peel said to eliminate wrinkles); St. Ives Laboratories, Inc., 115 F.T.C. 77, 1992 FTC LEXIS 40, 5 Trade Reg. Rep. (CCH) ¶ 23,088 (1992) (consent

against harmful ultraviolet rays,[3349] dyslexia treatments,[3350] a razor that was claimed to cure razor bumps,[3351] exercise machines,[3352] wheatgerm oil,[3353] electronic muscle stimulation treatment,[3354] and sun tanning.[3355]

It is deceptive to advertise denture cushions for long-term use when they should only be used temporarily until a dentist can be seen.[3356] "Denturists" (those who repair dentures) must disclose that they are not dentists and may not perform certain dental functions.[3357] It is deceptive to misrepresent that a water pik is recommended by dentists or prevents gum disease.[3358] Similarly deceptive are claims that a toothpaste cures gum disease.[3359]

Not surprisingly, it is unfair and deceptive for a home care medical equipment company to go into consumers' homes and remove equipment leased from competitors, and, without giving the consumer a choice, install new equipment.[3360] Part of this scheme was disparaging the competitor's equipment and claiming it needed to be replaced, while not identifying that it belonged to a competitor.

It is deceptive for an antiabortion group to lure women to their "clinic" on the promise of free pregnancy tests and the implication that they perform abortion services, when instead they counsel against abortion.[3361] Also deceptive are misrepresentations about a clinic's ability to help patients become pregnant,[3362] the success of an in vitro fertilization service[3363] or a company's ability to cure impotence.[3364] It is deceptive to misrepresent the effectiveness or performance characteristics of birth control devices, or to fail to disclose important directions in order to use the devices without side-effects.[3365]

False or unsubstantiated claims about the cancer-fighting properties[3366] or other health benefits[3367] of foods are deceptive, as are unsupported health claims for vitamins,[3368] bee pollen,[3369] nutritional supple-

---

order); Spinal Health Servs., Inc., 102 F.T.C. 1319 (1983) (consent order) (laser facelift).

3349 Site for Sore Eyes, Inc., 5 Trade Reg. Rep. (CCH) ¶ 23,273 (F.T.C. Dkt. C-3411 1993) (consent order).

3350 FTC v. Transformational Training Ctr., 5 Trade Reg. Rep. (CCH) ¶ 23,764 (C.D. Cal. 1995); Natural Organics, Inc., Dkt. No. 9294, 5 Trade Reg. Rep. (CCH) ¶ 15135 (Sept. 6, 2001) (proposed consent order) (dietary supplement that allegedly helped children overcome ADHD).

3351 McCaffrey & McCall, Inc., 101 F.T.C. 367 (1983) (consent order); North Am. Philips Corp., 101 F.T.C. 359 (1983) (consent order).

3352 Fitness Quest, Inc., 5 Trade Reg. Rep. (CCH) ¶ 24,601 (F.T.C. Dkt. C-3886 1999) (consent order) (exercise and weight loss equipment); Fleetwood Mfg., Inc., 5 Trade Reg. Rep. (CCH) ¶ 23,337 (F.T.C. Dkt. C-3428 1993) (consent order); Consumer Direct, Inc., 5 Trade Reg. Rep. (CCH) ¶ 22,863 (F.T.C. Dkt. 9236 1990) (consent order).

3353 Viobin Corp., 108 F.T.C. 385 (1986) (consent order); *In re* PLNP Holdings, Inc., 105 F.T.C. 291 (1985) (consent order).

3354 Nutritone, Inc., 112 F.T.C. 179, 1989 FTC LEXIS 65 (1989) (consent order).

3355 Haverhills, Inc., 114 F.T.C. 17 (1991), 1991 FTC LEXIS 26 (consent order) (safety claims for sunlamp); An-Mar Int'l, Ltd., 112 F.T.C. 72, 1989 FTC LEXIS 96 (1989) (consent order) (misrepresentations regarding the health benefits and lack of health risks of sun tanning).

3356 The Mentholatum Co., 96 F.T.C. 757 (1980) (consent order).

3357 Terry v. Hoden-Dhein Enterprises Ltd., 48 Or. App. 763, 618 P.2d 7 (1980).

3358 J. Walter Thompson Co., 97 F.T.C. 333 (1981) (consent order); Teledyne Inc., 97 F.T.C. 320 (1981) (consent order).

3359 Jerome Milton, Inc., 110 F.T.C. 104 (1987) (consent order).

3360 State v. Robertson, Clearinghouse No. 36,572 (Tenn. Ch. Ct. Davidson Cty. 1984).

3361 Mother & Unborn Baby Care v. State, 749 S.W.2d 533 (Tex. App. 1988) *cert. denied*, 490 U.S. 1090 (1989).

3362 FTC v. Jacobson, 5 Trade Reg. Rep. (CCH) ¶ 22,684 (E.D. Va. May 18, 1989) (consent decree); Fertility Institute of Western Massachusetts, 5 Trade Reg. Rep. (CCH) ¶ 22,893 (F.T.C. Dkt. C-3318 1990) (consent order).

3363 Arizona Institute of Reproductive Medicine, Ltd., 114 F.T.C. 802, 5 Trade Reg. Rep. (CCH) ¶ 23,844 (1995) (misleading success rate statutes); Reproductive Genetics In Vitro P.C., 114 F.T.C. 802, 5 Trade Reg. Rep. (CCH) ¶ 23,067 (F.T.C. C-3357 1991) (consent order); IVF Australia, Ltd., 5 Trade Reg. Rep. (CCH) ¶ 22,885 (F.T.C. Dkt. 9317 1990) (consent order). *See also* Karlin v. IVF Am., Inc., 93 N.Y.2d 282, 712 N.E.2d 662 (1999) (allowing private UDAP cause of action for fertility clinic's mispresentation of its success rate).

3364 FTC v. American Urological Corp., 5 Trade Reg. Rep. (CCH) ¶ 24,595 (N.D. Ga. 1999) (consent order) (impotence cures, use of name "Vaegra"); Genetus Alexandria, Inc., 5 Trade Reg. Rep. (CCH) ¶ 23,891 (F.T.C. C-3639 1996) (consent order) (treatment for impotence); Twin Star Productions, Inc., 5 Trade Reg. Rep. (CCH) ¶ 22,821 (F.T.C. C-3307 1990) (consent order).

3365 Johnson & Johnson Consumer Products, Inc., 5 Trade Reg. Rep. (CCH) ¶ 23,909 (F.T.C. C-3636 1996) (consent order); Benton & Bowles Inc., 97 F.T.C. 167 (1981) (consent order); Shaller Rubin Assocs., 97 F.T.C. 178 (1981) (consent order); Sorga Inc., 97 F.T.C. 205 (1981) (consent order); American Home Products Corp., 95 F.T.C. 884 (1980) (consent order); Jordan Simmer Inc., 95 F.T.C. 871 (1980) (consent order); Morton-Norwich Products Inc., 95 F.T.C. 899 (1980) (consent order).

3366 *Claims that food products are effective against cancer*: FTC v. Pharmtech Research, Inc., 576 F. Supp. 294 (D.D.C. 1983); Michael D. Miller, 5 Trade Reg. Rep. (CCH) ¶ 24,724 (F.T.C. Dkt. No. C-3941 2000) (consent order regarding herbal tea); Gracewood Fruit Co., 5 Trade Reg. Rep. (CCH) ¶ 23,359 (F.T.C. File No. 922 3056 1993) (consent order); National Media Corp., 5 Trade Reg. Rep. (CCH) ¶ 23,360 (F.T.C. File No. 902 3177 1993) (consent order); General Nutrition, Inc., 111 F.T.C. 387 (1988) (consent order); Pharmtech Research, 103 F.T.C. 448 (1984) (consent order).

3367 Pompeian, Inc., 115 F.T.C. 933, 1992 FTC LEXIS 267 (1992) (consent order) (unsubstantiated health claims for olive oil); Roy Brog, 108 F.T.C. 18 (1986) (consent order) (health claims for milk substitutes).

3368 Live-Lee Productions, Inc., 5 Trade Reg. Rep. (CCH) ¶ 23,842 (F.T.C. Dkt. No. C-3620 1995) (consent order) (vitamin spray to prevent wrinkles, treat hangovers and increase energy); Miles, Inc., 114 F.T.C. 31, 1991 FTC LEXIS 44, 5 Trade Reg. Rep. (CCH) ¶ 22,896 (F.T.C. Dkt. C-3323 1991) (consent order).

3369 Bee-Sweet, Inc., 5 Trade Reg. Rep. (CCH) ¶ 23,695 (F.T.C. C-3550 1995) (various health claims for bee pollen); CC Pollen Co., 5 Trade Reg. Rep. (CCH) ¶ 23,310 (F.T.C. Dkt. C-3419 1993) (consent order regarding claims that bee pollen would

ments,[3370] and the like.[3371] In 1994 Congress passed amendments to the Food, Drug, and Cosmetic Act to set standards for labeling of nutritional supplements,[3372] and the FTC has indicated that it may incorporate these standards into consent orders.[3373] Unsubstantiated or misleading claims that foods are fat free,[3374] low fat,[3375] low sodium,[3376] low calorie,[3377] low alcohol,[3378] sweetened with certain artificial sweeteners,[3379] low in sugar[3380] or cholesterol,[3381] high in calcium,[3382] or have other nutritional features are also deceptive. State attorney general offices have obtained settlements with Campbell's Soup concerning claims that soup can reduce the risk of heart disease or cancer,[3383] with Sara Lee Corp. concerning "light" cake that was not low in calories,[3384] with Carnation concerning infant formula that is not hypoallergenic,[3385] and with Nabisco concerning products' ability to reduce the risk of heart disease and claims that products are only sweetened with fruit juices.[3386]

5.11.3 Nursing Facilities

5.11.3.1 General

Nursing facilities provide room, board, and nursing services to disabled, elder, and other individuals needing intensive skilled care. A nursing facility may be a "stand

cure allergy symptoms, cause weight loss, and reverse the aging process).

3370 *Claims that nutritional supplements fight fatigue*: Metagenics, Inc., 5 Trade Reg. Rep. (CCH) ¶ 24,139 (F.T.C. Dkt. 9267 1996) (initial decision), The Winning Combination, Inc., 115 F.T.C. 831, 1992 FTC LEXIS 222, 5 Trade Reg. Rep. (CCH) ¶ 23,204 (1992) (consent order). *Nutritional supplements as body builders*: FTC v. AST Nutritional Concepts, Inc., 5 Trade Reg. Rep. (CCH) ¶ 24,671 (D. Colo. Nov. 15, 1999) (consent decree); RN Nutrition, 5 Trade Reg. Rep. (CCH) ¶ 23,658 (F.T.C. Dkt. C-3549 1995) (consent order) (calcium product); The Winning Combination, Inc., 115 F.T.C. 831, 1992 FTC LEXIS 222, 5 Trade Reg. Rep. (CCH) ¶ 23,204 (1992) (consent order); Great Earth Int'l Inc., 110 F.T.C. 188 (1988) (consent order); Weider Health & Fitness, Inc., 106 F.T.C. 584 (1985) (consent order). *Other claims*: MaxCell BioScience, Inc., Dkt. C-4017, www.ftc.gov/opa/2001/08/fyi0142.htm (Aug. 3, 2001) (consent order); FTC v. Rose Creek Health Prods., Inc., 5 Trade Reg. Rep. (CCH) ¶ 24,738 (E.D. Wash. Apr. 28, 2000) (consent order) (prevents cancer, heart and lung disease); Efanol Nutraceuticals, Inc., 5 Trade Reg. Rep. (CCH) ¶ 24,747 (F.T.C. Dkt. C-3958 2000) (consent order) (cures ADHD); Bogdana Corp., 5 Trade Reg. Rep. (CCH) ¶ 24,428 (F.T.C. Dkts. C-3820, C-3821, 1998) (consent orders) (dietary supplements purporting to reduce weight and cholesterol, strengthen immune systems, combat heart disease); New Vision Int'l, Inc., 5 Trade Reg. Rep. ¶ 24,537 (F.T.C. Dkts. C-3856, C-3857 1998) (consent orders) (nutritional supplement as cure for attention deficit disorder); American Life Nutrition, Inc., 5 Trade Reg. Rep. (CCH) ¶ 22,862 (F.T.C. Dkt C-3310 1990) (consent order). *See also* Venegas, Inc., 5 Trade Reg. Rep. (CCH) ¶ 24,342 (F.T.C. Dkt. No. C-3781 1998) (consent order); Global World Media Corp., 5 Trade Reg. Rep. (CCH) ¶ 24,306 (F.T.C. Dkt. C-3772 1997) (consent order); Health Mgmt. Resources Corp., 5 Trade Reg. Rep. (CCH) ¶ 23,356 (F.T.C. Dkt. C-3455 1993); Nature's Way Products, Inc., 5 Trade Reg. Rep. (CCH) ¶ 22,783 (F.T.C. C-3285 1990) (nutritional supplement claimed to prevent yeast infections); Nagel v. Twin Laboratories, Inc., 109 Cal. App. 4th 39, 134 Cal. Rptr. 2d 420 (2003) (affirming dismissal of defendant's challenge under anti-SLAPP suit law to plaintiff's claim that nutritional supplement ingredient label was deceptive).

3371 Body Sys. Technology, 5 Trade Reg. Rep. (CCH) ¶ 24622 (F.T.C. Dkt. No. C-3894, Sept. 7, 1999) (consent order regarding shark cartilege); Pain Stops Here!, 5 Trade Reg. Rep. (CCH) ¶ 24,624 (F.T.C. Dkt. No. C-3898, Sept. 7, 1999) (consent order regarding magnet therapy).

3372 21 U.S.C. § 343(s), *as amended by* Pub. Law No. 103-417, 108 Stat. 4329, Oct. 25, 1994; *cf.* Anthony v. Country Life Mfg., 2002 WL 31269621 (N.D. Ill. Oct. 9, 2002) (Food & Drug Act preempts private plaintiff's claim that sale of nutritional supplements with ingredients not approved by FDA was unfair), *aff'd*, 2003 WL 21540975 (7th Cir. July 2, 2003) (unpublished, citation limited).

3373 *See* General Nutrition Corp., 5 Trade Reg. Rep. (CCH) ¶ 24,701, F.T.C. Dkt. C-1517 and Dkt. 9175 (Jan. 31, 2000).

3374 The Clorox Co., 5 Trade Reg. Rep. (CCH) ¶ 23,269 (F.T.C. Dkt. C-3427 1993) (consent order).

3375 Uno Restaurant Corp., 5 Trade Reg. Rep. (CCH) ¶ 24,196 (F.T.C. Dkt. No. C-3730 1997) (consent order); Dannon Co., 5 Trade Reg. Rep. (CCH) ¶ 23,932 (F.T.C. C-3643 1996); Mrs. Fields Cookies, Inc., 5 Trade Reg. Rep. (CCH) ¶ 23,989 (F.T.C. C-3657 1996) (consent order); Haagen-Dazs Co., 5 Trade Reg. Rep. (CCH) ¶ 23,718 (F.T.C. Dkt. C-3582 1995); Nestle Food Co., 115 F.T.C. 67, 1992 FTC LEXIS 42, 5 Trade Reg. Rep. (CCH) ¶ 23,091 (1992) (consent order).

3376 Stouffer Foods Corp., 5 Trade Reg. Rep. (CCH) ¶ 23,686 (F.T.C. Dkt. 9250 1994) (final order).

3377 Mama Tish's Italian Specialties, Inc., 5 Trade Reg. Rep. (CCH) ¶ 23,943 (F.T.C. C-3644 1996) (consent order); Eskimo Pie Corp., 5 Trade Reg. Rep. (CCH) ¶ 23,819 (F.T.C. Dkt. No. C-3597 1995) (consent order).

3378 Canandaigua Wine Co., 114 F.T.C. 349 (1991) (consent order).

3379 Zapka v. Coca-Cola Co., 2001 U.S. Dist. LEXIS 20155 (N.D. Ill. Dec. 3, 2001) (denial of motion for summary judgment).

3380 Estee Corp., 102 F.T.C. 1804 (1983) (consent order) (claim that product is low in sugar and healthy for diabetics).

3381 Good News Products Inc., 5 Trade Reg. Rep. (CCH) ¶ 23,833 (F.T.C. Dkt. No. C-3642 1996) (consent order); Eggland's Best, Inc., 5 Trade Reg. Rep. (CCH) ¶ 23,551 (F.T.C. C-3520 1994) (consent order); Campbell Soup Co., 115 F.T.C. 788, 1992 FTC LEXIS 217 (1992) (consent order) (forbidding representations about health benefits of soup's low cholesterol and low fat level without disclosure of sodium content); CPC Int'l, Inc., 114 F.T.C. 1, 1991 FTC LEXIS 10 (1991) (consent order) (misrepresentation of effect of corn oil on cholesterol level).

3382 Kraft, Inc., 114 F.T.C. 40, 1991 FTC LEXIS 38, 5 Trade Reg. Rep. (CCH) ¶ 22,937 (1991) (deceptive to claim that cheese has more calcium than a non-dairy substitute), *aff'd*, Kraft, Inc. v. FTC, 970 F.2d 311 (7th Cir. 1992).

3383 Minnesota Attorney General News Release (May 10, 1989). *Accord* Campbell Soup Co., 115 F.T.C. 788, 1992 FTC LEXIS 217 (1992) (consent order) (forbidding representations about health benefits of soup's low cholesterol and low fat level without disclosure of sodium content).

3384 Minnesota Attorney General News Release (Sept. 5, 1989).

3385 *Id.* (July 6, 1989).

3386 *Id.* (Mar. 13, 1990).

alone" facility or it may be part of a larger continuing care retirement community.[3387]

Consumer protection laws provide a powerful tool to challenge unfair, deceptive, and unlawful nursing facility practices. Private litigation is particularly critical in this area because government enforcement of nursing facility protections is so sporadic.[3388]

Standards for proper nursing home conduct can be found in the federal Nursing Home Reform Law (NHRL).[3389] Although there is some support to the contrary in the legislative history, courts have held that the federal NHRL does not create a private right of action.[3390] However, the federal law is still relevant for setting the standard of care in negligence and tort actions against nursing facilities. In addition, violation of the NHRL should be a *per se* UDAP violation.[3391] State nursing facility laws may be clearer in providing for a private right of action.[3392]

5.11.3.2 Common Violations of the Federal Nursing Home Reform Law

5.11.3.2.1 Third-party guarantees

Nursing facilities commonly attempt to force a resident's family members or friends to become financially responsible for nursing facility expenses.[3393] Some facilities require these third-party financial guarantees of all residents, others only for residents not eligible for Medicaid.[3394] Facilities will also try to disguise third-party guarantees by calling them "responsible party" provisions. Regardless of what they are called, these types of financial guarantees violate federal law and the method of obtaining these guarantees may be a UDAP violation even if federal law is not violated.[3395]

Facilities will often require guarantees even for Medicaid recipients to ensure payment from family or friends if, for example, a resident's Medicaid application is mishandled or denied. In other cases, facilities will double-bill by forcing the friend or family member to make a separate payment for an item or service already covered by the Medicaid per-diem rate.[3396] Facilities are, however, permitted to obtain the signature of an individual acting as the resident's agent.

Numerous studies have found that nursing facility admission agreements routinely contain third-party financial guaranty provisions, even though these provisions clearly violate federal law.[3397]

5.11.3.2.2 Other common NHRL violations

Other common violations which can be the basis of a UDAP claim include:[3398]

3387 Assisted living facilities are discussed at § 5.11.4, *infra*.

3388 *See* General Accounting Office, Nursing Homes: Additional Steps Needed to Strengthen Enforcement of Federal Quality Standards, GAO/HEHS-99-46 (Mar. 1999) (finding that between January 1997 and July 1998, there were over 1500 substantiated cases of abuse and neglect in nursing homes, but there was no enforcement action in more than 90% of the cases).

3389 The Nursing Home Reform Law applies to any facility which is certified to accept any money from the Medicare program and/or the Medicaid program. The statutes linked to a facility's Medicare certification are located at 42 U.S.C. § 1395i-3, to Medicaid certification at 42 U.S.C. § 1396r, and regulations applicable to both Medicare-certified and Medicaid-certified facilities at 42 C.F.R. §§ 483.5–483.75.

3390 *See, e.g.*, Prince v. Dicker, 29 Fed. Appx. 52, 2002 WL 226492 (2d Cir. Feb. 14, 2002); Carroll v. Butterfield Health Care, Inc., 2003 WL 22462604 (N.D. Ill. Oct. 29, 2003); Tinder v. Lewis County Nursing Home Dist., 207 F. Supp. 2d 951 (E.D. Mo. 2001); Brodgon v. National Healthcare Corp., 103 F. Supp. 2d 1322 (N.D. Ga. 2000); Ayres v. Beaver, 48 F. Supp. 2d 1335 (M.D. Fla. 1999) (discussing issue only in context of whether federal court had removal jurisdiction; defendants were attempting to recharacterize plaintiffs' state law claims as federal claims); Nichols v. St. Luke Center, 800 F. Supp. 1564 (S.D. Ohio 1992). *See generally* Eric Carlson, Long-Term Care Advocacy § 10.06 (Matthew Bender 2003).

3391 For a discussion of whether UDAP statutes apply to regulated industries such as nursing facilities, see § 2.3.3, *supra*.

3392 See Eric Carlson, Long-Term Care Advocacy § 2.101 (Matthew Bender 2003) for a summary of each state statute. States may also have UDAP regulations specifically referring to nursing home practices.

3393 These types of requirements are prohibited by the NHRL, 42 U.S.C. §§ 1395i-3(c)(5)(A)(ii), 1396r(c)(5)(A)(ii); 42 C.F.R. § 483.12(d)(2).

3394 The relevant federal statutes do not make distinctions based on source of payment, 42 U.S.C. §§ 1395i-3(c)(5)(A)(ii), 1396r(c)(5)(A)(ii), and the corresponding federal regulation simply refers to the admission of a "resident." 42 C.F.R. § 483.12(d)(2).

3395 Podolsky v. First Healthcare Corp., 50 Cal. App. 4th 632, 58 Cal. Rptr. 2d 89 (1996); Manor of Lake City, Inc. v. Hinners, 548 N.W.2d 573 (Iowa 1996) (nursing home can not require third party guarantee of payment as condition of admission), *appeal after remand, remanded by* 576 N.W.2d 592 (Iowa 1998). *But see* Carroll v. Butterfield Health Care, Inc., 2003 WL 22462604 (N.D. Ill. Oct. 29, 2003) (violation of Medicaid Act not UDAP violation).

3396 *See generally* Eric Carlson, Long-Term Care Advocacy § 3.06[2] (Matthew Bender 2003); Eric Carlson, Illegal Guarantees in Nursing Homes: A Nursing Facility Can not Force a Resident's Family Members and Friends to Become Financially Responsible for Nursing Facility Expenses, 30 Clearinghouse Review 33 (May 1996); Charles Sabatino, *Nursing Home Admission Contracts: Undermining Rights the Old-Fashioned Way*, 24 Clearinghouse Rev. 553 (Oct. 1990).

3397 *See* Bet Tzedek Legal Services, If Only I Had Known: Misrepresentations by Nursing Homes Which Deprive Residents of Legal Protection (1998); Rebecca J. Benson, Check Your Rights at the Door: Consumer Protection Violations in Massachusetts Nursing Home Admission Agreements (Gerontology Institute, University of Massachusetts, Boston 1997); Anne Kisor, Nursing Facility Admission Agreements: An Analysis of Selected Content, 15 Journal of Applied Gerontology 294 (Sept. 1996).

3398 This is not an exhaustive list of violations. For more information, see Eric Carlson, Long-Term Care Advocacy § 3.06 (Mathew Bender 2003); National Consumer Law Center, "When

- Limiting visiting hours for immediate family or other relatives. Assuming the resident consents to the visit, the NHRL provides that a resident's immediate family or other relatives have the right to visit at any time.[3399]
- Evicting residents because they are considered to be difficult. The NHRL provides that transfer or discharge from a nursing facility is justified only under one of the following six circumstances: (1) to meet the resident's welfare and her welfare can not be met in the facility; (2) because the resident's health has improved sufficiently so that she no longer needs the services provided by the facility; (3) the safety of individuals in the facility is endangered; (4) the health of individuals in the facility would otherwise be endangered; (5) the resident has failed, after reasonable and appropriate notice, to pay, or to have Medicaid or Medicare pay on the resident's behalf; (6) the facility closes.[3400] Even if the problem does in fact justify the eviction, the facility is still required to make reasonable attempts to address the problem before evicting the resident.[3401]

UDAP claims may also be brought to challenge unfair and deceptive practices regardless of whether there is a violation of federal or state nursing home laws.[3402]

5.11.4 Assisted Living Facilities

A growing industry of assisted living facilities (ALFs) has developed to meet the needs of seniors who are unable to live alone but are still able to live somewhat independently.[3403] Assisted living initially was geared mostly at higher income seniors. However, more and more states are now incorporating assisted living into their publicly funded long-term care systems, usually through a Medicaid waiver.[3404] Medicaid only covers the services portion of an assisted living stay. A resident who is also receiving Supplemental Security Income (SSI) can use those funds to subsidize the assisted-living room and board costs.[3405]

ALFs differ from nursing facilities in a number of ways. Most important, not all assisted living facilities are licensed or regulated. As of 2002, thirty-two states and the District of Columbia had a licensing category or statute that used the term assisted living, and thirty-six states had requirements for facilities serving people with Alzheimer's disease or dementia.[3406] The rules that do exist vary widely by state, making it difficult to determine whether a particular regulation even applies to the facility in question.[3407] The regulations may be scattered across several programs and/or agencies. Even in states where regulations exist, they may not be very helpful in protecting facility residents.

In contrast to this patchwork of assisted living regulations, strong but under-enforced federal and state nursing facility laws have been on the books for years. Despite these differences in the degree of regulation, many of the con-

---

You Can't Go Home Again: Using Consumer Law to Protect Nursing Facility Residents" (2000); Horvath & Nemore, Nursing Home Abuses and Unfair Trade Practices, 20 Clearinghouse Review 801 (Nov. 1986).

3399 42 U.S.C. §§ 1395i-3(c)(3)(B), 1396r(c)(3)(B), 42 C.F.R. § 483.10(j)(1)(vii).

3400 42 U.S.C. §§ 1395i-3(c)(2)(A), 1396r(c)(2)(A); 42 C.F.R. § 483.12(a)(2).

3401 *See* In the Matter of the Involuntary Discharge or Transfer of J.S. by Ebenezer Hall, 512 N.W.2d 604 (Minn. 1994) (nursing facility can not discharge resident for refusing treatment unless the statutory discharge criteria are met; involuntary discharge or transfer must be a last resort).

3402 *See, e.g.*, Rohlfing v. Manor Care, 172 F.R.D. 330 (N.D. Ill. 1997) (UDAP cause of action based on allegations that the facility routinely misrepresented that their medication prices were lower than the prices offered by other suppliers); Arenson v. Whitehall Convalescent and Nursing Home, 164 F.R.D. 659 (N.D. Ill. 1996) (class certification granted in a UDAP claim against a nursing facility for assessment of excessive charges for medication); Chalfin v. Beverly Enterprises, 741 F. Supp. 1162 (E.D. Pa. 1989) (UDAP claims based on alleged facility practice of discharging residents who applied for Medicaid), *reconsideration denied*, 745 F. Supp. 1117 (E.D. Pa. 1990), *summary judgment granted in part, denied in part on other grounds*, 1991 U.S. Dist. LEXIS 937 (E.D. Pa.); People v. Casa Blanca Convalescent Homes, 206 Cal. Rptr. 164 (Cal. Ct. App. 1984) (UDAP claims based on allegations that the facility had employed inadequate numbers of staff members, falsified records, used rotting food, and failed to keep residents clean); Sullivan's Wholesale Drug v. Faryl's Pharmacy, Inc., 214 Ill. App. 3d 1073, 573 N.E.2d 1370 (1991) (facility may violate UDAP statute by billing patients for the full price of drugs, when the facility was charged only 85% of the price).

3403 In addition to the term "assisted living facility," other commonly used terms for the same types of facilities are "residential care facilities," "personal care homes," "catered living facilities," "retirement homes," "homes for adults," "board and cares" and "adult congregate living facilities."

3404 By October 2002, forty-one states had approval to cover services in residential settings, either assisted living or board-and-care licensing categories, through Medicaid. Robert L. Mollica, State Assisted Living Policy 2002, National Academy for State Health Policy 2002.

3405 *See* AARP, Public Policy Institute, "Assisted Living in the United States" (1998); Eric Carlson, Long-Term Care Advocacy § 5.05[2] (Matthew Bender 2003).

3406 Robert L. Mollica, State Assisted Living Policy 2002, National Academy for State Health Policy 2002. For a summary of state assisted-living facility statutes and regulations, see Eric Carlson, Long-Term Care Advocacy §§ 5.101 to 5.152 (Matthew Bender 2003). *See generally* Stephanie Edelstein, *Living Longer: A Legal Response to Aging in America*, 9 Stanford Law & Policy Rev. 373 (Spring 1998).

3407 The primary federal law relating to the quality of care in residential care facilities, the Keys amendment, is widely considered to be ineffective. The Keys amendment (42 U.S.C. § 1382e(e)) was a 1976 amendment to the Social Security Act. It requires each state to establish and enforce standards for any type of residential facility in which significant numbers of SSI recipients reside. If a facility does not meet state standards set pursuant to the amendment, SSI payments are reduced for recipients who reside in that facility. *See generally* Eric Carlson, Long-Term Care Advocacy § 5.04[2] (Matthew Bender 2003).

sumer remedies that apply to nursing facilities can also be used to challenge abusive and deceptive practices of assisted living facilities.[3408] UDAP claims based on violations of state regulations should be considered as well as general UDAP claims.

One source of UDAP claims is misleading advertisements, which frequently imply that residents can stay in the ALF for as long as they want, no matter how ill they become. In reality, about half of ALF residents eventually move into nursing homes because they need more help than the facility can provide. A large percentage of others end up in hospitals or in other ALFs.[3409] In other cases, facilities, contrary to advertising representations, simply do not have the capacity to meet the residents' needs. Other possible UDAP claims include unfair or deceptive billing practices, understaffing, and resident neglect.[3410]

Contract claims are also critical in the assisted living context. Assisted living facilities are frequently given substantial flexibility to negotiate individual agreements with prospective residents. The resulting contracts are supposed to be tailored to individual needs. The industry calls this practice "negotiated risk," generally described as an agreement between a resident and an assisted living facility regarding the services that the resident requires and the risks that the resident is willing to take.[3411] However, in nearly every case, residents are in fact waiving their right to sue or seek other redress if the facility can not care for them. A number of possible claims may arise from these negotiated risk "agreements," including inadequate capacity to contract and unequal bargaining claims.[3412]

3408 *See* § 5.11.3, *supra*.

3409 Dorothy Siemon, Stephanie Edelstein, & Zita Dresner, *Consumer Advocacy in Assisted Living*, 30 Clearinghouse Rev. 579 (Oct. 1996). *See also* U.S. General Accounting Office, GAO/HEHS-99-27, Assisted Living: Quality-Of-Care and Consumer Protection Issues in Four States (1999) (finding that written material provided by assisted living facilities often does not contain key information and that facilities do not routinely provide prospective residents with important documents, such as copies of admission contracts, to use in decision-making).

3410 *See, e.g.*, State of Minnesota v. Alterra Healthcare Corp., No. C1-00-6824 (1st Jud. Dist. Minn. Mar. 6, 2000) (allegations of consumer fraud, false advertising, and deceptive trade practices against facility that misrepresented that it would have 24 hour nursing staff and a 1:7 staff to resident ratio, and could provide all care "to the end" if necessary; settlement order dated March 29, 2000, is available as Clearinghouse No. 53,537); Elder v. Fischer, 717 N.E.2d 730 (Ohio Ct. App. 1998) (state UDAP statute applied to the billing practices of a residential care facility).

3411 *See* General Accounting Office, Long-Term Care Consumer Protection and Quality-of-Care Issues in Assisted Living (1997).

3412 *See* § 9.5.7, *infra*.

5.11.5 Funerals

5.11.5.1 The FTC Rule

Funeral and burial services are often high-priced packages purchased by bereaved relatives of the deceased under time pressures allowing little reflection. Religious, racial or ethnic preferences may create virtual local monopolies of services. Because of this market power, consumer vulnerability, and the prevalence of deception, the FTC has enacted a Funeral Practices Trade Regulation Rule.[3413] The rule requires funeral homes to offer itemized price information and to reveal prices over the telephone. The rule also prohibits misrepresentations and specifies disclosures concerning the need or legal requirements for embalming, a casket for cremation purposes, or an outer burial container. Also prohibited are misrepresentations about cemetery requirements and about the preservative or protective value of funeral goods. Funeral homes must disclose if they make a profit on cash-advance items and may not condition a funeral sale on the purchase of a casket or other items. Nor should a funeral home provide any funeral services without a family member's prior authorization.

Portions of the rule originally went into effect January 1, 1984, and the remainder on April 30, 1984. In 1994, concluding a lengthy review of the rule,[3414] the FTC promulgated a final amended rule.[3415] The amended rule made a number of minor changes and clarifications and also added a ban on fees for "handling" caskets purchased from third parties.[3416]

The Fourth Circuit rejected all challenges to the original rule in *Harry and Bryant Co. v. FTC*,[3417] holding that the rulemaking proceeding did not deny due process rights, the rule was within the Commission's statutory authority and the rule was supported by substantial evidence. The remedy of itemized price lists did not exceed the Commission's power under the FTC Improvements Act, and the rule did not violate First Amendment rights of commercial free speech. In 1994, the Third Circuit upheld the newly added ban on casket handling fees, finding that it was supported by

3413 16 C.F.R. § 453 [reprinted at Appx. B.5, *infra*].

3414 *See* Notice of Proposed Rulemaking, 53 Fed. Reg. 19864 (May 31, 1988). On July 30, 1990, the FTC published for comment a Final Staff Report and the Recommended Decision of the Presiding Officer. *See* 55 Fed. Reg. 30925.

3415 59 Fed. Reg. 1592 (Jan. 11, 1994). In 1998 the FTC began a review of the rule. 63 Fed. Reg. 62740 (Nov. 8, 1998). The FTC now projects that it will conclude the review by July 2005. *See* FTC, Semiannual Regulatory Agenda, 69 Fed. Reg. 38599 (June 28, 2004).

3416 16 C.F.R. § 453.4(b)(1)(ii). This subsection specifies the services for which a funeral home may charge. It does not list casket handling as one of the services for which a home may charge.

3417 726 F.2d 993 (4th Cir. 1982). *See also* FTC v. Hughes, 710 F. Supp. 1524 (N.D. Tex. 1989).

substantial evidence and not arbitrary or capricious.[3418]

The FTC staff has also issued staff compliance guidelines covering the rule. These guidelines do not represent the views of the Commission and are not binding on the Commission. The first set of guidelines explains staff views on who must comply with the rule, the type of representations that are prohibited, what price disclosures must be made, when disclosures are clear, when the purchase of one good is improperly conditioned on the purchase of another, and when services are charged to the consumer without prior approval.[3419] The second set of guidelines deals with the rule's state exemption provisions.[3420] The FTC's 1978 staff report is also useful background for understanding the FTC rule.[3421]

The FTC and an industry trade association have developed the Funeral Rule Offenders Program, which requires funeral providers who have violated the rule to make voluntary payments to the U.S. Treasury in an amount slightly less than the FTC would seek in an enforcement action, and to participate in a training and competency testing program. The FTC identifies non-complying providers through test shopping.[3422]

The FTC's rule on Cooling-Off Period for Door-to-Door Sales[3423] may also apply to some funeral contracts. "Pre-need" contracts are often sold in the consumer's home, thus mandating the right to cancel under the FTC rule and possibly state door-to-door sales laws as well.[3424]

State statutes and regulations may also provide protections for consumers. Some states have enacted special consumer protection statutes about funeral homes and cemetery sales. The Oklahoma UDAP statute specifically prohibits failure to perform cemetery services that are promised in the contract.[3425] Many states also have funeral director licensing laws, some of which include consumer protections. In two states, however, the portions of a licensing statute that required casket sellers to have funeral director licenses have been struck down on due process and equal protection grounds.[3426] The courts found that the licensing requirements just perpetuated a monopoly and allowed the maintenance of higher prices.

5.11.5.2 Case Law

FTC surveys of consumers show widespread violations of the rule by funeral parlors, and the FTC has brought a number of enforcement actions for rule violations.[3427] In an important FTC consent order, one of the major national chains of funeral homes agreed to cease misrepresenting the price the funeral home paid for third-party services (such as flowers or chaplains) and the quality and legal requirement for purchasing a casket and has agreed that the homes will disclose the availability of an immediate cremation service.[3428] Other cases have prohibited misrepresenting that burial vaults are impervious to all known elements,[3429] misrepresenting that tombstones are forever durable,[3430] misrepresenting synthetic tombstones to be made of granite or marble,[3431] and deceptive pricing practices concerning grave sites.[3432] Another FTC consent order involves a funeral director who failed to bury individuals with the purchased caskets or burial vaults and who desecrated the bodies and the graves.[3433]

In any case involving deceptive funeral practices, the consumer should stress the particularly vulnerable conditions under which the sale was made.[3434] In some states, consumer litigants dealing with burial space misrepresenta-

3418 Pennsylvania Funeral Directors Ass'n v. FTC, 41 F.3d 81 (3d Cir. 1994).

3419 50 Fed. Reg. 28062 (July 9, 1985).

3420 50 Fed. Reg. 12521 (Mar. 29, 1985). The State of Texas' application for an exemption from the rule was denied. *See* 56 Fed. Reg. 28829 (June 25, 1991). New York also applied for an exemption, but the FTC has not yet reached a decision. *See* 56 Fed. Reg. 11381 (Mar. 18, 1991); 57 Fed. Reg. 34532 (Aug. 5, 1992).

3421 Clearinghouse No. 31,044 (June, 1978).

3422 FTC Testifies on Funeral Rule Activities (Apr. 26, 2002), *available at* www.ftc.gov/opa/2002/04/funeralruletest.htm.

3423 16 C.F.R. § 429. *See* § 5.8.2, *supra*.

3424 United States v. Mission Plans, Inc., 5 Trade Reg. Rep. (CCH) ¶ 23,660 (S.D. Tex. Sept. 2, 1994) (consent decree requiring pre-need funeral contract seller to give notice of right to cancel).

3425 Okla. Stat. Ann. tit. 15, § 753(21).

3426 Craigmiles v. Giles, 312 F.3d 220 (6th Cir. 2002); Casket Royale, Inc. v. Mississippi, 124 F. Supp. 2d 434 (S.D. Miss. 2000).

3427 Recent actions include: Va. Bd. of Funeral Directors and Embalmers, File No. 041 0041 (Aug. 16, 2004) (proposed consent order), *available at* www.ftc.gov/ox/2004/08/index.htm; United States v. Hutchison, 5 Trade Reg. Rep. (CCH) ¶ 24,005 (D. Del. Mar. 26, 1996) (consent decree); United States v. Patton Brothers Funeral Homes, 5 Trade Reg. Rep. (CCH) ¶ 23,856 (M.D. Tenn. July 6, 1995) (proposed consent decree); United States v. Ruzich Funeral Home, Inc., 5 Trade Reg. Rep. (CCH) ¶ 23,855 (N.D. Ill. July 6, 1995) (proposed consent decree); A.H. Peters Funeral Home of Grosse Pointe, Inc., 5 Trade Reg. Rep. (CCH) ¶ 23,945 (E.D. Mich. 1995) (proposed consent order); United States v. Mission Plans, Inc., 5 Trade Reg. Rep. (CCH) ¶ 23,660 (S.D. Tex. Sept. 2, 1994) (consent decree) (failure to provide price lists); United States v. Macias Mortuary Servs., 5 Trade Reg. Rep. (CCH) ¶ 23,314 (N.D. Cal. 1993) (consent decree); United States v. Meyer Funeral Home, Inc., 5 Trade Reg. Rep. (CCH) ¶ 23,358 (S.D. Iowa 1993) (consent order); FTC v. Wetherill, 5 Trade Reg. Rep. (CCH) ¶ 23,403 (N.D. Cal. 1993) (consent decree).

3428 Service Corp. Int'l, 88 F.T.C. 530 (1976) (consent order).

3429 United States v. Wilbert, Inc., 5 Trade Reg. Rep. (CCH) ¶ 22,849 (N.D. Ill. 1990) (consent decree); Batesville Casket Co., 111 F.T.C. 112 (1988) (consent order); Egyptian Vault Co., 59 F.T.C. 1349 (1961) (consent order).

3430 Asa L. Wooten, 31 F.T.C. 508 (1940).

3431 Roy Burnsed, 30 F.T.C. 436 (1940).

3432 Olive v. Graceland Sales Corp., 61 N.J. 182, 293 A.2d 658 (1972).

3433 Wilks, 112 F.T.C. 526 (1989) (consent order).

3434 *See* § 4.2.11 *supra*.

tions may also face scope issues as to whether the sale of a burial space is the sale of "goods or services" within the scope of the statute. One court has said it is not.[3435] In contrast, the Oklahoma UDAP statute's coverage of these transactions is clearly demonstrated by its inclusion of specific prohibitions relating to cemetery services.[3436]

5.11.6 Hospital Treatment and Payment Issues

Medical bill payment issues may give rise to UDAP violations, especially given the growing number of uninsured and underinsured consumers in this country.[3437] Even some providers have brought UDAP claims against insurers.[3438]

However, some state UDAP statutes exempt transactions between consumers and physicians or members of learned professions in general.[3439] These exemptions might not apply to a transaction with a third party such as an HMO.[3440] Other courts have created an exception for the professional aspects of medical care, but not the entrepreneurial aspects, so misrepresentations about billing would probably not be exempt.[3441]

One practice that may potentially give rise to UDAP liability is "discriminatory pricing," whereby hospitals and other healthcare providers routinely charge uninsured consumers significantly higher prices than Medicaid, HMOs, and private insurers. This practice results when hospitals give significant discounts to private and public insurers, which causes them to inflate their "list" charges in light of these concessions.[3442] Several dozen lawsuits have been filed against hospitals for discriminatory pricing and hospital billing practices.[3443]

One reason for discriminatory pricing may be the hospitals' overly restrictive interpretations of Medicaid and Medicare requirements to charge "uniform rates" and to make reasonable collection efforts of Medicare co-payments and deductibles.[3444] The U.S. Department of Health and Human Services has issued guidance refuting that argument and permitting hospitals and other providers "provide discounts to uninsured and underinsured patients who can not afford their hospital bills and to Medicare beneficiaries who can not afford their Medicare cost-sharing obligations."[3445]

UDAP liability may also arise from a hospital's failure to inform a medical debtor of free care funds or to apply such funds to the debtor's bill.[3446] Because they are charitable organizations, hospitals in many states have some sort of "free care" obligation.[3447] In addition, the federal Hill-Burton Act[3448] made a health care facility's receipt of certain hospital construction funds contingent on the facility's assurance that it would provide a reasonable volume of services for persons unable to pay for them. UDAP litigation to enforce Hill-Burton's requirement enjoyed some success;[3449] unfortunately, these obligations generally lasted

3435 Hutchings v. Valhalla Cemetery, 622 S.W.2d 296 (Mo. Ct. App. 1981).

3436 Okla. Stat. Ann. tit. 15, § 753(21).

3437 For a discussion of medical debt collection issues, see National Consumer Law Center, Fair Debt Collection Ch. 14 (5th ed. 2004).

3438 Coast Plaza Doctors Hosp. v. UHP Healthcare, 129 Cal. Rptr. 2d 650 (Cal. App. 2002) (hospital alleged sufficient facts to state a claim for violation of California UDAP law with allegation that HMO caused patients to be transferred in violation of federal law).

3439 *See, e.g.*, Ohio Rev. Code Ann. § 1345.01 (transactions between attorneys, physicians or dentists and their clients or patients). *See generally* § 2.3.10, *supra*.

3440 Summa Health Sys. v. Viningre, 140 Ohio App. 3d 780, 749 N.E.2d 344 (2000) (HMO made misrepresentations about financial aspects of patient's care).

3441 *See* § 2.3.10, *supra*; National Consumer Law Center, Fair Debt Collection § 14.4.3 (5th ed. 2004).

3442 *See* National Consumer Law Center, Fair Debt Collection § 14.5.5.2 (5th ed. 2004).

3443 According to a press release by the private class action attorneys, over 50 lawsuits have been filed against hospitals and hospital systems for their pricing practices. Press Release, *Six More Class Action Lawsuits Filed Against Nonprofit Hospital Systems*, August 26, 2004, *available at* www.nfplitigation.com. At least one of these cases has settled. Memorandum of Understanding between North Mississippi Health Services and Uninsured Patients, August 5, 2004, *available on* companion CD-Rom.

3444 Carol Pryor and Robert Seifert, Unintended Consequences: How Federal Regulations and Hospital Policies Can Leave Patients in Debt, The Commonwealth Fund, May 2003.

3445 Letter from Tommy G. Thompson, Secretary of Health and Human Services to Richard J. Davidson, President, American Hospital Association, Feb. 19, 2004.

3446 Flagstaff Medical Center, Inc. v. Sullivan, 773 F. Supp. 1325 (D. Ariz. 1991), *rev'd in part on other grounds*, 962 F.2d 879 (9th Cir. 1992) (standing and attorney fees); Yale New Haven Hosp. v. Gargiulo, 1999 WL 989422 (Conn. Super. Oct. 18, 1999) (special defense of failure to mitigate sufficiently alleged: hospital failed to advise patient of Hill Burton or other aid programs, or to assist her in applying); Yale New Haven Hosp. Inc. v. Mitchell, 683 A.2d 1362 (Conn. Super. 1995) (holding that Hill-Burton Act does not preempt state UDAP claim).

3447 The website of Community Catalyst has several publications on free care programs. Community Catalyst, Free Care Monitoring Project, at www.communitycat.org/index.php?fldID=204. *See also* Access Project, Fact Sheet: The Free Care Safety Net (1999), *available at* www.accessproject.org. Many of the several dozen class action lawsuits filed in 2004 against hospitals included causes of action based upon the hospitals' alleged failure to fulfill their charitable or free care obligations arising from their tax exempt status. Press Release, *Six More Class Action Lawsuits Filed Against Nonprofit Hospital Systems*, August 26, 2004, *available at* www.nfplitigation.com.

3448 42 U.S.C. §§ 291 and 300.

3449 Flagstaff Medical Center, Inc. v. Sullivan, 773 F. Supp. 1325 (D. Ariz. 1991), *rev'd in part on other grounds*, 962 F.2d 879 (9th Cir. 1992) (standing and attorney fees); Yale New Haven Hosp. v. Gargiulo, 1999 WL 989422 (Conn. Super. Oct. 18, 1999) (special defense of failure to mitigate sufficiently alleged: hospital failed to advise patient of Hill Burton or other aid pro-

just twenty years, and very few hospitals are still subject to them.[3450]

Another federal statute, the Emergency Medical Treatment and Active Labor Act (EMTALA),[3451] prohibits hospitals participating in federal programs from turning away a patient in need of emergency medical treatment, because, for example, the patient may not be able to pay for care. It also prohibits premature discharge of a patient after emergency care is provided. It provides for a private cause of action for actual damages, attorney fees, and, in states where otherwise available, punitive damages. A parallel UDAP claim might also be available in states that recognize a violation of another statute as a UDAP violation.[3452]

Hospitals may also face UDAP liability if they misrepresent their payment policies. For example, it may be a UDAP violation for a hospital to advertise that it accepts HMO payments in full satisfaction of patients' bills, but then to place a lien for further payment on a patient's tort recovery.[3453]

5.11.7 Managed Care

More than 184 million Americans now get their medical care through managed care plans.[3454] Consumer disputes concerning managed care often involve difficulty getting access to specialists, problems with emergency care, and disputes over bills.

A number of states have enacted "patients' bills of rights" that provide for some protections for managed care consumers.[3455] Some of these statutes create a private right of action to sue plans for denial of care. In other states, UDAP statutes may create a right of action.[3456] However, the ability to sue managed care plans under state patients' rights laws is limited by the Employee Retirement Income Security Act,[3457] which regulates employee benefits plans, including health insurance plans.[3458]

The question of whether federal law preempts UDAP claims is complicated. In general, Medicare and Medicaid law does not preempt claims for deceptive advertising.[3459] However, ERISA preempts many UDAP claims, especially claims that arise from the administration of the managed care plan.[3460]

5.11.8 Tobacco

In 1999 Massachusetts adopted a UDAP regulation[3461] that prohibited or restricted a number of tobacco marketing practices, such as promotional give-aways and mail order sales without age verification, and outdoor advertising and point-of-sale advertising near schools and playgrounds. It also required health warnings on cigars similar to those that the federal Cigarette Labeling and Advertising Act[3462] requires for cigarettes.

---

grams, or to assist her in applying); Yale New Haven Hosp. Inc. v. Mitchell, 683 A.2d 1362 (Conn. Super. 1995) (holding that Hill-Burton Act does not preempt state UDAP claim).

3450 For a list of hospitals that still have Hill-Burton obligations, see www.hrsa.gov/osp/dfcr/obtain/hbstates.htm

3451 42 U.S.C. § 1395dd. *See* National Consumer Law Center, Fair Debt Collection § 14.3.2 (5th ed. 2004) for a further discussion of EMTALA.

3452 *See, e.g.*, Coast Plaza Doctors Hosp. v. UHP Healthcare, 129 Cal. Rptr. 2d 650 (Cal. App. 2002) (hospital stated a claim for violation of California UDAP law with allegation that HMO caused patients to be transferred in violation of EMTALA). *See generally* § 3.2.7, *supra*.

3453 Dorr v. Sacred Heart Hosp., 597 N.W.2d 462 (Wis. App. Ct. 1999).

3454 Managed Care On Line, Managed Care National Statistics, available at www.mcareol.com/factshts/factnati.htm. The term "managed care" encompasses a number of different types of health services organizations, including preferred provider organizations (PPOs) as well as all types of health maintenance organizations (HMOs). In general, all managed care organizations restrict services in some way, at a minimum by limiting consumers' choice of providers.

3455 *See, e.g.*, Ga. Code Ann. §§ 33-20A-20 to 33-20A-41, 51-1-148 and 57-1-48; N.C. Gen. Stat. §§ 90-21.50 to 90-21.56; Tex. Civ. Prac. & Rem. Code Ann. §§ 88.001–88.003. A chart of states with some form of patient protection legislation is available on AARP's website. States' Progress on Patients' Bill of Rights Measures, AARP Bulletin (Feb. 2002), *available at* www.aarp.org/bulletin/yourhealth/Articles/a2003-08-05-rights_measures.html.

3456 *See* § 3.2.7, *supra*.

3457 29 U.S.C. § 1001 *et seq*.

3458 Aetna v. Davila, 124 S. Ct. 2488 (2004) (ERISA completely preempts claims brought under Texas patients' rights law). For a discussion of ERISA preemption, see § 2.5.8, *supra*.

3459 Ardary v. Aetna Health Plans of California, Inc., 98 F.3d 496 (9th Cir. 1996), *cert. denied*, 520 U.S. 1251 (1997); Downhour v. Somani, 85 F.3d 261 (6th Cir. 1996) (no preemption by Medicare Act of Ohio statute's bar to balanced billing; Medicare Act and legislative history do not suggest Congress saw need for national uniformity as to balanced billing); Plocica v. Nylcare of Texas, Inc., 43 F. Supp. 2d 658 (N.D. Tex. 1999) (follows *Ardary*, no preemption of state tort claims of wrongful death and negligence); McCall v. Pacificare of Cal., Inc., 25 Cal. 4th 412, 21 P.3d 1189 (2001) (Medicare administrative review scheme does not displace traditional tort remedies for claims—such as quality of care, marketing problems, and forced disenrollment—that do not seek payment of claim); Solorzano v. Superior Court of Los Angeles, 10 Cal. App. 4th 1135, 13 Cal. Rptr. 2d 161 (1992), *review denied*, 1993 Cal. LEXIS 741 (Cal. Feb. 11, 1993), *cert. denied*, 510 U.S. 814 (1993) (federal law does not sufficiently occupy the field to displace state regulation of HMOs). For non-HMO cases where preemption arguments were defeated, see Pennsylvania Medical Soc. v. Marconis, 942 F.2d 842 (3d Cir. 1991); Massachusetts Medical Soc. v. Dukakis, 815 F.2d 790 (1st Cir. 1987), *cert. denied*, 484 U.S. 896 (1987). With respect to Medicaid, the *Solorzano* court speculated that the HMO may have dropped the Medicaid preemption claim because Medicaid is a joint state and federal program expressly subject to state regulations. *Solarzano* at 1139. For a general discussion of federal preemption of state consumer protections, see § 2.5.2, *supra*.

3460 *See generally* § 2.5.8, *supra*.

3461 940 Mass. Regs. Code §§ 21.00 to 21.07.

3462 15 U.S.C. §§ 1331–41.

The United States Supreme Court[3463] held that the regulations restricting outdoor and point-of-sale advertising of cigarettes near schools were preempted by the Federal Cigarette Labeling and Advertising Act (FCLAA).[3464] With respect to cigars and smokeless tobacco, which are not covered by the FCLAA, the Court analyzed the outdoor advertising regulations in light of the First Amendment. While it recognized the state's substantial interest in curbing youth tobacco use, it held that the regulations were overly restrictive. The Court upheld portions of the regulations requiring that tobacco products be placed out of the reach of customers in a location accessible only to salespersons.

The court of appeals had struck down two other restrictions—a requirement that cigar advertisements published in Massachusetts carry warnings and a requirement that any cigars shipped into the state carry labels—as unconstitutional burdens on interstate commerce.[3465] The Supreme Court did not review this ruling.

Even though the Supreme Court struck down many provisions of the regulation, it made it clear that tobacco restrictions designed to protect minors will pass First Amendment scrutiny as long as they are narrowly tailored. For example, the Court indicated that the state could target floor-level tobacco advertisements and displays that entice children, but could not prohibit all floor-level advertising. The Court also made it clear that the state has a relatively free hand in restricting sales practices as opposed to advertising.

Tobacco sales practices and advertisements have also been challenged under UDAP statutes that do not have special provisions dealing with tobacco. At least one court has held that such claims are not preempted by the FCLAA despite the fact that the claims are seemingly based on manufacturer's failure to warn consumers about the ill effects of smoking.[3466] The court reasoned that UDAP claims are not preempted by FCLAA because they do not seek to hold defendants liable for the health effects of smoking, but instead seek to hold defendants liable for deceptive or unfair business practices employed when marketing the cigarettes.

The FTC has obtained consent decrees from companies claiming that their tobacco products are safer because of fewer additives.[3467] Also, the FTC has brought suit against a cigarette manufacturer that engineered its cigarettes to give off low levels of tar and nicotine in laboratory tests.[3468] The District of Columbia Circuit upheld an injunction preventing the defendant from advertising its cigarettes as "light" because the manufacturer knew that when smoked by person as opposed to laboratory apparatus the cigarettes gave off no less tar and nicotine than many other cigarettes.[3469] The Massachusetts Supreme Court, affirming certification of a class of cigarette smokers in a case not governed by the state tobacco regulation, held that a UDAP violation would be established by proof that the manufacturer labeled its cigarettes "Lights" with "lowered tar and nicotine" while knowing that most smokers would not experience the advertised reduction.[3470]

5.12 Attorneys, Living Trusts, Other Fiduciaries

5.12.1 Attorneys

Attorney misconduct can be challenged by a UDAP statute in many states.[3471] An attorney's use of an illegal fee arrangement may be a *per se* UDAP violation.[3472] Massachusetts' highest court has found it unfair for an attorney, after a case is settled, to collect a contingency fee from the amount the client received when the settlement provided for attorney fees.[3473] Double billing or other abusive billing practices are also UDAP violations.[3474]

It is unconscionable for an attorney to refuse to return monies to a client where the attorney was holding the money as a deposit for future work which was not performed.[3475] A lawyer can be found to have engaged in a deceptive practice by failing to disclose material information the lawyer is aware of concerning his or her services.[3476] Also deceptive and unconscionable is for an attorney to fail to prosecute a case and then to fail to keep the client informed of that fact.[3477] An attorney's false representations to the client are

3463 Lorillard Tobacco Co. v. Reilly, 533 U.S. 525, 121 S. Ct. 2404, 150 L. Ed. 2d 532 (2001).

3464 15 U.S.C. § 1334(b). *See also* Cipollone v. Liggett Group, Inc., 505 U.S. 504, 112 S. Ct. 2608, 120 L. Ed. 2d 407 (1992) (holding that state law claims against cigarette manufacturers based on a failure to warn consumers of potential dangers are preempted by the FCLAA).

3465 Consolidated Cigar Corp. v. Reilly, 218 F.3d 30 (1st Cir. 2000).

3466 *See* Little v. Brown & Williamson Tobacco, 1999 WL 33291385, at *3, *5 (D.S.C. Mar. 3, 1999) (compiling cases that address the FCLAA preemption question with respect to UDAP claims).

3467 Alternative Cigarettes, Inc., 5 Trade Reg. Rep. (CCH) ¶ 24,736 (June 14, 2000) (consent order regarding claim that company's cigarettes were less hazardous); Santa Fe Natural Tobacco Co., 5 Trade Reg. Rep. (CCH) ¶ 24,736 (F.T.C. Dkt. No. C-3952, June 12, 2000) (same).

3468 FTC v. Brown & Williamson Tobacco Corp., 778 F.2d 35, 37 (D.C. Cir. 1985).

3469 *Id. See also* Watson v. Philip Morris Companies, Inc., 2003 WL 23272484 (E.D. Ark. Dec. 12, 2003).

3470 Aspinall v. Philip Morris Cos., 813 N.E.2d 476 (Mass. 2004).

3471 *See* § 2.3.9, *supra*.

3472 Guenard v. Burke, 387 Mass. 802, 443 N.E.2d 892 (1982).

3473 Doucette v. Kwiat, 392 Mass. 915, 467 N.E.2d 1374 (1984).

3474 Sears, Roebuck & Co. v. Goldstone & Sudalter, 128 F.3d 10 (1st Cir. 1997) (Mass. law).

3475 Barnard v. Mecom, 650 S.W.2d 123 (Tex. App. 1983).

3476 *See* Wright v. Lewis, 777 S.W.2d 520 (Tex. App. 1989) (no UDAP violation where no knowledge of material not disclosed).

3477 Wilson v. Rice, 807 S.W.2d 836 (Tex. App. 1991).

also actionable.[3478] The FTC has negotiated a consent order with an attorney who marketed professional services to immigrants interested in green cards. He falsely represented in advertisements and promotional materials that no customers had ever been rejected from the green card lottery and that his services satisfied the State Department's technical requirements and he unfairly submitted multiple entries to the lottery.[3479]

An appellate court in Connecticut has held, however, that an attorney's violation of the Rules of Professional Conduct does not give rise to a private UDAP cause of action.[3480] Nor is an attorney's saying "ready" at the beginning of a trial an actionable representation as to an attorney's quality of work.[3481] A letter from one party's attorney to the other side's attorney arguably containing misrepresentations about a co-defendant is not a UDAP violation.[3482] A number of courts have concluded that an attorney's negligence or malpractice is not actionable as a UDAP violation.[3483] Texas courts have held that a criminal defendant can not file a UDAP based claim arising out of a conviction based on a guilty plea, on the theory that a guilty plea admits the crime and thus defeats causation.[3484]

5.12.2 Nonattorney Legal Service Providers and the Unauthorized Practice of Law

5.12.2.1 Introduction

Scam nonattorney services are a growth industry nationwide. The problem is particularly prevalent in immigrant communities. For example, nonattorneys advertising as "*notarios*"[3485] in the Spanish-speaking community explicitly or implicitly represent that they can provide the same legal services to unsuspecting consumers as can attorneys.

The majority of fraudulent nonattorney practitioners and document preparers focus their efforts in certain areas of the law such as immigration, eviction defense, bankruptcy and living trusts.[3486]

There are special state or federal statutes that apply to some of these scams. In all cases, a UDAP cause of action should be available, based on unauthorized practice of law, violations of a specific state or federal statute, or general principles of deception or unfairness.[3487]

5.12.2.2 Immigration Consultants or Assistants

The number of scam artists preying upon immigrants seeking assistance in obtaining legal residence, work authorization, or citizenship has risen dramatically in recent years. Many unscrupulous consultants claim that they are attorneys or that they have close connections to the Immigration and Naturalization Service (INS). Others use titles such as notary public or *notario* to deceive people into believing that they are lawyers. In many Spanish-speaking countries, a *notario* is an attorney, often possessing more credentials than other lawyers.

In many areas, honest and responsible immigration consultants provide a real service. Unfortunately, there are almost always dishonest consultants and frequently dishonest attorneys as well. Victims of these scams not only lose large sums of money but also are likely to suffer serious harm to their immigration status.

Those seeking to adjust their legal status or obtain work authorization in the United States are often bewildered by the complex immigration laws in this country. Frequent changes and adjustments in these programs make understanding immigration law even more difficult. Unscrupulous immigration consultants take advantage of these circumstances in many different ways. Typical scams include:

- Charging exorbitant fees for immigration services and then failing to file any documents;
- Filing false asylum claims on behalf of victims who do not speak or read English and have no idea what the application contains;
- Charging fees to prepare applications for nonexistent

3478 *See* Johnson v. DeLay, 809 S.W.2d 552 (Tex. App. 1991).

3479 FTC v. Amkraut, 5 Trade Reg. Rep. (CCH) ¶ 24,198 (C.D. Cal. 1997) (proposed consent decree).

3480 Noble v. Marshall, 23 Conn. App. 227, 579 A.2d 594 (1990).

3481 Heath v. Herron, 732 S.W.2d 748 (Tex. App. 1987).

3482 Harris v. NCNB Nat'l Bank, 355 S.E.2d 838 (N.C. Ct. App. 1987).

3483 *See* § 2.3.9, *supra*.

3484 Van Polen v. Wisch, 23 S.W.3d 510 (Tex. App. 2000).

3485 In many Spanish-speaking countries a *notario publico* is a lawyer. Nonattorney providers in the United States often use such terms in order to mislead their clients into believing that they are attorneys. *See generally* Anne E. Langford, *What's In A Name?:* Notarios *in the United States and the Exploitation of a Vulnerable Latino Immigrant Population*, 7 Harv. Latino L. Rev. 115 (Spring 2004).

3486 For a more extensive analysis of these issues, see Deanne Loonin, Kathleen Michon, David Kinnecome, *Fraudulent Notarios, Document Preparers, and Other Nonattorney Service Providers: Legal Remedies for a Growing Problem*, 31 Clearinghouse Rev. 327 (Nov./Dec. 1997) and Katherine Brady, Immigrant Legal Resource Center, *Immigrant Consultant Fraud: Laws and Resources* (Mar. 2000). For information specifically on challenging living trust scams, see § 5.12.3, *infra*.

3487 *See* Francorp., Inc. v. Siebert, 2002 U.S. Dist. LEXIS 5232 (N.D. Ill. Mar. 27, 2002); Sussman v. Grado, 192 Misc. 2d 628, 746 N.Y.S.2d 548 (Dist. Ct. 2002) (unlicensed, unsupervised *notario*'s acceptance of legal work was UDAP violation); State *ex rel.* Stovall v. Martinez, 27 Kan. App. 2d 9, 996 P.2d 371 (2000) (upholding injunction against unauthorized practice of law granted under state UDAP statute).

immigration programs or for legitimate programs for which the client does not qualify, such as asylum or labor certification.

Several states have enacted statutes which regulate nonattorneys who assist consumers on immigration matters.[3488] Most of these statutes exempt accredited representatives[3489] and nonattorneys who work for nonprofit agencies or law school legal clinics.[3490]

All of the statutes prohibit immigration consultants from providing legal assistance.[3491] Many states also require nonattorney notaries who advertise in languages other than English to disclose, in both languages, that they are not attorneys and are not qualified to give legal advice.[3492] A number of statutes forbid "literal translations" or the use of the terms "*notario*" or "*notario* public."[3493]

Several statutes, such as those in California, Illinois and Washington, list specific limited services that the assistant may lawfully perform, such as transcribing responses onto forms, translating answers, or securing documents which support an immigration application.[3494] Many of the statutes also attempt to prevent some of the more common misrepresentations and abuses, prohibiting, for example, consultants from representing that they have special influence with the Immigration and Naturalization Service[3495] or charging for services not performed.[3496] Some states regulate immigration consultant services through laws governing the notary public profession.[3497] The remedies vary by state.

In a novel immigration consultant fraud-related suit, a class of immigrant plaintiffs sued the I.N.S. in 2002 challenging the agency's immigration application processing practices.[3498] The case centers on the Chicago I.N.S. office's practice of accepting untimely applications for legal permanent resident status prepared by *notarios*, retaining the fees for these applications, and then using information from the documents as a means to initiate removal proceedings against many of the applicants.[3499]

5.12.2.3 Bankruptcy Petition Preparers

Responding to the tremendous need for bankruptcy relief among many low-income debtors, various types of nonattorney operations have sprung up, purporting to offer assistance to debtors in filing bankruptcy petitions. Unfortunately many of these document preparers are either fraudulent or incompetent, making promises which they can not keep and extracting fees that far exceed the value of the work performed. As a result of these schemes, many victims file for bankruptcy with the hope of saving a home or other assets only to lose those assets due to the preparer's incompetence.

Bankruptcy Code section 110[3500] regulates nonattorneys

3488 Ariz. Rev. Stat. Ann. §§ 12-2701 to 12-2704; Cal. Bus. & Prof. Code § 22440 through -48; Colo. Rev. Stat. Ann. § 12-55-110.3; 815 Ill. Comp. Stat. 505/2AA; Ind. Code Ann. § 33-42-2-10; Mich. Comp. Laws Ann. § 55.291 (regulation of notaries), Mich. Comp. Laws Ann. § 338.3451 through 3471 (Immigration Clerical Assistant Act); Minn. Stat. § 325E.031; N.J. Stat. Ann. § 2C:21-31; N.M. Stat. Ann. §§ 36-3-1 to 36-3-10; N.C. Gen. Stat. Ann. § 10A-9; Okla. Stat. Ann. tit. 49, § 6; Or. Rev. Stat. § 9.280 (making it a violation of Oregon's unauthorized practice of law statute for any person to engage in the business or act in the capacity of an immigration consultant for compensation unless the person is an active member of the Oregon Bar; accredited representatives are specifically exempted); Tenn. Code Ann. § 8-16-402; Tex. Gov. Code § 406.017; Wash. Rev. Code §§ 19.154.010 to 19.154.902. Some states specifically regulate immigration consultant services as part of their UDAP regulations. *See, e.g.*, Ill. Admin. Code Part 485; Or. Admin. R. § 137-020-0600 (misrepresentation of notarial powers, including but not limited to immigration matters).

3489 An accredited representative is a nonattorney working for an organization accredited by the board of Immigration Appeals. 8 C.F.R. § 292.1(a)(4), 8 C.F.R. § 292.2. Accredited representatives should be immune from state prosecution for unauthorized practice of law. *See also* Oregon State Bar v. Ortiz, 713 P.2d 1068 (Or. Ct. App. 1986) (defendant nonattorney did not fit within federal attorney requirement exceptions and was subject to state law enforcement for unauthorized practice of immigration law).

3490 *E.g.*, Ariz. Rev. Stat. § 12-2702; Cal. Bus. & Prof. Code § 22440; 815 Ill. Comp. Stat. Ann. 505/2AA(a-5); Mich. Comp. Laws Ann. § 338.3455; Minn. Stat. § 325E.031(5); N.M. Stat. Ann. § 36-3-4; Wash. Rev. Code § 19.154.030.

3491 *E.g.*, Ariz. Rev. Stat. Ann. §§ 12-2702(B), 12-2703(A); Cal. Bus. & Prof. Code § 22441(d); 815 Ill. Comp. Stat. Ann. 505/2AA(j)(5),(b); Minn. Stat. § 325E.031, subdiv. § 3(1); Mich. Comp. Law Ann. § 338.3467(a); N.J. Stat. Ann. § 2C:21-31; N.M. Stat. Ann. § 36-3-5; Wash. Rev. Code §§ 19.154.060 & 19.154.080(6).

3492 Colo. Rev. Stat. Ann. § 12-55-110.3; Ind. Code Ann. § 33-42-2-10; Mich. Comp. Laws Ann. § 55.291; N.C. Gen. Stat. Ann. § 10A-9; Okla. Stat. Ann. tit. 49, § 6; Tex. Gov. Code § 406.017.

3493 Cal. Bus. & Prof. Code. § 22442.3; Colo. Rev. Stat. Ann. § 12-55-110.3; 815 Ill. Comp. Stat. Ann. § 505/2AA; Mich. Comp. Laws Ann. § 55.291; Minn. Stat. Ann. § 325E.031(3)(2); Okla. Stat. Ann. tit. 49, § 6; Tex. Gov. Code § 406.017; Wash. Rev. Code Ann. § 19.154.080(4).

3494 Cal. Bus. & Prof. Code § 22441; 815 Ill. Comp. Stat. Ann. 505/2AA(b); Wash. Rev. Code § 19.154.020.

3495 *E.g.*, Cal. Bus. & Prof. Code § 22444(c); 815 Ill. Comp. Stat. Ann. 505/2AA(j)(1); Mich. Comp. Laws Ann. § 338.3467(o); Wash. Rev. Code § 19.154.080(1).

3496 *E.g.*, 815 Ill. Comp. Stat. Ann. § 505/2AA(j)(2); Minn. Stat. § 325E.031, subdiv. 3(4); Wash. Rev. Code § 19.154.080(2). At least one state sets limits on the amounts immigration "clerical assistants" may charge for various services. Mich. Comp. Laws Ann. § 338.3461.

3497 *See, e.g.*, Colo. Rev. Stat. § 12-55-110.3 (notary publics that are not licensed attorneys are prohibited from representing themselves as immigration consultants or as experts on immigration matters); N.C. Gen. Stat. § 10A-9; Tenn. Code Ann. § 8-16-402.

3498 Ramos v. Ashcroft, 2004 WL 161520 (N.D. Ill. Jan. 16, 2004) (plaintiffs' APA claim survives motion to dismiss, but constitutional claims are dismissed).

3499 *Id.*

3500 11 U.S.C. § 110. *See generally* National Consumer Law Center, Consumer Bankruptcy Law and Practice § 15.6 (6th ed. 2000 and Supp.).

who, for compensation, prepare petitions or other documents in bankruptcy. The goal of section 110 is to create a paper trail to identify and monitor petition preparers. All documents filed must have the preparer's signature, printed name, address and Social Security number as well as the Social Security number of all other people who assisted in preparing the document.[3501] Among other requirements, preparers must file a declaration of the amount of any fees received from or on behalf of debtors and the amount of fees yet to be paid.[3502]

Any violation of section 110 gives rise to numerous remedies including damages, injunctive relief, and fines of up to $500.[3503] The debtor, trustee or a creditor may file a motion for damages, payable to the debtor, if the preparer violates any of the provisions of section 110, or commits any unfair, deceptive or fraudulent act.[3504] This permits private parties to bring violations to the attention of the court. In a successful action, the debtor is to be awarded actual damages plus the greater of $2000 or twice the amount paid to the petition preparer.[3505] The court must disallow and order disgorgement of any fees in excess of the value of services provided.[3506] A trustee or creditor moving for damages is entitled to an additional $1000 in statutory damages.[3507] Preparers may be enjoined from engaging in specific unfair or deceptive acts. In addition, if the court finds that such an injunction would not be sufficient to prevent the conduct, or if the preparer has not paid a fine imposed under section 110, the court may enjoin the person from acting as a petition preparer.[3508]

Several courts have held that evidence of unauthorized practice of law is sufficient to establish unfair and deceptive conduct in violation of section 110(i) or to justify injunctive relief under section 110(j).[3509] Parties, debtors, trustees or creditors bringing a successful action for damages or injunctive relief may recover attorney fees and costs.[3510] Even the "assistance" provided by a scrupulous nonattorney petition preparer is, in fact, the unauthorized practice of law.[3511]

3501 11 U.S.C. § 110(b), (c). *See In re* Paskel, 201 B.R. 511 (Bankr. E.D. Ark. 1996) (preparer fined $1500 for failing to place name and address on three documents); *In re* Bohman, 202 B.R. 179 (Bankr. S.D. Fla. 1996) (preparer fined for failing to sign dischargeability complaint prepared for debtor; preparation of complaint held to be unauthorized practice); *see also In re* Crawford, 194 F.3d 954 (9th Cir. 1999), *cert. denied*, 528 U.S. 1189 (2000) (requirement of Social Security number disclosure not unconstitutional); *In re* Graham, 2004 WL 1052963 (Bankr. M.D.N.C. Feb. 13, 2004) (rejecting the argument that § 110 is unconstitutional).

3502 11 U.S.C. § 110(h). *See In re* Moore, 290 B.R. 287 (Bankr. E.D.N.C. 2003) (fee of $199 was excessive and only $80 was permitted); *In re* Pavlis, 264 B.R. 57 (Bankr. D.R.I. 2001) (presumed reasonable fee was $30 per hour for no more than five hours); *In re* Moffett, 263 B.R. 805 (Bankr. W.D. Ky. 2001) (preparer enjoined from charging more than $20 per hour with maximum of $100); *In re* Guttierez, 248 B.R. 287 (Bankr. W.D. Tex. 2000) (reasonable fee for typing services was $50); *In re* Moran, 256 B.R. 842 (Bankr. D.N.H. 2000) (finding $20/hour to be reasonable hourly fee for petition preparer plus $10/hour overhead; preparer should be able to complete a routine petition in 5 hours).

3503 11 U.S.C. § 110(b)–(h). *See, e.g., In re* Fleet, 95 B.R. 319 (E.D. Pa. 1989); *In re* Moffett, 263 B.R. 805 (Bankr. W.D. Ky. 2001) (use of "paralegal" in advertisement violated § 110); Moore v. Jencks (*In re* Moore), 232 B.R. 1 (Bankr. D. Me. 1999) (awarding damages, injunction, and attorney fees, and issuing order to show cause why fine should not be ordered); *In re* Hobbs, 213 B.R. 207 (Bankr. D. Me. 1997) (nonattorney bankruptcy preparer enjoined from preparing chapter 13 petitions); *In re* Paskel, 201 B.R. 511 (Bankr. E.D. Ark. 1996) (preparer fined $1500 for failing to place name and address on three documents); *In re* Bohman, 202 B.R. 179 (Bankr. S.D. Fla. 1996) (preparer fined for failing to sign dischargeability complaint prepared for debtor; preparation of complaint held to be unauthorized practice); *In re* Cordero, 185 B.R. 882 (Bankr. M.D. Fla. 1995) (fine of $250 for each violation of statute); *In re* Samuels, 176 B.R. 616 (Bankr. M.D. Fla. 1994).

3504 11 U.S.C. § 110(i). *See In re* Moore, 290 B.R. 287 (Bankr. E.D.N.C. 2003) (inviting debtors to "chat" with a supervising attorney for "We the People" but not informing them that they can not rely on that attorney's advice and that attorney does not represent them, was unfair and deceptive).

3505 11 U.S.C. § 110(i)(1). *See In re* Gavin, 184 B.R. 670 (E.D. Pa. 1995); *In re* Kangarloo, 250 B.R. 115 (Bankr. C.D. Cal. 2000) (recommending $2050 actual damages for cost of property bankruptcy filing plus $2000 statutory damages and $1500 attorney fees); *In re* Murray, 194 B.R. 651 (Bankr. D. Ariz. 1996) (recommending that debtors be awarded actual damages, statutory damages and attorney fees for unfair and deceptive acts of preparer). The damages must be awarded by the district court, after the bankruptcy court certifies the underlying facts to that court and the moving party then moves for the award in district court. *See* Order Interpreting 11 U.S.C. § 110, 198 B.R. 604 (C.D. Cal. 1996).

3506 11 U.S.C. § 110(h). If the services have no value, or a negative value, the entire fee should be disgorged. *See, e.g., In re* Pillot, 286 B.R. 157 (Bankr. C.D. Cal. 2002); *In re* Bradshaw, 233 B.R. 315 (Bankr. D.N.J. 1999).

3507 11 U.S.C. § 110(i)(2).

3508 11 U.S.C. § 110(j)(2). *See In re* Schweitzer, 196 B.R. 620 (Bankr. M.D. Fla. 1996) (statewide injunction entered precluding preparer from acting as preparer in other bankruptcy cases due to numerous violations); *In re* Lyvers, 179 B.R. 837 (Bankr. W.D. Ky. 1995) (injunction against filing any petition or other papers in bankruptcy court for district); *In re* Gavin, 181 B.R. 814 (Bankr. E.D. Pa. 1995) (injunction against individual acting as a petition preparer in any jurisdiction). *See also In re* Graves, 279 B.R. 266 (B.A.P. 9th Cir. 2002) (court could issue injunction *sua sponte*, but petition preparer must be given notice and opportunity to be heard).

3509 *See, e.g., In re* Graham, 2004 WL 1052963 (Bankr. M.D.N.C. Feb. 13, 2004) (it is appropriate to look to state law in determining whether a petition preparer is seeking compensation for activities or services that constitute the unauthorized practice of law); *In re* Moore, 232 B.R. 1 (Bankr. D. Me. 1999); *In re* McDaniel, 232 B.R. 674 (Bankr. N.D. Tex. 1999); *In re* Hobbs, 213 B.R. 207 (Bankr. D. Me. 1997).

3510 11 U.S.C. § 110(i)(1)(C), (j)(3).

3511 *See, e.g., In re* Agyekum, 225 B.R. 695 (B.A.P. 9th Cir. 1998) (preprinted bankruptcy guide and questionnaire used by preparer to assist debtors constituted practice of law); *In re* Powell, 266 B.R. 450 (Bankr. N.D. Cal. 2001).

5.12.2.4 Unauthorized Practice of Law

Scams targeted at immigrants, tenants, debtors, and other consumers can often be challenged by unauthorized practice of law (UPL) statutes. Most states have UPL statutes which generally provide for criminal penalties but not for private rights of action in civil cases.[3512] Thus, violations of UPL statutes are most commonly brought as part of UDAP actions.[3513]

Almost universally, these states limit the practice of law to those who have been licensed and admitted to the state bar association.[3514] Exceptions to UPL statutes always include self-representation and sometimes include lay representation before certain local courts or state administrative agencies.[3515] A few states also carve out specific practices that nonattorneys may perform. For example, California's "Legal Document Assistants and Unlawful Detainer Assistants Act" allows nonattorneys to provide certain types of "self-help" services to the public.[3516] "Self-help" services include completing legal documents selected by a person representing himself in a legal matter, providing general published factual information that has been written or approved by an attorney, and filing and serving legal documents at the specific direction of someone representing himself in a legal matter.[3517] Another growing problem is the failure of most state unauthorized practice of law statutes to address possible exceptions for self-help interactive software and on-line programs.[3518]

The definition of "practice of law" varies greatly by state. In most cases, states will allow nonattorneys to make legal forms available to consumers and to complete those forms at the direction of the consumer but will not permit nonattorneys to give legal advice pertaining to the particular facts of an individual's case.[3519] There is a greater split on whether the provision of self-help kits by nonattorneys is considered UPL.[3520]

5.12.2.5 Tort and Other Causes of Action

Many common-law causes of action such as fraud, breach of contract, conversion and breach of fiduciary duty will also apply. Statutes requiring contracts to be written in languages other than English when negotiations are carried out in these languages should also be considered.[3521]

3512 Note that this almost universal prohibition against practicing law applies only to nonattorneys who are not agents of licensed attorneys. Whether a nonattorney is working independently or under the supervision of an attorney may not be readily apparent, warranting further factual investigation or discovery through litigation. There may be other remedies, not discussed here, generally against the attorney in cases where a nonattorney is acting as an attorney's agent. These remedies include possible bar disciplinary action as well as malpractice litigation.

3513 *See, e.g.*, First Am. Marketing Corp. v. Canella, 2004 WL 250537 (E.D. Pa. Jan. 26, 2004); Banks v. District of Columbia Dep't. of Consumer & Regulatory Affairs, 634 A.2d 433 (D.C. 1993), *cert. denied*, 513 U.S. 820, 115 S. Ct. 81 (1994); Bishop v. Jefferson Title Co., 28 P.3d 802 (Wash. App. 2001).

3514 *See generally* Derek A. Denckla, *Responses to the Conference: Nonlawyers and the Unauthorized Practice of Law: An Overview of the Legal and Ethical Parameters*, 67 Fordham L. Rev. 2581 (Apr. 1999).

3515 *See* ABA Commission on Nonlawyer Practice, 1994 Survey and Related Materials on the Unauthorized Practice of Law/Nonlawyer Practice; American Bar Association Center for Professional Responsibility, "1999 Survey of Unauthorized Practice of Law Committees" (1999).

3516 Cal. Bus. & Prof. Code §§ 6400–6415 *See* Brockey v. Moore, 107 Cal. App. 4th 86 (2003) (affirming jury award of damages under the Unlawful Detainer Assistants Act and UDAP law to customers of eviction "typing service" business that used names such as "Legal Aid" and "Legal Aid Services.").

3517 Cal. Bus. & Prof. Code § 6400(d).

3518 *See generally* Cristina L. Underwood, *Balancing Consumer Interests in a Digital Age: A New Approach to Regulating the Unauthorized Practice of Law*, 79 Wash. L. Rev. 437 (Feb. 2004).

3519 For a summary of UPL statutes and key legislation in all states, see ABA Commission on Nonlawyer Practice, Nonlawyer Activity in Law-Related Situations (Aug. 1995). *See also* Taub v. Weber, 366 F.3d 966 (9th Cir. 2004) (in Oregon, the "practice of law" at a minimum means the exercise of professional judgment in applying legal principles to address another person's individualized needs through analysis, advice, or other assistance); State Bar of Arizona v. Arizona Land Title & Trust Co., 366 P.2d 1 (Ariz. 1961); People v. Landlords Professional Servs., 264 Cal. Rptr. 548, 215 Cal. App. 3d 1599 (1989); Florida Bar v. Matus, 528 So. 2d 895 (Fla. 1988); State *ex rel.* Stovall v. Martinez, 27 Kan. App. 2d 9, 996 P.2d 371 (2000) (non-attorney engaged in unauthorized practice of law when he entered into contingent fee contracts to settle insurance claims, negotiated settlements, and advised claimants about the reasonableness of settlement offers); Dressel v. Ameribank, 664 N.W.2d 151 (Mich. 2003) (in defining the practice of law as counseling or assisting another in matters that require the use of legal discretion or profound legal knowledge, court found a bank's preparation of ordinary mortgage documents did not constitute UPL); Oregon State Bar v. Smith, 149 Or. App. 171, 942 P.2d 793 (1997), *cert. denied*, 522 U.S. 1117 (1998); Jones v. Allstate Ins. Co., 45 P.3d 1068 (Wash. 2002) (acts of claims adjuster for tortfeasor's insurance company in dealing with unrepresented victim amounted to practice of law); Perkins v. CTX Mortgage Co., 137 Wash. 2d 93, 969 P.2d 93 (1999) (lender's lay employees may prepare simple mortgage loan documents that do not involve exercise of legal discretion); Bishop v. Jefferson Title Co., 28 P.3d 802 (Wash. Ct. App. 2001) (reversing summary judgment for defendant on UDAP claims where non-attorney went beyond bounds of limited practice rule); State v. Hunt, 880 P.2d 96 (Wash. Ct. App. 1994).

3520 In New York, for example, courts have held that the mere selling of self-help kits is not UPL but becomes UPL when combined with legal advice. *See* New York County Lawyers' Ass'n v. Dacey, 234 N.E.2d 459 (N.Y. 1967); People v. Divorce Associated & Publishing Ltd., 407 N.Y.S.2d 142 (Sup. Ct. 1978); State v. Winder, 348 N.Y.S.2d 270 (App. Div. 1973). In contrast, in Texas, courts have expressly forbidden the dispensing of "will kits" by nonlawyers. *See* Palmer v. Unauthorized Practice Comm. of the State Bar of Texas, 438 S.W.2d 374 (Tex. Civ. App. 1969).

3521 *See* § 5.2.1, *supra*.

Malpractice actions against nonattorney providers may also be possible in some states. Several states hold nonattorneys who engage in the unauthorized practice of law to the same duty of care to which an attorney would be held in a negligence action.[3522] In other states, the standard of care is even higher. For example, in West Virginia, nonattorneys engaging in the unauthorized practice of law are considered negligent *per se*.[3523] In Arkansas, the state supreme court has stated that a nonattorney practicing law may even be subject to strict liability.[3524] Some states, however, have specially held that a nonattorney may not be liable for legal malpractice.[3525]

5.12.3 Living Trusts

A living trust is a legitimate estate planning device that, in appropriate situations and when properly implemented, can avoid probate and provide a consumer with other benefits. (A living trust must be distinguished from a living will, which is a communication to a doctor or others about an individual's wishes if that individual becomes terminally ill.)

Living trusts are more and more frequently being sold through high pressure door-to-door or seminar sales for as much as $5000 to $10,000. A recent study found that the average cost for the living trust forms alone was $2000.[3526] The seller is not an attorney and often has no relationship with an attorney in that state. The seller will often pose as a member of a seemingly legitimate organization (such as the "American Association of Senior Citizens,"[3527] thus imitating the name "American Association of Retired Persons") and even offer other membership privileges, but the sale of the living trust is the money-maker. The seller preys on many seniors' fears that the probate process will tie up property for years and needlessly dissipate assets built up over a lifetime. Despite evidence to the contrary, living trusts are also touted as a way to save taxes.[3528]

Not only are the prices for living trusts sold by con artists many times what an attorney would charge, but the living trusts often fail to meet that state's particular legal requirements (for example, a trust from a community property state may be sold in a non-community property state). Some living trust sellers even appoint themselves as the trustees. The primary goal of unscrupulous living trust salespeople is to gain access to the victim's assets. Once they have this information, they recommend that prospective buyers liquidate their assets and purchase insurance or annuity contracts.[3529]

Moreover, a trust has no impact unless assets are transferred into the trust and can not completely avoid probate unless all assets otherwise subject to probate are transferred into the trust. Nevertheless, many living trust sellers fail to help consumers to move assets into the trust or even fail to advise them of the need to do so.

Many consumers can benefit from use of a proper living trust. On the other hand, it is highly unlikely that such trusts sold door-to-door or through a seminar are ever a good idea. By contrast, many attorneys specializing in trusts and estates will provide a free consultation explaining the pros and cons of a living trust.

Probably the best approach to challenging a fraudulent sale of a living trust is through a state UDAP action, alleging various misrepresentations in the sale—deceptive pricing claims, overstatement of the cost of probate, misrepresentations as to endorsements or approvals, misrepresentations as to tax advantages, failure to disclose important information, etc. Advocates should also allege, where appropriate, high-pressure sales tactics, the unauthorized practice of law, significant errors in the forms, the failure to provide instructions as to moving property into the trust, and breach of fiduciary duty.

Unauthorized practice of law (UPL) claims often arise when nonattorneys sell self-help living trust kits. These kits are usually not a good idea because they are not tailored to individual needs. They also usually require consumers to transfer assets on their own. Sometimes the kits fail to even inform consumers that assets must be transferred. There is a

3522 Hermitage Corp. v. Contractors Adjustment Co., 637 N.E.2d 1201 (Ill. App. Ct. 1993) (the elements of a legal malpractice claim are relevant to a claim for negligent unauthorized practice of law), *aff'd in part and rev'd in part on other grounds*, 166 Ill. 2d 72, 651 N.E.2d 1132 (1995); Webb v. Pomeroy, 655 P.2d 465 (Kan. Ct. App. 1982), *reh'g denied*, 233 Kan. 1093 (1993); Busch v. Flangas, 837 P.2d 438 (Nev. 1992) (nonattorney working for attorney is subject to legal malpractice claim if he attempts to provide legal services); Bowers v. Transamerica Title Inc., 675 P.2d 193 (Wash. 1983) (escrow agent who engaged in the unauthorized practice of law is subject to the standard of care of an attorney).

3523 *See* Brammer v. Taylor, 338 S.E.2d 207 (W. Va. 1985).

3524 *See* Wright v. Langdon, 623 S.W.2d 823 (Ark. 1981) (a nonattorney practicing law should at least be held to the standard of care of an attorney and possibly should be strictly liable).

3525 *See* United Steelworkers of America v. Craig, 571 So. 2d 1101 (Ala. 1990) (nonlawyer's failure to adequately represent union member did not form a basis for legal malpractice suit); Palmer v. Westmeyer, 549 N.E.2d 1202 (Ohio Ct. App. 1988); Carstensen v. Chrisland Corp., 442 S.E.2d 660 (Va. 1994).

3526 See Angela M. Vallario, Living Trusts in the Unauthorized Practice of Law: A Good Thing Gone Bad, 59 Md. L. Rev. 595 (2000).

3527 *See* Stiegel, Norrgard & Talbert, *Scams in the Marketing and Sale of Living Trusts*, 26 Clearinghouse Rev. 609 n.2 (Oct. 1992).

3528 *See* People *ex rel.* MacFarlane v. Boyls, 591 P.2d 1315 (Colo. 1979) (en banc) (noting that neither the IRS nor any courts have found the trusts to be viable tax saving mechanisms).

3529 *See* People *ex rel.* Lockyer v. Fremont Life Ins. Co., 104 Cal. App. 4th 508, 128 Cal. Rptr. 2d 463, 469 (2002) (affirming civil penalties and restitution order where sales agents represented themselves as estate planning advisors when they were actually insurance agents seeking to sell annuities). *See generally* Angela M. Vallario, *Living Trusts in the Unauthorized Practice of Law: A Good Thing Gone Bad*, 59 Md. L. Rev. 595 (2000).

split among the states whether the mere provision of a self-help kit is the unauthorized practice of law.[3530] No jurisdiction to date has codified whether the preparation of a living trust by a nonattorney is *per se* the unauthorized practice of law. The question is generally determined by case law in each state. In most states that have considered this issue, courts have found that living trust marketing by nonlawyers does constitute the unauthorized practice of law.[3531]

Another tip is to look to see whether a door-to-door or even a seminar sale (if not conducted at the seller's principal place of business) complied with the FTC and state three-day cancellation laws.[3532] If not, this may provide an independent ground to cancel the sale or establish damages. If a telephone solicitation was involved in the sale, a state telemarketing law may also give the consumer a right to cancel the sale.[3533] States are also beginning to enact statutes aimed at living trust abuses, which may provide additional consumer remedies.[3534] In egregious cases, common law fraud claims seeking punitive damages should also be considered.

It is always a good idea to contact the state attorney general's consumer protection office. They have been active in suing these types of sellers in some states.[3535]

3530 *See* § 5.12.2, *supra*.

3531 *See, e.g.*, People *ex rel.* Lockyer v. Fremont Life Ins. Co., 104 Cal. App. 4th 508, 128 Cal. Rptr. 2d 463, 469 (2002); People *ex rel.* MacFarlane v. Boyls, 591 P.2d 1315 (Colo. 1979) (suspending a lawyer for aiding nonlawyers in the marketing of trusts); Florida Bar v. American Senior Citizens Alliance, Inc., 689 So. 2d 255 (Fla. 1997); Florida Bar re: Advisory Opinion, Non-Lawyer Preparation of Living Trusts, 613 So. 2d 426 (Fla. 1992) (court identified five steps in the process of creating a living trust: (1) gathering the necessary information; (2) assembling the document; (3) reviewing the document with the client; (4) properly executing the document; and (5) funding the trust document. Only #1 was considered appropriate for nonlawyers); Committee on Prof'l Ethics and Conduct v. Baker, 492 N.W.2d 695 (Iowa 1992) (a nonlawyer's advising of clients with respect to living trust constituted UPL); *In re* Mid-America Living Trust, 927 S.W.2d 855 (Mo. 1996); Cleveland Bar Ass'n v. Yurich, 642 N.E.2d 79 (Ohio Bd. Comm'rs on Unauthorized Practice of Law 1994).

3532 *See* § 5.8.2, *supra*.

3533 *See* § 5.9.2.5, *supra*.

3534 *See* Ark. Code Ann. § 4-88-107(a) (adding marketing of living trust documents by non-attorneys and non-banks to UDAP statute's list of violations); 815 Ill. Comp. Stat. Ann. § 505/2BB (same); Mont. Code Ann. § 30-10-909; Tenn. Code § 47-18-104(b)(36) (requiring disclosures in living trust advertisements).

3535 Prosecution of living trust mills remains low in most jurisdictions. A few states such as Florida and Texas, however, have aggressively pursued claims against nonattorney living trust providers. For a discussion of the enforcement efforts in the various states, see American Bar Ass'n, Standing Comm'n on Lawyers' Responsibility for Client Protection, Survey and Related Materials on the Unauthorized Practice of Law/Nonlawyer Practice (1994) (identifying each jurisdiction's definition of the practice of law and summarizing activity regarding UPL); American Bar Ass'n, 1999 Survey of Unauthorized Practice of Law Committees (1999).

5.12.4 Trustees, Escrow Agents, Other Fiduciaries

It is unfair for a bank to allow a trustee to use trust assets for personal purposes,[3536] or for a bank acting as an escrow agent to fail to answer inquiries, pay interest as required, or account for the money, in intentional disregard of its fiduciary status.[3537] Similarly, it is unconscionable for an escrow company to pay out money to the wrong party based on questionable documentation and to refuse to pay out the required amount to the correct party.[3538] An escrow agent must disclose to all parties any information as to whether the transaction is being closed in full compliance with escrow instructions.[3539] Courts have suggested that any breach of fiduciary duty is a UDAP violation.[3540]

5.12.5 Investigators and Other "Finders"

UDAP claims have also successfully challenged practices by companies that alleged they would collect delinquent child support payments due a client and owed by the client's spouse.[3541] The FTC has sued many ingenious telemarketers who falsely promised, for a fee, to obtain relief for past victims of telemarketing fraud, particularly in obtaining free gifts that were never delivered.[3542] When such a service is sold by telephone, the FTC's Telemarketing Sales Rule prohibits the seller from requesting or receiving any payment from the consumer until seven business days *after* recovering the money or property.[3543] However there is no automatic UDAP violation in a company contacting missing heirs, even though the heirs would probably have been found without the company's assistance.[3544]

3536 Dahlborg v. Middleborough Trust Co., 16 Mass. App. Ct. 481, 452 N.E.2d 281 (1983).

3537 United States v. U.S. Trust Co., 660 F. Supp. 1085 (D. Mass. 1986).

3538 Commercial Escrow Co. v. Rockport Rebel, Inc., 778 S.W.2d 532 (Tex. App. 1989).

3539 Styrk v. Cornerstone Investments, Inc., 61 Wash. App. 463, 810 P.2d 1366 (1991).

3540 *See* State Street Bank & Trust Co. v. Mutual Life Ins. Co. of New York, 811 F. Supp. 915 (S.D.N.Y. 1993). *See also* James L. Miniter Ins. Agency, Inc. v. Ohio Indemnity Co., 112 F.3d 1240 (1st Cir. 1997) (Mass. law); Sullivan's Wholesale Drug v. Faryl's Pharmacy, Inc., 214 Ill. App. 3d 1073, 573 N.E.2d 1370 (1991) (nursing home has enough of a fiduciary duty to its patients that it may commit a UDAP violation by billing patients the full price for drugs, while accepting a 15% kickback from the drug supplier).

3541 Ulberg v. Seattle Bonded Inc., 28 Wash. App. 762, 626 P.2d 522 (1981).

3542 *See* § 5.9.1, *supra*.

3543 16 C.F.R. § 310.4(b)(3). *See* § 5.9.4.7.4, *supra*.

3544 Guess v. Brophy, 164 Ill. App. 3d 75, 517 N.E.2d 693 (1987).

5.12.6 Accountants

An accountant may violate a UDAP statute by certifying financial statements that contain material misstatements and omissions.[3545] In general, the lack of privity between the consumer and the accountant does not prevent the UDAP claim.[3546] The public must be able to reasonably rely on financial statements certified by public accounting firms.[3547] It is a UDAP violation to hold oneself out as an accountant if not certified.[3548]

5.13 Opportunity Schemes and Other "Nonsale" Transactions

5.13.1 Franchises and Business Opportunities

5.13.1.1 FTC Franchising Rule

According to a 2004 FTC survey, almost half a million U.S. adults purchased business opportunities involving false earnings claims or false promises of assistance over a two-year period.[3549] The FTC has adopted a Trade Regulation Rule Concerning Franchising and Business Opportunities,[3550] and has brought many enforcement proceedings under it[3551] The FTC can also base charges against franchisors on its general authority to prohibit unfair and deceptive acts.[3552]

The rule requires franchisors to furnish prospective franchisees with a disclosure statement containing information on the franchise operation, including the franchisor's business experience, balance sheet, recurring fees, and conditions under which the franchise may be sold.[3553] The nature of the involvement of public figures in a franchise must be disclosed. The franchisor must also have substantiation for income and profit claims and inform prospects that these are only estimates.[3554] In the alternative, the franchisor has the option of making disclosures in accordance with the Uniform Franchise Offering Circulating Guidelines adopted by the North American Securities Administrators Association on April 25, 1993.[3555]

3545 Reisman v. KPMG Peat Marwick L.L.P., 965 F. Supp. 165 (D. Mass. 1997).

3546 *Id. See also* § 4.2.15.3, *supra. But see* Spencer v. Doyle, 733 N.E.2d 1082 (Mass. App. 2002) (investors can not sue accountant who issued favorable report on company in which they invested).

3547 United States v. Arthur Young, 465 U.S. 805 (1984); Reisman v. KPMG Peat Marwick L.L.P., 965 F. Supp. 165 (D. Mass. 1997).

3548 *See* § 4.7.7, *supra.*

3549 FTC, Consumer Fraud in the United Sates: An FTC Survey (Aug. 2004) at 30.

3550 16 C.F.R. Part 436 (effective Oct. 21, 1979). In 1993, after a review of the rule, the FTC decided not to initiate a rulemaking proceeding to amend the earnings claims and preemption provisions of the rule. 58 Fed. Reg. 69223 (Dec. 30, 1993). The FTC performs a Regulatory Flexibility Act review of its rules every ten years. The FTC requested comments on April 7, 1995, about whether the rule should be changed. 60 Fed. Reg. 17656. The Commission extended the comment period of its regulatory review until December 31, 1997, and has not yet acted based on this review. 63 Fed. Reg. 62743 (Nov. 9, 1998). As of mid-2004, the FTC staff was still preparing its report. *See* FTC, Semiannual Regulatory Agenda, 69 Fed. Reg. 38602 (June 28, 2004).

3551 Examples of the FTC's many enforcement proceedings include: FTC v. Marrone's Water Ice, Inc., 5 Trade Reg. Rep. (CCH) ¶ 15397 (E.D. Pa. Apr. 16, 2003) (proposed consent decree against defendants who sold business opportunity without adequate franchise disclosure statement and made false earnings claims); FTC v. Accent Marketing, Inc., 2002 WL 31257708 (S.D. Ala. July 1, 2002) (issuing preliminary injunction); U.S. v. Vaughan, 2001 WL 1526274 (D. Kan. Oct. 18, 2001) (denying motion to dismiss criminal contempt charges for violating consent order in franchise case); FTC v. Hart Marketing Enterprises Ltd., 5 Trade Reg. Rep. (CCH) ¶ 24,559 (M.D. Fla. 1999) (consent order) (Internet kiosk business opportunity scheme); FTC v. Independent Travel Agencies of Am., Inc., 5 Trade Reg. Rep. (CCH) ¶ 24,356 (S.D. Fla. 1998) (proposed consent decree); FTC v. Gulfstar Corp., 5 Trade Reg. Rep. (CCH) ¶ 24,534 (N.D. Tex. 1998) (consent order) (investments solicited for oil drilling ventures); FTC v. Electronic Filing Assoc., Ltd., 5 Trade Reg. Rep. (CCH) ¶ 24,549 (D. Ariz. 1998) (consent order) (promoters of home-based medical billing businesses); FTC v. Mackie Servs., Inc., 5 Trade Reg. Rep. (CCH) ¶ 23,981 (D. Colo. 1996) (proposed consent decree); FTC v. Fresh-O-Matic Corp., 5 Trade Reg. Rep. (CCH) ¶ 23,982 (E.D. Mo. 1996) (proposed consent decree); FTC v. Wolf, 5 Trade Reg. Rep. (CCH) ¶ 23,974 (S.D. Fla. 1996) (summary judgment); FTC v. Intellipay, Inc., 5 Trade Reg. Rep. (CCH) ¶ 23,382 (S.D. Tex. 1993) (consent decree); FTC v. Stricker, 5 Trade Reg. Rep. (CCH) ¶ 23,203 (C.D. Cal. 1992) (consent judgment); FTC v. Caribbean Clear, Inc., 5 Trade Reg. Rep. (CCH) ¶ 23,207 (D.S.C. 1992) (consent decree); United States v. WHY USA, Inc., 5 Trade Reg. Rep. (CCH) ¶ 23,221 (D. Ariz. 1992) (consent decree); United States v. TeleComm, Inc., 5 Trade Reg. Rep. (CCH) ¶ 23,260 (D.N.J. 1992) (consent judgment); FTC v. National Bus. Consultants, 781 F. Supp. 1136 (E.D. La. 1991); FTC v. American Marketing, Inc., 5 Trade Reg. Rep. (CCH) ¶ 23,790 (N.D. Ga. 1990) (consent judgment); FTC v. Investment Developments, Inc., 5 Trade Reg. Rep. (CCH) ¶ 22,788 (E.D. La. 1990) (injunction); FTC v. McKleans, Inc., 5 Trade Reg. Rep. (CCH) ¶ 22,762 (D. Conn. Nov. 15, 1989) (consent decree); U.S. Royce Automobile Parts, Inc., 3 Trade Reg. Rep. (CCH) ¶ 22,275 (M.D. Fla. 1985); Federal Energy Sys., 3 Trade Reg. Rep. (CCH) ¶ 22,290 (F.T.C. Dkt. #832-3063 1985) ($3 million redress and $1.6 million penalties for franchise rule violations).

3552 *See, e.g.*, FTC v. Tashman, 318 F.3d 1273 (11th Cir. 2003) (baseless sales estimates violated FTC Act).

3553 *See* FTC v. Accent Marketing, Inc., 2002 WL 31257708 (S.D. Ala. July 1, 2002) (issuing preliminary injunction against company that failed to make required disclosures).

3554 *See* FTC v. Tashman, 318 F.3d 1273 (11th Cir. 2003) (ordering entry of judgment for FTC where promoter had no basis for sales estimates).

3555 58 Fed. Reg. 69224 (Dec. 30, 1993).

As long as there are no questions about UDAP coverage, it should be a *per se* UDAP violation to violate the FTC rule.[3556] Even though franchise and business opportunity schemes do not exactly involve consumer sales, these schemes do take advantage of consumers, and most UDAP statutes cover these practices.[3557] States may also have their own consumer protection laws specifically directed at business opportunity promotions.[3558] The FTC rule does not preempt state laws that regulate the substantive terms of franchise contracts.[3559]

One interesting note about the FTC Franchise Rule is that the FTC has stated that it believes there is a private right of action for the violation of the FTC rule:

> The Commission believes that the courts should and will hold that any person injured by a violation of the rule has a private right of action against the violator under the Federal Trade Commission Act, as amended, and the rule. Such a private right of action is necessary to protect those meant to benefit from the rule. The FTC also finds this consistent with the legislative intent of the Congress in enacting the Federal Trade Commission Act, as amended, and is necessary to the FTC's enforcement scheme.[3560]

Nevertheless, federal district courts have consistently held that it is for Congress and the courts to make this decision, not the FTC, and that there is no congressional intent underlying the FTC position. Consequently, the longstanding position that there is no private right of action under the FTC Act will not be changed for a violation of the FTC Franchise Rule, despite the FTC position.[3561]

3556 Nieman v. DryClean U.S.A. Franchise Co., 178 F.3d 1126 (11th Cir. 1999) (violation is *per se* violation of Florida UDAP statute, but Franchise Rule did not apply here), *cert. denied*, 528 U.S. 1118 (2000); Aurigemma v. Arco Petroleum Products Co., 734 F. Supp. 1025 (D. Conn. 1990) (violation of FTC Franchise rule is *per se* violation of Connecticut's UDAP statute); Morgan v. Air Brook Limousine, Inc., Clearinghouse No. 40,640 (N.J. Super. Ct. Law Div. 1986); Texas Cookie Co. v. Hendricks & Peralta, 747 S.W.2d 873 (Tex. App. 1988) (deceptive to fail to disclose information required by FTC Franchise Rule). *Cf.* Lui Ciro, Inc. v. Ciro, Inc., 895 F. Supp. 1365 (D. Haw. 1995) (state franchise law does not create cause of action; consumers, but not business, may sue under UDAP statute). *But see* Leblanc v. Belt Center, Inc., 509 So. 2d 134 (La. Ct. App. 1987).

3557 *See* § 2.2.9.2, *supra*.

3558 *See* § 5.13.1.2, *infra*.

3559 H.R.R. Zimmerman v. Tecumseh Prods. Co., 2001 U.S. Dist. LEXIS 1920 (N.D. Ill. Feb. 15, 2001).

3560 43 Fed. Reg. 59614 (Feb. 10, 1978).

3561 FTC v. Davis, 5 Trade Reg. Rep. (CCH) ¶ 22,741 (D. Nev. Oct. 17, 1989); FTC v. McKleans, Inc., 5 Trade Reg. Rep. (CCH) ¶ 22,762 (D. Conn. Nov. 15, 1989) (consent order); Days Inn of Am. Franchising, Inc. v. Windham, 699 F. Supp. 1581 (N.D. Ga. 1988); Mon-Shore Mgmt., Inc. v. Family Media, Bus. Fran. Guide (CCH) ¶ 8494 (S.D.N.Y. 1985); Freedman v. Meldy's, Inc., 587 F. Supp. 658 (E.D. Pa. 1984); Chelson v. Oregonian Publishing Co., 1981-1 Trade Cas. (CCH) ¶ 64,031 (D. Or. 1981). *See generally* § 9.1, *infra*.

5.13.1.2 Other FTC, State UDAP Precedent

Some states have business opportunity laws or UDAP rules that specify certain unfair practices.[3562] Some business opportunities may also be considered securities that will be governed by the state's securities law.[3563] In other states, unfair practices will be determined under the more general standards of the state's UDAP statute, taking the prohibitions of the FTC rule into account. A state's regulation of business opportunities within its borders does not violate the Commerce Clause even though the franchise may make sales in other states.[3564]

FTC[3565] and state[3566] decisions hold that it is deceptive to

3562 *See, e.g.*, Ga. Code Ann. § 10-1-410 *et seq.*; Haw. Rev. Stat. ch. 482E; 940 Code Mass. Reg. § 3.11; Ohio Rev. Code Ch. 1334; Rules of the Utah Consumer Sales Practices Act, Utah Admin. Rules 152-11-11(B), Franchises, Distributorships, Referral Sales and Pyramid Codes Marketing Schemes. *See also* League v. U.S. Postmatic, Inc., 235 Ga. App. 171, 508 S.E.2d 210 (1998) (violation of Georgia business opportunity statute is *per se* UDAP violation); Williams, Ohio Consumer Law, Ch. 8 (2002 ed.) (analysis of Ohio's law). *See* § 2.2.9.4, *supra*.

3563 *See, e.g.*, State *ex rel.* Miller v. Pace, 677 N.W.2d 761 (Iowa 2004); State v. Justin, 2003 WL 23269283 (N.Y. Sup. Ct. Nov. 29, 2003). *See* § 9.4.10, *supra*.

3564 H.R.R. Zimmerman v. Tecumseh Prods. Co., 2001 U.S. Dist. LEXIS 1920 (N.D. Ill. Feb. 15, 2001).

3565 The following are among the many FTC cases on this topic: FTC v. End70 Corp., 2003 WL 21770837 (N.D. Tex. July 31, 2003) (preliminary injunction); FTC v. Accent Marketing, Inc., 2002 WL 31257708 (S.D. Ala. July 1, 2002); FTC v. Data Medical Capital, Inc., 5 Trade Reg. Rep. (CCH) ¶ 15129 (C.D. Cal. July 6, 2001) (work at home scheme); FTC v. Medicor L.L.C., 5 Trade Reg. Rep. (CCH) ¶ 24,883 (C.D. Cal. Mar. 1, 2001) (issuing TRO against at-home medical billing scam); FTC v. Vending Communications, Inc., 5 Trade Reg. Rep. (CCH) ¶ 24,876 (S.D. Fla. Feb. 8, 2001) (consent decree against business that advertised earnings without disclosing number and percentage of purchasers who made that much); FTC v. Five Star Auto Club, Inc., 97 F. Supp. 2d 502 (S.D.N.Y. 2000) ($2.9 million restitution order); FTC v. Chappie, 5 Trade Reg. Rep. (CCH) ¶ 24,062 (S.D. Fla. 1996) (issuing temporary restraining order against misrepresenting the profitability of business opportunities involving CD-Rom display racks); FTC v. Patriot Alcohol Testers, 798 F. Supp. 851 (D. Mass. 1992) (coin-operated blood alcohol testing, device); FTC v. Communidyne Inc., 5 Trade Reg. Rep. (CCH) ¶ 23,632 (N.D. Ill. July 12, 1994); FTC v. Digital Communications Corp., 5 Trade Reg. Rep. (CCH) ¶ 23,722 (C.D. Cal. 1994); FTC v. Davis, 5 Trade Reg. Rep. (CCH) ¶ 22,741 (D. Nev. Oct. 17, 1989); FTC v. TransAlaska Energy Corp., 3 Trade Reg. Rep. (CCH) ¶ 22,446 (C.D. Cal. 1987) ($2.1 million redress for worthless oil and gas leases); Akers v. Bonifasi, 629 F. Supp. 1212 (M.D. Tenn. 1985); FTC v. Leland Indus., Inc., 3 Trade Reg. Rep. (CCH) ¶ 22,297 (C.D. Cal. 1985) ($2.5 million redress for misrepresentations concerning oil and gas rights lotteries); U.S. Royce Automobile Parts, Inc., 3 Trade Reg. Rep. (CCH) ¶ 22,275 (M.D. Fla. 1985); FTC v. International Computer Concepts, Inc., 5 Trade Reg. Rep. (CCH) ¶ 23,927 (N.D. Ohio 1995) (permanent injunction); FTC v. Metropolitan Communications Corp., 5 Trade Reg. Rep. (CCH) ¶ 23,634 (S.D.N.Y. July 14, 1994), 5 Trade Reg. Rep. (CCH) ¶ 23,652 (N.D. Ohio Aug. 17,

misrepresent profits or earnings which may be anticipated by a prospective purchaser of a business opportunity or franchise. Thus it is deceptive to represent that a substantial number of distributors have made or can make the profits advertised when only a few have made that high a profit,[3567] when claimed earnings far exceed earnings normally received,[3568] or when the representation is made with only limited knowledge of actual profits received.[3569] Earnings figures, even those attributed to a specific distributor, unaccompanied by limiting or explanatory language, imply that a substantial number of distributors will earn the figure indicated.[3570] Franchise operators may not misrepresent a franchise location as profitable[3571] or the risk involved.[3572]

1994) (TRO); FTC v. Wolf, 5 Trade Reg. Rep. (CCH) ¶ 23,665 (S.D. Fla. Sept. 12, 1994) (consent order) (defendants must post $1 million bond before marketing franchises again); FTC v. Vendall Marketing Corp., 5 Trade Reg. Rep. (CCH) ¶ 23,671 (D. Or. Sept. 13, 1994) (consent order) (bars defendants from vending machine business in future); FTC v. National Bus. Consultants, 5 Trade Reg. Rep. (CCH) ¶ 22,816 (E.D. La. 1990) (permanent injunction); Blenheim Expositions, Inc., 5 Trade Reg. Rep. (CCH) ¶ 23,902 (F.T.C. C-3633 1995) (consent order) (misrepresentations made in ads promoting company's franchise trade shows); National Impulse Marketing Corp., 5 Trade Reg. Rep. (CCH) ¶ 23,014 (F.T.C. File No. 91 0005 1991) (consent order); National Dynamics Corp., 82 F.T.C. 488 (1973), *remanded in part*, 492 F.2d 1333 (2d Cir. 1974), *on remand*, 85 F.T.C. 391, 1052 (1975); Universal Credit Acceptance Corp., 82 F.T.C. 570 (1973), *rev'd in part sub nom.* Heater v. FTC, 503 F.2d 321 (9th Cir. 1974); Universal Electronics Corp., 78 F.T.C. 265 (1971); Windsor Distrib. Co., 77 F.T.C. 204 (1970) *aff'd*, 431 F.2d 443 (3d Cir. 1971); Waltham Watch Co., 60 F.T.C. 1692 (1962), *aff'd*, 318 F.2d 28 (7th Cir. 1963), *cert. denied*, 375 U.S. 944 (1963); La Notte, Inc. v. New Way Gourmet, Inc., 83 N.C. App. 480, 350 S.E.2d 889 (1986); Rendon v. Sanchez, 737 S.W.2d 122 (Tex. App. 1987); Staley v. Terns Serv. Co., 595 S.W.2d 882 (Tex. Civ. App. 1980); Woo v. Great Southwestern Acceptance Co., 565 S.W.2d 290 (Tex. Civ. App. 1978).

3566 La Notte, Inc. v. New Way Gourmet, Inc., 83 N.C. App. 480, 350 S.E.2d 889 (1986); Rendon v. Sanchez, 737 S.W.2d 122 (Tex. App. 1987); Staley v. Terns Serv. Co., 595 S.W.2d 882 (Tex. Civ. App. 1980); Woo v. Great Southwestern Acceptance Co., 565 S.W.2d 290 (Tex. Civ. App. 1978).

3567 Bailey Employment Sys., Inc. v. Hahn, 545 F. Supp. 62 (D. Conn. 1982); National Dynamics Corp., 82 F.T.C. 488 (1973), *remanded in part*, 492 F.2d 1333 (2d Cir. 1974), *on remand*, 85 F.T.C. 391, 1052 (1975); Woo v. Great Southwestern Acceptance Co., 565 S.W.2d 290 (Tex. Civ. App. 1978).

3568 Among the many consent decrees the FTC has obtained on this subject are: FTC v. Williams, 5 Trade Reg. Rep. (CCH) ¶ 24,813 (C.D. Cal. Sept. 25, 2000) (at home medical billing); FTC v. Mediworks, 5 Trade Reg. Rep. (CCH) ¶ 24,800 (C.D. Cal. Sept. 6, 2000) (at home medical billing); FTC v. Innovative Prods., Inc., 5 Trade Reg. Rep. (CCH) ¶ 24,797 (N.D. Tex. Aug. 16, 2000) (work at home scam advertised in employment want ads); FTC v. Vendors Fin. Servs., 5 Trade Reg. Rep. (CCH) ¶ 24,605 (D. Colo. 1999) (consent order) (vending machine franchises); U.S. v. Photo Vending Int'l, 5 Trade Reg. Rep. (CCH) ¶ 24,655 (S.D. Fla. 1999) (consent order) (photo machine franchises); FTC v. Hart Marketing Enterprises Ltd., 5 Trade Reg. Rep. (CCH) ¶ 24,559 (M.D. Fla. 1999) (consent decree) (Internet kiosks as business opportunity); FTC v. Intellicom Servs., Inc., 5 Trade Reg. Rep. (CCH) ¶ 24,556 (C.D. Cal. 1999) (consent decree) (Internet business profitability); FTC v. Robert Oliver, 5 Trade Reg. Rep. (CCH) ¶ 24,433 (N.D. Fla. 1998) (consent order) (Internet promoter of "consumer protection agency" franchises); FTC v. Inetintl.Com, Inc., 5 Trade Reg. Rep. (CCH) ¶ 24,413 (C.D. Cal. 1998) (preliminary injunction) (Internet-related business opportunity); FTC v. Electronic Filing Assocs., Ltd., 5 Trade Reg. Rep. (CCH) ¶ 24,549 (D. Ariz. 1998) (stipulated final judgment and consent decree) (promoters of a home-based medical billing business misrepresented earnings potential); FTC v. Shelton, 5 Trade Reg. Rep. (CCH) ¶ 24,529 (D. Nev. 1998) (consent decree) (medical and dental billing business opportunity); FTC v. Saffer, 5 Trade Reg. Rep. (CCH) ¶ 24,476 (S.D. Fla. 1998) (final judgment and permanent injunction) (leasing, transferring, or selling FCC paging licenses); FTC v. Bell Communications, Inc., 5 Trade Reg. Rep. (CCH) ¶ 24,177 (C.D. Cal. 1998) (final order and permanent injunction) (same); FTC v. National Consumer Consulting Group, 5 Trade Reg. Rep. (CCH) ¶ 24,432 (N.D. Ill. 1998) (proposed consent decree) (medical billing business); FTC v. Metropolitan Communications Corp., 5 Trade Reg. Rep. (CCH) ¶ 24,352 (S.D.N.Y. 1998) (proposed consent decree) (license application preparation service); FTC v. U.S.A. Channel Sys., Inc., 5 Trade Reg. Rep. (CCH) ¶ 24,180 (C.D. Cal. 1996) (final orders for permanent injunction) (leasing, transferring, or selling FCC paging licenses); National Dynamics Corp., 82 F.T.C. 488 (1973), *remanded in part*, 492 F.2d 1333 (2d Cir. 1974), *on remand*, 85 F.T.C. 391, 1052 (1975); Windsor Distrib. Co., 77 F.T.C. 204 (1970), *aff'd*, 431 F.2d 443 (3d Cir. 1971); Von Schroder Mfg. Co., 33 F.T.C. 58 (1941); *see also* Massachusetts Consumer Protection Regulations, Mass. Regs. Code tit. 940, § 3.11, Private Employment Agencies and Bus. Schemes; Kugler v. Koscot Interplanetary, Inc., 120 N.J. Super. 216, 293 A.2d 682 (Ch. Div. 1972).

3569 Von Schroder Mfg. Co., 33 F.T.C. 58 (1941); Massachusetts Consumer Protection Regulations, Mass. Regs. Code tit. 940, § 3.11, Private Employment Agencies and Bus. Schemes; Commonwealth v. Mirror World, Inc., No. 4058 June Term 1973, Clearinghouse No. 26,022 (C.P. Phila., Cty., Pa. Dec. 31, 1978); Kugler v. Koscot Interplanetary, Inc., 120 N.J. Super. 216, 293 A.2d 682 (Ch. Div. 1972).

3570 National Dynamics Corp., 82 F.T.C. 488 (1973), *remanded in part*, 492 F.2d 1333 (2d Cir. 1974), *on remand*, 85 F.T.C. 391, 1052 (1975); Massachusetts Consumer Protection Regulations, Mass. Regs. Code tit. 940, § 3.11, Private Employment Agencies and Bus. Schemes.

3571 United States v. C.D. Control Technology, Inc., 3 Trade Reg. Rep. (CCH) ¶ 22,267 (E.D.N.Y. 1985) (preliminary injunction); Cope Enterprises Ltd., 87 F.T.C. 129 (1976) (consent order); Consolidated Int'l Tool & Oil, Inc., 86 F.T.C. 947 (1975) (consent order); Multi-State Distrib., Inc., 80 F.T.C. 754 (1972) (consent order); Universal Electronics Corp., 78 F.T.C. 265 (1971); International Sales Co., 79 F.T.C. 159 (1971) (consent order); Youngstown Spectrum Corp., 75 F.T.C. 457 (1969) (consent order).

3572 Consolidated Chemical Corp., 84 F.T.C. 379 (1974) (consent order); Universal Credit Acceptance Corp., 82 F.T.C. 570 (1973), *rev'd in part sub nom.* Heater v. FTC, 503 F.2d 321 (9th Cir. 1974); Mercury Electronics, Inc., 74 F.T.C. 548 (1968) (consent order); Rules for the Utah Consumer Sales Practices Act, Utah Admin. Rules 152-11-11, Franchises, Distributorships Referral Sales and Pyramid Sales Marketing Schemes. *See also* United States v. Vaughan, 2001 U.S. Dist. LEXIS 20084 (D. Kan. Oct. 18, 2001) (denying motion to dismiss contempt

Misrepresentations concerning business arrangements, the goods to be distributed, operations, termination provisions, and benefits of a business opportunity are also deceptive.[3573] Franchisors can not misrepresent that the franchise is guaranteed to remain active for years.[3574] Franchisors may not exaggerate the assistance they will offer the franchisee in reselling the franchise and equipment, in advertising, and in training and other management assistance.[3575]

Franchise operations may not be advertised in help-wanted sections.[3576] The FTC has obtained a consent decree from a franchise seller that placed newspaper ads that appeared to be from individuals selling established local vending routes.[3577] Using shills as references is deceptive.[3578]

Equally deceptive are business opportunity offers to recruit other distributors or sell products where the market at the time of the offer is already saturated with such distributors.[3579] The same exclusive territory may not be assigned to two franchisees, and franchise agents may not assign territories without proper authority.[3580] The franchisor must also determine the ability of the prospective franchisee to run the business opportunity and may not falsely represent that no special ability is needed to be a success.[3581]

It is equally deceptive to represent that a franchisor is more selective than it actually is in choosing franchisees.[3582] Also deceptive is a franchisor's failure to provide all promised aspects of the franchise package to franchisees,[3583] to fail to disclose the attrition rate of franchisees,[3584] or to fail to disclose the franchisor's current involvement in lawsuits by or judgments in favor of the franchisees for fraud or UDAP violations.[3585] It is also deceptive to misrepresent the availability of government grants to start a business.[3586] The FTC has accepted a consent order from an idea promotion firm after complaining that the promotion firm did not

charges against defendant who misrepresented franchise failure rate); State *ex rel.* Miller v. Pace, 677 N.W.2d 761 (Iowa 2004) (misrepresentation and nondisclosure of investment's risk).

3573 FTC v. Richard J. Scott, 5 Trade Reg. Rep. (CCH) ¶ 15316 (D. Conn. Oct. 23, 2002) (proposed consent decree against sellers who marketed spam lists as business opportunity); FTC v. Davis, 5 Trade Reg. Rep. (CCH) ¶ 22,741 (D. Nev. Oct. 17, 1989) (consent order); Consolidated Chemical Corp., 84 F.T.C. 379 (1974) (consent order); Redi-Brew Corp., 83 F.T.C. 1347 (1974) (consent order); Universal Credit Acceptance Corp., 82 F.T.C. 570 (1973), *rev'd in part sub nom.* Heater v. FTC, 503 F.2d 321 (9th Cir. 1974); Universal Electronics Corp., 78 F.T.C. 265 (1971); Windsor Distrib. Co., 77 F.T.C. 204 (1970), *aff'd*, 431 F.2d 443 (3d Cir. 1971); Waltham Watch Co., 60 F.T.C. 1692 (1962), *aff'd*, 318 F.2d 28 (7th Cir. 1903), *cert. denied*, 375 U.S. 944 (1963), *rehearing denied*, 375 U.S. 998 (1964); Washington Mushroom Indus., Inc., 53 F.T.C. 368 (1956); Von Schroder Mfg. Co., 33 F.T.C. 58 (1941); Rules for the Utah Consumer Sales Practices Act, Utah Admin. Code 152-11-11(B), Franchises, Distributorships, Referral Sales and Pyramid Sales Marketing Schemes; Salkeld v. V.R. Bus. Brokers, 192 Ill. App. 3d 663, 548 N.E.2d 1151 (1989); State *ex rel.* Ashcroft v. Marketing Unlimited, 613 S.W.2d 440 (Mo. Ct. App. 1981); Potere, Inc. v. National Realty Serv., 667 S.W.2d 252 (Tex. App. 1984); Anhold v. Daniels, 94 Wash. 2d 40, 614 P.2d 184 (1980).

3574 Universal Credit Acceptance Corp., 82 F.T.C. 570 (1973), *rev'd in part sub nom.* Heater v. FTC, 503 F.2d 321 (9th Cir. 1974).

3575 FTC v. National Bus. Consultants, 5 Trade Reg. Rep. (CCH) ¶ 22,816 (E.D. La. 1990) (permanent injunction); FTC v. McKleans, Inc., 5 Trade Reg. Rep. (CCH) ¶ 22,762 (D. Conn. Nov. 15, 1989) (consent decree); United States v. C.D. Control Technology, Inc., 3 Trade Reg. Rep. (CCH) ¶ 22,267 (E.D.N.Y. 1985) (preliminary injunction); Leisure Time Electronics, 3 Trade Reg. Rep. (CCH) ¶ 22,369 (F.T.C. No. 812 3099, 1986) (consent order); Firestone Photographers, Inc., 91 F.T.C. 729 (1978) (consent order); Cope Enterprises, Ltd., 87 F.T.C. 129 (1976) (consent order); Career Academy, Inc., 84 F.T.C. 453 (1974) (consent order); Postage Stamp Serv. Bureau, Inc., 83 F.T.C. 319 (1973) (consent order); Universal Credit Acceptance Corp., 82 F.T.C. 570 (1973), *rev'd in part sub nom.* Heater v. FTC, 503 F.2d 321 (9th Cir. 1974); Universal Electronics Corp., 78 F.T.C. 265 (1971); Windsor Distrib. Co., 77 F.T.C. 204 (1970), *aff'd*, 431 F.2d 443 (3d Cir. 1971); Rules for the Utah Consumer Sales Practices Act, Utah Admin. Code § 152-11-11(B)(5); Distributorships Referral Sales and Pyramid Sales Marketing Schemes; Salkeld v. V.R. Bus. Brokers, 192 Ill. App. 3d 663, 548 N.E.2d 1151 (1989); Staley v. Terns Serv. Co., 595 S.W.2d 882 (Tex. Civ. App. 1980).

3576 Windsor Distrib. Co., 77 F.T.C. 204 (1970), *aff'd*, 431 F.2d 443 (3d Cir. 1971).

3577 N. Am. Marketing Sys., Inc., 5 Trade Reg. Rep. (CCH) ¶ 15111 (May 18, 2001) (proposed consent decree).

3578 FTC v. Universal Greeting Card Corp., 5 Trade Reg. Rep. (CCH) ¶ 15350 (M.D. Fla. Jan. 5, 2003) (proposed consent decree); FTC v. Affiliated Vendors Ass'n, Inc., 5 Trade Reg. Rep. (CCH) ¶ 15282 (N.D. Tex. July 25, 2002) (proposed consent decree against sham BBB-type organization); FTC v. International Computer Concepts, Inc., 5 Trade Reg. Rep. (CCH) ¶ 23,927 (N.D. Ohio 1995) (permanent injunction).

3579 Holiday Magic, 84 F.T.C. 748 (1974); Rules for the Utah Consumer Sales Practices Act, Utah Admin. Code 152-11-11(B)(3), Franchises, Distributorships Referral Sales and Pyramid Sales Marketing Schemes.

3580 FTC v. Stephen I. Tashman, 5 Trade Reg. Rep. (CCH) ¶ 24,511 (S.D. Fla. 1998) (TRO); FTC v. National Bus. Consultants, 5 Trade Reg. Rep. (CCH) ¶ 22,816 (E.D. La. 1990) (permanent injunction); United States v. C.D. Control Technology, Inc., 3 Trade Reg. Rep. (CCH) ¶ 22,267 (E.D.N.Y. 1985) (preliminary injunction); Rules for the Utah Consumer Sales Practices Act, Utah Admin. Code 152-11-11(B)(10), Franchises, Distributorships Referral Sales and Pyramid Sales Marketing Schemes. *See also* Universal Credit Acceptance Corp., 82 F.T.C. 570 (1973), *rev'd in part sub. nom.* Heater v. FTC, 503 F.2d 321 (9th Cir. 1974); Universal Electronics Corp., 78 F.T.C. 265 (1971).

3581 International Marketing Corp., 82 F.T.C. 1074 (1973) (consent order); Woo v. Great Southwestern Acceptance Co., 565 S.W.2d 290 (Tex. Civ. App. 1978).

3582 Meredith Corp., 101 F.T.C. 390 (1983) (consent order).

3583 State *ex rel.* Ashcroft v. Marketing Unlimited, 613 S.W.2d 440 (Mo. Ct. App. 1981).

3584 Aurigemma v. Arco Petroleum Products Co., 734 F. Supp. 1025 (D. Conn. 1990) (failure to disclose potential loss of franchise due to lease termination violates UDAP); Bailey Employment Sys., Inc. v. Hahn, 545 F. Supp. 62 (D. Conn. 1982).

3585 Bailey Employment Sys., Inc. v. Hahn, 545 F. Supp. 62 (D. Conn. 1982).

3586 Phillips, 114 F.T.C. 587, 1991 FTC LEXIS 465, 5 Trade Reg. Rep. (CCH) ¶ 23,029 (1991) (consent order).

produce promised results, did not evaluate the feasibility of ideas it agreed to promote, did not promote the ideas, misrepresented the nature of patent protections, and misrepresented the success of its clients and the financial gain applicants could realize.[3587] A franchise or investment operation that involves recruiting additional investors may run afoul of the state's pyramid sales law.[3588] Another FTC settlement involves a company that induced consumers to purchase travel tutorials that the company claimed allowed them to receive the professional courtesy discounts and upgrades traditionally available to travel agents. The company also misrepresented the earnings potential of a home-based travel business.[3589]

5.13.1.3 Investments

The FTC has also proceeded against promoters of many types of investments. It has successfully challenged misrepresentations concerning profits available through investments in oil and gas,[3590] precious metal and coins,[3591] telecommunications services,[3592] gems,[3593] films,[3594] buying and selling real estate,[3595] "error" postage stamps,[3596] mining ventures,[3597] day trading,[3598] art and other collectibles,[3599] and

3587 International Investors Inc., E., 94 F.T.C. 111 (1979) (consent order). *See also* FTC v. International Product Design Inc., 5 Trade Reg. Rep. (CCH) ¶ 24,528 (E.D. Va. 1998) (consent decree); FTC v. Eureka Solutions Int'l, Inc., 5 Trade Reg. Rep. (CCH) ¶ 24,423 (W.D. Pa. 1998) (proposed consent order); FTC v. National Idea Network, 5 Trade Reg. Rep. (CCH) ¶ 24,348 (W.D. Pa. 1998) (stipulated order for permanent injunction); FTC v. American Idea Mgmt., 5 Trade Reg. Rep. (CCH) ¶ 23,056 (D. Mass. 1991) (consent order).

3588 *See* Giarratano v. Midas Muffler, 630 N.Y.S.2d 656, 27 U.C.C. Rep. 2d 87 (City Ct. 1995); § 5.13.3, *infra*.

3589 FTC v. World Class Network, Inc., 5 Trade Reg. Rep. (CCH) ¶ 24,261 (C.D. Cal. 1997) (proposed consent decree).

3590 FTC v. Atlantex Assocs., 1987-2 Trade Cases ¶ 67,788 (S.D. Fla. 1987); FTC v. Alaska Land Leasing, Inc., 3 Trade Reg. Rep. (CCH) ¶ 22,459 (C.D. Cal. 1987) (consent order); FTC v. Leland Indus., Inc., 3 Trade Reg. Rep. (CCH) ¶ 22,297 (C.D. Cal. 1985); FTC v. U.S. Oil & Gas Group, 3 Trade Reg. Rep. (CCH) ¶ 22,182 (S.D. Fla. July 20, 1984). *See also* Albert Schneider, 107 F.T.C. 430 (1986).

3591 FTC v. Western Trading Group, Ltd., 5 Trade Reg. Rep. (CCH) ¶ 23,401 (C.D. Cal. 1993) (consent order); FTC v. Golden Oak Numismatics Inc., 5 Trade Reg. Rep. (CCH) ¶ 23,312 (C.D. Cal. 1993) (consent decree); FTC v. U.S. Rarities, Inc., 5 Trade Reg. Rep. (CCH) ¶ 23,199 (S.D. Fla. 1992) (consent judgment); FTC v. Hannes Tulving Rare Coin Investments, Inc., 5 Trade Reg. Rep. (CCH) ¶ 23,215 (C.D. Cal. 1992) (consent order); FTC v. Woodman Corp., 5 Trade Reg. Rep. (CCH) ¶ 23,009 (C.D. Cal. 1991) (consent order); FTC v. Morgan Whitney Trading Group, Inc., 5 Trade Reg. Rep. (CCH) ¶ 23,050 (C.D. Cal. 1991) (consent order); FTC v. Oak Tree Numismatics, Inc., 5 Trade Reg. Rep. (CCH) ¶ 23,058 (D.N.J. 1991) (consent order); FTC v. Uni-Vest Fin. Servs., 5 Trade Reg. Rep. (CCH) ¶ 23,076 (S.D. Fla. 1991) (consent order); FTC v. Security Rare Coins, Inc., 5 Trade Reg. Rep. (CCH) ¶ 22,801 (E.D.N.Y. 1990) (consent order); FTC v. Adler, 5 Trade Reg. Rep. (CCH) ¶ 22,770 (D.R.I. Nov. 22, 1989) (permanent injunction); FTC v. Pannor Mining Co., 5 Trade Reg. Rep. (CCH) ¶ 22,764 (C.D. Cal. Nov. 17, 1989) (settlement); FTC v. Numismatic Funding Corp., 5 Trade Reg. Rep. (CCH) ¶ 22,749 (E.D.N.Y. Oct. 25, 1989) (settlement); FTC v. Lynn Murphy & Co., 5 Trade Reg. Rep. (CCH) ¶ 22,714 (D. Ariz. Aug. 4, 1989) (injunction); FTC v. Rare Coins of Georgia, 5 Trade Reg. Rep. (CCH) ¶ 22,628 (N.D. Ga. Dec. 1, 1988) (consent decree); Schoolhouse Coins, Inc., 5 Trade Reg. Rep. (CCH) ¶ 22,602 (E.D. Cal. Sept. 28, 1988) (settlement of claims); Federal Coin Repository, Inc., 5 Trade Reg. Rep. (CCH) ¶ 23,436 (F.T.C. File No. 92 0021 1994) (consent order); Certified Rare Coin Galleries, 5 Trade Reg. Rep. (CCH) ¶ 22,875 (F.T.C. File No. X89 0035 1990) (consent order).

3592 FTC v. Satellite Broadcasting Corp., 5 Trade Reg. Rep. (CCH) ¶ 23,967 (C.D. Cal. 1996) (consent decree) (Direct Broadcast Satellite TV programming); FTC v. Chase McNulty Group, Inc., 5 Trade Reg. Rep. (CCH) ¶ 23,973 (M.D. Fla. 1996) (consent order) (wireless communications technology); Genesis One Corp., 5 Trade Reg. Rep. (CCH) ¶ 23,991 (C.D. Cal. 1996) (filing of complaints) (sale of 900 number business ventures).

3593 FTC v. Sweet Song, Inc., 5 Trade Reg. Rep. (CCH) ¶ 24,697 (C.D. Cal. Jan. 21, 2000) (consent decree); FTC v. International Assets Trading Co., 5 Trade Reg. Rep. (CCH) ¶ 23,252 (S.D. Cal. 1992) (preliminary injunction); FTC v. Newport Gems, Inc., 5 Trade Reg. Rep. (CCH) ¶ 23,023 (C.D. Cal. 1991) (consent order); FTC v. Newport Gems, Inc., 5 Trade Reg. Rep. (CCH) ¶ 22,914 (C.D. Cal. 1990) (consent judgments); Kimberly Int'l Gem Corp., 3 Trade Reg. Rep. (CCH) ¶ 22,282 (C.D. Cal. 1985) (settlement); International Diamond Corp., 3 Trade Reg. Rep. (CCH) ¶ 22,154 (F.T.C. File No. 822 3006 May 24, 1984) (consent order). *See also* FTC v. Thomas E. O'Day, 5 Trade Reg. Rep. (CCH) ¶ 23,698 (M.D. Fla. 1994) (complaint against defendants who contacted victims of gemstone investment fraud and promised to help them recoup their losses for a fee).

3594 FTC v. Dayton Family Productions, Inc., 5 Trade Reg. Rep. (CCH) ¶ 24,513 (D. Nev. 1998) (proposed consent decree); FTC v. Rosario Filosi, 5 Trade Reg. Rep. (CCH) ¶ 24,388 (D. Nev. 1998).

3595 Del Dotto Enterprises, Inc., 5 Trade Reg. Rep. (CCH) ¶ 23,378 (F.T.C. Dkt. 9257 1993) (infomercials).

3596 FTC v. Equifin Int'l, Inc., 5 Trade Reg. Rep. (CCH) ¶ 24,361 (C.D. Cal. 1998) (proposed consent decree); FTC v. World Wide Classics, Inc., 5 Trade Reg. Rep. (CCH) ¶ 23,377 (C.D. Cal. 1993) (consent decree) (stamps).

3597 FTC v. Tippecanoe Mining, Inc., 5 Trade Reg. Rep. (CCH) ¶ 24,378 (C.D. Cal. 1998) (proposed consent decree).

3598 FTC v. Ken Roberts Co., 276 F.3d 583 (D.C. Cir. 2001) (upholding FTC's jurisdiction to issue civil investigative demands to seller of courses in commodities trading); WFS Enterprises, Inc., 5 Trade Reg. Rep. (CCH) ¶ 24,852 (F.T.C. Dkt. C-3993 2001) (consent order); R.S. of Houstaon Workshop, 5 Trade Reg. Rep. (CCH) ¶ 24,853 (F.T.C. Dkt. C-3994 2001) (consent order); Indigo Investor Sys., Inc., 5 Trade Reg. Rep. (CCH) ¶ 24,854 (F.T.C. Dkt. C-4002 2001) (consent order); Michael G. Chrisman, 5 Trade Reg. Rep. (CCH) ¶ 24,739 (F.T.C. Dkt. C-3951 2000).

3599 FTC v. Ivory Jack's Trading Co., 5 Trade Reg. Rep. (CCH) ¶ 24,014 (W.D. Wash. 1996) (proposed consent decree); FTC v. Hang-Ups Art Enterprises, Inc., 5 Trade Reg. Rep. (CCH) ¶ 23,963 (C.D. Cal. 1996) (proposed consent decree); FTC v. All-Pro Sports, 5 Trade Reg. Rep. (CCH) ¶ 23,771 (D. Ariz. 1995) (proposed consent decree) (sports trading cards); FTC v. Wine Exchange, Inc., 5 Trade Reg. Rep. (CCH) ¶ 23,793 (C.D.

other investment strategies.[3600] Other FTC actions involve sellers who induced consumers to purchase application preparation services for the FCC's cellular license lottery.[3601] It is of course deceptive for an investment company to say it will invest in metals for the consumer and then never purchase the metals.[3602] Another FTC consent order dealt with a book's claims concerning how to easily obtain various government loans and grants.[3603] Selling shares in foreign lotteries that are illegal in the United States is an unfair and deceptive practice.[3604]

5.13.2 Employment Opportunities

As with business opportunities, consumers may wish to challenge deceptive employment opportunity claims, and UDAP statutes normally provide a cause of action.[3605] Companies must disclose if commissioned rather than salaried jobs are being offered.[3606] Companies may not bait consumers with salaried positions and switch them to commissioned positions.[3607]

Companies may not advertise atypical earnings,[3608] misrepresent sales territories as being exclusive,[3609] or misrepresent that the company will pay such business expenses as travel or advertising.[3610] Wisconsin UDAP regulations require that sales of goods in conjunction with employment offers must be evidenced by written contracts setting forth all provisions, costs, work to be performed by the employee, and the rate of pay.[3611] Companies may not misrepresent to potential employees the size and nature of the business,[3612] or the terms, conditions, or travel requirements of the job.[3613] Nor may employers force or induce employees to terminate employment in order to have the employees forfeit

---

Cal. 1995) (proposed consent decree) (wines); FTC v. Renaissance Fine Arts, Ltd., 5 Trade Reg. Rep. (CCH) ¶ 23,879 (N.D. Ohio 1995) (permanent injunction); FTC v. National Art Publishers & Distributors, Inc., 5 Trade Reg. Rep. (CCH) ¶ 23,655 (S.D. Cal. 1994) (proposed consent decree) (movie posters); FTC v. Michael L. Zabrin Fine Arts, Ltd., 5 Trade Reg. Rep. (CCH) ¶ 23,324 (N.D. Ill. 1993) (consent decree); FTC v. Cambridge Exchange Ltd., 5 Trade Reg. Rep. (CCH) ¶ 23,383 (S.D. Fla. 1993); FTC v. Solomon Trading Co., 5 Trade Reg. Rep. (CCH) ¶ 23,243 (D. Ariz. 1992) (consent decree); FTC v. Austin Galleries, 5 Trade Reg. Rep. (CCH) ¶ 22,819 (N.D. Ill. 1990) (consent decree).

3600 FTC v. Wade Cook Fin. Corp., 5 Trade Reg. Rep. (CCH) ¶ 15334 (W.D. Wash. Dec. 4, 2002) (proposed consent decree against investment seminar promoter); Ted Warren Corp., Dkt. C-4078, www.ftc.gov/opa/2003/05/fyi30331.htm (May 2, 2003) (consent order).

3601 FTC v. American Nat'l Cellular, Inc., 5 Trade Reg. Rep. (CCH) ¶ 23,098 (C.D. Cal. 1991) (consent order); Albert Schneider, 107 F.T.C. 430 (1986). *See also* United States v. Investment Update, Inc., 5 Trade Reg. Rep. (CCH) ¶ 23,396 (S.D. Fla. 1993) (consent decree) (wireless-cable television stations); FTC v. Foreman, 5 Trade Reg. Rep. (CCH) ¶ 23,256 (S.D. Cal. 1992) (consent order) (same); FTC v. Applied Telemedia Engineering & Mgmt., Inc., 5 Trade Reg. Rep. (CCH) ¶ 23,308 (S.D. Fla. 1992) (final judgment) (same).

3602 State *ex rel.* Corbin v. Goodrich, 151 Ariz. 118, 726 P.2d 215 (Ct. App. 1986).

3603 Wyatt Marketing Corp., 5 Trade Reg. Rep. (CCH) ¶ 23,605 (F.T.C. C-3510 1994) (consent order). *See also* FTC v. Hartbrodt, 5 Trade Reg. Rep. (CCH) ¶ 23,878 (C.D. Cal. 1995) (consent order) (telemarketing of information packages about how to get government real property, vehicles and personal property at auction).

3604 FTC v. World Media Brokers, Inc., 2004 WL 432475 (N.D. Ill. Mar. 2, 2004); FTC v. Canada Prepaid Legal Servs., Inc., 5 Trade Reg. Rep. (CCH) ¶ 15336 (W.D. Wash. Dec. 5, 2002) (proposed consent decree); FTC v. B.B.M. Investments, Inc., 5 Trade Reg. Rep. (CCH) ¶ 15154 (W.D. Wash. Sept. 18, 2001) (proposed consent decree).

3605 *See* § 2.2.9 *supra* for a discussion of UDAP scope issues concerning business and employment opportunities.

3606 Public Circulation Serv., Inc., 80 F.T.C. 187 (1972). *See also* FTC v. Century Direct Marketing, 5 Trade Reg. Rep. (CCH) ¶ 24,753 (W.D. Cal. May 2, 2000) (consent decree against company that advertised delivery job but work actually involved selling long-distance service).

3607 Grolier, Inc., 91 F.T.C. 315 (1978), *vacated on other grounds*, 615 F.2d 1215 (9th Cir. 1980); Encyclopedia Brittanica, 87 F.T.C. 421 (1976); Cromwell-Collier Publishing Co., 70 F.T.C. 977 (1966).

3608 FTC v. Medicor, 217 F. Supp. 2d 1048 (C.D. Cal. 2002) (work-at-home scheme); Homespun Products, Inc. 5 Trade Reg. Rep. (CCH) ¶ 23,518 (F.T.C. C-3482 1994) (consent order) (weekly earnings for assembling crafts); Grolier, Inc., 91 F.T.C. 315 (1978); *vacated on other grounds*, 615 F.2d 1215 (9th Cir. 1980); American Consumer Serv., 89 F.T.C. 492 (1977) (consent order); Encyclopedia Brittanica, 87 F.T.C. 421 (1976); Bill J. Robertson, 87 F.T.C. 255 (1976) (consent order); Library Marketing Serv., Inc., 85 F.T.C. 957 (1975) (consent order); Dixie Reader's Serv., Inc., 80 F.T.C. 215 (1972); Massachusetts Consumer Protection Regulations, Mass. Regs. Code tit. 940, § 3.11, Private Employment Agencies and Business Schemes; Wisconsin Dep't of Agriculture, Trade and Consumer Protection Rules Wis. Admin. Code §§ ATCP 116.04, 116.05, Work Recruitment Schemes; Commonwealth v. Tolleson, 14 Pa. Commw. Ct. 72, 321 A.2d 664 (1974).

3609 Grand Indus., 87 F.T.C. 47 (1976) (consent order); Grayco Chemical Corp., 84 F.T.C. 420 (1974) (consent order); Cromwell Oil Co., 81 F.T.C. 819 (1972) (consent order); Process Components, Inc. v. Baltimore Aircoil Co., 366 S.E.2d 907 (N.C. Ct. App. 1988); Wisconsin Dep't of Agriculture, Trade and Consumer Protection Rules, Wis. Admin. Code § ATCP 116.03(f), Work Recruitment Schemes.

3610 Commonwealth v. Tolleson, 14 Pa. Comm. Ct. 72, 321 A.2d 664 (1974); Publishers Continental Sales Corp., 80 F.T.C. 165 (1972) (consent order); Cromwell Oil Co., 81 F.T.C. 819 (1972) (consent order); Wisconsin Dep't of Agriculture, Trade and Consumer Protection Rules, Wis. Admin. Code §§ ATCP 116.03, 116.05, Work Recruitment Schemes.

3611 Wisconsin Dep't of Agriculture, Trade and Consumer Protection Rules, Wis. Admin. Code § ATCP 116.03, Work Recruitment Schemes.

3612 American Consumer Serv., Inc., 89 F.T.C. 492 (1977) (consent order); Interstate Publishers Serv., Inc., 82 F.T.C. 364 (1973) (consent order).

3613 Bill J. Robertson, 87 F.T.C. 255 (1976) (consent order); Circulation Builders, Inc., 87 F.T.C. 81 (1976) (consent order); Interstate Publishers Serv., Inc., 82 F.T.C. 364 (1973) (consent order); LRS Inc., 82 F.T.C. 1366 (1973) (consent order).

earned commissions,[3614] or continually promise to pay commissions with no right to do so.[3615] The FTC has proceeded against a number of sellers of fraudulent work-at-home schemes.[3616]

Employment agencies may not misrepresent their job placement service or misrepresent that advertised jobs are available, and must properly offer refunds.[3617] It is deceptive to claim that an employment agency has access to hidden jobs where the agency has no special knowledge, does not contact employers, and only provides applicants with a cover letter and list of employers, with little proven success.[3618] Employment counseling services may not misrepresent the basis upon which clients are accepted, the number of clients who have obtained jobs, or that the client's fee to the agency would be refunded by the new employer.[3619] Similarly deceptive is for a non-existent airline to promise high paying jobs if the prospective employee first pays a training fee.[3620] A related deceptive scam is for an "employment agency" for models or a screen test company really to be just be a front to get people to pay for expensive photographs or films for their portfolios.[3621] It is deceptive for a company to place advertisements in the Help Wanted sections of newspapers implying that it could place people in government jobs, when all it actually did was sell outdated test preparation booklets at inflated prices.[3622] Wisconsin UDAP regulations prohibit various practices related to requiring a consumer to make a purchase or investment as a precondition to finding employment.[3623]

A new type of employment opportunity scam has been created with the advent of "900" telephone numbers. It is

3614 Bell & Howell Co., 95 F.T.C. 761 (1980) (consent order).

3615 Business Brokers Int'l Corp., 24 Mass. App. Ct. 957, 510 N.E.2d 301 (1987).

3616 *See, e.g.*, FTC v. Stuffingforcash.com Corp., 5 Trade Reg. Rep. (CCH) ¶ 15432 (N.D. Ill. July 2, 2003) (proposed consent decree); FTC v. Electronic Medical billing, 5 Trade Reg. Rep. (CCH) ¶ 15399 (C.D. Cal. Apr. 22, 2003) (proposed consent decree against work-at-home medical billing scam); FTC v. Leading Edge Processing, Inc., 5 Trade Reg. Rep. (CCH) ¶ 15387 (M.D. Fla. Mar. 6, 2003) (proposed consent decree against work-at-home business opportunity sellers who sent e-mail messages claiming actual job opportunities to job seekers who had posted resumes on Internet); FTC v. Healthcare Claims Network, Inc., 5 Trade Reg. Rep. (CCH) ¶ 15380 (C.D. Cal. Mar. 14, 2003) (proposed consent decree against medical billing work-at-home scheme); FTC v. Domaco Int'l, Inc., 5 Trade Reg. Rep. (CCH) ¶ 15344 (C.D. Cal. Dec. 13, 2002) (consent decree against marketers of fraudulent work-at-home booklet-stapling opportunity); FTC v. Electronic Processing Servs., Inc., 5 Trade Reg. Rep. (CCH) ¶ 15312 (D. Nev. Sept. 27, 2002) (medical billing); FTC v. Int'l Trader, 5 Trade Reg. Rep. (CCH) ¶ 15302 (C.D. Cal. Sept. 13, 2002) (medical billing); FTC v. Medicor, L.L.C., 2002 WL 1925896 (C.D. Cal. July 18, 2002) (permanent injunction against at-home medical billing opportunity); FTC v. Para-Link Int'l, Inc., 2001 WL 1701537 (M.D. Fla. Feb. 28, 2001) (preliminary injunction against paralegal work-at-home scam); FTC v. SkyBiz.com, Inc., 2001 WL 1673645 (N.D. Okla. Aug. 31, 2001) (preliminary injunction at pyramid work-at-home scheme), *aff'd*, 2003 WL 202438 (10th Cir. Jan. 30, 2002) (unpublished, citation limited).

3617 FTC v. Am. Career Serv., Inc., 5 Trade Reg. Rep. (CCH) ¶ 15293 (S.D. Ala. Aug. 15, 2002) (proposed consent decree against operators of postal job scam); FTC v. Career Network, Inc., 5 Trade Reg. Rep. (CCH) ¶ 15171 (N.D. Ind. Oct. 17, 2001) (proposed consent decree against operators of postal job scam); FTC v. Screen Test USA, 5 Trade Reg. Rep. (CCH) ¶ 24,699 (D.N.J. 2000) (consent order) (training for acting and modeling careers); New England Tractor Trailer Training School, 5 Trade Reg. Rep. (CCH) ¶ 24,641 (F.T.C. Dkt. C-3916 2000) (consent order) (driver training); FTC v. Model 1, Inc., 5 Trade Reg. Rep. (CCH) ¶ 24,641 (E.D. Va. 1999) (consent order) (training for acting and modeling careers); FTC v. Afriat, 5 Trade Reg. Rep. (CCH) ¶ 24,524 (C.D. Cal. 1998) (consent order) (postal service career services); FTC v. Metro Data, Inc., 5 Trade Reg. Rep. (CCH) ¶ 24,355 (M.D. Fla. 1998) (consent decree); FTC v. Linc II, Inc., 5 Trade Reg. Rep. (CCH) ¶ 24,230 (M.D. Fla. 1997) (proposed consent decree); FTC v. Stratified Advertising & Marketing, Inc., 5 Trade Reg. Rep. (CCH) ¶ 24,249 (C.D. Cal. 1997) (proposed consent decree); FTC v. Stratified Advertising & Marketing, Inc., 5 Trade Reg. Rep. (CCH) ¶ 24,130 (C.D. Cal. 1996) (proposed consent decree); FTC v. Mink, 5 Trade Reg. Rep. (CCH) ¶ 23,903 (S.D. Mich. 1995) (judgment for $593,206 and permanent injunction against employment service work); State *ex rel.* Graddick v. Jim Lewis, CV No. 81-1681A (Ala. Cir. Ct. Montgomery Cty. 1982); *see also* Federal Trade Commission v. Para-Link Int'l, Inc., 2001 WL 1701537 (M.D. Fla. Feb. 28, 2001) (issuing preliminary injunction against deceptive work-at-home scheme).

3618 FTC v. Career Information Servs., Inc., 5 Trade Reg. Rep. (CCH) ¶ 24,234 (N.D. Ga. 1997) (proposed consent decree); State v. Management Transition Resources, Inc., 454 N.Y.S.2d 513 (Sp. Term 1982); *see also* FTC v. Overseas Unlimited Agency, Inc., 3 Trade Reg. Rep. (CCH) ¶ 22,552 (C.D. Cal. 1988) (consent order); John William Costello Assocs., 107 F.T.C. 32 (1986) (consent order).

3619 FTC v. Mink, 5 Trade Reg. Rep. (CCH) ¶ 23,903 (S.D. Mich. 1995) (judgment for $593,206 and permanent injunction against employment service work); Roy B. Kelly, 107 F.T.C. 26 (1986); John William Costello Assocs., 107 F.T.C. 32 (1986).

3620 State v. Hawaiian Pacific Airlines, Inc., Clearinghouse No. 40,639 (Minn. Dist. Ct. Sept. 5, 1985) (temporary injunction).

3621 FTC v. Screen Test U.S.A., 5 Trade Reg. Rep. (CCH) ¶ 24,699 (D.N.J. Jan. 21, 2000) (consent decree); FTC v. Model 1, Inc., 5 Trade Reg. Rep. (CCH) ¶ 24,641 (E.D. Va. Aug. 31, 1999) (consent decree); FTC v. Dupont Model Mgmt., Inc., 5 Trade Reg. Rep. (CCH) ¶ 23,139 (E.D. Pa. 1992) (consent order); State v. Keaton Model Mgmt., Inc., 1996 WL 146484, Clearinghouse No. 51,272 (Minn. App. Apr. 2, 1996) (unpublished, citation limited).

3622 FTC v. Think Achievement, 144 F. Supp. 2d 993 (N.D. Ind. 2000), *later op. at* 144 F. Supp. 2d 1029 (N.D. Ind. 2000) (issuing permanent injunction and awarding consumer restitution of $28,149,600), *aff'd in part, rev'd in part on other grounds*, 312 F.3d 259 (7th Cir. 2002). *See also* FTC v. Healthcare Claims Network, Inc., 5 Trade Reg. Rep. (CCH) ¶ 15380 (C.D. Cal. Mar. 14, 2003) (proposed consent decree against medical billing work-at-home scheme); FTC v. Vocational Guides, Inc., 5 Trade Reg. Rep. (CCH) ¶ 15138 (M.D. Tenn. July 27, 2001) (proposed consent decree against company that falsely advertised locally available postal jobs and misrepresented affiliation with postal service).

3623 Wisconsin Dep't of Agriculture, Trade, and Consumer Protection Rules, Wis. Admin. Code §§ ATCP 116.02, 116.03, 116.05.

deceptive to advertise job listings available by calling a 900 number but not to disclose the charge for use of the number or that most of the job opportunities were not offered in a timely fashion.[3624] An employment opportunity that involves payment of money by the consumer and recruitment of others to join the program may be actionable as a pyramid sales scheme.[3625]

5.13.3 Pyramid Sales

Pyramid sales involve schemes where, in the guise of selling a product, what is really being sold is the right to sell new memberships in the pyramid, so that investors make their return not through the sale of the product, but through encouraging others to invest. Pyramid schemes take many guises and are often marketed over the Internet.[3626] Sometimes they are marketed as if they were employment opportunities.[3627] The mathematical reality is that only early participants recoup their investment.

Some states have enacted specific legislation proscribing pyramid schemes, often found in the state code near the UDAP statute. In addition, other states have adopted UDAP regulations specifically prohibiting pyramid sales.[3628] Such statutes and regulations are constitutional even when they ban pyramid sales *per se*.[3629] Violations of these state statutes and regulations are generally found to be *per se* UDAP violations.[3630]

Even without a specific statutory prohibition, it is deceptive to fail to disclose that, because of the pyramid structure, most consumers will not receive the rewards touted by operators.[3631] The FTC has also successfully challenged a number of pyramid schemes as unfair and deceptive.[3632]

3624 FTC v. Career Information Servs., Inc., 5 Trade Reg. Rep. (CCH) ¶ 24,234 (N.D. Ga. 1997) (proposed consent decree); FTC v. Starlink, 5 Trade Reg. Rep. (CCH) ¶ 22,946 (E.D. Pa. 1991) (temporary restraining order). *See also* FTC v. Starlink, Inc., 5 Trade Reg. Rep. (CCH) ¶ 23,145 (E.D. Pa. 1992) (settlement). *See* § 5.9.3, *supra* for further discussion of 900-number fraud.

3625 *See* FTC v. Leading Edge Processing, Inc., 5 Trade Reg. Rep. (CCH) ¶ 15387 (M.D. Fla. Mar. 6, 2003) (proposed consent decree against work-at-home business opportunity sellers who sent e-mail messages claiming actual job opportunities to job seekers who had posted resumes on Internet); FTC v. Martinelli, 5 Trade Reg. Rep. (CCH) ¶ 24,830 (D. Conn. Nov. 14, 2000) (consent decree against company that advertised jobs in want ads but actually recruited people into pyramid scheme); Giarratano v. Midas Muffler, 630 N.Y.S.2d 656, 27 U.C.C. Rep. 2d 87 (City Ct. 1995); § 5.13.3, *infra*.

3626 FTC v. Mentor Network, Inc., 5 Trade Reg. Rep. (CCH) ¶ 24,233 (C.D. Cal. 1997) (proposed consent decree); FTC v. Fortuna Alliance, L.L.C., 5 Trade Reg. Rep. (CCH) ¶ 24,039 (W.D. Wash. 1996) (TRO); Kalvin Schmidt, 5 Trade Reg. Rep. (CCH) ¶ 24,462 (F.T.C. Dkt. No. C-3834, 1998) (consent decree).

3627 *See, e.g.*, FTC v. Leading Edge Processing, Inc., 5 Trade Reg. Rep. (CCH) ¶ 15387 (M.D. Fla. Mar. 6, 2003) (proposed consent decree against work-at-home business opportunity sellers who sent e-mail messages claiming actual job opportunities to job seekers who had posted resumes on Internet).

3628 *See, e.g.*, Idaho Consumer Protection Regulations, Idaho Admin. Code §§ 04.02,01,020(1), 04.02.01.190, Pyramid Sales and Chain Distribution Schemes; Louisiana Consumer Protection Division Rules and Regulations, La. Admin. Code tit. 16, pt. III, § 503, Multi-Level Distribution and Chain Distributor Marketing Schemes (chain distributor schemes are *per se* unfair and deceptive; other schemes are subject to regulations); Rules for the Utah Consumer Sales Practices Act, Utah Admin. R. 152-11-11, Franchises, Distributorships, Referral Sales and Pyramid Sales Marketing Schemes; Code Vt. Rules 06 031 002 Rule CF 101, Chain Distributor Schemes; Wisconsin Dep't of Agriculture, Trade and Consumer Protection Rules, Wis. Admin. Code § ATCP 122.02, Chain Distributor Schemes.

3629 People *ex rel.* Hartigan v. Dynasty Sys., 471 N.E.2d 236 (Ill. App. Ct. 1984); State *ex rel.* Turner v. Koscot Interplanetary, Inc., 191 N.W.2d 624 (Iowa 1971); State *ex rel.* Humphrey v. Computerized Markets Co., Clearinghouse No. 36,592 (Minn. Dist. Ct., 10th Jud. Dist., 1983); State *ex rel.* Stratton v. Sinks, 106 N.M. 213, 741 P.2d 435 (Ct. App. 1987); State v. Lambert, 68 Wis. 2d 523, 229 N.W.2d 622 (1978); HM Distributors of Milwaukee, Inc. v. Dep't of Agriculture, 55 Wis. 2d 261, 198 N.W.2d 598 (1972). *See also* State v. Irons, 254 Neb. 18, 574 N.W.2d 144 (1998) (rejecting vagueness challenge to state securities law as applied to criminal prosecution of pyramid scheme operator).

3630 Koscot Interplanetary, Inc., 86 F.T.C. 1106 (1975), *aff'd sub nom.* Turner v. FTC, 580 F.2d 701 (D.C. Cir. 1978); Holiday Magic, Inc., 84 F.T.C. 748 (1974); Bounds v. Figurettes, Inc., 135 Cal. App. 3d 1 (1982); People v. Bestline Products, Inc., 61 Cal. App. 3d 879, 132 Cal. Rptr. 767 (1976); People *ex rel.* Fahner v. Walsh, 122 Ill. App. 3d 481, 461 N.E.2d 78 (App. Ct. 1984) ("Circle of Platinum" chain letter is UDAP violation even if no misrepresentations; market becomes saturated, forcing the chain to end; scheme also has aspects of lottery); State v. Koscot Interplanetary Inc., 212 Kan. 668, 512 P.2d 416 (1973); Kugler v. Koscot Interplanetary, Inc., 120 N.J. Super. 216, 293 A.2d 682 (Ch. Div. 1972); State *ex rel.* Celebrezze v. Howard, 77 Ohio App. 3d 387, 602 N.E.2d 665 (1991); State *ex rel.* Medlock v. Nest Egg Society Today, Inc., 348 S.E.2d 381 (S.C. Ct. App. 1986); Wesware, Inc. v. State, 488 S.W.2d 844 (Tex. Civ. App. 1972). ***But see*** State *ex rel.* Ashcroft v. Wahl, 600 S.W.2d 175 (Mo. Ct. App. 1980) (pyramid scheme did not violate UDAP statute where no deception or misrepresentation was found).

3631 Neilson v. Union Bank, 2003 WL 22533553, at *30 (C.D. Cal. Oct. 20, 2003) (denying motion to dismiss investors' UDAP claims regarding Ponzi scheme); FTC v. Five-Star Auto Club, Inc., 97 F. Supp. 2d 502 (S.D.N.Y. 2000); State *ex rel.* Miller v. Pace, 677 N.W.2d 761 (Iowa 2004) (failure to disclose that investment is a Ponzi scheme is UDAP violation). *See also* State v. McLeod, 2003 WL 1711657 (Me. Super. Jan. 3, 2003) (misrepresentations regarding legality of scheme and availability of refunds).

3632 *See, e.g.*, FTC v. Affordable Media, 179 F.3d 1228 (9th Cir. 1999) (affirming contempt order for violation of preliminary injunction requiring defendants who telemarketed a Ponzi scheme to repatriate assets held outside U.S.); FTC v. Netforce Seminars, 5 Trade Reg. Rep. (CCH) ¶ 15278 (D. Ariz. July 22, 2002) (proposed consent decree) (Internet business opportunities were structured so that earnings depended on recruiting new members); FTC v. Streamline Int'l, Inc., 5 Trade Reg. Rep. (CCH) ¶ 15217 (S.D. Fla. Jan. 31, 2002); FTC v. SkyBiz.com,

Since most pyramid schemes will involve mail fraud, RICO claims are another possibility.[3633] Pyramid sales schemes may also violate state or federal securities laws.[3634]

Pyramid sellers' most common defense is that their particular sales arrangement does not fall within the scope of the state statute or UDAP regulation's definition of an illegal pyramid scheme. Nevertheless, courts generally find the statutory definition to apply.[3635] This is the case even when companies add distinguishing features to their plans that are typically not present in illegal pyramid schemes, attempting to make their pyramid sales look like legal multi-level distributorships.[3636]

Another possible defense to a UDAP challenge is that the pyramid scheme does not fall within the scope of a statute applying only to "consumer" transactions. (A pyramid scheme clearly falls within the scope of a statute applying to practices in trade or commerce.) Case law generally finding pyramid sales to involve consumer transactions is found at § 2.2.9.1, *supra*.

Inc., 2001 WL 1673645 (N.D. Okla. Aug. 31, 2001) (preliminary injunction) (discussing distinctions between pyramid scheme and legitimate multi-level marketing program), *aff'd*, 2003 WL 202438 (10th Cir. Jan. 30, 2002) (unpublished, citation limited); FTC v. Bigsmart.com L.L.C., 5 Trade Reg. Rep. (CCH) ¶ 15142 (D. Ariz. Aug. 8, 2001); FTC v. Five-Star Auto Club, Inc., 97 F. Supp. 2d 502 (S.D.N.Y. 2000); FTC v. Credit Development Int'l, 5 Trade Reg. Rep. (CCH) ¶ 24,564 (C.D. Cal. 1999) (consent order) (Internet pyramid scheme offering unsecured credit cards); FTC v. FutureNet, Inc., 5 Trade Reg. Rep. (CCH) ¶ 24,547 (C.D. Cal. 1998) (stipulated final judgment) (Internet pyramid scheme promoted as multi-level marketing program); Kalvin Schmidt, 5 Trade Reg. Rep. (CCH) ¶ 24,462 (F.T.C. Dkt. No. C-3834, 1998) (consent decree); FTC v. Mentor Network, Inc., 5 Trade Reg. Rep. (CCH) ¶ 24,233 (C.D. Cal. 1997) (proposed consent decree); FTC v. Global Assistance Network for Charities, 5 Trade Reg. Rep. (CCH) ¶ 24,265 (D. Ariz. 1997) (proposed consent decree).

3633 United States v. Gold Unlimited, Inc., 177 F.3d 472 (6th Cir. 1999) (affirming RICO criminal conviction against pyramid scheme operator). *But cf.* Ballard v. Royal Trust Bank, 1999 U.S. App. LEXIS 31595 (9th Cir. 1999) (bank that may have known about pyramid scheme but did not agree to further it had no RICO liability); Bald Eagle School Dist. v. Keystone Fin., Inc., 189 F.3d 321 (3d Cir. 1999) (securities fraud can not be predicate act for RICO claim against Ponzi scheme).

3634 *See, e.g.*, Rhodes v. Consumers' Buyline, Inc., 868 F. Supp. 368 (D. Mass. 1993) (ruling on motion to dismiss); State v. Irons, 254 Neb. 18, 574 N.W.2d 144 (1998) (affirming conviction of pyramid scheme operator under state securities law); State *ex rel.* Miller v. Pace, 677 N.W.2d 761 (Iowa 2004). *See also In re* Old Naples Securities, Inc., 223 F.3d 1296 (11th Cir. 2000) (individuals who lost money due to brokerage's Ponzi scheme were entitled to protection under Securities Investor Protection Act). *See* § 9.4.10, *infra* for a brief overview of securities law.

3635 Webster v. Omnitrition Int'l, Inc., 79 F.3d 776 (9th Cir. 1996) (business was illegal pyramid scheme because supervisors were compensated on basis of "downline" sales to other participants); State *ex rel.* Corbin v. Challenge, Inc., 151 Ariz. 20, 725 P.2d 727 (Ct. App. 1986); Bounds v. Figurettes, Inc., 135 Cal. App. 3d 1 (1982); People v. Bestline Products, Inc., 61 Cal. App. 3d 879, 132 Cal. Rptr. 767 (1976); People *ex rel.* Hartigan v. Unimax, Inc., 168 Ill. App. 3d 718, 523 N.E.2d 26 (1988) (overturning lower court decision holding that scheme did not fall within definition of illegal pyramid sale); People *ex rel.* Hartigan v. Dynasty Sys., 471 N.E.2d 236 (Ill. App. Ct. 1984) (illegal pyramid scheme found even where franchisees not required to pay money and where scheme tries to explain to court lack of retail sales); State *ex rel.* Stovall v. Cooper, 2001 WL 34117813 (Kan. Dist. Ct. May 15, 2001); Missouri *ex rel.* Nixon v. Consumer Automotive Resources, Inc., 882 S.W.2d 717 (Mo. Ct. App. 1994) (scheme in which members received one-time and monthly commissions for enrolling new members was illegal pyramid sales scheme as defined by Missouri law); State *ex rel.* Webster v. Membership Marketing, Inc., 766 S.W.2d 654 (Mo. Ct. App. 1989); State v. Irons, 254 Neb. 18, 574 N.W.2d 144 (1998) (detailed discussion of applicability of state securities law to pyramid scheme); Brown v. Hambric, 638 N.Y.S.2d 873 (N.Y. Yonkers City Ct. 1995) (travel agent training scheme); State *ex rel.* Edmisten v. Challenge, Inc., 54 N.C. App. 513, 284 S.E.2d 333 (1981); State *ex rel.* Fisher v. Harper, 83 Ohio App. 3d 754, 615 N.E.2d 733 (1993) (pyramid sales scheme involving travel discount coupons and membership in sales network violates Ohio's Anti-Pyramid Act and UDAP statute); Commonwealth v. Bell, 5 Va. Cir. 296 (Richmond Cir. 1985), *aff'd*, 236 Va. 298, 374 S.E.2d 13 (1988) ("Feelin' Great" pyramid scheme). *See also* People v. Knop, 619 N.E.2d 203 (Ill. App. Ct. 1993) (under criminal pyramid sales statute, scheme meets statutory definition if consumer pays for opportunity to participate, even if payment is not required). *Cf.* State v. Fortune in Motion, 214 Wis. 2d 148, 570 N.W.2d 875 (Ct. App. 1997) (question whether practice is covered as a pyramid sale remanded to trial court for further determination). *But see* State *ex rel.* Miller v. American Professional Marketing, Inc., 382 N.W.2d 117 (Iowa 1986) (practice does not fall within FTC definition of pyramid sale). For a discussion of the elements of a pyramid sale, see Stone & Steiner, The Federal Trade Commission and Pyramid Sales Schemes, 15 Pacific L.J. 879 (1984).

3636 United States v. Gold Unlimited, Inc., 177 F.3d 472 (6th Cir. 1999) (to differentiate between legal multilevel marketing programs and illegal pyramid schemes, courts evaluate whether the company stresses recruitment or sales as its marketing strategy, and the percentage of product sold compared with the percentage of commissions granted; cosmetic anti-saturation policies are insufficient to make scheme legal); FTC v. SkyBiz.com, Inc., 2001 WL 1673645 (N.D. Okla. Aug. 31, 2001) (pyramid scheme's primary purpose is to recruit new marketers, not to sell end product, and it ultimately collapses because of saturation; courts finds this scheme to be a pyramid scheme and issues preliminary injunction), *aff'd*, 2003 WL 202438 (10th Cir. Jan. 30, 2003) (unpublished, citation limited); Bounds v. Figurettes, Inc., 135 Cal. App. 3d 1 (1982) (the fact that some retail sales occurred did not mitigate the unlawful nature of the method of recruiting); Kugler v. Koscot Interplanetary, Inc., 120 N.J. Super. 216, 293 A.2d 682 (Ch. Div. 1972) (pyramid scheme was not saved by the imposition of a quota limiting the number of distributorships); Commonwealth by Zimmerman v. First Fin. Security, Inc., 564 A.2d 280 (Pa. Commw. Ct. 1989) (pyramid scheme was illegal despite defendant's efforts to separate the membership and distributorship aspects of the organization); Commonwealth v. Tolleson, 14 Pa. Commw. Ct. 72, 321 A.2d 664 (1974); State *ex rel.* McLeod v. VIP Enterprises, Inc., 335 S.E.2d 243 (S.C. Ct. App. 1985) (the fact that members received commissions from corporation instead of from other members did not place the plan beyond the reach of the UDAP statute).

Another pyramid sales issue is which members of the pyramid are liable under the UDAP statute for participating in the scheme. Even a one-time participation in a pyramid scheme may render a person liable where that person receives others' money.[3637]

The Nebraska Supreme Court has held that proof of specific intent, evil motive, or knowledge that the law was being violated is not necessary to sustain a pyramid scheme operator's conviction under state securities law.[3638] Willfulness, in the sense that the defendant was aware of what he or she was doing, is all that is necessary. UDAP statutes likewise usually do not require any showing of intent.[3639]

5.13.4 Contests and Game Promotions

It is deceptive, in connection with a game or contest promotion, to misrepresent the chances of winning[3640] or to use a sham contest to gain sales leads by failing to offer bona fide prizes and awards[3641] or by offering fictitious discounts as a prize to specially selected winners.[3642] Informing all entrants that they are "finalists," thereby falsely implying that they are members of a smaller group with a greater chance of winning, is deceptive.[3643] Prize promotion mailings are also deceptive if they implicitly misrepresent that it is necessary for an entrant to make a purchase to enter the contest, or that making a purchase will increase the chances of winning.[3644] It is deceptive to misrepresent the value of the prize to be offered,[3645] or the nature of offered prizes, for example, to offer a "frost-free refrigerator" with a fifty-dollar delivery charge, but deliver only a small plastic cooler with a cigarette lighter plug-in attachment.[3646] The promoter must disclose costs that the consumer must pay and conditions that must be satisfied to get or use the prize.[3647]

3637 Watkins v. Alvey, 549 N.E.2d 74 (Ind. Ct. App. 1990).

3638 State v. Irons, 254 Neb. 18, 574 N.W.2d 144 (1998).

3639 *See* § 4.2.4, *supra*.

3640 FTC v. Gem Merchandising Corp., 87 F.3d 466 (11th Cir. 1996); FTC v. International Charity Consultants, Inc., 5 Trade Reg. Rep. (CCH) ¶ 24,021 (D. Nev. 1996) (summary judgment); FTC v. Research Awards Center, Inc., 5 Trade Reg. Rep. (CCH) ¶ 23,990 (D. Md. 1996) (proposed consent decree) (promoters sold memberships in club that would enter consumers in independent sweepstakes, but entries violated sweepstakes rules or were received late); Oden Distrib. Co., 84 F.T.C. 1125 (1974) (consent order); Cal-Roof Wholesale, Inc., 81 F.T.C. 703 (1972) (consent order); Revere Chemical Corp., 80 F.T.C. 85 (1972) (consent order); Proctor & Gamble Co., 79 F.T.C. 589 (1971) (consent order); Brothers Int'l Corp. of California, 56 F.T.C. 434 (1959); Publishers Serv. Co., 44 F.T.C. 127 (1947); Connecticut Regulations for the Dep't of Consumer Protection, Conn. Agencies Regs. § 42-110b-23, Game Promotion (1977); Idaho Consumer Protection Regulations, Idaho Admin. Code §§ 04.02.01.081, .081, Promotional Games and Advertising and Deceptive Use of Gifts (1978); Code Miss. Rules 24 000 002, Rules 38, 39; N.M. Admin. Code §§ 12.2.2.9, 12.2.2.10; Code Vt. Rules 06 031 003 Rule CF 109, Contests and Prizes; State v. Imperial Marketing, 472 S.E.2d 792 (W. Va. 1996). *But cf.* Lamb v. United States Sales Corp., 194 Ga. App. 333, 390 S.E.2d 440 (1990) (offer was clearly initial solicitation and not offer to claim sweepstakes prize). *See also* Dep't of Legal Affairs v. Rogers, 329 So. 2d 257 (Fla. 1976) (upholding constitutionality of Florida's former regulations).

3641 Tri-State Distrib., Inc., 63 F.T.C. 788 (1963); Connecticut Regulations for the Department of Consumer Protection, Conn. Agencies Regs. § 42-110b-23, Game Promotion 1977); Idaho Consumer Protection Regulations, Idaho Admin. Code § 04.02.01.082, Promotional Games and Advertising and Deceptive Use of Gifts (1978); Code Vt. Rules 06 031 003 Rule CF 109.

3642 Tri-State Distrib., Inc., 63 F.T.C. 788 (1963); Connecticut Regulations for the Department of Consumer Protection, Conn. Agencies Regs. § 42-110b-23, Game Promotion 1977); Idaho Consumer Protection Regulations, Idaho Admin. Code §§ 04.02.01.081, 04.02.01.082, Promotional Games and Advertising and Deceptive Use of Gifts (1978); Code Vt. Rules 06 031 003 Rule CF 109.

3643 Miller v. American Family Publishers, 284 N.J. Super. 67, 663 A.2d 643 (Chancery Div. 1995); W. Va. Code § 46A-6D-5; State v. Imperial Marketing, 472 S.E.2d 792 (W. Va. 1996).

3644 FTC v. American Exchange Group, Inc., 5 Trade Reg. Rep. (CCH) ¶ 24,258 (D. Nev. 1997) (consent decree); FTC v. Oasis Southwest, Inc., 5 Trade Reg. Rep. (CCH) ¶ 24,281 (D. Nev. 1997) (consent decree); FTC v. Family Publishers Clearing Center, 5 Trade Reg. Rep. (CCH) ¶ 24,309 (C.D. Cal. 1997) (consent decree); FTC v. Lubell, 5 Trade Reg. Rep. (CCH) ¶ 24,274 (S.D. Iowa 1997) (proposed consent decree); Miller v. American Family Publishers, 284 N.J. Super. 67, 663 A.2d 643 (Chancery Div. 1995). *See also* Code Miss. Rules 024 000 002, Rules 37, 38.

3645 FTC v. Gem Merchandising Corp., 87 F.3d 466 (11th Cir. 1996); FTC v. United Holdings Inc., 5 Trade Reg. Rep. (CCH) ¶ 23,692 (D. Nev. Oct., 18 1994) (proposed consent decree); FTC v. World Wide Factors, Ltd., 5 Trade Reg. Rep. (CCH) ¶ 22,829 (D. Nev. 1990) (stipulated final judgment) (large "processing fee" and only received a catalog); FTC v. Creative Advertising Specialty House, 5 Trade Reg. Rep. (CCH) ¶ 22,740 (C.D. Cal. Oct. 10, 1989) ("shipping fee" for free "boat" exceeded value of boat); Sewing Distributors, Inc., 82 F.T.C. 380 (1973) (consent order); New Home Sewing Center, 76 F.T.C. 191 (1969); Household Sewing Machine Co., 76 F.T.C. 207 (1969); Atlas Sewing Centers, Inc., 57 F.T.C. 974 (1959); Monarch Sewing Centers, Inc., 57 F.T.C. 948 (1958); Connecticut Regulations for the Dep't of Consumer Protection, Conn. Agencies Regs. § 42-110b-23, Game Promotion (1977); Idaho Consumer Protection Regulations, Idaho Admin. Code § 04.02.01.081, .082, Promotional Games and Advertising and Deceptive Use of Gifts (1978); Code Miss. Rules 024 000 002, Rules 38, 39; N.M. Admin. Code §§ 12.2.2.9, 12.2.2.10; Rules for the Utah Consumer Sales Practices Act, Utah Admin. Rules 152-2-6, Prizes; Code Vt. Rules 06 031 003, Rule CF 109; Brown v. Miami Vacations, Inc., No. 75CV-12-5247, Clearinghouse No. 27,052 (C.P. Franklin Cty., Ohio Aug. 18, 1976). *See also* State *ex rel.* Webster v. Areaco Inv. Co., 756 S.W.2d 633 (Mo. Ct. App. 1988).

3646 FTC v. EDJ Communications, 5 Trade Reg. Rep. (CCH) ¶ 24,017 (D. Nev. 1996) (proposed consent decree) (prize worth less than consumers paid); State *ex rel.* Webster v. Areaco Inv. Co., 756 S.W.2d 633 (Mo. Ct. App. 1988); Rossi v. 21st Century Concepts, Inc., 162 Misc. 2d 932, 618 N.Y.S.2d 182 (Yonkers City Ct. 1994) (100 rolls of film not "free" when consumer required to develop one roll before getting the next; vacation offer misleading where hotels of poor quality).

3647 FTC v. Gem Merchandising Corp., 87 F.3d 466 (11th Cir. 1996);

Early FTC decisions held that the sale of merchandise by means of games of chance or lottery schemes was an unfair practice in and of itself under the FTC Act.[3648] However, after the FTC adopted a rule merely regulating deceptive aspects of games of chance in the food retailing and gasoline industries, the Second Circuit questioned whether a blanket prohibition of games of chance in other industries was justified.[3649] In 1996, the FTC repealed its rule, concluding that regulation of games of chance was best left to the states.[3650]

Promoters must disclose contest terms and conditions, including starting and ending dates, the nature and numbers of prizes to be awarded, the geographic area involved, and the criteria for judging winners.[3651] West Virginia's statute requires that prizes be delivered within ten days after the contact with the consumer.[3652]

Some jurisdictions prohibit entry fees, purchase requirements, and other consideration.[3653] Thus it is deceptive to misrepresent a vacation as free when there were significant expenses involved.[3654] It is deceptive to award a free gem, but to charge the consumer for the mounting, while making it cumbersome for the consumer to accept just the unmounted gem and leading the consumer to believe that the chances of winning a larger prize are higher if the mounting is purchased.[3655] Maryland prohibits prize promotions that require the consumer to purchase goods or services, pay money, or submit to a sales promotion effort.[3656] This prohibition did not apply, however, to a sales promotion involving free airfare that was disseminated to the public generally through advertisements rather than to specific individuals who were told they were specially selected.[3657]

Georgia's UDAP statute, a West Virginia statute, and an Ohio UDAP rule prohibit prizes or contests as sales promotions unless the dealer makes various disclosures, such as the market value of the prize and whether the consumer will be requested to listen to a sales pitch.[3658] A disclosure that the retail value of a prize is "up to" a stated amount is not a clear and meaningful disclosure.[3659] Regulations restricting prize or bonus promotions do not violate the First Amendment.[3660]

Contests involving 900 telephone numbers have sprung up in which consumers can telephone a pay number (e.g., at $.99 a minute) and answer questions, accumulating points toward a grand prize if they are successful. Where such a contest advertises cars, books, trips and other monthly grand prizes, but does not intend to award any prizes, this can be a UDAP violation.[3661] Other federal and state protections against 900-number frauds are discussed at § 5.9.8, *supra*.

If a contest is promoted by telephone, the FTC's Telemarketing Rule requires clear and conspicuous disclosure of the odds of winning the prize; that no purchase is required to win a prize and that any purchase or payment will not increase the chance of winning;[3662] the method of entering without making a purchase or an address or local or toll-free telephone number to contact to get this information; and all

FTC v. Marketing Response Group, 5 Trade Reg. Rep. (CCH) ¶ 23,958 (M.D. Fla. 1996) (filing of complaint) (consumers allegedly had to pay hundreds of dollars to get prize); Ohio Admin. Code § 109:4-3-06, Prizes.

3648 *See, e.g.*, Bear Sales Co. v. FTC, 362 F.2d 96 (7th Cir. 1966); Bear Sales Co., 68 F.T.C. 37 (1968); J.C. Martin Corp., 66 F.T.C. 1 (1964); Great Western Distrib. Co., 63 F.T.C. 2169 (1963). *See also* Marco Sales Co. v. FTC, 453 F.2d 1, 4 n.2 (2d Cir. 1971) (citing cases, but questioning whether blanket prohibition was appropriate).

3649 Marco Sales Co. v. FTC, 453 F.2d 1, 4 n.2 (2d Cir. 1971).

3650 61 Fed. Reg. 68143 (Dec. 27, 1996) (repealing former 16 C.F.R. Part 419, Trade Regulation Rules for Games of Chance in the Food Retailing and Gasoline Industries).

3651 Coca Cola Co., 88 F.T.C. 656 (1976) (consent order); Oden Distrib. Co., 84 F.T.C. 1125 (1974) (consent order); Cal-Roof Wholesale, Inc., 81 F.T.C. 703 (1972) (consent order); Revere Chemical Corp., 80 F.T.C. 85 (1972); Reuben H. Donnelley Corp., 79 F.T.C. 599 (1971); D'Aray Advertising Co., 78 F.T.C. 616 (1971) (consent order); McDonald's Corp., 78 F.T.C. 606 (1971) (consent order); Proctor & Gamble Co., 79 F.T.C. 589 (1971) (consent order); Connecticut Regulations for the Dep't of Consumer Protection, Conn. Agencies Regs. § 42-1106-23, Game Protection (1977); Idaho Consumer Protection Regulations, Idaho Admin. Code §§ 04.02.01.081, 04.02.01.082 Promotional Games and Advertising and Deceptive Use of Gifts (1978); People v. Columbia Research Corp., 71 Cal. App. 3d 607, 139 Cal. Rptr. 517 (1977). *See also* N.M. Admin. Code § 12.2.2.12.

3652 W. Va. Code § 46A-6D-3; State v. Imperial Marketing, 472 S.E.2d 792 (W. Va. 1996).

3653 16 C.F.R. §§ 310.3(a)(1)(iv), 310.4(d)(4) (telemarketing); Cal. Bus. & Prof. Code § 17539.15, *as amended by* S.B. No. 1780 (1998); Connecticut Regulations for the Dep't of Consumer Protection, Conn. Agencies Regs. § 42-110b-23, Game Promotion (1977); Ga. Code Ann. § 10-1-393(b)(16); Code Miss. Rules 024 000 002 Rule 37; Code Vt. Rules 06 031 003 Rule CF 109; Kugler v. Market Dev. Corp., 124 N.J. Super. 314, 306 A.2d 489 (Ch. Div. 1973); Brown v. Miami Vacations, No. 75CV-12-5247, Clearinghouse No. 27,052 (C.P. Franklin Cty., Ohio Aug. 18, 1976); State v. Reader's Digest Ass'n, Inc., 81 Wash. 2d 259, 501 P.2d 290 (1972). *See also* Idaho Consumer Protection Regulations, Idaho Admin. Code §§ 04.02.01.081, 04.02.01.082, Promotional Games and Deceptive Use of Gifts (1978).

3654 FTC v. Vacation Travel Club, Inc., 5 Trade Reg. Rep. (CCH) ¶ 22,822 (M.D. Fla. 1990) (consent order). *See also* Ga. Code Ann. § 10-1-393(b)(23) (deceptive to state that person has won prize unless the person will receive it without obligation).

3655 State v. Imperial Marketing, 472 S.E.2d 792 (W. Va. 1996).

3656 Md. Comm. Law Code Ann. § 13-305(b).

3657 Luskin's, Inc. v. Consumer Protection Div., 353 Md. 335, 726 A.2d 702 (1999).

3658 Ga. Code Ann. § 10-1-393(b)(16); Ohio Admin. Code § 109:4-3-06, Prizes; W. Va. Code §§ 46A-6D-1 to 46A-6D-10.

3659 State v. Imperial Marketing, 472 S.E.2d 792 (W. Va. 1996).

3660 North Am. Enterprises, Inc. v. State of Vermont, Clearinghouse No. 50,442 (Vt. Super. Oct. 11, 1994).

3661 *See* Wexler v. Brothers Entertainment Group, Inc., 457 N.W.2d 218 (Minn. Ct. App. 1990). *See also* FTC v. Wilcox, 926 F. Supp. 1091 (S.D. Fla. 1995) (consumers were notified that money or prizes were being held for them and would be sent upon payment of processing fee).

3662 This requirement was added effective March 31, 2003. *See* 16 C.F.R. § 310.3(a)(1)(iv), *as amended by* 68 Fed. Reg. 2580 (Jan. 29, 2003).

material costs or conditions to receive or redeem the prize.[3663] These disclosures must be made before the consumer pays. Misrepresentation of the nature or value of the prize, the odds of winning, that a purchase or payment is required, or any other material aspect of a prize promotion is also prohibited.[3664] Telemarketers who call consumers must, before or in conjunction with the description of the prize, orally disclose that no purchase is necessary and that any purchase or payment will not increase the chance of winning.[3665] If the consumer asks, they must describe the no-purchase/no-payment entry method.[3666] The rule also contains many general prohibitions of abusive and deceptive practices.[3667] Some state telemarketing statutes may have similar requirements.[3668]

A federal law places certain restrictions on sweepstakes that are promoted by mail.[3669] This law provides a private cause of action if a promoter continues to mail skill contest or sweepstakes promotions to a consumer who has registered with a do-not-mail list.[3670]

5.13.5 Charitable Solicitations

Many states, either as part of their UDAP statutes or as separate laws, require a charitable organization to register with the state, disclosing various types of information, such as its name and address, the amount of funds to be raised, estimated expenses, previous court actions, and the organization's tax status.[3671] In 2003, in response to a Congressional mandate,[3672] the FTC amended its Telemarketing Sales rule to apply to charitable solicitations conducted over the telephone by for-profit entities on behalf of non-profit organizations.[3673] These charitable solicitors are required to make various disclosures and avoid various deceptive and abusive practices.[3674] A state's telemarketing law may also apply to charitable solicitors, although many states exclude them from coverage.[3675] Coverage of non-profit organizations under state UDAP statutes and the FTC Act is discussed at § 2.3.5, *infra*.

A sales scheme is deceptive if it allows consumers to believe falsely that the seller is a charity or that sales are for the benefit of disabled persons.[3676] It is deceptive for an individual to misrepresent that he or she is acting for a charitable organization in selling advertising.[3677] Similarly deceptive are misrepresentations of the nature of the charity, the solicitor's relation to it, the use that will be made of collections, and the failure to disclose that most money collected would not be forwarded to the charity.[3678] It is deceptive to misrepresent that donations are tax-deductible[3679] or that an individual will receive a valuable prize upon making a donation to an alleged charity.[3680]

3663 16 C.F.R. § 310.3(a)(1)(iv) and (v). For the scope of the telemarketing sales rule, see 16 C.F.R. §§ 310.6 and 310.2(xx), discussed in § 5.9.2.3.2, *supra* and *reprinted in* Appx. D.2.1, *infra*. *See also* FTC v. First Impressions, Inc., 5 Trade Reg. Rep. (CCH) ¶ 24,774 (S.D. Fla. July 10, 2000) (consent decree against telemarketer who told consumers they had won free vacations without disclosing fees that were required).

3664 16 C.F.R. § 310.3(a)(2)(v).

3665 16 C.F.R. § 310.4(d)(4). These requirements apply to outbound calls and "upsells." *See* preliminary clause of 16 C.F.R. § 310.4(d).

3666 *Id.*

3667 *See* § 5.9.4.4, *supra*.

3668 *See* § 5.9.2.5, *supra*, Appx. E, *infra*.

3669 39 U.S.C. § 3001(k)(3).

3670 39 U.S.C. § 3017.

3671 *See, e.g.*, Ark. Stat. Ann. §§ 4-28-402, 4-28-403; Colo. Rev. Stat. § 6-16-101 *et seq.*; Pa. Stat. Ann. tit. 10, § 162.1 *et seq. See also* La. Admin. Code tit. 16, pt. III, § 515; Vt. Stat. Ann. tit. 9, § 2475.

3672 15 U.S.C. § 6106(4), *as amended by* Pub. L. No. 107-56, § 1011 (Oct. 25, 2001).

3673 16 C.F.R. § 310.2(f), (cc), *as amended by* 68 Fed. Reg. 2580 (Jan. 29, 2003). *See* 68 Fed. Reg. 4584–86 (discussion of scope of coverage of charitable solicitations).

3674 *See* § 5.9.3, *supra*.

3675 *See* § 5.9.2.5, *supra*; *see also* Nat'l Fed. of the Blind v. Pryor, 258 F.3d 851 (8th Cir. 2001) (state telemarketing law's requirement that solicitor discontinue call upon request does not violate First Amendment even as applied to charitable solicitations).

3676 State Blind Sales, Inc., 63 F.T.C. 2012 (1963) (consent order); Commonwealth v. Handicapped Indus., Inc., No. 74-11131-0-5, Clearinghouse No. 26,027 (C.P. Bucks Cty. Nov. 25, 1977). *See also* FTC v. Voices for Freedom, 5 Trade Reg. Rep. (CCH) ¶ 23,228 (E.D. Va. 1992) (Desert Storm bracelets); Missouri *ex rel.* Nixon v. Audley (*In re* Audley), 268 B.R. 279 (Bankr. D. Kan. 2001) (restitution order against company that falsely claimed that products were made by handicapped persons is nondischargeable); Benckiser Consumer Products, 5 Trade Reg. Rep. (CCH) ¶ 23,992 (F.T.C. C-3659 1996) (consent order); Commonwealth *ex rel.* Armstrong v. Biering Publishing Co., Clearinghouse No. 38,910 (Ky. Cir. Ct. Franklin Cty. July 10, 1984); Commonwealth *ex rel.* Beshear v. Silver Shield Publishing Co., Clearinghouse No. 36,574, (Ky. Cir. Ct., Fayette Cty. Jan. 12, 1984) (advertising revenues from magazine did not go to "Police Reserve Association"); State *ex rel.* Ashcroft v. Marketing Unlimited, 613 S.W.2d 440 (Mo. Ct. App. 1981).

3677 FTC v. Southwest Marketing Concepts, Inc., 5 Trade Reg. Rep. (CCH) ¶ 24,436 (S.D. Tex. 1998) (stipulated final judgment); FTC v. Baylis Co., 5 Trade Reg. Rep. (CCH) ¶ 23,707 (F.T.C. File No. 942 3021 1994) (consent decree); State *ex rel.* Webster v. Cornelius, 729 S.W.2d 60 (Mo. Ct. App. 1987).

3678 FTC v. Saja, 5 Trade Reg. Rep. (CCH) ¶ 24,483 (D. Ariz. 1998) (proposed consent decree); People v. Orange County Charitable Servs., 73 Cal. App. 4th 1054, 87 Cal. Rptr. 2d 253 (1999); Commonwealth *ex rel.* Zimmerman v. Society of the 28th Division, 538 A.2d 76 (Pa. Commw. Ct. 1987); West Virginia *ex rel.* McGraw v. Hanshaw, Clearinghouse No. 50,441 (W. Va. Cir. Ct. May 23, 1995).

3679 FTC v. Saja, 5 Trade Reg. Rep. (CCH) ¶ 24,483 (D. Ariz. 1998) (proposed consent decree); FTC v. International Charity Consultants, 5 Trade Reg. Rep. (CCH) ¶ 23,825 (D. Nev. 1995) (agreed permanent injunction); FTC v. Publishers Clearinghouse Inc., 5 Trade Reg. Rep. (CCH) ¶ 23,758 (D. Nev. 1995) (consent decree), ¶ 23,826 (summary judgment); FTC v. United Holdings Inc., 5 Trade Reg. Rep. (CCH) ¶ 23,692 (D. Nev. 1994) (consent decree).

3680 FTC v. International Charity Consultants, 5 Trade Reg. Rep. (CCH) ¶ 23,825 (D. Nev. 1995) (agreed permanent injunction);

The United States Supreme Court issued five important cases in the 1980s on the constitutional limits of the regulation of charitable fraud. Two cases hold that it is unconstitutional for a state to limit a charity's allowable expenses to a certain percentage of the contributions received.[3681] The third case struck down a state statute which required religious organizations to register with the state unless they received more than half of their total contributions from members or affiliates.[3682] The fourth case upholds state regulation of the time, place and manner of charitable solicitations.[3683] The last of this series of cases, *Riley v. National Federation of the Blind of North Carolina*,[3684] struck down not only limits on fundraisers' fees but also a requirement that these fees be disclosed. The Court held that these restrictions on fundraisers' speech were not narrowly tailored to accomplish the goal of preventing fraud. Lower courts have followed these decisions by striking down state statutes that placed similar restrictions on charitable solicitations.[3685]

These decisions still leave some room for states to take action against fraudulent charitable solicitations, however, even when the fraud is connected to the low percentage of contributions that go to charitable activities. In *Illinois ex rel. Madigan v. Telemarketing Assocs., Inc.*,[3686] the Supreme Court held that the state may proceed against a charitable solicitor who fraudulently misrepresents facts, even facts about the percentage of contributions that go to charity that the state can not require the solicitor to disclose. Thus, the state can proceed against solicitors who knowingly and falsely tell donors that a substantial portion of their contributions will fund specific programs. The state must prove all elements of common law fraud by clear and convincing evidence, however.[3687] Thus, while UDAP restrictions on deception and misstatements by charitable fundraisers are constitutionally permissible, they must be narrowly tailored to avoid infringement on the fundraisers' First Amendment rights.[3688]

5.13.6 Scholarship Location Services and Diploma Mills

Companies that take advance payment from consumers to find them scholarships and grants are another growing abuse. These companies send high school and college students postcards advertising that for an advance fee the service can find "unclaimed" scholarship and grant funds from private companies. They promise to refund the fee if the student does not receive a minimum amount. Nevertheless, these companies all too often provide neither the promised financial aid nor the promised refunds.[3689] Other times, they claim a refund is not owing because the small print places onerous conditions on receiving a refund.[3690] When they can not get the student to send money up front, the companies may discover the student's checking account number and take money out of the account with an unauthorized demand draft or telecheck.[3691]

Sometimes these companies merely provide consumers with lists of financial aid sources to whom the consumers must apply on their own.[3692] One company agreed to stop its practice of selling employment and financial aid directories that it misrepresented as programs that guaranteed students jobs with free room, board and transportation or free financial aid.[3693]

FTC v. Publishers Clearinghouse Inc., 5 Trade Reg. Rep. (CCH) ¶ 23,758 (D. Nev. 1995) (consent decree), ¶ 23,826 (summary judgment); FTC v. United Holdings Inc., 5 Trade Reg. Rep. (CCH) ¶ 23,692 (D. Nev. 1994) (consent decree).

3681 Secretary of Maryland v. Joseph H. Munson Co., 467 U.S. 947 (1984); Village of Schaumburg v. Citizens for a Better Environment, 444 U.S. 620 (1980).

3682 Larson v. Valente, 456 U.S. 228 (1982).

3683 Heffron v. Int'l Society for Krishna Consciousness, 452 U.S. 640 (1981).

3684 487 U.S. 781, 108 S. Ct. 2667, 101 L. Ed. 2d 669 (1988).

3685 Kentucky State Police Prof. Ass'n v. Gorman, 870 F. Supp. 166 (E.D. Ky. 1994).

3686 538 U.S. 600, 123 S. Ct. 1829, 155 L. Ed. 2d 793 (2003).

3687 *Id.*, 123 S. Ct. at 1841.

3688 *See also* Fraternal Order of Police v. Stenehjem, 287 F. Supp. 2d 1023 (D.N.D. 2003) (state's restrictions on commercial telemarketers does not violate 1st Amendment, but application of the law to outside solicitors of charitable contributions does); People v. Orange County Charitable Servs., 73 Cal. App. 4th 1054, 87 Cal. Rptr. 2d 253 (1999) (requiring solicitor to disclose truthful information if donor asks about percentage that goes to charity does not violate First Amendment); Commonwealth *ex rel.* Preate v. Pennsylvania Chiefs of Police Ass'n, Inc., 572 A.2d 256 (Pa. Commw. Ct. 1990); Commonwealth *ex rel.* Preate v. Watson & Hughey Co., 563 A.2d 1276 (Pa. Commw. Ct. 1989); Federal Trade Commission, Telemarketing Sales Rule, Final Rule, Statement of Basis and Purpose, 68 Fed. Reg. 4580, 4634–37 (Jan. 29, 2003) (discussing First Amendment considerations in do-not-call lists for commercial and non-profit telemarketers); § 7.10.2, *infra*.

3689 FTC v. National Scholarship Foundation, Inc., 5 Trade Reg. Rep. (CCH) ¶ 24,512 (S.D. Fla. 1998) (order for permanent injunction); FTC v. Deco Consulting Servs., Inc., 5 Trade Reg. Rep. (CCH) ¶ 24,363 (S.D. Fla. 1998) (consent decree); FTC v. National Grant Foundation, Inc., 5 Trade Reg. Rep. (CCH) ¶ 24,427 (S.D. Fla. 1998) (proposed consent decree); FTC v. College Assistance Servs., Inc., 5 Trade Reg. Rep. (CCH) ¶ 24,357 (S.D. Fla. 1998) (proposed consent decree); FTC v. Career Assistance Planning, Inc., 5 Trade Reg. Rep. (CCH) ¶ 24,218 (N.D. Ga. 1997) (consent decree); FTC v. Nwaigwe, 5 Trade Reg. Rep. (CCH) ¶ 24,253 (D. Md. 1997) (proposed consent decree).

3690 FTC v. Student Aid Inc., 5 Trade Reg. Rep. (CCH) ¶ 24,312 (S.D.N.Y. 1997) (proposed consent decree).

3691 *Id.* See § 5.1.10.3, *supra* for a discussion of demand drafts or telechecks.

3692 FTC v. National Grant Foundation, Inc., 5 Trade Reg. Rep. (CCH) ¶ 24,427 (S.D. Fla. 1998) (proposed consent decree).

3693 FTC v. Progressive Media, Inc., 5 Trade Reg. Rep. (CCH) ¶ 24,304 (W.D. Wash. 1997) (proposed consent decree). More

In some cases, the companies do not purport to offer scholarships or grants, but rather aggressively sell scholarship location services. The companies claim that these placement services can help students and their parents obtain more financial aid than they could on their own.[3694] The company may claim to be a non-profit information gathering service.[3695]

In 2000, Congress passed legislation specifically addressing this issue. The College Scholarship Fraud Prevention Act of 2000 requires the United States Sentencing Commission to provide enhanced penalties for financial aid fraud.[3696] The Act also requires the Departments of Education, Justice and the Federal Trade Commission to coordinate enforcement and outreach activities in this area.[3697] In addition to possible UDAP claims, advocates should investigate whether the state credit repair organizations law applies to the scholarship location service.[3698]

Another problem is the rise of so-called "diploma mills." "Diploma mills" and other unaccredited schools resemble the distance education programs that have managed to secure legitimate accreditation. Although there is no formal definition of a "diploma mill," it is generally an on-line operation that offers degrees for money alone or in some cases for money and a little work.[3699]

information on inter-agency enforcement actions against scholarship scams is available on the FTC website, www.ftc.gov.

3694 Federal Trade Commission v. College Resource Mgmt., Inc., Case No. 3-01CV08280G (N.D. Tex. complaint filed May 1, 2001). The complaint is available at www.ftc.gov/os/2001/05/crmcmp.pdf. The stipulated order filed on May 1, 2001 prohibits the defendants from making any false claims in connection with the marketing and sale of college financial services and from violating the Commission's Rule Concerning Cooling-Off Period for Sales Made at Home or at Certain Other Locations ("Cooling-Off Rule"). The order also requires the defendants to pay $40,000 in disgorgement.

3695 *See, e.g.*, *In the Matter of* Educational Research Center of America, Inc. et. al, File No. 022-3249 (proposed consent order filed Jan. 29, 2003). The consent order is available on-line at: www.ftc.gov/os/2003/01/ercaconsent.htm.

3696 Scholarship Fraud Prevention Act, Pub. Law No. 106-420, 114 Stat. 1867 (Nov. 1, 2000).

3697 *Id.* For a summary of enforcement efforts, see Department of Justice, Department of Education, Federal Trade Commission, *Scholarship Fraud Prevention Act of 2000: First Annual Report to Congress* (May 2002), available on-line at www.ftc.gov/os/2002/05/scholarshipfraudreport2001.pdf and Second Annual Report to Congress (May 2003), available on-line at www.ftc.gov/os/2003/05/collegesfpactreport.pdf

3698 *See* Hatch v. College Resource Mgmt., Clearinghouse No. 53,563 (Minn. Dist. Ct. Oct. 24, 2001) (denying scholarship location service's motion for summary judgment and concluding that state credit repair law applies to it). *See generally* § 5.1.2.2.3, *supra*.

3699 *See, e.g.*, General Accounting Office, "Diploma Mills: Federal Employees Have Obtained Degrees from Diploma Mills and Other Unaccredited Schools, Some at Government Expense," GAO-04-77IT, May 2004; Thomas Bartlett and Scott Smallwood, "Inside the Multimillion-Dollar World of Diploma Mills," Chronicle of Higher Education at A8 (June 25, 2004).

Chapter 6 Liability of Various Parties

6.1 Introduction

One of the most important practical decisions for a consumer litigant bringing a UDAP action is determining which parties to join as defendants. Those most responsible for deceptive practices may be the most difficult to serve with process and most unlikely to pay a monetary judgment. The parties with the "deepest pockets," such as shareholders of corporations or officers not directly involved with the deceptive scheme, may have legal defenses insulating them from liability.

This chapter outlines legal and certain practical implications in naming as defendants:

- Agents such as sales personnel and advertising agencies;[1]
- Principals and co-venturers, such as corporations and other business entities;[2]
- Directors, officers, managers, owners, parent corporations, franchisors, successor corporations, and estates of individuals;[3] and
- Third parties offering the means or assisting the deceptive scheme or conspiring with those engaged in the violation.[4]

An even more critical issue is the ability of a consumer to raise, against an assignee of the original seller or a financier closely connected to the seller, UDAP claims and defenses the consumer could raise against the seller.[5] This requires an understanding of the FTC Holder Rule and related legal theories.

Similar questions arise if the transaction is a straight loan of money rather than a financed sale. Can the consumer raise against the lender's assignee claims and defenses that could be brought against the originating lender?[6] Another issue discussed in this chapter is the rights of consumers where a local telephone company attempts to collect on other companies' 900-number or long-distance charges.[7]

1 *See* § 6.2, *infra.*
2 *See* § 6.3, *infra.*
3 *See* § 6.4, *infra.*
4 *See* § 6.5, *infra.*
5 *See* § 6.6, *infra.*
6 *See* § 6.7, *infra.*
7 *See* § 6.10, *infra.*

Even where a liable party has filed for bankruptcy, this does not foreclose a consumer's recovery. There are various steps a consumer can take to seek at least a partial recovery from the bankruptcy estate.[8] In addition, many sellers are bonded or insured, providing another source of compensation.[9]

UDAP statutes should be interpreted to reach as least as far as contract and tort law would. Thus, tort law theories such as liability based on ratification of another's wrongdoing should apply in UDAP cases.[10] But UDAP statutes were passed to overcome the limitations of contract and tort law and should not be limited by these doctrines.[11] Even if there would not be a basis under contract or tort law to hold a particular defendant liable, UDAP liability should attach if the defendant meets the statute's coverage requirements and performed or participated in an unfair or deceptive act as defined by the statute. UDAP statutes should be broadly applied to meet their remedial goals.

This chapter briefly outlines common law concepts and summarizes existing state UDAP case law in these areas. Attorneys should supplement this discussion with research in their own jurisdiction concerning the law of agency, piercing the corporate veil, close-connectedness theories, and related topics.

8 *See* § 6.7, *infra.*
9 *See* § 6.9, *infra. See also* National Consumer Law Center, Consumer Bankruptcy Law and Practice Ch. 17 (7th ed. 2004 and Supp.) (detailed discussion of consumer claims against bankrupt sellers and creditors).
10 *See* Banks v. Consumer Home Mortgs., Inc., 2003 WL 21251584 (E.D.N.Y. Mar. 28, 2003) (importing tort aiding and abetting standard for UDAP claim); Qantel Bus. Sys. v. Custom Controls, 761 S.W.2d 302 (Tex. 1988) (using tort law as guide for liability of parties in UDAP cases). *See also* Sweet v. Roy, 801 A.2d 694 (Vt. 2002) (applying general law of agency to UDAP liability questions). *But see* Zekman v. Direct Am. Marketers, 182 Ill. 2d 359, 695 N.E.2d 853 (1998) (declining to use tort theories).
11 Meyer v. Dygert, 156 F. Supp. 2d 1081 (D. Minn. 2001); Garcia v. Overland Bond & Inv. Co., 668 N.E.2d 199 (Ill. App. Ct. 1996).

6.2 Liability of Agents and Employees

While a UDAP claim will normally name a corporation as defendant, there may be reasons to add the corporation's agents as defendants as well. Both employees and non-employee agents of the corporation can be liable.[12] If both the agent and the corporation committed the deceptive acts, each is liable for the entire UDAP award.[13] An advertising agency responsible for deceptive advertising, an insurance agent, or sales personnel participating in the deception are possible candidates. Such agents may be easier to reach or may possess more assets than an out-of-state, fly-by-night, or bankrupt corporation. There may also be tactical, evidentiary, or discovery reasons to include agents as defendants.

The normal common law approach to agents' torts is that the principal's command of the agent's actions does not excuse an agent from liability for tortious conduct.[14] An agent is personally liable for misrepresentations he makes even when acting within the scope of employment.[15] Thus, in most jurisdictions, an agent is liable if the agent defrauds the consumer or knowingly participates in a transaction based upon the principal's misrepresentation. In addition, although an agent is not normally a party to a contract made for the principal, the agent is liable if the agent misrepresents its own authority or the existence of the principal.[16]

Existing UDAP case law on this issue is consistent with common law tort concepts. An individual can not escape liability for his or her deceptive practices by claiming to be only an agent for the seller.[17] An agent is liable under a UDAP count even if the agent was not the one who actually sold the property to the buyer, but only made representations concerning the product.[18]

Similarly, an agent is liable for its own misrepresentations even if the agent has no knowledge whether or not its representations are true, and is just relying on information supplied by the principal.[19] The lack of privity between consumer and agent is not a defense to a UDAP claim.[20] An agent, however, is not responsible for independent conduct by the principal.[21]

There is a split of opinion in Texas whether the state Unfair Insurance Practices (UNIP) Act applies to employees, or only to their employers. Federal courts have held that employees are not liable for unfair insurance practices under the Texas Insurance Code.[22] The reasoning behind this

---

12 FTC v. Windward Marketing, Ltd., 1997 U.S. Dist. LEXIS 17114 (N.D. Ga. Sept. 30, 1997) (non-employee accountant who acted as day-to-day manager is liable under FTC Act); People by Spitzer v. Telehublink, 756 N.Y.S.2d 285 (App. Div. 2003) (employee who carried out deceptive practices is liable, but mere knowledge is insufficient).

13 Inserra v. J.E.M. Building Corp., 2000 Ohio App. LEXIS 5447 (Nov. 22, 2000). *See also* FTC v. Verity Int'l, Ltd., 194 F. Supp. 2d 270 (S.D.N.Y. 2002) (individual who directed company's deceptive acts is jointly and severally liable for full amount of consumer redress, not just the amount he actually received).

14 Pretzel & Stouffer v. Imperial Adjusters, Inc., 28 F.3d 42 (7th Cir. 1994); Anden v. Litinsky, 472 So. 2d 825 (Fla. Dist. Ct. App. 1985); Laurents v. Louisiana Mobile Homes, Inc., 689 So. 2d 536 (La. Ct. App. 1997) (defining when employee or agent is liable); Brungard v. Caprice Records, Inc., 608 S.W.2d 585 (Tenn. 1980); Weitzel v. Barnes, 691 S.W.2d 598 (Tex. 1985); Wheeler v. Box, 671 S.W.2d 75 (Tex. App. 1984); Aungst v. Roberts Constr. Co., 95 Wash. 2d 439, 625 P.2d 167 (1981); Gould v. Mutual Life Ins. Co. of New York, 37 Wash. App. 756, 683 P.2d 207 (1984); Seavey, Agency § 129 (1975); Restatement (Second) of Agency § 343 (1958); Gregory, The Law of Agency and Partnership § 124 (3d ed. 2001).

15 Miller v. Keyser, 90 S.W.3d 712 (Tex. 2002). *See also* Texas v. American Blastfax, Inc., 164 F. Supp. 2d 892 (W.D. Tex. 2001) (decided under Telephone Consumer Protection Act) (agent liable if he knowingly participated).

16 Seavey, Agency § 124 (1975); Restatement (Second) of Agency § 330 (1958); Gregory, The Law of Agency and Partnership §§ 118, 119 (3d ed. 2001).

17 Walker v. FDIC, 970 F.2d 114 (5th Cir. 1992) (Texas law); Daniels v. Baritz, 2003 WL 21027238, at *5 (E.D. Pa. Apr. 30, 2003) (employees or agents are liable if they participated in unfair or deceptive acts); Frontier Mgmt. Co. v. Balboa Ins. Co., 658 F. Supp. 987 (D. Mass. 1986); Evans v. Taylor, 711 So. 2d 1317 (Fla. Dist. Ct. App. 1998) (agent for construction contract liable for his own UDAP violations); Anden v. Litinsky, 472 So. 2d 825 (Fla. Dist. Ct. App. 1985); Eastern Star, Inc. v. Union Building Materials, 712 P.2d 1148 (Haw. Ct. App. 1985); Elder v. Coronet Ins. Co., 201 Ill. App. 3d 733, 558 N.E.2d 1312 (1990); Bois v. Pendexter, 2002 WL 966128 (Me. Super. Apr. 12, 2002); Commonwealth v. Windsor of Dracut, Inc., Clearinghouse No. 52,034 (Mass. Super. Ct. Aug. 20, 1997); Kugler v. Koscot Interplanetary, Inc., 120 N.J. Super. 216, 293 A.2d 682 (Ch. Div. 1972); Hardy v. Toler, 288 N.C. 303, 218 S.E.2d 342 (1978); State *ex rel.* Medlock v. Nest Egg Society Today, Inc., 348 S.E.2d 381 (S.C. Ct. App. 1986); Brungard v. Caprice Records, Inc., 608 S.W.2d 585 (Tenn. 1980); Weitzel v. Barnes, 691 S.W.2d 598 (Tex. 1985); Guilbeau v. Anderson, 841 S.W.2d 517 (Tex. App. 1992); Great Am. Homebuilders, Inc. v. Gerhart, 708 S.W.2d 8 (Tex. App. 1986); Wheeler v. Box, 671 S.W.2d 75 (Tex. App. 1984); Aungst v. Roberts Constr. Co., 95 Wash. 2d 439, 625 P.2d 167 (1981); Gould v. Mutual Life Ins. Co. of New York, 37 Wash. App. 756, 683 P.2d 207 (1984). *Cf.* Industrias Magromer Cueros y Pieles v. Louisiana Bayou Furs Inc., 293 F.3d 912 (5th Cir. 2002) (requiring finding of common law fraud in commercial case before agent will be liable for UDAP violations); People *ex rel.* Spitzer v. Telehublink Corp., 301 A.D.2d 1006, 756 N.Y.S.2d 285 (2003) (non-officer employee will be liable only if he actually participated in the deception).

18 Frazer v. Choiniere, 133 Vt. 631, 350 A.2d 755 (1975).

19 *See* Keyser v. Miller, 90 S.W.3d 712 (Tex. 2002) (agent is liable for actions in scope of employment even if he does not know his actions are false); Cameron v. Terrell & Garrett, Inc., 618 S.W.2d 535 (Tex. 1981); Henry S. Miller Co. v. Bynum, 797 S.W.2d 51 (Tex. App. 1990).

20 Carter v. Taylor, 1999 Ohio App. LEXIS 6097 (Dec. 9, 1999); Maryland Ins. Co. v. Head Indus. Coatings & Servs., Inc., 906 S.W.2d 218 (Tex. App. 1995).

21 Cameron v. Terrell & Garrett Inc., 618 S.W.2d 535 (Tex. 1981).

22 Ayoub v. Baggett, 820 F. Supp. 298 (S.D. Tex. 1993); Arzehgar v. Dixon, 150 F.R.D. 92 (S.D. Tex. 1993). *See also* Cavallini v. State Farm Mut. Auto Ins. Co., 44 F.3d 256 (5th Cir. 1995) (Texas law) (insurance agent has no duty of good faith and fair dealing and therefore can not be sued for a breach of that duty);

exception to the usual rule is that the unfair insurance practices laws were intended to regulate the trade practices of the insurance industry, and that this intent would not be served by making individual employees at risk.[23] More recent Texas state court decisions have rejected these holdings and have held that employees are subject to UNIP claims for their own acts.[24]

6.3 Liability of Principals, Co-Venturers

6.3.1 Principals Liable for the Acts of Their Agents

The normal UDAP case seeks to hold the principal—that is, the corporation, employer, or other deep pocket—liable for the acts of such agents as sales personnel, commissioned salespersons, and other employees. The principal is usually a stable entity easily served with court papers and usually possesses sufficient assets to satisfy a judgment. Requests for injunctions or other nonmonetary relief may only be practical if the principal is joined as a party, and naming the principal may also enhance discovery.

Common law doctrine in most jurisdictions holds principals liable for misrepresentations made by agents who are acting within their actual or apparent authority.[25] For torts involving bodily injury, the doctrine of *respondeat superior* holds masters liable only for the acts of "servants," that is, for agents whose activity the principal controls. But principals are liable for the misrepresentations of all their agents, not just their servants.[26] An agency relationship is shown if: (1) the agent is subject to the principal's right to control; (2) the agent has a duty to act primarily for the benefit of the principal; and (3) the agent holds a power to alter the legal relations of the principal.[27]

Courts, in general, are even more likely to hold a principal liable for the acts of its agents under a UDAP statute than at common law. Courts interpreting UDAP statutes often begin with common law agency concepts that a principal is liable for the acts of its agents when such acts are within the scope of the agent's actual or apparent authority.[28] Thus, even if the predominant motive is the agent's self benefit, there is actual authority if the activity is of the kind the agent is employed to perform and if the motivation, at least in part, is to serve the employer.[29]

Nor will courts immunize a principal if the agent lacks actual authority.[30] Apparent authority is shown when a reasonable person would suppose the agent has the authority

Coffman v. Scott Wetzel Servs., Inc., 908 S.W.2d 516 (Tex. App. 1995) (same). *But see* Tenner v. Prudential Ins. Co. of Am., 872 F. Supp. 1571 (E.D. Tex. 1994) (insurance agent individually liable under UDAP for misrepresentations outside scope of his authority); *cf.* Maryland Ins. Co. v. Head Indus. Coatings & Servs., Inc., 906 S.W.2d 218 (Tex. App. 1995) (agent's actions bind the insurer).

23 Ayoub v. Baggett, 820 F. Supp. 298 (S.D. Tex. 1993), cited with approval in Arzehgar v. Dixon, 150 F.R.D. 92 (S.D. Tex. 1993). However, the validity of these holdings, by a district judge and magistrate in the same federal district court, should be in doubt, especially considering the magistrate's additional holding that an employee is also not liable under the Texas UDAP statute for his own actions. Arzehgar v. Dixon, 150 F.R.D. 92 (S.D. Tex. 1993). This holding is in clear conflict with a significant body of law to the contrary, as discussed earlier in this section.

24 Garrison Contractors, Inc. v. Liberty Mut. Ins. Co., 927 S.W.2d 296 (Tex. App. 1996); Southland Lloyd's Ins. Co. v. Tomberlain, 919 S.W.2d 822 (Tex. App. 1996).

25 Meyer v. Holley, 537 U.S. 280, 123 S. Ct. 824, 154 L. Ed. 2d 753 (2003); Burlington Industries, Inc. v. Ellerth, 524 U.S. 742 (1998); Restatement (Second) of Agency § 140 (1958). *See also* McRaild v. Shepard Lincoln Mercury, 141 Mich. App. 406, 367 N.W.2d 404 (1985).

26 Seavey, Agency §§ 83, 92 (1975); Restatement (Second) of Agency §§ 249, 257, 264 (1958).

27 State v. Cottman Transmissions Sys., Inc., 86 Md. App. 714, 587 A.2d 1190 (1991) (citing the Restatement (Second) of Agency).

28 Williams v. Ford Motor Co., 990 F. Supp. 551 (N.D. Ill. 1997); Fravel v. Commonwealth, Clearinghouse No. 49,161 (E.D. Va. Jan. 8, 1993); Southwest Sunsites, Inc., 105 F.T.C. 79 (1985), *aff'd*, 785 F.2d 1431 (9th Cir. 1986); Wang Laboratories, Inc. v. Business Incentives, Inc., 398 Mass. 854, 501 N.E.2d 1163 (1986); Rousseau v. Gelinas, 24 Mass. App. Ct. 154, 507 N.E.2d 265 (1987); Gennari v. Weichert Co. Realtors, 148 N.J. 582, 691 A.2d 350 (1997) (real estate company liable for UDAP treble damages for the acts of its brokers); Poor v. Hill, 138 N.C. App. 19, 530 S.E.2d 838 (2000) (evidence that wife was husband's business partner, was peripherally involved in the transaction, and retained the proceeds shows agency); Brown v. Deacon's Chrysler Plymouth, Inc., 14 Ohio Op. 3d 436 (Ct. App. 1979); Brown v. Lyons, 43 Ohio Misc. 14, 332 N.E.2d 380, 72 Ohio Op. 2d 216 (C.P. Hamilton Cty. 1974); Commonwealth v. Programmed Learning Sys., Inc., Clearinghouse No. 26,019 (Pa. C.P. Allegheny Cty. 1975); Commonwealth v. Koscot Interplanetary, Inc., Clearinghouse No. 26,024 (Pa. C.P. Erie Cty. 1970); State *ex rel.* McLeod v. C&L Corp., 313 S.E.2d 334 (S.C. Ct. App. 1984) (principal without knowledge of deception liable for misrepresentation of agent acting within agent's authority); England v. Select Sires, Inc., 1998 Tenn. App. LEXIS 372 (June 12, 1998) (rule that principal is liable for acts of agent applies to UDAP cases); Celtic Life Ins. Co. v. Coats, 885 S.W.2d 96 (Tex. 1994); Sweet v. Roy, 801 A.2d 694 (Vt. 2002) (principal is liable for agent's acts in scope of employment whether or not principal specifically authorized them). *Cf.* International Brotherhood of Police Officers Local 433 v. Memorial Press, Inc., 31 Mass. App. Ct. 138, 575 N.E.2d 376 (1991) (employer not liable for intentional act of employee acting outside scope of employment).

29 Wang Laboratories, Inc. v. Business Incentives, Inc., 398 Mass. 854, 501 N.E.2d 1163 (1986).

30 Royal Globe Ins. Co. v. Bar Consultants, Inc., 577 S.W.2d 688 (Tex. 1979); Insurance Co. of N. Am. v. Morris, 928 S.W.2d 133 (Tex. App. 1996) (insurance agent's acts do not bind insurer but can subject insurer to UDAP claim), *rev'd on other grounds*, 981 S.W.2d 667 (1998) (no evidence of apparent or actual authority to bind insurer for statements made by agents regarding third party's investment product rather than insurance product).

he or she purports to exercise.[31] In one interesting case, a federal court allowed a claim to proceed against an automobile manufacturer for the acts of a dealer on an apparent agency theory, where the manufacturer authorized the dealer to perform service contract work, but not to charge an inspection fee before performing that work. Even though there was no actual authority for the dealer to assess such a charge, it could appear to the consumer that the dealer had that authority.[32] But there is no liability if the buyer has notice the agent is not acting for the principal.[33] Regardless of the agent's authority or lack thereof, a principal who ratifies the agent's acts is liable for them.[34]

A Texas court has analyzed the liability of insurers for the acts of insurance agents. The company was found liable not only for the acts of the "local recording agents" (those agents delegated with extensive responsibilities by the insurer), but also for the acts of "soliciting agents" (whose function is merely to receive and forward applications for insurance).[35] On the other hand, a "servicing company" (which issues policies, pays claims, and performs other tasks on behalf of the actual insurer) may not be an agent of the insurer.[36] Further, even if a servicing company is not an agent, it is nonetheless subject to suit in its own capacity.[37] Even if there is no apparent authority, some state insurance laws or regulations hold an insurer liable for the acts of insurance agents selling policies for that insurer.[38]

Courts flexibly analyze liability issues to meet the purposes of the UDAP statute. "To allow an employer to escape liability under the [state UDAP statute] on a claim that it did not know of a specific violation committed by its employee would frustrate the Act itself."[39] Principals can not escape liability for independent acts of salesmen since the principal has a duty to monitor the salesmen's activities.[40] A principal with a duty to disclose a material fact can not avoid responsibility by keeping its agents in the dark and then rely on their ignorance as a defense.[41] A principal is liable for the deceptive acts of its agents even if the principal tries to limit the deception and diligently tries to prevent such unauthorized behavior.[42]

The principal is liable not only for actual damages but also the treble damages portion of a UDAP award based on the acts of its agents.[43] This is true even though under common law there are limits on the principal's liability for punitive damages awarded because of an agent's acts.

One example of a potential principal-agent relationship is that between a manufacturer and its dealers. A consumer who seeks to hold a manufacturer liable for the acts of its dealers should do more than just categorically state that a dealer is an agent of the manufacturer. Specific facts that can establish such an agency must be alleged, however.[44] For example, it may be that the manufacturer provides commissions or other payments to the dealer or its personnel to encourage it to engage in certain activity benefiting the manufacturer, or the dealer may act as the manufacturer's agent in selling a service contract or other ancillary product. Careful development of facts may also show that dealers are agents of the financing arm of a manufacturer, even though the financing arm is an independent corporation separate from both the manufacturer and the dealers. The financing arm may provide training to dealers, send employees to the dealership to observe and review the dealer's profitability in financing transactions, and provide temporary employees to assist dealers with financing transactions.[45] A dealer may

31 Holley v. Gurnee Volkswagen & Oldsmobile, Inc., 2001 U.S. Dist. LEXIS 7274 (N.D. Ill. Jan. 4, 2001) (dealer liable for UDAP violations and fraud committed by car salesmen who acted with apparent authority); Williams v. Ford Motor Co., 990 F. Supp. 551 (N.D. Ill. 1997) (car dealer acted as apparent agent for manufacturer in charging fees for repairs under service contract); England v. Select Sires, Inc., 1998 Tenn. App. LEXIS 372 (June 12, 1998) (company was liable by apparent agency (agency by estoppel) when it acquiesced in fraud artist's exercise of authority); Longoria v. Atlantic Gulf Enterprises, Inc., 572 S.W.2d 71 (Tex. Civ. App. 1978).

32 Williams v. Ford Motor Co., 990 F. Supp. 551 (N.D. Ill. 1997).

33 Parsons v. Bailey, 30 N.C. App. 497, 227 S.E.2d 166 (1976).

34 Medley v. Boomershine Pontiac-GMC Truck, 214 Ga. App. 795, 449 S.E.2d 128 (1994); Walker v. Sloan, 137 N.C. App. 387, 529 S.E.2d 236 (2000).

35 Celtic Life Ins. Co. v. Coats, 885 S.W.2d 96 (Tex. 1994).

36 Northwinds Abatement, Inc. v. Employers Ins. of Wausau, 258 F.3d 345 (5th Cir. 2001) (Texas law).

37 *Id.*

38 *See* Maccabees Mut. Life Ins. Co. v. McNiel, 836 S.W.2d 229 (Tex. App. 1992).

39 Brown v. Deacon's Chrysler Plymouth, Inc., 14 Ohio Op. 3d 436, 438–439 (Ct. App. 1979).

40 Commonwealth v. Gold Bond Industries, Inc., No. 569 April Term 1972, Clearinghouse No. 26,028 (C.P. Allegheny Cty., Pa. Apr. 26, 1972).

41 *In re* Brandywine Volkswagen, Ltd., 312 A.2d 632 (Del. 1973).

42 Southwest Sunsites, Inc., 105 F.T.C. 79 (1985), *aff'd*, 785 F.2d 1431 (9th Cir. 1986); *see also* Standard Distributors, Inc. v. FTC, 211 F.2d 7 (2d Cir. 1954).

43 Gennari v. Weichert Co. Realtors, 148 N.J. 582, 691 A.2d 350 (1997). *See also* Stuppy v. World Gym Int'l, Inc., 2003 WL 886724 (Cal. App. Mar. 7, 2003) (unpublished, citation limited) (licensor ratified the acts of its licensee agent so is liable for treble damages under health spa law; licensor was also directly involved in culpable acts). *But see* Augaut, Inc. v. Aegis, Inc., 631 N.E.2d 995 (Mass. 1994) (multiple damages portion of UDAP award can not be recovered from both agent and corporation where corporation's liability was based solely on the conduct of a single agent).

44 Emery v. VISA Int'l Serv. Ass'n, 95 Cal. App. 4th 952, 116 Cal. Rptr. 2d 25 (2002) (plaintiff presented no facts showing agency relationship between merchants and VISA); Connick v. Suzuki Motor Co., 174 Ill. 2d 482, 675 N.E.2d 584 (1996) (consumer never pleaded or presented such facts). *See also* Abraham v. North Ave. Auto, Inc., 2001 U.S. Dist. LEXIS 12990 (N.D. Ill. Aug. 23, 2001) (must allege facts showing that auto dealer was agent of bank).

45 Coleman v. GMAC, 196 F.R.D. 315 (M.D. Tenn. 2000), *vacated, remanded on other grounds*, 296 F.3d 443 (6th Cir. 2002) (grant of class certification reversed; predominance not shown). *But cf.* LaChapelle v. Toyota Motor Credit Corp., 102 Cal. App. 4th 977, 126 Cal. Rptr. 2d 32 (2002) (lease finance company's

also be the agent of a bank that gives it authority to arrange a purchase-money loan for a consumer.

One exception to the doctrine of *respondeat superior* is the *Merrill* doctrine that limits the liability of a government agency for the acts of its agents.[46] For example, a court has found Freddie Mac not liable under a UDAP statute for the acts of its servicing agents (e.g., banks that service its home mortgages).[47] The effect of a contract provision limiting the principal's liability for the acts of an agent is discussed at § 4.2.15.4, *supra*.

6.3.2 Principal's Liability for Actions of Independent Contractor

Companies commonly argue that salespersons guilty of deception are independent contractors, separate and apart from the company, and not agents. Contracts signed by salespersons indicating that they are independent contractors do not make them so where the salespersons were in substance agents.[48] The substance, not the form, of the relationship is the determining factor.[49]

Sellers are not independent contractors if they sell through the parent company and are compensated on a commission basis.[50] Even where real estate agents are described as independent brokers, they are the seller's agents where they sell land on a commission, the developer provides the brochures and contracts, and the money goes to the developer directly.[51] An individual hired to establish a contractual relationship between a third party and the principal is an agent, not an independent contractor.[52]

The Federal Trade Commission has obtained a consent decree against a creditor that hired debt collection firms and allegedly approved or assisted their use of deceptive debt collection practices.[53] The FTC's position was that the creditor's failure to oversee properly its collection agencies violated the FTC Act prohibition against unfair trade practices. This consent decree could be helpful precedent in UDAP cases not only against creditors but also against other principals whose independent contractors commit unfair or deceptive acts.[54]

State courts have also been careful not to excuse companies from liability under UDAP statutes even if their salespersons are independent contractors. An individual is responsible for tortious conduct of others which the individual intends to accomplish and in which his or her conduct is a causative factor.[55] Thus if a company distributes sales manuals to independent contractors, recommending deceptive sales techniques, and the company intends that the manuals be used, the company is liable. Moreover, a related company can be held liable under the UDAP statute if the company retained the benefits of sale after knowing of the independent contractor's deception[56] or after failing to take action against the independent contractor.[57]

Consequently, the central concern in making a company or other principal liable for the acts of sales personnel or independent contractors is a careful investigation of the facts. A consumer litigant should determine the exact relationship of the company to the individual salesperson, the type of training, manuals, and instructions provided the individual, independent action by the company to further the deception, and the nature of company supervision, review and control over the salesperson's action. Also important is the extent of company knowledge of the deception after the fact, steps the company took to deal both with the agent or contractor and the deceived consumer, and any other fact that would discredit the company so as to justify shifting the loss due to the salesperson's deception from the consumer to the company.

6.3.3 Liability of Co-Venturers, Partners

Where a company is organized as a joint venture, all co-venturers are jointly and severally liable for actions of other co-venturers.[58] Joint UDAP violators may have claims

provision of forms did not make dealer its agent).

46 Federal Crop Ins. Corp. v. Merrill, 332 U.S. 380 (1947).

47 Deerman v. Federal Home Loan Mortg. Corp., 955 F. Supp. 1393 (N.D. Ala. 1997), *aff'd without op.*, 140 F.3d 1043 (11th Cir. 1998).

48 Kugler v. Koscot Interplanetary, Inc., 120 N.J. Super. 216, 293 A.2d 682 (Ch. Div. 1972); Kugler v. Romain, 110 N.J. Super. 470, 266 A.2d 144 (Ch. Div. 1970), *modified on other grounds*, 58 N.J. 522, 279 A.2d 640 (1971). *But see* Melton v. Family First Mortg. Corp., 576 S.E.2d 365 (N.C. App. 2003) (giving effect to contract clause that original lender was not assignee's agent).

49 Goodman v. FTC, 244 F.2d 584 (9th Cir. 1957); Southwest Sunsites, Inc., 105 F.T.C. 79 (1985), *aff'd*, 785 F.2d 1431 (9th Cir. 1986); *see also* International Art Co. v. FTC, 109 F.2d 393 (7th Cir. 1940); Atlas Aluminum Co., 71 F.T.C. 762 (1967); Wilmington Chemical Corp., 69 F.T.C. 828 (1966).

50 Warren v. LeMay, 142 Ill. App. 3d 550, 491 N.E.2d 464 (1986); State *ex rel.* Spannus v. Mecca Enterprises, Inc., 262 N.W.2d 152 (Minn. 1978).

51 Southwest Sunsites, Inc., 105 F.T.C. 79 (1985), *aff'd*, 785 F.2d 1431 (9th Cir. 1986).

52 State *ex rel.* McLeod v. C&L Corp., 313 S.E.2d 334 (S.C. Ct. App. 1984).

53 Am. Family Publishers, 58 Fed. Reg. 8762, Clearinghouse No. 47,965 (F.T.C. Dkt. 9240, Feb. 17, 1993) (consent order).

54 *But cf.* Lowe v. Surpas Resource Corp., 253 F. Supp. 2d 1209 (D. Kan. 2003) (finding collection agent to be creditor's independent contractor; duty to comply with UDAP statute is not non-delegable).

55 Seavey, Agency § 82 (1975); Restatement (Second) of Agency § 212 (1958).

56 Southwest Sunsites, Inc., 105 F.T.C. 79 (1985), *aff'd*, 785 F.2d 1431 (9th Cir. 1986).

57 Kugler v. Romain, 110 N.J. Super. 470, 266 A.2d 144 (Ch. Div. 1970), *modified on other grounds*, 58 N.J. 522, 279 A.2d 640 (1971).

58 Wilkinson v. Smith, 31 Wash. App. 1, 639 P.2d 768 (1982). *See also* Meyers v. Postal Fin. Co., 287 N.W.2d 614 (Minn. 1979)

for indemnity or contribution against each other under state law,[59] but these claims should not affect their liability to the consumer. A partner is bound by another partner's actions, and is liable to the extent of that other partner, even for treble damages.[60] The Uniform Partnership Act, adopted in one version or another by most states, provides that all partners are liable jointly and severally for all obligations of the partnership unless otherwise agreed by the claimant or provided by law.[61]

6.4 Liability of Officers, Directors, Owners, Parent Companies, Franchisors, Successor Corporations, and an Individual's Estate

6.4.1 Introduction

In cases where neither the principal nor the agent is solvent, neither may be the preferred defendant. In these instances, the company may be little more than an empty shell, with assets and responsibility concentrated in one or a group of principal officers, directors, and/or shareholders; therefore this group is the preferred defendant. Even if a corporation is solvent at the initiation of the lawsuit, it may be prudent to join principal officers or owners in case the corporation is later dissolved. The officers and owners may be jointly and severally liable for disgorgement of all the profits obtained through the deceptive scheme, not just the portion they received.[62]

6.4.2 Liability for Own Actions

Corporate officers, managers, directors, shareholders, owners, and parent companies are liable, just as corporate agents are liable,[63] to the extent that they are directly involved in deceptive or unfair activity.[64] It is not necessary

(listing elements for joint venture, but finance company was not joint venturer).

59 *See, e.g.*, Framingham Union Hospital, Inc. v. Travelers Ins. Co., 744 F. Supp. 29 (D. Mass. 1990).

60 Dollar v. General Motors Corp., 814 F. Supp. 538 (E.D. Tex. 1993); Termeer v. Interstate Motors, Inc., 634 S.W.2d 12 (Tex. App. 1982); *see also* Jurgens v. Abraham, 616 F. Supp. 1381 (D. Mass. 1985); Salisbury v. Chapman Realty, 124 Ill. App. 3d 1057, 465 N.E.2d 127 (1984); Kansallis Fin. Ltd. v. Fern, 421 Mass. 659, 659 N.E.2d 731 (1996) (defendant liable for partner's UDAP violations if committed with apparent authority or to benefit the partnership, but may not be liable for treble damages without showing of culpability or involvement).

61 Uniform Partnership Act § 306 (text available at www.nccusl.org) (note that different rules apply to limited liability partnerships).

62 FTC v. Windward Marketing, Ltd., 1997 U.S. Dist. LEXIS 17114 (N.D. Ga. Sept. 30, 1997); People v. First Fed. Credit Corp., 104 Cal. App. 4th 721, 128 Cal. Rptr. 2d 542 (2002) (principals are jointly and severally liable for civil penalties).

63 *See* § 6.2, *supra*.

64 FTC v. Gem Merchandising Corp., 87 F.3d 466 (8th Cir. 1996) (individual liability under FTC Act); Daniels v. Baritz, 2003 WL 21027238, at *5 (E.D. Pa. Apr. 30, 2003); Knapp v. Americredit Fin. Servs., Inc., 245 F. Supp. 2d 841 (S.D. W. Va. 2003); Cooper v. First Gov't Mortg. and Investors Corp., 206 F. Supp. 2d 33 (D.D.C. 2002); FTC v. SkyBiz.com, Inc., 2001 WL 1673645 (N.D. Okla. Aug. 31, 2001), *aff'd*, 2003 WL 202438 (10th Cir. Jan. 30, 2003) (unpublished, citation limited); Meyer v. Dygert, 156 F. Supp. 2d 1081 (D. Minn. 2001) (liable if participated in, directed, or was negligent in learning of and preventing the fraud); Bolen v. Paragon Plastics, Inc., 754 F. Supp. 221 (D. Mass. 1990); *In re* Fleet, 95 B.R. 319 (E.D. Pa. 1989) (New Jersey law); Frontier Mgmt. Co. v. Balboa Ins. Co., 658 F. Supp. 987 (D. Mass. 1986); Griffin Sys., 5 Trade Reg. Rep. (CCH) ¶ 23,603 (F.T.C. Dkt. 9249 1994) (final decision); Hoang v. Arbess, 2003 WL 1842878 (Colo. App. Apr. 10, 2003); State *ex rel.* Brady v. Preferred Florist Network, 791 A.2d 8 (Del. Ch. 2001); State *ex rel.* Attorney General v. Wyndham Int'l, Inc., 869 So. 2d 592 (Fla. Dist. Ct. App. 2004); Anden v. Litinsky, 472 So. 2d 825 (Fla. Dist. Ct. App. 1985); Fuller v. Pacific Medical Collections, Inc., 891 P.2d 300 (Haw. Ct. App. 1995); Garcia v. Overland Bond & Inv. Co., 668 N.E.2d 199 (Ill. App. Ct. 1996); Stogsdill v. Cragin Federal Bank, 645 N.E.2d 564 (Ill. App. Ct. 1995); Central Collection Unit v. Kossol, 138 Md. App. 338, 771 A.2d 501 (2001); Standard Register Co. v. Bolton-Emerson, Inc., 38 Mass. App. Ct. 545, 649 N.E.2d 791 (1995); State by Humphrey v. Alpine Air Products, Inc., 490 N.W.2d 888 (Minn. Ct. App. 1992); State *ex rel.* Ashcroft v. Marketing Unlimited, 613 S.W.2d 440 (Mo. Ct. App. 1981); Polonetsky v. Better Homes Depot, Inc., 97 N.Y.2d 46, 760 N.E.2d 1274 (2001) (participation or knowledge makes officer or director liable); *In re* Spitzer v. All-Pro Telemarketing Assocs. Corp., 195 Misc. 2d 245, 758 N.Y.S.2d 775 (Sup. Ct. 2003); Meachum v. Outdoor World Corp., 652 N.Y.S.2d 749 (App. Div. 1997); People v. Empyre Inground Pools, 642 N.Y.S.2d 344 (App. Div. 1996) (corporate veil may be pierced to hold corporate officers personally liable for tortious conduct or knowing participation in fraudulent acts); People v. Concert Connection, Ltd., 629 N.Y.S.2d 254 (App. Div. 1995) (president of company liable for violations of which he was aware); People v. Apple Health & Sports Clubs, Ltd., Inc., 206 A.D.2d 266, 613 N.Y.S.2d 868 (1994) (company president's participation in UDAP violations creates liability); Allen v. Roberts Constr. Co., 532 S.E.2d 534 (N.C. App. 2000) (affirming UDAP judgment against company owner who concealed material facts and falsely represented that house had been constructed in accord with plans); Stultz v. Artistic Pools, Inc., 2001 Ohio App. LEXIS 4561 (Oct. 10, 2001); Inserra v. J.E.M. Building Corp., 2000 Ohio App. LEXIS 5447 (Nov. 22, 2000); Cremeans v. Robbins, 2000 Ohio App. LEXIS 2753 (June 12, 2000); Arales v. Furs by Weiss, Inc., 1999 Ohio App. LEXIS 125 (Jan. 21, 1999); State *ex rel.* Fisher v. Warren Star Theater, 84 Ohio App. 3d 435, 616 N.E.2d 1192 (1992); Gayer v. Ohio Bus. Trading Ass'n, 1988 Ohio App. LEXIS 2684 (Ohio Ct. App. July 7, 1988); Moy v. Schreiber Deed Security Co., 535 A.2d 1168 (Pa. Super. Ct. 1988); State *ex rel.* McLeod v. C&L Corp., 313 S.E.2d 334 (S.C. Ct. App. 1984) (controlling person liable where formulates and directs policy); Brungard v. Caprice Records, Inc., 608 S.W.2d 585 (Tenn. 1980); Kingston v. Helm, 82 S.W.3d 755 (Tex. App. 2002); Barclay v. Johnson, 686

for the plaintiff to meet the standards for piercing the corporate veil to establish the UDAP liability of these defendants for their own acts.[65]

Courts take a flexible view of what type of participation is sufficient to hold an officer liable under a UDAP statute.[66] Evidence indicating that an officer, director, or shareholder directed, participated in, or facilitated the challenged deceptive practice should be enough to join that individual in the UDAP action.[67] Officers do not need to make deceptive representations, as long as they knowingly entered into the deceptive scheme,[68] established the company policy[69] or approved of a UDAP violation,[70] such as approving an advertising brochure.[71] An officer in a position to control a company's activities is liable for deceptive practices, particularly if the conduct continues after the officer becomes aware of it.[72] A corporate officer's negligence in learning of

S.W.2d 334 (Tex. App. 1985); Norwood Builders, Inc. v. Toler, 609 S.W.2d 861 (Tex. Civ. App. 1981); Olson v. ML&D Builders, Inc., 1999 Wash. App. LEXIS 14 (Jan. 7, 1999). *See also* Texas v. American Blastfax, Inc., 164 F. Supp. 2d 892 (W.D. Tex. 2001) (decided under Telephone Consumer Protection Act). *Cf.* State *ex rel.* McLeod v. VID Enterprises, Inc., 335 S.E.2d 243 (S.C. Ct. App. 1985) (no liability for those who did not control or help formulate the scheme).

65 Meyer v. Dygert, 156 F. Supp. 2d 1081 (D. Minn. 2001); Central Collection Unit v. Kossol, 138 Md. App. 338, 771 A.2d 501 (2001); Inserra v. J.E.M. Building Corp., 2000 Ohio App. LEXIS 5447 (Nov. 22, 2000); Olson v. ML&D Builders, Inc., 1999 Wash. App. LEXIS 14 (Jan. 7, 1999) (corporate form can be disregarded when corporation used it to violate or evade a duty to another; even without piercing corporate veil, individual is liable if participated in corporation's UDAP violation). *But see* Unit Owners Ass'n v. Miller, 677 A.2d 138 (N.H. 1996) (New Hampshire UDAP plaintiff must not merely show participation by officer, but must pierce corporate veil); Davila v. Calo, 1985 Ohio App. LEXIS 9751 (Dec. 19, 1985) (Ohio UDAP statute does not cover corporate officers acting in their official capacity unless corporate veil is pierced).

66 *See* Petri v. Gatlin, 997 F. Supp. 956 (N.D. Ill. 1997).

67 DeLeon v. Beneficial Constr. Co., 998 F. Supp. 859 (N.D. Ill. 1998); Moore v. Fidelity Fin. Servs., Inc., 949 F. Supp. 673 (N.D. Ill. 1997) (parent corporation liable if part of joint scheme with subsidiary, even if only subsidiary dealt with consumer); FTC v. U.S. Sales Corp., 785 F. Supp. 737 (N.D. Ill. 1992); FTC v. Patriot Alcohol Testers, 798 F. Supp. 851 (D. Mass. 1992); *In re* Fleet, 95 B.R. 319 (E.D. Pa. 1989) (New Jersey law); Griffin Sys., 5 Trade Reg. Rep. (CCH) ¶ 23,603 (F.T.C. Dkt. 9249 1994) (final decision); Garcia v. Overland Bond & Inv. Co., 668 N.E.2d 199 (Ill. App. Ct. 1996); T-UP, Inc. v. Consumer Protection Div., 801 A.2d 173 (Md. App. 2002); State v. Keaton Model Mgmt., Inc., 1996 Minn. App. LEXIS 382 (Apr. 2, 1996) (unpublished, non-precedential); Polonetsky v. Better Homes Depot, 97 N.Y.2d 46, 760 N.E.2d 1274 (2001); Kidd v. Delta Funding Corp., 2000 N.Y. Misc. LEXIS 29 (Sup. Ct. Feb. 22, 2000); State *ex rel.* Fisher v. Am. Courts, Inc., 96 Ohio App. 3d 297 (1994) (allegation that corporate president specifically directed and ratified wrongful acts is sufficient to state UDAP claim); State *ex rel.* Fisher v. Harper, 83 Ohio App. 3d 754, 615 N.E.2d 733 (1993); Gayer v. Ohio Bus. Trading Ass'n, 1988 Ohio App. LEXIS 2684 (Ohio Ct. App. July 7, 1988); Fate v. Dick Callendar Buick, 1986 Ohio App. LEXIS 6878 (May 23, 1986) (owner and president of automobile dealership is covered by Ohio UDAP statute even though he did not deal directly with the consumer); Moy v. Schreiber Deed Security Co., 535 A.2d 1168 (Pa. Super. Ct. 1988); Commonwealth of Pennsylvania v. Diversified Chemicals, Inc., Clearinghouse No. 50,440 (Pa. C.P. Oct. 6, 1994); Brandon v. Winnett, 1995 Tenn. App. LEXIS 508 (Tenn. Ct. App. July 28, 1995) (company officer who made misrepresentations is liable); Plowman v. Bagnal, 450 S.E.2d 36 (S.C. 1994) (directors and officers are liable if they personally commit, participate in, direct or authorize UDAP violations; simply being in control is not enough); State *ex rel.* Medlock v. Nest Egg Society Today, Inc., 348 S.E.2d 381 (S.C. Ct. App. 1986); State *ex rel.* McLeod v. C&L Corp., 313 S.E.2d 334 (S.C. Ct. App. 1984); Vermont v. Gene Rosenberg, Clearinghouse No. 50,445 (Vt. Super. Ct. Apr. 26, 1995) (defendants hired sales staff and arranged for advertisements); State v. WWJ Corp., 941 P.2d 717 (Wash. Ct. App. 1997) (participation in or knowledge of wrongful conduct establishes liability). *But see* Saveall v. Adams, 36 Mass. App. 349, 631 N.E.2d 561 (1994) (allegations that company owner/officers had signed the contract documents and had failed to correct problems were insufficient to state UDAP claim against them); Davila v. Calo, 1985 Ohio App. LEXIS 9751 (Dec. 19, 1985) (Ohio UDAP statute does not cover corporate officers acting in their official capacity, unless corporate veil is pierced). *But cf.* Sunset Harbour North Condo. Ass'n v. Bedzow, 842 So. 2d 200 (Fla. Dist. Ct. App. 2003) (director and vice president of corporation not liable for acts in which she did not participate and from which she derived no special benefit); Rowe v. Hyatt, 468 S.E.2d 649 (S.C. 1996) (directed verdict appropriate if no evidence that person committed, participated in, directed or authorized alleged misrepresentation; mere status is insufficient).

68 People v. First Fed. Credit Corp., 104 Cal. App. 4th 721, 128 Cal. Rptr. 2d 542 (2002) (civil penalties properly imposed on principal who was in a position of control and had knowledge yet permitted unlawful activities to continue); Schmidt Enterprises, Inc. v. State, 170 Ind. Ct. App. 628, 354 N.E.2d 247 (1976); People *ex rel.* Spitzer v. Telehublink Corp., 301 A.D.2d 1006, 756 N.Y.S.2d 285 (2003) (knowledge of deceptive or illegal activities will make officer liable); People v. Apple Health & Sports Clubs, Ltd., Inc., 206 A.D.2d 266, 613 N.Y.S.2d 868 (1994) (corporate officer's knowledge and participation establish liability).

69 *In re* Fleet, 95 B.R. 319 (E.D. Pa. 1989) (New Jersey law); Moy v. Schreiber Deed Security Co., 535 A.2d 1168 (Pa. Super. Ct. 1988); Mother & Unborn Care v. State, 749 S.W.2d 533 (Tex. App. 1988). *See also* State *ex rel.* Miller v. Santa Rosa Sales & Marketing, Inc., 475 N.W.2d 210 (Iowa 1991).

70 Garcia v. Overland Bond & Inv. Co., 668 N.E.2d 199 (Ill. App. Ct. 1996); Grayson v. Nordic Constr. Co., 92 Wash. 2d 548, 599 P.2d 1271 (1979); State v. Ralph Williams' N.W. Chrysler Plymouth, Inc., 87 Wash. 2d 298, 553 P.2d 423 (1976); Olson v. ML&D Builders, Inc., 1999 Wash. App. LEXIS 14 (Jan. 7, 1999) (corporate form can be disregarded when corporation used it to violate or evade a duty to another; even without piercing corporate veil, individual is liable if participated in corporation's UDAP violation).

71 Petri v. Gatlin, 997 F. Supp. 956 (N.D. Ill. 1997); Garcia v. Overland Bond & Inv. Co., 668 N.E.2d 199 (Ill. App. Ct. 1996); Grayson v. Nordic Constr. Co., 92 Wash. 2d 548, 599 P.2d 1271 (1979).

72 FTC v. Windward Marketing, Ltd., 1997 U.S. Dist. LEXIS 17114 (N.D. Ga. Sept. 30, 1997); *In re* Fleet, 95 B.R. 319 (E.D. Pa. 1989) (New Jersey law); People v. Conway, 42 Cal. App. 3d 875, 117 Cal. Rptr. 251 (1974); Nader v. Citron, 372 Mass. 96,

and preventing the fraudulent conduct may be sufficient to create liability.[73]

An officer or director is personally liable if he or she personally derives benefits from and is central to the merchandising philosophy[74] or recruited the manager responsible for the deceptive practices and discussed the manager's sales presentation.[75] Officers have also been found liable under a UDAP statute if they had a duty to monitor salesmen and the deceptive practices permeated the sales organization.[76] The owner of a business may be held liable under a UDAP theory for failing to take reasonable steps to assure that all employees comply with UDAP regulations.[77]

There is no requirement that the officer had sole control of the scheme. All that needs to be shown is that the officer in some way participated with others in formulating, directing or controlling policy.[78] Knowledge or participation makes the officer liable even if he or she gains nothing personally from the deception.[79]

Under the FTC Act, a corporate officer can be held liable if the corporation committed misrepresentations or omissions of a kind usually relied on by reasonably prudent persons and the officer either participated directly in the acts or had authority to control them.[80] An individual's active involvement in the business or in corporate policy-making are indicators of this authority.[81] Corporate officers of a small closely-held corporation are presumed to control it.[82] A corporate officer can not avoid penalties for the corporation's violations by removing himself from its day-to-day operations and washing his hands of responsibility.[83] Reckless indifference to the truth or falsity of advertising claims is sufficient to establish personal liability.[84] An officer's knowledge of the deceptive nature of a scheme can be inferred from outlandish profitability claims that the officer makes to potential investors.[85] There is no requirement that the officer had sole control of the scheme. All that needs to be shown is that the officer in some way participated with

360 N.E.2d 870 (1977). *See also* People v. Toomey, 157 Cal. App. 3d 1, 203 Cal. Rptr. 642 (1984); State v. Keaton Model Mgmt., Inc., 1996 Minn. App. LEXIS 382 (Apr. 2, 1996) (unpublished, non-precedential) (knowledge of company's operations, material assistance in form of loans and contributions, and close family relationship with president can make officer liable); Hyland v. Aquarian Age 2000, Inc., 148 N.J. Super. 186, 372 A.2d 320 (Ch. Div. 1977); People by Spitzer v. Telehublink, 756 N.Y.S.2d 285 (App. Div. 2003) (stating that officers' and directors' participation in, or knowledge of, fraudulent acts creates liability); People by Abrams v. Am. Motor Club, Inc., 179 A.D.2d 277, 852 N.Y.S.2d 688 (1992); People v. 21st Century Leisure Spa, 153 Misc. 2d 938, 583 N.Y.S.2d 726 (Sup. Ct. 1991); Brown v. Wonderful World Publishing Co., No. 74CV-12-4741, Clearinghouse No. 27,055 (C.P. Franklin Cty., Ohio July 28, 1976); State *ex rel.* Medlock v. Nest Egg Society Today, Inc., 348 S.E.2d 381 (S.C. Ct. App. 1986).

73 Meyer v. Dygert, 156 F. Supp. 2d 1081 (D. Minn. 2001).

74 *In re* Fleet, 95 B.R. 319 (E.D. Pa. 1989) (New Jersey law); State *ex rel.* Sanborn v. Koscot Interplanetary, Inc., 212 Kan. 668, 512 P.2d 416 (1973); State *ex rel.* Fisher v. Harper, 83 Ohio App. 3d 754, 615 N.E.2d 733 (1993) (one-quarter owner of pyramid sales company who received share of company's earnings and made sales presentations on videotape held liable). *See also* People v. Toomey, 157 Cal. App. 3d 1, 203 Cal. Rptr. 642 (1984); Dare to Be Great, Inc. v. Commonwealth, 511 S.W.2d 224 (Ky. 1974); Kugler v. Koscot Interplanetary, Inc., 120 N.J. Super. 216, 293 A.2d 682 (Ch. Div. 1972); State *ex rel.* McLeod v. Whiteside, Clearinghouse No. 38,907 (S.C. C.P. July 16, 1981). *But see* State *ex rel.* Webster v. Eisenbeis, 775 S.W.2d 276 (Mo. Ct. App. 1989).

75 Commonwealth v. Programmed Learning Sys., Inc., Clearinghouse No. 26,019 (Pa. C.P. Allegheny Cty. 1975).

76 *In re* Fleet, 95 B.R. 319 (E.D. Pa. 1989) (New Jersey law); State *ex rel.* Miller v. Santa Rosa Sales & Marketing, Inc., 475 N.W.2d 210 (Iowa 1991); Commonwealth v. Gold Bond Industries, Inc., Clearinghouse No. 26,028 (Pa. C.P. Allegheny Cty. 1972).

77 Fate v. Dick Callendar Buick, 1986 Ohio App. LEXIS 6878 (May 23, 1986).

78 Griffin Sys., 5 Trade Reg. Rep. (CCH) ¶ 23,603 (F.T.C. Dkt. 9249 1994) (final decision).

79 Polonetsky v. Better Homes Depot, Inc., 97 N.Y.2d 46, 760 N.E.2d 1274 (2001). *See also* FTC v. Verity Int'l, Ltd., 194 F. Supp. 2d 270 (S.D.N.Y. 2002) (individual who directed company's deceptive acts is jointly and severally liable for full amount of consumer redress, not just the amount he actually received).

80 FTC v. Affordable Media, 179 F.3d 1228 (9th Cir. 1999), *subsequent appeal*, 2001 WL 583100 (9th Cir. May 30, 2001) (unpublished, citation limited) (affirming summary judgment ordering individuals to make restitution); FTC v. Publishing Clearing House, Inc., 104 F.3d 1168 (9th Cir. 1996); FTC v. World Media Brokers, Inc., 2004 WL 432475 (N.D. Ill. Mar. 2, 2004); FTC v. Consumer Alliance, Inc., 2003 WL 22287364 (N.D. Ill. Sept. 30, 2003); FTC v. Medicor, 217 F. Supp. 2d 1048 (C.D. Cal. 2002); FTC v. SkyBiz.com, Inc., 2001 WL 1673649 (N.D. Okla. Aug. 2, 2001) (authority to sign documents on company's behalf demonstrates control), *aff'd*, 2003 WL 202438 (10th Cir. Jan. 30, 2003) (unpublished, citation limited); FTC v. Crescent Publishing Group, 129 F. Supp. 2d 311 (S.D.N.Y. 2001).

81 FTC v. Amy Travel Service, Inc., 875 F.2d 564 (7th Cir. 1989).

82 FTC v. Windward Marketing, Ltd., 1997 U.S. Dist. LEXIS 17114 (N.D. Ga. Sept. 30, 1997).

83 FTC v. Kuykendall, 312 F.3d 1329 (10th Cir. 2002).

84 FTC v. Affordable Media, 179 F.3d 1228 (9th Cir. 1999) (for restitution order, FTC need only show officer's actual knowledge, recklessness as to the truth or falsity of representations, or awareness of a high probability of fraud and intentional avoidance of the truth), *subsequent appeal*, 2001 WL 583100 (9th Cir. May 30, 2001) (unpublished, citation limited) (affirming summary judgment ordering individuals to make restitution where they were recklessly indifferent to falsity of representations); FTC v. Pantron I Corp., 33 F.3d 1088 (9th Cir. 1994) (FTC Act); FTC v. Amy Travel Service, Inc., 875 F.2d 564 (7th Cir. 1989); FTC v. SkyBiz.com, Inc., 2001 WL 1673645 (N.D. Okla. Aug. 31, 2001) (preliminary injunction) (same as *Affordable Media*), *aff'd*, 2003 WL 202438 (10th Cir. Jan. 30, 2002) (unpublished, citation limited); FTC v. Medicor, 217 F. Supp. 2d 1048 (C.D. Cal. 2002).

85 FTC v. Affordable Media, 179 F.3d 1228 (9th Cir. 1999), *subsequent appeal*, 2001 WL 583100 (9th Cir. May 30, 2001) (unpublished, citation limited) (affirming summary judgment requiring individuals to make restitution).

others in formulating, directing, or controlling policy.[86] State courts may be willing to follow this FTC law in injunctive suits by state attorneys general.[87]

6.4.3 Piercing the Corporate Veil and Related Theories

Consumer litigants may also wish to join major shareholders of a corporation in an action if the corporation engaged in the UDAP violation is a mere shell, even if the shareholders were not directly involved in the deception. For the same reasons, litigants may also wish to join parent corporations. If these individuals or entities participated in the UDAP violations, it is not necessary to pierce the corporate veil to hold them liable.[88] But if they did not participate in the deceptive acts, they can still be held liable if the corporate veil can be pierced.[89]

The extent to which consumers will be able to pierce the corporate veil to recover against shareholders or parent corporations will be determined by a state's own statutory and judicially created law in this developing area. Inadequate capitalization, use of the corporate form to avoid obligations, and the "alter ego" doctrine,[90] where shareholders do not separate their affairs from those of the corporation, are legal theories successfully used in some jurisdictions.[91] Subpoenaing corporate documents such as bank records and minutes of board meetings may help establish these facts.

In Illinois, the corporate veil may be pierced if there is such unity of interest and ownership that the separate personalities of the corporation and the individual no longer exist, and adherence to the fiction of a separate corporate existence would, in the circumstances, sanction a fraud, promote injustice, or promote inequitable consequences.[92] Factors include: (1) inadequate capitalization; (2) failure to issue stock; (3) failure to observe corporate formalities; (4) payment of dividends; (5) the insolvency of the corporation; (6) whether other corporate officers or directors are functioning; (7) absence of corporate records; (8) whether the corporation is a mere facade for the operation of dominant stockholders.[93] Massachusetts includes many of the same factors in its list.[94] Not all factors need be present.[95]

An Ohio court held that a corporate entity could be disregarded where it was an implement for avoiding the UDAP statute's legislative purpose and where to honor the corporate entity would defeat public convenience, justify a wrong, or protect a fraud.[96] Another Ohio court held that the president and sole shareholder of a home improvement company could be personally liable for UDAP violations where he founded the company, did a substantial amount of the work, and approved the consumers' contract.[97] The court stated that the plaintiff must prove: (1) that those to be held liable exercised such complete control over the corporation that it did not have a separate mind, will, or existence of its own; (2) that they exercised this control in such a manner as to commit fraud or an illegal act against the plaintiff; and (3) that the plaintiff suffered injury or unjust loss as a result of such control and wrong.[98]

A Kentucky court indicates it will disregard the corporate entity only where the individual to be held personally liable actively participated in the scheme, or knew about it and did nothing.[99] But an Indiana court disregarded the corporate

---

86 Griffin Sys., 5 Trade Reg. Rep. (CCH) ¶ 23,603 (F.T.C. Dkt. 9249 1994) (final decision).

87 Plowman v. Bagnal, 450 S.E.2d 36, 38 (S.C. 1994).

88 Central Collection Unit v. Kossol, 138 Md. App. 338, 771 A.2d 501 (2001).

89 *See* Meyer v. Holley, 537 U.S. 280, 123 S. Ct. 824, 154 L. Ed. 2d 753 (2003); United States v. Bestfoods, 524 U.S. 51 (1998).

90 Petty v. Ferguson, 601 S.W.2d 782 (Tex. Civ. App. 1980). *Accord In re* Fleet, 95 B.R. 319 (E.D. Pa. 1989) (New Jersey law); Elite Towing, Inc. v. Hernandez, 2001 Tex. App. LEXIS 1971 (Mar. 28, 2001) (family members and a related corporation). *But see In re* Matthes, 23 B.R. 162 (Bankr. S.D. Tex. 1982) (no evidence that corporate form was mere conduit for violation or important public policy); Roy E. Thomas Constr. Co. v. Arbs, 692 S.W.2d 926 (Tex. App. 1985).

91 Lattin on Corporations § 14 *et seq.* (1971); Commonwealth of Pennsylvania Diversified Chemicals, Inc., Clearinghouse No. 50,440 (Pa. C.P. Oct. 6, 1994). *See also* Perry v. Household Retail Servs., Inc., 953 F. Supp. 1378 (M.D. Ala. 1996); Fravel v. Commonwealth, Clearinghouse No. 49,161 (E.D. Va. Jan. 8, 1993); *In re* Fleet, 95 B.R. 319 (E.D. Pa. 1989) (New Jersey law); Kelley v. Sclater (*In re* Slater), 40 B.R. 594 (E.D. Mich. 1984) (health spa owner); State *ex rel.* McLeod v. Whiteside, Clearinghouse No. 38,907 (S.C. C.P. July 16, 1981) (shareholders liable where corporate structure was mere umbrella for deceptive conduct and principals behaved as if corporation did not exist); Nelson v. Schanzer, 788 S.W.2d 81 (Tex. App. 1990).

92 Falcon Assocs., Inc. v. Cox, 699 N.E.2d 203 (Ill. App. Ct. 1998) (piercing corporate veil in UDAP case), *appeal denied*, 182 Ill. 2d 549, 707 N.E.2d 1239 (1999). *See also* Societa Bario E Derivati v. Kaystone Chem., Inc., 1998 U.S. Dist. LEXIS 23066 (D. Conn. Apr. 15, 1998) (similar test).

93 *Id.*

94 George Hyman Constr. Co. v. Gateman, 16 F. Supp. 2d 129 (D. Mass. 1998). *See also* Carte Blanche Pte., Ltd. v. Diners Club Int'l, Inc., 2 F.3d 24 (2d Cir. 1993) (listing factors for piercing veil between related corporations).

95 William Passalacqua Builders, Inc. v. Resnick Developers S., Inc., 933 F.2d 131, 139 (2d Cir. 1991).

96 Quality Carpet Co. v. Brown, 6 Ohio Op. 3d 185 (C.P. Franklin Cty. 1977).

97 Janos v. Murduck, 109 Ohio App. 3d 583, 672 N.E.2d 1021 (1996). *See also* Gale v. Ficke, 2001 Ohio App. LEXIS 1877 (Apr. 26, 2001) (individuals who controlled small family-run corporation and who received payments in their personal capacities are liable). *But cf.* Cremeans v. Robbins, 2000 Ohio App. LEXIS 2753 (June 12, 2000) (shareholder not liable without evidence of control).

98 *Accord* Becker v. Graber Builders, Inc., 149 N.C. App. 787, 561 S.E.2d 905 (2002).

99 Commonwealth *ex rel.* Beshear v. ABC Pest Control, Inc., 621 S.W.2d 705 (Ky. Ct. App. 1981). *Accord* People by Koppell v. Empyre Inground Pools Inc., 642 N.Y.S.2d 344 (App. Div. 1996) (corporate veil may be pierced where corporate officers

entity where there was deception, misrepresentation and injustice, and also on the alternative ground that the individual and entity were really one.[100]

A related situation is where a corporation most directly involved in the fraud has no assets, but where a related corporation is collectable. The collectable corporation may be a parent or affiliated by common directors, shareholders or managers. Some courts use a "piercing the corporate veil analysis" to reach the parent or affiliated corporation. Other courts use a "corporate disregard" theory where the representatives of one corporation exercise pervasive control of another corporation. Corporate entities can also be disregarded where there is a confused intermingling of activity of two or more corporations with substantial disregard of the separate nature of the corporate entities or when there is serious ambiguity as to the capacity in which the two corporations are acting.[101] Apparent, and not just actual intermingling, is sufficient to disregard the corporate structure, at least where actions by the collectable corporation have led consumers to believe the other corporation was merely a division of the collectable corporation, not a separate corporation.[102]

Where the corporate veil can not be pierced for a UDAP suit, consumers should investigate whether the liability sections of other consumer protection statutes cast a wider net. A state licensing law may, for example, make the party who holds the license broadly liable for deceptive acts.

6.4.4 Liability of Franchisors

Consumers may also find franchisees to be insolvent, with the franchisor being the deep pocket. Liability has been asserted where the franchisor failed to terminate a financially troubled franchisee which later went out of business without honoring consumer contracts, particularly where franchisor advertising implied financial solvency of its franchisees.[103]

Another approach is to find an actual or apparent agency relationship between the franchisor and franchisee.[104] Special consideration should be paid to advertising, brochures, or other claims made by the franchisor.

A franchisor is also liable if it instructed its franchisees to commit deceptive practices, whether or not an agency relationship is shown.[105] Evidence that the franchisor's operations managers visited franchises periodically to enforce the franchisor's instructions and practices demonstrate its control over the franchise's practices.[106] Since the franchisor itself met the statutory definition of a merchant, it was liable for the harm to consumers caused by these practices.[107]

6.4.5 Liability of Other Closely-Related Corporations

Closely related corporations other than parent companies and franchisors may also be liable for another company's UDAP violations. For example, where a company had the same two shareholders as another company, performed accounting and paperwork functions for the other company, and owned the real property in which the other company operated, it was liable for the other's UDAP violations.[108] This approach is particularly important where a fraudulent operator attempts to shield assets such as real estate by placing them in the name of a separate corporation. The theory that closely connected corporations can be held liable for each others' wrongs arises more commonly between seller and financer and is discussed more fully in § 6.6.5.4, *infra*.

6.4.6 Liability of Successor Corporations

A corporation that purchases the assets of another corporation is liable for the debts or liabilities of the transferor corporation if:

- There is an express agreement of assumption;
- The transaction amounts to a consolidation or merger of the buyer and seller corporations;
- The purchaser is merely a continuation of the seller;[109] or

---

acted tortiously or knowingly participated in fraud). *See also* Saveall v. Adams, 36 Mass. App. 349, 631 N.E.2d 561 (1994) (allegations that company owner/officers had signed the contract documents and had failed to correct problems were insufficient to pierce the corporate veil).

100 State v. McKinney, 508 N.E.2d 1319 (Ind. Ct. App. 1987).

101 *See* My Bread Baking Co. v. Cumberland Farms Co., 353 Mass. 614, 233 N.E.2d 748 (1968).

102 *Id.* (upholding judgment where evidence allowed jury to infer that corporation was liable for acts of related corporation).

103 *See* Cullen v. BMW of N. Am., Inc., 691 F.2d 1097 (2d Cir. 1982); Spartan Pools v. Royal, 386 So. 2d 421 (Ala. 1980).

104 *See* State v. Cottman Transmissions Sys., Inc., 86 Md. App. 714, 587 A.2d 1190 (1991) (legal standard discussed; agency relationship not shown but court cites cases where franchisees were held to be franchisor's agents).

105 State v. Cottman Transmissions Sys., Inc., 86 Md. App. 714, 587 A.2d 1190 (1991).

106 *Id.*

107 *Id.*

108 People v. Apple Health & Sports Clubs, Ltd., Inc., 206 A.D.2d 266, 613 N.Y.S.2d 868 (1994). *See also* Freeman v. Hubco Leasing, Inc., 253 Ga. 698, 324 S.E.2d 462 (1985) (estoppel prevents leasing company from accelerating balance where related company, owned by same parties, operating from the same location, and run by same officers, had breached warranty); Elite Towing, Inc. v. Hernandez, 2001 Tex. App. LEXIS 1971 (Mar. 28, 2001) (applying alter ego doctrine to impose liability upon related corporation owned by family member).

109 Green v. USA Energy Consultants, 1986 Ohio App. LEXIS 8309 (Ohio Ct. App. 1986) (successor corporation to which the original company has transferred all its assets and which is a mere continuation or reincarnation of the original company is liable for the original company's violations).

• The transaction is for the fraudulent purpose of escaping liability for the seller's obligations.[110]

A New Jersey appellate court has identified four factors for determining whether the purchaser corporation is liable for the seller's debts under the second and third of these tests. The transaction amounts to a *de facto* merger or a mere continuation of the seller's business if there is: (1) continuity of management, personnel, physical location, assets, and general business operations; (2) a cessation of ordinary business and dissolution of the predecessor as soon as practically and legally possible; (3) assumption by the successor of the liabilities ordinarily necessary for the uninterrupted continuation of the business of the predecessor; and (4) continuity of ownership/shareholders.[111]

Not all of the factors need be present for a *de facto* merger or continuation to have occurred, and a number of courts have held a purchasing corporation responsible for the seller's liabilities in a cash-for-assets transaction where there was no continuity of ownership.[112] Even if no *de facto* merger or continuation of business can be found, the successor corporation will be liable if it expressly or impliedly agrees to assume the transferor's debts and liabilities; if some of the elements of a purchaser in good faith are absent; or if the transaction is entered into fraudulently in order to escape responsibility for the seller's debts and liabilities.[113]

Advocates should also check their state's Bulk Sales Law in these situations. In states that have adopted Article 6 of the Uniform Commercial Code (UCC),[114] a bulk transfer is ineffective unless advance notice is sent to the transferor's known creditors, including those with disputed claims, as listed by the transferor. Another possibility is the state's fraudulent conveyance law, which may apply if the assets of the business were transferred to a straw party such as a relative or a related corporation. If the transfer is found to be fraudulent, the consumer can collect from those assets. Assets transferred in this manner may also be reachable under doctrines of unjust enrichment or constructive trust.[115]

6.4.7 Survival of Action After Defendant's Death

When a UDAP defendant dies during the pendency of a UDAP case, the state's general statute about survival of actions should be consulted. Even where the survival statute does not appear to apply to the UDAP claim, however, the court may hold that the claim survives because of the remedial purposes of the UDAP statute and the importance of preventing injustices.[116]

If the claim survives, the defendant's estate bears the burden of paying the judgment in the UDAP action. The deceased UDAP defendant's estate can be substituted as a party defendant.[117] The defendant's executor and distributee may also be substituted as a party, and be made liable to the extent of the assets in the estate.[118]

6.5 Those Aiding or Furnishing Means for Deception; Civil Conspiracy and Joint Enterprise

6.5.1 Types of Parties Who May Be Liable

A consumer litigant is not limited in a UDAP action to seeking damages from the company, its agents, officers, owners or related corporations. Third parties that furnish the means for or aid in the deception or join in a conspiracy[119] can also be held liable.

An important category of third parties who can be liable are creditors who are either related to or purchase consumer credit contracts from a seller. These creditors may be liable

110 Reavley v. Toyota Motor Sales US Corp., 2001 U.S. Dist. LEXIS 1555 (N.D. Ill. Feb. 14, 2001); Becker v. Graber Builders, Inc., 149 N.C. App. 787, 561 S.E.2d 905 (2002). *But cf.* Kondracky v. Crystal Restoration, Inc., 791 A.2d 482 (R.I. 2002) (successor corporation not liable where no assets were ever transferred).

111 Woodrick v. Jack J. Burke Real Estate, 306 N.J. Super. 61, 703 A.2d 306 (App. Div. 1997). *Accord* Reavley v. Toyota Motor Sales US Corp., 2001 U.S. Dist. LEXIS 1555 (N.D. Ill. Feb. 14, 2001) (finding factors not present).

112 *See* Woodrick v. Jack J. Burke Real Estate, 306 N.J. Super. 61, 703 A.2d 306 (App. Div. 1997) and cases cited therein.

113 Woodrick v. Jack J. Burke Real Estate, 306 N.J. Super. 61, 703 A.2d 306 (App. Div. 1997) (also identifying special rule for product liability cases); Green v. USA Energy Consultants, 1986 Ohio App. LEXIS 8309 (Ohio Ct. App. 1986).

114 The National Conference of Commissioners on Uniform State Law (NCCUSL) is currently recommending that the original version of Article 6 either be repealed or replaced by a revised version, and many states have taken one of these options. Details are available on NCCUSL's website, www.nccusl.org.

115 *See* FTC v. Think Achievement Corp., 144 F. Supp. 2d 1013 (N.D. Ind. 2000), *aff'd in part, rev'd in part on other grounds*, 312 F.3d 259 (7th Cir. 2002) (innocent party may be ordered to disgorge profits if they were illegally obtained and the innocent party has no legitimate claim to them). *But cf.* McGregor v. Chierico, 206 F.3d 1378 (11th Cir. 2000) (FTC can not get contempt order against party who did not violate decree, even as means of reaching assets held jointly with party who did violate it).

116 State v. Therrien, 633 A.2d 272 (Vt. 1993) (suit by attorney general to force developer to correct water and sewer problems survives developer's death).

117 *Id.*

118 *Id.*

119 Camp, Dresser & McKee, Inc. v. Steimle & Assocs., Inc., 652 So. 2d 44 (La. Ct. App. 1995); Strahan v. State *ex rel.* Dep't of Agriculture & Forestry, 645 So. 2d 1162 (La. App. 1994); Brooks v. Creech, 2003 WL 174805 (Tenn. App. Jan. 28, 2003) (misrepresentations of conspirator can be attributed to conspiracy partner, so defendant is liable on UDAP and fraud claims even though she never dealt directly with plaintiff).

to the consumer under two general theories. One is that they have derivative liability for the acts of their assignor or related seller because of the operation of the FTC Holder Rule or a related legal doctrine. This liability is discussed at §§ 6.6 and 6.7, *infra*.

In addition, creditors and other third parties can be directly liable if they participate with the seller or originating lender in the deceptive scheme.[120] Such direct liability for their actions in concert with the other party is discussed in this section.

Examples of third parties that can be liable for deceptive schemes conducted largely by others are:

- Wholesalers or manufacturers that aid deceptive retail sales by turning back odometers, concealing a vehicle's collision history, preticketing items with excessive prices that can be deceptively reduced by the retailer, or creating deceptive warranties;[121]
- Companies that create deceptive sales promotions and license them to auto dealers or other sellers, or that train sellers' sales staff;[122]
- The seller's attorney;[123]
- Distributors of standard form contracts;[124]
- Insurance agents and insurance companies;
- Those who write telemarketers' scripts;[125]
- Debt collectors who control or routinely participate in deceptive schemes with the seller.
- Companies that develop computer software to assist merchants to deceive consumers, such as a program that fictitiously represented car loans as advantageous over cash purchases.[126]
- Companies that help fraudulent sellers place charges on the consumer's credit card, bank account, or telephone bill.[127]

A $30 million UDAP settlement is a particularly vivid example of the potential payback when a consumer's attorney imaginatively and aggressively seeks recovery from *all* those who aid and abet a deceptive scheme.[128] A corporation had convinced numerous consumers that it would help them win lucrative oil and gas concessions from the federal government, and that a portion of their investment would go to purchase an annuity which would protect the investors from risk. The whole scheme was fraudulent, but by the time the FTC sought restitution, the corporate assets had been looted by the principals.

120 Vendall Marketing Corp. v. State, Clearinghouse No. 50,414 (D. Or. 1993) (refusing to allow a lender to enforce notes where the lender had an intimate knowledge of a related seller's operation); Smith v. Navistar Int'l Transp. Corp., 714 F. Supp. 303 (N.D. Ill. 1989) (buyer who obtains financing through an entity closely connected to the seller may use the seller's breach of its duties to the buyer as a defense to liability under the financing instrument); Vasquez v. Superior Court (Karp), 4 Cal. 3d 800, 484 P.2d 964, 94 Cal. Rptr. 796 (1977); King v. Central Bank, 135 Cal. Rptr. 771, 558 P.2d 857 (1977); Connor v. Great W. Sav. & L. Ass'n, 73 Cal. Rptr. 369, 447 P.2d 609 (1968); Budget Fin. Plan v. Superior Court (McDowell), 34 Cal. App. 3d 794, 110 Cal. Rptr. 302 (1973); Stotler v. Geibank Indus. Bank, 827 P.2d 608 (Colo. Ct. App. 1992) (court recognized the close-connectedness doctrine but concluded that there was no close connection based on the facts); Cessna Fin. Corp. v. Warmus, 159 Mich. App. 706. 407 N.W.2d 66 (Mich. Ct. App. 1987); Meyers v. Postal Fin. Co., 287 N.W.2d 614 (Minn. 1979) (explains at length various theories that would make an assignee affirmatively liable, not just liable for any set-off, but found the theories not to apply to the facts of that case); St. James v. Diversified Commercial Fin. Corp., 102 Nev. 23, 714 P.2d 179 (1986) (close-connectedness theory); Karmich Invest. Group v. W.M.R. Restaurant, 86 Ohio App. 3d 479, 621 N.E.2d 561 (1993) (court recognized the close-connectedness doctrine but concluded that there was no close connection based on the facts); Johntson v. Beneficial Mgmt. Corp., 85 Wash. 2d 637, 538 P.2d 510, (1975); State v. Excel Mgmt. Servs., 111 Wis. 2d 479, 331 N.W.2d 312 (1983); *see also* 2 White & Summers, Uniform Commercial Code § 17-7 (4th ed. 1995). *But see* Bankers Trust Co. v. Crawford, 781 F.2d 39 (3d Cir. 1986) (holding that the Pennsylvania Supreme Court would not adopt the doctrine of close-connectedness if given the opportunity to do so). In Texas, inextricably intertwined is not an additional theory of vicarious liability under the UDAP statute, but if the financer is inextricably intertwined with the seller of goods or services it will be subject to the UDAP statute and liable for its participation in the deception even though it does not sell goods or services: Qantel Bus. Sys. v. Custom Controls, 761 S.W.2d 302 (Tex. 1988) (inextricably intertwined is not additional theory of vicarious liability under UDAP statute).

121 Tandy v. Marti, Clearinghouse No. 54557 (S.D. Ill. Apr. 29, 2002) (allowing claim against wholesaler that sold car with wreck history to retail dealer, knowing it was unsafe and was likely to be sold to public). *See* § 2.3.8, *supra* for a discussion of whether manufacturers or wholesalers are within the scope of a UDAP statute.

122 *See, e.g.*, Knapp v. Americredit Fin. Servs., Inc., 245 F. Supp. 2d 841 (S.D. W. Va. 2003). *Cf.* General Motors Acceptance Corp. v. Laesser, 718 So. 2d 276 (Fla. Dist. Ct. App. 1998) (creditor's instruction of dealership employees in bait-and-switch tactics and methods of concealing transaction's true cost violates UDAP statute, but claim fails because causation not shown).

123 *See, e.g.*, Banks v. Consumer Home Mortg., Inc., 2003 WL 21251584 (E.D.N.Y. Mar. 28, 2003) (denial motion to dismiss attorney who represented home seller at closing and included backdated contract, remained silent about a conflict of interest, and presented documents without giving consumer time to review them).

124 *See* § 2.3.7, *supra* for a discussion of whether publishers are exempted by UDAP statutes. See, in particular, Commonwealth by Creamer v. Monumental Properties, Inc., 459 Pa. 450, 329 A.2d 812 (1974), holding that distributors of lease forms are exempt from the Pennsylvania UDAP statute.

125 FTC v. Consumer Alliance, Inc., 2003 WL 22287364 (N.D. Ill. Sept. 30, 2003); FTC v. Bruce Turianski, 5 Trade Reg. Rep. (CCH) ¶ 15341 (S.D. Fla. Dec. 10, 2002) (proposed consent decree).

126 *See* Automatic Data Processing, 5 Trade Reg. Rep. (CCH) ¶ 23,049 (F.T.C. 892 3107 1992) (consent order).

127 *See* § 5.9.6, *supra*.

128 U.S. Oil & Gas Corp., 5 Trade Reg. Rep. (CCH) ¶ 22,985 (F.T.C. File No. 812 3232 Apr. 30, 1991).

A trustee was appointed to try to recover the corporation's assets so they could be turned over to defrauded consumers. The trustee sued the following:

1. The insurance brokerage firm that helped promote the bogus annuity program;
2. The insurance company that issued the annuities knowing that they would be used as part of a scheme to defraud consumers;
3. The law firm that set up the annuity plan and helped the principals loot the corporation of its assets;
4. The accounting firm, whose services assisted the fraud;
5. Banks that were used as references in the company's sales materials where the banks should have known that the scheme was fraudulent;
6. The Better Business Bureau of South Florida, which also was used as a reference for the corporation; and
7. The Council of Better Business Bureaus for failing to supervise the Better Business Bureau of South Florida.

The matter was eventually settled with the trustee collecting $30 million from the various "aiders and abettors."

Another often overlooked party who may be liable is the seller's advertising agency. The FTC routinely sues both the seller and its advertising agency for deceptive advertising.[129] To the extent that false advertising is part of a deceptive scheme, then the advertising agency should be liable under the UDAP statute. In one case where one advertising agency produced the commercials and a second agency was only responsible for arranging air time for them, the court said the second agency could be liable if it failed in its duty to ascertain whether the ads were accurate.[130]

In a case with widespread implications, a court has found a UDAP violation where a car distributor failed to disclose to a consumer that the dealer with whom the consumer was dealing was in financial difficulty and that the consumer's payment to the dealer might not be forwarded to the distributor to pay for the car.[131] This was the holding even though the distributor had no direct relationship with the consumer.[132] Query whether the same rationale would apply to an aluminum siding distributor supplying products to a fly-by-night home improvement contractor.

A court has considered whether GMAC should be held liable for a consumer being switched from a credit sale to a lease of a vehicle because GMAC conducted training sessions for employees at the auto dealership. At the training sessions the employees were allegedly taught the bait and switch procedure used on the consumer and explained how the use of a lease agreement could lead to deceiving the consumer about the transaction's true cost. The court found this to be a clear UDAP violation by GMAC if proven, but the consumer had failed to show any connection between the training sessions and the harm caused to the consumer.[133]

6.5.2 Conduct Sufficient to Trigger Liability

6.5.2.1 General

Consumer litigants wishing to sue aiders and abettors face two separate issues. The first is whether these third parties and the practices they engaged in fall within the scope of a UDAP statute. These coverage issues are detailed in Chapter 2, *supra*. Even third parties who are not normally covered by the UDAP statute may, however, subject themselves to UDAP liability by conspiring with an entity that is covered.[134] For example, in Texas a financer that is inextricably intertwined with a seller of goods loses the UDAP statute's exemption for loans of money and is liable for deceptive acts in which it participated or aided.[135] Moreover, even if the third party is not subject to the UDAP statute, the third party can still be liable on a fraud or related common law claim.

Assuming that the third party and the practice engaged in by that party are covered by the statute, then at least the normal common law principles should apply, making all who knowingly enter a fraudulent scheme liable, even if they do not make fraudulent representations.[136] A corporation incorporated solely to issue certificates to individuals, so that these individuals could advertise themselves as "certified," is liable in a UDAP action, just as the "certified" individuals are liable.[137] Moreover, those who induce another to violate a UDAP statute and furnish the means are as guilty as the UDAP violator.[138]

---

129 *See, e.g.*, Scali, McCabe, Sloves, Inc., 115 F.T.C. 96 (1992) (consent order) (advertising agency ordered to pay $100,000 for creating advertisement that misrepresented crashworthiness of vehicle).

130 Aramowicz v. Bridges (*In re* Diamond Mortgage Corp.), 118 B.R. 575 (Bankr. N.D. Ill. 1989).

131 Temborius v. Slatkin, 157 Mich. App. 587, 403 N.W.2d 821 (1986).

132 *Id.*

133 General Motors Acceptance Corp. v. Laesser, 718 So. 2d 276 (Fla. Dist. Ct. App. 1998).

134 Camp, Dresser & McKee, Inc. v. Steimle & Assocs., Inc., 652 So. 2d 44 (La. Ct. App. 1995) (detective agency that conspires with a competitor is covered); Strahan v. State *ex rel.* Dep't of Agriculture & Forestry, 645 So. 2d 1162 (La. Ct. App. 1994).

135 Qantel Bus. Sys. v. Custom Controls Co., 761 S.W.2d 302 (Tex. 1988).

136 Schmidt Enterprises, Inc. v. State, 170 Ind. Ct. App. 628, 354 N.E.2d 247 (1976); Brooks v. Creech, 2003 WL 174805 (Tenn. App. Jan. 28, 2003) (unpublished, citation limited). *See also* Jurgens v. Abraham, 616 F. Supp. 1381 (D. Mass. 1985).

137 People *ex rel.* Lefkowitz v. Therapeutic Hypnosis, Inc., 83 Misc. 2d 1068, 374 N.Y.S.2d 576 (Sup. Ct. 1975). *See also* Alexander v. Certified Master Builders Corp., 268 Kan. 812, 1 P.3d 899 (Kan. 2000). *But cf.* Ambrose v. New England Ass'n of Schools and Colleges, 252 F.3d 488 (1st Cir. 2001) (company not liable for mere "negligent accreditation").

138 People *ex rel.* Lefkowitz v. Colorado State Christian College of

Individuals can not escape liability by putting into the hands of another the means to defraud.[139] While in Texas merely being "inextricably intertwined" with another party does not create liability for that party's deception, common law theories of vicarious liability are applicable to UDAP cases.[140] Thus, an assignee who drafted and supplied a credit agreement that contained unfair and deceptive terms was liable under the UDAP statute even though the consumer contracted only with the seller.[141]

The remainder of this section examines specific theories for establishing this third party liability, including aiding and abetting, civil conspiracy, ratification, acceptance of benefits, and concealment of fraud. The section then applies these principles to specific situations of particular relevance to today's consumer transactions, including the liability of credit card issuers, credit card intermediaries, and others who assist telemarketing fraud.

6.5.2.2 Aiding and Abetting

To aid and abet a fraud, the assisting party must act knowingly or recklessly in substantially assisting a fraud.[142] This assistance can be to further the fraud or to assist in the concealment of the fraud.[143] Since UDAP statutes are interpreted liberally, at least this same standard should apply to UDAP liability.[144] The Kansas Supreme Court identifies the following as the elements of a claim that one party aided and abetted another's fraud: (1) the party whom the defendant aids must perform a wrongful act causing injury; (2) at the time the defendant provides assistance, he or she must be generally aware of his or her role in part of an overall tortious or illegal activity; and (3) the defendant must knowingly and substantially assist in the principal violation.[145] The Connecticut Supreme Court has found that defendants who unite to commit a UDAP violation are jointly and severally liable for the entire injury caused by the concerted action.[146]

Other courts have found that a party engages in an unfair practice when it knowingly accepts the benefits of conduct which has fraudulently misled another.[147] A federal court has ruled that a financing entity which deliberately shuts its eyes to clues concerning fraud may be unable to enforce promissory notes signed as a result of the fraud.[148]

Of course, UDAP standards for liability may be even more expansive than those found at common law. The Vermont Supreme Court has found creditors directly liable for the practices of a home improvement contractor because the UDAP statute finds liable those "using" any unlawful act. The court found "using" to include the creditor's participation with the home improvement contractor in the transaction.[149]

Inner Power, Inc., 76 Misc. 2d 50, 346 N.Y.S.2d 482 (Sup. Ct. 1973).

139 Regina Corp. v. FTC, 322 F.2d 765 (3d Cir. 1963); Waltham Watch Co. v. FTC, 318 F.2d 28 (7th Cir. 1963); Irwin v. FTC, 143 F.2d 316 (8th Cir. 1944); Allen v. American Land Research, 95 Wash. 2d 841, 631 P.2d 930 (1981) (*citing to* FTC v. Winsted Hosiery Co., 258 U.S. 483 (1921)).

140 Qantel Bus. Sys. v. Custom Controls Co., 761 S.W.2d 302 (Tex. 1988).

141 Qantel Bus. Sys. v. Custom Controls Co., 761 S.W.2d 302 (Tex. 1988) (noting that the term "inextricably intertwined" applied in *Knight* is not an additional basis of vicarious liability under state UDAP statute); Knight v. International Harvester Credit Corp., 627 S.W.2d 382 (Tex. 1982).

142 Hashimoto v. Clark, 264 B.R. 585 (D. Ariz. 2001) (Cal. law) (reciting elements); Tew v. Chase Manhattan Bank, N.A., 728 F. Supp. 1551 (S.D. Fla. 1990). *See also* FTC v. Windward Marketing, Ltd., 1997 U.S. Dist. LEXIS 17114 (N.D. Ga. Sept. 30, 1997) (company that helped telemarketer obtain payment from consumers' banks is liable where it continued to do so despite high dishonor rate and information from law enforcement authorities about seller's fraud).

143 Tew v. Chase Manhattan Bank, N.A., 728 F. Supp. 1551 (S.D. Fla. 1990).

144 Banks v. Consumer Home Mortg., Inc., 2003 WL 21251584 (E.D.N.Y. Mar. 28, 2003) (UDAP liability sufficiently alleged as to mortgage lender's attorney who knew of the deception and lent substantial assistance).

145 York v. InTrust Bank, 265 Kan. 271, 962 P.2d 405 (1998). *See also* Vaughn v. Consumer Home Mortg., Inc., 2003 WL 21241669 (E.D.N.Y. Mar. 23, 2003) (reciting similar elements); Banks v. Consumer Home Mortg., Inc., 2003 WL 21251584 (E.D.N.Y. Mar. 28, 2003) (reciting elements).

146 Smith v. Snyder, 267 Conn. 456, 839 A.2d 589 (2004).

147 Mason v. Fieldstone Mortg. Co., 2000 U.S. Dist. LEXIS 16415 (N.D. Ill. Oct. 10, 2000); Armstrong v. Edelson, 718 F. Supp. 1372 (N.D. Ill. 1989); Heastie v. Community Bank, 690 F. Supp. 716 (N.D. Ill. 1988). *But see* Javorsky v. Freedom Driving Aids, Inc., 2001 U.S. Dist. LEXIS 14078 (N.D. Ill. Aug. 29, 2001) (following *Zekman, see below*); Jackson v. South Holland Dodge, Inc., 197 Ill. 2d 39, 755 N.E.2d 462, 258 Ill. Dec. 79 (2001) (knowing acceptance of benefits is insufficient for liability under Illinois UDAP statute); Zekman v. Direct Am. Marketers, Inc., 182 Ill. 2d 359, 695 N.E.2d 853, 231 Ill. Dec. 80 (1998) (Illinois UDAP statute does not incorporate common law fraud liability principles, so knowing acceptance of benefits of UDAP violation is insufficient for liability).

148 Estate of Sheradsky v. West One Bank, 817 F. Supp. 423 (S.D.N.Y. 1993). *But see* Armstrong v. Accrediting Council for Continuing Educ. & Training, Inc., 832 F. Supp. 419 (D.D.C. 1993) (finding that aiders and abettors are not subject to liability under DC UDAP statute). *Armstrong's* later history, none of which deals with aider and abettor liability, is *vacated and remanded*, 84 F.3d 1452 (D.C. Cir. 1996) (table, text on Westlaw) (remanding for consideration of whether to exercise pendent jurisdiction, and to determine which state law applies, whether provision is preempted by federal law, and interpretation of state law), *on remand*, 950 F. Supp. 1 (D.D.C. 1996) (court maintained jurisdiction of pendent claims and found case to be appropriate for declaratory relief), *later op. at* 961 F. Supp. 305 (D.D.C. 1997), *later op. at* 980 F. Supp. 53 (D.D.C. 1997) (holding that California law applies to other defendants), *aff'd*, 168 F.3d 1362 (D.C. Cir. 1999) (affirming district court's dismissal of claims), *cert. denied*, 528 U.S. 1073 (2000).

149 State v. Custom Pools, 556 A.2d 72 (Vt. 1988).

Lack of privity will not be a defense in a UDAP action.[150] For example, a pest inspector could be liable to a homebuyer for misrepresentations in its report to the seller and broker, even though the homebuyer never hired the pest inspector.[151]

On the other hand, consumers should carefully develop the facts to show the culpability of third parties. One court has held that a landlord who knows its commercial tenant is engaging in a deceptive scheme against other parties is not liable where the landlord did not conspire in or aid the scheme.[152]

A manufacturer is not liable for statements about its product that are accurate in the context of its brochure but are rendered misleading when taken out of context by a distributor.[153] A manufacturer is not liable if it recommends that a vehicle not be used for a certain purpose, and then refuses to cover, under its warranty, defects caused by such improper use, even where a car dealer represented that the car could be put to such improper use.[154] Nor is a supplier of raw materials liable for defects in medical implants, where it did not participate in the design, manufacture, sale, marketing, or labeling of the implants or make any representations about them.[155]

Innocent intermediaries will not be liable.[156] A company is not liable solely for letting an individual use its repair shop, thinking the car being repaired was the individual's personal car.[157] In Texas, the supreme court has held that it is not enough that two parties are inextricably intertwined, like a lessor and the supplier of the leased goods; the third party must either do something wrongful or ratify the acts of the other.[158] However, other jurisdictions recognize that where two entities are closely connected they may be treated as a single entity.[159]

6.5.2.3 Civil Conspiracy

Civil conspiracy targets an unnaturally close relationship between the party engaging in the misconduct and a lender or other party. In *Williams v. ITT Aetna Finance*,[160] the Ohio Supreme Court upheld a jury's award of $15,000 compensatory damages and $1.5 million in punitive damages against a lender who had financed a home improvement loan with a contractor who defaulted on the work. The court found that the lender had known that the contractor was in financial difficulty, and further knew that he was fraudulently using money from new contracts to pay for work on old ones, in a Ponzi-type scheme.[161] The lender furthered the conspiracy by providing customers access to the loan money necessary for the contractor to continue his fraud.[162] The court upheld the lender's liability even though the lender had not made any misrepresentations of its own, and the contractor was not the lender's agent and did not receive any payments directly from the lender.

The mere allegation of conspiracy, standing alone, is not recognized as a cause of action. The pleadings must include allegations of an underlying tort or unlawful act resulting in damage to the plaintiff.[163] All jurisdictions except Wyoming currently recognize civil conspiracy as a cause of action, provided that the elements are properly pleaded and the allegation of conspiracy does not stand alone.[164]

---

150 *See* § 4.2.15.3, *supra*.

151 Raudebaugh v. Action Pest Control, Inc., 59 Or. App. 166, 650 P.2d 1006 (1982). *See also* Tackling v. Shinerman, 42 Conn. Supp. 517, 630 A.2d 1381 (1993) (appraiser may be liable to homebuyers for negligence even though he was hired by bank).

152 People v. Louden, 148 Cal. App. 1147, 196 Cal. Rptr. 582 (1983).

153 Chattin v. Cape May Greene, Inc., 243 N.J. Super. 590, 581 A.2d 91 (1990).

154 Jeep Eagle Sales Corp. v. Mack Massey Motors, Inc., 814 S.W.2d 167 (Tex. App. 1991).

155 Parker v. E.I. DuPont de Nemours & Co., 121 N.M. 120, 909 P.2d 1 (App. 1995).

156 Strickland v. Kafko Mfg., Inc., 512 So. 2d 714 (Ala. 1987).

157 Simpson v. Smith, 34 Ohio Misc. 2d 7, 517 N.E.2d 276 (Mun. Ct. 1987).

158 Quantel Bus. Sys., Inc. v. Custom Controls, 761 S.W.2d 302 (Tex. 1988); Home Sav. Ass'n v. Guerra, 733 S.W.2d 134 (Tex. 1987); Eckler v. General Council of the Assemblies of God, 784 S.W.2d 935 (Tex. App. 1990); Home Sav. Ass'n Service Co. v. Martinez, 788 S.W.2d 52 (Tex. App. 1990); Colonial Leasing Co. v. Kinerd, 733 S.W.2d 671 (Tex. App. 1987), *rev'd on other grounds*, 800 S.W.2d 187 (1990). *But cf.* Elite Towing, Inc. v. Hernandez, 2001 Tex. App. LEXIS 1971 (Mar. 28, 2001) (other family-owned entities that were inextricably intertwined with sale are subject to buyer's claims regardless of privity).

159 *See* §§ 6.4.5, *supra*, 6.6.5.4, *infra*.

160 Williams v. Aetna Fin. Co., 700 N.E.2d 859 (Ohio 1998), *cert. denied*, 526 U.S. 1051 (1999).

161 *Id.* at 869. *See also* Weiss v. Winner's Circle of Chicago, Inc., 1995 U.S. Dist. LEXIS 18713 (N.D. Ill. 1995) (lenders may be subject to UDAP liability where they knew of scheme yet continued to advance funds).

162 *See also* Matthews v. New Century Mortg. Corp., 185 F. Supp. 2d 874 (S.D. Ohio 2002) (lender can be liable on civil conspiracy theory where it knowingly lent money for fraudulent and discriminatory loans).

163 Matthews v. New Century Mortg. Corp., 185 F. Supp. 2d 874 (S.D. Ohio 2002) (holding fraud sufficiently alleged as underlying tort); Hashimoto v. Clark, 264 B.R. 585 (D. Ariz. 2001) (Cal. law). *See, e.g.*, Powell v. Kopman, 511 F. Supp. 700 (S.D.N.Y. 1981) (collecting New York cases); Louisiana v. McIlhenny, 201 La. 78, 9 So. 2d 467 (La. 1942); Hoffman v. Stamper, 843 A.2d 153 (Md. Spec. App. 2004).

164 *See, e.g.*, Valdes v. Leisure Resource Group, 810 F.2d 1345 (5th Cir. 1987) (Texas law); Halberstam v. Welch, 705 F.2d 472 (D.C. Cir. 1983); Loughridge v. Goodyear Tire & Rubber Co., 192 F. Supp. 2d 1175 (D. Colo. 2002) (denying manufacturer's motion for summary judgment on claim it conspired with seller in fraudulent marketing of product); Haymond v. Lundy, 2001 U.S. Dist. LEXIS 630 (E.D. Pa. Jan. 29, 2001); Barman v. Union Oil Co., 2000 U.S. Dist. LEXIS 14157 (D. Or. Sept. 8, 2000), *aff'd in part, rev'd in part*, 2002 WL 31133363 (9th Cir. Sept. 26, 2002) (summary judgment for defendant on civil conspiracy claim; plaintiff provided "no evidentiary support");

A significant benefit of a civil conspiracy theory is that the plaintiff does not have to show that all conspirators committed the tort or the unlawful act. For example, an appraiser who issues inflated appraisals as part of a conspiracy with a real estate seller to foist properties off on unsophisticated first-time home buyers can be liable for civil conspiracy to defraud whether or not the appraiser's actions satisfy all the elements of fraud.[165] Although the specific elements of the tort of civil conspiracy vary among jurisdictions, one formal expression is as follows:

(1) there was a combination of two or more persons or entities;
(2) there was an oral or written agreement among those persons or entities for a common purpose;
(3) each of those persons or entities had knowledge of that purpose;
(4) each of those persons or entities intended to participate therein; and
(5) one or more overt acts were done in furtherance of the conspiracy.[166]

The tort, in essence, is a derivative one, one that serves to "enlarge the pool of potential defendants from whom a

---

Pescia v. Auburn Ford-Lincoln Mercury, Inc., 68 F. Supp. 2d 1269 (M.D. Ala. 1999), *aff'd without op. sub nom.* Pescia v. Ford Motor Credit Corp., 2001 WL 1711051 (11th Cir. Dec. 17, 2001); Hays v. Bankers Trust Co., 46 F. Supp. 2d 490 (S.D. W. Va. 1999); Nichols Motorcycle Supply, Inc. v. Dunlop Tire Corp., 1994 U.S. Dist. LEXIS 17761 (N.D. Ill. Dec. 12, 1994); Gray v. Laws, 915 F. Supp. 762 (E.D.N.C. 1994); Williams Elec. Co. v. Honeywell, Inc., 772 F. Supp. 1225, 1239 (N.D. Fla. 1991); Mason v. Funderburk, 247 Ark. 521, 446 S.W.2d 543 (1969); Summers v. Hagen, 852 P.2d 1165 (Alaska 1993); McElhanon v. Hing, 151 Ariz. 386, 728 P.2d 256 (1985); Lesperance v. North Am. Aviation, Inc., 217 Cal. App. 2d 336, 31 Cal. Rptr. 873 (1963); Magin v. DVCO Fuel Sys., Inc., 981 P.2d 673 (Colo. App. 1999); Barber v. Glick, 2000 Conn. Super. LEXIS 172 (Jan. 20, 2000); Connolly v. Labowitz, 519 A.2d 138, 143 (Del. Super. 1986); Alta Anesthesia Assocs. of Ga., P.C. v. Gibbons, 245 Ga. App. 79, 537 S.E.2d 388 (2000); Weinberg v. Mauch, 78 Haw. 40, 890 P.2d 277 (1995); Argonaut Ins. Co. v. White, 86 Idaho 374, 386 P.2d 964 (1963); Adcock v. Brakegate, Ltd., 164 Ill. 2d 54, 62–3, 645 N.E.2d 888, 894, 206 Ill. Dec. 636 (1994); Indianapolis Horse Patrol, Inc. v. Ward, 247 Ind. 519, 217 N.E.2d 626 (1966); Adam v. Mt. Pleasant Bank & Trust Co. 387 N.W.2d 771 (Iowa 1986); York v. InTrust Bank, 265 Kan. 271, 962 P.2d 405 (1998); Stoldt v. City of Toronto, 234 Kan. 957, 678 P.2d 153 (1984); Eustler v. Hughes, 267 Ky. 200, 101 S.W.2d 917 (1937); Louisiana v. McIlhenny, 201 La. 78, 9 So. 2d 467 (1942); Cohen v. Bowdoin, 288 A.2d 106 (Me. 1972); Hoffman v. Stamper, 843 A.2d 153 (Md. Spec. App. 2004) (conspiratorial agreement may be tacit); Alleco, Inc. v. Weinberg Foundation, 99 Md. App. 696, 639 A.2d 173 (1994); Alexander & Alexander v. B. Dixon Evander & Assocs., Inc., 88 Md. App. 672, 596 A.2d 687, 700 (Md. App. 1991)]; Kyte v. Philip Morris, Inc., 408 Mass. 162, 556 N.E.2d 1025 (1990); Admiral Ins. v. Columbia Ins., 194 Mich. App. 300, 486 N.W.2d 351, 359 (Mich. App. 1992); Harding v. Ohio Cas. Ins. Co., 230 Minn. 327, 41 N.W.2d 818 (1950); Williams v. Mercantile Bank of St. Louis, 845 S.W.2d 78, 85 (Mo. App. E.D. 1993); Bailey v. Richards, 236 Miss. 523, 111 So. 2d 402 (1959); Schumacher v. Meridian Oil Co., 288 Mont. 217, 956 P.2d 1370 (1998); Four R Cattle Co. v. Mullins, 570 N.W.2d 813 (Neb. 1997); Siragusa v. Brown, 114 Nev. 1384, 971 P.2d 801 (1998); Edwards v. Baker, 130 N.H. 41, 534 A.2d 706 (1987); Middlesex Concrete Products & Excavating Corp. v. Cartaret Indus. Assn., 37 N.J. 507, 181 A.2d 774 (1962); Ettenson v. Burke, 17 P.3d 440 (N.M. App. 2000); Hurt v. Freeland, 1999 N.D. 12, 589 N.W.2d 551 (1999); Barsh v. Mullins, 1959 Okla. 2, 338 P.2d 845 (1959); Granewich v. Harding, 150 Or. App. 34, 945 P.2d 1067 (1996); Paradis v. Zarella, 1996 R.I. Super. LEXIS 97 (Super. Ct. Apr. 2, 1996); LaMotte v. Punch Line of Columbia, Inc., 296 S.C. 66, 370 S.E.2d 711 (1988); Knott's Wholesale Foods, Inc. v. Azbell, 1996 Tenn. App. LEXIS 774 (Ct. App. Dec. 6, 1996); Estate of Pagan v. Cannon, 746 P.2d 785 (Utah 1987); Hunnewell v. Catamount Nat'l Bank, 137 Vt. 389, 406 A.2d 386 (1979); Citizens for Fauquier County v. SPR Corp., 37 Va. Cir. 44 (1995); Lindsey v. Organik Technologies, Inc., 1999 Wash. App. LEXIS 742 (Ct. App. Apr. 23, 1999) (unpublished); Onderdonk v. Lamb, 79 Wis. 2d. 241, 255 N.W.2d 507 (1977).

Although Wyoming has yet to squarely address the issue, caselaw indicates that it would not stand alone against the foregoing weight of authority. *Compare* Spear v. Nicholson, 882 P.2d 1237 (Wyo. 1994) (court declined to issue advisory opinion as to conspiracy cause of action) *with* Jurkovich v. Estate of Tomlinson, 843 P.2d 1166 (Wyo. 1992) (facts sufficient to allege civil conspiracy at summary judgment stage).

165 Hoffman v. Stamper, 843 A.2d 153 (Md. Spec. App. 2004).

166 Valdes v. Leisure Resource Group, 810 F.2d 1345 (5th Cir. 1987) (Texas law); Hashimoto v. Clark, 264 B.R. 585 (D. Ariz. 2001) (Cal. law) (elements are an agreement, a wrongful act by any of the conspirators pursuant to the agreement, and damages); *In re* Methyl Tertiary Butyl Ether Prods. Liab. Litigation, 175 F. Supp. 2d 593 (S.D.N.Y. 2001) (summarizing elements in California, Illinois, and New York as agreement to participate in an unlawful act or a lawful act in an unlawful means and an overt act performed in furtherance of scheme, causing an injury); Haymond v. Lundy, 2001 U.S. Dist. LEXIS 630 (E.D. Pa. Jan. 29, 2001) (elements are (1) an agreement by two or more persons to perform an unlawful act or perform an otherwise lawful act by unlawful means; (2) an overt act accomplished in pursuit of that common purpose; and (3) actual legal damage); Adcock v. Brakegate, Ltd., 164 Ill. 2d 54, 645 N.E.2d 888, 206 Ill. Dec. 636 (1994) (elements are (1) an agreement (2) by two or more persons (3) to perform an overt act or acts (4) in furtherance of the agreement/conspiracy (5) to accomplish an unlawful purpose or a lawful purpose by unlawful means (6) causing injury to another); York v. InTrust Bank, 265 Kan. 271, 962 P.2d 405 (1998) (finding that bank had conspired with real estate developers to extract higher sales commissions from buyers; elements are (1) two or more persons; (2) an object to be accomplished; (3) a meeting of minds in the object or course of action; (4) one or more unlawful overt acts; and (5) damages proximately caused by those acts); Simmons Oil Corp. v. Holly Corp., 258 Mont. 79, 852 P.2d 523 (1993) (elements are (1) two or more persons (including corporations); (2) an object to be accomplished; (3) a meeting of the minds on the object or course of action; (4) one or more unlawful overt acts; and (5) damages as the proximate result thereof); Williams v. Aetna Fin. Co., 83 Ohio St. 3d 464, 700 N.E.2d 859 (1998) (defining civil conspiracy as "a malicious combination of two or more persons to injure another in person or property, in a way not competent for one alone, resulting an actual damages").

plaintiff may recover for an underlying tort."[167] Thus, a claimant must generally show that one member of the conspiracy (usually the seller) committed a tort (for example, fraud) or other unlawful act as part of the conspiracy claim.[168] However, the plaintiff need not show that the defendant actually intended the tort so long as the defendant knew of the wrongdoing, and the nature of the defendant's relationship with the actual tortfeasor enabled the tort.

For example, in the *Williams* case, evidence that the lender "allow[ed] [the seller] to have access to loan money that was necessary to further his fraudulent actions against customers such as Williams"[169] supported the judgment. Another court found in a bait-and-switch loan case that evidence that the loan documents themselves showed fraudulent misrepresentations by a loan servicer precluded summary judgment in favor of the lender that contracted with the servicer.[170] An attorney for a fraudulent land development corporation who knew of the corporation's deceptive practices and who intended to share in the gains was liable under a UDAP statute as a participant in a civil conspiracy.[171] A loan officer and an appraiser who worked with a speculator to foist properties off on first-time home buyers at inflated prices were liable for civil conspiracy to commit fraud.[172] A federal court in West Virginia has found a joint venture or conspiracy claim can go forward where the creditor trained auto dealership employees and worked with them in perpetrating the scheme.[173]

6.5.2.4 Ratification, Acceptance of Benefits, and Concealment of Fraud

Even defendants who were not involved in the original fraud may be liable if they ratified others' fraud, accepted the benefits of the fraud, or assisted in continuing to conceal the fraud. For example, if a subsequent assignee of a contract has reason to know it was procured by fraud, yet takes the contract without investigating the fraud, the assignee can be found to have ratified the fraud and be liable for it.[174] Failure to disclose the fraud to the consumer may be sufficient for liability.[175] Another theory provides that one who knowingly receives the benefits of fraud can be held

167 Williams v. ITT Fin. Servs., 1997 Ohio App. LEXIS 2721 at *30 (June 25, 1997), *aff'd sub nom.* Williams v. Aetna Fin. Co., 83 Ohio St. 3d 464, 700 N.E.2d 859 (1998), *cert. denied*, 526 U.S. 1051 (1999).

168 *See* Beck v. Prupis, 529 U.S. 494, 120 S. Ct. 1608, 146 L. Ed. 2d 561 (2000) (extensive discussion of common law elements); Pescia v. Auburn Ford-Lincoln Mercury Inc., 68 F. Supp. 2d 1269 (M.D. Ala. 1999) (finding no civil conspiracy in yo-yo sales case where plaintiff failed to establish underlying tort), *aff'd without op. sub nom.* Pescia v. Ford Motor Credit Corp., 2001 WL 1711051 (11th Cir. Dec. 17, 2001); Hays v. Bankers Trust Co., 46 F. Supp. 2d 490, 497 (S.D. W. Va. 1999) ("A civil conspiracy is a combination of two or more persons by concerted action to accomplish an unlawful purpose or to accomplish some purpose, not in itself unlawful, by unlawful means. The cause of action is not created by the conspiracy but by the wrongful acts done by the defendants to the injury of the plaintiff"); Domchick v. Greenbelt Consumer Servs., Inc., 200 Md. 36, 87 A.2d 831 (1952) (to maintain an action for civil conspiracy under Maryland law, the acts committed must be such that if done by one person, would constitute a tort); Thompson Coal Co. v. Pike Coal Co., 488 Pa. 198, 412 A.2d 466 (1979) (to prove civil conspiracy under Pennsylvania law, a plaintiff must show "that two or more persons combined or agreed to do an unlawful act or to do an otherwise lawful act by unlawful means"); *In re* Thoma, 873 S.W.2d 477, 490 (Tex. 1994) ("an actionable civil conspiracy is a combination by two or more persons to accomplish an unlawful purpose or to accomplish a lawful purpose by unlawful means"). *See also* Champion Parts, Inc. v. Oppenheimer & Co., 878 F.2d 1003, 1008 (7th Cir. 1989) ("conspiracy becomes actionable only when the underlying conduct which is the subject of the conspiracy is independently tortious"); Nichols Motorcycle Supply, Inc. v. Dunlop Tire Corp., 1994 U.S. Dist. LEXIS 17761 (Dec. 12, 1994) (claim dismissed for failure to plead tortious or unlawful conduct); Williams Elec. Co. v. Honeywell, Inc., 772 F. Supp. 1225, 1239 (N.D. Fla. 1991) ("Under Florida law, actionable civil conspiracy must be based on an existing independent wrong or tort that would constitute a valid cause of action if committed by one actor"); Williams v. Mercantile Bank of St. Louis, 845 S.W.2d 78, 85 (Mo. App. 1993) ("Conspiracy is not itself actionable in the absence of an underlying wrongful act or tort.").

169 Williams v. Mercantile Bank of St. Louis, 700 N.E.2d 859, 868–69 (Ohio 1998). *See also* Weiss v. Winner's Circle of Chicago, Inc., 1995 U.S. Dist. LEXIS 18713 (N.D. Ill. 1995) (lender may be subject to UDAP liability where it knew of scheme yet continued to advance funds to defendants).

170 Hays v. Bankers Trust Co., 46 F. Supp. 2d 490 (S.D. W. Va. 1999).

171 Bourland v. State, 528 S.W.2d 350 (Tex. Civ. App. 1975). *See also* Jurgens v. Abraham, 616 F. Supp. 1381 (D. Mass. 1985); Elite Towing, Inc. v. Hernandez, 2001 Tex. App. LEXIS 1971 (Mar. 28, 2001) (holding family members and related corporations liable).

172 Hoffman v. Stamper, 843 A.2d 153 (Md. Spec. App. 2004) (also upholding liability on fraud and UDAP claims).

173 *See* Knapp v. Americredit Fin. Servs., Inc., 245 F. Supp. 2d 841 (S.D. W. Va. 2003).

174 *See* Pescia v. Auburn Ford-Lincoln Mercury, Inc., 68 F. Supp. 2d 1269, 1283–84 (M.D. Ala. 1999) (finance company ratified seller's fraud when called consumer and learned that seller had altered terms, yet accepted contract), *aff'd without op. sub nom.* Pescia v. Ford Motor Credit Corp., 2001 WL 1711051 (11th Cir. Dec. 17, 2001); Chavarria v. Fleetwood Retail Corp., Clearinghouse No. 54576 (N.M. Dist. Ct. Aug. 29, 2002) (employer ratified salesmen's fraud by paying commissions rather than terminating them after discovering the fraud, by covering up the fraud in order to make the contract more palatable to a lender, and by fighting the consumers in court). *But see* Luck v. Primus Auto. Fin. Servs., Inc., 763 So. 2d 243 (Ala. 2000) (finance company's right of approval and the appearance of its name on lease forms did not amount to a ratification of statements made by dealer to purchaser).

175 Williams v. ITT Fin. Servs., 1997 Ohio App. LEXIS 2721 (Ohio Ct. App. June 23, 1997), *aff'd on other grounds sub nom.* Williams v. Aetna Fin. Co., 83 Ohio St. 3d 464, 708 N.E.2d 859 (1998).

liable for it.[176] These theories are discussed in more detail in another manual.[177]

6.5.3 Liability of Credit Card Issuers as Aiders and Abettors

Federal law sets out when a consumer can refuse to pay a credit card charge based on the consumer's claims and defenses against the billing merchant. These consumer rights are described at § 6.6.5.6, *infra*. In addition, the credit card issuer or other intermediaries assisting the fraudulent merchant's access to the credit card charge system can be liable as aiders and abettors. This is important because the federal law protection relating to credit card charges only allows the consumer to stop payment, and then in only certain situations. On the other hand, credit card issuers or other intermediaries aiding and abetting a fraud can be found liable under the UDAP statute for consequential, multiple or punitive damages and attorney fees.

The Federal Trade Commission reached a consent order with a credit card issuer, Citibank Credit Services, Inc., on allegations that it engaged in unfair and deceptive conduct by aiding and abetting a fraudulent sales scheme.[178] The credit card issuer allegedly continued to process credit card sales when it knew or should have known that the seller was engaged in deceptive sales practices.

Indicators that should have warned the credit card issuer about possible merchant fraud, according to the FTC, were the high volume of consumer complaints, ongoing governmental investigations, and a twenty-five percent chargeback rate—about twenty times the industry average. A chargeback occurs when a consumer protects a credit charge and it is removed from the consumer's account and charged back to the merchant. Citicorp agreed to monitor its merchants to determine if any had chargeback rates over six percent for two months out of three, and then terminate or further investigate those merchants.

The consent order suggests ways that credit card issuers can investigate a merchant, including reviewing the merchant's advertising, sales scripts and promotional materials, the goods or services offered, and the truth of claims being made. They can also determine if other credit card issuers have terminated the merchant, whether government agencies are conducting investigations, and the nature of consumer complaints. Refusal by a merchant to cooperate with a card issuer's investigation should be taken as a possible indication of wrongdoing.

An implication of the Citicorp case is that defrauded consumers have a new remedy where they purchased a product through a credit card. Existing federal law allows consumers to challenge such charges if they exceed $50 and occur in the consumer's own state, and if certain other steps are properly taken.[179] Federal law also allows a consumer to challenge these charges under the Fair Credit Billing Act.[180] The Citicorp case offers a third avenue—that a card issuer is liable under a UDAP statute for aiding and abetting a deceptive scheme by not adequately investigating the merchant.

The same analysis should be applicable to other institutions that impose charges on consumers at the behest of third parties. For example, telephone companies impose charges submitted by telemarketers and 900-number providers. Banks pay money out of consumers' accounts based on demand drafts or "telechecks."[181] A high rate of dispute or rejection of these charges by consumers should place these institutions on notice of the probable fraud, and make them responsible for consumers' losses.

6.5.4 Credit Card ISOs and Other Intermediaries as Aiders and Abettors

To submit credit card charge slips for payment through a national credit card processing system, a merchant needs a "merchant account" at a bank. The bank then credits the merchant with the amount of the charges (minus a fee) and submits the charge slips to the customer's bank for reimbursement through the credit card processing system. If the customer cancels the transaction, the process is reversed: the merchant's bank has to reimburse the customer's bank, and then the merchant bank tries to get the money back from the merchant. Perhaps because of fear of liability similar to that of Citicorp discussed in the previous subsection, some banks refuse to open merchant accounts for sellers they fear will have a high level of chargebacks.

176 *See, e.g.*, Weiss v. Winner's Circle of Chicago, Inc., 1995 U.S. Dist. LEXIS 18713 (N.D. Ill. 1995); Duckworth v. National Bank of Commerce, 656 So. 2d 340 (Ala. 1994). *But see* Manufacturers and Traders Trust Co. v. Hughes, 2003 WL 21780956 (N.D. Ill. July 31, 2003) (following *Zekman*; assignee of fraudulent mortgage not liable for mortgagor's UDAP violations); Atilano v. Zero Plus Dialing, Inc., 2002 U.S. Dist. LEXIS 1561 (N.D. Ill. Feb. 4, 2002) (following *Zekman*); Jackson v. South Holland Dodge, Inc., 197 Ill. 2d 39, 755 N.E.2d 462, 258 Ill. Dec. 79 (2001) (knowing acceptance of benefits is insufficient for liability under Illinois UDAP statute); Zekman v. Direct Am. Marketers, Inc., 182 Ill. 2d 359, 695 N.E.2d 853 (1998) (plaintiff can not bring UDAP claim against one who did not directly participate in the alleged fraud, even if it knowingly received the benefits of the fraud); Saltzman v. Enhanced Servs. Billing, Inc., 811 N.E.2d 191 (Ill. App. 2003) (distinguishing *Zekman*; telecommunications billing intermediary may have participated actively enough to allow UDAP liability).

177 *See generally* National Consumer Law Center, Automobile Fraud § 9.4.3 (2d ed. 2003 and Supp.).

178 *See* Citicorp Credit Servs., Inc., 5 Trade Reg. Rep. (CCH) ¶ 23,280 (F.T.C. Dkt. C-3413 1993) (consent order).

179 *See* 15 U.S.C. § 1666i; *see also* § 6.6.5.6, *infra*.

180 *See* 15 U.S.C. § 1666; *see also* National Consumer Law Center, Truth in Lending § 5.8 (5th ed. 2003 and Supp.).

181 *See* § 5.9.2.3.6, *supra*.

Soon after the Citicorp case, the FTC followed up with an important action against an independent service organization (ISO) that acted as an intermediary between telemarketers and bank card issuers. The ISO processed credit card sales for telemarketers. It also agreed to indemnify banks against losses from these telemarketers, thereby enabling the telemarketers to get merchant accounts. The FTC alleged that the ISO's advice and assistance to the telemarketers made it aware of their deceptive practices, yet it continued to process their card sales.[182] The ISO settled the case by agreeing to investigate its participating telemarketers on a continual basis as to their sales scripts, offers, consumer complaints, charge card policies, and related matters before processing credit card charges.[183]

Another way to evade a bank's refusal to open a merchant account is to use a credit card factoring service—a third party that has its own merchant account and will, for a charge, submit another seller's charge slips through it. Often the factoring service conceals from the merchant bank the fact that it is submitting a different merchant's charge slips. Using or operating a factoring service to process a telemarketer's credit card payments without authorization of the bank and the credit card system violates the FTC's telemarketing rule.[184] Even outside the telemarketing context, a factoring service that gives a fraudulent merchant access to the credit card system in violation of bank rules should be liable for the merchant's fraud. The same analysis should also apply to other intermediaries, such as those who submit 900-number charges to local telephone providers to be included on consumers' bills.[185]

6.5.5 Those Assisting Telemarketing Fraud

An FTC rule promulgated pursuant to the Telemarketing and Consumer Fraud and Abuse Prevention Act declares it a deceptive act for a person to provide substantial assistance to a telemarketer while knowing, or consciously avoiding knowledge that, the telemarketer was violating the FTC rule.[186] The FTC recognizes the following as examples of substantial assistance: providing lists of contacts to a seller or telemarketer that identify people who are over age fifty-five, have bad credit histories, or have been victimized previously by deceptive telemarketing or direct sales;[187] providing certificates for travel-related services to be used as a sales promotion device; providing scripts, advertising, or other promotional material; or providing inflated appraisals or phony testimonials for goods or services sold through telemarketing.[188]

Pursuant to this rule, the FTC has proceeded against a company that masterminded real estate telemarketing schemes for various promoters by providing them mailing lists, promotional mailings, and a printing and mailing service;[189] a company that supplied the products that were sold, trained the telemarketers, and extended credit to the victims to buy the products;[190] and a company that assisted telemarketers in submitting demand drafts to banks.[191] A federal court held that a bank that approved telemarketers' scripts, allowed them to use its name, and benefited financially from their sales could be liable under the telemarketing rule.[192]

Violating the FTC telemarketing rule by provid ing substantial assistance will be a UDAP violation in most states.[193] In addition, some state telemarketing laws have a similar prohibition and also create a private cause of action.[194]

6.5.6 Endorsers and Accrediting Organizations

Those who endorse a product or company may be liable for their deceptive endorsements.[195] Other possible defen-

182 FTC v. Electronic Clearinghouse, Inc., 5 Trade Reg. Rep. (CCH) ¶ 23,517 (D. Nev. Dec. 21, 1993) (consent decree).

183 *Id. See also* FTC v. Productive Marketing, Inc., 136 F. Supp. 2d 1096 (C.D. Cal. 2001) (company that processed fraudulent seller's credit card payments and failed to turn over funds despite knowledge of injunction obtained by FTC can be held in contempt even though not a party to original suit); FTC v. Hold Billing Servs., 5 Trade Reg. Rep. (CCH) ¶ 24,659 (W.D. Tex. Oct. 6, 1999) (consent decree requiring $250,000 in consumer redress).

184 16 C.F.R. § 310.3(c).

185 *See, e.g.*, Saltzman v. Enhanced Servs. Billing, Inc., 811 N.E.2d 191 (Ill. App. 2003) (telecommunications billing intermediary may have participated actively enough to allow UDAP liability).

186 16 C.F.R. § 310.3(b).

187 *See, e.g.*, FTC v. Consumer Money Markets, Inc., 5 Trade Reg. Rep. (CCH) ¶ 24,796 (D. Nev. Sept. 6, 2000) (consent decree requiring list broker to disgorge $150,000).

188 Statement of Basis and Purpose, 60 Fed. Reg. 43852 (Aug. 23, 1995), *reproduced on* the companion CD-Rom to this volume. *See* § 5.9.2.3, *supra*, for further discussion of the FTC rule.

189 FTC v. Marketing Response Group, 1996 U.S. Dist. LEXIS 10589, 5 Trade Reg. Rep. (CCH) ¶ 23,958 (M.D. Fla. June 24, 1996) (filing of complaint).

190 FTC v. Unimet Credit Corp., 5 Trade Reg. Rep. (CCH) ¶ 23,730. *But cf.* Zekman v. Direct Am. Marketers, 182 Ill. 2d 359, 695 N.E.2d 853 (1998) (knowingly receiving benefits of another company's 900-number fraud insufficient for liability under UDAP statute; no discussion of FTC telemarketing rule).

191 FTC v. Cordeiro, 5 Trade Reg. Rep. (CCH) ¶ 24,870 (N.D. Cal. Feb. 5, 2001).

192 Minnesota *ex rel.* Hatch v. Fleet Mortg. Corp., 158 F. Supp. 2d 962 (D. Minn. 2001) (denial of motion to dismiss).

193 *See* §§ 3.2.6, 3.2.7, 5.9.2.3.8, *supra.*

194 *See, e.g.*, Haw. Rev. Stat. §§ 481P-2(b), 481P-6.

195 Ramson v. Layne, 668 F. Supp. 1162 (N.D. Ill. 1987); Aramowicz v. Bridges (*In re* Diamond Mortgage Corp.), 118 B.R. 575 (Bankr. N.D. Ill. 1989). *See also* FTC v. Universal Greeting Card Corp., 5 Trade Reg. Rep. (CCH) ¶ 15350 (M.D. Fla. Jan. 5, 2003) (proposed consent decree); Robert M. Currier, Dkt. C-4067, www.ftc.gov/opa/2002/12/fyi0267.htm (Dec. 20,

dants are those involved in the accrediting process. The FTC has sued a company for falsely accrediting a lab that tested the energy efficiency of windows and similar products.[196] Both the accrediting company and the lab in such a situation could be held liable for consumer injury that resulted from false energy efficiency claims.

The Kansas Supreme Court has ruled that a company that certified "master builders" was subject to a UDAP suit by consumers who selected a builder in reliance upon the certification, only to find that the builder had been grandfathered into the certifying organization without meeting its standards. The court stressed that one goal of the certifying organization was promotion of the home building industry, and it supplied promotional materials to members and distributed brochures to the general public.[197]

6.6 Liability of Assignees and Related Creditors for Seller's Misconduct Under the FTC Holder Rule

6.6.1 Overview

6.6.1.1 Rationale for FTC Holder Rule

In consumer transactions, one of the most important issues is whether a creditor is subject to the claims and defenses that the consumer has against the seller or original creditor. There are two reasons for the importance of this issue. First, the seller or original creditor may be judgment proof, so that consumers would be left without a remedy if they had to pay the holder of the note and then recover all or some of this amount from the original seller or creditor. As the West Virginia Supreme Court stated in construing a state law that incorporated the FTC Holder Rule, without such a rule a financial institution could "run in effect a 'laundry' for 'fly-by-night' retailers."[198]

Second, even if the seller is solvent, it is usually impractical to expect a consumer to defend a collection action and simultaneously bring an affirmative suit against the seller or original creditor. The collection suit may be resolved years before the affirmative suit, and it is often not feasible for a consumer to bring an affirmative action for the small amount of money at stake. By far the most practical action for the consumer is to defend the collection action by raising in that case the consumer's claims and defenses against the seller or original creditor.

Making creditors liable for the acts of the original seller serves the additional goal of establishing a market-based incentive for creditors to inquire into the merchants for whom they finance sales and to refuse to deal with those merchants whose conduct would subject the creditor to potential claims and defenses.[199] Forcing the market to police itself reduces unfair and deceptive practices.

Moreover, the creditor is in a much better position than the consumer to recover money from the seller. "Consumers are not in a position to police the market, exert leverage over sellers, or vindicate their legal rights in cases of clear abuse. . . . Redress via the legal system is seldom a viable alternative for consumers where problems occur."[200] On the other hand, "As a practical matter, the creditor is always in a better position than the buyer to return seller misconduct costs to sellers, the guilty party."[201]

The FTC emphasized in its *Statement of Basis and Purpose* for the rule that the holder is in an excellent position to recover money from the seller: the holder "has recourse to contractual devices which render the routine return of seller misconduct costs to sellers relatively cheap and automatic . . . The creditor may also look to a 'reserve' or 'recourse' arrangement or account with the seller for reimbursement."[202]

6.6.1.2 Credit-Sale Obligations Assigned to Creditor

Consumer attorneys must distinguish between three ways in which credit is extended. First is the installment contract, in which a seller sells goods or services on credit and then assigns the contract to a financing entity. The seller itself is named as the original payee of the installment contract. Examples are installment sales of cars in which the obligation is assigned to General Motors Acceptance Corp. or Ford Motor Credit Co. In this situation, the general rule is that the

2002) (consent order against doctor who made infomercials for anti-smoking ad without disclosing product's limitations or his relationship with seller); Glass, 95 F.T.C. 246 (1980) (consent order); Cooper, 94 F.T.C. 674 (1979) (consent order); Cooga Mooga, Inc., 92 F.T.C. 310 (1978) (consent order).

196 FTC v. American Architectural Manufacturers Ass'n, 5 Trade Reg. Rep. (CCH) ¶ 23,719 (N.D. Ill. 1994). *See also* § 4.7.7, *supra*.

197 Alexander v. Certified Master Builders Corp., 268 Kan. 812, 1 P.3d 899 (Kan. 2000). *See also* People *ex rel.* Lefkowitz v. Therapeutic Hypnosis, Inc., 83 Misc. 2d 1068, 374 N.Y.S.2d 576 (Sup. Ct. 1975).

198 Green Tree Acceptance, Inc. v. Pirtle, 1999 WL 33740367 (E.D. Mich. Mar. 1, 1999) (purpose of rule is to reallocate cost of seller misconduct to creditor); State *ex rel.* McGraw v. Scott Runyan Pontiac-Buick, Inc., 194 W. Va. 770, 461 S.E.2d 516, 526 (1995). *See also* Scott v. Mayflower Home Improvement Corp., 363 N.J. Super. 145, 831 A.2d 564, 569 (Law Div. 2001). *Accord* State *ex rel.* Easley v. Rich Food Servs., Inc., 535 S.E.2d 84 (N.C. App. 2000).

199 Bryant v. Mortgage Capital Resource Corp., 197 F. Supp. 2d 1357, 1364 n.23 (N.D. Ga. 2002).

200 Federal Trade Commission, Statement of Basis and Purpose, Trade Regulation Rule Concerning the Preservation of Consumers' Claims and Defenses, 40 Fed. Reg. 53523 (Nov. 18, 1975), reprinted on the companion CD-Rom.

201 *Id.*

202 *Id.*

seller's assignee, when it seeks collection of the obligation, is subject to defenses the consumer could raise against the seller.[203]

However, prior to the FTC Holder Rule, the general rule was virtually swallowed by two exceptions allowed by the Uniform Commercial Code. First, UCC § 9-206 (Revised UCC § 9-403) allowed contracts to contain a clause by which the buyer waived any defenses (with some exceptions) that the general rule might make available against the assignee.[204] Second, if the transaction included a promissory note governed by Article 3 of the UCC, the holder-in-due-course doctrine set forth at UCC § 3-302 insulated the holder of the note from defenses that consumers could raise against the assignor.[205] These defense cut-off devices were particularly onerous where the assignor had fled the jurisdiction or was judgment proof. The consumer would be liable on the contract or note, but would not be able to recover UDAP damages from the assignor.

In most consumer sales transactions involving assignment of installment contracts, these means of insulating assignors and holders no longer have any effect, because of the FTC's Rule Concerning the Preservation of Consumers' Claims and Defenses (the FTC Holder Rule).[206] This rule requires credit-sellers to include in consumer credit contracts (defined broadly to include both contracts and promissory notes)[207] a notice that any holder is subject to the consumer's claims and defenses against the seller. This effectively defeats the protections afforded the holder by the UCC. It subjects the holder, as a matter of contract law, to the consumer's claims and defenses.[208]

6.6.1.3 Loans to Purchase Goods or Services

In a second way of extending credit, the sale of goods is financed by a loan from a third party lender. Often the loan is arranged for the buyer by the seller from a third party lender. The lender then pays the seller in full. When financing is set up in this manner, the consumer's debt is owed to the lender from the outset. Prior to the FTC Holder Rule, these third party lenders and their assignees claimed insulation from the consumer's claims and defenses against the seller, but not because they were holders in due course. Instead, such third party creditors claimed they loaned money directly to the consumer and were not responsible for how the consumer spent the proceeds.

The FTC Holder Rule again offers consumers in this situation their best remedy. The rule requires sellers to arrange for the FTC Holder Notice to be present in all notes where the seller refers consumers to the lender or is affiliated with the lender by common control or contract or by any formal or informal business arrangement, understanding, course of dealing, or procedure.[209] The FTC Holder Rule language in the note must state that the holder is subject to all claims and defenses the consumer has against the related seller, up to the amount of the loan.

If the consumer arranges the loan on his or her own, however, the FTC Holder Rule does not apply. The FTC Holder Rule also does not apply if the consumer pays by credit card, but there are comparable provisions of the Truth in Lending Act that apply to credit cards.[210]

6.6.1.4 Straight Loans of Money

Another type of credit is a straight loan that is not related to a specific sales transaction. Examples are personal loans and home equity loans. For this type of credit, the consumer will deal directly with the lender (sometimes through a broker), but the original lender may assign the obligation to a different creditor. If the consumer has claims or defenses arising from the creation of the loan obligation, such as misrepresentation of credit terms or unfair creditor remedies, can these be raised against the lender's assignee? Unfortunately, the FTC Holder Rule only applies to "purchase money loans," so the Holder Notice need not be included in the note. If the consumer has claims and defenses against the original lender, but the original lender assigns the note to an assignee, the consumer will have to find grounds other than the FTC Holder Rule to defeat the assignee's claim of holder-in-due-course status. The key issue here will be whether the assignee can take advantage of the holder-in-due-course protections offered by the UCC. Theories for holding the holder of a straight loan obligation liable for the acts of the original lender are discussed in § 6.7, *infra*.

---

203 *See* § 6.6.5.6.4, *infra*.

204 This provision has been transferred to §§ 9-403 and 9-404 of Rev. Art. 9, effective in most states on July 1, 2001.

205 *See* Kurt Eggert, *Held Up In Due Course: Codification and the Victory of Form Over Intent in Negotiable Instrument Law*, 35 Creighton L. Rev. 364 (Feb. 2002) (history of negotiable instruments and HIDC rule and their role in encouraging deceptive practices).

206 16 C.F.R. § 433 [*reprinted at* Appx. B.2.1, *infra*]. The procedures and substance of the FTC Holder Rule resisted challenge in United States v. Hertz Corp., 1981-1 Trade Cases ¶ 64,023 (S.D. Fla. 1981). In 1988 the FTC initiated a review of the rule to determine the rule's cost to small entities, as a first step toward consideration if the rule should be amended or repealed. *See* 53 Fed. Reg. 44456 (Nov. 3, 1988). The FTC in 1992 announced that the rule will not be amended or repealed pursuant to this review. *See* 57 Fed. Reg. 28814 (June 29, 1992).

207 16 C.F.R. § 433.1(i).

208 *See* Hempstead Bank v. Babcock, 115 Misc. 2d 97, 453 N.Y.S.2d 557 (Sup. Ct. 1982); De La Fuente v. Home Savings Ass'n, 669 S.W.2d 137 (Tex. App. 1984).

209 16 C.F.R. § 433.1(d), (g) [*reprinted at* Appx. B.2.1, *infra*].

210 *See* § 6.6.5.6, *infra*.

6.6.1.5 Relationship to Lender's Direct Liability for Participation in Deception

The FTC Holder Rule and related theories of liability are not based on the holder's misconduct or participation in another's misconduct. Instead, the holder is subject to claims and defenses that can be brought against another because the very act of holding the note creates derivative liability, even if the holder is completely innocent of any knowledge of the seller or originating lender's misconduct.

This derivative liability that is the subject of this section and also of § 6.7, *infra*, must be kept distinct from a holder's liability for participating with the seller or originating lender in the misconduct. Such liability is examined earlier in this chapter, particularly at § 6.5, *supra*. While it is usually easier to establish a holder's liability pursuant to the FTC Holder Rule or another theory of derivative liability, establishing a holder's liability based on its own participation in the scheme has certain advantages.

Such liability is found irrespective of a note's failure to include the FTC Holder Notice, any waiver-of-defense clause agreed to by the consumer, the holder's alleged holder-in-due-course status, or other defense the holder might raise to avoid derivative liability. In addition, theories based on a holder's active participation create holder liability for the consumer's *full* damages, without regard to the FTC Holder Rule cap,[211] including liability for punitive damages.

6.6.1.6 Organization of This Section

This section details the FTC Holder Rule, its scope and how it operates at §§ 6.6.2, and 6.6.3, *infra*. Since the rule operates by the insertion of a notice in the loan documents making holders subject to seller-related claims and defenses, another issue analyzed at § 6.6.4, *infra*, is what happens when the rule is violated and the notice is not placed in the loan documents. The FTC Holder Rule is reproduced in Appx. B.2.1, *infra*. It is also on the companion CD-Rom to this volume, along with the FTC's original *Statement of Basis and Purpose, a Statement of Enforcement Policy* published in 1976, and Staff Guidelines published in the same year.

Other theories for holding a creditor liable for seller-related claims and defenses are detailed in § 6.6.5.6, *infra*. These theories are useful both when the Holder Notice has been wrongfully omitted and when, for one reason or another, the FTC Holder Rule does not apply to the transaction. One example is credit card transactions, which are covered by provisions of the Truth in Lending Act similar to the FTC Holder Rule rather than by the FTC Holder Rule itself. These provisions are covered in § 6.6.5.6, *infra*. The liability of a party financing a lease is examined in § 6.6.5.7, *infra*.

When claims relating to a direct lender's credit terms or the nature of a loan transaction that does not involve the sale of goods or services, consumers will want to consider theories of an assignee's derivative liability not based on the FTC Holder Rule. In practice, this will often involve issues of the definition and scope of the holder-in-due-course status as a means of insulating assignees. Questions as to an assignee's liability for the acts of an assignor lender are analyzed in § 6.7, *infra*.

Bounced or dishonored checks are subject to a different analysis. The FTC Holder Rule does not apply because there is no credit. The check is a negotiable instrument, and the bank is a holder in due course. As such, the consumer may have difficulty bringing seller-related defenses to the bank's collection on the check.[212] Consumer rights as to checks, money orders, electronic transfers, and similar payment devices are covered in another NCLC manual, *Consumer Banking and Payments Law* (2d ed. 2002 and Supp.).

As described in § 6.5.1.4, *supra*, a holder's liability can also be based on the holder's direct participation in the misconduct. This liability for direct participation is examined in § 6.5, *supra*.

6.6.2 *Scope of the FTC Holder Rule*

6.6.2.1 Operational Scope of the Holder Notice

The FTC Holder Rule is unique in that the scope of the rule is somewhat different from the scope of the rule's operational effect. The rule operates by a notice being placed in consumer credit agreements whereby, as a matter of the contract itself,[213] the parties agree that the consumer can raise seller-related claims and defenses against the holder of the note or contract. As such, the *effect* of the rule is directly felt by *any* agreement that includes the FTC Holder Notice.

Even if a transaction is beyond the scope of the FTC rule, if the credit agreement contains the FTC Holder *Notice*, the holder is subject to seller-related claims and defenses.[214]

---

211 *See* § 6.6.3.7, *infra*.

212 *See* First Nat'l Bank, Conway Springs v. Jones, 17 Kan. App. 2d 269, 839 P.2d 535 (1992).

213 Thomas v. Ford Motor Credit Co., 429 A.2d 277 (Md. App. 1981); Hempstead Bank v. Babcock, 115 Misc. 2d 97, 453 N.Y.S.2d 557 (Sup. Ct. 1982); De La Fuente v. Home Savings Ass'n, 669 S.W.2d 137 (Tex. App. 1984).

214 Gray v. Atlantic Permanent Savings & Loan Ass'n, Inc., 49 B.R. 540 (Bankr. E.D. Va. 1985); Music Acceptance Corp. v. Lofing, 32 Cal. App. 4th 610, 39 Cal. Rptr. 2d 159 (1995); Boden v. Atlantic Federal Savings & Loan Ass'n, 396 So. 2d 827 (Fla. Dist. Ct. App. 1981); Jefferson Bank & Trust Co. v. Stamiatiou, 384 So. 2d 388 (La. 1980); *cf.* International Harvester Credit Corp. v. Hill, 496 F. Supp. 329 (M.D. Tenn. 1979) (where form contract explicitly limits FTC Holder Rule language's applicability to consumer transactions, not business transactions, the notice is not effective as to a business transaction).

The very terms of the contract govern the relationship between the parties.[215] Even if the FTC notice was not required to be inserted, it is given full effect if it is inserted.

There is no requirement that the Holder Notice appear at any particular place in the loan documents,[216] so the consumer's attorney must carefully review all portions of all the documents for the notice. In open-end plans, the notice may be in the master credit agreement, in one or more monthly statements, or in charge slips.[217]

Creditors can not avoid the rule by stating in credit agreements that holders are subject to claims and defenses *if* the FTC Holder Rule applies to the transaction, but that holders are not subject to such claims if the rule is found not to apply. This is a rule violation and contrary to the FTC policies in enacting the rule.[218]

On the other hand, even if an agreement is within the scope of the FTC Holder Rule, and the FTC notice is required to be inserted in the agreement, this may not happen. Then the rule does not work as intended. Another subsection details a consumer's remedies and ability to raise seller-related claims and defenses if the notice is not in the contract.[219]

6.6.2.2 Scope of the Rule

6.6.2.2.1 Sales transactions covered

The FTC rule, in general, requires a notice to be inserted in credit agreements whenever the seller finances a sale or a creditor has a relationship with the seller and that creditor finances the sale. The rule applies broadly to "any sale or lease of goods or services to consumers in or affecting commerce."[220] The rule applies equally to the sale of services, such as home improvement contracting, vocational training, employment counseling, and health spa membership, as it does to the sale of tangibles.[221]

"Consumer" is defined as "a natural person who seeks or acquires goods or services for personal, family, or household use."[222] As such, the rule applies to virtually every type of consumer sales transaction. But the rule does not apply to the purchase of equipment for agricultural production, the purchase of securities, or purchases made by an organization.[223] Importantly, the rule does not apply to sales of real estate, although it does apply to loans where real estate is taken as security and to home improvement contracts.[224]

The rule also does not apply to a third party lender's direct loan to the consumer unrelated to a sale or seller.[225] There are times when a consumer will wish to raise against an assignee of that direct lender defenses that the consumer has concerning the creation of that loan. Even if the FTC notice is in the note, the FTC Holder Rule offers no protection to such consumers because the rule only allows the consumer to raise seller-related defenses, not lender-related defenses. The consumer must depend on theories other than the FTC Holder Rule to raise such defenses.[226]

6.6.2.2.2 Coverage of leases

It is unclear whether the FTC Holder Rule applies to leases. While the rule explicitly indicates that it applies to a "sale or lease," other aspects of the rule require the lease to involve a "consumer credit contract."[227] "Consumer credit contract" is a defined term that refers to the Truth in Lending Act definition of a finance charge and a credit sale. The rule clearly applies to a transaction structured as a lease, but which falls within Truth in Lending's definition of a credit transaction.[228] What is unclear is whether the rule applies to leases not within that definition.[229]

If the FTC Holder Rule does not apply, a state holder law

215 Kish v. Van Note, 692 S.W.2d 463 (Tex. 1985). *See also In re* Armor, 1999 U.S. Dist. LEXIS 5885 (E.D.N.C. Mar. 15, 1999), *aff'd without op.*, 232 F.3d 887 (4th Cir. 2000); Jackson v. CIT Group/Sales Financing Inc., 630 So. 2d 368 (Ala. 1994); Maxwell v. Fidelity Fin. Servs., Inc., 907 P.2d 51 (Ariz. 1995); BCS Fin. Corp. v. Sorbo, 444 S.E.2d 85 (Ga. Ct. App. 1994).

216 Staff Guidelines, 41 Fed. Reg. 20026, Placement of the Notice (May 14, 1976), *reproduced on* the companion CD-Rom to this volume.

217 *Id.*

218 Federal Trade Commission Advisory Letter by Eric Rubin, Assistant Director for Compliance, FTC Bureau of Consumer Protection (Sept. 17, 1976).

219 *See* § 6.6.4, *infra*.

220 16 C.F.R. § 433.2 [*reprinted at* Appx. B.2.1, *infra*].

221 Statement of Basis and Purpose for the Federal Trade Commission Rule Concerning the Preservation of Consumers' Claims and Defenses, 40 Fed. Reg. 53524 (Nov. 18, 1975), *reproduced on* the companion CD-Rom to this volume; Staff Guidelines, 41 Fed. Reg. 20024, Affected Transactions (May 14, 1976), *reproduced on* the companion CD-Rom to this volume.

222 16 C.F.R. § 433.1(b) [*reprinted at* Appx. B.2.1, *infra*]. *See* Drew v. Chrysler Corp., 596 F. Supp. 1371 (W.D. Mo. 1984) (adopting objective test for determining whether goods were acquired for consumer purposes).

223 Staff Guidelines, 41 Fed. Reg. 20024, Affected Transactions (May 14, 1976), *reproduced on* the companion CD-Rom to this volume.

224 *See* FTC Staff Guidelines, 41 Fed. Reg. 20024, Affected Transactions (May 14, 1976), *reproduced on* the companion CD-Rom to this volume.

225 16 C.F.R. § 433.1 [*reprinted at* Appx. B.2.1, *infra*].

226 *See* § 6.7, *infra.*

227 16 C.F.R. § 433.2(a), (b) [*reprinted at* Appx. B.2.1, *infra*].

228 For example, the rule refers to Truth in Lending's definition of a credit sale, which refers to certain nominal leases as credit sales where the consumer pays a sum equivalent to the value of the goods or services and has the option to become the owner for nominal consideration. 12 C.F.R. § 226.2(16).

229 *See* Bescos v. Bank of America, 129 Cal. Rptr. 2d 423 (Cal. App. 2003) (does not apply to leases); LaChappelle v. Toyota Motor Credit Corp., 126 Cal. Rptr. 2d (Cal. App. 2002); Jarvis v. South Oak Dodge, 319 Ill. App. 3d 509, 747 N.E.2d 383 (2000) (rule does not apply to true lease), *rev'd on other grounds*, 773 N.E.2d 641 (Ill. 2002); Marchionna v. Ford Motor

may. Many state holder laws cover leases that would not meet the TIL definition of credit sale.[230] These laws cover leases either by broadly defining a term such as "retail installment contract" to include leases, or by explicitly mentioning consumer leases in the holder statute. In addition, Connecticut has adopted a Consumer Leasing Act as proposed by the National Conference of Commissioners on Uniform State Laws that allows consumers to raise all dealer-related claims and defenses against the lessor, and other state leasing statutes provide similar protections.[231]

Of most general applicability, the typical automobile lease involves a transaction where the dealer is the originating lessor, and the lease is then assigned to a lender. In that situation, the lender steps into the shoes of the dealer, and is subject to all defenses the consumer could raise against the dealer. The lease does not qualify as a negotiable instrument, and the lender can not claim holder-in-due-course status, so is subject as assignee to all defenses that could be raised against the assignor.[232]

Co., 1995 U.S. Dist. LEXIS 11408 (N.D. Ill. Aug. 9, 1995) (rule does not apply to pure lease).

230 State holder laws that appear to cover at least some leases beyond those defined as credit transactions by Regulation Z include Alaska Stat. § 45.50.541(a); Ariz. Stat. § 44-145; Colo. Rev. Stat. § 5-3-303; Del. Code tit. 6, §§ 4312, 4301(6) (defining "retail installment contract" to include leases without a requirement that purchase option be for no or nominal additional consideration); Iowa Code §§ 537.3307, 537.3404; Kan. Stat. §§ 16a-3-307, 16a-3-404, 16a-3-405; Me. Rev. Stat. Ann. tit. 9-A, §§ 3-307, 3-403, 3-405; Md. Code Comm. Law §§ 12-628, 12-601(m)(1) (defining "installment sale agreement" to include all leases in which the lessee agrees to pay a sum substantially equal to or greater than the value of the goods); Mich. Comp. Laws Ann. §§ 492.114a, 492.102(9) (definition of "installment sale contract" for Motor Vehicle Sales Finance Act similar to Maryland's); Minn. Stat. Ann. §§ 325G.16, 325G.15(5) (defining "sale of goods" to include leases, even if terminable, and even if additional consideration for purchase option is more than nominal); Miss. Code Ann. §§ 63-19-41, 63-19-3 (defining "retail installment contract" for MVRISA to include leases in which lessee agrees to pay a sum substantially equivalent or greater than value of vehicle and has option of becoming owner); Mo. Stat. § 408.405 (applies broadly to leases); N.J. Stat. Ann. §§ 17:16C-38.1, 17:16C-38.2, 17:16C-1 (definition of "retail installment contract" similar to Minnesota's); N.C. Gen. Stat. §§ 25A-25, 25A-2(b) (defining "sale" to include leases where purchase option is up to 10% of cash price); Okla. Stat. tit. 14-A, § 2-403, 2-404; Or. Rev. Stat. § 83.820 (motor vehicle sales and leases); Pa. Stat. Ann. tit. 69, §§ 615(F), (G), 603(10) (definition of installment sale contract for Motor Vehicle Sales Finance Act), 1401, 1402, 1201(6) (definition of retail installment contract); S.C. Code §§ 37-2-403, 37-2-404; S.D. Codified Laws §§ 57A-3A-102–57A-3A-107; Vt. Stat. Ann. tit. 9, §§ 2455, 2451a(a) (definition of "consumer"); W. Va. Code § 46A-2-101, 46A-2-102, 46A-2-103a (finance leases and sale-leaseback agreements); Wis. Stat. Ann. §§ 422.406, 422.407, 421.301(10) (defining "consumer credit transaction" to include consumer leases); Wyo. Stat. §§ 40-14-237, 40-14-238. *See* § 6.6.3.11.1, *infra*.

231 *See* § 6.6.5.7, *infra*.

232 *See* § 6.7.2, *infra*.

6.6.2.2.3 Covered sellers

The rule places certain obligations on "sellers," defined as those in the ordinary course of business who sell or lease goods or services to consumers.[233] Since the rule only applies to sellers who sell in the ordinary course of their business, isolated sales by individuals are not covered.

Moreover, the rule only applies where a seller is within the scope of the FTC Act. This requires some explanation why it is the FTC Act's scope as to sellers, not creditors that is critical. The rule does not require creditors to place the Holder notice in their contracts. Nor does the rule place any obligations on assignees of a credit agreement. Instead, the rule requires that sellers place the notice in their credit sale contracts and that they arrange for the notice's inclusion when a loan is made by a related third party lender.[234] Then, as a matter of contract law, the notice is binding on all subsequent holders because the notice is a term of the credit agreement.

Since the FTC only has authority to impose requirements on sellers within the scope of the FTC Act, the FTC Holder Rule does not apply where the seller (not the assignee or related lender) is outside the scope of the FTC Act. Even if an entity is outside the scope of the FTC Act and does not have obligations under the rule as a "seller" to place or arrange for the notice to be included in the note, as a matter of contract law, the Holder notice is effective against that entity acting as a holder of the note if the notice is found in the note.

Public entities and truly nonprofit corporations are not within the scope of the FTC Act,[235] and the FTC Holder Rule does not obligate these entities as *sellers* to arrange for the notice to be placed in consumer credit agreements. For example, the FTC Holder Rule does not apply to loans involving public or nonprofit vocational schools. Other entities outside the scope of the FTC Act include banks, savings and loans, federal credit unions, and common carriers and air carriers subject to federal regulation.[236] The McCarran-Ferguson Act also prohibits FTC regulation of insurance where state law otherwise regulates the practice. It is possible that certain state regulation of unfair insurance practices would oust insurance transactions from the scope of the FTC Holder Rule.

233 16 C.F.R. § 433.1(j) [*reprinted at* Appx. B.2.1, *infra*].

234 The Commission in 1979 tentatively adopted an amendment that would have allowed FTC enforcement of the rule against assignees and lenders but the Commission never officially promulgated this amendment. After nine years of inaction, the FTC killed the amendment on the grounds that there was no evidence that the practice of creditors cutting off consumer defenses was prevalent. 53 Fed. Reg. 44457 (Nov. 3, 1988).

235 15 U.S.C. § 44 (definition of "corporation").

236 15 U.S.C. § 45(a)(2).

6.6.2.2.4 Covered credit transactions

The rule requires the FTC Holder Notice to be placed in any instrument evidencing a debt arising from a "financed sale" or a "purchase money loan."[237] A financed sale is the typical credit sale where the seller acts as the initial creditor. The term "purchase money loan" is a defined term that requires some explanation. The basic concept is that if a creditor is related in some fashion with the seller and makes a loan to the consumer to purchase goods or services from the seller, the FTC Holder Rule applies as if the financing came directly from the seller. Sellers can not avoid the rule by arranging with third parties to finance a sales transaction.

For a credit transaction to be a "purchase money loan," the transaction must meet four preconditions. First, there must be a cash advance received by the consumer in return for a finance charge within the meaning of the Truth in Lending Act. Since the Truth in Lending Act's definition of finance charge is very broad, this applies to virtually all credit transactions.

Second, the cash advance must be applied in whole or *substantial* part to a purchase of goods or services from the seller. A loan is still covered even if some part is kept by the consumer or goes to pay another debt, as long as a substantial part goes to purchase the goods or services from the seller.[238] The rule should thus apply to the refinancing of a note as long as a substantial part of the total proceeds can be traced back to the original sale. For example, where a seller offered initial financing, and then arranged permanent financing that paid off the original note owed the seller, this is covered by the FTC rule.[239]

Third, the seller must be related to the creditor, either by referring consumers to the creditor or by being affiliated with the creditor by common control, contract, or business arrangement.[240] This is an expansive definition.[241] The rule makes clear that the seller need not refer the particular consumer to the creditor as long as the seller refers consumers to the creditor. Moreover, "contract" and "business arrangement" are both defined terms that cover any formal or informal agreement between the creditor and seller, be it written or oral, or even an informal course of dealing, procedure, or arrangement.[242]

In short, the rule applies to any third party loan transaction used to purchase goods or services where the seller and creditor have virtually *any* form of a relationship with each other. A referral relationship may exist between dealer and creditor where a car dealership refers consumers to an insurance agent, and where the insurance agent then refers consumers to a creditor.[243]

Fourth, the rule only applies where the related creditor fits the rule's definition of "creditor." A creditor is a person who in the ordinary course of business makes purchase money loans or finances the sale of goods or services to consumers.[244] There is one important exception to this definition of creditor: the rule does not apply to a creditor who in the particular transaction at issue is acting as a credit card issuer.[245] A separate federal law analyzed later establishes consumer rights to raise seller-related claims and defenses against credit card issuers.[246]

While the FTC rule's definition of creditor does not include credit card issuers, the rule does not exempt credit card issuers from the definition of "*seller*." Sellers that have their own "house" credit cards must still comply with the rule. Moreover, the FTC rule applies to seller-provided open-end credit.[247] The rule will typically not apply to open-end credit provided by a lender because the consumer usually will use the money to purchase goods or services from various sellers not related to the lender.[248]

An issue arises whether the FTC Holder Rule applies to loans where the amount financed exceeds $25,000. 1976 staff guidelines on the rule state that terms used in the rule—financing a sale and purchase money loan—expressly refer to Truth in Lending (TIL) and Regulation Z, and "thus incorporate the limitations contained in these laws."[249] The guidelines then reach the conclusion that "a purchase involving an expenditure of more than $25,000 is not affected by the Rule."[250]

On its face, this staff statement clearly is in error and shows a lack of understanding of TIL. Even if the FTC Holder Rule's scope is limited to TIL's scope (which is a nonsensical position), TIL only exempts transactions where the *amount financed* exceeds $25,000, and then only where the credit is neither secured by real property or by personal property expected to be used as the consumer's principal

237 16 C.F.R. § 433.1(i), 433.2 [*reprinted at* Appx. B.2.1, *infra*].

238 Staff Guidelines, 41 Fed. Reg. 20025, Purchase Money Loans (May 14, 1976), *reproduced on* the companion CD-Rom to this volume.

239 Associates Home Equity Servs., Inc. v. Troup, 343 N.J. Super. 254, 778 A.2d 529 (App. Div. 2001).

240 16 C.F.R. § 433.1(d) [*reprinted at* Appx. B.2.1, *infra*].

241 *See* Associates Home Equity Servs., Inc. v. Troup, 343 N.J. Super. 254, 778 A.2d 529 (App. Div. 2001).

242 16 C.F.R. § 433.1(f), (g) [*reprinted at* Appx. B.2.1, *infra*]. *See also* Iowa Attorney General Informal Opinion Letter, Clearinghouse No. 53560 (May 22, 2001) (informal referral agreement qualifies).

243 Brown v. LaSalle Northwest Nat'l Bank, 820 F. Supp. 1078 (N.D. Ill. 1993).

244 16 C.F.R. § 433.1(c) [*reprinted at* Appx. B.2.1, *infra*].

245 *Id.*

246 *See* § 6.6.5.6, *infra*.

247 Staff Guidelines, 41 Fed. Reg. 20024, Financing a Sale (May 14, 1976), *reproduced on* the companion CD-Rom to this volume.

248 Staff Guidelines, 41 Fed. Reg. 20025, Purchase Money Loans (May 14, 1976), *reproduced on* the companion CD-Rom to this volume.

249 Staff Guidelines on Trade Regulation Rule Concerning Preservation of Consumers' Claims and Defenses, 41 Fed. Reg. 200022 (May 14, 1976), reprinted on the companion CD-Rom.

250 *Id.*

dwelling.[251] So, were the FTC Holder Rule to have the same scope as TIL, it would not be limited to where "expenditures" were under $25,000. Instead, it would be limited to transactions where the amount financed was under $25,000. For example, if a consumer expends $35,000 on an automobile, the amount financed may still be under $25,000 if sufficient down payments, trade-ins, and rebates are involved.

And, of course, the $25,000 limit would not apply to home improvement loans or any other loan where any real property is taken as security. Nor would it apply to loans taking a mobile home or motor home as security where the home was expected to be the consumer's principal dwelling.

The staff's 1976 view is also flawed in its totality. The FTC Holder Rule defines "financing a sale" as extending credit in connection with a credit sale "within the meaning of the Truth in Lending Act and Regulation Z."[252] TIL and Regulation Z define a credit sale as any sale in which the seller is a creditor. TIL and Regulation Z also define creditor and credit.[253] None of these definitions mentions a $25,000 limit.

The rule also defines "purchase money loan" as one involving a finance charge "within the meaning of the Truth in Lending Act and Regulation Z."[254] Finance charge is defined in Regulation Z as the cost of consumer credit as a dollar amount. Again, neither Regulation Z's definitions of consumer, consumer credit, or finance charge in any way refer to a dollar limit.[255]

Instead, TIL has a separate section that exempts certain transactions from the scope of the Act. One of these exemptions applies to certain transactions with an amount financed over $25,000. This exemption in no way refers to finance charges or the term "credit sale."[256] The exemption does not state that transactions over $25,000 are not credit sales or do not have finance charges. It simply states that TIL requirements are not applicable to that form of credit.

Why TIL excludes large transactions in an exemption section and not in the definition of finance charge and credit sale is obvious. Clearly a credit sale over $25,000 still involves a seller who is a creditor. A loan over $25,000 still has a finance charge. In fact, it has a larger finance charge, on average, than a smaller loan. Transactions over $25,000 thus should still be covered by the FTC Holder Rule, to the extent to which they have finance charges or are credit sales within TIL's definitions.

There is no indication that the FTC, in adopting the FTC Holder Rule, was seeking to make the scope of that rule exactly the same as the scope of TIL. Instead, the FTC was only adopting definitions found in TIL as a handy reference point, so that they did not have to be defined again in the FTC rule.

A $25,000 exemption from the FTC Holder Rule has never been announced by the full Federal Trade Commission. The exemption is found neither in the rule nor in the lengthy *Commission Statement of Basis and Purpose* for the rule. Instead, the exemption is found only in a 1976 staff interpretation.

Such staff statements are not binding on the Commission and may not reflect the views of the Commission. The statements are certainly not binding on a court. A court should not give credence to a staff statement so patently incorrect as not to even accurately track TIL's exemption language, nor which fails to explain how an exemption from TIL's scope has any relevance as to how credit sale and finance charge are defined in TIL.

Finally, where the Holder language is actually placed in credit documents for a loan exceeding $25,000, the scope of the FTC Holder Rule becomes irrelevant. The credit agreement as a matter of contract law states that the holder is subject to all seller related claims, whether or not the FTC Holder Rule applies to the transaction.[257]

6.6.2.2.5 Student loans

Truly nonprofit schools fall outside the FTC's jurisdiction and are not covered by the FTC Holder Rule.[258] On the other hand, there is no question that for-profit schools such as proprietary trade schools are covered when they extend credit themselves or refer the consumer to a particular lender. The FTC staff in charge of enforcing the FTC Holder Rule has unambiguously stated that the FTC Holder Rule applies to Federal Family Education Loans (FFELs).[259] The Secretary of Education[260] and a 1993 Congressional Con-

251 15 U.S.C. § 1603(3); 12 C.F.R. § 226.3(b).

252 16 C.F.R. § 433.1(e).

253 15 U.S.C. § 1602(e), (f), (g); 12 C.F.R. § 226.2(a)(14), (16), (17).

254 16 C.F.R. § 433.1(d).

255 12 C.F.R. § 226.2(a)(11), (12), 226.4(a). *See also* 15 U.S.C. § 1605(a).

256 15 U.S.C. § 1603(3); 12 C.F.R. § 226.2(a)(14), (16), (17).

257 *See* § 6.6.2.1, *supra.*

258 *See* § 6.6.2.2.3, *supra.*

259 *See* FTC Staff Letter from David Medine, Associate Director for Credit Practices, Clearinghouse No. 47,975 (Feb. 11, 1993); FTC Staff Opinion Letter to Jonathan Sheldon, National Consumer Law Center, Clearinghouse No. 46,752 (July 24, 1991). These letters reverse a prior letter on the subject, Esposito, FTC Informal Staff Letter, Clearinghouse No. 44,341 (Jan. 9, 1989). The full Federal Trade Commission, while not formally adopting the 1991 staff opinion, did refer to that opinion with apparent approval in 1992. In a Commission decision not to amend the FTC Holder Rule, the Commission stated that "the Commission staff has provided NCLC with an opinion letter stating that such educational loans are not exempt from the Rule." 57 Fed. Reg. 28815, n.11 (June 29, 1992). *But see* Armstrong v. Accrediting Council for Continuing Educ. & Training, Inc., 168 F.3d 1362 (D.C. Cir. 1999), *cert. denied*, 528 U.S. 1073 (2000).

260 The introductory material to the Department's common promissory note, at page 7, states "The Secretary of Education has determined that the Governing Law and Notices section of the

ference Report[261] reach the same conclusion. These 1991, 1992, and 1993 interpretations supersede a few earlier courts that ruled otherwise.[262] Subsequent court rulings agree that the FTC Holder Rule applies to FFELs.[263]

Despite the unequivocal application of the FTC Holder Rule, proprietary vocational schools routinely failed to include the Holder Notice in student loans they arranged prior to 1994. Unfortunately, courts have been leery of providing consumers with a *remedy* for the lenders' failure to include that notice. In other contexts, courts have had little difficulty finding a violation of an FTC rule to be a state UDAP violation.[264] Yet in the student loan context, courts have usually found ways to avoid UDAP liability for violating the FTC Holder Rule.[265]

The problems with raising defenses against holders of fraudulent student loans are reduced to some extent by regulations and forms promulgated by the Department of Education that provide at least some of the protections of the Holder Notice. These vary depending on the particular student loan program involved. For Direct Loans, Department of Education regulations state that in any collection proceeding, the borrower may assert as a defense against repayment any act or omission of the school that would give rise to a cause of action against the school under applicable state law.[266] As to Federally Insured Student Loans (FISLs), which were common in the 1970s and early 1980s, until 1986 (when it was dropped without comment), a regulation explicitly stated that the United States would not collect an FISL to the extent that a school had closed or students had certain school-related defenses.[267] As to Federal Family Education Loan (FFELs), starting on January 1, 1994, the Department of Education requires use of a common promissory note that includes an adaptation of the FTC Holder Notice.[268] For earlier FFELs, several statements by the Secretary of Education appear to recognize that students can

---

common promissory note must include the Federal Trade Commission (FTC) consumer defense clause as required by the FTC regulations, 16 CFR Section 433.2." *See* Common Application Material and Promissory Note, Clearinghouse No. 47,974 (Apr. 16, 1993).

261 "The Holder Rule applies to student loan borrowers attending for-profit institutions, and the new Federal Family Education Loan promissory note includes the required notice." Omnibus Budget Reconciliation Act of 1993, Conference Report to Accompany H.R. 2264, H.R. Rep. No. 213, 455, 103d Cong., 1st Sess. (Aug. 4, 1993). In addition, Congress, in the Higher Education Amendments of 1992, had an opportunity, by adopting the House version, to limit significantly the FTC rule's applicability to GSLs. Instead, Congress decided to adopt the Senate version that would not limit the FTC Holder Rule's applicability.

262 Veal v. First Am. Savings Bank, 914 F.2d 909 (7th Cir. 1990); *see also* McVey v. U.S. Training Academy, Clearinghouse No. 44,344 (Bankr. E.D. Ky. Aug. 25, 1988); Molina v. Crown Bus. Institute, Clearinghouse No. 45,920 (N.Y. Sup. Ct. 1990).

263 *See, e.g.*, Morgan v. Markerdowne Corp., 976 F. Supp. 301 (D.N.J. 1997); Jackson v. Culinary School of Washington, 788 F. Supp. 1233 (D.D.C. 1992), *vacated on other grounds*, 115 S. Ct. 2573 (1995) (appellate court used de novo instead of abuse of discretion standard to review district court's decision to decide state law issues in declaratory judgment action), *remanded to district court on state law claims, but affirming ruling on origination*, 59 F.3d 254 (D.C. Cir. 1995) (to determine on what basis federal court decided to rule on state law issues), *motion dismissed* 1995 U.S. App. LEXIS 22304 (D.C. Cir. 1995). *See also* Spinner v. Chesapeake Bus. Institute of Virginia, Clearinghouse No. 49,131A (E.D. Va. Feb. 5, 1993); C. Mansfield, *The Federal Trade Commission Holder Rule and its Applicability to Student Loans—Re-allocating the Risk of Proprietary School Failure*, 26 Wake Forest L. Rev. 635 (1991). *But cf.* Hernandez v. Alexander, Clearinghouse No. 46,792 (D. Nev. May 18, 1992).

264 *See* § 6.6.4.4, *infra.*

265 Armstrong v. Accrediting Council for Continuing Educ. & Training, Inc., 84 F.3d 1452 (D.C. Cir. 1996), *on remand*, 950 F. Supp. 1 (D.D.C. 1996) (court maintained jurisdiction of pendent claims and found case to be appropriate for declaratory relief), *on further remand*, 980 F. Supp. 53 (D.D.C. 1997) (court determined that California law controls and invited plaintiff to amend complaint to assert claims and defenses under California consumer protection laws), *aff'd*, 168 F.3d 1362 (D.C. Cir. 1999) (affirming district court's dismissal of claims), *cert. denied*, 528 U.S. 1073 (2000); Keams v. Tempe Technical Institute, Inc., 993 F. Supp. 714 (D. Ariz. 1997) (since student loan contracts did not include terms of FTC Holder Rule, former vocational school students were not able to assert claims and defenses arising from school's behavior against assignee), *claims against all defendants dismissed*, 16 F. Supp. 2d 1119 (D. Ariz. 1998); Morgan v. Markerdowne Corp., 976 F. Supp. 301 (D.N.J. 1997); United States v. Ornecipe, Clearinghouse No. 51,941 (S.D. Fla. 1995) (Florida UDAP statute does not apply to banks); Jackson v. Culinary School of Washington, 811 F. Supp. 714 (D.D.C. 1993) (summary judgment) (court found insufficient facts to find UDAP liability), *aff'd on other grounds*, 27 F.3d 573 (D.C. Cir. 1994) (court declined to consider complex state law issue in declaratory judgment action), *vacated,* 115 S. Ct. 2573 (1995) (appellate court used de novo instead of abuse of discretion standard to review district court's decision to decide state law issues in declaratory judgment action), *remanded to district court on state law claims* 59 F.3d 254 (D.C. Cir. 1995) (to determine on what basis federal court decided to rule on state law issues), *motion dismissed*, 1995 U.S. App. LEXIS 22304 (D.C. Cir. 1995); Williams v. National School of Health Technology, Inc., 836 F. Supp. 273 (E.D. Pa. 1993) (United States committed no wrongdoing, so no UDAP violation; court failed to consider that lender did engage in wrongdoing and that the United States is an assignee of the lender); Hernandez v. Alexander, Clearinghouse No. 46,792 (D. Nev. May 18, 1992). *See also* Armand v. Secretary of Educ., Clearinghouse No. 51,298 (S.D. Fla. July 19, 1995) (Florida UDAP statute does not apply to banks). *Cf.* Spinner v. Chesapeake Bus. Institute of Virginia, Clearinghouse No. 49,131A (E.D. Va. Feb. 5, 1993) (student loan contracts fall into UDAP exemption for practices authorized by federal laws or regulations, but claims of unconscionability and constructive fraud must go to trial).

266 34 C.F.R. § 685.206(c)(1). *See also* 20 U.S.C. § 1087e(h) (requiring regulations specifying when school misconduct may be asserted as defense to loan repayment).

267 34 C.F.R. § 518 (1985) (since rescinded). *See also* United States v. Griffin, 707 F.2d 1477 (D.C. Cir. 1983).

268 *See* National Consumer Law Center, Student Loan Law § 9.5.2.4 (2d ed. 2002 and Supp.).

raise school-related defenses to FFEL collection actions when the school was in an "origination relationship" with the lender.[269] All of these theories for raising school-related defenses are discussed in detail in National Consumer Law Center, *Student Loan Law* § 9.5 (2d ed. 2002 and Supp.).

6.6.3 Operation of the FTC Holder Rule

6.6.3.1 Seller-Related Claims Covered by the Rule

The holder of a credit agreement containing the Holder Notice is liable for all seller-related "claims or defenses connected with the transaction."[270] As a result, consumers may not only raise seller-related *defenses* against creditors, but also may bring *affirmative claims* against the creditor relating to the seller.[271] The FTC Holder Rule has the force of law.[272]

The FTC rule does not define what claims can be brought against the seller, and hence the holder. The consumer can bring all claims against the holder that are available under state and other applicable law against the seller.

Creditors are liable for *all* claims and defenses involving the seller, including those relating to the advertising, oral claims, sale, warranties, insurance, service contracts, financing, collection, servicing of warranty, and anything else connected with the transaction.[273] The creditor is liable even if it would be exempt from direct liability under the statute

269 A good enunciation of this policy is found in a letter from Acting Assistant Secretary Whitehead to Congressman Stephen Solarz, Clearinghouse No. 44,343 (May 19, 1988). In addition, a recent Department of Education regulation requires schools to warn students that students can not raise school-related defenses against lenders "other than a loan made or originated by the school." 34 C.F.R. § 682.604(f)(2)(iii). *See also* 41 Fed. Reg. 4496 (Jan. 29, 1976) for an explanation of the origins of this policy. *But see* Jackson v. Culinary School of Washington, 27 F.3d 573 (D.C. Cir. 1994) (Secretary's origination policy not enforceable by students), *vacated on other grounds,* 115 S. Ct. 2573 (1995) (appellate court used de novo instead of abuse of discretion standard to review district court's decision to decide state law issues in declaratory judgment action), *op. reinstated in relevant part, remanding in part on other grounds,* 59 F.3d 254 (D.C. Cir. 1995).

270 16 C.F.R. § 433.2 [*reprinted at* Appx. B.2.1, *infra*].

271 *See* Gonzalez v. Old Kent Mortgage Co., 2000 U.S. Dist. LEXIS 14530 (E.D. Pa. Sept. 19, 2000); Boggess v. Lewis Raines Motors, Inc., 20 F. Supp. 2d 979 (S.D. W. Va. 1998) (allowing used car buyer to assert claims against assignee arising from seller's misrepresentation of car's mileage); Cole v. Lovett, 672 F. Supp. 947 (S.D. Miss. 1987) (Holder Notice makes assignee liable for homeowner's claim under home solicitation sales law against contractor), *aff'd without op.*, 833 F.2d 1008 (5th Cir. 1987); Eachen v. Scott Housing Sys., Inc., 630 F. Supp. 162 (M.D. Ala. 1986); Maberry v. Said, 911 F. Supp. 1393 (D. Kan. 1995); Tinker v. De Maria Porsche Audi, Inc., 459 So. 2d 487 (Fla. Dist. Ct. App. 1984); Bennett v. D. L. Claborn Buick, Inc., 414 S.E.2d 12 (Ga. Ct. App. 1991); Taylor v. Trans Acceptance Corp., 267 Ill. App. 3d 562, 641 N.E.2d 907 (1994) (consumer can assert fraud claims against assignee); Thomas v. Ford Motor Credit Co., 429 A.2d 277 (Md. App. 1981); Ford Motor Credit Co. v. Morgan, 404 Mass. 537, 536 N.E.2d 587 (1989); Scott v. Mayflower Home Improvement Corp., 363 N.J. Super. 145, 831 A.2d 564 (App. Civ. 2001); Hempstead Bank v. Babcock, 115 Misc. 2d 97, 453 N.Y.S. 2d 557 (Sup. Ct. 1982).

272 Beemus v. Interstate Nat'l Dealer Servs., Inc., 823 A.2d 979 (Pa. Super. 2003).

273 FTC Staff Guidelines, 41 Fed. Reg. 20024 (May 14, 1976), *reproduced on* the companion CD-Rom to this volume; Alvizo v. Metro Ford Sales & Serv., Inc., 2001 U.S. Dist. LEXIS 21777 (N.D. Ill. Dec. 28, 2001) (holder liable for dealer's conversion of personal property in car after buyer returned it); Javorsky v. Freedom Driving Aids, Inc., 2001 U.S. Dist. LEXIS 14078 (N.D. Ill. Aug. 29, 2001); Morales v. Walker Motors Sales, Inc., 162 F. Supp. 2d 786 (S.D. Ohio 2000) (because of FTC Holder Rule, holder steps into shoes of seller); Gaddy v. Galarza Motor Sport L.T.D., 2000 U.S. Dist. LEXIS 13881 (N.D. Ill. Sept. 18, 2000) (warranty claims); Armstrong v. Edelson, 718 F. Supp. 1372 (N.D. Ill. 1989) (FTC Holder Rule applies to claims for fraud, not just contract claims); Cole v. Lovett, 672 F. Supp. 947 (S.D. Miss. 1987) (state home solicitation sales act claims), *aff'd without op.*, 833 F.2d 1008 (5th Cir. 1987); Gill v. Fidelity Fin. Servs., Inc., 631 So. 2d 913 (Ala. 1993); Condor Capital Corp. v. Michaud, 2000 Conn. Super. LEXIS 1894 (July 25, 2000) (RISA and U.C.C. claims); Ford Motor Credit Co. v. Britton, 1996 Conn. Super. LEXIS 504 (Feb. 23, 1996) (used car lemon law claims); Felde v. Chrysler Credit Corp., 219 Ill. App. 3d 530, 580 N.E.2d 191 (1991) (warranty breach); First Homestead Fed. Sav. & Loan v. Boudreaux, 450 So. 2d 995 (La. Ct. App. 1984) (buyer can assert contractual arbitration requirement against assignee); GMAC v. Johnson, 426 So. 2d 691 (La. Ct. App. 1982) (warranty claims); Aillet v. Century Fin. Co., 391 So. 2d 895 (La. Ct. App. 1980) (nonperformance of seller's obligations grounds for return of amounts paid); Jerry v. Second Nat'l Bank, 208 Mich. App. 87, 527 N.W.2d 788 (1994) (applying provision of Michigan law nearly identical to FTC Holder Rule and finding that buyer's claims and defenses arose out of the transaction); Alduridi v. Community Trust Bank, 1999 Tenn. App. LEXIS 718 (Tenn. Ct. App. Oct. 26, 1999) (consumer can raise against assignee claims against the dealer relating to the dealer's failure to pay off consumer's obligations on trade-in vehicles; this is not a separate transaction from the consumer's purchase of new vehicles from the dealer); *cf.* Provident Bank v. Barnhart, 445 N.E.2d 746 (Ohio Ct. App. 1982) (issue of fact whether claim connected with the credit transaction). *But cf.* Ford Motor Credit Co. v. Dunsmore, 374 Pa. Super. Ct. 303, 542 A.2d 1033 (1988) (where consumer has no cause of action against seller, consumer can not use the FTC Holder Rule to bring action against seller's assignee). *See generally* National Consumer Law Center, Consumer Law Pleadings, No. 1, §§ 3.1, 3.2, 3.8, and 3.9 (CD-Rom and Index Guide) (complaint, interrogatories, and briefs in a case in which the creditor's liability was based upon the contract's inclusion of the notice required by the FTC Holder Rule); National Consumer Law Center, Consumer Class Actions: A Practical Litigation Guide Appxs. D.1 (sample class action complaint in home improvement case in which the creditor's liability was based on the same clause), H.1 (motion and order for protection of class members' files), O.3.1 (class action settlement notice), P.1 (settlement stipulation), R.1 (memo in support of approval of settlement) (5th ed. 2003 and Supp.), also found on the CD-Rom accompanying this volume.

on which the consumer's claim against the seller is based.[274] As long as the creditor's liability is below the maximum cap under the FTC rule, the creditor should be liable for the consumer's claims against the seller, even if those claims involve attorney fees, statutory, treble, or punitive damages.[275]

On the other hand, if the consumer's claim against a seller is based on an entirely separate transaction with the seller, a transaction not involving the creditor, the creditor will have no liability since "the holder's obligations are limited to those arising from the transaction which he finances."[276]

6.6.3.2 Consumer's Claims Can Offset Remainder Due on the Note

Since the FTC Holder Rule limits the consumer's recovery from the creditor for seller-related claims to the "amounts paid by the debtor hereunder,"[277] sometimes there is confusion as to whether the consumer can also offset the remainder due on the note. The FTC Holder Rule statement that "recovery hereunder by the debtor shall not exceed amounts paid by the debtor hereunder" does *not* mean that the consumer can *only* get back payments already made on the loan. It means the consumer can get back these payments *plus* cancel all remaining indebtedness under the note.

According to the FTC, the consumer can "sue to liquidate the unpaid balance owed to the creditor and to recover the amounts paid under the contract."[278] "The consumer may assert, by way of claim or defense, a right not to pay all or part of the outstanding balance owed the creditor under the contract; but the consumer will not be entitled to receive from the creditor an affirmative recovery which exceeds the amounts of money the consumer had paid in."[279] In other words, the consumer can obtain a declaration that the remaining loan balance is unenforceable, if the consumer's claims and defenses merit such relief.[280] Likewise, if the consumer has the right under applicable law to withhold payment from the seller, the consumer may withhold payment from the assignee.[281]

6.6.3.3 Effect on Security Interest

In the typical consumer transaction, the entity that financed the sale will have a security interest in the items purchased and possibly other property as well. If the consumer has claims or defenses that offset the entire debt, then there is no longer any obligation for the collateral to secure. In this event, the secured party has a duty under Article 9 of the Uniform Commercial Code to document that the security interest has terminated.[282] Likewise, if the consumer's claims reduce the amount of the debt, the collateral secures only the reduced obligation, and the creditor must file a termination statement once the consumer pays the reduced amount. The consumer also has the right to deduct damages for breach of contract from the payments owing on the debt.[283]

Some courts have had difficulty with the analysis in the situation where the consumer revokes acceptance of the goods. Under Article 2 of the UCC, after revoking accep-

274 Milchen v. Bob Morris Pontiac-GMC Truck, 113 Ohio App. 3d 190, 680 N.E.2d 698 (1996). *See* § 2.2.1.5, *supra*.

275 Music Acceptance Corp. v. Lofing, 32 Cal. App. 4th 610, 39 Cal. Rptr. 2d 159 (1995) (warranty claims). *See also* Scott v. Mayflower Home Improvement Corp., 363 N.J. Super. 145, 831 A.2d 564 (App. Civ. 2001) (assignee liable for treble damages and attorney fees only if this is within the cap of the amount paid by the consumer). *But see* Hardeman v. Wheels, Inc., 56 Ohio App. 3d 142 (1988) (punitive and treble damages and attorney fees can not be set off against amount owed on debt where assignee is not subject to state UDAP statute). For a critique of *Hardeman*, see M. Greenfield & N. Ross, *Limits on a Consumer's Ability to Assert Claims and Defenses Under the FTC's Holder in Due Course Rule*, 46 Bus. Law. 1135 (May 1991).

276 FTC Staff Guidelines, 41 Fed. Reg. 20024 (May 14, 1976), *reproduced on* the companion CD-Rom to this volume. *But see* Jerry v. Second Nat'l Bank, 527 N.W.2d 788 (Mich. Ct. App. 1994) (applying provision of Michigan law nearly identical to FTC Holder Rule and finding that buyer's claims and defenses arose out of the transaction); Alduridi v. Community Trust Bank, 1999 Tenn. App. LEXIS 718 (Tenn. Ct. App. Oct. 26, 1999) (consumer can raise against assignee claims against the dealer relating to the dealer's failure to pay off consumer's obligations on trade-in vehicles; this is not a separate transaction from the consumer's purchase of new vehicles from the dealer).

277 16 C.F.R. § 433.2 [*reprinted at* Appx. B.2.1, *infra*].

278 FTC Staff Guidelines, 41 Fed. Reg. 20023 (May 14, 1976), *reproduced on* the companion CD-Rom to this volume.

279 *Id.*

280 Ellis v. General Motors Acceptance Corp., 160 F.3d 703, 709 (11th Cir. 1998) (Holder Notice gives buyer right to withhold payment if car is a lemon); Ransom v. Rohr-Gurnee Volkswagen, Inc., 2001 U.S. Dist. LEXIS 17363 (N.D. Ill. Oct. 22, 2001) (Holder Notice gives buyer the right to withhold payment if a car is a lemon); Mount v. LaSalle Bank Lake View, 926 F. Supp. 759 (N.D. Ill. 1996); Music Acceptance Corp. v. Lofing, 32 Cal. App. 4th 610, 39 Cal. Rptr. 2d 159 (1995); Tinker v. DeMaria Porsche Audi, Inc., 459 So. 2d 487 (Fla. Dist. Ct. App. 1984); Jackson v. South Holland Dodge, Inc., 197 Ill. 2d 39, 755 N.E.2d 462, 258 Ill. Dec. 79 (2001) (same); Ford Motor Credit Co. v. Morgan, 404 Mass. 537, 536 N.E.2d 587 (1989); Perez v. Briercroft Service Corp., 809 S.W.2d 216 (Tex. 1991); Home Sav. Ass'n v. Guerra, 733 S.W.2d 134 (Tex. 1987); Reliance Mortgage Co. v. Hill-Shields, 2001 Tex. App. LEXIS 140 (Tex. App. Jan. 10, 2001); Oxford Fin. Cos. v. Velez, 807 S.W.2d 460 (Tex. App. 1991); Green Tree Acceptance, Inc. v. Pierce, 768 S.W.2d 416 (Tex. App. 1989); Alvarez v. Union Mortgage Co., 747 S.W.2d 484 (Tex. App. 1988). *See also* Tinker v. DeMaria Porsche Audi, Inc., 459 So. 2d 487 (Fla. Dist. Ct. App. 1984); Shelter Am. Corp. v. Edwards, 1987 Tex. App. LEXIS 7954 (July 30, 1987); *cf.* Briercroft Service Corp. v. De Los Santos, 776 S.W.2d 198 (Tex. App. 1988).

281 FTC Advisory Op., 89 F.T.C. 675 (Apr. 6, 1977).

282 U.C.C. § 9-513 (formerly U.C.C. 9-404).

283 U.C.C. § 2-717. *See* National Consumer Law Center, Consumer Warranty Law § 8.5 (2d ed. 2001 and Supp.).

tance and canceling the sale, the consumer no longer owes any part of the purchase price to the seller.[284] Further, Article 2 gives the consumer a security interest in the goods until the seller refunds the purchase price and reimburses the consumer for the expenses reasonably incurred in inspecting, receiving, transporting, caring for, and holding the goods.[285] As the secured party, the consumer has the obligation to use reasonable care in the custody and preservation of the goods.[286]

Properly analyzed, the FTC Holder Rule places the assignee or related lender in exactly the same shoes as the seller: because of the revocation of acceptance and cancellation of the sale, the consumer's obligation to pay for the goods is cancelled, so there is no obligation for the collateral to secure. Since the assignee or related lender is subject to the same revocation claims as the dealer, the consumer owes no money and can not be in default. As the FTC stated in a formal opinion letter soon after the FTC Holder Rule was adopted: "if the consumer, under applicable law, is entitled to withhold payments from the seller, he may, pursuant to the notice, withhold payment from the holder."[287] The consumer has the right to retain possession of the collateral until any payments and expenses are refunded.

While one court has accepted this analysis,[288] other courts, primarily in Illinois, have confused the issue with an analysis of UCC Article 9's rules regarding the priority among competing security interests.[289] This approach is wrong, because after revocation both the obligation and the creditor's security interest cease to exist, so the only security interest is the consumer's.

The factor that may have troubled the Illinois courts was that the consumer's revocation of acceptance was unilateral, neither accepted by the seller or creditor nor approved by a court. But the UCC also gives creditors self-help remedies such as repossession, so the existence of a self-help remedy for consumers is perfectly consistent with the UCC's approach. Nonetheless, courts are more likely to accept the effect of the FTC Holder Rule on the creditor's security interest if the consumer is seeking or has obtained a court ruling upholding the claim or defense against the creditor.

6.6.3.4 Recovery of Amounts Already Paid

6.6.3.4.1 General

In addition to canceling all or part of the indebtedness, under the rule, the consumer can seek an affirmative cash recovery. In practice, in individual cases, the consumer's claim is usually applied first to reduce the indebtedness the consumer owes the holder. If the consumer's claim exceeds this amount, then the consumer can recover the difference affirmatively from the holder.[290]

The rule limits the consumer's affirmative recovery to the amount the consumer has already "paid in."[291] In other words, the consumer's maximum recovery under the rule is cancellation of all remaining indebtedness plus an affirmative recovery of the amount already paid in on the debt. Some state holder laws also make this an explicit rule, for example by limiting the creditor's liability to the amount owing on the credit contract.[292]

In calculating the amounts paid in, add both the amounts the consumer paid to the note holder and any amount paid to a prior holder of the note. The fact that a holder never received any money from the consumer is no defense to a judgment against that holder for amounts paid to other holders.[293] The FTC has made clear that the holder is in much better position than the consumer, through use of reserve and recourse arrangements, to easily recover any amounts owed from the holder's assignor.[294] While the holder can easily recover that amount paid to a prior holder, it may be practically impossible for the consumer to do so.

Where a credit sales contract is assigned to a creditor, the amount paid in by the consumer includes all deposits and

284 U.C.C. § 2-711.

285 U.C.C. § 2-711(3).

286 U.C.C. § 9-207(a).

287 Advisory Opinion, 89 F.T.C. 675, 1977 FTC LEXIS 233 (Apr. 6, 1977). *Accord* Ellis v. GMAC, 160 F.3d 703, 709 (11th Cir. 1998) (Holder Notice "affirms the right of buyers to withhold payment from sellers *or* assignees, if the cars they purchase turn out to be lemons"); Ransom v. Rohr-Gurnee Volkswagen, Inc., 2001 U.S. Dist. LEXIS 17363 (N.D. Ill. Oct. 22, 2001); Jackson v. South Holland Dodge, 197 Ill. 2d 39, 755 N.E.2d 462, 258 Ill. Dec. 79 (2001) (erroneously confining affirmative actions against assignees to those where seller's breach is so substantial that rescission is warranted, but confirming the right to withhold payment from the assignee if a car is a lemon).

288 Ford Motor Credit Co. v. Caiazzo, 387 Pa. Super. 561, 564 A.2d 931 (1989).

289 Ambre v. Joe Madden Ford, 881 F. Supp. 1182 (N.D. Ill. 1995); Valentino v. Glendale Nissan, Inc., 317 Ill. App. 3d 524, 740 N.E.2d 538 (2000). *But see* Jackson v. South Holland Dodge, Inc., 197 Ill. 2d 39, 755 N.E.2d 462, 258 Ill. Dec. 79 (2001) (erroneously confining affirmative actions against assignees to those where seller's breach warrants rescission, but confirming "the right of buyers to withhold payment from sellers or assignees, if it becomes apparent that the car purchased is a lemon").

290 *Cf.* Schauer v. GMAC, 819 So. 2d 809 (Fla. Dist. Ct. App. 2002) (no affirmative recovery where did not allege claim exceeded amount still owed the creditor).

291 *See* Resolution Trust Corp. v. Cook, 840 S.W.2d 42 (Tex. App. 1992); Oxford Fin. Cos. v. Velez, 807 S.W.2d 460 (Tex. App. 1991).

292 *See* § 6.6.3.11.1, *infra*.

293 Green Tree Acceptance, Inc. v. Pirtle, 1999 WL 33740367 (E.D. Mich. Mar. 1, 1999) (buyer may recover down payment from assignee even though assignee did not receive it); Alduridi v. Community Trust Bank, 1999 Tenn. App. LEXIS 718 (Tenn. Ct. App. Oct. 26, 1999) (creditor, not the consumer should bear the risk of recovering payments made to the dealer); Resolution Trust Corp. v. Cook, 840 S.W.2d 42 (Tex. App. 1992).

294 *See* § 6.6.1.1, *supra*.

trade-ins the consumer has given to the seller.[295] The consumer can thus recover affirmatively all periodic payments and late charges paid either to the seller or an assignee, and also the total amount of the consumer's down payment and the value of the trade-in. In determining the value of the trade-in, utilize the amount stated in the contract, even if the holder argues that this valuation was inflated.[296] After all, this is the value the parties agreed to after negotiation.

The amount paid in on a direct loan is calculated differently. This is the amounts paid to the originating lender and all subsequent assignees. Since in this type of loan, the trade-in and down payments go to the dealer, and not the originating lender, these amounts given to the *seller* are *not* amounts paid to the creditor.

For example, in a credit sale, if a consumer makes a $1000 down payment and trades in a car for a $3000 credit, and then purchases a $10,000 car, the amount financed will be $6000. The consumer, in an action against the seller's assignee, can seek a maximum of: (1) cancellation of the remaining indebtedness on the $6000 loan; *plus* (2) an affirmative recovery of monthly installment payments already paid to the dealer or assignee; *plus* (3) the $4000 trade-in and down payment. If this were a direct loan from a related creditor, the $6000 loan would be canceled, amounts paid the creditor could be returned, but the consumer could not recover the $4000 trade-in and down payment.

A creditor's maximum liability should also include the price which the creditor realizes when it sells collateral after repossession. This sale price reduces the size of the indebtedness and, in effect, is a payment on the loan. It should be treated as "an amount paid hereunder," and the creditor's maximum liability should include this amount.[297]

6.6.3.4.2 *Recovering from a prior holder*

In some cases, the consumer will want to bring into an action the prior holder in a case, and one of the claims against that party may be based on the seller's misconduct. In other words, the consumer may seek to recover affirmatively for the seller's misconduct not from the seller or the final holder, but from an intermediary holder. There is little case law in this area, but the decisions that do exist hold that the consumer can bring seller-related claims against intermediate holders.[298]

6.6.3.4.3 *Is recovery of amount paid only available where consumer could rescind sale or goods or services have no value?*

Although the FTC rule clearly states that consumers can recover on their claims all amounts the consumer has already paid, several courts, starting with *Ford Motor Credit Co. v. Morgan*,[299] have found otherwise. These courts acknowledge that consumers in a collection action can raise defenses that cancel the remainder of the amount due, and that they can sue affirmatively to both cancel the amount due and (at least in certain situations) to recover affirmatively. But these courts hold that consumers can only sue to recover the amount already paid where the consumer could rescind the sale or the goods or services have little or no value.

These courts reach this strange result based on a misinterpretation of two statements in the FTC's *Statement of Basis and Purpose* for the rule, to the effect that a consumer will obtain a positive recovery from the creditor only when the consumer rescinds or has received little or nothing of value.[300] These cases misconstrue these quotations as setting up a *legal* requirement that the consumer can recover affirmatively against a creditor only if the claim is for rescission or where the product has little or no value.

Instead, the quotations simply make the obvious *practical* point that consumers will only recover affirmatively where

295 Green Tree Acceptance, Inc. v. Pirtle, 1999 WL 33740367 (E.D. Mich. Mar. 1, 1999); Maberry v. Said, 911 F. Supp. 1393 (D. Kan. 1995); Featherlite Credit Corp. v. Caride, 2000 Del. Super. LEXIS 206 (Del. Super. Ct. May 30, 2000); Credit Acceptance Corp. v. Banks, 1999 Ohio App. LEXIS 6058 (Dec. 16, 1999); Credit Acceptance Corp. v. Smith, No. 96CVF01066, Clearinghouse No. 52,138 (Mun. Ct. of Vandalia, Ohio July 31, 1997); FTC Staff Guidelines, 41 Fed. Reg. 20023 (May 14, 1976), *reproduced on* the companion CD-Rom to this volume. *But see* General Motors Acceptance Corp. v. Grady, 27 Ohio App. 3d 321, 501 N.E.2d 68 (1985) (without discussion, court grants judgment against assignee only in amount of monthly payment, not in amount of down payment; consumer had requested judgment only in this amount).

296 Featherlite Credit Corp. v. Caride, 2000 Del. Super. LEXIS 206 (Del. Super. Ct. May 30, 2000).

297 Alduridi v. Community Trust Bank, 1999 Tenn. App. LEXIS 718 (Tenn. Ct. App. Oct. 26, 1999); *see also* BCS Fin. Corp. v. Sorbo, 444 S.E.2d 85 (Ga. Ct. App. 1994). *But cf.* Oxford Fin. Cos. v. Velez, 807 S.W.2d 460 (Tex. App. 1991) (proceeds of foreclosure sale not recoverable where court voids the foreclosure sale).

298 *In re* Barker, 306 B.R. 339, 350–51 (Bankr. E.D. Cal. 2004) (assignor's repurchase of debt does not relieve assignee of liability); Associates Home Equity Servs., Inc. v. Troup, 343 N.J. Super. 254, 778 A.2d 529 (App. Div. 2001); Resolution Trust Corp. v. Cook, 840 S.W.2d 42 (Tex. App. 1992).

299 404 Mass. 537, 536 N.E.2d 587 (1989). *Accord* Herrara v. North & Kimball Group, Inc., 2002 U.S. Dist. LEXIS 2640 (N.D. Ill. Feb. 15, 2002) (court also seems to indicate that forgery of contract is insufficient to warrant rescission); Crews v. Altavista Motors, Inc., 65 F. Supp. 2d 388 (W.D. Va. 1999); Boggess v. Lewis Raines Motors, Inc., 20 F. Supp. 2d 979 (S.D. W. Va. 1998); Taylor v. Bob O'Connor Ford, Inc., 1998 U.S. Dist. LEXIS 5095 (N.D. Ill. Apr. 10, 1998); Mount v. LaSalle Bank Lake View, 926 F. Supp. 759 (N.D. Ill. 1996); *In re* Hillsborough Holdings Corp., 146 B.R. 1015 (Bankr. M.D. Fla. 1992); Mardis v. Ford Motor Credit Co., 642 So. 2d 701 (Ala. 1994); Felde v. Chrysler Credit Corp, 219 Ill. App. 3d 530, 580 N.E.2d 191.

300 *See* 40 Fed. Reg. 53524, 53527 (Nov. 18, 1975).

their claims are serious enough to exceed the remainder of the debt owed.[301] For example, the FTC staff at the time stated "The vast majority of cases, in the staff's opinion, will involve a limited right of set-off against the unpaid balance. Most sellers do not do business in a way that creates a right to rescission or significant consequential damages."[302]

The FTC is observing that consumers can not receive an affirmative recovery until their claims are so large that the claims first wipe out the remainder of the debt. Then the claims can be used to obtain a positive recovery, capped by the amount the consumer has already paid on the loan.

Several factors support this conclusion. The rule itself indicates that holders are subject to *all* claims, and in no way limits such claims to those for rescission or to those where the product has no value. Several courts have relied on the plain language of the rule in rejecting the *Morgan* theory.[303] The same point is made in the FTC Staff's Guidelines for the rule:

> The Rule does apply to all claims or defenses connected with the transaction, whether in tort or contract. When, under state law, a consumer would have a tort claim against the seller that would defeat a seller's right to further payments or allow the consumer to recover affirmatively, this claim is preserved against the holder.[304]

The guidelines also state:

> This limits a consumer to a refund of monies paid under the contract, in the event that an affirmative money recovery is sought. In other words, the consumer may assert, by way of a *claim or defense*, a right not to pay all *or part* of the outstanding balance owed the creditor under the contract. . . .[305]

Moreover, to allow affirmative recovery only where a product has little or no value or where the claim is for "rescission" is too vague a standard to be administered. The FTC rule provides no guidance because there was no intent by the FTC to make this distinction.

Finally, this distinction lacks any rational basis for its different treatment of consumers with identical claims. To allow one consumer to recover for the claim by deducting its amount from the amount due on the contract, but to prevent affirmative recovery for the identical claim because a second consumer has already paid off most or all of the debt makes no sense.[306]

In an important development that will hopefully lay this issue to rest, a 1999 FTC staff interpretation explicitly states that *Morgan* and the cases that follow it incorrectly interpret the FTC rule and the FTC's language from the *Statement of Basis and Purpose*.[307] The FTC staff letter states that these cases are wrong, and that there is no restriction on when the consumer can obtain an affirmative recovery under the FTC rule.

The FTC letter states that the FTC's *Statement of Basis and Purpose* was merely making the practical point that an affirmative recovery requires a consumer claim large enough to first fully satisfy the remainder due on the debt, before the consumer is entitled to a positive recovery. The FTC Staff Letter states "the provision is quite clear. The consumer may recover his or her down payment (all deposits and trade-ins given to the seller), and all installment payments made pursuant to the contract, but no more. There are no other limitations on the creditor/assignee's liability under the required contract language."

Courts must give great weight not only to this FTC interpretation of its own rule, but even more so to its interpretation of its own *Statement of Basis and Purpose*—who better to determine what was meant by a statement than the entity that said it.[308]

Fortunately, a combination of this FTC staff letter and a growing understanding among courts of the issues involved has produced an impressive array of cases that reject *Morgan* and its progeny.[309]

301 *See* Lozada v. Dale Baker Oldsmobile, 91 F. Supp. 2d 1087 (W.D. Mich. 2000); Beemus v. Interstate Nat'l Dealer Servs., Inc., 823 A.2d 979 (Pa. Super. 2003); Oxford Fin. Cos. v. Velez, 807 S.W.2d 460 (Tex. App. 1991); M. Greenfield & N. Ross, *Limits on a Consumer's Ability to Assert Claims and Defenses Under the FTC's Holder in Due Course Rule*, 46 Bus. Law. 1135 (May 1991).

302 FTC Staff Guidelines, 41 Fed. Reg. 20024 (May 14, 1976), *reproduced on* the companion CD-Rom to this volume.

303 Lozada v. Dale Baker Oldsmobile, 91 F. Supp. 2d 1087, 1094 (W.D. Mich. 2000); Simpson v. Anthony Auto Sales, Inc., 32 F. Supp. 2d 405 (W.D. La. 1998); Beemus v. Interstate Nat'l Dealer Servs., Inc., 823 A.2d 979 (Pa. Super. 2003) (language of rule is unambiguous, so no need to refer to Statement of Basis and Purpose); Oxford Fin. Cos. v. Velez, 807 S.W.2d 460 (Tex. App. 1991).

304 41 Fed. Reg. 20024 (May 14, 1976). *See also* Lozada v. Dale Baker Oldsmobile, 91 F. Supp. 2d 1087 (W.D. Mich. 2000) (citing to other sections of staff guidelines as support for its criticism of the *Morgan* line of cases); Oxford Fin. Cos. v. Velez, 807 S.W.2d 460 (Tex. App. 1991).

305 41 Fed. Reg. 20222 at 20023–4 (May 14, 1976).

306 For a similar critique of Morgan, see M. Greenfield & N. Ross, Limits on a Consumer's Ability to Assert Claims and Defenses Under the FTC's Holder in Due Course Rule, 46 Bus. Law. 1135 (May 1991).

307 Letter of David Medine, Associate Director, Division of Financial Practices, to Jonathan Sheldon, National Consumer Law Center, Clearinghouse No. 52,487 (Sept. 25, 1999), *reprinted at* Appx. B.2.2, *infra*.

308 *See* Ford Motor Credit Co. v. Milhollin, 444 U.S. 555 (1980) (courts should show deference to FRB interpretations of Truth in Lending); Lozada v. Dale Baker Oldsmobile, 91 F. Supp. 2d 1087, 1096 (W.D. Mich. 2000) (citing Medine letter as part of analysis rejecting *Morgan*).

309 Gonzalez v. Old Kent Mortg. Co., 2000 U.S. Dist. LEXIS 14530 (E.D. Pa. Sept. 19, 2000); Lozada v. Dale Baker Oldsmobile, 91 F. Supp. 2d 1087 (W.D. Mich. 2000) (citing FTC staff letter); Riggs v. Anthony Auto Sales, Inc., 32 F. Supp. 2d 411 (W.D. La.

If a court adopts the *Morgan* approach, then the consumer should argue that *Morgan* only requires, for the consumer to recover affirmatively, that rescission be an available remedy in the facts of the case, not that the consumer must in fact have exercised the right to rescind the transaction.[310] If the court adopts this approach, then it is often easy for the consumer to show that the transaction could have been rescinded based on the seller's misrepresentation or because of substantial defects in the goods leading to revocation of acceptance. For example, one court found that fraudulent misrepresentation of odometer mileage is sufficient to justify rescission and restitution. Thus, the consumers could recover affirmatively from the holder.[311]

Another approach is to bring a claim under a state statute that makes lenders derivatively liable for a related seller's misconduct.[312] The FTC has explicitly stated that state law is preserved where it would provide a greater consumer recovery against a lender than is provided for by the FTC Holder Rule.[313] If a court were to determine that the state law provides for an affirmative consumer recovery, then that should be allowed despite any contrary interpretation the court might have under the FTC rule.

6.6.3.4.4 *Is recovery of amounts paid available only where otherwise permitted by state law?*

In *LaBarre v. Credit Acceptance Corp.*,[314] the Eighth Circuit seriously misinterpreted the operation of the FTC Holder Rule. It held that Minnesota law should decide when consumers under the FTC Holder Rule can raise seller-related claims against assignees. Relying on a Minnesota statute that limits a consumer to raising defenses, not claims, against an assignee, the court came to the conclusion that the FTC Holder Rule does not allow affirmative recovery for cases brought in Minnesota. That is, while consumers can raise seller-related misconduct defensively in response to an assignee's collection action, in Minnesota they can not do so affirmatively by bringing an action against the assignee to recover amounts already paid that assignee, all because a Minnesota statute predating the FTC Holder Rule did not offer consumers as much protection as the FTC Holder Rule.

The FTC Holder Notice states that the holder of the credit contract is subject to *all claims* the debtor can assert against the seller.[315] As the Eighth Circuit correctly noted, what claims the consumer can bring against the seller are not defined by the FTC rule, but include any legally sufficient claim the consumer may have in a sales transaction. State law is important in determining what claims can be brought against the *seller*, and hence the holder.

Where the Eighth Circuit made its fatal mistake was in confusing the relevance of state law limits on what claims can be brought against the seller with the relevance of state law limitations on what claims can be brought against an assignee. Minnesota law, enacted before promulgation of the FTC Holder Rule, allows consumers to raise seller-related defenses against an assignee, but not to raise those seller-related defenses as affirmative claims against the assignee. The Eighth Circuit applied this Minnesota limitation to what claims can be brought against the *assignee* to determine what claims can be brought, pursuant to the FTC Holder Notice, against the *seller*.

This is clearly wrong.[316] Taken to its logical extension, the ruling would make a nullity of the FTC Holder Rule, giving it no greater effect than already existing under state law. In other words, the *LaBarre* ruling not only eliminates any effect of the FTC Holder Rule, but creates deceptive notices in consumer contracts which indicate the consumer has rights that *LaBarre* would take away. More discussion of why this case is wrong can be found at § 6.6.3.11.2, *infra*.

1998); Simpson v. Anthony Auto Sales, Inc., 32 F. Supp. 2d 405 (W.D. La. 1998); Maberry v. Said, 911 F. Supp. 1393 (D. Kan. 1995) (holder rule permits affirmative claims); Scott v. Mayflower Home Improvement Corp., 363 N.J. Super. 145, 831 A.2d 564 (Law Div. 2001); Jaramillo v. Gonzales, 50 P.3d 554 (N.M. Ct. App. 2002) (purchaser of mobile home is not required to show that home had little or no value in order to recover affirmatively); Beemus v. Interstate Nat'l Dealer Servs., Inc., Beemus v. Interstate Nat'l Dealer Servs., Inc., 823 A.2d 979 (Pa. Super. 2003) (citing FTC staff letter); Homziak v. Gen. Elec. Capital Warranty Corp., Clearinghouse No. 54,551 (Pa. C.P. Ct. May 21, 2001); Resolution Trust Corp. v. Cook, 840 S.W.2d 42 (Tex. App. 1992); Oxford Fin. Cos. v. Velez, 807 S.W.2d 460 (Tex. App. 1991); M. Greenfield & N. Ross, *Limits on a Consumer's Ability to Assert Claims and Defenses Under the FTC's Holder in Due Course Rule*, 46 Bus. Law. 1135 (May 1991). *Cf.* Shelter Am. Corp. v. Edwards, 1987 Tex. App. LEXIS 7954 (July 30, 1987) (allowing consumer recovery where *Morgan* reasoning would deny affirmative recovery).

310 Eromon v. Grand Auto Sales, Inc., 2004 WL 1794916 (N.D. Ill. Aug. 4, 2004) (claim may be asserted against assignee if consumer would have been unlikely to enter into contract in absence of dealer's wrongdoing); Reavley v. Toyota Motor Sales U.S. Corp., 2001 WL 127662, at *4 (N.D. Ill. Feb. 14, 2001) (express claim of rescission is not required as long as breach was so substantial as to justify rescission). *See also* Boggess v. Lewis Raines Motors, Inc., 20 F. Supp. 2d 979 (S.D. W. Va. 1998); M. Greenfield & N. Ross, *Limits on a Consumer's Ability to Assert Claims and Defenses Under the FTC's Holder in Due Course Rule*, 46 Bus. Law. 1135 (May 1991).

311 Boggess v. Lewis Raines Motors, Inc., 20 F. Supp. 2d 979 (S.D. W. Va. 1998).

312 Such state statutes are examined at § 6.6.3.11, *infra*.

313 *See* § 6.6.3.11, *infra*.

314 175 F.3d 640 (8th Cir. 1999).

315 16 C.F.R. § 433.2.

316 *See* Milchen v. Bob Morris Pontiac-GMC Truck, 113 Ohio App. 3d 190, 680 N.E.2d 698 (1996) (FTC Holder Rule does not make creditor liable only for claims for which it would be liable under existing state law).

6.6.3.5 Are Attorney Fees Included Within the Cap?

The creditor's liability for the consumer's attorney fees should not be capped by the creditor's maximum liability for seller-related claims.[317] The consumer's right to recover the fees incurred in enforcing the creditor's liability is based on the UDAP statute, not on the Holder Notice, so it is not a "recovery hereunder" that is subject to the cap. In other words, the creditor's liability for fees is not a derivative liability, but is based on its own actions in refusing to resolve the consumer's claim. Attorney fees are not awarded because of the seller's conduct, but because of the creditor's conduct. It is the creditor who is refusing to settle the claim and who insists on litigating the issues. Even if the creditor's UDAP liability is based on the seller's misdeeds, its liability for attorney fees is based on its own actions in litigating the claim.[318]

The purpose of attorney fees is to encourage settlement, make it economically feasible for consumers to bring small claims, and to discourage sellers and creditors from using their superior legal resources to wear down the consumer. All of these purposes would be thwarted if attorney fees were lumped in with the recovery on the merits and capped at the amount of the creditor's maximum liability.

The argument for recovery of attorney fees above the cap is even stronger in those states, such as California, that treat fees as costs, incidental to a judgment, not as part of damages. Since the fees are in the nature of costs, they should be awarded separately from the issue of how much in damages can be provided under the cap.

6.6.3.6 Multiple or Punitive Damages

To the extent that treble or punitive damages are based on the seller's willful misconduct, the holder should be liable for those damages, but the holder's maximum liability for those damages should probably be capped under the FTC rule as with any other damages.[319] The fact that the holder did not authorize the willful conduct is irrelevant, because what is at issue is the holder's liability for all claims the consumer has against the seller, up to the cap.

There is one case where a holder might be liable for treble damages in excess of the cap. To the extent treble damages are awarded because the *creditor* has not engaged in a good faith attempt at settlement of seller-related claims,[320] such multiple damages should not be capped for the same reasons that attorney fees should not be capped.

6.6.3.7 No Limit on Creditor's Liability for Own Conduct

The FTC rule sets out a creditor's liability for the acts of the seller. The creditor is additionally liable for its own conduct,[321] or its own participation in another's misconduct.[322] The lender can even be independently liable for its own conduct in misleading the consumer as to the consumer's right to raise seller-related claims against the lender.[323] There are no limits under the FTC Holder Rule to the creditor's liability for its own conduct, and the amount of that liability is then added above and beyond its maximum liability for the seller's conduct.[324]

Some creditors argue that their liability for their own misconduct is limited to the FTC Holder Rule limits. They argue that as a contract term, the consumer has waived any right to recovery beyond the "amounts paid by the debtor

---

317 Kish v. Van Note, 692 S.W.2d 463 (Tex. 1985); *see also In re* Stewart, 93 B.R. 878 (Bankr. E.D. Pa. 1988); Home Savings Ass'n v. Guerra, 733 S.W.2d 134 (Tex. 1987); Reliance Mortgage Co. v. Hill-Shields, 2001 Tex. App. LEXIS 140 (Tex. App. Jan. 10, 2001); Oxford Fin. Cos. v. Velez, 807 S.W.2d 460 (Tex. App. 1991); Briercroft Service Corp. v. Perez, 820 S.W.2d 813 (Tex. App. 1990), *aff'd in relevant part, rev'd in part on other grounds*, 809 S.W.2d 216 (Tex. 1991); Green Tree Acceptance, Inc. v. Pierce, 768 S.W.2d 416 (Tex. App. 1989). *But see* Riggs v. Anthony Auto Sales, Inc., 32 F. Supp. 2d 411 (W.D. La. 1998); Simpson v. Anthony Auto Sales, Inc., 32 F. Supp. 2d 405 (W.D. La. 1998); Scott v. Mayflower Home Improvement Corp., 363 N.J. Super. 145, 831 A.2d 564 (Law Div. 2001) (plaintiffs may not recover attorney fees in excess of amounts they paid); Alduridi v. Community Trust Bank, 1999 Tenn. App. LEXIS 718 (Tenn. Ct. App. Oct. 26, 1999); Patton v. McHone, 1993 Tenn. App. LEXIS 212 (Tenn. Ct. App. 1993).

318 *But see* Alduridi v. Community Trust Bank, 1999 Tenn. App. LEXIS 718 (Tenn. Ct. App. Oct. 26, 1999) (holding that fees awarded in whole or in part for claims based on the seller's misconduct are subject to the cap).

319 Simpson v. Anthony Auto Sales, Inc., 32 F. Supp. 2d 405 (W.D. La. 1998); Music Acceptance Corp. v. Lofing, 32 Cal. App. 4th 610, 39 Cal. Rptr. 2d 159 (1995); Scott v. Mayflower Home Improvement Corp., 363 N.J. Super. 145, 831 A.2d 564 (Law Div. 2001) (treble damages barred if they would push recovery over cap); Briercroft Service Corp. v. Perez, 820 S.W.2d 813 (Tex. App. 1990), *rev'd in part on other grounds*, 809 S.W.2d 216 (Tex. 1991). *But see* Hardeman v. Wheels, Inc., 56 Ohio App. 3d 142, 565 N.E.2d 849 (1988) (punitive and treble damages and attorney fees can not be set off against amount owed on debt where assignee is not subject to state UDAP statute). For a critique of *Hardeman*, see M. Greenfield & N. Ross, *Limits on a Consumer's Ability to Assert Claims and Defenses Under the FTC's Holder in Due Course Rule*, 46 Bus. Law. 1135 (May 1991).

320 *See* § 6.6.3.13, *infra*.

321 See § 5.1, *supra* for an analysis of UDAP violations related to credit.

322 *See* § 6.5, *supra*.

323 *See* § 6.6.3.13, *infra*.

324 *See* Eremon v. Grand Auto Sales, Inc., 2004 WL 1794916, at *2 n.1 (N.D. Ill. Aug. 4, 2004) (if creditor actually participated in deceptive scheme, FTC Holder Rule cap is inapplicable); Briercroft Service Corp. v. Perez, 820 S.W.2d 813 (Tex. App. 1990) (court recognizes that independent wrongful conduct could be basis for recovery beyond amount paid to creditor), *rev'd in part on other grounds*, 809 S.W.2d 216 (Tex. 1991). *Cf.* Resolution Trust Corp. v. Cook, 840 S.W.2d 42 (Tex. App. 1992).

hereunder." What these arguments miss is that the provision states that recovery "hereunder" is so limited. But recovery on an independent theory clearly is not. The purpose of the FTC rule is to protect consumers, not to protect creditors. "The words 'recovery hereunder' . . . refer specifically to a recovery under the Notice. If a larger affirmative recovery is available against a creditor as a matter of state law, the consumer would retain this right."[325]

6.6.3.8 Relationship of FTC Rule and Federal Statutes Limiting Liability

6.6.3.8.1 Relation to TIL and ECOA limits on assignee liability

Another issue is the interplay among the FTC Holder Rule, the Truth in Lending Act (TILA), and the Equal Credit Opportunity Act (ECOA). The TILA explicitly limits an assignee's TIL liability to those TIL violations apparent on the face of the documents. But an assignee with no liability under the TILA arguably is liable under the FTC Holder Rule for the full amount of the *assignor's* TIL liability (subject, of course, to the maximum liability cap under the FTC Holder Rule). That is, since the contract explicitly states the assignee is liable for claims against the assignor, this contract clause must be given effect.

A few courts have followed this argument and found an assignee liable under the FTC Holder Rule for assignor-related TIL claims.[326] The trend, though, is for courts to reach the opposite conclusion.[327] One court has applied the same reasoning to an Equal Credit Opportunity Act claim, holding the FTC Holder Rule overridden by federal regulations that limit an assignee's liability to situations where the assignee knew or should have known of the assignor's violation.[328] Illinois courts have developed a unique doctrine as to the relationship of TIL and UDAP claims,[329] and, for this reason, sometimes hold that the TIL restrictions on assignee liability also shield the assignee from UDAP liability that is based on TIL violations.[330]

While courts often find the FTC Holder Rule not applicable to TIL claims, in some cases the consumer's recovery under TIL's assignee liability provisions can be greater than that under the FTC Holder Rule; the FTC Holder Rule's cap does not apply where the assignee is directly liable under the TILA for violations apparent on the face of the documents.[331] Creditors are liable above and beyond the FTC Holder cap for their own misconduct, and the TILA has expressly held assignees fully liable for any TIL violations apparent on the face of the documents.

One aberrant decision has held a New Jersey version of the FTC Holder Rule preempted because of inconsistency with the TILA not only as to TIL claims but also as to state law claims including unconscionability and deception.[332] Since the FTC Holder Rule primarily applies to the same consumer credit transactions as the TILA, this poorly-reasoned holding would make the FTC Holder Rule a nullity. By contrast, many other decisions correctly conclude that TILA's assignee liability provisions have no effect on preservation of non-TILA claims.[333]

---

325 Staff Guidelines, 41 Fed. Reg. 20023, Mechanism of the rule (May 14, 1976), *reproduced on* the companion CD-Rom to this volume.

326 Cox v. First Nat'l Bank of Cincinnati, 633 F. Supp. 236 (S.D. Ohio 1986); *In re* Stewart, 93 B.R. 878 (Bankr. E.D. Pa. 1988).

327 *See* Ramadan v. Chase Manhattan Corp., 229 F.3d 194 (3d Cir. 2000); Green v. Levis Motors, Inc., 179 F.3d 286 (5th Cir. 1999), *cert. denied*, 120 S. Ct. 528, 145 L. Ed. 2d 409 (1999); Ellis v. GMAC, 160 F.3d 703 (11th Cir. 1998); Taylor v. Quality Hyundai, Inc., 150 F.3d 689 (7th Cir. 1998), *cert. denied*, 119 S. Ct. 1043, 143 L. Ed. 2d 41 (1999) (TIL limit on assignee liability trumps the FTC Holder Notice found in the note); Walker v. Wallace Auto Sales, Inc., 155 F.3d 927 (7th Cir. 1998) (same); Javorsky v. Freedom Driving Aids, Inc., 2001 U.S. Dist. LEXIS 14078 (N.D. Ill. Aug. 29, 2001); Lacasse v. All Star Dodge, 2001 U.S. Dist. LEXIS 6590 (M.D. La. Feb. 2, 2001); Fillinger v. Willowbrook Ford, Inc., 1999 U.S. Dist. LEXIS 3629 (N.D. Ill. Mar. 22, 1999) (discussing assignee liability for UDAP claims based on TIL violations); Jordan v. Chrysler Credit Corp., 73 F. Supp. 2d 469 (D.N.J. Nov. 12, 1999); Franks v. Rockenbach Chevrolet Sales, Inc., 1999 U.S. Dist. LEXIS 3367 (N.D. Ill. Mar. 15, 1999) (same); Mayfield v. General Electric Capital Corp., 1999 U.S. Dist. LEXIS 4048 (S.D.N.Y. Mar. 31, 1999); Owens v. Tranex Credit Corp., Clearinghouse No. 52,129 (S.D. Ind. 1998) (TIL limit on assignee liability trumps the FTC Holder Notice found in the note); Young v. Ford Motor Co., 1998 U.S. Dist. LEXIS 15376 (N.D. Ill. Sept. 16, 1998) (same); Cemail v. Viking Dodge, Inc., 982 F. Supp. 1296 (N.D. Ill. 1997) (same); Lindsey v. Ed Johnson Oldsmobile, Inc., 1996 U.S. Dist. LEXIS 10236 (N.D. Ill. July 18, 1996), *aff'd on reconsideration*, 1996 U.S. Dist. LEXIS 13750 (N.D. Ill. Sept. 12, 1996) (same); Jackson v. South Holland Dodge, Inc., 197 Ill. 2d 39, 755 N.E.2d 462 (2001) (assignee not liable for TIL violation that is not apparent on face of disclosure statement, unless it actively participated in the fraud). *See* § 2.2.1.6.3, *supra* (discussion of relationship between TILA and UDAP claims), and National Consumer Law Center, Truth in Lending § 7.3 (5th ed. 2003 and Supp.) (discussion of TIL assignee liability rule).

328 Coleman v. GMAC, 196 F.R.D. 315 (M.D. Tenn. 2000), *vacated, remanded, on other grounds* 296 F.3d 443 (6th Cir. 2002) (class certification erroneous because predominance of common questions not shown).

329 *See* § 2.2.1.6.3, *supra*.

330 Jenkins v. Mercantile Mortg. Co., 231 F. Supp. 2d 737 (N.D. Ill. 2002); Jarvis v. South Oak Dodge, Inc., 201 Ill. 2d 81, 773 N.E.2d 641, 265 Ill. Dec. 877 (2002); Jackson v. South Holland Dodge, 197 Ill. 2d 39, 258 Ill. Dec. 79, 755 N.E.2d 462 (2001).

331 Shepeard v. Quality Siding & Window Factory, Inc., 730 F. Supp. 1295, n.8 (D. Del. 1990).

332 Alexiou v. Brad Benson Mitsubishi, 127 F. Supp. 2d 557 (D.N.J. 2000).

333 Taylor v. Quality Hyundai, Inc., 150 F.3d 689, 693 (7th Cir. 1998) (TILA assignee liability rule "limits only certain TILA claims"); Green v. Levis Motors, Inc., 179 F.3d 286, 296 (5th Cir. 1999) (TILA "limits assignee liability on only one set of claims (i.e., the specified TILA claims")); Irby-Greene v. M.O.R., Inc., 79 F. Supp. 2d 630, 633 (E.D. Va. 2000); Scott v.

6.6.3.8.2 Relation to the Magnuson-Moss Warranty Act

The federal Magnuson-Moss Warranty Act states that for purposes of civil liability under that Act, "only the warrantor actually making a written affirmation of fact, promise, or undertaking shall be deemed to have created a written warranty, and any rights arising thereunder may be enforced under this section only against such warrantor and no other person."[334] The question arises whether a claim under the Magnuson-Moss Warranty Act can be brought against an assignee of the warrantor, based on the FTC Holder language, or whether the above-quoted language restricts the consumer's ability to bring such a claim against anyone other than the warrantor.

It is important to note what the above-quoted language does *not* say. Since by its very terms it is limited to written warranties, a consumer can certainly bring a Magnuson-Moss Warranty Act claim against an assignee, that is not based on the enforcement of a written warranty. Examples of claims not based on a written warranty are claims for breach of an implied warranty, for breach of a service contract, for violation of various Magnuson-Moss disclosure requirements, or for violation of various substantive Magnuson-Moss Act restrictions, such as those dealing with tie-ins.[335] Warranty claims that are not based on the Magnuson-Moss Act are also not affected by this language.

The only issue is whether a claim based on a written warranty can be brought against the warrantor's assignee, based on the fact that the note contains the FTC Holder Notice. Two courts have suggested that the Magnuson-Moss language trumps the FTC Holder Notice.[336] In one of these cases, the court based its ruling on similar case law relating to the relationship of the FTC Holder Rule to TILA's limitation on assignee liability.[337] But TILA's limitation on assignee liability specifically restricts assignee liability, while the Magnuson-Moss Warranty Act limitation applies broadly to all third party liability, and does not even mention the issue of assignee liability. It thus leaves open the issue of whether the legislative intent was to limit third parties' direct liability only, or also their derivative liability. TIL case law is not helpful in making this decision.

The better view is that third parties do not have *direct* liability for breaches of the warrantor's written warranty. For example, a dealer is not liable if a manufacturer's written warranty is breached. But a third party can have derivative liability if that party is subject to claims the consumer can bring against the written warrantor.

6.6.3.9 Liability of Holders of Securitized Debt

A growing development among subprime car and mobile home dealers and other lenders is the securitization of debt. The lender or dealer groups consumers' obligations into pools, which are typically assigned to a trust. The trustee is then the legal owner of the obligation. Securities backed by this pool of obligations are then issued and sold by investment bankers to investors. Part of the interest paid by the consumers goes to the investors. The remainder covers the risk of loss for the pool of loans and then goes to the original lender or dealer.[338]

The original lender or dealer may remain involved as the servicer of the obligation, dealing with the consumer, collecting payments, and initiating collection actions. When the seller or loan originator is the servicer, the consumer may be unaware that the obligation has been assigned.

The Holder Notice applies to securitized transactions the same as to ordinary transactions. If the trustee is the holder of the note or contract, the trustee is liable for all claims and defenses that the consumer would have against the original seller or lender, up to the limit set by the FTC Holder Rule. However, investors who buy the securities backed by the obligations are probably not subject to the FTC Holder Rule.[339]

6.6.3.10 Liability of FDIC, RTC, or Holders Subsequent to Them

When a federally-insured bank or savings and loan is taken over by the Federal Deposit Insurance Corporation or the Resolution Trust Corporation, the consumer notes held by the institution transfer to the federal agency. To promote the goals of confidence and stability in the banking system, and efficiency in the trade of notes and other financial instruments, Congress and the courts have granted to the FDIC and the RTC unique powers to enforce such instruments.

Mayflower Home Improvement Corp., 363 N.J. Super. 145, 831 A.2d 564 (Law Div. 2001).

334 15 U.S.C. § 2310(f).

335 *See* National Consumer Law Center, Consumer Warranty Law Ch. 2 (2d ed. 2001 and Supp.).

336 Owens v. Tranex Credit Corp., Clearinghouse No. 52,129 (S.D. Ind. 1998); *see also* Patton v. McHone, 1993 Tenn. App. LEXIS 212, 40 U.C.C. Rep. Serv. 2d 299 (Tenn. Ct. App. 1993) (declining to make assignee subject to buyer's affirmative Magnuson-Moss claims, based on erroneous interpretation of FTC Holder Rule and on view that Magnuson-Moss does not impose obligation on party who did not make the warranty); *cf.* Gaddy v. Galarza Motor Sport L.T.D., 2000 U.S. Dist. LEXIS 13881 (N.D. Ill. Sept. 18, 2000) (finding that assignee was not liable because it did not meet definition of "supplier" and did not make a warranty; court also denies motion to dismiss a separate count that sought to impose liability against assignee based on Holder Notice, but does not say whether this count included a Magnuson-Moss claim).

337 Owens v. Tranex Credit Corp., Clearinghouse No. 52,129 (S.D. Ind. 1998).

338 *See* § 6.7.4, *infra.*

339 *See* Ross v. Thousand Adventures, 675 N.W.2d 812 (Iowa 2004) (FTC Holder Rule does not apply to bank that bought participation interest in pool of obligations held by a different bank).

When the FDIC or RTC collects on the note, the federal agency often will claim complete insulation from all claims and defenses relating to the note. Of even more significance, these defenses may transfer with the note to the benefit of a subsequent purchaser.[340] For example, when another bank purchases an insolvent bank from the FDIC or RTC, that purchasing bank may also claim insulation from all claims and defenses the consumer had against the seller related to the now insolvent bank.

The consumer's ability to raise defenses against the FDIC or RTC can be an issue both as to installment sales paper where the FTC Holder Notice will be present, as well as straight loans, where it will not. This subsection considers the first situation. A later section examines the second.[341]

There are three separate but overlapping doctrines that may insulate the FDIC and RTC from debtor defenses, and these are discussed in more detail in a later section.[342] One is federal common law starting with the Supreme Court's 1942 decision in *D'Oench, Duhme and Company v. FDIC*,[343] that the maker of the note could not raise an unrecorded side agreement as a defense on the note after the note was acquired by the FDIC. The second source of FDIC and RTC protection is 12 U.S.C. § 1823(e), which provides that no agreement that hinders a note shall be valid against the FDIC or RTC unless the agreement is in writing and was properly signed, approved, and recorded by the bank.

The third doctrine which may insulate the FDIC and RTC from debtors' claims is a common law "super" holder-in-due-course status that goes beyond the scope of section 1823(e) and *D'Oench.* Most courts have held that this doctrine only applies when the FDIC engages in a "purchase and assumption" transaction in which it transfers the failed bank's healthy assets to a viable banking institution. Although decisions are split, many cases hold that the FDIC must meet state law requirements for holder-in-due-course status,[344] and a number of courts indicate that the federal statute, 12 U.S.C. § 1823(e), has displaced the common law doctrines.[345]

The effect of *D'Oench* and related doctrines on sale-related consumer transactions may be negated by the FTC Holder Rule Notice. If the FTC Holder Rule Notice is in a note, it would appear that the FDIC and RTC can not avoid the impact of that notice. The notice is in writing and is incorporated into the note itself, and the federal agency and subsequent purchasers have adequate notice of that limitation on the note. Further, the inclusion of the Holder Notice makes a note non-negotiable, thus avoiding the "super holder-in-due-course" doctrine. Most *D'Oench, Duhme* litigation has dealt with large commercial transactions, so there is little case law on the effect of the FTC Holder Rule Notice.[346]

If the Holder Notice should have been inserted in the promissory note, but was not, it is probably not advisable to pursue seller-related claims against the FDIC or RTC based on the failure to include the FTC notice. There is little case law about using the failure to comply with the rule as a defense against even normal creditors. Consumer attorneys must carefully consider whether to bring a case of first impression in their jurisdiction and then to complicate it by bringing it against the FDIC or RTC where these entities are entitled to special consideration.

6.6.3.11 Relation of FTC Rule to State Law

6.6.3.11.1 FTC Rule overrides only less protective state laws

Virtually all states have statutes that subject creditors in at least some circumstances to claims or defenses that the

340 *See* § 6.7.5, *infra.*

341 *See id.*

342 *See id.*

343 315 U.S. 447 (1942).

344 *See* discussion in Desmond v. FDIC, 798 F. Supp. 829 (D. Mass. 1992). *See also* Sunbelt Savings, FSB Dallas, Texas v. Montross, 923 F.2d 353 (5th Cir. 1991), *reh'g granted*, 932 F.2d 363, *reinstated in part, and remanded*, 944 F.2d 227 (5th Cir. 1991) (en banc); St. Bernard Sav. & Loan Ass'n v. Cella, 826 F. Supp. 985, 987 (E.D. La. 1993) (holding RTC not entitled to summary judgment on a note which its predecessor bank had bought after maturity, reasoning that the government could not change "lead into gold"); *In re* Miraj & Sons, Inc., 192 B.R. 297 (Bankr. D. Mass. 1996) (no holder in due course when assignee purchased notes from FDIC knowing they were overdue), *amended by* 197 B.R. 737 (D. Mass. 1996); Rhode Island Depositors Economic Protection Corp. v. Ryan, 697 A.2d 1087 (R.I. 1997) (court noted that protection enjoyed by federal holder in due course was not absolute; most effective way to pierce protections would be for the party asserting the defense to establish that FDIC possessed actual knowledge of the defense before taking the note); Cadle Co. v. Patoine, 772 A.2d 544 (Vt. 2001) (reversing summary judgment in favor of plaintiff, who had purchased defendant's note from FDIC; neither FDIC nor its transferee were holders in due course under state law because the FDIC had purchased the note as part of a bulk transaction not in the ordinary course of the transferor's business). *But see* Joslin v. Friends of Wayne Babovich, 699 So. 2d 1107 (La. App. 1997) (court agrees that once the FDIC or RTC acquired the instrument, it was accorded the status of holder in due course vis-à-vis the borrower, irrespective of state law requirements), *review denied*, 706 So. 2d 456 (La. 1997); Rhode Island Depositors Economic Protection Corp. v. Ryan, 697 A.2d 1087 (R.I. 1997); Pinkston v. Diversified Fin. Sys., 2000 Tex. App. LEXIS 6962 (Tex. App. Oct. 16, 2000) (reaffirming federal holder-in-due-course doctrine to hold that assignee of note acquired from FDIC could claim holder-in-due-course status notwithstanding that note was overdue at time acquired).

345 *See* § 6.7.5, *infra.*

346 *See* Resolution Trust Corp. v. Cook, 840 S.W.2d 42 (Tex. App. 1992) (declining to apply *D'Oench* and section 1823(e) to claims based on original lender's torts; FTC Holder Rule notice allows affirmative recovery against Resolution Trust Corp.). *But see* Smania v. Mundaca Inv. Corp., 629 So. 2d 242 (Fla. Dist. Ct. App. 1993) (FTC Holder Rule notice on note is insufficient to prevent bar of claims that could have been asserted against seller since those claims are based on a different document).

consumer could assert against the seller. These statutes should be consulted whenever there is an issue of a creditor's derivative liability for acts or omissions of the seller.

Some of these state holder laws are broader than the FTC Holder Rule, covering more types of transactions[347] or making the holder liable even if the Holder Notice is omitted.[348] Even if the state law does no more than the FTC Holder Rule, a court may be more willing to enforce FTC Holder Rule liability if state law dictates the same result. The existence of the state law may deter the court from falling into an erroneous interpretation of the FTC Holder Rule.

The FTC Holder Notice states that the consumer's "recovery hereunder" is limited, i.e., recovery pursuant to the FTC rule is limited to certain amounts. The FTC rule does not limit a larger recovery under a different state or federal law. A consumer can recover more than that allowed under the FTC rule if state or federal law so allows. "The words 'recovery hereunder' . . . refer specifically to a recovery under the Notice. If a larger affirmative recovery is available against a creditor as a matter of state law, the consumer would retain this right."[349]

Conversely, state laws are typically more restrictive than the FTC rule. The state statute may impose a lower cap on the consumer's relief than the FTC Holder Rule, may be limited only to certain claims and defenses, or require the consumer to notify the creditor of particular claims and defenses within a specific period of time after the creditor sends the consumer a notice.

Such a more restrictive state law does not limit the application of the FTC rule. For example, Alabama law allows consumers to raise seller-related *defenses* against assignees, but not raise those claims affirmatively. Alabama consumers nevertheless can use the FTC Holder Rule to bring affirmative claims against assignees.[350] Michigan consumers can recover a down payment from an assignee even where the Michigan holder law would allow recovery only of the amounts paid to the assignee.[351] Consumers can recover under the FTC Holder Rule even if they could not recover under state law.

6.6.3.11.2 The **LaBarre** *court's misinterpretation*

Notwithstanding the language of the FTC Holder Rule and the FTC's multiple unequivocal statements that it is not limited by state holder law restrictions, the Eighth Circuit ruled to the contrary in *LaBarre v. Credit Acceptance Corp.*[352] The court held that state law should be used to determine what claims can be brought under the FTC Holder Rule, against assignees and related lenders. In that case, Minnesota law (and thus the FTC Holder Rule) was interpreted as allowing a consumer to raise seller-related claims only as a defense to the assignee's collection action, and not in an affirmative action.

The decision is patently absurd. It would mean that the FTC Holder Rule, enacted because state law was not adequate, would have only the same reach as state law. What the Eighth Circuit got wrong is that the FTC stated applicable state law determines what claims can be brought against the *seller* (not what claims that can be brought against the *assignee*).[353] *All* seller-related claims allowed by applicable law can then be brought against the assignee. Indeed, the Official Comment to Article 3 of the UCC clearly expresses this interpretation: "The effect of the FTC legend is to make the rights of a holder or transferee subject to *claims or defenses* that the issuer could assert *against the original payee* of the note."[354]

The *LaBarre* decision not only means that the FTC Holder Rule is a nullity (providing no greater rights than already provided by state law), but it is a deceptive nullity, because the notice mandated by the FTC Holder Rule clearly informs consumers they can bring all claims and defenses against the assignee, while *LaBarre* rules they can not. Hopefully, other courts that understand the FTC Holder Rule will reject *LaBarre*, and the Eighth Circuit will reconsider its ruling in another case.

---

347 *See, e.g.*, § 6.6.2.2.2, *supra* (leases).

348 *See* § 6.6.5.3, *infra*.

349 Staff Guidelines, 41 Fed. Reg. 20023, Mechanism of the Rule (May 14, 1976), *reproduced on* the companion CD-Rom to this volume. *See also* FTC Staff Advisory Letter, Diercks (Oct. 12, 1976), summarized at [1974–1980 Transfer Binder] Consumer Cred. Guide (CCH) ¶ 98,284; Resolution Trust Corp. v. Cook, 840 S.W.2d 42 (Tex. App. 1992).

350 Eachen v. Scott Housing Sys., Inc., 630 F. Supp. 162 (M.D. Ala. 1986); *see also* De La Fuente v. Home Savings Ass'n, 669 S.W.2d 137 (Tex. App. 1984); Hernandez v. Forbes Chevrolet Co., 680 S.W.2d 75 (Tex. App. 1984).

351 Green Tree Acceptance, Inc. v. Pirtle, 1999 WL 33740367 (E.D. Mich. Mar. 1, 1999).

352 175 F.3d 640 (8th Cir. 1999); *see also* Pescia v. Auburn Ford-Lincoln Mercury, 68 F. Supp. 2d 1269 (M.D. Ala. 1999) (construing FTC Holder Notice to nullify holder-in-due-course status, but holding that there still must be independent state grounds for holder's liability), *aff'd without op. sub nom.* Pescia v. Ford Motor Credit Corp., 2001 WL 1711051 (11th Cir. Dec. 17, 2001).

353 Federal Trade Commission Statement of Basis and Purpose for the Trade Regulation Rule Concerning Preservation of Consumers' Claims and Defenses, 40 Fed. Reg. 53524 (Nov. 18, 1975), *reproduced on* the companion CD-Rom to this volume. *See also* Letter from Christopher Keller, Federal Trade Commission to Jonathan Sheldon, Clearinghouse No. 52,159 (May 13, 1999) (citing sections in the FTC's Statement of Basis and Purpose showing the Commission's intent), *reprinted at* Appx. B.2.2, *infra*.

354 Official Comment 3 to U.C.C. § 3-106 (emphasis added). *See* World Wide Tracers, Inc. v. Metropolitan Protection, Inc., 384 N.W.2d 442, 447 (Minn. 1986) (illustrating the weight the Minnesota Supreme Court gives to the U.C.C. Official Comments).

The FTC rule and the credit agreement in *LaBarre* both state that the creditor is "subject to all claims and defenses which the debtor could assert against the seller." It is hard to see how this could be any clearer. The FTC itself in the *Statement of Basis and Purpose* for the rule indicates the consumer can "maintain an affirmative action"[355] and explicitly rejected a creditor proposal that the consumer only be able to use the FTC Holder Rule defensively.[356]

The Eighth Circuit ruling relied, not on the Commission's Statement, but on an FTC staff interpretation, and even then misinterpreted that interpretation. The staff interpretation cited by the Eighth Circuit in fact states the opposite of what it is cited for—applicable law controls what is a claim against the *seller*, not which seller-related claims can be brought against an assignee. As if to underscore this, the staff interpretation contains three examples of controlling applicable law, and all three relate to whether the claim could be brought against the seller, not whether valid seller-related claims can be brought against an assignee.[357] The very next paragraph in the staff interpretation states that the consumer can bring affirmatively *all* claims against the lender that could be brought against the seller.[358] The Eighth Circuit's interpretation of Minnesota law and the FTC Holder Rule is wrong. It should not be adopted by any court that is not bound by it, including Minnesota's state courts.

Fortunately, *LaBarre*'s misinterpretation of the FTC Holder Rule has rarely if ever been followed. One decision, *Pescia v. Auburn Ford-Lincoln Mercury*,[359] cites *LaBarre* in a seemingly favorable way, but also makes favorable reference to an earlier decision[360] that took the opposite approach. *Pescia* required the plaintiff to show independent state law grounds for asserting her claims against the creditor, but suggests that this ruling is based on the manner in which the plaintiff framed her complaint[361] rather than on an interpretation of the FTC Holder Rule. Another decision explicitly rejects *LaBarre*.[362] Other courts have implicitly rejected the *LaBarre* position, by recognizing that state law is relevant only to whether there is a claim against the seller, not whether the consumer can raise that seller-related claim against a holder.[363]

6.6.3.12 Consumer's Waiver of Claims Against Holder

Another issue is the effect of the FTC Holder Rule where the consumer signs a document indicating the work purchased with the loan proceeds has been completed and performed satisfactorily. Holders argue that they can rely on this statement and are not liable for consumer claims against the seller inconsistent with this statement. Nevertheless, this statement should be binding on the consumer in an action against the holder only to the extent the statement would have been binding on the consumer in the consumer's action against the seller.

It is unlikely that a court will give much credence to such a statement, particularly where it is part of boilerplate language the consumer is asked to sign.[364] Similarly, a court will not give much credence to a provision whereby the consumer waives his or her right to raise defenses against assignees where the contract also contains the FTC Holder Notice.[365]

---

355 Federal Trade Commission Statement of Basis and Purpose for the Trade Regulation Rule Concerning Preservation of Consumers' Claims and Defenses, 40 Fed. Reg. 53524 (Nov. 18, 1975), *reproduced on* the companion CD-Rom to this volume. *See also* Letter from Christopher Keller, Federal Trade Commission to Jonathan Sheldon, Clearinghouse No. 52,159 (May 13, 1999) (citing sections in the FTC's Statement of Basis and Purpose showing the Commission's intent as to affirmative claims against holders), *reprinted at* Appx. B.2.2, *infra*.

356 FTC Statement of Basis and Purpose, at 53526, 53527. *See also* Letter from Christopher Keller, Federal Trade Commission to Jonathan Sheldon, Clearinghouse No. 52,159 (May 13, 1999), *reprinted at* Appx. B.2.2, *infra*.

357 Staff Guidelines on Trade Regulation Rule Concerning Preservation of Consumers' Claims and Defenses, 41 Fed. Reg. 20024 (May 14, 1976), *reproduced on* the companion CD-Rom to this volume.

358 *Id.*

359 68 F. Supp. 2d 1269 (M.D. Ala. 1999), *aff'd without op. sub nom.* Pescia v. Ford Motor Credit Corp., 2001 WL 1711051 (11th Cir. Dec. 17, 2001). *See also* Brooks v. O'Connor Chevrolet, Inc., 2003 WL 22427795 (N.D. Ill. Oct. 23, 2003) (not citing *LaBarre*, but erroneously concluding that assignee's derivative UDAP liability is subject to same limits as would apply to liability for its own acts).

360 Eachen v. Scott Housing Sys., Inc., 630 F. Supp. 162 (M.D. Ala. 1986) (inclusion of FTC Holder Rule in contract means that consumer can assert seller-related claims affirmatively against creditor, even though Alabama law made creditor liable only for defensive claims).

361 Pescia v. Auburn Ford-Lincoln Mercury, 68 F. Supp. 2d 1269, 1282 (M.D. Ala. 1999) (the FTC Holder Rule "creates a federal right but that federal right has not been invoked in this case"), *aff'd without op. sub nom.* Pescia v. Ford Motor Credit Corp., 2001 WL 1711051 (11th Cir. Dec. 17, 2001).

362 Alduridi v. Community Trust Bank, 1999 Tenn. App. LEXIS 718 (Oct. 26, 1999).

363 Eachen v. Scott Housing Sys., Inc., 630 F. Supp. 162 (M.D. Ala. 1986); Thomas v. Ford Motor Credit Co., 429 A.2d 277 (Md. App. 1981); Credit Acceptance Corp. v. Banks, 1999 Ohio App. LEXIS 6058 (Dec. 16, 1999); Beemus v. Interstate Nat'l Dealer Servs., Inc., Clearinghouse No. 53,575 (Pa. C.P. Ct. Feb. 8, 2002) (citing *LaBarre* but nonetheless applying the correct rule), *aff'd on other grounds*, 823 A.2d 979 (Pa. Super. 2003); Homziak v. Gen. Elec. Capital Warranty Corp., Clearinghouse No. 54,551 (Pa. C.P. Ct. May 21, 2001) (citing *LaBarre* but nonetheless applying the correct rule); De La Fuente v. Home Savings Ass'n, 669 S.W.2d 137 (Tex. App. 1984); Hernandez v. Forbes Chevrolet Co., 680 S.W.2d 75 (Tex. App. 1984).

364 *See* Alvarez v. Union Mortgage Co., 747 S.W.2d 484 (Tex. App. 1988). *See also* Mahaffey v. Investor's Nat'l Security Co., 103 Nev. 615, 747 P.2d 890 (1987).

365 Hernandez v. Forbes Chevrolet Co., 680 S.W.2d 75 (Tex. App. 1984); Hinojosa v. Castellow Chevrolet Oldsmobile, 678 S.W.2d 707 (Tex. App. 1984).

A federal court in *Heastie v. Community Bank*[366] has found it to be a state UDAP violation for a creditor simultaneously to include in its loan agreements the FTC Holder notice and a statement indicating that the creditor "does not guarantee the material or workmanship or inspect the work performed" by the seller. The two statements in the loan agreement directly contradict each other.

There is no private right of action under the FTC Act for violation of the FTC Holder Rule, and, as the *Heastie* court noted, the FTC rule does not even apply to lenders, but only to sellers. Nevertheless, the *Heastie* court found that the state UDAP statute was not limited by the scope of the FTC rule, and that the creditor's inclusion in its loan agreement of a provision contradicting the FTC Holder notice was a UDAP violation. The *Heastie* court found the UDAP violation even though there was no evidence that the creditor intended to use the provision to insulate itself from liability for the seller's conduct; the mere inclusion of the provision was enough.

A Missouri middle-level appellate court has incorrectly interpreted the FTC Holder Rule. The court mistakenly thought that it was the FTC position that a provision in a contract conflicting with the FTC Holder notice negates the notice, and the lender would thus not be subject to the FTC notice.[367] In fact, in the FTC language the court quoted, the FTC was indicating that it would be a rule violation to insert both the FTC notice and the conflicting language in the same document because it would tend to negate the meaning of the holder notice for the consumer.

The FTC never indicated that a court confronted with such conflicting provisions should negate the legal effect of the FTC notice. In fact, it would almost certainly be the FTC's opinion that the FTC notice would negate the other language. Straight rules of contract construction should construe the ambiguous provisions against the drafter. No courts have ever followed this Missouri decision.

In any event, consumers faced with a waiver of rights under the FTC Holder Rule can allege that it is a state UDAP violation for a creditor to accept a consumer note containing such conflicting language. The consumer in the Missouri case never alleged such a state UDAP violation, so the court did not reach the issue.[368]

6.6.3.13 Holder's Refusal to Accept Liability Under Holder Rule as an Independent UDAP Violation

It is very common for holders to inform consumers that the holder is not subject to the consumer's claims and defenses against the seller, even where the FTC Holder Notice is in the loan documents. Instead, the holder tells the consumer to take up the dispute with the seller, but that the consumer must continue to pay the lender.

These representations by the holder mislead the consumer as to the status of the obligation and as to the consumer's legal rights.[369] As such, the holder's own conduct is a UDAP violation, and the holder is liable for that conduct over and above any derivative liability it has for the seller's conduct.[370] There should be no question as to the holder's liability for all UDAP remedies, including, attorney fees or multiple damages, for the holder's own conduct.

It may be possible to develop evidence that the defendant follows a pattern or practice of repudiating its obligations under the FTC Holder Rule.[371] Discovery on this issue could include questions such as:

- Whether the defendant has ever been a defendant in any similar claim in which the FTC Holder clause was asserted as a basis for a claim or defense against the defendant's;
- The defendant's procedure for collecting debts and investigating consumers' claims when the consumer has asserted a claim or defense similar to the plaintiff's;
- The defendant's procedure for collecting debts and investigating consumers' claims when the consumer has asserted claims or defenses based on the FTC Holder clause;
- Whether it is the defendant's procedure to insist that the consumer must pay regardless of any claim the consumer may have against the seller.

6.6.4 Theories of Recovery Where FTC Holder Notice Is Improperly Omitted

6.6.4.1 General

A major problem with the FTC Holder Rule is that if sellers violate the rule by failing to include the prescribed notice in the credit contract, the consumer's rights against creditors are muddied. If the notice is not placed in the consumer contract, then the consumer has no direct *contractual* right to raise seller-related defenses against the creditor. Nor can the consumer directly claim a violation of the FTC rule because only the FTC can directly enforce the FTC Holder Rule.[372] The FTC Holder Rule does not provide

366 727 F. Supp. 1133 (N.D. Ill. 1989).

367 Blackmon v. Hindrew, 824 S.W.2d 85 (Mo. Ct. App. 1992).

368 *Id.*

369 *See* § 5.2.8, *supra.*

370 *See* Jaramillo v. Gonzales, 50 P.3d 554 (N.M. Ct. App. 2002) (failure to concede liability under FTC Holder Rule is UDAP violation).

371 *See* § 7.9.1.2, *infra.*

372 Armstrong v. Accrediting Council for Continuing Educ. & Training, Inc., 832 F. Supp. 419 (D.D.C. 1993); Williams v. National School of Health Technology, 836 F. Supp. 273 (E.D. Pa. 1993); Jackson v. Culinary School of Washington, 788 F. Supp. 1233 (D.D.C. 1992), *aff'd in part, rev'd and remanded in*

a private right of action.[373]

There should be little doubt that the *seller's* violation of the FTC rule (by its failure to arrange for the Holder Notice to be included in the loan documents) is a state UDAP violation. In some states, this may even directly violate a state UDAP regulation.[374] But this UDAP claim against the *seller* rarely is of value to the consumer, since the failure to include the FTC Holder Notice is relevant because the consumer does not wish to bring a claim against the seller, but wishes instead to raise seller-related defenses to a *creditor's* collection action. (Nevertheless, a UDAP injunctive or class action claim against a seller for systematically violating the FTC Holder Rule may prevent fraud and protect future consumers.)[375]

The remainder of this section details five theories a consumer can use to press seller-related claims against a creditor under the FTC Holder Rule *even if* the seller has not placed the FTC Holder Notice in the contract:

- The absent holder notice is an implied contract term;
- Accepting the irregular contract or note deprives the lender of the insulation from defenses that the UCC provides;
- Omission of the Holder Notice is a UDAP violation by the creditor;
- The creditor has RICO liability for omitting the Holder Notice; and
- The contract or note is illegal and unenforceable.

Subsection 6.6.5.6 examines a related question: theories separate and apart from the FTC Holder Rule for holding creditors liable for seller-related claims. These theories are applicable both to transactions where the Holder Notice was wrongfully omitted from the contract documents, and to transactions to which the FTC Holder Rule is inapplicable.

part on other grounds, 27 F.3d 573 (D.C. Cir. 1994) (on de novo review, reversing district court's decision to issue declaratory judgment on state law issues), *vacated*, 515 U.S. 1139 (1995) (appellate court should have used abuse of discretion standard to review district court's decision to issue declaratory judgment on state law issues), *on remand*, 59 F.3d 254 (D.C. Cir. 1995) (remanding for district court to exercise its discretion about whether to issue declaratory judgment on state law issues); Vietnam Veterans of Am. v. Guerdon Industries, Inc., 644 F. Supp. 951 (D. Del. 1986); Capital Bank & Trust Co. v. Lacey, 393 So. 2d 668 (La. 1980). *See also* Blackmon v. Hindrew, 824 S.W.2d 85 (Mo. Ct. App. 1992).

373 *See* § 9.1, *infra*.

374 Georgia Office of Consumer Affairs Regulations, Ga. Comp. R. & Regs. Rule 122-5-.01 (state incorporates FTC Holder Rule as state UDAP regulation so that any violation of FTC Holder Rule is automatic Georgia UDAP violation); Massachusetts Consumer Protection Regulations, Mass. Regs. Code tit. 940, § 3.07, Advertising or Offering to Sell on an "Easy Credit" Basis.

375 *Cf.* FTC v. Med Resorts Int'l, Inc., 5 Trade Reg. Rep. (CCH) ¶ 15174 (N.D. Ill. Nov. 1, 2001) (proposed consent decree against seller of travel club memberships that did not include Holder Notice in contract).

6.6.4.2 Absent Holder Notice as an Implied Contract Term

6.6.4.2.1 Revised Article 9 requires notice to be implied

Revised Article 9 of the UCC makes an omitted Holder Notice part of the contract as a matter of law, allowing the consumer to utilize the Holder Notice as if it were included.[376] Under Revised Article 9, an assignee of a contract without the required notice is subject to a consumer account debtor's claims and defenses to the same extent as if the contract had contained the notice.[377] Neither the assignor nor the assignee can seek a waiver from the consumer avoiding this result.[378]

Revised Article 9 has been adopted by all fifty states. In most states it was effective July 1, 2001. It applies to enforcement of the consumer's rights after its effective date, even if the contract was created before that date. In other words, Revised Article 9 creates rights for the consumer raising claims and defenses in July 2001 against a holder even if the credit agreement was first entered into years earlier.[379]

This Revised Article 9 provision applies to any credit sales agreement assigned to a creditor. However, it does not apply to direct loans, even seller-referred purchase money loans that are covered by the FTC Holder Rule.[380] This is because such direct loans are usually negotiable instruments, and this Revised Article 9 provision does not apply to negotiable instruments.[381] In addition, the Revised Article 9 provision subjects assignees to claims the consumer could assert against the original *obligee* (the assignor),[382] while the consumer wants to use the FTC Holder Rule to bring claims and defenses against the seller. In a direct loan, the seller is not the original obligee, but the payee of the loan proceeds.

Revised Article 9 implies into the contract any holder notice required by either state or federal law, so if a notice is required by state law it also becomes part of the contract. In particular, certain state holder laws clearly cover

376 *See In re* Barker, 306 B.R. 339, 350 (Bankr. E.D. Cal. 2004).

377 Rev. U.C.C. §§ 9-403(d), 9-404(d). *See also* Official Comment 5, Rev. U.C.C. § 9-403.

378 *In re* Barker, 306 B.R. 339 (Bankr. E.D. Cal. 2004).

379 Rev. U.C.C. § 9-702; *In re* Barker, 306 B.R. 339, 350 (Bankr. E.D. Cal. 2004) (applying Rev. Art. 9's Holder Notice rule to pre-revision transaction). Note that there is an exception for cases commenced before the effective date, so that the new rights do not apply where the consumer brought a lawsuit to raise seller-related claims before July 1, 2001.

380 *See* §§ 6.6.1.2, 6.6.1.3, *supra* (difference between purchase money loans and assignment of installment contracts as ways of financing purchases).

381 *See* Rev. U.C.C. § 9-102(a)(3) (definition of "account debtor"); Official Comment 5(h), Rev. U.C.C. § 9-102; Official Comment 5, Rev. U.C.C. § 9-404.

382 U.C.C. § 9-403(d), (d)(2).

leases.[383] Revised Article 9's rule implying holder notices into contracts applies to "account debtors,"[384] a term that includes anyone liable under a property lease.[385] Consequently, if state law requires a holder notice be included in a lease, but the notice is not present, then Article 9 will imply its insertion.

6.6.4.2.2 Revised Article 3 will require the Holder Notice to be implied in negotiable instruments

In 2002, the National Conference of Commissioners on Uniform State Laws and the American Law Institute adopted revisions to UCC Article 3. By mid 2004, these revisions had only been adopted by Minnesota,[386] but were being considered by a few other states.

Revised Article 3 complements the Article 9 provisions discussed above[387] by stating that the FTC Holder Notice shall be implied into any promissory note whenever that notice should have been inserted into the note.[388] The consumer may assert against the holder all claims and defenses that would have been available against the "payee" if the note included the FTC Holder Notice.[389] A payee is the person who receives the funds from the loan, i.e., the seller.

Revised Article 3 thus insures that any transaction not covered by the FTC Holder Rule provision of Article 9 (because it involves a negotiable instrument or a purchase money loan) will be covered by the analogous Article 3 provision.[390] Thus, where the seller refers the consumer to the lender and the consumer then signs a note with the lender, the FTC requires the Holder Notice to be included in the note. If it is not, Revised Article 3 reads it into the note.

6.6.4.2.3 Court decisions prior to Revised Article 9 implying notice into contract

Even before enactment of Revised Article 9, a number of courts have been willing to imply the Holder Notice into an agreement where it is required to be placed.[391] This is particularly important in the case of negotiable instruments where Revised Article 9's protection does not apply.

In a recent New Jersey case, an appellate court found that "it is inconceivable to us that [the holders] may evade the remedial reach of the FTC Holder Rule simply because of that omission."[392] The appellate court found support for reading into the contract the FTC Holder language in that the "law is a silent factor in every contract" and "equity looks to substance rather than form." In that case, the seller had a business arrangement with the lender, but the Holder Notice was not found in the lender's direct loan with the consumer. This approach, though, has not been successful in the student loan context in arguing that students should be able to raise school-related defenses to student loan collection actions.[393]

---

383 *See* § 6.6.2.2.2, *supra*.

384 Rev. U.C.C. § 9-404(a).

385 Rev. U.C.C. §§ 9-102(a)(3) (definition of "account debtor"), (2) (definition of "account").

386 Minn. Stat. § 336.3-305(e).

387 *See* § 6.6.4.2.1, *supra*.

388 Rev. U.C.C. § 3-305(e).

389 Rev. U.C.C. § 3-305(e)(2).

390 Rev. U.C.C. § 3-305(e) applies to "instruments." There are two major types of instruments, drafts and notes. A check is a type of draft. The typical consumer loan involves a note.

391 Gonzalez v. Old Kent Mortgage Co., 2000 U.S. Dist. LEXIS 14530 (E.D. Pa. Sept. 19, 2000); Anderson v. Central States Waterproofing, Clearinghouse No. 40,627 (Minn. Dist. Ct. Hennepin Cty. 1982); Associates Home Equity Servs., Inc. v. Troup, 343 N.J. Super. 254, 778 A.2d 529 (App. Div. 2001). *See also* Xerographic Supplies Corp. v. Hertz Commercial Leasing Corp, 386 So. 2d 299 (Fla. Dist. Ct. App. 1980) (appellate court does not reach trial court's holding that Holder Notice must be implied into contract). *But see* Vietnam Veterans of Am., Inc. v. Guerdon Industries, 644 F. Supp. 951 (D. Del. 1986) (declining to read absent Holder Notice into contract); Crisomia v. Parkway Mortgage, Inc., 2001 Bankr. LEXIS 1469 (Bankr. E.D. Pa. Aug. 21, 2001); Hayner v. Old Kent Bank, 2002 Mich. App. LEXIS 190 (Feb. 12, 2002) (FTC Holder Rule places no duty upon lender who accepted contract without Holder Notice); Pratt v. North Dixie Manufactured Housing, Ltd., 2003 WL 21040658 (Ohio App. May 9, 2003) (unpublished, citation limited) (finding no basis for holder liability where assigned contract did not include Holder Notice).

392 Associates Home Equity Servs., Inc. v. Troup, 343 N.J. Super. 254, 778 A.2d 529 (App. Div. 2001).

393 Keams v. Tempe Technical Institute, Inc., 993 F. Supp. 714 (D. Ariz. 1997); Bartels v. Alabama Commercial College, 918 F. Supp. 1565 (S.D. Ga. 1995), *aff'd in part, rev'd in part, and remanded without op.*, 189 F.3d 483 (11th Cir. 1999), *cert. denied*, 528 U.S. 1074 (2000); Armstrong v. Accrediting Council for Continuing Educ. & Training, Inc., 832 F. Supp. 419 (D.D.C. 1993), *vacated and remanded*, 84 F.3d 1452 (D.C. Cir. 1996) (table, text available at 1996 U.S. App. LEXIS 12241) (remanding for further consideration of whether to exercise jurisdiction over state claims), *on remand*, 950 F. Supp. 1 (D.D.C. 1996) (maintaining jurisdiction of pendent claims and finding case appropriate for declaratory relief), *on further remand*, 980 F. Supp. 53 (D.D.C. 1997) (determining that California law controls and inviting plaintiff to amend complaint to assert claims and defenses under California consumer protection laws), *aff'd*, 168 F.3d 1362 (D.C. Cir. 1999) (affirming district court's dismissal of claims), *cert. denied*, 528 U.S. 1073 (2000); Spinner v. Chesapeake Bus. Institute of Virginia, Clearinghouse No. 49,131A (E.D. Va. Feb. 5, 1993); Jackson v. Culinary School of Washington, 788 F. Supp. 1233 (D.D.C. 1992), *aff'd in part, rev'd and remanded in part*, 27 F.3d 573 (D.C. Cir. 1994) (on de novo review, reversing district court's decision to issue declaratory judgment on state law issues), *vacated*, 515 U.S. 1139 (1995) (appellate court should have used abuse of discretion standard to review district court's decision to issue declaratory judgment on state law issues), *on remand*, 59 F.3d 254 (D.C. Cir. 1995) (remanding for district court to exercise its discretion about whether to issue declaratory judgment on state law issues); Hernandez v. Alexander, 1992 U.S. Dist. LEXIS 21930 (D. Nev. May 18, 1992); Shorter v. Alexander, Clearinghouse No. 47,950 (N.D. Ga. Dec. 8, 1992).

6.6.4.3 Creditor Who Accepts Contract or Note Without Required Holder Notice Loses UCC Protection Against Consumer's Defenses

Where a credit-seller fails to include the FTC Holder Notice, there should be little problem raising seller-related *defenses* against the assignee in a collection action. For an assignee of the credit-seller to claim insulation for defenses that could be raised against the assignor, it must claim it is a holder-in-due-course under Uniform Commercial Code (UCC) section 3-302 (if it holds a note that was transferred to it by a seller) or that a waiver-of-defense clause in the assigned contract is valid. The consumer should be able to defeat these arguments on a number of grounds.

UCC § 3-302(b) allows holder-in-due-course status only if the holder has taken a negotiable instrument "in good faith" and without notice of any claim by the consumer against the seller.[394] Acceptance of a contract or instrument that on its face violates the FTC Holder Rule should defeat any claim of good faith and should be notice of a consumer's claims against the seller, at least claims relating to this FTC rule violation.

Likewise, for transactions covered by Article 9, waiver-of-defense clauses in a credit contract are effective only if the assignee meets the same standards.[395] (These clauses are disfavored in any event, are rarely enforced by the courts,[396] and often violate specific state laws prohibiting such waivers.[397])

6.6.4.4 Omission of Holder Notice as UDAP Violation by Holder

6.6.4.4.1 General

Another approach for finding holder liability where the Holder Notice is missing applies both to assigned installment sales contract or a direct loan. The consumer's claim is that the creditor's attempt to enforce a note without the Holder Notice is a state UDAP violation. Under this theory, the creditor has engaged in an unfair or deceptive practice, and is thus liable to the consumer for the creditor's own misconduct. The consumer's damages equal the amount of the consumer's claim it could have raised against the creditor if the FTC Holder Notice had been included in the note. This approach should be successful in many instances because the creditor's actions are often clearly unfair or deceptive.

394 See § 6.7.2, *infra*, for further analysis of these requirements.

395 U.C.C. § 9-403 (formerly § 9-206(1)).

396 *See, e.g.*, Vasquez v. Superior Court (Karp), 4 Cal. 3d 800, 94 Cal. Rptr. 796, 484 P.2d 964 (1971); Fairfield Credit Corp. v. Donnelly, 158 Conn. 543, 264 A.2d 547 (1969); Unico v. Owen, 50 N.J. 101, 232 A.2d 405 (1967); Capital City Fin. Group, Inc. v. MAC Constr. Inc., 2002 WL 2016332 (Ohio App. Aug. 28, 2002) (unpublished, citation limited).

397 *See* § 6.6.5.6.5, *infra*.

6.6.4.4.2 Creditor's actions as a deceptive practice

Where a creditor's promissory note violates the FTC Holder Rule, the creditor is engaging in a deceptive practice. As one court has put it, the creditor engages in "fraudulent conduct which creates a likelihood of confusion or misunderstanding" since the "FTC Regulation preserving defenses serves to eliminate confusion and misunderstanding created through an artificial bifurcation of a transaction by an installment seller in an effort to insulate the duty to pay from the duty to perform."[398]

A creditor also violates the state UDAP statute by supplying other forms for the consumer to sign, such as completion certificates, that contain language sidestepping the FTC

398 Iron & Glass Bank v. Franz, 9 Pa. D. & C.3d 419, Clearinghouse No. 31,047 (Pa. C.P. Allegheny Cty. 1978). *See also* Keams v. Tempe Technical Institute, Inc., Clearinghouse No. 41,793J (D. Ariz. Oct. 19, 1995); Brown v. LaSalle Northwest Nat'l Bank, 820 F. Supp. 1078 (N.D. Ill. 1993) (complaint survives motion to dismiss); Spinner v. Chesapeake Bus. Institute of Virginia, Clearinghouse No. 49,131A (E.D. Va. Feb. 5, 1993) (practice may involve constructive fraud); Jackson v. Culinary School of Washington, 788 F. Supp. 1233 (D.D.C. 1992) (complaint survives motion to dismiss), *later dismissed on summary judgment on other grounds*, 811 F. Supp. 714 (D.D.C. 1993) (court found insufficient facts to find UDAP liability), *aff'd in part, rev'd and remanded in part on other grounds*, 27 F.3d 573 (D.C. Cir. 1994) (on de novo review, reversing district court's decision to issue declaratory judgment on state law issues), *vacated*, 515 U.S. 1139 (1995) (appellate court should have used abuse of discretion standard to review district court's decision to issue declaratory judgment on state law issues), *on remand*, 59 F.3d 254 (D.C. Cir. 1995) (remanding for district court to exercise its discretion about whether to issue declaratory judgment on state law issues); Shorter v. Alexander, Clearinghouse No. 47,950 (N.D. Ga. Dec. 8, 1992); Heastie v. Community Bank, 727 F. Supp. 1133 (N.D. Ill. 1989) (creditor liable under state UDAP statute for unfair practices in regard to FTC Holder Rule; creditor included a written notice in the contract in part contradicting the FTC Holder notice). *See also* Letter from Kathleen E. Keest, Deputy Administrator, Iowa Consumer Credit Code, Clearinghouse No. 53560 (May 22, 2001). *But see* Williams v. National School of Health Technology, 836 F. Supp. 273 (E.D. Pa. 1993) (only original seller, not seller's assignee, is liable for failure to include the FTC notice in the promissory note; decision ignores fact that if this UDAP violation is a defense against the lender, it is also a defense against the assignee); Capital Bank & Trust Co. v. Lacey, 393 So. 2d 668 (La. 1981) (only seller, not assignee, commits unfair act by failing to include Holder Notice in contract; assignee claimed transactions was commercial rather than consumer); Hayner v. Old Kent Bank, 2002 WL 227016 (Mich. App. Ct. Feb. 12, 2002) (unpublished, limited precedent) (no UDAP violation because FTC Holder Rule does not create a duty on the bank to place language in agreement, only on the seller); Nashville Electric Service v. Stone, 1998 Tenn. App. LEXIS 474 (Tenn. Ct. App. July, 15, 1998) (only seller, not lender from which seller arranged loan, is liable for failure to include Holder Notice in loan documents). *But cf.* Morales v. Walker Motors Sales, Inc., 162 F. Supp. 2d 786 (S.D. Ohio 2000) (failure to use type size specified by FTC Holder Rule not material, so not a UDAP violation).

Holder Rule by absolving the creditor of responsibility for some or all of the seller's liability.[399] This is the case even though the FTC rule only applies to the seller, placing no responsibility on the creditor to insure that the notice is inserted in the credit agreement.

It is also a material non-disclosure for the creditor to fail to inform the consumer that the creditor's loan documents violate federal law. A court thus let a case proceed where RICO and UDAP claims were brought against a creditor who failed to include the FTC Holder Notice in its documents. The omission was alleged to be mail fraud, wire fraud, and deception, particularly in that the creditor covered up its relationship to the seller and supplied the documents violating the FTC rule.[400]

Massachusetts UDAP regulations also indicate that creditors violate the state UDAP statute if they fail to comply with standards similar to the FTC Holder Notice. These standards are that lenders are subject to all defenses if they are related to the seller, they prepared the loan documents, they supplied the loan forms, the seller recommended the creditor and the creditor financed at least two consumer loans related to the seller in the calendar year, or the creditor issued a credit card used in the transaction.[401]

Wisconsin UDAP regulations are somewhat similar in that it is unfair and deceptive for assignees of home improvement contracts to take those contracts unless they are subject to the consumer's *claims* and defenses against the assignor.[402] (Normally, assignees are just subject to the consumer's defenses against the assignor.)

The situation in Georgia is slightly different because Georgia has enacted as a state UDAP regulation the exact wording of the FTC Holder Rule.[403] As a result, any violation of the FTC Holder Rule automatically violates the Georgia regulation and thus the Georgia UDAP statute. Similarly, a creditor using a promissory note failing to comply with Georgia UDAP regulations should violate the Georgia UDAP statute.

Idaho UDAP regulations prohibit a "seller" from receiving a contract without the Holder Notice, and the regulations define "seller" as anyone engaged in trade or commerce.[404] Thus a lender should be engaged in a *per se* UDAP violation in Idaho if the notice is not in the note.

Even apart from the FTC rule violation, the very practice of insulating closely connected creditors from seller-related claims is a deceptive trade practice. FTC case law decided before the enactment of the FTC Holder Rule holds as deceptive the use of holder-in-due-course status in consumer transactions, finding deceptive the failure to disclose the possibility of assignment where the seller habitually assigns paper.[405]

Finally, to the extent a creditor aids and abets the seller's scheme to avoid its responsibilities under the FTC Holder Rule, the creditor can be found directly liable under a UDAP statute for its conduct in furtherance of the fraud.[406] For example, does the creditor draft form loan documents knowing that in most cases the notes will violate the FTC Holder Rule? Does the lender participate in some subterfuge attempting to show the two are not related?

6.6.4.4.3 Creditor's actions as an unfair practice

The creditor's use of a contract violating the FTC Holder Rule fits neatly into the FTC's definition of an unfair practice. There is substantial consumer injury and the consumer could not reasonably avoid the practice. Nor can there be any countervailing business justification for a lender to engage in loan practices that involve a violation of a federal regulation.[407]

Perhaps the best place to start in arguing that a lender engages in an unfair practice by so insulating itself is the *Statement of Basis and Purpose* for the FTC Holder Rule:

> The Commission believes that relief under Section five of the FTC Act is appropriate where sellers or creditors impose adhesive contracts upon consumers, where such contracts contain

---

399 Heastie v. Community Bank, 727 F. Supp. 1133 (N.D. Ill. 1989). *See* § 6.6.3.12, *supra*.

400 Brown v. LaSalle Northwest Nat'l Bank, 820 F. Supp. 1078 (N.D. Ill. 1993).

401 Massachusetts Consumer Protection Regulations, Mass Regs. Code tit. 940, § 3.07, Advertising or Offering to Sell on an "Easy Credit" Basis.

402 Wisconsin Department of Agriculture, Trade and Consumer Protection Rules, Wis. Ad. Code, ATCP 110.06, Home Improvement Trade Practices. *See* Jackson v. DeWitt, 224 Wis. 2d 877, 592 N.W.2d 262 (1999) (home improvement UDAP regulation which subjected assignee to buyer's claims and defenses trumped more general statute that limited assignee's liability to amount still owing on date consumer gave notice of claim).

403 Georgia Office of Consumer Affairs Regulations, Ga. Comp. R. & Regs. 122-5-.01.

404 Idaho Consumer Protection Regulations, Idaho Admin. Code §§ 04.02.01.020(44), 04.02.01.210.

405 All-State Industries of North Carolina, Inc. v. FTC, 423 F.2d 423 (4th Cir. 1970), *cert. denied*, 400 U.S. 828 (1970); Certified Building Products, Inc., 83 F.T.C. 1004 (1973); Southern States Distributing Co., 83 F.T.C. 1125 (1973).

406 *See* § 6.5, *supra*.

407 See § 4.3, *supra* for further discussion of the FTC unfairness definition. *But see* Armstrong v. Accrediting Council for Continuing Educ. & Training, Inc., 832 F. Supp. 419 (D. D.C. 1993) (failure to include holder notice in student loan contract not unconscionable where federal government approved the contract form), *vacated and remanded*, 84 F.3d 1452 (D.C. Cir. 1996) (table, text available at 1996 U.S. App. LEXIS 12241) (remanding for further consideration of whether to exercise jurisdiction over state claims), *on remand*, 950 F. Supp. 1 (D.D.C. 1996) (maintaining jurisdiction of pendent claims and finding case appropriate for declaratory relief), *on further remand*, 980 F. Supp. 53 (D.D.C. 1997) (determining that California law controls and inviting plaintiff to amend complaint to assert claims and defenses under California consumer protection laws), *aff'd*, 168 F.3d 1362 (D.C. Cir. 1999) (affirming district court's dismissal of claims), *cert. denied*, 528 U.S. 1073 (2000).

terms which injure consumers, and where consumer injury is not off-set by a reasonable measure of value received in return. In this connection, the Commission's authority to examine and prohibit unfair practices in or affecting commerce in the manner of a commercial equity court is appropriately applied to this problem. Where one party to a transaction enjoys substantial advantages with respect to the consumers with whom he deals, it is appropriate for the Commission to conduct an inquiry to determine whether the dominant party is using an overabundance of market power, or commercial advantage, in an inequitable manner.

We have conducted the contemplated inquiry in this case. We have reached a determination that it constitutes an unfair and deceptive practice to use contractual boilerplate to separate a buyer's duty to pay from a seller's duty to perform. We are persuaded that this bifurcation of duties with its attendant externalization of costs injures both consumers and the market. We know of no substantial benefits which may be received by consumers in return for the valuable legal rights they are compelled to relinquish. We can imagine no reasonable measure of value which could justify requiring consumers to assume all risk of seller misconduct, particularly where creditors who profit from consumer sales have access to superior information combined with the means and capacity to deal with seller misconduct costs expeditiously and economically.

Our findings with respect to the use of vendor related loans to separate a consumer's duty to pay from his seller's duty to perform are detailed in Chapter IV. We are of the view that the use of direct loan agreements is no less adhesive than the use of installment sales contracts which incorporate waivers or promissory notes. We have received substantial evidence that sellers work cooperatively with lenders to foreclose consumer equities, and that such cooperation involves high-pressure sales tactics and deceptive and misleading statements. We have received substantial evidence that this rule would be seriously weakened by a failure to address the vendor related loan problem. We are therefore persuaded that the reasoning appearing above in this chapter applies with equal force to direct loan financing, and that our rule must apply to "purchase money" loan transactions.[408]

A federal court allowed a case to go to trial to determine if it was unconscionable or unfair to have a credit agreement without the Holder Notice.[409] But the court later found no evidence that a contract without the Holder Notice was unconscionable where the consumer offered no evidence that the contract unreasonably favored the creditor.[410]

6.6.4.4.4 Are the creditor's actions within the UDAP statute's scope?

Where the FTC Holder Notice is included in a contract or promissory note, the consumer can raise a seller-related UDAP claim against the creditor even if the creditor is not within the scope of the UDAP statute.[411] All that is required is that both the seller and the challenged practice are within the scope of the UDAP statute. But where a consumer is bringing a UDAP claim directly against the creditor for using a contract or note failing to contain the Holder Notice, both the creditor and the creditor's alleged violation must be within the scope of the UDAP statute. A number of UDAP statutes exclude credit from their scope or exempt banks or financial institutions.[412]

Most cases facing such a UDAP scope issue involve student loan notes where the bank and guaranty agency did not include the FTC Holder Notice in the loan documents. Many courts appear to be looking for ways of avoiding these complex cases, and a number of these cases have dismissed UDAP claims because of scope issues.

---

408 Statement of Basis and Purpose for the Federal Trade Commission Rule Concerning the Preservation of Consumers' Claims and Defenses, 40 Fed. Reg. 53524 (Nov. 18, 1975), *reproduced on* the companion CD-Rom to this volume.

409 Jackson v. Culinary School of Washington, 788 F. Supp. 1233 (D.D.C. 1992). *See also* Spinner v. Chesapeake Bus. Institute of Virginia, Clearinghouse No. 49,131A (E.D. Va. Feb. 5, 1993).

410 Jackson v. Culinary School of Washington, 811 F. Supp. 714 (D.D.C. 1993), *aff'd in part on other grounds, vacated and remanded in part on other grounds*, 27 F.3d 573 (D.C. Cir. 1994) (finding, on de novo review, that district court should have refused to issue declaratory judgment on state law issues), *vacated and remanded*, 115 S. Ct. 2573 (1995) (circuit court should have used abuse of discretion standard, not de novo review, in determining whether district court should have ruled on state law issues), *on remand*, 59 F.3d 255 (D.C. Cir. 1995) (remanding for district court to exercise its discretion about whether to issue declaratory judgment on state law issues). *See also* Armstrong v. Accrediting Council for Continuing Educ. & Training, Inc., 832 F. Supp. 419 (D.D.C. 1993) (not unconscionable where United States had approved the student loan note), *vacated and remanded*, 84 F.3d 1452 (D.C. Cir. 1996) (table, text available at 1996 U.S. App. LEXIS 12241) (remanding for further consideration of whether to exercise jurisdiction over state claims), *on remand*, 950 F. Supp. 1 (D.D.C. 1996) (maintaining jurisdiction of pendent claims and finding case appropriate for declaratory relief), *on further remand*, 980 F. Supp. 53 (D.D.C. 1997) (determining that California law controls and inviting plaintiff to amend complaint to assert claims and defenses under California consumer protection laws), *aff'd*, 168 F.3d 1362 (D.C. Cir. 1999) (affirming district court's dismissal of claims), *cert. denied*, 528 U.S. 1073 (2000).

411 Pratt v. North Dixie Manufactured Housing, Ltd., 2003 WL 21040658 (Ohio App. May 9, 2003) (unpublished, citation limited) (creditor is derivatively liable if Holder Notice is included in contract, but here it was not).

412 *See* §§ 2.2.1, 2.3.3, *supra*.

Thus in one case the consumer brought a UDAP action under the District of Columbia statute, alleging a violation of a specific UDAP provision prohibiting the sale of consumer goods in a condition or manner not consistent with that warranted by requirement of federal laws. The court dismissed the claim because the contract dealt with trade school *services*, and the court found that the particular UDAP provision only applied to goods, not services.[413]

In other cases, a UDAP claim was not available against a bank extending the student loan since the Florida UDAP statute specifically exempts banks.[414] In a Virginia student loan case, the court seized on the argument that the student loan note was authorized by the government, so that the practice was exempted from the UDAP statute under that statute's exclusion for practices authorized by federal laws or regulations.[415] A New Jersey court held that claims under New Jersey's consumer fraud statute relating to omission of the FTC Holder Notice from student loan documents were preempted by the federal Higher Education Act of 1965.[416] However, claims under a New Jersey state law similar to the FTC Holder Rule were not so barred.[417]

6.6.4.5 RICO Liability for Omitted Holder Notice

Where a creditor's participation in violating the FTC Holder Rule is deceptive, the practice may also involve mail or wire fraud, and thus lead to a RICO violation.[418] A failure to disclose can be enough to trigger mail fraud.[419]

6.6.4.6 Does Violation of FTC Rule Make Contract or Note Illegal and Thus Unenforceable?

Another approach is to argue that the whole contract or note is voidable where it fails to include a provision required by law.[420] A contract made in violation of a statute meant to protect the public—such as the FTC Holder Rule—is often found to be void, except when an innocent party to the contract maintains an action for its breach. But here the creditor should know that the Holder language should be included, and is thus not innocent.

A related argument arises where a related lender directly makes out the check to the seller. The seller, according to the rule, can not accept loan proceeds unless the notice is in the loan documents. Even though it is illegal for the seller to accept the proceeds, the creditor has delivered the proceeds to the seller. The creditor can not now seek repayment of proceeds it never should have disbursed.

Another way to make these arguments is that the creditor is estopped from claiming insulation from seller-related claims. Consumers relied on the loan documents including all terms required by law, and the creditor can not now renege on that implied promise.

These arguments, though, have generally not been successful in the student loan context.[421] Courts in this area appear to be loathe to prevent government collections based

---

413 Jackson v. Culinary School of Washington, 811 F. Supp. 714 (D.D.C. 1993), *aff'd in part on other grounds, vacated and remanded in part on other grounds*, 27 F.3d 573 (D.C. Cir. 1994) (finding, on de novo review, that district court should have refused to issue declaratory judgment on state law issues), *vacated and remanded*, 115 S. Ct. 2573 (1995) (circuit court should have used abuse of discretion standard, not de novo review, in determining whether district court should have ruled on state law issues), *on remand*, 59 F.3d 255 (D.C. Cir. 1995) (remanding for district court to exercise its discretion about whether to issue declaratory judgment on state law issues). *See also* Armstrong v. Accrediting Council for Continuing Educ. & Training, Inc., 832 F. Supp. 419 (D.D.C. 1993) (not unconscionable where United States had approved the student loan note), *vacated and remanded*, 84 F.3d 1452 (D.C. Cir. 1996) (table, text available at 1996 U.S. App. LEXIS 12241) (remanding for further consideration of whether to exercise jurisdiction over state claims), *on remand*, 950 F. Supp. 1 (D.D.C. 1996) (maintaining jurisdiction of pendent claims and finding case appropriate for declaratory relief), *on further remand*, 980 F. Supp. 53 (D.D.C. 1997) (determining that California law controls and inviting plaintiff to amend complaint to assert claims and defenses under California consumer protection laws), *aff'd*, 168 F.3d 1362 (D.C. Cir. 1999) (affirming district court's dismissal of claims), *cert. denied*, 528 U.S. 1073 (2000).

414 United States v. Ornecipe, Clearinghouse No. 51,941 (S.D. Fla. 1995); Armand v. Secretary of Educ., Clearinghouse No. 51,298 (S.D. Fla. July 19, 1995).

415 Spinner v. Chesapeake Bus. Institute of Virginia, Clearinghouse No. 49,131A (E.D. Va. Feb. 5, 1993).

416 Morgan v. Markerdowne Corp., 976 F. Supp. 301 (D.N.J. 1997).

417 *Id.*

418 Brown v. LaSalle Northwest Nat'l Bank, 820 F. Supp. 1078 (N.D. Ill. 1993).

419 *Id.*; *see also* § 9.2.4, *infra*.

420 *See, e.g.*, Virginia Attorney General Mary Terry Opinion Letter to Judge J. R. Zepkin, Clearinghouse No. 44,810 (Feb. 24, 1989).

421 Keams v. Tempe Technical Institute, Inc., 993 F. Supp. 714 (D. Ariz. 1997) (since student loan contracts did not include terms of FTC Holder Rule, former vocational school students were not able to assert claims and defenses arising from school's behavior against assignee); Armstrong v. Accrediting Council for Continuing Educ. & Training, Inc., 832 F. Supp. 419 (D.D.C. 1993), *vacated and remanded*, 84 F.39 1452 (D.C. Cir. May 3, 1996) (table, text on Westlaw) (ruling on state law claims must first determine whether district court should exercise pendent jurisdiction and consider possibility of declaratory relief; if district court decides to proceed, it must revisit state law issues as to which state law applies, whether provision is preempted by federal law, and interpretation of state law); *Armstrong's* later history is *on remand*, 950 F. Supp. 1 (D.D.C. 1996) (court maintained jurisdiction of pendent claims and found case to be appropriate for declaratory relief), *reinstated in relevant part*, 980 F. Supp. 53 (D.D.C. 1997) (state common law claim of illegality was preempted by Higher Education Act of 1965), *aff'd*, 168 F.3d 1362 (D.C. Cir. 1999) (affirming district court's dismissal of claims), *cert. denied*, 528 U.S. 1073 (2000); Spinner v. Chesapeake Bus. Institute of Virginia, Clearinghouse No. 49,131A (E.D. Va. Feb. 5, 1993).

on school misconduct, but may consider such arguments in other contexts.

6.6.5 Other Theories for Holding Assignees and Lenders Liable for Seller-Related Claims and Defenses

6.6.5.1 Introduction

If the Holder Notice has been wrongfully omitted from the loan or credit sale documents and the court refuses to read the notice into the contract or enforce it in one of the ways listed in the previous subsections, the creditor may still be held liable for the seller's misconduct on a number of theories. These theories also apply if the sales transaction falls into one of the exceptions to the FTC Holder Rule.[422] The subsections that follow discuss several of these theories:

- The general UCC rule that the assignee of a contract stands in the shoes of the assignor;
- State statutes that make creditors liable for seller-related claims;
- The close-connectedness doctrine;
- Protections provided by the federal Homeownership and Equity Protection Act (HOEPA) that allow consumers to raise claims and defenses against holders where a high-rate loan is secured by a residence.
- Provisions of the Truth in Lending Act for credit cards and open-end credit; and
- Liability of entities that finance consumer leases.

In addition, theories of agency and participation in the fraud discussed in §§ 6.3 and 6.5, *supra*, may be helpful in some circumstances to hold a creditor liable for a seller's misconduct. For example, the creditor may be liable under theories of aiding and abetting, co-conspiracy, joint enterprise, and the like if they participate with the seller in the illegal conduct.[423] Where the seller fills out the loan documents for the lender or otherwise acts as the lender's agent, then the consumer may be able to bring an action against the lender for the acts of its agent. In general, principles are liable for the acts of their agents,[424] and the lender should thus be liable for the actions of the seller within the scope of the agency.

Finally, § 6.7, *infra*, discusses theories for holding assignees liable for the acts of lenders who make straight loans of money, such as home equity loans and consolidation loans, that are not tied to the purchase of goods and services. That discussion will also have relevance to any credit sale where the assignee claims holder-in-due course status. Usually, however, sellers assign installment sales contracts rather than promissory notes to assignees,[425] in part because many state retail installment statutes prohibit sellers from taking promissory notes in consumer installment sales.[426] As a result, assignees can not claim holder-in-due course status in relationship to such installment sales contracts, but only for negotiable instruments.

422 *See* § 6.6.2.2, *supra*.

423 *See* § 6.5, *supra*.

424 *See* § 6.3.1, *supra*.

6.6.5.2 Assignee of Credit Contract Is Generally Subject to Seller-Related Defenses

If the seller assigned an installment sales contract to the creditor, the general rule is that the creditor stands in the shoes of the seller and is subject to seller-related *defenses* (although not affirmative claims).[427] Only if there is an enforceable waiver-of-defense clause can the creditor avoid the defenses that would be good against the seller.[428] Many installment contracts do not contain waiver-of-defense clauses, and many states prohibit them in at least some types of transactions.[429] As a result, even without the FTC Holder Rule, the assignee of an installment sales contract usually holds it subject to the defenses the consumer could raise against the seller.[430]

6.6.5.3 State Statute May Create Derivative Liability Independent of FTC Holder Rule

Virtually every state has enacted state "holder" laws.[431]

425 *See* § 6.6.1.2, 6.6.1.3, *supra*.

426 *See* § 6.6.5.6.5, *infra* (list of state holder laws).

427 Nat'l City Bank v. Columbian Mut. Life Ins. Co., 282 F.3d 407 (6th Cir. 2002); *In re* Shaw, 178 B.R. 380 (Bankr. D.N.J. 1994); Am. Transportation Corp. v. Exchange Capital Corp., 129 S.W.3d 312, 52 U.C.C. Rep. Serv. 2d 505 (Ark. App. 2003); Meyers v. Postal Fin. Co., 287 N.W.2d 614 (Minn. 1979); Capital City Fin. Group, Inc. v. MAC Constr. Inc., 2002 WL 2016332 (Ohio App. Aug. 28, 2002) (unpublished, citation limited); DaimlerChrysler Servs. N. Am., L.L.C. v. Ouimette, 830 A.2d 38 (Vt. 2003) (assignee of credit sale contract stands in shoes of seller); 9 Corbin, Corbin on Contracts §§ 892 (interim ed. 2002); 29 Lord, Williston on Contracts §§ 74.47, 74.49 (4th ed. 2003); Farnsworth, Farnsworth on Contracts § 11.8 (2d ed. 1998); Restatement (Second) of Contracts § 336 (1981).

428 U.C.C. § 9-403 (former § 9-206).

429 *See* § 6.6.5.6.5, *infra*.

430 See also § 6.7.3, infra.

431 *Alabama*: Ala. Code §§ 5-19-5, 5-19-8 (applicable to consumer credit sales).
Alaska: Alaska Stat. § 45.50.541 (contracts for sale or lease of consumer goods or services on credit).
Arizona: Ariz. Stat. §§ 44-145 (writings evidencing the obligation of a natural person as buyer, lessee, or borrower in connection with purchase or lease of goods or services), 45-5005 (home solicitation sales).
California: Cal. Civ. Code §§ 1747.90 (credit cards), 1804.1, 1804.2 (retail installment contracts), 1810.7 (retail installment accounts), 2982.5 (motor vehicle loans).

These laws though vary dramatically from state to state. One significant aspect of many of these laws is that they are not

Colorado: Colo. Rev. Stat. § 5-3-303 (consumer credit sales and leases).
Connecticut: Conn. Gen. Stat. § 52-572g (credit transactions covering consumer goods or services, other than credit card transactions).
Delaware: Del. Code tit. 6, §§ 4311, 4312 (retail installment sales), 4342 (retail installment accounts).
District of Columbia: D.C. Code §§ 28-3807, 28-3808 (consumer credit sales), 28-3809 (direct installment loan to purchase goods or services).
Florida: Fla. Stat. Ann. § 520.74 (home improvement contracts).
Georgia: Ga. Code Ann. §§ 10-1-9 (retail installment contracts), 10-1-33 (motor vehicle sales financing).
Hawaii: Haw. Rev. Stat. § 476-19 (credit sales).
Idaho: Idaho Code § 28-43-306 (no negotiable instruments in credit sales).
Illinois: 815 Ill. Comp. Stat. Ann. §§ 405/17, 405/18 (retail installment contracts), 375/16, 375/17 (motor vehicle retail installment sales).
Iowa: Iowa Code §§ 537.3307, 537.3404 (consumer credit sales and leases), 537.3403 (credit cards), 537.3405 (loans for property or services).
Kansas: Kan. Stat. §§ 16a-3-307, 16a-3-404 (consumer credit sales and leases), 16a-3-403 (credit cards), 16a-3-405 (loans for goods or services).
Maine: Me. Rev. Stat. Ann. tit. 9-A, §§ 3-307, 3-403 (consumer credit sales and leases), 3-404 (loans for goods or services), 3-405 (consumer leases).
Maryland: Md. Code, Comm. Law §§ 12-309 (loans to buy consumer goods or services), 12-628 (promissory notes in installment sales).
Massachusetts: Mass. Gen. Laws Ann. ch. 255, §§ 12C (promissory notes in credit sales of goods), 12F (consumer loan transactions connected to consumer sale or lease transactions), ch. 255B, § 19A (motor vehicle retail installment contracts), ch. 255D, §§ 10(6), 25A (retail installment sale agreements). *See also* Code Mass. Regs. tit. 940, § 3.07 (certain sellers).
Michigan: Mich. Comp. Laws Ann. §§ 445.865 (retail installment contracts), 445.1207 (home improvement contracts), 492.114a (motor vehicle installment sale contracts). *See* Cannoy v. Interstate Builders, Inc., 2003 WL 133063 (Mich. Ct. App. Jan. 3, 2003) (language of state law limits recovery to amount paid to specific holder, not to amount paid on the debt to all holders); Jerry v. Second Nat'l Bank, 208 Mich. App. 87, 527 N.W.2d 788 (1994) (finding assignee of retail installment contract liable for buyer's claims and defenses under Michigan statute similar to FTC Holder Rule).
Minnesota: Minn. Stat. Ann. § 325G.16 (consumer credit sales).
Mississippi: Miss. Code Ann. § 63-19-41 (motor vehicle retail installment contracts).
Missouri: Mo. Rev. Stat. Ann. §§ 408.405 (purchase or lease of consumer goods or services), 408.410 (exclusion for certain loans and credit card transactions).
Nevada: Nev. Rev. Stat. § 97.275 (retail installment contracts and retail charge agreements).
New Hampshire: N.H. Rev. Stat. §§ 320:21-a, 320:21-b (consumer credit sales and leases by hawker or peddler).
New Jersey: N.J. Stat. Ann. §§ 17:16C-38.1, 17:16C-38.2 (retail installment contracts), 17:16C-64.1, 17:16C-64.2 (home repair contracts).
New Mexico: N.M. Stat. Ann. §§ 56-1-5, 56-1-7 (retail installment contracts and retail charge agreements).
New York: N.Y. Pers. Prop. Law §§ 302(9) (motor vehicle retail installment contracts), § 403 (retail installment contracts), 413 (retail installment credit agreements), N.Y. Gen. Bus. Law § 253 (interlocking loans).
North Carolina: N.C. Gen. Stat. § 25A-25 (consumer credit sales). *See* State *ex rel.* Easley v. Rich Food Servs., Inc., 535 S.E.2d 84 (N.C. Ct. App. 2000) (attorney general can obtain cancellation of contracts and restitution from finance company based on Holder Notice required by state statute).
Ohio: Ohio Rev. Code §§ 1317.031, 1317.032 (purchase money loan installment notes and retail installment contracts in connection with consumer transactions). *But see* Abel v. Kaybank USA, 313 F. Supp. 2d 720 (N.D. Ohio 2004) (Ohio Rev. Code § 1317.032 conflicts with and is therefore preempted by National Bank Act; court fails to consider that the state statute is no greater impingement on the autonomy of national banks than is already imposed by the FTC Holder Rule).
Oklahoma: Okla. Stat. Ann. tit. 14-A, §§ 2-403, 2-404 (consumer credit sales and leases).
Oregon: Or. Rev. Stat. §§ 83.650 (retail installment contracts for motor vehicles and mobile homes), 83.820 (contracts for sale or lease of motor vehicles or consumer goods or services on credit), 83.850 (interlocking loans).
Pennsylvania: Pa. Stat. Ann. tit. 69, §§ 615 (motor vehicle installment sale contracts), 1401, 1402 (retail installment sales except motor vehicles), tit. 73, § 500-207 (home improvement contracts).
Puerto Rico: P.R. Laws Ann. tit. 10, §§ 748, 749 (retail installment contracts).
Rhode Island: R.I. Gen. Laws Ann. §§ 6-27-5 (promissory notes in retail contracts for goods or services; certain loans), 6-28-6 (home solicitation sales). *See also* R. I. Gen. Laws Ann. § 6-28.1-3 (liability of third parties for certain unfair home improvement loans to senior citizens).
South Carolina: S.C. Code §§ 37-2-403, 37-2-404 (consumer credit sales and leases), 37-3-410 (interlocking loans), 37-3-411 (credit cards).
South Dakota: S.D. Codified Laws Ann. §§ 57A-3A-102–57A-3A-107 (contracts for sale or lease of consumer goods or services on credit).
Texas: Tex. Fin. Code §§ 345.304 (retail installment transactions).
Utah: Utah Code §§ 70C-2-204, 70C-2-205 (consumer credit sales).
Vermont: Vt. Stat. Ann. tit. 9, § 2455 (consumer contracts), tit. 8, § 14303 (bank credit cards).
Washington: Wash. Rev. Code Ann. § 63.14.020 (retail installment contracts). *See also* Wash. Rev. Code Ann. § 63.14.145 (contract retains its character after assignment).
West Virginia: W. Va. Code §§ 46A-2-101 (consumer credit sales and leases), 46A-2-102 (instruments, contracts, and other writings evidencing obligations arising from consumer credit sales and leases), 46A-2-103 (claims and defenses of borrowers, arising from consumer sales, with respect to consumer loans), 46A-2-103a (consumer finance leases and sale-leaseback agreements). *See* McGraw v. Scott Runyan Pontiac-Buick, Inc., 194 W. Va. 770, 461 S.E.2d 516 (1995) (under West Virginia law, assignee takes note subject to all rights of the consumer).
Wisconsin: Wis. Stat. Ann. §§ 422.406 (consumer credit sales and leases and interlocking loans), 422.407 (certain consumer credit transactions), 422.408 (interlocking consumer loans); Wis. Admin. Code ATCP § 110.06 (home improvement contracts). *See also* Jackson v. DeWitt, 592 N.W.2d 262 (Wis. Ct. App. 1999) (Wis. Admin. Code applies even where installment sales agreement is not a negotiable instrument).

dependent on a notice being placed in a note—consumers can raise defenses and in some cases affirmative claims as a matter of the state's substantive law. This right is not just based on a contractual right derived from a notice included in the note and is not dependent on the seller or lender's insertion of the FTC Holder Notice into the note or contract.[432]

A number of state laws simply prohibit waivers of the consumer's rights to bring defenses against an assignee. On the other hand, about a third of the states have holder laws that usually allow a consumer to bring affirmative claims even where there is no assignment, but the seller instead is connected with lender in some way.[433] These statutes usually include a definition of the special relationship between the lender and seller that triggers this liability. Typically, it is enough if the seller gets a referral fee, the seller participates in the preparation of the loan documents, the loan is conditioned on a purchase from the seller, or the lender had knowledge of complaints against the seller. The state holder statute may require the consumer to first make a good faith effort to obtain satisfaction from the seller.

State holder statutes may not be as protective as the FTC Holder Rule. For example, some state statutes may have a lower maximum recovery than the FTC rule.[434] On the other

Wyoming: Wyo. Stat. §§ 40-14-237, 40-14-238 (consumer credit sales and consumer leases).

432 *See In re* Paradise Palms Vacation Club, 41 B.R. 916 (D. Haw. 1984) (interpreting Washington RISA); Gogola v. First South Savings & Loan of Pittsburgh, 1990 WL 312777 (Pa. Com. Pl. Dec. 10, 1990); Wash. Rev. Code § 63.14.020.

433 Ariz. Rev. Stat. Ann. § 44-145; Cal. Civ. Code § 2982.5(d)(4) (motor vehicle sales only); Conn. Gen. Stat. § 52-572g (allowing defenses to be raised where "in connection with a credit transaction covering consumer goods"; unclear whether this would apply to direct loans in connection with sale, or only to credit sales); D.C. Code Ann. § 28-3809; Iowa Code Ann. § 537.3405; Kan. Stat. Ann. §§ 16a-3-403, 16a-3-405; Me. Rev. Stat. Ann. tit. 9-A, §§ 3-404, 3-405 (interlocking loans and leases); Md. Comm. Law Code Ann. § 12-309; Mass. Gen. Laws Ann. ch. 255, § 12F; Massachusetts Consumer Protection Regulations, Mass Regs. Code tit. 940, § 3.07, Advertising or Offering to Sell on an "Easy Credit" Basis; Mo. Rev. Stat. §§ 408.400–408.410, 408.250; N.Y. Gen. Bus. Law § 253; N.C. Gen. Stat. § 25A-1 (exempting "bona fide direct loan transactions" from RISA; this language may not exempt lenders referred by seller); Ohio Rev. Code §§ 1317.01, 1317.031 (preserving defenses as to purchase money loans); Or. Rev. Stat. §§ 83.850, 83.860; 69 Pa. Stat. § 1402 (appears to apply to direct loans, based on applicable definition found at 69 Pa. Stat. § 1201(17), (18)); R.I. Gen. Laws § 6-27-5 (requiring holder-type notice on contract with lender to which seller regularly refers buyers); S.C. Code Ann. § 37-3-410; Vt. Stat. Ann. tit. 9, § 2455 (unclear whether applies to direct loans or just credit-sales); W. Va. Code § 46A-2-103; Wis. Stat. Ann. § 422.408. *See also* Gonzalez v. Old Kent Mortg. Co., 2000 U.S. Dist. LEXIS 14530 (E.D. Pa. Sept. 19, 2000) (loan not a direct loan where consumer asked contractor to obtain financing, and contractor contacted lender, even though eventual loan was for both the construction and other things such as debt consolidation); Heastie v. Community Bank, 727 F. Supp. 1133 (N.D. Ill. 1989) (UDAP violation where related lender included provision in contract which sought to disclaim any responsibility for seller's work); Drew v. Chrysler Credit Corp., 596 F. Supp. 1371 (W.D. Mo. 1984) (interpreting Missouri statute); *In re* Brown, 134 B.R. 134 (Bankr. E.D. Pa. 1991) (loan was covered by home improvement finance act where contractor agreed to arrange financing, drove consumer to lender's office, and stood by while she signed papers); Hernandez v. Atlantic Fin. Co., 105 Cal. App. 3d 65 (1980) ("direct loan" exception to MVRISA narrowly construed to cover only financing arranged independently by buyer); Halloran v. North Plaza State Bank, 17 Kan. App. 2d 840, 844 P.2d 764 (1993) (Kansas holder statute did not apply to loan taken out to pay taxes, as it was not for the purpose of enabling a consumer to buy or lease from a particular seller); Credit Fin. Co. v. Stevens, 221 Kan. 1, 558 P.2d 122 (1976) (Kansas holder statute did not apply to lender who had no relationship with the seller, where loan was not conditioned upon the consumer purchasing goods from a particular seller); Roosevelt Fed. Sav. & Loan Ass'n v. Crider, 722 S.W.2d 325 (Mo. Ct. App. 1986) (exterior siding is a "consumer good," therefore home improvement loan fell within state holder statute); Collins v. Horizon Housing, inc., 135 N.C. App. 227, 519 S.E.2d 534 (1999) (RISA did not impose liability on bank which financed purchase of defective mobile home, where borrowers directly approached bank; implication is that result might be different if seller and lender had business relationship); Turner v. Citywide Home Improvement, Inc., 2000 Ohio App. LEXIS 904 (Mar. 10, 2000) (state holder law allows debtor to raise seller-related claims against direct lender where loan meets statutory definition of "purchase money loan"); Bennett v. Reliable Credit Ass'n, Inc., 125 Or. App. 531, 865 P.2d 496 (1993); State *ex rel.* McGraw v. Scott Runyan Pontiac-Buick, Inc., 194 W. Va. 770, 461 S.E.2d 516 (1995) (West Virginia law allows attorney general to recover illegal charges from assignees even if they are free of wrongdoing); Gramatan Home Investors Corp. v. Starling, 143 Vt. 527, 470 A.2d 1157 (1983) (allowing siding purchaser to assert failure of consideration defense against note's assignee); Randolph Nat'l Bank v. Vail, 131 Vt. 390, 308 A.2d 588 (1973) (state holder statute did not apply to note given as security for a preexisting obligation); Jackson v. DeWitt, 224 Wis. 2d 877, 592 N.W.2d 262 (1999) (home improvement UDAP regulation which subjected assignee to buyer's claims and defenses trumped more general statute that limited assignee's liability to amount still owing on date consumer gave notice of claim); Letter from Kathleen E. Keest, Deputy Administrator, Iowa Consumer Credit Code, Clearinghouse No. 53560 (May 22, 2001). *Cf.* Beaudreau v. Chrysler Credit Corp., 1979 WL 195988 (R.I. Super. Ct. Feb. 13, 1979). *But see* Armstrong v. Accrediting Council for Continuing Educ. and Training, Inc., 168 F.3d 1362 (D.C. Cir. 1999) (D.C. statute preempted when applied to federally guaranteed student loans); Alexiou v. Brad Benson Mitsubishi, 127 F. Supp. 2d 557 (D.N.J. 2000) (taking the absurd position that the New Jersey holder statute is preempted by the limitations on assignee liability in the Truth in Lending Act, even as to state claims; taking extraordinary position that Congress, when it limited assignee liability for TIL violations, intended to immunize assignees from all state law consumer protection violations); Butz v. Society Nat'l Bank, 83 B.R. 459 (S.D. Ohio 1987) (RISA does not apply if consumer goes to lender, borrows money for car, and gives lender a security interest).

434 Wis. Stat. Ann. § 422.408. *See, e.g.*, Kan. Stat. § 16a-3-404 (cap is amount owing at time assignee has notice of the claims or defenses).

hand, state holder statutes may provide rights not available under the FTC rule. For example, where the consumer has a claim against the manufacturer, but not the dealer, the holder may have no liability under the FTC Holder Rule, but may have such liability under a state statute.[435] Where the consumer has more rights under state law than the FTC Holder Rule, the FTC Holder Rule does not preempt such rights.[436]

6.6.5.4 The Close-Connectedness Doctrine

The close-connectedness doctrine is a another basis on which an assignee's immunity from defenses can be challenged when the Holder Notice is omitted. This doctrine, also referred to as the "party-to-the-transaction" doctrine, contests a creditor's assertion of holder-in-due-course status by disputing the "good faith" and "without notice" requirements of UCC § 3-302 where the creditor played some part in the original transaction. It has also been used to allow a consumer to assert defenses to the enforcement of a non-negotiable instrument, such as a retail installment sales contract or a lease, against a third party who would not otherwise be subject to such defenses.[437] The doctrine can be thought of as a common law alternative to the FTC Holder Rule,[438] and is particularly suitable to cases where a seller arranged credit through a particular financer to finance the sale and the paper was assigned when executed.

The New Jersey Supreme Court stated the modern version of the doctrine in *Unico v. Owen*.[439] In holding that consumers who had executed a note along with a retail installment contract could assert the defense of failure of consideration against the note holder, the court stated that it was "impelled for reasons of equity and justice to join those courts which deny holder-in-due-course status in consumer goods sales cases to those financers whose involvement with the seller's business is as close, and whose knowledge of the extrinsic factors—i.e., the terms of the underlying sale agreement—is as pervasive, as it is in the present case."[440] Much of the evidence driving the court's conclusion derived from the agreement between the creditor, which was a partnership formed expressly for financing the seller's operations, and the seller. This evidence revealed that the creditor maintained substantial control over the seller by imposing credit qualifications for customer requirements, prescribing terms for making of notes and their indorsement, and dictating other provisions of the sales transaction.[441]

Generally, flags of close-connectedness between a financer and seller or lessor are as follows:

(1) the financer's drafting of the forms used by the seller;
(2) approval and/or establishment of the seller's procedures by the financer (e.g., setting the interest rate, approval of a referral sales plan);
(3) a direct contact between the financer and the debtor, such as an independent check on the debtor's creditworthiness by the financer;
(4) heavy financial reliance upon the financer by the seller (e.g., the transfer of all or most of the seller's paper to the financer); and

435 *See, e.g.*, Mich. Comp. Laws Ann. § 492.114a(b) (holder of installment sale contract is subject to all buyer's claims and defenses arising out of the transaction, with recovery capped at amount paid to holder). *Cf.* Chrysler Fin. Co. v. Flynn, 88 S.W.3d 142 (Mo. Ct. App. 2002) (seeming to assume this interpretation of the Missouri statute).

436 *See* § 6.6.3.11, *supra*.

437 *See, e.g.*, Mercedes-Benz Credit Corp. v. Lotito, 306 N.J. Super. 25, 703 A.2d 288 (App. Div. 1997) (allowing consumer to assert breach of warranty claims against assignee of automobile lease).

438 *See* §§ 6.6.1–6.6.2, *supra*.

439 50 N.J. 101, 232 A.2d 405 (1967). The court was particularly influenced by the executory contractual obligations of the seller, on which it had defaulted. *See also* Whitlock v. Midwest Acceptance Corp., 575 F.2d 652 (8th Cir. 1978) (Missouri law) (reversing summary judgment for defendants on grounds that financer with whom car seller had arranged financing for buyers, may have had a close connection with the seller that would deny holder-in-due-course status); Commercial Credit Co. v. Childs, 137 S.W.2d 260 (Ark. 1940) (consumer transaction for purchase of automobile; closely-connected assignee of note not a good faith holder in due course because for "all intents and purposes [it was] a party to the agreement and instrument from the beginning"); Gross v. Appelgren, 467 P.2d 789 (Colo. 1970) (allowing purchasers of kitchen equipment to rescind mortgages and return purchase money notes, on grounds that financer was subject to defense of fraud because of its close connection with the equipment's seller); Citicorp Acceptance Co. v. Bunnell, 1992 Conn. Super. LEXIS 172 (Jan. 23, 1992); Jones v. Approved Bancredit Corp., 256 A.2d 739 (Del. 1969) (allowing a purchaser of pre-cut house to assert defense of fraud against holder where the holder took immediate assignment of the note and mortgage, prescribed the sales documents, shared officers and directors with sellers, and was involved in the construction, both seller and financer were wholly-owned subsidiaries of parent pre-cut home company, and 99% of the financer's business came from wholly-owned subsidiaries of parents); Ramadan v. Equico Lessors, Inc., 448 So. 2d 60 (Fla. Dist. Ct. App. 1984) (holding that under close-connection theory, assignee's name on preprinted form and lessee's deposition testimony raised issue as to close connection; reversing summary judgment for assignee); Provident Bank v. Barnhart, 445 N.E.2d 746 (Ohio App. 1982) (interrelationship of ownership between seller and lender, approval or establishment or both of seller's business practices by the lender, reliance upon the lender by the seller amounting to a principal-agent relationship, or an independent check of the debtor's credit by the lender all indicate close-connection). *But see* Wilson v. Direct Cable Technologies, 964 F. Supp. 1548 (M.D. Ala. 1997) (finance company that extended open-end credit for consumer to finance purchase is generally not liable for a retailer's misconduct without further evidence of an agency relationship, which does not arise merely by the financer providing the retailer with credit application forms bearing the finance company's name, by retaining a right to approve a consumer's credit, and by dictating the terms of the consumer's payments).

440 *Unico*, 232 A.2d at 413.

441 *Id.* The lack of bargaining power typical of consumer contracts clearly influenced the court. *Id.* at 411.

(5) common or connected ownership or management of the seller and financer.[442]

To illustrate these factors, in one case[443] a court ruled that a bank's "closer than usual relationship" with a seller whose promissory note was taken by assignment justified denying holder-in-due-course status, after finding that: a former employee of the bank was a sales representative of the dealer; the bank had taken a substantial number of notes from the dealer by assignment; the bank had taken them with recourse and at a substantial discount rate; evidence indicated that the bank provided the note and security agreement used by the dealer; and significantly, "the type of business appeared to be almost inherently suspect."[444]

Courts may be particularly receptive to a consumer's use of the doctrine when the seller's behavior was egregious. For example, in *American Plan Corp. v. Woods*,[445] the court allowed the purchaser of a defective water softener machine to maintain a fraud in the factum defense against the note holder after finding that the seller had subjected the consumer to a two hour sales pitch in her home, had told her that the softener was being given to her for "advertising," and had otherwise misrepresented the terms of the contract to a woman described as being "with little if any business experience."[446] The court found the financer too closely connected to the transaction to be a holder-in-due-course because it was the sole assignee for all of the seller's contracts, reserved the right to refuse any note, and investigated the credit of each purchaser whose note was offered to it.

The financer need not actually know of fraud in the underlying sale, where the assignment was contemporaneous and the financer has reason, beyond mere negligence or suspicion, to know of some "infirmity."[447] Accordingly, in *United States Finance Co. v. Jones*,[448] where a home improvement contractor had sold aluminum siding to the consumer, then covered her house in tar paper sprayed with aluminum paint, the court applied the doctrine to deny the financer holder-in-due-course status. The court noted that even though the work could have been expected to take several days, the finance company got the mortgage executed and a certificate of completion signed at the time of the sale, which "smacks of bad faith."[449]

In opposing the close-connectedness doctrine, creditors may argue that holder-in-due-course status, which promotes free and stable commerce in negotiable instruments, should not be put at risk by the seller's bad behavior. However, "a proper balance must be struck between the commercial need for negotiability and the individual's need for relief against fraud."[450] The doctrine was intended to protect the truly independent assignee, not one who engaged in the original transaction, and furthermore, subsequent holders of the tainted assignee will still be protected by holder-in-due-course status, fulfilling the policies of the doctrine.[451]

Most cases applying this doctrine involve contracts or notes that were originally payable to the seller but then were assigned to the creditor. Courts may be willing to expand the doctrine to other financing arrangements, however. In *Mercedes-Benz Credit Corp. v. Lotito*,[452] the court broadened the doctrine to allow a lessee to assert a claim that the manufacturer's warranty had been breached against a financer attempting to enforce an automobile lease. In finding a close connection among the dealer (who was also the original lessor), the manufacturer, and the financer,[453] the court pointed out that the financer created the lease form and authorized dealerships to execute leases on its behalf, that it had a close relationship with the dealership from whom the lessee had leased the car, and that it had extensive knowledge of the underlying lease agreement.[454] This case also

442 Arcanum Nat'l Bank v. Hessler, 433 N.E.2d 204 (Ohio 1982) (citing White & Summers, Uniform Commercial Code 481 (1972)). *See also* Freeman v. Hubco Leasing, Inc., 253 Ga. 698, 324 S.E.2d 462 (1985) (company through which dealer arranged lease, which was owned by same shareholders, had same officers, and operated from same location as dealer, was liable for dealer's breach of warranty); Allis-Chalmers Credit Corp. v. Herbolt, 479 N.E.2d 293, 302 (Ohio Ct. App. 1984) (mere similarity in names of seller and creditor insufficient to invoke close-connectedness doctrine).

443 Security Central Nat'l Bank v. Williams, 368 N.E.2d 1264 (Ohio Ct. App. 1976).

444 *Id.* at 1266 (the seller sold equipment to appellee for making stereo tapes from master tapes and promised to furnish master tapes weekly from which 400 individual tapes could be made each week to be bought back by the seller).

445 240 N.E.2d 886 (Ohio Ct. App. 1968).

446 *Id.* at 888.

447 *See* Local Acceptance Co. v. Kinkade, 361 S.W.2d 830, 834 (Mo. 1962) (financer's knowledge that seller of sewing machines also executed a "sew" contract with buyers whereby the buyers were to sew pre-cut garments to make the payments was sufficient to raise issue of bad faith for jury).

448 229 So. 2d 495 (Ala. 1969).

449 *Id.* at 497 (noting that the finance company apparently wanted to guarantee its status as a holder in due course whether or not the work is ever completed).

450 Security Nat'l Bank v. Williams, 368 N.E.2d 1264 (Ohio Ct. App. 1976).

451 *See* Note, Harv. L. Rev. 1200 (1940) ("By abandoning the test of the 'white heart and the empty head' in the case of the transferee who is more like an original party to the transaction than a subsequent purchaser, this decision increases the protection afforded the consumer who has not received what he was promised.") .

452 306 N.J. Super. 25, 703 A.2d 288 (1997).

453 All three entities were subsidiaries of one company. 703 A.2d at 290.

454 Policy considerations guided the court: "This disposition recognizes the disparity in economic power a consumer like defendant and companies like the third party defendants [the financer]. The latter are clearly more able than an individual consumer to 'absorb the impact of a single imprudent or unfair exchange.' " *Id.*, 306 N.J. Super. at 36, 703 A.2d at 294 (quoting *Unico*, 232 A.2d at 410). *Accord* Freeman v. Hubco Leasing, Inc., 253 Ga. 698, 324 S.E.2d 462 (1985).

shows how the doctrine may be of particular use where the FTC Holder Rule for whatever reason—such as a lease, not sale, transaction—may not apply.[455] By the same token, it should be possible to apply the doctrine where the transaction is set up as a direct loan from the closely-connected creditor to the consumer to pay for the seller's goods.

6.6.5.5 HOEPA Liability

The Homeownership and Equity Protection Act of 1994 (HOEPA) has a broad assignee liability provision for certain high-cost credit transactions secured by the consumer's home. In the case of a credit sale of goods or services, such as home improvements where the finance charge or the points and fees are so high that HOEPA applies and there is a security interest in the consumer's home, the creditor will be liable for the claims and defenses that the consumer could raise against the home improvement contractor, subject to a cap.[456] HOEPA is significant, because the consumer can affirmatively raise claims against the holder, and because claims and defenses can be raised even if the required notice is not found in the note. For more on HOEPA, refer to § 6.7.3, *infra*, and also in even more detail at NCLC's *Truth in Lending* Ch. 9 (5th ed. 2003 and Supp.).

6.6.5.6 Liability of Credit Cards Issuers and Those Issuing Similar Devices

6.6.5.6.1 Introduction

The FTC Holder Rule explicitly excludes credit card transactions from the rule,[457] deferring instead to the provisions of the federal Truth in Lending Act (TILA) in this area. TILA provides that a credit card issuer is subject to all claims (except tort claims) and defenses of a consumer against a merchant when the consumer uses a credit card as a method of payment or extension of credit, if certain conditions are met.[458] This section summarizes these protections, but greater detail is found in NCLC's *Truth in Lending* § 5.9.5 (5th ed. 2003 and Supp.) and *Consumer Banking and Payments Law* Ch. 3 (2d ed. 2002 and Supp.).

6.6.5.6.2 What is a "credit card?"

For a card issuer to be subject to the consumer's claims and defenses against a merchant, a credit card must have been used to purchase goods or services, but the card need not have been physically presented in the course of the transaction.[459] For example, the consumer can assert claims or defenses even if the credit card was used in a mail, telephone, or Internet order.

In addition, in a surprising number of cases that appear to be closed-end credit, the merchant instead sets up as credit card transactions, such as the sale of satellite dishes or home improvements. If the characterization of the transaction as open-end credit is spurious, then the FTC Holder Rule should apply, although one would predict the FTC Holder Notice will be missing from the notes. If the transaction instead is treated as involving a credit card, then TIL's credit card protections would certainly apply.

The credit card must have been used directly to purchase the goods or services in dispute. If the consumer gets a cash advance from a teller machine located on the seller's premises and uses the cash advance to make the purchase, the transaction is not one in which the card has been used as a method of payment.[460]

A check guarantee card does not operate as a credit card for the purpose of this section. Nor does a debit card when used as a debit card. If the debit card also has credit card features and is used as a credit card, the protections of this section apply.[461]

As forms of payment continue to evolve, an increasing number of open-end transactions bear some similarity to credit cards, but are not standard credit cards. The question then arises as to whether TIL's credit card protections apply to, for example, the use of cell phones as payment devices to make purchases unrelated to the phone.

TIL applies to "a card issuer" who has issued a "credit card" to a "cardholder" pursuant to an "open end consumer credit plan."[462] The open-end consumer credit plan requirement is certainly met in open-end transactions. The question then is whether a transaction meets TIL's definition of a card issuer, a credit card, and a cardholder, even where the transaction does not match common usage as to what is a credit card transaction.

The key question is whether a transaction involves a "credit card" because card issuer is defined as any person who issues a credit card,[463] and cardholder is defined as any person to whom a credit card is issued.[464] Credit card is defined as "any card, plate, coupon book or other credit device existing for the purposes of obtaining money, property, labor, or services on credit."[465] Regulation Z similarly specifies that a credit card is "any card, plate, coupon book,

455 *See* § 6.6.2.2.2, *supra*.

456 *See* § 6.7.3, *infra*.

457 16 C.F.R. § 433.1(c) [*reprinted at* Appx. B.2.1, *infra*].

458 15 U.S.C. § 1666i. *See also In re* Standard Fin. Mgmt. Corp., 94 B.R. 231 (Bankr. D. Mass. 1988); Izraelewitz v. Manufacturers Hanover Trust, 120 Misc. 2d 125, 465 N.Y.S.2d 486 (Civ. Ct. 1983).

459 In an unauthorized use situation, in contrast, the card must have been presented. Federal Reserve Board Official Staff Commentary on Regulation Z § 226.12(c)(1)-1.

460 Federal Reserve Board Official Staff Commentary on Regulation Z § 226.12(c)(1)-1.

461 *Id.*

462 15 U.S.C. § 1666i(a).

463 15 U.S.C. § 1602(n).

464 15 U.S.C. § 1602(m).

465 15 U.S.C. § 1602(k).

or other single credit device that may be used from time to time to obtain credit."[466] The Commentary emphasizes that the credit card must be useable from time to time, and includes as examples an identification card that permits the consumer to defer payment on a purchase.[467]

While there is little case law in this area, it is clear that at least some forms of open-end credit will involve a "credit card" as defined by Truth in Lending, even if the card is not a VISA, Discover, or MasterCard. If so, then the consumer will be able to raise all seller-related claims and defenses against the lender.

6.6.5.6.3 Covered disputes; payment of disputed amount waives consumer rights

One important provision is that payment of a disputed balance waives the right to assert a claim or defense as to the card issuer.[468] In addition, the claims or defenses must have to do with the property or services purchased from the merchant with the credit card. The claims and defenses may include unauthorized use of the card or billing errors even though the Truth in Lending Act also sets out separate protections for both unauthorized use and billing errors.[469] For example, non-delivery can be asserted either as a billing error or as a claim or defense. But a dispute as to the quality of the merchandise can be asserted only as a claim or defense, since it is not within the billing error provisions. Truth in Lending billing error procedures are detailed in another NCLC manual.[470]

6.6.5.6.4 Three additional preconditions to asserting cardholder claims and defenses

There are three TIL conditions which must be met before a consumer who has used a credit card can assert merchant-related claims or defenses against the card issuer. The cardholder must have made a good faith attempt to resolve the matter with the merchant. Whether this has been done is a question of fact. No particular procedures are mandated.[471] The consumer does not have to go beyond the merchant to the manufacturer. If the merchant has filed for bankruptcy, the consumer need not file a claim.[472]

Second, the amount of credit involved in the disputed transaction must be more than $50.[473] Third, the transaction must have occurred in the same state as the cardholder's current address or within 100 miles from that address.[474] The location of a transaction is a matter of state law.[475] For example, a mail or telephone order may be deemed to have occurred at the consumer's home for purposes of state venue or usury provisions,[476] and would be treated as occurring at the consumer's home for TIL purposes as well.[477]

These three preconditions only apply where the card issuer and merchant are separate entities. The cardholder can still raise claims and defenses against the card issuer even if the amount in controversy is less than $50 or where the transaction occurs out of state where the merchant and card issuer are related by ownership.[478]

6.6.5.6.5 Mechanics of raising claims with card issuer

Once the cardholder has met the above three conditions, payment for the disputed transaction may be withheld to the extent of the credit outstanding on that transaction and finance charges attributable thereto.[479] If the consumer had made a partial or minimum payment on the transaction while trying to resolve the dispute, he or she can not withhold or set off the amount already paid against future payments. The consumer can withhold only the amount (with finance charge) remaining unpaid at the time he or she

466 12 C.F.R. § 226.2(a)(15).

467 Official Staff Commentary §§ 226.2(a)(15)-1, 226.2(a)(15)-2(i)(C).

468 15 C.F.R. § 1666i(b). Note that Federal Reserve Board Official Staff Commentary on Regulation Z provides that a consumer who has paid the disputed balance can still assert the dispute as a billing error pursuant to the independent procedures set forth in Regulation Z § 226.13.

469 *See* 15 U.S.C. §§ 1643, 1666.

470 *See* National Consumer Law Center, Truth in Lending § 5.8 (5th ed. 2003 and Supp.).

471 In Montgomery Ward v. Horgan, 448 A.2d 151 (Vt. 1982), the buyer had called and written notes on payment stubs. This was found to be a reasonable effort, even though the creditor claimed it had no record of the complaints.

472 12 C.F.R. § 226.12(c)(3)(i); Official Staff Commentary § 226.12(c)(3)(i)-1.

473 12 C.F.R. § 226.12(c)(3)(ii).

474 *Id. See also In re* Standard Fin. Mgmt. Corp., 94 B.R. 231 (Bankr. D. Mass. 1988); Singer v. Chase Manhattan Bank, 890 P.2d 1305 (Nev. 1995) (court declines to create an exception to the 100 mile limit of § 1666i); Plutchok v. European Am. Bank, 143 Misc. 2d 149, 540 N.Y.S.2d 135 (Dist. Ct. 1989); Izraelewitz v. Manufacturers Hanover Trust, 120 Misc. 2d 125, 465 N.Y.S.2d 486 (Civ. Ct. 1983).

475 Official Staff Commentary § 226.12(c)(3)(ii)-1; *In re* Standard Fin. Mgmt. Corp., 94 B.R. 231 (Bankr. D. Mass. 1988); Plutchok v. European Am. Bank, 143 Misc. 2d 149, 540 N.Y.S.2d 135 (Dist. Ct. 1989); Izraelewitz v. Manufacturers Hanover Trust, 120 Misc. 2d 125, 465 N.Y.S.2d 486 (Civ. Ct. 1983).

476 *See* Conn. Gen. Stat. §§ 36a-770(9) (when retail installment sale deemed made in Connecticut); 42-133c (when open-end credit plan deemed made in Connecticut); 51-345(d) (venue in consumer transactions).

477 *See In re* Standard Fin. Mgmt. Corp., 94 B.R. 231 (Bankr. D. Mass. 1988) (where the transaction involves a sale by telephone, social policy favors finding that the transaction took place in the customer's home). *But see* Plutchok v. European Am. Bank, 143 Misc. 2d 149, 540 N.Y.S.2d 135 (Dist. Ct. 1989) (transaction occurred in Florida where Florida company mailed offer to New York consumer, New York consumer offered to purchase item by telephone, and company accepted offer in Florida). *See* National Consumer Law Center, Truth in Lending § 5.9.5.3 (5th ed. 2003 and Supp.).

478 12 C.F.R. § 226.12 n.26.

479 *Id.* § 226.12(c)(1).

notifies the card issuer of his or her assertion of claims or defenses.[480]

If only part of a single extension of credit is in dispute (e.g., multiple purchases at the same time), payments shall be prorated according to prices and applicable taxes. For example, if the disputed transaction represents 60% of the credit, payments are to be attributed 60% to that transaction and 40% to the balance of the credit extended at the same time.[481]

The separate requirement of the Fair Credit Billing Act (FCBA) that the card holder notify the card issuer of billing errors within sixty days of the consumer's receipt of the relevant credit statement[482] is inapplicable to the consumer's right to raise claims and defenses against the card issuer.[483] The consumer is not complaining of a billing error, but is raising claims and defenses against the merchant.[484] The FCBA's requirement of notice within 60 days applies only to FCBA claims.

Nevertheless, there are two reasons why it is good practice to comply with the FCBA requirement in any event. One is that consumers should simultaneously assert an FCBA dispute as an alternative means of refusing to pay the credit card charge, since the FCBA provides for statutory damages and various other protections.[485] The other reason is to avoid wrong-headed decisions such as that made by the New York court.

6.6.5.6.6 Challenging credit card charges under the Fair Credit Billing Act

The provision of the Truth in Lending Act discussed in the previous sections, which makes the credit card issuer subject to claims and defenses that the consumer could assert against the merchant, is more sweeping than the Fair Credit Billing Act in that the TILA provision covers all types of claims and defenses that relate to the property or services purchased.[486] It also has the virtue of being self-enforcing: the consumer can simply withhold the money. But the consumer may not be able to use the TILA provision because the consumer paid the credit card bill before discovering the problem; the charge is less than $50; the transaction occurred in another state and more than 100 miles from the consumer's address; or the consumer's effort to resolve the dispute with the merchant is deemed insufficient. The Fair Credit Billing Act (FCBA)[487] is not limited by these restrictions.

The FCBA covers: extensions of credit that were not made, or not made in the amount reflected; unauthorized use; extensions of credit for property or services that were not delivered as agreed or that the consumer did not accept; and a variety of billing issues such as failure to credit payments.[488] To assert FCBA rights, the consumer must send written notice of the error, which must be received by the creditor no later than sixty days after the creditor first transmitted the first periodic statement that reflected the billing error.[489] The creditor than has the duty to acknowledge the billing error notice,[490] investigate the dispute,[491] and notify the consumer of the resolution.[492] Statutory damages of double the finance charge, plus attorney fees, are available.[493]

6.6.5.6.7 Other theories of card issuer liability

State statutory law or common law concepts may provide additional rights for consumers against card issuers. Credit card charge slips are not negotiable instruments.[494] As a result, Article 3's holder-in-due-course provisions do not apply to credit card charge slips. Instead, they are "accounts" whose assignment is governed by UCC Article 9.[495] The general rule under Article 9 is that an assignee is subject to all defenses that the debtor can assert against the assignor.[496] There is an exception as to certain defenses if the debtor has signed a waiver-of-defense clause and the assignee has taken the assignment for value, in good faith, and without notice.[497] Only if TILA's protections do not apply *and* the credit card issuer meets Article 9's waiver-of-defense requirements will the issuer be able to avoid the defenses that the consumer could assert against the seller.

---

480 *Id.* n.25; *see also* 15 U.S.C. § 1666i(b); *In re* Standard Fin. Mgmt. Corp., 94 B.R. 231 (Bankr. D. Mass. 1988) (credit card holder can not recover amounts already paid).

481 12 C.F.R. § 226.12, n.26

482 15 U.S.C. § 1666.

483 Citibank v. Mincks, 135 S.W.3d 545 (Mo. App. 2004). *Cf.* Lincoln First Bank, N.A. v. Carlson, 103 Misc. 2d 467, 426 N.Y.S.2d 433 (Sup. Ct. 1980) (treating billing error and right to raise defenses against card issuer as independent; consumer who enters into transaction more than 100 miles from home does not thereby lose right to raise billing error claims). *But see* Plutchok v. European Am. Bank, 143 Misc. 2d 149, 540 N.Y.S.2d 135 (Dist. Ct. 1989)

484 Federal Reserve Board Official Staff Commentary on Regulation Z § 226.12(c)-1 (billing error procedures operate independently).

485 *See* § 6.6.5.6.6, *infra*.

486 15 U.S.C. § 1666i; 12 C.F.R. § 226.12(c)(1).

487 15 U.S.C. § 1666.

488 12 C.F.R. § 226.13(a).

489 15 U.S.C. § 1666(a).

490 12 C.F.R. § 226.13(c)(1).

491 12 C.F.R. § 226.13(f).

492 12 C.F.R. § 226.13(e), (f), (g).

493 15 U.S.C. § 1640(a)(1). *See* National Consumer Law Center, Truth in Lending § 5.12 (5th ed. 2003 and Supp.).

494 First Nat'l Bank v. Fulk, 57 Ohio App. 3d 44, 566 N.E.2d 1270 (1989).

495 U.C.C. § 9-102(a)(2)(vii).

496 U.C.C. § 9-404(a).

497 U.C.C. § 9-403(b). *See* § 6.6.4.3, *supra*. Note that many states prohibit waiver-of-defense clauses for at least some types of credit transactions. *See* § 6.6.5.6.5, *supra* (listing state laws).

In addition, certain state statutes deal with a credit card issuer's liability for seller-related claims.[498] These statutes generally track the federal Truth in Lending Act on the subject, but in some cases allow consumer claims when not available under the federal law.[499]

6.6.5.7 Liability of Lessor for Consumer's Claims Against Dealer and Manufacturer

6.6.5.7.1 Raising dealer-related claims against the lessor

There is much confusion over the ability of a consumer to raise against the lessor claims the consumer has against the dealer or manufacturer. There is little precedent to argue that the FTC Holder Rule applies to leases, and lease agreements routinely fail to include that notice.[500]

Nevertheless, the typical lease is originated by the dealer. Even though the lease document may have the name of a auto finance company in big letters at the top, the lessor signing the lease typically will be the dealer, who then immediately assigns the lease to the auto finance company or other lender.

Thus, the dealer is the original lessor, and the finance company is an assignee lessor. In this situation, under standard assignment law, the consumer can raise as a defense against the assignee all claims and defenses the consumer could raise against the dealer.[501]

A lease is not a negotiable instrument, so the assignee can not claim holder-in-due-course status. The lease does not meet the UCC's definition of a negotiable instrument because it is not an unconditional promise to pay a fixed amount of money.[502] Most leases, for example, allow early termination if the liability is less than the original total of payments—and the total liability will include charges for excess mileage or wear and tear, which are not a fixed amount of money. Nor is a lease payable to bearer or to order.[503] Moreover, the typical consumer lease includes undertakings by both parties that would also take the lease out of the UCC's definition of negotiable instrument.[504]

While the consumer can thus raise dealer-related defenses against the assignee lessor, in most states, the common law doctrine that the assignee steps in the shoes of the assignor does not allow the consumer to raise affirmative claims against the lessor related to the dealer's conduct.[505] Nevertheless, some state statutes do allow consumers to raise such affirmative claims against the assignee lessor.[506]

Less common is for a finance company to be the originating lessor, with a dealer referring the consumer to that lessor. In that case, the lessor is not the dealer's assignee, the lessor does not step into the dealer's shoes, and it is not clear how the consumer can raise dealer-related defenses against such a lessor.

One answer in some states is that state law allows the consumer to raise dealer-related claims against such a lessor. For example, Connecticut's new leasing statute, patterned after the Uniform Consumer Leasing Act, provides that consumers can raise against holders the claims they could assert against the dealer even where the dealer was not the originating lessor.[507] Illinois has a state holder rule that applies explicitly to leases, but only applies where the violation was apparent on the face of the lease.[508]

Another answer is to examine whether the lessor aided and abetted the dealer in the dealer's misconduct. Such a lessor may assist the dealer with training, manuals, videos, and other aids that explicitly assist the dealer to deceive the consumer or engage in unfair practices.

6.6.5.7.2 Raising manufacturer-related claims against the lessor

A remaining question is whether the consumer can raise against the assignee-lessor the consumer's warranty claim against the manufacturer. The analysis of this issue is very similar to that in a credit-sale situation: can the consumer raise against the holder a motor vehicle installment sales agreement defenses that the consumer could raise against the manufacturer. Certainly, to the extent the dealer has adopted or is otherwise liable under the manufacturer's warranty, the consumer can raise that claim against the dealer's assignee.[509] In addition, some courts have been

498 *See, e.g.*, Cal. Civ. Code § 1747.90; Iowa Code Ann. § 537.3403; Kan. Stat. Ann. § 16a-3-403; Me. Rev. Stat. Ann. tit. 9A, §§ 3-403, 3-404; Mass. Gen. Laws Ann. ch. 255, § 12F; Vt. Stat. Ann. tit. 8, § 14303; Wis. Stat. Ann. Laws § 422.408.

499 *See, e.g.*, Mass. Gen. Laws Ann. ch. 255, § 12F; Vt. Stat. Ann. tit. 8, § 14303.

500 *See* § 6.6.2.2.2, *supra*.

501 *See* note 511, *infra*.

502 U.C.C. § 3-104(a).

503 U.C.C. § 3-104(a)(1).

504 U.C.C. § 3-104(a)(3).

505 *See* Bescos v. Bank of America, 129 Cal. Rptr. 2d 423 (Ct. App. 2003).

506 *See* 42 Conn. Gen. Stat. § 411(b) (effective July 1, 2003); 815 Ill. Comp. Stat. § 636/70 (notice must be included in consumer leases that holder subject to lessor-related claims apparent on face of the lease, with recovery not to exceed amounts paid by the lessee); Mich. Comp. Laws §§ 492.102, 492.114a (applies to motor vehicle leases, and allows consumer to recover up to the amount paid to a particular holder); N.Y. Pers. Property Law § 347 (claims for violation of the leasing statute apparent on the face of the lease can be brought against assignee). *See also* Jarvis v. South Oak Dodge, Inc., 773 N.E.2d 641 (Ill. 2002) (Illinois statute creates derivative liability for holder only where violation apparent on the face of the lease).

507 42 Conn. Gen. Stat. § 411(b) (effective July 1, 2003). *See also* Mo. Rev. Stat. § 408.405 (consumer can raise against holder all defenses arising out of a lease); § 6.6.3.11, *supra*.

508 815 Ill. Comp. Stat. § 636/70; *see also* Jarvis v. South Oak Dodge, Inc., 773 N.E.2d 641 (Ill. 2002).

509 Freeman v. Hubco Leasing, Inc., 324 S.E.2d 462 (Ga. 1985);

persuaded that the close connectedness of a manufacturer, its franchisee dealer, and its financing subsidiary is sufficient to allow the lessee to raise the manufacturer's breach as a defense against the finance arm of the same corporation.[510]

6.7 Raising Lender-Related Defenses Against the Lender's Assignee

6.7.1 General

The FTC Holder notice allows consumers to raise *seller-related* claims only, not claims concerning a direct lender's loan practices. For example, a finance company or other originating lender may engage in various unfair or deceptive loan practices, and then assign the note to a third party. The Holder Notice typically will not appear in the loan documents, so the consumer must find other theories in order to raise claims or defenses relating to the originating lender against that lender's assignee.

The common law rule is that an assignee is subject to all defenses that the consumer could raise against the assignor.[511] But Uniform Commercial Code (UCC) § 3-305 generally allows the assignee of a promissory note or other negotiable instrument to be free from those defenses if it has attained the status of a holder in due course. There are technical requirements as to when an assignee becomes a holder in due course, as set out in UCC § 3-302. So an important initial issue is whether an assignee has met those requirements.[512] Even if those requirements are met, consumers can still raise certain defenses against holders in due course.[513]

Another approach can be based on the federal Home Ownership and Equity Protection Act (HOEPA), which makes certain assignees of high-rate mortgages liable for all claims and defenses that the consumer could raise against the originating lender, up to a cap.[514]

In addition to the theories discussed in this section, advocates should explore whether the assignee's own conduct makes it liable on a theory such as civil conspiracy, as discussed in § 6.5, *infra*. Alternatively, a state consumer statute or the close-connectedness doctrine, discussed in §§ 6.6.5.6.4 and 6.6.5.6.5, *supra*, may provide grounds for finding assignees liable even if they would not be so under the UCC or HOEPA.[515]

Whether the holder of a note has holder-in-due-course status, and what insulation from defenses this status offers, is analyzed in § 6.7.2, *infra*. Liability under HOEPA is discussed in § 6.7.3, *infra*. Section 6.7.4 looks at a special, but increasingly important case where the notes are securitized. Section 6.7.5 discusses special issues when the note at some point in time was taken over by the FDIC or RTC.

6.7.2 Does Holder-In-Due-Course Status Exist and What Defenses Does It Bar?

6.7.2.1 Introduction

An assignee only attains holder-in-due-course status (and thus avoids defenses the consumer could raise against the assignor) if it is (1) assigned a negotiable instrument and (2) meets the holder-in-due-course requirements of Article 3 of the UCC.[516] Section 6.7.2.2, *infra*, deals with the question whether an instrument is a negotiable instrument. If it is not, then Article 3 does not govern it, and Article 3's holder-in-due-course rules are irrelevant. Section 6.7.2.3, *infra*, deals with the question whether a person to whom a negotiable instrument has been assigned is a holder in due course of that instrument.

In analyzing whether these requirements have been met, it is important to distinguish between the pre-1990 version and the current version of Article 3. Article 3 was revised in 1990, and the revised version has since been adopted by every state except New York and South Carolina.[517] However, instruments executed before the effective date of the adoption should be governed by the old version.[518] The effective date is the date that Article 3 revisions became effective in a particular state (as late as 2001 in some states), not the date that the UCC drafts issued the 1990 revisions.

Mercedes-Benz Credit Corp. v. Lotito, 306 N.J. Super. 25, 703 A.2d 288 (Super. Ct. App. Div. 1997).

510 Mercedes-Benz Credit Corp. v. Lotito, 306 N.J. Super. 25, 703 A.2d 288 (App. Div. 1997).

511 9 Corbin, Corbin on Contracts §§ 892 (interim ed. 2002); 29 Lord, Williston on Contracts §§ 74.47, 74.49 (4th ed. 2003); Farnsworth, Farnsworth on Contracts § 11.8 (2d ed 1998); Restatement (Second) of Contracts § 336 (1981).

512 *See* § 6.7.2, *infra*.

513 *See* § 6.7.2.5, *infra*.

514 15 U.S.C. § 1641(d)(1).

515 *See* § 6.7.4, *infra*.

516 As revised, U.C.C. § 3-305 also says that the right to enforce an instrument is subject to "a claim in recoupment" against the original payee, so long as the claim arose from the transaction that gave rise to the claim. U.C.C. § 3-305(a)(3). This might appear at first glance to reduce the scope of the holder-in-due-course doctrine, but a later section provides that a holder in due course is only subject to claims in recoupment that arise against it, not those that are based on the actions of the assignee. Official Comments 2, 3, U.C.C. § 3-305.

517 Rhode Island was the most recent enactment, in 2001.

518 *See, e.g.*, Universal Premium Acceptance Corp. v. York Bank & Trust Co., 69 F.3d 695, 699 n.1 (3d Cir. 1995) (Pennsylvania law); *In re* Ostrom-Martin, Inc., 192 B.R. 937 (Bankr. C.D. Ill. 1996); Barnsley v. Empire Mortgage Ltd. P'ship V, 142 N.H. 721, 720 A.2d 63 (1998); Trump Plaza Assocs. v. Haas, 300 N.J. Super. 113, 692 A.2d 86 (App. Div. 1997); Barclays Bank PLC v. Johnson, 499 S.E.2d 768 (N.C. Ct. App. 1998); Southwestern Resolution Corp. v. Watson, 964 S.W.2d 262 (Tex. 1997).

There is now also a 2002 version of Article 3. While it makes other important changes to Article 3, it does not affect the criteria for holder-in-due-course status discussed in this section. As of mid-2004 it had only been adopted by Minnesota. Unless otherwise indicated, this section's references to UCC Article 3 are to the post-1990, pre-2002 version that is in effect in every state except South Carolina, New York, and Minnesota.

6.7.2.2 Is There a Negotiable Instrument?

6.7.2.2.1 Overview of requirements for negotiable instruments

Before an assignee can be a holder in due course, the note must be a negotiable instrument. UCC § 3-104(a) sets out seven basic requirements for a note to be a negotiable instrument. The note must:

1. Be a writing that is signed.[519]
2. Contain an unconditional promise to pay.[520]
3. Be a fixed amount.[521]
4. Of money.[522]
5. Payable to bearer or to order.[523]
6. Payable on demand or at a definite time.[524]
7. Contain no other undertaking except as authorized by section 3-104(a)(3). (This last requirement has been called a requirement that the instrument be a "courier without baggage.")[525]

If any one of these seven requirements is not met, the instrument is not a negotiable instrument. If an instrument is not a negotiable instrument, there can not be a holder in due course of that instrument, since holder-in-due-course protection is a creature of UCC Article 3. Therefore, one way to defeat holder-in-due-course status is to demonstrate to the court that the instrument assigned was not a negotiable instrument. The following are the most common ways that an instrument's negotiability is defeated.

6.7.2.2.2 The fixed amount requirement

UCC § 3-104(a) requires the note to contain a promise to pay a fixed amount of money. Under the pre-1990 version of Article 3 many courts held that a variable-rate loan was not a promise to pay a fixed amount of money.[526] This rationale for attacking a note is still important for any note made prior to the effective date of the Article 3 changes in the relevant state.

However, under the revised Code[527] the fixed amount requirement relates only to principal. Therefore, a note can have a variable interest rate and still be negotiable, as long as the note was made after the effective date of the Article 3 amendments in the particular state. Similarly, a note can refer to an outside source for its interest rate (for example the Treasury rate) and still be negotiable.[528] Additionally, both the pre-revision and post-revision versions of the Code allow an instrument to state that it bears interest without stating an interest rate, and still retain its status as a negotiable instrument.[529] While New York still has the 1990 version of Article 3, it has adopted an amendment that allows a negotiable instrument to carry a variable rate of interest as long as it is readily ascertainable by a reference in the instrument to a published statute, regulation, rule of court, generally accepted commercial or financial index, compendium of interest rates, or announced rate of a named financial institution.[530]

The fixed amount requirement means that open-end loans can not be negotiable instruments. The amount of the loan is not known at the time it is made and can change over time. For an open-end loan to meet the UCC's requirements, each extension of credit must include a separate note for a fixed amount that otherwise meets all the UCC's requirements for a negotiable instrument and a holder in due course. Similarly, a home improvement loan is not a negotiable instrument if the amount of the loan is left uncertain, depending on charges assessed by the contractor.

A promissory note that offers the consumer a discount if some future event occurs can not be a negotiable instrument

519 U.C.C. §§ 3-104(a), 3-103(a)(6), (9).

520 U.C.C. §§ 3-104(a), 3-106.

521 U.C.C. §§ 3-104(a), 3-112.

522 U.C.C. §§ 3-104(a), 3-107.

523 U.C.C. §§ 3-104(a)(1), 3-109, 3-110.

524 U.C.C. §§ 3-104(a)(2), 3-108.

525 Overton v. Tyler, 3 Pa. 346, 342 (1846) (in reference to precursor of the U.C.C.'s Holder-in-Due-Course rule). *See also* Crandall, Herbert & Lawrence, Uniform Commercial Code § 14.5, *Courier Without Luggage* (1996).

526 Resolution Trust Corp. v. Maplewood Investments, 31 F.3d 1276 (4th Cir. 1994) (variable-rate note is a nonnegotiable instrument); Desmond v. FDIC, 798 F. Supp. 829 (D. Mass. 1992); *In re* Miraj & Sons, Inc., 192 B.R. 297 (Bankr. D. Mass. 1996) (variable-rate notes are nonnegotiable instruments); Morris v. Bank of Chicago, 79 B.R. 777 (Bankr. N.D. Ill. 1987); Johnson v. Johnson, 244 Ill. App. 3d 518, 614 N.E.2d 348 (1993); Army Nat'l Bank v. Equity Developers, Inc., 245 Kan. 3, 774 P.2d 919 (1989); Centerre Bank of Branson v. Campbell, 744 S.W.2d 490 (Mo. Ct. App. 1988); Taylor v. Roeder, 360 S.E.2d 191 (Va. 1987). *But see* Ackerman v. FDIC, 973 F.2d 1221 (5th Cir. 1992); Doyle v. Trinity Savings & Loan Ass'n, 940 F.2d 592 (10th Cir. 1991); Tanenbaum v. Agri-Capital, Inc., 885 F.2d 464 (8th Cir. 1989); FDIC v. Hershiser Signature Properties, 777 F. Supp. 539 (E.D. Mich. 1991); First City Federal Sav. Bank v. Bhogaonker, 715 F. Supp. 1216 (S.D.N.Y. 1989); Carnegie Bank v. Shalleck, 256 N.J. Super. 23, 606 A.2d 389 (App. Div. 1993); Goss v. Trinity Savings & Loan Ass'n, 813 P.2d 492 (Okla. 1991); Amberboy v. Societe de Banque Privee, 831 S.W.2d 793 (Tex. 1992).

527 U.C.C. § 3-112; Official Comment 1 to U.C.C. § 3-112.

528 U.C.C. § 3-112(b).

529 U.C.C. § 3-112(b).

530 N.Y. U.C.C. Law § 3-106.

either. A common example is if the consumer refers others to the lender.

Automobile leases typically are not negotiable instruments either. Leases usually provide the lessee with the opportunity to terminate early or exercise a purchase option, both of which change the amount owed. Furthermore, additional amounts may be assessed at scheduled termination for excess mileage or unusual wear and tear.

6.7.2.2.3 *Payable on demand or at a definite time*

To be negotiable, an instrument must be payable either on demand or at a definite time.[531] A demand instrument is created by words such as due on demand, due at sight, or by saying nothing about when an instrument is due. A time instrument is one that is due on a specified date or on a date that is readily ascertainable at the time the instrument is issued.[532]

The most common mistake defeating negotiability occurs when the drafter of an instrument tries to create a time instrument, but the due date is not readily ascertainable. In this case, the instrument is neither a time nor a demand instrument and negotiability is defeated. A note that contains an estimated payment schedule, with the lender later notifying the consumer of the first payment due date, does not meet this requirement.[533] A note where the payment schedule will be determined later based on when construction or other work is completed is not a negotiable instrument. Nor can a payment schedule be contingent on when a vehicle or other product is delivered to the consumer.

6.7.2.2.4 *Payable to bearer or to order*

Another important requirement is that the note be payable either to bearer or to order.[534] If a non-bearer note lacks the words "to the order of," it is not a negotiable instrument.[535] The most common mistake defeating negotiability occurs when the drafter of the instrument is attempting to create order paper but forgets the "to the order of" language. So, for example, if a promissory note said "payable to First National Bank," this would not be payable to *order*. However, if it said "payable to the order of First National Bank" it would be payable to order.[536]

6.7.2.2.5 *Unconditional promise to pay and no other undertaking*

These two distinct but related concepts were treated the same under the pre-revision Code. They are similar in the sense that they require a "naked promise to pay." But the revised Code treats these requirements as two distinct concepts.

In order to have an unconditional promise to pay, the note itself must not contain an express condition.[537] Additionally, the note itself can not be subject to or governed by another document or obligation. However, the fact that the note simply refers to another writing does not in itself make the promise or order conditional—it must be subject to or governed by that other document.[538] Magic words of "incorporation" that defeat negotiability include "subject to" or "governed by."[539] Additionally, the words "rights of the parties are stated in another agreement" are deemed an incorporation of another writing, and thereby defeat negotiability.[540] By contrast, under the pre-revision UCC, the words "in accordance with" and "as per" were deemed to be words of reference that did not defeat negotiability.[541] These words probably do not defeat negotiability under the revised version of section 3-106.[542]

Finally, a promise to pay which has an additional undertaking besides the promise to pay defeats negotiability and therefore eliminates the possibility of a holder in due course.[543] For example, if the maker of a promissory note

531 U.C.C. §§ 3-104(a); U.C.C. § 3-108. Note that the 1990 revision of Article 3 broadened the previous definition of "definite time" to include a time readily ascertainable at the time the promise or order is issued. *See* Official Comment to U.C.C. § 3-108. A due date that runs from a future event would still not meet this standard unless the date of the future event was known at the time the note was signed.

532 U.C.C. § 3-108(b).

533 *In re* Boardwalk Marketplace Securities Litigation, 668 F. Supp. 115 (D. Conn. 1987). *But cf. In re* AppOnline.com, Inc., 290 B.R. 1 (Bankr. E.D.N.Y. 2003) (acceleration language does not impair negotiability).

534 U.C.C. §§ 3-104, 3-109.

535 *See* Universal Premium Acceptance Corp. v. York Bank & Trust Co., 69 F.3d 695 (3d Cir. 1995) (drafts that stated "pay and deposit only to credit of" were not negotiable); Stone v. Mehlberg, 728 F. Supp. 1341 (W.D. Mich. 1989); Tompkins Printing Equipment Co. v. Almik, Inc., 725 F. Supp. 918 (E.D. Mich. 1989); Hall v. Westmoreland, Hall & Bryan, 123 Ga. App. 809, 182 S.E.2d 539 (1971). *Cf.* Lakhaney v. Anzelone, 788 F. Supp. 160 (S.D.N.Y. 1992) (note was negotiable where it was payable to "[plaintiff] or order"); Cooperatieve Centrale Raiffeisen-Boerenleenbank B.A. v. Bailey, 710 F. Supp. 737 (C.D. Cal. 1989) (note was negotiable where it obliged the maker to "pay to the order to payee;" the phrase could be construed only to mean "pay to the order of" payee).

536 This rule does not apply to checks, which under U.C.C. §§ 3-104(c) and 3-104(f) are negotiable even if they do not have order language.

537 U.C.C. § 3-106(a)(i). *See* American Plan Corp. v. Woods, 16 Ohio App. 2d 1, 240 N.E.2d 886 (1968) (instrument not negotiable where it made amount payable dependent on whether debtor referred other borrowers to lender).

538 U.C.C. § 3-106(a)(ii), (iii).

539 U.C.C. § 3-106(a)(ii).

540 U.C.C. § 3-106(a)(iii).

541 Pre-revision § 3-105(1)(b).

542 Official Comment 1 to U.C.C. § 3-106.

543 U.C.C. § 3-104(a)(3). *See* Reid v. Pyle, 51 P.3d 1064 (Colo. App. 2002) (language conditioning obligation upon transfer of property made note non-negotiable); Geiger Fin. Co. v. Graham, 123 Ga. App. 771, 182 S.E.2d 521 (1971); Chrysler Credit Corp.

promised in the note to pay and to do a commercial for the lender, this additional promise would defeat the negotiability of the note.

The only exceptions to this rule are contained in section 3-104(a)(3). An instrument in which a person promising to pay also agrees to give, maintain or protect collateral to secure payment, authorizes the holder to confess judgment or realize on or dispose of collateral, or waives the benefit of any law intended for the advantage or protection of the obligor, does not defeat negotiability.[544] However, any other undertaking does defeat negotiability.

Installment sales contracts do not meet these requirements.[545] The seller's performance will be part of the contract, for example, the delivery of the car or the performance of the home improvements. This baggage is sufficient in and of itself to prevent the contract from being a negotiable instrument. The drafters of Revised Article 3 stated:

> Article 3 is not meant to apply to contracts for the sale of goods or services or to the sale or lease of real property or similar writings that may contain a promise to pay money. The use of words of negotiability in such contracts would be an aberration.[546]
>
> Under the pre-1990 version of Article 3, an important example of excess baggage was the Holder Notice itself. Where a related creditor inserts the Holder language in a note, and then assigns the note to another creditor, the consumer can raise seller-related defenses against the assignee. Under the pre-1990 version of the UCC, this was enough to prevent the note from becoming a negotiable instrument, so the assignee could not qualify as a holder in due course under UCC § 3-302. As revised, Article 3 now provides that an instrument that contains the Holder Notice is still a negotiable instrument governed by Article 3, but since revised Article 3 still affirms that "there can not be a holder in due course of [such an] instrument," the end result appears unchanged.[547]

6.7.2.2.6 *Electronic negotiable instruments*

The Electronic Signatures in Global and National Commerce Act (E-Sign) validates electronic negotiable instruments that relate to loans secured by real property.[548] E-Sign refers to these as "transferable records." The issuer of the instrument must expressly agree that it is a transferable record.[549] If the transferable record meets various E-Sign requirements designed to ensure that multiple copies of the instrument are not created, then the holder can acquire holder-in-due-course status by meeting Article 3's requirements.[550] Delivery, possession, and indorsement are not required, however.[551]

6.7.2.3 Is the Holder of the Instrument a Holder in Due Course?

6.7.2.3.1 *General*

If an instrument meets Article 3's definition of a negotiable instrument, then it is governed by Article 3. The entity to which a negotiable instrument is transferred is not automatically a holder in due course, however. To qualify as a holder in due course under Article 3, the transferee must meet four requirements: It must be:

(1) A holder;
(2) For value;
(3) In good faith; and
(4) Without notice of a host of things delineated in the UCC § 3-302(a)(2).

These requirements are discussed below.

Even a holder who meets all of these requirements is not a holder in due course if it acquired the instrument in certain non-ordinary ways from someone who was not a holder in due course: by legal process; by purchase in an execution, bankruptcy, or creditors sale or similar proceeding; by purchase as part of a bulk transaction not in the transferor's ordinary course of business; or as the successor in interest to an estate or other organization.[552]

---

v. Friendly Ford, Inc., 535 S.W.2d 110 (Mo. Ct. App. 1976); P & K Marble, Inc. v. La Paglia, 537 N.Y.S.2d 682 (App. Div. 1989) (mortgage note not a negotiable instrument under pre-1990 version of Article 3 where it included numerous promises such as to keep the property insured); Ford v. Darwin, 767 S.W.2d 851 (Tex. App. 1989) (promissory note which also contained a promise to sell stock was not a negotiable instrument). *But see* Jenkins v. Karlton, 329 Md. 510, 620 A.2d 894 (1993) (negotiability of note was not destroyed by promise by endorser to pay collection fees, including attorney fees).

544 Wilson v. Toussie, 260 F. Supp. 2d 530, 542 (E.D.N.Y. 2003) (referring to a mortgage does not make a note non-negotiable); *In re* AppOnline.com, Inc., 290 B.R. 1 (Bankr. E.D.N.Y. 2003) (reference to separate mortgage agreement and inclusion of acceleration language do not impair negotiability under NY's 1990 version of Art. 3); Slutsky v. Blooming Grove Inn, Inc., 147 A.D.2d 208, 542 N.Y.S.2d 721, 723 (1989) (same). *But see In re* U.S. v. Bowman Poultry Farms, Inc., 1994 WL 577524, at *7 n.1 (W.D.N.Y. Sept. 30, 1992) (mortgage note is not negotiable); P & K Marble v. La Paglia, 147 A.D.2d 804, 537 N.Y.S.2d 682 (1989) (mortgage note is generally not negotiable).

545 Condor Capital Corp. v. Michaud, 2000 Conn. Super. LEXIS 1894 (July 25, 2000).

546 Official Comment 2 to U.C.C. § 3-104.

547 U.C.C. § 3-106(d).

548 15 U.S.C. § 7021.

549 15 U.S.C. § 7021(a)(1)(B).

550 15 U.S.C. § 7021(b), (c), (d).

551 15 U.S.C. § 7021(d).

552 U.C.C. § 3-302(c).

6.7.2.3.2 The holder requirement; indorsements and allonges

The first requirement to be a holder in due course is that the party be a holder of the instrument. This means essentially that it must have good title to the instrument. If an indorsement is forged, no one with possession of the instrument after the forgery has good title to the instrument. They are not holders, and therefore can not become holders in due course.

To become a holder, an assignee must have the instrument "negotiated" to it. Bearer paper can be negotiated simply by delivery of the instrument.[553] Today, bearer paper is often held by a custodian, who is an agent for the holder. When the bearer paper is "transferred" to a new party, physically all that may happen is that the custodian of the note acknowledges that it is now the agent of the new party in holding the note. Whether this is sufficient will depend on the facts of a case.

To negotiate order paper (instruments made payable to the order of an identified person),[554] the assignor has to indorse the instrument and give delivery of the instrument.[555] If the instrument is not negotiated properly, then the party seeking to enforce the instrument is not in fact a holder of the instrument. A holder must also have physical possession of the instrument.[556]

The most common mistake in this regard is for a transferor to forget to indorse the instrument, or for the wrong party to indorse the instrument. For example, if a note is made payable to a lender, and is then put into a securitization trust without indorsement by the lender, the securitization trust does not have "good title" to the instrument.[557] If the trust sued to enforce the note, the trust would not be a holder of the instrument and thus could not be a holder in due course. While the trust might be able to go back and obtain the missing indorsement, if by that time the trust had notice of the consumer's claims and defenses against the lender, its holder-in-due-course status would be defeated. The consumer's attorney should always require the holder to produce the original instrument itself, so that the existence of an indorsement can be verified.

Another error that can prevent an assignee from being a holder relates to the location of the indorsement on the instrument. A holder of a negotiable instrument payable to order must obtain that instrument via an indorsement either written on the instrument itself or on a paper affixed to the instrument.[558] Such a separate paper for an indorsement is called an allonge.[559]

Article 3 requires that, if an allonge is used, it must be "affixed" to the instrument.[560] Folding a promissory note around the purported indorsements lacks any physical attachment to the notes, so the assignee is not a holder and can not attain holder-in-due-course status.[561] The use of a separate assignment agreement, rather than the prescribed indorsement, likewise prevents the assignee from being a holder.[562] Allonges governed by the pre-1990 version of Article 3 must meet even stricter requirements: they must be so firmly attached to the instrument as to become a part of it,[563] and many cases held that an allonge could only be used

553 U.C.C. § 3-201(b).

554 U.C.C. § 3-109(b).

555 U.C.C. §§ 3-201(b), 3-204.

556 Provident Bank v. MorEquity, Inc., 585 S.E.2d 625 (Ga. App. 2003).

557 See Kurt Egger, Held Up In Due Course: Predatory Lending, Securitization, and the Holder In Due Course Doctrine, 35 Creighton L. Rev. 503, 566–570 (2002).

558 U.C.C. §§ 3-201(b) and 3-204(a). Note that if it is bearer paper, only delivery of the instrument is necessary.

559 *See* U.C.C. § 3-204 Comment 1.

560 U.C.C. § 3-204(a).

561 Adams v. Madison Realty & Development, Inc., 853 F.2d 163 (3d Cir. 1988) (decided under pre-1990 version of Art. 3, but interprets language that the 1990 version did not change).

562 Becker v. National Bank & Trust Co., 284 S.E.2d 793 (Va. 1981) (decided under pre-1990 version of Art. 3, but interprets language that the 1990 version did not change). Other decisions under the comparable language of the pre-1990 version include: *In re* Governor's Island, 39 B.R. 417 (Bankr. E.D.N.C. 1984) (where there is separate assignment and no indorsement on note, assignee is not holder in due course); Wear v. Farmers & Merchants Bank, 605 P.2d 27 (Alaska 1980) (Texas law; separate assignment not sufficient where actual note was not attached to the assignment agreement); Security Pacific Nat'l Bank v. Chess, 58 Cal. App. 3d 555, 129 Cal. Rptr. 852 (1976) (separate assignment agreement did not serve as an indorsement; thus, assignee did not become holder in due course); Billas v. Dwyer, 140 Ga. App. 774, 232 S.E.2d 102 (1976) (where purported transfer and assignment of note had never been attached to the note, it did not serve as an effective indorsement); Dyck-O'Neal, Inc. v. Pungitore, 52 U.C.C. Rep. Serv. 2d 717 (Mass. App. 2003) (unpublished) (plaintiff not a holder where assignment not affixed to note, but still obtained transferor's rights); Duxbury v. Roberts, 388 Mass. 385, 446 N.E.2d 401 (Mass. 1983); Bremen Bank & Trust Co. v. Muskopf, 817 S.W.2d 602 (Mo. Ct. App. 1991) (instrument was not effectively negotiated where separate assignment agreement was not attached to the note).

563 *See* pre-revision § 3-202(2). Decisions finding allonges defective under the pre-1990 version of Art. 3 include: Tallahassee Bank & Trust Co. v. Raines, 125 Ga. App. 263, 187 S.E.2d 320 (1972) (a separate paper pinned or clipped to an instrument is an insufficient indorsement); Illinois State Bank v. Yates, 678 S.W.2d 819 (Mo. Ct. App. 1984) (assignment stapled to note did not constitute negotiation of note); Estrada v. River Oaks Bank & Trust Co., 550 S.W.2d 719 (Tex. App. 1977) (one indorsement stapled to four notes not sufficient); Crossland Savings Bank v. Constant, 737 S.W.2d 19, 4 U.C.C. Rep. 2d 1479 (Tex. App. 1987) (stapling separate piece of paper to back of two long sets of loan documents insufficient where there was room on note for indorsement). *But see In re* Nash, 49 B.R. 254 (Bankr. D. Ariz. 1985), *aff'd on other grounds*, 60 B.R. 27 (B.A.P. 9th Cir. 1986) (physical separation of note and assignment within company's file did not prevent assignee from becoming a holder in due course given the parties' clear intent that the note and the assignment were to be physically attached); Lamson v. Com-

if there was no room on the instrument itself for an indorsement.[564] These stricter requirements still apply to notes made prior to the effective date of the Article 3 revisions in the relevant state.

6.7.2.3.3 Value

The second requirement for a holder in due course is that the holder must have given value for the instrument.[565] Value is defined in UCC § 3-303 and is different from the concept of consideration under contract law. A Hawaii court held that whether assignment of mortgage note for $1.00 was for value was a question of fact that precluded summary judgment for the assignee.[566]

6.7.2.3.4 Good faith

The third requirement is that a holder in due course must have taken the instrument in good faith.[567] The 1990 revision of Article 3, in effect in all states except New York and South Carolina, defines "good faith" as "honesty in fact and the observance of reasonable commercial standards of fair dealing."[568] Accordingly, subjective good faith is not enough; the holder must act in a way that is fair according to commercial standards that are reasonable.[569]

If the circumstances surround the acquisition of an instrument are unusual or suggest a need for caution, the holder will not achieve holder-in-due-course status.[570] The holder must make inquiry sufficient to satisfy the suspicions raised by such circumstances.[571] If the holder accepts the instrument while aware of a problem with it, the holder loses the protection of holder-in-due-course status as to all defenses, not just those that relate to the problem of which it knew.[572] The consumer will not have to show bad faith. Instead, the holder will have to establish good faith; the burden is on the assignee to show it has met the UCC's prerequisites for holder-in-due-course status.[573]

6.7.2.3.5 Without notice

The final requirement for holder-in-due-course status is that the holder must take the instrument without notice of any of the following problems:[574]

---

mercial Credit Corp., 531 P.2d 966 (Colo. 1975) (a two-page indorsement stapled to two checks was sufficient to constitute an allonge for both checks).

564 Official Comment 1 to the 1990 version of U.C.C. § 3-204 repudiates this position. *See* Winfield v. Dosohs I, 1998 Tex. App. LEXIS 4674 (July 30, 1998) (unpublished) (upholding indorsement in light of 1990 amendments where allonge was a paper "sticky" attached to note, even though note had room for indorsement). Decisions enforcing the restrictions of the pre-1990 version of Art. 3 include: *In re* Nash, 49 B.R. 254 (Bankr. D. Ariz. 1985), *aff'd on other grounds*, 60 B.R. 27 (B.A.P. 9th Cir. 1986); Pribus v. Bush, 118 Cal. App. 3d 1003, 173 Cal. Rptr. 747 (1981) (an allonge should only be used when there is no room for the indorsement on the note itself); Tallahassee Bank & Trust Co. v. Raines, 125 Ga. App. 263, 187 S.E.2d 320 (1972); Bremen Bank & Trust Co. v. Muskopf, 817 S.W.2d 602 (Mo. Ct. App. 1991); Federal Fin. Co. v. Delgado, 1 S.W.3d 181 (Tex. App. 1999) (indorsement on allonge invalid under pre-1990 version of Art. 3 where adequate space on original note, therefore holder was mere "transferee," not "holder in due course"); Estrada v. River Oaks Bank & Trust Co., 550 S.W.2d 719 (Tex. App. 1977). *But cf.* Southwestern Resolution Corp. v. Watson, 964 S.W.2d 262 (Tex. 1997) (staples can be used as an allonge under pre-1990 version of Art. 3 where no more room on note).

565 U.C.C. § 3-302(a)(2).

566 Ocwen Fed. Bank v. Russell, 53 P.3d 312 (Haw. App. 2002).

567 U.C.C. § 3-302(a)(2). *See also* Kennard v. Reliance, Inc., 264 A.2d 832 (Md. 1970); Norman v. Word Wide Distributors, Inc., 202 Pa. Super. 53, 195 A.2d 115 (1963); Arcanum Nat'l Bank v. Hessler, 69 Ohio St. 2d 549, 433 N.E.2d 204 (1982); Security Central Nat'l Bank v. Williams, 52 Ohio App. 2d 175, 368 N.E.2d 1264 (1976).

568 U.C.C. § 3-103(a)(4). *See also* Wachovia Bank, N.A. v. Fed. Reserve Bank, 338 F.3d 318 (4th Cir. 2003) (since good faith requires reasonable commercial standards of fair dealing, must be some unfairness, not mere negligence); Agriliance, L.L.C. v. Runnells Grain Elevator, Inc., 272 F. Supp. 2d 800 (S.D. Iowa 2003) (unless landlord had notice of farm creditor's claim of security interest in proceeds of crops, good faith did not require it to conduct lien search before accepting check); Jones v. Community Bank, 306 A.D.2d 679, 762 N.Y.S.2d 133 (2003) (bank's disregard of its rules and failure to make further inquiry about suspicious checks creates fact question as to its observance of reasonable commercial standards of fair dealing).

569 Agrilance, L.L.C. v. Farmpro Servs., Inc., 52 U.C.C. Rep. Serv. 2d 36 (S.D. Iowa 2003); Any Kind Checks Cashed, Inc. v. Talcott, 830 So. 2d 160 (Fla. App. 2002).

570 Any Kind Checks Cashed, Inc. v. Talcott, 830 So. 2d 160 (Fla. App. 2002). *See, e.g.*, Gerber & Gerber, P.C. v. Regions Bank, 2004 WL 287347 (Ga. App. Feb. 13, 2004) (fact question whether bank should have made inquiries in light of irregularities in indorsements on checks).

571 Agrilance, L.L.C. v. Farmpro Servs., Inc., 52 U.C.C. Rep. Serv. 2d 36 (S.D. Iowa 2003).

572 Fidelity Bank v. Avrutick, 740 F. Supp. 222, 238 (S.D.N.Y. 1990).

573 U.C.C. § 3-308(b). *See also* Greene v. Gibraltar Mortgage Investment Corp., 488 F. Supp. 177 (D.D.C. 1980).

574 U.C.C. §§ 3-302(a)(2). *See also* Agriliance, L.L.C. v. Runnells Grain Elevator, Inc., 272 F. Supp. 2d 800 (S.D. Iowa 2003) (payee was holder in due course even though it had notice that source of funds was crops, where it did not have notice of other creditor's security interest in crop proceeds); United States Fin. Co. v. Jones, 229 So. 2d 495 (Ala. 1969); Salter v. Vanotti, 599 P.2d 962 (Colo. App. 1979); Calvert Credit Corp. v. Williams, 244 A.2d 494 (D.C. 1968); Ocwen Fed. Bank v. Russell, 53 P.3d 312 (Haw. App. 2002) (denying summary judgment to assignee of mortgage note on claim to be holder in due course where assignment occurred after debtor had filed pleadings raising her defenses); Govoni & Sons Constr. Co. v. Mechanics Bank, 51 Mass. App. Ct. 35, 742 N.E.2d 1094, 43 U.C.C. Rep. 2d 1058 (2001) (bank's reason to know of irregularity deprived it of holder-in-due-course status); Arcanum Nat'l Bank v. Hessler, 69 Ohio St. 2d 549, 433 N.E.2d 204 (1982); Fairbanks Capital Corp. v. Summerall, 2003 WL 1700487 (Ohio App. Mar. 31,

- That the instrument is overdue;
- That it has been dishonored, or there that there is an uncured default on another instrument in the same series;
- That it lacks an authorized signature or has been altered;
- That someone else has a claim to the instrument; or
- That any party has a defense or a "claim in recoupment" (a claim arising out of the transaction that gave rise to the instrument).[575]

Defects apparent on the face of the documents, such as unfair contract terms, Truth in Lending violations, or usurious interest rates, should defeat holder-in-due-course status. Knowledge acquired simultaneously with the acquisition of the instrument defeats holder-in-due-course status.[576] Holder-in-due-course status is defeated even if the holder did not have actual knowledge of the defenses, as long as the holder had reason to know of a defense in light of all the other facts and circumstances the holder knew.[577]

Assignees with close business ties to assignors are particularly vulnerable to challenges that they are not holders in due course,[578] particularly where they supply forms, receive assignment of substantially all the originator's obligations, and have constructive knowledge of the originator's fraud.[579] A transferee does not take an instrument in good faith when the transferee is so closely connected with the transferor that the transferee may be charged with knowledge of the obligor's defenses.[580]

6.7.2.4 Rights of Transferees from Holders in Due Course

A holder can acquire the *rights* of a holder in due course, even if it does not itself qualify as a holder in due course in its own right. A transferee from a holder in due course acquires all the rights of a holder in due course, even where this transferee does not qualify on its own for that status.[581] For example, a transferee may not qualify as a holder in due course in its own right because it knew of a defense before it acquired the instrument,[582] or because the prior holder did not properly indorse the instrument.[583] Even though it is not a holder in due course, it acquires the *rights* of a holder in due course if its transferor is a holder in due course. Similarly, a subsequent transferee from that party also acquires the rights of a holder in due course.

There is one important exception to this "shelter rule." If the transferee from the holder in due course engaged in fraud or illegality affecting the instrument, it does not acquire the rights of a holder in due course.[584] "A person who is a party to fraud or illegality affecting the instrument is not permitted to wash the instrument clean by passing it into the hands of a holder in due course and then repurchasing it."[585]

2003) (unpublished, citation limited) (question of fact whether holder took instrument with notice of defenses, where debtor had rescinded the transaction and filed suit before holder acquired it). *Cf.* Triffin v. Quality Urban Housing Partners, 352 N.J. Super. 538, 800 A.2d 905 (App. Div. 2002) (holder in due course could assign claim on check stamped "stop payment"; assignee would not be holder in due course but would have right to enforce assignor's claims).

575 *See* U.C.C. § 3-305(a)(3); Official Comment 3 to U.C.C. § 3-305 (discussing meaning of "claim in recoupment").

576 Provident Bank v. MorEquity, Inc., 585 S.E.2d 625 (Ga. App. 2003).

577 U.C.C. § 1-201(25) (definition of "notice"); Pulphus v. Sullivan, 2003 WL 1964333, at *18 n.10 (N.D. Ill. Apr. 28, 2003); *In re* SGE Mortg. Funding Corp., 278 B.R. 653 (Bankr. M.D. Ga. 2001) (citing Art. 1 definition of notice; question of fact whether holder had notice). *See* Agrilance, L.L.C. v. Farmpro Servs., Inc., 52 U.C.C. Rep. Serv. 2d 36 (S.D. Iowa 2003); Beal Bank v. Siems, 670 N.W.2d 119 (Iowa 2003) (expert testimony about banks' customary practices established that bank had reason to know of debtor's discharge); Bay Shore Check Cashing Corp. v. Landscapes by North East Constr. Corp., 3 Misc. 3d 475 (N.Y. Dist. Ct. 2004) (irregularities in signature on check sufficient to give notice of defenses). *But see* Van Hattem v. Dublin Nat'l Bank, 47 U.C.C. Rep. 2d 1171 (Tex. App. 2002) (actual knowledge required; court relies on narrower Art. 1 definition of "good faith," apparently overlooking broader Art. 3 definition).

578 *See* Unico v. Owen, 50 N.J. 101, 232 A.2d 405 (1967). *See also* Greene v. Gibraltar Mortgage Investment Corp., 488 F. Supp. 177 (D.D.C. 1980); Commercial Credit Corp. v. Childs, 199 Ark. 1073, 137 S.W.2d 260 (1940); Jones v. Approved Bancredit Corp., 256 A.2d 739 (Del. 1969); Ramadan v. Equico Lessors, Inc., 448 So. 2d 60 (Fla. Dist. Ct. App. 1984); Rehurek v. Chrysler Credit Corp., 262 So. 2d 452 (Fla. Dist. Ct. App. 1972); HIMC Inv. Co. v. Siciliano, 103 N.J. Super. 27, 246 A.2d 502 (1968); Arcanum Nat'l Bank v. Hessler, 69 Ohio St. 2d 549, 433 N.E.2d 204 (1982); American Plan Corp. v. Woods, 16 Ohio App. 2d 1, 240 N.E.2d 886 (1968). *See generally* Annot. 36 A.L.R.4th 212 (1985) (good faith under U.C.C. § 3-302).

579 Vasquez v. Superior Court (Karp), 4 Cal. 3d 800, 484 P.2d 964, 94 Cal. Rep. 796 (1977). *See also* § 6.6.5.4, *supra*.

580 Arcanum Nat'l Bank v. Hessler, 69 Ohio St. 2d 549, 433 N.E.2d 204 (1982).

581 U.C.C. § 3-203; Official Comments 2, 4 to U.C.C. § 3-203. *See* Nat'l Union Fire Ins. Co. v. Turtur, 892 F.2d 199, 205–206 (2d Cir. 1989) (reviewing operation of shelter rule under similar provisions of pre-1990 version of Art. 3); Fidelity Bank v. Avrutick, 740 F. Supp. 222, 238 (S.D.N.Y. 1990) (same).

582 *See, e.g.*, Fidelity Bank v. Avrutick, 740 F. Supp. 222, 238 (S.D.N.Y. 1990).

583 *See, e.g.*, Piper v. Goodwin, 20 F.3d 216 (6th Cir. 1994); Bank of Am. v. Crumb, 1999 WL 435770 (Conn. Super. June 21, 1999); Triffin v. Somerset Valley Bank, 343 N.J. Super. 73, 777 A.2d 993 (App. Div. 2001).

584 U.C.C. § 3-203(b). *See* Nat'l Union Fire Ins. Co. v. Turtur, 892 F.2d 199 (2d Cir. 1989) (reversing summary judgment for creditor where debtors showed that creditor knew of and facilitated the initial fraud; case decided under comparable provisions of pre-1990 version of Art. 3).

585 Official Comment 2 to U.C.C. § 3-203.

6.7.2.5 Defenses the Consumer Can Raise Even Against a Holder in Due Course

Even if an instrument meets all the requirements of a negotiable instrument, and even if the holder meets the requirements for being a holder in due course or otherwise acquires the rights of a holder in due course, the holder is still subject to some defenses. Both the prior and current versions of UCC § 3-305 establish that a holder in due course takes an instrument free from all defenses *except*:

- Incapacity;
- Infancy;
- Duress;
- Illegality that is sufficient to nullify the obligation;
- Discharge in insolvency proceedings; or
- Fraud that induced the obligor to sign the instrument with neither knowledge nor reasonable opportunity to learn of its character or its essential terms.

For example, a consumer can raise fraud in the factum as a defense against a holder in due course.[586] The consumer never knew he or she was signing a binding agreement. Similarly, if finance company personnel put an elderly consumer in a room without food for four hours and use a relay system to break down resistance, that type of duress should provide a defense even against a holder in due course.

Another important application of UCC § 3-305 arises if a loan is usurious. For example, the Official Comments to section 3-305 state "Illegality is most frequently a matter of gambling or usury. . . . If under [local] law the effect of the duress or the illegality is to make the obligation entirely null and void, the defense may be asserted against the holder in due course."

In many states a usurious loan will be void in whole or in part. This should be an illegality that nullifies the obligation and should be available as a defense even against holders in due course.[587] Even if state law only voids the finance charge or some other part of the total obligation, it may be that the consumer has a defense as to this portion of the loan.[588] A similar result should be reached when a UDAP or other consumer protection statute authorizes the court to void an agreement where the statute is violated or the lender operates without a license.[589]

586 Official Comment 1 to U.C.C. § 3-305(a)(1)(iii) provides that the test of the defense is that of "excusable ignorance of the contents of the writing signed."

587 *See* National Consumer Law Center, The Cost of Credit: Regulation and Legal Challenges § 10.8.2 (2d ed. 2000 and Supp.).

588 *Id.*

589 *See* § 8.7, *infra*. *See also* Columbus Checkcashiers Inc. v. Stiles, 56 Ohio App. 3d 159, 565 N.E.2d 883 (1990) (contractor's failure to obtain a license sufficient defense to check casher who was holder in due course). *But see* Kedzie & 103d Currency Exchange, Inc. v. Hodge, 156 Ill. 2d 112, 619 N.E.2d 732 (1993) (plumber's noncompliance with plumbing license law not sufficient to void check).

6.7.3 Liability of Assignees of High-Rate Mortgages

6.7.3.1 General

The Home Ownership and Equity Protection Act of 1994 (HOEPA) provides consumers with the right to raise claims and defenses against assignees of certain home mortgages.[590] Of special note, this federal statute provides the consumer with the right to raise both *claims* and defenses against assignees, and provides this right whether or not the assignee is a holder in due course or has inserted a waiver-of-defense clause in the contract. Compare this with the consumer's rights under common law principles, where consumers can generally only raise defenses (not claims) against assignees, and then only against assignees that are not holders-in-due course.

Unlike the FTC Holder Notice, the HOEPA provision applies whether or not the originating lender places a notice in the loan documents. HOEPA provides that as a matter of substantive federal law the assignee is "subject to all claims and defenses with respect to that mortgage that the consumer could assert against the creditor."[591] While the statute also requires a notice to the consumer of this right,[592] the right itself is in no way contingent on this notice in fact being given. The HOEPA provision, even though it is part of the federal Truth in Lending Act, applies not just to the consumer's Truth in Lending claims, but to the consumer's UDAP, RICO, fraud, and all other claims against the originating mortgage lender.[593]

The HOEPA provision is similar to the FTC Holder Notice concerning the cap on assignee liability. The assign-

590 15 U.S.C. § 1641(d)(1).

591 *Id.*

592 15 U.S.C. § 1641(d)(4).

593 Pulphus v. Sullivan, 2003 WL 1964333, at *21 n.11 (N.D. Ill. Apr. 28, 2003); Bryant v. Mortgage Capital Resource Corp., 197 F. Supp. 2d 1357 (N.D. Ga. 2002); Cooper v. First Gov't Mortg. & Investors Corp., 238 F. Supp. 2d 50 (D.D.C. 2002); Mason v. Fieldstone Mortgage Co., 2000 U.S. Dist. LEXIS 16415 (N.D. Ill. Oct. 10, 2000); Vandenbroeck v. Contimortgage Corp., 53 F. Supp. 2d 965, 968 (W.D. Mich. 1999); Lewis v. Delta Funding Corp. (*In re* Lewis), 290 B.R. 541, 556 (Bankr. E.D. Pa. 2003); Rodrigues v. U.S. Bank, 278 B.R. 683, 688 (Bankr. D.R.I. 2002); Murray v. First Nat'l Bank, 239 B.R. 728, 732 (Bankr. E.D. Pa. 1999). *See also* Harvey v. EMC Mortg. Corp. (*In re* Harvey), 2003 WL 21460063 (E.D. Pa. June 9, 2003) (HOEPA abrogates holder-in-due-course defense and makes assignee liable for all claims except under laws that have conflicting assignee liability provisions). *But see* Dowdy v. Bankers Trust, 2002 U.S. Dist. LEXIS 3978 (N.D. Ill. Feb. 7, 2002) (erroneously confusing derivative liability created by HOEPA with the standard for liability for one's own acts under state UDAP statute).

ee's maximum liability for claims and defenses to which it is subject by virtue of the HOEPA provision is the remainder of the mortgage indebtedness plus the total amount paid by the consumer in the transaction.[594] The HOEPA provision does not, however, limit the assignee's liability for its own actions. Further, if the assignee would be liable for the assignor's actions even in the absence of the HOEPA provision, the HOEPA provision does not limit liability.

6.7.3.2 Loans Covered by HOEPA

The HOEPA provision giving consumers the right to raise claims and defenses against assignees applies only to transactions covered by HOEPA. HOEPA coverage is explored in detail in another NCLC manual, National Consumer Law Center, *Truth in Lending* § 9.2 (5th ed. 2003 and Supp.). This subsection provides only a summary of this topic.

HOEPA applies to closed-end consumer credit transactions secured by the consumer's principal dwelling, where the loan was entered into after October 1, 1995.[595] HOEPA explicitly excludes reverse mortgages, open-end loans, and mortgages to purchase or construct a home.[596] HOEPA thus applies primarily to home equity loans, second mortgages, refinancings of first mortgages, home improvement loans, and credit sales of goods or services in which a security interest in the home is taken.

Loans meeting this definition must still contain either one of two characteristics to be covered by HOEPA. One characteristic sufficient to trigger HOEPA coverage is if the loan's annual percentage rate exceeds by more than ten percentage points the yield on treasury securities having comparable maturities at the time the loan is made.[597] For first-lien mortgage credit extended after October 1, 2002, the FRB has reduced the trigger to eight percentage points above comparable Treasury securities.[598]

For example, where, in 2005, a five-year treasury note has a 5% yield, HOEPA applies to a five-year home improvement, second mortgage loan extended around that time with a 15.1% APR. If the home were to have no other mortgage, this home improvement loan becomes a first mortgage loan, and HOEPA would apply if the APR were 13.1%.

The alternative trigger for HOEPA coverage instead of a high APR is the charging of total points and fees that total in excess of $400 (this number is adjusted each year for inflation) and also in excess of 8% of the total loan amount.[599] Such points and fees include prepaid interest, points, origination fees, service charges and other creditor charges for costs of doing business, all compensation paid to mortgage brokers, certain real estate charges, and, for loans consummated after October 1, 2002, premiums for certain credit insurance products.[600]

6.7.3.3 Exemption Where Assignee Is Unaware of HOEPA Coverage

Assignees are exempt from HOEPA's assignee liability provision if the assignee "demonstrates, by a preponderance of the evidence, that a reasonable person exercising ordinary due diligence" could not have determined that the loan was covered by HOEPA.[601] Due diligence requires that the assignee examine all documentation required by TILA, the itemization of the amount financed, and other disclosures of disbursements.[602] But due diligence requires more than a mechanical comparison of the loan documents and the disbursement statement.[603] For example, if the loan documents show unfamiliar fees, the assignee must look into them to make sure that they are bona fide, reasonable in amount, and otherwise legitimate.[604] In addition, the assignee is responsible for any other information it actually possesses at the time of assignment. It would be difficult for an assignee to argue that a reasonable person exercising due diligence could not obtain such information when the assignee in fact had it.

In most cases, whether the loan is covered or not will be apparent on the face of the documents. The maker of a covered transaction is required to place notice of the fact that assignees are potentially liable prominently in the loan documents.[605] Alternatively, review of the APR and the points and fees charged should reveal whether or not the loan is covered, and the assignee has the responsibility to review that itself.

594 15 U.S.C. § 1641(d)(2).

595 15 U.S.C. § 1602(aa)(1). Pub. L. No. 103-325, Title I § 157 provides that it applies to qualifying mortgages consummated after the date that FRB regulations go into effect on this subject, which was October 1, 1995.

596 15 U.S.C. § 1602(aa)(1).

597 15 U.S.C. § 1602(aa)(1)(A); 12 C.F.R. § 226.32(a)(i). Note that the Federal Reserve Board has proposed an amendment to its regulations that would lower the trigger by two percentage points. 65 Fed. Reg. 81438 (Dec. 26, 2000).

598 12 C.F.R. § 226.32(a)(1)(i), *as amended by* 66 Fed. Reg. 65604 (Dec. 20, 2001).

599 15 U.S.C. § 1602(aa)(1)(B); 12 C.F.R. § 226.32(a)(ii). The $400 figure had risen to $499 by 2004. 68 Fed. Reg. 50965 (Aug. 25, 2003). *See generally* National Consumer Law Center, Truth in Lending § 9.2.4 (5th ed. 2003 and Supp.).

600 15 U.S.C. § 1602(aa)(4); 12 C.F.R. § 226.32(b).

601 15 U.S.C. § 1641(d)(1); Cooper v. First Gov't Mortg. & Investors Corp., 238 F. Supp. 2d 50 (D.D.C. 2002) (assignee failed to meet burden); Rodrigues v. U.S. Bank, 278 B.R. 683, 688 (Bankr. D.R.I. 2002) (assignee has burden).

602 15 U.S.C. § 1641(d)(1).

603 Cooper v. First Gov't Mortg. & Investors Corp., 238 F. Supp. 2d 50 (D.D.C. 2002).

604 *Id.*

605 15 U.S.C. § 1641(d)(4). *See* Reg. Z § 226.32(e)(3). Failure to include this notice should be grounds for enhanced damages and civil liability under 15 U.S.C. § 1640.

6.7.4 Special Issues Arising in Securitization Transactions

6.7.4.1 Introduction

Increasingly, the capital underlying consumer credit markets is coming from the financing mechanism known as "securitization." Securitization is the process by which lenders can transform their loans into marketable securities. This occurs by pooling a large volume of loans, with interests in the underlying cash flows being sold, usually, to insurance companies, mutual funds, and other large institutional investors. Known as "asset-backed securities" or "ABS," these bonds are characterized by the fact that their creditworthiness (usually AAA) derives not from the creditworthiness of the original lender or of the quality of the loans, but rather, from other sources. During the 1990s securitization exploded as a primary source of capital for home equity lending, car loans, and student loans.[606]

For several reasons, an understanding of securitization is becoming essential to the effective representation of consumer borrowers. First, because securitization results in a transfer of ownership of the underlying loans, usually to a trust entity, the concept of real party in interest is rendered more complex. Even where a consumer is being billed by the original lender, that lender may not actually hold the loan. Whether defending a collection action or contemplating affirmative litigation, knowing the real party in interest can be critical to the litigation.

Second, because it is often the case that wrongdoing lenders go out of business or become insolvent, the existence of a consumer remedy may depend on evaluating liability theories against other participants in a securitization transaction. Perhaps even more importantly, in defending a foreclosure or deficiency action, the consumer will want to raise defenses it could raise against the originating lender. Being forced to separately sue that lender is often impractical, and may provide little benefit after consumers have lost their homes.

Whether the consumer can raise defenses and claims against subsequent note holders in a securitization transaction requires an extremely complex analysis, since one of the very purposes of securitization is to attempt to insulate participants from legal responsibility for the liability-producing activity of the originating lender.[607] Third, securitizations generate extensive transactional documentation and extensive ongoing reporting. Reading this paperwork with an understanding of the securitization process can provide important sources of information about the companies involved and about the underlying loans.

6.7.4.2 The Different Players in a Securitization Transaction

This subsection lists various players in one type of securitization transaction. But it is important to note that securitizations can be structured in many different ways and the parties involved can be given many different names. It is equally important to realize that these different entities are not unrelated or independent of each other. Instead, a complex web of relationships was consciously worked out in an attempt to insulate various parties from the conduct of the originating lender.

Lender. The originator of the loans.

Seller/Wholesale Lender. The Seller is the party that sells the loans to the Issuer. (The term Seller is also used in a different context as the entity that sells securities certificates to investors.) The Seller can be the original Lender, or an affiliate of the original Lender. Alternatively, the original Lender can sell the loans to a Wholesale Lender who, in turn, becomes the Seller of the loans to an Issuer. Where the Seller is a Wholesale Lender, it may sell the loans to an Issuer that is a wholly owned subsidiary of the Seller or of the same parent company that owns the Seller.

Issuer/Depositor. The Seller transfers the notes to an Issuer, also sometimes called a Depositor, or a "Bankruptcy-Remote Entity" or a "Special Purpose Vehicle" (SPV). (Sometimes, though, the Trust is termed the SPV.) The Issuer is a temporary, intermediary owner of the mortgages, and issues securities that represent undivided interests in the cash flows from a particular pool of loans. The Issuer sells the securities and transfers legal title in the loans to a trust entity. Its primary function is to create a legal separation between the entity that is producing the loans (the Lender or Seller) and the Trust which ultimately holds the loans. This separation is referred to as "bankruptcy remoteness" and the Issuer is often referred to as a "bankruptcy remote entity" in that it attempting to insulate the financial integrity of the securities from any economic difficulties of the Seller.[608] This separation also is intended to create holder-in-due-course status.

---

606 For some easily accessible explanations of securitization concepts and terminology, see the "MBS/ABS Publications" available on-line at www.bondmarkets.com/publications.html. For more technical sources, see books published by Frank J. Fabozzi Associates, such as F. Fabozzi et al, (ed.), The Handbook of Nonagency Mortgage-Backed Securities (1999). *See also* Kurt Eggert, *Held Up in Due Course: Predatory Lending, Securitization, and the Holder in Due Course Doctrine*, 35 Creighton L. Rev. 507 (Apr. 2002).

607 *See* Kurt Eggert, *Held Up in Due Course: Predatory Lending, Securitization, and the Holder in Due Course Doctrine*, 35 Creighton L. Rev. 507 (Apr. 2002); LoPucki, *The Death of Liability*, 106 Yale L.J. 1 23–30 (1996) ("Asset securitization is both a substitute for borrowing and a powerful new strategy for judgment proofing"); Schwarcz, *The Alchemy of Asset Securitization*, 1 Stan. J.L.Bus. & Fin. 133 (1994).

608 See LoPucki, The Death of Liability, 106 Yale L.J. 1 23–30 (1996); Gordon, Securitization of Executory Future Flows as Bankruptcy-Remote True Sales, 67 U. of Chicago L.R. 1317 (2000).

Servicer. The entity that collects monthly payments from borrowers and passes on required cash flows to the Trustee. The Servicer must advance to the Trust payments due from delinquent borrowers, and also must advance the costs of foreclosure. The Servicer retains a fee from borrower payments, usually 0.5%, and can also pocket late charges, bad check charges and other costs. The right to service a portfolio of securitized loans is regarded as a valuable asset and has been traditionally reserved by the Seller for itself, so in many securitized transactions the Seller and the Servicer is the same company. When these companies file bankruptcy, it is often these servicing rights that are their principal assets. But there also is a growing trend to use third party servicers who are not affiliated with the Issuer.

Trustee. Usually a commercial bank, the Trustee acts on behalf of the Trust and the investors. It is essentially an administrative function, to represent the Trust, to monitor the effectiveness of the servicing, to manage and oversee the payments to the bondholders and to administer any reserve accounts. Should the Servicer fail, it is the Trustee's job to step in as temporary servicer until a replacement can be hired.

Custodian. Where a note is bearer paper, and not to the order of a named party, a custodian may hold onto the bearer paper for safekeeping as an agent for the Trust. This entity may be the originating Lender or the Servicer, but it does not own the notes, even though it possesses them and the notes are bearer paper.

Underwriter. The Wall Street investment firm(s) that provides the initial capital to purchase the securities from the Issuer and then, at a profit, sells them to its customers, institutional investors like insurance companies and mutual funds. As the initial purchaser of all of the bonds, the Underwriter plays a key role in structuring the entire transaction, including a role in determining the characteristics of the underlying loans.

Rating agency. Provides supposedly independent evaluation of the credit quality of the securities. There are four rating agencies: Standard & Poors, Moody's, Fitch and Duff & Phelps. One of them has to rate the bonds as having AAA quality in order for the transaction to be regarded as marketable. The agencies research the characteristics and performance of an ABS, and rating agency websites are a good source of information about ABS transactions.[609]

Insurer. In order for the asset-based securities to be graded as AAA, they have be "credit enhanced." Often these enhancements come in the form of bond insurance provided by firms that historically insured municipal bonds.[610]

Warehouse Lender/Facility. This financial entity provides the short-term capital a small lender needs to fund the mortgages initially, until the loans are securitized. Once the Underwriter purchases the securities, there should be enough cash to repay the Warehouse Lender. The warehouse role has been played by the large commercial banks, but the underwriting firms have provided warehouse funding as well, sometimes taking a security interest in the loans up until they are transferred to the securitization trust.

The existence of all of these entities underscores the complexity of the securitization process. The ability to securitize consumer loan obligations that become due years in the future provides an effective means by which an originating lender can sell all of its loans and receive cash immediately, allowing it to then seek out new loans. On the other hand, the securitization process attempts to insulate those supplying this capital from any wrongdoing of the originating lender.

6.7.4.3 Documentation Underlying a Securitization Transaction

The primary contractual document underlying a securitization transaction is the Pooling and Servicing Agreement (PSA). The PSA establishes the securitization loan trust and the various classes of bondholders, and it also contains the obligations of the servicer and the various "representations and warranties" of the parties to the transaction. In addition, there is often an underwriting agreement, a warehouse agreement, and an insurance agreement. If the securities are publicly sold, then all these documents are publicly available.[611] Searching SEC-filed documents requires the name of the actual loan trust in which the consumer's loan is contained.[612]

609 For more on rating agencies, see National Consumer Law Center, Cost of Credit Ch. 11 note 28.3 (2004 Supp.).

610 Bond insurance is an example of "external" credit enhancement. Even more common are methods of "internal" enhancement. One example of an internal credit enhancement is a "senior/subordinated structure," in which the securities are divided into *senior* and *subordinate* layers with the subordinate investors assuming a greater risk of loss in return for receiving a higher return than the senior bondholders. By illustration, a $100 million pool of 30-year fixed rate mortgages might require, in the judgment of a rating agency, a loss coverage of 8%, resulting in the issuance of $8 million in subordinate bonds in order to provide AAA rating to the remaining senior class of $92 million. Often, additional support is created during the early years of the security by diverting the subordinated share of principal repayments into *reserve funds*. When bond insurance is present, the insurers usually are not in first-loss position, often taking a risk position behind the subordinate bondholders.

611 Each securitization trust, once identified, will have web-accessible SEC forms, often with the above documents attached as exhibits. To locate documentation for a particular securitization, start with an "Edgar" search. Go to the SEC's homepage at www.sec.gov and click on "Search for company filings" under the section titled "Filings and Forms (EDGAR)." More detail about finding and analyzing documents in this database may be found at Kevin Byers, *Researching Subprime Residential Loan Securitizations*, The Consumer Advocate vol. 9, no. 1, at 15–20 (Jan./Feb./Mar. 2003) (newsletter of the Nat'l Ass'n of Consumer Advocates).

612 Through discovery, the name of the loan trust that actually owns

These documents often contain interesting information. The documents may make representations about the characteristics of the borrowers and of the loan pools. A prospectus may list such information as purported default rates.

6.7.4.4 Raising Defenses on a Securitized Loan

6.7.4.4.1 Introduction

This subsection examines the consumer's right to raise defenses on a securitized loan. Securitized mortgage and car loans can be enforced through judicial or non-judicial foreclosure, repossession, or deficiency suits. This subsection focuses on the right to raise defenses on the loan obligation, not on the right to bring an affirmative suit for actual, statutory, or punitive damages. Affirmative suits for damages related to securitized loans are discussed at § 6.7.4.5, *infra*.

6.7.4.4.2 Who is the proper party in interest in the enforcing the note?

Whether the consumer is opposing an action for money, a judicial foreclosure, or a non-judicial foreclosure, the first issue is in whose name is the note being enforced. If it is the servicer who is also the originating lender, then the consumer should raise all defenses the consumer has against that lender. Even if the servicer is not the originating lender, the servicer can not claim holder-in-due-course status, because it is not a holder of the note. It is only servicing the note for the real party in interest.

The servicer may respond that it is not bringing the action for itself, but on behalf of the trust, who is the real party in interest, and that the trust is a holder in due course. In that case, it may be possible to argue that the action can not go forward in the name of the servicer, but must be refiled in the name of the trust. Case law is divided at present as to whether the action must be brought in the name of the real party in interest.[613] In any event, use this as an opportunity to investigate the original note and all indorsements and all transfer documents.

6.7.4.4.3 Defenses that can be raised even against a holder in due course

Certain defenses are available even if the party enforcing the note has the rights of a holder in due course.[614] These defenses include duress, illegality, and fraud in the factum. Illegality may include usury and making a loan while the originating lender is unlicensed.

6.7.4.4.4 Holder-in-due-course status can only be raised where the note is a negotiable instrument

If a note is not a negotiable instrument, then no holder of that note can be a holder in due course or have the rights of a holder in due course.[615] Few if any automobile or mobile home installment contracts or leases originated by the dealer will qualify as instruments.[616] Moreover, such contracts and leases typically include the FTC Holder Notice, and that notice states that consumers can raise dealer-related claims and defenses against the holder.

Similarly, car loans made directly with a lender, but referred by the dealer, are covered by the FTC Holder Rule, and the Holder Notice again should allow the consumer to raise *seller* related claims and defenses against the holder. In addition, because the Holder Notice is in the direct loan, the trust or other assignee of the note can not raise holder-in-due-course status to prevent defenses the consumer has against the original lender.[617]

Even some mortgage notes will not qualify as instruments. The amount of the note and the payment schedule must be definite.[618] Where a note has a payment schedule to be determined later or the size of the payment is contingent on a future event, the note is not a negotiable instrument. Open-end loans can not be negotiable instruments because the amount of credit extended, by definition, changes over time.[619] In addition, with certain exceptions, a negotiable instrument can not contain any other undertaking. For example, a requirement that the consumer purchase insurance not related to protecting the home can be viewed as such an undertaking, defeating the note's status as a negotiable instrument.

Older notes must also meet additional standards. If a note was made before the relevant state enacted revised Article 3, then the trust can not be a holder in due course of a variable-rate loan,[620] or a loan where strict requirements regarding allonges have not been followed.[621]

6.7.4.4.5 No holder in due course in HOEPA loans

High-rate mortgage loans must comply with HOEPA, analyzed at § 6.7.3, *supra*. HOEPA states that consumers can raise all claims and defenses against assignees that they could against the original lender, whether or not the HOEPA

a particular loan can be learned by making a demand to the loan servicer under 15 U.S.C. § 1641(f)(2).

613 For more on defending on this basis, and tips on how to discover who really holds the note, see National Consumer Law Center, Repossessions and Foreclosures §§ 12.8.1, 16.3.4 (5th ed. 2002 and Supp.).

614 *See* § 6.7.2.5, *supra*.

615 *See* § 6.7.2.2.1, *supra*.

616 *See* § 6.7.2.2, *supra*.

617 U.C.C. § 3-106(d).

618 *See* § 6.7.2.2.2, *supra*.

619 *See id.*

620 *See id.*

621 *See* § 6.7.2.3.2, *supra*.

notice on assignee liability is included in the note. The only exception to assignee liability is where the assignee could not reasonably have known that HOEPA applied to the note, such as being unaware that hidden fees triggered HOEPA coverage. But if the APR rate or fees on their face are high enough to trigger HOEPA coverage, then the trust is subject to all claims and defenses the consumer has against the originating lender, even though the loan itself is not identified as a HOEPA loan and the HOEPA notice is not in the loan.

6.7.4.4.6 Does the trust acquire holder-in-due-course status?

Even if a note is a negotiable instrument, the party holding the note, in this case the trust, must still qualify as a holder in due course or qualify as having the rights of a holder in due course. Whether the trust acquires those rights can be complicated by the number of note transfers, the fact that some transfers do not involve proper indorsements, and the fact that some transferees may have notice of defenses, while other transferees may not.

Where the note has been properly indorsed at each step of the note's securitization, or where bearer paper is involved, then the primary question is whether the trust meets the standards for being a holder in due course. The trust must take the note in good faith, for value, and without notice of defenses or that the note is overdue. The trust must also physically possess the note. Typically, the trust attempts to accomplish this by having a custodian hold the note as an agent for the trust.

Where a note is order paper, and it has not been properly indorsed at each transfer, then the trust can still acquire the rights of a holder in due course. To have the rights of a holder in due course it must be a transferee from someone who has the rights of a holder in due course.

Consider a note made out to the order of the originating lender that is transferred from an originating lender to a wholesale lender to an issuer to the trust. (These terms are defined at § 6.7.4.2, *supra*.) For the trust to be a holder in due course, there must be a proper indorsement to the trust. This means that there must be proper indorsement from the originating lender to the wholesale lender to the issuer to the trust. If any of those indorsements is missing or not proper, then the trust is not a holder in due course. Sometimes, the transfer from the wholesale lender to the issuer or at least from issuer to the trust will not include a proper indorsement, because the volume of notes involved encourages parties to skip this step.

Nevertheless, the trust still has the *rights* of a holder in due course if it is a transferee from someone who has the rights of a holder in due course. Thus if the wholesale lender is a holder in due course, then the issuer and the trust have the rights of a holder in due course, even though there is no proper indorsement from seller to issuer and from issuer to the trust.[622]

There is an exception to this rule. A party can not acquire the rights of a holder in due course if it engaged in fraud or illegality affecting the instrument.[623] This means that if the trust engaged in fraud, it can not obtain these rights from the issuer.

Similarly, the issuer can not acquire rights of a holder in due course from the wholesale lender if the issuer engaged in fraud. If the issuer does not have the rights of a holder in due course, then the trust can not obtain rights from the issuer that the issuer does not have. Since securitizations often involve interconnected and affiliated parties, it may be possible to show that the issuer or the trust aided and abetted a pattern of fraud by the originating lender, and thus the trust can not acquire the rights of a holder in due course.

The next question is whether either the wholesale lender or issuer is a holder in due course, allowing that party to transfer those rights to subsequent transferees. Note that a holder-in-due-course issuer can transfer those rights to subsequent transferees even if the wholesale lender is not a holder in due course.

To be a holder in due course, a party must take in good faith, for value, without notice that the loan is overdue, and without notice that the consumer has a defense.[624] If no entity is a holder in due course, then the consumer can raise against the trust all defenses the consumer has against the originating lender.

6.7.4.5 Damage Claims in Securitization Transactions Against Parties Other Than the Original Lender

As predatory lenders rise and fall, it is becoming increasingly important to formulate liability theories that will reach subsequent holders of the loans, as well as more distant participants in these transactions. The prior subsection examines defenses consumers can raise against enforcement of such loans. This subsection considers affirmative claims for damages that can be brought against parties other than the originating lender.

Liability theories will vary dramatically depending on whether a transaction involves a sale or a straight loan. In a transaction involving the sale of goods or services, the FTC Holder Notice may be present in the loan documents, making subsequent holders, including trusts, subject to all of the consumer's claims and defenses. If the Holder Notice should be, but is not included in the documents, legal theories to bring affirmative claims against loan holders are set out in § 6.6.4, *supra*.

622 *See* § 6.7.2.4, *supra*.
623 *See id.*
624 *See* § 6.7.2.3, *supra*.

In a mortgage loan, liability theories are somewhat different. In the case of HOEPA loans, federal law allows the consumer to raise affirmative claims (up to a cap) against the note holder (in a securitized loan, this is usually the trust).[625] In addition, various parties that aid and abet in the fraud can be held liable for their participation.

Where the original lender sells the loan to a wholesale lender, which, in turn, securitizes the loan, the ultimate holder, while being more remote from the wrongdoing of the original lender, may still be liable, particularly where the original lender was making loans to the specifications of the purchaser.[626] Once it can be shown that the financial institutions that are providing the lending capital for a predatory lending scheme are dictating loan terms or, at least, are aware of the predatory characteristics of the loans, participation theories should be able to reach those entities, even where they do not take legal title to the loans.

In a recent decision, a federal district court held that the Wall Street underwriters for a bankrupt predatory lender could be liable to injured consumers on an aiding and abetting theory where consumers alleged that the underwriters knew of the lender's fraud and provided substantial assistance to the lender's scheme.[627] Civil conspiracy and RICO theories have also been upheld in such circumstances.[628] While those who construct securitization transactions go to great lengths to attempt to insulate participants in the transactions from liability for lender malfeasance, those very efforts can establish the absence of an arms length relationship.[629]

6.7.5 Raising Lender-Related Defenses Against the FDIC, RTC, and Subsequent Note Holders

6.7.5.1 Introduction

This section examines a consumer's ability to raise lender-related claims and defenses against a subsequent note holder where the note at some point has been assigned to the Federal Deposit Insurance Corporation (FDIC) or Resolution Trust Corporation (RTC). A prior subsection[630] reviews the consumer's ability to raise seller-related defenses against the FDIC or RTC in a credit-sale. This section focuses only on FDIC and RTC-related issues as to a straight loan from a lender to the consumer unrelated to a consumer purchase.

When a federally-insured bank or savings and loan is taken over by the Federal Deposit Insurance Corporation or the Resolution Trust Corporation, the consumer notes held by the institution transfer to the federal agency. To promote the goals of confidence and stability in the banking system, and efficiency in the trade of notes and other financial instruments, Congress and the courts have granted the FDIC and the RTC unique powers to enforce such instruments.

When the FDIC or RTC collects on the note, the federal agency often will claim complete insulation from all claims and defenses relating to the note. Of even more significance, these defenses may transfer with the note to the benefit of a subsequent purchaser.[631] For example, when another bank purchases an insolvent bank from the FDIC or RTC, that purchasing bank may also claim insulation from all claims and defenses the consumer had against the now insolvent bank.

Case law in this area has tailed off after a swell of litigation in the 1990s, following the wave of bank and savings and loan failures. Very little of the case law deals with consumer notes, but instead involves large commercial loans. As a result, this subsection will only sketch the central issues for consumers. A more detailed discussion of these doctrines is found in National Consumer Law Center's *The Cost of Credit: Regulation and Legal Challenges* § 10.7 (2d ed. 2000 and Supp.).

6.7.5.2 Three Doctrines Insulating FDIC and RTC

There are three separate but overlapping doctrines that may insulate the FDIC and RTC from debtor defenses. One is federal common law starting with the Supreme Court's

625 15 U.S.C. § 1641(d). *See* § 6.7.3, *supra*.

626 England v. MG Investments, Inc., 93 F. Supp. 2d 718 (S.D. W. Va. 2000) (original lender could be viewed as agent of secondary purchaser where Master Loan Purchase Agreement contained detailed requirements for loans and a purchase commitment regarding loans that met these requirements, despite language in agreement that attempted to create appearance of arms length relationship between the two parties).

627 Aiello v. Chisik, 2002 U.S. Dist. LEXIS 5858 (C.D. Cal. Jan. 10, 2002) (denying motion to dismiss of Lehman Bros.).

628 *See, e.g.*, Smith v. Berg, 247 F.3d 532 (3d Cir. 2001) (RICO); Williams v. ITT Aetna Fin. Co., 700 N.E.2d 859 (Ohio 1998), *cert. denied*, 526 U.S. 1051 (1999). *See generally* § 6.5, *supra*.

629 England v. MG Investments, Inc., 93 F. Supp. 2d 718 (S.D. W. Va. 2000).

630 *See* § 6.6.3.10, *supra*.

631 *See, e.g.*, UMLIC-Nine Corp. v. Lipan Springs Dev. Corp., 168 F.3d 1173 (10th Cir. 1999) (*D'Oench* applies to actions brought by FDIC's assignees as well as by FDIC itself); Ranger Portfolio, L.L.C. v. Greene, 1998 U.S. Dist. LEXIS 10347 (D. Mass. May 8, 1998) (*D'Oench* runs to successors of FDIC, otherwise FDIC's ability to market assets would be severely diminished); AAI Recoveries, Inc. v. Pijuan, 13 F. Supp. 2d 448 (S.D.N.Y. June 23, 1998) (successor in interest to FDIC could assert *D'Oench* to defeat defense of lack of consideration); RTC Mortgage Trust 1994-S2 v. Shlens, 72 Cal. Rptr. 2d 581 (App. 1998); Jackson v. Thweatt, 883 S.W.2d 171 (Tex. 1994) (FIRREA applies to assignees); Bosque Asset Corp. v. Greenberg, 19 S.W.3d 514 (Tex. App. 2000) (FIRREA's protections extend not just to first assignee of FDIC but to subsequent assignees as well, therefore subsequent assignee could claim benefit of FIRREA's six-year limitations period); Ross v. SMS Fin., II, L.L.C., 959 S.W.2d 343 (Tex. App. 1998).

1942 decision in *D'Oench, Duhme and Company v. FDIC*.[632] In that case, a note was executed in favor of a bank solely to inflate artificially the bank's assets. The bank in a side agreement not reflected in the bank's records agreed that the note need not be repaid. The Court held that the maker of the note could not raise this unrecorded side agreement as a defense on the note after the note was acquired by the FDIC. Since then, *D'Oench* has been expanded to cover affirmative claims as well as defenses which are premised on secret agreements, and to cover claims based both in tort and in contract.[633]

The second source of FDIC and RTC protection is 12 U.S.C. § 1823(e), which provides that no agreement that hinders a note shall be valid against the FDIC or RTC unless the agreement is in writing and was properly signed, approved, and recorded by the bank. This statute obviously responds to the same issues raised in *D'Oench*, but is not, as often misdescribed, a codification of *D'Oench*.[634] The Supreme Court has interpreted this statute broadly in *Langley v. FDIC*,[635] to apply not only to side agreements, but also to claims of misrepresentation in the inducement. In that case, the borrowers claimed that the bank had committed fraud by misrepresenting the acreage and mineral content of land they financed.

The Supreme Court held that the prohibition against claims based on unrecorded agreements in section 1823(e) covered more than just promises to perform an act in the future; the bank's alleged representations about the property were in the nature of warranties, the truthfulness of which was a condition of their obligation to repay the loan. As such, if these representations were not included in the written, approved agreement, section 1823(e) barred claims based on them. The debtors' claims were barred even though they were wholly innocent and had not, unlike the debtor in *D'Oench*, been involved in any scheme with the bank.

632 315 U.S. 447 (1942).

633 See *discussion in* In re *604 Columbus Avenue Realty Trust, 968 F.2d 1332 (1st Cir. 1992).*

634 As one court noted, with side-by-side analysis:

> Section 1823(e) specifically applies to "agreements" between the borrower and the bank, and thus, inapplication of section 1823(e), the borrower's conduct is irrelevant. The *D'Oench, Duhme* doctrine, however, is a rule of equitable estoppel and applies to any defense that a borrower may assert in which the borrower participated in a scheme, which tends to deceive bank examiners. . . . In this respect, the statute is both broader and narrower than *D'Oench, Duhme*. It is broader in that it applies to *any* agreement, whether or not it was secret and regardless of the maker's participation in a scheme; it is narrower in that it applies *only* to agreements, and not to other defenses the borrower might raise.

Tuxedo Beach Club Corp. v. City Fed. Sav. Bank, 749 F. Supp. 635, 642 (D.N.J. 1990) (emphasis in original).

635 484 U.S. 86, 108 S. Ct. 396, 98 L. Ed. 2d 340 (1987).

Section 1823(e) and the *D'Oench* doctrine bar debtors' claims whether or not the federal agency meets the UCC definition of holder in due course. In fact, being a bulk purchaser, the FDIC is clearly not a state law holder in due course.

The third doctrine which may insulate the FDIC and RTC from debtors' claims is a common law "super" holder-in-due-course status that goes beyond the scope of section 1823(e) and *D'Oench*. Most courts have held that this doctrine only applies when the FDIC engages in a "purchase and assumption" transaction in which it transfers the failed bank's healthy assets to a viable banking institution. The doctrine gives the FDIC a complete defense to state and common law fraud claims, and probably all other "personal defenses" as well, on such notes when it acquires them for value, in good faith, and without actual knowledge of the defense.[636] Although decisions are split, many cases hold that the FDIC must meet state law requirements for holder-in-due-course status.[637]

636 *See* discussion at *In re* 604 Columbus Avenue Realty Trust, 968 F.2d 1332 (1st Cir. 1992) and Desmond v. FDIC, 798 F. Supp. 829 (D. Mass. 1992).

637 *See* discussion in Desmond v. FDIC, 798 F. Supp. 829 (D. Mass. 1992). *See also* FDIC v. Houde, 90 F.3d 600, 604 (1st Cir. 1996) (following *O'Melveny*, holder-in-due-course status of FDIC determined by state law); Sunbelt Savings, FSB Dallas, Texas v. Montross, 923 F.2d 353 (5th Cir. 1991), *reh'g granted*, 932 F.2d 363, *reinstated in part, and remanded*, 944 F.2d 227 (5th Cir. 1991) (en banc); RTC v. A.W. Assocs., 869 F. Supp. 1503, 1510 (D. Kan. 1994) (state law governs holder-in-due-course status); St. Bernard Sav. & Loan Ass'n v. Cella, 826 F. Supp. 985, 987 (E.D. La. 1993) (holding RTC not entitled to summary judgment on a note which its predecessor bank had bought after maturity, reasoning that the government could not change "lead into gold"); *In re* Miraj & Sons, Inc., 192 B.R. 297 (Bankr. D. Mass. 1996) (no holder in due course when assignee purchased notes from FDIC knowing they were overdue), *amended by* 197 B.R. 737 (D. Mass. 1996); Jackson v. Mundaca Fin. Servs., Inc., 76 S.W.3d 819, 825 (Ark. 2002) (state rule of civil procedure barred raising of federal holder-in-due-course argument in motion for reconsideration); Bisson v. Eck, 430 Mass. 406, 720 N.E.2d 784, 789 (Mass. 1999); Sun NLF Ltd. P'ship v. Sasso, 313 N.J. Super. 546, 713 A.2d 538, 544 (App. Div. 1998) (rejecting federal holder-in-due-course doctrine); Rhode Island Depositors Economic Protection Corp. v. Ryan, 697 A.2d 1087 (R.I. 1997) (court noted that protection enjoyed by federal holder in due course was not absolute; most effective way to pierce protections would be for the party asserting the defense to establish that FDIC possessed actual knowledge of the defense before taking the note); Depositors Economic Protection Corp. v. Proacaccianti, 2002 WL 977496, at *8, *9 (R.I. Super. Ct. May 2, 2002) (state insurance corporation could assert holder-in-due-course status, where defendant failed to show that corporation had actual knowledge of defendant's right of setoff); Cadle Co. v. Patoine, 772 A.2d 544 (Vt. 2001) (reversing summary judgment in favor of plaintiff, who had purchased defendant's note from FDIC; neither FDIC nor its transferee were holders in due course under state law because the FDIC had purchased the note as part of a bulk transaction not in the ordinary course of the transferor's business). *But see* Joslin v. Babovich, 699 So. 2d 1107 (La. App. 1997) (court agrees that

An important and emerging issue is whether the common law *D'Oench* doctrine and the "super" holder-in-due-course status continue to exist. A number of courts have held that the federal statute, 12 U.S.C. § 1823(e), has displaced the common law doctrines.[638] These decisions rely on two United States Supreme Court decisions, *O'Melveny & Myers v. FDIC*,[639] and *Atherton v. FDIC*,[640] which hold that the Financial Institutions Recovery and Reform Act (FIRREA), of which section 1823(e) is a part, is a comprehensive statute which leaves no room for federal common law doctrines. Although many of the decisions in this area do not clearly distinguish between the statutory and common law doctrines, there is no doubt that displacement of the broad and expandable *D'Oench* doctrine by the more precise and limited immunity afforded by section 1823(e) would result in the preclusion of fewer debtor claims.[641]

6.7.5.3 Consumer Obligations Not Covered by the FTC Holder Rule

The effect of *D'Oench* and related doctrines on sale-related consumer transactions may be negated by the FTC Holder Rule Notice. If the FTC Holder Rule Notice is in a note, it would appear that the FDIC and RTC can not avoid the impact of that notice. But there are many consumer claims to which the FTC Holder Rule does not apply. For example, the FTC Holder Rule does not apply to claims arising from the bank's misconduct, rather than the seller's misconduct, whether or not the FTC Holder Rule Notice is included in the note. These cases present more difficult problems and must be analyzed under the same case law as has been applied to commercial transactions.

---

once the FDIC or RTC acquired the instrument, it was accorded the status of holder in due course vis-à-vis the borrower, irrespective of state law requirements), *review denied*, 706 So. 2d 456 (La. 1997); Rhode Island Depositors Economic Protection Corp. v. Ryan, 697 A.2d 1087 (R.I. 1997); Pinkston v. Diversified Fin. Sys., 2000 Tex. App. LEXIS 6962 (Tex. App. Oct. 16, 2000) (reaffirming federal holder-in-due-course doctrine to hold that assignee of note acquired from FDIC could claim holder-in-due-course status notwithstanding that note was overdue at time acquired).

638 FDIC v. Deglau, 207 F.3d 153 (3d Cir. 2000) (holding that *O'Melveny* overruled *D'Oench*); Kessler v. National Enters., Inc., 165 F.3d 596 (8th Cir. 1999) (*D'Oench* no longer in force); Murphy v. FDIC, 61 F.3d 34 (D.C. Cir. 1995); DiVall Insured Income Fund v. Boatmen's First Nat'l Bank, 69 F.3d 1398 (8th Cir. 1995); Nashville Lodging Co. v. Resolution Trust Corp., 59 F.3d 236 (D.C. Cir. 1995); Davidson v. FDIC, 44 F.3d 246 (5th Cir. 1995); Resolution Trust Corp. v. Miller, 67 F.3d 308 (9th Cir. 1995) (unpublished decision); DiVall Insured Income Fund v. Boatmen's First Nat'l Bank, 69 F.3d 1398 (8th Cir. 1995) (FIRREA excludes federal common law defenses not specifically mentioned). *See also* Fens v. RTC, 112 F.3d 569, 577 (1st Cir. 1997) (suggesting that the "FDIC's right to invoke [either *D'Oench* or federal holder in due course] doctrine[s] . . . is open to serious question" without deciding the issue); Ledo Fin. Corp. v. Summers, 122 F.3d 825 (9th Cir. 1997) (*D'Oench* doctrine not applicable in light of *O'Melveny* and *Atherton* but declining to reach whether *D'Oench* overruled); FDIC v. Houde, 90 F.3d 600 (1st Cir. 1996); DiMuzio v. RCT, 68 F.3d 777, 780 n.2 (3d Cir. 1995); RTC v. Maplewood Invs., 31 F.3d 1276 (4th Cir. 1994) (*O'Melveny* creates a heavy presumption in favor of applying state law rules of negotiability); Resolution Trust Corp. v. Maplewood Investments, 31 F.3d 1276 (4th Cir. 1994); Shapo v. Underwriters Mgmt. Corp., 2002 WL 31155059, at *18, *19 (N.D. Ill. Sept. 27, 2002) (questioning *D'Oench*'s continued viability, and refusing to extend it to bar enforcement of a side agreement entered into by insurance company in action by insurance company's liquidator); S.E.C. v. Capital Consultants, L.L.C., 2002 WL 31441215, at *4 (D. Or. Jan. 3, 2002) (declining to extend *D'Oench* to bar defenses of borrower who had borrowed from an entity that was not federally regulated); RTC v. Massachusetts Mut. Life Ins. Co., 93 F. Supp. 2d 300 (W.D.N.Y. 2000) (*O'Melveny* effectively ended use of common law in cases governed by FIRREA, therefore defendant could assert state law affirmative defenses based on the FDIC's discretionary activities that occurred post-receivership to professional malpractice action brought by RTC); Federal Deposit Ins. Corp. v. Healey, 991 F. Supp. 53 (D. Conn. 1998); Sun NLF L.P. v. Sasso, 713 A.2d 538 (N.J. Super. App. Div. 1998) (federal holder-in-due-course doctrine did not survive *O'Melveny*); Bisson v. Eck, 720 N.E.2d 784 (Mass. 1999); Calaska Partners, Ltd. v. Corson, 672 A.2d 1099 (Me. 1996); Stewart Title Guaranty Co. v. FDIC, 936 S.W.2d 266 (Tenn. App. 1996). *But see* Harrison v. Wahatoyas, 253 F.3d 552, 559 (10th Cir. 2001) (applying *D'Oench* without questioning its continued viability); Young v. FDIC, 103 F.3d 1180 (4th Cir. 1997) (*D'Oench* remains separate and independent ground for decision), *cert. denied*, 522 U.S. 928 (1997); First Union Nat'l Bank v. Hall, 123 F.3d 1374, 1379 (11th Cir. 1997), *cert. dismissed*, 523 U.S. 1135 (1998); Motorcity of Jacksonville, Ltd. v. Southeast Bank, N.A., 83 F.3d 1317 (11th Cir. 1996), *vacated sub nom.* Hess v. FDIC, 519 U.S. 1087, 117 S. Ct. 760, 136 L. Ed. 2d 708 (1997), *reinstated*, 120 F.3d 1140 (11th Cir. 1997), *cert. denied*, 523 U.S. 1093 (1998) (*O'Melveny* does not *preempt D'Oench* doctrine); Rankin v. Toberoff, 1998 U.S. Dist. LEXIS 9714 (S.D.N.Y. June 30, 1998) (concluding that *D'Oench* survives *O'Melveny* in Second Circuit); State St. Capital Corp. v. Gibson Tile, Inc., 1998 U.S. Dist. LEXIS 20104 (N.D. Tex. Dec. 16, 1998) (unpublished) (assuming *D'Oench* still good law); Bank of San Padro v. Schuette, 2002 WL 2017089, at *2–*4 (Cal. Ct. App. Sept. 4, 2002) (citing *D'Oench*); RTC Mortgage Trust 1994-S2 v. Shlens, 62 Cal. App. 4th 304, 72 Cal. Rptr. 2d 581 (1998); Republic Credit Corp. I v. Gallo *ex rel.* Trustee of Spaulding Realty Trust, 2002 WL 31862709, at *7 (Mass. Super. Ct. Oct. 21, 2002) (holding *D'Oench* barred enforcement of any oral amendments to construction loan agreement; no analysis of effect of *O'Melveny*); Depositors Economic Protection Corp. v. Proacaccianti, 2002 WL 977496, at *9 (R.I. Super. Ct. May 2, 2002) (neither letter to lender nor proof of claim met requirements of state version of § 1823(e)); Ray & Assocs., P.C. v. SMS Fin. II, L.L.C., 2002 WL 997663, at *2, *3 (Tex. App. May 15, 2002) (*D'Oench* doctrine applied to bar guarantor from asserting that guaranteed note was never funded and from claiming defense of failure of consideration).

639 512 U.S. 79, 114 S. Ct. 2048, 129 L. Ed. 2d 67 (1994).

640 519 U.S. 213, 117 S. Ct. 666, 136 L. Ed. 2d 656 (1997).

641 Section 1823(e) is narrower than the *D'Oench* doctrine in that it applies only to agreements, and not to other possible defenses, but it is broader in that it applies to any agreement, regardless of whether it was secret and whether the borrower participated in a scheme.

Where the FDIC or RTC becomes an assignee of such a note, the issue is whether these agencies or their assignees are subject to defenses the consumer could raise against the assignor. The import of *Langley v. FDIC*,[642] appears to be that the consumer could raise defenses that would void the original loan, such as fraud in the factum, duress, or perhaps usury.[643] Much more problematic would be the consumer raising other defenses against the "super" holder-in-due-course status of FDIC or RTC or against those who receive a note through them.[644]

Consumer claims will be much more likely to survive if their origin is remote from the consumer's agreement with the bank and from anything that could have been included in that agreement. Accordingly, claims of debt collection harassment,[645] payment,[646] violations of law at the point of a foreclosure sale,[647] and wrongful repossession[648] may survive. A claim that the consumer entered into the agreement because of duress may survive as long as the alleged duress is not based on any oral agreement, since duress would be external to the agreement and not normally recorded in an agreement.[649]

Claims should survive if they can meet the demands of *D'Oench* and section 1823(e) by being premised upon a written, approved agreement between the bank and the consumer.[650] Sometimes called a "bilateral agreement exception" to *D'Oench*, the exception allows borrowers to assert rights under an agreement in the bank's file that imposed duties on both parties.[651]

Thus, for example, a breach of contract claim may survive.[652] One case holds that *D'Oench* and the common law doctrines do not bar claims of fraudulent omissions that are not inconsistent with any written document, i.e., where the written document is silent also.[653]

Many courts, following *Langley*, have held that claims of fraud in the *inducement* are barred.[654] However, claims of fraud in the *factum*—fraud that procures a party's signature to an instrument without knowledge of its true nature or contents—are not barred, because such fraud renders the

642 484 U.S. 86, 108 S. Ct. 396, 98 L. Ed. 2d 340 (1987).

643 *See* FDIC v. Rusconi, 808 F. Supp. 30 (D. Me. 1992); Wilshire Credit Corp. v. Walsh, 1998 Conn. Super. LEXIS 2196 (July 30, 1998) (fraud in the factum). *But see* FSLIC v. Murray, 853 F.2d 1251 (5th Cir. 1988); FDIC v. McClanahan, 795 F.2d 512 (5th Cir. 1986) (promissory note executed in blank and later "altered" held enforceable); FDIC v. Dureau, 261 Cal. Rptr. 19 (Ct. App. 1989) (*D'Oench* available to FDIC despite fact obligor told he was signing a corporate resolution, which bank knew was a guaranty).

644 *See, e.g.*, Buchanan v. Federal Sav. & Loan Ins. Corp., 935 F.2d 83 (5th Cir. 1991). *See* Sweeney v. Resolution Trust Corp., 16 F.3d 1 (1st Cir. 1994); FDIC v. Rusconi, 808 F. Supp. 30 (D. Me. 1992). *But see* Resolution Trust Corp. v. Cook, 840 S.W.2d 42 (Tex. App. 1992) (*D'Oench* doctrine does not apply to claim for infliction of emotional distress).

645 Resolution Trust Corp. v. Cook, 840 S.W.2d 42 (Tex. App. Ct. 1992).

646 FDIC v. Rusconi, 808 F. Supp. 30 (D. Me. 1992); Resiventure, Inc. v. National Loan Investors, 480 S.E.2d 212 (Ga. App. 1996) (payment defense allowed). *But see* Carson Props., Inc. v. NAB Asset Venture, III, L.P., 1998 Tex. App. LEXIS 1619 (Mar. 17, 1998) (unpublished) (*D'Oench* barred payment defense).

647 *See* Resolution Trust Corp. v. Carr, 13 F.3d 425 (1st Cir. 1993).

648 FDIC v. Payne, 973 F.2d 403 (5th Cir. 1992).

649 FDIC v. Rusconi, 808 F. Supp. 30 (D. Me. 1992); Desmond v. FDIC, 798 F. Supp. 829 (D. Mass. 1992).

650 FSLIC v. Mackie, 962 F.2d 1144 (5th Cir. 1992).

651 FDIC v. McFarland, 33 F.3d 532 (5th Cir. 1994) (*D'Oench* doctrine does not apply when agreement FDIC seeks to avoid is spelled out in loan documents); Howell v. Continental Credit Corp., 655 F.2d 743, 746 (7th Cir. 1981) ("[*D'Oench* is inapplicable] where the document the FDIC seeks to enforce is one, such as the leases here, which facially manifests bilateral obligations and serves as the basis of the lessee's defense"); FDIC v. Glynn, 1995 U.S. Dist. LEXIS 13957 (N.D. Ill. Sept. 20, 1995) (*D'Oench* does not preclude argument about loan construction and capacity in which parties signed); *In re* Miraj & Sons, Inc., 192 B.R. 297 (Bankr. D. Mass. 1996) (*Howell* exception extended to apply when bilateral agreements contained in closely related or integral loan documents in bank's records), *amended by* 197 B.R. 737 (D. Mass. 1996); Diversified Fin. Sys., Inc. v. Miner, 713 N.E.2d 293 (Ind. Ct. App. 1999) (where loan agreement on its face referenced "floor plan agreement," a document which manifests bilateral obligations, *D'Oench* did not bar borrower's counterclaim that FDIC and assignee/plaintiff caused borrowers' business to fail because it did not comply with the floor plan agreement, affirming denial of summary judgment for plaintiff); Sun NLF L.P. v. Sasso, 713 A.2d 538 (N.J. Super. 1998) (affirming denial of summary judgment for assignee, where letter agreement by bank containing "take out" commitment was in bank's files, though not referenced in subsequent notes).

652 *See* Allied Elevator v. East Texas State Bank, 965 F.2d 34 (5th Cir. 1992); FDIC v. Parkway Exec. Office Ctr., 1997 U.S. Dist. LEXIS 12318 at 33–34 (E.D. Pa. Aug. 18, 1997) (where instrument imposed obligations on both parties § 1823(e)(1) did not apply); Diversified Fin. Sys., Inc. v. Miner, 713 N.E.2d 293 (Ind. Ct. App. 1999). *But see* Harrison v. Wahatoyas, 253 F.3d 552, 559 (10th Cir. 2001) (*D'Oench* barred borrower's breach of contract action based on settlement agreement to which borrower was a third party beneficiary where even though agreement was in bank's records, it was not clear on its face that it had been written to benefit the borrower); OCI Mortgage Corp. v. Marchese, 774 A.2d 940 (Conn. 2001) (unwritten understanding that bank would apply payments due under debenture agreement representing loan from mortgagors to bank against payments due under the mortgage was not bilateral with mortgage agreement executed sixteen months previous); Carson Props., Inc. v. NAB Asset Venture, III, L.P., 1998 Tex. App. LEXIS 1619 (Mar. 17, 1998) (unpublished) (simple note did not represent bilateral agreement).

653 John v. Resolution Trust Co., 39 F.3d 773 (7th Cir. 1994). *But see* McCullough v. FDIC, 987 F.2d 870 (1st Cir. 1993); Desmond v. FDIC, 798 F. Supp. 829, 835 (D. Mass. 1992) (deceitful omissions are barred).

654 *See, e.g.*, FDIC v. Rusconi, 808 F. Supp. 30 (D. Me. 1992). *But see* FSLIC v. Murray, 853 F.2d 1251 (5th Cir. 1988); FDIC v. McClanahan, 795 F.2d 512 (5th Cir. 1986) (promissory note executed in blank and later "altered" held enforceable); FDIC v. Dureau, 261 Cal. Rptr. 19 (Ct. App. 1989) (*D'Oench* available to FDIC despite fact obligor told he was signing a corporate resolution, which bank knew was a guaranty).

obligation entirely void rather than voidable. The bank has nothing that it can pass on to the RTC or FDIC.[655]

Another way to avoid the *D'Oench* doctrines is to argue that the doctrine is inapplicable to a particular type of transaction. The *D'Oench* doctrine may not apply where the consumer's claims against the original bank do not arise from a credit transaction. For example, where a bank owned a house and sold it to consumers without providing the financing for the purchase, the *D'Oench* doctrine and section 1823(e) do not prevent the consumers from asserting claims against the RTC that the bank fraudulently concealed defects in the house.[656] Nor does section 1823(e) apply where the bank is involved in a joint venture with the obligor, rather than in a creditor-debtor relationship.[657] Courts have also found that the *D'Oench* doctrine affords no protection to former officers of the failed bank.[658] The FDIC and RTC may be liable for their own conduct that violates UDAP standards.[659]

6.8 Raising Defenses to Local Telephone Company Collection of 900-Number and Long-Distance Charges

An increasingly important issue is the consumer's rights where a local telephone company attempts to collect on 900-number and long-distance charges. Numerous fraud claims have been alleged concerning 900 numbers, and consumers also find themselves charged for long-distance calls by unfamiliar companies at exorbitant rates. The consumer's right to contest these charges is weakened because these companies contract with the local telephone carrier to assess these charges in conjunction with the basic telephone bill, so that the consumer will not be able to simply defend against the 900-number or long-distance carrier. Instead, the consumer will have to deal with the local carrier, and perhaps face disconnection of local service if the consumer refuses to pay for long-distance or 900-number charges.

The consumer can certainly raise all valid defenses to payment against the local telephone company. That company is not a holder in due course, but is merely an agent for the 900-number or long-distance carrier. But a local telephone company is more likely to disconnect service for non-payment rather than bring a collection action.

Fortunately for consumers, federal and state legislation offers consumers increased protection for disconnection of their local service because of nonpayment of 900-number or long-distance service. The Telephone Disclosure and Dispute Resolution Act of 1992 prohibits common carriers from disconnecting a subscriber's long-distance or local service because of unpaid charges for any pay-per-call service.[660]

The Federal Communications Commission had also attempted to protect customers receiving discounted local phone service through federal Universal Service Funds from being disconnected for unpaid long-distance charges.[661] Unfortunately, the Fifth Circuit overturned this prohibition on disconnection on jurisdictional grounds in July 1999.[662] However, a number of states have Public Utility Commission regulations, policies or case law that prevent disconnection of any residential user's local service because of nonpayment of long-distance charges.[663]

---

655 Langley v. FDIC, 484 U.S. 86, 108 S. Ct. 396, 98 L. Ed. 2d 340 (1987); FDIC v. Kagan, 871 F. Supp. 1522 (D. Mass. 1995); RTC v. Davies, 824 F. Supp. 1002 (D. Kan. 1993) (fraud in the factum requires "excusable ignorance" of the contents of the writing and no reasonable opportunity to obtain knowledge); FDIC v. Rusconi, 808 F. Supp. 30 (D. Me. 1992). A recent decision finding circumstances to fall within the fraud in the factum exception to the *D'Oench* doctrine is FDIC v. Turner, 869 F.2d 270 (6th Cir. 1989) (bank officer fraudulently altered guaranty); Wilshire Credit Corp. v. Walsh, 1998 Conn. Super. LEXIS 2196 (July 30, 1998) (fraud in the factum rendered note void). *But see* FSLIC v. Murray, 853 F.2d 1251 (5th Cir. 1988); FDIC v. McClanahan, 795 F.2d 512 (5th Cir. 1986) (promissory note executed in blank and later "altered" held enforceable); FDIC v. Dureau, 261 Cal. Rptr. 19 (Ct. App. 1989) (*D'Oench* available to FDIC despite fact obligor told he was signing a corporate resolution, which bank knew was a guaranty).

656 John v. Resolution Trust Co., 39 F.3d 773 (7th Cir. 1994). *See also* Waynesboro Village, L.L.C. v. BMC Props., 496 S.E.2d 64 (Va. 1998) (restrictive covenants executed in conjunction with loan were enforceable against successor bank notwithstanding either *D'Oench* or section 1823(e)).

657 Resolution Trust Corp. v. Maplewood Investments, 31 F.3d 1276 (4th Cir. 1994).

658 *See* Crowe v. Smith, 848 F. Supp. 1248 (W.D. La. 1994) and cases cited therein.

659 FDIC v. Rusconi, 808 F. Supp. 30 (D. Me. 1992); Tuxedo Beach Club Corp. v. City Fed. Sav. Bank, 749 F. Supp. 635, 648 (D.N.J. 1990).

660 47 U.S.C. § 228(c)(4); 47 C.F.R. § 64.1507. *See also* 15 U.S.C. § 5721 and 16 C.F.R. § 308.7(g).

661 Federal Communications Commission, *Report and Order In the Matter of Federal-State Joint Board on Universal Service*, CC Docket No. 96-45, FCC 97-157 (May 8, 1997). This five-hundred-plus page report is available on-line in several formats at www.fcc.gov/wcb/universal_service/fcc97157/.

662 Texas Office of Public Utility Counsel v. FCC, 183 F.3d 393 (5th Cir. 1999). The FCC issued an order in October 1999 that implemented changes to the universal service rules to comply with the Fifth Circuit decision (Federal Communications Commission, *Sixteenth Order on Reconsideration in CC Docket No. 96-45, Eighth Report and Order in CC Docket 96-45, Sixth Report and Order in CC Docket 96-262 In the Matter of Federal-State Joint Board on Universal Service; Access Charge Reform*, CC Docket Nos. 96-45, 96-262 and FCC 99-290 (Oct. 8, 1999) at www.fcc.gov/Bureaus/Common_Carrier/Orders/1999/fcc99290.txt).

663 For example, in Washington state, residential consumers can not be disconnected for nonpayment of information service charges (e.g., 900 numbers) and can not be disconnected from local service for nonpayment of long-distance charges (but can lose long-distance service for nonpayment). Wash. Admin. Code §§ 480-120-254, 480-120-072(4). *See also* N.Y. Comp. Codes R. & Regs. tit. 16, § 606.4(a) (New York has similar protections

Federal law also provides special rights for consumers to challenge 900-number charges. Local carriers must establish a procedure for handling consumer complaints about 900-number charges, and have discretion to set standards for determining when a subscriber's complaint warrants forgiveness of the charges.[664] Carriers are required to forgive the debt and refund any payment if the FTC, the FCC, or a court finds that the 900-number service violated the federal law or regulations.[665] Vermont and Oregon statutes also require full refunds on 900-number charges upon request in several situations.[666]

A local carrier may also be liable not only for improper long-distance or 900-number charges, but also for consequential and punitive damages and attorney fees where the carrier aided and abetted a fraudulent scheme or otherwise directly engaged in misconduct. Such aiding and abetting may be provable since the local carrier assisted in the collection of the amount due and is likely to receive a number of complaints about the same company. FTC actions against credit card issuers and service bureaus may provide useful precedent.[667] But a phone company is not criminally or civilly liable solely because it provided transmission, billing and collection for a pay-per-call company unless the phone company reasonably should have known the service was in violation of the pay-per-call laws.[668]

for local phone service); 16 Tex. Admin. Code § 26.28(a)(4)(E) (Texas prohibits disconnection for nonpayment of non-tariffed charges but allows disconnection for nonpayment of long-distance charges incurred after toll blocking was imposed). Massachusetts does not have a formal tariff on this issue, but apparently has an established policy not to allow disconnection of local service for nonpayment of long-distance charges. *See* Letter from MA Dept. of Public Utilities to New England Tel. Co. (Dec. 5, 1985) ("the rights of the consumer to maintain access to the local network remain paramount" and that a local phone company's "right to disconnect for non-payment can not be transferred to another company by any contractual means"); Letter from MA Dept. of Public Utilities to New England Tel. Co. (June 26, 1987) (phone company can use toll denial for non-payment of long-distance only if it can selectively deny access to the specific long-distance carrier's network with whom the customer has unpaid charges); MA Dept. of Telecommunications and Energy, *Order on Motion for Reconsideration and Extension of the Judicial Appeal Period by Bell Atlantic-Mass.*, D.P.U./D.T.E. 96-AD-9-A (May 25, 2000) (MA D.P.U./D.T.E refuses to reconsider its policy prohibiting all-carrier toll denial) (available on the companion CD-Rom). *See also* National Consumer Law Center, Access to Utility Service § 11.4, Appx. A (3d ed. 2004).

664 47 C.F.R. § 64.1511(a) and 47 U.S.C. § 228(f).

665 47 U.S.C. § 228(f); 47 C.F.R. § 64.1511(a).

666 Or. Rev. Stat. § 759.720 (charges made by children or mentally disabled individuals); Vt. Stat. Ann. tit. 9, §§ 2505 (credit cards and loans), 2507 (prize promotions), 2508 (use by children), 2509 (charitable donations), 2516 (no sponsor shall bill or collect if pay-per-call service in violation of the provisions of the chapter).

667 *See* §§ 6.5.3, 6.5.4, *supra*.

668 47 U.S.C. § 228(e) (but the FCC can still impose sanctions and fines).

Federal law also makes companies known as "service bureaus," which provide access to telephone service and voice storage for 900-number operators, liable if they knew or should have known that the operators were violating applicable laws.[669] The FTC has accepted a consent order requiring a service bureau to pay $2 million in consumer redress because of its facilitation of a telephone scam.[670]

6.9 UDAP Claims Against Bankrupt Sellers

Frequently, a company engaging in unfair or deceptive practices will teeter on the brink of insolvency. The company may file for bankruptcy protection before the UDAP claim can be brought or will respond to UDAP actions or judgments by filing for bankruptcy. Consumers should not treat this as the end of the matter. While this chapter examines in detail claims and defenses against third parties, there are also a number of steps that can be taken that will provide the consumer with full or at least partial compensation directly from the seller's assets, even though the seller has filed for bankruptcy.

Chapter 17 of the National Consumer Law Center's *Consumer Bankruptcy Law and Practice* (7th ed. 2004) provides a detailed discussion of a consumer's strategies when a company files for bankruptcy and the consumer becomes the creditor. It includes in the appendices and also on a companion CD-Rom, the Bankruptcy Code, the Rules of Bankruptcy Procedure, and model forms for a consumer seeking to recover from a merchant or creditor in bankruptcy.

Once a defendant files bankruptcy, an automatic stay goes into effect that requires almost all legal proceedings and collection efforts to stop, on pain of contempt.[671] The consumer has the right to seek relief from the automatic stay in order to pursue litigation outside the bankruptcy court. If the consumer does not seek relief from the automatic stay, the bankruptcy court will determine the consumer's claim against the bankrupt.

Regardless of whether the consumer seeks relief from the automatic stay, the consumer should file a proof of claim, asserting any priorities that are applicable.[672] If there is a straight liquidation of the company's assets, the consumer likely will only recover a small percentage of the claim, at best, although asserting a "consumer" priority may improve the consumer's position somewhat. Some courts allow a proof of claim to be filed on behalf of a class of consumers.[673]

669 16 C.F.R. § 308.5(l).

670 United States v. American TelNet, 5 Trade Reg. Rep. (CHH) ¶ 23,723 (C.D. Cal. 1994).

671 11 U.S.C. § 362. *See* National Consumer Law Center, Consumer Bankruptcy Law and Practice Ch. 9, § 17.3 (7th ed. 2004).

672 *See* National Consumer Law Center, Consumer Bankruptcy Law and Practice 17.4 (7th ed. 2004).

673 *See id.* § 17.4.2.

The consumer should also try to identify assets, such as a deposit or personal property, that the bankrupt is arguably holding in trust for the consumer. It may be possible to exclude these assets from the bankruptcy estate so that the consumer can recover 100% of those assets, since they belong to the consumer and not the bankrupt.[674]

The consumer may also want to challenge the dischargeability of the consumer's claim where an individual is filing a chapter 7 bankruptcy.[675] Then, even though the consumer may not recover much from the bankruptcy proceeding, the consumer's claim survives the bankruptcy, and the consumer can recover assets whenever the individual acquires any in the future.

In a chapter 13 bankruptcy, the consumer might have grounds to object to the confirmation of the merchant's chapter 13 plan.[676] There are also steps that consumers can take to protect their interests when a defendant files a chapter 11 bankruptcy.[677]

In addition, the consumer can take a number of steps before the bankruptcy is filed to prepare for the possibility that a defendant will file bankruptcy:

- Naming as defendants any other individuals and corporations that may be liable;[678]
- Obtaining findings of fact, or stipulations in any settlement agreement, that establish grounds to contest dischargeability of the debt;[679]
- Moving promptly to collect a judgment as soon as it is rendered;
- Obtaining a stipulation, or a ruling from the court that hears the case, that property or other assets are held in constructive trust for the consumer.[680]

6.10 Merchant Bonding, Insurance, and Consumer Recovery Funds

6.10.1 Recovering on a Bond

A number of merchants are required by state law to post a bond as a precondition of doing business in that state. Important examples are car dealers,[681] manufacturers and dealers of mobile homes,[682] realtors, home improvement contractors,[683] and vocational schools. When the consumer has a claim against the merchant, and the merchant does not pay, the consumer can seek recovery from the company holding the merchant's bond. The consumer's rights, though, often depend on the exact language of the bond, and whether this language covers the consumer's claim against the merchant.

Assuming a seller is bonded, the key issue thus in recovering on the bond is whether the consumer's UDAP or other claim is within the scope of the bond. The bonding company will only pay losses that are explicitly covered by the language of the bond. In addition, even where a bonding company will pay out actual damages for a type of claim, it may balk at paying out punitive, treble, or statutory damages, or attorney fees, arguing that these are not within the scope of the bond.[684]

Consumers should distinguish between attorney fees expended in a lawsuit against the merchant from attorney fees required to press a demand against the bonding company. Even if the first type of attorney fee award is not within the scope of a bond, the public policy behind UDAP attorney fees requires that the consumer recover from the bonding company for work expended pressing the consumer's claim against the bonding company.[685]

Similarly, even if treble damages are not with the scope of a bond, the consumer will have a UDAP action in most states against the bonding company for that company's unreasonable refusal to pay on a bond. In a number of states, that unreasonable refusal to pay may lead to a trebling of the amount owed on the bond.[686]

Another problem with a merchant bond may be that the total amount recoverable on the bond is relatively small, and not adequate to pay all victimized consumers. In that case, the consumers that make their claims earliest may be the

674 *See id.* § 17.5.2.

675 *See id.* § 17.5.4.

676 *See id.* § 17.5.4.3.

677 *See id.* § 17.7.

678 *See* §§ 6.1–6.5, *supra.*

679 National Consumer Law Center, Consumer Bankruptcy Law and Practice § 17.5.4.2.1 (7th ed. 2004 and Supp.).

680 *See id.* § 17.5.2.

681 *See* National Consumer Law Center, Automobile Fraud § 9.13.4 (detailed discussion of claims under state motor vehicle dealer bonding statutes) and Appx. C (listing of state bonding statutes) (2d ed. 2003 and Supp.).

682 *See* National Consumer Law Center, Consumer Warranty Law § 15.4.2 (2d ed. 2001 and Supp.).

683 *See* National Consumer Law Center, Consumer Warranty Law § 17.7.4 (2d ed. 2001 and Supp.).

684 *See, e.g.*, Ames v. Commissioner of Motor Vehicles, 267 Conn. 524, 839 A.2d 1250 (Conn. 2004) (surety bond statute's coverage of "any loss" does not include treble damages and attorney fees); Hubbel v. Aetna Cas. & Sur. Co., 758 So. 2d 94 (Fla. 2000) (fees incurred in pursuing claim against bonded party not recoverable from bond); Tomlinson v. Camel City Motors, Inc., 330 N.C. 76, 408 S.E.2d 853 (1991) (where statute authorizes consumers who have "suffered" to recover from a bond, consumer can not recover treble damages, at least where no unusual effort expended to collect the judgment from surety). *See generally* National Consumer Law Center, Automobile Fraud §§ 9.13.4.4, 9.13.4.5 (2d ed. 2003 and Supp.).

685 Marshall v. W&L Enterprises Corp., 360 So. 2d 1147 (Fla. Dist. Ct. App. 1978). *But see* Brock v. American Mfrs. Mutual Ins. Co., 94 Md. App. 194, 616 A.2d 458 (1992) (bond posted under motor vehicle laws not available for attorney fees for UDAP claim).

686 *See* Lawyers Surety Corp. v. Royal Chevrolet, Inc., 847 S.W.2d 624 (Tex. App. 1993).

lucky ones. If a surety exhausts a bond by paying some claimants at a time when it has notice of others, however, its liability may be expanded beyond the amount of the bond.[687] Consumers should therefore take care that the surety has notice of the claim at the earliest possible moment.

6.10.2 Recovering from the Merchant's Insurance Policy

Another possibility is to recover from a seller's insurance company. Sellers typically purchase insurance on a voluntary basis to protect themselves from lawsuits and other potential losses. If the policy applies to the type of claims the consumer has against the merchant, the consumer may be able to recover even if the seller is otherwise judgment-proof.

For example, many companies purchase liability insurance policies that pay out claims based on the negligence of the seller's employees. If the seller's UDAP or similar violation can be labeled "negligence," this may assure the existence of a deep pocket. Often insurance policies exclude coverage for intentional fraudulent acts, but a UDAP claim does not require proof of intent, so that this exclusion should not apply.[688] An Oregon appellate court has held that coverage of UDAP misrepresentation claims was required by a seller's insurance policy that covered claims under "any federal, state, or local truth in lending law."[689] Some courts hold that insurance coverage for UDAP violations is not contrary to public policy.[690] But a court has found that a policy covering "occurrences," defined as accidents, did not cover UDAP violations that involved misrepresentations, using the wrong home improvement materials, and installing them improperly.[691] A court has also found various fraud counts not to be covered under a policy protecting the dealer from bodily injury or property damage caused by a specific event.[692]

A number of standard liability policies also cover "advertising injury," and define advertising injury to include "unfair competition." Courts generally find that UDAP claims based on deception or unfairness do not fall within this policy coverage.[693] But a claim that the insured sent junk faxes to consumers in violation of the Telephone Consumer Protection Act[694] did allege an advertising injury.[695] A court has also found that a UDAP claim is not covered by a medical malpractice policy where the state's UDAP statute requires an injury to business or property, while the malpractice policy only covers bodily or mental

687 Durant v. Changing, Inc., 891 P.2d 628 (Okla. App. 1995).

688 Sibley v. National Union Fire Ins., 921 F. Supp. 1526 (E.D. Tex. 1996). *See also* Pacific Ins. Co. v. Burnet Title, Inc., 2003 WL 22283355 (D. Minn. Sept. 24, 2003) (construing UDAP complaint to allege negligence, and finding that lender's insurance company has duty to defend lender). *Cf.* Conn. Indemnity Co. v. DER Travel Serv., Inc., 328 F.3d 347 (7th Cir. 2003) (Ill. law) (policy that covered negligence might have covered UDAP claims but not where plaintiffs alleged intentional overcharges). *But cf.* Travelers Indemnity Co. v. Jim Coleman Automotive, 236 F. Supp. 2d 513 (D. Md. 2002) (no coverage for UDAP claim alleging intentional acts); Upland Anesthesia Medical Group v. Doctors' Co., 100 Cal. App. 4th 1137, 123 Cal. Rptr. 2d 94 (2002) (no coverage where UDAP complaint alleged intentional acts).

689 Fredericks v. Universal Underwriters Ins. Co., 140 Or. App. 269, 915 P.2d 472 (1996). *But see* Landmark Chevrolet Corp. v. Universal Underwriters Ins. Co., 2003 WL 22809055 (Tex. App. Nov. 26, 2003) (no duty to defend as UDAP claim was not a claim of violation of a truth-in-lending or truth-in-leasing law).

690 State *ex rel.* Fisher v. Warren Star Theater, 84 Ohio App. 3d 435, 616 N.E.2d 1192 (1992). *But see* TIG v. Andrews Sporting Goods, Inc., 2002 Cal. App. Unpub. LEXIS 2105 (June 12, 2002) (unpublished, citation limited) (construing Cal. Ins. Code § 533.5 to prohibit insurance policy from covering fines, penalties or restitution in claims brought by certain public authorities under § 17200).

691 Brosnahan Builders, Inc. v. Harleysville Mut. Ins. Co., 137 F. Supp. 2d 517 (D. Del. 2001), *aff'd without op.*, 2003 WL 146486 (3d Cir. Jan. 21, 2003). *See also* Western Rim Investment Advisors, Inc. v. Gulf Ins. Co., 269 F. Supp. 2d 836 (N.D. Tex. 2003) (sending junk faxes not an "accident" covered by insurance policy).

692 Auto-Owners Ins. Co. v. Toole, 947 F. Supp. 1557 (M.D. Ala. 1996). *See also* Travelers Indemnity Co. v. Jim Coleman Automotive, 236 F. Supp. 2d 513 (D. Md. 2002) (dealer's liability for overcharging consumers not "property damage" resulting from an "accident").

693 *See* Granite State Ins. Co. v. Aamco Transmissions, Inc., 57 F.3d 316 (3d Cir. 1995) (Pennsylvania UDAP suit not covered by "unfair competition" provision); Alliance Ins. Co. v. Colella, 995 F.2d 944 (9th Cir. 1993) (California law); Keating v. National Union Fire Ins. Co., 995 F.2d 154 (9th Cir. 1993) (California law); *In re* San Juan DuPont Plaza Hotel Fire Litigation, 802 F. Supp. 624 (D. P.R. 1992); Globe Indem. Co. v. First Am. State Bank, 720 F. Supp. 853 (W.D. Wash. 1989); Pine Top Ins. v. Utility Dist. No. 1, 676 F. Supp. 212 (E.D. Wash. 1987); Bank of the West v. Superior Court (Industrial Indemnity Co.), 2 Cal. 4th 1254, 10 Cal. Rptr. 2d 538, 833 P.2d 545 (1992); Chatton v. National Union Fire Ins. Co., 13 Cal. Rptr. 2d 318 (Ct. App. 1992); Graham Resources, Inc. v. Lexington Ins. Co., 625 So. 2d 716 (La. Ct. App. 1993); Meyers & Sons v. Zurich Am. Ins., 74 N.Y.2d 298, 545 N.E.2d 1206, 546 N.Y.S.2d 818 (1989); Ruder & Finn, Inc. v. Seaboard Sur. Co., 52 N.Y.2d 663, 422 N.E.2d 518, 439 N.Y.S.2d 858 (1981); Seaboard Sur. Co. v. Ralph Williams' Northwest Chrysler-Plymouth, Inc., 81 Wash. 2d 740, 504 P.2d 1139 (1973); Boggs v. Whitaker, Lipp & Helen, Inc., 56 Wash. App. 583, 784 P.2d 1273 (1990). *See also* Cort v. St. Paul Fire & Marine Ins. Cos., 311 F.3d 979 (9th Cir. 2002) (painting over an exterior wall mural did not create an "advertising injury"); Wake Stone Corp. v. Aetna Cas. & Sur. Co., 995 F. Supp. 612 (E.D.N.C. 1998) (policy covering libel and slander did not cover UDAP violations even though they arose out of same statements that had been alleged to be libelous).

694 *See* § 5.9.3.3, *supra*.

695 TIG Ins. Co. v. Dallas Basketball, Ltd., 2004 WL 243773 (Tex. App. Feb. 11, 2004); Western Rim Investment Advisors, Inc. v. Gulf Ins. Co., 269 F. Supp. 2d 836 (N.D. Tex. 2003); Hooters of Augusta, Inc. v. Am. Global Ins. Co., 272 F. Supp. 2d 1365 (S.D. Ga. 2003).

injury.[696] An unpublished California decision concludes that restitution ordered under one of its UDAP statutes was not "damages" within the meaning of an insurance policy that covered damages.[697]

Even if an insurance policy will pay on the consumer's claim, another issue is whether the now insolvent company kept the insurance coverage in force. If the insurance coverage pays on claims arising during the insurance policy, then the question is whether the coverage was in force at the time of the UDAP violation. If the coverage pays only on claims filed during the policy period, then the coverage will have to be in force at the time the consumer files the UDAP claim in court.

It may be with a failing company that the company requests its agent to renew insurance coverage, but the agent fails to do so. In that case, it may be possible to sue the insurance agent who agreed but failed to obtain insurance coverage. The consumer must show that the agent was negligent, that the insurance would have covered the loss, and the amount of the loss.[698]

696 Podiatry Ins. Co. of Am. v. Isham, 828 P.2d 59 (Wash. Ct. App. 1992).

697 TIG v. Andrews Sporting Goods, Inc., 2002 Cal. App. Unpub. LEXIS 2105 (June 12, 2002) (unpublished, citation limited) (suit under § 17200).

698 State *ex rel.* Fisher v. Warren Star Theater, 84 Ohio App. 3d 435, 616 N.E.2d 1192 (1992).

6.10.3 Consumer Recovery Funds

A number of states have set up consumer recovery funds, either for particular industries or for all consumer transactions. One specific form of such funds, Student Tuition Recovery Funds, relating to trade school fraud, is discussed at National Consumer Law Center, *Student Loan Law* § 9.6 (2d ed. 2002 and Supp.).

Where a company is insolvent, consumer recovery funds are an excellent avenue to explore. Where the fund only provides payment for certain types of judgments—for example, where the court finds "improper or dishonest conduct"—the advocate should make sure the default judgment complies with those requirements.

Every state has insurance guaranty funds that reimburse consumers when insurance companies become insolvent. But it may be hard to fit a UDAP claim under the scope of that type of fund.[699] Of course, what claims a recovery fund should pay in the final analysis is a matter of the legislative intent in setting up that fund.

Another common pitfall is not bringing claims against the recovery fund in a timely fashion. For example, the Virginia Contractors Transaction Recovery Act Fund requires claims to be made within one year of a final judgment.[700] The legislation also limits recovery to licensed contractors, thus not covering many fraudulent fly-by-night operations.

699 Bentley v. North Carolina Ins. Guaranty Ass'n, 107 N.C. App. 1, 418 S.E.2d 705 (1992).

700 Va. Code § 54.1-1120.

Chapter 7 Litigating UDAP Cases

7.1 Introduction

Previous chapters have analyzed major issues facing UDAP litigants: whether the seller's unfair or deceptive actions fall within the scope of the statute, whether the challenged practice violates the UDAP statute, and who can be held liable for the UDAP violation. But a number of other issues are important when litigating UDAP cases. The first question, of course, is whether the state UDAP statute authorizes a private right of action. Timing issues such as the statute of limitations and the effective date of the statute and its amendments are also raised in many UDAP cases. Some statutes or courts also create special preconditions to a private action, such as requirements that the consumer plaintiff have suffered ascertainable damage, that the action be in the public interest, or that the consumer give notice or exhaust non-litigation approaches before court action.

Jurisdictional issues are important in any lawsuit. UDAP litigants must be especially concerned with problems of jurisdiction over out-of-state sellers, choices of the proper state court, and whether there is federal court jurisdiction. There are also issues concerning whether binding arbitration provisions prevent UDAP court actions.

Careful pleading avoids pretrial delays and frames the case in an attractive light. Prompt and aggressive discovery is often essential to document the defendant's unfair and deceptive practices. Jury trial is an option in a number of jurisdictions.

Sellers have often challenged UDAP statutes on various constitutional grounds. While consumer litigants need not worry that they are utilizing an unconstitutional statute, they must be able to respond to constitutional defenses, whether meritorious or used merely to delay and confuse.

In dealing with jurisdictional and procedural questions in a UDAP case, it is important to remember that UDAP statutes are remedial and must be liberally interpreted to accomplish their purposes.[1] This rule applies to procedural issues as well as to substantive issues.[2]

1 *See* §§ 2.1.3 and 3.1.2, *supra*.

2 *See, e.g.*, Avery v. Industry Mortg. Co., 135 F. Supp. 2d 840 (W.D. Mich. 2001) (construing loss requirement); Patterson v. Beall, 19 P.3d 839 (Okla. 2000) (declining to read public interest precondition into statute); Williams v. Hills Fitness Center, Inc., 705 S.W.2d 189 (Tex. App. 1985) (liberal construction of notice requirement); State v. Therrien, 633 A.2d 272 (Vt. 1993).

7.2 Is There a Private UDAP Right of Action?

7.2.1 *Private Right Unambiguously Exists in Every State Except Iowa*

The first issue in any private UDAP case is whether there is a private right of action under the statute. Allowing a private cause of action deters violations and allows consumers to serve as private attorneys general, a necessary supplement to state enforcement actions given the limited resources available to the state.[3] A private UDAP damages remedy clearly exists in every state except Iowa.

Most state UDAP statutes explicitly authorize a private right of action.[4] North Dakota, which formerly was an exception, amended its UDAP statute in 1991 to explicitly provide a private right of action.[5] Arkansas did the same in 1999, authorizing a private cause of action for actual damages and attorney fees for any person who suffers actual damage or injury as a result of a UDAP violation.[6] One of

3 *See* Baierl v. McTaggart, 629 N.W.2d 277 (Wis. 2001).

4 *See* Appendix A, *infra*. The availability of explicit private actions in two states requires special note. Nev. Rev. Stat. § 41.600 provides for a private damage action for violations of Nev. Rev. Stat. §§ 598.0915–.0925. Although Okla. Stat. Ann. tit. 15, § 761 was amended in 1980 with the apparent intent to add a private UDAP remedy, the Oklahoma Supreme Court interpreted the poorly drafted and inconsistent language of that amendment as not providing for a private right of action. *See* Holbert v. Echeveiria, 744 P.2d 960 (Okla. 1987) (interpreting § 761.1(A)). The Oklahoma legislature amended the statute again in 1988 to make clear that there is a private right of action under § 761.1(A). *See* 1988 Okla. Sess. Laws 161.

5 N.D. Cent. Code § 51-15-09, *as amended by* 1991 N.D. Laws 529 § 1 (effective July 7, 1991).

6 Ark. Stat. Ann. § 4-88-113(f). In 1993, the Arkansas legislature had amended the statute to provide a private cause of action for elderly or disabled individuals. Ark. Stat. Ann. § 4-88-204. Even before these amendments, the Arkansas Supreme Court had come very close to recognizing an implied right of action under the Arkansas UDAP statute. Berkeley Pump Co. v. Reed-Joseph Land Co., 279 Ark. 384, 653 S.W.2d 128 (1983). *See also* New Equity Security Holdings Committee for Golden Gulf v. Phillips, 97 B.R. 492 (E.D. Ark. 1989) (allowing consumer to raise Arkansas UDAP claim by way of defense to

Delaware's two UDAP statutes, the Deceptive Trade Practices Act,[7] explicitly provides a private injunctive remedy and treble damages, but the Delaware Supreme Court has held that these remedies are not available to retail consumers, but only to plaintiffs who have a business or trade interest at stake.[8] The other Delaware UDAP statute, the Consumer Fraud Act,[9] formerly did not explicitly provide for any type of private right of action, the Delaware Supreme Court[10] found an implied private damage remedy,[11] and in 2003 the legislature amended the statute to make this remedy explicit.[12] The Arizona UDAP statute does not explicitly authorize a private cause of action, but the Arizona Supreme Court has found an implied private UDAP damage remedy.[13] Hawaii interprets its UDAP statute in light of legislative history to allow a private cause of action for consumer claims of unfair and deceptive acts and practices, but not for anti-competitive conduct.[14] The entrustment of UDAP enforcement authority to a state official such as the state attorney general does not diminish the consumer's right to bring a private cause of action.[15]

7.2.2 *Implying a Private UDAP Right of Action in Iowa*

There is an implied private right of action in Iowa for violation of a criminal statute.[16] This principle has recently been codified, at least to a certain extent, at Iowa Code Ann. § 706A, the Iowa Ongoing Criminal Conduct Act. That statute is similar to the federal RICO statute, but is triggered by *any* act committed for financial gain on a continuing basis that is punishable in Iowa as an indictable offense.[17] It provides for treble damages, costs and attorney fees, injunctive relief, and even divestiture.

Unfortunately, however, the Iowa Supreme Court has ruled that a violation of its UDAP statute is not a crime.[18] Since the Ongoing Criminal Conduct Act provides a remedy only for acts that are indictable offenses, this decision appears to foreclose private UDAP suits except for acts that also violate some provision of the criminal code. The Iowa Supreme Court's decision also contrasts the UDAP statute with other consumer protection statutes that explicitly create a private right of action, and declines to find a private right of action implicit in Iowa's UDAP statute.[19]

Nevertheless, a number of Iowa consumer protection statutes *do* have criminal penalties, and may be the basis for private causes of action for conduct that also violates the UDAP statute.[20] In addition, some consumer frauds may amount to theft offenses.

There are also several consumer protection statutes in Iowa that overlap to some extent with the UDAP statute and that offer explicit private causes of action. For example, the health spa statute,[21] a statute relating to prize promotions,[22]

collection action); Lemarco v. Wood, 305 Ark. 1, 804 S.W.2d 724 (1991) (certifying class to litigate, *inter alia*, alleged violations of Arkansas UDAP statute).

7 Del. Code Ann. tit. 6, §§ 2531–2536.

8 Grand Ventures, Inc. v. Whaley, 632 A.2d 63 (Del. 1993); Crosse v. BCBSD, Inc., 2003 WL 22214021, at *4 (Del. Super. Sept. 22, 2003). *Accord* Calbert v. Volkswagen of Am., Inc., 634 A.2d 938 (Del. 1993) (table, text available at 1993 WL 478079) (consumer plaintiff has no standing to sue under DTPA, Del. Code tit. 6, §§ 2531–2536).

9 Del. Code Ann. tit. 6, §§ 2511–2527, 2580–2584.

10 Young v. Joyce, 351 A.2d 857 (Del. 1975). *Accord* Grand Ventures, Inc. v. Whaley, 632 A.2d 63 (Del. 1993); Crosse v. BCBSD, Inc., 2003 WL 22214021, at *4 (Del. Super. Sept. 22, 2003).

11 Del. Code Ann. tit. 6, §§ 2511–2527.

12 Del. Code Ann. tit. 6, § 2525(a).

13 Sellinger v. Freeway Mobile Home Sales, 110 Ariz. 573, 576, 521 P.2d 1119, 1122 (1974).

14 Robert's Hawaii School Bus, Inc. v. Laupahoehoe Transportation, Inc., 91 Haw. 224, 982 P.2d 853 (1999). This decision reaffirms the holding in Ai v. Frank Huff Agency Ltd., 61 Haw. 607, 607 P.2d 1304 (1980) that consumers have a private cause of action for unfair and deceptive acts that violate Haw. Rev. Stat. § 480-2, but overrules dictum in that case that extended the private cause of action to antitrust violations.

15 Fuller v. Pacific Medical Collections, Inc., 891 P.2d 300 (Haw. Ct. App. 1995).

16 Hall v. Montgomery Ward, 252 N.W.2d 421 (Iowa 1977).

17 Iowa Code § 706A does not directly prohibit these predicate offenses. Instead, like the federal RICO statute, it prohibits investing the proceeds of such activity, acquiring or maintaining an interest in or control of any enterprise through specified unlawful activity, knowingly conducting or participating in the affairs of any enterprise through specified unlawful activity, or conspiring to do any of the above.

18 Molo Oil Co. v. River City Ford Truck Sales, 578 N.W.2d 222 (Iowa 1998).

19 The court rejected the views of courts in other states that had found a private right of action in similar circumstances: Sellinger v. Freeway Mobile Home Sales, Inc., 110 Ariz. 573, 521 P.2d 1119 (1974); Young v. Joyce, 351 A.2d 857 (Del. 1975); Rice v. Snarlin, Inc., 131 Ill. App. 2d 434, 266 N.E.2d 183 (1970) (the Illinois UDAP statute has since been amended to explicitly provide a private right of action. 815 Ill. Comp. Stat. Ann. § 505/10a). *See also* Fargo Women's Health Organization v. FM Women's Help & Caring Connection, 444 N.W.2d 683 (N.D. 1989) (implying a private right of action under North Dakota false advertising statutes), *overruled by* Trade 'N Post v. World Duty Free Americas, Inc., 628 N.W.2d 707 (N.D. 2001) (finding no private cause of action under Unfair Discrimination Law or Unfair Trade Practice Law, both of which deal with anti-competitive conduct; interpreting *Fargo Women's Health* as merely providing that violation of false advertising law was evidence of negligence). *But see* Johnston v. Beneficial Mgmt. Corp., 85 Wash. 2d 637, 538 P.2d 510 (1975) (court refused to imply a private remedy for an early version of the Washington UDAP statute that did not expressly provide such a remedy).

20 *See, e.g.*, Iowa Code Ann. §§ 321.69 (damage disclosure law; violations is defined as "fraudulent practice," which is criminalized by Iowa Code §§ 714.8–714.13), 321.71 (odometer law; violation is fraudulent practice), 714.8(15) (telemarketing fraud; violation is fraudulent practice), and § 555A.6 (door-to-door sales).

21 Iowa Code Ann. § 552.13.

22 Iowa Code Ann. § 714B.8.

the Consumer Credit Code,[23] the telephone slamming and cramming law,[24] the state identity theft law,[25] the door-to-door sales and debt collection laws,[26] and a law prohibiting e-mail spamming[27] all explicitly authorize private causes of action.

Iowa consumers may also be able to raise UDAP claims defensively. Courts in other states have allowed consumers to raise UDAP claims by way of a defense to a collection action even when the statute did not authorize a private cause of action.[28] Similarly, a New York court in *Donnelly v. Mustang Pools, Inc.*[29] canceled a contract which did not contain notice, as required by a Federal Trade Commission rule, that the consumer has a three-day cooling-off period for door-to-door sales. This case is noteworthy because the Federal Trade Commission rule can not be privately enforced and New York's UDAP statute at the time did not provide either an express or a court-interpreted private right of action. Illegality is grounds at common law for refusing to enforce a contract, and if a bargain violates a UDAP statute, it should not be enforced.[30]

7.2.3 Can Consumers Bring Actions Under UDTPA-Type Statutes?

There is an issue as to whether consumers, or only business competitors, can bring actions under the nine UDAP statutes patterned after the Uniform Deceptive Trade Practices Act (UDTPA).[31] These statutes provide only a private injunctive remedy, without an explicit private damage remedy.[32] As a result, there is at least an appearance that the statutes were chiefly intended to stop unfair methods of competition, rather than provide consumer redress. Still the majority rule is that consumers *can* bring an action under those statutes patterned after the UDTPA.[33] While in each of these nine states a second UDAP statute provides an explicit damage remedy for consumers, the UDTPA statutes are sometimes useful in that their scope may be broader, or their remedy of attorney fees (typically attorney fees "may" be awarded in exceptional cases) and injunctive relief may be attractive.

---

23 Iowa Code Ann. §§ 537.5201–.5203.

24 Iowa Code Ann. § 714D.6.

25 Iowa Code Ann. § 714.16B.

26 Iowa Code § 537.5201 (allowing private cause of actions for violations of debt collection restrictions set forth at § 537.7103 and door-to-door sales restrictions set forth at § 537.3501).

27 Iowa Code Ann. § 714E.1.

28 New Equity Security Holders Committee for Golden Gulf v. Phillips, 97 B.R. 492 (E.D. Ark. 1989); *In re* Saler, 84 B.R. 45 (Bankr. E.D. Pa. 1988) (UDAP claim used by way of recoupment even where no private remedy for that type of claim); *In re* Jungkurth, 74 B.R. 323 (Bankr. E.D. Pa. 1987) (same).

29 84 Misc. 2d 28, 374 N.Y.S.2d 967 (Sup. Ct. 1975).

30 *See* Farnsworth on Contracts §§ 5.1, 5.5, 9.5 (2d ed. 1998). *See also* § 9.5.8, *infra*.

31 Del Code Ann. tit. 6, § 2531; Ga. Code Ann. § 10-1-370; Haw. Rev. Stat. § 481A; 815 Ill. Comp. Stat. Ann. § 510; Me. Rev. Stat. Ann. tit. 10, § 1211; Minn. Stat. Ann. § 325D.43; Neb. Rev. Stat. § 87-301; Ohio Rev. Code Ann. § 4165.01 (Baldwin); Okla. Stat. Ann. tit. 78, § 51 (West).

32 Gardner v. First Am. Title Ins. Co., 296 F. Supp. 2d 1011 (D. Minn. 2003); Lawyers Title Ins. Corp. v. Dearborn Title Corp., 904 F. Supp. 818 (N.D. Ill. 1995); Bentley v. Slavik, 663 F. Supp. 736 (S.D. Ill. 1987); Pain Prevention Lab v. Electronic Waveform Labs, 657 F. Supp. 1486 (N.D. Ill. 1987); National Educational Advertising Servs., Inc. v. Cass Student Advertising, 454 F. Supp. 71 (N.D. Ill. 1977); Glazewski v. Coronet Ins. Co., 108 Ill. 2d 243, 483 N.E.2d 1263 (1985); Empire Home Servs., Inc. v. Carpet Am., 653 N.E.2d 852 (Ill. App. Ct. 1995) (only injunctive relief and attorney fees are available in UDTPA suit between business competitors); Crinkley v. Dow Jones & Co., 67 Ill. App. 3d 869 (1979); Brooks v. Midas-Int'l Corp., 47 Ill. App. 3d 266, 361 N.E.2d 815 (1977); Simmons v. Modern Aero, Inc., 603 N.W.2d 336 (Minn. App. 1999) (Minnesota DTPA only authorizes injunctive relief; Minn. Stat. § 8.31 gives a private cause of action for damages for violation of other consumer protection statutes but not DTPA); Mountz v. Global Vision Prods., Inc., 770 N.Y.S.2d 603 (Sup. Ct. 2003) (no private cause of action for damages under Maine DTPA). *See also* Grand Ventures, Inc. v. Whaley, 632 A.2d 63 (Del. 1993) (Delaware DTPA was amended to allow treble damages, but suit is allowed only if defendant is interfering with plaintiff's business or trade interest). *But see* Duncavage v. Allen, 147 Ill. App. 3d 88, 497 N.E.2d 433 (1986) (court incorporates UDTPA itemized violations into other state UDAP statute that does provide private damage remedies).

33 Garland v. Mobile Oil Corp., 340 F. Supp. 1095 (N.D. Ill. 1972); Robinson v. Toyota Motor Credit Corp., 315 Ill. App. 3d 1086, 735 N.E.2d 724, 249 Ill. Dec. 120 (2000) (consumers can seek injunction but not damages under UDTPA), *aff'd in part, rev'd in part on other grounds*, 201 Ill. 2d 403, 775 N.E.2d 951 (2002); People v. Datacom Sys. Corp., 176 Ill. App. 3d 697, 531 N.E.2d 839 (1988), *aff'd on other grounds*, 146 Ill. 2d 1, 585 N.E.2d 51 (1991); Williams v. Bruno Appliance & Furniture Mart, 62 Ill. App. 3d 219, 379 N.E.2d 52 (1978); Brooks v. Midas-Int'l Corp., 47 Ill. App. 3d 266, 361 N.E.2d 815 (1977). *See also* State *ex rel.* Hatch v. Publishers Clearing House, Clearinghouse No. 53,567 (D. Minn. June 12, 2000) (DTPA protects consumers as well as competitors, so attorney general can sue to prevent harm to consumers); Glazewski v. Coronet Ins. Co., 108 Ill. 2d 243, 483 N.E.2d 1263 (1985) (consumers can bring injunctive action, but only if otherwise likely to be harmed). *But see* Grand Ventures, Inc. v. Whaley, 632 A.2d 63 (Del. 1993) (litigant has standing under UDTPA only when the litigant has a business or trade interest at stake which is the subject of interference by the unfair or deceptive trade practices of the defendant); Crosse v. BCBSD, Inc., 2003 WL 22214021, at *4 (Del. Super. Sept. 22, 2003) (consumers do not have standing to bring DTPA claims); S&R Assocs. v. Shell Oil Co., 725 A.2d 431 (Del. Super. 1998) (only competing businesses can sue); Wald v. Wilmington Trust Co., 552 A.2d 853 (Del. Super. Ct. 1988); Trabardo v. Kenton Ruritan Club Inc., 517 A.2d 706 (Del. Super. Ct. 1986); Galasso Import Co. v. Porter, CA No. 79A-JA-19 (Del. Super. Ct. 1978); Sexton v. J.C. Penney Co., CA 77C-DE-74 (Del. Super. Ct. 1978); Conatzer v. Am. Mercury Ins. Co., 15 P.3d 1252 (Okla. App. 2000) (UDTPA only applies to competing businesses).

7.3 Statutes of Limitations

7.3.1 Applicable Limitation Period

In analyzing statute of limitations issues, the first step is determining the applicable time period after which an action is barred. Some UDAP statutes of limitations are found in the UDAP statute itself. In that case, the specific UDAP limitations period should control, even if another limitation period also applies. For example, Massachusetts applies the four-year UDAP limitations period even where the challenged conduct is specifically prohibited by another statute more particularly regulating that conduct, and where the other statute has a one-year statute of limitations.[34] The California Supreme Court has reached the same conclusion.[35] Similarly, the Connecticut six-year UDAP statute of limitations, rather than the one-year limitation for suits on an insurance policy, applies to UDAP claims involving an insurer's unreasonable claims settlement procedures.[36]

In other jurisdictions where no limitation period is found in the UDAP statute and the state has several general statutes of limitations applying to differing categories of actions, the court must determine which statute of limitations applies to a UDAP action. Thus, there may be different limitations periods for an action arising from a nonpenal statutory right, a tort, a contract, or a penal statute. When a UDAP statute does not have a specific limitations period, consumer litigants must familiarize themselves with all of the state's general statutes of limitations and determine which applies.

Massachusetts' highest court, faced with a decision whether a general tort or contract limitations period applied to a UDAP action alleging emotional distress from a debt collection action, decided that the fact situation essentially involved personal injury and was thus tortious in nature. The longer contract period would apply to a UDAP claim to recover for money paid.[37] (Massachusetts has since enacted a four-year limitations period specifically for the UDAP statute.[38]) West Virginia has determined that claims under its Unfair Insurance Practices Act are tortious in nature and are therefore governed by a one-year statute of limitations.[39]

A 1979 amendment to the Texas UDAP statute explicitly provides for a two-year statute of limitations.[40] Use of this limitations period is mandatory for causes of action arising under the Texas UDAP statute, and the consumer may not elect to use a longer limitations period applicable under a different statute to seek relief under the Texas UDAP statute.[41] The specific tolling provision in the UDAP statute precludes application of other court-made exceptions to limitations.[42] But for actions before the effective date of that amendment, the Texas courts applied an approach similar to Massachusetts.[43]

Many states take a different approach, treating the UDAP action as one based on a statute and selecting the state's general limitations period or a period that the legislature creates for special statutes. An Arizona court has ruled that, where a state had a general statute of limitations applicable to actions created by statute, that period, and not the common law fraud limitation, should be used since the UDAP statute creates a new liability beyond common law fraud.[44]

---

34 Rita v. Carella, 394 Mass. 822, 477 N.E.2d 1016 (1985). *See also* Schwartz v. Travelers Indemnity Co., 740 N.E.2d 1039 (Mass. App. Ct. 2001) (UDAP limitations period applies even when case is based on violation of unfair insurance practices act); McAdams v. Capitol Products Corp., 810 S.W.2d 290 (Tex. App. 1991) (UDAP two year period applies for UDAP action based on breach of U.C.C. warranty, not U.C.C.'s four year limitations period). *But see* Nunheimer v. Continental Ins. Co., 68 F. Supp. 2d 75 (D. Mass. 1999) (2-year statute of limitations for insurance claims overrides UDAP statute's longer period); Walsh v. Barry-Harlem Corp., 649 N.E.2d 614 (Ill. App. Ct. 1995) (where both the UDAP and a more specific statute of limitations apply, the more specific statute prevails). *But cf.* Fine v. Huygens, DiMella, Shaffer & Assocs., 783 N.E.2d 842 (Mass. App. 2003) (applying 6-year statute of repose to UDAP claim against design professional arising out of improvement of real property).

35 Cortez v. Purolator Air Filtration Prods. Co., 23 Cal. 4th 163, 999 P.2d 706 (2000) (construing § 17200).

36 Lees v. Middlesex Ins. Co., 219 Conn. 644, 594 A.2d 952 (1991).

37 Baldassari v. Public Fin. Trust, 369 Mass. 33, 337 N.E.2d 701 (1975).

38 *See* Mass. Gen. Laws Ann. ch. 260, § 5A; *see also* Levin v. Berley, 728 F.2d 551 (1st Cir. 1984) (Massachusetts law).

39 Wilt v. State Automobile Mut. Ins. Co., 506 S.E.2d 608 (W. Va. 1998). *Accord* Klettner v. State Farm Mut. Automobile Ins. Co., 205 W. Va. 587, 519 S.E.2d 870 (1999).

40 Texas Soil Recycling, Inc. v. Intercargo Ins. Co., 273 F.3d 644 (5th Cir. 2001) (Texas law); Maltz v. Union Carbide Chemicals & Plastics Co., 992 F. Supp. 286 (S.D.N.Y. 1998); Milestone Properties, Inc. v. Federated Metals Corp., 867 S.W.2d 113 (Tex. App. 1993).

41 Smith v. Herco, Inc., 1995 Tex. App. LEXIS 965 (1995); Calabria v. Merrill, Lynch, Pierce, Fenner & Smith, Inc., 855 F. Supp. 172 (N.D. Tex. 1994).

42 Underkofler v. Vanasek, 53 S.W.3d 343 (Tex. 2001).

43 *Applying limitations period for contracts to UDAP sales and warranty claims*: Employees Cas. Co. v. Fambro, 694 S.W.2d 449 (Tex. App. 1985); Jim Walter Homes Inc. v. Castillo, 616 S.W.2d 630 (Tex. Civ. App. 1981); Jim Walter Homes Inc. v. Chapa, 614 S.W.2d 838 (Tex. Civ. App. 1981); Jim Walter Homes Inc. v. White, 617 S.W.2d 767 (Tex. Civ. App. 1981). *Applying limitations period for debts not in writing*: Marcotte v. American Motorists Ins. Co., 709 F.2d 378 (5th Cir. 1983). *But see* Holland Mortgage & Inv. Corp. v. Bone, 751 S.W.2d 515 (Tex. App. 1987) (applying instead Tex. Rev. Civ. Stat. Ann. art. 5529 (Vernon 1958)). *Applying limitations period for fraud to fraud-type UDAP claim*: Marcotte v. American Motorists Ins. Co., 709 F.2d 378 (5th Cir. 1983); Eagle Properties Ltd. v. Scharbauer, 758 S.W.2d 911 (Tex. App. 1988), *aff'd in part, rev'd in part, remanded*, 807 S.W.2d 714 (Tex. 1990), *on remand*, 816 S.W.2d 559 (Tex. App. 1991). *Applying six-year limitations period for mandatory arbitration to UDAP claim against securities dealer*: Calabria v. Merrill Lynch, Pierce, Fenner & Smith, Inc., 855 F. Supp. 172 (N.D. Tex. 1994).

44 Murry v. Western Am. Mortgage Co., 124 Ariz. 387, 604 P.2d

Similarly, the Montana Supreme Court applies the two-year limitations period for actions upon a liability created by statute other than a penalty or forfeiture.[45] Maine's highest court uses the state's general six-year limitations period for UDAP actions, and not the four-year limitations period for warranty actions.[46] Minnesota uses the six-year period for statutory actions, not the two-year limitations period for penalty actions, because the UDAP statute is remedial, not penal in nature.[47] But Maryland's highest court has rejected the argument that the twelve-year statute of limitations for statutory "specialties" applies to UDAP actions.[48] Instead, the state's general three-year statute of limitations applies.[49]

In North Carolina, before the state UDAP statute was amended to provide for a specific limitations period, a state court was faced with the choice of utilizing a three-year period for liabilities created by statute or the one-year period for penalty actions by individuals. The court's decision was complicated by the state UDAP statute's provision for mandatory treble damages. The court selected the three-year period, ruling, after extensive discussion, that the statute was not punitive.[50]

New York's highest court has held that its deceptive practices act is governed by a three-year statute of limitations for actions to recover upon a liability created by statute.[51] Resolving a series of conflicting lower court cases, the court rejected the state's limitation period for fraud because UDAP is broader than fraud.

In Kansas, courts were torn between the state's one-year statute of limitations for actions upon a statutory penalty or the three-year limitations period for actions upon a liability created by a statute until the Kansas Supreme Court ruled in 2000 that the three-year statute applies.[52] The Kansas UDAP statute allows the consumer to seek actual damages or a statutory penalty of $5000, whichever is greater. The court was particularly persuaded by the fact that the statutory penalty was not free-standing, but merely an alternative to actual damages, so the penalty provision was more remedial than punitive.

A Missouri court has held that where the state brings an action for restitution and injunctive relief, the statute is remedial and the three-year limitations period for statutory actions applies. Only where enforcement of a penalty is sought would the court consider using the limitations period for penal actions.[53]

In Oklahoma, an appellate court has adopted a similar approach, ruling that the three-year statute of limitations period for liabilities created by statute applies to UDAP damage claims, but a one-year period applies to claims seeking penalties.[54]

A Pennsylvania court has ruled that the two-year period for deceit is not applicable because the UDAP statute is broader than common law deceit. Instead, the state's general six-year limitations period should be used so that the limitations period will not depend on whether a UDAP action is based on deceit or some other theory.[55] A federal court has opined that Washington UDAP claims are governed by a catchall three-year statute of limitations for claims for injury to the person or rights.[56] The highest court in the District of Columbia has taken a similar approach, holding that a residual three-year statute of limitations rather than the UCC four-year statute of limitations for breach of contract applied to a UDAP claim that a cable television company charged excessive late fees.[57]

The Virginia UDAP statute was amended effective July 1, 1995, to set a two-year statute of limitations.[58] For actions that accrued before that date, two trial courts applied a one-year catchall statute of limitations.[59] The Virginia Supreme Court has held that claims under a different statute,

651 (Ct. App. 1979). *See also* Richards v. Powercraft Homes, Inc., 678 P.2d 449 (Ariz. Ct. App. 1983), *aff'd on this ground, but vacated in part on other grounds*, 678 P.2d 427 (Ariz. 1984).

45 Osterman v. Sears, Roebuck & Co., 80 P.3d 435 (Mont. 2003).

46 State v. Bob Chambers Ford, Inc., 522 A.2d 362 (Me. 1987) (applying Me. Rev. Stat. tit. 14, § 752).

47 Estate v. Life Care Retirement Communities, Inc., 505 N.W.2d 78 (Minn. Ct. App. 1993).

48 Greene Tree Home Owners Ass'n v. Greene Tree Assocs., 358 Md. 453, 749 A.2d 806 (2000).

49 Miller v. Pacific Shore Funding, 224 F. Supp. 2d 977 (D. Md. 2002).

50 Holley v. Coggin Pontiac, 43 N.C. App. 229, 259 S.E.2d 1 (1979). *Accord* Reid v. New Jersey Home Energy Center, Clearinghouse No. 46,800 (N.J. Super. Ct. Law Div. Sept. 6, 1991).

51 Gaidon v. Guardian Life Ins. Co., 96 N.Y.2d 201, 727 N.Y.S.2d 30 (2001) (§ 349 case).

52 Alexander v. Certified Master Builders Corp., 268 Kan. 812, 1 P.3d 899 (2000). For discussion of the division of opinion among lower courts prior to the Kansas Supreme Court's ruling, see Griffin v. Security Pacific Automotive Fin. Servs. Corp., 33 F. Supp. 2d 926 (D. Kan. 1998).

53 State *ex rel.* Webster v. Myers, 779 S.W.2d 286 (Mo. Ct. App. 1989). *Cf.* Alexander v. Certified Master Builders Corp., 268 Kan. 812, 1 P.3d 899 (2000) (rejecting use of different limitations period depending on whether suit seeks actual damages or statutory penalty; longer limitations period applies to all UDAP suits).

54 Fuller v. Sight N Sound Appliance Centers, Inc., 982 P.2d 528 (Okla. App. 1999).

55 Gabriel v. O'Hara, 534 A.2d 488 (Pa. Super. Ct. 1987). *Accord* Santana Prods., Inc. v. Bobrick Washroom Equipment, Inc., 249 F. Supp. 2d 463 (M.D. Pa. 2003); Algrant v. Evergreen Valley Nurseries Ltd. P'ship, 941 F. Supp. 495 (E.D. Pa. 1996), *aff'd on other grounds*, 126 F.3d 178 (3d Cir. 1997); *In re* Milbourne, 108 B.R. 522 (Bankr. E.D. Pa. 1989). *See also* Woody v. State Farm Fire & Cas. Co., 965 F. Supp. 691 (E.D. Pa. 1997) (applying six-year period to state unfair insurance practices statute).

56 Watkins v. Peterson Enterprises, Inc., 57 F. Supp. 2d 1102 (E.D. Wash. 1999).

57 District Cablevision Ltd. P'ship v. Bassin, 828 A.2d 714 (D.C. 2003).

58 Va. Code § 59.1-204.1(A).

59 Patterson v. Bob Wade Lincoln-Mercury, Inc., 48 Va. Cir. 471, 1999 Va. Cir. LEXIS 121 (1999); Byrd v. Crosstate Mortg. & Invs., 34 Va. Cir. 17, 1994 Va. Cir. LEXIS 38 (1994).

the false advertising statute, are different enough from fraud that the "catchall" statute of limitations, currently two years, rather than the limitations period for fraud, applies.[60]

One Illinois UDAP statute explicitly provides for a three-year limitations period.[61] Illinois courts apparently apply the same limitations period to the other Illinois UDAP statute,[62] even though that statute has no explicit limitations period.[63] The Eleventh Circuit, however, has reached the opposite result under Georgia law. While one UDAP statute had a two-year limitations period, the court did not use that period to determine the limitations period under the Georgia version of the Uniform Deceptive Trade Practices Act. Instead the court used the state's four-year period that applies to fraud and other injuries to personalty.[64] Nebraska's statute based on the Uniform Deceptive Trade Practices Act requires suit be to brought within four years of the date of purchase,[65] while its other UDAP statute requires suit within four years after the cause of action accrues.[66] New Jersey applies a six-year statute of limitations to UDAP claims.[67] A Georgia case holds that the consumer must file the UDAP suit, not merely give the mandatory thirty-day notice, within the limitations period.[68]

7.3.2 When Does the Period Start to Run?

7.3.2.1 Discovery Rule

The second step in analyzing statute of limitations issues is to determine when the time period starts to run. The general rule is that the limitations period begins from the time a reasonable person would be put on notice concerning the facts constituting the deception.[69] The burden is generally on the seller to plead and prove a statute of limitations

60 Parker-Smith v. Sto Corp., 262 Va. 432, 551 S.E.2d 615 (2001).

61 815 Ill. Comp. Stat. Ann. § 505/10a(e). *But see* Walsh v. Barry-Harlem Corp., 649 N.E.2d 614 (Ill. App. Ct. 1995) (where both the UDAP and the more specific statute of limitations for medical malpractice cases apply, the more specific statute prevails).

62 815 Ill. Comp. Stat. Ann. § 510.

63 Elrad v. United Life & Accident Ins. Co., 624 F. Supp. 742 (N.D. Ill. 1985). *See also* Juszczak v. Blommer Chocolate Co., 1999 U.S. Dist. LEXIS 17230 (N.D. Ill. Sept. 30, 1999) (applying 3-year statute of limitations to claims under both statutes).

64 Kason Indus., Inc. v. Component Hardware Group, Inc., 120 F.3d 1199 (11th Cir. 1997) (Georgia law).

65 Neb. Rev. Stat. § 87-303.10. *See* Meyer Brothers v. Travelers Ins. Co., 250 Neb. 389, 551 N.W.2d 1 (1996).

66 Neb. Rev. Stat. § 59-1612.

67 D'Angelo v. Miller Yacht Sales, 261 N.J. Super. 683, 619 A.2d 689 (1992).

68 Greene v. Team Properties, Inc., 247 Ga. App. 544, 544 S.E.2d 726 (2001).

69 Peter Farrell Supercars, Inc. v. Monsen, 2003 WL 22852654 (4th Cir. Dec. 3, 2003) (unpublished, citation limited) (Va. law); Mackey v. Judy's Foods, Inc., 867 F.2d 325 (6th Cir. 1989) (Tennessee law); Levin v. Berley, 728 F.2d 551 (1st Cir. 1984) (Massachusetts law); Chicago Board Options Exch. v. Conn. Gen. Life Ins., 713 F.2d 254 (7th Cir. 1983) (Illinois law) (period begins when plaintiff first experiences all the elements of injury stemming from deceptive acts); Marcotte v. American Motorists Ins. Co., 709 F.2d 378 (5th Cir. 1983) (Texas law) (period begins when became aware of deception); Zamboni v. Aladan Corp., 304 F. Supp. 2d 218 (D. Mass. 2004) (reasonable jury could find that plaintiff was not on notice of cause of action in light of conflicting medical diagnoses and lack of information that manufacturer's product caused illness); Terry v. Community Bank of Northern Virginia, 255 F. Supp. 2d 817 (W.D. Tenn. 2003); Hunton v. Guardian Life Ins. Co. of Am., 243 F. Supp. 2d 686 (S.D. Tex. 2002), *aff'd without op.*, 2003 WL 21418107 (5th Cir. June 10, 2003); Smith v. Brown & Williamson Tobacco Corp., 108 F. Supp. 2d 12 (D.D.C. 2000); Weil v. Long Island Sav. Bank, 77 F. Supp. 2d 313 (E.D.N.Y. 1999); Maltz v. Union Carbide Chemicals & Plastics Co., 992 F. Supp. 286 (S.D.N.Y. 1998) (Massachusetts law); Kuiper v. American Cyanamid Co., 913 F. Supp. 1236 (E.D. Wis. 1996), *aff'd*, 131 F.3d 656 (7th Cir. 1997); Liner v. Dicresce, 905 F. Supp. 280 (M.D.N.C. 1994); Pucci v. Litwin, 828 F. Supp. 1285 (N.D. Ill. 1993); Neill v. Rusk, 745 F. Supp. 362 (E.D. La. 1990); Prescott v. Morton Int'l Inc., 769 F. Supp. 404 (D. Mass. 1990); Attorney General v. Dickson, 717 F. Supp. 1090 (D. Md. 1989) (statute of limitations for AG's suit for restitution runs from AG's discovery of UDAP violation, but statute of limitations for civil fine runs from date violation is complete); Continental Grain Co. v. Pullman Standard, Inc., 690 F. Supp. 628 (N.D. Ill. 1988); Elrad v. United Life & Accident Ins. Co., 624 F. Supp. 742 (N.D. Ill. 1985) (period begins when should have known injury and known that it was wrongfully caused); Barr Co. v. Safeco Ins. Co., 583 F. Supp. 248 (N.D. Ill. 1984) (period begins when insurance company refuses claim); Curiakala v. Economy Autos, Ltd., 587 F. Supp. 1462 (N.D. Ind. 1984) (intentional concealment tolls statute of limitations); *In re* Gardner, 218 B.R. 338 (Bankr. E.D. Pa. 1998); London v. Green Acres Trust, 159 Ariz. 136, 765 P.2d 538 (Ct. App. 1988); Teran v. Citicorp Person-to-Person Fin. Center, 146 Ariz. 370, 706 P.2d 382 (Ct. App. 1985) (consumer should have discovered fraud in contract immediately, not three years later); Richards v. Powercraft Homes, Inc. 678 P.2d 449 (Ariz. Ct. App. 1983), *aff'd on this ground, vacated in part on other grounds*, 678 P.2d 427 (Ariz. 1984) (period begins to run when consumers learned facts that would cause a reasonable person to make an inquiry that would have led to discovery of the fraud); Clingerman v. Ford Motor Credit Co., Clearinghouse No. 50,427 (Ariz. Super. Ct. Nov. 1, 1994) (fraudulent concealment tolls UDAP statute of limitations); Stiff v. BilDen Homes, Inc., 2003 WL 22019865 (Colo. App. Aug. 28, 2003) (applying UDAP statute's explicit discovery rule but finding claim barred); Robinson v. Lynmar Racquet Club, Inc., 851 P.2d 274 (Colo. Ct. App. 1993); Pack & Process, Inc. v. Celotex Corp., 503 A.2d 646 (Del. Super. Ct. 1985); Leibert v. Finance Factors Ltd., 788 P.2d 833 (Haw. 1990); Gredell v. Wyeth Laboratories, Inc., 803 N.E.2d 541 (Ill. App. 2004); Harris Auction Galleries, Inc. v. Legum, Clearinghouse No. 36,565 (Md. Cir. Ct. Baltimore Cty. 1984); Fine v. Huygens, DiMella, Shaffer & Assocs., 783 N.E.2d 842 (Mass. App. Ct. 2003); Szymanski v. Boston Mut. Life Ins. Co., 778 N.E.2d 16 (Mass. App. Ct. 2002) (question of fact when reasonable consumer should have discovered that assurance of vanishing insurance premium was deceptive); Schwartz v. Travelers Indemnity Co., 740 N.E.2d 1039 (Mass. App. Ct. 2001) (discovery rule applies when the acts underlying the UDAP claims are tortious in nature); International Mobiles Corp. v. Corroon &

defense. But if the consumer is relying on an exception to the statute of limitations such as the discovery rule, it is prudent practice for the consumer to plead and prove that fact.[70] The date of a UDAP plaintiff's discovery of the violation is a question of fact.[71]

Black, 29 Mass. App. Ct. 215, 560 N.E.2d 122 (1990) (period begins to run when plaintiff knows or should know of loss due to unfair or deceptive act); Kidd v. Delta Funding Corp., 2000 N.Y. Misc. LEXIS 29 (Sup. Ct. Feb. 22, 2000) (applying statutory discovery rule where facts were analogous to fraud so fraud statute of limitations applied); Nash v. Motorola Communications & Electronics, Inc., 385 S.E.2d 537 (N.C. Ct. App. 1989), *aff'd without op.*, 400 S.E.2d 36 (N.C. 1991); Jennings v. Lindsey, 318 S.E.2d 318 (N.C. Ct. App. 1984); Johnson v. Phoenix Mut. Life Ins. Co., 44 N.C. App. 210, 261 S.E.2d 135 (1979), *rev'd on other grounds*, 300 N.C. 247, 266 S.E.2d 610 (1980); Jaquith v. Ferris, 64 Or. App. 508, 669 P.2d 334 (1983) (period begins when should have discovered fraud), *aff'd*, 297 Or. 783, 687 P.2d 1083 (1984); Bodin v. B & L Furniture Co., 42 Or. App. 731, 601 P.2d 848 (1979) (period begins when consumer knew or should have known of deception, to be determined by trier of facts); Heatherly v. Merrimack Mut. Fire Ins. Co., 43 S.W.3d 911 (Tenn. App. 2000); Newton v. Cox, 1992 Tenn. App. LEXIS 758, Clearinghouse No. 51,277 (Tenn. App. 1992) (Tennessee requires UDAP action to be brought within one year from discovery, but in no event more than four years after date of transaction), *rev'd on other grounds*, 878 S.W.2d 105 (Tenn. 1994); KPMG Peat Marwick v. Harrison County Hous. Fin. Corp, 988 S.W.2d 746 (Tex. 1999) (discovery rule applies but statute of limitations begins to run when plaintiff knows or should know of injury, not of the injury plus the specific nature of each wrongful act that may have caused the injury); Burns v. Thomas, 786 S.W.2d 266 (Tex. 1990) (burden is on defendant in its summary judgment action to prove that consumer knew of deception for a longer period than the limitations period); Eshleman v. Shield, 764 S.W.2d 776 (Tex. 1989); J.M. Krupar Const. Co. v. Rosenberg, 95 S.W.3d 322 (Tex. App. 2002); Bell v. Showa, 1995 Tex. App. LEXIS 1113 (Tex. App. 1995) (period begins when consumer acquires knowledge of facts that would cause reasonable person to make an inquiry leading to the cause of action); King v. David C. Holland, 1994 Tex. App. LEXIS 2426 (1994) (court may decide as a matter of law consumer's failure to exercise due diligence in discovering facts); Ben Fitzgerald Realty Co. v. Muller, 846 S.W.2d 110 (Tex. App. 1993); Fort Worth Mortgage Corp. v. Abercrombie, 835 S.W.2d 262 (Tex. App. 1992) (even though letter specified unconscionable practices, consumer successfully proved that did not understand letter); Bowe v. General Motors Corp./Pontiac Div., 830 S.W.2d 775 (Tex. App. 1992); Southwestern Bell Media, Inc. v. Lyles, 825 S.W.2d 488 (Tex. App. 1992); Parker v. Yen, 823 S.W.2d 359 (Tex. App. 1992); Milt Ferguson Motor Co. v. Zeretzke, 827 S.W.2d 349 (Tex. App. 1991); American Centennial Ins. Co. v. Canal Ins. Co., 810 S.W.2d 246 (Tex. App. 1991), *aff'd in relevant part, rev'd in part on other grounds*, 843 S.W.2d 480 (Tex. 1992); Neal v. Haley Imports, Inc., 55 Va. Cir. 152, 2001 Va. Cir. LEXIS 258 (Apr. 3, 2001) (interpreting Va. UDAP statute of limitations as incorporating discovery rule from another statute); Pickett v. Holland Am. Line-Westours, Inc., 101 Wash. App. 901, 6 P.3d 63 (2000) (applying discovery rule to contractual limitations period), *rev'd on other grounds*, 35 P.3d 351 (Wash. 2001); Cain v. Source One Mortgage Servs. Corp., 1999 Wash. App. LEXIS 1600 (Aug. 30, 1999) (UDAP claim accrues when plaintiff knows relevant facts, even if plaintiff does not know they create a cause of action). *See also* Hogan v. Valley Nat'l Fin. Servs. Co., Clearinghouse No. 50,428 (D. Colo. Feb. 1, 1995) (fraudulent concealment tolls TILA statute of limitations); Bartone v. Robert L. Day Co., 656 A.2d 221 (Conn. 1995) (court declines to extend statute of limitations because fraudulent concealment not shown); Kelly v. Primeline Advisory, Inc., 889 P.2d 130 (Kan. 1995) (adopting discovery rule for fraud-based statutory securities action); Osterman v. Sears, Roebuck & Co., 80 P.3d 435 (Mont. 2003) (statute of limitations tolled if the facts forming the basis for the fraud are, by their nature, concealed, or defendant takes affirmative action to prevent plaintiff from discovering injury). *But see* Klehr v. A.O. Smith Corp., 875 F. Supp. 1342 (D. Minn. 1995) (Minnesota UDAP statute of limitations begins to run from date of sale not date of discovery), *aff'd*, 87 F.3d 231 (8th Cir. 1996), *aff'd on other grounds*, 521 U.S. 179 (1997); Campbell v. Machias Savings Bank, 865 F. Supp. 26 (D. Me. 1994) (relying on Dugan v. Martel, 588 A.2d 744 (Me. 1991) and Kasu v. Blake, Hall & Sprague, Inc., 582 A.2d 978 (Me. 1990) to hold that discovery rule does not apply in Maine); Willow Springs Condominium Ass'n v. Seventh BRT Development Corp., 245 Conn. 1, 717 A.2d 77 (1998) (discovery rule does not apply to Connecticut UDAP claims); A. J.'s Automotive Sales, Inc. v. Freet, 725 N.E.2d 955 (Ind. App. 2000) (UDAP statute of limitations runs from occurrence of deceptive act); Morris v. Sears, Roebuck & Co., 765 So. 2d 419 (La. App. 2000) (statute of limitations runs from date of wrongful act even if victim is unaware of it); Wender v. Gilberg Agency, 716 N.Y.S.2d 40 (App. Div. 2000) (discovery rule does not apply to New York UDAP claim); Provident Life & Accident Ins. Co. v. Knott, 128 S.W.3d 211 (Tex. 2003) (statute of limitations for UDAP claim for wrongful denial of insurance benefits runs from date of denial); Kain v. Bluemound East Indus. Park, Inc., 635 N.W.2d 640 (Wis. App. 2001) (Wisconsin's 3-year statute of limitations is a statute of repose and runs from date of misrepresentation, not date of injury); Thurin v. A.O. Smith Harvestore Products, Inc., 221 Wis. 2d 220, 584 N.W.2d 233 (App. 1998) (statute of limitations for statutory false advertising claims begins with transaction itself, not with discovery that ad was false); Skrupky v. Elbert, 189 Wis. 2d 31, 526 N.W.2d 264 (Wis. App. 1994) (discovery rule does not apply to UDAP claims).

70 *See* Moore v. Liberty Nat'l Ins. Co., 267 F.3d 1209 (11th Cir. 2001) (to extend statute of limitations, fraudulent concealment must be pleaded with particularity); Zamboni v. Aladan Corp., 304 F. Supp. 2d 218, 224 (D. Mass. 2004) (plaintiff has burden of proving lack of knowledge and reasonableness in support of discovery rule); Woods v. William M. Mercer, Inc., 769 S.W.2d 515 (Tex. 1988); Bowe v. General Motors Corp./Pontiac Div., 830 S.W.2d 775 (Tex. App. 1992). *Cf.* KPMG Peat Marwick v. Harrison County Fin. Corp., 988 S.W.2d 746 (Tex. 1999) (defendant moving for summary judgment on affirmative defense of statute of limitations has burden of proving when cause of action accrued and negating discovery rule if it applies and has been raised; defendant must prove when plaintiff discovered or should have discovered the injury). *But see* Buffington v. Lewis, 834 S.W.2d 601 (Tex. App. 1992) (seller has burden of proving when consumer discovered UDAP violation).

71 Wolinetz v. Berkshire Life Ins. Co., 361 F.3d 44 (1st Cir. 2004) (date on which claims accrued against insurer presents a jury question); Clough v. Brown, 59 Mass. App. Ct. 405, 796 N.E.2d 415 (Mass. App. Ct. 2003) (whether insurance agent made misrepresentations about policy that were inherently unknowable to consumer was a question for the trier of fact); Chambers v. Airport Toyota, Inc., 1994 Tenn. App. LEXIS 60, Clearinghouse No. 51,278 (Tenn. App. 1994).

The effect of the discovery rule varies from state to state, and consumer advocates should not assume that the full statute of limitations always runs from the date of discovery. A court interpreting the Illinois UDAP statute's three-year limitations period takes the position that if the consumer discovers the UDAP violation before three years from the occurrence of the UDAP violation, then the action must be filed within that three year period.[72] The discovery rule only helps the consumer when the violation is discovered *more than* three years from the violation.

A few states apply stricter rules about when the statute of limitations begins to run. Several UDAP statutes contain limitations periods that explicitly begin when the practice occurs, not when the consumer discovers the practice.[73] An Ohio court has held that the limitations period for a UDAP damage action runs from the occurrence of the deceptive practice, not when the consumer discovers the deception. This decision is based on the Ohio UDAP statute's peculiar language that begins the limitations period for the rescission remedy when the consumer discovers the deception, and explicitly begins the limitations period for the damage remedy upon the occurrence of the deceptive act, even if the consumer has not discovered the deception.[74]

The most severe and problematic interpretation of a statute of limitations is that it begins to run on the date of the transaction, even if the deceptive or unfair act occurred later. New Hampshire's UDAP statute formerly provided that it did not apply to "transactions entered into more than two years prior to the complaint. . . ." The New Hampshire Supreme Court,[75] following an earlier federal court decision,[76] ruled that this language meant that the statute of limitations was not extended by the discovery rule or fraudulent concealment. This narrow interpretation was particularly ominous for plaintiffs because the statute listed the two-year period as beginning when a transaction was "entered into," so there would be no possible UDAP claim if a violation—*e.g.*, a failure to honor a warranty—occurred more than two years after the transaction was entered into. Two years after this ruling, the legislature adopted the discovery rule by amending the UDAP statute to state that it does not apply to transactions entered into more than three years prior to the time the plaintiff knew, or should have known, of the conduct constituting the UDAP violation.[77]

Texas has a rule that real estate purchasers are on notice concerning all aspects of their chain of title on file at the registry of deeds. As a result, the limitations period for a claim concerning the chain of title begins when the property is conveyed, not when the buyer discovers the defect. An exception to this rule triggers the limitations period when the buyer discovers the defect if the defendant had a fiduciary relationship with the buyer.[78]

7.3.2.2 Date of Injury

Some UDAP statutes specify that the statute of limitations begins to run from the date the cause of action accrues, which can be subject to varying interpretations. Texas has a rule that the time period in a UDAP malpractice claim against an attorney for work performed on a case does not begin to run until all legal appeals on that case are con-

72 Van Gessell v. Folds, 210 Ill. App. 3d 403, 569 N.E.2d 141 (1991). *Accord* Hermitage Corp. v. Contractors Adjustment Co., 637 N.E.2d 1201 (Ill. App. Ct. 1994).

73 *In re* Lutheran Brotherhood Variable Ins. Prods. Co. Sales Practices Litigation, 2002 U.S. Dist. LEXIS 9045 (D. Minn. May 17, 2002) (interpreting Minn. UDAP statute of limitations to run from date of misrepresentation); Maltz v. Union Carbide Chemicals & Plastics Co., 992 F. Supp. 286 (S.D.N.Y. 1998) (Connecticut law); Safford v. Painewebber, Inc., 730 F. Supp. 15 (E.D. La. 1990) (applicable limitations statute explicitly indicates period starts when violation occurs, not when individual discovers the violation); Agristor Leasing v. Meuli, 634 F. Supp. 1208 (D. Kan. 1986) (same), *aff'd on other grounds*, 865 F.2d 1150 (10th Cir. 1988); Fichera v. Mine Hill Corp., 207 Conn. 204, 541 A.2d 472 (1988) (same); Cummings v. Warren Henry Motors, Inc., 648 So. 2d 1230 (Fla. Dist. Ct. App. 1995) (same); State v. Classic Pool & Patio, 777 N.E.2d 1162 (Ind. App. 2002) (violations occurred both at time of solicitation and at time contract was signed, and suit can be filed within 2 years of either date); Mayo v. Simon, 646 So. 2d 973 (La. Ct. App. 1994) (same); Kuebler v. Martin, 610 So. 2d 270 (La. Ct. App. 1992) (same); Dufour v. U.S. Home Corp., 581 So. 2d 765 (La. Ct. App. 1991) (same); Spencer-Wallington v. Service Merchandise, Inc., 562 So. 2d 1060 (La. Ct. App. 1990) (same); Canal Marine Supply, Inc. v. Outboard Marine Corp., 522 So. 2d 1201 (La. Ct. App. 1988) (same); Kain v. Bluemound E. Indus. Park, Inc., 635 N.W.2d 640 (Wis. App. 2001) (statute of limitations runs from date of unlawful act and is statute of repose); Skrupky v. Elbert, 189 Wis. 2d 31, 526 N.W.2d 264 (App. 1994) (statute of limitations runs from occurrence of unlawful practice). *See also* Staudt v. Artifex, Ltd., 16 F. Supp. 2d 1023 (E.D. Wis. 1998) (statute of limitations runs from date of occurrence of unlawful practice; note that court also mischaracterizes Wisconsin rulings as holding that UDAP limitations period is a statute of repose); Herman v. McCarthy Enters., Inc., 61 Va. Cir. 697 (Nov. 26, 2002) (construing Va. UDAP limitations period as running from date of injury, not date of discovery).

74 *In re* Ford Motor Co. Ignition Switch Prods. Liability Litig., 1999 WL 33495352 (D.N.J. July 27, 1999), *as modified on reconsideration*, (July 27, 1999); Weaver v. Armando's, Inc., 2003 WL 22071470 (Ohio App. Sept. 3, 2003) (unpublished, citation limited); Lloyd v. Buick Youngstown GMC Truck Co., 686 N.E.2d 350 (Ohio App. 1996); Cypher v. Bill Swad Leasing Co., 36 Ohio App. 3d 200, 521 N.E.2d 1142 (1987).

75 Catucci v. Lewis, 665 A.2d 378 (N.H. 1995). *See also* Gautschi v. Auto Body Discount Center, Inc., 660 A.2d 1076 (N.H. 1995) (minor misstatement that occurred more than two years after the transaction did not revive the UDAP claim, since it was separate and distinct).

76 Zee-Bar Inc.-N.H. v. Kaplan, 792 F. Supp. 895 (D.N.H. 1992). *See also* Bacon v. Smith Barney Shearson, Inc., 938 F. Supp. 98 (D.N.H. 1996); City of Manchester v. National Gypsum Co., 637 F. Supp. 646 (D.R.I. 1986).

77 N.H. Rev. Stat. Ann. § 358-A:3.

78 Zimmerman v. First Am. Title Ins. Co., 790 S.W.2d 690 (Tex. App. 1990).

cluded.[79] In a UNIP case based on a breach of the duty of good faith and fair dealing, the period runs from the date the insurer denies the claim, absent fraudulent concealment.[80] A Connecticut case holds that a UDAP violation exists when the misrepresentation is made and that the statute of limitations commences running the moment the act or omission complained of occurs.[81]

An Ohio decision holds that a UDAP claim for defective installation of a household product runs from the date of installation, not the date the homeowner sustained an injury.[82] But in a different context, a Maryland appellate court has ruled that a UDAP claim does not arise until the consumer sustains a legally compensable injury.[83] Several Virginia trial courts have also adopted the date the injury is sustained.[84]

In another case a developer promised that amenities such as a pool would be provided at a condominium development. The buyers' UDAP claim did not accrue when the representations were made, but only at the later date when the developer abandoned these plans, because the representation became deceptive only on that date.[85] Likewise, a consumer's claim against an insurance company that sold a "vanishing premium" life insurance policy accrued only when the defendant caused injury to plaintiff by breaching its promises, not when it made the promises.[86]

79 Aduddell v. Parkhill, 821 S.W.2d 158 (Tex. 1991).

80 Douskos v. Eden Park Ins. Co., 2001 U.S. Dist. LEXIS 7953 (W.D. Tex. June 15, 2001); Kuzniar v. State Farm Lloyds, 52 S.W.3d 759 (Tex. App. 2001).

81 Timmons v. City of Hartford, 283 F. Supp. 2d 712 (D. Conn. 2003).

82 Spiroles v. Simpson Fence Co., 99 Ohio App. 3d 72, 649 N.E.2d 1297 (1994).

83 Berg v. Byrd, 124 Md. App. 208, 720 A.2d 1283 (1998) (question was whether claim accrued before or after enactment of a damages cap). *Accord* John Beaudette, Inc. v. Sentry Ins., 94 F. Supp. 2d 77 (D. Mass. 1999) (UDAP cause of action accrues when injury results).

84 Herman v. McCarthy Enters., Inc., 61 Va. Cir. 697 (Nov. 26, 2002); Glass v. Trafalgar House Property, Inc., 58 Va. Cir. 437 (2002). *See also* Fix v. Eakin/Youngtob Assocs., Inc., 59 Va. Cir. 22 (2002) (runs from date of closing on home, not date purchase contract signed).

85 PED, Inc. v. Loebel, 594 N.W.2d 418 (Wis. App. 1999) (unpublished, citation limited, text available on Lexis). *Cf.* Thurin v. A.O. Smith Harvestore Products, Inc., 221 Wis. 2d 220, 584 N.W.2d 233 (App. 1998) (statute of limitations for statutory false advertising claims begins with transaction itself, not with discovery that ad was false; no discussion of any allegation that representations became deceptive only at later date).

86 Gaidon v. Guardian Life Ins. Co., 96 N.Y.2d 201, 727 N.Y.S.2d 30 (2001). *See also* Heslin v. Metropolitan Life Ins. Co., 287 A.D.2d 113, 733 N.Y.S.2d 753 (2001) (dismissing vanishing premium claim as premature where plaintiffs had not yet been asked to pay); Ostrower v. Metropolitan Life Ins. Co., 730 N.Y.S.2d 452 (App. Div. 2001) (same). *But see In re* Lutheran Brotherhood Variable Ins. Prods. Co. Sales Practices Litigation, 2002 U.S. Dist. LEXIS 9045 (D. Minn. May 17, 2002) (statute of limitations in vanishing premium case runs from date of misrepresentation); Werner v. Pittway Corp., 90 F. Supp. 2d 1018 (W.D. Wis. 2000) (statute of limitations runs from date of deceptive act, even if it has not yet caused injury).

7.3.2.3 Series of Events

Another means by which the limitations period is extended is to show a series of deceptive practices continuing after the initial transaction.[87] For example, the limitations period can run not from the initial sale, but rather from subsequent promises to fix or deliver replacements.[88] Arguing that the seller has continued to withhold the consumer's money unlawfully or that the seller has deceptively or unfairly responded to a consumer's demand for relief may establish a continuing violation after the initial deceptive transaction.

In many situations, a seller will have a continuing duty to disclose certain facts, so continued silence within the statute of limitations period will prevent the action from being time-barred.[89] Each day that a person fails to make statutorily-mandated disclosures constitutes a new violation and begins the running of the statute of limitations anew.[90] Continuing noncompliance with a loan broker statute may

87 Tubos de Acero v. Am. Int'l Investment Corp., 292 F.3d 471 (5th Cir. 2002); City of West Haven v. Commercial Union Ins. Co., 894 F.2d 540 (2d Cir. 1990) (since insurer had continuing duty to defend plaintiff, statute of limitations for Connecticut UDAP violation was tolled until the duty ended); Anzai v. Chevron Corp., 168 F. Supp. 2d 1180 (D. Haw. 2001) (antitrust case) (if there is a continuing violation of Haw. Rev. Stat. § 480-2, attorney general can get damages on behalf of all state residents for the entire period of the violation); Full Draw Productions v. Easton Sports, Inc., 85 F. Supp. 2d 1001 (D. Colo. 2000); Willow Springs Condominium Ass'n v. Seventh BRT Development Corp., 245 Conn. 1, 717 A.2d 77 (1998); Benton, Benton & Benton v. Louisiana Public Facilities Authority, 672 So. 2d 720 (La. App. 1996). *See also* Connecticut Bank & Trust v. Reckert, 638 A.2d 44 (Conn. Ct. App. 1994) (continuing course of conduct might extend statute of limitations); Martin v. Servs. Corp. Int'l, 2001 Ohio App. LEXIS 2702 (June 20, 2001) (citing favorably the rule that statute of limitations begins to run from the time continuing UDAP violation ceases); Medicare Rentals, Inc. v. Advanced Servs., 460 S.E.2d 361 (N.C. Ct. App. 1995) (interpreting statute of limitations that provides that each week of a continuing violation is a separate offense). *But see* Pelman v. McDonald's Corp., 2003 WL 22052778 (S.D.N.Y. Sept. 3, 2003) (rejecting continuing practice rule).

88 Hofstetter v. Fletcher, 905 F.2d 897 (6th Cir. 1988) (Ohio law); Dreier Co. v. Unitronix Corp., 218 N.J. Super. 260, 527 A.2d 875 (App. Div. 1986); La Sara Grain Co. v. First Nat'l Bank of Mercedes, 673 S.W.2d 558 (Tex. 1984); *see also* Woods v. Littleton, 554 S.W.2d 662 (Tex. 1977) (utilizing version of statute in effect at time of subsequent repairs, not initial sales transaction); *cf.* Fichera v. Mine Hill Corp., 207 Conn. 204, 541 A.2d 472 (1988) (not sufficient evidence of continuing violation). *But see* Walker v. Sears, Roebuck & Co., 853 F.2d 355 (5th Cir. 1988) (Texas law).

89 Willow Springs Condominium Ass'n v. Seventh BRT Development Corp., 245 Conn. 1, 717 A.2d 77 (1998).

90 Wood v. Collins, 725 So. 2d 531 (La. App. 1998); Capitol House Preservation Co. v. Perryman Consultants, Inc., 745 So. 2d 1194 (La. App. 1999).

be a continuing UDAP violation, so the limitations period would only begin after the seller began complying.[91]

For a UDAP-based suit against an insurance company, the limitations period runs from the date the insurance company denies the claim.[92] The period begins on the date of the final denial of coverage, not the initial denial.[93] Where an insurer misrepresented the beneficiaries on a policy, the period does not begin until it is too late for the insured to change the beneficiaries.[94] But some courts have ruled that the limitations period will run from the date of the last deceptive practice, not from later dates when the consumer continues to suffer the injury from that earlier practice.[95]

In states that run the statute of limitations from the date of the deceptive act, the consumer's attorney may avoid problems by focusing the complaint on the latest stage of the defendant's deception. If a consumer complains of an unfair or deceptive collection practice, the time period begins from the date of the collection practice, and not from the date of earlier, related deception concerning the debt.[96] For example, if a debt includes improper amounts, the limitations period does not begin until collection begins, if the claim is that the creditor sought amounts not owed.[97] Likewise, even though the statute of limitations for challenging misconduct at the time of formation of a contract has passed, consumers can sue regarding the more recent imposition of fees under the contract.[98]

7.3.2.4 Other State Rules

Michigan's UDAP statute extends the statute of limitations until six years after the deceptive act or one year after the consumer makes the last payment in the transaction, whichever is earlier.[99] This provision did not, however, extend the statute of limitations while the consumer was making payments on a loan that financed the purchase, since the consumer was complaining about the purchase itself, not the loan.[100]

7.3.3 *Tolling*

7.3.3.1 General

In addition to the discovery rule, there are several ways that a limitations period can be extended in most states. Many states suspend the running of the statute of limitations during specific conditions such as infancy.

If the courts characterize the limitations period as a statute of repose, however, it will probably not be subject to tolling. A Connecticut appellate decision views the limitations period in Connecticut's UDAP statute as a statute of repose, placing a substantive and jurisdictional bar to a suit after three years.[101] Such an interpretation, if adopted by the Connecticut Supreme Court, would prevent extension of the limitations period, although in the case of continuing violations the period could be construed to begin to run from the date of the last violation.[102]

7.3.3.2 Fraudulent Concealment and Estoppel

The limitations period can be tolled even after the consumer discovers the fraud, if there is a false statement of a material fact that prevents the consumer from taking action and the statement was made to be acted upon, was relied upon, and was to the consumer's injury.[103] Thus, where a

91 Fox v. Dupree, 633 So. 2d 612 (La. Ct. App. 1994).

92 Burton v. State Farm Mut. Auto. Ins. Co., 1994 U.S. Dist. LEXIS 16776 (S.D. Tex. 1995). *Cf.* Klettner v. State Farm Mut. Automobile Ins. Co., 205 W. Va. 587, 519 S.E.2d 870 (1999) (for UNIP claim brought by third party against tortfeasor's insurer, limitations period begins to run only after underlying tort claim has gone to trial and appeal period has passed).

93 Pena v. State Farm Lloyds, 980 S.W.2d 949 (Tex. App. 1998); Duzich v. Marine Office of Am. Corp., 980 S.W.2d 857 (Tex. App. 1998).

94 Jefferson-Pilot Life Ins. Co. v. Spencer, 110 N.C. App. 194, 429 S.E.2d 583 (1993), *rev'd on other grounds*, 336 N.C. 49, 442 S.E.2d 316 (1994).

95 Mount v. LaSalle Bank Lake View, 886 F. Supp. 650 (N.D. Ill. 1995); Canal Marine Supply, Inc. v. Outboard Marine Corp., 522 So. 2d 1201 (La. Ct. App. 1988).

96 Bennett v. Reliable Credit Ass'n, Inc., 125 Or. App. 531, 865 P.2d 496 (1993).

97 *Id.*

98 Dwyer v. Barco Auto Leasing Corp., 903 F. Supp. 205 (D. Mass. 1995).

99 Mich. Comp. Laws Ann. § 445.911(7).

100 Snyder v. Boston Whaler, Inc., 892 F. Supp. 955 (W.D. Mich. 1994).

101 Avon Meadow Condominium Ass'n v. Bank of Boston Connecticut, 50 Conn. App. 688, 719 A.2d 66 (1998).

102 *Cf.* Navin v. Essex Sav. Bank, 82 Conn. App. 255, 843 A.2d 679 (Conn. App. Ct. 2004) (no continuing violation to support tolling of statute of limitations).

103 Gibbs v. Main Bank, 666 S.W.2d 554 (Tex. App. 1984) (note that the Texas statute of limitations has been amended since this decision to incorporate a version of this rule); Jim Walter Homes, Inc. v. Mora, 622 S.W.2d 878 (Tex. Civ. App. 1981). *See also* Walker v. Sears, Roebuck & Co., 853 F.2d 355 (5th Cir. 1988) (Texas law) (elements not met under facts of particular case); Williams v. Central Money Co., 974 F. Supp. 22 (D.D.C. 1997) (question is a factual one); Osterman v. Sears, Roebuck & Co., 80 P.3d 435 (Mont. 2003) (statute of limitations tolled if the facts forming the basis for the fraud are, by their nature, concealed, or defendant takes affirmative action to prevent plaintiff from discovering injury, but this consumer's lack of ordinary diligence precludes tolling); Donohue v. Mid-Valley Glass Co., 84 Or. App. 584, 735 P.2d 1 (1987) (must show defendant's actions stopped plaintiff from bringing lawsuit until after limitation period had expired); Zimmerman v. First Am. Title Ins. Co., 790 S.W.2d 690 (Tex. App. 1990). *Cf.* Kozikowski v. Toll Bros., Inc., 246 F. Supp. 2d 93 (D. Mass. 2003) (no equitable estoppel because reasonable reliance not shown); Krondes v. Norwalk Savings Soc., 53 Conn. App. 102, 728 A.2d 1103 (1999) (reciting standards for fraudulent con-

consumer was told the builder would take care of everything, but the builder did nothing as the house deteriorated, the builder was equitably estopped from raising the statute of limitations as a defense.[104] This principle is particularly compelling when the consumer has an ongoing relationship of trust and confidence with the defendant.[105]

7.3.3.3 Pendency of Another Suit

The Georgia, Hawaii, Illinois, Kentucky, Nebraska, North Carolina, Ohio, Oregon, Utah, Virginia, and Washington UDAP statutes toll the limitations period for a private action during the pendency of a state action against the challenged activity. Nevertheless, an Oregon court has ruled that the limitations period continues to run where the prosecutor only initiates an investigation and sends a notice to the seller, but does not file a legal complaint.[106] Under Ohio's UDAP statute, consumers can bring suit up to one year after attorney general proceedings regarding the same violation are terminated, notwithstanding the statute of limitations.[107] This extension of the statute of limitations does not, however, allow the attorney general an extra year to file suit after completing its own investigation.[108]

The statute of limitations may also be suspended while the consumer's own suit raising the claim is pending. Thus, if the consumer's timely UDAP claim is dismissed without prejudice by one court, the consumer will be able to refile the claim even if the statute of limitations would have run while the first suit was pending.[109]

In the federal system and many states the statute of limitations will also be tolled while a class action that includes an individual in the proposed class is pending.[110]

7.3.4 Limitations Period Where Complaint Amended to Add New Claims or Parties

Often a consumer will amend the complaint to add a UDAP claim, and the question arises whether to use the date of filing the original action or the amended UDAP claim in calculating whether the statute of limitations has run. The federal rules provide that an amendment relates back to the date of the original pleading if it arises out of the conduct, transaction, or occurrence that was set forth in the original pleading.[111] Texas courts find that the date of filing the original suit should be used, particularly where the UDAP claim "relates back" to the original complaint and is not based on a new, distinct or different transaction.[112] But Nebraska's highest court found a UDAP claim not to relate back to an earlier filed complaint where the consumer would need to prove a new set of facts not put in dispute by the prior complaint.[113]

Similarly, after a UDAP claim is filed, the consumer may discover that another party should be added to the suit. Even where that amendment to the complaint occurs after the limitations period has expired, the complaint can go forward if the amendment properly "relates back" to the original complaint.[114] For example, the amended complaint usually

---

cealment but finding that facts did not establish it); Gredell v. Wyeth Laboratories, Inc., 803 N.E.2d 541 (Ill. App. 2004) (misrepresentations about the product, which formed the basis of plaintiff's suit, were not designed to conceal the cause of action so were not fraudulent concealment); Gonzalez v. City of Harlingen, 814 S.W.2d 109 (Tex. App. 1991) (facts not alleged to justify this theory for extending limitations period). *But see In re* Lutheran Brotherhood Variable Ins. Prods. Co. Sales Practices Litig., 2002 U.S. Dist. LEXIS 9045 (D. Minn. May 17, 2002) (questioning whether fraudulent concealment extends UDAP statute of limitations, but finding it inapplicable on the facts); Fichera v. Mine Hill Corp., 207 Conn. 204, 541 A.2d 472 (1988).

104 Jim Walter Homes, Inc. v. Mora, 622 S.W.2d 878 (Tex. Civ. App. 1981). *Accord* Ohio *ex rel.* Celebrezze v. Grogan Chrysler-Plymouth, 73 Ohio App. 3d 792, 598 N.E.2d 796 (1991) (fraud may estop defendant from asserting statute of limitations, although mere stubbornness and dilatoriness will not). *See also* Thurin v. A. O. Smith Harvestore Products, Inc., 221 Wis. 2d 220, 584 N.W.2d 233 (App. 1998) (defendant will be estopped from asserting statute of limitations if plaintiff shows reasonable reliance on defendant's assurances, but on facts no estoppel here). *But cf.* Kozikowski v. Toll Bros., Inc., 354 F.3d 16 (1st Cir. 2003) (letter from builder with non-specific terms did not amount to a representation that would reasonably induce plaintiff to postpone bringing suit).

105 McCulloch v. Price Waterhouse, 157 Or. App. 237, 971 P.2d 414 (1998) (accountants' assurance that they would take care of problems may extend statute of limitations).

106 Myers v. M.H.I. Investments Inc., 44 Or. App. 467, 606 P.2d 652 (1980).

107 Ohio Rev. Code § 1345.10(C).

108 Ohio *ex rel.* Celebrezze v. Grogan Chrysler-Plymouth, 73 Ohio App. 3d 792, 598 N.E.2d 796 (1991).

109 Wood v. Collins, 725 So. 2d 531 (La. App. 1998).

110 Crown Cork & Seal Co. v. Parker, 462 U.S. 345, 103 S. Ct. 2392, 76 L. Ed. 2d 628 (1983); American Pipe & Constr. Co. v. Utah, 414 U.S. 538, 94 S. Ct. 756, 38 L. Ed. 2d 713 (1974); Grimes v. Housing Authority of New Haven, 698 A.2d 302 (Conn. 1997); Brashears v. Sight N Sound Appliance Centers, Inc., 981 P.2d 1270 (Okla. App. 1999) (UDAP statute tolled during pendency of class action that would have included plaintiff if originally proposed class definition had been approved); Fuller v. Sight N Sound Appliance Centers, Inc., 982 P.2d 528 (Okla. App. 1999) (same).

111 Fed. R. Civ. P. 15(c)(2).

112 Long v. State Farm Fire & Cas. Co., 828 S.W.2d 125 (Tex. App. 1992); Aetna Cas. & Surety Co. v. Martin Surgical Supply Co., 689 S.W.2d 263 (Tex. App. 1985); Providence Hosp. v. Truly, 611 S.W.2d 127 (Tex. Civ. App. 1981). *See also* McGowan v. Pride Chrylser-Plymouth, Inc., 160 B.R. 694 (Bankr. D.R.I. 1993).

113 Meyer Brothers v. Travelers Ins. Co., 250 Neb. 389, 551 N.W.2d 1 (1996).

114 Thibaut v. Thibaut, 607 So. 2d 587 (La. Ct. App. 1992); Stark v. Patalano Ford Sales, Inc., 30 Mass. App. Ct. 194, 567 N.E.2d 1237 (1991) (addition of party in UDAP suit related back to original complaint under Massachusetts statute even though demand letter was sent after statute of limitations ran).

will properly relate back where the new defendant had notice of the original claim so as not to be prejudiced by the untimely amendment.

Exact standards as to when adding a new defendant "relates back" to the original complaint vary from jurisdiction to jurisdiction. The federal rules provide that a party can be added if: (1) the claim arises out of the conduct, transaction, or occurrence set forth in the original pleading; (2) the new party, within the period provided by the rules for service of the complaint and summons,[115] receives notice of the original action such that it will not be prejudiced in maintaining a defense; and (3) the new party knew or should have known that, but for a mistake concerning the identity of the proper party, the action would have been brought against it.[116] Notice can be formal, informal, or imputed.[117] Some states adopt this same rule, but many still follow an earlier version of the federal rule, interpreted in *Schiavone v. Fortune*,[118] which required notice to the new defendant within the applicable limitations period rather than within the period for service.[119] The remaining states continue to maintain a 1938 version of Federal Rule 15, or apply a statute, a court rule, or a common law rule.

Courts may allow correction of misnomers, where the correct party is sued and served by an incorrect name, more liberally than addition of a party where the wrong party was named and served.[120] A Texas court held that an owner of a corporation could be added to a lawsuit as long as the action against the corporation was within the limitations period if it was alleged that the corporation is just an alter ego for the owner.[121]

7.3.5 UDAP Recoupment Claims After the Limitations Period Expires

The most common situation where the limitations period will have run involves a UDAP counterclaim to a collection action, since the collection action may be brought several years after the underlying sales transaction took place. But even where the UDAP limitations period has expired, the consumer may still be able to use the UDAP claim by way of recoupment against the seller's or assignee's recovery on the debt. As long as the UDAP claim arises out of the same transaction as the plaintiff's claim, recoupment is in the nature of a defense or an equitable reason why the plaintiff's claim should be reduced.[122] The recoupment claim will only allow the consumer to offset all or part of the plaintiff's claim, and will not allow the consumer a net positive recovery. (UDAP attorney fees should be awarded in excess of the creditor's recovery. Although there are no UDAP cases on point, this is the majority rule for Truth in Lending recoupment cases.[123]) But the recoupment claim is advantageous in that it survives after the limitations period has run.[124] The typical UDAP claim concerns the same transaction that is the subject of the collection action, and, consequently, a recoupment claim up to the amount of the plaintiff's claim will almost always be appropriate after the UDAP statute of limitations has run.

7.4 Retroactive Application of Statutory Provisions

A second timing issue is the extent to which a UDAP statutory provision applies to practices occurring before the effective date of the statutory provision. In the 1970s, a major impediment to private UDAP actions was that UDAP statutes often did not exist at the time of the deceptive practices. Today the continual amending of UDAP statutes has led to a more common problem: which version of the legislation should be used—that in effect at the time of the challenged practice, or that in effect at the time the consumer brings the claim? The answer differs depending on what type of provision is being analyzed.

The basic rule is that provisions that are procedural or remedial in nature are retroactively applied,[125] while those

115 The time limitations for service are set forth in Fed. R. Civ. P. 4(m) and can be extended for good cause.

116 Fed. R. Civ. P. 15(c).

117 Childs v. City of Philadelphia, 2000 U.S. Dist. LEXIS 6281 (E.D. Pa. May 9, 2000); Zimmer v. United Dominion Indus., Inc., 193 F.R.D. 620 (W.D. Ark. 2000).

118 477 U.S. 21, 106 S. Ct. 2379, 91 L. Ed. 2d 18 (1986).

119 See generally Carol M. Rice, Meet John Doe: It is Time for Federal Court Procedure to Recognize John Doe Parties, 57 U. Pitt. Law Rev. 883, n.227 (1996).

120 Roberts v. Michaels, 219 F.3d 775, 778 (8th Cir. 2000); Maro v. Gopez, 1993 Del. Super. LEXIS 128, at 6 (Mar. 31. 1993); Dougherty v. Gifford, 826 S.W.2d 668 (Tex. App. 1992) (relation back as to defendants allowed in misnomer cases but not misidentification cases).

121 Nelson v. Schanzer, 788 S.W.2d 81 (Tex. App. 1990).

122 Stone v. White, 301 U.S. 532, 57 S. Ct. 851, 81 L. Ed. 1265 (1936); Mbank Fort Worth N.A. v. Trans Meridian, Inc., 820 F.2d 716 (5th Cir. 1987) (Texas law) (UDAP claims may be raised by way of recoupment). It is possible that a general procedural rule will permit revival of the entire claim—not limited to recoupment—when the UDAP claim is brought as a counterclaim after limitations has run. Tex. Civ. Prac. & Rem. Code § 16.069; Barraza v. Koliba, 933 S.W.2d 164 (Tex. App. 1996). *See also* National Consumer Law Center, Truth in Lending § 7.2.5 (5th ed. 2003 and Supp.) (rescission in TIL cases).

123 *See* National Consumer Law Center, Truth in Lending § 8.9.2.2 (5th ed. 2003 and Supp). In a somewhat analogous situation, UDAP attorney fees have been awarded in excess of the note amount against an assignee even though the assignee's liability is limited by the amount of the note. *See* § 8.8.9, *infra*.

124 Stone v. White, 301 U.S. 532, 57 S. Ct. 851, 81 L. Ed. 1265 (1936); Bull v. United States, 295 U.S. 247, 55 S. Ct. 695, 79 L. Ed. 1421 (1935); Luckenbach Steamship Co. v. United States, 312 F.2d 545 (2d Cir. 1963); Wright, Miller, and Kane, Federal Practice and Procedure: Civil § 1409 (1990); 3 Moore's Federal Practice ¶ 13:11 (3d ed. 1997 with updates); Fridenthal, Kane, & Miller, Civil Procedure § 6.7 at pp.362–63 (1999).

125 State *ex rel.* Turner v. Limbrecht, 246 N.W.2d 330 (Iowa 1976);

creating substantive rights are not.[126] The Iowa Supreme Court has found that the whole UDAP statute is remedial in nature since only new remedies have been added to common law fraud.[127] Consequently, the whole statute is applied retroactively. This interpretation is not generally accepted; most courts find that new statutes can not be retroactively applied before their effective date because they are not merely remedial, but create new rights of action.[128]

In addition, various amendments to UDAP statutes generally have been found to be substantive, foreclosing retroactive application of the amendment. Thus a change in the scope of a statute,[129] and an amendment granting a private right of action,[130] have been held not to be applicable retroactively. Courts also will not give retroactive effect to changes in the statute's remedies, particularly where a remedy involves treble damages (and thus is quasi-punitive in nature), and where there is no legislative intent to apply a change in remedy retroactively.[131] Also not applied retroactively are amendments changing who are "consumers" able to bring actions under the statute;[132] eliminating a privity requirement;[133] eliminating a damage requirement for a private action;[134] giving sellers a *bona fide* error

---

Commonwealth v. DeCotis, 366 Mass. 234, 316 N.E.2d 748 (1974); Goes v. Feldman, 8 Mass. App. Ct. 84, 391 N.E.2d 943 (1979); Johnston v. Beneficial Mgmt. Corp., 85 Wash. 2d 637, 538 P.2d 510 (1975).

126 Point East One Condominium Corp. v. Point East Developers, Inc., 348 So. 2d 32 (Fla. Dist. Ct. App. 1977); Devine Seafood, Inc. v. Attorney General, 37 Md. App. 439, 377 A.2d 1194 (Ct. Spec. App. 1977); Baldassari v. Public Fin. Trust, 369 Mass. 33, 337 N.E.2d 701 (1975); Commonwealth v. DeCotis, 366 Mass. 234, 316 N.E.2d 748 (1974); Woods v. Littleton, 554 S.W.2d 662 (Tex. 1977); Johnston v. Beneficial Mgmt. Corp., 85 Wash. 2d 637, 538 P.2d 510 (1975); Kittilson v. Ford, 23 Wash. App. 402, 595 P.2d 944 (1979), *aff'd on other grounds*, 93 Wash. 2d 223, 608 P.2d 264 (1980).

127 State *ex rel.* Turner v. Limbrecht, 246 N.W.2d 330 (Iowa 1976).

128 Teltronics Servs., Inc. v. Anaconda-Ericson, Inc., 587 F. Supp. 724 (E.D.N.Y. 1984), *aff'd on other grounds*, 762 F.2d 185 (2d Cir. 1985); Buccino v. Continental Assurance Co., 578 F. Supp. 1518 (S.D.N.Y. 1983); Point East One Condominium Corp. v. Point East Developers, Inc., 348 So. 2d 32 (Fla. Dist. Ct. App. 1977); State v. Commemorative Servs. Corp., 16 Kan. App. 2d 389, 823 P.2d 831 (1992); Lewis v. Ariens Co., 434 Mass. 643, 751 N.E.2d 862, 868 n.19 (2001); Gopen v. American Supply Co., 10 Mass. App. Ct. 342, 407 N.E.2d 1255 (1980); Burns v. Volkswagen of Am., 468 N.Y.S.2d 1017 (App. Div. 1983); McKnight v. Hill & Hill Exterminators, Inc., 689 S.W.2d 206 (Tex. 1985); Woods v. Littleton, 554 S.W.2d 662 (Tex. 1977). *See also* State *ex rel.* Bryant v. Callan Publishing Inc., Clearinghouse No. 49,974 (Ark. Chanc. Cty. Pulaski Cty. July 22, 1993).

129 Guyana Tel. & Tel. Co. v. Melbourne Int'l Communications, Ltd., 329 F.3d 1241 (11th Cir. 2003); Dash v. Wayne, 700 F. Supp. 1056 (D. Haw. 1988); GWC Restaurants, Inc. v. Hawaiian Flour Mills, Inc., 691 F. Supp. 247 (D. Haw. 1987); Haberman v. Hustler Magazine, Inc., 626 F. Supp. 201 (D. Mass. 1986); Flotech, Inc. v. E.I. DuPont de Nemours Co., 627 F. Supp. 358 (D. Mass. 1985), *aff'd on other grounds*, 814 F.2d 775 (1st Cir. 1987); Reichelt v. Urban Inv. & Dev. Co., 577 F. Supp. 971 (N.D. Ill. 1984); State *ex rel.* Corbin v. Pickrell, 136 Ariz. 589, 667 P.2d 1304 (1983); Madsen v. Western Am. Mortg. Co., 694 P.2d 1228 (Ariz. Ct. App. 1985); Goldstein Oil Co. v. C. K. Smith Co., 20 Mass. App. Ct. 243, 479 N.E.2d 728 (1985); Gage v. Langford, 615 S.W.2d 934 (Tex. Civ. App. 1981); Lidstrand v. Silvercrest Indus., 28 Wash. App. 359, 623 P.2d 710 (1981); Kittilson v. Ford, 23 Wash. App. 402, 595 P.2d 944 (1979), *aff'd on other grounds*, 93 Wash. 2d 223, 608 P.2d 264 (1980).

130 Sabater v. Lead Indus. Ass'n, Inc., 183 Misc. 2d 759, 704 N.Y.S.2d 800 (Sup. Ct. 2000); Burns v. Volkswagen of Am., 118 Misc. 2d 289, 460 N.Y.S.2d 410 (Sup. Ct. 1982), *aff'd*, 97 A.D.2d 977, 468 N.Y.S.2d 1017 (1983); Giummo v. Citibank N.A., 107 Misc. 2d 895, 436 N.Y.S.2d 172 (Civ. Ct., N.Y. Cty. 1981); Walls v. American Tobacco Co., 11 P.3d 626 (2000); Johnston v. Beneficial Mgmt. Corp., 85 Wash. 2d 637, 538 P.2d 510 (1975).

131 Lowe v. Surpas Resource Corp., 253 F. Supp. 2d 1209, 1230 (D. Kan. 2003); Schorsch v. Fireside Chrysler-Plymouth, Mazda, Inc., 677 N.E.2d 976 (Ill. App. Ct. 1997) (amendment precluding fee award if consumer recovered less than defendant offered in settlement is not retroactive); Greelish v. Drew, 35 Mass. App. Ct. 541, 622 N.E.2d 1376 (1993) (statutory amendment affecting the method of calculating multiple damages could not be applied retroactively); State *ex rel.* Webster v. Cornelius, 729 S.W.2d 60 (Mo. Ct. App. 1987) (expanding attorney fees to cover cost of investigation; adding 10% to civil penalty); Osai v. A & D Furniture Co., 68 Ohio St. 2d 99, 428 N.E.2d 857, 22 Ohio Op. 3d 328 (1981); Texas Real Estate Comm'n v. Lamb, 650 S.W.2d 66 (Tex. 1983) (use bonding statute at time of practice, not time of judgment); Russell v. Campbell, 725 S.W.2d 739 (Tex. App. 1987); Honeywell v. Imperial Condominium Ass'n, 716 S.W.2d 75 (Tex. App. 1986) (some acts occurred before and some after amendment to statute's remedies; apply earlier and stronger remedies to all practices); Cocke v. White, 697 S.W.2d 739 (Tex. App. 1985) (where new statute explicitly states it should only be prospectively applied to actions occurring after effective date, use old treble damages provision); McAllen State Bank v. Linbeck Constr. Corp., 695 S.W.2d 10 (Tex. App. 1985) (uses old treble damages provision); Mytel Int'l, Inc. v. Turbo Refrigerating Co., 689 S.W.2d 315 (Tex. App. 1985) (uses old treble damages provision); Cuevas v. Montoya, 48 Wash. App. 871, 740 P.2d 858 (1987); Nyby v. Allied Fidelity Ins. Co., 42 Wash. App. 543, 712 P.2d 861 (1986); Payless Car Rental Sys., Inc. v. Draayer, 43 Wash. App. 240, 716 P.2d 929 (1986); Swain v. Colton, 44 Wash. App. 204, 721 P.2d 990 (1986). *But see* Robinson v. Lynmar Racquet Club, Inc., 851 P.2d 274 (Colo. Ct. App. 1993); Commonwealth v. DeCotis, 366 Mass. 234, 316 N.E.2d 748 (1974); Hale v. Basin Motor Co., 110 N.M. 314, 795 P.2d 1006 (1990).

132 Crossland v. Canteen Corp., 711 F.2d 714 (5th Cir. 1983) (Texas law); Dash v. Wayne, 700 F. Supp. 1056 (D. Haw. 1988); Klo-Zik Co. v. General Motors Corp., 677 F. Supp. 499 (E.D. Tex. 1987); PPG Indus., Inc. v. JMB/Houston Centers Partners Ltd. P'ship, 41 S.W.3d 270 (Tex. App. 2001) (applying treble damages rule that was in effect when claim arose), *rev'd on other grounds*, 2004 WL 1533274 (Tex. July 9, 2004); Wood v. Component Constr. Corp., 722 S.W.2d 439 (Tex. App. 1986); McAllen State Bank v. Linbeck Constr. Corp., 695 S.W.2d 10 (Tex. App. 1985); Gibbs v. Main Bank of Houston, 666 S.W.2d 554 (Tex. App. 1984).

133 Waterbury Petroleum Products, Inc. v. Canaan Oil & Fuel Co., 193 Conn. 208, 477 A.2d 988 (1984).

134 Williams v. Purdue Phama Co., 297 F. Supp. 2d 171 (D.D.C. 2003); Smith v. Caggiano, 12 Mass. App. Ct. 41, 421 N.E.2d 473 (1981).

defense;[135] or changing the statute of limitations.[136] Consumers are also not expected to comply with notice provisions not effective at the time an action was brought.[137] Instead, courts have ruled consumers should comply with the notice provision in effect at the time of the challenged practice.[138] However, there are exceptions. The Texas UDAP statute's notice provision was amended in 1995. The amended notice provision applies (1) to all causes of action that accrue on or after September 1, 1995, and (2) to all causes of action that accrued before September 1, 1995, but on which suit is filed on or after September 1, 1996.[139]

Other amendments to UDAP statutes, however, have been found to be only procedural or remedial, allowing retroactive application, such as the choice of courts in which to bring a UDAP action.[140] Other times there is a clear legislative intent that an amendment be retroactively applied. Where a state's courts read a public interest precondition to bringing a UDAP action and the legislature then specifically amends the statute to preclude such an interpretation, courts have applied that amendment retroactively.[141] Similarly, where a statute was amended to limit UDAP actions to in-state sellers and then the legislature immediately nullified that amendment, the nullification can be retroactively applied.[142]

Even when a statutory provision can not be retroactively applied to the initial stages of a deceptive practice, the UDAP violation may be a repeated or continuing one, lasting until after the date of the statute's amendment. The statute as amended can then be applied to those practices occurring after the amendment's effective date.[143] For example, even where a mobile home was sold before a UDAP statute's effective date, an action could be based upon the dealer's subsequent misrepresentations that its attempted repairs had cured all defects.[144] A home seller's failure to make promised repairs after the sale could be challenged, even when the sale itself occurred prior to the UDAP statute's effective date.[145] Even though contracts were entered into before the statute's effective date, a UDAP action could still be brought where the seller unfairly breached the contracts after the UDAP statute's effective date.[146]

135 Rotello v. Ring Around Products Inc., 614 S.W.2d 455 (Tex. Civ. App. 1981).

136 Marcotte v. American Motorists Ins. Co., 709 F.2d 378 (5th Cir. 1983) (Texas law); Robinson v. Lynmar Racquet Club, Inc., 851 P.2d 274 (Colo. Ct. App. 1993); Anderson v. Phoenix Inv. Counsel, 387 Mass. 444, 440 N.E.2d 1164 (1982) (not applied retroactively where would require plaintiff to act quickly after amendment's passage); Woods v. William M. Mercer, Inc., 769 S.W.2d 515 (Tex. 1988); Holland Mortgage & Inv. Corp. v. Bone, 751 S.W.2d 515 (Tex. App. 1987); Nash v. Carolina Cas. Ins. Co., 741 S.W.2d 598 (Tex. App. 1987); Mytel Int'l, Inc. v. Turbo Refrigerating Co., 689 S.W.2d 315 (Tex. App. 1985); Gibbs v. Main Bank of Houston, 666 S.W.2d 554 (Tex. App. 1984); Jim Walter Homes, Inc. v. Chapa, 614 S.W.2d 838 (Tex. Civ. App. 1981); Jim Walter Homes Inc. v. White, 617 S.W.2d 767 (Tex. Civ. App. 1981). *But see* Duco Assocs. Inc. v. Lipson, 11 Mass. App. Ct. 935, 416 N.E.2d 555 (1981); Ditommaso v. Laliberte, 9 Mass. App. Ct. 890, 402 N.E.2d 1079 (1980).

137 Schenck v. Ebby Halliday Real Estate, 803 S.W.2d 361 (Tex. App. 1990); Oil Country Haulers, Inc. v. Griffin, 668 S.W.2d 903 (Tex. App. 1984); Scholtz v. Sigel, 601 S.W.2d 516 (Tex. Civ. App. 1980); *see also* Lubbock Mortgage & Inv. Co. v. Thomas, 626 S.W.2d 611 (Tex. Civ. App. 1981); Petty v. Ferguson, 601 S.W.2d 782 (Tex. Civ. App. 1980).

138 Schenck v. Ebby Halliday Real Estate, 803 S.W.2d 361 (Tex. App. 1990); Oil Country Haulers, Inc. v. Griffin, 668 S.W.2d 903 (Tex. App. 1984); Wolfe Masonry Inc. v. Stewart, 664 S.W.2d 102 (Tex. App. 1983); Williams v. 3 Beally Brothers Inc., 628 S.W.2d 531 (Tex. App. 1982); *cf.* Reed v. Israel Nat'l Oil Co., 681 S.W.2d 228 (Tex. App. 1984) (where 1977 amendment required notice letter for causes of action filed after 1977, this did not apply to 1976 suit amended in 1983 to add UDAP count).

139 Acts of 74th Legis. (1995) Ch. 414,1 § 1.

140 Chakrabarti v. Marco S. Marinello Assocs., 12 Mass. App. Ct. 934, 425 N.E.2d 402 (1981); Goes v. Feldman, 8 Mass. App. Ct. 84, 391 N.E.2d 943 (1979); *see also* ABC Truck Rental & Leasing Co. v. Southern Cty. Mut. Ins. Co., 662 S.W.2d 132 (Tex. App. 1983) (venue provision change normally applied retroactively, but not where statute explicitly requires otherwise); Jim Walter Homes Inc. v. Douglas, 603 S.W.2d 255 (Tex. Civ. App. 1980) (applying venue provision at time of filing of the complaint, not at the time of the challenged practice, and not at the time the seller raises the venue issue during the litigation).

141 Carpentino v. Transport Ins. Co., 609 F. Supp. 556 (D. Conn. 1985); Citizens Bank & Trust Co. v. Grant, Clearinghouse No. 41,256 (Conn. Super. Ct. 1985); Flaumenhaft v. Forest Garage Used Cars, Inc., Clearinghouse No. 40,645 (Conn. Super. Ct. 1985); Dixico, Inc. v. R.J.R. Archer, Inc., Clearinghouse No. 40,644 (Super. Ct. 1985); Johnston v. Anchor Organization, 621 N.E.2d 137 (Ill. App. Ct. 1993) (deletion of public injury requirement applied retroactively); Zinser v. Rose, 614 N.E.2d 1259 (Ill. App. Ct. 1993) (elimination of public injury requirement merely clarified existing law and was retroactive). *See also* cases cited in § 7.5.3.1, *infra*, regarding retroactive application of a similar Illinois amendment. *But see* Aldridge v. Cosby, 1985 WL 5953 (D. Conn. Nov. 12, 1985); Hydro Air v. Versa Technologies, Inc., 599 F. Supp. 1119 (D. Conn. 1984); L. Cohen & Co. v. Dunn & Bradstreet, Inc., 12 Conn. Law Tribune 20 (D. Conn. Feb. 24, 1980); Lembo v. Schlesinger, 15 Conn. App. 150, 543 A.2d 780 (1988); O'Leary v. Indus. Park Corp., 14 Conn. App. 425, 542 A.2d 333 (1988); Rotophone, Inc. v. Danbury Hosp., 13 Conn. App. 230, 535 A.2d 830 (1988).

142 Nickerson v. Metco Tools Corp., 813 F.2d 529 (1st Cir. 1987) (Massachusetts law).

143 State *ex rel.* Guste v. Orkin Exterminating Co., 528 So. 2d 198 (La. Ct. App. 1988); La Sara Grain Co. v. First Nat'l Bank, 673 S.W.2d 558 (Tex. 1984); Woods v. Littleton, 554 S.W.2d 662 (Tex. 1977).

144 Town & Country Mobile Homes v. Stiles, 543 S.W.2d 664 (Tex. Civ. App. 1976).

145 MacDonald v. Mobley, 555 S.W.2d 916 (Tex. Civ. App. 1977). *Cf.* Crossland v. Canteen Corp., 711 F.2d 714 (5th Cir. 1983) (Texas law) (statute applicable at time representation made, not at time representation breached); Conann Constr. Inc. v. Muller, 618 S.W.2d 564 (Tex. Civ. App. 1981) (no deception found still occurring at time UDAP statute enacted, which was several years after original sale and deception).

146 State *ex rel.* Guste v. Orkin Exterminating Co., 528 So. 2d 198 (La. Ct. App. 1988).

7.5 Preconditions to Private Actions

7.5.1 Introduction

In some jurisdictions, state legislatures or courts hesitate to allow any consumer who wishes to complain about any deceptive practice to have immediate access to the state courts. This may be interpreted as a prejudice against cluttering the courts with "unimportant" matters or as a desire that consumers first attempt to settle disputes informally. These concerns are manifested in such preconditions to a UDAP action as a requirement that the consumer have suffered damage, that the consumer first attempt to settle the dispute informally, or that the action be in the public interest. Compliance with any preconditions to private actions that the state UDAP law imposes should be pleaded and proven.[147]

Even if none of such preconditions strictly applies in a jurisdiction, consumer litigants are well-advised to consider how their case will appear to an overworked judge more accustomed to large business disputes than to small consumer complaints. It is to consumers' tactical advantage to make clear that they have suffered real injury, that resolution of the matter is important to them and to the public, and that, despite their efforts with the seller and with other possible avenues of redress, only the court can provide effective relief.

7.5.2 Damage Precondition

7.5.2.1 Types of Damage Preconditions

UDAP statutes fall into several main patterns with respect to damage preconditions. The most explicit statutes condition the consumer's private cause of action upon suffering "an ascertainable loss," sometimes specifying that the loss must be "pecuniary" or "of money or property." Courts almost universally construe this language to impose a damage precondition,[148] although the loss may be slight and need not be quantifiable.[149] The second type of statute affords a private cause of action to persons who are "injured by" or "suffer a loss" due to a UDAP violation. Courts generally construe these statutes to require the plaintiff to have suffered some type of actual injury.[150] A third type of

147 Greenspan v. Allstate Ins. Co., 937 F. Supp. 288 (S.D.N.Y. 1996). *See* § 7.7.1, *infra*.

148 Alston v. Crown Auto, Inc., 224 F.3d 332 (4th Cir. 2000) (Virginia law); Jewell v. Medical Protective Co., 2003 WL 22682332 (D. Conn. Oct. 30, 2003) (plaintiff must allege some economic loss); Lester v. Percudani, 217 F.R.D. 345 (M.D. Pa. Sept. 2003) (need to prove fact of injury prevents class certification even though amount of injury need not be proven); Arsenault v. PNC Mortg. Corp., 2000 U.S. Dist. LEXIS 21667 (W.D. Ky. Nov. 3, 2000) (no UDAP claim where plaintiffs suffered no loss), *aff'd on other grounds*, 2002 WL 509402 (6th Cir. Nov. 1, 2002); Chisolm v. Transouth Fin. Corp., 194 F.R.D. 538 (E.D. Va. 2000) (private cause of action is afforded only to person who suffers loss); Tragianese v. Blackmon, 993 F. Supp. 96 (D. Conn. 1997); *In re* Derienzo, 254 B.R. 334 (Bankr. M.D. Pa. 2000); *In re* Galloway, 220 B.R. 236 (Bankr. E.D. Pa. 1998); *In re* Milbourne, 108 B.R. 522 (Bankr. E.D. Pa. 1989) (no UDAP claim on certain counts because consumer showed no actual damages); Moye v. Credit Acceptance Corp., 2000 Conn. Super. LEXIS 3072 (Nov. 3, 2000) (plaintiffs can not proceed with UDAP claim where no ascertainable loss alleged except in conclusory language); Silver v. Jacobs, 682 A.2d 551 (Conn. App. 1996); Yellowpine Water User's Ass'n v. Imel, 105 Idaho 349, 670 P.2d 54 (1983); Muss v. Driskell, Clearinghouse No. 47,931 (Ky. Ct. App. Sept. 20, 1991); Abbyad v. Mathes Group, 671 So. 2d 958 (La. App. 1996); Curtis v. Allstate Ins. Co., 787 A.2d 760 (Me. 2002); Mariello v. Giguere, 667 A.2d 588 (Me. 1995) (consumer met requirement of loss of money or property but denied UDAP recovery because of failure to meet now-repealed requirement that deceptive acts benefit the actor as well as harm the consumer); Meshinsky v. Nichols Yacht Sales, Inc., 110 N.J. 464, 541 A.2d 1063 (1988); Levy v. Edmund Buick-Pontiac, Ltd., 270 N.J. Super. 563, 637 A.2d 600 (1993) (assignee's lack of ascertainable damage deprived him of standing to bring a UDAP claim); Hedrick v. Spear, 138 Or. App. 53, 907 P.2d 1123 (1995) (UDAP claim dismissed for failure to prove ascertainable loss of money or property); Fields v. Yarborough Ford, Inc., 414 S.E.2d 164 (S.C. 1992); Eastlake Constr. Co. v. Hess, 102 Wash. 2d 30, 686 P.2d 465 (1984); Clark v. Luepke, 118 Wash. 2d 577, 826 P.2d 147 (1992); Anhold v. Daniels, 94 Wash. 2d 40, 614 P.2d 184 (1980); Thomas v. Wilfac, Inc., 828 P.2d 597 (Wash. Ct. App. 1992); Girard v. Myers, 694 P.2d 678 (Wash. Ct. App. 1985); Snyder v. Badgerland Mobile Homes, Inc., 659 N.W.2d 887 (Wis. App. 2003). *But see* Page & Wirtz Constr. Co. v. Solomon, 110 N.M. 206, 212, 794 P.2d 349 (1990) (injunctive relief allowed by statute if plaintiff is likely to suffer loss; ascertainable loss requirement does not apply to statutory damages); Jones v. General Motors Corp., 953 P.2d 1104 (N.M. App. 1998) (declining to find damage precondition for recovery of statutory damages). Illinois in 1996 amended one of its UDAP statutes to require a showing of actual damages *See* 815 Ill. Comp. Stat. 505/10a(a). At least one court has retroactively applied this requirement. *See* Greisz v. Household Bank, 8 F. Supp. 2d 1031 (N.D. Ill. 1998), *aff'd on other grounds*, 176 F.3d 1012 (7th Cir. 1999).

149 *See* §§ 7.5.2.4, 7.5.2.6, *infra*.

150 Heard v. Bonneville Billing and Collections, 2000 U.S. App. LEXIS 14625 (10th Cir. June 26, 2000) (unpublished, citation limited) (debtor did not have standing to bring challenge under Utah UDAP statute to collection attorney's unethical splitting of fees with collection agency where it caused her no injury); Ortho Pharmaceutical Corp. v. Cosprophar, Inc., 32 F.3d 690 (2d Cir. 1994) (UDAP plaintiff must prove injury in suit under N.Y. Gen. Bus. law § 349); Grantham & Mann v. American Safety Products, 831 F.2d 596 (6th Cir. 1987) (North Carolina law) (statute gives private cause of action to person whose business is broken up, destroyed, or injured); Anheuser-Busch, Inc. v. Caught-on-Bleu, Inc., 2003 WL 21715330 (D.N.H. July 22, 2003); King v. International Data Servs., 2002 WL 32345923 (D. Haw. Aug. 5, 2002); Sambor v. Omnia Credit Servs., 183 F. Supp. 2d 1234 (D. Haw. 2002); Basnight v. Diamond Developers, Inc., 146 F. Supp. 2d 754 (M.D.N.C. 2001); Avery v. Indus. Mortg. Co., 135 F. Supp. 2d 840 (W.D. Mich. 2001); Milford Power Ltd. P'ship v. New England Power Co., 918 F. Supp. 471 (D. Mass. 1996) (statute requires loss of money or property); Demitropoulos v. Bank One Milwaukee, N.A., 915 F.

statute does not say that the plaintiff must have suffered an injury, but works an injury or loss requirement into the statement of what the consumer can recover in a private suit.[151]

A fourth category comprises states that only require that the consumer be "aggrieved" by the UDAP violation. This language leaves more room for argument that actual damages are not a precondition, but courts have still generally construed it to require actual damage.[152]

The final type of statute has no language requiring actual loss.[153] Some courts have still read a damage precondition into these statutes on standing grounds,[154] but other courts have accepted the statutory language and allowed suit by

Supp. 1399 (N.D. Ill. 1996) (damage is a precondition of suit under Wisconsin UDAP statute, which affords private cause of action to person suffering pecuniary loss); Skinder-Strauss v. Massachusetts Continuing Legal Education, 914 F. Supp. 665 (D. Mass. 1995) (loss of money or property required under § 11); Weight Watchers Int'l v. Stouffer Corp., 744 F. Supp. 1259 (S.D.N.Y. 1990) (N.Y. Gen. Bus. Law § 349H requires plaintiff to have been injured by UDAP violation); *In re* Glaser, 2002 WL 32375007 (Bankr. E.D. Va. Oct. 25, 2002) (no UDAP claim where failure to list all items on pawn ticket caused no quantifiable loss); Citaramanis v. Hallowell, 613 A.2d 964 (Md. 1992) (loss required for private action but not public enforcement action); Billions v. White & Stafford Furniture Co., 528 So. 2d 878 (Ala. Civ. App. 1988); Beard v. Goodyear Tire & Rubber Co., 587 A.2d 195 (D.C. 1991) (suffering damage is a condition precedent to suit under former version of D.C. UDAP law); Osbourne v. Capital City Mortgage Corp., 667 A.2d 1321 (D.C. App. 1995) (consumer must have suffered damage in order to bring suit under D.C. UDAP law; note that D.C. Code has since been amended to eliminate damage requirement); Moore-Davis Motors, Inc. v. Joyner, 252 Ga. App. 617, 556 S.E.2d 137 (2001); Chancellor v. Gateway Lincoln-Mercury, Inc., 233 Ga. App. 38, 502 S.E.2d 799 (1998) (decision cites standing concepts rather than statutory language, but statute affords private cause of action only to persons "suffering injury or damages"); Agnew v. Great Atlantic & Pacific Tea Co., 502 S.E.2d 735 (Ga. App. Ct. 1998); Hall v. Lovell Regency Homes Ltd., 121 Md. App. 1, 708 A.2d 344 (1998) (UDAP claim dismissed for failure to prove actual injury or loss); Legg v. Castruccio, 100 Md. App. 748, 642 A.2d 906 (1994); Lord v. Commercial Union Ins. Co., 60 Mass. App. Ct. 309, 801 N.E.2d 303 (Mass. App. Ct. 2004); Walsh v. Atamian Motors Inc., 10 Mass App. Ct. 828, 406 N.E.2d 733 (1980); K.A.C. v. Benson, 527 N.W.2d 553 (Minn. 1995) (UDAP suit fails because plaintiff showed no injury); Sutton v. Viking Oldsmobile Nissan, Inc., 611 N.W.2d 60 (Minn. App. 2000), *vacated, remanded*, 623 N.W.2d 247 (Minn. 2001) (remanding for reconsideration in light of Group Health Plan v. Philip Morris, Inc., 621 N.W.2d 2 (Minn. 2001), which holds that plaintiff must show a causal connection between unlawful act and damages), *appeal after remand*, 2001 Minn. App. LEXIS 866 (July 31, 2001) (consumer raised genuine issue of fact about "legal nexus" between misconduct and injury, with allegation that if he had known dealer kept part of sum paid for service contract, he would have negotiated about price or refused to purchase); Goshen v. Mut. Life Ins. Co., 98 N.Y.2d 314, 774 N.E.2d 1190 (2002); Small v. Lorillard Tobacco Co., 94 N.Y.2d 43, 720 N.E.2d 892 (1999) (no UDAP claim unless plaintiff alleges injury where statute requires that plaintiff be "injured"); Oswego Laborers' Local 214 Pension Fund v. Marine Midland Bank, 85 N.Y.2d 20, 623 N.Y.S.2d 529, 647 N.E.2d 741 (1995) (must show injury but need not be pecuniary); Pearce v. American Defender Life Ins. Co., 343 S.E.2d 174 (N.C. 1986) (statute grants relief "if any person shall be injured"); Melton v. Family First Mortg. Corp., 576 S.E.2d 365 (N.C. App. 2003) (no UDAP liability where creditor's backdating of loan application documents caused no injury). *Cf.* LeSage v. Norwest Bank Calhoun-Isles, 409 N.W.2d 536 (Minn. Ct. App. 1987) (no loss necessary for injunction, but for damages must show legal nexus between acts and losses).

151 City of Marshall v. Bryant Air Conditioning, 650 F.2d 724 (5th Cir. 1981) (Texas law); McGraw v. Loyola Ford, Inc., 124 Md. App. 560, 723 A.2d 502 (1999) ("any person may bring an action to recover for injury or loss sustained" required actual injury or loss). Illinois cases prior to an amendment that made a damages requirement explicit also found a damage requirement implicit in the statute: Oliveira v. Amoco Oil Co., 201 Ill. 2d 134, 776 N.E.2d 151, 267 Ill. Dec. 14 (2002) (consumer must show proximate causation of actual damages; not shown where plaintiff never saw the deceptive ads); Petty v. Chrysler Corp., 799 N.E.2d 432 (Ill. App. 2003) (insufficient proof of damages; declining to recognize salesman's alleged loss of goodwill as damages); Smith v. Prime Cable, 658 N.E.2d 1325 (Ill. App. Ct. 1995) (no cause of action because consumers paid disputed charge); Tarin v. Pellonari, 253 Ill. App. 3d 542, 625 N.E.2d 739 (1993) (showing of damage necessary for private cause of action under Illinois Consumer Fraud Act); Roche v. Fireside Chrysler-Plymouth, 600 N.E.2d 1218 (Ill. App. Ct. 1992) (no UDAP claim where consumer suffered no damage); Duran v. Leslie Oldsmobile, 594 N.E.2d 1355 (Ill. App. Ct. 1992); Pioneer Bank & Trust Co. v. Mitchell, 126 Ill. App. 3d 870, 467 N.E.2d 1011 (1984); Beard v. Gress, 90 Ill. App. 3d 622, 413 N.E.2d 448 (1980).

152 Haun v. Don Mealy Imports, Inc., 285 F. Supp. 2d 1297 (M.D. Fla. 2003) (Fla. DTPA); Green v. Kansas City Power & Light Co. (*In re* Green), 281 B.R. 699 (D. Kan. 2002); Macias v. HBC of Florida, Inc., 694 So. 2d 88 (Fla. Dist. Ct. App. 1997) (Florida's requirement that plaintiff be "aggrieved" requires showing of actual loss); Finstad v. Washburn University of Topeka, 252 Kan. 465, 845 P.2d 685 (1993) ("aggrieved by" requires causal link between deception and damage); Patterson v. Beall, 19 P.3d 839 (Okla. 2000); Tibbetts v. Sight 'N Sound Appliance Centers, Inc., 77 P.3d 1042 (Okla. 2003); Walls v. American Tobacco Co., 2000 OK 66, 11 P.3d 626 (2000) (affording remedy to "aggrieved consumer" means actual damage is required).

153 *See* § 7.5.2.3, *infra*.

154 Williams v. Purdue Phama Co., 297 F. Supp. 2d 171 (D.D.C. 2003); Stein v. Sprint Corp., 22 F. Supp. 2d 1210, 1215 (D. Kan. 1998) (decision on reconsideration) (although Kansas UDAP statute does not require plaintiff in class action for injunction to be aggrieved, court implies such a requirement because of constitutional standing concerns); Lens Crafters, Inc. v. Vision World, Inc., 943 F. Supp. 1481 (D. Minn. 1996) (no mention of damage in false advertising statute, but court finds implicit requirement of damage); Hall v. Walter, 969 P.2d 224 (Colo. 1998) (implies damage requirement into silent statute because of standing concepts; plaintiff must have suffered injury in fact to a legally protected interest in order to have standing); Carter v. Lachance, 766 A.2d 717 (N.H. 2001). *See also* Nataros v. Fine Arts Gallery, 126 Ariz. 44, 612 P.2d 500 (App. Ct. 1980); Parks v. Macro Dynamics, Inc., 121 Ariz. 517, 591 P.2d 1005 (1979); Sellinger v. Freeway Mobile Home Sales, Inc., 110 Ariz. 573, 521 P.2d 1119 (1974) (implies private cause of action for those injured).

persons who have not been injured.[155]

7.5.2.2 Implications of Damage Precondition

A damage precondition has limited impact on private actions for actual or multiple damages, since such damages have to be shown at some point. But if it applies to injunctive relief, it may bar actions where citizens are acting as private attorneys general and seeking injunctive relief but have suffered no personal loss.[156]

Damage preconditions also make minimum, statutory damages more difficult to obtain.[157] Statutory provisions for minimum damages allow consumers to recover a specified damage amount (usually $100 or $200) based solely on evidence that the seller has violated the statute. Since a tendency or capacity to deceive, and not actual deception, may be sufficient to prove deception,[158] actual damage may not otherwise be an element of a UDAP action. But if the statute has a damage precondition, the consumer must prove some amount of actual damage before he or she can win statutory damages.

Particularly for class actions, damage preconditions can significantly complicate the plaintiff's burden of proof.[159] On the other hand, if the class can be certified and liability established without having to show injury, then the remedy part of the trial can proceed separately. Where the UDAP statute allows minimum damages for each class member, the class action may never even have to address the actual damage issue if damage is not a precondition to a UDAP action.

An interesting issue is whether an organization can bring an action in its own name where the organization itself is not directly injured by the practice. A New York court has held that where legislation protects a class, a bona fide and nationally recognized organization may represent the class of persons who can claim to be aggrieved under the legislation. In the alternative, the organization need only fall within the zone of interest to be protected by the statute.[160]

7.5.2.3 UDAP Statutes That Explicitly Dispense with Damage Preconditions

The District of Columbia's UDAP law authorizes, and a California UDAP statute formerly authorized, suits without any damage precondition. Any person, organization, or group, whether acting in its own interests, on behalf of its members, or for the general public, may bring suit under the District of Columbia law.[161] Notwithstanding this law, however, a federal district court has held that general standing requirements adopted by District of Columbia courts still preclude suit unless the consumer has suffered injury in fact.[162]

Until 2004, one California UDAP statute allowed suit for injunction, restitution, and other equitable remedies by "any person acting for the interests of itself, its members, or the general public."[163] A private plaintiff need not have been

155 Kraus v. Trinity Mgmt. Servs., Inc., 23 Cal. 4th 116, 999 P.2d 718, 739, 96 Cal. Rptr. 2d 485 (2000); Committee on Children's Television v. General Foods Corp., 35 Cal. 3d 197, 673 P.2d 660, 668, 197 Cal. Rptr. 783 (1983); Page & Wirtz Constr. Co. v. Solomon, 110 N.M. 206, 212, 794 P.2d 349 (1990) (injunctive relief allowed by statute if plaintiff is likely to suffer loss; ascertainable loss requirement does not apply to statutory damages); Jones v. General Motors Corp., 953 P.2d 1104 (N.M. App. 1998) (declining to find damage precondition for recovery of statutory damages); Peabody v. P.J.'s Auto Village, 569 A.2d 460 (Vt. 1989) (actual damages need not be shown, since tendency to deceive is sufficient; consumer could recover despite inability to show that clipped condition caused car's specific malfunctions).

156 Maguire v. Citicorp Retail Servs., Inc., 147 F.3d 232 (2d Cir. 1998) (failure of named plaintiff to show ascertainable loss precluded her claim for classwide injunctive relief under Connecticut UDAP statute). *See* Halloran's v. Spillane's Servicecenter, Inc., 41 Conn. Supp. 484, 587 A.2d 176 (1990) (two UDAP claims dismissed for failure to show ascertainable loss); LeSage v. Norwest Bank Calhoun-Isles, 409 N.W.2d 536 (Minn. Ct. App. 1987) (need not prove damage for injunctive action, but must do so for damage action); § 8.6.3.1, *infra*. *Cf.* Service Road Corp. v. Quinn, 241 Conn. 630, 698 A.2d 258 (1997) (plaintiffs able to obtain injunctive relief because they proved ascertainable loss).

157 *In re* Glaser, 2002 WL 32375007 (Bankr. E.D. Va. Oct. 25, 2002) (no statutory damages without some actual loss). *See* Jackson v. Wood, 859 P.2d 378 (Idaho Ct. App. 1993) (where statute requires ascertainable loss as a precondition of suit, statutory damages are unavailable unless some actual damage shown). *See also* § 8.4.1.1, *infra*. *But see* Carter v. Lachance, 766 A.2d 717 (N.H. 2001) (plaintiff may recover statutory damages without showing actual damage); Jones v. General Motors Corp., 953 P.2d 1104 (N.M. App. 1998) (plaintiff who has not suffered actual damage may recover statutory damages despite ascertainable loss requirement); Dantzig v. Sloe, 684 N.E.2d 715, 718 (Ohio App. 1996) (consumer may recover statutory damages without showing loss).

158 *See* § 4.2.9, *supra*.

159 *See, e.g.*, Lester v. Percudani, 217 F.R.D. 345 (M.D. Pa. Sept. 2003) (need to prove fact of injury prevents class certification even though amount of injury need not be proven).

160 NYPIRG v. Insurance Information Institute, 140 Misc. 2d 920, 531 N.Y.S.2d 1002 (Sup. Ct. 1988), *aff'd on other grounds*, 161 A.D.2d 204, 554 N.Y.S.2d 590 (1990).

161 D.C. Code § 28-3905(k) *as amended* effective Oct. 10, 2000. *See* Wells v. Allstate Ins. Co., 210 F.R.D. 1 (D.D.C. 2002) (noting that 2000 amendments eliminate injury in fact and causation requirements; declining to decide if amendments apply to suit filed before effective date). *But cf.* Athridge v. Aetna Cas. & Surety Co., 351 F.3d 1166, 1176 (D.C. Cir. 2003) (construing law to include damage requirement for private suits; claim arose when an earlier, narrower version of the law was in effect).

162 Williams v. Purdue Phama Co., 297 F. Supp. 2d 171 (D.D.C. 2003).

163 Cal. Bus. & Prof. Code § 17203. *See, e.g.*, Braco v. Superior Court, 2002 Cal. App. Unpub. LEXIS 2534 (Mar. 28, 2002) (unpublished, citation limited) (any person, even if not an

directly harmed by the defendant's practices in order to bring suit.[164] The court could order restitution to all injured individuals without the formality of class certification.[165] If the individuals who have been injured could not be identified, the court could order a fluid recovery, with the restitution funds used as much as possible to correct the harm done, but for this remedy a class action had to be formally certified.[166] In 2004, Proposition 64 added a requirement that the plaintiff suffer injury in fact and lose money or property. Even before this amendment, some federal courts imposed a standing requirement.[167]

Under California's other UDAP statute, the California Supreme Court interprets standing requirements liberally. If the defendant responds to a demand letter sent by the named plaintiff in a UDAP class action by fully remedying the injury of the named plaintiff (resulting in no damage to that individual), that party can continue a class action where the rest of the class still suffers injury.[168]

Ohio's UDAP statute does not have a damage precondition, and allows statutory damages even in the absence of actual injury.[169] In the event of a violation of the statute, a consumer "has a cause of action and is entitled to relief" of actual damages or, if the defendant violated a rule or the holding in a decision that has been made available for public inspection, statutory damages of $200.[170] While the violation must arise from a consumer transaction, that term is defined to include solicitations that do not result in a sale.[171]

Even if a UDAP statute has a damage precondition, its scope should be analyzed carefully. For example, the precondition may not apply to a claim for declaratory or injunctive relief[172] or rescission.[173]

7.5.2.4 Must the Amount of Damage Be Proved?

Courts generally do not require that the exact amount of damage be proved, only that it is clear there is some damage, particularly when the statute requires the consumer to show only "ascertainable" loss. The loss must merely be capable of being discovered, observed, or estimated.[174] Courts in Oregon,[175] Connecticut,[176] Pennsylvania,[177] West Vir-

altruistic crusader, can pursue action); Prata v. Superior Court, 91 Cal. App. 4th 1128, 111 Cal. Rptr. 2d 296 (2001) (restitution can be ordered without proof of reliance, actual deception, or actual damages). *Cf.* Rosenbluth Int'l, Inc. v. Superior Court, 101 Cal. App. 4th 1073, 124 Cal. Rptr. 2d 844 (2002) (statute does not allow individual to bring suit on behalf of Fortune 100 companies that were overbilled by travel agencies, as those companies are not the "general public").

164 Mass. Mut. Life Ins. Co. v. Superior Court, 97 Cal. App. 4th 1282, 119 Cal. Rptr. 2d 190 (2002).

165 Kraus v. Trinity Mgmt. Servs., 23 Cal. 4th 116, 999 P.2d 718 (2000); Kagan v. Gibralter Sav. & Loan Ass'n, 676 P.2d 1060, 200 Cal. Rptr. 38 (1984).

166 Kraus v. Trinity Mgmt. Servs., 23 Cal. 4th 116, 999 P.2d 718 (2000); Braco v. Superior Court, 2002 Cal. App. Unpub. LEXIS 2534 (Mar. 28, 2002) (unpublished, citation limited).

167 *See* Kennedy v. Unumprovident Corp., 2002 U.S. App. LEXIS 23191 (9th Cir. Nov. 4, 2002) (unpublished, citation limited) (while plaintiff may assert § 17200 claims on behalf of others in state court, prudential standing requirements preclude such a suit in federal court). *See also* Virgin Enterprises Ltd. v. American Longevity, 2001 WL 34142402 (S.D.N.Y. Mar. 1, 2001) (Cal. law) (plaintiff alleged injury so met Art. III standing requirements).

168 Kagan v. Gibralter Sav. & Loan Ass'n, 676 P.2d 1060, 200 Cal. Rptr. 38 (1984) (interpreting Cal. Civ. Code § 1750). *See also* Garcia v. ARCS Mortg., Inc., 2002 Cal. App. Unpub. LEXIS 9661 (Oct. 18, 2002) (unpublished, citation limited) (plaintiffs who no longer have individual claims may still appeal trial court's ruling on class issues). *Cf.* Hamelin v. Allstate Ins. Co., 2002 U.S. Dist. LEXIS 5093 (C.D. Cal. Mar. 12, 2002) (plaintiff would have standing to pursue claim in state court even though she does not meet federal standing requirements).

169 *See* Dantzig v. Sloe, 684 N.E.2d 715, 718 (Ohio App. 1996).

170 Ohio Rev. Code § 1345.09(A).

171 Ohio Rev. Code § 1345.01(A).

172 *See* § 8.6.3.1, *infra*. *Cf.* Weinberg v. Sprint Corp., 173 N.J. 233, 801 A.2d 281 (2002) (plaintiff need not prove ascertainable loss at trial in order to obtain injunctive relief, but proof must be sufficient to survive summary judgment). *But see* Haun v. Don Mealy Imports, Inc., 285 F. Supp. 2d 1297 (M.D. Fla. 2003) (dismissing DTPA claim for declaratory and injunctive relief because of failure to allege damage); Freeman Health Sys. v. Wass, 124 S.W.3d 504 (Mo. App. 2004) (construing UDAP statute to allow injunctive relief only if consumer successfully brings damages suit, which requires ascertainable loss).

173 *See, e.g.*, New Phila, Inc. v. Sagrilla, 2002 WL 1467771 (Ohio App. June 26, 2002) (unpublished, citation limited).

174 *In re* Wiggins, 273 B.R. 839, 856 (Bankr. D. Idaho 2001); Rein v. Koons Ford, Inc., 567 A.2d 101 (Md. 1989) (Va. law). *See also* Idaho Admin. Code § 04.02.01.020.05 (defining "ascertainable loss"). *But see* Criscuolo v. Shaheen, 736 A.2d 947, 953 (Conn. Super. 1999) (ascertainable loss necessary for injunctive relief); *In re* W. Va. Rezulin Litig., 585 S.E.2d 52 (W. Va. 2003).

175 Scott v. Western Int'l Surplus Sales, Inc., 267 Or. 512, 517 P.2d 661 (1973). *See also* Weigel v. Ron Tonkin Chevrolet Co., 298 Or. 127, 690 P.2d 488 (1984). *Accord* Feitler v. Animation Celection, Inc., 13 P.3d 1044 (Or. App. 2000).

176 Bruce v. Home Depot, USA, Inc., 308 F. Supp. 2d 72 (D. Conn. 2004) (plaintiff need not allege a specific ascertainable loss with respect to each public policy, common-law, and/or statutory violation on which UDAP claim is based); Locascio v. Imports Unlimited, Inc., 309 F. Supp. 2d 267 (D. Conn. 2004) (finding plaintiff to have proven ascertainable loss even though proof of actual damages was insufficient); Beverly Hills Concepts v. Schatz & Schatz, Ribicoff & Kotkin, 247 Conn. 48, 717 A.2d 724 (1998); Service Road Corp. v. Quinn, 241 Conn. 630, 698 A.2d 258 (1997); Hinchliffe v. American Motors Corp., 440 A.2d 810 (Conn. 1981); Larobina v. Home Depot, USA, Inc., 821 A.2d 283 (Conn. App. 2003); Johnson Elec. Co. v. Salce Contracting Assocs., 72 Conn. App. 342, 805 A.2d 735 (2002). *Accord* Aurigemma v. Arco Petroleum Products Co., 734 F. Supp. 1025 (D. Conn. 1990). *Cf.* Reader v. Cassarino, 51 Conn. App. 292, 721 A.2d 911 (1998) (while evidence of ascertainable loss need not be precise, there must be some evidence of nature and extent of injury).

177 Lester v. Percudani, 217 F.R.D. 345 (M.D. Pa. Sept. 2003); *In re* Milbourne, 108 B.R. 522 (Bankr. E.D. Pa. 1989) (statutory damages awarded even though consumer could not quantify actual damages).

ginia,[178] and New Jersey[179] agree that an ascertainable loss requirement does not necessitate proof of the amount of the loss, as long as the damages are measurable. "Loss" has a broader meaning than "damage."[180] Proof that would be sufficient for an award of damages is unnecessary.[181] Nonquantifiable injuries such as damage to a consumer's credit rating are sufficient.[182] The potential loss of confidence by regulators and investors in a business can satisfy the statutory requirement of a loss of money or property, even though calculating this damage in dollar terms would be difficult.[183] A New York court has interpreted the language "injured" in the UDAP statute as not requiring proof of actual damages, but just proof that the consumer was misled in a material way.[184]

7.5.2.5 Consumer Injuries That Satisfy the Damage Requirement

7.5.2.5.1 Non-pecuniary losses

The type of injury that is required depends first on the language of the statute. Some UDAP statutes specify that the consumer must have suffered a loss of "money or property." Courts in these states may preclude UDAP cases where the plaintiff has suffered personal injury but not other damage.[185] By contrast, a UDAP statute that only requires the consumer to suffer a loss or be aggrieved is properly interpreted not to be limited to pecuniary loss.[186] Thus, a consumer who was threatened with suit and criminal prosecution by a debt collector, causing him to undertake the burden of seeking assistance of third parties, was "aggrieved" and could bring a UDAP claim.[187] The Washington[188] and New York[189] injury requirements can be satisfied by non-pecuniary injuries. A consumer's wasted time can be an ascertainable loss.[190]

Massachusetts' highest court originally held that emotional distress and other injuries to the person satisfied its UDAP statute's requirement of an "injury."[191] When the statute was amended to require "loss of money or property," however, the courts reached the opposite conclusion.[192] The current Massachusetts UDAP statute requires only that a

178 *In re* W. Va. Rezulin Litig., 585 S.E.2d 52 (W. Va. 2003).

179 Talalai v. Cooper Tire & Rubber Co., 360 N.J. Super. 547, 823 A.2d 888 (Law Div. 2001); Miller v. American Family Publishers, 284 N.J. Super. 67, 663 A.2d 643 (Chancery Div. 1995). *See also* Weinberg v. Sprint Corp., 173 N.J. 233, 801 A.2d 281 (2002) (plaintiff need not prove ascertainable loss at trial in order to obtain injunctive relief, but proof must be sufficient to survive summary judgment).

180 Beverly Hills Concepts, Inc. v. Schatz & Scatz, Ribicoff & Kotkin, 247 Conn. 48, 79, 717 A.2d 724 (1998); Larobina v. Home Depot, USA, Inc., 821 A.2d 283 (Conn. App. 2003).

181 Service Road Corp. v. Quinn, 241 Conn. 630, 698 A.2d 258 (1997); Rizzo Pool Co. v. Del Grosso, 232 Conn. 666, 657 A.2d 1087 (1995) (evidence sufficient to estimate damages is sufficient); Feitler v. Animation Celection, Inc., 13 P.3d 1044 (Or. App. 2000) ("ascertainable loss" can include losses not actionable under common law). *Accord* Gadula v. Gen. Motors Corp., 2001 Mich. App. LEXIS 692 (Jan. 5, 2001) (unpublished, limited precedent); Zwiercan v. Gen. Motors Corp., 2002 WL 1472335 (Pa. Com. Pl. May 22, 2002). *See also* Clement v. St. Charles Nissan, Inc., 103 S.W.3d 898 (Mo. App. 2003) (ascertainable loss requirement satisfied even though amount of damages is somewhat nebulous); Weinberg v. Sprint Corp., 173 N.J. 233, 801 A.2d 281 (2002) (plaintiff need not prove ascertainable loss at trial in order to obtain injunctive relief, but proof must be sufficient to survive summary judgment).

182 Besel v. Viking Ins. Co., 105 Wash. App. 463, 21 P.3d 293 (2001), *rev'd on other grounds*, 49 P.3d 887 (Wash. 2002).

183 Bro-Vita, Ltd. v. Rausch, 759 F. Supp. 33 (D. Mass. 1991). *See also* Service Road Corp. v. Quinn, 241 Conn. 630, 698 A.2d 258 (1997) (business's loss of potential customers sufficient even without proof regarding any individual customer).

184 Geismar v. Abraham & Straus, 109 Misc. 2d 495, 439 N.Y.S.2d 1005 (Dist. Ct. 1981).

185 Association of Washington Public Hosp. Districts v. Philip Morris Inc., 241 F.3d 696 (9th Cir. 2001) (expenses for tobacco-related illnesses are personal injuries and do not qualify as injuries to business or property); Blowers v. Eli Lilly & Co., 100 F. Supp. 2d 1265 (D. Haw. 2000). *But cf.* Cosentino v. Philip Morris Inc., 1998 WL 34168879 (N.J. Super., Law Div., June 5, 1998) (cost of medical monitoring is "ascertainable loss of moneys or property" even though underlying condition is a non-economic injury).

186 Lowe v. Surpas Resource Corp., 253 F. Supp. 2d 1209, 1227–29 (D. Kan. 2003); Caputo v. Professional Recovery Servs., Inc., 261 F. Supp. 2d 1249 (D. Kan. 2003); Avery v. Indus. Mortg. Co., 135 F. Supp. 2d 840 (W.D. Mich. 2001); Oswego Laborers' Local 214 Pension Fund v. Marine Midland Bank, 85 N.Y.2d 20, 623 N.Y.S.2d 529, 647 N.E.2d 741 (1995) (must show injury but need not be pecuniary); Sorrel v. Eagle Healthcare, Inc., 110 Wash. App. 290, 38 P.3d 1024 (2002).

187 Caputo v. Professional Recovery Servs., Inc., 261 F. Supp. 2d 1249 (D. Kan. 2003).

188 Besel v. Viking Ins. Co., 105 Wash. App. 463, 21 P.3d 293 (2001) (non-quantifiable injuries such as diminution in value of property, loss of goodwill, or harm to credit rating sufficient), *rev'd on other grounds*, 49 P.3d 887 (Wash. 2002).

189 Anonymous v. CVS Corp., 188 Misc. 2d 616, 728 N.Y.S.2d 333 (Sup. Ct. 2001). *But see* Smith v. Chase Manhattan Bank, 293 A.D.2d 598, 741 N.Y.S.2d 100 (2002) (sale of plaintiff's personal information to telemarketers and direct mail solicitors, who then offered goods and services, does not constitute actual injury).

190 Bump v. Robbins, 24 Mass. App. Ct. 296, 509 N.E.2d 12 (1987); Brashears v. Sight 'N' Sound Appliance Centers, Inc., 981 P.2d 1270 (Okla. App. 1999). *See also* Sign-O-Life Signs, Inc. v. Delauventi Florists, Inc., 825 P.2d 714 (Wash. Ct. App. 1992) (businesswoman's time away from work to handle business dispute sufficient to show injury to business). *But see* Hedrick v. Spear, 138 Or. App. 53, 907 P.2d 1123 (1995) (loss of time from work while attending trial of UDAP claim is not an ascertainable loss).

191 Haddad v. Gonzalez, 410 Mass. 855, 576 N.E.2d 658 (1991). *See also* Delaney v. Budget Rent A Car, Clearinghouse No. 36,595 (Conn. Super. Ct. Oct. 11, 1983) (mental distress may be recognized as legal injury).

192 McGrath v. Mishara, 386 Mass. 74, 434 N.E.2d 1215 (1982); Baldassari v. Public Fin. Trust, 369 Mass. 33, 337 N.E.2d 701 (1975); *see also* Tower v. Hirschhorn, 397 Mass. 581, 492 N.E.2d 728 (1986).

consumer plaintiff be injured, without specifying the nature of the injury.[193] (Business plaintiffs must still show a "loss of money or property."[194])

7.5.2.5.2 Clauses that have not been enforced

In Massachusetts, the injury requirement for consumer cases is satisfied where a lease contains unenforceable terms even though the tenants have never read the lease and the landlord has never threatened to utilize those terms. The mere invasion of a legal right constitutes an "injury."[195] But courts in other states have found that consumers suffered no "ascertainable loss of money or property" where a confusing and unenforceable provision was included in a contract but was never used nor had any impact on the consumers.[196] These courts probably viewed loss of "money or property" as a more restrictive requirement than the Massachusetts "injury" precondition. Similarly, a court may find that including authority to charge an illegal fee in a contract does not cause a loss if the fee is never actually imposed.[197]

7.5.2.5.3 Temporary losses

A temporary deprivation of property[198] or loss of the use of money[199] can satisfy a damage requirement. Slow payment of owed money is loss of money or property, even if the money is eventually paid, because the consumer has lost the use of the money and expenses in trying to collect the money.[200] One court has held, however, that a consumer suffered no loss when illegal fees were collected but later refunded.[201] This decision is questionable, since the consumer clearly did suffer a temporary loss. The fact that the defendant made restitution with interest may preclude actual damages, but having suffered a loss at some point during the transaction, the plaintiff should be able to claim statutory damages.

7.5.2.5.4 Delivering product different than consumer bargained for

An ascertainable loss requirement is satisfied if the consumer has purchased an item that is different from or inferior to that for which the consumer bargained.[202] Whenever a product fails to measure up to representations, even if the product is actually more valuable than represented, the consumer has been injured.[203] Similarly, there is "ascertain-

193 Mass. Gen. Laws ch. 93A, § 9.

194 Mass. Gen. Laws ch. 93A, § 11. *See* Tech Plus, Inc. v. Ansel, 793 N.E.2d 1256 (Mass. App. 2003).

195 Leardi v. Brown, 394 Mass. 151, 474 N.E.2d 1094 (1985); Lord v. Commercial Union Ins. Co., 60 Mass. App. Ct. 309, 801 N.E.2d 303 (Mass. App. Ct. 2004) (nominal damages not available unless consumer has suffered some harm; insurer's failure to send a notice caused no injury where consumer already knew the information).

196 Orlando v. Finance One, 369 S.E.2d 882 (W. Va. 1988). *See also In re* Milbourne, 108 B.R. 522 (Bankr. E.D. Pa. 1989) (no actual damages shown from lender's failure to disclose that it retained multiple mortgages, where consumer already received TIL damages for this nondisclosure); Race v. Fleetwood Retail Corp., 2003 WL 1901274 (Wash. App. Apr. 17, 2003) (unpublished, citation limited) (failure to hold earnest money in trust account, in violation of statute, did not cause injury where buyers would not have had use of the money even if it had been properly deposited).

197 Polk v. Crown Auto, Inc., 228 F.3d 541 (4th Cir. 2000) (Virginia law).

198 Josey v. Filene's, Inc., 187 F. Supp. 2d 9 (D. Conn. 2002).

199 Arthur D. Little, Inc. v. Dooyang Corp., 147 F.3d 47 (1st Cir. 1998) (Mass. law) (temporary loss of use of money is a loss of money or property); Keith v. Howerton, 2001 Tenn. App. LEXIS 646 (Aug. 28, 2001) (unreported, citation limited); Mason v. Mortgage Am., Inc., 114 Wash. 2d 842, 792 P.2d 142 (1990) (temporary loss of title to property satisfies damage requirement); Sorrel v. Eagle Healthcare, Inc., 110 Wash. App. 290, 38 P.3d 1024 (2002) (denial of use of funds for two weeks). *See also In re* Wiggins, 273 B.R. 839 (Bankr. D. Idaho 2001) (denial of access to annuity payments for 2 years is ascertainable loss).

200 Arthur D. Little, Inc. v. Dooyang Corp., 147 F.3d 47 (1st Cir. 1998) (Mass. law).

201 Alston v. Crown Auto, Inc., 224 F.3d 332 (4th Cir. 2000) (Virginia law). *See also* Huss v. Sessler Ford, Inc., 343 Ill. App. 3d 835, 799 N.E.2d 444 (Ill. App. 2003) (pre-suit offer of refund moots case).

202 Locascio v. Imports Unlimited, Inc., 309 F. Supp. 2d 267 (D. Conn. 2004); Delahunt v. Cytodyne Technologies, 241 F. Supp. 2d 827 (S.D. Ohio 2003); Brunwasser v. Trans World Airlines, Inc., 541 F. Supp. 1338 (W.D. Pa. 1982) (airline advertised non-stop service but then cancelled it and offered only refund, flight on different day, or flight that was not non-stop); Craft v. Philip Morris Cos., Inc., 2003 WL 23139381 (Mo. Cir. Ct. Dec. 31, 2003); Union Ink Co. v. AT&T Corp., 352 N.J. Super. 617, 801 A.2d 361 (App. Div. 2002); Talalai v. Cooper Tire & Rubber Co., 360 N.J. Super. 547, 823 A.2d 888 (Law Div. 2001); Miller v. American Family Publishers, 284 N.J. Super. 67, 663 A.2d 643 (Chancery Div. 1995) (ascertainable loss shown where consumers thought they were getting both a magazine subscription and an enhanced chance of winning a sweepstakes, but actually got only the former); Zurakov v. Register.com, Inc., Mountz v. Global Vision Prods., Inc., 770 N.Y.S.2d 603 (Sup. Ct. 2003); 304 A.D.2d 176, 760 N.Y.S.2d 13 (2003) (not getting the service paid for meets injury requirement); Feitler v. Animation Celection, Inc., 13 P.3d 1044 (Or. App. 2000) (art collection sold to buyer did not include all known pieces, contrary to representations); *In re* W. Va. Rezulin Litig., 585 S.E.2d 52 (W. Va. 2003). *See also* Gadula v. Gen. Motors Corp., 2001 Mich. App. LEXIS 692 (Jan. 5, 2001) (unpublished, limited precedent) (where car did not live up to buyer's expectations, she was entitled to at least statutory damages). *See also* Larobina v. Home Depot, USA, Inc., 821 A.2d 283 (Conn. App. 2003) (loss of benefit of bargain due to bait and switch is ascertainable loss); Coley v. Champion Home Builders Co., 590 S.E.2d 20 (N.C. App. 2004) (cost of defective product, or cost to retrofit it, is actual injury). *But see* Green v. Gen. Motors Corp., 2003 WL 21730592 (N.J. Super., App. Div. July 10, 2003) (alleged safety defect in vehicle not ascertainable loss of money or property where vehicle met federal standards and had not yet malfunctioned).

203 Hinchliffe v. American Motors Corp., 440 A.2d 810 (Conn. 1981) (consumer suffers ascertainable loss if wants to buy energy saving subcompact but gets more valuable gas guzzler);

able loss" because of decreased market value of a slightly used car sold as new even though the car is just like new.[204]

A consumer suffers ascertainable loss even though a complained-of defect is covered by a written warranty.[205] Where substandard work has been performed that would require repairs to correct, the consumer has suffered ascertainable loss even if he or she does not have the repairs done[206] or continues to live in the home on which the work was done.[207] Receiving less than the consumer reasonably expected in light of the seller's representations is sufficient.[208]

7.5.2.5.5 Bait-and-switch cases

A consumer suffers injury when he or she is unable, because of the merchant's UDAP violations, to enter into a transaction at the advertised price.[209] "Injured" means misled in any material way, such as thinking a sale price is lower than it is, even though no sale takes place.[210] In a bait-and-switch sale, the difference between the "bait" and the less advantageous transaction the consumer was actually given is a loss sufficient to support a UDAP claim.[211] A New Jersey appellate court recognized the difference between the price advertised and the actual price offered as ascertainable loss even though the consumer rejected the transaction.[212] Loss of time, inconvenience, and travel and telephone expenses also may be legally cognizable in a bait and switch case.[213] But a Georgia court held that being drawn into a store by a false advertisement did not constitute an injury.[214]

7.5.2.5.6 Debts and litigation Expenses

The entry of a judgment against the consumer is a loss of property, even if the seller has not yet collected on the judgment, since loss does not turn on the flow of dollars, but on the obligation to pay.[215] Similarly, actual damages are suffered where the consumer owes a debt, even if the debt has not been collected.[216] The imposition of a burden or obligation on the consumer is sufficient.[217]

The attorney fees and other expenses incurred by the consumer in the UDAP suit are recoverable as costs in most

---

Nemore, Nemore & Silverman v. W.A. Austin Chevrolet, D.N.C.V. 81 0054979 S (Conn. Super. Ct. 1982). *See also* Mayhall v. A.H. Pond Co., 129 Mich. App. 178, 341 N.W.2d 268 (1983). *But see* Rizzo Pool Co. v. Del Grosso, 232 Conn. 666, 657 A.2d 1087 (1995) (where contractor did not do any work, and consumers paid nothing, their loss of the benefit of their bargain is not an ascertainable loss, where they did not show that they could not find another contractor to do the same work at the contract price). *But cf. In re* Paige, 106 B.R. 346 (Bankr. D. Conn. 1989) (finding that consumer got what was bargained for, so no ascertainable loss); 669 Atlantic Street Assocs. v. Atlantic-Rockland Stamford Assocs., 43 Conn. App. 113, 682 A.2d 572 (1996) (same).

204 Weigel v. Ron Tonkin Chevrolet, Co., 298 Or. 127, 690 P.2d 488 (1984). *Accord* Besel v. Viking Ins. Co., 105 Wash. App. 463, 21 P.3d 293 (2001) (diminution in value of property can be ascertainable loss), *rev'd on other grounds*, 49 P.3d 887 (Wash. 2002). *See also* Miller v. William Chevrolet/Geo, Inc., 326 Ill. App. 3d 642, 762 N.E.2d 1 (2001) (diminution in value satisfies damage precondition).

205 State v. Bob Chambers Ford, Inc., 522 A.2d 362 (Me. 1987).

206 Cox v. Sears, Roebuck & Co., 138 N.J. 2, 647 A.2d 454 (1994). *Accord* Zwiercan v. Gen. Motors Corp., 2002 WL 1472335 (Pa. Com. Pl. May 22, 2002) (defective product's need for repairs is sufficient). *Cf.* Green v. Gen. Motors Corp., 2003 WL 21730592 (N.J. Super. App. Div. July 10, 2003) (alleged safety defect in vehicle not ascertainable loss of money or property where vehicle met federal standards and had not yet malfunctioned); Jiries v. BP Oil, 682 A.2d 1241 (N.J. Super. Law Div. 1996) (payment for repairs was not ascertainable loss where plaintiff did not show that repairs were substandard).

207 Scott v. Mayflower Home Improvement Corp., 363 N.J. Super. 145, 831 A.2d 564 (Law Div. 2001).

208 Talalai v. Cooper Tire & Rubber Co., 360 N.J. Super. 547, 823 A.2d 888 (Law Div. 2001).

209 Geismar v. Abraham & Straus, 109 Misc. 2d 495, 439 N.Y.S.2d 1005 (Dist. Ct. 1981). *See also* Larobina v. Home Depot, USA, Inc., 821 A.2d 283 (Conn. App. 2003) (loss of bargain due to bait and switch is ascertainable loss); Johnson Elec. Co. v. Salce Contracting Assocs., 72 Conn. App. 342, 354-55, 805 A.2d 735 (2002) (loss of a contract is ascertainable loss); Winey v. William E. Dailey, Inc., 636 A.2d 744 (Vt. 1993) (bait and switch tactics are actionable under Vermont UDAP statute; consumer is damaged by loss of purchase opportunity).

210 Geismar v. Abraham & Straus, 109 Misc. 2d 495, 439 N.Y.S.2d 1005 (Dist. Ct. 1981).

211 Chandler v. Am. Gen. Fin., Inc., 329 Ill. App. 3d 729, 768 N.E.2d 60 (2002).

212 Truex v. Ocean Dodge, Inc., 219 N.J. Super. 44, 529 A.2d 1017 (App. Div. 1987).

213 Zanakis-Pico v. Cutter Dodge, Inc., 47 P.3d 1222 (Haw. 2002); Rein v. Koons Ford, Inc., 567 A.2d 101 (Md. 1989) (Va. law) (cost to travel to dealership); Brashears v. Sight 'N' Sound Appliance Centers, Inc., 981 P.2d 1270 (Okla. App. 1999).

214 Agnew v. Great Atlantic & Pacific Tea Co., 502 S.E.2d 735 (Ga. App. Ct. 1998). *See also* Moore-Davis Motors, Inc. v. Joyner, 252 Ga. App. 617, 556 S.E.2d 137 (2001) (no UDAP claim for unavailability of advertised item because plaintiff did not show damage; plaintiff did not brief this issue on appeal); Lauer v. McKean Corp., 2 Pa. D. & C.4th 394 (Pa. C.P. 1989) (buyer who bought more expensive vehicle from another dealer due to defendant's bait-and-switch tactics could not bring UDAP suit because loss did not result from a purchase from the defendant).

215 Smith v. Caggiano, 12 Mass. App. Ct. 41, 421 N.E.2d 473 (1981); Cox v. Sears, Roebuck & Co., 138 N.J. 2, 647 A.2d 454 (1994). *But see* Allen v. Ferrera, 540 S.E.2d 761 (N.C. App. 2000) (having guaranteed a loan does not meet injury requirement without present loss of money).

216 Andrews v. Fleet Real Estate Funding Corp. (*In re* Andrews), 78 B.R. 78 (Bankr. E.D. Pa. 1987); Oil Country Haulers, Inc. v. Griffin, 668 S.W.2d 903 (Tex. App. 1984). *See also In re* Wiggins, 273 B.R. 839 (Bankr. D. Idaho 2001) (ascertainable loss includes deficiency owed on car bought by mentally disabled man in spending binge after defendant purchased his structured settlement annuity for cash).

217 Lowe v. Surpas Resource Corp., 253 F. Supp. 2d 1209, 1227–29 (D. Kan. 2003) (consumer was aggrieved by having to obtain assistance of third parties to respond to collection calls, even though she did not hear the calls herself).

jurisdictions if the consumer prevails, but they do not constitute an ascertainable loss.[218] But the other costs of undoing the harm caused by the defendant's deceptive practices—such as attorney fees incurred in defending a lawsuit seeking to collect unlawful charges, or in establishing guardianship over the incompetent victim of the defendant's deception—are ascertainable losses.[219]

7.5.2.5.7 *Other losses*

A consumer is "adversely affected" where the creditor fails to register the consumer's automobile title, resulting in the consumer not getting notice of a mechanic's lien.[220] A defendant's misappropriation of confidential business information may satisfy a damage precondition.[221] Money spent on an attempt, frustrated by defendants' acts, to acquire a business license is an ascertainable loss even if the license itself would not constitute a property interest.[222] Loss of the opportunity to object to the dissemination of confidential medical information is a sufficient injury to allow suit under New York's UDAP statute.[223]

A consumer suffers an ascertainable loss if she continues to make payments under a lease agreement in order to avoid an early termination charge, after the dealer represented that she would be able to terminate the lease at any time without charge.[224] A loss still satisfies the ascertainable loss requirement after the court renders judgment for the amount of the loss on a common law count.[225]

An insurer's failure to investigate a claim properly had no adverse effect where there was no showing that the insurer would have had to pay a claim if it had properly investigated.[226] By contrast, an insurer's delay in disapproving coverage of medical treatment can cause compensable damage even if the insurer is correct in denying coverage, if the insured is left personally liable for treatment that he or she might have chosen to forego.[227] Without evidence of actual infection by the virus, a patient's fear of contracting AIDS due to exposure to the HIV virus was not an injury sufficient to support a UDAP claim against a physician.[228] Loss of the opportunity to enter a contest that might have resulted in prize money is also too speculative to allow a UDAP suit.[229] The fact that the market price that the plaintiffs paid was higher because of the defendant's deceptive advertising may be insufficient where the plaintiffs themselves were not deceived.[230] The New Jersey Supreme Court has held that a damage claim that is barred by the filed rate doctrine can not meet the ascertainable loss requirement.[231]

7.5.2.6 The Damage May Be Minimal

Statutory requirements that the consumer suffer a loss of money or property do not specify the amount of damage that must be proved. Consumer litigants should be able to meet this requirement by proving minimal injury,[232] such as the cost of a long-distance telephone call[233] or $11.89 in 900-

218 *In re* Wiggins, 273 B.R. 839 (Bankr. D. Idaho 2001); Hedrick v. Spear, 138 Or. App. 53, 907 P.2d 1123 (1995).

219 *In re* Wiggins, 273 B.R. 839, 857 (Bankr. D. Idaho 2001); Osbourne v. Capital City Mortgage Corp., 667 A.2d 1321 (D.C. App. 1995) (attorney fees paid to defend foreclosure case may be damages sufficient to sustain UDAP claim); Duran v. Leslie Oldsmobile, 594 N.E.2d 1355 (Ill. App. Ct. 1992) (attorney fee that consumer had to pay for defense of collection suit constitutes damages); Columbia Chiropractic Group, Inc. v. Trust Ins. Co., 430 Mass. 60, 712 N.E.2d 93 (1999) (where UDAP violation involves filing a lawsuit, attorney fees incurred in defending it are a loss of money or property). *But see* Lester E. Cox Medical Centers v. Huntsman, 2003 WL 22004998 (W.D. Mo. Aug. 5, 2003) (costs of defending suit are not ascertainable loss); Yellowpine Water User's Ass'n v. Imel, 105 Idaho 349, 670 P.2d 54 (1983); Tolve v. Ogden Chrysler Plymouth, Inc., 324 Ill. App. 3d 485, 755 N.E.2d 536, 258 Ill. Dec. 153 (2001); C.A.R. Tow, Inc. v. Corwin, 76 Or. App. 192, 708 P.2d 644 (1985); Sign-O-Life Signs, Inc. v. Delauventi Florists, Inc., 825 P.2d 714 (Wash. Ct. App. 1992) (rejecting earlier holding in St. Paul Fire & Marine Ins. Co. v. Updegrave, 656 P.2d 1130 (Wash. Ct. App. 1983)); Demopolis v. Galvin, 786 P.2d 804 (Wash. Ct. App. 1990).

220 Rein v. Koons Ford, Inc., 567 A.2d 101 (Md. 1989) (Va. law); Fortner v. Fannin Bank in Windom, 634 S.W.2d 74 (Tex. App. 1982). *Accord* Cox v. Sears, Roebuck & Co., 138 N.J. 2, 647 A.2d 454 (1994) (filing of lien for home improvement work creates ascertainable loss).

221 Warner-Lambert Co. v. Execuquest Corp., 691 N.E.2d 545 (Mass. 1998).

222 Copeland v. Treasure Chest Casino, 822 So. 2d 68 (La. App. 2002).

223 Anonymous v. CVS Corp., 188 Misc. 2d 616, 728 N.Y.S.2d 333 (Sup. Ct. 2001).

224 Clement v. St. Charles Nissan, Inc., 103 S.W.3d 898 (Mo. App. 2003).

225 Larobina v. Home Depot, USA, Inc., 821 A.2d 283 (Conn. App. 2003); Keith v. Howerton, 2001 Tenn. App. LEXIS 646 (Aug. 28, 2001) (unreported, citation limited).

226 Van Dyke v. St. Paul Fire & Marine Ins. Co., 388 Mass. 671, 448 N.E.2d 357 (1983); *In re* Conseco Fin. Servicing Corp., 19 S.W.3d 562 (Tex. App. 2000) (same).

227 Van Noy v. State Farm Mut. Automobile Ins. Co., 98 Wash. App. 487, 983 P.2d 1129 (1999), *aff'd on other grounds*, 16 P.3d 574 (Wash. 2001).

228 K.A.C. v. Benson, 527 N.W.2d 553 (Minn. 1995).

229 Macias v. HBC of Florida, Inc., 694 So. 2d 88 (Fla. Dist. Ct. App. 1997). *See also* Walker v. Branch Banking & Trust Co., 515 S.E.2d 727 (N.C. App. 1999) (vague and speculative allegations did not meet injury requirement).

230 William v. Purdue Pharma Co., 297 F. Supp. 2d 171 (D.D.C. 2003); Weinberg v. Sun Co., 565 Pa. 612, 777 A.2d 442 (2001).

231 Weinberg v. Sprint Corp., 173 N.J. 233, 801 A.2d 281 (2002). *See* § 5.6.10.1, *supra* (discussion of filed rate doctrine).

232 Park v. Ford Motor Co., 844 A.2d 687 (R.I. 2004) (any loss capable of measurement, no matter or large or small, is sufficient).

233 *See* Schubach v. Household Fin. Corp., 375 Mass. 133, 376 N.E.2d 140 (1978) (challenge to filing of collection suits in inconvenient venue); *see also* Bump v. Robbins, 24 Mass. App. Ct. 296, 509 N.E.2d 12 (1987).

number charges.[234] The additional sales tax a consumer had to pay because the price of a car was inflated to conceal a finance charge is an ascertainable loss.[235] But a Texas case holds that, although damages may be minimal, they must be more than "nominal."[236]

Some transportation expenses and lost interest income have been found to satisfy a damage requirement that the consumer show "loss of money."[237] Hawaii's UDAP damage requirement includes *de minimis* damages such as an extra $10 paid in material, $15 in expenses for a money order, gasoline, wear and tear on a car and parking expenses to consult an attorney.[238] Similarly, courts have found "ascertainable loss" when the consumer shows minimal expenses incurred while obtaining a loan[239] or having to initiate by motion a transfer of a case from an inconvenient venue. Even a minimal decrease in the consumer's property interest or money is enough.[240] "Pecuniary loss" is shown even where the creditor's counterclaims exceed the debtor's UDAP claim.[241]

7.5.2.7 Causation

Some evidence of causation must be presented to meet an injury precondition.[242] Evidence that the defendants' misrepresentations were material may be sufficient proof that they were the cause of the harm suffered by the plaintiffs.[243] A Maryland decision holds that a landlord did not cause loss or injury to tenants merely by renting them unlicensed premises, where the tenants did not complain of substandard conditions and the non-licensure did not cause any interruption in their occupancy.[244] A New Jersey court, stressing the consumer's need to prove causation, held that the amount the consumer paid for automobile repairs was not an ascertainable loss where the only UDAP violation was failure to give a written estimate, and the repairs were not substandard.[245] Perhaps the result would have been different if the consumer had testified that she would not have entered into the transaction if the likely cost had been disclosed. Another New Jersey court held that consumers may well have suffered ascertainable loss where a home improvement contractor used unlicensed salespersons, violated state requirements for specification of costs, finance charges, and the work to be done, charged unconscionably high prices, and performed shoddy work.[246]

A dealer's non-disclosure of an upcharge causes injury in that it causes the consumer either to overpay or to lose the opportunity to decline the purchase.[247] Consumers suffered

234 Wexler v. Brothers Entertainment Group, Inc., 457 N.W.2d 218 (Minn. Ct. App. 1990). *Accord* Thomas v. Busby, 670 So. 2d 603 (La. App.) (failure to refund $19.13 price of potting soil satisfied damage precondition), *vacated and remanded without op.*, 673 So. 2d 601 (La.), *same result reached on remand*, 682 So. 2d 1025 (La. App. 1996); *see also* Larsen Chelsey Realty Co. v. Larsen, 232 Conn. 480, 499, 656 A.2d 1009 (1995); Yost v. Millhouse, 373 N.W.2d 826 (Minn. Ct. App. 1985).

235 Knapp v. Americredit Fin. Servs., Inc., 245 F. Supp. 2d 841 (S.D. W. Va. 2003).

236 Gulf States Utilities Co. v. Low, 79 S.W.3d 561 (Tex. 2002).

237 Duran v. Leslie Oldsmobile, 594 N.E.2d 1355 (Ill. App. Ct. 1992) (rental of temporary transportation due to rescission of car sale constitutes damages sufficient to support UDAP claim); Bump v. Robbins, 24 Mass. App. Ct. 296, 509 N.E.2d 12 (1987); Homsi v. C.H. Babb Co., 10 Mass. App. Ct. 474, 409 N.E.2d 219 (1980).

238 Wiginton v. Pacific Credit Corp., 2 Haw. App. 435, 634 P.2d 111 (1981).

239 Riviera Motors Inc. v. Higbee, 45 Or. App. 545, 609 P.2d 369 (1980).

240 *See* Mason v. Mortgage Am., Inc., 114 Wash. 2d 842, 792 P.2d 142 (1990); Sing v. John L. Scott, Inc., 920 P.2d 589 (Wash. App. 1996), *rev'd on other grounds*, 134 Wash. 2d 24, 948 P.2d 816 (1997).

241 Moonlight v. Boyce, 125 Wis. 2d 298, 372 N.W.2d 479 (Ct. App. 1985). *But see* Lester E. Cox Medical Centers v. Huntsman, 2003 WL 22004998 (W.D. Mo. Aug. 5, 2003) (alleged overcharge not ascertainable loss where consumer still owed creditor the undisputed portion of bill); Freeman Health Sys. v. Wass, 124 S.W.3d 504 (Mo. App. 2004) (alleged overcharge not ascertainable loss where consumer had not paid any portion of bill).

242 Lester v. Percudani, 217 F.R.D. 345 (M.D. Pa. Sept. 2003) (denying class certification because of need to prove causation); Sambor v. Omnia Credit Servs., 183 F. Supp. 2d 1234 (D. Haw. 2002) (plaintiff did not show that defendant's lack of license caused her any loss); Cannon v. Cherry Hill Toyota, Inc., 161 F. Supp. 2d 362 (D.N.J. 2001) (no damages can be awarded for extended warranty upcharge without proof that consumer would have sought and obtained cheaper warranty); Sheppard v. GMAC Mortg. Corp., 299 B.R. 753 (Bankr. E.D. Pa. 2003) (causation not shown); Silver v. Jacobs, 43 Conn. App. 184, 682 A.2d 551 (1996) (UDAP claim properly dismissed where plaintiff's loss was caused by his own neglect rather than by alleged UDAP violation); DeReggi Constr. Co. v. Mate, 130 Md. App. 648, 747 A.2d 743 (2000); Cartiglia v. Johnson & Johnson Co., 2002 WL 1009473 (N.J. Super. Law Div. Apr. 24, 2002) (unpublished, citation limited); Roberts v. Cowgill, 316 N.J. Super. 33, 719 A.2d 668 (App. Div. 1998) (loss must be caused by the UDAP violation; failure to obtain final inspection had a sufficient causal relationship to the defects it would have revealed and to the costs of providing access to the inspector); Jiries v. BP Oil, 294 N.J. Super. 225, 682 A.2d 1241 (1996); Kline v. Benefiel, 2001 Tenn. App. LEXIS 14 (Jan. 9, 2001); Hangman Ridge Training Stables, Inc. v. Safeco Title Ins. Co., 105 Wash. 2d 778, 719 P.2d 531 (1986). *See also* § 8.3.5.1, *infra*.

243 Mass. Mut. Life Ins. Co. v. Superior Court, 97 Cal. App. 4th 1282, 119 Cal. Rptr. 2d 190 (2002).

244 Hallowell v. Citaramanis, 328 Md. 142, 613 A.2d 964 (1992). *See also* Sambor v. Omnia Credit Servs., 183 F. Supp. 2d 1234 (D. Haw. 2002) (no UDAP claim where plaintiff did not show that debt collector's lack of license caused her any loss).

245 Jiries v. BP Oil, 682 A.2d 1241 (N.J. Super. Law Div. 1996). *Accord* Cartiglia v. Johnson & Johnson Co., 2002 WL 1009473 (N.J. Super. Law Div. Apr. 24, 2002) (unpublished, citation limited) (suggesting that price paid for medication may not be ascertainable loss under the facts alleged).

246 Scott v. Mayflower Home Improvement Corp., 363 N.J. Super. 145, 831 A.2d 564 (Law Div. 2001).

247 Sutton v. Viking Oldsmobile Nissan, Inc., 611 N.W.2d 60 (Minn. App. 2000), *vacated, remanded*, 623 N.W.2d 247 (Minn.

damages by paying illegal late charges, even though they could have avoided the charge by paying on time.[248]

A Maryland tenant's losses were not caused by her landlord's UDAP violation and did not satisfy the damage requirement where she made a conscious decision to accept the terms of the lease once she learned of the violation.[249] By the same token, no damage could be attributed to the defendant's deceptive price advertisement where the true price was made known to the plaintiff before the purchase.[250] Payments made before the deception can not be causally tied to the deception.[251] Where a contractor did not do any work, and the consumers repudiated the contract and paid nothing, and they did not show that they could not find another contractor to do the same work at the contract price, their loss of the benefit of their bargain was not an ascertainable loss.[252] Merely paying the purchase price for a product is insufficient without a showing of a causal connection between the wrong and the loss.[253] But payment of the purchase price is a sufficient loss if the defendant's UDAP violation was part of the inducement for the consumer to enter into the transaction.[254]

Two Pennsylvania trial courts have ruled that, where the statute requires the consumer to have purchased goods or services and "thereby" suffer a loss, the consumer must have actually gone through with the unfair or deceptive purchase, and the loss must result from the purchase itself.[255] More persuasive Pennsylvania cases reject this overly restrictive view.[256]

7.5.2.8 Proof of Damage Precondition

Except in the few states where UDAP claims must be proven by clear and convincing evidence,[257] the plaintiff need only convince the trier of fact that it is more likely than not that the plaintiff suffered an ascertainable loss.[258] The trier of fact may draw reasonable and logical inferences from the facts proven. For example, if a competitor takes steps that would reasonably deter individuals from patronizing a business, the trier of fact can infer that some customers were actually deterred, and that the business suffered a loss.[259]

A damage precondition in a UDAP statute should be, like the rest of the UDAP statute, interpreted liberally in favor of consumers.[260] Courts may borrow contract principles to evaluate whether a consumer has met a damage precondition.[261]

7.5.3 Public Interest Precondition

7.5.3.1 Almost All States Reject a Public Interest Requirement

Courts in a number of states have considered whether a public interest requirement should be imposed on private UDAP damage actions. (Limits on state attorneys general bringing UDAP actions are discussed elsewhere.[262]) In all but eight states, there should be no issue of a consumer's right to seek relief for a single UDAP violation even though the practice is not part of a more general pattern.[263]

2001) (remanding for reconsideration in light of Group Health Plan v. Philip Morris, Inc., 621 N.W.2d 2 (Minn. 2001), which holds that plaintiff must show a causal connection between unlawful act and damages), *appeal after remand*, 2001 Minn. App. LEXIS 866 (July 31, 2001) (consumer raised genuine issue of fact about "legal nexus" between misconduct and injury, with allegation that if he had known dealer kept part of sum paid for service contract, he would have negotiated about price or refused to purchase), *opinion on remand*, 2001 Minn. App. LEXIS 866 (July 31, 2001) (reversing summary judgment for seller on UDAP claim where buyer testified that he would have bargained for lower price or declined to buy service contract if seller had not misrepresented that charge was paid to others).

248 District Cablevision Ltd. P'ship v. Bassin, 828 A.2d 714 (D.C. 2003).

249 Legg v. Castruccio, 100 Md. App. 748, 642 A.2d 906 (1994).

250 Agnew v. Great Atlantic & Pacific Tea Co., 502 S.E.2d 735 (Ga. App. Ct. 1998). *See also* McGraw v. Loyola Ford, Inc., 124 Md. App. 560, 723 A.2d 502 (1999) (no damage where dealer orally disclosed that vehicle was demonstrator and buyer was not deceived).

251 Gemignani v. Pete, 71 P.3d 87 (Or. App. 2003).

252 Rizzo Pool Co. v. Del Grosso, 232 Conn. 666, 657 A.2d 1087 (1995). *See also* Bruce v. Home Depot, USA, Inc., 308 F. Supp. 2d 72 (D. Conn. 2004) (plaintiff need not allege a specific ascertainable loss with respect to each public policy, common-law, and/or statutory violation on which UDAP claim is based).

253 Walls v. American Tobacco Co., 2000 OK 66, 11 P.3d 626 (2000).

254 Pliss v. Peppertree Resort Villas, Inc., 663 N.W.2d 851 (Wis. App. 2003).

255 Lauer v. McKean Corp., 2 Pa. D. & C.4th 394 (Pa. C.P. 1989) (buyer who bought more expensive vehicle from another dealer due to defendant's bait-and-switch tactics could not bring UDAP suit because loss did not result from a purchase from the defendant); Mason v. National Central Bank, 19 Pa. D. & C.3d 229 (Pa. C.P. 1980) (deceptive repossession not actionable under UDAP statute). *See also* Sam Bradley Realty Co. v. McNair, 644 S.W.2d 533 (Tex. App. 1982).

256 *In re* Smith, 866 F.2d 576, 582–83 (3d Cir. 1989) (Pennsylvania law); Laxson v. Lenger, 6 Pa. D. & C.4th 175 (C.P. 1990).

257 *See* § 7.9.1.1, *infra*.

258 Service Road Corp. v. Quinn, 241 Conn. 630, 698 A.2d 258 (1997).

259 Id.

260 Brunwasser v. Trans World Airlines, Inc., 541 F. Supp. 1338 (W.D. Pa. 1982); Andrews v. Fleet Real Estate Funding Corp. (*In re* Andrews), 78 B.R. 78 (Bankr. E.D. Pa. 1987); Miller v. American Family Publishers, 284 N.J. Super. 67, 663 A.2d 643 (Chancery Div. 1995); Feitler v. Animation Celection, Inc., 13 P.3d 1044 (Or. App. 2000).

261 Cox v. Sears, Roebuck & Co., 138 N.J. 2, 647 A.2d 454 (1994).

262 *See* § 10.3, *infra*.

263 Mercedes-Benz of N. Am., Inc. v. Garten, 94 Md. App. 547, 618

In Connecticut, the legislature has now made it clear that there is no public interest precondition to a UDAP action. At one point, however, the Connecticut Supreme Court had ruled that a UDAP action must have some nexus to the public interest.[264] The issue for the court was the potential effect on the consuming public[265] or whether public policy was at stake.[266] Thus, a UDAP action based solely on a law firm's suing a corporation for too many damages did not involve systematic abuse or implicate the public interest.[267]

In response to these court decisions, the Connecticut legislature amended the UDAP statute to state explicitly that no public interest or public injury need be shown.[268] Under the amended statute, a single act can create UDAP liability.[269] At least some Connecticut courts applied this amendment retroactively, since it clarified the statute's original intent.[270]

The Illinois UDAP statute has been amended twice to deal with the question of whether an effect on the public interest is required. In 1990, after some courts had read a public interest requirement into the statute,[271] the state legislature amended the statute to state explicitly that "proof of public injury, a pattern, or an effect on consumers generally shall not be required."[272] After this amendment, multiple violations need not be shown to establish UDAP liability.[273] A single violation is sufficient.[274] Courts have generally found that the amendment clarified the legislature's original intent, so there is no public interest requirement even where actions took place before the amendment.[275] A few Illinois courts have, however, attempted to reinsert a public interest requirement by requiring a show-

---

A.2d 233 (1993) (term "practice" does not imply a requirement of repetition); Patterson v. Beall, 19 P.3d 839 (Okla. 2000) (declining to read public interest precondition into statute).

264 Ivey, Barnum & O'Mara v. Indian Harbor Properties, Inc., 190 Conn. 528, 461 A.2d 1369 (1983); *see also* Fortini v. New England Log Homes, Inc., 4 Conn. App. 132, 492 A.2d 545 (1985).

265 *See* Boyce v. Hebert, Clearinghouse No. 41,255 (Conn. Super. Ct. 1985) (public interest in person remodeling homes without a license); Wilson v. Fireman's Fund Ins. Co., 40 Conn. Supp. 336, 499 A.2d 81 (Super. Ct. 1985) (public interest present where practice may affect other insureds).

266 Flaumenhaft v. Forest Garage Used Cars, Inc., Clearinghouse No. 40,645 (Conn. Super. Ct. 1985) (violation of other statutes shows public interest).

267 Ivey, Barnum & O'Mara v. Indian Harbor Properties, Inc., 190 Conn. 528, 461 A.2d 1369 (1983). *See also* Fortini v. New England Log Homes, Inc., 4 Conn. App. 132, 492 A.2d 545 (1985). *But see* Aurigemma v. Arco Petroleum Products Co., 734 F. Supp. 1025 (D. Conn. 1990) (sufficient public interest where franchisor failed to disclose possibility of termination of franchise); Delaney v. Budget Rent A Car, Clearinghouse No. 36,595 (Conn. Super. Ct. 1983) (sufficient public interest where consumer challenged manner of collecting debt, where potential for repetition, and where practice inimical to public interest).

268 Conn. Gen. Stat. § 42-110g(a), *as amended by* Connecticut Acts 467 (1984).

269 Locascio v. Imports Unlimited, Inc., 309 F. Supp. 2d 267 (D. Conn. 2004); Jewell v. Medical Protective Co., 2003 WL 22682332 (D. Conn. Oct. 30, 2003) (rejecting defendant's argument that conduct must be contrary to public policy); Johnson Elec. Co. v. Salce Contracting Assocs., 72 Conn. App. 342, 805 A.2d 735 (2002); Roncari Dev. v. GMG Enterprises, 45 Conn. Super. 408, 718 A.2d 1025 (1997); Johnson Elec. Co. v. Salce Contracting Assocs., 72 Conn. App. 342, 805 A.2d 735 (2002). *But see* Baghdady v. Baghdady, 2003 WL 202436 (2d Cir. Jan. 29, 2003) (unpublished, citation limited) (erroneously relying on pre-amendment decision to find public interest precondition).

270 Carpentino v. Transport Ins. Co., 609 F. Supp. 556 (D. Conn. 1985); Wilson v. Fireman's Fund Ins. Co., 40 Conn. Supp. 336, 499 A.2d 81 (Super. Ct. 1985); Citizens Bank & Trust Co. v. Grant, Clearinghouse No. 41,256 (Conn. Super. Ct. 1985); Flaumenhaft v. Forest Garage Used Cars, Inc., Clearinghouse No. 40,645 (Conn. Super. Ct. 1985); Dixico, Inc. v. R.J.R. Archer, Inc., Clearinghouse No. 40,644 (Super. Ct. 1985). *But see* Aurigemma v. Arco Petroleum Products Co., 734 F. Supp. 1025 (D. Conn. 1990); Sorisio v. Lenox, Inc., 701 F. Supp. 950 (D. Conn.), *aff'd per curiam*, 863 F.2d 195 (2d Cir. 1988); Aldridge v. Cosby, 1985 WL 5953 (D. Conn. Nov. 12, 1985); Hydro Air v. Versa Technologies, Inc., 599 F. Supp. 1119 (D. Conn. 1984); Lembo v. Schlesinger, 15 Conn. App. 150, 543 A.2d 780 (1988); O'Leary v. Industrial Park Corp., 14 Conn. App. 425, 542 A.2d 333 (1988); Rotophone, Inc. v. Danbury Hosp., 13 Conn. App. 230, 535 A.2d 830 (1988).

271 *See, e.g.*, Refco, Inc. v. Troika Investment Ltd., 702 F. Supp. 684 (N.D. Ill. 1988) (must show pattern of concealment); Venturi, Inc. v. Austin Co., 681 F. Supp. 584 (S.D. Ill. 1988); Frahm v. Urkovich, 113 Ill. App. 3d 580, 447 N.E.2d 1007 (1983) (UDAP not available to remedy purely private wrong). *But see* Hometown Savings & Loan Ass'n v. Moseley Securities Corp., 703 F. Supp. 723 (N.D. Ill. 1988) (citing cases on each side); Haroco, Inc. v. American Nat'l Bank & Trust Co., 647 F. Supp. 1026 (N.D. Ill. 1986) (detailed discussion); Century Universal Enterprises v. Triana Dev. Corp., 158 Ill. App. 3d 182, 510 N.E.2d 1260 (1987).

272 815 Ill. Comp. Stat. Ann. § 505/10a, *as amended* effective Jan. 1, 1990.

273 Fidelity Fin. Servs. v. Hicks, 214 Ill. App. 3d 398, 574 N.E.2d 15 (1991).

274 Ciampi v. Ogden Chrysler Plymouth, Inc., 634 N.E.2d 448 (Ill. App. Ct. 1994); Roche v. Fireside Chrysler-Plymouth, 600 N.E.2d 1218 (Ill. App. Ct. 1992). *But see* Golembiewski v. Hallberg Ins. Agency, Inc., 635 N.E.2d 452 (Ill. App. Ct. 1994) (consumer must show repeated practice of breach of contract to make out UDAP claim).

275 *See* Ryan v. Wersi Electronics GmbH & Co., 3 F.3d 174 (7th Cir. 1993) (Illinois law); Hardin, Rodriguez & Boivin Anesthesiologists v. Paradigm Ins. Co., 962 F.2d 628 (7th Cir. 1992) (Illinois law); Resolution Trust Corp. v. Krantz, 757 F. Supp. 915 (N.D. Ill. 1991) (applies amendment to pre-amendment violation); Reshal & Assocs., Inc. v. Long Grove Trading Co., 754 F. Supp. 1226 (N.D. Ill. 1990) (applies amendment to pre-amendment violation); Johnston v. Anchor Organization, 621 N.E.2d 137 (Ill. App. Ct. 1993); Royal Imperial Group, Inc. v. Joseph Blumberg & Assocs., Inc., 608 N.E.2d 178 (Ill. App. Ct. 1992) (applies amendment to pre-amendment violation); Rubin v. Marshall Field & Co., 597 N.E.2d 688 (Ill. App. Ct. 1992) (applies amendment deleting pattern requirement retroactively); Sullivan's Wholesale Drug v. Faryl's Pharmacy, Inc., 214 Ill. App. 3d 1073, 573 N.E.2d 1370 (1991). *But see* A Kush & Assocs. v. American States Ins. Co., 927 F.2d 929 (7th Cir. 1991) (holding that amendment deleting public interest require-

ing, at least in UDAP cases based on breach of contract, that the defendant's conduct implicates consumer protection concerns.[276] In addition, a number of courts have held that a consumer protection nexus must be shown when the plaintiff is not a consumer.[277]

In 1995, the Illinois legislature revisited the public interest issue and inserted a requirement of proof of a public injury, a pattern, or an effect on consumers and the public interest generally for UDAP claims against new and used vehicle dealers.[278] Eight years later, the Illinois Supreme Court held the legislative enactment that added this provision to the UDAP statute unconstitutional as a special law.[279] While it was in effect, an action was found in the public interest where a car dealer allegedly deceived car purchasers in a way that had a potential for repetition with other consumers.[280]

In Hawaii, an earlier version of the UDAP statute created a public interest precondition for actions brought against nonmerchants.[281] The Hawaii UDAP statute has now been amended to explicitly eliminate the public interest requirement, whether the action is against a merchant or nonmerchant. UDAP actions now, though, can only be brought by "consumers."[282]

New Mexico rejects a requirement that the consumer show a pattern of misconduct. There is no defense that the violation is an isolated occurrence.[283] Pennsylvania reaches the same conclusion.[284]

The Oklahoma Supreme Court has declined to read a public interest requirement into its statute.[285] Citing the requirement of liberal construction, the court found that decisions from other states finding a public interest precondition were based on language not present in the Oklahoma statute.

The Florida Supreme Court has rejected an interpretation of its UDAP statute that would have required the plaintiff to show a pattern of unfair or deceptive conduct by the defendant.[286] The defendant had argued that the statute's reference to unfair and deceptive "practices" meant that there had to be more than a single instance of misconduct. But, as the high court pointed out, the statute referred to not just to practices but also to "acts," and the remedy sections of the statute afforded relief to anyone injured by "a violation" of the statute. The court was not troubled by the fact that some sections of the statute referred to "acts" in the plural, since a rule of statutory construction provided that the plural includes the singular when the context allows, and other sections of the statute used the term in the singular.

The West Virginia Supreme Court has likewise concluded that the state UDAP statute does not require a showing of a pattern or practice.[287] Stressing that the statute makes either an act or a practice actionable, the court held that the attorney general could obtain an injunction without proving a pattern or practice of unfair or deceptive acts.

In arguing against a public interest requirement, the plain language of the statute is usually the strongest point. Most UDAP statutes spell out preconditions for suit fairly clearly, leaving no justification for a court to impose additional preconditions. Particularly in light of the mandate of liberal construction, the court should avoid reading in restrictions that the legislature has not chosen to express. The model statute on which the state's UDAP statute is based may also have helpful comments.[288] Many UDAP statutes specify that the attorney general must conclude that a suit is in the public interest before that office may sue; the fact that the statute specifies a public interest precondition for one type of suit but not for another supports the conclusion that it is only required for the first type.[289]

---

ment does not apply retroactively; the Seventh Circuit later reversed itself on this issue).

276 Dunn v. Pace Suburban Bus Serv., 2001 U.S. Dist. LEXIS 20156 (N.D. Ill. Dec. 3, 2001) (no UDAP claim for mental health provider's diagnosis of plaintiff because no impact on consumers); Scarsdale Builders, Inc. v. Ryland Group, Inc., 911 F. Supp. 337 (N.D. Ill. 1996); Brody v. Finch University of Health Sciences, 698 N.E.2d 257 (Ill. App. Ct. 1998) (reciting elements that must be shown); Golembiewski v. Hallberg Ins. Agency, Inc., 635 N.E.2d 452 (Ill. App. Ct. 1994) (applies amendment to pre-amendment violation, but finds that breach of contract violates UDAP statute only if it is a repeated practice).

277 *See* § 2.4.5.2, *infra*.

278 815 Ill. Comp. Stat. Ann. § 505/10a. *See* Norman, *Consumer Fraud Act Suits Against Car Dealers After the Public Injury Amendment*, 84 Ill. Bar Journal 84 (Feb. 1996) (extensive discussion of legislative history and judicial decisions).

279 Allen v. Woodfield Chevrolet, Inc., 208 Ill. 2d 12, 802 N.E.2d 752, 280 Ill. Dec. 501 (2003).

280 McNair v. McGrath Lexus-Colosimo, Ltd., 11 F. Supp. 2d 990 (N.D. Ill. 1998). *See also* Szwebel v. Pap's Auto Sales, Inc., 2003 WL 21750841 (N.D. Ill. July 29, 2003) (magistrate's report and recommendation) (violation of federal odometer act and potential for repetition satisfy public interest test).

281 Haw. Rev. Stat. § 480-13. For cases applying the former standard, see Kona Hawaiian Ass'n v. Pacific Group, 680 F. Supp. 1438 (D. Haw. 1988); Ai v. Frank Huff Agency, Ltd., 61 Haw. 607, 607 P.2d 1304 (1980); Wiginton v. Pacific Credit Corp., 2 Haw. App. 435, 634 P.2d 111 (1981).

282 *See* Haw. Rev. Stat. § 480-13, as amended.

283 Hale v. Basin Motor Co., 110 N.M. 314, 795 P.2d 1006 (1990); Ashlock v. Sunwest Bank of Roswell, 107 N.M. 100, 753 P.2d 346 (1988).

284 Wallace v. Pastore, 742 A.2d 1090 (Pa. Super. 1999).

285 Patterson v. Beall, 19 P.3d 839 (Okla. 2000).

286 PNR, Inc. v. Beacon Property Mgmt., Inc., 2003 WL 10885751 (Fla. Mar. 13, 2003).

287 State *ex rel.* McGraw v. Telecheck Servs., Inc., 582 S.E.2d 885 (W. Va. 2003).

288 *See* § 3.4.2, *supra*, for a discussion of the legislative history of UDAP statutes.

289 Patterson v. Beall, 19 P.3d 839 (Okla. 2000). *But see* Ly v. Nystrom, 615 N.W.2d 302 (Minn. 2000) (erroneously finding public interest requirement for private suits by analogizing to express precondition for attorney general suits).

7.5.3.2 The Washington State Standard

The Washington Supreme Court finds implicit in the state's UDAP statute a public interest condition.[290] This finding relies in part on the unique Washington UDAP statute language indicating the statute only applies to practices injurious to the public interest.[291]

The extensive case law in Washington and the complex standards that have evolved are unique to that state and are of limited legal relevance in other jurisdictions, but illustrate a problem to be avoided by other states. The complexity of the standards and the amount of judicial effort to establish them is a lesson in the problems a state's courts can create for themselves if they try to imply a public interest precondition into the UDAP statute.

Washington courts have had significant difficulty in defining what practices do and do not affect the public interest. Early cases were decided on an *ad hoc* basis.[292] Later the Washington Supreme Court developed a more elaborate formula.[293] Then, in 1986, in *Hangman Ridge*, the court rejected its previous formula and announced a new formula.[294]

The general requirements for a UDAP action, according to *Hangman Ridge*, are that there be: (1) an unfair or deceptive act or practice, (2) occurring in the conduct of trade or commerce, (3) affecting the public interest, (4) that injures the plaintiff's business or property, (5) with a causal connection between the act or practice and the injury.[295]

There are two ways that a case can meet the third element, the public interest requirement. First, a practice has a *per se* effect on the public interest if the actor violates a statute that has a specific legislative declaration of public interest impact.[296] The judiciary can not find this impact in the statute; the legislature itself must enunciate it.[297] Note that this issue is different from the question of whether the defendant's act amounts to a *per se* UDAP violation, which can be established when the defendant violates certain statutes.[298]

If the defendant did not violate a statute that includes a declaration of public interest impact, a more complex analysis is necessary to determine whether the practice affects the public interest. First, according to *Hangman Ridge*, the court must determine whether a transaction is a "consumer transaction" or a "private dispute." The difference between these two types of transactions is unclear. The prototype of a consumer transaction is a consumer buying a product in a store, and the court listed as examples the sale of a vehicle, the sale of seed, and the sale of a mobile home. A business-to-business transaction is clearly a private dispute,[299] but the Supreme Court also included transactions between attorneys and clients, between an insurer and an insured, and between realtors and purchasers as examples.[300] Failure to disclose that a product is not warranted has also been found to be a private dispute where there is no showing that the practice is a general one or that there is a potential for repetition.[301] But buying a horse at an auction has potential for repetition and is thus a consumer transaction.[302]

In determining whether a practice committed in a "consumer transaction" affects the public interest, *Hangman*

---

290 Seattle Endeavors, Inc. v. Mastro, 123 Wash. 2d 339, 868 P.2d 120 (1994); Hangman Ridge Training Stables, Inc. v. Safeco Title Ins. Co., 105 Wash. 2d 778, 719 P.2d 531 (1986).

291 *Id.*

292 Levy v. North Am. Co. for Life & Health Ins., 90 Wash. 2d 846, 586 P.2d 845 (1978); Salois v. Mutual of Omaha Ins. Co., 90 Wash. 2d 355, 581 P.2d 1349 (1978); Brown v. Charlton, 90 Wash. 2d 362, 583 P.2d 1188 (1978); Lightfoot v. MacDonald, 86 Wash. 2d 331, 544 P.2d 88 (1976); Pilch v. Hendrix, 22 Wash. App. 531, 591 P.2d 824 (1979); Rounds v. Union Bankers Ins. Co., 22 Wash. App. 613, 590 P.2d 1286 (1979); Lookebill v. Mom's Mobile Homes, Inc., 16 Wash. App. 817, 559 P.2d 600 (1977); Allen v. Anderson, 16 Wash. App. 446, 557 P.2d 241 (1976).

293 *See, e.g.*, Sato v. Century 21 Ocean Shores Real Estate, 101 Wash. 2d 599, 681 P.2d 242 (1984).

294 Hangman Ridge Training Stables, Inc. v. Safeco Title Ins. Co., 105 Wash. 2d 778, 719 P.2d 531 (1986).

295 The fourth and fifth of these requirements had formerly been subsumed, more or less, in the court's formulation of the public interest requirement.

296 Campbell v. Seattle Engine Rebuilders, 75 Wash. App. 89, 876 P.2d 948 (1994); Aubrey's R.V. Center, Inc. v. Tandy Corp., 46 Wash. App. 595, 731 P.2d 1124 (1987). *See also* Strother v. Capital Bankers Life Ins. Co., 68 Wash. App. 224, 842 P.2d 504 (1992) (insurance regulation), *rev'd on other grounds*, 124 Wash. 2d 1, 873 P.2d 1185 (1994); Henery v. Robinson, 67 Wash. App. 277, 834 P.2d 1091 (1992) (no *per se* public interest impact where statute is technically not violated); Evergreen Int'l, Inc. v. American Cas. Co., 52 Wash. App. 548, 761 P.2d 964 (1988); Cuevas v. Montoya, 48 Wash. App. 871, 740 P.2d 858 (1987). *Cf.* Svendsen v. Stock, 98 Wash. App. 498, 979 P.2d 476 (1999) (no UDAP liability where real estate seller disclosure statute provided that violations did not affect the public interest for UDAP purposes), *rev'd on other grounds*, 23 P.3d 455 (Wash. 2001) (agreeing that UDAP liability could not be based on violation of real estate seller disclosure statute, but finding independent basis for UDAP liability).

297 Hangman Ridge Training Stables, Inc. v. Safeco Title Ins. Co., 105 Wash. 2d 778, 719 P.2d 531 (1986).

298 Hangman Ridge Training Stables, Inc. v. Safeco Title Ins. Co., 105 Wash. 2d 778, 719 P.2d 531 (1986); Campbell v. Seattle Engine Rebuilders, 75 Wash. App. 89, 876 P.2d 948 (1994). *See* § 3.2.7.3, *supra*.

299 Goodyear Tire & Rubber Co. v. Whiteman Tire, Inc., 935 P.2d 628 (Wash. App. Ct. 1997).

300 Edmonds v. John L. Scott Real Estate, Inc., 942 P.2d 1072 (Wash. Ct. App. 1997) (refers to real estate sale as a "private dispute"); Hangman Ridge Training Stables, Inc. v. Safeco Title Ins. Co., 105 Wash. 2d 778, 719 P.2d 531 (1986); Pacific Northwest Life Ins. Co. v. Turnball, 51 Wash. App. 692, 754 P.2d 1262 (1988). *See also* Cotton v. Kronenberg, 111 Wash. App. 258, 44 P.3d 878 (2002) (treating attorney-client transaction as private transaction).

301 Aubrey's R.V. Center, Inc. v. Tandy Corp., 46 Wash. App. 595, 731 P.2d 1124 (1987). *See also* Banks v. Nordstrom, Inc., 787 P.2d 953 (Wash. Ct. App. 1990) (erroneous identification of woman as shoplifter not part of generalized course of conduct).

302 Travis v. Washington Horse Breeders, 111 Wash. 2d 396, 759 P.2d 418 (1988).

Ridge requires the court to consider the following factors, although no one factor is dispositive or necessary to find a public interest:

- The practice was committed in the course of the defendant's business;
- The practice was committed as part of a pattern or general course of conduct;
- There were repeated acts prior to the acts involving the plaintiff;
- There is a real and substantial potential for repetition;
- Many consumers are affected, even by only one instance of deception.

The presence of the relevant factors is a question of fact.[303] Practices committed in connection with private disputes are less likely to affect the public interest than those that are part of consumer transactions, according to the *Hangman Ridge* court. Breach of a private contract only involves the public interest if there is a potential for repetition. In considering whether a private dispute affects the public interest, courts should consider the following factors, although no one factor is dispositive or necessary to find a public interest:

- The practice was committed in the course of the defendant's business;
- The defendant advertised to the public in general;
- The defendant actively solicited this particular plaintiff, indicating potential solicitation of others;
- There is unequal bargaining power.

Even if a practice meets the *Hangman Ridge* public interest standard, it is not a UDAP violation if it is "reasonable in relation to the development and preservation of business."[304] This language tracks exactly language found in the Washington UDAP statute itself.[305]

The *Hangman Ridge* public interest standard has been applied in a number of cases. The following have been found not to affect the public interest: a title insurance company's dispute with a business;[306] a business dispute with a realtor;[307] an isolated oral representation in a mobile home sale;[308] an inadvertent infringement of a weak trademark;[309] a company's negotiation with an experienced investor to establish a partnership;[310] a dispute about a single business loan transaction;[311] a private placement offering, limited to investors with net worth exceeding $1 million and not communicated to the public;[312] a dispute between a tire company and a dealer;[313] a store's detention of a suspected shoplifter where there was no evidence of a generalized course of conduct;[314] and a dispute between brokers over a commission.[315]

On the other hand, purchasing a horse at auction meets the five-prong public interest requirement,[316] as does a case involving a consumer's mobile home purchase and financing.[317] A real estate agency's policy regarding forfeiture of earnest money, which it applied in "dozens, perhaps hundreds" of cases, has an impact on the public interest.[318] Concealment of a basement water problem in the sale of a home also affects the public interest, where the same seller made similar false statements to a subsequent purchaser of the same home.[319] Sale of seed by a seller who solicits the public and is acting in the scope of its business affects the public interest.[320] Whether an attorney's deceptive negotiation and collection of a fee met the public interest test was a question of fact.[321] A pattern or practice of deception of mobile home buyers meets the public interest requirement.[322] A seller's active solicitation of business makes that seller's practices implicate the public interest.[323] Solicitation

303 Cotton v. Kronenberg, 111 Wash. App. 258, 44 P.3d 878 (2002).

304 Travis v. Washington Horse Breeders, 111 Wash. 2d 396, 759 P.2d 418 (1988).

305 Wash. Rev. Code § 19.86.920.

306 Hangman Ridge Training Stables, Inc. v. Safeco Title Ins. Co., 105 Wash. 2d 778, 719 P.2d 531 (1986).

307 Pacific Northwest Life Ins. Co. v. Turnball, 51 Wash. App. 692, 754 P.2d 1262 (1988).

308 Henery v. Robinson, 67 Wash. App. 277, 834 P.2d 1091 (1992).

309 Seattle Endeavors, Inc. v. Mastro, 123 Wash. 2d 339, 868 P.2d 120 (1994); *cf.* Nordstrom, Inc. v. Tampourlos, 107 Wash. 2d 735, 733 P.2d 208 (1987) (in typical trademark case, likelihood of confusing the public will meet public interest requirement).

310 Reeves v. Teuscher, 881 F.2d 1495 (9th Cir. 1989). *See also* Goel v. Jain, 259 F. Supp. 2d 1128 (W.D. Wash. 2003) (dispute among parties to a business acquisition deal did not affect public interest).

311 Cimarron Enters., Inc. v. Mortg. Exchange Investments, Inc., 2000 Wash. App. LEXIS 1384 (Apr. 3, 2000) (unpublished, citation limited).

312 Tuscany, Inc. v. Paragon Capital Corp., 2000 Wash. App. LEXIS 1609 (Aug. 28, 2000) (unpublished, citation limited).

313 Goodyear Tire & Rubber Co. v. Whiteman Tire, Inc., 935 P.2d 628 (Wash. App. Ct. 1997).

314 Guijosa v. Wal-Mart Stores, Inc., 101 Wash. App. 777, 6 P.3d 583 (2000), *aff'd on other grounds*, 144 Wash. 2d 907, 32 P.3d 250 (2001).

315 Broten v. May, 49 Wash. App. 564, 744 P.2d 1085 (1987).

316 Travis v. Washington Horse Breeders, 111 Wash. 2d 396, 759 P.2d 418 (1988).

317 Mason v. Mortgage Am., Inc., 114 Wash. 2d 842, 792 P.2d 142 (1990). *But cf.* Race v. Fleetwood Retail Corp., 2003 WL 1901274 (Wash. App. Apr. 17, 2003) (unpublished, citation limited) (insufficient pleading and proof).

318 Edmonds v. John L. Scott Real Estate, Inc., 942 P.2d 1072 (Wash. Ct. App. 1997). *See also* Bynum v. Klentak, 1999 Wash. App. LEXIS 76 (Jan. 19, 1999) (misrepresentations and building code violations affect public interest where builder is continuing to build and sell homes).

319 *Id. See also* Collard v. Reagan, 2002 WL 1357052, at *3 n.4 (Wash. App. June 21, 2002) (unpublished, citation limited) (reciting elements of public impact test met by abusive landlord).

320 Cox v. Lewiston Grain Growers, 936 P.2d 1191 (Wash. Ct. App. 1997).

321 Cotton v. Kronenberg, 111 Wash. App. 258, 44 P.3d 878 (2002).

322 Ethridge v. Hwang, 105 Wash. App. 447, 20 P.3d 958 (2001).

323 Reeves v. Teuscher, 881 F.2d 1495 (9th Cir. 1989); Travis v.

of unsophisticated investors who occupy an unequal bargaining position has an impact on the public interest.[324]

One of two alternate tests under the pre-*Hangman Ridge* formulation of the public interest test focused, *inter alia*, on whether the defendant's deceptive practices had the potential for repetition.[325] Since the potential for repetition is also one of the *Hangman Ridge* factors for determining whether a consumer transaction affects the public interest, cases interpreting the "potential for repetition" factor under the old standard may still have some precedential value.[326]

Washington Horse Breeders, 111 Wash. 2d 396, 759 P.2d 418 (1988); Ahlborn v. Daley, 2001 Wash. App. LEXIS 2567 (Nov. 20, 2001) (unpublished, citation limited) (yellow pages ad meets public interest test because it has potential to affect public at large); Edmonds v. John L. Scott Real Estate, Inc., 942 P.2d 1072 (Wash. App. 1997); Sing v. John L. Scott, Inc., 920 P.2d 589 (Wash. App. 1996), *rev'd on other grounds*, 134 Wash. 2d 24, 948 P.2d 816 (1997); Sign-O-Life Signs, Inc. v. Delauventi Florists, Inc., 825 P.2d 714 (Wash. App. 1992).

324 Reeves v. Teuscher, 881 F.2d 1495 (9th Cir. 1989).

325 Anhold v. Daniels, 94 Wash. 2d 40, 614 P.2d 184 (1980). *Accord* Eastlake Constr. Co. v. Hess, 102 Wash. 2d 30, 686 P.2d 465 (1984); Sato v. Century 21 Ocean Shores Real Estate, 101 Wash. 2d 599, 681 P.2d 242 (1984); McRae v. Bolstad, 101 Wash. 2d 161, 676 P.2d 496 (Wash. 1984); Haner v. Quincy Farm Chemicals Inc., 97 Wash. 2d 753, 649 P.2d 828 (1982); Keyes v. Bollinger, 27 Wash. App. 755, 621 P.2d 168 (1981); Ulberg v. Seattle Bonded Inc., 28 Wash. App. 762, 626 P.2d 522 (1981).

326 *Finding potential for repetition*: McRae v. Bolstad, 101 Wash. 2d 161, 676 P.2d 496 (1984) (realtor's sale of single family house through multiple listing service without disclosing sewage defects); Bowers v. Transamerica Title Ins. Co., 675 P.2d 193 (Wash. 1983) (practice occurring in firm's escrow business has potential for repetition); Harstad v. Frol, 41 Wash. App. 294, 704 P.2d 638 (1985) (deception by real estate agent who had marketed several other properties); Luxon v. Caviezel, 42 Wash. App. 261, 710 P.2d 809 (1985) (listing house with multiple listing service); Wilkinson v. Smith, 31 Wash. App. 1, 639 P.2d 768 (1982) (real estate sale by regulated brokers); Kelley v. Dick Balch Chevrolet Co., 28 Wash. App. 1059 (1981) (dealer's sale of used car as new).
No potential for repetition: Burton v. Ascol, 105 Wash. 2d 344, 715 P.2d 110 (1986) (building contractor's construction practices); Rouse v. Glascam Builders, Inc., 677 P.2d 125 (Wash. 1984) (builder's deceptive representation that it would repair condo defect, where there was no evidence of similar acts toward other condo owners); Sato v. Century 21 Ocean Shores Real Estate, 101 Wash. 2d 599, 681 P.2d 242 (1984) (upholding finding of no public interest impact where couple thought they were buying one lot but actually bought a different one and there was no evidence to show that error was more than a simple misunderstanding); Baker Boyer Nat'l Bank v. Garner, 43 Wash. App. 673, 719 P.2d 583 (1986) (trustee's administration of trust); Blake v. Federal Way Cycle Center, 40 Wash. App. 302, 698 P.2d 578 (1985) (problems with repair of motorcycle); Jackson v. Harkey, 41 Wash. App. 472, 704 P.2d 687 (1985) (posting of deceptive sign in a single home); Nuttall v. Dowell, 31 Wash. App. 98, 639 P.2d 832 (1982) (isolated breach of private contract).

7.5.3.3 Colorado Requires a Significant Impact on the Public as Consumers

In 1998 the Colorado Supreme Court announced criteria for UDAP claims that include a requirement that the challenged practice significantly impact the public as actual or potential consumers of the defendant's goods, services, or property.[327] The court cited only the statute's title and the legislative purpose of preventing consumer fraud as authority for this conclusion. Factors to determine whether a case meets the public impact test include the number of consumers directly affected, their relative sophistication and bargaining power, and evidence that the practice has impacted other consumers in the past or has significant potential to do so in the future.[328]

So far, the Colorado Supreme Court has found the public impact test not met only in cases where the plaintiff was not a consumer of the defendant's goods or services, and it is possible that the court will presume public impact when a consumer is dealing with an entity that regularly sells to the public.[329] It held that a subdivision developer's misrepresentations that home buyers would be allowed to use a private road on the plaintiff's property implicated the public as consumers because the misrepresentations were directed to the market generally.[330] On the other hand, a doctor's misrepresentation of his qualifications to a large insurance company did not meet the public impact test in a suit brought by a disability claimant who was examined by the doctor.[331] The doctor's misrepresentation was not public and was limited to two private parties, neither of which was the consumer. Likewise, a manufacturer's misrepresentation about the exclusivity of a dealership, which affected only three dealers at most and was not communicated to the

327 Hall v. Walter, 969 P.2d 224 (Colo. 1998); Martinez v. Lewis, 969 P.2d 213 (Colo. 1998).

328 Rhino Linings USA, Inc. v. Rocky Mountain Rhino Lining, Inc., 62 P.3d 142 (Colo. 2003); Martinez v. Lewis, 969 P.2d 213 (Colo. 1998).

329 *But cf.* Coors v. Security Life of Denver Ins. Co., 2003 WL 22019815 (Colo. App. Aug. 28, 2003) (intermediate appellate court decision that insurance company's overcharges did not have a public impact even though it had overcharged 200 other consumers, where this was only 1% of policyholders, there was no evidence of the magnitude of the other overcharges, and the plaintiff was a sophisticated businessman who was accompanied by counsel when he purchased the policy).

330 Hall v. Walter, 969 P.2d 224 (Colo. 1998). *See also* Full Draw Productions v. Easton Sports, Inc., 85 F. Supp. 2d 1001 (D. Colo. 2000) (wide dissemination of falsehoods may meet Colorado public impact requirement even though recipients were primarily businesses). *See also* Loughridge v. Goodyear Tire & Rubber Co., 192 F. Supp. 2d 1175 (D. Colo. 2002) (manufacturer's mass marketing, including a website that targeted ultimate consumers, shows consumer impact); Wheeler v. T.L. Roofing, Inc., 74 P.3d 499 (Colo. App. 2003) (general contractor's claim that roofing contractor's breach of contract had public impact was frivolous).

331 Martinez v. Lewis, 969 P.2d 213 (Colo. 1998).

general public, did not meet the public interest test.[332] Similarly, an intermediate appellate court held that a misrepresentation by one builder to another about a unique defect in a parcel of land did not meet the consumer impact test.[333]

7.5.3.4 Minnesota Requires Private UDAP Actions to Meet a Public Interest Test

A divided Minnesota Supreme Court has also read a public interest requirement into the statute that creates a private cause of action for consumer protection violations.[334] The court, using statutory language that applies only to attorney general suits, ruled that private claimants must also demonstrate that their cause of action benefits the public. The court failed to consider the fact that public enforcement involves the expenditure of public resources and the assertion of the state's authority against the defendant, making an inquiry into the public interest important in a way that is irrelevant for private suits.

The case that announced the public interest requirement involved an isolated one-on-one business transaction, which the court clearly felt was not the kind of private UDAP suit the legislature intended to authorize. It is possible that the court will recognize a presumption that most or all consumer suits meet its new public interest test. In a later decision, the court intimated that offering a program to the public at large is sufficient to meet the public-interest test.[335] The court held that even though only a few people were injured by a trade school's deceptive practices, the school affected the public interest by obtaining a state license, offering its programs to the general public, making misrepresentations in TV ads, and giving misleading information and sales and information presentations.

In applying the public interest test, lower courts often compare the facts in the case at hand to those in the two cases the Minnesota Supreme Court has decided. One court held that the UDAP statute did not cover a commercial lease transaction because the representations were made only to the plaintiff and possibly a group of other tenants, so only a finite group was affected.[336] An Eighth Circuit decision holds that transactions between sophisticated gas traders in the wholesale commercial gas market are not covered by Minnesota's UDAP statute.[337] Whether a case meets the public interest test is a question of law, not fact.[338]

Several federal decisions erroneously require the plaintiff's suit, not just the defendant's actions, to impact the public.[339] This view would eliminate the UDAP statute as a vehicle for consumer redress except in class actions and perhaps the occasional test case. These decisions misconstrue the Minnesota Supreme Court's decisions. While in its first decision announcing the public interest test[340] the court stated that the plaintiff's "cause of action" must benefit the public, the court's specific concern was that the misrepresentations were made only to the buyer in a one-on-one transaction, not that the buyer was seeking only individual damages. In its second decision,[341] the court reiterated that the nature of the transaction was the critical factor, and the simple fact that the defendant made its misrepresentations to the public satisfied the public interest test. Notably, *Collins* was not a class action and the plaintiffs won relief only for themselves.

7.5.3.5 Nebraska Applies UDAP Statute Only to Transactions That Affect the Public Interest

The Nebraska Supreme Court has also ruled that the state UDAP statute does not apply to transactions that do not

---

332 Rhino Linings USA, Inc. v. Rocky Mountain Rhino Lining, Inc., 62 P.3d 142 (Colo. 2003).

333 Anson v. Trujillo, 56 P.3d 114 (Colo. App. 2002).

334 Ly v. Nystrom, 615 N.W.2d 302 (Minn. 2000).

335 Collins v. Minn. School of Bus., 655 N.W.2d 320 (Minn. 2003). *Cf.* Flora v. Firepond, Inc., 260 F. Supp. 2d 780 (D. Minn. 2003) (articulating similar test; no public interest where alleged fraud occurred in one-on-one communications); Scally v. Norwest Mortg., Inc., 2003 WL 22039526 (Minn. App. Sept. 2, 2003) (unpublished, citation limited) (no UDAP claim where consumer transaction was one-on-one and lender had terminated loan officer who made misrepresentations).

336 Heaven & Earth, Inc. v. Wyman Props. Ltd. P'ship, 2003 WL 22680935 (D. Minn. Oct. 21, 2003).

337 Gas Aggregation Servs., Inc. v. Howard Avista Energy, Inc., 319 F.3d 1060 (8th Cir. 2003). *See also* Stephenson v. Deutsche Bank, 282 F. Supp. 2d 1032 (D. Minn. 2003) (Act's substantive provisions do not apply to transactions between sophisticated traders).

338 Heaven & Earth, Inc. v. Wyman Props. Ltd. P'ship, 2003 WL 22680935 (D. Minn. Oct. 21, 2003).

339 Kalmes Farms, Inc. v. J-Star Indus., Inc., 2004 WL 114976 (D. Minn. Jan. 16, 2004) (fact that plaintiffs seek only damages is persuasive; no public interest where product no longer in production, even though misrepresentations were made to public at large); Zutz v. Case Corp., 2003 WL 22848943 (D. Minn. Nov. 21, 2003) (no UDAP claim even though misrepresentations were in promotional literature made available to public and product was still on market, since plaintiffs sought only compensatory damages); Berczyk v. Emerson Tool Co., 291 F. Supp. 2d 1004 (D. Minn. 2003) (no public benefit where suit sought money damages for personal injury caused by product that had already been recalled); Antioch Co. v. Scrapbook Borders, Inc., 291 F. Supp. 2d 980 (D. Minn. 2003) (no public benefit where one business sought damages for personal benefit from another business); Tuttle v. Lorillard Tobacco Co., 2003 WL 1571584 (D. Minn. Mar. 3, 2003); Davis v. U.S. Bancorp., 2003 WL 21730102 (D. Minn. July 23, 2003); Pecarina v. Tokai Corp., 2002 WL 1023153 (D. Minn. May 20, 2002) (no public benefit where plaintiff sought personal injury damages, even though suit related to product advertised and sold to public).

340 Ly v. Nystrom, 615 N.W.2d 302, 314 (Minn. 2000).

341 Collins v. Minnesota School of Bus., 655 N.W.2d 320 (Minn. 2003).

affect the public interest.[342] The court based its decision on the UDAP statute's definition of "trade or commerce" as a "sale of assets or services and any commerce directly or indirectly affecting the people of the State of Nebraska." The Nebraska decision deals only with the question of whether the UDAP statute applies to a private sale of a vehicle where the seller was not a vehicle dealer, however. Courts in many other states have excluded sales by non-merchants from UDAP coverage on a variety of rationales.[343] Whether the Nebraska Supreme Court will require a public interest showing in cases against defendants who deal with consumers on a regular basis is an open question, and advocates in Nebraska should stress the narrow focus of the court's decision.

7.5.3.6 Georgia Intermediate Appellate Courts Require Impact on Consumer Marketplace or Potential Harm to Consumer Public

Intermediate appellate courts in Georgia have expanded upon the notion that an isolated sale of real estate by one individual to another is not covered by the UDAP statute,[344] and have stated a more general requirement that a challenged practice must have potential harm for the consumer public, or must have an impact on the consumer marketplace.[345] So far, the question has not reached the state supreme court. A single instance of an unfair or deceptive act or practice can be sufficient to support a damage claim if the public consumer interest would be served thereby.[346] Placing a newspaper ad to sell the item shows an intent to reach the general consuming public.[347]

7.5.3.7 South Carolina Requires That Practice Have Impact on Public Interest

South Carolina courts have interpreted "trade or commerce affecting the people of the state" as requiring that a practice not just affect the parties to a transaction, but have an impact on the public interest, such as where there is a potential for repetition.[348] Among the ways of establishing

342 Nelson v. Lusterstone Surfacing Co., 258 Neb. 678, 605 N.W.2d 136 (2000). *See also* Arthur v. Microsoft Corp., 676 N.W.2d 29 (Neb. 2004) (discussing public interest test and applying it to antitrust claim).

343 *See* § 2.3.4, *supra.*

344 *See* § 2.2.5.1.3, *supra.*

345 Pryor v. CCEC, Inc., 257 Ga. App. 450, 571 S.E.2d 454 (2002) (UDAP statute inapplicable to private school's dismissal of student for misbehavior and denial of refund); Campbell v. Beak, 568 S.E.2d 801 (Ga. App. 2002) (statute covered individual who bought, repaired, and sold wrecked cars as hobby, where he placed ad in newspaper and had sold at least one other car with similar deception); Davis v. Rich's Dept. Stores, Inc., 248 Ga. App. 116, 545 S.E.2d 661 (2001) (store's attempt to collect from identity theft victim was isolated deviation from its policy with no impact on public in general); Chancellor v. Gateway Lincoln-Mercury, 502 S.E.2d 799 (Ga. App. Ct. 1998) (auto dealer's discounting of credit contract to financing company not covered, where price to consumer was not raised); Billy Cain Ford Lincoln Mercury v. Kaminski, 496 S.E.2d 521 (Ga. App. Ct. 1998) (advertisement of vehicle to the public, and sale to member of public, met public interest requirement); Lynas v. Williams, 454 S.E.2d 570 (Ga. Ct. App. 1995) (alleged deception that was not introduced into the stream of commerce and that was intended to have no impact on any market other than the plaintiff was not actionable under UDAP statute); Medley v. Boomershine Pontiac-GMC Truck, 214 Ga. App. 795, 449 S.E.2d 128 (1994) (car dealership not subject to UDAP suit for its salesman's unauthorized misdeeds where it committed no acts that potentially harmed public); Borden v. Pope Jeep-Eagle, Inc., 200 Ga. App. 176, 407 S.E.2d 128 (1991) (misrepresentation in negotiating car loan not part of wider practice); Burdakin v. Hub Motor Co., 183 Ga. App. 90, 357 S.E.2d 839 (1987) (no potential harmful effect on the consuming public from individual negligent repair); Waller v. Scheer, 175 Ga. App. 1, 332 S.E.2d 293 (1985); Zeeman v. Black, 156 Ga. App. 82, 273 S.E.2d 910 (1980); *see also* State v. Meredith Chevrolet, 145 Ga. App. 8, 244 S.E.2d 16, *aff'd per curiam*, 242 Ga. 294, 249 S.E.2d 87 (1978). *Cf.* Miles Rich Chrysler-Plymouth, Inc. v. Mass, 201 Ga. App. 693, 411 S.E.2d 901 (1991) (car dealer's bait and switch-type scheme within context of consumer marketplace).

346 Catrett v. Landmark Dodge, Inc., 253 Ga. App. 639, 560 S.E.2d 101 (2002) (dealer's misrepresentation of car as demonstrator); Crown Ford, Inc. v. Crawford, 473 S.E.2d 554 (Ga. App. Ct. 1996).

347 Campbell v. Beak, 568 S.E.2d 801 (Ga. App. 2002).

348 Liberty Mut. Ins. Co. v. Employee Resource Mgmt., Inc., 176 F. Supp. 2d 510 (D.S.C. 2001) (public impact shown where company withheld information from state regulator and insurance companies and exposed employees and other companies to risk of having no workers' compensation coverage); Craig v. Andrew Aaron & Assoc., Inc., 947 F. Supp. 208 (D.S.C. 1996); Wilson Group, Inc. v. Quorum Health Resources, Inc., 880 F. Supp. 416 (D.S.C. 1995) (UDAP claim denied because public injury too remote and no showing of real potential for repetition); Orangeburg Pecan Co. v. Farmers Inv. Co., 869 F. Supp. 359 (D.S.C. 1994) (commercial breach of contract case lacks public impact); Brown v. Goode, Peterson & Hemme (*In re* Brown), 270 B.R. 43 (Bankr. D. Or. 2001) (S.C. law) (deceptive practices shown, but no recovery because plaintiffs failed to show public impact); Singleton v. Stokes Motors, Inc., 2004 WL 764941 (S.C. Apr. 12, 2004) (proof that car dealer's actions were part of its standard business practices suffices); Crary v. Djebelli, 329 S.C. 385, 496 S.E.2d 21 (1998) (affirming finding of potential for repetition); Daisy Outdoor Advertising Co. v. Abbott, 473 S.E.2d 47 (S.C. 1996); Florence Paper Co. v. Orphan, 379 S.E.2d 289 (S.C. 1989); La Motte v. Punch Line, Inc., 370 S.E.2d 711 (S.C. 1988); Robertson v. First Union Nat'l Bank, 565 S.E.2d 309 (S.C. App. 2002) (making a commercial loan based on inflated appraisal does not affect public interest where no pattern shown); Global Protection Corp. v. Halbersberg, 503 S.E.2d 483 (S.C. App. 1998) (large number of glow-in-the-dark condoms sold in violation of competitor's trademark has impact on public interest); Burbach v. Investors Mgmt. Corp., 484 S.E.2d 119 (S.C. App. 1997) (problems with residential leases have impact on public interest; tenants also showed repeated violations by same landlord); Young v. Cen-

a potential for repetition are proof that the same kind of actions occurred in the past or that the company's procedures create a potential for repetition.[349] This proof should not be difficult when the defendant is an ongoing business that provides products or services to consumers.[350] The state law regulating motor vehicle manufacturers, distributors, and dealers offers an alternative cause of action for twice actual damages (treble if malice is shown) plus attorney fees for any unfair or deceptive act or practice, without requiring special proof of a public impact.[351]

7.5.3.8 New York Requires That Practices Impact Consumers at Large

In New York, according to that state's highest court, UDAP plaintiffs need not show repetition or a pattern of deceptive behavior,[352] but they must show that the acts or practices "have a broader impact on consumers at large."[353] A "single shot transaction" or a private contract dispute, unique to the parties, does not fall within the ambit of the statute.[354] Thus, a union pension fund's transaction with a

tury Lincoln-Mercury, Inc., 396 S.E.2d 105 (S.C. Ct. App. 1990) (collusion between auto body shop and insurer subject to repetition), *aff'd in part, rev'd in part on other grounds*, 309 S.C. 263, 422 S.E.2d 103 (1992); Columbia East Assoc. v. Bi-Lo, Inc., 386 S.E.2d 259 (S.C. Ct. App. 1989); Noack Enterprises, Inc. v. Country Corner Interior, 351 S.E.2d 347 (S.C. Ct. App. 1986). *See also In re* Daniel, 137 B.R. 884 (D.S.C. 1992) (practices relating to repossession of mobile home have potential for repetition); McTeer v. Provident Life & Acc. Ins., 712 F. Supp. 512 (D.S.C. 1989) (potential for repetition where practice part of company's standard practice); Haley Nursery Co. v. Forrest, 381 S.E.2d 906 (S.C. 1989) (disseminating disputed representation to all seller's customers creates public interest in action); First Union Mortgage Corp. v. Thomas, 451 S.E.2d 907 (S.C. Ct. App. 1994); Ardis v. Cox, 431 S.E.2d 267 (S.C. Ct. App. 1993); Perry v. Green, 437 S.E.2d 150 (S.C. Ct. App. 1993); Camp v. Springs Mortgage Corp., 414 S.E.2d 784 (S.C. Ct. App. 1991), *aff'd in part, rev'd in part on other grounds*, 310 S.C. 514, 426 S.E.2d 304 (1993); Dowd v. Imperial Chrysler-Plymouth, Inc., 381 S.E.2d 212 (S.C. Ct. App. 1989) (public interest where potential for car dealer to repeat sales misrepresentation); Barnes v. Jones Chevrolet Co., 358 S.E.2d 156 (S.C. Ct. App. 1987) (padding of auto repair bill affects public interest because it has the potential for repetition). *But see* Jefferies v. Phillips, 451 S.E.2d 21 (S.C. Ct. App. 1994) (proof of potential for repetition of a business practice is insufficient; note that this holding is undercut by Daisy Outdoor Advertising Co. v. Abbott, 473 S.E.2d 47 (S.C. 1996)).

349 Liberty Mut. Ins. Co. v. Employee Resource Mgmt., Inc., 176 F. Supp. 2d 510 (D.S.C. 2001); Williams-Garrett v. Murphy, 106 F. Supp. 2d 834 (D.S.C. 2000) (proof of deceptive acts in past); Singleton v. Stokes Motors, Inc., 2004 WL 764941 (S.C. Apr. 12, 2004) (proof that car dealer's actions were part of its standard business practices suffices); Crary v. Djebelli, 496 S.E.2d 21 (S.C. 1998) (showing that the defendants had several opportunities to engage in similar transactions is enough to show potential for repetition); Daisy Outdoor Advertising Co. v. Abbott, 473 S.E.2d 47 (S.C. 1996); Burbach v. Investors Mgmt. Corp., 484 S.E.2d 119 (S.C. App. 1997) (proof that landlords had withheld other tenants' security deposits was admissible).

350 York v. Conway Ford, Inc., 480 S.E.2d 726 (S.C. 1997) (car dealer's practices have impact on public interest); Taylor v. Medenica, 479 S.E.2d 35 (S.C. 1996) (medical laboratory's practices have impact on public interest).

351 S.C. Code §§ 56-15-30, 56-15-110. *See* Kucharski v. Rick Hendrick Chevrolet Ltd. P'ship, 2002 WL 31386090 (S.C. App. Sept. 18, 2002) (unpublished, citation limited).

352 Prior to this ruling, many federal courts and lower state courts had required New York UDAP plaintiffs to show that the defendant's practices not only had some effect on consumers at large but also were of a recurring nature. *See* Tinlee Enterprises, Inc. v. Aetna Cas. & Surety Co., 834 F. Supp. 605 (E.D.N.Y. 1993); EFS Marketing, Inc. v. Russ Berrie & Co., 836 F. Supp. 128 (S.D.N.Y. 1993), *aff'd in part, rev'd in part on other grounds*, 76 F.3d 487 (2d Cir. 1996); Franklin Electronic Publishers v. Unisonic Products Corp., 763 F. Supp. 1 (S.D.N.Y. 1991); Perfumer's Workshop v. Roure Bertrand du Pont, 737 F. Supp. 785 (S.D.N.Y. 1990); Azby Brokerage, Inc. v. Allstate Ins. Co., 681 F. Supp. 1084 (S.D.N.Y. 1988) (no showing of consumer injury or public interest); Nardella v. Braff, 621 F. Supp. 1170 (S.D.N.Y. 1985) (attorney-client relationship); Genesco Entertainment v. Koch, 593 F. Supp. 743 (S.D.N.Y. 1984); United Knitwear Co. v. North Sea Ins. Co., 203 A.D.2d 358, 612 N.Y.S.2d 597 (1994) (no UDAP claim in commercial insurance case because no showing of recurring nature of practice and harmfulness to public); Myers, Smith & Granady v. New York Property Ins. Underwriting Ass'n, 607 N.Y.S.2d 288 (App. Div. 1994), *aff'd on other grounds*, 85 N.Y.2d 832, 647 N.E.2d 1348 (1995); Holmes Protection of New York, Inc. v. Provident Loan Society of New York, 577 N.Y.S.2d 850 (App. Div. 1991) (no UDAP claim in commercial case without proof of recurring deceptive business practices harmful to the public at large); H2O Swimwear, Ltd. v. Lomas, 164 A.D. 2d 804, 560 N.Y.S.2d 19 (1990) (no UDAP claim in commercial case because transaction did not affect public interest since it was not of a recurring nature); 99 Realty Co. v. Wall Street Transcript Corp., 611 N.Y.S.2d 767 (N.Y. Civ. Ct. 1994), *rev'd per curiam on other grounds*, 165 Misc. 2d 454, 632 N.Y.S.2d 742 (App. Term 1995). *But see* Riordan v. Nationwide Mut. Fire Ins. Co., 756 F. Supp. 732 (S.D.N.Y. 1990) (distinguishing *Genesco* because defendant's deceptive claim settlement policy affects public at large); Schroders, Inc. v. Hogan Sys., Inc., 137 Misc. 2d 738, 522 N.Y.S.2d 404 (Sup. Ct. 1987); *cf.* Construction Technology v. Lockformer Co., 704 F. Supp. 1212 (S.D.N.Y. 1989) (distinguishing *Genesco* because of the effect on the public at large).

353 Oswego Laborers' Local 214 Pension Fund v. Marine Midland Bank, 85 N.Y.2d 20, 647 N.E.2d 741, 744 (1995) (basing conclusion on title and purpose of law). *Accord* New York University v. Continental Ins. Co., 87 N.Y.2d 308, 662 N.E.2d 763 (1995). *See also* Greenspan v. Allstate Ins. Co., 937 F. Supp. 288 (S.D.N.Y. 1996).

354 Oswego Laborers' Local 214 Pension Fund v. Marine Midland Bank, 85 N.Y.2d 20, 647 N.E.2d 741 (1995); New York University v. Continental Ins. Co., 87 N.Y.2d 308, 662 N.E.2d 763 (1995). *Accord* MaGee v. Paul Revere Life Ins. Co., 954 F. Supp. 582 (E.D.N.Y. 1997); Citipostal v. Unistar Leasing, 283 A.D.2d 916, 724 N.Y.S.2d 555 (2001) (acts that are limited to business leases, and that can not carry over to consumer transactions, are not consumer oriented).

bank was consumer-oriented where the parties had unequal bargaining power and the bank gave the fund the same standard forms and advice that it supplied to the public at large.[355] But a specially negotiated insurance transaction between a major university and a national insurance company in which each side was expertly represented was a private contract dispute that did not affect the consuming public at large.[356]

Adoption of this test has spawned extensive litigation. While the lower court cases that have interpreted and applied New York's consumer-oriented test can not be perfectly harmonized, some overriding themes have emerged. Some courts cite the focus of the statute to protect consumers as a group, rather than punish wrongdoers as individuals.[357] Accordingly, courts often stress the highest court's instructions that the plaintiff must show that "the acts or practices have a broader impact on the consumer at large" in that they are "directed to consumers" or "potentially affect similarly situated consumers."[358] While it is not necessary to show that the wrongdoing recurred, it helps to show that such recurrence is possible. This may be illustrated by characterizing the wrongdoing as part of the defendant's ordinary manner of doing business, that is, that the defendant dealt with the consumer as it would with any other similarly situated customer.[359] One manner of making this point is to show that the defendant used a marketing scheme, advertising or other publication related to the conduct.[360] Another is to show elements of the conduct embedded in a preprinted form or contract.[361]

Courts have seemed more willing to find the conduct consumer-oriented when the defendant represents an industry with high impact on consumers, such as managed health care,[362] no-fault insurance,[363] or mortgage lending.[364] A "vanishing premium" insurance misrepresentation case met the standard because the allegations were of "a national scope that have generated industry-wide litigation."[365] Courts are far less likely to find consumer-oriented conduct when the dispute is between two businesses, particularly if it involves a negotiated contract[366] or the effects on con-

355 Oswego Laborers' Local 214 Pension Fund v. Marine Midland Bank, 85 N.Y.2d 20, 647 N.E.2d 741 (1995).

356 New York University v. Continental Ins. Co., 87 N.Y.2d 308, 662 N.E.2d 763 (1995).

357 Devlin v. Transportation Communications Int'l Union, 2000 U.S. Dist. LEXIS 2441 (S.D.N.Y. Mar. 6, 2000); Smith v. Triad Mfg. Group, 255 A.D.2d 962, 681 N.Y.S.2d 710 (1998).

358 Oswego Laborers' Local 214 Pension Fund v. Marine Midland Bank, 85 N.Y.2d 20, 647 N.E.2d 741, 744–45 (1995). *See also* Cruz v. NYNEX, 703 N.Y.S.2d 103 (App. Div. 2000); McGill v. General Motors Corp., 231 A.D.2d 449, 647 N.Y.S.2d 209 (1996) (car manufacturer's concealment of its "secret warranty" for its defective brakes has a broad impact on the public at large). *But cf.* Daniels v. Provident Life & Cas. Ins. Co., 2001 U.S. Dist. LEXIS 11388 (W.D.N.Y. July 24, 2001) (bare allegation of repetition is insufficient).

359 G.E. Capital Fin., Inc. v. Bank Leumi Trust Co., 1999 U.S. Dist. LEXIS 485 (S.D.N.Y. Jan. 19, 1999). *See also* Bauer v. Mellon Mortg. Co., 178 Misc. 2d 234, 680 N.Y.S.2d 397 (1998) (bank failed to notify mortgagors that they no longer needed to carry PMI), *aff'd in relevant part sub nom.* Walts v. First Union Mortg. Corp., 259 A.D.2d 322, 686 N.Y.S.2d 428 (1999).

360 *See, e.g.*, Ansari v. New York Univ., 1997 U.S. Dist. LEXIS 6863 (S.D.N.Y. May 16, 1997) (dental program's promotional literature); Gaidon v. Guardian Life Ins. Co., 94 N.Y.2d 330, 704 N.Y.S.2d 177, 725 N.E.2d 598 (1999) (marketing scheme for life insurance); Karlin v. IVF Am., Inc., 93 N.Y.2d 282, 712 N.E.2d 662 (1999) (citing the defendant's "multi-media dissemination" of information to the public regarding its infertility treatments); Akgul v. Prime Time Transportation, Inc., 293 A.D.2d 631, 741 N.Y.S.2d 553 (2002) (franchise marketing scheme); People v. Empyre Inground Pools, Inc., 227 A.D.2d 731, 642 N.Y.S.2d 344 (1996) (newspaper advertisements); B.S.L. One Owners Corp. v. Key Int'l Mfg., Inc., 225 A.D.2d 643, 640 N.Y.S.2d 135 (1996) (advertisement of shares in cooperative association to residents); Griffin-Amiel v. Frank Terris Orchestras, 178 Misc. 2d 71, 677 N.Y.S.2d 908 (City Ct. 1998) (practices of company that marketed wedding services to public are consumer-oriented).

361 *See, e.g.*, Greenspan v. Allstate Ins. Co., 937 F. Supp. 288 (S.D.N.Y. 1996) (standard insurance company forms); Fava v. RRI, Inc., 1997 U.S. Dist. LEXIS 5630 (N.D.N.Y. Apr. 24, 1997) (defendant used preprinted form in attempting to collect a debt). *But see* Cruz v. Northwestern Chrysler Plymouth Sales, 179 Ill. 2d 271, 688 N.E.2d 653 (1997) (defendant's use of preprinted forms to sell yellow pages space did not make conduct "consumer-oriented" where plaintiff was a business purchasing the space for business use).

362 Payton v. Aetna/US Healthcare, 2000 N.Y. Misc. LEXIS 91 (Sup. Ct. Mar. 22, 2000).

363 Greenspan v. Allstate Ins. Co., 937 F. Supp. 288 (S.D.N.Y. 1996).

364 Banks v. Consumer Home Mortg., Inc., 2003 WL 21251584 (E.D.N.Y. Mar. 28, 2003); Vaughn v. Consumer Home Mortg., Inc., 2003 WL 21241669 (E.D.N.Y. Mar. 23, 2003); Negrin v. Norwest Mortg., Inc., 700 N.Y.S.2d 184 (App. Div. 1999).

365 Gaidon v. Guardian Life Ins. Co., 94 N.Y.2d 330, 704 N.Y.S.2d 177, 725 N.E.2d 598 (1999).

366 *See, e.g.*, Solar Travel Corp. v. Nachtomi, 2001 U.S. Dist. LEXIS 7549 (S.D.N.Y. June 8, 2001); Eua Cogenex Corp. v. North Rockland Central School Dist., 124 F. Supp. 2d 861 (S.D.N.Y. 2000) (business-to-business transaction can in rare cases be consumer-oriented, but not here); A. Lorenzo Barroso, S.A. v. Polymer Research Corp., 80 F. Supp. 2d 39 (E.D.N.Y. 1999) (chemistry company's misrepresentation to a manufacturer not consumer-oriented); International Sport Divers Ass'n, Inc. v. Marine Midland, 25 F. Supp. 2d 101 (W.D.N.Y. 1998) (private contract negotiated between two businesses was not consumer-oriented); Ivy Mar Co. v. C.R. Seasons Ltd., 1998 U.S. Dist. LEXIS 15902 (E.D.N.Y Oct. 7, 1998) (trade dress dispute between companies is not consumer-oriented); New York Univ. v. Continental Ins. Co., 87 N.Y.2d 308, 662 N.E.2d 763 (1995) (dispute under unique, negotiated insurance policy); Ludl Electronics Prods., Ltd. v. Wells Fargo Fin. Leasing, Inc., 775 N.Y.S.2d 59 (App. Div. 2004) (automatic renewal clause in lease of business equipment); Cruz v. NYNEX, 703 N.Y.S.2d 103 (App. Div. 2000) (business's purchase of yellow pages advertisements was not consumer-oriented); St. Patrick's Home for the Aged & Infirm v. Laticrete Int'l, Inc., 696 N.Y.S.2d 117 (App. Div. 1999) (manufacturer's sale of exterior wall panels to installer was not consumer-oriented); Jim & Phil's Family Pharmacy, Ltd. v. National Prescription Administrators, Inc.,

sumers are merely incidental.[367]

The following types of conduct have all been found, based on some of the factors described above, to be consumer-oriented for purposes of New York's UDAP statute: marketing of insurance policies as having a "vanishing premium," using unrealistic projections;[368] other deception in the sale of insurance;[369] deception with respect to the availability of health care benefits under a managed care health insurance policy;[370] a bank's protection of its larger but not its smaller depositors from the devaluation of a foreign currency;[371] an HMO's attempt to run competitors out of business, thereby limiting consumers' health care choices;[372] entering into contracts without intending to supply conforming goods, and then suing dissatisfied customers and threatening to invoke a liquidated damages clause;[373] misrepresentation of infertility treatment results;[374] defective design and construction of a new home;[375] selling foreclosed homes at inflated prices, and misleading buyers about repairs and financing;[376] rigging bids at a public auction;[377] a mortgagee's unlawful demand of fees as part of payoff;[378] a mortgagee's billing of mortgagors for PMI premiums after it was no longer required by the terms of the mortgage;[379] a mortgagee's improper application of a fluctuating interest rate;[380] deceptive debt collection;[381] an unlicensed, independent paralegal's acceptance of legal work from a member of the public;[382] deception in the advertisement and sale of cooperative shares to residents;[383] a bail bond company's charging of excessive and unlawful fees on bonds;[384] deceptive description of an educational program;[385] deception about the environmental hazards of a gasoline additive that ended up polluting the plaintiffs' water supply;[386] offering certain contract terms to the public at large and then unilaterally changing those terms;[387] mislabeling a consumer product;[388] a franchise marketing scheme;[389] copyright infringement;[390] and a car manufacturer's concealment of its "secret warranty" for its defective brakes.[391]

On the other hand, courts have found the following types of conduct not to be consumer-oriented under the specific circumstances alleged, but rather private disputes over behavior not likely to affect consumers at large: deception

233 A.D.2d 423, 649 N.Y.S.2d 481 (1996) (dispute between pharmacy and prescription claim program); Rosenberg & Estis, P.C. v. Chicago Ins. Co., 2003 WL 21665680 (N.Y. Sup. Ct. July 11, 2003) (insurance coverage dispute not consumer-oriented where insured did not have disparate bargaining power); Banc of Am. Commercial Fin. Corp. v. Issacharoff, 188 Misc. 2d 790, 728 N.Y.S.2d 861 (Sup. Ct. 2001) (negotiation about collection of commercial loan).

367 Savin Corp. v. Savin Group, 2003 WL 22451731, at *16 (S.D.N.Y. Oct. 24, 2003) (trademark infringement not covered even though consumer confusion might result). *But see* Kforce v. Alden Personnel, Inc., 2003 WL 22420455 (S.D.N.Y. Oct. 23, 2003) (defaming a competitor would not affect public interest even though it would reduce consumer choice).

368 Gaidon v. Guardian Life Ins. Co., 94 N.Y.2d 330, 704 N.Y.S.2d 177, 725 N.E.2d 598 (1999).

369 Brenkus v. Metropolitan Life Ins. Co., 309 A.D.2d 1260, 765 N.Y.S.2d 80 (2003) (denial of insurer's motion for summary judgment).

370 Payton v. Aetna/US Healthcare, 2000 N.Y. Misc. LEXIS 91 (Sup. Ct. Mar. 22, 2000).

371 Rey-Willis v. Citibank, N.A., 2003 WL 21714947, at *7 n.7 (S.D.N.Y. July 23, 2003).

372 Digigan, Inc. v. Ivalidate, Inc., 2004 WL 203010 (S.D.N.Y. Feb. 3, 2004) (no UDAP claim for deception of public about ownership of patent, where harm was primarily to plaintiff's business); Excellus Health Plan, Inc. v. Tran, 2003 WL 22382948 (W.D.N.Y. Aug. 29, 2003). *But see* Kforce v. Alden Personnel, Inc., 2003 WL 22420455 (S.D.N.Y. Oct. 23, 2003) (defaming a competitor would not affect public interest even though it would reduce consumer choice).

373 Morgan Servs., Inc. v. Episcopal Church Home & Affiliates Life Care Community, Inc., 305 A.D.2d 1105, 757 N.Y.S.2d 917 (2003).

374 Karlin v. IVF Am., Inc., 93 N.Y.2d 282, 712 N.E.2d 662 (1999).

375 Latiuk v. Faber Constr. Co., 703 N.Y.S.2d 645 (App. Div. 2000). *See also* People v. Empyre Inground Pools, Inc., 227 A.D.2d 731, 642 N.Y.S.2d 344 (1996) (home improvement contractor).

376 Banks v. Consumer Home Mortg., Inc., 2003 WL 21251584 (E.D.N.Y. Mar. 28, 2003) (ongoing predatory home sale scheme; home inspector's false statements also are consumer oriented); Vaughn v. Consumer Home Mortg., Inc., 2003 WL 21241669 (E.D.N.Y. Mar. 23, 2003) (same); Polonetsky v. Better Homes Depot, Inc., 185 Misc. 2d 282, 712 N.Y.S.2d 801 (Sup. Ct. 2000) (construing city UDAP ordinance in light of state UDAP precedent), *rev'd*, 279 A.D.2d 418, 720 N.Y.S.2d 59 (2001) (holding that city UDAP ordinance did not cover real estate sales), *rev'd, complaint reinstated*, 97 N.Y.2d 46, 760 N.E.2d 1274 (2001) (real estate sale that was bound up with services was covered by city UDAP ordinance).

377 New York v. Feldman, 210 F. Supp. 2d 294 (S.D.N.Y. 2002).

378 Negrin v. Norwest Mortg., Inc., 700 N.Y.S.2d 184 (App. Div. 1999).

379 Bauer v. Mellon Mortgage Co., 178 Misc. 2d 234, 680 N.Y.S.2d 397 (Sup. Ct. 1998).

380 G.E. Capital Fin., Inc. v. Bank Leumi Trust Co., 1999 U.S. Dist. LEXIS 485 (S.D.N.Y. Jan. 19, 1999).

381 Fava v. RRI, Inc., 1997 U.S. Dist. LEXIS 5630 (N.D.N.Y. Apr. 24, 1997).

382 Sussman v. Grado, 192 Misc. 2d 628, 746 N.Y.S.2d 548 (Dist. Ct. 2002).

383 B.S.L. One Owners Corp. v. Key Mfg., Inc., 225 A.D.2d 643, 640 N.Y.S.2d 135 (1996).

384 McKinnon v. International Fidelity Ins. Co., 182 Misc. 2d 517, 704 N.Y.S.2d 774 (N.Y. Sup. Ct. 1999).

385 Ansari v. New York Univ., 1997 U.S. Dist. LEXIS 6863 (S.D.N.Y. May 16, 1997).

386 *In re* Methyl Tertiary Butyl Ether Prods. Liab. Litigation, 175 F. Supp. 2d 593 (S.D.N.Y. 2001).

387 People v. Wilco Energy Corp., 284 A.D.2d 469, 728 N.Y.S.2d 471 (2001).

388 Singh v. Queens Ledger Newspaper Group, 2 A.D.3d 703, 770 N.Y.S.2d 99 (2003).

389 Akgul v. Prime Time Transportation, Inc., 293 A.D.2d 631, 741 N.Y.S.2d 553 (2002).

390 Capitol Records, Inc. v. Wings Digital Corp., 218 F. Supp. 2d 280 (E.D.N.Y. 2002).

391 McGill v. General Motors Corp., 231 A.D.2d 449, 647 N.Y.S.2d 209 (1996).

alleged with respect to the purchase of securities;[392] disputes in a variety of business transactions;[393] misrepresentations made to a single individual;[394] a dispute arising out of a model's contract with a modeling agency;[395] fraud arising out of a large-scale home remodeling contract;[396] a warranty claim arising from the sale and manufacture of a customized wheelchair;[397] a union's discriminatory changes to a medical benefits system, where the plan was offered only to its own members and not to the public at large;[398] an insurance company's mishandling of an insured's claim;[399] a litigation party's violation of a stay imposed by state procedural rules;[400] breach of a contract for purchase of yellow pages advertisements;[401] misappropriation of literary ideas; a manufacturer's sale of a surgical laser to a doctor who used it to operate on the consumers;[402] a property owner's rental of a single apartment contrary to local zoning law;[403] public officials' collection of fees for cars that had been towed because of unpaid parking tickets; a realtor's misrepresentation that affected only a single real estate transaction;[404] an alleged failure to disclose the lower cash value of a replacement life insurance policy;[405] and a prescription claim program's distribution to its members of an allegedly defamatory letter regarding the termination of a pharmacy from the program.[406]

392 Jordan (Bermuda) Investment Co. v. Hunter Green Investments Ltd., 2003 WL 1751780 (S.D.N.Y. Apr. 1, 2003); Smith v. Triad Mfg. Group, Inc., 255 A.D.2d 962, 681 N.Y.S.2d 710 (1998). *See also* Lynch v. McQueen, 309 A.D.2d 790, 765 N.Y.S.2d 645 (2003) (deception regarding financial management not consumer-oriented).

393 Digigan, Inc. v. Ivalidate, Inc., 2004 WL 203010 (S.D.N.Y. Feb. 3, 2004) (patent ownership dispute); Highlands Ins. Co. v. PRG Brokerage, Inc., 2004 WL 35439 (S.D.N.Y. Jan. 6, 2004) (commercial insurance dispute); Maharishi Hardy Blechman Ltd. v. Abercrombie & Fitch Co., 292 F. Supp. 2d 535 (S.D.N.Y. 2003) (trademark dispute); Pfizer, Inc. v. Stryker Corp., 2003 WL 21660339 (S.D.N.Y. July 15, 2003); Wells Fargo Bank v. TACA Int'l Airlines, 247 F. Supp. 2d 352 (S.D.N.Y. 2002); Shred-It USA, Inc. v. Mobile Data Shred, Inc., 228 F. Supp. 2d 455 (S.D.N.Y. 2002) (breach of non-compete agreement), *aff'd*, 2004 WL 350152 (2d Cir. Feb. 25, 2004) (unpublished, citation limited); Champion Home Builders Co. v. ADT Security Servs., Inc., 179 F. Supp. 2d 16 (N.D.N.Y. 2001) (faulty installation and servicing of fire alarm system in factory); Green Harbour Homeowners' Ass'n v. G.H. Development and Constr., Inc., 307 A.D.2d 465, 763 N.Y.S.2d 114 (2003); St. Patrick's Home for the Aged & Infirm v. Laticrete Int'l, Inc., 696 N.Y.S.2d 117 (App. Div. 1999) (deceptive nondisclosure in manufacturer's sale of exterior wall panels to installer).

394 Sutton Assocs. v. Lexis-Nexis, 761 N.Y.S.2d 800 (Sup. Ct. 2003).

395 Dove v. L'Agence, 250 A.D.2d 435, 671 N.Y.S.2d 661 (1998).

396 Teller v. Bill Hayes, Ltd., 630 N.Y.S.2d 769 (App. Div. 1995).

397 Parrino v. Sperling, 648 N.Y.S.2d 702 (App. Div. 1996).

398 Devlin v. Transportation Communications. Int'l Union, 2000 U.S. Dist. LEXIS 2441 (S.D.N.Y. Mar. 6, 2000).

399 Lava Trading, Inc. v. Hartford Fire Ins. Co., 2004 WL 555723 (S.D.N.Y. Mar. 19, 2004); DePasquale v. Allstate Ins. Co., 179 F. Supp. 2d 51 (E.D.N.Y. 2002) (dispute between policyholder and insurance company about scope of coverage), *aff'd*, 2002 WL 31520500 (2d Cir. Oct. 31, 2002) (unpublished, citation limited); Scherer v. Equitable Life Assurance Soc., 190 F. Supp. 2d 629 (S.D.N.Y. 2002), *vacated on other grounds*, 347 F.3d 394 (2d Cir. 2003); Sichel v. Unum Provident Corp., 230 F. Supp. 2d 325 (S.D.N.Y. 2002) (distinguishing claims denial from false marketing of insurance); Bologna v. Allstate Ins. Co., 138 F. Supp. 2d 310 (E.D.N.Y. 2001); Daniels v. Provident Life & Cas. Ins. Co., 2001 U.S. Dist. LEXIS 11388 (W.D.N.Y. July 24, 2001); 61 Jane St. Tenants Corp. v. Great Am. Ins. Co., 2001 U.S. Dist. LEXIS 265 (S.D.N.Y. Jan. 12, 2001); Abraham v. Penn Mut. Life Ins. Co., 2000 U.S. Dist. LEXIS 10625 (S.D.N.Y. July 28, 2000) (but selling insurance it never intended to provide, or using deceptive practices against other policyholders, would establish consumer-oriented conduct); Shapiro v. Berkshire Life Ins. Co., 1999 U.S. Dist. LEXIS 11789 (S.D.N.Y. Aug. 2, 1999) (ruling that plaintiff's proffered affidavits by four other insureds with similar complaints were insufficient to demonstrate that the defendant routinely denied claims without adequately investigating them or with full knowledge that the claims are meritorious); Allahabi v. New York Life Ins. Co., 1999 U.S. Dist. LEXIS 2662 (S.D.N.Y. Mar. 9, 1999); Harary v. Allstate Ins. Co., 983 F. Supp. 95 (E.D.N.Y. 1997), *aff'd*, 162 F.3d 1147 (2d Cir. 1998); MaGee v. Paul Revere Life Ins. Co., 954 F. Supp. 582 (E.D.N.Y. 1997); Northwestern Mut. Life Ins. Co. v. Wender, 940 F. Supp. 62 (S.D.N.Y. 1996); Infostar Inc. v. Worcester Ins. Co., 924 F. Supp. 25 (S.D.N.Y. 1996); New York Univ. v. Continental Ins. Co., 87 N.Y.S.2d 308, 662 N.E.2d 763 (1995) (tailored insurance policy negotiated between two business entities); Hassett v. N.Y. Central Mut. Fire Ins. Co., 302 A.D.2d 886, 753 N.Y.S.2d 788 (2003); Goldman v. GEICO Gen. Ins. Co., 292 A.D.2d 162, 739 N.Y.S.2d 360 (2002) (providing erroneous declaration page to arbitrator handling insurance claim not covered); Fekete v. GA Ins. Co., 279 A.D.2d 300, 719 N.Y.S.2d 52 (2001); Martin v. Group Health Inc., 767 N.Y.S.2d 803 (App. Div. 2003) (refusal of health insurer to cover dental work); Egan v. New York Care Plus Ins. Co., 716 N.Y.S.2d 430 (A.D. 2000) (dispute over whether insurance covered particular treatment); Korn v. First UNUM Life Ins. Co., 717 N.Y.S.2d 606 (A.D. 2000) (dispute over insurance coverage). *Cf.* Wiener v. Unumprovident Corp., 202 F. Supp. 2d 116 (S.D.N.Y. 2002) (stating that claim is consumer oriented, but dismissing it because it is a private dispute). *But see* Binder v. National Life, 2003 WL 21180417 (S.D.N.Y. May 20, 2003) (allegation that insurer made a practice of wrongfully denying claims is sufficient to withstand motion to dismiss); Monga v. Security Mut. Life Ins. Co., 2002 WL 31777872 (N.Y. Sup. Oct. 10, 2002) (practice of delaying and denying claims without regard to their viability is consumer-oriented); DiDonato v. INA Life Ins. Co., 1999 U.S. Dist. LEXIS 9410 (S.D.N.Y. June 24, 1999) (selling a disability insurance policy, but then failing to pay a legitimate claim, would be a UDAP violation). *But cf.* Medina v. State Farm Mut. Auto. Ins. Co., 303 A.D.2d 987, 757 N.Y.S.2d 178 (2003) (reversing dismissal of UDAP claim because defendant insurance company has exclusive control of information regarding its practices and procedures).

400 Karp v. Siegel, 1998 U.S. Dist. LEXIS 8806 (June 12, 1998).

401 Cruz v. NYNEX, 703 N.Y.S.2d 103 (App. Div. 2000).

402 Soule v. Norton, 750 N.Y.S.2d 692 (App. Div. 2002).

403 Cater v. Saunders, 2002 WL 31207219 (N.Y. Dist. Ct. Sept. 30, 2002).

404 Canario v. Gunn, 751 N.Y.S.2d 310 (App. Div. Dec. 9, 2002).

405 Berardino v. Ochlan, 2 A.D.3d 556, 770 N.Y.S.2d 75 (2003).

406 Jim & Phil's Family Pharmacy, Ltd. v. National Prescription Administrators, Inc., 233 A.D.2d 423, 649 N.Y.S.2d 481 (1996).

7.5.4 Notice Letters as Precondition

7.5.4.1 Is a Notice Letter a Precondition to a UDAP Action?

Nine state UDAP statutes[407] require consumers to send sellers notice or demand letters before initiating a UDAP action, and a tenth state, Mississippi, requires the consumer to utilize an informal dispute resolution procedure prior to suit. In addition, Indiana's statute requires notice to the defendant except where the act is part of a scheme, artifice, or device with intent to defraud or mislead.[408] Illinois formerly required notice for UDAP suits against car dealers and holders of motor vehicle installment contracts,[409] but the state supreme court struck down this statute as an unconstitutional special law.[410] Like the rest of the UDAP statute, a notice letter requirement must be construed liberally.[411]

This type of demand letter precondition must be distinguished from UDAP notice requirements that are not preconditions to a consumer's complaint. Maryland's UDAP statute encourages reconciliation in proceedings brought by the state, but this is not a precondition for suit.[412] Several states require that the UDAP complaint, and in some states the final judgment, be mailed to the attorney general, either by the plaintiff or by the clerk of court.[413] Some of these statutes specify that this requirement is not jurisdictional. Even without statutory language, courts have found these requirements not to be jurisdictional.[414] The case can proceed to trial without the notice, although judgment may not be entered until the attorney general receives notice.[415]

Demand letters are only a precondition to a UDAP suit if the statute explicitly creates a demand letter requirement. No court has ever considered implying a notice letter requirement into a UDAP statute.[416]

In addition, even statutes that create a notice letter requirement may limit their effect in certain situations. The Massachusetts notice letter requirement applies to consumer actions, but not to those by merchants under the statute's section 11.[417] In addition, the Massachusetts notice letter requirement does not apply where a seller has failed to pay a lemon law arbitration award or appeal in a timely fashion. The lemon law requirement of payment within twenty-one days and the arbitration decision itself are the statutorily designated equivalent of a demand letter.[418]

A consumer suing under the Texas Consumer Credit Code does not have to meet the Texas UDAP statute's notice requirements.[419] The Texas UDAP statute also excuses the demand letter requirement if the statute of limitations would expire before the demand letter period expires.[420] The Fifth Circuit has ruled that it would be an error to limit this exception only to instances where the consumer discovers the deception too late to allow the full notice period before the statute of limitations expires.[421] But the burden is on the consumer to show that the impending expiration of the limitations period rendered impracticable the giving of proper notice.[422]

Even if a demand letter is required, the requirement may not apply in federal court. The Seventh Circuit found that a thirty-day notice requirement in a state debt collection

See also Kforce v. Alden Personnel, Inc., 2003 WL 22420455 (S.D.N.Y. Oct. 23, 2003) (company's defamation of competitor not consumer-oriented).

407 Alabama, California (under CLRA, Cal. Civ. Code § 1782(a), but only prior to action for damages), Georgia, Indiana, Maine, Massachusetts, Texas, Virginia, and Wyoming.

408 Ind. Code § 24-5-0.5-2 (definition of "incurable deceptive act").

409 815 Ill. Comp. Stat. Ann. § 505/10a (1995).

410 Allen v. Woodfield Chevrolet, Inc., 208 Ill. 2d 12, 802 N.E.2d 752, 280 Ill. Dec. 501 (2003).

411 Stringer v. Bugg, 254 Ga. App. 745, 563 S.E.2d 447 (2002); Lynas v. Williams, 454 S.E.2d 570 (Ga. Ct. App. 1995).

412 Devine Seafood, Inc. v. Attorney General, 37 Md. App. 439, 377 A.2d 1194 (1977).

413 Alaska, Connecticut, Georgia, Illinois, Kansas, Massachusetts, Missouri, New Jersey, Oregon. Washington requires notice to the attorney general when the complaint seeks injunctive relief. In addition, Tex. Bus. & Com. Code § 17.501 requires the petition in a class action to be sent to the AG.

414 Cole v. Metropolitan Property & Liability Co., 1984 U.S. Dist. LEXIS 15914 (D. Conn. June 13, 1984); Pointer v. Edward L. Kuhs Co., 678 S.W.2d 836 (Mo. Ct. App. 1984); Bodin v. B & L Furniture Co., 42 Or. App. 731, 601 P.2d 848 (1979); Collard v. Reagan, 2002 WL 1357052 (Wash. App. June 21, 2002) (unpublished, citation limited). *See also* Mers v. Fry's Electronics, Inc., 2002 Cal. App. Unpub. LEXIS 11714 (Dec. 17, 2002) (unpublished, citation limited) (Cal. requirement that AG be notified of any appellate proceeding involving unfair competition law is not jurisdictional).

415 Cole v. Metropolitan Property & Liability Co., 1984 U.S. Dist. LEXIS 15914, Clearinghouse No. 41,252 (D. Conn. June 13, 1984); Bodin v. B & L Furniture Co., 42 Or. App. 731, 601 P.2d 848 (1979).

416 *See* Cannon v. Metro Ford, Inc., 242 F. Supp. 2d 1322, 1332 (S.D. Fla. 2002).

417 Fickes v. Sun Expert, Inc., 762 F. Supp. 998 (D. Mass. 1991); Multi Technology v. Mitchell Mgmt. Sys., Inc., 25 Mass. App. Ct. 333, 518 N.E.2d 854 (1988); American Mechanical Corp. v. Union Machine Co., 21 Mass. App. Ct. 97, 485 N.E.2d 680 (1985); Aetna Cas. & Surety Co. v. State Park Ins. Agency, Inc., 12 Mass. App. Ct. 985, 428 N.E.2d 377 (1981).

418 Latino v. Ford Motor Co., 403 Mass. 247, 526 N.E.2d 1282 (1988).

419 Bevers v. Soule, 909 S.W.2d 599 (Tex. App. 1995).

420 *See* Star Houston, Inc. v. Kundak, 843 S.W.2d 294 (Tex. App. 1992); Winkle Chevy-Olds-Pontiac v. Condon, 830 S.W.2d 740 (Tex. App. 1992).

421 Foster v. Daon Corp., 713 F.2d 148 (5th Cir. 1983) (Texas law); *see also* Henry S. Miller Co. v. Bynum, 797 S.W.2d 51 (Tex. App. 1990), *aff'd on other grounds*, 836 S.W.2d 160 (Tex. 1992); Russell v. Campbell, 725 S.W.2d 739 (Tex. App. 1987) (no notice letter required when statute of limitations about to expire).

422 HOW Ins. v. Patriot Fin. Serv., 786 S.W.2d 533 (Tex. App. 1990).

statute does not apply to a federal court class action.[423] State requirements only govern a federal court action if they are substantive, not procedural; procedural preconditions are governed by Federal Rule of Civil Procedure 23.[424] However, one federal court held that the notice requirement must be pleaded by the plaintiff and that the defendant may seek an abatement if proper notice was not given.[425]

7.5.4.2 Are Notice Letters Required for Counterclaims?

Where a demand letter is required, an issue arises as to how a consumer can bring UDAP counterclaims. When the consumer is sued and wishes to bring a UDAP counterclaim, the consumer clearly can send a demand, wait the notice period, and then file a UDAP counterclaim.[426] But what happens when court rules require that the counterclaim be brought before the notice period has expired since the notice letter was sent?

In some states, judicial decisions or the statute may make it clear that the notice requirement does not apply to counterclaims or cross-claims.[427] In the absence of such authority, the safest course is to send the notice letter immediately, but also to bring the UDAP counterclaim when court procedure requires, making sure that the counterclaim contains all the information required of a notice letter so that it can serve as a notice letter. Some courts have found that legal pleadings can serve as the notice letter.[428]

Another approach is to offer the plaintiff the option of holding the lawsuit in abeyance for the notice period, allowing the two sides to seek an informal settlement on the UDAP counterclaim. If the seller declines to wait the notice period, the seller may have waived its right to object to the period not having expired. In any event, after the notice period has expired, it may be prudent to ask the court for leave to amend the consumer's answer to replace the old counterclaim with a new counterclaim specifically alleging that the notice period has expired.

Another issue is whether a notice requirement prior to filing a UDAP claim applies to an amended claim replacing a prior UDAP claim. The only court to decide this issue takes the sensible position that proper notice prior to the first complaint is all that is necessary and that a second notice is not required prior to amending the UDAP claim.[429]

7.5.4.3 Form of the Notice Letter; Delivery

It is of course far safer to send a separate notice letter than to use the consumer's complaint or an amended complaint as the notice letter. The purpose of the demand letter requirement is to avoid a legal complaint by giving the seller an opportunity to resolve the dispute. Thus one court has ruled that one can not bring a suit, then send the demand letter, wait the notice period, and then amend the complaint.[430]

Nevertheless, another court has held that an amended complaint can serve as a notice letter, but must at least mention the state UDAP statute.[431] But a Georgia court has ruled that a consumer's mere attempt to amend the original complaint to add a UDAP claim was not itself sufficient notice before bringing a new action.[432] A court interpreting the former Illinois notice letter requirement for suits against car dealers has found that prior complaints mentioning UDAP claims are not sufficient notice to allow an amended complaint to go forward.[433]

Similarly, it is important to send a letter rather than rely on the seller's actual notice of the dispute. At least one court has held that actual notice is not sufficient; the consumer must actually send the notice letter.[434]

One Texas court has been very literal about a requirement that written notice be delivered. Notice was improper where the consumer sent the notice to the correct address by certified mail, the notice was returned undelivered, and the consumer made no further efforts to deliver the notice.[435] This suggests it is safer to send notice both by first class and certified mail, and to follow up on an undelivered certified mail notice.

A consumer gives notice "in person" when the consumer places the notice in the seller's mail slot or otherwise delivers the letter to the seller without intervention of a third party. But there can still be a factual question whether the consumer did in fact insert the notice in the mail slot when the seller denies receipt.[436]

---

423 Mace v. Van Ru Credit Corp., 109 F.3d 338 (7th Cir. 1997) (interpreting applicability of Wisconsin debt collection statute).

424 *Id.*

425 Patel v. Holiday Hospitality Franchising, Inc., 172 F. Supp. 2d 821 (N.D. Tex. 2001).

426 Capp Homes v. Duarte, 617 F.2d 900 (1st Cir. 1980) (interpreting Massachusetts law).

427 Tex. Bus. & Com. Code Ann. § 17.505(b). *Cf.* Crosby Yacht Yard, Inc. v. Yacht "Chardonnay," 159 F.R.D. 1 (D. Mass. 1994).

428 *See* Morse v. Mutual Federal Sav. & Loan Ass'n of Whitman, 536 F. Supp. 1271 (D. Mass. 1982). *But see* Boyd Int'l, Ltd. v. Honeywell, Inc., 837 F.2d 1312 (5th Cir. 1988) (Texas law); Remis v. Browning, 153 Ga. App. 352, 265 S.E.2d 316 (1980).

429 Minor v. Land, 775 S.W.2d 744 (Tex. App. 1989).

430 Boyd Int'l, Ltd. v. Honeywell, Inc., 837 F.2d 1312 (5th Cir. 1988) (Texas law).

431 Morse v. Mutual Federal Sav. & Loan Ass'n, 536 F. Supp. 1271 (D. Mass. 1982).

432 Remis v. Browning, 153 Ga. App. 352, 265 S.E.2d 316 (1980).

433 McNair v. McGrath Lexus-Colosimo, Ltd., 11 F. Supp. 2d 990 (N.D. Ill. 1998).

434 Moving Co. v. Whitten, 717 S.W.2d 117 (Tex. App. 1986). *See also* Tex. Bus. & Com. Code Ann. § 17.505(a) (requires written notice).

435 Hash v. Hines, 796 S.W.2d 312 (Tex. App. 1990), *rev'd on other grounds*, 843 S.W.2d 464 (Tex. 1992).

436 Gulf Indus. v. Hahn, 156 Ariz. 153, 750 P.2d 911 (Ct. App. 1988).

7.5.4.4 To Whom Must the Notice Letter Be Sent?

Statutes vary in specifying which parties must be sent the notice letter. The Massachusetts UDAP statute only requires that a notice letter be sent to parties who are residents of Massachusetts.[437] The old Texas notice requirement (since amended) was satisfied where the consumer sent the complaint letter not to the corporation, but to the sole shareholder of the corporation, with an offer of settlement.[438] The requirement is also satisfied in regard to a dealer where the dealer only received a copy of a notice letter sent to the manufacturer.[439] But a dealer is not an agent of the manufacturer for purposes of a notice letter, and thus a letter sent to the dealer is not sufficient notice to the manufacturer.[440] Notice to an escrow holder is not sufficient against a merchant where the escrow holder is not the merchant's agent.[441] It has also been held not sufficient against the manufacturer to send a notice letter to the retailer, even though the manufacturer admits receiving a copy of the letter, where the letter alleges only that the retailer, not the manufacturer, engaged in UDAP violations.[442]

It is always safer to send a demand letter to every possible defendant.[443] Each demand letter should state that the consumer has UDAP claims against that particular defendant.

7.5.4.5 Content of the Notice Letter

The Massachusetts and Georgia UDAP statutes require that the demand letter identify the claimant and reasonably describe the unfair or deceptive practice and the injury caused thereby.[444] A demand letter satisfies this requirement where it gives the defendants enough information to enable them to review the facts and the law, evaluate whether the requested relief should be granted, and make a reasonable tender of settlement.[445]

The consumer does not have to specify the section of the statute that has been violated and need not threaten suit.[446] The fact that other matters are raised in a demand letter does not invalidate the portion complaining of the UDAP violation.[447] Nor does the demand letter have to list the consumer's specific monetary loss.[448] But the letter should be specific enough so that the defendant can determine the plaintiff's damages in order to make a reasonable settlement offer—either by specifying an amount sought or by detailing the actual injury.[449] The defendant can not insist on being informed of facts it has deceptively failed to disclose.[450] It is prudent practice to allege all possible UDAP violations of which the consumer is aware, because failure to list in the demand letter certain claims may foreclose the consumer's

---

437 Hadar v. Concordia Yacht Builders, Inc., 886 F. Supp. 1082 (S.D.N.Y. 1995).

438 Petty v. Ferguson, 601 S.W.2d 782 (Tex. Civ. App. 1980); *see also* Debakey v. Staggs, 605 S.W.2d 631 (Tex. Civ. App. 1980); Travenol Laboratories Inc. v. Bailey Laboratories Inc., 608 S.W.2d 308 (Tex. Civ. App. 1980). *But see* Jim Walter Homes Inc. v. Geffert, 614 S.W.2d 843 (Tex. Civ. App. 1981).

439 Chrysler Corp. v. Roberson, 619 S.W.2d 451 (Tex. Civ. App. 1981).

440 Preiser v. Jim Letts Oldsmobile, Inc., 160 Ga. App. 658, 288 S.E.2d 219 (1981).

441 King v. Ladd, 624 S.W.2d 195 (Tex. Civ. App. 1981).

442 Wellborn v. Sears, Roebuck & Co., 970 F.2d 1420 (5th Cir. 1992) (Texas law).

443 *See* Rita v. Carella, 394 Mass. 822, 477 N.E.2d 1016 (1985).

444 Hadar v. Concordia Yacht Builders, Inc., 886 F. Supp. 1082 (S.D.N.Y. 1995) (letter inadequate because it did not refer to specific deceptive practices or inform defendants of intent to seek relief under UDAP statute); Paces Ferry Dodge, Inc. v. Thomas, 174 Ga. App. 642, 331 S.E.2d 4 (1985) (notice reasonably described deceptive practice and injury suffered, particularly under liberal construction courts should give the provision); Plaza Pontiac v. Shaw, 158 Ga. App. 799, 282 S.E.2d 383 (1981); Colonial Lincoln-Mercury Sales, Inc. v. Molina, 152 Ga. App. 379, 262 S.E.2d 820 (1979); Spring v. Geriatric Authority of Holyoke, 475 N.E.2d 727 (Mass. 1985) (damages requested should not be exorbitant, out of all proportion to the claim); Slaney v. Westwood Auto, Inc., 366 Mass. 688, 322 N.E.2d 768 (1975); Lord v. Commercial Union Ins. Co., 60 Mass. App. Ct. 309, 801 N.E.2d 303 (Mass. App. Ct. 2004) (notice letter identifying as unfair and deceptive defendant's refusal to honor property damage claim because coverage had been suspended was probably sufficient to implicate all aspects of the suspension).

445 York v. Sullivan, 369 Mass. 157, 338 N.E.2d 341 (1975); Piccuirro v. Gaitenby, 20 Mass. App. Ct. 286, 480 N.E.2d 30 (1985); U.S. Steel Corp. v. Fiberex, Inc., 751 S.W.2d 628 (Tex. App. 1988), *modified in part and rev'd in part on other grounds*, 772 S.W.2d 442 (Tex. 1989); *see also* Miles Rich Chrysler-Plymouth, Inc. v. Mass, 201 Ga. App. 693, 411 S.E.2d 901 (1991); Captain & Co. v. Stenberg, 505 N.E.2d 88 (Ind. Ct. App. 1987); McCann v. Brown, 725 S.W.2d 822 (Tex. App. 1987).

446 Stringer v. Bugg, 254 Ga. App. 745, 563 S.E.2d 447 (2002); Cohen v. Liberty Mutual Ins. Co., 41 Mass. App. Ct. 748, 673 N.E.2d 84 (1996); Lester v. Logan, 893 S.W.2d 570 (Tex. App. 1994); U.S. Steel Corp. v. Fiberex, Inc., 751 S.W.2d 628 (Tex. App. 1988), *modified in part and rev'd in part on other grounds*, 772 S.W.2d 442 (Tex. 1989); Village Mobile Homes, Inc. v. Porter, 716 S.W.2d 543 (Tex. App. 1986); Jim Walter Homes, Inc. v. Valencia, 679 S.W.2d 29 (Tex. App. 1984), *aff'd in relevant part as modified*, 690 S.W.2d 239 (Tex. 1985); North Am. Van Lines v. Bauerle, 678 S.W.2d 229 (Tex. App. 1984).

447 Douchette v. Kwiat, 392 Mass. 915, 467 N.E.2d 1379 (1984); Fredericks v. Rosenblatt, 40 Mass. App. Ct. 713, 667 N.E.2d 287 (1996).

448 Simas v. House of Cabinets, Inc., 757 N.E.2d 277 (Mass. App. Ct. 2001); Brandt v. Olympic Constr., Inc., 16 Mass. App. Ct. 913, 449 N.E.2d 1231 (1983); *see also* Tarpey v. Crescent Ridge Dairy, 47 Mass. App. Ct. 380, 713 N.E.2d 975 (1999); Fredericks v. Rosenblatt, 40 Mass. App. Ct. 713, 667 N.E.2d 287 (1996) (demand for 23 times the amount of damages proven at trial did not invalidate demand letter).

449 Thorpe v. Mutual of Omaha Ins. Co., 984 F.2d 541 (1st Cir. 1993) (Mass. law); Moynihan v. LifeCare Centers of America, Inc., 60 Mass. App. Ct. 1102, 798 N.E.2d 1045(Mass. App. Ct. 2003); Simas v. House of Cabinets, Inc., 757 N.E.2d 277 (Mass. App. Ct. 2001).

450 Cassano v. Gogos, 20 Mass. App. Ct. 348, 480 N.E.2d 649 (1985).

right later to raise those specific claims.[451] Violations that are not listed in the demand letter may still be admissible to establish that the defendant violated another statute, such as an unfair insurance practices statute, on which UDAP liability is based.[452]

The demand letter does not have to be drafted with absolute legal precision.[453] Nevertheless, because the purpose of a demand letter is to encourage settlement, the letter must not hide the fact that the consumer is writing the letter pursuant to the UDAP statute. A Massachusetts court has held that the letter should contain at least one of the following six indications that it is a UDAP demand letter:

1. Express reference to the statutory cite of the UDAP statute;
2. Express reference to the name of the UDAP statute;
3. An assertion that the rights of claimants as consumers have been violated;
4. An assertion that the practice is unfair or deceptive;
5. A request for a response within thirty days (the time specified by the UDAP statute); *or*
6. An assertion that the claimant will seek multiple damages and attorney fees (as provided by the UDAP statute).[454]

Alabama requires that a demand letter reasonably describe the unfair and deceptive practice and the injury suffered.[455] This has been found not satisfied where the consumer only informed the seller of her intention to institute a civil proceeding if no settlement could be reached.[456]

Of course, if a state UDAP statute (such as Texas's) specifically requires the notice to state the amount of damages sought, compliance with this requirement is a precondition to a UDAP action.[457] "Full purchase price" sufficiently states the amount of damages sought,[458] as does a request for damages in an amount not less than a specified amount.[459] But an Indiana case holds a demand letter insufficient if it fails to specify the deceptive practice or the damage attributed specifically to this deceptive practice as opposed to other claims.[460]

In demanding compensation in a demand letter, the consumer should not demand attorney fees or require the seller to sign a formal consent order.[461] The purpose of a demand letter is to facilitate settlement before incurring legal fees and without the need for a formal consent order. If state law so provides, the notice letter can inform the seller that, if the seller does not make an appropriate response, the consumer may seek multiple damages and attorney fees in a court action.[462]

The Texas UDAP statute allows the seller to limit its liability if it offers to reimburse the consumer for actual damages *and* attorney fees. In that situation, where the seller must make an offer of the consumer's attorney fees, sellers may be able to argue that the consumer's demand letter should specify the amount of attorney fees expended to date. But such information is not required if the consumer in the demand letter specifically requests only damages and not attorney fees by way of settlement.[463] Alternatively the requirement is met if the letter gives a total amount of damages and attorney fees, but does not itemize the amount of attorney fees separately.[464] Obviously, any statement of the consumer's attorney fees expended to date does not limit the eventual fee if the attorney incurs additional time after sending the notice letter.[465]

7.5.4.6 Notice Letters and Class Actions

The highest court in Massachusetts has held that a demand letter by one class member suffices for other members if no reasonable offer is made in response.[466] The Texas

---

451 Sharpe v. General Motors Corp., 401 S.E.2d 328 (Ga. App. Ct. 1991); Bressel v. Jolicoeur, 34 Mass. App. Ct. 205, 609 N.E.2d 94 (1993) (plaintiff can not rely on act not described in demand letter).

452 Clegg v. Butler, 424 Mass. 413, 676 N.E.2d 1134 (1997).

453 Cohen v. Liberty Mut. Ins. Co., 41 Mass. App. Ct. 748, 673 N.E.2d 84 (1996); Williams v. Hills Fitness Center, Inc., 705 S.W.2d 189 (Tex. App. 1985).

454 Cassano v. Gogos, 20 Mass. App. Ct. 348, 480 N.E.2d 649 (1985).

455 Ala. Code § 8-19-10(e).

456 Givens v. Rent-A-Center, Inc., 720 F. Supp. 160 (S.D. Ala. 1988), *aff'd without op.*, 885 F.2d 870 (11th Cir. 1989).

457 Hash v. Hines, 843 S.W.2d 464 (Tex. 1992). *Accord* International Nickel Co. v. Trammel Crow Distrib., 803 F.2d 150 (5th Cir. 1986) (Texas law); Certainteed Corp. v. Cielo Dorado Dev., Inc., 733 S.W.2d 247 (Tex. App. 1987), *rev'd on other grounds*, 744 S.W.2d 10 (Tex. 1988); Hollingsworth Roofing Co. v. Morrison, 668 S.W.2d 872 (Tex. App. 1984); Sunshine Datsun, Inc. v. Ramsey, 680 S.W.2d 652 (Tex. App. 1984).

458 Vista Chevrolet, Inc. v. Lewis, 704 S.W.2d 363 (Tex. App. 1985), *aff'd in part, rev'd in part on other grounds*, 709 S.W.2d 176 (Tex. 1986).

459 Williams v. Hills Fitness Center, Inc., 705 S.W.2d 189 (Tex. App. 1985); *see also* U.S. Steel Corp. v. Fiberex, Inc., 751 S.W.2d 628 (Tex. App. 1988) (loss of "more than $67,000" was sufficient), *modified in part and rev'd in part on other grounds*, 772 S.W.2d 442 (Tex. 1989).

460 A.B.C. Home & Real Estate Inspection v. Plummer, 500 N.E.2d 1257 (Ind. Ct. App. 1987).

461 Leardi v. Brown, 394 Mass. 151, 474 N.E.2d 1094 (1985) (court does not indicate whether letter demanded prospective fees or fees that had already been incurred).

462 *Id*; Cassano v. Gogos, 20 Mass. App. Ct. 348, 480 N.E.2d 649 (1985).

463 Silva v. Porowski, 695 S.W.2d 766 (Tex. App. 1985) (note that the statute has been amended and renumbered since this decision, but still requires demand letters and offers to specify the amount of fees).

464 Minor v. Land, 775 S.W.2d 744 (Tex. App. 1989).

465 *Id.*

466 Baldassari v. Public Fin. Trust, 369 Mass. 33, 337 N.E.2d 701 (1975); *In re* Alford Chevrolet-Geo, 997 S.W.2d 173 (Tex. 1999). *See also* Latman v. Costa Cruise Lines, 758 So. 2d 699 (Fla. App. 2000) (named plaintiff's compliance with contractual notice requirement suffices for class).

Supreme Court also holds that a consumer can give a mandatory pre-suit notice on behalf of a class.[467] If the class representative only gives individual notice, the defendant can tender an offer of settlement to the class representative alone.

One of California's UDAP statutes has separate rules for notice letters depending on whether the letter seeks class-wide or individual relief. The California Supreme Court has held that an individual consumer's vaguely worded notice letter was adequate to serve as a class action notice letter because the consumer had indicated a desire for widespread relief.[468] Consequently, the merchant's response to that letter remedying that consumer's injury, but not providing a class-wide recovery, was not sufficient to prevent that individual (even though now undamaged) from bringing a UDAP class action.

7.5.4.7 Pleading Notice and Proving Notice Was Sent

As a general rule, where a notice letter is a prerequisite to bringing a UDAP action, the timely sending of the notice should be pleaded and proven.[469] A Texas court has held that the seller has the burden of establishing that the notice is not adequate,[470] although the consumer must prove that the notice was received the proper number of days prior to suit.[471] The seller's failure to object to the lack of notice may waive that objection.[472] If the consumer pleads proper notice, this fact is taken as admitted if the merchant defaults, and the seller can not later claim lack of notice.[473] Even if the consumer does not plead notice, the court may allow evidence of the notice to be presented at trial.[474]

7.5.4.8 If Notice Was Not Sent

Unless the UDAP statute explicitly requires dismissal, failure to send a required notice letter should not bar the suit. Maine's Supreme Court has ruled that the failure to send the statutorily required notice letter is not a jurisdictional defect and does not preclude the plaintiff from maintaining a UDAP suit. The court suggested other remedies for failure to send the notice, such as imposing a delay in the suit or denying attorney fees and costs.[475]

By contrast, Massachusetts' Supreme Judicial Court[476] and an Indiana appellate court[477] ruled that the failure to allege violations in the demand letter bars relief for those violations in a subsequent UDAP action. The notice requirement does not preclude the consumer from bringing an action alleging non-UDAP claims within the notice period, however.[478] Nor is the notice requirement jurisdictional in

---

467 *In re* Alford Chevrolet-Geo, 997 S.W.2d 173 (Tex. 1999).

468 Kagan v. Gibralter Savings & Loan Ass'n, 676 P.2d 1060, 200 Cal. Rptr. 38 (1984), *interpreting* Cal. Civ. Code § 1750 (West).

469 McNair v. McGrath Lexus-Colosimo, Ltd., 11 F. Supp. 2d 990 (N.D. Ill. 1998) (dismissing suit where compliance with former notice requirement not pleaded); Brown Realty Assoc., Inc. v. Thomas, 193 Ga. App. 847, 389 S.E.2d 505 (1989); Spring v. Geriatric Authority of Holyoke, 475 N.E.2d 727 (Mass. 1985); Baldassari v. Public Fin. Trust, 369 Mass. 33, 337 N.E.2d 701 (1975); Entrialgo v. Twin City Dodge, Inc., 368 Mass. 812, 333 N.E.2d 202 (1975); Slaney v. Westwood Auto, Inc., 366 Mass. 688, 322 N.E.2d 768 (1975); Hash v. Hines, 843 S.W.2d 464 (Tex. 1992); Auto Ins. Co. of Hartford v. Davila, 805 S.W.2d 897 (Tex. App. 1991); HOW Ins. v. Patriot Fin. Servs., 786 S.W.2d 533 (Tex. App. 1990). *See also* Nader v. Citron, 372 Mass. 96, 360 N.E.2d 870 (1977). *But see* Miller v. Presswood, 743 S.W.2d 275 (Tex. App. 1988) (notice must be pleaded, but only proven if seller properly denies pleading); Pool Co. v. Salt Grass Exploration, Inc., 681 S.W.2d 216 (Tex. App. 1984).

470 Chrysler-Plymouth City, Inc. v. Guerrero, 620 S.W.2d 700 (Tex. Civ. App. 1981).

471 Blumenthal v. Ameritex Computer Corp., 646 S.W.2d 283 (Tex. App. 1983).

472 Outboard Marine Corp. v. Superior Court (Howarth), 52 Cal. App. 3d 30, 124 Cal. Rptr. 852 (1952); Gomez v. Moore, 2003 WL 21355973 (Tex. App. June 11, 2003); LaChalet Int'l, Inc. v. Nowik, 787 S.W.2d 101 (Tex. App. 1990); Investors, Inc. v. Hadley, 738 S.W.2d 737 (Tex. App. 1987); Brown Foundation Repair & Consulting v. McGuire, 711 S.W.2d 349 (Tex. App. 1986). *See* Tex. Bus. & Com. Code Ann. § 17.505(a) and Hash v. Hines, 843 S.W.2d 464 (Tex. 1992) for the mechanism of giving notice in Texas. *See also* Andrade Enterprises, Inc. v. Cinnaroll Bakeries, Ltd., 2003 WL 22736538 (W.D. Tex. Oct. 31, 2003) (a defense objection to inadequate notice must be verified).

473 Termeer v. Interstate Motors Inc., 634 S.W.2d 12 (Tex. App. 1982).

474 Vista Chevrolet, Inc. v. Lewis, 704 S.W.2d 363 (Tex. App. 1985), *rev'd in part on other grounds*, 709 S.W.2d 176 (Tex. 1986).

475 Oceanside at Pine Point Condominium Owners Ass'n v. Peachtree Doors, Inc., 659 A.2d 267 (Me. 1995). *Cf.* Mountz v. Global Vision Prods., Inc., 770 N.Y.S.2d 603 (Sup. Ct. 2003) (granting stay to allow defendants to respond to plaintiff's demand where not was not sent as required by Maine UDAP statute).

476 Entrialgo v. Twin City Dodge, Inc., 368 Mass. 812, 333 N.E.2d 202 (1975). *See also* Neuhoff v. Marvin Lumber & Cedar Co., 370 F.3d 197, 205–06 (1st Padilla v. Payco Gen. Am. Credits, Inc., 161 F. Supp. 2d 264 (S.D.N.Y. 2001) (granting summary judgment for failure to send notices); Ball v. Wal-Mart, Inc., 102 F. Supp. 2d 44 (D. Mass. 2000); Hadar v. Concordia Yacht Builders, Inc., 886 F. Supp. 1082 (S.D.N.Y. 1995); Spilios v. Cohen, 38 Mass. App. Ct. 338, 647 N.E.2d 1218 (1995). Some courts reached similar rulings under the former Illinois notice requirement: Rivera v. Grossinger Autoplex, Inc., 2000 U.S. Dist. LEXIS 11240 (N.D. Ill. June 14, 2000) (dismissing UDAP claim without prejudice because of failure to send notice letter; dismissal appropriate because purpose of notice requirement is to enable defendant to avoid suit), *aff'd in part, remanded on other grounds*, 274 F.3d 1118 (7th Cir. 2001); McNair v. McGrath Lexus-Colosimo, Ltd., 11 F. Supp. 2d 990 (N.D. Ill. 1998) (dismissing suit where compliance with notice requirement not pleaded).

477 Lehman v. Shroyer, 721 N.E.2d 365 (Ind. App. 1999) (dismissing UDAP claim where notice not given).

478 York v. Sullivan, 369 Mass. 157, 338 N.E.2d 341 (1975); Reichhold Chemicals, Inc. v. Puremco Mfg. Co., 854 S.W.2d 240 (Tex. App. 1993).

the sense that a judge can raise the issue where the defendant has failed to raise it.[479] In addition, if a consumer fails to comply with a notice letter requirement, that defect should be cured if the consumer can dismiss the UDAP action without prejudice, send a notice letter, and then file a new suit after waiting the appropriate time period.[480]

A consumer can also send a notice letter after filing a non-UDAP case, and then, after waiting out the notice period, amend the claim by adding a UDAP count.[481] Similarly, a court may abate the suit while the consumer sends a proper notice letter.[482] The Texas UDAP statute was amended in 1995 to provide specific procedures for the abatement of actions on notice grounds.[483] If notice is not sent and the defendant complies with these specific procedures, abatement is automatic.[484] It is error to abate the action *after* trial so that the plaintiff can give notice, and then to enter judgment on the original UDAP verdict.[485]

7.5.4.9 Seller's Responsibilities on Receiving Notice Letter

The often amended Texas UDAP statute allows the seller to limit its liability if it tenders an offer of settlement to the consumer within sixty days of receipt of the demand letter. The proposed settlement must include an offer to pay two separately stated amounts of money: (1) an amount of money (or other consideration) as settlement of the consumer's claim for damages, and (2) an amount of money to compensate the consumer for his or her reasonable and necessary attorney fees.[486] One federal court has held that the second prong is met by "an agreement to reimburse the consumer for attorneys' fees."[487] The Texas Supreme Court has strictly construed this requirement so that an offer of the consumer's damages without attorney fees is not sufficient.[488] A supposed offer that is contingent in nature amounts to no more than an offer to negotiate and does not constitute a proper response.[489]

Unless the UDAP statute specifically allows oral responses, many consumer attorneys insist in the demand letter that all responses be in writing. Otherwise, there can be disputes at trial about whether the defendant responded and what the defendant offered. A prior version of the Texas UDAP statute required the seller's response to be in writing. This had been strictly construed to nullify the effect of an oral settlement offer.[490] However, the most recent version dropped the requirement of a written offer, so it is probable that an oral offer is now acceptable.[491] Similarly, in Georgia, a seller's *written* tender of settlement can limit the eventual damage award. This requirement has been interpreted literally so that an oral settlement offer is of no effect.[492]

In Massachusetts, to avoid liability for multiple damages, the seller's response to a demand letter must be in writing[493] and must contain a "reasonable" settlement offer. The burden of proving reasonableness is on the seller.[494] An indefinite offer, ignoring requested relief, is unreasonable.[495] A settlement offer is in bad faith if it is really illusory, not benefiting the consumer at all.[496] Gross inadequacy makes an offer unreasonable—rather than promote settlement, such a response merely encourages litigation.[497] A settlement offer has also been found unreasonable where the seller

479 Lord v. Commercial Union Ins. Co., 60 Mass. App. Ct. 309, 801 N.E.2d 303 (Mass. App. Ct. 2004); Tarpey v. Crescent Ridge Dairy, 47 Mass. App. Ct. 380, 713 N.E.2d 975 (1999) (notice requirement not necessarily jurisdictional); Fredericks v. Rosenblatt, 40 Mass. App. Ct. 713, 667 N.E.2d 287 (1996).

480 Foster v. Daon Corp., 713 F.2d 148 (5th Cir. 1983) (Texas law); Towne v. North End Isuzu, Inc., 1999 Mass. Super. LEXIS 302, 10 Mass. L. Rep. 340 (June 17, 1999). *See* Chrysler Corp. v. McMorries, 657 S.W.2d 858 (Tex. App. 1983). *See also* Boyd Int'l, Ltd. v. Honeywell, Inc., 837 F.2d 1312 (5th Cir. 1988) (Texas law); International Nickel Co. v. Trammel Crow Distrib., 803 F.2d 150 (5th Cir. 1986) (Texas law); Hollingsworth Roofing Co. v. Morrison, 668 S.W 2d 872 (Tex. App. 1984).

481 Tarpey v. Crescent Ridge Dairy, 47 Mass. App. Ct. 380, 713 N.E.2d 975 (1999) (upholding award of UDAP damages in case where plaintiff amended complaint to include UDAP claim after sending notice); State Farm Fire & Cas. Co. v. Price, 845 S.W.2d 427 (Tex. App. 1993).

482 International Nickel Co. v. Trammel Crow Distrib., 803 F.2d 150 (5th Cir. 1986) (Texas law); Hash v. Hines, 843 S.W.2d 464 (Tex. 1992); HOW Ins. v. Patriot Fin. Servs., 786 S.W.2d 533 (Tex. App. 1990); Moving Co. v. Whitten, 717 S.W.2d 117 (Tex. App. 1986); Netterville v. Interfirst Bank, 718 S.W.2d 921 (Tex. App. 1986); Sunshine Datsun, Inc. v. Ramsey, 680 S.W.2d 652 (Tex. App. 1984). *See* Tex. Bus. & Com. Code Ann. § 17.505.

483 Tex. Bus. & Com. Code Ann. § 17.505. This statutory amendment slightly changes the holding of the Texas Supreme Court in Hines v. Hash, 843 S.W.2d 464 (Tex. 1992).

484 America Online, Inc. v. Williams, 958 S.W.2d 268 (Tex. App. 1997) (abatement prevented certification of class action during abatement period); K.C. Roofing Co. v. Abundis, 940 S.W.2d 375 (Tex. App. 1997).

485 Hines v. Hash, 843 S.W.2d 464 (Tex. 1992); Angelo Broadcasting v. Satellite Music, 836 S.W.2d 726 (Tex. App. 1992).

486 Tex. Bus. & Com. Code § 17.5052.

487 Stanley v. Wal Mart Stores, Inc., 839 F. Supp. 430 (N.D. Tex. 1993).

488 Cail v. Service Motors, Inc., 660 S.W.2d 814 (Tex. 1983).

489 Knowlton v. U.S. Brass Corp., 864 S.W.2d 585 S.W.2d 240 (Tex. App. 1993).

490 Chambless v. Barry Robinson Farm Supply, 667 S.W.2d 598 (Tex. App. 1984).

491 Tex. Bus. & Com. Code § 17.5052.

492 Regency Nissan, Inc. v. Taylor, 194 Ga. App. 645, 395 S.E.2d 665 (1990).

493 Mackesy v. Fotopoulos, 2002 WL 971812 (Mass. App. May 7, 2002).

494 Patry v. Harmony Homes, Inc., 10 Mass. App. Ct. 1, 404 N.E.2d 1265 (1980).

495 *Id.*

496 Leardi v. Brown, 394 Mass. 151, 474 N.E.2d 1094 (1985); Brandt v. Olympic Constr. Inc., 16 Mass. App. Ct. 913, 449 N.E.2d 1231 (1983); Patry v. Liberty Mobilehome Sales, Inc., 15 Mass. App. Ct. 701, 448 N.E.2d 405 (1983), *aff'd on other grounds*, 394 Mass. 270, 475 N.E.2d 392 (1985).

497 Calimlim v. Foreign Car Center, Inc., 392 Mass. 228, 467 N.E.2d 443 (1984).

offers not to enforce unenforceable clauses in a contract; instead, a reasonable offer would be to remove the clauses from the contract.[498] It can also be unreasonable to fail to comply with a reasonable request to make repairs.[499]

The requirement of notice provides a wily defendant the opportunity to engage in forum shopping by filing a declaratory judgment action in the court of its own choice. At least one federal court has expressed an intent to resolve this problem by staying the defendant's suit in favor of the consumer's separate state court action.[500]

7.6 Jurisdiction and Choice of Law Issues

7.6.1 Introduction

UDAP actions must comply with the state courts' normal jurisdictional requirements. Jurisdictional and choice-of-law issues often arise in cases with out-of-state features. Even when a case has no multi-state aspects, there may be questions about which state court has jurisdiction. In other cases, the consumer may wish to litigate the case in federal court or bankruptcy court, or the defendant may seek to force the case into arbitration. This section discusses these questions.

7.6.2 Jurisdiction over Out-Of-State Sellers

One issue in many UDAP actions is that potential defendants are out of state. In the typical consumer case, it is neither practical to bring an action in the seller's state nor to enforce, in the seller's state, a judgment obtained in the consumer's state. Consumer litigants are advised to name as defendants, in addition to the out-of-state corporation, other participants in the deceptive scheme who have assets in the consumer's state.[501] Litigants should supplement this section with an analysis of their own state long-arm statute and judicial decisions on issues of personal jurisdiction.

If the defendant is out of state, but has left assets in state, the consumer may attempt to bring a *quasi in rem* action against those assets. Since requirements for *quasi in rem* actions differ from state to state, and since there are few reported UDAP decisions in this area, consumer litigants should consult their own state law.[502] To subject a defendant to a state's *quasi-in-rem* jurisdiction, due process requires the same level of minimum contacts with the state as is required for *in personam* jurisdiction.[503]

Consumers can also bring *in personam* actions against out-of-state defendants. Personal jurisdiction will allow a judgment that can be enforced in another state and may facilitate actions against the seller's assets that are within the state. Courts must consider both the state's long-arm statute and due process principles when determining whether they can exercise jurisdiction over out-of-state defendants. Since many state long-arm statutes are interpreted to allow jurisdiction to the maximum extent allowed by the Constitution,[504] however, the constitutional and statutory analyses tend to merge. Due process requires that a defendant, if not present in the state, have certain minimum contacts with it such that maintaining the suit does not offend traditional notions of fair play and substantial justice.[505]

Courts have "general jurisdiction"—the constitutional authority to hear any cause of action—over a defendant who has continuous and systematic contacts with a state, regardless of whether the claim arose from the defendant's activities in the state.[506] For example, a company generally has continuous and systematic contact with the state where its headquarters are located, so it can be sued there on any claim.

Even if a defendant does not have continuous and systematic contact with a state, the Due Process Clause allows a court to exercise "specific jurisdiction" over a cause of action that arises directly from the defendant's contacts with the forum state.[507] Specific jurisdiction is permissible if the defendant has purposefully availed itself of the privilege of conducting activities in the forum state, as long as exercise of personal jurisdiction would comport with fair play and substantial justice.[508] Factors relevant to this latter determination include the burden on the defendant, the forum state's interest in adjudicating the dispute, the plaintiff's interest in obtaining convenient and effective relief, the interstate judicial system's interest in obtaining the most efficient resolution of controversies, and the shared interest of the states

498 Leardi v. Brown, 394 Mass. 151, 474 N.W.2d 1094 (1985).

499 Brown v. LeClair, 20 Mass. App. Ct. 976, 482 N.E.2d 870 (1985).

500 Primerica Life Ins. Co. v. Twyman, 2002 U.S. Dist. LEXIS 611 (N.D. Tex. Jan. 14, 2002).

501 *See* Chapter 6, *supra* for a discussion of the liability of various participants in a deceptive sales scheme: agents, principals, officers, directors, owners, third parties assisting the scheme, assignees, and related creditors.

502 *See* Longo v. AAA-Michigan, 201 Ill. App. 3d 543, 569 N.E.2d 927 (1990) (quasi-in-rem jurisdiction defeated where defendant owned no property in forum state).

503 Shaffer v. Heitner, 433 U.S. 186, 97 S. Ct. 2569, 53 L. Ed. 2d 683 (1977).

504 *See, e.g.,* Worthy v. Cyberworks Technologies, Inc., 835 So. 2d 972 (Ala. 2002); Aaronson v. Lindsay & Hauer Int'l Ltd., 235 Mich. App. 259, 597 N.W.2d 227, 231 n.1 (1999); State *ex rel.* Nixon v. Beer Nuts, Ltd., 29 S.W.3d 828 (Mo. App. 2000). *Cf.* Rose v. Rusnak Automotive Group, 2002 U.S. Dist. LEXIS 7369 (S.D. Ohio Apr. 11, 2002) (discussing conflicting interpretations of whether Ohio's long-arm statute extends to the limits of due process).

505 International Shoe v. Washington, 326 U.S. 310, 66 S. Ct. 154, 90 L. Ed. 95 (1945).

506 Helicopteros Nacionales de Colombia v. Hall, 466 U.S. 408, 104 S. Ct. 1868, 80 L. Ed. 2d 404 (1984).

507 *Id.*

508 Burger King v. Rudzewicz, 471 U.S. 462, 105 S. Ct. 2174, 85 L. Ed. 2d 528 (1985).

in furthering fundamental substantive social policies.[509]

Courts in UDAP cases consistently find that an out-of-state seller's deceptive sales activity within the state meets the minimal contacts requirement. The state has a manifest interest in providing effective means of redress for citizens who are defrauded by out-of-state sellers.[510] Direct mail solicitation,[511] unsolicited e-mail,[512] or other media[513] directed at state residents, shipment of goods to state residents,[514] doing business in-state under a fictitious name,[515] registering under a state statute and making telephone and mail contacts with residents,[516] conducting a lottery through the mail,[517] contacting those responding to advertisements and negotiating or taking deposits,[518] placing dummy ads in

509 Id.

510 Aaronson v. Lindsay & Hauer Int'l Ltd., 235 Mich. App. 259, 597 N.W.2d 227 (1999).

511 Heritage House Restaurants v. Continental Funding Group, Inc., 906 F.2d 276 (7th Cir. 1990) (letter and telephone calls to Illinois by out-of-state company gave Illinois court jurisdiction); Consumer Protection Div. v. Outdoor World Corp., 91 Md. App. 275, 603 A.2d 1376 (1992) (deceptive solicitations mailed to consumers in state sufficient, even though some of conduct making solicitations deceptive occurred out of state); Consumer Protection Div. v. Outdoor World Corp., 91 Md. App. 275, 603 A.2d 1376 (1992); State *ex rel.* Nixon v. Telco Directory Publishing, 863 S.W.2d 596 (Mo. 1993); Kugler v. Market Dev. Corp., 124 N.J. Super. 314, 306 A.2d 489 (Ch. Div. 1973); Meachum v. Outdoor World Corp., 652 N.Y.S.2d 749 (App. Div. 1997). *But cf.* Berliner v. Theater Development Fund, 1997 U.S. Dist. LEXIS 13655 (S.D.N.Y. 1997) (soliciting business by telephone and mailings to forum state and maintaining 800 number accessible by customers in forum state insufficient to confer jurisdiction).

512 Verizon Online Servs., Inc. v. Ralsky, 203 F. Supp. 2d 601 (E.D. Va. 2002) (in trespass to chattel case, transmission of unsolicited bulk e-mail through plaintiff ISP by out-of-state defendant is sufficient minimum contacts to satisfy personal jurisdiction requirements). *See also* Internet Doorway, Inc. v. Parks, 138 F. Supp. 2d 773 (S.D. Miss. 2001) (in suit by ISP for trespass to chattel, personal jurisdiction proper over defendant who sent e-mail to state resident; active nature of e-mail satisfies minimum contact with state; tort occurred when state resident opened e-mail). *But cf.* Hydro Engineering, Inc. v. Landa, Inc., 231 F. Supp. 2d 1130 (D. Utah 2002) (of 400 e-mail messages sent, only three could have reasonably been perceived as addressed to Utah residents, and plaintiff provided no evidence that a single e-mail actually reached a Utah resident); Machulsky v. Hall, 210 F. Supp. 2d 531 (D.N.J. 2002) (minimal e-mail, "by itself or even in conjunction with a single purchase, does not constitute sufficient minimum contacts").

513 Back Bay Farm, L.L.C. v. Collucio, 230 F. Supp. 2d 176 (D. Mass. 2002) (advertising on Internet, contacting and negotiating with in-state buyer); Covington & Burling v. International Marketing & Research, Inc., 2003 WL 21384825 (D.C. Super. Apr. 17, 2003) (sending junk faxes into jurisdiction); State v. Granite Gate Resorts, Inc., 568 N.W.2d 715 (Minn. App. 1997) (defendant placed ads on Internet, knowing they would reach Minn. consumers), *aff'd by equally divided court*, 576 N.W.2d 747 (Minn. 1998); State v. Western Capital Corp., 290 N.W.2d 467 (S.D. 1980) (advertising in state, mailing contracts into state, and sales personnel working in state); Siskind v. Villa Foundation For Education, Inc., 642 S.W.2d 434 (Tex. 1982) (advertising in national publications and state telephone directories and mailing contracts into state). *See also* American Rockwool, Inc. v. Owen Corning Fiberglass, 640 F. Supp. 1411 (E.D.N.C. 1986).

514 Back Bay Farm, L.L.C. v. Collucio, 320 F. Supp. 2d 176 (D. Mass. 2002) (contacting buyer in forum state through agent, shipping goods there, nationwide advertising, and other contacts with forum state were sufficient); Rose v. Rusnak Automotive Group, 2002 U.S. Dist. LEXIS 7369 (S.D. Ohio Apr. 11, 2002) (telephone calls and faxes to consumer in forum state, and delivery of goods there, sufficient); Carlson v. Petroske, 2002 WL 31061873 (Mass. App. July 11, 2002) (seller advertised in forum state and delivered the goods there); Aaronson v. Lindsay & Hauer Int'l Ltd., 235 Mich. App. 259, 597 N.W.2d 227 (1998) (communicating with buyer and shipping gemstones into state); People v. Concert Connection, Ltd., 211 A.D.2d 310, 629 N.Y.S.2d 254 (1995) (shipment of scalped tickets into New York State); People *ex rel.* Lefkowitz v. Colorado State Christian College, 76 Misc. 2d 50, 346 N.Y.S.2d 482 (Sup. Ct. 1973) (shipment of honorary degrees by an out-of-state company claiming to be an educational institution); Thomas v. Shair Laboratories, Inc., 1998 Tenn. App. LEXIS 780 (Nov. 23, 1998) (shipping of goods plus direct contact with buyer); Michiana Easy Livin' Country Inc. v. Holten, 127 S.W.3d 89 (Tex. App. 2003) (telephone misrepresentations and shipping of vehicle to forum state sufficient even though seller did not advertise in forum state, contract had forum selection clause requiring litigation to be in seller's home state, and buyer had initiated the contact with seller).

515 Commonwealth v. Tolleson (I), 14 Pa. Commw. Ct. 72, 321 A.2d 664 (1974), *aff'd on other grounds*, 462 Pa. 193, 340 A.2d 428 (1975).

516 McGowan v. Woodsmall Benefit Servs., Inc., 197 Ill. App. 3d 400, 554 N.E.2d 704 (1990). *See also* Kelly v. Nelson, Mullins, Riley & Scarborough, 2002 U.S. Dist. LEXIS 6430 (M.D. Fla. Mar. 20, 2002) (meeting with plaintiff in forum state and representing him in business transactions there is sufficient); Wendt v. Horowitz, 822 So. 2d 1252 (Fla. 2002) (telephone calls into state sufficient if tort claim arises from them). *Accord* North Am. Enterprises, Inc. v. Vermont, Clearinghouse No. 51,266 (Vt. Super. Ct. Aug. 31, 1994) (court had jurisdiction over out-of-state telemarketing company). *But cf.* Cinalli v. Kane, 191 F. Supp. 2d 601 (E.D. Pa. 2002) (defendants' follow-up contacts with plaintiffs in forum state insufficient where contract for sale of out-of-state property was negotiated and signed in other state); Worthy v. Cyberworks Tech., Inc., 835 So. 2d 972 (Ala. 2002) (two telephone calls to plaintiff insufficient because no clear, firm nexus between these acts and the consequences complained of).

517 State v. Reader's Digest Ass'n, Inc., 81 Wash. 2d 259, 501 P.2d 290 (1972).

518 Back Bay Farm, L.L.C. v. Collucio, 230 F. Supp. 2d 176 (D. Mass. 2002) (advertising on Internet, contacting and negotiating with in-state buyer); Haddad v. Taylor, 32 Mass. App. Ct. 332, 588 N.E.2d 1375 (1992) (use of telephone and mails to negotiate for sale of in-state property); Thomas v. Shair Laboratories, Inc., 1998 Tenn. App. LEXIS 780 (Nov. 23, 1998) (contacts with buyer, plus shipping of goods); Siskind v. Villa Foundation For Education, Inc., 642 S.W.2d 434 (Tex. 1982) (advertising in national publications and state telephone directories and mailing contracts into state); State v. Advance Marketing Consultants, Inc., 66 Wis. 2d 706, 225 N.W.2d 887 (1975). *But cf.* Worthy v. Cyberworks Technologies, Inc., 835 So. 2d 972 (Ala. 2002) (two telephone calls to in-state buyers insufficient).

the yellow pages within the state,[519] and entering into a contract within the state[520] have all been found sufficient contact with a state to allow jurisdiction over the seller.[521] Even where the consumer initiated the call, an out-of-state telemarketer subjected itself to jurisdiction in the consumer's state when it launched into a deceptive "upsell" and sold her an additional product.[522]

Personal jurisdiction is found where the defendant intentionally serves a particular state's market. Purchasing a car at a Missouri auction, arranging financing through a Missouri corporation, and advertising in Missouri newspapers was sufficient to give Missouri jurisdiction over a Kansas car dealer, even though it sold the car in Kansas to a Kansas resident.[523] Iowa had jurisdiction[524] over a seller who advertised in Nebraska media that foreseeably reached the adjacent area of Iowa.[525]

As to individuals, a court has jurisdiction over the owner of an out-of-state company where it is alleged that he knew or should have known of the company's fraudulent activities within the state.[526] Serving as a director of an in-state corporation is sufficient to establish jurisdiction in that state even without other contacts.[527] However, merely being listed as directors on a charitable organization's letterhead does not subject individuals to jurisdiction in a state where they had no other contacts.[528] Nor is it sufficient to be an investor in a business that has minimum contacts with the state.[529] Similarly, a court has jurisdiction over the out-of-state parent corporation of an in-state company if the two operate as one entity.[530]

Special tests may apply where out-of-state defendants engage in a conspiracy that violates UDAP statutes, and where there is jurisdiction over at least one co-conspirator. The Supreme Court of Delaware holds that a state court can exercise jurisdiction over other co-conspirators if the plaintiff shows that those defendants participated in a conspiracy to defraud; a substantial act or a substantial effect in furtherance of the conspiracy occurred in the forum state; the defendant knew or had reason to know of the act in the forum state or that acts outside the forum state would have an effect in the forum state; and the act in, or effect on, the forum state was a direct and foreseeable result of the conduct in furtherance of the conspiracy.[531] The Florida Supreme Court has gone even farther and approved long-arm jurisdiction over a company that caused injury in Florida through an out-of-state price-fixing conspiracy.[532]

Even when there is *in personam* jurisdiction over an out-of-state corporation, some courts adopt the "fiduciary shield" doctrine to protect individuals who are acting for the corporation. The doctrine finds no jurisdiction over non-resident corporate agents if that individual's only contact with the forum is by virtue of his or her acts as fiduciary of

519 State *ex rel.* Brady v. Preferred Florist Network, Inc., 791 A.2d 8 (Del. Ch. 2001).

520 FTC v. Productive Marketing, Inc., 136 F. Supp. 2d 1096 (C.D. Cal. 2001) (entering into contract with California corporations to process credit card payments for them from consumers, many of whom lived in California, was sufficient); Parks v. Macro Dynamics, Inc., 121 Ariz. 517, 591 P.2d 1005 (1979). *But cf.* Worthy v. Cyberworks Technologies, Inc., 835 So. 2d 972 (Ala. 2002) (subcontracting with another company to fulfill its contract for services to state resident insufficient where there is no evidence of agency relationship).

521 *See also* Richmar Dev. Inc. v. Midland Doherty Servs. Ltd., 717 F. Supp. 1107 (W.D.N.C. 1989) (plaintiff corporation's contacts with forum state sufficient to obtain jurisdiction over out-of-state corporation); Steed Realty v. Oveisi, 823 S.W.2d 195 (Tenn. Ct. App. 1991) (advertising out-of-state real estate, holding closings, and having an office within the state sufficient contacts).

522 West Corp. v. Superior Court, 116 Cal. App. 4th 1167, 11 Cal. Rptr. 3d 145 (Cal. App. 2004).

523 Sloan-Roberts v. Morse Chevrolet, Inc., 44 S.W.3d 402 (Mo. App. 2001).

524 State *ex rel.* Miller v. Baxter Chrysler Plymouth, Inc., 456 N.W.2d 371 (Iowa 1990).

525 *See also* Logan Productions, Inc. v. Optibase, Inc., 103 F.3d 49 (7th Cir. 1996); FTC v. 1492828 Ontario Inc., 2003 WL 21038578 (N.D. Ill. May 7, 2003) (finding jurisdiction over principal of Canadian telemarketing company); Zazove v. Pelikan, Inc., 761 N.E.2d 256, 260 Ill. Dec. 412 (2001) (sending advertising brochures and direct mail to state residents, advertising in local and nationwide magazines, and shipping product into state for sale is sufficient). *But cf.* Worthy v. Cyberworks Technologies, Inc., 835 So. 2d 972 (Ala. 2002) (no jurisdiction where defendant merely subcontracted to fulfill contracts that other company solicited in the state and there was no evidence of agency relationship); Kluin v. Am. Suzuki Motor Corp., 56 P.3d 829 (Kan. 2002) (manufacturer's national advertising, and sales to authorized dealers within state, insufficient where in-state buyer bought the product from out-of-state dealer).

526 North Am. Enterprises, Inc. v. Vermont, Clearinghouse No. 51,266 (Vt. Super. Ct. Aug. 31, 1994).

527 Florists' Transworld Delivery, Inc. v. Fleurop-Interflora, 261 F. Supp. 2d 837 (E.D. Mich. 2003).

528 People *ex rel.* Hartigan v. Kennedy, 215 Ill. App. 3d 880, 576 N.E.2d 107 (1991).

529 Ross v. Thousand Adventures, 675 N.W.2d 812 (Iowa Feb. 25, 2004) (out-of-state bank that bought participation interest in retail installment contracts not subject to jurisdiction in state where contracts originated).

530 N.C. Steel, Inc. v. National Council on Compensation Ins., 496 S.E.2d 369 (N.C. 1998) (extent of control by parent corporation is important factor).

531 Istituto Bancario Italiano v. Hunter Engineering Co., 449 A.2d 210 (Del. 1982). *Cf.* J.C. Whitney & Co. v. Renaissance Software Corp., 2000 U.S. Dist. LEXIS 6180 (N.D. Ill. Apr. 19, 2000) (magistrate's decision) (jurisdiction proper over out-of-state actor who committed tortious act in forum state through agent as part of scheme to defraud), *adopted in part, rejected in part on other grounds*, 98 F. Supp. 2d 981 (N.D. Ill. 2000) (rejecting conspiracy as basis for personal jurisdiction because there can be no actionable conspiracy between corporation's own officers and employees); Wilcox v. Stout, 637 So. 2d 335 (Fla. Dist. Ct. App. 1994) (need only show that jurisdiction proper as to a co-conspirator, without needing to show the other criteria listed in *Instituto Bancario Italiano*).

532 Execu-Tech Bus. Sys., Inc. v. New Oji Paper Co., 752 So. 2d 582 (Fla. 2000).

the corporation.[533] If, however, the individuals themselves are engaged in wrongful activity that is directed at the forum state, they are subject to the state's jurisdiction and the corporate shield doctrine will not protect them.[534] An individual who is serving his or her own interests in the state and who exercises discretion will probably not be allowed to claim the protection of this doctrine, especially if the individual has an ownership interest in the corporation.[535]

A state has no jurisdiction to regulate sales practices which occur entirely out of state.[536] Thus, where a state's residents travel to another state and are subjected to deceptive practices there, a court has held that there is no personal jurisdiction over an out-of-state seller.[537] The state does have jurisdiction, however, over deceptive in-state solicitations that induce consumers to travel to another state.[538] A restitution award in such circumstances must be limited to the damages caused by the in-state conduct.[539]

The basic analysis of jurisdictional issues applies equally well to UDAP violations engaged in over the Internet.[540] Maintaining a website that enables customers to place orders, and then shipping a product into the state, is likely to give the state jurisdiction.[541] Courts may examine the extent of interaction between the customer and the host computer to determine jurisdiction.[542] The Fourth Circuit finds jurisdiction when an out-of-state person directs electronic activity into a state with the manifested intention of engaging in business transactions in that state, and that activity creates a potential cause of action for a person within the state.[543] On the other hand, a passive website that does no more than post advertisements that are accessible by persons in the forum state will probably not allow jurisdiction.[544]

---

533 *See, e.g.*, LaVallee v. Parrot-Ice Drink Prods., 193 F. Supp. 2d 296 (D. Mass. 2002); People *ex rel.* Hartigan v. Kennedy, 215 Ill. App. 3d 880, 576 N.E.2d 107 (1991) (court applies fiduciary shield doctrine where defendants' only contact with forum state was membership on board of charitable corporation that operated in forum state); State *ex rel.* Miller v. Baxter Chrysler Plymouth, Inc., 456 N.W.2d 371 (Iowa 1990). *But see* Florists' Transworld Delivery, Inc. v. Fleurop-Interflora, 261 F. Supp. 2d 837 (E.D. Mich. 2003).

534 State *ex rel.* Brady v. Preferred Florist Network, Inc., 791 A.2d 8 (Del. Ch. 2001); Covington & Burling v. International Marketing & Research, Inc., 2003 WL 21384825 (D.C. Super. Apr. 17, 2003); State *ex rel.* Attorney General v. Wyndham Int'l, Inc., 869 So. 2d 592 (Fla. Dist. Ct. App. 2004); State *ex rel.* Miller v. Moneda Corp., 571 N.W.2d 1 (Iowa 1997).

535 J.C. Whitney & Co. v. Renaissance Software Corp., 2000 U.S. Dist. LEXIS 6180 (Apr. 19, 2000), *adopted in part, rejected in part on other grounds*, 98 F. Supp. 2d 981 (N.D. Ill. 2000) (rejecting conspiracy as basis for personal jurisdiction; finding long-arm jurisdiction but dismissing claims due to lack of complete diversity).

536 Consumer Protection Div. v. Outdoor World Corp., 91 Md. App. 275, 603 A.2d 1376 (1992).

537 Commonwealth v. Turner, Clearinghouse No. 26,034 (Pa. C.P. Erie Cty. 1971).

538 Consumer Protection Div. v. Outdoor World Corp., 91 Md. App. 275, 603 A.2d 1376 (1992).

539 *Id.*

540 ALS Scan v. Digital Service Consultants, Inc. 293 F.3d 707 (4th Cir. 2002); People v. Lipsitz, 174 Misc. 2d 571, 663 N.Y.S.2d 468 (Sup. Ct. 1997) (Internet sales company's presence in New York and targeting of New York consumers sufficient).

541 Gator.com Corp. v. L.L. Bean, Inc., 341 F.3d 1072 (9th Cir. 2003) (marketer's Internet presence amounted to virtual store and gave state general jurisdiction over it), *rehearing granted*, 2004 WL 928247 (9th Cir. Apr. 29, 2004); Lakin v. Prudential Securities, Inc., 348 F.3d 704 (8th Cir. 2003) (substantial and continuous contacts via Internet may support general jurisdiction, depending on quantity); Arnold v. Goldstar Fin. Sys., Inc., 2002 WL 1941546 at *6 (N.D. Ill. Aug. 22, 2002) (acceptance of payment on webpage is "roughly analogous to setting up a twenty-four hour storefront [in the forum state]"); Stuart v. Hennesey, 214 F. Supp. 1198 (D. Utah 2002); Mulcahy v. Cheetah Learning L.L.C., 2002 WL 31053211 (D. Minn. Sept. 4, 2002) (jurisdiction found where course advertised on-line and customers registered for course, regardless of whether course was actually held); Alitalia-Linee Aeree Italiane S.P.A. v. Casinoalitalia.com, 128 F. Supp. 2d 340 (E.D. Va. 2001) (allowing forum state residents to place bets through out of state website sufficient); Euromarket Designs, Inc. v. Crate & Barrel Ltd., 96 F. Supp. 2d 824 (N.D. Ill. 2000) (Illinois residents could browse defendant's on-line catalog and place orders via Internet); Thompson v. Handa-Lopez, Inc., 998 F. Supp. 738 (W.D. Tex. 1998); Zippo Mfg. Co. v. Zippo Dot Com, Inc., 952 F. Supp. 1119 (W.D. Pa. 1997); State *ex rel.* Nixon v. Beer Nuts, Ltd., 29 S.W.3d 828 (Mo. App. 2000) (product was alcoholic beverages, over which 21st amendment gives state special authority); Thompson v. Handa-Lopez, Inc., 998 F. Supp. 738 (W.D. Tex. 1998) (website through which Texas resident purchased game tokens and gambled gave Texas jurisdiction). *See also* Neogen Corp. v. Neo Gen Screening, Inc., 282 F.3d 883 (6th Cir. 2002) (largely passive website plus other interactions with state residents is sufficient). *Cf.* Molnlycke Health Care v. Dumex Medical Surgical Products Ltd., 64 F. Supp. 2d 448 (E.D. Pa. 1999) (website through which products can be ordered is sufficient to give specific jurisdiction but not general jurisdiction). *But see* Butler v. Beer Across Am., 83 F. Supp. 2d 1261 (N.D. Ala. 2000) (sale of beer to minor in forum state via Internet site not sufficient to allow jurisdiction). *See generally* National Consumer Law Center, The Cost of Credit: Regulation and Legal Challenges § 9.2.9.6 (2d ed. 2000 and Supp.).

542 Donmar, Inc. v. Swanky Partners, Inc., 2002 WL 1917258 (N.D. Ill. Aug. 20, 2002) (website not interactive enough to support finding of jurisdiction where customers view information and join mailing list on website, but out-of-state names are immediately removed from mailing list and advertisements are not directed to out-of-state consumers). *See also* Machulsky v. Hall, 210 F. Supp. 2d 531 (D.N.J. 2002). *Cf.* Stuart v. Hennesey, 214 F. Supp. 1198 (D. Utah 2002) (website containing advertisements, video clip, employment opportunities, and an on-line purchase option is sufficiently interactive to warrant jurisdiction); Mothers Against Drunk Driving v. DAMMADD, Inc., 2003 WL 292162 (N.D. Tex. Feb. 7, 2003) (website that allowed anonymous tip reporting, on-line donations, and the limited sale of merchandise held not sufficiently interactive to support specific jurisdiction).

543 ALS Scan v. Digital Service Consultants, Inc. 293 F.3d 707 (4th Cir. 2002).

544 Gorman v. Ameritrade, 293 F.3d 506 (D.C. Cir. 2002); GTE New Media Servs. v. BellSouth Corp., 199 F.3d 1343 (D.C. Cir. 2000); Mink v. AAAA Development L.L.C., 190 F.3d 333 (5th Cir. 1999) (website with information about products, a printable

The burden of proof on questions of personal jurisdiction can be complicated. The West Virginia Supreme Court adopts the view that the plaintiff has the burden of establishing sufficient facts to show jurisdiction over a nonresident defendant who has filed a motion to dismiss.[545] If the court conducts a full evidentiary hearing on the motion or the issue is decided at trial, this showing must be by a preponderance of the evidence. If the court resolves the motion merely on the complaint, motion papers, briefs, affidavits, other documents, and discovery, the plaintiff need only make *prima facie* showing of personal jurisdiction, and the court must view the allegations in the light most favorable to the plaintiff and draw all inferences in favor of jurisdiction.

A separate question, once jurisdiction is established, is whether the forum state's UDAP statute applies to the case. The UDAP statute itself may contain restrictions on coverage of out-of-state transactions or out-of-state defendants. These topics are discussed elsewhere in this manual.[546]

7.6.3 Choice of Law Issues

In a case involving activity in more than one state, a threshold issue is what state law applies. The analysis differs depending on whether there is an effective contractual choice of law clause. Whether the UDAP statute itself is limited to in-state acts or parties is a separate question, discussed at §§ 2.3.12 and 2.4.4, *supra.* Special issues regarding choice of law in multi-state class actions are discussed in § 8.5.5, *infra.*

If either of two states' UDAP statutes could govern a transaction, the courts will apply choice of law principles to determine which statute to apply. The mere fact that two states are involved does not automatically raise a conflict of law or choice of law problem, however.[547] If there is no conflict between the laws of the states, then a court should apply the law of the forum state.[548] In federal court, the law of the forum state supplies the applicable choice-of-law standard in diversity cases, nondiversity cases involving nonfederal questions, supplemental jurisdiction cases, and federal question cases where federal law does not provide an independent rule of decision.[549]

When the parties' contract does not contain a choice of law clause, courts differ in the choice of law analysis they use.[550] In some jurisdictions, the court will apply the law of the state that had the most significant relationship to the occurrences giving rise to the claim.[551] Others use a "*lex loci delicti*" or "place of the wrong" test.[552] The court may give a preference

mail-in order form, the company's telephone number, mailing address, and e-mail address, but no ability to take orders was a passive advertisement that did not meet the minimum contacts test); SCC Communications Corp. v. Anderson, 195 F. Supp. 2d 1257 (D. Colo. 2002); Millennium Enterprises, Inc. v. Millennium Music, 33 F. Supp. 2d 907 (D. Or. 1999) (surveying and describing cases); Hearst Corp. v. Goldberger, 1997 U.S. Dist. LEXIS 2065 (S.D.N.Y. Feb. 26, 1997) (website accessible by forum state residents did not create jurisdiction in trademark infringement case where no sales had been made to forum state residents); Bensusan Restaurant Corp. v. King, 937 F. Supp. 295 (S.D.N.Y. 1996) (website does not create long-arm jurisdiction for trademark infringement claim where infringing goods were not shipped into forum state and no infringing activity was directed at forum state), *aff'd on other grounds*, 126 F.3d 25 (2d Cir. 1997). *But cf.* State v. Granite Gate Resorts, Inc., 568 N.W.2d 715 (Minn. App. 1997), *aff'd by equally divided court*, 576 N.W.2d 747 (Minn. 1998) (Minnesota had jurisdiction over Las Vegas outfit that placed advertisements on the Internet, knowing that they would reach Minnesota consumers).

545 N.C. Steel, Inc. v. National Council on Compensation Ins., 496 S.E.2d 369 (N.C. 1998) (denying writ of prohibition).

546 *See* §§ 2.3.12 and 2.4.4, *supra*.

547 Washington Mut. Bank v. Superior Court, 24 Cal. 4th 906, 15 P.3d 1071, 1080–81 (2001).

548 *See, e.g.*, Ventura v. Home Servicing of Am., 1996 U.S. Dist. LEXIS 4583 (N.D. Ill. Apr. 9, 1996) (applying Illinois UDAP statute rather than California UDAP statute after both tort and contract choice of law analysis). *See also* Yu v. Signet Bank/Virginia, 69 Cal. App. 4th 1377, 82 Cal. Rptr. 2d 304 (1999) (applying California UDAP statute to creditor that took void default judgments in Virginia against California debtors). *See generally* 16 Am. Jur. 2d Conflict of Law § 85 (2d ed. 1998).

549 Klaxon Co. v. Stentor Elec. Mfg. Co., 313 U.S. 487 (1941) (diversity); Williams v. First Government Mortgage & Investors Corp., 176 F.3d 497 (D.C. Cir. 1999) (diversity); Wiggins v. Avco Fin. Servs., 62 F. Supp. 2d 90 (D.D.C. 1999) (pendent state claim removed to federal court along with federal claims). *See also* 19 Charles Alan Wright, Arthur R. Miller & Edward H. Cooper, Federal Practice and Procedure, §§ 4507, 4520 (2d ed. 1996); 16 Am. Jur. 2d Conflict of Laws § 8 (2d ed. 1998).

550 *See generally* Symeon C. Symeonides, *Choice of Law in the American Courts in 1999: One More Year*, 48 Am. J. Comp. L. 143 (2000); 16 Am. Jur. 2d Conflict of Laws § 1 et seq. (2d ed. 1998); Annotation, Modern Status of Rule that Substantive Rights of Parties to a Tort Action are Governed by the Law of the Place of the Wrong, 29 A.L.R.3d 603 (1970); Restatement (Second) of Conflict of Laws (1971).

551 16 Am. Jur. 2d Conflict of Law § 128 (2d ed. 1998); Restatement (Second) of Conflict of Laws §§ 6, 145 (1971). *See, e.g.*, Ventura v. Home Servicing of Am., 1996 U.S. Dist. LEXIS 4583 (N.D. Ill. Apr. 9, 1996) (applying Illinois UDAP statute rather than California UDAP statute after both tort and contract choice of law analysis); Jacobs v. Central Transport, Inc., 891 F. Supp. 1088 (E.D.N.C. 1995) (rejecting alternate test that chose the law of the jurisdiction in which the last act occurred giving rise to the injury), *aff'd in part, rev'd in part on other grounds*, 83 F.3d 415 (4th Cir. 1996). *See also* Edmondson v. Am. Motorcycle Ass'n, 2001 U.S. App. LEXIS 1506 (4th Cir. Feb. 2, 2001) (unpublished, citation limited) (under North Carolina rules, where place of injury is unclear, court should apply the law of the state with the most significant relationship to the transaction); Boyes v. Greenwich Boat Works, Inc., 27 F. Supp. 2d 543 (D.N.J. 1998) (N.J. applies a "government interest" test similar to most significant relationship test).

552 *See, e.g.*, Griffin v. Security Pacific Automotive Fin. Servs. Corp., 25 F. Supp. 2d 1214 (D. Kan. 1998) (applying Kansas law, court applied *lex loci delicti*, or "place of the wrong" analyses, and applied Kansas law to claim under Kansas consumer protection statute because plaintiff was a state resident and his vehicle was purchased and repossessed within Kansas).

to the forum state's substantive law in some circumstances.[553] Practitioners will have to research their own state's law to determine what analysis it uses. The law of different states may apply to different issues in the same case.

Where a contract clause specifies that the law of a particular state applies, courts applying the *Restatement (Second) of Conflict of Laws* will give effect to the clause unless it would violate fundamental public policy of the forum state and the forum state has a materially greater interest in the litigation than the state specified in the clause.[554] The Restatement further provides that the parties' choice is not to be enforced if: "(a) the chosen state has no substantial relationship to the parties or the transaction and there is no other reasonable basis for the parties' choice. . . ."[555] Whether such a contract clause controls may depend on whether the plaintiff's UDAP claim is based primarily on a breach of the contract rather than on more tort-like misdeeds.[556] Some courts maintain that choice-of-law clauses are inapplicable to tort claims, and a court may construe a contractual choice-of-law clause to be limited to contract claims, or only applicable to the construction of the contract and not the claim itself.[557] A state may also have a law that nullifies choice-of-law clauses that would prevent that state's consumer protection laws from applying.[558]

A company may be bound by its own contractual choice of law provision. Where a contract indicated that Illinois law applied to a transaction, the Seventh Circuit applied the Illinois UDAP statute even though the consumer did not reside in Illinois and the transaction did not take place in Illinois.[559] A choice of law clause in a contract may simplify certification of a nationwide class, because the court need not analyze and apply a variety of state laws.[560]

7.6.4 The Proper State Court

Several UDAP statutes authorize UDAP actions only in specified courts.[561] Normally, this is an intermediate-level trial court. Thus, in some states, UDAP actions are precluded in small claims or similar courts,[562] even though such courts may be best suited for small consumer claims.

Even if the UDAP statute itself does not prevent a UDAP claim in small claims court, there is an issue in some states whether a "statutory" claim is within a state's small claims court jurisdiction. The Massachusetts court has held that a UDAP action is in the "nature of contract or tort" and is thus within the small claims court's jurisdiction.[563] Certain

553 Williams v. First Government Mortgage & Investors Corp., 176 F.3d 497 (D.C. Cir. 1999) (under D.C. choice of law rules, if the two jurisdictions have equally strong interests in application of the law to the case, the law of the forum state will be applied); Wiggins v. Avco Fin. Servs., 62 F. Supp. 2d 90 (D.D.C. 1999) (same); Boyes v. Greenwich Boat Works, Inc., 27 F. Supp. 2d 543 (D.N.J. 1998).

554 Stone Street Servs., Inc. v. Daniels, 2000 WL 1909373 (E.D. Pa. Dec. 29, 2000) (finding that application of Pennsylvania's weaker UDAP law, as specified by contract, would violate strong public policy of Kansas, where transaction occurred); Schiff v. Rice Mazda Motor, 102 F. Supp. 2d 891 (S.D. Ohio 2000) (giving effect to choice of law clause where state chosen had materially greater interest); Demitropoulos v. Bank One Milwaukee, N.A., 915 F. Supp. 1399 (N.D. Ill. 1996) (giving effect to clause specifying that Wisconsin law would apply). *See also* 16 Am. Jur. 2d Conflict of Law §§ 89–91 (2d ed. 1998).

555 Restatement (Second) of Conflict of Laws § 187(2)(a) (1971).

556 Valley Juice, Ltd. v. Evian Waters of France, 87 F.3d 604 (2d Cir. 1996); Andrews v. Temple Inland Mortg. Corp., 2001 U.S. Dist. LEXIS 23613 (D. Minn. Sept. 24, 2001) (applying contract choice-of-law rules to UDAP claim that was closely related to contract interpretation); Amaro v. Capital One Bank, 1998 U.S. Dist. LEXIS 8373 (N.D. Ill. 1998) (upholding choice of Virginia law provision even though Virginia UDAP did not apply to defendant); Bradley v. Dean Witter Realty Inc., 967 F. Supp. 19 (D. Mass. 1997); Worldwide Commodities, Inc. v. J. Amicone Co., 630 N.E.2d 615 (Mass. App. Ct. 1994). *See also* Scully Signal Co. v. Joyal, 881 F. Supp. 727 (D.R.I. 1995) (analysis under Rhode Island choice of law rules).

557 *See, e.g.*, Thera-Kinetics, Inc. v. Managed Home Recovery, Inc., 1997 U.S. Dist. LEXIS 15352 (N.D. Ill. Sept. 29, 1997) (parties' choice of law language referred to construction of agreement but did not refer to tort claims); Tucker v. Scott, 1997 U.S. Dist. LEXIS 3856 (S.D.N.Y. Apr. 1, 1997) (choice of law language not broad enough to encompass tort claim); Kitner v. CTW Transport, Inc., 762 N.E.2d 867 (Mass. App. 2002) (construing clause not to cover UDAP claims).

558 *See, e.g.*, Va. Code § 59.1-501.9.

559 Cange v. Stotler & Co., 913 F.2d 1204 (7th Cir. 1990) (court determined that customer's acknowledgment in trading contract that customer is transacting business in Illinois was sufficient nexus to apply UDAP statute). *See also* Scully Signal Co. v. Joyal, 881 F. Supp. 727 (D.R.I. 1995) (contractual choice of law provision followed).

560 Pickett v. Holland Am. Line—Westours, Inc., 101 Wash. App. 901, 6 P.3d 63 (2000) (trial court abused its discretion in denying nationwide class certification where cause of action is based solely upon violation of Washington UDAP and contract contained both choice of law and choice of forum provisions), *rev'd on other grounds*, 35 P.3d 351 (Wash. 2001). *But cf.* Washington Mut. Bank v. Superior Court, 24 Cal. 4th 906, 15 P.3d 1071 (2001) (trial court must consider whether clause selecting law of jurisdiction in which property was located prevented certification of nationwide class). Nationwide class actions present unique issues regarding choice of law analyses. *See generally* Ryan Patrick Phair, *Resolving the "Choice-of-Law Problem" in Rule 23(b)(3) Nationwide Class Actions*, 67 U. Chi. L. Rev. 835 (Summer 2000); § 8.5.5, *infra*.

561 American Appliance, Inc. v. State, 712 A.2d 1001 (Del. 1998) (AG enforcement actions may be filed in Delaware Superior Court; AG injunctive suits may be filed in Chancery Court). *See also* Greenlining Institute v. Pub. Utilities Comm'n, 103 Cal. App. 4th 1324, 127 Cal. Rptr. 2d 736 (2002) (§ 17200 claims can only be filed in courts, not before administrative agencies).

562 The Massachusetts UDAP statute was interpreted to exclude UDAP actions in housing court, Chakrabarti v. Marinello Assocs., 377 Mass. 419, 386 N.E.2d 1248 (1979), but then was amended to overrule this decision. *See* Worcester Heritage Soc. v. Trussell, 31 Mass. App. Ct. 343, 577 N.E.2d 1009 (1991). *See also* Foreman v. Discount Motors, Inc., 629 S.W.2d 635 (Mo. App. 1982).

563 Travis v. McDonald, 397 Mass. 230, 490 N.E.2d 1169 (1986).

small claims courts also have jurisdiction to grant injunctive relief along with damages.[564] Ohio does not grant its small claims courts jurisdiction to recover "punitive" damages, but this has been interpreted not to bar multiple damages claims.[565]

When a consumer can bring a UDAP action in a small claims court, the litigant must be careful not to seek damages exceeding the court's jurisdictional maximum. While the consumer's damage may be less than the maximum, treble damages and attorney fees could exceed that maximum. It is unclear whether the court's jurisdiction is ousted when actual damages are less than, but treble damages are more than, the jurisdictional maximum. Courts whose statutes make treble damages mandatory have determined jurisdiction by looking at the amount requested in the pleading, including treble damages and in some cases, attorney fees.[566] The New Jersey Supreme Court holds that attorney fees are costs that do not count toward the jurisdictional limit, noting that a contrary ruling would bar consumers from a streamlined court that is well-suited to consumer cases, and would undercut the critical role of attorney fees in remedying consumer fraud.[567] A well-reasoned Ohio lower court opinion agrees, noting that the unpredictability of the size of an attorney fee award would exclude a great number of consumer cases from courts with jurisdictional maximums.[568] Courts in Wisconsin[569] and Virginia[570] reach the same conclusion.[571] An Ohio decision also holds that a consumer may seek rescission, which is specifically authorized by the state UDAP statute, in small claims court, even though that court does not have equitable jurisdiction.[572]

The Rhode Island UDAP statute authorizes any consumer who has been injured by a violation to bring suit in the state superior court.[573] The Rhode Island Supreme Court interpreted this language to relieve UDAP plaintiffs of the normal requirement of alleging more than $5000 in controversy.

Where the consumer is not authorized to bring a UDAP action in a particular court, but is sued in that court, can the consumer then bring UDAP counterclaims there? The Washington Supreme Court has held that consumers can, because the act must be construed liberally and because consumers' other remedies are not adequate.[574] Similar issues can arise when the consumer is a defendant in a limited proceeding such as an eviction or replevin action. A Wisconsin decision holds that, because of the limited scope of an eviction action, the tenant could not assert UDAP counterclaims but had to file a separate UDAP action.[575] Where a court lacks jurisdiction over some of a plaintiff's UDAP claims, it may sever those and proceed with the remaining claims.[576]

Questions of venue within a state's court system can also arise due to conflicting provisions in different statutes. For example, the special venue provision in Tennessee's UDAP act conflicts with the state's general venue provision that requires venue where the cause of action arose or where the defendant resides. A Tennessee court resolved the conflict by concluding that the special venue provision in the UDAP act constituted an exception to the state's general venue provision.[577]

7.6.5 Federal Court Jurisdiction

Consumer litigants bringing federal claims—such Truth-in-Lending, RICO, Fair Debt Collection Practices, or Odometer Act claims—in federal court may be able to join a state UDAP claim in the same federal action. Until 1990, federal courts took jurisdiction over related state claims under the doctrine of "pendent jurisdiction." The Judicial Improvements Act of 1990[578] codified this doctrine by conferring "supplemental" jurisdiction on the district courts, so that district courts have jurisdiction to hear all claims related to claims over which the district courts have original jurisdiction. If the state claim is part of the same

564 Herman v. Home Depot, 436 Mass. 210, 763 N.E.2d 512 (2002).

565 Klemas v. Flynn, 66 Ohio St. 3d 249, 611 N.E.2d 810 (1993) (double damages provision of landlord-tenant security deposit statute).

566 Wisser v. Kaufman Carpet Co., 188 N.J. Super. 574, 485 A.2d 119 (App. Div. 1983); Nieves v. Baron, 164 N.J. Super. 86, 359 A.2d 875 (App. Div. 1978); Long v. Fox, 625 S.W.2d 376 (Tex. Civ. App. 1981); *see also* Allright v. Guy, 590 S.W.2d 734 (Tex. Civ. App. 1979). *But see* Bittner v. Tri-County Toyota, Inc., 62 Ohio Misc. 2d 345, 598 N.E.2d 925 (Mun. 1992) (attorney fees not counted toward jurisdictional limit); Sears, Roebuck & Co. v. Big Bend Motor Inn, Inc., 818 S.W.2d 542 (Tex. App. 1991) (discretionary treble damages are a penalty and therefore excluded from amount in controversy under Texas statute).

567 Lettenmaier v. Lube Connection, Inc., 162 N.J. 134, 741 A.2d 591 (1999).

568 Bittner v. Tri-County Toyota, Inc., 62 Ohio Misc. 2d 345, 598 N.E.2d 925 (Mun. 1992).

569 Reusch v. Roob, 234 Wis. 2d 270, 610 N.W.2d 168 (App. 2000).

570 Vanderander v. Larry Homes of Va., Inc., 2001 Va. Cir. LEXIS 30 (Feb. 22, 2001).

571 *See also* Stokus v. Marsh, 217 Cal. App. 3d 647, 651, 266 Cal. Rptr. 90 (1990) (non-UDAP case; fees can be awarded even though fees by themselves would exceed the jurisdictional limit); Bakkebo v. Mun. Ct., 124 Ca. App. 3d 229, 236, 177 Cal. Rptr. 239 (1981) (court has jurisdiction to award fees even though aggregate award would exceed jurisdictional limit).

572 Ferrari v. Howard, 2002 WL 1500414 (Ohio App. July 11, 2002) (unpublished, citation limited).

573 Park v. Ford Motor Co., 844 A.2d 687 (R.I. 2004).

574 Strenge v. Clarke, 89 Wash. 2d 23, 569 P.2d 60 (1977).

575 Defoe v. Sigrist, 655 N.W.2d 546 (Wis. App. 2002) (unpublished, citation limited). *See also* National Consumer Law Center, Repossessions and Foreclosures §§ 5.5.5, 5.8.1 (5th ed. 2002 and Supp.) (discussion of ability to raise counterclaims in replevin cases).

576 Poteat v. St. Paul Mercury Ins. Co., 277 Mont. 117, 918 P.2d 677 (1996).

577 Netherland v. Hunter, 2003 WL 22383616 (Tenn. Ct. App. Apr. 5, 2004).

578 28 U.S.C. § 1367, *as enacted by* Pub. L. No. 101-650, 104 Stat. 5089 (1990).

case or controversy, the district court can decline jurisdiction over it only if it raises a novel issue of state law, substantially predominates over the federal claims, is joined to federal law claims that have been dismissed, or, in exceptional circumstances, presents other compelling reasons for denying jurisdiction.[579] The Act explicitly allows not only pendent-claim jurisdiction, but pendent-party jurisdiction as well. A party can be joined in a federal action even where there is no federal jurisdiction as to that particular party, as long as there is federal jurisdiction over a related party.[580]

Federal jurisdiction is also appropriate for UDAP claims where there is diversity of citizenship and the amount in controversy exceeds $75,000.[581] Potential UDAP attorney fees,[582] punitive damages,[583] and treble damages[584] are included for purposes of determining the amount in controversy. If the plaintiffs win less than the minimum amount in controversy, however, the court has discretion to tax costs against them.[585] Class actions raise complicated questions about the calculation of the amount in controversy that are discussed in another NCLC manual.[586]

Sometimes a defendant will prefer a federal forum and will seek to remove a state UDAP claim to federal court where the UDAP claim is based on the defendant's violation of a federal statute. A complaint that pleads no federal claims is not made removable by a reference to a violation of federal standards as part of a UDAP claim,[587] or by the anticipation of a defense based on federal law.[588] Where a claim is supported by alternate theories, removal is not proper unless federal law is essential to each theory.[589]

Likewise, removal is improper where the plaintiff has chosen to plead solely state law claims, even though federal claims might have been pleaded and even though federal law might preempt the state claims.[590] However, under the "artful pleading rule," a case is removable if a consumer's state law claim is really just a federal claim "artfully pled" as a state law claim.[591]

The only exception to the rule that well-pleaded state claims can not be removed is the very limited area of complete federal preemption, where Congress has preempted an area of law so completely that any claim is removable.[592] A state claim can be removed to federal court

579 28 U.S.C. § 1367(c). *See* Brophy v. Chase Manhattan Mortgage Co., 947 F. Supp. 879 (E.D. Pa. 1996) (dismissing UDAP claim after federal claims dismissed); Newman v. Checkrite California, Inc., 912 F. Supp. 1354 (C.D. Cal. 1995) (retaining jurisdiction over UDAP claims arising from common nucleus of operative fact as FDCPA claims); Hunter by Conyer v. Estate of Baecher, 905 F. Supp. 341 (E.D. Va. 1995) (retaining jurisdiction after weighing factors).

580 *Cf.* Smith v. Burdette Chrysler Dodge Corp., 774 F. Supp. 380 (D.S.C. 1991).

581 28 U.S.C. § 1332(a).

582 Miera v. Dairyland Ins. Co., 143 F.3d 1337 (10th Cir. 1998) (removal proper where attorney fees pushed amount in controversy above jurisdictional threshold); Gardiner Stone Hunter v. Iberia Lineas Aereas, 896 F. Supp. 125 (S.D.N.Y. 1995); Garcia v. General Motors Corp., 910 F. Supp. 160 (D.N.J. 1995).

583 Garcia v. General Motors Corp., 910 F. Supp. 160 (D.N.J. 1995).

584 Miera v. Dairyland Ins. Co., 143 F.3d 1337 (10th Cir. 1998); Payne v. Goodyear Tire & Rubber, 229 F. Supp. 2d 43 (D. Mass. 2002); Robinson v. Hyundai Motor Am., 683 F. Supp. 515 (E.D. Pa. 1988); Neff v. General Motors Corp., 163 F.R.D. 478 (E.D. Pa. 1995).

585 28 U.S.C. § 1332(b). *See* Mimaco L.L.C. v. Maison Faurie Antiquities, 2000 U.S. App. LEXIS 18335 (10th Cir. July 31, 2000) (unpublished, citation limited) (denial of costs is discretionary and does not affect right to attorney fees).

586 National Consumer Law Center, Consumer Class Actions: A Practical Litigation Guide § 2.2 (5th ed. 2002 and Supp.).

587 Savalle v. Nestle Waters N. Am., Inc., 289 F. Supp. 2d 31 (D. Conn. 2003) (borrowing federal bottled water standards for UDAP claim); Rubel v. Pfizer Inc., 276 F. Supp. 2d 904 (N.D. Ill. Aug. 12, 2003) (referring to federal statute that does not provide a private cause of action does not make complaint removable); Vermont v. Oncor Communications, 166 F.R.D. 313 (D. Vt. 1996); Kentucky v. Comcast Cable, 881 F. Supp. 285 (W.D. Ky. 1995); State v. TRW, Inc., Clearinghouse No. 46,798 (D. Vt. Dec. 20, 1991). *See also* Cook v. Chrysler Credit Corp., 174 B.R. 321 (M.D. Ala. 1994) (removal not proper although FTC's Holder Rule could have been basis for asserting state law claims against defendant).

588 Beneficial Nat'l Bank v. Anderson, 539 U.S. 1, 123 S. Ct. 2058, 2062, 156 L. Ed. 2d 1 (2003); Rivet v. Regions Bank, 522 U.S. 470, 118 S. Ct. 921, 139 L. Ed. 2d 912 (1998); Bauchelle v. AT&T Corp., 989 F. Supp. 636 (D.N.J. 1997); Vermont v. Oncor Communications, 166 F.R.D. 313 (D. Vt. 1996).

589 Cavette v. Mastercard Int'l, Inc., 282 F. Supp. 2d 813 (W.D. Tenn. 2003); Klussman v. Cross-Country Bank, 2002 U.S. Dist. LEXIS 9387 (N.D. Cal. May 10, 2002) (removal improper where violation of federal law was only one of 20 examples of acts supporting plaintiff's UDAP claim), *vacated, remanded on other grounds*, 2003 U.S. App. LEXIS 18716 (9th Cir. Sept. 8, 2003); Vermont v. Oncor Communications, 166 F.R.D. 313 (D. Vt. 1996). *Cf.* People *ex rel.* Lockyer v. Reliant Energy, Inc., 2002 U.S. Dist. LEXIS 15733 (N.D. Cal. Aug. 6, 2002) (UDAP claim premised solely on federal law is removable).

590 Hofler v. Aetna US Healthcare, 296 F.3d 764 (9th Cir. 2002); Aetna U.S. Healthcare Inc. v. Maltz, 1999 U.S. Dist. LEXIS 6708 (S.D.N.Y. May 4, 1999); Bauchelle v. AT&T Corp., 989 F. Supp. 636 (D.N.J. 1997); Weinberg v. Sprint Corp., 165 F.R.D. 431 (D.N.J. 1996). *See* § 2.5, *supra*, for a discussion of federal preemption of UDAP claims.

591 Rivet v. Regions Bank, 522 U.S. 470, 118 S. Ct. 921, 139 L. Ed. 2d 912 (1998). *See also* Moriconi v. AT&T Wireless PCS, 280 F. Supp. 2d 867 (E.D. Ark. 2003) (plaintiff's complaint alleging misrepresentation of rates and services by wireless carrier does not depend on resolution of federal question so not removable); Cavette v. Mastercard Int'l, Inc., 282 F. Supp. 2d 813 (W.D. Tenn. 2003) (claims against credit card company for failing to disclose currency conversion fee were not artfully pleaded to avoid federal jurisdiction); *In re* Comcast Cellular Telecom. Litigation, 949 F. Supp. 1193 (E.D. Pa. 1996).

592 Hofler v. Aetna US Healthcare, 296 F.3d 764 (9th Cir. 2002) (Medicare statute does not completely preempt state claims regarding false advertising about quality of medical care); Wayne v. DHL Worldwide Express, 294 F.3d 1179 (9th Cir. 2002) (Airline Deregulation Act does not completely preempt state claims); Marcus v. AT&T Corp., 138 F.3d 46 (2d Cir. 1998) (Federal Communications Act does not completely preempt state claims); Gattegno v. Sprint Corp., 297 F. Supp. 2d 372 (D. Mass. 2003) (Federal Communications Act did not completely

under this doctrine only when Congress has expressly so provided[593] or when a federal statute's preemptive force is so powerful that it displaces entirely any state cause of action.[594] The Supreme Court has applied the latter theory to find complete preemption only under ERISA, section 301 of the Labor-Management Relations Act, and the National Bank Act.[595]

To justify removal under the complete preemption doctrine, the federal statute must include civil enforcement provisions under which the plaintiff's state law claims could be brought.[596] The question is whether the federal law provides the exclusive cause of action for the plaintiff's claim.[597] If the federal statute explicitly preserves state statutory or common law remedies it is a strong indication that Congress did not intend to completely preempt state law claims.[598] Preemption of UDAP claims is discussed in more detail in § 2.5, *supra*.

In diversity cases, a plaintiff may be able to avoid removal by praying for less than the $75,000 jurisdictional amount. Only if the defendant shows to a legal certainty that the plaintiff's claim must exceed this amount will removal be allowed.[599]

In rare cases, a seller may be able to challenge UDAP regulations in federal court, where the seller raises federal questions.[600] Seller attempts to obtain a federal court injunction against state UDAP enforcement proceedings will, however, usually be barred by the abstention doctrine.[601]

7.6.6 Bankruptcy Court Jurisdiction

Another way to obtain federal court jurisdiction for a UDAP count is to litigate the claim in bankruptcy court.[602] There are two different situations where UDAP claims may arise in bankruptcy court. Where the seller has filed for bankruptcy, the consumer has no choice but to bring UDAP claims before the bankruptcy court or at least ask the bankruptcy court for relief from the automatic stay so the consumer can bring or continue a state UDAP action. This situation, where the seller is in bankruptcy, is discussed in another manual.[603]

This section discusses some of the advantages to a consumer of litigating claims in bankruptcy court. Filing bankruptcy may appear an extreme approach to obtaining federal court jurisdiction. But the consumer may be in financial distress in large part because of the seller's or creditor's

---

preempt state UDAP claims arising from wireless carrier's deceptive billing); Alport v. Sprint Corp., 2003 WL 22872134 (N.D. Ill. Dec. 4, 2003) (Federal Communications Act completely preempts challenge to rates); State *ex rel.* Nixon v. Nextel West Corp., 248 F. Supp. 2d 885 (E.D. Mo. 2003) (Federal Communications Act does not completely preempt claim that cell phone company deceptively characterized charges on bills); Moriconi v. AT&T Wireless PCS, 280 F. Supp. 2d 867 (E.D. Ark. 2003) (Federal Communications Act does not completely preempt UDAP claim against wireless telecommunications provider); Klussman v. Cross-Country Bank, 2002 U.S. Dist. LEXIS 9387 (N.D. Cal. May 10, 2002) (Fed. Deposit Ins. Act does not completely preempt UDAP claims), *vacated, remanded*, 2003 U.S. App. LEXIS 18716 (9th Cir. Sept. 8, 2003) (remanding for further consideration in light of Beneficial Nat'l Bank v. Anderson, 123 S. Ct. 2058 (2003)); TPS Utilicom Servs., Inc. v. AT&T Corp., 223 F. Supp. 2d 1089 (C.D. Cal. 2002) (Communications Act of 1934 does not completely preempt state claims); Farkas v. Bridgestone/Firestone, Inc., 113 F. Supp. 2d 1107 (W.D. Ky. 2000) (Motor Vehicle Safety Act does not completely preempt state claims); Shaw v. TCI/TKR, 67 F. Supp. 2d 712 (W.D. Ky. 1999) (Federal Cable Television Consumer Protection and Competition Act does not completely preempt state claims); Sanderson, Thompson, Ratledge & Zimny v. AWACS, Inc., 958 F. Supp. 947 (D. Del. 1997) (Federal Communications Act does not completely preempt UDAP claim regarding solicitation and disclosure of cellular phone rates); DeCastro v. AWACS, Inc., 935 F. Supp. 541 (D.N.J. 1996); Weinberg v. Sprint Corp., 165 F.R.D. 431 (D.N.J. 1996) (Federal Communications Act does not completely preempt state law claims); Vermont v. Oncor Communications, 166 F.R.D. 313 (D. Vt. 1996) (Federal Communications Act completely preempts state law claims and allows removal).

593 Beneficial Nat'l Bank v. Anderson, 539 U.S. 1, 123 S. Ct. 2058, 2062, 156 L. Ed. 2d 1 (2003) (citing as example the Price-Anderson Act's preemption of tort actions arising out of nuclear accidents). The effect of the Securities Litigation Uniform Standards Act, 15 U.S.C. § 78bb(f), on certain state law class actions can also probably be characterized as complete preemption, however. *See* Spielman v. Merrill Lynch, Pierce, Fenner & Smith, Inc., 332 F.3d 116, 123 (2d Cir. 2003); § 2.5.7, *supra*.

594 *Id.* at 2062–63.

595 *Id.* (at 2603 n.4 court also notes special case of complete preemption over Indian land claims).

596 Franchise Tax Bd. v. Construction Laborers Vacation Trust, 463 U.S. 1, 103 S. Ct. 2841, 2855, 77 L. Ed. 2d 420 (1985) (no preemption where ERISA did not provide alternative cause of action for this party); Sanderson, Thompson, Ratledge & Zimny v. AWACS, Inc., 958 F. Supp. 947 (D. Del. 1997); Weinberg v. Sprint Corp., 165 F.R.D. 431 (D.N.J. 1996).

597 Beneficial Nat'l Bank v. Anderson, 539 U.S. 1, 123 S. Ct. 2058, 2063, 156 L. Ed. 2d 1 (2003).

598 Marcus v. AT&T Corp., 138 F.3d 46 (2d Cir. 1998) (no complete preemption under Federal Communications Act of 1934); DeCastro v. AWACS, Inc., 935 F. Supp. 541 (D.N.J. 1996) (UDAP claim is not completely preempted by Federal Communications Act). *See also* Bauchelle v. AT&T Corp., 989 F. Supp. 636 (D.N.J. 1997).

599 Landrum v. Johnson Mobile Homes, 1999 U.S. Dist. LEXIS 1987 (S.D. Ala. Feb. 1, 1999).

600 State *ex rel.* Abrams v. Trans World Airlines, 728 F. Supp. 162 (S.D.N.Y. 1989).

601 Temple of the Lost Sheep, Inc. v. Abrams, 761 F. Supp. 237 (S.D.N.Y. 1989).

602 *See* National Consumer Law Center, Consumer Law Pleadings, No. 2, § 3.3 (CD-Rom and Index Guide) for a sample complaint, discovery requests, summary judgment motion, list of evidence, request for findings, briefs on liability and damages, and attorney fee petition, all filed in Bankruptcy Court in a case raising UDAP and other claims concerning a lender's assessment of illegal charges. These documents are also found on the CD-Rom accompanying this volume.

603 *See* National Consumer Law Center, Consumer Bankruptcy Law and Practice Ch. 17 (6th ed. 2000 and Supp.).

fraud. Of course, the consumer's overall financial picture must be analyzed in relation to the potential relief affordable in bankruptcy.[604] Often the best approach is filing for a chapter 13 bankruptcy, giving the debtor some immediate relief, and then filing a UDAP claim that can help fund the chapter 13 repayment plan.

Bankruptcy court may be the best forum for litigating a consumer claim, where there are other reasons for a consumer to file bankruptcy. For example, a chapter 13 debtor used the bankruptcy court's jurisdiction over "related" proceedings[605] to pursue a UDAP class action in bankruptcy court against a company that advertised that for a fee of $225 it would provide expert advice on how to save a debtor's home from foreclosure.[606] All the company did, however, was refer debtors to an expensive bankruptcy attorney who filed chapter 13 petitions for them.

Other advantages to the bankruptcy forum are that it offers simple nationwide service of process, liberal federal discovery and class action rules, no additional filing fees for related claims, and a speedier trial than may be available in other courts.[607]

Bankruptcy court also can be a favorable forum for defeating arbitration clauses so that consumer claims may be litigated in court. Because of the conflict between the Bankruptcy Code and the Federal Arbitration Act,[608] courts generally have held that bankruptcy judges have discretion to deny enforcement of an arbitration clause, particularly as to "core proceedings" such as lien avoidance or modification actions.[609]

A chapter 7 bankruptcy may be less desirable for consumers than a chapter 13 bankruptcy. In chapter 7, only the trustee, not the debtor, may have standing to bring claims for the bankruptcy estate, particularly if the judgment would yield nonexempt funds.[610] However, the trustee in chapter 7 may abandon the estate's UDAP claim, allowing the debtor to pursue the claim. Alternatively, any recovery by the trustee may be exempt.[611]

Several recent cases have misapplied the preemption doctrine in finding that state law claims involving actions related to a bankruptcy proceeding are preempted by the Bankruptcy Code.[612] The better view has been adopted by the Eighth Circuit in *Sears, Roebuck and Co. v. O'Brien*.[613] In that case the debtor alleged that Sears violated the Iowa Consumer Credit Code, which prohibits creditor contact with a debtor who is represented by counsel, by sending a copy of a letter soliciting a reaffirmation agreement directly to the debtor. In response, Sears sought a declaratory judgment that the Iowa statute was preempted. In finding for the debtor, the Eighth Circuit noted that while bankruptcy law is "expansive," Congress did not intend to "exclusively" regulate the area and therefore there could be no "field" preemption.[614]

7.6.7 The Enforceability of Binding Arbitration Agreements

The enforceability of binding arbitration agreements is analyzed in a separate NCLC volume, *Consumer Arbitration Agreements* (4th ed. 2004). That volume contains not only detailed analysis, but reprints the rules from major arbitration mechanisms, and includes sample complaints, discovery and briefs on this topic. The volume also contains a companion CD-Rom with a number of additional briefs and important information on arbitration service provider costs and bias.

604 *See Id.* at Ch. 6 (6th ed. 2000 and Supp.).

605 28 U.S.C. § 1334(b).

606 Fleet v. United States Consumer Council, Inc., 53 B.R. 833 (Bankr. E.D. Pa. 1985), *adopted by* 70 B.R. 845 (E.D. Pa. 1987).

607 *See* Fed. R. Bankr. P. 7004(b), 7023, and 7026. *See also* National Consumer Law Center, Consumer Bankruptcy Law and Practice Ch. 13 (6th ed. 2000 and Supp.).

608 The presumption under the Federal Arbitration Act that valid arbitration agreements should be enforced is often in direct conflict with the goal of bankruptcy jurisdiction to have one centralized forum for the prompt resolution of disputes affecting the bankruptcy estate. *See* Zimmerman v. Continental Airlines, Inc., 712 F.2d. 55 (3d Cir. 1983); *In re* Hemphill Bus Sales, Inc., 259 B.R. 865 (Bankr. E.D. Tex. 2001); *In re* Knepp, 229 B.R. 821 (Bankr. N.D. Ala. 1999) (court finds "inherent conflict" between FAA and Bankruptcy Code).

609 *See In re* Mintze, 288 B.R. 95 (Bankr. E.D. Pa. 2003) (court refused to enforce arbitration clause because of potential impact on other creditors and questions about arbitrator's neutrality); *In re* Larocque, 283 B.R. 640 (Bankr. D.R.I. 2002) (denying enforcement of arbitration clause to decide Truth in Lending rescission issues); *In re* Hicks, 285 B.R. 317 (Bankr. W.D. Okla. 2002) (potential costs of arbitration would adversely affect debtor and creditors); *In re* Cavanaugh, 271 B.R. 414 (Bankr. D. Mass. 2001).

610 *In re* Snyder, 61 B.R. 268 (Bankr. S.D. Ohio 1986).

611 *See* National Consumer Law Center, Consumer Bankruptcy Law and Practice § 13.4.4 (6th ed. 2000 and Supp.).

612 *See, e.g.*, Loussides v. Am. Online, Inc., 175 F. Supp. 2d 211 (D. Conn. 2001); Lenior v. GE Capital Corp., 231 B.R. 662 (Bankr. N.D. Ill. 1999) (state UDAP claim based on filing of inflated proofs of claim in chapter 13 bankruptcy preempted by Bankruptcy Code); Holloway v. Household Automotive Fin. Corp., 227 B.R. 501 (N.D. Ill. 1998) (same).

613 178 F.3d 962 (8th Cir. 1999). *See also* Sturm v. Providian Nat. Bank, 242 B.R. 599 (S.D. W. Va. 1999) (enforcement of West Virginia statute prohibiting direct communications with a debtor represented by counsel "in no way impedes administration of bankruptcy case"); Greenwood Trust Co. v. Smith, 212 B.R. 599, 603 (B.A.P. 8th Cir. 1997) (Iowa state collection law does not impede creditor's rights under Bankruptcy Code relating to negotiation of reaffirmation agreements); *In re* Walker, 180 B.R. 834 (Bankr. W.D. La. 1995) (violation of discharge injunction is unfair trade practice); *In re* Aponte, 82 B.R. 738 (Bankr. E.D. Pa. 1988) (debtor awarded damages under Pennsylvania Unfair Trade Practices and Consumer Protection Act for creditor's violation of the automatic stay).

614 Sears, Roebuck and Co. v. O'Brien, 178 F.3d 962, 966–67 (8th Cir. 1999).

The volume examines a number of important exceptions to the general rule that the Federal Arbitration Act (FAA) requires enforcement of arbitration agreements. The FAA states that arbitration agreements are enforceable "save upon such grounds as exist at law or in equity for the revocation of any contract."[615] In addition, while the FAA enforces agreements to arbitrate, it does not require arbitration where there is no agreement to arbitrate a dispute.[616] State contract law determines if there is a binding agreement to arbitrate, and whether an agreement that does exist is revocable.[617]

An arbitration clause thus is not enforceable if:

- A binding agreement has never been formed, such as where the document is not signed, it was not entered into voluntarily and knowingly, or the arbitration agreement was sent after the contract was consummated;[618]
- The dispute is outside the scope of the arbitration agreement;[619]
- The consumer is suing someone not a party to the arbitration agreement;[620]
- The consumer bringing the suit has not signed the arbitration agreement;[621]
- The arbitration clause is unconscionable, because it is not mutual, it restricts statutory remedies or rights, it creates excessive fees, involves arbitrator bias or an inconvenient venue, or the agreement involved procedural unconscionability;[622]
- The contract is void because of fraud in the factum, illegality, or because the contract has been cancelled;[623]
- The arbitration clause, not the whole contract, is induced by misrepresentation;[624]
- The corporation has waived its rights under the arbitration clause by instituting litigation or by waiting too long in a case to demand that it be sent to arbitration;[625] or
- Other standard contract defenses apply, such as duress, competency, or minority.[626]

Where an arbitration agreement limits federal statutory rights or remedies, a conflict is created between the federal statute and the FAA. A court may determine that the Congressional intent is that the other federal statute prevails over the FAA, and that the arbitration agreement should not be enforced. Important examples of this are:

- The Bankruptcy Code's requirement that claims be presented to the bankruptcy court;[627]
- Arbitration clauses that limit a federal law's statutory remedies, such as attorney fees, statutory damages, the right to bring a class action, injunctive relief and the statute of limitations;[628] and
- High arbitration fees that effectively prevent vindication of federal statutory rights.[629]

Courts reach differing conclusions as to whether the Magnuson-Moss Warranty Act's provisions for informal dispute resolution conflict with a binding arbitration requirement.[630] Even if warranty disputes can be resolved through binding arbitration, the Magnuson-Moss Warranty Act requires that the warrantor clearly disclose that requirement in the written warranty.[631]

The Federal Arbitration Act preempts state laws that limit the enforceability of arbitration agreements.[632] But there are important exceptions:

- State law may limit the enforceability of an arbitration agreement in an insurance transactions, because of the operation of the McCarran-Ferguson Act;[633]
- The FAA applies only to transactions in interstate commerce and some courts have found real estate sales, home improvements, or similar transactions not to be in interstate commerce;[634] and
- If the state law applies to any agreement, and not just to an arbitration agreement, then that state law is not preempted, even if its effect is to limit the enforceability of an arbitration agreement.[635]
- State law can regulate arbitration service providers, such as requiring certain disclosures, and prohibiting the provider from participating in arbitrations where there is a conflict of interest.[636]

NCLC's *Consumer Arbitration Agreements* also covers such key topics as:

- The consumer's right to discovery relating to the enforceability of the arbitration clause;[637]

615 9 U.S.C. § 2.
616 National Consumer Law Center, Consumer Arbitration Agreements § 2.4 (4th ed. 2004).
617 *Id.*
618 *Id.* at Ch. 3.
619 *Id.* § 6.2.5.
620 *Id.* § 6.3.
621 *Id.* § 6.4.
622 *Id.* §§ 4.2, 4.3.
623 *Id.* § 4.5.
624 *Id.* § 4.6.
625 *Id.* at Ch. 7.
626 *Id.* §§ 4.7, 4.8, 4.9.

627 *Id.* § 5.2.3.
628 *Id.* § 5.3.
629 *Id.* § 5.4.
630 *Id.* § 5.2.2.
631 *Id.*
632 *Id.* § 2.2.
633 *Id.* § 2.3.3.
634 *Id.* § 2.3.1.
635 *Id.* § 2.3.4.
636 *Id.* § 2.2
637 *Id.* § 9.1.

- The right for a jury to decide whether the clause is enforceable;[638]
- Whether the determination as to enforceability can be removed to federal court;[639]
- Whether arbitration claims can proceed on a classwide basis;[640]
- Appeals from judicial orders relating to arbitration;[641] and
- Judicial enforcement and modification of the arbitrator's decision.[642]

Another issue related to the enforceability of an arbitration agreement is whether use of an unenforceable arbitration provision is a UDAP violation. This would provide a claim affirmatively to enjoin the use of the provision for all of a company's customers. Such a UDAP claim is examined at § 5.2.3.5, *supra*.

In addition, issues arise as to availability in arbitration proceedings of UDAP class actions, UDAP multiple or punitive damages, UDAP injunctive relief, and UDAP attorney fees. These are examined at §§ 8.4.2.5, 8.4.3.5, 8.5.9, 8.6.4, and 8.8.5, *infra*.

7.7 Pleading and Framing UDAP Claims

7.7.1 Complying with Notice Letter, Public Interest, Damage, and Scope Requirements

A first step in drafting a UDAP complaint or counterclaim is to determine if the state UDAP statute has special provisions requiring the consumer to send a demand letter prior to filing suit. Such a requirement should be followed strictly, as failure to do so will have severe adverse consequences in some jurisdictions.[643]

Special care should be given to complying with any notice requirement, including the content of the notice, which parties should receive notice, and how and when the notice is to be delivered. Well-represented defendants will always question the adequacy of such notice, but a consumer's attorney, with a little care, can easily comply with such requirements beyond any possible challenge. Remember that requirements may apply not just to UDAP claims, but also to UDAP counterclaims.

It is prudent to allege clearly in the consumer's complaint that any applicable notice requirement has been met. Introduce the notice into evidence at the first opportunity, or even better, attach a copy of the notice to the complaint. Such specificity in the pleading may force the defendant to admit that proper notice was provided, making proof at trial unnecessary. If there is to be an issue over notice, it is best to discover this at the onset of the litigation. Place the burden on the defendant to dispute the adequacy of the notice. If the consumer sent notice prior to being represented, it is good practice to send a new notice before filing suit if there is any possible question as to the adequacy of the original notice.

A few states require, as another precondition to a UDAP claim, that the action be in the public interest.[644] In these states, it is important that the complaint allege facts, such as prior acts affecting other consumers, a potential for repetition, or the existence of a policy or standard practice on the defendant's part.[645]

Most UDAP statutes require, as a precondition of suit, that the consumer have suffered some damage.[646] Consumer advocates in these states should make sure to allege in the pleading that the consumer was damaged.[647] Normally a damage requirement is not a problem because consumers will only pursue claims where they can recover damages, but it can become an issue in class or injunctive actions, or in situations where minimum damages are sought. It is important to remember that damage requirements, where applicable, do not specify how much damage. Thus a long-distance telephone call to an attorney in an inconvenient venue case or bus fare for alternative transportation in a defective automobile case may be enough. Moreover, the damage probably need not be proven, just be "ascertainable," that is, capable of being discovered. Even in states where damage is not a precondition of suit, the rules of court may require some types of damages, such as "special damages," to be specifically pleaded if the consumer seeks to recover them.

The complaint should also specifically allege how the UDAP statute's scope requirements have been met.[648] This

638 *Id.* § 9.2.
639 *Id.* § 9.3.
640 *Id.* § 9.4.
641 *Id.* § 9.5.
642 *Id.* at Ch. 10.
643 *See* § 7.5.4, *supra*.

644 *See* § 7.5.3, *supra*.
645 Greenspan v. Allstate Ins. Co., 937 F. Supp. 288 (S.D.N.Y. 1996) (UDAP suit dismissed for failure to plead public injury); Brody v. Finch University of Health Sciences, 698 N.E.2d 257 (Ill. App. Ct. 1998) (judgment for defendant upheld because plaintiff failed to plead and prove consumer nexus).
646 *See* § 7.5.2, *supra*.
647 *See* Gonzalez v. Old Kent Mortgage Co., 2000 U.S. Dist. LEXIS 14530 (E.D. Pa. Sept. 19, 2000) (dismissing UDAP claim because ascertainable loss was pleaded only as a legal conclusion).
648 Pergament v. Green, 32 Conn. App. 644, 630 A.2d 615 (1993) (UDAP claim dismissed because complaint did not allege that acts were performed in trade or business); Connick v. Suzuki Motor Co., Ltd., 275 Ill. App. 3d 705, 656 N.E.2d 170 (1995) (Pennsylvania UDAP claim dismissed because of failure to allege that purchase was for personal, family, or household use), *aff'd in part, rev'd in part on other grounds*, 174 Ill. 2d 482, 675 N.E.2d 584, 221 Ill. Dec. 389 (1996); Cameron v. Terrell &

will defeat a Rule 12(b)(6)-type motion. More importantly, it will assist the consumer litigant, early in the litigation, to analyze and clarify scope issues carefully. In particular, the complaint should allege, as applicable, that the consumer is a consumer, that a consumer transaction is involved, or that "goods or services" have been sold or leased. The Texas Supreme Court, however, has ruled that the defendant has the burden of pleading and proving that the plaintiff falls within a specific exception to UDAP coverage.[649]

Some states may also have special pleading requirements that will apply to some types of UDAP claims. For example, a UDAP claim against a physician for misrepresenting the benefits of a silicone breast implant was dismissed for failure to comply with a Colorado requirement, applicable to malpractice-type claims, that the plaintiff certify that an expert had reviewed the claim and found it justifiable.[650] But this requirement is not applicable where the UDAP claim does not involve professional negligence.[651]

7.7.2 Choosing the Plaintiff

It is always preferable to bring a UDAP claim in the name of the person who made the actual purchase and received the deceptive sales presentation. Problems may arise if third-party beneficiaries or others bring an action.[652]

Bringing a claim as a class, not an individual action, complicates a case and adds to expenses, but if the class is certified, an agreed or litigated order for widespread and significant relief, including attorney fees, is possible. UDAP claims are more amenable to class actions than common law fraud claims because the elements of the claim are less strict.[653]

7.7.3 Choosing the Defendants

When bringing an affirmative suit, as a general rule, consumers are better off naming multiple defendants, particularly when a company's financial stability is questionable. The consumer's attorney should always look for the deep pocket, for the defendant with assets within the jurisdiction, and for the party who will remain in the state. Certain classes of sellers are notorious for financial instability and mobility. The advocate should bear in mind, however, that naming extra parties as defendants complicates and delays the litigation and increases the amount of legal talent for the opposition.

Consumers too often neglect one of the most important UDAP defendants—the creditor who is financing the transaction. In defending a collection action, the consumer can bring seller-related counterclaims and defenses against assignees and related creditors, particularly where the FTC Holder Rule notice is in the credit agreement.[654] The consumer's attorney should also consider adding new parties, such as the original seller, to the creditor's collection action. This may avoid statute of limitations problems that would prevent an affirmative action against the seller. Suing the seller may also result in a larger recovery, particularly where treble or punitive damages are awarded, because the creditor's derivative liability for the acts of the seller typically is capped at the amount of the debt.[655] Bringing in the seller also may lead to a situation where the creditor or assignee attempts to prove that the original seller was at fault, thus helping the consumer's case.

In naming a company as a defendant, care must be taken to name the right corporation, using its proper name. The attorney should check with the secretary of state or other agency for the proper name and address for service. The government agency can also tell whether the corporation is in good standing or has been involuntarily or voluntarily dissolved. This may affect the consumer's strategies in naming defendants. If a defendant's answer to the complaint leaves open any question about whether it was correctly named, early discovery is critical.

It is always worthwhile to check whether a company or individual is bonded. For example, in most states car dealers and vocational schools are required to be bonded, although the size of the bond is typically small. If a company disappears, the bond may be sufficient to cover some consumer claims. Recoveries, including multiple damages and attorney fees, may be allowed against sureties. But the bond may cover only certain types of claims, so counsel should make sure to plead and prove appropriate claims. State practice varies as to whether the surety and seller can be joined in the same UDAP action, or whether a judgment first must be separately obtained against the seller.[656] Another possibility is to consider a negligence or other claim that falls within the scope of a company's liability insurance policy.[657]

Garrett, Inc., 618 S.W.2d 535 (Tex. 1981); River Oaks Townhomes Owners' Ass'n v. Bunt, 712 S.W.2d 529 (Tex. App. 1986). *Cf.* Gapas v. Hambleton, 1980 Ohio App. LEXIS 11295, Clearinghouse No. 46,632 (Nov. 20, 1980) (consumer must prove personal, family, or household use at trial to establish UDAP coverage). *But see* Reed v. Israel Nat'l Oil Co., 681 S.W.2d 228 (Tex. App. 1984) (court may find that facts establish coverage even though it was not pleaded and may infer coverage from the totality of the pleadings); Ridco v. Sexton, 623 S.W.2d 792 (Tex. Civ. App. 1981) (court may infer coverage from the totality of the pleadings).

649 Eckman v. Centennial Savings Bank, 784 S.W.2d 672 (Tex. 1990) (exclusion for business consumers with assets of $25 million or more).

650 Teiken v. Reynolds, 904 P.2d 1387 (Colo. App. 1995).

651 Baumgarten v. Coppage, 15 P.3d 304 (Colo. App. 2000).

652 *See* § 2.4.1, *supra.*

653 *See* § 8.5.4.2, *infra.*

654 *See* § 6.6, *supra.*

655 *Id.*

656 *See* § 6.10, *supra.*

657 *Id.*

The consumer's attorney should not neglect as possible UDAP defendants individual sales representatives, corporate officers, owners, advertising agencies, and others who directly participated in or supervised a scheme.[658] Those who aid or abet a scheme may also be liable, such as wholesalers, financiers, lawyers, franchisors, advertising agents, accountants, and perhaps even standard form contract publishers.[659] Certainly anyone who actively participates in a scheme can be held liable.

Sellers often argue that the individual responsible for the UDAP violation is an independent contractor, not the seller's agent. But even separate entities can be the seller's agent. Substance prevails over form. Further, companies can be liable for the actions of their independent contractors.[660]

Shareholders, owners, and related corporations may be liable under a piercing of the corporate veil, corporate disregard, or related theory. Such a theory should be considered at the pleading stage if there is any suspicion that the corporation itself is thinly capitalized or that the principals might voluntarily dissolve the corporation or allow it to become involuntarily dissolved by failing to comply with state requirements.[661]

Not only assignees, but also related creditors and credit card issuers often are subject to the affirmative claims the consumer has against the seller.[662] Consequently, the consumer can bring affirmative actions against assignees and related creditors, at least in an amount equaling the debt. A creditor's liability may go beyond the amount of the debt if it knowingly aided the fraud by providing the seller access to loan money that enabled the seller to sign up new victims.[663] Intermediaries that assist sellers in processing consumer payments may also be liable for the seller's fraud.[664] In certain situations, franchisors are liable for the acts of their franchisees.[665]

7.7.4 *Framing the Nature of the Suit*

Early on in a case, the consumer's attorney should carefully consider the possible damage award. This will shape the complaint and help determine the legal resources devoted to a case. Not only out-of-pocket damages, but also loss-of-bargain damages and such consequential damages as emotional distress should be investigated. If an item is represented as worth $200, is sold for $50, and is worth $25, consider seeking $175 damages, not $25. For an emotional distress claim, the attorney should talk to relatives and friends, see if the client went to a clinic, and see if the client lost sleep or suffered headaches, nausea, or crying spells.[666]

One attorney uses what he calls the "smell test" to evaluate a case. On a Saturday, he rounds up five random people near his office, pays them each $20, and asks them to listen to mock arguments that he and a friend present for both sides of the case. After an hour or two of presentations, the audience gives candid feedback about the case over a pizza: what evidence they would want before they are willing to assess large punitive damages, what they think of the client (if the client's demeanor is an issue, they get to meet the client), and the like. This is much less expensive than a full mock jury trial, but the attorney reports that the results are useful.

Where individual consumer damage is minimal, but the practice is obnoxious and widespread, the attorney and the consumer should consider the availability of an injunction preventing the seller from engaging in a similar practice in the future. Such an injunction may be more threatening to a seller than a treble damages award.[667]

The consumer should also consider a temporary restraining order or a preliminary injunction. Aside from putting the seller immediately on the defensive, the motion can expedite discovery and settlement of the case. Consumer litigants will find that seeking immediate preliminary injunctions against the seller's system of doing business is a far more potent approach than bringing an individual damage action that will be resolved several years in the future.[668]

A class action is another worthwhile approach where the individual consumer's damages are small but the seller's practice is widespread.[669] An important advantage of the class action, noted by several courts, is that it allows consumers with relatively small claims, who would otherwise have no efficient remedy, to join together to pursue them.[670]

If the UDAP claim is being pleaded in the answer to a creditor's complaint, rather than as an affirmative suit, the attorney should keep in mind state pleading rules when framing the claim as an affirmative defense or a counterclaim. An Ohio court and an Indiana court have held that UDAP claims should not be pleaded as affirmative defenses, but only as counterclaims.[671] Whether UDAP counterclaims

658 *See* §§ 6.2, 6.4, *supra*.
659 *See* § 6.5, *supra*.
660 *See* § 6.3.2, *supra*.
661 *See* § 6.4.3, *supra*.
662 *See* § 6.6, *supra*.
663 *See* § 6.5, *supra*.
664 *See* §§ 6.5.3, 6.5.4, *supra*.
665 *See* § 6.4.4, *supra*.

666 *See* §§ 8.3.3.8, 8.3.3.9, *infra*.
667 *See* § 8.6.1, *infra*.
668 *Id.*
669 *See* National Consumer Law Center, Consumer Law Pleadings, No. 1, §§ 2.1, 3.1, 4.3, 9.1 (CD-Rom and Index Guide) for examples of class action complaints under the California, New Mexico, Illinois and Connecticut UDAP statutes and National Consumer Law Center, Consumer Law Pleadings, No. 2, §§ 1.4, 2.1, 4.2, and 11.2 (CD-Rom and Index Guide) for examples of class action complaints under the New York, Vermont, Pennsylvania, and New Mexico UDAP statutes. These pleadings are also found on the CD-Rom accompanying this volume.
670 *See* § 8.5.3, *infra*.
671 Johnson v. Anderson, 590 N.E.2d 1146 (Ind. Ct. App. 1992); Atelier Design, Inc. v. Campbell, 68 Ohio App. 3d 724, 589 N.E.2d 474 (1990).

can be asserted in response to a specialized type of suit such as an eviction depends on state law.[672]

7.7.5 Elements to Plead

Some state courts have developed standard lists of elements for a UDAP claim:

- *Colorado*: (1) the defendant engaged in an unfair or deceptive trade practice; (2) the challenged practice occurred in the course of defendant's business, vocation, or occupation; (3) it significantly impacts the public as actual or potential consumers of the defendant's goods, services, or property; (4) the plaintiff suffered injury in fact to a legally protected interest; and (5) the challenged practice caused the plaintiff's injury.[673]
- *Georgia*: A private claim under the Fair Business Practices Act has three essential elements: a violation of the act, causation, and injury.[674] Case law also requires a showing of potential harm to the consumer public or an impact on the consumer marketplace.[675]
- *Hawaii*: (1) a violation of Haw. Rev. Stat. § 480-2, *i.e.*, an unfair method of competition or unfair or deceptive act or practice; (2) injury to the consumer caused by such a violation; and (3) proof of the amount of damages.[676]
- *Illinois*: (1) a deceptive act or practice by the defendant; (2) an intent by the defendant that the plaintiff rely on the deception; and (3) that the deception occurred in the course of conduct involving trade or commerce.[677] Some cases add two more elements for a private cause of action: (4) actual damage to the plaintiff (5) proximately caused by the deception.[678]
- *Minnesota*: (1) there must be an intentional misrepresentation relating to the sale of merchandise, and (2) the misrepresentation must have caused damage to the plaintiff.[679] Case law also requires UDAP claims to meet a public interest test.[680]
- *New Hampshire*: (1) the defendant is a person; (2) the defendant used an unfair method of competition or a deceptive act or practice; and (3) the act occurred in trade or commerce.[681]
- *New Jersey*: (1) unlawful conduct by the defendants; (2) an ascertainable loss on the part of the plaintiff; and (3) a causal relationship between the defendants' unlawful conduct and the plaintiff's ascertainable loss.[682]
- *New York*: (1) the act or practice is deceptive or misleading in a material respect and (2) the plaintiff has been injured as a result.[683] A broader impact on consumers at large must also be shown.[684]
- *North Carolina*: (1) an unfair or deceptive act or practice (2) in or affecting commerce (3) which proximately caused injury to plaintiffs.[685]
- *Oklahoma*: (1) the defendant engaged in an unlawful practice as defined at 15 Okla. Stat. § 753; (2) the challenged practice occurred in the course of defendant's business; (3) the plaintiff, as a consumer, suffered an injury in fact; and (4) the challenged practice caused the plaintiff's injury.[686]
- *Oregon*: An intermediate appellate decision describes the elements as: (1) a violation of Or. Rev. Stat. § 646.608(1), which is the "laundry list" of prohibited acts and practices; (2) causation; and (3) damage.[687] A decision by the state supreme court adds that, for a private cause of action, there must be proof that the

672 Hoffer v. Szumski, 129 Or. App. 7, 877 P.2d 128 (1994) (UDAP counterclaim may be asserted if eviction suit also seeks money judgment). *See also* National Consumer Law Center, Truth in Lending § 7.6.8 (5th ed. 2003 and Supp.) (discussion of similar issue in context of raising TIL claims in foreclosure cases).

673 Martinez v. Lewis, 969 P.2d 213 (Colo. 1998); Hall v. Walter, 969 P.2d 224 (Colo. 1998).

674 Catrett v. Landmark Dodge, Inc., 253 Ga. App. 639, 560 S.E.2d 101 (2002); Moore-Davis Motors, Inc. v. Joyner, 252 Ga. App. 617, 556 S.E.2d 137 (2001).

675 *See* § 7.5.3.6, *supra*.

676 King v. International Data Servs., 2002 WL 32345923 (D. Haw. Aug. 5, 2002).

677 *See, e.g.*, Thacker v. Menard, Inc., 105 F.3d 382 (7th Cir. 1997) (Illinois law); Robinson v. Toyota Motor Credit Corp., 201 Ill. 2d 403, 775 N.E.2d 951, 266 Ill. Dec. 879 (2002); Weatherman v. Gary-Wheaton Bank, 186 Ill. 2d 472, 713 N.E.2d 543 (1999); Cripe v. Leiter, 184 Ill. 2d 185, 703 N.E.2d 100 (1998); Connick v. Suzuki Motor Co., 174 Ill. 2d 482, 675 N.E.2d 584 (1996). *See also* Jenkins v. Mercantile Mortg. Co., 213 F. Supp. 2d 737 (N.D. Ill. 2002).

678 Oliveira v. Amoco Oil Co., 201 Ill. 2d 134, 776 N.E.2d 151, 267 Ill. Dec. 14 (2002); Weis v. State Farm Mut. Auto. Ins. Co., 333 Ill. App. 3d 402, 776 N.E.2d 309, 267 Ill. Dec. 172 (2002).

679 Wiegand v. Walser Automotive Groups, Inc., 2003 WL 22434678 (Minn. App. Oct. 28, 2003).

680 *See* 7.5.3.4, *supra*.

681 Milford Lumber Co. v. RCB Realty, Inc., 780 A.2d 1259 (N.H. 2001).

682 N.J. Citizen Action v. Schering-Plough Corp., 367 N.J. Super. 8, 842 A.2d 174 (App. Div. 2003).

683 Goshen v. Mut. Life Ins. Co., 98 N.Y.2d 314, 774 N.E.2d 1190 (2002); Oswego Laborers' Local 214 Pension Fund v. Marine Midland Bank, N.A., 85 N.Y.2d 20, 647 N.E.2d 741 (1995); *see also* Steinmetz v. Toyota Motor Credit Corp., 963 F. Supp. 1294 (E.D.N.Y. 1997); Northwestern Mut. Life Ins. Co. v. Wender, 940 F. Supp. 62 (S.D.N.Y. 1996).

684 *See* § 7.5.3.8, *supra*.

685 Gray v. North Carolina Ins. Underwriting Ass'n, 352 N.C. 61, 529 S.E.2d 676 (2000).

686 Patterson v. Beall, 19 P.3d 839 (Okla. 2000).

687 Feitler v. Animation Celection, Inc., 13 P.3d 1044 (Or. App. 2000). *See also* Rathgeber v. James Hemenway, Inc., 69 P.3d 710 (Or. 2003) (describing elements in a particular factual context as (1) a representation by defendants, (2) in the course of defendants' business, (3) that an employee had qualifications, (4) which in fact he did not have, when (5) defendants knew or should have known that the representation would constitute a violation of the UDAP statute), *aff'd on other grounds*, 69 P.3d 710 (Or. 2003).

violation was willful, *i.e.*, that the defendant knew or should have known, at the time of the representations, that they would not be carried out.[688]

- *Pennsylvania*: (1) the plaintiff is a purchaser or lessee; (2) the transaction deals with goods or services; (3) the good or service was primarily for personal, family, or household purposes; (4) the plaintiff suffered damages arising from the purchase or lease of goods or services; (5) the defendant was engaged in unfair methods of competition and unfair or deceptive acts or practices; and (6) the transaction between plaintiff and defendant constituted trade or commerce.[689]
- *South Carolina*: The cases do not list elements, but do require a showing of impact on the public interest, such as a potential for repetition.[690]
- *Texas*: (1) the plaintiff is a "consumer" as defined by the act; (2) the defendant engaged in false, misleading, or deceptive acts; and (3) these acts constituted a "producing cause" of the plaintiff's damages.[691] Although failure to send a pre-suit notice is a defense, at least one federal court has held that the burden is on the plaintiff to plead that he gave the UDAP notice.[692]
- *Vermont*: a "deceptive act or practice" requires (1) a representation, omission, or practice likely to mislead consumers; (2) the consumer must be interpreting the message reasonably under the circumstances; and (3) the misleading effects must be material, *i.e.*, likely to affect the consumer's conduct or decision regarding the product.[693]
- *Washington*: (1) an unfair or deceptive act or practice, (2) occurring in the conduct of trade or commerce, (3) affecting the public interest, (4) that injures the plaintiff's business or property, (5) with a causal connection between the act or practice and the injury.[694]

7.7.6 Allegations Should Be Specific

General allegations avoid tipping the litigant's hand too early. However, a definite, specific, organized complaint assists the consumer litigant in organizing the case and increases the credibility of the consumer's case for the judge and opposing attorneys.[695] This is particularly important since many UDAP statutes themselves are so general and broad.

Even if the consumer litigant opts for a broad allegation of deception in the pleadings, the litigant should still, for internal use, draft a detailed, precise outline of the facts and the specific violations alleged. Be prepared for the local media, and not just the courts, to review and analyze UDAP pleadings. The impact of publicity on certain types of companies is easy to underestimate.

Where a UDAP statute prohibits specifically enumerated practices and also has a general "catch-all" prohibition, consumers should specify itemized prohibitions in which the seller has engaged, and also allege a violation of the "catch-all" prohibition. While violation of a specific prohibition may be easier to prove, "catch-all" allegations are more likely to survive motions for dismissal or summary judgment. They will also allow a wider range of proof, allow consumers to raise new facts at the summary judgment stage, and improve the chances that amendments to the complaint relate back to the first filing for purposes of the statute of limitations. Allegations of fraud, where appropriate, are also likely to avoid summary judgment.

Almost as persuasive as alleging a violation of a specific practice prohibited by a state UDAP statute is an allegation that the seller has violated a specified state UDAP regulation or state or federal law.[696] It is always best to plead the specific regulation that the defendant has violated, but a citation to the UDAP statute may be sufficient to bring UDAP regulations into issue as well.[697] In Delaware, Georgia, Hawaii, Illinois, Maine, Minnesota, Nebraska, Ohio, and Oklahoma, consumer litigants should also consider alleging violations of the laundry list found in the state's UDTPA statute as a violation of the other state UDAP statute.[698]

Since some courts still have to be educated to treat UDAP claims seriously, a brief but compelling recitation of seller abuses in the complaint may be appropriate to indicate that a wrong has been done that compels a remedy. For similar reasons, a consumer's attorney may decide to estimate in the pleadings as precisely as possible many of the damages being claimed. This also assists the consumer litigant to organize the case and prepare for discovery. Where available and appropriate, minimum, treble or punitive damages, attorney fees, and other special remedies should be clearly requested. If the seller defaults, the consumer can prove the

---

688 Rathgeber v. Hemenway, Inc., 69 P.3d 710 (Or. 2003).

689 Keller v. Volkswagen of Am., Inc., 733 A.2d 642 (Pa. Super. 1999).

690 *See* § 7.5.3.7, *supra.*

691 Doe v. Boys Clubs of Greater Dallas, Inc., 907 S.W.2d 472 (Tex. 1995); Roberts v. Healey, 991 S.W.2d 873 (Tex. App. 1999); *see also* Petri v. Gatlin, 997 F. Supp. 956 (N.D. Ill. 1997) (Texas law).

692 Patel v. Holiday Hospitality Franchising, Inc., 172 F. Supp. 2d 821 (N.D. Tex. 2001). *See* § 7.5.2, *supra.*

693 Carter v. Gugliuzzi, 716 A.2d 17 (Vt. 1998). *Accord* Jordan v. Nissan North America, Inc., 2004 WL 595413 (Vt. Mar. 26, 2004).

694 Hayden v. Mutual of Enumclaw Ins. Co., 141 Wash. 2d 55, 1 P.3d 1167 (2000). *See* § 7.5.3.2, *supra.*

695 See National Consumer Law Center, Consumer Law Pleadings, No. 1, §§ 2.1, 3.1, 4.3, 7.1 and 9.1 (CD-Rom and Index Guide) for examples of UDAP complaints from California, New Mexico, Illinois, Massachusetts and Connecticut. These pleadings are also found on the CD-Rom accompanying this volume.

696 *See* §§ 3.2.3, 3.2.7, *supra.*

697 Robinson v. McDougal, 62 Ohio App. 3d 253, 575 N.E.2d 469 (1988).

698 *See* § 3.2.5, *supra.*

prerequisites of and recover these remedies even though the seller never contests the case. A catch-all request for damages and such other relief as the court deems appropriate may protect litigants who leave out a potential remedy.[699]

In collection cases, UDAP counterclaims should be as specific as possible, as well as containing a catch-all allegation, citing to applicable statutory and regulatory violations. This increases the consumer litigant's credibility in pretrial negotiations. Otherwise, courts tend to regard such claims merely as attempts to delay judgment.

Care should also be taken to include all UDAP compulsory counterclaims; otherwise, the claims may be lost depending on the state's rules regarding compulsory counterclaims. Some states require UDAP claims to be raised as counterclaims rather than defenses.[700] Nevertheless, depending on a state's procedure and the facts of a case, consumer litigants may also wish to incorporate the UDAP counterclaim into the defenses so that an action for recoupment will survive as a defense if the counterclaim is dismissed.

Where it is clear that a state UDAP statute does not require intent, scienter, or reliance, the complaint should not plead these elements. When it is possible that such elements are required, they should be clearly pleaded. If intent or wrongful motive is relevant only to a claim for punitive damages, minimum damages or multiple damages, the pleading should phrase these allegations so that their purpose and relevance is clear.

Some courts apply Federal Rule of Civil Procedure 9(b) or a state equivalent to UDAP claims, requiring that averments of each element of the claim be pleaded with particularity.[701] This holding is unnecessarily restrictive, in light of the liberal construction required of UDAP statutes and the clear distinction between UDAP statutes and com-

699 *Cf.* Rowan Heating-Air Conditioning v. Williams, 580 A.2d 583 (D.C. 1990) (pleading a violation of the state UDAP statute was sufficient to put the dealer on notice that it was subject to all penalties provided for by the statute); Robinson v. McDougal, 62 Ohio App. 3d 253, 575 N.E.2d 469 (1988) (giving notice that consumer intended to rely on UDAP statute placed defendant on notice that UDAP regulations and other portions of UDAP statute would also be relevant).

700 *See* § 7.7.8, *supra*.

701 *In re* Rey-Willis v. Citibank, N.A., 2004 WL 315267 (S.D.N.Y. Feb. 18, 2004); Universal Service Fund Telephone Billing Practices Litig., 300 F. Supp. 2d 1107, 1150 (D. Kan. 2003); Ergonomic Lighting Sys., Inc. v. Commercial Petroleum Equipment/USALCO, 2003 WL 22436101 (W.D. Tex. Oct. 21, 2003); Rey-Willis v. Citibank, N.A., 2003 WL 21714947 (S.D.N.Y. July 23, 2003); Fidelity Mortg. Corp. v. Seattle Times Co., 213 F.R.D. 573 (W.D. Wash. 2003); Stephenson v. Hartford Life & Annuity Ins. Co., 2003 WL 22232968 (N.D. Ill. Sept. 26, 2003) (Colorado and Illinois UDAP statutes); Stires v. Carnival Corp., 243 F. Supp. 2d 1313, 1322 (M.D. Fla. 2002); Cannon v. Metro Ford, Inc., 242 F. Supp. 2d 1322, 1332 (S.D. Fla. 2002); Michalowski v. Flagstar Bank, 2002 U.S. Dist. LEXIS 1245 (N.D. Ill. Jan. 24, 2002) (finding plaintiff's allegations sufficiently specific); Lilly v. Ford Motor Co., 2002 U.S. Dist. LEXIS 910 (N.D. Ill. Jan. 17, 2002) (finding plaintiff's allegations sufficiently specific); Fisher v. Quality Hyundai, Inc., 2002 U.S. Dist. LEXIS 407 (N.D. Ill. Jan. 8, 2002) (finding allegations sufficient); Cinalli v. Kane, 191 F. Supp. 2d 601 (E.D. Pa. 2002); Patel v. Holiday Hospitality Franchising, Inc., 172 F. Supp. 2d 821 (N.D. Tex. 2001); Chatman v. Fairbanks Capital Corp., 2002 WL 1338492 (N.D. Ill. June 18, 2002); Bell Enterprises Venture v. Santanna Natural Gas Corp., 2001 U.S. Dist. LEXIS 23684 (N.D. Ill. Dec. 7, 2001); Williamson v. Allstate Ins. Co., 204 F.R.D. 641 (D. Ariz. 2001) (UDAP and UNIP claims must be pleaded with particularity and must identify specific statutory provision that defendant is alleged to have violated); Tuttle v. Lorillard Tobacco Co., 118 F. Supp. 2d 954 (D. Minn. 2000) (rejecting argument that Rule 9(b) should not apply because UDAP is less strict than fraud); Naporano Iron & Metal Co. v. American Crane Corp., 79 F. Supp. 2d 494 (D.N.J. 1999); Jackson v. Philip Morris Inc., 46 F. Supp. 2d 1217 (D. Utah 1998); Frith v. Guardian Life Ins. Co., 9 F. Supp. 2d 734 (S.D. Tex. 1998); Petri v. Gatlin, 997 F. Supp. 956 (N.D. Ill. 1997); Witherspoon v. Philip Morris Inc., 964 F. Supp. 455 (D.D.C. 1997); Brooks v. Bank of Boulder, 891 F. Supp. 1469 (D. Colo. 1995) (allegations regarding bank's promotion of pyramid scheme must be pleaded with particularity); Burton v. R.J. Reynolds Tobacco Co., 884 F. Supp. 1515 (D. Kan. 1995); Gerdes v. John Hancock Mut. Life Ins. Co., 712 F. Supp. 692 (N.D. Ill. 1989); Wislow v. Wong, 713 F. Supp. 1103 (N.D. Ill. 1989); NCC Sunday Inserts, Inc. v. World Color Press, Inc., 692 F. Supp. 327 (S.D.N.Y. 1988) (UDAP must be pleaded with particularity where the UDAP claim alleges fraudulent intent and where the action is brought in federal court); Duran v. Clover Club Foods, Co., 616 F. Supp. 790 (D. Colo. 1985); Connick v. Suzuki Motor Co., 174 Ill. 2d 482, 675 N.E.2d 584 (1996); People *ex rel.* Hartigan v. E&E Hauling, Inc., 153 Ill. 2d 473, 607 N.E.2d 165 (1992) (commercial case); Paul H. Schwendener, Inc. v. Larrabee Commons Partners, 338 Ill. App. 3d 19, 787 N.E.2d 192, 201 (2003); Elson v. State Farm Fire & Cas. Co., 691 N.E.2d 807 (Ill. App. Ct. 1998); Mitchell v. Normal James Constr. Co., 684 N.E.2d 872 (Ill. App. Ct. 1997); Spengler v. V&R Marathon, Inc., 162 Ill. App. 3d 715, 516 N.E.2d 787 (1987); Saladino v. Team Chevrolet, Inc., 611 N.E.2d 583 (Ill. App. Ct. 1993); Popp v. Cash Station Inc., 613 N.E.2d 1150 (Ill. App. Ct. 1992); State *ex rel.* Zimmerman v. National Apartment Leasing Co., 102 Pa. Commw. 623, 519 A.2d 1050 (1989); Lindstrom v. Pennswood Village, 612 A.2d 1048 (Pa. Super. Ct. 1992); Nelson v. Stine, Davis & Peck Ins., 7 Pa. D. & C.4th 415 (C.P. 1990); Vermont v. Rosenberg, Clearinghouse No. 51,264A (Vt. Super. Ct. Feb. 24, 1992) (court applies Rule 9(b) standard but holds that details of each transaction need not be pleaded). *See also* Grant v. Kingswood Apts., 2001 U.S. Dist. LEXIS 15815 (E.D. Pa. Oct. 2, 2001) (predicting that Pennsylvania Supreme Court will require UDAP claims to be pleaded with same specificity as fraud); DeLeon v. Beneficial Constr. Co., 998 F. Supp. 859 (N.D. Ill. 1998) (must be made with specificity); Cobb v. Monarch Fin. Co., 913 F. Supp. 1164 (N.D. Ill. 1995) (declining to decide whether Rule 9(b) applies to UDAP claims, but holding that it does not require more than usual detail in pleading damages); Moye v. Credit Acceptance Corp., 2000 Conn. Super. LEXIS 3072 (Nov. 3, 2000) (plaintiffs can not proceed with UDAP claim where no ascertainable loss alleged except in conclusory language); Harvey v. Ford Motor Credit Co., 8 S.W.3d 273 (Tenn. App. 1999). The Pennsylvania cases may no longer be controlling in light of 1997 statutory changes that make it clear that common-law fraud need not be shown under the "catch-all" UDAP prohibition.

mon law fraud,[702] and a number of courts have rejected it.[703] Other courts require UDAP claims to be pleaded, but not with the same particularity as fraud claims.[704] The California Supreme Court holds that "a plaintiff need not plead the exact language of every deceptive statement; it is sufficient for plaintiff to describe a scheme to mislead customers, and allege that each misrepresentation to each customer conforms to that scheme . . . [t]o require plaintiffs to plead the specifics of each advertisement would render a suit challenging the overall program impractical."[705] The Ninth Circuit agrees that the California UDAP statutes do not require a showing of fraud, but nonetheless holds that any averments of fraud in support of a UDAP claim must be pleaded with particularity.[706] The New Hampshire Supreme Court holds that the plaintiff's complaint need not plead the exact subsection of the UDAP statute that the defendant is alleged to have violated.[707] Even if a court applies Rule 9(b), the rule allows the defendant's state of mind to be averred generally.[708]

Where UDAP claims have been inadvertently omitted from a pleading, they may still be decided by the trial court if they are presented by consent or without objection.[709] A complaint that merely pleads fraud, but sets out facts sufficient to show a UDAP violation, may be held sufficient to raise the UDAP claim.[710] It is error, however, for a trial court to decide a case on UDAP issues the court raises *sua sponte*, since such a procedure denies litigants their due process right to be apprised of the nature of the claims against them and to be given the opportunity to address them fully.[711] Failure to plead UDAP claims or defenses may also waive them.[712]

In cases where the facts and claims are simple and straightforward, form pleadings can be used to minimize the attorney's time investment in the case, particularly at the beginning. The companion CD-Rom to this volume includes a wealth of sample UDAP pleadings and discovery.[713] After

702 Zinser v. Rose, 614 N.E.2d 1259 (Ill. App. Ct. 1993) (UDAP pleading requirements less stringent than fraud). *See* §§ 3.1.2, 4.2.3.1, *supra*. *But see* Tuttle v. Lorillard Tobacco Co., 118 F. Supp. 2d 954 (D. Minn. 2000) (rejecting argument that Rule 9(b) should not apply because UDAP is less strict than fraud).

703 Lava Trading, Inc. v. Hartford Fire Ins. Co., 2004 WL 555723 (S.D.N.Y. Mar. 19, 2004) (Rule 9(b) does not apply, but UDAP claim must be stated with some specificity); Banks v. Consumer Home Mortg., Inc., 2003 WL 21251584 (E.D.N.Y. Mar. 28, 2003); U.S. on behalf of Polied Environmental Servs., Inc. v. Incor Group, Inc., 238 F. Supp. 2d 456 (D. Conn. 2002); Martin v. Am. Equity Ins. Co., 185 F. Supp. 2d 162, 167 n.3 (D. Conn. 2002); Gaddy v. Galarza Motor Sport L.T.D., 2000 U.S. Dist. LEXIS 13881 (N.D. Ill. Sept. 18, 2000); Omega Engineering, Inc. v. Eastman Kodak Co., 908 F. Supp. 1084 (D. Conn. 1995); Hedaya Bros., Inc. v. Federal Ins. Co., 799 F. Supp. 13 (E.D.N.Y. 1992) (fraud, but not UDAP, must be pleaded with particularity); Federal Paper Bd. Co. v. Amata, 693 F. Supp. 1376 (D. Conn. 1988) (UDAP claims need not be pleaded with particularity); State *ex rel.* Brady v. Publishers Clearing House, 787 A.2d 111 (Del. Ch. 2001) (drawing distinction between UDAP and fraud claims).

704 Bruce v. Home Depot, USA, Inc., 308 F. Supp. 2d 72, 78 (D. Conn. 2004); Nigh v. Koons Buick Pontiac GMC, Inc., 143 F. Supp. 2d 535 (E.D. Va. 2001), *aff'd on other grounds*, 319 F.3d 119 (4th Cir. 2003), *cert. granted on other issues*, 124 S. Ct. 1144 (2004); Gonzalez v. Old Kent Mortgage Co., 2000 U.S. Dist. LEXIS 14530 (E.D. Pa. Sept. 19, 2000) (conclusory allegations of UDAP ascertainable loss requirement insufficient); Federal Paper Bd. Co. v. Amata, 693 F. Supp. 1376 (D. Conn. 1988); Committee on Children's Television, Inc. v. General Foods Corp., 35 Cal. 3d 197, 673 P.2d 660, 197 Cal. Rptr. 783 (1983); S.M.S. Textile Mills, Inc. v. Brown, Jacobson, Tillinghast, Lahan & King, P.C., 32 Conn. App. 786, 631 A.2d 340 (1993) (UDAP claim must be pleaded with particularity to allow evaluation of the legal theory on which it is based); U.S. Funding, Inc. v. Bank of Boston, 551 N.E.2d 922 (Mass. App. Ct. 1990); Trask v. Bulter, 123 Wash. 2d 835, 872 P.2d 1080 (1994) (pleading must make reference to UDAP statute). *See also* McKinney v. State, 693 N.E.2d 65 (Ind. 1998) (claims alleging knowing or intentional violations must be pleaded with particularity, but other claims need not be).

705 Committee on Children's Television, Inc. v. General Foods Corp., 35 Cal. 3d 197, 673 P.2d 660, 197 Cal. Rptr. 783, (1983). *Accord* Quelimane Co. v. Stewart Title Guaranty Co., 77 Cal. Rptr. 2d 709, 960 P.2d 513 (1998).

706 Vess v. Ciba-Geigy Corp., 317 F.3d 1097 (9th Cir. 2003).

707 Milford Lumber Co. v. RCB Realty, Inc., 780 A.2d 1259 (N.H. 2001).

708 Vaughn v. Consumer Home Mortg., Inc., 2003 WL 21241669 (E.D.N.Y. Mar. 23, 2003).

709 Lee v. Hodge, 180 Ariz. 97, 882 P.2d 408 (1994) (allegation not contained in complaint, but listed in joint pretrial statement, discovery, and pretrial motions in limine, was tried by consent); R. Wilson Plumbing & Heating Inc. v. Wademan, 246 N.J. Super. 615, 588 A.2d 444 (App. 1991); Robinson v. McDougal, 62 Ohio App. 3d 253, 575 N.E.2d 469 (1988). *See also* Gorton v. American Cyanamid Co., 533 N.W.2d 746 (Wis. 1995) (where all elements of UDAP claim were presented to jury, judge may grant UDAP attorney fees even though UDAP claim was not pleaded). *But see In re* Crown Auto Dealerships, Inc., 187 B.R. 1009 (Bankr. M.D. Fla. 1995) (failure to set forth UDAP claim along with common law theory results in bar of claim under bankruptcy rules).

710 Arales v. Furs by Weiss, Inc., 1999 Ohio App. LEXIS 125 (Jan. 21, 1999).

711 R. Wilson Plumbing & Heating Inc. v. Wademan, 246 N.J. Super. 615, 588 A.2d 444 (App. 1991), *overruling* Blake Constr. v. Pavlick, 236 N.J. Super. 73, 564 A.2d 130 (Law Div. 1989). *Accord* Halper v. Demeter, 34 Mass. App. Ct. 299, 610 N.E.2d 332 (1993) (plaintiff who pleaded only one, narrow UDAP claim can not win damages for earlier UDAP violations). *But see* Heller v. Lexton-Ancira Real Estate Fund, Ltd., 809 P.2d 1016 (Colo. Ct. App. 1990), *rev'd on other grounds*, 826 P.2d 819 (Colo. 1992).

712 Missouri *ex rel.* Nixon v. Consumer Automotive Resources, Inc., 882 S.W.2d 717 (Mo. Ct. App. 1994) (defendant failed to plead bona fide error defense); Castelli v. Lien, 910 S.W.2d 420 (Tenn. App. 1995).

713 Other extensive collections of pleadings can be found in National Consumer Law Center, Consumer Law Pleadings (CD-Rom and Index Guide) (includes the pleadings from all previous Consumer Law Pleadings books); National Consumer Law Center, Consumer Class Actions: A Practical Litigation Guide (5th ed. 2002 and Supp.); National Consumer Law Center, Truth in Lending (5th ed. 2003 and Supp.); National Consumer Law

adaptation to local law and practice, they can be entered into a word processing program with blanks at appropriate places for insertion of details relevant to the particular case. Used in combination with an intake form which sets out all the necessary information from the client interview,[714] form pleadings may even permit a paralegal, a secretary, or other support staff to put together an initial draft of a complaint or answer under the attorney's supervision. Setting up such a system allows immediate action on a case, which might otherwise have to wait until other pressures of the attorney's practice have subsided. Immediate action obviously increases the pressure on the opposing side and may lead to an early settlement.

7.7.7 *Adding Non-UDAP Counts*

The drafter of a UDAP pleading should always consider a common law deceit or fraud claim where a practice is egregious.[715] The UDAP claim may provide attorney fees, while the common law action may provide substantial punitive damages. An excellent example of the utility of adding a common law fraud claim is a used car case in which the individual plaintiff received $210,000 punitive damages on a fraud claim, plus attorney fees on the UDAP claim.[716]

Of course, the fraud claim usually will be harder to prove than the UDAP claim, but evidence necessary to establish punitive damages is usually identical to that necessary to prove common law deceit. The UDAP statute does not preempt a common law fraud claim.[717] Inconsistent causes of action may be pleaded in the alternative unless barred by the state's election of remedies doctrine.[718]

A federal or state racketeering (RICO) count is often a possible additional count.[719] Federal and some state RICO claims provide treble damages and attorney fees, which some UDAP statutes lack. Practices outside a UDAP statute's scope will typically still be covered by a RICO statute. A federal RICO claim also makes federal jurisdiction possible. But a RICO claim will complicate a case and may raise the stakes for a merchant. This may facilitate settlement or it may bog the case down because of the enormous complexities of federal RICO law.[720]

A count for breach of contract or warranty[721] will not generate multiple or punitive damages, but the claim may survive, providing the consumer with actual damages, if the UDAP count is dismissed for some technical reason. Attorney fees for breach of warranty are available if a claim under the Magnuson Moss Warranty Act is established.[722] Another advantage of warranty claims is that courts may find them more familiar than UDAP claims and therefore more attractive as a basis for damages.

A claim under a state "plain English" statute[723] can also be an attractive addition to a UDAP case. Even in states that do not have such a statute, it may be a UDAP violation not to make clear disclosure of important information. In many cases, documents and disclosures are incomprehensible to both the consumer and the jury, containing overly formal and legalistic language, even where they have been written in an attempt to comply with these requirements. Such a claim, even if worth only a minimal amount of damages, can be valuable if the case goes to the jury. By having the creditor read the document on the witness stand and then asking him or her whether it is clear, the consumer's attorney can usually score points with the jury. This testimony may color the rest of the case, especially where the other claims are not clear cut.

Statutory or common law grounds for rescission or cancellation are other potential additional counts in a UDAP action: three-day cooling-off periods,[724] Truth in Lending rescission, revocation of acceptance, incapacity, illegality, fraud, misrepresentation, mistake, duress, impracticability, or frustration.[725]

Center, Consumer Bankruptcy Law and Practice (6th ed. 2000 and Supp.); National Consumer Law Center, Fair Debt Collection (5th ed. 2004). Contact NCLC's Publication Department for ordering information and a current list.

714 *See, e.g.*, National Consumer Law Center, Consumer Warranty Law Appx. H (2d ed. 2001 and Supp.).

715 *See* § 9.6.3, *infra*; National Consumer Law Center, Consumer Law Pleadings, No. 1, § 7.1, No. 2, §§ 6.1.1, 6.2.1, 6.3.1, 12.2.1, 13.3 (CD-Rom and Index Guide) for examples of UDAP complaints that include fraud claims as well. These pleadings are also found on the CD-Rom accompanying this volume.

716 Grabinski v. Blue Springs Ford Sales, Inc., 203 F.3d 1024 (8th Cir. 2000). *See also* Robbins v. Lewis Rainer Motors, Inc., Clearinghouse No. 47,938 (S.D. W. Va. Apr. 8, 1992) ($75,000 punitive damages on fraud claim awarded to legal services client in used car case); DeLong v. Hilltop Lincoln-Mercury, 812 S.W.2d 834 (Mo. Ct. App. 1991) ($75,000 punitive damages on fraud claim in used car case).

717 *See* Wildstein v. Tru Motors, Inc., 227 N.J. Super. 331, 547 A.2d 340 (Law Div. 1988).

718 Gironda v. Paulsen, 605 N.E.2d 1089 (Ill. App. Ct. 1992); Stanley v. Moore, 454 S.E.2d 225 (N.C. 1995); Taylor v. Medenica, 479 S.E.2d 35 (S.C. 1996) (plaintiff must choose between UDAP claim and other claims that are based on same conduct). *See generally* §§ 8.4.3.8, 8.7.5, *infra*.

719 *See* §§ 9.2, 9.3, *infra*. *See also* National Consumer Law Center, Consumer Law Pleadings, No. 1, § 4.3 (CD-Rom and Index Guide) for an example of a UDAP complaint that includes a RICO count as well. This complaint is also found on the CD-Rom accompanying this volume.

720 *See* § 9.2, *infra*.

721 *See* §§ 9.6.1, 9.6.2, *infra*.

722 15 U.S.C. § 1310. *See* National Consumer Law Center, Consumer Warranty Law Ch. 2 (2d ed. 2001 and Supp.).

723 *See* § 5.2.2, *supra*.

724 States commonly require three-day or other cooling-off periods for door-to-door and other off-premises sales, health spa contracts, credit repair and some other credit contracts, and some other specific types of transactions. *See* §§ 5.1.2.2, 5.8.2, 5.10.3, *supra*.

725 *See* § 9.5, *infra*.

7.7.8 Filing a UDAP Suit After a Collection Action and Other Res Judicata Issues

Occasionally a client may have a strong UDAP claim, but has already lost a judgment in a collection action brought by the dealer. The options are to reopen the judgment in the collection action to assert the UDAP claims, or to file a separate affirmative suit. Res judicata may be a problem with the latter option, but only where the consumer had a full and fair opportunity to litigate the issues.[726] Whether the state treats counterclaims as compulsory will be an important factor.[727]

Res judicata will not bar claims over which the court in the collection action lacked jurisdiction.[728] Some courts, such as small claims courts, also have special rules that limit the res judicata effect of their judgments. Based on such a rule, an Indiana court held that a judgment for a creditor in a small claims court collection action does not preclude later UDAP claims against the same creditor, even though they could have been raised as counterclaims in the collection action.[729]

A North Carolina court has held that UDAP remedies are equitable and the statute should not be frustrated by narrow interpretation of procedural rules. Consequently, a UDAP claim was not barred even though it should have been raised in an earlier action as a compulsory counterclaim.[730] Where a prior suit between the parties did not resolve the issues raised in a second suit, the Fourth Circuit held that the second suit was not barred.[731] A RICO claim based on misrepresentations and threatening conduct after a loan agreement had been executed did not pertain to the loan agreement itself so was not barred by a judgment on the note in a collection action.[732]

Res judicata will also not bar a claim if the first jurisdiction did not have the power to award the full measure of relief sought in the second action.[733] Thus, consumers could assert a Tennessee UDAP claim in a Tennessee court after losing a collection action in Arkansas, where the Arkansas UDAP statute would not have afforded them a private cause of action, and Arkansas courts would probably not have allowed all the Tennessee UDAP remedies if the consumers had asserted a Tennessee UDAP counterclaim there.[734]

Res judicata only applies to a subsequent action, so does not apply to a later trial in the same case.[735] Where the state obtains an injunction against a company, and restitution for certain consumer victims, *res judicata* will not bar a class action by other victims.[736] The purposes of the two suits are fundamentally different, as the state's suit is a law enforcement action intended to protect the public. But where the consumer filed an affirmative small claims case, litigated the contractor's poor performance, and lost, an Ohio court ruled that a later UDAP claim was barred.[737]

7.7.9 Preparing for Settlement

Being prepared for settlement efforts is critical.[738] The consumer's attorney should be ready to take advantage of an opening to resolve the case favorably. Having an analysis of the settlement value of the case helps avoid settling it for much less than it is worth or much less than the opposing side is willing to pay. Analyzing the settlement value of the case in advance, and keeping the analysis current, is also important when dealing with Rule 68 offers, which require a response within just ten days and visit significant consequences upon rejection of an offer.[739]

It is helpful to keep in the case file an analysis of the claims in the case. In this way, when opposing counsel calls to discuss settlement, the consumer's attorney has a quick review at hand of what the claims are and what they are

726 Jackson v. R.G. Whipple, Inc., 225 Conn. 705, 627 A.2d 374 (1993). *Contra* Fuller v. Pacific Medical Collections, Inc., 891 P.2d 300 (Haw. Ct. App. 1995) (collateral estoppel applies to default judgments and confessed judgments).

727 Glasgow v. Eagle Pacific Ins. Co., 45 F.3d 1401 (10th Cir. 1995); Sheahy v. Primus Automotive Fin. Servs., Inc., 284 F. Supp. 2d 278 (D. Md. 2003). *See also* Egge v. Healthspan Servs. Co., 115 F. Supp. 2d 1126 (D. Minn. 2000) (FDCPA claim was not compulsory counterclaim in collection suit).

728 Yu v. Signet Bank/Virginia, 69 Cal. App. 4th 1377, 82 Cal. Rptr. 3d 304 (1999) (collection judgments entered by Virginia courts against California debtors over whom they lacked jurisdiction did not bar California UDAP suit against creditor for distant forum abuse), *decision on later appeal*, 103 Cal. App. 4th 298, 126 Cal. Rptr. 2d 516 (2002) (reaffirming original holding); Fuller v. Pacific Medical Collections, Inc., 891 P.2d 300 (Haw. Ct. App. 1995).

729 Johnson v. Anderson, 590 N.E.2d 1146 (Ind. Ct. App. 1992).

730 Morentz v. Northwestern Bank, 313 S.E.2d 8 (N.C. Ct. App. 1984). *See also* National Consumer Law Center, Truth in Lending § 7.6.5 (5th ed. 2003 and Supp.); National Consumer Law Center, Fair Debt Collection § 7.6 (5th ed. 2004).

731 Empire Funding Corp. v. Armor, 2000 U.S. App. LEXIS 26405 (4th Cir. Oct. 20, 2000) (unpublished, citation limited). *See also* Stringer v. Bugg, 254 Ga. App. 745, 563 S.E.2d 447 (2002).

732 Brown v. C.I.L., Inc., 1996 U.S. Dist. LEXIS 4053, Clearinghouse No. 51,255 (N.D. Ill. Jan. 28, 1990) (magistrate's report), *adopted by* 1996 U.S. Dist. LEXIS 4917 (N.D. Ill. Mar. 29, 1996). *See also* Stringer v. Bugg, 254 Ga. App. 745, 563 S.E.2d 447 (2002) (suit based on unlawful entry of and execution upon judgment in earlier eviction case not barred by res judicata since causes of action not identical).

733 Lien v. Couch, 993 S.W.2d 53 (Tenn. App. 1998).

734 *Id.*

735 Charleston Lumber Co. v. Miller Housing Corp., 338 S.C. 171, 525 S.E.2d 869 (2000).

736 Payne v. National Collection Sys., Inc., 91 Cal. App. 4th 1037, 111 Cal. Rptr. 2d 260 (2001).

737 McCory v. Clements, 2002 WL 857721 (Ohio App. Apr. 26, 2002).

738 A more detailed discussion of approaching settlement may be found in National Consumer Law Center, Automobile Fraud § 9.11 (2d ed. 2003 and Supp.).

739 *See* § 8.8.11.8, *infra*.

worth. This will enable the attorney to discuss intelligently with opposing counsel exactly what the consumer will be able to prove.

Each claim should be listed along with its full value for a total of what the case is worth. Along with this can be listed each claim's settlement value. This value will be based on the attorney's assessment of the relative strength of each claim and the evidence available to prove it, perhaps discounted by some amount or percentage for the savings in time, effort and risk involved in avoiding a trial. This latter amount will obviously be a function of the stage in the process at which the case is settled. Moreover, the strength of the claims and evidence will need to be reassessed after discovery.

In making such an assessment, it is obviously important to know what damages are available for each claim in that state. In addition, keep in mind the possibility of punitive damages and have an idea how much a jury might award, given the particular facts of the case.

Finally, do not forget attorney fees. Along with the settlement analysis, it is important to keep the attorney's time sheets containing the time spent on cases for which fees are available. It is important to inform opposing counsel of this element of settlement up front. The potential for even higher fees as the case continues can give additional settlement leverage.

7.8 Discovery and Factual Investigation

7.8.1 Starting Discovery Early

Immediately upon accepting a case, the consumer's advocate should begin to plan for discovery. The seller may be more cooperative at the early informal discovery stage than after a complaint or counterclaims have been filed. Sales representatives and even certain companies are highly mobile, and if discovery does not take place early, it may never take place. Decisions may have to be made early whether to depose or informally interview an individual. Not only good but potentially bad witnesses may leave town, and a deposition may be used by the opposing party. The advocate should determine the facts necessary to evaluate the reasonableness of any settlement offer *before* the other side makes the settlement offer. Early on, decide if punitive or treble damages are possible, or whether an action should be brought as a class.

Where cases are simple or involve routine issues, form interrogatories and document requests can be readied to send as soon as local practice rules allow. This increases pressure on the opposing side, gives the consumer additional settlement leverage and keeps the case moving, while requiring little of the consumer attorney's time in the early stages. Dozens of sample interrogatories, document requests, and requests for admissions are included on the companion CD-Rom to this volume.

Often merchants have a complex pattern of unfair and deceptive sales techniques. The longer the consumer litigant delays the deposition, the longer the seller's attorney and the seller have to review the company's business practices and identify the illegal aspects, and for the seller to cover them up or at least avoid discussing them at the deposition. A fraudulent dealer's fear of being examined at a deposition may also speed settlement.

Interrogatories, while useful to ferret out cut-and-dried facts such as dates, names, and addresses, are no substitute for depositions in UDAP cases, which are often highly fact dependent. Depositions allow the consumer to get the witness' answers in the witness' own words and to pin down the fraudulent seller with follow-up questions. Interrogatory answers, on the other hand, are usually artfully phrased by the defendant's attorney to give as little information as possible to the other side. Interrogatories can be useful, however, to gather basic facts such as the identities of former employees, a company's licensure, and dates.

Documents in the hands of the seller are often critical to proof of the consumer's case. Document discovery should begin immediately upon filing of the case. States that have adopted the federal rules allow two forms of document discovery: a request for production of documents or a subpoena *duces tecum* in connection with a deposition.

Depositions are most productive when the relevant documents are available and the witness can be questioned about them. If the defendant is recalcitrant about producing the necessary documents, the consumer's attorney will have to decide between proceeding with depositions without all the documents, or delaying depositions until the defendant can be compelled to produce the documents. Often the best course is to conduct the deposition with the documents that are available, but then, instead of terminating it, to adjourn it subject to reconvening when the document disputes are resolved.

When it is not clear what employee to depose, a deposition notice under federal Rule of Civil Procedure 30(b)(6) or a state equivalent can require the dealer to designate a deponent who is knowledgeable on a certain subject. Even when it is clear that a certain employee should be deposed, it may be helpful to include a Rule 30(b)(6) request in the deposition notice so that the deponent can not claim lack of knowledge.

There are several ways to minimize the expense of depositions. Most local practice rules allow attorneys to tape record or video tape depositions rather than have an expensive court reporter present. This may require a special notice to the other party, but usually can be done by agreement. Even if a court reporter must be present, the cost of attending the deposition is usually minimal—it is the cost of transcription that is significant. It is, thus, better to wait until it is clearly needed before requesting a copy of the deposition. The attorneys may want to agree to share a copy of any deposition which is later transcribed, thus saving the additional cost of a court reporter's copies.

If a deposition is taken by tape recorder, it is important to make sure that all parties speaking are adequately picked up by the recorder, so that a transcriber can recognize all the voices, and that only one person talks at a time. Nevertheless, fancy equipment is not necessary. Even some dictating machines can perform the function of recording a deposition. It will be important for the attorney or an assistant to pay some attention to the tape in the recorder to make sure the deposition testimony is halted when the tape is finished and until it is turned over or a new tape inserted.

Local rules probably require the person swearing in the witness to be someone qualified to administer oaths, such as a notary. An attorney or support staff member who is so qualified can thus swear in the witness. It is often possible to work out a stipulation allowing this even if local rules prohibit a party's attorney or office staff from administering the oath.

Sometimes the deposition of someone out of town or out of state would be helpful to the case but the expense of travel is a concern. In such cases another attorney in the city where the deposition is to be taken may be willing to take the deposition based on questions provided by the consumer's attorney. Legal services attorneys can call upon their colleagues in the distant city to aid them in this kind of deposition. Some rules of civil procedure also allow depositions to be taken by telephone.

The scope of pretrial discovery in jurisdictions that have adopted a version of the Federal Rules of Civil Procedure is much broader than the test for relevancy that is to be utilized at trial, and the party opposing discovery has the burden of showing that it is improper.[740] The scope of discovery under the federal rules was narrowed in 2000, however, from any matter relevant to the subject matter of the action to any matter "relevant to the claim or defense of any party,"[741] and some states may amend their rules to follow this lead. Individual consumers for whom the state attorney general seeks restitution in a UDAP case are not considered party-plaintiffs for purposes of discovery by the defendants.[742]

7.8.2 *Evidence to Look for*

The consumer's advocate should look for a pattern or practice. This is powerful evidence and will often be necessary for punitive or multiple damages. Admissibility of this evidence is discussed in § 7.9.1.2, *infra*.

Sales manuals, training materials, internal memos, and similar documents may establish such a pattern or practice. Fraudulent companies often develop a sales technique that is deceptive on its face and take great pains to make sure all employees follow the system closely.[743] Such companies resist supplying this important information and may be more willing to settle if they do not have to produce it.

Former employees who are disenchanted with a company may want to "tell all." Commissioned sales representatives, who may be involved in litigation against their old company over disputed commissions, can often be found through court records. Litigants may also request through discovery a list of former employees.

The defendant's advertising, sales brochures, and other written claims should be carefully scrutinized. These written materials may on their face be deceptive or fail to comply with applicable rules or regulations.

Another way to develop pattern evidence is to seek discovery of information on all persons who have purchased or borrowed from the opposing side within a specified time frame. The consumer's attorney should anticipate the need for a motion to compel, since fraudulent sellers and creditors generally will not give up such information voluntarily.[744] While courts have considerable discretion about whether to allow discovery, many have required defendants to produce customer lists.[745] The need to produce such information may spur settlement negotiations.

Evidence of the defendant's financial status may be discoverable and admissible if punitive damages are sought, since the defendant's wealth is one of the factors in determining the size of a punitive damage award.[746]

7.8.3 *Other Approaches to Obtaining Evidence*

The state attorney general, the FTC, local consumer or district attorney offices, Better Business Bureaus and, most importantly, the state, federal or local regulatory agencies with responsibility for the seller's activities may have col-

740 State *ex rel.* Fisher v. Rose Chevrolet, 82 Ohio App. 3d 520, 612 N.E.2d 782 (1992).

741 Fed. R. Civ. P. 26(b)(1). The revised rule preserves the rule that information is discoverable even if inadmissible, as long as it is reasonably calculated to lead to the discovery of admissible evidence.

742 People *ex rel.* Hartigan v. Lann, 587 N.E.2d 521 (Ill. App. Ct. 1992).

743 *See* § 3.3.2, *supra*.

744 *See* National Consumer Law Center, Consumer Class Actions: A Practical Litigation Guide § 6.11 (5th ed. 2002 and Supp.).

745 Salmeron v. Highlands Ford Sales, Inc., 220 F.R.D. 667 (D.N.M. 2003) (ordering defendant auto dealer to produce names and contact information for consumers who bought vehicles with daily rental history, where court-supervised questionnaire had produced only 14% response rate); Martino v. Barnett, 595 S.E.2d 65 (W. Va. 2004) (neither Gramm-Leach-Bliley Act nor state law precludes party from obtaining information regarding other customers through discovery). *See Ex parte* Ocwen Fed. Bank, 2003 WL 1595271 (Ala. Mar. 28, 2003) (requiring lender to produce customer lists).

746 Lenz v. CNA Assurance Co., 42 Conn. Supp. 514, 630 A.2d 1082 (1993).

lected consumer complaints, records, data, or reports concerning the seller and may also impose special requirements the seller must follow. If the state requires specific employees to be licensed, the licensing agency may have information that will enable the consumer's attorney to locate employees that have left the company. Freedom of Information Act requests, where available, should be used where government agencies are uncooperative. State law may also authorize the court in the pending litigation, upon a showing of good cause, to order the government agency to release the information.[747]

State and local enforcement agencies are a particularly valuable resource. Many state attorneys general maintain consumer complaint departments that solicit and accept consumer complaints on a broad range of consumer protection issues, including alleged UDAP violations. These complaint departments often report trends in consumer complaints to staff attorneys who have authority to bring and litigate UDAP and other consumer protection cases. In many instances, consumer advocates can use public records laws to request information from these departments on particular defendants or specific subjects. A reasonable fee is usually allowed for copying and other costs. Advocates may also explore collaboration opportunities with state and local law enforcement officials and, in appropriate circumstances, share information about a particular defendant or practice that constitutes a UDAP violation. Such collaboration can be beneficial, particularly in complex or large UDAP cases.

A growing number of Internet sites provide helpful information. A list of particularly useful websites may be found in Appendix H, *infra*, and as weblinks on the companion CD-Rom to this volume. The defendant may also have its own website, which may offer revealing information about its activities, products, locations, assets, and corporate structure. There may also be a website where consumers voice complaints about a particular company. Helpful websites relating to automobile fraud and to warranty cases are listed in other manuals.[748]

A search of court records may reveal whether other private litigation has been brought against the same seller. Locating other cases may lead to proof that the seller's acts are part of a pattern or practice. The information gained in other litigation can also be an excellent source of informal discovery. Criminal court records should also be checked; many "fly-by-night" dealers have convictions in their pasts.

Publicity about the consumer's plight is another way to find other victims or disgruntled employees, who may contact the consumer's attorney in response to stories in the media. Of course, attorneys must make sure not to violate the rules of professional responsibility when dealing with the media. Defendants have also challenged the admissibility of consumer complaints that were made in response to the attorney general's allegedly wrongful disclosure of the name of a dealer who was being investigated.[749]

Requesting the opposing party to admit certain facts may be a useful discovery technique. Typically, if the other party does not deny admissions within a certain period of time, they are treated as admitted. Denials may force the other party to pay the costs of establishing the denied facts, if they are true.

The consumer's attorney should determine whether expert testimony is necessary to establish any elements of the UDAP claim.[750] Even if expert testimony is not essential to the claim, it may be helpful on key issues such as whether the seller's price was reasonable, whether work was performed properly, or whether a service was necessary or valuable. Experts may testify for indigent clients free of charge or at low rates, particularly where they are concerned with abuses in their profession. Where an expert has never testified at a trial before, the expert may set a low fee because he or she is eager to establish some experience in litigation. Sources of cooperative experts may include vocational education teachers, graduate students, personal acquaintances, and retirees. Attorneys should be aware, however, that the federal courts and many state courts will play a gatekeeping role, as required by *Daubert v. Merrell Dow Pharmaceuticals, Inc.*[751]

7.9 Trial

7.9.1 Evidence and Proof Issues

7.9.1.1 Standard of Proof

Most courts hold that UDAP claims need be proven only by the preponderance of evidence,[752] but a few courts find

747 Novak v. Orca Oil Co., 875 P.2d 756 (Alaska 1994).

748 National Consumer Law Center, Automobile Fraud § 2.5.15 (2d ed. 2003 and Supp.); National Consumer Law Center, Consumer Warranty Law Chs. 10, 13 (2d ed. 2001 and Supp.).

749 Ohio *ex rel.* Celebrezze v. Grogan Chrysler-Plymouth, 73 Ohio App. 3d 792, 598 N.E.2d 796 (1991).

750 *See* Durbin v. Ross, 916 P.2d 758 (Mont. 1996) (expert testimony not necessary in case against real estate broker for misrepresentations).

751 509 U.S. 579, 113 S. Ct. 2786, 125 L. Ed. 2d 469 (1993). *See* National Consumer Law Center, Consumer Warranty Law § 10.1.7.5 (2d ed. 2001 and Supp.).

752 *In re* Cohen, 185 B.R. 180 (Bankr. D.N.J. 1995), *aff'd*, 191 B.R. 599 (D.N.J. 1996), *aff'd on other grounds*, 106 F.3d 52 (3d Cir. 1997), *aff'd*, 523 U.S. 213 (1998); Dunlop v. Jimmy GMC, Inc., 136 Ariz. 338, 666 P.2d 83 (Ct. App. 1983); Nielsen v. Wisniewski, 32 Conn. App. 133, 628 A.2d 25 (1993) (even where punitive damages are sought); Cuculich v. Thomson Consumer Electronics, Inc., 317 Ill. App. 3d 709, 739 N.E.2d 934, 251 Ill. Dec. 1 (2000); Regnier v. Payter, 2003 WL 21246635 (Mich. App. May 29, 2003) (unpublished, citation limited) (contrasting UDAP claims to fraud claims); State *ex rel.* Humphrey v. Alpine Air Products, Inc., 500 N.W.2d 788 (Minn. 1993) (even where state seeks civil penalties); Isla Fin. Servs. v. Sablan, 2001 N.

that statutory fraud must be proven by clear and convincing evidence.[753] To impose the higher standard of proof upon consumers without an explicit statutory requirement would be contrary to the principle that UDAP statutes are to be liberally construed to effect the purpose of protecting consumers.[754] Using the standard burden of proof for civil actions also promotes the goal of deterring violations and augmenting state enforcement of UDAP statutes.[755]

State courts vary as to which standard to utilize for common law fraud actions.[756] But even where fraud must be proven with clear and convincing evidence, a UDAP violation should only need to be proven by a preponderance of evidence.[757]

7.9.1.2 Other Bad Acts

Evidence of the seller's unfair or deceptive acts toward others is powerful evidence. How to introduce a defendant's other bad acts is examined in more detail in another NCLC manual, *Automobile Fraud* § 9.8.1 (2d ed. 2003 and Supp.). In brief, there are at least nine ways to introduce this evidence, even though the general rule is that a consumer can not introduce such evidence to prove the defendant's character:

1. *Other bad acts are admissible to show intent or motive*, which is relevant in many UDAP statutes to prove enhanced damages, and is certainly relevant to any fraud claim that is added to the UDAP claim.[758]

2. *Evidence of other bad acts may be admissible to show preparation or a plan* on the part of the defendants, particularly in cases alleging a civil conspiracy.[759] Proving preparation or a plan may also be an essential element of a claim against a principal who was not directly involved in the deception against the consumer, but who may be liable for directing others in their fraudulent activity.

3. *Evidence of other acts is admissible to show the defendants' knowledge*. A principal's knowledge of the fraudulent activities of the dealership's salespersons is relevant, for example, to establish the principal's liability for the fraud committed against a particular consumer[760] or that the defendants had the specialized knowledge necessary to run the fraudulent scheme.[761] Some courts require proof of the defendant's knowledge as a condition of UDAP liability for nondisclosure,[762] and treble damages or attorney fees

---

Mar. I. LEXIS 24 (N. Mariana Is. Dec. 14, 2001); State v. Eddy Furniture Co., 386 N.W.2d 901 (N.D. 1986); State *ex rel.* Fisher v. Rose Chevrolet, 82 Ohio App. 3d 520, 612 N.E.2d 782 (1992); Robinson v. McDougal, 62 Ohio App. 3d 253, 575 N.E.2d 469 (1988); Poulin v. Ford Motor Co., 513 A.2d 1168 (Vt. 1986); Benkoski v. Flood, 242 Wis. 2d 652, 626 N.W.2d 851 (App. 2001) (even if there are also possible criminal penalties). *See also* Weisblatt v. Minnesota Mut. Life Ins. Co., 4 F. Supp. 2d 371 (E.D. Pa. 1998) (preponderance of evidence standard for UDAP claims not based on fraud, clear and convincing standard for UDAP claims based on fraud).

753 Osbourne v. Capital City Mortgage Corp., 727 A.2d 322 (D.C. App. 1999) (claim for intentional misrepresentation under UDAP statute requires clear and convincing evidence); Pliss v. Peppertree Resort Villas, Inc., 663 N.W.2d 851, 856 (Wis. App. 2003); Snyder v. Badgerland Mobile Homes, Inc., 659 N.W.2d 887 (Wis. App. 2003) (plaintiff has burden of establishing statutory violation to a reasonable certainty by clear, satisfactory, and convincing evidence); State v. Fonk's Mobile Home Park & Sales, Inc., 395 N.W.2d 786 (Wis. App. 1986). *See* Munjal v. Baird & Warner, Inc., 138 Ill. App. 3d 172, 485 N.E.2d 855 (1985); Deer Creek Constr. Co. v. Peterson, 412 So. 2d 1169 (Miss. 1982).

754 Ray v. Ponca/Universal Holdings, Inc., 913 P.2d 209 (Kan. App. 1995).

755 Benkoski v. Flood, 242 Wis. 2d 652, 626 N.W.2d 851 (App. 2001).

756 *See* Weisblatt v. Minnesota Mut. Life Ins. Co., 4 F. Supp. 2d 371 (E.D. Pa. 1998) (clear and convincing standard); State v. Alpine Air Products, Inc., 500 N.W.2d 788 (Minn. 1993). *See generally* National Consumer Law Center, Automobile Fraud § 7.7.1 (2d ed. 2003 and Supp.).

757 Ray v. Ponca/Universal Holdings, Inc., 913 P.2d 209 (Kan. App. 1995); State v. Alpine Air Products, Inc., 500 N.W.2d 788 (Minn. 1993). *See also* Weisblatt v. Minnesota Mut. Life Ins. Co., 4 F. Supp. 2d 371 (E.D. Pa. 1998) (preponderance of evidence standard for UDAP claims not based on fraud, clear and convincing standard for UDAP claims based on fraud).

758 Bird v. John Chezik Homerun, Inc., 152 F.3d 1014 (8th Cir. 1998); United States v. Mora, 81 F.3d 781 (8th Cir. 1996), *cert. denied*, 519 U.S. 950 (1996); United States v. Guyon, 27 F.3d 723 (1st Cir. 1994); United States v. Harvey, 959 F.2d 1371 (7th Cir. 1992); United States v. Serian, 895 F.2d 432, 434–35 (8th Cir. 1990); United States v. Greenwood, 796 F.2d 49 (4th Cir. 1986); Kerr v. First Commodity Corp., 735 F.2d 281 (8th Cir. 1984); Austin v. Loftsgaarden, 675 F.2d 168 (8th Cir. 1982), *rev'd on other grounds*, 478 U.S. 647 (1986); Shoals Ford, Inc. v. McKinney (Ala. 1992); Lee v. Hodge, 180 Ariz. 97, 882 P.2d 408 (1994); Smith v. Walt Bennett Ford, Inc., 864 S.W.2d 817, 828 (Ark. 1993); Walter v. Hall, 940 P.2d 991 (Colo. Ct. App. 1996), *aff'd on other grounds*, 969 P.2d 224 (1998); Meyers v. Cornwell Quality Tools, Inc., 41 Conn. App. 19, 674 A.2d 444 (1996) (evidence of prior acts admissible to prove intent); Dix v. American Bankers Life Assurance Co., 429 Mich. 410, 415 N.W.2d 206 (1987); Cates v. Darland, 537 P.2d 336 (Okla. 1975); Rugemer v. Rhea, 153 Or. App. 400, 957 P.2d 184 (1997) (evidence that defendant told exactly the same lie on another occasion is admissible to show that he lied to plaintiff and that he acted in bad faith); Schmitt v. Lalancette, 830 A.2d 16 (Vt. 2003) (trial court abused discretion in ordering plaintiff not to contact other customers of defendant identified through investigation, and was unjustified in denying discovery of identities of other customers).

759 United States v. Gold Unlimited, Inc., 177 F.3d 472 (6th Cir. 1999) (prior acts admissible in pyramid scheme criminal case to show knowledge or plan); Duval v. Midwest Auto City, Inc., 425 F. Supp. 1381 (D. Neb. 1977), *aff'd*, 578 F.2d 721 (8th Cir. 1978); Shoals Ford, Inc. v. McKinney, 605 So. 2d 1197 (Ala. 1992).

760 *See, e.g.*, Parrish v. Luckie, 963 F.2d 201 (8th Cir. 1992); United States v. Hugh Chalmers Chevrolet-Toyota, Inc., 800 F.2d 737 (8th Cir. 1986).

761 *See* United States v. Massey, 48 F.3d 1560 (10th Cir. 1995), *cert. denied*, 515 U.S. 1167 (1995); Commonwealth v. Source One Assocs., 436 Mass. 118, 763 N.E.2d 42 (2002).

762 *See* §§ 4.2.14.3.4, 4.2.4.2, *supra*.

may also depend on proof that the violation was knowing.[763] Even a consent order can establish the defendant's knowledge.[764]

4. *Evidence of other bad acts is admissible to prove absence of mistake or accident.*[765] Even settlement of prior claims can be admissible for this purpose.[766]

5. *That the defendant's conduct against the consumer was in conformity with the defendant's habit or routine practice* is another basis to introduce evidence of other bad acts.[767] In other words, if there is a dispute as to how the defendant handled a transaction, the way it normally handled transactions is relevant evidence.

6. *Evidence of other bad acts is admissible in support of punitive damages.* In *BMW v. Gore*, the United States Supreme Court noted: "Certainly, evidence that a defendant has repeatedly engaged in prohibited conduct while knowing or suspecting that it was unlawful would provide relevant support for an argument that strong medicine is required to cure the defendant's disrespect for the law. . . . [R]epeated misconduct is more reprehensible than an individual instance of malfeasance."[768] This evidence is relevant for the same reason in states where the judge has discretion about whether to award multiple UDAP damages, depending on factors such as reprehensibility.[769]

7. *Evidence of other bad acts is required for claims under state and federal RICO statutes* because the elements of a RICO claim include showing of a *pattern* of racketeering activity.[770] The consumer not only can, but must introduce pattern evidence if such a claim is added as an additional count in a UDAP case.

8. *Evidence of prior bad acts is relevant where the state imposes a "public interest" requirement* on UDAP suits, requiring the consumer to show that the defendant's misdeeds have been repeated or affect others.[771]

9. *Certain prior convictions relate to a crime involving dishonesty or false statement*, and thus are admissible for use as impeachment evidence under Federal Rule of Evidence 609(a)(2).[772] It is helpful to have a certified copy of the court record of the conviction available for introduction.

One court has suggested that, in determining whether evidence of acts toward others is admissible, courts should consider the length of time between the past incidents and the current incident; the factual similarity of the incidents; the similarity of the defendant's conduct, the advantage the defendants secured, and the harm to the victims in the past incidents and the current incident; and the number of prior incidents as compared to the number of prior opportunities to conduct the unfair conduct.[773] The trial court has discretion to exclude evidence of satisfied customers offered by the defendant, as such evidence merely shows that the fraud is succeeding.[774]

7.9.1.3 Expert Testimony

Expert testimony may be admissible to offer an opinion about whether the defendant's practices are unfair.[775] Depending on state evidence rules, such testimony may be admissible even though it deals with a mixed question of law and fact.[776] Expert opinion may also be helpful on such issues as the ambiguity or deceptiveness of advertisements and notices.[777] However, in some cases, a court may be able to rule that a document is deceptive simply by analyzing it,

---

763 *See* §§ 8.4.2.3.1, 8.8.2.1 *infra*.

764 Kerr v. First Commodity Corp., 735 F.2d 281 (8th Cir. 1984).

765 United States v. Murphy, 935 F.2d 899 (7th Cir. 1991); United States v. Gomez, 927 F.2d 1530, 1534 (9th Cir. 1991); United States v. Greenwood, 796 F.2d 49, 53 (4th Cir. 1986); Orkin Exterminating Co. v. Jeter, 832 So. 2d 25 (Ala. 2001); Lee v. Hodge, 180 Ariz. 97, 882 P.2d 408 (1994).

766 Bradbury v. Phillips Petroleum Co., 815 F.2d 1356 (10th Cir. 1987).

767 *See* Fed. R. Evid. 406; *see also* Mobil Exploration & Producing U.S., Inc. v. Cajun Constr. Servs., 45 F.3d 96 (5th Cir. 1995).

768 517 U.S. 559, 116 S. Ct. 1589, 134 L. Ed. 2d 809, 827 (1996) (citations omitted). *Accord* State Farm Mut. Auto. Ins. Co. v. Campbell, 538 U.S. 408, 123 S. Ct. 1513, 155 L. Ed. 2d 585 (2003); TXO Production Corp. v. Alliance Resources Corp., 509 U.S. 443, 113 S. Ct. 2711, 125 L. Ed. 2d 366 (1993) (evidence of defendant's wrongdoing in other parts of the country was a proper factor for punitive damages); Pacific Mut. Life Ins. Co. v. Haslip, 499 U.S. 1, 111 S. Ct. 1032, 113 L. Ed. 2d 1 (1991) (frequency of similar past conduct is a proper factor for punitive damages); Bird v. John Chezik Homerun, Inc., 152 F.3d 1014 (8th Cir. 1998) (evidence of prior sales of concealed wrecks admissible in support of punitive damage claim); *Ex parte* National Security Ins. Co., 773 So. 2d 461 (Ala. 2000) (plaintiff who seeks punitive damages may discover names and addresses of consumers who entered into similar transactions); MacTools, Inc. v. Griffin, 126 Idaho 193, 879 P.2d 1126 (1994); Burbach v. Investors Mgmt. Corp., 484 S.E.2d 119 (S.C. App. 1997) (approving jury instructions). *See* National Consumer Law Center, Automobile Fraud § 7.10.6 (2d ed. 2003 and Supp.).

769 *See* § 8.4.2.3, *infra*.

770 *See* §§ 9.2, 9.3, *infra*.

771 Burbach v. Investors Mgmt. Corp., 484 S.E.2d 119 (S.C. App. 1997); Cotton v. Kronenberg, 111 Wash. App. 258, 44 P.3d 878 (2002). *See generally* § 7.5.3, *supra*.

772 *See* United States v. Harris, 512 F. Supp. 1174 (D. Conn. 1981).

773 Burbach v. Investors Mgmt. Corp., 484 S.E.2d 119 (S.C. App. 1997).

774 U.S. v. Ciccone, 219 F.3d 1078 (9th Cir. 2000). *See also* FTC v. Five-Star Auto Club, Inc., 97 F. Supp. 2d 502 (S.D.N.Y. 2000) (existence of satisfied customers is no defense).

775 Pieffer v. State Farm Mut. Automobile Ins. Co., 940 P.2d 967 (Colo. Ct. App. 1996), *aff'd on other grounds*, 955 P.2d 1008 (1998). Note that in federal courts and many state courts expert testimony must meet the tests set by Daubert v. Merrell Dow Pharmaceuticals, Inc., 509 U.S. 579, 113 S. Ct. 2786, 125 L. Ed. 2d 469 (1993). *See* National Consumer Law Center, Consumer Warranty Law § 10.1.7.5 (2d ed. 2001 and Supp.).

776 Pieffer v. State Farm Mut. Automobile Ins. Co., 940 P.2d 967 (Colo. Ct. App. 1996), *aff'd on other grounds*, 955 P.2d 1008 (1998).

777 *See* § 5.5.2.9, *supra*.

without extrinsic evidence such as expert testimony or surveys.[778]

7.9.1.4 Other Evidence Issues

Statements made to a detective as part of a plea bargain in a criminal case are admissible in a UDAP enforcement action.[779]

Ownership of the vehicle may be an issue in automobile repair cases. The safest course is to comply with state law requirements that the certificate of title be produced. One court has, however, held such formal proof unnecessary in the absence of competing claims to ownership.[780] Requests for admissions prior to trial should eliminate these issues.

7.9.2 Trial Before a Judge or Jury

7.9.2.1 Strategic Considerations

One of the greatest resources an attorney has in consumer cases is a jury. It is difficult to pick a jury where at least one member has not had some consumer problem or felt that he or she had been taken advantage of or defrauded. This is why juries are usually sympathetic to the consumer. Juries have awarded substantial punitive damages in UDAP cases.[781] Requesting a jury trial raises the stakes for both sides, in terms of the time, effort, and money necessary to try the case. The time and effort increase for the judicial system as well, which may prompt pressure by the judge to abandon the jury demand or settle the case.

In deciding between a jury trial and a non-jury trial, the attorney should consider whether jury members are more likely than the judge to have backgrounds similar to one party, or an attitude of deference toward one party. If the consumer's claim is technical, or if the plaintiff has a troubled background, the judge may be better able to apply the law than a jury.

7.9.2.2 Is a Jury Trial Available for UDAP Claims?

Some jurisdictions find a constitutional or statutory right to a jury trial in UDAP actions.[782] Others, however, conclude that a UDAP claim was not known at common law or is equitable in nature, so there is no right to a jury trial.[783] The South Carolina Supreme Court treats the UDAP claim as legal and thus there is a right to a jury trial.[784] Since UDAP statutes represent a liberalization of long-standing common law claims such as fraud,[785] for which a jury trial is clearly available, the South Carolina view is more solidly grounded.

A New Jersey appellate court allows UDAP jury trials as a matter of statutory construction, even if a UDAP counterclaim is brought to an equitable foreclosure action.[786] In North Carolina, the jury determines the facts, the amount of damages, and causation, but the judge decides whether the defendant's behavior was unfair or deceptive in violation of the UDAP statute.[787] In Connecticut, a

778 Commonwealth v. Amcan Enterprises, 47 Mass. App. Ct. 330, 712 N.E.2d 1205 (1999).

779 State *ex rel.* Celebrezze v. Howard, 77 Ohio App. 3d 387, 602 N.E.2d 665 (1991).

780 Calderone v. Jim's Body Shop, 75 Ohio App. 3d 506, 599 N.E.2d 848 (1991).

781 *See* §§ 8.4.3, 9.6.3, *infra.*

782 Stires v. Carnival Corp., 243 F. Supp. 2d 1313, 1322 (M.D. Fla. 2002) (right to jury trial); Waggener v. Seever Sys., Inc., 233 Kan. 517, 664 P.2d 813 (1983) (right to jury trial); Robinson v. McDougal, 62 Ohio App. 3d 253, 575 N.E.2d 469 (1988) (right to jury trial even though remedy sought was rescission); North Carolina Fed. Sav. & Loan v. DAV Corp., 381 S.E.2d 903 (S.C. 1989) (right to jury trial). See § 10.7.2.1, *infra* for cases regarding the right to a jury trial in a civil enforcement action. *See also* Meyers v. Cornwell Quality Tools, Inc., 41 Conn. App. 19, 674 A.2d 444 (1996) (no right to jury trial, but court has power to submit claim to jury if party requests); Ihnat v. Pover, 2003 WL 22319459 (Pa. Com. Pleas Aug. 4, 2003) (jury trial available only if UDAP claim has same elements as common law claim, and then judge would decide treble damages and attorney fees).

783 Gonzalez v. Old Kent Mortgage Co., 2000 U.S. Dist. LEXIS 12314 (E.D. Pa. Aug. 15, 2000); Bedford Computer Corp. v. Ginn Pub., Inc., 63 B.R. 79 (D.N.H. 1986) (no right to jury trial under Mass. UDAP statute); L.L. Bean, Inc. v. Drake Publishers, Inc., 629 F. Supp. 644 (D. Me. 1986) (UDTPA injunctive action is equitable in nature so no right to jury trial); Larsen Chelsey Realty Co. v. Larsen, 232 Conn. 480, 656 A.2d 1009 (1995) (no right to jury trial); Associated Investment Co. v. Williams Assocs., 230 Conn. 148, 645 A.2d 505 (1994); Martin v. Heinold Commodities, Inc., 163 Ill. 2d 33, 643 N.E.2d 734 (1994) (no right to jury trial); Richard/Allen/Winter, Ltd., 156 Ill. App. 3d 717, 509 N.E.2d 1078 (1987); Town of Norwood v. Adams-Russell Co., 401 Mass. 677, 519 N.E.2d 253 (1988) (no right to jury trial); Nei v. Burley, 388 Mass. 307, 446 N.E.2d 674 (1983) (no right to jury trial); Guity v. Commerce Ins. Co., 631 N.E.2d 75 (Mass. App. Ct. 1994); Chamberlayne School v. Banker, 30 Mass. App. Ct. 346, 568 N.E.2d 642 (1991); State v. Alpine Air Products, Inc., 490 N.W.2d 888 (Minn. Ct. App. 1992) (attorney general action for injunction, restitution, and fines essentially equitable in nature), *aff'd on other grounds*, 500 N.W.2d 788 (Minn. 1993); State *ex rel.* Douglas v. Schroeder, 222 Neb. 473, 384 N.W.2d 622 (1986) (UDAP equitable so no right to jury trial); Oppenheimer v. York Int'l, 2002 WL 31409949 (Pa. C.P. Oct. 25, 2002); State v. Ameritech Corp., 185 Wis. 2d 686, 517 N.W.2d 705 (App. 1994), *aff'd without op.*, 193 Wis. 2d 150, 532 N.W.2d 449 (1995).

784 North Carolina Federal Sav. & Loan v. DAV Corp., 381 S.E.2d 903 (S.C. 1989).

785 *See* § 4.2.3.1, *supra.*

786 Zorba Contractors, Inc. v. Housing Authority, 362 N.J. Super. 124, 827 A.2d 313 (App. Div. 2003).

787 South Atlantic Ltd. P'ship v. Riese, 284 F.3d 518 (4th Cir. 2002) (N.C. law); Dalton v. Camp, 353 N.C. 647, 548 S.E.2d 704 (2001); Gray v. North Carolina Ins. Underwriting Ass'n, 352 N.C. 61, 529 S.E.2d 676 (2000); Hardy v. Toler, 288 N.C. 303, 218 S.E.2d 342 (1975); Melton v. Family First Mortg. Corp., 576 S.E.2d 365 (N.C. App. 2003); Durling v. King, 554 S.E.2d

decision[788] finding no right to trial by jury has been overruled by an amendment to the statute.[789] Whether a jury trial is available may also depend on whether the consumer seeks equitable relief, such as rescission, or damages.[790]

In jurisdictions that do not allow jury trials of UDAP claims, there may still be a right to a jury trial on the plaintiff's non-UDAP counts.[791] Where there are both UDAP and non-UDAP counts, it is best for the court to try them simultaneously, submitting the non-UDAP counts to the jury if the jurisdiction so requires.[792] In ruling on the UDAP claims, the judge will not be bound by the jury's findings or damage award[793] on the non-UDAP claims.[794] The judge may also have discretion to submit the case to a jury,[795] or to impanel an advisory jury.[796] UDAP claims may also go to a jury if neither party moves to strike a jury demand.[797]

In federal court, the Seventh Amendment to the United States Constitution guarantees the right to jury trial in "suits at common law." This has been construed to cover statutory causes of action, state or federal, that are "at least analogous to" matters tried at common law, if a party seeks legal, as opposed to equitable, relief.[798] Actions that seek compensatory or punitive damages or statutory penalties will usually meet this standard.[799] Actions for rescission or injunction will not.[800] Actions seeking restitution may also be considered equitable if the focus is on compelling the defendant to disgorge ill-gotten gains rather than to compensate the plaintiff for a loss.[801] The Eighth Circuit has held

1 (N.C. App. 2001); Barbee v. Atlantic Marine Sales & Service, 115 N.C. App. 641, 446 S.E.2d 117 (1994). *Accord* United States *ex rel.* S&D Land Clearing v. D'Elegance Mgmt. Ltd., 2000 U.S. App. LEXIS 16173 (4th Cir. July 13, 2000) (North Carolina law).

788 Associated Investment Co. v. Williams Assocs. IV, 230 Conn. 148, 645 A.2d 505 (1994).

789 *See* Lorenzetti v. Jolles, 120 F. Supp. 2d 181 (D. Conn. 2000).

790 Merritt v. Craig, 130 Md. App. 350, 746 A.2d 923 (2000).

791 *See, e.g.*, Wyler v. Bonnell Motors, Inc., 35 Mass. App. Ct. 563, 624 N.E.2d 116 (1993); Bressel v. Jolicoeur, 34 Mass. App. Ct. 205, 609 N.E.2d 94 (1993) (judge can find facts on UDAP count contrary to jury's findings on non-UDAP counts); Chamberlayne School v. Banker, 30 Mass. App. Ct. 346, 568 N.E.2d 642 (1991) (judge can issue UDAP decision that is contrary to jury's findings on non-UDAP counts); International Totalizing Sys., Inc. v. Pepsico, Inc., 29 Mass. App. Ct. 424, 560 N.E.2d 749 (1990) (judge has option of having jury decide only non-UDAP claims or having jury decide non-UDAP claims and render advisory decision on UDAP claim).

792 Wyler v. Bonnell Motors, Inc., 35 Mass. App. Ct. 563, 624 N.E.2d 116 (1993). *Cf.* Ihnat v. Pover, 2003 WL 22319459 (Pa. Com. Pleas Aug. 4, 2003) (if UDAP claim has same elements as common law claim, jury trial is available but judge decides treble damages and attorney fee issues).

793 Grove v. Huffman, 634 N.E.2d 1184 (Ill. App. Ct. 1994) (judge can award damages on UDAP count contrary to jury's award on non-UDAP counts); Poly v. Moylan, 423 Mass. 141, 667 N.E.2d 250 (1996), *cert. denied*, 519 U.S. 1114 (1997).

794 Check v. Clifford Chrysler-Plymouth, 794 N.E.2d 829 (Ill. App. 2003); Guity v. Commerce Ins. Co., 631 N.E.2d 75 (Mass. App. Ct. 1994); Wyler v. Bonnell Motors, Inc., 35 Mass. App. Ct. 563, 624 N.E.2d 116 (1993); Chamberlayne School v. Banker, 30 Mass. App. Ct. 346, 568 N.E.2d 642 (1991).

795 Bonofiglio v. Commercial Union Ins. Co., 411 Mass. 31, 576 N.E.2d 680 (1991) (while no right to jury trial, no error in submitting case to jury); Service Publications, Inc. v. Goverman, 396 Mass. 567, 487 N.E.2d 520 (1986) (while no right to jury trial, no error in submitting case to jury); Melo-Tone Vending, Inc. v. Sherry, 39 Mass. App. Ct. 315, 656 N.E.2d 312 (1995) (trial court had discretion to have jury find the facts on UDAP claim); State v. Alpine Air Products, Inc., 490 N.W.2d 888 (Minn. Ct. App. 1992), *aff'd on other grounds*, 500 N.W.2d 788 (Minn. 1993).

796 Billingham v. Dornemann, 771 N.E.2d 166 (Mass. App. 2002); Strawn v. Canuso, 638 A.2d 141 (N.J. Super. 1994), *aff'd on other grounds*, 657 A.2d 420 (N.J. 1995). *But see* Falcon Assocs., Inc. v. Cox, 699 N.E.2d 203 (Ill. App. Ct. 1998) (by accepting jury's finding regarding intent, court improperly delegated its fact-finding function), *appeal denied*, 182 Ill. 2d 549, 707 N.E.2d 1239 (1999).

797 Larsen Chelsey Realty Co. v. Larsen, 232 Conn. 480, 656 A.2d 1009, 1017 (1995).

798 City of Monterey v. Del Monte Dunes, 526 U.S. 687, 119 S. Ct. 1624, 143 L. Ed. 2d 882 (1999) (§ 1983 action seeking damages for regulatory taking); Chauffers, Teamsters and Helpers Local No. 391 v. Terry, 494 U.S. 558, 110 S. Ct. 1339, 108 L. Ed. 2d 519 (1990) (NLRA; workers seeking money damages for wages lost due to union's failure to properly represent them); Tull v. United States, 481 U.S. 412, 107 S. Ct. 1831, 95 L. Ed. 2d 365 (1987) (Clean Water Act; liability for penalties); Curtis v. Loether, 415 U.S. 189, 94 S. Ct. 1005, 37 L. Ed. 2d 260 (1974) (private remedy provisions of Fair Housing Act). *See also* Feltner v. Columbia Pictures Television, Inc., 523 U.S. 340, 118 S. Ct. 1279, 140 L. Ed. 2d 438 (1998) (money damages for copyright infringement); Granfinanciera, S.A. v. Nordberg, 492 U.S. 33, 109 S. Ct. 2782, 106 L. Ed. 2d 26 (1989) (bankruptcy trustee suing transferee of allegedly fraudulent transfer).

799 City of Monterey v. Del Monte Dunes, 526 U.S. 287, 119 S. Ct. 1624, 143 L. Ed. 2d 882 (1999) (measure of damages for regulatory taking is landowner's loss, not city's gain); Chauffers, Teamsters and Helpers Local No. 391 v. Terry, 494 U.S. 558, 110 S. Ct. 1339, 108 L. Ed. 2d 519 (1990) (measure of damages was compensatory, *i.e.*, wages lost because of union's failure to properly represent workers); Tull v. United States, 481 U.S. 412, 107 S. Ct. 1831, 95 L. Ed. 2d 365 (1987) (money penalty to "punish a culpable individual" is legal remedy); Curtis v. Loether, 415 U.S. 189, 94 S. Ct. 1005, 37 L. Ed. 2d 260 (1974) (actual and punitive damages are "the traditional form of relief offered in courts of law).

800 Marseille Hydro-Power L.L.C. v. Marseille Land and Water Co., 299 F.3d 643 (7th Cir. 2002) (no right to jury trial where plaintiff sued on contract but sought only equitable remedy, *i.e.*, specific performance; right to jury trial accrued when defendant counterclaimed for money damages).

801 Great West Life & Annuity Ins. Co. v. Knudson, 534 U.S. 204, 122 S. Ct. 708, 151 L. Ed. 2d 635 (2002) (restitution may be either a legal or an equitable remedy; where action seeks to impose personal liability on defendant for a sum of money due under, for a example, a contract, the action is legal); Brown v. Sandimo Materials, 250 F.3d 120 (2d Cir. 2001) (court explains difference between legal and equitable remedies; where issue was whether company owed money to pension fund, not whether company had obtained or retained benefit it was not entitled to keep, remedy was legal); Gagne v. Vaccaro, 835 A.2d 491 (Conn. App. 2003) (restitution or unjust enrichment claim

that, if the Seventh Amendment standard is met, jury trial is available even in an action to enforce a state statutory right, for which state law explicitly excludes jury trial.[802]

7.9.2.3 Questions of Law vs. Questions of Fact

The question whether a practice is deceptive or unfair is generally treated as one of fact for the fact finder, not a question of law for the judge.[803] Whether an insurer had a "reasonable basis" under a state UNIP statute for denying a claim is a jury question.[804] It is for the jury to make the judgment whether an item sold as new was actually used, even where the basic facts are undisputed.[805] Where willfulness is an element of a UDAP claim, it is a question for the jury.[806]

On the other hand, where the UDAP statute specifies that the "court" will make a determination, this typically is interpreted as requiring the judge, not the jury, to make this finding. Thus punitive damages are to be determined by the judge where the UDAP statute commits this authority to the court.[807] Ohio,[808] New Mexico,[809] and Tennessee[810] courts have held that the judge should decide treble damages after the jury has found a UDAP violation and awarded actual damages. In Colorado, the court awards treble damages after the jury has separately determined liability.[811]

Where the UDAP statute authorizes the court to award attorney fees, this determination is for the judge rather than the jury,[812] as is the question of whether the defendant acted knowingly, which is a prerequisite to an attorney fee award under Ohio's statute.[813] Whether a Texas UDAP case has been filed in bad faith or for harassment, thereby requiring the consumer to pay the seller's attorney fees, is also a question for the court, not the jury, because of the specific wording of the Texas UDAP statute.[814]

Civil rules may require the judge to make specific findings of fact and conclusions of law on a plaintiff's UDAP claim, but failure to do so will be harmless error where the record, taken as a whole, provides an adequate basis to dispose of all the claims presented.[815]

---

may be action at law, if plaintiff seeks money damages; collection of cases). *Compare* Crocker v. Piedmont Aviation, 49 F.3d 735 (D.C. Cir. 1995) (action seeking, *inter alia*, back pay under Airline Deregulation Act; remedy was "compensatory," *i.e.*, determined by amount of plaintiff's loss; jury trial required); *with* Ramos v. Roche Products, Inc., 936 F.2d 43 (1st Cir. 1991) (Title VII of civil rights act; relief "primarily equitable; no jury trial, even though plaintiff sought back pay).

802 Grabinski v. Blue Springs Ford Sales, 136 F.3d 565 (8th Cir. 1998) (Missouri UDAP and common law fraud; jury trial available if plaintiff seeks, at least in part, legal remedy, even if court enforcing state-created right and state law would preclude jury trial in state court); Kampa v. White Consolidated Indus., Inc., 115 F.3d 585 (8th Cir. 1997) (Minnesota human rights act; plaintiff seeking money damages for gender discrimination; jury trial available notwithstanding provisions of state statute); Gipson v. KAS Snacktime Co., 83 F.3d 225 (8th Cir. 1996) (Missouri human rights act; state decisions hold that action is equitable; jury trial required where plaintiff sought money damages).

803 Tanpiengco v. Tasto, 72 Conn. App. 817, 806 A.2d 1080 (2002); Ray v. Ponca/Universal Holdings, Inc., 913 P.2d 209 (Kan. App. 1995); Leon v. Rite Aid Corp., 340 N.J. Super. 462, 774 A.2d 674 (App. Div. 2001). *Cf.* Wayman v. Amoco Oil, 923 F. Supp. 1322 (D. Kan. 1996) (deception is decided by jury, but unconscionability by judge), *aff'd without op.*, 145 F.3d 1347 (10th Cir. 1998). *But see* South Atlantic Ltd. P'ship v. Riese, 284 F.3d 518 (4th Cir. 2002) (N.C. law) (once jury finds facts it is question of law whether they amount to UDAP violation); State *ex rel.* Stovall v. Confirmed.com, 38 P.3d 707 (Kan. 2002) (unconscionability is question of law); Gray v. North Carolina Ins. Underwriting Ass'n, 352 N.C. 61, 529 S.E.2d 676 (2000) (jury determines facts, amount of damages, and causation, but judge decides whether defendant's behavior was unfair or deceptive); State Properties, L.L.C. v. Ray, 574 S.E.2d 180 (N.C. App. Dec. 31, 2002) (jury decides whether defendant committed the alleged acts, and judge determines whether those acts constitute unfair or deceptive practices); Hertzog v. WebTV Networks, 2002 WL 1609032 (Wash. App. July 22, 2002) (unpublished, citation limited) (whether an act gives rise to a UDAP violation is reviewed as a question of law). *But cf.* State *ex rel.* Stovall v. DVM Enters., Inc., 62 P.3d 653 (Kan. 2003) (unconscionability is question of law, but highly dependent on facts, so reviewing court will give deference to trial court's sound discretion).

804 DeBruycker v. Guaranty Nat'l Ins. Co., 880 P.2d 819 (Mont. 1994) (reversing lower court's substitution of its own findings of fact for those of the jury in UDAP and contract case).

805 Arales v. Furs by Weiss, Inc., 1999 Ohio App. LEXIS 125 (Jan. 21, 1999), *appeal after remand*, 2001 Ohio App. LEXIS 5515 (Dec. 13, 2001). *See also* Chrysler Corp. v. Schiffer, 736 So. 2d 538 (Ala. 1999) (jury determines new vs. used in contract and fraud case).

806 Griffin v. Security Pacific Automotive Fin. Servs. Corp., 33 F. Supp. 2d 926 (D. Kan. 1998).

807 Dover v. Stanley, 652 S.W.2d 258 (Mo. Ct. App. 1983).

808 Crow v. Fred Martin Motor Co., 2003 WL 1240119 (Ohio App. Mar. 19, 2003) (unpublished, citation limited); Fit 'N' Fun Pools, Inc. v. Shelly, 2001 Ohio App. LEXIS 3 (Jan. 3, 2001); Inserra v. J.E.M. Building Corp., 2000 Ohio App. LEXIS 5447 (Nov. 22, 2000); Snider v. Conley's Service, 2000 Ohio App. LEXIS 2601 (June 12, 2000); Green v. USA Energy Consultants, 1986 Ohio App. LEXIS 8309 (Sept. 18, 1986).

809 McLelland v. United Wisconsin Life Ins. Co., 980 P.2d 86 (N.M. App. 1999).

810 Concrete Spaces, Inc. v. Sender, 2 S.W.3d 901 (Tenn. 1999).

811 Heritage Village Owners Ass'n v. Golden Heritage Investors, Inc., 2004 WL 439425 (Colo. App. Mar. 11, 2004).

812 Gill v. Petrazzvoli Brothers, Inc., 10 Conn. App. 22, 521 A.2d 212 (1987).

813 Dotson v. Brondes Motor Sales, 90 Ohio App. 3d 206, 628 N.E.2d 137 (1993).

814 Donwerth v. Preston II Chrysler-Dodge, 775 S.W.2d 634 (Tex. 1989).

815 Finn v. Krumroy Constr. Co., 68 Ohio App. 3d 480, 589 N.E.2d 58 (1990).

7.9.2.4 *Voir Dire*, Opening and Closing Arguments, Jury Instructions, and Trial Strategy

If all or part of a UDAP case is tried to a jury, jury instructions must be drafted with care, and should clearly set forth all of the elements of each of the plaintiff's legal theories.[816] One court has ruled that the trial judge erred by using broad general language such as "unconscionable commercial practices" in the jury instructions, without explaining the relevance of this standard to the facts of the case.[817] The judge's general language could have led the jury to impose liability without proof of all the statutory elements. Sample jury instructions are included on the companion CD-Rom to this volume.

There are advantages to having the jury answer specific questions about each claim rather than render a general verdict. Specific questions on the verdict form can help the jury focus on the issues. Breaking down its findings by cause of action or even by specific UDAP violation can make it easier to win enhanced UDAP damages or preserve a verdict on appeal.[818] The consumer must take care to present questions to the jury that will allow unequivocal findings about the defendant's UDAP violations in order to preserve the right to any special relief the UDAP statute offers.[819]

It is reversible error for the court to allow the defense to mislead and confuse the jury with incorrect characterizations of the law during *voir dire* and closing argument. Incorrect statements by defense counsel that the UDAP statute only applied to "scammers and swindlers," and that a jury verdict would amount to a conviction and leave the defendant with a record, deprived the consumers of a fair trial where the judge did not give corrective instructions.[820]

Regardless of whether the case is tried to a judge or a jury, the plaintiff must take care to introduce proof of such preliminary matters as UDAP coverage, unless the defendant has admitted these matters or they have been established by partial summary judgment.[821] The trial should focus, however, on the unfairness of the defendant's acts and the extent to which they damaged the plaintiff.

Where issues of technical violations of consumer protection statutes are still present when a case goes to trial before a jury, the consumer's attorney should be careful. These violations will usually not impress a jury and may backfire by making the consumer's case seem weak in needing to rely on something so technical. They may also inspire sympathy for the creditor. If these issues can not be resolved on pre-trial motions, it may be better to save them for the jury instructions.

7.10 Constitutional Issues

7.10.1 Introduction

Constitutional challenges to UDAP statutes are rarely successful. The fundamental notion that UDAP statutes and regulations can provide a right of action with flexible remedies for unfair or deceptive sales conduct is unchallengeable. Consumer litigants may, nevertheless, need to be familiar with constitutional UDAP issues because intransigent merchants may raise constitutional defenses in order to complicate, confuse, or postpone UDAP actions.

This section will review possible constitutional defenses, such as vagueness, overbreadth, and the right against self-incrimination. The most fashionable constitutional UDAP defense today is a claim of First Amendment protection of the seller's speech. First Amendment issues that arise when the state proceeds against deceptive charitable solicitations are discussed in § 5.13.5, *supra*.

7.10.2 The First Amendment

7.10.2.1 Deceptive Commercial Speech

Merchants may argue incorrectly that advertising, sales brochures and even sales presentations are protected First Amendment expressions, and can not be restrained by UDAP actions or regulations. That sellers would even make this argument is caused by a misunderstanding of a series of United States Supreme Court cases. Earlier United States Supreme Court cases seemed to offer no First Amendment protection at all to commercial speech.[822] But a series of Supreme Court cases in the 1970s indicated that commercial

816 Chattin v. Cape May Greene, Inc., 243 N.J. Super. 590, 581 A.2d 91 (1990), *aff'd*, 124 N.J. 520, 591 A.2d 943 (1991). *See also* Concrete Spaces, Inc. v. Sender, 2 S.W.3d 901 (Tenn. 1999), *aff'g* 1998 Tenn. App. LEXIS 525 (July 31, 1998) (both decisions contain detailed guides for instructions and verdict forms in cases involving multiple claims).

817 *Id.*

818 *See* Brzezinski v. Feuerwerker, 2000 Ohio App. LEXIS 4145 (Sept. 14, 2000) (no treble damage award where jury rendered general verdict without specifying the claims on which it awarded damages).

819 Stultz v. Artistic Pools, Inc., 2001 Ohio App. LEXIS 4561 (Oct. 10, 2001).

820 Harne v. Deadmond, 954 P.2d 732 (Mont. 1998).

821 Gapas v. Hambleton, 1980 Ohio App. LEXIS 11295, Clearinghouse No. 46,632 (Nov. 20, 1980) (consumer must prove personal, family, or household use at trial to establish UDAP coverage); *see also* § 2.1.2, *supra*. *But cf.* Eckman v. Centennial Savings Bank, 784 S.W.2d 672 (Tex. 1990) (defendant has burden of pleading and proving that plaintiff falls within exclusion for business consumers with assets of $25 million or more).

822 Breard v. Alexandria, 341 U.S. 622, 71 S. Ct. 920, 95 L. Ed. 1233 (1951) (upholding an ordinance prohibiting selling of merchandise door-to-door); Valentine v. Chrestensen, 316 U.S. 52, 62 S. Ct. 920, 86 L. Ed. 1262 (1942) (upholding ordinance forbidding commercial advertising through distributions on public streets).

speech is not completely unprotected by the First Amendment.[823]

However, the Court has taken pains to state that false, deceptive, or misleading advertising is *not* protected speech,[824] and numerous cases have held that UDAP statutes can challenge such speech.[825] The First Amendment applies to commercial speech only if it concerns lawful activity and is not misleading.[826] The state can restrict deceptive or misleading commercial speech even if it is not provably false and even if it is partly true.[827] Even truthful commercial speech can be regulated if the government asserts a substantial interest in support of the regulation, the regulation directly and materially advances that interest, and there is a reasonable fit between the government's ends and the means chosen to accomplish those ends.[828]

Prophylactic orders or rules whose objective is the prevention of deception before it occurs are not unreasonable or overbroad, even if they prohibit actions that are not clearly deceptive.[829] Thus, an injunction that prohibits unsubstan-

---

823 Bates v. State Bar of Arizona, 433 U.S. 350, 97 S. Ct. 2691, 53 L. Ed. 2d 810 (1977) (voiding restrictions on truthful lawyer advertising); Linmark Assocs., Inc. v. Township of Willingboro, 431 U.S. 85, 97 S. Ct. 1614, 52 L. Ed. 2d 155 (1977) (voiding ban of all "for sale" signs on homes); Virginia Pharmacy Board v. Virginia Consumer Council, 425 U.S. 748, 96 S. Ct. 1817, 48 L. Ed. 2d 346 (1976) (voiding ban on prescription drug price advertising); Bigelow v. Virginia, 421 U.S. 809, 95 S. Ct. 2222, 44 L. Ed. 2d 600 (1975) (overturning prosecution for newspaper advertising of legal abortions). *See also* § 5.13.5, *supra* (1st Amendment issues in regulation of charitable solicitations).

824 Illinois *ex rel.* Madigan v. Telemarketing Assocs., Inc., 538 U.S. 600, 123 S. Ct. 1829, 1836, 155 L. Ed. 2d 793 (2003) (fraudulent charitable solicitation is unprotected speech); Greater New Orleans Broadcasting Assn. v. U.S., 527 U.S. 173, 119 S. Ct. 1923, 144 L. Ed. 2d 161 (1999) (reiterating *Central Hudson* test); Central Hudson Gas & Elec. Corp. v. Public Service Comm'n, 447 U.S. 557, 65 L. Ed. 2d 341, 100 S. Ct. 2343 (1980); Friedman v. Rogers, 440 U.S. 1, 99 S. Ct. 887, 59 L. Ed. 2d 100 (1979); Ohralik v. Ohio State Bar Ass'n, 436 U.S. 447, 98 S. Ct. 1912, 56 L. Ed. 2d 444 (1978); Bates v. State Bar of Arizona, 433 U.S. 350, 97 S. Ct. 2691, 53 L. Ed. 2d 810 (1977); Linmark Assocs., Inc. v. Township of Willingboro, 431 U.S. 85, 97 S. Ct. 1614, 52 L. Ed. 2d 155 (1977); Virginia Pharmacy Board v. Virginia Consumer Council, 425 U.S. 748, 96 S. Ct. 1817 48 L. Ed. 346 (1976); Gertz v. Robert Welch, Inc., 418 U.S. 323, 94 S. Ct. 2997, 41 L. Ed. 2d 789 (1974); Kasky v. Nike, Inc., 27 Cal. 4th 939, 45 P.3d 243, 119 Cal. Rptr. 2d 296, 304 (2002). *See also* Lorillard Tobacco Co. v. Reilly, 533 U.S. 525, 121 S. Ct. 2404, 150 L. Ed. 2d 532 (2001) (reiterating *Central Hudson* test but finding certain restrictions on tobacco advertising unconstitutional).

825 Central Hudson Gas & Elec. Corp. v. Public Service Comm'n, 447 U.S. 557, 100 S. Ct. 2343, 65 L. Ed. 2d 341 (1980) (for commercial speech to be protected it must concern lawful activity and not be misleading); Novartis Corp. v. FTC, 223 F.3d 783 (D.C. Cir. 2000); Association of Nat'l Advertisers, Inc. v. Lungren, 44 F.3d 726 (9th Cir. 1994); Virgin Enterprises Ltd. v. American Longevity, 2001 WL 34142402 (S.D.N.Y. Mar. 1, 2001); U.S. v. Federal Record Serv. Corp., 1999 U.S. Dist. LEXIS 7719, *62 (S.D.N.Y. May 21, 1999); Conte & Co. v. Stephan, 713 F. Supp. 1382 (D. Kan. 1989); People *ex rel.* Abrams v. Trans World Airlines, 728 F. Supp. 162 (S.D.N.Y. 1989); Caldor, Inc. v. Heslin, 215 Conn. 590, 577 A.2d 1009 (1990); State *ex rel.* Stovall v. Cooper, 2001 WL 34117813, at *22 (Kan. Dist. Ct. May 15, 2001); Adams Ford Belton, Inc. v. Missouri Motor Vehicle Comm'n, 946 S.W.2d 199 (Mo. 1997), *cert. denied*, 522 U.S. 952 (1997) (upholding regulations prohibiting motor vehicle dealers from referring to "invoice price" and from promising to match other dealers' prices without disclosing all conditions); Commonwealth *ex rel.* Zimmerman v. Bell Tel. Co., 121 Pa. Commw. 642, 551 A.2d 602 (1988); Mother & Unborn Baby Care v. State, 749 S.W.2d 533 (Tex. App. 1988), *cert. denied*, 490 U.S. 1090 (1989). *See also* FTC v. Brown & Williamson Tobacco Corp., 778 F.2d 35 (D.C. Cir. 1985); *In re* Air Crash Disaster at Stapleton Airport, 720 F. Supp. 1505 (D. Colo. 1989), *rev'd on other grounds*, 964 F.2d 1059 (10th Cir. 1992); State v. O'Neill Investigations, Inc., 609 P.2d 520 (Alaska 1980); Jewett v. Capitol One Bank, 113 Cal. App. 4th 805, 6 Cal. Rptr. 3d 675 (2003) (individually addressed credit card solicitations not free speech protected by anti-SLAPP suit law); People v. Superior Court (Olson), 96 Cal. App. 3d 181, 157 Cal. Rptr. 628 (1979); People v. Columbia Research Corp., 71 Cal. App. 3d 607, 139 Cal. Rptr. 517 (1977); Barry v. Arrow Pontiac, Inc., 100 N.J. 57, 494 A.2d 804 (1985); State *ex rel.* Stratton v. Sinks, 106 N.M. 213, 741 P.2d 435 (Ct. App. 1987); Driver v. J.C. Bradford & Co., Clearinghouse 38,904 (Tenn. Ch. Ct. 1984); State v. Lambert, 68 Wis. 2d 523, 229 N.W.2d 622 (1975). *But cf.* Lorillard Tobacco Co. v. Reilly, 533 U.S. 525, 121 S. Ct. 2404, 150 L. Ed. 2d 532 (2001) (striking down portions of UDAP regulation that restricted cigarette advertising, because of lack of close enough fit between goals and restrictions).

826 Central Hudson Gas & Elec. Corp. v. Public Service Comm'n, 447 U.S. 557, 100 S. Ct. 2343, 65 L. Ed. 2d 341 (1980).

827 Friedman v. Rogers, 440 U.S. 1, 99 S. Ct. 887, 59 L. Ed. 2d 100 (1979); Bates v. State Bar of Arizona, 433 U.S. 350, 97 S. Ct. 2691, 53 L. Ed. 2d 810 (1977); Virginia Pharmacy Board v. Virginia Consumer Council, 425 U.S. 748, 96 S. Ct. 1817, 48 L. Ed. 2d 346 (1976); Bristol-Myers Co. v. FTC, 738 F.2d 554 (2d Cir. 1984); Encyclopedia Britannica Inc. v. FTC, 605 F.2d 964 (7th Cir. 1979); Porter & Dietsch Inc. v. FTC, 605 F.2d 294 (7th Cir. 1979); Sterling Drug, 102 F.T.C. 395 (1983), *aff'd*, 741 F.2d 1146 (9th Cir. 1984); Scott v. Ass'n for Childbirth at Home Int'l, 88 Ill. 2d 279, 430 N.E.2d 1012 (1982); People *ex rel.* Hartigan v. Maclean Hunter Publishing Corp., 119 Ill. App. 1049, 457 N.W.2d 480 (1983); Quinn v. Aetna Life & Cas. Co., 96 Misc. 2d 545, 409 N.Y.S.2d 473 (Sup. Ct. 1978); North Am. Enterprises, Inc. v. Vermont, Clearinghouse No. 50,442 (Vt. Super. Ct. Oct. 11, 1994) (Vermont regulation regarding "bonus" promotions is constitutional); State v. Imperial Marketing, 472 S.E.2d 792 (W. Va. 1996); State v. Amoco Oil Co., 97 Wis. 2d 226, 293 N.W.2d 487 (1980).

828 Lorillard Tobacco Co. v. Reilly, 533 U.S. 525, 121 S. Ct. 2404, 150 L. Ed. 2d 532 (2001) (Massachusetts has substantial interest in regulating tobacco ads, but certain restrictions do not fit the state's goals closely enough); Central Hudson Gas & Elec. Corp. v. Public Service Comm'n, 447 U.S. 557, 100 S. Ct. 2343, 65 L. Ed. 2d 341 (1980) (utility company's advertisements promoting electric usage can be regulated as a means of promoting conservation, but complete suppression was overbroad); Desnick v. Department of Professional Regulation, 171 Ill. 2d 510, 665 N.E.2d 1346 (1996) (*citing* Florida Bar v. Went For It, Inc., 515 U.S. 618, 115 S. Ct. 2371, 132 L. Ed. 2d 541 (1995)), *cert. denied*, 519 U.S. 965 (1996).

829 Friedman v. Rogers, 440 U.S. 1, 99 S. Ct. 887, 59 L. Ed. 2d 100 (1979); Ohralik v. Ohio State Bar Ass'n, 436 U.S. 447, 98 S. Ct.

tiated advertising[830] or requires the seller to disclose the purpose of a door-to-door visit so as to prevent future deception[831] has been found to be constitutionally permissible. A regulation can prohibit all price comparisons to a dealer's cost where there is no clear understanding as to what dealer cost means.[832] But injunctions should be no broader than necessary to prevent future deception or correct past deception, or they may violate the First Amendment.[833]

7.10.2.2 Unfair Commercial Speech

Litigious sellers may raise constitutional defenses to UDAP actions restricting *unfair*, but not *deceptive*, commercial speech. (There is no real issue that a consumer can seek a damage award. The issue is whether a court or regulation can restrict certain speech.) The United States Supreme Court has responded that unfair trade practices may be restrained, even if they are not deceptive.[834]

Merchants may still argue that while unfair conduct and deceptive speech may be restrained, unfair speech is protected. The Court has made clear that while commercial speech is not excluded from First Amendment considerations, it deserves less protection than noncommercial speech.[835] The Court has not discarded the common sense distinction between commercial and noncommercial speech, finding commercial speech both "hardier" and less important than other forms of discourse. The Court has argued that commercial speech is important to business profits and that businesses thus carefully calculate the content of their advertising and other speech. This type of speech will not be easily inhibited by proper regulation. Commercial speech is also more objective and verifiable, thus less likely to be deterred by rational restrictions.

In determining whether commercial speech merits protection, the Court uses a balancing test to weigh the interest of the speech with the interest in restricting it. After determining that the First Amendment applies to the speech because it concerns lawful activity and is not misleading, the Court then asks whether the government interest is substantial, whether the restriction directly advances the governmental interest, and whether the restriction is more extensive than necessary.[836] The substantial nature of the government interest need not be shown by extensive empirical data, but can be justified by studies and anecdotes relating to different locales, or even by history, consensus, and common sense.[837] And the state need not choose the least restrictive means to accomplish its ends. All that is required is a reasonable fit between the legislature's ends and the means chosen to accomplish those ends.[838]

Since commercial speech is deemed of less value and hardier, the balancing test often results in the Court upholding restrictions on commercial speech. The Court has upheld a state restriction prohibiting businesses from using trade names,[839] the disbarment of an attorney unlawfully soliciting clients,[840] and a ban on a form of classified newspaper advertising violating equal employment laws.[841] A California court has held that a ban on unsubstantiated advertising does not violate First Amendment protections.[842] Minneso-

---

1912, 56 L. Ed. 2d 444 (1978); Bristol-Myers Co. v. FTC, 738 F.2d 554 (2d Cir. 1984); United States v. Readers Digest Ass'n, Inc., 662 F.2d 955 (3d Cir. 1981); U.S. v. Federal Record Serv. Corp., 1999 U.S. Dist. LEXIS 7719, *62 (S.D.N.Y. May 21, 1999) (requiring disclosures in ads); Caldor, Inc. v. Heslin, 215 Conn. 590, 577 A.2d 1009 (1990) (courts are reluctant to apply overbreadth analysis in the context of commercial speech); State v. Amoco Oil Co., 97 Wis. 2d 226, 293 N.W.2d 487 (1980). *See also* High Country Fashions, Inc. v. Marlenna Fashions, Inc., 257 Ga. 267, 357 S.E.2d 576 (1987) (no constitutional problem in enjoining business from deceptive speech). *But see* International Dairy Foods Ass'n v. Amestoy, 92 F.3d 67 (2d Cir. 1996) (statute requiring dairy manufacturers to identify products derived from cows treated with growth hormone violated First Amendment where state could not show any impact on public health).

830 People v. Custom Craft Carpets, Inc., 206 Cal. Rptr. 12 (Ct. App. 1984).

831 Encyclopedia Britannica v. FTC, 605 F.2d 964 (7th Cir. 1979).

832 Barry v. Arrow Pontiac, Inc., 100 N.J. 57, 494 A.2d 804 (1985). *See also* Thorn Americas, Inc. v. Vermont Attorney General, Clearinghouse No. 51,957 (Vt. Super. Ct. Mar. 7, 1997) (state can require disclosure of effective annual percentage rate for rent-to-own transactions).

833 Shapero v. Kentucky Bar Ass'n, 486 U.S. 466, 108 S. Ct. 1916, 100 L. Ed. 2d 475 (1988); FTC v. Brown & Williamson Tobacco Corp., 778 F.2d 35 (D.C. Cir. 1985); Encyclopedia Britannica v. FTC, 605 F.2d 964 (7th Cir. 1979); National Comm'n on Egg Nutrition v. FTC, 570 F.2d 157 (7th Cir. 1977); Beneficial Corp. v. FTC, 542 F.2d 611 (3d Cir. 1976), *cert. denied*, 430 U.S. 983 (1977).

834 FTC v. Sperry & Hutchinson Co., 405 U.S. 233 (1972).

835 Central Hudson Gas & Elec. Corp. v. Public Service Comm'n, 447 U.S. 557, 100 S. Ct. 2343, 65 L. Ed. 2d 341 (1980); Friedman v. Rogers, 440 U.S. 1, 99 S. Ct. 887, 59 L. Ed. 2d 100 (1979); Ohralik v. Ohio State Bar Ass'n, 436 U.S. 447, 98 S. Ct. 1912, 56 L. Ed. 2d 444 (1978); Bates v. State Bar of Arizona, 433 U.S. 350, 97 S. Ct. 2691, 53 L. Ed. 2d 810 (1977); Linmark Assocs., Inc. v. Township of Willingboro, 431 U.S. 85, 97 S. Ct. 1614, 52 L. Ed. 2d 155 (1977); Virginia Pharmacy Board v. Virginia Consumer Council, 425 U.S. 748, 96 S. Ct. 1817, 48 L. Ed. 2d 346 (1976).

836 Lorillard Tobacco Co. v. Reilly, 533 U.S. 525, 121 S. Ct. 2404, 150 L. Ed. 2d 532 (2001); Greater New Orleans Broadcasting Assn. v. U.S., 527 U.S. 173, 119 S. Ct. 1923, 144 L. Ed. 2d 161 (1999); Central Hudson Gas & Elec. Corp. v. Public Service Comm'n, 447 U.S. 557, 65 L. Ed. 2d 341, 100 S. Ct. 2343 (1980).

837 Lorillard Tobacco Co. v. Reilly, 533 U.S. 525, 121 S. Ct. 2404, 150 L. Ed. 2d 532 (2001).

838 *Id.*

839 Friedman v. Rogers, 440 U.S. 1, 99 S. Ct. 887, 59 L. Ed. 2d 100 (1979).

840 Ohralik v. Ohio State Bar Ass'n, 436 U.S. 447, 98 S. Ct. 1912, 56 L. Ed. 2d 444 (1978).

841 Pittsburgh Press Co. v. Human Relations Comm'n, 413 U.S. 376, 93 S. Ct. 2553, 37 L. Ed. 2d 669 (1973).

842 People v. Custom Craft Carpets, Inc., 206 Cal. Rptr. 12 (Ct. App. 1984).

ta's Supreme Court has upheld a state statute's restrictions on the time, place and manner of use of automatic dialing-announcement devices.[843] The Tenth Circuit has held that the FTC's nationwide do-not-call list rule does not violate the First Amendment.[844]

On the other hand, the Court has protected commercial speech where statutes sought to ban all prescription drug price advertising.[845] The Court has also overturned bans on lawyer advertising[846] and all "for sale" signs on homes.[847] It has found provisions of a UDAP regulation that restricted tobacco advertising unconstitutional because there was not a close enough fit between the regulation and the governmental interest.[848] The Court found that a state board's decision censuring a lawyer for advertising her credentials as a certified public accountant and a certified financial planner violated the First Amendment.[849] In two cases dealing with alcohol, the Court found that a federal regulation prohibiting beer labels from displaying alcohol content violated the First Amendment's protection of commercial speech[850] and that a state restriction on advertising retail prices of alcoholic beverages was invalid.[851] The Pennsylvania Supreme Court has struck down a law prohibiting public adjusters from soliciting clients during the twenty-four hours immediately after a disaster, in part because the statute's other anti-fraud provisions already protect disaster victims from unscrupulous practices.[852]

Based on these standards, individual consumer actions seeking only money damages against unfair, oppressive, or unconscionable sales practices should face no First Amendment problems. Even actions seeking injunctions or other broad consumer relief meet constitutional requirements since the seller's unfair commercial speech is harmful to consumers and will likely violate public policy, with little public interest in its dissemination.

843 State *ex rel.* Humphrey v. Casino Marketing Group, Inc., 491 N.W.2d 882 (Minn. 1992).

844 Mainstream Marketing Servs. v. FTC, 358 F.3d 1228 (10th Cir. 2004). *See also* Fraternal Order of Police v. Stenehjem, 287 F. Supp. 2d 1023 (D.N.D. 2003) (upholding application of state do-not-call list statute to commercial calls but not to charitable solicitations).

845 Virginia Pharmacy Board v. Virginia Consumer Council, 425 U.S. 748, 96 S. Ct. 1817, 48 L. Ed. 2d 346 (1976). *See also* 44 Liquormart v. Rhode Island, 517 U.S. 484, 116 S. Ct. 1495, 134 L. Ed. 2d 711 (1996) (striking down ban on truthful advertising of liquor prices).

846 Shapero v. Kentucky Bar Ass'n, 486 U.S. 466, 108 S. Ct. 1916, 100 L. Ed. 2d 475 (1988); Bates v. State Bar of Arizona, 433 U.S. 350, 97 S. Ct. 2691, 53 L. Ed. 2d 810 (1977).

847 Linmark Assocs., Inc. v. Township of Willingboro, 431 U.S. 85, 97 S. Ct. 1614, 52 L. Ed. 2d 155 (1977).

848 Lorillard Tobacco Co. v. Reilly, 533 U.S. 525, 121 S. Ct. 2404, 150 L. Ed. 2d 532 (2001).

849 Ibanez v. Florida Dep't of Bus. & Professional Regulation, 512 U.S. 136, 114 S. Ct. 2084, 129 L. Ed. 2d 118 (1994).

850 Rubin v. Coors Brewing Co., 514 U.S. 476, 115 S. Ct. 1585, 131 L. Ed. 2d 532 (1995).

851 44 Liquormart, Inc. v. Rhode Island, 517 U.S. 484, 116 S. Ct. 1495, 134 L. Ed. 2d 711 (1996).

852 Insurance Adjustment Bureau v. Pennsylvania Ins. Comm'r, 542 A.2d 1317 (Pa. 1988).

7.10.2.3 Determining Whether Speech Is Commercial or Political

Courts can not restrict even false *political* or "core" speech[853] and advertisers sometimes argue that their claims are political, not commercial speech. (The issue generally raised is not whether a consumer can seek damages for false political speech, but whether the state can enjoin such speech.) Unfortunately, since no clear-cut standards exist to determine whether speech is commercial or political, there is some uncertainty in borderline cases.[854]

Speech that does no more than propose a commercial transaction is commercial speech,[855] as is any expression related solely to the economic interests of the speaker and the speaker's audience.[856] For example, one Supreme Court decision upheld an order banning *all* advertising intended to promote the sale of utility services, since this was only commercial speech.[857] Speech is still commercial even if it

853 Meyer v. Grant, 486 U.S. 414, 108 S. Ct. 1886, 100 L. Ed. 2d 425 (1988); William O'Neil & Co. Inc. v. Validea.com Inc., 202 F. Supp. 2d 1113 (C.D. Cal. 2002) (contents of a book can not be basis for claim, but ads for the book may be); Keimer v. Buena Vista Books, Inc., 75 Cal. App. 4th 1220, 89 Cal. Rptr. 2d 781 (1999) (statements of objectively verifiable facts on book's cover were commercial because intended to promote sale of the book, even though content of book was fully protected by 1st Amendment); Lacoff v. Buena Vista Publ. Co., 183 Misc. 2d 600, 705 N.Y.S.2d 183 (Sup. Ct. 2000) (book and its cover were protected by 1st Amendment as they were not designed to sell another product). *But see* Del Tufo v. National Republican Senatorial Committee, 248 N.J. Super. 684, 591 A.2d 1040 (1991) (deceptive or misleading conduct by political fundraiser may be regulated).

854 *See* New York Magazine v. Metropolitan Transportation Authority, 136 F.3d 123 (2d Cir. 1998) (declining to decide whether advertisement for magazine that subtly criticized mayor is commercial speech); Kasky v. Nike, Inc., 27 Cal. 4th 939, 45 P.3d 243, 119 Cal. Rptr. 2d 296, 304 (2002) (the elements are the speaker, the intended audience, and the content of the message; athletic equipment manufacturer's statements about working conditions in its overseas factories were commercial speech).

855 Bolger v. Youngs Drug Products, 463 U.S. 60, 103 S. Ct. 2875, 77 L. Ed. 2d 469 (1983); *see also* Central Hudson Gas & Electric Corp. v. Public Service Comm'n, 447 U.S. 557, 115 S. Ct. 2371, 132 L. Ed. 2d 541 (1980); Linmark Assocs., Inc. v. Township of Willingboro, 431 U.S. 85, 97 S. Ct. 1614, 52 L. Ed. 2d 155 (1977); U.S. v. Federal Record Serv. Corp., 1999 U.S. Dist. LEXIS 7719, *62 (S.D.N.Y. May 21, 1999) (mailings that do no more than propose a commercial transaction are commercial speech).

856 Central Hudson Gas & Electric Corp. v. Public Service Comm'n, 447 U.S. 557, 115 S. Ct. 2371, 132 L. Ed. 2d 541 (1980).

857 Central Hudson Gas & Electric Corp. v. Public Service Comm'n, 447 U.S. 557, 115 S. Ct. 2371, 132 L. Ed. 2d 541 (1980).

links a product to important public issues or matters of current public debate.[858] But speech does not become commercial just because it concerns economic subjects or is sold for a profit.[859]

A first step in determining when speech is commercial is to look at the content of the speech, its "message." Does the speech contain a message promoting the demand for a product or service,[860] and does the speech refer to a specific product or service, or make a generic reference to a type of product?[861] For example, claims about a product's attributes or the health effects of using a product are an indication of commercial speech.[862]

A second step is to look at the "means" used to publish the speech. For example, commercial speech frequently takes the form of paid advertising.[863] Finally, the speaker's economic or commercial "motivation" is germane. Was the speech promotional in nature, seeking to benefit the economic interests of the speaker by promoting sales, or does the speech provide information relevant to political decisions or artistic or cultural choices?[864]

Using this three-step test—the "message," the "means," and the "motivation,"—the FTC overturned an administrative law judge's decision that had protected as political speech a tobacco company's commercial entitled "Of Cigarettes and Science."[865] Instead, the Commission remanded the case to the administrative law judge for a factual determination of the allegations in the complaint because the complaint alleged sufficient facts to indicate, if they were true, that the advertisement was commercial speech under the "message, means, and motivation" test.[866]

Of course, certain speech by corporations is protected political speech. Where an insurance trade association engaged in allegedly deceptive advertising concerning the liability insurance "crisis," a court found the advertisement to be protected political speech. The purpose of the advertising was not to sell insurance, but to influence legislation, persuade potential jurors to limit their damage awards, and improve the industry's image.[867] The courts also lack authority to enjoin fund solicitation by charitable organizations, although fraudulent and illegal acts by these organizations may be enjoined.[868]

---

858 Board of Trustees v. Fox, 492 U.S. 469, 109 S. Ct. 3028, 106 L. Ed. 2d 388 (1989) (Tupperware parties are commercial speech even though they also touch on subjects such as how to be financially responsible); Bolger v. Youngs Drug Products, 463 U.S. 60, 103 S. Ct. 2875, 77 L. Ed. 2d 469 (1983); Central Hudson Gas & Electric Corp. v. Public Service Comm'n, 447 U.S. 557, 562 n.5, 115 S. Ct. 2371, 132 L. Ed. 2d 541 (1980); *see also* Zauderer v. Office of Disciplinary Counsel of the Supreme Court of Ohio, 471 U.S. 626 (1985); National Comm'n on Egg Nutrition v. FTC, 570 F.2d 157 (7th Cir. 1977), *cert. denied*, 439 U.S. 821 (1978).

859 Riley v. National Fed'n of the Blind, 487 U.S. 781, 801, 108 S. Ct. 2667, 2680, 101 L. Ed. 2d 669 (1988) ("a speaker is no less a speaker because he or she is paid to speak"); Adventure Communications, Inc. v. Ky. Registry of Election Fin., 191 F.3d 429 (4th Cir. 1999) (paid political ads are non-commercial speech); Hoover v. Morales, 164 F.3d 221 (5th Cir. 1998) (serving as expert witness is non-commercial speech); Commodity Trend Serv., Inc. v. Commodity Futures Trading Comm'n, 149 F.3d 679 (7th Cir. 1998).

860 Central Hudson Gas & Electric Corp. v. Public Service Comm'n, 447 U.S. 557, 115 S. Ct. 2371, 132 L. Ed. 2d 541 (1980).

861 Bolger v. Youngs Drug Products, 463 U.S. 60, 103 S. Ct. 2875, 77 L. Ed. 2d 469 (1983); National Comm'n on Egg Nutrition v. FTC, 570 F.2d 157 (7th Cir. 1977), *cert. denied*, 439 U.S. 821 (1978).

862 Board of Trustees v. Fox, 492 U.S. 469, 109 S. Ct. 3028, 106 L. Ed. 2d 388 (1989) (Tupperware party is commercial speech even though it touches on subjects such as how to be financially responsible); Bolger v. Youngs Drug Products, 463 U.S. 60, 103 S. Ct. 2875, 77 L. Ed. 2d 469 (1983) (mailings promoting company's contraceptives are commercial speech even though they include discussions of public issues such as venereal disease and family planning); Friedman v. Rogers, 440 U.S. 1 (1979); National Comm'n on Egg Nutrition v. FTC, 570 F.2d 157 (7th Cir. 1977), *cert. denied*, 439 U.S. 821 (1978).

863 Bolger v. Youngs Drug Products, 463 U.S. 60, 103 S. Ct. 2875, 77 L. Ed. 2d 469 (1983); *see also* Bates v. State Bar of Arizona, 433 U.S. 350, 97 S. Ct. 2691, 53 L. Ed. 2d 810 (1977); Virginia State Board of Pharmacy v. Virginia Citizens Consumer Council, Inc., 425 U.S. 748, 96 S. Ct. 1817, 48 L. Ed. 2d 346 (1976).

864 R.J. Reynolds Tobacco Co., 111 F.T.C. 539 (1988) (interlocutory order); *see also* Bolger v. Youngs Drug Products, 463 U.S. 60, 103 S. Ct. 2875, 77 L. Ed. 2d 469 (1983); Consolidated Edison Co. of N.Y., Inc. v. Public Service Comm'n, 447 U.S. 530, 100 S. Ct. 2326, 65 L. Ed. 2d 319 (1980); First National Bank of Boston v. Bellotti, 435 U.S. 765 (1978); *In re* Primus, 436 U.S. 412, 98 S. Ct. 1893, 56 L. Ed. 2d 417 (1978); Proctor & Gamble Co. v. Haugen, 222 F.3d 1262 (10th Cir. 2000) (communication urging audience to buy one company's products because rival company is linked to Satan is commercial speech); U.S. West, Inc. v. FCC, 182 F.3d 1224 (10th Cir. 1999) (company's use of its own customer lists to market additional services to those customers is commercial speech; Bad Frog Brewery, Inc. v. N.Y. State Liquor Authority, 134 F.3d 87 (2d Cir. 1998) (product's satiric label is commercial speech because it is intended to sell product); National Comm'n on Egg Nutrition v. FTC, 570 F.2d 157 (7th Cir. 1977), *cert. denied*, 439 U.S. 821 (1978); Keimer v. Buena Vista Books, Inc., 75 Cal. App. 4th 1220, 89 Cal. Rptr. 2d 781 (1999) (statements of objectively verifiable facts on book's cover were commercial because intended to promote sale of the book). *See also* Kasky v. Nike, Inc., 27 Cal. 4th 939, 45 P.3d 243, 119 Cal. Rptr. 2d 296, 304 (2002) (adopting similar 3-part test under state constitution). *Cf.* Proctor & Gamble Co. v. Amway Corp., 242 F.3d 539 (5th Cir. 2001) (remanding case for further development of facts regarding speaker's motivation).

865 R.J. Reynolds Tobacco Co., 111 F.T.C. 539 (1988) (interlocutory order).

866 *Id.*

867 New York Public Interest Research Group, Inc. v. Ins. Information Inst., 161 A.D.2d 204, 554 N.Y.S.2d 590 (1990) (insurance company's expression of opinion in paid advertisements regarding social and financial costs of excessive litigation is fully protected by First Amendment).

868 Illinois *ex rel.* Madigan v. Telemarketing Assocs., Inc., 538 U.S. 600, 123 S. Ct. 1829, 155 L. Ed. 2d 793 (2003) (state may proceed against charitable fundraisers who make fraudulent misrepresentations); Riley v. National Fed'n of the Blind, 487

7.10.2.4 Attempts to Restrict Sale of Course Materials or Other Publications

Constitutional protections may severely limit the use of a UDAP statute where the *state* seeks to *enjoin* the sale of a publication or course materials, because the state is seeking to enjoin speech with an arguably political component. This situation must be distinguished from that where the state or a private plaintiff is seeking damages, restitution or penalties. The state's attempt to place pre-publication restraints on material is very different from an individual's claim for actual damages resulting from the publication. Restraint on the sale of publications or courses must also be distinguished from an attempt to enjoin the deceptive marketing of the publication or course. In the first situation, the state is seeking to prohibit the sale of the publication itself.

A deceptive commercial message may be enjoined.[869] But political or "core" speech—as opposed to commercial speech—may not be enjoined *even* if it is deceptive.[870] Where commercial and "core" speech are inextricably intertwined, the speech similarly can not be enjoined even if it is deceptive.[871] The commercial aspect of the speech must be separated, and only deceptive aspects of that commercial speech may be enjoined.[872]

Where the state seeks to enjoin the sale of written course materials—not just promotional materials about the product—these constitutional standards place a heavy burden on the state. The state must identify certain aspects of the course materials that are commercial speech and must then show which portions of those materials are deceptive. The court will only enjoin that subset of materials. An injunction will not issue where the state does not meet this burden.[873] This does *not* prevent the state from obtaining a monetary penalty or restitution if the course materials violate the UDAP statute, nor does it prevent the court from enjoining deceptive promotional practices for the written course materials.[874]

7.10.2.5 First Amendment Issues in Defamation Claims by Dealers

News media perform an important public service when they publicize information about consumer fraud. When a dealer who is the subject of such a report sues for defamation, First Amendment issues may arise. The United States Supreme Court has held that a libel plaintiff who is a public figure must show that a news media defendant acted with actual malice.[875] Even persons who are not public figures may have to show actual malice if they voluntarily thrust themselves into the vortex of a public issue. Then they are public figures for the limited purpose of that controversy.[876] If the plaintiff is not a public figure, however, the First Amendment does not require a showing of actual malice.[877] Most states require a showing only of negligence in this circumstance, but New Jersey requires a showing of actual malice where the challenged report addresses issues of consumer fraud.[878]

7.10.3 Vagueness

UDAP defendants often raise as a defense that the statute's broad prohibition against unfair or deceptive practices is unconstitutionally vague. This argument is consistently rejected by the courts.[879] The existence of FTC and other

U.S. 781, 108 S. Ct. 2667, 101 L. Ed. 2d 669 (1988); National Fed. of the Blind v. Pryor, 258 F.3d 851 (8th Cir. 2001) (requirement that solicitor discontinue call when asked does not violate First Amendment); Kentucky State Police Prof. Ass'n v. Gorman, 870 F. Supp. 166 (E.D. Ky. 1994) (striking down statute that prohibits representation that funds will go to charity if solicitor receives more than 50% of gross receipts, unless commission is disclosed to donor); State *ex rel.* Preate v. Pennsylvania Chiefs of Police, 572 A.2d 256 (Pa. Commw. Ct. 1990); State *ex rel.* Preate v. Watson & Hughey Co., 563 A.2d 1276 (Pa. Commw. Ct. 1989). *See* § 5.13.5, *supra*, for a fuller discussion of this issue.

869 Zauderer v. Office of Disciplinary Counsel, 471 U.S. 626, 105 S. Ct. 2265, 85 L. Ed. 2d 652 (1985); Marcus v. Jewish Nat'l Fund, 158 A.D.2d 101, 557 N.Y.S.2d 886 (1990).

870 Meyer v. Grant, 486 U.S. 414, 108 S. Ct. 1886, 100 L. Ed. 2d 425 (1988).

871 Riley v. National Fed'n of the Blind, 487 U.S. 781, 108 S. Ct. 2667, 101 L. Ed. 2d 669 (1988).

872 *Id.*

873 State *ex rel.* Corbin v. Tolleson, 160 Ariz. 385, 773 P.2d 490 (Ct. App. 1989).

874 *Id.*

875 Curtis Publishing Co. v. Butts, 388 U.S. 130, 87 S. Ct. 1975, 18 L. Ed. 2d 1094 (1967); New York Times Co. v. Sullivan, 376 U.S. 254, 84 S. Ct. 710, 11 L. Ed. 2d 686 (1964).

876 MacKay v. CSK Publishing, 693 A.2d 546 (N.J. Super. Ct. 1997) (citing Gertz v. Robert Welch, Inc., 418 U.S. 323, 94 S. Ct. 2997, 41 L. Ed. 2d 789 (1974)).

877 Gertz v. Robert Welch, Inc., 418 U.S. 323, 94 S. Ct. 2997, 41 L. Ed. 2d 789 (1974).

878 Turf Lawnmower Repair v. Bergen Record Corp., 139 N.J. 392, 655 A.2d 417 (1995); MacKay v. CSK Publishing, 693 A.2d 546 (N.J. Super. Ct. 1997).

879 United Companies Lending Corp. v. Sargeant, 20 F. Supp. 2d 192 (D. Mass. 1998); Carpets By the Carload, Inc. v. Warren, 368 F. Supp. 1075 (E.D. Wis. 1975); State v. O'Neill Investigations, Inc., 609 P.2d 520 (Alaska 1980); People v. Thomas Shelton Powers, M.D., Inc., 3 Cal. Rptr. 2d 34 (Ct. App. 1992) (no vagueness where seller claims surprise as to extent of restitution it must make); People v. Witzerman, 29 Cal. App. 3d 169, 105 Cal. Rptr. 284 (1972); People *ex rel.* Dunbar v. Gym of Am., Inc., 177 Colo. 97, 493 P.2d 660 (1972); State v. Leary, 217 Conn. 404, 587 A.2d 85 (1991); Department of Legal Affairs v. Rogers, 329 So. 2d 257 (Fla. 1976); Scott v. Ass'n for Childbirth at Home Int'l, 88 Ill. 2d 279, 430 N.E.2d 1012 (1982); State *ex rel.* Turner v. Koscot Interplanetary, Inc., 191 N.W.2d 624 (Iowa 1971); State v. Koscot Interplanetary Inc., 212 Kan. 668, 512 P.2d 416 (1973); Watkins v. Roach Cadillac, Inc., 7 Kan. App. 2d 8, 637 P.2d 458 (1981); Dare to Be Great, Inc. v. Commonwealth *ex rel.* Hancock, 511 S.W.2d 224 (Ky.

federal case law interpreting the terms "unfair and deceptive" is one factor preventing such statutes from being overly vague.[880] The Texas Supreme Court has found no constitutional defect even in mandatory treble damages for unintentional violations of the broad UDAP prohibitions.[881]

The Illinois Supreme Court has rejected an ophthalmologist's claim that a statute prohibiting solicitation of patients was unconstitutionally vague. While the term "solicitation" might be vague in other contexts, the ophthalmologist could not fail to know that his use of a telemarketing firm to promote his services fell under the statutory prohibition.[882]

A Missouri Supreme Court decision provides an extensive description of the vagueness argument in its most sympathetic guise—where a defendant was subject to criminal penalties of up to five years in prison for unfair practices. The court required a higher standard for criminal than civil cases, but still found no vagueness in a statute that provided criminal penalties for deceptive practices.[883] Deception has acquired a reasonable meaning over time. The court though was troubled by the broader and more evolving standard of unfair practices in a criminal action. But the court found no impermissible vagueness where criminal penalties were only available for knowing and willful violations.[884] If a defendant knew it was violating the law, the defendant can not argue that the law is too vague for the defendant to know when it is violating the law.[885]

7.10.4 Other Constitutional Challenges

Sellers have been uniformly unsuccessful in challenging UDAP regulations as invalid delegations of legislative authority,[886] as improper exercises of statutory authority by the state attorney general or other rule-making agency,[887] as violative of equal protection rights,[888] and as being uncon-

1974); Telcom Directories, Inc. v. Commonwealth *ex rel.* Cowan, 833 S.W.2d 848 (Ky. Ct. App. 1992); State v. Directory Publishing Servs., Inc., 1996 Minn. App. LEXIS 62 (Minn. App. Jan. 9, 1996) (unpublished, non-precedential); State *ex rel.* Nixon v. Telco Directory Publishing, 863 S.W.2d 596 (Mo. 1993); Kugler v. Market Dev. Corp., 124 N.J. Super. 314, 306 A.2d 489 (Ch. Div. 1973); Ran-Dav's County Kosher v. State, 243 N.J. 232, 579 A.2d 316 (App. Div. 1990), *rev'd on other grounds*, 129 N.J. 141, 608 A.2d 1353 (1992); State *ex rel.* Stratton v. Sinks, 106 N.M. 213, 741 P.2d 435 (Ct. App. 1987); State *ex rel.* Lefkowitz v. Fey, 87 Misc. 2d 987, 386 N.Y.S.2d 549 (Sup. Ct. 1976); Olivetti Corp. v. Ames Bus. Sys., Inc., 344 S.E.2d 82 (N.C. Ct. App. 1986), *aff'd in part, rev'd in part on other grounds*, 319 N.C. 534, 356 S.E.2d 578 (1987); Brown v. Barnum & Crow, Inc., 22 Ohio Op. 3d 24 (Lucas Cty. C.P. 1980); Brown v. United Laboratories of Am., Inc., Clearinghouse No. 27,056 (Ohio C.P. Portage Cty. 1975); Commonwealth *ex rel.* Zimmerman v. Bell Tel. Co., 121 Pa. Commw. 642, 551 A.2d 602 (1988); Commonwealth v. National Apartment Leasing Co., 529 A.2d 1157 (Pa. Commw. Ct. 1987); Commonwealth v. Pennsylvania Apsco Sys., Inc., 10 Pa. Commw. Ct. 138, 309 A.2d 184 (1973); Inman v. Ken Hyatt Chrysler Plymouth, Inc., 363 S.E.2d 691 (S.C. 1988); State *ex rel.* McLeod v. Whiteside, Clearinghouse No. 38,907 (S.C. C.P. 1981); Driver v. J.C. Bradford & Co., Clearinghouse No. 38,904 (Tenn. Ch. Ct. 1984); Mother & Unborn Baby Care v. State, 749 S.W.2d 533 (Tex. App. 1988), *cert. denied*, 490 U.S. 1090 (1988); Rotello v. Ring Around Products Inc., 614 S.W.2d 455 (Tex. Civ. App. 1981); Gold Kist v. Massey, 609 S.W.2d 645 (Tex. Civ. App. 1980); Thorn Americas, Inc. v. Vermont Attorney General, Clearinghouse No. 51957 (Vt. Super. Ct. Mar. 7, 1997); State v. Ralph Williams' N.W. Chrysler Plymouth, Inc., 82 Wash. 2d 265, 510 P.2d 233 (1972); State v. Reader's Digest Ass'n, Inc., 81 Wash. 2d 259, 501 P.2d 290 (1972); State v. Lambert, 68 Wis. 2d 523, 229 N.W.2d 622 (1975). *See also* State v. Direct Sellers Ass'n, 108 Ariz. 165, 494 P.2d 361 (1972) (upholding state cooling off statute); State *ex rel.* Bryant v. R&A Investment, 985 S.W.2d 299 (Ark. 1999) (rejecting argument that UDAP statute was too vague for enforcement).

880 State v. O'Neill Investigations, Inc., 609 P.2d 520 (Alaska 1980); Brown v. Barnum & Crow, Inc., 22 Ohio Op. 3d 24 (Lucas Cty. C.P. 1980); Inman v. Ken Hyatt Chrysler Plymouth, Inc., 363 S.E.2d 691 (S.C. 1988); State *ex rel.* McLeod v. Whiteside, Clearinghouse No. 38,907 (S.C. C.P. 1981); State v. Ralph Williams' N.W. Chrysler Plymouth, Inc., 82 Wash. 2d 265, 510 P.2d 233 (1972); State v. Reader's Digest Ass'n, Inc., 81 Wash. 2d 259, 501 P.2d 290 (1972).

881 Pennington v. Singleton, 606 S.W.2d 682 (Tex. 1980). *See also* State Farm Fire & Cas. Co. v. Price, 845 S.W.2d 427 (Tex. App. 1993).

882 Desnick v. Department of Professional Regulation, 171 Ill. 2d 510, 665 N.E.2d 1346 (1996).

883 State v. Shaw, 847 S.W.2d 768 (Mo. 1993). *See also* State v. Direct Sellers Ass'n, 108 Ariz. 165, 494 P.2d 361 (1972) (upholding state cooling off statute).

884 State v. Shaw, 847 S.W.2d 768 (Mo. 1993).

885 *See* Boyce Motor Lines v. United States, 342 U.S. 337, 72 S. Ct. 329, 96 L. Ed. 367 (1951).

886 Department of Legal Affairs v. Rogers, 329 So. 2d 257 (Fla. 1976); United Consumers Club, Inc. v. Attorney General, 119 Ill. App. 301, 456 N.E.2d 856 (1983); T&W Chevrolet v. Darvial, 641 P.2d 1368 (Mont. 1982); Brown v. Barnum & Crow, Inc., 22 Ohio Op. 3d 24 (Lucas Cty. C.P. 1980); Brown v. United Laboratories of Am., Inc., Clearinghouse No. 27, 056 (Ohio C.P. Portage Cty. 1975).

887 United Companies Lending Corp. v. Sargeant, 20 F. Supp. 2d 192 (D. Mass. 1998); Caldor, Inc. v. Heslin, 215 Conn. 590, 577 A.2d 1009 (1990); Purity Supreme, Inc. v. Attorney General, 380 Mass. 762, 407 N.E.2d 297 (1980); Commonwealth v. Mass. CRINC, Clearinghouse No. 40,637 (Mass. Super. Ct. 1984); Fenwick v. Kay Am. Jeep, Inc., 72 N.J. 372, 371 A.2d 13 (1977); HM Distributors of Milwaukee, Inc. v. Dep't of Agriculture, 55 Wis. 2d 261, 198 N.W.2d 598 (1972).

888 Pennsylvania Mortgage Bankers Ass'n v. Zimmerman, 664 F. Supp. 186 (M.D. Pa. 1987); State v. Leary, 217 Conn. 404, 587 A.2d 85 (1991) (ticket scalping prohibition's exception for owners of property on which the event is held does not violate equal protection); Purity Supreme, Inc. v. Attorney General, 380 Mass. 762, 407 N.E.2d 297 (1980); Adams Ford Belton, Inc. v. Missouri Motor Vehicle Comm'n, 946 S.W.2d 199 (Mo. 1997), *cert. denied*, 522 U.S. 952 (1997) (regulation that applied only to in-state dealers did not deny equal protection or rights under Privileges and Immunities clause); Fenwick v. Kay Am. Jeep, Inc., 72 N.J. 372, 371 A.2d 13 (1977); Pet Dealer's Ass'n v. Div. of Consumer Affairs, 149 N.J. Super. 235, 373 A.2d 688 (App.

stitutionally vague or overbroad.[889] UDAP statutes awarding attorney fees and costs to one side but not the other do not violate the Equal Protection Clause.[890]

A purported religious college guilty of UDAP violations failed in raising freedom of religion as a defense.[891] A state's UDAP regulations can not, however, impose substantive religious standards upon kosher food sellers without violating the establishment clause of the constitution.[892]

UDAP statutes have been consistently found not to unconstitutionally impair contracts or the right to conduct business.[893] A state UDAP statute is not an excessive burden on interstate commerce since it furthers a legitimate state interest and applies the same standard to interstate and intrastate commerce.[894] Nor does a UDAP claim involving the international sale of ancient coins violate the Commerce Clause as interfering with international trade.[895] But a section of a UDAP statute that was intended to protect in-state repair shops by preventing interstate repair networks from contracting with insurance companies to repair damaged vehicles violated the Commerce Clause.[896] A Delaware trial court, relying on inconsistencies in the geographical application of the law, has held that a statute that prohibited dummy yellow pages ads that implicitly misrepresented a supplier's location violated the Commerce Clause.[897] The First Circuit also struck down portions of a UDAP tobacco regulation that would have restricted advertising in national magazines that were sold in Massachusetts, and that would have made the manufacturer liable if any third party shipped cigars into the state that did not have the required labels.[898]

A UDAP guideline does not violate due process where it bears a rational relation to the constitutionally permissible objective of regulating business to prevent deception.[899] UDAP defendants are entitled to the usual procedural protections required by the Due Process Clause, such as notice and an opportunity to be heard before an impartial tribunal.[900] A dealer could not complain that the *ex parte* granting of a preliminary injunction and receivership denied him due process, where he had been served with notice of the

---

Div. 1977), *cert. denied*, 75 N.J. 16, 379 A.2d 247 (1977); State v. Concert Connection, 211 A.D.2d 310, 629 N.Y.S.2d 254 (1995) (ticket scalping law upheld), *appeal dismissed without op.*, 86 N.Y.2d 837, 658 N.E.2d 223 (1995); Brown v. United Laboratories of Am., Inc., Clearinghouse No. 27, 056 (Ohio C.P. Portage Cty. 1975); *see also* State v. Direct Sellers Ass'n, 108 Ariz. 165, 494 P.2d 361 (1972) (upholding state cooling off statute); Dee v. Sweet, 489 S.E.2d 823 (Ga. 1997) (attorney fee award provision in state RICO statute does not deny defendants equal protection). *But cf.* Craigmiles v. Giles, 312 F.3d 220 (6th Cir. 2002) (striking down statute requiring casket seller to have funeral director license); Casket Royale, Inc. v. Mississippi, 124 F. Supp. 2d 434 (S.D. Miss. 2000) (statute requiring casket seller to have funeral service director license did not advance state interests in speedy burial or consumer protection and violated equal protection and substantive due process).

889 United Companies Lending Corp. v. Sargeant, 20 F. Supp. 2d 192 (D. Mass. 1998); Caldor, Inc. v. Heslin, 215 Conn. 590, 577 A.2d 1009 (1990); Barry v. Arrow Pontiac, Inc. 100 N.J. 57, 494 A.2d 804 (1985); Brown v. United Laboratories of Am., Inc., Clearinghouse No. 27, 056 (Ohio C.P. Portage Cty. 1975); HM Distributors of Milwaukee, Inc. v. Dep't of Agriculture, 55 Wis. 2d 261, 198 N.W.2d 598 (1972); State v. Fonk's Mobile Home Park & Sales, 343 N.W.2d 820 (Wis. Ct. App. 1983). *But see* Christie v. Dalwig, Inc., 136 Vt. 597, 396 A.2d 1385 (1979) (regulation defining as a UDAP violation any failure to honor a warranty is too broad a regulation).

890 Dee v. Sweet, 489 S.E.2d 823 (Ga. 1997) (attorney fee award provision in state RICO statute does not deny defendants equal protection); State v. Directory Publishing Servs., Inc., 1996 Minn. App. LEXIS 62, Clearinghouse No. 51,274 (Minn. App. Jan. 9, 1996) (unpublished, non-precedential); Taylor v. Medenica, 331 S.C. 575, 503 S.E.2d 458 (1998).

891 People *ex rel.* Lefkowitz v. Colorado State Christian College, 76 Misc. 2d 50, 346 N.Y.S.2d 482 (Sup. Ct. 1973). *See also* State, Dep't of Legal Affairs v. Jackson, 576 So. 2d 864 (Fla. Dist. Ct. App. 1991).

892 Ran-Dav's County Kosher, Inc. v. State, 129 N.J. 141, 608 A.2d 1353 (1992).

893 Pennsylvania Mortgage Bankers Ass'n v. Zimmerman, 664 F. Supp. 186 (M.D. Pa. 1987); United Consumers Club, Inc. v. Attorney General, 119 Ill. App. 301, 456 N.W.2d 856 (1983); State *ex rel.* Turner v. Koscot Interplanetary, Inc., 191 N.W.2d 624 (Iowa 1971); State v. Koscot Interplanetary, Inc., 212 Kan. 668, 512 P.2d 416 (1973); Telcom Directories, Inc. v. Commonwealth *ex rel.* Cowan, 833 S.W.2d 848 (Ky. Ct. App. 1992) (restitution order); Brown v. Columbus Remodeling & Builders, Inc., Clearinghouse No. 27,064 (Ohio C.P. Franklin Cty. 1978); Commonwealth v. Gold Bond Indus., Inc., Clearinghouse No. 26,028 (Pa. C.P. Allegheny Cty. 1973); *see also* Ferguson v. Skrupa, 372 U.S. 726 (1963); Breard v. Alexandria, 341 U.S. 622 (1951).

894 Chesire v. Coca-Cola Bottling Affiliated, Inc., 758 F. Supp. 1098 (D.S.C. 1990); State v. Imperial Marketing, 472 S.E.2d 792 (W. Va. 1996); State v. Amoco Oil Co., 97 Wis. 2d 226, 293 N.W.2d 487 (1980); *see also* International Dairy Foods Ass'n v. Amestoy, Clearinghouse No. 51,265 (D. Vt. Aug. 9, 1995) (Vermont milk labeling law does not unduly burden interstate commerce); *In re* Air Crash Disaster at Stapleton Airport, 720 F. Supp. 1505 (D. Colo. 1989); People v. Western Airlines, Inc., 155 Cal. App. 3d 597, 202 Cal. Rptr. 237 (1984); People v. Concert Connection, Ltd., 211 A.D.2d 310, 629 N.Y.S.2d 254 (1995) (ticket scalping law not an unconstitutional burden on interstate commerce).

895 Republic of Turkey v. OKS Partners, 797 F. Supp. 64 (D. Mass. 1992).

896 Globe Glass & Mirror Co. v. Brown, 917 F. Supp. 447 (E.D. La. 1996).

897 State *ex rel.* Brady v. Preferred Florist Network, Inc., 791 A.2d 8 (Del. Ch. 2001).

898 Consolidated Cigar Corp. v. Reilly, 218 F.3d 30 (1st Cir. 2000), *aff'd in part, rev'd in part on other grounds sub nom.* Lorillard Tobacco Co. v. Reilly, 533 U.S. 525, 121 S. Ct. 2404, 150 L. Ed. 2d 532 (2001) (Commerce Clause issues were not before the Supreme Court).

899 Conte & Co. v. Stephan, 713 F. Supp. 1382 (D. Kan. 1989); State v. Amoco Oil Co., 97 Wis. 2d 226, 293 N.E.2d 487 (1980). *See also* Illinois v. Thompson, 656 N.E.2d 77 (Ill. App. Ct. 1995) (constitutionality of criminal home repair fraud statute upheld); People v. Concert Connection, Ltd., 211 A.D.2d 310, 629 N.Y.S.2d 254 (1995) (constitutionality of ticket scalping prohibition upheld against police power challenge).

900 Northview Motors, Inc. v. Commonwealth, 562 A.2d 977 (Pa. Commw. Ct. 1989).

hearing but failed to appear.[901] Nor does use of a preponderance of evidence standard, even in a civil penalty action, create constitutional problems.[902]

Generally, a treble damage award does not violate a state constitution's prohibition against "excessive fines"[903] or due process restrictions on disproportionate penalties.[904] But the damages and penalties available under UDAP statutes may be subject to review under the guideposts established for review of punitive damage awards by the Supreme Court in *BMW of North America, Inc. v. Gore*.[905] Although the Supreme Court has not yet addressed the issue, the majority of courts have held that successive punitive damages awards against the same defendant do not violate the due process clause, so successive UDAP awards should also not present a problem.[906]

While a corporate seller accused of fraudulent business practices may also be subject to criminal prosecution, corporations are not protected by the privilege against self-incrimination, so may not invoke the right to withhold evidence in a civil UDAP action.[907] When an individual is a defendant, then a protective order can be issued so that evidence obtained can not be used in a criminal proceeding.[908] Nevertheless, to protect the privilege against self-incrimination a seller may be able to get a stay of a civil UDAP suit if a related criminal prosecution is also pending.[909]

Courts have rejected arguments that state UDAP enforcement actions are based on arbitrary or discriminatory enforcement.[910] A defendant in a civil UDAP enforcement action does not have a due process right to appointed counsel.[911]

UDAP statutes have also been upheld against claims that they violate provisions of state constitutions. The Arizona statute does not violate a state constitutional requirement that a statute embrace only one subject.[912] Nebraska's provision for civil penalties does not violate the state's constitutional restrictions on to whom those penalties can be awarded.[913]

901 State *ex rel.* Hartigan v. Peters, 871 F.2d 1336 (7th Cir. 1989) (Illinois law).

902 State *ex rel.* Humphrey v. Alpine Air Products, Inc., 500 N.W.2d 788 (Minn. 1993).

903 Pennington v. Singleton, 606 S.W.2d 682 (Tex. 1980).

904 Gennari v. Weichert Co. Realtors, 288 N.J. Super. 504, 672 A.2d 1190 (App. 1996), *aff'd, modified on other grounds*, 148 N.J. 582, 691 A.2d 350 (1997). *See also In re* Air Crash Disaster at Stapleton Airport, 720 F. Supp. 1505 (D. Colo. 1989) (treble damages award in airline crash case does not violate 1st, 8th, or 14th Amendment).

905 517 U.S. 559, 116 S. Ct. 1589, 134 L. Ed. 2d 809 (1996). *See, e.g.*, State of Washington v. WWJ Corp., 138 Wash. 2d 595, 980 P.2d 1257 (1999) (civil penalties of $500,000 for 250 violations upheld against challenges under Eighth and Fourteenth Amendments). *Cf.* McCauslin v. Reliance Fin. Co., 2000 Pa Super. 134, 751 A.2d 683 (2000) (where actual damages were $5000 and lower court denied treble damages, court noted that award of attorneys fees greatly exceeding actual damages may implicate due process concerns). *See also* National Consumer Law Center, Automobile Fraud § 7.10.6 (2d ed. 2003 and Supp.).

906 *See, e.g.*, Owens-Corning Fiberglass Corp. v. Golightly, 976 S.W.2d 409, 412 (Ky. 1998), and cases cited therein. *See generally* § 8.4.3.6.3, *infra*.

907 *In re* O'Neill Investigations, Clearinghouse No. 26,039 (Alaska Super. Ct. 1976); State v. Koscot Interplanetary, Inc., 212 Kan. 668, 512 P.2d 416 (1973).

908 People v. Superior Court (Kaufman), 12 Cal. 3d 421, 115 Cal. Rptr. 812, 535 P.2d 716 (1974); People v. Kafka & Sons Building Supply, 625 N.E.2d 16 (Ill. App. Ct. 1993) (seller may assert privilege against self-incrimination in UDAP case to avoid involuntary disclosure of incriminating information).

909 People v. Kafka & Sons Building Supply, 625 N.E.2d 16 (Ill. App. Ct. 1993).

910 *See* State v. Shaw, 847 S.W.2d 768 (Mo. 1993).

911 Arizona *ex rel.* Woods v. Hameroff, 180 Ariz. 380, 884 P.2d 266 (App. 1994); Arizona *ex rel.* Corbin v. Horvatter, 144 Ariz. 430, 698 P.2d 225 (App. 1985).

912 State *ex rel.* Corbin v. Goodrich, 151 Ariz. 118, 726 P.2d 215 (Ct. App. 1986).

913 State *ex rel.* Stenberg v. American Midlands, Inc., 244 Neb. 887, 509 N.W.2d 633 (1994).

Chapter 8 Private UDAP Remedies

8.1 Nature and Liberal Interpretation of UDAP Remedies

The most important aspect of a UDAP action is the remedy. If the remedy does not justify the litigation effort, there is little reason to bring an action. Before initiating a UDAP action, consumer litigants must determine what remedy is feasible.

While this analysis may prove that the actual damages do not justify the litigation costs, the potential award of consequential, multiple, minimum, or punitive damages may still encourage consumers to press their UDAP claims. Moreover, even when these special damage awards produce only minimal relief, a private injunctive action, if available, may allow an individual litigant to stop a seller's deceptive practices, benefiting the public more widely. Further, when an individual action is not practical, consumer claims may be aggregated in a class action.[1]

One of the most significant impediments to a UDAP action based on a relatively small consumer claim is that the cost of an attorney may exceed the potential award.[2] Most UDAP statutes authorize the award of attorney fees to a prevailing consumer. Critics have alleged that judges historically were more reluctant to award reasonable attorney fees in consumer cases than in antitrust or civil rights actions. Nevertheless, courts are beginning to award large UDAP attorney fee awards, often in an amount several times the damage award.

This chapter examines state case law dealing with private UDAP remedies. The next chapter analyzes certain non-UDAP private remedies, such as the federal and state racketeering statutes, common law fraud, and common law rescission. Chapter 10 treats state agency UDAP remedies.

The remedy sections of UDAP statutes are entitled to the same liberal construction as the rest of the statute.[3] UDAP statutes should be construed to authorize the broadest remedy possible.[4] Without a liberal construction of UDAP remedies, deception is more likely to recur, the public will be less protected, and fraudulent practices will continue unchecked while a multiplicity of damage suits develops.[5]

A ruling on UDAP remedies should effect the statute's object to eradicate deception, protect consumers, and correct

---

1 *See* § 8.5, *infra*. *See generally* National Consumer Law Center, Consumer Class Actions: A Practical Litigation Guide (5th ed. 2002 and Supp.).

2 Sprovach v. Bob Ross Buick, Inc., 90 Ohio App. 3d 117, 628 N.E.2d 82 (1993).

3 *In re* Aponte, 82 B.R. 738 (Bankr. E.D. Pa. 1988); *In re* Andrews, 78 B.R. 78 (Bankr. E.D. Pa. 1987); State v. O'Neill Investigations, Inc., 609 P.2d 520 (Alaska 1980); Hayward v. Ventura Volvo, 108 Cal. App. 4th 509, 133 Cal. Rptr. 2d 514 (2003) (UDAP attorney fee provision); Yeong Gil Kim v. Magnotta, 249 Conn. 94, 733 A.2d 809 (1999); Lettenmaier v. Lube Connection, Inc., 162 N.J. 134, 741 A.2d 591 (1999); Tanksley v. Cook, 360 N.J. Super. 63, 821 A.2d 524 (App. Div. 2003); Parker v. I&F Insulation Co., 89 Ohio St. 3d 261, 730 N.E.2d 972 (2000); Sprovach v. Bob Ross Buick, Inc., 90 Ohio App. 3d 117, 628 N.E.2d 82 (1993); Liggins v. May Co., 53 Ohio Misc. 21, 373 N.E.2d 404, 7 Ohio Op. 3d 164 (C.P. Cuyahoga Cty. 1977), *related decision*, 44 Ohio Misc. 81, 337 N.E.2d 816 (C.P. Cuyahoga Cty. 1975); Brown v. Lancaster Chrysler-Plymouth, Inc., Clearinghouse No. 27,061 (Ohio C.P. Franklin Cty., 1976); Brown v. Market Dev., Inc., 41 Ohio Misc. 57, 322 N.E.2d 367, 68 Ohio Op. 2d 276, (C.P. Hamilton Cty. 1974); Commonwealth v. Monumental Properties, Inc., 459 Pa. 450, 329 A.2d 812 (1974); Commonwealth by Zimmerman v. Society of the 28th Div., A.E.F., 113 Pa. Commw. 456, 538 A.2d 76 (1987); Croom v. Selig, 318 Pa. Super. 206, 464 A.2d 1303 (1983); Wilkins v. Peninsula Motor Cars, Inc., 587 S.E.2d 581 (Va. 2003) (declining to give restrictive reading to UDAP statute since it is remedial); Holmes v. LG Marion Corp., 258 Va. 473, 521 S.E.2d 528 (1999). *See also* Celebrezze v. Hughes, 18 Ohio St. 3d 71, 479 N.E.2d 886 (1985).

4 *See, e.g.*, *In re* Bryant, 111 B.R. 474 (E.D. Pa. 1990); *In re* Jungkurth, 74 B.R. 323, 336 (Bankr. E.D. Pa. 1987), *aff'd*, 87 B.R. 333 (E.D. Pa. 1988); Young v. Joyce, 351 A.2d 857 (Del. 1975); Delgado v. J.W. Courtesy Pontiac GMC-Truck, Inc., 693 So. 2d 602 (Fla. Dist. Ct. App. 1997) (ruling that "economic loss doctrine" does not limit UDAP damages); Gour v. Daray Motor Co., 373 So. 2d 571 (La. Ct. App. 1979); Heller v. Silverbranch Constr. Corp., 376 Mass. 621, 382 N.E.2d 1065 (1978); Neveroski v. Blair, 141 N.J. Super. 365, 358 A.2d 473 (App. Div. 1976); Roane-Barker v. Southeastern Hosp. Supply Corp., 99 N.C. App. 30, 392 S.E.2d 663 (1990); Smith v. Herco, Inc., 900 S.W.2d 852 (Tex. App. 1995); March v. Thiery, 729 S.W.2d 889 (Tex. App. 1987) (greatest amount provable under any acceptable theory); Johnson v. Willis, 596 S.W.2d 256 (Tex. Civ. App. 1980); Woo v. Great Southwestern Acceptance Corp., 565 S.W.2d 290 (Tex. Civ. App. 1978); *see also* Barber v. Woodmen of the World Life Ins. Society, 382 S.E.2d 830 (N.C. Ct. App. 1989); Process Components, Inc. v. Baltimore Aircoil Co., 89 N.C. App. 649, 366 S.E.2d 907 (1988), *aff'd*, 323 N.C. 620, 374 S.E.2d 116 (1988); Bernard v. Central Carolina Trade Sales, 68 N.C. App. 228, 314 S.E.2d 582 (1984).

5 Hockley v. Hargitt, 82 Wash. 2d 337, 510 P.2d 1123 (1973).

marketplace imbalances.[6] The private cause of action provisions of UDAP statutes are not designed solely to remedy private wrongs, but to protect the public by enforcing sanctions for unlawful behavior.[7] For example, courts have recognized the beneficial deterrent value of multiple damage awards.[8]

8.2 Is There a Private UDAP Remedy?

There is a private UDAP remedy in every state except Iowa.[9] Alternative private remedy theories in Iowa are detailed in another section.[10] A number of states have two UDAP statutes, one with a private damage remedy, and a second one patterned after the Uniform Deceptive Trade Practices Act (UDTPA).[11] Statutes modeled after the UDTPA typically do not provide a private damage remedy, but only injunctive relief and attorney fees.[12] But a private damage remedy can be incorporated into these statutes by use of the state's other UDAP statute. A violation of the UDTPA statute's enumerated prohibitions should be a *per se* deceptive practice under the state's other UDAP statute that does provide a private damage remedy.[13]

One of California's two UDAP statutes provides for a private damage action.[14] The other, Cal. Bus. & Prof. Code § 17200, does not authorize damages,[15] but allows restitution.[16] The California Supreme Court defines restitution as "compelling a . . . defendant to return money obtained through an unfair business practice to those persons in interest from whom property was taken."[17] Restitution can include profits that the defendant obtained unfairly, but only to the extent that those profits represent monies taken from the plaintiff or benefits in which the plaintiff has an ownership interest.[18] Some courts also hold that a restitution award can include consumers' out-of-pocket losses even if the defendant did not benefit from those losses.[19] These remedies may be granted whether or not they are ancillary to an injunction.[20] The court can order restitution to all injured consumers, even if only one individual brings the UDAP

6 Sellinger v. Freeway Motor Home Sales, Inc., 110 Ariz. 573, 521 P.2d 1119 (1974); Dunlap v. Jimmy GMC Tucson, Inc., 136 Ariz. 338, 666 P.2d 83 (App. Ct. 1983); Young v. Joyce, 351 A.2d 857 (Del. 1975); Pearlman v. Time, Inc., 64 Ill. App. 3d 190, 380 N.E.2d 1040 (1978); American Buyers Club v. Hayes, 46 Ill. App. 3d 270, 361 N.E.2d 1383 (1977); Commonwealth v. Monumental Properties, Inc., 459 Pa. 450, 329 A.2d 812 (1974); Commonwealth v. Handicapped Indus., Inc., Clearinghouse No. 26,027 (C.P. Bucks City, Pa. 1977); Dick v. Attorney General, 83 Wash. 2d 684, 521 P.2d 702 (1974); Hockley v. Hargitt, 82 Wash. 2d 337, 510 P.2d 1123 (1973); State v. Ralph Williams' N.W. Chrysler Plymouth, Inc., 82 Wash. 2d 265, 510 P.2d 233 (1973); Testo v. Russ Dunmire Oldsmobile, Inc., 16 Wash. App. 39, 554 P.2d 349 (1976).

7 Haddad v. Gonzalez, 410 Mass. 855, 576 N.E.2d 658 (1991); Weigel v. Ron Tonkin Chevrolet Co., 298 Or. 127, 690 P.2d 488 (1984); Fisher v. World-Wide Trophy Outfitter Ltd., 15 Wash. App. 742, 551 P.2d 1398 (1976).

8 Haddad v. Gonzalez, 410 Mass. 855, 576 N.E.2d 658 (1991).

9 *See* § 7.2.1, *supra*; Appx. A, *infra*.

10 *See* § 7.2.2, *supra*.

11 *See* § 3.4.2.4, *supra*.

12 *See* Appx. A, *infra*. *See also* Jets Prolink Cargo, Inc. v. Brenny Transportation, Inc., 2003 WL 22047910 (D. Minn. Aug. 29, 2003); Greisz v. Household Bank, 8 F. Supp. 2d 1031 (N.D. Ill. 1998); Bentley v. Slavik, 663 F. Supp. 736 (S.D. Ill. 1987); Pain Prevention Lab v. Electronics Waveform Labs, 657 F. Supp. 1486 (N.D. Ill. 1987); Disc Jockey Referral Network, Ltd. v. Ameritech Publishing of Illinois, 596 N.E.2d 4 (Ill. App. Ct. 1992); Alsides v. Brown Institute, 592 N.W.2d 468 (Minn. App. Ct. 1999). *See also* Four D. v. Dutchland Plastics Corp., 2002 U.S. Dist. LEXIS 6669 (D. Minn. Apr. 15, 2002). *But see* Long v. E.I. duPont de Nemours & Co., 821 F. Supp. 956 (D. Del. 1993) (no damage remedy under Delaware UDTPA unless also seek injunctive relief); Grand Ventures, Inc. v. Whaley, 632 A.2d 63 (Del. 1993) (treble damages provision of Delaware UDTPA statute applies where plaintiff also seeks injunction).

13 *See* § 3.2.5, *supra*.

14 Cal. Civ. Code § 1780.

15 Cort v. St. Paul Fire & Marine Ins. Cos., 311 F.3d 979 (9th Cir. 2002); Heller v. Norcal Mut. Ins. Co., 8 Cal. 4th 30, 32 Cal. Rptr. 2d 200, 876 P.2d 999 (1994), *cert. denied*, 513 U.S. 1059 (1994); Rubin v. Green, 4 Cal. 4th 1187, 847 P.2d 1044 (1993); Committee on Children's Television, Inc. v. General Foods Corp., 35 Cal. 3d 197, 197 Cal. Rptr. 783, 673 P.2d 660 (1983); Chern v. Bank of Am., 15 Cal. 3d 866, 127 Cal. Rptr. 110, 544 P.2d 1310 (1976); *see also* Little Oil Co. v. Atlantic Richfield Co., 852 F.2d 441 (9th Cir. 1988) (California law); Kates v. Crocker Nat'l Bank, 776 F.2d 1396 (9th Cir. 1985) (Cal. law); Czechowski v. Tandy Corp., 731 F. Supp. 406 (N.D. Cal. 1990) (no punitive damages available); Southwest Marine, Inc. v. Triple A Machine Shop, Inc., 720 F. Supp. 805 (N.D. Cal. 1989) (no punitive damages available, just restitution).

16 Cel-Tech Communications, Inc. v. Los Angeles Cellular Tel. Co., 83 Cal. Rptr. 2d 548, 973 P.2d 527 (1999); Fletcher v. Security Pacific Nat'l Bank, 23 Cal. 3d 442, 153 Cal. Rptr. 28, 591 P.2d 51 (1979); People v. Superior Court (Jayhill Corp.), 9 Cal. 3d 283, 107 Cal. Rptr. 192, 507 P.2d 1400 (1973); Bank of the W. v. Superior Court, 2 Cal. 4th 1254, 10 Cal. Rptr. 2d 538, 833 P.2d 545 (1992); Korea Supply Co. v. Lockheed Martin Corp., 29 Cal. 4th 1134, 131 Cal. Rptr. 2d 29, 63 P.3d 937 (2003) (restitution allowed but not nonrestitutionary disgorgement of profits); People v. Thomas Shelton Powers, M.D., Inc., 2 Cal. App. 4th 330, 3 Cal. Rptr. 2d 34 (1992). *See also* Watson Laboratories, Inc. v. Rhone-Poulenc Rorer, Inc., 178 F. Supp. 2d 1099 (C.D. Cal. 2001) (restitution order can not order disgorgement of profits that were earned from entities other than plaintiff). *But cf.* Everett-Dicko v. Ogden Entertainment Servs., Inc., 2002 U.S. App. LEXIS 8602 (9th Cir. May 2, 2002) (unpublished, citation limited) (restitution is "an attempt to give the plaintiff the very thing to which he is entitled": since lost good will can not be returned, plaintiff's remedy is damages, which are unavailable under § 17200).

17 Kasky v. Nike, Inc., 27 Cal. 4th 939, 45 P.3d 243, 119 Cal. Rptr. 2d 296, 304 (2002) (quoting Kraus v. Trinity Mgmt. Servs., Inc., 23 Cal. 4th 116, 126, 127, 999 P.2d 718 (2000)).

18 Korea Supply Co. v. Lockheed Martin Corp., 29 Cal. 4th 1134, 131 Cal. Rptr. 2d 29, 63 P.3d 937 (2003).

19 Rosales v. Citibank, 133 F. Supp. 2d 1177 (N.D. Cal. 2001). *But cf.* Stationary Engineers Local 39 Health & Welfare Trust Fund v. Philip Morris, Inc., 1998 U.S. Dist. LEXIS 8302 (N.D. Cal. Apr. 30, 1998).

20 ABC Int'l Traders, Inc. v. Matsushita Electric Corp., 61 Cal. Rptr. 2d 112, 931 P.2d 290 (1997).

action.[21] But a "fluid recovery," in which some or all of the disgorged funds do not go to aggrieved consumers but are applied toward related goals, is permissible only if the case is formally certified as a class action,[22] and Proposition 64, passed in 2004, requires all representative actions to meet some minimal class action requirements set fourth in state law.

The only private damage remedy that Maine's UDAP statute provided until 1991 was restitution, which was only available where the dealer had benefited from the acts that harmed the consumer.[23] In 1991, the Maine UDAP statute was amended to provide for the recovery of actual damages.[24] Minnesota courts read its Consumer Sales Practices Act in conjunction with another statute to find a damages remedy.[25]

New York's UDAP statute is somewhat ambiguous as to whether a $1000 cap applies to actual damages or just to the trebled portion of a damages award. Courts have construed the language to be a cap only on the treble damages portion, an interpretation that is consistent with the legislative history and the purpose of the statute.[26]

8.3 Calculating Actual Damages

8.3.1 Introduction

Although courts often distinguish between types of damages, there is not always a clear dividing line. Direct or general damages are those directly and immediately resulting from the unfair or deceptive act or practice and pertain directly to the goods or services involved in the transaction. For example, if a used car dealer sells the consumer a defective automobile, direct damages relate to the decreased value of the automobile.

UDAP litigants may obtain relief based not just on these direct damages, but also consequential or special damages—damages flowing from an unfair or deceptive act or practice. Such consequential damages are often far greater than the direct damages from the UDAP violation. For example, in the case of a defective used car, consequential damages may include the costs of substitute transportation, repairs to the car, towing expenses, lost earnings due to the inability to drive to work, and the like.

In some states, UDAP damages case law is not fully developed, or is limited by confused or aberrational decisions. In these states, attorneys should explore other claims at the pleading stage, such as breach of warranty, fraud and rescission, in hopes of avoiding problems in establishing damages.

Section 8.3.2 discusses methods of computing direct UDAP damages. Consequential damages are treated at § 8.3.3. Prejudgment interest on actual damages is treated at § 8.3.4, and proving actual damages at § 8.3.5. Limitation of remedy clauses, the collateral source rule, mitigation of damages, and the relationship between UDAP actual damages and other remedies are discussed at §§ 8.3.6, 8.3.7, 8.3.8, and 8.3.9 respectively. Section 8.4 then examines other UDAP damage remedies—statutory minimum, multiple and punitive damages.

8.3.2 Direct Actual Damages

8.3.2.1 How Are Direct Damages Calculated: Out of Pocket, Loss of Bargain, or Cost to Repair?

UDAP statutes should be liberally construed to authorize the broadest damage remedy possible.[27] Because of UDAP statutes' remedial purpose, common law principles limiting damages between merchants are often inappropriate.[28] Just as courts fashioned different rules of damages for different types of contract, equity and tort actions, they should fashion new remedial rules of damages under UDAP statutes allowing recovery of "actual" damages or "restitution." UDAP awards should not be limited to contract damages.[29]

The type of damages awarded, of course, is limited by the language of the statute's remedial provisions, such as language authorizing only "restitution," instead of "actual damages." But judicial precedent indicates that courts normally construe expansively the statutory language and borrow from the state's common law on damages to authorize the broad choices of UDAP damage rules.

For example, in Texas, litigants with common law fraud actions can seek out-of-pocket damages, which are calculated as the difference between what consumers paid and received. At common law, warranty breaches are remedied by "loss-of-bargain" damages which are calculated as the difference between what consumers thought they were getting and what they got. A third measure of damages is "cost

21 Kraus v. Trinity Mgmt. Servs., Inc., 23 Cal. 4th 116, 999 P.2d 718 (2000); Fletcher v. Security Pacific Nat'l Bank, 23 Cal. 3d 442 (1979); People v. Thomas Shelton Powers, M.D., Inc., 2 Cal. App. 4th 330, 3 Cal. Rptr. 2d 34 (1992); People v. Toomey, 157 Cal. App. 3d 1, 203 Cal. Rptr. 642 (1985).

22 Kraus v. Trinity Mgmt. Servs., Inc., 23 Cal. 4th 116, 999 P.2d 718 (2000); Corbett v. Superior Court, 101 Cal. App. 4th 649, 125 Cal. Rptr. 2d 46 (2002).

23 Kleinschmidt v. Morrow, 642 A.2d 161 (Me. 1994); Dudley v. Wyler, 647 A.2d 90 (Me. 1994).

24 5 Me. Rev. Stat. Ann. § 213(1). *See* Mariello v. Giguere, 667 A.2d 588 (Me. 1995) (amendment is applicable only to cases filed after its effective date).

25 Alsides v. Brown Institute, 592 N.W.2d 468 (Minn. App. Ct. 1999) (reading §§ 325F.69 and 8.31 together).

26 Sulner v. General Accident Fire & Life Assurance Corp., 471 N.Y.S.2d 794 (Sup. Ct. 1984).

27 *See* § 8.1, *supra*.

28 Coley v. Champion Home Builders Co., 590 S.E.2d 20 (N.C. App. 2004).

29 *In re* Universal Service Fund Tel. Billing Practices Litig., 300 F. Supp. 2d 1107, 1151 (D. Kan. 2003); Poor v. Hill, 138 N.C. App. 19, 530 S.E.2d 838 (2000).

of repair" which is the cost to the consumer to alter the product or service so that the product or service matches what was promised.[30]

Texas courts in UDAP actions have interpreted the legislative intent to allow consumers to recover the cost to repair an item, out-of-pocket damages, or loss-of-bargain damages, whichever is the most.[31] However, a consumer may not obtain both loss-of-bargain damages and cost of repair for the same wrongful act.[32] Similarly, the Delaware Supreme Court allows the consumer to choose any of these types of damages.[33] A North Carolina court has approved of damages calculated as the cost to build a new deck instead of the diminished value to the consumer of a deck built smaller than promised.[34]

A Massachusetts appellate court has affirmed a trial court's award of the cost of replacing equipment that was represented to be in working order, even though this exceeded either measure of damages (out of pocket or loss of bargain) allowed at common law.[35] A Missouri court followed the state's approach for fraud claims and allowed recovery of loss-of-bargain damages.[36]

A court interpreting Connecticut law limits damages to out-of-pocket and not benefit-of-the-bargain damages where the consumer can also get punitive and multiple damages.[37] On the other hand, a Connecticut appellate court has construed the UDAP statute's provision allowing recovery of the consumer's "loss," more broadly than the term "damage," allowing the consumer to recover special damages as well as actual damages.[38]

The "economic loss doctrine," which denies recovery in tort for decreased value of a product and other economic losses, has no application to UDAP claims, even those that are founded upon contracts.[39] UDAP claims are statutory causes of action rather than tort claims, and the legislature's decision to grant expanded remedies to consumers should not be overridden by courts.[40]

8.3.2.2 Loss-of-Bargain Damages

Normally, loss-of-bargain damages are more than out-of-pocket damages. For example, consider a seller's claim that a product priced at $100 is really worth $200. If the product is actually worth $50, loss-of-bargain damages are $150 and out-of-pocket damages are $50.

Unless the language in the statute's damage provision specifically limits damages to "restitution,"[41] courts will normally grant loss-of-bargain damages. Thus, courts have awarded as loss-of-bargain damages the difference between the value of the product as represented and as sold,[42] an

30 For a Maryland case enunciating the same three rules, see Hall v. Lovell Regency Homes Ltd., 121 Md. App. 1, 708 A.2d 344 (1998).

31 Coghlan v. Wellcraft Marine Corp., 240 F.3d 449 (5th Cir. 2001) (Texas law); Hiller v. Manufacturers Product Research Group of N. Am., Inc., 59 F.3d 1514 (5th Cir. 1995) (Texas law) (lost profits); Kinerd v. Colonial Leasing Co., 800 S.W.2d 187 (Tex. 1990) (buyer awarded out-of-pocket expenses *plus* difference between purchase price and product's actual value); W.O. Bankston Nissan, Inc. v. Walters, 754 S.W.2d 127 (Tex. 1988); Leyendecker & Assoc., Inc. v. Wechter, 683 S.W.2d 369 (Tex. 1984); Houston Livestock Show and Rodeo, Inc. v. Hamrick, 125 S.W.3d 555 (Tex. App. 2003) (good discussion of wide variety of damages available under UDAP statute); Connell Chevrolet Co. v. Leak, 967 S.W.2d 888 (Tex. App. 1998); Clary Corp. v. Smith, 949 S.W.2d 452 (Tex. App. 1997); Hedley Feedlot, Inc. v. Weatherly Trust, 855 S.W.2d 826 (Tex. App. 1993); Integrated Title Data Sys. v. Dulaney, 800 S.W.2d 336 (Tex. App. 1990) (damages equaled purchase price because product was found to have no value). *Cf.* Albert v. Boatsmith Marine Service & Storage, Inc., 65 Ohio App. 3d 38, 582 N.E.2d 1023 (1989) (reasonable cost of repairs is recognized as a proper measure of damages).

32 Blackstock v. Dudley, 12 S.W.3d 131 (Tex. App. 1999); Norwest Mortgage, Inc. v. Salinas, 999 S.W.2d 846 (Tex. App. 1999).

33 Stephenson v. Capano Dev., Inc., 462 A.2d 1069 (Del. 1983).

34 Lapierre v. Samco Dev. Co., 103 N.C. App. 551, 406 S.E.2d 646 (1991).

35 Sargent v. Koulisas, 29 Mass. App. Ct. 956, 560 N.E.2d 569 (1990).

36 Sunset Pools v. Schaefer, 869 S.W.2d 883 (Mo. Ct. App. 1994).

37 Bailey Employment Sys. Inc. v. Hahn, 545 F. Supp. 62 (D. Conn. 1982), *aff'd*, 723 F.2d 895 (2d Cir. 1983).

38 Catucci v. Ouellette, 25 Conn. App. 56, 592 A.2d 962 (1991).

39 *See* § 4.2.16.2, *supra*.

40 Delgado v. J.W. Courtesy Pontiac GMC-Truck, Inc., 693 So. 2d 602 (Fla. Dist. Ct. App. 1997).

41 Bartner v. Carter, 405 A.2d 194 (Me. 1979); Wimmer v. Down East Properties, Inc., 406 A.2d 88 (Me. 1979).

42 Scott v. Bill Swad Datsun, Inc., 729 F.2d 1461 (6th Cir. 1984) (unpublished, full text available at 1984 U.S. App. LEXIS 14712) (measure of damages for false statements about quality or characteristics of vehicle is difference between value of vehicle if it had been as represented and its actual value); Aurigemma v. Arco Petroleum Products Co., 734 F. Supp. 1025 (D. Conn. 1990); H & J Paving of Fla., Inc. v. Nextel, Inc., 849 So. 2d 1099 (Fla. Dist. Ct. App. 2003); Fort Lauderdale Lincoln Mercury v. Corgnati, 715 So. 2d 311 (Fla. Dist. Ct. App. 1998) (measure of damages is difference between value of goods in condition promised and value in condition delivered); Haddad v. Gonzalez, 410 Mass. 855, 576 N.E.2d 658 (1991) (difference in actual value of apartment in its defective condition and its fair market value if it were as warranted); Sunset Pools v. Schaefer, 869 S.W.2d 883 (Mo. Ct. App. 1994); Chattin v. Cape May Greene, Inc., 243 N.J. Super. 590, 581 A.2d 91 (1990), *aff'd per curiam*, 591 A.2d 943 (N.J. 1991); Taylor v. Triangle Porsche Audi, Inc., 27 N.C. App. 711, 220 S.E.2d 806 (1975); Ford v. Brewer, 1986 Ohio App. LEXIS 9790 (Dec. 9, 1986); Oster v. Swad Chevrolet, 1982 Ohio App. LEXIS 15049 (June 17, 1982) (measure of damages for misrepresentation about qualities of vehicle is difference between its value if it had been as represented and its actual value); Scott v. Noland Co., 1995 Tenn. App. LEXIS 505, Clearinghouse No. 51,282 (Tenn. App. 1995) (court finds that $200 repair cost is difference between actual value and value as warranted); Leyendecker & Assocs., Inc. v. Wechter, 683 S.W.2d 369 (Tex. 1984) (difference in value of land as represented and as received); Howell Crude Oil Co. v. Donna Refinery Partners, Ltd., 928 S.W.2d 100 (Tex. App. 1996); Southland Lloyd's Ins. Co. v. Tomberlain, 919 S.W.2d 822 (Tex. App. 1996); McCann v. Brown, 725 S.W.2d 822 (Tex.

amount equaling the difference between the final sale price and the lower price originally agreed upon,[43] the lost profit from a purchase that the defendant's UDAP violations prevented,[44] or even the difference between the final sale price and the lower price originally advertised.[45]

Loss-of-bargain damages can be sizeable. A court has awarded as loss-of-bargain UDAP damage the difference between what an investment scheme was expected to be worth ($65,000) and what it was actually worth ($0.00).[46]

Loss-of-bargain damages are especially helpful in cases dealing with credit terms. Where a lessor promised a purchase option of $1.00, but then demanded the market value of the property, the measure of damages was calculated as the difference between the market value and the $1.00 price.[47] In another example, a creditor disclosed a stated interest rate that was lower than the actual rate because the amount financed was disbursed in two installments. The court calculated the consumer class' damages based on the class' loss-of-the-bargain damages assuming the class bargained for the interest rate stated in the loan documents. Damages were the difference between the actual total of payments and the total correctly adjusted for the two disbursements of the amount financed, assuming the interest rate remained constant.[48] Where a buyer could not obtain financing at the rates promised by the seller, the buyer's damages were the difference between the interest payments as promised and the rates then available.[49] Although the eventual length of the financing period can not be determined precisely by a court (the buyer may pre-pay or refinance the mortgage), this does not make damages too indeterminate to be reasonably calculable.[50]

Loss-of-bargain damages can also be helpful where the consumer does not want to repair a product and keep it. Where failure to make repairs lowers the market value more than the cost of those repairs, the consumer can recover the larger diminished market value.[51]

Where a seller loses or damages the consumer's property, the consumer will also want to use loss-of-bargain damages. For example, where a moving company caused the loss of a consumer's household goods and personal effects, a court has measured their worth not by market value (out-of-pocket damages), but by their actual value to the owner in the condition in which they were at the time.[52]

8.3.2.3 Cost-to-Repair Damages

Often, the consumer's best option is to receive damages based on the cost to repair the purchased item.[53] Such cost-to-repair damages are measured as the cost of making the repairs, not just the diminished value of the property left in an unrepaired state.[54] Damages are the amount necessary to repair property to meet the seller's representations.[55] For

---

App. 1987); Mercedes-Benz of N. Am. v. Dickenson, 720 S.W.2d 844 (Tex. App. 1986); Cheek v. Zalta, 693 S.W.2d 632 (Tex. App. 1985). *See also* Black v. Iovino, 580 N.E.2d 139 (Ill. App. Ct. 1991) (difference between price buyer paid and actual value of vehicle); Cardwell v. Henry, 549 S.E.2d 587 (N.C. App. 2001) (measure of UDAP damages for substandard housing conditions is difference between fair rental value of the property in warranted condition and actual fair rental value, but damages can not exceed total amount of rent paid by tenant); Fields v. Yarborough Ford, Inc., 414 S.E.2d 164 (S.C. 1992); Houston v. Mike Black Auto Sales, Inc., 788 S.W.2d 696 (Tex. App. 1990). *Cf.* Locascio v. Imports Unlimited, Inc., 309 F. Supp. 2d 267 (D. Conn. 2004) (adopting loss of bargain standard, but finding consumer's proof insufficient); Craft v. Philip Morris Cos., Inc., 2003 WL 23139381 (Mo. Cir. Ct. Dec. 31, 2003). *But cf.* Tucker v. Boulevard at Piper Glen, 150 N.C. App. 150, 564 S.E.2d 248 (2002) (no damages where townhome's actual value exceeded purchase price).

43 Creeger v. Betz, 1974 Ohio App. LEXIS 3458 (Dec. 27, 1974) (consumer entitled to damages equaling total charge for unauthorized repairs where state rule prohibits charging for unauthorized repairs; those damages are then trebled); Crawford Chevrolet, Inc. v. McLarty, 519 S.W.2d 656 (Tex. Civ. App. 1975). *See also* Myers v. Hexagon Co., 54 F. Supp. 2d 742 (E.D. Tenn. 1998) (consumers' damages are difference between financing terms they were led to believe they would get and those they actually got). *But see* Jiries v. BP Oil, 294 N.J. Super. 225, 682 A.2d 1241 (1996) (payment consumer made for unauthorized repairs not "ascertainable loss" where consumer presented no evidence that repairs were done improperly or not done).

44 Veranda Beach Club v. Western Surety Co., 936 F.2d 1364 (1st Cir. 1991) (Mass. law). *But see* Zanakis-Pico v. Cutter Dodge, Inc., 47 P.3d 1222 (Haw. 2002) (difference between advertised "bait" price and actual price not recoverable where consumer declined to buy).

45 Truex v. Ocean Dodge, Inc., 219 N.J. Super. 44, 529 A.2d 1017 (App. Div. 1987); Crow v. Fred Martin Motor Co., 2003 WL 1240119 (Ohio App. Mar. 19, 2003) (unpublished, citation limited) (affirming award of damages in amount of discount that seller advertised but then denied).

46 Nottingham v. General Am. Communications Corp., 811 F.2d 873 (5th Cir. 1987) (Texas law). *Accord* Anthony's Pier Four v. HBC Assocs., 411 Mass. 451, 583 N.E.2d 806 (1991) (damage award based on lost profits and fair market value of property if defendant had not breached contract). *But see* Schwanbeck v. Federal Mogul Corp., 31 Mass. App. Ct. 390, 578 N.E.2d 789 (1991) (in commercial case, court declines to award lost profits), *aff'd on other grounds*, 592 N.E.2d 1289 (Mass. 1992).

47 A.V.I., Inc. v. Heathington, 842 S.W.2d 712 (Tex. App. 1992).

48 Leibert v. Finance Factors Ltd., 788 P.2d 833 (Haw. 1990).

49 Stephenson v. Capano Dev., Inc., 462 A.2d 1069 (Del. 1983).

50 *Id.*

51 Brighton Homes, Inc. v. McAdams, 737 S.W.2d 340 (Tex. App. 1987).

52 American Transfer & Storage Co. v. Brown, 584 S.W.2d 284 (Tex. Civ. App. 1979), *rev'd on other grounds*, 601 S.W.2d 931 (Tex. 1980).

53 Simmons v. Simpson, 626 S.W.2d 315 (Tex. Civ. App. 1981).

54 Pierce v. Drees, 607 N.E.2d 726 (Ind. Ct. App. 1993); Fate v. Dick Callendar Buick, 1986 Ohio App. LEXIS 6878 (May 23, 1986); Seabury Homes, Inc. v. Burleson, 688 S.W.2d 712 (Tex. App. 1985); Jim Walter Homes, Inc. v. Mora, 622 S.W.2d 878 (Tex. Civ. App. 1981); Salais v. Martinez, 603 S.W.2d 296 (Tex. Civ. App. 1980).

55 Young v. Joyce, 351 A.2d 857 (Del. 1975); Deltona Corp. v. Jannetti, 392 So. 2d 976 (Fla. Dist. Ct. App. 1981); Heller v.

example, damages for failure to complete a contract are the cost of properly fulfilling the contract, minus any amount the consumer had not yet paid the other party.[56]

While cost of repair is a legitimate basis for awarding damages, courts may not award such damages where it will lead to economic waste. The courts will instead award loss-of-bargain or out-of-pocket damages. For example, where a $44,000 house is situated on a dangerous site, a court has refused to award $83,000, which would be the cost to move the house to another site. Instead, $44,000 is the proper damage award, where the consumer can then purchase a similar house with that award.[57]

8.3.2.4 Out-of-Pocket Damages or Restitution

8.3.2.4.1 General

In some cases, restitution or out-of-pocket damages may be preferable to the consumer over other forms of damage calculations. Courts are normally generous in allowing restitution,[58] although traditional equitable defenses such as laches may be available.[59]

Strictly speaking, restitution and disgorgement are not damages;[60] the term damages refers to compensation for an injury done,[61] as opposed to the refund of a sum paid. The remedy differs from ordinary damages and other theories in that it is a remedy measured by the benefit to the defendant, not the damage to the plaintiff. Nor is restitution a penalty.[62] However, like damages and penalties, restitution can serve to deter future violations.[63]

A state UDAP statute that authorizes restitution as a remedy is by far the most expedient basis through which to recover an illegitimate fee or overcharge. Not every state provides for restitution of such an assessment through its UDAP statute, however. Ten jurisdictions expressly name restitution as a remedy available to a private litigant (as opposed to a state attorney general).[64] Other states do not specifically authorize restitution as a remedy, but do authorize equitable relief in general terms or give judges broad discretion in fashioning an appropriate UDAP remedy.[65] Consumers who have suffered an illicit overcharge should argue that the judge should use that discretion to order restitution against an overreaching seller. Such provisions have been construed to permit restitution in appropriate circumstances.[66] Case law construing UDAP statutes as

Silverbranch Constr. Corp., 376 Mass. 621, 382 N.E.2d 1065 (1978); Plymouth Pointe Condominium Ass'n v. Delcor Homes-Plymouth Pointe, Ltd., 2003 WL 22439654 (Mich. App. Oct. 28, 2003) (unpublished, citation limited); Grossman v. Waltham Chemical Co., 14 Mass. App. Ct. 932, 436 N.E.2d 1243 (1982); Neveroski v. Blair, 141 N.J. Super. 365, 358 A.2d 473 (App. Div. 1976); Papp v. J&W Roofing & General Contracting, 1999 Ohio App. LEXIS 6042 (Dec. 17, 1999) (cost to repair is proper measure of damages for breach of home improvement contract); Jim Walter Homes Inc. v. Mora, 622 S.W.2d 878 (Tex. Civ. App. 1981) (cost of repair, and not just difference in value from what contracted for, will be used as measure of damages as long as does not involve unreasonable economic waste). *But cf.* Jordan Ford, Inc. v. Alsbury, 625 S.W.2d 1 (Tex. Civ. App. 1981) (mere recital of repair estimates not sufficient proof of cost to repair).

56 Pierce v. Drees, 607 N.E.2d 726 (Ind. Ct. App. 1993). *Accord* Cox v. Sears, Roebuck & Co., 138 N.J. 2, 647 A.2d 454 (1994).

57 Guest v. Phillips Petroleum Co., 981 F.2d 218 (5th Cir. 1993) (Texas law); Hall v. Lovell Regency Homes Ltd., 121 Md. App. 1, 708 A.2d 344 (1998).

58 Cortez v. Purolator Air Filtration Prods. Co., 23 Cal. 4th 163, 999 P.2d 706 (2000) (payment of wages that employees have already earned can be treated as restitution even though a money damage award would also make plaintiff whole). *See* § 10.7.4, *infra*, for additional cases on restitution in suits brought by a state attorney general or other state enforcement agency. *See also* State v. Cottman Transmissions Sys., Inc., 86 Md. App. 714, 587 A.2d 1190 (1991) (reverses trial court's refusal to award restitution). *But cf.* Watson Laboratories, Inc. v. Rhone-Poulenc Rorer, Inc., 178 F. Supp. 2d 1099 (C.D. Cal. 2001) (restitution order can not order disgorgement of defendant's profits that were earned from entities other than plaintiff).

59 Cortez v. Purolator Air Filtration Prods. Co., 23 Cal. 4th 163, 999 P.2d 706 (2000) (court notes that such defenses "may not be asserted to wholly defeat a UCL claim since such claims arise out of unlawful conduct").

60 *See* Korea Supply Co. v. Lockheed Martin Corp., 29 Cal. 4th 1134, 131 Cal. Rptr. 2d 29, 63 P.3d 937 (2003) (contrasting damages and restitution); Bank of the West v. Superior Ct., 10 Cal. Rptr. 2d 538, 545, 546, 833 P.2d 545 (Cal. 1992) (bank's insurance policy, which insured against "damages," did not cover UDAP restitution).

61 22 Am. Jur. 2d Damages § 1 (2003).

62 Commonwealth *ex rel.* Corbett v. Ted Sopko Auto Sales & Locator, 719 A.2d 1111, 1114 (Pa. Commw. Ct. 1998).

63 Irwin v. Mascott, 112 F. Supp. 2d 937, 956 (N.D. Cal. 2000).

64 Alaska Stat. § 45.50.531; Cal. Civ. Code § 1780; Cal. Bus. & Prof. Code § 17203; D.C. Code § 28-3905; Idaho Code § 48-608; Ind. Code § 24.5-0.5-4; Me. Rev. Stat. tit. 5, § 213; Neb. Rev. Stat. § 87-303.07; Tex. Bus. & Com. Code § 17.50; Vt. Stat. Ann. tit. 9, § 2461; Va. Code Ann. § 59.1-204.

65 Conn. Gen. Stat. Ann. § 42-110g; 815 Ill. Comp. Stat. 505/10a; Ky. Rev. Stat. § 367.220; Mass. Gen. Laws ch. 93A, § 9; Minn. Stat. § 8.31(32); Mo. Rev. Stat. § 407.025; Mont. Code Ann. § 30-14-133; N.H. Rev. Stat. Ann. § 358-A:10; N.J. Stat. Ann. § 56:8-19; Or. Rev. Stat. § 646.638; 73 Pa. Cons. Stat. § 201-9.2; R.I. Gen. Laws § 6-13.1-5.2; S.C. Code Ann. § 39-5-140; Tenn. Code Ann. § 47-18-109; W. Va. Code § 46A-6-106. *See also* Nev. Rev. Stat. § 598.0977 (authorizing suit by elderly or disabled person for actual damages, but also referring to this relief as "restitution"); Ohio Rev. Code § 1345.09(D) (authorizing "declaratory judgment, injunction, or other appropriate relief"); Utah Code § 13-11-19(3) (authorizing class action for "declaratory judgment, an injunction, and appropriate ancillary relief").

66 *See, e.g.*, Catucci v. Ouellette, 592 A.2d 962, 963 (Conn. Ct. App. 1991); Cohon v. Oscar, 149 N.E.2d 472; *see also* Aurigemma v. Arco Petroleum Prods. Co., 734 F. Supp. 1025, 1033 (D. Conn. 1990) (actual damages language in statute would permit order of restitution, but it was not appropriate under circumstances of case); Gour v. Daray Motor Co., 373 So. 2d 571, 578 (La. Ct. App. 1979) (actual damages language of statute permits order of restitution); Gross-Haentjens v. Leck-

remedial and subject to liberal construction may also support an argument that restitution is within the statute's scope.[67]

A UDAP provision requiring sellers to "restore money acquired in violation" of the act has been interpreted as allowing full restitution of all money paid for a franchise.[68] Even where a statute limited recovery to "actual damages," since there was a legislative intent to encourage private UDAP litigation, the court allowed a consumer to return a defective car and obtain a refund of the original purchase price, thereby depriving the seller of any profit.[69] In another case, a debtor who was induced to pay up the arrearage on a repossessed car by false promises that it would then be returned to her was able to recover as damages the amount she paid.[70] In granting restitution, courts may award both return of the purchase price plus the consumer's other out-of-pocket expenditures as damages.[71]

Courts have granted restitution or allowed the claim to go to trial in cases involving UDAP or other claims about a variety of illegitimate fees, including:

- Inflated port charges;[72]
- Excess towing fees;[73]
- Illegally assessed mobile home sales fees;[74]
- Invalid returned check fees;[75]
- Overreaching debt collector charges;[76]
- Fees for services not rendered;[77]
- Unlawful car warranty deductibles;[78]
- Fuel surcharges;[79]
- Mortgage recording taxes;[80]
- Retailers' occupation taxes;[81]
- Excessive interest and attorney fees;[82] and
- Retention of security deposits and interest thereon;[83]

Restitution is also appropriately asserted to recover profit padding in the form of:

- Car dealer price misrepresentations;[84]
- Mortgage lender overcharges;[85]
- Excessive insurance premiums;[86]
- Excessive drug prices;[87] and
- Secret discounts.[88]

Some courts may allow restitution only in the amount that the defendant has benefited from the unlawful act. For example, an earlier version of the Maine UDAP statute, which allowed a consumer to sue for "restitution" but not actual damages, was interpreted to require that the dealer benefit from the act that harmed the consumers.[89] Where the dealer had already tendered a complete refund before suit, thus foregoing all the benefit it had obtained from the deceptive transaction, the Maine Supreme Court declined to order further restitution.[90] On the other hand, a court has interpreted the restitution authority in one of California's UDAP statutes as allowing a court to order a bank to restore money that its unfair acts allowed a third party to take from the consumer.[91]

The common law may provide an alternate vehicle for obtaining restitution.[92] However, since UDAP statutes were enacted to remedy the defects in existing common law

enby, 589 P.2d 1209, 1210 (Or. Ct. App. 1979) (purpose of private enforcement provision is to provide consumers restitution).

67 *See* § 2.1.3, *supra*.

68 United Postage Corp. v. Kammeyer, 581 S.W.2d 716 (Tex. Civ. App. 1979).

69 Gour v. Daray Motor Co., 373 So. 2d 571 (La. Ct. App. 1979). *See also* Aurigemma v. Arco Petroleum Products Co., 734 F. Supp. 1025 (D. Conn. 1990) ("actual damages" language in statute authorized restitution, but not appropriate where it would be extremely difficult to unravel a five-year business relationship between plaintiffs and defendants). *But see* Colonial Lincoln-Mercury Sales, Inc. v. Molina, 152 Ga. App. 379, 262 S.E.2d 820 (1979).

70 Patterson v. Chrysler Fin. Co. (*In re* Patterson), 263 B.R. 82 (Bankr. E.D. Pa. 2001).

71 Catucci v. Ouellette, 25 Conn. App. 56, 592 A.2d 962 (1991).

72 Latman v. Costa Cruise Lines, N.V., 758 So. 2d 699 (Fla. Ct. App. 2000).

73 Lonergan v. A.J.'s Wrecker Serv. of Dallas, Inc., 1999 WL 462333 (N.D. Tex. July 6, 1999).

74 Commonwealth v. DeCotis, 316 N.E.2d 748 (Mass. 1974).

75 Ballard v. Equifax Check Servs., Inc., 158 F. Supp. 2d 1163 (E.D. Cal. 2001).

76 Irwin v. Mascott, 112 F. Supp. 2d 937 (N.D. Cal. 2000).

77 State v. Bob Chambers Ford, Inc., 522 A.2d 362 (Me. 1987) (rustproofing fees); Motzer Dodge Jeep Eagle, Inc. v. Ohio Attorney Gen., 642 N.E.2d 20 (Ohio Ct. App. 1994) (delivery and handling fees).

78 State v. Ford Motor Co., 526 N.Y.S.2d 637 (N.Y. App. Div. 1988).

79 Durant v. Servicemaster Co., 147 F. Supp. 2d 744 (E.D Mich. 2001).

80 Friar v. Vanguard Holding Corp., 434 N.Y.S.2d 698 (N.Y. App. Div. 1980).

81 Cohon v. Oscar L. Paris Co., 149 N.E.2d 472 (Ill. App. Ct. 1958).

82 Owl Constr. Co. v. Ronald Adams Contractor, Inc., 642 F. Supp. 475 (E.D. La. 1986).

83 Steinmetz v. Toyota Motor Credit Corp., 963 F. Supp. 1294 (E.D.N.Y. 1997); Fitzpatrick v. Scalzi, 806 A.2d 593 (Conn. Ct. App. 2002).

84 Northview Motors, Inc. v. Commonwealth, 562 A.2d 977 (Pa. Commw. Ct. 1989).

85 Century Bank v. Hymans, 905 P.2d 722 (N.M. Ct. App. 1995).

86 *In re* Prudential Ins. Co. of Am. Sales Practices Litig., 975 F. Supp. 584 (D.N.J. 1996).

87 F.T.C. v. Mylan Labs., Inc., 62 F. Supp. 2d 25 (D.D.C. 1999).

88 Unit Process Co. v. Raychem Corp., 2002 WL 173286 (Cal. Ct. App. Feb. 5, 2002).

89 Kleinschmidt v. Morrow, 642 A.2d 161 (Me. 1994); Dudley v. Wyler, 647 A.2d 90 (Me. 1994).

90 Drinkwater v. Patten Realty Corp., 563 A.2d 772 (Me. 1989). *See also* Perez v. Anderson, 98 B.R. 189 (E.D. Pa. 1989) (order of specific performance obviates other damages).

91 Rosales v. Citibank, 133 F. Supp. 2d 1177 (N.D. Cal. 2001).

92 *See* § 9.7, *infra*.

remedies,[93] restrictions on the common law remedy of restitution should not be imported into UDAP claims.

8.3.2.4.2 Need the court deduct the value of the product from the restitution amount?

Courts in defective car cases make no adjustment for the consumer's use of the car, but return to the consumer everything paid in, including the value of the trade-in, all monthly payments (including interest), and the down payment.[94] This is the case even when the vehicle was repossessed before the consumer could bring a UDAP claim.[95]

A North Carolina court has gone one step further and ruled that where a product is worthless, the consumer need not return the product to obtain full restitution.[96] Similarly, where a consumer was deceptively sold worthless land, the Washington Supreme Court calculated damages as the amount of money paid plus interest, and did not require return of the land.[97] A Minnesota court has ordered full restitution to 140,000 consumers (without the consumers having to return the product and without any offset against the amount paid) where an air purifier was found ineffective and dangerous.[98]

Maryland's highest court has ruled that rental of an unlicensed apartment is unfair, and that the landlord may not retain benefits from the rental. Restitution should equal total rent paid plus moving costs plus the increased cost of the new apartment, with no reduction for the value of the apartment during the rental period.[99]

93 *See* § 4.2.3.1, *supra*.

94 Gent v. Collinsville Volkswagon, 116 Ill. App. 3d 496, 451 N.E.2d 1385 (1983) (damages for defective car include purchase price plus towing, repair, interest, and substitute vehicle costs); Bernard v. Central Carolina Truck Sales, Inc., 314 S.E.2d 582 (N.C. Ct. App. 1984); Lone Star Ford, Inc. v. McGlashan, 681 S.W.2d 720 (Tex. App. 1984); North Star Dodge Sales, Inc. v. Luna, 653 S.W.2d 892 (Tex. App. 1983), *aff'd*, 667 S.W.2d 115 (Tex. 1984); Helfman Motors, Inc. v. Stockman, 616 S.W.2d 394 (Tex. Civ. App. 1981). *But see* Gour v. Daray Motor Co., 373 So. 2d 571 (La. Ct. App. 1979); David McDavid Pontiac, Inc. v. Nix, 681 S.W.2d 831 (Tex. App. 1984).

95 Bernard v. Central Carolina Truck Sales, 314 S.E.2d 582 (N.C. Ct. App. 1984).

96 State *ex rel.* Edmisten v. Zim Chemical Co., 45 N.C. App. 604, 263 S.E.2d 849 (1980). *See also* Briercroft Service Corp. v. Perez, 820 S.W.2d 813 (Tex. App. 1990), *aff'd in part, rev'd in part on other grounds*, 809 S.W.2d 216 (Tex. 1991).

97 Allen v. American Land Research, 95 Wash. 2d 841, 631 P.2d 930 (1981); *see also* Vick v. George, 671 S.W.2d 541 (Tex. App. 1983), *aff'd on other grounds*, 696 S.W.2d 160 (Tex. 1984).

98 State v. Alpine Air Products, Inc., 490 N.W.2d 888 (Minn. Ct. App. 1992), *aff'd on other grounds*, 500 N.W.2d 788 (Minn. 1993).

99 Golt v. Phillips, 308 Md. 1, 517 A.2d 328 (1986). *See also In re* Fleet, 95 B.R. 319 (E.D. Pa. 1989) (New Jersey law) (UDAP violation makes contract void, entitling consumers to full repayment of all amounts paid).

8.3.2.4.3 Restitution where consumers can not be located

A California UDAP statute formerly authorized anyone to bring a UDAP action, including for restitution, even if the plaintiff was not affected by the unlawful practice.[100] An appellate court extended this concept to allow a restitution recovery even if the damaged consumers could not be identified. The seller must repay the money illegally acquired, and the court could order its distribution in a way to correct as much as possible the harm done.[101] However, the plaintiff must go through the formalities of class certification before this type of fluid recovery will be approved.[102] In 2004, the statute was amended to require all representative suits to comply with a state class action statute, to require the representative plaintiff to have suffered a loss of money or property. The District of Columbia has amended the UDAP provisions of its code to be similar to the former version of California's statute in allowing these broad remedies.[103]

8.3.3 Consequential Damages

8.3.3.1 General

Direct damages are those directly and immediately resulting from the unfair or deceptive act or practice and pertain directly to the goods or services involved in the transaction. UDAP litigants may obtain relief based not just on these direct damages, but also from proximate or consequential damages—all damages foreseeably flowing from an unfair or deceptive act or practice.[104] Such consequential damages are often far greater than the direct damages from the UDAP violation. Court rules may require consequential damages to be pleaded specifically.

100 Cal. Bus. & Prof. Code § 17200.

101 People v. Thomas Shelton Powers, M.D., Inc., 3 Cal. Rptr. 2d 34 (Ct. App. 1992).

102 Kraus v. Trinity Mgmt. Servs., 23 Cal. 4th 116, 999 P.2d 718 (2000).

103 D.C. Code § 28-3905(k).

104 Jersild v. Aker, 775 F. Supp. 1198 (E.D. Wis. 1991); Gent v. Collinsville Volkswagon, 116 Ill. App. 3d 496, 451 N.E.2d 1385 (1983); State *ex rel.* Guste v. General Motors Corp., 354 So. 2d 770 (La. Ct. App. 1978), *rev'd on other grounds*, 370 So. 2d 477 (La. 1978); Haddad v. Gonzalez, 410 Mass. 855, 576 N.E.2d 658 (1991); Hale v. Basin Motor Co., 110 N.M. 314, 795 P.2d 1006 (1990); Quate v. Caudle, 381 S.E.2d 842 (N.C. Ct. App. 1989); Caldwell v. Pop's Home Inc., 54 Or. App. 104, 634 P.2d 471 (1981); Smith v. Baldwin, 611 S.W.2d 611 (Tex. 1980); Sing v. John L. Scott, Inc., 920 P.2d 589 (Wash. App. 1996), *rev'd on other grounds*, 948 P.2d 816 (Wash. 1997). *But see* Fort Lauderdale Lincoln Mercury v. Corgnati, 715 So. 2d 311 (Fla. Dist. Ct. App. 1998) (aberrational decision holding that consequential damages can not be considered in "actual damages" allowed by UDAP statute); Urling v. Helms Exterminators, Inc., 468 So. 2d 451 (Fla. Dist. Ct. App. 1985).

For example, in a defective car case, a consumer may be awarded as damages not only the appropriate part of the purchase price, but also the costs of repairs, towing, alternate transportation, storage, and various other inconveniences resulting from the UDAP violation.[105] Where a faulty car repair causes continuing damage, the diminished value of the car is not measured immediately after the repair, but after all damage caused by the repair is manifested.[106]

Where the consumer was misled about how long his mobile home could be kept in a park, the consumer could obtain damages for moving and storing the home because these costs flow from the misrepresentation and are a foreseeable consequence.[107] Consequential damages include the consumer's cost of improvements to land incurred before the consumer purchased the land, where the consumer relied upon promises that low-cost financing would be available to purchase the land.[108] The equity in a home that was lost when the consumer fell prey to a predatory lending scheme can be awarded as damages.[109] A doctor who had to retire early because he was wrongfully denied liability insurance suffered consequential damages.[110] If a misrepresentation caused a consumer not to act, the consumer can recover damages as a consequence of that inaction.[111]

8.3.3.2 Standards to Prove Consequential Damages

Courts differ as to proof requirements for recovery of consequential damages. Some courts require more than a causal connection between the deceptive practice and the consumer's damage.[112] A number of courts follow the common law rule that the damage must be a foreseeable consequence of the deception.[113] In one case, future damages and possible loss of workers' compensation insurance were found too conjectural to be awarded in a UDAP claim.[114]

In Texas, the damage need not be foreseeable, as long as the deceptive practice was the producing cause.[115] This standard is incorporated in the statute.[116] Showing that an act is a cause-in-fact of damages is all that is needed.[117] "Producing cause" means an "efficient, exciting, or contributing cause" and there may be more than one producing cause.[118] A producing cause is a substantial factor which brings about the injury and without which the injury would not have occurred.

---

105 Gent v. Collinsville Volkswagon, 116 Ill. App. 3d 496, 451 N.E.2d 1385 (1983); State *ex rel.* Guste v. General Motors Corp., 354 So. 2d 770 (La. Ct. App. 1978), *rev'd on other grounds*, 370 So. 2d 477 (La. 1978); Hyder-Inrgram Chevrolet Inc. v. Kutach, 612 S.W.2d 687 (Tex. Civ. App. 1981) ($875 for use of a rental car); *see also* Tri-West Constr. Co. v. Hernandez, 43 Or. App. 961, 607 P.2d 1375 (1979); Atlas Amalgamated Inc. v. Castillo, 601 S.W.2d 728 (Tex. Civ. App. 1980).

106 Robinson Machinery Co. v. Davis, 689 S.W.2d 286 (Tex. App. 1985).

107 Caldwell v. Pop's Home Inc., 54 Or. App. 104, 634 P.2d 471 (1981).

108 Danny Darby Real Estate, Inc. v. Jacobs, 760 S.W.2d 711 (Tex. App. 1988). *See also* York v. InTrust Bank, 265 Kan. 271, 962 P.2d 405 (1998) (buyers allowed to recover increased construction and financing costs caused by delays when they refused to pay deceptively inflated commission).

109 Opportunity Mgmt. Co. v. Frost, 1999 Wash. App. LEXIS 336 (Feb. 16, 1999).

110 Herrin v. Medical Protective Co., 89 S.W.3d 301 (Tex. App. 2002).

111 Nast v. State Farm Fire and Cas. Co., 82 S.W.3d 114 (Tex. App. 2002).

112 Rollins, Inc. v. Heller, 454 So. 2d 580 (Fla. Dist. Ct. App. 1984); Petrauskas v. Wexenthaller Realty Mgmt., Inc., 186 Ill. App. 3d 820, 542 N.E.2d 902 (1989) (unforeseeable independent criminal act of third person which causes the injury relieves a defendant of UDAP liability).

113 Dimarzo v. American Mut. Ins. Co., 389 Mass. 85, 449 N.E.2d 1189 (1983) (entitled to all losses foreseeable consequence of insurer failing to settle claim); Kohl v. Silver Lake Motors, Inc., 369 Mass. 795, 343 N.E.2d 375 (1976); International Totalizing Sys., Inc. v. Pepsico, Inc., 29 Mass. App. Ct. 424, 560 N.E.2d 749 (1990) (loss of business opportunity was a foreseeable consequence of defendant's deception); Brown v. LeClair, 20 Mass. App. Ct. 976, 482 N.E.2d 870 (1985); Taylor v. Medenica, 479 S.E.2d 35 (S.C. 1996); *see also* Collins v. Gulf Oil Corp., 605 F. Supp. 1519 (D. Conn. 1985) (injury too remote to be recoverable); Troxler v. Hartford Ins. Group, 7 Conn. L. Trib. No. 22 at 7 (D. Conn. 1981).

114 Higbie Roth Constr. Co. v. Houston Shell & Concrete, 1 S.W.3d 808 (Tex. App. 1999).

115 Blue Star Operating Co. v. Tetra Technologies, Inc., 119 S.W.3d 916 (Tex. App. 2003); West Anderson Plaza v. Exxon Mehdi Feyznia, 876 S.W.2d 528 (Tex. App. 1994); Pena v. Ludwig, 766 S.W.2d 298 (Tex. App. 1989); Danny Darby Real Estate, Inc. v. Jacobs, 760 S.W.2d 711 (Tex. App. 1988) (cost of improvements to land buyer incurred before real estate closing, even if not foreseeable); FDP Corp. v. Southwestern Bell Tel. Co., 749 S.W.2d 569 (Tex. App. 1988), *rev'd on other grounds*, 811 S.W.2d 572 (Tex. 1991); Metro Ford Truck Sales, Inc. v. Davis, 709 S.W.2d 785 (Tex. App. 1986); Hycel, Inc. v. Wittstruck, 690 S.W.2d 914 (Tex. App. 1985); Reliance Universal Inc. v. Sparks Industrial Servs., 688 S.W.2d 890 (Tex. App. 1985): Martin v. Lou Poliquin Enterprises, Inc., 696 S.W.2d 180 (Tex. App. 1985); Rotello v. Ring Around Products Inc., 614 S.W.2d 455 (Tex. Civ. App. 1981).

116 Tex. Bus. & Com. Code § 17.50. *See* Union Pump Co. v. Allbritton, 898 S.W.2d 773 (Tex. 1995) (contrasting proximate cause, which requires foreseeability, with producing cause, which does not). The "producing cause" standard is also used in Jones Act litigation and is described as a lighter standard than proximate cause. *See* Cella v. U.S., 998 F.2d 418 (7th Cir. 1993).

117 Smith v. Heard, 980 S.W.2d 693 (Tex. App. 1998). *See* Union Pump Co. v. Allbritton, 898 S.W.2d 773 (Tex. 1995) (contrasting proximate cause, which requires foreseeability, with producing cause, which does not); 2 Fat Guys Inv., Inc. v. Klaver, 928 S.W.2d 268 (Tex. App. 1996); Hall v. Stephenson, 919 S.W.2d 454 (Tex. App. 1996); Camden Mach. & Tool, Inc. v. Cascade Co., 870 S.W.2d 304 (Tex. App. 1993); Peeler v. Hughes & Luce, 868 S.W.2d 823 (Tex. App. 1993), *aff'd*, 909 S.W.2d 494 (Tex. 1995).

118 Haynes & Boone v. Bowser Bouldin, Ltd., 896 S.W.2d 179 (Tex. 1995); Bartlett v. Schmidt, 33 S.W.3d 35 (Tex. App. 2000); Hall v. Stephenson, 919 S.W.2d 454 (Tex. App. 1996); Camden Mach. & Tool, Inc. v. Cascade Co., 870 S.W.2d 304 (Tex. App. 1993).

8.3.3.3 Financing Costs as Consequential Damages

An important example of consequential damages are various financing costs that relate to the unfair or deceptive practice. Where the purchase price of a defective car is found to be actual damages, interest payments attributed to the car loan are also recoverable.[119]

Similarly, courts award as additional UDAP damages any interest or finance charges the consumer was forced to pay by reason of a deceptive sale.[120] Even where prejudgment interest is not allowed, a consumer can recover the interest lost when the consumer had to take money out of a savings account to perform repairs the seller failed to perform.[121] Consumers may also recover increased construction and financing costs caused when building of a home was delayed by the consumers refusal to pay a deceptively inflated real estate commission.[122]

8.3.3.4 Consequential Damages Based on Consumer's Lost Time or Earnings

Often consequential damage is not evidenced by payment of extra expenses, but by additional efforts the consumer must undertake. This lost time is a possible source of damages.[123] A consumer has been awarded $5000 for the consumer's own efforts in supervising construction work necessary because the builder failed to complete the work.[124] Another consumer was awarded $400 for conducting her own title search on a mobile home where this was necessary because of the seller's deception.[125] An appellate court has affirmed an award of $750 for ten hours of lost wages because the consumer had to use his lunch time to repair a damaged car, where there was evidence that the consumer, who was paid on commission, made about $75 an hour.[126] The Hawaii Supreme Court has ruled that out-of-pocket costs such as gasoline and parking incurred to respond to a deceptive ad are compensable even if the consumer declined to make the purchase.[127]

New Mexico's highest court has indicated it may consider a consumer's "lost paid vacation time" in calculating actual damages. This would be time the consumer had to take off from work to prepare for and appear at depositions and trial. While the consumer had unsuccessfully argued that the loss of paid vacation time should be assessed as court costs, the court was sympathetic to an argument that these costs should be treated as actual damages. "Certainly, high among the factors motivating legislatures to enact laws such as we are considering today is the frustration experienced by consumers having to run around to straighten out unfair or deceptive trade practices."[128]

Lost future earnings caused by the UDAP violation should be awarded as consequential damages. For example, in a personal injury action based on a UDAP theory, a court approved $92,500 for loss of future earning capacity (which was then trebled).[129] In a commercial UDAP case, a graphics business that purchased a printing system that did not perform as represented recovered $96,586 in lost profits.[130]

8.3.3.5 Lost Use of a Product or Service

An important issue concerning consequential damages is how to measure the consumer's damages for lost use of a defective car or when a car was delivered late, or repairs were slow. Actual car rental costs can certainly be considered within the contemplation of the parties and thus are appropriate for consequential damages.[131] Courts also will award the reasonable rental value of a substitute vehicle, even though there was no evidence that the consumer had in fact rented a substitute vehicle.[132]

The consumer may even be reimbursed for the cost of purchasing a substitute car, calculated as the down payment,

---

119 Gent v. Collinsville Volkswagon, 116 Ill. App. 3d 496, 451 N.E.2d 1385 (1983). *But see* Fort Lauderdale Lincoln Mercury v. Corgnati, 715 So. 2d 311 (Fla. Dist. Ct. App. 1998) (aberrant decision holding that financing costs and other consequential damages can not be included in UDAP award).

120 Jersild v. Aker, 775 F. Supp. 1198 (E.D. Wis. 1991); Antle v. Reynolds, 15 S.W.3d 762 (Mo. App. 2000); Quate v. Caudle, 381 S.E.2d 842 (N.C. Ct. App. 1989); Smith v. Baldwin, 611 S.W.2d 611 (Tex. 1980); Investors, Inc. v. Hadley, 738 S.W.2d 737 (Tex. App. 1987); Lone Star Ford, Inc. v. McGlashan, 681 S.W.2d 720 (Tex. App. 1984); Chrysler Corp. v. Scheunemann, 618 S.W.2d 799 (Tex. Civ. App. 1981).

121 Quate v. Caudle, 381 S.E.2d 842 (N.C. Ct. App. 1989); Orkin Exterminating Co. v. Lesassier, 688 S.W.2d 651 (Tex. App. 1985). *See also* Jersild v. Aker, 775 F. Supp. 1198 (E.D. Wis. 1991).

122 York v. InTrust Bank, 265 Kan. 271, 962 P.2d 405 (1998).

123 *See* Bump v. Robbins, 24 Mass. App. Ct. 296, 509 N.E.2d 12 (1987) (consumer awarded damages for lost time).

124 Ybarra v. Saldona, 624 S.W.2d 948 (Tex. Civ. App. 1981).

125 Village Mobile Homes, Inc. v. Porter, 716 S.W.2d 543 (Tex. App. 1986).

126 Allied Towing Serv. v. Mitchell, 833 S.W.2d 577 (Tex. App. 1992).

127 Zanakis-Pico v. Cutter Dodge, Inc., 47 P.3d 1222 (Haw. 2002).

128 Hale v. Basin Motor Co., 110 N.M. 314, 795 P.2d 1006 (1990).

129 Keller Indus., Inc. v. Reeves, 656 S.W.2d 221 (Tex. App. 1983).

130 Innovative Office Sys. v. Johnson, 906 S.W.2d 940 (Tex. App. 1995).

131 Centroplex Ford, Inc. v. Kirby, 736 S.W.2d 261 (Tex. App. 1987) (slow repairs); Bob Robertson, Inc. v. Webster, 679 S.W.2d 683 (Tex. App. 1984) (late delivery).

132 Burgess Constr. Co. v. Hancock, 514 P.2d 236 (Alaska 1973); Malinson v. Black, 83 Cal. App. 2d 375, 188 P.2d 788 (1948); Meakin v. Dreier, 209 So. 2d 252 (Fla. Dist. Ct. App. 1968); Chriss v. Manchester Ins. & Indemnity Co., 308 So. 2d 803 (La. Ct. App. 1975); Luna v. North Star Dodge Sales, Inc, 653 S.W.2d 892 (Tex. 1983), *aff'd*, 667 S.W.2d 115 (Tex. 1984); Milt Ferguson Motor Co. v. Zeretzke, 827 S.W.2d 349 (Tex. App. 1991); Metro Ford Truck Sales, Inc. v. Davis, 709 S.W.2d 785 (Tex. App. 1986); Holmes v. Raffo, 60 Wash. 2d 421, 374 P.2d 536 (1962).

and tax, title and license fees, plus the monthly car payments for the period involved.[133] This was found to be appropriate even when the defective, but running car was parked in the consumer's own garage, where the consumer was rightfully concerned with the car's safety and did not want to sell it to another, and the dealer would not take the car back.[134]

But a consumer should not obtain a double recovery for a replacement vehicle and for lost use. Lost-use damages should be calculated only until a replacement vehicle is purchased, and, from then on, the consumer should just recover for the cost of the replacement vehicle.[135]

8.3.3.6 Injury to Credit Rating

Consumers may also be able to recover damages for injury to their credit rating resulting from the deceptive practice. Thus where a trucker purchased a defective truck, leading to lost income, repossession of the truck and a bad credit rating, the trucker recovered $50,000 damages for loss of credit.[136] In some states, the consumer must plead specifically each type of consequential damages, including damage to her credit rating.[137] To recover more than nominal damages in Texas, a consumer must show that the injury to her credit rating resulted in either (1) a denial of credit and resulting damages or (2) a requirement of a higher interest rate.[138]

8.3.3.7 Attorney Fees as Consequential Damages

Often one of the greatest consequential costs to a consumer of a UDAP violation is the expense of hiring an attorney to untangle the problems caused by the deceptive practice. Most UDAP statutes authorize a prevailing consumer to recover attorney fees required to obtain the UDAP judgment, so that it will be unnecessary to recover these same costs as consequential damages. But some UDAP statutes do not do so, or make such an award discretionary with the court.

Moreover, even in states that provide statutory attorney fees, the consumer may have legal expenses relating to the UDAP violation that are in addition to legal costs to prosecute the UDAP case. Furthermore, being able to treat legal expenses as actual damages may allow the consumer to treble those costs in some circumstances.

In general, it will be difficult to receive attorney fees as consequential damages, instead of being based on a statutory authorization.[139] But there are situations where a court will award attorney fees as UDAP consequential damages. Attorney fees expended to collect money due from one party are recoverable as UDAP damages against the third party responsible for forcing the plaintiff to resort to a collection action.[140] Attorney fees paid to defend an earlier lawsuit are recoverable as actual damages where an insurer's unconscionable conduct required the expenditure of those fees.[141]

A bankruptcy court has also trebled attorney fees as a form of treble actual damages where the Bankruptcy Code allowed attorney fees as actual damages, and where the Bankruptcy Code violation was also a UDAP violation.[142] Where a UDAP statute did not authorize statutory attorney fees, but did authorize "additional relief as appropriate," a court has awarded the consumer attorney fees, although it did not specify whether it was treating them as damages.[143]

8.3.3.8 Physical Injuries

Some UDAP statutes specifically disallow damages for physical injuries.[144] Where, however, the statute allows the consumer to recover damages, without restricting the injury that is compensable, then the consumer can recover for physical injuries as well as monetary loss.[145]

133 Town East Ford Sales, Inc. v. Gray, 730 S.W.2d 796 (Tex. App. 1987).

134 *Id.*

135 Jeep Eagle Sales Corp. v. Mack Massey Motors, Inc., 814 S.W.2d 167 (Tex. App. 1991). *See also* Greelish v. Drew, 35 Mass. App. Ct. 541, 622 N.E.2d 1376 (1993) (interest actually earned and paid to the consumer on money that defendant wrongfully withheld must be deducted from consumer's damages for loss of use of the money).

136 Metro Ford Truck Sales, Inc. v. Davis, 709 S.W.2d 785 (Tex. App. 1986). *See also* Phillips v. David McDermott Chevrolet, Inc., 1992 Conn. Super. LEXIS 888 (Mar. 24, 1992) ($5000 for damage to credit rating); Smith v. Herco, Inc., 1995 Tex. App. LEXIS 965 (1995). *See also* City Nat'l Bank v. Wells, 384 S.E.2d 374 (W. Va. 1989) (damage to credit rating is a consequential damage recoverable under UCC). *But cf.* Page & Wirtz Constr. Co. v. Solomon, 110 N.M. 206, 794 P.2d 349 (1990) (no award where no evidence of UDAP violation).

137 *See* Boat Superstore, Inc. v. Haner, 877 S.W.2d 376 (Tex. App. 1994).

138 Provident Am. Ins. Co. v. Castaneda, 988 S.W.2d 189 (Tex. 1999); St. Paul Surplus Lines Ins. Co. v. Dal-Worth Tank Co., 974 S.W.2d 51 (Tex. 1998); Connell Chevrolet Co. v. Leak, 967 S.W.2d 888 (Tex. App. 1998).

139 Milam Dev. Corp. v. 7*7*0*1 Wurzbach Tower Council of Co-Owners, Inc., 789 S.W.2d 942 (Tex. App. 1990); Brown Foundation v. Friendly Chevrolet Co., 715 S.W.2d 115 (Tex. App. 1986).

140 Fraser Eng'g Co. v. Desmond, 26 Mass. App. Ct. 99, 524 N.E.2d 110 (1988).

141 Nationwide Mut. Ins. Co. v. Holmes, 842 S.W.2d 335 (Tex. App. 1992). *Accord* Columbia Chiropractic Group, Inc. v. Trust Ins. Co., 430 Mass. 60, 712 N.E.2d 93 (1999) (UDAP damages can include fees for defense of lawsuit that was filed to collect unreasonable and unnecessary charges).

142 Aponte v. Aungst, 82 B.R. 738 (Bankr. E.D. Pa. 1988).

143 Jungkurth v. Eastern Fin. Servs., Inc., 74 B.R. 323 (Bankr. E.D. Pa. 1987) (statute has since been amended to include explicit authority to award fees).

144 *See, e.g.*, T.W.M. v. American Medical Sys., Inc., 886 F. Supp. 842 (N.D. Fla. 1995) (denying recovery for personal injury because of Florida UDAP statute's explicit bar); Tex. Bus. & Com. Code Ann. §§ 17.50(b), (h), 17.49(e) (recovery limited to economic damages and mental anguish in some UDAP suits; damages for bodily injury or death excluded in most cases).

145 Maurer v. Cerkvenik-Anderson Travel, Inc., 181 Ariz. 294, 890

A number of states require, as a condition of a UDAP suit, that the consumer have suffered "an ascertainable loss of money or property."[146] Courts in several states have misinterpreted this language to restrict the type of damages for which a consumer can be compensated only to those involving loss of money or property, not physical injury.[147] Connecticut adopts a better interpretation, more consistent with the liberal construction due UDAP statutes, that once the threshold requirement of an ascertainable loss of money or property is met, the consumer's damages are measured and limited only by general damage law principles.[148] Massachusetts also recognizes that UDAP damages can include non-pecuniary losses.[149] Then damage for physical injury can be recovered *in addition to* recovery for the loss of money or property.

8.3.3.9 Pain and Suffering; Mental Anguish

8.3.3.9.1 General

An important form of consequential damages is pain and suffering or mental anguish. In general, these damages should be available in a UDAP case at least to the same extent that they are recoverable at common law.[150] States are even abandoning common law restrictions on the recovery of these damages.[151]

8.3.3.9.2 States where UDAP pain and suffering damages are never recoverable

The one exception where pain and suffering will not be available for a UDAP claim, even though such damages are recoverable at common law, is where the UDAP statute explicitly limits itself to economic damages. In practice few if any UDAP statutes explicitly limit the type of damages that are recoverable. More common is for a UDAP statute to limit recovery only to those situations where there is damage to money or property. That is, if the consumer's only injury is pain and suffering, UDAP damages are not recoverable. The logical extension to this limitation is that if there is damage to money or property, then the consumer can recover not only that damage, but, in appropriate circumstances, also for pain and suffering.

Nevertheless, several courts have failed to make this distinction, and find that pain and suffering is not recoverable under a UDAP statute that requires damage to money or property as a precondition to a private cause of action.[152] These courts fail to distinguish between a legislative intent to limit UDAP cases to situations where there is at least some monetary damage and a much broader limitation, not explicitly found in the statutes, that only economic injury be compensated. In addition, the Hawaii Supreme Court has concluded that emotional distress and other personal injury damages can not be awarded even though the UDAP statute does not have an explicit limit.[153]

8.3.3.9.3 Pain and suffering damages generally recoverable where there is physical injury

Where a UDAP statute does not explicitly limit the recovery of pain and suffering damages, such damages should be available in almost all states where there is also a

---

P.2d 69 (App. 1994) (California UDAP statute allows recovery for death of tourist caused by travel agency's failure to disclose risks of trip); Duncavage v. Allen, 147 Ill. App. 3d 88, 497 N.E.2d 433 (1986) (death claim allowed to proceed); Maillet v. ATF-Davidson Co., 407 Mass. 185, 552 N.E.2d 95 (1990). *See also* Kociemba v. G.D. Searle & Co., 680 F. Supp. 1293 (D. Minn. 1988) (Minnesota UDAP statute applies to product liability litigation); § 2.2.11, *supra*. *But see* Zanakis-Pico v. Cutter Dodge, Inc., 47 P.3d 1222 (Haw. 2002).

146 *See* § 7.5.2, *supra*.

147 Association of Washington Public Hosp. Dists. v. Philip Morris, 241 F.3d 696 (9th Cir. 2001); Blowers v. Eli Lilly & Co., 100 F. Supp. 2d 1265 (D. Haw. 2000); Northwest Laborers-Employers Health & Security Trust Fund v. Philip Morris, Inc., 58 F. Supp. 2d 1211 (W.D. Wash. 1999) (expenses for medical treatment paid by union health and welfare trust fund due to tobacco-related illnesses not compensable); *In re* Bryant, 111 B.R. 474 (E.D. Pa. 1990); *In re* Clark, 96 B.R. 569 (E.D. Pa. 1989); Beerman v. Toro Mfg. Corp., 1 Haw. App. 111, 615 P.2d 749 (1980); Gross-Haentjens v. Leckenby, 38 Or. App. 313, 589 P.2d 1209 (1979); Kirksey v. Overton Pub, Inc., 804 S.W.2d 68 (Tenn. App. 1990); Washington State Physicians Ins. Exchange v. Fisons Corp., 122 Wash. 2d 299, 858 P.2d 1054 (1993); Hiner v. Bridgestone/Firestone, Inc., 959 P.2d 1158 (Wash. App. 1998) (disallowing UDAP claim where property damage arose from automobile accident that caused personal injury), *rev'd in part on other grounds*, 138 Wash. 2d 248, 978 P.2d 505 (1999).

148 Simms v. Candela, 45 Conn. Super. 267, 711 A.2d 778 (1998).

149 American Shooting Sports Council v. Attorney General, 429 Mass. 871, 711 N.E.2d 899 (1999) (upholding attorney general's promulgation of handgun regulation).

150 Hart v. GMAC Mortgage Corp., 246 B.R. 709 (Bankr. D. Mass. 2000) (requiring proof of elements of intentional infliction of emotional distress in order to recover UDAP damages for emotional distress); Kish v. Van Note, 692 S.W.2d 463 (Tex. 1985); Brown v. American Transfer & Storage Co., 601 S.W.2d 931 (Tex. 1980); Mercedes-Benz of N. Am. v. Dickenson, 720 S.W.2d 844 (Tex. App. 1986).

151 *See* St. Elizabeth Hosp. v. Garrard, 730 S.W.2d 649 (Tex. 1987); Lone Star Ford, Inc. v. Howard R. Hill, Jr., 879 S.W.2d 116 (Tex. App. 1994); Milt Ferguson Motor Co. v. Zeretzke, 827 S.W.2d 349 (Tex. App. 1991); *see also* HOW Ins. v. Patriot Fin. Servs., 786 S.W.2d 533 (Tex. App. 1990).

152 *See In re* Bryant, 111 B.R. 474 (E.D. Pa. 1990); White River Estates v. Hiltbruner, 953 P.2d 796 (Wash. 1998); Keyes v. Bollinger, 31 Wash. App. 286, 640 P.2d 1077 (1982). *See also* Wenrich v. Robert E. Cole, P.C., 2000 U.S. Dist. LEXIS 18687 (E.D. Pa. Dec. 22, 2000) (emotional distress damages probably not available for Pennsylvania UDAP violation). *See generally* § 8.3.3.8, *supra*.

153 Zanakis-Pico v. Cutter Dodge, Inc., 47 P.3d 1222 (Haw. 2002).

showing of physical injury.[154] For example, UDAP damages have been awarded for physical pain and mental anguish where the consumer had to push a defective car, causing strain.[155] UDAP damages have been awarded against a landlord for a tenant's mental anguish associated with an assault and battery by a third person where the landlord installed a flimsy door that was easily forced open.[156]

In a case where misrepresentation concerning a burglar alarm system resulted in a woman being terrorized by burglars, $150,000 mental anguish damages were not excessive.[157] The requisite physical injury was found by the woman being tied up and pushed around.

8.3.3.9.4 Pain and suffering damages recoverable where deception intentional or grossly negligent

Some jurisdictions allow mental anguish damages where fraud is proven,[158] where there is an intentional invasion of the consumer's peace of mind, or where the deception was grossly negligent, made knowingly, or willfully.[159] Thus, pain and suffering damages have been awarded where a warrantor behaved unreasonably, and the consumer had to live with constant leaks, repair problems and defective windows.[160] Another court found unconscionability for slow auto repairs to be sufficient to trigger damages for pain and suffering, since a showing of unconscionability demonstrates wanton misconduct.[161]

A dealer's continual stalling in turning over proper title to a car was also found to be willful, triggering mental anguish damages.[162] An award of $50,000 for mental anguish was upheld where willful deception in the sale of a defective truck led to loss of job, lack of sleep, and the inability to repay friends.[163] Actual damages are recoverable for humiliation and mental anguish for the intentional filing of a suit in the wrong venue.[164]

8.3.3.9.5 Modern standards may be even more liberal

In a number of states, courts award pain and suffering damages even where there is no physical injury or intent to deceive. For example, Texas courts award UDAP pain and suffering damages without a showing of willfulness or intent.[165] Mental anguish damages are recoverable in Texas UDAP cases even in the absence of economic damages.[166] However, in the absence of physical injury, the consumer must show that the action was done "knowingly."[167] In this context, "knowingly" in Texas means a subjective awareness of the falsity or deception.[168] Nonetheless, the Texas

---

154 Pope v. Rollins Protective Servs. Co., 703 F.2d 197 (5th Cir. 1983) (Texas law); Am. Bankers' Ins. Co. v. Wells, 819 So. 2d 1196 (Miss. 2001) (emotional distress damages are recoverable for ordinary negligence only if there is physical manifestation of injury or demonstrable physical harm); American Nat'l Ins. Co. v. Paul, 927 S.W.2d 239 (Tex. App. 1996); Mahan Volkswagen Inc. v. Hall, 648 S.W.2d 324 (Tex. App. 1982); Farmers & Merchants Market State Bank v. Ferguson, 605 S.W.2d 320 (Tex. Civ. App. 1980), *modified on other grounds*, 617 S.W.2d 918 (Tex. 1981). *See also* National Consumer Law Center, Consumer Warranty Law § 10.6.3.3 (2d ed. 2001 and Supp.) (mental anguish damages in warranty actions).

155 Tom Benson Chevrolet v. Alvarado, 636 S.W.2d 815 (Tex. App. 1982).

156 Brown v. LeClair, 20 Mass. App. Ct. 976, 482 N.E.2d 870 (1985).

157 Pope v. Rollins Protective Servs., Co., 703 F.2d 197 (5th Cir. 1983) (Texas law).

158 *See* Dodds v. Frontier Chevrolet Sales & Service, Inc., 676 P.2d 1237 (Colo. Ct. App. 1983).

159 *See, e.g.*, Vercher v. Ford Motor Co., 527 So. 2d 995 (La. Ct. App. 1988); Am. Bankers' Ins. Co. v. Wells, 819 So. 2d 1196 (Miss. 2001) (unless there is physical harm, defendant's conduct must be malicious, intentional, willful, wanton, grossly careless, indifferent or reckless). Texas courts have held that mental anguish damages are available for a variety of claims if the defendant's conduct is grossly negligent, knowing, or willful: State Farm Life Ins. Co. v. Beaston, 907 S.W.2d 430 (Tex. 1995) (Insurance Code violations); Luna v. North Star Dodge Sales, Inc., 667 S.W.2d 115 (Tex. 1984) (UDAP violation; knowing violation is sufficient basis for mental anguish damages); American Nat'l Ins. Co. v. Paul, 927 S.W.2d 239 (Tex. App. 1996) (UDAP and Insurance Code violations); Guilbeau v. Anderson, 841 S.W.2d 517 (Tex. App. 1992) (on negligence claim, mental anguish damages can be based on gross negligence); American Commercial Colleges, Inc. v. Davis, 821 S.W.2d 450 (Tex. App. 1991); J.B. Custom Design & Bldg. v. Clawson, 794 S.W.2d 38 (Tex. App. 1990); HOW Ins. v. Patriot Fin. Servs., 786 S.W.2d 533 (Tex. App. 1990); National Van Lines v. Lifshen, 584 S.W.2d 298 (Tex. Civ. App. 1979). *See also* National Consumer Law Center, Consumer Warranty Law § 10.6.3.3 (2d ed. 2001 and Supp.) (mental anguish damages in warranty actions).

160 HOW Ins. v. Patriot Fin. Servs., 786 S.W.2d 533 (Tex. App. 1990).

161 Centroplex Ford, Inc. v. Kirby, 736 S.W.2d 261 (Tex. App. 1987).

162 Dan Boone Mitsubishi, Inc. v. Ebrom, 830 S.W.2d 334 (Tex. App. 1992).

163 Metro Ford Truck Sales, Inc. v. Davis, 709 S.W.2d 785 (Tex. App. 1986). *See also* Vercher v. Ford Motor Co., 527 So. 2d 995 (La. Ct. App. 1988).

164 Bank of New Orleans & Trust Co. v. Phillips, 415 So. 2d 973 (La. Ct. App. 1982) (Louisiana law is generally more generous toward allowing damages for mental anguish than other jurisdictions).

165 Stevens v. State Farm Fire & Cas. Co., 929 S.W.2d 665 (Tex. App. 1996); Milt Ferguson Motor Co. v. Zeretzke, 827 S.W.2d 349 (Tex. App. 1991). *Cf.* Town East Ford Sales, Inc. v. Gray, 730 S.W.2d 796 (Tex. App. 1987) (in a case decided before Texas liberalized its standards as to recovery of pain and suffering, no recovery where only showed mere worry, anger, resentment, and disappointment). *Contra* Beaston v. State farm Life Ins., 907 S.W.2d 430 (Tex. 1995).

166 Latham v. Castillo, 972 S.W.2d 66 (Tex. 1998); Gill v. Boyd Distribution Center, 64 S.W.3d 601 (Tex. App. 2001).

167 Verinakis v. Medical Profiles, Inc., 987 S.W.2d 90 (Tex. App. 1998).

168 For examples of Texas cases in which defendants were found to have acted knowingly, see Luna v. North Star Dodge Sales, Inc., 667 S.W.2d 115 (Tex. 1984); Connell Chevrolet Co. v. Leak,

Supreme Court holds that appellate courts should "closely scrutinize" mental anguish awards and allow them only when the plaintiff has introduced direct evidence of mental anguish that is sufficient to establish a "substantial disruption" in the plaintiff's daily routine.[169] Louisiana allows damages for mental anguish and humiliation in UDAP cases.[170] A federal court in Michigan has concluded that mental anguish damages can be awarded under its UDAP statute whenever they are the natural and legal consequence of the wrongful act and might reasonably have been anticipated.[171] Massachusetts' highest court has affirmed an award of treble a tenant's emotional distress damages in a UDAP case against a slumlord.[172] The landlord refused to make repairs, and threatened, abused, or harassed the tenant, causing her to feel angry, alone, helpless, withdrawn, tearful, and in physical pain.

8.3.3.9.6 Is mere aggravation enough?

In at least some jurisdictions, while damages for mental anguish are recoverable in proper circumstances, there can be no recovery for mere aggravation; aggravation should just be offered as evidence of mental anguish.[173] Thus, in Texas, a consumer may not recover damages for mere worry, but may do so where there is a relatively high degree of mental pain and distress.[174] Mental anguish is established by testimony that a consumer was "terrified," "devastated," sleepless, and using prescription medicine.[175] In the same case, a spouse's testimony that he "felt bad," was upset, and was mad did not establish mental anguish.[176] One court found that testimony that a consumer had "shut down," cried "a lot," and endured "extreme hardship" was insufficient to show mental anguish, and reversed the jury finding.[177] But an Illinois appellate court has affirmed a UDAP damage award for aggravation and inconvenience resulting from misrepresentations in a car sale.[178] Likewise, a New York court awarded $500 for disappointment, humiliation, and annoyance suffered when the defendant sent a different singer to the plaintiff's wedding than the one she had contracted for.[179] An Ohio decision,[180] several Oklahoma appellate decisions[181] and a Fourth Circuit decision based on West Virginia law[182] hold that losses such as annoyance, loss of time, inconvenience, travel, and telephone expenses are compensable.[183]

8.3.4 Prejudgment Interest

Whether a court will order prejudgment interest on a UDAP claim will normally depend on the state's general treatment of prejudgment interest. One court has ruled that the authority in the UDAP statute to award such equitable relief as the court deems proper was not, in itself, broad enough to allow an award of prejudgment interest.[184]

Where state law provides for such interest, a court certainly has the power to award prejudgment interest on its UDAP damages award.[185] While the Massachusetts UDAP

---

967 S.W.2d 888 (Tex. App. 1998); Smith v. Levine, 911 S.W.2d 427 (Tex. App. 1995); Sanchez v. Guerrero, 885 S.W.2d 487 (Tex. App. 1994); Dan Boone Mitsubishi v. Ebrom, 830 S.W.2d 334 (Tex. App. 1992); J.B. Custom Design & Bldg. v. Clawson, 794 S.W.2d 38 (Tex. App. 1990); HOW Ins. v. Patriot Fin. Servs., 786 S.W.2d 533 (Tex. App. 1990); Kold-Serve Corp. v. Ward, 736 S.W.2d 750 (Tex. App. 1987); Metro Ford Truck Sales, Inc. v. Davis, 709 S.W.2d 785 (Tex. App. 1986); West v. Carter, 712 S.W.2d 569 (Tex. App. 1986); Jasso v. Duron, 681 S.W.2d 279 (Tex. App. 1984); Miller v. Dickenson, 677 S.W.2d 253 (Tex. App. 1984).

169 Gunn Infiniti, Inc. v. O'Byrne, 18 S.W.3d 715 (Tex. App. 2000), *on remand from* Gunn Infiniti v. O'Byrne, 996 S.W.2d 854 (Tex. 1999). *See also* Anderson v. Long, 118 S.W.3d 806 (Tex. App. 2003).

170 Laurents v. Louisiana Mobile Homes, Inc., 689 So. 2d 536 (La. Ct. App. 1997) (upholding award of mental anguish damages where seller delivered defective mobile home).

171 Avery v. Industry Mortg. Co., 135 F. Supp. 2d 840 (W.D. Mich. 2001). *Accord* Lozada v. Dale Baker Oldsmobile, Inc., 136 F. Supp. 2d 719 (W.D. Mich. 2001).

172 Haddad v. Gonzalez, 410 Mass. 855, 576 N.E.2d 658 (1991); Grundberg v. Gill, 56 Mass. App. Ct. 1116, 780 N.E.2d 158 (Mass. App. Ct. 2002) (unpublished).

173 Town East Ford Sales, Inc. v. Gray, 730 S.W.2d 796 (Tex. App. 1987).

174 J.B. Custom Design & Bldg. v. Clawson, 794 S.W.2d 38 (Tex. App. 1990); Autohaus, Inc. v. Aguilar, 794 S.W.2d 459 (Tex. App. 1990).

175 Texas Farmers Ins. Co. v. Cameron, 24 S.W.3d 386 (Tex. App. 2000).

176 *Id.*

177 Woodlands Land Development Co., L.P. v. Jenkins, 48 S.W.3d 415 (Tex. App. 2001).

178 Roche v. Fireside Chrysler-Plymouth, 600 N.E.2d 1218 (Ill. App. Ct. 1992) (affirming award of $750 for aggravation and inconvenience).

179 Griffin-Amiel v. Frank Terris Orchestras, 178 Misc. 2d 71, 677 N.Y.S.2d 908 (City Ct. 1998).

180 Becker v. Montgomery, Lunch, 2003 WL 23335929 (N.D. Ohio Feb. 26, 2003) (frustration, aggravation, humiliation, embarrassment, inconvenience, humiliation, and upset).

181 Brashears v. Sight N Sound Appliance Centers, Inc., 981 P.2d 1270 (Okla. App. 1999); Fuller v. Sight N Sound Appliance Centers, Inc., 982 P.2d 528 (Okla. App. 1999). *But see* Hedrick v. Spear, 138 Or. App. 53, 907 P.2d 1123 (1995) (damages can not include work time lost to attend trial).

182 Mirandy v. Allstate Ins. Co., 151 F.3d 1029 (4th Cir. 1998) (table, text available at 1998 U.S. App. LEXIS 10915). *See also* National Consumer Law Center, Consumer Warranty Law § 10.6.3.3 (2d ed. 2001 and Supp.) (mental anguish damages in warranty actions).

183 *See also* Zanakis-Pico v. Cutter Dodge, Inc., 47 P.3d 1222 (Haw. 2002) (travel expenses compensable).

184 Nielsen v. Wisniewski, 32 Conn. App. 133, 628 A.2d 25 (1993).

185 Concorde Limousines, Inc. v. Moloney Coachbuilders, Inc., 835 F.2d 541 (5th Cir. 1987) (Texas law); Mill Pond Assocs. v. E&B Giftware, Inc., 751 F. Supp. 299 (D. Mass. 1990); District Cablevision Ltd. P'ship v. Bassin, 828 A.2d 714, 731–32 (D.C. 2003) (awarding interest); State v. Bob Chambers Ford, Inc., 522 A.2d 362 (Me. 1987); Luft v. Perry County Lumber &

statute could arguably be interpreted as allowing recovery of prejudgment interest twice when an insurer fails to pay a claim, a court has interpreted that statute as allowing the recovery of pre-judgment interest only once.[186] Whether prejudgment interest should be trebled with other UDAP damages is discussed in § 8.4.2.7.5, *infra*.

8.3.5 Proving Actual Damages and Causation

8.3.5.1 General Standards

Whatever theory a consumer uses in seeking damages, the consumer has the clear responsibility to prove the amount of those damages, and how they are related to the deceptive conduct.[187] While proof of damages does not require mathematical precision, it must be based on more than mere speculation.[188]

Thus where damage is to be based upon the difference between what was paid for a defective car and what it was

Supply Co., 2003 WL 21027291 (Ohio App. May 8, 2003) (unpublished, citation limited) (upholding denial of pre-judgment interest based on Ohio's specific statutory requirements); Quintero v. Jim Walter Homes, Inc., 709 S.W.2d 225 (Tex. App. 1986); Rotello v. Ring Around Products Inc., 614 S.W.2d 455 (Tex. Civ. App. 1981). *But see* American Baler Co. v. SRS Sys., Inc., 748 S.W.2d 243 (Tex. App. 1988).

186 Yeagle v. Aetna Casualty & Surety Co., 679 N.E.2d 248 (Mass. App. Ct. 1997).

187 Perry v. American Tobacco Co., Inc., 324 F.3d 845 (6th Cir. 2003) (increase in health insurance premiums due to smokers in pool of insureds not recoverable from tobacco companies because causation too remote); Pelman v. McDonald's Corp., 2003 WL 22052778 (S.D.N.Y. Sept. 3, 2003) (dismissing complaint because of failure to isolate the particular effect of defendant's acts upon plaintiffs' injuries); Anthony v. Country Life Mfg., 2002 WL 31269621 (N.D. Ill. Oct. 9, 2002) ("but for" causation insufficient), *aff'd*, 2003 WL 21540975 (7th Cir. July 2, 2003) (unpublished, citation limited); Conn. Pipe Trades Health Fund v. Philip Morris, Inc., 153 F. Supp. 2d 101 (D. Conn. 2001) (costs incurred by union health fund due to members' smoking-related illnesses too remote to satisfy proximate cause requirement in suit against tobacco companies); Lozada v. Dale Baker Oldsmobile, Inc., 136 F. Supp. 2d 719 (W.D. Mich. 2001) (finance charges for transaction not recoverable for failure to provide copy of contract without proof that they were incurred as a result of that violation); Werner v. Pittway Corp., 90 F. Supp. 2d 1018 (W.D. Wis. 2000) (no UDAP liability because plaintiffs did not prove causation between their injuries and deceptive ads they never saw); Smith v. Brown & Williamson Tobacco Corp., 108 F. Supp. 2d 12 (D.D.C. 2000) (UDAP claim denied where smoker failed to show reliance or any other causal connection between tobacco ads and her decision to start and continue smoking); W.D. Taylor & Co. v. Griswold & Bateman Warehouse Co., 742 F. Supp. 1398 (N.D. Ill. 1990) (plaintiff did not show that damages, which were not reasonably foreseeable, were proximately caused by defendant's alleged fraud); Hall v. Walter, 969 P.2d 224 (Colo. 1998) (defendant's deception toward others caused damage to UDAP plaintiff); Haesche v. Kissner, 229 Conn. 213, 640 A.2d 89 (1994) (UDAP suit fails because causation was not proven); Suarez v. Sordo, 43 Conn. App. 756, 685 A.2d 1144 (1996) (UDAP claim denied for failure to prove causation); Agnew v. Great Atlantic & Pacific Tea Co., 502 S.E.2d 735 (Ga. App. Ct. 1998) (deceptive advertising not proximate cause of plaintiff's loss where plaintiff knew true facts before making purchase); Oliveira v. Amoco Oil Co., 201 Ill. 2d 134, 776 N.E.2d 151, 267 Ill. Dec. 14 (2002) (consumer must show proximate causation of actual damages; not shown where plaintiff never saw the deceptive ads); Martin v. Heinold Commodities, Inc., 643 N.E.2d 734 (Ill. 1994) (consumer must prove causation); Weis v. State Farm Mut. Automobile Ins. Co., 333 Ill. App. 3d 402, 776 N.E.2d 309 (2002) (loss must relate to the specific misrepresentations alleged); Zankle v. Queen Anne Landscaping, 724 N.E.2d 988, 244 Ill. Dec. 100 (App. 2000) (no UDAP liability where defendant's failure to perform contract in manner promised was not the cause of the defects); Wheeler v. Sunbelt Tool Co., 181 Ill. App. 3d 1088, 537 N.E.2d 1332 (1989) (plaintiff did not show that misrepresentation was proximate cause of damages); Massachusetts Farm Bureau Fed'n v. Blue Cross, 403 Mass. 722, 532 N.E.2d 660 (1989) (plaintiff did not show causal relationship between unintelligible statement in contract and plaintiff's loss); Lord v. Commercial Union Ins. Co., 60 Mass. App. Ct. 309, 801 N.E.2d 303 (Mass. App. Ct. 2004) (defendant's failure to give timely notice to insured was not the reason for the insured's failure to have vehicle inspected within seven days so did not cause the insured's injury); Peterson v. BASF Corp., 675 N.W.2d 57 (Minn. 2004) (N.J. law) (causation established by evidence that buyers saw misleading ads and that seller was able to charge higher price when misleading ads were running); Colbert v. Bank Am., Inc., 295 A.D.2d 300, 743 N.Y.S.2d 150 (2002) (no UDAP claim where plaintiffs did not see deceptive ads until after purchase); Mitchell v. Linville, 557 S.E.2d 620 (N.C. App. 2001) (no UDAP claim where plaintiffs did not show causal connection between defects in the home and contractor's failure to obtain license); Chaucer v. Chapman, 1995 Tenn. App. LEXIS 150, Clearinghouse No. 51,285 (Tenn. Ct. App. 1995) (no proof of causation); Mackie v. McKenzie, 900 S.W.2d 445 (Tex. App. 1995); Dubow v. Dragon, 746 S.W.2d 857 (Tex. App. 1988) (consumer did not show that deception caused damages); Nelson v. Data Terminal Sys., Inc., 762 S.W.2d 744 (Tex. App. 1988) (same); Sparkman v. Presley Olds-Cadillac Inc., 616 S.W.2d 264 (Tex. Civ. App. 1981). *See also* Pritikin v. Liberation Publications, Inc., 83 F. Supp. 2d 920 (N.D. Ill. 1999) (plaintiff has no standing to bring UDAP claim where his injury is not traceable to defendant's deception); § 2.3.8, *supra*. *Cf.* Blue Cross & Blue Shield v. Philip Morris USA Inc., 344 F.3d 211 (2d Cir. 2003) (certifying question to N.Y. Court of Appeals whether third party payer of smokers' health care costs must present individualized proof of harm to subscribers from defendant tobacco companies' practices).

188 *In re* Wiggins, 273 B.R. 839 (Bankr. D. Idaho 2001); Conseco Fin. Serv. Corp. v. Hill, 556 S.E.2d 468 (Ga. App. 2001); Petty v. Chrysler Corp., 2003 WL 22240548 (Ill. App. Sept. 30, 2003) (evidence must include a basis for calculating damages with a fair degree of probability); Hall v. Lovell Regency Homes Ltd., 121 Md. App. 1, 708 A.2d 344 (1998) (expert testimony regarding value of property insufficient because it was speculative, and there was no evidence of actual value at time of sale); Squeri v. McCarrick, 32 Mass. App. Ct. 203, 588 N.E.2d 22 (1992). *But see* Fort Lauderdale Lincoln Mercury v. Corgnati, 715 So. 2d 311 (Fla. Dist. Ct. App. 1998) ("the amount of damages can not be based on speculation or conjecture, but must be proven with certainty").

worth, the consumer must offer evidence of what the car was actually worth when purchased, not the consumer's opinion of how much the car is now worth.[189] While the owner of property is competent to testify as to its value, such testimony can be disregarded if it is mere speculation.[190]

New Jersey courts hold that once the consumer establishes a significant relationship between the defendant's UDAP violations and the plaintiff's losses, it becomes the defendant's responsibility to isolate particular losses that do not have the requisite causal connection.[191] Where a consumer presented testimony about the aggregate cost of repairing defects in a home improvement job, the defendant had the burden of showing that some of them were not related to the UDAP violations.[192]

In a suit alleging deceptive sale of a car for more than the advertised cash price, contrary to the UDAP statute, the price advertised by the dealer establishes the cash price, even if the consumer never saw or relied on the advertisement.[193]

Some courts adopt a more relaxed version of causation in UDAP cases than in other cases.[194] For example, reliance is often an element of causation,[195] but many courts have held that proof of reliance is not always necessary in a UDAP case.[196] Some UDAP plaintiffs have attempted to establish causation without proving that the customer saw or relied on the deceptive advertisements by arguing that the deception increased the general demand for the product, thereby increasing the price for all buyers, even those who did not see the ads. The Illinois Supreme Court rejected such a suit on the ground that a UDAP plaintiff "must allege that he was, in some manner, deceived."[197] The ultimate consumer need not have seen the deceptive representations, though, if others who were acting for the plaintiff saw them and relied on them.[198]

In order to recover as damages the full costs of a transaction, the consumer may have to prove that the defendant withheld or misrepresented information that would have made a difference to the consumer in deciding whether to enter into the transaction.[199] Where no actual damages flowed from the failure to reduce an oral agreement to writing, the consumer could recover only nominal damages.[200] On the other hand, in a UDAP suit alleging unfair insurance claims settlement practices, the insured need not prove that he or she would have accepted the settlement if a reasonable offer had been made at the time liability became reasonably clear, but only that the insurer failed to make such an offer.[201] The UDAP plaintiffs must show at least that, but for the defendant's unlawful conduct, they would not have suffered the loss.[202] A plaintiff seeking

---

189 Fort Lauderdale Lincoln Mercury v. Corgnati, 715 So. 2d 311 (Fla. Dist. Ct. App. 1998) (damage award vacated because of failure to prove diminished value of car); Hall v. Lovell Regency Homes Ltd., 121 Md. App. 1, 708 A.2d 344 (1998) (UDAP claim dismissed where evidence of actual value related solely to present time, not time of sale); Town East Ford Sales, Inc. v. Gray, 730 S.W.2d 796 (Tex. App. 1987).

190 Locascio v. Imports Unlimited, Inc., 309 F. Supp. 2d 267 (D. Conn. 2004) (disregarding consumer's "self-serving, after-the-fact speculations" as to car's value); Hall v. Lovell Regency Homes Ltd., 121 Md. App. 1, 708 A.2d 344 (1998). *See generally* National Consumer Law Center, Consumer Warranty Law § 10.5.5 (2d ed. 2001 and Supp.).

191 Roberts v. Cowgill, 719 A.2d 668 (N.J. App. Ct. 1998).

192 *Id.*

193 Collins v. Fred Haas Toyota, 21 S.W.3d 606 (Tex. App. 2000).

194 *See, e.g.*, Pelman v. McDonald's Corp., 2003 WL 22052778, at *9–10 (S.D.N.Y. Sept. 3, 2003).

195 *See, e.g.*, Fozard v. Publishers Clearing House, Inc., 1999 U.S. Dist. LEXIS 22994 (M.D.N.C. Apr. 29, 1999), *aff'd without op.*, 205 F.3d 1333 (4th Cir. 2000).

196 *See* § 4.2.12.3, *supra*.

197 Oliveira v. Amoco Oil Co., 201 Ill. 2d 134, 776 N.E.2d 151, 164, 267 Ill. Dec. 14 (2002). *See also* Pelman v. McDonald's Corp., 2003 WL 22052778, at *9–10 (S.D.N.Y. Sept. 3, 2003) (causation requirements are relaxed for UDAP claims, but plaintiff must have seen the deceptive advertisements); N.J. Citizen Action v. Schering-Plough Corp., 367 N.J. Super. 8, 842 A.2d 174 (App. Div. 2003) (rejecting fraud-on-the-market and price inflation as UDAP damages); Fink v. Ricoh Corp., 365 N.J. Super. 520, 839 A.2d 942 (Law. Div. 2003) (rejecting price inflation theory of causation); Weinberg v. Sun Oil Co., 565 Pa. 612, 777 A.2d 442 (2001) (rejecting marketing theory of causation; plaintiff must prove that he purchased the product because he heard and believed the false advertising). *But cf.* Peterson v. BASF Corp., 675 N.W.2d 57 (Minn. 2004) (N.J. law) (causation established by evidence that buyers saw misleading ads and that seller was able to charge higher price when misleading ads were running).

198 Shannon v. Boise Cascade Corp., 208 Ill. 2d 517, 805 N.E.2d 213 (Ill. 2004); Shannon v. Boise Cascade, 783 N.E.2d 1105 (Ill. App. 2003), *appeal allowed*, 792 N.E.2d 314 (Ill. 2003).

199 *In re* Milbourne, 108 B.R. 522 (Bankr. E.D. Pa. 1989); Martin v. Heinold Commodities, Inc., 163 Ill. 2d 33, 643 N.E.2d 734 (1994) (securities fraud plaintiffs entitled to refund of concealed commissions, but not to all investment loses). *See* § 4.2.12, *supra* (discussion of whether proof of reliance is necessary).

200 Poncz v. Loftin, 607 N.E.2d 765 (Mass. App. Ct. 1993). *See also* Branigan v. Level on the Level, Inc., 326 N.J. Super. 24, 740 A.2d 643 (App. Div. 1999) (no damages resulted from failure to state starting date and completion date in contract); Josantos Constr. v. Bohrer, 326 N.J. Super. 42, 740 A.2d 653 (App. Div. 1999) (no causal connection between defects in one part of work and demand that homeowner sign completion certificate before another part of job was finished); Jakubowski v. Rock Valley Builders, 588 N.W.2d 928 (Wis. App. 1998) (*unpublished limited precedent opinion*, text available at 1998 Wisc. App. LEXIS 1363) (no damages resulted from contractor's failure to provide clear written contract); § 5.6.1.3, *supra*. *But cf.* Mullis v. Brennan, 716 N.E.2d 58 (Ind. App. 1999) (causation shown between lack of detail in contract and contractor's failure to cure deficiencies in work); William Mushero, Inc. v. Hull, 667 A.2d 853 (Me. 1995) (awarding homeowner damages for contractor's failure to perform according to specifications, where contract had not been reduced to writing).

201 Hopkins v. Liberty Mut. Ins. Co., 434 Mass. 556, 750 N.E.2d 943 (2001).

202 L.R.J. Ryan v. Wersi Electronic, 59 F.3d 52 (7th Cir. 1995); Adler v. William Blair & Co., 648 N.E.2d 226 (Ill. App. Ct. 1995); Aetna Fin. v. Gaither, 118 N.M. 246, 880 P.2d 857

consequential damages should also take care to introduce evidence that these damages were the foreseeable consequence of the UDAP violations or that other state standards for consequential damages are satisfied.[203] A UDAP violation need only be one of several causes of harm to be actionable, however.[204] Nor need the consumer show a link between a misrepresentation that induced a purchase and the subsequent discovery of a specific problem with the merchandise.[205] Thus, a misrepresentation concerning a car's odometer reading justifies a UDAP award even if the consumer can not point to a specific mechanical problem caused by the higher mileage.[206]

8.3.5.2 Damages and Causation in Bait and Switch Cases

Damages and causation issues sometimes arise in private suits challenging bait and switch tactics. If the consumer backed out of the sale after learning the true price, the seller may argue that the consumer has not suffered any loss. But at least one court has held that the difference between the advertised price and the actual price the seller demanded is an ascertainable loss even if the consumer did not enter into a transaction.[207] (Note, however, that the standards for meeting a statute's "ascertainable loss" requirement may be more lenient than for proving actual damages.[208])

Some courts are willing to recognize inconvenience, travel expenses, lost time, and loss of the opportunity to purchase as compensable losses.[209] If the consumer bought the same item elsewhere at a higher price, a court may be willing to consider the price differential a loss.[210]

If the consumer made the purchase after learning the true price, the seller is likely to argue that the disclosure of the true price corrected the deception. Courts have, however, rejected the argument that subsequent disclosure negates a deception.[211] Also, the seller may have disclosed the actual price in a way that impeded the consumer's ability to compare it to the price of the "bait."[212] The buyer may also be able to argue that such tactics are unfair, not just deceptive, in which case the subsequent disclosure would be less significant.

8.3.6 Contractual Limitations on Damages

A contractual provision limiting the consumer's remedies may be effective in limiting a consumer's damages resulting from a contract or warranty claim. A UDAP action, however, is not based on the contract or on a warranty but on the seller's unfair or deceptive practices.[213] Consequently, such limitations are inapplicable to UDAP claims.[214]

8.3.7 Collateral Source Rule

In states with a collateral source rule, insurance proceeds received by the consumer should not reduce the amount of recovery under a UDAP statute. The Texas Supreme Court has held that the collateral source rule applies to UDAP claims.[215]

8.3.8 Mitigation of Damages

Some courts may find that the consumer has a duty to mitigate damages,[216] but, even then, the defendant has the

(1994). *But see* Anthony v. Country Life Mfg., 2002 WL 31269621 (N.D. Ill. Oct. 9, 2002) ("but for" causation insufficient), *aff'd*, 2003 WL 21540975 (7th Cir. July 2, 2003) (unpublished, citation limited).

203 *See* § 8.3.3.2, *supra*.

204 Conatzer v. American Mercury Ins. Co., 15 P.3d 1252 (Okla. App. 2000).

205 Twardy v. L.B. Sales, Inc., 2000 Minn. App. LEXIS 636 (June 27, 2000).

206 *Id.*

207 Truex v. Ocean Dodge, Inc., 219 N.J. Super. 44, 529 A.2d 1017, 1021 (App. Div. 1987).

208 *See* § 7.5.2.4, *supra*.

209 Larobina v. Home Depot, USA, Inc., 821 A.2d 283 (Conn. App. 2003) (loss of bargain due to bait and switch is ascertainable loss); Zanakis-Pico v. Cutter Dodge, Inc., 47 P.3d 1222 (Haw. 2002) (travel costs due to bait and switch are compensable); Rein v. Koons Ford, Inc., 567 A.2d 101 (Md. 1989) (Va. law) (expense of traveling to dealership in response to deceptive ad is ascertainable loss); Brashears v. Sight N Sound Appliance, 981 P.2d 1270 (Okla. App. 1999). *See also* Geismar v. Abraham & Straus, 109 Misc. 2d 495, 439 N.Y.S.2d 1005 (Dist. Ct. 1981) (loss of opportunity to purchase is sufficient injury to support UDAP action; plaintiff entitled to statutory damages); § 7.5.2.5, *infra*.

210 Chandler v. Am. Gen. Fin., Inc., 329 Ill. App. 3d 729, 768 N.E.2d 60 (2002) (difference between cost of the bait and cost of the product to which the consumer was switched can be sufficient damage to support a UDAP claim).

211 *See* § 4.2.17, *supra*.

212 Chandler v. Am. Gen. Fin., Inc., 329 Ill. App. 3d 729, 768 N.E.2d 60 (2002).

213 *See* Standard Register Co. v. Bolton-Emerson, Inc., 38 Mass. App. Ct. 545, 649 N.E.2d 791 (1995) (contractual limitation on damages has no effect on tort-type UDAP claim, but may apply where UDAP claim is merely an alternative theory of recovery under a contract).

214 *See* § 4.2.15.4, *infra*.

215 Brown v. American Transfer & Storage Co., 601 S.W.2d 931 (Tex. 1980); *see also* Global Petrotech, Inc. v. Engelhard Corp., 824 F. Supp. 103 (S.D. Tex. 1993) (reluctantly following *Brown*; insurance proceeds will not reduce UDAP award).

216 Cambridge Plating Co. v. NAPCO, Inc., 85 F.3d 752 (1st Cir. 1996); Andrade Enterprises, Inc. v. Cinnaroll Bakeries, Ltd., 2003 WL 22736538 (W.D. Tex. Oct. 31, 2003); Texas Carpenters Health Ben. Fund v. Philip Morris, Inc., 21 F. Supp. 2d 664 (E.D. Tex. 1998); Gunn Infiniti, Inc. v. O'Byrne, 996 S.W.2d 854 (Tex. 1999) (common law mitigation duties apply to a UDAP claim); Doe v. Boys Clubs of Greater Dallas, Inc., 907 S.W.2d 472 (Tex. 1995); Southwell v. University of Incarnate Word, 974 S.W.2d 351 (Tex. App. 1998); Gillespie v. Century

burden of proving that the consumer has not used reasonable diligence to do so.[217] The defendant must also prove that the steps it claims the consumer should have taken would have been effective to remedy the damage.[218]

8.3.9 *Interrelation of UDAP Actual Damages and Damages on Other Claims*

A consumer is entitled to only one recovery for a single injury. Thus, a consumer may not recover actual damages for the same act that is both a breach of contract and a UDAP violation[219] or that is both fraud and a UDAP violation.[220] Nonetheless, there is nothing inconsistent or duplicative in recovering actual damages and attorney fees under a UDAP claim and punitive damages under a tort claim.[221] Since a fraud claim and a UDAP claim are consistent with each other rather than irreconcilable, the consumer need not elect between them, as long as duplicative awards are avoided.[222] Courts will also award actual UDAP damages on one count and statutory damages under the Truth in Lending Act under another count.[223] One federal court aggregated UDAP damages and contract damages to reach the amount in controversy requirement.[224]

Products Co., 936 S.W.2d 50 (Tex. App. 1996); Camden Mach. & Tool, Inc. v. Cascade Co., 870 S.W.2d 304 (Tex. App. 1993); Peeler v. Hughes & Luce, 868 S.W.2d 823 (Tex. App. 1993), *aff'd*, 909 S.W.2d 494 (Tex. 1995); McCulley Fine Arts Gallery, Inc. v. X Partners, 860 S.W.2d 473 (Tex. App. 1993).

217 Pierce v. Drees, 607 N.E.2d 726 (Ind. Ct. App. 1993); York v. InTrust Bank, 265 Kan. 271, 962 P.2d 405 (1998) (defendant's proof insufficient); Flym v. Blout, 2003 WL 22387141 (Mass. App. Div. Oct. 15, 2003) (consumer's two month delay in exercising rights under UDAP statute was not unreasonable).

218 Pierce v. Drees, 607 N.E.2d 726 (Ind. Ct. App. 1993).

219 Waite Hill Servs., Inc. v. World Class Metal Works, Inc., 959 S.W.2d 182 (Tex. 1998); Bekins Moving & Storage Co. v. Williams, 947 S.W.2d 568 (Tex. App. 1997).

220 Wilkins v. Peninsula Motor Cars, Inc., 587 S.E.2d 581 (Va. 2003).

221 United Laboratories v. Kuykendall, 335 N.C. 183, 437 S.E.2d 374 (1993); Wilkins v. Peninsula Motor Cars, Inc., 587 S.E.2d 581 (Va. 2003).

222 Wilkins v. Peninsula Motor Cars, Inc., 587 S.E.2d 581 (Va. 2003).

223 Douglas v. G.E.E.N. Corp., 415 So. 2d 130 (Fla. Dist. Ct. App. 1982); *see also* Burnett v. Ala Moana Pawn Shop, Clearinghouse No. 46,771 (D. Haw. 1991) (TIL statutory damages and UDAP treble damages for same TIL violation; court would have awarded both TIL and UDAP statutory damages if UDAP treble damages had been less than UDAP statutory damages), *aff'd*, 3 F.3d 1261 (9th Cir. 1993).

224 McCall v. UNUM Life Ins. Co. of Am., 2001 U.S. Dist. LEXIS 18132 (N.D. Tex. Nov. 6, 2001).

8.4 Statutory, Multiple, and Punitive Damages

8.4.1 *Statutory Minimum Damages*

8.4.1.1 General

About half the states authorize private litigants who have proven a UDAP violation to obtain minimum damage awards ranging from $25 to $5000, even if actual damages have not been proven.[225] Thus, even if actual damages are only one dollar, minimum damage provisions allow sizeable recoveries. In some cases, recoveries are as much as $2000 or higher.[226] Thus, $3000 minimum damages have been awarded where the actual damages established were only $200.[227]

Statutory damages are intended to encourage private litigation, and courts should award such damages whenever authorized to do so.[228] A trial court's award of statutory damages should be upheld on appeal unless the amount of the award shocks the conscience of the appellate court.[229]

Statutory minimum damages for a consumer litigant must be distinguished from provisions that allow the state attorney general to seek civil penalties ranging from $500 to $25,000 for initial UDAP violations. Private litigants can not seek such penalties but are limited to statutory minimum damages, if available, and other private remedies.[230] How-

225 *See* Appx. A, *infra*; *see also* Carter v. Lachance, 766 A.2d 717 (N.H. 2001) (statutory damages are required even without proof of actual damages); Dantzig v. Sloe, 115 Ohio App. 3d 64, 684 N.E.2d 715 (1996) (statutory damages required even if consumer proves no damages). *See also* United HealthCare Ins. Co. v. AdvancePCS, 2002 U.S. Dist. LEXIS 4676 (D. Minn. Mar. 18, 2002) (treating Minn. civil penalty as available to private litigants, not just AG), *aff'd on other grounds*, 316 F.3d 737 (8th Cir. 2002). *But see* Lord v. Commercial Union Ins. Co., 60 Mass. App. Ct. 309, 801 N.E.2d 303 (Mass. App. Ct. 2004) (rejecting award of minimum damages of $25 where plaintiff showed no injury).

226 *See, e.g.*, Maberry v. Said, 927 F. Supp. 1456 (D. Kan. 1996) ($1500 for one violation and $1500 for another violation); Ray v. Ponca/Universal Holdings, Inc., 913 P.2d 209 (Kan. App. 1995) ($2742 award); Bell v. Kent-Brown Chevrolet Co., 1 Kan. App. 2d 131, 561 P.2d 907 (1977) (authorizing a $2000 minimum damage award).

227 Watkins v. Roach Cadillac Inc., 7 Kan. App. 2d 8, 637 P.2d 458 (1981). *See also* Ray v. Ponca/Universal Holdings, Inc., 913 P.2d 209 (Kan. App. 1995) (upholding statutory damage award of 46 times actual damages).

228 Zanakis-Pico v. Cutter Dodge, Inc., 47 P.3d 1222 (Haw. 2002) (purpose is to encourage consumers to prosecute and deter violations); Geismar v. Abraham & Strauss, 109 Misc. 2d 495, 439 N.Y.S.2d 1005 (Dist. Ct. 1981).

229 Ray v. Ponca/Universal Holdings, Inc., 913 P.2d 209 (Kan. App. 1995).

230 Peery v. Hansen, 120 Ariz. 266, 585 P.2d 574 (Ct. App. 1978); Walls v. American Tobacco Co., 11 P.3d 626 (Okla. 2000); Gramaton Home Investors Corp. v. Starling, 470 A.2d 1157 (Vt. 1983); Stigall v. Courtesy Chevrolet-Pontiac, Inc., 15 Wash. App. 739, 551 P.2d 763 (1976).

ever, this distinction is complicated because the phrase "civil penalties" in a UDAP statute may refer to private, minimum damages.[231]

Statutory minimum damages not only allow consumers more sizeable recoveries when actual damage is small, but also avoid problems of proving damages. Minimum damages can be awarded even if the consumer can not prove the amount of his or her loss.[232] Even UDAP statutes that require a showing of "ascertainable loss" have been interpreted to mean capable of being discovered or established and not requiring that they actually be established.[233] Damage or ascertainable loss requirements also have been interpreted as being satisfied with only minimal consumer damages.[234] Thus, minimum damages are awarded even in states that require ascertainable loss where there are only slight damages, and these damages are only capable of being shown, but not proven.

California was the first state to provide special UDAP statutory minimum damages for elderly and handicapped consumers. In addition to restitution and punitive damages, statutory damages of $5000 are available where the consumer is elderly or handicapped and where certain criteria are met.[235] Hawaii has adopted a similar provision.[236]

The Kansas UDAP statute allows consumers to seek a civil penalty of "not more than $10,000," without any minimum amount.[237] The civil penalty can be up to $20,000 per violation if the victim is elderly or disabled.[238] The purpose of this civil penalty is remedial rather than punitive.[239]

231 *See* Bell v. Kent-Brown Chevrolet Co., 1 Kan. App. 2d 131, 561 P.2d 907 (1977).

232 Perez v. Anderson, 98 B.R. 189 (E.D. Pa. 1989) (statutory damages awarded despite no actual damages); Clayton v. McCary, 426 F. Supp. 248 (N.D. Ohio 1976); Swanston v. McConnell Air Force Base Federal Credit Union, 8 Kan. App. 2d 538, 661 P.2d 826 (1983); Jones v. General Motors Corp., 953 P.2d 1104 (N.M. App. 1998) (statutory damages allowed even if no actual damage shown); Dantzig v. Sloe, 115 Ohio App. 3d 64, 684 N.E.2d 715 (1996); Gaylan v. Dave Towell Cadillac, 15 Ohio Misc. 2d 1, 473 N.E.2d 64 (Mun. Ct. 1984). *See also* Page & Wirtz Constr. Co. v. Solomon, 110 N.M. 206, 794 P.2d 349 (1990); Couto v. Gibson, Inc., 1992 Ohio App. LEXIS 756 (Feb. 26, 1992); §§ 7.5.2.4, 7.5.2.5, *supra*. *But see* Shurtliff v. Northwest Pools, Inc., 120 Idaho 263, 815 P.2d 461 (Ct. App. 1991) (no statutory damages where no actual damages).

233 *See* § 7.5.2.4, *supra*.

234 *Id.*

235 Cal. Civ. Code § 1780(b).

236 Haw. Rev. Stat. § 480-13(b)(1).

237 Kan. Stat. Ann. §§ 50.634, 50.636, 50.677; *see* Lowe v. Surpas Resource Corp., 253 F. Supp. 2d 1209, 1230 (D. Kan. 2003); Maberry v. Said, 927 F. Supp. 1456 (D. Kan. 1996) (applying pre-amendment civil penalty amount).

238 Kan. Stat. Ann. § 50-677; *see* Lowe v. Surpas Resource Corp., 253 F. Supp. 2d 1209, 1227–29 (D. Kan. 2003); Caputo v. Professional Recovery Servs., Inc., 261 F. Supp. 2d 1249 (D. Kan. 2003) (finding consumer disabled).

239 Alexander v. Certified Master Builders Corp., 1 P.3d 899 (Kan. 2000).

8.4.1.2 Statutory Damages for Multiple Claims

While a consumer may not be able to recover UDAP actual damages and UDAP statutory damages for the same UDAP violation, multiple recoveries are possible for multiple violations. Thus, a court has awarded twelve different $100 statutory damages for twelve different illegal provisions in the same lease.[240] Another court awarded $200 statutory damages for each of thirty-six payments a consumer made on a usurious loan.[241] A federal decision suggests that minimum statutory damages are available in Kansas for each sale of the product to the consumer.[242]

8.4.1.3 Statutory Damages for Multiple Plaintiffs

An important question is whether UDAP statutory damages can be awarded to each member of a prevailing class or only once to the class as a whole. Massachusetts' highest court has held that each class member must receive the minimum damages because "dividing a single award of statutory damages among all class members would discourage the assertion of consumer class actions where injuries have taken place, though actual damages may be insignificant or nonexistent, and would thus be contrary to one of the basic purposes of the statute."[243] A federal decision also views statutory minimum damages under the District of

240 Upadhyay v. Anderson, Clearinghouse No. 49,148 (Va. Dist. Ct., Cty. of Colonial Heights Apr. 2, 1993). *See also* Griffin v. Bank of Am., 971 F. Supp. 492 (D. Kan. 1997) (jury could award multiple statutory damage awards for the nine violations alleged even though Kansas UDAP statute allows court to award statutory damages up to $5000 for each claim); *In re* Wiggins, 273 B.R. 839 (Bankr. D. Idaho 2001) ($1000 statutory damages for each of 6 violations in single transaction); Smith v. Stacy, 2001 Ohio App. LEXIS 3202 (June 19, 2001) (statutory damages of $200 available for each of four UDAP violations, but actual damages are greater so are awarded instead); Baker v. Tri-County Harley Davidson, Inc., 1999 Ohio App. LEXIS 5353 (Nov. 15, 1999) ($200 statutory damages awarded for each of three violations); Crye v. Smolak, 110 Ohio App. 3d 504, 674 N.E.2d 779 (1996) (three separate awards of statutory damages and one award of treble damages for four violations within one transaction). *But see* Ferrari v. Howard, 2002 WL 1500414 (Ohio App. July 11, 2002) (unpublished, citation limited) (only one statutory damage award possible for multiple violations in same transaction); Cummins v. Dave Fillmore Car Co., 1987 WL 19186 (Ohio App. Oct. 27, 1987) (only one statutory damage award allowed).

241 *In re* Arsenault, 184 B.R. 864 (Bankr. D.N.H. 1995). *See also* Lowe v. Surpas Resource Corp., 253 F. Supp. 2d 1209 (D. Kan. 2003) (multiple statutory damages are available for multiple violations, even if several violations occur in a single telephone call).

242 Burton v. R.J. Reynolds Tobacco Co., 205 F. Supp. 2d 1253, 1264 (D. Kan. 2002).

243 Leardi v. Brown, 394 Mass. 151, 474 N.E.2d 1094 (1985). *See also* Oslan v. Law Offices of Mitchell N. Kay, 232 F. Supp. 2d 436, 443 (E.D. Pa. 2002).

Columbia Code as available on a classwide basis.[244] There may be due process issues, however, if there is a massive aggregation of minimum statutory damages for a large group of people.[245]

8.4.1.4 Should Statutory Damages Be Trebled?

A number of UDAP statutes authorize both statutory damages and treble damages for certain types of violations, such as willful or knowing violations. The statutory language will often control whether the minimum statutory damages can also be trebled.

The Massachusetts statutory and multiple damage provisions are ambiguously drafted so it is unclear whether a consumer can obtain treble the minimum damages where the seller's practice is willful. The Massachusetts court has decided that the legislative intent is to award either treble or minimum damages, but not treble minimum damages.[246]

8.4.1.5 Interrelationship Between Statutory Damages and Other Awards

While a statutory provision allowing "actual damages or civil penalties" could be construed to authorize the award of only one or the other,[247] an Oregon court has found that a consumer can obtain actual damages for one UDAP violation and statutory minimum damages for another separate UDAP violation.[248] A court has also awarded actual UDAP damages on one count and statutory damages under the Truth in Lending Act under another count.[249] Other courts have awarded:

- Fair Debt Collection Practices Act statutory damages and UDAP statutory damages for similar collection agency misconduct;[250]
- $1000 statutory damages under a UDAP count and also $1000 tort damages for the infliction of emotional distress;[251]
- $1500 statutory damages for sending unsolicited faxes in violation of the Telephone Consumer Protection Act[252] plus $200 statutory damages on a parallel UDAP claim;[253]
- Statutory damages for each of two different UDAP violations, treble damages for a third UDAP violation, plus actual damages for a fourth violation.[254]

Statutory damages are not considered punitive, but compensatory, so that courts may award both statutory and punitive damages.[255]

8.4.2 Multiple Damages

8.4.2.1 General

About half of all UDAP statutes authorize treble or other multiple damage awards.[256] The actual damage award, under specified conditions, is multiplied (usually by three) to calculate treble damages. Unlike minimum damages, multiple damages are awarded only if actual damages are proven.[257] Where an individual consumer's actual damages are nominal, three times this amount will still be nominal. But where actual damages are substantial, the possibility of multiple damages should significantly affect settlement negotiations and a consumer litigant's willingness to press the action.[258]

Multiple damages have a number of purposes. They are an incentive for private individuals to ferret out deception and bring legal actions, they provide a remedy for those injured, they deter future seller misconduct, and they increase the incentive for the parties to reach a settlement.[259]

---

244 Wells v. Allstate Ins. Co., 210 F.R.D. 1 (D.D.C. 2002).

245 Parker v. Time Warner Entertainment Co., 331 F.3d 13, 22, 26 (2d Cir. 2003) (civil penalties for non-UDAP federal claims).

246 Leardi v. Brown, 394 Mass. 151, 474 N.E.2d 1094 (1985).

247 Bell v. Kent-Brown Chevrolet Co., 1 Kan. App. 2d 131, 561 P.2d 907 (1977).

248 Tri-West Constr. Co. v. Hernandez, 43 Or. App. 961, 607 P.2d 1375 (1979).

249 Douglas v. G.E.E.N. Corp., 415 So. 2d 130 (Fla. Dist. Ct. App. 1982). *See also* Burnett v. Ala Moana Pawn Shop, Clearinghouse No. 46,771 (D. Haw. 1991) (TIL statutory damages and UDAP treble damages for same TIL violation; court would have awarded both TIL and UDAP statutory damages if UDAP treble damages had been less than UDAP statutory damages), *aff'd*, 3 F.3d 1261 (9th Cir. 1993).

250 *In re* Belile, 209 B.R. 658 (Bankr. E.D. Pa. 1997).

251 Sherwood v. Bellevue Dodge, Inc., 35 Wash. App. 741, 669 P.2d 1258 (1983).

252 *See* § 5.9.3, *supra*.

253 Dubsky v. Advanced Cellular Communications, Inc., 2004 WL 503757 (Ohio Com. Pleas Feb. 24, 2004) (unpublished, citation limited).

254 Simpson v. Smith, 34 Ohio Misc. 2d 7, 517 N.E.2d 276 (Mun. Ct. 1987). *See also* Gaylan v. Dave Towell Cadillac, 15 Ohio Misc. 2d 1, 473 N.E.2d 64 (Mun. Ct. 1984) ($200 minimum damages for each of two separate deceptive practices arising in the same transaction). *But see* Couto v. Gibson, Inc., 1992 Ohio App. LEXIS 756 (Feb. 26, 1992) (no multiple statutory damages for different violations emanating from the same transaction).

255 Equitable Life Leasing Corp. v. Abbick, 243 Kan. 513, 757 P.2d 304 (1988); Riviera Motors, Inc. v. Higbee, 45 Or. App. 545, 609 P.2d 369 (1980).

256 *See* Appx. A, *infra*.

257 Faris v. Model's Guild, 297 So. 2d 536 (La. Ct. App. 1974); Schafer v. Conner, 805 S.W.2d 554 (Tex. App. 1991); Sign-O-Lite Signs, Inc. v. Delaurenti Florists, Inc., 825 P.2d 714 (Wash. Ct. App. 1992).

258 *See, e.g.*, Veranda Beach Club v. Western Surety Co., 936 F.2d 1364 (1st Cir. 1991) (Mass. law) (court doubles UDAP award of $2 million).

259 *See, e.g.*, Refuse & Environmental Sys., Inc. v. Industrial Servs., 932 F.2d 37 (1st Cir. 1991); Showpiece Homes Corp. v. Assurance Co. of Am., 38 P.3d 47 (Colo. 2001) (purposes are to

Multiple damages can also compensate consumers for injuries that the law of damages does not recognize, and for damages that the consumer, with only limited resources, is unable to prove at trial. Thus UDAP statutes' treble damage provisions are not penal, but remedial,[260] and should be liberally construed. There is no merit to the claim that treble damages should only be available where actual damages are small.[261]

8.4.2.2 Are Multiple Damages Mandatory?

Despite the clear policy underpinnings for multiple damage awards, individual courts may be reluctant to order merchants to pay consumers more than actual damages. In this situation, it is useful if the consumer litigant can argue that the award of multiple damages is not in the court's discretion, but is mandated if the statutory preconditions are met.

Whether multiple damages are mandatory will turn on the statutory language. The language for some statutes is unambiguously mandatory,[262] such as a statement that treble damages "shall" be awarded. In that case, courts will not infer limits on the award.

The North Carolina Supreme Court has refused to imply any intent or other precondition to the mandatory award of treble damages for any UDAP violation.[263] New Jersey courts also rule that treble damages are mandatory for any UDAP violation.[264] In Ohio, treble damages are authorized only if a consumer shows a violation of a rule or other clear standard,[265] but in that case they are mandatory[266] unless the seller proves a bona fide error.[267] Vermont's UDAP statute makes the award of treble damages (termed "exemplary damages" by the statute) mandatory if the seller acts willfully or with malice.[268]

Other UDAP statutes use the word "may," which is less clearly mandatory. Nevertheless, the Texas Supreme Court has ruled that where the statute stated that the consumer "may" obtain treble his or her damages, the award was not in the court's discretion, but was mandatory once a UDAP violation is proven, even if there was no unlawful intent.[269]

On the other hand, courts have interpreted language that "the court may award" multiple damages differently than language that the consumer "may recover" multiple damages. Where a statute states that the court may award treble damages, this means it is discretionary with the court.[270]

If treble damages are proper, the fact that treble damages will result in a recovery of hundreds of thousands of dollars should not prevent the award. UDAP cases have trebled a $150,000 award for pain and suffering,[271] awarded multiple damages exceeding $300,000 where an insurer's settlement

---

provide remedy and promote enforcement); Plath v. Schonrock, 64 P.3d 984 (Mont. 2003) (purpose is to encourage private enforcement by making it economically feasible to pursue small damage claims); Marshall v. Miller, 302 N.C. 539, 276 S.E.2d 397 (1981), *rev'd in part on other grounds*, 302 N.C. 539, 276 S.E.2d 397 (1981) (holding that intent is not an element); State *ex rel.* Easley v. Rich Food Servs., Inc., 535 S.E.2d 84 (N.C. App. 2000) (purpose of treble damages and fees is to enable private citizens to prosecute claims which might otherwise involve prohibitive expense); Jim Walter Homes, Inc. v. Valencia, 690 S.W.2d 239 (Tex. 1985); Pennington v. Singleton, 606 S.W.2d 682 (Tex. 1980); Wilder v. Aetna Life & Casualty Ins. Co., 140 Vt. 16, 433 A.2d 309 (1981).

260 Holley v. Coggin Pontiac, 43 N.C. App. 229, 259 S.E.2d 1 (1979). *But see* Jones v. Sportelli, 166 N.J. Super. 383, 399 A.2d 1047 (Law. Div. 1979).

261 Mosley & Mosley Builders v. Landin Ltd., 389 S.E.2d 576 (N.C. Ct. App. 1990).

262 South Atlantic Ltd. P'ship v. Riese, 284 F.3d 518, 529 n.13 (4th Cir. 2002) (N.C. law); District Cablevision Ltd. P'ship v. Bassin, 828 A.2d 714 (D.C. 2003); Colonial Lincoln-Mercury Sales, Inc. v. Molina, 152 Ga. App. 379, 262 S.E.2d 820 (1979); Marshall v. Miller, 302 N.C. 539, 276 S.E.2d 397 (1981); Dairs v. Sellers, 443 S.E.2d 879 (N.C. Ct. App. 1994); Schafer v. Conner, 805 S.W.2d 554 (Tex. App. 1991) (Texas UDAP statute now specifies that first $1000 of damages "shall" be trebled); National Bugmobiles, Inc. v. Jobi Properties, 773 S.W.2d 616 (Tex. App. 1989); Shands v. Castrovinci, 115 Wis. 2d 352, 340 N.W.2d 506 (1983); Armour v. Klecker, 169 Wis. 2d 692, 486 N.W.2d 563 (Ct. App. 1992).

263 Marshall v. Miller, 302 N.C. 539, 276 S.E.2d 397 (1981). *Accord In re* Bozzano, 183 B.R. 735 (Bankr. M.D.N.C. 1995). *See also* Kim v. Professional Bus. Brokers, Ltd., 328 S.E.2d 296 (N.C. Ct. App. 1985).

264 *In re* Fleet, 95 B.R. 319 (E.D. Pa. 1989) (New Jersey law); Huffmaster v. Robinson, 221 N.J. Super. 315, 534 A.2d 435 (Law Div. 1986); Ramanadham v. New Jersey Manufacturers Ins. Co., 188 N.J. Super. 30, 455 A.2d 1134 (App. Div. 1982); Skeer v. EMK Motors, 187 N.J. Super. 465, 455 A.2d 508 (App. Div. 1982).

265 *See* § 8.4.2.3.3, *infra*.

266 Bierlein v. Alex's Continental Inn, 16 Ohio App. 3d 294, 475 N.E.2d 1274 (1984). *See also* Crenshaw v. Simione, Clearinghouse No. 47,840, 1988 Ohio App. LEXIS 1953 (Ohio Ct. App. 1988).

267 Swift v. Allied Pest Control, Inc., 2001 Ohio App. LEXIS 3853 (Aug. 31, 2001) (remanding case because jury's finding that violation was knowing was inconsistent with its finding of bona fide error).

268 Bruntaeger v. Zeller, 515 A.2d 123 (Vt. 1986); Winton v. Johnson & Dix Fuel Corp., 515 A.2d 371 (Vt. 1986).

269 Pennington v. Singleton, 606 S.W.2d 682 (Tex. 1980); Woods v. Littleton, 554 S.W.2d 662 (Tex. 1977). Note that the treble damages language in the Texas statute has been amended since these decisions. Tex. Bus. & Com. Code Ann. § 17.50.

270 Teague-Strebeck Motors, Inc. v. Chrysler Ins. Co., 985 P.2d 1183 (N.M. App. 1999); Keith v. Howerton, 2002 WL 31840683 (Tenn. Ct. App. Dec. 19, 2002) (unpublished, citation limited) (a trial court may, at the upper limit, award treble damages, but the trial court may chose to award something less than treble damages under the appropriate circumstances); Baggett v. Crown Automotive Group, Inc., 1992 Tenn. App. LEXIS 464 (May 22, 1992); Holmes v. LG Marion Corp., 258 Va. 473, 521 S.E.2d 528 (1999).

271 Pope v. Rollins Protective Servs. Co., 703 F.2d 197 (5th Cir. 1983); *see also* Otero v. Midland Life Ins. Co., 753 So. 2d 579 (Fla. App. 1999) (mental distress damages are available for UNIP claim only if there is physical impact); Mahan Volkswagen Inc. v. Hall, 648 S.W.2d 324 (Tex. App. 1982).

offer was unreasonably low by $2000,[272] trebled $212,900 actual damages,[273] increased $250,000 actual damages for sale of a defective truck to $534,000,[274] and in commercial UDAP cases trebled actual damage recoveries of $960,000[275] and $113,630[276] and doubled damages of $2,336,742.[277] The Texas Supreme Court even trebled a $2,111,500 UDAP award.[278]

8.4.2.3 Limits on Treble Damages Award

8.4.2.3.1 Intent or knowledge preconditions

Courts will not infer an intent or knowledge precondition just because treble damages are mandatory.[279] Nevertheless, most UDAP statutes explicitly set preconditions for a treble damages recovery. A number of UDAP statutes limit multiple damage awards to situations where intent, willfulness, or bad faith is shown.[280] For example, the Texas statute was amended in 1995 to provide for recovery of treble the consumer's economic damages only if the defendant acted knowingly, and treble the consumer's economic damages and mental anguish damages only if the defendant acted intentionally.[281] Deception is "knowing" if the defendant had actual awareness that the act was false, deceptive or unfair.[282] Knowledge can be established by circumstantial evidence.[283]

In such states, even the knowing nondisclosure of a fact[284] or a representation with reckless disregard of whether it is true or false[285] can be enough to trigger multiple damages. Likewise, a conscious decision to remain uninformed about health and safety requirements is a willful and knowing UDAP violation that justifies treble damages.[286]

It is not necessary to show that the seller knew it was violating the UDAP statute or knew that its practice was illegal in some more general sense.[287] In addition, the accumulation of a large number of minor UDAP violations over a period of time can show willfulness.[288] A violation may be "grievous," however, without being willful or

272 Dimarzo v. American Mut. Ins. Co., 389 Mass. 85, 449 N.E.2d 1189 (1983).

273 Keller Indus., Inc. v. Reeves, 656 S.W.2d 221 (Tex. App. 1983).

274 Metro Ford Truck Sales, Inc. v. Davis, 709 S.W.2d 785 (Tex. App. 1986).

275 McAllen State Bank v. Linbeck Constr. Corp., 695 S.W.2d 10 (Tex. App. 1985).

276 Hundred East Credit Corp. v. Eric Shuster Corp., 212 N.J. Super. 350, 515 A.2d 246 (App. Div. 1986).

277 Computer Sys. Eng'g, Inc. v. Quantel Corp., 571 F. Supp. 1365 (D. Mass. 1983) (Massachusetts law), *aff'd*, 740 F.2d 59 (1st Cir. 1984).

278 Birchfield v. Texarkana Memorial Hosp., 747 S.W.2d 361 (Tex. 1987).

279 Marshall v. Miller, 302 N.C. 539, 276 S.E.2d 397 (1981); Pennington v. Singleton, 606 S.W.2d 682 (Tex. 1980); Barnett v. Coppell N. Texas Court, Ltd., 123 S.W.3d 804 (Tex. App. 2003); *see also* Indust-Ri-Chem Laboratory v. Par-Pak Co., 602 S.W.2d 282 (Tex. Civ. App. 1980).

280 Nelson v. Cowles Ford, Inc., 2003 U.S. App. LEXIS 20371 (4th Cir. Oct. 7, 2003) (unpublished, citation limited) (Va. law); Equitable Life Assurance Soc. v. Porter-Englehart, 867 F.2d 79 (1st Cir. 1989) (Mass. law); Rini v. United Van Lines, Inc., 903 F. Supp. 224 (D. Mass. 1995), *rev'd on other grounds*, 104 F.3d 502 (1st Cir. 1997) (willfulness shown); *In re* Globe Distributors, Inc., 129 B.R. 304 (Bankr. D.N.H. 1991) (violation must be willful or knowing); Kaiser v. Garrus, 617 So. 2d 107 (La. Ct. App. 1993); Faris v. Model's Guild, 297 So. 2d 536 (La. Ct. App. 1974); Avolizi v. Bradford White Corp., 2003 WL 21361781 (Mass. App. Div. June 10, 2003) (rejecting award of multiple damages where there was no evidence that the breach of warranty was a knowing or intentional one); V-Mark Software v. EMC Corp., 37 Mass. App. Ct. 610, 642 N.E.2d 587 (1994) (insincerity about product's performance ability not enough for multiple damages); Whelihan v. Markowski, 37 Mass. App. Ct. 209, 638 N.E.2d 927 (1994) (treble damages not allowable for negligent acts or relatively innocent UDAP violations); Stark v. Patalano Ford Sales, Inc., 30 Mass. App. Ct. 194, 567 N.E.2d 1237 (1991) (damages not trebled where defendant's UDAP violation was not knowing and willful); International Totalizing Sys., Inc. v. Pepsico, Inc., 29 Mass. App. Ct. 424, 560 N.E.2d 749 (1990); Oswego Laborers' Local 214 Pension Fund v. Marine Midland Bank, 85 N.Y.2d 20, 647 N.E.2d 741 (1995) (proof of scienter necessary); Gaylan v. Dave Towell Cadillac, 15 Ohio Misc. 2d 1, 473 N.E.2d 64 (Mun. Ct. 1984); Top Value Homes, Inc. v. Harden, 460 S.E.2d 427 (S.C. Ct. App. 1995) (treble damages properly denied where consumers did not prove willful or knowing violation); Payne v. Holiday Towers, Inc., 321 S.E.2d 179 (S.C. Ct. App. 1984). *See also* Cambridge Plating Co. v. NAPCO, Inc., 85 F.3d 752 (1st Cir. 1996) (Massachusetts law) (defendant's acts did not rise to the level of callousness or meretriciousness that would justify multiple damages); Smith Corona Corp. v. Pelikan, Inc., 784 F. Supp. 452 (M.D. Tenn. 1992), *aff'd*, 1 F.3d 1252 (1993).

281 Tex. Bus. & Com. Code Ann. § 17.50.

282 Streber v. Hunter, 221 F.3d 701, 730 (5th Cir. 2000) (Texas law); Blue Star Operating Co. v. Tetra Technologies, Inc., 119 S.W.3d 916 (Tex. App. 2003); Houston Livestock Show and Rodeo, Inc. v. Hamrick, 125 S.W.3d 555 (Tex. App. 2003); Allison v. Fire Ins. Exchange, 98 S.W.3d 227 (Tex. App. 2002).

283 Streber v. Hunter, 221 F.3d 701 (5th Cir. 2000) (Texas law).

284 Shawmut Community Bank v. Zagami, 30 Mass. App. Ct. 371, 568 N.E.2d 1163 (1991); Grossman v. Waltham Chemical Co., 14 Mass. App. Ct. 932, 436 N.E.2d 1243 (1982).

285 Computer Sys. Engineering, Inc. v. Quantel Corp., 571 F. Supp. 1365 (D. Mass. 1983), *aff'd*, 740 F.2d 59 (1st Cir. 1984); Kattar v. Demoulas, 433 Mass. 1, 739 N.E.2d 246 (2000) (recklessness is sufficient); Shawmut Community Bank v. Zagami, 30 Mass. App. Ct. 371, 568 N.E.2d 1163 (1991); Shaw v. Rodman Ford Truck Center, Inc., 19 Mass. App. Ct. 709, 477 N.E.2d 413 (1985).

286 Whelihan v. Markowski, 37 Mass. App. Ct. 209, 638 N.E.2d 927 (1994).

287 Computer Sys. Engineering, Inc. v. Quantel Corp., 571 F. Supp. 1365 (D. Mass. 1983), *aff'd*, 740 F.2d 59 (1st Cir. 1984); Whelihan v. Markowski, 37 Mass. App. Ct. 209, 638 N.E.2d 927 (1994). *But see* Haley Nursery Co. v. Forrest, 381 S.E.2d 906 (S.C. 1989).

288 Brown v. LeClair, 20 Mass. App. Ct. 976, 482 N.E.2d 870 (1985).

knowing.[289] The knowing misrepresentation of an agent is imputed to the principal.[290]

Under the Texas statute, the jury (if a case is tried before a jury) must determine not only that the practice was committed knowingly, but also that the damages should be trebled.[291] It is not enough just to submit to the jury the question of whether the practice was knowingly committed.[292] In Massachusetts, where UDAP claims are tried to the court, the judge must find that the defendant acted knowingly or willfully in order to award multiple damages, but an express finding is unnecessary as long as it is the clear implication from the court's factual findings.[293] In Ohio, the jury decides liability and actual damages, and the court decides whether there is a basis for treble damages.[294]

8.4.2.3.2 Bad faith refusal to settle as precondition

Other UDAP statutes trigger multiple damages not upon the seller's intent to deceive but upon the seller's bad faith refusal to grant the injured consumer relief after the consumer notifies the merchant of the deception. Thus some state UDAP statutes authorize treble damages even if a seller does not intend to deceive a consumer if, upon receiving a complaint, the seller does not investigate the facts, consider the legal precedents, and make a good faith offer to settle the problem.[295]

289 Shawmut Community Bank v. Zagami, 30 Mass. App. Ct. 371, 568 N.E.2d 1163 (1991).

290 Maryland Ins. Co. v. Head Indus. Coatings & Servs., Inc., 906 S.W.2d 218 (Tex. App. 1995), *rev'd on other grounds*, 938 S.W.2d 27 (Tex. 1996).

291 Martin v. McKee Realtors, Inc., 663 S.W.2d 446 (Tex. 1984); Leonard & Harral Packing Co. v. Ward, 883 S.W.2d 337 (Tex. App. 1994); J.B. Custom Design & Bldg. v. Clawson, 794 S.W.2d 38 (Tex. App. 1990). *See also* Boat Superstore, Inc. v. Haner, 877 S.W.2d 376 (Tex. App. 1994) (whether to award multiple damages after a finding of willfulness is question for the trier of fact).

292 Martin v. McKee Realtors, Inc., 663 S.W.2d 446 (Tex. 1984). Perhaps this distinction explains the seeming conflict between Leonard & Harral Packing Co. v. Ward, 883 S.W.2d 337 (Tex. App. 1994) and Boat Superstore, Inc. v. Haner, 877 S.W.2d 376 (Tex. App. 1994) (trial court's entry of default judgment improperly awarded additional damages because no evidence was presented to support additional damages, beyond judicial admission of knowledge of conduct in violation of UDAP).

293 Anthony's Pier Four v. HBC Assocs., 411 Mass. 451, 583 N.E.2d 806 (1991).

294 Fit 'N' Fun Pools, Inc. v. Shelly, 2001 Ohio App. LEXIS 3 (Jan. 3, 2001). *See also* § 7.9.2.3, *supra*; Crow v. Fred Martin Motor Co., 2003 WL 1240119 (Ohio App. Mar. 19, 2003) (unpublished, citation limited).

295 Heller v. Silverbranch Constr. Corp., 376 Mass. 621, 382 N.E.2d 1065 (1978); Stark v. Patalano Ford Sales, Inc., 30 Mass. App. Ct. 194, 567 N.E.2d 1237 (1991) (damages not trebled where defendant's response to demand letter was not in bad faith); Tate v. Wiggins, 583 S.W.2d 640 (Tex. Civ. App. 1979). *See also* Colo. Rev. Stat. § 13-20-806 (allowing multiple damages against construction professional only if defendant does not make or comply with settlement offer).

Conversely, a seller who intended to deceive the consumer can avoid liability for treble damages in these states by making a reasonable settlement offer.[296] In Massachusetts, a landlord met this standard when he made good-faith, albeit negligent, efforts to repair substandard housing conditions.[297]

To avoid liability for multiple damages, the seller's settlement offer must be reasonable.[298] The burden of proving reasonableness is on the seller.[299] In determining whether an offer was reasonable the court will consider the information given to and available to the defendant at the time.[300] An indefinite offer, ignoring requested relief, is unreasonable.[301]

A settlement offer is in bad faith if it is really illusory, not benefiting the consumer at all.[302] Gross inadequacy makes an offer unreasonable—rather than promoting settlement, such a response merely encourages litigation.[303] A settlement offer has been found unreasonable where the seller merely offered not to enforce unenforceable clauses in a contract; instead, a reasonable offer would be to remove the clauses from the contract.[304] It can also be unreasonable to fail to comply with a reasonable request to make repairs.[305]

8.4.2.3.3 Other preconditions to multiple damage awards

A few UDAP statutes trigger treble damages if the seller violates a UDAP rule or other clear standard.[306] In Ohio, a dealer is liable for treble damages only if it violated a rule adopted under the state UDAP statute or a decision interpreting the statute that was made available for public in-

296 Kohl v. Silver Lake Motors, Inc., 369 Mass. 795, 343 N.E.2d 375 (1976); Whelihan v. Markowski, 37 Mass. App. Ct. 209, 638 N.E.2d 927 (1994).

297 Cruz Mgmt. Co. v. Thomas, 417 Mass. 782, 633 N.E.2d 390 (1994).

298 Parker v. D'Avolio, 40 Mass. App. Ct. 394, 664 N.E.2d 858 (1996) (landlord's token offer to settle lead paint poisoning case not unreasonable in light of information available at time of demand); Williams v. Gulf Ins. Co., 39 Mass. App. Ct. 432, 657 N.E.2d 240 (1995); Burke v. Atamian Porsche Audi, Inc., Clearinghouse No. 25,841 (Mass. Super. Ct. 1978).

299 Patry v. Harmony Homes, Inc., 10 Mass. App. Ct. 1, 404 N.E.2d 1265 (1980).

300 Whelihan v. Markowski, 37 Mass. App. Ct. 209, 638 N.E.2d 927 (1994).

301 Patry v. Harmony Homes, Inc., 10 Mass. App. Ct. 1, 404 N.E.2d 1265 (1980).

302 Leardi v. Brown, 394 Mass. 151, 474 N.E.2d 1094 (1985); Brandt v. Olympic Constr. Inc., 16 Mass. App. Ct. 913, 449 N.E.2d 1231 (1983); Patry v. Liberty Mobilehome Sales, Inc., 15 Mass. App. Ct. 701, 448 N.E.2d 405 (1983).

303 Calimlim v. Foreign Car Center, Inc., 392 Mass. 228, 467 N.E.2d 443 (1984).

304 Leardi v. Brown, 394 Mass. 151, 474 N.W.2d 1094 (1985).

305 Brown v. LeClair, 20 Mass. App. Ct. 976, 482 N.E.2d 870 (1985).

306 *See* La. Rev. Stat. Ann. § 51:1409 (knowing violation after notice given by state official); Ohio Rev. Code Ann. § 1345.09.

spection.[307] The decision's availability for public inspection is treated as a question of fact that must be proven by admissible evidence.[308] The court must award treble damages even if the seller acted without knowledge of the rule or other clear standard.[309] Good faith, the fact that the consumer has already been adequately compensated, and equitable considerations are not grounds for denying treble damages.[310] But if the dealer proves that its violation was a bona fide error despite the maintenance of reasonable procedures to avoid such errors, its monetary liability is limited to actual damages.[311] The consumer must take care to present questions to the jury that will allow unequivocal findings about the defendant's UDAP violations and serve as a predicate for a treble damages award.[312]

Louisiana's UDAP statute makes a defendant liable for treble damages only if it knowingly used the unfair or deceptive practice after being put on notice by the director of consumer affairs or the attorney general.[313] The statute does not define being put on notice, so adoption of regulations and issuance of press releases or advisories, as well as individual notice to a particular dealer, should suffice.

Certain UDAP statutes further limit multiple damages to a certain class of litigants. For example, the Texas statute limits treble damages to "consumers," as defined in the statute, thus excluding purchasers of real property[314] and those making purchases for nonhousehold purposes.[315] Delaware's UDTPA statute, which provides for trebling of damages awarded under the common law or other state statutes, is interpreted to apply only to plaintiffs who have a trade or business interest at stake and who have standing to seek injunctive relief.[316] Delaware's other UDAP statute was amended in 2003 to allow any victim to seek damages, and elderly or disabled victims to seek treble damages.[317]

New York's UDAP statute allows treble damages only if the total award does not exceed $1000.[318] One court has found this means that treble damages can be awarded only where the total award, after trebling, is less than $1000.[319] There is some doubt whether this was legislative intent.

Tennessee's UDAP statute lists the factors a court should consider in determining whether to award treble damages. The Tennessee courts have had little difficulty awarding treble damages based on these factors.[320]

8.4.2.3.4 Standards where multiple damages are discretionary

In states that do not specify the standards for an award of treble damages, courts have looked to such factors as the

307 Ohio Rev. Code § 1345.09(B). *See* Lewis v. ACB Bus. Servs., 135 F.3d 389 (6th Cir. 1998) (to justify treble damages under Ohio statute, defendant's actions must be similar to specific conduct determined to be UDAP violation by prior court); Arales v. Furs by Weiss, Inc., 2003 WL 21469131 (Ohio App. June 26, 2003) (unpublished, citation limited) (violation of rule or prior decision is only required for treble, not actual damages); Dotson v. Brondes Motor Sales, 90 Ohio App. 3d 206, 628 N.E.2d 137 (1993) (no treble damages where no showing that seller violated UDAP rule or prior court decision); Mid Am. Acceptance Co. v. Lightle, 63 Ohio App. 3d 590, 579 N.E.2d 721 (1989) (treble damages only authorized where violation of UDAP rule or prior judicial declaration is shown); Gross v. Bildex, Inc., 647 N.E.2d 573 (Ohio Mun. 1994) (damages trebled where contractor's acts violated decisions made available for public inspection); Daniels v. True, 47 Ohio Misc. 2d 8, 547 N.E.2d 425 (Mun. Ct. 1988) (multiple damages available where decision prohibiting this type of conduct had been made available for public inspection and defendant had been convicted of consumer fraud).

308 White v. Hornbeck, 2002 WL 1363689 (Ohio App. June 19, 2002) (unpublished, citation limited); Fribourg v. Vandemark, 1999 Ohio App. LEXIS 3424 (July 26, 1999) (no evidence presented that decision was made available for public inspection). *See also* Fit 'N' Fun Pools, Inc. v. Shelly, 2001 Ohio App. LEXIS 3 (Jan. 3, 2001) (suggesting that court may take judicial notice that decision was made available for public inspection, but proper procedures for requesting judicial notice not followed here).

309 Bierlein v. Alex's Continental Inn, 16 Ohio App. 3d 294, 475 N.E.2d 1274 (1984).

310 Crow v. Fred Martin Motor Co., 2003 WL 1240119 (Ohio App. Mar. 19, 2003) (unpublished, citation limited) (whether violation was egregious not a factor); Stultz v. Artistic Pools, Inc., 2001 Ohio App. LEXIS 4561 (Oct. 10, 2001).

311 Frey v. Vin Devers, Inc., 80 Ohio App. 3d 1, 608 N.E.2d 796 (1992).

312 Stultz v. Artistic Pools, Inc., 2001 Ohio App. LEXIS 4561 (Oct. 10, 2001).

313 La. Rev. Stat. Ann. § 51:1409. *See* Jesco Constr. Corp. v. NationsBank Corp., 107 F. Supp. 2d 715 (E.D. La. 2000), *stay granted, interlocutory appeal allowed on other issue*, 2000 U.S. Dist. LEXIS 13256 (E.D. La. 2000), *question certified to Louisiana Supreme Court*, 2001 U.S. App. LEXIS 27530 (5th Cir. 2001), *certified question answered*, 830 So. 2d 989 (La. 2002) (claims barred on other grounds); Joseph v. Hendrix, 536 So. 2d 448 (La. Ct. App. 1988) (multiple damages not available because defendant had not been put on notice by director of consumer affairs or attorney general).

314 Trial v. McCoy, 553 S.W.2d 199 (Tex. Civ. App. 1977).

315 Cape Conroe Ltd. v. Specht, 525 S.W.2d 215 (Tex. Civ. App. 1975).

316 Grand Ventures, Inc. v. Whaley, 632 A.2d 63 (Del. 1993).

317 Del. Code Ann. tit. 6, §§ 2525, 2583.

318 Yochim v. McGrath, 165 Misc. 2d 10, 626 N.Y.S.2d 685 (Yonkers City Ct. 1995); Hairt v. Moore, 155 Misc. 2d 203, 587 N.Y.S.2d 477 (Sup. 1992).

319 Hart v. Moore, 587 N.Y.S.2d 477 (Sup. Ct. 1992).

320 *See* Myers v. Hexagon Co., 54 F. Supp. 2d 742 (E.D. Tenn. 1998) (concealing fact that consumers were given no credit for their trade-in justified treble damages); Akers v. Bonifasi, 629 F. Supp. 1212 (M.D. Tenn. 1985) (misrepresentation of franchise earnings justified treble damages); Brandon v. Winnett, 1995 Tenn. App. LEXIS 508, Clearinghouse No. 51,279 (Tenn. App. 1995) (double damages awarded for negligent misrepresentation); Ramey v. Kingsport Motors Inc., 1992 Tenn. App. LEXIS 316, Clearinghouse No. 51,280 (Tenn. App. 1991) (defendant's culpable intent and stonewalling justified treble damages); Tilson v. Buchanan, 1991 Tenn. App. LEXIS 99, Clearinghouse No. 51,281 (Tenn. App. 1991) (false statement of vehicle's mileage justified treble damages).

deterrent effect of an award and whether the defendant's acts were deliberate, unconscionable, obdurate, repeated, knowing, or otherwise aggravated.[321] A Pennsylvania appellate decision equates treble UDAP damages with punitive damages when the claim is based on breach of contract or warranty.[322] In such cases, the plaintiff must prove that the defendant's conduct was malicious, wanton, willful, or oppressive, or exhibited a reckless indifference to the rights of others. For other UDAP violations, a simple showing of fraudulent behavior is sufficient.[323]

The District of Columbia UDAP statute allows treble damages without any additional findings by the court.[324] Some multiple damages provisions are punitive in nature, but in the District of Columbia UDAP statute they are intended for remedial purposes of encouraging private enforcement and providing compensation for damages that are difficult to prove.[325] Likewise, the Montana Supreme Court ruled that intentional conduct was not necessary for a discretionary treble damages award.[326] Instead, the trial court should be guided by the purpose of the Act of protecting consumers and the purpose of the treble damage provision of encouraging consumers to bring UDAP actions.

8.4.2.3.5 Statutory standards as to the multiplier to be utilized

In some states, the multiple applied to actual damages will vary depending on certain conditions or on the court's discretion.[327] For example, actual damages may be doubled in some cases and trebled in others.

In Massachusetts[328] and New Hampshire,[329] the court must at least double, and may treble, the actual damage award if certain preconditions are met. The defendant's egregiousness, its failure to make a reasonable settlement offer, the probable effect of its practices on others, and the need for a deterrent are relevant to the determination whether to go up to treble damages.[330] A Tennessee decision interprets its UDAP statute to allow the trial court to augment the damage award by a factor less than trebling.[331]

8.4.2.4 Are Multiple Damages Available in Default Judgments?

Default judgments are subject to trebling just as litigated judgments are.[332] It is wise to put a defendant on notice through the complaint that treble damages are being sought. That way, if there is a default judgment, there will not be an issue of unfair surprise to the defendant. The complaint should clearly allege any preconditions to multiple damages and include them in the prayer for relief.[333]

8.4.2.5 Arbitration and Multiple Damages

8.4.2.5.1 Can UDAP multiple damages claims be forced into arbitration?

Whether an arbitration clause generally is enforceable is examined in another NCLC manual, *Consumer Arbitration Agreements* (4th ed. 2004).[334] This subsection reviews whether a claim for UDAP treble damages raises special issues as to the arbitration agreement's enforceability.

The United States Supreme Court has held that private parties can agree to arbitrate claims for multiple damages even though such claims also serve a public function. The Court found no inherent problem in plaintiffs being forced to arbitrate RICO treble damages claims as long as the arbitrator could award treble damages.[335] Similarly, an arbitra-

321 Refuse & Environmental Sys., Inc. v. Industrial Servs., 732 F. Supp. 1209 (D. Mass. 1990), *rev'd in part on other grounds*, 932 F.2d 37 (1st Cir. 1991); *In re* Bryant, 111 B.R. 474 (E.D. Pa. 1990); *In re* Globe Distributors, Inc., 129 B.R. 304 (Bankr. D.N.H. 1991) (choice between doubling and trebling damages depends on defendant's egregious willfulness and knowledge); Clarkson v. DeCaceres, 105 B.R. 266 (Bankr. E.D. Pa. 1989); Aponte v. Aungst, 82 B.R. 738 (Bankr. E.D. Pa. 1988); Russell v. Fidelity Consumer Discount Co., 72 B.R. 855 (Bankr. E.D. Pa. 1987); *In re* Andrews, 78 B.R. 78 (Bankr. E.D. Pa. 1987) (repeated violations); *cf. In re* Wernly, 91 B.R. 702 (Bankr. E.D. Pa. 1988) (conduct not outrageous, so treble damages denied); Cooper v. Pilgrim Life Ins. Co., 95 York Legal Record 121 (Pa. C.P. 1982) (double damages awarded).

322 Johnson v. Hyundai Motor Am., 698 A.2d 631 (Pa. Super. 1997).

323 Skurnowicz v. Lucci, 798 A.2d 788 (Pa. Super. 2002).

324 Williams v. First Government Mortgage & Investors Corp., 225 F.3d 738 (D.C. Cir. 2000); District Cablevision Ltd. P'ship v. Bassin, 828 A.2d 714 (D.C. 2003).

325 District Cablevision Ltd. P'ship v. Bassin, 828 A.2d 714, 726–29 (D.C. 2003).

326 Plath v. Schonrock, 64 P.3d 984 (Mont. 2003).

327 *See* Appx. A, *infra*.

328 Refuse & Environmental Sys., Inc. v. Industrial Servs. of Am., 732 F. Supp. 1209 (D. Mass. 1990), *rev'd in part on other grounds*, 932 F.2d 37 (1st Cir. 1991); Bonofiglio v. Commercial Union Ins. Co., 411 Mass. 31, 576 N.E.2d 680 (1991).

329 *In re* Globe Distributors, Inc., 129 B.R. 304 (Bankr. D.N.H. 1991) (violation must be willful or knowing).

330 Rini v. United Van Lines, Inc., 903 F. Supp. 224 (D. Mass. 1995), *rev'd on other grounds*, 104 F.3d 502 (1st Cir. 1997); Brown v. LeClair, 20 Mass. App. Ct. 976, 482 N.E.2d 870 (1985).

331 Keith v. Howerton, 2002 WL 31840683 (Tenn. App. Dec. 19, 2002).

332 Woodrick v. Jack J. Burke Real Estate, 306 N.J. Super. 61, 703 A.2d 306 (App. Div. 1997).

333 Multi Technology v. Mitchell Mgmt. Sys., Inc., 25 Mass. App. Ct. 333, 518 N.E.2d 854 (1988). *See also* Henry S. Miller Co. v. Hamilton, 813 S.W.2d 631 (Tex. App. 1991) (even alleging that conduct is knowing may not be sufficient to obtain treble damages where judgment obtained by default); Sunrizon Homes, Inc. v. Fuller, 747 S.W.2d 530 (Tex. App. 1988).

334 *See also* § 7.6.7, *supra*.

335 Shearson/American Express, Inc. v. McMahon, 482 U.S. 220, 107 S. Ct. 2332, 96 L. Ed. 2d 185 (1987).

tion agreement can require a UDAP multiple damages claim to be pursued through arbitration, as long as the arbitrator has authority to award such damages.[336]

On the other hand, an arbitration clause may not be enforceable if the consumer can not recover UDAP multiple damages—such as where such recovery is prohibited by the arbitration clause itself, the rules of the arbitration mechanism, or state law as to arbitrations. The Supreme Court, in *Mitsubishi Motors Corp. v. Soler Chrysler-Plymouth, Inc.*, stated that if an arbitration clause waives the plaintiff's "right to pursue statutory remedies [i.e., treble damages] for antitrust violations, we would have little hesitation in condemning the agreement as against public policy."[337]

The same Court stated, "so long as the prospective litigant effectively may vindicate [her] statutory cause of action in the arbitral forum, the statute will continue to serve both its remedial and deterrent function."[338] The clear implication is that if the consumer can not effectively utilize a statutory remedy in arbitration, the arbitration clause is ineffective. As a result, a number of cases have found the arbitration requirement unenforceable where the consumer's recovery of treble or punitive damages was limited.[339]

8.4.2.5.2 *Does an arbitrator have authority to award multiple damages?*

As described in the prior subsection, consumers may be better served if an arbitrator *can not* award UDAP multiple damages. Then the consumer can argue that the arbitration clause is unenforceable as to that claim, and the consumer can then bring the claim in court.

In general, an arbitrator should be free to award multiple damages.[340] But look for any limits on an award of multiple damages that may be found in the arbitration clause itself. The arbitrator can determine whether treble damages are allowed where the clause is ambiguous.[341] For example, where an arbitration agreement prohibits punitive damages, the Supreme Court has found this to be ambiguous as to whether treble damages can be awarded, and the arbitrator initially should interpret this ambiguous language.[342]

Also examine the current rules of any arbitration service provider specified in the arbitration clause. Major mechanisms such as the American Arbitration Association, JAMS (formerly, the Judicial Arbitration and Mediation Services) and the National Arbitration Forum have their rules on the Internet. At present, these rules appear not to limit the consumer's ability to obtain multiple damages.

It is also possible that the UDAP statute itself could limit the authority to award treble damages only to a court. Nevertheless, silence on this should be interpreted as allowing the arbitrator to award multiple damages. The Fourth Circuit has affirmed an arbitrator's award of treble damages under a UDAP claim, since the UDAP statute does not explicitly require that it be a court that makes the treble damages award.[343] A Massachusetts appellate court has interpreted ambiguous language in the Massachusetts UDAP statute as allowing an arbitrator to award multiple damages.[344]

There is very limited judicial review of an arbitrator's decision not to award treble damages, just as there is very limited judicial review of any aspect of an arbitrator's award.[345] Nevertheless, where the award of multiple damages is mandatory under a UDAP statute, and the arbitrator fails to award them, the consumer may prevail on judicial review. A New Jersey appellate court has found it to be reversible error for an arbitrator to fail to award UDAP treble damages where the statute mandated such relief upon a finding of UDAP liability.[346]

8.4.2.6 Interrelation of Treble Damages with Other Awards

Treble damages are both exemplary and compensatory damages. Accordingly, a consumer may not be permitted to receive both treble and actual damages.[347] Moreover, an

336 Stehli v. Action Custom Homes, Inc., 1999 Ohio App. LEXIS 4464 (Ohio Ct. App. Sept. 24, 1999).

337 473 U.S. 614, 105 S. Ct. 3346, 87 L. Ed. 2d 444 (1985).

338 *Id.*

339 *See* National Consumer Law Center, Consumer Arbitration Agreements §§ 4.3.6.1, 5.3.2.4 (4th ed. 2004).

340 Drywall Sys., Inc. v. ZVI Constr., Co., 747 N.E.2d 168 (Mass. App. Ct. 2001), *aff'd in part, rev'd in part on other grounds*, 435 Mass. 664, 761 N.E.2d 482 (2002).

341 *See* Pacificare Health Sys., Inc. v. Book, 123 S. Ct. 1531 (2003).

342 *Id.*

343 Peoples Security Life Ins. Co. v. Monumental Life Ins. Co., 991 F.2d 141 (4th Cir. 1993) (N.C. law).

344 Drywall Sys., Inc. v. ZVI Constr., Co., 747 N.E.2d 168 (Mass. App. Ct. 2001), *aff'd in part, rev'd in part on other grounds*, 435 Mass. 664, 761 N.E.2d 482 (2002).

345 *See* National Consumer Law Center, Consumer Arbitration Agreements Ch. 10 (4th ed. 2004).

346 Cybul v. Atrium Palace Syndicate, 272 N.J. Super. 330, 639 A.2d 1146 (App. Div. 1994).

347 LaBarre v. Shepard, 84 F.3d 496 (1st Cir. 1996) (New Hampshire law); Lexton-Ancira Real Estate Fund, 1972 v. Heller, 826 P.2d 819 (Colo. 1992); Leibert v. Finance Factors Ltd., 788 P.2d 833 (Haw. 1990); Han v. Yang, 931 P.2d 604 (Haw. Ct. App. 1997); Borne v. Haverhill Golf and Country Club, Inc., 58 Mass. App. Ct. 306, 791 N.E.2d 903 (Mass. App. Ct. 2003) (UDAP claims dismissed as duplicative since multiple damages factor in UDAP statute was satisfied by punitive damages awarded on discrimination claim); Poor v. Hill, 138 N.C. App. 19, 530 S.E.2d 838 (2000) (if same conduct gives rise to both UDAP and contract claims, plaintiffs must elect one or the other after verdict); Prince v. Campbell Roofing & Sheet Metal, 2002 WL 1728089 (Ohio App. July 26, 2002) (unpublished, citation limited); Estate of Cattano v. High Touch Homes, Inc., 2002 WL 1290411 (Ohio App. May 24, 2002) (unpublished, citation limited); Freitag v. Bill Swad Datsun, 3 Ohio App. 3d 83, 443 N.E.2d 988 (1981). *Cf.* Wilkins v. Peninsula Motor Cars, Inc., 587 S.E.2d 581, 584 (Va. 2003) (declining to decide whether

injured consumer can not recover twice for the same injury, by receiving treble damages under a UDAP count and compensatory damages under another statute or a common law fraud count.[348]

A consumer can, however, recover compensatory damages on non-UDAP counts, plus the punitive or exemplary component of UDAP damages.[349] Two recoveries can also be had if separate wrongs causing separate damage are alleged.[350] Thus, a consumer can recover both treble damages under a UDAP count and statutory damages under another statute,[351] or treble damages under a UDAP statute for deceptive sales practices and punitive damages for tortious malicious prosecution.[352]

For example, where a creditor fails to disclose important credit information, the consumer in appropriate situations could recover Truth in Lending statutory damages, treble actual damages under a UDAP claim, and attorney fees.[353] One court has even awarded two different statutory damage awards for two different UDAP counts, treble damages for a third UDAP count, and actual damages for a fourth.[354] A restriction on treble damages in actions brought under one statute does not prevent an award of treble damages on a separate UDAP count.[355] A consumer can recover the punitive or exemplary component of a UDAP award from each of multiple defendants who in some way contributed to the consumer's damages.[356] Consumers may be able to recover both treble damages and exemplary damages for the same UDAP violation under the Georgia statute.[357]

Another issue is whether a consumer can seek treble damages under a UDAP count and punitive damages under a common law fraud count. Arguably, these two forms of damages are not necessarily inconsistent, and while com-

---

UDAP treble damages are duplicative of punitive damages).

348 Edmondson v. Am. Motorcycle Ass'n, 2001 U.S. App. LEXIS 1506 (4th Cir. Feb. 2, 2001) (unpublished, citation limited) (N.C. law); LaBarre v. Shepard, 84 F.3d 496 (1st Cir. 1996); Refuse & Environmental Sys., Inc. v. Industrial Servs., 732 F. Supp. 1209 (D. Mass. 1990), *aff'd on this ground, rev'd and remanded on other grounds*, 932 F.2d 37 (1st Cir. 1991) (UDAP damages may not duplicate award of damages on other legal theory based on same facts); Williams v. Toyota of Jefferson, Inc., 655 F. Supp. 1081 (E.D. La. 1987); Shapiro v. American Home Assur. Co., 616 F. Supp. 906 (D. Mass. 1985); Lexton-Ancira Real Estate Fund, 1972 v. Heller, 826 P.2d 819 (Colo. 1992); Calimlim v. Foreign Car Center, Inc., 392 Mass. 228, 467 N.E.2d 443 (1984); Transmedia Restaurant Co. v. Devereaux, 821 A.2d 983 (N.H. 2003); Neveroski v. Blair, 141 N.J. Super. 365, 358 A.2d 473 (App. Div. 1976); Poor v. Hill, 138 N.C. App. 19, 530 S.E.2d 838 (2000) (plaintiff must elect between UDAP and contract recovery after verdict); Vazquez v. Allstate Ins. Co., 137 N.C. App. 741, 529 S.E.2d 480 (2000) (plaintiff must make election between contract and UDAP recovery); Barbee v. Atlantic Marine Sales & Service, 115 N.C. App. 641, 446 S.E.2d 117 (1994) (plaintiff can not recover UDAP treble damages plus warranty damages for same injury); Borders v. Newton, 315 S.E.2d 731 (N.C. Ct. App. 1984); Marshall v. Miller, 47 N.C. App. 530, 268 S.E.2d 97 (N.C. App. 1980), *rev'd in part on other grounds*, 302 N.C. 539, 276 S.E.2d 397 (1981) (holding that intent is not an element); Waite Hill Servs., Inc. v. World Class Metal Works, Inc., 959 S.W.2d 182 (Tex. 1998); Mayo v. John Hancock Mut. Life Ins. Co., 711 S.W.2d 5 (Tex. 1986); Lucas v. Nesbitt, 653 S.W.2d 883 (Tex. App. 1983); Smith v. Kinslow, 598 S.W.2d 910 (Tex. Civ. App. 1980); *see also* Taylor v. Hoppin' Johns, Inc., 405 S.E.2d 410 (S.C. Ct. App. 1991); Progressive County Mut. Ins. Co. v. Boman, 780 S.W.2d 436 (Tex. App. 1989); American Baler Co. v. SRS Sys., Inc., 748 S.W.2d 243 (Tex. App. 1988).

349 Cambridge Plating Co. v. NAPCO, Inc., 85 F.3d 752 (1st Cir. 1996) (affirming non-UDAP damages and single UDAP damages, vacating UDAP punitive damages).

350 Foster v. New Dimensions Funding, Clearinghouse No. 47,070 (D.N.H. Nov. 24, 1992); Refuse & Environmental Sys., Inc. v. Industrial Servs., 732 F. Supp. 1209 (D. Mass. 1990), *aff'd on this ground, rev'd and remanded on other grounds*, 932 F.2d 37 (1st Cir. 1991); Calimlim v. Foreign Car Center, Inc., 392 Mass. 228, 467 N.E.2d 443 (1984); Simpson v. Smith, 34 Ohio Misc. 2d 7, 517 N.E.2d 276 (Mun. Ct. 1987); Taylor v. Medenica, 479 S.E.2d 35 (S.C. 1996); Winkle Chevy-Olds-Pontiac v. Condon, 830 S.W.2d 740 (Tex. App. 1992); *see also* American Baler Co. v. SRS Sys., Inc., 748 S.W.2d 243 (Tex. App. 1988). *Cf.* Cherick Distributors, Inc. v. Polar Corp., 41 Mass. App. Ct. 125, 669 N.E.2d 218 (1996) (where UDAP claim derived from same wrongful acts as non-UDAP claim, only single award of damages should have been trebled).

351 Foster v. New Dimensions Funding, Clearinghouse No. 47,070 (D.N.H. Nov. 24, 1992); Burnett v. Ala Moana Pawn Shop, Clearinghouse No. 46,771 (D. Haw. 1991) (Truth in Lending statutory damages plus UDAP treble damages where UDAP violation is the violation of the Truth in Lending Act), *aff'd*, 3 F.3d 1261 (9th Cir. 1993); Washburn v. Vandiver, 379 S.E.2d 65 (N.C. Ct. App. 1989) (treble UDAP damages and statutory damages under *both* federal and state odometer acts); Freeman v. A&M Mobile Home Sales, Inc., 293 S.C. 255, 359 S.E.2d 532 (Ct. App. 1987); Mayo v. John Hancock Mut. Life Ins. Co., 711 S.W.2d 5 (Tex. 1986); Kish v. Van Note, 692 S.W.2d 463 (Tex. 1985); Jim Walter Homes, Inc. v. Mora, 622 S.W.2d 878 (Tex. Civ. App. 1981).

352 Medina v. Town & Country Ford, Inc., 335 S.E.2d 831 (N.C. Ct. App. 1987), *aff'd without op.*, 364 S.E.2d 140 (N.C. 1988); St. Gelais v. Jackson, 769 S.W.2d 249 (Tex. App. 1988); Advanced Marine Enters., Inc. v. PRC, Inc., 256 Va. 106, 501 S.E.2d 148, 159 (1998) (treble damages on non-UDAP statutory claim and punitive damages on common law claims involving different duties and injuries). *See also* Rhue v. Dawson, 173 Ariz. 220, 841 P.2d 215 (Ct. App. 1992) (state RICO treble damages and tort punitive damages); Winkle Chevy-Olds-Pontiac v. Condon, 830 S.W.2d 740 (Tex. App. 1992) (UDAP treble damages and punitive damages for conversion).

353 Foster v. New Dimensions Funding, Clearinghouse No. 47,070 (D.N.H. Nov. 24, 1992); Burnett v. Ala Moana Pawn Shop, Clearinghouse No. 46,771 (D. Haw. 1991) (Truth in Lending statutory damages plus UDAP treble damages where UDAP violation is the violation of the Truth in Lending Act), *aff'd*, 3 F.3d 1261 (9th Cir. 1993).

354 Simpson v. Smith, 34 Ohio Misc. 2d 7, 517 N.E.2d 276 (Mun. Ct. 1987).

355 Stanley v. Moore, 454 S.E.2d 225 (N.C. 1995).

356 *See* International Fidelity Ins. Co. v. Wilson, 443 N.E.2d 1308 (Mass. 1983); Mohamed v. Fast Forward, Inc., 682 N.E.2d 1363 (Mass. App. Ct. 1997).

357 Conseco Fin. Serv. Corp. v. Hill, 556 S.E.2d 468 (Ga. App. 2001).

pensatory damages should be awarded only once, proper deterrence may call for both treble and punitive damages.[358] The Montana Supreme Court holds that treble damages are compensatory or remedial rather than punitive in nature.[359] But other courts believe that one form of exemplary damage is enough.[360]

At one time the Texas UDAP statute mandated trebling of the first $1000 in damages, and, if the court found the practice was committed knowingly, then the court could award up to three times the actual damages in excess of $1000.[361] While this had been interpreted literally as allowing treble damages in addition to actual damages, the Texas Supreme Court has decided the legislative intent was not to allow quadruple, but only treble damages.[362] In addition, the maximum possible recovery is treble the actual damages, regardless of the number of defendants.[363]

Courts that allow only one recovery or the other usually allow the consumer to seek both treble and punitive damages, but require the consumer to elect only one award *after* the court has determined the size of these two awards.[364] Consumers must make sure they follow state procedural rules to make the election in a timely fashion.[365]

A further issue is whether a consumer, pursuant to a UDAP statute, can rescind the transaction and get treble actual damages. Some courts, while allowing the buyer to choose between either rescission or treble damages, will not award both.[366] But the policy behind the treble damages should apply whether the consumer retains the goods sold or returns them. Accordingly, other courts have refused to enforce the remaining obligation on the contract and have also awarded the consumer three times everything the consumer had lost.[367] Whether the consumer can recover three times the full obligation rescinded is discussed in § 8.4.2.7.4, *infra*.

358 Aponte v. Aungst, 82 B.R. 738 (Bankr. E.D. Pa. 1988) (treble UDAP damages and punitive damages under Bankruptcy Code); Colonial Lincoln-Mercury Sales, Inc. v. Molina, 152 Ga. App. 379, 262 S.E.2d 820 (1980) (for intentional violations treble damages mandatory and exemplary damages are permissible); Freeman v. A&M Mobile Home Sales, Inc., 293 S.C. 255, 359 S.E.2d 532 (Ct. App. 1987) (court awards both UDAP treble damages and punitive damages under fraud count even though actual damages identical under both counts). *See* § 8.4.3.8, *infra*.

359 Plath v. Schonrock, 64 P.3d 984 (Mont. 2003) (ruling on question whether intentional violation must be shown).

360 *See* Lexton-Ancira Real Estate Fund, 1972 v. Heller, 826 P.2d 819 (Colo. 1992); Walter v. Hall, 940 P.2d 991 (Colo. Ct. App. 1996), *aff'd on other grounds*, 969 P.2d 224 (Colo. 1998); Edwards v. William H. Porter, Inc., 1991 WL 165877, Clearinghouse No. 47,935 (Del. Super. Ct. July 26, 1991); 49 Prospect Street Tenants Ass'n v. Sheva Gardens, Inc., 227 N.J. Super. 449, 547 A.2d 1134 (App. Div. 1988) (where same practice results in award under different counts for treble and punitive damages, both awards may stand, but exemplary portion of treble damages (i.e., double damages) must be deducted from punitive damages award); Hale v. Basin Motor Co., 110 N.M. 314, 795 P.2d 1006 (1990); Hardy v. Toler, 288 N.C. 303, 218 S.E.2d 342 (1975); Smith v. Strickland, 442 S.E.2d 207 (S.C. Ct. App. 1994); Concrete Spaces, Inc. v. Sender, 2 S.W.3d 901 (Tenn. 1999); Birchfield v. Texarkana Memorial Hosp., 747 S.W.2d 361 (Tex. 1987). *Cf.* Ciampi v. Ogden Chrysler Plymouth, Inc., 634 N.E.2d 448 (Ill. App. Ct. 1994) (treble damages for odometer violation do not prevent punitive damages for other acts constituting common-law fraud).

361 Tex. Bus. & Com. Code § 17.50. *See* PPG Indus., Inc. v. JMB/Houston Centers Partners, 41 S.W.3d 270 (Tex. App. 2001) (reciting history of Texas treble damages provision), *rev'd on other grounds*, 2004 WL 1533274 (Tex. July 9, 2004); Lawyers Surety Corp. v. Royal Chevrolet, Inc., 847 S.W.2d 624 (Tex. App. 1993) (interpreting former provision).

362 Jim Walter Homes, Inc. v. Valencia, 690 S.W.2d 239 (Tex. 1985); *see also* March v. Thiery, 729 S.W.2d 889 (Tex. App. 1987).

363 Busse v. Pacific Cattle Feeding Fund #1, LTD., 896 S.W.2d 807 (Tex. App. 1995).

364 Roberts v. American Warranty Corp., 514 A.2d 1132 (Del. Super. Ct. 1986); Eastern Star, Inc. v. Union Bldg. Materials, 712 P.2d 1148 (Haw. Ct. App. 1985); Hale v. Basin Motor Co., 110 N.M. 314, 795 P.2d 1006 (1990); Volt Sys. Corp. v. Raytheon Corp., 547 N.Y.S.2d 280 (App. Div. 1989) (claims for punitive and treble damages under different laws may be pleaded, but plaintiff may have to make election of remedies later); Ellis v. Northern Star Co., 388 S.E.2d 127 (N.C. 1990); Mapp v. Toyota World, Inc., 344 S.E.2d 297 (N.C. Ct. App. 1986); Birchfield v. Texarkana Memorial Hosp., 747 S.W.2d 361 (Tex. 1987); Town East Ford Sales, Inc. v. Gray, 730 S.W.2d 796 (Tex. App. 1987); Hall v. Birchfreed, 718 S.W.2d 313 (Tex. App. 1986); *see also* Hajmm Co. v. House of Raeford Farms, Inc., 379 S.E.2d 868 (N.C. Ct. App. 1989). *But see* Concrete Spaces, Inc. v. Sender, 2 S.W.3d 901 (Tenn. 1999) (election must be made before jury sets the size of punitive damage award); Jim Walters Home, Inc. v. Reed, 703 S.W.2d 701 (Tex. App. 1985) (both punitive and treble damages awarded), *aff'd in part, rev'd in part*, 711 S.W.2d 617 (Tex. 1986) (reversing punitive damage award due to insufficient evidence).

365 Hall v. Birchfreed, 718 S.W.2d 313 (Tex. App. 1986) (consumer must elect type of damage award when submitting proposed judgment).

366 Winant v. Bostic, 5 F.3d 767 (4th Cir. 1993) (N.C. law) (UDAP statute trebles only actual damages, and no damages awarded where rescission remedy elected); Taylor v. Triangle Porsche-Audi, Inc., 27 N.C. App. 711, 220 S.E.2d 806 (1975) (must elect one or the other); Cremeans v. Robbins, 2000 Ohio App. LEXIS 2753 (June 12, 2000) (where remedy plaintiff sought was basically cancellation of the transaction and return of money paid, this was a prayer for rescission so she could not get treble damages; UDAP statute requires consumer to elect between rescission and damages); Eckman v. Columbia Oldsmobile, Inc., 65 Ohio App. 3d 719, 585 N.E.2d 451 (1989). *See also* § 8.7.5, *infra*, for cases dealing with whether actual damages are available in addition to rescission.

367 Huffmaster v. Robinson, 221 N.J. Super. 315, 534 A.2d 435 (Law Div. 1986); Washburn v. Vandiver, 379 S.E.2d 65 (N.C. Ct. App. 1989); Lorentz v. Deardan, 834 S.W.2d 316 (Tenn. Ct. App. 1992). *See also* Sherrod v. Holzshuh, 274 Or. 327, 546 P.2d 470 (1976) (buyer can both rescind and receive punitive damages).

8.4.2.7 How to Calculate Multiple Damages

8.4.2.7.1 Relationship to seller's recovery in the same case

It is not always clear how to compute multiple damage awards. Should a consumer's damage award be first trebled and then offset by any seller's recovery in the same action, or should the offset occur before the consumer's award is trebled? A number of courts treble the damages first,[368] while Texas courts and at least one Wisconsin court adopt the rule that the consumer's damages are reduced by set-offs before they are trebled.[369]

The Texas approach is questionable on both pragmatic and policy grounds. A consumer in Texas can avoid subtracting the seller's counterclaims before the consumer's recovery is trebled by voluntarily paying the seller the amount the seller claims before the lawsuit, thereby preventing the seller from bringing a counterclaim. The consumer's total recovery will then be trebled with no set-off.[370] Further, from a policy viewpoint, the legislative purpose of encouraging consumer litigation and deterring merchant misconduct are frustrated if the seller happens to have claims against the consumer.

Thus Massachusetts's highest court finds that, in a landlord-tenant situation where the consumer withheld rent, the amount the landlord owes the tenant should be trebled before deducting the rent the court determines the consumer owes the landlord. The difference between the rental value of the unit as warranted and its actual value is the amount that should be trebled, not just any excessive amount the consumer has actually paid.[371]

The District of Columbia's highest court held that, where plaintiffs paid excessive late fees, the court should have trebled the overcharge rather than the entire fee.[372] The court reasoned that the seller's claim for a reasonable late fee was a recoupment of damages intrinsic to the late fee rather than a setoff of an extrinsic claim. By contrast, the court indicated that a setoff should be assessed only after the initial damages are multiplied.

8.4.2.7.2 Relationship to settlement with other defendant in the same case or defendant's payments before judgment

If state law requires that the amount one defendant pays to the plaintiff in pre-trial should be deducted from the judgment awarded the plaintiff against another defendant, the settlement amount should be deducted after the damage award is trebled, not before, even in Texas.[373] Where two parties are jointly and severally liable for the consumer's damages, the court trebles the total, and does not have to separate the damages caused by each party.[374]

8.4.2.7.3 What awards should be trebled?

A similar issue arises where a defendant such as an insurance company that owes the consumer money initially stonewalls, but finally pays the consumer prior to the entry of judgment on the UDAP claim. Then the defendant may claim that the amount to be trebled should not include that payment, but only any damage the consumer suffers because of the delay in payment.

The Massachusetts legislature has responded to this issue by amending the UDAP statute so that the amount to be trebled includes the judgment on all claims arising out of the same underlying transaction or occurrence. This statute allows trebling of payments made pursuant to any judgment, regardless of whether the judgment is entered in the UDAP

368 Davis v. Wholesale Motors, Inc., 949 P.2d 1026 (Haw. App. 1997); Wolfberg v. Hunter, 385 Mass. 390, 432 N.E.2d 467 (1982); Brown v. LeClair, 20 Mass. App. Ct. 976, 482 N.E.2d 870 (1985); Olivetti Corp. v. Ames Bus. Sys., Inc., 344 S.E.2d 82 (N.C. Ct. App. 1986), *rev'd on other grounds*, 356 S.E.2d 578 (N.C. 1987); Benkoski v. Flood, 242 Wis. 2d 652, 626 N.W.2d 851 (App. 2001); Moonlight v. Boyce, 125 Wis. 2d 298, 372 N.W.2d 479 (Ct. App. 1985); Paulik v. Coombs, 120 Wis. 2d 431, 355 N.E.2d 357 (Ct. App. 1984).

369 Smith v. Baldwin, 611 S.W.2d 611 (Tex. 1980); Streeter v. Thompson, 751 S.W.2d 329 (Tex. App. 1988); Acco Constructors v. National Steel Products, Co., 733 S.W.2d 368 (Tex. App. 1987); Building Concepts, Inc. v. Duncan, 667 S.W.2d 897 (Tex. App. 1984); Birds Constr., Inc. v. McKay, 657 S.W.2d 514 (Tex. App. 1983) (damages trebled after counterclaims subtracted, but not subtracting voluntary payments made by consumer); Wolfe Masonry Inc. v. Stewart, 664 S.W.2d 102 (Tex. App. 1983); Guerra v. Brumlow, 630 S.W.2d 425 (Tex. App. 1982) (damages trebled only after counterclaims are subtracted) (vigorous dissent); Dickinson State Bank v. Ogden, 624 S.W.2d 214 (Tex. Civ. App. 1981), *rev'd on other grounds*, 662 S.W.2d 330 (Tex. 1983); Atlas Amalgamated Inc. v. Castillo, 601 S.W.2d 728 (Tex. Civ. App. 1980); Pierce v. Norwick, 550 N.W.2d 451 (Wis. App. 1996).

370 *See* Birds Constr., Inc. v. McKay, 657 S.W.2d 514 (Tex. App. 1983).

371 Tosi v. Adams, 424 Mass. 1001, 673 N.E.2d 1224 (1997).

372 District Cablevision Ltd. P'ship v. Bassin, 828 A.2d 714 (D.C. 2003).

373 Seafare Corp. v. Trenor Corp., 88 N.C. App. 404, 363 S.E.2d 643 ($400,000 verdict trebled before deducting $137,000 received from co-defendant); Reed v. Israel Nat'l Oil Co., 681 S.W.2d 228 (Tex. App. 1984); Stenderbach v. Campbell, 665 S.W.2d 557 (Tex. App. 1984); Providence Hosp. v. Truly, 611 S.W.2d 127 (Tex. Civ. App. 1980); *see also* Flintkote Co. v. Lysfjord, 246 F.2d 368 (9th Cir.), *cert. denied*, 355 U.S. 835 (1957) (award under federal Clayton Act); Vairo v. Clayden, 153 Ariz. 13, 734 P.2d 110 (Ct. App. 1987) (state RICO case).

374 International Fidelity Ins. Co. v. Wilson, 387 Mass. 841, 433 N.E.2d 1308 (1983); Piccuirro v. Gaitenby, 20 Mass. App. Ct. 286, 480 N.E.2d 30 (1985); Leibert v. Finance Factors Ltd., 788 P.2d 833 (Haw. 1990); Love v. Keith, 383 S.E.2d 674 (N.C. Ct. App. 1989).

case or in a prior case on which the UDAP case is based.[375] Thus, if a consumer wins a judgment on an insurance claim, the consumer can ask that the full amount of the judgment be the basis for treble damages in a subsequent UDAP suit claiming that the insurer's claims settlement practices were unfair. The amount of the valid insurance claim and the damage from lost use of the money (e.g., interest) are trebled, not just the damage from the lost use of the money.[376] If, however, the insurer pays the consumer's claim before any judgment is entered, only the amount of lost interest can be trebled in a UDAP suit.[377]

A North Carolina court has reached the same result in a case in which the trial was bifurcated into an initial phase in which the jury determined whether the plaintiff was entitled to insurance proceeds, and a second phase in which the jury determined whether the insurer had committed unfair and deceptive practices by refusing to pay. The insurer attempted to avoid treble damages by stipulating to the jury's award in Phase I immediately after it was rendered. The court rejected this ruse, holding that it would defeat the statutory goal of giving insurance companies an incentive to settle claims promptly.[378]

8.4.2.7.4 *Should the amount of a cancelled or rescinded debt be trebled?*

It is not uncommon in cases involving fundamental deception in a credit transaction for a court to order all consumer payments returned and cancellation of the remainder of the indebtedness to the creditor. An appellate court has considered whether both the amount paid and the amount canceled should be trebled. The court indicated that both could be trebled, but since treble damages were discretionary, it was not an abuse of discretion to treble only the amount the consumer had already paid.[379] A Tennessee decision holds that the entire purchase price can be trebled when the consumer rescinds, at least where the consumer paid the full purchase price.[380]

An alternate position is that the amount of debt that is cancelled can not be trebled, but the payments actually returned to the consumer can be. For example, a Pennsylvania case holds that the amount to be trebled in a rescission case is the consumer's out-of-pocket payments such as the down payment and transactional costs, plus consequential damages such as any increase in price for replacement goods or in interest.[381]

Massachusetts takes a more restrictive view, allowing only incidental and consequential damages to be trebled, not payments toward the purchase price that are returned to the consumer.[382] The courts reason that return of the purchase price is part of the equitable remedy of rescission, and the Massachusetts UDAP statute treats equitable remedies separately from the treble damages remedy. The result might be different under treble damages statutes that do not separate equitable relief from treble damages so explicitly. Consumers will probably face similar problems, however, in states that require the consumer to elect between rescission and damages.[383]

8.4.2.7.5 *Prejudgment and postjudgment interest; other financing costs*

Courts are split as to whether prejudgment interest should be trebled.[384] A court has attempted to resolve this split with the following reasoning. Prejudgment interest should not be allowed on treble damages. But where prejudgment interest is authorized in calculating actual damages, that amount

375 Clegg v. Butler, 424 Mass. 413, 676 N.E.2d 1134 (1997).

376 Cohen v. Liberty Mut. Ins. Co., 41 Mass. App. Ct. 748, 673 N.E.2d 84 (1996).

377 Hopkins v. Liberty Mut. Ins. Co., 434 Mass. 556, 750 N.E.2d 943 (2001).

378 Vazquez v. Allstate Ins. Co., 137 N.C. App. 741, 529 S.E.2d 480 (2000).

379 Baggett v. Crown Automotive Group, Inc., 1992 Tenn. App. LEXIS 464 (May 22, 1992).

380 Lorentz v. Deardan, 834 S.W.2d 316 (Tenn. Ct. App. 1992). *Accord* Pliss v. Peppertree Resort Villas, Inc., 663 N.W.2d 851 (Wis. App. 2003).

381 Metz v. Quaker Highlands, Inc., 714 A.2d 447 (Pa. Super. 1998).

382 Schwartz v. Rose, 418 Mass. 41, 634 N.E.2d 105 (1994); Ann & Hope, Inc. v. Muratore, 42 Mass. App. Ct. 223, 676 N.E.2d 478 (1997) (rescission damages can not be trebled, but any other losses can).

383 *See* § 8.7.5, *infra.*

384 *Compare* Market Am., Inc. v. Rossi, 104 F. Supp. 2d 606 (M.D.N.C. 2000) (damages should be trebled before prejudgment interest is calculated, and interest should be calculated only on base amount); Sampson-Bladen Oil Co. v. Walters, 356 S.E.2d 805 (N.C. Ct. App. 1987) (interest not trebled); Roberts v. Grande, 868 S.W.2d 956 (Tex. App. 1994) (interest not trebled); Benefit Trust Life Ins. Co. v. Littles, 869 S.W.2d 453 (Tex. App. 1993) (interest not trebled under either Texas UDAP or UNIP statutes); McCann v. Brown, 725 S.W.2d 822 (Tex. App. 1987) (interest not trebled); Precision Homes, Inc. v. Cooper, 671 S.W.2d 924 (Tex. App. 1984) (interest not trebled); Rotello v. Ring Around Products Inc., 614 S.W.2d 455 (Tex. Civ. App. 1981) (interest not trebled) *with* District Cablevision Ltd. P'ship v. Bassin, 828 A.2d 714 (D.C. 2003) (prejudgment interest added to actual damages and trebled along with actual damages); Beaston v. State Farm Life Ins. Co., 861 S.W.2d 268 (Tex. App. 1993) (interest trebled under Texas UNIP statute); Paramore v. Nehring, 792 S.W.2d 210 (Tex. App. 1990) (interest trebled); McGuire v. Texas Farmers Ins. Co., 727 S.W.2d 1 (Tex. App. 1987) (interest trebled); Indust-Ri-Chem Laboratory, Inc. v. Par-Pak Co., 602 S.W.2d 282 (Tex. Civ. App. 1980) (interest trebled); *see also* Vairo v. Clayden, 153 Ariz. 13, 734 P.2d 110 (Ct. App. 1987) (interest trebled in state RICO action); Murphy v. National Union Fire Ins. Co., 438 Mass. 529, 781 N.E.2d 1232, 1236 (2003) (where insurer paid arbitration award within 30 days, court may enter judgment only for post-award interest, not for amount of award; court suggests that this interest can be trebled); Wallace v. American Manufacturers Mut. Ins. Co., 22 Mass. App. Ct. 938, 494 N.E.2d 35 (1986) (interest based on delay in paying insurance claim should be doubled).

should be included in the actual damage award. This total award should then be trebled where appropriate.[385] The Massachusetts Supreme Judicial Court has ruled, however, that prejudgment interest runs only on the untrebled compensatory portion of the award.[386]

Despite the split in the courts about whether pre-judgment interest should be trebled, there should be no question that financing costs that are necessitated by the consumer's purchase of substitute goods and awarded as actual damages should be trebled like any other actual damages.[387] Likewise, where an element of actual damages is the amount of interest the plaintiff lost on money paid to the defendant, it can be trebled.[388]

Post-judgment interest should be computed on the whole award, including treble damages[389] and attorney fees.[390]

8.4.2.7.6 Multiple violations

Many UDAP complaints assert multiple violations of the UDAP statute. If there are several UDAP violations, each of which causes a separate injury, the court should treble the damages for each violation. If, however, multiple UDAP violations result in a single injury, the consumer may be limited to a single award of treble damages.[391] If the consumer prevails on both UDAP claims and non-UDAP claims, only the damages resulting from the UDAP claims should be trebled.[392]

8.4.2.8 Should the Jury Be Told That Actual Damages Will Be Trebled?

Some UDAP statutes mandate that actual damages be doubled or trebled.[393] In these states, the question arises whether the jury should be told that the court will double or treble any actual damages found by the jury.

In comparative negligence cases, some courts have ruled that the jury should be given an "ultimate outcome" charge—that is, it should be instructed that a finding that the plaintiff is more than fifty percent negligent will completely bar recovery.[394] These courts have reasoned that it is essential to the jury's role as fact finder to know that finding that a plaintiff was seventy-five percent at fault will mean that the plaintiff will receive nothing, not twenty-five percent of his or her actual damages.[395]

However, a UDAP statute more closely resembles other damage-multiplying statutes than it does comparative negligence laws, and cases involving federal antitrust,[396] state antitrust,[397] federal RICO,[398] state racketeering,[399] and labor statutes[400] have generally ruled that juries should *not* be told that their finding of actual damages will be multiplied. Most of these cases cite two main reasons for keeping quiet. First, while it is the jury's role to determine damages, it is the court's role to determine the judgment as dictated by the

385 Canady v. Mann, 107 N.C. App. 252, 419 S.E.2d 597 (1992).

386 City Coal Co. v. Noonan, 434 Mass. 709, 751 N.E.2d 894 (2001).

387 Quate v. Caudle, 381 S.E.2d 842 (N.C. Ct. App. 1989).

388 Schwartz v. Rose, 418 Mass. 41, 634 N.E.2d 105 (1994).

389 Leibert v. Finance Factors Ltd., 788 P.2d 833 (Haw. 1990); Custom Molders, Inc. v. American Yard Products, Inc., 463 S.E.2d 199 (N.C. 1995). *But see* Tex. Bus. & Com. Code Ann. § 17.50(f)(2) (no prejudgment interest on additional damages).

390 Parker v. I&F Insulation Co., 89 Ohio St. 3d 261, 730 N.E.2d 972 (2000).

391 Edmonds v. John L. Scott Real Estate, Inc., 942 P.2d 1072 (Wash. Ct. App. 1997).

392 Edmondson v. Am. Motorcycle Assn., 2001 U.S. App. LEXIS 1506 (4th Cir. Feb. 2, 2001) (unpublished, citation limited) (No. Car. law); Cannon v. Cherry Hill Toyota, Inc., 161 F. Supp. 2d 362 (D.N.J. 2001) (TIL statutory damages should not be included in amount trebled); Gray v. N. Carolina Ins. Underwriting Assoc., 352 N.C. 61, 529 S.E.2d 676 (2000); Cremeans v. Robbins, 2000 Ohio App. LEXIS 2753 (June 12, 2000).

393 *See* § 8.4.2.2, *supra*.

394 *See, e.g.*, Roman v. Mitchell, 82 N.J. 336, 413 A.2d 322 (1980) (jury should have been informed that if it found plaintiff had been 75% negligent, plaintiff could not recover damages); Durrenberger v. Ferris, 305 N.J. Super. 231, 701 A.2d 1322 (1997). *See also* Dimogerondakis v. Dimogerondakis, 197 N.J. Super. 518, 523, 485 A.2d 338 (1984) (jury should be instructed that any damages awarded to plaintiff in personal injury action would be molded to reflect only that percentage of liability that jury attributed to non-settling defendant).

395 *See, e.g.*, Roman v. Mitchell, 82 N.J. 336, 345, 413 A.2d 322 (1980). *But cf.* Brodsky v. Grinnell Haulers, Inc., 2004 WL 1774568 (N.J. Aug. 10, 2004) (error to give ultimate outcome instruction where question is apportionment of liability among defendants).

396 Pollock & Riley, Inc. v. Pearl Brewing Co., 498 F.2d 1240 (5th Cir. 1974) (jury hearing Clayton Act case should not be instructed as to statute's award of treble damages and attorney fees), *cert. denied*, 420 U.S. 992 (1975); Lehrman v. Gulf Oil Corp., 500 F.2d 659 (5th Cir. 1974) (trial judge properly did not instruct jury that pursuant to Clayton Act actual damages would be trebled); Noble v. McClatchy Newspapers, 533 F.2d 1081 (9th Cir. 1975) (trial court erred in instructing jury that pursuant to Clayton Act, actual damages would be trebled), *vacated on other grounds,* 433 U.S. 904 (1977); Webster Motor Car Co. v. Packard Motor Car Co., 135 F. Supp. 4 (D.D.C. 1955), *rev'd on other grounds*, 243 F.2d 418 (D.C. Cir. 1957).

397 Sharon Investment Corp. v. Spaghetti Place, 1981 Ohio App. LEXIS 12379 (Apr. 1, 1981) (holding that jury should not have been instructed that damages in state antitrust suit would be doubled, but held error harmless).

398 HBE Leasing Corp. v. Frank, 22 F.3d 41 (2d Cir. 1994) (upholding trial court's refusal to allow defendants to inform jury about RICO's treble damages and attorney fees provision, which would interfere with Congress's goal to deter racketeering).

399 Rhue v. Dawson, 173 Ariz. 220, 841 P.2d 215 (1992); St. James v. Future Fin., 342 N.J. Super. 310, 776 A.2d 849 (App. Div. 2001).

400 *See, e.g.*, Campos-Orrego v. Rivera, 175 F.3d 89 (1st Cir. 1999) (jury should not be instructed that pursuant to labor law the court would award plaintiff double her actual damages); Marshall v. Brown, 141 Cal. App. 3d 408, 190 Cal. Rptr. 392 (1983) (not error to fail to instruct jury that damages in state labor law case would be trebled).

statute.[401] Second, instructing the jury that actual damages will be multiplied could tempt the jury to adjust its verdict downward, thereby undermining the public policies underlying the multiplying provision.[402] Although a few courts have ruled that a jury should be instructed as to a statute's multiplier, those cases have involved statutes with a two-tier level of liability that imposed multiple damages only for willful violations, so the jury instruction as to the multiplier explained the reason they were being asked about different levels of culpability.[403]

The reasoning of the majority of cases on the multiple damages instruction fits UDAP cases, particularly in states that award multiple damages as a matter of law, not dependent upon a finding of fact or assessment of motive. Accordingly, the trebling belongs to the court's role in determining the judgment, not the jury's role in determining actual damages. Instructing the jury that actual damages will be trebled could invite the jury to modify its finding of actual damages to prevent a perceived windfall to the plaintiff. Such tinkering would thwart the public policies behind the damages multiplier, which is intended to deter wrongdoing, encourage private enforcement, and compensate plaintiffs for damages otherwise unrecognized.[404] Any concern that the jury's sense of outrage might be reflected in its assessment of actual damages can be allayed by an instruction that once the jury determines actual damages, the court will determine the judgment, including additional damages, but without identifying the formula for such damages.[405]

Perhaps the most compelling argument is that the statute's multiplication of damages is simply irrelevant to the determination of actual damages. Just as evidence that is irrelevant to liability is not allowed to be put before jurors,[406] the Second Circuit held that a trial court properly refused to instruct a RICO jury that actual damages would be trebled, because trebling was irrelevant to the questions of liability and actual damages.[407] Similarly, the New Jersey Supreme Court ruled that a jury should not be told, in a case that alleged malpractice by both a doctor and a hospital, that the hospital's liability would be capped at $10,000 by the state's Charitable Immunity Act.[408] The court distinguished comparative negligence cases by pointing out that this charge did not involve percentages of fault; rather the court likened the defendant's limited liability under the Act to information about a defendant's insurance, which is not allowed to be disclosed to a jury.[409]

Agreeing with these reasons, a Colorado intermediate appellate court has held that a trial court did not err in declining to instruct the jury that the court would treble the damage award.[410] The court reasoned that this information is irrelevant to the jury's function, may tend to confuse or prejudice the jury, and frustrates the goal of deterrence. On the other hand, the New Jersey Supreme Court held, over a strong dissent, that the jury should be given an ultimate outcome charge.[411] Such a charge, according to the court,

401 *See, e.g.*, Noble v. McClatchy Newspapers, 533 F.2d 1081 (9th Cir. 1975), *vacated on other grounds,* 433 U.S. 904 (1977); Pollock & Riley, Inc. v. Pearl Brewing Co., 498 F.2d 1240 (5th Cir. 1974) ("[It] is not for the jury to determine the amount of a judgment. Its function is to compute the amount of damages. Congress's authorization in 15 U.S.C.A. § 15 to triple the award of damages is a matter of law to be applied by the district court without interference from the jury"), *cert. denied*, 420 U.S. 992 (1975); Lehrman v. Gulf Oil Corp., 500 F.2d 659 (5th Cir. 1974); Webster Motor Car Co. v. Packard Motor Car Co., 135 F. Supp. 4 (D.D.C. 1955), *rev'd on other grounds*, 243 F.2d 418 (D.C. Cir. 1957); Rhue v. Dawson, 173 Ariz. 220, 841 P.2d 215 (1992); Marshall v. Brown, 141 Cal. App. 3d 408, 190 Cal. Rptr. 392 (1983); Sharon Investment Corp. v. Spaghetti Place, 1981 Ohio App. LEXIS 12379. *See also* Brooks v. Cook, 938 F.2d 1048 (9th Cir. 1991) (federal civil rights jury should not have been instructed that nominal damages could yield award of attorney fees).

402 *See, e.g.*, HBE Leasing Corp. v. Frank, 22 F.3d 41 (2d Cir. 1994) (upholding trial court's refusal to allow defendants to inform jury about RICO's treble damages and attorney fees provision, which would interfere with Congress's goal to deter racketeering); Noble v. McClatchy Newspapers, 533 F.2d 1081 (9th Cir. 1975), *vacated on other grounds,* 433 U.S. 904 (1977); Lehrman v. Gulf Oil Corp., 500 F.2d 659 (5th Cir. 1974) (purpose of treble damages was not compensation, but to deter antitrust violations); Webster Motor Car Co. v. Packard Motor Car Co., 135 F. Supp. 4 (D.D.C. 1955), *rev'd on other grounds*, 243 F.2d 418 (D.C. Cir. 1957); Rhue v. Dawson, 173 Ariz. 220, 841 P.2d 215 (1992) (jury might view state racketeering statute's trebling of damages as a windfall and reduce finding of actual damages, which would thwart purpose of the statute). *Cf.* Brooks v. Cook, 938 F.2d 1048 (9th Cir. 1991) (letting jury know that fees could be awarded would undermine public interests of civil rights law, which was to eliminate financial barriers to the vindication of constitutional rights).

403 Real v. Continental Group, Inc., 627 F. Supp. 434 (N.D. Cal. 1986) (not error to inform jury that finding of willfulness would result in double damages in age discrimination case where jury had found willful discrimination but had not imposed punitive damages; court distinguished treble damages antitrust cases on grounds that here served a useful purpose); Schweisberger v. Weiner, 1995 Ohio App. LEXIS 6101 (Dec. 12, 1995) (unpublished) (state racketeering statute, instruction explaining additional damages upon finding of willfulness not an abuse of discretion).

404 *See* § 8.4.2.1, *supra.*

405 *See* Marshall v. Brown, 141 Cal. App. 3d 408, 190 Cal. Rptr. 392 (1983) (instruction as to trebling was not necessary to "avoid an exaggerated finding of compensatory damages").

406 *See, e.g.*, Paige v. Manuzak, 57 Md. App. 621, 632, 471 A.2d 758, 763 (1984).

407 HBE Leasing Corp. v. Frank, 22 F.3d 41 (2d Cir. 1994). *See also* Pollock & Riley, Inc. v. Pearl Brewing Co., 498 F.2d 1240 (5th Cir. 1974) ("fact that the awarded amount will be tripled has no relevance in determining the amount a plaintiff was injured by the anti-trust violation"), *cert. denied*, 420 U.S. 992 (1975); Marshall v. Brown, 141 Cal. App. 3d 408, 190 Cal. Rptr. 392 (1983) (trebling irrelevant).

408 Weiss v. Goldfarb, 154 N.J. 468, 713 A.2d 427 (1998).

409 *Id.* at 433–34.

410 Heritage Village Owners Ass'n v. Golden Heritage Investors, Inc., 2004 WL 439425 (Colo. App. Mar. 11, 2004).

411 Wanetick v. Gateway Mitsubishi, 163 N.J. 484, 750 A.2d 79 (2000).

"will insure that the jury's sense of outrage will not be reflected either in its assessment of compensation or in some other aspect of the case."[412] The court made it clear, though, that in complex cases involving multiple questions and many parties, the court retains discretion to withhold the instruction if it would tend to confuse or mislead the jury or produce a manifestly unjust result.

8.4.2.9 Parties Liable for Treble Damages

An important question is whether a company is liable in treble damages for the acts of one of its agents even if the company does not approve of those acts. The company is liable in treble damages for acts its agents engaged in within the scope of employment.[413] Typically, an employer will be liable for treble damages whenever the employer would be vicariously liable for the tortious conduct of its employees.[414] But where a corporation and its employee did not participate through their own individual acts in a single wrong, but the corporation acted wrongfully only through its agent, multiple damages should not be awarded severally.[415]

Where treble damages are predicated on the seller's knowledge that a practice is deceptive, the corporation is assumed to possess whatever knowledge its employees possess.[416] Conversely, employees are assumed to have whatever knowledge the corporation possesses.[417] The knowing misrepresentation of an agent is imputed to the principal.[418] One court has also held that one business partner can be liable for treble damages for the actions of another partner.[419]

Where a statute allows consumers who have "suffered" to recover on a seller's bond, this has been interpreted narrowly. The consumer can recover only actual and not treble damages from the bonding company where the consumer had no special problems recovering the actual damages from the bonding company.[420] Another court has held that a consumer may only be able to get actual, not treble damages from a state fund where the defendant is insolvent.[421] Special problems arise where the FDIC or RTC has taken over a bank that is liable for treble damages. At least one court has found that sovereign immunity prevents such liability.[422]

412 *Id.*, 750 A.2d at 85.

413 Wang Laboratories, Inc. v. Business Incentives, Inc., 398 Mass. 854, 501 N.E.2d 1163 (1986).

414 *Id.*

415 Augat, Inc. v. Aegis, Inc., 631 N.E.2d 995 (Mass. 1994).

416 Green Tree Acceptance, Inc. v. Holmes, 803 S.W.2d 458 (Tex. App. 1991).

417 *Id.*

418 Maryland Ins. Co. v. Head Indus. Coatings & Servs., Inc., 906 S.W.2d 218 (Tex. App. 1995), *rev'd on other grounds*, 938 S.W.2d 27 (Tex. 1996).

419 Termeer v. Interstate Motors, Inc., 634 S.W.2d 12 (Tex. App. 1982).

420 Tomlinson v. Camel City Motors, Inc., 330 N.C. 76, 408 S.E.2d 853 (1991). *See also* Ames v. Comm'r of Motor Vehicles, 839 A.2d 1250 (Conn. 2004) (UDAP treble damages not recoverable from bond). *See* National Consumer Law Center, Automobile Fraud § 9.13.4.4 (2d ed. 2003 and Supp.) (standards for collection from dealer bonds).

421 State v. Pace, 650 S.W.2d 64 (Tex. 1983).

422 Bank One, Texas, N.A. v. Taylor, 970 F.2d 16 (5th Cir. 1992). *See also* § 6.7.5, *supra*.

8.4.3 Punitive Damages

8.4.3.1 Are Punitive Damages Available Under a UDAP Statute?

Ten UDAP statutes explicitly authorize punitive damages,[423] and a separate Minnesota statute authorizes punitive damages for UDAP and other claims.[424] The Illinois UDAP statute authorizes the court to award any other relief it deems proper, and then restricts the circumstances under which punitive damages can be awarded against car dealers, nec-

423 Cal. Civ. Code § 1780; Conn. Gen. Stat. § 42-110g; D.C. Code Ann. § 28-3905(k)(1)(C); Ga. Code Ann. § 10-1-399; Idaho Code § 48-608; Ky. Rev. Stat. § 367.220; Mo. Rev. Stat. § 407.025; Or. Rev. Stat. § 646.638; R.I. Gen. Laws § 6-13.1-5.2; Vt. Stat. Ann. tit. 9, § 2461 (exemplary damages capped at treble the consideration that consumer provides the merchant). *See In re* Wiggins, 273 B.R. 839 (Bankr. D. Idaho 2001) (awarding 5 times defendant's anticipated gross profit, totaling $184,910); Nielsen v. Wisniewski, 32 Conn. App. 133, 628 A.2d 25 (1993) (punitive damages against landlord of substandard housing); Neal Pope, Inc. v. Garlington, 245 Ga. App. 49, 537 S.E.2d 179 (2000) (*per se* UDAP violation was sufficient basis to allow discovery regarding punitive damages); Billy Cain Ford Lincoln Mercury v. Kaminski, 496 S.E.2d 521 (Ga. App. Ct. 1998); Kleczek v. Jorgensen, 328 Ill. App. 3d 1012, 767 N.E.2d 913, 263 Ill. Dec. 187 (2002) (upholding trial court's discretion in denying punitive damages); Miles Rich Chrysler-Plymouth, Inc. v. Mass, 201 Ga. App. 693, 411 S.E.2d 901 (1991); Colonial Lincoln-Mercury Sales, Inc. v. Molina, 152 Ga. App. 379, 262 S.E.2d 820 (1979); Parrott v. Carr Chevrolet, Inc., 331 Or. 537, 17 P.3d 473 (2001) (reinstating $1 million punitive damage award on UDAP claim); Byers v. Santiam Ford, Inc., 281 Or. 411, 574 P.2d 1122 (1978); Harris v. Chalet Car Co., 280 Or. 679, 572 P.2d 623 (1977); Wolverton v. Stanwood, 278 Or. 341, 563 P.2d 1203 (1977); Sherrod v. Holzshuh, 274 Or. 327, 546 P.2d 470 (1976); Allen v. Morgan Drive Away, Inc., 273 Or. 614, 542 P.2d 896 (1975); Teague Motor Co. v. Rowton, 84 Or. App. 72, 733 P.2d 93 (1987); Tri-West Constr. Co. v. Hernandez, 43 Or. App. 961, 607 P.2d 1375 (1979); Bisson v. Ward, 628 A.2d 1256 (Vt. 1993); Winton v. Johnson & Dix Fuel Corp., 515 A.2d 371 (Vt. 1986); Bruntaeger v. Zeller, 515 A.2d 123 (Vt. 1986). *See also* 815 Ill. Comp. Stat. Ann. § 505/10a(a) (limiting punitive damages against car dealers to extreme cases; necessary implication is that they are allowable as "other relief which the court deems proper").

424 Minn. Stat. § 549.20 ("upon clear and convincing evidence that the acts of the defendant show a deliberate disregard for the rights or safety of others"); *see also* Wexler v. Brothers Entertainment Group, Inc., 457 N.W.2d 218 (Minn. Ct. App. 1990); Yost v. Millhouse, 373 N.W.2d 826 (Minn. Ct. App. 1985).

essarily implying that they are allowed as "other relief."[425] (The Illinois Supreme Court has held the special protection for car dealers unconstitutional.[426]) Some additional states authorize punitive damages only for elderly or disabled victims.[427] Courts in other states may find such a remedy within their inherent authority, particularly where courts award punitive damages for common law fraud.[428]

425 Ill. Comp. Stat. Ann. § 505/10a.

426 Allen v. Woodfield Chevrolet, Inc., 208 Ill. 2d 12, 802 N.E.2d 752, 280 Ill. Dec. 501 (2003).

427 *See, e.g.*, Ark. Code Ann. § 4-88-204; Nev. Rev. Stat. § 598.0977.

428 Aronson v. Creditrust Corp., 7 F. Supp. 2d 589 (W.D. Pa. 1998) (construing language authorizing "such additional relief as [court] deems necessary and proper" to allow punitive damages); Sellinger v. Freeway Motor Home Sales, Inc., 110 Ariz. 573, 521 P.2d 1119 (1974); Parks v. Macro Dynamics, Inc., 121 Ariz. 517, 591 P.2d 1005 (App. Ct. 1979); Stephenson v. Capano Dev., Inc., 462 A.2d 1069 (Del. 1983); Nash v. Hoopes, 332 A.2d 411 (Del. Super. Ct. 1975); Martin v. Heinold Commodities, Inc., 163 Ill. 2d 33, 643 N.E.2d 734 (1994) (punitive damages awarded in suit alleging UDAP violations and breach of fiduciary duty); Ekl v. Knecht, 585 N.E.2d 156 (Ill. App. Ct. 1991); Warren v. LeMay, 142 Ill. App. 3d 550, 491 N.E.2d 464 (1986); Gent v. Collinsville Volkswagon, Inc., 116 Ill. App. 3d 496, 451 N.E.2d 1385 (1983); Kiser v. Gilmore, 2 Kan. App. 2d 683, 587 P.2d 911 (1978); Brown v. Lyons, 43 Ohio Misc. 14, 332 N.E.2d 380, 72 Ohio Op. 2d 216, 8 Clearinghouse Rev. 621, Clearinghouse No. 14,083 (C.P. Hamilton Cty. 1974). *But see* Tousley v. North Am. Van Lines, Inc., 752 F.2d 96 (4th Cir. 1985) (South Carolina law) (no punitive damages where statute already authorizes treble damages); Rollins, Inc. v. Heller, 454 So. 2d 580 (Fla. Dist. Ct. App. 1984) (punitive damages only for common law fraud action); Zanakis-Pico v. Cutter Dodge, Inc., 47 P.3d 1222 (Haw. 2002); Pinehurst, Inc. v. O'Leary Bros. Realty, Inc., 338 S.E.2d 918 (N.C. Ct. App. 1986) (no punitive damages where treble damages are mandatory); McCauslin v. Reliance Furniture Co., 751 A.2d 683 (Pa. Sup. Ct. 2000) (punitive damages not available under Pennsylvania UDAP statute); Wyman v. Terry Schulte Chevrolet, Inc., 584 N.W.2d 103 (S.D. 1998) (punitive damages not available on UDAP claim); Concrete Spaces, Inc. v. Sender, 2 S.W.3d 901 (Tenn. 1999) (holding that consumer can not recover both treble damages on UDAP claim and punitive damages on fraud claim, and implying that punitive damages are unavailable on UDAP claim), *aff'g in part, remanding*, 1998 Tenn. App. LEXIS 525 (1998) (punitive damages not available on UDAP claim); Paty v. Herb Adcox Chevrolet Co., 756 S.W.2d 697 (Tenn. Ct. App. 1988); Bayliner Marine Corp. v. Elder, 994 S.W.2d 439 (Tex. App. 1999) (no punitive damages under UDAP). *Cf.* Duncavage v. Allen, 147 Ill. App. 3d 88, 497 N.E.2d 433 (1986) (UDAP punitive damages claim does not survive consumer's death since no explicit right to such damages in statute). *But cf.* Stuppy v. World Gym Int'l, Inc., 2003 WL 886724 (Cal. App. Mar. 7, 2003) (unpublished, citation limited) (no punitive damages under Cal. Bus. & Prof. Code § 17200 unless plaintiff meets requirements of Civ. Code § 3294 by showing malice, oppression, or fraud).

8.4.3.2 Common Law Fraud Punitive Damages Where UDAP Punitive Damages Not Available

If a UDAP statute does not authorize punitive damages, in appropriate cases consumer attorneys should add a common law fraud count to their UDAP action and seek punitive damages under the common law fraud claim.[429]

There is no merit to the argument that the availability of UDAP remedies preempts common law tort claims or remedies.[430] Consumers can recover actual damages and attorney fees under a UDAP claim and punitive damages under a tort claim.[431]

Graphic examples of the importance of adding a common law fraud claim include multi-million dollar punitive damages awards against finance companies participating with home improvement contractors in various fraudulent schemes.[432] Defendants who sold vehicles with concealed wreck damage have been assessed punitive damages up to $1 million.[433]

8.4.3.3 Standards for Determining Whether UDAP Punitive Damages Should Be Awarded

Unless a UDAP statute specifies other standards, courts are likely to use a state's common law fraud standards in determining whether UDAP punitive damages are appropriate in a particular case.[434] Standards concerning when pu-

429 *See* § 9.6.3, *infra* (common law fraud claims); National Consumer Law Center, Automobile Fraud Ch. 7 (2d ed. 2003 and Supp.).

430 Wildstein v. Tru Motors, Inc., 227 N.J. Super. 331, 547 A.2d 340 (Law Div. 1988).

431 *See* § 8.3.9, *supra*.

432 *See* Union Mortgage Co. v. Barlow, 595 So. 2d 1335 (Ala. 1992) ($6 million in punitive damages); Williams v. Aetna Fin. Co., 83 Ohio St. 3d 64, 700 N.E.2d 859 (1998) ($1.5 million), *cert. denied*, 119 S. Ct. 1357, 143 L. Ed. 2d 518 (1999). It has also been reported that a jury in July, 1991 in Barbour County, Alabama, awarded five families $9 million each in a similar case against Union Mortgage. A May, 1992 Barbour county jury awarded $2.1 million in the case of Holiday v. Chrysler Fin. Servs.

433 Parrott v. Carr Chevrolet, 331 Or. 573, 17 P.3d 473 (2001) (case also involved odometer rollback); *see also* Grabinski v. Blue Springs Ford Sales, Inc., 203 F.3d 1024 (8th Cir. 2000) ($210,000 in punitive damages); Teague Motor Co. v. Rowton, 84 Or. App. 72, 733 P.2d 93 (1987) ($15,000 punitive damages for misrepresentations regarding used car).

434 Boulevard Assocs. v. Sovereign Hotels, Inc., 861 F. Supp. 1132 (D. Conn. 1994) (Connecticut's UDAP statute expands purpose of punitive damages to include deterrence as well as compensation), *rev'd on other grounds*, 72 F.3d 1029 (2d Cir. 1995); District Cablevision Ltd. P'ship v. Bassin, 828 A.2d 714 (D.C. 2003) (applying common law standards; defendant's imposition of excessive late charge, while illegal as a penalty, was for legitimate business reason of deterring delinquencies and does not justify punitive damages); Ford Motor Co. v. Mayes, 575

nitive damages are awarded vary from state to state. Common criteria for awarding punitive damages are malice, willful or wanton conduct, ill will, or reckless indifference to the interests of others.[435] Punitive damages are appropriate when an act involves a particularly aggravated disregard for the rights of the victim[436] or a grievous violation of societal interests.[437]

Other courts use as a standard whether the conduct is gross, oppressive, and breaches the consumer's trust or confidence.[438] Punitive damages may be awarded where the seller makes a deliberate and conscious effort to misrepresent the facts to the consumer.[439] Some Connecticut courts seem to require a pattern whereby other consumers are affected by the same practice.[440] Legislative history indicates that whether a punitive damage award will be made in the District of Columbia is to be determined by the amount of actual damages, the frequency, persistency and degree of intention in the merchant's unlawful trade practice, and the number of consumers adversely affected.[441] Applying these factors, the District's highest court held punitive damages appropriate where a dealer misrepresented material facts, supervised workers in a shoddy way, failed to admit its mistakes, and declined to rectify the situation.[442]

S.W.2d 480 (Ky. Ct. App. 1978); Deck & Decker Personnel Consultants, Ltd. v. Thomas, 623 S.W.2d 90 (Mo. Ct. App. 1981); Teague Motor Co. v. Rowton, 84 Or. App. 72, 733 P.2d 93 (1987); Dailey v. Sundance Ranches, Inc., 59 Or. App. 142, 650 P.2d 994 (1982); Mabin v. Tualatin Dev., 48 Or. App. 271, 616 P.2d 1196 (1980); Crooks v. Payless Drug Stores, 592 P.2d 196 (Or. 1979). *But see In re* Wiggins, 273 B.R. 839 (Bankr. D. Idaho 2001) (awarding $184,910 in punitive damages under Idaho's less strict statutory standards); MacTools, Inc. v. Griffin, 126 Idaho 193, 879 P.2d 1126 (1994) (court approves use of UDAP statute's "repeated or flagrant violations" standard, which is less strict than general standard).

435 Chong v. Parker, 361 F.3d 455 (8th Cir. 2004) (reckless indifference); Societa Bario E Derivati v. Kaystone Chem., Inc., 1998 U.S. Dist. LEXIS 23066 (D. Conn. Apr. 15, 1998) (Connecticut UDAP statute adopts common law standards for punitive damages but expands their nature to serve both compensatory and deterrent purposes); Boyes v. Greenwich Boat Works, Inc., 27 F. Supp. 2d 543 (D.N.J. 1998) (actual malice or wanton and willful disregard); Tillquist v. Ford Motor Credit Co., 714 F. Supp. 607 (D. Conn. 1989) (intentional violation or reckless indifference); Sellinger v. Freeway Motor Home Sales, Inc., 110 Ariz. 573, 521 P.2d 1119 (1974); Schmidt v. American Leasco, 139 Ariz. 509, 679 P.2d 532 (Ct. App. 1983); Dunlap v. Jimmy GMC Tucson, Inc., 136 Ariz. 338, 666 P.2d 83 (App. Ct. 1983); Witters v. Daniels Motors, Inc., 524 P.2d 632 (Colo. Ct. App. 1974); Gargano v. Heyman, 203 Conn. 616, 525 A.2d 1343 (1987); Advanced Fin. Servs., Inc. v. Associated Appraisal Servs., Inc., 79 Conn. App. 22, 830 A.2d 249 (2003) (reckless indifference to the rights of others or an intentional and wanton violation of those rights); Larobina v. Home Depot, USA, Inc., 821 A.2d 283 (Conn. App. 2003) (affirming award of punitive damages due to reckless indifference); Tanpiengco v. Tasto, 72 Conn. App. 817, 806 A.2d 1080 (2002) (reckless indifference to others' rights or intentional and wanton violation); Nielsen v. Wisniewski, 32 Conn. App. 133, 628 A.2d 25 (1993) (reckless indifference to rights of others or an intentional and wanton violation of those rights); Nash v. Hoopes, 332 A.2d 411 (Del. Super. Ct. 1975); Miles Rich Chrysler-Plymouth, Inc. v. Mass, 201 Ga. App. 693, 411 S.E.2d 901 (1991); Totz v. Continental DuPage Acura, 602 N.E.2d 1374 (Ill. App. Ct. 1992); Ekl v. Knecht, 585 N.E.2d 156 (Ill. App. Ct. 1991) (punitive damages awarded for conduct that is outrageous because acts are done with evil motive or with reckless indifference toward the rights of others); Overbey v. Illinois Farmers Ins. Co., 170 Ill. App. 3d 594, 525 N.E.2d 1076 (1988); Warren v. LeMay, 142 Ill. App. 3d 550, 491 N.E.2d 464 (1986); Hardy v. Toler, 288 N.C. 303, 218 S.E.2d 342 (1975); Allen v. Morgan Drive Away, Inc., 273 Or. 614, 542 P.2d 896 (1975); Tri-West Constr. Co. v. Hernandez, 43 Or. App. 961, 607 P.2d 1375 (1979); Leonard & Harral Packing Co. v. Ward, 971 S.W.2d 671 (Tex. App. 1998); Woo v. Great Southwestern Acceptance Corp., 565 S.W.2d 290 (Tex. Civ. App. 1978); L'Esperance v. Benware, 830 A.2d 675 (Vt. 2003) (malice, ill will, or wanton conduct necessary; exemplary damages properly awarded where landlord rented out house with knowledge it was unsafe); Bisson v. Ward, 628 A.2d 1256 (Vt. 1993); Fancher v. Benson, 580 A.2d 51 (Vt. 1990) (punitive damages allowed where malice, ill will, or wanton conduct is shown; award affirmed where seller delayed disclosure of report, lied about what report contained, and deceived buyer's agent into not promptly informing the buyer of the report's contents). *See also* Check v. Clifford Chrysler-Plymouth, 794 N.E.2d 829 (Ill. App. 2003) (evidence insufficient to show intentional, willful, or recklessly indifferent acts). *Cf.* Locascio v. Imports Unlimited, Inc., 309 F. Supp. 2d 267 (D. Conn. 2004) (recklessly indifferent, intentional and wanton, malicious, violent, or motivated by evil, but not shown here); Gibbs v. Southeastern Investment Corp., 705 F. Supp. 738 (D. Conn. 1989) (no punitive damages under UDAP statute where no blatantly intentional acts or long-term practices); Johnston v. Anchor Organization, 621 N.E.2d 137 (Ill. App. Ct. 1993) (no punitive damages where defendant was only negligent).

436 Crooks v. Payless Drug Stores, 592 P.2d 196 (Or. 1979); Abrams v. Mike Salta Pontiac Inc., 51 Or. App. 495, 625 P.2d 1383 (1981); Tri-West Constr. Co. v. Hernandez, 43 Or. App. 961, 607 P.2d 1375 (1979).

437 Weigel v. Ron Tonkin Chevrolet Co., 298 Or. 127, 690 P.2d 488 (1984); Schmidt v. Pine Tree Land Dev., 291 Or. 462, 631 P.2d 1373 (1981); Chamberlain v. Jim Fisher Motors, Inc., 282 Or. 229, 578 P.2d 1225 (1978); Dailey v. Sundance Ranches, Inc., 59 Or. App. 142, 650 P.2d 994 (1982); Abrams v. Mike Salta Pontiac Inc., 51 Or. App. 495, 625 P.2d 1383 (1981).

438 Stephenson v. Capano Dev., Inc., 462 A.2d 1069 (Del. 1983).

439 Piengco v. Tasto, 72 Conn. App. 817, 806 A.2d 1080 (2002) ($20,000 award upheld for deliberate misrepresentation); Mabin v. Tualatin Dev., 48 Or. App. 271, 616 P.2d 1196 (1980).

440 Gibbs v. Southeastern Investment Corp., 705 F. Supp. 738 (D. Conn. 1989); Bailey Employment Sys., Inc. v. Hahn, 545 F. Supp. 62 (D. Conn. 1982), *aff'd*, 723 F.2d 895 (2d Cir. 1983). *But see* Tingley Sys., Inc. v. Norse Sys., Inc., 49 F.3d 93 (2d Cir. 1995) (pattern unnecessary); Boulevard Assocs. v. Sovereign Hotels, Inc., 861 F. Supp. 1132 (D. Conn. 1994) (Connecticut UDAP statute expands purpose of common law punitive damages to include deterrence as well as compensation), *rev'd on other grounds*, 72 F.3d 1029 (2d Cir. 1995); Tillquist v. Ford Motor Credit Co., 714 F. Supp. 607 (D. Conn. 1989) (intentional violation or reckless indifference will support punitive damages award); Tanpiengco v. Tasto, 72 Conn. App. 817, 806 A.2d 1080 (2002) (punitive damages upheld for deliberate misrepresentation; no evidence of repetition cited).

441 Rowan Heating-Air Conditioning v. Williams, 580 A.2d 583 (D.C. 1990).

442 *Id.*

In a UDAP case of particular interest to consumer advocates, punitive damages were awarded where a repair shop maintained a pattern of inefficiency and incompetence and continually stalled and evaded its legal obligations to consumers.[443] A car dealer was ordered to pay $50,000 in punitive damages for failing to order a particular model for a customer, and then trying to sell the customer a more expensive model.[444] But, in another case, a mere breach of warranty was held insufficient to award punitive damages.[445] Whatever the standard used, the award of punitive damages is largely within the discretion of the trier of fact.[446]

8.4.3.4 Need Consumer Prove Actual Damages?

An important UDAP issue is whether punitive damages can be awarded where the consumer has not proven actual damages. Connecticut courts allow punitive damages in UDAP cases even where no actual damages are established.[447] This holding is consistent with the rule in at least some jurisdictions for common law fraud actions that punitive damages can be awarded even if actual damages are not proven.[448] Other courts refuse to award UDAP punitive damages unless and until compensatory damages are awarded.[449]

8.4.3.5 Arbitration and Punitive Damages

The interrelationship of arbitration and punitive damages is very similar to that between arbitration and multiple damages examined at § 8.4.2.5, *supra*. If a UDAP statute provides for punitive damages as a remedy and the arbitration agreement or rules prohibit such a recovery, then the agreement may be unenforceable.[450]

Consequently, consumers may be better served to find punitive damages *not* authorized in an arbitration proceeding, allowing them to proceed in court instead. Whether a consumer is authorized to recover punitive damages will be determined by the language of the arbitration agreement. The Federal Arbitration Act preempts any state law limiting the consumer's ability to recover punitive damages, where those damages are authorized by the arbitration agreement.[451]

If the arbitration clause prohibits punitive damages, that provision will generally be given effect (although a consequence may be that the arbitration provision as a whole becomes unenforceable); if the provision allows punitive damages, such a provision will also be given effect.[452]

In interpreting an ambiguous or generally silent provision, the Supreme Court favors allowing punitive damages. This is because in this case two important presumptions both point to interpreting the contract as allowing punitive damages: that ambiguous clauses are interpreted against their drafters and that arbitration clauses are interpreted not to limit the parties' rights to arbitrate.[453] Moreover, it will be up to the arbitrator to interpret ambiguous language.[454] Because of the limited nature of judicial review of an arbitration award, a finding that punitive damages are allowed is unlikely to be overturned by a court.[455] Punitive

443 Brown v. Lyons, 43 Ohio Misc. 14, 332 N.E.2d 380, 72 Ohio Op. 2d 216 (C.P. Hamilton Cty. 1974). *Accord* Rowan Heating-Air Conditioning v. Williams, 580 A.2d 583 (D.C. 1990) (dealer's misrepresentation of material facts, its continuing failure to admit to mistakes, and its unwillingness to rectify the situation justified punitive damages).

444 Miles Rich Chrysler-Plymouth, Inc. v. Mass, 201 Ga. App. 693, 411 S.E.2d 901 (1991).

445 Ford Motor Co. v. Mayes, 575 S.W.2d 480 (Ky. Ct. App. 1978).

446 Colonial Lincoln-Mercury Sales, Inc. v. Molina, 152 Ga. App. 379, 262 S.E.2d 820 (1979).

447 Bristol Technology v. Microsoft Corp., 114 F. Supp. 2d 59 (D. Conn. 2000) (awarding $1 million in punitive damages against Microsoft even though jury awarded $1 in actual damages), *vacated*, 250 F.3d 152 (2d Cir. 2001) (vacating judgment pursuant to settlement agreement; expressing doubt about whether district court had jurisdiction to consider punitive damages issues); Tillquist v. Ford Motor Credit Co., 714 F. Supp. 607 (D. Conn. 1989); Conway v. American Excavating, Inc., 41 Conn. App. 437, 676 A.2d 881 (1996). *See also* Jacques All Trades Corp. v. Brown, 42 Conn. App. 124, 679 A.2d 27 (1996), *aff'd on other grounds*, 692 A.2d 809 (Conn. 1997).

448 *See, e.g.*, Nappe v. Anschelewitz, Barr, Ansell & Bonello, 97 N.J. 37, 477 A.2d 1224 (Law. Div. 1984). *But see* Hauser Motor Co. v. Byrd, 377 So. 2d 773 (Fla. Dist. Ct. App. 1980) (no punitive damages where no award of compensatory or nominal damages); Equitable Life Leasing Corp. v. Abbick, 243 Kan. 513, 757 P.2d 304 (1988) (while actual damages necessary to obtain punitive damages under fraud count, this requirement met where court awarded actual damages under contract claim and would be duplicative to also award under fraud claim); Burns v. Walters, 1984 Ohio App. LEXIS 10312 (June 27, 1984) (punitive damages not allowed unless actual compensatory damages awarded); Twin City Fire Ins. Co. v. Davis, 904 S.W.2d 663 (Tex. 1995). *See generally* National Consumer Law Center, Automobile Fraud § 7.10.1 (2d ed. 2003 and Supp.).

449 Liggett Group Inc. v. Engle, 853 So. 2d 434 (Fla. Dist. Ct. App. 2003).

450 *See* § 8.4.2.5.1, *supra*.

451 Mastrobuono v. Shearson Lehman Hutton, 514 U.S. 52, 115 S. Ct. 1212, 131 L. Ed. 2d 76 (1995).

452 *Id.*

453 *Id. See also* Stark v. Sandberg, Phoenix & von Gontard P.C., 2004 WL 1900319 (8th Cir. Aug. 26, 2004); Baravati v. Josephthal, Lyon, & Ross, 28 F.3d 704 (7th Cir. 1994); Complete Interiors, Inc. v. Behan, 558 So. 2d 48 (Fla. Dist. Ct. App. 1990); Greenway Capital Corp. v. Schneider, 494 S.E.2d 287 (Ga. App. 1997); Regina Constr. Corp. v. Envirmech Contracting Corp., 565 A.2d 693 (Md. Ct. App. 1989); Kennedy, *et al.* v. Young, 524 N.W.2d 752 (Minn. Ct. App. 1994).

454 *See* Pacificare Health Sys., Inc. v. Book, 123 S. Ct. 1531 (2003). *See also* Stark v. Sandberg, Phoenix & von Gontard P.C., 2004 WL 1900319 (8th Cir. Aug. 26, 2004).

455 *See* Baravati v. Josephthal, Lyon, & Ross, 28 F.3d 704 (7th Cir. 1994); Greenway Capital Corp. v. Schneider, 494 S.E.2d 287 (Ga. App. 1997); Regina Constr. Corp. v. Envirmech Contracting Corp., 565 A.2d 693 (Md. Ct. App. 1989); Kennedy, *et al.*

damages should be available then, at least for those claims where a court could award such relief.[456]

It is important though to look both at the language of the arbitration clause and the rules of any arbitration service provider referenced in the arbitration agreement. For example, National Arbitration Forum Rule 37B states that the award can not exceed the amount requested in the claim. Since filing fees are based on the amount of the claim, a consumer seeking $11,000 in actual damages and $250,000 in punitive damages would have to pay a NAF *filing fee* of $2500. This is just the amount to initiate the proceeding and does not include fees to request an amendment, subpoena, discovery order, continuance, post-hearing memorandum, other orders, plus $3000 for the initial in-person session, plus $2000 for each additional session (a session apparently being one half day long). Where the consumer has limited financial means, such a fee structure may have the practical effect of making punitive damages unavailable, and such an arbitration process would then be subject to challenge, where the consumer would argue the agreement is unenforceable.[457]

If punitive damages are allowed, the consumer should present a strong case to the arbitrator that such damages should be awarded. Implicit in such an endeavor is the right to take extensive discovery from the defendant to show intent and whether the challenged practice is part of a pattern of conduct. While the consumer's ability to challenge an arbitrator's refusal to award punitive damages is quite limited, so too are a merchant's rights to seek judicial review of an arbitrator's decision to award punitive damages.[458]

8.4.3.6 Limits on the Amount of Punitive Damages

8.4.3.6.1 Constitutional limitations enunciated by the United States Supreme Court

While computation of punitive damages awards under state UDAP or other state law theories is fundamentally a state law issue, federal constitutional standards can limit the size of this award. These issues are discussed in greater detail in NCLC's *Automobile Fraud* § 7.10.6 (2d ed. 2003 and Supp.).

The United States Supreme Court in recent years has addressed the due process limitations on punitive damages on a number of occasions.[459] Two cases in particular, *BMW of North America, Inc. v. Gore*[460] and *State Farm Mutual Automobile Insurance Co. v. Campbell,*[461] articulate three guideposts for determining whether the amount of a punitive damage award falls within due process limits:

- The degree of reprehensibility of the conduct;
- The disparity between the actual harm and the punitive damages, generally expressed as a ratio; and
- A comparison of penalties that could be imposed for similar conduct in analogous cases.[462]

Of these three guideposts, the reprehensibility of the defendant's conduct is the most important.[463] In evaluating this factor, the Supreme Court requires courts to consider whether:

- The harm caused was physical as opposed to economic;
- The tortious conduct evinced an indifference to or a reckless disregard of the health or safety of others;
- The target of the conduct had financial vulnerability;
- The conduct involved repeated actions or was an isolated incident; and
- The harm was the result of intentional malice, trickery, or deceit, or mere accident.[464]

Evidence of repeated misconduct is relevant to the reprehensibility analysis only if it involves acts that are similar to those directed toward the plaintiff. Although the evidence of other acts need not be identical, general corporate wrongdoing can not be a basis for punitive damages.[465] Evidence of out-of-state acts is relevant to show the deliberateness and culpability of the defendant's in-state conduct.[466] On the

v. Young, 524 N.W.2d 752 (Minn. Ct. App. 1994); *see also* Complete Interiors, Inc. v. Behan, 558 So. 2d 48 (Fla. Dist. Ct. App. 1990).

456 Gateway Technologies, Inc. v. MCI Telecommunications Corp., 64 F.3d 993 (5th Cir. 1995) (arbitrator can award punitive damages under tort claim, not contract claim); Padilla v. D.E. Frey & Co., 939 P.2d 475 (Colo. App. 1997). *Cf.* Barnes v. Logan, 122 F.3d 820 (9th Cir. 1997), *cert. denied*, 523 U.S. 1059 (1998) (upholding arbitrator's award of punitive damages where Minnesota appellate courts were split as to whether punitive damages may be awarded in cases not involving personal injuries, and Minnesota law governed).

457 *See* National Consumer Law Center, Consumer Arbitration Agreements § 4.3.2 (4th ed. 2004).

458 *See* Stark v. Sandberg, Phoenix & von Gontard P.C., 2004 WL 1900319 (8th Cir. Aug. 26, 2004).

459 State Farm Mut. Auto. Ins. Co. v. Campbell, 538 U.S. 408, 123 S. Ct. 1513, 155 L. Ed. 2d 585 (2003); BMW of N. Am., Inc. v. Gore, 517 U.S. 559, 116 S. Ct. 1589, 134 L. Ed. 2d 809 (1996); Honda Motor Co. v. Oberg, 512 U.S. 415, 114 S. Ct. 2331, 129 L. Ed. 2d 336 (1994); TXO Production Corp. v. Alliance Resources Corp., 509 U.S. 443, 113 S. Ct. 2711, 125 L. Ed. 2d 366 (1993); Pacific Mut. Life Ins. Co. v. Haslip, 499 U.S. 1, 111 S. Ct. 1032, 113 L. Ed. 2d 1 (1991). *Cf.* Browning-Ferris Indus., Inc. v. Kelco Disposal Inc., 492 U.S. 257, 109 S. Ct. 2909, 106 L. Ed. 2d 219 (1989) (8th Amendment excessive fines clause does not apply to punitive damages).

460 517 U.S. 559, 116 S. Ct. 1589, 134 L. Ed. 2d 809 (1996).

461 538 U.S. 408, 123 S. Ct. 1513, 155 L. Ed. 2d 585 (2003).

462 BMW of N. Am., Inc. v. Gore, 517 U.S. 559, 574–75, 116 S. Ct. 1589, 1598–99, 134 L. Ed. 2d 809 (1996).

463 *State Farm*, 538 U.S. at 419.

464 *Id.*.

465 *Id.*, 538 U.S. at 423–24.

466 *Id.*, 538 U.S. at 421, 427.

other hand, a state can not punish a party for conduct that was lawful in the state where it occurred, or even, as a general rule, for unlawful acts committed outside the state's jurisdiction.[467]

UDAP cases will often have strong evidence of reprehensibility that will meet these standards. Once defendants master their techniques for defrauding consumers, they usually repeat them many times, so evidence of intentional, repeated actions is often available. It is also common for fraudulent or predatory sellers to target financially vulnerable consumers, such as the elderly, disabled, unemployed, or underemployed.[468] While often the harm is primarily economic, in many consumer cases—especially those involving defective home repairs, defective cars, and mislabeled products—the seller places the buyer at risk of physical injury as well.[469]

As to the second guidepost, the ratio of punitive damages to compensatory damages, both *Gore* and *State Farm* refused to establish a bright-line test. In *State Farm*, however, the Court stated that "few awards exceeding a single-digit ratio between punitive and compensatory damages, to a significant degree, will satisfy due process."[470] Nonetheless, the Court acknowledged that larger ratios may be appropriate where a particularly egregious act has resulted in only a small amount of economic damages,[471] which is typical of consumer cases. Since *State Farm*, a number of courts have upheld ratios larger than ten-to-one on this theory.[472] In

467 *Id.*

468 *See* Neibel v. Trans World Assurance, Co., 108 F.3d 1123 (9th Cir. 1997); Life Ins. Co. of Georgia v. Johnson, 701 So. 2d 524 (Ala. 1997) (intentional sale of unnecessary supplemental Medicare insurance policy to Medicaid recipient was particularly reprehensible given that victim was elderly and poor, and supported a ratio of punitive to compensatory damages of 12 to 1); Sheffield v. Andrews, 679 So. 2d 1052 (Ala. 1996); Waltson v. Monumental Life Ins. Co., 923 P.2d 456 (Idaho 1996); Williams v. ITT Fin. Servs., 1997 Ohio App. LEXIS 2721 (Ohio App. June 25, 1997) (home repair loan scam perpetrated on elderly victim supported punitive to compensatory damages ratio of 100 to 1), *aff'd,* 83 Ohio St. 3d 464, 700 N.E.2d 859 (1998). *See also* Watson v. Johnson Mobile Homes, 284 F.3d 568 (5th Cir. 2002) (affirming $150,000 of a $700,000 punitive damages award against mobile home dealer that refused to return $4000 deposit when financing fell through); Cooper v. Casey, 97 F.3d 914 (7th Cir. 1996) (court cited *Gore* in holding that punitive damage award was not excessive even though it was twelve times the amount awarded in compensatory damages). *Cf.* Dean v. Olibas, 129 F.3d 1001 (8th Cir. 1997) (punitive damages 14 times actuals not excessive for malicious prosecution action against bail bondsman); Parsons v. First Investors Corp., 122 F.3d 525 (8th Cir. 1997) (punitive damages award over 11 times the actual damages not excessive in investors' action for fraudulently inducing them to invest in junk bond mutual funds); Hampton v. Dillard Dept. Stores, Inc., 18 F. Supp. 2d 1256 (D. Kan. 1998) ($1,100,000 punitive damage award, at a 20-to-1 ratio to the $56,000 compensatory award, was justified due to the reprehensible pattern of discriminatory behavior against minorities); McDermott v. Party City Corp., 11 F. Supp. 2d 612 (E.D. Pa. 1998) (upholding 9 to 1 ration where breach of fiduciary duties).

469 *See* Grabinski v. Blue Springs Ford Sales, Inc., 203 F.3d 1024 (8th Cir. 2000) (sale of vehicle with concealed wreck damage showed "clear and disturbing disregard for [the buyer's] safety"; punitive damage awards ranging from 5 to 99 times actual damages upheld); Orkin Exterminating Co. v. Jeter, 832 So. 2d 25 (Ala. 2001) (concealing and failing to repair termite damage left home unsafe).

470 538 U.S. at 425.

471 *Id.*

472 Williams v. Kaufman County, 352 F.3d 994 (5th Cir. 2004) (affirming $15,000 punitive damages award when jury awarded $100 nominal damages, a 150-to-1 ratio, in § 1983 strip search case); Mathias v. Accor Econ. Lodging, Inc., 347 F.3d 672 (7th Cir. 2003) (upholding 37.2-to-1 ratio when compensatory damages to hotel guest bitten by bedbugs was $5000); Asa-Brandt, Inc. v. ADM Investor Servs., Inc., 344 F.3d 738 (8th Cir. 2003) ($1.25 million punitive damages award not excessive in light of potential harm of $3.9 million, even though jury awarded only nominal damages); Lincoln v. Case, 340 F.3d 283 (5th Cir. 2003) (ordering *remittur* of $100,000 punitive damages award to $55,000 on $500 compensatory damages, a 110-to-1 ratio, in housing discrimination case); Planned Parenthood v. Am. Coalition of Life Activists, 2004 WL 144204 (D. Or. Jan. 28, 2004) (upholding ratios ranging from 31.8-to-1 to 6.7-to-1 against defendants who blockaded abortion clinics and threatened physical harm against providers when defendants were unrelenting recidivists); Dunn v. Vill. of Put-in-Bay, 2004 WL 169788 (N.D. Ohio Jan. 26, 2004) (upholding $23,422.50 punitive damages award on $1577.50 compensatory damages, a 14.8-to-1 ratio, in light of small compensatory award in § 1983 excessive force case and difficulty of placing value on constitutional violation not accompanied by lasting physical consequences); Jones v. Rent-A-Center, Inc., 281 F. Supp. 2d 1277 (D. Kan. 2003) (upholding $290,000 punitive damages award on $10,000 compensatory damages in Title VII case because Title VII $300,000 damages cap gives defendants fair warning of potential liability); S. Union Co. v. Southwest Gas Corp., 281 F. Supp. 2d 1090 (D. Ariz. 2003) (upholding $60 million punitive damages award on $390,072.58 compensatory damages, a ratio of 153-to-1, when potential harm was high, some damage was unquantifiable, and defendant breached public trust); Simon v. San Paolo U.S. Holding Co., 7 Cal. Rptr. 3d 367 (Ct. App. 2003) (unpublished) (affirming $1,700,000 punitive damages award on $5000 compensatory damages, a 340-to-1 ratio, because of small compensatory award in land sale fraud case; court takes other harm not reflected in compensatory award into account and considers ratio to be 4-to-1), *review granted,* 2004 Cal. LEXIS 2548 (Cal. Mar. 24, 2004); Craig v. Holsey, 590 S.E.2d 742 (Ga. Ct. App. 2003) (upholding 22.7-to-1 ratio when drunk driver crashed into plaintiff's car, pushing her into oncoming traffic, but caused only $8801.40 actual damages); Phelps v. Louisville Water Co., 103 S.W.3d 46 (Ky. 2003) (affirming $2 million punitive damages award, an 11.3-to-1 ratio, because of low compensatory damages award of $176,361.64 for wrongful death); Werremeyer v. K.C. Auto Salvage Co., 2003 WL 21487311 (Mo. Ct. App. June 30, 2003), (approving a 13.9-to-1 ratio in consumer automobile fraud case when the fraud was difficult to detect), *aff'd in relevant part, rev'd in part on other grounds,* 134 S.W.3d 633 (Mo. App. 2004) (reversing denial of prejudgment interest; affirming fraud judgment and punitive damages award); Madeja v. MPB Corp., 821 A.2d 1034 (N.H. 2003) (upholding 35-to-1 punitive damages award in sexual harassment case); Hollock v. Erie Ins. Exch., 842 A.2d 409 (Pa. Super. 2004) (affirming 10-to-1 ratio,

determining the ratio, courts can consider not only actual harm but also harm that the defendant's actions could have caused[473] and future harm that may occur.[474] It may also be possible to consider harm to others.[475]

As to the third guidepost, comparable penalties for similar conduct, in consumer cases there are usually significant civil and criminal penalties to which a punitive damage award can be compared. UDAP statutes typically authorize the state to assess civil penalties of thousands of dollars per consumer per violation.[476] Additional penalties in certain states are available if the elderly are targeted.[477] The FTC Act is another useful analogy. It allows a civil penalty up to $10,000 per rule violation, with each day of noncompliance being treated as a separate violation.[478] The state may be able to impose the "civil death penalty"—revocation of the wrongdoer's business license—for violations of the UDAP or related consumer protection statutes.[479] Criminal penalties are also often available, either under a UDAP statute or a criminal theft or other statute.[480] The Supreme Court has, however, stressed that the remote possibility of a criminal sanction is insufficient to sustain a damage award, and criminal penalties can only be considered if they are applicable to the specific conduct toward the plaintiff.[481] It may also be appropriate to consider the availability of a private UDAP class action for actual or treble damages to see how that amount might compare to the punitive damages award.[482]

8.4.3.6.2 State statutory caps on punitive damages awards

In addition to the constitutional standards set by the Supreme Court, in many states there are statutory caps on

---

with compensatory damages of $278,825 and punitive damages of $2,800,000, in insurance bad faith case). *See also* Trinity Evangelical Lutheran Church v. Tower Ins. Co., 661 N.W.2d 789 (Wis. 2003) (upholding $3.5 million punitive damages award in insurance bad faith case, even though no actual damages were awarded, when ratio was 7-to-1 to harm that would have occurred if defendant's misconduct had succeeded).

473 Asa-Brandt, Inc. v. ADM Investor Servs., Inc., 344 F.3d 738 (8th Cir. 2003) ($1.25 million punitive damages award not excessive in light of potential harm of $3.9 million, even though jury awarded only nominal damages); *In re* Exxon Valdez, 296 F. Supp. 2d 1071, 1098, 1103, 1104 (D. Alaska 2004) (upholding $4.5 billion punitive damages award in environmental tort class action when compensatory damages were about $513 million but harm would have been much greater if pilot's boneheaded maneuver after crash had ripped larger hole in hull); Willow Inn v. Pub. Serv. Mut. Ins. Co., 2003 WL 21321370 (E.D. Pa. May 30, 2003); S. Union Co. v. Southwest Gas Corp., 281 F. Supp. 2d 1090, 1104 (D. Ariz. 2003) (taking potential harm into account in upholding $60 million punitive damages award on $390,072.58 compensatory damages, a ratio of 153 to 1); Craig v. Holsey, 590 S.E.2d 742 (Ga. Ct. App. 2003). *See also* Romo v. Ford Motor Co., 113 Cal. App. 4th 738, 6 Cal. Rptr. 3d 793 (2003) (approving ratios of 3-to-1 and 5-to-1 in wrongful death case even though actual damages were about $5 million; court takes into account that loss of life is undercompensated); Roberie v. VonBokern, 2003 WL 22976126 (Ky. Ct. App. Dec. 19, 2003) (unpublished) (punitive damages may be awarded even without actual damages; potential harm may be considered in ratio; remanding to trial court for *State Farm* analysis); Trinity Evangelical Lutheran Church v. Tower Ins. Co., 661 N.W.2d 789 (Wis. 2003) (upholding $3.5 million punitive damages award in insurance bad faith case even though no actual damages were awarded, when ratio was 7-to-1 to harm that would have occurred if defendant's misconduct had succeeded).

474 Planned Parenthood v. Am. Coalition of Life Activists, 2004 WL 144204 (D. Or. Jan. 28, 2004) (taking potential of future harm into account in upholding ratios ranging from 31.8-to-1 to 6.7-to-1 against defendants who blockaded abortion clinics and threatened physical harm against providers); *In re* Exxon Valdez, 296 F. Supp. 2d 1071, 1104, 1105 (D. Alaska 2004) (accommodating potential future harm by allowing higher ratio; upholding $4.5 billion punitive damages award on $513 million compensatory damages in environmental tort class action).

475 *Harm to others can be considered*: *In re* Exxon Valdez, 296 F. Supp. 2d 1071, 1103 (D. Alaska 2004) (potential harm to others can be included in ratio, but not necessary here); *see also* Roth v. Farner-Bocken Co., 667 N.W.2d 651 (S.D. 2003) (accepting that harm to others can be included in ratio, but not shown here); *cf.* S. Union Co. v. Southwest Gas Corp., 281 F. Supp. 2d 1090, 1101 (D. Ariz. 2003) (harm to public can justify higher ratio). *Harm to others can not be considered*: Bocci v. Key Pharm., Inc., 76 P.3d 669, 674 (Or. Ct. App.), *as amended by* 79 P.3d 908 (Or. Ct. App. 2003).

476 *See* Grabinski v. Blue Springs Ford Sales, Inc., 203 F.3d 1024 (8th Cir. 2000) (citing $1000 per violation UDAP civil penalty as reason to uphold punitive damage award); Burton v. R.J. Reynolds Tobacco Co., 205 F. Supp. 2d 1253, 1264 (D. Kan. 2002) (comparing $16 million punitive damages award to $10,000 civil penalty for each sale of cigarettes to plaintiff over 40-year period); State of Washington v. WWJ Corp., 138 Wash. 2d 595, 980 P.2d 1257 (1999) (civil penalty of $2000 for each of 250 UDAP violations upheld against Eighth and Fourteenth Amendment challenges). *See also* § 10.7.3 and Appx. A, *infra*. *Cf.* Watson v. Johnson Mobile Homes, 284 F.3d 568 (5th Cir. 2002) (taking UDAP penalties into account in upholding $150,000 of $700,000 punitive damages award, but citing only penalties for single violation even though plaintiff showed that many others had been victimized).

477 *See generally* § 10.7.3.7, *infra*.

478 15 U.S.C. § 45(m).

479 Grabinski v. Blue Springs Ford Sales, Inc., 203 F.3d 1024 (8th Cir. 2000) (state's authority to refuse to issue or renew motor vehicle dealer's license to anyone who has obtained money by fraud, deception, or misrepresentation "weigh[s] heavily in favor of an award of punitive damages"); United Technologies Corp. v. Am. Home Assurance Co., 118 F. Supp. 2d 174 (D. Conn. 2000) (taking into account losses that insurer would suffer if its right to do business in the state were revoked).

480 *See* Grabinski v. Blue Springs Ford Sales, Inc., 203 F.3d 1024 (8th Cir. 2000) (citing criminal penalties for UDAP violations as reason to uphold punitive damage award); Burton v. R.J. Reynolds Tobacco Co., 205 F. Supp. 2d 1253, 1264, 1265 (D. Kan. 2002) (fines and imprisonment, which could be imposed for multiple acts of deception in sale of cigarettes, justify $16 million punitive damages award).

481 State Farm Mut. Auto. Ins. Co. v. Campbell, 538 U.S. 408, 428, 123 S. Ct. 1513, 155 L. Ed. 2d 585 (2003).

482 *See* Ford Motor Co. v. Sperau, 708 So. 2d 111 (Ala. 1997) (using UDAP treble damages as a standard).

punitive damages awards.[483] These caps may apply to UDAP or fraud claims in some states, but not in others. For example, some caps apply only to product liability cases, while others apply to all civil actions. A state cap on punitive damages may not apply to UDAP treble damages.[484] These caps are discussed in more detail in NCLC's *Automobile Fraud* § 7.10.5 (2d ed. 2003 and Supp.).

8.4.3.6.3 Potential of multiple punitive damages awards against one defendant

Defendants often argue against punitive damages by raising the possibility that future or pending individual actions against the same company could result in future punitive damages awards. They argue that the total of awards could result in "overkill," violating the defendant's due process rights under the Fourteenth Amendment. The majority of courts have held that successive punitive damages awards against the same defendant do not violate the Due Process Clause.[485] The Sixth Circuit has rejected this argument, even in a case where punitive damages of $1.5 million were awarded against Johns-Manville in a product liability case while numerous other suits were pending against it.[486] The

483 *Alabama*: Ala. Stat. § 6-11-20. The state supreme court held a predecessor version of this statute unconstitutional in 1993: Henderson *ex rel.* Hartsfield v. Alabama Power Co., 627 So. 2d 878 (Ala. 1993) (a limitation on punitive damages clearly impairs the traditional function of the jury and is therefore unconstitutional); Blackburn v. Resolution Trust Corp., 627 So. 2d 915 (Ala. 1993) (section violates the right to a trial by jury as guaranteed by the Alabama Constitution); *see also* Foster v. Life Ins. Co., 656 So. 2d 333 (Ala. 1994) (based on the *Blackburn* decision, a $1 million verdict award of punitive damages in an action brought against a life insurance company for fraud in selling a worthless Medicare supplement policy to the insured would be reinstated). However, more recently the court has expressed doubt about whether its decision on the constitutionality of the statute was correct, liver v. Towns, 738 So. 2d 798, 804 n.7 (Ala. 1999), and it has cited the current revised statute with approval, Wal-Mart Stores, Inc. v. Goodman, 789 So. 2d 166 (Ala. 2000).

Alaska: Alaska Stat. § 09.17.020. The state supreme court upheld the constitutionality of this statute in Central Bering Sea Fishermen's Ass'n v. Anderson, 54 P.3d 271 (Alaska 2002).

Colorado: Colo. Rev. Stat. Ann. § 13-21-102.

Connecticut: Conn. Gen. Stat. § 52-240b (product liability actions only).

Florida: Fla. Stat. Ann. § 768.73.

Georgia: Ga. Code Ann. § 51-12-5.1. The state supreme court upheld the constitutionality of this statute in State v. Mosely, 436 S.E.2d 632 (Ga. 1993).

Idaho: Idaho Code § 6-1604.

Illinois: 735 Ill. Comp. Stat. Ann. § 5/2-1115.05. These caps were held unconstitutional in Best v. Taylor Machine Works, 179 Ill. 2d 367, 689 N.E.2d 1057, 228 Ill. Dec. 636 (1997). A separate statute, 735 Ill. Comp. Stat. Ann. § 5/2-1115, completely bars punitive damages in medical or legal malpractice actions.

Indiana: Ind. Code Ann. § 34-51-3-4. The state supreme court upheld the constitutionality of the statute's apportionment of 75% of the punitive damage award to the state in Cheatham v. Pohle, 789 N.E.2d 467 (Ind. 2003).

Kansas: Kan. Stat. Ann. § 60-3702. The state supreme court upheld the constitutionality of this statute in Smith v. Printup, 866 P.2d 985 (Kan. 1993).

Mississippi: Miss. Code Ann. § 11-1-65.

Missouri: Mo. Rev. Stat. § 537.675 (half of punitive damage award goes to state). The statute's constitutionality was upheld in Hoskins v. Bus. Men's Assurance, 79 S.W.3d 901 (Mo. 2002) and Fust v. Att'y Gen., 947 S.W.2d 424 (Mo. 1997).

Montana: Mont. Code Ann. § 27-1-220.

Nevada: Nev. Rev. Stat. Ann. § 42.005.

New Hampshire: N.H. Rev. Stat. Ann. § 507:16 (prohibiting punitive damages in any action, unless otherwise provided by statute).

New Jersey: N.J. Stat. Ann. § 2A:15-5.14.

North Carolina: N.C. Gen. Stat. § 1D-25. The constitutionality of this statute was upheld in Rhyne v. K-Mart Corp., 594 S.E.2d 1 (N.C. 2004).

North Dakota: N.D. Cent. Code § 32-03.2-11.

Ohio: Ohio Rev. Code § 2315.21. This statute was struck down as violative of the state constitution by State *ex rel.* Ohio Academy of Trial Lawyers v. Sheward, 86 Ohio St. 3d 451, 715 N.E.2d 1062 (1999).

Oklahoma: Okla. Stat. tit. 23, § 9.1.

Oregon: Or. Rev. Stat. § 18.540 (allocating 60% of any punitive damages award go to the state). *See also* Or. Rev. Stat. § 18.550 (baring punitive damages against licensed health care practitioners acting within the scope of their licenses and without malice).

Texas: Tex. Civ. Prac. & Rem. § 41.008(b). Intermediate appellate courts have held that the cap does not run afoul of the state constitution's guarantee of open courts or its requirement of separation of powers: Waste Disposal Center, Inc. v. Larson, 74 S.W.3d 578 (Tex. App. 2002); Hall v. Diamond Shamrock Refining Co., 82 S.W.3d 5 (Tex. App. 2001).

Utah: Utah Code Ann. § 78-18-1 (allowing punitive damages only if compensatory or general damages are awarded, and allocating 50% of punitive damage awards to state fund).

Virginia: Va. Code Ann. § 8.01-38.1. A Fourth Circuit decision, Wackenhut Applied Technologies Ctr., Inc. v. Sygnetron Protection Sys., 979 F.2d 980 (4th Cir. 1992), holds that this statute does not violate the due process guarantees of the U.S. or Virginia Constitution.

484 Advanced Marine Enters., Inc. v. PRC, Inc., 256 Va. 106, 501 S.E.2d 148 (1998) (non-UDAP case holding Virginia's cap inapplicable to treble damages).

485 *See, e.g.*, Owens-Corning Fiberglas Corp. v. Golightly, 976 S.W.2d 409, 412 (Ky. 1998), and cases cited therein. *See generally* Margaret Meriwether Cordray, The Limits of State Sovereignty and the Issue of Multiple Punitive Damages Awards, 78 Or. L. Rev. 275, 309 (1999).

486 Cathey v. Johns-Manville Sales Corp., 776 F.2d 1565 (6th Cir. 1985); Kociemba v. G.D. Searle & Co., 707 F. Supp. 1517 (D. Minn. 1989) (upholding $7 million punitive damages award despite 500 other pending cases against same defendant); Stevens v. Owens-Corning Fiberglas Corp., 57 Cal. Rptr. 2d 525 (Ct. App. 1996) (upholding $2 million punitive damage award); Owens-Corning Fiberglas Corp. v. Ballard, 739 So. 2d 603, 606 (Fla. Dist. Ct. App. 1998) ("where the defendant's conduct is considered tortious in all 50 states, as here, the same due process concerns implicated in BMW do not arise"), *aff'd on other grounds*, 749 So. 2d 483 (Fla. 1999); Owens-Corning Fiberglas Corp. v. Rivera, 683 So. 2d 154 (Fla. Dist. Ct. App. 1996)

Sixth Circuit found that the probability of such multiple damage awards did not violate constitutional due process or fundamental fairness standards because the presence of a judicial tribunal provides an adequate forum for the manufacturer to litigate the propriety of each punitive damages award. Defendants should not be relieved of liability because their outrageous conduct injures a large number of persons. A few states, however, have statutes restricting multiple awards of punitive damages against the same defendant under certain circumstances.[487]

(upholding $1.5 million punitive damage award); Owens-Corning Fiberglas Corp. v. Golightly, 976 S.W.2d 409 (Ky. 1998). *See also* Leonen v. Johns-Manville Corp., 717 F. Supp. 272 (D.N.J. 1989). *But see* Steans v. Combined Ins. Co. of Am., 1998 U.S. Dist. LEXIS 7494 (S.D. Ala. Apr. 2, 1998) (enjoining additional claims for punitive damages where defendant had already been assessed over $8 million), *vacated, remanded on other grounds*, 148 F.3d 1266 (11th Cir. 1998); Juzwin v. Amtorg Trading Corp., 705 F. Supp. 1053 (D.N.J. 1989) ("[i]f a defendant's conduct has been evaluated by a factfinder, and if that factfinder has made an assessment of the amount of punitive damages necessary to deter and punish that conduct, then this court concludes that any further punishment would be unnecessary, repetitive, and a violation of due process"), *vacated*, 718 F. Supp. 1233 (D.N.J. 1989) (vacating its earlier decision dismissing plaintiffs' claims for punitive damages, but maintaining its view "that multiple awards of punitive damages for a single course of conduct violate the fundamental fairness requirement of the Due Process Clause" and permitting defendants to file post-trial motions regarding any such awards), *rev'd on other grounds*, 900 F.2d 686 (3d Cir. 1990); *Ex parte* Ingram, 774 So. 2d 563 (Ala. 2000) (dismissing as premature petition for mandamus to vacate trial court's order precluding punitive damages). *But cf.* Morse v. Southern Union Co., 38 F. Supp. 2d 1120, 1126 n.12 (W.D. Mo. 1998) ("while the Missouri courts seem not to have considered whether the likelihood of multiple claims should limit punitive damages recovery, I believe such a factor may be required by Due Process;" granting remittur of punitive damages award), *aff'd*, 174 F.3d 917 (8th Cir. 1998); Owens-Corning Fiberglas Corp. v. Wasiak, 917 S.W.2d 883 (Tex. App. 1996) (applying Alabama law and upholding $3.7 million punitive damage award), *aff'd*, 972 S.W.2d 35 (Tex. 1998) (affirming but expressing concern that repeatedly imposing punitive damages on the same defendant for the same course of wrongful conduct may implicate substantive due process constraints," and fashioning a post-trial test for a court to evaluate multiple punitive damage awards).

487 Fla. Stat. Ann. § 768.73(2) (punitive damages may not be awarded where defendant establishes before trial that punitive damages have previously been awarded in any state or federal court in any action arising from the same act or single course of conduct, but court in subsequent action may permit jury to consider punitive damages if the court determines by clear and convincing evidence that the amount of prior punitive damages was insufficient); Ga. Code Ann. § 51-12-5.1 (in product liability cases only there is no limit to the award, but "only one award of punitive damages may be recovered in a court in this state from a defendant for any act or omission . . . , regardless of the number of causes of action which may arise from such act or omission"); Okla. Stat. Ann. tit. 23, § 9.1 (punitive damages to be reduced by awards previously paid by same defendant for same conduct in any Oklahoma state court).

8.4.3.7 Who Is Liable for Punitive Damages?

The common law approach is that principals are liable for punitive damages for the acts of their agents only where:

- The principal authorized the doing and the manner of the act;
- The agent was unfit and the principal was reckless in employing the agent;
- The agent was employed in a managerial capacity and was acting in the scope of employment; or
- The principal or a manager of the principal ratified or approved the act.[488]

For example, where a corporation encourages a real estate agent to make representations the corporation knows to be groundless, both parties are liable for punitive damages.[489] Some states have statutes that specifically address punitive damages awards against a principal for the acts of agents, and these contain one or more common law predicates for imposing such awards.[490]

Because UDAP statutes should be liberally construed to remedy marketplace imbalances and the common law approach was too permissive toward corporate irresponsibilities, many courts have rejected the limitations of the common law approach. Instead, a corporation can be liable for punitive damages for the actions of a nonmanagerial employee even without any of the above four criteria being met.[491]

---

488 Restatement (Second) of Torts § 909; Restatement (Second) of Agency, 217C; 3 Am. Jur. 2d *Agency* § 343 (2002); 22 Am. Jur. 2d *Damages* §§ 589–595 (2003); 25 C.J.S. *Damages* §§ 212 (2002). *See* Preston v. Income Producing Mgmt. Co., 871 F. Supp. 411 (D. Kan. 1994); Bates v. William Chevrolet/Geo, Inc., 337 Ill. App. 3d 151, 785 N.E.2d 53 (2003); Riley v. Fair & Co. Realtors, 150 Ill. App. 3d 597, 502 N.E.2d 45 (1986); Dahl v. Sittner, 474 N.W.2d 897 (S.D. 1991). *See also* N.D. Cent. Code § 32-03.2-11(8) (statute mirrors common law approach).

489 Mabin v. Tualatin Dev., 48 Or. App. 271, 616 P.2d 1196 (1980).

490 *See, e.g.*, Kan. Stat. Ann. § 60-3702(2); Nev. Rev. Stat. Ann. § 42.007; N.D. Cent. Code § 32-03.2-11(8) (must prove authority, ratification, recklessness in employing agent, managerial capacity of agent); Ohio Rev. Code Ann. § 2315.21 (must show authorization, participation or ratification). *See also* York v. InTrust Bank, 265 Kan. 271, 962 P.2d 405 (1998).

491 Allen v. Morgan Drive Away, Inc., 273 Or. 614, 542 P.2d 896 (1975); Teague Motor Co. v. Rowton, 84 Or. App. 72, 733 P.2d 93 (1987) (corporation may be liable for punitive damages if employee, acting within the scope of employment, commits an act which would subject employee personally to punitive damages). *See also* Abrams v. Mike Salta Pontiac Inc., 51 Or. App. 495, 625 P.2d 1383 (1981). *Cf.* Kansallis Fin. Ltd. v. Fern, 421 Mass. 659, 659 N.E.2d 731 (1996) (noting distinction between corporations and partnerships for purposes of vicarious liability for punitive damages, and holding that an innocent and uninvolved partner may be vicariously liable, but that a further showing of culpability or involvement must be made to justify punitive damages). *But cf.* Larsen Chelsey Realty Co. v. Larsen,

While an assignee finance company is not liable for punitive damages where there is no allegation that the assignee vicariously made any representations,[492] a series of Alabama cases has resulted in large punitive damages awards against creditors who were involved with fraudulent home improvement scams.[493] In these cases the home improvement contractors assigned all their loan payments to one creditor, worked closely with that creditor, and acted as the creditor's agent.

In one case against ITT Credit Corporation, the lower court awarded punitive damages against ITT even though it was the home improvement contractor's conduct which was fraudulent, and even though the contractor was not ITT's agent. The punitive damages award was based on the fact that ITT and the contractor engaged in a civil conspiracy to further the contractor's fraudulent practices. The Ohio Supreme Court upheld the $1.5 million punitive damages award because, based on the nature of the conspiracy, either party is fully liable for the acts of the other, including liability for punitive damages.[494]

ITT's role in the conspiracy was to allow the contractor access to loan money that was necessary to further the contractor's fraudulent practices against its customers. ITT made this money available even though it knew of the contractor's propensity for misconduct. This was found to be a sufficient basis to affirm the punitive damages award against ITT.[495]

8.4.3.8 Interrelation of Punitive Damages with Other Remedies

The issues surrounding the relationship between punitive damages and other remedies are similar to those the consumer faces when seeking treble damages.[496] Punitive damages are awarded in addition to compensatory damages. Actual UDAP damages can also be awarded in addition to punitive damages under a tort claim.[497] Some courts allow both treble and punitive damages recoveries.[498] This should be the case particularly where the UDAP treble damages and tort punitive damages recoveries relate to separate damages and separate violations.[499]

But other courts hold that a consumer can not receive both UDAP treble damages and punitive damages under a tort theory.[500] Instead, these courts usually allow the consumer to seek both treble and punitive damages, and after the court has set the size of both awards, the consumer can elect which award to accept.[501] Consumers should be careful to

---

232 Conn. 480, 656 A.2d 1009 (1995) (plaintiff must show that corporation's agents, acting on behalf of corporation, ratified or authorized the wrongful acts); York v. InTrust Bank, 265 Kan. 271, 307, 962 P.2d 405, 429 (1998) (plaintiff must show by clear and convincing evidence that principal "through a person expressly empowered to do so . . . , authorized the other party to engage in the fraudulent conduct"); Carter v. Gugliuzzi, 168 Vt. 48, 716 A.2d 17 (1998) (the knowledge of an authorized agent is chargeable to the principal, regardless of whether the agent actually communicates the knowledge to the principal, but punitive damages may not be awarded unless principal acted with malice, ill will, or wanton disregard of plaintiff's rights).

492 Anglin v. Household Retail Servs., Inc., 17 F. Supp. 2d 1251 (M.D. Ala. 1998) (finance company is generally not liable for retailer's misconduct without further evidence of agency relationship); Harris v. Chalet Car Co., 280 Or. 679, 572 P.2d 623 (1977). *But cf.* an assignee's liability pursuant to the FTC Holder Rule discussed at § 6.6, *supra.*

493 *See* Union Mortgage Co. v. Barlow, 595 So. 2d 1335 (Ala. 1992) (upholding $6 million in punitive damages).

494 Williams v. Aetna Fin. Co., 83 Ohio St. 3d 464, 700 N.E.2d 859 (1998), *cert. denied*, 119 S. Ct. 1357, 143 L. Ed. 2d 518 (1999).

495 *Id.*

496 *See* § 8.4.2.6, *supra.*

497 United Laboratories v. Kuykendall, 335 N.C. 183, 437 S.E.2d 374 (1993).

498 Aponte v. Aungst, 82 B.R. 738 (Bankr. E.D. Pa. 1988) (treble UDAP damages and punitive damages under Bankruptcy Code); Conseco Fin. Serv. Corp. v. Hill, 556 S.E.2d 468 (Ga. App. 2001) (treble and punitive damages may be allowed for same UDAP violation if intentional); Colonial Lincoln-Mercury Sales, Inc. v. Molina, 152 Ga. App. 379, 262 S.E.2d 820 (1979) (for intentional violations treble damages mandatory and exemplary damages are permissible); Crawford v. Bill Swad Chevrolet, Inc., 2000 Ohio App. LEXIS 4221 (Sept. 19, 2000) (allowing both punitive damages for fraud plus treble damages for UDAP violations); Mid Am. Acceptance Co. v. Lightle, 63 Ohio App. 3d 590, 579 N.E.2d 721 (1989) (punitive damages for fraud are recoverable along with UDAP treble damages); Freeman v. A&M Mobile Home Sales, Inc., 293 S.C. 255, 359 S.E.2d 532 (Ct. App. 1987) (court awards UDAP treble damages and punitive damages under common law fraud count). *See also* Rhue v. Dawson, 173 Ariz. 220, 841 P.2d 215 (Ct. App. 1992) (state RICO treble damages and tort punitive damages); Advanced Marine Enters., Inc. v. PRC, Inc., 256 Va. 106, 501 S.E.2d 148, 159 (1998) (treble damages on non-UDAP statutory claim and punitive damages on common law claims involving different duties and injuries).

499 Winkle Chevy-Olds-Pontiac v. Condon, 830 S.W.2d 740 (Tex. App. 1992).

500 *See* Lexton-Ancira Real Estate Fund, 1972 v. Heller, 826 P.2d 819 (Colo. 1992); Edwards v. William H. Porter, Inc., 1991 Del. Super. LEXIS 315, Clearinghouse No. 47,935 (July 26, 1991); Cieri v. Leticia Query Realty, Inc., 905 P.2d 29 (Haw. 1995) (consumer must elect between treble damages and attorney fees on a UDAP claim or punitive damages on a fraud claim); 49 Prospect Street Tenants Ass'n v. Sheva Gardens, Inc., 227 N.J. Super. 449, 547 A.2d 1134 (App. Div. 1988) (where same practice results in award under different counts for treble and punitive damages, both awards may stand, but exemplary portion of treble damages (i.e., double damages) must be deducted from punitive damages award); Hale v. Basin Motor Co., 110 N.M. 314, 795 P.2d 1006 (1990); Hardy v. Toler, 288 N.C. 303, 218 S.E.2d 342 (1975); Smith v. Strickland, 442 S.E.2d 207 (S.C. Ct. App. 1994); Concrete Spaces, Inc. v. Sender, 2 S.W.3d 901 (Tenn. 1999); Birchfield v. Texarkana Memorial Hosp., 747 S.W.2d 361 (Tex. 1987). *Cf.* Wilkins v. Peninsula Motor Cars, Inc., 587 S.E.2d 581, 584 (Va. 2003) (declining to decide whether UDAP treble damages are duplicative of punitive damages).

501 Roberts v. American Warranty Corp., 514 A.2d 1132 (Del. Super. Ct. 1986); Cieri v. Leticia Query Realty, Inc., 905 P.2d 29 (Haw. 1995) (consumer must choose larger award; in determin-

make this election in a timely fashion, as required by state procedure.[502]

A buyer may be able to rescind a purchase and also receive punitive damages.[503] This is consistent with the rule in many states that a buyer who rescinds a transaction because of fraud can recover punitive damages.[504] Punitive damages may be awarded in addition to statutory damages, since statutory damages can be viewed as in lieu of compensatory damages.[505]

Punitive damages and attorney fees can both be awarded even where the cost of litigation is one of the factors used to justify punitive damages.[506] A somewhat unique issue arises in Oregon because a state statute specifies that punitive damages awards first go to pay the consumers' attorneys and the remainder is split between the consumer and a special state fund.[507] Oregon's highest court has ruled that UDAP attorney fees should still be awarded on top of the punitive damages award that the total recovery should not be limited simply because the attorney can be paid out of the punitive damages award.[508]

8.5 Class Actions

8.5.1 General

Consumer class action practice issues are treated in another National Consumer Law Center publication.[509] This section briefly addresses the use of class actions as a means of challenging UDAP violations. Theoretically, class actions are well suited for securing wide-scale redress for marketplace deception. Class actions adjudicate numerous claims that individually damaged consumers would not pursue because they are uninformed of their rights, deterred from filing individual suits because of an ongoing relationship with the prospective defendant, or have claims too small to merit individual adjudication.[510]

A UDAP class action seeking damages allows the aggregation of many small consumer claims, thereby deterring merchant misconduct far more effectively than one individual damage action. Such an action makes it feasible for an attorney to handle the case, even though individual consumer injury is minimal. These factors lead some courts to look with particular favor on class actions in the consumer context.[511]

UDAP class actions may also prove to be useful vehicles to obtain injunctive relief.[512] Class injunctive actions face fewer procedural hurdles than do class damage actions. A court may be more willing to issue a broad injunction in a class action than in an individual action.[513]

Class actions may also simplify compliance with UDAP statutes' procedural requirements. For example, if a UDAP

---

ing which is larger, attorney fees are included in UDAP award); Eastern Star, Inc. v. Union Bldg. Materials, 712 P.2d 1148 (Haw. Ct. App. 1985); Hale v. Basin Motor Co., 110 N.M. 314, 795 P.2d 1006 (1990); McLelland v. United Wisconsin Life Ins. Co., 980 P.2d 86 (N.M. App. 1999); Volt Sys. Corp. v. Raytheon Corp., 547 N.Y.S.2d 280 (App. Div. 1989) (claims for punitive and treble damages under different laws may be pleaded, but plaintiff may have to make election of remedies later); Ellis v. Northern Star Co., 388 S.E.2d 127 (N.C. 1990); Mapp v. Toyota World, Inc., 344 S.E.2d 297 (N.C. Ct. App. 1986); Concrete Spaces, Inc. v. Sender, 2 S.W.3d 901 (Tenn. 1999) (plaintiff must make election before amount of punitive damages is awarded); Birchfield v. Texarkana Memorial Hosp., 747 S.W.2d 361 (Tex. 1987); Town East Ford Sales, Inc. v. Gray, 730 S.W.2d 796 (Tex. App. 1987); Hall v. Birchfreed, 718 S.W.2d 313 (Tex. App. 1986); *see also* Hajmm Co. v. House of Raeford Farms, Inc., 379 S.E.2d 868 (N.C. Ct. App. 1989); Inman v. Imperial Chrysler-Plymouth, Inc., 397 S.E.2d 774 (S.C. Ct. App. 1990). *But see* Jim Walters Home, Inc. v. Reed, 703 S.W.2d 701 (Tex. App. 1985) (both punitive and treble damages awarded); *aff'd in part, rev'd in part on other grounds*, 711 S.W.2d 617 (Tex. 1986) (evidence did not support punitive damage award).

502 Hall v. Birchfreed, 718 S.W.2d 313 (Tex. App. 1986) (must elect when submitting proposed judgment). *See also* Inman v. Imperial Chrysler-Plymouth, Inc., 397 S.E.2d 774 (S.C. Ct. App. 1990).

503 Sherrod v. Holzshuh, 274 Or. 327, 546 P.2d 470 (1976); Consolidated Texas Fin. v. Shearer, 739 S.W.2d 477 (Tex. App. 1987).

504 *See* National Consumer Law Center, Automobile Fraud § 7.10.2 (2d ed. 2003 and Supp.).

505 *See* Equitable Life Leasing Corp. v. Abbick, 243 Kan. 513, 757 P.2d 304 (1988) ($2000 statutory damages and $15,000 punitive damages); Riviera Motors Inc. v. Higbee, 45 Or. App. 545, 609 P.2d 369 (1980) ($200 statutory and $10,000 punitive damages awarded).

506 Equitable Life Leasing Corp. v. Abbick, 243 Kan. 513, 757 P.2d 304 (1988). *See also* United Laboratories v. Kuykendall, 335 N.C. 183, 437 S.E.2d 374 (1993) (UDAP attorney fees and tort punitive damages not inconsistent or duplicative); Wilkins v. Peninsula Motor Cars, Inc., 587 S.E.2d 581 (Va. 2003) (UDAP attorney fees and tort punitive damages not inconsistent or duplicative; they serve different purposes).

507 Or. Rev. Stat. § 31.735.

508 Honeywell v. Sterling Furniture Co., 310 Or. 206, 797 P.2d 1019 (1990). *But see* Ekl v. Knecht, 585 N.E.2d 156 (Ill. App. Ct. 1991) (no abuse of discretion to deny attorney fee where punitive damage award was sufficient to pay fee).

509 *See* National Consumer Law Center, Consumer Class Actions: A Practical Litigation Guide (5th ed. 2002 and Supp.).

510 Picciuto v. Dwyer, 32 Mass. App. Ct. 137, 586 N.E.2d 38 (1992).

511 Linder v. Thrifty Oil Co., 23 Cal. 4th 429, 2 P.3d 27 (2000) (class actions allow consumers to recover for modest individual damages, deter fraudulent practices, aid legitimate businesses by curtailing illegitimate competition, and avoid multiple suits); Carroll v. Cellco P'ship, 313 N.J. Super. 488, 713 A.2d 509 (1998) ("This preference for class certification applies especially for adjudication of multiple consumer-fraud claims."); Varacallo v. Massachusetts Mut. Life Ins. Co., 332 N.J. Super. 31, 752 A.2d 807 (App. Div. 2000) (courts should liberally allow UDAP class actions when individual actions would be uneconomical, as they promote efficient judicial administration, save time and money, and promote consistent decisions).

512 Section 8.6, *infra* discusses UDAP injunctions more generally.

513 The issue of standing to seek a UDAP injunction is dealt with at § 8.6.3.2, *infra*.

statute requires the plaintiff to give notice to the defendant before filing suit, a class representative may give the required prefiling notice on behalf of the entire class.[514]

Despite the advantages of a class action, an attorney should not initiate a UDAP class action lightly. Class actions demand a significant commitment of legal resources, and notice, discovery and other procedural requirements may prove costly to consumer litigants.[515] While the two parties to an individual action can often reach a quick compromise, class actions may be less prone to easy settlement. Nevertheless, once class certification has been granted, and the seller's inevitable summary judgment motion defeated, the class action may settle on favorable terms without a full trial.[516]

8.5.2 UDAP Class Action Procedures

Class action procedures are normally determined by a state's class action statute or rule, but a number of state UDAP statutes contain class action provisions that supplement or supersede the general class action rules.[517] Other UDAP statutes specifically foreclose the use of class actions to challenge UDAP violations.[518] But most UDAP statutes are silent concerning class actions, and consumer litigants can assume that state court class actions are appropriate if consistent with a state's general class action rules and precedent.[519] If a UDAP class action is in federal court (for example if there are related federal claims), then the procedure will be determined instead by Federal Rule of Civil Procedure 23 and by federal class action standards. But limitations found in the UDAP statute itself may still apply even to UDAP actions litigated in federal court.

8.5.3 UDAP Class Actions Where Individual Damage Is Minimal

One of the most important uses of a consumer class action is where individual damage is so minimal that there is no economic incentive for an individual UDAP action. Defendants argue that such actions should not proceed as class suits because individual damage is *de minimis*, but courts reject this argument because one legitimate purpose of a UDAP class action is to aggregate small claims.[520]

---

514 Baldassari v. Public Fin. Trust, 369 Mass. 33, 337 N.E.2d 701 (1975); *In re* Alford Chevrolet-Geo, 997 S.W.2d 173 (Tex. 1999); *see also* Latman v. Costa Cruise Lines, 758 So. 2d 699 (Fla. App. 2000) (named plaintiff's compliance with contractual notice requirement sufficed for class). *See generally* § 7.5.4.6, *supra*.

515 It may be possible to defer sending notice until the court decides an individual test case on the issue of liability. Fogie v. Rent-A-Center, Inc., 867 F. Supp. 1398 (D. Minn. 1993).

516 *See* National Consumer Law Center, Consumer Class Actions: A Practical Litigation Guide Ch. 11 (5th ed. 2002 and Supp.) (discussion of class action settlement terms, including the guidelines of the National Association of Consumer Advocates).

517 *See* Cal. Civ. Code §§ 1752, 1781; Conn. Gen. Stat. § 42-110g; Idaho Code § 48-608; Ind. Code Ann. § 24-5-0.5-4; Kan. Stat. Ann. § 50-634; Mass. Gen. Laws Ann. ch. 93A, § 9; Mich. Comp. Laws Ann. § 445.911; Mo. Rev. Stat. § 407.025; N.H. Rev. Stat. Ann. § 358-A:10-a; Ohio Rev. Code Ann. § 1345.09; R.I. Gen. Laws § 6-13.1-5.2; Wyo. Stat. § 40-12-108. *See also* Delahunt v. Cytodyne Technologies, 241 F. Supp. 2d 827 (S.D. Ohio 2003) (finding that proposed class action meets Ohio's requirement that practice have been determined by a rule or court decision to be a violation); Deadwyler v. Volkswagen of Am., Inc., 748 F. Supp. 1146 (W.D.N.C. 1990) (failure to submit class action complaint to attorney general grounds for dismissing UDAP class action in Alaska), *aff'd on other grounds*, 1992 U.S. App. LEXIS 14891 (4th Cir. June 25, 1992); Fletcher v. Cape Cod Gas Co., 394 Mass. 595, 477 N.E.2d 116 (1985) (in determining whether Massachusetts' UDAP statute's special class action requirements are met, court is not restricted to considering analogous factors set out in rule 23 on general class actions); Corbett v. Superior Court, 101 Cal. App. 4th 649, 125 Cal. Rptr. 2d 46 (2002).

518 *See* Ala. Code § 8-19-10 (attorney general or district attorney but not consumer may bring class action); Ga. Code Ann. § 10-1-399; La. Rev. Stat. Ann. § 51:1409(A); Miss. Code Ann. § 75-24-15; Mont. Rev. Code Ann. § 30-14-133; S.C. Code § 39-5-140; Tenn. Code § 47-18-109 (section that creates private cause of action allows consumer to bring suit individually). *See also* Landreneau v. Fleet Fin. Group, 197 F. Supp. 2d 551 (M.D. La. 2002); Durant v. ServiceMaster Co., 208 F.R.D. 228 (E.D. Mich. 2002) (Tenn. UDAP statute only allows individual actions); *In re* Microsoft Corp. Antitrust Litigation, 127 F. Supp. 2d 702 (D. Md. 2001) (South Carolina UDAP statute does not permit class actions); Cheminova Am. Corp. v. Corker, 779 So. 2d 1175 (Ala. 2000) (statutory ban on UDAP class action does not prevent certification of class on contract, warranty, and product liability claims); *Ex parte* Exxon Corp. (Lewis v. Exxon Corp.), 725 So. 2d 930 (Ala. 1998) (consumers could not circumvent Alabama's restrictions on UDAP class actions by bringing claims under New Jersey's UDAP statute); State *ex rel.* Guste v. General Motors Corp., 370 So. 2d 477 (La. 1978) (La. Rev. Stat. Ann. § 51:1409a prohibits UDAP class actions for damages, but apparently not for restitution); Morris v. Sears, Roebuck and Co., 765 So. 2d 419 (La. App. 2000) (interpreting Louisiana UDAP statute to bar private class actions for damages or restitution; only attorney general can seek restitution in class action); Burns v. Volkswagen of Am., 118 Misc. 2d 289, 460 N.Y.S.2d 410 (Sup. Ct. 1982), *aff'd*, 468 N.Y.S.2d 1017 (A.D. 4th Dept. 1983) (interpreting N.Y. Gen. Bus. Law § 349, class actions in New York authorized only for actual, not minimum or punitive damages).

519 Brooks v. Midas Int'l Corp., 47 Ill. App. 3d 266, 361 N.E.2d 815 (1977); Olive v. Graceland Sales Corp., 61 N.J. 182, 293 A.2d 658 (1972); Mahoney v. Cupp, 638 S.W.2d 257 (Tex. App. 1982) (legislature's repeal of UDAP class action means that consumers instead can use general class action provision).

520 Gilkey v. Central Clearing Co., 202 F.R.D. 515 (E.D. Mich. 2001); Arenson v. Whitehall Convalescent & Nursing Home, 164 F.R.D. 659 (N.D. Ill. 1996) (small amount at stake for each individual militates in favor of class action); Miner v. Gillette Co., 87 Ill. 2d 7, 428 N.E.2d 478 (1981), *cert. dismissed*, 459 U.S. 86 (1982); Hayna v. Arby's, 99 Ill. App. 3d 700, 425 N.E.2d 1174 (1981); Carroll v. Cellco P'ship, 313 N.J. Super. 488, 713 A.2d 509 (1998); Weinberg v. Hertz Corp., 69 N.Y.2d

The court in its discretion may not certify a class where the class is unidentifiable, where it will be difficult to award damages, and where the consequent high administrative costs in awarding damages to class members would consume the *de minimis* recoveries.[521] Courts can solve these problems, however, through the use of "fluid recovery," under which the unclaimed portion of the damages incurred by the class as a whole is applied to the benefit of the class.[522] Usually the unclaimed portion is distributed through the market in the form of reduced prices, or used to fund a project that will benefit class members.[523]

8.5.4 *Proving a UDAP Violation Is Common to the Class*

8.5.4.1 Comparison of UDAP and Fraud Class Actions

Before the enactment of UDAP statutes, few common law fraud or deceit cases were brought as class actions. Typically, the class would have to prove for each class member that the elements of common law fraud were met. Thus for each individual class member, the class would have to prove the consumer's reliance and the consumer's damage. The class action device was viewed by most courts as too cumbersome where a separate factual "trial" was thus necessary for each class member. There are obvious difficulties in getting hundreds of consumers to testify as to their reliance or damage.

UDAP statutes that prohibit deceptive, and not just fraudulent, practices radically alter this situation. In most states, deception can be proved even if the plaintiff does not prove intent,[524] knowledge,[525] actual deception as opposed to a tendency or likelihood to deceive,[526] reliance,[527] or materiality.[528] And even where reliance must be proven, where multiple plaintiffs, standing in the same shoes, are subject to a uniform deceptive practice, reliance can be inferred from the circumstances.[529] As a result, much individual proof can be avoided, particularly when liability and damages can be established by documentary evidence, e.g., advertising copy and form contracts. In fact, the differences between the minimum standards for common law fraud and deception become most apparent in the class action context.[530]

979, 509 N.E.2d 347 (1987); Roemisch v. Mutual of Omaha, 39 Ohio St. 2d 119, 314 N.E.2d 386, 390 (1975) (O'Neill, C.J., concurring); Washington v. Spitzer Mgmt., Inc., 2003 WL 1759617 (Ohio App. Apr. 3, 2003) (unpublished, citation limited); Pyles v. Johnson, 143 Ohio App. 3d 720, 758 N.E.2d 1182 (2001); Kelly v. Allegheny County, 519 Pa. 213, 546 A.2d 608 (1988).

521 Hayna v. Arby's, 99 Ill. App. 3d 700, 425 N.E.2d 1174 (1981). *But see* Weinberg v. Hertz Corp., 69 N.Y.2d 979, 509 N.E.2d 347 (1987) (class certified even though notice will be difficult).

522 Kraus v. Trinity Mgmt. Servs., Inc., 23 Cal. 4th 116, 999 P.2d 718 (2000) (fluid recovery may be ordered if class is certified); Corbett v. Superior Court, 101 Cal. App. 4th 649, 125 Cal. Rptr. 2d 46 (2002) (§ 17200 case may be certified as class action and fluid recovery ordered); Picciuto v. Dwyer, 32 Mass. App. Ct. 137, 586 N.E.2d 38 (1992).

523 Picciuto v. Dwyer, 32 Mass. App. Ct. 137, 586 N.E.2d 38 (1992). *See* National Consumer Law Center, Consumer Law Pleadings, No. 1, Ch. 12 (CD-Rom and Index Guide) for memoranda and orders on this subject. These pleadings are also found on the CD-Rom accompanying this volume.

524 *See* § 4.2.4, *supra*. If a UDAP statute does require that intent be shown, a pattern of misrepresentations may show intent without having to show the seller intended to deceive each individual class member. Dix v. American Bankers Life Assurance Co., 429 Mich. 410, 415 N.W.2d 206 (1987).

525 *See* § 4.2.5, *supra*.

526 *See* § 4.2.9, *supra*; *see also* Martin v. Dahlberg, Inc., 156 F.R.D. 207 (N.D. Cal. 1994); Eshaghi v. Hanley Dawson Cadillac Co., 214 Ill. App. 3d 995, 574 N.E.2d 760 (1991); Dix v. American Bankers Life Assurance Co., 429 Mich. 410, 415 N.W.2d 206 (1987); Weinberg v. Hertz Corp., 116 A.D.2d 1, 499 N.Y.S.2d 693 (1986) (no need to show reliance to certify class), *aff'd*, 69 N.Y. 2d 979, 509 N.E.2d 347 (1987); Shaver v. Standard Oil Co., 89 Ohio App. 3d 52, 623 N.E.2d 602 (1993); Amato v. General Motors Corp., 11 Ohio App. 3d 124, 463 N.E.2d 625 (1982).

527 *See* § 4.2.12, *supra*. *See also* Arenson v. Whitehall Convalescent & Nursing Home, 164 F.R.D. 659 (N.D. Ill. 1996) (no need to show reliance in Illinois UDAP class action); Martin v. Dahlberg, Inc., 156 F.R.D. 207 (N.D. Cal. 1994); Mass. Mut. Life Ins. Co. v. Superior Court, 97 Cal. App. 4th 1282, 119 Cal. Rptr. 2d 190 (2002); Gordon v. Boden, 586 N.E.2d 461 (Ill. App. Ct. 1991); Dix v. American Bankers Life Assurance Co., 429 Mich. 410, 415 N.W.2d 206 (1987) (no proof of individual reliance needed if reasonable person would have relied); Weinberg v. Hertz Corp., 116 A.D.2d 1, 499 N.Y.S.2d 693 (1986) (no need to show reliance to certify class); Amato v. General Motors Corp., 11 Ohio App. 3d 124, 463 N.E.2d 625 (1982). *But see* Elliot v. ITT Corp., 150 F.R.D. 569 (N.D. Ill. 1992) (magistrate's report & recommendation) (while oral representations are sufficiently common among class members, individual questions of reliance predominate over common questions of fact), *report and recommendation adopted at* 150 B.R. 36 (N.D. Ill. 1992); *In re* Woodward & Lothrop Holdings, Inc., 205 B.R. 365 (Bankr. S.D.N.Y. 1997); Prime Meats, Inc. v. Yochim, 619 A.2d 769 (Pa. Super. Ct. 1993) (proof of reliance requirement under Pennsylvania's restrictive interpretation of the relevant section of its UDAP statute defeats class certification).

528 *See* § 4.2.12, *supra*.

529 *See* §§ 4.2.12.3.6, *supra*, 8.5.4.2.1, *infra*.

530 W.S. Badcock Corp. v. Myers, 696 So. 2d 776 (Fla. Dist. Ct. App. 1996) (refusing to apply common law fraud cases to UDAP class action); Carroll v. Cellco P'ship, 313 N.J. Super. 488, 713 A.2d 509 (App. Div. 1998) (reversing class certification on fraud and negligent misrepresentation claims but remanding for further consideration of UDAP claims). *Cf.* Dix v. American Bankers Life Assurance Co., 367 N.W.2d 896 (Mich. Ct. App. 1985).

8.5.4.2 Showing a Common Deceptive Practice

8.5.4.2.1 General

The critical element to establish liability in a UDAP class action is the existence of a common deceptive practice involving each class member. The deception practiced against each different class member must not only be sufficiently alike so that there is a community of interest, but also questions common to the class must predominate.[531]

Proving damages for individual class members is not as critical. If the issues of liability are sufficiently common, courts will allow the liability issues to go forward as a class action, postponing to a later date the decision as to how the damage issues are to be treated.[532] Individual litigation as to the amount of damage can subsequently be handled through a variety of methods, such as special masters and affidavits.[533]

Proving the existence of a common deceptive scheme is not as difficult as it first appears. In many cases, media advertising, standard sales presentations, or similar methods have been used to disseminate the same deceptive message to all class members. Even where the unfair or deceptive representations are separately made to each class member, the possibility of a class action is not foreclosed as long as each class member is not required to litigate numerous and substantial issues.[534] It is enough to establish a pattern of conduct or policy by the seller.

8.5.4.2.2 Mass advertising

This pattern of conduct can be shown most easily by mass advertising read or seen by the public at large.[535] Advertising is deceptive and thus actionable under a UDAP statute even if it is subsequently clarified at the point of sale.[536] Even if class members do not focus their complaint initially on misleading advertising, investigation may reveal that an advertising campaign was directed to the class as a whole and involved deception. Thus, even if the class can not prove point-of-sale deception involving each class member, it is enough that the advertisement has a tendency or capacity to deceive consumers.

Proof of extensive advertising is sufficient to make a *prima facie* case that all class members were exposed to the deceptive advertising.[537] Proof of reliance, if required,[538] can be established by inference or presumption from circumstantial evidence without direct testimony from each class member.[539]

8.5.4.2.3 Standardized sales presentations

A pattern or policy of deception may also be shown even if sales are only made orally by different sales representatives. A single type of scheme with substantially similar sales representations is enough to make the action manageable.[540] A pattern of deception can be proven if the mis-

531 Petrolito v. Arrow Fin. Servs., 2004 WL 963962 (D. Conn. Apr. 8, 2004) (class certification allowed on whether defendant sought to collect on bad debt after original creditor had written off the debt); Heastie v. Community Bank, 125 F.R.D. 669 (N.D. Ill. 1989) (class certified based on plaintiffs' allegations of common scheme; court will reconsider if proof shows that misrepresentations were not common to all class members); Collins v. Anthem Health Plans, Inc., 266 Conn. 12, 835 A.2d 1124 (Conn. 2003) (upholding class certification of Connecticut UDAP claims concerning general practices of insurer and uniform methods of doing business that breached agreements with physicians). *See also* Elliot v. ITT Corp., 150 F.R.D. 569 (N.D. Ill. 1992) (U.S. Magistrates Report & Recommendation), *report and recommendation adopted at* 150 B.R. 36 (N.D. Ill. 1992). *See generally* National Consumer Law Center, Consumer Class Actions: A Practical Litigation Guide § 9.3 (5th ed. 2002 and Supp.).

532 Heastie v. Community Bank, 125 F.R.D. 669 (N.D. Ill. 1989) (opinion concerning class certification). *See also In re* Lutheran Brotherhood Variable Ins. Prods. Co. Sales Practices Litig., 2003 WL 21737528 (D. Minn. July 22, 2003) (individual damage issues do not prevent class certification).

533 Arenson v. Whitehall Convalescent & Nursing Home, 164 F.R.D. 659 (N.D. Ill. 1996).

534 Vasquez v. Superior Court (Karp), 4 Cal. 3d 800, 484 P.2d 964, 94 Cal. Rptr. 796 (1971). *Cf.* Elliot v. ITT Corp., 150 F.R.D. 569 (N.D. Ill. 1992) (Magistrate's Report & Recommendation) (while oral representations are sufficiently common among class members, individual questions of reliance predominate over common questions of fact), *report and recommendation adopted at* 150 B.R. 36 (N.D. Ill. 1992).

535 Miner v. Gillette Co., 87 Ill. 2d 7, 428 N.E.2d 478 (1981), *cert. dismissed*, 459 U.S. 86 (1982); Brooks v. Midas Int'l Corp., 47 Ill. App. 3d 266, 361 N.E.2d 815 (1977). *See also In re* Lutheran Brotherhood Variable Ins. Prods. Co. Sales Practices Litig., 2003 WL 21737528 (D. Minn. July 22, 2003) (upholding class certification where all plaintiffs were given similar deceptive illustrations of vanishing insurance premiums); Broder v. MBNA Corp., 722 N.Y.S.2d 524 (App. Div. 2001) (class certified where based on deceptive language in identical written credit card solicitations).

536 *See* § 4.2.17, *supra*.

537 Amato v. General Motors Corp., 11 Ohio App. 3d 124, 463 N.E.2d 625 (1982).

538 *See* § 4.2.12, *supra*.

539 *See* §§ 4.2.12.3.6, 8.5.4.1 *supra*.

540 Dix v. American Bankers Life Assurance Co., 429 Mich. 410, 415 N.W.2d 206 (1987); Varacallo v. Massachusetts Mut. Life Ins. Co., 332 N.J. Super. 31, 752 A.2d 807 (App. Div. 2000) (vanishing life insurance premium case); Pyles v. Johnson, 143 Ohio App. 3d 720, 758 N.E.2d 1182 (2001) (affirming certification of class on fraud and UDAP claims). *Cf.* Stephenson v. Bell Atlantic Corp., 177 F.R.D. 279 (D.N.J. 1997) (similarity of oral representations not shown). *But see* Szczubelek v. Cendant Mortg. Corp., 215 F.R.D. 107 (D.N.J. 2003) (denying class certification where claim was based on individualized oral statements); Gaidon v. Guardian Life Ins. Co., 2 A.D.3d 130, 767 N.Y.S.2d 599 (2003) (oral representations would require individualized proof). *But cf.* Markarian v. Conn. Mut. Life Ins. Co., 202 F.R.D. 60 (D. Mass. 2001) (existence of oral representations, not just omissions, by agents who were not uniformly trained and did not follow a script, makes vanishing premium case non-certifiable).

leading sales presentations were standard statements pursuant to the company's sales plan or learned by sales representatives through company training or other sales manuals.[541]

Thus, in class actions involving sophisticated sales presentations or high-pressure sales by commissioned sales representatives, consumer litigants should seek to discover all company sales manuals, training materials, directives, and instructions. Even if edited to meet regulatory scrutiny, these materials will often include clear-cut UDAP violations. If the standard sales presentation was kept only in an unwritten form, former employees may be able to testify to its content.

Companies guilty of abusing consumers often take advantage of their commissioned sales representatives as well. These disgruntled employees, particularly supervisors, make excellent witnesses. Lists of former employees can be obtained through discovery. In addition, former commissioned sales representatives may have initiated lawsuits to recover back commissions, and court records will reveal their identities.

8.5.4.2.4 Common problems with the product itself

A common pattern of deception can also be established if all class members purchased a similar product or service and if the UDAP violation involves not just product representations, but the nature of the product itself. Price unconscionability[542] or a product's inability to perform its normal function are defects common to all class members. Thus, a class allegation that General Motors placed Chevrolet engines in a large number of Oldsmobiles was allowed to continue as a class action.[543]

8.5.4.2.5 Common excess charges

Standardized overcharges can provide a basis for class certification. For example, where official fees or taxes are a specified amount, a seller accepting more than that amount from consumers to pay for those charges engages in a common UDAP violation, even if the sales presentations are different and even if the amount of the overcharge varies with the consumer.[544]

8.5.4.2.6 Standard form contract provisions

Unfair or deceptive standard form contract provisions and standard disclosures are ideal for class treatment.[545] It is easily proven that all class members signed the same standard form contract or were given the same written warranty. The class need only show that the contract or other document is unfair or deceptive on its face to establish liability.[546]

8.5.4.2.7 Standardized billing and collection practices

A company's uniform practice of billing consumers for an illegal[547] or deceptively disclosed[548] charge is well-suited for a class action. If the court finds that reliance is an element, it may be willing to presume reliance for consumers who paid the fee after receiving the bill.[549]

---

541 Vasquez v. Superior Court (Karp), 4 Cal. 3d 800, 484 P.2d 964, 94 Cal. Rptr. 796 (1971); Budget Fin. Plan v. Superior Court (McDonnell), 34 Cal. App. 3d 794, 110 Cal. Rptr. 302 (1973); Kugler v. Koscot Interplanetary, Inc., 120 N.J. Super. 216, 293 A.2d 682 (Ch. Div. 1972).

542 Vasquez v. Superior Court (Karp), 4 Cal. 3d 800, 484 P.2d 964, 94 Cal. Rptr. 796 (1971); Kugler v. Romain, 58 N.J. 522, 279 A.2d 640 (1971).

543 State *ex rel.* Guste v. General Motors Corp., 370 So. 2d 477 (La. 1978) (attorney general allowed to prosecute class action). *See also* Cheminova Am. Corp. v. Corker, 779 So. 2d 1175 (Ala. 2000) (class certified on contract, warranty, and product liability claims where product did not conform to standardized representations).

544 *See* Fielder v. Credit Acceptance Corp., 175 F.R.D. 313 (W.D. Mo. 1997), *rev'd in part on other grounds*, 188 F.3d 1031 (8th Cir. 1999); Duffy v. Jerry's Chevrolet, Inc., Clearinghouse No. 54,555 (Md. Cir. Ct. Aug. 27, 2001) (common issues where class members were all charged same charge, even though sales were separately negotiated); *In re* Coordinated Title Ins. Cases, 2004 WL 690380 (N.Y. Sup. Ct. Jan. 8, 2004). *See also* Violette v. P.A. Days, Inc., 214 F.R.D. 207 (S.D. Ohio 2003) (interest overcharges and charges for vehicle window etching); Washington v. Spitzer Mgmt., Inc., 2003 WL 1759617 (Ohio App. Apr. 3, 2003) (unpublished, citation limited) (inclusion of "dealer overhead" charge in preprinted form contracts).

545 Heastie v. Community Bank, 125 F.R.D. 669 (N.D. Ill. 1989) (opinion concerning class certification); Vasquez v. Superior Court (Karp), 4 Cal. 3d 800, 484 P.2d 964, 94 Cal. Rptr. 796 (1977); McGhee v. Bank of Am. Nat'l Trust & Savings Ass'n, 60 Cal. App. 3d 442, 131 Cal. Rptr. 482 (1976). *See also* National Consumer Law Center, Consumer Class Actions: A Practical Litigation Guide § 9.3.4.1 (5th ed. 2002 and Supp.).

546 Shields v. Lefta, Inc., 888 F. Supp. 891 (N.D. Ill. 1995) (class certified on claim that standard contract falsely represented that cost disclosed for extended warranty was actually paid to warranty company). *See also* § 5.2.3, *supra*.

547 P.J.'s Concrete Pumping Serv., Inc. v. Nextel West Corp., 803 N.E.2d 1020 (Ill. App. 2004); Kidd v. Delta Funding Corp., 2000 N.Y. Misc. LEXIS 378 (Sup. Ct. Sept. 18, 2000) (illegal loan processing fee), *aff'd*, 734 N.Y.S.2d 848 (A.D. 2001); Dwyer v. J. I. Kislak Mortgage Corp., 103 Wash. App. 542, 13 P.3d 240 (2000) (reversing dismissal of class action where lender included fee in payoff statement that could not legally be required as a condition of release of mortgage).

548 Latman v. Costa Cruise Lines, N.V., 758 So. 2d 699 (Fla. App. 2000) (cruise line falsely portrayed port charges as pass-through charges); Pickett v. Holland Am. Line—Westours, Inc., 101 Wash. App. 901, 6 P.3d 63 (2000) (same), *rev'd on other grounds*, 35 P.3d 351 (Wash. 2001) (in appeal of fairness of settlement, court of appeals should not have addressed merits of trial court's denial of class certification).

549 Latman v. Costa Cruise Lines, N.V., 758 So. 2d 699 (Fla. App. 2000); Pickett v. Holland Am. Line—Westours, Inc., 101 Wash.

Companies often use standard debt-collection procedures for a given class of customers, making class actions particularly appropriate.[550] Standard first and second notices may be sent. The same "lawyer's letter" may be used. Telephone collection activities may follow a standard script. A company may routinely sue all debtors in an inconvenient forum, establishing an unfair or deceptive practice common to the class.[551]

8.5.4.2.8 Common failure to disclose a material fact

A common pattern of conduct can also be shown by a seller's consistent failure to disclose a material fact.[552] Failure to disclose a material fact is a clear UDAP violation,[553] and it is often easier to show that a seller did not disclose specific information than it is to show that the seller consistently made the same affirmative misrepresentations to all members of a class. In most states, the class will not have to prove that individual class members were actually deceived[554] or actually relied on the incomplete representations.[555] All that need be shown is that the material omissions had a capacity to deceive.[556]

8.5.4.2.9 Do class issues predominate?

A related question is whether questions common to the class predominate over questions that affect only individual class members.[557] In states adopting the federal class action rule, this question is relevant only to class actions that primarily seek money damages. Careful drafting of the complaint and the prayer for relief may help avoid problems with this requirement. Where a class action primarily seeks equitable or injunctive relief, certification under the less stringent requirements of Rule 23(b)(2) may be granted even though the suit also seeks money damages.[558]

When arguing that a class has sufficient community of interest that questions common to the class predominate, and that the lawsuit should proceed as a class action, litigants should remember the legislative intent in enacting UDAP statutes. UDAP statutes attempt to provide consumers with a flexible and practical cause of action to remedy marketplace injustice, to deter future violations, and to return ill-gotten gains. Where a class action is the only effective means to satisfy the legislative intent, class action requirements should be liberally construed.[559] Particularly where a UDAP statute authorizes class actions, this should be taken as a legislative intent to liberally construe UDAP statutes to allow class actions to proceed.[560]

Thus, a court has allowed a class action to proceed where there was no evidence of individual class members being deceived, because the UDAP statute armed the trial court with "the cleansing power to order restitution to effect complete justice."[561] Similarly, a court has ruled that a UDAP class action does not have to produce evidence that each class member was exposed to the challenged advertising where there is proof the advertising was extensive.[562] Proof of reliance can be established by inference or presumption from circumstantial evidence without direct testimony from each class member,[563] both as to affirmative

App. 901, 6 P.3d 63 (2000) (same), *rev'd on other grounds*, 35 P.3d 351 (Wash. 2001) (in appeal of fairness of settlement, court of appeals should not have addressed merits of trial court's denial of class certification). *See also* Chisolm v. Transouth Fin. Corp., 194 F.R.D. 538 (E.D. Va. 2000) (reliance can be proven in RICO claim by consumers' payment of bill).

550 Baldassari v. Public Fin. Trust, 369 Mass. 33, 337 N.E.2d 701 (1975).

551 Zanni v. Lippold, 119 F.R.D. 32 (C.D. Ill. 1988); Santiago v. S.S. Kresge Co., 2 Ohio Op. 3d 54 (C.P. Cuyahoga Cty. 1976).

552 Heastie v. Community Bank, 125 F.R.D. 669 (N.D. Ill. 1989) (opinion concerning class certification); Fletcher v. Security Pacific Nat'l Bank, 23 Cal. 3d 442, 591 P.2d 51, 153 Cal. Rptr. 28 (1979) (bank's failure to disclose interest information); Mass. Mut. Life Ins. Co. v. Superior Court, 97 Cal. App. 4th 1282, 119 Cal. Rptr. 2d 190 (2002); Strawn v. Canuso, 140 N.J. 43, 657 A.2d 420 (1995) (failure to disclose existence of landfill near homes that were being sold); *see also* Elliot v. ITT Corp., 150 F.R.D. 569 (N.D. Ill. 1992) (U.S. Magistrate's Report & Recommendation), *report and recommendation adopted at* 150 B.R. 36 (N.D. Ill. 1992); Leibert v. Finance Factors Ltd., 788 P.2d 833 (Haw. 1990).

553 *See* § 4.2.14, *supra.*

554 *See* § 4.2.9, *supra.*

555 *See* § 4.2.12, *supra.*

556 *See* Fletcher v. Security Pacific Nat'l Bank, 23 Cal. 3d 442, 591 P.2d 51, 153 Cal. Rptr. 28 (1979).

557 Elder v. Coronet Ins. Co., 201 Ill. App. 3d 733, 558 N.E.2d 1312 (1990). *See generally* § National Consumer Law Center, Consumer Class Actions: A Practical Litigation Guide § 9.3 (5th ed. 2002 and Supp.).

558 Warehouse Home Furnishing Distributors, Inc. v. Whitson, 709 So. 2d 1144 (Ala. 1997). *See generally* National Consumer Law Center, Consumer Class Actions: A Practical Litigation Guide § 9.8 (5th ed. 2002 and Supp.).

559 Gilkey v. Central Clearing Co., 202 F.R.D. 515 (E.D. Mich. 2001).

560 Dix v. American Bankers Life Assurance Co., 429 Mich. 410, 415 N.W.2d 206 (1987).

561 Fletcher v. Security Pacific Nat'l Bank, 23 Cal. 3d. 442, 591 P.2d 51, 153 Cal. Rptr. 28, 32 (1979). *Accord* Perolito v. Arrow Fin. Servs., 2004 WL 963962 (D. Conn. Apr. 8, 2004) (whether or not the plaintiff paid and suffered actual damages does not affect his typicality as a class representative against illegal debt collection efforts); Eshaghi v. Hanley Dawson Cadillac Co., 214 Ill. App. 3d 995, 574 N.E.2d 760 (1991).

562 Amato v. General Motors Corp., 11 Ohio App. 3d 124, 463 N.E.2d 625 (1982).

563 *In re* Lutheran Brotherhood Variable Ins. Prods. Co. Sales Practices Litig., 2003 WL 21737528 (D. Minn. July 22, 2003) (vanishing insurance premium case; defendant's memos showing that it knew consumers were relying on the misrepresentations is sufficient to withstand summary judgment); Chisolm v. Transouth Fin. Corp., 194 F.R.D. 538 (E.D. Va. 2000) (reliance can be proven in RICO claim by consumers' payment of bill); Arenson v. Whitehall Convalescent & Nursing Home, 164 F.R.D. 659 (N.D. Ill. 1996) (no need to show reliance in Illinois UDAP class action); Sikes v. American Tel. & Tel. Co., Clearinghouse No. 50,437 (S.D. Ga. May 13, 1994) (reliance on promotional materials may be presumed where there was no

misrepresentations and as to material omissions.[564] Indeed, there is substantial authority that reliance is not required for a UDAP claim.[565]

Sellers may oppose a UDAP class certification motion for another reason. In states where only "consumers" can bring UDAP actions or where the sale must be a "consumer" transaction, the burden may be on the UDAP plaintiff to allege and prove that this requirement is met.[566] Since this issue may require an individual offer of proof as to whether a transaction was entered into for personal, family, or household use, sellers may argue that this individual proof requirement destroys the predominance of common questions of fact or law. Where the defendant's business was consumer sales, namely low-end used car sales, one court dismissed this objection as a makeweight.[567]

other way to learn of product); Latman v. Costa Cruise Lines, N.V., 758 So. 2d 699 (Fla. App. 2000) (it is sufficient to show that a reasonable person would have relied on the representation); Mass. Mut. Life Ins. Co. v. Superior Court, 97 Cal. App. 4th 1282, 119 Cal. Rptr. 2d 190 (2002); Duffy v. Jerry's Chevrolet, Inc., Clearinghouse No. 54,555 (Md. Cir. Ct. Aug. 27, 2001); Dix v. American Bankers Life Assurance Co., 429 Mich. 410, 415 N.W.2d 206 (1987); Varacallo v. Massachusetts Mut. Life Ins. Co., 332 N.J. Super. 31, 752 A.2d 807 (App. Div. 2000) (proof of causal nexus is sufficient for UDAP claims; reliance can be presumed for fraud claims); Washington v. Spitzer Mgmt., Inc., 2003 WL 1759617 (Ohio App. Apr. 3, 2003) (unpublished, citation limited); Amato v. General Motors Corp., 11 Ohio App. 3d 124, 463 N.E.2d 625 (1982); Pickett v. Holland Am. Line—Westours, Inc., 101 Wash. App. 901, 6 P.3d 63 (2000) (reliance can be shown by fact that class member parted with money to pay a deceptive charge), *rev'd on other grounds*, 35 P.3d 351 (Wash. 2001) (in appeal of fairness of settlement, court of appeals should not have addressed merits of trial court's denial of class certification). *See* § 4.2.12, *supra*. *But see* Stephenson v. Bell Atlantic Corp., 177 F.R.D. 279 (D.N.J. 1997) (individual proof of reliance defeats class certification); Buford v. H&R Block, 168 F.R.D. 340 (S.D. Ga. 1996) (finding that individual reliance issues predominated over class-wide issues); Elliot v. ITT Corp., 150 F.R.D. 569 (N.D. Ill. 1992) (U.S. Magistrate's Report & Recommendation), *report and recommendation adopted at* 150 B.R. 36 (N.D. Ill. 1992) (where written disclosure varies from oral representations, individual questions of consumer reliance on the oral claims prevent common questions from predominating); Gross v. Johnson & Johnson-Merck Consumer Pharmaceuticals Co., 303 N.J. Super. 336, 696 A.2d 793 (1997) (class action not allowed because causal connection between television advertisements, purchase, and loss required individual proof).

564 *In re* Great Southern Life Ins. Co. Sales Practices Litigation, 192 F.R.D. 212 (N.D. Tex. 2000).

565 *See* Wells v. Allstate Ins. Co., 210 F.R.D. 1 (D.D.C. 2002) (certifying class; no reliance required where defendants failed to disclose material facts); Varacallo v. Massachusetts Mut. Life Ins. Co., 332 N.J. Super. 31, 752 A.2d 807 (App. Div. 2000) (vanishing life insurance premium class action; proof of causal nexus is sufficient); Kidd v. Delta Fin. Corp., 2000 N.Y. Misc. LEXIS 378 (Sup. Ct. Sept. 18, 2000) (class action), *aff'd*, 734 N.Y.S.2d 848 (A.D. 2001). *See generally* § 4.2.12, *infra*.

566 *See* § 2.1.2, *supra*.

567 Chisolm v. TranSouth Fin. Corp., 194 F.R.D. 538, 567 (E.D. Va. 2000).

Since in most cases the majority of class members will be "consumers," the issue of whether a particular class member is a "consumer" is really an issue of distribution of damages *after* liability is determined. An order can easily be drafted providing UDAP relief to all class members found at a later hearing to be consumers. The law is clear that a class can proceed if common questions of law or fact predominate, even if the distribution of damages requires adjudication of individual issues of fact. It may also be possible to ascertain the consumer nature of the transaction from the documentation.[568]

In some class actions for damages, individual proof of such issues as causation, reliance and damages is unavoidable, but this should still not prevent class certification if the plaintiffs all seek to redress a common legal grievance.[569] A class action can also proceed even though individual class members may be differently affected by defenses such as laches, good faith, *res judicata*, or exhaustion of contract remedies.[570] Usually courts will also certify a class even if the defendant claims it has compulsory counterclaims it will have to raise against individual class members—such counterclaims are rarely compulsory.[571]

568 *See, e.g.*, Haynes v. Logan Furniture Mart, 503 F.2d 1161, 1165 n.4 (7th Cir. 1974) (TIL case). *See generally* National Consumer Law Center, Consumer Class Actions: A Practical Litigation Guide § 9.3.4.3 (5th ed. 2002 and Supp.).

569 Wells v. Allstate Ins. Co., 210 F.R.D. 1 (D.D.C. 2002) (certifying class; no reliance required where defendants failed to disclose material facts); Marr v. WMX Technologies, Inc., 244 Conn. 676, 711 A.2d 700 (1998) (class certification of UDAP suit against landfill not defeated by need to prove damages individually); Clark v. TAP Pharmaceuticals, Inc., 343 Ill. App. 3d 538, 798 N.E.2d 123 (2003); Strawn v. Canuso, 638 A.2d 141 (N.J. Super. 1994) (class action certified for damages for failure to disclose existence of nearby landfill to buyers of homes), *aff'd*, 657 A.2d 420 (N.J. 1995); *In re* W. Va. Rezulin Litig., 585 S.E.2d 52 (W. Va. 2003) (individual damage issues do not prevent certification). *See also* Gilkey v. Central Clearing Co., 202 F.R.D. 515 (E.D. Mich. 2001) (adopting simpler measure of damages that does not require individual determinations). *See generally* National Consumer Law Center, Consumer Class Actions: A Practical Litigation Guide §§ 9.3.4.2, 9.3.5 (5th ed. 2002 and Supp.). *But see* Lester v. Percudani, 217 F.R.D. 345 (M.D. Pa. Sept. 2003) (denying class certification where complicated fact pattern required individual proof of causation and fact of injury); Gross v. Johnson & Johnson-Merck Consumer Pharmaceuticals Co., 303 N.J. Super. 336, 696 A.2d 793 (1997) (need to prove that false advertisements caused loss defeats class certification).

570 Mass. Mut. Life Ins. Co. v. Superior Court, 97 Cal. App. 4th 1282, 119 Cal. Rptr. 2d 190 (2002) (individual statute of limitations issues do not prevent class certification); Eshaghi v. Hanley Dawson Cadillac Co., 214 Ill. App. 3d 995, 574 N.E.2d 760 (1991).

571 *See* Fielder v. Credit Acceptance Corp., 175 F.R.D. 313 (W.D. Mo. 1997), *vacated in part on other grounds*, 188 F.3d 1031 (8th Cir. 1999). *See also* Gilkey v. Central Clearing Co., 202 F.R.D. 515 (E.D. Mich. 2001) (presence of potential counterclaims does not defeat certification).

8.5.4.2.10 Is the class action superior?

Another requirement of Rule 23(b)(3) is that the class action be superior to other available methods for the fair and efficient adjudication of the controversy.[572] The fact that in some states treble damages are available only in individual actions does not defeat this requirement.[573] Since the class action mechanism allows small individual claims to be aggregated into a single larger claim, there is greater incentive to prosecute, so class members may be willing to accept the lower recovery. Moreover, they are free to opt out of the class and prosecute their claims individually.

8.5.5 Multi-State Class Actions

The starting point for analysis of multi-state class actions is *Phillips Petroleum Co. v. Shutts*.[574] That decision dealt with two issues: (1) whether a state court could constitutionally exercise jurisdiction over non-resident class members who did not have significant contacts with the forum state; and (2) in what circumstances the forum state could apply its law to non-resident class members.

On the jurisdictional question, the Supreme Court held that a forum state may exercise jurisdiction over the claims of absent class members even though they may not possess the minimum contacts with the forum state which would support personal jurisdiction over a defendant. Due process allows absent non-resident class members to be bound by a decision regarding a claim for money damages or similar relief as long as they are given notice, an opportunity to be heard and participate in the litigation, and an opportunity to opt out.

On the choice-of-law question, a class action plaintiff has the choice between arguing that the forum state's UDAP statute applies to all class members, or trying to apply each state's UDAP statute to its own residents. *Shutts* holds that the forum state's law may be applied to non-residents if it does not conflict in a material way with the other states' laws.[575] If there is a conflict, the forum state can apply its own law to non-residents only if it has a significant contact or significant aggregation of contacts to the claims asserted by each non-resident.[576] In *Shutts*, the fact that the defendant owned property and conducted substantial business in the forum state was not enough to allow the forum state's law to be applied to non-residents' claims.[577]

Since *Shutts*, courts in a number of states have approved UDAP class actions that applied the law of the forum state.[578] A California court has allowed its law to be applied in a nationwide class action where the defendant was located in California, prepared deceptive sales literature there, and disseminated it to other states from California.[579] In another case, the seller's form contract specified that it would be governed by Washington law, thus removing this impediment to class certification.[580]

Even when jurisdiction beyond the state borders is constitutionally permissible, the state's conflict-of-laws rules

---

572 *See* National Consumer Law Center, Consumer Class Actions: A Practical Litigation Guide § 9.9 (5th ed. 2002 and Supp.).

573 Pyles v. Johnson, 143 Ohio App. 3d 720, 758 N.E.2d 1182 (2001).

574 472 U.S. 797, 105 S. Ct. 2965, 86 L. Ed. 2d 628 (1985).

575 Phillips Petroleum Co. v. Shutts, 472 U.S. 797, 816, 105 S. Ct. 2965, 2976, 86 L. Ed. 2d 628 (1985).

576 *Id.*, 472 U.S. 797, 821, 105 S. Ct. 2965, 2979, 86 L. Ed. 2d 628 (1985). *See also* Montgomery v. New Piper Aircraft, 209 F.R.D. 221 (S.D. Fla. 2002) (finding insufficient contacts with forum state).

577 *See* § 7.6.3, *supra*. *See also* Norwest Mortgage, Inc. v. Superior Court, 72 Cal. App. 4th 214, 85 Cal. Rptr. 2d 18 (1999) (fact that defendant is incorporated in California and does business there gives California court personal jurisdiction over it but is insufficient to allow California law to be applied to nationwide class of customers).

578 *See, e.g.*, *In re* Lutheran Brotherhood Variable Ins. Prods. Co. Sales Practices Litig., 2003 WL 21737528 (D. Minn. July 22, 2003) (suit against in-state defendant); *In re* St. Jude Medical, Inc., Silzone Heart Valves Prods. Liability Litig., 2003 WL 1589527 (D. Minn. Mar. 27, 2003) (suit against in-state defendant); Martin v. Heinhold Commodities, Inc., 117 Ill. 2d 67, 510 N.E.2d 840 (1987); Clark v. TAP Pharmaceutical Prods., Inc., 343 Ill. App. 3d 538, 798 N.E.2d 123 (2003) (deceptive conduct that led to class members' injuries occurred at corporate headquarters in forum state). *See also* Weinberg v. Sun Co., 740 A.2d 1152 (Pa. Super. 1999) (concluding that state civil rules allow nationwide class actions), *rev'd on other grounds*, 777 A.2d 442 (Pa. 2001) (commonality not shown where individual reliance issues would predominate). *See generally* National Consumer Law Center, Consumer Class Actions: A Practical Litigation Guide § 3.6.2 (5th ed. 2002 and Supp.). *But see* Hutson v. Rexall Sundown, Inc., 837 So. 2d 1090 (Fla. Dist. Ct. App. 2003) (refusing to apply Florida law to nationwide sale of products with misleading label and point-of-sale advertising); Fink v. Ricoh Corp., 365 N.J. Super. 520, 839 A.2d 942 (Law. Div. 2003) (refusing to apply New Jersey law to a nationwide class of camera buyers). *But cf.* Miller v. Gen. Motors Corp., 2003 WL 168626 (N.D. Ill. Jan. 26, 2003) (declining to apply Illinois UDAP statute to residents of other states without state-by-state analysis of conflict with Illinois law).

579 Clothesrigger, Inc. v. GTE Corp., 191 Cal. App. 3d 605, 236 Cal. Rptr. 605 (1987). *Accord* Wershba v. Apple Computer, Inc., 91 Cal. App. 4th 224, 110 Cal. Rptr. 2d 145 (2001) (defendant had headquarters in state and some of the deceptive practices emanated from there). *See also* Rosen v. Fidelity Fixed Income Trust, 169 F.R.D. 295 (E.D. Pa. 1995) (court will apply Pennsylvania UDAP statute to nationwide class if that statute does not conflict with other states' laws or if Pennsylvania has sufficient contacts with non-resident class members' claims to meet *Shutts* test); Clark v. TAP Pharmaceuticals, Inc., 343 Ill. App. 3d 538, 798 N.E.2d 123 (2003) (affirming nationwide class where deception was initiated from defendant's in-state headquarters).

580 Pickett v. Holland Am. Line—Westours, Inc., 101 Wash. App. 901, 6 P.3d 63 (2000), *rev'd on other grounds*, 35 P.3d 351 (Wash. 2001) (in appeal of fairness of settlement, court of appeals should not have addressed merits of trial court's denial of class certification).

may not allow it.[581] Or the state UDAP statute may only apply to practices within the state or residents of the state.[582] This type of restriction has been interpreted to preclude a nationwide class action.[583] It also precluded a class action by out-of-state residents whose only in-state injury was that payments under an allegedly deceptive lease were sent to corporate headquarters in the state.[584]

Substantial problems can arise in nationwide class actions if the court uses each state's UDAP statute because of the variations among state statutes as to statute of limitations, notice requirements, special preconditions to class actions, private remedies, and the like.[585] Nonetheless, courts have certified class actions that have required the court to apply the UDAP laws of all fifty states. For example, the Illinois Supreme Court held that a trial court erred in denying certification of a nationwide class action against a company that had reneged on a free offer in a sales promotion.[586] Even though the laws of all fifty states might have to be considered, common questions would still predominate if those laws could be grouped into manageable subclasses.[587]

Attorneys must carefully review each state UDAP statute they wish to rely on in a multi-state class action.[588] In some states, prevailing sellers can be awarded attorney fees,[589] so that the class may have to pay attorney fees where a UDAP claim fails in one state for technical reasons even when the class generally prevails on the merits. Similarly, the attorney for the class may be held liable for Rule 11-type sanctions for bringing a nationwide class action where the claim of a sub-class is based on a clearly inapplicable statute.[590]

8.5.6 "Picking Off" Named Plaintiffs

A seller may try to "pick off" named plaintiffs in a UDAP class action by remedying their individual injuries, thereby arguably disqualify the individual from pursuing a UDAP class action because of the lack of personal damage.[591] The California Supreme Court interpreted the notice letter provision of one of its UDAP statutes to allow a merchant to respond to a classwide demand for relief (thus avoiding liability under the UDAP statute) only by remedying the alleged abuse classwide. Providing relief only for the named plaintiff is an inadequate response. The named plaintiff can pursue a UDAP class action even if he or she no longer meets the UDAP statute's damage precondition, as long as the named plaintiff continues to fairly and adequately protect the class.[592] The Texas Supreme Court has also held that if the named plaintiff properly gives notice on behalf of the entire class, the defendant can not moot the case by tendering only the damages of the named plaintiff.[593]

8.5.7 Statutory Damages for Each Class Member

A potent aspect of a UDAP class action is the possibility of minimum statutory damages for each class member in cases of minimal individual injury. This, of course, is only an issue in states whose UDAP statutes authorize minimum statutory damages.[594]

The Massachusetts Supreme Judicial Court has determined that statutory minimum damages under its UDAP statute should be awarded to each class member, and not just once to the class as a whole.[595] But the New York UDAP statute explicitly limits statutory damages to individual, not

581 Washington Mut. Bank v. Superior Court, 24 Cal. 4th 906, 15 P.3d 1071, 103 Cal. Rptr. 2d 320 (2001) (trial court must analyze contractual choice of law clause and California conflict of laws rules before determining whether class can be certified).

582 *See* §§ 2.3.12, 2.4.4 *supra*.

583 Durant v. Servicemaster Co., 208 F.R.D. 228 (E.D. Mich. 2002).

584 Highsmith v. Chrysler Credit Corp., 150 B.R. 997 (N.D. Ill. 1993), *aff'd in part and rev'd in part on other grounds*, 18 F.3d 434 (7th Cir. 1994).

585 Andrews v. American Tel. & Tel. Co., 95 F.3d 1014 (11th Cir. 1996) (certification of nationwide class denied where court might have to consider each state's gambling laws); Lilly v. Ford Motor Co., 2002 U.S. Dist. LEXIS 5698 (N.D. Ill. Apr. 2, 2002) (differences among UDAP statutes too great); Montgomery v. New Piper Aircraft, 209 F.R.D. 221 (S.D. Fla. 2002); *In re* Ford Motor Co. Ignition Switch Products Liability Litigation, 194 F.R.D. 484 (D.N.J. 2000) (certification denied despite attempt to narrow differences by using subclasses); Rosen v. Fidelity Fixed Income Trust, 169 F.R.D. 295 (E.D. Pa. 1995) (noting that if each state's law must be applied, a number of subclasses may be necessary, which may or may not be practical enough to permit class treatment); *Ex parte* Exxon Corp. (Lewis v. Exxon Corp.), 725 So. 2d 930 (Ala. 1998) (decertifying nationwide UDAP class; court disagrees with lower court's view that one state's law might apply to entire class); Fink v. Ricoh Corp., 365 N.J. Super. 520, 839 A.2d 942 (Law. Div. 2003) (declining to certify class where UDAP laws of all 50 states would have to be applied).

586 Miner v. Gillette Co., 87 Ill. 2d 7, 428 N.E.2d 478 (1981).

587 *See also* Elliot v. ITT Corp., 150 F.R.D. 569 (N.D. Ill. 1992) (U.S. Magistrate's Report & Recommendation), *report and recommendation adopted at* 150 B.R. 36 (N.D. Ill. 1992); Washington Mut. Bank v. Superior Court, 24 Cal. 4th 906, 15 P.3d 1071, 103 Cal. Rptr. 2d 320 (2001); Carroll v. Cellco P'ship, 313 N.J. Super. 488, 713 A.2d 509 (1998) (discussing New Jersey cases on multi-state class actions).

588 *See* Appx. A, *infra*.

589 *See* § 8.8.10, *infra*.

590 *Cf.* Deadwyler v. Volkswagen of Am., Inc., 134 F.R.D. 128 (W.D.N.C. 1991) (Rule 11 sanctions considered but not awarded for failed UDAP claims in multi-state class action claims), *aff'd on other grounds*, 1992 U.S. App. LEXIS 14891 (4th Cir. June 25, 1992).

591 Kagan v. Gibralter Sav. & Loan Ass'n, 676 P.2d 1060, 200 Cal. Rptr. 38 (1984).

592 *Id.*

593 *In re* Alford Chevrolet-Geo, 997 S.W.2d 173 (Tex. 1999). *See also* National Consumer Law Center, Consumer Class Actions: A Practical Litigation Guide § 6.3 (5th ed. 2002 and Supp.).

594 *See* § 8.4.1, *supra*.

595 Leardi v. Brown, 394 Mass. 151, 474 N.E.2d 1094 (1985).

class actions.[596] The class can waive its right to minimum or multiple damages, and still bring a UDAP class action in New York for actual damages.[597]

8.5.8 Settlements

Class action settlements will be subject to appellate court review to determine whether the settlement is fair, adequate, and reasonable to the class. Where it is not, the settlement will be rejected.[598]

8.5.9 Arbitration and Class Actions

Increasingly, merchants and creditors are including arbitration clauses in their consumer agreements, in large part to avoid exposure to class actions. Another NCLC manual, *Consumer Arbitration Agreements* (4th ed. 2004), examines three intertwined issues:

- Whether there are grounds to find the arbitration requirement unenforceable on grounds unrelated to the class action procedure;
- If not, whether the consumer can bring a class action in an arbitration proceeding; and
- If not, whether it is then unconscionable or against public policy to force a UDAP class action into a series of individual arbitrations.

As to the third issue, one factor the court will consider is whether the UDAP statute provides for a class action as a substantive right under the statute. Then the arbitration clause's waiver of a substantive statutory right is more likely to be viewed as unconscionable.[599]

596 Burns v. Volkswagen of Am., 118 Misc. 2d 289, 460 N.Y.S.2d 410 (Sup. Ct. 1982) (interpreting N.Y. Gen. Bus. Law § 349, class actions in New York authorized only for actual, not minimum or punitive damages), *aff'd*, 468 N.Y.S.2d 1017 (A.D. 4th Dept. 1983).

597 Weinberg v. Hertz Corp., 69 N.Y.2d 979, 509 N.E.2d 347, 516 N.Y.S.2d 652 (1987); Super Glue Corp. v. Avis Rent-a-Car Sys., Inc., 132 A.D.2d 604, 517 N.Y.S.2d 764 (1987).

598 *In re* General Motors Corp. Pick-Up Truck Fuel Tank Products Liability Litigation, 55 F.3d 768 (3d Cir. 1995); Bloyed v. GMC, 916 S.W.2d 949 (Tex. 1996). *See generally* National Consumer Law Center, Consumer Class Actions: A Practical Litigation Guide Ch. 11 (5th ed. 2002 and Supp.).

599 *See* National Consumer Law Center, Consumer Arbitration Agreements § 4.3.6 (4th ed. 2004).

8.6 Injunctions and Other Equitable Relief

8.6.1 Advantages of the Injunctive Remedy

One of the potentially most effective UDAP remedies against widespread marketplace misconduct is for a private individual to seek a court-ordered injunction preventing the seller from engaging in specified conduct in the future. A merchant may treat occasional damage awards, even if trebled or increased with punitive damages, as an acceptable cost of business, not deterring future misconduct. But a properly framed and monitored injunction can eliminate the seller's use of the challenged practice against all future customers. Many merchants will comply with court-ordered injunctions, and judges will deal harshly with those challenging the court's authority. A judge will be far more strict with a seller who violates the court's own order than with a company that just deceives consumers.

Consumer litigants can also seek temporary restraining orders or preliminary injunctions to halt deceptive practices. A consumer who quickly goes to court seeking such preliminary relief will put sellers on the defensive, expedite the case, obtain early discovery, and provide consumers with other tactical advantages. The ability of a wronged consumer to go into court immediately and seek a preliminary injunction offers consumers a powerful weapon when dealing with unscrupulous merchants or defendants with minimal resources.

While an injunction can be an effective remedy, it need not be an onerous one. It does not penalize a business for its misconduct, but solely orders the seller not to repeat the practice, putting the company on clear notice of specifically defined prohibited practices. In theory, judges should enjoin future conduct even if they are unwilling to order a company to pay for past conduct that was not clearly deceptive.

In every state, the state attorney general or similar state official can seek to enjoin UDAP violations. However, these state officials have limited resources and their own priorities. Attorney general offices must also make priority decisions regarding when to follow up to determine if a seller is complying with an injunctive order. Private litigants not wishing to be bound by state attorney general priority decisions find it useful to act as a "private attorneys general," bringing their own injunctive actions and monitoring the seller's compliance with the court order themselves. This section will explore the question of whether a private litigant can act as a private attorney general or otherwise seek injunctive relief.

8.6.2 Does a UDAP Statute Authorize Private Injunctive Relief?

8.6.2.1 Statutes that Explicitly Authorize Private Injunctive Relief

Most UDAP statutes explicitly authorize private injunctive actions. (A number of states have two different UDAP statutes authorizing injunctive relief.) Eleven UDAP statutes[600] modeled after the Uniform Deceptive Trade Practices Act (UDTPA)[601] provide that a "person likely to be damaged by deceptive practices of another" may seek injunctive relief. A primary function of the UDTPA is to provide businesses with a means of enjoining deceptive and thus unfairly competitive practices of other businesses. The UDTPA has also been found to provide injured consumers with an injunctive remedy.[602] Therefore, a private injunctive remedy is available for violations of the specific prohibitions of state UDAP statutes patterned after the UDTPA.

In Delaware, Georgia, Hawaii, Illinois, Maine, Minnesota, Nebraska, Ohio, and Oklahoma, consumer litigants should not confuse the UDAP statute patterned after the UDTPA[603] with the state's other UDAP statute that provides a private damages remedy, with which they may be more familiar.[604] Aggressive consumer litigants will select the more advantageous statute for a particular case, or will even bring claims under both statutes.

In addition, in twenty-two states, UDAP statutes not patterned after the UDTPA explicitly authorize a private injunctive remedy.[605] The Missouri UDAP statute explicitly authorizes private injunctions in class actions.[606] Since procedural requirements for class injunctive actions are less burdensome than for damage class actions, this may not significantly impair a litigant's ability to seek an injunction.

8.6.2.2 Implying an Injunctive Remedy in Other States

Private injunctions may also be available in most other states, particularly where the UDAP statute generally authorizes the court to grant other forms of relief. Often a UDAP statute will allow a court to grant private plaintiffs "other equitable relief" or "other relief the court deems appropriate."[607] These phrases may be terms of art in a particular state with specific state precedent as to their meaning. Where it is unclear whether injunctive relief is authorized, or where the statute is completely silent on the issue, consumer litigants should stress the legislative intent and liberal construction of UDAP statutes.

UDAP statutes are interpreted liberally to effect their objects of eradicating deception, protecting consumers, and correcting marketplace imbalances.[608] The statute's remedial nature also leads to a liberal construction.[609] Statutes are intended to prevent deception from recurring,[610] to protect the public, and to prevent fraudulent practices from continuing unchecked while a multiplicity of damage suits

600 Del. Code Ann. tit. 6, § 2531; Ga. Code § 10-1-370; Haw. Rev. Stat. § 481A; 815 Ill. Comp. Stat. § 510/1; Me. Rev. Stat. Ann. tit. 10, § 1211; Minn. Stat. Ann. § 325D.23; Neb. Rev. Stat. § 87-301; N.M. Stat. Ann. § 57-12-1; Ohio Rev. Code Ann. § 4165; Okla. Stat. Ann. tit. 78, § 51; Or. Rev. Stat. § 646.605.

601 *See* § 3.4.2.4, *supra*.

602 *See* § 7.2.3, *supra*.

603 Del. Code Ann. tit. 6, § 2531; Ga. Code Ann. § 10-1-370; Haw. Rev. Stat. § 481A; 815 Ill. Comp. Stat. 510/1 *et seq.*; Me. Rev. Stat. Ann. tit. 10, § 1211; Minn. Stat. Ann. § 325D.43; Neb. Rev. Stat. § 87-301; Ohio Rev. Code Ann. § 4165; Okla. Stat. Ann. tit. 78, § 51.

604 Del. Code Ann. tit. 6, § 2511; Ga. Code Ann. § 10-1-390; Haw. Rev. Stat. § 480-1; 815 Ill. Comp. Stat. 505/1 *et seq.*; Me. Rev. Stat. Ann. tit. 5, § 206; Minn. Stat. Ann. § 8.31; Neb. Rev. Stat. § 59-1601; Ohio Rev. Code Ann. § 1345.01; Okla. Stat. Ann. tit. 15, § 751. *See* Greenberg v. United Airlines, 206 Ill. App. 3d 40, 563 N.E.2d 1031 (1990) (comparison of the two statutes).

605 Ala. Code § 8-19-10; Cal. Civ. Code § 1780; Cal. Bus. & Prof. Code §§ 17203, 17204; Conn. Gen. Stat. § 42-110(g); D.C. Code Ann. § 28-3905(k); Fla. Stat. Ann. § 501.211(1); Ga. Code Ann. § 10-1-399; Haw. Rev. Stat. § 480-13; Idaho Code § 48-608; 815 Ill. Comp. Stat. 505/10a; Kan. Stat. Ann. § 50-634; Me. Rev. Stat. Ann. tit. 5, § 213; Mass. Gen. Laws Ann. ch. 93A, § 9; Mich. Comp. Laws § 445.911; Neb. Rev. Stat. § 59-1609; N.H. Rev. Stat. Ann. § 358-A:10; N.Y. Gen. Bus. Law § 349; Ohio Rev. Code Ann. § 1345.09; R.I. Gen. Laws § 6-13.1-5.2; Tenn. Code Ann. § 47-18-109; Tex. Bus. & Comm. Code Ann. tit. 2, § 17.50(b); Utah Code Ann. § 13-11-19; Wash. Rev. Code § 19.86.090. *See also* Mick v. Level Propane Gases, Inc., 168 F. Supp. 2d 804 (S.D. Ohio 2001) (consumer can seek injunction but must meet usual prerequisites for injunctive relief); Recreation Servs. v. Odyssey Fun World, Inc., 952 F. Supp. 594 (N.D. Ill. 1997); Wexler v. Brothers Entertainment Group, Inc., 457 N.W.2d 218 (Minn. Ct. App. 1990); Beslity v. Manhattan Honda, 113 Misc. 2d 888, 450 N.Y.S.2d 278 (N.Y. Cty. Civ. Ct. Small Claims 1982) (injunction not only permitted but required in any damage action), *rev'd*, 467 N.Y.S.2d 471 (Sup. Ct., App. Term 1983) (injunction not required in damage action); Washburn v. Krenek, 684 S.W.2d 187 (Tex. App. 1984); Keyes v. Bollinger, 31 Wash. App. 286, 640 P.2d 1077 (1982). *But see In re* Fredeman Litigation, 843 F.2d 821 (5th Cir.) (Texas law), *reh'g denied en banc*, 847 F.2d 840 (5th Cir. 1988) (since statute explicitly allows the state, but not private individuals, to seek sequestration of assets, private suits can seek injunctive relief, but can not seek sequestration of assets); *cf.* Girard v. Myers, 694 P.2d 678 (Wash. Ct. App. 1985) (no UDAP action for declaratory relief).

606 Mo. Rev. Stat. § 407.025(2).

607 *Cf.* Vineyard v. Varner, 2003 WL 22794467 (Tenn. Ct. App. Nov. 25, 2003) (unpublished, citation limited) (construing authority to grant "necessary and proper" relief to include the equitable remedy of rescission).

608 *See* § 3.1.2, *supra*.

609 *Id.*

610 State *ex rel.* Guste v. Crossroads Gallery, Inc., 357 So. 2d 1381 (La. Ct. App. 1978). *See generally* § 8.1, *supra*.

develops.[611] UDAP statutes are not designed solely to remedy private wrongs, but to protect the public.[612]

Thus, a strong argument can be made that in statutes that do not explicitly provide or deny injunctive relief, the legislative intent of eliminating deception from the marketplace can best be served by implying the availability of injunctive relief. Consumers can then serve as private attorneys general, bringing to the court's attention seller misconduct that the state attorney general does not have the resources to pursue.

Louisiana courts differ about whether a private party can obtain injunctive relief under the UDAP statute, with some courts holding that it is available.[613] In contrast, Illinois courts had interpreted old statutory language "such equitable relief which the court deems appropriate" as not authorizing an injunctive remedy.[614] This ruling may be partially explained by the fact that another Illinois UDAP statute provided for private injunctive relief. In any event, the Illinois legislature disagreed with these court interpretations of the UDAP statute, and promptly amended the statute to explicitly provide an injunctive remedy.[615]

Some statutes are drafted so that private injunctions are clearly foreclosed, as where a statute indicates that a damage award is the exclusive individual remedy.[616] Where a statute authorized the state to seek injunctive relief, but limits private remedies to actions for damages, a court refused to infer a private injunctive remedy.[617]

611 Hockley v. Hargitt, 82 Wash. 2d 337, 510 P.2d 1123 (1973).

612 Weigel v. Ron Tonkin Chevrolet Co., 298 Or. 127, 690 P.2d 488 (1984); Fisher v. World-Wide Trophy Outfitter Ltd., 15 Wash. App. 742, 551 P.2d 1398 (1976).

613 Oreck Corp. v. Bissell, Inc., 1999 U.S. Dist. LEXIS 3446 (E.D. La. Mar. 22, 1999) (citing cases). *But see* Family Resource Group v. Louisiana Parent Magazine, 818 So. 2d 28 (La. App. 2001) (only AG can seek injunctive relief).

614 Zanni v. Lippold, 119 F.R.D. 32 (C.D. Ill. 1988); Disc Jockey Referral Network, Ltd. v. Ameritech Publishing of Illinois, 596 N.E.2d 4 (Ill. App. Ct. 1992) (attorney general has sole power to obtain injunction under Illinois UDAP statute); Greenberg v. United Airlines, 206 Ill. App. 3d 40, 563 N.E.2d 1031 (1990) (same; consumers may seek injunction under UDTPA statute); Martin v. Eggert, 174 Ill. App. 3d 71, 528 N.E.2d 386, *appeal denied*, 123 Ill. 2d 559, 535 N.E.2d 403 (1988); Jones v. Eagle II, 99 Ill. App. 3d 64, 424 N.E.2d 1253 (1981); Brooks v. Midas Int'l Corp., 47 Ill. App. 3d 266, 361 N.E.2d 815 (1977); Bonner v. Westbound Records, Inc., 49 Ill. App. 3d 543, 364 N.E.2d 570 (1977).

615 815 Ill. Comp. Stat. § 505/10a. *See* Cobb v. Monarch Fin. Co., 913 F. Supp. 1164 (N.D. Ill. 1995).

616 *See* Wyo. Stat. § 40-12-114.

617 Monroe Medical Clinic, Inc. v. Hospital Corp. of Am., 522 So. 2d 1362 (La. Ct. App. 1988); Michaelson v. Motwani, 372 So. 2d 726 (La. Ct. App. 1979).

8.6.3 Preconditions for Private Injunctive Relief

8.6.3.1 Must the Plaintiff Be Injured?

Not every individual can seek an injunction against merchant misconduct. While some individuals or organizations may wish to act as private attorneys general to combat UDAP violations, UDAP statutes often specifically limit those who can seek relief to those who have suffered actual monetary loss, have been aggrieved, or have been adversely affected by a violation. Care must be taken in reviewing the UDAP statute for such limiting language, by scrutinizing not only the provision for injunctive relief but also other sections dealing with private remedies.[618]

A Missouri court construes its UDAP statute as allowing injunctive relief only if the consumer successfully brings a damages suit, so the consumer must meet the ascertainable loss requirement.[619] New Jersey requires UDAP litigants to allege a bona fide ascertainable loss, sufficient to withstand summary judgment, before they may obtain injunctive relief under the UDAP statute.[620] The plaintiff need not, however, succeed at trial on the damages claim in order to obtain injunctive relief.[621]

A notable exception was a California UDAP statute,[622] which allowed any person to bring an injunctive action against an unfair or unlawful practice. This had been interpreted as allowing organizations and others not specifically affected by the practice to bring the UDAP injunction action.[623] The plaintiffs need not have personally suffered damages.[624] Even where the UDAP claim was solely based on a violation of another statute, and the plaintiff would have no standing under that statute, the plaintiff could achieve standing in California by challenging the violation of that other statute under the UDAP statute.[625] This applied to violations

618 *See, e.g.*, Haun v. Don Mealy Imports, Inc., 285 F. Supp. 2d 1297 (M.D. Fla. 2003) (dismissing DTPA claim for declaratory and injunctive relief because of failure to allege damage).

619 Freeman Health Sys. v. Wass, 124 S.W.3d 504 (Mo. App. 2004).

620 Weinberg v. Sprint Corp., 173 N.J. 233, 801 A.2d 281 (2002).

621 *Id.*

622 Cal. Bus. & Prof. Code § 17200.

623 Stop Youth Addiction, Inc. v. Lucky Stores, Inc., 17 Cal. 4th 553, 71 Cal. Rptr. 2d 731, 950 P.2d 1086 (1998); Perdue v. Crocker Nat'l Bank, 38 Cal. 3d 913, 216 Cal. Rptr. 345, 702 P.2d 503 (1985); Midpeninsula Citizens for Fair Hous. v. Westwood Investors, 221 Cal. App. 3d 1377, 271 Cal. Rptr. 99 (1990); Consumers Union of U.S., Inc. v. Fisher Dev. Inc., 208 Cal. App. 3d 1433, 257 Cal. Rptr. 151 (1989); Hernandez v. Atlantic Fin. Co., 105 Cal. App. 3d 65, 164 Cal. Rptr. 279 (1980).

624 Quelimane Co. v. Stewart Title Guaranty Co., 77 Cal. Rptr. 2d 709, 960 P.2d 513 (1998); Braco v. Superior Court, 2002 Cal. App. Unpub. LEXIS 2534 (Mar. 28, 2002) (unpublished, citation limited).

625 Stop Youth Addiction, Inc. v. Lucky Stores, Inc., 17 Cal. 4th 553, 71 Cal. Rptr. 2d 731, 950 P.2d 1086 (1998); Midpeninsula Citizens for Fair Hous. v. Westwood Investors, 221 Cal. App. 3d

of criminal statutes as well as civil statutes.[626] The injunction must, however, be directed to ongoing conduct.[627] However, in 2004, the statute was amended to allow suit only by a person who had suffered injury in fact and had lost money or property. The District of Columbia Code was amended in 2000 to be very similar to the pre-2004 version of the California statute.[628] The Massachusetts UDAP statute allows a plaintiff to obtain an injunction before suffering actual damages, as long as the defendant's unfair practices may have the effect of causing a future loss of money or property.[629] The Alaska UDAP statute also provides, that with prior notice, any person who is a victim of a UDAP violation may bring an action for injunctive relief, whether or not that person suffered actual damages.[630]

8.6.3.2 Must the Plaintiff Benefit from the Injunction?

While federal issues of Article III case-or-controversy standing will not apply to state court actions, consumer litigants seeking a court injunction from which they will derive little or no individual benefit should carefully review any applicable state standing doctrines. It will also be important to review the language of the state UDAP statute itself.

The California UDAP statute does not limit who may bring injunctive actions, but allows litigants to seek such relief even if they have not and will not be adversely affected by a practice.[631] Any individual or group willing to expend the legal resources can seek to enjoin any form of marketplace abuse it chooses that falls within the UDAP statute's scope. The trial court has broad discretion in fashioning the breadth of the injunction.[632]

1377, 271 Cal. Rptr. 99 (1990); Consumers Union of U.S., Inc. v. Fisher Dev. Inc., 208 Cal. App. 3d 1433, 257 Cal. Rptr. 151 (1989); *see also* Committee on Children's Television, Inc. v. General Foods Corp., 35 Cal. 3d 197, 197 Cal. Rptr. 783, 673 P.2d 660 (1983); People v. McKale, 25 Cal. 3d 626, 159 Cal. Rptr. 811, 602 P.2d 731 (1979).

626 Stop Youth Addiction, Inc. v. Lucky Stores, Inc., 17 Cal. 4th 553, 71 Cal. Rptr. 2d 731, 950 P.2d 1086 (1998).

627 Pena v. McArthur, 889 F. Supp. 403 (E.D. Cal. 1994).

628 D.C. Code § 28-3905(k).

629 Warner-Lambert Co. v. Execuquest Corp., 691 N.E.2d 545 (Mass. 1998).

630 Alaska Stat. § 45.50.535.

631 Cal. Bus. & Prof. Code § 17200; Stop Youth Addiction, Inc. v. Lucky Stores, Inc., 17 Cal. 4th 553, 71 Cal. Rptr. 2d 731, 950 P.2d 1086 (1998); Mass. Mut. Life Ins. Co. v. Superior Court, 97 Cal. App. 4th 1282, 119 Cal. Rptr. 2d 190 (2002); Saunders v. Superior Court, 27 Cal. App. 4th 832, 33 Cal. Rptr. 2d 438 (1994); *see also* Perdue v. Crocker Nat'l Bank, 38 Cal. 3d 913, 702 P.2d 503, 216 Cal. Rptr. 345 (1985), *appeal dismissed*, 475 U.S. 1001 (1986); Committee on Children's Television, Inc. v. General Foods, Corp., 35 Cal. 3d 197, 197 Cal. Rptr. 783, 673 P.2d 660 (1983); Hernandez v. Atlantic Fin. Co., 105 Cal. App. 3d 65, 164 Cal. Rptr. 279 (1980).

632 Brockey v. Moore, 107 Cal. App. 4th 86, 131 Cal. Rptr. 2d 746 (2003).

The District of Columbia amended its Consumer Protection Act in 2000 to be similar to California's. Any person, organization, or group, whether acting in its own interests, on behalf of its members, or for the general public, may bring suit.[633] The plaintiff may seek treble damages or $1500 per violation, whichever is greater; punitive damages; an injunction against use of the unlawful practice; any additional relief necessary to implement restitution in a representative action; attorney fees; and any other relief that the court deems proper.

A Florida appellate court has interpreted its statute as requiring that the consumer be aggrieved by the practice, but not that the injunction would benefit the consumer.[634] Thus a person who has suffered damage due to a practice may pursue a claim for declaratory or injunctive relief, even if the effect of those remedies would be limited to consumers who have not yet been harmed by the practice.

More typical are statutes patterned after the UDTPA, which include language allowing private injunctions when a litigant is "likely to be damaged." The test is thus prospective, not retrospective. For a plaintiff to seek a UDAP injunction, the plaintiff must benefit from the injunction.[635] Legislative drafters may have had in mind businesses suing to halt competitors' deceptive practices that were placing the plaintiff at a competitive disadvantage. For private individu-

633 D.C. Code § 28-3905(k).

634 Davis v. Powertel, Inc., 776 So. 2d 971 (Fla. App. 2000).

635 Gardner v. First Am. Title Ins. Co., 296 F. Supp. 2d 1011 (D. Minn. 2003) (mere possibility that plaintiff will transact business with defendant in the future is insufficient); Jets Prolink Cargo, Inc. v. Brenny Transportation, Inc., 2003 WL 22047910 (D. Minn. Aug. 29, 2003) (no injunction where no risk of future harm to plaintiff); Greisz v. Household Bank, 8 F. Supp. 2d 1031 (N.D. Ill. 1998); Catrett v. Landmark Dodge, Inc., 253 Ga. App. 639, 560 S.E.2d 101 (2002); Robinson v. Toyota Motor Credit Corp., 315 Ill. App. 3d 1086, 735 N.E.2d 724, 249 Ill. Dec. 120 (2000), *aff'd in part, rev'd in part on other grounds*, 775 N.E.2d 951 (Ill. 2002); Smith v. Prime Cable, 658 N.E.2d 1325 (Ill. App. Ct. 1995) (no right to injunction where consumer could not show likelihood of future damage); Tarin v. Pellonari, 625 N.E.2d 739 (Ill. App. Ct. 1993) (plaintiff must show likelihood of future damage); Popp v. Cash Station Inc., 613 N.E.2d 1150 (Ill. App. Ct. 1992) (consumer is unlikely to be confused in the future and therefore can not seek injunction under Illinois Deceptive Trade Practices Act); Disc Jockey Referral Network, Ltd. v. Ameritech Publishing of Illinois, 596 N.E.2d 4 (Ill. App. Ct. 1992) (business can not win injunction under UDTPA because it is not likely to be happen in the future); Hayna v. Arby's, 99 Ill. App. 3d 700, 425 N.E.2d 1174 (1981) (injunction not appropriate because plaintiff knows of the deception and is thus unlikely to be deceived in future). *See also* Glazewski v. Coronet Ins. Co., 108 Ill. 2d 243, 483 N.E.2d 1263 (1985) (consumer can not bring UDTPA injunctive action where consumer will not be deceived by the practice in the future). *But see* Greenberg v. United Airlines, 206 Ill. App. 3d 40, 563 N.E.2d 1031 (1990); Lofquist v. Whitaker Buick-Jeep-Eagle, Inc., 2001 Minn. App. LEXIS 1291 (Dec. 4, 2001) (unpublished, citation limited); Coronado Products, Inc. v. Stewart, Clearinghouse No. 45,905 (Tenn. Ct. App. 1988) (available on LEXIS, 1988 Tenn. App. LEXIS 672).

als, the applicability of this standard may be confusing because a litigant who knows about a deceptive practice is unlikely to be damaged by it in the future.

There are obvious exceptions. Examples are when there is only one such merchant in the area or there is an ongoing contractual relationship with the seller and the plaintiff must continue to deal with it or when deceptive or abusive debt collection practices may continue.[636] Apartment rentals, mobile home parks, migrant farm camps, campground memberships, health spas and vocational schools are other areas where a consumer's injury may be continuing and injunctive relief particularly appropriate.

Thus in one UDAP case the court ordered the landlord not to evict any tenants without the court's prior approval.[637] Similarly, a developer's real estate practices may be subject to injunctive action, as where a court ordered a developer to use abutting property as conservation areas as was promised to the consumers.[638] A preliminary injunction to freeze the seller's assets should also be permitted where such assets may be necessary to satisfy an eventual judgment.[639]

Even where the UDAP statute does not expressly require that the plaintiff be likely to benefit from an injunction, sellers may argue that courts should not grant an injunction that will not benefit any named party to the action. This, of course, creates an anomalous situation. If only a consumer likely to suffer future damages from a deceptive practice can seek an injunction, then only those unaware of the deceptive practice could challenge it. Thus, a Texas court has stated that an injunction could be granted where other consumers were being injured or where the seller intended to repeat its deceptive practice.[640]

Moreover, judicial economy and the public interest in stopping a deceptive practice before a multiplicity of individual damage suits are filed outweighs any argument that the relief does not benefit any of the parties to the action.[641] Framing a lawsuit as a class action may ease this problem, and class injunctive actions pose fewer procedural problems than class damage actions.

8.6.3.3 Does an Adequate Remedy at Law Prevent Injunctive Relief?

Litigants who have been damaged by a practice and who seek to enjoin the seller's future use of that practice may have to respond to a defense that equitable relief is not appropriate where a damage remedy making them whole is adequate. This common law doctrine is being eroded and should not apply at all where equity jurisdiction is specifically conferred by the UDAP statute.[642] Thus, a court has ruled that recovery of even treble damages does not preclude injunctive relief.[643] Where the underlying transaction involves real property, an analogy to specific performance may help overcome any judicial reluctance to grant injunctive relief.[644]

8.6.4 Relationship of Injunctive Remedy to Arbitration Clause

Special issues arise where a consumer seeks a UDAP injunctive remedy, and the merchant seeks to enforce an agreement to submit the action to binding arbitration. Another NCLC manual, *Consumer Arbitration Agreements* (4th ed. 2004) examines a number of ways to challenge the enforceability of such arbitration agreements. The injunctive nature of the sought remedy provides another reason why the arbitration clause should not be enforced.

The injunctive nature of the action actually raises two problems with the arbitration agreement. The first is whether the arbitration agreement and the rules of the arbitration service provider allow the consumer to seek an injunctive remedy in arbitration. If not, then the fact that the consumer can not pursue UDAP statutory remedies may make the arbitration agreement unconscionable or against public policy.[645]

In addition, even if an arbitrator can issue an injunction, there is an issue whether a private arbitrator should be issuing orders that affect the public at large. The most detailed discussion of these issues in the context of a UDAP case is the California Supreme Court's decision in *Brough-*

636 Asch v. Teller, Levit & Silvertrust, P.C., 2003 WL 22232801 (N.D. Ill. Sept. 26, 2003) (consumer can obtain injunction against debt collector under Ill. DTPA).

637 Hernandez v. Stabach, 145 Cal. App. 3d 309, 193 Cal. Rptr. 350 (1983).

638 Brandt v. Olympic Constr., Inc., 16 Mass. App. Ct. 913, 449 N.E.2d 1231 (1983).

639 Finkelstein v. Southeast Bank, N.A., 490 So. 2d 976 (Fla. Dist. Ct. App. 1986).

640 David McDavid Pontiac, Inc. v. Nix, 681 S.W.2d 831 (Tex. App. 1984). *See also* Adkinson v. Harpeth Ford-Mercury, Inc., 1991 Tenn. App. LEXIS 114 (Feb. 15, 1991).

641 Courts finding that an injunction is appropriate to prevent future deception while other individual actions develop are: David McDavid Pontiac, Inc. v. Nix, 681 S.W.2d 831 (Tex. App. 1984); Hockley v. Hargitt, 82 Wash. 2d 337, 510 P.2d 1123 (1973); Connelly v. Puget Sound Collections, Inc., 16 Wash. App. 62, 553 P.2d 1354 (1976). *See also* Wiginton v. Pacific Credit Corp., 2 Haw. App. 435, 634 P.2d 111 (1981) (even cessation of the practice does not make a private injunction moot).

642 *See* Braco v. Superior Court, 2002 Cal. App. Unpub. LEXIS 2534 (Mar. 28, 2002) (unpublished, citation limited); Greenfield Country Estates Tenants Ass'n v. Deep, 423 Mass. 81, 666 N.E.2d 988 (1996). *But see* Watkins Inc. v. Lewis, 346 F.3d 841 (8th Cir. 2003) (must show absence of adequate remedy at law).

643 David McDavid Pontiac, Inc. v. Nix, 681 S.W.2d 831 (Tex. App. 1984).

644 *See* Greenfield Country Estates Tenants Ass'n v. Deep, 423 Mass. 81, 666 N.E.2d 988 (1996).

645 *See* National Consumer Law Center, Consumer Arbitration Agreements §§ 4.3.6, 5.3 (4th ed. 2004).

ton v. CIGNA Healthplans.[646] The court discussed the difficulty an arbitrator would encounter monitoring a UDAP injunction and issuing subsequent orders. The court especially found that private arbitration could not provide the type of equitable relief that the California legislature had intended in passing the Consumer Legal Remedies Act, which allows an individual to seek injunctive relief on behalf of a large number of consumers, acting as a private attorney general.

Such an injunction is for the benefit of the general public and not for the resolution of private disputes. The legislature did not intend injunctive relief under a private attorney general type of statute to be subject to arbitration. In that situation, arbitration of an injunctive action is inconsistent with the legislative intent and can not be enforced.[647] The California Supreme Court, in 2003, in *Cruz v. Pacificare Health Systems,* reaffirmed its 1999 *Broughton* ruling, and extended it to California's two other UDAP statutes.[648]

The results in *Broughton* and *Cruz* must be distinguished from *Gilmer v. Interstate/Johnson Lane Corp.*, in which an employee argued before the Supreme Court that Age Discrimination in Employment Act (ADEA) claims need not be submitted to arbitration. One of a number of arguments the employee made was that arbitration does not further the purposes of the ADEA, because it does not provide for equitable relief.[649]

The Supreme Court responded that in the arbitration at issue, the arbitrator had the capacity and authority to fashion equitable relief, and such authority was not restricted by the rules of the arbitration mechanism. In that case, the equitable relief most likely would have been simply to reinstate the employee's employment contract, with no need for ongoing monitoring of the employer. Compare this to a more complex injunction altering the way a corporation markets and conducts its business as to all consumers for the indefinite future, requiring far more pervasive and long-term monitoring, and perhaps rulings as to whether the injunction has been violated.

8.6.5 Other Equitable Relief

Equitable relief other than injunctions may also be available under the state UDAP statute, especially if it allows the court to grant "other relief" or "other equitable relief." For example, a court may have the authority to exercise the equitable power of reformation of a contract or to order specific performance in an appropriate UDAP case. In addition, some UDAP statutes specifically empower courts to award specific performance, and this remedy should also be considered authorized by general language allowing equitable relief.

The Connecticut Supreme Court has interpreted its UDAP statute's authorization of "such equitable relief as [the court] deems necessary or proper" in the broad spirit appropriate for a remedial statute.[650] Where a seller's deception led to his obtaining a stipulated judgment, the supreme court ruled that the trial court had authority to order the judgment reopened despite a general state procedural law that set a four-month period for reopening judgments. Recovery of real property can be ordered under the Massachusetts UDAP statute's authorization of equitable relief.[651]

8.7 Voiding and Rescinding Contracts

8.7.1 Introduction

In many states, the UDAP statute may be able to be used to void or rescind a sales transaction that involved deception or unfairness. A consumer may prefer this remedy over damages or an injunction, since it can result in the dismissal of a collection action by the seller or its assignees, without proof of the consumer's actual damages.

This section is limited to a discussion of whether violation of a state UDAP statute should lead to rescission or voiding of a transaction. A discussion of canceling contracts pursuant to the FTC Door-to-Door and Off-Premises Sales Rule and related state statutes can be found in § 5.8.2, *supra*. Section 9.5, *infra*, discusses canceling or voiding a contract or transaction under various other statutory and common law doctrines.

8.7.2 Statutory Language Authorizing Remedy

Relatively few state UDAP statutes explicitly provide rescission or voiding the transaction as a remedy. The Ohio UDAP statute allows consumers an election between rescinding the contract and damages.[652] Even if the UDAP

646 21 Cal. 4th 1066, 90 Cal. Rptr. 2d 334, 988 P.2d 67 (1999).

647 *Id.*

648 66 P.3d 1157 (Cal. 2003).

649 Gilmer v. Interstate/Johnson Lane Corp., 500 U.S. 20, 111 S. Ct. 1647, 114 L. Ed. 2d 26 (1991).

650 Yeong Gil Kim v. Magnotta, 249 Conn. 94, 733 A.2d 809 (1999).

651 Kattar v. Demoulas, 433 Mass. 1, 739 N.E.2d 246 (2000).

652 Ohio Rev. Code Ann. § 1345.09; Wenneman v. Sperano, 2001 Ohio App. LEXIS 1970 (May 3, 2001) (must elect between rescission and damages); Credit Acceptance Corp. v. Banks, 1999 Ohio App. LEXIS 6058 (Dec. 16, 1999) (ordering return of money paid is consistent with rescission remedy); Frey v. Vin Devers, Inc., 80 Ohio App. 3d 1, 608 N.E.2d 796 (1992); Eckman v. Columbia Oldsmobile, Inc., 65 Ohio App. 3d 719, 585 N.E.2d 451 (1989); *see also* Mid Am. Acceptance Co. v. Lightle, 63 Ohio App. 3d 590, 579 N.E.2d 721 (1989) (consumers entitled to rescind and recover the amount already paid on the contract, but not entitled to treble that amount); Bramley's Water Conditioning v. Hagen, 27 Ohio App. 3d 300, 501

violation resulted from a bona fide error, the consumer can still rescind the transaction.[653] Rescission pursuant to this statute is an action at law, not in equity.[654]

Idaho's UDAP statute allows the consumer to treat a contract as voidable if it is incident to a UDAP violation.[655] In the alternative, the consumer may seek actual and statutory damages.

The Hawaii UDAP statute specifically voids contracts that violate the statute.[656] A court has used this provision to void only the offending portion of a contract, and not the whole agreement.[657]

The Louisiana UDAP statute authorizes the court to refuse to enforce an unconscionable agreement. Where a credit insurance policy did not offer adequate coverage, a court has refused to enforce the consumer's obligation to pay on the contract, even though the consumer received benefits under the policy.[658]

The Texas UDAP statute provides that the court can issue orders necessary to restore money acquired through a UDAP violation.[659] This is generally interpreted as allowing rescission.[660] But at least one Texas court has ruled that the consumer's unclean hands can prevent utilization of this remedy.[661]

8.7.3 Where Statute Is Silent as to Availability of Remedy

The more typical UDAP statute does not explicitly state whether a court can void or rescind a transaction based on UDAP violations. Consumer litigants should begin by closely examining the remedy section of the UDAP statute to determine what remedies are specifically mentioned, such as "other equitable relief" or "other appropriate remedies."

Even if no statutory language suggests the availability of the rescission or voiding remedies, a number of courts have found such inherent authority. For example, a New Jersey case offers three theories for finding an automobile repair contract unenforceable where the repair shop violated UDAP regulations requiring written authorization for repairs.

First, the contract is void against public policy. Second, the contract is illegal and an illegal contract can not be enforced. Third, since the regulations specify that written authorization is a condition precedent to forming the contract, the contract was never consummated and is thus unenforceable.[662]

The Washington Supreme Court has found that rescinding a contract is within a court's inherent authority because of the legislative intent to have broad and effective private UDAP remedies.[663] Similarly, a Florida court found its authority in a UDAP case extended to voiding a note, mortgage, and agreement, where the transaction was unfair and the avoidance would restore the status quo.[664] Wisconsin courts void contractual provisions that limit the effectiveness of UDAP requirements.[665] Tennessee courts also find rescission an implicit remedy within the UDAP statute.[666]

Illinois courts are divided on whether there is implicit authority to rescind or void a contract as a UDAP remedy. On the one hand, Illinois courts have dismissed creditors' collection actions where the underlying transaction was deceptive.[667] Another federal court assumed that the Illinois Consumer Fraud Act allowed rescission, but declined to order it on equitable grounds.[668] But a federal court interpreting the Illinois UDAP statute indicated that the UDAP statute creates no right to rescind.[669] Similarly, a middle-level Georgia appellate court found no right to rescind implicit in that state's UDAP statute.[670] A bankruptcy court

N.E.2d 38 (1985); Bierlein v. Alex's Continental Inn, 16 Ohio App. 3d 294, 475 N.E.2d 1273 (1984).

653 Frey v. Vin Devers, Inc., 80 Ohio App. 3d 1, 608 N.E.2d 796 (1992).

654 Ferrari v. Howard, 2002 WL 1500414 (Ohio App. July 11, 2002) (unpublished, citation limited).

655 Idaho Code § 48-608(1).

656 Haw. Rev. Stat. § 480-12. *See* Hawaii Community Federal Credit Union v. Keka, 94 Haw. 213, 11 P.3d 1 (2000).

657 Ai v. Frank Huff Agency Ltd., 61 Haw. 607, 607 P.2d 1304 (1980).

658 Marshall v. Citicorp Mortgage Inc., 601 So. 2d 669 (La. Ct. App. 1992).

659 Tex. Bus. & Com. Code § 17.50(b)(3).

660 *See, e.g.*, Schenck v. Ebby Halliday Real Estate, 803 S.W.2d 361 (Tex. App. 1990).

661 *Id.*

662 Huffmaster v. Robinson, 221 N.J. Super. 315, 534 A.2d 435 (Law Div. 1986). *See also In re* Fleet, 95 B.R. 319 (E.D. Pa. 1989) (New Jersey law); § 9.5, *infra*. *But see* Rudy v. Hoffman-Brunner, 514 N.W.2d 422 (Wis. Ct. App. 1993) (unpublished limited precedent decision, text available at 1993 Wisc. App. LEXIS 1700).

663 Allen v. American Land Research, 95 Wash. 2d 841, 631 P.2d 930 (1980).

664 McLendon v. Metropolitan Mortgage Co., Clearinghouse No. 43,703G (Fla. Cir. Ct. Dade Cty. May 20, 1988).

665 Perma-Stone Corp. v. Merkel, 255 Wis. 565, 39 N.W.2d 730 (1949); Moonlight v. Boyce, 125 Wis. 2d 298, 372 N.W.2d 479 (Ct. App. 1985).

666 Vineyard v. Varner, 2003 WL 22794467 (Tenn. Ct. App. Nov. 25, 2003) (unpublished, citation limited) (the equitable remedy of rescission is an appropriate remedy under the state's Consumer Protection Act); Lorentz v. Deardan, 834 S.W.2d 316 (Tenn. Ct. App. 1992); Smith v. Scott Lewis Chevrolet, Inc., 843 S.W.2d 9 (Tenn. Ct. App. 1992).

667 American Buyers Club v. Hayes, 46 Ill. App. 3d 270, 361 N.E.2d 1383 (1977); American Buyers Club v. Honecker, 46 Ill. App. 3d 252, 361 N.E.2d 1370 (1977).

668 Walker v. Gateway Fin. Corp., 2003 WL 22318843 (N.D. Ill. Oct. 7, 2003).

669 April v. Union Mortg. Co., 709 F. Supp. 809 (N.D. Ill. 1989).

670 Little v. Paco Collection Servs., 156 Ga. App. 175, 274 S.E.2d 147 (1980).

in Pennsylvania has reached the same result,[671] but another Pennsylvania bankruptcy decision awarded a remedy similar to rescission: it basically rewrote a loan, disregarding all illegal and unconscionable charges, recalculating interest, and then subtracting the borrower's payments.[672]

8.7.4 Procedures to Rescind Contract

When a consumer seeks to rescind a contract, he or she should be careful to follow common law requirements concerning notice, tender, etc., if they are applied by the courts.[673] Courts may also apply UCC principles that relate to revocation of acceptance.[674] Where a contract has been assigned to another entity, the consumer should notify that entity of the rescission; while it is a good idea to notify the original seller also, it may not be legally necessary.[675] The seller may be entitled to a setoff for the rental value and any damages to the item purchased.[676]

In addition, several of the UDAP statutes that contain an explicit rescission remedy establish special procedures for rescission actions. The Ohio UDAP statute allows consumers to rescind a contract, but specifies that the consumer must rescind within a reasonable time of discovering the grounds for rescission and before any substantial change in the subject of the consumer transaction.[677] A consumer was not allowed to rescind after home improvements had been completed.[678] But a consumer was allowed to rescind a car sale after driving the car, and could even continue to make reasonable use of the car after rescinding.[679] If rescission itself is timely, any delay between the time of rescission and the filing of suit is irrelevant.[680]

671 *In re* Soto, 221 B.R. 343 (Bankr. E.D. Pa. 1998).

672 *In re* Fricker, 115 B.R. 809 (Bankr. E.D. Pa. 1990).

673 *See, e.g.*, David McDavid Pontiac, Inc. v. Nix, 681 S.W.2d 831 (Tex. App. 1984).

674 Peterman v. Waite, 1980 Ohio App. LEXIS 13565 (June 25, 1980) (buyer's continued use of vehicle, and failure to tender possession of it to seller, were inconsistent with revocation).

675 Nations Credit v. Pheanis, 102 Ohio App. 3d 71, 656 N.E.2d 998 (1995).

676 Davis v. Wholesale Motors, Inc., 949 P.2d 1026 (Haw. App. 1997).

677 Ohio Rev. Code Ann. § 1345.09; Wenneman v. Sperano, 2001 Ohio App. LEXIS 1970 (May 3, 2001) (rescission 11 months after purchase and only when vehicle needed repairs is too late); Lloyd v. Buick Youngstown GMC Truck Co., 686 N.E.2d 350 (Ohio App. 1996) (depreciation precluded rescission five years after purchase of car).

678 Reichert v. Ingersoll, 18 Ohio St. 3d 220, 480 N.E.2d 802 (1985).

679 Andrews v. Scott Pontiac Cadillac GMC, Inc., 71 Ohio App. 3d 613, 594 N.E.2d 1127 (1991). *But see* Cummins v. Dave Fillmore Car Co., 1987 WL 19186 (Ohio App. Oct. 27, 1987) (no right to rescind after buyer drove car two months and made repairs to it). *But see* Frey v. Vin Devers, Inc., 80 Ohio App. 3d 1, 608 N.E.2d 796 (1992) (rescission not allowed where consumers drove car for six months after learning of deceptive acts).

680 Nations Credit v. Pheanis, 102 Ohio App. 3d 71, 656 N.E.2d 998 (1995).

8.7.5 Relationship of Remedy with Other UDAP Remedies

Some UDAP statutes specify the relationship of the UDAP rescission remedy to other UDAP remedies. The Ohio UDAP statute specifically allows consumers only an election between rescinding the contract and damages.[681] If the consumer rescinds, the consumer can also recover any amount already paid on the contract, but the consumer can not treble that amount.[682] The consumer also can not recover statutory damages for the UDAP violations that led up to the transaction.[683] The election between rescission and a damage remedy must be made *prior* to going to trial.[684]

A Maryland appellate court also held that a consumer must make an election before trial between rescission on common law grounds and damages on UDAP theories.[685] By contrast, Texas courts allow a consumer to rescind a transaction and still obtain UDAP damages to the extent that rescission has not made the consumer whole.[686] A Wisconsin court allowed consumers to recover UDAP double damages even though they had rescinded the transaction on other grounds.[687]

Another issue is whether a UDAP provision that allows treble damages can be used in conjunction with a rescission remedy. Tennessee and Pennsylvania courts find that the UDAP statute authorizes a court to treble the amount returned to the consumer pursuant to the rescission.[688] A Hawaii appellate court has not only authorized damages in a case where the transaction was rescinded, but directed that any trebling of damages be calculated before setting off the seller's claim for rental value and damages to the item purchased.[689]

681 Ohio Rev. Code Ann. § 1345.09. *See also* Bramley's Water Conditioning v. Hagen, 27 Ohio App. 3d 300, 501 N.E.2d 38 (1985); Bierlein v. Alex's Continental Inn, 16 Ohio App. 3d 294, 475 N.E.2d 1274 (1984).

682 Mid Am. Acceptance Co. v. Lightle, 63 Ohio App. 3d 590, 579 N.E.2d 721 (1989). *See also* Credit Acceptance Corp. v. Banks, 1999 Ohio App. LEXIS 6058 (Dec. 16, 1999) (rescission award can include money judgment for return of buyer's payments); § 8.4.2.6, *supra*.

683 Eckman v. Columbia Oldsmobile, Inc., 65 Ohio App. 3d 719, 585 N.E.2d 451 (1989).

684 Williams v. Banner Buick, Inc., 60 Ohio App. 3d 128, 574 N.E.2d 579 (1989).

685 Merritt v. Craig, 746 A.2d 923 (Md. App. 2000).

686 LaChalet Int'l, Inc. v. Nowik, 787 S.W.2d 101 (Tex. App. 1990). *But see* Kargar v. Sorrentino, 788 S.W.2d 189 (Tex. App. 1990).

687 Pliss v. Peppertree Resort Villas, Inc., 663 N.W.2d 851 (Wis. App. 2003).

688 Metz v. Quaker Highlands, Inc., 714 A.2d 447 (Pa. Super. 1998); Lorentz v. Deardan, 834 S.W.2d 316 (Tenn. Ct. App. 1992). *See also* § 8.4.2.7.4, *supra*.

689 Davis v. Wholesale Motors, Inc., 949 P.2d 1026 (Haw. App. 1997).

8.8 Attorney Fees

8.8.1 Purpose of UDAP Attorney Fee Provisions

Virtually all UDAP statutes that authorize a private remedy offer attorney fees to successful consumer litigants. By requiring sellers that violate UDAP statutes to pay the consumer's legal expenses, UDAP statutes make it possible for attorneys to devote significant resources to a case, even if the consumer's dollar losses are relatively minor compared to commercial disputes.[690] This not only encourages consumers to remedy marketplace abuses, but also increases the sellers' maximum liability if they refuse to settle the consumers' just claims. A key purpose of UDAP fee-shifting provisions is to ensure that plaintiffs with bona fide claims are able to find lawyers to represent them.[691]

Courts should construe UDAP statutory attorney fee provisions in favor of consumers since such provisions promote the UDAP statute's underlying legislative purpose.[692] Consumers with legitimate UDAP claims would be deterred from enforcing their rights if they were required to absorb all costs of litigation.[693] Unless reasonable attorney fees are awarded in consumer protection cases, the doors to the courthouse will be closed to all but those with either potentially substantial damages or sufficient economic resources to afford the litigation expenses.[694] By encouraging consumers to act as private attorneys general, attorney fee awards reduce the burden on public enforcement agencies.[695] Attorney fee provisions also discourage tradesmen from engaging in unfair or deceptive practices, thereby enforcing the purpose of UDAP statutes.[696]

Attorney fees are discussed in other treatises, particularly as they relate to antitrust, civil rights, and Truth in Lending cases.[697] This section will analyze only UDAP cases dealing with attorney fees.

8.8.2 When Are UDAP Attorney Fees Available?

8.8.2.1 Statutory Preconditions to Attorney Fee Award

While most UDAP statutes specifically provide for awards of attorney fees, the statutory language differs from statute to statute, and consumer attorneys should be familiar with their own state's legislation. For example, at one time in Florida only consumers could obtain attorney fees, and not a buyer whose purchase was for business purposes.[698] The statute has since been amended to allow fees in non-consumer cases.

In Michigan, the defendant can assert a bona fide error defense to the award of attorney fees. This does not require a showing by the consumer that the seller's acts were willful. Instead, the burden is on the seller to show that its acts were in good faith and it had implemented reasonable procedures to avoid the UDAP violation.[699]

In North Carolina, fees are awarded only if conduct is willful and there is an unwarranted refusal to settle.[700] If the

690 *See, e.g.*, Tanksley v. Cook, 360 N.J. Super. 63, 821 A.2d 524 (App. Div. 2003); Parker v. I&F Insulation Co., 89 Ohio St. 3d 261, 730 N.E.2d 972 (2000).

691 Lettenmaier v. Lube Connection, Inc., 162 N.J. 134, 741 A.2d 591 (1999); Chattin v. Cape May Greene, Inc., 243 N.J. Super. 590, 581 A.2d 91 (1990), *aff'd per curiam*, 124 N.J. 943, 591 A.2d 943 (1991); Keith v. Howerton, 2002 WL 31840683 (Tenn. Ct. App. Dec. 19, 2002) (unpublished, citation limited); Wilkins v. Peninsula Motor Cars, Inc., 587 S.E.2d 581 (Va. 2003) (purpose is to encourage private enforcement). *See also* Showpiece Homes Corp. v. Assurance Co. of Am., 38 P.3d 47 (Colo. 2001) (purposes are to provide remedy and promote enforcement).

692 Hayward v. Ventura Volvo, 108 Cal. App. 4th 509, 133 Cal. Rptr. 2d 514 (2003) (applying rule of liberal construction to UDAP attorney fee statute); Jordan v. Transnational Motors, Inc., 537 N.W.2d 471 (Mich. Ct. App. 1995); Tanner v. Tom Harrigan Chrysler Plymouth, 82 Ohio App. 3d 764, 613 N.E.2d 649 (1991) (attorney fee provision should be construed liberally); Wilkins v. Peninsula Motor Cars, Inc., 587 S.E.2d 581 (Va. 2003).

693 Fabri v. United Techs. Int'l, Inc., 193 F. Supp. 2d 480 (D. Conn. 2002); Gibbs v. Southeastern Investment Corp., 705 F. Supp. 738 (D. Conn. 1989) (purpose of UDAP attorney fee provision is to encourage private UDAP litigation); Ford Motor Co. v. Mayes, 575 S.W.2d 480 (Ky. Ct. App. 1978); Beaulieu v. Dorsey, 562 A.2d 678 (Me. 1989) (attorney fee awards serve UDAP purpose of encouraging litigation which might otherwise be prohibited by economic concerns); Yost v. Millhouse, 373 N.W.2d 826 (Minn. Ct. App. 1985); Honeywell v. Sterling Furniture Co., 310 Or. 206, 797 P.2d 1019 (1990); Taylor v. Medenica, 331 S.C. 575, 503 S.E.2d 458 (1998).

694 Jordan v. Transnational Motors, Inc., 537 N.W.2d 471 (Mich. Ct. App. 1995). *See also* § 8.8.11.1, *infra*.

695 Blue Cross & Blue Shield of N.J., Inc. v. Philip Morris, Inc., 190 F. Supp. 2d 407 (E.D.N.Y. 2002), *rev'd in part on other grounds, questions certified by* 344 F.3d 211 (2d Cir. 2003).

696 Parker v. I&F Insulation Co., 89 Ohio St. 3d 261, 730 N.E.2d 972 (2000); Taylor v. Medenica, 331 S.C. 575, 503 S.E.2d 458 (1998).

697 *See, e.g.*, National Consumer Law Center, Credit Discrimination § 11.6.6 (3d ed. 2002 and Supp.) (ECOA); Fair Credit Reporting § 11.6 (5th ed. 2002 and Supp.) (FCRA); Fair Debt Collection § 6.8 (5th ed. 2004) (FDCPA); Truth in Lending § 8.9 (5th ed. 2003 and Supp.).

698 Darrell Swanson Consolidated Servs. v. Davis, 433 So. 2d 651 (Fla. Dist. Ct. App. 1983).

699 Temborius v. Slatkin, 157 Mich. App. 587, 403 N.W.2d 821 (1986).

700 N.C. Gen. Stat. § 75-16.1. *See also* Llera v. Security Credit Sys., Inc., 93 F. Supp. 2d 674 (W.D.N.C. 2000) (no unwarranted refusal to settle where defendant made several settlement offers greater than amount plaintiff won, and plaintiff delayed a year before making a counteroffer); Barbee v. Atlantic Marine Sales & Service, 115 N.C. App. 641, 446 S.E.2d 117 (1994) (award of fees upheld where defendant was intractable); Garlock v. Henson, 112 N.C. App. 243, 435 S.E.2d 114 (1993); Lapierre v.

court awards attorney fees, it must make findings on each of these elements.[701] Proof of fraud satisfies the willfulness criterion.[702] Of course, a defendant's offer to resolve a case can be found to be insufficient, justifying an award of attorney fees.[703] A reasonable settlement must reflect the seller's liability for treble damages.[704] Refusing plaintiffs' offer to settle for $50,000 less than was ultimately awarded justifies fees.[705]

In Massachusetts, the UDAP statute provides that the defendant be given an opportunity in all UDAP cases to make a reasonable settlement offer. If that offer is reasonable, but the consumer proceeds to trial, then a consumer's fee award is limited to fees incurred prior to the settlement offer, even if the consumer prevails at trial.[706] Recovery will be allowed for work after that point only if the settlement offer is unreasonable.[707] It is not necessary to show that the violation was intentional.[708]

A Tennessee court has reached the same conclusion. Relying on a section of the UDAP statute that allows recovery to be limited to the amount of a reasonable settlement offer, the court limited an attorney fee award to approximately the amount incurred at the time of the offer.[709] An Illinois UDAP provision (struck down in 2003 as unconstitutional)[710] provided that if a consumer failed to recover at trial an amount greater than the settlement offered by a new or used car dealer at least thirty days prior to trial, then the consumer could not recover for costs or attorney fees incurred after the offer was made.[711]

Under the Texas pre-litigation notice requirement, if the consumer rejects a settlement offer that is substantially the same as that awarded at trial, the consumer's right to recover treble damages is denied, but the consumer's attorney's right to recover fees is not affected.[712] Texas also has a generally-applicable statute that shifts litigation costs (including attorney fees) if the plaintiff rejects an offer and then recovers significantly less at trial.[713]

In Ohio attorney fees are only authorized if the seller knowingly violates the statute.[714] This is interpreted to mean knowingly engaging in the challenged practice, not knowingly engaging in an illegal practice.[715] The determination of whether the seller acted knowingly is for the judge, not the jury.[716] Attorney fees can be denied if the seller demonstrates that its violation resulted from a bona fide error notwithstanding the maintenance of procedures to avoid such errors.[717] While the trial court has discretion to deny fees,[718] it must state its reasons so that an appellate court can review its exercise of that discretion.[719]

Samco Dev. Co., 103 N.C. App. 551, 406 S.E.2d 646 (1991); Cotton v. Stanley, 380 S.E.2d 419 (N.C. Ct. App. 1989); Morris v. Bailey, 358 S.E.2d 120 (N.C. Ct. App. 1987).

701 United States *ex rel.* S&D Land Clearing v. D'Elegance Mgmt., 2000 U.S. App. LEXIS 16173 (4th Cir. July 13, 2000) (unpublished, citation limited) (trial court's findings sufficient); Torrance v. AS&L Motors, 459 S.E.2d 67 (N.C. Ct. App. 1995).

702 United States *ex rel.* S&D Land Clearing v. D'Elegance Mgmt., 2000 U.S. App. LEXIS 16173 (4th Cir. July 13, 2000) (unpublished, citation limited).

703 Lapierre v. Samco Dev. Co., 103 N.C. App. 551, 406 S.E.2d 646 (1991); Love v. Keith, 383 S.E.2d 674 (N.C. Ct. App. 1989).

704 Custom Molders, Inc. v. Roper Corp., 101 N.C. App. 606, 401 S.E.2d 96 (1991), *aff'd without op.*, 410 S.E.2d 55 (N.C. 1991).

705 United States *ex rel.* S&D Land Clearing v. D'Elegance Mgmt., 2000 U.S. App. LEXIS 16173 (4th Cir. July 13, 2000) (unpublished, citation limited). *But cf.* Volumetrics Medical Imaging, Inc. v. ATL Ultrasound, Inc., 2003 WL 21650004 (M.D.N.C. July 10, 2003) (defendant's settlement efforts sufficient to avoid fee award even though its highest offer was just 10% of jury's award).

706 Mass. Gen. Laws Ann. ch. 93A, § 9(4); *see also* Briggs v. Carol Cars, Inc., 407 Mass. 391, 553 N.E.2d 930 (1990).

707 Kohl v. Silver Lake Motors, Inc., 369 Mass. 795, 343 N.E.2d 375 (1976).

708 Garcia v. L&R Realty, Inc., 790 A.2d 936 (N.J. Super. App. Div. 2002) (Mass. law).

709 Scott v. Noland Co., 1995 Tenn. App. LEXIS 505, Clearinghouse No. 51,282 (Tenn. App. 1995).

710 Allen v. Woodfield Chevrolet, Inc., 208 Ill. 2d 12, 802 N.E.2d 752, 280 Ill. Dec. 501 (2003).

711 815 Ill. Comp. Stat. 505/10a(f).

712 Lone Star Ford, Inc. v. Howard R. Hill, Jr., 879 S.W.2d 116 (Tex. App. 1994).

713 Tex. Civ. Practice & Remedies Code §§ 42.001–42.005.

714 *See* Gadfield v. Ferris Chevrolet, Inc., 1992 Ohio App. LEXIS 2402 (Apr. 28, 1992); Brooks v. Hurst Buick-Pontiac-Olds-GMC, Inc., 23 Ohio App. 3d 85, 491 N.E.2d 345 (1985); Gross v. Bildex, Inc., 647 N.E.2d 573 (Ohio Mun. 1994); Gaylan v. Dave Towell Cadillac, 15 Ohio Misc. 2d 1, 473 N.E.2d 64 (Mun. Ct. 1984). *See also* Swift v. Allied Pest Control, Inc., 2001 Ohio App. LEXIS 3853 (Aug. 31, 2001) (remanding case because jury's finding that violation was knowing was inconsistent with its finding of bona fide error).

715 Einhorn v. Ford Motor Co., 48 Ohio St. 3d 27, 548 N.E.2d 933 (1990); Patterson v. Stockert, 2000 Ohio App. LEXIS 6004 (Dec. 13, 2000); Fletcher v. Don Foss of Cleveland, Inc., 90 Ohio App. 3d 82, 628 N.E.2d 60 (1993); Vannoy v. Capital Lincoln-Mercury Sales, Inc., 88 Ohio App. 3d 138, 623 N.E.2d 177 (1993) (seller was liable for fees because it intentionally followed its own policy). *See also* Gadfield v. Ferris Chevrolet, Inc., 1992 Ohio App. LEXIS 2402 (Apr. 28, 1992); Andrews v. Scott Pontiac Cadillac GMC, Inc., 71 Ohio App. 3d 613, 594 N.E.2d 1127 (1991) (seller's policy of not disclosing information that it knew entitles consumer to fees).

716 Buist v. Columbiana Buick Olds Cadillac Inc., 2001 Ohio App. LEXIS 384 (Feb. 1, 2001); Dotson v. Brondes Motor Sales, 90 Ohio App. 3d 206, 628 N.E.2d 137 (1993). *See also* Cain v. Pruett, 938 S.W.2d 152 (Tex. App. 1996) (settlement offer not sufficient to limit recovery of fees where offer did not include amount for the consumer's attorney fees). *But see* Prince v. Campbell Roofing & Sheet Metal, 2002 WL 1728089 (Ohio App. July 26, 2002) (unpublished, citation limited) (treating question as one for jury).

717 Swift v. Allied Pest Control, Inc., 2001 Ohio App. LEXIS 3853 (Aug. 31, 2001) (remanding case because jury's finding that violation was knowing was inconsistent with its finding of bona fide error); Frey v. Vin Devers, Inc., 80 Ohio App. 3d 1, 608 N.E.2d 796 (1992).

718 Brzezinski v. Feuerwerker, 2000 Ohio App. LEXIS 4145 (Sept. 14, 2000) (discretionary even if preconditions are met).

719 Snider v. Conley's Serv., 2000 Ohio App. LEXIS 2601 (June 12, 2000).

A number of UDAP statutes patterned after the Uniform Deceptive Trade Practices Act (UDTPA) award attorney fees only if the seller's practice is willful.[720] Oklahoma's version of the UDTPA makes attorney fees discretionary, but mandatory if the practice is willful, and "willful" has been interpreted as meaning the seller knew it was encroaching upon protected rights.[721] Colorado's UDAP statute provides for no attorney fees for class actions, only individual actions. Consequently, no attorney fee award should be made for work attempting to certify a UDAP class.[722] Other statutes patterned after the UDTPA only award attorney fees in "exceptional cases."[723]

8.8.2.2 Where No Explicit Statutory Authority for Fees

Where a statute provides for attorney fees for certain private actions, but is silent as to such fees for other types of actions, a court has found that authority to award fees should inferred for all actions under the statute.[724]

A number of Pennsylvania cases found authority to award UDAP attorney fees from a statutory provision allowing the court to provide "additional relief as appropriate,"[725] before an explicit provision for attorney fees was added to the statute. But where a UDAP statute is silent as to the availability of any private remedy, courts have been willing to imply a private right of action, but not the right to attorney fees.[726]

8.8.2.3 Availability of Other Remedies Does Not Limit Access to Fees

There is no merit to the claim that a punitive damages award in some way prevents the consumer from also receiving attorney fees.[727] To the contrary, excellent results justify a higher fee award.[728] For example, a consumer can obtain an actual damage award and attorney fees under a UDAP count and punitive damages under a tort claim.[729] Similarly, attorney fees are available even where there are significant actual damages—while attorney fees encourage suits where damages are only nominal, their recovery is not limited to such suits.[730] A ban on attorney fee awards in suits brought under one statute does not apply to a separate UDAP count.[731]

A somewhat unique issue has arisen in Oregon where a state statute specifies that punitive damages awards first go to pay the consumer's attorney.[732] The issue is whether UDAP attorney fees can be awarded in addition to the punitive damages award. The Oregon Supreme Court has held that attorney fees should be awarded on top of the punitive damages award, so that the distribution of part of the punitive damages to the attorney does not lessen the total allowed recovery under the UDAP statute.[733]

---

720 *See* Scott Fetzer Co. v. Williamson, 101 F.3d 549 (8th Cir. 1996) (no attorney fee award against defendant who was negligent); Bentley v. Slavik, 663 F. Supp. 736 (S.D. Ill. 1987); Edwards v. William H. Porter, Inc., 1991 Del. Super. LEXIS 315, Clearinghouse No. 47,935 (July 26, 1991) (fees awarded where violations found to be willful); Tarin v. Pellonari, 625 N.E.2d 739 (Ill. App. Ct. 1993) (no attorney fee award under Illinois UDTPA statute without proof of willfulness); Bingham v. Inter-Track Partners, 600 N.E.2d 70 (Ill. App. Ct. 1992).

721 Brunswick Corp. v. Spinit Reel Co., 832 F.2d 513 (10th Cir. 1987) (Oklahoma law).

722 Robinson v. Lynmar Racquet Club, Inc., 851 P.2d 274 (Colo. Ct. App. 1993).

723 *See, e.g.*, Del. Code Ann. tit. 6, § 2533(b). *See generally* Appx. A, *supra*.

724 United Postage Corp. v. Kammeyer, 581 S.W.2d 716 (Tex. Civ. App. 1979). *But cf.* Schultz v. Subaru of Am., Inc., 407 Mass. 1004, 553 N.E.2d 893 (1990) (where UDAP statute authorized attorney fee award for "actions," no award allowed for arbitration proceeding).

725 *In re* Bryant, 111 B.R. 474 (E.D. Pa. 1990); *In re* Wernly, 91 B.R. 702 (Bankr. E.D. Pa. 1988); *In re* Stewart, 93 B.R. 878 (Bankr. E.D. Pa. 1988); Andrews v. Fleet Real Estate Funding Corp., 78 B.R. 78 (Bankr. E.D. Pa. 1987); Jungkurth v. Eastern Fin. Servs., Inc., 74 B.R. 323 (Bankr. E.D. Pa. 1987), *aff'd on other grounds*, 87 B.R. 333 (E.D. Pa. 1988) (while the reviewing district court acknowledged the argument for UDAP attorney fees as "additional relief," it did not expressly affirm this part of the bankruptcy court's ruling). *See also* Hines v. Chrysler Corp., 971 F. Supp. 212 (E.D. Pa. 1997).

726 Sellinger v. Freeway Motor Home Sales, Inc., 110 Ariz. 573, 521 P.2d 1119 (1974); Stephenson v. Capano Dev., Inc., 462 A.2d 1069 (Del. 1983) (attorney fees are available under a different Delaware UDAP statute, Del. Code Ann. tit. 6, § 2511).

727 Grabinski v. Blue Springs Ford Sales, Inc., 203 F.3d 1024 (8th Cir. 2000); S&S Tobacco & Candy Co. v. Stop & Shop Cos., 815 F. Supp. 65 (D. Conn. 1992); Warren v. LeMay, 142 Ill. App. 3d 550, 491 N.E.2d 464 (1986); Equitable Life Leasing Corp. v. Abbick, 243 Kan. 513, 757 P.2d 304 (1988) (even though cost of litigation is one factor in determining size of punitive damages, one can also obtain full attorney fee award); Garcia v. Coffman, 1997 NMCA 092, 946 P.2d 216 (N.M. App. Ct. 1997) (attorney fees "not a surrogate for punitive damages"); United Laboratories v. Kuykendall, 335 N.C. 183, 437 S.E.2d 374 (1993); Honeywell v. Sterling Furniture Co., 310 Or. 206, 797 P.2d 1019 (1990) (must award both UDAP attorney fees and punitive damages even though state law requires punitive damages award first go to pay off consumer's attorney); Orkin Exterminating Co. v. Williamson, 785 S.W.2d 905 (Tex. App. 1990); Wilkins v. Peninsula Motor Cars, Inc., 587 S.E.2d 581 (Va. 2003). *But see* Ekl v. Knecht, 585 N.E.2d 156 (Ill. App. Ct. 1991) (no abuse of discretion to deny attorney fee where punitive damage award was sufficient to pay fee); Alexander v. S&M Motors, Inc., 28 S.W.3d 303 (Ky. 2000) (punitive damage award, out of which plaintiff could pay fees, justified denial of fee award).

728 *See* §§ 8.4.3.8, 8.8.2.3, *supra*.

729 *See* Grabinski v. Blue Springs Ford Sales, Inc., 203 F.3d 1024 (8th Cir. 2000); United Laboratories v. Kuykendall, 335 N.C. 183, 437 S.E.2d 374 (1993); Wilkins v. Peninsula Motor Cars, Inc., 587 S.E.2d 581 (Va. 2003).

730 Kronebusch v. MVBA Harvestore Sys., 488 N.W.2d 490 (Minn. Ct. App. 1992).

731 Stanley v. Moore, 454 S.E.2d 225 (N.C. 1995).

732 Or. Rev. Stat. § 31.735.

733 Honeywell v. Sterling Furniture Co., 310 Or. 206, 797 P.2d 1019 (1990).

8.8.3 Are Attorney Fees Mandatory?

The goal of an attorney fee award is to allow just and fair compensation for the services and efforts of counsel on the case viewed as a whole,[734] so as to encourage enforcement of UDAP protections. Thus where a UDAP statute indicates that attorney fees *shall* be awarded if damages are awarded to the consumer, a court can not refuse to award reasonable fees.[735] Similarly, where a statute says the consumer "may sue and recover . . . reasonable attorney fees," the award of attorney fees has been held to be mandatory.[736] "The interests of both the business community and the public at large are best served by shifting the burden of expense of consumer fraud litigation onto the shoulders of those whose unfair and fraudulent acts are responsible for the litigation in the first place."[737]

Some state UDAP statutes state that the court "may award" attorney fees to the prevailing party.[738] This language will likely be construed as making fees discretionary,[739] but there are strong arguments that the factors guiding the court's discretion should favor consumers. Many of these provisions are worded almost identically to the non-mandatory fee-shifting provisions in federal civil rights statutes,[740] and their underlying purposes—to encourage enforcement by "private attorneys general"[741] and to give aggrieved individuals access to the courts[742]—are also similar. For these reasons, courts should be encouraged to look to the analysis developed in civil rights matters when deciding whether to award fees under nonmandatory UDAP fee shifting provisions.[743]

As first articulated in *Newman v. Piggy Park Enterprises*,[744] and further developed in *Hensley v. Eckerhart*,[745] this analysis dictates that even where statutory language is

734 Hanner v. Classic Auto Body Inc., 10 Mass. App. Ct. 121, 406 N.E.2d 686 (1980).

735 Refuse & Environmental Sys., Inc. v. Industrial Servs., 732 F. Supp. 1209 (D. Mass. 1990), *rev'd and remanded on other grounds*, 932 F.2d 37 (1st Cir. 1991); *In re* Fleet, 95 B.R. 319 (E.D. Pa. 1989) (New Jersey law); Cieri v. Leticia Query Realty, Inc., 905 P.2d 29 (Haw. 1995); Moore v. Goodyear Tire & Rubber Co., 364 So. 2d 630 (La. Ct. App. 1978); Cox v. Sears, Roebuck & Co., 138 N.J. 2, 647 A.2d 454 (1994); Roberts v. Cowgill, 719 A.2d 668 (N.J. App. Ct. 1998) (attorney fees are required if a UDAP violation, even a technical one, is shown); Performance Leasing Corp. v. Irwin Lincoln-Mercury, 262 N.J. Super. 23, 619 A.2d 1024 (1993); BJM Insulation & Constr. v. Evans, 287 N.J. Super. 513, 671 A.2d 603 (App. Div. 1996); Huffmaster v. Robinson, 221 N.J. Super. 315, 534 A.2d 435 (Law Div. 1986); Griffith v. Porter, 817 S.W.2d 131 (Tex. App. 1991); National Bugmobiles, Inc. v. Jobi Properties, 773 S.W.2d 616 (Tex. App. 1989); Satellite Earth Stations East, Inc. v. Davis, 756 S.W.2d 385 (Tex. App. 1988); Mail Box, Inc. v. The Communicators, Inc., 703 S.W.2d 783 (Tex. App. 1985); Hennessey v. Skinner, 698 S.W.2d 382 (Tex. App. 1985); Joseph v. PPG Indus., Inc., 674 S.W.2d 862 (Tex. App. 1984); Potere, Inc. v. National Realty Service, 667 S.W.2d 252 (Tex. App. 1984); Doerfler v. Espensen Co., 659 S.W.2d 929 (Tex. App. 1983); Shands v. Castrovinci, 115 Wis. 2d 352, 340 N.W.2d 506 (1983); *cf.* Beaulieu v. Dorsey, 562 A.2d 678 (Me. 1989) (recognizes court's discretion in setting amount of fees where statute says the court "shall" award fees).

736 Bruntaeger v. Zeller, 515 A.2d 123 (Vt. 1986); Winton v. Johnson & Dix Fuel Corp., 515 A.2d 371 (Vt. 1986); Gramatan Home Indus. Corp. v. Starling, 470 A.2d 1157 (Vt. 1983); Tradewell Stores, Inc. v. TB&M, Inc., 7 Wash. App. 424, 500 P.2d 1290 (1972). *See also* Roustabouts v. Hamer, 447 So. 2d 543 (La. Ct. App. 1984) (seems to imply attorney fees are mandatory); State v. Black, 100 Wash. 2d 739, 676 P.2d 963 (1984); Clark v. Luepke, 60 Wash. App. 848, 809 P.2d 752 (1991). *See also* Kolupar v. Wilde Pontiac Cadillac, 683 N.W.2d 58 (Wis. 2004) (interpreting "may recover" in non-UDAP consumer statute to mandate fee award). *But see* Hutchinson Utilities Comm'n v. Curtiss-Wright Corp., 775 F.2d 231 (8th Cir. 1985) (Minnesota law).

737 Gramatan Home Indus. Corp. v. Starling, 470 A.2d 1157, 1162 (Vt. 1983).

738 *See, e.g.*, Mo. Rev. Stat. § 407.025 (the court "may award to the prevailing party attorney's fees"); 73 Pa. Stat. § 201-9.2(a) (court may award "reasonable" attorney fees).

739 Blue Cross & Blue Shield of N.J., Inc. v. Philip Morris, Inc., 190 F. Supp. 2d 407 (E.D.N.Y. 2002), *rev'd in part on other grounds, questions certified by* 344 F.3d 211 (2d Cir. 2003); Dobosz v. Barrington Dodge, Inc., 2002 WL 31248505 (N.D. Ill. Oct. 7, 2002) (fee award is discretionary; listing factors); Graunke v. Elmhurst Chrysler Plymouth, 617 N.E.2d 858 (Ill. App. Ct. 1993) (award of fees is discretionary as to both consumers and sellers under Illinois statute); Ekl v. Knecht, 585 N.E.2d 156 (Ill. App. Ct. 1991); Kleidon v. Rizza Chevrolet, Inc., 173 Ill. App. 3d 116, 527 N.E.2d 374 (1988) (attorney fees "may" be awarded means attorney fee award is discretionary); Tague v. Molitor Motor Co., 139 Ill. App. 3d 313, 487 N.E.2d 436 (1985); Carpenter v. Discount Motors, Inc., 652 S.W.2d 716 (Mo. Ct. App. 1983) (interpreting statutory language that "court may, in its discretion," award fees); Custom Molders, Inc. v. American Yard Products, Inc., 463 S.E.2d 199 (N.C. 1995) (interpreting statutory language that "judge may, in his discretion," award fees); Varnell v. Henry M. Milgrom, Inc., 337 S.E.2d 616 (N.C. Ct. App. 1985) (same); Borders v. Newton, 315 S.E.2d 731 (N.C. Ct. App. 1984); James v. Thermal Master, Inc., 55 Ohio App. 3d 51, 562 N.E.2d 917 (1988) (attorney fees are discretionary where statute says court "may" award them); Gadfield v. Ferris Chevrolet, Inc., Clearinghouse No. 1992 Ohio App. LEXIS 2402 (Apr. 28, 1992); Milliken v. Crye-Leike Realtors, 2001 Tenn. App. LEXIS 472 (July 5, 2001); Town East Ford Sales, Inc. v. Gray, 730 S.W.2d 796 (Tex. App. 1987).

740 *See, e.g.*, 42 U.S.C. § 1988 (the court, in its discretion, may allow the prevailing party a reasonable attorney fee); 42 U.S.C. § 2000e-5(k) (same).

741 Casey v. Yusim Nissan, 296 Ill. App. 3d 102, 694 N.E.2d 206 (1998).

742 AFSCME v. County of Nassau, 96 F.3d 644 (2d Cir. 1996) (interpreting 42 U.S.C. 2000e-5(k)); Casey v. Yusim Nissan, 296 Ill. App. 3d 102, 694 N.E.2d 206 (1998) (interpreting Illinois Consumer Fraud and Deceptive Business Practices Act, 815 Ill. Comp. Stat. 505/1 et. seq.).

743 Grabinski v. Blue Springs Ford Sales, Inc., 203 F.3d 1024 (8th Cir. 2000). *See also* § 8.8.10.3, *infra*.

744 390 U.S. 400, 402, 88 S. Ct. 964, 966, 19 L. Ed. 2d 1263 (1968).

745 461 U.S. 424, 103 S. Ct. 1933 (1983).

seemingly neutral and appears to grant discretion to the trial courts, prevailing civil rights plaintiffs should ordinarily be awarded attorney fees *except* in extraordinary circumstances.[746] In other words, the provisions directing that a court "*may* award" attorney fees are interpreted to mean "*shall* award" fees, except in unusual circumstances. The district court's discretion to *deny* plaintiffs' an award of attorney fees is narrow,[747] and the presumption in favor of an award to plaintiffs acting as private attorneys general is so strong that denial based on "special circumstances" is extremely rare. A defendant's good faith does not constitute a special circumstance.[748]

If attorney fees are discretionary, there is still an issue whether the court has discretion over the size of the award, or only as to whether to make the award. It has been held that if a fee award is made, it must be a reasonable one.[749] A federal court has also indicated that, even if fees are discretionary, the limited financial resources of the plaintiffs and the significance of the fraud "compel" reasonable fees.[750] Other factors that the courts may consider are the opposing party's culpability, bad faith, and ability to pay fees; the potential deterrent effect of a fee award; whether the suit sought to benefit others or resolve an important legal question; and the relative merits of the parties' positions.[751]

Where an award of fees is discretionary, the trial court's decision will not be disturbed on appeal absent an abuse of discretion.[752] A court has discretion to award attorney fees even when the defendant's misrepresentations were innocent.[753]

746 Hensley v. Eckerhart, 461 U.S. 424, 103 S. Ct. 1933 (1983). *See also* LeBlanc-Sternberg v. Fletcher, 143 F.3d 765, 769, 770 (2d Cir. 1998); Stocker v. Keith, 178 Or. App. 544, 38 P.3d 283 (2002) (articulating similar standard under state law).

747 New York Gaslight Club, Inc. v. Carey, 447 U.S. 54, 100 S. Ct. 2024, 64 L. Ed. 2d 723 (1980); *see also* Dahlem v. Bd. of Ed. Of Denver Public Schools, 901 F.2d 1508 (10th Cir. 1990); Chernin v. Welchans, 844 F.2d 322, 330 (6th Cir. 1988).

748 *See, e.g.*, Brown v. Culpeper, 559 F.2d 274, 278, *rehearing denied*, 561 F.2d 1177 (5th Cir. 1977); New York State NOW v. Terry, 737 F. Supp. 1350 (S.D.N.Y. 1990).

749 Steiger v. J.S. Builders, Inc., 39 Conn. App. 32, 663 A.2d 432 (1995) (even if trial court has discretion whether to award fees, it must apply the correct legal standard in setting the amount of fees); Custom Molders, Inc. v. American Yard Products, Inc., 463 S.E.2d 199 (N.C. 1995); Morris v. Bailey, 358 S.E.2d 120 (N.C. Ct. App. 1987).

750 Rosario v. Livaditis, Clearinghouse No. 47,927 (N.D. Ill. 1990).

751 Washington Courte Condominium Ass'n v. Washington-Golf Corp., 267 Ill. App. 3d 790, 643 N.E.2d 199 (1994); Graunke v. Elmhurst Chrysler Plymouth, 617 N.E.2d 858 (Ill. App. Ct. 1993). *See also* Stocker v. Keith, 178 Or. App. 544, 38 P.3d 283 (2002) (listing various factors).

752 Prior Plumbing & Heating Co. v. Hagins, 630 N.E.2d 1208 (Ill. App. Ct. 1994); Missi v. CCC Custom Kitchens, Inc., 731 N.E.2d 1037 (Ind. App. 2000).

753 Grove v. Huffman, 634 N.E.2d 1184 (Ill. App. Ct. 1994).

8.8.4 When Does a Consumer Prevail, Triggering UDAP Attorney Fees?

8.8.4.1 Must the Consumer Prove UDAP Damages?

The case law is divided as to whether a damage award is a precondition to the award of attorney fees. Some courts will award attorney fees even if the consumer is awarded no damages,[754] since "there is a benefit to the public where

754 Kennedy v. Sphere Drake Ins. P.L.C., 2002 U.S. App. LEXIS 6054 (9th Cir. Apr. 2, 2002) (unpublished, citation limited) (Wash. law); Refuse & Environmental Sys., Inc. v. Industrial Servs. of Am., 932 F.2d 37 (1st Cir. 1991) (Mass. law); Fabri v. United Techs. Int'l, Inc., 193 F. Supp. 2d 480 (D. Conn. 2002) (compensatory damages unnecessary; federal cases to the contrary are inapplicable to UDAP claims); Advanced Sys. Consultants v. EPM, 899 F. Supp. 832 (D. Mass. 1995) (attorney fees proper where injunctive relief is only award); Thames River Recycling, Inc. v. Gallo, 50 Conn. App. 767, 720 A.2d 242 (1998) (UDAP attorney fees can be awarded even without actual damages); Jacques of All Trades Corp. v. Brown, 679 A.2d 27 (Conn. App. 1996); Freeman v. Alamo Mgmt. Co., 24 Conn. App. 124, 586 A.2d 619 (1991) (attorney fee award proper even though no UDAP damages awarded); Raymer v. Bay State Nat'l Bank, 384 Mass. 310, 424 N.E.2d 515 (1981); Trempe v. Aetna Casualty & Surety Co., 20 Mass. App. Ct. 448, 480 N.E.2d 670 (1985); Shapiro v. Public Serv. Mut. Ins. Co., 19 Mass. App. Ct. 648, 477 N.E.2d 146 (1985); Weinberg v. Sprint Corp., 173 N.J. 233, 801 A.2d 281 (2002) (plaintiff must allege bona fide ascertainable loss, sufficient to withstand summary judgment, but need not prevail on damages claim at trial); Cox v. Sears, Roebuck & Co., 138 N.J. 2, 647 A.2d 454 (1994); Cuesta v. Classic Wheels, Inc., 358 N.J. Super. 512, 818 A.2d 448 (App. Div. 2003); Jiries v. BP Oil, 294 N.J. Super. 225, 682 A.2d 1241 (Law. Div. 1996); Branigan v. Level on the Level, Inc., 326 N.J. Super. 24, 740 A.2d 643 (App. Div. 1999) (attorney fees must be awarded even where plaintiff won no damages, but trial court should consider level of success in setting amount); BJM Insulation & Constr. v. Evans, 287 N.J. Super. 513, 671 A.2d 603 (App. Div. 1996); Cybul v. Atrium Palace Syndicate, 272 N.J. Super. 330, 639 A.2d 1146 (App. Div. 1994) (no actual UDAP damages because seller mooted damage claim by returning deposit before hearing); Performance Leasing Corp. v. Irwin Lincoln-Mercury, 262 N.J. Super. 23, 619 A.2d 1024 (1993); Jones v. General Motors Corp., 953 P.2d 1104 (N.M. App. 1998) (attorney fees awarded even though plaintiff recovered only statutory damages); Pinehurst, Inc. v. O'Leary Bros. Realty, Inc., 338 S.E.2d 918 (N.C. Ct. App. 1986); Vineyard v. Varner, 2003 WL 22794467 (Tenn. App. Nov. 25, 2003) (unpublished, citation limited) (trial court had discretion to award rescission and UDAP attorney fees where jury found UDAP violation but no damages); Tallmadge v. Aurora Chrysler Plymouth, 25 Wash. App. 90, 605 P.2d 1275 (1979). *See also* Shapiro v. American Home Assurance Co., 616 F. Supp. 906 (D. Mass. 1985) (note that the Supreme Judicial Court has, in Jet Line Servs., Inc. v. American Employers Ins. Co., 404 Mass. 706, 537 N.E.2d 107 (1989), held that proof of some adverse effect on the plaintiff is required, and that any suggestion to the contrary in *Shapiro* was error); Jacques All Trades Corp. v. Brown, 42 Conn. App. 124, 679 A.2d 27 (1996), *aff'd on other grounds*, 692 A.2d 809 (Conn. 1997); Love v.

deception in the marketplace is brought to light (and thereby corrected) by an individual who has been deceived even though his actual damages were not proved."[755] One case even awarded attorney fees even where there were no damages and the finding of a UDAP violation was not based on the evidence, but was imposed as a sanction for the defendant's failure to respond to discovery.[756]

Some UDAP statutes require injury to the consumer as a precondition to prevailing on a UDAP claim. In that situation, the court may find that sufficient injury to prevail on the UDAP claim is also sufficient to trigger UDAP attorney fees, even when no actual damages are proven.

For example, Washington case law requires a causal link between the UDAP violation and some injury suffered.[757] Injury is thus a precondition for an attorney fee award, because it is a precondition to a UDAP violation. The injury, however, can be nonmonetary and nonquantifiable, such as loss of goodwill.[758] Even a minimal or temporary loss of money or property is enough.[759] *Any* injury meeting the Washington test is sufficient to trigger attorney fees.[760]

On the other hand, a number of cases rule that attorney fees are available only if the consumer both shows a UDAP violation and proves damages.[761] The United States Supreme Court ruled on this issue as it relates to federal Civil Rights Act cases. A unanimous Court found that recovery of nominal damages (such as $1.00) is sufficient to be a "prevailing party" eligible for attorney fees.[762] But a five to four split Court found that attorney fees will often not be awarded in such a situation because the degree of success is the most critical factor in determining the reasonableness of a fee award. In the case before the Court, the plaintiff sought $17 million but recovered $1.00, and the Court found no fee award to be merited.[763]

It is important to note, however, that this Supreme Court holding in a Civil Rights Act case is not binding on courts interpreting state UDAP statutes. For example, degree of success may not be viewed as a critical factor in recovery of fees under a state UDAP statute.

Where a case involves multiple counts, a jury may decide that actual damages should be awarded under a common law fraud count, and then not award damages under the UDAP count. But if the jury finds a UDAP violation, a court should reform the jury verdict.[764] Even though the consumer should not receive double actual damages, the fact that actual damages are recoverable under either the fraud or UDAP count should be enough to trigger UDAP attorney fees.

Even if a court would otherwise require a damage award for attorney fees, certain other relief will be treated as the equivalent, such as an injunction ordering the seller to sign a certificate of title.[765] Where there is unlikely to be an

---

Amsler, 441 N.W.2d 555 (Minn. Ct. App. 1989); Couto v. Gibson, Inc., 1992 Ohio App. LEXIS 756 (Feb. 26, 1992); St. Paul Fire & Marine Ins. Co. v. Updegrave, 656 P.2d 1130 (Wash. Ct. App. 1983) (minimal damage of having to defend a lawsuit is enough to trigger attorney fees).

755 Trempe v. Aetna Casualty & Surety Co., 20 Mass. App. Ct. 448, 480 N.E.2d 670 (1985).

756 Shapiro v. Public Service Mut. Ins. Co., 19 Mass. App. Ct. 648, 477 N.E.2d 146 (1985).

757 *See* Hangman Ridge Training Stables, Inc. v. Safeco Title Ins. Co., 105 Wash. 2d 778, 719 P.2d 531 (1986).

758 *See* Mason v. Mortgage Am., Inc., 114 Wash. 2d 842, 792 P.2d 142 (1990); Nordstrom, Inc. v. Tampourlos, 107 Wash. 2d 735, 733 P.2d 208 (1987).

759 *See* Mason v. Mortgage Am., Inc., 114 Wash. 2d 842, 792 P.2d 142 (1990) (temporary loss of title to property).

760 *Id.*

761 Nasco, Inc. v. Public Storage, Inc., 127 F.3d 148 (1st Cir. 1997) (Mass. law); Llera v. Security Credit Sys., Inc., 93 F. Supp. 2d 674 (W.D.N.C. 2000) (plaintiff who won only statutory damages was not prevailing party); Witters v. Daniels Motors, Inc., 524 P.2d 632 (Colo. Ct. App. 1974); Maroone Chevrolet, Inc. v. Nordstrom, 587 So. 2d 514 (Fla. Dist. Ct. App. 1991); Abbyad v. Mathes Group, 671 So. 2d 958 (La. Ct. App. 1996); Faris v. Model's Guild, 297 So. 2d 536 (La. Ct. App. 1974); VanVoorhees v. Dodge, 679 A.2d 1077 (Me. 1996); Jet Line Servs., Inc. v. American Employers Ins. Co., 404 Mass. 706, 537 N.E.2d 107 (1989); Martha's Vineyard Auto Village v. Newman, 30 Mass. App. Ct. 363, 569 N.E.2d 401 (1991); Tibbetts v. Sight 'N Sound Appliance Centers, Inc., 77 P.3d 1042 (Okla. 2003); Martin v. American Appliance, 174 N.J. Super. 382, 416 A.2d 933 (Law Div. 1980) (now overruled by Performance Leasing Corp. v. Irwin Lincoln-Mercury, 262 N.J. Super. 23, 619 A.2d 1024 (1993)); Poor v. Hill, 138 N.C. App. 19, 530 S.E.2d 838 (2000); Eckman v. Columbia Oldsmobile, Inc., 65 Ohio App. 3d 719, 585 N.E.2d 451 (1989) (court did not abuse discretion in denying attorney fee where seller agreed to rescission after suit filed and consumer lost on UDAP damages claims); Charleston Lumber Co. v. Miller Housing Corp., 458 S.E.2d 431 (S.C. App. 1995) (proof of damages necessary for UDAP claim); Milliken v. Crye-Leike Realtors, 2001 Tenn. App. LEXIS 472 (July 5, 2001); Nabours v. Longview Sav. & Loan Ass'n, 700 S.W.2d 901 (Tex. 1986); Jackson Law Office, P.C. v. Chappell, 37 S.W.3d 15 (Tex. App. 2000) (deceptive actions alone insufficient; the actions must cause damage); American Nat'l Ins. Co. v. Paul, 927 S.W.2d 239 (Tex. App. 1996); Ebby Halliday Real Estate, Inc. v. Murnan, 916 S.W.2d 585 (Tex. App. 1996); Scharer v. John's Cars, Inc., 776 S.W.2d 228 (Tex. App. 1989); Reuben H. Donnelley Corp. v. McKinnon, 688 S.W.2d 612 (Tex. App. 1985); Goodwin Construction Co. v. Schardt, 2002 WL 1825424 (Wash. App. Aug. 9, 2002) (unpublished, citation limited); Clark v. Luepke, 60 Wash. App. 848, 809 P.2d 752 (1991). *See also* Shurtliff v. Northwest Pools, Inc., 120 Idaho 263, 815 P.2d 461 (Ct. App. 1991) (court has discretion to find consumer has not prevailed where no damages awarded); Mancorp Inc. v. Culpepper, 802 S.W.2d 226 (Tex. 1990).

762 Farrar v. Hobby, 506 U.S. 103, 113 S. Ct. 566, 121 L. Ed. 2d 494 (1992).

763 *Id.*

764 Bird v. John Chezik Homerun, Inc., 152 F.3d 1014 (8th Cir. 1998) (Missouri law).

765 Hanover Ins. Co. v. Sutton, 46 Mass. App. Ct. 153, 705 N.E.2d 279. (1999); IFG Leasing Co. v. Ellis, 748 S.W.2d 564 (Tex. App. 1988). *But see* Eckman v. Columbia Oldsmobile, Inc., 65 Ohio App. 3d 719, 585 N.E.2d 451 (1989) (court did not abuse discretion in denying attorney fees where seller agreed to rescission after suit filed and consumer lost on UDAP damages claims).

actual damage award for a UDAP violation, consumers might be prudent to seek injunctive relief on an individual or class basis. Having obtained protection from UDAP violations for a wide group of consumers, the consumer will be more likely to be awarded attorney fees.

Incurring bills with a third party because of the defendant's UDAP violations is a sufficient loss on which to base an award of fees, even if the plaintiff never becomes financially able to pay the bills.[766] Attorney fees are to be awarded if the defendant's acts had some adverse effect on the consumer, even if it is not quantifiable in dollars.[767]

8.8.4.2 Must the Consumer's Recovery Exceed the Creditor's?

In many cases, the consumer's UDAP claim is a counterclaim to a collection action by the creditor. In such instances, the consumer may prevail on the UDAP counterclaim, but the damage recovery may be smaller than the amount that the creditor recovers, resulting in a positive recovery for the creditor.

Even some of the courts that require the consumer to prove actual damages find this requirement satisfied where the consumer recovers damages on the UDAP claim that are lower than the seller's recovery in the same case.[768] "A consumer victimized by a deceptive practice can seldom be certain that the lawsuit will yield a net recovery. Nevertheless, in order to give real meaning to the Act and to penalize deceptive practices, the consumer must have uninhibited access to the courts."[769]

Where the consumer prevailed on a UDAP count, but the damage award was less than a settlement with another party, a Texas court held that the consumer was entitled to a zero recovery and no attorney fees.[770] Nevertheless, Washington's highest court has ruled that the consumer's attorney fees should first be added to the judgment and the consumer should receive the amount by which this combined figure of damages and fees exceeds the amount recovered from the other party.[771]

8.8.4.3 Multiple Claims or Multiple Parties

In the typical lawsuit, the consumer will allege a number of UDAP and non-UDAP claims against a number of different defendants. The court may rule for the consumer without reaching some of these claims, may rule for the consumer without clarifying on which claims the decision is based, or may reject certain UDAP claims, but allow others. The court may rule against certain defendants, but in favor of others. The court may rule for the consumer, but in an amount less than the consumer sought.

In which of these situations has the consumer "prevailed" on a UDAP claim sufficient to trigger UDAP attorney fees? Section 8.8.11.4, *infra*, discusses how to compute the size of the attorney fee award in such situations—what attorney time on the case can and can not be compensated through the fee award. This subsection examines whether the consumer has sufficiently prevailed to trigger a fee award, whatever its size.

In general, courts are liberal in allowing UDAP attorney fees as long as the consumer has prevailed in some way on at least some of the claims against at least one defendant. Consumers do not have to recover on all counts of their complaint to receive attorney fees for all their efforts,[772] and an award of damages against only some of the defendants for a mere fraction of the amount sought is sufficient to justify attorney fees.[773]

For example, the Idaho Supreme Court approved an attorney fee award for all work expended on a case even though the consumer prevailed on only six of twenty-eight counts, the consumer was awarded in damages only three percent of what he requested, and the seller prevailed on its counterclaims. It is in the trial court's discretion to determine who prevailed, and the prevailing party can obtain all

766 Nasco, Inc. v. Public Storage, Inc., 127 F.3d 148 (1st Cir. 1997) (Mass. law).

767 Hanover Ins. Co. v. Sutton, 46 Mass. App. Ct. 153, 705 N.E.2d 279 (1999).

768 Matthews v. Candlewood Builders, 685 S.W.2d 649 (Tex. 1985); McKinley v. Drozd, 685 S.W.2d 7 (Tex. 1985); Buccaneer Homes of Alabama, Inc. v. Pelis, 43 S.W.3d 586 (Tex. App. 2001); Hamra v. Gulden, 898 S.W.2d 16 (Tex. App. 1995); Hartnett v. Hampton Inns, Inc., 870 S.W.2d 162 (Tex. App. 1993); Green Tree Acceptance, Inc. v. Pierce, 768 S.W.2d 416 (Tex. App. 1989); Satellite Earth Stations East, Inc. v. Davis, 756 S.W.2d 385 (Tex. App. 1988); Badtke v. Grant, 495 N.W.2d 527 (Wis. Ct. App. 1992) (unpublished limited precedent opinion, text available at 1992 Wisc. App. LEXIS 1119); Moonlight v. Boyce, 125 Wis. 2d 298, 372 N.W.2d 479 (Ct. App. 1985); Paulik v. Coombs, 120 Wis. 2d 431, 355 N.W.2d 357 (Ct. App. 1984).

769 Building Concepts, Inc. v. Duncan, 667 S.W.2d 897 (Tex. App. 1984); *see also* Paulik v. Coombs, 120 Wis. 2d 431, 355 N.W.2d 357 (Ct. App. 1984) (public policy of encouraging UDAP actions and deterring misconduct requires attorney fees award even where seller's counterclaim exceeds UDAP recovery).

770 Buccaneer Homes v. Pelis, 43 S.W.3d 586 (Tex. App. 2001) (no attorney fees where jury award was entirely offset by settlement with other defendant); Hamra v. Gulden, 898 S.W.2d 16 (Tex. App. 1995). *See, e.g.*, Wash. Rev. Code § 4.22.060.

771 Schmidt v. Cornerstone Investments, Inc., 115 Wash. 2d 148, 795 P.2d 1143 (1990).

772 Knight v. Snap-On Tools Corp., 3 F.3d 1398 (10th Cir. 1993) (N.M. law); Boulevard Assocs. v. Sovereign Hotels, Inc., 868 F. Supp. 70 (S.D.N.Y. 1994), *rev'd on other grounds*, 72 F.3d 1029 (2d Cir. 1995); State *ex rel.* Douglas v. Schroeder, 222 Neb. 473, 384 N.W.2d 626 (1986); Stocker v. Keith, 178 Or. App. 544, 38 P.3d 283 (2002) (plaintiffs who won one UDAP claim prevailed even though they lost on others); Greene v. Bearden Enterprises Inc., 598 S.W.2d 649 (Tex. Civ. App. 1980); Barnhouse Motors, Inc. v. Godfrey, 577 S.W.2d 378 (Tex. Civ. App. 1979).

773 Tate v. Wiggins, 583 S.W.2d 640 (Tex. Civ. App. 1979).

its attorney fees.[774] However, in a later case it upheld the trial court's discretion in ruling that a consumer who won on a UDAP claim but lost on other claims was not the prevailing party.[775]

The consumer has also prevailed, entitling the consumer to attorney fees, where the consumer wins on a UDAP count but elects to recover on a different count instead.[776] The court in making this ruling was influenced in part by the fact that UDAP remedies are in addition to those provided by other law. But consumers in electing recovery under a non-UDAP count should be careful to make clear to the court that they nevertheless intend to collect their UDAP attorney fees.

On the other hand, despite a similar provision in the Texas UDAP statute, a court held that a consumer could not elect to recover exemplary damages under a common law theory, which does not provide for attorney fees, and also recover UDAP attorney fees for the same conduct and damages.[777] Perhaps the court was influenced by fact that the consumer received common law damages totaling $5,796,109.49 for an extremely hard sell technique at a car dealer.

The Montana Supreme Court went one step further and awarded UDAP attorney fees even where the consumer lost on the UDAP claim but recovered on other claims. The consumer brought a UDAP action and prevailed and is entitled to attorney fees.[778] Where a consumer accepted an offer of judgment that did not specify the counts to which it related, and a fee-generating UDAP claim was one of the counts, the Minnesota Supreme Court held that the plaintiffs had prevailed on the UDAP claim.[779]

A federal statute allows the district court to deny costs to a party who recovers less than the $75,000 jurisdictional requirement in a diversity suit.[780] This rule only applies to costs, however, not UDAP attorney fees.[781] Further, even denial of costs is discretionary rather than mandatory.[782]

It is proper for a court to award a consumer attorney fees for defending a related counterclaim.[783] But courts have also held that no attorney fees should be awarded for work on other claims before an action was amended to include a UDAP count.[784] Where only one of two defendants is found to have violated the UDAP statute, only that defendant can be found liable for UDAP attorney fees.[785]

8.8.4.4 Attorney Fees for Work on Default Judgments and Protecting a Judgment

Attorney fees should be recoverable for work performed on a default judgment.[786] Attorney fees are also recoverable for time spent opposing a motion to set aside a default,[787] or to defend on appeal the propriety of the court's refusal to set aside the default.[788] The consumer should receive attorney fees for any effort required to protect a judgment.[789]

8.8.4.5 Settlements

8.8.4.5.1 Are fees available after settlement?

The United States Supreme Court recognizes that a plaintiff who wins a favorable consent order is a prevailing party, even though the court never considers the merits of the case.[790] The federal rule, however, is that in suits for equitable relief, the defendant's mere cessation of the challenged conduct, without a litigated or consent order, does not entitle the plaintiff to fees even if the suit was the catalyst for the change.[791] State courts are, of course, free to interpret their own UDAP statutes differently. However, UDAP litigants who are seeking solely equitable relief should not assume that the defendant's unilateral change of its practices after suit will entitle them to fees.

Complex issues arise where a UDAP action is settled without mention of attorney fees, particularly where the action involves UDAP and non-UDAP claims, and the settlement does not admit the seller's liability on any of these claims. Maine's highest court has held in such a

774 Decker v. Homeguard Sys., 105 Idaho 158, 666 P.2d 1169 (Ct. App. 1983); *see also* Nalen v. Jenkins, 113 Idaho 79, 741 P.2d 366 (Ct. App. 1987).

775 Israel v. Leachman, 72 P.3d 864 (Idaho 2003).

776 Gardner v. Nimnicht Chevrolet Co., 532 So. 2d 26 (Fla. Dist. Ct. App. 1988); Garcia v. Coffman, 1997 NMCA 092, 946 P.2d 216 (N.M. App. Ct. 1997); Standard Fire Ins. Co. v. Stephenson, 963 S.W.2d 81 (Tex. App. 1997).

777 George Grubbs Enterprises v. Bien, 881 S.W.2d 843 (Tex. App. 1994), *rev'd on other grounds*, 900 S.W.2d 337 (Tex. 1995).

778 Dillree v. Devoe, 724 P.2d 171 (Mont. 1986).

779 Collins v. Minn. School of Bus., 655 N.W.2d 320 (Minn. 2003).

780 28 U.S.C. § 1332(b).

781 Mimaco L.L.C. v. Maison Faurie Antiquities, 2000 U.S. App. LEXIS 18335 (10th Cir. July 31, 2000) (unpublished, citation limited).

782 *Id.*

783 Building Concepts, Inc. v. Duncan, 667 S.W.2d 897 (Tex. App. 1984); Benkoski v. Flood, 242 Wis. 2d 652, 626 N.W.2d 851 (App. 2001).

784 Hundred East Credit Corp. v. Eric Schuster Corp., 212 N.J. Super. 350, 515 A.2d 246 (App. Div. 1986).

785 Taylor v. Foy, 91 N.C. App. 82, 370 S.E.2d 442 (1988), *aff'd*, 324 N.C. 331, 377 S.E.2d 745 (1989).

786 City Fin. Co. v. Boykin, 358 S.E.2d 83 (N.C. Ct. App. 1987); Blumenthal v. Ameritex Computer Corp., 646 S.W.2d 283 (Tex. App. 1983).

787 City Fin. Co. v. Boykin, 358 S.E.2d 83 (N.C. Ct. App. 1987); Rodriguez v. Holmstrom, 627 S.W.2d 198 (Tex. Civ. App. 1981).

788 City Fin. Co. v. Boykin, 358 S.E.2d 83 (N.C. Ct. App. 1987).

789 *Id. See also* § 8.8.6, *infra* (fees for appellate work).

790 Maher v. Gagne, 448 U.S. 122, 100 S. Ct. 2570, 65 L. Ed. 2d 653 (1980). *See also* Buckhannon Board & Care Home, Inc. v. W. Va. Dept. of Health and Human Resources, 532 U.S. 598, 121 S. Ct. 1835, 149 L. Ed. 2d 855 (2001).

791 Buckhannon Board & Care Home, Inc. v. W. Va. Dept. of Health and Human Resources, 532 U.S. 598, 121 S. Ct. 1835, 149 L. Ed. 2d 855 (2001).

situation that attorney fees should be awarded where the settlement gives the consumer a positive recovery.[792] "To hold otherwise would compel either the submission of each case to a full trial for the purpose of effectuating the fee provision or the loss to the consumer of the full measure of protection afforded by the legislation."[793]

In Connecticut, the award of attorney fees after a settlement is within the sound discretion of the trial court, and the consumer is entitled to an evidentiary hearing on the question.[794] In Massachusetts, however, an attorney fee award may not be available unless the settlement so stipulates or includes a finding of a UDAP violation.[795] Similarly, a North Carolina court has ruled that a UDAP plaintiff who accepted an offer of judgment prior to trial was not a prevailing party and could not recover fees, although she could have bargained for fees as part of the settlement.[796]

A federal bankruptcy court has upheld another approach. The bankruptcy court looked behind the settlement and determined on its own—without argument from the parties—which claims had merit and which did not. Finding Truth in Lending claims (that authorize attorney fees) to have merit, but finding the RICO and UDAP claims not to have merit, the court awarded only some of the fees requested. This was based in part on the fact that work on Truth in Lending claims was separate from work on the UDAP and RICO claims.[797]

8.8.4.5.2 *Can a seller ask the consumer to waive fees in a settlement?*

Problems of attorney fees in settlements become even more complex when the seller seeks to have the consumer waive his or her attorney fees as part of the settlement agreement. These issues are treated in another NCLC manual.[798] One case is of special importance to public interest attorneys. The New Jersey Supreme Court in *Coleman v. Fiore Brothers, Inc.*[799] held that sellers can not insist that public interest attorneys simultaneously negotiate the claims on the merits and the consumer's attorney fee award settlement. The legal services or other public interest attorney can inform the seller that the consumer is waiving attorney fees, but the seller can not ask the consumer to do so until after the claims on the merits have been settled.

The consumer's attorney should advise the seller's attorney that the consumer's settlement on the merits will not preclude a subsequent request for fees. The consumer attorney's silence on this matter may in fact foreclose the ability to subsequently seek fees.[800] If asked, the consumer's attorney should also indicate the number of hours expended and the hourly rate at which the consumer's attorney believes the services should be compensated.

Coleman is particularly interesting in light of the United States Supreme Court's decision in *Evans v. Jeff D.*,[801] holding that a plaintiff in a Civil Rights Act action could be forced to waive attorney fees during the settlement on the merits. *Coleman* distinguished *Jeff D.* because *Jeff D.* only holds that Congress did not intend to require in Civil Rights Act cases separate negotiations for the merits and attorney fees. The New Jersey Supreme Court still had to determine the intent of the New Jersey legislature in enacting the New Jersey UDAP statute. The New Jersey court was particularly impressed that the UDAP statute primarily provided for damage awards, while injunctive relief was an important component of Civil Rights Act cases.

The *Coleman* court made an important distinction between public interest attorneys and other attorneys. Public interest attorneys are not paid by their clients and simultaneous negotiation of fees and the merits places them in a particularly difficult position. Other attorneys are paid by their clients and can deduct their fee from the settlement, as long as the retainer is appropriately drafted. By contrast, public interest attorneys generally do not collect a fee from the consumer's settlement. Consequently, the *Coleman* court only requires a bifurcation of negotiations between the merits and fees when a public interest attorney is bringing the action.

8.8.4.5.3 *The catalyst theory and how to preserve a fee claim when settling a case*

Until 2001, federal courts accepted the "catalyst" rule, which held that a plaintiff prevails and is therefore entitled to recover under a federal fee-shifting statute when the lawsuit causes a change of conduct by the defendant, even if a favorable order on the merits is never entered. In *Buckhannon Board & Care Home, Inc. v. West Virginia Department of Health and Human Resources*,[802] the Court

792 Poussard v. Commercial Credit Plan, 479 A.2d 881 (Me. 1984); *see also* Bittner v. Tri-County Toyota, Inc., 58 Ohio St. 3d 143, 569 N.E.2d 464 (1991) (award of fees after settlement where settlement based on consumer's UDAP and contract claims).

793 Poussard v. Commercial Credit Plan, 479 A.2d 881 (Me. 1984). *Accord* Hernandez v. Monterey Village Assocs. Ltd. P'ship, 17 Conn. App. 421, 553 A.2d 617 (1989).

794 Hernandez v. Monterey Village Assocs. Ltd. P'ship (Hernandez II), 24 Conn. App. 514, 589 A.2d 888 (1991).

795 Riedle v. Peterson, 29 Mass. App. Ct. 966, 560 N.E.2d 724 (1990).

796 Evans v. Full Circle Productions, Inc., 114 N.C. App. 777, 443 S.E.2d 108 (1994). *But see* Collins v. Minn. School of Bus., 655 N.W.2d 320 (Minn. 2003).

797 *In re* Mattera, 144 B.R. 687 (E.D. Pa. 1992).

798 *See* National Consumer Law Center, Consumer Class Actions: A Practical Litigation Guide §§ 11.9, 15.3 (5th ed. 2002 and Supp.).

799 113 N.J. 594, 552 A.2d 141 (1989).

800 *Id. But see* Muckleshoot Tribe v. Puget Sound Power & Light Co., 875 F.2d 695 (9th Cir. 1989) (U.S. Civil Rights Act case); Ashley v. Atlantic Richfield Co., 794 F.2d 128 (3d Cir. 1986).

801 475 U.S. 717, 106 S. Ct. 1531, 89 L. Ed. 2d 747 (1986).

802 532 U.S. 598, 121 S. Ct. 1835, 149 L. Ed. 2d 855 (2001).

rejected this rule and held that a plaintiff can achieve prevailing party status only by obtaining a "material alteration of the legal relationship of the parties."[803]

The Court stated that a "private settlement" that does not "entail the judicial approval and oversight involved in consent decrees" is insufficient.[804] For a party to be entitled to fees, a final order must be entered in the case which permits the court to retain jurisdiction for enforcement purposes under the standards set forth in *Kokkonen v. Guardian Life Ins. Co.*[805] This standard can be met by "enforceable judgments on the merits and court-ordered consent decrees."[806]

While the Supreme Court made it clear in *Buckhannon* that it was announcing a general rule that applied to most, if not all, federal fee-shifting statutes,[807] the decision only controls as to federal law. Courts interpreting state fee-shifting statutes may find *Buckhannon* persuasive[808] but are free to adopt their own views about the catalyst theory and the formal requirements of settlements. Some states may have statutes or rules of court that define "prevailing party" more generously than *Buckhannon*.[809] Nonetheless, it is prudent to assume that state courts will impose the same requirements and to draft settlement documents accordingly.

For courts that follow *Buckhannon*, the following ways of settling a case are likely to preserve entitlement to fees:

- Negotiation of payment of fees in an acceptable amount as part of the settlement on the merits.[810]
- An agreed judgment for money, as long as it is clear that fees have not been waived. The ability to enforce a money judgment by judicial process should be considered the functional equivalent of the judicial oversight that was the hallmark of a court-ordered consent decree for the *Buckhannon* court.
- An agreed order that specifies the steps the defendant will take (e.g., repair of a vehicle, cancellation of a contract), as long as the court retains jurisdiction to enforce it. It is clearer that the plaintiff is the prevailing party if the order the court signs actually recites the steps the defendant will take, rather than referring to a separately filed document, although the latter format is probably also sufficient.[811]
- An agreed order of any sort that includes a finding or stipulation that the plaintiff is the prevailing party.[812] Such a stipulation is probably sufficient even if it is not signed by the court. While *Buckhannon* does not explicitly endorse this method of preserving the right to attorney fees, the court never indicated that winning an enforceable judgment or a court-ordered consent decree is a jurisdictional requirement that can not be satisfied by a stipulation. At least one court has held, however, that merely reserving the issue of attorney fees for the court, without stipulating that the plaintiff is the prevailing party, is insufficient.[813]

---

803 *Id.*, 121 S. Ct. at 1840.

804 *Id.*, 121 S. Ct. at 1840 n.7.

805 *Id.*; Tisdale v. Dept. of Developmental Servs., 317 F.3d 1000 (9th Cir. 2003); Truesdell v. Philadelphia Hous. Auth., 290 F.3d 159 (3d Cir. 2002) (district court's order incorporating plaintiff's settlement in mandatory terms is sufficient); Smyth v. Rivero, 282 F.3d 268 (4th Cir. 2002) (consent decree on which fees can be based is one that is enforceable as a judicial decree by the court that entered it); Am. Disability Ass'n v. Chmielarz, 289 F.3d 1315 (11th Cir. 2002); Vasquez v. County of Lake, 2002 WL 31256166 (N.D. Ill. Oct. 7, 2002).

806 532 U.S. 598, 121 S. Ct. 1835, 1840, 149 L. Ed. 2d 855 (2001).

807 *Id.*, 121 S. Ct. at 1838 ("Numerous federal statutes allow courts to award attorney's fees and costs to the 'prevailing party.' The question presented here is whether this term includes a party that has failed to secure a judgment on the merits or a court-ordered consent decree. . . ."), 1839, n.4 (citing various fee-shifting statutes, referring to list of additional statutes in Marek v. Chesny, 473 U.S. 1, 105 S. Ct. 3012 87 L. Ed. 2d 1 (1985), and saying that all are interpreted consistently).

808 *Compare* Graham v. Daimlerchrysler Corp., 2002 WL 31732556 (Cal. App. Dec. 16, 2002) (unpublished, citation limited) (rejecting *Buckhannon* and adhering to catalyst theory for state law warranty claim), *review granted* (Cal. Feb. 19, 2003) *and* Moedt v. Gen. Motors Corp., 60 P.3d 240 (Ariz. App. 2002) (awarding fees for settlement of state lemon law claim even though *Buckhannon* might have precluded fees for federal claim) *with* Pitchford v. Oakwood Mobile Homes, Inc., 212 F. Supp. 2d 613 (W.D. Va. 2002) (adopting interpretation of Virginia UDAP fee award standard similar to *Buckhannon*) *and* Wallerstein v. Stew Leonard's Dairy, 258 Conn. 299, 780 A.2d 916 (2001) (citing *Buckhannon* as authority that judgment entered under Connecticut equivalent of Rule 68 made plaintiff the prevailing party); Tibbetts v. Sight 'N Sound Appliance Centers, Inc., 77 P.3d 1042 (Okla. 2003) (adopting *Buckhannon* standard); Chase v. DaimlerChrysler Corp., 587 S.E.2d 521 (Va. 2003) (adopting interpretation of "successful" party in Virginia lemon law similar to *Buckhannon*).

809 *See* Arvetis v. Euro Classic Body Shop, 2003 WL 22120939 (Cal. App. Sept. 15, 2003) (unpublished, citation limited) (plaintiff who settled case met civil procedure code's definition of prevailing party as one who has obtained net recovery).

810 *See* Am. Disability Ass'n v. Chmielarz, 289 F.3d 1315 (11th Cir. 2002) (dismissal order that approved, adopted, and ratified settlement, and retained jurisdiction to enforce it, was consent decree and plaintiff was prevailing party).

811 Labotest, Inc. v. Bonta, 297 F.3d 892 (9th Cir. 2002).

812 *See* Pitchford v. Oakwood Mobile Homes, Inc., 212 F. Supp. 2d 613 (W.D. Va. 2002) (settlement that merely reserved fee issue for court insufficient; court says that it would have sufficed if parties had stipulated that plaintiff was entitled to fees and that court would decide amount); Blaylock v. Johns Hopkins Fed. Credit Union, 831 A.2d 1120 (Md. Spec. App. 2003) (finding stipulation sufficient); Chase v. DaimlerChrysler Corp., 587 S.E.2d 521 (Va. 2003) (lemon law case) (consent order stating that plaintiff was the prevailing party would be sufficient).

813 Dorfsman v. Law Sch. Admission Council, 2001 U.S. Dist. LEXIS 24044 (E.D. Pa. Nov. 28, 2001); *see also* Oil, Chem. & Atomic Workers Int'l Union v. Dep't of Energy, 288 F.3d 452 (D.C. Cir. 2002) (no fees despite stipulation that dismissal is "without prejudice to the right of plaintiff to obtain . . . an award of attorney's fees"; court does not discuss whether this provision amounted to a stipulation that plaintiff was the prevailing party); Pitchford v. Oakwood Mobile Homes, Inc., 212 F. Supp.

Settlement methods that are less likely to preserve the right to fees are:

- A stipulation resolving the merits that is filed with the court but is signed only by the parties and does not state that the plaintiff is the prevailing party.
- A dismissal entry, even if the case is dismissed pursuant to an agreement signed by the parties under which the defendant agrees to the relief the plaintiff sought.[814]

This topic is discussed in more detail in another manual.[815]

8.8.4.6 Collateral Proceedings, Including Proceedings Relating to the Fee Award

Attorney fees should also be available for the consumer's defense of the seller's declaratory action where the defense was related to the consumer's eventual UDAP counterclaim filed in a later damage action.[816] Fees should also be awarded for actions necessary to collect UDAP judgments.[817]

A Florida court has worked out a rule for determining if attorney work expended solely for the purpose of obtaining court-awarded attorney fees should be reimbursed by a higher fee award. Attorney work is not recoverable if it will not help the client. But where the consumer is obligated to pay the attorney fee, the attorney's work to obtain the fee award helps the consumer and should be recovered.[818] An Ohio appellate court, however, has held that a trial court acted within its discretion in denying a request for attorney fees incurred by the consumer for defense of the defendant's appeal of an award of fees for work on the underlying case.[819]

8.8.5 Attorney Fees in Arbitration Proceedings

8.8.5.1 Where Arbitration Restricts Prevailing Consumer's Right to Fees

Where a UDAP statute authorizes a prevailing consumer to recover attorney fees, but the arbitration clause or the rules of the applicable arbitration service provider restrict the award of such fees, then this limitation should be against public policy and unconscionable.[820] The result should be the same where an award of UDAP attorney fees to a prevailing consumer is mandatory under the statute, but where the arbitration service provider rules make this discretionary with the arbitrator.

The issue becomes more complex where state arbitration law restricts the prevailing consumer's right to fees. Most state versions of the Uniform Arbitration Act indicate that, unless otherwise agreed, the arbitrators' expenses and fees, together with other expenses, *not* including counsel fees, incurred in the conduct of the arbitration, shall be paid as provided in the award. In other words, the arbitrator has discretion to apportion between the parties the responsibility for various expenses, but *not* for attorney fees, unless the parties so agree.[821]

Look for an agreement that a prevailing consumer recover statutory fees not only in the arbitration clause itself, but also in the rules of any arbitration service provider referenced in the arbitration clause. Courts may also view UDAP language explicitly providing for attorney fees as overruling arbitration statutes that generally limit the award of such fees.[822] On the other hand, in Maryland the UDAP statute is

---

2d 613 (W.D. Va. 2002) (settlement that reserved fee issue for court insufficient; court says that it would have sufficed if settlement had said plaintiff was entitled to fees and that court would decide amount). *But cf.* Tisdale v. Dept. of Developmental Servs., 317 F.3d 1000 (9th Cir. 2003) (stipulation that court retained jurisdiction to resolve attorney fee issues was sufficient where settlement agreement was binding and enforceable by court order).

814 *See* Smyth v. Rivero, 282 F.3d 268 (4th Cir. 2002) (dismissal order that merely acknowledges, refers to, or approves settlement agreement is insufficient). A federal court does not have jurisdiction to enforce a settlement agreement once a case is dismissed, unless the dismissal entry embodies the settlement agreement or retains jurisdiction to enforce it. Kokkonen v. Guardian Life Ins. Co., 511 U.S. 375, 114 S. Ct. 1673, 128 L. Ed. 2d 391 (1994).

815 National Consumer Law Center, Consumer Warranty Law § 2.7.6.5 (2d ed. 2001 and Supp.).

816 Safeco Ins. Co. of Am. v. JMG Restaurants, 37 Wash. App. 1, 680 P.2d 409 (1984).

817 Oshry v. Statewide Auto Sales, 2002 WL 104422 (Cal. App. Jan. 28, 2002) (unpublished, citation limited) (based on California statute); Dee v. Sweet, 489 S.E.2d 823 (Ga. 1997) (fees awarded for work necessary to collect civil RICO judgment); Tanksley v. Cook, 360 N.J. Super. 63, 821 A.2d 524 (App. Div. 2003). *See also* Nunez v. Interstate Corporate Sys., Inc., 799 P.2d 30 (Ariz. App. 1990) (awarding fees under Fair Debt Collection Practices Act for collection of judgment; otherwise would defeat purpose of fee-shifting provision to encourage suits by small claimants as a means of deterring abusive debt collection). *But see* A&M Ins., Inc. v. Compass Software, Inc., 2000 Wash. App. LEXIS 938 (June 19, 2000).

818 B&L Motors, Inc. v. Bignotti, 427 So. 2d 1070 (Fla. Dist. Ct. App. 1983).

819 Tanner v. Tom Harrigan Chrysler Plymouth, 82 Ohio App. 3d 767, 613 N.E.2d 650 (1992).

820 *See* National Consumer Law Center, Consumer Arbitration Agreements § 4.3.6.2 (4th ed. 2004).

821 But the Texas Uniform Arbitration Act specifically allows attorney fees in arbitration proceedings. Moreover, an indication in the UDAP statute itself as to whether such fees are allowed in arbitration should control over contrary language of more general applicability in the state arbitration statute.

822 *See* Drywall Sys., Inc. v. Zvi Constr. Co., 435 Mass. 664, 761 N.E.2d 482 (2002) (where UDAP statute provided for attorney fees, arbitrator can award fees even where state statute otherwise limits fees); *see also* Kamakazi Music Corp. v. Robbins Music Corp., 684 F.2d 228 (2d Cir. 1982) (attorney fees awarded in arbitration).

interpreted as only authorizing a court to award fees, not an arbitrator.[823]

Where state law prevents a consumer from recovering attorney fees in an arbitration, there is a strong argument that a court should be able to award the fees when the consumer seeks to confirm the award in court.[824] If neither the arbitrator nor the court can award UDAP attorney fees to a prevailing consumer, then it should be unconscionable to force a consumer to litigate UDAP claims in arbitration. The legislative intent behind the UDAP statute has been frustrated.[825]

8.8.5.2 Where Arbitrator with Authority to Do So Fails to Award Fees to Prevailing Consumer

If, under a UDAP statute, attorney fees are discretionary with the court, then there may be little a consumer can do if the arbitrator decides not to award such fees. But under many state UDAP statutes, attorney fees are mandatory, and must be reasonable.[826] Where an arbitrator fails to award fees or an award is unreasonable, one possible option is for the consumer immediately (state statutes may require this within 90 days of an award) to go into state court and ask the court to modify the award to include reasonable fees. While courts generally do not review the merits of an arbitration decision, courts do so where there is a manifest disregard of a statutory right. Courts differ as to standards they will employ in reviewing an arbitrator's decision as to manifest disregard of the law, but will more closely scrutinize disregard of statutory law than common law. The law in this area is examined in another NCLC manual.[827]

Of course, the consumer's challenge is even more difficult if the arbitrator's ruling does not specify upon which claims the consumer has prevailed, but only issues a decision as to the amount the consumer is owed. Then the consumer does not even know if the UDAP claim prevailed, authorizing the fee award.[828] In response to this problem, the California Supreme Court construes the state arbitration statute as requiring an arbitrator in a discrimination claim to issue a written decision. That decision must reveal the essential findings and conclusions on which the award is based.[829]

8.8.5.3 Where Arbitration Agreement Provides Consumer Must Pay Prevailing Defendants' Fees

Many arbitration clauses and rules of arbitration service providers contain a "loser pays rule" that requires non-prevailing consumer plaintiffs to pay the attorney fees and expenses of the prevailing defendant. These "loser-pays" provisions often have the effect of substantially re-writing the attorney fee provisions of the UDAP statute involved, which typically only authorizes attorney fees and costs for a prevailing consumer, not for a prevailing defendant.

Such arbitration clauses have a profound effect on the risks a consumer takes in bringing a UDAP action, even though the statute was enacted to encourage consumers to bring even small claims. In the related context of civil rights statutes, which also provide remedies for individuals wronged by more powerful corporations, the Supreme Court in *Christiansburg Garment Co. v. EEOC* enunciated the rationale behind the UDAP statute: "To take the further step of assessing attorney's fees against plaintiffs simply because they do not finally prevail would substantially add to the risks inherent in most litigation and would undercut the efforts of Congress to promote the vigorous enforcement of the provisions of Title VII."[830]

When arbitration clauses impose "loser pays rules," it directly interferes with the legislative intent in enacting UDAP statutes, and should thus make the arbitration clause against public policy, unconscionable, and unenforceable. Nevertheless, courts are divided as to whether a loser pay rule makes an arbitration requirement unenforceable.[831]

823 Curtis G. Testerman Co. v. Buck, 340 Md. 569, 667 A.2d 649 (1995).

824 Ins. Co. of No. Am. v. Accousti Engineering Co., 579 So. 2d 77 (Fla. 1991); Charbonneau v. Morse Operations, Inc., 727 So. 2d 1017 (Fla. Dist. Ct. App. 1999); Raymond James & Assoc., Inc. v. Wieneke, 556 So. 2d 800 (Fla. Dist. Ct. App. 1990); Fewox v. McMerit Constr. Co., 556 So. 2d 419 (Fla. Dist. Ct. App. 1989).

825 *See* National Consumer Law Center, Consumer Arbitration Agreements § 4.3.6.2 (4th ed. 2004).

826 *See* § 8.8.3, *supra.*

827 *See* National Consumer Law Center, Consumer Arbitration Agreements § 10.5 (4th ed. 2004).

828 Bennett v. California Custom Coach, 234 Cal. App. 3d 333, 285 Cal. Rptr. 649 (1991) (where consumer pleaded various theories, and an arbitrator ruled in the consumer's favor, but with no mention of a UDAP recovery, the consumer was not entitled to UDAP attorney fees). *See also* Cruz v. Northwestern Chrysler Plymouth Sales, 674 N.E.2d 871 (Ill. App. Ct. 1996), *aff'd on other grounds*, 179 Ill. 2d 271, 688 N.E.2d 653 (1997).

829 Armendariz v. Foundation Health Psychare Servs., Inc., 24 Cal. 4th 83, 6 P.3d 669 (2000). *See also* Halligan v. Piper Jaffray, Inc., 148 F.3d 197 (2d Cir. 1998) (failure to provide reasoning relevant to whether the decision is in manifest disregard of the law). *But see* Merrill Lynch, Pierce, Fenner & Smith, Inc. v. Jaros, 70 F.3d 418 (6th Cir. 1995) and other cases cited at NCLC's Consumer Arbitration Agreements § 10.5.4 (4th ed. 2004).

830 434 U.S. 412, 422, 98 S. Ct. 694, 700, 54 L. Ed. 2d 648 (1978).

831 See National Consumer Law Center, Consumer Arbitration Agreements §§ 4.3.8, 5.3.2.3 (4th ed. 2004).

8.8.6 Attorney Fees for Appellate Work

8.8.6.1 When Are Such Fees Awarded?

Attorney fees can be awarded for appellate work,[832] as long as the consumer's judgment is preserved in at least some respect on appeal.[833] In one case, the seller prevailed on most issues on appeal, but the consumer did prevail on some and saved a positive UDAP recovery. The consumer received fees for the appeal, but not as much as if the consumer had prevailed on all appellate issues.[834] The seller, on the other hand, should receive no fees even if it prevails on UDAP issues on appeal.[835]

Where the consumer wins by a default judgment, consumer attorneys should obtain their attorney fees if the merchant appeals the denial of the reopening of the default judgment.[836] Similarly, a court has found that a contingent award of attorney fees for appellate work applies to the consumer's legal expenses to object to the reopening of a default judgment and the consumer's successful appeal of the court's decision to reopen the default judgment.[837]

832 Cange v. Stotler & Co., 913 F.2d 1204 (7th Cir. 1990) (Illinois law); Bandura v. Orkin Exterminating Co., 865 F.2d 816 (7th Cir. 1988) (Illinois law); State *ex rel.* Corbin v. Tucson Public Auction, 147 Ariz. 213, 709 P.2d 570 (Ct. App. 1985); Oshry v. Statewide Auto Sales, 2002 WL 104422 (Cal. App. Jan. 28, 2002) (unpublished, citation limited); Rocky Mtn. Rhino Lining, Inc. v. Rhino Linings USA, Inc., 37 P.3d 458 (Colo. App. 2001), *rev'd on other grounds*, 62 P.2d 142 (Colo. 2003); Bert Smith Oldsmobile, Inc. v. Franklin, 400 So. 2d 1235 (Fla. Dist. Ct. App. 1981); Nalen v. Jenkins, 113 Idaho 79, 741 P.2d 366 (Ct. App. 1987); Affrunti v. Village Ford Sales, Inc., 597 N.E.2d 1242 (Ill. App. Ct. 1992); Chesrow v. DuPage Auto Brokers, Inc., 200 Ill. App. 3d 72, 557 N.E.2d 1301 (1990); Warren v. LeMay, 142 Ill. App. 3d 550, 491 N.E.2d 464 (1986); Laurents v. Louisiana Mobile Homes, Inc., 689 So. 2d 536 (La. Ct. App. 1997); Bryant v. Sears Consumer Fin. Corp., 617 So. 2d 1191 (La. Ct. App. 1993); Chrysler Credit Corp. v. Walker, 488 So. 2d 209 (La. Ct. App. 1986); Beaulieu v. Dorsey, 562 A.2d 678 (Me. 1989); Linkage Corp. v. Trustees of Boston University, 425 Mass. 1, 679 N.E.2d 191 (1997), *cert. denied*, 522 U.S. 1015 (1997); Bonofiglio v. Commercial Union Ins. Co., 412 Mass. 612, 591 N.E.2d 197 (1992) (fees awarded for consumer's successful defense of cross-appeal); Haddad v. Gonzalez, 410 Mass. 855, 576 N.E.2d 658 (1991); Yorke Mgmt. v. Castro, 406 Mass. 17, 546 N.E.2d 342 (1989); Manzaro v. McCann, 401 Mass. 880, 519 N.E.2d 1337 (1988); Patry v. Liberty Mobilehome Sales, Inc., 475 N.E.2d 392 (Mass. 1985); Linthicum v. Archambault, 379 Mass. 381, 398 N.E.2d 482 (1979); O'Connor v. Brophy, 773 N.E.2d 474 (Mass. App. 2002) (reversing denial of appellate fees); Jordan v. Transnational Motors, Inc., 537 N.W.2d 471 (Mich. Ct. App. 1995) (plaintiff entitled to fees for time spent pursuing trial fees in appellate court); Smolen v. Dahlmann Apartments, Ltd., 186 Mich. App. 292, 463 N.W.2d 261 (1990); Temborius v. Slatkin, 157 Mich. App. 587, 403 N.W.2d 821 (1986) (while appellate attorney fees are available, none will be awarded in this case because of the particular facts of the case); Hale v. Basin Motor Co., 110 N.M. 314, 795 P.2d 1006 (1990); Garlock v. Henson, 112 N.C. App. 243, 435 S.E.2d 114 (1993); Cotton v. Stanley, 380 S.E.2d 419 (N.C. Ct. App. 1989) (fees should be awarded for appellate work, not just work preparing for new trial); City Fin. Co. v. Boykin, 358 S.E.2d 83 (N.C. Ct. App. 1987); Parker v. I&F Insulation Co., 89 Ohio St. 3d 261, 730 N.E.2d 972 (2000); Tanner v. Tom Harrigan Chrysler Plymouth, Inc., 82 Ohio App. 3d 764, 613 N.E.2d 649 (1991); Kish v. Van Note, 692 S.W.2d 463 (Tex. 1985); Mouton v. Cassello, 693 S.W.2d 556 (Tex. App. 1985); North Star Dodge Sales, Inc. v. Luna, 653 S.W.2d 892 (Tex. App. 1983); Chrysler-Plymouth City Inc. v. Guerrero, 620 S.W.2d 700 (Tex. Civ. App. 1981); Long v. Fox, 625 S.W.2d 376 (Tex. Civ. App. 1981); Rodriguez v. Holmstrom, 627 S.W.2d 198 (Tex. Civ. App. 1981); Lerma v. Brecheizen, 602 S.W.2d 318 (Tex. Civ. App. 1980) ($2000 to defend appeal to appellate court, another $1750 if seller also appeals to Texas Supreme Court); Riverside Nat'l Bank v. Lewis, 572 S.W.2d 553 (Tex. Civ. App. 1978); Volkswagen of Am., Inc. v. Licht, 544 S.W.2d 442 (Tex. Civ. App. 1976); Bruntaeger v. Zeller, 515 A.2d 123 (Vt. 1986); Washington State Physicians Ins. Exchange & Ass'n v. Fisons Corp., 122 Wash. 2d 299, 858 P.2d 1054 (1993); Mason v. Mortgage Am., Inc., 114 Wash. 2d 842, 792 P.2d 142 (1990); Olson v. M. L. & D. Builders, Inc., 1999 Wash. App. LEXIS 14 (Jan. 7, 1999); Sing v. John L. Scott, Inc., 920 P.2d 589 (Wash. App. 1996), *rev'd on other grounds*, 948 P.2d 816 (Wash. 1997); Shands v. Castrovinci, 115 Wis. 2d 352, 340 N.W.2d 506 (1983) (consumer's attorney fees to appeal or to oppose appeal); Harris, Luck, Rubin v. Turenske, 1996 Wisc. App. LEXIS 1424 (Nov. 12, 1996); Mulligan v. Koehler, 557 N.W.2d 257 (Wis. App. 1996) (unpublished and non-precedential, text available at 1996 Wisc. App. LEXIS 1241); Prestien v. Roets, 477 N.W.2d 363 (Wis. Ct. App. 1991) (unpublished and non-precedential, text available at 1991 Wisc. App. LEXIS 1296). *See also* Baird v. Norwest Bank, 843 P.2d 327 (Mont. 1992). *Contra* Decker v. Homeguard Sys., 105 Idaho 158, 666 P.2d 1169 (Ct. App. 1983) (no appellate attorney fees where seller's appeal brought in good faith and where a genuine issue of law presented); M&W Gear Co. v. A.W. Dynamometer Inc., 97 Ill. App. 3d 904, 424 N.E.2d 356 (1981). *But cf.* Sunset Pools v. Schaefer, 869 S.W.2d 883 (Mo. Ct. App. 1994) (attorney fees on appeal discretionary and not awarded in this case); Tanner v. Tom Harrison Chrysler Plymouth, Inc., 82 Ohio App. 3d 767, 613 N.E.2d 650 (1992) (award discretionary with trial court).

833 *See* Robinwood Building & Dev. Co. v. Pettigrew, 737 S.W.2d 110 (Tex. App. 1987) (implicit in court's attorney fee award for appellate work was condition that consumer preserve judgment); Radford v. J.J.B. Enterprises, Ltd., 163 Wis. 2d 534, 472 N.W.2d 790 (1991). *But see* Parker v. I&F Insulation Co., 89 Ohio St. 3d 261, 730 N.E.2d 972 (2000) (consumer not entitled to fees for seller's appeal in which seller won 63% reduction of trial court's UDAP award).

834 Town East Ford, Sales, Inc v. Gray, 730 S.W.2d 796 (Tex. App. 1987) ($15,000 award reduced to $5000); *see also* Golber v. BayBank Valley Trust Co., 46 Mass. App. Ct. 256, 704 N.E.2d 1191 (1999) (UDAP plaintiffs entitled to fees for defending against defendant's unsuccessful appeal but not for pursuing their own unsuccessful cross-appeal); Schmidt v. Cornerstone Investments, Inc., 115 Wash. 2d 148, 795 P.2d 1143 (1990) (consumer can not receive fees for all work where 13 issues were not related to UDAP claim); Sign-O-Lite Signs, Inc. v. Delaurenti Florists, Inc., 825 P.2d 714 (Wash. Ct. App. 1992); Nguyen v. Glendale Constr. Co., 56 Wash. App. 196, 782 P.2d 1110 (1989).

835 Sign-O-Lite Signs, Inc. v. Delaurenti Florists, Inc., 825 P.2d 714 (Wash. Ct. App. 1992).

836 *See* § 8.8.4.4, *supra*.

837 Rodriguez v. Holmstrom, 627 S.W.2d 198 (Tex. Civ. App. 1981).

There are strong policy arguments why a consumer should be awarded attorney fees for appellate work, particularly where the seller is appealing the lower court's finding of a deceptive trade practice. It makes no sense to balance the seller's superior legal resources and encourage consumers to press small claims (by awarding attorney fees to successful consumer litigants) only at the trial level, while allowing the seller to wear down a consumer through a costly appellate process.[838]

8.8.6.2 Who Determines Appellate Attorney Fees?

Be sure to comply with any appellate rules as to preserving the right to attorney fee awards for appellate work. For example, in Washington attorneys must submit an affidavit ten days *prior* to oral argument to obtain attorney fees for appellate work in some situations.[839] Failure to do so may prevent any attorney fee award for appellate work.[840]

Where consumer attorneys can receive fees for appellate work, they should consider developing a strategy for calculating such an award at the trial level, and should not just wait for an appeal to materialize. In Texas and a few other jurisdictions, UDAP judgments typically specify not only the size of the attorney fee award, but also an additional attorney fee if the seller appeals.[841] The trial court also has the option of awarding appellate attorney fees subject to a remittitur.[842] The advantage of calculating the fee in advance at the trial stage is that the trial court will be accustomed to awarding such fees, and has already ruled for the consumer, and is thus likely to grant a sizeable fee if the seller tries to appeal the court's own judgment.

In some states, the trial court will not be authorized to determine appellate fees prior to the appeal. The Massachusetts Supreme Judicial Court[843] and a Wisconsin appellate court[844] have ruled that a trial court on its own may not award attorney fees for appellate work. The appellate court must specifically direct the trial court to calculate attorney fees for the appellate work.

If the trial court does not specify an amount for appellate attorney fees, the appeals court may determine the amount itself.[845] But appellate courts, not examining the factual details of the case and unaccustomed to awarding attorney fees, may be less sympathetic than trial courts. An appellate court may also remand a case to the trial court to determine the proper size of fees for appellate work, thereby delaying the fee award.[846]

838 Warren v. LeMay, 142 Ill. App. 3d 550, 491 N.E.2d 464 (1986); Bonofiglio v. Commercial Union Ins. Co., 412 Mass. 612, 591 N.E.2d 197 (1992); O'Connor v. Brophy, 773 N.E.2d 474 (Mass. App. 2002); Shands v. Castrovinci, 115 Wis. 2d 352, 340 N.W.2d 506 (1983); *see also* Nalen v. Jenkins, 113 Idaho 79, 741 P.2d 366 (Ct. App. 1987); Hale v. Basin Motor Co., 110 N.M. 314, 795 P.2d 1006 (1990).

839 Wash. R. App. P. 18.1

840 Mason v. Mortgage Am., Inc., 114 Wash. 2d 842, 792 P.2d 142 (1990); Schmidt v. Cornerstone Investments, Inc., 115 Wash. 2d 148, 795 P.2d 1143 (1990).

841 *See, e.g.*, McGuire v. Texas Farmers Inc., 727 S.W.2d 1 (Tex. App. 1987) (attorney fees set out for appeals to state middle-level appellate court and to state supreme court); E.F. Hutton & Co. v. Youngblood, 708 S.W.2d 865 (Tex. App. 1986) ($5000 attorney fee if merchant appeals to middle-level appellate court, $2000 if appeal to state supreme court, and $800 if writ is granted); Jasso v. Duron, 681 S.W.2d 279 (Tex. App. 1984) ($3750 attorney fees it merchant appeals to middle-level appellate court; another $2250 if appeals to state supreme court); North Star Dodge Sales, Inc. v. Luna, 653 S.W.2d 892 (Tex. App. 1983), *aff'd*, 667 S.W.2d 115 (Tex. 1984) ($5000 attorney fees if merchant appeals to middle-level appellate court; another $5000 if appeals to state supreme court); Cameo Constr. Co. v. Campbell, 642 S.W.2d 10 (Tex. App. 1982) ($15,000 attorney fees if merchant appeals); Chrysler-Plymouth City Inc. v. Guerrero, 620 S.W.2d 700 (Tex. Civ. App. 1981) ($2000 attorney fees if merchant appeals); Wilkinson v. Smith, 31 Wash. App. 1, 639 P.2d 768 (1982).

842 *See, e.g.*, Long v. Fox, 625 S.W.2d 376 (Tex. Civ. App. 1981).

843 Patry v. Liberty Mobilehome Sales, Inc., 475 N.E.2d 392 (Mass. 1985); *see also* Picciuto v. Dwyer, 32 Mass. App. Ct. 137, 586 N.E.2d 38 (1992) (appellate court directs party to submit fee request to it); Trempe v. Aetna Casualty & Surety Co., 20 Mass. App. Ct. 448, 480 N.E.2d 670 (1985).

844 Mulligan v. Koehler, 557 N.W.2d 257 (Wis. App. 1996) (unpublished and non-precedential, text available at 1996 Wisc. App. LEXIS 1241).

845 *See, e.g.*, Chrysler Credit Corp. v. Walker, 488 So. 2d 209 (La. Ct. App. 1986) ($1000 for appellate attorney fees); Yorke Mgmt. v. Castro, 406 Mass. 17, 546 N.E.2d 342 (1989); Picciuto v. Dwyer, 32 Mass. App. Ct. 137, 586 N.E.2d 38 (1992); Chattin v. Cape May Greene, Inc., 243 N.J. Super. 590, 581 A.2d 91 (1990), *aff'd per curiam*, 124 N.J. 943, 591 A.2d 943 (1991) (in New Jersey, applications for attorneys fees for appellate work must be presented to the appellate court); Safeco Ins. Co. of Am. v. JMG Restaurants, 37 Wash. App. 1, 680 P.2d 409 (1984) ($12,600 for appellate attorney fees); Sherwood v. Bellevue Dodge, Inc., 35 Wash. App. 741, 669 P.2d 1258 (1983); Kelly v. Dick Balch Chevrolet Co., No. 7263-1-I (Wash. Ct. App. 1981).

846 Taylor v. Medenica, 332 S.C. 324, 504 S.E.2d 590 (1998). *See* Garlock v. Henson, 112 N.C. App. 243, 435 S.E.2d 114 (1993); Washington State Physicians Ins. Exchange & Ass'n v. Fisons Corp., 122 Wash. 2d 299, 858 P.2d 1054 (1993). *See, e.g.*, Bandura v. Orkin Exterminating Co., 865 F.2d 816 (7th Cir. 1988) (Illinois law); Bert Smith Oldsmobile, Inc. v. Franklin, 400 So. 2d 1235 (Fla. Dist. Ct. App. 1981); Warren v. LeMay, 142 Ill. App. 3d 550, 491 N.E.2d 464 (1986); Fraser Eng'g Co. v. Desmond, 26 Mass. App. Ct. 99, 524 N.E.2d 110 (1988); Dorgan v. Loukas, 473 N.E.2d 1151 (Mass. App. Ct. 1985); Thomas v. French, 30 Wash. App. 811, 638 P.2d 613 (1981), *rev'd on other grounds*, 659 P.2d 1097 (Wash. 1983).

8.8.7 Types of Representation Entitled to Fees

8.8.7.1 Attorney Fees for Legal Services Attorneys

Legal services attorneys receiving funds from the Legal Services Corporation (LSC) have restrictions on their ability to seek attorney fees. On the other hand, there are many different types of legal services offices, and only some of these are LSC-funded.

Legal services attorneys not subject to the current LSC restrictions have consistently been held entitled to attorney fees in Truth-in-Lending litigation.[847] While there are fewer cases in the UDAP context, courts invariably hold that attorney fees can be awarded to legal services attorneys who bring successful UDAP actions.[848] For example, the Wisconsin Supreme Court, in *Shands v. Castrovinci*,[849] has detailed how the same policy justifications for attorney fees generally should also apply to legal services offices. Legal services offices have finite resources, and can not absorb litigation costs without limiting the number of other cases handled. Issues as to calculating the amount of attorney fees for legal services attorneys are discussed in § 8.8.11.5, *infra*.

Legal services offices funded by the Legal Services Corporation must comply with LSC regulations that prohibit programs from claiming or collecting and retaining attorney fees in any cases undertaken on behalf of clients.[850] Nonetheless, LSC-funded programs may co-counsel cases with private attorneys or attorneys from non-LSC funded programs, and those attorneys may claim and seek fees for their own time. In addition, according to an opinion letter from LSC's General Counsel's office, if the fee award under the particular statute is interpreted as belonging to the client rather than to the attorney,[851] the client may authorize a non-LSC funded attorney to seek fees for the time spent by the LSC-funded attorney, and the LSC-funded attorney may turn over his or her time records to facilitate this claim.[852] Any fees that are awarded based on the LSC-funded attorney's time belong to the client, and the client can not turn them over to the LSC-funded program because of the prohibition against collecting and retaining attorney fees. If an LSC-funded program asserts an attorney fee claim in this manner on behalf of the client, the complaint should make it clear that only the non-LSC funded attorney is representing the consumer on the attorney fee claim.

8.8.7.2 Paralegals and Law Clerks

UDAP cases generally hold that work by paralegals, law clerks, and law students can be compensated separately under an attorney fee award.[853] This is consistent with the Supreme Court's ruling that, at least under federal attorney fee statutes, work by paralegals and law clerks should be separately compensated where that is the standard billing practice in the relevant legal community.[854] Since this is almost universally the standard billing practice,[855] work by law students, law clerks, and paralegals should be separately accounted for in an attorney fee award.

On the other hand, if attorneys' prevailing hourly rates already reflect within that hourly rate the contribution of paralegals or other staff members, they should not bill separately. For example, often courts will view secretarial and similar clerical work as being part of the attorney's overhead. Thus it is reimbursed under the attorney's hourly rate.

8.8.7.3 Expert Witnesses

Another important issue is whether attorney fee awards will reimburse expert witness expenses. Courts on this

847 *See* National Consumer Law Center, Truth in Lending § 8.9.3.2 (5th ed. 2003 and Supp.).

848 Rosario v. Livaditis, Clearinghouse No. 47,927 (N.D. Ill. 1990); *In re* Bryant, 111 B.R. 474 (E.D. Pa. 1990); *In re* Samuels, Clearinghouse No. 50,439 (Bankr. M.D. Fla. 1995); Wiginton v. Pacific Credit Corp., 2 Haw. App. 435, 634 P.2d 111 (1981) (attorney fees designed as deterrent and to induce settlement); Linthicum v. Archambault, 379 Mass. 381, 398 N.E.2d 482 (1979); Coronado Products, Inc. v. Stewart, Clearinghouse No. 45,905 (Tenn. Ct. App. 1988) (available on LEXIS, 1988 Tenn. App. LEXIS 672); Bisson v. Ward, 628 A.2d 1256 (Vt. 1993); Shands v. Castrovinci, 115 Wis. 2d 352, 340 N.W.2d 506 (1983).

849 115 Wis. 2d 352, 340 N.W.2d 506 (1983).

850 45 C.F.R. § 1642.3.

851 *Cf.* § 8.8.8, *infra*.

852 Letter from Suzanne B. Glasow, Senior Assistant General Counsel, Legal Services Corporation, November 12, 1999; *see also* Legal Services Corporation, Office of Legal Affairs, External Opinion # EX-2003-1005 (Mar. 20. 2003). Both of these documents are included on the companion CD-Rom to NCLC's Truth in Lending manual.

853 *See* Blue Cross & Blue Shield of N.J., Inc. v. Philip Morris, Inc., 190 F. Supp. 2d 407 (E.D.N.Y. 2002); Computer Sys. Engineering v. Quantel Corp., 571 F. Supp. 1379 (D. Mass. 1983), *aff'd*, 740 F.2d 59 (1st Cir. 1984) (compensating paralegals $40 an hour); State v. Fuchs, Clearinghouse No. 49,158 (Colo. Dist. Ct., Denver Cty. 1992) (paralegal fees found to be included within term "attorney fees"; paralegal fees of $8980 awarded, calculated at $40 an hour); Clary Corp. v. Smith, 949 S.W.2d 452 (Tex. App. 1997). *See also* United Laboratories v. Kuykendall, 335 N.C. 183, 437 S.E.2d 374 (1993) (approving upward award of fees based on paralegal efforts or efforts of secretaries acting as paralegals).

854 Missouri v. Jenkins, 491 U.S. 274, 109 S. Ct. 2463, 105 L. Ed. 2d 229 (1989).

855 *See id.* at n.11, citing a study that for 77% of legal assistants surveyed, their firms billed for paralegal time on an hourly basis. *But see* Bryant v. Walt Sweeney Automotive, Inc., 2002 WL 1071943 (Ohio App. May 31, 2002) (unpublished, citation limited) (no award for paralegal fees where they were not separately billed to consumer).

subject may rely on general state rules or federal cases dealing with federal fee-generating statutes.[856] However, the legislative purpose of the UDAP statute will be better served by awarding the consumer his or her expert witness costs, irrespective of the general state or federal rule.

Thus, in Massachusetts "reasonable expert witness fees should normally be recoverable . . . in order to vindicate the policies of the act."[857] Such fees are within the court's discretion.[858] A Connecticut court held, however, that fees could only be awarded for the categories of experts listed in a state statute.[859]

Even where a court will not award an expert's time testifying at trial, there is an argument that the expert's time spent preparing the attorney should be compensated.[860] Moreover, where the UDAP statute authorizes consumers to recover the "costs of investigation," this should be interpreted to include expert witness fees and transcript costs.[861] Similarly, expert witness fees may be considered "costs" which may be recoverable.

A federal court has awarded expert witness fees under the Pennsylvania UDAP statute's authorization for additional relief as the court deemed necessary. The court reasoned that Pennsylvania courts had already decided to award expert witness fees in lemon law cases, and the UDAP statute should be interpreted in the same way.[862]

8.8.7.4 *Pro Se* Representation

A Minnesota appellate court has ruled that a licensed attorney acting as his own attorney in a case is still entitled to UDAP costs and fees.[863] The United States Supreme Court has reached an opposite conclusion regarding fees under the U.S. Civil Rights Attorney's Fees Award Act,[864] but this decision can be distinguished in that the Court was interpreting congressional intent in enacting the federal statute, not a state legislature's intent in enacting its UDAP statute.

8.8.8 Who Receives the Fees?

Some courts will award attorney fees directly to the counsel, rather than the consumer.[865] This avoids various practical problems which might occur if the consumer received the award.

The issue of who should receive the fees has special relevance where the consumer's obligation to the merchant exceeds the consumer's UDAP recovery. Should the fees be used to offset this merchant's net recovery, or should the fees go to the attorney, with the merchant left to collect its judgment from the consumer? Case law is split on this issue, and the exact language of the UDAP statute may be determinative. Some Texas cases pay the attorney ahead of the UDAP defendant.[866] However, other Texas courts may hold the opposite—that attorney fees must be offset against *all* other awards of damages and interest, particularly since the statute states that the consumer should be awarded attorney fees.[867]

8.8.9 Who Is Liable for Attorney Fees?

All defendants who participate in the deception, including corporate officers as well as the companies themselves, can be liable for UDAP attorney fees.[868] Defendants are jointly and severally liable for fees.[869] But the Florida[870] and

856 *See* West Virginia University Hosps., Inc. v. Casey, 499 U.S. 83, 111 S. Ct. 1138, 113 L. Ed. 2d 68 (1991) (fees for expert's testimonial or non-testimonial services may not be recovered as attorney fees under 43 U.S.C. § 1988; Congress overruled this decision as to civil rights cases by enacting 42 U.S.C. § 1988(c)).

857 Linthicum v. Archambault, 379 Mass. 381, 398 N.E.2d 482 (1979). *See also* Krewson v. City of Quincy, 74 F.3d 15 (1st Cir. 1996) (interpreting Massachusetts Civil Rights Act).

858 Charles River Constr. Co. v. Kirksey, 20 Mass. App. Ct. 333, 480 N.E.2d 315 (1985); Geraci v. Crown Chevrolet, Inc., 15 Mass. App. Ct. 935, 444 N.E.2d 1308 (1983).

859 Miller v. Guimaraes, 78 Conn. App. 760, 829 A.2d 422 (Conn. App. Ct. 2003).

860 *See* Friedrich v. City of Chicago, 888 F.2d 511 (7th Cir. 1989); Denny v. Westfield State College, 880 F.2d 1465 (1st Cir. 1989) (no award for expert's appearance at trial; but reserved question of award for time expert spent preparing attorney for trial). *But see* West Virginia University Hosps., Inc. v. Casey, 499 U.S. 83, 111 S. Ct. 1138, 113 L. Ed. 2d 68 (1991) (rejecting distinction between expert's testimonial and non-testimonial services).

861 Love v. Amsler, 441 N.W.2d 555 (Minn. Ct. App. 1989).

862 Hines v. Chrysler Corp., 971 F. Supp. 212 (E.D. Pa. 1997).

863 Wexler v. Brothers Entertainment Group, Inc., 457 N.W.2d 218 (Minn. Ct. App. 1990). *But see* Lawson v. Whitey's Frame Shop, 42 Conn. App. 599, 682 A.2d 1016 (1996) (*pro se* plaintiffs not entitled to attorney fees under state UDAP statute). *But cf.* Krause v. Myre Electric, 616 N.W.2d 524 (Wis. App. 2000) (unpublished, limited precedent opinion, text available at 2000 Wisc. App. LEXIS 354) (specific statute precludes award of fees to attorney representing himself).

864 Kay v. Ehrler, 499 U.S. 432, 111 S. Ct. 1435, 113 L. Ed. 2d 486 (1991) (under 42 U.S.C. § 1988 neither nonattorney nor an attorney *pro se* litigant is entitled to attorney fees).

865 Yorfino v. Ferguson, 552 S.W.2d 563 (Tex. Civ. App. 1977); Connelly v. Puget Sound Collections, Inc., 16 Wash. App. 62, 553 P.2d 1354 (1976). *See also* McKinley v. Drozd, 685 S.W.2d 7, 9–10 (Tex. 1985). *But see* Hartnett v. Hampton Inns, Inc., 870 S.W.2d 162 (Tex. App. 1993) (attorney fee belongs to the party, not to the attorney, absent special authorization).

866 Roberts v. Grande, 868 S.W.2d 956 (Tex. App. 1994). *See also* McKinley v. Drozd, 685 S.W.2d 7, 9–10 (Tex. 1985).

867 Hartnett v. Hampton Inns, Inc., 870 S.W.2d 162 (Tex. App. 1993); Satellite Earth Stations East, Inc. v. Davis, 756 S.W.2d 385 (Tex. App. 1988).

868 Grayson v. Nordic Constr. Co., 92 Wash. 2d 548, 599 P.2d 1271 (1979).

869 Cogar v. Monmouth Toyota, 331 N.J. Super. 197, 751 A.2d 599 (App. Div. 2000).

870 Hubbel v. Aetna Cas. & Sur. Co., 758 So. 2d 94 (Fla. 2000). *See* § 6.9.1, *supra*; National Consumer Law Center, Automobile Fraud § 9.13.4.5 (2d ed. 2003 and Supp.).

Connecticut[871] Supreme Courts have held that a surety company bonding a seller is liable only for the consumer's damages, not the attorney fee award. This issue will turn on the specific language of the state bonding statute and the bond itself.

Under the FTC's Holder Rule, holders are subject to the consumer's UDAP claims against the seller, but the holder's liability can not exceed the amount of the debt due the holder.[872] If this limit applied to attorney fees as well, this would effectively insulate holders from such awards, even if they refused to reach reasonable settlements of UDAP claims. Courts have thus found that the holder is liable for the consumer's attorney fees, even if these fees exceed the amount of the debt, at least for attorney fees incurred to overcome the holder's denial of liability.[873]

8.8.10 Attorney Fees for Prevailing Sellers

8.8.10.1 Introduction

In most states a UDAP statute will only authorize attorney fees for prevailing consumers, but some UDAP statutes explicitly provide for attorney fees for either prevailing party, and consumers in those states must understand the risks involved in litigation.[874] There are several arguments a consumer can make as to why a prevailing seller should not be awarded attorney fees pursuant to the UDAP statute.

8.8.10.2 Has the Seller Prevailed?

Generally, a seller will only be awarded fees if it "prevails," so that the seller's request for fees can be challenged by arguing that the seller has not prevailed. Where attorney fees are awarded the prevailing party "after judgment," this has been interpreted as preventing the seller from obtaining attorney fees where the consumer has voluntarily dismissed the UDAP action, and where there is thus no judgment.[875] Similarly, after a court dismissed a UDAP claim without prejudice, an appellate court ruled that the trial court loses its jurisdiction to award the seller attorney fees.[876]

At least some courts rule that the seller is not entitled to attorney fees as the "prevailing" party where it wins the UDAP count, but judgment is entered against it on other counts; for the seller to "prevail," it must have a net positive recovery on all the claims.[877] Certainly, if the seller recovers UDAP attorney fees, these should be limited to expenses to defend the consumer's UDAP claim, and not to defend other of the consumer's claims.[878] Nor does the seller prevail where the consumer wins only the amount the seller was willing to pay before suit.[879]

Florida courts, before the attorney fee provision was amended to make fees to the prevailing seller discretionary rather than mandatory, found that a seller prevailed in a UDAP case even where the court found the action outside the UDAP statute's scope.[880] A Florida court, also before the

871 Ames v. Comm'r of Motor Vehicles, 839 A.2d 1250 (Conn. 2004).

872 *See* § 6.6, *supra.*

873 *In re* Stewart, 93 B.R. 878 (Bankr. E.D. Pa. 1988) (seller and assignee jointly and severally liable for fees); Kish v. Van Note, 692 S.W.2d 463 (Tex. 1985) (same); *see also* Home Savings Ass'n v. Guerra, 733 S.W.2d 134 (Tex. 1987); Green Tree Acceptance, Inc. v. Pierce, 768 S.W.2d 416 (Tex. App. 1989) (attorney fee award seems to be independent of FTC Holder Rule cap).

874 *See* Deadwyler v. Volkswagen of Am., Inc., 748 F. Supp. 1146 (W.D.N.C. 1990), *aff'd on other grounds*, 1992 U.S. App. LEXIS 14891 (4th Cir. June 25, 1992); Arbuckle Broadcasters v. Rockwell Int'l Corp., 513 F. Supp. 412 (N.D. Texas 1981); Miami Lincoln Mercury v. Kramer, 399 So. 2d 1003 (Fla. Dist. Ct. App. 1981); Johnny Crews Ford, Inc. v. Llewellyn, 353 So. 2d 606 (Fla. Dist. Ct. App. 1977); Haskell v. Blumthal, 204 Ill. App. 3d 596, 561 N.E.2d 1315 (1990) (defendant who wins UDAP case is the "prevailing party" for purposes of attorney fee award); Deer Creek Constr. Co. v. Peterson, 412 So. 2d 1169 (Miss. 1982); Selig v. BMW of N. Am., Inc., 832 S.W.2d 95 (Tex. App. 1992); Texas Am. Corp. v. Woodbridge, 809 S.W.2d 299 (Tex. App. 1991); Elbaor v. Sanderson, 817 S.W.2d 826 (Tex. App. 1991); Flukinger v. Straughan, 795 S.W.2d 779 (Tex. App. 1990); Howell v. Homecraft Land Dev., Inc., 749 S.W.2d 103 (Tex. App. 1987); Preston II Chrysler-Dodge, Inc. v. Donewerth, 775 S.W.2d 634 (Tex. 1989); Wickersham Ford, Inc. v. Orange County, 701 S.W.2d 344 (Tex. App. 1986); Brunstetter v. Southern, 619 S.W.2d 557 (Tex. Civ. App. 1981); Genico Distributors Inc. v. First Nat'l Bank of Richardson, 616 S.W.2d 418 (Tex. Civ. App. 1981).

875 Nolan v. Altman, 449 So. 2d 898 (Fla. Dist. Ct. App. 1984). *See also* Kohn v. Mug-A-Bug, 380 S.E.2d 548 (N.C. Ct. App. 1989); Hansel v. Creative Concrete & Masonry Constr. Co., 772 N.E.2d 138 (Ohio App. 2002); Continental Savings Ass'n v. Maheney, 641 S.W.2d 290 (Tex. App. 1982). *But see* Haskell v. Blumthal, 204 Ill. App. 3d 596, 561 N.E.2d 1315 (1990) (under Illinois statute, seller may be prevailing party after voluntary dismissal of buyer's UDAP claim).

876 Peters v. United Consumers Club, 786 S.W.2d 192 (Mo. Ct. App. 1990). *See also* Poindexter v. Morse Chevrolet, Inc., 282 F. Supp. 2d 1232 (D. Kan. 2003) (defendant not entitled to fees after plaintiff's suit dismissed on jurisdictional grounds); Knudson v. LeMarr, 787 F. Supp. 835 (N.D. Ill. 1992).

877 Ghodrati v. Miami Paneling Corp., 770 So. 2d 181 (Fla. App. 2000); Heindel v. Southside Chrysler-Plymouth, Inc., 476 So. 2d 266 (Fla. Dist. Ct. App. 1985). *But see* Deer Creek Constr. Co. v. Peterson, 412 So. 2d 1169 (Miss. 1982); Dillree v. Devoe, 223 Mont. 47, 724 P.2d 171 (1986).

878 Hamilton v. Palm Chevrolet-Oldsmobile Inc., 388 So. 2d 638 (Fla. Dist. Ct. App. 1980); Deer Creek Constr. Co. v. Peterson, 412 So. 2d 1169 (Miss. 1982). *Cf.* Estate of Smith v. Ware, 307 Or. 478, 769 P.2d 773 (1989) (error to give seller no fees for work needed to defend both UDAP and other count). *But see* Caplan v. 1616 E. Sunrise Motors, Inc., 522 So. 2d 920 (Fla. Dist. Ct. App. 1988) (common core of facts and related theories); Smith v. Bilgin, 534 So. 2d 852 (Fla. Dist. Ct. App. 1988).

879 Ghodrati v. Miami Paneling Corp., 770 So. 2d 181 (Fla. App. 2000).

880 Smith v. Bilgin, 534 So. 2d 852 (Fla. Dist. Ct. App. 1988); Brown v. Gardens By the Sea South Condominium Ass'n, 424 So. 2d 181 (Fla. Dist. Ct. App. 1983); Rustic Village, Inc. v. Friedman, 417 So. 2d 305 (Fla. Dist. Ct. App. 1982).

amendment, held that if the consumer prevailed against one defendant, but not against another defendant, the consumer might be liable for that other defendant's attorney fees.[881]

8.8.10.3 Tougher Standard for Sellers' Fees Where Award Is Discretionary for Either Party

No state UDAP statute now mandates attorney fees for a prevailing seller,[882] but a number of UDAP statutes indicate that attorney fees may be awarded, in the court's discretion, to the prevailing party.[883] In these states, the United States Supreme Court's ruling in *Christiansburg Garment Co. v. Equal Employment Opportunity Commission*,[884] indicates that a different standard should be used to award fees to prevailing consumers than to prevailing merchants.

Christiansburg Garment interprets Title VII of the U.S. Civil Rights Act,[885] which provides that the court in its discretion may allow the prevailing party a reasonable attorney fee. The unanimous Supreme Court, while noting that prevailing plaintiffs should recover "in all but special circumstances,"[886] ruled that prevailing defendants should not routinely recover fees, and should only do so where the plaintiff's claim was frivolous, unreasonable or without foundation.[887]

Courts have followed the *Christiansburg Garment* holding in UDAP cases. For example, an Illinois appellate court has ruled that attorney fees should not be awarded to a prevailing seller unless the plaintiff's suit was frivolous or filed in bad faith, applying standards similar to those in Rule 11 of the Federal Rules of Civil Procedure.[888] A federal court has reached the same conclusion with respect to the UDAP statutes of Colorado, Illinois, Indiana, Kentucky, and Missouri.[889] The Seventh Circuit in a commercial case has departed from the *Christiansburg Garment* holding in interpreting the Illinois UDAP statute, and found the defendant entitled to fees in situations where the plaintiff's claim had been oppressive, even if not in bad faith.[890] But that decision explicitly stated that it was based on the fact that the plaintiff was not a consumer and there was no gross disparity of resources between the parties. It specifically stated that all plaintiffs should not face the same standard. The Seventh Circuit thus did not exactly state, but it can be implied, that it intended the *Christiansburg Garment* standard to apply to most consumer claims under the Illinois UDAP statute.

The purpose of fee awards to consumers is to encourage plaintiffs to sue even if recovery would be small. The purpose of fee awards to sellers is to deter abuses and bad-faith conduct by plaintiffs.[891] A stricter standard should be applied when defendants seek attorney fees, since routinely subjecting plaintiffs to liability for defendants' fees would deter consumers' suits, defeating the purpose of UDAP statutes.[892]

---

881 Caplan v. 1616 E. Sunrise Motors, Inc., 522 So. 2d 920 (Fla. Dist. Ct. App. 1988).

882 Until recently both Florida and Mississippi UDAP statutes mandated fees to prevailing sellers. *See* Fla. Stat. Ann. § 501.201; Miss. Code Ann. § 75-24-1; *see also* Donald Frederich Evans & Assocs., Inc. v. Continental Homes, Inc., 785 F.2d 897 (11th Cir. 1986) (Florida law); Deadwyler v. Volkswagen of Am., Inc., 748 F. Supp. 1146 (W.D.N.C. 1990), *aff'd on other grounds*, 1992 U.S. App. LEXIS 14891 (4th Cir. June 25, 1992); Target Trailer v. Feingold, 632 So. 2d 198 (Fla. Dist. Ct. App. 1994); Deer Creek Constr. Co. v. Peterson, 412 So. 2d 1169 (Miss. 1982).

Pursuant to a 1994 amendment, the Mississippi statute, Miss. Code Ann. § 75-24-15, no longer states that the prevailing party shall recover fees, but states that a prevailing defendant may recover fees if action was frivolous, harassing, or dilatory. *See* Wilson v. William Hall Chevrolet, Inc., 871 F. Supp. 279 (S.D. Miss. 1994). Similarly, the Florida statute is now amended to provide that the court may in its discretion award attorney fees.

883 *See, e.g.*, Fla. Stat. Ann. 501.2105; 815 Ill. Comp. Stat. 505/10a; Ind. Code § 24-5-0.5-4(b); Ky. Rev. Stat. § 367.220(3); Mo. Rev. Stat. § 407.025(1); Mont. Code Ann. § 30-14-133(3); Or. Rev. Stat. § 646.638. *See also* Deadwyler v. Volkswagen of Am., Inc., 748 F. Supp. 1146 (W.D.N.C. 1990) (court in its discretion denies fees for UDAP claims in Colorado, Illinois, Indiana, Kentucky and Missouri where claims not frivolous or brought in bad faith; court takes different view for claim brought pursuant to Montana UDAP statute), *aff'd on other grounds*, 1992 U.S. App. LEXIS 14891 (4th Cir. June 25, 1992). Alaska Stat. § 45.50.531 formerly included such language, but it was deleted in 1998. Attorney fees can now be awarded to a prevailing defendant only pursuant to court rule or if the action is found to be frivolous. *See* Alaska Stat. § 45.50.537. The former language was interpreted in Garrison v. Dixon, 19 P.3d 1229 (Alaska 2001). *But cf.* Wagner v. Fleming, 2004 WL 32379 (Tenn. Ct. App. Jan. 6, 2004) (unpublished, citation limited) (remanding case for trial court to determine whether to award fees where plaintiff's UDAP claim was without legal merit).

884 434 U.S. 412, 98 S. Ct. 694, 54 L. Ed. 2d 648 (1978). *See also* § 8.8.3, *supra*.

885 42 U.S.C. § 2000e-5(k).

886 434 U.S. 412 at 417.

887 *Id.* at 421. *See also* Knudson v. LeMarr, 787 F. Supp. 835 (N.D. Ill. 1992).

888 Haskell v. Blumthal, 204 Ill. App. 3d 596, 561 N.E.2d 1315 (1990); Krautsack v. Anderson, 329 Ill. App. 3d 666, 768 N.E.2d 133, 263 Ill. Dec. 373 (2002). *Accord* Casey v. Jerry Yusim Nissan, Inc., 694 N.E.2d 206 (Ill. App. Ct. 1998) (including discussion of factors to consider in determining bad faith). *But see* Graunke v. Elmhurst Chrysler Plymouth, 617 N.E.2d 858 (Ill. App. Ct. 1993) (interpreting *Haskell* as merely identifying bad faith as one of the several factors guiding the discretionary award of attorney fees to prevailing consumers or sellers).

889 Deadwyler v. Volkswagen of Am., Inc., 748 F. Supp. 1146 (W.D.N.C. 1990) ("may" award defendant attorney fees interpreted as requiring fees only when action frivolous), *aff'd on other grounds*, 1992 U.S. App. LEXIS 14891 (4th Cir. June 25, 1992).

890 Door Sys., Inc. v. Pro-Line Door Sys., Inc., 126 F.3d 1028 (7th Cir. 1997) (Illinois law).

891 Graunke v. Elmhurst Chrysler Plymouth, 617 N.E.2d 858 (Ill. App. Ct. 1993).

892 Casey v. Jerry Yusim Nissan, Inc., 694 N.E.2d 206 (Ill. App. Ct. 1998).

The next subsection discusses whether a consumer's UDAP claim is frivolous or groundless for purposes of state UDAP statutes that explicitly provide seller's attorney fees for frivolous or groundless UDAP claims. This discussion should apply as well to whether a consumer's claim is frivolous, groundless, or the like for purposes of the *Christiansburg* standard. Consequently, refer to the next subsection for an analysis of when a seller should receive fees in a state allowing the court in its discretion to award fees.

8.8.10.4 Where a UDAP Statute Explicitly Limits Fees to Frivolous or Bad Faith Actions

8.8.10.4.1 Importance of the exact statutory language

Many UDAP statutes are explicit that a seller may obtain attorney fees only when the consumer's claim was frivolous, groundless, in bad faith, or similarly wrongful.[893] The exact language of these statutes is often critical in determining whether the seller is entitled to fees.

Of particular note is whether the various terms triggering a seller's attorney fees are linked by an "or" or by an "and." If the statute indicates, the seller receives attorney fees if the consumer's claim "was groundless *and* brought in bad faith;" the merchant must show both.[894]

Where a statute provides for the seller's attorney fees when an action is "groundless and brought in bad faith, or brought for the purpose of harassment," the better interpretation is that the seller must show the action either is groundless and in bad faith or is groundless and meant to harass. The mere showing that it is brought for the purposes of harassment is insufficient.[895] It is a much tougher standard to prove that a UDAP claim was frivolous *and* brought for purposes of harassment than that the claim was frivolous *or* brought for purposes of harassment.

Where a statute says the court *may* award attorney fees if the action is groundless and in bad faith, the court has discretion whether to make the award. Where the statute says the court *shall* make the award, the court has no discretion as long as the action was groundless and in bad faith.[896]

Oklahoma's UDAP statute allows the prevailing party to recover fees where the non-prevailing party asserted a claim in bad faith, that was not well grounded in fact, or that was unwarranted by existing law or a good faith argument for the extension, modification, or reversal of existing law.[897] Oklahoma's Supreme Court has interpreted the language "not well-grounded in fact" narrowly to apply only on a showing of bad faith.[898] The court was concerned that a broader interpretation would have a chilling effect on the right of access to the courts, posing an impediment to arguably meritorious but ultimately unsuccessful cases.

8.8.10.4.2 Meaning of "for purposes of harassment"

"For purposes of harassment" has been interpreted as for the *sole* purpose of harassment; the consumer's additional motivation of recovering even minimal damages should defeat a finding of harassment.[899] As a consequence, any requirement that a UDAP claim be brought for purposes of harassment will be hard for a seller to prove.

8.8.10.4.3 Meaning of "bad faith"

To prove "bad faith," the seller must show malice by the consumer.[900] That a case is groundless does not show that it was brought in bad faith.[901] Bad faith implies intent and knowledge that the suit is groundless, and the seller must offer evidence of this intent and knowledge.[902] Bad faith can

---

893 *See* Ala. Code § 8-19-10; Cal. Civ. Code § 1780; Colo. Rev. Stat. § 6-1-113; Ga. Code Ann. §§ 10-1-373, 10-1-399; Haw. Rev. Stat. § 481A-4; Idaho Code § 48-608; Kan. Stat. Ann. § 50-634; La. Rev. Stat. Ann. § 51:1409; Md. Comm. Law Code Ann. § 13-408; Minn. Stat. Ann. § 325D.45; Miss. Code § 75-24-15; Neb. Rev. Stat. § 87-303; N.M. Stat. Ann. § 57-12-10; N.C. Gen. Stat. § 75-16.1; Ohio Rev. Code Ann. §§ 1345.09, 4165.03; Okla. Stat. Ann. tit. 15, § 761.1, tit. 78, § 54; Tenn. Code Ann. § 47-18-109; Tex. Bus. & Com. Code Ann. § 17.50; Utah Code Ann. § 13-11-19.

894 Jones v. Smith, 649 S.W.2d 29 (Tex. 1983); Chambless v. Barry Robinson Farm Supply, 667 S.W.2d 598 (Tex. App. 1984); Jernigan v. Page, 662 S.W.2d 760 (Tex. App. 1983); LaChance v. McKown, 649 S.W.2d 658 (Tex. App. 1983). Note that the Texas statute was amended in 1995 to substitute "or" for "and." Tex. Bus. & Com. Code Ann. § 17.50(c).

895 Myer v. Splettstosser, 759 S.W.2d 514 (Tex. App. 1988), *rev'd on other grounds*, 779 S.W.2d 806 (Tex. 1989); Carrington v. Hart, 703 S.W.2d 814 (Tex. App. 1986). *But see* Shenandoah Assocs. v. J&K Properties, Inc., 741 S.W.2d 470 (Tex. App. 1987); Schott v. Leissner, 659 S.W.2d 752 (Tex. App. 1983). Note that the Texas statute was amended in 1995 to substitute "or" for "and." Tex. Bus. & Com. Code Ann. § 17.50(c).

896 Intertex, Inc. v. Cowden, 728 S.W.2d 813 (Tex. App. 1987).

897 Okla. Stat. tit. 15, § 761.1(A).

898 Whitlock v. Bob Moore Cadillac, Inc., 938 P.2d 737 (Okla. 1997).

899 Donwerth v. Preston II Chrysler-Dodge, 775 S.W.2d 634 (Tex. 1989); Splettstosser v. Myer, 779 S.W.2d 806 (Tex. 1989); Webb v. International Trucking Co., 909 S.W.2d 220 (Tex. App. 1995); Rutherford v. Riata Cadillac Co., 809 S.W.2d 535 (Tex. App. 1991).

900 Schlager v. Clements, 939 S.W.2d 183 (Tex. App. 1996); Central Texas Hardware, Inc. v. First City Texas-Bryan, N.A., 810 S.W.2d 234 (Tex. App. 1991); Perma Stone-Surfa Shield Co. v. Merideth, 752 S.W.2d 224 (Tex. App. 1988); Hill v. Pierce, 729 S.W.2d 340 (Tex. App. 1987); Brunstetter v. Southern, 619 S.W.2d 557 (Tex. Civ. App. 1981).

901 Walker v. Cadillac Motor Car Div., 63 Ohio App. 3d 220, 578 N.E.2d 524 (1989); Chambless v. Barry Robinson Farm Supply, 667 S.W.2d 598 (Tex. App. 1984).

902 Bohls v. Oakes, 75 S.W.3d 473 (Tex. App. 2002) (bad faith shown when statute of limitations had run at time of suit); Group Hosp. Servs., Inc. v. One & Two Brookriver Center, 704 S.W.2d 886 (Tex. App. 1986); Glasgow v. Hall, 668 S.W.2d 863 (Tex. App. 1984); *see also* Fichtner v. Richardson, 708 S.W.2d 479

be found where a consumer makes demands more to punish the seller than to resolve differences.[903] Bad faith has been found where major corporations brought UDAP actions even though it was clear that the UDAP statute explicitly excluded actions by large corporate plaintiffs.[904]

Obviously, the consumer's conduct after filing suit will be important in determining if an action is in bad faith.[905] If a consumer drops a suit as soon as it appears groundless, this should be an indicator of good faith.

8.8.10.4.4 Meaning of "groundless"

"Groundless" does not mean that the consumer fails to recover, but instead means "no arguable basis for the cause of action."[906] Under the definition used by most courts, a claim is "groundless" only if "there is no arguable basis in law or fact to support the cause of action and the claim is not supported by a good-faith argument for the extension, modification, or reversal of existing law."[907] If there are few or no decisions on an issue, the court is less likely to find that raising the issue is groundless.[908]

If a UDAP action is not initiated in bad faith and there are colorable arguments in favor of the plaintiff's position, the action is not groundless.[909] A case is not groundless if the consumer would have recovered if the jury had believed the consumer instead of the seller.[910] A consumer's claim is not groundless if the consumer had some evidence to support it, even if the evidence was hearsay which could not be admitted at trial.[911]

Where a consumer alleges multiple UDAP theories, a court may sustain certain theories, but reject others. The Tenth Circuit has refused to examine each theory separately to see if that part of the UDAP action was groundless. Instead, the court looked at the case as a whole. Since the consumer won on at least part of the UDAP claims, no part of the complaint could be considered groundless.[912]

The Texas Supreme Court has rejected a standard that would find a suit not groundless where the claim survives a motion for a directed verdict. Instead, it adopts a test as to whether the totality of the evidence demonstrates an arguable basis in law or fact for the claim.[913]

8.8.10.4.5 Meaning of "frivolous"

In determining whether an action is frivolous, unreasonable, or without foundation, the United States Supreme Court in *Christiansburg Garment Co.* discourages hindsight logic just because the plaintiff loses. Decisive facts may not have emerged until after the complaint was filed or the law may have changed or been clarified during the course of litigation.[914] "Even when the law or facts appear questionable or unfavorable at the outset, a party may have an entirely reasonable ground for bringing suit."[915] Other courts have

---

(Tex. App. 1986) (burden on seller, but in this case the burden was met).

903 Zak v. Parks, 729 S.W.2d 875 (Tex. App. 1987).

904 Transport Indemnity Co. v. Orgain, Bell & Tucker, 846 S.W.2d 878 (Tex. App. 1993).

905 *See* Schlager v. Clements, 939 S.W.2d 183 (Tex. App. 1996); Fichtner v. Richardson, 708 S.W.2d 479 (Tex. App. 1986).

906 Hill Wholesale Distributing Co. v. Louis W. Howat & Son, 666 So. 2d 1252 (La. App. 1996) (rejection of plaintiff's claim does not mean claim was groundless); Jones v. Beavers, 116 N.M. 634, 866 P.2d 362 (N.M. App. 1993) (claim not groundless simply because consumer did not prevail); Davis v. Axelrod Chrysler Plymouth, Inc., 2003 WL 194888 (Ohio App. Jan. 30, 2003) (UDAP action not groundless even though it had insufficient legal basis); Couto v. Gibson, Inc., 67 Ohio App. 3d 407, 587 N.E.2d 336 (1990) (prayer for treble damages for each UDAP violation not groundless where statute was ambiguous and susceptible to an interpretation allowing such relief); Preston II Chrysler-Dodge, Inc. v. Donewerth, 775 S.W.2d 634 (Tex. 1989); Rutherford v. Riata Cadillac Co., 809 S.W.2d 535 (Tex. App. 1991); Hill v. Pierce, 729 S.W.2d 340 (Tex. App. 1987); Xarin Real Estate, Inc. v. Gamboa, 715 S.W.2d 80 (Tex. App. 1986); LaChance v. McKown, 649 S.W.2d 658 (Tex. App. 1983); *see also* Waggener v. Seever Sys., Inc., 233 Kan. 517, 664 P.2d 813 (1983); C.S.R., Inc. v. Industrial Mechanical, Inc., 698 S.W.2d 213 (Tex. App. 1985); Allright, Inc. v. Burgard, 666 S.W.2d 515 (Tex. App. 1984).

907 Ameristar Jet Charter, Inc. v. Signal Composites, Inc., 271 F.3d 624 (5th Cir. 2001) (Texas law); Marchman v. NCNB Texas Nat'l Bank, 898 P.2d 709 (N.M. 1995); Donwerth v. Preston II Chrysler-Dodge, 775 S.W.2d 634 (Tex. 1989); Riddick v. Quail Harbor Condominium Ass'n, Inc., 7 S.W.3d 663 (Tex. App. 1999); Hartman v. Urban, 946 S.W.2d 546 (Tex. App. 1997); Schlager v. Clements, 939 S.W.2d 183 (Tex. App. 1996); Webb v. International Trucking Co., 909 S.W.2d 220 (Tex. App. 1995); Central Texas Hardware, Inc. v. First City Texas-Bryan, N.A., 810 S.W.2d 234 (Tex. App. 1991); Ceda Corp. v. City of Houston, 817 S.W.2d 846 (Tex. App. 1991); *see also* G.E.W. Mechanical Contractors, Inc. v. Johnston Co., 115 N.M. 727, 858 P.2d 103 (Ct. App. 1993); Splettstosser v. Myer, 779 S.W.2d 806 (Tex. 1989).

908 Snyder v. Badgerland Mobile Homes, Inc., 659 N.W.2d 887 (Wis. App. 2003).

909 Marchman v. NCNB Texas Nat'l Bank, 898 P.2d 709 (N.M. 1995). *Accord* Jones v. Beavers, 116 N.M. 634, 866 P.2d 362 (N.M. App. 1993).

910 Knebel v. Port Enterprises, Inc., 760 S.W.2d 829 (Tex. App. 1988); Xarin Real Estate, Inc. v. Gamboa, 715 S.W.2d 80 (Tex. App. 1986); LaChance v. McKown, 649 S.W.2d 658 (Tex. App. 1983).

911 Donwerth v. Preston II Chrysler-Dodge, 775 S.W.2d 634 (Tex. 1989).

912 Knight v. Snap-On Tools Corp., 3 F.3d 1398 (10th Cir. 1993) (N.M. law). *See also* Draper v. Allen's Auto Serv. & Repair, Inc., 2003 WL 22532946 (Kan. App. Nov. 7, 2003) (entire action must be groundless, but this one was).

913 Splettstosser v. Myer, 779 S.W.2d 806 (Tex. 1989). *See also* Maronge v. Cityfed Mortgage Co., 803 S.W.2d 393 (Tex. App. 1991).

914 Christiansburg Garment Co. v. Equal Employment Opportunity Comm'n, 434 U.S. 412, 422 (1978).

915 *Id.*; Bakhico Co. v. Shasta Beverages, Inc., 1998 U.S. Dist. LEXIS 7564 (N.D. Tex. May 14, 1998); Ostrow v. United Bus. Machines, Inc., 982 S.W.2d 101 (Tex. App. 1998); Sifuentes v. Carrillo, 982 S.W.2d 500 (Tex. App. 1998).

found a case not "frivolous" where the consumer's claim withstood an initial summary judgment motion.[916]

8.8.10.4.6 Issue for the judge or jury?

The Texas Supreme Court has held that whether the seller is awarded attorney fees is for the court, not the jury, to decide.[917] In considering a "bad faith" claim, the court may consider evidence not otherwise admissible.[918] However, a hearing is unnecessary if adequate grounds exist in the existing record.[919]

8.8.10.5 Authority for Seller's Attorney Fees Where No Explicit Authorization in UDAP Statute

Where a UDAP statute does not explicitly provide for a seller's attorney fees, the court should not find that such a recovery is implied.[920] A seller may, however, claim attorney fees based on other grounds. For example, a creditor may seek fees for defending a UDAP counterclaim based on a provision in the credit contract providing for the creditor's attorney fees in any collection action.

Such an attempt should be resisted because a UDAP counterclaim is not asserted as a defense to the collection action, nor is it a contractual claim, i.e., it is not based on whether the consumer is obligated on the contract. Instead, the UDAP claim is a separate statutory cause of action. A contractual provision authorizing recovery of attorney fees for collection efforts should not apply to actions required to defend a non-contractual counterclaim.

But in at least one case between two businesses, where the UDAP counterclaim was so intertwined with the collection claim that they involved the same facts, the creditor was awarded contractual attorney fees for work on both claims even though it had not met the UDAP standards for attorney fees for prevailing sellers.[921] On the other hand, a trial court had discretion not to award attorney fees to the defendant where the fundamental nature of the consumers' suit was a UDAP claim, not a claim under the contract.[922]

Consumer attorneys should also be aware of any other special grounds in their state for a seller's recovery of fees. For example, an Alaska statute provides for the award of attorney fees, in the court's discretion, to the prevailing party in any civil action.[923] This has been interpreted as providing the defendant with fees only if the plaintiff's claim is frivolous.[924] There is some authority that federal courts have inherent authority to assess attorney fees against counsel, but only in narrowly defined circumstances.[925] Hawaii provides mandatory attorney fees for the prevailing party in all actions in the nature of assumpsit,[926] but UDAP claims are apparently not in the nature of assumpsit.[927]

Finally, Federal Rule of Civil Procedure 11 or similar state rules of procedure may provide a defendant with fees.[928] As with many of the other provisions for defendants' recovery of fees, Rule 11 provides fees where the plaintiff's claim is not well grounded in fact, not warranted by existing law or a good faith argument for the extension, modification,

916 Scott v. Mego Int'l Inc., 524 F. Supp. 74 (D. Minn. 1981). *Cf.* Deadwyler v. Volkswagen of Am., Inc., 748 F. Supp. 1146 (W.D.N.C. 1990) (action frivolous where did not comply with requirement that private litigants obtain state attorney general's approval before filing class action), *aff'd on other grounds*, 1992 U.S. App. LEXIS 14891 (4th Cir. June 25, 1992).

917 Donwerth v. Preston II Chrysler-Dodge, 775 S.W.2d 634 (Tex. 1989) (overruling cases that had drawn a distinction between the question whether the action was groundless and whether it was filed in bad faith or for harassment); Texas Am. Corp. v. Woodbridge, 809 S.W.2d 299 (Tex. App. 1991); *see also* Hartman v. Urban, 946 S.W.2d 546 (Tex. App. 1997) (appellate review of determination of groundlessness is a question of law, determined by an abuse of discretion standard); Blizzard v. Nationwide Mut. Fire Ins. Co., 756 S.W.2d 801 (Tex. App. 1988); Myer v. Splettstosser, 759 S.W.2d 514 (Tex. App. 1988); Schlager v. Clements, 939 S.W.2d 183 (Tex. App. 1996); Webb v. International Trucking Co., 909 S.W.2d 220 (Tex. App. 1995); Geotech Energy Corp. v. Gulf States, 788 S.W.2d 386 (Tex. App. 1990).

918 Davila v. World Car Five Star, 75 S.W.3d 537 (Tex. App. 2002).

919 Vu v. Rosen, 2004 WL 612832 (Tex. App. Mar. 30, 2004) (unpublished, citation limited).

920 Ramos v. District of Columbia Dep't of Consumer & Regulatory Affairs, 601 A.2d 1069 (D.C. 1992); Vogt v. Seattle-First Nat'l Bank, 117 Wash. 2d 541, 817 P.2d 1364 (1991); Sato v. Century 21 Ocean Shares Real Estate, 101 Wash. 2d 599, 681 P.2d 242 (1984).

921 Flint & Assocs. v. Intercontinental Pipe & Steel, Inc., 739 S.W.2d 622 (Tex. App. 1987). *Accord* Diamond D. Enterprises USA, Inc. v. Steinsvaag, 979 F.2d 14 (2d Cir. 1992) (New York). *See also* Keeper v. First Care, Inc., 794 S.W.2d 879 (Tex. App. 1990).

922 Walker v. Countrywide Home Loans, Inc., 98 Cal. App. 4th 1158, 121 Cal. Rptr. 2d 79 (2002). *See also* Testan v. Carlsen Motor Cars, Inc., 2002 Cal. App. LEXIS 1837 (Feb. 19, 2002) (unpublished, citation limited) (awarding fees to defendants based on clause in auto sales contract; dispute involved post-sale repairs to vehicle).

923 *See* Alaska Stat. § 09.60.010; Alaska Civ. R. 82.

924 *See* Deadwyler v. Volkswagen of Am., Inc., 748 F. Supp. 1146 (W.D.N.C. 1990) (nationwide class action analyzing the law in a number of states concerning defendant's attorney fees), *aff'd on other grounds*, 1992 U.S. App. LEXIS 14891 (4th Cir. June 25, 1992).

925 Ramos v. District of Columbia Dep't of Consumer & Regulatory Affairs, 601 A.2d 1069 (D.C. 1992).

926 Haw. Rev. Stat. § 607-14.

927 *See* Deadwyler v. Volkswagen of Am., Inc., 748 F. Supp. 1146 (W.D.N.C. 1990) (nationwide class action analyzing the law in a number of states concerning defendant's attorney fees), *aff'd on other grounds*, 1992 U.S. App. LEXIS 14891 (4th Cir. June 25, 1992). *But cf.* Schulz v. Honsador, Inc., 67 Haw. 433, 690 P.2d 279 (1984) (warranty action is action for assumpsit for purposes of Haw. Rev. Stat. § 607-14).

928 *See, e.g.*, Wheeler v. T.L. Roofing, Inc., 74 P.3d 499 (Colo. App. 2003) (awarding fees under Rule 11-type statute where commercial plaintiff's UDAP claim was frivolous).

or reversal of existing law, or is interposed for an improper purpose, such as to harass, cause unnecessary delay or needlessly increase the cost of litigation.

28 U.S.C. § 1927 also holds, for cases in federal court, that an attorney who multiplies the proceedings unreasonably and vexatiously may be required to satisfy personally the excess costs and fees incurred because of such conduct. The standard applied by courts in this situation is generally whether the attorney acts "recklessly or with indifference to the law, as well as by acting in the teeth of what he knows to be the law."[929]

8.8.11 How Attorney Fees Are Calculated

8.8.11.1 Why UDAP Attorney Fee Awards Must Be Adequate

A major attorney fee issue in any UDAP case is how the fee award should be calculated. UDAP litigants face a particular problem of judicial aversion to granting large attorney fees where the consumer damage award is minimal.[930] However, in many cases courts have awarded UDAP attorney fees that were many times more than the damages awarded in the same case.[931]

The size of a damage award should not limit the size of an attorney fee award, since this would frustrate the legislative intent in providing consumers with UDAP attorney fees.[932] Without adequate fees, attorneys may not accept

929 Miera v. Dairyland Ins. Co., 143 F.3d 1337 (10th Cir. 1998) (overturning district court award of sanctions).

930 *See* Morse v. Mutual Federal Sav. & Loan Ass'n, 536 F. Supp. 1271 (D. Mass. 1982) (court criticized attorney's request for exorbitant attorney fees in relatively small matter, but agrees to reimburse attorney for time); Lord v. Commercial Union Ins. Co., 60 Mass. App. Ct. 309, 801 N.E.2d 303 (Mass. App. Ct. 2004) (rejecting award of attorney fees when plaintiff suffered no injury or loss); Stark v. Patalano Ford Sales, Inc., 30 Mass. App. Ct. 194, 567 N.E.2d 1237 (1991); Cox v. Sears, Roebuck & Co., 138 N.J. 2, 647 A.2d 454 (1994) (court disapproves of $56,000 fee request as disproportionate to actual damages of $6800); Chattin v. Cape May Greene, Inc., 243 N.J. Super. 590, 581 A.2d 91 (1990), *aff'd per curiam*, 124 N.J. 943, 591 A.2d 943 (1991) (amount of damage award is relevant to amount of attorney fee award); James v. Thermal Master, Inc., 55 Ohio App. 3d 51, 562 N.E.2d 917 (1988) (court's award of low fee upheld in light of jury's low award and low actual amount in controversy); Tibbetts v. Sight 'N Sound Appliance Centers, Inc., 77 P.3d 1042 (Okla. 2003) (no fee can be awarded where plaintiffs won verdict on liability but zero damages).

931 Williams v. First Gov't Mortg. & Inv. Corp., 225 F.3d 738 (D.C. Cir. 2000) (affirming fees of $199,340 for UDAP recovery of $25,200); Peckham v. Continental Cas. Ins. Co., 895 F.2d 830 (1st Cir. 1990) (Massachusetts law) (successful plaintiff entitled to fee award even if damage award is nominal); Cange v. Stotler & Co., 913 F.2d 1204 (7th Cir. 1990) (attorney fee award larger than compensatory damage award justified where appeal, reward, and trial necessary); Evans v. Yegen Assocs., 556 F. Supp. 1219 (D. Mass. 1982) ($21,000 attorney fees); Hayward v. Ventura Volvo, 108 Cal. App. 4th 509, 133 Cal. Rptr. 2d 514 (2003) (fees of $103,419 on recovery of $44,436); Dodds v. Frontier Chevrolet Sales & Service, 676 P.2d 1237 (Colo. Ct. App. 1983) ($800 damages and $2700 attorney fees); B&L Motors, Inc. v. Bignotti, 427 So. 2d 1070 (Fla. Dist. Ct. App. 1983) ($7272 attorney fees and $6500 damages); LaFerney v. Scott Smith Oldsmobile Inc., 410 So. 2d 534 (Fla. Dist. Ct. App. 1982); Miles Rich Chrysler-Plymouth, Inc. v. Mass, 201 Ga. App. 693, 411 S.E.2d 901 (1991) ($36,000 in attorney fees where actual damages less than $2000); Cieri v. Leticia Query Realty, Inc., 905 P.2d 29 (Haw. 1995) (fees of $12,252 for recovery of $10,878); Grove v. Huffman, 634 N.E.2d 1184 (Ill. App. Ct. 1994) (fees of $21,073.46 upheld for work winning UDAP damages of $12,500); Totz v. Continental Du Page Acura, 602 N.E.2d 1374 (Ill. App. 1992) (affirming $17,625 in fees where consumer was awarded $407.50 compensatory and $5000 punitive damages); Wadkins v. Roach Cadillac Inc., 7 Kan. App. 2d 8, 637 P.2d 458 (1981) ($3000 fees where $200 actual damage but $2000 statutory damage award); Bank of New Orleans & Trust Co. v. Phillips, 415 So. 2d 973 (La. Ct. App. 1982) ($700 attorney fees where damages $250); Beaulieu v. Dorsey, 562 A.2d 678 (Me. 1989) ($18,000 in fees for $610 recovery); Dimarzo v. American Mut. Ins. Co., 389 Mass. 85, 449 N.E.2d 1189 (1983) ($71,962 in attorney fees); McGrath v. Mishara, 386 Mass. 74, 434 N.E.2d 1215 (1982) ($2950 attorney fees for $25 damages); Dorgan v. Loukas, 473 N.E.2d 1151 (Mass. App. Ct. 1985) ($3450 treble damages and $9695 attorney fees); Geraci v. Crown Chevrolet, Inc., 15 Mass. App. Ct. 935, 444 N.E.2d 1308 (1983) ($1000 attorney fees for $100 damages); Paschal v. Bristol Window & Door, Inc., 2001 Mich. App. LEXIS 1131 (Mar. 16, 2001) (unpublished, limited precedent) (affirming fee award of $11,000 where damages were $5000); Luft v. Perry County Lumber & Supply Co., 2003 WL 21027291 (Ohio App. May 8, 2003) (unpublished, citation limited) (affirming $86,115.95 in fees for judgment of $24,000); Gaskill v. Doss, 2000 Ohio App. LEXIS 6185 (Dec. 26, 2000) (affirming fees of $8331 for $1495 damage award); Crye v. Smolak, 110 Ohio App. 3d 504, 674 N.E.2d 779 (1996) ($2700 in attorney fees where treble damages plus statutory damages equaled $1008); Cardwell v. Tom Harrigan Oldsmobile, Inc., 1984 Ohio App. LEXIS 10104 (June 27, 1984) (upholding fee award of $1935 where consumer defeated a $500 claim and won an order requiring transfer of car title); Sherrod v. Holzshuh, 274 Or. 327, 546 P.2d 470 (1976); Duncan v. Luke Johnson Ford Inc., 603 S.W.2d 777 (Tex. 1980) ($3500 attorneys fees, actual damages $150); Cain v. Pruett, 938 S.W.2d 152 (Tex. App. 1996) ($29,250 in attorney fees where actual damages equaled $1525); Seabury Homes, Inc. v. Burleson, 688 S.W.2d 712 (Tex. App. 1985) ($15,000 attorney fees where actual damages equaled $2000); Cameo Constr. Co. v. Campbell, 642 S.W.2d 10 (Tex. App. 1982) ($36,600 attorney fees for $25,400 damages); Rotello v. Ring Around Products Inc., 614 S.W.2d 455 (Tex. Civ. App. 1981) (attorney fee award exceeded $35,000); Dillon v. Troublefield, 601 S.W.2d 141 (Tex. Civ. App. 1980) ($1500 attorney fees for $459 damage award); Tate v. Wiggins, 583 S.W.2d 640 (Tex. Civ. App. 1979); Mallory v. Custer, 537 S.W.2d 141 (Tex. Civ. App. 1976); L'Esperance v. Benware, 830 A.2d 675 (Vt. 2003); Travis v. Washington Horse Breeders Ass'n, 111 Wash. 2d 396, 759 P.2d 418 (1988); Keyes v. Bollinger, 31 Wash. App. 286, 640 P.2d 1077 (1982) (attorney fees reasonable even if exceed damage award).

932 Williams v. First Government Mortgage and Investors Corp., 225 F.3d 738 (D.C. Cir. 2000); Fabri v. United Techs. Int'l, Inc., 193 F. Supp. 2d 480 (D. Conn. 2002); Thames River Recycling, Inc. v. Gallo, 50 Conn. App. 767, 720 A.2d 242 (1998) (attorney

cases where the recovery is small.[933] Moreover, UDAP fees are intended to discourage misconduct by other sellers. Limiting attorney fees under a UDAP statute would undermine the statute's deterrent effect.[934]

When awarding UDAP attorney fees, the court must also consider the public interest policies underlying the statute.[935] These results are in keeping with the purpose of attorney fees, which is to provide successful litigants with adequate compensation for their legal representation when the potential size of the damage award is insufficient to justify the attorney's time. Attorney fees, of course, will not be granted if the consumer's complaint is ill-founded. But where the consumer's complaint is meritorious, the consumer litigant should not also have to bear the cost of attorney fees. Instead, the seller who has deceived the consumer and who has refused to settle informally should bear the cost of the consumer's legal representation. One purpose for UDAP attorney fees is to encourage individuals to bring valid actions to enforce the statute by making such actions economically feasible.[936]

A fully compensatory award is not a windfall. Indeed, there are strong arguments that a multiplier is often necessary to take into account the risk involved. It should be remembered that, with a fee-shifting statute, the consumer's attorney will be paid only at the very end of the case and then only if the defendant turns out to be collectable. This delay in payment is a significant deterrent to handling consumer cases, especially since it creates a risk of nonpayment due to disappearance or bankruptcy of defendants. Delay also increases the financial pressure on the consumer victim, who may be forced to accept a minimal settlement. In most cases the consumer's attorney will also be paid only if the case is successful, so there is another element of risk. These factors may persuade courts to treat fee requests with the seriousness they deserve.[937]

Some UDAP statutes explicitly indicate that the size of attorney fees should not be limited by the size of the damage award. For example, language in the Georgia UDAP statute that fees should be awarded "irrespective of the amount in controversy"[938] has been used to justify a $36,000 fee award where actual damages were less than $2000.[939]

While the size of attorney fees is initially in the court's discretion,[940] reviewing courts have overturned awards as

---

fees are based on attorney's work, not on amount of recovery); Jacques All Trades Corp. v. Brown, 42 Conn. App. 124, 679 A.2d 27 (1996); Totz v. Continental DuPage Acura, 602 N.E.2d 1374 (Ill. App. Ct. 1992) (attorney fee award that was 40 times greater than actual damage award is not excessive); Blaylock v. Johns Hopkins Fed. Credit Union, 831 A.2d 1120 (Md. Spec. App. 2003); Paschal v. Bristol Window & Door, Inc., 2001 Mich. App. LEXIS 1131 (Mar. 16, 2001) (unpublished, limited precedent) (allowing fees greater than judgment is consistent with remedial purposes); Jordan v. Transnational Motors, Inc., 537 N.W.2d 471 (Mich. Ct. App. 1995); Plath v. Schonrock, 64 P.3d 984 (Mont. 2003) (trial court erred in basing fees solely on result obtained); Jones v. General Motors Corp., 953 P.2d 1104 (N.M. App. 1998); Bittner v. Tri-County Toyota, Inc., 58 Ohio St. 3d 143, 569 N.E.2d 464 (1991); Ferrari v. Howard, 2002 WL 1500414 (Ohio App. July 11, 2002) (unpublished, citation limited); Taylor v. Medenica, 331 S.C. 575, 503 S.E.2d 458 (1998) (no requirement that fees be less than damage award; fees of $500,000 affirmed on $108,726 recovery); Keith v. Howerton, 2002 WL 31840683 (Tenn. Ct. App. Dec. 19, 2002) (unpublished, citation limited); Kalnes v. Monnier, 203 Wis. 2d 271, 551 N.W.2d 870 (table), 1996 Wisc. App. LEXIS 737 (Wis. App. 1996) (unpublished and non-precedential). *See also* Riverside v. Rivera, 477 U.S. 561, 106 S. Ct. 2686, 91 L. Ed. 2d 466 (1986) (§ 1988 decision); Gonzales v. Transfer Technologies, Inc., 301 F.3d 608 (7th Cir. 2002) ("willful infringements [of copyright laws] involving small amounts of money can not be adequately deterred . . . without an award of attorneys' fees. . . . The effect of [denial of attorneys' fees] if universalized would be to allow minor infringements, though willful, to be committed with impunity, to be in effect privileged, immune from legal redress."); Steiger v. J.S. Builders, Inc., 39 Conn. App. 32, 663 A.2d 432 (1995) (size of damage award may be considered, but should not be the controlling factor); National Consumer Law Center, Fair Credit Reporting § 11.6.2.1 (5th ed. 2002 and Supp.) (similar cases under Fair Credit Reporting Act); National Consumer Law Center, Truth in Lending § 8.9.4.1 (5th ed. 2003 and Supp.) (similar cases under Truth in Lending Act). *But see* Tibbetts v. Sight 'N Sound Appliance Centers, Inc., 77 P.3d 1042 (Okla. 2003) (no fee can be awarded where plaintiffs won verdict on liability but zero damages).

933 Blaylock v. Johns Hopkins Fed. Credit Union, 831 A.2d 1120 (Md. Spec. App. 2003); Bittner v. Tri-County Toyota, Inc., 58 Ohio St. 3d 143, 569 N.E.2d 464 (1991); Luft v. Perry County Lumber & Supply Co., 2003 WL 21027291 (Ohio App. May 8, 2003) (unpublished, citation limited); Parrott v. Carr Chevrolet, 156 Or. App. 257, 965 P.2d 440 (1998), *rev'd in part on other grounds*, 331 Or. 537, 17 P.3d 473 (2001) (reinstating full punitive damages); *see also* Riverside v. Rivera, 477 U.S. 561 (1986).

934 Bittner v. Tri-County Toyota, Inc., 58 Ohio St. 3d 143, 569 N.E.2d 464 (1991).

935 Wexler v. Brothers Entertainment Group, Inc., 457 N.W.2d 218 (Minn. Ct. App. 1990); *see also* Liess v. Lindemyer, 354 N.W.2d 556 (Minn. Ct. App. 1984). *See* § 8.8.1, *supra*.

936 Steiger v. J.S. Builders, Inc., 39 Conn. App. 32, 663 A.2d 432 (1995) (inadequate fees would frustrate the purpose of creating a climate in which private litigants help to enforce the UDAP statute's ban on unfair or deceptive trade practices); Cieri v. Leticia Query Realty, Inc., 905 P.2d 29 (Haw. 1995); Silva v. Autos of Amboy, 267 N.J. Super. 546, 632 A.2d 291 (1993); Jones v. General Motors Corp., 953 P.2d 1104 (N.M. App. 1998) (one purpose of attorney fee award is to reimburse individuals for enforcing the UDAP statute on behalf of the general citizenry); Winston Realty Co. v. G.H.G., Inc., 314 N.C. 90, 331 S.E.2d 677 (1985); Cotton v. Stanley, 380 S.E.2d 419 (N.C. Ct. App. 1989); L'Esperance v. Benware, 830 A.2d 675 (Vt. 2003).

937 *See* Ketchum v. Moses, 24 Cal. 4th 1122, 17 P.3d 735, 104 Cal. Rptr. 2d 377 (2001) (spelling out reasons for contingency enhancement).

938 Ga. Code Ann. § 10-1-399.

939 Miles Rich Chrysler-Plymouth, Inc. v. Mass, 201 Ga. App. 693, 411 S.E.2d 901 (1991).

940 Witters v. Daniels Motors, Inc., 524 P.2d 632 (Colo. Ct. App. 1974); Black v. Iovino, 580 N.E.2d 139 (Ill. App. Ct. 1991); Kleidon v. Rizza Chevrolet, Inc., 173 Ill. App. 3d 116, 527 N.E.2d 374 (1988); Wadkins v. Roach Cadillac Inc., 7 Kan. App. 2d 8, 637 P.2d 458 (1981); Bell v. Kent-Brown Chevrolet

being so inadequate as to be an abuse of discretion where $500 was awarded for twenty-five hours of work[941] and where $200 was awarded for a case that went to trial.[942] The court's discretion may go only to whether to award attorney fees; if it does make an award, that award must be reasonable.[943] An award is not reasonable if it does not assure competent legal representation for a consumer.[944]

8.8.11.2 Examples of Significant UDAP Attorney Fee Awards

Courts have awarded substantial attorney fees under state UDAP statutes. UDAP attorney fee awards have been made in the following amounts: $915,000,[945] $900,000,[946] $556,962,[947] $500,000,[948] $271,711,[949] $267,000,[950] and $208,333.[951]

Legal services attorneys have been awarded as much as $271,711 in attorney fees in a class action against a trade school.[952] A state attorney general has obtained an award of $389,258 in attorney fees from each of three defendants.[953] An appeals court in 1981 upheld an attorney fee award of $17,685 as reasonable even though the consumer obtained a default judgment.[954]

Hourly rates vary by community standards and the year of the award, but attorneys have received UDAP attorney fee awards based on significant hourly rates. A 1998 decision awarded fees ranging from $170 to $325 an hour.[955] In 1996 the First Circuit upheld an award at the rate of $235 an hour.[956] A federal court approved an hourly rate for a legal services attorney of $170 for 1986 and $180 for 1987.[957] Courts have awarded $50 and $65 an hour for paralegal or law clerk services.[958]

8.8.11.3 Factors Used to Calculate Fees

8.8.11.3.1 Standards vary by state

Courts and attorneys may be most accustomed to the lodestar methodology (discussed at § 8.8.11.3.2, *infra*) that courts use to calculate fees for federal fee-shifting statutes—the Civil Rights Acts, Truth in Lending, Fair Debt Collection, RICO, Fair Credit Reporting, Equal Credit Opportunity Act, the Odometer Act, and the like. Nevertheless, UDAP attorney fees are pursuant to *state* statutes, and federal interpretations of how to calculate fees under federal statutes are not controlling. Federal courts and lower state courts should follow the most recent standards set out by that state's appellate courts in interpreting the state's UDAP statute.[959]

Co., 1 Kan. App. 2d 131, 561 P.2d 907 (1977); VanVoorhees v. Dodge, 679 A.2d 1077 (Me. 1996); Olivetti Corp. v. Ames Bus. Sys., Inc., 344 S.E.2d 82 (N.C. Ct. App. 1986); Stone v. Paradise Park Homes, Inc., 37 N.C. App. 97, 245 S.E.2d 801 (1978); Bryant v. Walt Sweeney Automotive, Inc., 2002 WL 1071943 (Ohio App. May 31, 2002) (unpublished, citation limited); Hardeman v. Wheeler, Inc., 56 Ohio App. 3d 142, 565 N.E.2d 849 (1988) (amount of UDAP fee award is within discretion of trial court); Brooks v. Hurst Buick-Pontiac-Olds-GMC, Inc., 23 Ohio App. 3d 85, 491 N.E.2d 345 (1985); Sewak v. Lockhart, 699 A.2d 755 (Pa. Super. 1997); Keith v. Howerton, 2002 WL 31840683 (Tenn. App. Dec. 19, 2002); Minor v. Land, 775 S.W.2d 744 (Tex. App. 1989); Pontiac v. Elliot, 775 S.W.2d 395 (Tex. App. 1989).

941 Marchion Terrazo, Inc. v. Altman, 372 So. 2d 512 (Fla. Dist. Ct. App. 1979).

942 Connelly v. Puget Sound Collections, Inc., 16 Wash. App. 62, 553 P.2d 1354 (1976); *see also* Hanner v. Classic Auto Body Inc., 10 Mass. App. Ct. 121, 406 N.E.2d 686 (1980).

943 Cotton v. Stanley, 380 S.E.2d 419 (N.C. Ct. App. 1989); Morris v. Bailey, 358 S.E.2d 120 (N.C. Ct. App. 1987).

944 Connelly v. Puget Sound Collections, Inc., 16 Wash. App. 62, 553 P.2d 1354 (1976).

945 Arthur D. Little Int'l, Inc. v. Dooyang Corp., 995 F. Supp. 217 (D. Mass. 1998), *aff'd on other grounds*, 147 F.3d 47 (1st Cir. 1998).

946 Linkage Corp. v. Trustees of Boston University, 425 Mass. 1, 679 N.E.2d 191 (1997), *cert. denied*, 522 U.S. 1015 (1997).

947 Benefit Trust Life Ins. Co. v. Littles, 869 S.W.2d 453 (Tex. App. 1993).

948 Taylor v. Medenica, 331 S.C. 575, 503 S.E.2d 458 (1998).

949 Rosario v. Livaditis, Clearinghouse No. 47,927 (N.D. Ill. 1990).

950 Computer Sys. Engineering v. Quantel Corp., 571 F. Supp. 1379 (D. Mass. 1983), *aff'd*, 740 F.2d 59 (1st Cir. 1984).

951 Bandura v. Orkin Exterminating Co., 865 F.2d 816 (7th Cir. 1988) (Illinois law). *See also* Williams v. First Government Mortgage and Investors Corp., 225 F.3d 738 (D.C. Cir. 2000) ($199,340); Cashman v. Allied Products Corp., 761 F.2d 1250 (8th Cir. 1985) (Minnesota law) ($82,000); Advanced Sys. Consultants v. EPM, 899 F. Supp. 832 (D. Mass. 1995) ($150,000); Dimarzo v. American Mut. Ins. Co., 389 Mass. 85, 449 N.E.2d 1189 (1983) ($71,962); Jillian's Billiard v. Beloff Billiards, 35 Mass. App. Ct. 372, 619 N.E.2d 635 (1993) (business case; $180,000 fee award upheld even though no actual damages were shown and only injunctive relief was granted); Church of the Nativity of Our Lord v. Watpro, 491 N.W.2d 1 (Minn. 1992) ($109,000); Keller Indus., Inc. v. Reeves, 656 S.W.2d 221 (Tex. App. 1983) ($97,000); Travis v. Washington Horse Breeding Ass'n, 47 Wash. App. 361, 734 P.2d 956 (1987) ($95,000); Safeco Ins. Co. of Am. v. JMG Restaurants, 37 Wash. App. 1, 680 P.2d 409 (1984) ($83,000).

952 Rosario v. Livaditis, Clearinghouse No. 47,927 (N.D. Ill. 1990).

953 State v. Ralph Williams' Northwest Chrysler Plymouth, Inc., 87 Wash. 2d 298, 553 P.2d 423 (1976).

954 Helfman Motors Inc. v. Stockman, 616 S.W.2d 394 (Tex. Civ. App. 1981).

955 Arthur D. Little Int'l v. Dooyang Corp., 995 F. Supp. 217, 224 n.1 (D. Mass. 1998), *aff'd on other grounds*, 147 F.3d 47 (1st Cir. 1998).

956 Damon v. Sun Co., 87 F.3d 1467 (1st Cir. 1996) (Massachusetts law). *See also* Computer Sys. Engineering v. Quantel Corp., 571 F. Supp. 1379 (D. Mass. 1983) ($200/hour for lead attorney, $150 for associate counsel, $40 for paralegal), *aff'd*, 740 F.2d 59 (1st Cir. 1984).

957 Jungkurth v. Eastern Fin. Servs., Inc., 87 B.R. 333 (E.D. Pa. 1988).

958 Gibbs v. Southeastern Investment Corp., 705 F. Supp. 738 (D. Conn. 1989) ($50/hour); Arthur D. Little Int'l, Inc. v. Dooyang Corp., 995 F. Supp. 217 (D. Mass. 1998) ($65/hour), *aff'd on other grounds*, 147 F.3d 47 (1st Cir. 1998).

959 Davis v. Mutual Life Ins. Co., 6 F.3d 367 (6th Cir. 1993) (Ohio law).

Courts often use methods other than the lodestar formula in calculating the proper award of UDAP attorney fees, and even state courts that adopt the lodestar approach are not bound to follow all federal interpretations of that method. While the elements may not be that different from state to state, practitioners will obviously have to be familiar with the exact standards set for their state:

Alabama: There are no reported Alabama decisions concerning the calculation of attorney fees under its UDAP statute, but in other cases Alabama courts calculate attorney fees based on twelve criteria: "(1) the nature and value of the subject matter of the employment; (2) the learning, skill and labor requisite to its proper discharge; (3) the time consumed; (4) the professional experience and reputation of the attorney; (5) the weight of his responsibilities; (6) the measure of success achieved; (7) the reasonable expenses incurred; (8) whether a fee is fixed or contingent; (9) the nature and length of the professional relationship; (10) the fee customarily charged in the locality for similar services; (11) the likelihood that a particular employment may preclude other employment; and (12) the time limitations imposed by the client or by the circumstances."[960] Not all of these criteria must apply in a case in order for an attorney fee to be deemed reasonable, but these criteria will be used as an evaluative tool.[961] Opinion evidence offered by qualified experts may also be considered.[962]

Alaska: In Alaska, prevailing consumers are entitled to "full reasonable attorney fees at the prevailing reasonable rate."[963] The same standard applies if the defendant prevails and the consumer's case was frivolous.[964] There are no cases interpreting this standard. If the consumer's case was not frivolous but the defendant prevails, the defendant is entitled to fees under a civil rule, which allows 10% to 20% of any money judgment, or, if there is no monetary recovery, 20% to 30% of actual fees incurred.[965] This amount can be adjusted based on a list of factors such as the complexity of the litigation, the length of trial, and the attorney's efforts to minimize fees.

Arkansas: Arkansas courts have not reported any cases concerning the calculation of attorney fees in UDAP cases, but in other cases the courts consider seven factors: "the experience and ability of the attorney, the time and labor required to perform the legal service properly, the amount involved in the case and the results obtained, the novelty and difficulty of the issues involved, the fee customarily charged in the locality for similar legal services, whether the fee is fixed or contingent, the time limitations imposed upon the client or by the circumstances, and the likelihood, if apparent to the client, that the acceptance of the particular employment will preclude other employment by the lawyer."[966]

California: An intermediate appellate court cited the following factors for determining the amount of a fee award: the nature of the litigation; its difficulty; the amount involved; the skill required and the skill employed in handling the litigation; the attention given; the success of the attorney's efforts; the attorney's age, learning, and experience in the particular type of work demanded; the intricacies and importance of the litigation; the labor and necessity for skilled legal training; and the time consumed.[967] Fees are not limited by the amount the attorney would receive under a contingent fee agreement.[968] California has endorsed the lodestar method under other fee-shifting statutes.[969] The lodestar figure can be adjusted based on factors such as novelty, difficulty, skill, preclusion of other employment, and the contingent nature of the fee.[970] Courts may apply this analysis to UDAP cases also.[971] It may be possible to seek a fee award by submitting a cost bill with itemized fees.[972]

Colorado: Given the lack of a specific definition of "reasonable" attorney fees by the statute, a court found that "compensation should be determined in light of all circumstances for the time and effort reasonably expended by the prevailing party's attorney. The trial court may consider, among other factors, the amount in controversy, the length of time required to represent the client effectively, the complexity of the case, and the value of the legal services to the client."[973] A court will find an award of attorney fees appropriate if the amount is "reasonable and supported by the evidence."[974]

---

960 Beal Bank, SSB v. Schilleci, 2004 WL 870446 at *7–8, (Ala. Apr. 23, 2004) *citing* Van Schaack v. AmSouth Bank, N.A., 530 So. 2d 740, 749 (Ala. 1988).

961 *Beal Bank*, 2004 WL 870446 at *8.

962 *Id.*

963 Alaska Stat. § 45.50.537(a).

964 Alaska Stat. § 45.50.537(b).

965 Alaska R. Civ. P. 82(b)(1).

966 Chrisco v. Sun Indus., Inc., 800 S.W.2d 717, 718–19 (Ark. 1990) (citations omitted).

967 Cortez v. Purolator Air Filtration Prods. Co., 64 Cal. App. 4th 882, 75 Cal. Rptr. 2d 551 (1998) (fee award entered pursuant to Labor Code in suit that also asserted § 17200 claims), *aff'd on other grounds, superseded by, remanded*, 23 Cal. 4th 163, 999 P.2d 706, 96 Cal. Rptr. 2d 518 (2000); Stokus v. Marsh, 217 Cal. App. 3d 647, 266 Cal. Rptr. 90 (1990) (fee award under reciprocal fee statute).

968 Hayward v. Ventura Volvo, 108 Cal. App. 4th 509, 133 Cal. Rptr. 2d 514 (2003) (Cons. Legal Remedies Act).

969 Ketchum v. Moses, 24 Cal. 4th 1122, 17 P.3d 735, 104 Cal. Rptr. 2d 377 (2001); Serrano v. Unruh, 32 Cal. 3d 621, 186 Cal. Rptr. 754 (1982).

970 Ketchum v. Moses, 24 Cal. 4th 1122, 17 P.3d 735, 104 Cal. Rptr. 2d 377 (2001); Thayer v. Wells Fargo Bank, 92 Cal. App. 4th 819, 112 Cal. Rptr. 2d 284 (2001).

971 Thayer v. Wells Fargo Bank, 92 Cal. App. 4th 819, 112 Cal. Rptr. 2d 284 (2001).

972 Reveles v. Toyota By the Bay, 57 Cal. App. 4th 1139, 1148, 67 Cal. Rptr. 2d 543 (1997) (Cal. Civ. Code § 1780, Song-Beverly Act, and reciprocal fee statute).

973 Robinson v. Lynmar Racquet Club, Inc., 851 P.2d 274, 280 (Col. Ct. App. 1993) (using lodestar method; reducing hours because plaintiff's attorney unnecessarily complicated case).

974 Dodds v. Frontier Chevrolet Sales & Service, Inc., 676 P.2d 1237, 1237–38 (Colo. Ct. App. 1983) (allowing $2700 in attorney fees where plaintiff recovered $800 in actual damages).

Connecticut: UDAP attorney fees in Connecticut are based on the attorney's work, not on the amount of the recovery.[975] A federal court has applied the lodestar analysis in a Connecticut UDAP case.[976] There must be a clearly stated and described factual predicate for attorney fees in order for the court to determine the reasonableness of the request.[977] A Connecticut court, citing federal equal employment law precedent, has listed the following factors to be considered in awarding UDAP attorney fees: the time and labor required; the novelty and difficulty of the questions; the skill level required; the preclusion of other employment by the attorney due to acceptance of the case; the customary fee for similar work in the community; whether the fee is fixed or contingent; time limitations imposed by the client or the circumstances; the amount involved and the results obtained; the experience, reputation and ability of the attorneys; the undesirability of the case; the nature and length of the professional relationship with the client; and awards in similar cases.[978] The court can subtract unnecessary hours, or, in dealing with such surplus, simply reduce the hours by a reasonable percentage.[979]

Delaware: Although there is limited jurisprudence on UDAP attorney fees, one court looked to the value of the attorney's services, and seemed particularly impressed that a UDAP case involved a novel approach, justifying a higher fee award.[980]

District of Columbia: Statutory fee awards are not measurable so much by the amount of the recovery of damages as by the value of the services.[981] When computing a fair market hourly rate for an attorney, it is appropriate for a court to consider how the market place would react to "a fee grossly in excess of the values at stake."[982] It is not necessary for a party seeking attorney fees to submit an "accounting" to the court before such fees are awarded.[983] The District of Columbia Circuit upheld a lower court's attorney fee award even though the plaintiff won less than originally sought.[984]

Florida: Courts apply the lodestar approach to Florida's attorney fee provision, which was amended in 1995.[985] Since the statute authorizes an award of fees for "the hours actually spent on the case," an intermediate appellate court has disapproved the use of a contingency risk multiplier.[986]

Georgia: The Georgia UDAP statute specifies that reasonable attorney fees are to be awarded "irrespective of the amount in controversy." An intermediate appellate court has characterized as not excessive or improper an award of attorney fees that was thirteen times more than actual damages.[987] Fees may be awarded for work on both fraud and UDAP counts where they are intertwined, even though the consumer prevails only on the UDAP claim.[988]

Hawaii: A federal court listed the following guidelines for determining the amount of an attorney fee award: (1) the time and labor required; (2) the novelty and difficulty of the questions involved; (3) the skill requisite to perform the legal service properly; (4) the preclusion of other employment by the attorney due to acceptance of the case; (5) the customary fee; (6) whether the fee is fixed or contingent; (7) time limitations imposed by the client or the circumstances; (8) the amount involved and the results obtained; (9) the experience, reputation, and ability of the attorneys; (10) the undesirability of the case; (11) the nature and length of the professional relationship with the client; and (12) awards in

---

975 Conn. Gen. Stat. § 42-110g(d). *See* Fabri v. United Techs. Int'l, Inc., 193 F. Supp. 2d 480 (D. Conn. 2002); Thames River Recycling, Inc. v. Gallo, 50 Conn. App. 767, 720 A.2d 242 (1988).

976 Gervais v. O'Connell, Harris & Assocs., Inc., 297 F. Supp. 2d 435 (D. Conn. 2003) (adopting lodestar but rejecting fees requested for future work to enforce judgment); Societa Bario E Derivati v. Kaystone Chem., Inc., 1998 U.S. Dist. LEXIS 23066 (D. Conn. Apr. 15, 1998).

977 Smith v. Snyder, 267 Conn. 456, 839 A.2d 589 (2004).

978 Steiger v. J.S. Builders, Inc., 39 Conn. App. 32, 663 A.2d 432 (1995). *Accord* Fabri v. United Techs. Int'l, Inc., 193 F. Supp. 2d 480 (D. Conn. 2002). *Cf.* Bristol Technology v. Microsoft Corp., 127 F. Supp. 2d 64 (D. Conn. 2000) (adopting lodestar method), *vacated*, 250 F.3d 152 (2d Cir. 2001) (vacated pursuant to settlement).

979 Fabri v. United Techs. Int'l, Inc., 193 F. Supp. 2d 480 (D. Conn. 2002).

980 Roberts v. American Warranty Corp., 514 A.2d 1132 (Del. Super. Ct. 1986).

981 Freeman v. B&B Assocs., 595 F. Supp. 1338, 1344 (D.D.C. 1984), *rev'd on other grounds*, 790 F.2d 145 (D.C. Cir. 1986).

982 *Id.*

983 Rowan Heating-Air Conditioning-Sheet Metal, Inc. v. Williams, 580 A.2d 583, 586 (D.C. 1990).

984 Williams v. First Gov't Mortg. & Investing Corp., 225 F.3d 738, 747 (D.C. Cir. 2000) (affirming $199,340 attorney fee where plaintiff won $25,200).

985 Nutrivida, Inc. v. Inmuno Vital, Inc., 46 F. Supp. 2d 1310, 1318 (S.D. Fla. 1998) (awarding double lodestar amount because of excellent results and partial contingency nature of fee agreement); *In re* Samuels, Clearinghouse No. 50,439 (Bankr. M.D. Fla. 1995); Mclendon v. Metropolitan Mortgage Co., Clearinghouse No. 43,703 (Fla. Cir. Ct. Dade Cty. Dec. 18, 1989). *See also* Florida Patient's Compensation Fund v. Rowe, 472 So. 2d 1145 (Fla. 1985) (adopting lodestar approach in non-UDAP case and listing 8 factors to determine reasonableness of fees); Gen. Motors Acceptance Corp. v. Laesser, 791 So. 2d 517 (Fla. App. 2001) (using lodestar calculation for fees awarded to prevailing seller under prior version of statute).

986 Corvette Shop & Supplies, Inc. v. Coggins, 779 So. 2d 529, 530 (Fla. Dist. Ct. App. 2000). *But see* Nutrivida, Inc. v. Inmuno Vital, Inc., 46 F. Supp. 2d 1310, 1318 (S.D. Fla. 1998) (awarding double lodestar amount because of excellent results and partial contingency nature of fee agreement; case involved both UDAP and Lanham Act claims); Mclendon v. Metropolitan Mortgage Co., Clearinghouse No. 43,703 (Fla. Cir. Ct. Dade Cty. Dec. 18, 1989) ($30,000 UDAP award multiplied by 2.5 because success was unlikely at the time the case was initiated).

987 Miles Rich Chrysler-Plymouth v. Mass, 411 S.E.2d 901, 905 (Ga. Ct. App. 1991) (fees of $36,362.90 for actual damages of $2000).

988 Campbell v. Beak, 568 S.E.2d 801 (Ga. App. 2002).

similar cases.[989] Fees need not be limited to the amount of actual damages.[990] A lower court did not abuse its discretion in reducing a fee award by 50% where the plaintiff prevailed against only one of two defendants.[991]

Idaho: Idaho courts rely on standards set out in the state's rules of civil procedure.[992] The consumer's recovery of attorney fees is not necessarily limited to the amount the consumer is contingently obligated to pay his or her attorney.

Illinois: Illinois courts consider the skill and standing of the attorney, the nature of the case, the novelty and difficulty of the question at issue, the amount and importance of the subject matter, the degree of responsibility, the usual and customary charges, and the benefits to the client.[993] They may also consider a contingency fee agreement in computing fees.[994] One court declined to allow pre-judgment interest on attorney fees, but noted that such an award might be appropriate on other facts.[995]

Indiana: The factors for determining the reasonableness of the attorney fee are: (1) the time, labor, and skill required to perform the legal service properly; (2) the difficulty of the issue involved; (3) the fee customarily charged in the locality for similar legal services; (4) the amount involved, and (5) the time limitations imposed by the circumstances.[996]

Kansas: A Kansas appellate court calculated attorney fees based on the attorney's normal rate for work reasonably performed.[997] A second appellate decision relies on factors set forth in the Rules of Professional Conduct: the time and labor required; the novelty and difficulty of the questions; the skill needed; whether other employment is precluded; the customary fee for similar services in the locality; the amount involved and results obtained; the experience and ability of the lawyer; and whether the fee is fixed or contingent.[998]

Kentucky: Under the Kentucky Consumer Protection Act, courts consider the "purpose and intent of providing an award of attorney's fees and costs."[999] In consumer protection cases undue focus on small monetary awards would defeat the purpose of awarding attorney fees.[1000] Instead, the court should focus on the "expense of bringing an action under the statute . . . [and] provide attorneys with incentive for representing litigants who assert claims which serve an ultimate public purpose."[1001]

Louisiana: Louisiana courts have indicated that the following factors should be weighed in determining the size of an award: the number of hours spent; the ultimate result; the responsibility incurred; the importance of the litigation; the amount involved; the extent and character of labor; the skill of the attorney; the number of appearances made; the novelty and intricacies of the facts and law involved; the diligence of the attorney; the court's own knowledge; and the ability of the liable party to pay.[1002]

Maine: Maine apparently uses the factors spelled out in *Johnson v. Georgia Highway Express*,[1003] rather than the lodestar rate.[1004] In federal courts, most of these factors are usually subsumed in the initial calculation of the lodestar rate.[1005]

Maryland: Maryland courts base fee awards on factors similar to those in Rule of Professional Conduct 1.5: (1) the time and labor required, the novelty and difficulty of the questions, and the skill required; (2) preclusion of other employment; (3) the fee customarily charged; (4) the amount involved and results obtained; (5) time limitations imposed by the client or the circumstances; (6) the nature and length of the professional relationship with the client; (7) the experience, reputation, and ability of the lawyer; and (8) whether the fee is fixed or contingent.[1006] The fact that the fee is disproportionate to the recovery on the merits is not a basis for reducing the fee.[1007] An intermediate appellate court affirmed a trial court's reduction of hours to those reasonably necessary to try the case, and its elimination of time spent on unsuccessful claims.[1008]

989 Bulgo v. Munoz, 1987 U.S. Dist. LEXIS 15832, at *7 (1987) (D. Haw. Aug. 13, 1987).
990 Cieri v. Leticia Query Realty, 905 P.2d 29 (Haw. 1995).
991 *Id.*
992 Decker v. Homeguard Sys., 105 Idaho 158, 666 P.2d 1169 (Ct. App. 1983).
993 Hoke v. Beck, 587 N.E.2d 4 (Ill. App. Ct. 1992); Black v. Iovino, 580 N.E.2d 139 (Ill. App. Ct. 1991).
994 *See* § 8.8.11.3.3, *infra*.
995 Prior Plumbing & Heating Co. v. Hagins, 630 N.E.2d 1208 (Ill. App. Ct. 1994).
996 Lystarczyk v. Smits, 435 N.E.2d 1011, 1017 (Ind. Ct. App. 1982).
997 Bell v. Kent-Brown Chevrolet Co., 1 Kan. App. 2d 131, 561 P.2d 907 (1977).
998 DeSpiegelaere v. Killion, 947 P.2d 1039 (Kan. App. 1997).
999 Alexander v. S&M Motors, Inc., 28 S.W.3d 303, 305 (Ky. 2000).
1000 *Id.*
1001 *Id.* at 306.
1002 Roustabouts, Inc. v. Hamer, 447 So. 2d 543 (La. Ct. App. 1984); General Inv. Inc. v. Thomas, 400 So. 2d 1081 (La. Ct. App. 1981). *See also* Morrison v. Allstar Dodge, Inc., 792 So. 2d 9 (La. App. 2001) (reciting similar but shorter list of factors for award of fees in redhibition case).
1003 488 F.2d 714 (5th Cir. 1974): the time and labor required; the novelty and difficulty of the questions; the skill needed; the preclusion of other employment; the customary fee; whether the fee is fixed or contingent; time limitations imposed by the client or the circumstances; the amount involved and results obtained; the attorney's experience, reputation, and ability; the undesirability of the case; the nature and length of the professional relationship; and awards in similar cases.
1004 Poussard v. Commercial Credit Plan, 479 A.2d 881 (Me. 1984).
1005 Hensley v. Eckerhart, 461 U.S. 424, 434, 103 S. Ct. 1933, 1940, 76 L. Ed. 2d 40 n.9 (1983). *See* § 8.8.11.3.2, *infra*.
1006 Blaylock v. Johns Hopkins Fed. Credit Union, 831 A.2d 1120 (Md. Spec. App. 2003).
1007 *Id.*
1008 Barnes v. Rosenthal Toyota, Inc., 727 A.2d 431, 434 (Md. Ct. Spec. App. 1999).

Massachusetts: Courts should consider the nature of the case and issues involved; the attorney's time and labor; the size of the case, the damages awarded, and the result; the experience, reputation, and ability of the attorneys; and the price charged by other attorneys in the area for similar services.[1009] The amount received in damages is not the fundamental factor in determining the attorney fee size.[1010] The trial court should reduce the award where the fees sought are plainly excessive given the length of trial and the difficulty of the issues.[1011] If the defendant makes a reasonable settlement offer, then a fee award is limited to fees incurred prior to the offer.[1012]

Michigan: Michigan courts consider the experience of the attorney, the skill and time involved, the amount in question and the results achieved, the difficulty of the case, the expenses incurred, and the nature and length of the professional relationship with the client.[1013] Apparently no prejudgment interest will be allowed on an attorney fee award,[1014] although courts might consider the delay in compensation in setting the amount to be awarded.

Minnesota: A Minnesota appellate decision affirms a trial court's award of fees based on (1) the time and labor involved; (2) the nature and difficulty of the responsibility assumed; (3) the amount involved and the result obtained; (4) fees customarily charged for similar legal services; and (5) the experience and reputation of counsel.[1015] Another decision lists a similar but not identical set of factors.[1016] An earlier federal decision used the lodestar approach.[1017] The Minnesota Supreme Court has stated that the court should take into account the degree to which the public interest is advanced by the suit or else "every artful counsel could dress up his dog bite case to come under an attorney's fees statute."[1018] While the primary purpose of the statute is to encourage lawyers to accept cases where nominal damages erect financial barriers to litigation, this does not limit the statute to cases with only nominal damages.[1019]

Mississippi: Mississippi's deceptive trade practices act only allows attorney fees to prevailing defendants.[1020] If the plaintiff's action was frivolous or filed for the purpose of delay or harassment the defendant is entitled to reasonable attorney fees which are calculated by reference to Mississippi Rule of Professional Conduct.[1021] There are no reported Mississippi cases concerning the calculation of attorney fees under the deceptive trade practices act, but in other cases courts have used the following factors: "(1) the time and labor required, the novelty and difficulty of the questions involved, and the skill requisite to perform the legal service properly; (2) the likelihood, if apparent to the client, that the acceptance of the particular employment will preclude other employment by the lawyer; (3) the fee customarily charged in the locality for similar legal services; (4) the amount involved and the results obtained; (5) the time limitations imposed by the client or by the circumstances; (6) the nature and length of the professional relationship with the client; (7) the experience, reputation, and ability of the lawyer or lawyers performing the services; and (8) whether the fee is fixed or contingent."[1022]

Missouri: Missouri courts have not reported any decisions concerning the calculation of attorney fees under the Merchandising Practices Act, but in other cases courts begin by considering the rates usually charged by other attorneys involved in the subject litigation and the rates charged by other attorneys in the community for similar services, plus the amount involved in the litigation and the results ob-

---

1009 Linthicum v. Archambault, 379 Mass. 381, 389 N.E.2d 482 (1979); *see also* Arthur D. Little Int'l, Inc. v. Dooyang Corp., 995 F. Supp. 217 (D. Mass. 1998), *aff'd on other grounds*, 147 F.3d 47 (1st Cir. 1998); Heller v. Silverbranch Constr. Corp., 376 Mass. 621, 382 N.E.2d 1065 (1978) (basing the award not on the attorney's usual charge, but the objective worth of the attorney's services, including the length and difficulty of the trial and the attorney's displayed competence); Stark v. Patalano Ford Sales, Inc., 30 Mass. App. Ct. 194, 567 N.E.2d 1237 (1991).

1010 Homsi v. C. H. Babb Co., 10 Mass. App. Ct. 474, 409 N.E.2d 219 (1980). *See also* Arthur D. Little Int'l, Inc. v. Dooyang Corp., 995 F. Supp. 217 (D. Mass. 1998) ($915,000 attorney fee award), *aff'd on other grounds*, 147 F.3d 47 (1st Cir. 1998); Refuse & Environmental Sys., Inc. v. Industrial Servs., 732 F. Supp. 1209 (D. Mass. 1990) (fees of $80,260 awarded), *rev'd in part on other grounds*, 932 F.2d 37 (1st Cir. 1991); Computer Sys. Eng'g v. Quantel Corp., 571 F. Supp. 1379 (D. Mass. 1983), *aff'd*, 740 F.2d 59 (1st Cir. 1984) ($267,025 in attorney fees).

1011 Rex Lumber Co. v. Acton Block Co., 29 Mass. App. Ct. 510, 562 N.E.2d 845 (1990).

1012 Mass. Gen. Laws Ann. ch. 93A, § 9(3); Briggs v. Carol Cars, Inc., 407 Mass. 391, 553 N.E.2d 930 (1990); Kohl v. Silver Lake Motors, Inc., 369 Mass. 795, 343 N.E.2d 375 (1976). *See* § 8.2.1, *supra*.

1013 Paschal v. Bristol Window & Door, Inc., 2001 Mich. App. LEXIS 1131 (Mar. 16, 2001) (unpublished, limited precedent); Smolen v. Dahlmann Apartments, Ltd., 186 Mich. App. 292, 463 N.W.2d 261 (1990), *citing* Crawley v. Schick, 48 Mich. App. 728, 211 N.W.2d 217 (1973).

1014 Harvey v. Gerber, 153 Mich. App. 528, 396 N.W.2d 470 (1986).

1015 State *ex rel.* Humphrey v. Alpine Air Products, Inc., 490 N.W.2d 888, 896 (Minn. App. 1992) ($104,165.20 in costs and attorney fees for $70,000 in damages), *aff'd on other grounds*, 500 N.W.2d 788 (Minn. 1993).

1016 Sibley v. Bauers, 1999 Mich. App. LEXIS 1267 (July 16, 1999) (unpublished, limited precedent) (attorney's professional standing and experience; skill, time, and labor; amount in question and results achieved; difficulty; expense; nature and length of professional relationship with client).

1017 Bryant v. TRW, Inc., 689 F.2d 72, 80 (6th Cir. 1982).

1018 Ly v. Nystrom, 615 N.W.2d 302, 312 (Minn. 2000); *see also* Liess v. Lindemyer, 354 N.W.2d 556, (Minn. App. 1984).

1019 Kronebusch v. MVBA Harvestore Sys., 488 N.W.2d 490 (Minn. App. 1992).

1020 Miss. Code Ann. § 75-24-15.

1021 Wilson v. William Hall Chevrolet, Inc., 871 F. Supp. 279, 280 (S.D. Miss. 1994); Smith v. Parkerson Lumber, Inc., 2004 WL 835878 at *6, (Miss. Ct. App. Apr. 20, 2004).

1022 Smith v. Parkerson Lumber, Inc., 2004 WL 835878 at *6 (Miss. Ct. App. Apr. 20, 2004), *quoting* Miss. R. Prof. Conduct 1.5.

tained.[1023] In the context of consumer protection, the courts determine fees while keeping in mind the statutory policy of private enforcement.[1024] Fees must bear some relation to the damage award, but courts are cognizant that expense should not stand in the way of the private enforcement that is essential to the operation of consumer protection statutes.[1025] Fees are not limited to a percentage of the consumer's recovery, even if the consumer has entered into a contingency fee agreement.[1026] Applying the Missouri UDAP statute, the Eighth Circuit held that a generous punitive damage award on a fraud count is not a basis for reducing the attorney fee award on a UDAP count.[1027]

Montana: The Montana Supreme Court requires consideration of seven factors: (1) the amount and character of the services; (2) the labor, time, and trouble involved; (3) the character and importance of the litigation; (4) the amount of money or value of property affected; (5) the professional skill and experience called for; (6) the attorneys' character and standing in their profession; and (7) the results obtained.[1028] Trial courts have discretion to consider other factors as well.[1029]

Nebraska: There are no reported Nebraska decisions concerning the calculation of attorney fees under the Consumer Protection Act or the Deceptive Trade Practices Act, but in other cases, courts have considered the following factors: "the nature of the proceeding, the time and labor required, the novelty and difficulty of the questions raised, the skill required to properly conduct the case, the responsibility assumed, the care and diligence exhibited, the result of the suit, the character and standing of the attorney, and the customary charges of the bar for similar services."[1030]

Nevada: There are no reported cases concerning the calculation of attorney fees under the Nevada Trade Regulation and Practices Act, but in other cases courts have considered numerous factors, none of which should predominate in the decision. The factors are: "(1) the qualities of the advocate: his ability, his training, education, experience, professional standing and skill; (2) the character of the work to be done: its difficulty, its intricacy, its importance, time and skill required, the responsibility imposed and the prominence and character of the parties where they affect the importance of the litigation; (3) the work actually performed by the lawyer: the skill, time and attention given to the work; (4) the result: whether the attorney was successful and what benefits were derived."[1031]

New Hampshire: There appears to be limited jurisprudence in New Hampshire on how to compute UDAP attorney fees. A bankruptcy court adopted the federal lodestar formula discussed at § 8.8.11.3.2, *infra*, but doubled the lodestar to account for the case's contingent nature.[1032]

New Jersey: The New Jersey Supreme Court has adopted the lodestar method as the general rule for determining fees under fee-shifting statutes.[1033] Courts can also consider other factors, such as the damages sought compared to the damages recovered; the interest to be vindicated in the context of the statutory objectives; any circumstances directly or indirectly affecting the extent of counsel's efforts; and whether the hours expended are in excess of those which competent counsel would have expended to achieve a comparable result.[1034] The same case states that where there are interrelated claims, the basic lodestar rate may be excessive only if there is partial or limited success. Even before the state supreme court's ruling, New Jersey courts applied the lodestar formula and also followed federal cases in allowing fees for work on non-UDAP claims that are intertwined with UDAP claims.[1035]

New Mexico: Attorney fees should reflect the full amount of fees fairly and reasonably incurred by a party in securing an award under the statute,[1036] and is not limited to a specific percentage of the recovery.[1037]

New York: One case has held the existence of a contingency fee agreement does not force the attorney to take fees out of the client's recovery instead of seeking an award from the opposing party.[1038] Nor is a contingency fee agreement a cap on UDAP fees, although the court may consider the agreement as one factor in determining the fee award.[1039] A federal court has listed the factors as the time and skill required in litigating the case; the complexity of issues; the customary fee for the work; the results achieved; the law-

1023 Williams v. Finance Plaza, Inc., 78 S.W.3d 175, 184 (Mo. App. 2002); O'Brien v. B.L.C. Ins. Co., 768 S.W.2d 64 (Mo. 1989) (Odometer Act).

1024 Williams v. Finance Plaza, Inc., 78 S.W.3d 175, 187 (Mo. App. 2002).

1025 *Id.*

1026 O'Brien v. B.L.C. Ins. Co., 768 S.W.2d 64 (Mo. 1989) (Odometer Act).

1027 Grabinski v. Blue Springs Ford Sales, Inc., 203 F.3d 1024 (8th Cir. 2000).

1028 Osterman v. Sears, Roebuck & Co., 80 P.3d 435 (Mont. 2003) (court appears to be stating general rule applicable to UDAP and non-UDAP fee claims).

1029 *Id.*

1030 *In re* Donley, 631 N.W.2d 839, 846 (Neb. 2001), *citing* Schirber v. State, 581 N.W.2d 873 (1998).

1031 Bruznell v. Golden Gate Nat'l Bank, 455 P.2d 31, 33 (Nev. 1969); *see also* Hornwood v. Smith's Food King No. 1, 807 P.2d 208, 213 (Nev. 1991).

1032 *In re* Globe Distributors, Inc., 145 B.R. 728 (Bankr. D.N.H. 1992).

1033 Packard-Bamberger & Co. v. Collier, 167 N.J. 427, 771 A.2d 1194 (2001).

1034 *Id.*

1035 Silva v. Autos of Amboy, 267 N.J. Super. 546, 632 A.2d 291 (1993); Chattin v. Cape May Greene, Inc., 243 N.J. Super. 590, 581 A.2d 91 (1990), *aff'd mem.*, 591 A.2d 943 (N.J. 1991).

1036 Jones v. GMC, 953 P.2d 1104 (N.M. App. 1998).

1037 Candelaria v. General Elec. Co., 730 P.2d 470, 479 (N.M. App. 1986).

1038 Boulevard Assocs. v. Sovereign Hotels, Inc., 868 F. Supp. 70 (S.D.N.Y. 1994), *rev'd on other grounds*, 72 F.3d 1029 (2d Cir. 1995).

1039 Blue Cross & Blue Shield of N.J., Inc. v. Philip Morris, Inc., 190 F. Supp. 2d 407 (E.D.N.Y. 2002).

yer's experience; ability and reputation; the amount in dispute; and the benefit to the client.[1040] Another federal decision endorses use of the lodestar method.[1041] Where successful and unsuccessful claims intertwine to a great extent and the plaintiff wins substantial relief, full fees can be awarded.[1042] Fees may exceed the underlying recovery.[1043] Paralegal work is compensable.[1044]

North Carolina: The North Carolina Supreme Court has suggested that courts consider, in awarding UDAP attorney fees, the novelty and difficulty of the questions of law, the adequacy of representation, the difficulty of the problems faced by the attorney, especially any unusual difficulties, the kind of case, and the results obtained.[1045] In determining whether fees are reasonable, North Carolina courts must include findings of fact as to the time and labor expended, the skill required, the customary fee for like work, and the experience or ability of the attorney.[1046]

North Dakota: North Dakota has no reported decisions concerning the calculation of attorney fees under its consumer protection statute, but to determine the reasonableness of attorney fees in other cases, courts evaluate the fee in light of North Dakota Rule of Professional Conduct 1.5(a).[1047] The courts should determine the amount of time reasonably expended by the attorney and determine a reasonable hourly rate by considering: "(1) the time and labor required, the novelty and difficulty of the questions involved, and the skill requisite to perform the legal service properly; (2) the likelihood, if apparent to the client, that the acceptance of the particular employment will preclude other employment by the lawyer; (3) the fee customarily charged in the locality for similar legal services; (4) the amount involved and the results obtained; (5) the time limitations imposed by the client or by the circumstances; (6) the nature and length of the professional relationship with the client; (7) the experience, reputation, and ability of the lawyer or lawyers performing the services; and (8) whether the fee is fixed or contingent."[1048] Each factor must be considered, but no one factor should dominate the court's determination.[1049]

1040 *Id. See also* Riordan v. Nationwide Mut. Fire Ins. Co., 977 F.2d 47, 53 (2d Cir. 1992) (listing just the first four of these factors); Independent Living Aids, Inc. v. Maxi-Aids, Inc., 25 F. Supp. 2d 127, 132 (E.D.N.Y. 1998).

1041 Wilson v. Car Land Diagnostics Center, Inc., 2001 U.S. Dist. LEXIS 19760 (S.D.N.Y. Nov. 15, 2001).

1042 Blue Cross & Blue Shield of N.J., Inc. v. Philip Morris, Inc., 190 F. Supp. 2d 407 (E.D.N.Y. 2002).

1043 *Id.*

1044 *Id.*

1045 United Laboratories v. Kuykendall, 335 N.C. 183, 437 S.E.2d 374 (1993).

1046 Pierce v. Reichard, 593 S. E. 2d 787 (N.C. Ct. App. 2004).

1047 T.F. James Co. v. Vakoch, 628 N.W.2d 298, 304 (N.D. 2001).

1048 *Id.* at 304–05; *see also* State Farm Fire and Casualty Co. v. Sigman, 508 N.W.2d 323, 327 (N.D. 1993).

1049 T.F. James Co. v. Vakoch, 628 N.W.2d 298, 305 (N.D. 2001).

Ohio: The Ohio Supreme Court adopts the federal lodestar formula discussed at § 8.8.11.3.2, *infra*,[1050] taking into account a list of factors set forth in a bar disciplinary rule.[1051] Ohio courts have not yet adopted recent United States Supreme Court rulings limiting the use of multipliers, however.[1052]

Oklahoma: In awarding fees, courts should consider (1) the time and labor required; (2) the novelty and difficulty of the question; (3) the skill requisite to perform the legal service properly; (4) the preclusion of other employment by the attorney due to acceptance of the case; (5) the customary fee; (6) whether the fee is fixed or contingent; (7) time limitations imposed by the client or the circumstances; (8) the amount involved and the results obtained; (9) the experience, reputation and ability of the attorneys; (10) the "undesirability" of the case, i.e., the risk of non-recovery; (11) the nature and length of the professional relationship with the client; and (12) awards in similar cases.[1053] The degree of success obtained is especially important.[1054]

Oregon: An Oregon appellate decision upholds UDAP attorney fees based on the number of hours multiplied by a reasonable hourly rate.[1055] The decision cites the risk involved in the contingency fee case and the defendant's obstinacy as well as the prevailing market rates in the community.

Pennsylvania: In awarding UDAP fees, the courts should consider the time and labor involved; the novelty and difficulty of the questions; the skill required to handle the case; lawyers' customary charges for similar services; the amount in controversy; the benefits resulting to the clients; and the contingency or certainty of compensation.[1056] Prior to a 1997 amendment that explicitly authorized fees, a number of courts found authority to award attorney fees implicit in the statute,[1057] and at least one bankruptcy court[1058] adopted the federal lodestar formula discussed at § 8.8.11.3.2, *infra*.

Rhode Island: Courts in Rhode Island have not reported any cases concerning the calculation of fees under the

1050 Bittner v. Tri-County Toyota, Inc., 58 Ohio St. 3d 143, 569 N.E.2d 464 (1991).

1051 Ferrari v. Howard, 2002 WL 1500414 (Ohio App. July 11, 2002) (unpublished, citation limited).

1052 Davis v. Mutual Life Ins. Co., 6 F.3d 367 (6th Cir. 1993) (Ohio law) (federal court will not apply latest federal interpretations of lodestar multiplier where Ohio courts have not similarly ruled).

1053 State *ex rel.* Burk v. City of Oklahoma City, 598 P.2d 659, 661 (Okla. 1979).

1054 Tibbetts v. Sight 'N Sound Appliance Centers, Inc., 77 P.3d 1042 (Okla. 2003).

1055 Parrott v. Carr Chevrolet, 156 Or. App. 257, 965 P.2d 440 (1998), *rev'd in part on other grounds*, 331 Or. 537, 17 P.3d 473 (2001) (reinstating full punitive damages award).

1056 Sewak v. Lockhart, 699 A.2d 755 (Pa. Super. 1997).

1057 *See, e.g.*, Gabriel v. O'Hara, 368 Pa. Super. 383, 534 A.2d 488 (1987); Hammer v. Nikol, 659 A.2d 617 (Pa. Commw. 1995).

1058 *In re* Bryant, 111 B.R. 474 (E.D. Pa. 1990). *See also* Hines v. Chrysler Corp., 971 F. Supp. 212 (E.D. Pa. 1997) (lodestar method used where fees primarily awarded under Magnuson-Moss Warranty Act, but also awarded under state UDAP statute).

Unfair Trade Practice and Consumer Protection Act, but in other cases, Rhode Island courts consider the factors set out Supreme Court Rule Article V, Rule of Professional 1.5 (2002) to determine whether an attorney fee authorized by statute is reasonable.[1059] These factors are: "(1) the time and labor required, the novelty and difficulty of the questions involved, and the skill requisite to perform the legal service properly; (2) the likelihood, if apparent to the client, that the acceptance of the particular employment will preclude other employment by the lawyer; (3) the fee customarily charged in the locality for similar legal services; (4) the amount involved and the results obtained; (5) the time limitations imposed by the client or by the circumstances; (6) the nature and length of the professional relationship with the client; (7) the experience, reputation, and ability of the lawyer or lawyers performing the services; and (8) whether the fee is fixed or contingent."[1060]

South Carolina: South Carolina courts consider the following factors in determining attorney fees: (1) the nature, extent, and difficulty of the case; (2) the time necessarily devoted to the case; (3) the professional standing of counsel; (4) the contingency of compensation; (5) the beneficial results obtained; and (6) the customary legal fees for similar services.[1061] In a commercial case, a court placed considerable weight on a contingent fee contract in determining the amount of a fee award.[1062] But in a consumer case a court held that it was error to limit the fee award to the amount set by the contingent fee contract.[1063]

Tennessee: Tennessee courts use a list of factors in the Code of Professional Responsibility to determine a reasonable attorney fee.[1064] A court can award attorney fees in excess of a contingency fee arrangement.[1065] The fee award need not be proportionate to the recovery on the merits.[1066]

Texas: Texas courts look to the entire record, the amount in controversy, the nature of the case, and judges' common knowledge and experience as lawyers and judges.[1067] The court may discount hours for duplicative time with co-counsel.[1068] An award will not be based on the amount specified in a contingency fee agreement.[1069] However, a fee award can be based on a percentage if the plaintiff proves that it is reasonable.[1070] If reasonableness is proven, a fee award that is nine times actual damages is not excessive.[1071] While one court would not allow prejudgment interest on an attorney fee award,[1072] another court allowed such interest for the consumer where the consumer had paid the attorney in advance.[1073]

U.S. Virgin Islands: Courts in the Virgin Islands have not reported any decisions concerning the calculation of attorney fees under the Consumer Protection Law of 1973, but in other cases courts have used the lodestar approach. To determine whether the amount of counsel fees requested by an attorney in a civil action under Virgin Islands law is reasonable, the court must first determine the lodestar amount by multiplying the attorney's billing rate by the number of hours expended.[1074] Next, the court must determine what portion of the lodestar amount is a reasonable fee by considering several factors. These factors are: "the time and labor required, the novelty and difficulty of the questions involved, the skill requisite to properly conduct the cause, the customary charges of the bar for similar services, the amount involved in the controversy, the benefits resulting to the client from the services, and the contingency or certainty of the compensation."[1075]

Utah: There are no reported Utah decisions concerning the calculation of reasonable attorney fees under the Consumer Sales Practices Act, but the Utah Supreme Court has held that fee awards in other cases should be determined by answering four questions: what legal work was actually performed; how much of that work was reasonably necessary to prosecute the matter; whether the billing rate is consistent with the rates charged in locality for similar services; and whether the circumstances require consider-

1059 Keystone Elevator Co. v. Johnson & Wales University, 850 A.2d 912, 921 (R.I. 2004), *citing* Colonial Plumbing & Heating Supply Co. v. Contemporary Constr. Co., 464 A.2d 741, 743 (R.I. 1983).

1060 Sup. Ct. R. Art. V, R. Prof. Conduct 1.5 (2002).

1061 Taylor v. Medenica, 331 S.C. 575, 503 S.E.2d 458 (1998) (affirming award of $500,000 in fees on $108,726 recovery).

1062 Global Protection Corp. v. Halbersberg, 503 S.E.2d 483 (S.C. App. 1998).

1063 Kucharski v. Rick Hendrick Chevrolet Ltd. P'ship, 2002 WL 31386090 (S.C. App. Sept. 18, 2002) (unpublished, citation limited).

1064 Killingsworth v. Ted Russell Ford, Inc., 104 S.W.3d 530 (Tenn. App. 2002); Keith v. Howerton, 2002 WL 31840683 (Tenn. App. Dec. 19, 2002).

1065 Adkinson v. Harpeth Ford-Mercury, Inc., 1991 Tenn. App. LEXIS 114 (Feb. 15, 1991). *Accord* Killingsworth v. Ted Russell Ford, Inc., 104 S.W.3d 530 (Tenn. App. 2002).

1066 Keith v. Howerton, 2002 WL 31840683 (Tenn. Ct. App. Dec. 19, 2002) (unpublished, citation limited).

1067 Keith v. Howerton, 2002 WL 31840683 (Tenn. App. Dec. 19, 2002). *See* Star Houston, Inc. v. Kundak, 843 S.W.2d 294 (Tex. App. 1992); *see also* Arthur Anderson & Co. v. Perry Equipment Corp., 945 S.W.2d 812 (Tex. 1997).

1068 Galveston County Fair & Rodeo, Inc. v. Kauffman, 910 S.W.2d 129 (Tex. App. 1995) (Texas UDAP permits payment of fees to two independent attorneys provided that there is no "impermissible double dipping" by duplicate billing).

1069 Arthur Anderson & Co. v. Perry Equipment Corp., 945 S.W.2d 812 (Tex. 1997).

1070 Northwinds Abatement, Inc. v. Employers Ins. of Wausau, 258 F.3d 345 (5th Cir. 2001) (Texas law); PPG Indus., Inc. v. JMB/Houston Centers Partners Ltd. P'ship, 41 S.W.3d 270 (Tex. App. 2001), *rev'd on other grounds*, 2004 WL 1533274 (Tex. July 9, 2004).

1071 Northwinds Abatement, Inc. v. Employers Ins. of Wausau, 258 F.3d 345 (5th Cir. 2001) (Texas law).

1072 McCann v. Brown, 725 S.W.2d 822 (Tex. App. 1987).

1073 A.V.I., Inc. v. Heathington, 842 S.W.2d 712 (Tex. App. 1992).

1074 Gardiner v. Virgin Islands Water and Power Authority, 32 F. Supp. 2d 816, 819 (D. V.I. 1999).

1075 *Id.*; *See also* Lucerne Investment Co. v. Estate Belvedere, Inc., 411 F.2d 1205, 1207 (3d Cir. 1969).

ation of additional factors such as the amount in controversy, the extent of the attorney's services, the relationship of the requested fee to the amount recovered, the novelty and difficulty of the issues confronted (the difficulty of the litigation), the efficiency of the attorneys, the results attained and the expertise and experience of counsel.[1076]

Vermont: It is within the trial court's discretion to determine reasonable attorney fees.[1077] Vermont courts start with a lodestar figure, computed by multiplying the number of hours reasonably expended on the case by a reasonable hourly rate, and then adjust that figure upward or downward based on various factors.[1078] Where the plaintiff's UDAP claim and a non-fee shifting claim arise from a common core of facts, and the plaintiff achieves excellent results on the UDAP claim, the court may award fees for all hours.[1079] Plaintiff's counsel has the burden of proving what services were provided and the reasonableness of the fees sought, and a fee bill must break down the time spent on each task.[1080]

Virginia: The Virginia Supreme Court has not decided whether it will adopt the lodestar method, but has approved several factors that it considers to be included within the lodestar approach, such as the novelty and difficulty of the questions raised, the skill required, and the overall relief obtained by the plaintiff in relation to the hours expended on the litigation.[1081]

Washington: Washington adopts the federal lodestar formula discussed at § 8.8.11.3.2, *infra*.[1082] Unlike federal courts, however, Washington courts continue to endorse the use of multipliers, at least for contingency.[1083]

Wisconsin: Wisconsin courts look to the amount and character of services rendered, the labor involved, the character and importance of the litigation, the amount at stake, the experience and skill required, the attorney's standing in the profession, the client's ability to pay, and how much the client benefited from the services.[1084] A reduced award was upheld in one case where the time expended was excessive and the parties had disregarded opportunities to settle the case.[1085]

Wyoming: No reported decisions discuss the calculation of attorney fees under the Wyoming Consumer Protection Act, but in other cases Wyoming courts determine the lodestar value of the attorney's services by deciding whether the fee charged represents a reasonable amount of time spent on the case at a reasonable hourly rate and whether this lodestar value should be adjusted upward or downward by considering discretionary factors found in Wyo. Stat. § 1-14-126(b).[1086] These factors are: "(i) The time and labor required, the novelty and difficulty of the questions involved, and the skill requisite to perform the legal service properly; (ii) The likelihood that the acceptance of the particular employment precluded other employment by the lawyer; (iii) The fee customarily charged in the locality for similar legal services; (iv) The amount involved and the results obtained; (v) The time limitations imposed by the client or by the circumstances; (vi) The nature and length of the professional relationship with the client; (vii) The experience, reputation and ability of the lawyer or lawyers performing the services; and (viii) Whether the fee is fixed or contingent."[1087]

8.8.11.3.2 The lodestar formula

All UDAP practitioners should be familiar with the federal lodestar formula.[1088] The method is obviously central in any state adopting the lodestar approach. (States adopting this approach for awarding UDAP attorney fees are listed in § 8.8.11.3.1, *supra*.) In addition, courts in other states may

1076 Dixie State Bank v. Bracken, 764 P.2d 985, 990 (Utah 1988); *see also* Brown v. Richards, 840 P.2d 143, 155 (Utah Ct. App. 1992).

1077 Bruntaeger v. Zeller, 515 A.2d 123, 128 (Vt. 1986).

1078 L'Esperance v. Benware, 830 A.2d 675 (Vt. 2003).

1079 *Id.*

1080 *Id.*

1081 Holmes v. LG Marion Corp., 258 Va. 473, 521 S.E.2d 528 (1999) (approving reduction of fees due to unnecessary time and time on unsuccessful issues).

1082 Washington State Physicians Ins. Exchange & Ass'n v. Fisons Corp., 122 Wash. 2d 299, 858 P.2d 1054 (1993); Bowers v. Transamerican Title Ins. Co., 675 P.2d 193 (Wash. 1983); Bishop v. Jefferson Title Co., 28 P.3d 802 (Wash. App. 2001); Edmonds v. John L. Scott Real Estate, Inc., 942 P.2d 1072 (Wash. Ct. App. 1997) (trial court should have used lodestar approach rather than simply doubling the amount of fees incurred at arbitration). *See also* Schmidt v. Cornerstone Investments, Inc., 115 Wash. 2d 148, 795 P.2d 1143 (1990); Travis v. Washington Horse Breeders Ass'n, 111 Wash. 2d 396, 759 P.2d 418 (1988); Evergreen Int'l Inc. v. American Casualty Co., 52 Wash. App. 548, 761 P.2d 964 (1988). *Cf.* Connelly v. Puget Sound Collections, Inc., 16 Wash. App. 62, 553 P.2d 1354 (1976) (taking into consideration the public benefit of a case).

1083 Washington State Physicians Ins. Exchange & Ass'n v. Fisons Corp., 122 Wash. 2d 299, 858 P.2d 1054 (1993); Smith v. Behr Process Corp., 113 Wash. App. 306, 54 P.3d 665 (2002); Bishop v. Jefferson Title Co., 28 P.3d 802 (Wash. Ct. App. 2001); Ethridge v. Hwang, 105 Wash. App. 447, 20 P.3d 958 (2001); Edmonds v. John L. Scott Real Estate, Inc., 942 P.2d 1072 (Wash. Ct. App. 1997).

1084 Three & One Co. v. Geilfuss, 178 Wis. 2d 400, 504 N.W.2d 393 (1993). *Cf.* Kolupar v. Wilde Pontiac Cadillac, 683 N.W.2d 58 (Wis. 2004) (non-UDAP consumer case adopting lodestar approach to determine reasonable attorney fees; lodestar amount is then evaluated based on factors listed in a bar disciplinary rule).

1085 Pierce v. Norwick, 550 N.W.2d 451 (Wis. App. 1996).

1086 Johnston v. Stevenson, 938 P.2d 861, 862 (Wyo. 1997).

1087 Wyo. Stat. § 1-14-126.

1088 This formula is enunciated in Blum v. Stenson, 465 U.S. 886, 104 S. Ct. 1541, 79 L. Ed. 2d 891 (1984), Hensley v. Eckerhart, 461 U.S. 424, 103 S. Ct. 1933 (1983), Lindy Bros. Bldrs., Inc. v. American Radiator & Standard Sanitary Corp., 487 F.2d 161 (3d Cir. 1973), and in more detail in Copeland v. Marshall, 641 F.2d 880 (D.C. Cir. 1980). *See* National Consumer Law Center, Truth in Lending § 8.9.4 (5th ed. 2003 and Supp.).

still turn to lodestar cases to decide how to compute attorney fees.

Nevertheless, federal attorney fee statutes are not controlling for state UDAP cases. The federal lodestar formula was designed for federal fee-shifting statutes. Even in states generally adopting a lodestar approach, federal courts and lower state courts should follow the most recent standards set out by that state's appellate courts in interpreting the state's UDAP statute.[1089] A state may, for example, generally follow the lodestar standard, yet allow multipliers not allowed by the federal standard. This subsection sets out the federal lodestar formula, as supplemented by case law interpreting that formula for purposes of state UDAP statutes.

The first step in the lodestar calculation is establishing a "lodestar"[1090] figure based on the number of attorney hours reasonably expended in the litigation times a reasonable hourly rate for this attorney work. The attorney must provide reasonable, although not exhaustive, documentation for this number, including the number of hours worked, the type of work performed, and the category of attorney who performed the work (i.e., senior partner, associate).[1091] Attorneys can be compensated even for travel time.[1092] The court must discount hours on unsuccessful claims, unproductive time, or duplicative time with co-counsel and may reduce the award where the fees sought are plainly excessive for the length of trial, the difficulty of the issues, and the amount at stake.[1093] The total reasonable hours is multiplied by a reasonable hourly rate of compensation, varying with each attorney and the type of work involved.[1094] This establishes the lodestar figure.

Either party can then attempt to carry the burden of justifying an adjustment to this figure. Although awards under federal fee shifting statutes can not be adjusted upward due to contingency,[1095] state courts may still follow older cases that allowed such adjustments.[1096] These courts reason that, if an attorney will receive no fee from his or her client if the claim is not successful, the lodestar figure should be adjusted up based on the risk involved that the attorney will receive no fee in the case.[1097] Thus in one case, the Washington Supreme Court approved a 50% increase in the lodestar figure to account for the contingent nature of the case.[1098] An upward adjustment is particularly appropriate if the attorney has taken the case pro bono, without requiring or expecting payment, and then prevails on a claim that allows fees.[1099]

The lodestar figure can also be adjusted to reflect the quality of work performed, that is whether the quality is higher or lower than one would expect for the hourly rate used to compute the lodestar figure.[1100] When courts men-

1089 Davis v. Mutual Life Ins. Co., 6 F.3d 367 (6th Cir. 1993) (Ohio law).

1090 Lodestar refers to a star that is used as a point of reference, such as the North Star.

1091 Bowers v. Transamerican Title Ins. Co., 675 P.2d 193 (Wash. 1983).

1092 Planned Parenthood v. Attorney General, 297 F.3d 253 (3d Cir. 2002) (§ 1988 case); Henry v. Webermeier, 738 F.2d 188 (7th Cir. 1984); *In re* Pine, 705 F.2d 936 (7th Cir. 1983).

1093 Rex Lumber Co. v. Acton Block Co., 29 Mass. App. Ct. 510, 562 N.E.2d 845 (1990); James v. Thermal Master, Inc., 55 Ohio App. 3d 51, 562 N.E.2d 917 (1988); Bittner v. Tri-County Toyota, Inc., 62 Ohio Misc. 2d 345, 598 N.E.2d 925 (Mun. Ct. 1992); Galveston County Fair & Rodeo, Inc. v. Kauffman, 910 S.W.2d 129 (Tex. App. 1995) (Texas UDAP statute permits payment of fees to two independent attorneys provided that there is no "impermissible double dipping" by duplicate billing); Bowers v. Transamerican Title Ins. Co., 675 P.2d 193 (Wash. 1983).

1094 Bowers v. Transamerican Title Ins. Co., 675 P.2d 193 (Wash. 1983). *See* § 8.8.11.2, *supra*, for examples of hourly rates authorized in UDAP cases.

1095 City of Burlington v. Dague, 505 U.S. 557, 112 S. Ct. 2638, 120 L. Ed. 2d 449 (1992).

1096 Davis v. Mutual Life Ins. Co., 6 F.3d 367 (6th Cir. 1993) (Ohio law); Washington State Physicians Ins. Exchange & Ass'n v. Fisons Corp., 122 Wash. 2d 299, 858 P.2d 1054 (1993); Ethridge v. Hwang, 105 Wash. App. 447, 20 P.3d 958 (2001); Edmonds v. John L. Scott Real Estate, Inc., 942 P.2d 1072 (Wash. Ct. App. 1997).

1097 Bowers v. Transamerican Title Ins. Co., 675 P.2d 193 (Wash. 1983). *See also* Mclendon v. Metropolitan Mortgage Co., Clearinghouse No. 43,703 (Fla. Cir. Ct. Dade Cty. Dec. 18, 1989) ($30,000 UDAP award multiplied by 2.5 because success was unlikely at the time the case was initiated). *But see* City of Burlington v. Dague, 505 U.S. 557, 112 S. Ct. 2638, 120 L. Ed. 2d 449 (1992); Computer Sys. Engineering v. Quantel Corp., 740 F.2d 59 (1st Cir. 1984).

1098 Bowers v. Transamerican Title Ins. Co., 675 P.2d 193 (Wash. 1983). *Accord In re* Globe Distributors, Inc., 145 B.R. 728 (Bankr. D.N.H. 1992) (doubling lodestar because of case's contingent nature); Sing v. John L. Scott, Inc., 920 P.2d 589 (Wash. App. 1996), *rev'd on other grounds*, 948 P.2d 816 (Wash. 1997). *See also* Washington State Physicians Ins. Exchange & Ass'n v. Fisons Corp., 122 Wash. 2d 299, 858 P.2d 1054 (1993). *But cf.* Travis v. Washington Horse Breeders Ass'n, 47 Wash. App. 361, 734 P.2d 956 (1987) (lodestar upward adjustment overturned because the case was not risky), *aff'd*, 111 Wash. 2d 396, 759 P.2d 418 (1988) (attorney's hiring another trial counsel on a non-contingent hourly rate basis belied claim that case was highly risky).

1099 Opportunity Mgmt. Co. v. Frost, 1999 Wash. App. LEXIS 336 (Feb. 16, 1999).

1100 Washington State Physicians Ins. Exchange & Ass'n v. Fisons Corp., 122 Wash. 2d 299, 858 P.2d 1054 (1993); Bowers v. Transamerican Title Ins. Co., 675 P.2d 193 (Wash. 1973); *see also* Computer Sys. Eng'g v. Quantel Corp., 571 F. Supp. 1379 (D. Mass. 1983), *aff'd*, 740 F.2d 59 (1st Cir. 1984) (hourly rates of $200 and $150 an hour increased by 25% to account for various factors in case other than uncertainty over whether attorney fees will be paid); Chattin v. Cape May Greene, Inc., 243 N.J. Super. 590, 581 A.2d 91 (1990), *aff'd per curiam*, 124 N.J. 943, 591 A.2d 943 (1991) (upward adjustment may be based on quality of services but should be reserved for rare and exceptional cases); Kolupar v. Wilde Pontiac Cadillac, 683 N.W.2d 58 (Wis. 2004) (non-UDAP consumer case; lists factors for adjusting lodestar amount). *But see* Travis v. Washington Horse Breeders Ass'n, 47 Wash. App. 361, 734 P.2d 956 (1987) (upward adjustment for quality overturned because quality was already accounted for by the numbers chosen for an hourly rate and for the number of hours billed), *aff'd*, 111 Wash. 2d 396, 759 P.2d 418 (1988) (attorney did not display "exceptional" quality).

tion adjusting the fee award to account for the "results obtained," this does not mean reducing fees if the damage award is small in relation to the fee award.[1101] Instead, it means that the fee should be adjusted to reflect the degree of success enjoyed by the prevailing party in recovering the amount requested in the complaint.[1102] For example, even if a damage award is small in absolute terms, the consumer's attorney may have recovered the full amount sought, and this should be an excellent result indicating an upward adjustment of the fee, not a downward adjustment.

The lodestar should also be adjusted upward to account for the delay between the attorney's performance of the work and receipt of payment.[1103] The Seventh Circuit suggests either of two methods to increase the lodestar to adjust for this delay.[1104] One is to add interest to the award to reflect the delay between when the work was performed and when the attorney fee was awarded. The other is to use as an hourly rate, the attorney's current rate or a rate based on current rates in the community, not the rates in effect when the work was performed.[1105] Regardless of whether prejudgment interest is added to adjust for delay, post-judgment interest should accrue on fee awards.[1106]

8.8.11.3.3 Fees calculated based on contingency fee agreement

As with other attorney fee issues, courts are not bound by interpretations of federal fee-shifting statutes in determining the use of a contingency fee agreement in calculating an attorney fee award. Thus, the Seventh Circuit, in interpreting the Illinois UDAP statute, has approved a $208,333.33 lump sum fee award calculated on a total damages recovery of $625,000. The attorney presented, as evidence, a one-third contingent fee agreement with his client, and the court found this to be a reasonable measure of the prevailing market rate because it was a standard contingent fee.[1107] Although the agreement with the client increased the contingency to 50% if the case was appealed, even the consumer's attorney admitted that an extra $104,167 to do the appeal was excessive, and this amount was not allowed.[1108] However, fees will usually not be calculated on a contingent fee basis where the attorney does not have a contingent fee contract with the consumer.[1109]

In addition, the Texas Supreme Court refuses to base UDAP attorney fees *solely* on a contingency fee agreement.[1110] Although the contingency fee agreement may be considered, the reasonableness of the fee, expressed as a dollar amount, must be proven by evidence extrinsic to the agreement.[1111] An Ohio decision reaches the same conclusion.[1112] Similarly, a New Hampshire bankruptcy court refused to award fees commensurate with a contingency fee agreement (where this would have been twenty-eight times the amount of time actually put into a case). The court instead multiplied the lodestar (reasonable hourly rate times hours reasonably expended) by two.[1113]

In other cases, where damages may be less, the consumer's recovery of attorney fees is not necessarily limited to the amount the consumer is contingently obligated to pay his or her attorney. A court can award attorney fees in excess of a contingency fee arrangement.[1114] The existence of a contingency fee agreement also does not force the attorney to take fees out of the client's recovery instead of seeking an award from the opposing party.[1115] But a Massachusetts appellate

1101 Wilson v. Car Land Diagnostics Center, Inc., 2001 U.S. Dist. LEXIS 19760 (S.D.N.Y. Nov. 15, 2001); Bittner v. Tri-County Toyota, Inc., 58 Ohio St. 3d 143, 569 N.E.2d 464 (1991). *Cf.* James v. Thermal Master, Inc., 55 Ohio App. 3d 51, 562 N.E.2d 917 (1988) (amount in controversy and amount of verdict are two of factors to be considered in calculating fee award).

1102 Wilson v. Car Land Diagnostics Center, Inc., 2001 U.S. Dist. LEXIS 19760 (S.D.N.Y. Nov. 15, 2001); Silva v. Autos of Amboy, 267 N.J. Super. 546, 632 A.2d 291 (1993) (downward adjustment of fee award justified where plaintiff won only nominal damages); Bittner v. Tri-County Toyota, Inc., 58 Ohio St. 3d 143, 569 N.E.2d 464 (1991).

1103 Missouri v. Jenkins, 491 U.S. 274, 109 S. Ct. 2463, 105 L. Ed. 2d 229 (1989) (Civil Rights Act case); Smith v. Village of Maywood, 17 F.3d 219 (7th Cir. 1994) (Civil Rights Act case).

1104 Smith v. Village of Maywood, 17 F.3d 219 (7th Cir. 1994) (Civil Rights case).

1105 *Id.*

1106 Parker v. I&F Insulation Co., 89 Ohio St. 3d 261, 730 N.E.2d 972 (2000).

1107 Bandura v. Orkin Exterminating Co., 865 F.2d 816 (7th Cir. 1988) (Illinois law); Global Protection Corp. v. Halbersberg, 503 S.E.2d 483 (S.C. App. 1998) (court considers contingent fee agreement in awarding UDAP fees in commercial case with large recovery).

1108 Bandura v. Orkin Exterminating Co., 865 F.2d 816 (7th Cir. 1988) (Illinois law).

1109 GMAC Mortgage Corp. v. Larson, 597 N.E.2d 1245 (Ill. App. Ct. 1992).

1110 Arthur Anderson & Co. v. Perry Equipment Corp., 945 S.W.2d 812 (Tex. 1997). *Accord* Purina Mills, Inc. v. Odell, 948 S.W.2d 927 (Tex. App. 1997).

1111 Keeton v. Wal-Mart Stores, Inc., 21 F. Supp. 2d 653 (E.D. Tex. 1998); Mid-Century Ins. Co. of Texas v. Boyte, 49 S.W.3d 408 (Tex. App. 2001), *rev'd on other grounds*, 80 S.W.3d 546 (Tex. 2002); Dunn v. Southern Farm Bureau Cas. Ins. Co., 991 S.W.2d 467 (Tex App. 1999).

1112 Crawford v. Bill Swad Chevrolet, Inc., 2000 Ohio App. LEXIS 4221 (Sept. 19, 2000).

1113 *In re* Globe Distributors, Inc., 145 B.R. 728 (Bankr. D.N.H. 1992).

1114 Fabri v. United Techs. Int'l, Inc., 193 F. Supp. 2d 480 (D. Conn. 2002); Blue Cross & Blue Shield of N.J., Inc. v. Philip Morris, Inc., 190 F. Supp. 2d 407 (E.D.N.Y. 2002), *rev'd in part on other grounds, questions certified by* 344 F.3d 211 (2d Cir. 2003); Hayward v. Ventura Volvo, 108 Cal. App. 4th 509, 133 Cal. Rptr. 2d 514 (2003) (Consumers Legal Remedies Act); Decker v. Homeguard Sys., 105 Idaho 158, 666 P.2d 1169 (1983); Adkinson v. Harpeth Ford-Mercury, Inc., 1991 Tenn. App. LEXIS 114 (Feb. 15, 1991); Evergreen Int'l Inc. v. American Casualty Co., 52 Wash. App. 548, 761 P.2d 964 (1988).

1115 Boulevard Assocs. v. Sovereign Hotels, Inc., 868 F. Supp. 70 (S.D.N.Y. 1994), *rev'd on other grounds*, 72 F.3d 1029 (2d Cir. 1995).

court has ruled that a UDAP fee award can not operate as a cap; if there is a contingent fee contract that would allow a greater fee, the attorney can recover the remainder from the client.[1116]

8.8.11.4 Awards for Work on Non-UDAP Counts and on Unsuccessful UDAP Counts

The typical UDAP case will include multiple UDAP and non-UDAP counts. For many non-UDAP counts, such as breach of warranty or common law fraud, there will be no attorney fees available. A prevailing consumer may be awarded damages based on some but not all UDAP counts and on some of the non-UDAP counts. The question will then arise whether the consumer should receive attorney fees for all work done on the case, just on prevailing UDAP counts, just on prevailing counts, or just on UDAP counts.

A good place to start is the United States Supreme Court's treatment of the issue in *Hensley v. Eckerhart*.[1117] *Hensley*, of course is not a UDAP case, and has direct applicability only to federal attorney fee statutes, such as the U.S. Civil Rights Act. *Hensley* indicates that attorney fees will not reimburse work on unsuccessful claims where those claims are totally unrelated to the successful claim allowing attorney fees. That is, fees will not be paid for work on claims where those claims are based on different facts and legal theories. Attorney fees will not be awarded where work on one claim does not help the attorney prepare for the successful claim, and the number of hours working on unsuccessful claims can be differentiated from work spent on the successful claims.[1118]

Conversely, where there is a common core of facts or where the legal theories are related, it is impractical to separate the attorney fees for each claim. Where an attorney has obtained excellent results, the award should cover all attorney work on all claims, even claims not providing attorney fees and unsuccessful claims. The result is what matters and the consumer's attorney should not be penalized for raising alternative claims that the court dismisses or does not reach.[1119] But if the degree of success is limited, attorney fees should not be awarded for totally unsuccessful claims, even if related to the successful claim. A reduced fee is appropriate if the relief is limited in comparison to the scope of the litigation as a whole.[1120]

This approach to fees under federal fee-generating statutes should be compared with what state courts have done in state UDAP cases. State courts have ruled, particularly where the UDAP and non-UDAP claims are intertwined, that the consumer can obtain attorney fees for work on all claims, successful and unsuccessful.[1121] A consumer who

---

1116 Graves v. R.M. Packer Co., 45 Mass. App. Ct. 760, 702 N.E.2d 21 (1998).

1117 461 U.S. 424, 103 S. Ct. 1933, 76 L. Ed. 2d 40 (1983).

1118 *See also* Matter of Mattera, 144 B.R. 687 (E.D. Pa. 1992).

1119 Hensley v. Eckerhart, 461 U.S. 424, 103 S. Ct. 1933, 76 L. Ed. 2d 40 (1983); KPS Assocs., Inc. v. Designs by FMC, Inc., 2003 WL 1538540 (D. Mass. Mar. 25, 2003) (unsuccessful contract claims and UDAP claims are inextricably intertwined and apportionment is neither feasible nor appropriate since plaintiff proceeded almost exclusively on the UDAP claims); L'Esperance v. Benware, 830 A.2d 675 (Vt. 2003). *See also* Rosario v. Livaditis, 963 F.2d 1013 (7th Cir. 1992) (Illinois law).

1120 Hensley v. Eckerhart, 461 U.S. 424, 103 S. Ct. 1933, 76 L. Ed. 2d 40 (1983). *See also* Rudy v. Hoffman-Brunner, 514 N.W.2d 422 (Wis. Ct. App. 1993) (unpublished limited precedent decision, text available at 1993 Wisc. App. LEXIS 1700).

1121 Williams v. First Government Mortgage and Investors Corp., 225 F.3d 738 (D.C. Cir. 2000) (fees should cover time spent on unsuccessful claims unless they are distinctly different in all respects from the UDAP claims); Concorde Limousines, Inc. v. Moloney Coachbuilders, Inc., 835 F.2d 541 (5th Cir. 1987) (Texas law); Nottingham v. General Am. Communications Corp., 811 F.2d 873 (5th Cir. 1987) (Texas law); Arthur D. Little Int'l, Inc. v. Dooyang Corp., 995 F. Supp. 217 (D. Mass. 1998), *aff'd on other grounds*, 147 F.3d 47 (1st Cir. 1998); *In re* Globe Distributors, Inc., 145 B.R. 728 (Bankr. D.N.H. 1992); Caplan v. 1616 E. Sunrise Motors, Inc., 522 So. 2d 920 (Fla. Dist. Ct. App. 1988); Campbell v. Beak, 568 S.E.2d 801 (Ga. App. 2002); Ciampi v. Ogden Chrysler Plymouth, Inc., 634 N.E.2d 448 (Ill. App. Ct. 1994) (court affirms awards of fees for all work on case where evidence was same for UDAP and non-UDAP counts); York v. InTrust Bank, 265 Kan. 271, 962 P.2d 405 (1998); DeSpiegelaere v. Killion, 947 P.2d 1039 (Kan. App. 1997) (court can award fees for all work on a case if UDAP and non-UDAP claims are intertwined to the point of being inseparable; otherwise work on the various claims must be segregated in fee petition); State *ex rel.* Douglas v. Schroeder, 222 Neb. 473, 384 N.W.2d 626 (1986); Luft v. Perry County Lumber & Supply Co., 2003 WL 21027291 (Ohio App. May 8, 2003) (unpublished, citation limited); Budner v. Lake Erie Homes, 2001 Ohio App. LEXIS 4446 (Sept. 28, 2001) (plaintiff entitled to fees for entire case where UDAP and contract claims arose from common facts); Fit 'N' Fun Pools, Inc. v. Shelly, 2001 Ohio App. LEXIS 3 (Jan. 3, 2001); Arthur Andersen & Co. v. Perry Equip. Corp., 945 S.W.2d 812 (Tex. 1997); Texas Cookie Co. v. Hendricks & Peralta, 747 S.W.2d 873 (Tex. App. 1988); Greene v. Bearden Enterprises Inc., 598 S.W.2d 649 (Tex. Civ. App. 1980); Barnhouse Motors, Inc. v. Godfrey, 577 S.W.2d 378 (Tex. Civ. App. 1979); Collard v. Reagan, 2002 WL 1357052 (Wash. App. June 21, 2002) (unpublished, citation limited) (fees may be awarded for all hours where claims intertwined and segregation of UDAP hours not feasible); Opportunity Mgmt. Co. v. Frost, 1999 Wash. App. LEXIS 336 (Feb. 16, 1999); Radford v. J.J.B. Enterprises, Ltd., 163 Wis. 2d 534, 472 N.W.2d 790 (1991). *See also* Rosario v. Livaditis, Clearinghouse No. 47,927 (N.D. Ill. 1990); Kleczek v. Jorgensen, 328 Ill. App. 3d 1012, 767 N.E.2d 913, 263 Ill. Dec. 187 (2002) (allowing fees for claims closely related to successful UDAP claim, but not for less-closely related claims); Briercroft Service Corp. v. Perez, 820 S.W.2d 813 (Tex. App. 1990). *Cf.* Schorsch v. Fireside Chrysler-Plymouth, Mazda, Inc., 677 N.E.2d 976 (Ill. App. Ct. 1997) (where UDAP claims and common law claims were tried separately, time spent on each must be differentiated). *But see* VanVoorhees v. Dodge, 679 A.2d 1077 (Me. 1996) (attorney fees are recoverable pursuant to the UDAP statute only to the extent that the fees were earned pursuing a UDAP claim); Hoke v. Beck, 587 N.E.2d 4 (Ill. App. Ct. 1992) (court may award fees only for work on UDAP count); William Mushero, Inc. v. Hull,

wins on both UDAP and non-UDAP claims, but elects recovery under the non-UDAP claim, is still entitled to all fees related to the UDAP claim.[1122]

The Idaho Supreme Court approved an attorney fee award for all work expended on a case even where the consumer prevailed on only six of twenty-eight counts; the consumer was awarded in damages only three percent of what he requested; and the seller prevailed on its counterclaims. It is in the trial court's discretion to determine who prevailed, and the prevailing party can obtain all its attorney fees.[1123]

In another case, where a UDAP claim was only one of eight counts, but all counts were intermingled and the consumer's attorney had spent most of his time on the UDAP claim, the trial court abused its discretion in awarding fees for only one-fifth of the work on the case.[1124] Instead, the appellate court ruled the attorney should recover for 85% of his work.[1125] Another court has awarded fees for essentially all work on a case, even for non-UDAP claims and for UDAP claims that did not prevail.[1126] Similarly, it was proper for a court to award attorney fees for the consumer's defense of a preliminary declaratory action where that defense was related to the eventual UDAP counterclaim filed in the later damage action,[1127] and for a court to award a consumer attorney fees for defending a related counterclaim.[1128]

The Montana Supreme Court has held that attorney fees should be awarded even where the consumer loses the UDAP claim, as long as the consumer prevails on other counts.[1129] Similarly, where a UDAP claim is brought against multiple defendants, and several of those defendants are eventually dropped from the suit, attorney fees can be awarded for all work on the case where the cases against each of the initial defendants were interrelated and involved the same set of circumstances.[1130]

Other courts find that it is not unreasonable for a trial court to award fees to the consumer's attorney only for work on counts that were successfully prosecuted.[1131] Appellate

667 A.2d 853 (Me. 1995); Silva v. Autos of Amboy, 267 N.J. Super. 546, 632 A.2d 291 (1993) (partially prevailing plaintiff should be awarded the legal expenses he would have borne if his suit had been confined to the ground on which he prevailed plus related grounds). *But cf.* Refuse & Environmental Sys., Inc. v. Industrial Servs., 732 F. Supp. 1209 (D. Mass. 1990) (fee award reduced to account for time spent on related, successful tort claims), *rev'd in part on other grounds*, 932 F.2d 37 (1st Cir. 1991); 49 Prospect Street Tenants Ass'n v. Sheva Gardens, Inc., 227 N.J. Super. 449, 547 A.2d 1134 (App. Div. 1988).

1122 Standard Fire Ins. Co. v. Stephenson, 963 S.W.2d 81 (Tex. App. 1997).

1123 Decker v. Homeguard Sys., 105 Idaho 158, 666 P.2d 1169 (Ct. App. 1983); *see also* Nalen v. Jenkins, 113 Idaho 79, 741 P.2d 366 (Ct. App. 1987).

1124 LaFerney v. Scott Smith Oldsmobile, Inc., 410 So. 2d 534 (Fla. Dist. Ct. App. 1982). *See also* Heindel v. Southside Chrysler-Plymouth, Inc., 476 So. 2d 266 (Fla. Dist. Ct. App. 1985); Wasserman v. Agnastopoulos, 22 Mass. App. Ct. 672, 497 N.E.2d 19 (1986) (defending against seller's collection action so intertwined with UDAP counterclaim that all but nominal hours worked on case qualify for attorney fees); Osterman v. Sears, Roebuck & Co., 80 P.3d 435 (Mont. 2003) (error to make mechanical, pro rata reduction of attorney fees where consumer won only 1 of 7 claims); Silva v. Autos of Amboy, 267 N.J. Super. 546, 632 A.2d 291 (1993) (trial court erred in dividing attorney fee award by seven where consumer won on one of seven counts); Briercroft Service Corp. v. Perez, 820 S.W.2d 813 (Tex. App. 1990). *But see* Satterwhite v. Safeco Land Title of Tarrant, 853 S.W.2d 202 (Tex. App. 1993) (affirming a trial court's reduction of fees that deducted from total fees the time spent in successfully pursuing fraud and fiduciary duty claims in addition to winning on Texas UDAP statute claims, because Texas law does not permit recovery of attorney fees for those claims).

1125 LaFerney v. Scott Smith Oldsmobile, Inc., 410 So. 2d 534 (Fla. Dist. Ct. App. 1982).

1126 Arthur D. Little Int'l, Inc. v. Dooyang Corp., 995 F. Supp. 217 (D. Mass. 1998), *aff'd on other grounds*, 147 F.3d 47 (1st Cir. 1998). *Accord* Bryant v. Walt Sweeney Automotive, Inc., 2002 WL 1071943 (Ohio App. May 31, 2002) (unpublished, citation limited).

1127 Safeco Ins. Co. of Am. v. JMG Restaurants, 37 Wash. App. 1, 680 P.2d 409 (1984).

1128 Arthur D. Little Int'l, Inc. v. Dooyang Corp., 995 F. Supp. 217 (D. Mass. 1998), *aff'd on other grounds*, 147 F.3d 47 (1st Cir. 1998); Building Concepts, Inc. v. Duncan, 667 S.W.2d 897 (Tex. App. 1984).

1129 Dillree v. Devoe, 724 P.2d 171 (Mont. 1986). *See also* Chattin v. Cape May Greene, Inc., 243 N.J. Super. 590, 581 A.2d 91 (1990), *aff'd per curiam*, 124 N.J. 943, 591 A.2d 943 (1991) (where consumers won on non-UDAP counts in first trial but lost on UDAP count, they may still be entitled to fee award for that work, but loss on UDAP counts should be taken into account in determining reasonable fee).

1130 Green Tree Acceptance, Inc. v. Pierce, 768 S.W.2d 416 (Tex. App. 1989). *But see* Cieri v. Leticia Query Realty, Inc., 905 P.2d 29 (Haw. 1995) (trial court did not abuse discretion in reducing fees 50% where plaintiffs prevailed against only one of two defendants).

1131 Refuse & Environmental Sys., Inc. v. Industrial Servs., 732 F. Supp. 1209 (D. Mass. 1990) (fee award reduced to account for time spent on related tort claims), *rev'd in part on other grounds*, 932 F.2d 37 (1st Cir. 1991); Morse v. Mutual Federal Sav. & Loan Ass'n, 536 F. Supp. 1271 (D. Mass. 1982); Roche v. Fireside Chrysler-Plymouth, 600 N.E.2d 1218 (Ill. App. Ct. 1992); Poussard v. Commercial Credit Plan, 479 A.2d 881 (Me. 1984) (no award for work to certify class where court denied certification); Barnes v. Rosenthal Toyota, Inc., 126 Md. App. 97, 727 A.2d 431 (1999) (affirming trial court's apportionment of fees between successful UDAP and unsuccessful non-UDAP claims); Jet Line Servs., Inc. v. American Employers Ins. Co., 404 Mass. 706, 537 N.E.2d 107 (1989); Cremeans v. Robbins, 2000 Ohio App. LEXIS 2753 (June 12, 2000) (affirming reduction of fees to reflect percentage of claims on which consumer prevailed); Sing v. John L. Scott, Inc., 920 P.2d 589 (Wash. App. 1996), *rev'd on other grounds*, 948 P.2d 816 (Wash. 1997); Styrk v. Cornerstone Investments, Inc., 61 Wash. App. 463, 810 P.2d 1366 (1991) (lodestar reduced 60% so as not to compensate consumer for unsuccessful claims and claims against defendants not found liable); Nuttall v. Dowell, 31 Wash. App. 98, 639 P.2d 832 (1982); Kestel-Rauls v. Moore, 586 N.W.2d 699 (Wis. App. 1998) (unpublished limited precedent opinion, text available at 1998 Wisc. App. LEXIS 992); Moonlight v. Boyce, 125 Wis. 2d 298, 372 N.W.2d 479 (Ct.

courts may urge trial courts to attempt to segregate work performed solely for non-UDAP counts.[1132] Not all work on other counts is intertwined or overlapping. A court has also held that no attorney fees should be awarded for work on other claims before an action was amended to include a UDAP count.[1133]

8.8.11.5 Calculating Fees for Public Interest Attorneys

The Wisconsin Supreme Court has issued perhaps the best opinion on UDAP attorney fees for legal services attorneys.[1134] The court finds that legal services attorneys should be paid at the same hourly rate as others, since this agrees with the purpose of UDAP attorney fees of encouraging litigants to seek redress of consumer wrongs involving small dollar amounts, where the amount at stake may not justify the attorney's time.

This is also in accord with the Supreme Court's decision in *Blum v. Stenson*,[1135] where the court upheld a $79,312 award to the Legal Aid Society of New York for 809 hours of work in a federal civil rights action (performed in 1979 and 1980) at rates ranging from $95 to $105 an hour for attorneys averaging one-and-a-half years practical legal experience. The Supreme Court explicitly rejected the argument that the rate for legal services attorneys should reflect only the cost of their service to their program; rather the hourly rate should be based on the prevailing market rate.

The Court grounded its ruling on the legislative history of the federal civil rights statute's provision for "reasonable attorney fees." The Court expressly stated that legal services attorneys paid at market rates would not produce windfall profits contrary to the Congressional intent.

One method for legal services attorneys to assure they are paid market rates is to establish an attorney fee committee. For example, Community Legal Services in Philadelphia, Pennsylvania has established a committee that sets hourly rates for each attorney in the program, and periodically changes these rates as required. The committee surveys rates in the community for various types of attorneys and then matches attorneys with similar experience, expertise, and responsibility. The program's Board of Directors approves the fee schedule. This fee schedule gives the court a specific starting point in determining an hourly rate, and at least one court has referred to it explicitly in awarding fees in a consumer case.[1136]

A 1989 case awarded Legal Services of Greater Miami $75,000 in attorney fees in a UDAP case where the court found $150 an hour to be reasonable because it was at the low end of the market range for such services in the Miami area. The court then multiplied this by the 200 hours expended on the case and multiplied the resulting $30,000 by a factor of 2.5 because success was unlikely at the time the case was initiated.[1137] A federal court awarded a legal services office $271,711 in attorney fees for work by attorneys and clerks on a class action against a trade school.[1138]

8.8.11.6 Fees for Paralegals, Law Clerks

Paralegal and law clerk rates should be calculated using prevailing market rates, not the cost to a firm of these staff.[1139] Where a market bills paralegal time at an hourly rate, that is the rate to use.[1140] Thus the Supreme Court has approved an award of $35 an hour for law clerks, $40 for paralegals, and $50 for recent law graduates as consistent with the then (early 1980s) Kansas City area market.[1141] Decisions from the 1990s and late 1980s have awarded $65 and $50 an hour for paralegal or law clerk work on UDAP cases.[1142]

App. 1985) (no attorney fees for work defending against creditor's successful counterclaims).

1132 Equitable Life Assurance Soc. v. Porter-Englehart, 867 F.2d 79 (1st Cir. 1989) (Mass. law); Grove v. Huffman, 634 N.E.2d 1184 (Ill. App. Ct. 1994); Hoke v. Beck, 587 N.E.2d 4 (Ill. App. Ct. 1992) (trial court must apportion fees between UDAP counts and non-UDAP counts); Chesrow v. DuPage Auto Brokers, Inc., 200 Ill. App. 3d 72, 557 N.E.2d 1301 (1990); Werdann v. Mel Hambelton Ford, Inc., 79 P.3d 1081 (Kan. App. 2003) (where plaintiff did not claim that it was impossible to separate out time on UDAP claim, must do so or no fees will be awarded); VanVoorhees v. Dodge, 679 A.2d 1077 (Me. 1996) (fees are allowed only for the costs of pursuing the UDAP claim); Bittner v. Tri-County Toyota, Inc., 58 Ohio St. 3d 143, 569 N.E.2d 464 (1991); Travis v. Washington Horse Breeders Ass'n, 111 Wash. 2d 396, 759 P.2d 418 (1988); Smith v. Behr Process Corp., 113 Wash. App. 306, 54 P.3d 665 (2002) (reversing and remanding to trial court to attempt to segregate hours); Sing v. John L. Scott, Inc., 83 Wash. App. 55, 920 P.2d 589 (1996), *rev'd on other grounds*, 948 P.2d 816 (Wash. 1997).

1133 Hundred East Credit Corp. v. Eric Schuster Corp., 212 N.J. Super. 350, 515 A.2d 246 (App. Div. 1986).

1134 Shands v. Castrovinci, 115 Wis. 2d 352, 340 N.W.2d 506 (1983). *See also* Prestien v. Roets, 477 N.W.2d 363 (Wis. Ct. App. 1991) (unpublished and non-precedential, text available at 1991 Wisc. App. LEXIS 1296) (following *Shands*, appellate court overturns $35 an hour calculation, and awards legal services attorney $75 an hour, considered the standard rate in the community). *See* § 8.8.7.1, *supra*, for a discussion of whether legal services attorneys are entitled to fees.

1135 465 U.S. 886 (1984).

1136 Laubach v. Fidelity Consumer Discount Co., 1988 U.S. Dist. LEXIS 12690, Clearinghouse No. 44,820 (E.D. Pa. Nov. 10, 1988).

1137 *See also* McLendon v. Metropolitan Mortgage Co., Clearinghouse No. 43,703 (Fla. Cir. Ct. Dade Cty. Dec. 18, 1989).

1138 Rosario v. Livaditis, Clearinghouse No. 47,927 (N.D. Ill. 1990).

1139 *See* § 8.8.7.2, *supra*, for a discussion of whether the work of these staff members can be compensated separately in a UDAP fee award).

1140 Missouri v. Jenkins, 491 U.S. 274, 109 S. Ct. 2463, 105 L. Ed. 2d 229 (1989).

1141 *Id.*

1142 Gibbs v. Southeastern Investment Corp., 705 F. Supp. 738 (D. Conn. 1989) ($50/hour); Arthur D. Little Int'l, Inc. v. Dooyang Corp., 995 F. Supp. 217 (D. Mass. 1998) ($65/hour), *aff'd on other grounds*, 147 F.3d 47 (1st Cir. 1998).

8.8.11.7 Out-of-Pocket Expenses

There is little UDAP case law concerning supplementing an attorney's hourly rate with out-of-pocket expenses. The clear import of the Supreme Court approach to these questions[1143] is that a court should follow the prevailing billing practice of a community. If certain items are typically included in an hourly rate, they should not also be reimbursed separately. However, if attorneys typically bill for these items separately, the attorney fee award should include separate provisions for these expenses. In non-UDAP cases, courts have awarded out-of-pocket expenses for travel, investigations and other trial preparations.[1144] But a New Jersey court held that its UDAP statute's authorization of "reasonable costs of suit" did not give the court authority to order reimbursement of expert witness fees.[1145]

8.8.11.8 Effect of Federal Rule of Civil Procedure 68 and Similar State Rules

Federal Rule of Civil Procedure 68 allows parties to a lawsuit to minimize their liability for costs by making an offer to allow judgment for a set amount, including costs then accrued. If the offeree rejects the offer, and the eventual judgment is for a lesser amount, the offeror is not liable for post-offer costs and, instead, the offeree becomes liable for those costs.

In *Marek v. Chesny*,[1146] the plaintiff had rejected a lump sum Rule 68 offer of $100,000 that included damages, costs, and attorney fees. At that point, the plaintiff's costs and attorney fees totaled $32,000, so the plaintiff's net recovery would have been $68,000. The plaintiff then went to trial, won $60,000 in damages, and moved for an award of attorney fees under 42 U.S.C. § 1988. The Court held that the rejection of the Rule 68 offer precluded an award of post-offer fees. To reach this conclusion, the Court looked at section 1988, the fee-shifting statute. Since it defined attorney fees as a part of costs, the plaintiff's rejection of the offer meant that post-offer attorney fees would, along with other post-offer costs, be barred.

The question then becomes, in federal court cases and in states following the federal rule, whether UDAP attorney fees should be considered "costs" for purposes of Rule 68. If so, UDAP defendants could use this technique to shift attorney fees to the consumer, even if the consumer prevails, as long as the judgment is for less than the offer. The Tenth Circuit has decided that it is a matter of a state's interpretation of its own UDAP statute whether attorney fees are considered costs. The Tenth Circuit concluded that attorney fees under the New Mexico statute were not costs, so that attorney fees could be awarded even if a judgment was for less than the defendant's offer.[1147]

A related question involves the interpretation of Rule 68 offers, particularly the question whether fees can be awarded separately if the consumer accepts the offer.[1148] A Maine trial court found attorney fees not to be costs under that state's UDAP statute, so an offer that provided for costs but was silent as to fees did not preclude a fee award.[1149] But the Minnesota Supreme Court concluded that attorney fees are included as "costs and disbursements" under its UDAP statute, so fees may be awarded under the state version of Rule 68 after a plaintiff accepts an offer of judgment for $200,000 plus costs and disbursements.[1150] If a Rule 68 offer is ambiguous (for example, by not making clear whether the sum mentioned includes attorney fees), and the defendant will not clarify it voluntarily, the appropriate procedure appears to be a motion to strike.[1151]

Many states have rules or statutes similar to Rule 68.[1152] In addition, a number of state UDAP statutes require notice to the defendant and an opportunity to settle the case before the consumer files suit.[1153] If the consumer rejects an offer but then recovers less at trial, fees are limited to those incurred before the offer was rejected. Texas has both a pre-suit offer provision in its UDAP statute and a separate, generally-applicable Rule 68-type statute.[1154]

Even without a rule similar to Rule 68, courts may hold that a tender to the named plaintiff moots a class action.[1155] The court may find that the action is not moot, however, if a class certification motion is pending at the time of the tender, or if a new named plaintiff is substituted after the tender.[1156]

1143 *Id.*

1144 Henry v. Webermeier, 738 F.2d 188 (7th Cir. 1984); *In re* Pine, 705 F.2d 936 (7th Cir. 1983); York v. InTrust Bank, 265 Kan. 271, 962 P.2d 405 (1998) (affirming award of expenses as part of attorney fee award; case probably *sub silentio* overrules DeSpiegelaere v. Killon, 947 P.2d 1039 (Kan. App. 1997), which held that the UDAP statute did not authorize an award of expenses).

1145 Josantos Constr. v. Bohrer, 326 N.J. Super. 42, 740 A.2d 653 (App. Div. 1999). *Accord* Bryant v. Walt Sweeney Automotive, Inc., 2002 WL 1071943 (Ohio App. May 31, 2002) (unpublished, citation limited) (no statutory authority to tax expert witness fees and other litigation expenses as costs).

1146 473 U.S. 1, 105 S. Ct. 3012, 87 L. Ed. 2d 1 (1985).

1147 Knight v. Snap-On Tools Corp., 3 F.3d 1398 (10th Cir. 1993) (N.M. law).

1148 *See, e.g.*, Keeton v. Wal-Mart Stores, Inc., 21 F. Supp. 2d 653 (E.D. Tex. 1998).

1149 Townsend v. S.K.R. Distributors, 2002 WL 32068356 (Me. Super. Dec. 26, 2002).

1150 Collins v. Minn. School of Bus., 655 N.W.2d 320 (Minn. 2003).

1151 Taylor v. Unifund, 1999 U.S. Dist. LEXIS 13657 (N.D. Ill. Apr. 30, 1999); Christian v. R. Wood Motors, 1995 U.S. Dist. LEXIS 5560 (N.D.N.Y. Apr. 21, 1995).

1152 *See, e.g.*, People *ex rel.* Lockyer v. Fremont Gen. Corp., 89 Cal. App. 4th 1260, 108 Cal. Rptr. 2d 127 (2001) (applying rule that shifts expert witness fees if plaintiff wins less than rejected offer).

1153 *See* § 7.5.4, *supra*.

1154 Tex. Civ. Prac. & Rem. Code §§ 42.001–42.005.

1155 Bruemmer v. Compaq Computer Corp., 329 Ill. App. 3d 755, 768 N.E.2d 276, 263 Ill. Dec. 516 (2002).

1156 *Id.*

8.8.12 Judicial Procedure for Seeking Attorney Fees

The resolution of a UDAP fee claim is often just as important as the resolution of the substantive claim, since the consumer will not be made whole if a contingent fee eats into the recovery on the merits. The consumer's attorney should approach the fee hearing with the same attitude as any other trial. Defendants are often obdurate in their opposition to fee claims, and tenacious prosecution of the claim is necessary.

The fee applicant has the burden of documenting the amount of time spent on the case and the reasonableness of the fee sought.[1157] As soon as a file is opened, consumer attorneys are well advised to begin keeping careful records, detailing all work and time devoted to a UDAP case. Attorney fee requests can then be based on these records. Otherwise, attorneys may find themselves being examined at the fee hearing concerning the dates and substance of all work supporting the attorney fee request. Where such examination takes place several years after the initiation of the case, failure to keep adequate records will result in memory lapses that may significantly reduce the fee award.[1158] Courts may also take differing views on submissions for attorney fees which are based on reconstructed rather than contemporaneous time records.[1159] Some courts demand considerable detail about the activities represented by the time records, so "block billing," i.e., aggregation of a number of activities into a single time entry, should be avoided. If an activity took an unusually long time or is inadequately documented, it is better to discount it before submitting the petition than to give the court reason to scrutinize every entry. Many attorneys automatically deduct 5% or 10% of their time, and mention this deduction in their fee petitions. Sometimes a defendant will agree not to challenge a fee petition in return for such a deduction. The request for attorney fees should be specifically mentioned in the prayer for relief, although a court may be willing to construe a pleading liberally to include such a claim.[1160]

While several courts have held that a separate evidentiary hearing is not necessary to determine the proper size of attorney fees,[1161] other courts have required the consumer to offer evidence of the reasonableness of the attorney fee award.[1162] Even where there is a default judgment, this proof may be necessary.[1163] The prudent course is to establish with the court the proper time to offer evidence of the amount and type of attorney and paralegal time expended in the case. Then follow up at the appropriate time with a thorough presentation of the attorney time expended and the reasons why those hours were necessary. Proof of the attorney fee that the consumer has agreed to pay may not be sufficient to show the reasonableness of the fee, without evidence of the number of hours the attorney spent on the case and the reasonable rate for the attorney's time.[1164] In determining the reasonableness of the consumer's attorney's hours and fees, the court may consider the defense attorney's hours and

1157 Fabri v. United Techs. Int'l, Inc., 193 F. Supp. 2d 480 (D. Conn. 2002).

1158 *See* Chesrow v. DuPage Auto Brokers, Inc., 200 Ill. App. 3d 72, 557 N.E.2d 1301 (1990) (attorney's vague records resulted in denial of attorney fee award for appellate work). *See also* Prior Plumbing & Heating Co. v. Hagins, 630 N.E.2d 1208 (Ill. App. Ct. 1994) (time records need not break down time performed on each of several tasks done on same date).

1159 *See* Riordan v. Nationwide Mut. Fire Ins. Co., 977 F.2d 47 (2d Cir. 1992) (New York law) (refusing to apply federal rule against reconstructed time records to New York UDAP claim).

1160 Killingsworth v. Ted Russell Ford, Inc., 2002 WL 31718030 (Tenn. App. Dec. 4, 2002) (unpublished, citation limited).

1161 Heller v. Silverbranch Constr. Corp., 376 Mass. 621, 382 N.E.2d 1065 (1978); Brandt v. Olympic Constr., Inc., 16 Mass. App. Ct. 913, 449 N.E.2d 1231 (1983); Goes v. Feldman, 8 Mass. App. Ct. 84, 391 N.E.2d 943 (1979); State *ex rel.* Douglas v. Schroeder, 222 Neb. 473, 384 N.W.2d 626 (1986); Fletcher v. Don Foss of Cleveland, Inc., 90 Ohio App. 3d 82, 628 N.E.2d 60 (1993) (evidentiary hearing not required where seller's counsel did not object or seek cross-examination when consumer's attorney argued issue of fees); Wallace v. Pastore, 1999 Pa. Super. 297, 742 A.2d 1090 (1999) (memo presented to trial court at end of trial, listing number of hours and requested rate, and post-trial motion were sufficient basis for fee award); Vu v. Rosen, 2004 WL 612832 (Tex. App. Mar. 30, 2004) (unpublished, citation limited) (court may make finding that plaintiff's suit was in bad faith without evidentiary hearing); *see also* Ford Motor Co. v. Mayes, 575 S.W.2d 480 (Ky. Ct. App. 1978); Chrysler Corp. v. Scheunemann, 618 S.W.2d 799 (Tex. Civ. App. 1981) (attorney's testimony as to hours spent and sum he considered reasonable held sufficient).

1162 Smith v. Snyder, 267 Conn. 456, 839 A.2d 589 (2004) (there must be a clearly stated and described factual predicate for attorney fees in order for the court to determine the reasonableness of the request); Barco Auto Leasing Corp. v. House, 202 Conn. 106, 520 A.2d 162 (1987); Levesque Builders v. Hoerle, 49 Conn. App. 751, 717 A.2d 252 (1998) (improper for trial court to award fees without hearing evidence at trial; remanded for hearing); Family Fin. Servs., Inc. v. Spencer, 41 Conn. App. 754, 677 A.2d 479 (1996) (trial court erred in ruling on attorney fee claim on affidavits where losing party requested hearing); Pierce v. Reichard, 593 S. E. 2d 787 (N.C. Ct. App. 2004) (must be sworn motion, affidavit, or testimony); Morris v. Bailey, 358 S.E.2d 120 (N.C. Ct. App. 1987); Freitag v. Bill Swad Datsun, 3 Ohio App. 3d 83, 443 N.E.2d 988 (1981); Gaylan v. Dave Towell Cadillac, 15 Ohio Misc. 2d 1, 473 N.E.2d 64 (Mun. Ct. 1984); American Commercial Colleges, Inc. v. Davis, 821 S.W.2d 450 (Tex. App. 1991); King v. Ladd, 624 S.W.2d 195 (Tex. Civ. App. 1981); Small v. Baker, 605 S.W.2d 401 (Tex. Civ. App. 1980); National Van Lines v. Lifshen, 584 S.W.2d 298 (Tex. Civ. App. 1979); Bruntaeger v. Zeller, 515 A.2d 123 (Vt. 1986).

1163 Blumenthal v. Ameritex Computer, Corp., 646 S.W.2d 283 (Tex. App. 1983).

1164 Conseco Fin. Serv. Corp. v. Hill, 556 S.E.2d 468 (Ga. App. 2001) (client's testimony regarding number of hours attorneys said they had worked and rate they were charging is insufficient); Crawford v. Bill Swad Chevrolet, Inc., 2000 Ohio App. LEXIS 4221 (Sept. 19, 2000) (evidence of contingency fee agreement was insufficient); Albert v. Boatsmith Marine Service & Storage, Inc., 65 Ohio App. 3d 38, 582 N.E.2d 1023 (1989).

fees[1165] and, in appropriate circumstances, should allow discovery on this issue.[1166]

Expert testimony about the reasonableness of the rate is desirable, although some courts hold that it is not necessary.[1167] The expert should give an opinion not only about the lodestar rate, dealing with all factors that the state's courts have identified, but also about other issues that are likely to come up, such as whether paralegal services are customarily billed separately, whether the attorney's charges for customizing standardized documents are reasonable, the quality of the work, whether local or out-of-town rates are customarily used for out-of-town attorneys, and whether the allocation of tasks between senior attorneys, junior attorneys, and non-attorney assistants was reasonable. Periodicals such as the National Law Journal publish annual surveys of attorney fees that the expert can refer to, or that can be attached to the fee motion.

The consumer client is often an excellent lay witness at the fee hearing. Clients can testify about their futile efforts to resolve the matter and the stress and aggravation they suffered before they retained the attorney. If the attorney has kept the client informed of the progress of the case, the client can also substantiate the attorney's time records. The client's personal appearance in support of the fee petition also helps dispel the perception that the lawyer is merely using the case as a vehicle for a fee award.

Exhibits can be persuasive at fee hearings. Courts are especially impressed with documentation of early and persistent efforts to settle the case on reasonable terms. It is also helpful to document the defendant's resistance to discovery or other defense tactics that prolonged and complicated the case.

Where the judge, rather than the jury, has the duty of ruling on a fee petition, jurisdictions differ as to when the fee petition must be filed.[1168] In Wisconsin, the petition must only be filed a reasonable time after the court enters the judgment.[1169]

1165 Gaines v. Doughterty County Bd. of Ed., 775 F.2d 1565, 1571 n.12 (11th Cir. 1985) (§ 1988); Duchscherer v. W.W. Wallwork, Inc., 534 N.W.2d 13, 19 (N.D. 1995) (odometer rollback case).

1166 Henson v. Columbus Bank & Trust Co., 770 F.2d 1566, 1575 (11th Cir. 1985) (Truth in Lending case; consumer showed need for this information because there were unanswered questions about the reasonableness of the fee request); Gaines v. Doughterty County Bd. of Ed., 775 F.2d 1565, 1571 n.12 (11th Cir. 1985) (desegregation case; court requires disclosure of defense's hours but not rate since evidence about rate was already adequate).

1167 *In re* Moon, 1998 Bankr. LEXIS 1919 (Bankr. E.D. Va. June 22, 1998).

1168 *See* Barnes v. Rosenthal Toyota, Inc., 126 Md. App. 97, 727 A.2d 431 (1999) (attorney fees are a collateral matter and may be sought after judgment).

1169 Gorton v. American Cyanamid Co., 533 N.W.2d 746 (Wis. 1995) (holding that rule requiring motions to be filed within 20 days after the verdict only applies to trial-related motions, not attorney fee petitions).

Even after judgment, it may not be too late to request attorney fees. Courts have awarded fees requested after judgment[1170] or even after judgment has been satisfied.[1171] Thus, it may not be unreasonable to seek supplemental attorney fees for work performed collecting a judgment. An Ohio court has held that it was not improper for a consumer to seek fees only after the trial court's judgment was affirmed on appeal, and that the trial court judgment entry's silence about fees did not bar a later award of fees.[1172] Timing and evidentiary requirements for fee petitions should be interpreted in light of the general mandate of liberal construction of UDAP statutes.[1173]

Where a statute specifies that the "court" may award attorney fees, this is usually construed as a determination for the judge, not the jury.[1174] A Kentucky court holds that the amount of the fee award is an issue of law.[1175] The Texas rule seems to be that the amount of a reasonable attorney fee is a fact question to be determined by the jury,[1176] while the appellate court is entitled to determine whether the amount is excessive based on the entire record, the amount in controversy, the nature of the case, and the common knowledge and experience of the judges as lawyers and judges.[1177] Ohio[1178] and North Carolina[1179] courts are required to state

1170 Jeffcoat v. Heinicka, 436 So. 2d 1042 (Fla. Dist. Ct. App. 1983); Wiginton v. Pacific Credit Corp., 2 Haw. App. 435, 634 P.2d 111 (1981); Gaskill v. Doss, 2000 Ohio App. LEXIS 6185 (Dec. 26, 2000) (court's entry of judgment on jury verdict did not prevent it from later ruling on attorney fee motion).

1171 B&L Motors Inc. v. Bignotti, 427 So. 2d 1070 (Fla. Dist. Ct. App. 1983).

1172 Sprovach v. Bob Ross Buick, Inc., 90 Ohio App. 3d 117, 628 N.E.2d 82 (1993).

1173 Crawford v. Bill Swad Chevrolet, Inc., 2000 Ohio App. LEXIS 4221 (Sept. 19, 2000) (trial court should have conducted further hearing after consumer failed to introduce sufficient evidence of fees at first hearing).

1174 Gill v. Petrazzoli Brothers, Inc., 10 Conn. App. 22, 521 A.2d 212 (1987).

1175 Inn-Group Mgmt. Servs., Inc v. Greer, 71 S.W.3d 125 (Ky. App. 2002).

1176 Doerfler v. Espensen Co., 659 S.W.2d 929 (Tex. App. 1983); Jack Roach Ford v. De Urdanavia, 659 S.W.2d 725 (Tex. App. 1983).

1177 Morgan v. Ebby Halliday Real Estate, 873 S.W.2d 385 (Tex. App. 1993); David McDavid Pontiac, Inc. v. Nix, 681 S.W.2d 831 (Tex. App. 1984) ($100 an hour for all work expended reduced to $75 an hour where attorney had only recently increased rate from $75 to $100 an hour); Jack Roach Ford v. De Urdanavia, 659 S.W.2d 725 (Tex. App. 1983) (award of $28,500 attorney fees where damages only $500 overturned subject to remittitur of $8500 attorney fees).

1178 Fletcher v. Don Foss of Cleveland, Inc., 90 Ohio App. 3d 82, 628 N.E.2d 60 (Ohio App. 8 Dist. 1993).

1179 Lapierre v. Samco Dev. Corp., 103 N.C. App. 551, 406 S.E.2d 646 (N.C. Ct. App. 1991); Pierce v. Reichard, 593 S. E. 2d 787 (N.C. Ct. App. 2004); Viswanathan v. Chrysler Fin. Co., L.L.C., 161 N.C. App. 182, 588 S.E.2d 86 (N.C. Ct. App. 2003) (unpublished); Winston-Salem Wrecker Assn., Inc. v. Barker, 557 S.E.2d 614 (N.C. Ct. App. 2001) (sufficient if trial court merely states that it is adopting grounds set forth in moving papers).

the basis for their fee awards so that appellate review is possible.

In some jurisdictions (such as Illinois) certain claims must go to mandatory arbitration, although the consumer can reject the award and proceed to trial. A consumer who accepts the award must seek fees before the arbitration panel. If the consumer fails to seek fees in the arbitration proceeding, the court does not have jurisdiction to award fees.[1180]

1180 Cruz v. Northwestern Chrysler Plymouth Sales, 179 Ill. 2d 271, 688 N.E.2d 653 (1997). *Accord* Conner v. Daimlerchrysler Corp., 820 A.2d 1266 (Pa. Super. 2003) (failure to present fee claim to arbitration panel is waiver).

Chapter 9 Other Private Remedies

9.1 No Private Remedy Under the FTC Act

The Federal Trade Commission Act[1] prohibits unfair methods of competition and unfair or deceptive acts or practices. The FTC Act gives the FTC various powers to enforce this standard, but does not explicitly provide for private remedies. Private litigants have attempted to bring individual enforcement actions under the FTC Act, but judicial precedent, with only a few exceptions, indicates that there is no implied private right of action under the FTC Act.[2]

Similarly, a consumer does not have standing to sue under the Federal Lanham Trademark Act,[3] or under a uniform statute derived from the FTC Act that has not been enacted in that state.[4]

In 1978 the FTC attempted to carve an exception to the line of cases that find no private right of action under the FTC Act. It explicitly stated in the Statement of Basis and Purpose to its Franchise Rule that there is a private right of action at least to enforce the Franchise Rule.[5] Nevertheless, courts have consistently held that it is for Congress and the courts, not the FTC, to decide if there is a private right of action under an FTC rule, and since there is no evidence that Congress changed its mind, the FTC Statement of Basis and Purpose should be given no effect.[6]

Even though the FTC Act itself does not provide a private means of enforcement, the FTC Act decisions provide guidance in interpreting state UDAP statutes. Therefore, violations of the FTC Act may be challenged indirectly through a state UDAP cause of action. That is, an individual can not bring a claim specifically founded upon a violation of the FTC Act. But an individual may bring a claim based on a violation of the state UDAP statute and then argue that the court should be guided in its determination whether a practice violates the state statute by the fact that the practice violates the FTC standard.[7] In addition, the requirements of an FTC rule or consent decree may be, in certain circumstances, implied contract terms, so a violation would be a breach of contract.[8]

---

1 15 U.S.C. § 45.

2 Baum v. Great Western Cities, Inc., 703 F.2d 1197 (10th Cir. 1983); Dreisbach v. Murphy, 658 F.2d 720 (9th Cir. 1981); Fulton v. Hecht, 580 F.2d 1243 (5th Cir. 1978), *cert. denied*, 440 U.S. 981 (1979); Alfred Dunhill Ltd. v. Interstate Cigar Co., 499 F.2d 232 (2d Cir. 1974); Holloway v. Bristol-Myers Corp., 485 F.2d 986 (D.C. Cir. 1973); Carlson v. Coca Cola Co., 483 F.2d 279 (9th Cir. 1973); Haun v. Don Mealy Imports, Inc., 285 F. Supp. 2d 1297 (M.D. Fla. 2003); Morales v. Walker Motors Sales, Inc., 162 F. Supp. 2d 786 (S.D. Ohio 2000) (no private cause of action to enforce FTC Holder Rule); Tacker v. Wilson, 830 F. Supp. 422 (W.D. Tenn. 1993); Dash v. Wayne, 700 F. Supp. 1056 (D. Haw. 1988); Days Inn of Am. Franchising, Inc. v. Windham, 699 F. Supp. 1581 (N.D. Ga. 1988); Waldo v. North Am. Van Lines, Inc., 669 F. Supp. 722 (W.D. Pa. 1987); Freedman v. Meldy's, Inc., 587 F. Supp. 658 (E.D. Pa. 1984); First Phone Co. of New England v. New England Tel. & Tel. Co., 1981 U.S. Dist. LEXIS 11538 (D. Mass. Mar. 31, 1981); Greenberg v. Michigan Optometric Ass'n Inc., 483 F. Supp. 142 (E.D. Mich. 1980); Meyer v. Bell & Howell Co., 453 F. Supp. 801 (D. Mo. 1978), *appeal dismissed*, 584 F.2d 291 (8th Cir. 1978); Summey v. Ford Motor Credit Co., 449 F. Supp. 132 (D.S.C. 1976), *aff'd without op.*, 573 F.2d 1306 (4th Cir. 1978); Culbreth v. Lawrence J. Miller, Inc., 477 A.2d 491 (Pa. Super. Ct. 1984). *But see* Guernsey v. Rich Plan of the Midwest, 408 F. Supp. 582 (N.D. Ind. 1976); Donnelly v. Mustang Pools, Inc., 84 Misc. 2d 28, 374 N.Y.S.2d 967 (Sup. Ct. 1975).

3 Bacon v. Southwest Airlines Co., 997 F. Supp. 775 (N.D. Tex. 1998).

4 *Id.* (the Uniform Deceptive Trade Practices Act).

5 43 Fed. Reg. 59614 (Feb. 10, 1978).

6 FTC v. Davis, 5 Trade Reg. Rptr. (CCH) ¶ 22,741 (D. Nev. Oct. 17, 1989); Days Inn of Am. Franchising, Inc. v. Windham, 699 F. Supp. 1581 (N.D. Ga. 1988); Mon-Shore Mgmt., Inc. v. Family Media, 1985 U.S. Dist. LEXIS 12407, Bus. Fran. Guide (CCH) ¶ 8494 (S.D.N.Y. Dec. 23, 1985); Freedman v. Meldy's, Inc., 587 F. Supp. 658 (E.D. Pa. 1984); Chelson v. Oregonian Publishing Co., 1981 U.S. Dist. LEXIS 12488, 1981-1 Trade Cas. (CCH) ¶ 64,031 (D. Or. Mar. 4, 1981).

7 The use of FTC precedent in state court actions is analyzed in more detail at §§ 3.2.7 and 3.4.5, *supra*.

8 *See* § 6.6.4.4, *supra* (FTC Holder Rule as implied contract term); 16 C.F.R. § 455.3(b) (information on final version of Buyers Guide required by FTC Used Car Rule is incorporated into contract).

9.2 The Racketeer Influenced & Corrupt Organizations Act (RICO)

9.2.1 Overview of RICO and Its Application to Consumer Fraud

9.2.1.1 Advantages and Disadvantages of RICO Claims

The private remedies authorized by the Federal Racketeer Influenced and Corrupt Organization provisions of the Organized Crime Control Act of 1970 (RICO)[9] offer important alternatives to state UDAP remedies in cases of consumer fraud, and several state RICO statutes provide potential claims to defrauded consumers as well. Although federal RICO was primarily devised as a weapon against organized crime, its broad provisions for criminal and civil liability were deliberately drawn to encompass types of business-related misconduct that are not peculiar to gangsters.[10] Civil RICO creates a federal civil action for damages (and, arguably, for private injunctive relief)[11] based on the existence of a pattern of enumerated federal and state crimes or on the collection of an unlawful debt.[12] Most importantly, RICO provides prevailing plaintiffs with treble damages plus attorney fees and costs[13] for violations of underlying predicate statutes that themselves might provide only compensatory damages or no damages at all.[14] Because of the increased monetary exposure resulting from the threat of treble damages and attorney fees, a RICO claim may cause a defendant to settle more quickly or for more money than it might do in the ordinary civil lawsuit, where the defendant might only have to return what was wrongfully received.

While RICO claims give a powerful boost to many types of consumer claims, attorneys should be aware that a RICO claim—even if technically available—may not always be a wise addition to a complaint. Including a RICO claim in a simple lawsuit may needlessly complicate the case and lead to numerous procedural motions. In addition, even though many defendants will be more reasonable about settlement when they face potential treble damages and attorney fees, some defendants will see the added exposure as justifying a more vigorous defense.

As additional considerations, the RICO statute is complex and important ambiguities remain to be resolved by the courts.[15] The law is in flux, the volume of civil RICO litigation is high, and practitioners must keep abreast of recent developments.[16]

For all its possible pitfalls, however, RICO has great potential as a consumer protection statute.[17] Some of the difficulties that have generated the most controversy will not normally arise in a consumer case. The following discussion is a general overview of RICO as judicially construed, which attempts to pinpoint aspects of the law that may be most pertinent to the use of civil RICO on behalf of consumer plaintiffs. For an exhaustive treatment of the statute and its fate in the courts, the reader is referred to other useful sources.[18]

9.2.1.2 Liberal Construction

Many federal courts initially reacted with hostility to civil RICO actions in areas remote from organized crime conducted by professional criminals. Courts interpreted RICO—especially civil RICO—restrictively, dismissing many actions at the pleading stage. However, by its own terms, RICO "shall be liberally construed to effectuate its remedial purposes,"[19] and the Supreme Court has rebuffed several lower court efforts to limit its scope, supporting an expansive construction of the statute.[20] It has done this despite acknowledging the fact that civil RICO has been

9 18 U.S.C. §§ 1961–1968 (reprinted at Appx. C.1, *infra*).

10 For the legislative history of RICO, see 115 Cong. Rec. 6994, 6995, 9567 (1969); 1970 U.S.C.C.A.N. 4007, 4032–4036; Blakey, *The RICO Civil Fraud Action in Context: Reflections on Bennett v. Berg*, 58 Notre Dame L. Rev. 237 (1982) (Prof. G. Robert Blakey, the author of this article, was principal draftsman of RICO) and sources cited in Strafer, Massumi & Skolnick, *Civil RICO in the Public Interest: "Everybody's Darling,"* 19 Am. Crim. L. Rev. 655, 680 n.193 (1982).

11 *See* § 9.2.5.3.4, *infra*.

12 18 U.S.C. § 1961(1).

13 18 U.S.C. § 1964(c).

14 For instance, there is no private cause of action for damages under the federal mail fraud statute, 18 U.S.C. § 1341, but because it is a RICO predicate offense, a defrauded victim may be able to recover for a violation of the statute through RICO's remedies. *See, e.g.*, Wisdom v. First Midwest Bank of Poplar Bluff, 167 F.3d 402, 408 (8th Cir. 1999) (en banc) (applying factors of Cort v. Ash, 422 U.S. 66, 78 (1975)), Moss v. Morgan Stanley, Inc., 553 F. Supp. 1347, 1361 (S.D.N.Y.), *aff'd*, 719 F.2d 5 (2d Cir. 1983), *cert. denied*, 465 U.S. 1025 (1984).

15 *See, e.g.*, § 9.2.5.3.4 (injunctive relief for private plaintiffs), *infra*.

16 Three reporting services, RICO Law Reporter, Civil RICO Reporter (BNA), and RICO Business Disputes Guide (CCH), are devoted exclusively to RICO. RICO cases are regularly featured in bar journals and the legal press.

17 *See, e.g.*, National Senior Citizens Law Center, *Applying Racketeering Laws to Nursing Homes*, 19 Clearinghouse Rev. 1306 (1986).

18 *See, e.g.*, Gregory P. Joseph, Civil RICO: A Definitive Guide (2d ed. 1999).

19 Organized Crime Control Act of 1970, Pub. L. No. 91-452, tit. IX, § 304(a), 84 Stat. 92, 947 (1970) (uncodified provision). The Supreme Court quoted this provision to support its holding that a RICO plaintiff need only show injury from the predicate acts themselves, and not a "racketeering injury." Sedima, S.P.R.L. v. Imrex Co., 473 U.S. 479, 497–98 (1985). *See also* Biasch v. Gallina, 346 F.3d 366, 372 (2d Cir. 2003) (quoting provision in holding that civil RICO plaintiff had standing).

20 *See* Sedima, S.P.R.L. v. Imrex Co., 473 U.S. 479, 497–499, 105 S. Ct. 3275, 87 L. Ed. 2d 346 (1985); United States v. Turkette, 452 U.S. 576, 586, 587 (1981).

used far more often against "legitimate" businesses than against "the archetypal, intimidating gangster."[21] Among the limitations that have been rejected by the Supreme Court or the great weight of authority are:

- *Organized Crime Nexus*: The defendant need not be a member of or involved with "organized crime."[22]
- *Racketeering Enterprise Injury*: The injury to the plaintiff need not derive from the racketeering enterprise instead of resulting simply from the predicate offenses themselves.[23]
- *Criminal Conviction*: The defendant need not have been criminally convicted of the acts alleged as predicate offenses.[24]
- *Association for Wholly Criminal Purposes*: RICO applies not only to racketeering in relation to otherwise lawful enterprises, but to associations whose purposes are wholly criminal.[25]
- *Commercial or Competitive Injury*: A RICO action does not require a distinctively commercial or competitive injury.[26]
- *"Garden-Variety" Fraud*: Perhaps most important in consumer cases, RICO does not exclude "garden variety" business or consumer fraud that otherwise satisfies the requirements of a RICO cause of action.[27]

Plaintiffs' attorneys should be alert to defense attempts to interject new substantive RICO limitations that may be only relabeled versions or minor variants of discredited restrictions. For example, the Supreme Court in *American Bank & Trust Co. v. Haroco* rejected a proposed limitation revolving around whether the defendant enterprise was "conducted" through a pattern of racketeering activity.[28] This, held the Court, was essentially a restatement of the "racketeering injury" restriction it had just rejected in *Sedima*: "The submission that the injury must flow not from the predicate acts themselves but from the fact that they were performed as part of the conduct of an enterprise suffers from the same defects as the amorphous and unfounded restrictions on the RICO private action we rejected in [*Sedima*]."[29] Any proposed limitation, old or new, without explicit support in the language of the statute should be vigorously contested on the basis of the liberal construction that Congress mandated[30] and that the Supreme Court has consistently avowed. The expansive use of civil RICO against "legitimate" businesses has aroused widespread criticism and occasioned various proposals to restrict its scope;[31] nonetheless, civil RICO survives as a potent tool with which to combat corporate abuses of consumers.

---

21 Sedima, S.P.R.L. v. Imrex Co., 473 U.S. 479, 499, 105 S. Ct. 3275, 87 L. Ed. 2d 346 (1985).

22 The U.S. Supreme Court, in reiterating this position, has stated that Congress' failure to limit the application of RICO to organized crime resulted from its acknowledgment that organized crime is heavily involved in legitimate enterprises, making it impossible to adequately define organized crime. H.J. Inc. v. Northwestern Bell Tel. Co., 492 U.S. 229, 109 S. Ct. 2893, 106 L. Ed. 2d 195 (1989). *See also* United States v. Hunt, 749 F.2d 1078, 1088 (4th Cir. 1984), *cert. denied*, 472 U.S. 1018 (1985); Owl Constr. Co. v. Ronald Adams Contractors, Inc., 727 F.2d 540, 542 (5th Cir.), *cert. denied*, 469 U.S. 831 (1984); Schacht v. Brown, 711 F.2d 1343, 1353 (7th Cir. 1983), *cert. denied*, 464 U.S. 1002 (1983); Bennett v. Berg, 685 F.2d 1053, 1063 (8th Cir. 1982), *aff'd en banc*, 710 F.2d 1361 (8th Cir.), *cert. denied*, 464 U.S. 1008 (1983); United States v. Campanale, 518 F.2d 352, 363, 364 (9th Cir. 1975), *cert. denied sub nom.* Matthews v. United States, 423 U.S. 1050 (1976); Prudential Ins. Co. v. U.S. Gypsum Co., 711 F. Supp. 1244 (D.N.J. 1989) (suit for property damage caused by asbestos in buildings).

23 Sedima, S.P.R.L. v. Imrex Co., 473 U.S. 479, 495, 105 S. Ct. 3275, 87 L. Ed. 2d 346 (1985). According to this theory, now rejected, an injury "caused by the defendant's predicate acts, rather than by its use of a pattern of racketeering injury in connection with a RICO enterprise," was not considered to be caused by a violation of § 1962. Bankers Trust Co. v. Rhoades, 741 F.2d 511, 517 (2d Cir. 1984), *vacated and remanded*, 473 U.S. 922 (1985).

24 Sedima, S.P.R.L. v. Imrex Co., 473 U.S. 479, 493, 105 S. Ct. 3275, 87 L. Ed. 2d 346 (1985). A criminal conviction, though not a requirement, is not an impediment either. Conduct resulting in convictions for predicate offenses may be used in subsequent RICO proceedings. United States v. Persico, 774 F.2d 30 (2d Cir. 1985) (criminal case).

25 United States v. Turkette, 452 U.S. 576, 584, 585 (1981).

26 Callan v. State Chem. Mfg. Co., 584 F. Supp. 619, 622, 623 (E.D. Pa. 1984) (mem.); Crocker Nat'l Bank v. Rockwell Int'l Corp., 555 F. Supp. 47, 49 (N.D. Cal. 1982). As a commentator has pointed out, "[t]here appears to be some overlap between the concepts of a 'racketeering enterprise injury' and a 'commercial injury.' " Litigation Research Group, Civil RICO: A Review of the Case Law 20 (1985). *See also* Strafer, Massumi & Skolnick, *Civil RICO in the Public Interest: "Everybody's Darling,"* 79 Am. Crim. L. Rev. 655, 689–91 (1982).

27 Tabas v. Tabas, 47 F.3d 1280 (3d Cir. 1995); Schacht v. Brown, 711 F.2d 1343, 1353–56 (7th Cir.), *cert. denied*, 464 U.S. 1002 (1983).

28 473 U.S. 606, 607 (1985) (*per curiam*).

29 *Id.* at 609.

30 *See* § 9.2.1, *supra*. *See also* Note, *Civil RICO: The Temptation and the Impropriety of Judicial Restriction*, 95 Harv. L. Rev. 1101 (1982).

31 *See, e.g.*, The Private Securities Litigation Reform Act of 1995, 104 Pub. L. No. 104-67, 109 Stat. 758 (1995) (amending 18 U.S.C. § 1964(a) to exclude "any conduct that would have been actionable as fraud in the purchase or sale of securities" as the basis of a civil RICO action); Howard v. Am. Online Inc., 208 F.3d 741, 749 (9th Cir. 2000) (PSLRA bars claim where it was "actionable" as securities fraud even if plaintiffs themselves would not have standing to bring such a claim); Bald Eagle Area Sch. Dist. v. Keystone Fin., Inc., 189 F.3d 321, 329 (3d Cir. 1999) (affirming dismissal on basis of PSLRA). *See also* Grell, *Exorcising RICO from Product Litigation*, 24 Wm. Mitchell L. Rev. 1089 (1998); Bradley, *Long Arm of the Rackets Law Draws Fire From White-Collar Targets*, Christian Science Monitor, Feb. 7, 1986, at 21, col. 1; Zimroth, *Legislative Proposals to Amend the Civil RICO Statute*, in Practicing Law Institute, 1985 Civil RICO at 427–444.

9.2.1.3 Scope, Preemption, and Immunity

UDAP practitioners should consider RICO claims in many consumer cases, which have previously been characterized only in terms of UDAP, tort or contract.[32] However, specific statutes may be found to bar RICO claims based on conduct regulated by such statutes. For example, whistleblower claims arising in the nuclear industry are preempted by the Energy Reorganization Act.[33] Some RICO claims relating to workers' benefits have been deemed preempted by the National Labor Relations Act,[34] while others have survived preemption.[35] RICO itself now excludes securities fraud claims from its scope.[36]

RICO claims based on fraud in the insurance industry will generally survive, notwithstanding the reverse preemption provisions of the McCarran-Ferguson Act.[37] In *Humana Inc. v. Forsyth*[38] the Supreme Court ruled that the reverse preemption provision does not apply to federal RICO claims unless the RICO statute invalidates, impairs, or supersedes a state insurance statute. "When federal law does not directly conflict with state regulation, and when application of the federal law would not frustrate any declared state policy or interfere with a State's administrative regime, the McCarran-Ferguson Act does not preclude its application."[39] Accordingly, even if state insurance law provides a remedial scheme for insurance fraud, the additional availability of RICO remedies for the same misconduct does not "impair" the insurance regulatory scheme.

Until *Humana* clarified RICO's applicability to insurance, insurance fraud litigation generally had to be brought in state court on a UDAP, breach of contract, or bad faith tort claim.[40] Such claims were inadequate because state insurance statutes rarely provide for a private right of action, and, in some states, the state insurance regulation may even prevent a private UDAP or bad faith tort claim. Following *Humana*, RICO provides an alternative that allows federal court jurisdiction, mandatory treble damages, and attorney fees that is not preempted by state insurance regulation, so long as it does not impair a state regulation.

Municipalities and municipal corporations such as school boards are immune from suit,[41] either on the theory that they can not form the necessary criminal intent[42] or because treble damages would punish the very taxpayers that RICO was designed to protect.[43] General immunity principles prevent RICO suits against the Internal Revenue Service,[44] tribal councils,[45] legislators,[46] and the FDIC.[47] As with other federal statutes, the Eleventh Amendment may bar claims against state agencies or state officials.[48]

32 So long as a claim has not been established as clearly nonviable, courts in RICO cases have been reluctant to impose Rule 11 sanctions against lawyers using RICO in novel ways. *See* § 9.2.5.1, *infra*.

33 Norman v. Niagara Mohawk Power Corp., 873 F.2d 634, 637 (2d Cir. 1989); Masters v. Daniel Int'l Corp., 1991 U.S. Dist. LEXIS 7595 (D. Kan. May 3, 1991).

34 Tamburello v. Comm-Tract Corp., 67 F.3d 973 (1st Cir. 1995), *cert. denied*, 517 U.S. 1222 (1996); Brennan v. Chestnut, 973 F.2d 644 (8th Cir. 1992); Mann v. Air Line Pilots Ass'n, 848 F. Supp. 990 (S.D. Fla. 1994); Graveley Roofing Corp. v. United Union of Roofers, Waterproofers & Allied Workers Local Union No. 30, 1994 U.S. Dist. LEXIS 7489 (E.D. Pa. June 2, 1994); Domestic Linen Supply & Laundry Co. v. Int'l Bhd. of Teamsters, 1992 U.S. Dist. LEXIS 22201 (E.D. Mich. Oct. 30, 1992); Butchers' Union, Local 498 v. SDC Inv., Inc., 631 F. Supp. 1001 (E.D. Cal. 1986); *see also* Danielson v. Burnside-Ott Aviation Training Ctr., Inc., 941 F.2d 1220 (D.C. Cir. 1991) (Service Contract Act preempts RICO); Goulart v. United Airlines, Inc., 1996 U.S. Dist. LEXIS 2894 (N.D. Ill. Mar. 8, 1996) (Railway Labor Act). *But see* Hood v. Smith's Transfer Corp., 762 F. Supp. 1274 (W.D. Ky. 1991) (suit by employee participants in ESOP plan against their company not preempted by National Labor Relations Act).

35 Trollinger v. Tyson Foods, Inc., 370 F.3d 602, 610 (6th Cir. 2004) (holding that suit by workers who were union members that alleged that their employer had violated RICO in scheming to depress their wage scale was not preempted by the NLRA).

36 18 U.S.C. § 1964(a), *as amended by* the Private Litig. Sec. Reform Act of 1995, Pub. L. No. 104-67, 109 Stat. 758 (1995).

37 15 U.S.C. § 1012(b).

38 525 U.S. 299, 119 S. Ct. 710, 142 L. Ed. 2d 753 (1999).

39 525 U.S. at 310. *See also* National Consumer Law Center, The Cost of Credit § 8.5.2.5.3 (2d ed. 2000 & Supp.).

40 *See* § 2.3.1.3, *supra*.

41 *See, e.g.*, Ochoa v. Housing Auth. of City of Los Angeles, 47 Fed. Appx. 484, 486 (9th Cir. 2002) (neither a municipal corporation nor its employees in their official capacities are subject to RICO liability); Wood v. Incorporated Village of Patchogue, 11 F. Supp. 2d 344, 354 (E.D.N.Y. 2004); Dickerson v. City of Denton, 298 F. Supp. 2d 537, 549 (C.D. Tex. 2004); Frooks v. Town of Cortlandt, 997 F. Supp. 438, 457 (S.D.N.Y. 1998), *aff'd without op.*, 182 F.3d 899 (2d Cir. 1999); Dammon v. W.L. Folse, 846 F. Supp. 36, 37–38 (E.D. La. 1994); Nu-Life Constr. Corp. v. Bd. of Educ. of the City of N.Y., 779 F. Supp. 248, 252 (E.D.N.Y. 1991).

42 *See, e.g.*, Interstate Flagging, Inc. v. Town of Darien, 283 F. Supp. 2d 641, 645–46 (D. Conn. 2003); Lancaster Cmty. Hosp. v. Antelope Valley Hosp. Dist., 940 F.2d 397, 404 (9th Cir. 1991); Nu-Life Constr. Corp. v. Bd. of Educ. of the City of N.Y., 779 F. Supp. 248, 251 (E.D.N.Y. 1991).

43 Genty v. Resolution Trust Corp., 937 F.2d 899, 914 (3d Cir. 1991) (township).

44 Chow v. Giordano, 24 F.3d 245 (9th Cir.) (unpublished disposition, text at 1994 U.S. App. LEXIS 11048), *cert. denied*, 513 U.S. 989 (1994) (relying on agency's sovereign immunity).

45 Smith v. Babbitt, 875 F. Supp. 1353 (D. Minn. 1995), *cert. denied*, 522 U.S. 807 (1997) (relying on tribe's sovereign immunity).

46 Chappell v. Robbins, 73 F.3d 918 (9th Cir. 1995).

47 McNeily v. United States, 6 F.3d 343 (5th Cir. 1993) (relying on misrepresentation exception of the Federal Tort Claims Act, 28 U.S.C. § 2680(h)).

48 Bair v. Krug, 853 F.2d 672, 675 (9th Cir. 1988) (action against state officials acting in their official capacities barred); Rogers v. Mitchell, 2003 WL 21976743, at *1–2 (N.D. Tex. Aug. 19, 2003) (action against state lottery commission barred).

9.2.2 The Structure of RICO

To recover on a RICO count, the plaintiff must show that the defendant engaged in at least one of the four prohibited activities spelled out in section 1962, subsections (a) through (d):

> (a) It shall be unlawful for any person who has received any income derived, directly or indirectly, from a pattern of racketeering activity or through collection of an unlawful debt . . . to use or invest, directly or indirectly, any part of such income, or the proceeds of such income, in acquisition of any interest in, or the establishment or operation of, any enterprise which is engaged in, or the activities of which affect, interstate or foreign commerce. . . .
>
> (b) It shall be unlawful for any person through a pattern of racketeering activity or through collection of an unlawful debt to acquire or maintain, directly or indirectly, any interest in or control of any enterprise which is engaged in, or the activities of which affect, interstate or foreign commerce.
>
> (c) It shall be unlawful for any person employed by or associated with any enterprise engaged in, or the activities of which affect, interstate or foreign commerce, to conduct or participate, directly or indirectly, in the conduct of such enterprise's affairs through a pattern of racketeering activity or collection of unlawful debt.
>
> (d) It shall be unlawful for any person to conspire to violate any of the provisions of subsections (a), (b), or (c) of this section.[49]

These four prohibited practices are triggered by *either* a pattern of racketeering activity or the "collection of an unlawful debt."

"Racketeering activity" is defined in the statute to include nine generic state crimes and a longer list of specified federal offenses such as bribery, extortion, narcotics, and obstruction of justice.[50] The crimes are called predicate offenses, and only the enumerated crimes can be used to show racketeering activity.[51] Mail fraud[52] and wire fraud[53] are the most significant predicate offenses, especially for consumer plaintiffs.[54]

To prevail on a RICO claim, one must show either a "pattern of racketeering activity" or the "collection of an unlawful debt." A "pattern of racketeering activity" requires at least two acts of "racketeering activity" within ten years of each other.[55] Pattern, in RICO, is a complex and intensely fact-specific element that has been the subject of abundant litigation. This topic is covered in § 9.2.3.4, *infra*.

An "unlawful debt" is defined as either illegal gambling debts or usury, under either state or federal law, at a rate at least twice the enforceable rate.[56] For a violation based on collection of an unlawful debt, there need be no racketeering activity and no pattern of abuse, just one instance of collection of a debt.[57]

RICO is somewhat confusing to deal with, partly because RICO does not prohibit racketeering activity directly. Rather, its provisions deal with the peripheral aspects of racketeering—use of money made through racketeering, control of businesses affecting interstate commerce by racketeers, and conspiracy to do either. Each element of a RICO claim is discussed below.

Violators of RICO are subject to criminal penalties,[58] to forfeiture of their interest in the enterprise,[59] and to other sanctions.[60] Significant for consumer attorneys, however, RICO also provides private litigants with federal court jurisdiction for actions seeking treble damages plus attorney fees:

---

49 18 U.S.C. § 1962.

50 18 U.S.C. § 1961(1).

51 Consumer attorneys should note that since deceptive trade act violations are not RICO predicate offenses, they will not support a RICO claim. Zito v. Leasecomm Corp., 2003 WL 22251352, at *9 (S.D.N.Y. Sept. 30, 2003). That court also held that the plaintiff's alleged predicate act of obstruction of justice for failing to comply with state subpoenas could not support a RICO claim because to violate the listed predicate offense of obstruction of justice, 18 U.S.C. § 1503, the act must relate to a federal court proceeding; obstruction of state justice will not suffice. *Id.* at 8.

52 18 U.S.C. § 1341. *See* § 9.2.4, *infra*.

53 18 U.S.C. § 1343. *See* § 9.2.4, *infra*.

54 Prior to 1995, securities fraud was often cited as a RICO predicate act, but the Private Securities Litigation Reform Act of 1995 amended civil RICO to exclude as an underlying predicate "any conduct that would have been actionable as fraud in the purchase or sale of securities."

55 18 U.S.C. § 1961(5). At least one of the acts must have taken place after the statute took effect in 1970. *Id.*

56 18 U.S.C. § 1961(6).

57 18 U.S.C. §§ 1961(6), 1962(a)–(c) (pattern of racketeering *or* collection of unlawful debt); *see* § 9.2.3.5, *infra*. One state case reached the opposite conclusion, that a pattern of unlawful debts must be shown. Bandas v. Citizens State Bank of Silver Lake, 412 N.W.2d 818 (Minn. Ct. App. 1987), *remanded on other grounds sub nom.* VanderWeyst v. First State Bank, 425 N.W.2d 803 (Minn. 1988), *cert. denied*, 488 U.S. 943 (1988). This holding is clearly wrong, and the Minnesota Supreme Court on appeal made a special effort in dicta to point out the error of the holding in *Bandas*. However, in doing so, *VanderWeyst* dicta may have suggested another route to a similar requirement by noting that the bank was not alleged to be "in the business" of lending money at usurious rates. *Id.* at 812. (*Cf.* 18 U.S.C. § 1961(6) (definition of unlawful debt).) *See* § 9.2.3.5.3, *infra*.

58 18 U.S.C. § 1963.

59 *Id. See* U.S. Dept. of Justice, Criminal Div., Criminal Forfeitures Under the RICO and Continuing Enterprise Statutes (1980).

60 *E.g.*, 18 U.S.C. § 1964(a) (court-ordered restrictions on future business activities, dissolution or reorganization of any enterprise).

> Any person injured in his business or property by reason of a violation of section 1962 of this chapter may sue therefor in any appropriate United States district court and shall recover threefold the damages he sustains and the cost of the suit, including a reasonable attorney fee.[61]

9.2.3 Elements of the Civil RICO Action

9.2.3.1 Introduction

Some of the essential elements of a civil RICO action depend upon which of the four subsections of section 1962 is the subject of the alleged violation. However, to state any civil RICO a plaintiff must show the following:

- That an "enterprise" engaged in or affecting interstate commerce existed;
- That there was a nexus between the pattern of racketeering activity or collection of an unlawful debt and the enterprise; and
- That an injury to business or property occurred as a result of the above two factors.[62]

Additionally, every RICO violation involves either a "collection of an unlawful debt"[63] or a "pattern of racketeering activity"[64] by the defendant that is related to the enterprise in the particular manner described in each subsection. The pattern of racketeering activity—the most common allegation—includes a pattern of two or more predicate offenses whose elements must also be specified.[65]

Subsection 1962(c) is so far the most commonly used basis for alleging activities prohibited by RICO. Its particular elements, in addition to the elements common to all RICO claims, are as follows:

- The defendant is either employed by, or associated with, the enterprise;
- The defendant conducted or participated in, directly or indirectly, the conduct of the enterprise's affairs; and
- The participation was through a pattern of racketeering activity (or collection of an unlawful debt).[66]

9.2.3.2 The Defendant "Person" and the "Enterprise"

9.2.3.2.1 Identifying appropriate defendants and enterprises

A critical decision in any RICO case is identifying the appropriate characters for the role of "person," i.e., the defendant, and the "enterprise," i.e., the vehicle through which the "person" committed the unlawful activity. RICO defines "person" as "including any individual or entity capable of holding a legal or beneficial interest in property."[67] This is the character that is identified as the wrongdoer, as the defendant in the RICO claim.[68]

Often, a given set of facts can offer a number of arrangements of the involved parties. Although the concept of a "person" under RICO is straightforward, the concept of the "enterprise" is far less so, and it in turn influences the identification of the defendant. As discussed below, an enterprise—the key to any properly pleaded RICO allegation—can be "any individual, partnership, corporation, association, or other legal entity, and any union or group of individuals associated in fact although not a legal entity."[69]

---

61 18 U.S.C. § 1962(c).

62 *See* VanDenBroeck v. Common Point Mortg. Co., 210 F.3d 696, 699 (6th Cir. 2000); Wilcox v. First Interstate Bank, 815 F.2d 522, 531 n.7 (9th Cir. 1987); R.A.G.S. Couture, Inc. v. Hyatt, 774 F.2d 1350, 1352 (5th Cir. 1985); Haroco, Inc. v. Am. Nat'l Bank & Trust Co. of Chicago, 747 F.2d 384, 387 (7th Cir. 1984), *aff'd per curiam*, 473 U.S. 606 (1985); Martin-Trigona v. Smith, 712 F.2d 1421, 1426 n.6 (D.C. Cir. 1983); Singh v. Parnes, 199 F. Supp. 2d 152, 160 (S.D.N.Y. 2002); Al-Kazemi v. Gen. Acceptance & Inv. Corp., 633 F. Supp. 540, 542 (D.D.C. 1986); Cole v. Circle R. Convenience Stores, Inc., 602 F. Supp. 1108, 1112 (M.D. La. 1985). The elements have been spelled out more distinctly by the Second Circuit: (1) that the defendant (2) through the commission of two or more acts (3) constituting a pattern (4) of "racketeering activity" (5) directly or indirectly invests in, or maintains an interest in, or participated in (6) an "enterprise" (7) the activities of which affect interstate or foreign commerce. Moss v. Morgan Stanley, Inc., 719 F.2d 5, 17 (2d Cir. 1983), *cert. denied*, 465 U.S. 1025 (1984). The elements of criminal and civil RICO are the same; only the standard of proof is different. Hudson v. LaRouche, 579 F. Supp. 623, 626 n.2 (S.D.N.Y. 1983).

63 18 U.S.C. § 1961(6) (definition). *See* Blount Fin. Servs., Inc. v. Walter E. Heller & Co., 632 F. Supp. 240, 243 (E.D. Tenn. 1986) (complaint must specify the lawful rate of interest which the defendant has exceeded), *aff'd*, 819 F.2d 151 (6th Cir. 1987).

64 18 U.S.C. §§ 1961(1), (5). *See* § 9.2.3.4, *infra*.

65 *See* §§ 9.2.3.4 (pattern of racketeering activity) and 9.2.4 (predicate mail fraud and wire fraud offenses) *infra*.

66 *Id.*

67 *Id.* § 1961(3).

68 Each of the four subsections defining the conduct prohibited by RICO begin "[i]t shall be unlawful for *any person* to. . . ." 18 U.S.C. § 1962(a)–(d) (emphasis added). *See also* St. Paul Mercury Ins. Co. v. Williamson, 224 F.3d 425, 440 (5th Cir. 2000) (a RICO person is the defendant, while a RICO enterprise can be either a legal entity or an association in fact). An individual or entity may meet the definition of "person" but nonetheless be immune from liability. *See, e.g.*, Ochoa v. Housing Auth. of City of Los Angeles, 47 Fed. Appx. 484, 486 (9th Cir. 2002) (neither a municipal corporation nor its employees in their official capacities are subject to RICO liability); *see also* § 9.2.1.3, *supra*.

69 18 U.S.C. § 1961(4).

Often the most attractive candidate for the role of enterprise will be an association in fact of some of the parties involved, but to qualify as an association in fact the relationship among the parties must meet certain case law requirements. Furthermore, in a section 1962(c) case, the most commonly selected RICO allegation, most circuits require the enterprise to be "distinct" from the person/defendant, and meeting that requirement requires both careful thought about the roles of defendant and enterprise and precise pleading of their relationship.

Furthermore, under RICO an appropriate enterprise is not just an entity that fulfills the definition, but one that the plaintiff can demonstrate the defendant used in a way that the statute prohibits. In a section 1962(c) case, for example, the plaintiff must show that the person operated or managed the enterprise.[70] In a section 1962(a) case, the defendant must have used or invested illegally-gained income in an enterprise. In a section 1962(b) case, the defendant must have acquired or maintained an interest in that enterprise.[71]

9.2.3.2.2 Alleging an appropriate enterprise

The enterprise element of RICO is considerably more complicated, and the subject of considerably more litigation, than the person element. Under RICO, an enterprise includes "any individual, partnership, corporation, or other legal entity, and any union or group of individuals associated in fact although not a legal entity."[72] In *Scheidler*, the Supreme Court characterized the "enterprise" as the vehicle through which the unlawful pattern of racketeering is committed.[73] However, a court might not allow a corporation that is actually a victim of its officers or employees to serve as the enterprise through which they conducted racketeering activity.[74]

It is usually not difficult to plead and prove that a legal entity is an enterprise; courts are to construe the term broadly.[75] However, often the logical subject for the role of enterprise is not a single legal entity, but a group of the characters that are associated with each other not as a single legal entity, but as an association in fact. For RICO purposes, an association in fact is "a group of persons associated together for a common purpose of engaging in a course of conduct."[76] Thus, to show an association in fact a plaintiff must allege component entities—the associates—and a relationship—the association.

70 Reves v. Ernst & Young, 507 U.S. 170, 179, 113 S. Ct. 1163, 1170 122 L. Ed. 2d 525, 536–37 (1993).

71 *See* § 9.2.3.7, *infra*.

72 18 U.S.C. § 1961 (4).

73 National Organization for Women v. Scheidler, 510 U.S. 249, 259, 114 S. Ct. 748, 804, 127 L. Ed. 2d 99, 109 (1994).

74 *See* LaSalle Bank Lake View v. Seguban, 54 F.3d 387, 393 (7th Cir. 1995) (questioning whether bank, which was the victim of an employee's embezzlement, could be an enterprise).

75 U.S. v. Connolly, 341 F.3d 16, 28 (1st Cir. 2003) (upholding conviction of FBI agent).

76 United States v. Turkette, 452 U.S. 576, 583 (1981).

The enterprise may thus be an association in fact of a corporation with one or more individuals or corporations. A group of corporations, for instance, can be an association in fact,[77] as can a group of individuals associated with several corporations.[78] An institution and its customer may form an association in fact: one court found that a lender had worked closely enough with a development company it financed to create an association in fact enterprise.[79] A complaint that names a discreet and specific number of constituents to the enterprise, as opposed to an amorphous group as a whole (such as all members of the secondary market) is more likely to succeed.[80] An association in fact enterprise may include nonculpable associates that do not have a criminal purpose in common with the other entities included in the enterprise.[81]

Once the associates have been identified, a plaintiff must show an association among them to fully establish an association in fact enterprise. Critical to demonstrating that a group of persons and/or entities functioned as an association in fact is showing some sort of structure among them.[82] Courts have varied on just what type of, and how much,

77 *See, e.g.*, Shearin v. E.F. Hutton Group, Inc., 885 F.2d 1162, 1165 (3d Cir. 1989). *But see* Roberts v. Heim, 670 F. Supp. 1466 (N.D. Cal. 1987) (association in fact can only comprise of natural persons).

78 United States v. London, 66 F.3d 1227, 1244 (1st Cir. 1995) (business owner can be enterprise with corporation), *cert. denied*, 517 U.S. 1155 (1996); Ocean Energy II, Inc. v. Alexander & Alexander, Inc., 868 F.2d 740 (5th Cir. 1989) (individuals and corporations who attempted to sell worthless and illegal insurance policies on at least one occasion may be deemed association in fact); United States v. Thevis, 665 F.2d 616, 625, 626 (5th Cir.), *cert. denied*, 456 U.S. 1008 (1982); *see also* United States v. Benny, 786 F.2d 1410 (9th Cir.) (sole proprietor can associate with enterprise consisting of sole proprietorship and other individuals working for the proprietorship), *cert. denied*, 479 U.S. 1017 (1986); Am. Manufacturers' Mut. Ins. Co. v. Townson, 912 F. Supp. 291 (E.D. Tenn. 1995) (marriage can be an enterprise/association in fact for insurance fraud purposes); Allstate Ins. Co. v. A.M. Pugh Assocs., Inc., 604 F. Supp. 85, 100 (M.D. Pa. 1984) (mem.). *But see* Foval v. First Nat'l Bank of Commerce in New Orleans, 841 F.2d 126 (5th Cir. 1988) (no association in fact if no continuing relationship).

79 Rodriguez v. Banco Central, 777 F. Supp. 1043 (D. P.R. 1991), *aff'd on other grounds*, 990 F.2d 7 (1st Cir. 1993).

80 *See, e.g.*, VanDenBroeck v. CommonPoint Mortg. Co., 210 F.3d 696, 700 (6th Cir. 2000); Dirt Hogs, Inc. v. Natural Gas Pipeline Co., 2000 U.S. App. LEXIS 6463, at *9 (10th Cir. Apr. 10, 2000) (criticizing allegations of a string of participants, known and unknown, as a "moving target" approach); Richmond v. Nationwide Cassel L.P. 52 F.3d 640, 645 (7th Cir. 1995) ("a nebulous, open-ended description of the enterprise does not sufficiently identify this essential element").

81 U.S. v. Cianci, 210 F. Supp. 2d 71, 73–75 (D.R.I. 2002) (a legitimate organization, such as a city agency, may be a nonculpable member of a RICO enterprise operated by a defendant for criminal purposes).

82 United States v. Turkette, 452 U.S. 576, 583, 101 S. Ct. 2524, 2528 (1981) (entity is proved by existence of an ongoing organization, formal or informal, and by evidence that the various associates function as a continuing unit).

structure must be shown. Clearly the group can not simply comprise random parties, but neither need it be as organized as a corporate family.

The most widely accepted organizational requirements of an association in fact demand allegations of the following characteristics: (1) an ongoing organization with a decision-making framework or mechanism for controlling the group; (2) with associates that function as a continuing unit; and (3) that is separate and apart from the pattern of racketeering activity.[83]

To satisfy the first characteristic, the decision-making framework, some jurisdictions require the plaintiff to show that the enterprise had a hierarchical or consensual decision-making structure with evidence of a chain of command or similar evidence.[84] Corporate affiliations, such as those between a corporation and its parent, its subsidiaries, or its officers may establish this structure.[85] However, such overt structure is not necessary; the plaintiff need only show some sort of organization.[86] Nor must the organization be formalized; an "informal consortium" will suffice.[87] Nonetheless, courts have consistently held that mere contractual relationships, without more, do not satisfy this structural element of

83 *See* Dirt Hogs, Inc. v. Natural Gas Pipeline Co., 2000 U.S. App. LEXIS 6463, at *7 (10th Cir. Apr. 10, 2000); Frank v. D'Ambrosi, 4 F.3d 1378, 1386 (6th Cir. 1993) (plaintiff must show that the persons engaged in "ongoing, coordinated behavior"); United States v. Sanders, 928 F.2d 940, 943, 944 (10th Cir. 1991), *cert. denied*, 502 U.S. 845 (1991); United States v. Riccobene, 709 F.2d 214, 223, 224 (3d Cir. 1983), *cert. denied*, 464 U.S. 849 (1983); *see also* U.S. v. Kehoe, 310 F.3d 579, 586 (8th Cir. 2002) (RICO enterprise must have a common purpose or goal, a continuity of persons with an ongoing origination, and a structure distinct from the pattern of racketeering); Stachon v. United Consumers Club, Inc., 229 F.3d 673, 675–76 (7th Cir. 2000) (distinguishing a mere conspiracy from an association in fact); Begala v. PNC Bank, 214 F.3d 776, 781, 782 (6th Cir. 2000) (complaint must contain facts suggesting that the business of the listed entities is coordinated in such a way that they function as a continuing unit), *cert. denied*, 121 S. Ct. 1082 (2001); United States v. Nabors, 45 F.3d 238, 240 (8th Cir. 1995) (enterprise must have a common or shared purpose, some continuity of structure and personnel, and an ascertainable structure distinct from that inherent in a pattern of racketeering), *cert. denied*, 525 U.S. 1032 (1998); Richmond v. Nationwide Cassel, L.P., 52 F.3d 640, 645 (7th Cir. 1995) (a RICO enterprise has "an ongoing 'structure' of persons associated through time, joined in purpose, and organized in a manner amenable to hierarchical or consensual decision-making") (quoting Jennings v. Emry, 910 F.2d 1434 1440 (7th Cir. 1990); Martinez v. Martinez, 207 F. Supp. 2d 1303, 1306 (D.N.M. 2002), *aff'd in part, vacated in part on other grounds*, 2003 WL 1904807 (10th Cir. 2003) (unpublished, citation limited); Broad, Vogt & Conant, Inc. v. Alsthom Automation, Inc., 200 F. Supp. 2d 756, 759–61 (E.D. Mich. 2002) (allegations of strings of entities and activities did not fulfill organizational requirement for association in fact enterprise); Singh v. Parnes, 199 F. Supp. 2d 152, 163 (S.D.N.Y. 2002) (no RICO claim where evidence only showed defendants carried on their own affairs as opposed to those of an unlawful enterprise); Walsh v. America's Tele-Network Corp., 195 F. Supp. 2d 840 (E.D. Tex. 2002) (granting motion to dismiss); Purdie v. Ace Cash Express, Inc., 2002 WL 31730967, at *4, *5 (N.D. Tex. Oct. 29 (2002) (must show enterprise existed for purpose other than simply to commit predicate acts), *vacated on other grounds*, 2003 WL 21447854 (N.D. Tex. June 13, 2003) (vacating prior order due to settlement); Manhattan Telecomms. Corp. v. DialAmerica Mktg., 156 F. Supp. 2d 376, 381–82 (S.D.N.Y. 2001) (RICO enterprise must have structural continuity that incorporates a mechanism for directing the group's affairs on a continuing basis); Emcore Corp. v. PricewaterhouseCoopers L.L.P., 102 F. Supp. 2d 237 (D.N.J. 2000). *But see* Pavlov v. Bank of New York Co., 2002 WL 63576 (2d Cir. Jan. 14, 2002) (unpublished, citation limited) (enterprise sufficiently alleged; continuity need not extend beyond acts forming pattern), *vacating and remanding* 135 F. Supp. 2d 426 (S.D.N.Y. 2001).

84 *See, e.g.*, VanDenBroeck v. CommonPoint Mortg. Co., 210 F.3d 696, 700 (6th Cir. 2000); Simon v. Value Behavioral Health, Inc., 208 F.3d 1073, 1083 (9th Cir. 2000), *cert. denied*, 531 U.S. 1104 (2001) (allegations that merely show collaboration or collective activity will not support enterprise element); Chang v. Chen, 80 F.3d 1293, 1295 (9th Cir. 1996) (dismissing complaint that did not allege a "system of authority" among the members of the association in fact); Crowe v. Henry, 43 F.3d 198, 205 (5th Cir. 1995) (association in fact enterprise must have an existence separate and apart from the pattern of racketeering, must be an ongoing organization, and have members that function as a continuing unit as shown by a hierarchical or consensual decision making structure); Landry v. Air Line Pilots Ass'n Int'l AFL-CIO, 901 F.2d 404 (5th Cir. 1990), *cert. denied*, 498 U.S. 895 (1991); State Farm Mut. Auto Ins. Co. v. Giventer, 212 F. Supp. 2d 639, 650 (N.D. Tex. 2002); Wagh v. Metris Direct, Inc., 2002 U.S. Dist. LEXIS 2905, at *6 (N.D. Cal. Feb. 20, 2002), *aff'd*, 348 F.3d 1102 (9th Cir. 2003); *In re* Mastercard Int'l Inc., 132 F. Supp. 2d 468, 484–85 (E.D. La. 2001) (enterprise must have an existence separate from the pattern itself; test is whether enterprise would continue if pattern of racketeering ceased), *aff'd*, 313 F.3d 257 (5th Cir. 2003).

85 *See, e.g.,* Majchrowski v. Norwest Mortg., Inc. 6 F. Supp. 2d 946, 954 (N.D. Ill. 1998) (plaintiff met characteristic in case alleging that mortgage service company, its parent, and its parent's parent formed an enterprise that the mortgage company used to charge improper fees to borrowers).

86 VanDenBroeck v. CommonPoint Mortg. Co., 210 F.3d 696, 700 (6th Cir. 2000).

87 United States v. Masters, 924 F.2d 1362, 1366 (7th Cir. 1991) ("informal consortium" of a law firm, two police departments, an attorney, and two law enforcement officers could fulfill enterprise element). *See also* U.S. v. Connolly, 341 F.3d 16, 25–26 (1st Cir. 2003) (enterprise must be an " 'ongoing organization' " but need not have a former or " 'ascertainable structure' ") (quoting United States v. Patrick, 248 F.3d 11, 19 (1st Cir. 2001)); VanDenBroeck v. CommonPoint Mortg. Co., 210 F.3d 696, 699 (6th Cir. 2000) (relationship between lender and its secondary lenders "too unstable and fluid an entity" to fulfill enterprise element, affirming dismissal of plaintiffs' claim); Wiwa v. Royal Dutch Petroleum Co., 2002 WL 319887, at *23 (S.D.N.Y. Feb. 28, 2002) (denying motion to dismiss where plaintiff alleged defendants attended meetings and coordinated activities); Eva v. Midwest Nat'l Mortg. Banc, Inc., 143 F. Supp. 2d 862 (N.D. Ohio 2001) (holding that plaintiff properly alleged an enterprise comprising banks and individual defendants by alleging activity showing ongoing, coordinated behavior among the members in a scheme to charge excessive fees and interest rates on loans).

an association in fact enterprise.[88] A plaintiff can use evidence of acts other than predicate offenses to demonstrate the decision-making framework of the association in fact.[89] Furthermore, the plaintiff need not prove that the members' whole purpose in organizing together was to engage in *prohibited* conduct, so long as the members intended to engage together in *some* form of conduct.[90]

To satisfy the second characteristic the plaintiff must show that the association's associates functioned as a "continuing unit," identifiable over a period of time.[91] Such continuity can be shown from a pre-existing corporate relationship, such as among a corporation and its parent or subsidiaries.[92] Accordingly, legitimate associations in fact may serve as enterprises.

As for the third characteristic, although the *association* must exist separate from the pattern of racketeering activity in order to keep the two elements of "enterprise" and "pattern" from collapsing into one, the plaintiff should not have to show that the enterprise had any *purposes* or *goals* (as opposed to structures) separate from the pattern of racketeering activity.[93] In other words, the whole *raison d'etre* for the enterprise can be the goal sought to be achieved by the pattern of racketeering activity. In analyzing whether the enterprise is separate and apart from the racketeering, the Eighth Circuit asks whether the "the enterprise would still exist were the predicate acts removed from the equation."[94] A more conservative approach toward the third characteristic harkens back to the image of a Mafia crime family, looking for evidence that a group engaged in a diverse number of predicate acts or had an organizational system of authority beyond what was purely necessary to commit the predicate acts.[95] However, that analogy can ease the structural characteristic; the Seventh Circuit has noted that criminal gangs "have a less formal, a less reticulated and differentiated structure" than do formal enterprises,[96]

---

88 *See, e.g.*, VanDenBroeck v. CommonPoint Mortg. Co., 210 F.3d 696, 700 (6th Cir. 2000) (that mortgage lender had business relationship with secondary lenders to whom it sold loans did not establish an association in fact enterprise); Wagh v. Metris Direct, Inc., 2002 U.S. Dist. LEXIS 2905, at *8 (N.D. Cal. Feb. 20, 2002) (finding that what were characterized as "normal credit card transaction[s]" among the members of the enterprise fell short of establishing an association in fact), *aff'd*, 348 F.3d 1102 (9th Cir. 2003); Manhattan Telecomms. Corp. v. DialAmerica Mktg., 156 F. Supp. 2d 376, 382 (S.D.N.Y. 2001) (rejecting enterprise made up of vendor and its customers where no evidence that they were connected in any manner beyond ordinary business relationship); *In re* Mastercard Int'l Inc., 132 F. Supp. 2d 468 (E.D. La. 2001), *aff'd*, 313 F.3d 257 (5th Cir. 2003) (contractual arrangements among credit card companies, their issuing banks, and on-line casinos demonstrated nothing more than ordinary business relationships); 800537 Ont., Inc. v. Auto Enters., 113 F. Supp. 2d 1116 (E.D. Mich. 2000); Jubelirer v. MasterCard Int'l, Inc., 68 F. Supp. 2d 1049, 1053 (W.D. Wis. 1999); Williams v. Ford Motor Co., 11 F. Supp. 2d 983, 986 (N.D. Ill. 1998) (in suit alleging dealer and Ford misrepresented extended service warranty, mere allegation of association in fact of Ford and its affiliated dealers and servicers did not sufficiently fulfill requirements of structure, continuity, and common course of conduct to be an enterprise).

89 U.S. v. Connolly, 341 F.3d 16, 26 (1st Cir. 2003) (testimony of several payments made to FBI agent that were not part of the alleged predicate acts supported jury's finding that agent had participated in an ongoing association in fact).

90 Richmond v. Nationwide Cassel L.P. 52 F.3d 640, 644 (7th Cir. 1995). *See also In re* Pharmaceutical Indus. Average Wholesale Price Litig., 263 F. Supp. 2d 172, 184 (D. Mass. 2003) (mere awareness by participants in fraudulent scheme that there were others in parallel schemes did not sufficiently establish an association in fact); *In re* Lupron Mktg. & Sales Practices Litig., 295 F. Supp. 2d 148, 173–74 (D. Mass. 2001) (holding that plaintiff failed to show that doctors made up an association in fact where, though they may have individually benefited from defendants' fraudulent drug scheme, there was no evidence that they "were associated together in any meaningful sense, or were even aware of one another's existence as participants in a scheme to defraud"; the court noted that such "hub-and-spoke" enterprises rarely satisfy the enterprise requirement); Manhattan Telecomms. Corp. v. DialAmerica Mktg., 156 F. Supp. 2d 376, 382 (S.D.N.Y. 2001) (dismissing complaint on grounds that plaintiff failed to demonstrate that members of the enterprise functioned as a continuing unit).

91 Burdett v. Miller, 957 F.3d 1375, 1379 (7th Cir. 1992). *See also* Landry v. Air Line Pilots Ass'n Int'l AFL-CIO, 901 F.2d 404, 433 (5th Cir. 1990) (no continuing unit where the alleged enterprise "briefly flourished and faded"), *cert. denied*, 498 U.S. 895 (1991).

92 *See, e.g.*, Majchrowski v. Norwest Mortg., Inc. 6 F. Supp. 2d 946, 954 (N.D. Ill. 1998) (plaintiff met characteristic in case alleging that mortgage service company, its parent, and its parent's parent formed an enterprise that the mortgage company used to charge improper fees to borrowers).

93 United States v. Phillips, 239 F.3d 829, 844 (7th Cir. 2001).

94 Handeen v. Lemaire, 112 F.3d 1339, 1351–52 (8th Cir. 1997) (enterprise must have a common or shared purpose, continuity of personnel, and an ascertainable structure distinct from the pattern of racketeering activity). *See also* Williams Elec. Games, Inc. v. Garrity, 366 F.3d 569, 579 (7th Cir. 2004) (rejecting enterprise comprising briber and the corporation he bribed); Asa-Brandt, Inc. v. ADM Investor Servs., Inc., 344 F.3d 738, 752–753 (8th Cir. 2003) (citing *Handeen* in affirming summary judgment for defendants); Harwood v. Int'l Estate Planners, 33 Fed. Appx. 903, 905 (9th Cir. 2002); Crowe v. Henry, 43 F.3d 198, 205 (5th Cir. 1995) (finding enterprise existed beyond the alleged predicate acts); Landry v. Airline Pilots Assoc., 901 F.2d 404 (5th Cir. 1990) (when only purpose is to commit predicate acts, no separate enterprise).

95 Gunderson v. ADM Investor Servs., Inc., 2001 U.S. Dist. LEXIS 3383, at *58, *59 (N.D. Iowa Feb. 13, 2001). *See also* Ochoa v. Housing Auth. of City of Los Angeles, 47 Fed. Appx. 484, 486 (9th Cir. 2002) (dismissing claim where plaintiffs did not allege an organization with a structure outside of that inherent in the alleged predicate acts); State Farm Mut. Auto Ins. Co. v. Giventer, 212 F. Supp. 2d 639, 650 (N.D. Tex. 2002) (no enterprise where nothing held constituent members together beyond the predicate acts themselves).

96 Burdett v. Miller, 957 F.2d 1375, 1379 (7th Cir. 1992) (rejecting argument of defendants, investment advisors to the plaintiff, that though they may have conspired to defraud the plaintiff they did not form an enterprise); *see also* Carnegie v. Household Intl, Inc., 220 F.R.D. 542, 546 (N.D. Ill. 2004) (in case by taxpayer against tax service based on alleged fraud in refund anticipation loans, suggesting that the plaintiff has a lighter burden in

concluding that while "[t]here must be some structure . . . there need not be much." In any event, the enterprise need not have had an economic goal that was separate from the commission of the racketeering acts.[97]

The evidence of illegal activity should be able to serve dual, albeit separate, functions: pattern and enterprise.[98] Enterprise is proved by evidence that the participants functioned as a continuing unit, while pattern is proved by evidence of the requisite number of acts of racketeering committed by the participants in the enterprise.[99] The Supreme Court has acknowledged that "the proof used to establish these separate elements may in particular cases coalesce."[100] Accordingly, a plaintiff should not have to offer different evidence to meet the element of pattern. Nonetheless, because a plaintiff must show that the organization's structure existed separate from the pattern, plaintiffs should carefully distinguish the function of evidence offered to show the purpose of the enterprise's existence from the function of that same evidence offered to show the racketeering activity itself.[101]

9.2.3.2.3 Alleging an enterprise distinct from the defendant for section 1962(c) claims

Subsection 1962(c) prohibits one "employed by or associated with" an enterprise from "[conducting or participating] . . . in the conduct of such enterprise's affairs" in a defined manner. The other three subsections of 1962 do not have comparable language, and this has led the Supreme Court to construe subsection (c) as imposing a "distinctness" requirement[102] that subsections (a) and (b) and (d) do not necessarily have.[103] The theory is that the language of subsection 1962(c) clearly envisions a person separate and apart from the subject enterprise, a distinction between the two. Only the Eleventh Circuit has held that a corporate defendant, in association with itself, can be both person and enterprise under section 1962(c).[104] Thus, ordinarily in a section 1962(c) case one can not simply allege that a defendant conducted the defendant's own affairs through a pattern of racketeering activity or collection of an unlawful debt, but rather must allege that the defendant conducted someone *else's* affairs that way.[105]

The distinctness requirement between enterprise and person in a section 1962(c) case does not lack case law, but it does lack consistent interpretation. Among the many issues are: whether an enterprise in which the defendant person is one member is sufficiently distinct from the defendant; whether an enterprise that consists of nothing but defendant persons is sufficiently distinct; whether an enterprise that consists of a defendant along with that defendant's employees or agents is sufficiently distinct; and whether an enterprise that consists of a defendant's subsidiary or parent is sufficiently distinct.

The issue arises often because the most attractive defendant may well be a corporation that has been active in the commission of the unlawful activity within a sphere in which the only obvious characters to fill out an association in fact are in fact related in some way to that corporation.

At the strictest interpretation of the distinctness requirement, some early cases appeared to construe *any* overlap between the defendant and the enterprise as failing the requirement. Thus, the Fifth Circuit held that an alleged enterprise consisting of the plaintiff and the defendant person did not satisfy the distinctness requirement.[106] However, the Fifth Circuit later stepped back from such a constrained interpretation of subsection 1962(c) to hold that "[a]lthough a defendant may not be both a person and an enterprise, a

---

establishing an enterprise at the pleading stage of the litigation).

97 *In re* Sumitomo Copper Litig., 104 F. Supp. 2d 314 (S.D.N.Y. 2000); Moss v. Morgan Stanley, 719 F.2d 5, 22 (2d Cir. 1983).

98 *In re* Sumitomo Copper Litig., 104 F. Supp. 2d 314, 318 (S.D.N.Y. 2000) (the same evidence may be offered to prove both the enterprise and the pattern of racketeering, so long as the plaintiff shows an ascertainable structure that is more than the sum of the predicate acts); Schmidt v. Fleet Bank, 16 F. Supp. 2d 340, 349 n.5 (S.D.N.Y. 1998). *See also* U.S. v. Ganim, 225 F. Supp. 2d 145, 161 (D. Conn. 2002) (rejecting argument that proof of enterprise must be distinct from proof of pattern).

99 United States v. Turkette, 452 U.S. 576, 583 (1981).

100 *Id. See also* United States v. Phillips, 239 F.3d 829, 844 (7th Cir. 2001); United States v. Rogers, 89 F.3d 1326, 1337 (7th Cir. 1997) ("it would be nonsensical to require proof that an enterprise had purposes or goals separate and apart from the pattern of racketeering activity"; finding evidence sufficient); Moss v. Morgan Stanley, 719 F.2d 5, 22 (2d Cir. 1983) (evidence offered to prove racketeering acts and that offered to prove the existence of an enterprise will not always be distinct).

101 *Cf.* Wagh v. Metris Direct, Inc., 363 F.3d 821, 831 (9th Cir. 2003) (dismissing complaint where plaintiff did not allege that defendants "established a system of making decisions in furtherance of their alleged criminal activities, independent from their respective regular business practices," practices such as routine credit card transactions), *cert. denied*, 124 S. Ct. 2176 (2004).

102 Cedric Kushner Promotions Ltd. v. King, 533 U.S. 158, 161, 121 S. Ct. 2087, 2090, 150 L. Ed. 2d 198 (2001); Switzer v. Coan, 261 F.3d 985, 992 (10th Cir. 2000) (affirming dismissal of claim); Bessette v. Arco Fin. Servs., Inc., 230 F.3d 439, 449 (1st Cir. 2000); Begala v. PNC Bank, Ohio, N.A., 214 F.3d 776, 781 (6th Cir. 2000), *cert. denied*, 531 U.S. 1145 (2001); Jaguar Cars, Inc. v. Royal Oaks Motor Car Co., 46 F.3d 258, 268 (3d Cir. 1995); Crowe v. Henry, 43 F.3d 198, 205, 206 (5th Cir. 1995); Puckett v. Tennessee Eastman Co., 889 F.2d 1481, 1489 (6th Cir. 1989).

103 *See* § 9.2.3.2.3, *infra. But see* Kredietbank, N.V. v. Joyce Morris, Inc., 1986 WL 5926, at *5 (D.N.J. Jan. 9, 1986), *aff'd*, 808 F.2d 1516 (3d Cir. 1986) ("person" and "enterprise" must be distinct under each subsection of § 1962).

104 United States v. Hartley, 678 F.2d 961, 988, 989 (11th Cir. 1982), *cert. denied*, 459 U.S. 1183 (1983), *abrogated by* U.S. v. Goldin Indus., Inc., 219 F.3d 1268, 1271 (11th Cir. 2000).

105 *See* Reves v. Ernst & Young, 507 U.S. 170, 113 S. Ct. 1163, 122 L. Ed. 2d 525 (1993).

106 Crowe v. Henry, 43 F.3d 198, 206 (5th Cir. 1995).

defendant may be both a person and a *part* of an enterprise. In such a case, the individual defendant is distinct from the organizational entity."[107] Thus, if the RICO persons have a different role and function as defendants than they serve in the enterprise, a court may find that they were sufficiently separate from the enterprise to satisfy distinctness.[108] The Third Circuit has upheld distinctness even where the defendants completely overlapped with the alleged members of the association in fact enterprise.[109]

The Supreme Court held in *Cedric Kushner Promotions Ltd. v. King*[110] that the distinctness requirement is satisfied where the person and the corporation are distinctly different legal entities, even though they may be connected. The decision respects legal formalities, holding that for purposes of subsection 1962(c), an employee person is distinct from a corporation enterprise notwithstanding that the employee is the president and sole shareholder of the corporation.[111] However, the Supreme Court expressly chose not to decide the merits of those cases where the defendant person was also a member of an association in fact enterprise along with other parties related to that person;[112] decisions addressing these sorts of enterprises are discussed below. The decision may signal, however, that a legal distinction will satisfy the requirement of a distinction between the person and the enterprise, notwithstanding some substantive identification between those serving the roles.[113]

Defendant-employees enterprise. Some courts appear to hold that the legal distinction between a corporation and its employees is sufficient to meet the distinctness requirement, so long as the corporation's actions can be shown to be separate from those of its agents.[114] Showing that the two had different goals for their actions may be one way to demonstrate this separation. However, in general an enterprise that consists of a defendant corporation along with its employees may not be sufficiently distinct from the defendant itself, at least where the employees were acting within the scope of their employment.[115] Courts reason that a

---

107 St. Paul Mercury Ins. Co. v. Williamson, 224 F.3d 425, 447 (5th Cir. 2000) (emphasis added) (reversing summary judgment in favor of three individual defendants who were also alleged to be the RICO enterprise); *see also In re* Lupron Mktg. & Sales Practices Litig., 295 F. Supp. 2d 148, 173 (D. Mass. 2001) ("[t]he basic idea is that while one basketball player does not constitute a team, an association of five players does, without each losing his identity as a distinct person.").

108 *Id.*; Riverwoods Chappaqua Corp. v. Marine Midland Bank, 30 F.3d 339, 344 (2d Cir. 1994) ("a section 1962(c) claim may be sustained where there is only partial overlap between the RICO person and the RICO enterprise, and . . . a defendant may be a RICO 'person' and one of a number of members of the RICO 'enterprise' "); Charleswell v. Chase Manhattan Bank, N.A., 308 F. Supp. 2d 545, 576 (D. V.I. 2004) (entity can be both the RICO person and part of the RICO enterprise); Sony Music Entertainment Inc. v. Robison, 2002 WL 272406, at *5 (S.D.N.Y. Feb. 26, 2002) (defendant could be RICO person notwithstanding that it was also a part owner of one member of the enterprise), *reconsideration granted*, 2002 WL 550967 (S.D.N.Y. Apr. 11, 2002); *In re* Mastercard Int'l Inc., 132 F. Supp. 2d 468 (E.D. La. 2001), *aff'd*, 313 F.3d 257 (5th Cir. 2003) (finding distinctness satisfied where defendant bank and charge card company were alleged to be both the RICO defendants and part of an association in fact enterprise along with casinos that contracted for the charge card services). *But see* Durant v. ServiceMaster Co., 159 F. Supp. 2d 977 (E.D. Mich. 2001) (dismissing RICO claim that alleged enterprise consisting solely of the three named defendants); Manhattan Telecomms. Corp. v. DialAmerica Mktg., 156 F. Supp. 2d 376, 382 (S.D.N.Y. 2001) (enterprise may not consist solely of the named defendants).

109 *See, e.g.*, Shearin v. E.F. Hutton Group, Inc., 885 F.2d 1162, 1165, 1166 (3d Cir. 1989) (three corporate defendants could form a valid association in fact enterprise); Perlberger v. Perlberger, 1999 U.S. Dist. LEXIS 1407, at *8 (E.D. Pa. Feb 12, 1999) (denying defendants' motion for summary judgment where they were alleged to comprise an association in fact enterprise; "[a]lthough the enterprise is comprised of the named Defendants, it is separate and distinct from its constituent members"), *aff'd without op.*, 262 F.3d 404 (3d Cir. 2001).

110 533 U.S. 158, 121 S. Ct. 2087, 150 L. Ed. 2d 198 (2001).

111 533 U.S. at 163–65.

112 *Id.* (calling it "less natural to speak of a corporation as 'employed by' or 'associated with' [such an] oddly constructed entity").

113 *See, e.g.*, Ad-X Int'l., Inc. v. Kolbjornsen, 97 Fed. Appx. 263, 266-267 (10th Cir. 2004) (debtor is distinct from debtor's bankruptcy estate for purposes of RICO, citing *Cedric Kushner*); Chen v. Mayflower Transit, Inc., 315 F. Supp. 2d 886, 903 (N.D. Ill. 2004) (defendant could be sufficiently distinct from enterprise comprising defendant and affiliates); Craford & Sons, Ltd. Profit Sharing Plan v. Besser, 216 F.R.D. 228, 237 (E.D.N.Y. 2003) (shareholder and officer of corporation were sufficiently distinct from corporation itself); G-I Holdings, Inc. v. Baron & Budd, 238 F. Supp. 2d 521 (S.D.N.Y. 2002) (name partners of law firm were separate and distinct entities from firm, citing *Cedric Kushner*); Wilson v. De Angelis, 156 F. Supp. 2d 1335, 1338 (S.D. Fla. 2001) (relying on *Cedric Kushner* to hold that the legal distinction between a corporation and its officer suffices to establish RICO distinctness); Eva v. Midwest Nat'l Mortgage Banc, Inc., 143 F. Supp. 2d 862, 871 (N.D. Ohio 2001) (allowing enterprise of association in fact comprising all the named defendants); *see also* Fleischhauer v. Feltner, 879 F.2d 1290, 1297 (6th Cir. 1989) (earlier case allowing plaintiff to plead as enterprise a corporation whose stock was wholly owned by the named person), *cert. denied*, 493 U.S. 1074 (1990). *But see* Wagh v. Metris Direct, Inc., 2002 U.S. Dist. LEXIS 2905, at *6 (N.D. Cal. Feb. 20, 2002) (that association members are entities legally distinct from the defendant person does not alone satisfy the distinctness requirement; case does not acknowledge *Cedric Kushner*), *aff'd*, 2003 WL 22519429 (9th Cir. Nov. 7, 2003).

114 *See, e.g.*, Jaguar Cars, Inc. v. Royal Oaks Motor Car Co., 46 F.3d 258, 268 (3d Cir. 1995) ("[a] corporation is an entity legally distinct from its officers or employees, which satisfies the 'enterprise' definition of [RICO]"); Emcore Corp. v. PricewaterhouseCoopers L.L.P., 102 F. Supp. 2d 237, 257 (D.N.J. 2000) (defendant partners were distinct from association in fact enterprise comprising partners and the partnership, however, partners were not distinct from enterprise consisting of nothing but the partnership).

115 Anatian v. Coutts Bank (Switz.) Ltd., 193 F.3d 85 (2d Cir. 1999), *cert. denied*, 528 U.S. 1188 (2000); Bachman v. Bear, Stearns & Co., 178 F.3d 930, 932 (7th Cir. 1999); Riverwoods

corporation must always act through its employees and agents, and accordingly any corporate act will be accomplished through an association of the employees or subsidiaries and their corporation.[116] Nonetheless, a RICO plaintiff may be able to satisfy the distinctness requirement by showing that the corporation's agents included in the enterprise took separate roles in the racketeering activities, such as by showing the agents conducted racketeering acts in their private capacity and to their own benefit, as opposed to within the scope of their employment.[117]

Defendant-employer enterprise. Where employees are the named defendants and the employing corporation is the alleged enterprise, some courts find no distinctness problem,[118] while others require the plaintiff to show that the employees were somehow acting outside the scope of their authority while engaging in the predicate acts in order to establish that they were distinct from the enterprise they were conducting.[119]

Defendant-parent corporation enterprise. Many courts will also not find a parent corporation to be a distinct enterprise from subsidiary defendants, at least where the plaintiff fails to allege that the enterprise included some person or entity operating outside of the defendant's normal scope of business.[120] However, other courts have ruled that a subsidiary can be sufficiently distinct from a parent to satisfy the requirement, where the parent is alleged to be the enterprise.[121] The subsidiary-as-defendant scenario has been

---

Chappaqua Corp. v. Marine Midland Bank, 30 F.3d 339, 344 (2d Cir. 1994) ("plain language" of subsection 1962(c) requires that the defendant be distinct from the enterprise); Brittingham v. Mobil Corp., 943 F.2d 297, 300, 301 (3d Cir. 1991) (distinctness not met where enterprise alleged to consist of defendant corporation and its subsidiary together with advertising agencies); Eva v. Midwest Nat'l Mortgage Banc, Inc., 143 F. Supp. 2d 862, 874 (N.D. Ohio 2001) (individual defendants who are employees or agents of enterprise are too identified with it to be considered distinct).

116 Brittingham v. Mobil Corp., 943 F.2d 297, 300 (3d Cir. 1991), *criticized by* Emcore Corp. v. PricewaterhouseCoopers L.L.P., 102 F. Supp. 2d 237, 261 (D.N.J. 2000) ("the conception that a corporation must always act through its agents has become outdated").

117 Emcore Corp. v. PricewaterhouseCoopers L.L.P., 102 F. Supp. 2d 237, 258 (D.N.J. 2000).

118 *See, e.g.*, United States v. Najjar, 300 F.3d 466, 485 (4th Cir. 2002) (so long as employee is a distinct legal entity, employee is sufficiently distinct from corporation); Oklahoma *ex rel.* AG v. Stifel, Nicolaus & Co., 1998 U.S. App. LEXIS 18291 (10th Cir. Aug. 7, 1998); Khurana v. Innovative Health Care Sys., Inc., 130 F.3d 143, 155 (5th Cir. 1997), *vacated as moot sub nom.* Teel v. Khurana, 525 U.S. 979 (1998); Eva v. Midwest Nat'l Mortgage Banc, Inc., 143 F. Supp. 2d 862 (N.D. Ohio 2001) (distinctness requirement satisfied where alleged enterprise consisted of more than the defendant corporation associated with individual defendant employees, mere affiliation with third-party corporation completing the enterprise did not destroy distinctness).

119 *See, e.g.*, George Lussier Enters., Inc. v. Subaru of New England, Inc., 2002 WL 1349523, at *2 (D.N.H. June 3, 2002) (executive vice president and general manager could be RICO person conducting employer-enterprise); Allen v. New World Coffee, Inc., 2001 U.S. Dist. LEXIS 3269, at *27 (S.D.N.Y. Mar. 27, 2001) (complaint that alleged that employee defendants associated together in the course of their employment and on behalf of the corporation was insufficient to establish the corporation as a distinct enterprise); Emcore Corp. v. PricewaterhouseCoopers L.L.P., 102 F. Supp. 2d 237, 261 (D.N.J. 2000) (defendant partners were not distinct from enterprise consisting of nothing but partnership). *See also* Kovian v. Fulton County Nat'l Bank & Trust Co., 100 F. Supp. 2d 129 (N.D.N.Y. 2000) (dismissing claim against defendant bank and two of its employees where enterprise alleged to be association in fact among the three on grounds that if employees acted outside of the scope of their employment, than claim against defendant bank failed).

120 *See, e.g.*, Fogie v. THORN Ams., Inc., 190 F.3d 889, 897, 898 (8th Cir. 1999) (subsidiary not liable for conducting an enterprise comprising solely of the parent of the subsidiary and related businesses; however, court suggests that if sufficient evidence of distinction beyond the mere fact of legal entities were offered, liability might arise); Brannon v. Boatmen's First Nat'l Bank, 153 F.3d 1144, 1149 (10th Cir. 1998) (bank's holding company was not a distinct enterprise plaintiff showed nothing more than ordinary parent-subsidiary relationship); Discon, Inc. v. NYNEX Corp., 93 F.3d 1055, 1064 (2d Cir. 1996), *rev'd on other grounds*, 525 U.S. 128 (1998) (distinctness requirement not satisfied where NYNEX Group was alleged to be the RICO enterprise and its subsidiaries were named the defendants where they "were acting within the scope of a single corporate structure, guided by a single corporate consciousness"); NCNB Nat'l Bank v. Tiller, 814 F.2d 931, 936 (4th Cir. 1987) (defendant bank was not distinct from its holding company, the alleged enterprise); *overruled on other grounds*, Busby v. Crown Supply, Inc., 896 F.2d 833 (4th Cir. 1990); Atkinson v. Anadarko Bank & Trust Co., 808 F.2d 438, 441 (5th Cir.), *cert. denied*, 483 U.S. 1032 (1987) (no evidence that defendant bank was distinct from the alleged enterprise, its holding company); Panix Promotions v. Lewis, 2002 U.S. Dist. LEXIS 784, at *19 (S.D.N.Y. Jan 15, 2002) (a division or subsidiary of an alleged enterprise may not serve as the RICO "person"); Dow Chem. Co. v. Exxon Corp., 30 F. Supp. 2d 673, 700, 701 (D. Del. 1998); Metcalf v. Painewebber Inc., 886 F. Supp. 503, 513 (W.D. Pa. 1995) (defendant corporation was not distinct from enterprise alleged to comprise corporation with its subsidiaries and agents where all the members of the alleged enterprise were acting in furtherance of the defendant's business), *aff'd without op.*, 79 F.3d 1138 (3d Cir. 1996) (table); Nebraska Sec. Bank v. Dain Bodsworth, Inc., 838 F. Supp. 1362, 1369 (D. Neb. 1993) (neither a parent nor its wholly owned subsidiary can constitute a § 1962(c) enterprise if the other is named as the defendant person). *See also* Bodam v. GTE Corp, 197 F. Supp. 2d 1225 (C.D. Cal. 2002) (units within enterprise were not sufficiently distinct to be RICO person); Pavlov v. Bank of N.Y. Co., 135 F. Supp. 2d 426, *vacated and remanded on other grounds*, 2002 WL 63576 (2d Cir. Jan. 14, 2002) (unpublished, citation limited) (enterprise sufficiently alleged; continuity need not extend beyond acts forming pattern) (division of defendant corporation is not a distinct enterprise).

121 *See, e.g.*, Begala v. PNC Bank, Ohio, N.A., 214 F.3d 776, 781 (6th Cir. 2000) (a corporation may not be liable under subsection 1962(c) for participating in the affairs of an enterprise that consists only of its own subdivisions, agents or members), *cert. denied*, 531 U.S. 1145 (2001); Dirt Hogs, Inc. v. Natural Gas Pipeline Co., 2000 U.S. App. LEXIS 6463, at *9, *10 (10th Cir. Apr. 10, 2000); Haroco v. Am. Nat'l Bank, 747 F.2d 384, 402

distinguished from that of parent-as-defendant on the grounds that while ordinarily a subsidiary is the agent of its parent, the reverse is not true.[122] In this framework, courts appear to look for an irregular relationship, something beyond the ordinary corporate activities of a corporation acting through its employees or a parent controlling the affairs of its subsidiary. Thus, in the Seventh Circuit one may be able to fulfill the distinctness requirement by showing that the parent corporation "somehow made it easier to commit or conceal the fraud of which the plaintiff complains."[123] The expressed fear of some courts, that allowing a claim against a subsidiary conducting the affairs of its parent corporation will allow unintended RICO liability,[124] is constrained by subsection 1962(c)'s separate requirement that the defendant must have conducted or participated in the conduct of the enterprise, and not just its own affairs.[125] To read distinctness expansively does not correspondingly expand RICO liability for corporations, as a plaintiff must still show that the subsidiary corporation itself engaged in racketeering activity.

Defendant-subsidiary enterprise. Where the parent corporation serves the role of defendant and one or more of its subsidiaries as the enterprise, courts are also reluctant to find a distinct enterprise without some evidence that the subsidiary acted outside an ordinary parent/subsidiary relationship,[126] unless additional parties had roles in the enterprise. Correspondingly, a principal and its agent who do not have a corporate relationship may be separate persons in a RICO enterprise where the agent is not acting in the scope of the agency relationship.[127]

(7th Cir. 1984) (§ 1962(c) "requires only some separate and distinct existence for the person and the enterprise, and a subsidiary is certainly a legal entity distinct from its parent"), *aff'd on other grounds*, 473 U.S. 606 (1985); Majchrowski v. Norwest Mort., 6 F. Supp. 2d 946, 956 (N.D. Ill. 1998) (*Haroco* dictates that a subsidiary is presumptively distinct from its parent in a case where a subsidiary is cast as the defendant, and its parent as the enterprise, therefore manufacturer's dealer alleged to have fraudulently sold an extended service contract to the plaintiff was distinct from enterprise comprising manufacturer and its dealers).

122 Majchrowski v. Norwest Mort., 6 F. Supp. 2d 946, 956. (N.D. Ill. 1998).

123 Emery v. Am. Gen. Fin., Inc., 134 F.3d 1321, 1324 (7th Cir. 1998), *cert. denied*, 525 U.S. 818 (1998); Fitzgerald v. Chrysler Corp., 116 F.3d 225, 227 (7th Cir. 1997). The author of these two decisions, Chief Judge Posner, describes the appropriate analysis as the "family resemblance" test to "determine how close to the prototype the case before the court is." *Fitzgerald*, 116 F.3d at 227. As examples of such a prototype he cited:

> [O]ne in which a person bent on criminal activity seizes control of a previously legitimate firm and uses the firm's resources, contacts, facilities, and appearance of legitimacy to perpetrate more, and less easily discovered, criminal acts than he could do in his own person, that is, without channeling his criminal activities through the enterprise that he has taken over.

Id. As another example, a criminal might seize control over a subsidiary of a corporation and pervert the subsidiary into a criminal enterprise that in turn wrests control over the parent corporation sufficient to use it to commit criminal acts. *Id.* In *Fitzgerald*, the Seventh Circuit rejected a claim against Chrysler corporation, as the person, where the enterprise was alleged to be Chrysler with its subsidiaries and dealers, because Chrysler had not established dealerships in order to perpetrate the fraud alleged by the plaintiff, that of failing to fulfill extended warranties. *Id.* at 228. *See also* Bessette v. Avco Fin. Servs., Inc., 230 F.3d 439, 449 (1st Cir. 2000) (applying test of whether parent's activities are sufficiently distinct from those of the subsidiary at the time the alleged RICO violations occurred to dismiss complaint); Brannon v. Boatmen's First Nat'l Bank, 153 F.3d 1144, 1147, 1148 (10th Cir. 1998); Majchrowski v. Norwest Mort., 6 F. Supp. 2d 946, 956 (N.D. Ill. 1998) (complaint satisfied distinctness where alleged that the parent enterprise has some part in masking the fraudulent scheme perpetrated by the subsidiary, that parent received the profits from the fraud and reported them on the parent's financial statement supported finding that subsidiary "integrally involved" the parent).

124 Brannon v. Boatmen's First Nat'l Bank, 153 F.3d 1144, 1147 (10th Cir. 1998); Bodtker v. Forest City Trading Group, 1999 U.S. Dist. LEXIS 15345, at *20 (D. Or. Sept. 9, 1999).

125 *See* § 9.2.3.7, *infra*. Indeed, some courts confuse the distinctness requirement with this separate element of RICO.

126 *See, e.g.*, Bucklew v. Hawkins, Ash, Baptie & Co., 329 F.3d 923, 934 (7th Cir. 2003) (affirming dismissal of complaint against parent and subsidiary); Brannon v. Boatmen's First Nat'l Bank, 153 F.3d 1144, 1148 (10th Cir. 1998); Emery v. Am. Gen. Fin., Inc., 134 F.3d 1321, 1324 (7th Cir. 1998) (no distinctness where defendant corporation was merely exercising power that is inherent in its ownership of wholly-owned subsidiaries), *cert. denied*, 525 U.S. 818 (1998); Khurana v. Innovative Health Care Sys., Inc., 130 F.3d 143, 155 (5th Cir. 1997); Fitzgerald v. Chrysler Corp., 116 F.3d 225, 227 (7th Cir. 1997); Compagnie de Reassurance d'Ile de France v. New England Reinsurance Corp., 57 F.3d 56, 92 (1st Cir. 1995) (distinctness not met where alleged enterprise, a subsidiary, took no actions independent of its defendant parent), *cert. denied*, 516 U.S. 1009 (1995); Lorenz v. CSX Corp., 1 F.3d 1406, 1412 (3d Cir. 1993) (subsidiary not a distinct enterprise when it "merely acts on behalf of, or to the benefit of, its parent"); Waddell & Reed Fin., Inc. v. Torchmark Corp., 2004 WL 1877744, *28 (D. Kan. Aug. 20, 2004) (subsidiary not distinct without allegation that parent corporation was able to more easily commit or conceal the fraud by using the subsidiary); Blue Cross & Blue Shield of N.J., Inc v. Philip Morris, Inc., 113 F. Supp. 2d 345, 368 (E.D.N.Y. 2000) (distinctness not met where enterprise consisted solely of defendant corporation's subsidiaries, where they and the corporation "operated within a generally unified corporate structure and were guided by a single corporate consciousness"). *But see* Fleischhauer v. Feltner, 879 F.2d 1290, 1297 (6th Cir. 1989) (that one of the individual defendants alleged to be part of the enterprise owned 100% of the corporate defendants alleged to be part of the same enterprise did not vitiate distinctness, corporations were separate legal entities), *cert. denied*, 493 U.S. 1027 (1990).

127 Wiwa v. Royal Dutch Petroleum Co., 2002 WL 319887, at *23 (S.D.N.Y. Feb. 28, 2002) (denying motion to dismiss); *see also* Chen v. Mayflower Transit, Inc., 315 F. Supp. 2d 886, 903 (N.D. Ill. 2004) (corporation and its affiliates).

9.2.3.2.4 Subsections 1962(a), (b), and (d) generally do not require a distinct enterprise

The issue of distinct entities generally arises only in claims brought under subsection 1962(c). Since subsections 1962(a) and 1962(b) do not refer to the liable "person" as being "employed by or associated with" an enterprise, no need for the distinction arises from their language.[128] Under subsection (a), most courts have accepted the argument that the liable "person" and the affected "enterprise" may be the same.[129] Subsection 1962(a) may be useful in consumer situations where a business invests the proceeds of mail fraud in its own operations,[130] for instance, or where a bank converts the contents of a customer's IRA for its own use, that is to pay off a defaulted loan of which it was guarantor.[131]

Under subsection (b), the "distinct" requirement has been the subject of conflicting judicial opinions.[132] With respect to subsection (d), at least one court has ruled that the defendant and the enterprise need not be distinct where the substantive provision subject to the conspiracy, subsection 1962(b), did not require such distinction.[133]

9.2.3.2.5 Strategies to find the corporation liable

The major implication for consumer attorneys of having to plead an enterprise distinct from the "person" being sued when alleging a violation of subsection 1962(c) is that the corporation involved in a scheme will often present itself as the obvious enterprise, and corporate employees or officers will be the apparent defendants. Unfortunately, the corporation may be the party with the deep pocket, and the individuals largely judgment proof.

There are a few ways to avoid this result. The corporation may be vicariously liable under principles of *respondeat superior*,[134] but several decisions have held that *respondeat*

---

128 *See* Bowman v. Western Auto Supply Co., 773 F. Supp. 174 (W.D. Mo. 1991) (§ 1962(a) and (b) do not require enterprise distinct from person), *rev'd on other grounds*, 985 F.2d 383 (8th Cir. 1993), *cert. denied*, 508 U.S. 957 (1993); Gervase v. Superior Ct., 37 Cal. Rptr. 875, 889 (Cal. App. 1995) (no other subsection requires distinction).

129 Busby v. Crown Supply, Inc., 896 F.2d 833 (4th Cir. 1990), *overruling* United States v. Computer Sciences Corp., 689 F.2d 1181 (4th Cir. 1982); Petro-Tech, Inc. v. Western Co., 824 F.2d 1349 (3d Cir. 1987); Schreiber Distributing Co. v. Serv-Well Furniture, 806 F.2d 1393 (9th Cir. 1986); Prodex, Inc. v. Legg Mason Wood Walker, Inc., 1987 U.S. Dist. LEXIS 866 (E.D. Pa. Feb. 5, 1987); Smith v. MCI Telecommunications Corp., 678 F. Supp. 823 (D. Kan. 1987); Welek v. Solomon, 650 F. Supp. 972 (E.D. Mo. 1987); *In re* Dow Co. "Sarabond" Prods. Liability Litigation, 660 F. Supp. 270 (D. Colo. 1987), *aff'd in part, rev'd in part on other grounds*, 875 F.2d 278 (10th Cir. 1989); Conan Properties, Inc. v. Mattel, 619 F. Supp. 1167, 1171 (S.D.N.Y. 1985); Gervase v. Superior Ct., 37 Cal. Rptr. 875, 889 (Cal. App. 1995). *But see* McEvoy Travel Bureau, Inc. v. Heritage Travel, Inc., 721 F. Supp. 15 (D. Mass. 1989), *aff'd on other grounds*, 904 F.2d 786 (1st Cir. 1990), *cert. denied*, 498 U.S. 992 (1990); Garbade v. Great Divide Mining & Milling Corp., 645 F. Supp. 808 (D. Colo. 1986), *aff'd*, 831 F.2d 212 (10th Cir. 1987).

130 Haroco, Inc. v. Am. Nat'l Bank & Trust Co., 747 F.2d 384, 401 (7th Cir. 1984), *aff'd per curiam*, 473 U.S. 606 (1985) ("under subsection (a), therefore, the liable person may be a corporation using the proceeds of a pattern of racketeering activity in its operations"). *See also* Gutierrez v. Givens, 1 F. Supp. 2d 1077 (S.D. Cal. 1998) (reasonable to infer from allegations that bank received beneficial income from alleged racketeering activities which was likely invested in the bank's operations in violation of § 1962(a)).

131 Masi v. Ford City Bank & Trust Co., 779 F.2d 397, 401, 402 (7th Cir. 1985).

132 Landry v. Air Line Pilots Ass'n Int'l AFL-CIO, 901 F.2d 404 (5th Cir. 1990), *cert. denied*, 498 U.S. 895 (1991) (two may be the same); Hillard v. Shell Western E & P, Inc., 836 F. Supp. 1365, 1374 (W.D. Mich. 1993), *rev'd on other grounds*, 149 F.3d 1183 (6th Cir.) (table), *cert. denied*, 525 U.S. 1048 (1998); Prodex, Inc. v. Legg Mason Wood Walker, Inc., 1987 U.S. Dist. LEXIS 866 (E.D. Pa. Feb. 5, 1987); Robinson v. City Colleges of Chicago, 656 F. Supp. 555, 560 (N.D. Ill. 1987); Medallion TV Enters. Inc. v. SelecTV of California, 627 F. Supp. 1290, 1294–95 (C.D. Cal. 1985) (distinction required), *aff'd*, 833 F.2d 1360 (9th Cir. 1987), *cert. denied*, 492 U.S. 917 (1989). *But see* Vietnam Veterans of Am. v. Guerdon Indus., 644 F. Supp. 951, 957 (D. Del. 1986) (distinct entities not required); Commonwealth of Pa. v. Perry Constr. Co., 617 F. Supp. 940, 943 (W.D. Pa. 1985).

133 Gordon v. Tyndall, 1987 U.S. Dist. LEXIS 13664, at *3 (N.D. Cal. Feb. 5, 1987).

134 Oki Semiconductor Co. v. Wells Fargo Bank, N.A., 298 F.3d 768, 775–76 (9th Cir. 2002) (*respondeat superior* liability may be imposed if employer benefited from acts); Crowe v. Henry, 43 F.3d 198, 206 (5th Cir. 1995) (law firm could be vicariously liable under § 1962(a) and (b) where it was alleged to have derived some benefit from its agent's wrongdoing in the form of unauthorized legal fees); Cox v. Administrator, United States Steel & Carnegie, 17 F.3d 1386, 1407 (corporation could be liable where union negotiators fraudulently received pension benefits from corporation in exchange for concessions which ultimately damaged the union), *op. amended*, 30 F.3d 1347 (11th Cir. 1994); Davis v. Mutual Life Ins. Co. of New York, 6 F.3d 367 (6th Cir. 1993), *cert. denied*, 510 U.S. 1193 (1994) (vicarious liability under RICO against insurer for fraudulent actions of one of its agents; no prohibition against such liability where corporation benefited from agent's acts); Quick v. Peoples Bank of Cullman County, 993 F.2d 793, 798 (11th Cir. 1993) (*respondeat superior* liability where bank benefited from loan officer's wrongdoing and some evidence of acquiescence); Brady v. Dairy Fresh Prods. Co., 974 F.2d 1149, 1153–54 (9th Cir. 1992) (*respondeat superior* allowed where corporation is not the enterprise and the employer receives some benefit from the employee's actions); Petro-Tech, Inc. v. Western Co., 824 F.2d 1349, 1361 (3d Cir. 1987) (*respondeat superior* liability may be imposed for violations of subsection 1962(a)); Moy v. Adelphi Institute, 866 F. Supp. 696 (E.D.N.Y. 1994) (vocational school could be vicariously liable for statements made by its recruiters); Western Auto Supply Co. v. Northwestern Mut. Life Ins. Co., 1994 U.S. Dist. LEXIS 13574 (W.D. Mo. Apr. 25, 1994) (insurer could be liable for acts of its agents where it was named as part of association in fact, had not been named as the enterprise, and was alleged to have benefited from the agent's actions); Mylan Labs., Inc. v. Akzo, N.V., 770 F. Supp. 1053 (D. Md. 1991); Connors v. Lexington Ins. Co., 666 F. Supp. 434

superior should not be available to circumvent the section 1962(c) requirement that the "person" and the "enterprise" be distinct.[135] Where the employer is not the alleged enterprise, however, other courts have pointed out that *respondeat superior* liability can both motivate employers to monitor their employees and keep them from engaging in racketeering activity, and force employers who have benefited from their employee's illegal activity to compensate the victims.[136]

Courts that have ruled against *respondeat superior* liability in section 1962(c) cases have often cited to the congressional intent behind that subsection, which was to protect corporations from criminal infiltration; to hold them liable would be to use RICO to hold liable the very entities it was designed to protect.[137] However, other courts have held that this intent is not subverted when the defendant corporation is not the same as the section 1962(c) enterprise, and accordingly *respondeat superior* may be appropriate in those cases.[138] The non-identity concerns are not raised in a

(E.D.N.Y. 1987); Temple Univ. v. Salla Bros., 656 F. Supp. 97 (E.D. Pa. 1986); Bernstein v. IDT Corp., 582 F. Supp. 1079, 1082–84 (D. Del. 1984); *see also* Clark v. Sec. Life Ins. Co., 270 Ga. 165, 509 S.E.2d 602 (1998) (vicarious liability in civil suit under RICO law should be decided under criminal law principles rather than tort law; superior is liable for agent's act if superior authorized, requested, commanded, performed, or recklessly tolerated it); Brian & Lee, *Vicarious Liability of Corporations and Corporate Enterprises Under RICO*, 7 RICO Law Rep. 560 (1988); Dwyer & Kelly, *Vicarious Civil Liability Under the Racketeer-Influenced and Corrupt Organizations Act*, 21 Cal. W. L. Rev. 324 (1985). *But see* Laro, Inc. v. Chase Manhattan Bank, 866 F. Supp. 132 (S.D.N.Y. 1994) (no corporate liability for independent fraudulent acts of its employees unless corporation actually benefited), *aff'd without op.*, 60 F.3d 810 (1995); Jeffreys v. Exten, 784 F. Supp. 146 (D. Del. 1992) (defendant which has itself been victimized not liable for third party RICO violation); Albert Einstein Med. Ctr. v. Physicians Clinical Servs., Ltd., 1991 U.S. Dist. LEXIS 13302 (E.D. Pa. Sept. 18, 1991) (same).

135 Miller v. Yokohama Tire Corp., 358 F.3d 616, 620 (9th Cir. 2004) (no vicarious liability where the employer is not distinct from the RICO enterprise); Gasoline Sales, Inc. v. Aero Oil Co. 39 F.3d 70, 73 (3d Cir. 1994) (subsidiary corporation could not be held vicariously liable for actions of subsidiary's vice president); Brady v. Dairy Fresh Prods. Co., 974 F.2d 1149 (9th Cir. 1992) (vicarious liability not allowed where it would violate the distinctness requirement or if the company was not benefited); Miranda v. Ponce Fed. Bank, 948 F.2d 41 (1st Cir. 1991) (attempt to invoke *respondeat superior* "lame"—§ 1962(c) does not recognize corporate liability on that basis); D&S Auto Parts, Inc. v. Schwartz, 838 F.2d 964, 967 (7th Cir.) (imposing vicarious liability would defeat the purposes of RICO), *cert. denied*, 486 U.S. 1061 (1988); Luthi v. Tonka Corp., 815 F.2d 1229 (8th Cir. 1987) (no vicarious liability); Liquid Air Corp. v. Rogers, 834 F.2d 1297 (7th Cir. 1987), *cert. denied*, 492 U.S. 917 (1989); Schofield v. First Commodity Corp., 793 F.2d 28 (1st Cir. 1986) (*respondeat superior* at odds with Congressional intent behind § 1962(c)); Williams Elecs. Games, Inc. v. Barry, 42 F. Supp. 2d 785, 791 (N.D. Ill. 1999), *aff'd*, 366 F.3d 569 (7th Cir. 2004); Sea-Land Serv. v. Atlantic Pac. Int'l, 61 F. Supp. 2d 1102 (D. Haw. 1999) (vicarious liability not appropriate where would impose liability on the enterprise); Soanes v. Empire Blue Cross/Blue Shield, 26 RICO L. Rep. 241, No. 91 Civ. 8698 (S.D.N.Y. July 3, 1997) (union and its welfare fund not vicariously liable for local's president's participation in fraudulent insurance brokerage transaction); Pollack v. Laidlaw Holdings, Inc., 1993 U.S. Dist. LEXIS 459 (S.D.N.Y. Jan. 19, 1993), *rev'd on other grounds*, 27 F.3d 808 (2d Cir. 1994), *cert. denied*, 115 S. Ct. 425 (1995), *on remand* 1995 U.S. Dist. LEXIS 15935 (S.D.N.Y. Oct. 30, 1995); Ram Inv. Assocs. v. Citizens Fid. Bank & Trust Co., 1992 WL 240581 (S.D.N.Y. 1992) (if no apparent authority, no *respondeat superior*); Metro Furniture Rental, Inc. v. Alessi, 770 F. Supp. 198 (S.D.N.Y. 1991) (bank could not be liable for actions of low-level employee where no corporate policy shown); First Nat'l Bank v. Lustig, 727 F. Supp. 276 (E.D. La. 1989); Grimsley v. First Alabama Bank, 1988 WL 156777, 1988 U.S. Dist. LEXIS 16042 (S.D. Ala. 1988); Am. Bonded Warehouse Corp. v. Compagnie Nationale Air France, 653 F. Supp. 861 (N.D. Ill. 1987); Banque Worms v. Luis A. Duque Pena E Hijos Ltd., 652 F. Supp. 770 (S.D.N.Y. 1987); Gilbert v. Prudential Bache Sec., 643 F. Supp. 107 (E.D. Pa. 1986); Lynn Elecs. v. Automation Mach. & Dev. Corp., 1986 U.S. Dist. LEXIS 19433 (E.D. Pa. Oct. 6, 1986); *see also* D&S Auto Parts, Inc. v. Schwartz, 838 F.2d 964 (7th Cir. 1988) (principal liable under § 1962(a) only if principal also is perpetrator), *cert. denied*, 486 U.S. 1061 (1988); *In re* Citisource, Inc., Sec. Litig., 694 F. Supp. 1069 (S.D.N.Y. 1988) (municipal corporation can not be held vicariously liable under RICO); Gruber v. Prudential-Bache Sec., 679 F. Supp. 165 (D. Conn. 1987) (non-enterprise vicariously liable under § 1962(c) only where it is central figure in the alleged scheme); Kovian v. Fulton County Nat'l Bank, 647 F. Supp. 830 (N.D.N.Y. 1986) (limited vicarious liability in unlawful debt collection action); Sea State Bank v. Visiting Nurses Ass'n of Telfair Cty., Inc., 568 S.E.2d 491, 492 (Ga. App. 2002) (no *respondeat superior* liability unless evidence that employer profited from acts).

136 *See, e.g.*, Thomas v. Ross & Hardies, 9 F. Supp. 2d 547, 557 (D. Md. 1998) (holding law firm partnership could be held liable under RICO under traditional partnership agency principles for racketeering acts of partner); Baker *ex rel.* Hall Brake Supply, Inc. v. Stewart Title & Trust, Inc., 197 Ariz. 535, 5 P.3d 249, 259 (2000).

137 Landry v. Air Line Pilots Ass'n Int'l AFL-CIO, 901 F.2d 404 (5th Cir. 1990), *cert. denied*, 498 U.S. 895 (1991); Yellow Bus Lines, Inc. v. Drivers, Chauffeurs & Helpers Local Union 639, 883 F.2d 132, 140 (D.C. Cir. 1989), *rev'd in part on other grounds*, 913 F.2d 948 (D.C. Cir. 1990) (en banc), *cert. denied*, 501 U.S. 1222 (1991); D&S Auto Parts, Inc. v. Schwartz, 838 F.2d 964, 967 (7th Cir. 1988); Liquid Air Corp. v. Rogers, 834 F.2d 1297, 1306 (7th Cir. 1987); Luthi v. Tonks Corp., 815 F.2d 1229, 1230 (8th Cir. 1987); Kovian v. Fulton County Nat'l Bank & Trust Co., 100 F. Supp. 2d 129, 133 (N.D.N.Y. 2000); Qatar Nat'l Navigation & Transp. Co. v. Citibank, N.A., 1992 U.S. Dist. LEXIS 14784 (S.D.N.Y. Sept. 29, 1992), *aff'd*, 182 F.3d 901 (2d Cir. 1999); Kahn v. Chase Manhattan Bank, N.A., 760 F. Supp. 369, 373 (S.D.N.Y. 1991) ("the independent acts of an employee not acting in his employer's interest are not a sufficient basis to hold the employer liable under RICO"); Schofield v. First Commodity Corp. of Boston, 793 F.2d 28, 32–34 (1st Cir. 1986); Banque Worms v. Luis A. Duque Pena E Hijos, Ltda., 652 F. Supp. 770, 772 (S.D.N.Y. 1986); Rush v. Oppenheimer & Co., 628 F. Supp. 1188, 1194, 1195 (S.D.N.Y. 1985).

138 *See, e.g.*, Davis v. Mut. Life Ins. Co., 6 F.3d 367, 379, 380 (6th Cir.), *cert. denied*, 510 U.S. 1193 (1994) (where defendant is not the enterprise, and "knowingly sponsored and benefited from

section 1962(d) case, and accordingly *respondeat superior* liability may be less controversial there.[139]

To avoid undermining congressional intent, some courts have sought to distinguish those cases where the defendant corporation was a "central figure" or "aggressor" in the scheme, where *respondeat superior* liability may be appropriate,[140] from those cases where the corporation was merely passive, even though perhaps benefiting from the scheme. To show that the defendant was a central figure or aggressor, the plaintiff may have to show that one of the officers or directors either knew of, or was recklessly indifferent to, the illegal activities.[141] It may be sufficient in other courts to show that the defendant corporation's agents actively promoted the scheme.[142] The question is fact-specific, and therefore not appropriate for a 12(b)(6) motion.[143]

In pleading *respondeat superior*, it is wise to plead both that the employee took the alleged action on behalf of the employer and that the employer benefited from the action.[144] If there is evidence of ratification by the principal, that should be pleaded as well.

Alternatively, the corporation may be required to indemnify the individual employees. Indemnification is not always favored.[145] Consequently, care should be taken to name as the defendant an officer, director, or agent of an enterprise for whose actions the enterprise is responsible or whom it will indemnify. Similarly, the individual defendant may have liability insurance. Liability insurance normally does not cover intentional wrongdoing, so it is important to plead a RICO claim in a manner designed to maximize the chance of recovery by incorporating such considerations.

Another approach is to make the corporation the defendant and argue that the enterprise is an "association in fact" between the corporation and its officers.[146] This approach may raise concerns about whether the defendant and the enterprise are sufficiently distinct, however.[147]

Yet another course would be to argue that the defendant is liable under RICO for aiding and abetting the RICO violation even if the defendant did not have the requisite participation in the enterprise. However, before asserting and aider and abettor claim, a practitioner must consider the Supreme Court's decision in *Central Bank v. First Interstate Bank*.[148] *Central Bank* held that civil liability under the Securities Exchange Act of 1934 did not include those who merely aid and abet a section 10(b) violation because the act does not provide for aider and abettor liability.

Some RICO courts have ruled that *Central Bank* does not

---

the activity," vicarious liability may be appropriate); Brady v. Dairy Fresh Prods. Co., 974 F.2d 1149, 1154 (9th Cir. 1992); Petro-Tech, Inc. v. Western Co. of N. Am., 824 F.2d 1349, 1361, 1362 (3d Cir. 1987); Connors v. Lexington Ins. Co., 666 F. Supp. 434, 453 (E.D.N.Y. 1987) (ordinary rules of agency apply to RICO cases); Bernstein v. IDT Corp., 582 F. Supp. 1079, 1083 (D. Del. 1984) (same).

139 *See, e.g.*, Baker *ex rel.* Hall Brake Supply, Inc. v. Stewart Title & Trust, Inc., 197 Ariz. 535, 5 P.3d 249, 259 (2000).

140 *See* USA Certified Merchs., L.L.C. v. Koebel, 273 F. Supp. 2d 501, 504 (S.D.N.Y. 2003); Dubai Islamic Bank v. Citibank, N.A., 256 F. Supp. 2d 158, 165 (S.D.N.Y. 2003); Kovian v. Fulton County Nat'l Bank & Trust Co., 100 F. Supp. 2d 129, 133 (N.D.N.Y. 2000) (not enough to show that employer benefited from the scheme); Nystrom v. Associated Plastic Fabricators, Inc., 1999 U.S. Dist. LEXIS 9480 (N.D. Ill. June 1999) (same); Schmidt v. Fleet Bank, 16 F. Supp. 2d 340, 352 (S.D.N.Y. 1998) (must show employer was more than mere beneficiary); Gruber v. Prudential-Bache Sec. Inc., 679 F. Supp. 165, 181 (D. Conn. 1987).

141 Kovian v. Fulton County Nat'l Bank & Trust Co., 100 F. Supp. 2d 129, 133 (N.D.N.Y. 2000).

142 Gunderson v. ADM Investor Servs., Inc., 2001 U.S. Dist. LEXIS 3383, at *72, *73 (N.D. Iowa Feb. 13, 2001). *But see* Kovian v. Fulton County Nat'l Bank & Trust Co., 100 F. Supp. 2d 129, 133 (N.D.N.Y. 2000) (respondeat superior liability inappropriate where high-ranking officers were acting outside the scope of their employment).

143 Bank Brussels Lambert v. Credit Lyonnais (Suisse) S.A., 2000 U.S. Dist. LEXIS 16399, at *33 (S.D.N.Y. Nov. 13, 2000).

144 Pollack v. Laidlaw Holdings, Inc., 1995 U.S. Dist. LEXIS 15935 (S.D.N.Y. Oct. 30, 1995) (corporation could be liable where these two elements proved). *See also In re* Hydrox Chem. Co., 194 B.R. 617, 627–28 (Bankr. N.D. Ill. 1996) (while no vicarious liability for actions of corporate officers, corporation that benefited could be directly liable).

145 Andrews v. Fitzgerald, 1992 U.S. Dist. LEXIS 9315 (M.D.N.C. Feb. 7, 1992) and Friedman v. Hartmann, 787 F. Supp. 411, 415 (S.D.N.Y. 1992) have held that contribution and indemnity are not available as to RICO violations. *See also* Sequa v. Gelmin, 851 F. Supp. 106, 108 (S.D.N.Y. 1994) (corporation did not have to indemnify person it sued, despite indemnification agreement); Sequa Corp. v. Gelmin, 828 F. Supp. 203, 205–06 (S.D.N.Y. 1993) (indemnification for costs of defense only); Sikes v. AT&T Co., 841 F. Supp. 1572 (S.D. Ga. 1993) (contribution, but not indemnification, rights will be honored). *But see* Vanguard Sav. & Loan Ass'n v. Banks, 1995 U.S. Dist. LEXIS 961 (E.D. Pa. Jan. 26, 1995) (contribution is not available to a RICO defendant).

146 Jaguar Cars Inc. v. Royal Oaks Motor Car Co., 46 F.3d 258, 261 (3d Cir. 1995) (officers and directors of a corporation can be named as RICO persons where the corporation is named as the enterprise); *see also* Miranda v. Ponce Fed. Bank, 948 F.2d 41, 45 (1st Cir. 1991) (officers of corporate enterprise can be personally liable for RICO violations on behalf of corporation); United States v. Perholtz, 842 F.2d 343, 354 (D.C. Cir.), *cert. denied*, 488 U.S. 821 (1988); Cullen v. Margiotta, 811 F.2d 698 (2d Cir.), *cert. denied*, 483 U.S. 4021 (1987); United States v. Local 560, IBT, 780 F.2d 267 (3d Cir. 1985), *cert. denied*, 476 U.S. 1140 (1986); Petro-Tech v. Western Co. of N.A., 824 F.2d 1349 (3d Cir. 1987); United States v. Benny, 786 F.2d 1410 (9th Cir.), *cert. denied*, 479 U.S. 1017 (1986); Gassner v. Stotler & Co., 671 F. Supp. 1187 (N.D. Ill. 1987); Portnoy v. E.F. Hutton & Co., 1987 U.S. Dist. LEXIS 17337 (D.N.J. Jan. 15, 1987); Huntsman-Christensen Corp. v. Mountain Fuel Supply Co., 1986 U.S. Dist. LEXIS 17337 (D. Utah Nov. 24, 1986); Brainerd & Bridges v. Weingeroff Enters., Inc., 1986 U.S. Dist. LEXIS 22478 (N.D. Ill. July 21, 1986); Chicago HMO v. Trans Pac. Life Ins. Co., 622 F. Supp. 489, 494, 495 (N.D. Ill. 1985) (mem.). *But see* Rhodes v. Consumers' Buyline, 868 F. Supp. 368 (D. Mass. 1993) (directors and officers acting on behalf of corporate enterprise are not distinct from it).

147 *See* § 9.2.3.2.4, *supra*.

148 511 U.S. 164, 114 S. Ct. 1439, 128 L. Ed. 2d 119 (1994).

affect RICO aider and abettor liability because RICO liability depends on whether the defendant is criminally liable for the predicate act, and one who aids and abets a federal crime is principally liable.[149] However, recent opinions have agreed almost universally that *Central Bank* destroyed any aider and abettor cause of action under RICO, at least with respect to actions brought under subsection 1962(c).[150]

Nonetheless, an aiding and abetting claim may still be viable under subsection 1962(a), for the reason that unlike the other subsections, 1962(a) incorporates by reference the general criminal aiding and abetting statute, 18 U.S.C. § 2.[151] To state a claim of aider and abettor liability under RICO, the plaintiff must allege (1) the existence of an independent wrong committed by the primary offender; (2) the rendering of substantial assistance to the primary wrongdoer by the aider and abettor; and (3) the requisite scienter of the aider and abettor.[152]

9.2.3.3 Interstate or Foreign Commerce

To state a RICO claim the plaintiff must allege that the asserted enterprise "is engaged in, or [that] the activities of which affect, interstate or foreign commerce."[153] This is an easy requirement to meet, especially at the pleading stage. The requisite connection with commerce need only be "minimal"[154] or "insubstantial."[155] Use of the mail to execute a fraudulent scheme satisfies the requirement; in other words, predicate acts of mail fraud are sufficient in and of themselves.[156] The effects of the enterprise itself can also provide the nexus to commerce.[157] Sufficient effects will be found where the enterprise utilizes the interstate mails or wires[158] or where supplies are shipped through interstate commerce.[159]

---

149 Crowe v. Henry, 43 F.3d 198 (5th Cir. 1995); First Am. Corp. v. Al-Nahyan, 17 F. Supp. 2d 10 (D.D.C. 1998) (finding RICO sufficiently different from the Securities Exchange Act that *Central Bank* did not control); *In re* Am. Honda Motor Co. Dealership Relations Litig., 958 F. Supp. 1045 (D. Md. 1997); Am. Auto. Accessories, Inc. v. Fishman, 1996 U.S. Dist. LEXIS 12207 (N.D. Ill., Aug. 22, 1996); Dayton Monetary Assocs. v. Donaldson, Lufkin & Jenrette Sec. Corp., RICO Business Disputes Guide (CCH) ¶ 8748, 1995 U.S. Dist. LEXIS 1198 (S.D.N.Y. Feb. 1, 1995); Standard Chlorine of Delaware, Inc. v. Sinibaldi, RICO Business Disputes Guide (CCH) ¶ 8780, 1994 U.S. Dist. LEXIS 20541 (D. Del. Dec. 8, 1994); Succession of Lula Belle Wardlaw v. Whitney Nat'l Bank, RICO Business Disputes Guide (CCH) ¶ 8711, 1994 U.S. Dist. LEXIS 15215 (E.D. La. Oct. 17, 1994).

150 Pa. Ass'n of Edwards Heirs v. Rightenour, 235 F.3d 839, 844 (3d Cir. 2001) (no aiding and abetting liability under RICO after Central Bank); Rolo v. City Investing Co. Liquidating Trust, 155 F.3d 644 (3d Cir. 1998) (relying on *Central Bank*, no aiding and abetting liability); Wiwa v. Royal Dutch Petroleum Co., 2002 WL 319887, at *25 n.33 (S.D.N.Y. Feb. 28, 2002) (no aider-and-abettor liability); Goldfine v. Sichenzia, 118 F. Supp. 2d 392, 406 (S.D.N.Y. 2000) (no aiding and abetting liability under § 1962(c)); *In re* Mastercard Int'l Inc., 132 F. Supp. 2d 468 (E.D. La. 2001); Niles v. Palmer, 1999 U.S. Dist. LEXIS 17759, at *28 (S.D.N.Y. Oct. 26, 1999); Jubelirer v. Mastercard Int'l, 68 F. Supp. 2d 1049 (W.D. Wis. 1999) (no aiding and abetting liability under RICO after *Central Bank*); Soranno v. New York Life Ins. Co., 1999 U.S. Dist. LEXIS 1963 (N.D. Ill. Feb. 22, 1999) (no aiding and abetting liability under § 1962(d)); Touhy v. Northern Trust Bank, 1999 U.S. Dist. LEXIS 7967, at *7 (N.D. Ill. May 17, 1999) (no aiding and abetting liability for § 1962(c)); Hayden v. Paul, Weiss, Rifkind, Wharton & Garrison, 955 F. Supp. 248 (S.D.N.Y. 1997); Kaiser v. Stewart, 1997 U.S. Dist. LEXIS 12788 (E.D. Pa. Aug. 19, 1997); *In re* Lake States Commodities, Inc., 936 F. Supp. 1461 (N.D. Ill. 1996) (no aiding and abetting liability under § 1962(c)); Department of Economic Dep't v. Arthur Andersen & Co., 924 F. Supp. 449 (S.D.N.Y. 1996) (no aiding and abetting liability under civil RICO); Rosenheck v. Rieber, 932 F. Supp. 626 (S.D.N.Y. 1996); Bowdoin Constr. Corp. v. Rhode Island Hosp. Trust Nat'l Bank, N.A., 869 F. Supp. 1004 (D. Mass. 1994) (aiding and abetting securities fraud can not be a predicate act for RICO; under *Reves*, to be liable under § 1962(c), a defendant must participate in the operation or management of the enterprise itself), *aff'd on other grounds*, 94 F.3d 721 (1st Cir. 1996).

151 18 U.S.C. § 1962(a). However, the reference is made specifically with respect to collection of an unlawful debt, so arguably only those actions will be eligible for an aiding and abetting claim.

152 Touhy v. Northern Trust Bank, 1999 U.S. Dist. LEXIS 7967 (N.D. Ill. May 14, 1999) (unpublished) (deliberate indifference to scheme insufficient for aider and abettor liability) (citing R.E. Davis Chem. Corp. v. Nalco Chem. Co., 757 F. Supp. 1499 (N.D. Ill. 1990)).

153 18 U.S.C. § 1962(a), (b), (c).

154 U.S. v. Chance, 306 F.3d 356, 373 (6th Cir. 2002) (need only show a *de minimis* connection with interstate commerce); United States v. Juvenile Male, 118 F.3d 1344 (9th Cir. 1997); United States v. Miller, 116 F.3d 641 (2d Cir. 1997), *cert. denied*, 524 U.S. 905 (1998); R.A.G.S. Couture, Inc. v. Hyatt, 774 F.2d 1350, 1353 (5th Cir. 1985); United States v. Robinson, 763 F.2d 778, 781 (6th Cir. 1985); United States v. Rone, 598 F.2d 564, 573 (9th Cir. 1979), *cert. denied*, 445 U.S. 946 (1980).

155 United States v. Qaoud, 777 F.2d 1105, 1116 (6th Cir. 1985), *cert. denied*, 475 U.S. 1098 (1986); Owl Constr. Co. v. Ronald Adams Contractors, Inc., 642 F. Supp. 475 (E.D. La. 1986).

156 *See* United States v. Maloney, 71 F.3d 645, 663–64 (7th Cir. 1995), *cert. denied*, 519 U.S. 927 (1996); Illinois Dep't of Revenue v. Phillips, 771 F.2d 312, 313 (7th Cir. 1985). However, allegations of intrastate mail may not be sufficient. Calica v. Independent Mortgage Bankers, Ltd., 1989 WL 117057, at *2 (E.D.N.Y. Sept. 28, 1989); *see also* Utz v. Correa, 631 F. Supp. 592, 596 (S.D.N.Y. 1986) (intrastate telephone calls did not violate wire fraud statute).

157 United States v. Conn, 769 F.2d 420, 423, 424 (7th Cir. 1985); United States v. Murphy, 768 F.2d 1518, 1531 (7th Cir. 1985), *cert. denied*, 475 U.S. 1012 (1986); Wiwa v. Royal Dutch Petroleum Co., 2002 WL 319887, at *22 (S.D.N.Y. Feb. 28, 2002) (claim that unlawful exploitation of Nigerian oil fields resulted in an unfair advantage in the United States oil market established commercial nexus); Karel v. Kroner, 635 F. Supp. 725, 728 (N.D. Ill. 1986).

158 *See* United States v. Bagnariol, 665 F.2d 877, 892, 893 (9th Cir. 1981), *cert. denied*, 456 U.S. 962 (1982). *But see* Utz v. Correa, 631 F. Supp. 592, 596 (S.D.N.Y. 1986) (intrastate phone calls do not satisfy interstate commerce requirement of wire fraud statute).

159 *See* Meineke Discount Muffler Shops, Inc. v. Noto, 548 F. Supp. 352, 354 (E.D.N.Y. 1982) (mem.).

9.2.3.4 "Pattern" of Racketeering Activity

9.2.3.4.1 Introduction

The racketeering activities prohibited by RICO all involve acting through, or deriving income from "a pattern of racketeering activity,"[160] or conspiring to do so.[161] A pattern of racketeering activity "requires at least two acts of racketeering activity"[162]—though it does not require more than one criminal scheme.[163] Courts have great difficulty defining "pattern" of racketeering activity, and this remains one of the haziest aspects of RICO law. The United States Supreme Court has addressed the issue twice, but uncertainty still remains. The same set of acts will look like a pattern to one court, but not to another.

9.2.3.4.2 Supreme Court guidance

The first Supreme Court case to address the "pattern" requirement was *Sedima, S.P.R.L. v. Imrex Co.*[164] That case, without adopting a definition of pattern, indicated that the commission of two predicate offenses is necessary but may not be sufficient to establish a pattern:

> As many commentators have pointed out, the definition of a "pattern of racketeering activity" differs from the other provisions in § 1961 in that it states that a pattern "requires at least two acts of racketeering activity," . . . not that it "means" two such acts. The implication is that while two acts are necessary, they may not be sufficient. Indeed, in common parlance two of anything do not generally form a "pattern."[165]

The Court quoted from RICO's Senate Report: "[t]he target of [RICO] is thus not sporadic activity. The infiltration of legitimate business normally requires more than one "racketeering activity" and the threat of continuing activity to be effective. It is this factor of continuity plus relationship which combines to produce a pattern."[166] The Court also pointed out a non-RICO provision of the Organized Crime Control Act which defined pattern: "criminal conduct forms a pattern if it embraces criminal acts that have the same or similar purposes, results, participants, victims, or methods of commission, or otherwise are interrelated by distinguishing characteristics and are not isolated events."[167] The Supreme Court, by deploring "the failure of Congress and the courts to develop a meaningful concept of 'pattern,' "[168] in effect invited the lower courts to redress their neglect of the problem.

The second Supreme Court case to consider the pattern requirement provides more direction for the lower courts. *H.J. Inc. v. Northwestern Bell Telephone Co.*[169] specifically states that a pattern of racketeering need not involve organized crime, can not be shown merely by proving two predicate acts, and does not require predicate acts that are part of separate illegal schemes.[170]

The Court noted that the dictionary definition of pattern is "an arrangement or order of things or activity."[171] Therefore, the Court reasoned, it does not matter how many predicate acts there are, unless they are related to one another in some order or arrangement.[172]

In *H.J.*, the Supreme Court held that the concept of "pattern" has two separate properties that must be established: relationship and continuity.[173] The relationship criterion is met if the acts have " 'the same or similar purposes, results, participants, victims, or methods of commission, or are otherwise interrelated.' "[174] As for continuity, while the Court declined to express a specific test, it roughed out the requirement by providing that a plaintiff could meet the requirement by showing either closed-ended or open-ended continuity.[175] Closed-ended continuity could be shown "by proving a series of related predicates extending over a substantial period of time."[176] Alternatively, a plaintiff could show "open-ended" continuity by proving a threat of continued racketeering activity.[177] These different means of

160 18 U.S.C. § 1962(a), (b), (c).

161 18 U.S.C. § 1962(d).

162 18 U.S.C. § 1961(5).

163 Blake v. Dierdorff, 856 F.2d 1365, 1368 (9th Cir. 1988); Madden v. Gluck, 815 F.2d 1163, 1164 (8th Cir. 1987), *cert. denied*, 484 U.S. 823 (1987).

164 473 U.S. 479 (1985).

165 *Id.* at 496 n.14 (1985).

166 *Id.* (quoting S. Rep. No. 617, 91st Cong., 1st Sess. 158 (1969)).

167 *Id.* (quoting 18 U.S.C. § 3575(e)).

168 *Id.* at 500.

169 492 U.S. 229, 109 S. Ct. 2893, 106 L. Ed. 2d 195 (1989). After remand, the district court again dismissed this case because of the court's unwillingness to second guess the state public utility commission's authority. H.J. Inc. v. Northwestern Bell Tel. Co., 734 F. Supp. 879 (D. Minn. 1990), *aff'd*, 954 F.2d 485 (8th Cir. 1992), *cert. denied*, 504 U.S. 957 (1992).

170 492 U.S. 229, 236–327, 109 S. Ct. 2893, 106 L. Ed. 2d 195 (1989).

171 *Id.* at 238.

172 *Id.*

173 492 U.S. at 239.

174 *Id.* at 240 (quoting 18 U.S.C. § 3575(e)).

175 *Id.* at 241.

176 *Id.* at 242 (emphasis added). Predicate acts committed over just a few weeks or months would not satisfy closed-ended continuity, in such a case the plaintiff would have to show "open-ended" continuity to meet the continuity property of the pattern element. *Id.*

177 *Id.* at 242. While declining to define open-ended continuity, the Court offered a couple of examples: open-ended continuity could be met if the racketeering acts themselves included a specific threat of repetition, extending indefinitely into the future, as with a "protection" racket, or if the predicate acts or offenses were part of an ongoing entity's regular way of doing business. *Id.* at 242, 243. Given the facts alleged by the plaintiffs, that the defendants had paid five bribes to a utility commission over the course of six years, the Court reversed the lower court's dismissal of the claim and remanded. The court

establishing the continuity criterion have received significant attention from the courts.

9.2.3.4.3 Closed-ended continuity

The length of time of the scheme is the primary factor in closed-ended continuity. Courts rarely find that a scheme, measured from first predicate act to last,[178] that lasted less than two years qualifies for closed-ended continuity.[179] However, though closed-ended continuity is primarily a temporal concept, time span alone does not necessarily determine its existence; the number and variety of predicate acts, the number of both participants and victims, and the presence of separate schemes are also relevant in determining whether closed-ended continuity exists.[180] A scheme aimed at only a handful of victims may be less likely to meet the closed-ended continuity requirement of pattern.[181] In any event, these factors can be particularly influential when the time span falls on the short side of two years.[182]

---

held that the bribes could be found to be related for a common purpose, meeting the relationship property, and the plaintiffs could meet the continuity property either under a closed-ended analysis, given the frequency of the acts, or under an open-ended analysis, either by showing that the bribes were a regular way of conducting the defendant's ongoing business, or that bribery was a regular way of conducting or participating in the conduct of the alleged RICO enterprise, the utility company. *Id.* at 250.

178 *See* Cofacredit, S.A. v. Windsor Plumbing Supply Co., 187 F.3d 229, 243 (2d Cir. 1999) (acts that do not constitute RICO predicate acts are not included in the calculation, refusing to consider later acts that did not involve interstate commerce).

179 *See, e.g.*, Jackson v. BellSouth Telecomms. 2004 WL 1301078, at *1–14 (11th Cir. June 14, 2004) (nine months insufficient, given that allegations related to a single scheme); Turner v. Cook, 362 F.3d 1219, 1230 (9th Cir. 2004) (in suit by judgment debtor against judgment creditors, no closed-ended continuity when bulk of alleged predicate acts took place in two-month period with remaining acts occurring in the preceding year); Soto-Negron v. Taber Partners I, 339 F.3d 35, 38–39 (1st Cir. 2003) (wrongful cashing of six checks within days of one another did not satisfy continuity requirement); Pizzo v. Bekin Van Lines Co., 258 F.3d 629, 633 (7th Cir. 2001) (consumer who received substandard furniture could not demonstrate pattern of fraud by store with evidence of only one other dissatisfied customer); GE Inv. Private Placement Partners II v. Parker, 247 F.3d 543, 550 (4th Cir. 2001) (two years insufficient, in light of other circumstances); GICC Capital Corp. v. Tech. Fin. Group, Inc., 67 F.3d 463, 467 (2d Cir. 1992), *cert. denied*, 518 U.S. 1017 (1996); Metromedia Co. v. Fugazy, 983 F.2d 350, 369 (2d Cir. 1992) (over two years), *cert. denied*, 508 U.S. 952 (1993); Jacobson v. Cooper, 882 F.2d 717, 720 (2d Cir. 1989) ("matter of years"); *see also* De Falco v. Bernas, 2001 U.S. App. LEXIS 5256, at *92 (2d Cir. Mar. 13, 2001) (year and a half insufficient for closed-ended continuity); Wisdom v. First Midwest Bank, 167 F.3d 402, 407 (8th Cir. 1999) (six months insufficient); GICC Capital Corp. v. Tech. Fin. Group, Inc., 67 F.3d 463, 468 (2d Cir. 1992) (less than one year insufficient), *cert. denied*, 518 U.S. 1017 (1996); Hughes v. Consol-Pa. Coal Co., 945 F.2d 594, 611 (3d Cir. 1991) (twelve months insufficient), *cert. denied*, 504 U.S. 955 (1992); J.D. Marshall Int'l, Inc. v. Redstart, Inc., 935 F.2d 815, 821 (7th Cir. 1991) (thirteen months insufficient); Monasco v. Wasserman, 886 F.2d 681, 684 (4th Cir. 1989) (one year insufficient); Metcalf v. Death Row Records, Inc., 2003 WL 22097336, at *3 (N.D. Cal. Sept. 3, 2003) (no closed-ended continuity where scheme spanned only one to two months); Maryland-Nat'l Capital Park & Planning Comm'n v. Boyle, 203 F. Supp. 2d 468, 478 (D. Md. 2002) (eighteen months insufficient), *aff'd*, 2003 WL 1879017 (4th Cir. Apr. 16, 2003) (unpublished, citation limited); Special Purpose Accounts Receivable Co-op Corp. v. Prime One Capital Co. L.L.C., 202 F. Supp. 2d 1339, 1350 (S.D. Fla. 2002) (five and a half months insufficient); Vicon Fiber Optics Corp. v. Scrivo, 201 F. Supp. 2d 216, 220 (S.D.N.Y. 2002) (four months insufficient); Shapo v. O'Shaugnessy, 246 F. Supp. 2d 935 (N.D. Ill. 2002) (seven years sufficed); G-I Holdings, Inc. v. Baron & Budd, 238 F. Supp. 2d 521 (S.D.N.Y. 2002) (seven months insufficient); Arboireau v. Adidas Salomon AG, 2002 WL 31466557 (D. Or. Mar. 19, 2002), *aff'd in part, vacated in part on other grounds*, 347 F.3d 1158 (4th Cir. 2003); First Capital Asset Mgmt. v. Brickelbush, Inc., 150 F. Supp. 2d 624, 635 (S.D.N.Y. 2001) (less than a year insufficient); Dempsey v. Sanders, 132 F. Supp. 2d 222, 228 (S.D.N.Y. 2001); Oak Bevs., Inc. v. TOMRA of Mass., L.L.C., 96 F. Supp. 2d 336 (S.D.N.Y. 2000) (14 months insufficient); Staiger v. Bentley Mortg. Corp., 1999 Conn. Super. LEXIS 2407, at *14, *15 (Sept. 7, 1999) (one year insufficient where single scheme). *But see* Wilson v. De Angelis, 156 F. Supp. 2d 1335, 1339 (S.D. Fla. 2001) (refusing to dismiss RICO claim based on ten acts over ten months); Williams v. Waldron, 14 F. Supp. 2d 1334, 1340 (N.D. Ga. 1998) (one year sufficient), *aff'd without op.*, 248 F.3d 1180 (11th Cir. 2001).

180 Cofacredit, S.A. v. Windsor Plumbing Supply Co., 187 F.3d 229, 242 (2d Cir. 1999) (citing GICC Capital Corp. v. Tech. Fin. Group, Inc., 67 F.3d 463, 468 (2d Cir. 1992)); Vicom, Inc. v. Harbridge Merchant Servs., 20 F.3d 771, 780 (7th Cir. 1994); Brandon Apparel Group v. Quitman Mfg. Co., 52 F. Supp. 2d 913, 918 (N.D. Ill. 1999) (court should consider (1) the number and variety of predicate acts; (2) the length of time over which the predicate acts were committed; (3) the number of victims; (4) the presence of separate schemes; and (5) the occurrence of distinct injuries) (citing Morgan v. Bank of Waukegan, 804 F.2d 970, 975 (7th Cir. 1986). *See also* Efron v. Embassy Suites (P.R.), Inc., 223 F.3d 12, 19 (1st Cir. 2000) (where alleged scheme involved only one venture against three plaintiffs, it was merely a 'single effort' and did not have closed-ended continuity), *cert. denied*, 121 S. Ct. 1228 (2001); Vicom v. Harbridge Merch. Servs., Inc., 20 F.3d 771, 780 (7th Cir. 1994); Javitch v. Capwill, 284 F. Supp. 2d 848, 855–56 (N.D. Ohio 2003); Meyer Material Co. v. Mooshol, 188 F. Supp. 2d 936, 941 (N.D. Ill. 2002) (citing factors to find pattern); Teti v. Towamencin Township, 2001 U.S. Dist. LEXIS 15600, at *24–25 (E.D. Pa. Aug. 17, 2001), *aff'd without op.*, 2002 WL 31758388 (3d Cir. Nov. 6, 2002); Regency Communications v. Cleartel Communications. Inc., 160 F. Supp. 2d 36, 46 (D.D.C. 2001); Jordan (Berm.) Inv. Co. v. Hunter Green Invs. Ltd., 154 F. Supp. 2d 682, 694 (S.D.N.Y. 2001).

181 *See, e.g.*, Lefkowitz v. Bank of New York, 2003 WL 22480049, at *8 (S.D.N.Y. Oct. 31, 2003).

182 *See, e.g.*, Roger Whitmore's Automotive Servs., Inc. v. Lake County, IL, 2002 WL 959587, at *5 (N.D. Ill. May 9, 2002) (short duration of scheme outweighed by the number of victims, number of injuries, variety of predicate acts and existence of two separate schemes); Kayne v. MTC Elecs. Techs. Co. 74 F. Supp. 2d 276, 286 (E.D.N.Y. 1998) (rejecting "bright line test"

9.2.3.4.4 Open-ended continuity

To show open-ended continuity, the plaintiff must establish a threat that the defendant will continue its criminal activity.[183] Courts will examine the nature of the predicate acts alleged or the nature of the enterprise on whose behalf the predicate acts were performed.[184] To show open-ended continuity where the enterprise is primarily a legitimate business, a plaintiff should show that the predicate acts were the regular way of running the business, or that the acts were of a sort that imply a threat of continued criminal activity,[185] for instance, that they would require additional criminal activity to complete their purpose. So, for example, the Second Circuit has held that plaintiffs sufficiently pleaded pattern where they alleged that defendants, owners of apartments being offered as condominiums, mailed 8000 copies of a single marketing letter that allegedly misrepresented the condition of the apartments.[186] Although the mailing was a single act, because the defendants owned several other apartments in the same complex that remained to be sold, they could be expected to offer them with similar fraudulent letters.[187] Showing that the defendants have committed similar predicate acts with regard to other consumers can also establish open-ended continuity.[188]

Lower court decisions reveal a good deal of doctrinal confusion with respect to the meaning of pattern, some of which may be particularly important in some consumer cases that are framed around a single fraudulent scheme. For instance, a typical consumer case might involve identical fraudulent representations that are made to a large number of potential purchasers.[189] These facts may generate multiple mail and wire fraud violations to serve as predicate offenses, but a restrictively-minded court might hold that there is only one scheme and one criminal episode, and, therefore, no threat of continued criminal activity and no pattern.[190] How-

---

in favor of evaluation of factors, ruling that plaintiffs adequately alleged open-ended continuity of scheme that spanned fifteen months).

183 *H.J., Inc.*, 492 U.S. at 242, 243; *see also* Turner v. Cook, 362 F.3d 1219, 1229 (9th Cir. 2004) (plaintiff must allege misconduct that threatens to repeat in the future); U.S. v. Connolly, 341 F.3d 16, 30 (1st Cir. 2003) (finding threat of future criminal conduct fulfilled where the racketeering acts were part of an ongoing criminal enterprise); Jordan (Berm.) Inv. Co. v. Hunter Green Invs. Ltd., 154 F. Supp. 2d 682, 694 (S.D.N.Y. 2001).

184 GICC Capital Corp. v. Tech. Fin. Group, Inc., 67 F.3d 463, 468 (2d Cir. 1992), *cert. denied*, 518 U.S. 1017 (1996).

185 *See H.J., Inc.*, 492 U.S. at 242, 243 (such a threat exists when there is "a specific threat of repetition," "the predicates are a regular way of conducting [an] ongoing legitimate business," or "the predicates can be attributed to a defendant operating as part of a long-term association that exists for criminal purposes."); Jackson v. BellSouth Telecomms. 2004 WL 1301078, at *1–14 (11th Cir. June 14, 2004) (no open-ended continuity in case brought by plaintiffs against their former attorneys arising from defendants' allegedly unethical settlement of plaintiffs' employment discrimination suit, where plaintiffs did not show that the predicate acts were part of defendants' usual way of doing business or that acts might be repeated in the future); GE Inv. Private Placement Partners II v. Parker, 247 F.3d 543, 549 (4th Cir. 2001); Heaven & Earth, Inc. v. Wyman Props. Ltd. P'ship, 2003 WL 22680935, at *9 (D. Minn. Oct. 21, 2003) (finding continuity where plaintiff alleged that defendants' fraudulent billing practices were part of their regular business practice); First Guar. Mortgage Corp. v. Procopio, 217 F. Supp. 2d 633, 637 (D. Md. 2002); First Capital Asset Mgmt. v. Brickelbush, Inc., 150 F. Supp. 2d 624, 633–34 (S.D.N.Y. 2001). *See also Cofacredit*, 187 F.3d at 243; GICC Capital Corp. v. Tech. Fin. Group, Inc., 67 F.3d 463, 466 (2d Cir. 1992), *cert. denied*, 518 U.S. 1017 (1996) (holding that plaintiffs' evidence of a "discrete and relatively short-lived scheme to defraud a handful of victims" did not sufficiently demonstrate that such fraud was an ordinary part of the operations of the enterprise, a plumbing supply company; accordingly, no open-ended continuity); Lefkowitz v. Bank of New York, 2003 WL 22480049, at *9 (S.D.N.Y. Oct. 31, 2003) (plaintiff, the beneficiary of her parents' estates, failed to show that the defendants, the estates' executor and its counsel, regularly used fraud to administer estates).

186 Beauford v. Helmsley, 865 F.2d 1386, 1392 (2d Cir.) (en banc), *vacated and remanded*, 492 U.S. 914, *adhered to on remand*, 843 F.2d 1433, *cert. denied*, 443 U.S. 992 (1989).

187 *Id.* at 1391, 1392; *see also* De Falco v. Bernas, 244 F.3d 286 (2d Cir. 2001) (open-ended continuity sufficiently pleaded where escalating nature of defendants' extortion demands implied a threat that the demands would continue); G-I Holdings, Inc. v. Baron & Budd, 238 F. Supp. 2d 521 (S.D.N.Y. 2002) (finding threat of continuing illegal activity in scheme to fix affidavits).

188 *See, e.g.*, Corley v. Rosewood Care Ctr., Inc., 142 F.3d 1041, 1046 (7th Cir. 1998) (reversing summary judgment for defendant, which operated a number of nursing homes, and remanding to allow further discovery to substantiate the pattern element because plaintiff alleged that there were other victims, in other nursing homes, of the defendant's bait and switch scheme who taken together would establish continuity), *on remand*, Corley v. Rosewood Care Ctr., Inc., 152 F. Supp. 2d 1099, 1110 (C.D. Ill. 2001) (again entering summary judgment, on ground that plaintiff had still failed to show that misrepresentations regarding the nursing homes were a regular activity of the defendants in their transactions with other customers); Ifill v. West, 1999 U.S. Dist. LEXIS 21320, *20, *21 (E.D.N.Y. Aug. 24, 1999) (open-ended continuity sufficiently pleaded where plaintiffs alleged an ongoing agreement between defendants to continue the scheme, and alleged that the defendant had used the same modus operandi to defraud other consumers); *see also* G-I Holdings, Inc. v. Baron & Budd, 238 F. Supp. 2d 521 (S.D.N.Y. 2002) (threat of criminal activity by law firm who allegedly falsified affidavits continued while asbestos litigation existed, therefore pattern element satisfied).

189 *E.g.*, Hofstetter v. Fletcher, 905 F.2d 897 (6th Cir. 1988) (injuring numerous investors over the course of several years sufficient); Terre Du Lac Ass'n, Inc. v. Terre Du Lac, Inc., 772 F.2d 467 (8th Cir. 1985) (suit against subdivision promoters by land purchasers alleging unfulfilled promises to pave roads), *cert. denied*, 475 U.S. 1082 (1986); *see also* Lawaetz v. Bank of Nova Scotia, 653 F. Supp. 1278 (D. V.I. 1987) (bank's fraudulent promise to extend credit through phone calls and letters to six plaintiffs constitutes pattern).

190 *See* GE Inv. Private Placement Partners II v. Parker, 247 F.3d 543, 549 (4th Cir. 2001) (no pattern where scheme had single goal of defrauding investors in the sale of a single enterprise); Sagliocolo v. Eagle Ins. Co., 112 F.3d 226 (6th Cir. 1997)

ever, consumer attorneys should argue that such identical fraudulent representations may actually establish open-ended continuity under the criteria established in *H.J. Inc.*, because they reveal the defendant's regular manner of doing business and thus establish the future threat that is key to proving open-ended continuity. Where a lender was accused of using a fraudulent loan agreement and extortionate means of collection, a court found that allegations of identical fraudulent documents and letters could establish the continuity aspect of pattern by showing that they were part of the defendant's regular way of conducting business.[191] Other courts have also held that multiple acts arising from one criminal episode can form a pattern.[192]

Consumer cases that involve a scheme that by its nature projects into the future, a "recidivist" scheme, may well meet the requirements of an "open-ended" type pattern. For example, homeowners who pleaded that they had been victimized by a scheme through which a finance company illegally diverted loan proceeds successfully argued that the scheme, which took place over just nine months, satisfied the pattern requirement by virtue of being "open-ended."[193] In contrast, a case alleging a single transaction with a single victim, such as in the sale of a piece of real estate, may have more difficulty meeting the continuity requirement, even where the plaintiff alleges several predicate acts.[194]

(insurer's refusal to provide documentation needed to sell cab medallions due to unpaid premiums on cab's insurance not pattern where it took place over one month); Leonard v. J.C. Pro Wear, Inc., 64 F.3d 657 (4th Cir. 1995) (unpublished disposition text available on Westlaw) (single purpose, single set of victims, seven months insufficient; Fourth Circuit refused, however, to hold that a seven month scheme is *per se* insufficient); Tudor Assocs. Ltd., II v. AJ & AJ Servicing, Inc., 36 F.3d 1094 (4th Cir. 1994) (no pattern where scheme lasted more than ten years and involved many predicates, but single injury and single victim), *cert. denied*, 514 U.S. 1107 (1995); Vemco, Inc. v. Camardella, 23 F.3d 129 (6th Cir. 1994) (17 month scheme, one goal and one victim, is not a pattern), *cert. denied*, 513 U.S. 1017 (1994); Primary Care Investors v. PHP Healthcare Corp., 986 F.2d 1208 (8th Cir. 1993) (no continuity where less than one year); Wade v. Hopper, 993 F.2d 1246 (7th Cir. 1993) (same), *cert. denied*, 510 U.S. 868 (1993); 420 E. Ohio Ltd. P'ship v. Cocose, 980 F.2d 1122 (7th Cir. 1992) (despite high number of mail and wire fraud predicate acts, six months is not a substantial period of time under *H.J., Inc.*); Fleet Credit Corp. v. Sion, 893 F.2d 441 (1st Cir. 1990) (95 predicate acts of mail fraud over four and a half years is not a pattern); *see also* Schroeder v. Acceleration Life Ins. Co., 972 F.2d 41 (3d Cir. 1992) (reversing summary judgment for defendant on grounds that an alleged "benefits reduction scheme" based on a large number of credit disability insurance policies issued over a long period of time met definition of "pattern"); Johnson v. Andrews, RICO Business Disputes Guide (CCH) ¶ 8643, 1994 U.S. Dist. LEXIS 11880 (D. Mass. Aug. 17, 1994) (with mail and wire fraud, sheer numbers do not make a pattern). *But see* Libertad v. Welch, 53 F.3d 428 (1st Cir. 1995) (abortion protestors' three month campaign could be long enough where it was its regular way of doing business).

191 Brown v. C.I.L., Inc., 1996 U.S. Dist. LEXIS 4917 (N.D. Ill. Jan. 26, 1996) (unpublished); *see also* Arenson v. Whitehall Convalescent & Nursing Home, 880 F. Supp. 1202 (N.D. Ill. 1995) (allegations that nursing home sent 75 bills fraudulently overcharging for drugs over five year period established closed-end continuity, and additionally established open-ended continuity by showing such fraud was part of defendant's regular way of conducting business); Robinson v. Empire of Am. Realty Credit Corp., 1991 U.S. Dist. LEXIS 2084 (N.D. Ill. Feb. 20, 1991) (unpublished) (allegations that mortgagor sent thousands of statements over a period of several years demanding excess escrow deposits met continuity requirement).

192 Young v. Hamilton, 92 Fed. Appx. 389, 392 (9th Cir. 2003) (predicate acts that related to a single fraudulent investment scheme could establish pattern); Corley v. Rosewood Care Ctr., Inc., 142 F.3d 1041 (7th Cir. 1998) (plaintiff's allegations that nursing home's alleged bait and switch scheme involved not just the plaintiff but many other residents over a period of 12 to 14 months were sufficient evidence of pattern to withstand summary judgment); Busby v. Crown Supply, Inc., 896 F.2d 833 (4th Cir. 1990) (scheme to defraud salesmen of their commissions, which extended over 10 years, sufficient). *See also* U.S. v. Connolly, 341 F.3d 16, 30 (1st Cir. 2003) (stating that a "single criminal episode" is "narrow in scope and purpose"); Walk v. Baltimore & Ohio Railroad, 847 F.2d 1100 (4th Cir. 1988) (not necessary to show more than one fraudulent scheme to establish a pattern), *vacated*, 492 U.S. 914 (1989), *on remand*, 890 F.2d 698 (4th Cir. 1989); Heaven & Earth, Inc. v. Wyman Props. Ltd. P'ship, 2003 WL 22680935, at *6–7 (D. Minn. Oct. 21, 2003) (plaintiffs could establish pattern based on acts committed as part of single scheme to overcharge tenant for utility charges); Matthews v. New Century Mortg. Corp., 185 F. Supp. 2d 874, 892 (S.D. Ohio 2002) (finding that plaintiffs had adequately alleged pattern in state RICO claim brought against defendants who had allegedly been part of a fraudulent home improvement loan scheme targeted toward elderly women). *But see* GE Inv. Private Placement Partners II v. Parker, 247 F.3d 543, 550 (4th Cir. 2001) (lender fraud that stopped with plaintiff's investment did not demonstrate that defendants regularly did business that way); Eastern Pub'g & Adver., Inc. v. Chesapeake Pub'g & Advert., Inc., 895 F.2d 971 (4th Cir. 1990) (single closed-ended scheme, which posed no threat of continuity and lasted only 3 months, insufficient), *cert. denied*, 497 U.S. 1025 (1990).

193 Thomas v. Ross & Hardies, 9 F. Supp. 2d 547, 553 (D. Md. 1998) (the plaintiffs alleged that the principals had targeted minority homeowners and had convinced them to mortgage their homes for the maximum amount possible in return for paying off prior mortgages and extending a line of credit, then failed to pay off the prior loans). *But see* Corley v. Rosewood Care Ctr., Inc., 152 F. Supp. 2d 1099, 1110 (C.D. Ill. 2001) (court would not infer that if nursing home company misrepresented prices in one home, it must have made the same misrepresentations with respect to other homes).

194 *See, e.g.*, Soto-Negron v. Taber Partners I, 339 F.3d 35, 38–39 (1st Cir. 2003) (wrongful cashing of six checks within days of one another did not satisfy continuity requirement); Nugent v. Saint Agnes Medical Ctr., 53 Fed. Appx. 828, 829 (9th Cir. 2002) (no threat of continuity when scheme involves single fraud with single victim); Martinez v. Martinez, 207 F. Supp. 2d 1303, 1306 (D.N.M. 2002) (no pattern where scheme involved only ex-wife and ran only over the course of divorce litigation), *aff'd in part, vacated in part on other grounds*, 2003 WL 1904807 (10th Cir. 2003) (unpublished, citation limited); Singh v. Parnes, 199 F. Supp. 2d 152, 161, 162 (S.D.N.Y. 2002) (no pattern where all activities related to purchase and sale of one

Where a scheme is "inherently terminable," such as where it plots the looting of funds that have already been exhausted, there is no threat of continued activity and accordingly no open-ended continuity.[195] Where the scheme involves representations made to many consumers, courts should allow plaintiffs the opportunity to discover other targets of the scheme and the representations made to them in order to establish a threat of continued crimes, that is, open-ended continuity.[196]

property); Mathon v. Marine Midland Bank, 875 F. Supp. 986 (E.D.N.Y. 1985) (no continuity). *See also* GE Inv. Private Placement Partners II v. Parker, 247 F.3d 543, 550 (4th Cir. 2001) (fraud in association with sale of single enterprise did not satisfy continuity); GICC Capital Corp. v. Tech. Fin. Group, 67 F.3d 463, 468 (2d Cir. 1995) (where just one victim, continuity not established); Welch v. Centex Home Equity Co., 2004 WL 1486310, at *7 (D. Kan. June 30, 2004) (no continuity where fraud arose from a single scheme, the forgery of plaintiff's signature on loan documents for the purchase of a home); Dempsey v. Sanders, 132 F. Supp. 2d 222, 227 (S.D.N.Y. 2001) (thirteen predicate acts comprising a single scheme to defraud a single victim were not sufficiently continuous); Hobson v. Lincoln Ins. Agency, Inc., 2000 U.S. Dist. LEXIS 13314 (N.D. Ill. Sept. 7, 2000) (plaintiff's allegations of ten payments made over a ten month period as part of a single, allegedly fraudulent, insurance transaction do not constitute a "pattern"); China Trust Bank v. Standard Chartered Bank, PLC, 981 F. Supp. 282, 287–88 (S.D.N.Y. 1997) (predicate acts by single defendant against single victim met neither open-ended nor closed-ended continuity tests); Travis v. Boulevard Bank, 1994 U.S. Dist. LEXIS 14615 (N.D. Ill. Oct. 14, 1994) (where alleged acts of mail fraud all related to the single alleged wrongful act of defendant's procurement of force-placed insurance on plaintiff's RISC, no continuity).

195 Turner v. Cook, 362 F.3d 1219, 1229 (9th Cir. 2004) (no open-ended continuity in suit against judgment creditors "since the alleged activities were finite in nature [and] would cease once appellees collected the outstanding tort judgment"); Kenda Corp. v. Pot O'Gold Money Leagues, Inc., 329 F.3d 216, 233 (1st Cir. 2003) (no open-ended continuity where all acts directed toward one transaction); GICC Capital Corp. v. Tech. Fin. Group, Inc., 67 F.3d 463, 467 (2d Cir. 1992), *cert. denied*, 518 U.S. 1017 (1996); GE Inv. Private Placement Partners II v. Parker, 247 F.3d 543, 549 (4th Cir. 2001) (where fraud limited to the sale of a single enterprise, no threat of continued criminal activity); First Capital Asset Mgmt. v. Brickelbush, Inc., 150 F. Supp. 2d 624, 634 (S.D.N.Y. 2001) (bankruptcy fraud scheme inherently terminable by the conclusion of the case). *See also* Howard v. America Online, Inc., 208 F.3d 741, 750 (9th Cir. 2000) (no open-ended continuity where basis of plaintiff's complaint was an advertising program to promote a one-time change in pricing policy, no threat that would be repeated in the future), *cert. denied*, 531 U.S. 828 (2000); Metcalf v. Death Row Records, Inc., 2003 WL 22097336, at *4 (N.D. Cal. Sept. 3, 2003) (no open-ended continuity where only one scheme with one victim).

196 *See* Corley v. Rosewood Care Ctr., 142 F.3d 1041, 1049 (7th Cir. 1998) (reversing summary judgment in favor of defendant, a nursing home owner, where plaintiff alleged that there were other victims of the defendant's bait and switch scheme). *But see* Pizzo v. Bekin Van Lines Co., 258 F.3d 629 (7th Cir. 2001) (refusing plaintiff the opportunity to discover additional fraud victims).

9.2.3.4.5 Relationship aspect of pattern

The relationship property is usually less tricky than the continuity property. Predicate acts of racketeering satisfy the relationship test if they "have the same or similar purposes, results, participants, victims, or methods of commission, or otherwise are interrelated by distinguishing characteristics and are not isolated events."[197] This criterion "exists to ensure that RICO is not used to penalize a series of disconnected criminal acts."[198]

Until further guidance from the Supreme Court, the pleader must try to come within the terms of whatever theories of relationship and continuity prevail in his or her jurisdiction. The more predicate offenses of the same or similar character, the better; and they should be pleaded so far as possible in enough detail to warrant the inference that they are related to one another above and beyond the fact that they are the work of the same culprit. This is an area where judicial hostility to broad uses of civil RICO may yet manifest itself as narrow construction of an element not fully defined by the language of the statute.[199]

197 *H.J., Inc.*, 492 U.S. at 240 (internal quotation omitted); *see also* Heller Fin., Inc. v. Grammco Computer Sales, Inc., 71 F.3d 518, 524 (5th Cir. 1996) (relationship requirement not met where "[t]he purposes of the alleged predicate acts were distinct and dissimilar"); Vild v. Visconsi, 956 F.2d 560 (6th Cir.) (relationship requirement met), *cert. denied*, 506 U.S. 832 (1992); U.S. v. Eufrasio, 935 F.2d 553, 565 (3d Cir.) (finding requirement met, affirming defendants' convictions), *cert. denied*, 502 U.S. 925 (1991); Anderson v. Smithfield Foods, Inc., 207 F. Supp. 2d 1358, 1363 (M.D. Fla. 2002); Maryland-Nat'l Capital Park & Planning Comm'n v. Boyle, 203 F. Supp. 2d 468, 475 (D. Md. 2002), *aff'd*, 2003 WL 1879017 (4th Cir. Apr. 16, 2003) (unpublished, citation limited); Meyer Material Co. v. Mooshol, 188 F. Supp. 2d 936, 941 (N.D. Ill. 2002) (relationship element satisfied where acts related to common purpose of embezzlement); Wilson v. De Angelis, 156 F. Supp. 2d 1335, 1340 (S.D. Fla. 2001) (fraud in connection with ten purchases of gold bullion coins over ten-month period was sufficiently related for purposes of fulfilling pattern element); Dempsey v. Sanders, 132 F. Supp. 2d 222, 227 (S.D.N.Y. 2001); Ifill v. West, 1999 U.S. Dist. LEXIS 21320, at *19 (E.D.N.Y. Aug. 24, 1999) (where refinancing and foreclosure scheme designed to acquire inflated, federally insured mortgages had common participants and common goals, relationship established).

198 U.S. v. Eufrasio, 935 F.2d 553, 565 (3d Cir.) (finding requirement met, affirming defendants' convictions), *cert. denied*, 502 U.S. 925 (1991).

199 For example, in Brown v. Coleman Invs., Inc., 993 F. Supp. 416, 430 (M.D. La. 1998), the court took a miserly view of the pattern requirement, finding that there is no pattern of racketeering activity if the alleged acts are part of the usual endeavors of the enterprise; thus, a RICO claim could not be based on a loan funded by an enterprise to a dealer even though the loan necessarily included funding upcharges for license fees and taxes wrongfully charged by the dealer. *See also* Maryland-Nat'l Capital Park & Planning Comm'n v. Boyle, 203 F. Supp. 2d 468, 476 (D. Md. 2002) (suggesting caution about finding RICO claims in episodes of "garden variety fraud") (citations omitted), *aff'd*, 2003 WL 1879017 (4th Cir. Apr. 16, 2003) (unpub-

9.2.3.4.6 *Proving a "pattern"*

There are at least two special issues in proving a "pattern." Although the "pattern" and "enterprise" elements of a RICO claim are distinct and each must be proven, the same evidence may prove both.[200] Another issue is whether an individual can plead, as part of a pattern of racketeering, acts committed by the defendant that do not affect the plaintiff. Most courts hold that a plaintiff need not be injured by a practice to plead it as part of the pattern of racketeering activity,[201] so long as the plaintiff otherwise meets the requirement of injury to business or property.[202]

Specificity in pleading and proof is also important. When alleging that a defendant made fraudulent representations to a pool of consumers, it is critical to substantiate to the court the details of those representations and the victims to whom they were made in order to avoid summary dismissal.[203]

9.2.3.5 Collection of an Unlawful Debt

9.2.3.5.1 *General*

RICO provides an alternative to proof of a pattern of racketeering in establishing a substantive violation. The statute provides that it is illegal to associate in various specified ways with an enterprise *either* through a pattern of racketeering activity *or* through collection of an unlawful debt.[204] The latter is one of the most overlooked RICO provisions.[205] An unlawful debt is defined to include a usurious debt which is unenforceable in whole or in part as to interest or principal, and which bears an interest rate of at least twice the enforceable rate.[206]

Virtually all usury laws specify that usurious loans are unenforceable, at least as to the portion of interest exceeding the enforceable rate. Consequently, the key to proving a RICO violation based on collection of an unlawful debt is showing that a creditor collected a debt where the interest rate exceeded twice the enforceable rate.[207]

It is not enough to show that a creditor violated a lending law—the law must set a maximum amount of interest that can be charged and the creditor must have charged more than twice that set amount. Collection of an unlawful debt thus can not be based merely on violations of laws dealing with the method of collecting interest or the kind of property that can be received for a loan.[208]

Furthermore, it is interest, and not other lending-related charges, that must have been overcharged. For example, the District of Columbia Circuit has disallowed a RICO claim based on a mortgage lender's practice of charging more than twice the legally allowable points on a mortgage loan, because the total amount charged was not more than the legally permissible interest rate of 24%.[209] The plaintiffs argued that the District of Columbia usury law states a maximum interest rate and a maximum points rate, so that violation of either could form the basis of a RICO claim.

---

lished, citation limited); Majchrowski v. Norwest Mort., 6 F. Supp. 2d 946, 946 (N.D. Ill. 1998) (describing plaintiff's claim that mortgagee imposed fraudulent fees against mortgagors as illustrating that "the line between civil RICO, a formidable weapon authorizing treble damages and attorneys' fees, and conventional breach of contract actions, has faded considerably.").

200 United States v. Turkette, 452 U.S. 576, 582, 583 (1981); United States v. Qaoud, 777 F.2d 1105, 1115 (6th Cir. 1985), *cert. denied*, 475 U.S. 1098 (1986); United States v. Mazzei, 700 F.2d 85, 89 (2d Cir.), *cert. denied*, 461 U.S. 945 (1983); United States v. Bagnariol, 665 F.2d 877, 890, 891 (9th Cir. 1981), *cert. denied*, 456 U.S. 962 (1982); United States v. Perholtz, 657 F. Supp. 603 (D.D.C. 1988); *see also* § 9.2.3.2.2, *supra*.

201 Marshall v. Ilsley Trust Co. v. Pate, 819 F.2d 806, 809 (7th Cir. 1987); Town of Kearney v. Hudson Meadows Urban Renewal Corp., 829 F.2d 1263, 1268 (3d Cir. 1987).

202 *See* § 9.2.3.6, *infra*.

203 *See, e.g.*, Corley v. Rosewood Care Ctr., Inc., 152 F. Supp. 2d 1099, 1113 (C.D. Ill. 2001) (granting summary judgment to defendant, which operated nursing homes, where plaintiff failed to present sufficient evidence of his claim that the defendant made the same misrepresentations to other consumers as were made to the plaintiff).

204 18 U.S.C. § 1962.

205 *See* Ukwuoma v. Marine, No. CV-85-6557 DWW (KX), 6 RICO L. Rep. 94,220 (C.D. Cal. verdict June 9, 1987) ($1.1 million for collection of unlawful debt and pattern of lender fraud involving 36% loan to restaurant owners).

206 The following language was deemed sufficient pleading of unlawful debt in Merly v. D'Arcangelo, 1992 WL 11182, at *1 (Conn. Super. Ct. Jan. 16, 1992): "that the plaintiff was associated with the Gambino crime family, that each defendant was engaged in interstate commerce, and that the notes called for usurious interest (104%)." The plaintiff should also plead that the usury laws affect the enforceability of the loans. In Cannarozzi v. Fiumara, the First Circuit ruled that because the allegedly unlawful loans could be enforced through an exception to the usury laws, they could not support the plaintiff's RICO claims. 371 F.3d 1, 6 (1st Cir. 2004).

207 Bellizan v. Easy Money of Louisiana, Inc., 2002 WL 1611648, at *6 (E.D. La. July 19, 2002) (rejecting argument that where loan was illegally split into two transactions to avoid interest rate limitations, allowable interest on second loan was zero for purposes of RICO's interest rate element). The Second Circuit has held that a person can be liable for aiding and abetting collection of an unlawful debt without proof that the defendant knew that the rates of interest charged were usurious. United States v. Biasucci, 786 F.2d 504, 512–13 (2d Cir.), *cert. denied*, 479 U.S. 827 (1986). However, that decision preceded the Supreme Court's decision in Central Bank v. First Interstate Bank, 511 U.S. 164, 114 S. Ct. 1439, 128 L. Ed. 2d 119 (1994), and the near consensus that aiding and abetting is no longer viable under RICO. *See* §§ 9.2.3.2.4, *supra*, 9.2.4.3, *infra*.

208 Sundance Land Corp. v. Cmty. First Fed. Sav. & Loan Ass'n, 840 F.2d 653, 666–67 (9th Cir. 1988).

209 Reidy v. Meritor Sav., 888 F.2d 898 (table), 1989 WL 132673, at *1 (D.C. Cir. 1989). Similarly, in Johnson v. Fleet Fin., Inc., 785 F. Supp. 1003, 1010 (S.D. Ga. 1992) the court dismissed federal and state RICO claims by mortgagors against lenders because, although the first month's interest rate exceeded the permitted percentage, the interest calculated over the life of the loan did not.

The court rejected this view, holding that charging more than twice the allowable points was not twice the allowable "rate." The court held that the RICO statute, in referring to twice the allowable rate, referred to the total of all interest-related charges, and not just the rate for a component of the total interest charge.[210]

9.2.3.5.2 Potential RICO claims based on the collection of an unlawful debt; payday lenders

Consumers should consider alleging a RICO violation based on the collection of an unlawful debt in the following situations:

- If a rent-to-own appliance transaction is treated under state law as a disguised credit transaction, the imputed interest rate (calculated by assigning a fair market value for the appliance and dividing lease payments between principal and interest) will probably exceed twice the allowed rate.[211]
- Interest hidden or mislabeled in a sham "post-dated check-cashing" loan scheme may affect the relevant interest rate.[212]
- If a house sale and lease-back arrangement can be treated instead as a direct loan with an imputed interest rate, this may significantly exceed the allowable rate.
- A number of installment sales acts only allow creditors to exceed the general usury rate (e.g., 8%) with a higher rate (e.g., 18%) where the installment sales act is complied with. Failure to comply should make the general rate, and not the higher installment sales rate, the "enforceable" rate for purposes of RICO.
- Federal law allows mobile home lenders to charge rates far in excess of the rate allowed by state usury law, but only if the creditor complies with certain OTS regulations; noncompliance makes the state usury rate applicable.[213]
- If hidden interest, such as fictitious fees, broker's commissions, inflation of the cash sales price for credit customers, or points are treated as interest under state law, the actual rate may exceed twice the allowable rate.[214]
- Where an auto pawnbroker or other pawnbroker incorrectly believes that state usury rates do not apply, the customer may be charged effective interest rates as high as 200 or 300%;[215]
- Where a creditor thinks it is not, but actually is, covered by a state credit limit, the creditor may exceed twice the enforceable rate.[216]

9.2.3.5.3 Is an isolated collection of an unlawful debt actionable?

A plaintiff asserting collection of an unlawful debt must demonstrate that the unlawful debt (if not from gambling) was "incurred in connection with . . . the business of lending money or a thing of value, at a rate usurious under State or Federal law, where the usurious rate is at least twice the enforceable rate."[217] The RICO statute does not explicitly require either a pattern of unlawful debt collection[218] or a

---

210 *See* Nolen v. Nucentrix Broadband Networks, Inc., 293 F.3d 926, 929 (5th Cir.) (late fee not interest under Texas law), *cert. denied*, 537 U.S. 1047 (2002).

211 *See* Starks v. Rent-A-Center, 1990 U.S. Dist. LEXIS 20099, Clearinghouse No. 45,215 (D. Minn. May 15, 1990), *aff'd on other grounds*, 58 F.3d 358 (8th Cir. 1995); Miller v. Colortyme, Inc., 518 N.W.2d 544, 548 (Minn. 1994) (Minnesota's usury statute applies to rent-to-own contracts); Fogie v. Rent-A-Center, Inc., 518 N.W.2d 544, 548 (Minn. 1994) (rent-to-own contracts are consumer credit sales under Minnesota law).

212 *See* Arrington v. Colleen, Inc., 2000 WL 34001056, at *6 (D. Md. Aug. 7, 2000) (denying lender's motion for summary judgment); Cashback Catalog Sales, Inc. v. Price, 102 F. Supp. 2d 1375, 1380 (S.D. Ga. Mar. 20, 2000) (denying summary judgment to defendant who took post-dated checks in return for a reduced amount of cash plus an allegedly valueless certificate to a mail-order catalog company for the difference); Burden v. York, Clearinghouse No. 52,502, Civil Action No. 98–268 (E.D. Ky. Sept. 29, 1999); Hamilton v. HLT Check Exchange, 987 F. Supp. 953, 957–58 (E.D. Ky. 1997) (denying the motion of the defendant, a check cashing business, to dismiss RICO claim alleging the collection of an unlawful debt). *See also* Henry v. Cash Today, Inc., 199 F.R.D. 566, 572–73 (S.D. Tex. 2000) (class certification granted in cash back ad sale case). *See also* National Consumer Law Center, The Cost of Credit: Regulation and Legal Challenges § 7.5.5 (2d ed. 2000 & Supp.).

213 *See* National Consumer Law Center, The Cost of Credit: Regulation and Legal Challenges § 3.5.3.4 (2d ed. 2000 and Supp.).

214 *Id.* at Ch. 5. *See also* Faircloth v. Certified Fin. Inc., 2001 U.S. Dist. LEXIS 6793 (E.D. La. May 15, 2001) (approving settlement agreement in class action that alleged defendants flipped loans to impose excessive interest). *But see* Rivera v. AT&T Corp., 141 F. Supp. 2d 719, 723–25 (S.D. Tex. 2001) (since late fee was not interest under state law, no usury that would establish collection of an unlawful debt), *aff'd without op.*, 2002 WL 663707 (5th Cir. Mar. 25, 2002).

215 *See* Burnett v. Ala Moana Pawn Shop, Clearinghouse No. 46,771 (D. Haw. 1991) (RICO not pleaded), *aff'd*, 3 F.3d 1261 (9th Cir. 1993).

216 *See* National Consumer Law Center, The Cost of Credit: Regulation and Legal Challenges §§ 9.1.2.2.1, 9.1.2.2.2 (2d ed. 2000 and Supp.). *But see* State v. Roderick, 704 So. 2d 49, 54 (Miss. 1997) (holding Mississippi RICO statute void for vagueness as applied to a criminal prosecution of check cashing business for violation of usury law), *cert. denied*, 524 U.S. 926 (1998).

217 18 U.S.C. § 1961(6)(B).

218 The statute mentions pattern of racketeering activity and collection of unlawful debt three times. 18 U.S.C. § 1962(a) specifies a violation where income is received "from a pattern of racketeering activity or through collection of an unlawful debt." By the grammar it is clear that pattern refers only to racketeering activity and not to collection of an unlawful debt. 18 U.S.C. § 1962(b) also specifies that it is unlawful for a person "through a pattern of racketeering activity or through collection of an unlawful debt. . . ." Again the grammar is clear that a pattern is not required for collection of an unlawful debt. 18 U.S.C. § 1961(c) prohibits participation "through a pattern of rack-

defendant's being in the business of unlawful debt collection, and courts have held that the provision can apply to an occasional instance of loansharking.[219] Nonetheless, some courts have expressly or implicitly created such a requirement. A Minnesota state court held that a plaintiff must show not just one collection of an unlawful debt but a pattern of collection of unlawful debts.[220] This holding was clearly wrong, and the Minnesota Supreme Court in dicta on appeal made a special effort to point out the error of the holding.[221] However, in doing so, the high court may have suggested another route to a similar requirement by noting that the bank was not alleged to be "in the business of lending money at usurious rates."[222]

A few other courts have followed the same route, holding that the scope of RICO does not extend to occasional usurious transactions by one not in the business of loansharking.[223] For example, in a Rhode Island district court case, two individuals filed a RICO claim against the president of a car dealership, alleging that he had twice loaned them money at usurious rates.[224] The court stated that two incidents of lending did not demonstrate that the defendant was in the business of lending money, so an unlawful debt could not have occurred. The court reasoned that Congress did not intend RICO to penalize isolated instances of usury—only the business of gambling or the business of lending.[225] In another case, the plaintiff was beaten by a law enforcement officer who was trying to collect a debt the plaintiff owed to a private creditor. The court held that a single, isolated event, which did not result in financial gain to the officer, could not constitute collection of an unlawful debt for RICO purposes.[226]

9.2.3.6 The "Injury" Element

9.2.3.6.1 Introduction

"Any person injured in his business or property" may sue for treble damages under RICO.[227] Constrictive constructions of this language—confining civil RICO plaintiffs to those who could plead and prove "racketeering" or "competitive" or "commercial" injury—were rejected by the Supreme Court in *Sedima*.[228] Nonetheless, the plaintiff must establish both the injury[229] and that the defendant's violation of a substantive RICO provision proximately caused the injury. The injury must be sufficiently concrete as well. However, mere pleading that the plaintiff has suffered an injury caused by the violations should suffice; the plaintiff need not plead factual detail such as the components of the damages.[230] While a plaintiff must have suffered an injury, that plaintiff need not have been injured by each predicate

---

eteering activity or collection of an unlawful debt." While this grammar is somewhat ambiguous, the clear import of subsections (a) and (b) is that Congress did not intend a pattern requirement for collection of an unlawful debt under (a), (b) or (c). *See* United States v. Oreto, 37 F.3d 739 (1st Cir. 1994) (unlawful debt section does not require pattern—that does not render the statute unconstitutional), *cert. denied*, 513 U.S. 1177 (1995); Ballen v. Prudential Bache Sec., 23 F.3d 335 (10th Cir. 1994); United States v. Weiner, 3 F.3d 17 (1st Cir. 1993); Davis v. Mutual Life Ins. Co. of New York, 6 F.3d 367 (6th Cir. 1993), *cert. denied*, 510 U.S. 1193 (1994); United States v. Giovanelli, 945 F.2d 479 (2d Cir. 1991) (only single collection of unlawful debt need be proved).

219 *See, e.g.*, Cashback Catalog Sales, Inc. v. Price, 102 F. Supp. 2d 1375 (S.D. Ga. 2000) (denying summary judgment on RICO claim); Arrington v. Colleen, Inc., 2000 WL 34001056, at *7 (D. Md. Aug. 7, 2000) (denying lender's motion for summary judgment); Burden v. York, Clearinghouse No. 52,502, Civil Action No. 98-268 (E.D. Ky. Sept. 29, 1999); Hamilton v. HLT Check Exchange, 987 F. Supp. 953 (E.D. Ky. 1997) (denying the motion of the defendant, a check cashing business, to dismiss RICO claim alleging the collection of an unlawful debt). *See also* Henry v. Cash Today, Inc., 199 F.R.D. 566 (S.D. Tex. 2000) (class certification granted in cash back ad sale case).

220 Bandas v. Citizens State Bank of Silver Lake, 412 N.W.2d 818, 821 (Minn. Ct. App. 1987), *remanded on other grounds sub nom.* VanderWeyst v. First State Bank, 425 N.W.2d 803 (Minn.), *cert. denied*, 488 U.S. 943 (1988).

221 425 N.W.2d 803 (Minn.), *cert. denied*, 488 U.S. 943 (1988).

222 425 N.W.2d at 812.

223 Cannarozzi v. Fiumara, 371 F.3d 1, 4 n.4 (1st Cir. 2004); Durante Bros. & Sons, Inc. v. Flushing Nat'l Bank, 755 F.2d 239 (2d Cir.), *cert. denied*, 473 U.S. 906 (1985); Weisel v. Pischel, 197 F.R.D. 231 (E.D.N.Y. 2000). The *Weisel* court granted summary judgment to defendants on this basis, reasoning that RICO's legislative history justified limiting the statute to loansharkers, not ordinary businessmen who might make a usurious loan: "[t]he requirement that the loan have been incurred in connection with 'the business of' making usurious loans is aimed at . . . 'the exclusion from the scope of the statute of occasional usurious transactions by one not in the business of loan sharking.' " *Id.* at 241 (quoting S. Rep. No. 91-617, 91st Cong., 1st Sess. 158 (1969)).

224 Robidoux v. Conti, 741 F. Supp. 1019 (D.R.I. 1990).

225 *Id.* at 1022.

226 Wright v. Sheppard, 919 F.2d 665 (11th Cir. 1990).

227 18 U.S.C. § 1964(c). The injury need not be direct, but it must satisfy the traditional "but for" analysis. Ocean Energy II, Inc. v. Alexander & Alexander, Inc., 868 F.2d 740 (5th Cir. 1989). So, for example, in Corley v. Rosewood Care Ctr., Inc., 152 F. Supp. 2d 1099, 1112 (C.D. Ill. 2001) the court held that though the defendant nursing home company's representations regarding continuing care might have formed a pattern of racketeering activity, the plaintiff failed to show requisite injury because the guaranty neither factored in decision to place mother in home nor was tested by need for such aid.

228 Sedima, S.P.R.L. v. Imrex Co., 473 U.S. 479, 495, 105 S. Ct. 3275, 87 L. Ed. 2d 346 (1985).

229 18 U.S.C. § 1962(c); Sedima, S.P.R.L. v. Imrex Co., 473 U.S. 479, 496, 105 S. Ct. 3275, 87 L. Ed. 2d 346 (1985) (a "plaintiff only has standing if, and can only recover to the extent that, he has been injured in his business or property by the conduct constituting the violation."). *See also* Price v. Pinnacle Brands, Inc., 138 F.3d 602, 606, 607 (5th Cir. 1998) (injury to plaintiff's business or property is a prerequisite under § 1964); Nodine v. Textron, Inc., 819 F.2d 347, 348, 349 (1st Cir. 1987) (a plaintiff who can not show injury to business or property lacks standing).

230 Zito v. Leasecomm Corp., 2003 WL 22251352, at *18–19 (S.D.N.Y. Sept. 30, 2003).

act alleged, but only by one of the defendant's predicate acts.[231]

9.2.3.6.2 Standing

Subsection 1964(c)'s term "business or property" limits compensable injuries to those that are proprietary in nature. Personal injury and mental suffering do not confer RICO standing.[232] Nonetheless, the defendant need not have had an economic motive in order to cause an actionable injury.[233] Furthermore, the plaintiff must allege that the defendant's specific violation of the substantive provision caused the injury.

The plaintiff in a RICO action must have suffered direct injury; indirectly injured third parties do not have RICO standing. Consequently, creditors do not have standing to sue for injury to the direct victim[234] and union members do not have standing to sue for injuries to the union.[235] An employee who is fired for his alleged refusal to participate in a fraudulent scheme may or may not be able to bring a RICO claim.[236] Depositors in a failed financial institution lack standing to sue because of the derivative nature of their injuries.[237] Hospitals and insurers may not recover their expenses incurred for the medical care of smokers who were allegedly injured by RICO violations.[238] Similarly, those

231 Terminate Control Corp. v. Horowitz, 28 F.3d 1335 (2d Cir. 1994); Town of Kearny v. Hudson Meadows Urban Renewal Corp., 829 F.2d 1263 (3d Cir. 1987); Marshall & Ilsley Trust Co. v. Pate, 819 F.2d 806 (7th Cir. 1987); Hunt v. Gouverneur Townhouse Partners, 1991 U.S. Dist. LEXIS 16749 (S.D.N.Y. Nov. 18, 1991).

232 *See, e.g.*, Ove v. Gwinn, 264 F.3d 817, 825 (9th Cir. 2001) (deprivation of "honest services" that does not constitute concrete financial loss was not a RICO injury); Fleischhauer v. Feltner, 879 F.2d 1290, 200 (6th Cir. 1989), *cert. denied*, 493 U.S. 1027 (1990); Grogan v. Platt, 835 F.2d 844, 847 (1st Cir. 1988), *cert. denied*, 488 U.S. 981 (1988) (income lost by FBI agents who were shot by defendants was not injury to "business or property" because they derived from personal injuries); Burnett v. Al Baraka Inv. and Dev. Corp., 274 F. Supp. 2d 86, 101 (D.D.C. 2003) (losses suffered on September 11, 2001 from terrorist attacks did not grant standing to victims' family members and representatives in suit against entities that allegedly supported the terrorists); Giannone *ex rel.* Giannone v. Ayer Inst., 290 F. Supp. 2d 553, 565 (E.D. Pa. 2003) (neither frostbite nor emotional distress suffered by student in a wilderness camp fulfilled RICO's requirement of injury to "business or property"); LaBarbera v. Angel, 2000 U.S. Dist. LEXIS 1195, at *8, 9 (E.D. Tex. Jan. 20, 2000). A California district court has expanded the personal injury disqualification to include those pecuniary losses suffered by reason of a personal injury. Walker v. Gates, 2002 WL 1065618, at *8 (C.D. Cal. May 28, 2002) (finding that plaintiff's lost wages and other pecuniary losses resulting from allegedly illegal incarceration did not meet injury requirement because they derived from a personal, not proprietary, injury). Addicted smokers' attempts to characterize their wages, medical expenses, costs of tobacco, and other expenses as business or property damages have not been successful. *E.g.*, Ehrich v. B.A.T. Indus. PLC, 964 F. Supp. 164 (D.N.J. 1997). *See also* Curtin v. Tilley Fire Equip. Co., 1999 U.S. Dist. LEXIS 19467 (E.D. Pa. 1999) (unpublished) (personal and emotional injuries not compensable under RICO).

233 The United States Supreme Court has made clear that an economic motive on the defendant's part is not required for the plaintiff to have a compensable RICO injury. The Court reversed the dismissal of a section 1962(c) claim against several anti-abortion groups that allegedly conspired to close clinics through a pattern of extortion. National Organization for Women, Inc. v. Scheidler, 510 U.S. 249, 114 S. Ct. 798, 127 L. Ed. 2d 99 (1994).

234 National Enters., Inc. v. Mellon Fin. Servs. Corp., 847 F.2d 251 (5th Cir. 1988). *But see* Bauder v. Ralston Purina Co., 1989 U.S. Dist. LEXIS 14091, 1989 U.S. Dist. LEXIS 14091 (E.D. Pa. Nov. 21, 1989) (puppy food buyers who relied on ads had RICO claim against dog food manufacturer which misrepresented beneficial effects of dog food).

235 Adams-Lundy v. Association of Professional Flight Attendants, 844 F.2d 245 (5th Cir. 1988); *see also* Commer v. Am. Fed'n of State, County and Mun. Employees, 2003 WL 21697873, at *3–4 (S.D.N.Y. July 22, 2003) (acts that caused removal of plaintiff from presidency of union damaged union, not plaintiff). *But see* Trollinger v. Tyson Foods, Inc., 370 F.3d 602, 617 (6th Cir. 2004) (plaintiffs, unionized employees who sued employer claiming that employer schemed to depress wages by transporting and hiring illegal immigrants, had standing, rejecting defendant's argument that only union could bring the suit).

236 Courts split on this issue. *Compare* Schiffels v. Kemper Fin. Servs., Inc., 978 F.2d 344 (7th Cir. 1992) (whistleblower's termination and removal from executive bonus pool is injury to property), *appeal after remand*, 1993 U.S. Dist. LEXIS 6283 (N.D. Ill. May 10, 1993); Miranda v. Ponce Fed. Bank, 948 F.2d 41 (1st Cir. 1991) (standing); Reddy v. Litton Indus., Inc., 912 F.2d 291 (9th Cir. 1990) (standing), *cert. denied*, 502 U.S. 921 (1991); Shearin v. E.F. Hutton Group, Inc., 885 F.2d 1162 (3d Cir. 1989) (standing); Mruz v. Caring, Inc., 991 F. Supp. 701 (D.N.J. 1998) (fired whistleblower employees had suffered RICO injury) *with* Bowman v. Western Auto Supply Co., 985 F.2d 383 (8th Cir.) (no standing, noting that firing an employee is not a predicate act, and that it is irrelevant that the employer engaged in predicate acts which did not injure the employee), *cert. denied*, 508 U.S. 957 (1993); Hecht v. Commerce, 897 F.2d 21 (2d Cir. 1990) (no standing); O'Malley v. O'Neill, 887 F.2d 1557 (11th Cir. 1989), *cert. denied*, 496 U.S. 926 (1990) (no standing); Cullom v. Hibernia National Bank, 859 F.2d 1211, 1214, 1215 (5th Cir. 1988) (no standing); Hjermastad v. Central Livestock Ass'n, Inc., 2003 WL 21658260, at *3–4 (D. Minn. 2003) (employee fired after he refused to participate in an allegedly illegal scheme of his employer's did not have standing); Dunn v. Board of Incorporators of African Methodist Episcopal Church, 2002 WL 1000920, at *2, *3 (N.D. Tex. May 14, 2002) (no standing); Dugan v. Bell Tel. of Pa., 876 F. Supp. 713 (W.D. Pa. 1994) (former employee had no standing to sue where his alleged injury stemmed from his firing and not from the predicate act he alleged); Hoydal v. Prime Opportunities, Inc., 856 F. Supp. 327 (E.D. Mich. 1994) (employee who resigned rather than engaging in what she saw as fraudulent acts has no standing); Nicholson v. Windham, 571 S.E.2d 466, 469 (Ga. Ct. App. 2002) (plaintiff's injury from being fired did not meet state RICO's injury requirement).

237 *In re* Sunrise Sec. Litig., 916 F.2d 874 (3d Cir. 1990).

238 *See, e.g.*, Association of Wash. Pub. Hosp. Dists. v. Philip Morris, Inc., 241 F.3d 696 (9th Cir. 2001); Blue Cross & Blue Shield of N.J., Inc v. Philip Morris, Inc., 113 F. Supp. 2d 345, 369 (E.D.N.Y. 2000).

who have suffered increased health care costs from the effects of others' smoking have been unable to assert standing.[239] Though shareholders may not have standing to sue for their own injuries from racketeering activity conducted through the corporation, they have standing to sue derivatively on behalf of the corporation.[240] The Ninth Circuit considers three factors in evaluating whether an injury is too remote to state a RICO claim: (1) whether more direct victims of the alleged wrongful conduct exist; (2) whether the amount of damages attributable to the conduct will be too difficult to ascertain; and (3) whether courts will have to use complicated apportioning rules to avoid awarding multiple recoveries.[241]

The injury must be sufficiently concrete, or ripe, to confer RICO standing.[242] Injury to mere expectancy interests will not confer RICO standing, such as where one purchases a pack of trading cards in the hope that it holds a special promotional card, where the plaintiff can not show that the value of the pack was less than what was paid.[243] The increased risk of loss suffered by a lender who made loans secured by artificially inflated collateral was not sufficiently ripe to confer standing.[244]

Likewise, the Second Circuit has refused to recognize as compensable the injury of receiving a product less valuable than that paid for. So, for example, car buyers who had purchased vehicles equipped with defective Firestone tires were held not to have suffered a RICO injury merely because the value of their vehicles had diminished.[245] Similarly, in *Maio v. Aetna Inc.*,[246] the court ruled that insurance purchasers, who alleged that the health insurance plan the defendant provided was inferior to that which had been advertised, could not demonstrate that they had received something worth less than they paid unless they could show some sort of adverse medical consequences, such as denial of benefits or medical malpractice.[247] However, one court recently distinguished *Maio* where a plaintiff alleged not that she was given an inferior insurance policy, but that she would not have purchased the policy in the first place but for the defendant's fraudulent misrepresentations, finding that the plaintiff had sufficiently alleged that the defendants had caused her injury of lost monies spent on premiums.[248]

Nonetheless, a cause of action can be a form of "property," the loss of which will confer RICO standing.[249] Similarly, the loss of a right to compete is an injury to "business."[250]

However, in one unique case, the Third Circuit expanded usual notions of who qualifies as a victim for RICO purposes. An American businessman had bribed Nigerian officials to get a contract with Nigeria. The Third Circuit held

239 *See, e.g.*, Perry v. Am. Tobacco Co., 324 F.3d 845, 850 (6th Cir. 2003); Service Employees Int'l Union Health & Welfare Fund v. Philip Morris Inc., 249 F.3d 1068 (D.C. Cir.), *cert. denied*, 534 U.S. 994 (2001); Texas Carpenters Health Benefit Fund v. Philip Morris Inc., 199 F.3d 788 (5th Cir. 2000); Lyons v. Philip Morris Inc., 225 F.3d 909 (8th Cir. 2000); Steamfitters Local Union No. 420 Welfare Fund v. Philip Morris Inc., 171 F.3d 912 (3d Cir. 1999); Int'l Bhd. of Teamsters, Local 734 Health & Welfare Trust Fund v. Philip Morris Inc., 196 F.3d 818 (7th Cir. 1999); Or. Laborers-Employers Health & Welfare Trust Fund v. Philip Morris Inc., 185 F.3d 957 (9th Cir. 1999); Laborers Local 17 Health & Benefit Fund v. Philip Morris Inc., 191 F.3d 229 (2d Cir. 1999).

240 Bivens Gardens Office Bldg., Inc. v. Barnett Banks of Fla., Inc., 140 F.3d 898 (11th Cir. 1998) ("[a]llowing shareholders to state a RICO claim on behalf of the corporation functions as an important safety valve, because otherwise executives looting a corporation would be insulated from RICO liability as a result of no one having standing to sue them").

241 Mendoza v. Zirkle Fruit Co., 301 F.3d 1163, 1169 (9th Cir. 2002) (finding that plaintiffs who alleged an illegal scheme to hire illegal immigrants in order to depress the labor market stated a claim).

242 For example, the loss of *potential* business does not satisfy RICO's injury requirement. Imagineering, Inc. v. Kiewit Pac. Co., 976 F.2d 1303, 1312 (9th Cir. 1992), *cert. denied*, 507 U.S. 1004 (1993). Likewise, the possibility of a future injury is not a present injury compensable under RICO. Calobrace v. Am. Nat'l Can Co., 1995 U.S. Dist. LEXIS 915 (N.D. Ill. Jan. 25, 1995). Lost opportunity does not qualify as a RICO injury. *In re* Taxable Municipal Bond Sec. Litig., 51 F.3d 518 (5th Cir. 1995); *see also* Kaplan v. Prolife Action League, 475 S.E.2d 247 (N.C. App. 1996) (loss of use of property is not an injury to property under North Carolina RICO), *aff'd*, 347 N.C. 342, 493 S.E.2d 416 (1997).

243 Price v. Pinnacle Brands, 138 F.3d 602, 604, 605 (5th Cir. 1998). *See also* Chaset v. Fleer/Skybox Int'l, L.P., 300 F.3d 1083, 1087 (9th Cir. 2002) (no injury from trading card purchase); Moccio v. Cablevision Sys. Corp. 208 F. Supp. 2d 361, 373 (E.D.N.Y. 2002) (plaintiffs who complained that cable company failed to broadcast every Yankee game broadcast failed to state an injury because they did not allege a right to all such games); Dumas v. Major League Baseball Props., Inc., 104 F. Supp. 2d 1220 (S.D. Cal. 2000).

244 First Nationwide Bank v. Gelt Funding Corp, 27 F.3d 763, 769 (2d Cir. 1994), *cert. denied*, 513 U.S. 1079 (1995).

245 *In re* Bridgestone/Firestone Inc. v. Wilderness Tires Prods. Liab. Litig., 155 F. Supp. 2d 1069, 1090–91 (S.D. Ind. 2001). The court further ruled that even those plaintiffs who had expended money in replacing the allegedly defective tires did not establish a RICO injury. Apparently the court reasoned that notwithstanding the plaintiff's actual expense, without actual failure by the tire—as opposed to the mere expectancy that it might fail—the plaintiffs did not show that the defendant's representations proximately caused that expense. *Id.*

246 221 F.3d 472 (3d Cir. 2000).

247 *Id.* at 483. *But see In re* Managed Care Litig., 185 F. Supp. 2d 1310 (S.D. Fla. 2002) (plaintiffs who alleged that they were injured by paying more for insurance coverage than they would have absent the defendants' alleged omissions and misrepresentations established RICO standing).

248 McClain v. Coverdell & Co., 272 F. Supp. 2d 631, 637–38 (E.D. Mich. 2003).

249 *See, e.g.*, Deck v. Engineered Laminates, 349 F.3d 1253, 1259 (10th Cir. 2003) (plaintiff alleged standing by claiming that settlement agreement reached in prior litigation with the defendant, in which the plaintiff relinquished certain claims, arose from mail fraud).

250 *Id.* (plaintiff fulfilled RICO's standing requirement by alleging that plaintiff relinquished right to compete in fraudulently induced settlement agreement).

that the victims of the scheme included American and foreign citizens who suffered no economic injury, on the theory that bribery of foreign officials injures the people whose officials accepted bribes and diminishes the stature and influence of the United States abroad.[251]

When a RICO case is based on mail or wire fraud, the circuits are split on whether a plaintiff must assert that he or she relied on the false statement, as opposed to suffering injury from a third party's reliance.[252] Thus, a New York district court upheld the standing of a company that refused to go along with a price-fixing scheme, where competitors did rely on the defendant's fraudulent statements which in turn diverted business from the plaintiff.[253]

9.2.3.6.3 Proximate cause

Once the plaintiff has demonstrated an injury that is sufficiently direct and concrete, the plaintiff must then show that the defendant's RICO violation proximately caused that injury. In *Holmes v. Securities Investor Protection Corp.*,[254] the Court rejected a construction of RICO that would have allowed a plaintiff to recover simply by showing that the plaintiff was injured, that the defendant had violated section 1962, and that "but for" that violation, the plaintiff would not have suffered the injury.[255] Rather, a RICO plaintiff may not recover unless the plaintiff can demonstrate that the injuries were directly and proximately caused by a defendant's racketeering activity.[256] Many lawyers view this decision as the first significant attempt by the Supreme Court

251 Environmental Tectonics v. W.S. Kirkpatrick, Inc., 847 F.2d 1052 (3d Cir. 1988) (number of victims considered in deciding whether acts constituted a pattern), *aff'd on other grounds*, 493 U.S. 400 (1990).

252 *Compare* Ideal Steel Supply Corp. v. Anza, 2004 WL 1475497, at *10 (2d Cir. July 2, 2004); Cty. of Suffolk v. Long Island Lighting Co., 907 F.2d 1295, 1311, 1312 (2d Cir. 1990) *and* Sterling Interiors Group v. Haworth, Inc., 1996 U.S. Dist. LEXIS 13908 (S.D.N.Y. Sept. 19, 1996) (third party reliance that caused injury to plaintiff adequate for standing) *with* Pelletier v. Zweifel, 921 F.2d 1465, 1499 (11th Cir.), *cert. denied*, 502 U.S. 855 (1991) (must have suffered injury from direct reliance); Allocco v. City of Coral Gables, 221 F. Supp. 2d 1317, 1363 (S.D. Fla. 2002) (plaintiff can not base RICO claim on representations made to third parties) *and* Grantham & Mann, Inc. v. Am. Safety Prods., Inc., 831 F.2d 596, 606 (6th Cir. 1987) (same).

253 Sterling Interiors Group v. Haworth, Inc., 1996 U.S. Dist. LEXIS 13908, at *4, *5 (S.D.N.Y. Sept. 19, 1996). *See also* Ifill v. West, 1999 U.S. Dist. LEXIS 21320, at 35, 36 (E.D.N.Y. Aug. 24, 1999) (plaintiffs, who'd lost their homes in a refinancing fraud, could satisfy RICO's standing requirement by pleading that they were injured as a proximate result of defendants' bank fraud directed at third parties).

254 503 U.S. 258, 112 S. Ct. 1311, 117 L. Ed. 2d 532 (1992).

255 *Id.* at 265, 266.

256 *See* Green Leaf Nursery v. E.I. DuPont De Nemours and Co., 41 F.3d 1292, 1306–07 (11th Cir. 2003), *cert. denied*, 124 S. Ct. 2094 (2004) (owners of nursery who alleged that defendant falsified evidence and tampered with witnesses could not establish proximate cause); Oki Semiconductor Co. v. Wells Fargo Bank, N.A., 298 F.3d 768, 774 (9th Cir. 2002) (plaintiff failed to show that defendant's money laundering of proceeds from armed robbery proximately caused loss); Ove v. Gwinn, 264 F.3d 817, 825 (9th Cir. 2001) (plaintiffs, whose blood was taken by defendant's employees upon arrest for driving under the influence, could not show causation as they did not allege that the fact that employees were unlicensed caused their blood alcohol levels to register above the legal limit); Byrne v. Nezhat, 261 F.3d 1075, 1111 (11th Cir. 2001) (injury to plaintiff arising from surgery by defendant did not result from misrepresentations allegedly made in medical journals or on bills, therefore no RICO injury); Proctor & Gamble Co. v. Amway Corp., 242 F.3d 539, 565 (5th Cir. 2001) (company could not demonstrate that competitor's alleged illegal pyramid structure proximately caused its injury); Summit Props. v. Hoechst Celanese Corp., 214 F.3d 556, 561 (5th Cir. 2000) (rejecting "fraud on the market" theory of causation for RICO injury); Maio v. Aetna Inc., 221 F.3d 472, 483 (3d Cir. 2000) (a RICO plaintiff must show that suffered an injury to business or property, and that that injury was proximately caused by the defendant's violation of section 1962); Steamfitters Local Union No. 420 Welfare Fund v. Phillip Morris, Inc., 171 F.3d 912, 933 (3d Cir. 1999) (union health and welfare funds did not have standing to sue tobacco companies to recover monies paid for funds' participants' smoking-related illnesses; causation "much too speculative and attenuated to support a RICO claim"), *cert. denied*, 528 U.S. 1105 (2000); Bonilla v. Volvo Car Corp., 150 F.3d 62 (1st Cir. 1998), *cert. denied*, 119 S. Ct. 1574 (1999) (defendant's excise fraud, which presumably lowered the cost of cars purchased by plaintiffs, could not support a RICO claim because plaintiffs were not injured by reason of the fraud); Price v. Pinnacle Brands, Inc., 138 F.3d 602 (5th Cir. 1998) (no RICO injury where plaintiffs, purchasers of trading cards packages manufactured by defendant, alleged that defendant's practice of randomly inserting limited edition cards in packages was illegal gambling; plaintiffs had mere expectancy interests, not tangible property interests, declining to follow Schwartz v. Upper Deck Co., 967 F. Supp. 405 (S.D. Cal. 1997)); First Nationwide Bank v. Gelt Funding Corp., 27 F.3d 763 (2d Cir. 1994), *cert. denied*, 513 U.S. 1079 (1995); George Lussier Enters., Inc. v. Subaru of New England, Inc., 286 F. Supp. 2d 86 (D.N.H. 2003) (injuries of car dealers from alleged scheme by distributor to pack options onto vehicles were not caused by any misrepresentations and therefore did not support RICO claim); Anglo-Iberia Underwriting Mgmt. Co. v. Lodderhose, 282 F. Supp. 2d 126, 133 (S.D.N.Y. 2003) (defamation damages too speculative to be recoverable, and therefore trebleable, under RICO); Evans v. City of Chicago, 2003 WL 22232963, at *6 (N.D. Ill. Sept. 16, 2003) (plaintiff, who had allegedly been wrongfully imprisoned, could not base standing on the income lost from being incarcerated where he could not show that he had been gainfully employed before his arrest); First Capital Asset Mgmt., Inc. v. Brickelbush, Inc., 218 F. Supp. 2d 369, 381 (S.D.N.Y. 2002) (plaintiffs failed to show that their inability to collect debts was proximately caused by defendants' predicate acts of bankruptcy crimes); Anderson v. Smithfield Foods, Inc., 207 F. Supp. 2d 1358, 1364 (M.D. Fla. 2002) (plaintiffs failed to allege causation where did not allege that defendants targeted plaintiffs with scheme to defraud); G-I Holdings, Inc. v. Baron & Budd, 238 F. Supp. 2d 521 (S.D.N.Y. 2002) (plaintiffs who alleged that they paid higher settlements to defendants' clients due to defendants' fraud alleged RICO injury); Emcore Corp. v. Pricewaterhouse-Coopers L.L.P., 102 F. Supp. 2d 237, 243 (D.N.J. 2000); Line v. Astro Mfg. Co., 993 F. Supp. 1033 (E.D. Ky. 1998) (plaintiff

to limit the scope of RICO, although it is not yet clear how much it will affect common RICO claims.

The decision is more likely to discourage "fringe"-type claims than the normal RICO case that includes the element of causation. Some RICO plaintiffs allege that the injury they suffered was their being forced to pay legal fees in prior litigation involving the RICO defendant. One court considering this claim stated that including attorney fees incurred in prior litigation can meet the RICO injury requirement only if the defendants' RICO violations caused the plaintiffs to incur the fees.[257]

A plaintiff shows proximate cause by showing that the violation was both the factual and proximate cause of the plaintiff's injury: the violation was a substantial factor in the sequence of responsible causation and the injury was reasonably foreseeable or a natural consequence of the violation.[258]

A liberal view of proximate cause requires only that it "be a substantial cause of a succession of events that in a logical sequence ultimately causes a plaintiff injury."[259] In a RICO case based on fraud, a court may require a plaintiff to prove both transaction and loss causation to demonstrate proximate cause. That is, the plaintiff may be required to show that but for the defendant's misrepresentations the transaction would not have come about, and also that the misstatements were the reason the transaction turned out to be a losing one.[260]

In some circuits, a RICO plaintiff may establish proximate cause by showing either that the plaintiff relied upon the fraud or that the plaintiff was the target of a fraud, regardless of whether the plaintiff relied upon any misrepresentation.[261] The target theory allows a plaintiff to establish proximate cause when a third party relies upon a fraudulent statement in a way that injures the plaintiff.[262]

The Second Circuit recently clarified that contrary to earlier precedent that had suggested that plaintiffs would have to pass a zone-of-interests test in addition to showing proximate cause in order to demonstrate standing,[263] the

---

who had paid no more than fair market value for manufactured home did not suffer an injury from the manufacturer's alleged concealment of the fire hazards of such homes); Medgar Evers Houses Tenants Ass'n v. Medgar Evers Houses Assocs., L.P., 25 F. Supp. 2d 116 (E.D.N.Y. 1998) (plaintiffs who alleged that housing management company made fraudulent statements to HUD had not suffered an injury proximately caused by the fraud; plaintiffs must show that their injuries are the "preconceived purpose," "specifically intended consequence," "necessary result" or "foreseeable consequences" of the racketeering); Skeete v. IVF Am., Inc., 972 F. Supp. 206 (S.D.N.Y. 1997) (no standing where injury did not arise from claimed predicate acts); Moore v. Painewebber, Inc., 1997 U.S. Dist. LEXIS 13884 (S.D.N.Y. Sept. 9, 1997) (investor who sued brokerage firm alleging misrepresentation could not proceed without alleging either "transaction causation" (would not have purchased but for the misrepresentations) or "loss causation" (misrepresentations were the reason the transaction turned out to be a losing one)); Red Ball Interior Demolition Corp. v. Palmadessa, 874 F. Supp. 576 (S.D.N.Y. 1995) (plaintiff must show direct relationship between plaintiff's injury and defendant's conduct). Where mail fraud is involved, plaintiffs must show not only that they relied on fraudulent representations, but that their reliance was the cause of their injury. Red Ball Interior Demolition Corp. v. Palmadessa, 874 F. Supp. 576 (S.D.N.Y. 1995).

257 Payment of attorney fees incurred by a judgment creditor as a result of allegedly fraudulent claims made by the debtor was considered an injury to business or property by one court. Handeen v. Lemaire, 112 F.3d 1339 (8th Cir. 1997); *see also* Miller Hydro Group v. Popovitch, 851 F. Supp. 7, 13–14 (D. Me. 1994) (plaintiff failed to establish that RICO violation caused plaintiff's litigation costs in previous suit). *But see* Deck v. Engineered Laminates, 349 F.3d 1253, 1259 (10th Cir. 2003) (plaintiff alleged standing by claiming that settlement agreement reached in prior litigation with the defendant, in which the plaintiff relinquished certain claims, arose from mail fraud, distinguishing this injury from that arising from payment of attorney fees).

258 Baisch v. Gallina, 346 F.3d 366, 369–71 (2d Cir. 2003); Lerner v. Fleet Bank, N.A., 318 F.3d 113, 116–30 (2d Cir. 2003); Brittingham v. Mobil Corp., 943 F.2d 297, 304 (3d Cir. 1991). *See also* Brandenburg v. Seidel, 859 F.2d 1179, 1189 (4th Cir. 1988) (proximate cause inquiry considers factors such as the foreseeability of the particular injury, the intervention of other independent causes, and the factual directness of the causal connection); Dale v. Ala Acquisitions, Inc., 203 F. Supp. 2d 694, 702 (S.D. Miss. 2002) (plaintiffs sufficiently pleaded standing).

259 *In re* Lupron Mktg. & Sales Practices Litig., 295 F. Supp. 2d 148, 175 (D. Mass. 2003); *see also* Trollinger v. Tyson Foods, Inc., 370 F.3d 602, 619 (6th Cir. 2004) (overturning dismissal of complaint by plaintiffs, unionized employees who alleged that their wages were depressed by employer's transportation and employment of illegal immigrants); Heaven & Earth, Inc. v. Wyman Props. Ltd. P'ship, 2003 WL 22680935 at *1–2 (D. Minn. Oct. 21, 2003) (denying motion to dismiss).

In proposing a more restrictive construction of standing, Justice Scalia has argued that a plaintiff has RICO standing only by meeting the traditional elements of statutory standing under the predicate acts giving rise to the claim. Holmes v. Securities Investor Protection Corp., 503 U.S. 258, 287–89 (1992) (Scalia, J., concurring). One such element is the "zone-of-interests" test, which asks, apart from the directness of the injury, whether the plaintiff is in the class of persons that Congress intended the statute to benefit. *Id.* at 287 (Scalia, J., concurring).

260 First Nationwide Bank v. Gelt Funding Corp., 27 F.3d 763, 769 (2d Cir. 1994), *cert. denied*, 513 U.S. 1079 (1995).

261 *See, e.g.*, Summit Props. v. Hoechst Celanese Corp., 214 F.3d 556, 561 (5th Cir. 2000).

262 *See, e.g.*, Ideal Steel Supply Corp. v. Anza, 2004 WL 1475497, at *10 (2d Cir. July 2, 2004) (holding that a business could demonstrate proximate cause based on a competitor's tax fraud scheme that the plaintiff alleged was implemented to draw customers away from it); Proctor & Gamble Co. v. Amway Corp., 242 F.3d 539, 564–65 (5th Cir. 2001) (reversing dismissal of RICO claim where plaintiff alleged injury arising from customers' reliance on defendants' misrepresentations of plaintiff's links to Satanism). *But see* Sandwich Chef of Tex., Inc. v. Reliance Nat'l Indem. Ins. Co., 319 F.3d 205 (5th Cir. 2003).

263 *See, e.g.*, Baisch v. Gallina, 346 F.3d 366, 369–71 (2d Cir. 2003) (lender to construction firm that allegedly sought to defraud county could not establish RICO standing because county, not lender, was the "target of the racketeering enterprise"); Abrahams v. Young & Rubicam Inc., 79 F.3d 234, 239 (2d Cir. 1996);

Second Circuit's proximate cause analysis adequately incorporated zone-of-interest concerns and therefore plaintiffs need not pass such an independent test.[264] Nonetheless, some other decisions have required plaintiffs to pass such a test, which serves to sideline those who are foreseeable, yet still collateral, victims of an illegal scheme.[265] However, a plaintiff who bases the claim on a representation to a third party may be able to use the "intended target" test to establish the proximate cause that might be in question given the indirect communication.[266]

9.2.3.6.4 *Provision-specific standing—injuries from subsection 1962(a), (b), and (d) violations*

The nature of the violation that proximately caused the injury depends upon which subsection the plaintiff alleges the defendant violated. One great advantage of subsection 1962(c) is that a plaintiff can demonstrate standing by showing that the plaintiff was injured by reason of a predicate act.[267] However, if the plaintiff asserts that the defendant violated subsection 1962(a), most circuits require the plaintiff to show that the injury was proximately caused by the use or investment of racketeering income that the subsection specifically prohibits.[268] In these circuits, the plaintiff has to show that the use or investment of the income was a "substantial factor" in causing the plaintiff's injury; simply showing that the racketeering activity continued through the reinvestment of racketeering proceeds will be considered too remote an injury to establish standing.[269]

In re Am. Express Co. Shareholder Litig., 39 F.3d 395, 400 (2d Cir. 1994); *see also* Hamm v. Rhone-Poulenc Rorer Pharms., 187 F.3d 941 (8th Cir. 1999) (where plaintiffs were not the intended target of the RICO scheme, they did not have standing), *cert. denied*, 528 U.S. 1117; Vicon Fiber Optics Corp. v. Scrivo, 201 F. Supp. 2d 216, 219 (S.D.N.Y. 2002) (injury to plaintiff would have occurred regardless of whether alleged predicate acts had occurred, dismissing claim); Kaplan v. Prolife Action League, 475 S.E.2d 247 (N.C. App. 1996) (proof that pecuniary gain was derived from the organized unlawful activity is required under North Carolina RICO), *aff'd*, 347 N.C. 342 (1997).

264 Baisch v. Gallina, 346 F.3d 366, 372–73 (2d Cir. 2003); *see also* Lerner v. Fleet Bank, N.A., 318 F.3d 113, 116–30 (2d Cir. 2003) (investors, who lost money when attorney wrongfully took money from escrow accounts, could not establish that their losses were proximately caused by the failure of the depository banks to notify state attorney disciplinary program that attorney's checks had been dishonored, rejecting argument that such reporting would have resulted in attorney's disbarment, which in turn would have caused the investors to pull their money from the investment before they lost it).

Accordingly, previous decisions from the Second Circuit that purportedly required plaintiffs to meet the zone-of-interests test should no longer be precedent. *See, e.g., In re* Am. Express Co. Shareholder Litig., 39 F.3d 395, 400 (2d Cir. 1994) (shareholders who brought a derivative suit against a corporation for its scheme to injure competitors could not show proximate cause because they were not the intended targets, and were even, arguably, the intended beneficiaries, of the scheme); BCCI Holdings (Luxembourg), Societe Anoyme v. Pharaon, 43 F. Supp. 2d 359, 366 (S.D.N.Y. 1999); Medgar Evers Houses Tenants Ass'n v. Medgar Evers Houses Assocs., 25 F. Supp. 2d 116, 122 (S.D.N.Y. 1998).

265 Regency Communications, Inc. v. Cleartel Communications, Inc., 212 F. Supp. 2d 1, 4, 5 (D.D.C. 2002) (finding that plaintiffs could be viewed as the intended targets of the RICO scheme); Regency Communications v. Cleartel Communications Inc., 160 F. Supp. 2d 36, 44–45 (D.D.C. 2001); Meng v. Schwartz, 116 F. Supp. 2d 92, 96 (D.D.C. 2000), *aff'd*, 2002 WL 31248491 (D.C. Cir. Oct. 7, 2002).

266 *See, e.g.*, Summit Props. v. Hoechst Celanese Corp., 214 F.3d 556, 561 (5th Cir. 2000).

267 Sedima, S.P.R.L. v. Imrex, Co., 473 U.S. 479, 497, 105 S. Ct. 3275, 87 L. Ed. 2d 346 (1985) (under § 1962(c), "the compensable injury necessarily is the harm caused by predicate acts sufficiently related to constitute a pattern, for the essence of the violation is the commission of those acts in connection with the conduct of an enterprise.").

268 *See, e.g.*, St. Paul Mercury Ins. Co. v. Williamson, 224 F.3d 425, 443 (5th Cir. 2000); Fogie v. THORN Ams., Inc., 190 F.3d 889, 894 (8th Cir. 1999); Parker & Parsley Petroleum Co. v. Dresser Indus., 972 F.2d 580, 584 (5th Cir. 1992); Vemco, Inc. v. Camardella, 23 F.3d 129, 132 (6th Cir. 1994), *cert. denied*, 513 U.S. 1017 (1994); Nugget Hydroelec. L.P. v. Pacific Gas & Elec. Co., 981 F.2d 429, 437, 438 (9th Cir. 1992), *cert. denied*, 508 U.S. 908 (1993); Glessner v. Kenny, 952 F.2d 702, 708–10 (3d Cir. 1991); Danielsen v. Burnside-Ott Aviation Training Ctr., Inc., 941 F.2d 1220, 1229, 1230 (D.C. Cir. 1991); Ouaknine v. McFarlane, 897 F.2d 75, 82 (2d Cir. 1990); Grider v. Texas Oil & Gas Corp., 868 F.2d 1147, 1150 (10th Cir.), *cert. denied*, 493 U.S. 820 (1989); *see also* Carnegie v. Household Int'l, Inc., 220 F.R.D. 542, 546 (N.D. Ill. 2004) (noting that while the Seventh Circuit has not ruled on the issue, following the majority to hold that a plaintiff "must allege an investment injury which can be distinguished from the injuries resulting from the predicate acts of fraud"); Allen v. New World Coffee, Inc., 2002 WL 432685, at *3, *4 (S.D.N.Y. Mar. 19, 2002) (claim that alleged injury arose from reinvestment of racketeering income into the enterprise did not state § 1962(a) claim). *But see* Busby v. Crown Supply, Inc., 896 F.2d 833, 836–40 (4th Cir. 1990) (rejecting "investment injury" rule).

269 Wagh v. Metris Direct, Inc., 363 F.3d 821, 829 (9th Cir. 2003) (rejecting argument that a plaintiff need only allege an injury caused by the use or investment of funds received from anyone through racketeering activity, *cert. denied*, 124 S. Ct. 2176 (2004); R.R. Brittingham v. Mobil Corp. 943 F.2d 297, 304 (3d Cir. 1991) ("[i]f this remote connection were to suffice, the use-or-investment injury requirement would be almost completely eviscerated where the alleged pattern of racketeering is committed on behalf of a corporation."); Carnegie v. Household Int'l, Inc., 220 F.R.D. 542, 546 (N.D. Ill. 2004) (dismissing § 1962(a) claim arising from alleged kickbacks for refund anticipation loans on grounds that the plaintiff alleged only that the enterprise, rather than the defendants' ownership of the enterprise, caused her injuries); Charleswell v. Chase Manhattan Bank, N.A., 308 F. Supp. 2d 545, 575 (D. V.I. 2004) (dismissing § 1962(a) claim arising from mortgagee's procurement of forced placed hazard insurance that did not insure the plaintiffs' equity in their homes on grounds that the plaintiffs failed to distinguish the harm resulting from the defendants' reinvestment of proceeds from the harm that was caused by their allegedly fraudulent activities); Calabrese v. CSC Holdings, Inc., 283 F. Supp. 2d 797, 812 (E.D.N.Y. 2003) (dismissing § 1962(a) claim

This interpretation of the injury element will hamper use of the subsection in typical consumer cases. For example, a plaintiff who alleged that a bank violated subsection 1962(a) by collecting improper late charges through mail fraud, then reinvesting those charges to finance the bank's operations, was deemed to have failed to allege that he was injured by reason of the investment.[270] In *Brittingham v. Mobil Corp.*,[271] a Third Circuit panel affirmed the dismissal of a class action brought by plaintiffs who alleged that the defendants had fraudulently marketed a type of garbage bag as being degradable, when in fact it was not. The court ruled that the injury alleged, the excessive prices paid by plaintiffs for the bags, was caused by the use or investment of the racketeering income only to the extent that the reinvestment of the proceeds of the prior frauds permitted the defendants to continue their fraudulent scheme, and that was not a sufficient connection to create standing under subsection 1962(a).[272]

Similarly, those courts that have addressed the issue have held that when alleging a violation of subsection 1962(b), the plaintiff must plead that the injury suffered was caused by the defendant's acquisition of an interest in an enterprise, as distinct from an injury resulting from the predicate acts.[273]

As for subsection 1962(d), the conspiracy subsection, the Supreme Court held in *Beck v. Prupis*[274] that a plaintiff must show that his or her injury was caused by an overt act that is an act of racketeering or otherwise wrongful under RICO, and not just injury from an act that furthered the conspiracy. The Court affirmed the dismissal of the case of a former employee who alleged that his firing was part of the defendant's conspiracy to violate RICO. The firing itself was not an overt act of racketeering or otherwise prohibited by the statute and therefore the claim failed to meet RICO's injury requirement.[275]

---

against cable company on plaintiffs' failure to specifically allege how racketeering income was invested and how that investment directly caused their injuries); Dangerfield v. Merrill Lynch, Pierce, Fenner & Smith, Inc., 2003 WL 22227956, at *10 (S.D.N.Y. Sept. 26, 2003); Berk v. Tradewell, Inc., 2003 WL 21664679, at *1–4 (S.D.N.Y. July 16, 2003) (section 1962(a) requires a plaintiff to allege an injury caused by the defendant's investment of racketeering income, dismissing claim against offices of employee that allegedly underpaid commissions and issued false W-2 statements); Roger Whitmore's Automotive Servs., Inc. v. Lake County, IL, 2002 WL 959587, at *7 (N.D. Ill. May 9, 2002) (mere reinvestment insufficient); Bodtker v. Forest City Trading Group, 1999 U.S. Dist. LEXIS 15345, at *11, *12 (D. Or. Sept. 9, 1999) (dismissing § 1962(a) claim where plaintiff alleged that the defendant reinvested racketeering proceeds back into parent corporation, which allowed the racketeering activities to continue through "normal business operations"); Birnbaum v. Law Offices of G. David Westfall, P.C., 120 S.W.3d 470, 475 (Tex. App. 2003) (affirming summary judgment in favor of law firm on counterclaim brought by former client).

270 Turner v. Union Planters Bank, 974 F. Supp. 890, 893, 894 (S.D. Miss. 1997).

271 943 F.2d 297 (3d Cir. 1991).

272 *Id.* at 303, 304; Bellizan v. Easy Money of La., Inc., 2001 U.S. Dist. LEXIS 1731, at *10 (E.D. La. Feb. 12, 2001) (since the injury suffered by plaintiff borrowers arose from payday lender's collection of allegedly usurious loans and not from the reinvestment of the profits from those loans in the business, their § 1962(a) claim failed).

273 *See, e.g.*, Discon, Inc. v. Nynex Corp., 93 F.3d 1055, 1062, 1063 (2d Cir. 1996); Compagnie de Reassurance d'Ile de France v. New England Reinsurance Corp., 57 F.3d 56, 92 (1st Cir.), *cert. denied*, 516 U.S. 1009 (1995); Lightning Lube, Inc. v. Witco Corp., 4 F.3d 1153, 1191 (3d Cir. 1993); Danielson v. Burnside-Ott-Aviation Training Ctr., Inc., 941 F.2d 1220, 1229, 1230 (D.C. Cir. 1991); Old Time Enters., Inc. v. Int'l Coffee Corp., 862 F.2d 1213, 1219 (5th Cir. 1989); Carnegie v. Household Int'l, Inc., 220 F.R.D. 542, 546 (N.D. Ill. 2004) (dismissing § 1962(b) claim arising from alleged kickbacks for refund anticipation loans on grounds that the plaintiff failed to allege a separate injury arising from the defendants' ownership of the enterprise); Crawford & Sons, Ltd. Profit Sharing Plan v. Besser, 216 F.R.D. 228, 238 (E.D.N.Y. 2003); Berk v. Tradewell, Inc., 2003 WL 21664679, at *1–4 (S.D.N.Y. July 16, 2003) (holding that the plaintiff failed to allege acquisition or maintenance injuries under § 1962(b)); Allen v. New World Coffee, Inc., 2002 WL 432685, at *3, *4 (S.D.N.Y. Mar. 19, 2002) (plaintiff who failed to allege injury from defendant's acquisition or maintenance of an interest in the enterprise, but who only alleged injury from predicate acts, could not sustain § 1862(b) claim); Roger Whitmore's Automotive Servs., Inc. v. Lake County, IL, 2002 WL 959587, at *8 (N.D. Ill. May 9, 2002) (dismissing plaintiffs' claim that failed to allege racketeering activity was a "but-for" cause of injury); Bellizan v. Easy Money of La., Inc., 2001 U.S. Dist. LEXIS 1731 (E.D. La. Feb. 12, 2001) (dismissing claim against payday lender because plaintiffs were injured only by the predicate acts, not by the defendant's acquiring or maintaining an interest or control in the enterprise); *In re* Motel 6 Sec. Litig., 161 F. Supp. 2d 227 (S.D.N.Y. 2001); Redtail Leasing v. Bellezza, 1997 U.S. Dist. LEXIS 14821, at *3 (S.D.N.Y. Sep. 30, 1997); Domberger v. Metropolitan Life Ins. Co., 961 F. Supp. 506, 525 (S.D.N.Y. 1997).

274 529 U.S. 494, 120 S. Ct. 1608, 146 L. Ed. 2d 561 (2000).

275 529 U.S. at 507. However, the Court expressly declined to decide whether "whether a plaintiff suing under § 1964(c) for a RICO conspiracy must allege an actionable violation under § 1962(a)–(c), or whether it is sufficient for the plaintiff to allege an agreement to complete a substantive violation and the commission of at least one act of racketeering that caused him injury." *Id.* at 506, n.10. Based on dicta, it does not appear that a plaintiff must necessarily have a claim under § 1962(c) in order to allege a violation of § 1962(d), which would functionally render § 1962(d) superfluous: "a plaintiff could, through a § 1964(c) suit for a violation of § 1962(d), sue co-conspirators who might not themselves have violated one of the substantive provisions of § 1962." The Third Circuit subsequently upheld such an interpretation, ruling that a defendant alleged to have conspired to violate § 1962(c) did not have to commit or agree to commit predicate acts to be liable for conspiracy under § 1962(d), so long as he knowingly agreed to facilitate a scheme which included operation or management of a RICO enterprise. Smith v. Berg, 247 F.3d 532, 538 (3d Cir. 2001).

9.2.3.7 The Prohibited Conduct

9.2.3.7.1 Subsection 1962(a)—prohibited investments

Subsection 1962(a) addresses the investment of ill-gotten gains in an enterprise, specifically prohibiting any person who receives income from a pattern of racketeering activity from using that income to acquire any interest in, or to establish or operate any enterprise engaged in, interstate or foreign commerce.[276] "This provision was primarily directed at halting the investment of racketeering proceeds into legitimate businesses, including the practice of money laundering."[277] Under this section, a plaintiff must allege the following: (1) that the defendant has received money from a pattern of racketeering activity; (2) that the defendant invested that money in an enterprise; and (3) that the enterprise affected interstate commerce.[278]

9.2.3.7.2 Subsection 1962(b)—prohibited acquisitions

Subsection 1962(b) prohibits a person from acquiring or maintaining directly or indirectly, through a pattern of racketeering activity, any interest in or control of an enterprise engaged in interstate or foreign commerce.[279] The purpose of subsection 1962(b) is "to prohibit the takeover of a legitimate business through racketeering, typically extortion or loansharking."[280] To establish a claim the plaintiffs must allege that (1) the defendants acquired or maintained an interest in or control of the enterprise through a pattern of racketeering activity, and (2) the plaintiffs suffered injury as a result.[281] One court has held that acquiring control through legal means, such as a legitimate stock purchase, will nullify the first element.[282]

"Interest" means a proprietary interest,[283] and the element can be satisfied with the purchase of stock,[284] or any other property right in the enterprise.[285] However, a plaintiff who seeks to show that a defendant acquired control through racketeering activity must show more than mere influence. "[T]he 'control' contemplated is in the nature of the control one gains through the acquisition of sufficient stock to affect the composition of a board of directors."[286] Or, even more restrictively, "control connotes domination. It signifies the kind of power that an owner of 51% or more of an entity would normally enjoy."[287] But once the plaintiff has shown the acquisition of an interest in or control of the enterprise, the plaintiff must further demonstrate a relationship between the pattern of racketeering activity and the acquisition or maintenance of the interest.[288]

9.2.3.7.3 Subsection 1962(c)—prohibited association; conduct or participation and the **Reves** *test*

Subsection 1962(c) declares it unlawful for "any person *employed by* or *associated with* any enterprise . . . *to conduct or participate*, directly or indirectly, in the conduct of

276 18 U.S.C. § 1962(a). *See also* Kauthar SDN BHD v. Sternberg, 149 F.3d 659, 672 (7th Cir. 1998) (affirming dismissal of RICO claims), *cert. denied*, 525 U.S. 1114 (1999); Kashelkar v. Rubin & Rothman, 97 F. Supp. 2d 383, 394 (S.D.N.Y. 2000) (section 1962(a) complaint dismissed for failing to allege that the defendant received income from racketeering activity, acquired an interest in an enterprise, or established an enterprise), *aff'd*, 242 F.3d 365 (2d Cir. 2001); Morin v. Trupin, 835 F. Supp. 126, 131, 132 (S.D.N.Y. 1985). *See also* Tran v. Tran, 2000 U.S. Dist. LEXIS 10946, at *43 (S.D.N.Y. Aug. 4, 2000) (plaintiff proved violation of subsection 1962(a) by showing that the defendant, who owned hotels, underpaid their employees, the savings from which could be considered income which the defendants than used or invested in the enterprise comprising the hotels), *aff'd in part, reversed in part on other grounds*, 281 F.3d 23 (2d Cir. 2002) (holding that RICO claim was timebarred).

277 Brittingham v. Mobil Corp., 943 F.2d 297, 303 (3d Cir. 1991).

278 Nolen v. Nucentrix Broadband Networks, Inc., 293 F.3d 926, 929, 930 (5th Cir. 2002) (injury from allegedly illegal late fees did not arise from use or investment of racketeering income); Shearin v. E.F. Hutton Group, Inc., 885 F.2d 1162, 1165 (3d Cir. 1989) (citing B.F. Hirsch, Inc. v. Enright Refining Co., 617 F. Supp. 49, 51, 52 (D.N.J. 1985)); Allen v. New World Coffee, Inc., 2002 WL 432685 (S.D.N.Y. Mar. 19, 2002) (investment of racketeering income is essence of § 1962(a) violation).

279 18 U.S.C. § 1962(b). *See also* Kauthar SDN BHD v. Sternberg, 149 F.3d 659, 672 (7th Cir. 1998) (affirming dismissal of RICO claims), *cert. denied*, 525 U.S. 1114 (1999); Kashelkar v. Rubin & Rothman, 97 F. Supp. 2d 383, 394 (S.D.N.Y. 2000) (section 1962(b) complaint dismissed for failing to allege that the defendant acquired or maintained an interest in an enterprise), *aff'd*, 242 F.3d 365 (2d Cir. 2001); Morin v. Trupin, 835 F. Supp. 126, 133 (S.D.N.Y. 1985).

280 David B. Smith & Terrance G. Reed, Civil RICO, P 5.01, p.5-2 (1997).

281 Jordan (Berm.) Inv. Co. v. Hunter Green Invs. Ltd., 154 F. Supp. 2d 682 (S.D.N.Y. 2001); Morin v. Trupin, 832 F. Supp. 93, 99 (S.D.N.Y. 1993).

282 Acro-Tech, Inc. v. Robert Jackson Family Trust, 84 Fed. Appx. 747, 750, 2003 WL 22783349, at *2 (9th Cir. Sept. 12, 2003).

283 Guerrier v. Advest, Inc., 1993 U.S. Dist. LEXIS 3975, at *30, *31 (D.N.J. Mar. 25, 1993).

284 Moffatt Enters., Inc. v. Borden, Inc., 763 F. Supp. 143, 147 (W.D. Pa. 1990).

285 *See* Welch Foods, Inc. v. Gilchrist, 1996 U.S. Dist. LEXIS 15819, at *7 (W.D.N.Y. Oct. 18, 1996).

286 Moffatt Enters., Inc. v. Borden, Inc., 763 F. Supp. 143, 147 (W.D. Pa. 1990). *But see* Kukuk v. Fredal, 2001 U.S. Dist. LEXIS 16419, at *27–28 (E.D. Mich. Aug. 1, 2001) (refusing to dismiss § 1962(b) claim against defendant who did not own stock in allegedly sham fund and was employed by fund, but who had simply earned commissions on sales of interests in the fund).

287 Kaiser v. Stewart, 1997 U.S. Dist. LEXIS 12788, at *9 (E.D. Pa. Aug. 19, 1997). *See also* Browne v. Abdelhak, 2000 U.S. Dist. LEXIS 12064, at *30, *31 (E.D. Pa. Aug. 23, 2000) (plaintiff failed to sufficiently allege control where only alleged that the defendants were officers of the corporation who had received large bonuses, salary increases, and payments from the enterprise's stock option plan).

288 Browning Ave. Realty Corp. v. Rosenshein, 774 F. Supp. 129, 140 (S.D.N.Y. 1991); Litton Indus., Inc. v. Lehman Bros. Kuhn Loeb Inc., 709 F. Supp. 438, 452 (S.D.N.Y. 1989).

such enterprise's affairs through a pattern of racketeering activity or collection of unlawful debt."[289] After identifying the appropriate defendant as someone employed by or associated with the enterprise and the enterprise itself, and after establishing their respective roles in the RICO scheme while ensuring that they are sufficiently distinct from each other,[290] the plaintiff must demonstrate that the relationship between the defendant person and the enterprise meets the requirements of subsection 1962(c). That is, the plaintiff must show that the defendant conducted or participated in the conduct of the enterprise's affairs.

For many years, courts differed widely in their assessment of what constituted the requisite participation in an enterprise's affairs. Although it was clear that mere employment by the enterprise was not enough,[291] it was not clear what amount of participation was required.

In *Reves v. Ernst & Young*,[292] the Supreme Court interpreted the meaning of the phrase "to conduct or participate, directly or indirectly, in the conduct of such enterprise's affairs." In that case, the defendants were auditors who had issued a series of false financial statements, but who did not otherwise participate in the enterprise's affairs. "Conduct," stated the majority, "requires an element of direction."[293] To participate, the defendant must have had "*some* part in directing the enterprise's affairs."[294] The requirement is not control, but direction.[295] Although the Court held that the behavior of the third-party professionals in this case did not rise to this level, the Court stressed that subsection 1962(c) does not limit liability to upper-level professionals:

> An enterprise is "operated" not just by upper management but also by lower rung participants in the enterprise who are under the direction of upper management. An enterprise also might be "operated" or "managed" by others "associated with" the enterprise who exert control over it as, for example, by bribery.[296]

While acknowledging that the interpretation limits the liability of "outsiders" who have no official position within the enterprise, the Court noted that its test allowed outsiders to be liable if they conducted or participated in the enterprise's affairs, consistent with the limiting language of that subsection. The Court also pointed out that that limiting language is specific to subsection 1962(c), and accordingly had no effect on subsections 1962(a) and (b), which were still appropriate for the infiltration of legitimate organizations by "outsiders."[297]

The *Reves* case has severely limited the liability of outside professionals for RICO violations of enterprises with which they do business. Since *Reves*, plaintiffs have not had great success with claims against outside professionals.[298] However, it does not answer all questions about what constitutes conducting the enterprise's affairs. *Reves* was concerned with those cases where the defendant had a horizontal relationship with the enterprise. It has less of a limiting effect on those cases where the defendant is within the

289 Emphasis added.

290 *See* § 9.2.3.2.1, *supra*.

291 United States v. Cryan, 490 F. Supp. 1234, 1243 (D.N.J. 1980), *aff'd without op.*, 636 F.2d 1211 (3d Cir. 1980). *But see* United States v. Yonan, 800 F.2d 164 (7th Cir. 1986) (defendant not required to have stake or interest in enterprise or contact with management), *cert. denied*, 475 U.S. 1055 (1987); State of New York v. O'Hara, 652 F. Supp. 1049 (W.D.N.Y. 1987) (private contractor's mere bidding on contracts satisfied "associated with" language); Ashland Oil, Inc. v. Arnett, 656 F. Supp. 950 (N.D. Ind. 1987), *aff'd in part, rev'd in part on other grounds*, 875 F.2d 1271 (7th Cir. 1989) (mere servant or employee having no part in management of enterprise may be found to conduct or participate).

292 507 U.S. 170, 113 S. Ct. 1163, 122 L. Ed. 2d 525 (1993).

293 *Id.* at 178.

294 *Id.* at 179 (emphasis in original).

295 *Id.*

296 *Id.* at 184 (footnotes deleted).

297 *Id.* at 185.

298 *See, e.g.*, Azrielli v. Cohen Law Offices, 21 F.3d 512 (2d Cir. 1994) (attorneys); Nolte v. Pearson, 994 F.2d 1311 (8th Cir. 1993) (preparer of opinion letters); McNew v. People's Bank of Ewing, 999 F.2d 540 (6th Cir. 1993) (bank); Baumer v. Pachl, 8 F.3d 1341 (9th Cir. 1993) (attorney); United States v. Quintanilla, 25 F.3d 694 (8th Cir. 1993) (attorneys), *cert. denied*, 513 U.S. 978 (1994); Jordan (Berm.) Inv. Co. v. Hunter Green Invs. Ltd., 154 F. Supp. 2d 682, 693 (S.D.N.Y. 2001) (law firm and lawyer); Feirstein v. Nanbar Realty Corp., 963 F. Supp. 254 (S.D.N.Y. 1997); Vickers Stock Research Corp. v. Quotron Sys., Inc., 26 RICO L. Rep. 246, No. 96 Civ. 2269 (HB) (S.D.N.Y. July 22, 1997); Hayden v. Paul, Weiss, Rifkind, Wharton & Garrison, 955 F. Supp. 248 (S.D.N.Y. 1997) (auditor); Resolution Trust Corp. v. S&K Chevrolet Co., 918 F. Supp. 1235 (C.D. Ill.) (outside insurance broker who just provided services for a car dealership did not operate or manage it; encouraging fraudulent scheme is not enough), *vacated in part on other issues*, 923 F. Supp. 135 (C.D. Ill. 1996); Reynolds v. Condon, 908 F. Supp. 1494 (N.D. Iowa 1995) (lawyer who merely did work for client did not participate in the conduct of its affairs); *In re* Phar-Mor, Inc. Sec. Litig., 893 F. Supp. 484 (W.D. Pa. 1995) (auditors who ignored fraudulent financials of client did not manage or operate it for RICO purposes); Succession of Lula Belle Wardlaw v. Whitney Nat'l Bank, RICO Business Disputes Guide (CCH) ¶ 8711, 1994 U.S. Dist. LEXIS 15215 (E.D. La. Oct. 17, 1994) (lender did not meet RICO's participation requirement when all it did was honor withdrawal requests even if it knew they were fraudulent; it had no duty to watch for breach of fiduciary duty). *But see* Resolution Trust Corp. v. Stone, 998 F.2d 1534 (10th Cir. 1993) (insurance group liable because participation sufficient).

In one post-*Reves* case, the court considered the possible liability of a lender which did not exercise direct control over the enterprise, and ruled that it is not enough that the enterprise might not have been able to function without the financing—provision of services essential to the operation of the RICO enterprise is not the same as participating in the conduct of its affairs. De Wit v. Firstar Corp., 879 F. Supp. 947 (N.D. Iowa 1995). The quality of job done by the professional is irrelevant. Baumer v. Pachl, 8 F.3d 1341 (9th Cir. 1993); University of Maryland at Baltimore v. Peat, Marwick, Main & Co., 996 F.2d 1534 (3d Cir. 1993).

structure of the enterprise, that is, where the defendant has a vertical relationship with the enterprise.

Several courts have applied *Reves* in cases against outsiders to give further detail to the Supreme Court's test. Some courts have stated that the plaintiff must show more than a legitimate business relationship between the defendant and the enterprise, that is, where the defendant is outside the enterprise's chain of command, an ordinary contractual relationship will not be considered conduct or participation.[299] So, for example, where a bank's involvement with the enterprise was limited to processing deposits and withdrawals, it did not sufficiently participate for section 1962(c) liability, even though it knew the deposits and withdrawals were fraudulent.[300] Similarly, a lender that had financed a real estate developer that was accused of defrauding lot buyers evaded liability under the *Reves* test.[301] Even where the outside professional had influence over the enterprise,[302] and even when the goods or services provided benefited the enterprise, the element will not be satisfied without additional evidence of actual direction.[303] Allegations of assistance that do not show direction will not suffice.[304] However, when the defendants do more than just provide services, but participate in the functions of the allegedly illegal activity, then they come within subsection 1962(c).[305] Accordingly, attorneys can be liable under RICO if they participated in the fraud, as opposed to merely providing the traditional functions of giving legal advice.[306]

---

299 *See, e.g.*, Brannon v. Boatmen's First Nat'l Bank, 153 F.3d 1144, 1148 (10th Cir. 1998); *In re* Mastercard Int'l Inc., 132 F. Supp. 2d 468,489 (E.D. La. 2001).

300 Goren v. New Vision Int'l Inc., 156 F.3d 721, 728 (7th Cir. 1998) ("simply performing services for an enterprise, even with knowledge of the enterprise's illicit nature, is not enough to subject an individual to RICO liability under § 1962(c)"); Jubelirer v. MasterCard Int'l, 68 F. Supp. 2d 1049, 1053 (W.D. Wis. 1999) (merely having a business relationship with and performing services for an enterprise does not give rise to RICO liability); Succession of Wardlaw v. Whitney Nat'l Bank, 1994 U.S. Dist. LEXIS 15215, at *5 (E.D. La. 1994).

301 Dongelewicz v. PNC Bank Nat'l Ass'n., 2004 WL 1661863, *5 (3d Cir. July 23, 2004) (affirming summary judgment in favor of lender).

302 *In re* Taxable Municipal Bond Sec. Litig., 1993 U.S. Dist. LEXIS 17978, at *14 (E.D. La. 1993) (attorney not liable even though had influence in the enterprise).

303 Slaney v. Int'l Amateur Athletic Fed'n, 244 F.3d 580, 598 (7th Cir.) (U.S. Olympic Committee did not engage in conduct of alleged enterprise merely by providing drug testing services), *cert. denied*, 534 U.S. 828 (2001); The Univ. of Maryland v. Peat, Marwik, Main & Co., 996 F.2d 1534, 1539 (3d Cir. 1993) (auditor); *see also* Paycom Billing Servs., Inc. v. Payment Resources Int'l, 212 F. Supp. 2d 732, 740 (W.D. Mich. 2002) (mere participation of non-employee is not enough, must show some exertion of control); Roger Whitmores Auto. Servs., Inc. v. Lake County, IL, 2002 WL 959587, at *6 (N.D. Ill. May 9, 2002); Brown v. Coleman Invs., Inc., 993 F. Supp. 416 (M.D. La. 1998) (automobile credit corporation who merely made and approved loans had no part in directing affairs of enterprise that included dealer alleged to have charged inflated fees and taxes).

304 Mayo, Lynch & Assocs., Inc. v. Pollack, 799 A.2d 12, 21, 22 (N.J. Super. App. Div. 2002) (attorney who issued opinion letters only gave routine legal services that did not constitute direction of the enterprise's affairs, and therefore did not violate RICO regardless of whether letters were fraudulent). *See also* Javitch v. Capwill, 284 F. Supp. 2d 848, 854 (D.N.D. 2003) (allegations that defendant acted pursuant to instructions of others while ignoring illicit nature of scheme did not meet *Reves*' operation or management test); Schmidt v. Fleet Bank, 16 F. Supp. 2d 340, 347 (S.D.N.Y. 1998) (allegations that bank allowed defrauder access to escrow accounts, approving overdrafts, and helping him to conceal scheme did not sufficiently allege conduct or participation).

305 *See, e.g.*, Roger Whitmores Auto. Servs., Inc. v. Lake County, IL, 2002 WL 959587, at *5 (N.D. Ill. May 9, 2002) (defendants' accompaniment of allegedly corrupt sheriff on visits to extort campaign contributions could satisfy conduct element where defendants knew the purpose of the visits); *In re* Lupron Mktg. & Sales Practices Litig., 295 F. Supp. 2d 148, 172 n.25 (D. Mass. 2001) (rejecting defendant's argument that *Reves'* required the defendant to have had "control" of the enterprise); Ifill v. West, 1999 U.S. Dist. LEXIS 21320, at *27, 28 (E.D.N.Y. Aug. 24, 1999) (denying motion to dismiss RICO claim against lender, where plaintiff alleged that lender recruited prospective targets for the fraudulent scheme by distributing brochures and giving seminars, and applied to HUD before making loans for protection from possible losses from the contemplated mortgages); Sikes v. Am. Tel. & Tel., 179 F.R.D. 342, 353 (S.D. Ga. 1998) (denying summary judgment to AT&T for its part in operating a 900-number game, where defendant had not just rendered telephone services, but had allegedly approved and edited the scripts and advertising used in the game, and reviewed and altered the prize structure and game rules, and exercised control over the length and price of calls to the game); Heller v. First Town Mortg. Corp., 1998 U.S. Dist. LEXIS 14427, at *24, 25 (S.D.N.Y. Sept. 14, 1998) (declining to dismiss RICO claim against mortgage escrow account servicer, finding that the functions that the defendant performed for the enterprise, which comprised investors or lenders who pool their mortgages, rose to level of participation in the operation and management of the enterprise's affairs); Bowdoin Constr. Corp. v. Rhode Island Hosp. Trust Nat'l Bank, N.A., 869 F. Supp. 1004 (D. Mass. 1994) (developer and lead lender for a resort exercised actual control over the resort), *aff'd on other grounds*, 94 F.3d 721 (1st Cir. 1996). *See also* Phila. Reserve Supply Co. v. Nowalk & Assocs., Inc., 864 F. Supp. 1456 (E.D. Pa. 1994) (under N.J. RICO statute, accountants who assisted in formulation and implementation of fraudulent scheme operated or managed the RICO enterprise; went well beyond the normal provision of accounting services).

306 Thomas v. Ross & Hardies, 9 F. Supp. 2d 547 (D. Md. 1998) (*Reves* did not limit liability of attorney who allegedly persuaded homeowners to obtain mortgages and then diverted proceeds to enterprise instead of paying prior mortgagors, as agreed); Arons v. Lalime, 3 F. Supp. 2d 314 (W.D.N.Y. 1998) (document that showed that defendant attorney helped establish and create procedures for fraudulent "roll program" which would pay attorney percentage of financial benefits raised factual question as to whether attorney exercised sufficient control over the enterprise to incur RICO liability); Mruz v. Caring, Inc., 991 F. Supp. 701 (D.N.J. 1998) (plaintiffs, whistleblower employees, overcame *Reves* by alleging that attorneys seized power and control of enterprise for purposes of dissuading plaintiffs from revealing fraud and to defame and intimidate them; alleged behavior was more than the mere provision of

The question of just how much participation the outside professional had is not usually appropriate to resolve at the pleadings stage.[307]

When the defendant is within the enterprise, however, "[s]pecial care is required in translating *Reves*' concern with 'horizontal' connections—focusing on the liability of an outside adviser—to the 'vertical' question of how far RICO liability may extend within the enterprise but down the organizational ladder."[308] Courts have repeated the Supreme Court's instruction that lower rung participants may be liable, for example by "knowingly implementing decisions, as well as by making them."[309] Evidence that a defendant had decision-making power can show that a defendant participated in the operation of an enterprise, but *Reves* does not require such evidence.[310] On the other hand, the commission of crimes by lower level employees may be found to indicate participation in the operation or management of the enterprise, but does not prove it.[311] The plaintiff must demonstrate that the defendant's conduct related to the enterprise and was not just the defendant's own wrongdoing.[312]

Where the enterprise is alleged to be an association in fact of which the defendants are alleged to be members, the structure is vertical, not horizontal, and the level of the defendant's participation should be judged accordingly.[313] By knowingly implementing management's decisions, and thereby enabling the enterprise to achieve its goals, the defendants meet the participation test of *Reves*.[314] Similarly, in a case against a subsidiary, a plaintiff may be able to meet its burden of establishing conduct by showing that the subsidiary used its responsibilities to commit fraud and then upstreamed that income to the corporate group enterprise in a manner that influenced the operation of the enterprise beyond a mere financial benefit.[315]

9.2.3.7.4 Subsection 1962(d)

Subsection 1962(d) declares it unlawful for any person to conspire to violate any of the provisions of subsections (a), (b), or (c) of section 1962. *Salinas v. United States*[316] resolved a split in the circuits as to the requirements of subsection 1962(d) by choosing the broader of two possible readings. Relying on traditional conspiracy law which provides that so long as they share a common purpose, conspirators are liable for the acts of their co-conspirators, the Court ruled that RICO does not require that the defendant must commit or agree to commit two or more predicate acts in order to violate sub-

---

legal services); Mathon v. Marine Midland Bank, N.A., 875 F. Supp. 986 (E.D.N.Y. 1995); Tribune Co. v. Purcigliotti, 869 F. Supp. 1076 (S.D.N.Y. 1994) (attorneys who assisted in filing and prosecution false workers' compensation claims participated in the operation or management of an enterprise comprising their law firm, several unions, and a doctor, where they were alleged to have conceived of and executed the scheme), *aff'd*, 66 F.3d 12 (2d Cir. 1995). *See also* Mayo, Lynch & Assocs., Inc. v. Pollack, 799 A.2d 12, 18 (N.J. Super. App. Div. 2002) (jury could conclude that attorney's failure to comply with bid law indicated an intent to participate in illegal scheme in violation of state RICO statute); Roger Whitmores Auto. Servs., Inc. v. Lake County, IL, 2002 WL 959587, at *6 (N.D. Ill. May 9, 2002) (dismissing attorneys from suit).

307 *See, e.g.*, MCM Partners, Inc. v. Andrews-Bartlett & Assoc., Inc., 62 F.3d 967 (7th Cir. 1995) (lower level employees can be deemed to participate in RICO enterprise even if participation was coerced); United States v. Starrett, 55 F.3d 1525 (11th Cir. 1995) (lower level employees can be liable if they knowingly implement management decisions), *cert. denied*, 517 U.S. 1111 (1996); Ifill v. West, 1999 U.S. Dist. LEXIS 21320, at *25 (E.D.N.Y. Aug. 24, 1999); Friedman v. Hartmann, 1994 U.S. Dist. LEXIS 9727, at *2 (S.D.N.Y. July 15, 1994); LaVornia v. Rivers, 669 So. 2d 288 (Fla. Dist. Ct. App. 1996) (employee does not have to be in control of decisions to be deemed to have participated).

308 United States v. Oreto, 37 F.3d 739, 750 (1st Cir. 1994), *cert. denied*, 513 U.S. 1177 (1995).

309 United States v. Diaz, 176 F.3d 52, 93 (2d Cir.), *cert. denied*, 528 U.S. 875 (1999) (affirming convictions of gang members where "the record makes clear that [the defendants] were both on the ladder, rather than under it"); MCM Partners, Inc. v. Andrews-Bartlett & Assocs., Inc., 62 F.3d 967, 978 (5th Cir. 1995) (citing United States v. Oreto, 37 F.3d 739, 750 (1st Cir. 1994), *cert. denied*, 513 U.S. 1177 (1995)).

310 DeFalco v. Bernas, 244 F.3d 286, 312 (2d Cir. 2001) (affirming verdict in case arising from alleged corruption in town affairs against defendants who did not have any official role in managing the town where there was sufficient evidence that the defendants participated in that management); United States v. Posada-Rios, 158 F.3d 832, 856 (5th Cir. 1998), *cert. denied, sub nom.* Grajales-Murga v. United States, 526 U.S. 1031 (1999); Dale v. Frankel, 131 F. Supp. 2d 852 (S.D. Miss. 2001). *See also* Baisch v. Gallina, 346 F.3d 366, 376 (2d Cir. 2003) (vacating summary judgment for a defendant, a shareholder and officer of participant in an allegedly fraudulent financing scheme, because the plaintiff "demonstrated his discretionary authority and direction of the enterprise"); United States v. Shifman, 124 F.3d 31, 36 (1st Cir. 1997) (a defendant who is plainly integral to carrying out the enterprise's activities may be liable; denying summary judgment to defendant, an indebted borrower, who allegedly made referrals to his loansharker in exchange for relief on his debts), *cert. denied*, 522 U.S. 1116 (1998).

311 United States v. Allen, 155 F.3d 35, 42 (2d Cir. 1998) (denying summary judgment where evidence could show that defendant's acts of bribery could be found to be participation).

312 *See, e.g.*, Williams v. Ford Motor Co., 11 F. Supp. 2d 983, 986 (N.D. Ill. 1998) (dismissing complaint against Ford Motor Company based on dealer's fraudulent charges under extended service plan, dealer's fraud was its own act, not that of the enterprise consisting of Ford and dealership).

313 *See* MCM Partners v. Andrews-Bartlett & Assocs., 62 F.3d 967, 979 (7th Cir. 1995) (reversing dismissal of claims against defendant).

314 *Id. See also* United States v. Oreto, 37 F.3d 739, 750, 751 (1st Cir. 1994) (section 1962(c) applies to foot soldiers as well as to generals), *cert. denied*, 513 U.S. 1177 (1995).

315 *See* Miller v. Chevy Chase Bank, 1998 U.S. Dist. LEXIS 3651, at *3 (N.D. Ill. Mar. 24, 1998); Majchrowski v. Norwest Mortg., 6 F. Supp. 2d 946, at 44, 45 (N.D. Ill. 1998).

316 522 U.S. 52, 118 S. Ct. 469, 139 L. Ed. 2d 352 (1997).

section 1962(d).[317] Rather, the conspirator need only "intend to further an endeavor which, if completed, would satisfy all of the elements of a substantive criminal offense, . . . it suffices that he adopt the goal of furthering or facilitating the criminal endeavor."[318] While the commission of two predicate acts may prove this intent, it is not the only means of proving it.[319] Based on this holding, the Court affirmed the conviction of a sheriff's deputy who knew about and agreed to facilitate a bribery scheme but who had not accepted or agreed to accept two bribes.

Lower court decisions since *Salinas* have generally held that the plaintiff or prosecutor need only show that the defendant agreed that predicate acts would be committed on behalf of the conspiracy.[320] The Eleventh Circuit has taken the expansive view that such an agreement can be shown by proving an agreement on an overall objective, which in turn can be proven by circumstantial evidence that each defendant must reasonably have known that others were also conspiring to participate in the same enterprise through a pattern of racketeering activity.[321] However, a few courts have ruled that a RICO civil conspiracy claim can stand only if the plaintiff proves that the defendant agreed to commit predicate acts.[322] Given that these cases did not analyze the impact of *Salinas*, their holdings are frail.

The issue that arises most often under subsection 1962(d) is whether a corporation can be deemed to conspire with its own parent, subsidiaries, officers, or directors. While some courts have ruled that a corporation can not, in effect, conspire with itself for RICO purposes,[323] other courts accept intracorporate conspiracies.[324]

---

317 522 U.S. at 65 ("[t]he interplay between subsections (c) and (d) does not permit us to excuse from the reach of the conspiracy provision an actor who does not himself commit or agree to commit the two or more predicate acts requisite to the underlying offense.").

318 *Id.*

319 *Id.*

320 U.S. v. Corrado, 286 F.3d 934, 937 (6th Cir. 2002) (§ 1962(d) does not require an overt or specific act to further the RICO enterprise); Smith v. Berg, 247 F.3d 532, 538 (3d Cir. 2001) (defendant may be liable under § 1962(d) if he knowingly agrees to facilitate a scheme that includes the operation or management of an enterprise; rejecting construction that would require defendants to have conspired to do something for which the defendant would, if successful, be liable under § 1962(c)); Goren v. New Vision Int'l, Inc., 156 F.3d 721 (7th Cir. 1998) (defendant must agree that someone would commit two predicate acts on behalf of the enterprise); United States v. To, 144 F.3d 737 (11th Cir. 1998); Roger Whitmore's Automotive Servs., Inc. v. Lake County, IL, 2002 WL 959587, at *10 (N.D. Ill. May 9, 2002) (conspiracy claim could survive if one of the defendants agreed that someone else should commit two predicate acts constituting a pattern); Wiwa v. Royal Dutch Petroleum Co., 2002 WL 319887, at *26 (S.D.N.Y. Feb. 28, 2002) (co-conspirators need not know of all violations by the other conspirators in furtherance of the conspiracy, finding plaintiff alleged RICO conspiracy claim); Eva v. Midwest Nat'l Mortgage. Banc, Inc., 143 F. Supp. 2d 862, 880 (N.D. Ohio 2001) (refusing to dismiss conspiracy claim, since it could be logically inferred from plaintiff's allegations that the defendant voluntarily involved itself in the scheme); BCCI Holdings v. Khalil, 56 F. Supp. 2d 14 (D.D.C. 1999) (co-conspirator need only agree to a scheme that will violate § 1962(c), need not commit or agree to commit the predicate acts himself), *aff'd in part, rev'd in part on other grounds*, 214 F.3d 168 (D.C. Cir. 2000); Am. Auto. Accessories, Inc. v. Fishman, 991 F. Supp. 995 (N.D. Ill. 1998).

321 United States v. To, 144 F.3d 737 (11th Cir. 1998). Alternatively, a violation of § 1962(d) can be shown by proving the defendant agreed to commit two predicate acts. *Id. But see* Zito v. Leasecomm Corp., 2003 WL 22251352, at *20 (S.D.N.Y. Sept. 30, 2003) (allegation that defendant should have known of fraudulent scheme insufficient to support conspiracy claim because a RICO plaintiff must show that a defendant joined the conspiracy with the intent to commit the offenses that are the object of the scheme) (citing United States v. Ceballos, 340 F.3d 115, 123–24 (2d Cir. 2003)).

322 Jordan (Berm.) Inv. Co. v. Hunter Green Invs. Ltd., 154 F. Supp. 2d 682, 695 (S.D.N.Y. 2001) (holding, contrary to *Salinas*, that defendants must have agreed to commit two predicate acts in order to sustain § 1962(d) liability); First Capital Asset Mgmt. v. Brickelbush, Inc., 150 F. Supp. 2d 624, 636 (S.D.N.Y. 2001) (no conspiracy without claim that defendants agreed to commit predicate acts sufficient for a pattern).

323 Fogie v. THORN Americas, Inc., 190 F.3d 889 (8th Cir. 1999) (as a matter of law, a parent corporation and its wholly-owned subsidiaries are incapable of forming a conspiracy with one another); Broussard v. Meineke Discount Muffler Shops, Inc., 903 F. Supp. 16 (W.D.N.C. 1996); Brown v. Siegel, 1995 U.S. Dist. LEXIS 1945 (E.D. Pa. Feb. 14, 1995); Rosemount Cogeneration Joint Venture v. Northern States Power Co., 1991 U.S. Dist. LEXIS 1504, 1991-1 Trade Cas. (CCH) ¶ 69,351 (D. Minn. Jan. 18, 1991); Northeast Jet Ctr., LTD. v. Lehigh-Northampton Airport Authority, 767 F. Supp. 672 (E.D. Pa. 1991); U.S. Concord, Inc. v. Harris Graphics Corp., 757 F. Supp. 1053 (N.D. Cal. 1991); Gaudette v. Panos, 650 F. Supp. 912 (D. Mass. 1987), *rev'd on other grounds*, 852 F.2d 30 (1st Cir. 1988); Satellite Fin. Planning Corp. v. First Nat'l Bank, 633 F. Supp. 386 (E.D. Pa. 1986); Yancoski v. E.F. Hutton, 581 F. Supp. 88 (E.D. Pa. 1983). *See also* Bellizan v. Easy Money of La., Inc., 2001 U.S. Dist. LEXIS 1731 (E.D. La. Feb. 12, 2001) (refusing to dismiss conspiracy claim where plaintiff avoided self-conspiracy problem by excluding primary defendant, a payday loan company, from the conspiracy claims).

324 Webster v. Omnitriton Int'l, Inc., 79 F.3d 776 (9th Cir.), *cert. denied*, 519 U.S. 865 (1996) (extends § 1962(d) liability to a wholly intracorporate conspiracy); Webster v. Omnitrition Int'l, Inc., 79 F.3d 776 (9th Cir. 1996), *cert. denied* 117 S. Ct. 174 (1996); Shearin v. E.F. Hutton Group, Inc., 885 F.2d 1162 (3d Cir. 1989); Fleischhauer v. Feltner, 879 F.2d 1290 (6th Cir. 1989), *cert. denied*, 494 U.S. 1027 (1990); Haroco, Inc. v. Am. Nat'l Bank & Trust Co. of Chicago, 747 F.2d 384, 403 n.22 (7th Cir. 1984), *aff'd on other grounds*, 473 U.S. 606 (1985); United States v. Hartley, 678 F.2d 961, 970–72 (11th Cir. 1982) (dicta), *cert. denied*, 459 U.S. 1183 (1983); District 65 Retirement Trust v. Prudential Sec. Inc., 925 F. Supp. 1551 (N.D. Ga. 1996); Ashland Oil, Inc. v. Arnett, 656 F. Supp. 950 (N.D. Ind. 1987), *aff'd in part, rev'd in part on other grounds*, 875 F.2d 1271 (7th Cir. 1989); Pappas v. NCNB, 653 F. Supp. 699 (M.D.N.C. 1987); Pandick v. Rooney, 632 F. Supp. 1430, 1435 (N.D. Ill. 1986); Callan v. State Chem. Mfg. Co., 584 F. Supp. 619, 623 (E.D. Pa. 1984). *Cf.* Hoxworth v. Blinder, Robinson & Co., 903 F.2d 186 (3d Cir. 1990) (leaving issue unresolved). *See generally* D. Abrams, The Law of Civil RICO § 4.8 (1995).

A plaintiff pleading a violation of subsection 1962(d) must meet the restrictive injury pleading rules for that section in addition to pleading the substantive violation.[325]

9.2.4 Predicate Offenses: Mail Fraud and Wire Fraud

9.2.4.1 Elements of Mail Fraud

The elements of mail fraud are: (1) a scheme to defraud, and (2) a mailing made for the purpose of executing the scheme.[326] The mail and wire fraud statutes address a broader scope of fraud than common law fraud does.[327] It is not necessary that anyone actually be defrauded.[328] Nor is it necessary that the mailings themselves include any misrepresentations or contribute directly to the deception of the plaintiffs, so long as they are part of a scheme to defraud.[329] A half-truth will suffice as an actionable misrepresentation.[330] As always under RICO, the plaintiff must have suffered injury to business or property "by reason of" the RICO violation.[331]

Courts are split as to whether a plaintiff must show detrimental reliance on the misrepresentation to sustain a RICO claim based on mail fraud.[332] However, even in

325 *See* § 9.2.3.6.4, *supra*.

326 Schmuck v. United States, 489 U.S. 705, 109 S. Ct. 1443, 103 L. Ed. 2d 734 (1989) (mailing incidental to fraudulent scheme sufficient); Pereira v. United States, 347 U.S. 1, 8, 74 S. Ct. 358, 98 L. Ed. 2d 435 (1954); United States v. Dick, 744 F.2d 546, 550 (7th Cir. 1984); Anderson v. Smithfield Foods, Inc., 207 F. Supp. 2d 1358, 1362 (M.D. Fla. 2002); Jordan (Berm.) Inv. Co. v. Hunter Green Invs. Ltd., 154 F. Supp. 2d 682, 691 (S.D.N.Y. 2001); Emcore Corp. v. PricewaterhouseCoopers L.L.P., 102 F. Supp. 2d 237, 245 (D.N.J. 2000); Polycast Tech. Corp. v. Uniroyal, Inc., 728 F. Supp. 926 (S.D.N.Y. 1989); Austin v. Merrill Lynch, Pierce, Fenner & Smith, 570 F. Supp. 667, 669 (W.D. Mich. 1983); *see also* Manax v. McNamara, 660 F. Supp. 657 (W.D. Tex. 1987) (no scheme to defraud), *aff'd*, 842 F.2d 808 (5th Cir. 1988).

327 Regency Communications v. Cleartel Communications Inc., 160 F. Supp. 2d 36, 44 (D.D.C. 2001) (breach of contract accompanied by use of mail to deceive plaintiffs could fulfill mail fraud statute's requirements) (citing McEvoy Travel Bureau, Inc. v. Heritage Travel, Inc., 904 F.2d 786 (1st Cir. 1990)). Furthermore, the party deprived of money or property need not be the same person who was deceived. *In re* Lupron Mktg. & Sales Practices Litig., 295 F. Supp. 2d 148, 168 (D. Mass. 2001) (citing United States v. Evans, 844 F.2d 36, 39 (2d Cir. 1988)).

328 United States v. Reid, 533 F.2d 1255, 1264 n.34 (D.C. Cir. 1976); United States v. Andreadis, 366 F.2d 423, 431 (2d Cir. 1966), *cert. denied*, 385 U.S. 1001 (1967); Unocal Corp. v. Superior Court, 244 Cal. Rptr. 540 (Ct. App. 1988) (unpublished).

329 Schmuck v. United States, 489 U.S. 705, 714 (1989); Charleswell v. Chase Manhattan Bank, N.A., 308 F. Supp. 2d 545, 577 (D. V.I. 2004) Shapo v. O'Shaugnessy, 246 F. Supp. 2d 935 (N.D. Ill. 2002); Silvershein v. Fruman, 1997 WL 531310 (S.D.N.Y. 1997) (mailings may constitute mail fraud even if they occur after the fraud is completed). *See also* Eva v. Midwest Nat'l Mortgage. Banc, Inc., 143 F. Supp. 2d 862, 877 (N.D. Ohio 2001) (incidental use of the mail sufficient).

330 *In re* Lupron Mktg. & Sales Practices Litig., 295 F. Supp. 2d 148 (D. Mass. 2001).

331 18 U.S.C. § 1962(c); § 9.2.3.6, *supra*.

332 *Compare* Green Leaf Nursery v. E.I. DuPont De Nemours and Co., 41 F.3d 1292, 1306–08 (11th Cir. 2003) (holding that since state law fraud required justifiable reliance, plaintiffs had to establish justifiable reliance under federal mail and wire fraud statutes as well); GE Inv. Private Placement Partners II v. Parker, 247 F.3d 543, 548 (4th Cir. 2001) (plaintiff must demonstrate justifiable reliance); Chisolm v. Charlie Falk's Auto Wholesale, Inc., 95 F.3d 331 (4th Cir. 1996); Appletree Square I v. W.R. Grace & Co., 29 F.3d 1283 (8th Cir. 1994) (detrimental reliance necessary where mail and wire fraud are predicate acts); Central Distributors of Beer, Inc. v. Conn, 5 F.3d 181 (6th Cir. 1993), *cert. denied*, 512 U.S. 1207 (1994); Caviness v. Derand Resources Corp., 983 F.2d 1295 (4th Cir. 1993); Metromedia Co. v. Fugazy, 983 F.2d 350 (2d Cir. 1992), *cert. denied*, 508 U.S. 952 (1993); Pelletier v. Zweifel, 921 F.2d 1465 (11th Cir.), *cert. denied*, 502 U.S. 855 (1991); Blount Fin. Servs., Inc. v. Walter E. Heller & Co., 819 F.2d 151 (6th Cir. 1987) (reasonable reliance required for RICO mail fraud); Grantham & Mann v. Am. Safety Prods., 831 F.2d 596 (6th Cir. 1987); Allocco v. City of Coral Gables, 221 F. Supp. 2d 1317 (S.D. Fla. 2002) (requiring reliance under state RICO statute where mail and wire fraud are predicate acts); Special Purpose Accounts Receivable Co-op Corp. v. Prime One Capital Co. L.L.C., 202 F. Supp. 2d 1339, 1350 (S.D. Fla. 2002) (plaintiffs can not rely on statements made to third parties); Lodal, Inc. v. Great Am. Ins. Cos., 2001 U.S. Dist. LEXIS 22123, at *16–17 (W.D. Mich. Sept. 19, 2001) (mail and wire fraud allegations deficient because they failed to allege reliance); and Long Island Lighting Co. v. Transamerica Delaval, 646 F. Supp. 1442, 1453 (S.D.N.Y. 1986) (claim dismissed for failing to plead justifiable reliance) *with* Tabas v. Tabas, 47 F.3d 1280, 1294 n.18 (3d Cir. 1995) (victim of fraud need not have relied on mailings to establish RICO claim); Akin v. Q-L Inv., Inc., 959 F.2d 521 (5th Cir. 1992) (reliance not element of mail and wire fraud); Abell v. Potomac Ins. Co., 858 F.2d 1104 (5th Cir. 1988) (need not show materiality or reliance in mail fraud case), *vacated, remanded on other grounds*, 492 U.S. 914, 109 S. Ct. 3236, 106 L. Ed. 2d 584 (1989); *In re* Lupron Mktg. & Sales Practices Litig., 295 F. Supp. 2d 148, 175 (D. Mass. 2001) (since federal mail fraud statute does not require reliance, RICO does not either); Corley v. Rosewood Care Ctr., Inc., 152 F. Supp. 2d 1099, 1108 (C.D. Ill. 2001) (plaintiff did not need to prove injury or reliance to establish mail fraud); System Mgmt., Inc. v. Loiselle, 112 F. Supp. 2d 112, 114 (D. Mass. 2000), *rev'd on other grounds*, 303 F.3d 100 (1st Cir. 2002) (reliance need not be shown, but pattern not shown where all acts of mail fraud occurred in context of one contract over limited time); Kaiser v. Stewart, 1997 U.S. Dist. LEXIS 12788 (E.D. Pa. Aug. 19, 1997); Perlman v. Zell, 938 F. Supp. 1327, 1344 (N.D. Ill. 1996) (scheme need not have actually fooled victim), *aff'd*, 185 F.3d 850 (7th Cir. 1999); Estate of Ltc William Lewis Scott v. Scott, 907 F. Supp. 1495 (M.D. Ala. 1995); B.V. Optische Industrie de Oude Delft v. Hologic, Inc., 909 F. Supp. 162 (S.D.N.Y. 1995); Prudential Ins. Co. of Am. v. United States Gypsum Co., 828 F. Supp. 287 (D.N.J. 1993) (judge can not see why courts have been reading detrimental reliance requirement into RICO); Winsome Shoppe, Inc. v. Cynwyd Inv., 1992 U.S. Dist. LEXIS 16715 (E.D. Pa. Nov. 3, 1992); Shaw v. Rolex Watch, 726 F. Supp. 969

jurisdictions that do not hold that reliance is an element of mail or wire fraud, reliance may resurface as part of the proximate cause question of RICO standing, discussed above.[333] The majority of Circuits hold that the party injured need not be the party deceived.[334]

A scheme to defraud encompasses anything "designed to defraud as to representation as to the past or present, or suggestions and promises as to the future."[335] It includes the assertion of "half-truths" or the concealment of material facts.[336] Misappropriation of confidential information may involve mail fraud.[337]

In 1987, the Supreme Court ruled that mail and wire fraud are limited to the protection of money and property and do not apply to violations of intangible rights such as the public's right to an "impartial government."[338] Congress has since amended the mail and wire fraud statutes to include schemes to defraud a person of intangible rights, thereby overruling that Supreme Court decision.[339] Nonetheless, a RICO plaintiff must meet RICO's requirement of "injury to business or property."[340]

Mail fraud requires specific intent to defraud.[341] This includes not just intentional deception but also the making of representations in reckless disregard for their truth or falsity.[342] The intent requirement is satisfied by the existence of a scheme reasonably calculated to deceive persons of ordinary prudence and comprehension, which can be shown by examining the scheme itself.[343]

Claims based on negligent or unintentional conduct will not meet the intent requirement. The defendant's good faith belief in even an impractical or "somewhat visionary"

(S.D.N.Y. 1989); Mid-State Fertilizer Co. v. Exchange Bank of Chicago, 693 F. Supp. 666 (N.D. Ill. 1988) (materiality an element of RICO mail fraud), *aff'd*, 877 F.2d 1333 (7th Cir. 1989); and Wooten v. Loshbough, 649 F. Supp. 531 (N.D. Ind. 1986) (justifiable reliance not an element of RICO mail or wire fraud claim), *aff'd on other grounds*, 951 F.2d 768 (7th Cir. 1991). Courts may require the plaintiff to prove reliance when using mail fraud in a civil case even where they would not require reliance in a criminal mail fraud case. *See, e.g.*, State Farm Mut. Auto. Ins. Co. v. Abrams, 2000 U.S. Dist. LEXIS 6837, at *57, *58 (N.D. Ill. May 11, 2000) (holding plaintiff required to show reliance because a civil case).

333 *See* § 9.2.3.6, *supra*.

334 United States v. Christopher, 142 F.3d 46, 54 (1st Cir. 1998) ("[n]othing in the mail and wire fraud statutes requires that the party deprived of money or property be the same party who is actually deceived), *cert. denied*, 525 U.S. 1054 (1998); United States v. Blumeyer, 114 F.3d 758 (8th Cir. 1997), *cert. denied*, 522 U.S. 938 (1997) (fraudulent misrepresentations need not have been directed at the victims); Corcoran v. American Plan Corp., 886 F.2d 16 (2d Cir. 1989); Prince Heaton Enters., Inc. v. Buffalo's Franchise Concepts, Inc., 117 F. Supp. 2d 1357 (N.D. Ga. 2000) (no detrimental reliance where contract said defendants had not made any statements regarding profits or sales and that plaintiffs had conducted independent investigation); System Mgmt., Inc. v. Loiselle, 112 F. Supp. 2d 112, 116 (D. Mass. 2000) (declining to adopt "convergence theory," that the scheme must deceive the same person that it deprives of money or property), *rev'd on other grounds*, 303 F.3d 100 (1st Cir. 2002) (reliance need not be shown, but pattern not shown where all acts of mail fraud occurred in context of one contract over limited time); *In re* American Express Co. Shareholder Litig., 840 F. Supp. 260 (S.D.N.Y. 1993) (party deceived need not be party injured), *aff'd*, 39 F.3d 395 (2d Cir. 1994). *But see* Israel Travel Advisory Serv., Inc. v. Israel Identity Tours, Inc., 61 F.3d 1250 (7th Cir. 1995), *cert. denied*, 116 S. Ct. 1847 (1996) (only the person defrauded can claim mail fraud).

335 Durland v. United States, 161 U.S. 306, 313 (1896); *see also* Williams v. Aztar Ind. Gaming Corp., 351 F.3d 294, 299 (7th Cir. 2003) (plaintiff must allege a misrepresentation in order to allege mail fraud). *But see* D'Orange v. Feely, 894 F. Supp. 159 (S.D.N.Y. 1995) (mailings sent by attorney regarding pending litigation can not be mail fraud predicates even if contain fraudulent material), *aff'd on other grounds*, 101 F.3d 1393 (2d Cir. 1996) (table).

336 Emery v. American General Fin., Inc., 71 F.3d 1343 (7th Cir. 1995) (omission or concealment of loan information can constitute mail fraud); United States v. Beecroft, 608 F.2d 753, 757 (9th Cir. 1979); Parish v. Beneficial Illinois, Inc., 1996 U.S. Dist. LEXIS 4453 (N.D. Ill. Apr. 10, 1996) (loan refinancing forms which were misleading as to costs were basis for mail fraud). *But see* Nolan v. Galaxy Scientific Corp., 269 F. Supp. 2d 635, 640 (E.D. Pa. 2003) (no RICO liability based on omission in mailed literature where "the causal link between the alleged mail fraud and the purported fraudulent activity [was] too attenuated"); Pappas v. NCNB, 653 F. Supp. 699 (M.D.N.C. 1987) (no mail fraud where no fiduciary duty existed to disclose prime lending rate).

337 United States v. Cherif, 943 F.2d 692 (7th Cir. 1991), *cert. denied*, 503 U.S. 961 (1992).

338 McNally v. United States, 483 U.S. 350, 107 S. Ct. 2875, 97 L. Ed. 292 (1987). Note, however, that the scheme may be designed either to obtain money or property or to deprive one of it. Shaw v. Rolex Watch, 726 F. Supp. 969 (S.D.N.Y. 1989).

339 Pub. L. No. 100-690, § 7603(a), 102 Stat. 4508 (1988) (codified at 18 U.S.C. § 1346). The section reads "[f]or the purposes of this chapter, the term 'scheme or artifice to defraud' includes a scheme or artifice to deprive another of the intangible right of honest services."

340 *See* § 9.2.3.6, *supra*.

341 Blu-J, Inc. v. Kemper C.P.A. Group, 916 F.2d 637 (11th Cir. 1990); Abell v. Potomac Ins. Co., 858 F.2d 1104 (5th Cir. 1988) (fraudulent intent required; materiality and reliance not required); Haroco v. American Nat'l Bank & Trust Co., 747 F.2d 384, 403 (7th Cir. 1984), *aff'd per curiam*, 473 U.S. 606 (1985); United States v. Rasheed, 663 F.2d 843, 847 (9th Cir. 1981), *cert. denied*, 454 U.S. 1137 (1982); Mount Prospect State Bank v. Grossman, 1989 U.S. Dist. LEXIS 2086 (N.D. Ill. Feb. 24, 1989) (default on loans not sufficient to make RICO claim because no showing of intent to defraud at time loans made); *see also* Selman v. American Sports Underwriters, Inc., No. 84-0099C (W.D. Va. Mar. 23, 1987) (plaintiff's mail and wire fraud allegations insufficient to show specific intent to defraud).

342 United States v. Munoz, 233 F.3d 1117, 1136 (9th Cir. 2000); United States v. Cogle, 63 F.3d 1239 (3d Cir. 1995); United States v. Dick, 744 F.2d 546, 551 (7th Cir. 1984); United States v. Hopkins, 744 F.2d 716, 717, 718 (10th Cir. 1984); United States v. Farris, 614 F.2d 634, 638 (9th Cir. 1979), *cert. denied*, 447 U.S. 926 (1980).

343 Berent v. Kemper Corp., 973 F.2d 1291 (6th Cir. 1992); Sun Sav. & Loan Ass'n v. Dierdorff, 825 F.2d 187 (9th Cir. 1987); United States v. Green, 745 F.2d 1205 (9th Cir. 1984), *cert. denied*, 474 U.S. 925 (1985).

scheme is a defense;[344] however, this belief will not be determined by a purely subjective standard of sincerity. Honest belief does not justify baseless, false, or reckless representations or promises.[345] Thus mail fraud includes more conduct than covered by common law fraud, but probably somewhat less conduct than covered by the UDAP "deception" standard.

9.2.4.2 The Mailing Requirement

The mailing need not be made by the defendant so long as he or she causes it to be made.[346] Nor need the mailing contain the fraudulent representation itself; it is enough if the mailing somehow aids in the execution of the fraudulent scheme.[347] An example would be mailings made after the commission of fraud and acquisition of its proceeds which prevent or postpone its detection by the victims.[348]

Under the mail fraud statute, each mailing in furtherance of a scheme to defraud is a separate offense, separately punishable.[349] It does not follow, though, for purposes of RICO, that two or more acts indictable as mail fraud will always establish a "pattern" of racketeering activity.[350] But, so far as the mail fraud statute itself is concerned, multiple mailings in furtherance of a single scheme to defraud provide multiple RICO predicate offenses: the mail fraud statute punishes not the "scheme to defraud" but *mailings* which further it.[351] For mail fraud, unlike wire fraud, the communication need not have been interstate.[352]

9.2.4.3 Aiding and Abetting Mail Fraud

While most Circuits that have addressed the issue recently have ruled that there is no aiding and abetting liability under, at least, subsection 1962(c), a different question is whether aiding and abetting mail fraud can itself be a predicate act under RICO.[353] RICO defines, as a predicate offense, "any act which is indictable under . . . § 1341 (relating to mail fraud), [or] § 1343 (relating to wire fraud). . . ."[354] One who aids and abets a federal crime is treated as a principal.[355] Accordingly, aiding and abetting mail fraud or one of the other federal offenses listed should constitute a predicate offense under RICO.[356] However, in a section 1962(c) claim one will still have to prove that the defendant, in addition to aiding and abetting the underlying crime, "conduct[ed] or participate[d] . . . in the conduct of [the] enterprise's affairs" through the pattern of racketeering activity or collection of an unlawful debt, so the broader scope of the mail fraud statute may be of little ultimate use.

9.2.4.4 Wire Fraud

Insofar as RICO is concerned, wire fraud[357] and mail

---

344 South Atlantic Ltd. P'ship v. Riese, 284 F.3d 518, 531 (4th Cir. 2002); United States v. Smith, 13 F.3d 1421, 1426 (10th Cir. 1994); United States v. Hopkins, 744 F.2d 716, 717, 718 (10th Cir. 1984).

345 United States v. Smith, 13 F.3d 1421, 1426 (10th Cir. 1994); United States v. Stoll, 743 F.2d 439, 445, 446 (6th Cir. 1984), *cert. denied*, 470 U.S. 1112 (1985); Sparrow v. United States, 402 F.2d 826, 828, 829 (10th Cir. 1968).

346 United States v. Maze, 414 U.S. 395, 399, 400, 94 S. Ct. 645, 38 L. Ed. 2d 603 (1974); Pereira v. United States, 347 U.S. 1, 8, 74 S. Ct. 358, 98 L. Ed. 2d 435 (1954); Dale v. Ala Acquisitions, Inc., 203 F. Supp. 2d 694, 702 (S.D. Miss. 2002) (defendant need not have made the communication personally, enough whether the use of the mail was reasonably foreseeable). The mailing must have been made by the defendant or its agent. Armbruster v. K-H Corp., 206 F. Supp. 2d 870, 897 (E.D. Mich. 2002).

347 Schmuck v. United States, 489 U.S. 705, 109 S. Ct. 1443, 103 L. Ed. 2d 734 (1989) (mailing incidental to fraudulent scheme sufficient); Hofstetter v. Fletcher, 905 F.2d 897 (6th Cir. 1988) (mailings after initial sales based on fraud may be considered to show scheme existed); United States v. Reid, 533 F.2d 1255, 1265 (D.C. Cir. 1976). *See also* American Eagle Credit Corp. v. Gaskins, 920 F.2d 352 (6th Cir. 1990) (mailings need not be essential element of scheme).

348 United States v. Brutzman, 731 F.2d 1449, 1454 (9th Cir. 1984); United States v. Jones, 712 F.2d 1316, 1320, 1321 (9th Cir.), *cert. denied*, 464 U.S. 986 (1983).

349 United States v. Stoll, 743 F.2d 439, 444, 445 (6th Cir.), *cert. denied*, 470 U.S. 1062 (1984); United States v. Ledesma, 632 F.2d 670, 679 (7th Cir.), *cert. denied*, 449 U.S. 998 (1980).

350 *See* § 9.2.3.4, *supra*; *see also* Anton Motors, Inc. v. Powers, 644 F. Supp. 299 (D. Md. 1986); Millers Cove Energy Co. v. Domestic Energy Servs. Co., 646 F. Supp. 520 (E.D. Mich. 1986).

351 United States v. Weatherspoon, 581 F.2d 595, 601, 602 (7th Cir. 1978).

352 United States v. Cady, 567 F.2d 771, 776 n.7 (8th Cir. 1977), *cert. denied*, 435 U.S. 944 (1978); Hinsdale Women's Clinic v. Women's Health Care of Hinsdale, 690 F. Supp. 658 (N.D. Ill. 1988).

353 *See also* § 9.2.3.6, *supra*.

354 18 U.S.C. § 1961(B).

355 18 U.S.C. § 2. *See also* Petro-Tech, Inc. v. Western Co., 824 F.2d 1349, 1357 (3d Cir. 1987) (one who has aided and abetted the commission of two predicate offenses is guilty of those offenses).

356 *See, e.g.*, Aetna Cas. Sur. Co. v. P&B Autobody, 1994 U.S. App. LEXIS 36770, at *94 (1st Cir. Dec. 29, 1994) (aiding or abetting mail fraud is also a "predicate act," because aiding and abetting mail fraud is a violation of the mail fraud statute itself). *See also* Dayton Monetary Assocs. v. Donaldson, Lufkin, & Jenrette Sec. Corp., 1995 U.S. Dist. LEXIS 1198, at *12 (S.D.N.Y. Feb. 2, 1995) (holding that Supreme Court's decision in Central Bank v. Interstate Bank did not affect whether aiding and abetting mail fraud was a predicate act, but whether aiding and abetting a RICO violation was a RICO violation).

357 18 U.S.C. § 1343. The statute states:

> Whoever, having devised or intending to devise any scheme or artifice to defraud, or for obtaining money or property by means of false or fraudulent pretenses, representations, or promises, transmits or causes to be transmitted by means of wire, radio, or television communication in interstate or foreign commerce, any writings, signs, signals, pictures, or sounds for

fraud are treated in virtually identical fashion.[358] The only difference is that wire fraud requires an interstate communication,[359] typically by telephone. The requirement is met if a telephone call, though originating and arriving in the same state, is routed out of the state along the way.[360] The element of specific intent is the same,[361] and it is enough if the defendant foreseeably caused the telephone call, whether or not he or she placed it.[362] As with mail fraud, each use of the wires is a separate offense, even if they all facilitate the same scheme.[363] Again the same as mail fraud, schemes to defraud a person of intangible rights are actionable.[364]

9.2.5 RICO Pleading

9.2.5.1 Avoiding Rule 11 Claims

There are numerous practical matters to consider when contemplating a RICO claim. Careful drafting, an understanding of the RICO statute and its elements, and knowledge of local requirements will all help the practitioner establish valid RICO claims efficiently. Following these guidelines will also help protect a consumer attorney against a Rule 11 claim.[365] So long as a claim has not been established as clearly non-viable, courts in RICO cases have been reluctant to impose Rule 11 sanctions against lawyers using RICO in novel ways.[366]

A few of the highest exposure missteps are easy to avoid. Be careful to plead only those predicate acts that are recognized by the statute, as including other acts may lead to sanctions.[367] Also, when pleading fraud, an attorney's failure to plead with particularity in accordance with Rule 9(b) can lead to sanctions.[368] Finally, be sure to allege each

the purpose of executing such scheme or artifice, shall be fined not more than $1000 or imprisoned not more than five years, or both. If the violation affects a financial institution, such person shall be fined not more than $1,000,000 or imprisoned not more than 20 years, or both.

358 *See* Carpenter v. United States, 484 U.S. 19, 108 S. Ct. 316, 98 L. Ed. 2d 275 (1987); United States v. Giovengo, 637 F.2d 941, 944 (3d Cir. 1980), *cert. denied*, 450 U.S. 1032 (1981); D'Iorio v. Adonizio, 554 F. Supp. 222, 264 n.3 (M.D. Pa. 1982) (mem.).

359 Smith v. Ayres, 845 F.2d 1360 (5th Cir. 1988); First Pac. Bancorp, Inc. v. Bro, 847 F.2d 542 (9th Cir. 1988); Harris Trust & Sav. Bank v. Ellis, 609 F. Supp. 1118, 1122 (N.D. Ill. 1985) (mem.), *aff'd on other grounds*, 810 F.2d 700 (7th Cir. 1987); Efron v. Embassy Suites (P.R.), Inc., 47 F. Supp. 2d 200, 205 (D. P.R. 1999) (allegations of facsimile transmissions without allegations of use of telephone lines were insufficient to allege predicate act of wire fraud), *aff'd*, 223 F.3d 12 (1st Cir. 2000), *cert. denied*, 121 S. Ct. 1228 (2001); Utz v. Correa, 631 F. Supp. 592 (S.D.N.Y. 1986); Gitterman v. Vitoulis, 579 F. Supp. 423 (S.D.N.Y. 1983).

360 *See, e.g.*, United States v. Davila, 592 F.2d 1261, 1263, 1264 (5th Cir.), *reh'g denied en banc*, 597 F.2d 283 (5th Cir.), *cert. denied*, 435 U.S. 944 (1978).

361 United States v. Cusino, 694 F.2d 185, 187 (9th Cir. 1982), *cert. denied*, 461 U.S. 932 (1983).

362 *Id.* at 188.

363 United States v. Benmuhar, 658 F.2d 14, 16 (1st Cir. 1981), *cert. denied*, 457 U.S. 1117 (1982).

364 Pub. L. No. 100-690, § 7603(a), 102 Stat. 4508 (1988) (codified at 18 U.S.C. § 1346). The section reads "[f]or the purposes of this chapter, the term 'scheme or artifice to defraud' includes a scheme or artifice to deprive another of the intangible right of honest services."

365 Fed. R. Civ. P. 11.

366 *E.g.*, Official Pub'ns, Inc. v. Kable News Co., 884 F.2d 664 (2d Cir. 1989) (reversing award of sanctions); Smith Int'l, Inc. v. Texas Commerce Bank, 844 F.2d 1193 (5th Cir. 1988); Beeman v. Fiester, 852 F.2d 206 (7th Cir. 1988); Clifford v. Hughson, 992 F. Supp. 661 (S.D.N.Y. 1998) (no Rule 11 sanctions where plaintiffs amended complaint each time with leave of court, in a good faith effort to supply missing RICO elements); Arnold v. Moran, 687 F. Supp. 232 (E.D. Va. 1988); Rochester Midland Corp. v. Mesko, 696 F. Supp. 262 (E.D. Mich. 1988); Design Time, Inc. v. Synthetic Diamond Tech., Inc., 674 F. Supp. 1564 (N.D. Ind. 1987). *See also* Blakey, *How to Tell If You Have a RICO Case*, 5 Law. Alert (Oct. 28, 1985), at 27. *But see* Avirgan v. Hull, 932 F.2d 1572 (11th Cir. 1991) (affirming award of one million dollars in sanctions and fees where no proof established of RICO claim after two years of discovery and no basis for original claim), *cert. denied*, 502 U.S. 1048 (1992); Hartz v. Friedman, 919 F.2d 469 (7th Cir. 1990) (sanctions for filing frivolous appeal); O'Malley v. New York City Transit Authority, 896 F.2d 704 (2d Cir. 1990) (sanctions are mandatory if court finds suit baseless); Lodal, Inc. v. Great Am. Ins. Cos., 2001 U.S. Dist. LEXIS 22123, at *28 (W.D. Mich. Sept. 19, 2001) (awarding sanctions against attorney for RICO claims that "lacked any factual or legal basis and were asserted for an improper basis" in case arising from dispute between manufacturer and two insurers over coverage of policies); Brandt v. Schal Assocs., Inc., 131 F.R.D. 512 (N.D. Ill. 1990) ($350,000 sanctions awarded against plaintiff's lawyer for turning simple contract case into RICO claim); Wardwell v. Metmor Fin., Inc., 1988 WL 156801 (D. Mass. 1988) (sanctions imposed where no reasonable investigation into the law prior to bringing baseless RICO claim); Davies v. Thiessen, 1999 Wash. App. LEXIS 1242 (Wash. App. July 6, 1999) (unpublished) (upholding sanctions against attorney who filed UDAP and RICO claims arising from sale of an allegedly defective house; court found suit baseless and filed for an improper purpose). One development RICO's drafters probably did not expect is that several marital disputes have resulted in RICO litigation. *See* Grimmett v. Brown, 75 F.3d 506 (9th Cir. 1996) (spouse claimed to have been defrauded out of assets), *cert. granted*, 518 U.S. 1003 (1996), *cert. dismissed*, 519 U.S. 233 (1997); Reynolds v. Condon, 908 F. Supp. 1494 (N.D. Iowa 1995) (man sued former wife and others alleging they defrauded him out of marital home and other assets).

367 Binghamton Masonic Temple, Inc. v. Bares, 1999 U.S. App. LEXIS 18139, at *4 (2d Cir. July 30, 1999) (affirming sanctions against attorney who pleaded non-recognized acts in addition to the recognized predicate acts of mail fraud, wire fraud, bank fraud and Sec. fraud); Browning v. Weichert, 1999 U.S. App. LEXIS 2307, at *3 (9th Cir. Feb. 12, 1999) (affirming sanctions where plaintiff pleaded slander as a predicate act).

368 *See, e.g.*, Binghamton Masonic Temple, Inc. v. Bares, 1999 U.S. App. LEXIS 18139, at *4 (2d Cir. July 30, 1999) (affirming sanctions against attorney where, among other defects, he failed to plead scienter with particularity). *See also* Gerstenfeld v. Nitsberg, 190 F.R.D. 127 (S.D.N.Y. 1999) (denying sanctions in

element of a RICO claim; omitting an element may lead to sanctions.[369]

A RICO claim should not be omitted if there is a good faith basis for it at the time the complaint is filed, but attorneys should reevaluate the RICO claim as the case progresses.[370] Courts in two circuits have affirmed Rule 11 sanctions for failure to dismiss a RICO claim when it was clear after discovery that the claim was not valid[371] and one circuit has imposed sanctions against attorneys for filing a class action securities fraud suit based on a *Wall Street Journal* article and an earlier-filed complaint, without conducting their own investigation.[372] In a borderline case which is not being received well by the judge hearing it, consider that a federal district judge's sanctions will be reviewed only for abuse of discretion on appeal.[373] On appeal, Federal Rule of Appellate Procedure 38 allows an appellate court to impose sanctions for frivolously filed claims as well.[374]

9.2.5.2 Pleading Fraud—Rule 9(b)'s Particularity Requirement

Pleading a RICO claim properly requires reasonably detailed allegations of fraud and a multi-faceted claim for relief. Many local courts have their own special requirements for pleading RICO cases, and these should be followed carefully.[375]

Most consumer RICO cases assert the predicate acts of mail fraud or wire fraud, and for purposes of RICO, the Federal Rules of Civil Procedure apply, requiring that fraud be pleaded with particularity.[376] The rule's purposes include

---

dismissal of RICO claim for failure to comply with Rule 9(b), but warning that sanctions could be imposed if the attorney reasserted the claim without pleading facts supporting both particularity and substantive RICO elements). *See also* § 9.2.5.2, *infra*.

369 *See, e.g.,* Dangerfield v. Merrill Lynch, Pierce, Fenner & Smith, Inc., 2003 WL 22227956, at *13 (S.D.N.Y. Sept. 26, 2003) (imposing sanctions in light of court's conclusion that "no attorney conducting a reasonable inquiry into the legal viability of [the plaintiff's] RICO claim could have thought that it had any chance to succeed").

370 *See* Smith v. Our Lady of the Lake Hosp., Inc., 960 F.2d 439 (5th Cir. 1992) (while attorney's Rule 11 duty is particularly strong in RICO cases, sanctions for withdrawn RICO claim were inappropriate because law was not clear when complaint was filed in good faith); Divot Golf Corp. v. Citizens Bank of Mass., 2003 WL 61287, at *2, 3 (D. Mass. Jan. 8, 2003) (imposing sanctions, noting that plaintiffs repeated factual misstatements and failed to properly allege pattern even after put on notice of complaint's deficiencies by defendants); Anderson v. Smithfield Foods, Inc., 209 F. Supp. 2d 1278, 1281 (S.D. Fla. 2002) (imposing sanctions for failing to make a "reasonable inquiry" before filing second amended complaint after previous two complaints had been dismissed); Miller v. Norfolk Southern Ry. Co., 208 F. Supp. 2d 851, 852 (N.D. Ohio 2002) (ordering reprimand against attorney who filed motion to reconsider that contained no new facts or legal theories); Martinez v. Martinez, 207 F. Supp. 2d 1303, 1309 (D.N.M. 2002) (imposing sanctions where attorney failed to follow court's explicit warnings upon dismissing initial complaint, but rather filed amended complaint that still failed to properly allege RICO claim), *aff'd in part, vacated in part on other grounds*, 2003 WL 1904807 (10th Cir. 2003) (unpublished, citation limited). *See also* Byrne v. Nezhat, 261 F.3d 1075, 1116 (11th Cir. 2001) ("any doubt" as to meritlessness of state RICO claim dissolved when state court dismissed similar action brought on behalf of a different client against same defendants; affirming sanctions against attorney who nonetheless continued to pursue claim).

371 Fahrenz v. Meadow Farm P'ship, 850 F.2d 207 (4th Cir. 1988) (affirming sanctions against attorney for unreasonable opposition to summary judgment motion after three key deponents repudiated critical facts); Flip Side Productions, Inc. v. Jam Productions, Ltd., 843 F.2d 1024, 1037 (7th Cir. 1988) (affirming sanctions for failure to dismiss after discovery showed no claim); Fred A. Smith Lumber Co. v. Edidin, 845 F.2d 750 (7th Cir. 1988) (law clearly against plaintiff). *See also In re* Taxable Municipal Bond Sec. Litig., 1994 U.S. Dist. LEXIS 1072 (E.D. La. Feb. 3, 1994) (court imposed sanctions where plaintiff refused to dismiss claims which were clearly invalidated by new case).

372 Garr v. U.S. Healthcare, Inc., 22 F.3d 1274, 1279, 1280 (3d Cir. 1994). Now that securities fraud no longer serves as a predicate act such a case would have further reason to draw sanctions. *See* The Private Sec. Litig. Reform Act of 1995, 104 Pub. L. No. 104-67, 109 Stat. 758 (1995) (amending 18 U.S.C. § 1964(a) to exclude "any conduct that would have been actionable as fraud in the purchase or sale of securities" as the basis of a civil RICO action).

373 *See, e.g.*, Olson Farms, Inc. v. Barbosa, 134 F.3d 933, 936 (9th Cir. 1998). *See also* Byrne v. Nezhat, 261 F.3d 1075, 1116–17 (11th Cir. 2001) (affirming sanctions against attorney but vacating sanctions against client in medical malpractice case framed as a RICO claim, finding record "replete with instances of bad faith and dilatory tactics"); Birnbaum v. Law Offices of G. David Westfall, P.C., 120 S.W.3d 470, 476 (Tex. App. 2003) (affirming sanctions against plaintiff where plaintiff failed to properly specify his objections to the order in the lower court).

374 *See, e.g.*, Horoshko v. Citibank, N.A., 2004 WL 1472680, at *2 (2d Cir. July 2, 2004) (*per curiam*) (awarding fees for "gross[]" abuse of the appellate process); Williams v. Aztar Ind. Gaming Corp., 351 F.3d 294, 300 (7th Cir. 2003) (finding that RICO claim was filed solely to invoke federal court jurisdiction and directing plaintiff to show cause as to why he should not be sanctioned).

375 *See* § 9.2.5.4, *infra*.

376 Lum v. Bank of Am., 361 F.3d 217, 223–24 (3d Cir. 2003) (complaint must put the defendants " 'on notice of the precise misconduct with which they are charged,' " holding that "conclusory" allegations that do not state the date, time, or place of the alleged misrepresentations do not satisfy the rule) (quoting Seville Indus. Mach. Corp. v. Southmost Mach. Corp., 742 F.2d 786, 791 (3d Cir. 1984)); Murr Plumbing Inc. v. Scherer Brothers Fin. Servs. Co., 48 F.3d 1066 (8th Cir. 1995) (while mail and wire fraud statutes do not require proof of a misrepresentation of fact, still must be specificity regarding the elements of the statutory fraud); Mills v. Polar Molecular Corp., 12 F.3d 1170 (2d Cir. 1993); Farlow v. Peat, Marwick, Mitchell & Co., 956 F.2d 982 (10th Cir. 1992); Cayman Exploration Corp. v. United Gas Pipe Line Corp., 873 F.2d 1357 (10th Cir. 1989); Durham v. Business Mgmt. Assocs., 847 F.2d 1505, 1512 (11th Cir.

providing defendants with fair notice of the claims against them, protecting defendants from harm to their reputations by unfounded fraud allegations, and reducing the number of strike suits.[377] Many cases with potentially valid RICO claims are dismissed each year because the complaints do not explain clearly and in sufficient detail the fraudulent behavior allegedly constituting the RICO predicate acts.[378] Some courts now require that all predicate acts—not just those based on fraud—be pleaded with equal particularity.[379] However, the plaintiff need not plead damages with the particularity of Rule 9(b).[380] Furthermore, a plaintiff need only plead the intent element of fraud in general terms.[381]

The degree of pleading that constitutes particularity varies, depending on the type of fraud. However, generally courts require a RICO plaintiff to plead the time, place, and particular context of the false representations as well as the identity of the party making the representations and the consequences of making them.[382] The consumer lawyer

1988) (allegations necessary to fulfill Rule 9(b) need not necessarily be in complaint, finding rule satisfied by allegations in filed affidavit along with complaint); Flowers v. Continental Grain Co., 775 F.2d 1051, 1054 (8th Cir. 1985) (mail fraud); Allen v. New World Coffee, Inc., 2001 U.S. Dist. LEXIS 3269, at *13 (S.D.N.Y. Mar. 27, 2001); Brown v. Coleman Invs., Inc., 993 F. Supp. 416 (M.D. La. 1998) (in case against assignee of retail installment sales contract, plaintiff's complaint failed to adequately plead fraud where alleged only that defendant knew assignor had inflated fees but did not allege defendant had specific intent); Prudential Ins. Co. v. U.S. Gypsum Co., 711 F. Supp. 1244 (D.N.J. 1989) (fraud sufficiently pleaded where plaintiff alleged that defendants conspired in printing materials of various sorts which hid the dangers of asbestos); Wabash Valley Power Ass'n v. Public Serv. Co., 678 F. Supp. 757 (S.D. Ind. 1988); McLendon v. Continental Group, Inc., 602 F. Supp. 1492, 1507 (D.N.J. 1985); Saine v. A.I.A., Inc., 582 F. Supp. 1299, 1303 (D. Colo. 1984); Doxieu v. Ford Motor Credit Co., 603 F. Supp. 624, 627, 628 (S.D. Ga. 1984) (mem.); Taylor v. Bear Stearns & Co., 572 F. Supp. 667, 682 (N.D. Ga. 1983). *See also* Chang v. California Canadian Bank, 823 F.2d 554 (9th Cir. 1987) (holding that Rule 9(b) is not satisfied by conclusory allegation of "intimate knowledge"). If it is impossible to meet specificity requirements because the necessary information is in the defendant's control, one might request limited discovery for the purpose of refining the RICO claim. Blue Line Coal Co. v. Equibank, 683 F. Supp. 493 (E.D. Pa. 1988).

377 DiVittorio v. Equidyne Extractive Indus., Inc., 822 F.2d 1242, 1247 (2d Cir. 1987); New England Data Servs., Inc. v. Becher, 829 F.2d 286, 288 (1st Cir. 1987) (the court decided, however, that when mail and wire fraud are pleaded as predicate acts in RICO cases, the court should follow a more lenient process of dismissal, in light of the probability that the information needed to satisfy Rule 9(b) will be in the exclusive control of a defendant; *id.* at 290); G-I Holdings, Inc. v. Baron & Bodd, 238 F. Supp. 2d 521 (S.D.N.Y. 2002). *See also In re* Lupron Mktg. & Sales Practices Litig., 295 F. Supp. 2d 148, 171 (D. Mass. 2001) (suggesting that given the improbability that the defendants communicated without using the mail or interstate wires, the plaintiffs should be able to cure their pleading deficiencies in an amended complaint).

378 *See* National Consumer Law Center, Consumer Law Pleadings, No. 3, § 9.3 (CD-Rom and Index Guide) also found on the CD-Rom accompanying this volume. Courts may use Rule 9(b) aggressively to move RICO cases off their dockets. *See also* Smith v. Figa & Burns, 69 Fed. Appx. 922, 926 (10th Cir. 2003) (affirming dismissal of RICO counterclaim where pleading contained no details about the timing and nature of the predicate acts alleged); Int'l Telecom, Inc. v. Generadora Electrica del Oriente S.A., 2002 WL 465291, at *7 (S.D.N.Y. Mar. 27, 2002) (noting trend to apply the rule "strictly" to dismiss civil RICO claims).

379 *See* Shapo v. O'Shaugnessy, 246 F. Supp. 2d 935 (N.D. Ill. 2002) (plaintiff must meet Rule 9(b) for all underlying predicate acts); Jordan (Berm.) Inv. Co. v. Hunter Green Invs. Ltd., 154 F. Supp. 2d 682, 692 (S.D.N.Y. 2001); Brooks v. Bank of Boulder, 891 F. Supp. 1469 (D. Colo. 1995) ("a charge of racketeering should not be easier to make than an allegation of fraud"); Biddle Sawyer Corp. v. Charket Chem. Corp., 1991 U.S. Dist. LEXIS 4599 (S.D.N.Y. Apr. 2, 1991); Market Servs., Inc. v. Ying, No. 90-CIV-3152 (S.D.N.Y. Feb. 1, 1991); . *Accord* Holbrook v. Master Protection Corp., 883 P.2d 295 (Utah App. 1994) (unlawful activity under Utah's RICO statute must be pleaded with particularity). *But see* Abels v. Farmers Commodities Corp., 259 F.3d 910, 919 (8th Cir. 2001) (plaintiff need not meet Rule 9(b) when pleading non-fraud predicate offenses); Panix Promotions v. Lewis, 2002 U.S. Dist. LEXIS 784, at *26 (S.D.N.Y. Jan 15, 2002) (allegations of a RICO conspiracy need not meet Rule 9(b)'s heightened pleading allegations); CNBC v. Alvarado, RICO Business Disputes Guide (CCH) ¶ 8629, 1994 U.S. Dist. LEXIS 11505 (S.D.N.Y. Aug. 17, 1994) (specificity not required when pleading commercial bribery as predicate act); Towers Fin. Corp. v. Solomon, 126 F.R.D. 531 (N.D. Ill. 1989) (only fraud allegations, not whole RICO claim, need meet Rule 9(b) specificity requirements); Gentry v. Yonce, 522 S.E.2d 137 (S.C. 1999) (pleading need not comply with state Rule 9's particularity requirements unless fraud is alleged as a predicate act).

380 Robbins v. Wilkie, 300 F.3d 1208, 1211 (10th Cir. 2002).

381 Jordan (Berm.) Inv. Co. v. Hunter Green Invs. Ltd., 154 F. Supp. 2d 682 (S.D.N.Y. 2001) (plaintiff pleads fraudulent intent adequately either by pleading that the defendants consciously engaged in fraudulent behavior or that they had both the motive and the "clear opportunity" to commit fraud).

382 *E.g.*, Lum v. Bank of Am., 361 F.3d 217, 223–24 (3d Cir. 2003); Walls v. Int'l Longshoremen's & Warehousemen's Union, 2001 U.S. App. LEXIS 9746, at *4–5 (9th Cir. May 11, 2001) (dismissing RICO complaint that contained only "general and conclusory allegations" regarding the predicate acts of fraud); Corley v. Rosewood Care Ctr., 142 F.3d 1041, 1050 (7th Cir. 1998); Emery v. Am. General Fin., Inc., 134 F.3d 1321 (7th Cir. 1998), *cert. denied*, 525 U.S. 818 (1998); Murr Plumbing Inc. v. Scherer Brothers Fin. Servs. Co., 48 F.3d 1066 (8th Cir. 1995); Bankers Trust Co. v. Rhoades, 859 F.2d 1096 (2d Cir. 1988), *cert. denied*, 490 U.S. 1007 (1989); Schreiber Distrib. Co. v. Serv Well Furniture Co., 806 F.2d 1393 (9th Cir. 1986); Haroco v. Am. Nat'l Bank & Trust Co., 747 F.2d 384, 405 (7th Cir. 1984), *aff'd*, 473 U.S. 606 (1985); Moss v. Morgan Stanley, Inc., 719 F.2d 5, 19 (2d Cir. 1983), *cert. denied*, 465 U.S. 1025 (1984); Bennett v. Berg, 685 F.2d 1053, 1062 (8th Cir. 1982), *aff'd en banc*, 710 F.2d 1361 (8th Cir.), *cert. denied*, 464 U.S. 1008 (1983); Welch v. Centex Home Equity Co., 2004 WL 1486310, at *6 (D. Kan. June 30, 2004) (dismissing complaint of borrower arising from forgery of plaintiff's name on loan documents because plaintiff had alleged fraud "conclusorily"); Crawford & Sons, Ltd. Profit Sharing Plan v. Besser, 216 F.R.D. 228, 234 (E.D.N.Y. 2003) (stating that allegations of intent need

should be as factually specific as possible about the fraud.

In alleging mail fraud, the plaintiff should outline the fraud by delineating the sender and recipient, the date and location of mailing and receipt, the contents of the mailings and their relationship to the fraud, and the consequences of the mailings.[383] Mere recitation of the time and place letters were sent is not enough.[384] Nonetheless, a plaintiff may be able to avoid identifying specific instances of mailings if the plaintiff does identify the specific details of the nature of the materials that allegedly furthered the scheme. Some courts read Rule 9(b) as requiring the plaintiff to plead the purpose of the mailing within the defendant's scheme.[385]

In the case of wire fraud, the plaintiff must provide similarly detailed information, and also must allege an interstate telephone call or other interstate wire communication in the furtherance of the fraudulent scheme.[386] Where the predicate offense is the collection of an unlawful debt, the plaintiff must, in addition to specifying the details of the transaction, specify the prescribed interest rate which the defendant has exceeded.[387]

It is clear that a plaintiff may not plead fraud simply on information and belief without some elaboration of the facts supporting that belief, subject to two primary exceptions.[388] First, many courts will make an exception to the rule of pleading fraud with particularity when the information needed to do so is within the exclusive control of the defendant, and will permit the plaintiff to conduct discovery in order to plead more specifically.[389] Second, the pleading

not meet such a high standard; holding that plaintiff met rule's requirements); Tierney and Partners, Inc. v. Rockman, 274 F. Supp. 2d 693, 699 (E.D. Pa. 2003) (RICO plaintiff alleging mail or wire fraud must plead the means of transmission of the material in complaint, along with the material's date, sender, recipient, and an explanation of its relationship to the pattern); DeNune v. Consol. Capital of N. Am., Inc., 288 F. Supp. 2d 844, 857 (N.D. Ohio 2003) (holding plaintiff pleaded RICO allegations with sufficient particularity); Paycom Billing Servs., Inc. v. Payment Resources Int'l, 212 F. Supp. 2d 732, 735 (W.D. Mich. 2002); Sony Music Entertainment Inc. v. Robison, 2002 WL 272406, at *5 (S.D.N.Y. Feb. 26, 2002), *reconsideration granted*, 2002 WL 550967 (S.D.N.Y. Apr. 11, 2002); Eva v. Midwest Nat'l Mortgage. Banc, Inc., 143 F. Supp. 2d 862, 877 (N.D. Ohio 2001). *But see* Perlberger v. Caplan & Luber, L.L.P., 152 F. Supp. 2d 650, 653 (E.D. Pa. 2001) (in case involving pro se plaintiff's claim against attorneys who had represented her, Rule 9(b)'s requirements "must be read in conjunction with the liberal pleading rules that the Rules embrace"; denying motion to dismiss); Metro Furniture Rental, Inc. v. Alessi, 770 F. Supp. 198 (S.D.N.Y. 1991); Azurite Corp. Ltd. v. Amster Co., 730 F. Supp. 571 (S.D.N.Y. 1990); Frank E. Basil, Inc. v. Leidesdorf, 713 F. Supp. 1194 (N.D. Ill. 1989); UNR Indus., Inc. v. Continental Ins. Co., 623 F. Supp. 1319, 1329 (N.D. Ill. 1985) (mem.); Mitchell Energy Corp. v. Martin, 616 F. Supp. 924 (S.D. Tex. 1985); Harris Trust & Sav. Bank v. Ellis, 609 F. Supp. 1118, 1123 (N.D. Ill. 1985) (mem.), *aff'd on other grounds*, 810 F.2d 700 (7th Cir. 1987); Rudolph v. Merrill Lynch, Pierce, Fenner & Smith, Inc., 100 F.R.D. 807, 809 (N.D. Ill. 1984).

383 First Guar. Mortgage Corp. v. Procopio, 217 F. Supp. 2d 633, 637 (D. Md. 2002); Int'l Telecom, Inc. v. Generadora Electrica del Oriente S.A., 2002 WL 465291, at *7 (S.D.N.Y. Mar. 27, 2002) (plaintiff failed to show the whom, what, where, when and why surrounding the allegedly fraudulent communications); Kukuk v. Fredal, 2001 U.S. Dist. LEXIS 16419, at *16 (E.D. Mich. Aug. 1, 2001) (plaintiffs, who set forth the months and years of alleged misrepresentations, sufficiently described the time-period requirement of Rule 9(b)); Kerby v. Mortgage Funding Corp., 992 F. Supp. 787 (D. Md. 1998) (in claim by borrowers alleging initial mortgage funder had received a kickback from the subsequent purchaser of the mortgage, plaintiffs sufficiently pleaded fraud by producing internal document listing payments passed from purchaser to funder to mortgage broker and by showing that funder failed to timely provide the Good Faith Estimate required by RESPA and received compensation for holding a risk-free note two weeks; not fatal that funder was not differentiated in the generalized descriptions of the acts of mail and wire fraud); Grafman v. Century Broadcasting Corp., 727 F. Supp. 432 (N.D. Ill. 1989); Tkaczuk v. Weil, 1988 U.S. Dist. LEXIS 14080, 1988 U.S. Dist. LEXIS 14080, Fed. Sec. L. Rep. (CCH) ¶ 94,347 (N.D. Ill. Dec. 9, 1988). *See also* Martinez v. Martinez, 207 F. Supp. 2d 1303, 1307 (D.N.M. 2002), *aff'd in part, vacated in part on other grounds*, 2003 WL 1904807 (10th Cir. 2003) (unpublished, citation limited); Karreman v. Evergreen Int'l Spot Trading, Inc., 2002 WL 31119429, at *6 (S.D.N.Y. Sept. 24, 2002).

384 DeLorean v. Cork Gully, 118 B.R. 932 (E.D. Mich. 1990); *see also* Schweitzer v. Testaverde, 1990 U.S. Dist. LEXIS 1672 (S.D.N.Y. Feb. 15, 1990) (must set forth contents of the items mailed and specify how each item was false and misleading).

385 Allen v. New World Coffee, Inc., 2001 U.S. Dist. LEXIS 3269, at *12 (S.D.N.Y. Mar. 27, 2001) (citing McLaughlin v. Anderson, 962 F.2d 187, 191 (2d Cir. 1992)).

386 DeLorean v. Cork Gully, 118 B.R. 932 (E.D. Mich. 1990); Harris Trust & Sav. Bank v. Ellis, 609 F. Supp. 1118, 1122 (M.D. Ill. 1985) (mem.), *aff'd on other grounds*, 810 F.2d 700 (7th Cir. 1987).

387 Blount Fin. Servs., Inc. v. Walter E. Heller & Co., 632 F. Supp. 240 (E.D. Tenn. 1986), *aff'd*, 819 F.2d 151 (6th Cir. 1987).

388 *See* Saporito v. Combustion Eng'g, Inc., 843 F.2d 666 (3d Cir. 1988), *remanded on other grounds*, 489 U.S. 1049 (1989), *remanded in part to district court*, 879 F.2d 859 (3d Cir. 1989).

389 Corley v. Rosewood Care Ctr., 142 F.3d 1041, 1050 (7th Cir. 1998); New England Data Serv., Inc. v. Becher, 829 F.2d 286 (1st Cir. 1987); Saporito v. Combustion Eng'g, Inc., 843 F.2d 666 (3d Cir. 1988), *remanded on other grounds*, 489 U.S. 1049 (1989), *remanded in part to district court*, 879 F.2d 859 (3d Cir. 1989); *Berk v. Tradewell, Inc.*, 2003 WL 21664679, at *13 (S.D.N.Y. July 16, 2003) (Rule 9(b) should be read permissively when the relevant information is in the defendant's exclusive possession or when the complaint is filed against a corporate insider); Shapo v. O'Shaugnessy, 246 F. Supp. 2d 935, 956 (N.D. Ill. 2002) (appropriate to loosen particularity requirement when information on extent of defendants' use of wires and mails exclusively in their control); Taylor v. Bob O'Connor Ford, Inc., 1999 U.S. Dist. LEXIS 4028, at *11 (N.D. Ill. Mar. 26, 1999); Spira v. Nick, 876 F. Supp. 553 (S.D.N.Y. 1995); CNBC v. Alvarado, RICO Business Disputes Guide (CCH) ¶ 8629, 1994 U.S. Dist. LEXIS 11505 (S.D.N.Y. Aug. 17, 1994); Official Pub'ns, Inc. v. Kable News Co., 775 F. Supp. 631 (S.D.N.Y. 1991); Economou v. Physicians Weight Loss Ctrs., 756 F. Supp. 1024 (N.D. Ohio 1991); Vista Co. v. Columbia Pictures Indus., Inc. 725 F. Supp. 1286 (S.D.N.Y. 1989); Philan Ins. Ltd. v. Frank B. Hall Co., 712 F. Supp. 339 (S.D.N.Y. 1989);

based on information and belief may be sufficient if the "information and belief" pertains to information from a pending criminal complaint.[390] A RICO claim that alleges mail fraud against third parties in addition to the plaintiff may also be subject to more lenient particularity requirements.[391] However, mere allegations that a defendant also defrauded unidentified others will not suffice.[392]

The safest approach is to draft the civil RICO complaint so as to resemble, as closely as possible, a criminal indictment.[393] Claims should be framed as specifically as possible, including particular factual allegations that establish two or more predicate acts. While most courts have rejected this as a legal requirement,[394] a few older federal district court decisions held that RICO claims based on predicate offenses of fraud must be pleaded with as much detail as a bill of particulars in a federal criminal indictment, sufficient to furnish probable cause to conclude that the predicate offenses were committed.[395] In any event, the closer to a criminal indictment, the less potential there is for the defendant to even raise the issue. Similarly, drafting a complaint in close compliance with any required RICO case statement (or, if the jurisdiction does not require such a statement, in line with one of the more detailed case statements required by other jurisdictions)[396] should forestall allegations that the complaint fails to meet Rule 9(b).

9.2.5.3 Pleading the Relief Sought

9.2.5.3.1 Actual damages

Although the Supreme Court has not established a measure of damages available in RICO claims,[397] it has stated that "the compensable injury necessarily is the harm caused by predicate acts sufficiently related to constitute a pattern."[398] Accordingly, a court should consider any reasonable basis for assessing the injury. A plaintiff injured by a RICO violation is entitled to a complete recovery.[399] Nevertheless, an important exclusion from RICO's general availability to remedy injury is personal injury.[400] Personal injury—whether manifested by physical injury or emotional distress—is neither directly nor indirectly compensable.[401]

Blue Line Coal Co. v. Equibank, 683 F. Supp. 493 (E.D. Pa. 1988). *But see* Denison v. Kelly, 759 F. Supp. 199 (M.D. Pa. 1991) (plaintiff not allowed to do discovery as to elements of complaint; reasonable investigations to be completed *before* complaint is filed).

390 Epstein v. Haas Sec. Corp., 731 F. Supp. 1166, 1183 (S.D.N.Y. 1990).

391 Corley v. Rosewood Care Ctr., Inc., 142 F.3d 1041, 1050 (7th Cir. 1998) (in case alleging that nursing home company ran bait-and-switch scheme, Rule 9(b)'s particularity requirement "must be relaxed where the plaintiff lacks access to all facts necessary to detail his claim, and that is most likely to be the case where, as here, the plaintiff alleges a fraud against one or more third parties [other residents]").

392 Goren v. New Vision Int'l, Inc., 156 F.3d 721 (7th Cir. 1998) (affirming dismissal of RICO claim that alleged defendants had sold bogus health products not just to the plaintiff but to other, unidentified, customers); Emery v. Am. General Fin., Inc., 134 F.3d 1321 (7th Cir. 1998) (affirming dismissal of RICO claim based on the defendant's alleged loan-flipping scheme where the plaintiff had failed to produce fraud-containing solicitation letters mailed to other borrowers), *cert. denied*, 525 U.S. 818 (1998).

393 Blakey, *How to Tell If You Have a RICO Case*, 5 Law. Alert, Oct. 28, 1985, at 28; Harris, *A Framework for Pleading Civil RICO*, in Practicing Law Institute, Civil RICO 1985, at 165. Five examples of RICO civil complaints and criminal indictments are reproduced in Harris, *A Framework for Pleading Civil RICO*, in Practicing Law Institute, 1985 Civil RICO, at 189-318.

394 Haroco v. Am. Nat'l Bank & Trust Co., 747 F.2d 384, 403, 404 (1984) *aff'd per curiam*, 473 U.S. 606 (1985); Cincinnati Gas & Elec. Co. v. General Elec. Co., 656 F. Supp. 49 (S.D. Ohio 1986); Kamin v. Colorado Nat'l Bank of Denver, 648 F. Supp. 52 (D. Colo. 1986); *In re* National Mortgage Equity Corp., 636 F. Supp. 1138 (C.D. Cal. 1986); Chicago HMO v. Trans Pac. Life Ins. Co., 622 F. Supp. 489, 494, 495 (N.D. Ill. 1985); Electronic Relays (India) Pvt. Ltd. v. Pascente, 610 F. Supp. 648, 649 (N.D. Ill. 1985) (mem.).

395 Rhoades v. Powell, 644 F. Supp. 645 (E.D. Cal. 1986), *aff'd without op.*, 961 F.2d 217 (9th Cir. 1992); Gregoris Motors v. Nissan Motor Corp., 630 F. Supp. 902 (E.D.N.Y. 1986); Beauregard Sav. & Loan Ass'n v. First Louisiana Fed. Sav. Bank, No. 86-0566-0 (W.D. La. Dec. 9, 1986); Allington v. Carpenter, 619 F. Supp. 474 (C.D. Cal. 1985); Bennett v. E.F. Hutton Co., 597 F. Supp. 1547, 1560 (N.D. Ohio 1984); Taylor v. Bear Stearns & Co., 572 F. Supp. 667 (N.D. Ga. 1983); Bache Halsey Stuart Shields, Inc. v. Tracy Collins Bank & Trust Co., 558 F. Supp. 1042, 1045, 1046 (D. Utah 1983).

396 *See* § 9.2.5.4, *infra*.

397 Fleischhauer v. Feltner, 879 F.2d 1290 (6th Cir. 1989), *cert. denied*, 494 U.S. 1027 (1990).

398 Sedima, S.P.R.L. v. Imrex Co., 473 U.S. 479, 497, 105 S. Ct. 3275, 87 L. Ed. 2d 346 (1985) (rejecting requirement of a racketeering injury); Liquid Air Corp. v. Rogers, 834 F.2d 1297, 1310 (7th Cir. 1987), *cert. denied*, 492 U.S. 917 (1989); City of Chicago Heights v. Lobue, 914 F. Supp. 279, 283 (N.D. Ill. 1996) (plaintiff failed to show causation); County of Oakland by Kuhn v. Vista Disposal, 900 F. Supp. 879, 890 (E.D. Mich. 1995) (plaintiff showed injury caused by RICO conspiracy). *See also* D'Orange v. Feely, 894 F. Supp. 159, 163 (S.D.N.Y. 1995) (damages sustained by RICO victim were, at a minimum, equal to the damages resulting from the sum of the predicate acts of mail fraud).

399 Liquid Air Corp. v. Rogers, 834 F.2d 1297, 1310 (7th Cir. 1987) (citing Carter v. Berger, 777 F.2d 1173, 1176 (7th Cir. 1985), *cert. denied*, 492 U.S. 917 (1989)).

400 Grogan v. Platt, 835 F.2d 844 (11th Cir.), *cert. denied*, 488 U.S. 981 (1988); Bankers Trust Co. v. Rhoades, 741 F.2d 511, 515 (2d Cir. 1984), *vacated and remanded on other grounds*, 473 U.S. 922 (1985); East v. A.H. Robins Co., 616 F. Supp. 333, 335 (E.D. Wis. 1985).

401 Maio v. Aetna Inc., 221 F.3d 472, 482 (3d Cir. 2000); Hamm v. Rhone-Poulenc Rorer Pharms., 187 F.3d 941, 948 (8th Cir. 1999), *cert. denied*, 528 U.S. 1117 (2000); Price v. Pinnacle Brands, 138 F.3d 602, 607 n.20 (5th Cir. 1998) (no recovery for gambling addiction injury); Pilkington v. United Airlines, 112 F.3d 1532, 1526 (11th Cir. 1997); Genty v. Resolution Trust Corp., 937 F.2d 899 (3d Cir. 1991); Berg v. First State Ins. Co.,

Nor are pecuniary losses connected with physical injury or emotional distress.[402] The Ninth Circuit requires the plaintiff to prove "concrete financial loss."[403] Injury as a standing issue is discussed in § 9.2.3.6, *supra*.

The attorney should take care when establishing damages in a complicated case to break the damages claim down as clearly as possible. Despite the liberal damages provisions of RICO, courts do analyze the damages carefully to prevent windfall recovery, so it is important to delineate the source of various categories of damages and to be prepared to show the court that the various components are not duplicative.[404]

9.2.5.3.2 Attorney fees, costs, and interest

The amount of attorney fees awarded to a successful RICO plaintiff can be substantial, even in a case with relatively small damages. The attorney fees awarded need not be in proportion to the amount of damages.[405] Singling out RICO defendants for the imposition of attorney fee liability does not deny them equal protection of the laws.[406]

The fees will often be calculated by the court after it asks for an affidavit of counsel as to the fees incurred. But beware, if a RICO case is settled without explicit provision for attorney fees, the plaintiff may face the argument that attorney fees have been waived.[407]

It is important to itemize the time spent and the work performed during the course of investigation and litigation, and, to the extent possible, to separate work done on the RICO claim from work done on other aspects of the case. Under *Hensley v. Eckerhart* a plaintiff who is entitled to fees arising from a successful RICO claim may also obtain fees for other claims arising from the same common nucleus of facts.[408] Nonetheless, since the party seeking to recover attorney fees bears the burden of "[d]ocumenting the appropriate hours expended and hourly rates," it is best to present the court with a detailed affidavit rather than to leave the matter to conjecture. It is the plaintiff's job to establish what fees are being sought and to justify them, and courts occasionally refuse to award fees if they are not presented with proper evidence of the appropriate dollar amount.

The costs awarded can be substantial. One court included among recoverable costs all of the following: photocopying, paralegal assistance, travel, telephone, videotaped depositions, postage, investigative fees, process server fees, witness fees, delivery, and any other costs for which an attorney generally bills the client separately. The court drew the line at parking and office supplies, however, finding that they are items of overhead.[409]

Consumer attorneys should always request prejudgment interest in a RICO case. The United States Supreme Court let stand a Fourth Circuit denial of prejudgment interest on the basis that the district courts have discretion to award prejudgment interest to RICO plaintiffs.[410] One district court

---

915 F.2d 460 (9th Cir. 1990); Fleischhauer v. Feltner, 879 F.2d 1290 (6th Cir. 1989), *cert. denied*, 494 U.S. 1027 (1990); Grogan v. Platt, 835 F.2d 844 (11th Cir.), *cert. denied*, 488 U.S. 982 (1988); LaBarbera v. Angel, 2000 U.S. Dist. LEXIS 1195, at *8, 9 (E.D. Tex. Jan. 20, 2000); *see also* § 9.2.3.6.2, *supra*. In two cases, RICO claims filed by former users of defective medical devices were dismissed on the grounds that the financial cost to the users did not constitute a RICO injury because it was too closely tied to personal injuries. Borskey v. Medtronics, Inc., RICO Business Disputes Guide (CCH) ¶ 8811, 1995 U.S. Dist. LEXIS 3749 (E.D. La. Mar. 13, 1995) and *In re* Orthopedic Bone Screw Prods. Liability Litig., 1995 U.S. Dist. LEXIS 21525 (E.D. Pa. Mar. 2, 1995).

402 Grogan v. Platt, 835 F.2d 844 (11th Cir. 1988), *cert. denied*, 488 U.S. 982 (1988). *See also* Rodriguez v. Quinones, 813 F. Supp. 924 (D. P.R. 1993) (reputation injury not RICO injury).

403 Imagineering, Inc. v. Kiewit Pac. Co., 976 F.2d 1303, 1310 (9th Cir. 1992) (affirming dismissal), *cert. denied*, 507 U.S. 1004 (1993); Oscar v. University Students Co-Op Ass'n, 965 F.2d 783, 785–87 (9th Cir. 1992) (en banc) ("injury" must consist of concrete financial loss, and not injury to a valuable, but intangible, property interest), *cert. denied*, 506 U.S. 1020 (1996).

404 *See* Alcorn County v. U.S. Interstate Supplies, Inc., 731 F.2d 1160, 1171 (5th Cir. 1984) (court should not allow duplicative damages under RICO and state common law); Interpool Ltd. v. Patterson, 1994 U.S. Dist. LEXIS 16897 (S.D.N.Y. Nov. 28, 1994); Burdett v. Miller, 1990 U.S. Dist. LEXIS 16098 at *34 (N.D. Ill. Nov. 28, 1990) (declining to award damages for breach of fiduciary duty as those would be duplicative of RICO damages), *vacated on other grounds*, 957 F.2d 1375 (7th Cir. 1992).

405 Rosario v. Livaditis, 963 F.2d 1013 (7th Cir. 1992), *cert. denied*, 506 U.S. 1051 (1993); FMC Corp. v. Varonos, 892 F.2d 1308 (7th Cir. 1990); Northeast Women's Ctr. v. McMonagle, 889 F.2d 466 (3d Cir. 1989), *cert. denied*, 494 U.S. 1068 (1990); Nu-Life Constr. Corp. v. Board of Educ., 795 F. Supp. 602 (E.D.N.Y. 1992). One court has held that adding a multiplier to the attorney fee is inappropriate. Burdett v. Miller, 957 F.2d 1375 (7th Cir. 1992).

406 Dee v. Sweet, 489 S.E.2d 823 (Ga. 1997) (upholding state RICO statute).

407 *See* Buckhannon Bd. & Care Home v. W. Va. Dept. of Health & Human Resources, 532 U. S. 598, 121 S. Ct. 1835, 149 L. Ed. 2d 855 (2001) (plaintiff who obtains enforceable judgment on merits or court-ordered consent decree is prevailing party and may seek fee award, but "private settlement" is insufficient); Nusom v. COMH Woodburn, Inc., 122 F.3d 830 (9th Cir. 1997) (construing acceptance of Rule 68 offer for money judgment "together with costs" not to be waiver of TIL and state RICO attorney fees). *See also* § 8.8.4.5.3, *supra*.

408 461 U.S. 424, 435 (1983). *See also* Uniroyal Goodrich Tire Co. v. Mutual Trading Corp., 63 F.3d 516, 525 (7th Cir. 1995) (citing *Hensley* in reversing the trial court's refusal to award fees in case that alleged a RICO violation along with state unfair trade practices and other state claims); Tran v. Tran, 2002 WL 31108362, at *3 (S.D.N.Y Sept. 23) (refusing to reduce award of fees notwithstanding that the plaintiff failed to prevail on her RICO count given that she prevailed on her Fair Labor Standards Act count, the facts of which were "inextricably intertwined" with those of the RICO count), *aff'd*, 67 Fed. Appx. 40, 2003 WL 21308620 (2d Cir. June 3, 2003); § 8.8.11.4, *supra*.

409 Hertz Corp. v. Caulfied, 796 F. Supp. 225 (E.D. La. 1992).

410 *See* Bseirani v. Abou-Khadra, 4 F.3d 1071 (4th Cir. 1993), *cert. denied*, 114 S. Ct. 1835 (1994). *See also* Securitron Magnalock Corp. v. Schnabolk, 1994 U.S. Dist. LEXIS 14894 (S.D.N.Y. Oct. 18, 1994) (prejudgment interest not available under RICO

imposed prejudgment interest because the defendants had unreasonably delayed and obstructed the course of litigation.[411] Another district court ruled that prejudgment interest should only be awarded under special circumstances.[412]

9.2.5.3.3 Treble and punitive damages

A successful RICO claimant will be awarded treble damages. The jury will not normally be told about either the triple damages provision or the attorney fee provision.[413]

It can not hurt, if the case seems appropriate, to add a claim for punitive damages in excess of the triple damages available under RICO. The courts are divided as to availability of punitive damages.[414] One would argue that the treble damage provision does not replace a punitive damages remedy because it is remedial rather than punitive.[415] However, in the Fifth Circuit only one-third of RICO's trebled damages are deemed compensatory, and the other two-thirds are penal.[416]

9.2.5.3.4 Injunctive and other equitable relief

The district courts have jurisdiction to prevent and restrain RICO violations by means including, but not limited to, the compelled divestiture of interests in an enterprise, reasonable restrictions on a person's future activities or investments, and even the dissolution or reorganization of an enterprise.[417] The United States Attorney General is expressly authorized to seek such relief,[418] but whether private civil litigants may obtain it is a question that has divided the courts and the Supreme Court recently declined to resolve the circuits' split on the issue.[419] Some have indicated that such relief is available,[420] often in dictum; others have said that it was not, again usually in dictum.[421] The Ninth Circuit

except in the most unusual case), *aff'd on other grounds*, 65 F.3d 256 (2d Cir. 1995), *cert. denied*, 116 S. Ct. 916 (1996).

411 Miltland Raleigh-Durham v. Myers, 807 F. Supp. 1025 (S.D.N.Y. 1993). *See also* D'Orange v. Feely, 894 F. Supp. 159 (S.D.N.Y. 1995) (prejudgment interest awarded), *aff'd*, 101 F.3d 1393 (2d Cir. 1996) (table).

412 Farberware, Inc. v. Groben, 1995 U.S. Dist. LEXIS 15409 (S.D.N.Y. Sept. 15, 1995) (magistrate's recommendation), *adopted by* 1995 U.S. Dist. LEXIS 14492 (Oct. 4, 1995).

413 HBE Leasing Corp. v. Frank, 22 F.3d 41, 45 (2d Cir. 1994); St. James v. Future Fin., 776 A.2d 849, 870 (N.J. Super. 2001).

414 *Compare* Com-Tech Assocs. v. Computer Assocs. Int'l, Inc., 753 F. Supp. 1078 (E.D.N.Y. 1991) (declining to strike a claim for punitive damages "at the pleading stage"), *aff'd on other grounds*, 938 F.2d 1574 (2d Cir. 1991); Ross v. Jackie Fine Arts, Inc., 1991 U.S. Dist. LEXIS 13535 (D.S.C. Sept. 4, 1991) (awarding actual, trebled, *and* punitive damages); Al-Kazemi v. General Acceptance & Inv. Corp., 633 F. Supp. 540 (D.D.C. 1986) (same) *with* Toucheque v. Price Bros. Co., 5 F. Supp. 2d 341, 350 (D. Md. 1998) (RICO does not authorize punitive damages); Galerie Furstenberg v. Coffaro, 697 F. Supp. 1282, 1289 (S.D.N.Y. 1998) (dismissing punitive damages claim); Bingham v. Zolt, 823 F. Supp. 1126, 1135 (S.D.N.Y. 1993) (RICO does not authorize punitive damages), *aff'd*, 66 F.3d 553 (2d Cir. 1995); Standard Chlorine of Del., Inc. v. Sinibaldi, 821 F. Supp. 232, 252–53 (D. Del. 1992) (RICO does not authorize punitive damages); Mylan Labs., Inc. v. Akzo, N.V., 770 F. Supp. 1053 (D. Md. 1991) (striking RICO punitive damages claim); *In re* VMS Sec. Litig., 752 F. Supp. 1373 (N.D. Ill. 1990) (treble damages are outer limit); Southwest Marine, Inc. v. Triple A Mach. Shop, Inc., 720 F. Supp. 805 (N.D. Cal. 1989) (same).

415 *See* Rhue v. Dawson, 841 P.2d 215 (Ariz. Ct. App. 1992) (allowing punitive damages in addition to treble damages under Arizona RICO statute; jury not to be told of trebling when it determines amount of punitive damages). Many courts recognize that RICO is a remedial statute, not punitive. *See, e.g.*, Agency Holding Corp. v. Malley-Duff & Assocs., 483 U.S. 143, 107 S. Ct. 2759, 2764, 97 L. Ed. 2d 121 (1987) (RICO was designed to remedy injury); County of Oakland v. City of Detroit, 784 F. Supp. 1275, 1285 (E.D. Mich. 1992).

416 Abell v. Potomac Ins. Co., 858 F.2d 1104, *vacated on other grounds sub. nom.* Fryar v. Abell, 492 U.S. 914 (1989).

417 18 U.S.C. § 1964(a).

418 18 U.S.C. § 1964(b).

419 Scheidler v. National Organization for Women, Inc., 537 U.S. 393 (2003) (finding that ruling on Hobbs Act that reversed judgment against petitioners rendered decision on the injunction issue unnecessary).

420 *See* Aetna v. Liebowitz, 730 F.2d 905 (2d Cir. 1984) (suggesting private injunctive relief available); Trane Co. v. O'Connor Sec., 718 F.2d 26, 28, 29 (2d Cir. 1983); Dan River, Inc. v. Icahn, 701 F.2d 278, 290 (4th Cir. 1983); United States v. Philip Morris USA, 316 F. Supp. 2d 6, 12 (D.D.C. 2004) (denying defendants' motion for partial summary judgment); Motorola Credit Corp. v. Uzan, 202 F. Supp. 2d 239, 243 (S.D.N.Y. 2002) (injunctive relief available), *remanded on other grounds*, 322 F.3d 130 (2d Cir. 2003); NOW, Inc. v. Scheidler, 267 F.3d 687 (7th Cir. 2001) (affirming injunction against abortion protestors), *cert. granted*, 122 S. Ct. 1604 (2002); Bernard v. Taub, 1990 WL 34680 (E.D.N.Y. 1990); Abel v. Bonfanti, 625 F. Supp. 263 (S.D.N.Y. 1986) (court assumed availability based on traditional equitable factors); FDIC v. Antonio, 649 F. Supp. 1352 (D. Colo. 1986) (discussed, but did not decide availability), *aff'd*, 843 F.2d 1311 (10th Cir. 1988); Miller v. Affiliated Fin. Corp., 600 F. Supp. 987, 994 (N.D. Ill. 1984) (denying injunction and declaratory relief); Kaufman v. Chase Manhattan Bank, 581 F. Supp. 350, 359 (S.D.N.Y. 1984); DeMent v. Abbott Capitol Corp., 589 F. Supp. 1378, 1382–84 (N.D. Ill. 1984) (mem.) (denying equitable relief except forms amounting to monetary payment); Kaushal v. State Bank of India, 556 F. Supp. 576, 581–84 (N.D. Ill. 1983) (denying orders for divestiture and against sale of business); Nakash v. Superior Court, 196 Cal. App. 3d 59, 241 Cal. Rptr 578 (1987) (state not bound by Ninth Circuit). For arguments in favor of the availability of injunctive relief to private civil plaintiffs, see Blakey, *The RICO Civil Fraud Action in Context: Reflections on Bennett v. Berg*, 58 Notre Dame L. Rev. 237, 330–41 (1982); Note, *The Availability of Equitable Relief in Causes of Action in RICO*, 59 Notre Dame L. Rev. 945 (1984).

421 Matek v. Murat, 862 F.2d 720 (9th Cir. 1988); Religious Tech. Ctr. v. Wollersheim, 796 F.2d 1076 (9th Cir. 1986), *cert. denied*, 479 U.S. 1103 (1987); USACO Coal Co. v. Carbomin Energy, 689 F.2d 94, 97, 98 (6th Cir. 1982); Sterling Suffolk Racecourse Ltd. P'ship v. Burrillville Racing Assoc., Inc., 802 F. Supp. 662

has expressly considered the issue and held that it was not available.[422] The Sixth Circuit has ruled that injunctive relief is available in private RICO actions, without commenting on its reasons for departing from the more usual rule.[423] Some inclination to avoid the issue is discernible.[424] Without ruling on the issue of equitable relief as such, the Fifth Circuit has held that disgorgement is not a remedy available under civil RICO where it is sought only to compensate losses, not to prevent future misconduct.[425]

(D.R.I. 1992); P.R.F., Inc. v. Philips Credit Corp., 1992 U.S. Dist. LEXIS 19696 (D. P.R. 1992); Mississippi Women's Medical Ctr. v. Operation Rescue, No. J90-0052 (S.D. Miss. Apr. 6, 1990); Town of West Hartford v. Operation Rescue, 726 F. Supp. 371 (D. Conn. 1989), *vacated, remanded on other grounds*, 915 F.2d 92 (2d Cir. 1990); Birmingham Medical Ctr. v. Operation Rescue, No. CV-89-P-1261-S (N.D. Ala. Aug. 2, 1989); Curley v. Cumberland Farms Dairy, Inc., 728 F. Supp. 1123 (D.N.J. 1989); Raymark Indus., Inc. v. Stemple, 714 F. Supp. 460 (D. Kan. 1988); First Nat'l Bank & Trust Co. v. Hollingsworth, 701 F. Supp. 701 (W.D. Ark. 1988); Anderson-Myers Co. v. Roach, 660 F. Supp. 106 (D. Kan. 1987); Leff v. Olympic Fed. S&L, No. 86 C 3026 (N.D. Ill. June 18, 1987); Vietnam Veterans of Am., Inc. v. Guerdon Indus., 644 F. Supp. 951 (D. Del. 1986); Philatelic Foundation v. Alan Kaplan, 647 F. Supp. 1344 (S.D.N.Y. 1986); Chambers Dev. Co. v. Browning-Ferris Indus., 590 F. Supp. 1528, 1540, 1541 (W.D. Pa. 1984); Vietnamese Fishermen's Ass'n v. Knights of the Ku Klux Klan, 518 F. Supp. 993, 1014 (S.D. Tex. 1981); United States v. Barber, 476 F. Supp. 182, 189 (S.D. W. Va. 1979); United States v. Mandel, 415 F. Supp. 997, 1021 (D. Md. 1976), *aff'd on other grounds by equally divided court*, 602 F.2d 653 (4th Cir. 1979). *See also* Burnham Broadcasting Co. v. Williams, 629 So. 2d 1335 (La. Ct. App. 1993) (Louisiana appellate court affirmed preliminary injunction in private RICO action without comment).

422 Or. Laborers-Employers Health & Welfare Trust Fund v. Philip Morris, Inc., 185 F.3d 957, 967 (9th Cir. 1999), *cert. denied*, 528 U.S. 1075 (2000); Ganey v. Raffone, 91 F.3d 143 (6th Cir. 1988) (noting in dictum that it is questionable whether injunctions are available to RICO private plaintiffs); Religious Tech. Ctr. v. Wollersheim, 796 F.2d 1076 (9th Cir. 1986), *cert. denied*, 479 U.S. 1103 (1987). *See also In re* Fredeman Litig., 843 F.2d 821 (5th Cir. 1988) (court could not use general equitable powers to enjoin sale of assets in RICO case). *But cf.* Nakash v. Superior Court, 196 Cal. App. 3d 59, 241 Cal. Rptr 578 (1987) (state court is not bound by Ninth Circuit precedent).

423 NCR Corp. v. Feltz, 983 F.2d 1068 (table), 1993 WL 11876 (6th Cir. Jan. 21, 1993).

424 *E.g.*, Northeast Women's Ctr., Inc. v. McMonagle, 813 F.2d 53 (3d Cir. 1987) (vacated denial of preliminary injunction due to failure to make factual findings of irreparable harm without mentioning whether private injunctive relief is available); Revlon, Inc. v. Pantry Pride, Inc., 621 F. Supp. 804, 816 (D. Del. 1985) (denying a preliminary injunction on the ground of lack of probability of success on the merits without deciding whether such relief is available); McLendon v. Continental Group, Inc., 602 F. Supp. 1492, 1518, 1519 (D.N.J. 1985) (reviewing the arguments and reserving decision as "the law is in great flux"). *See also In re* Fredeman Litig., 843 F.2d 821 (5th Cir. 1988) (court declines to decide whether all forms of injunctive relief are foreclosed to private RICO plaintiffs).

425 Richard v. Hoechst Celanese Chem. Group, Inc., 355 F.3d 345, 354–55 (5th Cir. 2003) (reasoning that equitable relief under RICO would only be available to address future violations); U.S. v. Carson, 52 F.3d 1173, 1182 (2d Cir. 1995) (disgorgement limited to those funds "being used to fund or promote the illegal conduct, or [that] constitute capital available for that purpose"). *But see* United States v. Philip Morris USA, Inc., 2004 WL 1161455, at *7–8 (D.D.C. May 21, 2004) (rejecting *Carson*'s strict limitations on disgorgement and denying defendant's motion for partial summary judgment).

9.2.5.3.5 Preserving assets

One issue that arises in RICO cases, as in all litigation, is how to ensure that a defendant will not dissipate its assets during the course of the lawsuit so that there is nothing left by the time a judgment is obtained. To prevent such dissipation, lawyers can ask the court to freeze assets of the defendant for the pendency of the litigation.

The circuits differ on whether such a freeze is permissible. The Third Circuit concluded that the district court may order assets frozen to prevent dissipation, so long as there is a relationship established between the amount sought and the amount sought to be detained.[426] The Sixth Circuit affirmed preliminary injunctive relief to freeze assets which were likely to be taken out of the country while suit was pending.[427] The First Circuit has taken the opposite view,[428] and the Eleventh Circuit refused to permit injunctions to accomplish an asset freeze.[429] The Eleventh Circuit stated that prejudgment attachment could accomplish the same result, and if a forum state does not allow prejudgment attachment, the federal court should not circumvent that rule by issuing an injunction.

In arguing for such a freeze, the consumer attorney should be prepared to show why there is a danger that the defendant will dissipate assets so as to make a judgment uncollectible. The amount of the defendant's assets will obviously be important—a billion dollar company, for example, would hardly be likely to dissipate its assets. Discovery may be needed in order to learn enough to make a reasonable argument on this issue. The consumer attorney should also be prepared to argue to the court regarding the justification for such discovery, as it, too, is likely to be resisted.

9.2.5.4 Local Requirements for Case Statements

Prior to filing any RICO claim, check to see if the relevant court has issued a standing order or a local court rule that requires a plaintiff to file a RICO case statement. The popularity and complexity of RICO claims have led many

426 Hoxworth v. Blinder, Robinson & Co., 903 F.2d 186 (3d Cir. 1990).

427 NCR Corp. v. Feltz, 983 F.2d 1068 (table), 1993 WL 11876 (6th Cir. Jan. 21, 1993).

428 Teradyne, Inc. v. Mostek Corp., 797 F.2d 43 (1st Cir. 1986).

429 Rosen v. Cascade Int'l, Inc., 21 F.3d 1520 (11th Cir. 1994). The Eleventh Circuit stated that prejudgment attachment could accomplish the same result, and if a forum state does not allow prejudgment attachment, the federal court should not circumvent that rule by issuing an injunction.

courts to institute special procedures specific to cases including RICO counts. Failing to file the required statement can lead to dismissal of the RICO claim.[430] Some of the case statements are extremely detailed, and may impose a set outline that demands the attorney to pinpoint each element of the RICO claim.[431]

The RICO case statement requirement was recently unsuccessfully challenged in New Jersey.[432] The plaintiff alleged alternatively that the RICO case statement was an impermissibly heightened pleading standard or court-issued discovery. The court found it was neither, but was simply a case management tool.[433] At least one plaintiff has argued that the Supreme Court's decision in *Swierkiewicz v. Sorema N.A.*,[434] which held that courts may not require a plaintiff to plead a *prima facie* case in an employment discrimination suit, prohibits the heightened pleading requirements of RICO standing orders.[435] The court avoided the issue by finding that the plaintiff's complaint failed to meet even the basic requirements of Rule 8(a).

Even should such a case statement not be required by the relevant jurisdiction, running through such a statement before filing a RICO claim can be a good exercise, to help ensure that every element of the RICO claim has been properly pleaded, to expose potential points of litigation such as identity between enterprise and defendant,[436] to try out different organizations as enterprise and defendants, and to organize a presentation of evidence.

430 *See, e.g.*, Ruiz v. Alegria, 905 F.2d 545 (1st Cir. 1990) (dismissal with prejudice); Pierce v. Ritter, 133 F. Supp. 2d 1344, 1346 (S.D. Fla. 2001) (dismissing both federal and state RICO claims for failing to comply with local rule). *But see* Commercial Cleaning Servs., L.L.C. v. Colin Serv. Sys., 271 F.3d 374 (2d Cir. 2001) (complaint's failure to allege an essential element of the RICO predicate offense was not fatal, allowing plaintiff to cure by repleading).

431 *See, e.g.*, General Order #34, U.S. District Court for the Northern District of New York; RICO Standing Order, U.S. District Court for the Eastern District of Louisiana; RICO Case Statement, U.S. District Court for the Southern District of California; Greer v. Stulp, 2002 U.S. Dist. LEXIS 1482 (N.D. Ill. Feb. 1, 2002) (listing elements of required case statement).

432 Northland Ins. Co. v. Shell Oil Co., 930 F. Supp. 1069 (D.N.J. 1996).

433 *See also* Figueroa Ruiz v. Alegria, 896 F.2d 645, 646 (1st Cir. 1990) (affirming dismissal for failure to comply with order); Old Time Enters. v. Int'l Coffee Corp., 862 F.2d 1213, 1217 (5th Cir. 1989) (affirming dismissal); Elliott v. Foufas, 867 F.2d 877 (5th Cir. 1989) (rejecting argument that standing order conflicted with Federal Rule of Civil Procedure 8(a)). *But see* Commercial Cleaning Servs., L.L.C. v. Colin Serv. Sys., Inc., 271 F.3d 374, 385–86 (2d Cir. 2001) (finding that the standing order called for more than the "essential elements of a RICO claim").

434 534 U.S. 506, 511 (2002).

435 Wagh v. Metris Direct, Inc., 363 F.3d 821, 826–27 (9th Cir. 2003), *cert. denied*, 124 S. Ct. 2176 (2004).

436 *See* § 9.2.3.2.3, *supra*.

9.2.6 Procedural Issues

9.2.6.1 Service of Process and Venue

Most courts have construed RICO as having a nationwide service of process provision,[437] so that suit can be brought in a convenient forum without concern for whether the defendant has minimum contacts with the state.[438] Where a federal statute explicitly provides for nationwide service of process, personal jurisdiction is not constrained by *International Shoe*'s minimum contact standards.[439] Circuits split on whether a defendant need only have minimum contacts with the United States,[440] or whether the Fifth Amendment requires a court to consider issues of fairness and reason-

437 Although courts agree that the nationwide service of process provision is found within 18 U.S.C. § 1965, some base the finding on § 1965(b), which allows nationwide service where required for "ends of justice," while others base it on § 1965(d). *Compare* PT United Can Co. v. Crown Cork & Seal Co., 138 F.3d 65, 71 (2d Cir. 1998) (§ 1965(b), but nationwide service only authorized where ends of justice require it); Stauffacher v. Bennett, 969 F.2d 455, 460 (7th Cir. 1992) (§ 1965(b)), *cert. denied*, 506 U.S. 1034 (1992); Butcher's Union Local No. 498 v. SDC Inv., Inc., 788 F.2d 535, 538 (9th Cir. 1986) (§ 1965(b), however court must have personal jurisdiction over at least one of the participants in the alleged multidistrict conspiracy and the plaintiff must show that there is no other district in which a court will have personal jurisdiction over all of the alleged co-conspirators) *and* Suarez Corp. Indus. v. McGraw, 71 F. Supp. 2d 769, 777 (N.D. Ohio 1999) (§ 1965(b)) *with* ESAB Group, Inc. v. Centricut, Inc., 126 F.3d 617, 626 (4th Cir. 1997) (§ 1965(d)), *cert. denied*, 523 U.S. 1048 (1998) *and* Republic of Panama v. BCCI Holdings (Luxembourg) S.A., 119 F.3d 935, 942 (11th Cir. 1997) (§ 1965(d)); *see also* Gatz v. Ponsoldt, 271 F. Supp. 2d 1143, 1153 (D. Neb. 2003) (finding personal jurisdiction appropriate). *But see* 800537 Ont., Inc. v. Auto Enters., 113 F. Supp. 2d 1116, 1128 (E.D. Mich. 2000) (§ 1965 authorizes nationwide service of process only when plaintiff shows court has personal jurisdiction over at least one of the defendants).

438 ESAB Group, Inc. v. Centricut, Inc., 126 F.3d 617 (4th Cir. 1997), *cert. denied*, 523 U.S. 1048 (1998); Lisak v. Mercantile Bancorp, Inc., 834 F.2d 668, 671 (7th Cir. 1987), *cert. denied*, 485 U.S. 1007 (1988); Sadighi v. Daghighfekr, 36 F. Supp. 2d 267, 274 (D.S.C. 1999); Monarch Normandy Square Partners v. Normandy Square Assocs. Ltd. P'ship, 817 F. Supp. 896 (D. Kan. 1993).

439 Trustees of the Nat'l Elevator Pension, Health Benefit & Educ. Funds v. Continental Elevator Co., 1999 U.S. Dist. LEXIS 7062, at *4 (E.D. Pa. May 12, 1999).

440 *See, e.g.*, Busch v. Buchman, Buchman & O'Brien, Law Firm, 11 F.3d 1255, 1258 (4th Cir. 1994); United States v. Tillem, 906 F.2d 814 (2d Cir. 1990); Go-Video, Inc. v. Akai Elec. Co., 885 F.2d 1406, 1416 (9th Cir. 1989); Lisak v. Mercantile Bancorp, Inc., 834 F.2d 668, 671 (7th Cir. 1987) (RICO), *cert. denied*, 485 U.S. 1007 (1988); BankAtlantic v. Coast to Coast Contractors, Inc., 947 F. Supp. 480 (S.D. Fla. 1996); Headwear, U.S.A., Inc. v. Stange, 166 F.R.D. 36 (D. Kan. 1996). However, notwithstanding the nationwide service provisions, a court will most likely not exercise jurisdiction over a potential RICO claim involving an Indian intra-tribal dispute.

ableness after the defendant has shown that litigating in the plaintiff's chosen forum will implicate the liberty interests of the defendant.[441] RICO does not authorize international service.[442]

As for venue, section 1965(a) provides that venue is proper in any district in which the defendant resides, is found, has an agent, or transacts his affairs. This section has been ruled to supplement, without nullifying, general venue provisions, so the court will weigh all relevant factors.[443] One court found that a defendant can not succeed on a venue defense on the basis that he merely conducted the affairs of his employer in the forum.[444]

9.2.6.2 RICO Standard of Proof

Since civil RICO claims are essentially fraud claims, at least one commentator has suggested they should be proven by clear and convincing evidence, the traditional standard of proof in fraud cases.[445] However, federal courts have ruled with near universal agreement that civil RICO claims, even those based on mail and wire fraud, need only be established by a preponderance of the evidence.[446] These courts have found support in *Sedima*, in which the Supreme Court, while refusing to decide the issue, strongly suggested that the ordinary civil standard of preponderance of the evidence should apply to civil RICO:

> In a number of settings, conduct that can be punished as criminal only upon proof beyond a reasonable doubt will support civil sanctions under a preponderance standard. [Citations omitted.] There is no indication that Congress sought to depart from this general principle here.[447]

9.2.6.3 RICO Concurrent Jurisdiction

While the RICO statute expressly confers jurisdiction upon the federal district courts,[448] it says nothing about whether state courts have concurrent jurisdiction. However, the United States Supreme Court resolved this issue in *Tafflin v. Levitt*,[449] holding that state courts have concurrent jurisdiction with federal courts over civil RICO claims.

While the Supreme Court decided in *Tafflin* that state courts have jurisdiction over RICO claims, it did not speak to the issue of removability. Since there is no express statutory prohibition on removal of RICO claims, defendants may remove them to federal court pursuant to 28 U.S.C. § 1441.[450]

---

441 *See, e.g.*, Republic of Panama v. BCCI Holdings (Luxembourg) S.A., 119 F.3d 935, 945, 946 (11th Cir. 1997).

442 Forbes v. Eagleson, 1996 U.S. Dist. LEXIS 10583 (E.D. Pa. July 23, 1996).

443 *See* Bigham v. Envirocare of Utah, Inc., 123 F. Supp. 2d 1046 (S.D. Tex. 2000) (though venue proper in forum sought by plaintiff, court transferred venue to another district after balancing the statutory factors and finding that action overwhelmingly involved conduct in and persons situated in transferee district); Kunkler v. Palko Mgmt. Corp., 992 F. Supp. 780, 781, 782 (E.D. Pa. 1998) (transferring venue); Cobra Partners L.P. v. Liegl, 990 F. Supp. 332, 335 (S.D.N.Y. 1998); BankAtlantic v. Coast to Coast Constr., 947 F. Supp. 480, 485 (S.D. Fla. 1996) (denying motion to dismiss); Quirk v. Gilsenan, RICO Business Disputes Guide (CCH) ¶ 8666, 1994 U.S. Dist. LEXIS 14041, at *6, *7 (S.D.N.Y. Sept. 29, 1994) (transferring venue).

444 Phoenix Home Mut. Ins. Co. v. Brown, 857 F. Supp. 7 (W.D.N.Y. 1994).

445 Strafer, Massumi & Skolnick, *Civil RICO in the Public Interest: "Everybody's Darling,"* 19 Am. Crim. L. Rev. 655, 715–17 (1985). *See also* Hofstetter v. Fletcher, 905 F.2d 897 (6th Cir. 1988) (court explicitly refused to adopt clear and convincing standard, rejecting argument that standard should be higher because finding of RICO liability implied criminal wrongdoing).

446 NMB Air Operations Corp. v. McEvoy, 194 F.3d. 1317 (table), 1999 U.S. App. LEXIS 22991 (9th Cir. 1999) (preponderance of evidence is the proper standard of proof for RICO claims based on predicate acts of mail and wire fraud, rejecting claim that trial court should have held plaintiff to a clear and convincing standard); Fleischhauer v. Feltner, 879 F.2d 1290 (6th Cir. 1989), *cert. denied*, 494 U.S. 1027 (1990); Liquid Air Corp. v. Rogers, 834 F.2d 1297 (7th Cir. 1987), *cert. denied*, 492 U.S. 917 (1989); Cullen v. Margiotta, 811 F.2d 698 (2d Cir. 1987), *cert. denied*, 483 U.S. 1021 (1987); Wilcox v. First Interstate Bank of Or., 815 F.2d 522, 532 (9th Cir. 1987); Armco Industrial Credit Corp. v. SLT Warehouse Co., 782 F.2d 475, 481 (5th Cir. 1986); United States v. Local 560 of Int'l Brotherhood of Teamsters, 780 F.2d 267, 279 n.12 (3d Cir. 1985), *cert. denied*, 476 U.S. 140 (1987); United States v. Capetto, 502 F.2d 1351, 1358 (7th Cir. 1974), *cert. denied*, 420 U.S. 925 (1975); City of New York v. Liberman, 1988 U.S. Dist. LEXIS 580 (S.D.N.Y. Jan. 25, 1988); Asher v. Bear, Stearns & Co., No. CA 4-85-603K (N.D. Tex. Apr. 22, 1987); Eaby v. Richmond, 561 F. Supp. 131, 133, 134 (E.D. Pa. 1983); Heinhold Commodities, Inc. v. McCarty, 513 F. Supp. 311, 313 (N.D. Ill. 1979); Farmers Bank of Delaware v. Bell Mortgage Corp., 452 F. Supp. 1278, 1280 (D. Del. 1978).

447 Sedima, S.P.R.L. v. Imrex Co., 473 U.S. 479, 491, 105 S. Ct. 3275, 87 L. Ed. 2d 346 (1985).

448 18 U.S.C. §§ 1964(a), (c).

449 493 U.S. 455, 110 S. Ct. 792, 107 L. Ed. 2d 887 (1990).

450 Emrich v. Touche Ross & Co., 846 F.2d 1190, 1195, 1196 (9th Cir. 1988) (RICO claims are removable pursuant to 28 U.S.C. § 1441(a), federal court may exercise jurisdiction over pendent state claims); Kabealo v. Davis, 829 F. Supp. 923, 927 (S.D. Ohio 1993), *aff'd without op.*, 72 F.3d 129 (6th Cir. 1995); Lichtenberger v. Prudential-Bache Sec., Inc., 737 F. Supp. 43 (S.D. Tex. 1990). *See also* Bass v. First Pac. Networks, Inc., 219 F.3d 1052 (9th Cir. 2000) (RICO claim that had been filed in state court removed to federal court, district court retained jurisdiction over pendent state claim after dismissing federal RICO claim). *But see* Murphy v. Bank of Am. Nat'l Trust & Sav. Ass'n, 1999 U.S. App. LEXIS 3575, at *7 (9th Cir. Mar. 4, 1999) (holding it was without jurisdiction to review district court's remand order that RICO claim did not meet section 1331(c)'s statutory requirement of being a "separate and independent" cause of action because it was too inextricably intertwined with the state causes of action).

It is also worth noting that a federal court to which a RICO claim has been removed may abstain from hearing it if there is a pending state action. Farkas v. D'Oca, 857 F. Supp. 300

9.2.6.4 RICO Statute of Limitations

The Supreme Court has ruled that the statute of limitations in RICO cases is four years.[451] When the statute of limitations begins to run remains a question answered differently in different jurisdictions.

The first issue to determine is whether the claim is yet in existence. In this connection, the Second Circuit holds that where a separate bankruptcy proceeding is pending in which the plaintiff stands to recover all or some of his or her damages, a RICO claim has yet to accrue.[452]

The next issue is to determine when the claim, if in existence, has accrued. While the Supreme Court has yet to sanction a specific accrual method, it has expressly disapproved of two of them. In *Klehr v. A.O. Smith Corp.*,[453] the Court outlawed the Third Circuit's "last predicate act" approach, which provided that so long as any predicate act causing injury occurred within the limitations period, the RICO claim will have accrued within the statute of limitations.[454] The next year, in *Rotella v. Wood*,[455] the Court eliminated an even more popular rule, the "injury and pattern" discovery rule, which had been used by the Sixth,[456] Eighth,[457] Tenth,[458] and Eleventh[459] Circuits, and which provided that a RICO claim accrues when the claimant discovers, or should have discovered, both an injury and a pattern of racketeering activity. The Court reasoned that "[b]y tying the start of the limitations period to a plaintiff's reasonable discovery of a pattern rather than to the point of injury or its reasonable discovery, the rule would extend the potential limitations period for most civil RICO cases well beyond the time when a plaintiff's cause of action is complete," which would undercut the principal policies behind a statute of repose.[460]

While expressly refusing to endorse a final rule,[461] the Court left open the possibility that two remaining rules may be valid. One, the "injury discovery" rule, provides that the cause of action accrues as soon as the plaintiff knew, or should have known, that the plaintiff had been injured, regardless of the plaintiff's knowledge of the pattern. This rule has been used by the First,[462] Second,[463] Third,[464] Fourth,[465] Fifth,[466] Seventh[467] and Ninth[468] Circuits. The

---

(S.D.N.Y. 1994) (abstention proper where state case involving difficult marital issues was pending); Lawrence v. Cohn, 778 F. Supp. 678 (S.D.N.Y. 1991). *But see* New Beckley Mining Corp. v. Int'l Union, United Mine Workers of Am., 946 F.2d 1072 (4th Cir. 1991), *cert. denied*, 503 U.S. 971 (1992) (abuse of discretion for federal court judge to abstain in favor of state court action). One federal court declined to abstain from hearing a RICO claim filed in federal court that duplicated a state court action, stating that federal courts should decide RICO claims. Macy's E., Inc. v. Emergency Environmental Servs., Inc., 925 F. Supp. 191 (S.D.N.Y. 1996). One federal court remanded to state court a case that was removed on the basis of the RICO count in the counterclaim, deciding that the complaint was essentially state-based and that it is the complaint, not the counterclaim, that determines whether a case is removable. Barnhart-Graham Auto Inc. v. Green Mountain Bank, 786 F. Supp. 394 (D. Vt. 1992).

451 Agency Holding Corp. v. Malley-Duff & Assocs., 483 U.S. 143, 107 S. Ct. 2759, 2764, 97 L. Ed. 2d 121 (1987).

452 *See* Bankers Trust v. Rhodes, 859 F.2d 1096, 1106 (2d Cir. 1988), *cert. denied*, 490 U.S. 1007 (1989); *see also* First Nationwide Bank v. Gelt Funding Corp., 27 F.3d 763 (2d Cir. 1994), *cert. denied*, 513 U.S. 1079 (1995); Lincoln House v. Dupree, 903 F.3d 845 (1st Cir. 1990); Barnett v. Stern, 909 F.2d 973, 977 n.4 (7th Cir. 1990). *But cf.* Grimmett v. Brown, 75 F.3d 506 (9th Cir. 1996), *cert. granted, then dismissed as improvidently granted*, 65 U.S.L.W. 4068 (1997).

453 521 U.S. 179, 117 S. Ct. 1984, 138 L. Ed. 2d 373 (1997).

454 Keystone Ins. Co. v. Houghton, 863 F.2d 1125 (3d Cir. 1988); Norris v. Wirtz, 703 F. Supp. 1322 (N.D. Ill. 1989); Armbrister v. Roland Int'l Corp., 667 F. Supp. 802 (M.D. Fla. 1987); Wabash Pub. Co. v. Dermer, 650 F. Supp. 212 (N.D. Ill. 1986).

455 528 U.S. 549, 120 S. Ct. 1075, 145 L. Ed. 2d 1047 (1998).

456 Caproni v. Prudential Sec., Inc., 15 F.3d 614, 619, 620 (6th Cir. 1994).

457 Granite Falls Bank v. Henrikson, 924 F.2d 150 (8th Cir. 1991).

458 Bath v. Bushkin, Gaims, Gaines, & Jonas, 913 F.2d 817 (10th Cir. 1990).

459 Bivens Gardens Office Bldg., Inc. v. Barnett Bank of Florida, Inc., 906 F.2d 1546 (11th Cir. 1990), *cert. denied*, 500 U.S. 910 (1991).

460 528 U.S. at 558.

461 *Id.* at 554 n.2.

462 Lares Group, II v. Tobin, 221 F.3d 41, 44 (1st Cir. 2000); Rodriguez v. Banco Central, 917 F.2d 664 (1st Cir. 1990).

463 Riverwoods Chappaqua Corp. v. Marine Midland Bank, 30 F.3d 339 (2d Cir. 1994) (concluding that federal, not state tolling rules apply to civil RICO and overruling *Cullen* in this regard; holding that federal tolling rule does not apply on the facts); Bankers Trust Co. v. Rhoades, 859 F.2d 1096 (2d Cir. 1988), *cert. denied*, 490 U.S. 1007 (1989); Lapides v. Tarlow, 2002 WL 31682382, at *2 (S.D.N.Y. Nov. 27, 2002); Strother v. Harte, 171 F. Supp. 2d 203, 209 (S.D.N.Y. 2001).

464 Mathews v. Kidder, Peabody & Co., 260 F.3d 239, 247 (3d Cir. 2001) (RICO injury from overpriced securities occurs at time of purchase); Forbes v. Eagleson, 228 F.3d 471, 482 (3d Cir. 2000), *cert. denied*, 121 S. Ct. 2551 (2001); Annulli v. Panikkar, 200 F.3d 189, 195 (3d Cir. 1995).

465 Detrick v. Panalpina, Inc., 108 F.3d 529 (4th Cir. 1997) (4th Circuit declines to reconsider its accrual rule), *cert. denied sub nom. Gold v. Panalpina, Inc.* 522 U.S. 810 (1997); Pocahontas Supreme Coal Co. v. Bethlehem Steel Corp., 828 F.2d 211 (4th Cir. 1987).

466 Rotella v. Wood, 147 F.3d 438 (5th Cir.), *aff'd*, 528 U.S. 549 (1998).

467 Graves v. Combined Ins. Co., 95 F.3d 1154 (7th Cir. 1996) (accrual when plaintiff discovers or should have discovered, his injury); McCool v. Strata Oil Co., 972 F.2d 1452 (7th Cir. 1992); *see also* Heaven & Earth, Inc. v. Wyman Props. Ltd. P'ship, 2003 WL 22680935, at *6–7 (D. Minn. Oct. 21, 2003) (each of landlord's allegedly fraudulent billing statements that over-charged for utilities was a separate act of fraud for purposes of the statute of limitations); Quanstrom v. Kirkwood, 2002 WL 1770526, at *5 (N.D. Ill. July 31, 2002) (dismissing suit).

468 Grimmett v. Brown, 75 F.3d 506 (9th Cir. 1996) (9th Circuit declines to change from discovery of injury rule to knowledge of extent to damage rule; must be clear and definite damages before statute will begin to run), *cert. granted*, 518 U.S. 1003 (1996), *then dismissed as improvidently granted*, 519 U.S. 233 (1997).

other, the more draconian "injury" rule, would deem the action accrued as soon as the injury occurred, with discovery of that injury irrelevant.[469]

The injury discovery rule provides that a civil RICO claim accrues when the plaintiff discovers, or should have discovered, the injury. When a pattern of RICO activity causes a continuing series of separate injuries, the "separate accrual" rule allows a civil RICO claim to accrue for each injury when the plaintiff discovers, or should have discovered, that injury.[470] Under the "separate accrual" rule, which has been adopted by the Second,[471] Third,[472] and Seventh[473] Circuits, discovery of each separate RICO violation triggers a new limitations period. The Fifth Circuit recently adopted the separate accrual rule after analyzing *Rotella* and finding that it did not bar adoption of the rule.[474]

The Supreme Court conceded that the "injury discovery" rule leaves open the possibility that the four-year period could expire before a second predicate act—necessary for a RICO violation—occurred, but declined to rule on that contingency because it was not a part of the case before it.[475] The Sixth Circuit has since rejected the argument that the "injury discovery" period could begin to run before the RICO cause of action accrued.[476]

With respect to RICO conspiracy actions, most courts follow the "conspiracy" rule, under which the limitation period runs from the date of the last predicate act.[477] The First Circuit's conspiracy rule provides that the statute of limitations does not begin to run until the objectives of the conspiracy are either accomplished or abandoned.[478]

An additional statute of limitations issue involves the situation where, although the RICO statute of limitations has not run, the statute of limitations *has* expired as to the predicate acts underlying the RICO claim. Two courts have held that so long as the RICO statute of limitations has not run, the predicate acts can be proved.[479]

The doctrine of equitable tolling is also relevant to limitations issues. To raise equitable tolling as a statute of limitations defense, the plaintiff must be prepared to plead and prove the following elements: (1) the use of fraudulent means by the party raising the statute of limitations; (2) successful concealment from the injured party; and (3) evidence that the party claiming fraudulent concealment did not know or by the exercise of due diligence could not have known that he might have a cause of action.[480] At least one court has stated that the doctrine of equitable tolling may well delay the running of the RICO statute of limitations while the victim diligently investigates the possible existence and extent of a pattern of racketeering.[481] In *Rotella*, the Supreme Court responded to concerns that the "injury discovery" rule might bring Rule 9(b) fraud pleading problems by stating that their decision did not disturb general equitable principles of tolling.[482]

One form of equitable tolling, based on a defendant's fraudulent concealment, can toll a RICO limitations period.[483] Fraudulent concealment refers to a defendant's active steps to prevent the plaintiff from suing in time, such as by hiding evidence or promising not to plead the statute of

469 Rotella, 528 U.S. at 554 n.2.

470 Bankers Trust Co. v. Rhoades, 859 F.2d 1096, 1102 (2d Cir. 1988), *cert. denied*, 490 U.S. 1007 (1989).

471 Bingham v. Zolt, 66 F.3d 553 (2d Cir. 1995), *cert. denied*, 517 U.S. 1134 (1996); Bankers Trust Co. v. Rhoades, 859 F.2d 1096 (2d Cir. 1988), *cert. denied*, 490 U.S. 1007 (1989).

472 Annulli v. Panikkar, 200 F.3d 189, 197, 198 (3d Cir. 1999); Keystone Ins. Co. v. Houghton, 863 F.2d 1125 (3d Cir. 1988).

473 McCool v. Strata Oil Co., 972 F.2d 1452 (7th Cir. 1992). This approach was specifically rejected by the Fourth Circuit in Cherrey v. Diaz, 991 F.2d 787 (4th Cir. 1993), *cert. denied*, 510 U.S. 863 (1993).

474 Love v. National Med. Enters., 230 F.3d 765, 774 (5th Cir. 2000).

475 *Rotella*, 528 U.S. at 559.

476 Bygrave v. Van Reken, 238 F.3d 419 (6th Cir. 2000), *reported in full at* 2000 U.S. App. LEXIS 29377 (Nov. 14, 2000) (dismissing plaintiff's case on other grounds).

477 Charter Oak Fire Ins. Co. v. Domberg, 1987 WL 15413, 1987 U.S. Dist. LEXIS 7153 (N.D. Ill. Aug. 3, 1987); Citicorp Sav. of Illinois v. Streit, 1987 WL 9318, 1987 U.S. Dist. LEXIS 2860 (N.D. Ill. Apr. 6, 1987); Carlstead v. Holiday Inns, Inc., 1987 WL 9024, 1987 U.S. Dist. LEXIS 2546 (N.D. Ill. Mar. 26, 1987). The Sixth Circuit rejected the last predicate act rule in Agristor Fin. Corp. v. Van Sickle, 967 F.2d 233 (6th Cir. 1992), and the Seventh Circuit rejected it in McCool v. Strata Oil Co., 972 F.2d 1452 (7th Cir. 1992).

478 United States v. Lopez, 851 F.2d 520 (1st Cir. 1988), *cert. denied*, 489 U.S. 1021 (1989).

479 Hoxworth v. Blinder, Robinson & Co., 980 F.2d 912 (3d Cir. 1992); Leroy v. Paytel III Mgmt. Assocs., 1992 U.S. Dist. LEXIS 17864 (S.D.N.Y. 1992). *See also* Toto v. McMahan, Brafman, Morgan & Co., RICO Business Disputes Guide (CCH) ¶ 8761, 1995 U.S. Dist. LEXIS 1399 (S.D.N.Y. Feb. 7, 1995) (even though underlying Sec. fraud predicates untimely, RICO claims viable); Kress v. Hall-Houston Oil Co., 1993 U.S. Dist. LEXIS 6350 (D.N.J. May 12, 1993) (same).

480 Klehr v. A.O. Smith Corp., 521 U.S. 179, 117 S. Ct. 1984, 138 L. Ed. 2d 373 (1997) (requiring exercise of due diligence); *see also* Ballen v. Prudential Bache Sec., 23 F.3d 335 (10th Cir. 1994).

481 McCool v. Strata Oil Co., 972 F.2d 1452 (7th Cir. 1992). *See also* Shapo v. O'Shaugnessy, 246 F. Supp. 2d 935 (N.D. Ill. 2002) (recognizing tolling doctrine); G-I Holdings, Inc. v. Baron & Bodd, 238 F. Supp. 2d 521 (S.D.N.Y. 2002) (standard tolling exceptions apply to civil RICO claims). *But see* Graves v. Combined Ins. Co., 95 F.3d 1154 (7th Cir. 1996) (no equitable tolling of claims of life insurance purchasers where original contract and mailed policies put them on notice of possible fraud); Bontknowski v. First Nat'l Bank, 998 F.2d 459 (7th Cir.) (no equitable tolling where with due diligence the plaintiff could have discovered the facts), *cert. denied*, 510 U.S. 1012 (1993); Calabrese v. State Farm Mut. Automobile Ins. Co., 996 F.2d 1219 (7th Cir. 1993) (to show equitable tolling, plaintiff must allege affirmative acts of concealment; inadequate responses to discovery in earlier litigation do not constitute such acts).

482 528 U.S. at 560.

483 *See, e.g.*, Love v. National Med. Enters., 230 F.3d 765, 780 (5th Cir. 2000) (finding material fact as to issue of fraudulent concealment).

limitations.[484] However, the Supreme Court ruled in *Klehr* that to assert fraudulent concealment, the plaintiff must have been reasonably diligent in seeking to discover the injury.[485] The plaintiff must also show that he or she was actively misled by the defendant.[486]

9.2.6.5 Offensive and Defensive Collateral

9.2.6.5.1 Is offensive collateral estoppel available?

RICO subsection 1964(d) specifically allows a successful government prosecutor to prevent the defendant from denying a final criminal judgment in a subsequent civil RICO action based on the same issues. So, it appears possible that in government actions, a civil RICO action would follow automatically from a successful criminal prosecution.[487]

However, the RICO statute does not specifically allow private parties to use offensive collateral estoppel in civil suits following criminal convictions.[488] The few applicable federal district court cases split on whether offensive collateral estoppel is available to the private RICO claimant. Thus one case finds it available on the grounds that collateral estoppel is an existing civil remedy and an uncodified RICO section provides that RICO does not supplant existing federal or state civil remedies.[489] The court also argued that Congress intended RICO to have a liberal construction to "seek the eradication of organized crime in the United States . . . by providing enhanced sanctions and new remedies."[490] Without analyzing the issue of applicability, another district court relied on collateral estoppel to grant a plaintiff summary judgment on RICO claims.[491]

But another federal court argued that since the liberal use of offensive collateral estoppel was not allowed until 1979, and RICO was enacted in 1970, it would be "a strange result" to allow the use of the doctrine.[492]

A third district court ruled that collateral estoppel was not available in a bank fraud case.[493] There, the FDIC filed a civil RICO case and moved for summary judgment on the basis of collateral estoppel. The judge decided that the RICO claim should be left for the jury, mentioning as reasons the more extensive discovery and the additional defenses available in civil actions.

9.2.6.5.2 Elements of offensive collateral estoppel if it applies to RICO

Assuming offensive collateral estoppel is available to private RICO plaintiffs, its normal principles should apply. Thus the private plaintiff (1) must allege that issues in the subsequent civil case were actually litigated and necessary to the outcome of the first criminal case;[494] and (2) must show that, under the doctrine of *Parklane Hosiery*, use of offensive collateral estoppel would not involve any of the following four situations unfair to the defendant:

- It would have been practical to join the civil plaintiff in the prior action;
- Judgment in the first case was inconsistent with any prior decisions;
- The defendant in the first case lacked the incentive to litigate vigorously;

484 Reeves v. Frierdich, 2000 U.S. App. LEXIS 416, at *16 (7th Cir. Jan. 4, 2000) (citing Hentosh v. Herman M. Finch Univ., 167 F.3d 1170, 1174 (7th Cir. 1999)).

485 *Klehr*, 521 U.S. 179, 194, 195 (1997). *See also* Rolo v. City Investing Co. Liquidating Trust, 155 F.3d 644, 656 n.12 (3d Cir. 1998) (plaintiff did not meet burden of showing diligence); Whitehall Tenants Corp. v. Whitehall Realty Co., 1997 U.S. App. LEXIS 30264, at *5, *6 (2d Cir. Oct. 31, 1997) (same).

486 Forbes v. Eagleson, 228 F.3d 471, 486 (3d Cir. 2000) (refusing to toll period), *cert. denied*, 533 U.S. 929 (2001).

487 *See* United States v. Ianniello, 808 F.2d 184 (2d Cir. 1986) (criminal RICO acquittal does not estop government civil RICO action), *cert. denied*, 483 U.S. 1006 (1987); County of Cook v. Lynch, 560 F. Supp. 136 (N.D. Ill. 1982) (county successfully used offensive collateral estoppel after criminal conviction in United States v. Marubeni Am. Corp., 611 F.2d 763 (9th Cir. 1980)), *aff'd*, United States v. Lynch, 692 F.2d 759 (7th Cir. 1982); Maryland v. Buzz Berg Wrecking Co., 496 F. Supp. 245 (D. Md. 1980) (civil suit following criminal conviction in United States v. Grande, 620 F.2d 1026 (4th Cir. 1980)). *But see In re* Lewisville Properties, Inc., 849 F.2d 946 (5th Cir. 1988) (no collateral estoppel where civil pleading identified different enterprises and patterns of racketeering).

488 *Cf.* 18 U.S.C. § 1964(d) (only specifies the United States may estop denials in civil actions following criminal convictions).

489 Anderson v. Janovich, 543 F. Supp. 1124, 1128, 1129 (W.D. Wash. 1982) (§ 904(b) provides saving clause for existing criminal and civil remedies). *See also* Parklane Hosiery Co. v. Shore, 439 U.S. 322, 326–28, 99 S. Ct. 645, 58 L. Ed. 2d 552 (1979) (use of offensive collateral estoppel is within the broad discretion of the trial court, and even strangers to the original suit may rely on it); County of Oakland v. City of Detroit, 776 F. Supp. 1211 (E.D. Mich. 1991) (convicted sewage haulers collaterally estopped from relitigating issues necessarily decided in prior judgments).

490 *See* Anderson v. Janovich, 543 F. Supp. 1124, 1129 (W.D. Wash. 1982) (quoting Pub. L. No. 91-452, Stat. 922 (1970)).

491 Ross v. Jackie Fine Arts, Inc., 1991 U.S. Dist. LEXIS 13535, at *3 (D.S.C. Sept. 4, 1991).

492 Henry v. Farmer City State Bank, 808 F.2d 1228 (7th Cir. 1987); *see also* City of New York v. Liberman, 1988 U.S. Dist. LEXIS 580 (S.D.N.Y. Jan. 25, 1988). Yet another decision barring offensive collateral estoppel may be distinguishable since the court holding was limited to the finding that offensive collateral estoppel may not be used against a defendant where the prior criminal conviction against him was abated due to his death; the court left open the possibility that "upon appropriate motion collateral estoppel may be available against [other] defendants." State Farm Fire & Cas. Co. v. Estate of Caton, 540 F. Supp. 673, 683 (N.D. Ind. 1982); *cf.* Moss v. Morgan Stanley, 719 F.2d 5, 22 (2d Cir. 1983), *cert. denied*, 465 U.S. 1025 (1984).

493 FDIC v. Bayles & Co. of Am., 1992 U.S. Dist. LEXIS 10138 (M.D. Fla. June 30, 1992).

494 *See, e.g.*, Schaafsma v. Marriner, 641 F. Supp. 576 (D. Vt. 1986) (no bar to RICO suit where predicate acts not at issue in earlier proceeding and controlling law changed).

- The first case did not provide procedural opportunities that are available to the defendant in the second case and that could readily cause a different result.[495]

9.2.6.5.3 Defensive collateral estoppel

Conversely, plaintiffs may also find that *res judicata* (claim preclusion)[496] and collateral estoppel (issue preclusion)[497] may be used defensively against them. The doctrine of *res judicata* requires that the parties in the present suit be the same as those in the prior suit.[498] However, identification of parties is not necessarily an element of collateral estoppel,[499] so that doctrine may be used to bar a RICO claim even when the defendant in the present suit was not a party to the prior suit.[500]

As examples, the Second Circuit has held that plaintiffs who failed to raise fraud and forgery as defenses in an earlier state foreclosure action had their federal RICO claim, based on the same allegations, barred by *res judicata*.[501] The Sixth Circuit has held that a breach-of-contract arbitration panel's decision precluded the plaintiff from litigating a related RICO claim.[502] The Ninth Circuit barred a RICO claim by a women's health clinic against anti-abortion protestors because of an earlier state court suit, even though the law on state court jurisdiction over RICO claims was not clear when the state court suit was pending.[503]

9.2.7 RICO Consumer Cases in the Courts

9.2.7.1 Introduction

There are quite a few reported consumer cases involving RICO claims. In this section, a number of them, successful and unsuccessful, are summarized. A review of these cases will give the consumer attorney some idea of the variety of possible uses of civil RICO in the consumer interest and some of the traps to be avoided by the careful pleader. RICO is doubtless adaptable to many other consumer fraud contexts. It has been suggested, for instance, that civil RICO is a suitable vehicle for litigating some typical claims against nursing homes by their residents.[504] False advertising, a chronic consumer abuse, has become a far more common subject of RICO claims in recent years.[505]

9.2.7.2 Examples of Successful Consumer RICO Cases

Decisions that are more or less favorable to consumer civil RICO plaintiffs or potentially of value to them include the following:

- The Seventh Circuit reversed the dismissal of RICO claims by a loan applicant against a lender in which she

495 Parklane Hosiery Co. v. Shore, 439 U.S. 322, 330, 99 S. Ct. 645, 58 L. Ed. 2d 552 (1979); *see also* Narumanchi v. Adanti, 101 F.3d 108 (2d Cir. 1996) (table; text at 1996 U.S. App. LEXIS 39274) (*res judicata* barred RICO claims that could have been asserted in prior action); County of Cook v. Lynch, 648 F. Supp. 738 (N.D. Ill. 1986) (collateral estoppel precludes defendant who vigorously contested her guilt of mail fraud and bribery from relitigating issues in civil suit).

496 To establish a defense of *res judicata*, defendants must show (1) identity of claims; (2) identity of parties; and (3) a prior final judgment on the merits. Perry v. Globe Auto Recycling, Inc., 227 F.3d 950, 952 (7th Cir. 2000).

497 Defendants, to establish the defense of collateral estoppel, must show that (1) the issue sought to be precluded was the same as that involved in the prior action; (2) the issue was actually litigated; (3) the determination of the issue was essential to the final judgment; and (4) the party against whom estoppel is invoked fully represented in the prior action. Haroco of Am., Ltd. v. Freeman, Atkins & Coleman, Ltd., 58 F.3d 303, 307 (7th Cir. 1995).

498 Saboff v. St. John's River Water Mgmt. Dist., 200 F.3d 1356, 1360 (11th Cir. 2000), *cert. denied*, 531 U.S. 823 (2000). *See also* Pierce v. Ritter, 133 F. Supp. 2d 1344 (S.D. Fla. 2001) (refusing to apply doctrine of *res judicata* where defendants in present suit were the attorneys for the defendants in the prior suit, not those defendants themselves).

499 Blonder-Tongue Lab. v. University of Illinois Found., 402 U.S. 313, 91 S. Ct. 1434, 28 L. Ed. 2d 788 (1970).

500 *See, e.g.*, Pierce v. Ritter, 133 F. Supp. 2d 1344, 1347 (S.D. Fla. 2001) (holding that collateral estoppel doctrine barred plaintiff's RICO action).

501 Saud v. Bank of New York, 929 F.2d 916 (2d Cir. 1991); Miller Hydro Group v. Popovitch, 851 F. Supp. 7 (D. Me. 1994); State Farm Fire & Cas. Co. v. Estate of Caton, 540 F. Supp. 673, 682, 683 (N.D. Ind. 1982); *see also* Wyckoff v. Zaiderman, 1987 WL 14295 (D.D.C. June 3, 1987). *Res judicata* can preclude litigation of all claims that could have been raised in the earlier proceeding, even if they were not. Greenberg v. Board of Governors of the Federal Reserve Sys., 968 F.2d 164, 168 (2d Cir. 1992).

502 Central Transport, Inc. v. Four Phase Sys., Inc., 936 F.2d 256 (6th Cir. 1991). *But see* Green Tree Fin. Corp. v. Honeywood Dev. Corp., 2001 U.S. Dist. LEXIS 654, at *18–20 (where prior arbitration demand did not specifically assert a RICO conspiracy violation nor use the word conspiracy, collateral estoppel would not bar plaintiff's RICO conspiracy claim).

503 Feminist Women's Health Ctr. v. Codispoti, 63 F.3d 863 (9th Cir. 1995). *See also* Cahill v. Jewell, 1999 U.S. App. LEXIS 9268 (6th Cir. May 12, 1999) (unpublished) (plaintiff's RICO action against insurance seller barred by *res judicata* effect of prior state court class action, where plaintiffs were members of the class); Miller Hydro Group v. Popovitch, 851 F. Supp. 7 (D. Me. 1994) (dismissing plaintiff's RICO claims on grounds of defensive collateral estoppel).

504 National Senior Citizens Law Ctr., *Applying Racketeering Laws to Nursing Homes*, 19 Clearinghouse Rev. 1306 (1986). *See also* Arenson v. Whitehall Convalescent & Nursing Home, 880 F. Supp. 1202 (N.D. Ill. 1995) (denying motion to dismiss RICO claim based on nursing home president's use of dummy drug invoices to overbill patients).

505 A.B. Weissman, Watch Out Joe Isuzu, the Civil RICO Police Are on Your Trail: Misleading Advertising as a Potential Civil RICO Growth Industry, 13 RICO L. Rep. 5 (May 1991).

alleged that the lender fraudulently induced her to refinance her existing personal loan at exorbitant rates. She did not allege that Truth-in-Lending requirements or other statutory requirements were violated, but the lender did not make clear that it would be less expensive to take out a new loan than to refinance the old one. The Seventh Circuit noted that a careful reading of the Truth-in-Lending statement would have shown that the refinancing was not a good deal, but noted that not everyone is capable of being a careful reader. It summarized the allegation as being that the complainant belonged to a class of borrowers who are not competent interpreters of Truth-in-Lending forms and that the lender took advantage of that fact.[506]

- The Fourth Circuit twice reversed the district court's dismissal of RICO claims by a class of used car buyers against a car wholesaler and a related finance company. The consumer alleged that the defendants had engaged in a fraudulent "churning" scheme to sell cars at inflated rates, repossess them, conduct sham repossession sales, and bill consumers for alleged deficiencies.[507]
- A RICO class action against a lender that charged interest rates between 179% and 557% and used threats in the collection process withstood a motion to dismiss.[508]
- A criminal conviction was upheld under a state RICO statute against parties engaged in an automobile brokerage scam in which a company "took over" car loans or leases, reselling the cars to other parties, without first paying off the lessor or creditor.[509]
- A court refused to dismiss a class action brought against a finance company for failing to include a provision in car loan documents that would allow the debtor to raise seller-related defenses to any attempt to collect the loan. The court ruled that the plaintiff had alleged a sufficient pattern.[510]
- A complaint by borrowers victimized by a mortgage lender survived a motion to dismiss. The plaintiffs alleged that the lender, among other abuses, padded loans with fraudulent charges. The borrowers sued the subsequent holders of the notes who had purchased them on the secondary mortgage market. (The lender itself was in bankruptcy.) The defendant had sought to dismiss the claims based on mail fraud to the extent the suit alleged the note purchasers knew of the mortgage lender's fraudulent conduct. The lenders subsequently settled the case by agreeing to reform the borrower's notes, for a savings to the class conservatively estimated at $2.5 million, plus attorney fees.[511]
- Where the implicit interest in rent-to-own (RTO) contracts was usurious under state law and was more than twice the applicable rate, the RICO predicate element of "unlawful debt" was established.[512]
- The Eighth Circuit held that plaintiffs had sufficiently alleged injury in a case where an association of purchasers of land in a subdivision sued the developer, relying upon mail fraud predicate offenses, alleging that the developer had not lived up to its promises. The alleged failure to pave roads as promised, and the sale of additional lots by a mail fraud scheme, leading to heavier road use and greater need for maintenance (which was the landowners' responsibility) were held to be sufficient direct or indirect injury under the statute.[513]
- Past and present residents sued the corporation which owned and operated their retirement community for fraudulently inducing them to purchase lifetime occupancy agreements by misrepresenting the financial soundness of the corporation and falsely promising affordable "life care." In a wide-ranging opinion, the Eighth Circuit rejected the district court's imposition of commercial or competitive racketeering injury requirements. The court also allowed the corporations' mortgage lender and former accountant to be sued as persons "associated with" the enterprise, rejecting any "RICO relationship" requirement linking these defendants to the enterprise; and held that an enterprise had been alleged which was sufficiently distinct from the "pattern of racketeering activity." However, the court called for greater particularity in the pleading of the predicate acts of mail fraud, and for pleading of a culpable "person" apart from the corporate "enterprise."[514] On remand, the owner of the retirement community turned out to be judgment-proof, but its

506 Emery v. Am. General Fin., Inc., 71 F.3d 1343 (7th Cir. 1995).

507 Chisolm v. TranSouth Fin. Corp., 95 F.3d 331 (4th Cir. 1996), *appeal after remand*, 164 F.3d 623 (4th Cir. 1998) (table, full text at 1998 U.S. App. LEXIS 24632), *on remand*, 184 F.R.D. 556 (E.D. Va. 1999) (certifying class), *later op. at* 194 F.R.D. 538 (E.D. Va. 2000) (defining subclasses and ruling on trial plans).

508 Brown v. C.I.L., Inc., 1996 WL 164294, 1996 U.S. Dist. LEXIS 4053, Clearinghouse No. 51,255 (N.D. Ill. Mar. 29, 1996).

509 Thompson v. State, 211 Ga. App. 887, 440 S.E.2d 670 (1994).

510 Brown v. LaSalle Northwest Nat'l Bank, 820 F. Supp. 1078 (N.D. Ill. 1993).

511 Anderson v. FNMA, Clearinghouse No. 42,568 (E.D. Va. Nov. 25, 1987) (order denying motion to dismiss).

512 *See* Fogie v. Rent-A-Center, Inc., 1995 WL 649575 (D. Minn. 1995), *aff'd sub nom.* Fogie v. Thorn Americas, Inc., 95 F.3d 645 (8th Cir. 1996) (RICO issue was not addressed on appeal), *cert. denied*, 520 U.S. 1166 (1997). *See also* Starks v. Rent-A-Center, 1990 U.S. Dist. LEXIS 20099, Clearinghouse No. 45,215 (D. Minn. May 15, 1990), *aff'd on other grounds*, 58 F.3d 358 (8th Cir. 1995).

513 Terre Du Lac Ass'n, Inc. v. Terre Du Lac, Inc., 772 F.2d 467 (8th Cir. 1985), *cert. denied*, 475 U.S. 1082 (1986).

514 Bennett v. Berg, 685 F.2d 1053 (8th Cir. 1982), *aff'd en banc*, 710 F.2d 1361 (8th Cir.), *cert. denied*, 464 U.S. 1008 (1983). *See* Blakey, *The RICO Civil Fraud Action in Context: Reflections on Bennett v. Berg*, 58 Notre Dame L. Rev. 237 (1982).

mortgagee, a defendant "associated with" the enterprise and alleged to have known of and concealed its mismanagement, settled the case for $62.8 million.[515]

- A court tentatively certified a class of students on a RICO claim they brought against the former president of a trade school. The students alleged that the defendant had fraudulently caused them to get student loans while misrepresenting their qualifications to the government.[516]
- A court ruled that several policyholders had alleged sufficient injury in a suit against an insurance agent that alleged that he fraudulently induced them to buy life insurance policies by misrepresenting the benefits. The issue was whether the plaintiffs, who were proceeding under subsection 1962(a), had to prove they were injured because of the defendant's investment of the racketeering proceeds.[517]
- A district court's dismissal on the ground that there was no RICO injury, separate from the injury caused by the predicate offenses,[518] was reversed by the Seventh Circuit[519] in a case where corporations sued a bank alleging that it had fraudulently charged an excessive interest rate on loans by lying about the prime rate to which the interest rates were pegged; the deceptive statements, sent by mail, were the predicate acts of mail fraud. The decision was, in turn, affirmed by the Supreme Court.[520]
- A court refused to dismiss a case brought by a class of AT&T calling card holders against AT&T, claiming AT&T said the cards were "free" without disclosing that there was a substantial fee for using them. The lawsuit alleged fraud, RICO violation, deceptive acts, and false advertising. The RICO predicate acts alleged were mail and wire fraud.[521]
- A court refused to dismiss RICO claims brought by a class of loan applicants against a lender and affiliated mortgage brokers, alleging that the lender bribed the brokers to induce their business. The court said the alleged association in fact was sufficiently distinct from the defendants itself where the brokers were an integral part of the scheme and indeed benefited from it.[522]
- A court refused to dismiss a complaint brought by homeowners who had allegedly been victimized by a scheme by which a financial services company convinced them to mortgage their homes for the maximum amount possible in return for paying off prior loans and extending a line of credit. The homeowners sued the company, its principals, and its attorney. The court ruled that the plaintiffs had sufficiently alleged a pattern of racketeering activity.[523]
- A court certified a class of persons in a suit against an insurance company that alleged that the company charged the insureds a copayment for the generic drug Tamoxifen as if it were a prescription drug; the court refused to dismiss the case, ruling that the plaintiff had adequately alleged a pattern to defraud.[524]
- The Second Circuit overturned the dismissal of a claim by life insurance policy buyers who alleged that the defendant had marketed the policy as a kind of IRA. If the plaintiff were able to prove that the defendant had "misdescribed the economic value of the bargain," and that foregone returns of an IRA or other similar savings plan would have been greater than the investment plaintiffs selected and the difference was a foreseeable consequence of the misrepresentation, the court ruled that the allegations would show loss causation and confer standing under RICO.[525]
- A RICO class was certified against a vocational school and its parent company, where the class alleged that the defendants had fraudulently represented to students the education they would receive.[526]
- A RICO class was certified against an auto dealership and finance company in a case where the plaintiffs alleged that the defendants had violated both RICO and TILA in connection with discounts associated with certain retail installment sales contracts, and sales of extended warranties.[527]
- A court refused to dismiss a claim by mortgage loan customers against a bank that they alleged charged inflated legal fees. The court found that the plaintiffs had sufficiently alleged an enterprise, an association in

515 "Indirect" RICO Defendant Settles for $62.8 Million, 5 Law. Alert, Feb. 24, 1986, at 5.

516 Rodriguez v. McKinney, 156 F.R.D. 112 (E.D. Pa. June 6, 1994).

517 Pinski v. Adelman, 1995 U.S. Dist. LEXIS 16550 (N.D. Ill. Nov. 2, 1995). This issue of whether a § 1962(a) injury may arise from the predicate acts or must arise from the investment of the proceeds of the predicate acts has arisen in many cases. *See* Compagnie de Reassurance D'Ille de France v. New England Reinsurance Corp., 57 F.3d 56 (1st Cir. 1995), *cert. denied*, 116 S. Ct. 564 (1995) (Supreme Court let stand First Circuit ruling which required injury from the investment of the proceeds, not just from the predicate acts). *See also* R.C.M. Executive Gallery Corp. v. ROLS Capital Corp., 901 F. Supp. 630 (S.D.N.Y. 1995) (§ 1962(a) action by restaurant investors dismissed where they did not allege injury from investment of the proceeds of usurious loan).

518 Haroco, Inc. v. Am. Nat'l Bank & Trust Co., 577 F. Supp. 111, 114 (N.D. Ill. 1983).

519 Haroco, Inc. v. Am. Nat'l Bank & Trust Co., 747 F.2d 384, 387–398 (7th Cir. 1984).

520 Am. Nat'l Bank & Trust Co. v. Haroco, Inc., 473 U.S. 606, 105 S. Ct. 3291, 87 L. Ed. 2d 437 (1985) (per curiam).

521 Gelb v. Am. Tel. & Tel., 813 F. Supp. 1022 (S.D.N.Y. 1993).

522 Epps v. The Money Store, No. 96 C 2703, 26 RICO L. Rep. 631 (N.D. Ill. Sept. 30, 1997).

523 Thomas v. Ross & Hardies, 9 F. Supp. 2d 547 (D. Md. 1998).

524 Morse v. Bankers Life & Cas. Co., 2000 U.S. Dist. LEXIS 2211 (N.D. Ill. Feb. 24, 2000) (finding that two acts could form a pattern).

525 Moore v. PaineWebber, Inc., 189 F.3d 165 (2d Cir. 1999).

526 Cullen v. Whitman Med. Corp., 188 F.R.D. 226 (E.D. Pa. 1999).

527 Johnson v. Rohr-Ville Motors, Inc., 189 F.R.D. 363 (N.D. Ill. 1999).

fact comprising the bank and a law firm, and that the bank conducted a pattern of racketeering activity consisting in part of a scheme to defraud by means of affirmative representations that the legal fees were genuine and not excessive.[528]

- A court refused to dismiss a claim brought by homeowners against their mortgagee and related entities that alleged that the mortgagee had charged unauthorized and illicit fees related to the plaintiffs' bankruptcy.[529]
- A court refused to dismiss claims brought by former residential property owners against a Christian corporation, a mortgage company and others alleging a scheme to defraud the plaintiffs of their property and profit from inflated mortgages. The court found that the plaintiffs had sufficiently alleged an enterprise, a pattern of racketeering activity and proximate cause of their injuries, which included the loss of their home equity and the amount of their monthly rent payments that exceeded their prior mortgage obligations.[530] At least one other RICO claim against such equity strippers has survived a motion to dismiss.[531]
- A court of appeals panel affirmed a district court's ruling that a title insurance agency and lending companies, who allegedly conspired with another defendant to defraud the plaintiffs into purchasing homes they could not afford by misrepresenting that the homes would be entitled to tax abatements and mortgage credit certificates, could be liable under RICO's conspiracy provision by knowingly agreeing to facilitate a scheme which included operation or management of a RICO enterprise, even if they did not commit or agree to commit predicate acts.[532]
- A Third Circuit panel upheld a lower court's decision that refused to dismiss a class action RICO conspiracy claim by plaintiff home buyers against several realty-related corporations. The plaintiffs alleged that the corporations had conspired with another defendant, a developer, to induce the plaintiffs to purchase homes they could not afford, by using fraudulent financial incentives. On appeal, the court held that the plaintiffs need not show that the defendant corporations committed a substantive violation of RICO, but only that the defendant knowingly agreed to assist a scheme that included the operation or management of a RICO enterprise.[533]
- A complaint by a taxpayer against a tax return preparation service and lender based on alleged fraud in refund anticipation loans survived a motion to dismiss.[534]

9.2.7.3 Examples of Unsuccessful Consumer RICO Cases

Consumer cases in which the plaintiffs were for one reason or another unsuccessful include the following:

- Three circuits have ruled that telephone ratepayers do not have the right to have courts award damages that effectively reset filed rates.[535]
- A court dismissed a class action that credit card holders filed against three financial institutions which gave credit cards to bad credit risks upon payment of a deposit. The deposits were misused and the marketer went bankrupt. The court held that the 16–18% interest rate charged was not twice the allowable credit card rate of 24%, so the RICO claim for unlawful debt collection was dismissed.[536]
- The Ninth Circuit held that tenants near a drug den do not suffer a RICO injury to property when their right to quiet enjoyment is encroached upon.[537]
- A court dismissed a suit filed by a charge card holder that claimed mail and wire fraud as to a scheme to waive fees for some cardholders. The court dismissed the case, stating that even if the claims were true, there was no mail fraud. RICO, the court said, was not meant to protect consumers against the irritation of learning that others have gotten a better deal.[538]
- A court held that a bank's practice of buying insurance which protected its loan at the expense of automobile purchasers who did not produce evidence of insurance did not violate RICO where the three plaintiffs (who owned one car) did not produce evidence of a pattern or of continuity.[539] The plaintiffs argued that there were numerous events of mail fraud because the bank sent several letters, but the court said that the Seventh

528 Weil v. Long Island Sav. Bank, FSB, 77 F. Supp. 2d 313 (E.D.N.Y. 1999).

529 Majchrowski v. Norwest Mort., 6 F. Supp. 2d 946 (N.D. Ill. 1998).

530 Ifill v. West, 1999 U.S. Dist. LEXIS 21320 (E.D.N.Y. Aug. 24, 1999).

531 Bryant v. Bigelow, 311 F. Supp. 2d 666, 671 (S.D. Ohio 2004) (holding that the plaintiffs had properly alleged predicate acts of mail fraud and an association in fact enterprise).

532 Smith v. Berg, 247 F.3d 532 (3d Cir. 2001).

533 Smith v. Berg, 247 F.3d 532, 538 (3d Cir. 2001). The trial court later declined to certify the class of homebuyers, but on other grounds. Smith v. Berg, 2001 U.S. Dist. LEXIS 15814 (E.D. Pa. Oct. 1, 2001).

534 Carnegie v. Household Intl, Inc., 220 F.R.D. 542 (N.D. Ill. 2004).

535 Wegoland, Ltd. v. NYNEX Corp., 27 F.3d 17 (2d Cir. 1994); Taffet v. Southern Co., 967 F.2d 1483 (11th Cir.), *cert. denied*, 506 U.S. 1021 (1992); H.J. Inc. v. Northwestern Bell Tel. Co., 954 F.2d 485 (8th Cir. 1992), *cert. denied*, 504 U.S. 957 (1992).

536 Iacobucci v. Universal Bank of Maryland, 1991 WL 10246 (S.D.N.Y. 1991).

537 Oscar v. University Students Coop. Ass'n, 965 F.2d 783 (9th Cir.), *cert. denied*, 506 U.S. 1020 (1992).

538 Litwin v. Am. Express Co., 838 F. Supp. 855 (S.D.N.Y. 1993).

539 Travis v. Boulevard Bank, N.A., No. 93 C 6847 (N.D. Ill. Oct. 7, 1994).

Circuit does not look favorably on relying on many instances of mail fraud to establish a pattern of racketeering activity.

- In a suit brought by survivors of deceased people against a number of funeral homes based on the funeral homes' knowing dealings with a cemetery with a reputation for mistreating corpses, the court found no RICO violation. It said that while the funeral homes may have been negligent, there was no pattern to defraud, the plaintiffs having shown no motive and no benefit to the funeral homes.[540]
- The Seventh Circuit declined to find mail fraud where consumers complained that their insurance certificates said they would receive unearned premiums back on prepayment, but the insurer did not pay the premiums back until asked to do so. The court found that the insurance certificates did not say anything incorrect, and that the complaint did not state a cause of action for mail fraud.[541]
- Where a car buyer claimed that the assignee of her finance contract bought more insurance than necessary and demanded that she pay for it, a court found that there was no mail fraud because there was no allegation of a misrepresentation. The assignee said it was going to buy the insurance and did so. The car buyer did not allege any intent to defraud. The allegations were not sufficient for mail fraud.[542]
- The Sixth Circuit granted summary judgment to a bank on RICO claims brought by a class of automobile purchasers who alleged that the bank had fraudulently purchased unauthorized insurance coverage on their loans. The court found the language of the loan documents not sufficiently misleading to constitute fraud. It also found that allegations of kickbacks the bank received from the insurance company were not sufficiently particularized.[543]
- A court dismissed the case of frustrated former property owners who had sued their mortgage holder, alleging that it had a practice of fraudulently imposing early payoff charges. The enterprises alleged, consisting of the defendants' corporate parents, were insufficiently distinct from the defendant itself where there was an integrated operational relationship between the three entities.[544]
- A consumer class action for warranty fraud brought by two purchasers of automobile service contracts against Chrysler, alleging fraudulent inducement by misrepresentation of coverage, was dismissed because Chrysler was insufficiently distinct from a claimed enterprise consisting of its affiliates and agents.[545]
- A RICO claim filed by allegedly defrauded franchisees was deemed barred by a waiver of liability signed by franchisees.[546]
- A used car buyer brought section 1962(a) claim against the financier of his vehicle, alleging that the defendant had fraudulently charged excessive late fees which were later used to replenish, in part, the general operating funds of the enterprise so the scheme could continue. Requisite investment injury was lacking. If there was any claim it was based on predicate acts, not investment injury.[547]
- A court dismissed a claim against the successor to a company that had allegedly lent money to the plaintiffs at usurious rates, ruling that the plaintiffs can not claim themselves as part of an associated-in-fact enterprise where the group existed to defraud them.[548]
- A court found that a claimed association in fact was indistinct from the alleged pattern where the only activities alleged were the scheme itself. Homebuyers brought a RICO claim against parties who participated in selling them unstable homes built over a landfill. The court ruled that the enterprise was the same as the pattern of activity, and must be proved separately.[549]
- The First Circuit overturned a $43 million RICO verdict against Volvo Car Corp., ruling that there was insufficient evidence that Volvo knew of fraud by a Volvo dealer and distributor, and that Monroney Act violations by Volvo could not support the verdict because they are not predicate offenses.[550]
- A court dismissed a claim that due to the defendant's allegedly fraudulent forced placement of collateral protection insurance (CPI), the plaintiffs had lost money spent on overpriced insurance that insured only the defendant's interest. The court held that the injury alleged did not arise from the reinvestment of racketeering proceeds, and that the claim was insufficient to allege that the defendant invested the money obtained in the alleged enterprise.[551]

---

540 *In re* Cedar Hill Cemetery Litig., 853 F. Supp. 706 (S.D.N.Y. 1994).

541 Richards v. Combined Ins. Co. of Am., 55 F.3d 247 (7th Cir. 1995). *See also* Hoban v. USLIFE Credit Life Ins. Co., 163 F.R.D. 509 (N.D. Ill. 1995), a similar case.

542 Dixon v. TCF Bank Illinois, FSB, 1995 U.S. Dist. LEXIS 15706 (N.D. Ill. 1995).

543 Kenty v. Bank One, Columbus, N.A., 92 F.3d 384 (6th Cir. 1996).

544 Deane v. Weyerhaeuser Mortgage Co., 967 F. Supp. 30 (D. Mass. 1997).

545 Fitzgerald v. Chrysler Corp., 116 F.3d 225 (7th Cir. 1997).

546 Williams v. Stone, 109 F.3d 890 (3d Cir. 1997), *cert. denied*, 522 U.S. 956 (1997).

547 Turner v. Union Planters Bank, 974 F. Supp. 890 (S.D. Miss. 1997) (class action alleging RICO violations and violations of Mississippi Motor Vehicle Sales Finance Act).

548 R.C.M. Executive Gallery Corp. v. Rols Capital Co., 1997 U.S. Dist. LEXIS 565 (S.D.N.Y. Jan. 23, 1997).

549 McDonough v. National Home Ins. Co., 108 F.3d 174 (8th Cir. 1997).

550 Bonilla v. Volvo Car Corp., 150 F.3d 62 (1st Cir. 1998), *cert. denied*, 119 S. Ct. 1574 (1999).

551 Weathersby v. Associated Fin. Servs. Co., 1999 U.S. Dist. LEXIS 6392 (E.D. La. Apr. 28, 1999) (unpublished).

9.3 State RICO Statutes

9.3.1 Overview of State RICO Statutes

Approximately half the states have enacted legislation similar to the federal RICO statute.[552] These statutes have been upheld against a variety of constitutional challenges.[553] All but a few of these statutes[554] create a private civil cause of action.

State RICO statutes differ from federal RICO, and each other, in various respects, which are discussed in the following subsections. One universal difference is that state RICO statutes do not require a nexus between racketeering activity and interstate commerce.[555] Although state courts have not hesitated to reject federal RICO cases when interpreting state RICO provisions that appear to have a different legislative intent,[556] state courts will often look to federal court decisions in interpreting state RICO provisions that track federal RICO closely.[557]

---

552 State RICO statutes are summarized in Appx. C.2, *infra*. Some states also have forfeiture laws that are similar in some ways to RICO statutes but apply only to drug offenses. *See, e.g.*, 725 Ill. Comp. Stat. Ann. §§ 175/1 to 175/9.

553 Ft. Wayne Books, Inc. v. Indiana, 489 U.S. 46, 109 S. Ct. 916, 103 L. Ed. 2d 34 (1989) (state RICO statute is not unconstitutionally vague and does not violate First Amendment, but pretrial seizure of adult bookstore's entire stock was unconstitutional prior restraint); Lemaster v. Ohio, 119 F. Supp. 2d 754 (S.D. Ohio Oct. 20, 2000) (not unconstitutionally vague); Freeman v. State, 554 So. 2d 621 (Fla. Dist. Ct. App. 1989) (state RICO statute not unconstitutionally vague); State v. Bates, 933 P.2d 48 (Haw. 1997) (term "associated with any enterprise" is not unconstitutionally vague, and RICO statutes do not implicate freedom of association); State v. Passante, 542 A.2d 952 (N.J. 1987) (state RICO act constitutional); State v. Romig, 73 Or. App. 780, 700 P.2d 293 (1985) (state RICO Act constitutional); State v. Thompson, 751 P.2d 805 (Utah Ct. App. 1988) (same); Wisconsin v. O'Connell, 179 Wis. 2d 598 (Ct. App. 1993). *But cf.* State v. Feld, 155 Ariz. 88, 745 P.2d 147 (Ct. App. 1987) (certain remedies given to state under state RICO constitutional, certain are not); State v. Roderick, 704 So. 2d 49 (Miss. 1997), *cert. denied*, 524 U.S. 926 (1998) (state RICO statute's predicate offense of usury is unconstitutionally vague as applied to check cashing fees); State v. Thomas, 103 Wash. App. 800, 14 P.3d 854 (2000) (finding repeal of state RICO statute's sunset provision void because of violation of state constitution's procedural requirements, so entire statute except for certain severable insurance fraud provisions is no longer in effect; legislature responded by enacting Laws 2001, Ch. 222, effective May 9, 2001, which reenacted the RICO statute without substantive change).

554 Statutes that do not provide a private cause of action include: Cal. Penal Code §§ 186 to 186.8 (West); Conn. Gen. Stat. § 53-393; Minn. Stat. Ann. § 609.901; Mich. Comp. Laws Ann. §§ 750.159f to 750.159x; N.Y. Penal Law art. 460; Okla. Stat. Ann. tit. 22, §§ 1401–1419; 18 Pa. Cons. Stat. § 911. *See also* Federal Ins. Co. v. Ayers, 741 F. Supp. 1179 (E.D. Pa. 1990) (no private cause of action under Pennsylvania RICO); Odesser v. Continental Bank, 676 F. Supp. 1305 (E.D. Pa. 1987) (no private right of action under state RICO); D'Iorio v. Adonizio, 554 F. Supp. 222, 232 (M.D. Pa. 1982) (mem.) (Pennsylvania statute is similar to RICO but appears not to create a private cause of action); Town of West Hartford v. Dadi, 2002 Conn. Super. LEXIS 325 (Feb. 1, 2002); Machnicz v. Property Pros, Inc., 1999 Conn. Super. LEXIS 3239 (1999) (Connecticut statute does not contain provision authorizing civil action).

555 Baines v. Superior Court, 142 Ariz. 145, 149, 688 P.2d 1037, 1041 (Ct. App. 1984).

556 F.D.I.C. v. First Interstate Bank of Denver, 937 F. Supp. 1461 (D. Colo. 1996) (declining to follow federal RICO precedent in interpreting Colorado RICO statute); Philadelphia Reserve Supply Co. v. Nowalk & Assocs., Inc., 864 F. Supp. 1456 (E.D. Pa. 1994) (finding New Jersey RICO statute to have less strict definition of "pattern" than federal RICO); People v. James, 40 P.3d 36 (Colo. App. 2001) (declining to follow federal precedent because of differences between federal and Colorado RICO); Southern-Intermodal Logistics, Inc. v. D.J. Powers Co., 251 Ga. App. 865, 555 S.E.2d 478 (2000) (U.S. Supreme Court ruling on RICO statute of limitations has no bearing on interpretation of Georgia RICO); Franklin Medical Assocs. v. Newark Public Schools, 362 N.J. Super. 494, 828 A.2d 966 (App. Div. 2003) (construing N.J. RICO definition of enterprise more broadly than federal); State v. Wilson, 113 Ohio App. 3d 737, 682 N.E.2d 5 (1996) (declining to follow federal precedent about whether the enterprise must be separate and apart from the corrupt activity); Bowcutt v. Delta N. Star Corp., 976 P.2d 643 (Wash. Ct. App. 1999) (declining to follow federal precedent where state statutory language differed from federal).

557 Acro-Tech, Inc. v. Robert Jackson Family Trust, 2003 WL 22783349 (9th Cir. Nov. 24, 2003) (unpublished, citation limited); DeNune v. Consolidated Capital, 2003 WL 22435772 (N.D. Ohio Sept. 23, 2003); Allocco v. City of Coral Gales, 221 F. Supp. 2d 1317 (S.D. Fla. 2002) (following federal RICO decisions that require reliance where mail and wire fraud are predicate acts); Matthews v. New Century Mortg. Corp., 185 F. Supp. 2d 874 (S.D. Ohio 2002); Jackson v. Bellsouth Telecommunications, Inc., 181 F. Supp. 2d 1345 (S.D. Fla. 2001) (treating federal and state RICO statutes as identical); Wilson v. De Angelis, 156 F. Supp. 2d 1335 (S.D. Fla. 2001); National Union Fire Ins. Co. v. Kozeny, 115 F. Supp. 2d 1210 (D. Colo. 2000), *aff'd*, 2001 WL 1149327 (10th Cir. Sept. 28, 2001); Planned Parenthood v. American Coalition, 945 F. Supp. 1355 (D. Or. 1996); Lifeflite Medical Air Transport, Inc. v. Native Am. Air Servs., Inc., 7 P.3d 158 (Ariz. App. 2000); Gross v. State, 765 So. 2d 39 (Fla. 2000); O'Malley v. St. Thomas University, 599 So. 2d 999 (Fla. Dist. Ct. App. 1992) (federal decisions should be accorded great weight); Simpson Consulting, Inc. v. Barclays Bank, 490 S.E.2d 184 (Ga. App. Ct. 1997) (Georgia will follow federal RICO interpretations except where Georgia's public policy differs); State v. Bates, 933 P.2d 48 (Haw. 1997); State v. Ontai, 929 P.2d 69 (Haw. 1996) (following federal interpretations about how much structure an enterprise must have); Allum v. Valley Bank, 849 P.2d 297 (Nev. 1993) (Nevada will impose proximate causation requirement because United States Supreme Court did so), *cert. denied*, 510 U.S. 857 (1993); State v. Bisaccia, 319 N.J. Super. 1, 724 A.2d 836 (App. Div. 1999) (following federal court rules that conspiracy can be a predicate offense; court notes that New Jersey RICO statute covers broader spectrum of behavior than federal RICO); State v. Schlosser, 79 Ohio St. 3d 329, 681 N.E.2d 911 (1997); Loewen v. Galligan, 130 Or. App. 222, 882 P.2d 104 (1994) (federal decisions persuasive); Beckett v. Computer Career Institute, Inc., 120 Or. App. 143, 852 P.2d 840 (1993) (same);

9.3.2 Predicate Acts

The typical state RICO statute lists a variety of state offenses that constitute predicate acts. Some state statutes allow both state and federal crimes as predicate offenses. Many include the same offenses as federal RICO, providing a parallel cause of action to a federal RICO claim. Ohio's RICO statute requires that at least one predicate act not be a form of securities fraud, mail fraud, or wire fraud.[558] Generally, state RICO statutes recognize only the more serious crimes as predicate offenses.[559]

State RICO statutes are particularly useful for consumer claims because they often include consumer fraud offenses as predicate acts. Many state RICO statutes explicitly list fraud and usury as predicate offenses.[560] Some list violations of specific consumer protection laws, such as those that prohibit equity skimming or telemarketing fraud.[561] Ohio's RICO statute includes operation of an unregistered credit service organization as a predicate offense.[562] Wisconsin has added its new crime of identity theft[563] to its list of predicate offenses.[564] Even if specific consumer fraud offenses are not among the listed predicate offenses, theft offenses are often included and will be applicable to many types of consumer fraud.[565] New Jersey RICO claims can be based on securities fraud even though the Private Securities Litigation Reform Act bars this for federal RICO claims.[566]

Generally, there is no requirement that the defendant be criminally convicted of the acts alleged as predicate offenses,[567] although the plaintiff must prove all elements of the predicate offenses, including any required mental state.[568] Only a corporation's agents, not the corporation itself, can be prosecuted criminally in Georgia, so a state RICO claim based on state crimes can not be asserted against a corporation.[569] Some state RICO statutes require that economic gain motivate the commission of the predicate crimes.[570]

Commonwealth v. Donahue, 630 A.2d 1238 (Pa. Super. Ct. 1993) (federal decisions persuasive); Sanchez v. Guerrero, 885 S.W.2d 487 (Tex. App. 1994); State v. Evers, 163 Wis. 2d 725, 472 N.W.2d 828 (Wis. Ct. App. 1991). *See also* Altamont Summit Apts. v. Wolff Properties L.L.C., 2002 U.S. Dist. LEXIS 2761 (D. Or. Feb. 13, 2002).

558 Ohio Rev. Code § 2923.34. *See* Rahimi v. St. Elizabeth Medical Center, 1997 WL 33426269 (S.D. Ohio July 16, 1997).

559 Byrne v. Nezhat, 261 F.3d 1075 (11th Cir. 2001) (misdemeanors are not predicate offenses under Georgia RICO).

560 *But cf.* State v. Roderick, 704 So. 2d 49 (Miss. 1997), *cert. denied*, 524 U.S. 926 (1998) (where usury is not listed in RICO statute as a predicate offense, and is a civil rather than a criminal offense under Mississippi law, check casher's charging of interest in excess of allowable amount will not constitute a RICO violation).

561 Fla. Stat. Ann. § 895.02 (lists telemarketing fraud as a predicate offense); Wash. Rev. Code Ann. § 9A.82.010 (includes equity skimming as a predicate offense). *See also* Iowa Code Ann. § 706A.1 (any indictable offense committed for financial gain on a continuing basis); Or. Rev. Stat § 166.715(6)(a)(ss) (offenses involving real estate and escrow); Canterbury v. Columbia Gas, 2001 WL 1681132 (S.D. Ohio Sept. 25, 2001) (telecommunication fraud is predicate offense but plaintiff must plead detrimental reliance). *But see* State v. Gusow, 724 So. 2d 135 (Fla. Dist. Ct. App. 1998) (loan broker fraud and violations of advance fee prohibitions not predicate offenses since they did not involve interest or usurious practices); Clark v. Security Life Ins. Co., 270 Ga. 165, 509 S.E.2d 602 (1998) (failure to file insurance policy with state insurance department is not a predicate offense); State v. Roderick, 704 So. 2d 49 (Miss. 1997), *cert. denied*, 524 U.S. 926 (1998) (state RICO statute's predicate offense of usury is unconstitutionally vague as applied to check cashing fees).

562 State v. Schlosser, 79 Ohio St. 3d 329, 681 N.E.2d 911 (1997).

563 Wis. Stat. § 943.201.

564 Wis. Stat. § 946.82.

565 *Cf.* Blanton v. Bank of America, 256 Ga. App. 103, 567 S.E.2d 313 (2002) (theft by conversion is predicate offense, but not shown by bank's disregard of oral escrow agreement).

566 Metz v. United Counties Bancorp, 61 F. Supp. 2d 364 (D.N.J. 1999).

567 Black v. State, 819 So. 2d 208, 212 n.2 (Fla. App. 2002) (criminal case); Harvey v. State, 617 So. 2d 1144 (Fla. Dist. Ct. App. 1993); 4447 Corp. v. Goldsmith, 504 N.E.2d 559 (Ind. 1987), *aff'd in relevant part, rev'd in part on other grounds*, 489 U.S. 46, 109 S. Ct. 916, 103 L. Ed. 2d 34 (1989) (liability despite lack of conviction is constitutional); Com. v. Stocker, 424 Pa. Super. 189, 622 A.2d 333 (1993); Baxter v. Jones, 83 Ohio App. 3d 314, 614 N.E.2d 1094 (1992); Computer Concepts v. Brandt, 310 Or. 706, 801 P.2d 800 (1990) (interpreting version of Oregon statute before 1995 amendment). *But see* Or. Rev. Stat. § 166.725(6), (7) (allowing RICO suit based on certain predicate offenses only after conviction); Rolin Mfg. Inc. v. Mosbrucker, 544 N.W.2d 132 (N.D. 1996) (under North Dakota's RICO statute either a prior conviction or probable cause must be alleged with reference to the predicate acts); Black v. Arizala, 182 Or. App. 16, 48 P.3d 843 (2002) (amendment requiring conviction for certain offenses should not apply retroactively), *review granted*, 335 Or. 104 (2002).

568 Occidental Fire & Cas. Co. v. Great Plains Capital Corp., 1999 U.S. App. LEXIS 3070 (9th Cir. 1999) (company owner's civil liability as principal for acts of agent does not create state RICO liability where owner not shown to have criminal intent); *In re* Caribbean K Line, Ltd., 288 B.R. 908 (S.D. Fla. 2002) (felonious intent is element of Fla. Civil Theft claim); Arwood v. Dunn (*In re* Caribbean K Line, Ltd.), 2002 WL 31966573 (S.D. Fla. Dec. 26, 2002) (finding allegation of felonious intent sufficient at pleading stage); Mayo, Lynch & Assocs. v. Pollack, 351 N.J. Super. 486, 799 A.2d 12 (App. Div. 2002) (trier of fact may infer defendant attorney's knowledge of bid-rigging scheme from his egregiously wrong legal advice approving the rigged bid).

569 Byrne v. Nezhat, 261 F.3d 1075 (11th Cir. 2001).

570 *See* Occidental Fire & Cas. Co. v. Great Plains Capital Corp., 1999 U.S. App. LEXIS 3070 (9th Cir. Feb. 22, 1999) (unpublished, citation limited) (Arizona requires that offense be committed for financial gain); Kaplan v. Prolife Action League, 347 N.C. 342, 493 S.E.2d 416 (1997) (No. Car. RICO statute requires causal nexus between racketeering activity and pecuniary gain); Winchester v. Stein, 135 Wash. 2d 835, 959 P.2d 1077 (1998).

9.3.3 Pattern Requirements

Some state RICO statutes are explicit about matters as to which federal RICO is silent or ambiguous, such as the meaning of a "pattern of racketeering activity."[571] Thus, several state statutes have no pattern requirement,[572] whereas others require at least three predicate offenses.[573] Hawaii's RICO statute only requires one predicate offense.[574] A pattern under the Florida RICO statute is at least two predicate acts.[575] The Nevada RICO statute does not require a "pattern of racketeering," and instead defines racketeering as "two predicate acts of the type described" in the state statute.[576] Proof of two predicate acts is also sufficient under the Oregon RICO statute.[577]

Some courts also interpret "pattern" for purposes of a state RICO statute more liberally than courts interpret the term under federal RICO.[578] For example, the Colorado RICO statute does not require that proof of a pattern include proof that predicate acts are related to another or proof of continuity.[579] Continuity is similarly not required in Georgia, New Jersey, Ohio, and Oregon.[580] In Oklahoma, however, there must be proof of a relationship between the predicate acts and that the acts pose a threat of continuing activity.[581] In Georgia, the pattern of racketeering activity can consist of two acts that harm the same individual and that are linked to each other.[582] But in Ohio conduct that involves a single victim and a single transaction and takes place over a short period of time does not constitute a pattern.[583] A federal court likewise held that a series of predicate acts that were part of a single fraudulent scheme to sell a single property to a single buyer did not constitute a pattern under Oregon's RICO statute.[584]

9.3.4 Enterprise Requirements

Some courts have rejected the position that a "distinct" or "ascertainable" structure is a necessary component of a state RICO enterprise.[585] In New Jersey, the enterprise

---

571 *See, e.g.*, Idaho Code § 18-7803(d); Ind. Code Ann. § 35-45-6-1 (West); N.M. Stat. Ann. § 30-42-3(D); Wis. Stat. Ann. § 946.82 (West). *See also* Patterson v. Proctor, 514 S.E.2d 37 (Ga. App. 1999) (thefts may be considered separate transactions, even though related, to meet Georgia's requirement of at least two offenses).

572 *See, e.g.*, R.I. Gen. Laws § 7-15-2. *See* State *ex rel.* Corbin v. Pickrell, 136 Ariz. 589, 667 P.2d 1304 (1983); Siragusa v. Brown, 971 P.2d 801 (Nev. 1998) (Nevada requires 2 predicate acts but does not require pattern); Commonwealth v. Peetros, 535 A.2d 1026 (Pa. 1987); State v. Brown, 486 A.2d 595 (R.I. 1985); *see also* Design Shelters Inc. v. Pizzeria Enterprises, Inc., 1988 WL 391256 (Wis. Civ. Ct. Feb. 1, 1988) (evidence did not show sufficient pattern for federal RICO action, but did for state RICO action).

573 *E.g.*, Minn. Stat. Ann. § 609.902(6); Wash. Rev. Code Ann. § 9A.82.010(12); Wis. Stat. Ann. § 946.82(3); *see also* State v. Huynh, 519 N.W.2d 191 (Minn. 1994).

574 Hawaii v. Ontai, 929 P.2d 69 (Haw. 1996).

575 Watts v. Dep't of Professional Regulation, 571 So. 2d 483 (Fla. Dist. Ct. App. 1990) (table).

576 *See* Siragusa v. Brown, 971 P.2d 801 (Nev. 1998).

577 Computer Concepts v. Brandt, 801 P.2d 800 (Or. 1990). *See also* Larson v. Smith, 194 Ga. App. 698, 391 S.E.2d 686 (1990).

578 *See, e.g.*, Emcore Corp. v. PricewaterhouseCoopers L.L.P., 102 F. Supp. 2d 237 (D.N.J. 2000) (New Jersey RICO definition of pattern is more flexible and generous to plaintiffs than federal definition, and requires only relatedness among incidents; continuity may be considered as a circumstance favoring finding of relatedness); State v. Pierce, 153 Or. App. 569, 962 P.2d 35 (1998) (separate acts taking place within a very short period of time, even a few minutes, can establish a pattern, and thus eight identical letters sent by attorney constituted pattern of mail fraud, not single episode). *But cf.* Perimeter Realty v. GAPI, Inc., 243 Ga. App. 584, 533 S.E.2d 136 (2000) (two real estate closings, part of a single transaction, constitute just one predicate act). *But see* Lifeflite Medical Air Transport, Inc. v. Native Am. Air Servs., Inc., 7 P.3d 158 (Ariz. App. 2000) (interpreting Arizona's RICO statute, which had been amended to parallel federal RICO more closely, to require that related predicate acts extend over a substantial period of time); Gross v. State, 765 So. 2d 39 (Fla. 2000) (Florida requires continuity, similarity, and interrelatedness).

579 People v. Chausee, 880 P.2d 749 (Colo. 1994).

580 Marshall v. City of Atlanta, 195 B.R. 156 (N.D. Ga. 1996); Philadelphia Reserve Supply Co. v. Nowalk & Assocs., Inc., 864 F. Supp. 1456 (E.D. Pa. 1994) (New Jersey law); Newman v. Comprehensive Care Corp., 794 F. Supp. 1513 (D. Or. 1992); Dover v. State, 385 S.E.2d 417 (Ga. Ct. App. 1989); State v. Ball, 141 N.J. 142, 661 A.2d 251 (1995), *cert. denied*, 516 U.S. 1075 (1996); Computer Concepts v. Brandt, 801 P.2d 800 (Or. 1990); State v. Hicks, 2003 WL 23095414 (Ohio App. Dec. 31, 2003). *See also* Altamont Summit Apts. v. Wolff Properties L.L.C., 2002 U.S. Dist. LEXIS 2761 (D. Or. Feb. 13, 2002). *But cf.* Metz v. United Counties Bancorp, 61 F. Supp. 2d 364 (D.N.J. 1999) (acts must be related and pose a threat of continued criminal activity, but New Jersey stresses continuity less than relatedness); Colonial Penn Ins. Co. v. Value Rent-A-Car, Inc., 814 F. Supp. 1084 (S.D. Fla. 1992) (Florida RICO statute requires continuity).

581 Miskovsky v. State, 31 P.3d 1054 (Okla. Crim. App. 2001) (note that Oklahoma RICO does not explicitly afford a private cause of action).

582 Brown v. Freedman, 474 S.E.2d 73 (Ga. App. 1996). *See also* O'Neal v. Garrison, 263 F.3d 1317 (11th Cir. 2001) (pattern established by two related acts toward plaintiff plus a similar act toward another person), *amended on other grounds and rehearing denied*, 270 F.3d 1323 (11th Cir. 2001). *Accord* Colonial Penn Ins. Co. v. Value Rent-A-Car, Inc., 814 F. Supp. 1084 (S.D. Fla. 1992) (Florida RICO statute requires continuity).

583 Hanlin v. Ohio Builders & Remodelers, Inc., 196 F. Supp. 2d 572 (S.D. Ohio 2001).

584 Altamont Summit Apts. L.L.C. v. Wolff Props. L.L.C., 2002 WL 31972359 (D. Or. Aug. 21, 2002).

585 Acro-Tech, Inc. v. Robert Jackson Family Trust, 2003 WL 22783349 (9th Cir. Nov. 24, 2003) (unpublished, citation limited); Martin v. State, 189 Ga. App. 483, 376 S.E.2d 888 (1988); State v. Ball, 141 N.J. 142, 661 A.2d 251 (1995) (enterprise must have an "organization," but this organization need not feature an ascertainable structure or a structure with a particular configuration), *cert. denied*, 516 U.S. 1075 (1996); State v. Hughes, 108 N.M. 143, 767 P.2d 382 (Ct. App. 1988); State v. Cheek, 100 Or. App. 501, 786 P.2d 1305 (1990). *See* § 9.2.3.2,

element is satisfied if there is a group of people, no matter how loosely defined, whose existence or association provides or implements the common purpose of committing one or more predicate acts.[586] In defining the term "enterprise" under its RICO statute, the Minnesota Supreme Court has required a showing of "an organizational set-up, whether formal or informal, that not only exists to commit the predicate acts but also does more, such as coordinating those acts into an overall pattern of criminal activity."[587] In Florida, the evidence of the existence of the enterprise may be the same as the evidence that establishes the pattern.[588] In Oklahoma, the enterprise must have some structure apart from the crimes it is alleged to have committed, and separate proof is required.[589]

Ohio's RICO statute requires that the defendant be associated with an enterprise, but one court holds that the enterprise need not have an existence separate and apart from the corrupt activity.[590] A New Jersey RICO defendant need not have played a part in directing the enterprise's affairs; providing advice is sufficient.[591] Idaho, on the other hand, has determined that a defendant must have some level of managerial control over the enterprise in order to implicate the state statute.[592] In Colorado, the enterprise must include at least one person or entity besides the defendant,[593] but it can be a corporation over which the defendant has some control.[594] Colorado follows federal cases that hold that when a separate entity is formed by the act of incorporation, the corporation constitutes an enterprise within the meaning of the state RICO law, separate from the person engaged in the pattern of racketeering activity.[595] But the jury need not be instructed that the enterprise must be an ongoing organization, operate as a continuing unit, and be separate and apart from the pattern of activity in which it engages.[596]

Many state RICO statutes have simplified requirements about the relationship between the defendant's racketeering acts and an enterprise. Some allow suit by anyone who suffers damage as a result of the racketeering acts, without any requirement that those acts have an effect on an enterprise. Georgia's counterpart to section 1962(b) of the federal RICO statute is broader than the federal statute in that it outlaws the use of a pattern of racketeering activity to acquire or maintain an interest in any property, not just in an enterprise.[597] Under Rhode Island's statute, however, the plaintiff must have suffered harm from the defendant's acquisition or maintenance of an interest in or control of an enterprise, or from the defendant's conduct or participation in the conduct of the affairs of an enterprise.[598] Ohio's RICO statute specifically includes governmental agencies in the definition of enterprise.[599]

9.3.5 *Timing of Offenses and Statute of Limitations*

Most state RICO statutes set forth a statute of limitations period as well as a requirement for the timing between predicate offenses. Statutes of limitations vary from one year to ten years, and are typically about five years.[600] Most are

---

supra, for a discussion of related issues under the federal RICO statute. *See also* Wesleyan Pension Fund, Inc. v. First Albany Corp., 964 F. Supp. 1255 (S.D. Ind. 1997) (association in fact consisting of a corporation, its officers, and either two sister corporations or a parent and subsidiary and their officers and employees are sufficiently distinct from the named defendants); Gross v. State, 765 So. 2d 39 (Fla. 2000); Helmadollar v. State, 811 So. 2d 819 (Fla. App. 2002) (short term informal organization is enterprise); State v. Wilson, 113 Ohio App. 3d 737, 682 N.E.2d 5 (1996) (enterprise need not have an existence separate and apart from defendant's corrupt activity). *But see* State v. Ontai, 929 P.2d 69 (Haw. 1996) (requiring proof of ongoing organization with a structure distinct from that inherent in the conduct of the racketeering activity); Knutson v. County of Barnes, 642 N.W.2d 910 (N.D. 2002) (enterprise must be distinct); Carlsten v. Widecom Group, Inc., 2003 WL 21688263 (R.I. Super. July 1, 2003) (unpublished, citation limited). *But cf.* Colonial Penn Ins. Co. v. Value Rent-A-Car, Inc., 814 F. Supp. 1084 (S.D. Fla. 1992) (a corporation and its officers can not conspire with each other for purposes of a RICO violations); State v. Gertsch, 2000 Ida. App. LEXIS 92 (Dec. 5, 2000) (sole proprietorship made up of single person is not an enterprise with which that person may be associated).

586 Franklin Medical Assocs. v. Newark Public Schools, 362 N.J. Super. 494, 828 A.2d 966 (App. Div. 2003).

587 State v. Huynh, 519 N.W.2d 191, 196 (Minn. 1994).

588 Gross v. State, 765 So. 2d 39 (Fla. 2000).

589 Miskovsky v. State, 31 P.3d 1054 (Okla. Crim. App. 2001) (note that Oklahoma RICO does not explicitly afford a private cause of action).

590 State v. Wilson, 113 Ohio App. 3d 737, 682 N.E.2d 5 (1996). *But see* Patton v. Wilson, 2003 WL 21473566 (Ohio App. June 26, 2003) (unpublished, citation limited).

591 Mayo, Lynch & Assocs. v. Pollack, 351 N.J. Super. 486, 799 A.2d 12 (App. Div. 2002).

592 *See* State of Idaho v. Nunez, 981 P.2d 738 (Idaho 1999) (concluding officer who stole money and drugs from police station was not involved in a criminal enterprise because he was not conducting his employer's affairs when he committed his crimes).

593 People v. James, 40 P.3d 36 (Colo. App. 2001). *See also* Miskovsky v. State, 31 P.3d 1054 (Okla. Crim. App. 2001) (enterprise need not be incorporated but can be a sole proprietorship that the defendant owns and works for).

594 National Union Fire Ins. Co. v. Kozeny, 2001 U.S. App. LEXIS 21211 (10th Cir. Sept. 28, 2001).

595 People v. Pollard, 3 P.3d 473 (Colo. App. 2000).

596 People v. James, 40 P.3d 36 (Colo. App. 2001).

597 Reaugh v. Inner Harbour Hosp., Ltd., 214 Ga. App. 259, 447 S.E.2d 248 (1994). *See also* National Union Fire Ins. Co. v. Kozeny, 2001 U.S. App. LEXIS 21211 (10th Cir. Sept. 28, 2001) (applying Colorado's version, which prohibits use of proceeds to acquire interest in enterprise or real property).

598 Carlsten v. Widecom Group, Inc., 2003 WL 21688263 (R.I. Super. July 1, 2003) (unpublished, citation limited).

599 Bratton v. Couch, 2003 WL 21652166 (Ohio App. July 8, 2003) (unpublished, citation limited).

600 *See* Burr v. Kulas, 564 N.W.2d 631 (N.D. 1997) (applying state RICO statute's 7-year limitations period instead of other limitations period urged by defendant).

tolled while related cases are pending. Some state RICO statutes also extend the time allowed between predicate offenses when the offender has been incarcerated. North Dakota's RICO statute has a discovery rule[601] and Georgia[602] and Florida[603] also recognize the rule. An Ohio court, following federal decisions, adopts an injury discovery rule.[604]

Colorado's RICO statute does not specify a limitations period, but a court has used the two year Colorado general limitations period, and ruled the two years do not begin to run until the plaintiff knew or should have known of all elements of the RICO claim, including the existence of a pattern.[605] A New Jersey appellate court has suggested that either a four-year or a five-year statute of limitations applies to New Jersey civil RICO claims.[606]

9.3.6 Jurisdictional and Procedural Issues

State RICO actions will generally be tried in state court.[607] State RICO claims can probably be brought into federal district court along with related federal RICO claims.[608] The Eleventh Circuit has held that federal courts have original jurisdiction over a state RICO claim that alleges only federal crimes as predicate offenses and raises very substantial federal questions, so such a case is removable to federal court.[609]

Most states will require the same degree of specificity in pleading fraud that exists under the federal RICO statute.[610] Nevada requires that claims under its RICO statute be as specific as would be required in a criminal indictment or information.[611]

An out-of-state resident has the right to file a state RICO case.[612] The fact that some acts occurred outside the state does not make the RICO statute inapplicable as long as acts in furtherance of the conspiracy occurred in the state.[613] A Georgia appellate court has ruled that a plaintiff who alleges Insurance Code violations in a RICO suit need not exhaust administrative remedies.[614]

Some state RICO statutes specify a standard of proof.[615] Georgia's statute is silent on this issue, but an appellate court has held that proof must be by clear and convincing evidence because of the significance of the consequences to the defendant.[616]

9.3.7 Private Remedies Under State RICO Statutes

Most state RICO statutes, like federal RICO, provide for treble damages, costs, and attorney fees,[617] but several

601 *See* N.D. Cent. Code § 12.1-06.1-05(7); *see also* Burr v. Kulas, 564 N.W.2d 631 (N.D. 1997).

602 Southern-Intermodal Logistics, Inc. v. D.J. Powers Co., 251 Ga. App. 865, 555 S.E.2d 478 (2000).

603 Huff Groves Trust v. Caulkins Indiantown Citrus Co., 829 So. 2d 923 (Fla. Dist. Ct. App. 2002).

604 Tri-State Computer Exchange, Inc. v. Burt, 2003 WL 21414688 (Ohio App. June 20, 2003) (unpublished, citation limited).

605 FDIC v. Refco Group, Ltd., 989 F. Supp. 1052 (D. Colo. 1997).

606 Fraser v. Bovino, 317 N.J. Super. 23, 721 A.2d 20 (1998).

607 *See* § 9.2.6.3, *supra*. *But see* Ayres v. General Motors Corp., 234 F.3d 514 (11th Cir. 2000) (state RICO case based on predicate acts of federal mail and wire fraud was removable because plaintiff's claims required resolution of substantial, disputed questions of federal law).

608 *See, e.g.*, Doxieu v. Ford Motor Credit Co., 603 F. Supp. 624 (S.D. Ga. 1984) (mem.) (Georgia and federal RICO claims by automobile buyer against assignee under retail installment contract); Bache Halsey Stuart Shields Inc. v. Tracy Collins Bank & Trust Co., 558 F. Supp. 1042 (D. Utah 1983) (mem.) (Utah, federal RICO claims). *But see* Chas. Kurtz Co. v. Lombardi, 595 F. Supp. 373 (E.D. Pa. 1984) (discretionary refusal to exercise pendent jurisdiction over state claims related to RICO claim).

609 Ayres v. General Motors Corp., 234 F.3d 514 (11th Cir. 2000). *But cf. In re* United Container L.L.C., 284 B.R. 162, 173 (Bankr. S.D. Fla. 2002) (removal not allowed where complaint alleged both federal and state predicate acts). *But see* Local 1 FLM-FJC UFCWIV v. Caputo, 1988 U.S. Dist. LEXIS 1253 (S.D.N.Y. Feb. 18, 1988).

610 Knutson v. County of Barnes, 642 N.W.2d 910 (N.D. 2002); Canterbury v. Columbia Gas, 2001 WL 1681132 (S.D. Ohio Sept. 25, 2001); National Credit Union Board v. Regine, 749 F. Supp. 401 (D.R.I. 1990) (applying rule that Rhode Island's RICO statute is to be construed liberally, court finds that complaint adequately pleads enterprise of racketeering activity); Cobb County v. Jones Group P.L.C., 218 Ga. App. 149, 460 S.E.2d 516 (1995) (claim dismissed because complaint did not contain specific allegations of fraud); Rolin Mfg., Inc. v. Mosbrucker, 544 N.W.2d 132 (N.D. 1996); Patton v. Wilson, 2003 WL 21473566 (Ohio App. June 26, 2003) (unpublished, citation limited); Kondrat v. Morris, 118 Ohio App. 3d 198, 692 N.E.2d 246 (1997) (conclusory allegations of corrupt activity do not satisfy requirement that claim alleging state civil RICO violation be pleaded with particularity). *See also* Altamont Summit Apts. v. Wolff Properties L.L.C., 2002 U.S. Dist. LEXIS 2761 (D. Or. Feb. 13, 2002) (specifying elements that must be pleaded).

611 Cummings v. Charter Hosp. of Las Vegas, Inc., 111 Nev. 639, 896 P.2d 1137 (1995); Hale v. Burkhardt, 764 P.2d 866 (Nev. 1988).

612 State *ex rel.* Corbin v. Pickrell, 136 Ariz. 589, 597, 667 P.2d 1304, 1312 (1983).

613 Black v. State, 819 So. 2d 208 (Fla. App. 2002) (criminal case).

614 Provident Indemnity Life Ins. Co. v. James, 506 S.E.2d 892 (Ga. App. 1998).

615 *See, e.g.*, Arwood v. Dunn (*In re* Caribbean K Line, Ltd.), 2002 WL 31966573 (S.D. Fla. Dec. 26, 2002) (applying Florida's statutory requirement of clear and convincing evidence).

616 Simpson Consulting, Inc. v. Barclays Bank, 490 S.E.2d 184 (Ga. App. Ct. 1997).

617 *See, e.g.*, Ariz. Rev. Stat. Ann. § 13-2314; Fla. Stat. Ann. § 895.04(7); R.I. Gen. Laws § 7-15-4(c). *See also* Altamont Summit Apts. v. Wolff Properties L.L.C., 2002 U.S. Dist. LEXIS 2761 (D. Or. Feb. 13, 2002) (deferring question whether to award attorney fees to prevailing defendants in state RICO case); Dial Mfg. Int'l, Inc. v. McGraw-Edison Co. Int'l, 657 F. Supp. 248 (D. Ariz.) (discussion of apportionment of state RICO attorney fees relating to non-RICO counts), *aff'd without op.*, 833 F.2d 1015 (9th Cir. 1987); Vairo v. Clayden, 153 Ariz. 13, 734 P.2d 110 (Ct. App. 1987) (treble damages mandatory;

provide for double damages[618] or just compensatory damages.[619] Additional punitive damages are often authorized.[620] Some state statutes, unlike federal RICO, allow recovery for injury to the person as well as to property or business.[621] In some states, the statute sets a cap on damage awards. The plaintiff may have to show that the injury flowed directly from the racketeering activity.[622] Florida courts disagree about whether the economic loss doctrine limits state RICO claims.[623] A New Jersey court has ruled that the plaintiff can not get both punitive damages on a non-RICO claim and treble damages on a state RICO claim.[624] At least one court in a state RICO case has followed the federal rule that the jury should not be told that its compensatory damages award will be trebled.[625]

Many state RICO statutes expressly authorize injunctive relief for private plaintiffs.[626] A Washington court ordered an injunction to be issued without bond under the state RICO law to prevent a predatory lender from foreclosing on a home, even though the state Deeds of Trust Act authorized an injunction against foreclosure only upon posting a substantial bond.[627]

9.3.8 Application of State RICO Statutes to Consumer Fraud

Courts construing state RICO statutes have rejected some of the same limitations on RICO liability that the United States Supreme Court and the federal courts have rejected with regard to the federal RICO statute. For example, there is no requirement that the defendant be a member of or involved with organized crime.[628] Like federal RICO, state RICO is a proper weapon for use against "garden variety" fraud.[629] Indeed, many state RICO statutes explicitly list

treble *before* deducting amount received in settlement; treble pre-judgment interest); Daggett v. Jackie Fine Arts, Inc., 152 Ariz. 559, 733 P.2d 1142 (Ct. App. 1986) (treble damages mandatory); Sullivan v. Metro Productions, Inc., 150 Ariz. 573, 724 P.2d 1242 (Ct. App. 1986) (treble damages and attorney fees are mandatory); Tallitsch v. Child Support Servs., Inc., 926 P.2d 143 (Colo. App. 1996) (discussing calculation of attorney fees under Colorado RICO statute); RLS Bus. Ventures v. Second Chance Wholesale, Inc., 784 So. 2d 1194 (Fla. App. 2001) (denying prevailing defendant's claim for fees because plaintiffs were advancing in good faith a novel but credible interpretation); Dee v. Sweet, 489 S.E.2d 823 (Ga. 1997) (upholding award of fees and finding fee award provision constitutional); Dee v. Sweet, 218 Ga. App. 18, 460 S.E.2d 110 (1995) (damages award of one dollar sufficient to justify awarding of attorney fees; discussion of apportionment of state RICO attorney fees relating to non-RICO counts); Franklin Medical Assocs. v. Newark Public Schools, 362 N.J. Super. 494, 828 A.2d 966 (App. Div. 2003) (error for trial court to disallow attorney fee petition because it was filed after judgment); Nelson v. Taff, 499 N.W.2d 685 (Wis. Ct. App. 1993) (treble damages). *Cf.* Bronson v. Bronson, 685 So. 2d 994 (Fla. Dist. Ct. App. 1997) (interpreting provision of Florida's civil theft statute that allows defendants to recover attorney fees if plaintiff's claim was without substantial fact or legal support); Holbrook v. Master Protection Corp., 883 P.2d 295 (Utah Ct. App. 1994) (no error in awarding attorney fees to the defendant on state RICO claim).

618 *See, e.g.*, Utah Code Ann. § 76-10-1605(1); Wis. Stat. Ann. § 946.87(4) (West).

619 *See, e.g.*, Wash. Rev. Code Ann. § 9A.82.100(1)(a).

620 *See, e.g.*, Del. Code Ann. tit. 11, § 1505; Ga. Code Ann. § 16-14-6; Ind. Code Ann. § 34-24-2-6; Miss. Code Ann. § 97-43-9(6); Or. Rev. Stat. § 166.725(7)(a); Wis. Stat. Ann. § 946.87(4). *See also* Rhue v. Dawson, 841 P.2d 215 (Ariz. Ct. App. 1992).

621 *See, e.g.*, Ariz. Rev. Stat. Ann. § 13-2314.04(A); Idaho Code § 18-7805; N.M. Stat. Ann. § 30-42-6(A); Utah Code Ann. § 76-10-1605(1). *See also* Southern-Intermodal Logistics, Inc. v. D.J. Powers Co., 251 Ga. App. 865, 555 S.E.2d 478 (2000) (Georgia RICO allows suit by any person who has been injured, with no requirement that injury be to person or property).

622 Nicor Int'l Corp. v. El Paso Corp., 292 F. Supp. 2d 1357, 1378 (S.D. Fla. 2003) (dismissing claim because of failure to show causation); Nicholson v. Windham, 257 Ga. App. 429, 571 S.E.2d 466 (2002) (causation too remote where injury was termination of employment because employee refused to participate in criminal activity); Franklin Medical Assocs. v. Newark Public Schools, 362 N.J. Super. 494, 828 A.2d 966 (App. Div. 2003) (must show that predicate acts were proximate cause of the harm).

623 *See* Wilson v. De Angelis, 156 F. Supp. 2d 1335 (S.D. Fla. 2001) (economic loss doctrine is no bar). *Contra* Delgado v. J.W. Courtesy Pontiac GMC-Truck, Inc., 693 So. 2d 602 (Fla. Dist. Ct. App. 1997); Sarkis v. Pafford Oil Co., 697 So. 2d 524 (Fla. Dist. Ct. App. 1997).

624 St. James v. Future Fin., 342 N.J. Super. 310, 776 A.2d 849 (App. Div. 2001).

625 *Id. See also* § 8.4.2.8, *supra*.

626 *See, e.g.*, Ind. Code Ann. § 34-24-2-6(a); Or. Rev. Stat. § 166.725(6). *See* FDIC v. Antonio, 843 F.2d 1311 (10th Cir. 1988) (injunction preventing dissipation of assets not traceable to alleged racketeering permitted under Colorado RICO statute); National Union Fire Ins. Co. v. Kozeny, 115 F. Supp. 2d 1210 (D. Colo. 2000) (granting injunctive relief to prevent dissipation of assets), *aff'd*, 2001 U.S. App. LEXIS 21211 (10th Cir. Sept. 28, 2001); Marsellis-Warner Corp. v. Rabens, 51 F. Supp. 2d 508 (D.N.J. 1999) (stating New Jersey statute does not expressly preclude equitable actions by private plaintiffs and that its plain language appears to allow courts authority to grant such equitable relief); Bowcutt v. Delta N. Star Corp., 976 P.2d 643 (Wash. Ct. App. 1999) (interpreting the Washington statute as allowing private plaintiffs the right to obtain injunctive relief). *But see* Curley v. Cumberland Farms Dairy, Inc., 728 F. Supp. 1123 (D.N.J. 1989) (no injunctions for private litigants under N.J. RICO statute).

627 Bowcutt v. Delta N. Star Corp., 976 P.2d 643 (Wash. Ct. App. 1999).

628 Doxieu v. Ford Motor Credit Co., 603 F. Supp. 624 (S.D. Ga. 1984); Banderas v. Banco Cent. del Ecuador, 461 So. 2d 265 (Fla. Dist. Ct. App. 1985); Patterson v. Proctor, 514 S.E.2d 37 (Ga. App. 1999) (Georgia RICO statute does not require conspiracy or connection to organized crime); Dee v. Sweet, 218 Ga. App. 18, 460 S.E.2d 110 (1995) (need not demonstrate a nexus with organized crime in order to prevail on a Georgia RICO claim); Larson v. Smith, 194 Ga. App. 698, 391 S.E.2d 686 (1990) *But see* Georgia Gulf Corp. v. Ward, 701 F. Supp. 1556 (N.D. Ga. 1987) (plaintiff must allege organized crime nexus under Georgia RICO statute).

629 *See, e.g.*, Matthews v. New Century Mortg. Corp., 185 F. Supp. 2d 874 (S.D. Ohio 2002) (predatory lending and home improve-

fraud, usury, and violations of certain consumer protection statutes as predicate offenses.[630] These statutes demonstrate the legislative intent to treat consumer fraud as organized crime, and to afford victimized consumers the powerful remedies of the RICO laws. If the predicate offenses impose strict liability, without the need to prove criminal intent, state RICO liability may also be possible to establish without any showing of intent.[631]

The objection that federal RICO was not intended to federalize state tort law can not be used to confine the impact of state RICO.[632] State courts had rejected some of the proposed limitations on RICO, like the "racketeering injury" requirement, even before the Supreme Court disapproved them.[633] The formulation of consumer fraud claims as state RICO claims has great potential for strengthening many consumer cases.

9.3.9 Strategic Advantages of State RICO Laws as Compared to UDAP Statutes

State RICO laws offer a number of strategic advantages when compared to state UDAP statutes. UDAP statutes are broad and flexible, but in some states they have certain limitations. Not all state UDAP statutes authorize multiple damages or attorney fees; some exclude significant actors such as banks, insurance companies, and landlords; and some have short statutes of limitations. Litigation under state RICO statutes may be a way to fill some of these gaps. Attorneys in the twenty-four jurisdictions[634] that have civil RICO statutes that afford the consumer a private cause of action should consider whether a RICO cause of action might fill any of these voids.

Private right of action. The Iowa UDAP statute does not provide an explicit private right of action, and the Iowa Supreme Court has declined to find a private action implicit in the statute.[635] The RICO statute can fill this void, at least in part. The state RICO statute should also be investigated as an alternative in any other situation where a private right of action is denied, for example because the case involves a non-consumer transaction.

Scope restrictions. A number of state UDAP statutes exclude banks, insurance companies, utilities, landlords, or others. While state RICO statutes have their own coverage complexities, they do not exclude whole categories of potential defendants. Any defendant who commits the required number of predicate offenses, has the involvement with an enterprise that the statute requires, and causes damage to the victim is covered by the state RICO statute. State RICO laws also cover both business and consumer transactions. In Florida, Louisiana, Ohio, Oregon, and Utah, where the state UDAP statutes have significant coverage gaps, a private cause of action under the state RICO statute can be a particularly attractive alternative.

On the other hand, some states may make it harder to use RICO than UDAP in some instances. For example, Wisconsin prohibits RICO actions against an estate of a deceased defendant.[636] The Georgia Supreme Court has refused to apply to state RICO claims the rule that an employer is liable for its employees' tortious acts committed within the scope of their employment.[637] Instead, the criteria for criminal liability must be applied.

Exhaustion of administrative remedies. Plaintiffs may not be subject to an exhaustion of administrative remedies requirement in a RICO action that they might face with another type of claim. In a Georgia case, the court ruled that the plaintiffs did not have to exhaust Insurance Department administrative remedies when making a RICO claim based on violation of insurance laws and other fraudulent acts.[638]

Substantive prohibitions. While the substantive prohibitions

---

ment fraud); Eva v. Midwest Nat'l Mortg. Banc, Inc., 143 F. Supp. 2d 862 (N.D. Ohio 2001) (denying motion to dismiss state RICO claim against predatory lender based on wire fraud); Bandaras v. Banco Central del Ecuador, 461 So. 2d 265, 269–70 (Fla. Dist. Ct. App. 1985); Reaugh v. Inner Harbour Hosp., Ltd., 214 Ga. App. 259, 447 S.E.2d 248 (1994) (suit against juvenile treatment center for abuse and failure to provide treatment); Larson v. Smith, 194 Ga. App. 698, 391 S.E.2d 686 (1990); Sanchez v. Guerrero, 885 S.W.2d 487 (Tex. App. 1994); State v. Thompson, 751 P.2d 805 (Utah Ct. App. 1988); Dorr v. Sacred Heart Hosp., 597 N.W.2d 462 (Wis. App. Ct. 1999) (hospital's filing of false lien on consumer's tort recovery could be criminal slander of title, which would support RICO suit). *But see* Daniels v. True, 47 Ohio Misc. 2d 8, 547 N.E.2d 425 (Mun. Ct. 1988) (state RICO statute not intended to reach contractor's use of false name and failure to perform work); Griswold v. U.S. Sprint Communications Co., 506 N.W.2d 426 (Wis. Ct. App. 1993) (no fraud claims allowed for simple refusal to do business in manner claimant wanted).

630 *But cf.* State v. Roderick, 704 So. 2d 49 (Miss. 1997), *cert. denied*, 524 U.S. 926 (1998) (where usury is not listed in RICO statute as a predicate offense, and is a civil rather than a criminal offense under Mississippi law, check casher's charging of interest in excess of allowable amount will not constitute a RICO violation).

631 State v. Schlosser, 79 Ohio St. 3d 329, 681 N.E.2d 911 (1997) (Ohio's RICO statute allows a strict liability statute).

632 State *ex rel.* Corbin v. Pickrell, 136 Ariz. 589, 596, 667 P.2d 1304 (1983).

633 *Id.* at 667 P.2d 1309–10.

634 Arizona, Colorado, Delaware, Florida, Georgia, Hawaii, Idaho, Indiana, Iowa, Louisiana, Mississippi, Nevada, New Jersey, New Mexico, North Carolina, North Dakota, Ohio, Oregon, Puerto Rico, Rhode Island, Utah, Virgin Islands, Washington, and Wisconsin.

635 *See* § 7.2.2, *supra*.

636 *See* Schimpf v. Gerald, Inc., 2 F. Supp. 2d 1150 (E.D. Wis. 1998) (concluding state RICO action is punitive in nature and so can not survive defendant's death).

637 Clark v. Security Life Ins. Co., 270 Ga. 165, 509 S.E.2d 602 (1998).

638 Provident Indemnity Life Ins. Co. v. James, 234 Ga. App. 403, 506 S.E.2d 892 (1998).

of most UDAP statutes are broad, cases sometimes arise that do not fit cleanly into any UDAP substantive prohibition. This is particularly true in states where the UDAP statute does not prohibit unfair conduct, or has a limited "catch-all" for acts that are not specifically listed. The state RICO law is worth investigating in these cases. While all state RICO laws require proof of acts that would constitute a criminal offense, many include such offenses as fraud, usury, violation of certain consumer protection laws, and federal mail and wire fraud.

Treble damages provisions. The UDAP statutes in Arizona, Florida, Idaho, Indiana, Michigan, Oregon, and Rhode Island do not authorize treble damages. Yet each of those states has a RICO statute that authorizes a private cause of action for treble damages.

In Arizona, for example, a private cause of action under the state UDAP statute is available only because the courts have implied one, and the courts have not implied a treble damages remedy. The state RICO statute, on the other hand, allows suit for treble damages, costs, and attorney fees. Predicate offenses include usury, fraud, and extortionate extensions of credit.

Attorney fee provisions. A number of state UDAP statutes do not provide for an award of attorney fees, or make the award discretionary. Most state RICO statutes, by contrast, mandate an award of attorney fees if the plaintiff is successful.

Statutes of limitations. Many state RICO statutes have more generous statutes of limitations than the state UDAP statute. For example, the statute of limitations is just one year for Louisiana and Oregon UDAP claims, but five years for a state RICO suit. Even where the UDAP and state RICO statutes of limitations are similar, the state RICO statute may have better rules about tolling; most state RICO statutes of limitations are tolled during the pendency of a related criminal or civil action.

9.3.10 Strategic Advantages of State RICO Statutes as Compared to Federal RICO

Defrauded consumers in any state can, of course, take advantage of the private cause of action afforded by the federal RICO statute. State RICO laws, however, offer a number of strategic advantages. The consumer may prefer to stay in state court, while a federal RICO complaint can be removed to federal court. Many state RICO statutes explicitly afford a right to trial by jury. Filing a claim under a state rather than the federal RICO statute may trigger less of a "full battle" response on the defendant's part.

Further, many state RICO statutes have simplified versions of federal RICO's complex requirements about how the defendant's acts have affected an enterprise. For example, many state RICO statutes allow a civil suit if the defendant used the proceeds of racketeering activity to acquire an interest in either an enterprise or real property, in contrast to federal RICO's requirement that the defendant acquire an interest in an enterprise.[639] Several state RICO statutes allow suit whenever the plaintiff has suffered damage due to a pattern of racketeering activity on the part of the defendant, without any requirement of an effect on an enterprise.[640] Georgia[641] and Nevada[642] courts have interpreted such departures from federal RICO as intentional and significant, and have given them their plain meaning. A federal court in New Jersey has concluded that the state legislature wrote the statute to be broader than the federal RICO, and that courts are constrained to interpret the statute such that it encompasses more violations than does the federal statute.[643]

Another possible advantage is that most state RICO statutes set forth a specific, concrete pattern requirement that may be easier to deal with than federal RICO's standard.[644] Some specifically allow recovery for personal injury as well as financial losses. Many state RICO statutes explicitly state that a civil RICO defendant who has been criminally convicted is precluded from denying commission of the criminal acts. Finally, the additional predicate offenses that state RICO statutes list may allow a RICO recovery where federal mail fraud or wire fraud can not be proven.

9.3.11 State Civil Theft Laws

A few states have civil theft laws that offer a cause of action that is similar to but less complex than a state RICO claim. These statutes also usually cover a greater range of fraud and theft offenses than federal RICO does.

In Indiana, a person who has suffered a pecuniary loss as a result of a theft or fraud crime, or certain other types of crimes, may sue for treble damages, costs, attorney fees, certain travel expenses and court costs, and collection costs.[645] Ohio offers a private cause of action for damages, attorney fees, costs, and, in certain cases, punitive damages to anyone injured in person or property by a criminal act.[646] The statute also provides for treble damages and statutory

639 *See, e.g.*, Fla. Stat. Ann. § 895.03; Miss. Code Ann. § 97-43-5. Some state RICO statutes, such as Ga. Code Ann. § 16-14-4, allow a private RICO suit where the defendant has acquired an interest in an enterprise, real property, or personal property. *See* Cobb County v. Jones Group P.L.C., 218 Ga. App. 149, 460 S.E.2d 516 (1995).

640 *See, e.g.*, Ariz. Rev. Stat. Ann. § 13-2314.04.

641 Reaugh v. Inner Harbour Hosp., Ltd., 214 Ga. App. 259, 447 S.E.2d 248 (1994).

642 Siragusa v. Brown, 971 P.2d 801 (Nev. 1998).

643 *See* Metz v. United Counties Bancorp, 61 F. Supp. 2d 364 (D.N.J. 1999).

644 *See* § 9.2.3.4, *supra* (federal RICO pattern requirement).

645 Ind. Code § 34-24-3-1.

646 Ohio Rev. Code § 2307.60.

damages in some circumstances[647] if the defendant does not respond properly to a thirty-day demand letter.[648] Rhode Island provides a private cause of action for damages to any person who suffers injury to the person, reputation, or estate by reason of the commission of any crime or offense, and specifies that it is not a defense that no criminal complaint has been filed.[649]

9.4 Other Federal Causes of Action

9.4.1 Introduction

This manual focuses on state UDAP claims. Where federal court is the preferred forum for the consumer's case, the consumer's attorney will usually have to utilize a federal claim in addition to the UDAP claim. One important example of such a federal claim is a federal RICO claim, analyzed in § 9.2, *supra*. The RICO statute potentially applies to almost all types of consumer transactions. Nevertheless, there are drawbacks to a RICO claim, not the least of which is that the claim can greatly complicate a case. This section briefly lists other approaches to obtaining federal court jurisdiction in consumer protection cases.

9.4.2 United States Bankruptcy Code

The United Bankruptcy Code[650] provides an important avenue for obtaining federal jurisdiction in consumer cases. Filing a bankruptcy case allows the consumer to litigate any of the consumer's claims—whether they are federal or state claims—in the bankruptcy forum before a United States bankruptcy judge. Appeals are to a federal district court judge. Bankruptcy court litigation is discussed in detail in another NCLC manual, *Consumer Bankruptcy Law and Practice* (6th ed. 2000 and Supp.).

9.4.3 Federal Anti-Discrimination Laws

When a deceptive scheme targets minorities or certain categories of vulnerable consumers, a possible claim involves one of the various federal anti-discrimination laws. The three major federal anti-discrimination laws relevant to consumer transactions are the Equal Credit Opportunity Act (ECOA),[651] the Fair Housing Act,[652] and the Civil Rights Acts.[653]

These statutes vary depending on their scope—for example the Fair Housing Act applies only to housing and housing-related loans. The ECOA applies only to the extension of credit. The Civil Rights Acts apply to any form of contract or adverse treatment.

The statutes also vary as to what bases for discrimination are prohibited. For example, the federal Civil Rights Acts apply only to discrimination based on race and (to a certain extent) ethnicity. The ECOA and Fair Housing Act prohibits discrimination on the basis of race, religion, national origin, and sex. The ECOA also prohibits discrimination on the basis of marital status, age, public assistance status, and good faith exercise of certain consumer protection statutes. While not containing these prohibited bases, the Fair Housing Act prohibits discrimination on the basis of familial or disability status.

These statutes may apply where a seller treats different categories of consumers differently and those categories are among the prohibited bases listed above. For example, charging higher prices or denying credit based on race will most likely be violations. It may even be a violation for an unscrupulous seller to defraud all its consumers alike, but especially to target sales to minorities.

It is important to compare the basis for discrimination and the type of transaction with the coverage of the various federal anti-discrimination statutes. If one of the federal anti-discrimination statutes applies, then violations generally lead to actual and punitive damages and attorney fees. For more details on these statutes, see National Consumer Law Center, *Credit Discrimination* (3d ed. 2002 and Supp.).

9.4.4 Federal Magnuson-Moss Warranty Act

The federal Magnuson-Moss Warranty Act[654] provides a private right of action for actual damages and attorney fees whenever a product breaches its implied or written warranty and also whenever a warrantor engages in certain disclosure or other violations relating to a written warranty.

While the Magnuson-Moss Act thus has broad applicability in consumer sales transactions, federal court jurisdiction is limited to cases where the amount in controversy is $50,000 or more. This amount can be reached by joining together a number of individual claims, and perhaps by alleging punitive damages or personal injury damages under the Act. For more on the Magnuson-Moss Warranty Act, see National Consumer Law Center, *Consumer Warranty Law* Ch. 2 (2d ed. 2001 and Supp.).

647 Ohio Rev. Code § 2307.61.

648 *See* Buckeye Check Cashing, Inc. v. Proctor, 1999 Ohio App. LEXIS 2678 (June 15, 1999) (interpreting ambiguous statutory language).

649 R.I. Gen. Laws § 9-1-2.

650 11 U.S.C. §§ 101–1330.

651 15 U.S.C. § 1691.

652 42 U.S.C. §§ 3601–3631.

653 42 U.S.C. §§ 1981, 1982, 1988.

654 15 U.S.C. §§ 2301–2312.

9.4.5 Federal Odometer Act

The federal Odometer Act[655] is not only an important federal cause of action for odometer tampering and misdisclosure on odometer statements, but also for misrepresentations outside the odometer statement. Any type of oral or written misrepresentations is a violation if it is made in connection with the odometer disclosure.[656] The federal odometer law provides for mandatory treble actual damages or $1500, whichever is greater, plus attorney fees for prevailing consumers.

Application of this federal law to automobile mileage misrepresentations conveyed orally or through documents in addition to the federal odometer statement is set out at § 5.4.6.5.2, *supra*. The federal law is considered in detail in National Consumer Law Center, *Automobile Fraud* (2d ed. 2003 and Supp.).

9.4.6 Federal Telemarketing Statutes and the Federal Credit Repair Organizations Act

Two federal statutes provide private remedies specifically concerning telemarketing fraud. These statutes are detailed at §§ 5.9.2, 5.9.4, *supra*. The federal Telephone Consumer Protection Act of 1991[657] and the accompanying FCC regulations prohibit junk faxes, telemarketing calls before 8:00 A.M. and after 9:00 P.M., telemarketing calls to consumers who register on the nationwide do-not-call list, and a variety of other abuses. The Act authorizes a private right of action in state court for actual damages or up to $500 statutory damages. Treble damages are available for knowing violations.

The Telemarketing and Consumer Fraud Abuse Prevention Act[658] and the accompanying FTC Telemarketing Rule contain a number of important prohibitions concerning telemarketing fraud. The Act provides a private right of action in federal court, but only where each plaintiff's damages exceed $50,000.[659]

The federal Credit Repair Organizations Act provides a potent private remedy for various credit repair abuses by anyone who performs or offers to perform any service for a fee for purposes of improving the consumer's credit record, history, or rating.[660] Credit repair contracts in violation of the Act are void and unenforceable, and consumers can also recover actual and punitive damages and attorney fees.[661] The Act does not provide an explicit grant of federal jurisdiction, but federal jurisdiction is probably available under the general federal question statute.[662]

9.4.7 Truth in Lending, Consumer Leasing, HOEPA, and RESPA

The federal Truth in Lending Act[663] provides a federal remedy for misdisclosure of credit terms. In addition, it requires creditors to provide a right of rescission for certain loans secured by the consumer's residence, and violations of this right—such as beginning home improvements before the three-day period has expired—are actionable under the statute. Remedies include actual damages plus statutory damages and attorney fees.[664] This statute is examined in detail at National Consumer Law Center, *Truth in Lending* (5th ed. 2003 and Supp.).

The Truth in Lending Act also includes the Home Ownership and Equity Protection Act (HOEPA), which provides special protections concerning high-rate home equity loans, that is certain home equity loans with high interest rates or a large number of points. For these high-rate loans, HOEPA requires special disclosures, limits prepayment penalties, prohibits rate increases on default, limits balloon payments, prohibits negative amortization, prohibits engaging in a pattern or practice of extending credit without regard to the consumer's ability to pay, and restricts certain other practices. Remedies are the same as under Truth in Lending, and, in addition, the creditor forfeits all finance charges for specified violations. This statute is briefly summarized at § 6.7.3, *supra*, and examined in detail at National Consumer Law Center, *Truth in Lending* Ch. 9 (5th ed. 2003 and Supp.).

The Real Estate Settlement Procedures Act (RESPA)[665] prohibits kickbacks and unearned fees for the referral of a settlement service, including certain fees to mortgage brokers. The remedy is treble damages and attorney fees.[666]

RESPA requires lenders to properly forward amounts paid in escrow.[667] RESPA also contains provisions protecting consumers where a mortgage is assigned to another lender and consumer payments get lost between the two lenders. Violations of any of these provisions lead to a private action for actual and statutory damages and attorney fees.[668]

655 49 U.S.C. §§ 32701–32711.

656 49 U.S.C. § 32705(a)(2).

657 47 U.S.C. § 227.

658 15 U.S.C. § 6101. *See* § 5.9.4, *supra*, for a discussion of this statute.

659 15 U.S.C. § 6104(a). *See* § 5.9.4.9.2, *supra*, for a discussion of this remedy.

660 15 U.S.C. § 1679. *See generally* § 5.1.2.2.2, *supra*. *See also* National Consumer Law Center, Fair Credit Reporting Ch. 15 (5th ed. 2002 and Supp.).

661 15 U.S.C. §§ 1679f(c), 1679g.

662 28 U.S.C. § 1331.

663 15 U.S.C. § 1601 *et seq.*

664 15 U.S.C. § 1640.

665 12 U.S.C. § 2601.

666 *See* National Consumer Law Center, The Cost of Credit: Regulation and Legal Challenges § 11.3.1 (2d ed. 2000 and Supp.).

667 12 U.S.C. § 2605. *See* National Consumer Law Center, Repossessions and Foreclosures Ch. 19 (5th ed. 2002 and Supp.).

668 *Id.*

The federal Consumer Leasing Act[669] provides a federal remedy for misdisclosure of lease terms and also for unreasonable early termination, default, excess mileage, or excess wear and tear charges. Remedies include actual damages plus (in the typical car lease) $1000 statutory damages plus attorney fees. This statute is examined in detail at National Consumer Law Center, *Truth in Lending* Ch. 10 (5th ed. 2003 and Supp.).

9.4.8 Fair Debt Collection Practices Act

The federal Fair Debt Collection Practices Act prohibits unfair and deceptive debt collection practices by collection agencies, proscribes certain practices by repossessors, and prohibits creditors from misrepresenting their identity when they collect a debt.[670] The Act provides up to $1000 statutory damages plus actual damages plus attorney fees. For a detailed analysis of this Act, see National Consumer Law Center, *Fair Debt Collection* (5th ed. 2004 and Supp.).

9.4.9 Fair Credit Reporting Act

The Fair Credit Reporting Act places certain restrictions on suppliers of information to consumer reporting agencies, on the consumer reporting agencies themselves, and on those using information from the reporting agencies.[671] Remedies include actual and punitive damages and attorney fees.

Of special note is the Act's provision of a private remedy where suppliers of information, such as creditors who furnish reporting agencies with the consumer's payment history, fail to comply with the Act. The Act does not provide the consumer with a private cause of action where a creditor or other party initially supplies inaccurate information to the reporting agency. Instead, the cause of action is provided where the consumer disputes the information and the supplier of the information fails to participate in a dispute resolution process concerning the accuracy of information or fails to properly re-investigate the information it supplies.

The FCRA was amended extensively in 2003 by the Fair and Accurate Credit Transactions Act (FACTA).[672] Many of the consumer protection provisions contained in the FCRA prior to FACTA were unchanged, but FACTA extends existing preemption provisions and adds other provisions that place limitations on liability.[673] The full impact of these provisions on UDAP claims is uncertain and advocates should use caution when considering a combination of FCRA and UDAP claims together. FACTA also added new provisions to the FCRA that will allow for additional consumer claims, including claims against credit reporting agencies for failing place blocks on consumer information that resulted from identity theft; claims against debt collectors for failing to notify creditors that the underlying debt is fraudulent or the result of identity theft; and claims against furnishers for failing to block unverifiable information.

For more on the Fair Credit Reporting Act generally and the specific requirements of FACTA, see National Consumer Law Center, Fair Credit Reporting (5th ed. 2002 and Supp.).[674]

9.4.10 Federal Securities Legislation

The federal securities laws[675] provide a private right of action that can apply in certain consumer cases, particularly those involving pyramid sales and sales of multi-level distributorships. The statutes provide a private right of action for damages for the sale of unregistered securities, certain untrue statements or the failure to disclose material facts, and deceptive devices or contrivances.[676] The test for determining whether a particular scheme is an investment contract is "whether the scheme involves an investment of money in a common enterprise with profits to come solely from the efforts of others."[677]

These securities laws have been found to apply to pyramid schemes and multi-level marketing programs, even though the sellers never issued securities. Investments in pyramid schemes are "investment contracts" which are subject to the securities laws.[678] Once the pyramid scheme is recognized as covered by the securities laws, then there is little difficulty finding a violation, particularly since the scheme does not disclose the fact that it is bound eventually to collapse.[679]

State securities law also may apply to some consumer cases. For example, a Michigan appellate court has ruled that its securities law applies to the sale of gemstones because they are commonly offered to the public as investments and meet the statutory definition of a commodity contract.[680] Violation of federal securities law may also be a violation of the state UDAP statute.[681]

669 15 U.S.C. § 1667.

670 15 U.S.C. § 1692.

671 15 U.S.C. § 1681.

672 Pub. L. No. 108-159 (2003). NCLC's analysis of FACTA is available at www.consumerlaw.org.

673 *See* National Consumer Law Center, Fair Credit Reporting, §§ 10.3 and 10.4 (Supp. 2004).

674 NCLC analysis of FACTA is also available on the Internet at www.consumerlaw.org.

675 In addition, most states have enacted their own state securities laws, but these statutes do not provide federal court jurisdiction.

676 15 U.S.C. §§ 77k, 77*l*. *See also* 15 U.S.C. § 77e(c).

677 SEC v. W.J. Howey Co., 328 U.S. 293, 301, 66 S. Ct. 1100, 90 L. Ed. 1244 (1946).

678 *See, e.g.*, SEC v. Glenn W. Turner Enterprises, 474 F.2d 476 (9th Cir.), *cert. denied*, 414 U.S. 821 (1973).

679 *See, e.g.*, Webster & Ligon v. Omnitoron, 79 F.3d 776 (9th Cir. 1995), *cert. denied*, 519 U.S. 865 (1996).

680 Aaronson v. Lindsay & Hauer Int'l Ltd., 235 Mich. App. 259, 597 N.W.2d 227 (1998). *See also* State *ex rel.* Miller v. Pace, 677 N.W.2d 761 (Iowa 2004).

681 *See* § 3.2.7, *supra*.

More on securities law can be found in treatises on the subject. See, for example, Budnitz, *Lender Liability* Ch. 10 (1998); Hazen, *Securities Regulation* (4th ed. 2001); Ratner, *Securities Regulation in a Nutshell* (7th ed. 2001); Commerce Clearinghouse, Federal Securities Law Reporter; BNA, Securities Regulation and Law Report.

9.4.11 Federal Antitrust Law

Federal law provides a private, federal court right of action for treble damages, attorney fees, and injunctive relief for violations of any of four federal antitrust statutes.[682] The Sherman Act prohibits contracts or combinations in restraint of trade, including price fixing, illegal tie-ins, and monopolization of trade.[683] The Clayton Act prohibits seller requirements that purchasers not contract with certain other competitors where the effect is to reduce competition, and also prohibits certain other forms of anti-competitive conduct.[684] The Wilson Tariff Act prohibits anti-competitive behavior regarding imports into the United States.[685] The Robinson-Patman Act prohibits price discrimination that has the effect of reducing competition.[686]

One area of consumer abuse where the antitrust laws have been applied involves mobile home parks that require tenants to purchase their homes from particular dealers or utility service from particular providers.[687] Such illegal tie-ins also may be found in other consumer transactions.

One significant limitation to consumer use of the federal antitrust statutes is the *Illinois Brick* doctrine: the requirement that the consumer's injury be directly caused by the defendant's conduct.[688] It is not always easy to draw a line as to whether an injury is sufficiently direct, but this requirement may prevent a consumer from bringing an action where a manufacturer's anti-competitive conduct directly impacts only a retailer who eventually sells the product to the consumer. If the retailer participated in the price-fixing conspiracy, however, this doctrine should not bar suit.

An excellent example of the creative use of the Clayton Act price-fixing prohibition is a class action seeking treble damages and attorney fees and alleging that the Louisiana automobile dealership association colluded with the state's automobile dealers to create a separate charge added to each car sale to reimburse dealers for the inventory tax dealers must pay the state. The allegation was not that the dealers had fixed prices, but that they had engaged in concerted action that had an impact on prices. The federal court certified a plaintiff class of all Louisiana car purchasers over a ten year period and a defendant class of all Louisiana car dealers, and rejected the defendants' summary judgment motions. A settlement was reached valued at several hundred million dollars.[689]

Consumer advocates should also examine their state antitrust laws, many of which are not limited by the *Illinois Brick* doctrine. These statutes generally apply just to in-state activities, however, so would be applicable only to the most small-scale conspiracies.

Some courts have ruled that state UDAP statutes can be used to redress anti-competitive activity without the constraints of *Illinois Brick*. This topic is discussed in § 4.10, *supra*. Standard antitrust treatises explore antitrust issues in more detail.

9.4.12 Banking Holding Company Anti-Tying Act

The Bank Holding Company Act provides a private right of action for treble damages and attorney fees[690] for violation of its anti-tying provisions.[691] One of these provisions prohibits banks, as defined by the statute,[692] from conditioning an extension of credit upon the borrower's obtaining some additional credit, property, or service from the bank or certain affiliated entities.[693] Consumers have not been successful in using this act against banks that required the consumer to purchase insurance as a condition of an extension of credit, however.[694]

682 15 U.S.C. §§ 15, 26. *See* 15 U.S.C. § 12(a) for a listing of the antitrust statutes to which these remedies apply.

683 15 U.S.C. §§ 1–7.

684 15 U.S.C. §§ 12–27.

685 15 U.S.C. §§ 8–11.

686 15 U.S.C. §§ 13, 13a, 13b, 21a.

687 *See* National Consumer Law Center, Consumer Law Pleadings, No. 2, § 2.2 (CD-Rom and Index Guide) also found on the CD-Rom accompanying this volume.

688 *See* Illinois Brick Co. v. Illinois, 431 U.S. 720 (1977). *See also* § 4.10, *supra* (discussion of *Illinois Brick* issues in UDAP cases).

689 *See* Cook v. Powell Buick, Inc., Clearinghouse No. 52,030 (W.D. La. complaint filed 1994). Documents available through the Clearinghouse number include the First Amended Complaint, Findings and Recommendation (concerning class certification and defendants' motion for partial summary judgment), The Proposed Settlement Agreement, and The Notice of Settlement. *See* 155 F.3d 758 (5th Cir. 1998) (affirming approval of settlement).

690 12 U.S.C. §§ 1975, 1976.

691 12 U.S.C. § 1972.

692 12 U.S.C. § 1971.

693 12 U.S.C. § 1972(1).

694 *See* § 5.3.11.10, *supra*; National Consumer Law Center, The Cost of Credit: Regulation and Legal Challenges § 8.4.1.5.2 (2d ed. 2000 and Supp.).

9.4.13 Federal False Claims Act[695]

9.4.13.1 Overview

The federal False Claims Act (FCA) imposes liability on government contractors who make false or fraudulent claims for payment of services and products.[696] Although the False Claims Act has traditionally been used against defense and health care contractors and suppliers, it is expanding into other areas—such as insurance, housing, government entitlement programs, government loan programs and environmental and labor laws—that offer potential use by consumer lawyers.

Unlike almost all other federal fraud statutes or common law causes of action, the False Claims Act,[697] with its unique *qui tam*[698] provisions, allows consumers to file and prosecute a lawsuit in the name of the United States. Because False Claims Act cases are brought on behalf of the government, the plaintiff—or relator—need not suffer any individual or direct harm to bring the action.[699] By authorizing suits in these situations, the False Claims Act offers a tremendous opportunity for individuals and organizations to effectuate significant public policy changes.

The False Claims Act empowers individuals and organizations with knowledge of private fraud against the government to file lawsuits to recover damages and penalties for the government. Its express intent is to encourage *qui tam* suits by giving consumers the tools and incentive to represent the government in actions against individuals and organizations who falsely bill for services not rendered or goods not delivered. A number of states have their own *qui tam* statutes.

Knowledge of the statute and compliance with its sometimes strict procedural requirements are a necessary first step for consumer attorneys seeking to use the False Claims Act as a tool for consumer protection.

9.4.13.2 Features of the False Claims Act

Almost any action that involves fraud in trying to obtain payment of government funds or avoid lawful payment of government funds may impose liability under the Act.[700] The False Claims Act is "intended to reach all types of fraud, without qualification, that might result in financial loss to the Government."[701] The most common are "mischarge" cases in which the government has been overcharged for a service not rendered, or charged more than it should have been. Other types of false claims include the submission of false claims for payment or in contract negotiations, the submission of false statements to create eligibility for federal programs, and supplying substandard services or products.[702] Importantly, the False Claims Act also imposes liability where the contractor has certified explicitly or implicitly that it will comply with federal statutes and laws, but fails to do so.[703] The Act excludes claims that a person or company failed to pay federal taxes.[704]

The Act allows for treble damages, plus civil penalties of $5000 to $10,000 per false claim.[705] The relator is entitled to a percentage of the proceeds of the case. If the government intervenes in the case, the minimum award to the relator is 15% (but not more than 25%). If the government declines to intervene, the minimum award is 25% (but not more than 30%).[706]

The standard for liability under the Act makes it clear that it is not a fraud statute to which common law fraud principles apply, although the requirements of Federal Rule of Civil Procedure 9(b) to plead with particularity are imposed.[707] Instead, it is a false claim or false statement statute, which imposes liability based upon a scienter standard.[708] Before 1986, some courts had incorrectly interpreted the Act to require intentional acts to find a contractor liable for submission of false claims.[709] In 1986 Congress

695 This discussion is based on an article written by Thomas Grande, a partner in Davis Levin Livingston Grande in Honolulu, Hawaii, for the *Consumer Advocate*, the newsletter of the National Association of Consumer Advocates. Mr. Grande represents *qui tam* relators and consumers in class and group actions.

696 *See generally* Claire M. Slvia, The False Claims Act: Fraud Against the Government (2004) For an overview of the statute, see Grande, *An Overview of the Federal False Claims Act*, Ann. 2002 ATLA-CLE 1177 (July 2002).

697 31 U.S.C. § 3729 (1983). The Act, originally known as the "Informer's Act" or the "Lincoln Law," was enacted during the Civil War to deal with widespread fraud by private military supply contractors. U.S. *ex rel.* Newsham v. Lockheed Missiles and Space Co., 722 F. Supp. 607, 609 (N.D. Cal. 1989).

698 *Qui tam* is the abbreviation of the Latin phrase "*qui tam pro domino rege quam pro si ipso in hac parte sequitur*," which means, "Who sues on behalf of the King as well as for himself." Black's Law Dictionary 1282 (8th ed. 2004).

699 The False Claims Act does contain a prohibition on discriminatory or retaliatory acts against an employee who takes actions in furtherance of a False Claims Act case. 31 U.S.C. § 3730(h). The FCA also allows for supplemental jurisdiction over related state law claims, including wrongful termination claims and claims that may be brought under the various state false claims acts. 31 U.S.C. § 3732(b).

700 *See* John T. Boese, Civil False Claims and *Qui Tam* Actions § 1-4 (2d ed. 2000).

701 U.S. v. Neifert-White Co., 390 U.S. 228, 232 (1968)

702 31 U.S.C. § 3730(a)(1)–(7).

703 *See* Slvia, The False Claims Act: Fraud Against the Government § 4:43 (2004).

704 31 U.S.C. § 3729(e).

705 31 U.S.C. § 3729(a).

706 31 U.S.C. § 3730(d)(1), (2).

707 *See* Claire M. Slvia, The False Claims Act: Fraud Against the Government § 10-59 (2004).

708 *See* John T. Boese, Civil False Claims and *Qui Tam* Actions § 1-3, 2-5 (2d ed. 2000).

709 *Compare* United States v. Hughes, 585 F.2d 284, 286–88 (7th Cir. 1978) (no specific intent to defraud required to satisfy

clarified the standard and imposed liability where the defendant knows the information is false or acts in deliberate ignorance or reckless disregard of its truth or falsity.[710] The intent of these amendments was to impose liability for conduct that was more than merely negligent but less than intentional.[711] Congress wanted to impose liability where "an individual 'buried his head in the sand' and failed to make simple inquiries which would alert him that false claims are being submitted."[712]

The pre-1986 Act precluded a private cause of action where the government had any prior knowledge of the fraud. The 1986 amendments eliminated this bar. The current version of the Act specifically allows *qui tam* actions to be pursued even after public disclosure of false billings from a criminal, civil or administrative hearing, or other public sources. Such cases can only be brought, however, where the relator was an "original source" of the allegations and has direct and independent knowledge of the fraudulent activity.[713]

In order to prevail on a False Claims Act claim, the fraud must be proven by a preponderance of the evidence.[714] The statute of limitations is six years from the date of the violation, but a tolling provision can extend the period to as long as ten years.[715]

9.4.13.3 Who May File a False Claims Act Case

The current version of the Act contains virtually no restrictions on who may be a relator, other than the requirement that the relator be an "original source" of the allegations and have direct and independent knowledge of the fraudulent activity if the fraud has already been publicly disclosed.[716] Often relators are employees or former employees who have direct knowledge of fraudulent activity and have complained directly or indirectly to their company. Relators may also be outside consultants or even competitors who have discovered fraudulent activity by another company. The Act gives relators an independent cause of action in the event of retaliation for reporting fraudulent claims or taking actions in pursuit of a *qui tam* complaint.[717]

9.4.13.4 Procedure Under the False Claims Act

To commence a False Claims Act case, the relator files a complaint under seal and serves a copy on the United States Attorney.[718] Unlike any other civil action, the relator and relator's attorney are acting on behalf of two interests-that of the person filing the complaint and that of the United States.[719]

The complaint, which must be accompanied by a written disclosure of evidence and information possessed by the relator, is then evaluated by government attorneys who decide whether or not to intervene in the case.[720] Although the statute requires the government to make its decision to intervene within sixty days,[721] the government often seeks multiple extensions[722] and may possibly take two or three years to decide whether to intervene in the action.

If the government chooses to intervene, the U.S. Attorney's Office will either attempt to settle the action or ask that the complaint be unsealed. When the complaint is unsealed, it is served on the defendant and the government will have primary responsibility for prosecuting the action.[723] The relator, however, still has a statutory right to participate in the lawsuit, unless the government seeks to limit the relator's involvement by court order.[724] Congress wanted the relator to stay in the case to make sure that the government did not neglect evidence, cause undue delay, or drop the case without legitimate reason.[725]

If the government declines to intervene, the relator may continue the action on his or her own, while continuing to inform the government of the course of the litigation.[726] The government also retains its right to intervene at a later stage in the case. Regardless of whether the government decides to intervene, court approval must be sought for any settlement.[727] While the relator's percentage of the proceeds is greater if the government does not intervene, the vast majority of *qui tam* recoveries have occurred in cases in which the government has intervened.[728]

Venue is proper in the judicial district where any defendant can be found, resides, transacts business, or in which any act alleged as a violation is alleged to have occurred.[729] The Act provides for international service of process[730] and

knowing violation) *with* United States v. Mead, 426 F.2d 118, 122, 123 (9th Cir. 1970) (specific intent to defraud required to show knowing violation) *and* United States v. Ekelman & Assocs., Inc., 532 F.2d 545, 548 (6th Cir. 1976) (actual knowledge of falsity of claims required).

710 31 U.S.C. § 3729(b).

711 S. Rep. No. 99-345, at 21 (1986), *reprinted in* 1986 U.S.C.C.A.N. 5266, 5286.

712 S. Rep. No. 99-345, at 20, 21 (1986), *reprinted in* 1986 U.S.C.C.A.N. 5266, 5285, 5286.

713 31 U.S.C. § 3730(e)(1) (as amended, Oct. 27, 1986).

714 31 U.S.C. § 3731(c).

715 31 U.S.C. § 3731(b).

716 31 U.S.C. § 3730(e)(1).

717 31 U.S.C. § 3730(h).

718 31 U.S.C. § 3730(b)(1).

719 31 U.S.C. § 3730(b).

720 31 U.S.C. § 3730(b)(2).

721 *Id.*

722 *See* 31 U.S.C. § 3730(b)(3), (4).

723 31 U.S.C. § 3730(c).

724 31 U.S.C. § 3730(c)(1), (2)(C).

725 S. Rep. No. 99-345, at 26 91986), reprinted in 1986 U.S.C.C.A.N. 5266, 5291.

726 31 U.S.C. § 3730(c)(3).

727 *Id.*

728 *See* Taxpayers Against Fraud: Qui Tam Statistics, *posted at* www.taf.org/statistics.html.

729 31 U.S.C. § 3732(a).

730 *Id.*

national service of trial and hearing subpoenas.[731]

9.4.13.5 Examples of False Claims Act Cases

The fact patterns giving rise to False Claims Act liability are extremely varied. Traditional areas such as Medicare and Medicaid fraud by health care providers, health care contractors and private insurance companies administering government health insurance programs, offer tremendous opportunity for a consumer attorney seeking to establish a false claims act practice. However, the following less traditional areas should also provide a focus for potential use of the Act:

FDCPA: A law firm that acted as a collection agency for the federal government has been sued under the False Claims Act for failing to credit consumers accounts on the day that payment was received. The firm was collecting student loans on behalf of the Illinois Student Assistance Commission. The failure to credit the accounts resulted in excessive interest payments by the students and an inflated fee earned by the law firm because its fees were based upon the a percentage of the amount collected.[732]

Long-Distance Carriers: The False Claims Act was used to reach a settlement with MCI for improperly overbilling the General Services Administration for communications charges.[733]

Insurance: Where the government agrees to provide insurance and applications for either coverage or benefits are fraudulent, a False Claims Act claim may be brought. For example, the Third Circuit has held that a lender's claim for mortgage insurance benefits is a false claim, where the lender fraudulently induced the government to issue the insurance policy.[734] Another example is a settlement against Bankers Insurance Company, where Bankers, authorized to collect flood insurance premiums for deposit into the U.S. Treasury's national flood insurance fund and to use federal money to pay flood insurance claims, submitted monthly statements that failed to report $1.1 million in interest due the government.[735]

Loan Applications: A false application for a government loan is a false claim.[736] For example, if there are false representations made to obtain a government loan, the False Claims Act may impose liability.[737]

Banks: A False Claims Act settlement was recently reached with Gold Bank–Oklahoma for charging excessive interest rates. The bank charged excessive interest rates and fees on agricultural loans guaranteed by the Farm Service Agency.[738]

Environmental Statutes: The False Claims Act imposes liability where a contractor knowingly fails to satisfy the environmental requirements of a government contract, but seeks payment even though it has not complied with the contractual requirements.[739]

Education: A False Claims Act case was recently settled by the City of San Francisco against Strategic Resource Solutions, a city contractor that was supposed to install energy efficient equipment in San Francisco Schools.[740] The government has also settled cases with school counseling programs whose payments were made in part with Medicaid funds.[741]

9.4.13.6 FCA Checklist

Because of the procedural and substantive differences in the FCA, it is extremely important that any attorney considering filing an FCA case associate or at the least consult with an experienced practitioner. However, the following checklist should provide some guidance in assessing whether a potential False Claims Act cause of action is possible:

(1) Is there government funding involved?
(2) Does the false or fraudulent action involve a claim for payment or involve a certification of compliance with governmental statutes?
(3) Is the conduct of the contract knowing or in reckless disregard (as opposed to merely negligent)?
(4) Has the government suffered actual or potential loss as a result of the false or fraudulent action?
(5) Is the problem systemic or systematic in nature?

If the answers to these five questions are "yes," then the procedural aspects of the statute must be analyzed:

(1) Has there been a public disclosure of the basis of the fraudulent activity?
(2) If there has been a public disclosure, is the relator the original source of the publicly disclosed information?
(3) What documentation does the relator have to support the claim?
(4) Are there sufficient facts to plead the fraud with particularity as required under Federal Rule of Civil Procedure 9(b)?
(5) What is the proper venue for the case?

731 *Id.*
732 8 Consumer Fin. Servs. Law Report, No. 1 (June 2, 2004).
733 Los Angeles Times, May 5, 2004.
734 United States v. Venziale, 268 F.2d 504 (3d Cir. 1959).
735 The Daily Record (Baltimore, MD) July 2, 2004.
736 United States v. Neifer-White Co., 390 U.S. 228 (1968).
737 United States v. Entin, 750 F. Supp. 512 (S.D. Fla. 1990).
738 See *Gold Banc Reaches Agreement in Principle to Settle Qui Tam Lawsuit,* Business Wire, August 9, 2004.
739 *See, e.g.*, United States *ex rel.* Made in the USA Foundation v. Billington, 985 F. Supp. 604 (D. Md. 1997).
740 Bay City News, June 30, 2004.
741 New Jersey Express Times, May 7, 2004.

(6) Is it a case in which the government is likely to intervene?
(7) Are there other individual claims that the relator has (wrongul termination, retaliation)?

9.5 Cancellation and Rescission

9.5.1 *Introduction*

In general, UDAP actions are for money damages. But for many consumers, the preferred remedy is merely canceling the contract. Canceling a contract may be available even when damages are not. Cancellation may also be easier to accomplish than recovering money from a merchant. In some cases, the consumer can both cancel the transaction and seek money damages. Many UDAP statutes allow cancellation as a remedy.[742] This section lists various other approaches a consumer can take to cancel an agreement.

9.5.2 *Cooling-Off Period for Door-to-Door and Certain Other Sales*

The FTC and all states require door-to-door and other off-premises sellers to give consumers a three-day cancellation right.[743] This right to cancel may be a continuing one even after three days if the seller does not properly notify the consumer of the right to cancel.[744] The FTC cooling-off period applies not just to door-to-door sales, but to any sale away from the seller's principal place of business.[745] Consequently, sales in motels, at the consumer's place of work, or in booths set up in shopping center parking lots, should be covered. Some state cooling-off laws apply to telephone sales.[746] These statutes are examined in detail at § 5.8.2, *supra*.

In addition, certain other legislation provides three-day cooling-off periods for certain specific types of sales. State health spa legislation is the most common example of a statute that allows a consumer to back out of a long term membership agreement.[747]

9.5.3 *Truth in Lending Rescission for Home Secured Loans*

The Truth in Lending Act provides a three-day right to rescind a loan where the consumer's residence is taken as security and the loan is not used to purchase the home. This right extends up to three years until proper disclosures are given to the consumer. This important consumer cancellation right is discussed in detail in another NCLC manual, *Truth in Lending* Ch. 6 (5th ed. 2003 and Supp.).

742 *See* § 8.7, *infra*.
743 *See* § 5.8.2, *supra*.
744 *See* § 5.8.2.6.3, *supra*.
745 *See* § 5.8.2.4.1, *supra*.
746 *Id*.
747 *See* § 5.10.3, *supra*.

9.5.4 *Cancellation Under Federal and State Credit Repair Laws*

Cancellation under a state or federal credit repair law should be investigated whenever a seller, broker, or other middleman has offered to improve the consumer's credit rating or arrange credit for the consumer. Many entities subject to these laws choose to ignore them, and others mistakenly believe the laws do not apply to them. As a result, if it can be established that these laws apply to a particular seller, the seller has usually committed a number of violations.

Most state credit repair statutes cover not only organizations that offer to improve an individual's credit rating, but also organizations that assist or offer to assist consumers in obtaining extensions of credit (usually limited to credit for personal, family, or household use), in return for the payment of money or other consideration. In determining whether an organization is covered by a state credit repair law, it is important to pay attention to the statutory exemptions. State statutes vary in the parties they exempt, but most exempt non-profit organizations; licensed real estate brokers and attorneys when acting within the scope of their licenses;[748] broker-dealers registered with the SEC or CFTC; consumer reporting agencies; credit unions; banks eligible for FDIC or FSLIC insurance; banks and other lenders authorized under federal or state law; and lenders approved by HUD for participation in federal mortgage insurance.

The federal and most state credit repair statutes require the provider to afford the consumer a three- or five-day right to cancel. In addition, these laws typically require disclosures and a written contract with specified provisions, and prohibit certain misrepresentations and deceptive acts. State credit repair laws often require registration and bonding as well.

The federal statute and almost all state credit repair laws provide a private right of action to consumers. Some state laws do so both by making a violation actionable under the state UDAP statute and by creating a special cause of action, which may include minimum damages and attorney fees. These laws are discussed in more detail at § 5.1.2.2, *supra*, and analyzed in depth in National Consumer Law Center, *Fair Credit Reporting* Ch. 15 (5th ed. 2002 and Supp.).

748 *See* King v. Rubin, 35 Phila. 571, 1998 Phila. Cty. Rptr. LEXIS 73 (Pa. C.P. July 1, 1998) (licensed real estate brokers were exempt even when holding credit workshops, as this was related to their real estate business).

9.5.5 Right to Reject or Revoke Acceptance of Purchased Goods; Automobile Lemon Laws

The Uniform Commercial Code provides consumers with the right to reject an offered good as nonconforming or to revoke acceptance of the good if a substantial defect is later discovered. These UCC rights apply to the sale of all goods, and are analyzed in detail in another NCLC manual.[749]

The federal Magnuson-Moss Warranty Act also gives consumers a right, where the seller offers a "full" written warranty, to receive a new product or a refund if the seller is not able to repair the purchased item.[750] Full written warranties are relatively rare, however.

More important for consumers are new car lemon laws that all states have enacted and that give the consumer a right to a replacement car or refund in the case of automobile defects that the dealer can not repair.[751] A few states have similar legislation providing the right to cancel used car sales in specified circumstances.[752] New and used car lemon laws are discussed in detail in NCLC's *Consumer Warranty Law* §§ 13.2, 14.6 (2d ed. 2001 and Supp.).

9.5.6 Unconscionable Contracts

UCC §§ 2-302 and 2A-108 allow courts to refuse to enforce unconscionable contracts or contract terms. State credit codes based on the Uniform Consumer Credit Code generally have a similar provision.[753] A number of other states have statutes prohibiting unconscionable contract terms in certain types of transactions.[754] Unconscionability is also a common law doctrine.[755] Generally a consumer is allowed to cancel an unconscionable contract,[756] although this may not result in the return of monies already paid. Unconscionability is discussed in § 4.4, *supra*, and is more fully analyzed in NCLC's *Consumer Warranty Law*.[757]

9.5.7 The Consumer's Incapacity—Minority, Mental Incompetence, or Intoxication

9.5.7.1 General

An otherwise valid contract may be voidable because one party does not have the capacity to make the contract.[758] The parties must be capable of intelligent assent in order to make a valid contract, and there can be no contract where there is no capacity to understand or agree.[759]

There are three conditions which give rise to questions about a person's capacity to contract: minority, mental disability, and intoxication. When the party with the defective capacity seeks to cancel the contract, that person is entitled to have the other party return whatever the incompetent party gave under the contract, and must usually restore to the other party what the incompetent party received under the contract.[760]

9.5.7.2 Minority

The legal age of minority is determined by the law of the state in which the contract is made. A minor may void a contract whether or not the other party knew of the minority and whether or not the consumer understood the nature of the contract.[761] Among other things, this rule protects the minor from being bound by contracts he or she may not understand, or may have entered into at the insistence of an overzealous or intimidating seller.

The contract may be disaffirmed by the minor during his or her minority. It also may be disaffirmed within a reason-

---

749 National Consumer Law Center, Consumer Warranty Law Ch. 8 (2d ed. 2001 and Supp.).

750 15 U.S.C. § 2301; *see* National Consumer Law Center, Consumer Warranty Law Ch. 2 (2d ed. 2001 and Supp.).

751 15 U.S.C. § 2301; *see* National Consumer Law Center, Consumer Warranty Law Ch. 13, Appx. F (2d ed. 2001 and Supp.).

752 National Consumer Law Center, Consumer Warranty Law Ch. 14 (2d ed. 2001 and Supp.).

753 *See, e.g.*, Iowa Code § 537.5108.

754 *See, e.g.*, Ala. Code § 5-19-16; Alaska Stat. § 45.12.108 (leases); Cal. Civ. Code § 1670.5; Cal. Fin. Code § 22302 (consumer loans by finance lenders); D.C. Code § 28-3812 (consumer credit transactions or direct installment loans); Ind. Code § 24-7-6-5 (rental purchase agreements); Kan. Stat. § 58-2544 (residential rental agreements); La. Rev. Stat. § 9:3551 (consumer credit transactions); Mont. Code Ann. § 70-24-404 (residential rental agreements); N.Y. Gen. Bus. Law § 396-r (sale of goods or services at unconscionably excessive price during period of abnormal disruption of market due to disaster, strike, etc.); N.C. Gen. Stat. § 25A-43 (consumer credit sales); Vt. Stat. Ann. tit. 9, § 2485 (agricultural finance leases); W. Va. Code § 46B-2-2 (rent-to-own).

755 Besta v. Beneficial Loan Co., 855 F.2d 532 (8th Cir. 1988); Matthews v. New Century Mortg. Corp., 185 F. Supp. 2d 874 (S.D. Ohio 2002) (denying motion to dismiss). *See generally* National Consumer Law Center, The Cost of Credit: Regulation and Legal Challenges § 11.7 (2d ed. 2000 and Supp.).

756 *See, e.g.*, Eva v. Midwest Nat'l Mortg. Banc, Inc., 143 F. Supp. 2d 862 (N.D. Ohio 2001).

757 *See* National Consumer Law Center, Consumer Warranty Law § 11.2 (2d ed. 2001 and Supp.).

758 D. Dobbs, Remedies § 13.4.1 (1993).

759 17A Am. Jur. 2d *Contracts* § 28 (2004).

760 *Id.* §§ 28, 580.

761 *See* Keser v. Chagnon, 159 Colo. 209, 410 P.2d 637 (1966) (minor's absolute right to disaffirm is not diminished by minor's false representation of age); Gillis v. Whitley's Discount Auto Sales, Inc., 70 N.C. App. 270, 319 S.E.2d 661 (1984) (fraudulent misrepresentation would not be valid defense to minor's action to disaffirm). There seems to be some move away from this rule in some jurisdictions. *See, e.g.*, Annot., *Infant's Misrepresentation as to His Age as Estopping Him from Disaffirming His Voidable Transaction*, 29 A.L.R.3d 1270 (1970).

able period after the minor reaches majority, unless ratified when of legal age.[762] The minor disaffirms by giving the seller notice of his age or by offering to return to the seller any goods the minor may still have. A disaffirming minor need only return the goods in their present condition. If the goods have been damaged or dissipated, the seller must bear the loss.[763] Some states have modified this result by statute, by requiring the minor to restore the value received.[764]

Despite the general rule about contracts entered into by minors, a minor may be liable for the fair market value of goods that are necessaries.[765] The disaffirming minor is not liable for the contract price of these goods, but only for their fair market value. Whether goods are necessaries is determined by the facts of each case, depending upon the person and the circumstances, being relative to the minor's actual needs and status in life.[766]

Courts generally limit necessaries to food or clothing of a reasonable kind purchased for the minor or the minor's family and to medical and dental services. A house is probably not a necessary. It has also generally been held that an automobile is not a necessary,[767] but there are occasions where it may be, such as when a twenty year-old needs a car for school and work.[768] If goods are not necessaries, then the general rule applies, and the contract can be disaffirmed.

9.5.7.3 Mental Incompetency

The general rule for a mentally incompetent person is that the incompetent person may avoid the contract upon proof of mental incapacity, provided the incompetent can fully restore the other party to its position before the contract.[769] If the incompetent no longer has the consideration received, the incompetent can not rescind the contract.[770]

This rule applies only if the seller did not know about the incapacity. If the seller is aware of the incompetency, the incompetent person may rescind the contract upon returning whatever is left of the consideration.[771]

The Restatement (Second) of Contracts finds a person mentally incompetent if that person is unable to understand in a reasonable manner the nature and consequence of a transaction *or* if the person is unable to act in a reasonable manner in relation to the transaction and the other party has reason to know of the condition.[772]

An important difference between incapacity due to mental incompetence and incapacity due to minority is that the mental incompetence defense requires a showing that the party actually did not understand the nature and consequences of the contract.[773] As with minors, though, a person deemed mentally incompetent is still liable for the fair market value of necessaries.[774]

One who is no longer deemed incompetent because of mental illness or other disability may ratify a contract by indicating assent to it.[775] In addition, if the person, upon regaining legal competence, is aware of the contract made while legally incompetent, and delays in disaffirming, this delay may constitute ratification.[776] This is not true if the person was under guardianship when the contract was made, as such a contract is totally void.[777]

9.5.7.4 Intoxication

Persons who make contracts when they are so intoxicated that they can not understand the nature and consequences of their act may be treated in the same manner as mentally disabled persons.[778] Disaffirmance and ratification would occur in the manner described at § 9.5.7.3, *supra*. Presumably, drug abusers will be treated similarly to intoxicated persons, and, in jurisdictions following the *Restatement* view, unreasonable contracts they make when incompetent by reason of drug use will be voidable.

9.5.8 Illegality in the Transaction

An illegal contract is generally void and unenforceable.[779]

762 Keser v. Chagnon, 159 Colo. 209, 410 P.2d 637 (1966). *See also* Gillis v. Whitley's Discount Auto Sales, Inc., 70 N.C. App. 270, 319 S.E.2d 661 (1984).

763 Restatement (Second) of Contracts, § 14 comment (c) (1981).

764 *Id.*

765 Webster Street P'ship, Ltd. v. Sheridan, 220 Neb. 9, 368 N.W.2d 439 (1985) (liability based not on contractual but upon quasi-contract theory); *see also* G. Calamari & J. Perillo, Contracts § 8-8 (5th ed. 2003).

766 Webster Street P'ship, Ltd. v. Sheridan, 220 Neb. 9, 368 N.W.2d 439 (1985).

767 Star Chevrolet Co. v. Green, 473 So. 2d 157 (Miss. 1985) (car usually not a necessary for a minor).

768 Rose v. Sheehan Buick, Inc., 204 So. 2d 903 (Fla. Dist. Ct. App. 1967).

769 D. Dobbs, Remedies § 13.4(3) (1993).

770 *Id. See, e.g.*, Young v. Lujan, 11 Ariz. App. 47, 461 P.2d 691 (1969); Davis v. Colorado Kenworth Corp., 156 Colo. 98, 396 P.2d 958 (1964); Sjulin v. Clifton Furniture Co., 241 Iowa 761, 41 N.W.2d 721 (1950); Lawson v. Bennett, 240 N.C. 52, 81 S.E.2d 162 (1954).

771 D. Dobbs, Remedies § 13.4(3) (1993); Sjulin v. Clifton Furniture Co., 241 Iowa 761, 41 N.W.2d 721 (1950).

772 Restatement (Second) of Contracts § 15 (1981).

773 *In re* Estate of Hendrickson, 248 Kan. 72, 805 P.2d 20 (1991) (courts will apply presumption in favor of mental capacity to contract and place burden of proof on those claiming incapacity to rebut that presumption); Restatement (Second) of Contracts § 15 (1981). *See also* 17A Am. Jur. 2d *Contracts* § 28 (2004) and 53 Am. Jur. 2d *Mentally Impaired* §§ 155–166 (1996).

774 Williston on Contracts § 10.7 (4th ed. 1990).

775 G. Calamari & J. Perillo, Contracts §§ 8.12, 8.4 (5th ed. 2003).

776 Williston on Contracts §§ 10.5, 10.12 (4th ed. 1990).

777 Restatement (Second) of Contracts § 13 (1981).

778 *Id.* § 16.

779 RCDI Constr., Inc. v. Spaceplan/Architecture, Planning, & Interiors, P.A., 148 F. Supp. 2d 607 (W.D.N.C. 2001), *aff'd*, 2002 WL 53927 (4th Cir. Jan. 15, 2002) (unpublished, citation limited); Dornberger v. Metropolitan Life Ins. Co., 961 F. Supp.

This section deals with contracts that were unlawful when made. If the contract was legal when made, but became illegal due to supervening events, its performance is considered impossible and this may be grounds to void the contract.[780] That situation is examined at § 9.5.13, *infra.*

One important example of a contract that is illegal when made is where a seller enters into a consumer contract without the proper licensing required by state law, particularly where the licensing statute was enacted for the protection of the public, not just to raise revenue.[781] Similarly, a contract may be unenforceable or void where the contracting corporation is not qualified to do business in the state.[782] Courts, however, may refuse relief based on illegality where the seller of goods or services has substantially complied with the licensing requirements, has caused no harm to the consumer, or poses no grave threat to the public.[783] Not only is an illegal contract unenforceable, but the consumer may be able to recover payments made.[784]

A contract can also be illegal if a consumer protection statute prohibits a contractual provision found in the contract. Thus a security agreement violating the FTC Credit Practices Rule is unlawful and unenforceable.[785] A contract that does not include language or terms required by state law, such as a three-day cooling-off period or a specific description of the work to be performed, may also be void.[786] The Wisconsin Supreme Court has held that a lease is unenforceable in its entirety if it includes a prohibited clause.[787] Merely severing the illegal clause and allowing the rest of the lease to be enforced would mean that a landlord would suffer no consequences for including the illegal clause yet would reap the benefits of its chilling effects. Connecticut's Home Improvement Act offers a remedy similar to rescission in that it precludes recovery by a contractor for breach of an oral contract. The Connecticut Supreme Court has ruled that a contractor who has not entered into a written contract with the consumer is also barred from recovery under a *quantum meruit* theory.[788]

A person who is responsible for an illegal contract should be denied restitution for any benefits already conferred upon the consumer under the contract.[789] Thus an unlicensed seller can not recover on its contracts or in a *quantum meruit* action.[790] Similarly, a seller violating a state consumer protection statute should not be able to recover in *quantum meruit*.[791]

---

506 (S.D.N.Y. 1997); Davis v. Pennzoil Co., 438 Pa. 194, 264 A.2d 597 (1970); Blick v. Marks, Stokes & Harrison, 234 Va. 60, 360 S.E.2d 345 (1987); Bowen Electric Co. v. Foley, 194 Va. 92, 72 S.E.2d 388 (1952); Letter from Virginia Attorney General Mary Terry to Judge J. R. Zepkin, Clearinghouse No. 44,810 (Feb. 24, 1989); Restatement (Second) of Contracts §§ 178, 179 (1981).

780 *See* 17A Am. Jur. 2d *Contracts* § 678 (2004).

781 *See, e.g.,* Dornberger v. Metropolitan Life Ins. Co., 961 F. Supp. 506 (S.D.N.Y. 1997); *In re* Anderson, 79 B.R. 482 (Bankr. S.D. Cal. 1987); Cevern, Inc. v. Ferbish, 666 A.2d 17 (D.C. App. 1995); Mincks Agri Center, Inc. v. Bell Farms, Inc., 611 N.W.2d 270 (Iowa 2000); Kowalski v. Cedars of Portsmouth Condominium Ass'n, 769 A.2d 344 (N.H. 2001); Scott v. Mayflower Home Improvement Corp., 363 N.J. Super. 145, 831 A.2d 564 (Law Div. 2001) (home improvement contract void where salesperson was unlicensed); Community Nat'l Bank & Trust Co. v. McClammy, 138 A.D.2d 339, 525 N.Y.S.2d 629 (1988); Columbus Checkcashiers v. Stiles, 565 N.E.2d 883 (Ohio App. 1990); Grenco v. Greene, 218 Va. 228, 237 S.E.2d 107 (1977); Colbert v. Ashland Constr. Co., 176 Va. 500, 11 S.E.2d 612 (1940). *But cf.* DeReggi Constr. Co. v. Mate, 130 Md. App. 648, 747 A.2d 743 (2000) (contract is enforceable where builder complied substantially with licensing law and did not knowingly ignore its requirements). *See also* National Consumer Law Center, The Cost of Credit: Regulation and Legal Challenges § 9.2.4.5.2 (2d ed. 2000 and Supp.) (consumer remedies when creditor lacks required license).

782 Brogdon v. Exterior Design, 781 F. Supp. 1396 (W.D. Ark. 1992); Green Tree Acceptance, Inc. v. Blalock, 525 So. 2d 1366 (Ala. 1988).

783 J. Calamari & J. Perillo, Contracts § 22-3 (5th ed. 2003). *But see* Cevern, Inc. v. Ferbish, 666 A.2d 17 (D.C. App. 1995) (contract unenforceable even though contractor obtained license shortly after beginning work). *Cf.* Dornberger v. Metropolitan Life Ins. Co., 961 F. Supp. 506 (S.D.N.Y. 1997).

784 Nadoff v. Club Central, 2003 WL 21537405 (N.Y. Dist. Ct. June 27, 2003) (payments may be recovered if contract is unenforceable on grounds of public policy and consumer is not equally culpable).

785 *In re* Raymond, 103 B.R. 846 (Bankr. W.D. Ky. 1989); Boyer v. ITT Fin. Servs. (*In re* Boyer), 63 B.R. 153 (Bankr. E.D. Mo. 1986). *See* §§ 5.1.1.2.7, 5.1.1.2.10, *supra.*

786 Letter from Virginia Attorney General Mary Terry to Judge J.R. Zepkin, Clearinghouse No. 44,810 (Feb. 24, 1989); Scott v. Mayflower Home Improvement Corp., 363 N.J. Super. 145, 831 A.2d 564 (Law Div. 2001) (home improvement contract void where salesperson unlicensed and contract did not state costs, finance charges, and specific description of work as required by state law). *See also* Donnelly v. Mustang Pools, Inc., 84 Misc. 2d 28, 374 N.Y.S.2d 967 (Sup. Ct. 1975); Brown v. Banks, Clearinghouse No. 27,065 (Ohio C.P. Cuyahoga Cty. 1976). *But see* Wowaka & Sons, Inc. v. Pardell, 242 A.D.2d 1, 672 N.Y.S.2d 358 (1998) (failure of home improvement contract to contain all the information required by statute does not render it unenforceable).

787 Baierl v. McTaggart, 629 N.W.2d 277 (Wis. 2001).

788 A. Secondino & Son, Inc. v. LoRicco, 215 Conn. 336, 576 A.2d 464 (1990).

789 Restatement of Restitution § 140 (1939). The Restatement (3d) of Restitution and Unjust Enrichment § 32 (discussion draft 2000) allows the person responsible for an illegal contract to obtain restitution if it is necessary to prevent unjust enrichment and will not defeat or frustrate the policy of the underlying prohibition.

790 *See, e.g., In re* Anderson, 79 B.R. 482 (Bankr. S.D. Cal. 1987); Community Nat'l Bank & Trust Co. v. McClammy, 138 A.D.2d 339, 525 N.Y.S.2d 629 (1988); Grenco v. Greene, 218 Va. 228, 237 S.E.2d 107 (1977); Colbert v. Ashland Constr. Co., 176 Va. 500, 11 S.E.2d 612 (1940).

791 Letter from Virginia Attorney General Mary Terry to Judge J.R. Zepkin, Clearinghouse No. 44,810 (Feb. 24, 1989); *see also* Donnelly v. Mustang Pools, Inc., 84 Misc. 2d 28, 374 N.Y.S.2d 967 (Sup. Ct. 1975); Brown v. Banks, Clearinghouse No. 27,065 (Ohio C.P. Cuyahoga Cty. 1976).

9.5.9 Misrepresentation or Fraud

9.5.9.1 General

Fraud is probably the most common ground for canceling a contract.[792] Contracts induced by fraud entitle the defrauded party to rescind the transaction, even though the contract has been executed.[793] The defrauded party is also entitled to be restored to the position he or she was in before the contract was made.[794] Fraud is discussed in more detail in another NCLC manual.[795]

While only a minority of courts do away with the intent requirement where the consumer brings a deceit action for damages, it is much more common to allow the consumer to rescind a contract even if no intent by the other party to defraud is proved. Mere misrepresentation may be grounds for rescission. If A misrepresents a material fact to B in the course of negotiation and B accepts the statement as true and acts on it, then B is entitled to a remedy.[796] If A's representation was intended to be false, B has an action for damages on a deceit theory or one for rescission for the fraud. Even an innocent misstatement, however, may be grounds for rescission.[797]

To be effective as a contract defense, misrepresentation must be either fraudulent or material. It can not relate to a minor point unless there is also fraud, that is, unless there is an intent that the consumer rely on the statement and the maker either knows or believes the assertion is not true.[798] A misrepresentation is material if a reasonable person would act on it or if the maker knows the particular consumer involved will act on it.[799]

9.5.9.2 Actionable Misrepresentations

The *Restatement (Second) of Contracts* defines a misrepresentation as "an assertion that is not in accord with the facts."[800] A statement need not be fraudulent to be a misrepresentation. A simple typing error which changes a number is a misrepresentation. Nor is there any requirement that the misrepresentation be made in any particular form. A seller who, seeking to induce a buyer to buy a used car, turns back the odometer makes a misrepresentation to the same extent that a used car salesman mistakenly says that a car has had only one owner when it has had two. A misrepresentation does not have to be oral; it can be in the form of active concealment or simply, in some cases, nondisclosure.[801] Half-truths, i.e., statements that are literally true but fail to include qualifying matter necessary to prevent a false implication with respect to other facts, are also misrepresentations.[802]

The assertion must relate to a fact which was in existence at the time the contract was made. Future events can not be

792 *See* National Consumer Law Center, Automobile Fraud Ch. 7 (2d ed. 2003 and Supp.) and National Consumer Law Center, Consumer Warranty Law Ch. 11 (2d ed. 2001 and Supp.) for a fuller discussion of the law of fraud.

793 D. Dobbs, Remedies §§ 9.1, 9.2 (1993).

794 *Id.*

795 National Consumer Law Center, Automobile Fraud Ch. 7 (2d ed. 2003 and Supp.).

796 *Id.* §§ 9.1, 9.2. *See also* Coronado Products, Inc. v. Stewart, 1988 Tenn. App. LEXIS 672, Clearinghouse No. 45,905 (Tenn. Ct. App. Nov. 2, 1988) (contract misrepresented as estimate and approval of credit check is rescinded).

797 A little fewer than half of the states recognize responsibility in tort without fault for false statements made to induce a transaction. *See, e.g.*, Schwartz v. Electronic Data Sys., Inc., 913 F.2d 279 (6th Cir. 1990) (Michigan law); Stein v. Treger, 182 F.2d 696 (D.C. Cir. 1950); Logan Equip. Corp. v. Simon Aerials, Inc., 736 F. Supp. 1188 (D. Mass. 1990); Associated Bus. Tel. Sys. Corp. v. Greater Capital Corp., 729 F. Supp. 1488 (D.N.J. 1990) (Ill. law), *aff'd without op.*, 919 F.2d 133 (3d Cir. 1990); Resolution Trust Corp. v. Mooney, 592 So. 2d 186 (Ala. 1991); Smith v. Reynolds Metals Co., 497 So. 2d 93 (Ala. 1986); Bevins v. Ballard, 655 P.2d 757 (Alaska 1982); Hale v. George A. Hormel Co., 121 Cal. Rptr. 144 (Ct. App. 1975); Richard v. A. Waldman & Sons, Inc., 155 Conn. 343, 232 A.2d 307 (1967); Norton v. Poplos, 443 A.2d 1 (Del. 1982); Pusker v. Hughes, 179 Ill. App. 3d 522, 533 N.E.2d 962 (1989); Clarke Auto Co. v. Reynolds, 119 Ind. App. 586, 88 N.E.2d 775 (1949); Roome v. Sonora Petroleum Co., 111 Kan. 633, 208 P. 255 (1922); Zimmerman v. Kent, 575 N.E.2d 70 (Mass. App. Ct. 1991); Mitchell v. Dahlberg, 547 N.W.2d 74 (Mich. Ct. App. 1996); Osborn v. Will, 183 Minn. 205, 236 N.W. 197 (1931); Osterman v. Sears, Roebuck & Co., 80 P.3d 435 (Mont. 2003) (recognizing tort of negligent misrepresentation); Paul v. Cameron, 127 Neb. 510, 256 N.W. 11 (1934); Liebling v. Garden State Indem., 337 N.J. Super. 447, 767 A.2d 515 (App. Div. 2001); Wolf & Klar Cos. v. Garner, 101 N.M. 116, 679 P.2d 258 (1984); Archuleta v. Kopp, 90 N.M. 273, 562 P.2d 834 (1977); Bloomquist v. Farson, 222 N.Y. 375, 118 N.E. 855 (1918); Albany Motor Inn & Restaurant, Inc. v. Watkins, 85 A.D.2d 797, 445 N.Y.S.2d 616 (1981); Bourgois v. Montana-Dakota Utils. Co., 466 N.W.2d 813 (N.D. 1991); Doyle v. Fairfield Mach. Co., 697 N.E.2d 667 (Ohio Ct. App. 1997); Lesher v. Strid, 165 Or. App. 34, 996 P.2d 988 (2000); Sullivan v. Allegheny Ford Truck Sales, Inc., 283 Pa. Super. 351, 423 A.2d 1292 (1980); Estate of Braswell v. People's Credit Union, 602 A.2d 510 (R.I. 1992); Cannon v. Chadwell, 25 Tenn. App. 42, 150 S.W.2d 710 (1940); Wilson v. Jones, 45 S.W.2d 572 (Tex. Comm. App. 1932); Trust Co. of Norfolk v. Fletcher, 152 Va. 868, 148 S.E. 785 (1929); Pratt v. Thompson, 133 Wash. 218, 233 P. 637 (1925); Lengyel v. Lint, 280 S.E.2d 66 (W. Va. 1981); Whipp v. Iverson, 43 Wis. 2d 166, 168 N.E.2d 201 (1969); D. Dobbs, Remedies §§ 9.1, 9.2 (1993).

States that have not recognized responsibility in tort without fault or false statements, or that have not resolved the issue are: Arizona, Arkansas, Colorado, Delaware, Florida, Georgia, Hawaii, Idaho, Illinois, Iowa, Kentucky, Louisiana, Maine, Maryland, Mississippi, Nevada, New Hampshire, New York, North Carolina, Oklahoma, South Carolina, South Dakota, Tennessee, Utah, Vermont and Wyoming.

798 Restatement (Second) of Contracts § 162 (1981).

799 *Id.*

800 Restatement (Second) of Contracts § 159 (1981).

801 *Id.* §§ 160, 161.

802 Restatement (Second) of Contracts § 159, Comment b.

the subject of a misrepresentation. On the other hand, factual statements about a product's capacity to do something in the future can be misrepresentations, either because the assertion concerns the product's present characteristics or because it involves assertions known at the time they were said to be false.

Many states recognize a cause of action for promissory fraud, which is simply ordinary fraud where the fact that is misrepresented is the promisor's present intent to fulfill the promise.[803] However, since an erroneous forecast that a future event will occur is not actionable, it is essential that the plaintiff put forth evidence that at the time of the promise the promisor had no intention to perform the agreement or meet its obligations.[804] While mere evidence that the promisor later breached a contract will not suffice to prove this element,[805] circumstantial evidence of the promisor's failure to act in good faith to perform its obligations, such as similar treatment of other customers, can uphold a finding of promissory fraud.[806] The intent element can also be satisfied with evidence that the promisor knew, at the time the promise was made, that it would not be able to fulfill the promise or had made other arrangements inconsistent with fulfilling the promise.[807]

Concealing a fact from a buyer is a misrepresentation. According to the *Restatement*, concealment is an affirmative act intended or known to be likely to keep another person from learning a fact which he or she would otherwise have learned.[808] Nondisclosure of a fact is a misrepresentation in four types of cases:

- Where disclosure is necessary to prevent a previous assertion from being a misrepresentation;
- Where disclosure would correct a mistake of the other party as to a basic assumption on which the party is making the contract, and non-disclosure amounts to a failure to act in good faith and in accordance with reasonable standards of fair dealing;
- Where the person knows that disclosure of the fact would correct a mistake as to the effect or contents of a written contract; or
- Where there is a relation of trust and confidence between the two parties involved.[809]

Nondisclosure as misrepresentation arises frequently in residential real estate cases, where the seller neglects to mention something like termite infestation, which has a substantial effect on the value of the property.[810]

803 *See, e.g.*, Chedick v. Nash, 151 F.3d 1077 (D.C. Cir. 1998); Desnick v. American Broadcasting Cos., 44 F.3d 1345, 1354 (7th Cir. 1995) (under Illinois law, plaintiff must additionally show that the alleged promissory fraud was part of a "scheme" to defraud); Intercorp, Inc. v. Pennzoil Co., 877 F.2d 1524 (11th Cir. 1989) (Alabama law; citing Ala. Code § 65-104); Blanton v. Mobil Oil Corp., 721 F.2d 1207 (9th Cir. 1983) (Washington law), *cert. denied*, 471 U.S. 1120 (1985); Salstein v. HA-Lo Indus., Inc., 82 F. Supp. 2d 1080, 1085 (N.D. Cal. 1999); Hayes v. Northwood Panelboard Co., 415 N.W.2d 687, 690 (Minn. Ct. App. 1987); Graubard Mollen Dannett & Horowitz v. Moskovitz, 86 N.Y.2d 112, 629 N.Y.S.2d 1009, 653 N.E.2d 1179, 1184 (1995); Steed Realty, Inc. v. Oveisi, 823 S.W.2d 195 (Tenn. Ct. App. 1991). *Cf.* Chicago Messenger Serv., Inc. v. Nextel Communications, Inc., 2003 WL 22225619 (N.D. Ill. Sept. 24, 2003) (discussing ambiguities in Illinois rule).

804 Chedick v. Nash, 151 F.3d 1077, 1081, 82 (1998) (upholding verdict against lender on evidence that lender had repeatedly miscalculated the borrower's monthly obligation, that it forced her into default by capitalizing costs that should have been assessed as separate fees, that its conduct was consistent with how it had treated other customers, and that it significantly overestimated the amount required to pay off the mortgage).

805 *See, e.g.*, Sanders v. First Nat'l Bank & Trust Co., 936 F.2d 273 (6th Cir. 1991) (plaintiff's mere subjective suspicion that bank did not intend to fulfill contractual obligation insufficient to establish promissory fraud); Jabour v. Aetna U.S. Healthcare, Inc., 2000 U.S. Dist. LEXIS 3683, at *26 (M.D. Ala. Feb. 15, 2000); Francis v. Bankcard America, Inc., 2000 U.S. Dist. LEXIS 40, at *25 (N.D. Ill. Jan. 3, 2000).

806 Chedick v. Nash, 151 F.3d at 1082; Heineman v. S&S Machinery Corp., 750 F. Supp. 1179 (E.D.N.Y. 1990) (evidence of defendant's subsequent actions may show intent not to perform promise); *Ex parte* Grand Manor, Inc., 778 So. 2d 173, 183 (Ala. 2000) (circumstantial evidence supported inference that seller of mobile home who promised to make repairs had no intention of completing the repairs); Steed Realty, Inc. v. Oveisi, 823 S.W.2d 195, 200 (Tenn. Ct. App. 1991) (property seller's repeated promises to make improvements, along with failure to provide reasons for not keeping promise and evidence that seller had means to fulfill promise supported action for promissory fraud).

807 International Travel Arrangers v. NWA, Inc., 991 F.2d 1389, 1402 (8th Cir. 1993); Palm Harbor Homes, Inc. v. Crawford, 689 So. 2d 3, 9 (Ala. 1997) (that seller of mobile home was not licensed to set it up for buyer supported verdict of promissory fraud based on seller's promise to do so), *cert. denied*, 510 U.S. 932 (1993).

808 *Id.* § 160. *See also* Greene v. Gibraltar Mortgage Investment Corp., 488 F. Supp. 177 (D.D.C. 1980). Two common examples of concealment, as distinguished from nondisclosure, are "half-truth" representations and affirmative concealment. A half truth is a partial disclosure, that, although literally true, creates a false impression, such as a claim that a car is new when it is actually incurred substantial mileage through demonstration use. *See, e.g.*, Wolfe v. Chrysler Corp., 734 F.2d 701 (11th Cir. 1984) (Georgia law). Affirmative concealment is a positive act by a seller to hide the truth, through either words, or conduct, such as turning back the odometer of a used car offered for sale. *See, e.g.*, Crown Ford, Inc. v. Crawford, 221 Ga. App. 881, 473 S.E.2d 554 (1996) (defendant replaced odometer and did not reflect old mileage on odometer statement).

809 Restatement (Second) of Contracts § 161 (1981). *See also* Bodiford v. Nabors, 2002 Tenn. App. LEXIS 35 (Jan. 15, 2002) (seller has duty to disclose basic, material information about the product if the seller knows that the buyer is about to act without knowledge of the information and is without reasonable means to acquire the information).

810 *See, e.g.*, Hill v. Jones, 151 Ariz. 81, 725 P.2d 1115 (1986); Lanier Home Ctr., Inc. v. Underwood, 252 Ga. App. 745, 557 S.E.2d 76 (2001) (misrepresentation as to septic system could give rise to claim for "passive concealment"); *see also* National Consumer Law Center, Consumer Warranty Law § 11.4.4 (2d ed. 2001 and Supp.).

9.5.9.3 Reliance

To successfully raise a contract defense of misrepresentation, the consumer must show either fraudulent intent or that the misrepresentation substantially contributed to the consumer's decision to enter the contract.[811] In such a case, the contract is voidable.[812] The misrepresentation does not have to be the only or even the predominant factor in influencing the consumer; it need only be a substantial factor.[813]

The consumer must also have justifiably relied on the misrepresentation.[814] Whether reliance is reasonable is usually a factual issue. Issues of reliance are most troubling regarding reliance on opinion, matters of law, and stated intentions.

A representation is an opinion if it is a statement of belief, without certainty, or a judgment as to quality, value, authenticity, or similar matters.[815] If a seller gives an opinion to a consumer, the consumer is justified in assuming that the seller knows no facts inconsistent with the opinion and that the seller has some basis for making the statement.[816] A seller's "puffing," on the other hand, is not a representation on which a consumer can reasonably rely.[817] A statement is puffing if it is imprecise or vague.[818] A specific representation about the performances of a product can not be considered "puffing."[819] The fundamental test is whether the seller states a fact of which the buyer is ignorant, or merely gives an opinion on a matter as to which the seller and the buyer have good knowledge. The fact is actionable, but the opinion may be puffery.[820]

Consumers can not rely on simple opinions unless the consumer is in a position of trust and confidence with the speaker, reasonably believes that the speaker has some special knowledge of the subject matter,[821] or has some other special reason for being particularly susceptible to the opinion involved.[822] The *Restatement* gives the following example as a situation in which the consumer *is* entitled to rely on what appears to be merely slight flattery:

> A, the proprietor of a dance studio, seeking to induce B, a 60-year-old widow with no background in dancing, to make a contract for dance lessons, tells B that she has "dance potential" and would develop into a "beautiful dancer." A knows that B has little aptitude as a dancer. B is induced by A's statement of opinion to make the proposed contract.[823]

Under the *Restatement* the same rules apply regarding misrepresentations of the law and of facts with regard to whether the consumer is justified in relying on a statement. For example, if a car salesman told a buyer that a certain expensive add-on was required by law in that state, knowing that his statement was false, the contract would be voidable by the consumer if the consumer justifiably relied on the statement.

Usually, a consumer is not entitled to rely on a seller's stated intention of doing something in the future. To defend on such a basis, the consumer would have to show that the seller, at the time of making the statement, had no plan to do what he said he would do, and said it only to cause the consumer to enter into the contract.[824]

9.5.9.4 Misrepresentation of the Nature of the Contract Document

The preceding sections describe circumstances in which a contract is voidable. In some cases there is simply no contract. If the misrepresentation is such that the contract the consumer believes he is assenting to and the contract he is in fact assenting to are not the same contract, there really is no assent, and a contract is not formed.[825] For example, suppose a consumer hires a workman to do home repair work, and the workman presents a contract for the consumer to read, then without the consumer's knowledge substitutes a different contract for signing. The consumer has not assented to the different contract he signed, so no contract was formed. In the same setting, if the consumer's eyesight is impaired and he asks the workman to read the contract to him, there is no contract if the workman reads the contract

---

811 Restatement (Second) of Contracts §§ 162, 164, 167 (1981).

812 *Id.* § 164.

813 *Id.* § 167.

814 *Id.* § 164.

815 *Id.* § 168(a).

816 *Id.*

817 Helena Chemical Co. v. Wilkins, 18 S.W.3d 744 (Tex. App. 2000), *aff'd*, 47 S.W.3d 486 (Tex. 2001). *See, e.g.*, Nigh v. Koons Buick Pontiac GMC, Inc., 143 F. Supp. 2d 535 (E.D. Va. 2001) (salesman who, when asked by truck buyer about the vehicle's accident history, responded that "[i]t doesn't look like it's been in any accident to me" had merely expressed an opinion, not represented a fact), *aff'd on other grounds*, 319 F.3d 119 (4th Cir. 2003), *cert. granted on other issues*, 124 S. Ct. 1144 (2004).

818 Helena Chemical Co. v. Wilkins, 47 S.W.3d 486 (Tex. 2001).

819 *Id.*

820 Restatement (Second) of Contracts § 168 (1981). *See also* § 4.2.10, *supra* (puffery in UDAP cases).

821 *See, e.g.*, Bareham & McFarland v. Kane, 228 App. Div. 396, 240 N.Y.S. 123 (1930) (representation that oil burner was capable of heating residence to 70°F in zero degree weather at a specified cost per season is statement of quality by a person of superior knowledge, not a prediction). *See also* Porreco v. Porreco, 811 A.2d 566, 572 (Pa. 2002) (woman's reliance on fiancé's representation that engagement ring's stone was a diamond was not justifiable, unreasonable for her to fail to independently investigate ring's value; case remanded for determination of whether a confidential relationship existed between the parties).

822 Restatement (Second) of Contracts § 169 (1981).

823 *Id.* at comment d.

824 *See* § 9.5.9.2, *supra.*

825 Restatement (Second) of Contracts § 163 (1981).

incorrectly. The same may be the case if key terms are buried in fine print legalese.[826]

9.5.9.5 Nature of the Cancellation Remedy

A consumer who has been the victim of a fraudulent or material misrepresentation may seek to avoid the contract and obtain restitution of the value conferred upon the seller.[827] In most jurisdictions, the party seeking avoidance and restitution must offer to return that which he received under the contract.[828] The consumer's offer may be conditioned upon the seller's return of consideration.[829] In some jurisdictions, failure to tender before filing suit will result in dismissal of the suit.[830] Upon discovering a fraudulent or material misrepresentation, the aggrieved party must act with reasonable promptness to avoid the contract, or he will be held to have ratified the contract.[831] In many jurisdictions, punitive damages are available even when the consumer wins cancellation of the contract.[832]

Though the general rule is that rescission will not be ordered where a party can not be returned to the *status quo*, that rule will not always be strictly enforced. Where, for example, the party resisting rescission is a wrongdoer who is exploiting its change of position, courts may allow rescission despite the inability to place the parties where they were.[833]

9.5.10 Mistake

9.5.10.1 When Is a Mistake Sufficient to Cancel the Contract?

Equity will rescind a contract for a simple mistake concerning facts or the law, if it is substantial and serious. (When a mistake involves only minor terms, courts generally will conclude that a contract was formed and enforce the contract.) Where parties enter into an agreement under a misunderstanding, or under certain serious and mistaken assumptions of fact, courts may either rescind the contract or declare that, due to the mistake, there was never any contract formed at all.[834]

Thus, where the contract is ambiguous and the consumer understands the contract to mean something different than what the seller understands concerning a term central to the deal, the contract may be rescinded. Where a consumer does not read the contract for justifiable reasons, such as where the consumer can not read English and has asked the seller for assistance or where the seller pressures the consumer not to read the contract, there may be a rescindable contract if the consumer is mistaken as to its terms.

Nevertheless, some courts distinguish between mistakes that are unilateral, that is, made by one person, and those that are mutual, that is, made by both parties, and allow relief in the form of rescission or reformation only for mutual mistakes.[835] Other courts may emphasize the relative sophistication of the parties, which party drafted the contract, or other factors. The different evaluation of mistakes among different courts—and even in different cases in the same court—suggests that in any case where consumer attorneys see a possible mistake defense, they should not hesitate to use it, even if strict application of textbook definitions would not result in a finding of mistake.

Some mistakes arise because an offer is ambiguous and the buyer and seller have different subjective interpretations of the ambiguous term. For example, a mobile home seller

---

826 *See* Marine Bank Nat'l Ass'n v. Meat Counter, Inc., 826 F.2d 1577 (7th Cir. 1987) (remanding for trial on question whether man who had not read a contract he signed was bound by it where other party misrepresented terms hidden in fine print legalese).

827 Restatement (Second) of Contracts § 376 (1981). *See, e.g.*, Bodiford v. Nabors, 2002 Tenn. App. LEXIS 35 (Jan. 15, 2002).

828 J. Calamari & J. Perillo, Contracts § 9-23 (5th ed. 2003). *See also* Weed Wizard Acquisition Corp. v. A.A.B.B., Inc., 201 F. Supp. 2d 1252, 1259 (N.D. Ga. 2002) (plaintiff's delay in seeking rescission deemed to have affirmed the contract, precluding rescission); Riley v. Hoisington, 96 S.W.3d 743 (Ark. Ct. App. 2003) (home buyers could rescind sales contract notwithstanding that they had made some changes to the house; house remained substantially same structure).

829 *Id.*; *see also* Karapetian v. Carolan, 83 Cal. App. 2d 344, 188 P.2d 809 (1948).

830 J. Calamari & J. Perillo, Contracts § 9-23 (5th ed. 2003) *See also* A.L. Williams Corp. v. Faircloth, 652 F. Supp. 51 (N.D. Ga. 1986); Cutler v. Sugarman Organization, Ltd., 88 Md. App. 567, 596 A.2d 105 (1991).

831 *Id. See, e.g.*, Merritt v. Craig, 130 Md. App. 350, 746 A.2d 923 (2000).

832 Smith v. Walt Bennett Ford, Inc., 864 S.W.2d 817 (Ark. 1993) (odometer rollback case; defrauded party may recover punitive damages in addition to either affirmance or disaffirmance remedies); Bickerstaff Automotive, Inc. v. Tsepas, 574 S.E.2d 322 (Ga. Ct. App. 2002) (affirming rescission of lease of car that had been represented as new though it had been previously wrecked, and affirming $53,000 punitive damages award); Golconda Screw, Inc. v. West Bottoms, Ltd., 20 Kan. App. 2d 1002, 894 P.2d 260 (1995) (punitive damages may be awarded in action to set aside conveyance due to fraud); Seaton v. Lawson Chevrolet-Mazda, Inc., 821 S.W.2d 137 (Tenn. 1991) (concealed wreck case; plaintiff may recover punitive damages where rescission is based on fraud).

833 *See, e.g.*, Bland v. Freightliner L.L.C., 206 F. Supp. 2d 1202, 1208, 1209 (M.D. Fla. 2002) (rescission may be ordered even though parties can not be returned to their *status quo*, if the balance of equities justifies it); Weed Wizard Acquisition Corp. v. A.A.B.B., Inc., 201 F. Supp. 2d 1252, 1259 (N.D. Ga. 2002); Sokolow, Dunaud, Mercadier & Carreras L.L.P. v. Lacher, 747 N.Y.S.2d 441, 447 (N.Y. App. Div. 2002).

834 D. Dobbs, Remedies §§ 11.3, 11.4 (1993). *See* Nelson v. Cowles Ford, Inc., 2003 U.S. App. LEXIS 20371 (4th Cir. Oct. 7, 2003) (unpublished, citation limited) (mutual mistake allows injured party to void the contract).

835 *But see* Donovan v. RRL Corp., 26 Cal. 4th 261, 27 P.3d 702 (2001) (rescission can be based on unilateral mistake of fact even when other party is unaware of mistake and did not cause it).

may show a buyer two mobile homes, Explorer I and Explorer II, which are made by the same manufacturer and are very similar in size and quality, except that Explorer I is more luxurious. If the buyer, intending to buy Explorer II, and the seller, intending to sell Explorer I, sign a contract for the purchase of "the Explorer," there is no contract because the parties are in subjective disagreement as to the meaning of the term "Explorer" and neither knew or had reason to know that they were in disagreement.[836] There is no mutual assent and neither party is at fault. If, by "Explorer," both parties had meant Explorer I, the fact that "Explorer" is ambiguous would not matter; the contract would be enforceable as the sale of an Explorer I.

If one party knows or should know that the other party has a different understanding as to the meaning of the term, a contract will be formed on the term as understood by the other, unknowing, party.[837] The first party knew what was happening, did not object, and can not later complain. The same rule applies if one party should, but does not actually, know of the ambiguity.[838]

Sometimes the buyer will inadvertently sign a writing which does not accurately state the agreement because the buyer does not understand it or has not read it. For example, the buyer signs a contract for an Explorer I, thinking it is a contract to buy an Explorer II. Whether the buyer can claim there was no contract because there was no mutual assent or can void the contract for mistake depends in part on whether the buyer was negligent or whether the seller misrepresented the contents of the writing.

If the buyer's failure to ascertain the contents of the offer is due solely to negligence, including lack of education if the buyer fails to ask for assistance, some courts hold the buyer bound by the terms of the contract as stated. Other courts say that ordinary negligence is not a bar to relief, but gross negligence is. If the buyer fails to understand the contents of the writing because the seller misrepresented the contents and the buyer relied on the misrepresentation, the modern cases[839] and the *Restatement (Second) of Contracts*[840] state that there is a contract on the terms understood by the innocent party. When the circumstances suggest the possibility that the buyer is mistaken, such as when the buyer does not read English and the contract is in English, or when the seller pressures the buyer into signing the contract without reading it, the court should allow the buyer to avoid the contract.[841]

An unexpected or oppressive provision in a standard form contract may be unenforceable for lack of assent. The *Restatement* indicates that a provision in a form that a party uses regularly in its dealings with others is invalid if it should reasonably know that the other contracting party would not agree to the contract if the provision were known.[842] This invalidity may arise because the provision is not commercially reasonable as well as because it is unexpected.[843] This standard is similar to that for unconscionability under the Uniform Commercial Code (UCC).

A different kind of mistake occurs when both parties make the same incorrect assumption at the time the contract is formed. For instance, the parties might both be mistaken about the value of the subject matter of the contract, its existence, or its identity.[844] The seller and buyer may agree to the sale of a 2004 car which they both think is a 2004 model and describe as a 2003 model in the contract. In this case, the contract is sometimes voidable at the option of the party harmed because things were not as they seemed. In the sale of the 2004 car, the seller, who sold the car for less than he otherwise would have, is the party harmed.

9.5.10.2 Who Incurs the Costs of Cancellation

When a court concludes that there was a mistake that justifies rescission, it must then determine who incurs the costs of the mistake. One approach is to let the losses remain with the party incurring them, because rescission can leave the parties as the court finds them. A second approach is to award restitution, making the party at fault suffer the loss. If neither party is at fault, the court can order the parties to split the loss, thus putting them as much as possible in a position they would have been in had the transaction never taken place.

In a consumer situation, a court may be more inclined to let the seller bear the cost on the theory that the seller, being a merchant, is held to a higher standard of behavior and is more at fault when a misunderstanding occurs. A court may also let the seller bear the cost on an insurance theory, that

836 *See* Restatement (Second) of Contracts § 20(1)(a) (1981). *See also* Konic Int'l Corp. v. Spokane Computer Servs., Inc., 109 Idaho 527, 708 P.2d 932 (1985) (seller quoted fifty-six twenty as price; no contract where seller meant $5620 and buyer heard $56.20).

837 A. Corbin, Contracts § 28.29 (2002). *See also* Exxon Corp. v. Bell, 695 S.W.2d 788 (Tex. 1985) (where seller knew buyer's interpretation of "waterwell" included pump, contract made on buyer's terms).

838 A. Corbin, Contracts § 28.41 (2002).

839 Quillen v. Twin City Bank, 253 Ark. 169, 485 S.W.2d 181 (1972) (substantial issue whether defendants were induced to sign guaranty without reading it because of fraudulent assurance that guaranty contract related only to original note and not to later advances; summary judgment precluded); Toker v. Perl, 103 N.J. Super. 500, 247 A.2d 701 (Law Div. 1968), *aff'd*, 108 N.J. Super. 129, 260 A.2d 244 (App. Div. 1970) (buyers signed contract for sale of freezer after being led to believe that freezer was included in food plan contract; contract unenforceable because procured by fraud).

840 Restatement (Second) of Contracts § 20 (1981).

841 *See* A. Corbin, Contracts § 28.38 (2002).

842 Restatement (Second) of Contracts § 211 (1981).

843 C. & J. Fertilizer, Inc. v. Allied Mut. Ins. Co., 227 N.W.2d 169 (Iowa 1975).

844 The mistake must involve facts as they existed when the contract was made, not future expectations or opinions. Opsahl v. Pinehurst, Inc., 81 N.C. App. 56, 344 S.E.2d 68 (1986).

is, when no one is at fault the cost should be borne by all. This is achieved by placing the loss on the seller because it is the only party with the ability to distribute the loss among all buyers in the form of higher sales prices.

9.5.10.3 Burden of Proof

Most of the time, a consumer asserting the defense of mistake will be attempting to rescind or reform a written agreement. Parties attempting to overcome written agreements on the basis of mistake or other equitable grounds generally must prove such conduct by clear and convincing evidence.[845] Courts differ in their definitions of clear and convincing, but most construe it to be a significantly greater evidentiary burden than that of a preponderance of the evidence.[846]

9.5.11 Restitution

Courts at law imported certain equitable principles into legal actions and gave them a slight twist. For example, there is an action in many states for restitution at law, allowing the consumer to recover for unjust enrichment. That is, the consumer returns what the consumer received and gets back what the consumer had paid. To establish restitution, it may be sufficient to show an honest misrepresentation or a mere mistake, but the consumer may waive this cause of action by conduct affirming the transaction or by nonaction for an unreasonable length of time after discovering the facts.[847] Restitution is discussed in more detail in § 9.6A, *infra*.

9.5.12 Duress, Coercion, Oppression, and Undue Influence

9.5.12.1 Introduction

Duress, coercion, oppression, and undue influence are grounds for rescinding a contract. An essential element in the formation of a contract is the parties' exercise of free will.[848] If one party overpowers the will of another, the contract is not binding on the second party. The force can be physical or psychological.

9.5.12.2 Duress, Coercion, Oppression

Duress involves the use of improper threats or economic pressure to coerce a person to enter a contract.[849] The coercion involved in duress must involve a wrongful act, although it does not have to be unlawful or even tortious.[850] It is difficult to define the kind of coercive conduct that is sufficiently improper as to constitute duress. Duress includes not only threats of physical violence, but also economic or even emotional pressure. The threat to institute legal proceedings, even if based on a colorable claim, can constitute duress if made with the intent to force a party to enter into a transaction not related to the legal proceedings.[851]

Duress may occur, for example, in the making of a contract to repair. A consumer may take his car to a mechanic for repairs at an agreed price. When the consumer returns to pick up the car, however, the mechanic states that the cost of repairs is much higher and the car will not be released until the higher price is paid. Duress exists because the mechanic wrongfully holds the property of the consumer to force payment of a price higher than the contract price.[852] Duress could also exist if a consumer were required to sign a release before being allowed to retrieve goods or an automobile after repairs.[853] Similarly, there is duress when a seller requires the buyer to purchase additional goods or services before the seller will perform repairs on the purchased goods. Oppression and coercion are similar to duress.

9.5.12.3 Undue Influence

Undue influence occurs where the wrongdoer misuses his or her position of trust and confidence to gain personal

845 *See* A. Corbin, § 28.47 (2002.).

846 *See id.* for several descriptions of the clear and convincing evidentiary standard. *See also* McCormick on Evidence, § 340(b) (2d ed. 1972) where clear and convincing proof is described as that which makes the truth of the contention "highly probable."

847 D. Dobbs, The Law of Torts § 483, p. 1382 (2000).

848 *See* G. Calamari & J. Perillo, Contracts § 9-2 (5th ed. 2003). *See also* 17A Am. Jur. 2d *Contracts* §§ 218–221 (2004).

849 D. Dobbs, Remedies § 10.2(1) (1993). *See also* National Consumer Law Center, Fair Debt Collection § 14.3 (4th ed. 2000 and Supp.) (duress in hospital contracts).

850 Restatement (Second) of Contracts § 176 (1981) ("wrongful" act or threat).

851 Link v. Link, 278 N.C. 181, 179 S.E.2d 697 (1971) (jury question whether assignment of securities to husband by wife upon husband's threat of child custody suit constituted duress); Germantown Mfg. Co. v. Rawlinson, 341 Pa. Super. 42, 491 A.2d 138 (1985) (insurer threatened woman with criminal action if she did not sign confessions of judgment); Warner v. Warner, 394 S.E.2d 74 (W. Va. 1990) (threat to prosecute criminal claim, irrespective of individual's guilt or innocence constitutes duress). *See also* National Consumer Law Center, Fair Debt Collection Ch. 14 (5th ed. 2004) (duress by hospital). *But see* Texas Com. Bank v. United Sav. Ass'n, 789 F. Supp. 848 (S.D. Tex. 1992) (threat that unless senior managers signed releases they would never work in savings and loan industry again was not duress).

852 G. Calamari & J. Perillo, Contracts § 9-5 (5th ed. 2003).

853 *Cf.* Hall v. Ochs, 623 F. Supp. 367 (D. Mass. 1987) (waiver signed under duress invalid), *aff'd in relevant part, rev'd in part on other grounds*, 817 F.2d 920 (1st Cir. 1987); International Paper Co. v. Whilden, 469 So. 2d 560 (Ala. 1985) (commercial parties; requiring signing of release for faulty work constituted economic duress).

advantage.[854] Undue influence exists when one party is so influential that the other person is unable to exercise independent judgment.[855] For example, if an elderly woman who can not read or write trusts her daughter to handle her affairs and the daughter has the mother sign over a deed to the family homestead to the daughter, then the mother can avoid the transaction because of the daughter's undue influence.[856]

Similarly, a woman was induced by a bank officer, who was a longtime family friend, to sign a mortgage and note on the home she shared with her hospitalized husband.[857] The note and mortgage were intended to guarantee the husband's defaulted business debts. Given the circumstances, the court found that the bank officer's actions constituted undue influence, especially because he did not tell the woman that the mortgage would destroy her judgment-proof status.

9.5.12.4 Mechanics of Cancellation

A contract entered into as a result of duress, coercion, oppression, or undue influence is voidable by the victim of the coercion.[858] To avoid the contract, the coerced party must elect to rescind and communicate that election to the other party.

A contract entered into under duress may be ratified by accepting the benefits of the contract, by remaining silent, or by acquiescing in the contract for too long after the coercion is removed.[859] Retention and use of the goods for a substantial time will usually constitute acquiescence and thus ratification.

9.5.13 Impossibility of Performance, Impracticability, and Frustration of Purpose

If performance of a contract becomes impossible or impracticable, then performance may be excused, unless the parties, in the contract, have specifically allocated this risk. For example, a contract might indicate that a sale of a ski ticket is final whether or not there is snow, thus allocating the risk to the consumer.

A contract may be impossible for any number of reasons, including a change in the law or an intervening calamity.[860] During the performance of a contract, events may occur which were unexpected by either of the parties at the time of contracting, and which affect the feasibility, or even the possibility, of performing the contract. A contract to repair a roof is impossible if in the intervening time before the repair, the house burns downs. Increased costs alone do not constitute impracticability; instead, the intervening difficulty must change the essential nature of performance.[861] Sufficient impracticability will excuse both parties from performing under the contract, although a party may have an action in *quantum meruit* for benefits already conferred.[862]

Destruction or unavailability of the subject matter of a contract makes performance of the contract impossible. The most difficult issue is determining whether the contract calls for a particular subject matter or merely a kind of subject matter.[863] If a seller agrees to sell the buyer a car of a particular make and model and containing certain options, and a car of that description is on the lot but is stolen before it can be delivered, the question is whether the parties intended that the seller provide that particular car or that it sell any car fitting that description.

An event which justifies discharge for impossibility is failure of the agreed-upon means of performance. The agreed-upon means of performance can depend upon a third person, a particular means of delivery, or a particular method of payment.[864] Another event justifying discharge for impossibility is death or incapacity of a party,[865] but only if the contract calls for personal services.[866] Otherwise the buyer's estate is still bound by the contract. A contract can also be discharged by virtue of the death or illness of a third party who is necessary to the performance of the contract but who is not a party to it.

Performance may be discharged due to impossibility because of supervening illegality.[867] If the contract is legal when it is entered into, but its performance is prevented by a subsequent change in the law making the contract illegal, the contract is discharged. This is the common law rule.

854 D. Dobbs, Remedies § 10.3 (1993).

855 G. Calamari & J. Perillo, Contracts §§ 9-9 to 9-11 (5th ed. 2003) (due to the party's use of his dominant psychological position or his position of trust and confidence).

856 Fritz v. Mazurek, 156 Conn. 555, 244 A.2d 368 (1968).

857 Peoples Bank & Trust Co. v. Lala, 392 N.W.2d 179 (Iowa 1986).

858 Williston on Contracts § 3.4 (4th ed. 1990).

859 *Id.*

860 *See* J. Calamari & J. Perillo, Contracts Ch. 13 (5th ed. 2003).

861 U.C.C. § 2-615, Comment 4.

862 In Latin, *quantum meruit* means "as much as deserved." When parties have not made a contract, but one party has performed services or taken action that has benefited the other party, the court may require the second party to pay the first party for the value of his services. The claim is for work and labor and is based on the second party's implied promise to pay the first party reasonable compensation for services rendered. The obligation is imposed by law without regard to intention or assent of the parties "for reasons dictated by reason and justice." Black's Law Dictionary 1276 (8th ed. 2004).

863 *See* G. Calamari & J. Perillo, Contracts § 13-3 (5th ed. 2003).

864 *See* Wickliffe Farms, Inc. v. Owensboro Grain Co., 684 S.W.2d 17 (Ky. Ct. App. 1984).

865 Paramount Supply Co. v. Sherlin Corp., 16 Ohio App. 3d 176, 475 N.E.2d 197 (1984).

866 *Id.* (government seizure of truck turbochargers as a result of possible illegal exportation into Iran prevented seller from delivering goods and thus discharged his delivery obligation under doctrine of impossibility of performance); *see also* G. Calamari & J. Perillo, Contracts §§ 13-1, 13-7 (5th ed. 2003).

867 *See* G. Calamari & J. Perillo, Contracts § 13-5 (5th ed. 2003).

Section 2-615(a) of the UCC makes this supervening illegality defense available only to the seller, not to the buyer.[868]

Temporary impossibility suspends the duty of performing until the impossibility ends.[869] For example, a seller may not be able to supply goods because of a strike, temporary trade embargo, or inclement weather. However, if at the time the impossibility ends, performance would be much more burdensome on either party than had it occurred on time, the contract may be completely discharged under the doctrine of impracticability.

Courts, following the common law, will excuse performance when it, although not impossible, becomes too costly, time-consuming, or otherwise impracticable.[870] The courts reason that, had the conditions rendering performance impracticable been foreseen, the parties would never have entered into the contract.

Frustration refers to a situation in which both parties contract with reference to a stated purpose and that purpose is substantially defeated by some supervening event.[871] In that case, the frustration of the purpose excuses performance. Frustration cases present three types of difficulties:[872] determining the main purpose,[873] determining whether the purpose has been seriously frustrated,[874] and determining whether the party claiming frustration assumed the risk of any frustration of purpose.[875]

9.5.14 Failure of Consideration

To be binding and enforceable, the parties' promises must generally be supported by consideration.[876] If both parties do not give up something of legal value, the contract is unenforceable because no contract was ever really formed.[877]

In a surprising number of consumer contracts, only the consumer is really obligated to do anything of value. For example, a buyer may pay for a service contract that merely duplicates the consumer's existing rights. The consumer has paid for the contract, but the seller has given up nothing. Although a distinction exists between want of consideration and failure of consideration, both generally are an excuse for nonperformance of a promise.[878]

As a general rule, courts will not substitute their opinions as to what is adequate consideration for the opinions of the parties. The issue is not whether both sides made a reasonable bargain, but whether there was *any* consideration.[879] Nevertheless, an exception may be made when a gross inequality between the things exchanged suggests fraud, duress, unconscionability, or mistake.

Under the preexisting duty rule, no consideration is provided where a party gives up something or agrees to do something which the party was already bound to give up or to do.[880] A car seller who refuses to transfer certificate of title unless the buyer pays more than the agreed-upon price gives no consideration for the buyer's additional money, and has no right to it.

The UCC has, to a limited extent, abolished the preexisting duty rule for cases within Article 2. Under UCC § 2-209, an agreement modifying a contract to sell goods needs no consideration to be binding. The *Restatement (Second) of Contracts* also limits the preexisting duty rule—a promise modifying a contract needs no consideration to be binding and equitable in light of unanticipated circumstances arising during the course of performance of the contract.[881] The promise must be voluntary.[882] Thus, coercive conduct inducing the promise, even though falling short of duress, will prevent enforcement of the promise.[883]

There is no consideration when one party's promise is illusory, i.e., it appears to, but does not, in fact, commit the promisor.[884] If a prospective car buyer agrees to pay an extra $100 for a thirty-day warranty on the car and the seller takes the $100 saying, "If anything goes wrong in the first thirty days, I'll take a look at it," the seller's promise is illusory. The seller is not giving a real warranty, but only a promise to look at the car at a later date and decide then whether it will repair it. If a promise is conditional upon the happening of a future event that is completely within the seller's control, the promise may be illusory.[885]

A promise which consists of several alternative performances is consideration only if each of the alternatives constitutes consideration. For example, if a car seller said, "Give me $100. If I get a car in, I may or may not call you first," the seller has not made any commitments and the promise lacks consideration.

868 Supervening illegality must be distinguished from contracts that, at the time of contracting, are prohibited by law. *See* § 9.5.8, *supra* (discussion of contracts illegal at time of contracting).

869 *See* A. Corbin, Contracts § 76.7 (2002).

870 *See* 17A Am. Jur. 2d *Contracts* § 676 (1991).

871 D. Dobbs, Remedies §§ 11.1, 13.3 (1993).

872 D. Dobbs, Remedies § 13.3 (1993).

873 *Id.*

874 *Id.*

875 *Id.*

876 The exceptions, not discussed here, include contracts under seal, promises which induce substantial reliance, and promises made from moral obligations.

877 Failure of consideration is different from failure to meet a condition. *See* § 9.5.15, *infra.*

878 17A Am. Jur. 2d *Contracts* §§ 648–650 (2004).

879 Williston on Contracts § 7.3 (4th ed. 1990).

880 G. Calamari & J. Perillo, Contracts § 4-9 (5th ed. 2003).

881 Restatement (Second) of Contracts § 89 (1981).

882 Angel v. Murray, 113 R.I. 482, 332 A.2d 630 (1974).

883 *See* Roth Steel Products v. Sharon Steel Corp., 705 F.2d 134 (3d Cir. 1983); Morgan Bros., Inc. v. Haskell Corp., Inc., 24 Wash. App. 773, 604 P.2d 1294 (1979).

884 G. Calamari & J. Perillo, Contracts § 4-12(b)(4) (5th ed. 2003).

885 *But see* G. Calamari & J. Perillo, Contracts § 4-12(b)(6) (5th ed. 2003) (where the contingency is controlled by one party, the better line of decisions holds that the promise is not illusory; rather the party in control has made an implied promise to use his best efforts to bring about the happening of the condition to his promise).

9.5.15 *Failure of Condition*

Where a consumer's duty under the contract is not intended to arise until one or more events have occurred, the event is called a condition of his performance. Until such a condition has been met, the consumer can not be said to bound by the contract.[886]

For example, payment may be conditioned upon the seller's delivery of a second product or service, upon the buyer's satisfaction with the product, or upon the buyer's securing financing or sending a letter approving the contract. The fact that these conditions do not appear in the writing is generally no bar to their assertion, at least under the UCC version of the parol evidence rule.[887]

It is important to distinguish between conditions and promises because failure of a promise may not lead to contract cancellation, but only to an action for damages. In determining whether an event is a condition or a promise, the intent of the parties is of paramount importance.[888] The intent to create a condition is shown by use of such words as "provided that," "unless," "if," or "on the condition that." The intent to create a promise is shown by use of such words as "I stipulate" or "I agree." The action or conduct of the parties is also important. When language is ambiguous, the court will follow the interpretation that is most just and reasonable.[889] Interpretation of a provision as a promise rather than as a condition is preferred because then both parties are protected through an action for breach of contract for any damages suffered because of the other party's failure to comply with the agreement.

Courts also distinguish between express and constructive conditions. An *express* condition is any one to which the parties agree, regardless of whether this agreement is made explicitly or implicitly from their conduct. An express condition, therefore, can be implied or include implied conditions.

A *constructive* condition is not agreed to by the parties but is imposed as a matter of law to insure fairness. For example, a contractor and homeowner might enter into a written agreement for the repair of the homeowner's roof, but say nothing about the time for payment. If the contract is assigned to a bank, which seeks to enforce it against the buyer even though the contractor never furnished the work, a court would probably hold that the contractor's repair is a constructive condition to the homeowner's duty to pay. The court would so hold not because the parties have agreed that the work must be done before payment, but out of a sense of fairness and a business tradition, that a homeowner should not be required to pay for services not received.

A *concurrent condition* exists when the parties are to exchange performances at the same time. For example, when a seller agrees to deliver a car on a certain date and the buyer agrees to pay for it at that time, each performance is a concurrent condition. If there is an agreed-upon order of performance, the party whose performance is due first must perform before performance can be demanded of the other.

If the parties have not agreed to an order of performance, when one party's performance requires a period of time and the other's does not, the performance requiring time must ordinarily occur first and is a constructive condition to the other's performance. If a buyer and mechanic agree to the repair of the buyer's car, a court will normally hold that the mechanic's performance is due before payment is due. If, on the other hand, both promised performances can occur at the same time, a court will normally require that the two occur simultaneously.[890]

9.6 Contract, Warranty, and Tort Damage Actions

9.6.1 *Breach of Contract*

An important alternative remedy in many UDAP cases is an action for breach of contract. The contract claim will usually not lead to an attorney fee award for the consumer (although in some jurisdictions a consumer will be awarded attorney fees for prevailing in a contract action if the contract provides for attorney fees for the seller).[891] While punitive damages are not ordinarily available for breach of contract, some states will award them when the breach is particularly egregious.[892] The contract action has the advantage of applying in cases outside a UDAP statute's scope and in situations where the court finds no deception or unfairness. The statute of limitations may also be longer for the contract action. This manual will not analyze state contract law issues. Sources for this law are well-known treatises (e.g., *Corbin on Contracts*), the state's UCC, and state practice manuals.

---

886 *See* Haraka v. Datry, 148 Ga. App. 642, 252 S.E.2d 71 (1979) (buyer successfully defends breach of contract suit by seller of real property on grounds that sale was conditional upon buyer's receipt of advance alimony payments). Conditions precedent and subsequent are discussed in the context of yo-yo sales at § 5.4.5.5, *supra*.

887 *See* National Consumer Law Center, Consumer Warranty Law § 3.7 (2d ed. 2001 and Supp.).

888 A. Corbin, Contracts § 30.14 (rev. ed. 1999).

889 *Id.* § 30.14.

890 *Compare* U.C.C. § 2-507(1) *with* U.C.C. § 2-511(1).

891 Ark. Code § 16-22-308; Cal. Civ. Code § 1717; Conn. Gen. Stat. § 42-150bb; Fla. Stat. Ann. § 57.105(7); Haw. Rev. Stat. § 607-14; Mont. Code Ann. § 28-3-704; N.H. Rev. Stat. Ann. § 361-C:2; N.Y. Gen. Oblig. Law § 5-327; Or. Rev. Stat. § 20.096; Utah Code § 78-27-26.5; Wash. Rev. Code § 4.84.330. *See also* Mo. Stat. Ann. § 408.092 (allows fees to enforce a credit agreement).

892 *See* National Consumer Law Center, Automobile Fraud § 8.2.9.2 (2d ed. 2003 and Supp.).

9.6.2 Breach of Warranty

Warranty law provides another important consumer remedy. A state's version of Uniform Commercial Code Article 2 is the prime source of this law. However, in cases of leases UCC Article 2A will apply, and in the case of services, the applicable law may be a state's common law of warranties. The federal Magnuson-Moss Act provides further protection where there is an implied warranty or a "written warranty," as defined by that Act.[893] Many states have statutes that provide further regulation of warranties, or that require warranties for particular types of transactions.

With the exception of the availability of attorney fees under the Magnuson-Moss Act and some lemon laws, warranty law remedies do not include multiple, minimum, or punitive damages or attorney fees. Nevertheless, as with breach of contract claims, in some situations warranty damage actions will be useful. A breach of warranty claim will be available even where there is no deception or unfairness. The four-year limitations period may be longer than the UDAP period. UDAP scope problems may be avoided.

Another NCLC manual, *Consumer Warranty Law* (2d ed. 2001 and Supp.) extensively analyzes private consumer warranty remedies under the UCC, common law warranty theories, the Magnuson-Moss Act, and other state statutes. That analysis is not duplicated here.

9.6.3 Common Law Deceit and Other Tort Actions

There are two major advantages of a deceit or other tort action over a UDAP claim. First, only some UDAP statutes authorize punitive damages, while common law fraud actions will lead to punitive damages in many cases in most states. The second advantage of a tort action is that it will apply even in cases outside the UDAP statute's scope. UDAP remedies complement, but do not eliminate, common law tort remedies.[894]

Common law torts of fraud, deceit or misrepresentation are the ones most commonly used in UDAP-type cases. As with other tort theories, these misrepresentation theories fall within three categories: actions based on an intent to deceive, upon negligence, and upon a policy of defendant's strict liability, despite intent or negligence. For the most part, courts limit misrepresentation actions to those involving an intent to deceive.[895] The classic elements of the common law action for deceit are:

- A false representation of fact made by the defendant orally, in writing, by conduct, or by concealing the truth. False statements of opinion are not actionable.
- Scienter, or defendant's knowledge or belief that the representation is false, or defendant's insufficient basis or information to make the representation.
- An intent to induce the plaintiff to act in reliance upon the representation.
- Plaintiff's justifiable reliance. The representation must have played a material and substantial part in leading the plaintiff to adopt his or her course of action, and that reliance must have been justifiable under the circumstances.
- Damage to the plaintiff resulting from the reliance. Damages must be established with reasonable certainty.[896]

In comparison with the elements of UDAP deception, this classic definition of deceit is significantly more cumbersome to prove. However, in practice, a number of factors mitigate the significance of this difference. Some jurisdictions modify these classic elements of deceit, making the cause of action easier to prove. Intent and scienter requirements are often liberalized.[897] Other jurisdictions hold that deceit will lie for negligent statements, finding sufficient knowledge when the defendant fails in his or her duty to learn the facts before making the representations. Some jurisdictions hold that a common law negligence action is appropriate not only for tangible injuries, but for economic loss.[898] In yet other states, in at least some contexts, defendants have been held strictly liable for false representations concerning a matter as to which the defendant purports to have knowledge, so that the defendant may be taken to have assumed responsibility.[899]

Even in jurisdictions that require a showing of intent in a deceit action, this requirement is not burdensome on the consumer because the consumer already wants to prove evil intent or at least reckless conduct so as to be eligible for punitive damages. In fact, proof of the classic elements of deceit includes proof of intentional wrongdoing and should thus automatically lead to eligibility for punitive damages.[900] Attorneys in states where the UDAP statute does

---

893 15 U.S.C. §§ 2301–2312. *See also* National Consumer Law Center, Consumer Warranty Law Ch. 2 (2d ed. 2001 and Supp.).

894 Richard Wolf Medical Instruments Corp. v. Dory, 723 F. Supp. 37 (N.D. Ill. 1989); Mid Am. Acceptance Co. v. Lightle, 63 Ohio App. 3d 590, 579 N.E.2d 721 (1989); *see also* Wildstein v. Tru Motors, Inc., 227 N.J. Super. 331, 547 A.2d 340 (Law Div. 1988). *See generally* §§ 8.3.9, 8.4.2.6, 8.4.3.2, 8.4.3.8, 8.8.2.3, *supra*.

895 Prosser and Keeton, Law of Torts § 105 (5th ed. 1984); D. Dobbs, The Law of Torts §§ 469-483 (2000).

896 D. Dobbs, The Law of Torts §§ 470, 472 (2000).

897 *Id.* §§ 470-471; Prossser and Keeton, Law of Torts § 107 (5th ed. 1984).

898 D. Dobbs, The Law of Torts § 472 (2000).

899 *Id.* § 473.

900 Black v. Iovino, 580 N.E.2d 139 (Ill. App. Ct. 1991); Swift v. Allied Pest Control, Inc., 2001 Ohio App. LEXIS 3853 (Aug. 31, 2001). *See* Newton v. Standard Fire Ins. Co., 291 N.C. 105, 229 S.E.2d 297 (1976). *But see* Watson v. Johnson Mobile

not authorize UDAP punitive damages should always consider adding a common law fraud count even if a UDAP count is available. Even a UDAP deception count seeking treble or punitive damages will usually require the same proof of intent or willfulness.[901]

Nondisclosure may be the basis of a fraud-type claim. This may be based on either active concealment or even just fraud by silence. Courts today find nondisclosure fraudulent where the seller has a fiduciary duty to the consumer, where speech is necessary to make full a half truth, or where one party has superior knowledge not available to the other party.[902] Nondisclosure as a basis for fraud is examined in more detail in another NCLC manual: National Consumer Law Center, *Automobile Fraud* §§ 7.3.4, 7.3.5 (2d 2003 and Supp.).

Several keys to a large punitive damage award are:

- *Bringing the story before a jury*. Because fraud claims are so fact intensive, it is hard for a defendant to succeed in dismissing a case before it gets to the jury.
- *Proving a truly heinous practice*. Unfortunately, in today's deregulated credit market, fraudulent sales and lending practices are all too common.
- *Showing a pattern of similar misconduct*. Most lending, leasing, and other types of consumer fraud are systematic, with large corporations stealing small amounts from large numbers of consumers pursuant to a standardized practice. Key to large punitive damage awards is the introduction of evidence as to the scope of consumers victimized by a practice, with an estimate of the dollar impact.
- *Showing especially vulnerable consumers as targets*. All too commonly fraud schemes target the most vulnerable—the elderly, the illiterate, non-English speakers, immigrants, minorities, and the poor. A sympathetic plaintiff, one who is retired or works hard for minimal pay, and is taken advantage of by a major corporation, can underscore the heightened immorality of the defendant's practices.
- *Finding a deep pocket*. In today's consumer marketplace, it is not difficult to find major corporations engaging in the worst fraud, although it may require an examination of all those who directly or indirectly profit from a scheme. For example, a seller may be a small-time player, but financing may be provided by a national entity that is involved in the fraud or ratifies it.

While not every consumer case will result in a multi-million dollar punitive damage award, it is not uncommon for the addition in a used car case of a common law fraud count to result in significant punitive damages in addition to actual damages.[903] Here are four recent examples:

- In *Chrysler Corp. v. Schiffer*,[904] the Alabama Supreme Court, although reducing the award from $325,000 to $150,000, upheld an award of punitive damages against the manufacturer and dealer for the manufacturer's sale of new car with undisclosed wreck damage and the dealer's closing its eyes to the manufacturer's actions.
- In *Parrott v. Carr Chevrolet, Inc.*,[905] a consumer brought a UDAP claim based on failure to disclose wreck damage. The jury's award of $1 million in punitive damages was reduced by the trial court to $50,000, but then reinstated by the Oregon Supreme Court.
- In *Grabinski v. Blue Springs Ford Sales, Inc.*,[906] after finding that a dealer had misrepresented a vehicle previously totaled in a rollover accident as being "very nice" and "driving fine," a jury awarded a total of $7835 in actual damages and $210,000 in punitive damages to the vehicle's ultimate purchaser. The Eighth Circuit has upheld the constitutionality of this award after reviewing the three *Gore* factors.[907]
- In *Watson v. Johnson Mobile Homes*,[908] the Fifth Circuit upheld $150,000 of a $700,000 punitive damages award against a mobile home dealer who had refused to return a $4000 deposit for a mobile home to a financially vulnerable, unsophisticated consumer after financing fell through. The consumer had shown that the dealer had withheld deposits from forty-five other buyers.

Punitive damages, including constitutional restrictions on the size of awards, are discussed in more detail in § 8.4.3, *supra*, and in National Consumer Law Center, *Automobile Fraud* § 7.10 (2d 2003 and Supp.). Other NCLC manuals and the companion CD-Rom to this volume include a number of sample complaints that combine UDAP claims with fraud claims.

Homes, 284 F.3d 568 (5th Cir. 2002) (must show malice, gross negligence, or recklessness in addition to elements of fraud); Mid Am. Acceptance Co. v. Lightle, 63 Ohio App. 3d 590, 579 N.E.2d 721 (1989) (to recover punitive damages, plaintiff must show that fraud was aggravated by malice or ill will, or that it was particularly gross or egregious).

901 *See* §§ 8.4.2.3.1, 8.4.3.3, *supra*.

902 *See, e.g.*, Streeks v. Diamond Hill Farms, Inc., 258 Neb. 581, 605 N.W.2d 110 (2000).

903 *See, e.g.*, Robbins v. Lewis Rainer Motors, Inc., Clearinghouse No. 47,938 (S.D. W. Va. Apr. 8, 1992) (legal services client); Tague v. Molitor Motor Co., 139 Ill. App. 3d 313, 487 N.E.2d 436 (1985) ($1125 actual and $17,000 punitive damages for used auto dealer's practices); Delong v. Hilltop Lincoln-Mercury, 812 S.W.2d 834 (Mo. Ct. App. 1991); Freeman v. A&M Mobile Home Sales, Inc., 293 S.C. 255, 359 S.E.2d 532 (Ct. App. 1987) ($1750 actual and $40,000 punitive damages).

904 736 So. 2d 538 (Ala. 1999).

905 331 Or. 537, 17 P.3d 473 (2001).

906 1998 U.S. Dist. LEXIS 17015 (W.D. Mo. 1998).

907 203 F.3d 1024 (8th Cir. 2000), *cert. denied*, 121 S. Ct. 70, 148 L. Ed. 2d 35 (2000).

908 284 F.3d 568 (5th Cir. 2002).

There is no merit to the argument that the UDAP statute preempts a common law fraud or deceit claim.[909] Similarly, consumers should not have to elect between UDAP and tort remedies. There is nothing inconsistent or duplicative in recovering actual damages and attorney fees under a UDAP claim and punitive damages under a tort claim.[910]

Conversion, while not strictly speaking a tort remedy, may be another alternate remedy for victims of consumer fraud.[911] A conversion action is available where a person knowingly or intentionally exerts unauthorized control over property of another person.[912] Cases particularly appropriate for a conversion count include those where a dealer refuses to return a trade-in vehicle or where a repair shop refuses to return articles left there.[913] Punitive damages are available for conversion.[914]

The tort claim of conversion should also be considered to recover misrepresented charges. In short, a conversion claim would assert that the merchant's collection of the sums is an unlawful exercise of control that is inconsistent with the consumer's rights.[915] One court has held that a finance company's retention of interest on a security deposit could support a claim for conversion.[916] Another allowed a conversion claim against a utility company that overbilled its customers in excess of its filed rate.[917] Though some jurisdictions maintain the historical rule that, in general, money may not be the subject of a conversion claim,[918] most will allow such a claim if the funds can be sufficiently identified as to resemble a specific chattel.[919]

9.7 Unjust Enrichment, Restitution, and Similar Equitable Theories

9.7.1 Introduction

Unjust enrichment is an equitable doctrine that provides a remedy—restitution—when a party receives benefits that would be unjust for that party to retain under the circumstances. Unjust enrichment is the source of the liability, and restitution is the consequence of—or remedy for—the liability.[920]

A claim for restitution may be a useful approach when a seller or lender collects funds that it is not entitled to. For example:

- A car dealer or mortgage lender may charge a consumer a fee or tax when in fact the actual amount due to the state is only a small fraction of the charge;
- A mobile home park may demand a fee for the sale of a home in the park, notwithstanding that state law prohibits such a fee;
- A merchant may disclose and collect a fee that the merchant does not have the authority to collect, for example, an unlicensed real estate broker is not entitled to command and keep a commission;
- A seller may charge a consumer a higher price than agreed to or allowed by law.

---

909 Wildstein v. Tru Motors, Inc., 227 N.J. Super. 331, 547 A.2d 340 (Law Div. 1988); *see also* Richard Wolf Medical Instruments Corp. v. Dory, 723 F. Supp. 37 (N.D. Ill. 1989).

910 United Laboratories v. Kuykendall, 335 N.C. 183, 437 S.E.2d 374 (1993). *See* §§ 8.3.9, 8.4.3.8, 8.8.2.3, *supra.*

911 Watkins v. Alvey, 549 N.E.2d 74 (Ind. Ct. App. 1990).

912 *Id.*

913 Conversion is discussed in more detail in National Consumer Law Center, Repossessions and Foreclosures §§ 13.6.2–13.6.5 (5th ed. 2002 and Supp.).

914 Watson v. Johnson Mobile Homes, 284 F.3d 568 (5th Cir. 2002) (dealer's refusal to return deposit after financing fell through).

915 W. Page Keeton, Prosser and Keeton on Torts 92 (5th ed. 1984).

916 Steinmetz v. Toyota Motor Credit Corp., 963 F. Supp. 1294, 1307 (E.D.N.Y. 1997).

917 Walsh v. America's Tele-Network Corp., 195 F. Supp. 2d 840, 850 (E.D. Tex. 2002).

918 *See, e.g.*, Reliance Ins. Co. v. U.S. Bank of Washington, 143 F.3d 502, 505 (9th Cir. 1998) (Washington law); Southwest When, Inc. v. Nutrition 101, Inc, 155 F. Supp. 2d 1003, 1007 (C.D. Ill. 2001); Farey-Jones v. Buckingham, 132 F. Supp. 2d 92, 106 (E.D.N.Y. 2001); *In re* McWeeney, 255 B.R. 3, 6 (Bankr. S.D. Ohio 2000) (plaintiff must show defendant owed an obligation to deliver "identical" money as opposed to a certain sum of money); Macomber v. Travelers Prop. & Cas. Corp., 804 A.2d 180, 1999 (Conn. 2002). Not every state restricts conversion claims based on money. *See, e.g., In re* Halmar Distribs., Inc., 232 B.R. 18, 22 (Bankr. D. Mass. 1999) (allowing claim for conversion of funds).

919 *See, e.g.*, Canawill, Inc. v. EMAR Group, Inc., 230 B.R. 533, 550 (M.D.N.C. 1999) (bank that specifically identified and designated funds as belonging to the plaintiff could be liable for conversion); Florida Dept. Ins. v. Debenture Guar., 921 F. Supp. 750, 757 (M.D. Fla. 1996); Wachovia Bank v. Decatur Auto Ctr., Inc., 583 S.E.2d 6 (Ga. 2003); *In re* Estate of Boatcrest, 88 S.W.3d 500, 506 (Mo. Ct. App. 2002) (affirming judgment on claim that proceeds received from sale were wrongfully converted). *But see* NPF IV, Inc. v. Transitional Health Servs., 922 F. Supp. 77, 81, 82 (S.D. Ohio 1996) (dismissing claim where plaintiff could not show that its overpayments were specifically identifiable and not commingled with the rest of the defendant's funds).

920 Restatement (Third) of Restitution & Unjust Enrichment § 2 at comment a (discussion draft 2000). The Restatement carefully circumscribes the situations of unjust enrichment that will yield restitution, providing as follows:

(1) Liability in restitution is based on and measured by the receipt of a benefit, but the receipt of a benefit does not of itself make the recipient liable in restitution.

(2) The transactions that give rise to a liability in restitution are primarily nonconsensual. They take place outside the framework of an enforceable contract, or otherwise without the effective consent of one or both parties.

(3) The fact that a person has received or obtained a benefit without paying for it does not of itself establish that the recipient has been unjustly enriched.

(4) There is no liability in restitution in respect of a benefit intentionally conferred by the claimant on the recipient, unless the circumstances of the transaction are such as to excuse the claimant from the necessity of basing a claim to payment on a contract with the recipient.

In some jurisdictions, "unjust enrichment" is a cause of action in and of itself, sounding in equity, that has distinct elements to prove and results in an award of restitution.[921] In other jurisdictions, unjust enrichment serves as the basis for imposing liability through another cause of action, and it must be proven as an element of the overriding claim. Typically such a claim is labeled restitution,[922] "money had and received,"[923] *assumpsit*,[924] or recoupment.[925]

9.7.2 Unjust Enrichment

In general, the elements of a claim of unjust enrichment include the following:

- The defendant received a benefit;
- The defendant's failure to pay was to the plaintiff's detriment; and
- The circumstances are such that it would be unjust for the defendant to fail to return the benefit to the plaintiff.[926]

Jurisdictions that have a more conservative approach to the doctrine may also require a plaintiff to show not just that the defendant obtained a benefit, but that the defendant obtained the benefit by fraud, duress, or the taking of an undue advantage.[927]

The injustice element, the core of the unjust enrichment doctrine, is circumstance-specific. It may be met by showing that the defendant has not provided services in exchange for the benefit, such as where a seller charged for services it never performed. It may also exist where the defendant was not authorized to earn the benefit, such as where an unlicensed real estate broker collects a commission.[928] In *Cohon v. Oscar L. Paris Co.*,[929] plaintiffs brought suit against a carpet installer to recover the retailers' occupation tax they had paid to the installer, which had been refunded to the installer by the state after the tax had been declared illegal. Reversing the lower court's dismissal of the suit, the court held that the plaintiffs presented a legitimate equitable claim to the funds, notwithstanding that the funds had not been paid under duress.[930] A Texas district court recently upheld a claim for unjust enrichment based on a telecommunications services provider's assessment of charges in excess of its filed tariff.[931]

Since the cause of action lies in an episode of enrichment to the defendant, a claim may fail if the collector has transferred the funds to a third party, such as where a merchant overcharges a consumer for sales tax, but passes the whole of the collected sum to the taxing authority.[932] Even if the defendant collected the money unlawfully, if the defendant turned the money over, it is the transferee who benefits and against whom the claim should be brought.

921 Restatement (Third) of Restitution & Unjust Enrichment § 1 (discussion draft 2000) provides: "A person who is unjustly enriched at the expense of another is liable in restitution to the other."

922 Kowalski v. Cedars of Portsmouth Condo. Ass'n, 769 A.2d 344, 346 (N.H. 2001); Oxford Fin. Cos. v. Velez, 807 S.W.2d 460, 465 (Tex. App. 1991) (while unjust enrichment is not an independent cause of action, an action for restitution based on unjust enrichment will lie to recover money that it would be unconscionable for the defendant to retain); *see also* Century Bank v. Hymans, 905 P.2d 722, 726, 727 (N.M. Ct. App. 1995) (allowing restitution claim based on mortgagee's overpayment to mortgagor).

923 *See, e.g.*, Lonergan v. A.J.'s Wrecker Serv. of Dallas, Inc., 1999 WL 462333, at *2 (N.D. Tex. July 6, 1999) (describing claim for money had and received as an equitable doctrine used to prevent unjust enrichment).

924 *See, e.g.*, Cohon v. Oscar L. Paris Co., 149 N.E.2d 472, 475 (Ill. App. Ct. 1958) (the action of *assumpsit*, under the common counts for money had and received, is an appropriate remedy to enforce the equitable obligation arising from the receipt of money by one person which belongs to another and which in equity and justice should be returned).

925 *See* Pension Benefit Guar. Corp. v. White Consol. Indus. Inc., 72 F. Supp. 2d 547, 550 (W.D. Pa. 1999).

926 *See, e.g.*, White v. Smith & Wesson Corp., 97 F. Supp. 2d 816 (N.D. Ohio 2000); Steinmetz v. Toyota Motor Credit Corp., 963 F. Supp. 1294, at 1307 (E.D.N.Y. 1997) (interest earned on lessee's security deposits could be basis of claim for unjust enrichment against lessor); Gary v. D. Agustini & Asociados, S.A., 865 F. Supp. 818 (S.D. Fla. 1994); Fitzpatrick v. Scalzi, 806 A.2d 593 (Conn. Ct. App. 2002); Clark v. TAP Pharmaceuticals, Inc., 343 Ill. App. 3d 538, 798 N.E.2d 123 (2003) (upholding certification of class action); Dominiack Mechanical, Inc. v. Dunbar, 757 N.E.2d 186, 190 (Ind. Ct. App. 2001). *See also* Union Nat'l Life Ins. Co. v. Crosby, 2004 WL 253557 (Miss. Feb. 12, 2004) (reciting elements of unjust enrichment).

927 Lonergan v. A.J.'s Wrecker Serv. of Dallas, Inc., 1999 WL 462333, at *2 (N.D. Tex. July 6, 1999) (fees paid to defendant's towing companies, for the nonconsensual towing and storage of vehicles sufficed as payment of money under duress); Friar v. Vanguard Holding Corp., 434 N.Y.S.2d 698, 702 (N.Y. App. Div. 1980) (action for money had and received arises when money was paid by mistake, upon consideration that failed, or under duress). *See also* Restatement (Third) of Restitution & Unjust Enrichment § 2 comment a (discussion draft 2000) ("the concern of restitution is with nonconsensual transactions and not (for example) with the fairness of a valid contractual exchange").

928 Kowalski v. Cedars of Portsmouth Condo. Ass'n, 769 A.2d 346 (N.H. 2001).

929 149 N.E.2d 472 (Ill. App. Ct. 1958).

930 *Id.* at 478.

931 Walsh v. America's Tele-Network Corp., 195 F. Supp. 2d 840, 852 (E.D. Tex. 2002).

932 *See, e.g.*, Epps Aircraft, Inc. v. Exxon Corp., 859 F. Supp. 533, 536 (M.D. Ala. 1993) (plaintiff must show that defendant holds its money to prove enrichment; where defendant had remitted disputed municipal taxes to the taxing entity, plaintiff's claim failed), *aff'd without op.*, 30 F.3d 1499 (11th Cir. 1994); Parker v. Giant Eagle, Inc., 2002 WL 31168571, at *4 (Ohio Ct. App. Sept. 26, 2002) (holding that since plaintiff's restitution claim had to be asserted against the State of Ohio, the court lacked subject matter jurisdiction to hear it); Winey v. William E. Dailey, Inc., 636 A.2d 744, 751 (Vt. 1993) (unjust enrichment claim for construction overcharges failed against wife of contractor even though she may have had access to the funds).

9.7.3 Money Had and Received

"Money had and received" is a cause of action that arises, where recognized, when "one person obtains money that in equity and good conscience belongs to another."[933] Conceptually it is an equitable doctrine that encompasses those unjust enrichment claims where the benefit retained by the defendant is cash, as opposed to services or some other subject. In some jurisdictions, it may be captioned as an action *in assumpsit*.[934]

9.7.4 Constructive Trust

One advantage of asserting a claim in equity is that a plaintiff able to prove entitlement to restitution may take the further step of seeking a constructive trust on the funds. Not a remedy or a cause of action, not even a genuine trust, a constructive trust is a legal concept that attaches to the property held unjustly by the defendant, to protect it until it is returned.[935] Like unjust enrichment, the concept of the constructive trust stems from property being in the wrong hands: "Where a person holding title to property is subject to an equitable duty to convey it to another on the ground that he would be unjustly enriched if he were permitted to retain it, a constructive trust arises."[936]

The fundamental element of a constructive trust is that the property at issue—the *res* of the trust—is held under circumstances in which it would be unjust for the holder to retain it.[937] Some states have codified the remedy.[938] An advantage of the constructive trust is that a plaintiff usually need not show that the holder behaved wrongfully, just that the holder has property that the plaintiff rightfully should have.[939] However, one drawback of the device is that a court may require the plaintiff to prove, in the case of sums of money, that the sums are in an identifiable fund that can be traced to the plaintiff; such a court will not impose a constructive trust on the defendant's general assets, however wrongful the original conduct might have been.[940]

9.7.5 Obstacles to Equitable Remedies

9.7.5.1 Introduction

Traditionally, actions in equity such as those seeking restitution for unjust enrichment have been burdened with

933 Phippen v. Deere & Co., 965 S.W.2d 713, 725 n.1 (Tex. App. 1998). *See also* Lonergan v. A.J.'s Wrecker Serv. of Dallas, Inc., 1999 WL 462333, at *1 (N.D. Tex. 1999) (claim of money had and received is an equitable doctrine used to prevent unjust enrichment); Epps Aircraft, Inc. v. Exxon Corp., 859 F. Supp. 533, 536 (M.D. Ala. 1993) (claim for money had and received requires plaintiff to show that the defendant holds money which "in equity and good conscience, belongs to plaintiff") (quoting Hancock-Hazlette General Constr. Co., 499 So. 2d 1385, 1387 (Ala. 1986)), *aff'd without op.*, 30 F.3d 1499 (11th Cir. 1994); Butitta v. First Mortgage Corp., 578 N.E.2d 116, 118 (Ill. App. Ct. 1991) (plaintiffs' money wrongfully had and received action against mortgage company based on allegedly illegal tax service and recording assignment fees sought money belonging to class members *in assumpsit*); Citipostal, Inc. v. Unistar Leasing, 724 N.Y.S.2d 555, 559 (N.Y. App. Div. 2001) (money had and received is a cause of action to obtain restitution from one who has been unjustly enriched); Friar v. Vanguard Holding Corp., 434 N.Y.S.2d 698, 700 (N.Y. App. Div. 1980) (action against lender who assessed an additional mortgage tax from plaintiff homeseller at closing by misrepresenting that the tax had to be paid by the seller; described as a restitutory remedy for recovery upon a quasi-contractual obligation for repayment of funds paid by mistake, failure of consideration, though extortion or oppression or undue advantage which the defendant is obliged under "the ties of natural justice and equity" to refund) (quoting Mansfield, Moses v. Macferlan, 2 Burr. 1005, 1 Wm. Bl. 219, 97 Eng. Rep. 676, All Eng. Law Rep. Reprint, 1598–1774 (1760), 581, 585); Winey v. William E. Dailey, Inc., 636 A.2d 744, 751 (Vt. 1993) (action against a person who received money to which another was entitled's covered by an action in assumpsit for money had and received).

934 An action to recover damages for breach or non-performance of a promise or contract. The New Shorter Oxford English Dictionary 133 (1993).

935 *See, e.g.*, Orud v. Groth, 652 N.W.2d 447, 452 n.2 (Iowa 2002); Union Nat'l Life Ins. Co. v. Crosby, 2004 WL 253557 (Miss. Feb. 12, 2004).

936 Restatement (First) of Restitution § 160 (1937). The Restatement (Third) of Trusts defines the concept as follows:

> A constructive trust is a relationship with respect to property usually subjecting the person by whom its title is held to an equitable duty to convey the property to another on the ground that the title holder's acquisition or retention of the property is wrongful and that unjust enrichment would occur if the title holder was permitted to retain the property.

§ 1 cmt. e.

937 *See, e.g.*, Eychaner v. Gross, 779 N.E.2d 1115, 1143 (Ill. 2002) (constructive trust may be imposed to redress unjust enrichment); United Carolina Bank v. Brogan, 574 S.E.2d 112 (N.C. Ct. App. 2002); University Hosps. of Cleveland, Inc. v. Lynch, 772 N.E.2d 105, 129, 130 (Ohio 2002) (constructive trust arises by equity against one who holds legal title to property that he should not, in equity and conscience, be allowed to hold and enjoy); Faulknier v. Shafer, 563 S.E.2d 755, 758 (Va. 2002) (constructive trust arises by construction of law where it would be inequitable for acquirer of property to keep it); Sulzer v. Diedrich, 664 N.W.2d 641 (Wis. 2003) (imposing constructive trust on former spouse's share of decedent's retirement benefits that were wrongfully distributed to decedent's second wife).

938 *See* Ga. Code Ann. § 53-12-93; Iowa Code § 633.2107; Mont. Code Ann. §§ 72-33-219, 220.

939 *See, e.g.*, *In re* Estate of McDermott, 51 P.3d 486, 491 (Mont. 2002) (plaintiff need not show fraud or other wrongful acts as a prerequisite to imposing a trust, citing Mont. Code Ann. § 72-33-219); Sulzer v. Diedrich, 664 N.W.2d 641 (Wis. 2003) (trust may be imposed against a person who did not know of or participate in the original wrongful conduct).

940 *See, e.g.*, Eychaner v. Gross, 779 N.E.2d 1115, 1143 (Ill. 2002) (plaintiff's plea for a constructive trust failed because plaintiff could not identify a fund traceable to the wrongful conduct).

extra requirements that would not be imposed in an action for damages. These restrictive elements are designed to favor legal remedies, so that equitable actions are a last resort for one who has suffered a wrong. So, for example, in some jurisdictions a plaintiff seeking restitution must show that no adequate remedy for the wrong exists at law, or that the parties had no express contract that could serve as the grounds of an action for damages.

These rules have grown somewhat stale, but are still observed vigorously in some jurisdictions. However, the rules should be treated as guidelines, not absolute proscriptions, and when blind adherence to the rule would produce injustice, they should be ignored.

9.7.5.2 Requirement of No Adequate Remedy at Law

Many jurisdictions require a plaintiff who seeks restitution in equity for unjust enrichment must demonstrate that no adequate remedy at law exists. This is a tenet of the law of equity in general,[941] though it may be fading as time passes. Claims for unjust enrichment, restitution or money had and received based on illegitimate fees have fallen afoul of this rule in some jurisdictions.[942]

The requirement that the plaintiff be without an adequate legal remedy has much less justification in a case seeking the return of illicitly collected funds than in other equity actions, such as those for an injunction[943] or for specific performance.[944] In those cases, the plaintiff is seeking to direct and control the defendant's behavior, and it may be justified to allow such control only when legal damages will not do. In the case of restitution, however, the plaintiff only seeks a refund of what was wrongfully received.

If faced with this requirement, the consumer may still be able to argue that no adequate remedy at law exists, because "adequate remedy" does not mean "any remedy." If a legal remedy would not be as certain, complete, prompt or efficient as an equitable remedy, it should not be preferred.[945] In the words of the Georgia Supreme Court, an adequate remedy at law is one "that is 'as practical and as efficient to the ends of justice and its prompt administration as the remedy in equity.' "[946] In the case of a wrongful overcharge, restitution may well be the most efficient method of righting the wrong. If an action in equity for restitution is superior to any potential action at law in terms of efficiency and practicality, the action at law, by comparison, is not adequate.

Aside from questions of judicial efficiency, the adequate remedy at law defense may be given less attention when a claim, though based on an underlying contract, asserts misrepresentation, concealment, or fraud.[947] It can be argued that equity should not allow a deliberate wrongdoer to resist restitution through this doctrine by forcing a plaintiff to go to another court to try to obtain a different remedy by a different cause of action.

9.7.5.3 Existence of an Express Contract

An express contract between the parties may also bar a plaintiff from obtaining an equitable remedy like restitution. This is another ancient rule retained by some jurisdictions, apparently on the grounds that plaintiffs who are parties to a contract should be restricted to contract actions at law.[948]

---

941 *See, e.g.*, Root v. Lake Shore & M.S. Ry., 105 U.S. 189, 207 (1881) ("[i]t is the fundamental characteristic and limit of the jurisdiction in equity that it can not give relief when there is a plain and adequate and complete remedy at law"); Bland v. Freightliner L.L.C., 206 F. Supp. 2d 1202, 1209 (M.D. Fla. 2002); Wilkison v. Wiederkehr, 124 Cal. Rptr. 2d 631, 639 (Cal. Ct. App. 2002); Kakaes v. George Washington Univ., 790 A.2d 581, 583 (D.C. 2002); Sullivan v. Board of Comm'rs of Oak Lawn Park Dist., 743 N.E.2d 1057 (Ill. App. Ct. 2001); DiMarzo v. Fast Trak Structures, Inc., 747 N.Y.S.2d 637, 638 (N.Y. App. Div. 2002); American Towers Owners Ass'n, Inc. v. CCI Mech., Inc., 930 P.2d 1182, 1193 (Utah 1996) (possibility of contractual remedy precluded equitable remedy); Kohlbeck v. Reliance Constr. Co., 647 N.W.2d 277, 285 (Wis. Ct. App. 2002); Texaco, Inc. v. State Bd. of Equalization, 845 P.2d 398, 401 (Wyo. 1993) (court would not allow suit in equity while remained opportunity for plaintiff to seek remedy at law).

942 *See, e.g.*, Lozada v. Dale Baker Oldsmobile, Inc., 145 F. Supp. 2d 878, 892 (W.D. Mich. 2001) (plaintiffs who claimed dealer wrongfully collected undisclosed finance charges had statutory cause of action that precluded claim for unjust enrichment); Brown v. Coleman Invs., Inc., 993 F. Supp. 432 (M.D. La. 1998) (state Motor Vehicle Sales Finance Act provided remedy at law, accordingly court granted summary judgment against plaintiff who claimed that dealer had charged excess fees for license, *ad valorem* taxes); Brister v. All Star Chevrolet, Inc., 986 F. Supp. 1003, 1010, 1011 (E.D. La. 1997) (plaintiffs' claim for restitution of license and tax fees that exceeded what dealer paid to the state dismissed because plaintiff could seek remedy at law based on contract misrepresentations); Martinez v. Weyerhaseuser Mortgage Co., 959 F. Supp. 1511, 1518 (S.D. Fla. 1996) (plaintiff's claim based on mortgagee's fees for services that may not have been performed could be remedied by TILA); Gary v. D. Agustini & Asociados, S.A., 865 F. Supp. 818 (S.D. Fla. 1994) (existence of contractual remedy precluded claim for unjust enrichment); Washington Suburban Sanitary Comm'n v. C.I. Mitchell & Best Co., 495 A.2d 30, 46 (Md. 1985) (plaintiff could not pursue claim against taxing authority for questionable sewer and water hook-up fees because they could have sought an injunction against the charging of those fees prior to paying them).

943 *See, e.g.*, DiMarzo v. Fast Trak Structures, Inc., 747 N.Y.S.2d 637, 638 (N.Y. App. Div. 2002).

944 *See, e.g.*, Wilkison v. Wiederkehr, 124 Cal. Rptr. 2d 631, 639 (Cal. Ct. App. 2002); Kakaes v. George Washington Univ., 790 A.2d 581, 583 (D.C. 2002).

945 McGrath v. C.T. Sherer Co., 195 N.E. 913, 917 (Mass. 1935).

946 Sherrer v. Hale, 285 S.E.2d 714, 718 (Ga. 1982).

947 *See In re* Brown, 287 B.R. 676, 682 (E.D. Mich. 2001).

948 *See, e.g.*, Daenzer v. Wayland Ford, Inc., 193 F. Supp. 2d 1030, 1041 (W.D. Mich. 2002) (plaintiff who had alleged that she had paid finance charges to defendant dealer to which dealer was not entitled could not assert claim of unjust enrichment, because the benefit plaintiff claimed defendant had received was within the

Courts adhering to this rule may find that any contract between the parties that relates to the substance underlying the collected charge will bar any unjust enrichment action to recover it. However, a breach of contract action may not be suitable to recovering a fee disclosed and collected but misused, and enforcing the express contract rule in such circumstances can lead to a defendant unjustly enriched to the detriment of a plaintiff left without a remedy. Enforcing the rule can even reward a defendant for flouting the law.[949]

A consumer may also argue that a defendant's misrepresentation should prevent the express contract rule from barring an equitable claim. For example, it could be argued that a contract that misrepresents the character of an assessed fee does not qualify as the sort of contract that the rule should attach to. In effect, the argument is that as to the fee, no valid contract provision exists to which the express contract rule can attach. So, for example, one district court held that plaintiffs who alleged that they were fraudulently induced into insurance contracts could maintain an action for unjust enrichment for restitution of excess premiums paid, because the written contract would not preclude a claim in equity if it was unenforceable.[950]

The rule should be narrowly construed, and accordingly should not bar a claim that, though arising out of a contract, is asserted against an entity that was not a party to that contract.[951] Furthermore, even if an express contract between the parties existed, the rule should not prevent restitution of a fee collected outside of the contract, because the contract would not embody the entire transaction between the parties.[952]

Not all courts reject equitable claims for restitution simply on the basis that the parties have a contract. For example, a lessee was allowed to assert a claim for money had and received against the lessee's former lessor, for payments made after the lease had expired and the leased property had become the plaintiff's.[953] In a case where telecommunications customers sued their provider for billing over the amount of the filed tariff, the court ruled that a claim in unjust enrichment for overbilling is an exception to the express contract rule, relying on a previous Texas Supreme

contract); Taylor Inv. Corp. v. Weil, 169 F. Supp. 2d 1046, 1060 (D. Minn. 2001) (express contract precludes recovery under quasi-contract, unjust enrichment, or *quantum meruit*); Lozada v. Dale Baker Oldsmobile, Inc., 145 F. Supp. 2d 878, 892 (W.D. Mich. 2001) (retail installment sales contract between the parties barred unjust enrichment claim of plaintiff who claimed that car dealer failed to fully disclose finance charges as required by statute; plaintiff limited to statutory remedies); *In re* Air Transp. Excise Tax Litig., 37 F. Supp. 2d 1133, 1143 (D. Minn. 1999) (shippers' customers who claimed that shipper had charged them for a federal excise tax that had expired could not assert equitable claims for unjust enrichment and money had and received because their rights were solely determined by the contract between the parties); Brown v. Coleman Invs., Inc., 993 F. Supp. 432, 438 (M.D. La. 1998) (contract between the parties precluded car buyer's claim for equitable restitution of $72 upcharge in dealer's assessment purportedly for state license fee and *ad valorem* taxes); Nicolas v. Deposit Guar. Nat'l Bank, 182 F.R.D. 226, 234 (S.D. Miss. 1998) (bank customer's claim that bank overcharged her insufficient fund fees was precluded by the depository agreement that authorized them); Green v. Levis Motors, Inc., 994 F. Supp. 735, 742 (M.D. La. 1997) (contract between the parties barred car buyer's unjust enrichment claim based on $18 upcharge dealer had included into license fee), *aff'd*, 179 F.3d 286 (5th Cir.), *cert. denied*, 528 U.S. 1020 (1999); Brister v. All Star Chevrolet, Inc., 986 F. Supp. 1003, 1011 (E.D. La. 1997) (claim that fees in contract exceeded those actually paid by dealer to state was precluded by contract between the parties); Noel v. Fleet Fin., Inc., 971 F. Supp. 1102, 1114 (E.D. Mich. 1997) (plaintiff's unjust enrichment claim against mortgage broker and lender to recover yield spread premium precluded by contract); Shvarts v. Budget Group, Inc., 97 Cal. Rptr. 2d 722, 727 (Cal. Ct. App. 2000) (plaintiffs who asserted that car rental company had overcharged for fuel replacement could not maintain action for money had and received and restitution because the parties had an express contract); Strategic Risk Mgmt., Inc. v. Federal Express Corp., 665 N.Y.S.2d 799, 801, 802 (N.Y. Sup. Ct. 1997) (parties' contract precluded plaintiff's unjust enrichment claim for the return of expired federal excise tax that plaintiff had paid to air delivery service), *aff'd*, 686 N.Y.S.2d 35 (N.Y. App. Div. 1999); Abrams v. Toyota Motor Credit Corp., 2001 WL 1807357, at *10, *11 (Pa. Com. Pl. Dec. 5, 2001); American Towers Owners Ass'n, Inc. v. CCI Mech., Inc., 930 P.2d 1182, 1193 (Utah 1996) (construction contract precluded unjust enrichment claim). *But see* Durant v. ServiceMaster Co., 159 F. Supp. 2d 977, 983 (E.D. Mich. 2001) (plaintiffs who claimed defendant wrongfully assessed a fuel surcharge fee could assert theories of both unjust enrichment and breach of contract).

Whether a fee was paid pursuant to a contract is sometimes a matter of construction. In *Cohon* the court held that the suit to recover a retailers' occupation tax, declared illegal, was distinguishable from a case where an overpayment was made by virtue of the contract, but it is clear that the original agreement pursuant to which the customers paid the tax was a contract. 149 N.E.2d 472, 477.

949 *In re* Smith, 280 B.R. 436, 444 (Bankr. N.D. Ill. 2002).

950 *In re* Prudential Ins. Co. of Am. Sales Practices Litig., 975 F. Supp. 584, 621, 622 (D.N.J. 1996). *But see* Green v. Levis Motors, Inc., 994 F. Supp. 735, 742 (M.D. La. 1997) (contract between car buyer and dealer barred plaintiff's equitable restitution claim to recover dealer's upcharge notwithstanding contract's deceitful inclusion of upcharge in "license fee").

951 Noel v. Fleet Fin., Inc., 971 F. Supp. 1102, 1114, 1115 (E.D. Mich. 1997) (plaintiffs' unjust enrichment claim to recover yield spread premium paid in mortgage transaction could stand against mortgage broker if that broker was not a party to the loan contract).

952 *Cf.* Daenzer v. Wayland Ford, Inc., 193 F. Supp. 2d 1030, 1041 (W.D. Mich. 2002) (plaintiff could not maintain unjust enrichment action for allegedly unlawful finance charges because she did not allege that the benefit to the defendant transpired outside the contract).

953 Citipostal, Inc. v. Unistar Leasing, 724 N.Y.S.2d 555, 559, 560 (N.Y. App. Div. 2001). *See also* Owl Constr. Co. v. Ronald Adams Contractor, Inc., 642 F. Supp. 475, 479 (E.D. La. 1986) (party to construction contract entitled to recover attorney fees and interest charged by defendant that were not authorized by the contract); Cohon v. Oscar L. Paris Co., 149 N.E.2d 472 (Ill. App. Ct. 1958) (allowing suit by carpet purchasers against seller to recover retailers' occupation tax paid to seller but later refunded to seller by the state).

Court decision that a claim for money had and received should look solely to whether the defendant holds money that belongs to the plaintiff.[954] Furthermore, authority exists for pleading unjust enrichment in the alternative to a breach of contract or other action at law.[955]

9.7.5.4 The Voluntary Payment Defense

A third obstacle to an equitable action for unjust enrichment is the voluntary payment defense. Many jurisdictions recognize this defense to an action for restitution of funds paid, whether framed as an action in equity or one at law for breach of contract.[956] Where recognized, the defense almost completely eradicates the claim. In such jurisdictions, a court may deem a consumer's payment voluntary even if the consumer did not realize that he or she was being tricked into paying a fee not legitimately owing, or even if the consumer fought the fee but nevertheless paid it in order to prevent unpleasant consequences threatened by the defendant. Whether the voluntary payment doctrine applies to UDAP claims, as opposed to equitable actions for unjust enrichment, is discussed at § 4.2.15.5, *supra*.

The defense has little discernable justification, and may even promote the practice of assessing illegitimate charges. The justifications cited for the voluntary payment defense are that it allows one who receives payment to rely upon those funds, and that it operates as a means to settle disputes without resort to courts by requiring the person asserting an overcharge to notify the payee.[957] These are, essentially, arguments of economic and judicial efficiency, concerns that should not trump a legitimate claim that one was tricked, defrauded, or otherwise overcharged by a party that knew that it was not entitled to the fee.

Some jurisdictions reject the voluntary payment defense out-of-hand, with the sensible view that one who receives that which is not properly due must return it.[958] Even in those jurisdictions that recognize the rule, though, counsel may be able to show that its use would not be appropriate under the particular circumstances of the overcharge. A full and proper statement of the defense provides that only money paid "with full knowledge of all facts and without fraud, deception, duress, or coercion," can not be refunded.[959] Accordingly, the voluntary payment defense fails if the payment was not, in fact, voluntary.

Nonetheless, a few courts apply the coercion qualification quite stringently. Some courts hold that to establish coercion sufficient to avoid the defense, the plaintiff must show that the pressure to pay was sufficient to " 'interfere with free enjoyment of his rights of person or property.' "[960] Courts that take a realistic view of the relationship between a consumer and a large entity demanding payment have given a broader reading to the meaning of "coercion" and a correspondingly narrower reading of the word "voluntary." So, for example, one New York court recognized that where a plaintiff paid overreaching recording fees to a mortgage company at closing after the company threatened to abort the sale, the plaintiff had alleged sufficient duress to maintain a money had and received action.[961] In a case where plaintiffs who had sued for money had and received to recover allegedly illegal towing fees, the court rejected the towing companies' defense that by paying the fees the plaintiffs had waived their claim, accepting the car owners' claim that they were forced to pay the fees in order to recover their vehicles.[962] The Indiana Supreme Court holds that the doctrine does not apply if the consumer is threatened with any loss of goods or services.[963]

The voluntary payment defense should also fail if the plaintiff can show that he or she did not have full knowledge of all the material facts—thereby establishing that the payment was not fully "voluntary."[964] One such material fact may be that the bill included sums that were not properly due and owing.[965] Nonetheless, a court may characterize the

954 Walsh v. America's Tele-Network Corp., 195 F. Supp. 2d 840, 852 (Tex. 1951) (citing Staats v. Miller, 243 S.W.2d 686, 687, 688 (Tex. 1951)); *see also* Webcon Group, Inc. v. S.M. Props., L.P., 1 S.W.3d 538, 542 (Mo. Ct. App. 1999) (court that has concurrent jurisdiction may invoke equitable principles regardless of whether an adequate remedy at law exists).

955 *See, e.g.*, United States v. Kensington Hosp., 760 F. Supp. 1120, 1135 (E.D. Pa. 1991); Quadion Corp. v. Mache, 738 F. Supp. 270, 278 (N.D. Ill. 1990).

956 *See, e.g.*, Jenkins v. Concorde Acceptance Corp., 802 N.E.2d 1270 (Ill. App. 2003), *app. granted*, 2004 Ill. LEXIS 583 (Mar. 24, 2004).

957 Putnam v. Time Warner Cable of Southeastern Wis., Ltd., 649 N.W.2d 626, 633 (Wis. 2002).

958 *See, e.g.*, Owl Constr. Co. v. Ronald Adams Contractor, Inc., 642 F. Supp. 2d 475, 480 (E.D. La. 1986) (citing La. Civ. Code Ann. arts. 2301, 2302); *In re* Barry, 170 B.R. 179, 183 (Bankr. S.D. Fla. 1994) ("[A]s far as equity is concerned, where one party has been unjustly enriched, the plaintiff's right to recover rests both on money paid by mistake of fact and by mistake of law"), *aff'd*, 184 B.R. 611 (S.D. Fla. 1995).

959 Sanders v. Republic Nat'l Bank of Dallas, 389 S.W.2d 551, 554 (Tex. Ct. App. 1965).

960 Smith v. Prime Cable of Chicago, 658 N.E.2d 1325, 1331 (Ill. App. Ct. 1995) (quoting Illinois Glass Co. v. Chicago Tel. Co., 85 N.E. 200, 201 (1908)).

961 Friar v. Vanguard Holding Corp., 434 N.Y.S.2d 698, 702 (N.Y. App. Div. 1980).

962 Lonergan v. A.J.'s Wrecker Serv. of Dallas, Inc., 1999 WL 462333, at *2 (N.D. Tex. 1999) (refusing to dismiss claim).

963 Time Warner Entertainment Co. v. Whiteman, 802 N.E.2d 886 (Ind. 2004).

964 *See, e.g.*, Allstate Life Ins. Co. v. Yurgil, 632 N.E.2d 282, 286 (Ill. App. Ct. 1994).

965 *See, e.g.*, Durant v. ServiceMaster Co., 159 F. Supp. 2d 977, 981 (E.D. Mich. 2001) (rejecting voluntary payment defense where plaintiffs alleged that defendant overbilled them for a fuel surcharge to which it was not entitled); TCI Cablevision of Dallas, Inc. v. Owens, 8 S.W.3d 837, 845 (Tex. App. 2000) (refusing to dismiss cable user's recoupment claim for excess late fees where plaintiff alleged that he did not pay with full knowledge of material facts because he did not know whether

consumer's ignorance of the fee's illegitimacy as a "mistake of law" that did not render the consumer's payment involuntary.[966] This view undercuts the force of the law by allowing the defendant to keep the full benefits of breaking it, and putting the full burden of knowing the law on the consumer, the party who in most cases will be far less likely apprised of it. A payment made under the mistake that the defendant is entitled to it may be characterized as a mistake of fact, not law. For example, a Missouri court upheld a party's right to recover payments that it had made pursuant to the "mistake of fact" that the contracts under which it made the payment were legally enforceable.[967]

As a pleading matter, to avoid the rule a complaint should carefully detail not just the illegitimacy of the charges themselves, but the plaintiff's own attempts to avoid them and the particular pressures exerted by the payee. In two Illinois cases that applied the voluntary payment defense, the courts zeroed in on the plaintiffs' failure to allege that they had refused to pay the demanded charges or that refusal to pay would have drawn specific consequences from the defendant.[968] A different presentation of the underlying facts might have passed muster.

the late fees were reasonably related to the costs of late payment, as opposed to amounting to unlawful liquidated damages).

966 *See, e.g.*, Abrams v. Toyota Motor Credit Corp., 2001 WL 1807357, at *10, *11 (Pa. Com. Pl. Dec. 5, 2001). *See also* Chris Albritton Constr. Co. v. Pitney Bowes Inc., 304 F.3d 527 (5th Cir. 2002) (voluntary-payment doctrine prevents breach of contract claim where commercial party failed to use reasonable diligence before paying bills that included fees that were not owed).

967 Missouri Ins. Guar. Ass'n v. Wal-Mart Stores, Inc., 811 S.W.2d 28, 35 (Mo. Ct. App. 1991). *See also* Time Warner Entertainment Co. v. Whiteman, 802 N.E.2d 886 (Ind. 2004) (doctrine only applies if consumer paid in face of recognized uncertainty about existence or extent of obligation).

968 Smith v. Prime Cable of Chicago, 658 N.E.2d 1325, 1334 (Ill. App. Ct. 1995) (condemning complaint for failing to allege that the plaintiffs had "availed themselves of all options to resist payment"); Butitta v. First Mortgage Corp., 578 N.E.2d 116, 119 (Ill. App. Ct. 1991) (condemning complaint for failing to include "any allegations that plaintiffs refused to pay the fees and that defendant retaliated by refusing to proceed with the closing").

9.8 Referral to a Government Agency

An alternative approach in cases where a private UDAP remedy is not available, or where an individual action is not practical, is to refer the consumer complaint to a government agency. This may be an unsatisfactory alternative because these agencies have limited resources, have their own priorities, and are often unable to handle cases that involve only compensating individual complainants.

Some local offices (e.g., state attorney general and city consumer protection offices) are geared toward mediating consumer disputes. They may effectively and quickly deal with some cases but rarely satisfy consumers if the seller is uncooperative. The Federal Trade Commission and state attorney general offices will initiate law enforcement investigations against suspected wrongdoers, especially if the scheme has an important economic impact on consumers or receives extensive publicity. However, these investigations, particularly at the FTC, often take years to complete and may result in agreements in which the merchant consents to cease the challenged practice, but the consumer is awarded little or no restitution.

Contacting a government agency, while not guaranteeing a client full and prompt restitution, may serve several valuable functions. It can assist the agency in preventing similar abuses in the future, by drawing the agency's attention to the problem, its prevalence, and its significance, thus providing a basis for agency action or legislative reform. Some dealers and creditors are very responsive to the government agencies that regulate them, particularly if the agency has the power to revoke a business license. Consumer enforcement agencies are also a useful source of information about the offending seller and the deceptive sales scheme. These agencies may be able to point to a pattern of deceptive conduct and may already possess useful evidence that can be used in private litigation.

Contact information for federal, state, and local consumer protection agencies, national consumer organizations, and Better Business Bureaus is included on the companion CD-Rom to this volume. It is also available on-line from the Federal Consumer Information Center, www.pueblo.gsa.gov.

Chapter 10 State Agency Enforcement

10.1 Introduction

This chapter analyzes special topics concerning state agency enforcement of UDAP statutes. State agency enforcement provisions of UDAP statutes are to be given a liberal construction consistent with their remedial purposes.[1]

Those interested in state enforcement of UDAP statutes should use this chapter in conjunction with other chapters. In particular, Chapters 1 through 7 consider issues important to both private litigants and enforcement officials, such as when a practice is unfair or deceptive, the scope of the state statute, how to research UDAP law, and constitutional and jurisdictional issues. This chapter discusses state investigatory powers and remedies, and special issues of standing, scope, and statutory standards when the state, not a private individual, brings a UDAP action. The chapter's primary focus is state UDAP law, and does not cover state prosecution powers under other statutes. The ability of private UDAP litigants to access complaints and other information gathered by state enforcement authorities is discussed in § 7.9.3, *supra*.

10.2 Civil Investigative Demands, Subpoenas, and Other Investigative Issues

10.2.1 Introduction

State agencies enforcing the UDAP statute generally have authority to use compulsory process in an investigation prior to filing a complaint. The two types of process are a civil investigation demand (CID) or a subpoena. These are powerful investigation tools that can compel production of documents and sworn testimony prior to any lawsuit being filed by law enforcement officials. This section will also consider other investigational issues, such as the state's use of test shoppers, the respondent's ability to discover the nature of the state's case, and the state's ability to use FTC investigational files.

The section is largely limited to an analysis of precedent dealing with UDAP investigations. Case law dealing with other forms of civil or criminal law enforcement investigations is not covered. Consequently, state enforcement officials should supplement this section with their state's own case law concerning state law enforcement investigations.

10.2.2 Standards of Review for Compulsory Process

The fundamental standards courts utilize in determining the propriety of a civil investigation demand or subpoena are whether "the inquiry is within the authority of the agency, the demand is not too indefinite, and the information sought is reasonably relevant."[2] These standards should be con-

1 Shiffrin v. I.V. Servs. of Am., Inc., 53 Conn. App. 129, 729 A.2d 784 (1999); State *ex rel.* Brady v. Publishers Clearing House, 787 A.2d 111 (Del. Ch. 2001); *In re* Attorney General's Investigative Demand, 493 A.2d 972 (Del. Super. Ct. 1985); Idaho *ex rel.* Lance v. Hobby Horse Ranch Tractor & Equip. Co., 929 P.2d 741 (Idaho 1996); Iowa *ex rel.* Campbell v. C-Pals Corp., Clearinghouse No. 50,444 (Iowa Dist. Ct. Dec. 19, 1994); *In re* Yankee Milk, Inc., 372 Mass. 353, 362 N.E.2d 207 (1977); Charlie's Dodge, Inc. v. Celebrezze, 72 Ohio App. 3d 744, 596 N.E.2d 486 (1991); Windsor Tower, Inc. v. Eaden, Clearinghouse No. 36,570 (Tenn. Ct. App. Jan. 28, 1983); State v. Custom Pools, 556 A.2d 72 (Vt. 1988). *See also* State *ex rel.* Div. of Consumer Protection v. GAF Corp., 760 P.2d 310 (Utah 1988) (construing statute to avoid subverting its purpose of protecting consumers).

2 United States v. Powell, 379 U.S. 48 (1964); United States v. Morton Salt Co., 338 U.S. 632 (1950); United States v. Litton Indus., 462 F.2d 14 (9th Cir. 1972); Tesoro Petroleum Corp. v. State, 42 P.3d 531 (Alaska 2002) (antitrust case); People *ex rel.* Babbitt v. Herndon, 119 Ariz. 454, 581 P.2d 688 (1978); Shiffrin v. I.V. Servs. of Am., Inc., 53 Conn. App. 129, 729 A.2d 784 (1999); Heslin v. Liberty Bank for Savings, 1977-1 Trade Cases ¶ 61,311 (Conn. C.P. 1977); *In re* Attorney General's Investigative Demand, 493 A.2d 972 (Del. Super. Ct. 1985); Idaho *ex rel.* Lance v. Hobby Horse Ranch Tractor & Equip. Co., 929 P.2d 741 (Idaho 1996); Scott v. Association for Childbirth at Home Int'l, 88 Ill. 2d 279, 430 N.E.2d 1012 (1981); Gumpty Corp. v. State, Clearinghouse No. 43,076 (Md. Ct. Spec. App. 1988); *In re* Yankee Milk, Inc., 372 Mass. 353, 362 N.E.2d 207 (1977); Kohn v. State *ex rel.* Humphrey, 336 N.W.2d 292 (Minn. 1983) (adding requirement that investigation not be undertaken for improper purpose such as harassment); Commonwealth v. Shults, 26 Pa. Commw. 129, 362 A.2d 1129 (1976); Commonwealth v. Miller Chrysler-Plymouth, Inc., 30 Pa. D. & C.3d 226 (C.P. Erie Cty. 1982); Commonwealth v. Smith, Clearinghouse No. 26,018 (Pa. C.P. Montgomery Cty. 1977); Windsor Tower,

strued liberally in favor of the government because of the remedial purposes of UDAP legislation.[3]

The first standard the compulsory process must meet is that the inquiry is within the authority of the agency.[4] Where such authority is uncertain, however, government agencies may argue successfully that the requested information is needed to help the agency and the court determine whether the inquiry is within the authority of the agency.[5] The applicability of the UDAP statute to the conduct of the party subject to the subpoena is not an issue at the investigative stage.[6] Even if the state agency has no authority to prosecute the recipient of the subpoena, the subpoena should still be enforced if the information will lead to prosecution of others within the agency's authority.[7] The fact that another state agency also has authority over the same business, and is investigating it, does not affect the attorney general's authority.[8] Nor can respondents argue that an investigation is outside the scope of the enforcing agency's authority just because the challenged practice has been followed in the industry for some time and has never previously been declared in violation of the state UDAP statute or the FTC Act.[9] A state UDAP statute's reach is a broad and evolving one.

The second standard, that the inquiry not be too indefinite or vague, is a broad standard, but there are limits. For example, a court has refused to enforce a CID that requires a company to produce virtually all its documents and that would substantially interfere with the operation of the company's business.[10] Unless compliance threatens to unduly disrupt or seriously hinder normal operations of a business, the compulsory process is not unreasonable.[11] While the compilation of the material requested should not substantially interfere with the operation of the respondent's business, a subpoena is not too indefinite even if it imposes considerable expense on the business.[12] Since the attorney general does not know what it will receive in response to a demand, it need only give a "reasonably informative description."[13]

The definitive requirement will be satisfied if the party subpoenaed knows precisely what is sought and good faith compliance will not be unduly burdensome.[14] It is often advisable to limit a CID by requesting documents produced during a specified time period, or by precisely identifying the documents requested.[15] A subpoena may go back in time for a reasonable period to determine the extent of noncompliance with UDAP requirements,[16] and may even seek information regarding transactions that are beyond the statute of limitations for suit.[17] If the state seeks information about transactions outside the state, it should be prepared to

Inc. v. Eaden, Clearinghouse No. 36,570 (Tenn. Ct. App. 1983); Steele v. State, 85 Wash. 2d 585, 537 P.2d 782 (1975).

3 Heslin v. Liberty Bank for Savings, 1977-1 Trade Cases ¶ 61,311 (C.P. Conn. 1977); *In re* Attorney General's Investigative Demand, 493 A.2d 972 (Del. Super. Ct. 1985); Idaho *ex rel.* Lance v. Hobby Horse Ranch Tractor & Equip. Co., 929 P.2d 741 (Idaho 1996); *In re* Yankee Milk, Inc., 372 Mass. 353, 362 N.E.2d 207 (1977); Charlie's Dodge, Inc. v. Celebrezze, 72 Ohio App. 3d 744, 596 N.E.2d 486 (1991); Windsor Tower, Inc. v. Eaden, Clearinghouse No. 36,570 (Tenn. Ct. App. Jan. 28, 1983).

4 Commonwealth v. Shults, 26 Pa. Commw. 129, 362 A.2d 1129 (1976); *see also* Ports Petroleum Co. v. Nixon, 37 S.W.3d 237 (Mo. 2001) (AG can not use UDAP CID authority to investigate violations of statute which prohibits price cutting); Hertz Corp. v. Attorney General, 136 Misc. 2d 420, 518 N.Y.S.2d 704 (Sup. Ct. 1987).

5 *See* Oklahoma Press Publishing Co. v. Walling, 327 U.S. 186 (1946); Vendall Marketing Corp. v. State, 318 Or. 189, 863 P.2d 1263 (1993); Windsor Tower, Inc. v. Eaden, Clearinghouse No. 36,570 (Tenn. Ct. App. 1983); *In re* Stifel, Nicholaus & Co., Clearinghouse No. 38,906 (Tenn. Ch. Ct. 1984). *See also* Department of Legal Affairs v. Jackson, 576 So. 2d 864 (Fla. Dist. Ct. App. 1991).

6 State *ex rel.* Kulongoski v. Cunning, 139 Or. App. 515, 912 P.2d 958 (1996).

7 Atlanta Auto Auction v. Ryles, 148 Ga. App. 20, 251 S.E.2d 28 (1978); *In re* Yankee Milk, Inc., 372 Mass. 353, 362 N.E.2d 207 (1977); Attorney General v. Bodimetric Profiles, 404 Mass. 152, 533 N.E.2d 1364 (1989); Vendall Marketing Corp. v. State, 318 Or. 189, 863 P.2d 1263 (1993).

8 Carrington v. Arizona Corp. Comm'n, 199 Ariz. 303, 18 P.3d 97 (App. 2000). *See also* State v. Ralph Williams' N.W. Chrysler Plymouth, Inc., 87 Wash. 2d 298, 553 P.2d 423 (1976) (fact that another state agency also has authority to enforce laws applicable to particular industry does not oust AG's authority)

9 Heslin v. Liberty Bank for Savings, 1977-1 Trade Cases ¶ 61,311 (C.P. Conn. 1977).

10 Check 'N Go of Fla., Inc. v. State, 790 So. 2d 454 (Fla. App. 2001) (subpoena under state RICO statute seeking substantial part of company's books and records was overbroad; should have focused on transactions that demonstrated the specific problem being investigated); *In re* Yankee Milk, Inc., 372 Mass. 353, 362 N.E.2d 207 (1977).

11 FTC v. Jim Walter Corp., 651 F.2d 251 (5th Cir. 1981); Attorney General v. Bodimetric Profiles, 404 Mass. 152, 533 N.E.2d 1364, 1368 (1989) (investigative demands exceed reasonable limits only when they "seriously interfere with functioning of the investigated party by placing excessive burdens on manpower or requiring removal of critical records"); Windsor Tower, Inc. v. Eaden, Clearinghouse No. 36,570 (Tenn. Ct. App. 1983).

12 *In re* Attorney General's Investigative Demand, 493 A.2d 972 (Del. Super. Ct. 1985); *In re* Yankee Milk, Inc., 372 Mass. 353, 362 N.E.2d 207 (1977); Wiener v. State *ex rel.* Abrams, 119 Misc. 2d 970, 464 N.Y.S.2d 919 (Sup. Ct. 1983).

13 Scott v. Ass'n for Childbirth at Home Int'l, 88 Ill. 2d 279, 430 N.E.2d 1012 (1981); Heritage House of Glamour, Inc. v. Attorney General, 179 Ill. App. 3d 336, 534 N.E.2d 648 (1989).

14 People *ex rel.* MacFarlane v. American Banco Corp., 194 Colo. 32, 570 P.2d 825 (1977).

15 *In re* O'Neill Investigations, Clearinghouse No. 26,039 (Alaska Super. Ct. 1976); *In re* Attorney General's Investigative Demand, 493 A.2d 972 (Del. Super. Ct. 1985); Check 'N Go of Fla., Inc. v. State, 790 So. 2d 454 (Fla. App. 2001) (subpoena under state RICO statute was overbroad where it requested documents created prior to company's incorporation).

16 Abrams v. Thruway Food Market, 147 A.D.2d 143, 541 N.Y.S.2d 856 (1989).

17 Auto-Owners Ins. Co. v. State, 692 N.E.2d 935 (Ind. App. 1998).

show why these transactions are within its authority or are relevant to in-state transactions.[18]

In interpreting the third standard, that the information is "reasonably relevant," a CID or subpoena is not limited to significant or material documents; the test is "simply one of relevance."[19] Courts take a deferential approach to the state enforcement agency's determination of relevance.[20] The state enforcement agency can examine any document relevant to its investigation, not just particularly useful documents. All that must be shown is a relationship between the documents and the purpose of the inquiry,[21] or that the information sought is not plainly incompetent or irrelevant to any lawful purpose.[22] The burden is on the party opposing the subpoena to show that the information sought is so irrelevant as to fail to comply with these standards.[23]

The party moving to set aside a CID bears a heavy burden to show good cause why it should not be compelled to respond.[24] A party who remains passive and does not utilize a statutory procedure for challenging a civil investigative demand may be barred from challenging it when the state enforcement agency seeks a court order enforcing the CID.[25]

The party being investigated has standing to challenge a CID or subpoena that has been issued to it.[26] It may also challenge CIDs or subpoenas issued to third parties that seek documents that are its property or that impinge on its privileges, but it only has standing to challenge the substance rather than the form of the subpoena.[27]

A company should not be able to raise defenses to a UDAP action in a hearing to determine whether compulsory process will be enforced. Factual and legal issues pertaining to the defendant's defense are better treated in later proceedings if the state pursues the action.[28]

10.2.3 Constitutional Issues

10.2.3.1 Due Process

Courts consistently uphold subpoenas and CID's against due process challenges.[29] Procedural due process is satisfied where there is specific notice of documents to be produced and a meaningful opportunity to be heard.[30] Court review of the state's subpoena is sufficient protection against unconstitutional searches.[31] While a subpoena ordering production of records "forthwith" without sufficient opportunity to consult counsel may deny the respondent due process, this defect can be cured by a state official's subsequent oral offer to allow additional time to produce the records.[32] Nevertheless, it is good practice to give a respondent a reasonable time to respond to the request. It may also be good practice not to place onerous and unnecessary travel requirements on a small defendant. The Illinois Supreme Court has found unconstitutional an attorney general's subpoena requiring the respondent to travel several hundred miles. The court indicated it would be more reasonable to investigate the matter more thoroughly before inflicting this hardship on the individual respondent.[33]

18 Check 'N Go of Fla., Inc. v. State, 790 So. 2d 454 (Fla. App. 2001) (subpoena under state RICO statute seeking information about transactions occurring outside Florida was overbroad).

19 *In re* O'Neill Investigations, Clearinghouse No. 26,039 (Alaska Super. Ct. 1976); Heslin v. Liberty Bank for Savings, 1977-1 Trade Cases ¶ 61,311 (C.P. Conn. 1977); *In re* Attorney General's Investigative Demand, 493 A.2d 972 (Del. Super. Ct. 1985); CUNA Mut. Ins. Society v. Attorney General, 380 Mass. 539, 404 N.E.2d 1219 (1980); *In re* Yankee Milk, Inc., 372 Mass. 353, 362 N.E.2d 207 (1977); Wiener v. State *ex rel.* Abrams, 119 Misc. 2d 970, 464 N.Y.S.2d 919 (Sup. Ct. 1983); Commonwealth v. Miller Chrysler-Plymouth, Inc., 30 Pa. D. & C.3d (C.P. Erie Cty. 1982).

20 Tesoro Petroleum Corp. v. State, 42 P.3d 531 (Alaska 2002) (antitrust case).

21 People *ex rel.* MacFarlane v. American Banco Corp., 194 Colo. 32, 570 P.2d 825 (1977); *In re* Attorney General's Investigative Demand, 493 A.2d 972 (Del. Super. Ct. 1985); Wiener v. State *ex rel.* Abrams, 119 Misc. 2d 970, 464 N.Y.S.2d 919 (Sup. Ct. 1983); Steele v. State, 85 Wash. 2d 585, 537 P.2d 782 (1975).

22 Heslin v. Liberty Bank for Savings, 1977-1 Trade Cases 61,311 (C.P. Conn. 1977); Abrams v. Thruway Food Market, 147 A.D.2d 143, 541 N.Y.S.2d 856 (1989) (person opposing subpoena *duces tecum* must show that documents sought are "utterly irrelevant").

23 Abrams v. Thruway Food Market, 147 A.D.2d 143, 541 N.Y.S.2d 856 (1989).

24 Attorney General v. Bodimetric Profiles, 404 Mass. 152, 533 N.E.2d 1364 (1989) (party resisting civil investigative demand has burden of showing good cause to modify it or set it aside); CUNA Mut. Ins. Society v. Attorney General, 380 Mass. 539, 404 N.E.2d 1219 (1980); *In re* Yankee Milk, Inc., 372 Mass. 353, 362 N.E.2d 207 (1977).

25 Idaho *ex rel.* Lance v. Hobby Horse Ranch Tractor & Equip. Co., 929 P.2d 741 (Idaho 1996); Attorney General v. Bodimetric Profiles, 404 Mass. 152, 533 N.E.2d 1364 (1989).

26 Oncor Communications v. State of New York, 165 Misc. 2d 262, 626 N.Y.S.2d 369 (Sup. 1995).

27 *Id.*

28 FTC v. Feldman, 532 F.2d 1092 (7th Cir. 1976); Attorney General v. Bodimetric Profiles, 404 Mass. 152, 533 N.E.2d 1364 (1989) (whether party is covered by the law is not at issue in enforcement of civil investigative demand); National Apartment Leasing Co. v. Commonwealth *ex rel.* Zimmerman, 519 A.2d 1055 (Pa. Commw. Ct. 1986); Windsor Tower, Inc. v. Eaden, Clearinghouse No. 36,570 (Tenn. Ct. App. 1983).

29 People *ex rel.* MacFarlane v. American Banco Corp., 194 Colo. 32, 570 P.2d 825 (1977); Scott v. Ass'n for Childbirth at Home Int'l, 88 Ill. 2d 279, 430 N.E.2d 1012 (1981); Commonwealth *ex rel.* Hancock v. Pineur, 533 S.W.2d 527 (Ky. 1976); State *ex rel.* Ashcroft v. Goldberg, 608 S.W.2d 385 (Mo. 1980); Lewandowski v. Danforth, 547 S.W.2d 470 (Mo. 1977), *cert. denied*, 434 U.S. 832 (1977).

30 *Id.*

31 People *ex rel.* MacFarlane v. American Banco Corp., 194 Colo. 32, 570 P.2d 825 (1977); Commonwealth *ex rel.* Hancock v. Pineur, 533 S.W.2d 527 (Ky. 1976).

32 *In re* Attorney General of New Jersey, 116 N.J. Super. 143, 281 A.2d 284 (1971).

33 People v. McWhorter, 113 Ill. 2d 374, 498 N.E.2d 1154 (1986).

10.2.3.2 Self-Incrimination

Respondents' constitutional protection against self-incrimination is a stronger ground for resisting a subpoena. But a business entity (such as a corporation or partnership), as opposed to an individual, has no right against self-incrimination, and can be compelled to produce records and other documents.[34] One commentator has explained: "A corporation can not take advantage of the fact that individual officers may be incriminated by the answers. It must find an agent who will not be so incriminated, and he must give what information the corporation may have."[35] Moreover, "an individual can not rely upon the privilege to avoid producing the records of a collective entity which are in his possession in a representative capacity, even if these records might incriminate him personally."[36]

It is thus good practice when seeking business documents to address the subpoena to the business or to an individual in a representative capacity. However, where a subpoena does not make clear whether it is addressed to the individual in a representative or private capacity, a court has looked at the circumstances of the case to determine that the subpoena was addressed to the individual in a representative capacity.[37]

An individual's claim against self-incrimination can be defeated by a grant of transactional immunity.[38] This grant prevents any of the information the respondent divulges from being used in a criminal action. Since a UDAP action, even one seeking civil penalties, is not criminal, the information can be utilized in a UDAP enforcement case.[39] The state can still bring a UDAP action for civil penalties or an injunction against the individual granted immunity.[40]

Even if there is an argument that a UDAP action is "criminal," thus preventing utilization of the immunized testimony, this argument goes to the propriety of the eventual UDAP prosecution, and can not be utilized as grounds to refuse to testify once immunity has been granted.[41] Prosecutors must be careful to grant broad enough immunity to stop any form of criminal prosecution; otherwise the respondent can argue that the testimony is still privileged because of the resulting danger of use in some form of criminal prosecution.[42] The grant of immunity "is not sufficient to compel testimony over a claim of the privilege, unless the scope of the grant of immunity is coextensive with the scope of the privilege."[43] Thus immunity is not adequate where the state only agrees not to use the compelled testimony in certain criminal prosecutions.[44]

If there are both criminal and civil proceedings against a defendant for the same acts, the court in the civil case may be faced with the question whether to stay the case until the criminal charges are resolved. A federal court ruled that the constitution does not require a stay of a civil suit brought by the FTC even though the defendant was asserting the Fifth Amendment in a parallel criminal case.[45] The court weighed the interest of the plaintiff in an expeditious resolution, the burden to the defendant, the convenience of the court and the efficient use of judicial resources, and the interests of non-parties and the public. The court was particularly swayed by the FTC's interest in proceeding expeditiously because of the defendant telemarketer's history of hiding assets and the continuing detriment to banks and credit card issuers due to charge-backs.

Even though the court may have discretion not to stay the civil case, it is usually best to allow the criminal charges to be resolved first. The criminal charges will be subject to speedy trial rules, so it is risky to try to postpone them until after the civil matters are tried. Also, trying the criminal charges first minimizes the grounds for asserting the Fifth Amendment privilege in the civil case. The criminal case may also resolve or moot many of the issues in the civil case.

---

34 Doe v. United States, 487 U.S. 201, 206, 108 S. Ct. 2341, 101 L. Ed. 2d 184 (1988); Fisher v. United States, 425 U.S. 391, 408 (1976); Bellis v. United States, 417 U.S. 85, 88 (1974); United States v. Morton Salt Co., 338 U.S. 632 (1950); Oklahoma Press Publishing Co. v. Walling, 327 U.S. 186 (1946); People *ex rel.* MacFarlane v. American Banco Corp., 194 Colo. 32, 570 P.2d 825 (1977); Attorney General v. Genie Project, Inc., Clearinghouse No. 41,257 (Conn. Super. Ct. 1986); Heslin v. Liberty Bank for Savings, 1977-1 Trade Cases ¶ 61,311 (C.P. Conn. 1977); *In re* Attorney General's Investigative Demand, 493 A.2d 972 (Del. Super. Ct. 1985); Kohn v. State *ex rel.* Humphrey, 336 N.W.2d 292 (Minn. 1983).

35 6 Moore's Federal Practice § 26.51(2), note 12 (3d ed. 1997).

36 Bellis v. United States, 417 U.S. 85, 88 (1974). *See also* Kohn v. State *ex rel.* Humphrey, 336 N.W.2d 292 (Minn. 1983).

37 Kohn v. State *ex rel.* Humphrey, 336 N.W.2d 292 (Minn. 1983).

38 Kastigar v. United States, 406 U.S. 441 (1972); Counselman v. Hitchcock, 142 U.S. 547 (1892); *see also* People *ex rel.* Smith v. Jordan, 689 P.2d 1172 (Colo. Ct. App. 1984).

39 Duncan v. Norton, 974 F. Supp. 1328 (D. Colo. 1997); People v. Superior Court (Kaufman), 12 Cal. 3d 421, 115 Cal. Rptr. 812, 525 P.2d 716 (1974); People *ex rel.* Smith v. Jordan, 689 P.2d 1172 (Colo. Ct. App. 1984); State *ex rel.* Ashcroft v. Goldberg, 608 S.W.2d 385 (Mo. 1980); State *ex rel.* Celebrezze v. Hughes, 58 Ohio St. 3d 273, 569 N.E.2d 1059 (1991). *But cf.* People v. Fleming, 804 P.2d 231 (Colo. Ct. App. 1990) (potential use of records for civil UDAP action does not justify prosecutor seizing records in criminal case), *rev'd on other grounds*, 817 P.2d 985 (Colo. 1991) (error, if any, was harmless), *cert. denied*, 502 U.S. 1113 (1992).

40 Duncan v. Norton, 974 F. Supp. 1328 (D. Colo. 1997); People *ex rel.* Smith v. Jordan, 689 P.2d 1172 (Colo. Ct. App. 1984); People *ex rel.* Fahner v. Walsh, 122 Ill. App. Ct. 481, 461 N.E.2d 78 (1984); State *ex rel.* Celebrezze v. Hughes, 58 Ohio St. 3d 273, 569 N.E.2d 1059 (1991).

41 People *ex rel.* Scott v. Walsh, 89 Ill. App. Ct. 3d 831, 412 N.E.2d 208 (1980).

42 Kastigar v. United States, 406 U.S. 441 (1972); People *ex rel.* MacFarlane v. Sari, 196 Colo. 235, 585 P.2d 591 (1978); *see also* People *ex rel.* Smith v. Jordan, 689 P.2d 1172 (Colo. Ct. App. 1984).

43 Kastigar v. United States, 406 U.S. 441, 450 (1972).

44 Attorney General v. Colleton, 387 Mass. 790, 444 N.E.2d 915 (1982).

45 F.T.C. v. J.K. Publications, 99 F. Supp. 2d 1176 (C.D. Cal. 2000).

If a respondent declines to testify in a civil proceeding based on the Fifth Amendment, a negative inference can be drawn by the trier of fact from the refusal to answer a specific question.[46]

10.2.3.3 Unreasonable Search and Seizure

Respondents may try to quash a subpoena by raising the Constitution's protection against unreasonable search and seizure. This protection applies in only a limited way to corporations: it is a protection against unreasonable requests for disclosures. Courts rely on a three-part test to determine whether an agency's request is reasonable: is the request within the authority of the agency; is the request too indefinite; and is the information sought reasonably relevant?[47]

10.2.4 Preconditions

10.2.4.1 Reasonable Cause

In a number of states, enforcement officials must have "reasonable cause" to believe the UDAP statute has been violated before they can issue a CID or subpoena. As a general rule, the state need not have such reasonable cause unless there is an express requirement in the authorizing statute.[48] Nevertheless, some state courts do infer a reasonable cause requirement into the UDAP legislation.[49]

Reasonable cause is a lower standard than probable cause.[50] Reasonable cause does not require actual belief that violations have occurred.[51] The state need not have definitive proof of a violation before issuing subpoenas; the attorney general is merely required to look at the evidence and rely on good judgment in deciding whether to issue subpoenas.[52]

The state's reasonable cause to believe that a law violation has occurred can be based on consumer complaints or informal inquiries, and the state does not need to have direct knowledge of the law violation.[53] This reasonable cause can be based on a small number of consumer complaints that represent only a tiny portion of the respondent's total customers.[54] The state does not have to investigate the accuracy of these complaints before having reasonable cause to pursue compulsory process.[55]

Reasonable cause can be based on evidence developed by the state attorney general's office.[56] But the state must have more than just a belief that if the subpoenaed documents were obtained, then at that time the state would have

46 *See* Mitchell v. United States, 526 U.S. 314, 328, 119 S. Ct. 1307, 1315, 143 L. Ed. 2d 424 (1999); Baxter v. Palmigiano, 425 U.S. 308, 318, 96 S. Ct. 1551, 47 L. Ed. 2d 810 (1976); United States v. Stein, 233 F.3d 6 (1st Cir. 2000); FTC v. Crescent Publ. Group, 129 F. Supp. 2d 311, 320 n.56 (S.D.N.Y. 2001) (case brought under FTC Act and N.Y. UDAP statute).

47 G.M. Leasing v. U.S., 429 U.S. 338 (1977) (corporations have 4th amendment right to freedom from unreasonable searches); California Bankers Assn. v. Shultz, 416 U.S. 21 (1974); United States v. Morton Salt Co., 338 U.S. 632 (1950); Oklahoma Press Publishing Co. v. Walling, 327 U.S. 186 (1946); Heslin v. Liberty Bank for Savings, 1977-1 Trade Cases ¶ 61,311 (C.P. Conn. 1977); Check 'N Go of Fla., Inc. v. State, 790 So. 2d 454 (Fla. App. 2001); Steele v. State, 85 Wash. 2d 585, 537 P.2d 782 (1975); *see also* New York v. Burger, 482 U.S. 691 (1987) (warrantless search of auto junkyard was constitutional; 4th amendment rights are particularly attenuated for commercial property used in closely regulated industries); Kohn v. State *ex rel.* Humphrey, 336 N.W.2d 292 (Minn. 1983).

48 Scott v. Ass'n for Childbirth at Home Int'l, 88 Ill. 2d 279, 430 N.E.2d 1012 (1981); Gumpty Corp. v. State, Clearinghouse No. 43,076 (Md. Ct. Spec. App. 1988); Little v. Department of Justice, 130 Or. App. 668, 883 P.2d 272 (1994) (court declines to read in probable cause requirement); Commonwealth v. Miller Chrysler-Plymouth, Inc., 30 Pa. D. & C.3d (C.P. Erie Cty. 1982); Commonwealth v. Gibson, Clearinghouse No. 26,029 (Pa. C.P. Allegheny Cty. 1974); *see also* United States v. Powell, 379 U.S. 48 (1964); Oklahoma Press Publishing Co. v. Walling, 327 U.S. 186 (1946); United States v. DeGrosa, 405 F.2d 926 (3d Cir. 1969), *cert. denied*, 374 U.S. 973 (1969).

49 People *ex rel.* MacFarlane v. American Banco Corp., 194 Colo. 32, 570 P.2d 825 (1977); Ward v. Commonwealth, 566 S.W.2d 426 (Ky. Ct. App. 1978); *see also* Windsor Tower, Inc. v. Eaden, Clearinghouse No. 36,570 (Tenn. Ct. App. 1983) (reason to believe statute violated *or* where it is in the public interest to determine whether the statute is being violated).

50 Paramount Builders, Inc. v. Commonwealth, 260 Va. 22, 530 S.E.2d 142 (2000); *In re* American Dollar Exchange, Inc., 27 Va. Cir. 428 (1992). *See* Check 'N Go of Fla., Inc. v. State, 790 So. 2d 454 (Fla. App. 2001) (interpreting subpoena authority of state RICO statute).

51 Paramount Builders, Inc. v. Commonwealth, 260 Va. 22, 530 S.E.2d 142 (2000); *In re* American Dollar Exchange, Inc., 27 Va. Cir. 428 (1992).

52 Charlie's Dodge, Inc. v. Celebrezze, 72 Ohio App. 3d 744, 596 N.E.2d 486 (1991). *See also* Check 'N Go of Fla., Inc. v. State, 790 So. 2d 454 (Fla. App. 2001) (test of "reason to believe" under state RICO statute is whether reasonably prudent person would be warranted in the belief that subject of subpoena had or was engaging in violation).

53 Kohn v. State *ex rel.* Humphrey, 336 N.W.2d 292 (Minn. 1983); Oncor Communications v. State of New York, 165 Misc. 2d 262, 626 N.Y.S.2d 369 (Sup. 1995); Commonwealth v. Lackey, Clearinghouse No. 26,037 (Pa. Commw. Ct. 1974); Windsor Tower, Inc. v. Eaden, Clearinghouse No. 36,570 (Tenn. Ct. App. 1983); Paramount Builders, Inc. v. Commonwealth, 260 Va. 22, 530 S.E.2d 142 (2000). *See also* Auto-Owners Ins. Co. v. State, 692 N.E.2d 935 (Ind. App. 1998) (pointing out absurdity of requiring reasonable cause to believe a violation occurred before an investigation is even initiated).

54 Kohn v. State *ex rel.* Humphrey, 336 N.W.2d 292 (Minn. 1983). *See also* Check 'N Go of Fla., Inc. v. State, 790 So. 2d 454 (Fla. App. 2001) (admissions by company, one customer affidavit, a survey, and a log from a county consumer protection office's investigation of a second customer's complaint held sufficient). *Cf.* Oncor Communications v. State of New York, 165 Misc. 2d 262, 626 N.Y.S.2d 369 (Sup. 1995) (basis for subpoena must be more than isolated or rare complaints by disgruntled persons).

55 Kohn v. State *ex rel.* Humphrey, 336 N.W.2d 292 (Minn. 1983).

56 *In re* Capital Minnesota Rents, Inc., Clearinghouse No. 45,906 (Minn. Dist. Ct. Ramsey Cty. Apr. 2, 1990); *In re* American Dollar Exchange, Inc., 27 Va. Cir. 428 (1992).

evidence allowing it to have reasonable cause.[57] When the statute requires that the state have reason to believe that the UDAP statute has been violated before the state can conduct an investigation, the state may not be able to conduct random test shopping.[58]

The state does not have to have reasonable cause to believe that the party to whom the subpoena is directed has violated the law, only that the law has been violated and that the subpoenaed information is relevant to the conduct of that investigation. Thus the state is not limited in issuing a CID or subpoena only to the person being investigated.[59]

Where an enforcement agency must have reasonable cause to believe the law has been violated before initiating compulsory process, that agency would be wise, and may even be required, to include in the subpoena or a supporting affidavit facts sufficient to demonstrate probable cause.[60] The state need not, however, make a factual showing of the violations themselves. Attaching copies of consumer complaints is sufficient.[61] The respondent also has a right to a hearing to raise lack of probable cause as a defense in any subpoena enforcement action.[62] However, at least some courts find that this hearing can be summary and need not comply with the state's rules of procedure,[63] and that the respondent has no right before such hearing to discover from the state what evidence the state has accumulated.[64]

Some state statutes also explicitly require more than just "reasonable cause," such as that the attorney general have evidence of unlawful activity before a CID is issued.[65] In that case, reasonable cause is not enough, and the state must allege material facts upon which its evidence of unlawful activity is based.[66] In some states, the UDAP statute may only require the attorney general to have reasonable cause to believe that the respondent has information that is relevant to an investigation, a lower standard than reasonable cause to believe that the respondent has committed UDAP violations.[67] In Massachusetts, the attorney general must have a belief that a person has violated the law before issuing a civil investigative demand, but the burden is on the party opposing the demand to show the attorney general acted arbitrarily or capriciously.[68]

10.2.4.2 Other Preconditions

The UDAP statute may require other conditions to be met for the issuance of a CID or subpoena. Virginia's statute, for example, allows a court to issue an investigative order if the attorney general is unable to obtain the information after a good faith effort, or it is impractical for the attorney general to do so. These are alternative, mutually exclusive options.[69] The attorney general need not make a factual showing that these conditions are met, but need only set forth the grounds in the petition.[70] The attorney general's belief that the respondent is likely to destroy the documents if given advance notice is sufficient to establish that it is impractical to obtain the documents without a court order.[71]

10.2.5 Defects on the Face of a Subpoena

State enforcement officials should be careful in drafting CIDs and subpoenas to make sure that the compulsory process fulfills all statutory requirements. Litigious respondents will scrutinize the process hoping to find a technical defect. While it is good practice not to give respondents grounds for objecting to the form of the subpoena, courts will usually enforce compulsory process even if there are complaints as to form.

A subpoena need not be personally signed by the state's attorney general,[72] the subpoena need not allege the grounds for its issuance or the illegal activity being investigated[73] (unless the statute requires this to establish the state's reasonable cause to believe a violation exists), and the sub-

57 Commonwealth v. Lackey, Clearinghouse No. 26,037 (Pa. Commw. Ct. 1974); *see also* Ward v. Commonwealth, 566 S.W.2d 426 (Ky. Ct. App. 1978).

58 Schweitzer v. State *ex rel.* Macy, No. 60,708 (Okla. Feb. 7, 1989) (unpublished opinion); State *ex rel.* Macy v. T.G. & Y. Stores Co., No. 59,085, (Okla. Nov. 18, 1986) (unpublished opinion).

59 Attorney General v. Bodimetric Profiles, 404 Mass. 152, 533 N.E.2d 1364 (1989); CUNA Mut. Ins. Society v. Attorney General, 380 Mass. 539, 404 N.E.2d 1219 (1980); *see also* Atlanta Auto Auction v. Ryles, 148 Ga. App. 20, 251 S.E.2d 28 (1978).

60 Diamond v. Vickrey, 134 Vt. 585, 367 A.2d 668 (1976).

61 Paramount Builders, Inc. v. Commonwealth, 260 Va. 22, 530 S.E.2d 142 (2000). *See also* Kasha v. Dept. of Legal Affairs, 375 So. 2d 43 (Fla. Dist. Ct. App. 1979) (affidavits could be admitted to supplement other evidence to show that the state had probable cause to institute enforcement proceeding).

62 People *ex rel.* Babbitt v. Herndon, 119 Ariz. 454, 581 P.2d 688 (1978); People *ex rel.* MacFarlane v. American Banco Corp., 194 Colo. 32, 570 P.2d 825 (1977); Ward v. Commonwealth, 566 S.W.2d 426 (Ky. Ct. App. 1978).

63 State *ex rel.* MacFarlane v. American Banco Corp., 194 Colo. 32, 570 P.2d 825 (1977).

64 State *ex rel.* Babbitt v. Herndon, 119 Ariz. 454, 581 P.2d 688 (1978).

65 Humphreys v. State *ex rel.* Guste, 377 So. 2d 88 (La. 1979).

66 *Id.*

67 Auto-Owners Ins. Co. v. State, 692 N.E.2d 935 (Ind. App. 1998).

68 Attorney General v. Bodimetric Profiles, 404 Mass. 152, 533 N.E.2d 1364 (1989).

69 Paramount Builders, Inc. v. Commonwealth, 260 Va. 22, 530 S.E.2d 142 (2000).

70 *Id.*

71 *Id.*

72 *In re* Western Acceptance Corp., 788 P.2d 214 (Idaho 1990); Scott v. Ass'n for Childbirth at Home Int'l, 88 Ill. 2d 279, 430 N.E.2d 1012 (1981).

73 Commonwealth *ex rel.* Hancock v. Pineur, 533 S.W.2d 527 (Ky. 1976); Commonwealth v. Gibson, Clearinghouse No. 26,029 (Pa. C.P. Allegheny Cty. 1974).

poena need not identify the specific person whose conduct is being investigated.[74] Even a statutory requirement that the names of persons being examined must be identified does not require that the subject of the investigation be identified.[75]

10.2.6 *Trade Secrets, Confidential Information*

Particularly when the state seeks to obtain a company's customer lists or sensitive financial information, the company may seek to quash the process on the basis of confidentiality or trade secrets. Massachusetts' highest court has listed six common law criteria for determining when information is exempt from discovery as a trade secret: the extent of the knowledge of the information outside the business; the extent of the knowledge of the information within the business; the measures taken to guard its secrecy; the value of the information to the business and its competitors; the efforts taken to develop the information; and the difficulty of acquiring or duplicating the information.[76]

Based on these criteria, the Massachusetts court set aside CID demands for the names and addresses of all members of the respondent's association, and the names of the association's major customers.[77] But other state courts have allowed discovery of customer lists[78] and membership lists[79] over objections that they are confidential. An Arizona court has also required an attorney to produce a client list over objections based on the attorney-client privilege.[80] The court also required the attorney to produce documents that the clients had provided him through a non-lawyer third party.

Even assuming that the confidentiality of a customer list is a valid objection, a court has ordered the production of the list where the state will use the list to contact individuals, and will not otherwise disclose the names on the list.[81] Any interest a company has in not having its customers contacted by the state is outweighed by the state interest in contacting the customers.[82] The state, when determining what size civil penalties to seek from the court, can also obtain data concerning the respondent's financial worth.[83]

One method of dealing with a respondent that argues that requested data is a trade secret or confidential is to require production of all documents, but allow the respondent to indicate which specific portions are confidential, with the state giving notice to the respondent before making that specific information public. It should be at that time that the company raises its objections, not before the information has been produced.[84] The court can also limit the experts employed by the state who have access to the documents.[85] The CID statute may also limit disclosure of information produced in response to a CID.[86]

Alternatively, the state should request that the court inspect *in camera* any documents alleged to be trade secrets before ruling on their nature. That is, the court should not rely just on the respondent's affidavits to determine a document's confidentiality.[87] Courts should not restrict the attorney general's ability to share confidential information with out-of-state law enforcement agencies.[88]

It is a common practice by state attorneys general to enter into confidentiality agreements to govern the handling and maintenance of documents that may be confidential or are considered trade secrets. This practice also occurs in multi-state enforcement actions when two or more states are pursuing the same respondent for similar UDAP and other violations. Although it is preferable not to have such agreements, government attorneys must weigh the benefits of having access to the materials and information against any adverse consequences of a confidentiality agreement.

A party who is subject to a civil investigative demand may not be allowed to assert the rights of others. Thus, the fact that the information is a trade secret of another entity or

74 CUNA Mut. Ins. Society v. Attorney General, 380 Mass. 539, 404 N.E.2d 1219 (1980).

75 *Id.*

76 *In re* Yankee Milk, Inc., 372 Mass. 353, 362 N.E.2d 207 (1977). *See also* State *ex rel.* Miller v. National Dietary Research, Inc., 454 N.W.2d 820 (Iowa 1990).

77 *In re* Yankee Milk, Inc., 372 Mass. 353, 362 N.E.2d 207 (1977).

78 *In re* Attorney General's Investigative Demand, 493 A.2d 972 (Del. Super. Ct. 1985); Harrington Mfg. Co. v. Powell Mfg. Co., 26 N.C. App. 414, 216 S.E.2d 379 (1975); *In re* American Dollar Exchange, Inc., 27 Va. Cir. 428 (1992). *See also* Attorney General v. Bodimetric Profiles, 404 Mass. 152, 533 N.E.2d 1364 (1989).

79 Straw v. State, Clearinghouse No. 26,038 (Tenn. Ch. & P. Ct. 1977).

80 Little v. Department of Justice, 130 Or. App. 668, 883 P.2d 272 (1994).

81 *In re* Attorney General's Investigative Demand, 493 A.2d 972 (Del. Super. Ct. 1985).

82 *Id.*

83 People v. Superior Court (Kardon), 35 Cal. App. 3d 710, 111 Cal. Rptr. 14 (1973).

84 *See, e.g.*, Lewandowski v. Danforth, 547 S.W.2d 470 (Mo. 1977). *See also* Attorney General v. Bodimetric Profiles, 404 Mass. 152, 533 N.E.2d 1364 (1989).

85 *See Ex parte* General Motors Acceptance Corp., 631 So. 2d 990 (Ala. 1994). *See also* Shiffrin v. I.V. Servs. of Am., Inc., 53 Conn. App. 129, 729 A.2d 784 (1999) (allowing defendant to redact information in pharmacy records that might disclose customer's physical or mental condition avoided confidentiality concerns; decision also rejects contention that there is a general pharmacist-patient privilege).

86 *See* Mass. Gen. Laws ch. 93A, § 6(6) (documentary material or other information produced shall not, unless ordered by a court for good cause shown, be disclosed to any person other than the authorized agent or representative of the attorney general, unless with consent of person producing the information); Tesoro Petroleum Corp. v. State, 42 P.3d 531 (Alaska 2002) (state may disclose information to specially-engaged outside counsel).

87 *See In re* Yankee Milk, 372 Mass. 353, 362 N.E.2d 207 (1977).

88 State *ex rel.* Salazar v. Publishers Clearing House, Clearinghouse No. 53,562 (Colo. Dist. Ct. Dec. 8, 2000).

that another person could claim that it is confidential is not grounds for resisting a subpoena.[89]

10.2.7 *Different Forms of Discovery Distinguished*

State enforcement officials must be careful to keep in mind the requirements and limitations of the particular type of discovery they are using. Each discovery technique, even though closely resembling another investigatory method, will have its own unique rules and requirements. In some states, agencies must distinguish between the power to compel production of documents for purely investigatory purposes and the power to compel production of documents for eventual law enforcement purposes. State legislation may specify that the latter form of subpoena is more restrictive.[90] In these states, information obtained through an investigative subpoena may have to be requested again using the proper CID for an enforcement action.[91]

Louisiana distinguishes between prerequisites for a subpoena and a CID. A CID is, in effect, the commencement of a civil action against the person on whom it is served. The demand should state not that the attorney general *may* have evidence of violations, but that the attorney general has such evidence, and the state must allege as in a civil suit the material facts upon which the demand is based.[92] A Connecticut court, however, construed a civil investigative demand as the equivalent of a subpoena in determining whether to apply a rule that allowed production of confidential information in response to a subpoena.[93]

Similarly, there may be distinctions between discovery under a state's rules of civil procedure and rules specified in a UDAP or other statute for law enforcement investigations. Where the special enforcement authority conflicts with general rules of civil procedure, the special authority should take precedence.[94] Thus a state's rules of civil procedure prohibiting pre-complaint depositions do not apply where the UDAP statute allows the attorney general to take such depositions.[95] Iowa's UDAP statute has been liberally construed to allow the attorney general to subpoena documents as well as witnesses and to compel testimony under oath.[96]

89 Attorney General v. Bodimetric Profiles, 404 Mass. 152, 533 N.E.2d 1364 (1989).

90 Commonwealth v. Shults, 26 Pa. Commw. 129, 362 A.2d 1129 (1976).

91 *Id.*

92 Humphreys v. State *ex rel.* Guste, 377 So. 2d 88 (La. 1979).

93 Shiffrin v. I.V. Servs. of Am., Inc., 53 Conn. App. 129, 729 A.2d 784 (1999).

94 *In re* Western Beef Packers Inc., Clearinghouse No. 26,446 (Mich. Cir. Ct. 1977). *But see* State *ex rel.* Ieyoub v. Racetrac Petroleum, Inc., 790 So. 2d 673 (La. App. 2001) (AG can not use CID to get information from parties once suit commenced but may be able to use CID as to non-parties).

95 *Id.*

96 Iowa *ex rel.* Campbell v. C-Pals Corp., Clearinghouse No. 50,444 (Iowa Dist. Ct. Dec. 19, 1994).

Discovery by the attorney general is not objectionable simply because it seeks the same information as was obtained through civil investigation prior to suit; the statutory protection against disclosure of information obtained through civil investigations does not protect the information from discovery once suit is filed.[97]

10.2.8 *Respondent's Discovery of the State's Case*

Courts consistently find that investigated companies do not have a right to compel the state to produce the evidence it is accumulating against that company.[98] One rationale preventing discovery against an attorney general's office is that the attorney general is not a party to the action, but the "people" are plaintiffs for whom the attorney general sues in a protective capacity.[99] Also, work product for impending litigation from an investigatory file is usually protected from disclosure.[100]

Enforcement officials should be familiar with their own state freedom of information acts, however. Both respondents and members of the public often seek information via public records requests and many of the requests may apply to information obtained in an investigation and state UDAP compulsory processes. Some statutes provide that public records may not be withheld unless a specific statutory exemption applies.[101]

The individual consumers for whom the attorney general is seeking restitution are not considered party-plaintiffs for purposes of discovery by the defendants, so the attorney general can not be required to produce the individual consumers for depositions and answer interrogatories on their behalf.[102] The attorney general acts on behalf of the public and does not have an attorney-client relationship with individual consumers.[103]

97 Vermont v. Rosenberg, Clearinghouse No. 51,264B (Vt. Super. Ct. Aug. 12, 1992).

98 People *ex rel.* Babbitt v. Herndon, 119 Ariz. 454, 581 P.2d 688 (1978); People v. Superior Court (Lyons-Buick-Opel-GMC, Inc.), 70 Cal. App. 3d 341, 138 Cal. Rptr. 791 (1977); People v. Volkswagen of Am., Inc., 41 A.D.2d 827, 342 N.Y.S.2d 749 (1973).

99 People v. Volkswagen of Am., Inc. 41 A.D.2d 827, 342 N.Y.S.2d 749 (1973).

100 *Id. Cf.* State *ex rel.* Brady v. Ocean Farm Ltd. P'ship, 2002 Del. Ch. LEXIS 16 (Feb. 14, 2002) (governmental privilege only protects reports prepared for criminal prosecution; work product doctrine only protects reports of investigations in preparation of litigation).

101 *See* General Electric v. Department of Environmental Protection, 429 Mass. 798, 805–806 (1999) (materials privileged as work product under Mass. R. Civ. P. 26(b)(3) are not protected from disclosure under public record statute unless they fall within the scope of an express statutory exemption).

102 People *ex rel.* Hartigan v. Lann, 587 N.E.2d 521 (Ill. App. Ct. 1992).

103 *Id.*

A respondent in a contempt case does not have the right to discover the state's policies and recommendations in similar cases against other dealers. Much of this information is protected from discovery as work product, and it has little or no relevance to the size of the penalty imposed on the respondent.[104]

On the other hand, a different standard may prevail where the plaintiff in a private UDAP case wants access to the state's non-privileged materials from a civil investigation of the defendant. Where the private suit is compatible with the underlying purposes of the state's investigation, a court may order release of the materials upon a showing of relevance.[105]

10.2.9 Test Purchases

An important investigative technique is for an enforcement agency investigator to pose as a consumer and witness the seller's practices. Common examples are taking a pre-inspected automobile or appliance to a repair shop, or shopping at a supermarket to determine if goods are available and sold at advertised sale prices.

Courts have found such test shopping not only to be authorized, but also to be a "consumer transaction" within the scope of the UDAP statute.[106] Consequently, investigators' testimony concerning such test sales is sufficient evidence upon which to base a UDAP prosecution.[107] In one case, however, while not reaching the question whether investigators could be considered consumers, the court relied heavily on the fact that they were not harmed as support for its conclusion that the sale was not unconscionable as prohibited by the UDAP statute.[108]

Testers are also used in civil rights and disability rights cases to test for discrimination in public accommodations. These issues are beyond the scope of this manual, but it is worth noting that testers can be used to test for a variety of reasons and that UDAP claims may also arise in other contexts like discrimination in public accommodations. For example, when testers find that stores discriminate based on race (racial profiling) or disability (lack of accessibility), it is arguable that these are unfair practices and constitute violations of state UDAP laws, as well as state and federal discrimination laws.[109]

104 Commonwealth v. Fall River Motor Sales, Inc., 409 Mass. 302, 565 N.E.2d 1205 (1991). *See also* § 10.8, *infra* (discussion of defense of selective enforcement).

105 Novak v. Orca Oil Co., 875 P.2d 756 (Alaska 1994).

106 *See* § 2.4.6, *supra*.

107 *See, e.g.*, Brown v. Spitzer Ford, Inc., 11 Ohio Op. 3d 84 (Ct. App. 1978).

108 State *ex rel.* Stovall v. Confirmed.com, 38 P.3d 707 (Kan. 2002).

109 *See* § 4.3.9, *supra*.

10.2.10 When Can the State Initiate an Investigation?

The state can investigate a UDAP violation at any time, subject to any reasonable cause requirement.[110] The attorney general does not have to wait for a case to be referred by a state consumer agency or wait to receive written complaints.[111] The state can issue a civil investigative demand even if suit on the act triggering the investigation would be barred by the statute of limitations.[112] Subpoenas do not have to allege a specific violation, but can be based on official curiosity.[113] The subpoena need not even be addressed to an individual who may have violated the UDAP statute, but can be directed to one who may have information concerning other parties' law violations.[114] Even where the statute requires the attorney general's office to inform other state regulatory agencies immediately about allegations of UDAP violations, its failure to do so does not detract from its authority to issue subpoenas, at least where the other agency had no authority over the specific practice being investigated.[115]

10.2.11 Access to FTC Investigational Records

The FTC Act specifies the limitations on the Commission's authority to release investigatory documents to state attorneys general. The FTC Act also sets requirements concerning use of such documents by state attorneys general that contain trade secrets or other confidential information.

Section 6(f) of the FTC Act (15 U.S.C. § 46(f)), as amended, states:

> [T]he Commission shall not have any authority to make public any trade secret or any commercial or financial information which is obtained from any person and which is privileged or confidential, except that the Commission may disclose such

110 Reasonable case as a precondition is analyzed in § 10.2.4, *supra*.

111 Scott v. Ass'n for Childbirth at Home Int'l, 88 Ill. 2d 279, 430 N.E.2d 1012 (1981); People by Spitzer v. Network Assocs., Inc., 195 Misc. 2d 384, 758 N.Y.S.2d 466, 469 (2003) (state may institute proceeding without having received complaints); Brown v. Howe Motor Co., Clearinghouse No. 26,474 (Ohio C.P. Butler Cty. 1977); *see also* Consumer Protection Div. v. Consumer Publishing Co., 304 Md. 731, 501 A.2d 48 (1985).

112 Auto-Owners Ins. Co. v. State, 692 N.E.2d 935 (Ind. App. 1998).

113 Commonwealth v. Gibson, Clearinghouse No. 26,029 (Pa. C.P. Allegheny Cty. 1974).

114 Attorney General v. Bodimetric Profiles, 404 Mass. 152, 533 N.E.2d 1364 (1989); CUNA Mut. Ins. Society v. Attorney General, 380 Mass. 539, 404 N.E.2d 1219 (1980).

115 Charlie's Dodge, Inc. v. Celebrezze, 72 Ohio App. 3d 744, 596 N.E.2d 486 (1991).

> information to . . . any officer or employee of any State law enforcement agency upon the prior certification of an officer of any such . . . State law enforcement agency that such information will be maintained in confidence and will be used only for official law enforcement purposes.

The Conference Report on this provision explained:

> A "law enforcement agency" is an agency that has the legal authority to engage in activities "for official law enforcement purposes." The phrase "law enforcement purposes," in turn, has the same meaning as it does in Exemption 7 of the Freedom of Information Act. That is, the Commission is permitted to provide documents to another agency . . . if the agency requests the material in connection with any criminal, civil, or administrative proceeding, or any investigation potentially resulting in such a proceeding.[116]

The FTC has adopted a rule concerning the procedure that state law enforcement agencies should follow in requesting FTC information.[117] Requests should be directed to the FTC liaison officer, or, if there is none, to the FTC General Counsel. The FTC will send the law enforcement agency a form on which to describe the nature of its activity and the reason the FTC information is relevant, and to certify that it will maintain the information in confidence and use it only for official law enforcement purposes. Before certain non-public information can be used in court, the person or entity that submitted it must be notified and given an opportunity to seek a protective order, if desired.[118]

The Seventh Circuit has ruled that the FTC decision to disclose investigative files to state attorneys general is not judicially reviewable if the statutory prerequisites of confidentiality and official law enforcement purposes are satisfied.[119] The court quoted approvingly from the legislative history: "[T]he purpose of these provisions is to make it crystal clear that the Commission has this authority, and that it should be able to exercise it without undue delay and restraint."[120]

116 H. Conf. Rep. No. 917, 96 Cong., 2d Sess. 33 (1980) *reprinted in* 1980 U.S.C.C.A.N. 1073, 1150.

117 16 C.F.R. § 4.11(c).

118 16 C.F.R. § 4.10(g).

119 Jaymar-Ruby, Inc. v. FTC, 651 F.2d 506 (7th Cir. 1981).

120 *Id.* at 508 quoting statement of Rep. Preyer (126 Cong. Rec. 3870 (daily ed. May 20, 1980)).

10.3 Special Preconditions to a State Enforcement Action

10.3.1 Prior Attempt to Obtain Voluntary Compliance

A number of state UDAP statutes require as a precondition to an enforcement action that the state notify the target of the investigation and permit that person to execute an assurance of voluntary compliance. While the state should strictly comply with this requirement, if the seller offers an assurance of voluntary compliance that is inadequate, the state can reject the offer and instead bring the enforcement action.[121] Moreover, having obtained an assurance of voluntary compliance, the state need not give the defendant further notice when it seeks an injunction against continuing violations of that assurance.[122] The state statute may also provide that notice may be omitted altogether if it is not in the public interest.[123]

The Ohio UDAP statute requires that the respondent be given an opportunity to offer an assurance of voluntary compliance only where the relief sought is more than a simple injunction. A number of cases have held that such assurance need not be sought where only an injunctive remedy is requested.[124] This applies whether the injunction is prohibitory or even if the injunction mandates affirmative actions.[125]

Where the UDAP statute requires the state to give sellers an opportunity to offer an assurance of voluntary compliance, the question may arise whether this opportunity must be afforded to new parties added to a lawsuit after the action has already commenced. The Idaho Supreme Court has ruled that, where these additional parties had actual knowledge of the investigation, and where there was a principal-agent relationship between the original and additional parties, no additional opportunity for voluntary compliance need be offered.[126] An Ohio court has gone one step further and ruled that officers and employees of a corporation need not be given an independent opportunity for voluntary compliance before they are named as additional defendants in a suit against the corporation.[127] It would be needlessly burdensome to have to offer this opportunity to each indi-

121 State v. Meredith Chevrolet, Inc., 145 Ga. App. 8, 244 S.E.2d 15 (1978).

122 Nunley v. State, 628 So. 2d 619 (Ala. 1993).

123 *See, e.g.*, FTC v. Crescent Publ. Group, 129 F. Supp. 2d 311, 320 n.56 (S.D.N.Y. 2001).

124 Brown v. Borchers Ford, Inc., 62 Ohio St. 2d 1, 402 N.E.2d 527, 16 Ohio Op. 3d 1 (1980); Brown v. Spitzer Ford, Inc., 11 Ohio Op. 3d 84 (Ct. App. 1978).

125 Brown v. Waddell, 3 Ohio Op. 3d 357 (C.P. Greene Cty. 1976).

126 State *ex rel.* Kidwell v. Master Distributors, 101 Idaho 447, 615 P.2d 116 (1980).

127 Quality Carpet Co. v. Brown, 6 Ohio Op. 3d 185 (C.P. Franklin Cty. 1977).

vidual in addition to the corporation.

The Texas UDAP statute requires the state to "contact such person to inform him in general of the alleged unlawful conduct" before bringing suit. In one case this requirement was satisfied where the seller met with enforcement officials who told the seller its scheme could get it into trouble and that the seller was being investigated, even though the enforcement officials did not state the specific law violations being committed. Preliminary legal proceedings in the case could also act as sufficient notice of unlawful conduct.[128]

New York's notice requirement has been found to be satisfied even though only a very brief time elapsed between notice and suit.[129] Actual notice of the state's investigation may be sufficient.[130]

In some states, the UDAP statute authorizes attempted reconciliation or assurances of voluntary compliance, while not specifically requiring the state to take these steps. This authorization should not be turned on its head to become a requirement that the state exhaust these avenues before bringing suit.[131] Maryland's conciliation requirement has been held to apply only to investigations of complaints filed by consumers, and not to cases the state enforcement agency initiates.[132]

If, as part of an assurance of voluntary compliance, the attorney general releases the business from all claims, the release may bar other public authorities such as district attorneys from bringing the same claims.[133]

10.3.2 Reason to Believe the Act Has Been Violated

Some statutes require that the state institute enforcement proceedings only if it has cause to believe that the statute has been violated.[134] This is not an essential element of the action that must be proved at trial. Instead, the requirement only forces the state to show the evidence leading it to believe a deceptive practice has occurred if the defendant raises this issue early in the proceedings.[135] Where an administrative proceeding must determine if there is probable cause to bring an enforcement action, it has been held that hearsay affidavits can be admitted in that proceeding.[136] The state's belief that the statute has been violated need not be based on consumer complaints.[137]

10.3.3 Preconditions to Private Actions Do Not Apply

Many of the limitations on private UDAP actions do not apply to state actions. In some states private actions may be brought only by "consumers." This limitation may prohibit actions by franchisees, purchasers of business opportunities, or small businesses. But the same UDAP statute is unlikely to place similar limitations on state actions on behalf of these same small businesses. Enforcement officials should thus carefully examine any case precedent that limits the types of actions that can be brought under a UDAP statute to determine if the precedent can be interpreted as applying only to private actions, and not state actions.

Certain UDAP statutes require consumers to suffer actual damage before bringing UDAP actions. This limitation should not apply to an action brought by the state, which need only show that a practice has a capacity or tendency to deceive, not that there is any actual deception.[138] However, a Tennessee court upheld the dismissal of a state UDAP claim for restitution against a health club operator when the state failed to produce consumers who suffered any ascertainable harm.[139]

128 Kirk v. State, 651 S.W.2d 840 (Tex. App. 1983).

129 State *ex rel.* Abrams v. Abandoned Funds Information Center, Inc., 129 Misc. 2d 614, 493 N.Y.S.2d 907 (Sup. Ct. 1985); *see also* State *ex rel.* Abrams v. Kase, Clearinghouse No. 43,079 (N.Y. Sup. Ct. 1986).

130 FTC v. Crescent Publ. Group, 129 F. Supp. 2d 311, 320 n.56 (S.D.N.Y. 2001).

131 Devine Seafood, Inc. v. Attorney General, 37 Md. App. 439, 377 A.2d 1194 (Ct. Spec. App. 1977). *See also* State *ex rel.* Miller v. Pace, 677 N.W.2d 761 (Iowa 2004) (no constitutional requirement to issue cease and desist order before bringing civil enforcement action under state securities law).

132 Consumer Protection Div. v. Consumer Publishing Co., 304 Md. 731, 501 A.2d 48 (1985).

133 People *ex rel.* Devine v. Time Consumer Marketing, Inc., 782 N.E.2d 761 (Ill. App. 2002).

134 *See* State *ex rel.* Celebrezze v. Grogan Chrysler-Plymouth, Inc., 73 Ohio App. 3d 792, 598 N.E.2d 796 (1991) (applying Ohio's "reasonable cause" requirement).

135 State *ex rel.* Douglas v. Ledwith, 204 Neb. 6, 281 N.W.2d 729 (1979).

136 Kasha v. Dept. of Legal Affairs, 375 So. 2d 43 (Fla. Dist. Ct. App. 1979).

137 State v. Leary, 217 Conn. 404, 587 A.2d 85 (1991); People by Spitzer v. Network Assocs., Inc., 195 Misc. 2d 384, 758 N.Y.S.2d 466, 469 (2003) (state may institute proceeding without having received complaints).

138 *See* Northwest Laborers-Employers Health & Security Trust Fund v. Philip Morris, Inc., 58 F. Supp. 2d 1211 (W.D. Wash. 1999) (dictum); Oliveira v. Amoco Oil Co., 201 Ill. 2d 134, 776 N.E.2d 151, 267 Ill. Dec. 14 (2002); People *ex rel.* Hartigan v. E&E Hauling, Inc., 577 N.E.2d 1262 (Ill. App. Ct. 1991) (no allegation of harm to consumers is necessary when Attorney General brings UDAP suit), *aff'd on other grounds*, 153 Ill. 2d 473, 607 N.E.2d 165 (1992); McGraw v. Loyola Ford, Inc., 124 Md. App. 560, 723 A.2d 502 (1999); Legg v. Castruccio, 100 Md. App. 748, 642 A.2d 906 (1994) (no allegation of actual deception or damage necessary); Hallowell v. Citaramanis, 88 Md. App. 160, 594 A.2d 591 (1991); Weinberg v. Sprint Corp., 173 N.J. 233, 801 A.2d 281 (2002); Cox v. Sears Roebuck & Co., 138 N.J. 2, 647 A.2d 454 (1994); Goshen v. Mut. Life Ins. Co., 98 N.Y.2d 314, 774 N.E.2d 1190, 1195 (2002); Rathgeber v. Hemenway, Inc., 69 P.3d 710, 715 n.5 (Or. 2003); § 4.2.9, *supra*.

139 State v. Thompson, 2003 WL 1442414 (Tenn. Ct. App. Mar. 20, 2003) (unpublished, citation limited).

Other UDAP statutes provide that private litigants must notify the seller before instituting private actions. Again, such a requirement invariably applies only to private and not state actions[140] (although there may be separate notice requirements applicable to the state).[141] Oregon's requirement of a showing that the defendant acted willfully applies only to private litigants, not to the state.[142] The state also need not exhaust administrative remedies.[143] When dealing with issues of preemption by federal law, however, courts may apply the same analysis to state enforcement actions as they do to private actions.[144]

Another restriction on private UDAP actions is the statute of limitations, described in detail in another section.[145] These limitation periods are usually not applicable to state actions,[146] even ones for restitution.[147] This is because the state is the real party in interest and the prosecution is exercising a governmental function.[148] The UDAP statute may set a special limitations period for state enforcement actions.[149]

There is one precondition that may be more applicable to the state than a private litigant—that the action be in the public interest. Although there appear to be no state UDAP cases explicitly requiring that a state action be in the public interest (there are a few cases requiring that a private action be in the public interest),[150] it may be a good strategy for a state enforcement agency to indicate to the court why its action is in the public interest. But the Washington Supreme Court has indicated (by way of dicta in a private action) that it is solely within the discretion of the attorney general whether an action is in the public interest.[151]

10.3.4 Standing Issues

The attorney general has standing to bring UDAP claims even where the entity that suffered damage would not have the right to sue.[152] The attorney general need not join as parties the individual consumers who have been affected.[153] Whether the attorney general has an interest in the litigation that is distinct from that of private parties is also irrelevant to the attorney general's standing.[154]

More complex standing issues may arise where the attorney general seeks to assert non-UDAP claims along with UDAP claims. The Illinois Supreme Court holds that the attorney general has common law authority to assert claims on behalf of the people and taxpayers of the state.[155] This authority allows the attorney general to sue a company that defrauded a public authority, even where the public authority has not authorized the suit.[156] The Arkansas Attorney General has standing to bring a UDAP action as a means of enforcing state usury laws, even though only a borrower has standing to bring a usury action.[157]

The New York Attorney General's authority to take action against persons engaged in fraudulent or illegal business practices is not limited to acts defined as fraudulent or illegal under state law, but also allows enforcement of federal law.[158] Likewise, the Tennessee Attorney General has a wide range of common law powers, and may bring suits in the public interest even under statutes that do not expressly confer this authority. The attorney general has broad discretion to decide what matters are of public interest.[159]

The fact that another state agency also has authority to enforce the laws applicable to a particular industry does not oust the attorney general of authority.[160] Nor does the

---

140 *See* Nunley v. State, 628 So. 2d 619 (Ala. 1993).

141 *See* § 10.3.1, *supra.*

142 Rathgeber v. Hemenway, Inc., 69 P.3d 710, 715 n.5 (Or. 2003).

143 State v. Ritz Realty Corp., 63 Conn. App. 544, 776 A.2d 1195 (2001) (state has option of either commencing administrative proceeding or suing directly in court); Commonwealth *ex rel.* Chandler v. Anthem Ins. Cos., 8 S.W.3d 48 (Ky. App. 1999).

144 *See, e.g.*, Minnesota *ex rel.* Hatch v. Fleet Mortg. Co., 158 F. Supp. 2d 962 (D. Minn. 2001) (state's suit against bank for deceptive telemarketing not preempted by OCC regulation); State *ex rel.* Hatch v. Worldcom, Inc., 125 F. Supp. 2d 365 (D. Minn. 2000) (state's suit against telecommunications provider for deception not preempted).

145 *See* § 7.3, *supra.*

146 State *ex rel.* Guste v. Orkin Exterminating Co., 528 So. 2d 198 (La. Ct. App. 1988); State v. Deltron Record Pressing Co., Clearinghouse No. 36,567 (Tenn. Ch. Ct., Davidson Cty. 1983); State v. Fuller, Clearinghouse No. 36,569 (Tenn. Ch. Ct. Shelby Cty. 1983); State v. Largo Enterprises Inc., Clearinghouse No. 36,568 (Tenn. Ch. Ct., Davidson Cty. 1981).

147 State *ex rel.* Stephan v. Brotherhood Bank & Trust Co., 649 P.2d 419 (Kan. Ct. App. 1982); State *ex rel.* Guste v. Orkin Exterminating Co., 528 So. 2d 198 (La. Ct. App. 1988).

148 State *ex rel.* Stephan v. Brotherhood Bank & Trust Co., 649 P.2d 419 (Kan. Ct. App. 1982).

149 *See* § 10.8, *infra.*

150 *See* § 7.5.3, *supra.*

151 Anhold v. Daniels, 94 Wash. 2d 40, 614 P.2d 184 (1980).

152 State *ex rel.* Hatch v. Publishers Clearing House, Clearinghouse No. 53,567 (D. Minn. June 12, 2000); People *ex rel.* Hartigan v. E&E Hauling, Inc., 153 Ill. 2d 473, 607 N.E.2d 165 (1992); People *ex rel.* Daley v. Datacom Sys. Corp., 146 Ill. 2d 1, 585 N.E.2d 51 (1991) (compare to Norton v. City of Chicago, 267 Ill. App. 3d 507, 642 N.E.2d 839 (1994); state's attorney has standing to sue even though individuals affected do not have standing as consumers).

153 State *ex rel.* Hatch v. Publishers Clearing House, Clearinghouse No. 53,567 (D. Minn. June 12, 2000).

154 State *ex rel.* Ieyoub v. Classic Soft Trim, Inc., 663 So. 2d 835 (La. App. 1995).

155 People *ex rel.* Hartigan v. E&E Hauling, Inc., 153 Ill. 2d 473, 607 N.E.2d 165 (1992).

156 *Id.*

157 State *ex rel.* Bryant v. R & A Investment Co., 985 S.W.2d 299 (Ark. 1999). *See also* State v. Thompson, 2003 WL 1442414 (Tenn. Ct. App. Mar. 20, 2003) (unpublished, citation limited) (AG may enforce health club law through UDAP action).

158 Oncor Communications v. State of New York, 165 Misc. 2d 262, 626 N.Y.S.2d 369 (Sup. 1995).

159 State v. Heath, 806 S.W.2d 535 (Tenn. App. 1990).

160 People *ex rel.* Orloff v. Pacific Bell, 31 Cal. 4th 1132, 7 Cal. Rptr. 3d 315, 80 P.3d 201 (2003) (interpreting Cal. statutes to allow District Attorneys to sue public utilities for deceptive practices unless suit would interfere with a PUC enforcement

existence of a complex regulatory scheme bar the attorney general from suing the regulated industry.[161] But a California court interpreted its public utilities code to allow the attorney general to bring suit against regulated utilities only if there was not a parallel proceeding pending before the public utilities commission.[162]

The attorney general has the authority to sue assignees who have collected illegal charges, even if they are free of wrongdoing, where state law makes assignees liable for claims that could be asserted against the original dealer.[163] The attorney general can sue agents, officers, and employees as well as the company in whose name the business was conducted.[164]

The attorney general may have authority under the UDAP statute to sue on behalf of non-residents who are injured by wrongdoing that occurs in the state.[165] Even if the attorney general does not have standing to sue on behalf of out-of-state residents, the attorney general may be able to get information about a company's transactions with out-of-state residents through discovery. In an Illinois case, the court held that this information might show that in-state businesses, on whose behalf the attorney general had standing to sue, were suffering a competitive injury due to the defendant's deceptive practices with out-of-state consumers.[166]

10.4 Special UDAP Scope Issues for State Enforcement Actions

Chapter 2 of this manual analyzes UDAP scope issues in detail. As a general rule, scope issues are the same whether the state or a private party brings the UDAP action. There are situations, however, where scope issues differ depending on who brings the action, the state or an individual, and this section discusses instances where this occurs.

A UDAP statute may broadly prohibit deceptive practices in one section, but limit the scope of the statute in another section by specifying that remedies or actions can be sought only by "consumers," against "suppliers," or concerning "consumer transactions" or "sales of goods or services." The scope of these statutes can differ depending on who enforces the statute or even depending on what remedy is sought.

For example, under Indiana's statute, if the consumer transaction is in real property, the attorney general may bring an action even though consumers can not.[167] The Texas UDAP statute was similar at one time: while it applied to "trade or commerce," which included real estate sales, *private* actions could only be brought by a "consumer," which was defined not to include real estate purchasers.[168] But state enforcement officials in Texas could bring suit even for non-consumer purchasers. Similarly, Missouri,[169] Vermont,[170] Texas,[171] Kentucky[172] and Illinois[173] cases hold that even if those injured are not "consumers," and could not bring a private action, the state attorney general has authority to bring an action on their behalf. The Delaware Unfair Trade Practices Act, one of Delaware's two UDAP-type statutes, was originally held to apply only to business-to-business deception,[174] but has since been amended to allow the attorney general to enforce it in favor of consumers also.[175]

In fact, most cases limiting the type of "consumers" that can bring an action—*e.g.*, not recipients of insurance payments or third party beneficiaries,[176] not loan guarantors,[177] or not merchants or corporations[178]—will not apply to state enforcement actions. The language "consumer" or similar language will limit parties eligible to bring a *private* action, but will not be found in statutory provisions dealing with state enforcement actions.

---

proceeding); State *ex rel.* Hatch v. American Family Mut. Ins. Co., 609 N.W.2d 1 (Minn. App. 2000) (insurance commissioner does not have exclusive authority). *But see* California v. Altus Fin., 2002 WL 1377711, 2002 U.S. Dist. LEXIS 8260 (C.D. Cal. May 8, 2002) (insurance commissioner has exclusive jurisdiction over disposition of assets of insurance company, so AG can not pursue UDAP claim).

161 State *ex rel.* Hatch v. American Family Mut. Ins. Co., 609 N.W.2d 1 (Minn. App. 2000).

162 People *ex rel.* Orloff v. Pacific Bell, 89 Cal. App. 4th 844, 108 Cal. Rptr. 2d 48 (2001), *depublished, review granted*, 31 P.3d 1271 (Cal. 2001).

163 State *ex rel.* Easley v. Rich Food Servs., Inc., 535 S.E.2d 84 (N.C. App. 2000); State v. Custom Pools, 150 Vt. 533, 556 A.2d 72 (1988); State *ex rel.* McGraw v. Scott Runyan Pontiac-Buick, Inc., 194 W. Va. 770, 461 S.E.2d 516 (1995); State v. Excel Mgmt. Servs., 111 Wis. 2d 479, 331 N.W.2d 312 (1983).

164 State *ex rel.* Easley v. Rich Food Servs., Inc., 535 S.E.2d 84 (N.C. App. 2000).

165 New York v. Feldman, 210 F. Supp. 2d 294 (S.D.N.Y. 2002); People *ex rel.* Spitzer v. Telehublink Corp., 301 A.D.2d 1006, 756 N.Y.S.2d 285 (2003).

166 Illinois v. Tri-Star Indus. Lighting, Inc., 2000 U.S. Dist. LEXIS 15376 (N.D. Ill. Oct. 5, 2000).

167 McKinney v. State, 693 N.E.2d 65 (Ind. 1998) (also holding that AG must show intent to defraud or mislead).

168 *See, e.g.*, Ferguson v. Beal, 588 S.W.2d 651 (Tex. Civ. App. 1979); Cape Conroe, Ltd. v. Specht, 525 S.W.2d 215 (Tex. Civ. App. 1975).

169 State *ex rel.* Nixon v. Telco Directory Publishing, 863 S.W.2d 596 (Mo. 1993).

170 State v. International Collection Service, 594 A.2d 426 (Vt. 1991).

171 Household Retail Servs. v. State, 2001 Tex. App. LEXIS 5893 (Aug. 29, 2001).

172 Commonwealth *ex rel.* Stephens v. North Am. Van Lines Inc., 600 S.W.2d 459 (Ky. Ct. App. 1980).

173 People *ex rel.* Fahner v. Walsh, 122 Ill. App. Ct. 481, 461 N.E.2d 78 (1984).

174 Grand Ventures, Inc. v. Whaley, 632 A.2d 63 (Del. 1993).

175 Del. Code Ann. tit 6, § 2533(d). *See* State *ex rel.* Brady v. Fallon, 1998 Del. Super. LEXIS 186 (Feb. 27, 1998).

176 *See* § 2.4.1, *supra.*

177 *See* § 2.4.3, *supra.*

178 *See* § 2.4.5.2, *supra.*

A few UDAP statutes have, or once had, a narrower scope for purposes of state enforcement. For example, the Florida UDAP statute applies to practices in trade or commerce, thus applying to real estate sales. But a former version of the statute authorized the state to enjoin only a "supplier," defined as someone involved in a "consumer transaction," which was interpreted not to include real estate sales.[179] Two Delaware courts have interpreted its Consumer Fraud Act as barring UDAP suits against insurance companies only when brought by the attorney general, not when brought by consumers.[180] A 1999 Michigan Supreme court decision suggested a similar result,[181] but the statute was amended soon afterward to overrule the decision.[182]

Typically the UDAP statute's scope limitations apply both to private and state actions. This is particularly the case for scope limitations found in the statute's exemption section. One of the most important such exemptions is for practices regulated or permitted by another state agency or law. This exclusion is fully discussed in § 2.3.3, *supra*. The important point here is that state attorney general offices and other enforcement officials have options in dealing with this exclusion that are typically not open to private litigants. For example, if a finance company's practices are excluded from the UDAP statute because of the state banking department's regulation of finance companies, the private litigant can do little more than complain to the banking department. However, the state UDAP enforcement official's request that the state banking department take legal action against the finance company should have more weight. Alternatively, an opinion by the regulatory agency or the state attorney general that the regulatory agency does not regulate the challenged practice will help persuade the court that the practice is not exempt from UDAP enforcement.

10.5 Special Standards for State Enforcement Actions to Determine Whether There Is a UDAP Violation

10.5.1 Introduction

For the most part, the same standards as to whether a practice is unfair or deceptive apply whether the state or a private individual brings the UDAP claim. (These standards are examined in detail in other chapters of this manual.[183]) This section considers the few differences that may exist in these standards depending on whether the state or a private individual brings the UDAP action.

10.5.2 Deception

State courts follow FTC precedent and hold that actual deception is unnecessary for a UDAP claim; only that a practice has a capacity or is likely to deceive need be shown.[184] Most courts find this standard to apply to both private and state actions.[185] But even if a court finds that actual deception is necessary to bring a private action,[186] the same court is likely to take a different view for a state action.[187]

Since the capacity to deceive the public, as opposed to actual damage to the private litigant, is paramount in a state action, state enforcement officials should be particularly aware that vulnerable consumers are specially considered. Courts will consider whether the ignorant, the unthinking, the credulous or the least sophisticated would be deceived.[188] Thus state enforcement officials should not apply a reasonable man standard, but determine if any potential consumers are especially vulnerable and would be misled (such as the elderly, the hard-of-hearing, the young, the less educated, etc.).

State courts may also have differing views for private as opposed to state actions as to whether reliance or materiality are necessary elements to a deception claim. The FTC standard is that the Commission generally can infer materiality and usually does not need independent evidence.[189] Some state courts in both private and state UDAP actions hold that proof of reliance is unnecessary.[190] Other state courts find that reliance must be proved,[191] but these cases are invariably private actions. Thus courts have ruled that reliance must be shown for a private action, but not for a state action.[192]

179 *See* State *ex rel.* Herring v. Murdock, 345 So. 2d 759 (Fla. Dist. Ct. App. 1977).

180 Crowhorn v. Nationwide Mut. Ins. Co., 2001 Del. Super. LEXIS 358 (Apr. 26, 2001); Mentis v. Delaware Am. Life Ins. Co., 1999 Del. Super. LEXIS 419 (July 28, 1999).

181 Smith v. Globe Life Ins. Co., 597 N.W.2d 28 (Mich. 1999). *See* § 2.3.1.2, *supra*.

182 Mich. Comp. Laws Ann. § 445.904 (2001).

183 *See* §§ 4.2, 4.3, *supra*.

184 *See* § 4.2.9, *supra*; *see also* FTC v. Crescent Publ. Group, 129 F. Supp. 2d 311, 320 n.56 (S.D.N.Y. 2001) (case brought under both FTC Act and N.Y. UDAP statute); Consumer Protection Div. v. Consumer Publishing Co., 304 Md. 731, 501 A.2d 48 (1985).

185 *See* § 4.2.9, *supra*.

186 *See, e.g.*, Bartner v. Carter, 405 A.2d 194 (Me. 1979).

187 *Id.* Knapp v. Patomkin Motors Corp., 253 N.J. Super. 502, 602 A.2d 302 (1991) (Attorney General need not show actual deception in UDAP suit, although private plaintiff may have to).

188 *See* § 4.2.11, *supra*.

189 *See* § 4.2.12.2, *supra*.

190 *See* § 4.2.12.3, *supra*. *See also* Elipas Enterprises, Inc. v. Silverstein, 612 N.E.2d 9 (Ill. App. Ct. 1993) (state need not prove reasonable reliance under Illinois Consumer Fraud Act).

191 *See* § 4.2.12.3, *supra*.

192 Commonwealth v. Percudani, 844 A.2d 35, 48 (Pa. Commw. Ct. 2004) (Commonwealth need not prove reliance on appraisals when it has reason to believe that the law is or was being

10.5.3 *Unfairness, Unconscionability, Unsubstantiated Claims*

There is no reported UDAP case finding a different standard in private versus state actions as to whether a practice is unfair or unconscionable. Consequently, state enforcement agencies are directed to the standards detailed in the appropriate sections of this manual.[193] It is arguable that a state attorney general's office may be able to successfully pursue a novel unfairness approach that a court would reject if brought by a private litigant. This is, however, more a function of the respect the court may pay to a state agency specializing in consumer issues, than to any legal doctrine.

State attorneys general in about half the states wishing to attack new schemes have one option open to them that private litigants do not have. Many state UDAP statutes authorize a state agency to adopt UDAP regulations defining unfair or deceptive practices.[194] By first declaring a practice unfair in a regulation, the state may be more successful in challenging the practice in a court action.

There are few state UDAP cases dealing with the substantiation standard—that unsubstantiated claims are unfair or deceptive. FTC precedent in this area[195] should apply equally to private as well as state cases. However, because state enforcement responsibilities more clearly parallel those of the FTC, state officials may find this standard of special utility in enforcing state UDAP laws.

10.6 Persons Liable in State Enforcement Actions

While Chapter 6 of this manual provides a detailed analysis as to what persons are liable under a state UDAP statute, this section examines certain cases which have dealt specially with this issue in state enforcement actions. The Vermont Supreme Court has ruled that the attorney general's authority to sue persons "using" any unlawful act allows suit against a finance company and a bank that extended credit for transactions with a home improvement company.[196] Construing the UDAP statute liberally to effect its purpose of protecting the public, the court interpreted the phrase "using" to include making use of, converting to one's service, availing oneself of, or employing. The Vermont court held that the legislature intended to place the cost of seller misconduct on financing parties, who can police sellers, even in an action by the state attorney general.

Wisconsin's Supreme Court has found inclusion of the language required by the FTC Holder Rule in a seller's contracts as grounds to bring a *state* enforcement action against the assignee creditor. Since individual consumers can bring claims against the assignee, the state should have the same right.[197]

State enforcement agencies may be able to get injunctive relief against individual corporate officers or owners without showing that they participated in or directed the company's UDAP violations. Merely showing that the individual defendant is in charge and in control of the affairs of the company may be sufficient.[198] A franchisor that participated in the deceptive acts of its franchisees can be held liable in a state enforcement action.[199]

10.7 Enforcement Remedies

10.7.1 *Cease and Desist Orders, Injunctions*

10.7.1.1 Introduction

A UDAP statute in all fifty states allows government enforcement officials to seek a cease and desist order or injunction to prevent merchants from engaging in deceptive practices. The standard for determining whether an injunction should be issued is whether it is designed to protect the public interest.[200] This section analyzes the common injunction issues confronting attorney general offices and other enforcement agencies, such as whether an injunction is still appropriate if the challenged practice has stopped, how broad and far-reaching the order can be, what preconditions there are to an order or a preliminary injunction, and who can be covered by the injunction.

10.7.1.2 Mootness

By the time the state brings a court action against a merchant, the seller often has discontinued the challenged practice. The seller may then defend the UDAP action by arguing that no injunction is necessary because the unlawful practice has already stopped.

violated); Nuttall v. Dowell, 31 Wash. App. 98, 639 P.2d 832 (1982).

193 *See* §§ 4.3, 4.4, *supra*.

194 *See* § 3.4.4.1, *supra*.

195 *See* § 4.5, *supra*.

196 State v. Custom Pools, 556 A.2d 72 (Vt. 1988).

197 State v. Excel Mgmt. Servs., Inc., 111 Wis. 2d 479, 331 N.W.2d 312 (1983). *Accord* State v. DeFranco Ford, Inc., 609 N.Y.S.2d 266 (App. Div. 1994). *See also* State *ex rel.* McGraw v. Scott Runyan Pontiac-Buick, Inc., 194 W. Va. 770, 461 S.E.2d 516 (1995) (West Virginia law allows attorney general to recover illegal charges from assignees even if they are free of wrongdoing).

198 Plowman v. Bagnal, 450 S.E.2d 36 (S.C. 1994).

199 State v. Cottman Transmission Sys., Inc., 86 Md. App. 714, 587 A.2d 1190 (1991).

200 Commonwealth v. Elm Medical Laboratories, Inc., 33 Mass. App. Ct. 71, 596 N.E.2d 376 (1992).

State courts invariably reject this defense.[201] Otherwise the seller would be free at no additional risk to revert to its old scheme after the case was dismissed. An injunction is a remedy designed to control future behavior, and whether that behavior is occurring at the time of the injunction is generally irrelevant.[202] Similarly, it should be no defense to a state agency's injunctive action that the respondent has recently entered into a similar consent agreement with a federal agency.[203]

On the other hand, the court has discretion as to whether it will issue an injunction or not.[204] Thus a court may not grant injunctive relief where it believes there is little likelihood that the challenged conduct will ever be repeated, such as where a deceptive advertisement was immediately corrected and the offense was not repeated for three years.[205] In another case, where the legislature, after the suit was initiated, enacted criminal penalties for those engaging in the challenged conduct, a court found the criminal sanction a sufficient deterrent to make a civil injunction unnecessary.[206]

201 State *ex rel.* Babbitt v. Goodyear Tire & Rubber Co., 128 Ariz. 483, 626 P.2d 1115 (Ct. App. 1981); People *ex rel.* Babbitt v. Green Acres Trust, 127 Ariz. 160, 618 P.2d 1086 (Ct. App. 1980); Commonwealth *ex rel.* Stephens v. Isaacs, 577 S.W.2d 617 (Ky. Ct. App. 1979); State *ex rel.* Guste v. Crossroads Gallery Inc., 357 So. 2d 1381 (La. Ct. App. 1978); Lowell Gas Co. v. Attorney General, 377 Mass. 37, 385 N.E.2d 240 (1979); State *ex rel.* Douglas v. Ledwith, 204 Neb. 6, 281 N.W.2d 729 (1979); People *ex rel.* Spitzer v. Gen. Electric Co., 302 A.D.2d 314, 756 N.Y.S.2d 520 (2003); People by Spitzer v. Network Assocs., Inc., 195 Misc. 2d 384, 758 N.Y.S.2d 466, 469 (2003); People *ex rel.* Lefkowitz v. Therapeutic Hypnosis Inc., 83 Misc. 2d 1068, 374 N.Y.S.2d 576 (Sup. Ct. 1975); State v. Ralph Williams' N.W. Chrysler Plymouth, Inc., 87 Wash. 2d 298, 553 P.2d 423 (1976); State v. Ralph Williams' N.W. Chrysler Plymouth, Inc., 82 Wash. 2d 265, 510 P.2d 233 (1973); State v. Fonk's Mobile Home Park & Sales, 343 N.W.2d 820 (Wis. Ct. App. 1983); Weller v. Dept. of Agriculture, Trade and Consumer Protection, 95 Wis. 2d 739, 293 N.W.2d 180 (Wis. Ct. App. 1980), *aff'd*, 109 Wis. 2d 665, 327 N.W.2d 172 (1982). *Accord* FTC v. Crescent Publ. Group, 129 F. Supp. 2d 311, 320 n.56 (S.D.N.Y. 2001) (case brought under both FTC Act and N.Y. UDAP statute).

202 State *ex rel.* Douglas v. Ledwith, 204 Neb. 6, 281 N.W.2d 729 (1979); *see also* State *ex rel.* Babbitt v. Goodyear Tire & Rubber Co., 128 Ariz. 483, 626 P.2d 1115 (Ct. App. 1981).

203 Consumer Protection Div. v. Consumer Publishing Co., 304 Md. 731, 501 A.2d 48 (1985).

204 State *ex rel.* Johnson v. International Harvester Co., 25 Or. App. 9, 548 P.2d 176 (1976).

205 People *ex rel.* Lefkowitz v. Volkswagen of Am., Inc., 47 A.D. 868, 366 N.Y.S.2d 157 (1975); *see also* State v. Wolowitz, 96 A.D.2d 47, 468 N.Y.S.2d 131 (1983) (acts must be repeated but statute amended to make requirement less strict); State by Lefkowitz v. Italian Line, 56 A.D.2d 533, 391 N.Y.S.2d 132 (1977) (interpreting pre-amendment version of statute). *But see* State v. Fonk's Mobile Home Park & Sales, 343 N.W.2d 820 (Wis. Ct. App. 1983) (threat of future harm not prerequisite for state injunctive action).

206 Bowles v. Blue Lake Dev. Corp., 504 F.2d 1094 (5th Cir. 1974) (Florida law).

10.7.1.3 Breadth of the Order

10.7.1.3.1 General considerations

Courts must determine how broad an injunctive order to approve. While there is little argument that the court can enjoin the specific unfair or deceptive conduct engaged in by the seller, state enforcement officials, like the FTC, will usually request a broader order to "fence in" the seller. Otherwise the merchant could continue its improper conduct by making only slight modifications in its misleading scheme that would result in the conduct falling outside the scope of the injunction. On the other hand, an appellate court is more likely to uphold an order if the state can show a clear relationship between the order and the type of deceptive acts the defendant committed.[207]

Consequently, state enforcement agencies should seek an injunction broad enough to ensure that future misconduct is prevented, but not so overly broad as to unreasonably impair the seller's right to conduct a legitimate business.[208] State enforcement officials should justify a broad order not as a punitive measure for past misconduct, but as a necessary precaution to prevent evasion of the order by the seller engaging in similar, but different practices in the future.[209] While the enforcement agency should not be discouraged from seeking a broad order, the order should be as precise as possible so that the seller knows what conduct will lead to future penalties and what conduct will not. A typical order will delineate specific acts and practices that are prohibited and other acts and practices that the respondent must follow to avoid further UDAP violations.[210] A general prohibition against unfair advertising may be insufficiently precise.[211]

10.7.1.3.2 First Amendment considerations

While the terms of an injunction should be plain enough

207 Luskin's, Inc. v. Consumer Protection Div., 353 Md. 335, 726 A.2d 702 (1999).

208 State *ex rel.* Stovall v. Martinez, 27 Kan. App. 2d 9, 996 P.2d 371 (2000) (order prohibiting non-attorney who had engaged in authorized practice of law from providing specific insurance consulting services to individual consumers, but allowing him to provide the same services to an insurance company, was narrowly tailored to prevent future violations while allowing him to use his training and experience).

209 *See* FTC v. Think Achievement Corp., 144 F. Supp. 2d 1013 (N.D. Ind. 2000) (federal courts have broad authority to restrain acts which are of same class or type as the unlawful acts defendant has committed), *aff'd in relevant part, rev'd in part on other grounds*, 312 F.3d 259 (7th Cir. 2002).

210 FTC v. Direct Marketing Concepts, Inc., 2004 WL 1399185 (D. Mass. June 23, 2004) (specifically identifying prohibited labeling, advertising and promotional practices).

211 *See, e.g.*, Luskin's, Inc. v. Consumer Protection Div., 353 Md. 335, 726 A.2d 702 (1999) (order should have been limited to statutory provisions that defendant had been charged with violating).

so that a person of common intelligence can understand them, a California middle-level appellate court has stated:

> However, there is a crucial distinction between "vague and indefinite" and "broad and general." The injunction need not etch forbidden actions with microscopic precision, but may instead draw entire categories of proscribed conduct. Thus, an injunction may have wide scope, yet if it is reasonably possible to determine whether a particular act is included within its grasp, the injunction is valid.[212]

The circumstances of each case will determine how broad an order the court will allow. On one extreme, in certain circumstances where the seller's conduct is egregious and its whole manner of business is deceptive, courts have revoked the seller's license and enjoined the company from doing business in the state.[213] The United States Supreme Court has ruled that "even a legitimate occupation may be restricted or prohibited in the public interest,"[214] and that if a claim can not be presented in a particular medium (*e.g.*, television) without deception, the seller must abandon use of that medium.[215]

Supreme Court First Amendment cases indicate that a certain degree of protection is given even to commercial activities.[216] Nonetheless, a remedy that is reasonably necessary to prevent future violations does not impinge upon constitutionally protected free speech.[217] In particular, an order requiring that all advertising claims be substantiated does not impinge on First Amendment guarantees.[218] A more detailed analysis of First Amendment limitations on UDAP orders, including special limitations where the state seeks to enjoin the sale of a publication or course materials, is found at § 7.10.1, *supra*.

212 People v. Custom Craft Carpets, Inc., 206 Cal. Rptr. 12 (Ct. App. 1984).

213 State *ex rel.* Sanborn v. Koscot Interplanetary Inc., 212 Kan. 668, 512 P.2d 416 (1973) (pyramid sale company ordered not to do business in state); Kugler v. Haitian Tours, Inc., 120 N.J. Super. 260, 293 A.2d 706 (1972) (company enjoined from selling foreign divorces); People *ex rel.* Abrams v. Helena VIP Personal Introductions Servs. of New York, Inc., 608 N.Y.S.2d 58 (App. Div. 1993); People *ex rel.* Lefkowitz v. Therapeutic Hypnosis, Inc., 83 Misc. 2d 1068, 374 N.Y.S.2d 576 (Sup. Ct. 1975) (hypnosis corporation ordered dissolved); Commonwealth v. Commercial Enterprises Inc., Clearinghouse No. 26,036 (Pa. C.P. Erie Cty. 1972) (swimming pool seller enjoined from ever doing any type of business in the state).

214 Breard v. Alexandria, 341 U.S. 622 (1951); *see also* Ferguson v. Skrupa, 372 U.S. 726 (1963); Kugler v. Haitian Tours, Inc., 120 N.J. Super. 260, 293 A.2d 706 (1972). *See generally* §§ 10.7.1.3.3, 10.7.1.4, *infra*.

215 FTC v. Colgate-Palmolive Co., 380 U.S. 374 (1965).

216 *See* § 7.10.1, *supra*.

217 United States v. Reader's Digest Ass'n, Inc., 662 F.2d 955 (3d Cir. 1981); People v. Custom Craft Carpets, Inc., 206 Cal. Rptr. 12 (Ct. App. 1984).

218 People v. Custom Craft Carpets, Inc., 206 Cal. Rptr. 12 (Ct. App. 1984).

10.7.1.3.3 Judicial discretion

Whatever the constitutional limits on injunctions, courts will often find that a UDAP statute calls for a narrower response than a total ban on the defendant's business operation. Thus the Nevada Supreme Court has refused to enjoin a company from any form of leasing, repairing or selling motor vehicles, but only from specific deceptive practices.[219] Similarly, a Pennsylvania court would not enjoin future sales of a hearing aid device, but only deceptive advertising of the device.[220] The Wisconsin Supreme Court has found that permanently enjoining a landlord from the residential rental business was broader than necessary because the landlord had already sold all existing residential property.[221] An Ohio court has held that the trial court has discretion to find that civil penalties and damages are an adequate remedy, and declined to issue an injunction.[222]

While courts are reluctant, except in extreme cases, to order a company to cease conducting business altogether, courts have no difficulty enjoining conduct that as a practical matter will put an end to the business. The fact that an injunction will prevent a business from being successfully continued is no defense in a UDAP action.[223] Thus courts have enjoined the selling of a worthless product even though that was the seller's whole business,[224] have enjoined a home improvement contractor from doing business unless it disclosed to each consumer that the company has been found to have engaged in deceptive, unconscionable and fraudulent practices,[225] and have enjoined a seller from offering certified copies of deeds until six months after the deed had been recorded.[226] The Maine Supreme Court approved an order enjoining a motel owner from having any contact with the public, where he had repeatedly abused and terrorized potential customers, conduct which the court held to be an unfair practice.[227]

219 State *ex rel.* List v. AAA Auto Leasing & Rental, 93 Nev. 483, 568 P.2d 1230 (1977).

220 Commonwealth v. Hush-Tone Indus. Inc., 4 Pa. Commw. 1 (1971).

221 State v. Weller, 109 Wis. 2d 665, 327 N.W.2d 172 (1982).

222 State *ex rel.* Fisher v. Rose Chevrolet, Inc., 98 Ohio App. 3d 611, 649 N.E.2d 50 (1994).

223 Slough v. Federal Trade Comm'n, 396 F.2d 870 (1968); Commonwealth v. Foster, 57 Pa. D. & C.2d 203 (Pa. C.P. Allegheny Cty. 1972).

224 Kugler v. Haitian Tours, Inc., 120 N.J. Super. 260, 293 A.2d 706 (1972). *See also* Federal Trade Commission v. Para-Link Int'l, Inc., 2001 WL 1701537 (M.D. Fla. Feb. 28, 2001).

225 Brown v. Columbus Remodeling & Builders Inc., Clearinghouse No. 27,064 (Ohio C.P. Franklin Cty. 1978).

226 Commonwealth v. Foster, 57 Pa. D. & C.2d 203 (Pa. C.P. Allegheny Cty. 1972).

227 State v. Shattuck, 747 A.2d 174 (Me. 2000).

10.7.1.3.4 Special statutory limitations to injunctive remedy

In a few states, the UDAP statute itself places limits on the injunctive remedy. Where a UDAP statute authorizes an injunction prohibiting a person from "continuing such practices or engaging therein or doing any acts in furtherance thereof," courts will only enjoin practices found to have been committed or previously connected with those violations.[228] Similarly, where a UDAP statute authorizes an attorney general to bring an injunction only against continuance of fraud, a court has held this does not authorize an injunction against eviction proceedings, where those proceedings are not fraudulent.[229]

10.7.1.4 Innovative Orders

State enforcement officials are not limited to requesting simple orders prohibiting specified practices. Injunctive orders can be innovative, and require affirmative actions that will prevent future deception. An injunctive order that requires a dealer to comply with specific requirements does not amount to illegal rulemaking by the court.[230] A court may apply the general standards of a UDAP statute to a specific factual situation by imposing specific requirements on the dealer.[231]

Courts have specified that the seller's violation of the court's order will result in the seller's sales contracts becoming null and void, thus protecting those victimized by the order violation.[232] In one case the respondent was ordered to consent to vacate and dismiss without prejudice more than 100 court judgments improperly obtained and to notify all its customers.[233] The Maine Supreme Court has upheld a trial court's order that a car dealer re-rustproof customers' cars.[234] Sellers have also been required to keep detailed records to accommodate compliance investigations.[235] In a private action, a court has also ordered that a seller include on the product a warning label setting out various hazards connected with its use.[236]

In a private UDAP injunctive action, the court has ordered a landlord not to evict any tenants, even for nonpayment of rent, without first getting the court's prior approval.[237] Another ordered an abusive landlord not to be personally involved in renting out his properties in the future.[238] Settlements between states and defendants sometimes include requirements that the defendants make monetary contributions to nonprofit organizations, usually organizations that assist consumers who are affected by the unfair or deceptive practice of the defendants. A Minnesota voluntary assurance required a seller to contribute $100,000 in home improvement products to Habitat for Humanity, and established special protections for senior citizens such as an extended right to cancel and prohibitions against specific high-pressure sales tactics.[239]

An appellate court has upheld as necessary to prevent future violations an injunction that: required the seller to establish an impound fund to be used to provide refunds to consumers; precluded the seller from selling products supplied by a third party unless there is a contract between the seller and third party; barred the seller from using any business name without first notifying the attorney general's office; mandated the maintenance of records of complaints, refunds, and customer correspondence; and required the seller to submit to warrantless searches and seizures.[240] Other cases have prohibited individuals from conducting their former business for a set period of years,[241] until they make restitution to consumers,[242] or until they post a $100,000 bond.[243] A number of FTC orders require a $1

228 State *ex rel.* Danforth v. Independence Dodge, Inc., 494 S.W.2d 362 (Mo. Ct. App. 1973). Note that Missouri's UDAP statute has been broadened since this decision, and now allows an injunction if the defendant is "about to engage" in a UDAP violation. *See* Mo. Rev. Stat. § 407.100.

229 State by Abrams v. Magley, 484 N.Y.S.2d 251 (App. Div. 1984).

230 State v. Cottman Transmissions Sys., Inc., 86 Md. App. 714, 587 A.2d 1190 (1991).

231 *Id.*

232 Commonwealth by Packel v. Tolleson, 14 Pa. Commw. Ct. 140, 321 A.2d 664 (1974).

233 State v. Cohen, N.Y.L.J., Feb. 6, 1984, at 7, col. 2 (Sup. Ct. 1984).

234 State v. Bob Chambers Ford, 522 A.2d 362 (Me. 1987).

235 *See, e.g.*, State *ex rel.* Douglas v. Ledwith, 204 Neb. 6, 281 N.W.2d 729 (1979).

236 Consumers Union of U.S., Inc. v. Alta-Dena Certified Dairy, 4 Cal. App. 4th 963, 6 Cal. Rptr. 2d 193 (1992).

237 Hernandez v. Stabach, 145 Cal. App. 3d 309, 193 Cal. Rptr. 350 (1983).

238 Collard v. Reagan, 2002 WL 1357052 (Wash. App. June 21, 2002) (unpublished, citation limited).

239 *In re* Pacesetter Corp., Clearinghouse No. 50,446 (Minn. Dist. Ct. June 23, 1995) (voluntary assurance).

240 People v. Toomey, 157 Cal. App. 3d 1, 203 Cal. Rptr. 642 (1984).

241 Commonwealth v. Elm Medical Laboratories, Inc., 33 Mass. App. Ct. 71, 596 N.E.2d 376 (1992). *See also* People v. First Fed. Credit Corp., 104 Cal. App. 4th 721, 128 Cal. Rptr. 2d 542 (2002) (affirming injunction that prohibited mortgage loan company principal from performing mortgage loan services without obtaining real estate license); Collard v. Reagan, 2002 WL 1357052 (Wash. App. June 21, 2002) (unpublished, citation limited) (affirming order in private injunctive action that prohibited abusive landlord from being personally involving in renting out his properties in the future).

242 State *ex rel.* Fisher v. Warren Star Theater, 84 Ohio App. 3d 435, 616 N.E.2d 1192 (1992); Brown v. Bredenbeck, 2 Ohio Op. 3d 286 (Franklin Cty. C.P. 1975); Brown v. Cole, Clearinghouse No. 27,057 (Ohio C.P. Richland Cty. 1976). *See also* Commonwealth v. Empire Express Inc., Clearinghouse No. 11,729 (Pa. C.P. Erie Cty. 1972) (injunction until company properly registers its name).

243 State v. Polley, 2 S.W.3d 887 (Mo. App. 1999) (interpreting statute to give court authority to require defendant to post bond before conducting further business); People *ex rel.* Vacco v. Lipsitz, 174 Misc. 2d 571, 663 N.Y.S.2d 468 (Sup. Ct. 1997); People *ex rel.* Abrams v. Robbins, Clearinghouse No. 50,409

million bond before the individual defendants can engage in the same line of business in the future.[244] FTC orders that base the amount of penalties or restitution on financial disclosures from the defendant often include an "avalanche" clause whereby a large sum will become due if it is discovered that there were misrepresentations in the financial disclosures.[245]

Another approach, particularly for a consent agreement, is for the cease and desist order to include an agreement by the respondent to pay a large civil penalty, that penalty being stayed as long as the respondent complies with the order. Courts are unlikely to give much leeway in avoiding the penalty to a respondent who violates such a cease and desist order.[246]

10.7.1.5 Asset Attachment Orders

In extremely egregious cases, state enforcement agencies may seek judicial orders for attachments or freezes on bank accounts or other assets that can be specifically identified. States must be prepared to justify the use of such a drastic remedy, but under the right circumstances, especially if there is evidence that the defendant will conceal or dissipate assets during the pendency of the action, courts will grant such relief.[247] Some states may have specific authority for such relief, but often state law enforcement officials rely on general grants of equitable authority to the courts to order relief that is just and reasonable or necessary to protect consumers who have ascertained losses as a result of an unfair or deceptive practice. The FTC also relies on the general inherent authority of federal courts to grant any ancillary relief necessary to accomplish justice.[248]

A freeze on a bank account or asset attachment will usually trigger immediate responses from the defendants and often will bring defendants to the negotiating table since their income is no longer available to them and they can not operate without it. This tactic is often and effectively used by the FTC.[249]

Where a court preliminarily freezes the defendant's assets, defendants may argue their assets are needed to pay their attorneys to defend the state's enforcement action. A preliminary freeze order can be drafted to allow the assets to be used for this purpose, but only after the court approves each payment. There is no foundation to a defendant's due process argument that freezing of assets deprived the defendant of expert witnesses to defend the case where the defendant had the right under the freeze order, but never asked the court, to release funds for those purposes.[250]

10.7.1.6 Preliminary Injunctions

State enforcement officials should always consider seeking a preliminary injunction against a challenged practice to stop its recurrence as soon as possible. The preliminary injunction also has tactical merit. Without a preliminary injunction, the defendant may attempt to prolong the litigation as long as possible, and will be in no rush to settle. Once the deceptive scheme is preliminarily enjoined, the burden shifts. Now the defendant's position can only be improved by a favorable judgment on the merits or by a settlement.

Although the trial court has discretion whether to grant a preliminary injunction, the court must at least grant a hearing on the preliminary injunction request.[251] In the hearing, the state should show by its pleadings and affidavits a reasonable probability of ultimate success in the legal action.[252] Where the defendant has alleged it will voluntarily terminate the challenged practice, the state should have little trouble obtaining an injunction since the defendant will not be prejudiced.[253]

Although the preliminary injunction is equitable in nature, courts take two approaches to avoid the normal requirement that the plaintiff show irreparable injury. One approach argues that future deceived consumers might not have an adequate remedy at law if their damages are uncertain.[254] The other approach convincingly claims that irreparable injury need not be shown where a preliminary injunction is authorized by statute.[255] Nor is a preliminary

(N.Y. Sup. Ct. Mar. 14, 1994) (prohibition against engaging in any business involving the public without posting $50,000 bond); State *ex rel.* Abrams v. Chalmers, Clearinghouse No. 43,075 (N.Y. Sup. Ct. 1987).

244 *See, e.g.*, FTC v. Wolf, 5 Trade Reg. Rep. (CCH) ¶ 23,665 (S.D. Fla. Sept. 12, 1994) (consent order); FTC v. United Holdings Inc., 5 Trade Reg. Rep. (CCH) ¶ 23,692 (D. Nev. Oct., 18 1994) (proposed consent decree).

245 *See, e.g.*, FTC v. The Kohn Group, Trade Reg. Rptr. (CCH) ¶ 24,836 (C.D. Cal. Nov. 29, 2000).

246 Begin v. State, 1996 Minn. App. LEXIS 1103 (Minn. Ct. App. Sept. 17, 1996) (unpublished).

247 FTC v. Singer, Inc., 668 F.2d 1107 (9th Cir. 1982).

248 *Id.*

249 FTC v. Direct Marketing Concepts, Inc., 2004 WL 1399185 (D. Mass. June 23, 2004).

250 FTC v. Atlantex Assoc., 872 F.2d 966 (11th Cir. 1989).

251 Commonwealth v. Schall, 6 Pa. Commw. 578, 297 A.2d 190 (1972).

252 People *ex rel.* Hartigan v. Peters, 871 F.2d 1336 (7th Cir. 1989) (Illinois law) (affidavits were sufficient to prove that defendant violated UDAP statute where defendant did not appear); People v. Sangiacomo, 128 Cal. App. 3d 942, 180 Cal. Rptr. 594 (1982). *Cf.* State *ex rel.* Attorney General v. NOS Communications, Inc., 84 P.3d 1052 (Nev. 2004) (state must assert claim for injunctive relief in its pleadings and support its motion with admissible evidence).

253 State *ex rel.* Lefkowitz v. Interstate Tractor Trailer Training, Inc., 66 Misc. 2d 678, 321 N.Y.S.2d 147 (Sup. Ct. 1971); Commonwealth v. Lenny Levy's Chrysler Plymouth, Clearinghouse No. 26,023 (Pa. C.P. Allegheny Cty. 1971).

254 State v. Quality Meats of Concord, Inc., Clearinghouse No. 44,812 (Alaska Super. Ct. 1988) (preliminary injunction); Commonwealth v. Lenny Levy's Chrysler Plymouth, Clearinghouse No. 26,023 (Pa. C.P. Allegheny Cty. 1971).

255 *See* § 10.7.1.7, *supra*.

injunction objectionable because it grants as much relief as would be available upon a final hearing.[256]

A Minnesota court has listed five factors for evaluating the propriety of a temporary UDAP injunction: (1) the nature of the two parties; (2) the relative harm to the two parties if an injunction is or is not granted; (3) the likelihood that one party or the other will prevail; (4) consideration of public policy as expressed in state and federal law; and (5) the administrative burdens involved in judicial supervision and enforcement of the temporary decree.[257]

As to the breadth of the preliminary injunction, the clearest statement is found in a Texas appellate case:

> The injunction decree must be as definite, clear and precise as possible. . . . But obviously the injunction must be in broad enough terms to prevent repetition of the evil sought to be stopped. . . . Otherwise it would probably take longer to write the decree than it would to try the case and the injunction might well become unintelligible and self-destructive.[258]

A preliminary injunction should attempt to preserve the status quo *not* before the state enforcement action was initiated, but the status quo before the seller engaged in the challenged practice.[259]

10.7.1.7 Preconditions to an Injunctive Order

The state does not need to show irreparable injury or that there is no adequate remedy at law before seeking an injunction under a UDAP statute.[260] This is in accord with the general rule that "[w]here an injunction is authorized by statute and the statutory conditions are satisfied, the usual grounds for injunctive relief need not be established."[261] Maryland requires, however, that the state show that the misrepresentation is material, *i.e.*, that it is likely to affect the purchasing decision.[262]

An injunction can be issued if the statute is violated even if the violation is not repeated.[263] No "balancing of equities" is necessary.[264] The fact that another state agency can revoke the seller's license does not prevent the state from instead utilizing a UDAP cease and desist order.[265] The state need only show by a preponderance of the evidence that the UDAP statute has been violated.[266] Indeed, for a preliminary injunction, the state need only present some credible evidence, even if disputed, that reasonable cause exists that the respondent is engaging in or is likely to engage in a UDAP violation.[267]

The merchant has no right to a jury trial in an injunctive action. The action is equitable in nature, and enforces a statute creating new rights not available at common law.[268]

256 Wesware, Inc. v. State, 488 S.W.2d 844 (Tex. Civ. App. 1972).

257 State *ex rel.* Humphrey v. Dynasty Sys. Corp., Clearinghouse No. 36,591 (Minn. Dist. Ct. 10th Jud. Dist. 1983), *relying on* Dahlberg Bros., Inc. v. Ford Motor Co., 272 Minn. 264, 137 N.W.2d 314 (1965).

258 Wesware, Inc. v. State, 488 S.W.2d 844 (Tex. Civ. App. 1972).

259 People v. Hill, 66 Cal. App. 3d 320, 136 Cal. Rptr. 30 (1977).

260 Henderson v. Burd, 133 F.2d 515 (2d Cir. 1943); S.E.C. v. Torr, 87 F.2d 446 (2d Cir. 1937); State v. Quality Meats of Concord, Inc., Clearinghouse No. 44,812 (Alaska Super. Ct. 1988) (preliminary injunction); People *ex rel.* Hartigan v. Stianos, 475 N.E.2d 1024 (Ill. App. Ct. 1985); People *ex rel.* Hartigan v. Dynasty Sys., 471 N.E.2d 236 (Ill. App. Ct. 1984); State *ex rel.* Stovall v. Cooper, 2001 WL 34117813, at *21 (Kan. Dist. Ct. May 15, 2001); Commonwealth *ex rel.* Chandler v. Anthem Ins. Cos., 8 S.W.3d 48 (Ky. App. 1999) (construing explicit provision of Kentucky UDAP statute); Reed v. Allison & Perrone, 376 So. 2d 1067 (La. Ct. App. 1979); State *ex rel.* Nixon v. Telco Directory Publishing, 863 S.W.2d 596 (Mo. 1993); State *ex rel.* Webster v. Milbourn, 759 S.W.2d 862 (Mo. Ct. App. 1988); State *ex rel.* Attorney General v. NOS Communications, Inc., 84 P.3d 1052 (Nev. 2004); Brown v. East Ohio Heating Co., 1981 Ohio App. LEXIS 13691 (Sept. 23, 1981); Brown v. Deacon's Chrysler Plymouth, Inc., 14 Ohio Op. 3d 436 (Ct. App. 1979); Brown v. Bob Kay, Inc., 14 Ohio Op. 3d 329 (Ct. App. 1979); Brown v. Spitzer Ford, Inc., 11 Ohio Op. 3d 84 (Ct. App. 1978); State *ex rel.* Edmisten v. Challenge, Inc., 54 N.C. App. 513, 284 S.E.2d 333 (1981) (preliminary injunction); Commonwealth *ex rel.* Fisher v. Cole, 709 A.2d 994 (Pa. Commw. Ct. 1998); Commonwealth v. Burns, 663 A.2d 308 (Pa. Commw. 1995); Household Retail Servs. v. State, 2001 Tex. App. LEXIS 5893 (Aug. 29, 2001); State v. Fonk's Mobile Home Park & Sales, 343 N.W.2d 820 (Wis. Ct. App. 1983). A number of UDAP statutes even state explicitly that the action can proceed even if there are other adequate remedies of law.

261 42 Am. Jur. 2d, *Injunctions* § 12 (2000 and 2001 Supp.). *See also* People *ex rel.* Hartigan v. Peters, 871 F.2d 1336 (7th Cir. 1989) (Illinois law) (harm to public is presumed under UDAP statute); S.E.C. v. Torr, 87 F.2d 446 (2d Cir. 1937); FTC v. Accent Marketing, Inc., 2002 WL 31257708 (S.D. Ala. July 1, 2002) (FTC need not show irreparable injury); FTC v. SkyBiz.com, Inc., 2001 WL 1673649 (N.D. Okla. Aug. 2, 2001) (FTC need not show irreparable injury), *aff'd*, 2003 WL 202438 (10th Cir. Jan. 30, 2003) (unpublished, citation limited); People *ex rel.* Hartigan v. Stianos, 475 N.E.2d 1024 (Ill. App. Ct. 1985); State *ex rel.* Nixon v. Telco Directory Publishing, 863 S.W.2d 596 (Mo. 1993).

262 Luskin's, Inc. v. Consumer Protection Div., 353 Md. 335, 726 A.2d 702 (1999).

263 Brown v. Bob Kay, Inc., 14 Ohio Op. 3d 329 (Ct. App. 1979); State *ex rel.* McGraw v. Telecheck Servs., Inc., 582 S.E.2d 885 (W. Va. 2003) (no need to show pattern or practice).

264 Brown v. Bob Kay, Inc., 14 Ohio Op. 3d 329 (Ct. App. 1979).

265 State v. Ralph Williams' N.W. Chrysler Plymouth, Inc., 87 Wash. 2d 298, 553 P.2d 423 (1976).

266 People *ex rel.* Hartigan v. Stianos, 475 N.E.2d 1024 (Ill. App. Ct. 1985); People *ex rel.* Hartigan v. Dynasty Sys., 471 N.E.2d 236 (Ill. App. Ct. 1984); State *ex rel.* Webster v. Milbourn, 759 S.W.2d 862 (Mo. Ct. App. 1988); State *ex rel.* Attorney General v. NOS Communications, Inc., 84 P.3d 1052 (Nev. 2004); Brown v. Barnum & Crow, Inc., 22 Ohio Op. 3d 24 (Lucas Cty. C.P. 1980).

267 State *ex rel.* McGraw v. Imperial Marketing, 472 S.E.2d 792 (W. Va. 1996).

268 Nunley v. State, 628 So. 2d 619 (Ala. 1993); State by Humphrey v. Alpine Air Products, Inc., 490 N.W.2d 888 (Minn. Ct. App.

10.7.1.8 Who Should Be Named in an Injunctive Order

The traditional wisdom is for state enforcement officials to name as defendants the corporation, individual officers and owners, and any other party involved in the deception. Naming individuals prevents them from avoiding the reach of the injunction by setting up a new corporation. Nevertheless, joining too many parties complicates the litigation, brings in additional attorneys for the defense, and may result in a more vigorous defense with less chance of a consent agreement.

An injunction may be issued not only against the defendants named in the UDAP action but also against its past, present, and future employees, agents, transferees, assigns, and beneficiaries.[269] However, a court may exercise its discretion to decline to subject an individual to an injunction where there is little possibility of that person engaging in deceptive conduct under a new corporate identity.[270] Injunctions also often apply to anyone "acting in concert or participating with" the named defendants. Moreover, it is not imperative that individuals be named in the injunction for the order to apply to them. A later section discusses how individuals not named in, but with knowledge of an order, can be found in contempt for violating the order.[271]

A court may not name someone in an injunction if that person is not liable for the deceptive practices. Issues as to which parties can be held liable in a damage action for the acts of individual agents and officers—the company itself, the company's parent corporation or other shareholders, other company officers, or third parties offering the means or assisting the deception—are detailed in Chapter 6, *supra*. But FTC precedent dealing with who can be made a party to a cease and desist order may be more useful for determining who can be named in a state UDAP enforcement action seeking injunctive relief.

An injunction is appropriate to prevent companies that are on the periphery of a fraudulent scheme from serving as conduits for improper transfers of funds, even though ultimately they may not be liable for consumer redress.[272] Courts have found that an FTC cease and desist order can apply to a parent corporation, even though the normal common law rule is that parent corporations are not liable for the acts of subsidiaries.[273] Companies can also be enjoined from future actions on the basis of acts committed by their agents, even if the company has taken steps to dismiss or discipline the agents for their deceptive practices.[274] Corporate officers who formulated, directed and controlled the company's practices can also be named in the order.[275]

10.7.1.9 Effect of Bankruptcy Stay on Injunction

The state may seek an injunction against a party even after that party has filed bankruptcy and the automatic stay is in effect. The U.S. Bankruptcy Code[276] states that the automatic stay does not apply to proceedings by a governmental unit to enforce such unit's police or regulatory power. This has been interpreted as authorizing the state to seek injunctive relief under a UDAP statute despite an automatic stay.[277] Even a suit seeking restitution for consumers may be exempt from the automatic stay.[278] But at least one bankruptcy court believes that an injunctive order prohibiting the merchant from conducting any form of business at all and an order appointing a state receiver for the merchant's business would interfere with the bankruptcy court's jurisdiction over the merchant.[279] Whenever there is doubt about the applicability of the automatic stay, it is wisest to seek a determination by the bankruptcy court before proceeding.[280]

10.7.1.10 Judicial Modification of Consent Decrees

An agreement between the parties that is not adopted by the court as a consent decree is governed by contract

---

1992) (even if restitution also sought, since restitution is equitable in nature), *aff'd on other grounds*, 500 N.W.2d 788 (Minn. 1993); State v. State Credit Ass'n, 33 Wash. App. 617, 657 P.2d 327 (1983); *see also* FTC v. Kitco of Nevada, Inc., 612 F. Supp. 1280 (D. Minn. 1985) (FTC action seeking injunctive relief).

269 *See* State v. Fonk's Mobile Home Park & Sales, 133 Wis. 2d 287, 395 N.W.2d 786 (Ct. App. 1986).

270 State *ex rel.* Danforth v. W.E. Constr. Co., 552 S.W.2d 72 (Mo. Ct. App. 1977).

271 *See* § 10.7.2.3, *infra*.

272 FTC v. SkyBiz.com, Inc., 2001 WL 1673649 (N.D. Okla. Aug. 2, 2001), *aff'd*, 2003 WL 202438 (10th Cir. Jan. 30, 2003) (unpublished, citation limited).

273 P.F. Collier & Son Corp. v. FTC, 427 F.2d 261 (6th Cir. 1970).

274 FTC v. Standard Educ. Society, 148 F.2d 931 (2d Cir. 1945); Perma-Maid Co. v. FTC, 121 F.2d 282 (6th Cir. 1941); FTC v. Five-Star Auto Club, Inc., 97 F. Supp. 2d 502 (S.D.N.Y. 2000); *see also* U.S. v. Phelps Dodge, 589 F. Supp. 1340 (S.D.N.Y. 1984) (antitrust suit).

275 FTC v. Standard Educ. Society, 302 U.S. 112 (1937); Standard Distributors Inc. v. FTC, 211 F.2d 7 (2d Cir. 1954).

276 11 U.S.C. § 362(b)(4).

277 *In re* Liss, 59 B.R. 556 (Bankr. N.D. Ill. 1986) (injunctive action and civil penalty action not stayed, but civil penalty award can not be enforced in state court); *In re* Charter First Mortgage, Inc., 42 B.R. 380 (Bankr. D. Or. 1984) (injunctive action and civil penalty action not stayed); Cannon v. State (*In re* Cannon), 30 B.R. 565 (Bankr. E.D. Mo. 1983); State v. Carlyle (*In re* Carlyle), Clearinghouse No. 36,571 (Bankr. M.D. Tenn. 1982).

278 *In re* First Alliance Mortg. Co., 263 B.R. 99 (B.A.P. 9th Cir. 2001); FTC v. First Alliance Mortg. Co. (*In re* First Alliance Mortg. Co.), 264 B.R. 634 (C.D. Cal. 2001); *In re* Nelson, 240 B.R. 802 (Bankr. D. Me. 1999) (automatic stay does not affect state's UDAP suit seeking injunction, penalties or fines, and restitution order); *In re* Family Vending, Inc., 171 B.R. 907 (Bankr. N.D. Ga. 1994); *see also* § 10.7.4.2, *infra*.

279 *In re* Liss, 59 B.R. 556 (Bankr. N.D. Ill. 1986).

280 *In re* Family Vending, Inc., 171 B.R. 907 (Bankr. N.D. Ga. 1994).

principles, and modification of the agreement will be governed by contract standards.[281] Once an agreement is adopted by a court as a consent decree, however, courts hold that it becomes a judgment of the court and can be modified like any other order.[282] Modification can be based on a finding of changed circumstances or the defendant's violation of the original order.[283]

10.7.1.11 Public Disclosure of Consent Agreements

As a general rule, consent agreements are public actions, and the public should have full access to such information. Nevertheless in special cases, a trial court may have authority to suppress a consent agreement from public disclosure until the defendant violates that order, if such arrangement is part of the agreement.[284] If the attorney general does not agree to suppress information pertaining to an investigation, the attorney general has an absolute privilege to disseminate information to the public concerning matters within the performance of the attorney general's official duties.[285]

10.7.2 Violations of Cease and Desist Orders, Injunctions, Assurances of Voluntary Compliance

10.7.2.1 Standard of Proof; Right to Jury Trial

Penalties for violation of an injunction are civil in nature and need not be proven beyond a reasonable doubt,[286] even where contempt leads to a jail sentence.[287] A violation need not be a knowing violation.[288] A court has also ruled that "a consent order is merely a recitation of the settlement agreement between the parties. Like any other agreement, the law of contract controls its interpretation, and its meaning should be determined by the language chosen by the parties."[289]

The Texas Constitution, which offers a broader guarantee to a jury trial than the federal Constitution, requires a jury trial for a defendant in a civil penalty action for violations of a consent agreement.[290] Other courts take the opposite view.[291]

10.7.2.2 Violations of Assurances of Voluntary Compliance

Unless a UDAP statute provides otherwise, the state can not seek civil penalties where a seller violates an assurance of voluntary compliance, even if the court approves the assurance.[292] Nonetheless, where a violation of an assurance of voluntary compliance constitutes a separate violation of a UDAP statute, then separate penalties may be sought. In some states, a violation of an assurance of voluntary compliance is prima facie evidence of a violation of the state's UDAP statute.[293] Whether a defendant can withdraw consent to an assurance of voluntary compliance will probably be governed by contract law.[294]

10.7.2.3 Who Must Comply with the Injunction and Has the Injunction Been Violated?

Even when an individual is not named in an injunction, that individual may have to comply with the order. Where a party participates in the proceedings and has actual knowl-

281 *See In re* People by Spitzer v. Condor Pontiac, Cadillac, Buick & GMC Trucks, Inc., 2003 WL 21649689 (N.Y. Sup. Ct. July 2, 2003) (whether assurance of voluntary compliance will be set aside is governed by contract standards).

282 People *ex rel.* Fahner v. Colorado City Lot Owners & Taxpayers Ass'n, 106 Ill. 2d 1, 476 N.E.2d 409 (1985); State v. Shattuck, 747 A.2d 174 (Me. 2000); State v. Peppertree Resort Villas, Inc., 651 N.W.2d 345 (Wis. App. 2002) (upholding trial court's decision that defendant's bad guess about the number of consumers who would choose private litigation over acceptance of partial restitution is not grounds to modify consent order).

283 State v. Shattuck, 747 A.2d 174 (Me. 2000).

284 People *ex rel.* MacFarlane v. A Delaware Corp., 626 P.2d 1144 (Colo. Ct. App. 1980).

285 State v. Ryan, Clearinghouse No. 38,908 (Minn. Dist. Ct. 1984).

286 Commonwealth v. Turner, Clearinghouse No. 26,034 (Pa. C.P. Erie Cty. 1973); *see also* People v. Toomey, 157 Cal. App. 3d 1, 203 Cal. Rptr. 642 (1984). *But see* Iowa *ex rel.* Campbell v. Runza, Clearinghouse No. 50,443 (Iowa Dist. Ct. Jan. 12, 1994) (proof beyond reasonable doubt necessary for contempt conviction).

287 American Security Benevolent Ass'n, Inc. v. District Court, 259 Iowa 983, 147 N.W.2d 55 (1966).

288 State v. Bachynsky, 770 S.W.2d 563 (Tex. 1989); Credit Bureau of Laredo, Inc. v. State, 515 S.W.2d 706 (Tex. Civ. App. 1974), *aff'd on other grounds*, 530 S.W.2d 288 (Tex. 1975). *But see* Iowa *ex rel.* Campbell v. Runza, Clearinghouse No. 50,443 (Iowa Dist. Ct. Jan. 12, 1994) (defendant found not in contempt because violation not willful).

289 People *ex rel.* Fahner v. Colorado City Lot Owners & Taxpayers Ass'n, 119 Ill. App. 3d 691, 456 N.E.2d 943 (1983), *rev'd on other grounds*, 106 Ill. 2d 1, 476 N.E.2d 409 (1985).

290 State v. Credit Bureau of Laredo, Inc., 530 S.W.2d 288 (Tex. 1975). *See also* FTC v. Kuykendall, 312 F.3d 1329 (10th Cir. 2002) (jury trial may be required on civil contempt charges for violation of complex FTC injunction where substantial sanctions are at stake).

291 People v. Toomey, 157 Cal. App. 3d 1, 203 Cal. Rptr. 642 (1984); People v. Bestline Products, Inc., 61 Cal. App. 3d 879, 132 Cal. Rptr. 767 (1976).

292 State v. McPherson, 208 Kan. 511, 493 P.2d 228 (1972); State *ex rel.* Danforth v. European Health Spa, Inc., 611 S.W.2d 259 (Mo. App. 1980).

293 *See* Wash. Rev. Code § 19.86.100.

294 *In re* People by Spitzer v. Condor Pontiac, Cadillac, Buick & GMC Trucks, Inc., 2003 WL 21649689 (N.Y. Sup. Ct. July 2, 2003) (denying petition to set assurance of voluntary compliance aside on grounds of fraud).

edge of the injunction, the party is bound by the order.[295] Individuals taking over a business that is subject to an injunction are liable for any violations they commit.[296] It is also irrelevant that an employee is unaware of the terms of an injunction where the employer has been notified of the injunction; the employee's violation makes the employer liable for penalties for violation of the injunction.[297]

The filing of an appeal from an injunction does not immunize the defendant from continuing violations of the order, unless the court specifically stays the injunction.[298] Nor is the defendant entitled, in a contempt proceeding, to attack the basis for the underlying order.[299]

Courts will also look dimly upon subterfuges to avoid the scope of an injunction. Thus flying prospective buyers to other states to sign purchase agreements could not be used to avoid liability.[300] Nor can changing the name of the challenged promotion, the name the company does business under, or other minor operating changes avoid an injunction where the essential deceptive scheme remains intact.[301] It is not necessary for the state to show that the defendant's violations of the UDAP decree injured consumers; the simple fact of a violation is sufficient to support the imposition of penalties.[302]

10.7.2.4 Size of Penalty for Violations

Where a UDAP statute establishes a specific dollar penalty for violations of cease and desist orders, an important issue is whether the penalty should be assessed for each separate violation, and, if so, what is a separate violation.[303] Courts have assessed $5000 penalties for each sales meeting in violation of an order,[304] $200 for each of 600 different violations,[305] $1000 for each of 500 violations,[306] and $1 for each of 150,000 solicitations and sales in violation of an order.[307] Massachusetts' highest court has affirmed the imposition of multiple penalties where a dealer ran three advertisements that violated a consent decree, even though all three were identical and were purchased in a single transaction.[308] Other times courts, in their discretion, have not awarded the maximum penalty for each violation, but only for a number of general violations.[309]

Particularly where a statute is not explicit as to the size of a penalty, courts will consider payments the defendant received in violation of court orders, and what amount is sufficient to compel compliance, deter noncompliance, and prevent the penalty from being just an acceptable cost of doing business.[310] Where a corporation willfully violates a UDAP decree, there is every reason to impose a penalty at or near the maximum.[311] It may help the trial court if the state can show an approximate amount of money that the defendant gained due to the violation.[312] State courts also cite approvingly to FTC Act criteria that include ability to pay, degree of harm, and seller's good faith.[313]

Where a seller's conduct warrants it, courts have ordered penalties as high as $1,000,000 (in addition to $6,000,000

295 Credit Bureau of Laredo, Inc. v. State, 515 S.W.2d 706 (Tex. Civ. App. 1974), *aff'd on other grounds*, 530 S.W.2d 288 (Tex. 1975); State v. Ralph Williams' N.W. Chrysler Plymouth, Inc., 87 Wash. 2d 327, 553 P.2d 442 (1976). *See also* FTC v. Standard Educ. Society, 302 U.S. 112 (1937); FTC v. Productive Marketing, Inc., 136 F. Supp. 2d 1096 (C.D. Cal. 2001) (company that processed fraudulent seller's credit card payments and failed to turn over funds despite knowledge of injunction obtained by FTC can be held in contempt even though not a party to original suit).

296 Americans Be Independent v. Commonwealth, 14 Pa. Commw. Ct. 179, 321 A.2d 721 (1974).

297 State v. Bachynsky, 770 S.W.2d 563 (Tex. 1989).

298 Bachynsky v. State, 747 S.W.2d 847 (Tex. App. 1988), *rev'd on other grounds*, 770 S.W.2d 563 (Tex. 1989); Allen v. American Land Research, 95 Wash. 2d 841, 631 P.2d 930 (1981); State v. Ralph Williams' N.W. Chrysler Plymouth Inc., 87 Wash. 2d 327, 553 P.2d 442 (1976).

299 Commonwealth v. Fall River Motor Sales, Inc., 409 Mass. 302, 565 N.E.2d 1205 (1991).

300 Commonwealth v. Koscot Interplanetary Inc., Clearinghouse No. 26,024 (Pa. C.P. Erie Cty. 1970).

301 State *ex rel.* Abrams v. East Coast Auto Consultants Corp., 472 N.Y.S.2d 1010 (Sup. 1984).

302 Commonwealth v. Fall River Motor Sales, Inc., 409 Mass. 302, 565 N.E.2d 1205 (1991).

303 *See also* § 10.7.3.2, *infra* (multiple civil penalties for initial violations).

304 Commonwealth by Packel v. Tolleson, 14 Pa. Commw. 140, 321 A.2d 701 (1974).

305 Commonwealth v. Turner, Clearinghouse No. 26,034 (Pa. C.P. Erie Cty. 1973).

306 State v. J&B Assocs., Clearinghouse No. 36,573 (Tenn. Ch. Ct. Shelby Cty. 1983).

307 People v. Toomey, 157 Cal. App. 3d 1, 203 Cal. Rptr. 642 (1984).

308 Commonwealth v. Fall River Motor Sales, Inc., 409 Mass. 302, 565 N.E.2d 1205 (1991); *see also* Commonwealth v. Ted Sopko Auto Sales & Locator, 719 A.2d 1111 (Pa. Commw. 1998) (separate civil penalty imposed for each violation, even though all occurred in same transaction). *But cf.* People v. Superior Court (Jayhill), 9 Cal. 3d 283, 507 P.2d 1400 (1973) (civil penalty for initial violations can be based on number of persons involved, but only one penalty allowed per victim regardless of number of violations).

309 Commonwealth by Packel v. Tolleson, 14 Pa. Commw. 140, 321 A.2d 701 (1974) (10 general instances instead of each violation).

310 Commonwealth v. Fall River Motor Sales, Inc., 409 Mass. 302, 565 N.E.2d 1205 (1991); Commonwealth v. Flick, 33 Pa. Commw. 553, 382 A.2d 762 (1978).

311 Commonwealth v. Fall River Motor Sales, Inc., 409 Mass. 302, 565 N.E.2d 1205 (1991).

312 *Id.*

313 Commonwealth v. Fall River Motor Sales, Inc., 409 Mass. 302, 565 N.E.2d 1205 (1991); Commonwealth v. Flick, 33 Pa. Commw. 553, 382 A.2d 762 (1978), *citing* United States v. J.B. Williams Co., 354 F. Supp. 521 (S.D.N.Y. 1973); *see also* Commonwealth v. Gold Bond Indus. Inc., Clearinghouse No. 26,028 (Pa. C.P. Allegheny Cty. 1972).

in restitution)[314] and jail terms[315] for UDAP order violations. A trial court's determination of the size of the penalty for violating a UDAP decree will be upheld on appeal in the absence of an abuse of discretion.[316] An important consideration for the state in seeking penalties for a violation of an injunction is to seek those penalties in a trial court with jurisdiction to make an award in the requested amount.[317] The state's policies and recommendations in similar cases against other dealers are not relevant to the size of the penalty imposed against a respondent in a contempt case, so this information is not discoverable by the respondent.[318]

10.7.3 Civil Penalties for Initial Violations

10.7.3.1 Criteria for Civil Penalties

In a majority of states, enforcing authorities can seek civil or criminal penalties for initial UDAP violations. That is, the state does not have to wait for the merchant to violate a cease and desist order, but can seek penalties immediately upon the first UDAP violation.[319]

The defendant's bad faith is not required for the assessment of a civil penalty.[320] A showing of intentional wrongdoing is not required unless the statute so specifies.[321] Where a statute requires "willful violations," civil penalties may be awarded where the seller knew or should have known that its actions were a UDAP violation (due diligence could have ascertained that the actions were illegal).[322] In the absence of a specific statutory requirement, actual knowledge that the acts were UDAP violations is not required.[323]

The attorney general can seek civil penalties for initial violations even after winning civil penalties for violation of an injunction involving different aspects of the defendant's business practices.[324] It is not necessary to show that anyone was actually harmed by the practice.[325] Generally only the attorney general or other designated enforcement authority can seek civil penalties.[326] Where the UDAP claim is based on conduct that also violates a separate statute that provides its own civil penalties, a New York court held that UDAP civil penalties could not also be imposed.[327]

10.7.3.2 Multiple Civil Penalties

The state is not limited to seeking only one penalty in each lawsuit.[328] Courts have awarded the stated penalty for each victimized consumer.[329] One court refused to abandon a per victim test even though it resulted in a million-dollar penalty.[330] A $221,700 civil penalty has been upheld where it was based on violations affecting almost 4500 consumers.[331] Similarly, appeals have upheld a $167,500 award

314 People v. Bestline Products, Inc., 61 Cal. App. 3d 879, 132 Cal. Rptr. 767 (1976); *see also* State v. J&B Assocs., Clearinghouse No. 36,573, No. 89635-2 (Tenn. Ch. Ct. Shelby Cty. Sept. 22, 1983) ($500,000 penalty for one defendant, $250,000 for another).

315 Commonwealth v. Ziomek, 352 A.2d 235 (Pa. Commw. Ct. 1976); State v. J&B Assocs., Clearinghouse No. 36,573 (Tenn. Ch. Ct. Shelby Cty. 1983) (175 days incarceration plus $500,000 penalty); State v. Keehn, 74 Wis. 2d 218, 246 N.W.2d 547 (1976).

316 Commonwealth v. Fall River Motor Sales, Inc., 409 Mass. 302, 565 N.E.2d 1205 (1991).

317 *See* State *ex rel.* Webster v. San Juan Products, Inc., 728 S.W.2d 735 (Mo. Ct. App. 1987).

318 Commonwealth v. Fall River Motor Sales, Inc., 409 Mass. 302, 565 N.E.2d 1205 (1991).

319 State *ex rel.* Nixon v. Telco Directory Publishing, 863 S.W.2d 596 (Mo. 1993) (need not pursue other remedies first).

320 *See* State *ex rel.* Humphrey v. Alpine Air Products, Inc., 490 N.W.2d 888 (Minn. Ct. App. 1992) ($70,000 penalty awarded with no finding of bad faith), *aff'd on other grounds*, 500 N.W.2d 788 (Minn. 1993).

321 People *ex rel.* Lockyer v. Fremont Life Ins. Co., 104 Cal. App. 4th 508, 128 Cal. Rptr. 2d 463, 478 (2002) (reprehensibility need not be shown); Motzer Dodge Jeep Eagle, Inc. v. Ohio Attorney General, 95 Ohio App. 3d 183, 642 N.E.2d 20 (1994). *But see* McKinney v. State, 693 N.E.2d 65 (Ind. 1998) (Indiana statute allows civil penalty only if knowledge and intent shown); Commonwealth v. Source One Assocs., 436 Mass. 118, 763 N.E.2d 42 (2002) (knowledge must be shown; defendants' lies about their tactics demonstrated their knowledge of illegality).

322 State *ex rel.* Brady v. Fallon, 1998 Del. Super. LEXIS 186 (Feb. 27, 1998) (statute defines act as willful if party knew or should have known that it was prohibited); State *ex rel.* Medlock v. Nest Egg Society Today, Inc., 348 S.E.2d 381 (S.C. Ct. App. 1986).

323 State *ex rel.* Woodard v. May Dep't Stores Co., 849 P.2d 802 (Colo. Ct. App. 1992), *rev'd in part on other grounds*, 863 P.2d 967 (Colo. 1993); State v. Cardwell, 246 Conn. 721, 718 A.2d 954 (1998).

324 State v. Polley, 2 S.W.3d 887 (Mo. App. 1999).

325 *Id*; People *ex rel.* Lockyer v. Fremont Life Ins. Co., 104 Cal. App. 4th 508, 128 Cal. Rptr. 2d 463, 479 (2002); State *ex rel.* Woodard v. May Dep't Stores Co., 849 P.2d 802 (Colo. Ct. App. 1992), *rev'd in part on other grounds*, 863 P.2d 967 (Colo. 1993).

326 Walls v. American Tobacco Co., 11 P.3d 626 (Okla. 2000). *See also* § 8.4.1.1, *supra*.

327 Gift & Luggage Outlet, Inc. v. People, 756 N.Y.S.2d 717 (N.Y. Sup. Ct. 2003). *But see* People v. Murrison, 101 Cal. App. 4th 349, 124 Cal. Rptr. 2d 68 (2002) (affirming award of UDAP civil penalties in addition to civil penalties imposed under separate statute).

328 *See also* § 10.7.2.4 (multiple civil penalties for violations of orders).

329 State *ex rel.* Corbin v. United Energy Corp. of Am., 151 Ariz. 45, 725 P.2d 752 (Ct. App. 1986) ($5000 penalty for each of 11 victims); People v. Toomey, 157 Cal. App. 3d 1, 203 Cal. Rptr. 642 (1984) ($1 penalty for each of 50,000 victims); State *ex rel.* Medlock v. Econotovistic Assoc., Inc., Clearinghouse No. 38,911 (S.C. C.P. 1984); State v. Packard, Clearinghouse No. 27,066 (Vt. Super. Ct. 1977) ($500 penalty for each of 3 UDAP violations).

330 People v. Bestline Products, Inc., 61 Cal. App. 3d 879, 132 Cal. Rptr. 767 (1976).

331 People *ex rel.* Smith v. Parkmerced Co., 198 Cal. App. 3d 683, 244 Cal. Rptr. 22 (1988); *see also* People v. First Fed. Credit

against a nursing home chain ($2500 each for sixty-seven violations),[332] a $500,000 award against a mortgage broker ($2000 for each of 250 violations),[333] penalties of $250 to $2000 per violation, totaling $289,250,[334] $1000 for each of 788 illegal transactions,[335] $200 for each of 1368 memberships sold in an illegal pyramid scheme,[336] a $2,543,000 penalty against a deceptive marketer of *inter vivos* trusts and annuities ($210 for each violation, enhanced by $210 per violation because senior citizens were targeted),[337] and a $55,000 award against a company ($5000 for each of eleven violations), even where the company had no knowledge of the law violations of its agent.[338]

One trial court, upon finding that the defendants committed at least one UDAP violation a day for 100 days, imposed a $10,000 fine ($100 for each violation) on the corporation, a $25,000 fine ($250 per violation) on the corporation's president, a $2500 fine ($25 per violation) on the store manager, and a $1000 fine ($10 per violation) on an employee.[339] This case indicates that a UDAP statute may authorize not only the maximum penalty per violation, but also per violation per perpetrator. The Washington Supreme Court has made this clear, that liability is not joint, but individual, and that liability for the penalty thus extends to every person committing a violation.[340] All those who formulate and direct corporate policy may be held individually liable for UDAP violations of the corporation and may be assessed penalties.[341] Moreover, the one penalty per violation per perpetrator standard is not limited to one penalty per victimized consumer, but one penalty for each cause of action for each consumer.[342]

A Wisconsin case has dealt extensively with issues of multiple civil penalties for multiple instances of deceptive advertising, finding one violation for each publication of each advertisement.[343] Thus running the same advertisement in several newspapers involves multiple violations, as does running the same ad on succeeding days.[344] This result withstood a series of constitutional objections as to due process, equal protection, vagueness, and double forfeiture.[345] A Colorado court awarded civil penalties for each day a newspaper or other media outlet ran an ad, and also for each individual who was affected by the misleading advertising.[346]

One important issue is what type of evidence is necessary to prove the number of violations. A Florida decision holds that it is a jury question whether a series of television broadcasts was one continuing act or a series of separate acts.[347] A New Jersey trial court ruled that penalties assessed per transaction should only apply to transactions where the consumer involved testified in court.[348] But the state supreme court reversed other portions of the trial court's order that had restricted relief to the consumers who testified, holding that relief could be ordered for all consumers since the defendant systematically used unfair practices.[349] While the limitation on civil penalties was not before the supreme court, its opinion rejects the trial court's rationale for having limited them.

Whether a separate penalty can be imposed for each day of a continuing violation will probably depend on the language of the statute. Some consumer protection laws, such as the FTC Act,[350] specifically authorize daily penalties. A Florida court held that daily penalties could not be imposed

Corp., 104 Cal. App. 4th 721, 128 Cal. Rptr. 2d 542 (2002) ($200,000 penalty for 700 violations); People v. Dollar Rent-A-Car Sys., Inc., 259 Cal. Rptr. 191 (Ct. App. 1989) ($100,000 civil penalty).

332 People v. Casa Blanca Convalescent Homes, 206 Cal. Rptr. 164 (Ct. App. 1984).

333 State v. WWJ Corp., 138 Wash. 2d 595, 980 P.2d 1257 (1999).

334 State v. Ralph Williams' N.W. Chrysler Plymouth, Inc., 87 Wash. 2d 298, 553 P.2d 423 (1976).

335 State *ex rel.* Stenberg v. American Midlands, Inc., 244 Neb. 887, 509 N.W.2d 633 (1994).

336 State *ex rel.* Nixon v. Consumer Automotive Resources, Inc., 882 S.W.2d 717 (Mo. Ct. App. 1994) (civil penalties totaling $237,600 upheld).

337 People *ex rel.* Lockyer v. Fremont Life Ins. Co., 104 Cal. App. 4th 508, 128 Cal. Rptr. 2d 463 (2002). *See also* Burton v. R.J. Reynolds Tobacco Co., 205 F. Supp. 2d 1253, 1264 (D. Kan. 2002) (civil penalty may be appropriate for each sale of the product).

338 State *ex rel.* McLeod v. C&L Corp., 313 S.E.2d 334 (S.C. Ct. App. 1984).

339 Devine Seafood Inc. v. Attorney General, 37 Md. App. 439, 377 A.2d 1194 (Ct. Spec. App. 1977).

340 State v. Ralph Williams' N.W. Chrysler Plymouth, Inc., 87 Wash. 2d 298, 553 P.2d 423 (1976); *see also* State *ex rel.* Corbin v. United Energy Corp. of Am., 151 Ariz. 45, 725 P.2d 752 (Ct. App. 1986); State *ex rel.* Doi v. Shasteen, 826 P.2d 879 (Haw. Ct. App. 1992).

341 People v. Dollar Rent-A-Car Sys., Inc., 259 Cal. Rptr. 191 (Ct. App. 1989); Central Collection Unit v. Kossol, 138 Md. App. 338, 771 A.2d 501 (2001) (corporate officer who participated in creation, development, and deceptive practices of corporation); State *ex rel.* Medlock v. Nest Egg Society Today, Inc., 348 S.E.2d 381 (S.C. Ct. App. 1986); Mother & Unborn Baby Care, Inc. v. State, 749 S.W.2d 533 (Tex. App. 1988), *cert. denied*, 490 U.S. 1090; *see also* State v. McKinney, 508 N.E.2d 1319 (Ind. Ct. App. 1987).

342 State v. Ralph Williams' N.W. Chrysler Plymouth, Inc., 87 Wash. 2d 298, 553 P.2d 423 (1976) (awarding penalties for each of 10 distinct violations per consumer).

343 State v. Menard, Inc., 121 Wis. 2d 199, 358 N.W.2d 813 (Ct. App. 1984).

344 *Id.*

345 *Id.*

346 State *ex rel.* Woodard v. May Dep't Stores Co., 849 P.2d 802 (Colo. Ct. App. 1992), *rev'd in part on other grounds*, 863 P.2d 967 (Colo. 1993). *See also* People *ex rel.* Vacco v. Lipsitz, 174 Misc. 2d 571, 663 N.Y.S.2d 468 (Sup. Ct. 1997) ($500 civil penalty appropriate for each improper ad and each improper consumer transaction).

347 3B TV, Inc. v. State, 794 So. 2d 744 (Fla. App. 2001).

348 Kugler v. Romain, 110 N.J. Super. 470, 266 A.2d 144 (Ch. Div. 1970).

349 Kugler v. Romain, 58 N.J. 522, 279 A.2d 640 (1971).

350 15 U.S.C. § 45(l).

without explicit statutory authority.[351] Statutory authority to impose a penalty for each day of a continuing violation does not protect a defendant from more than one fine per day if the defendant commits multiple violations in a single day.[352]

10.7.3.3 Factors for Determining Amount of Civil Penalties

Trial courts have considerable discretion in determining the amount of a civil penalty.[353] Defendants who act together can be held jointly and severally liable for civil penalties.[354] Courts can limit a penalty to less than the legal maximum. Thus a $1000 penalty may be reduced to $100 where it is a seller's first offense and the consumer was made whole.[355] Courts look to the magnitude and seriousness of the violations, the lack of a bona fide error and the need to deter similar schemes in determining the size of the penalty.[356] A Massachusetts court uses the following standards to determine the size of a civil penalty: the defendant's good faith and ability to pay; the injury to the public good; the desire to eliminate the benefits derived by the UDAP violation; and the need to vindicate the state's authority.[357] In a case involving overcharges, the Kansas Supreme Court borrowed guidelines from a weights and measures statute: the extent of harm caused by the violation, the nature and persistence of the violation, the length of time over which the violation occurred, any corrective actions taken, and any other relevant circumstances.[358] A California appellate court identified the following factors before the statute was amended to include an explicit list:

- The number of violations of specific regulations;
- The number of persons damaged;
- The number of institutions involved in the violations (the case involved a chain of nursing homes);
- The nature, seriousness, and detrimental effect of particular violations;
- The kind, nature, and extent of deceptive misrepresentations;
- The nature and extent of public injury; and
- The size and wealth of the defendant.[359]

Where the statute lists various factors that the court may consider, the state need not present evidence on every factor in order to justify an award.[360]

The civil penalty need not be proportionate to the defendant's financial gain from the transaction.[361] However, gross disproportionality may be a factor in finding a civil penalty excessive.[362] California courts interpreting the language "any person who violates [the Act] shall be liable for a civil penalty not to exceed $2500 for each violation" hold that a court only has discretion as to the size of the award, and not whether a penalty should be ordered.[363] The court has no discretion, but must order a penalty for each violation.[364]

10.7.3.4 Procedures for Imposing Civil Penalties

Although significant civil penalties for initial violations are sought, a UDAP action is not transformed into a criminal one, but remains essentially equitable in nature. Thus a jury trial is not necessitated,[365] unless otherwise required by state law or constitution. Nor is the defendant protected by other constitutional safeguards for a criminal action, since the civil penalties are remedial in nature and not a fine.[366] A defendant granted transactional immunity can still be held

351 3B TV, Inc. v. Office of Att'y Gen., 794 So. 2d 744 (Fla. App. 2001).

352 State *ex rel.* Morrison v. Oshman Sporting Goods Co., 69 P.3d 1087 (Kan. 2003).

353 People v. First Fed. Credit Corp., 104 Cal. App. 4th 721, 128 Cal. Rptr. 2d 542 (2002).

354 *Id.*

355 Hyland v. Zuback, 146 N.J. Super. 407, 370 A.2d 20 (1976).

356 State *ex rel.* Nixon v. Consumer Automotive Resources, Inc., 882 S.W.2d 717 (Mo. Ct. App. 1994).

357 Commonwealth v. AmCan Enterprises, 47 Mass. App. Ct. 330, 712 N.E.2d 1205 (1999) (awarding civil penalties of $733,000); *see also* State *ex rel.* Woodard v. May Dept. Stores Co., 849 P.2d 802 (Colo. Ct. App. 1992) (citing same factors except vindication of state's authority), *rev'd in part on other grounds*, 863 P.2d 967 (Colo. 1993); State *ex rel.* Brady v. Wellington Homes, Inc., 2001 Del. Super. LEXIS 73 (Jan. 23, 2001) (ability to pay and financial gain from deceptive practices are relevant factors).

358 State *ex rel.* Morrison v. Oshman Sporting Goods Co., 69 P.3d 1087 (Kan. 2003).

359 People v. Casa Blanca Convalescent Homes, 206 Cal. Rptr. 164 (Ct. App. 1984). *See also* People *ex rel.* Lockyer v. Fremont Life Ins. Co., 104 Cal. App. 4th 508, 128 Cal. Rptr. 2d 463 (2002) (discussing and applying factors).

360 People v. First Fed. Credit Corp., 104 Cal. App. 4th 721, 128 Cal. Rptr. 2d 542 (2002).

361 People *ex rel.* Lockyer v. Fremont Life Ins. Co., 104 Cal. App. 4th 508, 128 Cal. Rptr. 2d 463 (2002).

362 State *ex rel.* Morrison v. Oshman Sporting Goods Co., 69 P.3d 1087 (Kan. 2003) ($50,000 civil penalty for point-of-sale overcharges reversed as excessive where overcharges totaled only $144.64 and were less than undercharges).

363 People v. First Fed. Credit Corp., 104 Cal. App. 4th 721, 732, 128 Cal. Rptr. 2d 542 (2002); People v. Custom Craft Carpets, Inc., 206 Cal. Rptr. 12 (Ct. App. 1984); People v. National Ass'n of Realtors, 155 Cal. App. 3d 578, 202 Cal. Rptr. 243 (1984).

364 People v. Custom Craft Carpets, Inc., 206 Cal. Rptr. 12 (Ct. App. 1984).

365 People v. Bestline Products, Inc., 61 Cal. App. 3d 879, 132 Cal. Rptr. 767 (1976); People v. Witzerman, 29 Cal. App. 3d 169, 105 Cal. Rptr. 284 (1972); *see also* State *ex rel.* Douglas v. Schroeder, 222 Neb. 473, 384 N.W.2d 626 (1986). *But see* Tull v. United States, 481 U.S. 412, 107 S. Ct. 1831, 95 L. Ed. 2d 365 (1987).

366 State *ex rel.* Corbin v. Hovatter, 144 Ariz. 430, 698 P.2d 225 (App. 1985) (no right to appointed counsel); State *ex rel.* Woods v. Hameroff, 180 Ariz. 380, 884 P.2d 266 (App. 1994) (same); State v. Western Capital Corp., 290 N.W.2d 467 (S.D. 1980).

liable for civil penalties.[367] Even penalties of $25,000 per violation are civil, not criminal, and the standard of proof is a preponderance of the evidence, and not clear and convincing evidence.[368]

The state is not required to prove the defendant's financial condition, although the defendant can introduce evidence of inability to pay in mitigation.[369] An interesting issue is whether the state can seek discovery of a defendant's financial worth as an aid to determining how high a penalty to seek. One court permitted discovery of the defendant's financial worth by analogizing civil penalties to punitive damages.[370]

10.7.3.5 Constitutional Challenges to Civil Penalties

A civil penalty is unlikely to be considered punishment that implicates double jeopardy concerns under the standards announced by the United States Supreme Court in *Hudson v. United States*.[371] That case, which overruled a 1989 decision[372] that broadened the circumstances under which a civil penalty could create double jeopardy problems, sets forth a two-party inquiry. First, the court should determine whether the legislature indicated a preference for the civil or criminal label. Second, the court should determine whether the statutory scheme is so punitive in purpose or effect as to transform what was intended as a civil remedy into a criminal penalty. In making this second determination, the court should consider seven factors: (1) whether the sanction involves an affirmative disability or restraint; (2) whether it has historically been regarded as a punishment; (3) whether it comes into play only on a finding of *scienter*; (4) whether its operation will promote the traditional aims of punishment—retribution and deterrence; (5) whether the behavior to which it applies is already a crime; (6) whether an alternative purpose to which it may rationally be connected is assignable for it; and (7) whether it appears excessive in relation to the alternative purposes assigned. Applying these principles, the Court concluded that penalties between $12,500 and $16,500 and debarment from the banking business were not criminal sanctions so did not bar a bank fraud prosecution.

A Missouri court rejected a challenge that multiple civil penalties violated the Eighth Amendment's excessive fines prohibition.[373] Civil penalties may have to meet the due process standards set forth in *BMW v. Gore*,[374] but even an award of $500,000 in civil penalties was not excessive under these standards where the defendant had committed 250 violations of the state mortgage broker statute and had acted willfully, egregiously, and repeatedly.[375] A California decision holds that *BMW v. Gore* does not apply to civil penalties, but the due process clause requires that defendants have fair notice that specific conduct may subject them to substantial penalties.[376]

10.7.3.6 Civil Penalties in Bankruptcy

A UDAP defendant may attempt to escape civil penalties through bankruptcy or by passing the burden onto some other entity. Bankruptcy courts have found that UDAP civil penalty awards are a "penalty payable to or for the benefit of a governmental unit" within the meaning of 11 U.S.C. § 523(a)(7) and thus nondischargeable.[377] Since civil penalties serve the purposes of punishing the wrongdoer and deterring the wrongdoer from similar acts, a UDAP defendant does not have the right to seek indemnification for civil penalties from other participants.[378] Responsibility for payment of civil penalties can not be shifted to the defendant's insurer, because insurance coverage of civil penalties is against public policy.[379]

367 People *ex rel.* Fahner v. Walsh, 122 Ill. App. 3d 481, 461 N.E.2d 78 (1984).

368 State *ex rel.* Redden v. Discount Fabrics, Inc., 289 Or. 375, 615 P.2d 1034 (1980). *Accord* State *ex rel.* Humphrey v. Alpine Air Products, Inc., 500 N.W.2d 788 (Minn. 1993) (civil penalty claims need only be proven by preponderance of the evidence).

369 People v. First Fed. Credit Corp., 104 Cal. App. 4th 721, 128 Cal. Rptr. 2d 542 (2002).

370 People v. Superior Court (Kardon), 35 Cal. App. 3d 710, 111 Cal. Rptr. 14 (1973); State *ex rel.* Brady v. Wellington Homes, Inc., 2001 Del. Super. LEXIS 73 (Jan. 23, 2001).

371 Hudson v. United States, 522 U.S. 93, 118 S. Ct. 488, 139 L. Ed. 2d 450 (1997).

372 United States v. Halper, 490 U.S. 435, 109 S. Ct. 1892, 104 L. Ed. 2d 487 (1989).

373 State v. Polley, 2 S.W.3d 887 (Mo. App. 1999). *Accord* State v. WWJ Corp., 138 Wash. 2d 595, 980 P.2d 1257 (1999) (upholding civil penalties under manifest error standard). *See also* State v. Menard, Inc., 121 Wis. 2d 199, 358 N.W.2d 813 (Ct. App. 1984) (upholding multiple civil penalties against due process, equal protection, vagueness, and double forfeiture challenges).

374 517 U.S. 559, 116 S. Ct. 1589, 134 L. Ed. 2d 809 (1996). *See* § 8.4.3.6.1, *supra*.

375 State v. WWJ Corp., 138 Wash. 2d 595, 980 P.2d 1257 (1999) (manifest error standard).

376 People *ex rel.* Lockyer v. Fremont Life Ins. Co., 104 Cal. App. 4th 508, 128 Cal. Rptr. 2d 463 (2002). *See also* Parker v. Time Warner Entertainment Co., 331 F.3d 13, 22, 26 (2d Cir. 2003) (massive aggregation of civil penalties in private non-UDAP suit may violate due process); People v. First Fed. Credit Corp., 104 Cal. App. 4th 721, 128 Cal. Rptr. 2d 542 (2002) (listing differences between punitive damages and civil penalties).

377 Missouri *ex rel.* Nixon v. Audley (*In re* Audley), 268 B.R. 279 (Bankr. D. Kan. 2001); State v. Edwards (*In re* Edwards), 233 B.R. 461 (Bankr. D. Idaho 1999); *In re* Tapper, 123 B.R. 594 (Bankr. N.D. Ill. 1991); *In re* Taite, 76 B.R. 764 (Bankr. C.D. Cal. 1987).

378 *In re* Consolidated Vista Hills Retaining Wall Litigation, 893 P.2d 438 (N.M. 1995).

379 State Farm Fire & Cas. Co. v. Martinez, 26 Kan. App. 2d 869, 995 P.2d 890 (2000).

10.7.3.7 Enhanced Penalties Where Victim Is Elderly or Disabled

A number of UDAP statutes provide for enhanced penalties where the victim is elderly or disabled,[380] typically in the $2500 to $10,000 range. In addition, Georgia's statute allows enhanced penalties if the violation was committed during a declared emergency.[381] Minnesota's statute lists four factors for determining whether enhanced damages are appropriate, one of which is whether the defendant knew the practices were directed toward senior citizens, but the state need only show one of these factors.[382]

The Arkansas UDAP statute also expands the private cause of action to include punitive damages if the consumer is elderly or disabled.[383] Indiana's UDAP statute offers treble damages only to elderly consumers.[384]

10.7.4 Restitution

10.7.4.1 State Authority to Seek Restitution

Most state UDAP statutes authorize the state to seek restitution for injured consumers. In some states, the state may obtain a restitution order through an administrative proceeding. The respondent has the right to seek review by filing a timely appeal to court.[385]

Where a statute is amended to allow restitution, the state can seek such relief for consumers injured before the date of the amendment because the legislative change was procedural, not substantive.[386] In addition, the overwhelming majority of courts find it within their equitable powers to grant restitution as relief even when this is not provided for in the UDAP statute.[387] Whether to request restitution is entirely within the discretion of the attorney general.[388]

Assuming the state can seek restitution, questions arise as to whether the seller must compensate all victimized consumers, or only those named in the complaint. Some statutes specifically limit restitution to named parties, and courts will not expand on this statutory limit.[389] The Utah statute limits restitution to those complaining within a reasonable time after the state institutes its action, but this has been interpreted liberally to include also those who complained before the suit was instituted.[390] If a statute does allow restitution for all aggrieved consumers, and not just consumers appearing in the action, this does not violate the seller's due process rights or subject the seller to double liability.[391] Nor does a restitution award violate a state constitutional requirement forbidding lending "the credit of the state . . . to any individual . . ." since it was not the improper use of public money *solely* for private purposes.[392] However, a

380 *See, e.g.*, Ark. Code Ann. §§ 4-88-201–4-88-207; Cal. Bus. & Prof. Code § 17206.1; Fla. Stat. Ann. § 501.2077; Ga. Code Ann. § 10-1-851; Haw. Rev. Stat. §§ 480, 480-13–480-13.5, 487-14; 815 Ill. Comp. Stat. Ann. § 505/7; Iowa Code Ann. § 714.16A; Minn. Stat. § 325F.71; Nev. Rev. Stat. §§ 598.093, .0933, .0973; N.Y. Gen. Bus. Law § 349-c; Pa. Stat. Ann. tit. 73, § 201-8(b); Tenn. Code Ann. § 47-18-125; Tex. Bus. & Com. Code § 17.47(c)(2) (additional civil penalty up to $250,000 for initial violation if victim is over 65); Wis. Stat. Ann. § 100.264; Wyo. Stat. § 40-12-111 (effective July 1, 2000). *See also* United HealthCare Ins. Co. v. AdvancePCS, 2002 U.S. Dist. LEXIS 4676 (D. Minn. Mar. 18, 2002) (treating Minn. civil penalty as available to private litigants, not just AG), *aff'd on other grounds*, 2002 U.S. App. LEXIS 22707 (8th Cir. Nov. 1, 2002); People *ex rel.* Lockyer v. Fremont Life Ins. Co., 104 Cal. App. 4th 508, 128 Cal. Rptr. 2d 463 (2002) (affirming award of enhanced civil penalties).

381 Ga. Code Ann. § 10-1-438.

382 State *ex rel.* Hatch v. Publishers Clearing House, Clearinghouse No. 53,567 (D. Minn. June 12, 2000).

383 Ark. Stat. Ann. § 4-88-204.

384 Ind. Code Ann. § 24-5-0.5-4(h).

385 Central Collection Unit v. Kossol, 138 Md. App. 338, 771 A.2d 501 (2001) (administrative law judge's unappealed factual findings have preclusive effect); Dept. of Law v. Contemporary Communities, 337 N.J. Super. 177, 766 A.2d 818 (App. Div. 2001) (defendant's appeal dismissed as untimely).

386 Commonwealth v. De Cotis, 366 Mass. 234, 316 N.E.2d 748 (1974).

387 State *ex rel.* Hatch v. Publishers Clearing House, Clearinghouse No. 53,567 (D. Minn. June 12, 2000) (restitution and disgorgement of profits); American Marketing Ass'n v. State (*In re* American Marketing Ass'n), Clearinghouse No. 36,597 (Bankr. S.D. Ind. 1983); Nunley v. State, 628 So. 2d 619 (Ala. 1993); People v. Superior Court (Jayhill Corp.), 9 Cal. 3d 283, 107 Cal. Rptr. 192, 507 P.2d 1400 (1973); People v. Toomey, 157 Cal. App. 3d 1, 203 Cal. Rptr. 642 (1984); People v. Thomas Shelton Powers, M.D., Inc., 3 Cal. Rptr. 2d 34 (Ct. App. 1992); State *ex rel.* Guste v. Orkin Exterminating Co., 528 So. 2d 198 (La. Ct. App. 1988); State *ex rel.* Humphrey v. Ri-Mel, Inc., 417 N.W.2d 102 (Minn. Ct. App. 1987); Kugler v. Romain, 58 N.J. 522, 279 A.2d 640 (1971); Celebrezze v. Hughes, 18 Ohio St. 3d 71, 479 N.E.2d 886 (1985); Commonwealth v. Ted Sopko Auto Sales & Locator, 719 A.2d 1111 (Pa. Commw. 1998) (attorney general can seek restitution under UDAP statute's general authorization of equitable relief). *See also* New York v. Feldman, 210 F. Supp. 2d 294 (S.D.N.Y. 2002) (attorney general can seek restitution under UDAP statute for antitrust violations even though defendant's conduct also violates another law that does not provide for restitution); State *ex rel.* Guste v. General Motors Corp., 370 So. 2d 477 (La. 1978) (attorney general's power to use all enforcement powers under statute is interpreted to include restitution). *But see* Commonwealth by Packel v. Tolleson, 14 Pa. Commw. Ct. 140, 321 A.2d 664 (1974) (decided prior to 1976 statutory amendment that added explicit restitution authority); Commonwealth by Creamer v. Pennsylvania Apsco Sys., Inc., 10 Pa. Commw Ct. 138, 309 A.2d 184 (1973) (same).

388 State *ex rel.* Nixon v. American Tobacco Co., 34 S.W.3d 122 (Mo. 2000).

389 State *ex rel.* Reno v. Barquet, 358 So. 2d 230 (Fla. Dist. Ct. App. 1978).

390 State *ex rel.* Division of Consumer Protection v. GAF Corp., 760 P.2d 310 (Utah 1988).

391 State v. Ralph Williams' N.W. Chrysler Plymouth, Inc., 87 Wash. 2d 298, 553 P.2d 423 (1976).

392 State v. Ralph Williams' N.W. Chrysler Plymouth, Inc., 82

Tennessee court has held that the state must produce at least some consumers who suffered ascertainable harm in order to pursue claims of restitution.[393]

Courts usually interpret ambiguous language as allowing restitution for the full class of aggrieved consumers, and not just named parties.[394] Thus language that the "court may restore to any person in interest any money" has been interpreted to allow the state to obtain restitution, because only by this interpretation would effect be given to the legislative intent to provide strong consumer protection.[395] Restitution is still available for consumers who have their own judgments against the seller.[396] The state can also get a restitution order for an indirect purchaser, *e.g.*, a homeowner who dealt with the defendant through a builder.[397] The seller can seek a credit for restitution payments when paying a consumer's judgment, but the restitution order should still include all members of the restitution class.

Where the state obtains an injunction against a company and restitution for certain consumer victims, *res judicata* will not bar a class action by other victims.[398] The purposes of the two suits are fundamentally different, as the state's suit is a law enforcement action intended to protect the public.

The state need not prove the seller's intent before obtaining restitution, and an assignee who is innocent of wrongdoing can be ordered to refund money that consumers should not have paid.[399] Even though state courts will be guided by FTC decisions, the preconditions that the FTC Act requires before the FTC may seek a federal court restitution order are not controlling as to a state restitution action.[400] Except under the most extraordinary circumstances, a court will not enjoin the attorney general from seeking a restitution order.[401] Delays in seeking a restitution award do not preclude such an award, since the doctrine of laches does not apply to the attorney general.[402]

10.7.4.2 Restitution Where Seller Files for Bankruptcy

If the defendant has filed bankruptcy, courts are divided as to whether the automatic stay[403] stops a state court restitution proceeding.[404] But, even if the automatic stay does apply to the restitution action, the state can then either transfer the restitution action to the bankruptcy court or request the bankruptcy court to lift the automatic stay. In *In re First Alliance Mortgage Co.*,[405] the Ninth Circuit Bankruptcy Appellate Panel thoroughly discussed the policy and legal questions and concluded that an attorney general's restitution action against a predatory lender could proceed in state court notwithstanding the automatic stay.

However, where a restitution order indicates that the seller must pay certain consumers, and the company has filed bankruptcy, there are not only legal but practical

Wash. 2d 265, 510 P.2d 233 (1973).

393 State v. Thompson, 2003 WL 1442414 (Tenn. Ct. App. Mar. 20, 2003) (unpublished, citation limited).

394 State *ex rel.* Kidwell v. Master Distributors, 101 Idaho 447, 615 P.2d 116 (1980); Commonwealth *ex rel.* Beshear v. ABAC Pest Control, Inc., 621 S.W.2d 705 (Ky. Ct. App. 1981); Commonwealth v. De Cotis, 366 Mass. 234, 316 N.E.2d 748 (1974); Kugler v. Romain, 58 N.J. 522, 279 A.2d 640 (1971); State v. Ralph Williams' N.W. Chrysler Plymouth, Inc., 87 Wash. 2d 298, 553 P.2d 423 (1976); State v. Fonk's Mobile Home Park & Sales, Inc., 133 Wis. 2d 287, 395 N.W.2d 786 (Ct. App. 1986); *see also* People v. Toomey, 157 Cal. App. 3d 1, 203 Cal. Rptr. 642 (1984).

395 Commonwealth *ex rel.* Beshear v. ABAC Pest Control, Inc., 621 S.W.2d 705 (Ky. Ct. App. 1981).

396 State v. Maiorano, 592 N.Y.S.2d 409 (App. Div. 1993); Matter of State of New York, Clearinghouse No. 49,150 (N.Y. App. Div. Jan. 15, 1993).

397 State v. Polley, 2 S.W.3d 887 (Mo. App. 1999).

398 Payne v. National Collection Sys., Inc., 91 Cal. App. 4th 1037, 111 Cal. Rptr. 2d 260 (2001).

399 State *ex rel.* Easley v. Rich Food Servs., 139 N.C. App. 691, 535 S.E.2d 84 (2000); State *ex rel.* McGraw v. Scott Runyan Pontiac-Buick, Inc., 194 W. Va. 770, 461 S.E.2d 516 (1995). *Cf.* FTC v. Think Achievement Corp., 144 F. Supp. 2d 1013 (N.D. Ind. 2000) (non-wrongdoer who is holding funds can be ordered to make restitution under FTC Act), *aff'd in part, rev'd in part on other grounds*, 312 F.3d 259 (7th Cir. 2002). *But cf.* McGregor v. Chierico, 206 F.3d 1378 (11th Cir. 2000) (FTC can not get contempt order against party who did not violate decree, even as means of reaching assets held jointly with party who did violate it).

400 State v. Bob Chambers Ford, Inc., 522 A.2d 362 (Me. 1987).

401 Western Food Plan, Inc. v. District Court, 198 Colo. 251, 598 P.2d 1038 (1979).

402 State *ex rel.* Vacco v. Astro Shuttle Arcades, Inc., 633 N.Y.S.2d 304 (App. Div. 1995).

403 *See* 11 U.S.C. § 362(b)(4), (5).

404 *Compare In re* First Alliance Mortgage Co., 263 B.R. 99 (B.A.P. 9th Cir. 2001) (portion of state's suit seeking restitution not stayed); FTC v. First Alliance Mortg. Co. (*In re* First Alliance Mortg. Co.), 264 B.R. 634 (C.D. Cal. 2001) (state suits not stayed, even the restitution portion; also reverses bankruptcy court's grant of injunction against state suits); *In re* Nelson, 240 B.R. 802 (Bankr. D. Me. 1999) (state court action seeking restitution order not stayed; any restitution ordered will be paid through Chapter 13 plan); *In re* Family Vending, Inc., 171 B.R. 907 (Bankr. N.D. Ga. 1994) (restitution action not stayed); Kelley v. Sclater (*In re* Sclater), 40 B.R. 594 (E.D. Mich. 1984) (implying restitution action would not be stayed if it had been brought in state court); *In re* Cannon, 30 B.R. 565 (Bankr. E.D. Mo. 1983) (lifting stay); American Marketing Ass'n v. State (*In re* American Marketing Ass'n), Clearinghouse No. 36,597 (Bankr. S.D. Ind. Aug. 15, 1983) (restitution action not stayed); Gebelein v. Four State Builders, 1982 Del. Ch. LEXIS 479 (Oct. 8, 1982) *with In re* Poule, 91 B.R. 83 (Bankr. 9th Cir. 1988) (restitution action barred by stay); *In re* Liss, 59 B.R. 556 (Bankr. N.D. Ill. 1986) (restitution action stayed, but civil penalty and injunction action not stayed; in addition, restitution action can go forward for practices engaged in *after* bankruptcy petition filed); *In re* Charter First Mortgage, Inc., 42 B.R. 380 (Bankr. D. Or. 1984) (restitution action stayed, but civil penalty and injunction action not stayed); *In re* Cannon, 30 B.R. 565 (Bankr. E.D. Mo. 1983) (restitution action stayed, but stay lifted).

405 263 B.R. 99 (B.A.P. 9th Cir. 2001).

problems for individual consumers in collecting from the bankrupt debtor. It would be useful for the attorney general to intervene before the bankruptcy court on behalf of the individuals owed restitution.[406] Two courts have ruled that the state does not have standing to sue in bankruptcy court to determine the dischargeability of the debts owed the individual consumers pursuant to the restitution order, where the state attorney general does not have legislative authority to collect restitution for the class of deceived consumers.[407] But courts will usually rule otherwise where the state is specifically authorized to bring a restitution action on behalf of consumers.[408] Bankruptcy courts also rule that the attorney general has standing under a *parens patriae* theory.[409]

There is also an issue whether a restitution debt is nondischargeable in bankruptcy.[410] The United States Supreme Court has held criminal restitution debts to be automatically nondischargeable in chapter 7 and 11, but not in chapter 13 proceedings.[411]

10.7.4.3 Relation of Restitution to Other Remedies

State UDAP statutes should not be interpreted as requiring the state to choose between an injunction and restitution; the court can award both remedies.[412] Restitution can also be awarded in addition to civil penalties.[413] A UDAP defendant may be enjoined from resuming business until full restitution is made.[414] The fact that the use of sequestered funds for restitution will reduce the defendants' civil damages liability does not mean that restitution should not be ordered.[415]

The state may allow individuals to opt out of a restitution program in favor of private suits, and the state may then have larger amounts available for the consumers who do not opt out.[416] When individuals ask for a private attorney, it is not an act of bad faith for the state agency to refer them to the state bar referral service and to attorneys who practice in the substantive area.[417]

10.7.4.4 Establishing Evidence Sufficient to Require Restitution

Calculating a restitution award is relatively straightforward where the seller never delivers paid for goods or services, or where those goods or services are worthless. The state need only establish that the product was never delivered or was worthless, that the UDAP statute was violated, and that a certain class of individuals paid for the product. The restitution order then requires the seller to return the money paid.

Courts find that the restitution award need not be adjusted for expenses the merchant had in allegedly servicing con-

406 Alternatively, it is important that individual consumers be counseled to protect their own rights individually by filing claims with the bankruptcy court. *See* National Consumer Law Center, Consumer Bankruptcy Law and Practice Ch. 17 (6th ed. 2000 and Supp.).

407 *In re* Cannon, 36 B.R. 450 (Bankr. E.D. Mo. 1983), *aff'd*, 741 F.2d 1139 (8th Cir. 1984); State *ex rel.* Spire v. Bazemore (*In re* Bazemore), Clearinghouse No. 43,074 (D. Neb. 1986).

408 Edmond v. Consumer Protection Div., 934 F.2d 1304 (4th Cir. 1991) (Maryland law); Fravel v. Commonwealth, Clearinghouse No. 49,161 (E.D. Va. Jan. 8, 1993); People v. Taite (*In re* Taite), 76 B.R. 764 (Bankr. C.D. Cal. 1987); State *ex rel.* Abrams v. DeFelice (*In re* DeFelice), 77 B.R. 376 (Bankr. D. Conn. 1987) (New York law); Kelley v. Sclater (*In re* Sclater), 40 B.R. 594 (E.D. Mich. 1984); *In re* Tapper, 123 B.R. 594 (Bankr. N.D. Ill. 1991); People *ex rel.* Fahner v. Smith (*In re* Smith), 39 B.R. 690 (Bankr. N.D. Ill. 1984); Sacks v. Anthony Plumbing, Inc. (*In re* Klein) 39 B.R. 927 (Bankr. E.D. Pa. 1984) (interpreting Maryland UDAP statute); Degnan v. Ackerman (*In re* Ackerman), No. B-79-0697 (Bankr. D.N.J. Mar. 3, 1980); Kansas *ex rel.* Miller v. Bradbury, 4 B.C.D. 263 (Bankr. D. Kan. 1978).

409 Edmond v. Consumer Protection Div., 934 F.2d 1304 (4th Cir. 1991) (Maryland law); Fravel v. Commonwealth, Clearinghouse No. 49,161 (E.D. Va. Jan. 8, 1993); *In re* Tapper, 123 B.R. 594 (Bankr. N.D. Ill. 1991); State *ex rel.* Abrams v. DeFelice (*In re* DeFelice), 77 B.R. 376 (Bankr. D. Conn. 1987) (New York law); Kelley v. Sclater (*In re* Sclater), 40 B.R. 594 (E.D. Mich. 1984).

410 11 U.S.C. § 523(a)(7) makes certain penalties and restitution debts nondischargeable.

411 Kelly v. Robinson, 479 U.S. 36, 107 S. Ct. 353, 93 L. Ed. 2d 216 (1986) (debts nondischargeable in chapter 7 and 11 proceedings); Pennsylvania Dep't of Pub. Welfare v. Davenport, 495 U.S. 552, 110 S. Ct. 2126, 109 L. Ed. 2d 588 (1990) (chapter 13 debt may be discharged). *Davenport* was partially overruled legislatively in 1991 by an amendment creating new Bankruptcy Code section 1328(a)(3), 11 U.S.C. § 1328(a)(3), making certain restitution debts nondischargeable. The only restitution debts nondischargeable under a chapter 13 proceeding are those included in a sentence upon the debtor's conviction of a crime. For a more detailed discussion of dischargeability issues, see National Consumer Law Center, Consumer Bankruptcy Law and Practice § 14.4.3.7 (6th ed. 2000 and Supp.). Note that bills pending in Congress in mid-200 would, if passed, impose greater restrictions on dischargeability of restitution debts.

412 Western Food Plan, Inc. v. District Court, 198 Colo. 251, 598 P.2d 1038 (1979); State *ex rel.* Turner v. Limbrecht, 246 N.W.2d 330 (Iowa 1976); Commonwealth *ex rel.* Beshear v. ABAC Pest Control, Inc., 621 S.W.2d 705 (Ky. Ct. App. 1981); People *ex rel.* Abrams v. Chalmers, Clearinghouse No. 43,075 (N.Y. Sup. Ct. 1987).

413 People *ex rel.* Lockyer v. Fremont Life Ins. Co., 104 Cal. App. 4th 508, 128 Cal. Rptr. 2d 463 (2002); People v. Toomey, 157 Cal. App. 3d 1, 203 Cal. Rptr. 642 (1984); State v. McKinney, 508 N.E.2d 1319 (Ind. Ct. App. 1987); Kugler v. Market Dev. Corp., 124 N.J. Super. 314, 306 A.2d 489 (Ch. Div. 1973); People *ex rel.* Abrams v. Chalmers, Clearinghouse No. 43,075 (N.Y. Sup. Ct. 1987); Commonwealth v. Ted Sopko Auto Sales & Locator, 719 A.2d 1111 (Pa. Commw. 1998).

414 State *ex rel.* Fisher v. Warren Star Theater, 84 Ohio App. 3d 435, 616 N.E.2d 1192 (1992); Commonwealth of Pennsylvania v. Diversified Chemicals, Inc., Clearinghouse No. 50,440 (Pa. C.P. Oct. 6, 1994).

415 State *ex rel.* Nixon v. Consumer Automotive Resources, Inc., 882 S.W.2d 717 (Mo. Ct. App. 1994).

416 State v. Peppertree Resort Villas, Inc., 651 N.W.2d 345 (Wis. App. 2002) (interpreting terms of consent order).

417 *Id.*

sumers.[418] Where restitution is ordered for consumers' purchase of a worthless product, consumers do not have to return the product.[419] Where a health spa closes without giving consumers refunds, a restitution action can order the health spa to make these refunds.[420] Where a product is not only ineffective, but dangerous, a court can order restitution of the full purchase price to all 140,000 customers.[421] Full restitution is also appropriate where consumers were induced through deception to pay for services. It is irrelevant that they actually did get the services for their money.[422] The fact that the defendant has promised to make restitution voluntarily, but has not yet done so, is no defense to a restitution order.[423]

More difficult are restitution awards where the deception is more individualized to each consumer, and where consumers did receive something of value, even though the deceptive practice caused injury. Problems of having to prove that each member of the restitution class was in fact deceived can be eliminated where there is a standard sales script, sales presentation, sales manual or training.[424] Some courts look at a restitution action as not for the benefit of victimized consumers, but as a means of deterring seller misconduct. Consequently, the state need not show that individual consumers relied on seller representations or were damaged by them, only that the deception was standard practice in the seller's business.[425]

Maryland's highest court takes a similar view, allowing the court to infer, without evidence, that consumers actually relied on the deceptive claims; a restitution order can thus include all purchasers without proof of individual consumer reliance.[426] Nevertheless, a restitution award in Maryland will not just be mailed out to consumers; instead consumers must be told they can obtain a refund if they relied on the deceptive claims. No attempt will be made to verify the consumer's statement that he or she had relied on the claims.[427] The court will, however, scrutinize consumers' reliance claims and reject those that seem insufficiently related to the deceptive conduct in question.[428] Similarly, all health spa members should receive an owed refund, as part of a restitution order without any individual proof of reliance, but a mailing must be made to the class members to ascertain if any memberships had been transferred (where the refund should thus go only to the transferee).[429]

The state in bringing a restitution action need not comply with the procedural requirements imposed in private class actions. For example, the state need not give notice to class members.[430] As to proving the proper amount of relief to individual class members where damages vary, the court can avoid this problem by deferring it to a later procedure. The restitution order can establish a procedure by which individual hearings or affidavits can determine the proper size of the award for individual consumers.[431] Appointment of an administrator, at the defendants' expense, to identify victims and distribute restitution funds is appropriate and does not improperly delegate judicial power.[432]

Courts have discretion whether to order restitution where there has been a UDAP violation.[433] But courts should have a good reason not to order restitution because there is a legislative intent that the UDAP statute will deter merchant misconduct and provide relief for victimized consumers.[434]

418 State v. Midland Equities of New York, Inc., 117 Misc. 2d 203, 458 N.Y.S.2d 126 (Sup. Ct. 1982); State v. Western Capital Corp., 290 N.W.2d 467 (S.D. 1980).

419 State *ex rel.* Edmisten v. Zim Chemical Co., 45 N.C. App. 604, 263 S.E.2d 849 (1980). *See also* § 8.3.2.4, *supra*. *But see* Attorney General v. Dickson, 717 F. Supp. 1090 (D. Md. 1989) (restitution not awarded in odometer rollback case where consumers used cars for years and did not return them).

420 State v. Andrews, 73 Md. App. 80, 533 A.2d 282 (1987).

421 State *ex rel.* Humphrey v. Alpine Air Products, Inc., 490 N.W.2d 888 (Minn. Ct. App. 1992), *aff'd on other grounds*, 500 N.W.2d 788 (Minn. 1993).

422 State v. Cottman Transmissions Sys., Inc., 86 Md. App. 714, 587 A.2d 1190 (1991).

423 People *ex rel.* Vacco v. Lipsitz, 174 Misc. 2d 571, 663 N.Y.S.2d 468 (Sup. Ct. 1997).

424 State *ex rel.* Kidwell v. Master Distributors, 101 Idaho 447, 615 P.2d 116 (1980); Consumer Protection Div. v. Consumer Publishing Co., 304 Md. 731, 501 A.2d 48 (1985); Kugler v. Koscot Interplanetary, Inc., 120 N.J. Super. 216, 293 A.2d 682 (Ch. Div. 1972).

425 People *ex rel.* Lockyer v. Fremont Life Ins. Co., 104 Cal. App. 4th 508, 128 Cal. Rptr. 2d 463 (2002) (rejecting argument that across-the-board restitution can not be ordered without proof that all consumers lost money or property because of unfair practice); People v. Toomey, 157 Cal. App. 3d 1, 203 Cal. Rptr. 642 (1984); State *ex rel.* Webster v. Areaco Inv. Co., 756 S.W.2d 633 (Mo. Ct. App. 1988).

426 Consumer Protection Div. v. Consumer Publishing Co., 304 Md. 731, 501 A.2d 48 (1985); *see also* State v. Andrews, 73 Md. App. 80, 533 A.2d 282 (1987).

427 Consumer Protection Div. v. Consumer Publishing Co., 304 Md. 731, 501 A.2d 48 (1985).

428 *Id.*

429 State v. Andrews, 73 Md. App. 80, 533 A.2d 282 (1987).

430 Kugler v. Koscot Interplanetary, Inc., 120 N.J. Super. 216, 293 A.2d 682 (Ch. Div. 1972).

431 State *ex rel.* Nixon v. Consumer Automotive Resources, Inc., 882 S.W.2d 717 (Mo. Ct. App. 1994).

432 State v. Directory Publishing Servs., Inc., 1996 Minn. App. LEXIS 62 (Jan. 9, 1996) (unpublished and non-precedential under Minnesota rules).

433 State *ex rel.* Kidwell v. Master Distributors, 101 Idaho 447, 615 P.2d 116 (1980); State *ex rel.* Abrams v. Ford Motor Co., 74 N.Y.2d 495, 549 N.Y.S.2d 368 (1989) (trial court and appellate division have authority to order restitution). *But see* State v. Cottman Transmissions Sys., Inc., 86 Md. App. 714, 587 A.2d 1190 (1991) (trial court reversed because it should have ordered restitution once it found a UDAP violation that caused consumers damage).

434 State *ex rel.* Kidwell v. Master Distributors, 101 Idaho 447, 615 P.2d 116 (1980); State v. Cottman Transmissions Sys., Inc., 86 Md. App. 714, 587 A.2d 1190 (1991) (reverses trial court's refusal to award restitution); Motzer Dodge Jeep Eagle, Inc. v. Ohio Attorney General, 95 Ohio App. 3d 183, 642 N.E.2d 20 (1994) (reversing trial court's refusal to award restitution). *See also* State *ex rel.* Nixon v. Continental Ventures, Inc., 84 S.W.3d

Injunctive relief with no civil penalty or restitution award allows the seller to retain its ill-gotten gains.

10.7.4.5 Types of Restitution Awards

State enforcement agencies settle numerous cases that contain various types of restitution for consumers. When seeking far-reaching or innovative forms of restitution, enforcement agencies should stress not only the necessity of the remedy to adequately compensate victimized consumers, but also its necessity to insure adequate deterrence by not allowing the seller to retain its ill-gotten gains. For example, restitution payments should not be based on whether consumers respond to notification that they have a right to restitution. A very small percentage of consumers respond to such notification and unless defendants are required to pay specific monetary sums, they will benefit by the lack of consumer response to notices of refunds or restitution.

Courts have displayed significant flexibility in making restitution awards. Restitution is primarily an equitable proceeding and the court can fashion such remedies as necessary to provide justice for consumers as well as to create an effective deterrent against future illegal activity. Thus the onus can be placed on the seller to compile names of the restitution class by a certain date and distribute the money to that class. The state enforcement official can supervise the process and the seller's failure to comply by a fixed date can result in a contempt of court award.[435] It is no defense to a restitution order that the defendant will go out of business if it must comply.[436]

Where a danger that the merchant will continue its deceptive practices and skip town before it can be held in contempt for failing to pay restitution exists, the court can order that the restitution amount be placed in escrow immediately, and that the seller not engage in any further business until full restitution is made.[437] Where the state can not trust the seller to make the proper refunds, the money can be paid to the state enforcement agency, which can take the responsibility of distributing the restitution money.[438]

Where a company may go bankrupt before a restitution award can be made, the attorney general alternatively can seek to freeze the company's checking account and other assets, and have them turned over to a receiver.[439] A state court receiver holding funds obtained by fraud has priority over a federal bankruptcy trustee, even if the receiver can not trace the funds to show exactly which funds came from which consumer.[440]

Where the seller is judgment proof or for some other reason the state does not wish to seek restitution from the seller, the state can seek restitution from a creditor to whom the seller had assigned the credit contract, even if the assignee did not participate in the prohibited conduct, but knew of the UDAP violations.[441] Since a private individual could sue the assignee, the state can also.[442] A franchisor that exercises a significant level of control over the day-to-day operations of its franchisees can also be required to pay restitution for their deceptive acts.[443]

Where return of all monies paid is not adequate restitution, courts have not hesitated to order full and complete restoration of the status quo. Thus a swimming pool seller was required to return all monies paid with interest and to remove all pools installed and return the premises to their original condition.[444] An appellate court expanded the trial court's restitution award in a pyramid sales case so that the award was not limited to those who could show they lost money directly to the defendant, that is, those who were directly below the defendant in the pyramid. Instead, the total amount the defendant earned from the scheme must be turned over, to be paid to anyone in the pyramid scheme whose loss can be traced up the pyramid back to the named defendant.[445] Pyramid scheme victims who also fraudulently recruited others to the scheme may be entitled to restitution if they can show that their losses resulted from the defendants' unlawful practices.[446]

Other restitution orders have included pre-judgment interest[447] and reinstatement of old contracts that had lapsed when the seller had illegally raised prices and where that might have caused consumers to cancel the contracts.[448] A

114 (Mo. App. 2002) (trial court's discretion to deny restitution is limited, but issue not preserved here).

435 *See* Brown v. Wonderful World Publishing Co., Clearinghouse No. 27,055 (Ohio C.P. Franklin Cty. 1976).

436 *See* State *ex rel.* Humphrey v. Alpine Air Products, Inc., 490 N.W.2d 888 (Minn. Ct. App. 1992), *aff'd on other grounds*, 500 N.W.2d 788 (Minn. 1993).

437 *See* State *ex rel.* Nixon v. Consumer Automotive Resources, Inc., 882 S.W.2d 717 (Mo. Ct. App. 1994) (funds sequestered because of fear that defendant would waste, expend, or remove them); Brown v. Miami Vacations Inc., Clearinghouse No. 27,052 (Ohio C.P. Franklin Cty. 1976).

438 *See* Brown v. Cole, Clearinghouse No. 27,057 (Ohio C.P. Richland Cty. 1976).

439 *See In re* Teltronics, Ltd. (Heyman v. Kemp), 649 F.2d 1236 (7th Cir. 1981) (Illinois law). *See* § 10.7.5, *infra*.

440 *Id.*

441 State v. Excel Mgmt. Servs., Inc., 111 Wis. 2d 479, 331 N.W.2d 312 (1983) (court notes that assignee knew of the illegal conduct, but does not base its decision on assignee's knowledge). *See also* § 10.3.4, *supra*.

442 *Id.*

443 State v. Cottman Transmission Sys., Inc., 86 Md. App. 714, 587 A.2d 1190 (1991).

444 Commonwealth v. Commercial Enterprises Inc., Clearinghouse No. 26,036 (Pa. C.P. Erie Cty. 1972).

445 People *ex rel.* Fahner v. Walsh, 122 Ill. App. 3d 481, 461 N.E.2d 78 (1984).

446 State *ex rel.* Nixon v. Consumer Automotive Resources, Inc., 882 S.W.2d 717 (Mo. Ct. App. 1994).

447 State *ex rel.* Guste v. Orkin Exterminating Co., 528 So. 2d 198 (La. Ct. App. 1988); State v. Bob Chambers Ford, 522 A.2d 362 (Me. 1987).

448 State *ex rel.* Guste v. Orkin Exterminating Co., 528 So. 2d 198 (La. Ct. App. 1988).

California case held that the trial court could order unclaimed restitution funds to be paid to a tenant association in a case brought by a public enforcement authority.[449] A more recent California Supreme Court decision recognizes that the state's Unfair Competition Law allows such a remedy, but restricts it to certified class actions.[450] The Massachusetts Attorney General settled a false advertising case against a mattress company where part of the relief was $100,000 in bedding for homeless shelters.[451] One court limited restitution to disgorgement of the profits the defendant earned through the deceptive acts.[452] It held benefit of the bargain damages inappropriate in the facts of that case.

The Minnesota UDAP statute has been amended to allow monies from a restitution award to go to a consumer education account. Monies go to the fund when they can not be distributed to victims because the victims can not be located or identified or where the cost of distributing the money would outweigh the benefit to the victims.[453] In the absence of such statutory authority, the state is required to distribute sequestered funds to victims.[454]

Creditors of the defendant may be entitled to payment from sequestered funds under Missouri's UDAP law if they can show that their losses resulted from the defendant's unlawful practices.[455] An Arizona court has analyzed the question more thoroughly, and ruled that, under its statute, restitution is available only to people who lose money or property by means of the UDAP violations.[456] While general creditors may be entitled to payment if a receiver is appointed, they are not entitled to share in the restitution fund. The law firm that defends the UDAP suit therefore can not recover its unpaid fees from the restitution fund.[457] State law regarding survival of actions may bar restitution where the consumer dies while the case is pending.[458]

In another innovative case, Ohio's highest court has affirmed a $1500 statutory damage award for *each* injured consumer even though no actual damage was shown and the case was brought by the attorney general as a restitution action and not as a class action.[459]

10.7.5 Receivership

A number of state UDAP statutes allow the state attorney general to seek an order appointing a receiver to administer a violator's assets.[460] This is a most effective remedy against a recalcitrant seller, but courts will employ it only with caution.[461] The Seventh Circuit has disapproved of the breadth of a preliminary injunction and receivership arrangement which would essentially prohibit the seller from engaging in any unsupervised conduct.[462] Where a statute allows the court to place in receivership only those funds of a seller connected with the UDAP violation, it is an error for the court to fail to determine that all the funds placed into receivership were connected to the UDAP violation.[463] Once appointed, a receiver has the power, subject to court approval, to collect the defendants' assets and distribute them for the benefit of both victims of the unlawful practices and the defendants' general creditors.[464] Non-parties who are given notice of the receivership order may be held in contempt if they knowingly aid or abet a violation.[465] A court-appointed receiver in a consumer-protection case has absolute derivative judicial immunity.[466]

There is no denial of a right to an attorney where all a seller's assets are frozen, as long as the freeze order authorizes disbursal of the seller's attorney fees from those assets.[467] The court can, however, deny payment of the de-

449 People *ex rel.* Smith v. Parkmerced Co., 198 Cal. App. 3d 683, 244 Cal. Rptr. 22 (1988); *see also* People v. Thomas Shelton Powers, M.D., Inc., 3 Cal. Rptr. 2d 34 (Ct. App. 1992) (restitution should still be ordered even if victims can not be identified; funds should be used to correct harm as much as possible). *But see* State *ex rel.* Miller v. Santa Rosa Sales & Marketing, Inc., 475 N.W.2d 210 (Iowa 1991) (no authority for unclaimed portion of restitution award to go to attorney general's Consumer Education and Litigation Fund).

450 Kraus v. Trinity Mgmt. Servs., Inc., 23 Cal. 4th 116, 999 P.2d 718 (2000).

451 *See* Massachusetts Office of Attorney General, News Release (Dec. 9, 1992).

452 Luskin's, Inc. v. Consumer Protection Div., 353 Md. 335, 726 A.2d 702 (1999).

453 Minn. Stat. Ann. § 8.31(2c).

454 State *ex rel.* Nixon v. Consumer Automotive Resources, Inc., 882 S.W.2d 717 (Mo. Ct. App. 1994).

455 *Id.*

456 State *ex rel.* Woods v. Hameroff, 180 Ariz. 380, 884 P.2d 266 (App. 1994).

457 *Id.*

458 Motzer Dodge Jeep Eagle, Inc. v. Ohio Attorney General, 95 Ohio App. 3d 183, 642 N.E.2d 20 (1994).

459 Celebrezze v. Hughes, 18 Ohio St. 3d 71, 479 N.E.2d 886 (1985). *Accord* Attorney General v. Dickson, 717 F. Supp. 1090 (D. Md. 1989).

460 *See* Commonwealth *ex rel.* Terry v. United Members Loan Ass'n, Clearinghouse No. 45,936 (Va. Cir. Ct. Nov. 9, 1990) (as part of temporary injunction, all company's and principal's assets to be held by receiver).

461 People *ex rel.* Hartigan v. Peters, 871 F.2d 1336 (7th Cir. 1989) (Illinois law); *see also* FTC v. Crescent Publ. Group, 129 F. Supp. 2d 311, 320 n.56 (S.D.N.Y. 2001) (case brought under both FTC Act and N.Y. UDAP statute; court declines to impose receivership, but enjoins transfers of money, requires bond, and requires all funds in foreign accounts to be transferred to U.S. banks).

462 People *ex rel.* Hartigan v. Peters, 871 F.2d 1336 (7th Cir. 1989) (Illinois law).

463 *Id.*

464 State *ex rel.* Woods v. Hameroff, 180 Ariz. 380, 884 P.2d 266 (App. 1994).

465 FTC v. Productive Marketing, Inc., 136 F. Supp. 2d 1096 (C.D. Cal. 2001) (granting contempt order where non-party aided violation of receivership order obtained by FTC). *See* § 10.7.2.3, *supra*.

466 Perry Center v. Heitkamp, 576 N.W.2d 505 (N.D. 1998).

467 FTC v. Amy Travel Service, Inc., 875 F.2d 564 (7th Cir. 1989). *See also* FTC v. Think Achievement Corp., 312 F.3d 259 (7th Cir. 2002) (court may allow defendant to use sequestered funds

fendant's attorney fees from the assets placed in receivership if the defendant did not act in good faith in defending the suit.[468] Since there is no due process right to appointed counsel to defend civil UDAP enforcement actions,[469] concerns about protecting the defendants' ability to pay their attorneys are less applicable than in criminal cases.

While a court may grant a preliminary freeze of the defendant's assets, it is quite another question whether a court can order the defendant preliminarily to place all amounts received from consumers immediately in escrow. One court has found no authority under the state UDAP statute for such an order without a trial.[470]

10.7.6 Attorney Fees and Other Litigation Costs for the State and for the Respondent

Some state UDAP statutes provide that, in a state enforcement action, attorney fees may, at the court's discretion, go to the prevailing party.[471] One case has analyzed the standards the judge should use in exercising this discretion, pointing out different standards depending on whether the award goes to the state or to the respondent. There is a public interest for the state to receive attorney fees, but that interest is not present for the respondent. Instead, the factors to be weighed in giving an award to the respondent are:

- The need to curb serious abuses of government power;
- Fair treatment to vindicated defendants;
- The strong public interest in continued state prosecution of consumer protection violations; and
- Avoiding hindsight logic in deciding if a case should have been brought.[472]

Other UDAP statutes state that the attorney general is "entitled to recover" fees upon prevailing in a case. Under this language, a court has no discretion to deny a fee award where the attorney general prevails.[473] Attorney fee awards to the state should be computed at market rates, rather than the state's cost.[474]

Of course, not all UDAP statutes provide attorney fees for the state. Where the statute provides for attorney fees in private actions, but not in a state enforcement action, one court has ruled that no attorney fees may be awarded the state, particularly to enforce a civil investigative demand where there is a significant question as to the state's authority to issue the demand.[475] On the other hand, Massachusetts' highest court has read its UDAP statute broadly to authorize an award of attorney fees to the state in contempt actions as well as civil enforcement actions.[476] A former version of the Arkansas UDAP statute allowed fees only when the attorney general sought revocation of the defendant's corporate license,[477] but the statute has since been broadened.[478]

Court costs can probably be awarded to the state under general law if the UDAP statute does not specifically provide for them. Some UDAP statutes allow, or even mandate, an award of investigatory costs to the state. A court may decline to award expert witness fees, however, without explicit authority in the UDAP statute.[479]

Non-UDAP statutes may also allow an award of fees or costs against the state.[480] A California statute allows the costs of expert witnesses to be shifted to any party, including the state that rejects a settlement offer and then recovers less.[481]

10.8 Challenges and Defenses to State Enforcement Actions

A common challenge to a state enforcement action is that the state's selective enforcement action violates the Equal Protection Clause. But there is no merit to such a charge unless the seller can show deliberate discrimination based on an unjustifiable standard or an arbitrary classification such as race, gender, religion, or the exercise of constitu-

---

to pay attorney, but not after final judgment is entered that the funds are the fruit of fraud).

468 People *ex rel.* Hartigan v. Great Am. Homes of Illinois, Inc., 179 Ill. App. 3d 876, 535 N.E.2d 59 (1989); *see also* State *ex rel.* Woods v. Hameroff, 180 Ariz. 380, 884 P.2d 266 (App. 1994) (UDAP defendant's law firm can not recover its fees from restitution fund).

469 State *ex rel.* Woods v. Hameroff, 180 Ariz. 380, 884 P.2d 266 (App. 1994); Arizona *ex rel.* Corbin v. Hovatter, 144 Ariz. 430, 698 P.2d 225 (App. 1985).

470 State v. Gartenberg, 488 N.W.2d 496 (Minn. Ct. App. 1992).

471 *See* State v. Alpine Air Products, Inc., 490 N.W.2d 888 (Minn. Ct. App. 1992) (more than $100,000 awarded the state in fees), *aff'd on other grounds*, 500 N.W.2d 788 (1993).

472 State v. State Credit Ass'n, 33 Wash. App. 617, 657 P.2d 327 (1983).

473 State *ex rel.* Miller v. Fiberlite Int'l, Inc., 476 N.W.2d 46 (Iowa 1991).

474 Commonwealth v. Source One Assocs., Inc., 2000 Mass. Super. LEXIS 90 (Jan. 13, 2000) (analogizing to cases involving pro bono attorneys), *aff'd*, 436 Mass. 118, 763 N.E.2d 42 (2002). *See also* Ammex Inc. v. Granholm, Clearinghouse No. 53,565 (D. Minn. Aug. 17, 2001) (awarding fees at market rate for opposing overbroad subpoena issued to attorney general in case in which it was not a party).

475 *In re* Western Acceptance Corp., 788 P.2d 214 (Idaho 1990).

476 Commonwealth v. Fall River Motor Sales, Inc., 409 Mass. 302, 565 N.E.2d 1205 (1991).

477 State *ex rel.* Bryant v. McLeod, 318 Ark. 781 (Ark. 1994).

478 Ark. Code Ann. § 4-88-113(e).

479 State *ex rel.* Bryant v. McLeod, 318 Ark. 781 (Ark. 1994).

480 State v. Thompson, 2003 WL 1442414 (Tenn. Ct. App. Mar. 20, 2003) (unpublished, citation limited) (affirming award of fees against state under state Equal Access to Justice Act).

481 People *ex rel.* Lockyer v. Fremont Gen. Corp., 89 Cal. App. 4th 1260, 108 Cal. Rptr. 2d 127 (2001).

tional rights.[482] An enforcement agency "can not be expected to bring simultaneous proceedings against all of those engaged in identical practices."[483] It is rational for an agency to target one company, and use that prosecution to induce voluntary compliance or ease subsequent enforcement actions.[484]

A related argument is that a state enforcement agency should not bring individual actions against a practice that is industry-wide, and previously thought permissible, but should instead proceed through industry-wide rulemaking. This argument was successfully made before the Ninth Circuit in *Ford Motor Credit v. FTC*,[485] but enforcement officials are well advised to consider this case an aberration. The guiding law should still be the United States Supreme Court's standard that an agency has the discretion whether to enunciate new principles through adjudication or rulemaking.[486] Thus Maryland's highest court has upheld a state UDAP action against such a challenge.[487]

In some states, the state enforcement agency conducts the investigation, files charges, and holds hearings to determine whether the UDAP statute has been violated. Such a combination of powers has been held to meet due process standards,[488] as set out in the leading United States Supreme Court case of *Withrow v. Larkin*.[489] Attorney general press releases announcing the filing of charges have also resisted due process challenges.[490]

The filing of a private suit by an individual does not stop an attorney general enforcement action. The only consequence is that the individual can not obtain a recovery through both suits.[491] There is authority that estoppel can not be applied against the state, even for its own acts.[492]

An Ohio appellate court has dealt with the question of whether the attorney general is barred from introducing consumer complaints that were made in response to the attorney general's wrongful disclosure of the name of a dealer who was being investigated.[493] The court found that the attorney general had not disclosed the dealer's name, so did not reach the issue of whether suppression of the evidence in the complaints would be a proper remedy.

One ingenious but unsuccessful attempt to stop an attorney general enforcement action occurred when the respondent claimed it would call the attorney general's staff as adverse witnesses (because of certain alleged improprieties). The respondent then argued that the state's Code of Professional Responsibility required that a law office disqualify itself from a case if any attorneys in the office have to testify against the office's client. A trial court order barring an attorney general enforcement action based on this argument was overturned because there was no evidence the attorney general's staff testimony would be prejudicial to the office's clients.[494]

In another case, a UDAP defendant asserted a libel counterclaim against the attorney general, based on statements made to the press in connection with the UDAP action.[495] The court held that the attorney general was immune from such a claim, and that his statements were privileged:

> It is the function of the Attorney General to bring consumer fraud actions without fear of personal liability. Educating and informing the public is just as much a part of the Attorney General's function as prosecuting fraudulent and deceptive practices.[496]

---

482 Consumer Protection Div. v. Consumer Publishing Co., 304 Md. 731, 501 A.2d 48 (1985); *see also* Wayte v. United States, 470 U.S. 598, 105 S. Ct. 1524, 84 L. Ed. 2d 547 (1985); United States v. Berrios, 501 F.2d 1207 (2d Cir. 1974); National Loans, Inc. v. Tennessee Dept. of Fin. Institutions, 1997 Tenn. App. LEXIS 276 (Apr. 23, 1997); *see generally* Charles H. Koch, Jr., Administrative Law and Practice § 5.30[3][b] (2d. ed. 1997).

483 Ger-Ro-Mar, Inc. v. FTC, 518 F.2d 33, 35 (2d Cir. 1975).

484 Consumer Protection Div. v. Consumer Publishing Co., 304 Md. 731, 501 A.2d 48 (1985); *see also* National Loans, Inc. v. Tennessee Dept. of Fin. Institutions, 1997 Tenn. App. LEXIS 276 (Apr. 23, 1997) ("there is no right to have the law go unenforced even if other persons who may be equally or more culpable have gone unpunished").

485 673 F.2d 1008 (9th Cir. 1981), *cert. denied*, 459 U.S. 999 (1982).

486 NAACP v. Federal Power Comm'n, 425 U.S. 662 (1976); NLRB v. Bell Aerospace Co., 416 U.S. 267 (1974); SEC v. Chenery Corp., 332 U.S. 194 (1947). As one leading commentator notes, a person "interested only in the present state of the law need go no further" than the *Chenery* opinion. Richard J. Pierce, Jr., Administrative Law Treatise § 6.9 (4th ed. 2002).

487 Consumer Protection Div. v. Consumer Publishing Co., 304 Md. 731, 501 A.2d 48 (1985) (noting that the *Ford Motor Co.* decision is the most restrictive minority view); *see also* Consumer Protection Div. v. Luskin's, Inc., 120 Md. App. 1, 706 A.2d 102 (1998), *aff'd in part, rev'd in part on other grounds*, 353 Md. 335, 726 A.2d 702 (1999).

488 *Id.*

489 421 U.S. 35 (1975).

490 Consumer Protection Div. v. Consumer Publishing Co., 304 Md. 731, 501 A.2d 48 (1985).

491 Commonwealth *ex rel.* Zimmerman v. National Apartment Leasing Co., 519 A.2d 1050 (Pa. Commw. Ct. 1986).

492 State *ex rel.* Easley v. Rich Food Servs., Inc., 535 S.E.2d 84 (N.C. App. 2000) (rejecting argument that state should be estopped from bringing UDAP suit against assignees because it had not informed them that it was investigating assignors).

493 State *ex rel.* Celebrezze v. Grogan Chrysler-Plymouth, Inc., 73 Ohio App. 3d 792, 598 N.E.2d 796 (1991).

494 People *ex rel.* Woodard v. District Court, 704 P.2d 851 (Colo. 1985).

495 People *ex rel.* Hartigan v. Knecht Servs., Inc., 216 Ill. App. 3d 843, 575 N.E.2d 1378 (1991). *See also* Am. Consumer Publishing Ass'n v. Margosian, 2003 WL 22705492 (9th Cir. Nov. 18, 2003) (dismissing § 1983 defamation claim); Turf Lawnmower Repair v. Bergen Record Corp., 139 N.J. 392, 655 A.2d 417 (1995) (discussing whether plaintiff must show actual malice or merely negligence in libel suit arising out of a report of consumer fraud).

496 People *ex rel.* Hartigan v. Knecht Servs., Inc., 216 Ill. App. 3d 843, 575 N.E.2d 1378, 1391 (1991).

The Ninth Circuit rejected a seller's claim that negative statements made to the press by an investigator in the attorney general's office caused it injury to a constitutionally protected liberty or property interest.[497]

A Massachusetts court has ruled that a company can not use the state's civil rights act to cross-claim against the state for alleged due process violations in connection with a UDAP investigation.[498] The court concluded that the state's sovereign immunity protected it. The North Dakota Supreme Court has ruled that attorney general staff members are entitled to absolute prosecutorial immunity from section 1983 claims when they bring civil consumer protection enforcement actions.[499]

Another unusual challenge to an attorney general civil UDAP action is that the respondent has a constitutional right to a court-appointed attorney. But even in a case where an individual was ordered to pay over $4 million in civil UDAP and RICO penalties, a court has found no such right.[500]

Where the state enforcement agency begins administrative proceedings against an unfair or deceptive practice, the doctrine of primary jurisdiction may prevent the supplier from pursuing a parallel case seeking a declaratory judgment.[501] The courts may also reject such a suit on the grounds that a declaratory judgment would not end the controversy.[502] If a potential defendant files a suit for declaratory judgment at a point when the state has only threatened proceedings, the court may reject the suit on the ground that there is no case or controversy.[503] The abstention doctrine may also bar a federal challenge to a state enforcement proceeding.[504] Removal to federal court on diversity grounds is not available to a defendant sued by the state, because a state is not a "citizen" for diversity purposes.[505] The Louisiana UDAP statute specifies that a forum selection clause is unenforceable, at least in attorney general suits.[506]

Another special limit on a UDAP state enforcement action may be a different limitation period than that provided for in a private action. This, of course, will depend on the specific nature of a state's limitations statutes. The attorney general may be subject to a longer statute of limitations than private litigants, or to no statute of limitations at all.[507] On the other hand, it is possible that a UDAP suit by the state attorney general may be subject to a shorter statute of limitations than a suit by a consumer.[508] An Ohio court has rejected the argument that the statute of limitations for UDAP suits brought by the attorney general's office should be tolled while the attorney general investigates the violation, even though the defendant's stubbornness prolonged the investigation.[509] The doctrine of laches does not apply against the attorney general.[510]

497 Am. Consumer Publishing Ass'n, Inc. v. Margosian, 349 F.3d 1122 (9th Cir. 2003).

498 Commonwealth v. Elm Medical Laboratories, Inc., 33 Mass. App. Ct. 71, 596 N.E.2d 376 (1992).

499 Perry Center v. Heitkamp, 576 N.W.2d 505 (N.D. 1998) (also holding that state law precludes state law claims against AG staff and that a court-appointed receiver is also immune).

500 State *ex rel.* Corbin v. Hovatter, 144 Ariz. 430, 698 P.2d 225 (Ct. App. 1985).

501 Luskin's, Inc. v. Consumer Protection Div., 338 Md. 188, 657 A.2d 788 (1995).

502 Consumer Protection Div. v. Luskin's, Inc., 100 Md. App. 104, 640 A.2d 217 (1994), *aff'd on other grounds*, Luskin's, Inc. v. Consumer Protection Div., 338 Md. 188, 657 A.2d 788 (1995).

503 National Travel Servs., Inc. v. State *ex rel.* Cooper, 569 S.E.2d 667 (N.C. App. 2002).

504 Am. Consumer Publishing Ass'n, Inc. v. Margosian, 349 F.3d 1122 (9th Cir. 2003); Cedar Rapids Cellular Tel. v. Miller, 280 F.3d 874 (8th Cir. 2002) (affirming decision to abstain as to claims by providers against whose parent company the attorney general had filed suit, but not as to claims by other entities).

505 State *ex rel.* Stovall v. Home Cable Inc., 35 F. Supp. 2d 783 (D. Kan. 1998).

506 Rodriguez v. Class Travel Worldwide, 2000 U.S. Dist. LEXIS 1926 (E.D. La. Feb. 17, 2000) (finding forum selection clause enforceable in private cause of action; court construes statutory bar as applicable only to attorney general suits).

507 Illinois v. Tri-Star Indus. Lighting, Inc., 2000 U.S. Dist. LEXIS 14948 (N.D. Ill. Oct. 11, 2000) (no statute of limitations for telemarketing and UDAP claims filed by state, and state's request for restitution did not transform suit into a private action subject to a statute of limitations).

508 *Compare* Attorney General v. Dickson, 717 F. Supp. 1090 (D. Md. 1989) *with* Harris Auction Galleries, Inc. v. Legum, Clearinghouse No. 36,565 (Md. Cir. Ct. Baltimore Cty. 1984).

509 State *ex rel.* Celebrezze v. Grogan Chrysler-Plymouth, Inc., 73 Ohio App. 3d 792, 598 N.E.2d 796 (1991).

510 State *ex rel.* Vacco v. Astro Shuttle Arcades, Inc., 633 N.Y.S.2d 304 (App. Div. 1995).

Appendix A Statute-By-Statute Analysis of State UDAP Statutes

All cited web links are found as hyperlinks on the companion CD-Rom, allowing easy access to the cited address.

This appendix is a statute-by-statute analysis of all state UDAP legislation. Practitioners should use this for easy reference to their own UDAP statute, and to compare their statute with other states' legislation. But practitioners should not use this analysis to the exclusion of the actual statutory materials. This appendix only provides a summary of the most current version of each statute and of any state regulations enacted pursuant to that statute. Because many UDAP provisions are not retroactively applied, practitioners will have to refer for many cases to earlier statutory versions in effect at the time the challenged practice occurred. Similarly, while this appendix will be useful in understanding the type of statute a court from another state is interpreting in a particular case, that court may be interpreting an earlier version of the UDAP statute found in this appendix. In fact, UDAP statutes are often amended in response to such judicial interpretations, making that case's holding no longer applicable to the new statute. Note also that this appendix only analyzes the statutory language itself, and does not include judicial interpretations of that language. Such interpretations are found at the applicable sections of the manual's text.

Ala. Code §§ 8-19-1 through 8-19-15 Deceptive Trade Practices Act

Prohibited Practices: 27 enumerated practices, plus a catchall provision prohibiting other unconscionable or deceptive practices.
Scope: "Trade or commerce" includes advertising, buying, offering for sale, sale or distribution, or performance of any service, goods, article, commodity, or other thing of value. Goods include real estate, intangibles, and franchises. Leases and consignments are included. Private cause of action is limited to consumers, except for certain violations involving pyramid sales and seller-assisted marketing plans.
Exclusions: Advertisements by publisher, radio, television, or telephone media, with no knowledge of falsity; any person or activity subject to state insurance code, or bank or affiliate regulated by State Banking Department of Alabama, U.S. Comptroller of Currency, FDIC or Federal Reserve; violations of federal Consumer Credit Protection Act or Alabama Securities or Sales of Checks Act; violations of statute for issuance of certain industrial revenue bonds; utility, telephone company or railway regulated by state public service commission; health care service plans (subject to §§ 10-4-100 through 10-4-115; seller of goods or services who disseminated material from manufacturer or distributor without knowing false or misleading and per attorney general request provides name and address of manufacturer, distributor, and in writing agrees to stop disseminating the materials.
Private Remedies: Actual damages, $100 minimum damages; treble damages are discretionary based on amount of actual damages, frequency, number of persons affected, and intent; shall award attorney fees to successful consumer, or to respondent if suit frivolous or brought in bad faith or to harass; injunctive relief; class actions specifically prohibited.
Limitations: Monetary damage required; claimant must elect between UDAP remedies and certain fraud-type common law claims; 15-day notice letter is required; consumer who rejects settlement officer loses right to additional damages, costs, and attorney fees in some circumstances; statute of limitations is 1 year from date violation should have been discovered, but in no event more than 4 years from date of transaction, but no statute of limitation for counterclaim, and 1-year period from expiration of long-term contract or warranties. It is a defense if the defendant did not knowingly commit an act or knowingly engage in an activity that violates the statute. "Knowingly" is defined to include such awareness as a reasonable person should have in the circumstances.
State Remedies: Attorney general or district attorney enforces; $2000 per initial violation if knowing; injunctive relief; sequestration of assets; license suspension; other relief; may represent a class of claimants for actual damages, costs and attorney fees; contempt and $25,000 per violation of injunction; business dissolution after second violation of any injunction; misdemeanor penalties for continuous, willful violations.
Precedential Value of FTC Interpretations: FTC interpretations are given "great weight."
Web Link to UDAP Statute:
www.legislature.state.al.us/codeofalabama/1975/146208.htm

Alaska Stat. §§ 45.50.471 through 45.50.561 Unfair Trade Practices and Consumer Protection Act

Prohibited Practices: Unfair methods of competition and unfair or deceptive acts or practices, including 48 enumerated practices, plus restrictions on several specific industries.
Scope: Trade or commerce.
Exclusions: Advertisement by disinterested publisher, radio or television media without knowledge of falsity; act or transaction regulated under laws administered by state, regulatory board, or U.S. or state officer, unless law does not prohibit the UDAP violation; act or transaction regulated under Alaska Stat.

§§ 21.36.010 through 21.36.460 governing trade practices in insurance; act or transaction regulated under Alaska Stat. §§ 06.05.005 through 06.05.995, Alaska Banking Code, except for transaction between a bank and its borrowers, depositors, or other customers or potential customers.
Private Remedies: Treble actual damages; $500 minimum damages; treble damages; other relief the court considers necessary and proper; full reasonable attorney fees shall be awarded prevailing plaintiff; prevailing defendant also entitled to full reasonable attorney fees if the action was frivolous or brought to obtain a competitive business advantage, otherwise is entitled to fees as provided by court rule. A former provision about class actions has been eliminated so that attorney general approval is unnecessary and class actions are now brought pursuant to Alaska Rules of Civil Procedure Rule 23, not directly under § 45.50.471. With prior notice, any person who is a victim of an act violation may bring an action for injunctive relief, whether or not that person suffered actual damages.
Limitations: Ascertainable loss of money or property required for private damage actions; statute of limitations is 2 years from date violation was or should have been discovered.
State Remedies: Attorney general has substantive and procedural rulemaking powers and enforces; injunction; restitution; $5000 per initial violation; $25,000 per violation of injunction.
State UDAP Regulations: Alaska Admin. Code tit. 9, §§ 05.010 through 05.900, 12.010 through 12.900, 14.010 through 14.900—pricing; availability of advertised goods; charitable solicitations; telephone sellers.
Precedential Value of FTC Interpretations: Great weight.
Web Link to UDAP Statute:
http://old-www.legis.state.ak.us/cgi-bin/folioisa.dll/stattx99/query=[jump!3A!27as4550471!27]/doc/{@17081}?

Ariz. Rev. Stat. Ann. §§ 44-1521 through 44-1534 (West) Consumer Fraud Act
Prohibited Practices: Deception, omission of material fact with intent that others rely on it.
Scope: Sale, offer for sale, advertisement, or lease of goods, intangibles, real estate or services.
Exclusions: Advertisements of publisher, radio or television media without knowledge; advertising complying with FTC regulations.
Private Remedies: None specified. (Courts imply private right of action.)
Limitations: None specified.
State Remedies: Attorney general specifically and county attorney by delegation given enforcement powers; procedural rulemaking in attorney general; injunction; receiver, $10,000 per willful initial violation; $25,000 per violation of injunction; court costs, with attorney fees discretionary.
Precedential Value of FTC Interpretations: Used as a guide.
Web Link to UDAP Statute:
www.azleg.state.az.us/arizonarevisedstatutes.asp?title=44
www.azleg.state.az.us/ars/44/title44.htm

Ark. Code Ann. §§ 4-88-101 through 4-88-207 (Michie) Deceptive Trade Practices Act
Prohibited Practices: Deceptive and unconscionable practices, including but not limited to 11 enumerated practices; concealment of material fact with intent that others rely on it in sale or advertisement of goods, services, or charitable contributions; pyramid schemes.
Scope: Sale or advertisement of goods, services, or charitable solicitations.
Exclusions: Advertising complying with FTC standards; acts or transactions permitted by laws administered by state departments of insurance, securities, highways, public service, and banking or any other U.S. or state regulatory body acts by a public utility that have been authorized by certain regulatory authorities; broadcasters, printers, publishers and others who disseminate information without actual knowledge of intent, design, purpose or deceptive nature of advertising or practice.
Private Remedies: Any person who suffers actual damage or injury as result of violation has cause of action to recover actual damages, if appropriate, and reasonable attorney fees. Elder or disabled person may also recover punitive damages.
Limitations: Five years for any civil action.
State Remedies: Injunction, restitution, attorney fees, costs, and civil penalties of up to $10,000 per violation; up to $10,000 for injunction violation; forfeiture of licenses. An additional $10,000 per violation may be assessed if conduct is directed at the elderly or disabled; criminal penalties.
Precedential Value of FTC Interpretations: Not mentioned.
Web Link to UDAP Statute:
www.arkleg.state.ar.us/nxt/gateway.dll?f=templates&fn=default.htm&vid=blr:code

Cal. Civ. Code §§ 1750 through 1784 (West) Consumers Legal Remedies Act
Prohibited Practices: 23 enumerated unfair methods of competition and unfair or deceptive practices.
Scope: Transactions that are intended to result or which result in sale or lease of goods or services to any consumer.
Exclusions: Construction and/or sale of entire residence or all or part of commercial or industrial structure; sales of realty, including site preparation; dissemination of advertisements by any advertising medium with no knowledge of falsity; non-consumer transactions.
Private Remedies: Actual damages, injunction; restitution of property; punitive damages; any other relief court deems proper; up to $5000 additional award in certain individual or class actions where consumer is elderly or disabled; restitution; attorney fees to prevailing consumers, attorney fees for defendant if prosecution of action not in good faith. Class actions specifically authorized and in no class action may actual damage award be less than $1000.
Limitations: Consumer must suffer damages; give 30 day notice letters if seeks damages; no damages if correction or replacement given after notice sent; 3-year statute of limitation from commission of act. No violation if act unintentional, resulted from bona fide error notwithstanding reasonable procedures, *and* defendant appropriately cures.
State Remedies: None specified.
Precedential Value of FTC Interpretations: None specified.
Web Link to UDAP Statute:
www.leginfo.ca.gov/cgi-bin/calawquery?codesection=civ&codebody=&hits=20

Cal. Bus. & Prof. Code §§ 17200 through 17594 (West) Unfair Competition Law [includes Prop. 64 changes (Nov. 2004)]
Prohibited Practices: Unfair, deceptive, untrue or misleading advertisements and unfair methods of competition, i.e. unfair, fraudulent or unlawful business acts or practices. Statute also restricts

home solicitation sales, referral sales, charitable solicitations, and many other specific acts and practices.
Scope: Unfair, fraudulent and unlawful acts and practices by natural persons, corporations, firms, partnerships, joint stock companies, associations, and other organizations. Section 17500 applies to persons, firms, or associations and their employees who directly or indirectly dispose of real or personal property or perform services or anything of any nature or induce the public to enter into an obligation relating thereto, or make or disseminate or cause others to make or disseminate statements about these matters.
Exclusions: None.
Private Remedies: Injunction; receiver; restitution; other orders necessary to prevent unfair competition. Any person acting for the interest of itself, its members, or the general public may sue for these remedies, but must have suffered injury in fact and lost money or property. Certain prohibitions carry additional remedies, such as treble or punitive damages. Prevailing plaintiff may seek attorney fees as private attorney general under Cal. Civ. Proc. Code § 1021.5.
Limitations: Statute of limitations is 3 years from discovery of untrue or misleading statements and for § 17500 causes of action, and 4 years for § 17200 causes of action.
State Remedies: Enforced by attorney general and district attorney, and, in some circumstances, by city attorney or prosecutor or county counsel. Injunction, civil penalties up to $2500 per violation; additional civil penalties up to $2500 for violation against senior citizen or disabled person; receiver; restitution; orders necessary to prevent unfair competition; $6000 per day for intentional violation of injunction.
Precedential Value of FTC Interpretation: None specified.
Web Link to UDAP Statute:
www.leginfo.ca.gov/cgi-bin/calawquery?codesection=bpc&codebody=&hits=20

Colo. Rev. Stat. §§ 6-1-101 through 6-1-115 Consumer Protection Act
Prohibited Practices: 39 enumerated deceptive practices, plus separate sections on specific industries.
Scope: Practices in course of a person's business, vocation or occupation. The term "property," used in many substantive prohibitions, is broadly defined to include real property, personal property, intangible property, or services.
Exclusions: Conduct complying with rules or orders of or statute administered by state, federal, or local governmental agency; publishers, advertising agencies, broadcasters or printers who disseminate information without knowledge of deception.
Private Remedies: Private cause of action granted to actual or potential consumer of defendant's goods, services, or property; residential subscriber who receives unlawful telephone solicitation; successor in interest to consumer who made purchase; and person who is injured in course of business or occupation by deceptive trade practice. May recover greater of actual damages, $500, or, if defendant acted in bad faith, treble damages, plus attorney fees and costs for a successful action. Attorney fees and costs for seller if action in bad faith and groundless or for purposes of harassment. Special restrictions on treble damages in cases against construction professionals are found at Colo. Rev. Stat. § 13-20-806.
Limitations: Statute of limitation is 3 years from occurrence or discovery; may be extended one year if defendant engaged in conduct calculated to induce plaintiff to postpone action.
State Remedies: Attorney general or district attorney enforces; injunction; restitution; orders necessary to prevent unjust enrichment; civil penalty of up to $2000 for each violation with a maximum of $100,000 for a related series of violations; civil penalty up to $10,000 per violation if elderly victim; up to $10,000 for violation of injunction; rulemaking; attorney fees and costs where successful; criminal penalties for certain violations.
Precedential Value of FTC Interpretations: None specified.
Web Link to UDAP Statute:
http://198.187.128.12/colorado/lpext.dll?f=templates&fn=fs-main.htm&2.0http://64.78.178.12/cgi-dos/stattocp.exe?P&ttl=6&art=1

Conn. Gen. Stat. §§ 42-110a through 42-110q Connecticut Unfair Trade Practices Act
Prohibited Practices: Unfair methods of competition and unfair or deceptive acts or practices.
Scope: Trade or commerce means the advertising, sale, lease, offer for sale or lease, or distribution of any services or property, real, personal or intangible, or anything else of value.
Exclusions: Transactions or actions permitted under law as administered by board or officer of state or U.S.; advertisements by publisher, radio and television media, with no knowledge of falsity, and with no direct financial interest in the sale of the product.
Private Remedies: Actual damages; punitive damages in court's discretion; injunctive or other equitable relief in court's discretion; class actions; court "may" award costs and attorney fees to consumer, even if granted only non-monetary relief in class action. Right to jury trial except for equitable relief, punitive damages, and attorney fees.
Limitations: Ascertainable loss of money or property required for private cause of action; mail complaint and any judgment or decree to attorney general and commissioner of consumer protection; 3-year limitation period. Proof of public interest for private action shall *not* be required.
State Remedies: Enforced by commissioner of consumer protection or attorney general; injunction; restitution; receivership; accounting; equitable relief; $5000 civil penalty per initial violation if willful; up to $25,000 per injunction violation; dissolution of corporation that violates injunction; rulemaking by commissioner.
State UDAP Regulations: Connecticut Regulations for the Department of Consumer Protection, Conn. Agencies Regs. § 42-110b—bait and switch; contests; comparison price advertising; failure to disclose; disparaging competitors; misrepresentations of approval, affiliation, characteristics, uses, benefits, manufacture, quantity, quality, and seller's status; refunds; motor vehicle sales; used for new; warranties; price gouging of petroleum products; refusal to sell home heating fuel; foreign language advertising; limitations of offers; use of word "free"; posting of prescription drug prices; packaging and sales of commodities; packaging of meat; labeling.
Precedential Value of FTC Interpretations: Guided by FTC.
Web Link to UDAP Statute:
www.cga.state.ct.us/2001/pub/chap735a.htm

Del. Code Ann. tit. 6, §§ 2511 through 2527, 2580 through 2584 Consumer Fraud Act
Prohibited Practices: Deceptive practices; omission of material fact with intent that others rely.
Scope: Sale, offer of sale, attempt to sell, lease, or advertisement of merchandise, including objects, wares, commodities, goods, services, real estate or intangibles.

Exclusions: Advertisement by publisher, radio and television media, with no knowledge of falsity; advertisement complying with FTC rules; matters regulated by state commissioner of insurance or public service commission.
Private Remedies: In 2003 the statute was amended to provide an explicit private cause of action to any victim of a violation. Under Del. Code Ann. tit. 6, § 2583, victims who are over 65 or disabled are entitled to treble damages in addition to any other damages provided by common law or other provisions of the Delaware Code. Prior to 2003, courts had implied a private cause of action.
Limitations: None specified.
State Remedies: Attorney general enforces; injunction; annul corporate charter; suspend state license for failure to respond to investigative demand; restitution; receiver; civil penalty up to $10,000 per willful violation; costs.
Precedential Value of FTC Interpretations: None specified.
Web Link to UDAP Statute:
www.delcode.state.de.us/

Del. Code Ann. tit. 6, §§ 2531 through 2536 Uniform Deceptive Trade Practices Act
Prohibited Practices: 12 enumerated deceptive practices, including other conduct creating likelihood of confusion or misunderstanding.
Scope: In course of business, vocation or occupation.
Exclusions: Conduct complying with local, state or federal statute, order, or rule; publishers, broadcasters, printers or other persons who disseminate information without knowledge of deception.
Private Remedies: Injunction; attorney fees "may" be awarded prevailing party in exceptional cases; treble any actual damages awarded under common law or other Delaware statute. Attorney fees may be assessed against defendant if conduct is willful. Proof of monetary damage is not required. Courts have held that this private cause of action is not available to retail customers, but only to plaintiffs who have a business or trade interest at stake.
Limitations: None specified.
State Remedies: Attorney general may seek on behalf of state any of the remedies listed in private remedies for violations that are likely to harm any person, including but not limited to consumer purchasers.
Precedential Value of FTC Interpretations: None specified.
Web Link to UDAP Statute:
www.delcode.state.de.us/

D.C. Code Ann. § 28-3901
Prohibited Practices: 31 enumerated deceptive, unfair or unlawful trade practices, including unconscionable terms.
Scope: Private cause of action must relate to trade practice, defined as any act which does or would create, alter, repair, furnish, make available, provide information about, or, directly or indirectly, solicit or offer for or effectuate a sale, lease, or transfer of consumer goods or services.
Exclusions: Persons subject to regulations of public service commission; professional services of clergy, lawyers, Christian Science practitioners; advertisements by publisher, radio and television media of others' goods with no knowledge of falsity; acts of government agency. Department of consumer and regulatory affairs may not order damages for personal injury of a tortious nature or apply its complaint procedures to landlord-tenant relations.
Private Remedies: Any person, whether acting for the interests of itself, its members, or the general public, may sue for treble damages or $1500 per violation, whichever is greater, payable to the consumer, attorney fees, punitive damages, an injunction against the use of the practice, and any other relief the court deems proper. In a representative action, the consumer may also recover any other relief necessary for restitution.
Limitations: Corporation counsel may seek injunction if in public interest.
State Remedies: Department of consumer and regulatory affairs has primary responsibility for enforcement but its enforcement activities have been suspended by the D.C. Code. The D.C. corporation counsel has authority to seek injunction, restitution, civil penalty up to $1000 per violation, costs, and attorney fees; rulemaking; order restitution, rescission, reformation, repairs and replacement; suspend license if no other board oversees it; up to $1000 for each violation of order or consent decree; court "may" order injunction; treble damages, attorney fees.
Precedential Value of FTC Interpretations: None specified.
Web Link to UDAP Statute:
http://dccode.westgroup.com/home/dccodes/default.wl
Click on "Division V," then click on "Title 28," then click on "Subtitle II."

Fla. Stat. Ann. §§ 501.201 through 501.213 (West) Deceptive and Unfair Trade Practices Act
Prohibited Practices: Unfair methods of competition, unconscionable acts or practices, and unfair or deceptive acts or practices. Violations may be based on violation of FTC rules, FTC standards of unfairness and deception, or any statute, rule, regulation or ordinance proscribing unfair, deceptive, or unconscionable practices. Special restrictions on motor vehicle sales, added in 2001, are found at Fla. Stat. Ann. §§ 501.975 to 501.976 (West) and are explicitly made actionable.
Scope: Trade or commerce, defined as advertising, soliciting, providing, offering, or distributing, by sale, rental, or otherwise, any good or service, or any tangible or intangible property, or anything else of value. Includes nonprofit activities. "Consumer" is defined to include wide variety of businesses and commercial entities.
Exclusions: Act or practice required or specifically permitted by federal or state law; personal injury or death actions; actions for damage to property other than subject of consumer transactions; banking and insurance entities and activities regulated by state or federal agencies; publisher, broadcaster, printer or other person who disseminates information for others without actual knowledge of violation; activities regulated under laws administered by public service commission; some real estate sales, leases, rentals or appraisals by licensed persons.
Private Remedies: Any person aggrieved by a violation may seek injunction and declaratory relief; person who has suffered loss may seek actual damages, unless retailer disseminated manufacturer's claims in good faith and without knowledge of violation; damaged person may be reimbursed by Consumer Fraud Trust Fund; attorney fees and costs may be awarded to prevailing party.
Limitations: Although a probable cause hearing is not required, the head of the enforcing authority must determine in writing that declaratory or damages action serves the public interest. Statute of limitations for state or department is later of 4 years from violation or 2 years from last payment of consumer transaction.

State Remedies: Enforced by department of legal affairs or state attorney; substantive rulemaking in department; declaratory judgment; injunction; action on behalf of one or more consumers or governmental entities for actual damages, except against retailer who disseminated manufacturer's claims in good faith and without knowledge; receiver; strike unconscionable contract clauses; order performance of transaction in accordance with consumers' reasonable expectations; order divestiture of defendant's interest in enterprise or real estate; restrict defendant's future activity; order dissolution or reorganization of an enterprise; civil penalty of $10,000 per willful violation ($15,000 for victimizing senior citizens or disabled persons); other relief. Relief limited to unjust enrichment damages if violator committed bona fide error with reasonable procedures. Department may bring cease and desist order if in public interest, with $5000 for each violation of order. Attorney fees to prevailing party in civil litigation initiated by enforcing authority, but only if there was a complete absence of justiciable issue of law or fact or party acted in bad faith.
State UDAP Regulations: Florida repealed the majority of its UDAP rules effective June 19, 1996, on the ground that it was neither possible nor necessary to codify every conceivable deceptive and unfair trade practice. Two rules remain in effect: Fla. Admin. Code Ann. r. 2-9.003 (advertising "free," "discount," or "below cost") and r. 2-18.002 (disclosure and cancellation of future service contracts).
Precedential Value of FTC Interpretations: Due consideration and great weight.
Web Link to UDAP Statute:
www.leg.state.fl.us/statutes/index.cfm?app_mode=display_statute&search_string=&url=ch0501/part02.htm
Web Link to UDAP Regulation:
http://fac.dos.state.fl.us/faconline/chapter02.pdf

Ga. Code Ann. §§ 10-1-370 through 10-1-375 Uniform Deceptive Trade Practices Act
Prohibited Practices: 12 enumerated deceptive practices and conduct likely to create confusion or misunderstanding.
Scope: Action in course of business, vocation or occupation.
Exclusions: Conduct which complies with federal, state or local rules, orders, or statutes; publishers, broadcasters, printers or other persons who disseminate information without knowledge of deceptive character.
Private Remedies: Injunction; costs to prevailing party; attorney fees to prevailing party in court's discretion if consumer's case groundless or seller knew of deception.
Limitations: None specified.
State Remedies: None specified.
Precedential Value of FTC Interpretations: None specified.
Web Link to UDAP Statute:
www.legis.state.ga.us/cgi-bin/gl_codes_detail.pl?code=1-1-1

Ga. Code Ann. §§ 10-1-390 through 10-1-407 Fair Business Practices Act
Prohibited Practices: Unfair or deceptive acts or practices in consumer transaction, including 32 itemized examples and special provisions for office supply transactions, health spas, telemarketing, Internet activities, home repair, pre-need funeral contracts, and price-gouging in emergencies.
Scope: Consumer transactions, defined as sale, purchase, lease, or rental of goods, services, or real or personal property primarily for personal, family, household purposes; must be in trade or commerce, defined as advertising, sale, lease, or offering for distribution, sale, or lease, of any goods, services, real or personal property, intangibles, or thing of value. Consumer must be a natural person.
Exclusion: Actions or transactions specifically authorized under laws administered or rules promulgated by state or U.S. regulatory agency; advertisements by publisher, radio and television media, with no knowledge of falsity, did not prepare advertisement, or no direct financial interest in product.
Private Remedies: Injunction; general damages; exemplary and treble damages for intentional violations; costs and attorney fees to successful consumer (but no award for fees incurred after rejection of reasonable settlement offer); fees to respondent if case continues in bad faith or for purposes of harassment past rejection of settlement offer; recovery limited to actual damages if violation result of non-negligent bona fide error notwithstanding reasonable procedures. No class actions are authorized. Section 10-1-853 also gives elderly or disabled person right to bring action for actual damages, punitive damages, and attorney fees.
Limitations: Plaintiff must have suffered injury or damage; notice letter 30 days before suit and relief limited to offer if plaintiff rejects offer but court finds offer reasonable; 2-year statute of limitations after knew or should have known of violation or after state action terminated; no statute of limitations for set off.
State Remedies: Administrator enforces when deems in public interest and can issue cease and desist orders and order civil penalty of $200 per initial violation if willful. May bring suit for $5000 civil penalty per initial violation; declaratory judgment; injunction; restitution; receiver; damages action on behalf of others in representative capacity; $25,000 per violation of injunction; additional civil penalty up to $10,000 per violation if committed against elderly or disabled person. Must give written notice in most circumstances before proceeding.
State UDAP Regulations: Georgia Office of Consumer Affairs Regulations, Ga. Comp. R. & Regs. r.r. 122-1 through 122-14—door-to-door sales; mail order sales; refunds; negative option plans; home insulation; motor vehicle warranties.
Precedential Value of FTC Interpretations: Construction to be interpreted consistently with FTC. Administrator may adopt FTC rules.
Web Link to UDAP Statute:
www.legis.state.ga.us/cgi-bin/gl_codes_detail.pl?code=1-1-1

5 Guam Code Ann. §§ 32101 through 32603 Deceptive Trade Practices—Consumer Protection Act
Prohibited Practices: False, misleading or deceptive trade practices, including 50 enumerated practices. Additional provisions regarding vehicle warranties, telemarketing, prizes and gifts, homeowners' warranties, and cable television.
Scope: Very broad. Protects business consumers (including corporations and the government) as well as individuals purchasing goods or services for personal use.
Exclusions: Newspaper, magazine, broadcasting station, billboard, unless the owners had actual knowledge of falsity or a financial interest in the unlawfully advertised goods or services. Acts or practices authorized under specific rules of the FTC.
Private Remedies: Private right of action for actual and exemplary and punitive damages. If misconduct was knowing and a regular business practice, then damages may be trebled. Also temporary or permanent injunction, restitution, any orders necessary to restore

money or property acquired in violation of this chapter, other relief at law or equity, including appointment of a receiver and revocation of business license. Consumer who prevails in action under this section entitled to costs and attorney fees. A sale of goods in violation of this chapter is not enforceable by party responsible for the violation. Consumer may revoke if there was reasonable reliance on or material damage to the consumer from the false, misleading, deceptive or prohibited act or practice.
Limitations: Three years after consumer knew or should have known of the occurrence of the false, misleading, deceptive or prohibited act or practice. 180-day extension if delay caused by defendant's knowingly engaging in conduct to cause plaintiff to refrain from or delay commencement of the action. Before filing a suit for damages, consumer must give 30-day notice to prospective defendant. Defendant may inspect the goods, and may make an offer of settlement. If offer of settlement is rejected, it may be filed with court, and if trier of fact finds that actual damages were no more than settlement offer, consumer may recover only lesser of actual damages or amount offered.
State Remedies: Attorney general must receive notice of private actions, and may intervene. Attorney general may also sue on behalf of individual consumers or a class, or the government of Guam, for equitable relief, rescission, damages, restitution, and civil penalties. If attorney general prevails, entitled to costs and attorney fees. Attorney general may accept assurance of voluntary compliance, if restitution is made. Civil penalty of up to $5000 for violation of this chapter. Penalty of up to $10,000 for violation of injunction. Penalties of up to $5000 for concealing evidence, up to $50,000 for destroying or falsifying evidence.
Precedential Value of FTC Interpretations: None specified.
Web Link to UDAP Statute:
www.guam.net/gov/guam-law/05/5gc32.94u.html

Haw. Rev. Stat. §§ 480-1 through 480-24
Prohibited Practices: Unfair methods of competition and unfair or deceptive trade practices; antitrust violations.
Scope: Trade or commerce. Private action extended to consumer, defined to be natural person who primarily for personal, family or household purposes attempts to purchase, purchases, or is solicited to purchase goods or services or who commits money, property, or services in a personal investment. "Purchase" includes leasing and licensing.
Exclusions: Acts permitted by state insurance law.
Private Remedies: Consumer may sue for $1000 or treble actual damages, whichever is greater; attorney fees and costs; injunction with attorney fees and costs for successful plaintiff; class actions; contract in violation of statute void and unenforceable. Plaintiff over 62 years of age may, in the alternative, be awarded the greater of $5000 or treble damages, plus attorney fees and costs.
Limitations: Consumer must have been injured by unlawful practice. Limitation period is four years, but tolled for actions by state when defendant out of state, while defendant's bankruptcy case is pending, and during pendency of criminal proceeding arising out of same occurrence.
State Remedies: If state is injured party, attorney general may sue for treble damages. Where injury is to consumer, office of consumer protection or attorney general can file suit for injunction or damages, including class actions for threefold damages suffered by consumers. State can also seek civil penalties of not less than $500 or more than $10,000 per violation, plus an additional civil penalty of $10,000 if the victim is over 62 years of age,. State can obtain penalties of $500 to $10,000 for violations of injunction. Attorney fees.
State UDAP Regulations: Hawaii Rules Relating to Unfair or Deceptive Practices in Advertising, Haw. Admin. R. §§ 16-86-1 through 16-86-35, 16-106-1 through 16-106-58, 16-303-1 through 16-303-10 (motor vehicle dealers and salespersons; time sharing; availability of merchandise; limitations of offers; bait and switch; deceptive pricing; use of the word "free").
Precedential Value of FTC Interpretations: Give due consideration to FTC interpretations.
Web Link to UDAP Statute:
www.capitol.hawaii.gov/site1/docs/docs.asp?press1=docs
http://hawaii.gov/dcca/pdf/har_86-c.pdf
http://hawaii.gov/dcca/pdf/har_106-c.pdf
Web Link to UDAP Regulation:
http://hawaii.gov/dcca/pdf/har_303-c.pdf

Haw. Rev. Stat. §§ 481A-1 through 481A-5 Uniform Deceptive Trade Practice Act
Prohibited Practices: 12 enumerated deceptive practices and catchall prohibiting conduct creating confusion or misunderstanding.
Scope: Actions in course of business, vocation or occupation by individuals, corporations, partnerships, trusts, estates, governmental agency or subdivision, unincorporated association, or any other legal or commercial entity.
Exclusions: Conduct complying with orders or rules of, or statutes administered by, federal, state or local government; publishers, broadcasters, printers or others who disseminate information without knowledge of deceptive character.
Private Remedies: Injunction; costs unless court directs otherwise; attorney fees to prevailing party "may" be awarded if violation is willful or suit is groundless.
Limitations: None specified.
Precedential Value of FTC Interpretations: None specified.
Web Link to UDAP Statute:
www.capitol.hawaii.gov/site1/docs/docs.asp?press1=docs

Idaho Code §§ 48-601 through 48-619 (Michie) Consumer Protection Act
Prohibited Practices: 19 enumerated unfair methods of competition and unfair or deceptive acts or practices including catchalls prohibiting misleading consumer practices and unconscionable practices, except the latter catchall does not apply to regulated lenders; special restrictions specific industries.
Scope: Trade or commerce, defined as advertising, offering for sale, selling, leasing, renting, collecting debts arising out of, or distributing any goods or services. Goods include any property, tangible or intangible, real, personal, or mixed, and any other article, commodity, or thing of value.
Exclusions: Actions or transactions permitted under laws administered by public utility or state or U.S. regulatory body; advertisements by publisher, broadcasters, printers or retailers in good faith based on material supplied by others and without knowledge of deceptive or misleading character; persons subject to unfair insurance practices statute; actions complying with applicable FTC statutes or regulations.
Private Remedies: Void contract for purchase or lease of goods or services; greater of actual damages or minimum $1000 damages,

but a class action may only obtain actual damages or $1000 for the whole class, whichever is greater; punitive damages in court's discretion; restitution; injunction; other equitable relief if repeated or flagrant violations; any other appropriate relief; attorney fees to prevailing plaintiff, to defendant in court's discretion if action spurious or to harass.
Limitations: Must suffer ascertainable loss of money or property; statute of limitations for private action is 2 years after cause accrues. Acts are violations only if respondent knows or should know of violation.
State Remedies: Attorney general enforces and has substantive rulemaking authority; may bring action if has reason to believe in public interest for declaratory judgment, injunction, actual damages or restitution for consumers, specific performance, revocation of state license, receiver; up to $10,000 and dissolution of corporation, in court's discretion, for violation of injunction, specific performance, $5000 per violation as civil penalty for initial violations; attorney fees, expenses, and investigative costs; court may make additional orders "as may be necessary". Attorney general must, with certain exceptions, give notice before suit.
State UDAP Regulations: Idaho Consumer Protection Regulations, Idaho Admin. Code r.r. 04.02.01.020 through 04.02.02.999—definition of deception; bait and switch; contests; deceptive pricing; delay and nondelivery; failure to disclose; door-to-door sales; home improvements; layaway plans; mail order; misrepresentations of method of selecting consumer and of legal rights; pyramid sales; referral sales; used for new; standards of deception; defenses against assignees; automobile advertising and sales; loan broker fees; preservation of consumer claims and defenses (holder rule); subsequent correction; unordered goods or services; unsubstantiated claims; violation of FTC consent and other orders; telephone solicitation and pay per call; use of the word "free"; going out of business sales; insufficient supply/limitation of offers; estimates.
Precedential Value of FTC Interpretations: Due consideration and great weight; construe statute uniformly with federal law and regulations.
Web Link to UDAP Statute:
http://www3.state.id.us/idstat/toc/48ftoc.html

815 Ill. Comp. Stat. Ann. 505/1 through 505/12 Consumer Fraud and Deceptive Business Practices Act
Prohibited Practices: Unfair methods of competition and unfair or deceptive acts or practices including concealment or omission of any material fact with intent to cause reliance, including 44 enumerated prohibitions; violation of UDTPA.
Scope: Trade or commerce, defined as advertising, sale, offering for sale, or distribution of any real, personal or intangible property or services, and any other thing of value.
Exclusions: Actions or transactions specifically authorized by state or U.S. laws administered by regulatory body; trademark laws; advertisements by publisher, radio and television media, that had no knowledge of falsity, did not prepare the ad, or had no direct financial interest; unknowing deceptive communication by licensed realtor. The statute also states that it does not apply to claims seeking damages for conduct that results in bodily injury, death, or damage to property not the subject of the alleged unlawful practice, but this language had been added by the civil justice reform act, an act declared unconstitutional by *Best v. Taylor Machine Works*, 689 N.E.2d 1057 (Ill. 1997).
Private Remedies: Actual economic damages, injunctive relief, or other relief court deems proper; court "may" award attorney fees and costs to prevailing party.
Limitations: Plaintiff must have suffered actual damage. Attorney general action in public interest; statute of limitations for private suit is 3 years from accrual, action by attorney general tolls private action for pendency of suit and one year after. If defendant is motor vehicle dealer or holder of motor vehicle installment contract, must give 30-day notice before suit and show public injury, pattern, or effect on consumers and public interest, and punitive damages are barred unless conduct willful or intentional and done with evil motive or reckless indifference, but these provisions were struck down as unconstitutional special legislation by *Allen v. Woodfield Chevrolet, Inc.*, 208 Ill. 2d 12, 802 N.E.2d 752, 280 Ill. Dec. 501 (2003). Private plaintiff must mail complaint and judgment or order to attorney general. Three-year limitation period does not apply to state attorney general actions.
State Remedies: Attorney general enforces and has rulemaking power; court has discretion to exercise all powers necessary including injunction, revoke license, receiver; restitution; $50,000 civil penalty ($50,000 per violation if intent to defraud shown); costs; forfeiture or suspension of any authority for person to do business in the state. The penalty can be enhanced by $10,000 if the victim is elderly.
State UDAP Regulations: Illinois Attorney General Consumer Protection Rules, Ill. Admin. Code tit. 14, §§ 460.5 through 460.460, 470.110 through 470.310, 475.110 through 475.810, 485.10 through 485.60—buyers clubs, price comparisons, availability of advertised merchandise, motor vehicle advertising (including credit sales advertising and leasing advertising), immigration services.
Precedential Value of FTC Interpretations: Consideration to be given.
Web Link to UDAP Statute:
www.legis.state.il.us/legislation/ilcs/ilcs.asp
Web Link to UDAP Regulation:
www.legis.state.il.us/commission/jcar/admincode/titles.html

815 Ill. Comp. Stat. Ann. 510/1 through 510/7 Uniform Deceptive Trade Practices Act
Prohibited Practices: 11 enumerated deceptive trade practices plus a catchall prohibiting any conduct likely to cause confusion or misunderstanding.
Scope: In course of business, vocation or occupation.
Exclusions: Conduct complying with orders or rules of or statute administered by federal, state, or local agency; publishers, broadcasters, printers or other persons who disseminate information without knowledge of its deceptive character.
Private Remedies: Injunctive relief; costs or attorney fees if defendant willfully violated act.
Limitations: None specified.
State Remedies: None specified.
Precedential Value of FTC Interpretations: Construed to promote uniformity among states enacting.
Web Link to UDAP Statute:
www.legis.state.il.us/legislation/ilcs/ilcs.asp

Ind. Code Ann. §§ 24-5-0.5-1 to 24-5-0.5-12 (Michie) Deceptive Consumer Sales Act
Prohibited Practices: 18 enumerated deceptive acts, including transactions involving contracts with unconscionable clauses, plus

special provisions for specific industries.
Scope: Most substantive provisions apply to consumer transactions, defined as sale, lease, assignment, award by chance, or other disposition of real or personal property, intangibles, or services, with or without an extension of credit, to a person for purposes that are primarily personal, familial, charitable, agricultural or household, or solicitations to supply any of these things. Specifically includes transfer of a structured settlement payment.
Exclusions: Supplier in good faith reliance on representation made by another if discloses source to consumer; acts or practices required or expressly permitted by federal or state law or regulation; insurance, securities. Telephone company or other directory provider not liable for misleading business name in directory.
Private Remedies: Actual damages in individual or class actions; attorney fees "may" be awarded prevailing party; court may void contracts; security for costs may be imposed. While private remedies are not available for real estate transactions, they *are* available for practices involving timeshares and camping club memberships. Elderly victims may seek treble damages.
Limitations: No private action unless plaintiff relied on incurable or uncured deceptive act (i.e. one done with intent to defraud or mislead, or not cured after notice within specific time limits); bond fide error despite reasonable procedures to avoid error is defense; statute of limitations 2 years after act.
State Remedies: Attorney general enforces; injunction; restitution; court may void or limit contract; $15,000 plus costs per violation of injunction; up to $500 per knowing initial violation of most prohibitions; up to $500 per incurable violation (i.e. one done with intent to defraud). Rulemaking (*see* Ind. Code Ann. § 4-6-9-8 (Michie)); costs of prosecution; restitution where contracts are voided.
Precedential Value of FTC Interpretations: None specified.
Web Link to UDAP Statute:
www.in.gov/legislative/ic/code/title24/ar5/ch0.5.html
www.in.gov/legislative/ic/code/title24/ar5/ch0.5.pdf

Iowa Code Ann. §§ 714.16 through 714.16A (West)
Prohibited Practices: Unfair or deceptive acts, including 13 enumerated practices; concealment, suppression or omission of material fact with intent to cause reliance.
Scope: Lease, sale, offer of sale, attempt to sell, or advertisement of any objects, wares, goods, commodities, intangibles, stocks, bonds, securities, debentures, realty or services, or solicitation of charitable contributions.
Exclusions: Advertisements by publisher, radio, television, and other electronic media, with no knowledge of falsity; advertisements that comply with FTC rules, regulations and statutes; retailer not liable for using certain ads prepared by supplier except in certain circumstances.
Private Remedies: None specified. *See* **§ 7.2.2**, *supra.*
Limitations: None specified.
State Remedies: Attorney general enforces; injunction; $40,000 penalty for initial violations; $5000 per day of violation of injunction; restitution; receiver for substantial and willful violation; costs and attorney fees; rulemaking. If costs of administering restitution order outweigh the benefits to consumers or the consumers entitled to restitution cannot be located, the restitution amount may be used for implementation of state's consumer fraud act. If violation committed against a person 65 years of age or older, additional penalties up to $5000 per violation.
State UDAP Regulations: Iowa Admin. Code r.r. 61-25.1 through 61-34.2—membership campgrounds, health spas, salvaged vehicles, automobile repair, price gouging during an emergency, prize promotions. The Iowa Department of Justice has also issued guidelines for motor vehicle advertising.
Precedential Value of FTC Interpretations: None specified.
Web Link to UDAP Statute:
www.legis.state.ia.us/iacode/2001supplement/714/16.html
www.legis.state.ia.us/iacode/2001supplement/714/16a.html
Web Link to UDAP Regulation:
www.legis.state.ia.us/rules/current/iac/gnac/gnac291/gna292.pdf

Kan. Stat. Ann. §§ 50-623 through 50-640 and 50-675a through 50-679a Consumer Protection Act
Prohibited Practices: Any deceptive acts or practices including but not limited to 12 enumerated prohibitions, one of which is willful concealment of material fact; unconscionable practice, determined by considering 7 enumerated factors.
Scope: Consumer transaction, defined as sale, lease, assignment, or other disposition for value of property or services, including real estate and intangibles, or solicitation by supplier, to individual, sole proprietor, or family partnership for personal, family, household, business or agricultural purposes. Prohibitions apply only to suppliers, defined as manufacturers, distributors, dealers, sellers, lessors, assignors, or other persons who, in the ordinary course of business, solicit, engage in or enforce consumer transactions, whether or not dealing directly with a consumer.
Exclusions: Insurance contracts regulated under state law; publisher, broadcaster, printer or other person who disseminates information without actual knowledge of violation.
Private Remedies: In individual action, consumer may seek greater of actual damages or civil penalty up to $10,000 per violation (additional $10,000 under Kan. Stat. Ann. § 50-677 if victim is elderly or disabled); if consumer suffers loss from a specific act proscribed by statute, judgment or consent decree, then class action allowed for actual damages. Aggrieved consumer can seek declaratory or injunctive relief in individual or class action regardless of whether entitled to damages or has adequate remedy at law or equity. Reasonable attorney fees to prevailing party, to supplier if suit groundless. Elderly or disabled person can also recover punitive damages under Kan. Stat. Ann. § 50-679.
Limitations: Must give notice of certain suits to attorney general. Most enumerated deceptive prohibitions require seller know or have reason to know of violation or require intent.
State Remedies: Attorney general or local prosecuting attorney enforces; procedural rulemaking by attorney general; declaratory judgment; injunction; damages for consumers; reasonable expenses and investigation fees; court may make other orders "necessary"; receiver; revoke licenses; order transactions carried out in accordance with consumers' reasonable expectations; grant other appropriate relief; civil penalty up to $10,000 per violation, up to $20,000 per willful violation of court order in addition to other penalties court may deem proper. Under Kan. Stat. Ann. § 50-677, the penalty can be enhanced by $10,000 if the victim is elderly or disabled.
Precedential Value of FTC Interpretations: None specified.
Web Link to UDAP Statute:
www.kslegislature.org/cgi-bin/statutes/index.cgi

Ky. Rev. Stat. Ann. §§ 367.110 to 367.990 (Michie) Consumer Protection Act

Prohibited Practices: Unfair, false, misleading, or deceptive acts or practices; unfair construed to mean unconscionable; antitrust violations.

Scope: In trade or commerce defined as the advertising, offer for sale, or distribution of any service, real, personal, tangible or intangible property and any other thing of value.

Exclusions: Advertisements by publisher, radio and television media, with no knowledge of falsity; activities authorized or approved under federal or state law or regulation.

Private Remedies: Actual damages; equitable relief court deems "necessary or proper"; attorney fees and costs may be awarded to prevailing party. Statute does not limit right to seek punitive damages where appropriate.

Limitations: Private cause of action extended only to persons who purchase or lease goods or services primarily for personal, family, or household purposes and thereby suffer ascertainable loss of money or property as result of unlawful act; statute of limitations is 1 year after end of attorney general suit or 2 years after violation.

State Remedies: Attorney general, and, in certain situations, commonwealth and county attorneys have enforcement authority; injunction; restitution; receiver; revoke license; up to $2000 civil penalty per initial violation ($10,000 in some circumstances if elderly victim); up to $25,000 per injunction violation. Ky. Rev. Stat. Ann. § 15.180 (Michie) gives general rulemaking authority to attorney general.

State UDAP Regulations: Kentucky Division of Consumer Protection Rules and Regulations, 40 Ky. Admin. Regs. 2:001—recreational and retirement use land.

Precedential Value of FTC Interpretations: None specified.

Web Link to UDAP Statute:
http://162.114.4.13/krs/367-00/chapter.htm

La. Rev. Stat. Ann. §§ 51:1401 through 51:1420 (West) Unfair Trade Practices and Consumer Protection Law

Prohibited Practices: Unfair methods of competition and unfair or deceptive acts or practices.

Scope: Trade or commerce defined as advertising, sale, offers of sale, or distribution of any service, property (corporeal or incorporeal, movable or immovable), and any thing of value.

Exclusions: Actions or transactions subject to state public service commission, other public utility regulatory body, commissioner of financial institutions, or insurance commissioner; certain banks; advertisements by publisher, radio, television, or other media, with no knowledge of falsity, no direct financial interest, and no participation in preparation of ad; acts complying with FTC Act, rules and court interpretations; seller of products or services who disseminates advertisements or promotional material and agrees to assurance of voluntary compliance, unless refuses attorney general request to reveal name and address of advertiser, but this exception does not limit consumer's right of action.

Private Remedies: Actual damages; treble damages for knowing violation done after notice given by director or attorney general; attorney fees and costs to successful consumer, to defendant if suit groundless and brought in bad faith or for harassment. No class action for damages.

Limitations: Need ascertainable loss of money or movable property for private action; statute of limitations one year from transaction for private action; investigation by attorney general if in public interest. Consumer must mail copy of complaint and any judgment or order to attorney general.

State Remedies: Governor's assistant in charge of consumer affairs has rulemaking authority, subject to attorney general approval; attorney general and district attorneys enforce; injunction; restitution; court "may" issue additional relief necessary to compensate aggrieved party; up to $5000 per violation of injunction.

State UDAP Regulations: Louisiana Consumer Protection Division Rules and Regulations, La. Admin. Code tit. 3, § II.5007, La. Admin. Code tit. 16, §§ III.501–III.515—bait and switch; charitable solicitations; damaged goods; deceptive pricing; endorsements; magazine subscriptions; multi-level distribution and chain distributor marketing schemes; used for new; distressed goods.

Precedential Value of FTC Interpretations: Statute does not apply to conduct that complies with FTC Act, rules, and court decisions.

Web Link to UDAP Statute:
www.legis.state.la.us/tsrs/tsrs.asp?lawbody=rs&title=51§ion=1401

Me. Rev. Stat. Ann. tit. 5, §§ 205A through 214 (West) Unfair Trade Practices Act

Prohibited Practices: Unfair methods of competition and unfair or deceptive acts or practices.

Scope: Trade or commerce defined as advertising, sale, offer for sale, or distribution of any services, real or personal property, intangibles or any thing of value.

Exclusions: Transactions or actions permitted under laws administered by state or U.S. regulatory board. A separate banking law, Me. Rev. Stat. Ann. tit. 9-B, § 244 (West), exempts banks and credit unions.

Private Remedies: Restitution; actual damages; injunction; other equitable relief court may deem necessary; attorney fees and costs if violation proven. Right to jury trial if action brought in superior court.

Limitations: Attorney general acts in public interest and in most cases must give prior notice. Private actions require consumer transaction resulting in ascertainable loss of money or property. Consumer must give 30-day notice attempting to settle before bringing suit; no post-offer fees if rejects offer and then does not recover more at trial.

State Remedies: Attorney general enforces and has rulemaking power; injunction; restitution if defendant violates injunction; up to $10,000 per violation of injunction; costs of investigation and suit if permanent injunction granted to Attorney general; costs of defense to prevailing defendant if action frivolous; up to $10,000 civil penalty for intentional initial violation involving unfair or deceptive conduct.

State UDAP Regulations: Maine Unfair Trade Practices Act Regulations, Code Me. R. §§ 26-239-100, 102, 105, and 109—urca formaldehyde foam insulation; motor vehicle sales; sale of residential heating oil; charitable solicitations by law enforcement.

Precedential Value of FTC Interpretations: Guided by FTC interpretations of FTC Act. State regulations may not be inconsistent with FTC rules.

Web Link to UDAP Statute:
http://janus.state.me.us/legis/statutes/5/title5ch10sec0.html

Web Link to UDAP Regulation:
www.state.me.us/sos/cec/rcn/apa/26/chaps26.htm
Scroll down to appropriate sections.

Me. Rev. Stat. Ann. tit. 10, §§ 1211 through 1216 (West) Uniform Deceptive Trade Practices Act
Prohibited Practices: 12 enumerated deceptive practices including a catchall provision prohibiting any conduct likely to create confusion or misunderstanding.
Scope: In course of business, vocation or occupation.
Exclusions: Conduct complying with orders, rules, or statute administered by federal, state or local agency; publishers, broadcasters, printers or other persons who disseminate information without knowledge of deceptive character.
Private Remedies: Injunction; court "may" award attorney fees to prevailing party in exceptional cases; costs or attorney fees against defendant only if willful violation.
Limitations: None specified.
State Remedies: None specified.
Precedential Value of FTC Interpretations: Construed to create uniformity among states which enact statute.
Web Link to UDAP Statute:
http://janus.state.me.us/legis/statutes/10/title10ch206sec0.html

Md. Code Ann. Com. Law §§ 13-101 to 13-501 Maryland Consumer Protection Act
Prohibited Practices: Numerous enumerated unfair or deceptive trade practices. *See also* Md. Code Ann. Com. Law §§ 14-101 through 14-3202 for additional consumer protection provisions regarding unit pricing, guaranties, door-to-door sales, debt collection, and other topics.
Scope: Trade practices in sale, lease, rental, loan, or bailment of consumer goods, realty or services, or offers of same; extension of consumer credit or collection of consumer debts.
Exclusions: Professional services by insurance company authorized to do business in the state, insurance agent or broker licensed by state, real estate brokers and salespersons, CPA, lawyer, medical or dental practitioner, or certain other professionals; a public service company to the extent its services and operations are regulated by public service commission; publisher, printer, radio, television, or newspaper that disseminates advertising with no knowledge of falsity and not involving its own goods. No private cause of action for injuries sustained as a result of professional services provided by a health care provider.
Private Remedies: Actual damages; attorney fees "may" be awarded if plaintiff recovers damages; seller receives attorney fees if action in bad faith or is frivolous.
Limitations: Must sustain loss or injury for private action.
State Remedies: Division of consumer protection may issue cease and desist order, which may include restitution, and may seek injunction in court; has rulemaking power; attorney general may seek injunction, receiver, and costs; both agencies can obtain civil penalty up to $1000 civil fine per initial violation by merchant, $5000 per repeat violation.
State UDAP Regulations: Maryland Regulations of the Consumer Protection Division, Md. Regs. Code tit. 2, §§ 01.01.99 through 01.01.15, 01.05.00 through 01.05.05, and 01.07.00 through 01.07.10—invention services; refunds; unit pricing. Md. Regs. Code tit. 2, §§ .01.08.01 through 01.08.04 (kosher food), 01.04.01 through 01.04.04 (new home builder registration), 01.09.01 through 01.09.03 (warranty disclosures for new home builders). The statute (§ 13-103) allows counties and municipalities to adopt more stringent provisions.
Precedential Value of FTC Interpretations: Due consideration and weight.
Web Link to UDAP Statute:
http://mlis.state.md.us/#stat
Click on "Maryland Code Online."
Web Link to UDAP Regulation:
www.dsd.state.md.us/comar/subtitle_chapters/02_chapters.htm
Scroll down to consumer protection division regulations.

Mass. Gen. Laws Ann. ch. 93A, §§ 1 through 11 (West) Regulation of Business Practice and Consumer Protection Act
Prohibited Practices: Unfair methods of competition and unfair or deceptive acts or practices.
Scope: Trade or commerce includes advertising, distribution, offers or consummation of sale, rent or lease, of any services, real or personal property, commodity for future delivery, intangibles, or any other article of value; securities explicitly included.
Exclusions: Transactions or actions permitted under laws administered by regulatory board or officer.
Private Remedies: Section 9 allows actual damages and equitable relief, including injunction, as court deems necessary and proper; class actions; minimum $25 damages; double or treble damages for willful or knowing violation or bad faith refusal to settle with reason to know of violation; attorney fees and costs to prevailing plaintiff unless rejected reasonable offer of settlement. Persons engaged in conduct of trade or commerce who are injured by persons who also engage in trade or commerce have right to bring private action but must proceed under somewhat different provisions of § 11.
Limitations: Attorney general acts in public interest and must give prior notice except when seeking temporary restraining order; consumer action if injured and provides notice letter; consumer must give notice prior to suit and is limited to reasonable relief tendered if rejects a settlement offer; court may suspend court action to bring action before appropriate regulatory board if court action would require acts inconsistent with regulatory scheme or regulatory board had substantial interest court may issue interlocutory orders to preserve status quo.
State Remedies: Attorney general has rulemaking power consistent with FTC and federal court interpretations of FTC Act; attorney general enforces; injunction; restitution; special penalties, damages, and restitution provisions for securities violations; civil penalty of $5000 per violation and costs of investigation and litigation if the defendant knew or should have known it was violating the act; $10,000 penalty for each violation of injunction or court order; corporation may be dissolved or banned from doing business for habitual injunction violations.
State UDAP Regulations: Massachusetts Consumer Protection Regulations, Mass. Regs. Code tit. 940, §§ 3.01 through 3.19, 4.01 through 4.11, 5.01 through 5.06, 6.01 through 6.15, 7.01 through 7.11, 8.01 through 8.08, 9.01 through 9.07, 15.01 through 15.08, 16.01 through 16.09, 18.01 through 18.08, 19.01 through 19.07, 21.01 through 21.07, 22.01 through 22.09—advertising practices; automobile repair; automobile sales; bait-and-switch advertising; business opportunities; credit; debt collection; deceptive pricing; delay and nondelivery; failure to disclose; door-to-door sales; vocational schools; home improvements; landlord-tenant; layaway plans; magazine subscriptions; mail order; nursing homes; misrepresentations of methods of manufacture and quantity; mortgage brokers and mortgage lenders; other prohibited practices; petro-

leum product price gouging; referral sales; refunds; repairs and services; used for new; liability disclaimers; warranties; leases; rent to own; termination of group health insurance; mobile home parks; travel services; retail marketing and sale of electricity; handgun sales; smokeless tobacco; viatical settlements and viatical loans.
Precedential Value of FTC Interpretations: Guided by FTC interpretations; rules cannot be inconsistent with FTC rules.
Web Link to UDAP Statute:
www.state.ma.us/legis/laws/mgl/gl%2d93a%2dtoc.htm
Web Link to UDAP Regulation:
www.ago.state.ma.us/sp.cfm?pageid=1133
Scroll down to consumer protection division regulations.

Mich. Comp. Laws Ann. §§ 445.901 through 445.922 (West) Consumer Protection Act
Prohibited Practices: 33 enumerated unfair, unconscionable or deceptive practices, plus specific provisions for business opportunities and ads in telephone directories.
Scope: Trade or commerce defined as conduct of business providing goods, property, or service primarily for personal, family, household purposes, including advertising, solicitation, sale or offer for sale, rent, lease or distribution of service, real or personal property, intangible, or any other article. Includes business opportunities and pyramid schemes but not franchises.
Exclusions: A transaction or conduct specifically authorized under laws administered by state or U.S. regulatory board; advertisements by disinterested publisher, radio, television station, or other communications medium without knowledge of falsity or financial interest in sale; violations of 5 enumerated Michigan statutes except for private actions; certain acts made unlawful by insurance code.
Private Remedies: Declaratory judgment and injunction regardless of whether consumer seeks damages or has adequate remedy at law; if consumer has suffered loss, may seek greater of actual damages or $250 minimum damages, plus attorney fees, or may file class action for actual damages, restitution, performance of transaction in accord with consumer's reasonable expectations, striking of unconscionable clauses, receiver, or other appropriate relief.
Limitations: Attorney general acts upon probable cause with notice given; statute of limitations for private actions or class action by attorney general is later of 6 years from act or 1 year from last payment; consumer may raise defense or counterclaim regardless of statute of limitations; if violation occurs by bona fide error despite reasonable procedures, then limited to actual damages.
State Remedies: Attorney general enforces and has rulemaking power; injunction with costs to prevailing party; up to $5000 per injunctive or judgment violation; restitution; criminal penalties; class actions for actual damages or restitution, strike unconscionable contract clause, order transaction carried out in accordance with aggrieved persons' expectations, or other appropriate relief; receiver; civil penalty up to $25,000 for persistent and knowing violations.
State UDAP Regulations: Michigan Regulations of the Consumer Protection Division, Mich. Admin. Code r. 14.202 through 14.204, 14.206 through 14.208—sale advertisements; disclosure of limitations; successive advertisements; catalogs, circulars; clearance sales; disclaimers.
Precedential Value of FTC Interpretations: None specified.
Web Link to UDAP Statute:
www.michiganlegislature.org/

Minn. Stat. Ann. § 8.31
Prohibited Practices: Unfair, discriminatory and other unlawful practices including, without limitation, §§ 317A.001 through 317A.909 (nonprofit corporation act), §§ 325D.01 through 325D.07 (unfair discrimination and competition), §§ 325D.09 through 325D.16 (unlawful trade practices), §§ 325D.49 through 325D.66 (antitrust), § 325F.67 (false and fraudulent advertising), § 325D.67 (petroleum price discrimination), § 325D.68 (monopolization of food products), §§ 325F.69 through 325F.70 (prevention of consumer fraud), § 325E.39 (telephone advertising services), § 53A (currency exchanges).
Scope: In business, commerce or trade.
Exclusions: None specified.
Private Remedies: Any person injured by violation of certain specified laws, including §§ 325D.67 and 325F.68 through 325F.70, may sue for actual damages; costs and disbursements, including costs of investigation and attorney fees; equitable relief as court determines.
Limitations: Consumer must sustain injury to sue.
State Remedies: Attorney general enforces; injunction; civil penalties up to $25,000 per initial violation, if attorney general sues for consumer may obtain damages, equitable relief, costs and attorney fees.
State UDAP Regulations: None.
Precedential Value of FTC Interpretations: None specified.
Web Link to UDAP Statute:
www.revisor.leg.state.mn.us/stats/8/31.html

Minn. Stat. §§ 325D.43 through 325D.48 Uniform Deceptive Trade Practices Act
Prohibited Practices: 13 enumerated deceptive practices, including a catchall provision prohibiting any other conduct which similarly creates a likelihood of confusion or misunderstanding.
Scope: In course of business, vocation or occupation.
Exclusions: Publishers, broadcasters, printers or other persons who disseminate information without knowledge of deception or financial interest in goods or services; conduct in compliance with orders or rules of, or statute administered by, federal state or local agency.
Private Remedies: Injunction; costs to prevailing party unless court directs otherwise; court "may" award attorney fees to prevailing party if plaintiff brings suit knowing it to be groundless or defendant's willful violation found.
Limitations: None specified.
State Remedies: State remedies through Minn. Stat. § 8.31, i.e. attorney general enforces; injunction; civil penalties up to $25,000 per violation, if attorney general sues for consumer may obtain restitution, equitable relief, costs, and attorneys fees. Where conduct perpetrated against elderly or handicapped, Minn. Stat. § 325F.71 provides for an additional $10,000 civil penalty per violation is available in certain cases.
Precedential Value of FTC Interpretations: Construe to create uniformity among states which enact statute.
Web Link to UDAP Statute:
www.revisor.leg.state.mn.us/stats/325d/

Minn. Stat. § 325F.67 False Statement in Advertising Act
Prohibited Practices: Untrue, deceptive or misleading advertising.
Scope: Advertising in relation to merchandise, securities, service, or anything offered directly or indirectly to the public for sale or distribution.
Exclusions: None specified.
Private Remedies: *See* Minn. Stat. § 8.31. *See also* § 325F.71(4) (creating special cause of action for senior citizens and disabled persons for damages, costs, attorney fees, and other equitable relief).
Limitations: *See* Minn. Stat. § 8.31.
State Remedies: *See* Minn. Stat. § 8.31. Where conduct perpetrated against elderly or handicapped, Minn. Stat. § 325F.71 provides for an additional $10,000 civil penalty per violation is available in certain cases.
Precedential Value of FTC Interpretations: None specified.
Web Link to UDAP Statute:
www.revisor.leg.state.mn.us/stats/325f/67.html

Minn. Stat. §§ 325F.68 through 325F.70 Prevention of Consumer Fraud Act
Prohibited Practices: Fraud, misrepresentation, false promise, false pretense, misleading statement, or deceptive practice with intent that others rely thereon in connection with sale, whether or not person in fact is misled, deceived or damaged; special restrictions on deceptive billing, pyramid sales, and other specific industries.
Scope: Sale, offer for sale, or attempt to sell merchandise, defined as objects, wares, goods, commodities, intangibles, real estate, loans, or services.
Exclusions: Owners or employees of print, broadcast or other advertising media, unless owner or employee has knowledge of falsity or financial interest in sale of merchandise.
Private Remedies: As specified in Minn. Stat. § 8.31, i.e. actual damages, costs, and attorney fees, and equitable relief as court determines. *See also* § 325F.71(4) (creating special cause of action for senior citizens and disabled persons for damages, costs, attorney fees, and other equitable relief.
Limitations: None specified, but under § 8.31 consumer must sustain injury to sue.
State Remedies: Attorney general or county attorney may seek injunction. See also attorney general's remedies under § 8.31. Where conduct perpetrated against elderly or handicapped, an additional $10,000 civil penalty per violation is available in certain cases.
Precedential Value of FTC Interpretation: None specified.
Web Link to UDAP Statute:
www.revisor.leg.state.mn.us/stats/325f/

Miss. Code Ann. §§ 75-24-1 through 75-24-27 Consumer Protection Act
Prohibited Practices: Unfair methods of competition and unfair or deceptive trade practices, including but not limited to 12 enumerated practices and special restrictions on price gouging in emergency.
Scope: Trade or commerce, defined as advertising, offering for sale, or distribution of any service, any tangible, intangible, personal, real, or mixed property, or any other thing of value.
Exclusions: Advertisements by disinterested publisher, printer, radio or television media, with no knowledge of falsity and no financial interest in product; officer acting under court order.
Private Remedies: Actual damages; attorney fees and costs allowed to prevailing defendant for frivolous, dilatory or harassing suits.
Limitations: Attorney general action in public interest; private action allowed only to person who purchases or leases goods or services primarily for personal, family, or household purposes and thereby suffers ascertainable loss of money or property as a result of violation; in any private action must make resolution attempt through informal dispute settlement program approved by attorney general; no class actions.
State Remedies: Attorney general and district and county attorneys enforce; injunction; attorney general has rulemaking authority; court may make judgments necessary including restitution, receiver, revocation of license; civil penalty up to $10,000 per injunction violation, up to $10,000 per knowing and willful initial violation; criminal penalties.
State UDAP Regulations: Code of Miss. Rules 24-000-002—false, misleading conduct in general, bait and switch, deceptive pricing, use of the word free, promotional games and deceptive gifts, estimates, repairs and improvements, disclosure of prior use, door-to-door sales, per se violations, unconscionable practices, going out of business sales.
Precedential Value of FTC Interpretations: Guided by FTC and federal court interpretations.
Web Link to UDAP Statute:
www.ms.gov/frameset.jsp?url=http%3a%2f%2fwww.sos.state.ms.us%2fpubs%2fmscode%2f

Mo. Rev. Stat. §§ 407.010 through 407.307 Merchandising Practices Act
Prohibited Practices: Deception, fraud, false pretenses, false promises, misrepresentations, unfair practices, or concealment or omission of material fact.
Scope: Sale, lease, offer for sale or lease, attempt to sell or lease, distribution, or advertisement of any merchandise including goods, commodities, intangibles, realty or services. Also includes solicitation of funds for any charitable purpose.
Exclusions: Advertisements by publisher, radio and television media, with no knowledge of falsity; institutions supervised by director of insurance, credit unions, or finance unless director authorizes attorney general to act or a statute authorizes attorney general or a private citizen to act.
Private Remedies: Actual damages, punitive damages discretionary; court "may" award attorney fees to prevailing party; equitable relief as is necessary or proper; class action for actual and punitive damages, injunction or other equitable relief; injunction; attorney fees.
Limitations: For private action, must purchase or lease goods or services for personal, family, household purposes and thereby suffer ascertainable loss of money or property.
State Remedies: Attorney general enforces; may issue cease and desist order after giving notice; may seek injunction; court may make necessary orders including receiver, restitution, up to $5000 civil penalty per violation of injunction or restitution order; costs; up to $1000 civil penalty for initial violations, unless defendant shows bona fide error despite procedures; rulemaking authority. Criminal penalties are available for willful conduct.
State UDAP Regulations: Mo. Code Regs. Ann. tit. 15, §§ 60-3, 60-4, 60-6 through 60-9—deception; omission of material fact; substantiation for claims; price comparisons; bait and switch;

availability of advertised goods; unsolicited merchandise; unfair practices, including price gouging, duty of good faith, duress, breach of contract, unconscionable practices, illegal conduct; time-share rules; health spas; charitable solicitations; sale prices.
Precedential Value of FTC Interpretations: Interpretive rules make reference to FTC decisions.
Web Link to UDAP Statute:
www.moga.state.mo.us/statutes/c407.htm

Mont. Code Ann. §§ 30-14-101 through 30-14-142 Unfair Trade Practices and Consumer Protection Act
Prohibited Practices: Unfair methods of competition and unfair or deceptive acts or practices.
Scope: Trade or commerce defined to include advertising, sale, offering for sale, or distribution of any services, real or personal property, intangibles, or any thing of value.
Exclusions: Actions or transactions permitted under laws administered by state public service commission or state auditor; advertisements by publishers, radio and television media, advertising agency or retail merchants with no knowledge of falsity; national advertising.
Private Remedies: Actual damages or $500, whichever is greater; treble damages discretionary; court may provide equitable relief necessary or proper; attorney fees "may" be awarded prevailing party; no class actions.
Limitations: Consumer must purchase or lease goods or services primarily for personal or family purposes and suffer an ascertainable loss of money or property as a result of violation.
State Remedies: Rulemaking in department of administration consistent with FTC rules and decisions; enforcement by department of administration and county attorney or attorney general if requested; injunction if in public interest and upon notice; court may make additional orders necessary, including restitution, receiver, revoke license, and other relief required by equity; court has discretion to dissolve corporate franchise if defendant violates injunction; civil fine of up to $10,000 per injunction violation, up to $10,000 per initial violation if willful; criminal penalties for fraudulent conduct.
State UDAP Regulations: Mont. Admin. R. 2.61.101, 2.61.201 through .204, 2.61.301, 2.61.901 through .906—general advertising; motor vehicle sales and repairs; consumer reporting agencies; telemarketing.
Precedential Value of FTC Interpretations: Due consideration and great weight; rules may not be inconsistent with FTC rules and decisions.
Web Link to UDAP Statute:
http://data.opi.state.mt.us/bills/mca_toc/30_14_1.htm
Web Link to UDAP Regulation:
http://arm.sos.state.mt.us/8/8-2261.htm
This links to an index which indicates the former numbering of the sections and links to the renumbered sections.

Neb. Rev. Stat. §§ 59-1601 through 59-1623 Consumer Protection Act
Prohibited Practices: Unfair methods of competition and unfair or deceptive acts or practices; antitrust violations.
Scope: Trade or commerce defined as sale of assets or services and any commerce affecting people of the state. "Assets" includes real or personal property, intangibles and anything of value.
Exclusions: Nonprofit labor, agricultural or horticultural organizations in lawful pursuits; civil penalties do not apply to advertisements by publishers, radio, television, or other advertising media, with no knowledge of falsity; actions and transactions permitted, prohibited, or regulated under laws administered by public service commission, Federal Energy Regulatory Commission, or regulatory body acting under state or U.S. authority, except that insurance transactions, loan brokers, and transactions regulated by funeral board or agriculture department are not exempt; a variety of utility service providers including public power district, irrigation district, electric membership association, joint public power authority, cooperative, municipalities or associations furnishing electricity to consumers.
Private Remedies: Injunction, actual damages; attorney fees and costs; court has discretion to increase damages up to $1000 to include actual damages that are difficult to measure.
Limitations: Must be injured in business or property for private remedy; statute of limitations 4 years after cause accrues.
State Remedies: Attorney general enforces; injunction; attorney fees and costs discretionary to prevailing party; court may make additional orders for restitution; if state has suffered damages it may sue for actual damages and attorney fee; dissolution of franchise for injunction violation; civil penalty up to $25,000 for injunction violation, up to $2000 per initial violation.
Precedential Value of FTC Interpretations: None specified.
Web Link to UDAP Statute:
http://statutes.unicam.state.ne.us/corpus/chapall/chap59.html

Neb. Rev. Stat. §§ 87-301 through 87-306 Uniform Deceptive Trade Practices Act
Prohibited Practices: 14 enumerated deceptive trade practices; unconscionable acts in connection with consumer transaction.
Scope: In course of business, vocation or occupation.
Exclusions: Conduct complying with orders, rules, or statute administered by federal, state or local agency; publishers, broadcasters, printers or others who disseminate information without knowledge of deceptive character.
Private Remedies: Injunction; attorney fees in court's discretion to prevailing party if violation was willful and knowing, to prevailing defendant if plaintiff knew suit was groundless; if entered sale or lease, may rescind contract or retain merchandise or service without paying; costs to prevailing party unless court otherwise directs.
Limitations: Four-year statute of limitations from date of purchase.
State Remedies: Attorney general, or county attorney with consent of attorney general enforces; rulemaking in attorney general; revoke license or other relief if necessary to force defendant to provide information or obey attorney general order; injunction; restitution; criminal penalties for initial violation or willful violation of injunction or assurance of voluntary compliance; up to $2000 civil penalty per initial violation or willful violation of injunction or assurance of voluntary compliance. Attorney general may seek revocation of privilege of conducting business or dissolution of corporation in certain circumstances.
Precedential Value of FTC Interpretations: Construe to create uniformity among states enacting statute.
Web Link to UDAP Statute:
http://statutes.unicam.state.ne.us/corpus/chapall/chap87.html

Nev. Rev. Stat. §§ 598.0903 through 598.0999 Trade Regulation and Practices Act; Nev. Rev. Stat. § 41.600
Prohibited Practices: Numerous enumerated deceptive trade prac-

tices, including knowing failure to disclose material fact in connection with sale or lease of goods or services; knowing violation of state or federal statute relating to the sale or lease of goods or services.
Scope: In course of business or occupation.
Exclusions: Conduct complying with orders, rules, or statute administered by federal, state or local agency; publisher, advertising agencies, broadcasters and printers who disseminate information without knowledge of deceptive character.
Private Remedies: Actual damages; costs and reasonable attorney fees if victim of consumer fraud prevails (§ 41.600). Elderly or disabled person suffering injury sue for actual damages, punitive damages, and attorney fees (§ 598.0977).
Limitations: District attorney shall not institute actions until state agency or regulatory authority has reasonable time to investigate or within 30 days if immediate action not mandated by circumstances.
State Remedies: Commissioner of consumer affairs, director of department of commerce, the attorney general, or district attorney enforces; commissioner may issue cease and desist orders; court may order cease and desist order enforced; attorney general may seek injunction; court may make orders necessary including restitution; civil penalty up to $10,000 for violation of injunction, up to $2500 plus costs and attorney fees per initial violation if willful; criminal penalties; rulemaking in commission and director. Additional civil penalty of up to $10,000 for each violation if practice directed toward elderly or disabled.
State UDAP Regulations: Nev. Admin. Code ch. 119B, §§ 260 through 440, ch. 598, §§ 200 through 560, ch. 599B §§ 011 through 091—comparative price advertising; sellers of travel; tour brokers and tour operators; telephone solicitation; campground memberships.
Precedential Value of FTC Interpretations: None specified.
Web Link to UDAP Statute:
www.leg.state.nv.us/nrs/nrs-598.html
www.leg.state.nv.us/nrs/nrs-041.html#nrs041sec600

N.H. Rev. Stat. Ann. §§ 358-A:1 through 358-A:13 Consumer Protection Act
Prohibited Practices: Unfair method of competition or any unfair or deceptive acts or practices including but not limited to 13 enumerated prohibitions.
Scope: Trade or commerce defined to include advertising, sale, offer of sale, or distribution of any service, real or personal property, intangibles and any other thing of value.
Exclusions: Trade or commerce subject to the jurisdiction of the banking commissioner, the director of securities regulation, the insurance commissioner, the public utilities commissioner, the financial institutions and insurance regulators of other states, or federal banking or securities regulators who possess the authority to regulate unfair or deceptive practices, including trade or commerce under the jurisdiction of and regulated by the bank commissioner relative to retail installment sales of motor vehicles; defendants against whom FTC action is pending for same trade or commerce; publishers, broadcasters, printers or others engaged in dissemination of information without knowledge of its deceptive character.
Private Remedies: Person injured by violation may sue for actual damages and equitable relief including injunction as court deems necessary and proper; $1000 minimum damages; at least double, no more than treble damages for willful or knowing violation; costs and attorney fees to prevailing plaintiff; class action for actual damages, injunctive or equitable relief, and attorney fees.
Limitations: Statute does not apply to transactions entered into more than three years prior to time plaintiff knew or should have known of conduct violating statute; attorney general must send notice letter prior to suit except in emergency circumstances.
State Remedies: Rulemaking by attorney general under attorney general's general rulemaking power; administered by consumer protection and antitrust division of justice department; attorney general may seek injunction, restitution; court may make necessary orders, may award up to $10,000 civil penalty per initial violation, unless defendant shows good faith misunderstanding; receiver; criminal penalties for violation of act or injunction; legal costs and expenses may be awarded state; court may dissolve corporate franchise for habitual injunction violations.
Precedential Value of FTC Interpretations: Guided by FTC and judicial interpretations.
Web Link to UDAP Statute:
http://gencourt.state.nh.us/rsa/html/indexes/358-a.html

N.J. Stat. Ann. §§ 56:8-1 through 56:8-91 (West)
Prohibited Practices: Unconscionable commercial practice, deception, fraud, false pretense, false promise, or misrepresentation; knowing concealment, suppression or omission of material fact with intent to cause reliance; numerous enumerated prohibitions.
Scope: In connection with sale or advertisement of any merchandise or real estate; sale defined to include rental, distribution, and offer or attempt to sell, rent, or distribute; merchandise includes goods, commodities, services or anything offered to the public for sale; real estate specifically mentioned in prohibition section.
Exclusions: Advertisements by publisher, radio and television media, with no knowledge of advertiser's intent; restrictions on liability of realtors for unknowing communication of false information.
Private Remedies: Actual and treble damages; attorney fees and costs; refund of money; other appropriate legal or equitable relief.
Limitations: Must suffer ascertainable loss of money or property; must mail copy of pleading to attorney general.
State Remedies: Attorney general enforces; attorney general may issue cease and desist order; rulemaking in attorney general; restitution; injunction; receiver; annul corporate charter; revoke license; enjoin from managing or owning business or serving as officer or director; costs to attorney general; penalty up to $7500 for first offense, up to $15,000 for each subsequent offense; cease and desist orders; up to $25,000 per violation of such order. Additional civil penalty of up to $10,000 if defendant knew or should have known injured victim was elderly or disabled, up to $30,000 if violation part of a scheme directed at elderly or disabled people.
State UDAP Regulations: New Jersey Administrative Rules of the Division of Consumer Affairs, N.J. Admin. Code tit. 13, §§ 45A-1.1 through 45A-28.8—mail order; freezer meats; sale of unsafe products; furniture delivery; availability of advertised items; deceptive advertising, deceptive pricing; unsubstantiated claims; home appliance repair; pet dealers; unit pricing; refunds; home improvement practices; plain language; entertainment ticket sales; kosher food; toy and bicycle safety; health clubs; motor vehicle advertising; automobile sales; automobile repairs; tires; motor vehicle leasing.

Precedential Value of FTC Interpretations: None specified.
Web Link to UDAP Statute:
http://lis.njleg.state.nj.us/cgi-bin/om_isapi.dll?clientID=732939997&depth=2&expandheadings=off&headingswithhits=on&infobase=statutes.nfo&softpage=toc_frame_Pg42

N.M. Stat. Ann. §§ 57-12-1 through 57-12-22 Unfair Practices Act
Prohibited Practices: Unfair or deceptive trade practices (deception must be knowing), including 17 enumerated prohibitions; unconscionable trade practices that, to a person's detriment, take advantage of the knowledge, experience, ability or capacity of a person to a grossly unfair degree, or result in gross disparity between price and value received; referral sales; willful misrepresentation of age or condition of motor vehicle; other specific prohibitions.
Scope: Trade or commerce includes advertising, offering for sale, or distribution of any services, property, commodity or thing of value. Unfair or deceptive practice and unconscionable trade practice must be in connection with sale, lease, rental or loan of goods or services, extension of credit or debt collection in regular course of trade.
Exclusions: Actions or transactions expressly permitted under laws administered by state or U.S. regulatory body, but acts forbidden by that body, or about which it remains silent, are actionable; publishers, broadcasters, printers or others who reproduce material without knowledge of deceptive or unconscionable character.
Private Remedies: $100 minimum damages; $300 minimum damages or treble damages if willful; actual damages; person likely to be damaged may seek injunction; attorney fees mandatory if consumer prevails, to defendant if suit groundless; class actions for actual damages.
Limitations: Attorney general must act in public interest; acceptance of restitution pursuant to assurance bars any damage recovery on same practice; actual or minimum damages only if private party suffered loss of money or property.
State Remedies: Attorney general, or district attorney if delegated by attorney general enforces; injunction; restitution; civil penalty up to $5000 per violation if willful; rulemaking in attorney general; writ of *ne exeat* may be granted.
State UDAP Regulations: N.M. Admin. Code §§ 12.2.1.1 through 12.27.20—game promotions; motor vehicle advertising and sales; promotion and advertising of subdivided land, timeshares, condominium, and membership campgrounds; environmental marketing claims; automotive repair; Native American crafts.
Precedential Value of FTC Interpretations: Guided by FTC and judicial interpretations.
Web Link to UDAP Statute:
www.conwaygreene.com/newmexico.htm

N.Y. Exec. Law § 63(12) (McKinney)
Prohibited Practices: Repeated fraudulent or illegal acts, including deception, suppression, and unconscionable contractual provisions.
Scope: Conduct or transaction of business.
Exclusions: None specified.
Private Remedies: None specified.
Limitations: Attorney general must give notice 5 days before suit.
State Remedies: Attorney general enforces; injunction; restitution; damages; cancel filed certificate; court may award other relief proper.
Precedential Value of FTC Interpretations: None specified.
Web Link to UDAP Statute:
http://assembly.state.ny.us/leg/?cl=39&a=8

N.Y. Gen. Bus. Law §§ 349 and 350 (McKinney)
Prohibited Practices: Deceptive acts or practices and false advertising.
Scope: In conduct of business, trade or commerce or furnishing of any service in state.
Exclusions: Action subject to and in compliance with rules of FTC or other federal agency; any broadcaster or printer of advertising.
Private Remedies: Any person who has been injured may seek injunction for deceptive act; actual damages with $50 minimum; treble damages discretionary up to $1000 if willful or knowing violation; court "may" award attorney fees to prevailing plaintiff.
Limitations: Attorney general must give notice before suing, unless not in public interest; private action predicated on injury.
State Remedies: Attorney general enforces; injunction, restitution available for deceptive act; $500 civil penalty per initial violation; up to $10,000 additional civil penalty for consumer frauds against elderly persons.
Precedential Value of FTC Interpretations: None specified.
Web Link to UDAP Statute:
http://assembly.state.ny.us/leg/?cl=44&a=46
§§ 349 to 350-f
http://assembly.state.ny.us/leg/?cl=44&a=47
§§ 350-g to 350-i
www.nycourts.gov/courts/9jd/taxcert.shtml
Summary of New York UDAP law and decisions

N.C. Gen. Stat. §§ 75-1.1 through 75-35
Prohibited Practices: Unfair methods of competition and unfair or deceptive acts or practices; antitrust violations; special provisions for specific industries.
Scope: In or affecting commerce, which includes all business activities.
Exclusions: Professional services by member of learned profession; advertisements by a disinterested publisher, radio or television media, with no knowledge of falsity.
Private Remedies: Actual damages; treble damages; attorney fees may be awarded in court's discretion to prevailing plaintiff in case of willful violation and unwarranted refusal by defendant to resolve suit, to prevailing defendant if action frivolous and malicious.
Limitations: Private action based on injury to person or business; statute of limitations is 4 years after cause accrues, but tolled for private action while state action pending and 1 year afterwards.
State Remedies: Attorney general enforces; injunction; court "may" order restitution or cancel contracts; court has discretion to impose up to $5000 civil penalty per knowing violation or violation of court order.
Precedential Value of FTC Interpretations: None specified.
Web Link to UDAP Statute:
www.ncga.state.nc.us/gascripts/statutes/statutestoc.pl?0075

N.D. Cent. Code §§ 51-15-01 through 51-15-11
Prohibited Practices: Deceptive acts or practices, fraud, false pretense, false promise, or misrepresentation with intent others rely on.
Scope: Sale or advertisement of any merchandise, or any charitable solicitation; sale includes offers for and attempts to sell; merchandise includes goods, commodities, intangibles, realty, charitable contributions or services.

Exclusions: Advertisements by publisher, radio and television media, with no knowledge of advertiser's intent.
Private Remedies: Actual damages; discretionary treble damages and mandatory costs and attorney fees where violation knowingly committed.
Limitations: Attorney general must give notice before seeking injunction.
State Remedies: Attorney general enforces and has rulemaking power; injunction; cease and desist order; receiver; restitution; costs, investigation fees; expenses and attorney fees to attorney general; attorney general may impose civil penalty up to $1000 for violation of cease and desist order; court "may" assess statutory penalty of up to $5000 per initial violation.
State UDAP Regulations: N.D. Admin. Code § 10-15-01—retail price advertising.
Precedential Value of FTC Interpretations: None specified.
Web Link to UDAP Statute:
www.state.nd.us/lr/information/statutes/cent-code.html
Web Link to UDAP Regulation:
www.ag.state.nd.us/cpat/pdffiles/retailad.pdf

Ohio Rev. Code Ann. §§ 1345.01 through 1345.13 (West) **Consumer Sales Practices Act**
Prohibited Practices: Unfair and deceptive act or practice including but not limited to 10 enumerated prohibitions; any unconscionable act or practice, determined by considering 7 enumerated factors.
Scope: Applies to acts by supplier, defined as seller, lessor, assignor, franchisor, or other person engaged in the business of effecting or soliciting consumer transactions, whether or not the person deals directly with consumer. Must also be consumer transaction, defined as sale, lease, assignment, award by chance or transfer of goods, service, franchise or intangible to individual for personal, family, household purpose.
Exclusions: Transactions between entities regulated by public utilities commission and their customers; between financial institutions, dealers in intangibles, or insurance companies and their customers; between CPAs, public accounts, attorneys, physicians or dentists and clients or patients; transactions between veterinarians and patients for medical treatment; acts required or specifically permitted by federal or state law except attorney general may seek injunction in some circumstances; personal injury or death claims; publisher, broadcaster, printer or other person who disseminates information or reproduces printed matter if done for another and without knowledge; purely real estate transactions (exempt by judicial decision).
Private Remedies: Rescind transaction; actual damages; treble damages or minimum $200 for certain violations; declaratory judgment; injunction; class action for actual damages or "other appropriate relief" for certain violations; court may award attorney fees to prevailing party if consumer action is groundless and in bad faith or supplier commits a knowing violation.
Limitations: Attorney general brings actions in public interest; 2-year statute of limitations after occurrence for attorney general actions, 2 years after occurrence or 1 year after attorney general action terminates for private action; consumer may assert counterclaim in supplier's suit without regard to statute of limitations; in action for rescission, revocation must occur within reasonable time after discovers or should have discovered violation and before substantial change in condition of subject of transaction; private action by consumer precludes inclusion in subsequent class action by attorney general on same transaction. No civil penalties, attorney fees or amounts over actual damages if supplier proves bona fide error despite reasonable procedures; if acts were permitted by FTC rule, trade regulation or federal court interpretation of FTC Act and not prohibited by rule adopted before occurrence, no private action allowed and attorney general is limited to injunctive relief; in private action, consumer must choose between rescission and damages.
State Remedies: Attorney general has substantive and procedural rulemaking powers and acts upon petition of any person; attorney general enforces; may seek declaratory judgment; injunction; $5000 per each day injunction is violated if supplier has notice; class actions for consumers damaged by certain violations; receiver; restitution; performance of transaction in accord with consumer's reasonable expectations; strike unconscionable clauses; other appropriate relief; court may impose up to $25,000 civil penalty for certain initial violations; criminal penalties available for "slamming" by natural gas or public telecommunications services.
State UDAP Regulations: Ohio Attorney General Consumer Protection Rules, Ohio Admin. Code § 109:4-3—automobile sales; bait and switch; contests; deceptive pricing; delay and nondelivery; failure to disclose; door-to-door sales; insulation; misrepresentations of method of selecting consumer and seller's status; other prohibited practices; repairs and services; used for new; advertisement and sale of motor vehicles (amended); motor vehicle rust inhibitors; sale of gasoline containing alcohol; distress sales; motor vehicle repairs and services; use of the word "free."
Precedential Value of FTC Interpretations: Due consideration and great weight in interpretation of deceptive acts and in rulemaking.
Web Link to UDAP Statute:
http://onlinedocs.andersonpublishing.com
Click on Revised Code; click on Title XIII, 1345.
Web Link to UDAP Regulation:
http://onlinedocs.andersonpublishing.com
Click on Administrative Code, select chapter from tab at left of screen and then click on button labeled "chapter."

Ohio Rev. Code Ann. §§ 4165.01 through 4165.04 (West) **Deceptive Trade Practices Act**
Prohibited Practices: 13 enumerated deceptive trade practices.
Scope: In course of business, vocation or occupation.
Exclusions: Conduct complying with orders, rules, or laws administered by government agency; publishers, broadcasters, printers or other persons who disseminate information without knowledge of deception.
Private Remedies: Injunction; actual damages; court may award attorney fees to plaintiff if willful and knowing violation, to defendant if plaintiff knew action to be groundless. No requirement of monetary damage.
Limitations: None specified.
State Remedies: None specified.
Precedential Value of FTC Interpretations: None specified.
Web Link to UDAP Statute:
http://onlinedocs.andersonpublishing.com
Click on Revised Code; click on Title XLI, 4165.

Okla. Stat. tit. 15, §§ 751 through 763 Consumer Protection Act
Prohibited Practices: 30 enumerated unlawful practices.
Scope: In course of person's business. Many substantive prohibitions apply only to consumer transactions, defined as advertising, offering for sale, purchase, sale, or distribution of services, real or personal property, intangibles, or other thing of value, for purposes that are personal, household, or business oriented.
Exclusions: Advertisements by publisher, radio and television media, with no knowledge of unlawful practice; actions or transactions regulated under laws administered by corporation commission, or state or U.S. regulatory body; acts by retailers or others in good faith and without knowledge, if based on information supplied by others.
Private Remedies: Aggrieved consumer may sue for actual damages, costs and attorney fees. Costs and attorney fees to either party up to $10,000 if a claim or defense is in bad faith or groundless. Civil penalties up to $2000 per violation recoverable in individual action for unconscionable conduct.
Limitations: None specified.
State Remedies: Attorney general or district attorney enforces; declaratory judgment; injunction; actual damages; expenses and investigation fees; restitution; order that defendant carry out transaction in accord with consumer's reasonable expectations; receiver; revocation of license; other appropriate relief; civil penalty up to $10,000 per initial violation if willful, $10,000 per willful violation of injunction or court order plus other penalties as court deems necessary and proper; costs, investigation expenses, and attorney fees; criminal penalties.
Precedential Value of FTC Interpretations: None specified.
Web Link to UDAP Statute:
www.oscn.net/applications/oscn/index.asp?ftdb=stokst15&level=1

Okla. Stat. tit. 78, §§ 51 through 55 Deceptive Trade Practices Act
Prohibited Practices: 14 enumerated deceptive trade practices.
Scope: In course of business, vocation or occupation.
Exclusions: Conduct complying with order, rules, or statute administered by federal, state or local agency; advertisements by publisher, radio and television media, with no knowledge of falsity; new car franchise dealers covered by motor vehicle commission law.
Private Remedies: Injunction; actual damages; court has discretion to award attorney fees to prevailing party, with fees mandatory to prevailing party if suit based on willful violation or plaintiff acting in bad faith; trade associations may bring suit for injunction on behalf of its members. No requirement of monetary damage.
Limitations: None specified.
State Remedies: Attorney general may seek injunction, restitution, and reasonable expenses, plus attorney fees under same rules as private suits, for violation of telephone directory prohibitions.
Precedential Value of FTC Interpretations: None specified.
Web Link to UDAP Statute:
www.oscn.net/applications/oscn/index.asp?ftdb=stokst78&level=1

Or. Rev. Stat. §§ 646.605 through 646.656 Unlawful Trade Practices Law
Prohibited Practices: Numerous enumerated unlawful practices, including general prohibitions of unconscionable acts and unfair or deceptive conduct as defined by attorney general rule.
Scope: Trade or commerce, defined as advertising, offering, or distributing, by sale, rental, or otherwise, any real estate, goods or services, which include only those obtained primarily for personal, family or household purposes or as a result of a telephone solicitation; franchises, distributorship, and other similar business opportunities. Acts are violations if done in the course of the person's business, vocation, or occupation.
Exclusions: Insurance; conduct complying with orders, rules, or statute administered by federal, state or local agency; advertisements by publisher, radio and television media, with no knowledge of falsity; landlord-tenant matters.
Private Remedies: Actual damages; $200 minimum damages; punitive damages; equitable relief; court may award costs and attorney fees to prevailing party, but not to prevailing defendant in class action.
Limitations: Attorney general or district attorney acts upon probable cause; private action must be based on ascertainable loss of money or property as result of willful violation; no judgment rendered for plaintiff until plaintiff sends copy of complaint to attorney general; private action statute of limitations is one year from discovery, tolled during state prosecution of violation, limitations waived for counterclaims against seller or lessor of realty, goods, or services; does not create private cause of action for violation of certain vehicle registration, odometer disclosure, and odometer tampering laws.
State Remedies: Attorney general has rulemaking power; attorney general or district attorney enforces; injunction; notice letter required before seeking injunction except in specified circumstances; court may award attorney fees to prevailing party, and shall award fees to prevailing defendant if district attorney or attorney general did not have reasonable grounds or defendant offered to agree to satisfactory assurance of voluntary compliance before suit; court may make additional orders including restitution; civil penalty up to $25,000 per willful violation of act, injunction or assurance of compliance; court has discretion to order dissolution of license or franchise for injunction violation.
State UDAP Regulations: Or. Admin. R. 137-020-010 through 137-020-600—deceptive advertising; free offers; motor vehicle sales, motor vehicle advertising; mobile home consignments; federal credit and leasing laws; plain language; gasoline advertising; telemarketing; advance fee loan broker solicitations; unordered property; prize promotions; manufactured dwellings; *notarios*.
Precedential Value of FTC Interpretations: None specified.
Web Link to UDAP Statute:
www.doj.state.or.us

Pa. Stat. Ann. tit. 73, §§ 201-1 through 201-9.3 (West) Unfair Trade Practices and Consumer Protection Law
Prohibited Practices: 21 enumerated unfair methods of competition and unfair or deceptive acts or practices, including a catchall prohibiting any other fraudulent or deceptive conduct likely to create confusion or misunderstanding; separate sections providing cancellation rights for home solicitation sales and protections for dog purchasers.
Scope: Trade and commerce means advertising, sale, offering for sale, or distribution of any service, real or personal property, intangibles and any other thing of value.
Exclusions: Advertisements in good faith by publisher, radio and television media, with no knowledge of falsity.
Private Remedies: Actual damages; $100 minimum damages; treble damages discretionary; "may" award attorney fees and costs; may provide additional relief if proper.

Limitations: State action for injunction must be in public interest; private action authorized only for persons who purchase or lease goods or services primarily for personal, family or household purposes and thereby suffer ascertainable loss of money or property as a result of unlawful act.
State Remedies: Attorney general has rulemaking power; attorney general or district attorney enforces; injunction; court has discretion to award restitution; civil penalty up to $5000 per violation of injunction or assurance of compliance, $1000 per willful initial violation ($3000 if victim is 60 years or older); equitable relief deemed proper; court has discretion to dissolve business for violation of injunction; may appoint a receiver.
State UDAP Regulations: Pa. Regulations of the Bureau of Consumer Protection, 37 Pa. Code §§ 301.1 through 309.2—automotive industry, loan broker practices, plain language; sale of dogs.
Precedential Value of FTC Interpretations: None specified.
Web Link to UDAP Statute:
http://members.aol.com/statutesp8/73.cp.1.html

3 P.R. Laws Ann. §§ 341 through 341w Department of Consumer Affairs Organic Act
Prohibited Practices: Fraud, deceit, or misrepresentation of brand, price, quantity, size, quality, guaranty, or wholesomeness of a product, article, or service.
Scope: Not specified.
Exclusions: None specified.
Private Remedies: Consumer may make administrative complaint to department of consumer affairs. Any party adversely affected by department's ruling may appeal to court.
Limitations: None specified.
State Remedies: Department of consumer affairs may issue cease and desist orders and impose fines up to $10,000 for initial violation or violation of order.
State UDAP Regulations: Department of consumer affairs has rulemaking authority.
Precedential Value of FTC Interpretations: None specified.

10 P.R. Laws Ann. §§ 257 through 273 Fair Competition Act
Prohibited Practices: Unfair methods of competition and unfair or deceptive acts and practices in trade or commerce.
Scope: Applies to any natural or artificial person who draws substantial income from used or consumed goods or services rendered in Puerto Rico and/or receives substantial income within the scope of the economy of Puerto Rico or from any impact or effect in a specific local market.
Exclusions: None.
Private Remedies: No private remedy for violation of § 259, the section which forbids unfair and deceptive acts and practices.
Limitations: Statute of limitations for criminal proceedings is four years after commission of last act constituting in whole or in part the violation charged.
State Remedies: Office of monopolistic affairs may bring administrative complaints before the department of consumer affairs. Judicial review available. Civil penalties of up to $5000 for violation of department of consumer affairs order of knowing violation of regulations. Certain violations are misdemeanors, punishable by a fine of $5000 to $50,000 or up to one year in jail. Secretary of justice may sue to enjoin or punish violations. Violation of court order is contempt, punishable by fine up to $25,000 or one year in jail.
State UDAP Regulations: Office of monopolistic affairs has rulemaking authority.
Precedential Value of FTC Interpretations: None specified.

R.I. Gen. Laws §§ 6-13.1-1 through 6-13.1-27 Unfair Trade Practice and Consumer Protection Act
Prohibited Practices: 19 enumerated unfair methods of competition and unfair or deceptive practices, plus special provisions for specific industries.
Scope: Trade or commerce, defined as advertising, sale, offering for sale, or distribution of any service, real or personal property, intangibles, and any other thing of value.
Exclusions: Actions or transactions permitted under laws administered by department of business regulation or other state or federal regulatory body.
Private Remedies: Actual damages; minimum $200; punitive damages; equitable relief as court deems proper; class action for actual, minimum, and punitive damages and court has discretion to award injunction or other equitable remedy; court may award attorney fees and costs.
Limitations: Attorney general action for injunction if in public interest and notice given; private action authorized only for person who purchases or leases goods or services primarily for personal, family, or household purposes and thereby suffers ascertainable loss of money or property as result of unlawful act.
State Remedies: Attorney general enforces; injunction; court may make additional orders necessary including restitution, receiver, revocation of license; civil penalty up to $10,000 per injunction violation and court may order dissolution of corporation.
State UDAP Regulations: R.I. Department of Attorney General, Consumer Protection Division Rules & Regulations, R.I. Code R. 30 010 001 through 002 and 90 000 016 through 018—odometer tampering; time shares; nonregulated power producers.
Precedential Value of FTC Interpretations: Due consideration and great weight.
Web Link to UDAP Statute:
www.rilin.state.ri.us/statutes/statutes.html

S.C. Code Ann. §§ 39-5-10 to 39-5-160 (Law. Co-op) Unfair Trade Practices Act
Prohibited Practices: Unfair methods of competition and unfair or deceptive acts or practices.
Scope: Trade or commerce defined to include advertising, sale, offering for sale, or distribution of any service, real or personal property, intangible or any other thing of value.
Exclusions: Actions or transactions permitted under laws administered by state or federal regulatory body, or permitted by any other state law; advertisements by disinterested publisher, radio and television media, with no knowledge of falsity; actions governed by §§ 38-55-10 through 38-55-410 relating to regulation of insurance; actions that comply with FTC rules, decisions, and statutes.
Private Remedies: Actual damages; treble damages for willful or knowing violation and court "may" provide other relief deemed proper; attorney fees and costs to successful plaintiff.
Limitations: Attorney general action for injunction if in public interest and upon notice; private action predicated on ascertainable loss of money or property; private action may not be brought in representative capacity; statute of limitations is 3 years after discovery.

State Remedies: Attorney general, county or city attorney. upon attorney general approval enforces; injunction with costs to state; court may make additional orders necessary including restitution, revocation of license; rulemaking; civil penalty up to $5000 per initial violation if willful, up to $15,000 per injunction violation; court may dissolve corporation that violates injunction.
Precedential Value of FTC Interpretations: Guided by FTC interpretations.
Web Link to UDAP Statute:
www.scstatehouse.net/code/statmast.htm
www.scstatehouse.net/code/t39c005.doc

S.D. Codified Laws §§ 37-24-1 through 37-24-35 (Michie) Deceptive Trade Practices and Consumer Protection Law
Prohibited Practices: 12 enumerated deceptive practices, including knowing and intentional omission of material fact in connection with sale or advertisement of merchandise.
Scope: No scope limitations.
Exclusions: Advertisements by publisher, radio and television media, with no knowledge of falsity; acts permitted by state or U.S. laws or regulations.
Private Remedies: Actual damages.
Limitations: Statute of limitations is 2 years after discovery.
State Remedies: Director of Consumer Protection has rulemaking power; attorney general or state's attorney with attorney general approval has enforcement power; injunction; civil penalty up to $5000 per violation of injunction, up to $2000 per intentional initial violation; court may make necessary additional orders including restitution and receiver. For state actions, engaging in a practice is *prima facie* evidence that it is done knowingly and intentionally; criminal penalties.
Precedential Value of FTC Interpretations: None specified.
Web Link to UDAP Statute:
http://legis.state.sd.us/statutes/index.cfm?fuseaction=displaystatute&findtype=statute&txtstatute=37-24

Tenn. Code Ann. §§ 47-18-101 through 47-18-125 Consumer Protection Act
Prohibited Practices: Unfair or deceptive acts or practices, including but not limited to 36 enumerated prohibitions; special provisions for specific practices.
Scope: Trade, commerce, or consumer transaction, defined as advertising, offering for sale, lease, rental, or distribution of any goods, services, or property, tangible or intangible, real, personal, or mixed, and other articles, commodities, or things of value wherever situated.
Exclusions: Acts or transactions required or specifically authorized by laws administered by, or rules promulgated by, state or federal regulatory body or officer; advertisements by publisher, radio and television media, who have not been notified of falsity by division of consumer affairs; credit terms except insofar as state equal consumer credit act applies; retailer disseminating manufacturer's claims in good faith and without actual knowledge of violation.
Private Remedies: Actual damages; if willful or knowing violation, court may award treble damages and grant other relief necessary and proper; declaratory judgment; injunction provided no state action filed; court "may" award attorney fees and costs to prevailing plaintiff, and to defendant if action frivolous, without merit, or for purposes of harassment.
Limitations: Injunction if in public interest and upon notice; private action if suffered ascertainable loss of money or property, but anyone "affected by" violation may seek injunction; court may set aside unreasonable settlement 1 year from making; court may limit private party to terms of reasonable offer of settlement; statute of limitations for private rights of action is 1 year from discovery but in no event more than 5 years from transaction. No statute of limitations mentioned for actions brought by state. No private damages remedy for violation of state equal consumer credit act.
State Remedies: Attorney general and reporter at request of consumer affairs division enforces; injunction; costs and attorney fees; restitution; revoke license for knowing and persistent violation; civil penalty up to $1000 per initial violation or knowing violation of assurance of voluntary compliance, up to $2000 for knowing violation of injunction, up to $10,000 per initial violation that targets persons 60 years old or older; criminal penalties.
Precedential Value of FTC Interpretations: Interpreted and construed consistently with FTC.
Web Link to UDAP Statute:
www.tennesseeanytime.org/laws/laws.html

Tex. Bus. & Com. Code Ann. §§ 17.41 through 17.63 (Vernon) Deceptive Trade Practices—Consumer Protection Act
Prohibited Practices: Deceptive acts or practices, including but not limited to 26 enumerated prohibitions; also creates cause of action for breach of warranty, certain insurance violations, and unconscionable acts, defined as those that, to the consumer's detriment, take advantage of lack of knowledge, ability, experience, or capacity to a grossly unfair degree.
Scope: Trade or commerce, defined as advertising, offer for sale, sale, lease, or distribution of any service, good, real or personal property, intangible or any other thing of value.
Exclusions: Financially disinterested owners or employees of newspaper, magazine, telephone directory, billboard, broadcast station who advertise without knowledge; acts authorized by FTC rules or regulations; claims for bodily injury or death, or mental anguish other than specifically provided. Limited exemption for certain kinds of professional services, certain written contracts for more than $100,000, and all written contracts for more than $500,000 not involving a consumer's residence.
Private Remedies: Consumer may seek economic damages, injunction, restitution, other relief including receiver and, in some circumstances, license revocation; if the acts were "knowingly" committed, consumer may recover for mental anguish and treble economic damages; if "intentionally," both types of damages may be trebled. Prevailing consumer entitled to costs and fees; defendant if suit was groundless, in bad faith, or brought for purposes of harassment. Either party may demand mediation. For deceptive practices claim, consumer must show detrimental reliance on one of the specifically enumerated deceptive acts.
Limitations: Consumer may bring deceptive practices suit only for enumerated practices, and only if detrimental reliance. Consumer may sue only if violation is producing cause of economic damages or mental anguish. No double recovery of actual damages and penalties for same act; state acts in public interest and upon notice for injunction; consumer must give specific notice 60 days prior to damages action unless statute of limitations would run. Statute creates defense if defendant tenders full amount of economic and mental anguish damages claimed, plus reasonable attorney fees, within 30 days after notice letter; if plaintiff rejects an offer made within 60 days of notice letter, 90 days after answer filed, or 20

days after mediation, and court finds plaintiff not entitled to larger amount, plaintiff's recovery is limited and only attorney fees incurred before offer may be awarded; defense also exists if proves gave plaintiff written notice of defendant's reliance without knowledge on false information, provided in government records, tests, or another source; in addition, a general post-offer fee-shifting statute, Tex. Civ. Prac. & Rem. Code §§ 42.001 through 42.005, makes consumer who rejects defendant's offer and then wins significantly less at trial in a non-class action liable for defendant's post-offer litigation expenses, including attorney fees, up to a cap. Statute of limitations 2 years from discovery of violation; additional 180 days given if consumer proves defendant knowingly induced postponement of action. Waivers authorized under specified circumstances. Consumer filing class action must notify consumer protection division and give it opportunity to intervene.
State Remedies: Consumer protection division and district attorney or county attorney upon notice to division enforces; injunction; restitution; receiver; civil penalty up to up to $20,000 per initial violation, plus up to $250,000 more if victim was 65 or older; up to $10,000 per violation of injunction (not to exceed total of $50,000); criminal penalties. Attorney general may intervene in private class actions.
Precedential Value of FTC Interpretations: Guided by FTC Act and interpretations.
Web Link to UDAP Statute:
www.capitol.state.tx.us/statutes/statutes.html

Utah Code Ann. §§ 13-2-1 through 13-2-8 and 13-5-1 through 13-5-8 Unfair Practices Act
Prohibited Practices: Unfair methods of competition, including many enumerated unlawful practices primarily relating to antitrust, but also including advertising goods, wares, or merchandise without being prepared to supply them.
Scope: In trade or commerce defined as intrastate commerce.
Exclusions: Banks, common carriers and other public utilities subject to regulation; sales made to close out stock upon notice to public; sales of damaged goods upon notice to public; sales made to meet price competition; sale under court order; sales at prices set by interstate competition.
Private Remedies: Injunction; actual damages; treble damages, minimum $2000 damages; court costs; contract made in violation is illegal and no recovery may be had on it.
Limitations: Division acts in public interest; actual damages given only if injury occurred.
State Remedies: State may seek injunction; civil penalty up to $2000 per day of injunction violation upon notice of injunction; criminal penalties.
Precedential Value of FTC Interpretations: None specified.
Web Link to UDAP Statute:
www.le.state.ut.us/~code/title13/title13.htm

Utah Code Ann. §§ 13-11-1 through 13-11-23 Consumer Sales Practices Act
Prohibited Practices: Deceptive acts or practices by a supplier in consumer transaction, including but not limited to 19 enumerated prohibitions, and unconscionable practices.
Scope: Consumer transactions, defined as offers or solicitations and sale, lease, assignment, award by chance, or other transfer or disposition of goods, services, or other tangible or intangible property for primarily personal, family or household purposes, including business opportunity requiring expenditure of money or property and personal services on continuing basis and charitable solicitations.
Exclusions: Securities and insurance; act or practice required or specifically permitted by or under state or federal law; claims for personal injury, death, or damage to property other than subject of consumer transaction; credit terms; public utilities regulated by state public service commission; publisher, broadcaster, printer or other person who disseminates information for others if done without actual knowledge of violation.
Private Remedies: Declaratory judgment and injunction regardless of whether consumer has suffered actual damages or has adequate remedy at law, actual damages with minimum of $2000 plus court costs; class actions for declaratory judgment, injunction and appropriate ancillary relief or, in specified circumstances, actual damages; court "may" award attorney fees to consumer if violation shown, to defendant if consumer's action is groundless.
Limitations: If supplier proves bona fide error despite reasonable procedures, damages in class action brought by state or consumer are limited to unjust enrichment; statute of limitations is 2 years from violation, extended in private actions to 1 year after state action terminates; no statute of limitations on consumer counterclaims; detailed special provisions for consumer class actions; consumer action predicated upon loss suffered.
State Remedies: Division of consumer protection or state official (*see* Utah Code Ann. § 13-2-1) or agency with supervisory authority over supplier enforces; division of consumer protection may issue cease and desist order and impose administrative fine of $2500 per initial violation; civil penalty up to $5000 per day of injunction violation; substantive and procedural rulemaking; declaratory judgment; injunction; actual damages for consumers who complained; class action for actual damages for consumers in specified circumstances; reasonable attorney fees and costs; court may make appropriate orders, including receiver, reimbursement, carry out transaction in accord with consumer's reasonable expectations, strike unconscionable clauses, grant other relief.
State UDAP Regulations: Rules for the Utah Consumer Sales Practices Act, Utah Admin. Code 152-11-1 through 152-11-13—exclusions and limitations in advertising; bait advertising; use of the word "free"; repairs and services; prizes; new for used; substitution of goods; door-to-door sales; deposits and refunds; franchises, distributorships, and referral sales; travel packages; negative option sales.
Precedential Value of FTC Interpretations: Construe to avoid inconsistency with FTC policies and to create uniformity among states enacting similar statutes.
Web Link to UDAP Statute:
www.le.state.ut.us/~code/title13/13_0B.htm

Utah Code Ann. §§ 13.11a-1 through 13.11a.-5 Truth in Advertising
Prohibited Practices: Twenty enumerated deceptive practices.
Scope: Practices in course of defendant's business, trade, or occupation. Most substantive prohibitions involve "goods or services," which are broadly defined.
Exclusions: Conduct in compliance with orders or rules of, or statute administered by, a federal, state, or local governmental agency; publishers and others who disseminate information without knowledge of deception.
Private Remedies: Any person may sue for injunction and, if

injured, for actual damages or $2000, whichever is greater. Court may award costs and shall award attorney fees to prevailing party.
Limitations: No action for injunctive relief may be brought unless plaintiff first gives notice to defendant and allows defendant an opportunity to publish a correction notice.
State Remedies: State may seek injunction and same remedies as private plaintiff.
Precedential Value of FTC Interpretations: None specified.

Vt. Stat. Ann. tit. 9, §§ 2451 through 2480g Consumer Fraud Act
Prohibited Practices: Unfair methods of competition and unfair or deceptive acts or practices.
Scope: In commerce.
Exclusions: Advertisements by publisher, radio and television media, with no knowledge of fraudulent intent.
Private Remedies: Equitable relief; actual damages; restitution; attorney fees; exemplary damages not exceeding treble the consideration given.
Limitations: State acts in public interest. Private action limited to consumers, defined as those who purchase goods or services (defined as objects, wares, goods, commodities, work, labor, intangibles, courses of instruction or training, securities, bonds, debentures, stocks, real estate, or other property or services of any kind) for specified purposes other than resale; for private action plaintiff must show injury or reliance.
State Remedies: Attorney general rulemaking consistent with FTC Act; attorney general, or state's attorney if authorized by attorney general, enforces; injunction; dissolution of corporation; civil penalty up to $10,000 per initial violation or violation of injunction; restitution to consumer; expenses and reasonable value of attorney general's services; court may authorize any relief in public interest.
State UDAP Regulations: Vt. Consumer Fraud Rules, Vt. Code R. 06 031 001 through 019—automobile sales; bait advertising, contests and prizes; debt collection; deceptive pricing; delay and nondelivery; credit reporting; chain distribution schemes (pyramids); refunds; telephonic home solicitation sales; rent-to-own disclosures; sale of vacation packages; LPG gas sales; distress sales; charitable solicitations; seller's warranty obligations; odometers; statements of origin of fruits and vegetables.
Precedential Value of FTC Interpretations: Guided by FTC construction.
Web Link to UDAP Statute:
www.leg.state.vt.us/statutes/statutes2.htm
Web Link to UDAP Regulation:
www.atg.state.vt.us/display.php?smod=97

Va. Code Ann. §§ 59.1-196 through 59.1-207 (Michie) Consumer Protection Act
Prohibited Practices: 39 prohibited fraudulent acts, including catchall for any other deceptive practices. *See also* § 18.2-216 (false advertising), enforceable under § 59.1-68.3.
Scope: Committed by a supplier (including sellers, lessors, licensors, manufacturers, and distributors) in connection with a consumer transaction, defined as the advertisement, sale, lease or offer for sale or lease of goods or services for personal, family or household purposes, certain business opportunities, layaway agreements, and goods or services relating to finding or obtaining of employment; "goods" defined to include all real, personal, or mixed property, tangible or intangible, plus computer information and informational rights.
Exclusions: Aspects of consumer transactions authorized under state or U.S. laws, regulations or advisory opinions; advertisements by publisher, owner, agent or employee of a newspaper, periodical or radio or television station, or other advertising media, with no knowledge of falsity; aspects regulated by federal Consumer Credit Protection Act; banks, savings institutions, credit unions, small loan companies, and public service corporations; mortgage lenders as defined in § 6.1-409, broker-dealers as defined in § 13.1-501 and insurance companies regulated and supervised the state corporation commission or a comparable federal regulating body; any aspect of a consumer transaction subject to the landlord and tenant act, § 55-217 *et seq.* or the residential landlord and tenant act, § 55-248.2 *et seq.* unless the act or practice of a landlord constitutes misrepresentation or fraudulent act or practice under § 59.1-200; and real estate licensees who are licensed under § 54.1-2100 *et seq.*
Private Remedies: Actual damages or $500, whichever is greater, or in the case of a willful violation, damages may be increased to three times actual damages or $1000 whichever is greater; court "may" award reasonable attorney fees and court costs; court may make additional orders for restitution.
Limitations: State must give pre-suit notice in most cases; private action based on loss suffered; restitution allowed only to consumers identified within 180 days from grant of permanent injunction. No liability imposed upon a supplier who proves violation was act or practice of a manufacturer or distributor over which the supplier had no control or resulted from bona fide error despite procedures, but court may still order restitution and payment of reasonable attorney fees and court costs to individuals aggrieved by unintentional violation. Statute of limitations is two years from accrual, but tolled during government suit. If defendant delivers written cure offer including at least $500 for attorney fees and inconvenience before filing answer, it may be introduced into evidence at trial, and supplier is not liable for consumer's attorney fees and court costs unless the actual damages awarded, without consideration of attorney fees and court costs, exceed the offer.
State Remedies: Attorney general, commonwealth attorney, city, county, or town attorney enforces; injunction; restitution; civil penalty up to $2500 plus up to $1000 for expenses per initial violation if willful, up to $5000 plus up to $1000 for expenses per violation of injunction or assurance of voluntary compliance; contempt for violation of any court order.
Precedential Value of FTC Interpretations: None specified.
Web Link to UDAP Statute:
http://leg1.state.va.us/cgi-bin/legp504.exe?000+cod+TOC59010000017000000000000

12A V.I. Code Ann. §§ 101 through 123 and 180 through 185 Consumer Protection Law of 1973
Prohibited Practices: Deceptive or unconscionable trade practice in the sale, lease, rental or loan or in the offering for sale, lease, rental, or loan of any consumer goods or services, or in the collection of consumer debts, including but not limited to 16 enumerated practices. Additional prohibitions on deceptive pricing in § 121. Additional requirements for price disclosure of prescription drugs. Prohibited practices by motor vehicle dealers and repair shops enumerated at §§ 183 and 184.
Scope: Covers sale, lease, rental or loan, or the offer of sale, lease, rental or loan of consumer goods, or collection of consumer debt. Defined to mean goods, services, credit, and debts primarily for personal, household or family purposes.

Exclusions: None specified.
Private Remedies: Consumer who suffers a loss as a result of violation of this chapter may sue for the greater of actual damages or $250 in individual action. May also seek declaratory judgment or injunction regardless of whether has suffered damages or has adequate remedy at law. Consumer class actions available for declaratory judgment, injunction, ancillary relief other than damages, and, in some circumstances, damages. Criteria for class certification similar to federal. Attorney fees to prevailing party, if merchant violated this chapter or consumer brought action known to be groundless.
Limitations: For private action, statute of limitations is 2 years after violation, 1 year after last payment, or 1 year after termination of state proceedings, whichever is later; for commissioner's class action, 2 years. If merchant shows bona fide error despite reasonable procedures, recovery is limited to amount by which merchant was unjustly enriched. Before bringing civil action against motor vehicle dealer or repair shop, consumer must submit the dispute to the department of licensing and consumer affairs.
State Remedies: Director of consumer services administration has rulemaking power. Commissioner of licensing and consumer affairs, after a hearing, may impose administrative fines of up to $5000 per violation. May petition court for enforcement; court may impose up to $5000 additional fine for noncompliance. In case of repeated violation may petition for court order requiring violator to pay all proceeds of violations into court for consumer redress, and court may revoke business's license. Commissioner may sue to enjoin violations. Court may award costs and attorney fees to prevailing party. Commissioner may bring class action on behalf of consumers.
State UDAP Regulations: 12A V.I. R. & and Regs. §§ 101-1 *et seq.*—car rentals, refund policy disclosure, truth-in-pricing, layaway plans, jewelry repair and appraisals, sale of furniture, posting of prescription drug prices, deceptive price marking, display of octane rating and price.
Precedential Value of FTC Interpretations: Construe to supplement FTC rules, regulations, and decisions. State regulations may supplement but shall not be inconsistent with UCC, UCCC, and FTC Act rules, regulations and decisions.
Web Link to UDAP Statute:
http://198.187.128.12/virginislands/lpext.dll?f=templates&fn=fs-main.htm&2.0

Wash. Rev. Code Ann. §§ 19.86.010 through 19.86.920 (West) Consumer Protection Act
Prohibited Practices: Unfair methods of competition and unfair or deceptive acts; monopolization and restraint of trade. Violations of numerous other statutes are per se violations of § 19.86.
Scope: Trade and commerce; defined as sale of services or assets including any real or personal property, intangible and any other thing of value.
Exclusions: Nonprofit labor, agricultural or horticultural organization; civil penalties do not apply to advertisements by publisher, radio and television media, in good faith and with no knowledge of falsity; actions or transactions permitted, prohibited, or regulated by the state insurance commissioner (with significant exceptions), utilities and transportation commission, or federal power commission; actions or transactions permitted by other state or federal regulatory body or officer.
Private Remedies: Injunction; actual damages; costs and attorney fees; treble damages at court's discretion, not to exceed $10,000.
Limitations: Private action predicated upon injury to business or property; statute of limitations is 4 years after cause accrues, but tolled during pendency of attorney general action in most circumstances. Act must be injurious to public interest.
State Remedies: Attorney general enforces; injunction; restitution; court has discretion to award prevailing party costs and attorney fees; civil penalty of up to $2000 per initial violation (up to $500,000 for certain antitrust violations), up to $25,000 for injunction violation; court may order dissolution of corporation that violates injunction.
Precedential Value of FTC Interpretations: Guided by FTC interpretations.
Web Link to UDAP Statute:
www.leg.wa.gov/rcw/index.cfm?fuseaction=chapterdigest&chapter=19.86

W. Va. Code §§ 46A-6-101 through 46A-6-110
Prohibited Practices: Unfair methods of competition and unfair or deceptive practices, including 16 enumerated prohibitions.
Scope: Trade or commerce, defined as advertising, sale, offering for sale, or distribution of any goods or services.
Exclusions: Acts reasonable to develop and preserve business; acts not injurious to public interest; not to be interpreted to repeal §§ 47-11A-1 through 47-11A-14 (antitrust) or §§ 47-11B-1 through 47-11B-17 (closeout sales, fire sales and defunct business sales); advertisements by disinterested publisher, radio and television media, with no knowledge of falsity and without involvement in preparation.
Private Remedies: $200 minimum damages; actual damages; equitable relief in court's discretion if deemed necessary or proper; court may reform a consumer contract if defendant refuses to change contract to plain language after consumer so requests.
Limitations: Private action allowed only to persons who purchase or lease goods or services and thereby suffer an ascertainable loss of money or property as result of violation.
State Remedies: Attorney general has rulemaking power; injunction action, other equitable relief, other appropriate relief (W. Va. Code § 46A-7-108).
State UDAP Regulations: W. Va. Code St. R. §§ 142-5-1 through 142-5-4, 142-6-1 through 142-6-4, 142-8-1 through 142-8-17, 142-13-1 through 142-13-8, and 142-22-1 through 142-22-6—home improvements; sale of damaged goods; health spas; pre-need burial contracts; rent-to-own transactions.
Precedential Value of FTC Interpretations: Guided by federal court interpretations; regulations should conform as nearly as practicable with FTC's.
Web Link to UDAP Statute:
www.legis.state.wv.us/legishp.html

Wis. Stat. Ann. § 100.18 (West)
Prohibited Practices: Untrue, deceptive or misleading advertisements and representations, including numerous itemized deceptive representations.
Scope: Detailed scope provision applying to virtually any transaction.
Exclusions: Insurance; statements made by licensed real estate brokers and salespersons without knowledge of falsity; publishers, radio, and TV stations who publish advertisements in good faith without knowledge of falsity.

Private Remedies: Any person suffering pecuniary loss may sue for the loss, plus costs and attorney fees. Double damages are available if the defendant violated an injunction issued under the UDAP statute. Attorney fees are not recoverable from licensed real estate brokers.
Limitations: 3-year limitations period, running from occurrence of unlawful act.
State Remedies: Department of agriculture, trade and consumer protection has rulemaking authority; it, the department of justice, and district attorneys have enforcement powers; injunction; court has discretion to make other orders, including restitution; court may award costs of investigation and attorney fees; fines and civil forfeiture in varying amounts ranging from $100 to $10,000 for violations of statute, rule, or order; civil forfeiture of $100 to $10,000 for violation of injunction; supplemental forfeiture up to $10,000 in some cases if victim is elderly or disabled.
Precedential Value of FTC Interpretations: None specified.
Web Link to UDAP Statute:
http://folio.legis.state.wi.us/cgi-bin/om_isapi.dll?clientid=104903&infobase=stats.nfo&j1=100.18&jump=100.18

Wis. Stat. Ann. §§ 100.20 to 100.264 (West)
Prohibited Practices: Unfair methods of competition and unfair trade practices; special sections on specific industries.
Scope: Business.
Exclusions: None specified.
Private Remedies: Double pecuniary loss, costs and attorney fees, but private remedies available only for violation of general orders (i.e. regulations) or special orders (i.e. cease and desist orders) issued by department of agriculture, trade and consumer protection.
Limitations: Department of agriculture, trade and consumer protection acts after public hearing for rulemaking and injunction and cancellation; must give notice; private actions require pecuniary loss. Violations must be knowing.
State Remedies: Department of agriculture, trade and consumer protection has rulemaking and enforcement powers; injunction to enforce regulation or order; restitution; court may award costs of investigation and attorney fees; cancel corporate certificate if in public interest for substantial and willful violation; $25 to $5000 and/or imprisonment for failure to obey regulation or order; civil forfeiture of $100 to $10,000 for rule, order, or injunction violation; enhanced penalties if engage in acts against the elderly or disabled.
State UDAP Regulations: Wis. Department of Agriculture, Trade and Consumer Protection Rules, Wis. Admin. Code ATCP 109–137—home improvements; referral sales; pyramid sales; deceptive pricing; price comparison advertising; mobile home parks; door-to-door sales; automobile repairs; automobile rentals; landlord-tenant; environmental labeling of products; freezer meats; basement waterproofing; gasoline advertising; real estate advertising, advance fees; art prints; academic material; coupon sales; work recruitment schemes; telecommunications and cable TV billing practices; hazardous substances.
Precedential Value of FTC Interpretations: None specified.
Web Link to UDAP Statute:
http://folio.legis.state.wi.us/cgi-bin/om_isapi.dll?clientid=104903&infobase=stats.nfo&j1=100.20&jump=100.20

Wyo. Stat. Ann.§§ 40-12-101 to 40-12-114 (Michie) Consumer Protection Act
Prohibited Practices: 15 enumerated practices, including a catchall generally prohibiting unfair or deceptive acts or practices.
Scope: In course of business and in connection with a consumer transaction, defined as the advertising, sale, offering for sale, or distribution of any merchandise, defined to include real or personal property, services, intangibles or any article of value, for purposes that are primarily personal, family or household.
Exclusions: Acts or practices required or permitted by state or federal law, regulation or decision; advertisements by publisher, radio and television media, with no knowledge of falsity.
Private Remedies: Class actions or individual actions for actual damages; attorney fees to prevailing plaintiff in class action.
Limitations: Attorney general may seek injunction in public interest and upon notice; private action authorized only if person relies on uncured violation and suffers damages as result, "uncured" defined as notice given of violation and no offer of cure made within 15 days or no cure within reasonable time; consumer must give written notice to alleged violator within 1 year of discovery of violation or 2 years after consumer transaction, whichever first, and must file suit within 1 year of giving notice; remedies in act are exclusive remedies for actions brought pursuant to this act.
State Remedies: Attorney general enforces; injunction; restitution (including attorney fees if victim is elderly or disabled and violation was willful and knowing); up to $10,000 civil penalty for willful violations (up to $15,000 for willful and knowing violations that victimize or attempt to victimize older or disabled person), up to $5000 for violation of injunction.
Precedential Value of FTC Interpretations: None specified.
Web Link to UDAP Statute:
http://legisweb.state.wy.us/statutes/titles/title40/c12a01.htm

Appendix B Selected Federal Trade Commission Rules

The full text of this appendix and additional FTC interpretations relating to the FTC Rules reprinted in this appendix are found on the companion CD-Rom.

B.1 FTC Credit Practices Rule

16 C.F.R. 444

Source: 49 Fed. Reg. 7740 (Mar. 1, 1984), *effective* March 1, 1985

§ 444.1 Definitions.

(a) *Lender.* A person who engages in the business of lending money to consumers within the jurisdiction of the Federal Trade Commission.

(b) *Retail installment seller.* A person who sells goods or services to consumers on a deferred payment basis or pursuant to a lease-purchase arrangement within the jurisdiction of the Federal Trade Commission.

(c) *Person.* An individual corporation, or other business organization.

(d) *Consumer.* A natural person who seeks or acquires goods, services, or money for personal, family, or household use.

(e) *Obligation.* An agreement between a consumer and a lender or retail installment seller.

(f) *Creditor.* A lender or a retail installment seller.

(g) *Debt.* Money that is due or alleged to be due from one to another.

(h) *Earnings.* Compensation paid or payable to an individual or for his or her account for personal services rendered or to be rendered by him or her, whether denominated as wages, salary, commission, bonus, or otherwise, including periodic payments pursuant to a pension, retirement, or disability program.

(i) *Household goods.* Clothing, furniture, appliances, one radio and one television, linens, china, crockery, kitchenware, and personal effects (including wedding rings) of the consumer and his or her dependents, provided that the following are not included within the scope of the term *household goods*:

(1) Works of art;

(2) Electronic entertainment equipment (except one television and one radio);

(3) Items acquired as antiques; and

(4) Jewelry (except wedding rings).

(j) *Antique.* Any item over one hundred years of age, including such items that have been repaired or renovated without changing their original form or character.

(k) *Cosigner.* A natural person who renders himself or herself liable for the obligation of another person without compensation. The term shall include any person whose signature is requested as a condition to granting credit to another person, or as a condition for forbearance on collection of another person's obligation that is in default. The term shall not include a spouse whose signature is required on a credit obligation to perfect a security interest pursuant to state law. A person who does not receive goods, services, or money in return for a credit obligation does not receive compensation within the meaning of this definition. A person is a cosigner within the meaning of this definition whether or not he or she is designated as such on a credit obligation.

§ 444.2 Unfair credit practices.

(a) In connection with the extension of credit to consumers in or affecting commerce, as commerce is defined in the Federal Trade Commission Act, it is an unfair act or practice within the meaning of Section 5 of that Act for a lender or retail installment seller directly or indirectly to take or receive from a consumer an obligation that:

(1) Constitutes or contains a cognovit or confession of judgment (for purposes other than executory process in the State of Louisiana), warrant of attorney, or other waiver of the right to notice and the opportunity to be heard in the event of suit or process thereon.

(2) Constitutes or contains an executory waiver or a limitation of exemption from attachment, execution, or other process on real or personal property held, owned by, or due to the consumer, unless the waiver applies solely to property subject to a security interest executed in connection with the obligation.

(3) Constitutes or contains an assignment of wages or other earnings unless:

(i) The assignment by its terms is revocable at the will of the debtor, or

(ii) The assignment is a payroll deduction plan or preauthorized payment plan, commencing at the time of the transaction, in which the consumer authorizes a series of wage deductions as a method of making each payment, or

(iii) The assignment applies only to wages or other earnings already earned at the time of the assignment.

(4) Constitutes or contains a nonpossessory security interest in household goods other than a purchase money security interest.

(b) [Reserved]

§ 444.3 Unfair or deceptive cosigner practices.

(a) In connection with the extension of credit to consumers in or affecting commerce, as commerce is defined in the Federal Trade Commission Act, it is:

(1) A deceptive act or practice within the meaning of section 5 of that Act for a lender or retail installment seller, directly or indirectly, to misrepresent the nature or extent of cosigner liability to any person.

(2) An unfair act or practice within the meaning of section 5 of that Act for a lender or retail installment seller, directly or indirectly, to obligate a cosigner unless the cosigner is informed prior to becoming obligated, which in the case of

open end credit shall mean prior to the time that the agreement creating the cosigner's liability for future charges is executed, of the nature of his or her liability as cosigner.

(b) Any lender or retail installment seller who complies with the preventive requirements in paragraph (c) of this section does not violate paragraph (a) of this section.

(c) To prevent these unfair or deceptive acts or practices, a disclosure, consisting of a separate document that shall contain the following statement and no other, shall be given to the cosigner prior to becoming obligated, which in the case of open end credit shall mean prior to the time that the agreement creating the cosigner's liability for future charges is executed:

NOTICE TO COSIGNER

You are being asked to guarantee this debt. Think carefully before you do. If the borrower doesn't pay the debt, you will have to. Be sure you can afford to pay if you have to, and that you want to accept this responsibility.

You may have to pay up to the full amount of the debt if the borrower does not pay. You may also have to pay late fees or collection costs, which increase this amount.

The creditor can collect this debt from you without first trying to collect from the borrower. The creditor can use the same collection methods against you that can be used against the borrower, such as suing you, garnishing your wages, etc. If this debt is ever in default, that fact may become a part of *your* credit record.

This notice is not the contract that makes you liable for the debt.

§ 444.4 Late charges.

(a) In connection with collecting a debt arising out of an extension of credit to a consumer in or affecting commerce, as commerce is defined in the Federal Trade Commission Act, it is an unfair act or practice within the meaning of section 5 of that Act for a creditor, directly or indirectly, to levy or collect any delinquency charge on a payment, which payment is otherwise a full payment for the applicable period and is paid on its due date or within an applicable grace period, when the only delinquency is attributable to late fee(s) or delinquency charge(s) assessed on earlier installment(s).

(b) For purposes of this section, *collecting a debt* means any activity other than the use of judicial process that is intended to bring about or does bring about repayment of all or part of a consumer debt.

§ 444.5 State exemptions.

(a) If, upon application to the Federal Trade Commission by an appropriate State agency, the Federal Trade Commission determines that:

(1) There is a State requirement or prohibition in effect that applies to any transaction to which a provision of this rule applies; and

(2) The State requirement or prohibition affords a level of protection to consumers that is substantially equivalent to, or greater than, the protection afforded by this rule;

Then that provision of the rule will not be in effect in that State to the extent specified by the Federal Trade Commission in its determination, for as long as the State administers and enforces the State requirement or prohibition effectively.

(b) [Reserved]

B.2 FTC Rule Concerning Preservation of Consumers' Claims and Defenses

B.2.1 The Rule

16 C.F.R. 433

§ 433.1 Definitions.

(a) *Person.* An individual, corporation, or any other business organization.

(b) *Consumer.* A natural person who seeks or acquires goods or services for personal, family, or household use.

(c) *Creditor.* A person who, in the ordinary course of business, lends purchase money or finances the sale of goods or services to consumers on a deferred payment basis; *Provided,* such person is not acting, for the purposes of a particular transaction, in the capacity of a credit card issuer.

(d) *Purchase money loan.* A cash advance which is received by a consumer in return for a "Finance Charge" within the meaning of the Truth in Lending Act and Regulation Z, which is applied, in whole or substantial part, to a purchase of goods or services from a seller who (1) refers consumers to the creditor or (2) is affiliated with the creditor by common control, contract, or business arrangement.

(e) *Financing a sale.* Extending credit to a consumer in connection with a "Credit Sale" within the meaning of the Truth in Lending Act and Regulation Z.

(f) *Contract.* Any oral or written agreement, formal or informal, between a creditor and a seller, which contemplates or provides for cooperative or concerted activity in connection with the sale of goods or services to consumers or the financing thereof.

(g) *Business arrangement.* Any understanding, procedure, course of dealing, or arrangement, formal or informal, between a creditor and a seller, in connection with the sale of goods or services to consumers or the financing thereof.

(h) *Credit card issuer.* A person who extends to cardholders the right to use a credit card in connection with purchases of goods or services.

(i) *Consumer credit contract.* Any instrument which evidences or embodies a debt arising from a "Purchase Money Loan" transaction or a "financed sale" as defined in paragraphs (d) and (e) of this section.

(j) *Seller.* A person who, in the ordinary course of business, sells or leases goods or services to consumers.

[40 Fed. Reg. 53506 (Nov. 18, 1975)]

§ 433.2 Preservation of consumers' claims and defenses, unfair or deceptive acts or practices.

In connection with any sale or lease of goods or services to consumers, in or affecting commerce as "commerce" is defined in the Federal Trade Commission Act, it is an unfair or deceptive act or practice within the meaning of Section 5 of that Act for a seller, directly or indirectly, to:

(a) Take or receive a consumer credit contract which fails to contain the following provision in at least ten point, bold face, type:

NOTICE

ANY HOLDER OF THIS CONSUMER CREDIT CONTRACT IS SUBJECT TO ALL CLAIMS AND DEFENSES WHICH THE DEBTOR COULD ASSERT AGAINST THE SELLER OF GOODS OR SERVICES

OBTAINED PURSUANT HERETO OR WITH THE PROCEEDS HEREOF. RECOVERY HEREUNDER BY THE DEBTOR SHALL NOT EXCEED AMOUNTS PAID BY THE DEBTOR HEREUNDER.

or,

(b) Accept, as full or partial payment for such sale or lease, the proceeds of any purchase money loan (as purchase money loan is defined herein), unless any consumer credit contract made in connection with such purchase money loan contains the following provision in at least ten point, bold face, type:

NOTICE

ANY HOLDER OF THIS CONSUMER CREDIT CONTRACT IS SUBJECT TO ALL CLAIMS AND DEFENSES WHICH THE DEBTOR COULD ASSERT AGAINST THE SELLER OF GOODS OR SERVICES OBTAINED WITH THE PROCEEDS HEREOF. RECOVERY HEREUNDER BY THE DEBTOR SHALL NOT EXCEED AMOUNTS PAID BY THE DEBTOR HEREUNDER.

[49 Fed. Reg. 53506 (Nov. 18, 1975); 40 Fed. Reg. 58131 (Dec. 15, 1975)]

§ 433.3 Exemption of sellers taking or receiving open end consumer credit contracts before November 1, 1977 from requirements of § 433.2(a).

(a) Any seller who has taken or received an open end consumer credit contract before November 1, 1977, shall be exempt from the requirements of 16 C.F.R. Part 433 with respect to such contract provided the contract does not cut off consumers' claims and defenses.

(b) *Definitions*. The following definitions apply to this exemption:

(1) All pertinent definitions contained in 16 C.F.R. 433.1.

(2) *Open end consumer credit contract*: a consumer credit contract pursuant to which "open end credit" is extended.

(3) *Open end credit*: consumer credit extended on an account pursuant to a plan under which a creditor may permit an applicant to make purchases or make loans, from time to time, directly from the creditor or indirectly by use of a credit card, check, or other device, as the plan may provide. The term does not include negotiated advances under an open-end real estate mortgage or a letter of credit.

(4) *Contract which does not cut off consumers' claims and defenses*: a consumer credit contract which does not constitute or contain a negotiable instrument, or contain any waiver, limitation, term, or condition which has the effect of limiting a consumer's right to assert against any holder of the contract all legally sufficient claims and defenses which the consumer could assert against the seller of goods or services purchased pursuant to the contract.

[42 Fed. Reg. 19490 (Apr. 14, 1997), *as amended at* 42 Fed. Reg. 46510 (Sept. 16, 1997)]

B.2.2 FTC Staff Letters

The FTC staff in 1999 issued two important letters concerning interpretation of the FTC Rule Concerning Preservation of Consumers' Claims and Defenses. These letters are dated September 25, 1999 and May 13, 1999. Both counter recent judicial decisions that would limit the Rule's effect.

UNITED STATES OF AMERICA
FEDERAL TRADE COMMISSION
WASHINGTON, D.C. 20580

Bureau of Consumer Protection

May 13, 1999

By Facsimile Transmission to (617) 523-7398

Jonathan Sheldon
National Consumer Law Center
18 Tremont Street, Suite 400
Boston, MA 02108

Dear Mr. Sheldon:

I am providing the following citations in response to your inquiry regarding the stated intent of the Federal Trade Commission ("Commission" or "FTC"), in adopting its Trade Regulation Rule concerning Preservation of Consumers' Claims and Defenses ("Rule"), to provide consumers with an affirmative right to bring seller-related claims against holders of credit agreements that comply with the Rule and contain the FTC-mandated "Holder" notice. At the outset, I note that the purpose of the Commission's Statement of Basis and Purpose for the Rule (Preservation of Consumers' Claims and Defenses), 40 Federal Register 53506 (November 18, 1975) ["SBP"], notes that the Commission's aim in publishing the SBP is "to state, with particularity, the purpose of each provision of the rule . . . ". SBP at 53506. This objective of the Statement of Basis and Purpose is reiterated in the "History of the Proceeding" (id. at 53506 - 53507).

Language in Chapter III, *passim*, addresses the Commission's findings and concern regarding consumers' loss of claims and defenses. See, *e.g.*, SBP at 53510.

With respect to the specific intent of the Commission to enable consumers affirmatively to assert sales-related claims, the clearest Commission statements are in Chapter VII, starting at 53522, and in Chapter VIII, A. For example, "This rule is directed at the preservation of consumer claims and defenses. It will require that all consumer credit contracts generated by consumer sales include a provision which allows the consumer to assert his sale-related claims and defenses against any holder of the credit obligation. From the consumer's standpoint, this means that a consumer can (1) defend a creditor suit for payment of an obligation by raising a valid claim against the seller as a set-off, and (2) maintain an affirmative action against a creditor who has received payments for a return of monies paid on account." SBP at 53524.

Chapter VIII, Section A., specifically states that the Commission rejected the notion that the consumer should be limited to a defense or set-off, and explains at length the reason for not adopting that limitation. (SBP at 53526 - 53527.)

Thank you for your continued interest in the Commission's work.

Very truly yours,

Christopher W. Keller
Attorney

UNITED STATES OF AMERICA
FEDERAL TRADE COMMISSION
WASHINGTON, D.C. 20580

David Medine
Associate Director
Division of Financial Practices

Direct Dial: 202-326-3224
Fax: 202-326-2558
E-mail: dmedine@ftc.gov

September 25, 1999

Jonathan Sheldon, Esq.
National Consumer Law Center
18 Tremont Street, Suite 400
Boston, Massachusetts 02108

Dear Mr. Sheldon:

This responds to your request for our views as to the application of the Commission's trade regulation rule titled *Preservation of Consumers' Claims and Defenses* (16 CFR Part 433, the "Rule" or "Holder Rule") to cases where the consumer asserts a claim that exceeds the amount remaining to be paid on an installment loan or sales contract covered by the Rule.

The Holder Rule is designed to allow consumers to assert, against third party creditors, any claims they may have against merchants from whom they buy goods or services. To that end, it requires that any seller that arranges for (or offers) credit to finance consumers' purchases of goods or services must include in its form contracts the following provision:

> ANY HOLDER OF THIS CONSUMER CREDIT CONTRACT IS SUBJECT TO ALL CLAIMS AND DEFENSES WHICH THE DEBTOR COULD ASSERT AGAINST THE SELLER OF GOODS OR SERVICES OBTAINED [PURSUANT HERETO OR] WITH THE PROCEEDS HEREOF. RECOVERY HEREUNDER BY THE DEBTOR SHALL NOT EXCEED AMOUNTS PAID BY THE DEBTOR HEREUNDER. 16 CFR § 433.2 (emphasis added).

In our view, the provision is quite clear. The consumer may recover his or her down payment (all deposits and trade-ins given to the seller),[1] and all instalment payments made pursuant to the contract, but no more. There are no other limitations on the creditor/assignee's liability under the required contractual language. The line of cases stemming from Ford Motor Co. v. Morgan, 536 N.E.2d 587, 589-90 (Mass. 1989),[2] interpreting the provision to allow a consumer an affirmative recovery only if he or she is entitled to rescission or similar relief under state law, are inconsistent

[1] Guidelines on Trade Regulation Rule Concerning Preservation of Consumers' Claims and Defenses, 41 Fed. Reg. 20022, 20023 (May 14, 1976).

[2] The court faced extensive misconduct by the debtor in that case. Mr. Morgan concealed the automobile, removed the battery, removed or deflated the tires, and surrendered the vehicle only after being found in contempt by the trial judge. He then managed to delay the sale of the vehicle, during which time the vehicle was extensively vandalized. It resulted in a total loss, which was not recoverable due to the consumer's failure to obtain insurance. 536 N.E.2d at 588.

Jonathan Sheldon, Esq.
September 25, 1999
Page 2

with our position. Although no "rescission" (or similar) limitation can be found in either the contractual provision or the text of the Holder Rule, the Morgan court (and its successors)[3] instead quote from the Statement of Basis and Purpose ("SBP") issued at the time the Rule was promulgated. The SBP asserts that an affirmative claim by a consumer (as opposed to a defense in the nature of a set-off against a creditor claim for payment of the balance due) "will only be available where a seller's breach is so substantial that rescission and restitution are justified"[4] and that consumers "will not be in a position to obtain an affirmative recovery from a creditor unless they have actually commenced payments and received little or nothing of value from the seller."[5] We believe that the point made in these SBP excerpts is simply that affirmative recoveries will be rare because they occur only if only if the consumer has a claim large enough to more than extinguish the balance due. If the Commission had meant to limit recovery to claims subject to "rescission" or similar remedy, it would have said so in the text of the Rule and drafted the contractual provision accordingly.

Our view is best stated by the court in Oxford Finance Companies v. Velez, 807 S.W.2d 460, 463 (Tex. App. 1991):

> The clear and unambiguous language of the contractual provision notifies all potential holders that, if they accept an assignment of the contract, they will be "stepping into the seller's shoes." The creditor/assignee will become "subject to" *any* claims or defenses the debtor can assert against the seller. The (provision) does not say that a seller will be liable for the buyer's damages only if the buyer received little or nothing of value under the contract. Nor does the (provision) purport to limit a creditor/assignee's liability in such fashion." (Emphasis in original)

The views set forth in this informal staff opinion letter are not binding on the Commission.

Yours truly,

David Medine

---

[3] Mount v. LaSalle Bank Lake View, 926 F. Supp. 759, 763-64 (N.D. Ill. 1996); In re Hillsborough Holdings Corp., 146 B.R. 1015, 1021 (M.D. Fla. 1992); Felde v. Chrysler Credit Corp., 580 N.E.2d 191, 197 (Ill. App. 1991); Mardis v. Ford Motor Credit Co., 642 So.2d 701, 703 (Ala.1994).

[4] 40 Fed. Reg. 53506, 53524 (Nov. 18, 1975).

[5] Id. at 53527.

B.3 FTC Rule Concerning Cooling-Off Period For Sales Made at Homes or at Certain Other Locations

16 C.F.R. 429

Source: 37 Fed. Reg. 22,934 (Oct. 26, 1972), *as amended at* 38 Fed. Reg. 30105 (Nov. 1, 1973); 38 Fed. Reg. 31828 (Nov. 19, 1973); 53 Fed. Reg. 45459 (Nov. 10, 1988); 60 Fed. Reg. 54186 (Oct. 20, 1995)

§ 429.0 Definitions.

For the purposes of this part the following definitions shall apply:

(a) *Door-to-Door Sale*—A sale, lease, or rental of consumer goods or services with a purchase price of $25 or more, whether under single or multiple contracts, in which the seller or his representative personally solicits the sale, including those in response to or following an invitation by the buyer, and the buyer's agreement or offer to purchase is made at a place other than the place of business of the seller (*e.g.*, sales at the buyer's residence or at facilities rented on a temporary or short-term basis, such as hotel or motel rooms, convention centers, fairgrounds and restaurants, or sales at the buyer's workplace or in dormitory lounges). The term *door-to-door sale* does not include a transaction:

(1) Made pursuant to prior negotiations in the course of a visit by the buyer to a retail business establishment having a fixed permanent location where the goods are exhibited or the services are offered for sale on a continuing basis; or

(2) In which the consumer is accorded the right of rescission by the provisions of the Consumer Credit Protection Act (15 U.S.C. 1635) or regulations issued pursuant thereto; or

(3) In which the buyer has initiated the contact and the goods or services are needed to meet a bona fide immediate personal emergency of the buyer, and the buyer furnishes the seller with a separate dated and signed personal statement in the buyer's handwriting describing the situation requiring immediate remedy and expressly acknowledging and waiving the right to cancel the sale within 3 business days; or

(4) Conducted and consummated entirely by mail or telephone; and without any other contact between the buyer and the seller or its representative prior to delivery of the goods or performance of the services; or

(5) In which the buyer has initiated the contact and specifically requested the seller to visit the buyer's home for the purpose of repairing or performing maintenance upon the buyer's personal property. If, in the course of such a visit, the seller sells the buyer the right to receive additional services or goods other than replacement parts necessarily used in performing the maintenance or in making the repairs, the sale of those additional goods or services would not fall within this exclusion; or

(6) Pertaining to the sale or rental of real property, to the sale of insurance, or to the sale of securities or commodities by a broker-dealer registered with the Securities and Exchange Commission.

(b) *Consumer Goods or Services*—Goods or services purchased, leased, or rented primarily for personal, family, or household purposes, including courses of instruction or training regardless of the purpose for which they are taken.

(c) *Seller*—Any person, partnership, corporation, or association engaged in the door-to-door sale of consumer goods or services.

(d) *Place of Business*—The main or permanent branch office or local address of a seller.

(e) *Purchase Price*—The total price paid or to be paid for the consumer goods or services, including all interest and service charges.

(f) *Business Day*—Any calendar day except Sunday or any federal holiday (*e.g.*, New Year's Day, President's Day, Martin Luther King's Birthday, Memorial Day, Independence Day, Labor Day, Columbus Day, Veterans' Day, Thanksgiving Day, and Christmas Day.)

[60 Fed. Reg. 54186 (Oct. 20, 1995)]

§ 429.1 The Rule.

In connection with any door-to-door sale, it constitutes an unfair and deceptive act or practice for any seller to:

(a) Fail to furnish the buyer with a fully completed receipt or copy of any contract pertaining to such sale at the time of its execution, which is in the same language, e.g., Spanish, as that principally used in the oral sales presentation and which shows the date of the transaction and contains the name and address of the seller, and in immediate proximity to the space reserved in the contract for the signature of the buyer or on the front page of the receipt if a contract is not used and in bold face type of a minimum size of 10 points, a statement in substantially the following form:

"You, the buyer, may cancel this transaction at any time prior to midnight of the third business day after the date of this transaction. See the attached notice of cancellation form for an explanation of this right."

The seller may select the method of providing the buyer with the duplicate notice of cancellation form set forth in paragraph (b) of this section, *provided however*, that in the event of cancellation the buyer must be able to retain a complete copy of the contract or receipt. Furthermore, if both forms are not attached to the contract or receipt, the seller is required to alter the last sentence in the statement above to conform to the actual location of the forms.

(b) Fail to furnish each buyer, at the time the buyer signs the door-to-door sales contract or otherwise agrees to buy consumer goods or services from the seller, a completed form in duplicate, captioned either "NOTICE OF RIGHT TO CANCEL" or "NOTICE OF CANCELLATION," which shall (where applicable) contain in ten point bold face type the following information and statements in the same language, *e.g.*, Spanish, as that used in the contract.

Notice of Cancellation

[enter date of transaction]

____

(Date)

You may CANCEL this transaction, without any Penalty or Obligation, within THREE BUSINESS DAYS from the above date.

If you cancel, any property traded in, any payments made by you under the contract or sale, and any negotiable instrument executed by you will be returned within TEN BUSINESS DAYS following receipt by the seller of your cancellation notice, and any security interest arising out of the transaction will be canceled.

If you cancel, you must make available to the seller at your residence, in substantially as good condition as when received, any goods delivered to you under this contract or sale, or you may, if you wish, comply with the instructions of the seller regarding the return shipment of the goods at the seller's expense and risk.

If you do make the goods available to the seller and the seller does not pick them up within 20 days of the date of your Notice of Cancellation, you may retain or dispose of the goods without any further obligation. If you fail to make the goods available to the seller, or if you agree to return the goods to the seller and fail to do so, then you remain liable for performance of all obligations under the contract.

To cancel this transaction, mail or deliver a signed and dated copy of this Cancellation Notice or any other written notice, or send a telegram, to [*Name of seller*], at [*address of seller's place of business*] NOT LATER THAN MIDNIGHT OF [*date*].

I HEREBY CANCEL THIS TRANSACTION.

(Date)____________________

(Buyer's signature)____________________

(c) Fail, before furnishing copies of the "Notice of Cancellation" to the buyer, to complete both copies by entering the name of the seller, the address of the seller's place of business, the date of the transaction, and the date, not earlier than the third business day following the date of the transaction, by which the buyer may give notice of cancellation.

(d) Include in any door-to-door contract or receipt any confession of judgment or any waiver of any of the rights to which the buyer is entitled under this section including specifically the buyer's right to cancel the sale in accordance with the provisions of this section.

(e) Fail to inform each buyer orally, at the time the buyer signs the contract or purchases the goods or services, of the buyer's right to cancel.

(f) Misrepresent in any manner the buyer's right to cancel.

(g) Fail or refuse to honor any valid notice of cancellation by a buyer and within 10 business days after the receipt of such notice, to: (i) Refund all payments made under the contract or sale; (ii) return any goods or property traded in, in substantially as good condition as when received by the seller; (iii) cancel and return any negotiable instrument executed by the buyer in connection with the contract or sale and take any action necessary or appropriate to terminate promptly any security interest created in the transaction.

(h) Negotiate, transfer, sell, or assign any note or other evidence of indebtedness to a finance company or other third party prior to midnight of the fifth business day following the day the contract was signed or the goods or services were purchased.

(i) Fail, within 10 business days of receipt of the buyer's notice of cancellation, to notify the buyer whether the seller intends to repossess or to abandon any shipped or delivered goods.

[37 Fed. Reg. 22934 (Oct. 26, 1972), *as amended at* 38 Fed. Reg. 30105 (Nov. 1, 1973); 38 Fed. Reg. 31828 (Nov. 19, 1973); 53 Fed. Reg. 45459 (Nov. 10, 1988); 60 Fed. Reg. 54186 (Oct. 20, 1995)]

§ 429.2 Effect on State laws and municipal ordinances.

(a) The Commission is cognizant of the significant burden imposed upon door-to-door sellers by the various and often inconsistent State laws that provide the buyer the right to cancel a door-to-door sales transaction. However, it does not believe that this constitutes sufficient justification for preempting all of the provisions of such laws and the ordinances of the political subdivisions of the various States. The rulemaking record in this proceeding supports the view that the joint and coordinated efforts of both the Commission and State and local officials are required to insure that consumers who have purchased from a door-to-door seller something they do not want, do not need, or cannot afford, be accorded a unilateral right to rescind, without penalty, their agreement to purchase those goods or services.

(b) This part will not be construed to annul, or exempt any seller from complying with, the laws of any State or the ordinances of a political subdivision thereof that regulate door-to-door sales, except to the extent that such laws or ordinances, if they permit door-to-door selling, are directly inconsistent with the provisions of this part. Such laws or ordinances which do not accord the buyer, with respect to the particular transaction, a right to cancel a door-to-door sale that is substantially the same or greater than that provided in this part, which permit the imposition of any fee or penalty on the buyer for the exercise of such right, or which do not provide for giving the buyer a notice of the right to cancel the transaction in substantially the same form and manner provided for in this part, are among those which will be considered directly inconsistent.

[60 Fed. Reg. 54187 (Oct. 20, 1995)]

§ 429.3 Exemptions.

(a) The requirements of this part do not apply for sellers of automobiles, vans, trucks or other motor vehicles sold at auctions, tent sales or other temporary places of business, provided that the seller is a seller of vehicles with a permanent place of business.

(b) The requirements of this part do not apply for sellers of arts or crafts sold at fairs or similar places.

[60 Fed. Reg. 54187 (Oct. 20, 1995)]

B.4 FTC Mail or Telephone Order Merchandise Rule

16 C.F.R. 435

Source: 40 Fed. Reg. 29492 (Oct. 22, 1975), *as amended at* 58 Fed. Reg. 49121 (Sept. 21, 1993); 60 Fed. Reg. 56949 (Nov. 13, 1995)

§ 435.1 The Rule.

In connection with mail or telephone order sales in or affecting commerce, as "commerce" is defined in the Federal Trade Commission Act, it constitutes an unfair method of competition, and an unfair or deceptive act and practice for a seller:

(a)(1) To solicit any order for the sale of merchandise to be ordered by the buyer through the mails or by telephone unless, at the time of the solicitation, the seller has a reasonable basis to expect that it will be able to ship any ordered merchandise to the buyer:

(i) Within that time clearly and conspicuously stated in any such solicitation, or

(ii) if no time is clearly and conspicuously stated, within thirty (30) days after receipt of a properly completed order from the buyer. *Provided, however,* where, at the time the merchandise is ordered the buyer applied to the seller for credit to pay for the merchandise in whole or in part, the seller shall have 50 days, rather than 30 days, to perform the actions required in § 435.1(a)(1)(ii) of this part.

(2) To provide any buyer with any revised shipping date, as provided in paragraph (b) of this section, unless, at the time any such revised shipping date is provided, the seller has a reasonable basis for making such representation regarding a definite revised shipping date.

(3) To inform any buyer that it is unable to make any representation regarding the length of any delay unless

(i) the seller has a reasonable basis for so informing the buyer and

(ii) the seller informs the buyer of the reason or reasons for the delay.

(4) In any action brought by the Federal Trade Commission, alleging a violation of this part, the failure of a respondent-seller to have records or other documentary proof establishing its use of systems and procedures which assure the shipment of merchandise in the ordinary course of business within any applicable time set forth in this part will create a rebuttable presumption that the seller lacked a reasonable basis for any expectation of shipment within said applicable time.

(b)(1) Where a seller is unable to ship merchandise within the applicable time set forth in paragraph (a)(1) of this section, to fail to offer to the buyer, clearly and conspicuously and without prior demand, an option either to consent to a delay in shipping or to cancel his order and receive a prompt refund. Said offer shall be made within a reasonable time after the seller first becomes aware of its inability to ship within the applicable time set forth in paragraph (a)(1) of this section, but in no event later than said applicable time.

(i) Any offer to the buyer of such an option shall fully inform the buyer regarding the buyer's right to cancel the order and to obtain a prompt refund and shall provide a definite revised shipping date, but where the seller lacks a reasonable basis for providing a definite revised shipping date the notice shall inform the buyer that the seller is unable to make any representation regarding the length of the delay.

(ii) Where the seller has provided a definite revised shipping date which is thirty (30) days or less later than the applicable time set forth in paragraph (a)(1) of this section, the offer of said option shall expressly inform the buyer that, unless the seller receives, prior to shipment and prior to the expiration of the definite revised shipping date, a response from the buyer rejecting the delay and cancelling the order, the buyer will be deemed to have consented to a delayed shipment on or before the definite revised shipping date.

(iii) Where the seller has provided a definite revised shipping date which is more than thirty (30) days later than the applicable time set forth in paragraph (a)(1) of this section or where the seller is unable to provide a definite revised shipping date and therefore informs the buyer that it is unable to make any representation regarding the length of the delay, the offer of said option shall also expressly inform the buyer that the buyer's order will automatically be deemed to have been cancelled unless:

(A) The seller has shipped the merchandise within thirty (30) days of the applicable time set forth in paragraph (a)(1) of this section, and has received no cancellation prior to shipment, or

(B) the seller has received from the buyer within thirty (30) days of said applicable time, a response specifically consenting to said shipping delay. Where the seller informs the buyer that it is unable to make any representation regarding the length of the delay, the buyer shall be expressly informed that, should the buyer consent to an indefinite delay, the buyer will have a continuing right to cancel the buyer's order at any time after the applicable time set forth in paragraph (a)(1) of this section by so notifying the seller prior to actual shipment.

(iv) Nothing in this paragraph shall prohibit a seller who furnishes a definite revised shipping date pursuant to paragraph (b)(1)(i) of this section, from requesting, simultaneously with or at any time subsequent to the offer of an option pursuant to paragraph (b)(1) of this section, the buyer's express consent to a further unanticipated delay beyond the definite revised shipping date in the form of a response from the buyer specifically consenting to said further delay. *Provided, however*, that where the seller solicits consent to an unanticipated indefinite delay the solicitation shall expressly inform the buyer that, should the buyer so consent to an indefinite delay, the buyer shall have a continuing right to cancel the buyer's order at any time after the definite revised shipping date by so notifying the seller prior to actual shipment.

(2) Where a seller is unable to ship merchandise on or before the definite revised shipping date provided under paragraph (b)(1)(i) of this section and consented to by the buyer pursuant to paragraph (b)(1)(ii) or (iii) of this section, to fail to offer to the buyer, clearly and conspicuously and without prior demand, a renewed option either to consent to a further delay or to cancel the order and to receive a prompt refund. Said offer shall be made within a reasonable time after the seller first becomes aware of its inability to ship before the said definite revised date, but in no event later than the expiration of the definite revised shipping date: *Provided, however*, that where the seller previously has obtained the buyer's express consent to an unanticipated delay until a specific date beyond the definite revised shipping date, pursuant to paragraph (b)(1)(iv) of this section or to a further delay until a specific date beyond the definite revised shipping date pursuant to this paragraph (b)(2) of this section, that date to which the buyer has expressly consented shall supersede the definite revised shipping date for purposes of paragraph (b)(2) of this section.

(i) Any offer to the buyer of said renewed option shall provide the buyer with a new definite revised shipping date, but where the seller lacks a reasonable basis for providing a new definite revised shipping date, the notice shall inform the buyer that the seller is unable to make any representation regarding the length of the further delay.

(ii) The offer of a renewed option shall expressly inform the buyer that, unless the seller receives, prior to the expiration of the old definite revised shipping date or any date superseding the old definite revised shipping date, notification from the buyer specifically consenting to the further delay, the buyer will be deemed to have rejected any further delay, and to have cancelled the order if the seller is in fact unable to ship prior to the expiration of the old definite revised shipping date or any date superseding the old definite revised shipping date: *Provided, however*, that where the seller offers the buyer the option to consent to an indefinite delay the offer shall expressly inform the buyer that, should the buyer so consent to an indefinite delay, the buyer shall have a continuing right to cancel the buyer's order at any time after the old definite revised shipping date or any date superseding the old definite revised shipping date.

(iii) This paragraph (b)(2) shall not apply to any situation where a seller, pursuant to the provisions of paragraph (b)(1)(iv) of this section, has previously obtained consent from the buyer to an indefinite extension beyond the first revised shipping date.

(3) Wherever a buyer has the right to exercise any option under this part or to cancel an order by so notifying the seller prior to shipment, to fail to furnish the buyer with adequate means, at the seller's expense, to exercise such option or to notify the seller regarding cancellation.

Nothing in paragraph (b) of this section shall prevent a seller, where it is unable to make shipment within the time set forth in paragraph (a)(1) of this section or within a delay period consented to by the buyer, from deciding to consider the order cancelled and providing the buyer with notice of said decision within a reasonable time after it becomes aware of said inability to ship, together with a prompt refund.

(c) To fail to deem an order cancelled and to make a prompt refund to the buyer whenever:

(1) The seller receives, prior to the time of shipment, notification from the buyer cancelling the order pursuant to any option, renewed option or continuing option under this part;

(2) The seller has, pursuant to paragraph (b)(1)(iii) of this section, provided the buyer with a definite revised shipping date which is more than thirty (30) days later than the applicable time set forth in paragraph (a)(1) of this section or has notified the buyer that it is unable to make any representation regarding the length of the delay and the seller

(i) has not shipped the merchandise within thirty (30) days of the applicable time set forth in paragraph (a) (1) of this section, and

(ii) has not received the buyer's express consent to said shipping delay within said thirty (30) days;

(3) The seller is unable to ship within the applicable time set forth in paragraph (b)(2) of this section, and has not received, within the said applicable time, the buyer's consent to any further delay;

(4) The seller has notified the buyer of its inability to make shipment and has indicated its decision not to ship the merchandise;

(5) The seller fails to offer the option prescribed in paragraph (b)(1) of this section and has not shipped the merchandise within the applicable time set forth in paragraph (a)(1) of this section.

(d) In any action brought by the Federal Trade Commission, alleging a violation of this part, the failure of a respondent-seller to have records or other documentary proof establishing his use of systems and procedures which assure compliance, in the ordinary course of business, with any requirement of paragraphs (b) or (c) of this section will create a rebuttable presumption that the seller failed to comply with said requirements.

§ 435.2 Definitions.

For purposes of this part:

(a) *Mail or telephone order sales* shall mean sales in which the buyer has ordered merchandise from the seller by mail or telephone, regardless of the method of payment or the method used to solicit the order.

(b) *Telephone* refers to any direct or indirect use of the telephone to order merchandise, regardless of whether the telephone is activated by, or the language used is that of human beings, machines, or both.

(c) *Shipment* shall mean the act by which the merchandise is physically placed in the possession of the carrier.

(d) *Receipt of a properly completed order* shall mean, where the buyer tenders full or partial payment in the proper amount in the form of cash, check, money order or authorization from the buyer to charge an existing charge account, the time at which the seller receives both said payment and an order from the buyer containing all the information needed by the seller to process and ship the order. *Provided, however,* that where the seller receives notice that the check or money order tendered by the buyer has been dishonored or that the buyer does not qualify for a credit sale, *receipt of a properly completed order* shall mean the time at which:

(i) the seller receives notice that a check or money order for the proper amount tendered by the buyer has been honored,

(ii) the buyer tenders cash in the proper amount, or

(iii) the seller receives notice that the buyer qualifies for a credit sale.

(e) *Refund* shall mean:

(1) Where the buyer tendered full payment for the unshipped merchandise in the form of cash, check or money order, a return of the amount tendered in the form of cash, check or money order;

(2) Where there is a credit sale:

(i) And the seller is a creditor, a copy of a credit memorandum or the like or an account statement reflecting the removal or absence of any remaining charge incurred as a result of the sale from the buyer's account;

(ii) And a third party is the creditor, a copy of an appropriate credit memorandum or the like to the third party creditor which will remove the charge from the buyer's account or a statement from the seller acknowledging the cancellation of the order and representing that it has not taken any action regarding the order which will result in a charge to the buyer's account with the third party;

(iii) And the buyer tendered partial payment for the unshipped merchandise in the form of cash, check or money order, a return of the amount tendered in the form of cash, check or money order.

(f) *Prompt refund* shall mean:

(1) Where a refund is made pursuant to paragraphs (e)(1) or (2)(iii) of this section, a refund sent to the buyer by first class mail within seven (7) working days of the date on which the buyer's right to refund vests under the provisions of this part;

(2) Where a refund is made pursuant to paragraph (e)(2)(i) or (ii) of this section, a refund sent to the buyer by first class mail within one (1) billing cycle from the date on which the buyer's right to refund vests under the provisions of this part.

(g) The *time of solicitation* of an order shall mean that time when the seller has:

(1) Mailed or otherwise disseminated the solicitation to a prospective purchaser,

(2) Made arrangements for an advertisement containing the solicitation to appear in a newspaper, magazine or the like or on radio or television which cannot be changed or cancelled without incurring substantial expense, or

(3) Made arrangements for the printing of a catalog, brochure or the like which cannot be changed without incurring substantial expense, in which the solicitation in question forms an insubstantial part.

[58 Fed. Reg. 49121 (Sept. 21, 1993), *as amended at* 60 Fed. Reg. 56950 (Nov. 13, 1995)]

§ 435.3 Limited applicability.

(a) This part shall not apply to:

(1) Subscriptions, such as magazine sales, ordered for serial delivery, after the initial shipment is made in compliance with this part.

(2) Orders for seeds and growing plants.

(3) Orders made on a collect-on-delivery (C.O.D.) basis.

(4) Transactions governed by the Federal Trade Commission's Trade Regulation Rule entitled "Use of Negative Option Plans by Sellers in Commerce," 16 C.F.R. part 425.

(b) By taking action in this area:

(1) The Federal Trade Commission does not intend to preempt action in the same area, which is not inconsistent with this part, by any State, municipal or other local government. This part does not annul or diminish any rights or remedies provided to consumers by any State law, municipal ordinance, or other local regulation, insofar as those rights or remedies are equal to or greater than those provided by this part. In addition, this part does not supersede those provisions of any State law, municipal ordinance, or other local regulation which impose obligations or liabilities upon sellers, when sellers subject to this part are not in compliance therewith.

(2) This part does supersede those provisions of any State law, municipal ordinance, or other local regulation which are inconsistent with this part to the extent that those provisions do not provide the buyer with rights which are equal to or greater than those rights granted a buyer by this part. This part also supersedes those provisions of any State law, municipal ordinance, or other local regulation requiring that a buyer be notified of a right which is the same as a right provided by this part but requiring that a buyer be given notice of this right in a language, form, or manner which is different in any way from that required by this part. In those instances where any State law, municipal ordinance, or other local regulation contains provisions, some but not all of which are partially or completely superseded by this part, the provisions or portions of those provisions which have not been superseded retain their full force and effect.

(c) If any provision of this part, or its application to any person, partnership, corporation, act or practice is held invalid, the remainder of this part or the application of the provision to any other person, partnership, corporation, act or other practice shall not be affected thereby.

§ 435.4 Effective date of the rule.

The original rule, which became effective 100 days after its promulgation on October 22, 1975, remains in effect. The amended rule, as set forth in this part, became effective March 1, 1994.

B.5 FTC Funeral Industry Practices Rule

16 C.F.R. 453

Source: 47 Fed. Reg. 42299 (Sept. 24, 1982), *as amended at* 49 Fed. Reg. 563 (Jan. 5, 1984); 54 Fed. Reg. 19360 (May 5, 1989); 59 Fed. Reg. 1611 (Jan. 11, 1994)

§ 453.1 Definitions.

(a) *Alternative container.* An "alternative container" is an unfinished wood box or other non-metal receptacle or enclosure, without ornamentation or a fixed interior lining, which is designed for the encasement of human remains and which is made of fiberboard, pressed-wood, composition materials (with or without an outside covering) or like materials.

(b) *Cash advance item.* A "cash advance item" is any item of service or merchandise described to a purchaser as a "cash advance," "accommodation," "cash disbursement," or similar term. A cash advance item is also any item obtained from a third party and paid for by the funeral provider on the purchaser's behalf. Cash advance items may include, but are not limited to, the following items: cemetery or crematory services; pallbearers; public transportation; clergy honoraria; flowers; musicians or singers; nurses; obituary notices; gratuities and death certificates.

(c) *Casket.* A "casket" is a rigid container which is designed for the encasement of human remains and which is usually constructed of wood, metal, fiberglass, plastic or like material, and ornamented and lined with fabric.

(d) *Commission.* "Commission" refers to the Federal Trade Commission.

(e) *Cremation.* "Cremation" is a heating process which incinerates human remains.

(f) *Crematory.* A "crematory" is any person, partnership or corporation that performs cremation and sells funeral goods.

(g) *Direct cremation.* A "direct cremation" is a disposition of human remains by cremation, without formal viewing, visitation, or ceremony with the body present.

(h) *Funeral goods.* "Funeral goods" are the goods which are sold or offered for sale directly to the public for use in connection with funeral services.

(i) *Funeral provider.* A "funeral provider" is any person, partnership or corporation that sells or offers to sell funeral goods and funeral services to the public.

(j) *Funeral services.* "Funeral services" are any services which may be used to:

(1) care for and prepare deceased human bodies for burial, cremation or other final disposition; and

(2) arrange, supervise or conduct the funeral ceremony or the final disposition of deceased human bodies.

(k) *Immediate burial.* An "immediate burial" is a disposition of human remains by burial, without formal viewing, visitation, or ceremony with the body present, except for a grave-side service.

(l) *Memorial service.* A "memorial service" is a ceremony commemorating the deceased without the body present.

(m) *Funeral ceremony.* A "funeral ceremony" is a service commemorating the deceased with the body present.

(n) *Outer burial container.* An "outer burial container" is any container which is designed for placement in the grave around the casket including, but not limited to, containers commonly known as burial vaults, grave boxes, and grave liners.

(o) *Person.* A "person" is any individual, partnership, corporation, association, government or governmental subdivision or agency, or other entity.

(p) *Services of funeral director and staff.* The "services of funeral director and staff" are the services, not included in prices of other categories in § 453.2(b)(4) that are furnished by a funeral provider in arranging any funeral, such as conducting the arrangements conference, planning the funeral, obtaining necessary permits, and placing obituary notices.

§ 453.2 Price disclosures.

(a) *Unfair or deceptive acts or practices.* In selling or offering to sell funeral goods or funeral services to the public, it is an unfair or deceptive act or practice for a funeral provider to fail to furnish accurate price information disclosing the cost to the purchaser for each of the specific funeral goods and funeral services used in connection with the disposition of deceased human bodies, including at least the price of embalming, transportation of remains, use of facilities, caskets, outer burial containers, immediate burials, or direct cremations, to persons inquiring about the purchase of funerals. Any funeral provider who complies with the preventive requirements in paragraph (b) of this section is not engaged in the unfair or deceptive acts or practices defined here.

(b) *Preventive requirements.* To prevent these unfair or deceptive acts or practices, as well as the unfair or deceptive acts or practices defined in § 453.4(b)(1), funeral providers must:

(1) *Telephone price disclosures.* Tell persons who ask by telephone about the funeral provider's offerings or prices any accurate information from the price lists in paragraphs (b)(2) through (4) of this section and any other readily available information which reasonably answers the question.

(2) *Casket price list.* (i) Give a printed or typewritten price list to people who inquire in person about the offerings or prices of caskets or alternative containers. The funeral provider must offer the list upon beginning discussion of, but in any event before showing caskets. The list must contain at least the retail prices of all caskets and alternative containers offered which do not require special ordering, enough information to identify each, and the effective date for the price list. In lieu of a written list, other formats, such as notebooks, brochures, or charts may be used if they contain the same information as would the printed or typewritten list, and display it in a clear and conspicuous manner. *Provided, however*, that funeral providers do not have to make a casket price list available if the funeral providers place on the general price list, specified in paragraph (b)(4) of this section, the information required by this section.

(ii) Place on the list, however produced, the name of the funeral provider's place of business and a caption describing the list as a "casket price list."

(3) *Outer burial container price list.* (i) Give a printed or typewritten price list to persons who inquire in person about outer burial container offerings or prices. The funeral provider must offer the list upon beginning discussion of, but in any event before showing the containers. The list must contain at least the retail prices of all outer burial containers offered which do not require special ordering, enough information to identify each container, and the effective date for the prices listed. In lieu of a written list, the funeral provider may use other formats, such as notebooks, brochures, or charts, if they contain the same information as the printed or typewritten list, and display it in a clear and conspicuous manner. *Provided, however*, that funeral providers do not have to make an outer burial container price list available if the funeral providers place on the general price list, specified in paragraph (b)(4) of this section, the information required by this section.

(ii) Place on the list, however produced, the name of the funeral provider's place of business and a caption describing the list as an "outer burial container price list."

(4) *General price list.* (i)(A) Give a printed or typewritten price list for retention to persons who

inquire in person about the funeral goods, funeral services or prices of funeral goods or funeral services offered by the funeral provider. The funeral provider must give the list upon beginning discussion of any of the following:

(1) the prices of funeral goods or funeral services;

(2) the overall type of funeral service or disposition; or

(3) specific funeral goods or funeral services offered by the provider.

(B) The requirement in paragraph (b)(4)(i)(A) of this section applies whether the discussion takes place in the funeral home or elsewhere. *Provided, however*, that when the deceased is removed for transportation to the funeral home, an in-person request at that time for authorization to embalm, required by § 453.5(a)(2), does not, by itself, trigger the requirement to offer the general price list if the provider in seeking prior embalming approval discloses that embalming is not required by law except in certain special cases, if any. Any other discussion during that time about prices or the selection of funeral goods triggers the requirement under paragraph (b)(4)(i)(A) of this section to give consumers a general price list.

(C) The list required in paragraph (b)(4)(i)(A) of this section must contain at least the following information:

(1) the name, address, and telephone number of the funeral provider's place of business;

(2) a caption describing the list as a "general price list";

(3) the effective date for the price list;

(ii) Include on the price list, in any order, the retail prices (expressed either as the flat fee, or as the price per hour, mile or other unit of computation) and the other information specified below for at least each of the following items, if offered for sale:

(A) Forwarding of remains to another funeral home, together with a list of the services provided for any quoted price;

(B) Receiving remains from another funeral home, together with a list of the services provided for any quoted price;

(C) The price range for the direct cremations offered by the funeral provider, together with:

(1) A separate price for a direct cremation where the purchaser provides the container;

(2) separate prices for each direct cremation offered including an unfinished wood box or alternative container; and

(3) a description of the services and container (where applicable), included in each price;

(D) The price range for the immediate burials offered by the funeral provider, together with:

(1) A separate price for an immediate burial where the purchaser provides the casket;

(2) separate prices for each immediate burial offered including a casket or alternative container; and

(3) a description of the services and container (where applicable) included in that price;

(E) Transfer of remains to funeral home;

(F) Embalming;

(G) Other preparation of the body;

(H) Use of facilities and staff for viewing;

(I) Use of facilities and staff for funeral ceremony;

(J) Use of facilities and staff for memorial service;

(K) Use of equipment and staff for grave-side service;

(L) Hearse; and

(M) Limousine.

(iii) Include on the price list, in any order, the following information:

(A) Either of the following:

(1) the price range for the caskets offered by the funeral provider, together with the statement: "A complete price list will be provided at the funeral home."; or

(2) the prices of individual caskets, disclosed in the manner specified by paragraph (b)(2)(i) of this section; and

(B) Either of the following:

(1) the price range for the outer burial containers offered by the funeral provider, together with the statement: "A complete price list will be provided at the funeral home."; or

(2) the prices of individual outer burial containers, disclosed in the manner specified by paragraph (b)(3)(i) of this section; and

(C) Either of the following:

(1) the price for the basic services of funeral director and staff, together with a list of the principal basic services provided for any quoted price and, if the charge cannot be declined by the purchaser, the statement: "This fee for our basic services will be added to the total cost of the funeral arrangements you select. (This fee is already included in our charges for direct cremations, immediate burials, and forwarding or receiving remains.)". If the charge cannot be declined by the purchaser, the quoted price shall include all charges for the recovery of unallocated funeral provider overhead, and funeral providers may include in the required disclosure the phrase "and overhead" after the word "services"; or

(2) the following statement: "Please note that a fee of (*specify dollar amount*) for the use of our basic services is included in the price of our caskets. This same fee shall added to the total cost of your funeral arrangements if you provide the casket. Our services include (specify)." The fee shall include all charges for the recovery of unallocated funeral provider overhead, and the funeral providers may include in the required disclosure the phrase "and overhead" after the word "services." The statement must be placed on the general price list together with casket price range, required by paragraph (b)(4)(iii)(A)(1) of this section, or together with the prices of individual caskets, required by (b)(4)(iii)(A)(2) of this section.

(iv) The services fee permitted by § 453.2(b)(4)(iii)(C)(1) or (C)(2) is the only funeral provider fee for services, facilities or unallocated overhead permitted by this part to be non-declinable, unless otherwise required by law.

(5) *Statement of funeral goods and services selected.* (i) Give an itemized written statement for retention to each person who arranges a funeral or other disposition of human remains, at the conclusion of the discussion of arrangements. The statement must list at least the following information:

(A) The funeral goods and funeral services selected by that person and the prices to be paid for each of them;

(B) Specifically itemized cash advance items. (These prices must be given to the extent then known or reasonably ascertainable. If the prices are not known or reasonably ascertainable, a good faith estimate shall be given and a written statement of the actual charges shall be provided before the final bill is paid.); and

(C) The total cost of the goods and services selected.

(ii) The information required by this paragraph (b)(5) of this section may be included on any contract, statement, or other document which the funeral provider would otherwise provide at the conclusion of discussion of arrangements.

(6) *Other pricing methods.* Funeral providers may give persons any other price information, in any other format, in addition to that required by paragraphs (b)(2), (3), and (4) of this section so long as the statement required by § 453.2(b)(5) is given when required by the rule.

§ 453.3 Misrepresentations.

(a) *Embalming Provisions*—(1) *Deceptive acts or practices.* In selling or offering to sell funeral goods or funeral services to the public, it is a deceptive act or practice for a funeral provider to:

(i) Represent that State or local law requires that a deceased person be embalmed when such is not the case;

(ii) Fail to disclose that embalming is not required by law except in certain special cases.

(2) *Preventive requirements.* To prevent these deceptive acts or practices, as well as the unfair or deceptive acts or practices defined in §§ 453.4(b)(1) and 453.5(2), funeral providers must:

(i) Not represent that a deceased person is required to be embalmed for:

(A) Direct cremation;

(B) Immediate burial; or

(C) A closed casket funeral without viewing or visitation when refrigeration is available and when State or local law does not require embalming; and

(ii) Place the following disclosure on the general price list, required by § 453.2(b)(4), in immediate conjunction with the price shown for embalming: "Except in certain special cases, embalming is not required by law. Embalming may be necessary, however, if you select certain funeral arrangements, such as a funeral with viewing. If you do not want embalming, you usually have the right to choose an arrangement that does not require you to pay for it, such as direct cremation or immediate burial." The phrase "except in certain special cases" need not be included in this disclosure if State or local law in the area(s) where the provider does business does not require embalming under any circumstances.

(b) *Casket for cremation provisions.*—(1) *Deceptive acts or practices.* In selling or offering to sell funeral goods or funeral services to the public, it is a deceptive act or practice for a funeral provider to:

(i) Represent that State or local law requires a casket for direct cremations;

(ii) Represent that a casket is required for direct cremations.

(2) *Preventive requirements.* To prevent these deceptive acts or practices, as well as the unfair or deceptive acts or practices defined in § 453.4(a)(1), funeral providers must place the following disclosure in immediate conjunction with the price range shown for direct cremations: "If you want to arrange a direct cremation, you can use an alternative container. Alternative containers encase the body and can be made of materials like fiberboard or composition materials (with or without an outside covering). The containers we provide are (specify containers)." This disclosure only has to be placed on the general price list if the funeral provider arranges direct cremations.

(c) *Outer burial container provisions*—(1) *Deceptive acts or practices.* In selling or offering to sell funeral goods and funeral services to the public, it is a deceptive act or practice for a funeral provider to:

(i) Represent that State or local laws or regulations, or particular cemeteries, require outer burial containers when such is not the case;

(ii) Fail to disclose to persons arranging funerals that State law does not require the purchase of an outer burial container.

(2) *Preventive requirement.* To prevent these deceptive acts or practices, funeral providers must place the following disclosure on the outer burial container price list, required by § 453.2(b)(3)(i), or, if the prices of outer burial containers are listed on the general price list, required by § 453.2(b)(4), in immediate conjunction with those prices: "In most areas of the country, State or local law does not require that you buy a container to surround the casket in the grave. However, many cemeteries ask that you have such a container so that the grave will not sink in. Either a grave liner or a burial vault will satisfy these requirements." The phrase "in most areas of the country" need not be included in this disclosure if State or local law in the area(s) where the provider does business does not require a container to surround the casket in the grave.

(d) *General provisions on legal and cemetery requirements*—(1) *Deceptive acts or practices.* In selling or offering to sell funeral goods or funeral services to the public, it is a deceptive act or practice for funeral providers to represent that federal, state, or local laws, or particular cemeteries or crematories, require the purchase of any funeral goods or funeral services when such is not the case.

(2) *Preventive requirements.* To prevent these deceptive acts or practices, as well as the deceptive acts or practices identified in §§ 453.3(a)(1), 453.3(b)(1), and 453.3(c)(1), funeral providers must identify and briefly describe in writing on the statement of funeral goods and services selected (required by § 453.2(b)(5)) any legal, cemetery, or crematory requirement which the funeral provider represents to persons as compelling the purchase of funeral goods or funeral services for the funeral which that person is arranging.

(e) *Provisions on preservative and protective value claims.* In selling or offering to sell funeral goods or funeral services to the public, it is a deceptive act or practice for a funeral provider to:

(1) Represent that funeral goods or funeral services will delay the natural decomposition of human remains for a long-term or indefinite time;

(2) Represent that funeral goods have protective features or will protect the body from grave site substances, when such is not the case.

(f) *Cash advance provisions*—(1) *Deceptive acts or practices.* In selling or offering to sell funeral goods or funeral services to the public, it is a deceptive act or practice for a funeral provider to:

(i) Represent that the price charged for a cash advance item is the same as the cost to the funeral provider for the item when such is not the case;

(ii) Fail to disclose to persons arranging funerals that the price being charged for a cash advance item is not the same as the cost to the funeral provider for the item when such is the case.

(2) *Preventive requirements.* To prevent these deceptive acts or practices, funeral providers must place the following sentence in the itemized statement of funeral goods and services selected, in immediate conjunction with the list of itemized cash advance items required by § 453.2(b)(5)(i)(B): "We charge you for our services in obtaining (specify cash advance items)," if the funeral provider makes a charge upon, or receives and retains a rebate, commission or trade or volume discount upon a cash advance item.

§ 453.4 Required purchase of funeral goods or funeral services.

(a) *Casket for cremation provisions*—(1) *Unfair or deceptive acts or practices.* In selling or offering to sell funeral goods or funeral services to the public, it is an unfair or deceptive act or practice for a funeral provider, or a crematory, to require that a casket be purchased for direct cremation.

(2) *Preventive requirement.* To prevent this unfair or deceptive act or practice, funeral providers must make an alternative container available for direct cremations, if they arrange direct cremations.

(b) *Other required purchases of funeral goods or funeral services*—(1) *Unfair or deceptive acts or practices.* In selling or offering to sell funeral goods or funeral services, it is an unfair or deceptive act or practice for a funeral provider to:

(i) Condition the furnishing of any funeral good or funeral service to a person arranging a funeral upon the purchase of any other funeral good or funeral service, except as required by law or as otherwise permitted by this part;

(ii) Charge any fee as a condition to furnishing any funeral goods or funeral services to a person arranging a funeral, other than the fees for: (1) Services of funeral director and staff, permitted by § 453.2(b)(4)(iii)(C); (2) other funeral services and funeral goods selected by the purchaser; and (3) other funeral goods or services required to be purchased, as explained on the itemized statement in accordance with § 453.3(d)(2).

(2) *Preventive requirements.* (i) To prevent these unfair or deceptive acts or practices, funeral providers must:

(A) Place the following disclosure in the general price list, immediately above the prices required by § 453.2(b)(4)(ii) and (iii): "The goods and services shown below are those we can provide to our customers. You may choose only the items you desire. If legal or other requirements mean you must buy any items you did not specifically ask for, we will explain the reason in writing on the statement we provide describing the funeral goods and services you selected." *Provided, however,* that if the charge for "services of funeral director and staff" cannot be declined by the purchaser, the statement shall include the sentence: "However, any funeral arrangements you select will include a charge for our basic services" between the second and third sentences of the statement specified above herein. The statement may include the phrase "and overhead" after the word "services" if the fee includes a charge for the recovery of unallocated funeral provider overhead;

(B) Place the following disclosure on the statement of funeral goods and services selected, required by § 453.2(b)(5)(i): "Charges are only for those items that you selected or that are required. If we are required by law or by a cemetery or crematory to use any items, we will explain the reasons in writing below."

(ii) A funeral provider shall not violate this section by failing to comply with a request for a combination of goods or services which would be impossible, impractical, or excessively burdensome to provide.

§ 453.5 Services provided without prior approval.

(a) *Unfair or deceptive acts or practices.* In selling or offering to sell funeral goods or funeral services to the public, it is an unfair or deceptive act or practice for any provider to embalm a deceased human body for a fee unless:

(1) State or local law or regulation requires embalming in the particular circumstances regardless of any funeral choice which the family might make; or

(2) Prior approval for embalming (expressly so described) has been obtained from a family member or other authorized person; or

(3) The funeral provider is unable to contact a family member or other authorized person after exercising due diligence, has no reason to believe the family does not want embalming performed, and obtains subsequent approval for embalming already performed (expressly so described). In seeking approval, the funeral provider must disclose that a fee will be charged if the family selects a funeral which requires embalming, such as a funeral with viewing, and that no fee will be charged if the family selects a service which does not require embalming, such as direct cremation or immediate burial.

(b) *Preventive requirement.* To prevent these unfair or deceptive acts or practices, funeral providers must include on the itemized statement of funeral goods and services selected, required by § 435.2(b)(5) the statement: "If you selected a funeral that may require embalming, such as a funeral with viewing, you may have to pay for embalming. You do not have to pay for embalming you did not approve if you selected arrangements such as a direct cremation or immediate burial. If we charged for embalming, we will explain why below."

§ 453.6 Retention of documents.

To prevent the unfair or deceptive acts or practices specified in § 453.2 and § 453.3 of this rule, funeral providers must retain and make available for inspection by Commission officials true and accurate copies of the price lists specified in §§ 453.2(b)(2) through (4), as applicable, for at least one year after the date of their last distribution to customers, and a copy of each statement of funeral goods and services selected, as required by § 453.2(b)(5) for at least one year from the date of the arrangements conference.

§ 453.7 Comprehension of disclosures.

To prevent the unfair or deceptive acts or practices specified in § 453.2 through § 453.5, funeral providers must make all disclosures required by those sections in a clear and conspicuous manner. Providers shall not include in the casket, outer burial container, and general price lists, required by §§ 453.2(b)(2)–(4), any statement or information that alters or contradicts the information required by this part to be included in those lists.

§ 453.8 Declaration of intent.

(a) Except as otherwise provided in § 453.2(a), it is a violation of this rule to engage in any unfair or deceptive acts or practices specified in this rule, or to fail to comply with any of the preventive requirements specified in this rule;

(b) The provisions of this rule are separate and severable from one another. If any provision is determined to be invalid, it is the Commission's intention that the remaining provisions shall continue in effect.

(c) This rule shall not apply to the business of insurance or to acts in the conduct thereof.

§ 453.9 State exemptions.

If, upon application to the Commission by an appropriate State agency, the Commission determines that:

(a) There is a State requirement in effect which applies to any transaction to which this rule applies; and

(b) That State requirement affords an overall level of protection to consumers which is as great as, or greater than, the protection afforded by this rule;

then the Commission's rule will not be in effect in that state to the extent specified by the Commission in its determination, for as long as the state administers and enforces effectively the state requirement.

B.6 FTC Used Car Rule

16 C.F.R. 455

Source: 49 Fed. Reg. 45692 (Nov. 19, 1984)

§ 455.1 General duties of a used vehicle dealer; definitions.

(a) It is a deceptive act or practice for any used vehicle dealer, when that dealer sells or offers for sale a used vehicle in or affecting commerce as *commerce* is defined in the Federal Trade Commission Act:

(1) To misrepresent the mechanical condition of a used vehicle;

(2) To misrepresent the terms of any warranty offered in connection with the sale of a used vehicle; and

(3) To represent that a used vehicle is sold with a warranty when the vehicle is sold without any warranty.

(b) It is an unfair act or practice for any used vehicle dealer, when that dealer sells or offers for sale a used vehicle in or affecting commerce as *commerce* is defined in the Federal Trade Commission Act:

(1) To fail to disclose, prior to sale, that a used vehicle is sold without any warranty; and

(2) To fail to make available, prior to sale, the terms of any written warranty offered in connection with the sale of a used vehicle.

(c) The Commission has adopted this Rule in order to prevent the unfair and deceptive acts or practices defined in paragraphs (a) and (b). It is a violation of this Rule for any used vehicle dealer to fail to comply with the requirements set forth in §§ 455.2 through 455.5 of this part. If a used vehicle dealer complies with the requirements of §§ 455.2 through 455.5 of this part, the dealer does not violate this Rule.

(d) The following definitions shall apply for purposes of this part:

(1) *Vehicle* means any motorized vehicle, other than a motorcycle, with a gross vehicle weight rating (GVWR) of less than 8500 lbs., a curb weight of less than 6,000 lbs., and a frontal area of less than 46 sq. ft.

(2) *Used vehicle* means any vehicle driven more than the limited use necessary in moving or road testing a new vehicle prior to delivery to a consumer, but does not include any vehicle sold only for scrap or parts (title documents surrendered to the state and a salvage certificate issued).

(3) *Dealer* means any person or business which sells or offers for sale a used vehicle after selling or offering for sale five (5) or more used vehicles in the previous twelve months, but does not include a bank or financial institution, a business selling a used vehicle to an employee of that business, or a lessor selling a leased vehicle by or to that vehicle's lessee or to an employee of the lessee.

(4) *Consumer* means any person who is not a used vehicle dealer.

(5) *Warranty* means any undertaking in writing, in connection with the sale by a dealer of a used vehicle, to refund, repair, replace, maintain or take other action with respect to such used vehicle and provided at no extra charge beyond the price of the used vehicle.

(6) *Implied warranty* means an implied warranty arising under state law (as modified by the Magnuson-Moss Act) in connection with the sale by a dealer of a used vehicle.

(7) *Service contract* means a contract in writing for any period of time or any specific mileage to refund, repair, replace, or maintain a used vehicle and provided at an extra charge beyond the price of the used vehicle, provided that such contract is not regulated in your state as the business of insurance.

(8) *You* means any dealer, or any agent or employee of a dealer, except where the term appears on the window form required by § 455.2(a).

§ 455.2 Consumer sales—window form.

(a) *General duty.* Before you offer a used vehicle for sale to a consumer, you must prepare, fill in as applicable and display on that vehicle a "Buyers Guide" as required by this Rule.

(1) The Buyers Guide shall be displayed prominently and conspicuously in any location on a vehicle and in such a fashion that both sides are readily readable. You may remove the form temporarily from the vehicle during any test drive, but you must return it as soon as the test drive is over.

(2) The capitalization, punctuation and wording of all items, headings, and text on the form must be exactly as required by this Rule. The entire form must be printed in 100% black ink on a white stock no smaller than 11 inches high by 7 1/4 inches wide in the type styles, sizes and format indicated.

BUYERS GUIDE

28 pt Triumvirate Bold caps

2 pt Rule

IMPORTANT: Spoken promises are difficult to enforce. Ask the dealer to put all promises in writing. Keep this form.

10/12 Triumvirate Bold c & lc flush left ragged right maximum line 42 picas

______ ______ ______ ______

VEHICLE MAKE MODEL YEAR VIN NUMBER

10 pt Baseline Rule
6 pt Triumvirate Bold caps

______

DEALER STOCK NUMBER (Optional)

10 pt Baseline Rule
6 pt Triumvirate Bold caps

WARRANTIES FOR THIS VEHICLE:

10 pt Triumvirate Bold caps

2 pt Rule

☐ AS IS - NO WARRANTY

54 pt Box
42 Pt Triumvirate Bold caps

YOU WILL PAY ALL COSTS FOR ANY REPAIRS. The dealer assumes no responsibility for any repairs regardless of any oral statements about the vehicle.

10/10 Triumvirate Bold c & lc flush left ragged right maximum line 42 picas

1 pt Rule

☐ WARRANTY

54 pt Box
42 pt Triumvirate Bold caps

☐ FULL ☐ LIMITED WARRANTY. The dealer will pay ______% of the labor and ______% of the parts for the covered systems that fail during the warranty period. Ask the dealer for a copy of the warranty document for a full explanation of warranty coverage, exclusions, and the dealer's repair obligations. Under state law, "implied warranties" may give you even more rights.

10/10 Triumvirate Bold c & lc 4½ picas indent on 2nd line

SYSTEMS COVERED:	DURATION:

10 pt Triumvirate Bold caps

10 pt Baseline Rile

☐ SERVICE CONTRACT. A service contract is available at an extra charge on this vehicle. Ask for details as to coverage, deductable, price, and exclusions. If you buy a service contract within 90 days of the time of sale, state law "implied warranties" may give you additional rights.

10/10 Triumvirate Bold c & lc maximum line 42 picas

PRE PURCHASE INSPECTION: ASK THE DEALER IF YOU MAY HAVE THIS VEHICLE INSPECTED BY YOUR MECHANIC EITHER ON OR OFF THE LOT.

10/10 Triumvirate Bold caps flush left ragged right maximum line 42 picas

SEE THE BACK OF THIS FORM for important additional information, including a list of some major defects that may occur in used motor vehicles.

10/10 Triumvirate Bold c & lc flush left ragged right maximum line 42 picas

12 pt Triumvirate Bold lc
flush left ragged right
maximum line 42 pixas

Below is a list of some major defects that may occur in used motor vehicles.

2 pt Rule

8/9 Triumvirate Bold c & lc
flush left ragged right
maximum line 20 picas
1 em indent on 2nd line

Frame & Body
Frame-cracks, corrective welds, or rusted through
Dogtracks—bent or twisted frame

Engine
Oil leakage excluding normal seepage
Cracked block or head
Belts missing or inoperable
Knocks or misses related to camshaft lifters and push rods
Abnormal exhaust discharge

Transmission & Drive Shaft
Improper fluid level or leakage, excluding normal seepage
Cracked or damaged case which is visible
Abnormal noise or vibration caused by faulty transmission or drive shaft
Improper shifting or functioning in any gear
Manual clutch slips or chatters

Differential
Improper fluid level or leakage excluding normal seepage
Cracked or damaged housing which is visible
Abnormal noise of vibration caused by faulty differential

Cooling System
Leakage including radiator
Improperly functioning water pump

Electrical System
Battery leakage
Improperly functioning alternator, generator, battery, or starter

Fuel System
Visible leakage

Inoperable Accessories
Gauges or warning devices
Air conditioner
Heater & Defroster

Brake System
Failure warning light broken
Pedal not firm under pressure (DOT spec.)
Not enough pedal reserve (DOT spec.)
Does not stop vehicle in straight (DOT spec.)
Hoses damaged
Drum or rotor too thin (Mfgr Specs.)
Lining or pad thickness less than 1/32 inch
Power unit not operating or leaking
Structural or mechanical pans damaged

Steering System
Too much free play at steering wheel (DOT specs.)
Free play in linkage more than 1/4 inch
Steering gear binds or jams
Front wheels aligned improperly (DOT specs.)
Power unit belts cracked or slipping
Power unit fluid level improper

Suspension System
Ball joint seals damaged
Structural parts bent or damaged
Stabilizer bar disconnected
Spring broken
Shock absorber mounting loose
Rubber bushings damaged or missing
Radius rod damaged or missing
Shock absorber leaking or functioning improperly

Tires
Tread depth less than 2/32 inch
Sizes mismatched
Visible damage

Wheels
Visible cracks, damage, or repairs
Mounting bolts loose or missing

Exhaust System
Leakage

2 pt Rule

10 pt Baseline Rule
6 pt Triumvirate Bold caps

____
DEALER

____
ADDRESS

____

____
SEE FOR COMPLAINTS

2 pt Rule

10/12 Triumvirate Bold c & lc
maximum line 42 picas

IMPORTANT: The information on this form is part of any contract to buy this vehicle. Removal of this label before consumer purchase (except for purpose of test-driving) is a violation of federal law (16 C.F.R. 455).

When filling out the form, follow the directions in (b) through (e) of this section and § 455.4 of this part.

(b) *Warranties*—(1) *No Implied Warranty—"As Is"/No Warranty.* (i) If you offer the vehicle without any implied warranty, *i.e.*, "as is," mark the box provided. If you offer the vehicle with implied warranties only, substitute the disclosure specified below, and mark the box provided. If you first offer the vehicle "as is" or with implied warranties only but then sell it with a warranty, cross out the "As Is—No Warranty" or "Implied Warranties Only" disclosure, and fill in the warranty terms in accordance with paragraph (b)(2) of this section.

(ii) If your state law limits or prohibits "as is" sales of vehicles, that state law overrides this part and this rule does not give you the right to sell "as is." In such states, the heading "As Is—No Warranty" and the paragraph immediately accompanying that phrase must be deleted from the form, and the following heading and paragraph must be substituted. If you sell vehicles in states that permit "as is" sales, but you choose to offer implied warranties only, you must also use the following disclosure instead of "As Is—No Warranty":[1]

IMPLIED WARRANTIES ONLY

This means that the dealer does not make any specific promises to fix things that need repair when you buy the vehicle or after the time of sale. But, state law "implied warranties" may give you some rights to have the dealer take care of serious problems that were not apparent when you bought the vehicle.

(2) *Full/Limited Warranty.* If you offer the vehicle with a warranty, briefly describe the warranty terms in the space provided. This description must include the following warranty information:

(i) Whether the warranty offered is "Full" or "Limited."[2] Mark the box next to the appropriate designation.

(ii) Which of the specific systems are covered (for example, "engine, transmission, differential"). You cannot use shorthand, such as "drive train" or "power train" for covered systems.

(iii) The duration (for example, "30 days or 1,000 miles, whichever occurs first").

(iv) The percentage of the repair cost paid by you (for example, "The dealer will pay 100% of the labor and 100% of the parts."

(v) If the vehicle is still under the manufacturer's original warranty, you may add the following paragraph below the "Full/Limited Warranty" disclosure: MANUFACTURER'S WARRANTY STILL APPLIES. The manufacturer's original warranty has not expired on the vehicle. Consult the manufacturer's warranty booklet for details as to warranty coverage, service location, etc.

If, following negotiations, you and the buyer agree to changes in the warranty coverage, mark the changes on the form, as appropriate. If you first offer the vehicle with a warranty, but then sell it without one, cross out the offered warranty and mark either the "As Is—No Warranty" box or the "Implied Warranties Only" box, as appropriate.

(3) *Service contracts.* If you make a service contract (other than a contract that is regulated in your state as the business of insurance) available on the vehicle, you must add the following heading and paragraph below the "Full/Limited Warranty" disclosure and mark the box provided.[3]

[ ] Service Contract

A service contract is available at an extra charge on this vehicle. If you buy a service contract within 90 days of the time of sale, state law "implied warranties" may give you additional rights.

(c) *Name and Address.* Put the name and address of your dealership in the space provided. If you do not have a dealership, use the name and address of your place of business (for example, your service station) or your own name and home address.

(d) *Make, Model, Model Year, VIN.* Put the vehicle's name (for example, "Chevrolet"), model (for example, "Vega"), model year, and Vehicle Identification Number (VIN) in the spaces provided. You may write the dealer stock number in the space provided or you may leave this space blank.

(e) *Complaints.* In the space provided, put the name and telephone number of the person who should be contacted if any complaints arise after sale.

(f) *Optional Signature Line.* In the space provided for the name of the individual to be contacted in the event of complaints after sale, you may include a signature line for a buyer's signature. If you opt to include a signature line, you must include a disclosure in immediate proximity to the signature line stating: "I hereby acknowledge receipt of the Buyers Guide at the closing of this sale." You may pre-print this language on the form if you choose.

[49 Fed. Reg. 45725 (Nov. 19, 1984), *as amended at* 60 Fed. Reg. 62205 (Dec. 5, 1995)]

§ 455.3 Window form.

(a) *Form given to buyer.* Give the buyer of a used vehicle sold by you the window form displayed under § 455.2 containing all of the disclosures required by the Rule and reflecting the warranty coverage agreed upon. If you prefer, you may give the buyer a copy of the original, so long as that copy accurately reflects all of the disclosures required by the Rule and the warranty coverage agreed upon.

(b) *Incorporated into contract.* The information on the final version of the window form is incorporated into the contract of sale for each used vehicle you sell to a consumer. Information on the window form overrides any contrary provisions in the contract of sale. To inform the consumer of these facts, include the following language conspicuously in each consumer contract of sale:

The information you see on the window form for this vehicle is part of this contract. Information on the window form overrides any contrary provisions in the contract of sale.

§ 455.4 Contrary statements.

You may not make any statements, oral or written, or take other actions which alter or contradict the disclosures required by §§ 455.2 and 455.3. You may negotiate over warranty coverage, as provided in § 455.2(b) of this part, as long as the final warranty terms are identified in the contract of sale and summarized on the copy of the window form you give to the buyer.

§ 455.5 Spanish language sales.

If you conduct a sale in Spanish, the window form required by § 455.2 and the contract disclosures required by § 455.3 must be in that language. You may display on a vehicle both an English language window form and a Spanish language translation of that form. Use the following translation and layout for Spanish language sales:[4]

---

1 See § 455.5 n.4 for the Spanish version of this disclosure.

2 A "Full" warranty is defined by the Federal Minimum Standards for Warranty set forth in 104 of the Magnuson-Moss Warranty Act, 15 U.S.C. 2304 (1975). The Magnuson-Moss Warranty Act does not apply to vehicles manufactured before July 4, 1975. Therefore, if you choose not to designate "Full" or "Limited" for such cars, cross out both designations, leaving only "Warranty".

3 See § 455.5 n.4 for the Spanish version of this disclosure.

4 Use the following language for the "Implied Warranties Only" disclosure when required by § 455.2(b)(1):

Garantias implicitas solamente Este termino significa que el vendedor no hace promesas especificas de arreglar lo que requiera reparacion cuando usted compra el vehiculo o despues del momento de la venta. Pero, las "garantias implicitas" de la ley estatal pueden darle a usted algunos derechos y hacer que el vendedor resuelva problemas graves que no fueron evidentes cuando usted compro el vehiculo.

Use the following language for the "Service Contract" disclosure required by § 455.2(b)(3):

CONTRATO DE SERVICIO. Este vehiculo tiene disponible un contrato de servicio a un precio adicional. Pida los detalles en cuanto a cobertura, deducible, precio y exclusiones. Si adquiere usted un contrato de servicio dentro de los 90 dias del momento de la venta, las "garantias implicitas" de acuerdo a la ley del estado pueden concederle derechos adicionales.

GUÍA DEL COMPRADOR

28 pt Triumvirate Bold caps

2 pt Rule

IMPORTANTE: Las promesas verbales son dificiles de hacer cumplir. Solicité al vendedor que ponga todas las promesas por escrito. Conserve este formulario.

10/10 Triumvirate Bold c & lc maximum line 38 picas

MARCA DEL VEHÍCULO	MODELO	AÑO	NUMERO DE IDENTIFICACIÓN

Hairline Rule
6/8 pt Triumvirate Bold caps

NUMERO DE ABASTO DEL DISTRIBUDOR (Opcional)

Hairline Rule
6/8 pt Triumvirate Bold caps

GARANTÍAS PARA ESTE VEHÍCULO:

10 pt Triumvirate Bold caps

2 pt Rule

☐ COMO ESTÁ – SIN GARANTÍA

28 pt Box
24 Pt Triumvirate Bold c & lc

USTED PAGARÁ TODOS LOS GASTOS DE CUALQUIER REPARACIÓN QUE SEA NECESARIA. El vendedor no asume ninguna responsabilidad por cualquier reparación, sean cuales sean las declaraciones verbales que haya hecho acerca del vehículo.

10/10 Triumvirate Bold c & lc maximum line 38 picas

1 pt Rule

☐ GARANTÍA

28 pt Box
24 pt Triumvirate Bold c & lc

☐ COMPLETA ☐ LIMITADA. El vendedor pagará el ______% de la mano de obra y el ______% de los repuestos de los sistemas cubiertos que dejen de funcionar durante el período de garantía. Pida al vendedor una copía del documento de garantía donde se explican detalladamente la cobertura de le garantía, exclusiones y las obligaciones que tiene el vendedor de realizar reparaciones. Conforme a la ley estatal, las "garantías implicitas" pueden darle a usted incluso más derechos.

10/10 Triumvirate Bold c & lc
7½ picas indent
on runovers

SISTEMAS CUBIERTOS POR GARANTÍA:	DURACÍON:

10/10 Triumvirate Bold caps

10/12 Hairline Rile

CONTRATO DE SERVICIO. Este vehículo tiene disponible un contrato de servicio a un precio adicional. Pida los detalles en cuanto a cobertura, deducible, precio y exclusiones. Si adquiere usted un contrato de servicio dentro de los 90 días del momento de la venta, las 'garantías implícitas' de acuerdo a la ley del estado pueden concederle derechos adicionales.

10/10 Triumvirate Bold c & lc maximum line 38 picas

INSPECCIÓN PREVIA A LA COMPRA: PREGUNTE AL VENDEDOR SI PUEDE USTED TRAER UN MECÁNICO PARA QUE INSPECCIONE EL AUTOMÓVIL O LLEVAR EL AUTOMÓVIL PARA QUE ÉSTE LO INSPECCIONE EN SU TALLER.

10/10 Triumvirate Bold caps maximum line 38 picas

VÉASE EL DORSO DE ESTE FORMULARIO donde se proporciona información adicional importante, incluyendo una lista de algunos de los principales defectos que pueden ocurrir en vehículos usados.

10/10 Triumvirate Bold c & lc maximum line 38 picas

12 pt Triumvirate Bold lc flush left ragged right maximum line 42 pixas

A continuación presentamos una lista de algunos de los principales defectos que pueden ocurrir en vehiculos usados.

2 pt Rule

8/9 Triumvirate Bold c & lc flush left ragged right maximum line 20 picas 1 em indent on 2nd line

Chasis y carrocería
Chasis-grietas, soldaduras corractivas u oxidado
Chasis doblado o torcido

Motor
Fuga de aceite excluyendo el escape normal
Bloque o tapa de recamara agrietados
Correas que faltan o no funcionan
Falto o pistoneo
Emision excesiva de humo por el sistema de escape

Transmisión y eje de cordan
Nivel de liquido inadecuado o fuga, excluyendo filtración normal
Cubierta agrielada o dañada visible
Vibración o ruido anormal ocasion do por una transmisión o eje de cordan defectuoso
Cambio de marchas o funcionmiento inadecuado en cualquier marcha
Embraque manual patina o vibra

Diferencial
Nivel de liquido inadecuado o fuga excluyendo filtracion normal
Cubierta agrietada o dañada visible
Ruido o vibración anormal ocasionado por diferencial defectuoso

Sistema de refrigeración
Fuga, incluido el radiador
Bomba de agua defectuosa

Sistema electrico
Fuga en las baterías
Alternador generador batería o motor de arranque defectuosos

Sistema de combustible
Escape visible de combustible

Accesorios averiados
Indicadores o medidores del cuadro de instrumentos
Acondicionador de aire
Calefactor y descarchador

Sistema de frenos
Luz de advertencia de talla dañada
Pedal no firma bajo presión (Especif. del Dpto de Transp.)
Juego insuficiente en el pedal (Especif. Dpto de transp.)
No detiene el vehiculo en linea recta (Especif. del Dpto de Transp.)
Conductos dañados
Tambor o disco muy delgados (Especif. del fabricante)
Grosor de las bandas del los frenos menor de 1/32 de pulgada
Sistema de servofreno dañado o con escape
Partes estructurales o mecánicas danadas

Sistema de dirección
Juego excesivo en el volante (Especif. del Dpto de Transp.)
Juego en el varillaje en eaxceso de 1/4 pulgada
Engranaje del volante de dirección se agarrota
Ruedas delanteras mal alineadas (Especif. del Dpto de Transp.)
Correas del sistema de servodirección agrietadas o flojas
Nivel del liquido del sistema de servodirección inadecuado

Sistema de suspensión
Sellos de conexion de rodamientos defectuosos
Piezas estructurales dobladas o dañadas
Barra de estabilizacion desconectada
Resorte roto
Montura del amortiguador floja
Bujes de goma dañadas o avisantes
Estabilizador para curvas dañadas o ausente
Amortiguador tiene fuga o funciona defectuosamente

Llantas
Profundidad de la banda de rodamiento menor de 2/32 de pulgada
Diferentes tamaños de llanta
Daños visibles

Ruedas
Grietas visibles, daños, o reparaciones
Pernos de montaje sueltos o ausentes

Sistama de Escape
Fuga

2 pt Rule

10 pt Baseline Rule
6 pt Triumvirate Bold caps

____
VENDEDOR

____
DIRECCION

____

____
VEASE PARA RECLAMACIONES

2 pt Rule

10/12 Triumvirate Bold c & lc maximum line 42 picas

IMPORTANTE: La informacion contenida en este formulario forma parte de todo contrato de compra de este vehiculo. Constituye una contravencion de la leyy federal (16 C.F.R. 455) quitar este rotulo antes de la compra del vehiculo por el consumidor (salvo para conducir el automovil en calidad de prueba).

§ 455.6 State exemptions.

(a) If, upon application to the Commission by an appropriate state agency, the Commission determines, that—

(1) There is a state requirement in effect which applies to any transaction to which this rule applies; and

(2) That state requirement affords an overall level of protection to consumers which is as great as, or greater than, the protection afforded by this Rule; then the Commission's Rule will not be in effect in that state to the extent specified by the Commission in its determination, for as long as the State administers and enforces effectively the state requirement.

(b) Applications for exemption under Subsection (a) should be directed to the Secretary of the Commission. When appropriate, proceedings will be commenced in order to make a determination described in paragraph (a) of this section, and will be conducted in accordance with Subpart C of Part 1 of the Commission's Rules of Practice.

§ 455.7 Severability.

The provisions of this part are separate and severable from one another. If any provision is determined to be invalid, it is the Commission's intention that the remaining provisions shall continue in effect.

Appendix C Federal and State RICO Statutes

C.1 Federal RICO Statutes

C.1.1 Full Text of Federal RICO Statute

Title 18—Crimes and Criminal Procedure
Chapter 96—Racketeer Influenced and Corrupt Organizations

Sec.

18 U.S.C. § 1961. Definitions

As used in this chapter—

(1) "racketeering activity" means (A) any act or threat involving murder, kidnapping, gambling, arson, robbery, bribery, extortion, dealing in obscene matter, or dealing in a controlled substance or listed chemical (as defined in section 102 of the Controlled Substances Act), which is chargeable under State law and punishable by imprisonment for more than one year; (B) any act which is indictable under any of the following provisions of title 18, United States Code: Section 201 (relating to bribery), section 224 (relating to sports bribery), sections 471, 472, and 473 (relating to counterfeiting), section 659 (relating to theft from interstate shipment) if the act indictable under section 659 is felonious, section 664 (relating to embezzlement from pension and welfare funds), section 1028 (relating to fraud and related activity in connection with identification documents), sections 891–894 (relating to extortionate credit transactions), section 1029 (relating to fraud and related activity in connection with access devices), section 1084 (relating to the transmission of gambling information), section 1341 (relating to mail fraud), section 1343 (relating to wire fraud), section 1344 (relating to financial institution fraud), section 1425 (relating to the procurement of citizenship or nationalization unlawfully), section 1426 (relating to the reproduction of naturalization or citizenship papers), section 1427 (relating to the sale of naturalization or citizenship papers), sections 1461–1465 (relating to obscene matter), section 1503 (relating to obstruction of justice), section 1510 (relating to obstruction of criminal investigations), section 1511 (relating to the obstruction of State or local law enforcement), section 1512 (relating to tampering with a witness, victim, or an informant), section 1513 (relating to retaliating against a witness, victim, or an informant), section 1542 (relating to false statement in application and use of passport), section 1543 (relating to forgery or false use of passport), section 1544 (relating to misuse of passport), section 1546 (relating to fraud and misuse of visas, permits, and other documents), sections 1581–1591 (relating to peonage and slavery, and trafficking in persons), section 1951 (relating to interference with commerce, robbery, or extortion), section 1952 (relating to racketeering), section 1953 (relating to interstate transportation of wagering paraphernalia), section 1954 (relating to unlawful welfare fund payments), section 1955 (relating to the prohibition of illegal gambling businesses), section 1956 (relating to the laundering of monetary instruments), section 1957 (relating to engaging in monetary transactions in property derived from specified unlawful activity), section 1958 (relating to use of interstate commerce facilities in the commission of murder-for-hire), sections 2251, 2251A, 2252, 2260 (relating to sexual exploitation of children), sections 2312 and 2313 (relating to interstate transportation of stolen motor vehicles), sections 2314 and 2315 (relating to interstate transportation of stolen property), section 2318 (relating to trafficking in counterfeit labels for phonorecords, computer programs or computer program documentation or packaging and copies of motion pictures or other audiovisual works), section 2319 (relating to criminal infringement of a copyright), section 2319A (relating to unauthorized fixation of and trafficking in sound recordings and music videos of live musical performances), section 2320 (relating to trafficking in goods or services bearing counterfeit marks), section 2321 (relating to trafficking in certain motor vehicles or motor vehicle parts), sections 2341–2346 (relating to trafficking in contraband cigarettes), sections 2421–24 (relating to white slave traffic), (C) any act which is indictable under title 29, United States Code, section 186 (dealing with restrictions on payments and loans to labor organizations) or section 501(c) (relating to embezzlement from union funds), (D) any offense involving fraud connected with a case under title 11 (except a case under section 157 of this title), fraud in the sale of securities, or the felonious manufacture, importation, receiving, concealment, buying, selling, or otherwise dealing in controlled substance or listed chemical (as defined in section 102 of the Controlled Substances Act), punishable under any law of the United States, or (E) any act which is indictable under the Currency and Foreign Transactions Reporting Act, (F) any act which is indictable under the Immigration and Nationality Act, section 278 (relating to importation of alien for immoral purpose) if the act indictable under such section of such Act was committed for the purpose of financial gain, or (G) any act that is indictable under any provision listed in section 2332b(g)(5)(B);

(2) "State" means any State of the United States, the District of Columbia, the Commonwealth of Puerto Rico, any territory or possession of the United States, any political subdivision, or any department, agency, or instrumentality thereof;

(3) "person" includes any individual or entity capable of holding a legal or beneficial interest in property;

(4) "enterprise" includes any individual, partnership, corporation, association, or other legal entity, and any union or group of individuals associated in fact although not a legal entity;

(5) "pattern of racketeering activity" requires at least two acts of racketeering activity, one of which occurred after the effective date of this chapter and the last of which occurred within ten years (excluding any period of imprisonment) after the commission of a prior act of racketeering activity;

(6) "unlawful debt" means a debt (A) incurred or contracted in gambling activity which was in violation of the law of the United States, a State or political subdivision thereof, or which is unenforceable under State or Federal law in whole or in part as to principal or interest because of the laws relating to usury, and (B) which was incurred in connection with the business of gambling in violation of the law of the United States, a State or political subdivision thereof, or the business of lending money or a thing of value at a rate usurious under State or Federal law, where the usurious rate is at least twice the enforceable rate;

(7) "racketeering investigator" means any attorney or investigator so designated by the Attorney General and charged with the duty of enforcing or carrying into effect this chapter;

(8) "racketeering investigation" means any inquiry conducted by any racketeering investigator for the purpose of ascertaining whether any person has been involved in any violation of this chapter or of any final order, judgment, or decree of any court of the United States, duly entered in any case or proceeding arising under this chapter;

(9) "documentary material" includes any book, paper, document, record, recording, or other material; and

(10) "Attorney General" includes the Attorney General of the United States, the Deputy Attorney General of the United States, the Associate Attorney General of the United States, any Assistant Attorney General of the United States, or any employee of the Department of Justice or any employee of any department or agency of the United States so designated by the Attorney General to carry out the powers conferred on the Attorney General by this chapter. Any department or agency so designated may use in investigations authorized by this chapter either the investigative provisions of this chapter or the investigative power of such department or agency otherwise conferred by law.

[Added Pub. L. No. 91-452, Title IX, § 901(a), 84 Stat. 941 (Oct. 15, 1970), and amended Pub. L. No. 95-575, § 3(c),92 Stat. 2465 (Nov. 2, 1978); Pub. L. No. 95- 598, Title III, § 314(g), 92 Stat. 2677 (Nov. 6, 1978); Pub. L. No. 98-473, Title II, §§ 901(g), 1020, 98 Stat. 2136, 2143 (Oct. 12, 1984); Pub. L. No. 98-547, Title II, § 205, 98 Stat. 2770 (Oct. 25, 1984); Pub. L. No. 99-570, Title XIII, § 1365(b), 100 Stat. 3207-35 (Oct. 27, 1986); Pub. L. No. 99-646, § 50(a), 100 Stat. 3605 (Nov. 10, 1986); Pub. L. No. 100-690, Title VII, §§ 7013, 7020(c), 7032, 7054, 7514, 102 Stat. 4395, 4396, 4398, 4402, 4489 (Nov. 18, 1988); Pub. L. No. 101-73, Title IX, § 968, 103 Stat. 506 (Aug. 9, 1989); Pub. L. No. 101-647, Title XXXV, § 3560, 104 Stat. 4927 (Nov. 29, 1990); Pub. L. No. 103-322, Title IX, § 90104, Title XVI, § 160001(f), Title XXXIII, § 330021(1), 108 Stat. 1987, 2037, 2150 (Sept. 13, 1994); Pub. L. No. 103-394, Title III, § 312(b), 108 Stat. 4140 (Oct. 22, 1994); Pub. L. No. 104-132, Title IV, § 433, 110 Stat. 1274 (Apr. 24, 1996); Pub. L. No. 104-153, § 3, 110 Stat. 1386 (July 2, 1996); Pub. L. No. 104- 208, Div. C, Title II, § 202, 110 Stat. 3009-565 (Sept. 30, 1996); Pub. L. No. 104-294, Title VI, §§ 601(b)(3), (i)(3), 604(b)(6), 110 Stat. 3499, 3501, 3506 (Oct. 11, 1996); Pub. L. No. 107-56, Title VIII, § 813, 115 Stat. 382 (Oct. 26, 2001); Pub. L. No. 107-273, Div. B, Title IV, § 4005(f)(1), 116 Stat. 1813 (Nov. 2, 2002); Pub. L. No. 108-193, § 5(b), 117 Stat. 2879 (Dec. 19, 2003)]

18 U.S.C. § 1962. Prohibited activities

(a) It shall be unlawful for any person who has received any income derived, directly or indirectly, from a pattern of racketeering activity or through collection of an unlawful debt in which such person has participated as a principal within the meaning of section 2, title 18, United States Code, to use or invest, directly or indirectly, any part of such income, or the proceeds of such income, in acquisition of any interest in, or the establishment or operation of, any enterprise which is engaged in, or the activities of which affect, interstate or foreign commerce. A purchase of securities on the open market for purposes of investment, and without the intention of controlling or participating in the control of the issuer, or of assisting another to do so, shall not be unlawful under this subsection if the securities of the issuer held by the purchaser, the members of his immediate family, and his or their accomplices in any pattern or racketeering activity or the collection of an unlawful debt after such purchase do not amount in the aggregate to one percent of the outstanding securities of any one class, and do not confer, either in law or in fact, the power to elect one or more directors of the issuer.

(b) It shall be unlawful for any person through a pattern of racketeering activity or through collection of an unlawful debt to acquire or maintain, directly or indirectly, any interest in or control of any enterprise which is engaged in, or the activities of which affect, interstate or foreign commerce.

(c) It shall be unlawful for any person employed by or associated with any enterprise engaged in, or the activities of which affect, interstate or foreign commerce, to conduct or participate, directly or indirectly, in the conduct of such enterprise's affairs through a pattern of racketeering activity or collection of unlawful debt.

(d) It shall be unlawful for any person to conspire to violate any of the provisions of subsection (a), (b), or (c) of this section.

[Added Pub. L. No. 91-452, Title IX, § 901(a), 84 Stat. 942 (Oct. 15, 1970), and amended Pub. L. No. 100-690, Title VII, § 7033, 102 Stat. 4398 (Nov. 18, 1988)]

18 U.S.C. § 1963. Criminal penalties

(a) Whoever violates any provision of section 1962 of this chapter shall be fined under this title or imprisoned not more than 20 years (or for life if the violation is based on a racketeering activity for which the maximum penalty includes life imprisonment), or both, and shall forfeit to the United States, irrespective of any provision of State law—

(1) any interest the person has acquired or maintained in violation of section 1962;

(2) any—

(A) interest in;

(B) security of;

(C) claim against; or

(D) property or contractual right of any kind affording a source of influence over;

any enterprise which the person has established, operated, controlled, conducted, or participated in the conduct of, in violation of section 1962; and

(3) any property constituting, or derived from, any proceeds which the person obtained, directly or indirectly, from racketeering activity or unlawful debt collection in violation of section 1962.

The court, in imposing sentence on such person shall order, in addition to any other sentence imposed pursuant to this section, that the person forfeit to the United States all property described in this subsection. In lieu of a fine otherwise authorized by this section, a defendant who derives profits or other proceeds from an offense may be fined not more than twice the gross profits or other proceeds.

(b) Property subject to criminal forfeiture under this section includes—

(1) real property, including things growing on, affixed to, and found in land; and

(2) tangible and intangible personal property, including rights, privileges, interests, claims, and securities.

(c) All right, title, and interest in property described in subsection (a) vests in the United States upon the commission of the act giving rise to forfeiture under this section. Any such property that is subsequently transferred to a person other than the defendant may be the subject of a special verdict of forfeiture and thereafter shall be ordered forfeited to the United States, unless the transferee establishes in a hearing pursuant to subsection (l) that he is a bona fide purchaser for value of such property who at the time of purchase was reasonably without cause to believe that the property was subject to forfeiture under this section.

(d)(1) Upon application of the United States, the court may enter a restraining order or injunction, require the execution of a satisfactory performance bond, or take any other action to preserve the availability of property described in subsection (a) for forfeiture under this section—

(A) upon the filing of an indictment or information charging a violation of section 1962 of this chapter and alleging that the property with respect to which the order is sought would, in the event of conviction, be subject to forfeiture under this section; or

(B) prior to the filing of such an indictment or information, if, after notice to persons appearing to have an interest in the property and opportunity for a hearing, the court determines that—

(i) there is a substantial probability that the United States will prevail on the issue of forfeiture and that failure to enter the order will result in the property being destroyed, removed from the jurisdiction of the court, or otherwise made unavailable for forfeiture; and

(ii) the need to preserve the availability of the property through the entry of the requested order outweighs the hardship on any party against whom the order is to be entered:

Provided, however, That an order entered pursuant to subparagraph (B) shall be effective for not more than ninety days, unless extended by the court for good cause shown or unless an indictment or information described in subparagraph (A) has been filed.

(2) A temporary restraining order under this subsection may be entered upon application of the United States without notice or opportunity for a hearing when an information or indictment has not yet been filed with respect to the property, if the United States demonstrates that there is probable cause to believe that the property with respect to which the order is sought would, in the event of conviction, be subject to forfeiture under this section and that provision of notice will jeopardize the availability of the property for forfeiture. Such a temporary order shall expire not more than ten days after the date on which it is entered, unless extended for good cause shown or unless the party against whom it is entered consents to an extension for a longer period. A hearing requested concerning an order entered under this paragraph shall be held at the earliest possible time, and prior to the expiration of the temporary order.

(3) The court may receive and consider, at a hearing held pursuant to this subsection, evidence and information that would be inadmissible under the Federal Rules of Evidence.

(e) Upon conviction of a person under this section, the court shall enter a judgment of forfeiture of the property to the United States and shall also authorize the Attorney General to seize all property ordered forfeited upon such terms and conditions as the court shall deem proper. Following the entry of an order declaring the property forfeited, the court may, upon application of the United States, enter such appropriate restraining orders or injunctions, require the execution of satisfactory performance bonds, appoint receivers, conservators, appraisers, accountants, or trustees, or take any other action to protect the interest of the United States in the property ordered forfeited. Any income accruing to, or derived from, an enterprise or an interest in an enterprise which has been ordered forfeited under this section may be used to offset ordinary and necessary expenses to the enterprise which are required by law, or which are necessary to protect the interests of the United States or third parties.

(f) Following the seizure of property ordered forfeited under this section, the Attorney General shall direct the disposition of the property by sale or any other commercially feasible means, making due provision for the rights of any innocent persons. Any property right or interest not exercisable by, or transferable for value to, the United States shall expire and shall not revert to the defendant, nor shall the defendant or any person acting in concert with or on behalf of the defendant be eligible to purchase forfeited property at any sale held by the United States. Upon application of a person, other than the defendant or a person acting in concert with or on behalf of the defendant, the court may restrain or stay the sale or disposition of the property pending the conclusion of any appeal of the criminal case giving rise to the forfeiture, if the applicant demonstrates that proceeding with the sale or disposition of the property will result in irreparable injury, harm or loss to him. Notwithstanding 31 U.S.C. 3302(b), the proceeds of any sale or other disposition of property forfeited under this section and any moneys forfeited shall be used to pay all proper expenses for the forfeiture and the sale, including expenses of seizure, maintenance and custody of the property pending its disposition, advertising and court costs. The Attorney General shall deposit in the Treasury any amounts of such proceeds or moneys remaining after the payment of such expenses.

(g) With respect to property ordered forfeited under this section, the Attorney General is authorized to—

(1) grant petitions for mitigation or remission of forfeiture, restore forfeited property to victims of a violation of this chapter, or take any other action to protect the rights of innocent persons which is in the interest of justice and which is not inconsistent with the provisions of this chapter;

(2) compromise claims arising under this section;

(3) award compensation to persons providing information resulting in a forfeiture under this section;

(4) direct the disposition by the United States of all property ordered forfeited under this section by public sale or any other commercially feasible means, making due provision for the rights of innocent persons; and

(5) take appropriate measures necessary to safeguard and maintain property ordered forfeited under this section pending its disposition.

(h) The Attorney General may promulgate regulations with respect to—

(1) making reasonable efforts to provide notice to persons who may have an interest in property ordered forfeited under this section;

(2) granting petitions for remission or mitigation of forfeiture;

(3) the restitution of property to victims of an offense petitioning for remission or mitigation of forfeiture under this chapter;

(4) the disposition by the United States of forfeited property by public sale or other commercially feasible means;

(5) the maintenance and safekeeping of any property forfeited under this section pending its disposition; and

(6) the compromise of claims arising under this chapter.

Pending the promulgation of such regulations, all provisions of law relating to the disposition of property, or the proceeds from the sale thereof, or the remission or mitigation of forfeitures for violation of the customs laws, and the compromise of claims and the award of compensation to informers in respect of such forfeitures shall apply to forfeitures incurred, or alleged to have been incurred, under the provisions of this section, insofar as applicable and not inconsistent with the provisions hereof. Such duties as are imposed upon the Customs Service or any person with respect to the disposition of property under the customs law shall be performed under this chapter by the Attorney General.

(i) Except as provided in subsection (l), no party claiming an interest in property subject to forfeiture under this section may—

(1) intervene in a trial or appeal of a criminal case involving the forfeiture of such property under this section; or

(2) commence an action at law or equity against the United States concerning the validity of his alleged interest in the property subsequent to the filing of an indictment or information alleging that the property is subject to forfeiture under this section.

(j) The district courts of the United States shall have jurisdiction to enter orders as provided in this section without regard to the location of any property which may be subject to forfeiture under this section or which has been ordered forfeited under this section.

(k) In order to facilitate the identification or location of property declared forfeited and to facilitate the disposition of petitions for remission or mitigation of forfeiture, after the entry of an order declaring property forfeited to the United States the court may, upon application of the United States, order that the testimony of any witness relating to the property forfeited be taken by deposition and that any designated book, paper, document, record, recording, or other material not privileged be produced at the same time and place, in the same manner as provided for the taking of depositions under Rule 15 of the Federal Rules of Criminal Procedure.

(l)(1) Following the entry of an order of forfeiture under this section, the United States shall publish notice of the order and of its intent to dispose of the property in such manner as the Attorney General may direct. The Government may also, to the extent practicable, provide direct written notice to any person known to have alleged an interest in the property that is the subject of the order of forfeiture as a substitute for published notice as to those persons so notified.

(2) Any person, other than the defendant, asserting a legal interest in property which has been ordered forfeited to the United States pursuant to this section may, within thirty days of the final publication of notice or his receipt of notice under paragraph (1), whichever is earlier, petition the court for a hearing to adjudicate the validity of his alleged interest in the property. The hearing shall be held before the court alone, without a jury.

(3) The petition shall be signed by the petitioner under penalty of perjury and shall set forth the nature and extent of the petitioner's right, title, or interest in the property, the time and circumstances of the petitioner's acquisition of the right, title, or interest in the property, any additional facts supporting the petitioner's claim, and the relief sought.

(4) The hearing on the petition shall, to the extent practicable and consistent with the interests of justice, be held within thirty days of the filing of the petition. The court may consolidate the hearing on the petition with a hearing on any other petition filed by a person other than the defendant under this subsection.

(5) At the hearing, the petitioner may testify and present evidence and witnesses on his own behalf, and cross-examine witnesses who appear at the hearing. The United States may present evidence and witnesses in rebuttal and in defense of its claim to the property and cross-examine witnesses who appear at the hearing. In addition to testimony and evidence presented at the hearing, the court shall consider the relevant portions of the record of the criminal case which resulted in the order of forfeiture.

(6) If, after the hearing, the court determines that the petitioner has established by a preponderance of the evidence that—

(A) the petitioner has a legal right, title, or interest in the property, and such right, title, or interest renders the order of forfeiture invalid in whole or in part because the right, title, or interest was vested in the petitioner rather than the defendant or was superior to any right, title, or interest of the defendant at the time of the commission of the acts which gave rise to the forfeiture of the property under this section; or

(B) the petitioner is a bona fide purchaser for value of the right, title, or interest in the property and was at the time of purchase reasonably without cause to believe that the property was subject to forfeiture under this section;

the court shall amend the order of forfeiture in accordance with its determination.

(7) Following the court's disposition of all petitions filed under this subsection, or if no such petitions are filed following the expiration of the period provided in paragraph (2) for the filing of such petitions, the United States shall have clear title to property that is the subject of the order of forfeiture and may warrant good title to any subsequent purchaser or transferee.

(m) If any of the property described in subsection (a), as a result of any act or omission of the defendant—

(1) cannot be located upon the exercise of due diligence;
(2) has been transferred or sold to, or deposited with, a third party;
(3) has been placed beyond the jurisdiction of the court;
(4) has been substantially diminished in value; or
(5) has been commingled with other property which cannot be divided without difficulty;

the court shall order the forfeiture of any other property of the defendant up to the value of any property described in paragraphs (1) through (5).

[Added Pub. L. No. 91-452, Title IX, § 901(a), 84 Stat. 943 (Oct. 15, 1970), and amended Pub. L. No. 98-473, Title II, §§ 302, 2301(a)–(c), 98 Stat. 2040, 2192 (Oct. 12, 1984); Pub. L. No. 99-570, Title XI, § 1153(a), 100 Stat. 3207-13 (Oct. 27, 1986); Pub. L. No. 99-646, § 23, 100 Stat. 3597 (Nov. 10, 1986); Pub. L. No. 100-690, Title VII, §§ 7034, 7058(d), 102 Stat. 4398, 4403 (Nov. 18, 1988); Pub. L. No. 101-647, Title XXXV, § 3561, 104 Stat. 4927 (Nov. 29, 1990)]

18 U.S.C. § 1964. Civil remedies

(a) The district courts of the United States shall have jurisdiction to prevent and restrain violations of section 1962 of this chapter by issuing appropriate orders, including, but not limited to: ordering any person to divest himself of any interest, direct or indirect, in any enterprise; imposing reasonable restrictions on the future activities or investments of any person, including, but not limited to, prohibiting any person from engaging in the same type of endeavor as the enterprise engaged in, the activities of which affect interstate or foreign commerce; or ordering dissolution or reorganization of any enterprise, making due provision for the rights of innocent persons.

(b) The Attorney General may institute proceedings under this section. Pending final determination thereof, the court may at any time enter such restraining orders or prohibitions, or take such other actions, including the acceptance of satisfactory performance bonds, as it shall deem proper.

(c) Any person injured in his business or property by reason of a violation of section 1962 of this chapter may sue therefor in any appropriate United States district court and shall recover threefold the damages he sustains and the cost of the suit, including a reasonable attorney's fee, except that no person may rely upon any conduct that would have been actionable as fraud in the purchase or sale of securities to establish a violation of section 1962. The exception contained in the preceding sentence does not apply to an action against any person that is criminally convicted in connection with the fraud, in which case the statute of limitations shall start to run on the date on which the conviction becomes final.

(d) A final judgment or decree rendered in favor of the United States in any criminal proceeding brought by the United States under this chapter shall estop the defendant from denying the essential allegations of the criminal offense in any subsequent civil proceeding brought by the United States.

[Added Pub. L. No. 91-452, Title IX, § 901(a), 84 Stat. 943 (Oct. 15, 1970), and amended Pub. L. No. 98-620, Title IV, § 402(24)(A), 98 Stat. 3359 (Nov. 8, 1984); Pub. L. No. 104-67, Title I, § 107, 109 Stat. 758 (Dec. 22, 1995)]

18 U.S.C. § 1965. Venue and process

(a) Any civil action or proceeding under this chapter against any person may be instituted in the district court of the United States for any district in which such person resides, is found, has an agent, or transacts his affairs.

(b) In any action under section 1964 of this chapter in any district court of the United States in which it is shown that the ends of justice require that other parties residing in any other district be brought before the court, the court may cause such parties to be summoned, and process for that purpose may be served in any judicial district of the United States by the marshal thereof.

(c) In any civil or criminal action or proceeding instituted by the United States under this chapter in the district court of the United States for any judicial district, subpoenas issued by such court to compel the attendance of witnesses may be served in any other judicial district, except that in any civil action or proceeding no such subpena shall be issued for service upon any individual who resides in another district at a place more than one hundred miles from the place at which such court is held without approval given by a judge of such court upon a showing of good cause.

(d) All other process in any action or proceeding under this chapter may be served on any person in any judicial district in which such person resides, is found, has an agent, or transacts his affairs.

[Added Pub. L. No. 91-452, Title IX, § 901(a), 84 Stat. 944 (Oct. 15, 1970)]

18 U.S.C. § 1966. Expedition of actions

In any civil action instituted under this chapter by the United States in any district court of the United States, the Attorney General may file with the clerk of such court a certificate stating that in his opinion the case is of general public importance. A copy of that certificate shall be furnished immediately by such clerk to the chief judge or in his absence to the presiding district judge of the district in which such action is pending. Upon receipt of such copy, such judge shall designate immediately a judge of that district to hear and determine action.

[Added Pub. L. No. 91-452, Title IX, § 901(a), 84 Stat. 944 (Oct. 15, 1970), and amended Pub. L. No. 98-620, Title IV, § 402(24)(B), 98 Stat. 3359 (Nov. 8, 1984)]

18 U.S.C. § 1967. Evidence

In any proceeding ancillary to or in any civil action instituted by the United States under this chapter the proceedings may be open or closed to the public at the discretion of the court after consideration of the rights of affected persons.

[Added Pub. L. No. 91-452, Title IX, § 901(a), 84 Stat. 944 (Oct. 15, 1970)]

18 U.S.C. § 1968. Civil investigative demand

(a) Whenever the Attorney General has reason to believe that any person or enterprise may be in possession, custody, or control of any documentary materials relevant to a racketeering investigation, he may, prior to the institution of a civil or criminal proceeding thereon, issue in writing, and cause to be served upon such person, a civil investigative demand requiring such person to produce such material for examination.

(b) Each such demand shall—

(1) state the nature of the conduct constituting the alleged racketeering violation which is under investigation and the provision of law applicable thereto;

(2) describe the class or classes of documentary material produced thereunder with such definiteness and certainty as to permit such material to be fairly identified;

(3) state that the demand is returnable forthwith or prescribe a return date which will provide a reasonable period of time within which the material so demanded may be assembled and made available for inspection and copying or reproduction; and

(4) identify the custodian to whom such material shall be made available.

(c) No such demand shall—

(1) contain any requirement which would be held to be unreasonable if contained in a subpena duces tecum issued by a court of the United States in aid of a grand jury investigation of such alleged racketeering violation; or

(2) require the production of any documentary evidence which would be privileged from disclosure if demanded by a subpena duces tecum issued by a court of the United States in aid of a grand jury investigation of such alleged racketeering violation.

(d) Service of any such demand or any petition filed under this section may be made upon a person by—

(1) delivering a duly executed copy thereof to any partner, executive officer, managing agent, or general agent thereof, or to any agent thereof authorized by appointment or by law to receive service of process on behalf of such person, or upon any individual person;

(2) delivering a duly executed copy thereof to the principal office or place of business of the person to be served; or

(3) depositing such copy in the United States mail, by registered or certified mail duly addressed to such person at its principal office or place of business.

(e) A verified return by the individual serving any such demand or petition setting forth the manner of such service shall be prima facie proof of such service. In the case of service by registered or certified mail, such return shall be accompanied by the return post office receipt of delivery of such demand.

(f)(1) The Attorney General shall designate a racketeering investigator to serve as racketeer document custodian, and such additional racketeering investigators as he shall determine from time to time to be necessary to serve as deputies to such officer.

(2) Any person upon whom any demand issued under this section has been duly served shall make such material available for inspection and copying or reproduction to the custodian designated therein at the principal place of business of such person, or at such other place as such custodian and such person thereafter may agree and prescribe in writing or as the court may direct, pursuant to this section on the return date specified in such demand, or on such later date as such custodian may prescribe in writing. Such person may upon written agreement between such person and the custodian substitute for copies of all or any part of such material originals thereof.

(3) The custodian to whom any documentary material is so delivered shall take physical possession thereof, and shall be responsible for the use made thereof and for the return thereof pursuant to this chapter. The custodian may cause the preparation of such copies of such documentary material as may be required for official use under regulations which shall be promulgated by the Attorney General. While in the possession of the custodian, no material so produced shall be available for examination, without the consent of the person who produced such material, by any individual other than the Attorney General. Under such reasonable terms and conditions as the Attorney General shall prescribe, documentary material while in the possession of the custodian shall be available for examination by the person who produced such material or any duly authorized representatives of such person.

(4) Whenever any attorney has been designated to appear on behalf of the United States before any court or grand jury in any case or proceeding involving any alleged violation of this chapter, the custodian may deliver to such attorney such documentary material in the possession of the custodian as such attorney determines to be required for use in the presentation of such case or proceeding on behalf of the United States. Upon the conclusion of any such case or proceeding, such attorney shall return to the custodian any documentary material so withdrawn which has not passed into the control of such court or grand jury through the introduction thereof into the record of such case or proceeding.

(5) Upon the completion of—

(i) the racketeering investigation for which any documentary material was produced under this chapter, and

(ii) any case or proceeding arising from such investigation, the custodian shall return to the person who produced such material all such material other than copies thereof made by the Attorney General pursuant to this subsection which has not passed into the control of any court or grand jury through the introduction thereof into the record of such case or proceeding.

(6) When any documentary material has been produced by any person under this section for use in any racketeering investigation, and no such case or proceeding arising therefrom has been instituted within a reasonable time after completion of the examination and analysis of all evidence assembled in the course of such investigation, such person shall be entitled, upon written demand made upon the Attorney General, to the return of all documentary material other than copies thereof made pursuant to this subsection so produced by such person.

(7) In the event of the death, disability, or separation from service of the custodian of any documentary material produced under any demand issued under this section or the official relief of such custodian from responsibility for the custody and control of such material, the Attorney General shall promptly—

(i) designate another racketeering investigator to serve as custodian thereof, and

(ii) transmit notice in writing to the person who produced such material as to the identity and address of the successor so designated. Any successor so designated shall have with regard to such materials all duties and responsibilities imposed by this section upon his predecessor in office with regard thereto, except that he shall not be held responsible for any default or dereliction which occurred before his designation as custodian.

(g) Whenever any person fails to comply with any civil investigative demand duly served upon him under this section or whenever satisfactory copying or reproduction of any such material cannot be done and such person refuses to surrender such material, the Attorney General may file, in the district court of the United States for any judicial district in which such person resides, is found, or transacts business, and serve upon such person a petition for an order of such court for the enforcement of this section, except that if such person transacts business in more than one such district such petition shall be filed in the district in which such person maintains his principal place of business, or in such other district in which such person transacts business as may be agreed upon by the parties to such petition.

(h) Within twenty days after the service of any such demand upon any person, or at any time before the return date specified in the demand, whichever period is shorter, such person may file, in the district court of the United States for the judicial district within which such person resides, is found, or transacts business, and serve upon such custodian a petition for an order of such court modifying or setting aside such demand. The time allowed for compliance with the demand in whole or in part as deemed proper and ordered by the court shall not run during the pendency of such petition in the court. Such petition shall specify each ground upon which the petitioner relies in seeking such relief, and may be based upon any failure of such demand to comply with the provisions of this section or upon any constitutional or other legal right or privilege of such person.

(i) At any time during which any custodian is in custody or control of any documentary material delivered by any person in compliance with any such demand, such person may file, in the district court of the United States for the judicial district within which the office of such custodian is situated, and serve upon such custodian a petition for an order of such court requiring the performance by such custodian of any duty imposed upon him by this section.

(j) Whenever any petition is filed in any district court of the United States under this section, such court shall have jurisdiction to hear and determine the matter so presented, and to enter such order or orders as may be required to carry into effect the provisions of this section.

[Added Pub. L. No. 91-452, Title IX, § 901(a), 84 Stat. 944 (Oct. 15, 1970)]

C.1.2 Federal Wire and Mail Fraud Statutes

18 U.S.C. § 1341. Frauds and swindles

Whoever, having devised or intending to devise any scheme or artifice to defraud, or for obtaining money or property by means of false or fraudulent pretenses, representations, or promises, or to sell, dispose of, loan, exchange, alter, give away, distribute, supply, or furnish or procure for unlawful use any counterfeit or spurious coin, obligation, security, or other article, or anything represented to be or intimated or held out to be such counterfeit or spurious article, for the purpose of executing such scheme or artifice or attempting so to do, places in any post office or authorized depository for mail matter, any matter or thing whatever to be sent or delivered by the Postal Service, or deposits or causes to be deposited any matter or thing whatever to be sent or delivered by any private or commercial interstate carrier, or takes or receives therefrom, any such matter or thing, or knowingly causes to be delivered by mail or such carrier according to the direction thereon, or at the place at which it is directed to be delivered by the person to whom it is addressed, any such matter or thing, shall be fined under this title or imprisoned not more than 20 years, or both. If the violation affects a financial institution, such person shall be fined not more than $1,000,000 or imprisoned not more than 30 years, or both.

[June 25, 1948, ch. 645, 62 Stat. 763; May 24, 1949, ch. 139, § 34, 63 Stat. 94; Pub. L. No. 91-375, § (6)(j)(11), 84 Stat. 778 (Aug. 12, 1970); Pub. L. No. 101-73, tit. IX, § 961(i), 103 Stat. 500 (Aug. 9, 1989); Pub. L. No. 101-647, tit. XXV, § 2504(h), 104 Stat. 4861 (Nov. 29, 1990); Pub. L. No. 103-322, tit. XXV, § 250006, tit. XXXIII, § 330016(1)(H), 108 Stat. 2087, 2147 (Sept. 13, 1994); Pub. L. No. 107-204, 116 Stat. 745 (July 30, 2002)]

18 U.S.C. § 1343. Fraud by wire, radio, or television

Whoever, having devised or intending to devise any scheme or artifice to defraud, or for obtaining money or property by means of false or fraudulent pretenses, representations, or promises, transmits or causes to be transmitted by means of wire, radio, or television communication in interstate or foreign commerce, any writings, signs, signals, pictures, or sounds for the purpose of executing such scheme or artifice, shall be fined under this title or imprisoned not more than 20 years, or both. If the violation affects a financial institution, such person shall be fined not more than $1,000,000 or imprisoned not more than 30 years, or both.

[Added July 16, 1952, ch. 879, § 18(a), 66 Stat. 722; amended July 11, 1956, ch. 561, 70 Stat. 523; Pub. L. No. 101-73, tit. IX, § 961(j), 103 Stat. 500 (Aug. 9, 1989); Pub. L. No. 101-647, tit. XXV, § 2504(i), 104 Stat. 4861 (Nov. 29, 1990); Pub. L. No. 103-322, tit. XXXIII, § 330016(1)(H), 108 Stat. 2147 (Sept. 13, 1994); Pub. L. No. 107-204, 116 Stat. 745 (July 30, 2002).)

C.2 Statute-By-Statute Analysis of State RICO Statutes

This appendix summarizes the features of state RICO statutes. Most are modeled after the federal RICO statute, but many differ significantly from that statute.

Ariz. Rev. Stat. Ann. §§ 13-2301 through 13-2318 (West)

Predicate offenses: List of state offenses, including usury, extortionate extensions of credit, fraud, restraint of trade, and some securities offenses.

Pattern: Although only one offense is needed for the statutory definition of racketeering, or for a state criminal RICO conviction, a pattern is required for a civil RICO cause of action. A pattern requires either two or more related acts of racketeering within five years of each other, which were continuous or exhibit a threat of being continuous, or one single predicate act, if it is one of certain listed serious felonies (murder, kidnapping, drug offenses, etc.).

Does statute explicitly provide for private cause of action? Yes, for treble damages plus costs and attorney fees. No punitive damages or damages for emotional distress unless there is bodily injury. Enterprise requirements may be entirely available.

Statute of limitations: Three years after actual discovery of violation, or ten years after events giving rise to cause of action, whichever comes first.

Special procedural provisions: Preponderance of the evidence required for civil cases. The extensive 1993 revisions of the private RICO statute added a long list of protections against abuse, including sanctions for frivolous or oppressive actions and requirements that complaints be verified, that fraud be pleaded with particularity, and that the words "racketeer" or "racketeering activity" not be used unless one of the predicate acts is a crime of violence.

Cal. Penal Code §§ 186.1 through 186.8 (West)
Predicate offenses: List of state offenses, including securities offenses.
Pattern: Two or more interrelated predicate offenses that are committed as a criminal activity of organized crime. Most recent act must be within ten years, excluding periods of imprisonment, of prior act, and one offense must have occurred after enactment of the state RICO law.
Does statute explicitly provide for private cause of action? No.

Colo. Rev. Stat. §§ 18-17-101 through 18-17-109
Predicate offenses: List of state offenses, including some securities offenses, telecommunications offenses, felony charitable fraud, extortionate credit collections, and usury, plus those listed in federal RICO.
Pattern: Two predicate offenses related to the conduct of the enterprise. The last offense must have occurred no more than ten years, excluding periods of imprisonment, after a prior act, and one offense must have occurred after enactment of the statute.
Does statute explicitly provide for private cause of action? Yes, for treble damages plus costs and attorney fees. Enterprise requirements are less strict than in federal RICO.
Statute of limitations: Not specified.
Special procedural provisions: Standard of proof is clear and convincing evidence. Jury trial is available. Civil action may be brought by prosecutor or any aggrieved person.

Conn. Gen. Stat. Ann. §§ 53-393 through 53-403 (West)
Predicate offenses: List of state offenses, including extortionate credit transactions and securities offenses; also collection of unlawful debt.
Pattern: Two or more interrelated offenses. Last offense must have occurred within five years of a prior offense and at least one offense must have occurred after October 1, 1982.
Does statute explicitly provide for private cause of action? No. Forfeiture can be ordered by the court upon conviction of defendant. Court can direct transfer of assets to innocent persons or entities.
Statute of limitations: Five years after termination of unlawful conduct.

Del. Code Ann. tit. 11, §§ 1501 through 1511
Predicate offenses: List of state offenses, including all felonies and certain misdemeanors, plus those listed in federal RICO; also collection of unlawful debt.
Pattern: Two or more interrelated predicate offenses; must not be so closely related as to constitute a single event. The last offense must occur within ten years of the prior incident and at least one must occur after July 9, 1986.
Does statute explicitly provide for private cause of action? Yes, for treble damages plus costs and attorney fees; punitive damages are recoverable "when appropriate." Private action is allowed only against a defendant who has been convicted of a racketeering offense. Injured person can also intervene in an action to claim property that is forfeited. Enterprise requirements are less strict than in federal RICO.
Statute of limitations: Private civil action must be brought within one year of defendant's conviction of a racketeering activity; must also be brought within five years of the unlawful activity itself, but this limitation is tolled during any attorney general proceeding and for two years after its termination.

Fla. Stat. Ann. §§ 895.01 through 895.09 (West)
Predicate offenses: List of state offenses, including usury, securities offenses, telemarketing offenses, time-share escrow offenses, extortion, fraud, and telemarketing offenses (as of October 1, 1996), plus those listed in federal RICO; also collection of unlawful debt.
Pattern: Two or more related predicate offenses. Last predicate offense must have occurred within five years of a prior offense and at least one must have occurred after statute's effective date.
Does statute explicitly provide for private cause of action? Yes, but only for equitable relief. (*But see* Fla. Stat. Ann. §§ 772.101 through 772.190 (West), *infra*.) Plaintiff has claim to forfeited property superior to right or claim of state. Enterprise requirements are less strict than in federal RICO. Equitable relief is available without showing of special or irreparable damage. State and governmental subdivisions may sue for treble damages.
Statute of limitations: Five years, but suspended during prosecution for underlying offense and for two years thereafter.
Special procedural provisions: Standard of proof is clear and convincing evidence. Jury trial available.

Fla. Stat. Ann. §§ 772.101 through 772.19 (West)
Predicate offenses: List of state offenses, including securities offenses, telemarketing offenses, usury, fraud, extortion, exploitation of an elderly person, and time share escrow offenses, plus most offenses listed in federal RICO.
Pattern: Two related predicate offenses. Last act must be no more than five years after a prior act. Acts of fraud arising out of the same contract are treated as one offense.
Does statute explicitly provide for private cause of action? Yes, for treble damages, with a minimum of $200, plus costs and attorney fees. Punitive damages are not allowed. Enterprise requirements are less strict than in federal RICO.
Statute of limitations: Five years, but suspended during prosecution for underlying offense and for two years thereafter.
Special procedural provisions: Civil action can be pursued whether or not defendant is convicted of a predicate offense. Proof must be by clear and convincing evidence.

Ga. Code Ann. §§ 16-14-1 through 16-14-15
Predicate offenses: List of state offenses, including identity fraud and payday lending, plus those listed in federal RICO, plus certain crimes which carry a sentence of at least one year imprisonment according to U.S. or any state's laws (must involve extortion, theft, securities fraud, or various kinds of violence or illegal drugs.).
Pattern: Two similar or interrelated predicate offenses required. Last offense must have occurred within four years, excluding periods of imprisonment, of a prior act, and one offense must have occurred after July 1, 1980. The statute states that the legislative intent is to include only an interrelated pattern of criminal activity, the motive or effect of which is to derive pecuniary gain.
Does statute explicitly provide for private cause of action? Yes, for treble damages plus costs and attorney fees; punitive damages allowed, where appropriate. Enterprise requirements are less strict than in federal RICO. Injured person may also sue for injunctive relief and divestiture, without need to show irreparable harm. Injured person also can claim forfeited property, but must intervene in forfeiture proceeding.

Statute of limitations: Five years, suspended during pendency of related criminal prosecution or civil action and for two years thereafter.
Special procedural provisions: Jury trial available.

Haw. Rev. Stat. §§ 842-1 through 842-12
Predicate offenses: List of offenses, including extortion; must be punishable by at least one year in jail. Also collection of unlawful debt.
Pattern: Statute silent.
Does statute explicitly provide for private cause of action? Yes, any person injured in business or property by a violation may seek actual damages, costs, and attorney fees. Enterprise requirements are less strict than in federal RICO.
Statute of limitations: Statute silent.

Idaho Code §§ 18-7801 through 18-7805 (Michie)
Predicate offenses: List of state offenses, including fraud and usury; equivalent offenses under other states' laws.
Pattern: Two or more similar or related offenses. Last offense must have occurred within five years of a prior offense, and at least one offense must have occurred after July 1, 1981.
Does statute explicitly provide for private cause of action? Yes, for treble damages, plus costs and attorney fees. Enterprise requirements are less strict than in federal RICO.
Statute of limitations: Statute silent.

Ind. Code §§ 34-24-2-1 through 34-24-2-8 and 35-45-6-1 through 35-45-2
Predicate offenses: List of state offenses, including fraud.
Pattern: Two similar or interrelated incidents. The last must be within five years of a prior incident, and one must have occurred after August 31, 1980. *See Kollar v. State*, 556 N.E.2d 936 (Ind. App. 1990) for detail re elements of proof of pattern.
Does statute explicitly provide for private cause of action? Yes, for treble damages, plus costs and attorney fees. Punitive damages allowed. Enterprise requirements are less strict than in federal RICO. Victim also may sue for injunctive relief, and need not show special or irreparable damage. Victim also may make a claim to forfeited property.
Statute of limitations: Statute silent.
Special procedural provisions: Jury trial available. Burden of proof is preponderance of the evidence.

Iowa Code §§ 706A.1 through 706A.5
Predicate Offenses: "Specified unlawful activity" defined as any act, committed for financial gain on a continuing basis that is punishable as an indictable offense under the laws of the state in which it occurred and under the laws of Iowa.
Pattern: Statute silent.
Does statute explicitly provide for private cause of action? Yes, for treble damages plus costs and attorney fees. No recovery for pain and suffering. Aggrieved person may sue for injunction and divestiture.
Statute of limitations: Statute silent.
Special procedural provisions: Upon filing pleading, aggrieved person must notify the state attorney general. No need to show special injury to obtain an injunction. Standard of proof is preponderance of evidence. Criminal conviction or indictment not necessary. Pleadings must be verified. Fraud, coercion, and vicarious liability must be pled with particularity. Double damages plus attorney fees as sanction for frivolous pleading.

La. Rev. Stat. Ann. §§ 15:1351 through 15:1356 (West)
Predicate offenses: List of state offenses, focusing on crimes of violence and drug offenses, but also including theft and extortion.
Pattern: Two or more similar or related offenses. Last offense must have occurred within five years of a prior offense, and at least one offense must have occurred after July 22, 1983.
Does statute explicitly provide for private cause of action? Yes, for treble damages or $10,000, whichever is greater, plus costs and attorney fees. Enterprise requirements are less strict than in federal RICO. Injured person also has *in rem* claim to forfeited property.
Statute of limitations: Five years, suspended during pendency of related civil or criminal action and for two years thereafter.

Mich. Comp. Laws §§ 750.159f through 750.159x
Predicate offenses: List of state offenses, including securities fraud, extortion, false pretenses, federal RICO offenses, and similar offenses in other states.
Pattern: Two similar or interrelated incidents which pose a threat of continued criminal activity. The last must have occurred within 10 years, excluding periods of imprisonment, after a prior incident, and one must have been committed within the state after April 1, 1996.
Does statute explicitly provide for private cause of action? No. Statute explicitly states that it does not create a private cause of action. Forfeited property can be used to pay claims of victims.
Statute of limitations: Six years.

Minn. Stat. §§ 609.901 through 609.912
Predicate offenses: List of state felonies, including identity theft.
Pattern: Three or more related predicate offenses, two of which must be felonies other than conspiracy; offenses must not be so closely related as to constitute a single offense. Offenses must have been committed within ten years of commencement of criminal proceedings.
Does statute explicitly provide for private cause of action? No.
Statute of limitations: Ten years from commencement of criminal activity.

Miss. Code Ann. §§ 97-43-1 through 97-43-11
Predicate offenses: List of state offenses, including securities offenses. Also collection of unlawful debt.
Pattern: Two or more similar or related predicate offenses. Last offense must have occurred within five years of a prior act, and at least one offense must have occurred after the effective date of the statute.
Does statute explicitly provide for private cause of action? Yes, injured person has cause of action for treble damages plus costs and attorney fees against person or enterprise convicted of violation. Enterprise requirements are less strict than in federal RICO. Injured person can also seek injunction and divestiture; a showing of immediate or irreparable injury is not required for an injunction. Aggrieved person can also claim forfeited property.
Statute of limitations: Five years, suspended during pendency of related criminal prosecution or civil action and for two years thereafter.
Special procedural provisions: Jury trial available.

Nev. Rev. Stat. 207.350 through 207.520
Predicate offenses: List of state offenses, including extortion, extortionate collection of debt, obtaining money or property by false pretenses, and some securities offenses.
Pattern: Two or more similar or interrelated predicate offenses. Last offense must occur within five years of a prior act, and at least one offense must occur after July 1, 1983.
Does statute explicitly provide for private cause of action? Yes, for treble damages plus costs and attorney fees. Enterprise requirements are different than federal RICO. Injured person may also claim forfeited property.
Statute of limitations: Five years, suspended during pendency of related criminal prosecution or civil action and for two years thereafter.
Special procedural provisions: Jury trial available. Judicial decisions hold that predicate acts must be pleaded with same degree of specificity as in criminal indictment and that criminal conviction of the defendant is not a prerequisite to a civil action.

N.J. Stat. Ann. §§ 2C:41-1 through 2C:41-6.2 (West)
Predicate offenses: List of state offenses, including extortion, usury, and fraudulent practices, plus most of those listed in federal RICO. Also collection of unlawful debt.
Pattern: Two or more interrelated predicate offenses. Last act must have occurred within ten years (excluding periods of imprisonment) of a prior act. One offense must have occurred after effective date of statute.
Does statute explicitly provide for private cause of action? Yes, for treble damages plus costs and attorney fees.
Statute of limitations: Statute is silent, but judicial decisions say four years.

N.M. Stat. Ann. §§ 30-42-1 through 30-42-6 (Michie)
Predicate offenses: List of state offenses punishable by at least one year imprisonment, including fraud, extortion, securities offenses, and loan sharking.
Pattern: Two or more predicate offenses. Last offense must be within five years of a prior act and at least one offense must have occurred after the statute's effective date.
Does statute explicitly provide for private cause of action? Yes, for treble damages plus costs and attorney fees. Enterprise requirements are different than in federal RICO.
Statute of limitations: Statute silent.

N.Y. Penal Law §§ 460.00 through 460.80 (McKinney)
Predicate offenses: List of state offenses, including false statements, criminal usury, schemes to defraud, and certain securities offenses.
Pattern: Three or more related predicate offenses, but not so closely related as to constitute a single offense; at least two offenses must be felonies other than conspiracy; one felony within 5 years of commencement of action, and each act within 3 years of a prior act; many other requirements.
Does statute explicitly provide for private cause of action? No.
Statute of limitations: Ten years.

N.C. Gen. Stat. §§ 75D-1 through 75D-14
Predicate offenses: Most state offenses if chargeable by indictment, plus those listed in federal RICO. To maintain a civil RICO action, at least one offense must be other than federal mail fraud, federal wire fraud, or a securities offense.
Pattern: Two or more similar or interrelated offenses. One offense must have occurred no more than four years after a prior offense, excluding any period of imprisonment, and one offense must have occurred after October 1, 1986.
Does statute explicitly provide for private cause of action? Yes, for treble damages plus costs and attorney fees. Enterprise requirements are less strict than in federal RICO. Victim can also claim forfeited assets but must intervene in forfeiture proceeding.
Statute of limitations: Five years, suspended during pendency of civil action by state and for two years thereafter.
Special procedural provisions: Jury trial available. Plaintiff must notify attorney general of filing of suit, and attorney general can seek a stay of the action.

N.D. Cent. Code §§ 12.1-06.1-01 through 12.1-06.1-08
Predicate offenses: List of offenses including usury, extortion, fraud, and securities violations. If offense occurred in another state, it must be punishable by imprisonment for more than one year. Offenses must have been committed for financial gain.
Pattern: Two or more predicate offenses. Last offense must have occurred within 10 years, excluding periods of imprisonment, of a prior offense, and one offense must have occurred after July 8, 1987.
Does statute explicitly provide for private cause of action? Yes, for treble damages plus costs and attorney fees. Enterprise requirements may be entirely avoidable.
Statute of limitations: Seven years from discovery of violation.
Special procedural provisions: Plaintiff must notify attorney general of filing of suit. Burden of proof is preponderance of the evidence.

Ohio Rev. Code Ann. §§ 2923.31 through 2923.36 (West)
Predicate offenses: List of state offenses, including extortion, usury, credit repair clinic registration law, and mortgage broker registration law, plus those listed in federal RICO.
Pattern: Two or more related predicate offenses, but not so closely related as to constitute a single event. For civil suit, at least one offense must be other than federal mail fraud, federal wire fraud, or a securities offense. Unless one of the incidents was murder, last offense must be within six years, not including periods of imprisonment, of a prior offense. One offense must have occurred after January 1, 1986.
Does statute explicitly provide for private cause of action? Yes, for treble damages plus costs and attorney fees. Enterprise requirements are less strict than in federal RICO. Victim can also sue for equitable relief including injunction and divestiture. Victims also have right to forfeited property, if civil action is brought within 180 days after entry of sentence of forfeiture.
Statute of limitations: Five years after conduct terminated or cause of action accrued, or any longer statute which may be applicable. Suspended during pendency of civil or criminal proceedings and for two years thereafter.
Special procedural provisions: Proof by clear and convincing evidence required for treble damages. Special or irreparable injury need not be shown to get injunctive relief. Statute explicitly states that it is not necessary that defendant have been convicted of the predicate offenses.

Okla. Stat. Ann. tit. 22, §§ 1401 through 1419 (West)
Predicate offenses: List of state offenses, including extortion, fraud, and securities offense.
Pattern: Two or more predicate offenses within three years, excluding periods of imprisonment, at least one after November 1, 1988, related to the affairs of the enterprise, neither isolated nor so closely related as to constitute a single event. Criminal charge or indictment not required.
Does statute explicitly provide for private cause of action? No. The attorney general or a district attorney can seek injunctive relief and forfeiture.
Statute of limitations: Five years, suspended during pendency of related criminal or civil action and for two years thereafter.

Or. Rev. Stat. §§ 166.715 through 166.735
Predicate offenses: List of state offenses, including securities offenses and usury, offenses involving real estate and escrow, outfitters and guides, mortgage bankers and mortgage brokers, business and commercial offenses, communications crimes, plus some offenses listed in federal RICO; also, collection of unlawful debt.
Pattern: Two or more similar or interrelated predicate offenses. Last offense must have occurred within five years of a prior offense and at least one must have occurred after November 1, 1981.
Does statute explicitly provide for private cause of action? Yes, for treble damages plus costs and attorney fees; punitive damages allowed when appropriate. Criminal conviction of defendant is necessary in some cases. Enterprise requirements are less strict than in federal RICO. Victim may also sue for injunction and divestiture. Victim has claim to forfeited property.
Statute of limitations: Five years, suspended during pendency of a related civil action or criminal prosecution.
Special procedural provisions: No need to show special or irreparable injury to get injunction. Jury trial available.

18 Pa. Cons. Stat. § 911
Predicate offenses: List of state offenses, including charging more than 25% APR for debt unless otherwise authorized by law.
Pattern: Two or more predicate offenses, one after effective date of statute.
Does statute explicitly provide for private cause of action? No. Attorney general may seek divestiture.
Statute of limitations: Statute silent.

25 P.R. Laws Ann. §§ 971 through 971p
Predicate offenses: List of state offense, including extortion; also, collection of illegal debt.
Pattern: Two acts of organized criminal activity within a ten year period, excluding any period of imprisonment, at least one of which occurred after June 19, 1987.
Does statute explicitly provide for private cause of action? Yes, for treble damages, costs and attorney fees.
Statute of limitations: Ten years, except where other statute establishes longer limitations period.

R.I. Gen. Laws §§ 7-15-1 through 7-15-11
Predicate offenses: List of state offenses, including extortion; also, collection of unlawful debt.
Pattern: None required.
Does statute explicitly provide for private cause of action? Yes, for treble damages plus costs and attorney fees. Victim may also intervene in forfeiture proceeding and seek escrow of forfeited assets. Statute explicitly states that criminal conviction of defendant is unnecessary.
Statute of limitations: Statute silent.

Utah Code Ann §§ 76-10-1601 through 76-10-1609
Predicate offenses: List of state offenses, including theft by deception, theft by extortion, usury, confidence game, false statements, deceptive business practices, and identity fraud, plus most offenses listed in federal RICO.
Pattern: Three or more similar or interrelated offenses, demonstrating continuing unlawful conduct. Last offense must have occurred within five years of a prior offense and at least one offense must have occurred after July 31, 1981.
Does statute explicitly provide for private cause of action? Yes, for double damages plus costs and attorney fees. Victim may also request injunctive relief.
Statute of limitations: Three years.
Special procedural provisions: Statute explicitly states that criminal conviction of defendant is unnecessary. Fraud cases are subject to arbitration. Proof must be by clear and convincing evidence.

14 V.I. Code Ann. §§ 600 through 614
Predicate offenses: List of state offenses, including statutes regulating loans, disclosure of finance charges, extortion, fraud and false statements.
Pattern: Two or more offenses, not isolated, related to the conduct of the enterprise, at least one of which occurred after November 9, 1990.
Does statute explicitly provide for private cause of action? Yes, for treble damages (not including pain and suffering), costs and reasonable attorney fees. Victim has a claim to forfeited property.
Statute of limitations: Five years, excluding any period of imprisonment, unless a longer statute applies.
Special procedural provisions: Fraud, coercion or conspiracy must be pleaded with particularity. Showing of special or irreparable injury not required for injunction. Pleadings must be verified and signed by plaintiff's attorney, if any.

Wash. Rev. Code §§ 9A.82.010 through 9A.82.901
Predicate offenses: List of state offenses, including extortion, collection of unlawful debt, collection of extortionate extension of credit, telephone solicitation violations, securities fraud, pursuing a pattern of skimming homeowners' equity, identity theft, and unlicensed practice of profession or business. Securities fraud may be a predicate offense only if defendant has been convicted criminally.
Pattern: Three or more similar or interrelated offenses. The last must have occurred within five years, excluding periods of imprisonment, of the earliest, and one must have occurred after July 1, 1985.
Does statute explicitly provide for private cause of action? Yes, for actual damages, which may, in the court's discretion, be trebled, plus costs and attorney fees. Enterprise requirements may be entirely avoidable. Victim also has a claim on forfeited property.
Statute of limitations: Three years from discovery, or from when discovery reasonably should have occurred.

Special procedural provisions: Standard of proof is preponderance of evidence. Plaintiff must serve notice of suit on attorney general.

Wis. Stat. §§ 946.80 through 946.88
Predicate offenses: List of state offenses, including securities offenses, franchise law violations, loan sharking, identity theft and some frauds, plus offenses listed in federal RICO.
Pattern: Three or more similar or related predicate offenses, the motive of which is to derive pecuniary gain. Last offense must have occurred within seven years of the first, and at least one must have occurred after April 27, 1982.
Does statute explicitly provide for private cause of action? Yes, for double damages plus costs and attorney fees; punitive damages allowed when appropriate. Enterprise requirements are less strict than in federal RICO. Victim may also claim assets in forfeiture proceeding.
Statute of limitations: Six years, but suspended during pendency of related criminal or civil case and for two years thereafter.
Special procedural provisions: Jury trial is available.

Appendix D Federal Telemarketing Statutes and Regulations

The full text of this appendix and additional agency interpretations relating to the regulations reprinted in this appendix are found on the companion CD-Rom.

D.1 Federal Telemarketing Statutes

D.1.1 Telemarketing and Consumer Fraud and Abuse Prevention—15 U.S.C. §§ 6101–6108

§ 6101. Findings

The Congress makes the following findings:

(1) Telemarketing differs from other sales activities in that it can be carried out by sellers across State lines without direct contact with the consumer. Telemarketers also can be very mobile, easily moving from State to State.

(2) Interstate telemarketing fraud has become a problem of such magnitude that the resources of the Federal Trade Commission are not sufficient to ensure adequate consumer protection from such fraud.

(3) Consumers and others are estimated to lose $40 billion a year in telemarketing fraud.

(4) Consumers are victimized by other forms of telemarketing deception and abuse.

(5) Consequently, Congress should enact legislation that will offer consumers necessary protection from telemarketing deception and abuse.

[Pub. L. No. 103-297, § 2, 108 Stat. 1545 (Aug. 16, 1994)]

§ 6102. Telemarketing rules

(a) In general

(1) The Commission shall prescribe rules prohibiting deceptive telemarketing acts or practices and other abusive telemarketing acts or practices.

(2) The Commission shall include in such rules respecting deceptive telemarketing acts or practices a definition of deceptive telemarketing acts or practices which may include acts or practices which shall include fraudulent charitable solicitations, and of entities or individuals that assist or facilitate deceptive telemarketing, including credit card laundering.

(3) The Commission shall include in such rules respecting other abusive telemarketing acts or practices—

(A) a requirement that telemarketers may not undertake a pattern of unsolicited telephone calls which the reasonable consumer would consider coercive or abusive of such consumer's right to privacy,

(B) restrictions on the hours of the day and night when unsolicited telephone calls can be made to consumers,

(C) a requirement that any person engaged in telemarketing for the sale of goods or services shall promptly and clearly disclose to the person receiving the call that the purpose of the call is to sell goods or services and make such other disclosures as the Commission deems appropriate, including the nature and price of the goods and services;

(D) a requirement that any person engaged in telemarketing for the solicitation of charitable contributions, donations, or gifts of money or any other thing of value, shall promptly and clearly disclose to the person receiving the call that the purpose of the call is to solicit charitable contributions, donations, or gifts, and make such other disclosures as the Commission considers appropriate, including the name and mailing address of the charitable organization on behalf of which the solicitation is made.

In prescribing the rules described in this paragraph, the Commission shall also consider recordkeeping requirements.

(b) Rulemaking

The Commission shall prescribe the rules under subsection (a) of this section within 365 days after August 16, 1994. Such rules shall be prescribed in accordance with section 553 of Title 5.

(c) Enforcement

Any violation of any rule prescribed under subsection (a) of this section shall be treated as a violation of a rule under section 57a of this title regarding unfair or deceptive acts or practices.

(d) Securities and Exchange Commission rules

(1) Promulgation

(A) In general

Except as provided in subparagraph (B), not later than 6 months after the effective date of rules promulgated by the Federal Trade Commission under subsection (a) of this section, the Securities and Exchange Commission shall promulgate, or require any national securities exchange or registered securities association to promulgate, rules substantially similar to such rules to prohibit deceptive and other abusive telemarketing acts or practices by persons described in paragraph (2).

(B) Exception

The Securities and Exchange Commission is not required to promulgate a rule under subparagraph (A) if it determines that—

(i) Federal securities laws or rules adopted by the Securities and Exchange Commission thereunder provide protection from deceptive and other abusive telemarketing by persons described in paragraph (2) substantially similar to that provided by rules promulgated by the Federal Trade Commission under subsection (a) of this section; or

(ii) such a rule promulgated by the Securities and Exchange Commission is not necessary or appropriate in the public interest, or for the protection of investors, or would be inconsistent with the maintenance of fair and orderly markets.

If the Securities and Exchange Commission determines that an exception described in clause (i) or (ii) applies, the Securities and Exchange Commission shall publish in the Federal Register its determination with the reasons for it.

(2) Application

(A) In general

The rules promulgated by the Securities and Exchange Commission under paragraph (1)(A) shall apply to a broker, dealer, transfer agent, municipal securities dealer, municipal securities broker, government securities broker, government securities dealer, investment adviser or investment company, or any individual associated with a broker, dealer, transfer agent, municipal securities dealer, municipal securities broker, government securities broker, government securities dealer, investment adviser or investment company. The rules promulgated by the Federal Trade Commission under subsection (a) of this section shall not apply to persons described in the preceding sentence.

(B) Definitions

For purposes of subparagraph (A)—

(i) the terms "broker", "dealer", "transfer agent", "municipal securities dealer", "municipal securities broker", "government securities broker", and "government securities dealer" have the meanings given such terms by paragraphs (4), (5), (25), (30), (31), (43), and (44) of section 78c(a) of this title;

(ii) the term "investment adviser" has the meaning given such term by section 80b-2(a)(11) of this title; and

(iii) the term "investment company" has the meaning given such term by section 80a-3(a) of this title.

(e) Commodity Futures Trading Commission rules

(1) Application

The rules promulgated by the Federal Trade Commission under subsection (a) of this section shall not apply to persons described in section 9b(1) of Title 7.

(2) Omitted

[Pub. L. No. 103-297, § 3, 108 Stat. 1545 (Aug. 16, 1994); Pub. L. No. 107-56, Title X, § 1011(b)(1), (2), 115 Stat. 396 (Oct. 26, 2001)]

§ 6103. Actions by States

(a) In general

Whenever an attorney general of any State has reason to believe that the interests of the residents of that State have been or are being threatened or adversely affected because any person has engaged or is engaging in a pattern or practice of telemarketing which violates any rule of the Commission under section 6102 of this title, the State, as parens patriae, may bring a civil action on behalf of its residents in an appropriate district court of the United States to enjoin such telemarketing, to enforce compliance with such rule of the Commission, to obtain damages, restitution, or other compensation on behalf of residents of such State, or to obtain such further and other relief as the court may deem appropriate.

(b) Notice

The State shall serve prior written notice of any civil action under subsection (a) or (f)(2) of this section upon the Commission and provide the Commission with a copy of its complaint, except that if it is not feasible for the State to provide such prior notice, the State shall serve such notice immediately upon instituting such action. Upon receiving a notice respecting a civil action, the Commission shall have the right (1) to intervene in such action, (2) upon so intervening, to be heard on all matters arising therein, and (3) to file petitions for appeal.

(c) Construction

For purposes of bringing any civil action under subsection (a) of this section, nothing in this chapter shall prevent an attorney general from exercising the powers conferred on the attorney general by the laws of such State to conduct investigations or to administer oaths or affirmations or to compel the attendance of witnesses or the production of documentary and other evidence.

(d) Actions by the Commission

Whenever a civil action has been instituted by or on behalf of the Commission for violation of any rule prescribed under section 6102 of this title, no State may, during the pendency of such action instituted by or on behalf of the Commission, institute a civil action under subsection (a) or (f)(2) of this section against any defendant named in the complaint in such action for violation of any rule as alleged in such complaint.

(e) Venue; service of process

Any civil action brought under subsection (a) of this section in a district court of the United States may be brought in the district in which the defendant is found, is an inhabitant, or transacts business or wherever venue is proper under section 1391 of Title 28. Process in such an action may be served in any district in which the defendant is an inhabitant or in which the defendant may be found.

(f) Actions by other State officials

(1) Nothing contained in this section shall prohibit an authorized State official from proceeding in State court on the basis of an alleged violation of any civil or criminal statute of such State.

(2) In addition to actions brought by an attorney general of a State under subsection (a) of this section, such an action may be brought by officers of such State who are authorized by the State to bring actions in such State on behalf of its residents.

[Pub. L. No. 103-297, § 4, 108 Stat. 1548 (Aug. 16, 1994)]

§ 6104. Actions by private persons

(a) In general

Any person adversely affected by any pattern or practice of telemarketing which violates any rule of the Commission under section 6102 of this title, or an authorized person acting on such person's behalf, may, within 3 years after discovery of the violation, bring a civil action in an appropriate district court of the United States against a person who has engaged or is engaging in such pattern or practice of telemarketing if the amount in controversy exceeds the sum or value of $50,000 in actual damages for each person adversely affected by such telemarketing. Such an action may be brought to enjoin such telemarketing, to enforce compliance with any rule of the Commission under section 6102 of this title, to obtain damages, or to obtain such further and other relief as the court may deem appropriate.

(b) Notice

The plaintiff shall serve prior written notice of the action upon the Commission and provide the Commission with a copy of its complaint, except in any case where such prior notice is not feasible, in which case the person shall serve such notice immediately upon instituting such action. The Commission shall have the right (A) to intervene in the action, (B) upon so intervening, to be heard on all matters arising therein, and (C) to file petitions for appeal.

(c) Action by the Commission

Whenever a civil action has been instituted by or on behalf of the Commission for violation of any rule prescribed under section 6102 of this title, no person may, during the pendency of such action instituted by or on behalf of the Commission, institute a civil action against any defendant named in the complaint in such action for violation of any rule as alleged in such complaint.

(d) Cost and fees

The court, in issuing any final order in any action brought under subsection (a) of this section, may award costs of suit and reasonable fees for attorneys and expert witnesses to the prevailing party.

(e) Construction

Nothing in this section shall restrict any right which any person may have under any statute or common law.

(f) Venue; service of process

Any civil action brought under subsection (a) of this section in a district court of the United States may be brought in the district in which the defendant is found, is an inhabitant, or transacts business or wherever venue is proper under section 1391 of Title 28. Process in such an action may be served in any district in which the defendant is an inhabitant or in which the defendant may be found.

[Pub. L. No. 103-297, § 5, 108 Stat. 1549 (Aug. 16, 1994)]

§ 6105. Administration and applicability of chapter

(a) In general

Except as otherwise provided in sections 6102(d), 6102(e), 6103, and 6104 of this title, this chapter shall be enforced by the Commission under the Federal Trade Commission Act [15 U.S.C. § 41 et seq.]. Consequently, no activity which is outside the jurisdiction of that Act shall be affected by this chapter.

(b) Actions by the Commission

The Commission shall prevent any person from violating a rule of the Commission under section 6102 of this title in the same manner, by the same means, and with the same jurisdiction, powers, and duties as though all applicable terms and provisions of the Federal Trade Commission Act [15 U.S.C. § 41 et seq.] were incorporated into and made a part of this chapter. Any person who violates such rule shall be subject to the penalties and entitled to the privileges and immunities provided in the Federal Trade Commission Act [15 U.S.C.A. § 41 et seq.] in the same manner, by the same means, and with the same jurisdiction, power, and duties as though all applicable terms and provisions of the Federal Trade Commission Act [15 U.S.C.A. § 41 et seq.] were incorporated into and made a part of this chapter.

(c) Effect on other laws

Nothing contained in this chapter shall be construed to limit the authority of the Commission under any other provision of law.

[Pub. L. No. 103-297, § 6, 108 Stat. 1549 (Aug. 16, 1994)]

§ 6106. Definitions

For purposes of this chapter:

(1) The term "attorney general" means the chief legal officer of a State.

(2) The term "Commission" means the Federal Trade Commission.

(3) The term "State" means any State of the United States, the District of Columbia, Puerto Rico, the Northern Mariana Islands, and any territory or possession of the United States.

(4) The term "telemarketing" means a plan, program, or campaign which is conducted to induce purchases of goods or services, or a charitable contribution, donation, or gift of money or any other thing of value, by use of one or more telephones and which involves more than one interstate telephone call. The term does not include the solicitation of sales through the mailing of a catalog which—

- **(A)** contains a written description, or illustration of the goods or services offered for sale,
- **(B)** includes the business address of the seller,
- **(C)** includes multiple pages of written material or illustrations, and
- **(D)** has been issued not less frequently than once a year,

where the person making the solicitation does not solicit customers by telephone but only receives calls initiated by customers in response to the catalog and during those calls takes orders only without further solicitation.

[Pub. L. No. 103-297, § 7, 108 Stat. 1550 (Aug. 16, 1994); Pub. L. No. 107-56, Title X, § 1011(b)(3), 115 Stat. 396 (Oct. 26, 2001)]

§ 6107. Enforcement of orders

(a) General authority

Subject to subsections (b) and (c) of this section, the Federal Trade Commission may bring a criminal contempt action for violations of orders of the Commission obtained in cases brought under section 53(b) of this title.

(b) Appointment

An action authorized by subsection (a) of this section may be brought by the Federal Trade Commission only after, and pursuant to, the appointment by the Attorney General of an attorney employed by the Commission, as a special assistant United States Attorney.

(c) Request for appointment

(1) Appointment upon request or motion

A special assistant United States Attorney may be appointed under subsection (b) of this section upon the request of the Federal Trade Commission or the court which has entered the order for which contempt is sought or upon the Attorney General's own motion.

(2) Timing

The Attorney General shall act upon any request made under paragraph (1) within 45 days of the receipt of the request.

(d) Termination of authority

The authority of the Federal Trade Commission to bring a criminal contempt action under subsection (a) of this section expires 2 years after the date of the first promulgation of rules under section 6102 of this title. The expiration of such authority shall have no effect on an action brought before the expiration date.

[Pub. L. No. 103-297, § 9, 108 Stat. 1550 (Aug. 16, 1994)]

§ 6108. Review

Upon the expiration of 5 years following the date of the first promulgation of rules under section 6102 of this title, the Commission shall review the implementation of this chapter and its effect on deceptive telemarketing acts or practices and report the results of the review to the Congress.

[Pub. L. No. 103-297, § 10, 108 Stat. 1551 (Aug. 16, 1994)]

D.1.2 Telephone Disclosure and Dispute Resolution—15 U.S.C. § 5711

§ 5711. Federal Trade Commission regulations

(a) In general

(1) Advertising regulations

The Commission shall prescribe rules in accordance with this subsection to prohibit unfair and deceptive acts and practices in any advertisement for pay-per-call services. Such rules shall require that the person offering such pay-per-call services—

(A) clearly and conspicuously disclose in any advertising the cost of the use of such telephone number, including the total cost or the cost per minute and any other fees for that service and for any other pay-per-call service to which the caller may be transferred;

(B) in the case of an advertisement which offers a prize or award or a service or product at no cost or for a reduced cost, clearly and conspicuously disclose the odds of being able to receive such prize, award, service, or product at no cost or reduced cost, or, if such odds are not calculable in advance, disclose the factors determining such odds;

(C) in the case of an advertisement that promotes a service that is not operated or expressly authorized by a Federal agency but that provides information on a Federal program, include at the beginning of such advertisement a clear disclosure that the service is not authorized, endorsed, or approved by any Federal agency;

(D) shall not direct such advertisement at children under the age of 12, unless such service is a bona fide educational service;

(E) in the case of advertising directed primarily to individuals under the age of 18, clearly and conspicuously state in such advertising that such individual must have the consent of such individual's parent or legal guardian for the use of such services;

(F) be prohibited from using advertisements that emit electronic tones which can automatically dial a pay-per-call telephone number;

(G) ensure that, whenever the number to be called is shown in television and print media advertisements, the charges for the call are clear and conspicuous and (when shown in television advertisements) displayed for the same duration as that number is displayed;

(H) in delivering any telephone message soliciting calls to a pay-per-call service, specify clearly, and at no less than the audible volume of the solicitation, the total cost and the cost per minute and any other fees for that service and for any other pay-per-call service to which the caller may be transferred; and

(I) not advertise an 800 telephone number, or any other telephone number advertised or widely understood to be toll free, from which callers are connected to an access number for a pay-per-call service.

(2) Pay-per-call service standards

The Commission shall prescribe rules to require that each provider of pay-per-call services—

(A) include in each pay-per-call message an introductory disclosure message that—

(i) describes the service being provided;

(ii) specifies clearly and at a reasonably understandable volume the total cost or the cost per minute and any other fees for that service and for any other pay-per-call service to which the caller may be transferred;

(iii) informs the caller that charges for the call begin at the end of the introductory message;

(iv) informs the caller that parental consent is required for calls made by children; and

(v) in the case of a pay-per-call service that is not operated or expressly authorized by a Federal agency but that provides information on any Federal program, a statement that clearly states that the service is not authorized, endorsed, or approved by any Federal agency;

(B) enable the caller to hang up at or before the end of the introductory message without incurring any charge whatsoever;

(C) not direct such services at children under the age of 12, unless such service is a bona fide educational service;

(D) stop the assessment of time-based charges immediately upon disconnection by the caller;

(E) disable any bypass mechanism which allows frequent callers to avoid listening to the disclosure message described in subparagraph (A) after the institution of any price increase and for a period of time sufficient to give such frequent callers adequate and sufficient notice of the price change;

(F) be prohibited from providing pay-per-call services through an 800 number or other telephone number advertised or widely understood to be toll free;

(G) be prohibited from billing consumers in excess of the amounts described in the introductory message and from billing for services provided in violation of the rules prescribed by the Commission pursuant to this section;

(H) ensure that any billing statement for such provider's charges shall—

(i) display any charges for pay-per-call services in a part of the consumer's bill that is identified as not being related to local and long distance telephone charges; and

(ii) for each charge so displayed, specify, at a minimum, the type of service, the amount of the charge, and the date, time, and duration of the call;

(I) be liable for refunds to consumers who have been billed for pay-per-call services pursuant to programs that have been found to have violated the regulations prescribed pursuant to this section or subchapter II of this chapter or any other Federal law; and

(J) comply with such additional standards as the Commission may prescribe to prevent abusive practices.

(3) Access to information

The Commission shall by rule require a common carrier that provides telephone services to a provider of pay-per-call services to make available to the Commission any records and financial information maintained by such carrier relating to the arrangements (other than for the provision of local exchange service) between such carrier and any provider of pay-per-call services.

(4) Evasions

The rules issued by the Commission under this section shall include provisions to prohibit unfair or deceptive acts or practices that evade such rules or undermine the rights provided to customers under this subchapter, including through the use of alternative billing or other procedures.

(5) Exemptions

The regulations prescribed by the Commission pursuant to paragraph (2)(A) may exempt from the requirements of such paragraph—

(A) calls from frequent callers or regular subscribers using a bypass mechanism to avoid listening to the disclosure message required by such regulations, subject to the requirements of paragraph (2)(E); or

(B) pay-per-call services provided at nominal charges, as defined by the Commission in such regulations.

(6) Consideration of other rules required

In conducting a proceeding under this section, the Commission shall consider requiring, by rule or regulation, that providers of pay-per-call services—

(A) automatically disconnect a call after one full cycle of the program; and

(B) include a beep tone or other appropriate and clear signal during a live interactive group program so that callers will be alerted to the passage of time.

(7) Special rule for infrequent publications

The rules prescribed by the Commission under subparagraphs (A) and (G) of paragraph (1) may permit, in the case of publications that are widely distributed, that are printed annually or less frequently, and that have an established policy of not publishing specific prices, advertising that in lieu of the cost disclosures required by such subparagraphs, clearly and conspicuously disclose that use of the telephone number may result in a substantial charge.

(8) Treatment of rules

A rule issued under this subsection shall be treated as a rule issued under section 57a(a)(1)(B) of this title.

(b) Rulemaking

The Commission shall prescribe the rules under subsection (a) of this section within 270 days after October 28, 1992. Such rules shall be prescribed in accordance with section 553 of title 5.

(c) Enforcement

Any violation of any rule prescribed under subsection (a) of this section shall be treated as a violation of a rule respecting unfair or deceptive acts or practices under section 45 of this title. Notwithstanding section 45(a)(2) of this title, communications common carriers shall be subject to the jurisdiction of the Commission for purposes of this subchapter.

[Pub. L. No. 102-556, Title II, § 201, 106 Stat. 4187 (Oct. 28, 1992)]

D.1.3 Restrictions on Use of Telephone Equipment—47 U.S.C. § 227

§ 227. Restrictions on the use of telephone equipment

(a) Definitions

As used in this section—

(1) The term "automatic telephone dialing system" means equipment which has the capacity—

(A) to store or produce telephone numbers to be called, using a random or sequential number generator; and

(B) to dial such numbers.

(2) The term "telephone facsimile machine" means equipment which has the capacity (A) to transcribe text or images, or both, from paper into an electronic signal and to transmit that signal over a regular telephone line, or (B) to transcribe text or images (or both) from an electronic signal received over a regular telephone line onto paper.

(3) The term "telephone solicitation" means the initiation of a telephone call or message for the purpose of encouraging the purchase or rental of, or investment in, property, goods, or services, which is transmitted to any person, but such term does not include a call or message (A) to any person with that person's prior express invitation or permission, (B) to any person with whom the caller has an established business relationship, or (C) by a tax exempt nonprofit organization.

(4) The term "unsolicited advertisement" means any material advertising the commercial availability or quality of any property, goods, or services which is transmitted to any person without that person's prior express invitation or permission.

(b) Restrictions on the use of automated telephone equipment

(1) Prohibitions

It shall be unlawful for any person within the United States, or any person outside the United States if the recipient is within the United States—

(A) to make any call (other than a call made for emergency purposes or made with the prior express consent of the called party) using any automatic telephone dialing system or an artificial or prerecorded voice—

(i) to any emergency telephone line (including any "911" line and any emergency line of a hospital, medical physician or service office, health care facility, poison control center, or fire protection or law enforcement agency);

(ii) to the telephone line of any guest room or patient room of a hospital, health care facility, elderly home, or similar establishment; or

(iii) to any telephone number assigned to a paging service, cellular telephone service, specialized mobile radio service, or other radio common carrier service, or any service for which the called party is charged for the call;

(B) to initiate any telephone call to any residential telephone line using an artificial or prerecorded voice to deliver a message without the prior express consent of the called party, unless the call is initiated for emergency purposes or is exempted by rule or order by the Commission under paragraph (2)(B);

(C) to use any telephone facsimile machine, computer, or other device to send an unsolicited advertisement to a telephone facsimile machine; or

(D) to use an automatic telephone dialing system in such a way that two or more telephone lines of a multi-line business are engaged simultaneously.

(2) Regulations; exemptions and other provisions

The Commission shall prescribe regulations to implement the requirements of this subsection. In implementing the requirements of this subsection, the Commission—

(A) shall consider prescribing regulations to allow businesses to avoid receiving calls made using an artificial or prerecorded voice to which they have not given their prior express consent;

(B) may, by rule or order, exempt from the requirements of paragraph (1)(B) of this subsection, subject to such conditions as the Commission may prescribe—

(i) calls that are not made for a commercial purpose; and

(ii) such classes or categories of calls made for commercial purposes as the Commission determines—

(I) will not adversely affect the privacy rights that this section is intended to protect; and

(II) do not include the transmission of any unsolicited advertisement; and

(C) may, by rule or order, exempt from the requirements of paragraph (1)(A)(iii) of this subsection calls to a telephone number assigned to a cellular telephone service that are not charged to the called party, subject to such conditions as the Commission may prescribe as necessary in the interest of the privacy rights this section is intended to protect.

(3) Private right of action

A person or entity may, if otherwise permitted by the laws or rules of court of a State, bring in an appropriate court of that State—

(A) an action based on a violation of this subsection or the regulations prescribed under this subsection to enjoin such violation,

(B) an action to recover for actual monetary loss from such a violation, or to receive $500 in damages for each such violation, whichever is greater, or

(C) both such actions.

If the court finds that the defendant willfully or knowingly violated this subsection or the regulations prescribed under this subsection, the court may, in its discretion, increase the amount of the award to an amount equal to not more than 3 times the amount available under subparagraph (B) of this paragraph.

(c) Protection of subscriber privacy rights

(1) Rulemaking proceeding required

Within 120 days after December 20, 1991, the Commission shall initiate a rulemaking proceeding concerning the need to protect residential telephone subscribers' privacy rights to avoid receiving telephone solicitations to which they object. The proceeding shall—

(A) compare and evaluate alternative methods and procedures (including the use of electronic databases, telephone network technologies, special directory markings, industry-based or company-specific "do not call" systems, and any other alternatives, individually or in combination) for their effectiveness in protecting such privacy rights, and in terms of their cost and other advantages and disadvantages;

(B) evaluate the categories of public and private entities that would have the capacity to establish and administer such methods and procedures;

(C) consider whether different methods and procedures may apply for local telephone solicitations, such as local telephone solicitations of small businesses or holders of second class mail permits;

(D) consider whether there is a need for additional Commission authority to further restrict telephone solicitations, including those calls exempted under subsection (a)(3) of this section, and, if such a finding is made and supported by the record, propose specific restrictions to the Congress; and

(E) develop proposed regulations to implement the methods and procedures that the Commission determines are most effective and efficient to accomplish the purposes of this section.

(2) Regulations

Not later than 9 months after December 20, 1991, the Commission shall conclude the rulemaking proceeding initiated under paragraph (1) and shall prescribe regulations to implement methods and procedures for protecting the privacy rights described in such paragraph in an efficient, effective, and economic manner and without the imposition of any additional charge to telephone subscribers.

(3) Use of database permitted

The regulations required by paragraph (2) may require the establishment and operation of a single national database to compile a list of telephone numbers of residential subscribers who object to receiving telephone solicitations, and to make that compiled list and parts thereof available for purchase. If the Commission determines to require such a database, such regulations shall—

(A) specify a method by which the Commission will select an entity to administer such database;

(B) require each common carrier providing telephone exchange service, in accordance with regulations prescribed by the Commission, to inform subscribers for telephone exchange service of the opportunity to provide notification, in accordance with regulations established under this paragraph, that such subscriber objects to receiving telephone solicitations;

(C) specify the methods by which each telephone subscriber shall be informed, by the common carrier that provides local exchange service to that subscriber, of (i) the subscriber's right to give or revoke a notification of an objection under subparagraph (A), and (ii) the methods by which such right may be exercised by the subscriber;

(D) specify the methods by which such objections shall be collected and added to the database;

(E) prohibit any residential subscriber from being charged for giving or revoking such notification or for being included in a database compiled under this section;

(F) prohibit any person from making or transmitting a telephone solicitation to the telephone number of any subscriber included in such database;

(G) specify (i) the methods by which any person desiring to make or transmit telephone solicitations will obtain access to the database, by area code or local exchange prefix, as required to avoid calling the telephone numbers of subscribers included in such database; and (ii) the costs to be recovered from such persons;

(H) specify the methods for recovering, from persons accessing such database, the costs involved in identifying, collecting, updating, disseminating, and selling, and other activities relating to, the operations of the database that are incurred by the entities carrying out those activities;

(I) specify the frequency with which such database will be updated and specify the method by which such updating will take effect for purposes of compliance with the regulations prescribed under this subsection;

(J) be designed to enable States to use the database mechanism selected by the Commission for purposes of administering or enforcing State law;

(K) prohibit the use of such database for any purpose other than compliance with the requirements of this section and any such State law and specify methods for protection of the privacy rights of persons whose numbers are included in such database; and

(L) require each common carrier providing services to any person for the purpose of making telephone solicitations to notify such person of the requirements of this section and the regulations thereunder.

(4) Considerations required for use of database method

If the Commission determines to require the database mechanism described in paragraph (3), the Commission shall—

(A) in developing procedures for gaining access to the database, consider the different needs of telemarketers conducting business on a national, regional, State, or local level;

(B) develop a fee schedule or price structure for recouping the cost of such database that recognizes such differences and—

(i) reflect the relative costs of providing a national, regional, State, or local list of phone numbers of subscribers who object to receiving telephone solicitations;

(ii) reflect the relative costs of providing such lists on paper or electronic media; and

(iii) not place an unreasonable financial burden on small businesses; and

(C) consider (i) whether the needs of telemarketers operating on a local basis could be met through special markings of area white pages directories, and (ii) if such directories are needed as an adjunct to database lists prepared by area code and local exchange prefix.

(5) Private right of action

A person who has received more than one telephone call within any 12-month period by or on behalf of the same entity in violation of the regulations prescribed under this subsection may, if otherwise permitted by the laws or rules of court of a State bring in an appropriate court of that State—

(A) an action based on a violation of the regulations prescribed under this subsection to enjoin such violation,

(B) an action to recover for actual monetary loss from such a violation, or to receive up to $500 in damages for each such violation, whichever is greater, or

(C) both such actions.

It shall be an affirmative defense in any action brought under this paragraph that the defendant has established and implemented, with due care, reasonable practices and procedures to effectively prevent telephone solicitations in violation of the regulations prescribed under this subsection. If the court finds that the defendant willfully or knowingly violated the regulations prescribed under this subsection, the court may, in its discretion, increase the amount of the award to an amount equal to not more than 3 times the amount available under subparagraph (B) of this paragraph.

(6) Relation to subsection (b)

The provisions of this subsection shall not be construed to permit a communication prohibited by subsection (b) of this section.

(d) Technical and procedural standards

(1) Prohibition

It shall be unlawful for any person within the United States—

(A) to initiate any communication using a telephone facsimile machine, or to make any telephone call using any automatic telephone dialing system, that does not comply with the technical and procedural standards prescribed under this subsection, or to use any telephone facsimile machine or automatic telephone dialing system in a manner that does not comply with such standards; or

(B) to use a computer or other electronic device to send any message via a telephone facsimile machine unless such person clearly marks, in a margin at the top or bottom of each transmitted page of the message or on the first page of the transmission, the date and time it is sent and an identification of the business, other entity, or individual sending the message and the telephone number of the sending machine or of such business, other entity, or individual.

(2) Telephone facsimile machines

The Commission shall revise the regulations setting technical and procedural standards for telephone facsimile machines to require that any such machine which is manufactured after one year after December 20, 1991, clearly marks, in a margin at the top or bottom of each transmitted page or on the first page of each transmission, the date and time sent, an identification of the business, other entity, or individual sending the message, and the telephone number of the sending machine or of such business, other entity, or individual.

(3) Artificial or prerecorded voice systems

The Commission shall prescribe technical and procedural standards for systems that are used to transmit any artificial or prerecorded voice message via telephone. Such standards shall require that—

(A) all artificial or prerecorded telephone messages (i) shall, at the beginning of the message, state clearly the identity of the business, individual, or other entity initiating the call, and (ii) shall, during or after the message, state clearly the telephone number or address of such business, other entity, or individual; and

(B) any such system will automatically release the called party's line within 5 seconds of the time notification is transmitted to the system that the called party has hung up, to allow the called party's line to be used to make or receive other calls.

(e) Effect on State law

(1) State law not preempted

Except for the standards prescribed under subsection (d) of this section and subject to paragraph (2) of this subsection, nothing in this section or in the regulations prescribed under this section shall preempt any State law that imposes more restrictive intrastate requirements or regulations on, or which prohibits—

(A) the use of telephone facsimile machines or other electronic devices to send unsolicited advertisements;

(B) the use of automatic telephone dialing systems;

(C) the use of artificial or prerecorded voice messages; or

(D) the making of telephone solicitations.

(2) State use of databases

If, pursuant to subsection (c)(3) of this section, the Commission requires the establishment of a single national database of telephone numbers of subscribers who object to receiving telephone solicitations, a State or local authority may not, in its regulation of telephone solicitations, require the use of any database, list, or listing system that does not include the part of such single national database that relates to such State.

(f) Actions by States

(1) Authority of States

Whenever the attorney general of a State, or an official or agency designated by a State, has reason to believe that any person has engaged or is engaging in a pattern or practice of telephone calls or other transmissions to residents of that State in violation of this section or the regulations prescribed under this section, the State may bring a civil action on behalf of its residents to enjoin such calls, an action to recover for actual monetary loss or receive $500 in damages for each violation, or both such actions. If the court finds the defendant willfully or knowingly violated such regulations, the court may, in its discretion, increase the amount of the award to an amount equal to not more than 3 times the amount available under the preceding sentence.

(2) Exclusive jurisdiction of Federal courts

The district courts of the United States, the United States courts of any territory, and the District Court of the United States for the District of Columbia shall have exclusive jurisdiction over all civil actions brought under this subsection. Upon proper application, such courts shall also have jurisdiction to issue writs of mandamus, or orders affording like relief, commanding the defendant to comply with the provisions of this section or regulations prescribed under this section, including the requirement that the defendant take such action as is necessary to remove the danger of such violation. Upon a proper showing, a permanent or temporary injunction or restraining order shall be granted without bond.

(3) Rights of Commission

The State shall serve prior written notice of any such civil action upon the Commission and provide the Commission with a copy of its complaint, except in any case where such prior notice is not feasible, in which case the State shall serve such notice immediately upon instituting such action. The Commission shall have the right (A) to intervene in the action, (B) upon so intervening, to be heard on all matters arising therein, and (C) to file petitions for appeal.

(4) Venue; service of process

Any civil action brought under this subsection in a district court of the United States may be brought in the district wherein the defendant is found or is an inhabitant or transacts business or wherein the violation occurred or is occurring, and process in such cases may be served in any district in which the defendant is an inhabitant or where the defendant may be found.

(5) Investigatory powers

For purposes of bringing any civil action under this subsection, nothing in this section shall prevent the attorney general of a State, or an official or agency designated by a State, from exercising the powers conferred on the attorney general or such official by the laws of such State to conduct investigations or to administer oaths or affirmations or to compel the attendance of witnesses or the production of documentary and other evidence.

(6) Effect on State court proceedings

Nothing contained in this subsection shall be construed to prohibit an authorized State official from proceeding in State court on the basis of an alleged violation of any general civil or criminal statute of such State.

(7) Limitation

Whenever the Commission has instituted a civil action for violation of regulations prescribed under this section, no State may, during the pendency of such action instituted by the Commission, subsequently institute a civil action against any defendant named in the Commission's complaint for any violation as alleged in the Commission's complaint.

(8) Definition

As used in this subsection, the term "attorney general" means the chief legal officer of a State.

[June 19, 1934, ch. 652, tit. II, § 227, as added Dec. 20, 1991, Pub. L. No. 102-243, § 3(a), 105 Stat. 2395, and amended Pub. L. No. 102-556, tit. IV, § 402, 106 Stat. 4194 (Oct. 28, 1992); Pub. L. No. 103-414, tit. III, § 303(a)(11), (12), 108 Stat. 4294 (Oct. 25, 1994); Pub. L. No. 108-187, § 12, 117 Stat. 2717 (Dec. 16, 2003)]

D.1.4 Regulation of Carrier Offering of Pay-Per-Call Services—47 U.S.C. § 228

§ 228. Regulation of carrier offering of pay-per-call services

(a) Purpose

It is the purpose of this section—

(1) to put into effect a system of national regulation and review that will oversee interstate pay-per-call services; and

(2) to recognize the Commission's authority to prescribe regulations and enforcement procedures and conduct oversight to afford reasonable protection to consumers of pay-per-call services and to assure that violations of Federal law do not occur.

(b) General authority for regulations

The Commission by regulation shall, within 270 days after October 28, 1992, establish a system for oversight and regulation of pay-per-call services in order to provide for the protection of consumers in accordance with this chapter and other applicable Federal statutes and regulations. The Commission's final rules shall—

(1) include measures that provide a consumer of pay-per-call services with adequate and clear descriptions of the rights of the caller;

(2) define the obligations of common carriers with respect to the provision of pay-per-call services;

(3) include requirements on such carriers to protect against abusive practices by providers of pay-per-call services;

(4) identify procedures by which common carriers and providers of pay-per-call services may take affirmative steps to protect against nonpayment of legitimate charges; and

(5) require that any service described in subparagraphs (A) and (B) of subsection (i)(1) of this section be offered only through the use of certain telephone number prefixes and area codes.

(c) Common carrier obligations

Within 270 days after October 28, 1992, the Commission shall, by regulation, establish the following requirements for common carriers:

(1) Contractual obligations to comply

Any common carrier assigning to a provider of pay-per-call services a telephone number with a prefix or area code designated by the Commission in accordance with subsection (b)(5) of this section shall require by contract or tariff that such provider comply with the provisions of titles II and III of the Telephone Disclosure and Dispute Resolution Act [15 U.S.C.A. § 5711 et seq. and § 5721 et seq.] and the regulations prescribed by the Federal Trade Commission pursuant to those titles [15 U.S.C.A. § 5711 et seq. and § 5721 et seq.].

(2) Information availability

A common carrier that by tariff or contract assigns a telephone number with a prefix or area code designated by the Commission in accordance with subsection (b)(5) of this section to a provider of a pay-per-call service shall make readily available on request to Federal and State agencies and other interested persons—

(A) a list of the telephone numbers for each of the pay-per-call services it carries;

(B) a short description of each such service;

(C) a statement of the total cost or the cost per minute and any other fees for each such service;

(D) a statement of the pay-per-call service's name, business address, and business telephone; and

(E) such other information as the Commission considers necessary for the enforcement of this section and other applicable Federal statutes and regulations.

(3) Compliance procedures

A common carrier that by contract or tariff assigns a telephone number with a prefix or area code designated by the Commission in accordance with subsection (b)(5) of this section to a provider of pay-per-call services shall terminate, in accordance with procedures specified in such regulations, the offering of a pay-per-call service of a provider if the carrier knows or reasonably should know that such service is not provided in compliance with title II or III of the Telephone Disclosure and Dispute Resolution Act [15 U.S.C.A. § 5711 et seq. and § 5721 et seq.] or the regulations prescribed by the Federal Trade Commission pursuant to such titles [15 U.S.C.A. § 5711 et seq. and § 5721 et seq.].

(4) Subscriber disconnection prohibited

A common carrier shall not disconnect or interrupt a subscriber's local exchange telephone service or long distance telephone service because of nonpayment of charges for any pay-per-call service.

(5) Blocking and presubscription

A common carrier that provides local exchange service shall—

(A) offer telephone subscribers (where technically feasible) the option of blocking access from their telephone number to all, or to certain specific, prefixes or area codes used by pay-per-call services, which option—

(i) shall be offered at no charge (I) to all subscribers for a period of 60 days after the issuance of the regulations under subsection (b) of this section, and (II) to any subscriber who subscribes to a new telephone number until 60 days after the time the new telephone number is effective; and

(ii) shall otherwise be offered at a reasonable fee; and

(B) offer telephone subscribers (where the Commission determines it is technically and economically feasible), in combination with the blocking option described under subparagraph (A), the option of presubscribing to or blocking only specific pay-per-call services for a reasonable one-time charge.

The regulations prescribed under subparagraph (A)(i) of this paragraph may permit the costs of such blocking to be recovered by contract or tariff, but such costs may not be recovered from local or long-distance ratepayers. Nothing in this subsection precludes a common carrier from filing its rates and regulations regarding blocking and presubscription in its interstate tariffs.

(6) Verification of charitable status

A common carrier that assigns by contract or tariff a telephone number with a prefix or area code designated by the Commission in accordance with subsection (b)(5) of this section to a provider of pay-per-call services that the carrier knows or reasonably should know is engaged in soliciting charitable contributions shall obtain from such provider proof of the tax exempt status of any person or organization for which contributions are solicited.

(7) Billing for 800 calls

A common carrier shall prohibit by tariff or contract the use of any 800 telephone number, or other telephone number advertised or widely understood to be toll free, in a manner that would result in—

(A) the calling party being assessed, by virtue of completing the call, a charge for the call;

(B) the calling party being connected to a pay-per-call service;

(C) the calling party being charged for information conveyed during the call unless—

(i) the calling party has a written agreement (including an agreement transmitted through electronic medium) that meets the requirements of paragraph (8); or

(ii) the calling party is charged for the information in accordance with paragraph (9);

(D) the calling party being called back collect for the provision of audio information services or simultaneous voice conversation services; or

(E) the calling party being assessed, by virtue of being asked to connect or otherwise transfer to a pay-per-call service, a charge for the call.

(8) Subscription agreements for billing for information provided via toll-free calls

(A) In general

For purposes of paragraph (7)(C)(i), a written subscription does not meet the requirements of this paragraph unless the agreement specifies the material terms and conditions under which the information is offered and includes—

(i) the rate at which charges are assessed for the information;

(ii) the information provider's name;

(iii) the information provider's business address;

(iv) the information provider's regular business telephone number;

(v) the information provider's agreement to notify the subscriber at least one billing cycle in advance of all future changes in the rates charged for the information; and

(vi) the subscriber's choice of payment method, which may be by direct remit, debit, prepaid account, phone bill, or credit or calling card.

(B) Billing arrangements

If a subscriber elects, pursuant to subparagraph (A)(vi), to pay by means of a phone bill—

(i) the agreement shall clearly explain that the subscriber will be assessed for calls made to the information service from the subscriber's phone line;

(ii) the phone bill shall include, in prominent type, the following disclaimer:

"Common carriers may not disconnect local or long distance telephone service for failure to pay disputed charges for information services."; and

(iii) the phone bill shall clearly list the 800 number dialed.

(C) Use of PINS to prevent unauthorized use

A written agreement does not meet the requirements of this paragraph unless it—

(i) includes a unique personal identification number or other subscriber-specific identifier and requires a subscriber to use this number or identifier to obtain access to the information provided and includes instructions on its use; and

(ii) assures that any charges for services accessed by use of the subscriber's personal identification number or subscriber-specific identifier be assessed to subscriber's source of payment elected pursuant to subparagraph (A)(vi).

(D) Exceptions

Notwithstanding paragraph (7)(C), a written agreement that meets the requirements of this paragraph is not required—

(i) for calls utilizing telecommunications devices for the deaf;

(ii) for directory services provided by a common carrier or its affiliate or by a local exchange carrier or its affiliate; or

(iii) for any purchase of goods or of services that are not information services.

(E) Termination of service

On receipt by a common carrier of a complaint by any person that an information provider is in violation of the provisions of this section, a carrier shall—

(i) promptly investigate the complaint; and

(ii) if the carrier reasonably determines that the complaint is valid, it may terminate the provision of service to an information provider unless the provider supplies evidence of a written agreement that meets the requirements of this section.

(F) Treatment of remedies

The remedies provided in this paragraph are in addition to any other remedies that are available under subchapter V of this chapter.

(9) Charges by credit, prepaid, debit, charge, or calling card in absence of agreement

For purposes of paragraph (7)(C)(ii), a calling party is not charged in accordance with this paragraph unless the calling party is charged by means of a credit, prepaid, debit, charge, or calling card and the information service provider includes in response to each call an introductory disclosure message that—

(A) clearly states that there is a charge for the call;

(B) clearly states the service's total cost per minute and any other fees for the service or for any service to which the caller may be transferred;

(C) explains that the charges must be billed on either a credit, prepaid, debit, charge, or calling card;

(D) asks the caller for the card number;

(E) clearly states that charges for the call begin at the end of the introductory message; and

(F) clearly states that the caller can hang up at or before the end of the introductory message without incurring any charge whatsoever.

(10) Bypass of introductory disclosure message

The requirements of paragraph (9) shall not apply to calls from repeat callers using a bypass mechanism to avoid listening to the introductory message: Provided, That information providers shall disable such a bypass mechanism after the institution of any price increase and for a period of time determined to be sufficient by the Federal Trade Commission to give callers adequate and sufficient notice of a price increase.

(11) Definition of calling card

As used in this subsection, the term "calling card" means an identifying number or code unique to the individual, that is issued to the individual by a common carrier and enables the individual to be charged by means of a phone bill for charges incurred independent of where the call originates.

(d) Billing and collection practices

The regulations required by this section shall require that any common carrier that by tariff or contract assigns a telephone number with a prefix or area code designated by the Commission in accordance with subsection (b)(5) of this section to a provider of a pay-per-call service and that offers billing and collection services to such provider—

(1) ensure that a subscriber is not billed—

(A) for pay-per-call services that such carrier knows or reasonably should know was provided in violation of the regulations issued pursuant to title II of the Telephone Disclosure and Dispute Resolution Act [15 U.S.C.A. § 5711 et seq.]; or

(B) under such other circumstances as the Commission determines necessary in order to protect subscribers from abusive practices;

(2) establish a local or a toll-free telephone number to answer questions and provide information on subscribers' rights and obligations with regard to their use of pay-per-call services and to provide to callers the name and mailing address of any provider of pay-per-call services offered by the common carrier;

(3) within 60 days after the issuance of final regulations pursuant to subsection (b) of this section, provide, either directly or through contract with any local exchange carrier that provides billing or collection services to the common carrier, to all of such common carrier's telephone subscribers, to all new subscribers, and to all subscribers requesting service at a new location, a disclosure statement that sets forth all rights and obligations of the subscriber and the carrier with respect to the use and payment for pay-per-call services, including the right of a subscriber not to be billed and the applicable blocking option; and

(4) in any billing to telephone subscribers that includes charges for any pay-per-call service—

(A) display any charges for pay-per-call services in a part of the subscriber's bill that is identified as not being related to local and long distance telephone charges;

(B) for each charge so displayed, specify, at a minimum, the type of service, the amount of the charge, and the date, time, and duration of the call; and

(C) identify the toll-free number established pursuant to paragraph (2).

(e) Liability

(1) Common carriers not liable for transmission or billing

No common carrier shall be liable for a criminal or civil sanction or penalty solely because the carrier provided transmission or billing and collection for a pay-per-call service unless the carrier knew or reasonably should have known that such service was provided in violation of a provision of, or regulation prescribed pursuant to, title II or III of the Telephone Disclosure and Dispute Resolution Act [15 U.S.C.A. § 5711 et seq. and § 5721 et seq.] or any other Federal law. This paragraph shall not prevent the Commission from imposing a sanction or penalty on a common carrier for a violation by that carrier of a regulation prescribed under this section.

(2) Civil liability

No cause of action may be brought in any court or administrative agency against any common carrier or any of its affiliates on account of any act of the carrier or affiliate to terminate any pay-per-call service in order to comply with the regulations prescribed under this section, title II or III of the Telephone Disclosure and Dispute Resolution Act [15 U.S.C.A. § 5711 et seq. and § 5721 et seq.], or any other Federal law unless the complainant demonstrates that the carrier or affiliate did not act in good faith.

(f) Special provisions

(1) Consumer refund requirements

The regulations required by subsection (d) of this section shall establish procedures, consistent with the provisions of titles II and III of the Telephone Disclosure and Dispute Resolution Act [15 U.S.C.A. § 5711 et seq. and § 5721 et seq.], to ensure that carriers and other parties providing billing and collection services with respect to pay-per-call services provide appropriate refunds to subscribers who have been billed for pay-per-call services pursuant to programs that have been found to have violated this section or such regulations, any provision of, or regulations prescribed pursuant to, title II or III of the Telephone Disclosure and Dispute Resolution Act [15 U.S.C.A. § 5711 et seq. and § 5721 et seq.], or any other Federal law.

(2) Recovery of costs

The regulations prescribed by the Commission under this section shall permit a common carrier to recover its cost of complying with such regulations from providers of pay-per-call services, but shall not permit such costs to be recovered from local or long distance ratepayers.

(3) Recommendations on data pay-per-call

The Commission, within one year after October 28, 1992, shall submit to the Congress the Commission's recommendations with respect to the extension of regulations under this section to persons that provide, for a per-call charge, data services that are not pay-per-call services.

(g) Effect on other law

(1) No preemption of election law

Nothing in this section shall relieve any provider of pay-per-call services, common carrier, local exchange carrier, or any other person from the obligation to comply with Federal, State, and local election statutes and regulations.

(2) Consumer protection laws

Nothing in this section shall relieve any provider of pay-per-call services, common carrier, local exchange carrier, or any other person from the obligation to comply with any Federal, State, or local statute or regulation relating to consumer protection or unfair trade.

(3) Gambling laws

Nothing in this section shall preclude any State from enforcing its statutes and regulations with regard to lotteries, wagering, betting, and other gambling activities.

(4) State authority

Nothing in this section shall preclude any State from enacting and enforcing additional and complementary oversight and regulatory systems or procedures, or both, so long as such systems and procedures govern intrastate services and do not significantly impede the enforcement of this section or other Federal statutes.

(5) Enforcement of existing regulations

Nothing in this section shall be construed to prohibit the Commission from enforcing regulations prescribed prior to October 28, 1992 in fulfilling the requirements of this section to the extent that such regulations are consistent with the provisions of this section.

(h) Effect on dial-a-porn prohibitions

Nothing in this section shall affect the provisions of section 223 of this title.

(i) Definition of pay-per-call services

For purposes of this section—

(1) The term "pay-per-call services" means any service—

(A) in which any person provides or purports to provide—

(i) audio information or audio entertainment produced or packaged by such person;

(ii) access to simultaneous voice conversation services; or

(iii) any service, including the provision of a product, the charges for which are assessed on the basis of the completion of the call;

(B) for which the caller pays a per-call or per-time-interval charge that is greater than, or in addition to, the charge for transmission of the call; and

(C) which is accessed through use of a 900 telephone number or other prefix or area code designated by the Commission in accordance with subsection (b)(5) of this section.

(2) Such term does not include directory services provided by a common carrier or its affiliate or by a local exchange carrier or its affiliate, or any service for which users are assessed charges only after entering into a presubscription or comparable arrangement with the provider of such service.

[June 19, 1934, ch. 652, tit. II, § 228, as added Pub. L. No. 102-556, tit. I, § 101, 106 Stat. 4182 (Oct. 28, 1992), and amended Pub. L. No. 103-414, tit. III, § 303(a)(13), (14), 108 Stat. 4294 (Oct. 25, 1994); Pub. L. No. 104-104, tit. VII, § 701(a)(1), (b)(2), 110 Stat. 145, 148 (Feb. 8, 1996)]

D.2 Federal Telemarketing Rules and Regulations

D.2.1 Telemarketing Sales Rule—16 C.F.R. § 310

Sec.

Authority: 15 U.S.C. 6101–6108.

Source: 68 Fed. Reg. 4669 (Jan. 29, 2003)

§ 310.1 Scope of regulations in this part.

This part implements the Telemarketing and Consumer Fraud and Abuse Prevention Act, 15 U.S.C. 6101–6108, as amended.

§ 310.2 Definitions.

(a) *Acquirer* means a business organization, financial institution, or an agent of a business organization or financial institution that has authority from an organization that operates or licenses a credit card system to authorize merchants to accept, transmit, or process payment by credit card through the credit card system for money, goods or services, or anything else of value.

(b) *Attorney General* means the chief legal officer of a state.

(c) *Billing information* means any data that enables any person to access a customer's or donor's account, such as a credit card, checking, savings, share or similar account, utility bill, mortgage loan account, or debit card.

(d) *Caller identification service* means a service that allows a telephone subscriber to have the telephone number, and, where available, name of the calling party transmitted contemporaneously with the telephone call, and displayed on a device in or connected to the subscriber's telephone.

(e) *Cardholder* means a person to whom a credit card is issued or who is authorized to use a credit card on behalf of or in addition to the person to whom the credit card is issued.

(f) *Charitable contribution* means any donation or gift of money or any other thing of value.

(g) *Commission* means the Federal Trade Commission.

(h) *Credit* means the right granted by a creditor to a debtor to defer payment of debt or to incur debt and defer its payment.

(i) *Credit card* means any card, plate, coupon book, or other credit device existing for the purpose of obtaining money, property, labor, or services on credit.

(j) *Credit card sales draft* means any record or evidence of a credit card transaction.

(k) *Credit card system* means any method or procedure used to process credit card transactions involving credit cards issued or licensed by the operator of that system.

(l) *Customer* means any person who is or may be required to pay for goods or services offered through telemarketing.

(m) *Donor* means any person solicited to make a charitable contribution.

(n) *Established business relationship* means a relationship between a seller and a consumer based on:

(1) the consumer's purchase, rental, or lease of the seller's goods or services or a financial transaction between the consumer and seller, within the eighteen (18) months immediately preceding the date of a telemarketing call; or

(2) the consumer's inquiry or application regarding a product or service offered by the seller, within the three (3) months immediately preceding the date of a telemarketing call.

(o) *Free-to-pay conversion* means, in an offer or agreement to sell or provide any goods or services, a provision under which a customer receives a product or service for free for an initial period and will incur an obligation to pay for the product or service if he or she does not take affirmative action to cancel before the end of that period.

(p) *Investment opportunity* means anything, tangible or intangible, that is offered, offered for sale, sold, or traded based wholly or in part on representations, either express or implied, about past, present, or future income, profit, or appreciation.

(q) *Material* means likely to affect a person's choice of, or conduct regarding, goods or services or a charitable contribution.

(r) *Merchant* means a person who is authorized under a written contract with an acquirer to honor or accept credit cards, or to transmit or process for payment credit card payments, for the purchase of goods or services or a charitable contribution.

(s) *Merchant agreement* means a written contract between a merchant and an acquirer to honor or accept credit cards, or to transmit or process for payment credit card payments, for the purchase of goods or services or a charitable contribution.

(t) *Negative option feature* means, in an offer or agreement to sell or provide any goods or services, a provision under which the customer's silence or failure to take an affirmative action to reject goods or services or to cancel the agreement is interpreted by the seller as acceptance of the offer.

(u) *Outbound telephone call* means a telephone call initiated by a telemarketer to induce the purchase of goods or services or to solicit a charitable contribution.

(v) *Person* means any individual, group, unincorporated association, limited or general partnership, corporation, or other business entity.

(w) *Preacquired account information* means any information that enables a seller or telemarketer to cause a charge to be placed against a customer's or donor's account without obtaining the account number directly from the customer or donor during the telemarketing transaction pursuant to which the account will be charged.

(x) *Prize* means anything offered, or purportedly offered, and given, or purportedly given, to a person by chance. For purposes of this definition, chance exists if a person is guaranteed to receive an item and, at the time of the offer or purported offer, the telemarketer does not identify the specific item that the person will receive.

(y) *Prize promotion* means:

(1) A sweepstakes or other game of chance; or

(2) An oral or written express or implied representation that a person has won, has been selected to receive, or may be eligible to receive a prize or purported prize.

(z) *Seller* means any person who, in connection with a telemarketing transaction, provides, offers to provide, or arranges for others to provide goods or services to the customer in exchange for consideration.

(aa) *State* means any state of the United States, the District of Columbia, Puerto Rico, the Northern Mariana Islands, and any territory or possession of the United States.

(bb) *Telemarketer* means any person who, in connection with telemarketing, initiates or receives telephone calls to or from a customer or donor.

(cc) *Telemarketing* means a plan, program, or campaign which is conducted to induce the purchase of goods or services or a charitable contribution, by use of one or more telephones and which involves more than one interstate telephone call. The term does not include the solicitation of sales through the mailing of a catalog which: contains a written description or illustration of the goods or services offered for sale; includes the business address of the seller; includes multiple pages of written material or illustrations; and has been issued not less frequently than once a year, when the person making the solicitation does not solicit customers by telephone but only receives calls initiated by customers in response to the catalog and during those calls takes orders only without further solicitation. For purposes of the previous sentence, the term "further solicitation" does not include providing the customer with information about, or attempting to sell, any other item included in the same catalog which prompted the customer's call or in a substantially similar catalog.

(dd) *Upselling* means soliciting the purchase of goods or services following an initial transaction during a single telephone call. The upsell is a separate telemarketing transaction, not a continuation of the initial transaction. An "external upsell" is a solicitation made by or on behalf of a seller different from the seller in the initial transaction, regardless of whether the initial transaction and the subsequent solicitation are made by the same telemarketer. An "internal upsell" is a solicitation made by or on behalf of the same seller as in the initial transaction, regardless of whether the initial transaction and subsequent solicitation are made by the same telemarketer.

§ 310.3 Deceptive telemarketing acts or practices.

(a) *Prohibited deceptive telemarketing acts or practices.* It is a deceptive telemarketing act or practice and a violation of this Rule for any seller or telemarketer to engage in the following conduct:

(1) Before a customer pays[1] for goods or services offered, failing to disclose truthfully, in a clear and conspicuous manner, the following material information:

(i) The total costs to purchase, receive, or use, and the quantity of, any goods or services that are the subject of the sales offer;[2]

(ii) All material restrictions, limitations, or conditions to purchase, receive, or use the goods or services that are the subject of the sales offer;

(iii) If the seller has a policy of not making refunds, cancellations, exchanges, or repurchases, a statement informing the customer that this is the seller's policy; or, if the seller or telemarketer makes a representation about a refund, cancellation, exchange, or repurchase policy, a statement of all material terms and conditions of such policy;

(iv) In any prize promotion, the odds of being able to receive the prize, and, if the odds are not calculable in advance, the factors used in calculating the odds; that no purchase or payment is required to win a prize or to participate in a prize promotion and that any purchase or payment will not increase the person's chances of winning; and the no-purchase/no-payment method of participating in the prize promotion with either instructions on how to participate or an address or local or toll-free telephone number to which customers may write or call for information on how to participate;

(v) All material costs or conditions to receive or redeem a prize that is the subject of the prize promotion;

(vi) In the sale of any goods or services represented to protect, insure, or otherwise limit a customer's liability in the event of unauthorized use of the customer's credit card, the limits on a cardholder's liability for unauthorized use of a credit card pursuant to 15 U.S.C. 1643; and

(vii) If the offer includes a negative option feature, all material terms and conditions of the negative option feature, including, but not limited to, the fact that the customer's account will be charged unless the customer takes an affirmative action to avoid the charge(s), the date(s) the charge(s) will be submitted for payment, and the specific steps the customer must take to avoid the charge(s).

(2) Misrepresenting, directly or by implication, in the sale of goods or services any of the following material information:

(i) The total costs to purchase, receive, or use, and the quantity of, any goods or services that are the subject of a sales offer;

(ii) Any material restriction, limitation, or condition to purchase, receive, or use goods or services that are the subject of a sales offer;

(iii) Any material aspect of the performance, efficacy, nature, or central characteristics of goods or services that are the subject of a sales offer;

(iv) Any material aspect of the nature or terms of the seller's refund, cancellation, exchange, or repurchase policies;

(v) Any material aspect of a prize promotion including, but not limited to, the odds of being able to receive a prize, the nature or value of a prize, or that a purchase or payment is required to win a prize or to participate in a prize promotion;

(vi) Any material aspect of an investment opportunity including, but not limited to, risk, liquidity, earnings potential, or profitability;

(vii) A seller's or telemarketer's affiliation with, or endorsement or sponsorship by, any person or government entity;

(viii) That any customer needs offered goods or services to provide protections a customer already has pursuant to 15 U.S.C. 1643; or

(ix) Any material aspect of a negative option feature including, but not limited to, the fact that the customer's account will be charged unless the customer takes an affirmative action to avoid the charge(s), the date(s) the charge(s) will be submitted for payment, and the specific steps the customer must take to avoid the charge(s).

(3) Causing billing information to be submitted for payment, or collecting or attempting to collect payment for goods or services or a charitable contribution, directly or indirectly, without the customer's or donor's express verifiable authorization, except when the method of payment used is a credit card subject to protections of the Truth in Lending Act and Regulation Z,[3] or a debit card subject to the protections of the Electronic Fund Transfer Act and Regulation E.[4] Such authorization shall be deemed verifiable if any of the following means is employed:

(i) Express written authorization by the customer or donor, which includes the customer's or donor's signature;[5]

(ii) Express oral authorization which is audio-recorded and made available upon request to the customer or donor, and the customer's or donor's bank or other billing entity, and which evidences clearly both the customer's or donor's authorization of payment for the goods or services or charitable contribution that are the subject of the telemarketing transaction and the customer's or donor's receipt of all of the following information:

(A) The number of debits, charges, or payments (if more than one);

(B) The date(s) the debit(s), charge(s), or payment(s) will be submitted for payment;

(C) The amount(s) of the debit(s), charge(s), or payment(s);

1 When a seller or telemarketer uses, or directs a customer to use, a courier to transport payment, the seller or telemarketer must make the disclosures required by § 310.3(a)(1) before sending a courier to pick up payment or authorization for payment, or directing a customer to have a courier pick up payment or authorization for payment.

2 For offers of consumer credit products subject to the Truth in Lending Act, 15 U.S.C. 1601 *et seq.*, and Regulation Z, 12 C.F.R. 226, compliance with the disclosure requirements under the Truth in Lending Act and Regulation Z shall constitute compliance with § 310.3(a)(1)(i) of this Rule.

3 Truth in Lending Act, 15 U.S.C. 1601 *et seq.*, and Regulation Z, 12 C.F.R. part 226.

4 Electronic Fund Transfer Act, 15 U.S.C. 1693 *et seq.*, and Regulation E, 12 C.F.R. part 205.

5 For purposes of this Rule, the term "signature" shall include an electronic or digital form of signature, to the extent that such form of signature is recognized as a valid signature under applicable federal law or state contract law.

(D) The customer's or donor's name;

(E) The customer's or donor's billing information, identified with sufficient specificity such that the customer or donor understands what account will be used to collect payment for the goods or services or charitable contribution that are the subject of the telemarketing transaction;

(F) A telephone number for customer or donor inquiry that is answered during normal business hours; and

(G) The date of the customer's or donor's oral authorization; or

(iii) Written confirmation of the transaction, identified in a clear and conspicuous manner as such on the outside of the envelope, sent to the customer or donor via first class mail prior to the submission for payment of the customer's or donor's billing information, and that includes all of the information contained in §§ 310.3(a)(3)(ii)(A)–(G) and a clear and conspicuous statement of the procedures by which the customer or donor can obtain a refund from the seller or telemarketer or charitable organization in the event the confirmation is inaccurate; provided, however, that this means of authorization shall not be deemed verifiable in instances in which goods or services are offered in a transaction involving a free-to-pay conversion and preacquired account information.

(4) Making a false or misleading statement to induce any person to pay for goods or services or to induce a charitable contribution.

(b) *Assisting and facilitating*. It is a deceptive telemarketing act or practice and a violation of this Rule for a person to provide substantial assistance or support to any seller or telemarketer when that person knows or consciously avoids knowing that the seller or telemarketer is engaged in any act or practice that violates §§ 310.3(a), (c) or (d), or § 310.4 of this Rule.

(c) *Credit card laundering*. Except as expressly permitted by the applicable credit card system, it is a deceptive telemarketing act or practice and a violation of this Rule for:

(1) A merchant to present to or deposit into, or cause another to present to or deposit into, the credit card system for payment, a credit card sales draft generated by a telemarketing transaction that is not the result of a telemarketing credit card transaction between the cardholder and the merchant;

(2) Any person to employ, solicit, or otherwise cause a merchant, or an employee, representative, or agent of the merchant, to present to or deposit into the credit card system for payment, a credit card sales draft generated by a telemarketing transaction that is not the result of a telemarketing credit card transaction between the cardholder and the merchant; or

(3) Any person to obtain access to the credit card system through the use of a business relationship or an affiliation with a merchant, when such access is not authorized by the merchant agreement or the applicable credit card system.

(d) *Prohibited deceptive acts or practices in the solicitation of charitable contributions*. It is a fraudulent charitable solicitation, a deceptive telemarketing act or practice, and a violation of this Rule for any telemarketer soliciting charitable contributions to misrepresent, directly or by implication, any of the following material information:

(1) The nature, purpose, or mission of any entity on behalf of which a charitable contribution is being requested;

(2) That any charitable contribution is tax deductible in whole or in part;

(3) The purpose for which any charitable contribution will be used;

(4) The percentage or amount of any charitable contribution that will go to a charitable organization or to any particular charitable program;

(5) Any material aspect of a prize promotion including, but not limited to: the odds of being able to receive a prize; the nature or value of a prize; or that a charitable contribution is required to win a prize or to participate in a prize promotion; or

(6) A charitable organization's or telemarketer's affiliation with, or endorsement or sponsorship by, any person or government entity.

§ 310.4 Abusive telemarketing acts or practices.

(a) *Abusive conduct generally*. It is an abusive telemarketing act or practice and a violation of this Rule for any seller or telemarketer to engage in the following conduct:

(1) Threats, intimidation, or the use of profane or obscene language;

(2) Requesting or receiving payment of any fee or consideration for goods or services represented to remove derogatory information from, or improve, a person's credit history, credit record, or credit rating until:

(i) The time frame in which the seller has represented all of the goods or services will be provided to that person has expired; and

(ii) The seller has provided the person with documentation in the form of a consumer report from a consumer reporting agency demonstrating that the promised results have been achieved, such report having been issued more than six months after the results were achieved. Nothing in this Rule should be construed to affect the requirement in the Fair Credit Reporting Act, 15 U.S.C. 1681, that a consumer report may only be obtained for a specified permissible purpose;

(3) Requesting or receiving payment of any fee or consideration from a person for goods or services represented to recover or otherwise assist in the return of money or any other item of value paid for by, or promised to, that person in a previous telemarketing transaction, until seven (7) business days after such money or other item is delivered to that person. This provision shall not apply to goods or services provided to a person by a licensed attorney;

(4) Requesting or receiving payment of any fee or consideration in advance of obtaining a loan or other extension of credit when the seller or telemarketer has guaranteed or represented a high likelihood of success in obtaining or arranging a loan or other extension of credit for a person;

(5) Disclosing or receiving, for consideration, unencrypted consumer account numbers for use in telemarketing; provided, however, that this paragraph shall not apply to the disclosure or receipt of a customer's or donor's billing information to process a payment for goods or services or a charitable contribution pursuant to a transaction;

(6) Causing billing information to be submitted for payment, directly or indirectly, without the express informed consent of the customer or donor. In any telemarketing transaction, the seller or telemarketer must obtain the express informed consent of the customer or donor to be charged for the goods or services or charitable contribution and to be charged using the identified account. In any telemarketing transaction involving preacquired account information, the requirements in paragraphs (a)(6)(i) through (ii) of this section must be met to evidence express informed consent.

(i) In any telemarketing transaction involving preacquired account information and a free-to-pay conversion feature, the seller or telemarketer must:

(A) obtain from the customer, at a minimum, the last four (4) digits of the account number to be charged;

(B) obtain from the customer his or her express agreement to be charged for the goods or services and to be charged using the account number pursuant to paragraph (a)(6)(i)(A) of this section; and,

(C) make and maintain an audio recording of the entire telemarketing transaction.

(ii) In any other telemarketing transaction involving preacquired account information not described in paragraph (a)(6)(i) of this section, the seller or telemarketer must:

(A) at a minimum, identify the account to be charged with sufficient specificity for the customer or donor to understand what account will be charged; and

(B) obtain from the customer or donor his or her express agreement to be charged for the goods or services and to be charged using the account number identified pursuant to paragraph (a)(6)(ii)(A) of this section; or

(7) Failing to transmit or cause to be transmitted the telephone number, and, when made available by the telemarketer's carrier, the name of the telemarketer, to any caller identification service in use by a recipient of a telemarketing call; provided that it shall not be a violation to substitute (for the name and phone number used in, or billed for, making the call) the name of the seller or charitable organization on behalf of which a telemarketing call is placed, and the seller's or charitable organization's customer or donor service telephone number, which is answered during regular business hours.

(b) *Pattern of calls.*

(1) It is an abusive telemarketing act or practice and a violation of this Rule for a telemarketer to engage in, or for a seller to cause a telemarketer to engage in, the following conduct:

(i) Causing any telephone to ring, or engaging any person in telephone conversation, repeatedly or continuously with intent to annoy, abuse, or harass any person at the called number;

(ii) Denying or interfering in any way, directly or indirectly, with a person's right to be placed on any registry of names and/or telephone numbers of persons who do not wish to receive outbound telephone calls established to comply with § 310.4(b)(1)(iii);

(iii) Initiating any outbound telephone call to a person when:

(A) that person previously has stated that he or she does not wish to receive an outbound telephone call made by or on behalf of the seller whose goods or services are being offered or made on behalf of the charitable organization for which a charitable contribution is being solicited; or

(B) that person's telephone number is on the "do-not-call" registry, maintained by the Commission, of persons who do not wish to receive outbound telephone calls to induce the purchase of goods or services unless the seller

(i) has obtained the express agreement, in writing, of such person to place calls to that person. Such written agreement shall clearly evidence such person's authorization that calls made by or on behalf of a specific party may be placed to that person, and shall include the telephone number to which the calls may be placed and the signature[6] of that person; or

(ii) has an established business relationship with such person, and that person has not stated that he or she does not wish to receive outbound telephone calls under paragraph (b)(1)(iii)(A) of this section; or

(iv) Abandoning any outbound telephone call. An outbound telephone call is "abandoned" under this section if a person answers it and the telemarketer does not connect the call to a sales representative within two (2) seconds of the person's completed greeting.

(2) It is an abusive telemarketing act or practice and a violation of this Rule for any person to sell, rent, lease, purchase, or use any list established to comply with § 310.4(b)(1)(iii)(A), or maintained by the Commission pursuant to § 310.4(b)(1)(iii)(B), for any purpose except compliance with the provisions of this Rule or otherwise to prevent telephone calls to telephone numbers on such lists.

(3) A seller or telemarketer will not be liable for violating § 310.4(b)(1)(ii) and (iii) if it can demonstrate that, as part of the seller's or telemarketer's routine business practice:

(i) It has established and implemented written procedures to comply with § 310.4(b)(1)(ii) and (iii);

(ii) It has trained its personnel, and any entity assisting in its compliance, in the procedures established pursuant to § 310.4(b)(3)(i);

(iii) The seller, or a telemarketer or another person acting on behalf of the seller or charitable organization, has maintained and recorded a list of telephone numbers the seller or charitable organization may not contact, in compliance with § 310.4(b)(1)(iii)(A);

6 For purposes of this Rule, the term "signature" shall include an electronic or digital form of signature, to the extent that such form of signature is recognized as a valid signature under applicable federal law or state contract law.

(iv) The seller or a telemarketer uses a process to prevent telemarketing to any telephone number on any list established pursuant to § 310.4(b)(3)(iii) or 310.4(b)(1)(iii)(B), employing a version of the "do-not-call" registry obtained from the Commission no more than thirty-one (31) days prior to the date any call is made, and maintains records documenting this process;

(v) The seller or a telemarketer or another person acting on behalf of the seller or charitable organization, monitors and enforces compliance with the procedures established pursuant to § 310.4(b)(3)(i); and

(vi) Any subsequent call otherwise violating § 310.4(b)(1)(ii) or (iii) is the result of error.

(4) A seller or telemarketer will not be liable for violating 310.4(b)(1)(iv) if:

(i) the seller or telemarketer employs technology that ensures abandonment of no more than three (3) percent of all calls answered by a person, measured per day per calling campaign;

(ii) the seller or telemarketer, for each telemarketing call placed, allows the telephone to ring for at least fifteen (15) seconds or four (4) rings before disconnecting an unanswered call;

(iii) whenever a sales representative is not available to speak with the person answering the call within two (2) seconds after the person's completed greeting, the seller or telemarketer promptly plays a recorded message that states the name and telephone number of the seller on whose behalf the call was placed;[7] and

(iv) the seller or telemarketer, in accordance with § 310.5(b)–(d), retains records establishing compliance with § 310.4(b)(4)(i)–(iii).

(c) *Calling time restrictions.* Without the prior consent of a person, it is an abusive telemarketing act or practice and a violation of this Rule for a telemarketer to engage in outbound telephone calls to a person's residence at any time other than between 8:00 a.m. and 9:00 p.m. local time at the called person's location.

(d) *Required oral disclosures in the sale of goods or services.* It is an abusive telemarketing act or practice and a violation of this Rule for a telemarketer in an outbound telephone call or internal or external upsell to induce the purchase of goods or services to fail to disclose truthfully, promptly, and in a clear and conspicuous manner to the person receiving the call, the following information:

(1) The identity of the seller;

(2) That the purpose of the call is to sell goods or services;

(3) The nature of the goods or services; and

(4) That no purchase or payment is necessary to be able to win a prize or participate in a prize promotion if a prize promotion is offered and that any purchase or payment will not increase the person's chances of winning. This disclosure must be made before or in conjunction with the description of the prize to the person called. If requested by that person, the telemarketer must disclose the no-purchase/no-payment entry method for the prize promotion; *provided*, however, that, in any internal upsell for the sale of goods or services, the seller or telemarketer must provide the disclosures listed in this section only to the extent that the information in the upsell differs from the disclosures provided in the initial telemarketing transaction.

(e) *Required oral disclosures in charitable solicitations.* It is an abusive telemarketing act or practice and a violation of this Rule for a telemarketer, in an outbound telephone call to induce a charitable contribution, to fail to disclose truthfully, promptly, and in a clear and conspicuous manner to the person receiving the call, the following information:

(1) The identity of the charitable organization on behalf of which the request is being made; and

(2) That the purpose of the call is to solicit a charitable contribution.

[68 Fed. Reg. 16414 (Apr. 4, 2003); 69 Fed. Reg. 16373 (Mar. 29, 2004)]

§ 310.5 Recordkeeping requirements.

(a) Any seller or telemarketer shall keep, for a period of 24 months from the date the record is produced, the following records relating to its telemarketing activities:

(1) All substantially different advertising, brochures, telemarketing scripts, and promotional materials;

(2) The name and last known address of each prize recipient and the prize awarded for prizes that are represented, directly or by implication, to have a value of $25.00 or more;

(3) The name and last known address of each customer, the goods or services purchased, the date such goods or services were shipped or provided, and the amount paid by the customer for the goods or services;[8]

(4) The name, any fictitious name used, the last known home address and telephone number, and the job title(s) for all current and former employees directly involved in telephone sales or solicitations; *provided*, however, that if the seller or telemarketer permits fictitious names to be used by employees, each fictitious name must be traceable to only one specific employee; and

(5) All verifiable authorizations or records of express informed consent or express agreement required to be provided or received under this Rule.

(b) A seller or telemarketer may keep the records required by § 310.5(a) in any form, and in the same manner, format, or place as they keep such records in the ordinary course of business. Failure to keep all records required by § 310.5(a) shall be a violation of this Rule.

7 This provision does not affect any seller's or telemarketer's obligation to comply with relevant state and federal laws, including but not limited to the TCPA, 47 U.S.C. 227, and 47 C.F.R. part 64.1200.

8 For offers of consumer credit products subject to the Truth in Lending Act, 15 U.S.C. 1601 *et seq.*, and Regulation Z, 12 C.F.R. 226, compliance with the recordkeeping requirements under the Truth in Lending Act, and Regulation Z, shall constitute compliance with § 310.5(a)(3) of this Rule.

(c) The seller and the telemarketer calling on behalf of the seller may, by written agreement, allocate responsibility between themselves for the recordkeeping required by this Section. When a seller and telemarketer have entered into such an agreement, the terms of that agreement shall govern, and the seller or telemarketer, as the case may be, need not keep records that duplicate those of the other. If the agreement is unclear as to who must maintain any required record(s), or if no such agreement exists, the seller shall be responsible for complying with §§ 310.5(a)(1)–(3) and (5); the telemarketer shall be responsible for complying with § 310.5(a)(4).

(d) In the event of any dissolution or termination of the seller's or telemarketer's business, the principal of that seller or telemarketer shall maintain all records as required under this Section. In the event of any sale, assignment, or other change in ownership of the seller's or telemarketer's business, the successor business shall maintain all records required under this Section.

§ 310.6 Exemptions.

(a) Solicitations to induce charitable contributions via outbound telephone calls are not covered by § 310.4(b)(1)(iii)(B) of this Rule.

(b) The following acts or practices are exempt from this Rule:

(1) The sale of pay-per-call services subject to the Commission's Rule entitled "Trade Regulation Rule Pursuant to the Telephone Disclosure and Dispute Resolution Act of 1992," 16 CFR Part 308, *provided*, however, that this exemption does not apply to the requirements of §§ 310.4(a)(1), (a)(7), (b), and (c);

(2) The sale of franchises subject to the Commission's Rule entitled "Disclosure Requirements and Prohibitions Concerning Franchising and Business Opportunity Ventures," ("Franchise Rule") 16 CFR Part 436, *provided*, however, that this exemption does not apply to the requirements of §§ 310.4(a)(1), (a)(7), (b), and (c);

(3) Telephone calls in which the sale of goods or services or charitable solicitation is not completed, and payment or authorization of payment is not required, until after a face-to-face sales or donation presentation by the seller or charitable organization, *provided*, however, that this exemption does not apply to the requirements of §§ 310.4(a)(1), (a)(7), (b), and (c);

(4) Telephone calls initiated by a customer or donor that are not the result of any solicitation by a seller, charitable organization, or telemarketer, *provided*, however, that this exemption does not apply to any instances of upselling included in such telephone calls;

(5) Telephone calls initiated by a customer or donor in response to an advertisement through any medium, other than direct mail solicitation, *provided*, however, that this exemption does not apply to calls initiated by a customer or donor in response to an advertisement relating to investment opportunities, business opportunities other than business arrangements covered by the Franchise Rule, or advertisements involving goods or services described in §§ 310.3(a)(1)(vi) or 310.4(a)(2)–(4); or to any instances of upselling included in such telephone calls;

(6) Telephone calls initiated by a customer or donor in response to a direct mail solicitation, including solicitations via the U.S. Postal Service, facsimile transmission, electronic mail, and other similar methods of delivery in which a solicitation is directed to specific address(es) or person(s), that clearly, conspicuously, and truthfully discloses all material information listed in § 310.3(a)(1) of this Rule, for any goods or services offered in the direct mail solicitation, and that contains no material misrepresentation regarding any item contained in § 310.3(d) of this Rule for any requested charitable contribution; *provided*, however, that this exemption does not apply to calls initiated by a customer in response to a direct mail solicitation relating to prize promotions, investment opportunities, business opportunities other than business arrangements covered by the Franchise Rule, or goods or services described in §§ 310.3(a)(1)(vi) or 310.4(a)(2)–(4); or to any instances of upselling included in such telephone calls; and

(7) Telephone calls between a telemarketer and any business, except calls to induce the retail sale of nondurable office or cleaning supplies; *provided*, however, that § 310.4(b)(1)(iii)(B) and § 310.5 of this Rule shall not apply to sellers or telemarketers of nondurable office or cleaning supplies.

§ 310.7 Actions by states and private persons.

(a) Any attorney general or other officer of a state authorized by the state to bring an action under the Telemarketing and Consumer Fraud and Abuse Prevention Act, and any private person who brings an action under that Act, shall serve written notice of its action on the Commission, if feasible, prior to its initiating an action under this Rule. The notice shall be sent to the Office of the Director, Bureau of Consumer Protection, Federal Trade Commission, Washington, D.C. 20580, and shall include a copy of the state's or private person's complaint and any other pleadings to be filed with the court. If prior notice is not feasible, the state or private person shall serve the Commission with the required notice immediately upon instituting its action.

(b) Nothing contained in this Section shall prohibit any attorney general or other authorized state official from proceeding in state court on the basis of an alleged violation of any civil or criminal statute of such state.

§ 310.8 Fee for access to the National Do Not Call Registry.

(a) It is a violation of this Rule for any seller to initiate, or cause any telemarketer to initiate, an outbound telephone call to any person whose telephone number is within a given area code unless such seller, either directly or through another person, first has paid the annual fee, required by § 310.8(c), for access to telephone numbers within that area code that are included in the National Do Not Call Registry maintained by the Commission under § 310.4(b)(1)(iii)(B); *provided*, however, that such payment is not necessary if the seller initiates, or causes a telemarketer to initiate, calls solely to persons pursuant to Sec. Sec. 310.4(b)(1)(iii)(B)(*i*) or (*ii*), and the seller does not access the National Do Not Call Registry for any other purpose.

(b) It is a violation of this Rule for any telemarketer, on behalf of any seller, to initiate an outbound telephone call to any person whose telephone number is within a given area code unless that seller, either directly or through another person, first has paid the annual fee, required by § 310.8(c), for access to the telephone numbers within that area code that are included in the National Do

Not Call Registry; *provided*, however, that such payment is not necessary if the seller initiates, or causes a telemarketer to initiate, calls solely to persons pursuant to §§ 310.4(b)(1)(iii)(B)(*i*) or (*ii*), and the seller does not access the National Do Not Call Registry for any other purpose.

(c) The annual fee, which must be paid by any person prior to obtaining access to the National Do Not Call Registry, is $25 per area code of data accessed, up to a maximum of $7,375; provided, however, that there shall be no charge for the first five area codes of data accessed by any person, and *provided further*, that there shall be no charge to any person engaging in or causing others to engage in outbound telephone calls to consumers and who is accessing the National Do Not Call Registry without being required under this Rule, 47 CFR 64.1200, or any other federal law. Any person accessing the National Do Not Call Registry may not participate in any arrangement to share the cost of accessing the registry, including any arrangement with any telemarketer or service provider to divide the costs to access the registry among various clients of that telemarketer or service provider.

(d) After a person, either directly or through another person, pays the fees set forth in § 310.8(c), the person will be provided a unique account number which will allow that person to access the registry data for the selected area codes at any time for twelve months following the first day of the month in which the person paid the fee ("the annual period"). To obtain access to additional area codes of data during the first six months of the annual period, the person must first pay $25 for each additional area code of data not initially selected. To obtain access to additional area codes of data during the second six months of the annual period, the person must first pay $15 for each additional area code of data not initially selected. The payment of the additional fee will permit the person to access the additional area codes of data for the remainder of the annual period.

(e) Access to the National Do Not Call Registry is limited to telemarketers, sellers, others engaged in or causing others to engage in telephone calls to consumers, service providers acting on behalf of such persons, and any government agency that has law enforcement authority. Prior to accessing the National Do Not Call Registry, a person must provide the identifying information required by the operator of the registry to collect the fee, and must certify, under penalty of law, that the person is accessing the registry solely to comply with the provisions of this Rule or to otherwise prevent telephone calls to telephone numbers on the registry. If the person is accessing the registry on behalf of sellers, that person also must identify each of the sellers on whose behalf it is accessing the registry, must provide each seller's unique account number for access to the national registry, and must certify, under penalty of law, that the sellers will be using the information gathered from the registry solely to comply with the provisions of this Rule or otherwise to prevent telephone calls to telephone numbers on the registry.

[68 Fed. Reg. 45144 (July 31, 2003); 69 Fed. Reg. 45585 (July 30, 2004)]

§ 310.9 Severability.

The provisions of this Rule are separate and severable from one another. If any provision is stayed or determined to be invalid, it is the Commission's intention that the remaining provisions shall continue in effect.

D.2.2 Telephone Disclosure and Dispute Resolution Rule—16 C.F.R. § 308

Sec.

Authority: Pub. L. No. 102-556, 106 Stat. 4181 (15 U.S.C. 5701, et seq.)

Source: 58 Fed. Reg. 42400 (Aug. 9, 1993), unless otherwise noted.

§ 308.1 Scope of regulations in this part.

This rule implements titles II and III of the Telephone Disclosure and Dispute Resolution Act of 1992, to be codified in relevant part at 15 U.S.C. 5711–14, 5721–24.

§ 308.2 Definitions.

(a) *Bona fide educational service* means any pay-per-call service dedicated to providing information or instruction relating to education, subjects of academic study, or other related areas of school study.

(b) *Commission* means the Federal Trade Commission.

(c) *Pay-per-call service* has the meaning provided in section 228 of the Communications Act of 1934, 47 U.S.C. 228.[9]

---

9 Section 228 of the Communications Act of 1934 states:
(1) The term *pay-per-call services* means any service—
(A) In which any person provides or purports to provide—
(i) Audio information or audio entertainment produced or packaged by such person;
(ii) Access to simultaneous voice conversation services; or
(iii) Any service, including the provision of a product, the charges for which are assessed on the basis of the completion of the call;
(B) For which the caller pays a per-call or per-time-interval charge that is greater than, or in addition to, the charge for transmission of the call; and

(d) *Person* means any individual, partnership, corporation, association, government or governmental subdivision or agency, or other entity.

(e) (1) *Presubscription or comparable arrangement* means a contractual agreement in which

- **(i)** The service provider clearly and conspicuously discloses to the consumer all material terms and conditions associated with the use of the service, including the service provider's name and address, a business telephone number which the consumer may use to obtain additional information or to register a complaint, and the rates for the service;
- **(ii)** The service provider agrees to notify the consumer of any future rate changes;
- **(iii)** The consumer agrees to utilize the service on the terms and conditions disclosed by the service provider; and
- **(iv)** The service provider requires the use of an identification number or other means to prevent unauthorized access to the service by nonsubscribers.

(2) Disclosure of a credit card or charge card number, along with authorization to bill that number, made during the course of a call to a pay-per-call service shall constitute a presubscription or comparable arrangement if the credit or charge card is subject to the dispute resolution requirements of the Fair Credit Billing Act and the Truth in Lending Act, as amended. No other action taken by the consumer during the course of a call to a pay-per-call service can be construed as creating a presubscription or comparable arrangement.

(f) *Program-length commercial* means any commercial or other advertisement fifteen (15) minutes in length or longer or intended to fill a television or radio broadcasting or cablecasting time slot of fifteen (15) minutes in length or longer.

(g) *Provider of pay-per-call services* means any person who sells or offers to sell a pay-per-call service. A person who provides only transmission services or billing and collection services shall not be considered a provider of pay-per-call services.

(h) *Reasonably understandable volume* means at an audible level that renders the message intelligible to the receiving audience, and, in any event, at least the same audible level as that principally used in the advertisement or the pay-per-call service.

(i) *Service bureau* means any person, other than a common carrier, who provides, among other things, access to telephone service and voice storage to pay-per-call service providers.

(j) *Slow and deliberate manner* means at a rate that renders the message intelligible to the receiving audience, and, in any event, at a cadence or rate no faster than that principally used in the advertisement or the pay-per-call service.

(k) *Sweepstakes*, including games of chance, means a game or promotional mechanism that involves the elements of a prize and chance and does not require consideration.

§ 308.3 Advertising of pay-per-call services.

(a) *General requirements.* The following requirements apply to disclosures required in advertisements under §§ 308.3(b)–(d), and (f):

- **(1)** The disclosures shall be made in the same language as that principally used in the advertisement.
- **(2)** Television video and print disclosures shall be of a color or shade that readily contrasts with the background of the advertisement.
- **(3)** In print advertisements, disclosures shall be parallel with the base of the advertisement.
- **(4)** Audio disclosures, whether in television or radio, shall be delivered in a slow and deliberate manner and in a reasonably understandable volume.
- **(5)** Nothing contrary to, inconsistent with, or in mitigation of, the required disclosures shall be used in any advertisement in any medium; nor shall any audio, video or print technique be used that is likely to detract significantly from the communication of the disclosures.
- **(6)** In any program-length commercial, required disclosures shall be made at least three times (unless more frequent disclosure is otherwise required) near the beginning, middle and end of the commercial.

(b) *Cost of the call.* **(1)** The provider of pay-per-call services shall clearly and conspicuously disclose the cost of the call, in Arabic numerals, in any advertisement for the pay-per-call service, as follows:

- **(i)** If there is a flat fee for the call, the advertisement shall state the total cost of the call.
- **(ii)** If the call is billed on a time-sensitive basis, the advertisement shall state the cost per minute and any minimum charges. If the length of the program can be determined in advance, the advertisement shall also state the maximum charge that could be incurred if the caller listens to the complete program.
- **(iii)** If the call is billed on a variable rate basis, the advertisement shall state, in accordance with §§ 308.3(b)(1)(i) and (ii), the cost of the initial portion of the call, any minimum charges, and the range of rates that may be charged depending on the options chosen by the caller.
- **(iv)** The advertisement shall disclose any other fees that will be charged for the service.

(C) Which is accessed through use of a 900 telephone number or other prefix or area code designated by the (Federal Communications) Commission in accordance with subsection (b)(5) (47 U.S.C. 228(b)(5)).

(2) Such term does not include directory services provided by a common carrier or its affiliate or by a local exchange carrier or its affiliate, or any service the charge for which is tariffed, or any service for which users are assessed charges only after entering into a presubscription or comparable arrangement with the provider of such service.

(v) if the caller may be transferred to another pay-per-call service, the advertisement shall disclose the cost of the other call, in accordance with §§ 308.3(b)(1)(i), (ii), (iii), and (iv).

(2) For purposes of § 308.3(b), disclosures shall be made "clearly and conspicuously" as set forth in § 308.3(a) and as follows:

(i) In a television or videotape advertisement, the video disclosure shall appear adjacent to each video presentation of the pay-per-call number. However, in an advertisement displaying more than one pay-per-call number with the same cost, the video disclosure need only appear adjacent to the largest presentation of the pay-per-call number. Each letter or numeral of the video disclosure shall be, at a minimum, one-half the size of each letter or numeral of the pay-per-call number to which the disclosure is adjacent. In addition, the video disclosure shall appear on the screen for the duration of the presentation of the pay-per-call number. An audio disclosure shall be made at least once, simultaneously with a video presentation of the disclosure. However, no audio presentation of the disclosure is required in: (A) An advertisement fifteen (15) seconds or less in length in which the pay-per-call number is not presented in the audio portion, or (B) an advertisement in which there is no audio presentation of information regarding the pay-per-call service, including the pay-per-call number. In an advertisement in which the pay-per-call number is presented only in the audio portion, the cost of the call shall be delivered immediately following the first and last delivery of the pay-per-call number, except that in a program-length commercial, the disclosure shall be delivered immediately following each delivery of the pay-per-call number.

(ii) In a print advertisement, the disclosure shall be placed adjacent to each presentation of the pay-per-call number. However, in an advertisement displaying more than one pay-per-call number with the same cost, the disclosure need only appear adjacent to the largest presentation of the pay-per-call number. Each letter or numeral of the disclosure shall be, at a minimum, one-half the size of each letter or numeral of the pay-per-call number to which the disclosure is adjacent.

(iii) In a radio advertisement, the disclosure shall be made at least once, and shall be delivered immediately following the first delivery of the pay-per-call number. In a program-length commercial, the disclosure shall be delivered immediately following each delivery of the pay-per-call number.

(c) *Sweepstakes; games of chance.* **(1)** The provider of pay-per-call services that advertises a prize or award or a service or product at no cost or for a reduced cost, to be awarded to the winner of any sweepstakes, including games of chance, shall clearly and conspicuously disclose in the advertisement the odds of being able to receive the prize, award, service, or product at no cost or reduced cost. If the odds are not calculable in advance, the advertisement shall disclose the factors used in calculating the odds. Either the advertisement or the preamble required by § 308.5(a) for such service shall clearly and conspicuously disclose that no call to the pay-per-call service is required to participate, and shall also disclose the existence of a free alternative method of entry, and either instructions on how to enter, or a local or toll-free telephone number or address to which consumers may call or write for information on how to enter the sweepstakes. Any description or characterization of the prize, award, service, or product that is being offered at no cost or reduced cost shall be truthful and accurate.

(2) For purposes of § 308.3(c), disclosures shall be made "clearly and conspicuously" as set forth in § 308.3(a) and as follows:

(i) In a television or videotape advertisement, the disclosures may be made in either the audio or video portion of the advertisement. If the disclosures are made in the video portion, they shall appear on the screen in sufficient size and for sufficient time to allow consumers to read and comprehend the disclosures.

(ii) In a print advertisement, the disclosures shall appear in a sufficient size and prominence and such location to be readily noticeable, readable and comprehensible.

(d) *Federal programs.* **(1)** The provider of pay-per-call services that advertises a pay-per-call service that is not operated or expressly authorized by a Federal agency, but that provides information on a Federal program, shall clearly and conspicuously disclose in the advertisement that the pay-per-call service is not authorized, endorsed, or approved by any Federal agency. Advertisements providing information on a Federal program shall include, but not be limited to, advertisements that contain a seal, insignia, trade or brand name, or any other term or symbol that reasonably could be interpreted or construed as implying any Federal government connection, approval, or endorsement.

(2) For purposes of § 308.3(d), disclosures shall be made "clearly and conspicuously" as set forth in § 308.3(a) and as follows:

(i) In a television or videotape advertisement, the disclosure may be made in either the audio or video portion of the advertisement. If the disclosure is made in the video portion, it shall appear on the screen in sufficient size and for sufficient time to allow consumers to read and comprehend the disclosure. The disclosure shall begin within the first fifteen (15) seconds of the advertisement.

(ii) In a print advertisement, the disclosure shall appear in a sufficient size and prominence and such location to be readily noticeable, readable and comprehensible. The disclosure shall appear in the top one-third of the advertisement.

(iii) In a radio advertisement, the disclosure shall begin within the first fifteen (15) seconds of the advertisement.

(e) *Prohibition on advertising to children.* **(1)** The provider of pay-per-call services shall not direct advertisements for such pay-per-call services to children under the age of 12, unless the service is a bona fide educational service.

(2) For the purposes of this regulation, advertisements directed to children under 12 shall include: any pay-per-call advertisement appearing during or immediately adjacent to programming for which competent and reliable audience composition data demonstrate that more than 50% of the audience is composed of children under 12, and any pay-per-call advertisement appearing in a periodical for which competent and reliable readership data demonstrate that more than 50% of the readership is composed of children under 12.

(3) For the purposes of this regulation, if competent and reliable audience composition or readership data does not demonstrate that more than 50% of the audience or readership is composed of children under 12, then the Commission shall consider the following criteria in determining whether an advertisement is directed to children under 12:

(i) Whether the advertisement appears in a publication directed to children under 12, including, but not limited to, books, magazines and comic books;

(ii) Whether the advertisement appears during or immediately adjacent to television programs directed to children under 12, including, but not limited to, children's programming as defined by the Federal Communications Commission, animated programs, and after-school programs;

(iii) Whether the advertisement appears on a television station or channel directed to children under 12;

(iv) Whether the advertisement is broadcast during or immediately adjacent to radio programs directed to children under 12, or broadcast on a radio station directed to children under 12;

(v) Whether the advertisement appears on the same video as a commercially-prepared video directed to children under 12, or preceding a movie directed to children under 12 shown in a movie theater;

(vi) Whether the advertisement or promotion appears on product packaging directed to children under 12; and

(vii) Whether the advertisement, regardless of when or where it appears, is directed to children under 12 in light of its subject matter, visual content, age of models, language, characters, tone, message, or the like.

(f) *Advertising to individuals under the age of 18.* **(1)** The provider of pay-per-call services shall ensure that any pay-per-call advertisement directed primarily to individuals under the age of 18 shall contain a clear and conspicuous disclosure that all individuals under the age of 18 must have the permission of such individual's parent or legal guardian prior to calling such pay-per-call service.

(2) For purposes of § 308.3(f), disclosures shall be made "clearly and conspicuously" as set forth in § 308.3(a) and as follows:

(i) In a television or videotape advertisement, each letter or numeral of the video disclosure shall be, at a minimum, one-half the size of each letter or numeral of the largest presentation of the pay-per-call number. The video disclosure shall appear on the screen for sufficient time to allow consumers to read and comprehend the disclosure. An audio disclosure shall be made at least once, simultaneously with a video presentation of the disclosure. However, no audio presentation of the disclosure is required in: (A) An advertisement fifteen (15) seconds or less in length in which the pay-per-call number is not presented in the audio portion, or (B) an advertisement in which there is no audio presentation of information regarding the pay-per-call service, including the pay-per-call number.

(ii) In a print advertisement, each letter or numeral of the disclosure shall be, at a minimum, one-half the size of each letter or numeral of the largest presentation of the pay-per-call number.

(3) For the purposes of this regulation, advertisements directed primarily to individuals under 18 shall include: Any pay-per-call advertisement appearing during or immediately adjacent to programming for which competent and reliable audience composition data demonstrate that more than 50% of the audience is composed of individuals under 18, and any pay-per-call advertisement appearing in a periodical for which competent and reliable readership data demonstrate that more than 50% of the readership is composed of individuals under 18.

(4) For the purposes of this regulation, if competent and reliable audience composition or readership data does not demonstrate that more than 50% of the audience or readership is composed of individuals under 18, then the Commission shall consider the following criteria in determining whether an advertisement is directed primarily to individuals under 18:

(i) Whether the advertisement appears in publications directed primarily to individuals under 18, including, but not limited to, books, magazines and comic books;

(ii) Whether the advertisement appears during or immediately adjacent to television programs directed primarily to individuals under 18, including, but not limited to, mid-afternoon weekday television shows;

(iii) Whether the advertisement is broadcast on radio stations that are directed primarily to individuals under 18;

(iv) Whether the advertisement appears on a cable or broadcast television station directed primarily to individuals under 18;

(v) Whether the advertisement appears on the same video as a commercially-prepared video directed primarily to individuals under 18, or preceding a movie directed primarily to individuals under 18 shown in a movie theater; and

(vi) Whether the advertisement, regardless of when or where it appears, is directed primarily to individuals under 18 in light of its subject matter, visual content, age of models, language, characters, tone, message, or the like.

(g) *Electronic tones in advertisements.* The provider of pay-per-call services is prohibited from using advertisements that emit electronic tones that can automatically dial a pay-per-call service.

(h) *Telephone solicitations.* The provider of pay-per-call services shall ensure that any telephone message that solicits calls to the pay-per-call service discloses the cost of the call in a slow and deliberate manner and in a reasonably understandable volume, in accordance with §§ 308.3(b)(1)(i)–(v).

(i) *Referral to toll-free telephone numbers.* The provider of pay-per-call services is prohibited from referring in advertisements to an 800 telephone number, or any other telephone number advertised as or widely understood to be toll-free, if that number violates the prohibition concerning toll-free numbers set forth in § 308.5(i).

§ 308.4 Special rule for infrequent publications.

(a) The provider of any pay-per-call service that advertises a pay-per-call service in a publication that meets the requirements set forth in § 308.4(c) may include in such advertisement, in lieu of the cost disclosures required by § 308.3(b), a clear and conspicuous disclosure that a call to the advertised pay-per-call service may result in a substantial charge.

(b) The provider of any pay-per-call service that places an alphabetical listing in a publication that meets the requirements set forth in § 308.4(c) is not required to make any of the disclosures required by §§ 308.3 (b), (c), (d), and (f) in the alphabetical listing, provided that such listing does not contain any information except the name, address and telephone number of the pay-per-call provider.

(c) The publication referred to in § 308.4(a) and (b) must be:

(1) Widely distributed;

(2) Printed annually or less frequently; and

(3) One that has an established policy of not publishing specific prices in advertisements.

§ 308.5 Pay-per-call service standards.

(a) *Preamble message.* The provider of pay-per-call services shall include, in each pay-per-call message, an introductory disclosure message ("preamble") in the same language as that principally used in the pay-per-call message, that clearly, in a slow and deliberate manner and in a reasonably understandable volume:

(1) Identifies the name of the provider of the pay-per-call service and describes the service being provided;

(2) Specifies the cost of the service as follows:

(i) If there is a flat fee for the call, the preamble shall state the total cost of the call;

(ii) If the call is billed on a time-sensitive basis, the preamble shall state the cost per minute and any minimum charges; if the length of the program can be determined in advance, the preamble shall also state the maximum charge that could be incurred if the caller listens to the complete program;

(iii) If the call is billed on a variable rate basis, the preamble shall state, in accordance with §§ 308.5(a)(2)(i) and (ii), the cost of the initial portion of the call, any minimum charges, and the range of rates that may be charged depending on the options chosen by the caller;

(iv) Any other fees that will be charged for the service shall be disclosed, as well as fees for any other pay-per-call service to which the caller may be transferred;

(3) Informs the caller that charges for the call begin, and that to avoid charges the call must be terminated, three seconds after a clearly discernible signal or tone indicating the end of the preamble;

(4) Informs the caller that anyone under the age of 18 must have the permission of parent or legal guardian in order to complete the call; and

(5) Informs the caller, in the case of a pay-per-call service that is not operated or expressly authorized by a Federal agency but that provides information on a Federal program, or that uses a trade or brand name or any other term that reasonably could be interpreted or construed as implying any Federal government connection, approval or endorsement, that the pay-per-call service is not authorized, endorsed, or approved by any Federal agency.

(b) *No charge to caller for preamble message.* The provider of pay-per-call services is prohibited from charging a caller any amount whatsoever for such a service if the caller hangs up at any time prior to three seconds after the signal or tone indicating the end of the preamble described in § 308.5(a). However, the three-second delay, and the message concerning such delay described in § 308.5(a)(3), is not required if the provider of pay-per-call services offers the caller an affirmative means (such as pressing a key on a telephone keypad) of indicating a decision to incur the charges.

(c) *Nominal cost calls.* The preamble described in § 308.5(a) is not required when the entire cost of the pay-per-call service, whether billed as a flat rate or on a time sensitive basis, is $2.00 or less.

(d) *Data service calls.* The preamble described in § 308.5(a) is not required when the entire call consists of the non-verbal transmission of information.

(e) *Bypass mechanism.* The provider of pay-per-call services that offers to frequent callers or regular subscribers to such services the option of activating a bypass mechanism to avoid listening to the preamble during subsequent calls shall not be deemed to be in violation of § 308.5(a), *provided that* any such bypass mechanism shall be disabled for a period of no less than 30 days immediately after the institution of an increase in the price for the service or a change in the nature of the service offered.

(f) *Billing limitations.* The provider of pay-per-call services is prohibited from billing consumers in excess of the amount described in the preamble for those services and from billing for any services provided in violation of any section of this rule.

(g) *Stopping the assessment of time-based charges.* The provider of pay-per-call services shall stop the assessment of time-based charges immediately upon disconnection by the caller.

(h) *Prohibition on services to children.* The provider of pay-per-call services shall not direct such services to children under the age of 12, unless such service is a bona fide educational service. The Commission shall consider the following criteria in determining whether a pay-per-call service is directed to children under 12:

(1) Whether the pay-per-call service is advertised in the manner set forth in §§ 308.3(e)(2) and (3); and

(2) Whether the pay-per-call service, regardless of when or where it is advertised, is directed to children under 12, in light of its subject matter, content, language, featured personality, characters, tone, message, or the like.

(i) *Prohibition concerning toll-free numbers.* Any person is prohibited from using an 800 number or other telephone number advertised as or widely understood to be toll-free in a manner that would result in:

(1) The calling party being assessed, by virtue of completing the call, a charge for the call;

(2) The calling party being connected to an access number for, or otherwise transferred to, a pay-per-call service;

(3) The calling party being charged for information conveyed during the call unless the calling party has a presubscription or comparable arrangement to be charged for the information; or

(4) The calling party being called back collect for the provision of audio or data information services, simultaneous voice conversation services, or products.

(j) *Disclosure requirements for billing statements.* The provider of pay-per-call services shall ensure that any billing statement for such provider's charges shall:

(1) Display any charges for pay-per-call services in a portion of the consumer's bill that is identified as not being related to local and long distance telephone charges;

(2) For each charge so displayed, specify the type of service, the amount of the charge, and the date, time, and, for calls billed on a time-sensitive basis, the duration of the call; and

(3) Display the local or toll-free telephone number where consumers can obtain answers to their questions and information on their rights and obligations with regard to their use of pay-per-call services, and can obtain the name and mailing address of the provider of pay-per-call services.

(k) *Refunds to consumers.* The provider of pay-per-call services shall be liable for refunds or credits to consumers who have been billed for pay-per-call services, and who have paid the charges for such services, pursuant to pay-per-call programs that have been found to have violated any provision of this rule or any other Federal rule or law.

(l) *Service bureau liability.* A service bureau shall be liable for violations of the rule by pay-per-call services using its call processing facilities where it knew or should have known of the violation.

§ 308.6 Access to information.

Any common carrier that provides telecommunication services to any provider of pay-per-call services shall make available to the Commission, upon written request, any records and financial information maintained by such carrier relating to the arrangements (other than for the provision of local exchange service) between such carrier and any provider of pay-per-call services.

§ 308.7 Billing and collection for pay-per-call services.

(a) *Definitions.* For the purposes of this section, the following definitions shall apply:

(1) *Billing entity* means any person who transmits a billing statement to a customer for a telephone-billed purchase, or any person who assumes responsibility for receiving and responding to billing error complaints or inquiries.

(2) *Billing error* means any of the following:

(i) A reflection on a billing statement of a telephone-billed purchase that was not made by the customer nor made from the telephone of the customer who was billed for the purchase or, if made, was not in the amount reflected on such statement.

(ii) A reflection on a billing statement of a telephone-billed purchase for which the customer requests additional clarification, including documentary evidence thereof.

(iii) A reflection on a billing statement of a telephone-billed purchase that was not accepted by the customer or not provided to the customer in accordance with the stated terms of the transaction.

(iv) A reflection on a billing statement of a telephone-billed purchase for a call made to an 800 or other toll free telephone number.

(v) The failure to reflect properly on a billing statement a payment made by the customer or a credit issued to the customer with respect to a telephone-billed purchase.

(vi) A computation error or similar error of an accounting nature on a billing statement of a telephone-billed purchase.

(vii) Failure to transmit a billing statement for a telephone-billed purchase to a customer's last known address if that address was furnished by the customer at least twenty days before the end of the billing cycle for which the statement was required.

(viii) A reflection on a billing statement of a telephone-billed purchase that is not identified in accordance with the requirements of § 308.5(j).

(3) *Customer* means any person who acquires or attempts to acquire goods or services in a telephone-billed purchase, or who receives a billing statement for a telephone-billed purchase charged to a telephone number assigned to that person by a providing carrier.

(4) *Preexisting agreement* means a "presubscription or comparable arrangement," as that term is defined in § 308.2(e).

(5) *Providing carrier* means a local exchange or interexchange common carrier providing telephone services (other than local exchange services) to a vendor for a telephone-billed purchase that is the subject of a billing error complaint or inquiry.

(6) *Telephone-billed purchase* means any purchase that is completed solely as a consequence of the completion of the call or a subsequent dialing, touch tone entry, or comparable action of the caller. Such term does not include:

(i) A purchase by a caller pursuant to a preexisting agreement with a vendor;

(ii) Local exchange telephone services or interexchange telephone services or any service that the Federal Communications Commission determines by rule—

(A) Is closely related to the provision of local exchange telephone services or interexchange telephone services; and

(B) Is subject to billing dispute resolution procedures required by Federal or state statute or regulation; or

(iii) The purchase of goods or services that is otherwise subject to billing dispute resolution procedures required by Federal statute or regulation.

(7) *Vendor* means any person who, through the use of the telephone, offers goods or services for a telephone-billed purchase.

(b) *Initiation of billing review.* A customer may initiate a billing review with respect to a telephone-billed purchase by providing the billing entity with notice of a billing error no later than 60 days after the billing entity transmitted the first billing statement that contains a charge for such telephone-billed purchase. If the billing error is the reflection on a billing statement of a telephone-billed purchase not provided to the customer in accordance with the stated terms of the transaction, the 60-day period shall begin to run from the date the goods or services are delivered or, if not delivered, should have been delivered, if such date is later than the date the billing statement was transmitted. A billing error notice shall:

(1) Set forth or otherwise enable the billing entity to identify the customer's name and the telephone number to which the charge was billed;

(2) Indicate the customer's belief that the statement contains a billing error and the type, date, and amount of such; and

(3) Set forth the reasons for the customer's belief, to the extent possible, that the statement contains a billing error.

(c) *Disclosure of method of providing notice; presumption if oral notice is permitted.* A billing entity shall clearly and conspicuously[10] disclose on each billing statement or on other material accompanying the billing statement the method (oral or written) by which the customer may provide notice to initiate review of a billing error in the manner set forth in § 308.7(b). If oral notice is permitted, any customer who orally communicates an allegation of a billing error to a billing entity shall be presumed to have properly initiated a billing review in accordance with the requirements of § 308.7(b).

(d) *Response to customer notice.* A billing entity that receives notice of a billing error as described in § 308.7(b) shall:

(1) Send a written acknowledgement to the customer including a statement that any disputed amount need not be paid pending investigation of the billing error. This shall be done no later than forty (40) days after receiving the notice, unless the action required by § 308.7(d)(2) is taken within such 40-day period; and

(2)(i) Correct the billing error and credit the customer's account for any disputed amount and any related charges, and notify the customer of the correction. The billing entity also shall disclose to the customer that collection efforts may occur despite the credit, and shall provide the names, mailing addresses, and business telephone numbers of the vendor and providing carrier, as applicable, that are the subject of the telephone-billed purchase, or provide the customer with a local or toll-free telephone number that the customer may call to obtain this information directly. However, the billing entity is not required to make the disclosure concerning collection efforts if the vendor, its agent, or the providing carrier, as applicable, will not collect or attempt to collect the disputed charge; or

(ii) Transmit an explanation to the customer, after conducting a reasonable investigation (including, where appropriate, contacting the vendor or providing carrier),[11] setting forth the reasons why it has determined that no billing error occurred or that a different billing error occurred from that asserted, make any appropriate adjustments to the customer's account, and, if the customer so requests, provide a written explanation and copies of documentary evidence of the customer's indebtedness.

(3) The action required by § 308.7(d)(2) shall be taken no later than two complete billing cycles of the billing entity (in no event later than ninety (90) days) after receiving the notice of the billing error and before taking any action to collect the disputed amount, or any part thereof. After complying with § 308.7(d)(2), the billing entity shall:

(i) If it is determined that any disputed amount is in error, promptly notify the appropriate providing carrier or vendor, as applicable, of its disposition of the customer's billing error and the reasons therefor; and

(ii) Promptly notify the customer in writing of the time when

10 The standard for "clear and conspicuous" as used in this section shall be the standard enunciated by the Board of Governors of the Federal Reserve System in its Official Staff Commentary on Regulation Z, which requires simply that the disclosures be in a reasonably understandable form. *See* 12 C.F.R. part 226, Supplement I, Comment 226.5(a)(1)-1.

11 If a customer submits a billing error notice alleging either the nondelivery of goods or services or that information appearing on a billing statement has been reported incorrectly to the billing entity, the billing entity shall not deny the assertion unless it conducts a reasonable investigation and determines that the goods or services were actually delivered as agreed or that the information was correct. There shall be a rebuttable presumption that goods or services were actually delivered to the extent that a vendor or providing carrier produces documents prepared and maintained in the ordinary course of business showing the date on, and the place to, which the goods or services were transmitted or delivered.

payment is due of any portion of the disputed amount determined not to be in error, which time shall be the longer of ten (10) days or the number of days the customer is ordinarily allowed (whether by custom, contract or state law) to pay undisputed amounts, and that failure to pay such amount may be reported to a credit reporting agency or subject the customer to a collection action, if that in fact may happen.

(e) *Withdrawal of billing error notice.* A billing entity need not comply with the requirements of § 308.7(d) if the customer has, after giving notice of a billing error and before the expiration of the time limits specified therein, agreed that the billing statement was correct or agreed to withdraw voluntarily the billing error notice.

(f) *Limitation on responsibility for billing error.* After complying with the provisions of § 308.7(d), a billing entity has no further responsibility under that section if the customer continues to make substantially the same allegation with respect to a billing error.

(g) *Customer's right to withhold disputed amount; limitation on collection action.* Once the customer has submitted notice of a billing error to a billing entity, the customer need not pay, and the billing entity, providing carrier, or vendor may not try to collect, any portion of any required payment that the customer reasonably believes is related to the disputed amount until the billing entity receiving the notice has complied with the requirements of § 308.7(d). The billing entity, providing carrier, or vendor are not prohibited from taking any action to collect any undisputed portion of the bill, or from reflecting a disputed amount and related charges on a billing statement, provided that the billing statement clearly states that payment of any disputed amount or related charges is not required pending the billing entity's compliance with § 308.7(d).

(h) *Prohibition on charges for initiating billing review.* A billing entity, providing carrier, or vendor may not impose on the customer any charge related to the billing review, including charges for documentation or investigation.

(i) *Restrictions on credit reporting*—**(1)** *Adverse credit reports prohibited.* Once the customer has submitted notice of a billing error to a billing entity, a billing entity, providing carrier, vendor, or other agent may not report or threaten directly or indirectly to report adverse information to any person because of the customer's withholding payment of the disputed amount or related charges, until the billing entity has met the requirements of § 308.7(d) and allowed the customer as many days thereafter to make payment as prescribed by § 308.7(d)(3)(ii).

(2) *Reports on continuing disputes.* If a billing entity receives further notice from a customer within the time allowed for payment under § 308.7(i)(1) that any portion of the billing error is still in dispute, a billing entity, providing carrier, vendor, or other agent may not report to any person that the customer's account is delinquent because of the customer's failure to pay that disputed amount unless the billing entity, providing carrier, vendor, or other agent also reports that the amount is in dispute and notifies the customer in writing of the name and address of each person to whom the vendor, billing entity, providing carrier, or other agent has reported the account as delinquent.

(3) *Reporting of dispute resolutions required.* A billing entity, providing carrier, vendor, or other agent shall report in writing any subsequent resolution of any matter reported pursuant to § 308.7(i)(2) to all persons to whom such matter was initially reported.

(j) *Forfeiture of right to collect disputed amount.* Any billing entity, providing carrier, vendor, or other agent who fails to comply with the requirements of § 308.7(c), (d), (g), (h), or (i) forfeits any right to collect from the customer the amount indicated by the customer, under § 308.7(b)(2), to be in error, and any late charges or other related charges thereon, up to $50 per transaction.

(k) *Prompt notification of returns and crediting of refunds.* When a vendor other than the billing entity accepts the return of property or forgives a debt for services in connection with a telephone-billed purchase, the vendor shall, within seven (7) business days from accepting the return or forgiving the debt, either:

(1) Mail or deliver a cash refund directly to the customer's address, and notify the appropriate billing entity that the customer has been given a refund, or

(2) Transmit a credit statement to the billing entity through the vendor's normal channels for billing telephone-billed purchases. The billing entity shall, within seven (7) business days after receiving a credit statement, credit the customer's account with the amount of the refund.

(l) *Right of customer to assert claims or defenses.* Any billing entity or providing carrier who seeks to collect charges from a customer for a telephone-billed purchase that is the subject of a dispute between the customer and the vendor shall be subject to all claims (other than tort claims) and defenses arising out of the transaction and relating to the failure to resolve the dispute that the customer could assert against the vendor, if the customer has made a good faith attempt to resolve the dispute with the vendor or providing carrier (other than the billing entity). The billing entity or providing carrier shall not be liable under this paragraph for any amount greater than the amount billed to the customer for the purchase (including any related charges).

(m) *Retaliatory actions prohibited.* A billing entity, providing carrier, vendor, or other agent may not accelerate any part of the customer's indebtedness or restrict or terminate the customer's access to pay-per-call services solely because the customer has exercised in good faith rights provided by this section.

(n) *Notice of billing error rights.*—**(1)** *Annual statement.*

(i) A billing entity shall mail or deliver to each customer, with the first billing statement for a telephone-billed purchase mailed or delivered after the effective date of these regulations, a statement of the customer's billing rights with respect to telephone-billed purchases. Thereafter the billing entity shall mail or deliver the billing rights statement at least once per calendar year to each customer to whom it has mailed or delivered a billing statement for a telephone-billed purchase during the previous twelve months. The billing rights statement shall disclose that the rights and obligations of the customer and the billing entity, set forth therein, are provided under the federal Telephone Disclosure and Dispute Resolution Act. The statement shall describe the procedure that the customer must follow to notify the billing entity of a billing error and the steps that the billing entity must take in response to the customer's notice. If the customer is permitted to provide oral notice of a billing error, the statement shall disclose that a customer who orally communicates an allegation of a billing error is presumed to have provided sufficient notice to initiate a billing review. The statement shall also disclose the customer's right to withhold payment of any disputed amount, and that any action to collect any disputed amount will be suspended, pending completion of the billing review. The statement shall further disclose the customer's rights and obligations if the billing entity determines that no billing error occurred, including what action the billing entity may take if the customer continues to withhold payment of the disputed amount. Additionally, the statement shall inform the customer of the billing entity's obligation to forfeit any disputed amount (up to $50 per transaction) if the billing entity fails to follow the billing and collection procedures prescribed by § 308.7 of this rule.

(ii) A billing entity that is a common carrier may comply with § 308.7(n)(1)(i) by, within 60 days after the effective date of these regulations, mailing or delivering the billing rights statement to all of its customers and, thereafter, mailing or delivering the billing rights statement at least once per calendar year, at intervals of not less than 6 months nor more than 18 months, to all of its customers.

(2) Alternative summary statement. As an alternative to § 308.7(n)(1), a billing entity may mail or deliver, on or with each billing statement, a statement that sets forth the procedure that a customer must follow to notify the billing entity of a billing error. The statement shall also disclose the customer's right to withhold payment of any disputed amount, and that any action to collect any disputed amount will be suspended, pending completion of the billing review.

(3) *General disclosure requirements.* **(i)** The disclosures required by § 308.7(n)(1) shall be made clearly and conspicuously on a separate statement that the customer may keep.

(ii) The disclosures required by § 308.7(n)(2) shall be made clearly and conspicuously and may be made on a separate statement or on the customer's billing statement. If any of the disclosures are provided on the back of the billing statement, the billing entity shall include a reference to those disclosures on the front of the statement.

(iii) At the billing entity's option, additional information or explanations may be supplied with the disclosures required by § 308.7(n), but none shall be stated, utilized, or placed so as to mislead or confuse the customer or contradict, obscure, or detract attention from the information required to be disclosed. The disclosures required by § 308.7(n) shall appear separately and above any other disclosures.

(o) *Multiple billing entities.* If a telephone-billed purchase involves more than one billing entity, only one set of disclosures need by given, and the billing entities shall agree among themselves which billing entity must comply with the requirements that this regulation imposes on any or all of them. The billing entity designated to receive and respond to billing errors shall remain the only billing entity responsible for complying with the terms of § 308.7(d). If a billing entity other than the one designated to receive and respond to billing errors receives notice of a billing error as described in § 308.7(b), that billing entity shall either: (1) Promptly transmit to the customer the name, mailing address, and business telephone number of the billing entity designated to receive and respond to billing errors; or (2) transmit the billing error notice within fifteen (15) days to the billing entity designated to receive and respond to billing errors. The time requirements in § 308.7(d) shall not begin to run until the billing entity designated to receive and respond to billing errors receives notice of the billing error, either from the customer or from the billing entity to whom the customer transmitted the notice.

(p) *Multiple customers.* If there is more than one customer involved in a telephone-billed purchase, the disclosures may be made to any customer who is primarily liable on the account.

§ 308.8 Severability.

The provisions of this rule are separate and severable from one another. If any provision is stayed or determined to be invalid, it is the Commission's intention that the remaining provisions shall continue in effect.

§ 308.9 Rulemaking review.

No later than four years after the effective date of this Rule, the Commission shall initiate a rulemaking review proceeding to evaluate the operation of the rule.

D.2.3 Restrictions on Telephone Solicitation—47 C.F.R. § 64.1200

§ 64.1200 Delivery restrictions.

(a) No person or entity may:

(1) Initiate any telephone call (other than a call made for emergency purposes or made with the prior express consent of the called party) using an automatic telephone dialing system or an artificial or prerecorded voice,

(i) To any emergency telephone line, including any 911 line and any emergency line of a hospital, medical physician or service office, health care facility, poison control center, or fire protection or law enforcement agency;

(ii) To the telephone line of any guest room or patient room of a hospital, health care facility, elderly home, or similar establishment; or

(iii) To any telephone number assigned to a paging service, cellular telephone service, specialized mobile radio service, or other radio common carrier service, or any service for which the called party is charged for the call.

(2) Initiate any telephone call to any residential line using an artificial or prerecorded voice to deliver a message without the prior express consent of the called party, unless the call,

(i) Is made for emergency purposes,

(ii) Is not made for a commercial purpose,

(iii) Is made for a commercial purpose but does not include or introduce an unsolicited advertisement or constitute a telephone solicitation,

(iv) Is made to any person with whom the caller has an established business relationship at the time the call is made, or

(v) Is made by or on behalf of a tax-exempt nonprofit organization.

(3) Use a telephone facsimile machine, computer, or other device to send an unsolicited advertisement to a telephone facsimile machine,

(i) For purposes of paragraph (a)(3) of this section, a facsimile advertisement is not "unsolicited" if the recipient has granted the sender prior express invitation or permission to deliver the advertisement, as evidenced by a signed, written statement that includes the facsimile number to which any advertisements may be sent and clearly indicates the recipient's consent to receive such facsimile advertisements from the sender.

(ii) A facsimile broadcaster will be liable for violations of paragraph (a)(3) of this section if it demonstrates a high degree of involvement in, or actual notice of, the unlawful activity and fails to take steps to prevent such facsimile transmissions.

(4) Use an automatic telephone dialing system in such a way that two or more telephone lines of a multi-line business are engaged simultaneously.

(5) Disconnect an unanswered telemarketing call prior to at least 15 seconds or four (4) rings.

(6) Abandon more than three percent of all telemarketing calls that are answered live by a person, measured over a 30-day period. A call is "abandoned" if it is not connected to a live sales representative within two (2) seconds of the called person's completed greeting. Whenever a sales representative is not available to speak with the person answering the call, that person must receive, within two (2) seconds after the called person's completed greeting, a prerecorded identification message that states only the name and telephone number of the business, entity, or individual on whose behalf the call was placed, and that the call was for "telemarketing purposes." The telephone number so provided must permit any individual to make a do-not-call request during regular business hours for the duration of the telemarketing campaign. The telephone number may not be a 900 number or any other number for which charges exceed local or long distance transmission charges. The seller or telemarketer must maintain records establishing compliance with paragraph (a)(6) of this section.

(i) A call for telemarketing purposes that delivers an artificial or prerecorded voice message to a residential telephone line that is assigned to a person who either has granted prior express consent for the call to be made or has an established business relationship with the caller shall not be considered an abandoned call if the message begins within two (2) seconds of the called person's completed greeting.

(ii) Calls made by or on behalf of tax-exempt nonprofit organizations are not covered by paragraph (a)(6) of this section.

(7) Use any technology to dial any telephone number for the purpose of determining whether the line is a facsimile or voice line.

(b) All artificial or prerecorded telephone messages shall:

(1) At the beginning of the message, state clearly the identity of the business, individual, or other entity that is responsible for initiating the call. If a business is responsible for initiating the call, the name under which the entity is registered to conduct business with the State Corporation Commission (or comparable regulatory authority) must be stated, and

(2) During or after the message, state clearly the telephone number (other than that of the autodialer or prerecorded message player that placed the call) of such business, other entity, or individual. The telephone number provided may not be a 900 number or any other number for which charges exceed local or long distance transmission charges. For telemarketing messages to residential telephone subscribers, such telephone number must permit any individual to make a do-not-call request during regular business hours for the duration of the telemarketing campaign.

(c) No person or entity shall initiate any telephone solicitation, as defined in paragraph (f)(9) of this section, to:

(1) Any residential telephone subscriber before the hour of 8 a.m. or after 9 p.m. (local time at the called party's location), or

(2) A residential telephone subscriber who has registered his or her telephone number on the national do-not-call registry of persons who do not wish to receive telephone solicitations that is maintained by the federal government. Such do-not-call registrations must be honored for a period of 5 years. Any person or entity making telephone solicitations (or on whose behalf telephone solicitations are made) will not be liable for violating this requirement if:

(i) It can demonstrate that the violation is the result of error and that as part of its routine business practice, it meets the following standards:

(A) *Written procedures.* It has established and implemented written procedures to comply with the national do-not-call rules;

(B) *Training of personnel.* It has trained its personnel, and any entity assisting in its compliance, in procedures established pursuant to the national do-not-call rules;

(C) *Recording.* It has maintained and recorded a list of telephone numbers that the seller may not contact;

(D) *Accessing the national do-not-call database.* It uses a process to prevent telephone solicitations to any telephone number on any list established pursuant to the do-not-call rules, employing a version of the national do-not-call registry obtained from the administrator of the registry no more than three months prior to the date any call is made, and maintains records documenting this process; and

(E) *Purchasing the national do-not-call database.* It uses a process to ensure that it does not sell, rent, lease, purchase or use the national do-not-call database, or any part thereof, for any purpose except compliance with this section and any such state or federal law to prevent telephone solicitations to telephone numbers registered on the national database. It purchases access to the relevant do-not-call data from the administrator of the national database and does not participate in any arrangement to share the cost of accessing the national database, including any arrangement with telemarketers who may not divide the costs to access the national database among various client sellers; or

(ii) It has obtained the subscriber's prior express invitation or permission. Such permission must be evidenced by a signed, written agreement between the consumer and seller which states that the consumer agrees to be contacted by this seller and includes the telephone number to which the calls may be placed; or

(iii) The telemarketer making the call has a personal relationship with the recipient of the call.

(d) No person or entity shall initiate any call for telemarketing purposes to a residential telephone subscriber unless such person or entity has instituted procedures for maintaining a list of persons who request not to receive telemarketing calls made by or on behalf of that person or entity. The procedures instituted must meet the following minimum standards:

(1) *Written policy.* Persons or entities making calls for telemarketing purposes must have a written policy, available upon demand, for maintaining a do-not-call list.

(2) *Training of personnel engaged in telemarketing.* Personnel engaged in any aspect of telemarketing must be informed and trained in the existence and use of the do-not-call list.

(3) *Recording, disclosure of do-not-call requests.* If a person or entity making a call for telemarketing purposes (or on whose behalf such a call is made) receives a request from a residential telephone subscriber not to receive calls from that person or entity, the person or entity must record the request and place the subscriber's name, if provided, and telephone number on the do-not-call list at the time the request is made. Persons or entities making calls for telemarketing purposes (or on whose behalf such calls are made) must honor a residential subscriber's do-not-call request within a reasonable time from the date such request is made. This period may not exceed thirty days from the date of such request. If such requests are recorded or maintained by a party other than the person or entity on whose behalf the telemarketing call is made, the person or entity on whose behalf the telemarketing call is made will be liable for any failures to honor the do-not-call request. A person or entity making a call for telemarketing purposes must obtain a consumer's prior express permission to share or forward the consumer's request not to be called to a party other than the person or entity on whose behalf a telemarketing call is made or an affiliated entity.

(4) *Identification of sellers and telemarketers.* A person or entity making a call for telemarketing purposes must provide the called party with the name of the individual caller, the name of the person or entity on whose behalf the call is being made, and a telephone number or address at which the person or entity may be contacted. The telephone number provided may not be a 900 number or any other number for which charges exceed local or long distance transmission charges.

(5) *Affiliated persons or entities.* In the absence of a specific request by the subscriber to the contrary, a residential subscriber's do-not-call request shall apply to the particular business entity making the call (or on whose behalf a call is made), and will not apply to affiliated entities unless the consumer reasonably would expect them to be included given the identification of the caller and the product being advertised.

(6) *Maintenance of do-not-call lists.* A person or entity making calls for telemarketing purposes must maintain a record of a caller's request not to receive further telemarketing calls. A do-not-call request must be honored for 5 years from the time the request is made.

(7) Tax-exempt nonprofit organizations are not required to comply with 64.1200(d).

(e) The rules set forth in paragraph (c) and (d) of this section are applicable to any person or entity making telephone solicitations or telemarketing calls to wireless telephone numbers to the extent described in the Commission's Report and Order, CG Docket No. 02-278, FCC 03-153, "Rules and Regulations Implementing the Telephone Consumer Protection Act of 1991."

(f) As used in this section:

(1) The terms *automatic telephone dialing system* and *autodialer* mean equipment which has the capacity to store or produce telephone numbers to be called using a random or sequential number generator and to dial such numbers.

(2) The term *emergency purposes* means calls made necessary in any situation affecting the health and safety of consumers.

(3) The term *established business relationship* means a prior or existing relationship formed by a voluntary two-way communication between a person or entity and a residential subscriber with or without an exchange of consideration, on the basis of the subscriber's purchase or transaction with the entity within the eighteen (18) months immediately preceding the date of the telephone call or on the basis of the subscriber's inquiry or application regarding products or services offered by the entity within the three months immediately preceding the date of the call, which relationship has not been previously terminated by either party.

(i) The subscriber's seller-specific do-not-call request, as set forth in paragraph (d)(3) of this section, terminates an established business relationship for purposes of telemarketing and telephone solicitation even if the subscriber continues to do business with the seller.

(ii) The subscriber's established business relationship with a particular business entity does not extend to affiliated entities unless the subscriber would reasonably expect them to be included given the nature and type of goods or services offered by the affiliate and the identity of the affiliate.

[**Note to paragraph (f)(3)**: Paragraph 64.1200(f)(3) is stayed as of October 14, 2003, as it applies to the time limitations on facsimile advertisements. The Federal Communications Commission will publish a document in the Federal Register when the stay is lifted. [68 Fed. Reg. 59130 (Oct. 14, 2003)]]

(4) The term *facsimile broadcaster* means a person or entity that transmits messages to telephone facsimile machines on behalf of another person or entity for a fee.

(5) The term *seller* means the person or entity on whose behalf a telephone call or message is initiated for the purpose of encouraging the purchase or rental of, or investment in, property, goods, or services, which is transmitted to any person.

(6) The term *telemarketer* means the person or entity that initiates a telephone call or message for the purpose of encouraging the purchase or rental of, or investment in, property, goods, or services, which is transmitted to any person.

(7) The term *telemarketing* means the initiation of a telephone call or message for the purpose of encouraging the purchase or rental of, or investment in, property, goods, or services, which is transmitted to any person.

(8) The term *telephone facsimile machine* means equipment which has the capacity to transcribe text or images, or both, from paper into an electronic signal and to transmit that signal over a regular telephone line, or to transcribe text or images (or both) from an electronic signal received over a regular telephone line onto paper.

(9) The term *telephone solicitation* means the initiation of a telephone call or message for the purpose of encouraging the purchase or rental of, or investment in, property, goods, or services, which is transmitted to any person, but such term does not include a call or message:

(i) To any person with that person's prior express invitation or permission;

(ii) To any person with whom the caller has an established business relationship; or

(iii) By or on behalf of a tax-exempt nonprofit organization.

(10) The term *unsolicited advertisement* means any material advertising the commercial availability or quality of any property, goods, or services which is transmitted to any person without that person's prior express invitation or permission.

(11) The term *personal relationship* means any family member, friend, or acquaintance of the telemarketer making the call.

(g) Beginning January 1, 2004, common carriers shall:

(1) When providing local exchange service, provide an annual notice, via an insert in the subscriber's bill, of the right to give or revoke a notification of an objection to receiving telephone solicitations pursuant to the national do-not-call database maintained by the federal government and the methods by which such rights may be exercised by the subscriber. The notice must be clear and conspicuous and include, at a minimum, the Internet address and toll-free number that residential telephone subscribers may use to register on the national database.

(2) When providing service to any person or entity for the purpose of making telephone solicitations, make a one-time notification to such person or entity of the national do-not-call requirements, including, at a minimum, citation to 47 CFR 64.1200 and 16 CFR 310. Failure to receive such notification will not serve as a defense to any person or entity making telephone solicitations from violations of this section.

(h) The administrator of the national do-not-call registry that is maintained by the federal government shall make the telephone numbers in the database available to the States so that a State may use the telephone numbers that relate to such State as part of any database, list or listing system maintained by such State for the regulation of telephone solicitations.

[57 Fed. Reg. 53293 (Nov. 9, 1992); 60 Fed. Reg. 42069 (Aug. 15, 1995); 68 Fed. Reg. 44177 (July 25, 2003); 68 Fed. Reg. 50978, (Aug. 25, 2003); 68 Fed. Reg. 56764 (Oct. 1, 2003); 68 Fed. Reg. 59131 (Oct. 14, 2003)]

Appendix E State Telemarketing and State "900-Number" Statutes Summarized

This appendix summarizes the main features of state telemarketing laws and state laws regulating pay-per-call ("900-number") services. These summaries should only be used as a general guide. Advocates should consult the statutes themselves for details and precise statutory language.

These summaries include only state statutes that are clearly directed, at least in part, toward telemarketing or pay-per-call services. Some states have home solicitation sales statutes that do not specifically mention telephone sales but might be interpreted to cover such sales. If a state does not have a telemarketing statute listed in this appendix, the advocate should consult the state's home solicitation sales law to see if it might apply to the transaction.

These summaries do not describe attorney general enforcement authority that is derived from the state UDAP statute, but mention attorney general enforcement authority only where the telemarketing statute itself specifically provides for the role that the attorney general is to play. Similarly, the summaries only list penalties that are specifically provided by the telemarketing statute, and do not describe UDAP penalties that may be incorporated by reference into the telemarketing statute.

ALABAMA

Telemarketing Statute: **Ala. Code §§ 8-19A-1 through 8-19A-24 (Telemarketing) and 8-19C-1 through 8-19C–12 (Do-Not-Call list).**

Scope: Defines telemarketing broadly but lists 25 exceptions, such as persons calling for charitable donations or other non-commercial purposes, sales by established businesses, sales that involve face-to-face contact, and sales of securities, insurance, cable TV, newspapers or magazines. Do-not-call provisions apply to persons or entities making telephone solicitations, as defined in §§ 8-19A-3 and 8-19A-4, above, to residential subscribers in Alabama. Local or long distance telephone companies and providers of Caller ID service may not be held liable for violations committed by other persons or entities.

Registration Requirements: Telephone solicitors must obtain a license, pay an annual fee, maintain a surety bond, and submit information about prizes to the state agency.

Substantive Law: Solicitors must identify themselves, their company and the goods being sold, inform the consumer of cancellation rights, and reduce all sales transactions to a written contract. Solicitor must identify self, and may not block Caller ID. May not call residential subscribers who register on do-not-call list, which is to be coordinated with nationwide list.

Private Right of Action: Yes. A violation is a UDAP violation. The statute also provides a private cause of action for actual damages, court costs, and attorney fees. Statute also gives the attorney general specific enforcement powers. Individual who receives more than one telephone solicitation within twelve months from, or on behalf of, same individual in violation of do-not-call statute, may sue for the greater of actual monetary loss or $2000 per knowing violation, and for a cease and desist order. (Bona fide error defense available.) Remedies are in addition to any other causes of action, penalties and remedies provided by law.

Special Penalties: Civil penalty of up to $10,000 for each violation, and violations may also be a Class C felony. For violation of do-not-call statute, Public Service Commission may seek civil penalties of up to $2000 per violation, and cease and desist orders.

ALASKA

Telemarketing Statute: **Alaska Stat. §§ 45.63.010 through 45.63.100 (Michie).**

Scope: Defines telemarketing broadly but lists 19 exceptions, such as sales made by licensed real estate brokers, funeral directors and insurance agents, and the sale of items "made by hand."

Registration Requirements: Telephone solicitors must register with the Department of Law.

Substantive Law: Solicitors must receive a signed written contract from the consumer before they collect payment and provide a refund if consumer returns the goods and makes written request within seven days after receiving property, or if services have not been provided and consumer makes written request within seven days after payment; may not state or imply that they are licensed by the state unless asked by the consumer; waiver prohibited. State regulations at 9 Alaska Admin. Code Ch. 14 require specific disclosures for certain types of sales, including prize or gift promotions, sales of metals, stones, minerals, oil wells, gas wells, some office supply sales, and sales of yellow pages advertising. Alaska Stat. § 45.50.475 also makes it a UDAP violation use recorded messages in telephonic solicitations or engage in telephonic solicitations of residential customers who have told the company not to call or are on state or federal do-not-call list.

Private Right of Action: Violation is a UDAP violation.

Special Penalties: Certain violations are a Class C felony, certain others are a Class A misdemeanor.

900-Number Regulation: **Alaska Admin. Code tit. 3, §§ 53.500 through 53.599.**

Scope: Applies to local exchange carriers and interexchange carriers which provide transmission or billing and collection services to information providers (intrastate transactions only).

Exceptions: Preamble requirement does not apply to calls costing less than $2.00.

Substantive Law: May not disconnect or threaten to disconnect basic local or interexchange service for nonpayment of pay-per-call charges. May not include pay-per-call charges in amount to be paid to avoid disconnection, or amount used to calculate deposit to establish or reconnect basic service. On phone bills, pay-per-call charges must be separately listed and customers must be notified that local service cannot be disconnected for nonpayment. Bill must include customer service number for questions about pay-per-call charges, and carrier must provide customer, upon request, with name address and phone number of information provider. When a customer questions or complains about pay-per-call charges, customer must be informed of blocking options. Certain charges must be waived if inadvertent, mistaken or unauthorized. Charges must be waived if information provider did not comply with certain standards, i.e., price of call misrepresented or not disclosed, preamble was confusing or deceptive, information was garbled, out-of-date or inaudible, customer disconnected after preamble but was charged. Carrier must offer blocking, first time free, but may charge for reconnection on subsequent blocking. Carrier must notify customers of blocking options. May not provide transmission unless customer affirmatively indicates acceptance of charges. Preamble requirements: must be clearly understandable and audible, disclose name of service provider, nature of service, charge for call. Preambles directed at children must include parental permission warning. Carriers may not provide transmission services to information provider that fails to comply with preamble requirement or that uses broadcasting of tones to dial pay-per-call number.

ARIZONA

***Telemarketing Statute*: Ariz. Rev. Stat. §§ 44-1271 through 44-1282.**

Scope: Covers "sellers," broadly defined as persons who, directly or through solicitors, initiate telephone calls to provide or arrange to provide goods or services to consumers in return for payment. Also covers solicitations in response to inquiries by consumers generated by certain advertisements, direct mail solicitations, and other solicitations. Partial exemptions for certain catalog sellers, some sellers with established retail locations, some business-to-business solicitations, sales in which seller provides descriptive literature before consumer pays (some exceptions), calls that are followed up by face-to-face meeting, and solicitors for certain businesses, except all are required to comply with § 1278, which prohibits unlawful practices.

Registration Requirements: Telephone sellers must register with secretary of state, and provide detailed information, including scripts, and details about prize promotions.

Substantive Law: Three-day right to cancel. Seller must identify self and company, state sales purpose of call, and disclose all charges. May not block Caller ID; may not call any person on national do-not-call list also forbidden); may not make unsolicited call to mobile phone or paging device; may not deliver prerecorded message to residential number except by prior consent or for certain emergency purposes; may not use automatic dialing device unless it is able to exclude emergency numbers (fire, police, etc.), patient rooms at a hospital, nursing home, or similar facility, any number at which called party must pay for call, and numbers on seller's do-not-call list. Seller offering a recovery service may not charge or receive any consideration before full and complete performance of the service.

Private Right of Action: A violation is a UDAP violation, which carries an implied private cause of action. Purchaser may also rescind a sale by an unregistered seller and recover financial damages and attorney fees. Statute also gives attorney general specific enforcement powers. Consumer also recovers costs.

Special Penalties: Failure to register is a Class 5 felony.

***900-Number Statute*: Ariz. Rev. Stat. § 13-2920.**

Substantive Law: Advertisements must clearly disclose the price of the call; a preamble message at the beginning of each call must state the price of the call and how it is calculated; 900-number services that depict sexual conduct must be restricted to people 18 or older; consumers have a one-time right to avoid paying 900-number charges incurred by unauthorized minors or through fraud or misrepresentation.

Private Right of Action: None specified. Violation is Class 3 misdemeanor.

ARKANSAS

***Telemarketing Statute*: Ark. Code Ann. §§ 4-99-101 through 4-99-408 (Michie).**

Scope: Defines specific types of telemarketing that are covered, and excludes persons selling securities, insurance, newspapers, magazines or memberships in book or record clubs, sales to previous customers, sales that involve face-to-face contact, and sales made by supervised financial institutions or burial associations, or public utilities.

Registration Requirements: Telephone solicitors must register with the Consumer Protection Division, pay a fee, and maintain a surety bond. Must provide information, including sales scripts and detailed information about any gift or prizes. Additional bond required for person offering prize promotion.

Substantive Law: Any solicitor who implies the consumer has won a prize must provide the consumer with certain information, including the location of the seller, the odds of winning, any rules or regulations, and the number of consumers who have won the prize in the past. Use of couriers is prohibited, and the consumer's express written authorization is required before telemarketer may submit check, draft, or other negotiable instrument to consumer's bank. Telemarketers may not block Caller ID or transmit fictitious or misleading Caller ID information. Establishes state do-not-call list and prohibits violation of FTC do-not-call rule. Solicitors must identify themselves and their company and the goods being sold. Telemarketers are prohibited from calling people who have listed themselves on a statewide database as not wanting to receive telephone solicitations. Telemarketers must quit providing information or attempting to sell immediately upon notice that the called party is not interested. A separate statute, Ark. Code Ann. § 4-28-401, requires registration of charitable organizations and professional telemarketers who solicit funds for charities. Certain willful violations are a Class D felony.

Private Right of Action: A violation is a UDAP violation. The statute gives attorney general specific enforcement powers.

Special Penalties: A knowing and willful violation is a Class A misdemeanor; enhanced penalty for targeting the elderly or disabled based on five identified factors. Knowing and willful requirement does not apply to disclosure violations. Certain willful violations are Class D felonies.

***900-Number Statute*: Ark. Code Ann. §§ 4-98-101 through 4-98-105 (Michie).**

Substantive Law: Advertisements must clearly disclose costs, any limitations on the offer, and a requirement that minors get parental permission; a 12-second preamble message must disclose the

nature of the service, the cost of the call, and that the caller can avoid charges by hanging up within three seconds after the preamble is completed.
Exceptions: The preamble is not required if total cost of 900-number call is less than $2.00 or if call is for polling services, political fundraising, or asynchronous or computerized data transmission technology.
Private Right of Action: Violation is UDAP violation. Statute also authorizes suit for three times amount of actual damages recoverable, plus costs and attorney fees; action must be brought within 2 years. Attorney general can invoke UDAP enforcement powers.

CALIFORNIA

***Telemarketing Statute*: Cal. Bus. & Prof. Code §§ 17511 through 17513 (West) and Cal. Bus. & Prof. Code §§ 17591 through 17595 (West).**
Scope: Defines specific types of telemarketing that are covered, and lists 22 exceptions such as the sale of securities, sales made to previous customers, and sales that involve face-to-face contact. Exception for solicitations by certain tax exempt organizations. Covers Internet transactions.
Registration Requirements: Solicitors must register, pay a fee, and maintain a bond. Must provide detailed information, including sales scripts and information about gifts or prizes.
Substantive Law: Solicitors must provide consumers with certain information, including the solicitor's address and oral and written notification of the consumer's cancellation rights, and detailed information about gifts or prizes. Non-attorneys are prohibited from requesting or receiving payment for recovery of money or item of value paid for by, or promised to, the consumer in a previous telemarketing transaction, until 7 business days after that money or other item is delivered to the consumer. Third-party collections are prohibited unless goods are delivered before or at the same time the purchaser's payment is obtained. May not call consumer listed on FTC's do-not-call list.
Private Right of Action: For violation of do-not-call list provisions, recipient of prohibited call may bring action in small claims court for injunction; violation of injunction carries civil penalty of up to $1000, payable to the person who sought the injunction.
Special Penalties: Fine up to $10,000 and/or imprisonment up to one year, for each willful violation.

***900-Number Statute*: Cal. Bus. & Prof. Code §§ 17539.5 through 17539.6 (West).**
Substantive Law: Advertisements must clearly disclose the cost of the call, the identity of the provider, a description of the services, and, if the service is directed toward minors, a statement that parental consent is required; sweepstakes must offer a free alternative method of entering, disclose the odds of winning, provide refunds, and meet other requirements; providers may not solicit callers by outbound calls; there are protections against switching from non-900-number calls to 900-number calls and restrictions on "games of skill" and on incentives that are offered to induce calls; specific deceptive tactics such as use of the word "free" are prohibited. Advertisement containing 900 number must be written or spoken in same language as used by recorded announcement or live operator of the 900-number call.
Registration Requirement: Information provider who operates sweepstakes through 900 number must register and provide detailed information to state Department of Justice, including scripts, videotapes, or copies of all promotional materials.
Private Right of Action: The remedies allowed by California Bus. & Prof. Code § 17200 should be available.

COLORADO

***Telemarketing Statute*: Colo. Rev. Stat. § 6-1-301; Colo. Rev. Stat. §§ 6-1-901 through 6-1-908; 4 Colo. Code Regs. § 723-22.**
Scope: Defines telemarketing broadly but lists 20 exceptions, such as the sale of securities, newspapers or insurance, sales involving face-to-face contact, sales made by supervised financial institutions, and catalog sales.
Registration Requirements: Solicitors must register with the attorney general and file an application.
Substantive Law: Consumers may cancel transactions within 3 days, solicitors must refund payment to the consumers within 30 days of cancellation, and solicitors must disclose to consumers their cancellation rights. May not block Caller ID May not call person on Colorado do-not-call list. (Charitable and political organizations, which are exempt for free speech reasons, are encouraged to comply voluntarily.)
Private Right of Action: Yes. A violation is a UDAP violation.
Special Penalties: Violations are Class 1 misdemeanors.

CONNECTICUT

***Telemarketing Statute*: Conn. Gen. Stat. §§ 42-284 through 42-289.**
Scope: Initiating a sale, lease or rental of consumer goods or offering gifts or prizes with intent to sell, lease, or rent consumer goods by telephonic means, or by other advertising which invites consumer to telephone seller. Excludes sales involving prior negotiations at seller's place of business, prior business relationship, sale of newspapers by publisher, certain banking transactions, certain catalog sales, sales in which seller allows cancellation and refund, certain sales regulated under other statutes, including utilities and securities, sales by business which sells same goods from fixed location and does more than 50% if its business at that location.
Registration Requirements: None specified.
Substantive Law: Written contract required, which discloses all terms of the sale. Telemarketer may not accept payment nor charge consumer's credit card until telemarketer receives signed copy of contract. May not block Caller ID. May not call person on do-not-call list (Conn. Gen. Stat. § 42-288a). Compilers or sellers of lists for telephone solicitation must delete names found on do-not-call list (does not apply to telephone directories).
Private Right of Action: Violation is a UDAP violation.
Special Penalties: None specified.

DISTRICT OF COLUMBIA

***Telemarketing Statute:* D.C. Code Ann. §§ 22-3226.01 through 22-3226.15.**
Scope: Telemarketing is broadly defined, with exceptions for one-time or infrequent calls; information calls during which payment is not accepted; calls leading to face-to-face presentation; calls requested by consumer; servicing existing accounts; religious, political, charitable, educational or other non-profits; sales of newspapers; various sales regulated under other law, including securities, cable TV, insurance, travel; sales if seller offers 7-day inspection and full refund.
Registration Requirements: Must register with mayor, and post bond for $50,000.
Substantive Law: Within first 30 seconds of call must identify self

and company, and nature of goods being sold. Must disclose true name of solicitor, and total cost of goods or services. Forbids operating without a license, using name of charity without permission, knowing misrepresentations, false pretenses, charging a customer's account without express written authorization, using a courier to pick up payment before goods delivered with opportunity to inspect, causing a phone to ring more than 15 times, contacting a consumer who has expressly stated that he or she does not wish to receive calls from seller, calling between 9 p.m. and 8 a.m.

Private Right of Action: Yes, for actual and punitive damages, attorney fees and costs, declaratory judgment or injunction and any other equitable relief the court deems proper. This section is in addition to any other rights or remedies to which consumer may be entitled. Statute of limitations 3 years from date of call.

Special Penalties: Civil penalties of up to $1000 per violation; may be trebled for knowingly targeting elderly or disabled persons. Criminal penalties.

DELAWARE

***Telemarketing Statute*: Del. Code Ann. tit. 6, §§ 2501A through 2509A.**

Scope: Defines telemarketing broadly, and lists 10 exemptions such as sales involving a face-to-face pre-sale presentation, customer-initiated calls that are not a result of a telemarketing solicitation, business-to-business transactions, solicitations by charities and non-profits, insurance, securities, certain catalog sales, calls by supervised financial institutions, and goods or services regulated by PUC or FCC.

Registration Requirements: With certain exceptions, any person transacting business with a customer located in Delaware through telemarketing as a seller or a telemarketing business must register and post $50,000 bond.

Substantive Law: At beginning of call, telemarketer must disclose name, name of seller, purpose of call, and nature of product; must make additional disclosures prior to payment or conclusion of call, including price, basic characteristics of the product, restrictions and limitations, refund policy, and information about prize promotions. Buyer has right to cancel within 7 days after receiving written confirmation of the order unless seller offers full money-back guarantee. Telemarketer must obtain buyer's express verifiable authorization before obtaining or submitting check, draft, or other negotiable paper. Telemarketers must discontinue calls for 10 years after request. Statute prohibits advance payment for recovery services; provision of substantial assistance to telemarketer violating statute; use of courier to pick up payment before merchandise is delivered with an opportunity to inspect it; and various deceptive acts.

Private Right of Action: Yes, for actual and punitive damages, attorney fees, court costs, and any other remedies provided by law, including equitable relief.

Special Penalties: None stated.

FLORIDA

***Telemarketing Statute*: Fla. Stat. Ann. § 501.059 (West) and Fla. Stat. Ann. §§ 501.601 through 501.626 (West) (Florida Telemarketing Act).**

Scope: Defines telemarketing broadly. Numerous exemptions including single transaction, charitable or political, calls leading to face-to-face transaction, securities, newspapers, certain book or recording clubs, insurance, cable TV, certain business-to-business transactions, certain catalog sales, periodicals.

Registration Requirements: Sellers and salespersons must be licensed. Sellers must post bond or other acceptable security.

Substantive Law: Telephone solicitors must identify themselves and their companies, within the first 30 seconds of the call, must advise consumer of cancellation rights: cancellation by written notice within three business days of contract confirmation; refund, credit or replacement if goods returned within 7 business days after receipt. Certain provisions of this section do not apply if sellers offer full refund within 30 days if goods returned within 7 days of receipt. May not call consumers who place themselves on a "no-call" list, and must receive a signed written contract from the consumer before they collect payment. If a gift or premium is offered, caller must disclose value of item, odds if ascertainable, and any restrictions or conditions on the offer. It is unlawful to demand payment by credit card authorization or indicate a preference for that method of payment. All oral disclosures must be clear and intelligible. May not call between 9 p.m. and 8 a.m.; may not block Caller ID.

Private Right of Action: Any person injured by violation may bring civil action for actual and/or punitive damages, costs and attorney fees. Contract made pursuant to telemarketing call is unenforceable unless it complies with statutory requirements, and the prevailing party in any civil litigation under this section (§ 501.059) is entitled to costs and attorney fees. Statute also gives attorney general specific enforcement powers.

Special Penalties: Civil penalty of up to $10,000 for each violation and attorney fees and costs. Certain violations are third degree felonies. Enforcing authority may petition for appointment of receiver or sequestration of assets.

***900-Number Regulation*: Fla. Admin. Code r. 25-4.110(15).**

Substantive Law: Applies to local exchange carriers providing transmission or billing and collection services to information providers. Local exchange carriers must itemize pay-per-call charges separately. Must advise customers that nonpayment of pay-per-call charges will not result in disconnection of basic service, that free blocking is available, the phone number for disputing a pay-per-call bill, and the name of the pay-per-call service and the interexchange carrier. Local exchange carriers must adjust the bill if customer claims lack of knowledge (first time only) or if pay-per-call service misled or deceived customer, failed to disclose price, provided incomplete, garbled, or out-of-date information, or charged a customer who disconnected during the grace period. Local exchange carriers may impose pay-per-call blocking on customer who refuses to pay valid pay-per-call charges. Local exchange carriers may not bill for disputed pay-per-call charges, or report non-payment of pay-per-call charges to credit bureau. Local exchange carriers may provide transmission or billing and collection service only if pay-per-call service: provides a preamble disclosing the cost of the call (except for certain calls under $3.00); states parental permission requirement for calls likely to interest minors; provides an opportunity to disconnect; includes parental permission notice in advertising; does not use autodialers or broadcast tones; and discloses charges in advertising. Pay-per-call service may not offer children's programs costing more than $5.00 or offering the enticement of a gift or premium. Detailed disclosure requirements for advertising of pay-per-call services.

GEORGIA

***Telemarketing Statute*: Ga. Code Ann. §§ 10-5B-1 through 105B-8.**

Scope: Defines telemarketing broadly.

Registration Requirements: None.

Substantive Law: Caller must identify company and provide a telephone number or address at which it can be contacted before beginning sales solicitation, and may not block consumer's Caller ID. Secretary of state is authorized to promulgate rules concerning telemarketing. Note that a separate statute, Ga. Code Ann. § 10-1-393.5 and -393.6, makes it a UDAP violation to engage in fraud or deceit or commit a theft offense while engaged in telemarketing or use a courier to pick up payment before goods delivered with opportunity to inspect; that prohibition adopts the FTC rule's definition of telemarketing, but includes intrastate as well as interstate calls, and explicitly includes Internet transactions and imposes an enhanced penalty for deliberate targeting of elderly or disabled. Unlawful to demand advance payment for removing derogatory information from consumer's credit record, improving consumer's credit rating, or recovering money or goods lost in previous telemarketing transaction (except for services of licensed attorney).

Private Right of Action: Private right of action under § 10-1-399. A violation of Ga. Code Ann. § 10-1-393.5 is a UDAP violation.

Special Penalties: Willful violation is a felony; double applicable civil and criminal penalties for intentional targeting of elderly or disabled.

***900-Number Statute*: Ga. Code Ann. § 10-1-393(b)(21).**

Substantive Law: Advertisements must disclose name, address, telephone number of the person responsible for the advertisement and the per-call charge.

Exceptions: Applies only to telephone numbers with "976" prefix.

Private Right of Action: Yes. A violation is a UDAP violation.

HAWAII

***Telemarketing Statute*: Haw. Rev. Stat. §§ 481P-1 through 481P-8.**

Scope: Telemarketing broadly defined, including investment opportunities and recovery services. Exemptions include polling, political or charitable calls, certain catalog sales, certain businesses regulated under other laws, i.e. securities, real estate, insurance.

Registration Requirements: None specified.

Substantive Law: Telemarketers must not call numbers listed on nationwide do-not-call registry. Within the first minute of the call, and before any sales solicitation, caller must disclose own name and that of company, and sales purpose of call. Must disclose full cost of goods, any restrictions or limitations, seller's cancellation or refund policy. No payment required until express verifiable contract confirmation received. Must allow 7 days after receipt of goods to review goods and return for cancellation if desired. Detailed recordkeeping requirements, including scripts, contracts and training materials, extensive information about prize promotions, and evidence to substantiate claims for health, nutrition or diet-related goods and services. May not use a courier to pick up immediate payment. Abusive practices explicitly prohibited. May not demand advance payment for credit repair, recovery services, or obtaining a loan. May not call before 8 a.m. or after 9 p.m., or cause telephone to ring more than 10 times. May not call a consumer who has requested not to be called; bona fide error a defense, must keep do-not-call list. Noncomplying contracts are voidable; debt resulting from these contracts may not be reported to credit bureau.

Private Right of Action: Violation is a UDAP violation.

Special Penalties: *See* Haw. Rev. Stat. § 708-835.6. It is a Class B Felony to misrepresent, with intent to defraud, that person contacted will or is about to receive anything of value, or may be able to recover any losses suffered in connection with a prize promotion.

***900-Number Statute*: Haw. Rev. Stat. § 481B-1.6(c)(1).**

Substantive Law: Offer of gift, prize or award must disclose all material terms of the transaction, including handling, shipping, delivery or any other fee, if the consumer is requested to further the transaction by calling a 900 number or "pay per call".

Private Right of Action: Yes. A violation is a UDAP violation.

IDAHO

***Telemarketing Statute*: Idaho Code §§ 48-1001 through 48-1108 (Michie).**

Scope: Defines telemarketing broadly, but lists 10 exemptions, including isolated transactions, sales to previous customers, sales involving face-to-face contact, the sale of newspapers, magazines or periodicals, sales by licensed businesses or businesses that conduct 90% of their sales on location, and catalog sales.

Registration Requirements: Solicitors must register with the attorney general and pay a fee.

Substantive Law: Consumers can cancel purchases within 3 days and minors can cancel within a reasonable time; solicitors must also orally inform consumers of their right to cancel, disclose their street address and number, hang up immediately if requested, and send a written confirmation which includes the consumer's right to cancel. Solicitors cannot use devices that block consumers' Caller ID capacity. Various misrepresentations also prohibited. Abuse and intimidation explicitly prohibited. May not send unsolicited advertisement to fax machine. May not call persons on do-not-call list (home, mobile or pager numbers only). Nationwide do-not-call list may serve as Idaho's. Local exchange telephone companies must inform consumers of the provisions of this statute, either by annual bill stuffer or by information in phone directory. Written or tape-recorded verification required before telemarketer may charge a consumer's previously obtained account number.

Private Right of Action: Yes. A violation is a UDAP violation. Action must be brought within 2 years after party knows violation occurred. Noncomplying contracts are also null, void, and unenforceable.

Special Penalties: For calling persons on do-not-call list, penalties ranging from up to $500 for a first offense to up to $5000 for repeat violations.

***900-Number Statute*: Idaho Code §§ 48-1101 through 48-1108 (Michie).**

Substantive Law: Advertisements must clearly disclose the price of the service; a preamble message must disclose the nature of the service, the price, the identity of the provider, and the option to avoid charges by terminating the call; in 900-number services directed toward children, the preamble must also state that callers under 18 should hang up unless they have parental permission. Pre-subscription allowed, but agreement must be in writing and disclose all terms. Pre-subscription or comparable agreement required for adult entertainment calls.

Exceptions: Statute does not apply if total charge for the call is less than $2.00.

Private Right of Action: Violations of this statute are UDAP violations; must bring action within 2 years. If provider does not comply with the statute, the consumer's debt for the call is void. The statute also authorizes the attorney general to invoke UDAP enforcement powers.

ILLINOIS

***Telemarketing Statute*: 815 Ill. Comp. Stat. §§ 413/1 through 413/27; 815 Ill. Comp. Stat. §§ 402/1 through 402/99 (Restricted Call Registry, i.e., do-not-call list); 815 Ill. Comp. Stat. § 505/2P.1.**

Scope: Defines telemarketing broadly, with exceptions for calls made by autodialers, registered securities dealers, registered investment advisers, registered sellers of securities, or licensed insurance agents. Also exceptions for banks and credit unions.

Registration Requirements: None.

Substantive Law: Prohibits calls to emergency telephone numbers, and prohibits callers from continuing with a solicitation without the consumer's consent. Solicitors must identify themselves and their companies, and are prohibited from calling consumers who place themselves on a "no-call" list (45 or more days after obtaining copy of list containing consumer's name). National do-not-call registry will serve as Illinois do-not-call list. May not call between 9 p.m. and 8 a.m. May not block Caller ID. Express written consent required before presenting check, draft, etc. on consumer's account. Requires seller to send invoice with cancellation option at end of any free trial period.

Private Right of Action: Yes, for treble damages, costs and attorney fees. A violation is a UDAP violation.

Special Penalties: For calls to persons on no-call list, civil fines of up to $1000 first offense to $2500 subsequent offense.

***900-Number Statute*: 815 Ill. Comp. Stat. §§ 520/1 through 520/15.**

Substantive Law: Advertisements must describe cost, message content, terms and conditions of the service, and require that children under 12 get parental permission; a 12-second preamble message must disclose the nature of the service, the price, and the option to avoid charges by terminating the call; specific requirements apply to "games of chance," including a restriction that the prize amount cannot depend on the number of entries received and that there must be a no-purchase alternative method of entering. Carriers must give consumers the provider's name, address, and telephone number upon request.

Exceptions: The preamble is not required if the call costs less than $1.00 per minute or $5.00 total or the call relates to polling services, asynchronous technology or political fundraising.

Private Right of Action: Yes. Three times amount of actual damages recoverable, plus attorney fees. The statute also provides that a violation is a UDAP violation, and the attorney general can invoke UDAP enforcement powers.

INDIANA

***Telemarketing Statute*: Ind. Code §§ 24-5-12-1 through 24-5-12-25.**

Scope: Solicitors who sell precious metals, precious stones, minerals, mineral rights or, in some circumstances, office equipment or supplies; who make false representations about prizes or identity of solicitor, manufacturer, or supplier; or who offer vacations at a reduced price that are contingent on attending certain time-share or membership campground sales presentations.

Registration Requirements: Solicitors must register and pay a fee to the attorney general.

Substantive Law: Contracts are voidable if the solicitor fails to properly register, if the solicitor uses misleading or deceptive statements or if the solicitor fails to deliver an ordered item within 4 weeks. Requires disclosures about gift or prize promotions. Prohibits solicitors from knowingly or intentionally blocking or attempting to block the display of their telephone number or identity by a Caller ID service.

Private Right of Action: Yes, for actual damages, court costs and attorney fees. Contract is also voidable in case of deception or failure to deliver within four weeks.

Special Penalties: Failure to register is a Class D felony; attorney general may seek UDAP penalties. Caller ID blocking violation is a misdemeanor.

***Telemarketing Statute*: Ind. Code §§ 24-4.7-1-1 through 24-4.7-5-6.**

Scope: Defines "telephone sales call" and "telephone solicitor" broadly, but excludes calls regarding existing debts or contracts, sales of insurance or newspapers, calls by licensed real estate brokers and salespersons, certain calls on behalf of charitable organizations, and calls in response to a request.

Registration Requirements: None specified.

Substantive Law: Telemarketers must disclose their true names and the name of the business on whose behalf they are calling at the outset of the call. Contract that results from sales call (except certain sales in which consumer is allowed to return goods without payment, or for full refund) must be reduced to writing and signed, must include name, address and phone number of seller, price and description of goods, and notice that consumer is not obligated to pay unless he or she signs contract and returns it to seller. Contract may not exclude from its terms any written or oral representation made by telephone solicitor in connection with the transaction. Merchant may not charge consumer's credit card or cause any electronic transfer until signed contract is received. (Exemption for certain catalog sales.) May not call number on do-not-call list maintained by consumer protection division of attorney general's office. Telephone solicitor or other who collects consumer information (except for telephone directory) must omit telephone numbers of listed consumers. Regulations are found at Ind. Admin. Code tit. 11, r. 1-1-1 through 2-82.

Private Right of Action: Contracts that violate this statute are voidable.

Special Penalties: Civil penalties of up to $10,000 for first violation; $25,000 for second and subsequent violations; repayment of all funds obtained by the violation; costs of the investigation and the action and state's reasonable attorney fees. Court may void contracts made in violation of this chapter, and order restitution to consumers.

IOWA

***Telemarketing Statute*: Iowa Code § 714.8(15).**

Scope: Applies to persons who obtain or attempt to obtain another's property by deception through telephone communications involving direct or implied claims that the other person has won, or is about to win, a prize or may be able to recover losses suffered in connection with a prize promotion.

Registration Requirements: None.

Substantive Law: Criminalizes deceptive telemarketing prize pro-

motions and recovery room operations.
Private Right of Action: None specified, but Iowa recognizes a private cause of action for violation of a criminal statute.
Special Penalties: Criminal penalties.

***900-Number Statute*: Iowa Code §§ 714A.1 through 714A.5.**
Substantive Law: A preamble message must disclose the price and the option to avoid charges by terminating the call; advertisements must clearly state the price of the call. May not bill for pay-per-call services with actual knowledge that this section was not complied with; must cease billing efforts within 30 days of learning of non-compliance. May not bill or collect for any pay per service if call was not completed. Billing and collection contracts must reference this section's preamble requirements.
Exceptions: The preamble message is not required if the total charge for the call is less than $1.00.
Private Right of Action: Violations are UDAP violations; however, there is no explicit private right of action under Iowa's UDAP statute.

KANSAS
***Telemarketing Statute*: Kan. Stat. Ann. §§ 50-670 through 50-679a.**
Scope: Defines telemarketing broadly, but excludes nonprofit organizations, newspaper publishers, calls made pursuant to prior negotiations or an existing business relationship unless the consumer has objected to these calls and asked that they cease, some sales in response to advertisements or catalogs, and sales in which the consumer may obtain a full refund.
Registration Requirements: None.
Substantive Law: Solicitors must follow up all sales transactions with a written confirmation, containing specific information, including the name and address of the solicitor; solicitors cannot charge the consumer until they receive an original copy of the confirmation signed by the consumer. Other prohibitions, which apply more broadly, require callers to identify themselves and the purpose of the call, and terminate the call immediately if the consumer expresses disinterest. May not send unsolicited fax after consumer requests orally or in writing that such transmissions cease; may not use courier to pick up payment before goods delivered, with opportunity to inspect; may not block Caller ID (grace period until 2005 for technical obstacles). Prohibits solicitors from blocking display of telephone number by a Caller ID service when the solicitor's service or equipment is capable of allowing the display of such number. Telephone solicitors may not call consumers on do-not-call list. Attorney general may designate nationwide do-not-call list as Kansas list.
Private Right of Action: Yes. A violation is a UDAP violation. Bona fide error defense available for violations of no-call list violations.
Special Penalties: Elderly or disabled consumers may recover punitive damages.

KENTUCKY
***Telemarketing Statute*: Ky. Rev. Stat. Ann. §§ 367.461 through 367.46999 (Michie).**
Scope: Defines telemarketing broadly, but lists several exceptions, including calls made by licensed real estate brokers, insurance agents, nonprofit organizations, and persons soliciting the sale of a subscription to a newspaper, magazine or cable TV service.
Registration Requirements: Solicitors must obtain a permit from the attorney general. Merchant must post bond. Additional bond required for promotions which offer premium.
Substantive Law: Solicitors must immediately identify themselves, the goods being sold, and terminate the call if the consumer is disinterested; solicitors cannot request or accept payment until they receive a signed copy of a written contract from the consumer, unless consumer is given a notice of a 14-day right to cancel; also, several prohibitions apply to solicitors using automated messages. Harassment specifically forbidden, including causing phone to ring for more than 30 seconds, calling between 9 p.m. and 10 a.m., or calling consumers on do-not-call list. May not seek payment in advance for credit repair, finding a loan, or recovering funds lost to previous telemarketer. Detailed disclosure requirements for gifts and prizes, and business opportunities. May not: charge consumer's bank account without express written authorization, or charge credit card or make electronic funds transfer except in conformity with Ky. Rev. Stat. § 367.46963; use courier to obtain payment before goods delivered with opportunity for inspection; solicit person under 18 (must ask age, but may accept answer); block Caller ID; contact credit card issuer seeking consumer's credit card number, (and issuer may not provide number to telemarketer); call person listed on zero-call list maintained by attorney general. Automatic dialing device message must be preceded with live message, or message which allows consumer to respond with use of keypad, to determine if consumer wishes to hear message; must disconnect within ten seconds if consumer declines; may not call unlisted numbers, or hospital, nursing home or emergency numbers; may not use device between 9 p.m. and 8 a.m. (exceptions for certain calls to which consumer has consented, calls regarding previously ordered goods or pre-existing debt, calls regarding school attendance). May not use automatic dialing device to solicit persons to call a pay-per-call number. Phone company must discontinue pay-per-call line if it learns that automatic device is being used to solicit calls (§ 367.465).
Private Right of Action: Yes. Violation is UDAP violation (Ky. Rev. Stat. § 367.170). Actual damages recoverable, plus court costs and attorney fees. Bona fide error defense for no-call-list violations.
Special Penalties: Criminal penalties.

LOUISIANA
***Telemarketing Statute*: La. Rev. Stat. Ann. §§ 45:821 through 45:833 (West).**
Scope: Defines specific types of telemarketing that are covered and lists 20 exceptions, such as sales to previous customers, sales involving face-to-face contact, sales made by supervised financial institutions, and the sale of newspapers and securities.
Registration Requirements: Solicitors must register and maintain a bond.
Substantive Law: Solicitors must provide consumers with their street location and other information depending on the nature of the solicitation; consumers can cancel within 3 days of the sale; and contracts must be written, signed by the consumer, and contain specific information including the consumers right to cancel.
Private Right of Action: Violation is a UDAP violation.
Special Penalties: Up to $10,000 fine and 1 year in jail for specified violations.

***Telemarketing Statute*: La. Rev. Stat. §§ 45:844.11 through 45:844.15 (West) (Telephone Solicitation Relief Act).**
Scope: Unsolicited voice or data communications to residential

telephone subscribers. Exceptions for existing debt or contract, existing or recent prior (within 6 months) business relationship, polling, certain charitable solicitations, political activity, periodic healthcare reminders from physician, dentist, optometrist, chiropractor or veterinarian.
Registration Requirements: Telemarketers register with Public Service Commission and pay fee for use of do-not-call database.
Substantive Law: May not call person listed on do-not-call database. Compiler or seller of lists of names for telephone solicitation (except telephone directories) must delete names of those listed on do-not-call database.
Private Right of Action: None specified.
Special Penalties: Administrative penalty of up to $1500 per violation, $3000 if called party is age 65 or over.

***900-Number Statute*: La. Rev. Stat. Ann. §§ 51:1730 through 51:1735 (West).**
Substantive Law: Advertisements must accurately describe the service provided and the price, and identify the provider; services providing games of chance, sweepstakes, prizes, job lines, and loans must register with the attorney general; the statute prohibits false or misleading advertising, repetition of information to prolong calls, provision of unintelligible or out-of-date information, failure to disconnect the call immediately when the consumer hangs up, and advertising sexually explicit 900-numbers on television between 6:00 PM and midnight; providers cannot collect 900-number charges if consumer no longer wishes to make a political or charitable contribution pledged through the call.
Private Right of Action: Violation is a UDAP violation. The consumer's debt for a call is unenforceable and cannot be reported to any credit reporting agency if the price was not prominently disclosed in the advertisement.
Special Penalties: Civil penalty of $5000 for first violation, and $10,000 for second.

MAINE

***Telemarketing Statute*: Me. Rev. Stat. Ann. tit. 10, §§ 1498, 1499, 1499-A (West).**
Scope: Section 1498 governs automated telephone solicitation in which a recorded message is played. Section 1499 governs all other telephone solicitation, broadly defined.
Registration Requirements: Solicitors using automated messages must register with the secretary of state (§ 1498).
Substantive Law: Solicitors using automated calling devices must identify themselves within the first minute of the call, and are prohibited from calling outside the hours of 9 a.m. to 5 p.m., may not call emergency numbers, cell phones, pagers, unlisted or unpublished numbers, or make more than one call to the same number during any one eight-hour period. Must assure that call disconnects within 5 seconds after consumer hangs up (§ 1498). Solicitors not using automated messages are prohibited from calling individuals who have notified them of their desire not to be called (§ 1499), and Caller ID blocking prohibited. *See also* Me. Rev. Stat. Ann. tit. 32, § 14716 (violation of FTC's Telemarketing Rule by a transient seller of consumer goods also violates this subchapter (regulating sales by personal or telephone contact by seller who does not have a permanent place of business in Maine). Transient seller must follow Direct Marketing Association's do-not-call list. Transient seller may not use courier to pick up payment before goods delivered, with opportunity to inspect.).
Private Right of Action: Under § 1498, a violation is a UDAP violation. Under § 1499, after two violations, individuals can bring a private right of action for injunction and the greater of actual damages or $500, which can be trebled if violation was willful or knowing. Statute authorizes attorney general to seek similar remedies.
Special Penalties: Violation of § 1498 (prerecorded messages) is a UDAP violation.

***900-Number Statute*: Me. Rev. Stat. Ann. tit. 35-A, §§ 801 through 808.**
Substantive Law: Prohibits disconnection of basic telephone service for failure to pay 900-number charges; consumers must be allowed to block access to 900-numbers if feasible; telephone bills must itemize 900-number charges and disclose customer's rights; if consumer objects to 900-number charges, carrier must delete the charges or attempt in good faith to resolve the dispute; unintelligible messages and steps that create delays in the message are prohibited.
Private Right of Action: A violation is a UDAP violation.

MARYLAND

***Telemarketing Statute*: Md. Code Ann., Com. Law §§ 14-2201 through 14-2205 and Md. Code Ann., Pub. Util. Law §§ 8-204 and 8-205.**
Scope: Telemarketing statute covers sales made entirely by telephone and initiated by the solicitor; excludes catalog sales, sales where there is a pre-existing business relationship between the consumer and the solicitor, bona fide charities, and instances where the consumer can obtain a full refund. Public utility statute covers use of automatic dialing device, and telephone solicitation, broadly defined to include pollsters.
Registration Requirements: None.
Substantive Law: Contracts must be reduced to writing, signed by the consumer, and contain the name and address of the solicitor. Merchant may not submit charge to consumer's account before receiving signed contract that complies with this section. Public utility law forbids use of automated dialing to solicit the purchase, lease or rental of goods or services; offer a gift or prize; conduct a poll; or request information that will be used to solicit the purchase, lease, or rental of goods or services. Exception for pre-existing business relationship. Caller must disconnect within 5 seconds after termination of the call by either party. Telephone solicitor may not block Caller ID.
Private Right of Action: Violation of telemarketing statute is UDAP violation. Non-complying contracts are also unenforceable.
Special Penalties: Caller ID blocking by telephone solicitors or misuse of automatic dialing device is a misdemeanor.

MASSACHUSETTS

***Telemarketing Statute*: Mass. Gen. Laws ch. 159, § 19E.**
Scope: Statute covers all sales of goods or services made by telephone to the consumer's residence.
Registration Requirements: None.
Substantive Law: Solicitors must immediately disclose their identity, the trade name of the person they represent, and the kinds of goods or services being offered for sale. Solicitors are prohibited from using a plan or scheme which misrepresents their true purpose.
Private Right of Action: None specified.
Special Penalties: None specified.

***Telemarketing Statute*: Mass. Gen. Laws ch. 159C, §§ 1 through 14 (Telemarketing Solicitation).**
Scope: Unsolicited sales calls from a location in Massachusetts, or to a consumer in Massachusetts, for consumer goods and services, including stocks, bonds and mutual funds. Exceptions for calls requested by consumer; calls regarding existing contract or debt (performance not complete at time of call); calls to an existing customer, unless customer has requested no further calls; calls that lead to face-to-face meeting before sale is consummated; calls by non-profits; polls and surveys for non-commercial purposes.
Registration Requirements: None specified.
Substantive Law: Must disclose at beginning of call the sales purpose of the call, the name of the telemarketer and the prospective seller, and an accurate description of the goods. Before requesting payment, must disclose the cost of goods, including taxes, shipping and handling, any restrictions or limitations on an offer, the seller's return, refund and cancellation policy, and all "material aspects" of an investment opportunity. May not call between 8 p.m. and 8 a.m., send unsolicited faxes, use a recorded message device, block Caller ID, or call consumer listed on do-not-call list, maintained by Office of Consumer Affairs and Business Regulation and coordinated with nationwide list. Compilers and sellers of mailing lists for telephone sales must remove names of consumers on do-not-call list.
Private Right of Action: Consumer who receives more than one sales call in 12 months from same telemarketer in violation of this chapter has private right of action for the greater of actual monetary damages or $5000, and for injunctive relief. Bona fide error defense available. Prevailing party entitled to costs and reasonable attorney fees. Remedy is not exclusive, but is in addition to other remedies including chapter 93A.
Special Penalties: Attorney general may seek civil penalties of up to $5000 per violation ($1500 minimum for knowing violation involving consumer age 65 or over).

MICHIGAN

***Telemarketing Statute*: Mich. Comp. Laws §§ 445.111 through 445.111e. *See also* Mich. Comp. Laws §§ 445.113 and 445.116.**
Scope: Telemarketing is covered by the state's home solicitation sales law. "Home solicitation sale" does not include: (1) sales for less than $25.00; (2) sales pursuant to a preexisting revolving charge account agreement; (3) sales made at or pursuant to prior negotiations at a business establishment; (4) sales made pursuant to a general circulation printed advertisement; (5) sales by licensed insurance agents or licensed real estate professionals; (6) sales of agricultural equipment; (7) loans or extensions of credit that are regulated under other specified statutes; or (8) certain charitable or public safety solicitations covered by other statutes. Telephone solicitor code of conduct and do-not-call provisions apply to a "telephone solicitation," even when made by licensed insurance or real estate professional. Prescribed notice of cancellation language does not apply to telephone solicitation by telecommunications provider, if these comply with Telecommunications Act, Mich. Comp. Laws §§ 484.2505 to 484.2507.
Registration Requirements: None.
Substantive Law: Sales may not be made by telephone solicitations that use recorded messages. All agreements must be reduced to writing, be signed by the consumer and include a prescribed notice of cancellation; the consumer can cancel the transaction within 3 days of signing the agreement; and the solicitor must return payment to the consumer within 10 days of cancellation. At beginning of call, solicitor must identify self and company. On request, must provide a company phone number that will be answered by a natural person. May not block Caller ID. May not call person on the do-not-call list maintained by the Public Service Commission. Federal do-not-call list serves as state list. Before receipt of payment, seller must disclose total price of goods; any conditions or limitations on offers; seller's refund and cancellation policy; costs or conditions of winning a prize, including the odds; that no purchase is required to enter contest, and the no-purchase method of entry; any "material aspect" of a business opportunity; consumer's cancellation rights. May not accept payment, or charge consumer's bank account or credit card without "verifiable authorization" as defined. May not offer prize promotion for which purchase is necessary. May not use courier to pick up payment during period when consumer is entitled to cancel.
Private Right of Action: Violation is a UDAP violation. Person damaged by violation may sue for larger of actual damages or $250, and reasonable attorney fees.
Special Penalties: Knowing violation of certain provisions is a misdemeanor.

MINNESOTA

***Telemarketing Statute*: Minn. Stat. §§ 325E.26 through 325E.31, and 325E.395 (Automatic Dialing-Announcing Devices).**
Scope: Automatic dialing and announcing devices. Exemptions for prior business relationship, messages from school districts and messages advising employees of work schedules.
Registration Requirements: None.
Substantive Law: Automatic dialing and announcing devices may not be used without consent or between 9 p.m. and 9 a.m.; there must be a live operator, who discloses the name of the company, the sales purpose of the call, the identity of the goods or services offered and, if applicable, that the message solicits payment or commitment of funds; calling system must disconnect within ten seconds when the customer hangs up. Unsolicited advertising faxes include a toll-free number and a mailing address which the recipient may use to request that no more faxes be sent.
Private Right of Action: A violation is actionable under Minn. Stat. § 8.31.
Special Penalties: None specified.

***Telemarketing Statute*: Minn. Stat. §§ 325E.311 through 325E.316 (Telephone Solicitation).**
Scope: Voice communication over a telephone line to a residential subscriber, for purpose of encouraging the purchase, sale or rental of or investment in, property, goods or services. Exceptions for calls initiated by buyer, prior business or personal relationship, non-profits, and calls which result in face-to-face negotiations before sale is completed.
Registration Requirements: None.
Substantive Law: Must identify self at beginning of call; may not block Caller ID; may not call consumer listed on do-not-call list, established by Commissioner of Commerce and coordinated with federal list.
Private Right of Action: None specified, but this statute is in addition to other law.
Special Penalties: Civil penalties of up to $1000 per violation. Bona fide error defense available.

***Telemarketing Statute*: Minn. Stat. §§ 325G.12 through 325G.14 (Personal Solicitation of Sales).**
Scope: Sellers who regularly engage in transactions of the kind at issue and who use personal or telephone contact at place other than seller's place of business to sell personal, family, or household goods or services. Buyer-initiated calls, calls to buyers where the parties already know each other, and sales of newspapers by minors who also deliver papers are excluded.
Registration Requirements: None.
Substantive Law: Requires initial disclosure of seller's name, business name, type of goods or services being sold, and purpose of contact.
Private Right of Action: A violation is actionable under Minn. Stat. § 8.31.
Special Penalties: None.

MISSISSIPPI
***Telemarketing Statute*: Miss. Code Ann. §§ 77-3-601 through 77-3-619.**
Scope: Defines telemarketing broadly, but excludes isolated transactions, supervised financial institutions, non-commercial calls, sales that involve face-to-face contact, sales of securities, food, newspapers, magazines, memberships in book or record clubs, non-profits, certain catalog sales, sales resulting from prior negotiations, and several other enumerated exceptions. Statute covers some sales resulting from call by buyer in response to flyer, notice, or postcard delivered to home.
Registration Requirements: Telephone solicitors must register with the attorney general and post a surety bond or other acceptable security.
Substantive Law: Solicitors may call only between the hours of 8:00 a.m. and 9:00 p.m. (no Sunday calls), must identify themselves, terminate the call if the consumer expresses disinterest, and provide the consumer with a written contract pursuant to the telephone call. Merchant may not submit charge to consumer's account until it receives signed contract.
Private Right of Action: None specified, but the language of the statute suggests there is a private right of action. Noncomplying contracts are unenforceable. Statute also gives attorney general specific enforcement powers.
Special Penalties: Civil penalty of up to $10,000 for each violation.

***Telemarketing Statute:* Miss. Code Ann. §§ 77-3-701 through 77-3-737 (Mississippi Telephone Solicitation Act).** *Note: this statute sunsets on July 1, 2005.*
Scope: Telephone solicitation broadly defined, with exemptions for pre-existing business relationship; religious, charitable or bona fide non-profit; sales calls leading to face-to-face presentation, calls which do not make the "major sales presentation," sales of newspapers, various businesses regulated under law including real estate, insurance, motor vehicles, financial institutions.
Registration Requirement: Telephone solicitors must register with Public Service Commission, and pay fee for access to do-not-call database.
Substantive Law: May not call consumers listed on no-call database established by Public Service Commission and coordinated with federal do-not-call list. Telephone solicitors must begin calls by identifying self and company, and disclosing purpose of call. May call only between 8 a.m. and 8 p.m. May not block Caller ID. May not used automated dialing system to deliver prerecorded message except in context of established business relationship.
Private Right of Action: None specified.
Special Penalties: Administrative penalty of up to $5000 per violation. Bona fide error defense available.

***Telemarketing Statute*: Miss. Code Ann. §§ 77-3-451 through 77-3-459 (Automatic Dialing and Announcing Devices).**
Scope: Any automatic dialing and announcing device connected to telephone line.
Substantive Law: Forbids use of autodialer with prerecorded message for sales purposes, except with prior permission of person called or pursuant to established business relationship. Must be operated by person who states identity of caller and purpose of message, and disconnects if recipient declines. Forbids prerecorded message that will be received between 9 p.m. and 9 a.m. local time.
Special Penalties: Fine of up to $500 per violation, and disconnection for period specified by Public Service Commission.

MISSOURI
***Telemarketing Statute*: Mo. Rev. Stat. §§ 407.1070 through 407.1090 (Telemarketing Practices); Mo. Rev. Stat. §§ 407.1095 through 407.1110 (Telemarketing No-Call List).**
Scope: Telemarketing defined as plan, program or campaign, conducted to induce purchase or lease of merchandise, by use of one or more telephones, which involves more than one telephone call. Statute also covers investment opportunities. Exemptions for calls that will be followed by face-to-face negotiation before completion of sale; certain consumer-initiated calls; calls where consumer may return merchandise within 14 days for full refund; certain catalog sales, calls to consumer with established business relationship, certain calls by sellers who are regulated by other state or federal agency, business-to-business calls—but no exemption for sale of nondurable office supplies or cleaning supplies. Provider of telephone services not liable for violations of act by another.
Registration Requirements: None specified.
Substantive Law: Telemarketer must promptly disclose sales purpose of call, identity of telemarketer and seller, nature of merchandise or investment opportunity being sold, and, if a prize is being offered, that no purchase or payment is necessary to win. If call is by recorded or electronically generated voice, must disclose this at beginning. Before requesting payment, caller must disclose address or phone number where seller may be contacted, the cost and quantity of the merchandise, any material limitations or restrictions, material information about cancellation and other policies, material information about an investment opportunity, or a prize promotion (including the odds). Misrepresentations forbidden. Intimidation, harassment, night calls (9 p.m. to 8 a.m.) forbidden. May not request advance payment for credit repair, or for recovery of property lost to prior telemarketing scam. Verifiable authorization and confirmation required before payment by check, draft, or other means of access to consumer's account. May not use courier to obtain payment before goods or investment opportunity delivered, with opportunity to inspect. May not block consumer's Caller ID. Detailed record keeping requirements: advertising materials, verifiable authorizations, statistics on prizes, information about current and former employees, names and addresses of customers, and dates when goods shipped. Calls to persons on do-not-call list forbidden.
Private Right of Action: Violation is UDAP violation. Consumer also has right of action for actual and punitive damages, reasonable attorney fees, court costs and "any other remedy permitted by law." Consumer who receives two or more calls within a year from

same seller in violation of no-call statute may bring action for injunction and the greater of actual monetary loss or $5000 per violation.
Special Penalties: Violations are Class A misdemeanors or Class D felonies. Attorney general may seek injunction or civil penalties (up to $5000 per violation) for calls to persons on no-call list.

MONTANA

Montana has two applicable statutes. The provisions of one statute do not apply to a claim brought under the other.

***Telemarketing Statute*: Mont. Code Ann. §§ 30-14-1401 through 30-14-1606.**
Scope: Defines telemarketing broadly, but exempts calls initiated by a consumer without prior solicitation by telemarketer and calls in which a sale is not completed until after a face-to-face sales presentation. Also lists 18 exemptions from registration and bonding requirements, including: nonprofit organizations; business-to-business sales; licensed realtors, insurers, and securities dealers; solicitations for magazines, newspapers, satellite or cable television systems; businesses that publish certain types of catalogs; retail businesses that make most of their sales at their retail sites; food transactions of less than $100 per address; book, video or record clubs.
Registration Requirements: Telephone solicitors must register with the Department of Administration and maintain a bond.
Substantive Law: Telemarketers must promptly disclose their identity, purpose of call, nature of goods or services and inform consumer that purchases are not required to win a prize. A telemarketer may not block the called party's Caller ID. Prior to requesting any payment, telemarketers must disclose the total cost and any material restrictions, limitations or conditions pertaining to the purchase. Unless exception applies, sales are not final until purchaser receives notice of cancellation provisions. Repeated calls and other abusive practices are prohibited. Special restrictions on credit repair services, recovery of funds or property lost in prior telemarketing scams, use of telechecks, and use of couriers to pick up payments. Records must be kept for two years. Unsolicited advertising faxes prohibited. May not call consumer on do-not-call list, established by Department of Administration and coordinated with national list. (Exceptions for existing business relationship, non-profits, certain regulated entities, and licensed tradespeople or professionals setting up appointments.)
Private Right of Action: Yes, for actual damages or $500, whichever is greater, plus attorney fees. A violation is also a UDAP violation. Sales by unlicensed telemarketers are void. For violations of no-call list statute, consumer who receives more than one forbidden call within 12 months has right of action for greater of actual damages or $5000 for each knowing violation. Bona fide error defense available.
Special Penalties: Criminal penalties.

***Telemarketing Statute*: Mont. Code Ann. §§ 30-14-501 through 30-14-508 (Personal Solicitation Sales).**
Scope: Telemarketing is covered. The statute excludes sales where the consumer personally knows the seller, sales where the consumer initiates contact with the seller, the sale of insurance and newspaper subscriptions, and sales involving less than $25.
Registration Requirements: None.
Substantive Law: Solicitors must identify themselves, their company, and the goods being sold at the time of initial contact; consumers may cancel transactions within 3 days of signing a contract; solicitors must provide consumers with a notice of their right to cancel; and solicitors must return payment to the consumer within 10 days of cancellation.
Private Right of Action: Yes. A violation is a UDAP violation. If seller fails to comply with requirement to return downpayment, seller is liable for entire downpayment and if buyer prevails in court action for recovery, $500 plus costs and reasonable attorney fees.
Special Penalties: Civil fine of up to $1000 for failure to make required initial disclosures.

NEBRASKA

***Telemarketing Statute*: Neb. Rev. Stat. §§ 86-212 through 86-235 (Telemarketing and Prize Promotions).**
Scope: Covers seller-initiated calls soliciting the sale, lease or rental of consumer goods or services, or extension of consumer credit, or seeking information to be used to directly solicit consumer sales or extensions of credit, or offering gifts or prizes with intent to solicit consumer sale. Also covers prize promotions in which consumer is notified by mail to call seller. Excludes calls in response to express request of called party, calls regarding existing contract or debt, clearly established business relationship, sales of periodicals by publisher. Telecommunications company offering services subject to the verification provisions of the Telephone Consumer Slamming Prevention Act.
Registration Requirements: None specified.
Substantive Law: Seller may not debit consumer's bank account without verifiable (written or tape recorded) authorization from consumer. Written confirmation must be sent to consumer, including terms of sale and procedure for obtaining a refund if confirmation is inaccurate. Five-day cooling-off period, measured from receipt of written notice. Cancellation rights must be disclosed orally during phone call, and in writing with any advertising or with delivery of the product. Must refund within 30 days after cancellation. Use of courier to pick up payment forbidden, unless goods delivered at same time. Advance payment for recovery service prohibited (except for services of attorney). Detailed disclosure requirements for prize promotion, including odds, value of prizes, and no-purchase option for entry. Seller in prize promotion may not misrepresent value of prize, or falsely state that consumer has already won, or request any payment from consumer prior to delivery of written disclosures. Record-keeping requirements same as 16 C.F.R. § 310.5.
Private Right of Action: For actual damages, costs and attorney fees.
Special Penalties: Violation is a Class 1 misdemeanor. Certain violations in prize promotion punishable by civil penalty of up to $2000.

***Telemarketing Statute*: Neb. Rev. Stat. §§ 86-236 through 86-257.**
Scope: Statute covers solicitations using an automatic dialing-announcing device in which a recorded message is played; excludes calls made with consumer's prior invitation or permission; calls where there is an established business relationship between the consumer and the solicitor; tax-exempt nonprofit organizations; calls not made for commercial purposes, or made for commercial purposes but which do not include the transmission of an unsolicited advertisement.
Registration Requirements: Solicitors using automatic dialing-an-

nouncing devices must obtain permit from the Public Service Commission and pay $500 fee for each device.
Substantive Law: Requires disclosure of caller's identity at beginning of message; caller's telephone number (other than that of the device which made the call) or address must be disclosed during or after message. Calls may be made only between the hours of 8 a.m. and 9 p.m. Solicitors may not call consumers who place themselves on a "no-call" list. May not call any emergency number, pager, cellphone, guest or patient room at hospital or nursing home. May not engage two or more lines of business with multilane system. Must disconnect within five seconds after called party hangs up. Unsolicited advertising faxes prohibited.
Private Right of Action: None specified.
Special Penalties: Public Service Commission may administratively fine violator up to $1000 per violation after notice and hearing. Violations are Class II misdemeanors.

***900-Number Statute*: Neb. Rev. Stat. §§ 86-258 through 86-270.**
Scope: Statute explicitly states that it applies only to intrastate calls.
Substantive Law: Preambles must be consistent with the FTC requirements for preambles; carriers must provide consumers with the 900-number provider's name, address, and customer service number upon request, at no charge; carriers must offer customers a 900-number blocking option if feasible; tones to complete a 900-number call may not be broadcast; carriers may not disconnect basic phone service for failure to pay 900-number charges.
Private Right of Action: None Specified.
Special Penalties: Violations are Class II misdemeanors and can entail a fine of up to $1000.

NEVADA
***Telemarketing Statute*: Nev. Rev. Stat. §§ 597.814, 598.0918 and Nev. Rev. Stat. §§ 228.500 through 228.640.**
Scope: Section 597.814 applies to "any person"; § 598.0918 applies to any person during a solicitation by telephone or sales presentation. Other provisions apply to "telephone solicitors," broadly defined, with exceptions for delinquent debt, established business relationship, calls on behalf of tax-exempt charitable organizations, religious organizations, and political organizations.
Registration Requirements: None.
Substantive Law: Section 597.814 requires autodialed pre-recorded messages to include initial disclosures and prohibits calls between 8:00 p.m. and 9:00 a.m. and call-backs to people who terminate the first call. Section 598.0918 prohibits threatening, intimidating, profane, obscene language; harassment by repeat calls; calls between 8:00 p.m. and 9:00 a.m.; Caller ID blocking. Remaining provisions establish do-not-call rule and allow attorney general to use FTC's national do-not-call registry or establish state registry; requires telephone solicitors to maintain company-specific do-not-call lists.
Private Right of Action: Violation of do-not-call rule is UDAP violation.
Special Penalties: None.

***Telemarketing Statute*: Nev. Rev. Stat. §§ 599B.005 through 599B.300.**
Scope: Defines specific types of telemarketing that are covered, including prize promotions, the sale of information relating to sporting events, and recovery services (solicitors that promise, for a fee, to recover goods that the consumer never received from a different solicitor). There are 26 exceptions, such as sales made by licensed broadcasters, insurance brokers, the sale of newspapers and magazines, and some charitable solicitations.
Registration Requirements: Telemarketers must register with the Consumer Affairs Division of the Department of Business and Industry, pay a fee, and deposit a bond.
Substantive Law: Telemarketer must disclose true name, identity of seller, purpose of call, all charges, and all restrictions and conditions; specific restrictions on prize promotions and chance promotions; consumer has 30-day right to refund; delivery of goods or services must be accompanied by a prescribed form; recovery service solicitors cannot receive payment until their services are performed; and solicitors cannot disclose the name or address of any consumer.
Private Right of Action: Injured consumer may bring action against the bond. Elderly or disabled consumer can sue for actual damages, punitive damages, and attorney fees. Statute also gives attorney general specific enforcement powers.
Special Penalties: Criminal penalties. Enhanced penalty for deceptive practices directed towards the elderly or disabled.

NEW HAMPSHIRE
***Telemarketing Statute*: N.H. Rev. Stat. Ann. §§ 359-E:1 through 359-E:11 (Telemarketing).**
Scope: Applies to telemarketing, broadly defined, with exceptions for calls in response to requests, in connection with established business relationship, or on behalf of a non-profit charity, and political calls other than those using autodialers, plus a partial temporary exception for calls by newspapers. Also applies to use of automatic dialing system to place unsolicited recorded message calls to residential subscribers, seeking to give, sell, or lease goods or services, or obtain pledges, contributions, or information.
Exceptions: Pre-existing relationship.
Registration Requirements: Anyone wishing to use automatic dialing device for solicitation must register and pay a $20 per year fee.
Substantive Law: Requires compliance with FCC and FTC do-not-call list and FTC Telemarketing Rule. May not call emergency lines (911 or seven digit police, fire or ambulance numbers designated as emergency numbers). Must immediately disclose identity of caller and purpose of call. Must disconnect within 30 seconds after called party hangs up. May not block Caller ID, and number displayed on Caller ID must be one at which solicitor receives phone calls. Note that N.H. Rev. Stat. Ann. § 361-B:2-a also requires some telephone sellers to disclose a legal name, a street address from which the business is actually conducted, and a telephone number for inquiries and complaints.
Private Right of Action: Violation is a UDAP violation. Any person injured by violation of telemarketing provisions has private cause of action for actual damages or $1000, which may be doubled or trebled if willful or knowing, plus attorney fees; may also seek injunctive relief; good faith error defense.
Special Penalties: None specified.

***900-Number Regulation*: N.H. Code Admin. R. Ann. PUC 1306.01. *See also* N.H. Rev. Stat. Ann. § 358-O:4 (Prizes and Gifts).**
Substantive Law: Basic local telephone service must include a blocking option for 900-number calls. Disclosure of costs, required by prizes and gifts act, must include costs of any 900-number call required to claim the prize, and if a contest may be entered either

by written entry or 900-number call, the written entry method be disclosed as conspicuously as the 900 number.

NEW JERSEY

Telemarketing Statute: **N.J. Stat. Ann. §§ 56:8-119 through 56:8-135 (West).** ***See also*** **N.J. Stat. Ann. § 48:17-25 (West).**
Scope: Telemarketing broadly defined with exceptions for customer-requested call, established business relationship.
Registration Requirements: Telemarketer must register with Consumer Affairs Division of Department of Law and Public Safety, pay a fee, and post bond for $25,000.
Substantive Law: Telemarketer must identify self, company, and purpose of call within first thirty seconds. May not call between 9 p.m. and 8 a.m., block Caller ID, call commercial mobile phones, or call person on do-not-call list established by Consumer Affairs Division. *See also* N.J. Admin. Code tit. 13, §§ 45D-1.1 through 45D-5.2.
Private Right of Action: Violation is a UDAP violation. Bona fide error defense available. Also no liability for isolated (i.e. only one within 12 months) call.
Special Penalties: None specified.

Telemarketing Regulations**: N.J. Admin. Code tit. 13, § 45A-1.1.**
Scope: Merchandise ordered by telephone from a person conducting a "mail order or catalog business."
Exceptions: Merchandise ordered pursuant to an open-end credit plan opened prior to the sale in question; merchandise such as quarterly magazines that cannot be produced until a future date; merchandise such as magazines that are ordered for serial delivery.
Registration Requirements: None specified.
Substantive Law: Seller cannot accept money through the mail or any electronic transfer medium and then allow six weeks to pass without delivering or mailing the merchandise, making a refund, sending the consumer a notice with specified content, or sending merchandise of similar or superior quality with a refund offer. Does not apply if seller discloses specific longer delivery period and complies with other requirements.
Private Right of Action: Violation is UDAP violation.
Special Penalties: None.

900-Number Statute**: N.J. Stat. Ann. §§ 56:8-54 through 56:8-61 (West).**
Substantive Law: Advertising and preamble must disclose total cost of service (or price per minute) and include parental permission warning for minors. Caller must be given opportunity to disconnect after preamble. Preamble requirement does not apply to calls costing $5.00 or less. Use of automatic dialing and announcing devices or broadcast tones forbidden. Telephone carriers must offer blocking. Division of Consumer Affairs may promulgate regulations requiring information providers to register, and setting fees sufficient to pay for registration program.
Private Right of Action: Violation is UDAP violation. Attorney general may sue to enjoin violations.

900-Number Regulation**: N.J. Admin. Code tit. 14, § 3-7.17.**
Substantive Law: Applies to carriers which provide services to information providers. Basic service may not be terminated for nonpayment of charges for non-basic service, which is defined to include audio text and pay-per-call service. Non-basic service may be blocked or denied, after prescribed notice. Provider may offer a credit-limit option for non-basic service. Partial payments will be applied first to basic service.

NEW MEXICO

Telemarketing Statute**: N.M. Stat. Ann. §§ 57-12-22 through 57-12-24 (Michie).**
Scope: Defines telemarketing broadly. Faxes explicitly included. Exceptions for established business relationship; expression of political opinions; licensed real estate brokers.
Registration Requirements: None.
Substantive Law: Solicitors must promptly disclose the purpose of their call, fully disclose all costs associated with their goods, and may call only between the hours of 9:00 a.m. and 9:00 p.m.; they may not ask for credit card numbers unless the consumer has committed to making a purchase and expressed a desire to pay with a credit card, nor can solicitors use a pre-recorded message unless there is an existing business relationship and the consumer consents to hear the message. Prohibits misrepresenting call as courtesy call, survey, etc.; restricts abandoned calls; prohibits calls to residential subscribers who have registered on national do-not-call list; prohibits Caller ID blocking. Unsolicited fax or e-mail advertisements must conspicuously include a toll-free number which recipient may use to forbid further contacts.
Private Right of Action: Yes. Violation is UDAP violation. For fax or e-mail sent to person who has requested removal from mailing list, private right of action for greater of actual damages (including lost profits), $25 per fax or e-mail, or $5000 per day of violation, plus costs and reasonable attorney fees.
Special Penalties: None.

NEW YORK

Telemarketing Statute**: N.Y. Gen. Bus. Law §§ 399-p, 399-pp and 399-z (McKinney); N.Y. Pers. Prop. Law §§ 440 through 448 (McKinney) (Telephone Sales Protection Act).** ***See also*** **N.Y. Pub. Serv. Law § 92-d (McKinney).**
Scope: *Telephone Sales Act*: Seller's solicitation by telephone of sales of merchandise or certain travel services, paid for by credit card authorization. *Telemarketing Act*: "Telemarketing" means any plan, program or campaign which is conducted to induce payment or the exchange of any other consideration for any goods or services by use of one or more telephones and which involves more than one telephone call by a telemarketer in which the customer is located within the state at the time of the call.
Exceptions: *Telephone Sales Act*: Sales under $25, sale or rental of real property, regulated sales of insurance, securities, or commodities, certain catalog sales, prior relationship. *Telemarketing Act*: Debt collection in compliance with FDCPA, calls leading to face-to-face negotiation, buyer initiated calls which do not result from any solicitation by seller, certain calls to for-profit businesses, calls pursuant to prior contractual relationship; businesses licensed under other law; non-profits; certain calls made in effort to develop new business.
Registration Requirements: *Telephone Sales Act*: None. *Telemarketing Act*: Must register with secretary of state (detailed information requirements), pay $500 fee, and post $25,000 bond or other acceptable form of security (letter of credit, CD, etc).
Substantive Law: *Telephone Sales Act*: Written notice required, must be in same language as sales presentation, and disclose right to cancel; 3-day cooling-off period, begins to run when buyer receives written notice of right to cancel; upon cancellation, seller must recredit consumer's credit card for down payment and return any trade-ins; buyer must make goods available at buyer's residence; if seller does not collect them within a reasonable time,

buyer owns goods without obligation. Seller may not assign obligation until five days after notice of right to cancel. *Telemarketing Act*: At beginning of call, must disclose name of company, purpose of call, cost of goods offered; additional disclosure requirements for prize promotions; abuse and harassment prohibited; may call residence only between 8 a.m. and 9 p.m.; may not call consumer who has requested not to be called; may not request advance fee for credit repair or recovery services (except services of licensed attorney), must obtain written authorization for any draw on buyer's bank account; detailed recordkeeping requirements; waivers forbidden; may not block Caller ID; may not call number on do-not-call list; automatic dialing device that disseminates prerecorded message must announce purpose of call and disconnect promptly if call terminated, and may not use a random or sequential number generator, or make calls to certain emergency numbers, hospitals, nursing homes, etc.
Private Right of Action: *Telephone Sales Act*: If seller fails to refund payments upon cancellation, buyer may sue for the amount of payment, plus $100; reasonable costs and attorney fees within the discretion of the court; or consumer may recover against seller's bond. *Telemarketing Act*: Violation is a UDAP violation; private right of action for greater of actual damages or $50 per violation; may increase treble damages, up to $1000, in court's discretion, if violation is knowing or willful; attorney fees at court's discretion.
Special Penalties: *Telephone Sales Act*: Attorney general may seek injunction or civil penalty of up to $500 per violation. *Telemarketing Act*: Civil penalties of $1000 to $2000; denial or termination of registration; certain knowing violations are Class A or Class B misdemeanors; bona fide error defense available for violations of no-call list statute.

***900-Number Statute*: N.Y. Gen. Bus. Law § 336-b (McKinney).**
Substantive Law: Applies to any person or business entity advertising an interactive information network service (including games and contests, with or without prizes), except broadcasters or publishers who publish or print the advertisements. Advertising must conspicuously disclose all costs.
Private Right of Action: Attorney general may sue to enjoin violations. Civil penalties up to $500 per violation.

NORTH CAROLINA

***Telemarketing Statute*: N.C. Gen. Stat. §§ 66-260 through 66-266.**
Scope: Applies to telephone sellers who attempt to convince the consumer to buy goods or services, enter a contest, or contribute to a charity, with over twenty-five explicit exemptions, including non-profits, various businesses licensed under other law, certain catalog sales, certain book, record or video clubs, calls leading to face-to-face presentation.
Registration Requirements: Annual registration and filing of basic information required.
Substantive Law: All promoted gifts and prizes must be awarded, seller must provide evidence of that fact, and must take out a bond in the amount of the value of the promoted gifts and prizes. Seller must determine if the consumer contacted is under 18 years of age and discontinue the call if the consumer is under that age. Seller cannot require consumer to make payment or call 900 number to obtain prize.
Private Right of Action: Violation is a state UDAP violation.
Special Penalties: State can seek up to $25,000 penalty for each violation where consumer is over 65 years of age.

***Telemarketing Statute*: N.C. Gen. Stat. §§ 75-100 through 75-105 (Telephone Solicitations).**
Scope: Telephone solicitation broadly defined, with exceptions for small businesses averaging no more than 10 telephone solicitations per week; telephone solicitation for sole purpose of arranging face-to-face meeting; newspaper subscription sales; non-profits.
Registration Requirements: None.
Substantive Law: Prohibits calls to numbers registered on FTC's do-not-call list; allows state attorney general to create state do-not-call list if FTC's list ceases to operate; requires company-specific do-not-call lists; requires telemarketers to give identifying information at outset of call; requires compliance with most provisions of FTC telemarketing rule; prohibits calls before 8:00 a.m. or after 9:00 p.m.; prohibits calls to telephone subscribers under age 18; prohibits threats, profanity, etc.; prohibits Caller ID blocking; prohibits autodialing to play recorded message with exceptions for non-profit, political organization or candidate, or poll-taker (if caller identifies self and purpose of call, and no solicitation is made).
Private Right of Action: Telephone subscriber may sue for injunction, statutory damages of $500 for first violation, $1000 for second, $5000 for third or additional violation within two years; attorney fees to prevailing plaintiff if defendant acted willfully, to defendant if plaintiff knew or should have known that action was malicious and frivolous. Contract is invalid, and no money is due thereunder, if contract or sales representations were deceptive or abusive as defined by FTC Telemarketing Rule, or violated other state or federal law. Statute also authorizes suit in state courts under Telephone Consumer Protection Act.
Special Penalties: Attorney general may seek civil penalties in same amounts as telephone subscriber, but amount is reduced to $100 if solicitor shows mistake and meets certain other conditions.

***900-Number Regulation*: N.C. Admin. Code tit. 4, r. 11.R17-2.**
Substantive Law: Applies to local exchange carriers which provide services to information providers. Carriers must offer free pay-per-call blocking (and certain other per call or per line blocking if required by commission order) and advise customers of blocking options at least once a year. May not disconnect basic local or interexchange service for nonpayment for nonregulated services (which includes pay per call), and must state on bill that nonpayment for these services (which must be separately listed) will not result in disconnection. Carrier must follow Commission provisions for resolution of disputes over 900-number billing.

NORTH DAKOTA

***Telemarketing Statute*: N.D. Cent. Code §§ 51-18-01 through 51-18-09.**
Scope: Statute governs home solicitation sales and telemarketing. Defines telemarketing broadly, but excludes nonprofit and charitable organizations, the sale of insurance, cable TV and newspapers, sales of less than $25, sales by licensed broadcasters, and sales by telecommunications companies. Some restrictions apply only to "telepromoters," defined more narrowly.
Registration Requirements: None.
Substantive Law: Consumers have the right to cancel transactions within 3 days, or 15 days if they are 65 or older; solicitors must inform consumers of their right to cancel; all agreements must be reduced to writing, conform with specific font-size requirements, contain certain information regarding the goods and the solicitor,

and be signed by the consumer; solicitors must return payment to consumers within 10 days of cancellation.
Private Right of Action: None specified. Noncomplying contracts are unenforceable.
Special Penalties: Violations are Class B misdemeanors.

***Telemarketing Statute*: N.D. Cent. Code §§ 51-28-01 through 51-28-22.**
Scope: Telephone solicitation, broadly defined, for the purpose of encouraging charitable contributions or the purchase or rental of, or investment in, property, goods, services, or merchandise, with exceptions for calls in response to prior express written requests, established personal or business relationships, some solicitations by tax exempt charities, polls unless conducted by autodialers, political calls, and calls in which sales presentation is completed only at a later face-to-face meeting.
Registration Requirements: None.
Substantive Law: No calls before 8:00 a.m. or after 9:00 p.m. Requires compliance with state or national do-not-call list. Attorney general establishes state do-not-call list, but may designate federal list as state list. At beginning of call, telephone solicitors must identify themselves and the business on whose behalf they are calling. Prohibits Caller ID blocking. Prerecorded messages prohibited unless called party consents, with some exceptions; must be preceded by live operator who discloses name of company and purpose of message; must disconnect within 10 seconds after subscriber hangs up; and must exclude emergency numbers, cell phones, pagers, or other calls for which called party must pay, guest or patient rooms at healthcare facilities, numbers on do-not-call list.
Private Right of Action: Any person who receives telephone solicitation or message in violation of this chapter may sue for injunction or damages or both. Court may award actual damages or up to $2000 for each violation, whichever is greater, plus costs, expenses, and attorney fees.
Special Penalties: Attorney general may impose civil penalties up to $2000 per violation.

OHIO
***Telemarketing Statute*: Ohio Rev. Code Ann. §§ 4719.01 through 4719.99 (West).**
Scope: Defines telemarketing broadly, but lists 28 exceptions, such as solicitations by charitable organizations, one-time or infrequent solicitations, solicitations that involve face-to-face contact, numerous businesses licensed under other law, certain catalog sales, certain book, record and video clubs.
Registration Requirements: Solicitors must register and pay a fee with the attorney general, and also obtain a $50,000 surety bond.
Substantive Law: Within the first 60 seconds of the call, solicitors must identify themselves and the goods being sold, along with certain other information; transactions are not valid unless the solicitor receives a signed, written contract from the consumer. Contract must include notice of cancellation rights (7-day cooling-off period). Specific disclosure requirements for gift and prize promotions. Prohibits solicitor from intentionally blocking disclosure of telephone number from which call is made.
Private Right of Action: Yes. A violation is a UDAP violation. Statute also authorizes private suit for damages and/or injunction, plus costs and attorney fees; punitive damages are authorized for knowing violations; two-year statute of limitations. Statute also gives attorney general specific enforcement powers.
Special Penalties: Violations are 5th degree felonies.

***900-Number Regulation*: Ohio Admin. Code § 4901:1-5-06 Appx. A (West).**
Substantive Law: Phone bill must separately itemize and identify pay-per-call services. Local service can be disconnected only for non-payment of regulated local service charges.

OKLAHOMA
***Telemarketing Statute*: Okla. Stat. tit. 15, §§ 775A.1 through 775A.5.**
Scope: Defines telemarketing broadly but lists 21 exceptions, such as the sale of securities, newspapers, magazines, food, memberships in book or record clubs, and sales that involve face-to-face contact.
Registration Requirements: Telephone solicitors must register with the attorney general and post $10,000 bond.
Substantive Law: Solicitors must allow the consumer to cancel any sales transaction within three business days after receipt of goods, refund payments upon purchaser's cancellation, and disclose cancellation rights, and cannot misrepresent that the consumer won a contest or will receive "free" goods. May not block Caller ID. May not use an automatic dialing system that results in abandoned calls that are more than 5% of the answered calls. May not engage in any other deceptive trade practice, as defined in § 752 of this title.
Private Right of Action: Yes. A violation is a UDAP violation.
Special Penalties: None.

***Telemarketing Statute*: Okla. Stat. tit. 15, §§ 775B.1 through 775B.7 (Telemarketer Restriction Act).**
Scope: Solicitations for the sale of goods or services. Does not include solicitation for religious, charitable or political purposes, or for any non-profit organization. Exceptions for established business relationship or for calls that will lead to face-to-face negotiations.
Registration Requirements: None specified.
Substantive Law: May not call numbers on do-not-call list established by attorney general.
Private Right of Action: Willful violation is UDAP violation.
Special Penalties: For inadvertent violation, attorney general may assess an administrative fine. Bona fide error defense available.

***900-Number Statute*: Okla. Stat. tit. 17, §§ 140.1 through .6.**
Substantive Law: Prohibits telephone carriers from billing subscribers for 900-number calls that provide vulgar, violent, obscene or racist information or false or misleading advertising; the statute also includes several requirements for 900-number services that are directed towards children under 12.
Private Right of Action: None specified.

OREGON
***Telemarketing Statute*: Or. Rev. Stat. §§ 646.551 through 646.578.**
Scope: Defines specific types of telemarketing that are covered, and excludes the sale of securities, burial services, newspapers or cable TV, sales by supervised financial institutions, sales that involve face-to-face contact, sales to previous customers, and several other exceptions.
Registration Requirements: Telephone solicitors must register with the Department of Justice and pay a fee.
Substantive Law: Solicitors must disclose certain information to

consumers if they are selling oil, gas, stone or metal, or if they represent to consumers that they have won a prize. May not call number listed on do-not-call list, or person who has requested telemarketer not to call.
Private Right of Action: Violation is UDAP violation.
Special Penalties: None specified.

***900-Number Statute*: Or. Rev. Stat. §§ 759.700 through 759.720.**
Substantive Law: Advertisements must clearly disclose the nature of the service and the price of the call; a preamble message must disclose the nature of the service, the price, and the option to avoid charges by terminating the call; consumers must be allowed to block access to 900-numbers if feasible; prohibits disconnection of telephone service for failure to pay 900-number charges.
Exceptions: The preamble is not required in the case of polling services and calls that result in a flat charge of $2.00 or less.
Private Right of Action: Yes, for three times actual damages or $500, whichever is greater, plus attorney fees; injunctions and restitution are also available. The debt is void if the call was made by an unemancipated child under age 18 or by a person with a diagnosed mental or emotional disorder, or if the provider violated the statute.
Special Penalties: Telephone carrier may be liable for certain violations of this statute. Certain violations punishable by fines, or as a Class A violation.

***900-Number Regulations*: Or. Admin. R. 860-021-0620, 860-034-0290.**
Substantive Law: Utility which provides billing services for information provider must advise customer of availability of blocking, that local or long distance service may not be disconnected for nonpayment of pay per call, and of various rights under 900-number statute. Notice must be given to all new customers, and annually in bill stuffers and the informational pages of the phone directory.

PENNSYLVANIA
***Telemarketing Statute*: Pa. Stat. Ann. tit. 73, §§ 2241 through 2249 (West).**
Scope: Defines telemarketing broadly, but lists 12 exceptions, including catalog sales, newspaper and magazine sales, sales of food, and book, video and record club sales that meet certain criteria; most sales that involve a face-to-face contact; some business-to-business sales; sales by businesses that are licensed by, certified by, or registered with the federal or state government; solicitations by some nonprofit organizations; some sales to existing customers; some sales by established businesses that make most of their sales at a retail outlet in the state; some securities transactions; existing debt, contract payment or performance. The state's home solicitation sales law, Pa. Stat. Ann. tit. 73, § 201-7, also applies to telemarketing, broadly defined.
Registration Requirements: Telemarketers must register with attorney general, pay a fee, and post a bond.
Substantive Law: Calls between 9:00 p.m. and 8:00 a.m. prohibited; telemarketer must disclose purpose of call and identity of caller and seller; must terminate call upon consumer's request; cannot make repeat calls if consumer requests; signed written contract or opportunity to cancel required in most cases; safeguards against unauthorized submission of demand drafts; special disclosures and no-purchase entry option required for prize promotions; advance payment for recovery rooms prohibited. May not block Caller ID; may not call residential or wireless numbers listed on Bureau of Consumer Protection do-not-call list. (Bona fide error defense available.) Solicitation using auto-dialer or pre-recorded message player may not include 900- or other pay-per-call number. Prohibits violation of FTC telemarketing rule. State home solicitation sales law, Pa. Stat. Ann. tit. 73, § 201-7, also provides a right to cancel telemarketing sales, and state UDAP statute, Pa. Stat. Ann. tit. 73, § 201-2(4)(xvii) and (xix) also requires disclosures and prompt delivery in telemarketing sales.
Private Right of Action: Violation is UDAP violation.
Special Penalties: Attorney general may seek revocation of telemarketer's registration after second violation. Failure to register is a misdemeanor.

***900-Number Statute*: 66 Pa. Cons. Stat. § 2905.**
Substantive Law: A preamble message at the beginning of each call, informing the caller that the cost of the call will be charged and itemized on the caller's telephone bill, is required; if the service contains sexual material, the preamble must contain a warning message, and the caller must obtain an access code through written application; the 900-number carriers must itemize all 900-number calls on bills, and, upon request, identify the provider; consumers must have the option to block access to 900-number service.
Private Right of Action: Violations are UDAP violations.

RHODE ISLAND
***Telemarketing Statute*: R.I. Gen. Laws §§ 5-61-1 through 5-61-6.**
Scope: Defines specific types of telemarketing that are covered, and exempts persons selling securities, farm products, telephone answering services, cable TV, newspapers, magazines or memberships in book or record clubs, sales to previous customers, sales involving face-to-face contact, and sales by supervised financial institutions.
Registration Requirements: Telephone solicitors must register and pay a fee and post a $30,000 bond or other acceptable form of security.
Substantive Law: Telephone solicitor must identify self, company, and product being sold. If consumer wishes to buy, solicitor must inform consumer of cancellation rights, seller's and salesperson's registration numbers, and company's street address. Oral disclosures must be clear and intelligible. Use of automatic dialing-announcing devices prohibited (except from employers about work schedules and from school districts) unless consumer has given consent or live operator obtains consent, and must disconnect within five seconds after consumer hangs up. Sellers must maintain do-not-call lists. Sellers may call only between 9 a.m. and 6 p.m. on weekdays, 10 a.m. and 5 p.m. on Saturdays. Also restricts text message advertisements sent to cell phones or pagers.
Private Right of Action: Private right of action for treble damages, costs and reasonable attorney fees, or for injunction.
Special Penalties: Violations can entail a fine of up to $10,000 and a year imprisonment.

***900-Number Statute*: R.I. Gen. Law § 39-3-41.**
Substantive Law: Authorizes the public utility commission to adopt regulations for 900-number services, including advertising standards, and any other restrictions or requirements deemed necessary.

SOUTH CAROLINA

***Telemarketing Statute*: S.C. Code Ann. §§ 16-17-445 and 16-17-446 (Law. Co-op).**

Scope: Unsolicited calls by telephone solicitor seeking to sell consumer goods or services or an extension of consumer credit. Excludes calls in response to request by called party, calls regarding existing debt or contract, preexisting business relationship, services sold by institutions licensed and regulated under title 38. Telephone companies are not responsible for enforcing this section.

Registration Requirements: None specified.

Substantive Law: Seller must promptly and clearly disclose the seller's identity, the sales purpose of the call and the nature of the goods or services offered, the cost, payment plan, and any extra charges (shipping, handling, taxes). Must remove consumer's name from list if consumer asks not to be called, and maintain system to prevent calls to consumers who ask not to be called. May not call between 9 p.m. and 8 a.m. For prize promotion, must disclose that no purchase or payment is necessary to win and, if requested, the no-payment method of entry. Autodialed prerecorded messages prohibited except for existing debt or contract, or existing or previous business relationship; may not be made between 7 p.m. and 8 a.m.; must disconnect within 5 seconds after called party hangs up; may not ring hospitals, police stations, fire departments, nursing homes, hotels, or vacation rental units. *See also* S.C. Code Ann. §§ 15-75-50 and 15-75-51 (Law. Co-op) (forbids use of fax machine to send unsolicited advertising. Exceptions for existing business relationship, follow-up on prior contact.).

Private Right of Action: None specified, except for unsolicited fax advertising statute, which gives private remedy for injunction and actual damages, costs and attorney fees, or $200, applicable only after sender has been notified not to transmit to recipient.

Special Penalties: Civil penalties of up to $100 for first violation, $200 for second, $1000 for third and subsequent. Violation is a misdemeanor.

***900-Number Regulation*: S.C. Code Regs. 103-632.**

Scope: Carriers providing services to information providers.

Substantive Law: Preambles required for all calls over $2.00 and any calls directed to children. Calls directed at children shall not include offer of gift or premium. New customers must be offered choice of access or blocking; if customer does not choose, 900 numbers will be blocked. May impose blocking on customer who does not pay 900-number charges. Telecommunications carriers may not provide billing services to 900-number-type services which are fraudulent, unfair, deceptive, or advertised promoted or marketed in violation of S.C. or federal law.

SOUTH DAKOTA

***Telemarketing Statute*: S.D. Codified Laws §§ 37-30A-1 through 37-30A-17 (Michie) and S.D. Codified Laws §§ 49-31-101 through 49-31-108 (Michie) (Do-Not-Call Register).**

Scope: Unsolicited calls by telephone solicitor or telemarketer to South Dakota consumer soliciting sale, lease or rental of consumer goods or extension of consumer credit, or to obtain information used to solicit consumer sale or extension of credit. Excludes calls made in response to request by consumer, prior business relationship, pre-existing debt or contract, sale of newspaper by publisher, calls by merchant with fixed location from which goods are sold, sales made after consumer has examined catalog or other advertising which discloses price and description of goods and terms of sale, and certain transactions in which consumer has right to return goods for a refund.

Registration Requirements: Telephone solicitor must register with Public Service Commission and pay $500 fee.

Substantive Law: Caller must immediately identify self and company, and sales purpose of call, and ask within 30 seconds if consumer is interested in listening. Must hang up if consumer says no, or at any time if consumer expresses disinterest. May not call between 9 p.m. and 9 a.m., or engage in unfair, deceptive or harassing conduct. Verbal agreements not binding until confirmed by written agreement which discloses all terms of sale and is signed by consumer. Telemarketer may not debit consumer's bank account or credit card until written and signed confirmation received. Goods sent without this written confirmation are unordered merchandise, for which consumer is not obligated to pay. Consumer who makes payment without written confirmation may cancel by giving written notice and returning goods. Seller must then return any payments and trade-ins and cancel any evidence of indebtedness. Ten-day cooling-off period, during which consumer may cancel by giving notice and returning the goods. Seller must provide refund and return payments within 30 days and terminate any indication of indebtedness. May not call consumer listed on do-not-call list, to be maintained by Public Service Commission and coordinated with or replaced by national list.

Private Right of Action: For willful act or practice, action for greater of $500 or double damages, plus costs and attorney fees. Willful violation is UDAP violation.

Special Penalties: Willful and knowing violation with intent to defraud a consumer is a misdemeanor. Administrative fine of up to $5000 per violation of do-not-call statute.

***900-Number Regulations*: S.D. Admin. R. 20:10:09:03, 20:10:10:04, 20:10:05:05, and 20:10:10:10.**

Substantive Law: Telephone service may not be refused or disconnected for nonpayment of pay-per-call services.

TENNESSEE

***Telemarketing Statute*: Tenn. Code Ann. §§ 47-18-1501 through 47-18-1527.**

Scope: Covers telephonic sales calls, broadly defined.

Registration Requirements: Autodialers that provide pre-recorded messages must obtain permit from Tennessee Regulatory Authority and post $10,000 bond or letter of credit.

Substantive Law: Prohibits solicitors from calling unlisted numbers and blocking Caller ID function on consumer's telephone equipment. Prohibits solicitors from making unsolicited calls unless they maintain a "no-call" list. Unsolicited calls exclude calls made in response to consumer's express request, calls made in connection with an existing debt or contract, and calls where there is a prior or existing business relationship. With certain exceptions, autodialers that provide pre-recorded messages may not be used between 9 p.m. and 8 a.m.; may not operate unattended, nor use random nor sequential dialing; must hang up within 10 seconds after called party hangs up or declines to hear message; must state name and telephone number of caller within first 25 seconds and again at the end of the call, and the telephone number must be answered during business hours by live operator; may not call unlisted numbers, hospitals, nursing homes, law enforcement or fire protection agencies; may not call without consent, but consent may be given in response to live operator; may not use to solicit pay-per-call call. Special provisions for credit card companies making telephone

offers of services to cardholders: must prove that services were authorized, and if cardholder claims lack of authorization within three months after charges appear on bill, credit card company must refund amount equal to three months charges if it cannot prove authorization.
Private Right of Action: Individual or group that receives pre-recorded calls in violation of this section may seek injunction.
Special Penalties: Civil penalty of up to $1000 per call (both pre-recorded and general sales call provisions), waiveable if violator has made restitution to consumers. Violation of prohibitions against Caller ID blocking and calling unlisted numbers is Class A misdemeanor. Other violations are punishable by civil penalty up to $1000.

***Telemarketing Statute*: Tenn. Code Ann. §§ 65-4-401 through 65-4-408 (Telephone Solicitation).**
Scope: Sales calls to residential subscribers, except calls with subscriber's permission, calls to existing customers, certain charitable solicitations, and occasional calls (not more than three per week, and not part of a telemarketing plan) to specific persons whom the business reasonably believes to be interested in purchasing.
Registration Requirements: None.
Substantive Law: At beginning of call, must disclose identity of telemarketer and company. May not call between 9 p.m. and 8 a.m. May not block Caller ID. (Provider of Caller ID service not liable for violations of this part by others.) May not call numbers in do-not-call database maintained by the Tennessee Regulatory Authority.
Private Right of Action: *See* Consumer Telemarketing Act. The provisions of this act are in addition to that act and any other causes of action, remedies and penalties provided by law.
Special Penalties: Civil penalties of up to $2000 per knowing violation. Authority may issue cease and desist orders. Attorney general may seek injunction. Bona fide error defense available if defendant has established and implemented with due care reasonable practices and procedures to prevent violations.

***900-Number Regulation*: Tenn. Comp. R. and Regs. 1220-4-2-.58.**
Substantive Law: Carriers must provide blocking option for 900 numbers and advise consumers twice a year of its availability.

TEXAS

***Telemarketing Statute*: Tex. Bus. & Com. Code Ann. §§ 38.001 through 38.305 (Vernon).**
Scope: Defines telemarketing broadly and includes calls made by a purchaser in response to a mail or any other form of solicitation. The statute exempts a number of entities from its coverage including sellers of securities, publicly traded companies, insurance agents, financial institutions, public utilities, sellers of commodities futures and tax-exempt nonprofit and educational institutions. Other exempt transactions include sales of newspapers, magazines, cable television services, certain catalog sales and sales of food items, solicitation of present or former customers, and isolated transactions.
Registration Requirements: Telemarketers must obtain a local business certificate from each location within the state from which they plan to conduct business, and must meet extensive registration requirements with the secretary of state. Telemarketers must maintain a bond, letter of credit, or certificate of deposit in the amount of $10,000.
Substantive Law: Telemarketers must make certain disclosures before completing any telephone sale, including their street address, and, if an item is being offered for sale at a price less than is usually charged, the manufacturer of the item. If any free gift, premium, bonus or prize is being offered, the telemarketer must disclose the number of persons who have received both the highest valued item and the item with the lowest odds of being received during the previous 12 months. Where any free gift, premium, bonus or prize is being offered, telemarketer may not require giving a credit card or checking account number as a precondition to receiving the item. Unsolicited fax must disclose the name, address and phone number of sender, and include a toll-free telephone number at which recipient may speak to a person during business hours, or which allows recipient to automatically delete his or her name from sender's list.
Private Right of Action: Violation is a UDAP violation. Recipient of fax that violates this section may sue for injunction and damages, the greater of actual damages or $500; may be trebled if court finds violation was willful or knowing.
Special Penalties: Attorney general may enforce the statute directly. Civil penalty of up to $5000 per violation ($25,000 per violation, up to $50,000 total for violation of injunction). Knowing violation of specified provisions is Class A misdemeanor.

***Telemarketing Statute*: Tex. Bus. & Com. Code §§ 44.001 through 44.253 (Vernon) (Telemarketing Disclosure and Privacy Act).**
Scope: Unsolicited calls soliciting the sale of consumer goods or services, an extension of credit for consumer goods or services, or information to be used to solicit these things. Does not include calls initiated by consumer in response to advertising or direct mail that complies with state and federal law; existing business relationship; business relationship terminated within past year unless consumer is on do-not-call list; calls (but not faxes) to a business unless it requests no further calls; calls to collect a debt; calls by licensed telemarketers without automatic dialing device that will result in face-to-face negotiations before a sale is consummated, unless consumer has requested no further calls.
Registration Requirements: None specified.
Substantive Law: Waiver forbidden. May not block Caller ID. May not call number on do-not-call list established by Public Service Commission. Bona fide error defense available.
Private Right of Action: Consumer may bring action for second or subsequent call in violation of do-not-call list, if consumer has notified telemarketer about violation and filed verified complaint with Public Service Commission, attorney general, or appropriate licensing agency, and agency has failed to bring enforcement action within 121 days. If court finds violation to be knowing, damages of up to $500 per violation.
Special Penalties: Public Service Commission may assess fines of up to $1000 per violation. For any violator except a telecommunications provider (over which PSC has exclusive jurisdiction) attorney general may seek civil penalty ($1000, or for knowing violations $3000). Any state licensing agency may impose civil penalty on its licensees who violate this statute. May suspend or revoke license if violation was knowing.

***Telemarketing Statute*: Tex. Util. Code Ann. §§ 55.121 through 55.138 (Vernon) (Automatic Dialing and Announcing Devices). *See also* 16 Tex. Admin. Code § 26.125 (West).**

Scope: Use of autodialers for pre-recorded messages, except certain emergency, public service, and school uses.
Registration Requirements: Users must obtain permit from Public Service Commission, and pay a fee.
Substantive Law: User must notify every telecommunications utility over whose system the device is to be used. May not use device to dial random or sequential numbers; may be used only between 9 a.m. and 9 p.m. weekdays and Saturdays and between noon and 9 p.m. on Sundays. May not make collection call at hours forbidden by FDCPA. Must either disconnect within five seconds after termination of call, or be introduced by live operator who secures called party's permission before beginning the recorded message. First 30 seconds of message must include nature of call, identity of person making call, and the telephone number from which the call is made. Special requirements for cross-promotion of pay per call. Automatic dialing and announcing device may not be used to deliver message of more than 30 seconds unless it is capable of recognizing a telephone answering device and disconnecting within 30 seconds. Regulations also ban automatic dialing and announcing devices calls to emergency numbers, patient or guest rooms at hospitals or nursing homes, and cell phones, pagers or other numbers where called party is charged for the call.
Special Penalties: Administrative penalties of up to $1000 per day. Court or commission may require utility to disconnect service to user who violates this chapter. Willful violation is Class A misdemeanor.

***900-Number Statute*: Tex. Util. Code Ann. § 55.127 (Vernon).**
Substantive Law: Applies to calls made with the use of an automated dial announcing device which plays recorded messages and cross-promotes or references a pay-per-call information service. During the first 30 seconds of call, recorded message must disclose nature of the call, identity of the person or organization making the call, and telephone number from which the call is made. Calls must also disclose that consumers who call a pay-per-call number will be charged for that call, the amount of the flat-rate or cost-per-minute charge the consumer will incur, and the estimated amount of time required to receive all the information offered by the service during a call.
Private Right of Action: None specified.

***900-Number Regulations*: 16 Tex. Admin. Code §§ 26.124 and 26.125 (West).**
Substantive Law: Dominant carriers must offer 900-number blocking. First request free, may charge for reconnection or subsequent blocking. May not disconnect local telephone service for nonpayment of pay-per-call charges, but may impose involuntary 900-number blocking. If a message from an automatic dialing and announcing device includes reference to a 900 number, the message must disclose what charge will be incurred (or a charge per minute and an estimated time for the call).

UTAH
***Telemarketing Statute*: Utah Code Ann. §§ 13-25a-101 through 13-25a-111 (Telephone and Facsimile Solicitation Act).**
Scope: Telephone solicitation, broadly defined to include call encouraging the purchase, lease, rental or investment in property, goods or services, an extension of credit or certain charitable donations. Exceptions for established business relationship, call requested by consumer, existing debt or contract, call required by law for medical purpose. Certain sections do not apply to charities or to various businesses regulated under other law.
Registration Requirements: None specified.
Substantive Law: Telephone solicitations: Caller must promptly identify self, and company, state purpose of call, discontinue call if requested, disconnect within 25 seconds of termination of call. No telephone solicitation between 9 p.m. and 8 a.m. or anytime on Sunday or legal holiday. May send faxes only to person with established business relationship, or who has given prior written permission. May not call Utah number included in federal do-not-call database. May not block Caller ID. May not use automatic dialing device to deliver pre-recorded message, except for calls requested by recipient, existing debt or contract, existing business relationship, or certain emergency notifications.
Private Right of Action: For greater of actual damages or $500, injunctive relief, costs and reasonable attorney fees. For faxes that violate this section, sent after recipient advised sender of objection to previous fax, for greater of $500 or actual pecuniary loss, plus costs and attorney fees.
Special Penalties: Administrative fines of $100 to $1000 per violation. Intentional violation, after having been notified by enforcing authority that conduct violates this statute, is Class A misdemeanor. Attorney general may sue for injunction, consumer restitution or enforcement of fines.

***Telemarketing Statute*: Utah Code Ann. §§ 13-26-1 through 13-26-11.**
Scope: Telemarketing is defined broadly, but there are several exemptions from the registration requirement, including sales by nonprofit organizations, sales by licensed brokers, or certain other businesses licensed under other law, newspapers, catalog sales, isolated transactions, solicitation of present or former customers.
Registration Requirements: Solicitors must register with the attorney general and maintain a bond or other satisfactory security, in amounts ranging from $25,000 to $75,000, depending on size of business and whether it or any affiliated person have violated this chapter within the past 3 years.
Substantive Law: Consumers can cancel within 3 days of the sale or longer, depending on whether the solicitor disclosed their cancellation rights; use of fictitious names, false statements, failure to disclose material facts, and failure to refund payment within 30 days after cancellation are prohibited. May not use inmates in telephone soliciting operations if inmates would have access to personal data about an individual sufficient to physically locate or contact that individual.
Private Right of Action: None specified.
Special Penalties: Violation is either a Class A or B misdemeanor, or a third degree felony; also, civil penalty of up to $2000 for each unlawful transaction.

VERMONT
***Telemarketing Statute*: Vt. Stat. Ann. tit. 9, §§ 2464 through 2464d (Telemarketing Transactions).**
Scope: "Telemarketer" means any person who initiates telephone calls to, or who receives telephone calls from, a consumer in connection with a plan, program or campaign to market goods and services.
Exceptions: Section 2464: Banks, when obtaining or submitting for payment checks, drafts, etc.; certain credit card transactions; other exemptions as attorney general may provide by rule. Sections 2464a through 2464d: calls in response to inquiry by customer, established business relationship, calls by organization that has

applied for non-profit status, and calls by person not regularly engaged in telephone solicitation.
Registration Requirements: Telemarketers must register with secretary of state.
Substantive Law: May not use services of courier to pick up consumer's payment unless courier delivers goods at time of payment; may not obtain or submit for payment a check, draft or other form of negotiable instrument drawn on a person's checking, savings, share or other depository account without consumer's express written authorization. Courier service or telemarketer's financial institution may not knowingly (includes willful blindness) assist telemarketer to violate this section. May not call numbers on federal do-not-call list.
Private Right of Action: Section 2464: Violation is UDAP violation. Sections 2464a to 2464d: For greater of actual damages or $500 per call (first offense), $1000 (repeat offense), costs and attorney fees, with punitive damages if violation willful.
Special Penalties: None specified. Failing to register is a crime.

***900-Number Statute*: Vt. Stat. Ann. tit. 9, §§ 2501 through 2516.**
Scope: Any entity that sells or offers to sell pay-per-call services; does not include regulated utility or interexchange carrier that provides transport or billing, unless the utility or carrier actually produces or advertises the pay-per-call service. Preamble not required if cost of call cannot exceed $2.00.
Substantive Law: Advertisements must clearly disclose costs, message content, material terms and conditions, and the identity of the provider; advertisements for services directed toward minors must state that parental consent is necessary; use of the word "free" to describe a 900-number service is prohibited; advertisements for services directed at minors must state that parental consent is necessary; a preamble message must disclose the nature of the service, the price, and the option to avoid charges by terminating the call; telephone service may not be disconnected for failure to pay 900-number charges, and bills must itemize 900-number calls and disclose consumer rights; there are strict requirements for 900-number services that offer extensions of credit, employment opportunities, "free" items, or prizes, that solicit charitable contributions, or that are directed towards children; chain 900-numbers and the use of autodialing to promote or initiate calls are prohibited; charges cannot be imposed for calls made to the consumer or as a result of a call to a regular or non-charged telephone number.
Private Right of Action: A violation is a UDAP violation. The statute also authorizes suit for three times amount of actual damages recoverable, plus attorney fees. Providers may not bill consumers for noncomplying service, or report debt to credit reporting agencies. Attorney general has enforcement authority.

VIRGINIA

***Telemarketing Statute*: Va. Code §§ 59.1-21.1 through 59.1-21.7 (Michie).**
Scope: Telemarketing, broadly defined, is covered by the state's home solicitation sales law, which excludes sales of less than $25, sales pursuant to a preexisting charge account or prior negotiations, and sale or lease of farm equipment.
Registration Requirements: None.
Substantive Law: Consumer has right to cancel the transaction within 3 days after the sale, or 30 days after the sale if solicitor misrepresents nature of transaction, except in certain emergencies complying with specified safeguards.
Private Right of Action: Yes. Violation is UDAP violation.
Special Penalties: None.

***Telemarketing Statute*: Va. Code Ann. §§ 59.1-510 through 59.1-518 (Michie).**
Scope: Calls to natural person's home, or any wireless telephone with a Virginia area code, offering or advertising any property, goods or services for sale, lease, license or investment, including an extension of credit. Exempts calls requested by consumer, or established business relationship.
Registration Requirements: None specified.
Substantive Law: Must promptly identify self and company. May not call between 9 p.m. and 8 a.m. May not block Caller ID. The number disclosed must enable the called party, during business hours, to request that no further calls be made. If a live sales representative is not available to speak to the customer within 2 seconds after the greeting, a message must be played with the identity of the caller and a phone number which recipient may call to request no further contact. May not call consumer who has requested not to be called; telemarketer must keep record of requests for 10 years. May not call number listed on federal do-not-call registry. (Bona fide error defense available.)
Private Right of Action: Private right of action for $500 per violation (up to $1500 if courts finds violation to be knowing), costs and reasonable attorney fees, and injunctive relief. Does not limit rights under other law.
Special Penalties: Attorney general may sue for civil penalties of $500 per violation ($1000 if knowing), plus costs of investigation and action, and attorney fees.

***900-Number Statute*: Va. Code Ann. §§ 59.1-429 through 59.1-434 (Michie).**
Substantive Law: Advertisements must clearly disclose costs, and contain information about the provider; a preamble message must disclose the name of the program, the date the information was recorded, the option to avoid charges by terminating the call, and, if the cost is $2.00 or more per minute or a flat rate of $5.00 or more or the service is directed at children under age 12, the cost of the call; the preamble must also tell children under age 12 that parental permission is required; telephone bills must itemize 900-number charges.
Private Right of Action: Violation is UDAP violation.

WASHINGTON

***Telemarketing Statute*: Wash. Rev. Code §§ 19.158.010 through 19.158.901.**
Scope: Defines telemarketing broadly, but lists 20 exceptions, such as isolated transactions, sales by supervised financial institutions, persons calling for charitable, political or other non-commercial purposes, sales that involve face-to-face contact, sales to prior customers, and sales of newspapers, magazines, or memberships in book or record clubs.
Registration Requirements: Telephone solicitors must register with the department of licensing.
Substantive Law: Solicitors must call between the hours of 8:00 a.m and 9:00 p.m., identify themselves and the goods being sold, terminate the call if the consumer is disinterested, and follow up sales transactions with a written confirmation (allowing the purchaser to cancel), and cannot require that payment be made by credit card. Harassment explicitly forbidden.
Private Right of Action: Violation is UDAP violation. Statute also provides a private cause of action for actual damages, court costs

and attorney fees. Statute also gives attorney general specific enforcement powers.
Special Penalties: $500 to $2000 civil penalty for each violation; criminal penalties.

***900-Number Statute*: Wash. Rev. Code §§ 19.162.01 through 19.162.070.**
Substantive Law: Advertisements must clearly disclose the price of the service; except in the case of polling services, a preamble message describing the service and the cost is required if the call is more than $5.00 per minute or the potential total cost is greater than $10; there are specific requirements for services directed at children under age 12.
Private Right of Action: Yes, for three times amount of actual damages or $500, whichever is greater, plus costs and attorney fees; also, equitable relief is available. A violation of the statute is also a defense to the debt for the call. Violation is a UDAP violation.

WEST VIRGINIA

***Telemarketing Statute*: W. Va. Code §§ 46A-6F-101 through 46A-6F-703 (Telemarketing).**
Scope: Unsolicited call from telemarketer to consumer, or telemarketer's invitation to call telemarketer with intent to sell or attempt to sell goods or services. Exceptions for sales to be completed at later face-to-face meeting (which may be regulated under home solicitation sales act)—this exemption does not apply to courier sent to collect payment; certain catalog sales; business-to-business sales; maintenance or repair contracts for goods previously purchased from seller; cable TV; certain book and record clubs; newspapers and magazines; certain small scale sales of food; regulated sales of securities, investments, commodities, insurance, utilities, real estate; sales by businesses who do more than 50% of their sales at permanent place of business. Registration and bonding requirements do not apply to charitable organizations.
Registration Requirements: Telemarketers must register, pay a fee and post bond.
Substantive Law: Must disclose identity of company and sales purpose of call, cost of goods, restrictions and limitations. Additional disclosures for prize promotions or investment opportunities. Must provide for cancellation and refund for 7 days after goods received. Recordkeeping requirements (including copies of brochures, scripts, and advertising). Additional requirements for prize promotions. May not demand advance payment for credit repair. Verifiable authorization (written or tape recorded) required before debiting consumer's bank account. Use of courier forbidden unless requested by consumer, and unless consumer can inspect goods before paying courier. Abuse and harassment forbidden. May not call consumer who requests not to be called. May call only between 8 a.m. and 9 p.m.
Private Right of Action: Violation is UDAP violation. Actual damages. Non-complying contract is void.
Special Penalties: Civil penalties of $100 to $3000. Operation of fraudulent recovery service is a felony. Civil penalty of up to $5000 for failure to register.

WISCONSIN

***Telemarketing Statute*: Wis. Stat. §§ 423.201 through 423.205, 100.52.**
Scope: Consumer transactions initiated by mail or telephone solicitation directed at particular customer or by face-to-face meeting away from merchant's place of business, if offer or agreement to purchase is made at a place other than merchant's place of business; applies to all persons who make or solicit consumer approval transactions, directly collect payments or enforce debts arising from consumer approval transactions, or act as credit services organizations. Exceptions for cash transaction under $25, sale, lease or listing of real estate, auction sale, certain catalog sales, loan conducted and consummated entirely by mail, bona fide emergency (separate writing required). Do-not-call list statute does not apply to nonprofit organizations, consumer-requested calls, and certain calls to current clients.
Registration Requirements: Telephone solicitors must register and pay a fee.
Substantive Law: 3-day cooling-off period; do-not-call list; no pre-recorded messages without consent of called party.
Private Right of Action: None specified, but note that these provisions are part of the Wisconsin Consumer Act.
Special Penalties: For violation of do-not-call statute, $100 per violation.

***Telemarketing Regulation*: Wis. Admin. Code §§ 127.02 through 127.20.**
Scope: Telemarketing, broadly defined as solicitation made by seller to consumer through any interactive electronic voice communication.
Registration Requirements: None.
Substantive Law: Calls between 9:00 p.m. and 8:00 a.m. prohibited; telemarketers must inform consumers of their right to cancel within 3 days of their receiving required, written cancellation rights; telemarketers must promptly disclose their name, the company for which they are selling, that they are offering or promoting goods or services and the nature of those goods or services; prior to accepting payment, the telemarketer must inform the consumer of the nature and quantity of goods or services involved, the total cost, all material terms and conditions, and either the seller's mailing address or a phone number at which the consumer may contact the seller during business hours to obtain the seller's address. If sales presentation is in a language other than English, then required disclosures must be made in that language. (Contract must be in both English and other language.) Express verifiable authorization (defined) required before presenting check, draft or other negotiable instrument. Misrepresentation and harassment explicitly forbidden. Assisting others to commit violations (including credit card laundering) forbidden.
Private Right of Action: None Specified.

***900-Number Statute*: Wis. Stat. § 196.208.**
Substantive Law: A preamble is required at the beginning of each call which discloses the nature of the services, the cost of the call, the name of the provider, and the option to avoid charges by terminating the call; prohibits transferring a calling party from a toll-free service to a pay-per-call service, and restricts the imposition of charges in connection with a toll-free call; advertisements must not be deceptive and must clearly disclose the name of the provider, all conditions on prizes and gifts, and the price of the call; consumers must be allowed to block access to 900-numbers if feasible; telephone service may not be disconnected for failure to pay 900-number charges, and bills must itemize 900-number calls and disclose consumers' rights; if consumer reasonably disputes a 900-number change, it must be removed.

Exceptions: Preamble is not required unless the total cost of service exceeds $2.00.
Private Right of Action: Yes, for damages, specific performance, rescission, injunctions and declaratory relief, plus costs, disbursements and attorney fees; class actions specifically recognized. Attorney general and district attorneys have enforcement authority and can seek forfeitures of up to $5000 for each offense.

WYOMING
***Telemarketing Statute*: Wyo. Stat. Ann. §§ 40-12-301 through 40-12-305 (Telephone Solicitation) (Michie).**
Scope: Unsolicited call to consumer, to solicit sale of consumer goods or services (broadly defined), extension of credit for consumer goods or services, or information to be used in soliciting these things. Exceptions for calls at consumers request; existing debt or contract; existing business relationship; caller who makes fewer than 225 unsolicited calls per year.
Registration Requirements: Solicitors and merchants must register with attorney general.
Substantive Law: Must promptly identify self and company, disclose sales purpose of call, and nature of goods or services being offered. May not block Caller ID or call number on national do-not-call list, specifically defined as the list maintained by the Direct Marketing Association or successor organization. Automatic dialing devices banned, except for automatic dialing followed by live messages, if numbers have been screened to exclude unlisted numbers or numbers listed on do-not-call list, or calls at request of consumer or to consumer with established business relationship. No calls before 8:00 a.m. or after 8:00 p.m.
Private Right of Action: None specified.
Special Penalties: Enforcing authority may seek civil penalty up to $500 for first violation, $2500 for second, $5000 for third or subsequent, waiveable if telemarketer makes full restitution to injured consumers. Attorney fees to prevailing party. Bona fide error defense available.

***Telemarketing Statute*: Wyo. Stat. Ann. §§ 40-14-251 through 40-14-255 (Michie) (Home Solicitation Sales).**
Scope: Consumer credit sale of goods or services, with price of $25 or more (single or multiple contracts) if seller or seller's representative solicits buyer either face to face or by telephone, at a place other than seller's place of business and agreement or offer to purchase is made at place other than seller's place of business.
Exceptions: Buyer initiated transactions which take place entirely by mail or phone, preexisting charge account, prior negotiations at seller's place of business, bona fide emergency (writing required).
Registration Requirements: None specified.
Substantive Law: Written agreement required, in same language as sales presentation, including date of transaction and conspicuous notice of cancellation rights; 3-day cooling-off period.
Private Right of Action: None specified.
Special Penalties: None specified.

Appendix F UCC Holder-in-Due-Course Provisions

This appendix reproduces the provisions of the 1990 version of UCC Article 3 and the 1999 version of Article 9 that are most relevant to holder-in-due-course issues. Significant changes that would be made by the 2002 revision of Article 3 are indicated in footnotes or brackets.*

ARTICLE 3 NEGOTIABLE INSTRUMENTS

Part 1. General Provisions and Definitions

§ 3-104. Negotiable Instrument.

(a) Except as provided in subsections (c) and (d), "negotiable instrument" means an unconditional promise or order to pay a fixed amount of money, with or without interest or other charges described in the promise or order, if it:

(1) is payable to bearer or to order at the time it is issued or first comes into possession of a holder;

(2) is payable on demand or at a definite time; and

(3) does not state any other undertaking or instruction by the person promising or ordering payment to do any act in addition to the payment of money, but the promise or order may contain (i) an undertaking or power to give, maintain, or protect collateral to secure payment, (ii) an authorization or power to the holder to confess judgment or realize on or dispose of collateral, or (iii) a waiver of the benefit of any law intended for the advantage or protection of an obligor.

(b) "Instrument" means a negotiable instrument.

(c) An order that meets all of the requirements of subsection (a), except paragraph (1), and otherwise falls within the definition of "check" in subsection (f) is a negotiable instrument and a check.

(d) A promise or order other than a check is not an instrument if, at the time it is issued or first comes into possession of a holder, it contains a conspicuous statement, however expressed, to the effect that the promise or order is not negotiable or is not an instrument governed by this Article.

(e) An instrument is a "note" if it is a promise and is a "draft" if it is an order. If an instrument falls within the definition of both "note" and "draft," a person entitled to enforce the instrument may treat it as either.

(f) "Check" means (i) a draft, other than a documentary draft, payable on demand and drawn on a bank or (ii) a cashier's check or teller's check. An instrument may be a check even though it is described on its face by another term, such as "money order."

* * *

Official Comment

1. The definition of "negotiable instrument" defines the scope of Article 3 since Section 3-102 states: "This Article applies to negotiable instruments." The definition in Section 3-104(a) incorporates other definitions in Article 3. An instrument is either a "promise," defined in Section 3-103(a)(9), or "order," defined in Section 3-103(a)(6). A promise is a written undertaking to pay money signed by the person undertaking to pay. An order is a written instruction to pay money signed by the person giving the instruction. Thus, the term "negotiable instrument" is limited to a signed writing that orders or promises payment of money. "Money" is defined in Section 1-201(24) and is not limited to United States dollars. It also includes a medium of exchange established by a foreign government or monetary units of account established by an intergovernmental organization or by agreement between two or more nations. Five other requirements are stated in Section 3-104(a): First, the promise or order must be "unconditional." The quoted term is explained in Section 3-106. Second, the amount of money must be "a fixed amount * * * with or without interest or other charges described in the promise or order." Section 3-112(b) relates to "interest." Third, the promise or order must be "payable to bearer or to order." The quoted phrase is explained in Section 3-109. An exception to this requirement is stated in subsection (c). Fourth, the promise or order must be payable "on demand or at a definite time." The quoted phrase is explained in Section 3-108. Fifth, the promise or order may not state "any other undertaking or instruction by the person promising or ordering payment to do any act in addition to the payment of money" with three exceptions. The quoted phrase is based on the first sentence of N.I.L. Section 5 which is the precursor of "no other promise, order, obligation or power given by the maker or drawer" appearing in former Section 3-104(1)(b). The words "instruction" and "undertaking" are used instead of "order" and "promise" that are used in the N.I.L. formulation because the latter words are defined terms that include only orders or promises to pay money. The three exceptions stated in Section 3-104(a)(3) are based on and are intended to have the same meaning as former Section 3-112(1)(b), (c), (d), and (e), as well as N.I.L. § 5(1), (2), and (3). Subsection (b) states that "instrument" means a "negotiable instrument." This follows former Section 3-102(1)(e) which treated the two terms as synonymous.

2. Unless subsection (c) applies, the effect of subsection (a)(1) and Section 3-102(a) is to exclude from Article 3 any promise or

order that is not payable to bearer or to order. There is no provision in revised Article 3 that is comparable to former Section 3-805. The comment to former Section 3-805 states that the typical example of a writing covered by that section is a check reading "Pay John Doe." Such a check was governed by former Article 3 but there could not be a holder in due course of the check. Under Section 3-104(c) such a check is governed by revised Article 3 and there can be a holder in due course of the check. But subsection (c) applies only to checks. The comment to former Section 3-805 does not state any example other than the check to illustrate that section. Subsection (c) is based on the belief that it is good policy to treat checks, which are payment instruments, as negotiable instruments whether or not they contain the words "to the order of." These words are almost always pre-printed on the check form. Occasionally the drawer of a check may strike out these words before issuing the check. In the past some credit unions used check forms that did not contain the quoted words. Such check forms may still be in use but they are no longer common. Absence of the quoted words can easily be overlooked and should not affect the rights of holders who may pay money or give credit for a check without being aware that it is not in the conventional form.

Total exclusion from Article 3 of other promises or orders that are not payable to bearer or to order serves a useful purpose. It provides a simple device to clearly exclude a writing that does not fit the pattern of typical negotiable instruments and which is not intended to be a negotiable instrument. If a writing could be an instrument despite the absence of "to order" or "to bearer" language and a dispute arises with respect to the writing, it might be argued that the writing is a negotiable instrument because the other requirements of subsection (a) are somehow met. Even if the argument is eventually found to be without merit it can be used as a litigation ploy. Words making a promise or order payable to bearer or to order are the most distinguishing feature of a negotiable instrument and such words are frequently referred to as "words of negotiability." Article 3 is not meant to apply to contracts for the sale of goods or services or the sale or lease of real property or similar writings that may contain a promise to pay money. The use of words of negotiability in such contracts would be an aberration. Absence of the words precludes any argument that such contracts might be negotiable instruments.

An order or promise that is excluded from Article 3 because of the requirements of Section 3-104(a) may nevertheless be similar to a negotiable instrument in many respects. Although such a writing cannot be made a negotiable instrument within Article 3 by contract or conduct of its parties, nothing in Section 3-104 or in Section 3-102 is intended to mean that in a particular case involving such a writing a court could not arrive at a result similar to the result that would follow if the writing were a negotiable instrument. For example, a court might find that the obligor with respect to a promise that does not fall within Section 3-104(a) is precluded from asserting a defense against a bona fide purchaser. The preclusion could be based on estoppel or ordinary principles of contract. It does not depend upon the law of negotiable instruments. An example is stated in the paragraph following Case # 2 in Comment 4 to Section 3-302.

Moreover, consistent with the principle stated in Section 1-102(2)(b), the immediate parties to an order or promise that is not an instrument may provide by agreement that one or more of the provisions of Article 3 determine their rights and obligations under the writing. Upholding the parties' choice is not inconsistent with Article 3. Such an agreement may bind a transferee of the writing if the transferee has notice of it or the agreement arises from usage of trade and the agreement does not violate other law or public policy. An example of such an agreement is a provision that a transferee of the writing has the rights of a holder in due course stated in Article 3 if the transferee took rights under the writing in good faith, for value, and without notice of a claim or defense.

Even without an agreement of the parties to an order or promise that is not an instrument, it may be appropriate, consistent with the principles stated in Section 1-102(2), for a court to apply one or more provisions of Article 3 to the writing by analogy, taking into account the expectations of the parties and the differences between the writing and an instrument governed by Article 3. Whether such application is appropriate depends upon the facts of each case.

3. Subsection (d) allows exclusion from Article 3 of a writing that would otherwise be an instrument under subsection (a) by a statement to the effect that the writing is not negotiable or is not governed by Article 3. For example, a promissory note can be stamped with the legend NOT NEGOTIABLE. The effect under subsection (d) is not only to negate the possibility of a holder in due course, but to prevent the writing from being a negotiable instrument for any purpose. Subsection (d) does not, however, apply to a check. If a writing is excluded from Article 3 by subsection (d), a court could, nevertheless, apply Article 3 principles to it by analogy as stated in Comment 2.

4. Instruments are divided into two general categories: drafts and notes. A draft is an instrument that is an order. A note is an instrument that is a promise. Section 3-104(e). The term "bill of exchange" is not used in Article 3. It is generally understood to be a synonym for the term "draft."

* * *

§ 3-106. Unconditional Promise or Order.[1]

(a) Except as provided in this section, for the purposes of Section 3-104(a), a promise or order is unconditional unless it states (i) an express condition to payment, (ii) that the promise or order is subject to or governed by another writing, or (iii) that rights or obligations with respect to the promise or order are stated in another writing. A reference to another writing does not of itself make the promise or order conditional.

(b) A promise or order is not made conditional (i) by a reference to another writing for a statement of rights with respect to collateral, prepayment, or acceleration, or (ii) because payment is limited to resort to a particular fund or source.

1 In 2002, the National Conference of Commissioners on Uniform State Laws (NCCUSL) approved a revision to Article 3 that would replace "writing" in this section with "record," in order to accommodate electronic commerce. As of mid-2004, only Minnesota had enacted this revision.

* * *

(d) If a promise or order at the time it is issued or first comes into possession of a holder contains a statement, required by applicable statutory or administrative law, to the effect that the rights of a holder or transferee are subject to claims or defenses that the issuer could assert against the original payee, the promise or order is not thereby made conditional for the purposes of Section 3-104(a); but if the promise or order is an instrument, there cannot be a holder in due course of the instrument.

Official Comment

1. This provision replaces former Section 3-105. Its purpose is to define when a promise or order fulfills the requirement in Section 3-104(a) that it be an "unconditional" promise or order to pay. Under Section 3-106(a) a promise or order is deemed to be unconditional unless one of the two tests of the subsection make the promise or order conditional. If the promise or order states an express condition to payment, the promise or order is not an instrument. For example, a promise states, "I promise to pay $100,000 to the order of John Doe if he conveys title to Blackacre to me." The promise is not an instrument because there is an express condition to payment. However, suppose a promise states, "In consideration of John Doe's promise to convey title to Blackacre I promise to pay $100,000 to the order of John Doe." That promise can be an instrument if Section 3-104 is otherwise satisfied. Although the recital of the executory promise of Doe to convey Blackacre might be read as an implied condition that the promise be performed, the condition is not an express condition as required by Section 3-106(a)(i). This result is consistent with former Section 3-105(1)(a) and (b). Former Section 3-105(1)(b) is not repeated in Section 3-106 because it is not necessary. It is an example of an implied condition. Former Section 3-105(1)(d), (e), and (f) and the first clause of former Section 3-105(1)(c) are other examples of implied conditions. They are not repeated in Section 3-106 because they are not necessary. The law is not changed.

Section 3-106(a)(ii) and (iii) carry forward the substance of former Section 3-105(2)(a). The only change is the use of "writing" instead of "agreement" and a broadening of the language that can result in conditionality. For example, a promissory note is not an instrument defined by Section 3-104 if it contains any of the following statements: 1. "This note is subject to a contract of sale dated April 1, 1990 between the payee and maker of this note." 2. "This note is subject to a loan and security agreement dated April 1, 1990 between the payee and maker of this note." 3. "Rights and obligations of the parties with respect to this note are stated in an agreement dated April 1, 1990 between the payee and maker of this note." It is not relevant whether any condition to payment is or is not stated in the writing to which reference is made. The rationale is that the holder of a negotiable instrument should not be required to examine another document to determine rights with respect to payment. But subsection (b)(i) permits reference to a separate writing for information with respect to collateral, prepayment, or acceleration.

Many notes issued in commercial transactions are secured by collateral, are subject to acceleration in the event of default, or are subject to prepayment. A statement of rights and obligations concerning collateral, prepayment, or acceleration does not prevent the note from being an instrument if the statement is in the note itself. See Section 3-104(a)(3) and Section 3-108(b). In some cases it may be convenient not to include a statement concerning collateral, prepayment, or acceleration in the note, but rather to refer to an accompanying loan agreement, security agreement or mortgage for that statement. Subsection (b)(i) allows a reference to the appropriate writing for a statement of these rights. For example, a note would not be made conditional by the following statement: "This note is secured by a security interest in collateral described in a security agreement dated April 1, 1990 between the payee and maker of this note. Rights and obligations with respect to the collateral are [stated in] [governed by] the security agreement." The bracketed words are alternatives, either of which complies.

Subsection (b)(ii) addresses the issues covered by former Section 3-105(1)(f), (g), and (h) and Section 3-105(2)(b). Under Section 3-106(a) a promise or order is not made conditional because payment is limited to payment from a particular source or fund. This reverses the result of former Section 3-105(2)(b). There is no cogent reason why the general credit of a legal entity must be pledged to have a negotiable instrument. Market forces determine the marketability of instruments of this kind. If potential buyers don't want promises or orders that are payable only from a particular source or fund, they won't take them, but Article 3 should apply.

* * *

3. Subsection (d) concerns the effect of a statement to the effect that the rights of a holder or transferee are subject to claims and defenses that the issuer could assert against the original payee. The subsection applies only if the statement is required by statutory or administrative law. The prime example is the Federal Trade Commission Rule (16 C.F.R. Part 433) preserving consumers' claims and defenses in consumer credit sales. The intent of the FTC rule is to make it impossible for there to be a holder in due course of a note bearing the FTC legend and undoubtedly that is the result. But, under former Article 3, the legend may also have had the unintended effect of making the note conditional, thus excluding the note from former Article 3 altogether. Subsection (d) is designed to make it possible to preclude the possibility of a holder in due course without excluding the instrument from Article 3. Most of the provisions of Article 3 are not affected by the holder-in-due-course doctrine and there is no reason why Article 3 should not apply to a note bearing the FTC legend if holder-in-due-course rights are not involved. Under subsection (d) the statement does not make the note conditional. If the note otherwise meets the requirements of Section 3-104(a) it is a negotiable instrument for all purposes except that there cannot be a holder in due course of the note. No particular form of legend or statement is required by subsection (d). The form of a particular legend or statement may be determined by the other statute or administrative law. For example, the FTC legend required in a note taken by the seller in a consumer sale of goods or services is tailored to that particular transaction

and therefore uses language that is somewhat different from that stated in subsection (d), but the difference in expression does not affect the essential similarity of the message conveyed. The effect of the FTC legend is to make the rights of a holder or transferee subject to claims or defenses that the issuer could assert against the original payee of the note.

§ 3-108. Payable on Demand or at Definite Time.

(a) A promise or order is "payable on demand" if it (i) states that it is payable on demand or at sight, or otherwise indicates that it is payable at the will of the holder, or (ii) does not state any time of payment.

(b) A promise or order is "payable at a definite time" if it is payable on elapse of a definite period of time after sight or acceptance or at a fixed date or dates or at a time or times readily ascertainable at the time the promise or order is issued, subject to rights of (i) prepayment, (ii) acceleration, (iii) extension at the option of the holder, or (iv) extension to a further definite time at the option of the maker or acceptor or automatically upon or after a specified act or event.

(c) If an instrument, payable at a fixed date, is also payable upon demand made before the fixed date, the instrument is payable on demand until the fixed date and, if demand for payment is not made before that date, becomes payable at a definite time on the fixed date.

Official Comment

This section is a restatement of former Section 3-108 and Section 3-109. Subsection (b) broadens former Section 3-109 somewhat by providing that a definite time includes a time readily ascertainable at the time the promise or order is issued. Subsection (b)(iii) and (iv) restates former Section 3-109(1)(d). It adopts the generally accepted rule that a clause providing for extension at the option of the holder, even without a time limit, does not affect negotiability since the holder is given only a right which the holder would have without the clause. If the extension is to be at the option of the maker or acceptor or is to be automatic, a definite time limit must be stated or the time of payment remains uncertain and the order or promise is not a negotiable instrument. If a definite time limit is stated, the effect upon certainty of time of payment is the same as if the instrument were made payable at the ultimate date with a term providing for acceleration.

§ 3-109. Payable to Bearer or to Order.

(a) A promise or order is payable to bearer if it:

(1) states that it is payable to bearer or to the order of bearer or otherwise indicates that the person in possession of the promise or order is entitled to payment;

(2) does not state a payee; or

(3) states that it is payable to or to the order of cash or otherwise indicates that it is not payable to an identified person.

(b) A promise or order that is not payable to bearer is payable to order if it is payable (i) to the order of an identified person or (ii) to an identified person or order. A promise or order that is payable to order is payable to the identified person.

(c) An instrument payable to bearer may become payable to an identified person if it is specially indorsed pursuant to Section 3-205(a). An instrument payable to an identified person may become payable to bearer if it is indorsed in blank pursuant to Section 3-205(b).

Official Comment

1. Under Section 3-104(a), a promise or order cannot be an instrument unless the instrument is payable to bearer or to order when it is issued or unless Section 3-104(c) applies. The terms "payable to bearer" and "payable to order" are defined in Section 3-109. The quoted terms are also relevant in determining how an instrument is negotiated. If the instrument is payable to bearer it can be negotiated by delivery alone. Section 3-201(b). An instrument that is payable to an identified person cannot be negotiated without the indorsement of the identified person. Section 3-201(b). An instrument payable to order is payable to an identified person. Section 3-109(b). Thus, an instrument payable to order requires the indorsement of the person to whose order the instrument is payable.

* * *

§ 3-112. Interest.

(a) Unless otherwise provided in the instrument, (i) an instrument is not payable with interest, and (ii) interest on an interest-bearing instrument is payable from the date of the instrument.

(b) Interest may be stated in an instrument as a fixed or variable amount of money or it may be expressed as a fixed or variable rate or rates. The amount or rate of interest may be stated or described in the instrument in any manner and may require reference to information not contained in the instrument. If an instrument provides for interest, but the amount of interest payable cannot be ascertained from the description, interest is payable at the judgment rate in effect at the place of payment of the instrument and at the time interest first accrues.

Official Comment

1. Under Section 3-104(a) the requirement of a "fixed amount" applies only to principal. The amount of interest payable is that described in the instrument. If the description of interest in the instrument does not allow for the amount of interest to be ascertained, interest is payable at the judgment rate. Hence, if an instrument calls for interest, the amount of interest will always be determinable. If a variable rate of interest is prescribed, the amount of interest is ascertainable by reference to the formula or index described or referred to in the instrument. The last sentence of subsection (b) replaces subsection (d) of former Section 3-118.

2. The purpose of subsection (b) is to clarify the meaning of "interest" in the introductory clause of Section 3-104(a). It is not intended to validate a provision for interest in an instrument if that provision violates other law.

§ 3-113. Date of Instrument.

(a) An instrument may be antedated or postdated. The date stated determines the time of payment if the instrument is payable at a fixed period after date. Except as provided in Section 4-401(c), an instrument payable on demand is not payable before the date of the instrument.

(b) If an instrument is undated, its date is the date of its issue or, in the case of an unissued instrument, the date it first comes into possession of a holder.

Official Comment

This section replaces former Section 3-114. Subsections (1) and (3) of former Section 3-114 are deleted as unnecessary. Section 3-113(a) is based in part on subsection (2) of former Section 3-114. The rule that a demand instrument is not payable before the date of the instrument is subject to Section 4-401(c) which allows the payor bank to pay a postdated check unless the drawer has notified the bank of the postdating pursuant to a procedure prescribed in that subsection. With respect to an undated instrument, the date is the date of issue.

Part 2. Negotiation, Transfer, and Indorsement

§ 3-201. Negotiation.

(a) "Negotiation" means a transfer of possession, whether voluntary or involuntary, of an instrument by a person other than the issuer to a person who thereby becomes its holder.

(b) Except for negotiation by a remitter, if an instrument is payable to an identified person, negotiation requires transfer of possession of the instrument and its indorsement by the holder. If an instrument is payable to bearer, it may be negotiated by transfer of possession alone.

Official Comment

1. Subsections (a) and (b) are based in part on subsection (1) of former Section 3-202. A person can become holder of an instrument when the instrument is issued to that person, or the status of holder can arise as the result of an event that occurs after issuance. "Negotiation" is the term used in Article 3 to describe this post-issuance event. Normally, negotiation occurs as the result of a voluntary transfer of possession of an instrument by a holder to another person who becomes the holder as a result of the transfer. Negotiation always requires a change in possession of the instrument because nobody can be a holder without possessing the instrument, either directly or through an agent. But in some cases the transfer of possession is involuntary and in some cases the

person transferring possession is not a holder. In defining "negotiation" former Section 3-202(1) used the word "transfer," an undefined term, and "delivery," defined in Section 1-201(14) to mean voluntary change of possession. Instead, subsections (a) and (b) use the term "transfer of possession" and, subsection (a) states that negotiation can occur by an involuntary transfer of possession. For example, if an instrument is payable to bearer and it is stolen by Thief or is found by Finder, Thief or Finder becomes the holder of the instrument when possession is obtained. In this case there is an involuntary transfer of possession that results in negotiation to Thief or Finder.

* * *

3. Other sections of Article 3 may modify the rule stated in the first sentence of subsection (b). See for example, Sections 3-404, 3-405 and 3-406.

§ 3-203. Transfer of Instrument; Rights Acquired by Transfer.

(a) An instrument is transferred when it is delivered by a person other than its issuer for the purpose of giving to the person receiving delivery the right to enforce the instrument.

(b) Transfer of an instrument, whether or not the transfer is a negotiation, vests in the transferee any right of the transferor to enforce the instrument, including any right as a holder in due course, but the transferee cannot acquire rights of a holder in due course by a transfer, directly or indirectly, from a holder in due course if the transferee engaged in fraud or illegality affecting the instrument.

(c) Unless otherwise agreed, if an instrument is transferred for value and the transferee does not become a holder because of lack of indorsement by the transferor, the transferee has a specifically enforceable right to the unqualified indorsement of the transferor, but negotiation of the instrument does not occur until the indorsement is made.

* * *

Official Comment

1. Section 3-203 is based on former Section 3-201 which stated that a transferee received such rights as the transferor had. The former section was confusing because some rights of the transferor are not vested in the transferee unless the transfer is a negotiation. For example, a transferee that did not become the holder could not negotiate the instrument, a right that the transferor had. Former Section 3-201 did not define "transfer." Subsection (a) defines transfer by limiting it to cases in which possession of the instrument is delivered for the purpose of giving to the person receiving delivery the right to enforce the instrument.

Although transfer of an instrument might mean in a particular case that title to the instrument passes to the transferee, that result does not follow in all cases. The right to enforce an instrument and ownership of the instrument are two different concepts. A thief who steals a check payable to bearer becomes the holder of the check and a person entitled to enforce it, but does not become the owner of the check. If the thief transfers the check to a purchaser the transferee obtains the right to enforce the check. If the purchaser is not a holder in due course, the owner's claim to the check may be asserted against the purchaser. Ownership rights in instruments may be determined by principles of the law of property, independent of Article 3, which do not depend upon whether the instrument was transferred under Section 3-203. Moreover, a person who has an ownership right in an instrument might not be a person entitled to enforce the instrument. For example, suppose X is the owner and holder of an instrument payable to X. X sells the instrument to Y but is unable to deliver immediate possession to Y. Instead, X signs a document conveying all of X's right, title, and interest in the instrument to Y. Although the document may be effective to give Y a claim to ownership of the instrument, Y is not a person entitled to enforce the instrument until Y obtains possession of the instrument. No transfer of the instrument occurs under Section 3-203(a) until it is delivered to Y.

An instrument is a reified right to payment. The right is represented by the instrument itself. The right to payment is transferred by delivery of possession of the instrument "by a person other than its issuer for the purpose of giving to the person receiving delivery the right to enforce the instrument." The quoted phrase excludes issue of an instrument, defined in Section 3-105, and cases in which a delivery of possession is for some purpose other than transfer of the right to enforce. For example, if a check is presented for payment by delivering the check to the drawee, no transfer of the check to the drawee occurs because there is no intent to give the drawee the right to enforce the check.

2. Subsection (b) states that transfer vests in the transferee any right of the transferor to enforce the instrument "including any right as a holder in due course." If the transferee is not a holder because the transferor did not indorse, the transferee is nevertheless a person entitled to enforce the instrument under Section 3-301 if the transferor was a holder at the time of transfer. Although the transferee is not a holder, under subsection (b) the transferee obtained the rights of the transferor as holder. Because the transferee's rights are derivative of the transferor's rights, those rights must be proved. Because the transferee is not a holder, there is no presumption under Section 3-308 that the transferee, by producing the instrument, is entitled to payment. The instrument, by its terms, is not payable to the transferee and the transferee must account for possession of the unindorsed instrument by proving the transaction through which the transferee acquired it. Proof of a transfer to the transferee by a holder is proof that the transferee has acquired the rights of a holder. At that point the transferee is entitled to the presumption under Section 3-308.

Under subsection (b) a holder in due course that transfers an instrument transfers those rights as a holder in due course to the purchaser. The policy is to assure the holder in due course a free market for the instrument. There is one exception to this rule stated in the concluding clause of subsection (b). A person who is party to fraud or illegality affecting the instrument is not permitted to wash the instrument clean by passing it into the hands of a holder in due course and then repurchasing it.

3. Subsection (c) applies only to a transfer for value. It applies only if the instrument is payable to order or specially indorsed to the transferor. The transferee acquires, in the absence of a contrary agreement, the specifically enforceable right to the indorsement of the transferor. Unless otherwise agreed, it is a right to the general indorsement of the transferor with full liability as indorser, rather than to an indorsement without recourse. The question may arise if the transferee has paid in advance and the indorsement is omitted fraudulently or through oversight. A transferor who is willing to indorse only without recourse or unwilling to indorse at all should make those intentions clear before transfer. The agreement of the transferee to take less than an unqualified indorsement need not be an express one, and the understanding may be implied from conduct, from past practice, or from the circumstances of the transaction. Subsection (c) provides that there is no negotiation of the instrument until the indorsement by the transferor is made. Until that time the transferee does not become a holder, and if earlier notice of a defense or claim is received, the transferee does not qualify as a holder in due course under Section 3-302.

4. The operation of Section 3-203 is illustrated by the following cases. In each case Payee, by fraud, induced Maker to issue a note to Payee. The fraud is a defense to the obligation of Maker to pay the note under Section 3-305(a)(2).

Case # 1. Payee negotiated the note to X who took as a holder in due course. After the instrument became overdue X negotiated the note to Y who had notice of the fraud. Y succeeds to X's rights as a holder in due course and takes free of Maker's defense of fraud.

Case # 2. Payee negotiated the note to X who took as a holder in due course. Payee then repurchased the note from X. Payee does not succeed to X's rights as a holder in due course and is subject to Maker's defense of fraud.

Case # 3. Payee negotiated the note to X who took as a holder in due course. X sold the note to Purchaser who received possession. The note, however, was indorsed to X and X failed to indorse it. Purchaser is a person entitled to enforce the instrument under Section 3-301 and succeeds to the rights of X as holder in due course. Purchaser is not a holder, however, and under Section 3-308 Purchaser will have to prove the transaction with X under which the rights of X as holder in due course were acquired.

Case # 4. Payee sold the note to Purchaser who took for value, in good faith and without notice of the defense of Maker. Purchaser received possession of the note but Payee neglected to indorse it. Purchaser became a person entitled to enforce the instrument but did not become the holder because of the missing indorsement. If Purchaser received notice of the defense of Maker before obtaining the indorsement of Payee, Purchaser cannot become a holder in due course because at the time notice was received the note had not been negotiated to Purchaser. If indorsement by Payee was made after Purchaser received notice, Purchaser had notice of the defense when it became the holder.

* * *

§ 3-204. Indorsement.

(a) "Indorsement" means a signature, other than that of a signer as maker, drawer, or acceptor, that alone or accompanied by other words is made on an instrument for the purpose of (i) negotiating the instrument, (ii) restricting payment of the instrument, or (iii) incurring indorser's liability on the instrument, but regardless of the intent of the signer, a signature and its accompanying words is an indorsement unless the accompanying words, terms of the instrument, place of the signature, or other circumstances unambiguously indicate that the signature was made for a purpose other than indorsement. For the purpose of determining whether a signature is made on an instrument, a paper affixed to the instrument is a part of the instrument.

(b) "Indorser" means a person who makes an indorsement.

(c) For the purpose of determining whether the transferee of an instrument is a holder, an indorsement that transfers a security interest in the instrument is effective as an unqualified indorsement of the instrument.

(d) If an instrument is payable to a holder under a name that is not the name of the holder, indorsement may be made by the holder in the name stated in the instrument or in the holder's name or both, but signature in both names may be required by a person paying or taking the instrument for value or collection.

Official Comment

* * *

2. Assume that Payee indorses a note to Creditor as security for a debt. Under subsection (b) of Section 3-203 Creditor takes Payee's rights to enforce or transfer the instrument subject to the limitations imposed by Article 9. Subsection (c) of Section 3-204 makes clear that Payee's indorsement to Creditor, even though it mentions creation of a security interest, is an unqualified indorsement that gives to Creditor the right to enforce the note as its holder.

* * *

Part 3. Enforcement of Instruments

§ 3-301. Person Entitled to Enforce Instrument.

"Person entitled to enforce" an instrument means (i) the holder of the instrument, (ii) a nonholder in possession of the instrument who has the rights of a holder, or (iii) a person not in possession of the instrument who is entitled to enforce the instrument pursuant to Section 3-309 or 3-418(d). A person may be a person entitled to enforce the instrument even though the person is not the owner of the instrument or is in wrongful possession of the instrument.

Official Comment

This section replaces former Section 3-301 that stated the rights of a holder. The rights stated in former Section 3-301 to transfer, negotiate, enforce, or discharge an instrument are stated in other sections of Article 3. In revised Article 3, Section 3-301 defines "person entitled to enforce" an instrument. The definition recognizes that enforcement is not limited to holders. The quoted phrase includes a person enforcing a lost or stolen instrument. Section 3-309. It also includes a person in possession of an instrument who is not a holder. A nonholder in possession of an instrument includes a person that acquired rights of a holder by subrogation or under Section 3-203(a). It also includes any other person who under applicable law is a successor to the holder or otherwise acquires the holder's rights.

§ 3-302. Holder in Due Course.

(a) Subject to subsection (c) and Section 3-106(d), "holder in due course" means the holder of an instrument if:

(1) the instrument when issued or negotiated to the holder does not bear such apparent evidence of forgery or alteration or is not otherwise so irregular or incomplete as to call into question its authenticity; and

(2) the holder took the instrument (i) for value, (ii) in good faith, (iii) without notice that the instrument is overdue or has been dishonored or that there is an uncured default with respect to payment of another instrument issued as part of the same series, (iv) without notice that the instrument contains an unauthorized signature or has been altered, (v) without notice of any claim to the instrument described in Section 3-306, and (vi) without notice that any party has a defense or claim in recoupment described in Section 3-305(a).

(b) Notice of discharge of a party, other than discharge in an insolvency proceeding, is not notice of a defense under subsection (a), but discharge is effective against a person who became a holder in due course with notice of the discharge. Public filing or recording of a document does not of itself constitute notice of a defense, claim in recoupment, or claim to the instrument.

(c) Except to the extent a transferor or predecessor in interest has rights as a holder in due course, a person does not acquire rights of a holder in due course of an instrument taken (i) by legal process or by purchase in an execution, bankruptcy, or creditor's sale or similar proceeding, (ii) by purchase as part of a bulk transaction not in ordinary course of business of the transferor, or (iii) as the successor in interest to an estate or other organization.

(d) If, under Section 3-303(a)(1), the promise of performance that is the consideration for an instrument has been partially performed, the holder may assert rights as a holder in due course of the instrument only to the fraction of the amount payable under the instrument equal to the value of the partial performance divided by the value of the promised performance.

(e) If (i) the person entitled to enforce an instrument has only a security interest in the instrument and (ii) the person obliged to pay the instrument has a defense, claim in recoupment, or claim to the instrument that may be asserted against the person who granted the security interest, the person entitled to enforce the instrument may assert rights as a holder in due course only to an amount payable under the instrument which, at the time of enforcement of the instrument, does not exceed the amount of the unpaid obligation secured.

(f) To be effective, notice must be received at a time and in a manner that gives a reasonable opportunity to act on it.

(g) This section is subject to any law limiting status as a holder in due course in particular classes of transactions.

Official Comment

1. Subsection (a)(1) is a return to the N.I.L. rule that the taker of an irregular or incomplete instrument is not a person the law should protect against defenses of the obligor or claims of prior owners. This reflects a policy choice against extending the holder in due course doctrine to an instrument that is so incomplete or irregular "as to call into question its authenticity." The term "authenticity" is used to make it clear that the irregularity or incompleteness must indicate that the instrument may not be what it purports to be. Persons who purchase or pay such instruments should do so at their own risk. Under subsection (1) of former Section 3-304, irregularity or incompleteness gave a purchaser notice of a claim or defense. But it was not clear from that provision whether the claim or defense had to be related to the irregularity or incomplete aspect of the instrument. This ambiguity is not present in subsection (a)(1).

2. Subsection (a)(2) restates subsection (1) of former Section 3-302. Section 3-305(a) makes a distinction between defenses to the obligation to pay an instrument and claims in recoupment by the maker or drawer that may be asserted to reduce the amount payable on the instrument. Because of this distinction, which was not made in former Article 3, the reference in subsection (a)(2)(vi) is to both a defense and a claim in recoupment. Notice of forgery or alteration is stated separately because forgery and alteration are not technically defenses under subsection (a) of Section 3-305.

3. Discharge is also separately treated in the first sentence of subsection (b). Except for discharge in an insolvency proceeding, which is specifically stated to be a real defense in Section 3-305(a)(1), discharge is not expressed in Article 3 as a defense and is not included in Section 3-305(a)(2). Discharge is effective against anybody except a person having rights of a holder in due course who took the instrument without notice of the discharge. Notice of discharge does not disqualify a person from becoming a holder in due course. For example, a check certified after it is negotiated by the payee may subsequently be negotiated to a holder. If the holder had notice that the certification occurred after negotiation by the payee, the holder necessarily had notice of the discharge of the payee as indorser. Section 3-415(d). Notice of that discharge does not prevent the holder from becoming a holder in due course, but the discharge is effective against the holder. Section 3-601(b). Notice of a defense under Section 3-305(a)(1) of a maker, drawer or acceptor based on a bankruptcy discharge is different. There is no reason to give holder in due course status to a person with notice of that defense. The second sentence of subsection (b) is from former Section 3-304(5).

* * *

5. Subsection (c) is based on former Section 3-302(3). Like former Section 3-302(3), subsection (c) is intended to state existing case law. It covers a few situations in which the purchaser takes an instrument under unusual circumstances. The purchaser is treated as a successor in interest to the prior holder and can acquire no better rights. But if the prior holder was a holder in due course, the purchaser obtains rights of a holder in due course.

Subsection (c) applies to a purchaser in an execution sale or sale in bankruptcy. It applies equally to an attaching creditor or any other person who acquires the instrument by legal process or to a representative, such as an executor, administrator, receiver or assignee for the benefit of creditors, who takes the instrument as part of an estate. Subsection (c) applies to bulk purchases lying outside of the ordinary course of business of the seller. For example, it applies to the purchase by one bank of a substantial part of the paper held by another bank which is threatened with insolvency and seeking to liquidate its assets. Subsection (c) would also apply when a new partnership takes over for value all of the assets of an old one after a new member has entered the firm, or to a reorganized or consolidated corporation taking over the assets of a predecessor.

In the absence of controlling state law to the contrary, subsection (c) applies to a sale by a state bank commissioner of the assets of an insolvent bank. However, subsection (c) may be preempted by federal law if the Federal Deposit Insurance Corporation takes over an insolvent bank. Under the governing federal law, the FDIC and similar financial institution insurers are given holder in due course status and that status is also acquired by their assignees under the shelter doctrine.

6. Subsections (d) and (e) clarify two matters not specifically addressed by former Article 3:

Case # 5. Payee negotiates a $1,000 note to Holder who agrees to pay $900 for it. After paying $500, Holder learns that Payee defrauded Maker in the transaction giving rise to the note. Under subsection (d) Holder may assert rights as a holder in due course to the extent of $555.55 ($500 ÷ $900 = .555 × $1,000 = $555.55). This formula rewards Holder with a ratable portion of the bargained for profit.

Case # 6. Payee negotiates a note of Maker for $1,000 to Holder as security for payment of Payee's debt to Holder of $600. Maker has a defense which is good against Payee but of which Holder has no notice. Subsection (e) applies. Holder may assert rights as a holder in due course only to the extent of $600. Payee does not get the benefit of the holder-in-due-course status of Holder. With respect to $400 of the note, Maker may assert any rights that Maker has against Payee. A different result follows if the payee of a note negotiated it to a person who took it as a holder in due course and that person pledged the note as security for a debt. Because the defense cannot be asserted against the pledgor, the pledgee can assert rights as a holder in due course for the full amount of the note for the benefit of both the pledgor and the pledgee.

7. There is a large body of state statutory and case law restricting the use of the holder in due course doctrine in consumer transactions as well as some business transactions that raise similar issues. Subsection (g) subordinates Article 3 to that law and any other similar law that may evolve in the future. Section 3-106(d) also relates to statutory or administrative law intended to restrict use of the holder-in-due-course doctrine. See Comment 3 to Section 3-106.

§ 3-303. Value and Consideration.

(a) An instrument is issued or transferred for value if:

(1) the instrument is issued or transferred for a promise of performance, to the extent the promise has been performed;

(2) the transferee acquires a security interest or other lien in the instrument other than a lien obtained by judicial proceeding;

(3) the instrument is issued or transferred as payment of, or as security for, an antecedent claim against any person, whether or not the claim is due;

(4) the instrument is issued or transferred in exchange for a negotiable instrument; or

(5) the instrument is issued or transferred in exchange for the incurring of an irrevocable obligation to a third party by the person taking the instrument.

(b) "Consideration" means any consideration sufficient to support a simple contract. The drawer or maker of an instrument has a defense if the instrument is issued without consideration. If an instrument is issued for a promise of performance, the issuer has a defense to the extent performance of the promise is due and the promise has not been performed. If an instrument is issued for value as stated in subsection (a), the instrument is also issued for consideration.

Official Comment

1. Subsection (a) is a restatement of former Section 3-303 and subsection (b) replaces former Section 3-408. The distinction between value and consideration in Article 3 is a very fine one. Whether an instrument is taken for value is relevant to the issue of whether a holder is a holder in due course. If an instrument is not issued for consideration the issuer has a defense to the obligation to pay the instrument. Consideration is defined in subsection (b) as "any consideration sufficient to support a simple contract." The definition of value in Section 1-201(44), which doesn't apply to Article 3, includes "any consideration sufficient to support a simple contract." Thus, outside Article 3, anything that is consideration is also value. A different rule applies in Article 3. Subsection (b) of Section 3-303 states that if an instrument is issued for value it is also issued for consideration.

Case # 1. X owes Y $1,000. The debt is not represented by a note. Later X issues a note to Y for the debt. Under subsection (a)(3) X's note is issued for value. Under subsection (b) the note is also issued for consideration whether or not, under contract law, Y is deemed to have given consideration for the note.

Case # 2. X issues a check to Y in consideration of Y's promise to perform services in the future. Although the executory promise is consideration for issuance of the check it is value only to the extent the promise is performed. Subsection (a)(1).

Case # 3. X issues a note to Y in consideration of Y's promise to perform services. If at the due date of the note Y's performance is not yet due, Y may enforce the note because it was issued for consideration. But if at the due date of the note, Y's performance is due and has not been performed, X has a defense. Subsection (b).

2. Subsection (a), which defines value, has primary importance in cases in which the issue is whether the holder of an instrument is a holder in due course and particularly to cases in which the issuer of the instrument has a defense to the instrument. Suppose Buyer and Seller signed a contract on April 1 for the sale of goods to be delivered on May 1. Payment of 50% of the price of the goods was due upon signing of the contract. On April 1 Buyer delivered to Seller a check in the amount due under the contract. The check was drawn by X to Buyer as payee and was indorsed to Seller. When the check was presented for payment to the drawee on April 2, it was dishonored because X had stopped payment. At that time Seller had not taken any action to perform the contract with Buyer. If X has a defense on the check, the defense can be asserted against Seller who is not a holder in due course because Seller did not give value for the check. Subsection (a)(1). The policy basis for subsection (a)(1) is that the holder who gives an executory promise of performance will not suffer an out-of-pocket loss to the extent the executory promise is unperformed at the time the holder learns of dishonor of the instrument. When Seller took delivery of the check on April 1, Buyer's obligation to pay 50% of the price on that date was suspended, but when the check was dishonored on April 2 the obligation revived. Section 3-310(b). If payment for goods is due at or before delivery and the buyer fails to make the payment, the seller is excused from performing the promise to deliver the goods. Section 2-703. Thus, Seller is protected from an out-of-pocket loss even if the check is not enforceable. Holder-in-due-course status is not necessary to protect Seller.

3. Subsection (a)(2) equates value with the obtaining of a security interest or a nonjudicial lien in the instrument. The term "security interest" covers Article 9 cases in which an instrument is taken as collateral as well as bank collection cases in which a bank acquires a security interest under Section 4-210. The acquisition of a common-law or statutory banker's lien is also value under subsection (a)(2). An attaching creditor or other person who acquires a lien by judicial proceedings does not give value for the purposes of subsection (a)(2).

4. Subsection (a)(3) follows former Section 3-303(b) in providing that the holder takes for value if the instrument is taken in payment of or as security for an antecedent claim, even though

there is no extension of time or other concession, and whether or not the claim is due. Subsection (a)(3) applies to any claim against any person; there is no requirement that the claim arise out of contract. In particular the provision is intended to apply to an instrument given in payment of or as security for the debt of a third person, even though no concession is made in return.

5. Subsection (a)(4) and (5) restate former Section 3-303(c). They state generally recognized exceptions to the rule that an executory promise is not value. A negotiable instrument is value because it carries the possibility of negotiation to a holder in due course, after which the party who gives it is obliged to pay. The same reasoning applies to any irrevocable commitment to a third person, such as a letter of credit issued when an instrument is taken.

§ 3-304. Overdue Instrument.

(a) An instrument payable on demand becomes overdue at the earliest of the following times:

(1) on the day after the day demand for payment is duly made;

(2) if the instrument is a check, 90 days after its date; or

(3) if the instrument is not a check, when the instrument has been outstanding for a period of time after its date which is unreasonably long under the circumstances of the particular case in light of the nature of the instrument and usage of the trade.

(b) With respect to an instrument payable at a definite time the following rules apply:

(1) If the principal is payable in installments and a due date has not been accelerated, the instrument becomes overdue upon default under the instrument for nonpayment of an installment, and the instrument remains overdue until the default is cured.

(2) If the principal is not payable in installments and the due date has not been accelerated, the instrument becomes overdue on the day after the due date.

(3) If a due date with respect to principal has been accelerated, the instrument becomes overdue on the day after the accelerated due date.

(c) Unless the due date of principal has been accelerated, an instrument does not become overdue if there is default in payment of interest but no default in payment of principal.

Official Comment

1. To be a holder in due course, one must take without notice that an instrument is overdue. Section 3-302(a)(2)(iii). Section 3-304 replaces subsection (3) of former Section 3-304. For the sake of clarity it treats demand and time instruments separately. Subsection (a) applies to demand instruments. A check becomes stale after 90 days.

Under former Section 3-304(3)(c), a holder that took a demand note had notice that it was overdue if it was taken "more than a reasonable length of time after its issue." In substitution for this test, subsection (a)(3) requires the trier of fact to look at both the circumstances of the particular case and the nature of the instrument and trade usage. Whether a demand note is stale may vary a great deal depending on the facts of the particular case.

2. Subsections (b) and (c) cover time instruments. They follow the distinction made under former Article 3 between defaults in payment of principal and interest. In subsection (b) installment instruments and single payment instruments are treated separately. If an installment is late, the instrument is overdue until the default is cured.

§ 3-305. Defenses and Claims in Recoupment.

(a) Except as stated in subsection (b), the right to enforce the obligation of a party to pay an instrument is subject to the following:

(1) a defense of the obligor based on (i) infancy of the obligor to the extent it is a defense to a simple contract, (ii) duress, lack of legal capacity, or illegality of the transaction which, under other law, nullifies the obligation of the obligor, (iii) fraud that induced the obligor to sign the instrument with neither knowledge nor reasonable opportunity to learn of its character or its essential terms, or (iv) discharge of the obligor in insolvency proceedings;

(2) a defense of the obligor stated in another section of this Article or a defense of the obligor that would be available if the person entitled to enforce the instrument were enforcing a right to payment under a simple contract; and

(3) a claim in recoupment of the obligor against the original payee of the instrument if the claim arose from the transaction that gave rise to the instrument; but the claim of the obligor may be asserted against a transferee of the instrument only to reduce the amount owing on the instrument at the time the action is brought.

(b) The right of a holder in due course to enforce the obligation of a party to pay the instrument is subject to defenses of the obligor stated in subsection (a)(1), but is not subject to defenses of the obligor stated in subsection (a)(2) or claims in recoupment stated in subsection (a)(3) against a person other than the holder.

(c) Except as stated in subsection (d), in an action to enforce the obligation of a party to pay the instrument, the obligor may not assert against the person entitled to enforce the instrument a defense, claim in recoupment, or claim to the instrument (Section 3-306) of another person, but the other person's claim to the instrument may be asserted by the obligor if the other person is joined in the action and personally asserts the claim against the person entitled to enforce the instrument. An obligor is not obliged to pay the instrument if the person seeking enforcement of the instrument does not have rights of a holder in due course and the obligor proves that the instrument is a lost or stolen instrument.

(d) In an action to enforce the obligation of an accommodation party to pay an instrument, the accommodation party may assert against the person entitled to enforce the instrument any defense or claim in recoupment under subsection (a) that the accommodated party could assert against the person entitled to enforce the instrument, except the defenses of discharge in insolvency proceedings, infancy, and lack of legal capacity.

[*(e) In a consumer transaction, if law other than this article requires that an instrument include a statement to the effect that the rights of a holder or transferee are subject to a claim or defense that the issuer could assert against the original payee, and the instrument does not include such a statement:*

(1) the instrument has the same effect as if the instrument included such a statement;

(2) the issuer may assert against the holder or transferee all claims and defenses that would have been available if the instrument included such a statement; and

(3) the extent to which claims may be asserted against the holder or transferee is determined as if the instrument included such a statement.

(f) This section is subject to law other than this article that establishes a different rule for consumer transactions.][2]

Official Comment

1. Subsection (a) states the defenses to the obligation of a party to pay the instrument. Subsection (a)(1) states the "real defenses" that may be asserted against any person entitled to enforce the instrument.

Subsection (a)(1)(i) allows assertion of the defense of infancy against a holder in due course, even though the effect of the defense is to render the instrument voidable but not void. The policy is one of protection of the infant even at the expense of occasional loss to an innocent purchaser. No attempt is made to state when infancy is available as a defense or the conditions under which it may be asserted. In some jurisdictions it is held that an infant cannot rescind the transaction or set up the defense unless the holder is restored to the position held before the instrument was taken which, in the case of a holder in due course, is normally impossible. In other states an infant who has misrepresented age may be estopped to assert infancy. Such questions are left to other law, as an integral part of the policy of each state as to the protection of infants.

Subsection (a)(1)(ii) covers mental incompetence, guardianship, ultra vires acts or lack of corporate capacity to do business, or any other incapacity apart from infancy. Such incapacity is largely statutory. Its existence and effect is left to the law of each state. If

2 These two new subsections are added by the revision to Article 3 that NCCUSL approved in 2002 for consideration by state legislatures. The effect of new (e) will be to read the FTC Holder Notice and any comparable notices required by state law into a promissory note that should have included the notice. As of mid-2004, only Minnesota had adopted this revised version of Article 3.

under the state law the effect is to render the obligation of the instrument entirely null and void, the defense may be asserted against a holder in due course. If the effect is merely to render the obligation voidable at the election of the obligor, the defense is cut off.

Duress, which is also covered by subsection (a)(ii), is a matter of degree. An instrument signed at the point of a gun is void, even in the hands of a holder in due course. One signed under threat to prosecute the son of the maker for theft may be merely voidable, so that the defense is cut off. Illegality is most frequently a matter of gambling or usury, but may arise in other forms under a variety of statutes. The statutes differ in their provisions and the interpretations given them. They are primarily a matter of local concern and local policy. All such matters are therefore left to the local law. If under that law the effect of the duress or the illegality is to make the obligation entirely null and void, the defense may be asserted against a holder in due course. Otherwise it is cut off.

Subsection (a)(1)(iii) refers to "real" or "essential" fraud, sometimes called fraud in the essence or fraud in the factum, as effective against a holder in due course. The common illustration is that of the maker who is tricked into signing a note in the belief that it is merely a receipt or some other document. The theory of the defense is that the signature on the instrument is ineffective because the signer did not intend to sign such an instrument at all. Under this provision the defense extends to an instrument signed with knowledge that it is a negotiable instrument, but without knowledge of its essential terms. The test of the defense is that of excusable ignorance of the contents of the writing signed. The party must not only have been in ignorance, but must also have had no reasonable opportunity to obtain knowledge. In determining what is a reasonable opportunity all relevant factors are to be taken into account, including the intelligence, education, business experience, and ability to read or understand English of the signer. Also relevant is the nature of the representations that were made, whether the signer had good reason to rely on the representations or to have confidence in the person making them, the presence or absence of any third person who might read or explain the instrument to the signer, or any other possibility of obtaining independent information, and the apparent necessity, or lack of it, for acting without delay. Unless the misrepresentation meets this test, the defense is cut off by a holder in due course.

Subsection (a)(1)(iv) states specifically that the defense of discharge in insolvency proceedings is not cut off when the instrument is purchased by a holder in due course. "Insolvency proceedings" is defined in Section 1-201(22) and it includes bankruptcy whether or not the debtor is insolvent. Subsection (2)(e) of former Section 3-305 is omitted. The substance of that provision is stated in Section 3-601(b).

2. Subsection (a)(2) states other defenses that, pursuant to subsection (b), are cut off by a holder in due course. These defenses comprise those specifically stated in Article 3 and those based on common law contract principles. Article 3 defenses are nonissuance of the instrument, conditional issuance, and issuance for a special purpose (Section 3-105(b)); failure to countersign a traveler's check (Section 3-106(c)); modification of the obligation by a separate agreement (Section 3-117); payment that violates a restrictive indorsement (Section 3-206(f)); instruments issued without consideration or for which promised performance has not been given (Section 3-303(b)), and breach of warranty when a draft is accepted (Section 3-417(b)). The most prevalent common law defenses are fraud, misrepresentation or mistake in the issuance of the instrument. In most cases the holder in due course will be an immediate or remote transferee of the payee of the instrument. In most cases the holder-in-due-course doctrine is irrelevant if defenses are being asserted against the payee of the instrument, but in a small number of cases the payee of the instrument may be a holder in due course. Those cases are discussed in Comment 4 to Section 3-302.

Assume Buyer issues a note to Seller in payment of the price of goods that Seller fraudulently promises to deliver but which are never delivered. Seller negotiates the note to Holder who has no notice of the fraud. If Holder is a holder in due course, Holder is not subject to Buyer's defense of fraud. But in some cases an original party to the instrument is a holder in due course. For example, Buyer fraudulently induces Bank to issue a cashier's check to the order of Seller. The check is delivered by Bank to Seller, who has no notice of the fraud. Seller can be a holder in due course and can take the check free of Bank's defense of fraud. This case is discussed as Case # 1 in Comment 4 to Section 3-302. Former Section 3-305 stated that a holder in due course takes free of defenses of "any party to the instrument with whom the holder has not dealt." The meaning of this language was not at all clear and if read literally could have produced the wrong result. In the hypothetical case, it could be argued that Seller "dealt" with Bank because Bank delivered the check to Seller. But it is clear that Seller should take free of Bank's defense against Buyer regardless of whether Seller took delivery of the check from Buyer or from Bank. The quoted language is not included in Section 3-305. It is not necessary. If Buyer issues an instrument to Seller and Buyer has a defense against Seller, that defense can obviously be asserted. Buyer and Seller are the only people involved. The holder-in-due-course doctrine has no relevance. The doctrine applies only to cases in which more than two parties are involved. Its essence is that the holder in due course does not have to suffer the consequences of a defense of the obligor on the instrument that arose from an occurrence with a third party.

3. Subsection (a)(3) is concerned with claims in recoupment which can be illustrated by the following example. Buyer issues a note to the order of Seller in exchange for a promise of Seller to deliver specified equipment. If Seller fails to deliver the equipment or delivers equipment that is rightfully rejected, Buyer has a defense to the note because the performance that was the consideration for the note was not rendered. Section 3-303(b). This defense is included in Section 3-305(a)(2). That defense can always be asserted against Seller. This result is the same as that reached under former Section 3-408.

But suppose Seller delivered the promised equipment and it was accepted by Buyer. The equipment, however, was defective. Buyer retained the equipment and incurred expenses with respect to its repair. In this case, Buyer does not have a defense under Section 3-303(b). Seller delivered the equipment and the equipment was accepted. Under Article 2, Buyer is obliged to pay the price of the equipment which is represented by the note. But Buyer may have a claim against Seller for breach of warranty. If Buyer has a warranty claim, the claim may be asserted against Seller as a counterclaim or as a claim in recoupment to reduce the amount owing on the note. It is not relevant whether Seller is or is not a holder in due course of the note or whether Seller knew or had notice that Buyer had the warranty claim. It is obvious that holder-in-due-course doctrine cannot be used to allow Seller to cut off a warranty claim that Buyer has against Seller. Subsection (b) specifically covers this point by stating that a holder in due course is not subject to a "claim in recoupment * * * against a person other than the holder."

Suppose Seller negotiates the note to Holder. If Holder had notice of Buyer's warranty claim at the time the note was negotiated to Holder, Holder is not a holder in due course (Section 3-302(a)(2)(iv)) and Buyer may assert the claim against Holder (Section 3-305(a)(3)) but only as a claim in recoupment, i.e. to reduce the amount owed on the note. If the warranty claim is $1,000 and the unpaid note is $10,000, Buyer owes $9,000 to Holder. If the warranty claim is more than the unpaid amount of the note, Buyer owes nothing to Holder, but Buyer cannot recover the unpaid amount of the warranty claim from Holder. If Buyer had already partially paid the note, Buyer is not entitled to recover the amounts paid. The claim can be used only as an offset to amounts owing on the note. If Holder had no notice of Buyer's claim and otherwise qualifies as a holder in due course, Buyer may not assert the claim against Holder. Section 3-305(b).

The result under Section 3-305 is consistent with the result reached under former Article 3, but the rules for reaching the result are stated differently. Under former Article 3 Buyer could assert rights against Holder only if Holder was not a holder in due course, and Holder's status depended upon whether Holder had notice of a defense by Buyer. Courts have held that Holder had that notice if Holder had notice of Buyer's warranty claim. The rationale under former Article 3 was "failure of consideration." This rationale does not distinguish between cases in which the seller fails to perform and those in which the buyer accepts the performance of seller but makes a claim against the seller because the performance is faulty. The term "failure of consideration" is subject to varying interpretations and is not used in Article 3. The use of the term "claim in recoupment" in Section 3-305(a)(3) is a more precise statement of the nature of Buyer's right against Holder. The use of the term does not change the law because the treatment of a defense under subsection (a)(2) and a claim in recoupment under subsection (a)(3) is essentially the same.

Under former Article 3, case law was divided on the issue of the extent to which an obligor on a note could assert against a transferee who is not a holder in due course a debt or other claim that the obligor had against the original payee of the instrument. Some courts limited claims to those that arose in the transaction that gave rise to the note. This is the approach taken in Section 3-305(a)(3). Other courts allowed the obligor on the note to use any debt or other claim, no matter how unrelated to the note, to offset the amount owed on the note. Under current judicial authority and non-UCC statutory law, there will be many cases in which a transferee of a note arising from a sale transaction will not qualify as a holder in due course. For example, applicable law may require the use of a note to which there cannot be a holder in due course. See Section 3-106(d) and Comment 3 to Section 3-106. It is reasonable to provide that the buyer should not be denied the right to assert claims arising out of the sale transaction. Subsection (a)(3) is based on the belief that it is not reasonable to require the transferee to bear the risk that wholly unrelated claims may also be asserted. The determination of whether a claim arose from the transaction that gave rise to the instrument is determined by law other than this Article and thus may vary as local law varies.

4. Subsection (c) concerns claims and defenses of a person other than the obligor on the instrument. It applies principally to cases in which an obligation is paid with the instrument of a third person. For example, Buyer buys goods from Seller and negotiates to Seller a cashier's check issued by Bank in payment of the price. Shortly after delivering the check to Seller, Buyer learns that Seller had defrauded Buyer in the sale transaction. Seller may enforce the check against Bank even though Seller is not a holder in due course. Bank has no defense to its obligation to pay the check and it may not assert defenses, claims in recoupment, or claims to the instrument of Buyer, except to the extent permitted by the "but" clause of the first sentence of subsection (c). Buyer may have a claim to the instrument under Section 3-306 based on a right to rescind the negotiation to Seller because of Seller's fraud. Section 3-202(b) and Comment 2 to Section 3-201. Bank cannot assert that claim unless Buyer is joined in the action in which Seller is trying to enforce payment of the check. In that case Bank may pay the amount of the check into court and the court will decide whether that amount belongs to Buyer or Seller. The last sentence of subsection (c) allows the issuer of an instrument such as a cashier's check to refuse payment in the rare case in which the issuer can prove that the instrument is a lost or stolen instrument and the person seeking enforcement does not have rights of a holder in due course.

* * *

§ 3-309. Enforcement of Lost, Destroyed, or Stolen Instrument.[3]

(a) A person not in possession of an instrument is entitled to enforce the instrument if (i) the person was in possession of the instrument and entitled to enforce it when loss of possession occurred, (ii) the loss of possession was not the result of a transfer by the person or a lawful seizure, and (iii) the person cannot reasonably obtain possession of the instrument because the instrument was destroyed, its whereabouts cannot be determined, or it is in the wrongful possession of an unknown person or a person that cannot be found or is not amenable to service of process.

(b) A person seeking enforcement of an instrument under subsection (a) must prove the terms of the instrument and the person's right to enforce the instrument. If that proof is made, Section 3-308 applies to the case as if the person seeking enforcement had produced the instrument. The court may not enter judgment in favor of the person seeking enforcement unless it finds that the person required to pay the instrument is adequately protected

3 In 2002, NCCUSL approved an amendment to this subsection that would ease the requirements for transferees of instruments. As of mid-2004, only Minnesota had adopted this amendment.

against loss that might occur by reason of a claim by another person to enforce the instrument. Adequate protection may be provided by any reasonable means.

* * *

ARTICLE 9. SECURED TRANSACTIONS

* * *

Part 4. Rights of Third Parties

* * *

Section 9-403. Agreement Not to Assert Defenses Against Assignee.

(a) **["Value."]** In this section, "value" has the meaning provided in Section 3-303(a).

(b) **[Agreement not to assert claim or defense.]** Except as otherwise provided in this section, an agreement between an account debtor and an assignor not to assert against an assignee any claim or defense that the account debtor may have against the assignor is enforceable by an assignee that takes an assignment:

(1) for value;

(2) in good faith;

(3) without notice of a claim of a property or possessory right to the property assigned; and

(4) without notice of a defense or claim in recoupment of the type that may be asserted against a person entitled to enforce a negotiable instrument under Section 3-305(a).

(c) **[When subsection (b) not applicable.]** Subsection (b) does not apply to defenses of a type that may be asserted against a holder in due course of a negotiable instrument under Section 3-305(b).

(d) **[Omission of required statement in consumer transaction.]** In a consumer transaction, if a record evidences the account debtor's obligation, law other than this article requires that the record include a statement to the effect that the rights of an assignee are subject to claims or defenses that the account debtor could assert against the original obligee, and the record does not include such a statement:

(1) the record has the same effect as if the record included such a statement; and

(2) the account debtor may assert against an assignee those claims and defenses that would have been available if the record included such a statement.

(e) **[Rule for individual under other law.]** This section is subject to law other than this article which establishes a different rule for an account debtor who is an individual and who incurred the obligation primarily for personal, family, or household purposes.

(f) **[Other law not displaced.]** Except as otherwise provided in subsection (d), this section does not displace law other than this article which gives effect to an agreement by an account debtor not to assert a claim or defense against an assignee.

Official Comment

1. **Source.** Former Section 9-206.

2. **Scope and Purpose.** Subsection (b), like former Section 9-206, generally validates an agreement between an account debtor and an assignor that the account debtor will not assert against an assignee claims and defenses that it may have against the assignor. These agreements are typical in installment sale agreements and leases. However, this section expands former Section 9-206 to apply to all account debtors; it is not limited to account debtors that have bought or leased goods. This section applies only to the obligations of an "account debtor," as defined in Section 9-102. Thus, it does not determine the circumstances under which and the extent to which a person who is obligated on a negotiable instrument is disabled from asserting claims and defenses. Rather, Article 3 must be consulted. See, e.g., Sections 3-305, 3-306. Article 3 governs even when the negotiable instrument constitutes part of chattel paper. See Section 9-102 (an obligor on a negotiable instrument constituting part of chattel paper is not an "account debtor").

3. **Conditions of Validation; Relationship to Article 3.** Subsection (b) validates an account debtor's agreement only if the assignee takes an assignment for value, in good faith, and without notice of conflicting claims to the property assigned or of certain claims or defenses of the account debtor. Like former Section 9-206, this section is designed to put the assignee in a position that is no better and no worse than that of a holder in due course of a negotiable instrument under Article 3. However, former Section 9-206 left open certain issues, e.g., whether the section incorporated the special Article 3 definition of "value" in Section 3-303 or the generally applicable definition in Section 1-201(44). Subsection (a) addresses this question; it provides that "value" has the meaning specified in Section 3-303(a). Similarly, subsection (c) provides that subsection (b) does not validate an agreement with respect to defenses that could be asserted against a holder in due course under Section 3-305(b) (the so-called "real" defenses). In 1990, the definition of "holder in due course" (Section 3-302) and the articulation of the rights of a holder in due course (Sections 3-305 and 3-306) were revised substantially. This section tracks more closely the rules of Sections 3-302, 3-305, and 3-306.

4. **Relationship to Terms of Assigned Property.** Former Section 9-206(2), concerning warranties accompanying the sale of goods, has been deleted as unnecessary. This Article does not regulate the terms of the account, chattel paper, or general intangible that is assigned, except insofar as the account, chattel paper, or general intangible itself creates a security interest (as often is the case with chattel paper). Thus, Article 2, and not this Article, determines whether a seller of goods makes or effectively disclaims warranties, even if the sale is secured. Similarly, other law, and not this Article, determines the effectiveness of an account debtor's undertaking to pay notwithstanding, and not to assert, any defenses or claims against an assignor-e.g., a "hell-or-high-water" provision in the underlying agreement that is assigned. If other law gives effect to this undertaking, then, under principles of *nemo dat*, the undertaking would be enforceable by the assignee (secured party). If other law prevents the assignor from enforcing the undertaking, this section nevertheless might permit the assignee to do so. The right of the assignee to enforce would depend upon whether, under the particular facts, the account debtor's undertaking fairly could be construed as an agreement that falls within the scope of this section and whether the assignee meets the requirements of this section.

5. **Relationship to Federal Trade Commission Rule.** Subsection (d) is new. It applies to rights evidenced by a record that is required to contain, but does not contain, the notice set forth in Federal Trade Commission Rule 433, 16 C.F.R. Part 433 (the "Holder-in-Due-Course Regulations"). Under this subsection, an assignee of such a record takes subject to the consumer account debtor's claims and defenses to the same extent as it would have if the writing had contained the required notice. Thus, subsection (d) effectively renders waiver-of-defense clauses ineffective in the transactions with consumers to which it applies.

6. **Relationship to Other Law.** Like former Section 9-206(1), this section takes no position on the enforceability of waivers of claims and defenses by consumer account debtors, leaving that question to other law. However, the reference to "law other than this article" in subsection (e) encompasses administrative rules and regulations; the reference in former Section 9-206(1) that it replaces ("statute or decision") arguably did not.

This section does not displace other law that gives effect to a non-consumer account debtor's agreement not to assert defenses against an assignee, even if the agreement would not qualify under subsection (b). See subsection (f). It validates, but does not invalidate, agreements made by a non-consumer account debtor. This section also does not displace other law to the extent that the other law permits an assignee, who takes an assignment with notice of a claim of a property or possessory right, a defense, or a claim in recoupment, to enforce an account debtor's agreement not to assert claims and defenses against the assign*or* (e.g., a "hell-or-high-water" agreement). See Comment 4. It also does not displace an assignee's right to assert that an account debtor is estopped from asserting a claim or defense. Nor does this section displace other law with respect to waivers of potential future claims and defenses that are the subject of an agreement between the account debtor and the assign*ee*. Finally, it does not displace Section 1-107, concerning waiver of a breach that allegedly already has occurred.

Section 9-404. Rights Acquired by Assignee; Claims and Defenses Against Assignee.

(a) **[Assignee's rights subject to terms, claims, and defenses; exceptions.]** Unless an account debtor has made an enforceable agreement not to assert defenses or claims, and subject to subsections (b) through (e), the rights of an assignee are subject to:

(1) all terms of the agreement between the account debtor and assignor and any defense or claim in recoupment arising from the transaction that gave rise to the contract; and

(2) any other defense or claim of the account debtor against the assignor which accrues before the account debtor receives a notification of the assignment authenticated by the assignor or the assignee.

(b) **[Account debtor's claim reduces amount owed to assignee.]** Subject to subsection (c) and except as otherwise provided in subsection (d), the claim of an account debtor against an assignor may be asserted against an assignee under subsection (a) only to reduce the amount the account debtor owes.

(c) **[Rule for individual under other law.]** This section is subject to law other than this article which establishes a different rule for an account debtor who is an individual and who incurred the obligation primarily for personal, family, or household purposes.

(d) **[Omission of required statement in consumer transaction.]** In a consumer transaction, if a record evidences the account debtor's obligation, law other than this article requires that the record include a statement to the effect that the account debtor's recovery against an assignee with respect to claims and defenses against the assignor may not exceed amounts paid by the account debtor under the record, and the record does not include such a statement, the extent to which a claim of an account debtor against the assignor may be asserted against an assignee is determined as if the record included such a statement.

(e) **[Inapplicability to health-care-insurance receivable.]** This section does not apply to an assignment of a health-care-insurance receivable.

Official Comment

1. **Source.** Former Section 9-318(1).

2. **Purpose; Rights of Assignee in General.** Subsection (a), like former Section 9-318(1), provides that an assignee generally takes an assignment subject to defenses and claims of an account debtor. Under subsection (a)(1), if the account debtor's defenses on an assigned claim arise from the transaction that gave rise to the contract with the assignor, it makes no difference whether the defense or claim accrues before or after the account debtor is notified of the assignment. Under subsection (a)(2), the assignee takes subject to other defenses or claims only if they accrue before the account debtor has been notified of the assignment. Of course, an account debtor may waive its right to assert defenses or claims against an assignee under Section 9-403 or other applicable law. Subsection (a) tracks Section 3-305(a)(3) more closely than its predecessor.

3. **Limitation on Affirmative Claims.** Subsection (b) is new. It limits the claim that the account debtor may assert against an assignee. Borrowing from Section 3-305(a)(3) and cases construing former Section 9-318, subsection (b) generally does not afford the account debtor the right to an affirmative recovery from an assignee.

4. **Consumer Account Debtors; Relationship to Federal Trade Commission Rule.** Subsections (c) and (d) also are new. Subsection (c) makes clear that the rules of this section are subject to other law establishing special rules for consumer account debtors. An "account debtor who is an individual" as used in subsection (c) includes individuals who are jointly or jointly and severally obligated. Subsection (d) applies to rights evidenced by a record that is required to contain, but does not contain, the notice set forth in Federal Trade Commission Rule 433, 16 C.F.R. Part 433 (the "Holder-in-Due-Course Regulations"). Under subsection (d), a consumer account debtor has the same right to an affirmative recovery from an assignee of such a record as the consumer would have had against the assignee had the record contained the required notice.

5. **Scope; Application to "Account Debtor."** This section deals only with the rights and duties of "account debtors"—and for the most part only with account debtors on accounts, chattel paper, and payment intangibles. Subsection (e) provides that the obligation of an insurer with respect to a health-care-insurance receivable is governed by other law. References in this section to an "account debtor" include account debtors on collateral that is proceeds. Neither this section nor any other provision of this Article, including Sections 9-408 and 9-409, provides analogous regulation of the rights and duties of other obligors on collateral, such as the maker of a negotiable instrument (governed by Article 3), the issuer of or nominated person under a letter of credit (governed by Article 5), or the issuer of a security (governed by Article 8). Article 9 leaves those rights and duties untouched; however, Section 9-409 deals with the special case of letters of credit. When chattel paper is composed in part of a negotiable instrument, the obligor on the instrument is not an "account debtor," and Article 3 governs the rights of the assignee of the chattel paper with respect to the issues that this section addresses. See, e.g., Section 3-601 (dealing with discharge of an obligation to pay a negotiable instrument).

Appendix G UDAP Pleadings

UDAP pleadings can apply to a myriad of fact situations and must comply with different state UDAP procedural requirements. As a consequence, rather than offering one sample complaint or set of discovery as a print appendix, this manual provides over 150 sample UDAP pleadings, of different types, covering different fact situations, and from different jurisdictions on the companion CD-Rom.

A complete listing of these 150 pleadings is found at the CD-Rom Contents at the beginning of this volume. The CD-Rom uses Internet-style navigation to facilitate browsing through a list of the pleadings organized by type. The CD-Rom also allows keyword searches to pinpoint appropriate pleadings.

All pleadings are on the CD-Rom both in PDF format and MS Word. The PDF format facilitates Internet-style navigation and keyword searches. The Word format works somewhat better than PDF format for copying and pasting pleadings into Word or WordPerfect documents.

The pleadings are from federal and state courts all over the country and are organized in the following categories:

- Demand letters;
- Complaints;
- Objection to Creditor's Bankruptcy Claim;
- Intervention in State Attorney General Suits;
- Temporary Restraining Orders;
- Remand to State Court After Removal to Federal Court;
- Discovery;
- Motion to Compel Discovery;
- Consumer's Response to Motion to Dismiss;
- Class Certification Pleadings;
- Summary Judgment Motions;
- Expert Testimony;
- Settlements;
- Trial Briefs;
- Jury Instructions;
- Request for Findings and Rulings;
- Requests for Attorney Fees;
- Appellate Briefs;
- *Certiorari* and Petitions for Review;
- *Cy Pres* Remedy.

Just some of the subject areas included are:

- Auto Churning;
- Auto Defects;
- Auto Financing;
- Auto Leases;
- Auto Pawn;
- Auto Rebate Theft;

- Auto Sales;
- Bankruptcy Reaffirmations Illegally Obtained;
- Campground Memberships;
- Credit Bureaus, Furnishing of Information to;
- Credit Card Billing;
- Debt Collection Harassment;
- Distant Forum Abuse;
- Forced Placed Insurance;
- Foreclosure, False Threat of;
- FTC Holder Rule;
- Furniture Sales;
- Home Improvement Fraud;
- Home Solicitation Sales;
- Infertility Clinics;
- Land Installment Sales;
- Landlord-Tenant;
- Lender's Improvident Extension of Credit;
- Loan Flipping;
- Mandatory Arbitration Included in Credit Card "Stuffer";
- Mobile Home Parks;
- Mobile Home Sales and Defects;
- Mortgage Loans and Foreclosure Defense;
- Mortgage Servicers;
- Nursing Homes;
- Odometer Fraud;
- Payday Loans;
- Real Estate Broker Fraud;
- Rent to Own;
- Repossessions;
- Satellite Dish;
- Storage of Property;
- Trade School Fraud;
- Travel Fraud.

Appendix H Useful Websites

Consumer Protection Agencies

Federal Trade Commission
www.FTC.gov

Consumer Product Safety Commission
www.cpsc.gov

Other Governmental and Quasi-Governmental Websites

U.S. House of Representatives
www.house.gov

General website for federal legislative information
http://thomas.loc.gov

Comptroller of the Currency
www.occ.treas.gov

Office of Thrift Supervision
www.ots.treas.gov

National Credit Union Administration
www.ncua.gov

Department of Housing and Urban Development
www.hud.gov

Department of the Interior
www.doi.gov

Department of Labor
www.dol.gov

Department of Transportation
www.dot.gov

Federal Communications Commission
www.fcc.gov

National Conference of Commissioners on Uniform State Laws
www.nccusl.org

Consumer Information

www.consumeraffairs.com (links to other consumer sites)
www.consumerworld.com (consumer information and links to other sites)

Federal Consumer Information Center (part of the General Services Administration)
www.pueblo.gsa.gov

Investigation

Public record information about corporations
www.incspot.com
www.hoovers.com

Links to Secretary of State websites (to find a company's legal name, status, and agent for service of process)
www.nass.org/sos/sos.html

Consumer Advocacy Organizations

National Consumer Law Center
www.consumerlaw.org

National Association of Consumer Advocates
www.naca.net

Consumers Union
www.consumersunion.org

Trial Lawyers for Public Justice
www.tlpj.org

American Trial Lawyers Association
www.atlanet.org

Center for Auto Safety
www.autosafety.org

Consumers for Auto Reliability and Safety (CARS)
www.carconsumers.com

Immigrant Legal Resource Center
www.ilrc.org

National Association of Attorneys General
www.naag.org

False Claims Act Legal Center
www.taf.org

National Center on Poverty Law (source for ordering Clearinghouse documents)
www.povertylaw.org

Vehicle Financing Information

www.FinanCenter.com
www.TValue.com
www.auto-loan.com
www.edmunds.com
www.carinfo.com
www.autoweb.com

Other Vehicle Information

www.autopedia.com
www.cartalk.msn.com
www.essential.org/cas
www.nhtsa.dot.gov
www.alldata.com/consumer/TSB/yr.html (service bulletins)
www.carfax.com (vehicle history reports)
www.kbb.com (Kelley Blue Book)
www.nada.org (National Automobile Dealers Association)

Telemarketing and E-mail

www.spamlaws.com
www.junkfax.com
www.TCPALaw.com

National Fraud Information Center
www.fraud.org

Direct Marketing Association (offering a voluntary do-not-call list)
www.the-dma.org

State UDAP Statutes and Regulations

The companion CD-Rom contains links to free websites reprinting all state UDAP statutes. In addition, the CD-Rom contains the full text or links to websites reprinting a number of states' UDAP regulations.

Index

References are to sections

References are to sections

References are to sections

References are to sections

References are to sections

References are to sections

References are to sections

References are to sections

References are to sections

References are to sections

References are to sections

References are to sections

References are to sections

References are to sections

References are to sections

References are to sections

References are to sections

References are to sections

References are to sections

References are to sections

References are to sections

References are to sections

Quick Reference to the Consumer Credit and Sales Legal Practice Series

References are to sections in *all* manuals in NCLC's Consumer Credit and Sales Legal Practice Series. References followed by "S" appear only in a supplement.

> Readers should also consider another search option available at ***www.consumerlaw.org/keyword***. There, users can search all sixteen NCLC manuals for a case name, party name, statutory or regulatory citation, or *any* other word, phrase, or combination of terms. The search engine provides the title and page number of every occurrence of that word or phrase within each of the NCLC manuals. Further search instructions and tips are provided on the web site.

The Quick Reference to the Consumer Credit and Sales Legal Practice Series pinpoints where to find specific topics analyzed in the NCLC manuals. References are to individual manual or supplement sections. For more information on these volumes, see *What Your Library Should Contain* at the beginning of this volume, or go to www.consumerlaw.org.

This Quick Reference is a speedy means to locate key terms in the appropriate NCLC manual. More detailed indexes are found at the end of the individual NCLC volumes. Both the detailed contents pages and the detailed indexes for each manual are also available at NCLC's web site, www.consumerlaw.org.

NCLC *strongly recommends,* when searching for PLEADINGS on a particular subject, that users refer to the *Index Guide* accompanying *Consumer Law Pleadings on CD-Rom*, and not to this *Quick Reference*. Another option is to search for pleadings directly on the *Consumer Law Pleadings* CD-Rom or on the *Consumer Law in a Box* CD-Rom, using the finding tools that are provided on the CD-Roms themselves.

The finding tools found on *Consumer Law in a Box* are also an effective means to find statutes, regulations, agency interpretations, legislative history, and other primary source material found on NCLC's CD-Roms. Other search options are detailed at page vii, *supra*.

Abbreviations

AUS = Access to Utility Service (3d ed. 2004)

Auto = Automobile Fraud (2d ed. 2003 and 2004 Supp.)

Arbit = Consumer Arbitration Agreements (4th ed. 2004)

CBPL = Consumer Banking and Payments Law (2d ed. 2002 and 2004 Supp.)

Bankr = Consumer Bankruptcy Law and Practice (7th ed. 2004)

CCA = Consumer Class Actions: A Practical Litigation Guide (5th ed. 2002 and 2004 Supp.)

CLP = Consumer Law Pleadings, Numbers One Through Ten (2004)

COC = The Cost of Credit (2d ed. 2000 and 2004 Supp.)

CD = Credit Discrimination (3d ed. 2002 and 2004 Supp.)

FCR = Fair Credit Reporting (5th ed. 2002 and 2004 Supp.)

FDC = Fair Debt Collection (5th ed. 2004)

Repo = Repossessions and Foreclosures (5th ed. 2002 and 2004 Supp.)

Stud = Student Loan Law (2d ed. 2002 and 2004 Supp.)

TIL = Truth in Lending (5th ed. 2003 and 2004 Supp.)

UDAP = Unfair and Deceptive Acts and Practices (6th ed. 2004)

Warr = Consumer Warranty Law (2d ed. 2001 and 2004 Supp.)

References are to sections in *all* manuals in NCLC's Consumer Credit and Sales Legal Practice Series

References are to sections in *all* manuals in NCLC's Consumer Credit and Sales Legal Practice Series

References are to sections in *all* manuals in NCLC's Consumer Credit and Sales Legal Practice Series

References are to sections in *all* manuals in NCLC's Consumer Credit and Sales Legal Practice Series

References are to sections in *all* manuals in NCLC's Consumer Credit and Sales Legal Practice Series

References are to sections in *all* manuals in NCLC's Consumer Credit and Sales Legal Practice Series

References are to sections in *all* manuals in NCLC's Consumer Credit and Sales Legal Practice Series

References are to sections in *all* manuals in NCLC's Consumer Credit and Sales Legal Practice Series

References are to sections in *all* manuals in NCLC's Consumer Credit and Sales Legal Practice Series

NOTES

NOTES

NOTES

NOTES

NOTES

NOTES

NOTES

NOTES

NOTES

NOTES

NOTES

About the Companion CD-Rom

CD-Rom Supersedes All Prior CD-Roms

This CD-Rom supersedes the CD-Roms accompanying the Fifth Edition of *Unfair and Deceptive Acts and Practices* (2001) and all its supplements. Discard all prior CD-Roms. The 2004 CD-Rom contains everything found on the earlier CD-Roms and contains much additional material.

What Is on the CD-Rom

For a detailed listing of the CD's contents, see the CD-Rom Contents section on page xlvii of this book. Highlights and new additions include:

- Over 90 sample UDAP complaints and demand letters;
- Over 80 sample discovery requests and motions to compel discovery;
- Over 30 responses to motions to dismiss or summary judgment motions;
- Over 20 jury instructions, requests for findings, and trial briefs;
- Attorney fee requests;
- Temporary restraining orders, foreclosure defenses, class certification pleadings, expert testimony, settlements, appellate briefs, and more;
- Useful internet links to pleadings and reports relating to two auto finance upcharge cases, as well as links to summaries of Ohio and New York UDAP cases;
- The FTC Credit Practices, Holder, Used Car, and Door-to-Door Rules, with selected hard-to-find statements of basis and purpose, staff interpretations and opinion letters, and enforcement guidelines;
- The FTC Mail or Telephone Order, Funeral, and Franchise Rules and FTC Guides on Deceptive Pricing, Bait Advertising, Advertising of Warranties, Use of the Word "Free," Vocational Schools, and Endorsements;
- Summaries of all state UDAP statutes, selected legislative history of model UDAP statutes, and free links to the full text of most state UDAP statutes;
- Internet links to most state UDAP regulations;
- NAAG rental car guidelines;
- Federal RICO statute and summaries of state RICO statutes;
- Federal telemarketing statutes and regulations, including 2003 amendments;
- Summaries of state telemarketing and "900 Number" statutes; and
- Useful and up-to-date addresses for state attorney general and other state, county, and city government consumer protection offices, FTC regional offices, national consumer organizations, better business bureaus, HUD and state administrative agencies on mobile home defects, car manufacturers, and mobile home manufacturers.

How to Use the CD-Rom

The CD's pop-up menu quickly allows you to use the CD—just place the CD into its drive and click on the "Start NCLC CD" button that will pop up in the middle of the screen. You can also access the CD by clicking on a desktop icon that you can create using the pop-up menu.[1] For detailed installation instructions, see *One-Time Installation* below.

All the CD-Rom's information is available in PDF (Acrobat) format, making the information:

- Highly readable (identical to the printed pages in the book);
- Easily navigated (with bookmarks, "buttons," and Internet-style forward and backward searches);
- Easy to locate with keyword searches and other quick-search techniques across the whole CD-Rom; and
- Easy to paste into a word processor.

While much of the material is also found on the CD-Rom in word processing format, we strongly recommend you use the material in PDF format—not only because it is easiest to use, contains the most features, and includes more material, but also because you can easily switch back to a word processing format when you prefer.

Acrobat Reader 5 and 6.0.1 come free of charge with the CD-Rom. **We strongly recommend that new Acrobat users read the Acrobat tutorial on the Home Page. It takes two minutes and will really pay off.**

1 Alternatively, click on the D:\Start.pdf file on "My Computer" or open that file in Acrobat—always assuming "D:" is the CD-Rom drive on your computer.

How to Find Documents in Word Processing Format

Most pleadings and other practice aids are also available in Microsoft Word format to make them more easily adaptable for individual use. (Current versions of WordPerfect are able to convert the Word documents upon opening them.) The CD-Rom offers several ways to find those word processing documents. One option is simply to browse to the folder on the CD-Rom containing all the word processing files and open the desired document from your standard word processing program, such as Word or WordPerfect. All word processing documents are in the D:\WP_Files folder, if "D:" is the CD-Rom drive,[2] and are further organized by book title. Documents that appear in the book are named after the corresponding appendix; other documents have descriptive file names.

Another option is to navigate the CD in PDF format, and, when a particular document is on the screen, click on the corresponding bookmark for the "Word version of . . ." This will automatically run Word, WordPerfect for Windows, or *any other word processor* that is associated with the ".DOC" extension, and then open the word processing file that corresponds to the Acrobat document.[3]

Important Information Before Opening the CD-Rom Package

Before opening the CD-Rom package, please read this information. Opening the package constitutes acceptance of the following described terms. In addition, the *book* is not returnable once the seal to the *CD-Rom* has been broken.

The CD-Rom is copyrighted and all rights are reserved by the National Consumer Law Center, Inc. No copyright is claimed to the text of statutes, regulations, excerpts from court opinions, or any part of an original work prepared by a United States Government employee.

You may not commercially distribute the CD-Rom or otherwise reproduce, publish, distribute or use the disk in any manner that may infringe on any copyright or other proprietary right of the National Consumer Law Center. Nor may you otherwise transfer the CD-Rom or this agreement to any other party unless that party agrees to accept the terms and conditions of this agreement. You may use the CD-Rom on only one computer and by one user at a time.

The CD-Rom is warranted to be free of defects in materials and faulty workmanship under normal use for a period of ninety days after purchase. If a defect is discovered in the CD-Rom during this warranty period, a replacement disk can be obtained at no charge by sending the defective disk, postage prepaid, with information identifying the purchaser, to National Consumer Law Center, Publications Department, 77 Summer Street, 10th Floor, Boston, MA 02110. After the ninety-day period, a replacement will be available on the same terms, but will also require a $20 prepayment.

The National Consumer Law Center makes no other warranty or representation, either express or implied, with respect to this disk, its quality, performance, merchantability, or fitness for a particular purpose. In no event will the National Consumer Law Center be liable for direct, indirect, special, incidental, or consequential damages arising out of the use or inability to use the disk. The exclusion of implied warranties is not effective in some states, and thus this exclusion may not apply to you.

System Requirements

Use of this CD-Rom requires a Windows-based PC with a CD-Rom drive. (Macintosh users report success using NCLC CDs, but the CD has been tested only on Windows-based PCs.) The CD-Rom's features are optimized with Acrobat Reader 5 or later. Acrobat Reader versions 5 and 6.0.1 are included free on this CD-Rom, and either will work with this CD-Rom as long as it is compatible with your version of Windows. Acrobat Reader 5 is compatible with Windows 95/98/Me/NT/2000/XP, while Acrobat Reader 6.0.1 is compatible with Windows 98SE/Me/NT/2000/XP. If you already have Acrobat Reader 6.0, we *highly* recommend you download and install the 6.0.1 update from the Adobe web site at www.adobe.com because a bug in version 6.0 interferes with optimum use of this CD-Rom. The Microsoft Word versions of pleadings and practice aids can be used with any reasonably current word processor (1995 or later).

One-Time Installation

When the CD-Rom is inserted in its drive, a menu will pop up automatically. (Please be patient if you have a slow CD-Rom drive; this will only take a few moments.) If you do not already have Acrobat Reader 5 or 6.0.1, first click the "Install Acrobat Reader" button. Do not reboot, but then click on the "Make Shortcut Icon" button. (You need not make another shortcut icon if you already have done so for another NCLC CD.) Then reboot and follow the *How to Use the CD-Rom* instructions above.

[*Note*: If the pop-up menu fails to appear, go to "My Computer," right-click "D:" if that is the CD-Rom drive, and select "Open." Then double-click on "Read_Me.txt" for alternate installation and use instructions.]

2 The CD-Rom drive could be any letter following "D:" depending on your computer's configuration.

3 For instructions on how to associate WordPerfect to the ".DOC" extension, go to the CD-Rom's home page and click on "How to Use/Help," then "Word Files."